# THE OFFICIAL® 2002 PRICE GUIDE TO BASEBALL CARDS

BY

DR. JAMES BECKETT

TWENTY-FIRST EDITION

HC

HOUSE OF COLLECTIBLES

The Crown Publishing Group • New York

Important Notice: All of the information, including valuations, in this book has been compiled from the most reliable sources, and every effort has been made to eliminate errors and questionable data. Nevertheless, the possibility of error in a work of such scope always exists. The publisher will not be held responsible for losses which may occur in the purchase, sale or other transaction of items because of information contained herein. Readers who feel they have discovered errors are invited to *write* and inform us, so that they may be corrected in subsequent editions. Those seeking further information on the topics covered in this book are advised to refer to the complete line of *Official Price Guides* published by the House of Collectibles.



Published by:
House of Collectibles
The Crown Publishing Group
New York, New York

Distributed by The Crown Publishing Group,
a division of Random House, Inc.,
New York, and simultaneously in Canada by
Random House of Canada Limited, Toronto.

www.randomhouse.com

Manufactured in the United States of America

ISSN: 1062-7138

ISBN: 0-609-80764-1

10 9 8 7 6 5 4 3 2 1

Twenty-first Edition: April 2001

# Table of Contents


About the Author....10
How to Use This Book....10
How to Collect....11
  Obtaining Cards....11
  Preserving Your Cards....12
  Collecting vs. Investing....12
Terminology....13
Glossary/Legend....14
Understanding Card Values....18
  Determining Value....18
  Regional Variation....18
  Set Prices....19
  Scarce Series....19
Grading Your Cards....20
  Centering....20
  Corner Wear....20
  Creases....21
  Alterations....21
  Categorization of Defects....21
Condition Guide....22
  Grades....22
Selling Your Cards....23
Interesting Notes....26
History of Baseball Cards....26
  Increasing Popularity....27
  Intensified Competition....29
  Sharing the Pie....30
  Finding Out More....33
Additional Reading....34
Advertising....34
Prices in This Guide....34

1998 Aurora....35
1999 Aurora....35
2000 Aurora....36
1999 Black Diamond....37
2000 Black Diamond....38
2000 Black Diamond Rookie Edition....38
1948 Bowman....39
1949 Bowman....39
1950 Bowman....40
1951 Bowman....41
1952 Bowman....43
1953 Bowman B/W....44
1953 Bowman Color....44
1954 Bowman....45
1955 Bowman....46
1989 Bowman....47
1990 Bowman....49
1991 Bowman....51
1992 Bowman....54
1993 Bowman....57
1994 Bowman....60
1995 Bowman....63
1996 Bowman....65
1997 Bowman....66
1998 Bowman....68
1999 Bowman....70
2000 Bowman....72
2000 Bowman Draft Picks....74
1997 Bowman Chrome....74
1998 Bowman Chrome....75
1999 Bowman Chrome....77
2000 Bowman Chrome....79
2000 Bowman Chrome Draft Picks....81
1994 Bowman's Best....81
1995 Bowman's Best....82
1996 Bowman's Best....83
1997 Bowman's Best....84
1998 Bowman's Best....85
1999 Bowman's Best....86

2000 Bowman's Best ....87
1996 Circa ....87
1997 Circa ....88
1998 Circa Thunder ....90
1994 Collector's Choice ....91
1995 Collector's Choice ....94
1996 Collector's Choice ....96
1997 Collector's Choice ....100
1998 Collector's Choice ....102
1995 Collector's Choice SE ....104
1998 Crown Royale ....105
1999 Crown Royale ....106
2000 Crown Royale ....106
1981 Donruss ....107
1982 Donruss ....110
1983 Donruss ....113
1984 Donruss ....116
1985 Donruss ....119
1986 Donruss ....122
1986 Donruss Rookies ....125
1987 Donruss ....125
1987 Donruss Rookies ....128
1988 Donruss ....128
1988 Donruss Rookies ....131
1989 Donruss ....131
1989 Donruss Rookies ....134
1990 Donruss ....134
1990 Donruss Rookies ....138
1991 Donruss ....138
1991 Donruss Rookies ....142
1992 Donruss ....142
1992 Donruss Rookies ....145
1993 Donruss ....146
1994 Donruss ....149
1995 Donruss ....152
1996 Donruss ....154
1997 Donruss ....156
1998 Donruss ....158
1998 Donruss Collections Donruss ..160
1997 Donruss Elite ....161
1998 Donruss Elite ....161
1997 Donruss Limited ....162
1997 Donruss Preferred ....163
1998 Donruss Preferred ....164
1997 Donruss Signature ....165
1998 Donruss Signature ....166
1995 Emotion ....166
1996 Emotion-XL ....167
1997 E-X2000 ....169
1998 E-X2001 ....169
1999 E-X Century ....170
2000 E-X ....170
1993 Finest ....171
1994 Finest ....171
1995 Finest ....173
1996 Finest ....175
1997 Finest ....176
1998 Finest ....178
1999 Finest ....179
2000 Finest ....180
1993 Flair ....182
1994 Flair ....183
1995 Flair ....185
1996 Flair ....186
1997 Flair Showcase Row 2 ....188
1998 Flair Showcase Row 3 ....189

1999 Flair Showcase Row 3 ............190
1963 Fleer ............190
1981 Fleer ............191
1982 Fleer ............194
1983 Fleer ............197
1984 Fleer ............200
1984 Fleer Update ............202
1985 Fleer ............203
1985 Fleer Update ............206
1986 Fleer ............207
1986 Fleer Update ............209
1987 Fleer ............210
1987 Fleer Update ............213
1988 Fleer ............214
1988 Fleer Update ............217
1989 Fleer ............217
1989 Fleer Update ............221
1990 Fleer ............221
1990 Fleer Update ............225
1991 Fleer ............225
1991 Fleer Update ............229
1992 Fleer ............229
1992 Fleer Update ............232
1993 Fleer ............233
1993 Fleer Final Edition ............236
1994 Fleer ............237
1994 Fleer Update ............240
1995 Fleer ............241
1995 Fleer Update ............243
1996 Fleer ............244
1996 Fleer Update ............247
1997 Fleer ............248
1998 Fleer ............251
1998 Fleer Update ............253
1999 Fleer ............254
1999 Fleer Update ............256
2000 Fleer ............257
2000 Fleer Glossy ............259
2000 Fleer Update ............259
1999 Fleer Brilliants ............260
2000 Fleer Focus ............261
2000 Fleer Gamers ............262
2000 Fleer Greats of the Game ............263
1999 Fleer Mystique ............263
2000 Fleer Mystique ............264
2000 Fleer Showcase ............265
2000 Impact ............265
1949 Leaf ............266
1990 Leaf ............267
1991 Leaf ............269
1992 Leaf ............271
1993 Leaf ............273
1994 Leaf ............276
1995 Leaf ............277
1996 Leaf ............279
1997 Leaf ............280
1998 Leaf ............282
1994 Leaf Limited ............283
1994 Leaf Limited Rookies ............283
1995 Leaf Limited ............284
1996 Leaf Limited ............285
1998 Leaf Rookies and Stars ............285
1996 Leaf Signature ............286
1996 Metal Universe ............287
1997 Metal Universe ............288
1998 Metal Universe ............289

1999 Metal Universe ....290
2000 Metal ....291
2000 MLB Showdown 1st Edition ....293
2000 MLB Showdown Pennant Run 1st Edition ....294
1994 Pacific ....295
1995 Pacific ....298
1996 Pacific ....300
1997 Pacific ....302
1998 Pacific ....303
1999 Pacific ....305
2000 Pacific ....307
2001 Pacific ....309
1999 Pacific Crown Collection ....311
2000 Pacific Crown Collection ....313
1998 Pacific Invincible ....314
1999 Pacific Invincible ....315
2000 Pacific Invincible ....315
1998 Pacific Omega ....316
1999 Pacific Omega ....317
2000 Pacific Omega ....318
1998 Pacific Online ....320
1995 Pacific Prisms ....323
1996 Pacific Prisms ....323
1997 Pacific Prisms ....324
1999 Pacific Prism ....325
2000 Pacific Prism ....325
1999 Pacific Private Stock ....326
2000 Pacific Private Stock ....327
2001 Pacific Private Stock ....328
2000 Pacific Vanguard ....328
1998 Paramount ....329
1999 Paramount ....330
2000 Paramount ....331
2000 Paramount Update ....332
1992 Pinnacle ....332
1993 Pinnacle ....335
1994 Pinnacle ....337
1995 Pinnacle ....340
1996 Pinnacle ....342
1997 Pinnacle ....343
1998 Pinnacle ....344
1998 Revolution ....345
1999 Revolution ....346
2000 Revolution ....346
1988 Score ....347
1988 Score Rookie/Traded ....350
1989 Score ....351
1989 Score Rookie/Traded ....354
1990 Score ....354
1990 Score Rookie/Traded ....357
1991 Score ....358
1991 Score Rookie/Traded ....362
1992 Score ....363
1992 Score Rookie/Traded ....366
1993 Score ....367
1994 Score ....369
1994 Score Rookie/Traded ....372
1995 Score ....373
1996 Score ....375
1997 Score ....377
1998 Score ....380
1998 Score Rookie/Traded ....381
1993 Select ....382
1993 Select Rookie/Traded ....384
1994 Select ....384

1995 Select ....................386
1996 Select ....................387
1997 Select ....................388
1995 Select Certified ....................389
1996 Select Certified ....................390
2000 SkyBox ....................390
2000 Skybox Dominion ....................392
1993 SP ....................393
1994 SP ....................394
1995 SP ....................395
1996 SP ....................396
1997 SP ....................397
1998 SP Authentic ....................398
1999 SP Authentic ....................399
2000 SP Authentic ....................399
1999 SP Signature ....................400
1996 SPx ....................401
1997 SPx ....................401
1998 SPx Finite ....................402
1999 SPx ....................403
2000 SPx ....................404
1991 Stadium Club ....................405
1992 Stadium Club Dome ....................407
1992 Stadium Club ....................408
1993 Stadium Club Murphy ....................412
1993 Stadium Club ....................413
1994 Stadium Club ....................416
1995 Stadium Club ....................419
1996 Stadium Club ....................421
1997 Stadium Club ....................423
1998 Stadium Club ....................425
1999 Stadium Club ....................426
2000 Stadium Club ....................428
2000 Stadium Club Chrome ....................429
2001 Stadium Club ....................430
1991 Studio ....................431
1992 Studio ....................432
1993 Studio ....................433
1994 Studio ....................434
1995 Studio ....................435
1996 Studio ....................436
1997 Studio ....................437
1998 Studio ....................438
1952 Topps ....................439
1953 Topps ....................441
1954 Topps ....................442
1955 Topps ....................443
1956 Topps ....................444
1957 Topps ....................446
1958 Topps ....................448
1959 Topps ....................450
1960 Topps ....................453
1961 Topps ....................455
1962 Topps ....................458
1963 Topps ....................461
1964 Topps ....................465
1965 Topps ....................468
1966 Topps ....................471
1967 Topps ....................474
1968 Topps ....................478
1969 Topps ....................481
1970 Topps ....................484
1971 Topps ....................488
1972 Topps ....................492
1973 Topps ....................495
1974 Topps ....................499

1974 Topps Traded ....503
1975 Topps ....503
1976 Topps ....507
1976 Topps Traded ....510
1977 Topps ....510
1978 Topps ....513
1979 Topps ....517
1980 Topps ....520
1981 Topps ....524
1981 Topps Traded ....527
1982 Topps ....528
1982 Topps Traded ....532
1983 Topps ....532
1983 Topps Traded ....536
1984 Topps ....537
1984 Topps Traded ....540
1985 Topps ....541
1985 Topps Traded ....544
1986 Topps ....545
1986 Topps Traded ....548
1987 Topps ....549
1987 Topps Traded ....552
1988 Topps ....553
1988 Topps Traded ....556
1989 Topps ....557
1989 Topps Traded ....561
1990 Topps ....561
1990 Topps Traded ....565
1991 Topps ....565
1991 Topps Traded ....569
1992 Topps ....570
1992 Topps Traded ....573
1993 Topps ....574
1993 Topps Traded ....577
1994 Topps ....578
1994 Topps Traded ....581
1995 Topps ....582
1995 Topps Traded ....585
1996 Topps ....586
1997 Topps ....588
1998 Topps ....590
1999 Topps ....593
1999 Topps Traded ....595
2000 Topps ....596
2000 Topps Limited ....598
2000 Topps Traded ....598
2001 Topps ....599
1996 Topps Chrome ....601
1997 Topps Chrome ....602
1998 Topps Chrome ....602
1999 Topps Chrome ....605
1999 Topps Chrome Traded ....607
2000 Topps Chrome ....608
2000 Topps Chrome Traded ....610
1996 Topps Gallery ....611
1997 Topps Gallery ....612
1998 Topps Gallery ....612
1999 Topps Gallery ....613
2000 Topps Gallery ....614
1998 Topps Gold Label Class 1 ....614
1999 Topps Gold Label Class 1 ....615
2000 Topps Gold Label Class 1 ....615
2000 Topps HD ....616
1998 Topps Opening Day ....616
1999 Topps Opening Day ....617
2000 Topps Opening Day ....618

1997 Topps Stars ....619
1998 Topps Stars ....619
1999 Topps Stars ....620
2000 Topps Stars ....621
1998 Topps Tek ....622
1999 Topps Tek ....622
2000 Topps Tek ....622
1997 UD3 ....623
1998 UD3 ....623
1999 UD Ionix ....624
2000 UD Ionix ....625
1991 Ultra ....625
1991 Ultra Update ....627
1992 Ultra ....627
1993 Ultra ....630
1994 Ultra ....633
1995 Ultra ....635
1996 Ultra ....637
1997 Ultra ....639
1998 Ultra ....642
1999 Ultra ....644
2000 Ultra ....645
2001 Ultra ....646
1989 Upper Deck ....647
1990 Upper Deck ....651
1991 Upper Deck ....655
1991 Upper Deck Final Edition ....658
1992 Upper Deck ....659
1993 Upper Deck ....662
1994 Upper Deck ....666
1995 Upper Deck ....668
1996 Upper Deck ....670
1997 Upper Deck ....672
1998 Upper Deck ....674
1999 Upper Deck ....677
2000 Upper Deck ....680
2001 Upper Deck ....682
2000 Upper Deck Gold Reserve ....683
2000 Upper Deck Hitter's Club ....684
1999 Upper Deck HoloGrFX ....685
2000 Upper Deck HoloGrFX ....685
2000 Upper Deck Legends ....686
1999 Upper Deck MVP ....686
2000 Upper Deck MVP ....687
1999 Upper Deck Ovation ....688
2000 Upper Deck Ovation ....689
1999 Upper Deck PowerDeck ....689
2000 Upper Deck PowerDeck ....689
2000 Upper Deck Pros and Prospects ....689
1999 Upper Deck Ultimate Victory ....690
2000 Upper Deck Ultimate Victory ....691
1999 Upper Deck Victory ....691
2000 Upper Deck Victory ....693

# About the Author

Jim Beckett, the leading authority on sports card values in the United States, maintains a wide range of activities in the world of sports. He possesses one of the finest collections of sports cards and autographs in the world, has made numerous appearances on radio and television, and has been frequently cited in many national publications. He was awarded the first Special Achievement Award for Contributions to the Hobby by the National Sports Collectors Convention in 1980, the Jock-Jaspersen Award for Hobby Dedication in 1983, and the Buck Barker, Spirit of the Hobby Award in 1991.

Dr. Beckett is the author of *Beckett Baseball Card Price Guide, The Official Price Guide to Baseball Cards, Beckett Almanac of Baseball Cards and Collectibles, Beckett Football Card Price Guide,The Official Price Guide to Football Cards, Beckett Hockey Card Price Guide and Alphabetical Checklist, Beckett Basketball Card Price Guide, The Official Price Guide to Basketball Cards, Beckett Racing Collectibles and Die-Cast Price Guide, Beckett Baseball Card Alphabetical Checklist, Beckett Football Card Alphabetical Checklist, and Beckett Basketball Card Alphabetical Checklist.* In addition, he is the founder, publisher, and editor of *Beckett Baseball Card Monthly, Beckett Basketball Card Monthly, Beckett Football Card Monthly, Beckett Hockey Collector, Beckett Sports Collectibles,* and *Beckett Racing & Motorsports Marketplace* magazines.

Jim Beckett received his Ph.D. in Statistics from Southern Methodist University in 1975. Prior to starting Beckett Publications in 1984, Dr. Beckett served as an Associate Professor of Statistics at Bowling Green State University and as a vice president of a consulting firm in Dallas, Texas.

# How to Use This Book

Isn't it great? Every year this book gets bigger and bigger with all the new sets coming out. But even more exciting is that every year there are more collectors, more shows, more stores, and more interest in the cards we love so much. This edition has been enhanced and expanded from the previous edition. The cards you collect — who appears on them, what they look like, where they are from, and (most important to most of you) what their current values are — are enumerated within. Many of the features contained in the other *Beckett Price Guides* have been incorporated into this volume since condition grading, terminology, and many other aspects of collecting are common to the card hobby in general. We hope you find the book both interesting and useful in your collecting pursuits.

The *Beckett Guide* has been successful where other attempts have failed because it is complete, current, and valid. This Price Guide contains not just one, but two prices by condition for all the baseball cards listed. The prices were added to the card lists just prior to printing and reflect not the author's opinions or desires but the going retail prices for each card, based on the marketplace (sports memorabilia conventions and shows, sports card shops, hobby papers, current mail-order catalogs, local club meetings, auction results, and other firsthand reportings of actually realized prices).

What is the best price guide available on the market today? Of course, card sellers prefer the price guide with the highest prices, while card buyers naturally prefer the one with the lowest prices. Accuracy, however, is the true test. Use the price guide trusted by more collectors and dealers than all the others combined. Look for the *Beckett®* name. I won't put my name on anything I won't stake my reputation on. Not the lowest and not the highest—but the most accurate, with integrity.

To facilitate your use of this book, read the complete introductory section on the following pages before going to the pricing pages. Every collectible field has its own terminology; we've tried to capture most of these terms and definitions in our glossary. Please read carefully the section on grading and the condition of your cards, as you cannot determine which price column is appropriate for a given card without first knowing its condition.

Welcome to the world of baseball cards.

# How to Collect

Each collection is personal and reflects the individuality of its owner. There are no set rules on how to collect cards. Since card collecting is a hobby or leisure pastime, what you collect, how much you collect, and how much time and money you spend collecting are entirely up to you. The funds you have available for collecting and your own personal taste should determine how you collect. Information and ideas presented here are intended to help you get the most enjoyment from this hobby.

It is impossible to collect every card ever produced. Therefore, beginners as well as intermediate and advanced collectors usually specialize in some way. One of the reasons this hobby is popular is that individual collectors can define and tailor their collecting methods to match their own tastes. To give you some ideas of the various approaches to collecting, we will list some of the more popular areas of specialization.

Many collectors select complete sets from particular years. For example, they may concentrate on assembling complete sets from all the years since their birth or since they became avid sports fans. They may try to collect a card for every player during that specified period of time.

Many others wish to acquire only certain players. Usually such players are the superstars of the sport, but occasionally collectors will specialize in all the cards of players who attended a particular college or came from a certain town. Some collectors are only interested in the first cards or Rookie Cards of certain players. A handy guide for collectors interested in pursuing the hobby this way is the *Beckett Baseball Card Alphabetical Checklist.*

Another fun way to collect cards is by team. Most fans have a favorite team, and it is natural for that loyalty to be translated into a desire for cards of the players on that favorite team. For most of the recent years, team sets (all the cards from a given team for that year) are readily available at a reasonable price.

### Obtaining Cards

Several avenues are open to card collectors. Cards still can be purchased in the traditional way: by the pack at the local candy, grocery, drug or major discount stores.

But there are also thousands of card shops across the country that specialize in selling cards individually or by the pack, box, or set. Another alternative is the thousands of card shows held each month around the country, which feature anywhere from eight to 800 tables of sports cards and memorabilia for sale.

For many years, it has been possible to purchase complete sets of baseball cards through mail-order advertisers found in traditional sports media publications, such as *The Sporting News, Baseball Digest, Street & Smith* yearbooks, and others. These sets also are advertised in the card collecting periodicals. Many collectors will begin by subscribing to at least one of the hobby periodicals, all with good up-to-date information. In fact, subscription offers can be found in the advertising section of this book.

Most serious card collectors obtain old (and new) cards from one or more of several main sources: (1) trading or buying from other collectors or dealers; (2) responding to sale or auction ads in the hobby publications; (3) buying at a local hobby store; and/or (4) attending sports collectibles shows or conventions.

We advise that you try all four methods since each has its own distinct advantages: (1) trading is a great way to make new friends; (2) hobby periodicals help you keep up with what's going on in the hobby (including when and where the conventions are happening); (3) stores provide the opportunity to enjoy personalized service and consider a great diversity of material in a relaxed sports-oriented atmosphere; and (4) shows allow you to choose from multiple dealers and thousands of cards under one roof in a competitive situation.

## Preserving Your Cards

Cards are fragile. They must be handled properly in order to retain their value. Careless handling can easily result in creased or bent cards. It is, however, not recommended that tweezers or tongs be used to pick up your cards since such utensils might mar or indent card surfaces and thus reduce those cards' conditions and values.

In general, your cards should be handled directly as little as possible. This is sometimes easier to say than to do.

Although there are still many who use custom boxes, storage trays, or even shoe boxes, plastic sheets are the preferred method of many collectors for storing cards.

A collection stored in plastic pages in a three-ring album allows you to view your collection at any time without the need to touch the card itself. Cards can also be kept in single holders (of various types and thickness) designed for the enjoyment of each card individually.

For a large collection, some collectors may use a combination of the above methods. When purchasing plastic sheets for your cards, be sure that you find the pocket size that fits the cards snugly. Don't put your 1951 Bowman in a sheet designed to fit 1981 Topps.

Most hobby and collectibles shops and virtually all collectors' conventions will have these plastic pages available in quantity for the various sizes offered, or you can purchase them directly from the advertisers in this book.

Also, remember that pocket size isn't the only factor to consider when looking for plastic sheets. Other factors such as safety, economy, appearance, availability, or personal preference also may indicate which types of sheets a collector may want to buy.

Damp, sunny and/or hot conditions — no, this is not a weather forecast — are three elements to avoid in extremes if you are interested in preserving your collection. Too much (or too little) humidity can cause the gradual deterioration of a card. Direct, bright sun (or fluorescent light) over time will bleach out the color of a card. Extreme heat accelerates the decomposition of the card. On the other hand, many cards have lasted more than 75 years without much scientific intervention. So be cautious, even if the above factors typically present a problem only when present in the extreme. It never hurts to be prudent.

## Collecting vs. Investing

Collecting individual players cards and collecting complete sets are both popular vehicles for investment and speculation.

Most investors and speculators stock up on complete sets or on quantities of individual players cards they think have good investment potential.

There is obviously no guarantee in this book, or anywhere else for that matter, that cards will outperform the stock market or other investment alternatives in the future. After all, baseball cards do not pay quarterly dividends and cards cannot be sold at their "current values" as easily as stocks or bonds.

Nevertheless, investors have noticed a favorable long-term trend in the past performance of baseball and other sports collectibles, and certain cards and sets have outperformed just about any other investment in some years.

Many hobbyists maintain that the best investment is and always will be the building of a collection, which traditionally has held up better than outright speculation.

Some of the obvious questions are: Which cards? When to buy? When to sell? The best investment you can make is in your own education.

The more you know about your collection and the hobby, the more informed the decisions you will be able to make. We're not selling investment tips. We're selling information about the current value of baseball cards. It's up to you to use that information to your best advantage.

# Terminology

Each hobby has its own language to describe its area of interest. The nomenclature traditionally used for trading cards is derived from the American Card Catalog, published in 1960 by Nostalgia Press. That catalog, written by Jefferson Burdick (who is called the "Father of Card Collecting" for his pioneering work), uses letter and number designations for each separate set of cards. The letter used in the ACC designation refers to the generic type of card. While both sport and non-sport issues are classified in the ACC, we shall confine ourselves to the sport issues. The following list defines the letters and their meanings as used by the American Card Catalog.

**(none) or N** - 19th Century U.S. Tobacco
**B** - Blankets
**D** - Bakery Inserts Including Bread
**E** - Early Candy and Gum
**F** - Food Inserts
**H** - Advertising
**M** - Periodicals
**PC** - Postcards
**R** - Candy and Gum since 1930

Following the letter prefix and an optional hyphen are one-, two-, or three-digit numbers, R(-)999. These typically represent the company or entity issuing the cards. In several cases, the ACC number is extended by an additional hyphen and another one- or two-digit numerical suffix. For example, the 1957 Topps regular-series baseball card issue carries an ACC designation of R414-11. The "R" indicates a Candy or Gum card produced since 1930. The "414" is the ACC designation for Topps Chewing Gum baseball card issues, and the "11" is the ACC designation for the 1957 regular issue (Topps' eleventh baseball set). Like other traditional methods of identification, this system provides order to the process of cataloging cards; however, most serious collectors learn the ACC designation of the popular sets by repetition and familiarity, rather than by attempting to "figure out" what they might or should be. From 1948 forward, collectors and dealers commonly refer to all sets by their year, maker, type of issue, and any other distinguishing characteristic. For example, such a characteristic could be an unusual issue or one of several regular issues put out by a specific maker in a single year. Regional issues are usually referred to by year, maker, and sometimes by title or theme of the set.

# Glossary/Legend

Our glossary defines terms used in the card collecting hobby and in this book. Many of these terms are also common to other types of sports memorabilia collecting. Some terms may have several meanings depending on use and context.

**ACETATE** - A transparent plastic.

**AS** - All-Star card. A card portraying an All-Star Player of the previous year that says "All-Star" on its face.

**ATG** - All-Time Great card.

**ATL** - All-Time Leaders card.

**AU(TO)** - Autographed card.

**BC** - Bonus Card.

**BL** - Blue letters.

**BOX CARD** - Card issued on a box (i.e., 1987 Topps Box Bottoms).

**BRICK** - A group of 50 or more cards having common characteristics that is intended to be bought, sold or traded as a unit.

**CABINETS** - Popular and highly valuable photographs on thick card stock produced in the 19th and early 20th century.

**CHECKLIST** - A list of the cards contained in a particular set. The list is always in numerical order if the cards are numbered. Some unnumbered sets are artificially numbered in alphabetical order, by team and alphabetically within the team, or by uniform number for convenience.

**CL** - Checklist card. A card that lists in order the cards and players in the set or series. Older checklist cards in Mint condition that have not been marked are very desirable and command premiums.

**CO** - Coach.

**COMM** - Commissioner.

**COMMON CARD** - The typical card of any set; it has no premium value accruing from subject matter, numerical scarcity, popular demand, or anomaly.

**CONVENTION** - A gathering of dealers and collectors at a single location for the purpose of buying, selling, and trading sports memorabilia items. Conventions are open to the public and sometimes feature autograph guests, door prizes, contests, seminars, etc. They are frequently referred to simply as "shows."

**COOP** - Cooperstown.

**COR** - Corrected card.

**CY** - Cy Young Award.

**DEALER** - A person who engages in buying, selling, and trading sports collectibles or supplies. A dealer may also be a collector, but as a dealer, his main goal is to earn a profit.

**DIE-CUT** - A card with part of its stock partially cut, allowing one or more parts to be folded or removed. After removal or appropriate folding, the remaining part of the card can frequently be made to stand.

**DK** - Diamond King.

**DL** - Division Leaders.

**DP** - Double Print (a card that was printed in double the quantity compared to the other cards in the same series) or a Draft Pick card.

**DUFEX** - A method of card manufacturing technology patented by Pinnacle Brands, Inc. It involves a refractive quality to a card with a foil coating.

**ERA** - Earned Run Average.

**ERR** - Error card. A card with erroneous information, spelling, or depiction on either side of the card. Most errors are not corrected by the producing card company.

**FDP** - First or First Round Draft Pick.

**FOIL** - Foil embossed stamp on card.

**FOLD** - Foldout.

**FS** - Father/son card.

**FUN** - Fun Cards.

**GL** - Green letters.

**GLOSS** - A card with luster; a shiny finish as in a card with UV coating.

**HIGH NUMBER** - The cards in the last series of numbers in a year in which such higher-numbered cards were printed or distributed in significantly lesser amounts than the lower-numbered cards. The high-number designation refers to a scarcity of the high-numbered cards. Not all years have high numbers in terms of this definition.

**HL** - Highlight card.

**HOF** - Hall of Fame, or a card that portrays a Hall of Famer (HOFer).

**HOLOGRAM** - A three-dimensional photographic image.

**HOR** - Horizontal pose on card as opposed to the standard vertical orientation found on most cards.

**IA** - In Action card.

**IF** - Infielder.

**INSERT** - A card of a different type or any other sports collectible (typically a poster or sticker) contained and sold in the same package along with a card or cards of a major set. An insert card is either unnumbered or not numbered in the same sequence as the major set. Sometimes the inserts are randomly distributed and are not found in every pack.

**INTERACTIVE** - A concept that involves collector participation.

**ISSUE** - Synonymous with set, but usually used in conjunction with a manufacturer, e.g., a Topps issue.

**LHP** - Lefthanded pitcher.

**LL** - League leaders or large letters on card.

**MAJOR SET** - A set produced by a national manufacturer of cards containing a large number of cards. Usually 100 or more different cards comprise a major set.

**MEM** - Memorial card. For example, the 1990 Donruss and Topps Bart Giamatti cards.

**METALLIC** - A glossy design method that enhances card features.

**MG** - Manager.

**MINI** - A small card; for example, a 1975 Topps card of identical design but smaller dimensions than the regular Topps issue of 1975.

**ML** - Major League.

**MULTI-PLAYER CARD** - A single card depicting two or more players (but not a team card).

**MVP** - Most Valuable Player.

**NAU** - No autograph on card.

**NH** - No-Hitter.

**NNOF** - No Name on Front.

**NOF** - Name on Front.

**NOTCHING** - The grooving of the card, usually caused by fingernails, rubber bands, or bumping card edges against other objects.

**OF** - Outfield or Outfielder.

**OLY** - Olympics Card.

**P** - Pitcher or Pitching pose.

**P1** - First Printing.

**P2** - Second Printing.

**P3** - Third Printing.

**PACKS** - A means by which cards are issued in terms of pack type (wax, cello, foil, rack, etc.) and channels of distribution (hobby, retail, etc.).

**PARALLEL**- A card that is similar in design to its counterpart from a basic set, but offers a distinguishing quality.

**PF** - Profiles.

**PLASTIC SHEET** - A clear, plastic page that is punched for insertion into a binder (with standard three-ring spacing) containing pockets for displaying cards. Many different styles of sheets exist with pockets of varying sizes to hold the many differing card formats. Also called a display sheet or storage sheet.

**PLATINUM** - A metallic element used in the process of creating a glossy card.

**PR** - Printed name on back.

**PREMIUM** - A card, sometimes on photographic stock, that is purchased or obtained in conjunction with, or redemption for, another card or product. The premium is not packaged in the same unit as the primary item.

**PRES** - President.

**PRISMATIC/PRISM** - A glossy or bright design that refracts or disperses light.

**PUZZLE CARD** - A card whose back contains a part of a picture which, when joined correctly with other puzzle cards, forms the completed picture.

**PUZZLE PIECE** - A die-cut piece designed to interlock with similar pieces (e.g., early 1980s Donruss).

**PVC** - Polyvinyl chloride, a substance used to make many of the popular card display protective sheets. Non-PVC sheets are considered preferable for long-term storage of cards by many.

**RARE** - A card or series of cards of very limited availability. Unfortunately, "rare" is a subjective term frequently used indiscriminately to hype value. "Rare" cards are harder to obtain than "scarce" cards.

**RB** - Record Breaker.

**REDEMPTION** - A program established by multiple card manufacturers that allows collectors to mail in a special card (usually a random insert) in return for special cards, sets or other prizes not available through conventional channels.

**REFRACTORS** - A card that features a design element which enhances (distorts) its color/appearance through deflecting light.

**REV NEG** - Reversed or flopped photo side of the card. This is a major type of error card, but only some are corrected.

**RHP** - Right-handed pitcher.

**ROY** - Rookie of the Year.

**RP** - Relief pitcher.

**SA** - Super Action card.

**SASE** - Self-Addressed, Stamped Envelope.

**SB** - Stolen Bases.

**SCARCE** - A card or series of cards of limited availability. This subjective term is sometimes used indiscriminately to hype value. "Scarce" cards are not as difficult to obtain as "rare" cards.

**SCR** - Script name on back.

**SD** - San Diego Padres.

**SEMI-HIGH** - A card from the next-to-last series of a sequentially issued set. It has more value than an average card and generally less value than a high number. A card is not called a semi-high unless the next-to-last series in which it exists has an additional premium attached to it.

**SERIES** - The entire set of cards issued by a particular producer in a particular year; e.g., the 1971 Topps series. Also, within a particular set, series can refer to a group of (consecutively numbered) cards printed at the same time; e.g., the first series of the 1957 Topps issue (#1 through #88).

**SET** - One each of the entire run of cards of the same type produced by a particular manufacturer during a single year. In other words, if you have a complete set of 1976 Topps then you have every card from #1 up to and including #660, i.e., all the different cards that were produced.

**SF** - Starflics.

**SHEEN** - Brightness or luster emitted by a card.

**SKIP-NUMBERED** - A set that has many unissued card numbers between the lowest number in the set and the highest number in the set; e.g., the 1948 Leaf baseball set contains 98 cards skip-numbered from #1 to #168. A major set in which a few numbers were not printed is not considered to be skip-numbered.

**SP** - Single or Short Print (a card which was printed in lesser quantity compared to the other cards in the same series; see also DP and TP).

**SPECIAL CARD** - A card that portrays something other than a single player or team; for example, a card that portrays the previous year's statistical leaders or the results from the previous year's World Series.

**SS** - Shortstop.

**STANDARD SIZE** - Most modern sports cards measure 2-1/2 by 3-1/2 inches. Exceptions are noted in card descriptions throughout this book.

**STAR CARD** - A card that portrays a player of some repute, usually determined by his ability; however, sometimes referring to sheer popularity.

**STOCK** - The cardboard or paper on which the card is printed.

**SUPERIMPOSED** - To be affixed on top of something, i.e., a player photo over a solid background.

**SUPERSTAR CARD** - A card that portrays a superstar; e.g., a Hall of Famer or player with strong Hall of Fame potential.

**TC** - Team Checklist.

**TEAM CARD** - A card that depicts an entire team.

**THREE-DIMENSIONAL (3D)** - A visual image that provides an illusion of depth and perspective.

**TOPICAL** - A subset or group of cards that have a common theme (e.g., MVP award winners).

**TP** - Triple Print (a card that was printed in triple the quantity compared to the other cards in the same series).

**TRANSPARENT** - Clear, see-through.

**TR** - Trade reference on card.

**UDCA** - Upper Deck Classic Alumni.

**UER** - Uncorrected Error.

**UMP** - Umpire.

**USA** - Team USA.

**UV** - Ultraviolet, a glossy coating used in producing cards.

**VAR** - Variation card. One of two or more cards from the same series with the same number (or player with identical pose if the series is unnumbered) differing from one another by some aspect, the different feature stemming from the printing or stock of the card. This can be caused when the manufacturer of the cards notices an error in one or more of the cards, makes the changes, and then resumes the print run. In this case there will be two versions or variations of the same card. Sometimes one of the variations is relatively scarce.

**VERT** - Vertical pose on card.
**WAS** - Washington National League (1974 Topps).
**WC** - What's the Call?
**WL** - White letter on front.
**WS** - World Series card.
**YL** - Yellow letters on front
**YT** - Yellow team name on front.
* - To denote multi-sport sets.

# Understanding Card Values

## Determining Value

Why are some cards more valuable than others? Obviously, the economic laws of supply and demand are applicable to card collecting just as they are to any other field where a commodity is bought, sold or traded in a free, unregulated market.

Supply (the number of cards available on the market) is less than the total number of cards originally produced since attrition diminishes that original quantity. Each year a percentage of cards is typically thrown away, destroyed or otherwise lost to collectors. This percentage is much, much smaller today than it was in the past because more and more people have become increasingly aware of the value of their cards.

For those who collect only Mint condition cards, the supply of older cards can be quite small indeed. Until recently, collectors were not so conscious of the need to preserve the condition of their cards. For this reason, it is difficult to know exactly how many 1953 Topps are currently available, Mint or otherwise. It is generally accepted that there are fewer 1953 Topps available than 1963, 1973 or 1983 Topps cards. If demand were equal for each of these sets, the law of supply and demand would increase the price for the least available sets. Demand, however, is never equal for all sets, so price correlations can be complicated. The demand for a card is influenced by many factors. These include: (1) the age of the card; (2) the number of cards printed; (3) the player(s) portrayed on the card; (4) the attractiveness and popularity of the set; and (5) the physical condition of the card.

In general, (1) the older the card, (2) the fewer the number of the cards printed, (3) the more famous, popular and talented the player, (4) the more attractive and popular the set, and (5) the better the condition of the card, the higher the value of the card will be. There are exceptions to all but one of these factors: the condition of the card. Given two cards similar in all respects except condition, the one in the best condition will always be valued higher.

While those guidelines help to establish the value of a card, the countless exceptions and peculiarities make any simple, direct mathematical formula to determine card values impossible.

## Regional Variation

Since the market varies from region to region, card prices of local players may be higher. This is known as a regional premium. How significant the premium is — and if there is any premium at all — depends on the local popularity of the team and the player.

The largest regional premiums usually do not apply to superstars, who often are so well known nationwide that the prices of their key cards are too high for local dealers to realize a premium.

Lesser stars often command the strongest premiums. Their popularity is concentrated in their home region, creating local demand that greatly exceeds overall demand.

Regional premiums can apply to popular retired players and sometimes can be found in the areas where the players grew up or starred in college.

A regional discount is the converse of a regional premium. Regional discounts occur when a player has been so popular in his region for so long that local collectors and dealers have accumulated quantities of his key cards. The abundant supply may make the cards available in that area at the lowest prices anywhere.

## Set Prices

A somewhat paradoxical situation exists in the price of a complete set vs. the combined cost of the individual cards in the set. In nearly every case, the sum of the prices for the individual cards is higher than the cost for the complete set. This is prevalent especially in the cards of the last few years. The reasons for this apparent anomaly stem from the habits of collectors and from the carrying costs to dealers. Today, each card in a set normally is produced in the same quantity as all other cards in its set.

Many collectors pick up only stars, superstars, and particular teams. As a result, the dealer is left with a shortage of certain player cards and an abundance of others. He therefore incurs an expense in simply "carrying" these less desirable cards in stock. On the other hand, if he sells a complete set, he gets rid of large numbers of cards at one time. For this reason, he generally is willing to receive less money for a complete set. By doing this, he recovers all of his costs and also makes a profit.

The disparity between the price of the complete set and the sum of the individual cards also has been influenced by the fact that some of the major manufacturers now are pre-collating card sets. Since "pulling" individual cards from the sets involves a specific type of labor (and cost), the singles or star card market is not affected significantly by pre-collation.

Set prices also do not include rare card varieties, unless specifically stated. Of course, the prices for sets do include one example of each type for the given set, but this is the least expensive variety.

## Scarce Series

Scarce series occur because cards issued before 1974 were made available to the public each year in several series of finite numbers of cards, rather than all cards of the set being available for purchase at one time. At some point during the year, usually toward the end of the baseball season, interest in current year baseball cards waned. Consequently, the manufacturers produced smaller numbers of these later-series cards.

Nearly all nationwide issues from post–World War II manufacturers (1948 to 1973) exhibit these series variations. In the past, Topps, for example, may have issued series consisting of many different numbers of cards, including 55, 66, 80, 88 and others. Recently, Topps has settled on what is now its standard sheet size of 132 cards, six of which comprise its 792-card set.

While the number of cards within a given series is usually the same as the number of cards on one printed sheet, this is not always the case. For example, Bowman used 36 cards on its standard printed sheets, but in 1948 substituted 12 cards during later print runs of that year's baseball cards. Twelve of the cards from the initial sheet of 36 cards were removed and replaced by 12 different cards giving, in effect, a first series of 36 cards and a second series of 12 new cards. This replacement produced a scarcity of 24 cards — the 12 cards removed from the original sheet and the 12 new cards added to the sheet. A full sheet of 1948 Bowman cards (second printing) shows that card numbers 37 through 48 have replaced 12 of the cards on the first printing sheet.

The Topps Company also has created scarcities and/or excesses of certain cards in many of its sets. Topps, however, has most frequently gone in the other direction by double printing some of the cards. Double printing causes an abundance of cards of the players who are on the same sheet more than one time. During the years from 1978 to 1981, Topps double printed 66 cards out of their large 726-card set. The Topps practice of double printing cards in earlier years is the most logical explanation for the known scarcities of particular cards in some of these Topps sets.

From 1988 through 1990, Donruss short printed and double printed certain cards in its major sets. Ostensibly this was because of its addition of bonus team MVP cards in its regular-issue wax packs. In the last couple of years, card companies have been printing specific subsets (usually young players or rookie cards) in shorter supply than the regular cards.

We are always looking for information or photographs of printing sheets of cards for research. Each year, we try to update the hobby's knowledge of distribution anomalies. Please let us know at the address in this book if you have firsthand knowledge that would be helpful in this pursuit.

# Grading Your Cards

Each hobby has its own grading terminology — stamps, coins, comic books, record collecting, etc. Collectors of sports cards are no exception. The one invariable criterion for determining the value of a card is its condition: The better the condition of the card, the more valuable it is. Condition grading, however, is subjective. Individual card dealers and collectors differ in the strictness of their grading, but the stated condition of a card should be determined without regard to whether it is being bought or sold.

No allowance is made for age. A 1952 card is judged by the same standards as a 1992 card. But there are specific sets and cards that are condition sensitive (marked with "!" in the Price Guide) because of their border color, consistently poor centering, etc. Such cards and sets sometimes command premiums above the listed percentages in Mint condition.

## Centering

Current centering terminology uses numbers representing the percentage of border on either side of the main design. Obviously, centering is diminished in importance for borderless cards such as Stadium Club.

Slightly Off-Center (60/40): A slightly off-center card is one that, upon close inspection, is found to have one border bigger than the opposite border. This degree was once offensive only to purists, but now some hobbyists try to avoid cards that are anything other than perfectly centered.

Off-Center (70/30): An off-center card has one border that is noticeably more than twice as wide as the opposite border.

Badly Off-Center (80/20 or worse): A badly off-center card has virtually no border on one side of the card.

Miscut: A miscut card actually shows part of the adjacent card in its larger border and consequently a corresponding amount of its card is cut off.

## Corner Wear

Corner wear is the most scrutinized grading criterion in the hobby. These are the major categories of corner wear:

**Corner with a slight touch of wear:** The corner is still sharp, but there is a slight touch of wear showing. On a dark-bordered card, this shows as a dot of white.

**Fuzzy corner:** The corner still comes to a point, but the point has just begun to fray. A slightly "dinged" corner is considered the same as a fuzzy corner.

**Slightly rounded corner:** The fraying of the corner has increased to where there is only a hint of a point. Mild layering may be evident. A "dinged" corner is considered the same as a slightly rounded corner.

**Rounded corner:** The point is completely gone. Some layering is noticeable.

**Badly rounded corner:** The corner is completely round and rough. Severe layering is evident.

## Creases

A third common defect is the crease. The degree of creasing in a card is difficult to show in a drawing or picture. On giving the specific condition of an expensive card for sale, the seller should note any creases additionally. Creases can be categorized as to severity according to the following scale:

**Light crease:** A light crease is a crease that is barely noticeable upon close inspection. In fact, when cards are in plastic sheets or holders, a light crease may not be seen (until the card is taken out of the holder). A light crease on the front is much more serious than a light crease on the card back only.

**Medium crease:** A medium crease is noticeable when held and studied at arm's length by the naked eye, but does not overly detract from the appearance of the card. It is an obvious crease, but not one that breaks the picture surface of the card.

**Heavy crease:** A heavy crease is one that has torn or broken through the card's picture surface, e.g., puts a tear in the photo surface.

## Alterations

**Deceptive trimming:** This occurs when someone alters the card in order (1) to shave off edge wear, (2) to improve the sharpness of the corners, or (3) to improve centering — obviously their objective is to falsely increase the perceived value of the card to an unsuspecting buyer. The shrinkage usually is evident only if the trimmed card is compared to an adjacent full-sized card or if the trimmed card is itself measured.

**Obvious trimming:** Obvious trimming is noticeable and unfortunate. It is usually performed by non-collectors who give no thought to the present or future value of their cards.

**Deceptively retouched borders:** This occurs when the borders (especially on those cards with dark borders) are touched up on the edges and corners with magic marker or crayons of appropriate color in order to make the card appear Mint.

## Categorization of Defects—Miscellaneous Flaws

The following are common minor flaws that, depending on severity, lower a card's condition by one to four grades and often render it no better than Excellent-Mint: bubbles (lumps in surface), gum and wax stains, diamond cutting (slanted borders), notching, off-centered backs, paper wrinkles, scratched-off cartoons or puzzles on back, rubber band marks, scratches, surface impressions, and warping.

## Centering

Well-centered

Slightly Off-centered

Off-centered

Badly Off-centered

Miscut

## Corner Wear

**The partial cards here have been photographed at 300%. This was done in order to magnify each card's corner wear to such a degree that differences could be shown on a printed page.**

**The 1962 Topps Mickey Mantle card definitely has a rounded corner. Some may say that this card is badly rounded, but that is a judgment call.**

**The 1962 Topps Hank Aaron card has a slightly rounded corner. Note that there is definite corner wear evident by the fraying and that there is no longer a sharp point to which the corner converges.**

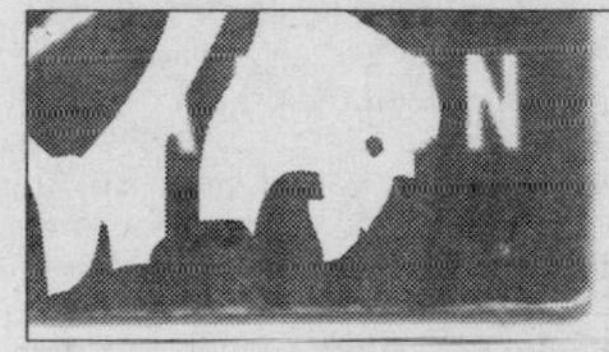

**The 1962 Topps Gil Hodges card has corner wear; it is slightly better than the Aaron card above. Nevertheless, some collectors might classify this Hodges corner as slightly rounded.**

**The 1962 Topps Manager's Dream card showing Mantle and Mays has slight corner wear. This is not a fuzzy corner as very slight wear is noticeable on the card's photo surface.**

**The 1962 Topps Don Mossi card has very slight corner wear such that it might be called a fuzzy corner. A close look at the original card shows that the corner is not perfect, but almost. However, note that corner wear is somewhat academic on this card. As you can plainly see, the heavy crease going across his name breaks through the photo surface.**

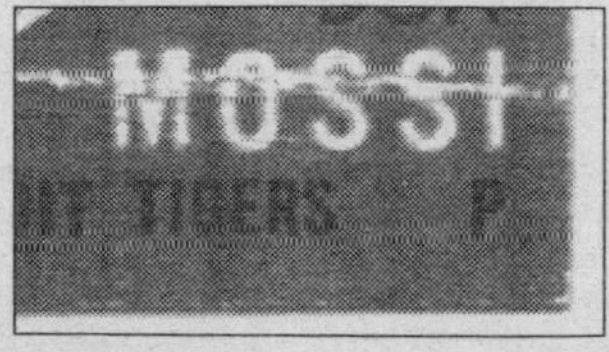

The following are common serious flaws that, depending on severity, lower a card's condition at least four grades and often render it no better than Good: chemical or sun fading, erasure marks, mildew, miscutting (severe off-centering), holes, bleached or retouched borders, tape marks, tears, trimming, water or coffee stains and writing.

# Condition Guide

## Grades

**Mint (Mt)** - A card with no flaws or wear. The card has four perfect corners, 60/40 or better centering from top to bottom and from left to right, original gloss, smooth edges and original color borders. A Mint card does not have print spots, color or focus imperfections.

**Near Mint-Mint (NrMt-Mt)** - A card with one minor flaw. Any one of the following would lower a Mint card to Near Mint-Mint: one corner with a slight touch of wear, barely noticeable print spots, color or focus imperfections. The card must have 60/40 or better centering in both directions, original gloss, smooth edges and original color borders.

**Near Mint (NrMt)** - A card with one minor flaw. Any one of the following would lower a Mint card to Near Mint: one fuzzy corner or two to four corners with slight touches of wear, 70/30 to 60/40 centering, slightly rough edges, minor print spots, color or focus imperfections. The card must have original gloss and original color borders.

**Excellent-Mint (ExMt)** - A card with two or three fuzzy, but not rounded, corners and centering no worse than 80/20. The card may have no more than two of the following: slightly rough edges, very slightly discolored borders, minor print spots, color or focus imperfections. The card must have original gloss.

**Excellent (Ex)** - A card with four fuzzy but definitely not rounded corners and centering no worse than 80/20. The card may have a small amount of original gloss lost, rough edges, slightly discolored borders and minor print spots, color or focus imperfections.

**Very Good (Vg)** - A card that has been handled but not abused: slightly rounded corners with slight layering, slight notching on edges, a significant amount of gloss lost from the surface but no scuffing and moderate discoloration of borders. The card may have a few light creases.

**Good (G), Fair (F), Poor (P)** - A well-worn, mishandled or abused card: badly rounded and layered corners, scuffing, most or all original gloss missing, seriously discolored borders, moderate or heavy creases, and one or more serious flaws. The grade of Good, Fair or Poor depends on the severity of wear and flaws. Good, Fair and Poor cards generally are used only as fillers.

The most widely used grades are defined above. Obviously, many cards will not perfectly fit one of the definitions.

Therefore, categories between the major grades known as in-between grades are used, such as Good to Very Good (G-Vg), Very Good to Excellent (VgEx), and Excellent-Mint to Near Mint (ExMt-NrMt). Such grades indicate a card with all qualities of the lower category but with at least a few qualities of the higher category.

*The Official Price Guide to Baseball Cards* lists each card and set in two grades, with the second grade valued at about 40-45% of the top grade.

The value of cards that fall between the listed columns can also be calculated using a percentage of the top grade. For example, a card that falls between the top and middle grades (ExMt or NrMt in most cases) will generally be valued at anywhere from 50% to 90% of the top grade.

Similarly, a card that falls between the middle and bottom grades (Vg or VgEx in most cases) will generally be valued at anywhere from 20% to 40% of the top grade.

There are also cases where cards are in better condition than the top grade or worse than the bottom grade. Cards that grade worse than the lowest grade are generally valued at 5-10% of the top grade.

When a card exceeds the top grade by one — such as NrMt-Mt when the top grade is NrMt, a premium of up to 50% is possible, with 10-20% the usual norm.

When a card exceeds the top grade by two — such as Mint when the top grade is NrMt, a premium of 25-50% is the usual norm. But certain condition sensitive cards or sets, particularly those from the pre-war era, can bring premiums of up to 100% or even more.

Unopened packs, boxes and factory-collated sets are considered Mint in their unknown (and presumed perfect) state. Once opened, however, each card can be graded (and valued) in its own right by taking into account any defects that may be present in spite of the fact that the card has never been handled.

## Selling Your Cards

Just about every collector sells cards or will sell cards eventually. Someday you may be interested in selling your duplicates or maybe even your whole collection. You may sell to other collectors, friends or dealers. You may even sell cards you purchased from a certain dealer back to that same dealer. In any event, it helps to know some of the mechanics of the typical transaction between buyer and seller.

Dealers will buy cards in order to resell them to other collectors who are interested in the cards. Dealers will always pay a higher percentage for items that (in their opinion) can be resold quickly, and a much lower percentage for those items that are perceived as having low demand and hence are slow moving. In either case, dealers must buy at a price that allows for the expense of doing business and a margin for profit.

If you have cards for sale, the best advice we can give is that you get several offers for your cards — either from card shops or at a card show — and take the best offer, all things considered. Note, the "best" offer may not be the one for the highest amount. And remember, if a dealer really wants your cards, he won't let you get away without making his best competitive offer. Another alternative is to place your cards in an auction as one or several lots.

Many people think nothing of going into a department store and paying $15 for an item of clothing for which the store paid $5. But if you were selling your $15 card to a dealer and he offered you $5 for it, you might consider his mark up unreasonable. To complete the analogy: Most department stores (and card dealers) that consistently pay $10 for $15 items eventually go out of business. An exception is when the dealer has lined up a willing buyer for the item(s) you are attempting to sell, or if the cards are so hot that it's likely he'll likely have to hold the cards for just a short period of time.

In those cases, an offer of up to 75% of book value will still allow the dealer to make a reasonable profit considering the short time he will need to hold the merchandise. In general, however, most cards and collections will bring offers in the range of 25% to 50% of retail price. Also consider that most material from the last five to 10 years is plentiful. If that's what you're selling, don't be surprised if your best offer is well below that range.

# Interesting Notes

The first card numerically of an issue is the single card most likely to obtain excessive wear.

Consequently, you typically will find the price on the #1 card (in NrMt or Mint condition) somewhat higher than might otherwise be the case.

Similarly, but to a lesser extent (because normally the less important, reverse side of the card is the one exposed), the last card numerically in an issue is also prone to abnormal wear. This extra wear and tear occurs because the first and last cards are exposed to the elements (human element included) more than any of the other cards. They are generally end cards in any brick formations, rubber bandings, stackings on wet surfaces, and like activities.

Sports cards have no intrinsic value. The value of a card, like the value of other collectibles, can be determined only by you and your enjoyment in viewing and possessing these cardboard treasures.

Remember, the buyer ultimately determines the price of each baseball card. You are the determining price factor because you have the ability to say No to the price of any card by not exchanging your hard-earned money for a given issue. When the cost of a trading card exceeds the enjoyment you will receive from it, your answer should be No. We assess and report the prices. You set them!

We are always interested in receiving the price input of collectors and dealers. We happily credit major contributors.

We welcome your opinions, since your contributions assist us in ensuring a better guide each year.

If you would like to join our survey list for the next editions of this book and others authored by Dr. Beckett, please send your name and address to Dr. James Beckett, 15850 Dallas Parkway, Dallas, TX 75248.

# History of Baseball Cards

Today's version of the baseball card, with its colorful and ofttimes high-tech fronts and backs, is a far cry from its earliest predecessors. The issue remains cloudy as to which was the very first baseball card ever produced, but the institution of baseball cards dates from the latter half of the 19th century, more than 100 years ago. Early issues, generally printed on heavy cardboard, were of poor quality, with photographs, drawings, and printing far short of today's standards.

Goodwin & Co., of New York, makers of Gypsy Queen, Old Judge, and other cigarette brands, is considered by many to be the first issuer of baseball and other sports cards. Its issues, predominantly sized 1-1/2 by 2-1/2 inches, generally consisted of photographs of baseball players, boxers, wrestlers, and other subjects mounted on stiff cardboard. More than 2,000 different photos of baseball players alone have been identified. These "Old Judges," a collective name commonly used for the Goodwin & Co. cards, were issued from 1886 to 1890 and are treasured parts of many collections today.

Among the other cigarette companies that issued baseball cards still attracting attention today are Allen & Ginter, D. Buchner & Co. (Gold Coin Chewing Tobacco), and P.H. Mayo & Brother. Cards from the first two companies bear colored line drawings, while the Mayos are sepia photographs on black cardboard. In addition to the small-size cards from this era, several tobacco companies issued cabinet-size baseball cards. These "cabinets" were considerably larger than the small cards, usually about 4-1/4 by 6-1/2 inches, and were printed on heavy stock. Goodwin & Co.'s Old Judge cabinets and the

National Tobacco Works' "Newsboy" baseball photos are two that remain popular today.

By 1895, the American Tobacco Company began to dominate its competition. They discontinued baseball card inserts in their cigarette packages (actually slide boxes in those days). The lack of competition in the cigarette market had made these inserts unnecessary. This marked the end of the first era of baseball cards. At the dawn of the 20th century, few baseball cards were being issued. But once again, it was the cigarette companies — particularly, the American Tobacco Company — followed to a lesser extent by the candy and gum makers that revived the practice of including baseball cards with their products. The bulk of these cards, identified in the American Card Catalog (designated hereafter as ACC) as T or E cards for 20th century "Tobacco" or "Early Candy and Gum" issues, respectively, were released from 1909 to 1915.

This romantic and popular era of baseball card collecting produced many desirable items. The most outstanding is the fabled T-206 Honus Wagner card. Other perennial favorites among collectors are the T-206 Eddie Plank card, and the T-206 Magee error card. The former was once the second-most valuable card and only recently relinquished that position to a more distinctive and aesthetically pleasing Napoleon Lajoie card from the 1933-34 Goudey Gum series. The latter misspells the player's name as "Magie," the most famous and most valuable blooper card.

The ingenuity and distinctiveness of this era has yet to be surpassed. Highlights include:

• the T-202 Hassan triple-folders, one of the best-looking and the most distinctive cards ever issued;

• the durable T-201 Mecca double-folders, one of the first sets with players' records on the reverse;

• the T-3 Turkey Reds, the hobby's most popular cabinet card;

• the E-145 Cracker Jacks, the only major set containing Federal League player cards;

• the T-204 Ramlys, with their distinctive black-and-white oval photos and ornate gold borders.

These are but a few of the varieties issued during this period.

## Increasing Popularity

While the American Tobacco Company dominated the field, several other tobacco companies, as well as clothing manufacturers, newspapers and periodicals, game makers, and companies whose identities remain anonymous, also issued cards during this period. In fact, the Collins-McCarthy Candy Company, makers of Zeenuts Pacific Coast League baseball cards, issued cards yearly from 1911 to 1938. Its record for continuous annual card production has been exceeded only by the Topps Chewing Gum Company. The era of the tobacco card issues closed with the onset of World War I, with the exception of the Red Man chewing tobacco sets produced from 1952 to 1955.

The next flurry of card issues broke out in the roaring and prosperous 1920s, the era of the E card. The caramel companies (National Caramel, American Caramel, York Caramel) were the leading distributors of these E cards. In addition, the strip card, a continuous strip with several cards divided by dotted lines or other sectioning features, flourished during this time. While the E cards and the strip cards generally are considered less imaginative than the T cards or the recent candy and gum issues, they still are pursued by many advanced collectors.

Another significant event of the 1920s was the introduction of the arcade card. Taking its designation from its issuer, the Exhibit Supply Company of

Chicago, it is usually known as the "Exhibit" card. Once a trademark of the penny arcades, amusement parks and county fairs across the country, Exhibit machines dispensed nearly postcard-size photos on thick stock for one penny. These picture cards bore likenesses of a favorite cowboy, actor, actress or baseball player. Exhibit Supply and its associated companies produced baseball cards during a longer time span, although discontinuous, than any other manufacturer. Its first cards appeared in 1921, while its last issue was in 1966. In 1979, the Exhibit Supply Company was bought and somewhat revived by a collector/dealer who has since reprinted Exhibit photos of the past.

If the T card period, from 1909 to 1915, can be designated the Golden Age of baseball card collecting, then perhaps the "Silver Age" commenced with the introduction of the Big League Gum series of 239 cards in 1933 (a 240th card was added in 1934). These are the forerunners of today's baseball gum cards, and the Goudey Gum Company of Boston is responsible for their success. This era spanned the period from the Depression days of 1933 to America's formal involvement in World War II in 1941.

Goudey's attractive designs, with full-color line drawings on thick card stock, greatly influenced other cards being issued at that time. As a result, the most attractive and popular vintage cards in history were produced in this Silver Age. The 1933 Goudey Big League Gum series also owes its popularity to the more than 40 Hall of Fame players in the set. These include four cards of Babe Ruth and two of Lou Gehrig. Goudey's reign continued in 1934, when it issued a 96-card set in color, together with the single remaining card from the 1933 series, #106, the Napoleon Lajoie card.

In addition to Goudey, several other bubblegum manufacturers issued baseball cards during this era. DeLong Gum Company issued an extremely attractive set in 1933. National Chicle Company's 192-card Batter-Up series of 1934-1936 became the largest die-cut set in card history. In addition, that company offered the popular Diamond Stars series during the same period. Other popular sets included the Tattoo Orbit set of 60 color cards issued in 1933 and Gum Products' 75-card Double Play set, featuring sepia depictions of two players per card.

In 1939, Gum Inc., which later became Bowman Gum, replaced Goudey Gum as the leading baseball card producer. In 1939 and the following year, it issued two important sets of black-and-white cards. In 1939, its Play Ball America set consisted of 162 cards. The larger, 240-card Play Ball set of 1940 is still considered by many to be the most attractive black-and-white cards ever produced. That firm introduced its only color set in 1941, consisting of 72 cards titled Play Ball Sports Hall of Fame. Many of these were colored repeats of poses from the black-and-white 1940 series.

In addition to regular gum cards, many manufacturers distributed premium issues during the 1930s. These premiums were printed on paper or photographic stock, rather than card stock. They were much larger than the regular cards and were sold for a penny across the counter with gum (which was packaged separately from the premium). They were often redeemed at the store or through the mail in exchange for the wrappers of previously purchased gum cards, like proof-of-purchase box-top premiums today. The gum premiums are scarcer than the card issues of the 1930s and in most cases no manufacturer's name is present.

World War II brought an end to this popular era of card collecting when paper and rubber shortages curtailed the production of bubblegum baseball cards. They were resurrected again in 1948 by the Bowman Gum Company (the direct descendant of Gum, Inc.) This marked the beginning of the modern era of card collecting.

In 1948, Bowman Gum issued a 48-card set in black and white consisting of one card and one slab of gum in every 1-cent pack. That same year, the Leaf Gum Company also issued a set of cards. Although rather poor in quality, these cards were issued in color. A squabble over the rights to use players' pictures developed between Bowman and Leaf. Eventually Leaf dropped out of the card market, but not before it had left a lasting heritage to the hobby by issuing some of the rarest cards now in existence. Leaf's baseball card series of 1948-49 contained 98 cards, skip-numbered to #168 (not all numbers were printed). Of these 98 cards, 49 are relatively plentiful; the other 49, however, are rare and quite valuable.

Bowman continued its production of cards in 1949 with a color series of 240 cards. Because there are many scarce "high numbers," this series remains the most difficult Bowman regular issue to complete. Although the set was printed in color and commands great interest due to its scarcity, it is considered aesthetically inferior to the Goudey and National Chicle issues of the 1930s. In addition to the regular issue of 1949, Bowman also produced a set of 36 Pacific Coast League players. While this was not a regular issue, it is still prized by collectors. In fact, it has become the most valuable Bowman series.

In 1950 (representing Bowman's one-year monopoly of the baseball card market), the company began a string of top quality cards that continued until its demise in 1955. The 1950 series was itself something of an oddity because the low numbers, rather than the traditional high numbers, were the more difficult cards to obtain.

The year 1951 marked the beginning of the most competitive and perhaps the highest quality period of baseball card production. In that year, Topps Chewing Gum Company of Brooklyn entered the market. Topps' 1951 series consisted of two sets of 52 cards each, one set with red backs and the other with blue backs. In addition, Topps also issued 31 insert cards, three of which remain the rarest Topps cards ("Current All-Stars" Konstanty, Roberts and Stanky). The 1951 Topps cards were unattractive and paled in comparison to the 1951 Bowman issues. They were successful, however, and Topps has continued to produce cards ever since.

## Intensified Competition

Topps issued a larger and more attractive card set in 1952. This larger size became standard for the next five years. (Bowman followed with larger-size baseball cards in 1953.) This 1952 Topps set has become, like the 1933 Goudey series and the T-206 white border series, the classic set of its era. The 407-card set is a collector's dream of scarcities, rarities, errors and variations. It also contains the first Topps issues of Mickey Mantle and Willie Mays.

As with Bowman and Leaf in the late 1940s, competition over player rights arose. Ensuing court battles occurred between Topps and Bowman. The market split due to stiff competition, and in January 1956, Topps bought out Bowman. (Topps, using the Bowman name, resurrected Bowman as a later label in 1989.) Topps remained essentially unchallenged as the primary producer of baseball cards through 1980. So, the story of major baseball card sets from 1956 through 1980 is by and large the story of Topps' issues. Notable exceptions include the small sets produced by Fleer Gum in 1959, 1960, 1961 and 1963, and the Kellogg's Cereal and Hostess Cakes baseball cards issued to promote their products.

A court decision in 1980 paved the way for two other large gum companies to enter (or reenter, in Fleer's case) the baseball card arena. Fleer, which had last made photo cards in 1963, and the Donruss Company (then a division of General Mills) secured rights to produce baseball cards of current players, thus breaking Topps' monopoly. Each company issued major card sets in 1981 with bubblegum products.

Then a higher court decision in that year overturned the lower court ruling against Topps. It appeared that Topps had regained its sole position as a producer of baseball cards. Undaunted by the revocation ruling, Fleer and Donruss continued to issue cards in 1982 but without bubblegum or any other edible product. Fleer issued its current player baseball cards with "team logo stickers," while Donruss issued its cards with a piece of a baseball jigsaw puzzle.

### Sharing the Pie

From 1981 to 1987, the three major companies solidified their leadership position. The growth and popularity of these newer cards helped in bringing along two new companies by 1989: Score (debut set in 1988) and Upper Deck (debut set in 1989). These five companies were about to embark on a wild ride through the 1990s.

Upper Deck's successful entry into the market turned out to be very important. The company's card stock, photography, packaging and marketing gave baseball cards a new standard for quality, and began the "premium card" trend that continues today. The second premium baseball card set to be issued was the 1990 Leaf set, named for and issued by the parent company of Donruss. To gauge the significance of the premium card trend, one need only note that two of the most valuable post-1986 regular-issue cards in the hobby are the 1989 Upper Deck Ken Griffey Jr. and 1990 Leaf Frank Thomas Rookie Cards.

The impressive debut of Leaf in 1990 was followed by Studio, Ultra, and Stadium Club in 1991. Of those, Stadium Club with its dramatic borderless photo and uncoated card fronts made the biggest impact. In 1992, Bowman and Pinnacle joined the premium fray. In 1992, Donruss and Fleer abandoned the traditional 50-cent-pack market and instead produced premium sets comparable to (and presumably designed to compete against) Upper Deck's set. Those moves, combined with the almost instantaneous spread of premium cards to the other major team sports cards, served as strong indicators that premium cards were here to stay. Bowman had been a lower-level product from 1989 to '91.

In 1993, Fleer, Topps and Upper Deck produced the first super-premium cards with Flair, Finest and SP, respectively. The success of all three products was an indication the baseball card market was headed toward even higher price levels, and that turned out to be the case in 1994 with the introduction of Bowman's Best (a Topps hybrid of prospect-oriented Bowman and the super-premium Finest) and Leaf Limited. Other 1994 debuts included Upper Deck's entry-level Collector's Choice and Pinnacle's hobby-only Select.

Overall, inserts continued to dominate the hobby scene. Specifically, the parallel chase cards first introduced in 1992 with Topps Gold became the latest major hobby trend. Topps Gold was followed by 1993 Finest Refractors (at the time the scarcest insert ever produced and still a landmark set), and the one-per-box Stadium Club First Day Issue.

Of course, the biggest on-field news of 1994 was the owner-provoked players strike that halted the season prematurely. While the baseball card hobby suffered noticeably from the strike, there was no catastrophic market crash as some had feared. However, the strike pulled the plug on a market that was both strong and growing, and contributed to a serious hobby contraction that continues to this day.

By 1995, parallel insert sets were commonplace and had taken on a new complexion: the most popular ones were those that had announced (or at least suspected) print runs of 500 or less, such as Finest Refractors and Select Artist's Proofs.

This trend continued in 1996, with several parallel inserts that were printed in quantities of 250 or less such as Finest Gold Refractors, Fleer Circa Rave, Studio Silver Press Proofs and three of the six Select Certified parallels. It could be argued that the high price tags on these extremely limited parallel cards (many exceeded the $1000 plateau) were driving many single-player collectors to frustration, and even completely out of the hobby. At the same time, average pack prices soared while average number of cards per pack dropped, making the baseball card hobby increasingly more expensive.

On the positive side, two trends from 1996 clearly brought in new collectors: Topp's Mickey Mantle retrospective inserts in both series of Topps and Stadium Club; and Leaf's Signature Series, which included one certified autograph per pack. While the Mantle craze following his passing seemed to be a short-term phenomenon, the inclusion of autographs in packs seemed to have more long-term significance.

In 1997 the print runs in selected sets got even lower. Both Fleer/SkyBox and Pinnacle brands issued cards of which only one exists.

The growth in popularity of autographs also continued. Many products had autographed cards in their packs. A very positive trend was a return to basics. Many collectors bought Rookie Cards as they understood that concept and worked on finishing sets.

There was also an increase in international players collecting. Hideo Nomo was incredibly popular in Japan while Chan Ho Park was in demand in Korea. This bodes well for an international growth in the hobby.

1998 was a year of rebirth and growth for the hobby, led by the home run chase of Mark McGwire and Sammy Sosa as well as the continued brilliance of stalwarts like Ken Griffey Jr. and Roger Clemens. The baseball card hobby got a considerable boost and positive publicity it had not seen in many years.

The Rookie Cards of these players as well as many others showed significant gains as the hobby started accepting Rookie Cards again as the most popular trend in collecting. Also, cards which were professionally graded by companies such as PSA and SGC (and in 1999, BGS) were becoming more heavily traded for both older and newer cards.

In addition, the Internet and various services (eBay, Beckett Auction Services, part of the burgeoning Beckett online service, as well as many others) contributed to the strong growth in collecting interest in 1998.

There were some downsides in 1998, though. Pinnacle brands went out of business, leaving a legacy of innovation and promotions not seen by the other companies. In addition, there was still the problem of collectors being frustrated by the extremely short-printed cards of their favorite players, making completion almost impossible.

During 1998, Pacific received a full baseball license and added many innovations to the card market. Their 1998 OnLine set, for example, is the most comprehensive set issued in the last five years and many veteran collectors applauded Pacific's continuing attempts to get as many different players as possible into their sets.

In the last couple of years, card companies have been printing specific subsets (usually young players or Rookie Cards) in shorter supply than the regular cards. This is not in every set, but in many sets produced since 1998.

In 1999, many of the trends of the last couple of years continued to gain strength. Buying, selling and trading cards over the Internet became a dominant factor in the secondary market. Beckett Publications began its own Marketplace, offering the collectors a chance to search across inventory from many of the finest dealers nationwide in one comprehensive online database. eBay continued to flourish, while many other parties began to reap the benefits of the burgeoning online auction market.

Also, the boom in Internet trading created a perfect fit for professionally graded cards as buyers and sellers traded cards sight unseen with the confidence established by a third-party grader.

From a field of almost a dozen contenders, three companies emerged in 1999 to dominate the field of professional grading–BGS (Beckett Grading Services), PSA (Professional Sports Authenticator), and SGC (Sportscard Guaranty L.L.C.). In 1999 these companies made dramatic expansions in on site grading and submissions at card shows throughout the nation. In response to the widespread acceptance of graded cards, the line of monthly Beckett Price Guides each added a separate section within the price guide area for professionally graded cards.

As was similar to 1998, four licensed manufacturers (Fleer/SkyBox, Pacific, Topps and Upper Deck) produced slightly more than fifty different products for 1999.

Perhaps the biggest hit of the 1999 card season was created by Topps. Card #220 within the basic issue first series 1999 Topps brand featured home run king Mark McGwire in 70 variations, one for each homer he slugged in 1998, and many collectors went after the whole set. Continuing a legacy as strong as the Yankees, the basic Topps issue was one of the most popular sets released in 1999.

Closely trailing the Topps McGwire promotion was Upper Deck's dynamic A Piece of History bat card promotion. The card that kicked off the frenzy was the Babe Ruth A Piece of History distributed in 1999 Upper Deck series 1 packs. Upper Deck actually purchased a cracked game-used Babe Ruth bat for $24,000 and proceeded to cut it up into approximately 350-400 chips of wood to create the now famous Ruth bat card. The card instantly created polar opposites of opinion amongst hobbyists. Traditional collectors howled at the sacrilegious act of destroying such a historic piece of memorabilia while more open-minded collectors jumped at the opportunity to chase such an important card. The Ruth card was followed up by the cross-brand "500 Club" bat card promotion, whereby UD produced bat cards from every major league ballplayer that hit 500 or more home runs in their career (except for Mark McGwire, who hit his 500th in the midst of the 1999 season and promptly stated that he did not support Upper Deck's promotion).

More memorabilia cards than ever were offered to collectors in 1999 as Fleer/SkyBox kicked up their efforts to match the standards set by Upper Deck in previous years. Batting gloves, hats and shoes joined the typical bats and jerseys as pieces of game-used equipment to be featured on trading cards. Sets like E-X Century Authen-Kicks and Fleer Mystique Feel the Game typified the new offerings.

Topps only dabbled with memorabilia cards in 1999, but continued to offer some of the hottest autographed inserts, highlighted by the Topps Stars Rookie Reprint Autographs and the Topps Nolan Ryan Autographs.

Pacific made a clear decision to steer free of memorabilia and autograph inserts, instead focusing on offering collectors a wide selection of beautifully designed insert and parallel cards. Those themes worked beautifully with their established presence for making comprehensive sets–providing collectors with the necessary challenge to pursue regional stars and a favorite team in addition to the typical superstars.

An astounding total of 264 different players made their first appearance on a major league licensed trading card in 1999. What may go down as the deepest class of Rookie Cards of all time features a cornucopia of talented youngsters led by Rick Ankiel, Josh Beckett, Pat Burrell, Josh Hamilton, Eric Munson, Corey Patterson and Alfonso Soriano.

As in years past, Topps continued to provide collectors with a fistful of Rookie Cards within their Bowman, Bowman Chrome and Bowman's Best brands. In a trend established in 1998 by Fleer when they released their Fleer Update set (fueled largely by a J.D. Drew Rookie Card), hobbyists enjoyed a bevy of late-season sets chock full of RC's. Fleer/SkyBox made an all-out effort by stuffing more than 100 Rookie Cards into their 1999 Fleer Update set. Topps produced their first boxed Traded set since 1994. Each 1999 Topps Traded set contained one of 75 different cards autographed by a rookie prospect. Considering how much wider the selection of Rookie Cards became in 1999, it's amazing to see that so few of these RC's were serial numbered. When one looks at the success established with serial-numbered Rookie Cards in the basketball and football card markets with brands like SP Authentic and SPx Finite, one can only scratch one's head when realizing that Fleer Mystique was the only brand to offer baseball collectors serial-numbered RC's. Thus, it's not surprising to see that despite having twenty-five different Rookie Cards issued in 1999, Pat Burrell's Fleer Mystique RC (#'d of 2,999) had been established as his "best" RC by year's end.

Youngsters weren't the only players in the limelight last year as retired stars and Hall of Famers were featured on more cards than any other year in the '90s. Upper Deck's Century Legends brand, featuring the top 50 active and top 50 retired players of the decade as chosen by *The Sporting News was* a runaway hit.

Perhaps the most popular insert set of the year, outpacing all of the dazzling high dollar memorabilia cards, was Topps Gallery Heritage. Utilizing the design and painting style of artist Gerry Dvorak from the classic 1953 Topps set, these modern masterpieces proved that insert cards can still be a hot commodity in the secondary market—albeit assuming they're well conceived and well made—an unfortunate rarity these days.

The spate of basic issue sets with short-printed subsets continued across many brands in 1999. In reaction to many frustrated dealers and collectors struggling to complete these sets, Fleer/SkyBox created dual versions of each prospect card for the 1999 SkyBox Premium set—an action shot was short-printed and a posed shot was seeded at the same rate as other basic issue cards. The idea was well received by collectors, but enjoyed a surprisingly short-lived period of active trading in the secondary market.

Unfortunately, such positives were clearly overshadowed by the industry's overriding problem: too many products costing too much money, with fewer and fewer buyers willing to ante up. The result? Many dealers going out of business, and a buyer's market in which new products usually were available cheaper to the consumer than original dealer cost from the factory. The hobby still faces this very complex problem with no easy solutions in sight.

## Finding Out More

The above has been a thumbnail sketch of card collecting from its inception in the 1880s to the present. It is difficult to tell the whole story in just a few pages — there are several other good sources of information. Serious collectors should subscribe to at least one of the excellent hobby periodicals. We also suggest that collectors visit their local card shop(s) and also attend a sports collectibles show in their area. Card collecting is still a young and informal hobby. You can learn more about it in either place. After all, smart dealers realize that spending a few minutes teaching beginners about the hobby often pays off in the long run.

# Additional Reading

Each year Beckett Publications produces comprehensive annual price guides for each of the four major sports: *Beckett Baseball Card Price Guide, Beckett Basketball Card Price Guide, Beckett Football Card Price Guide, Beckett Hockey Card Price Guide, Beckett Racing Collectibles and Die-Cast Price Guide* and a line of Beckett Alphabetical Checklists books have been released as well. The aim of these annual guides is to provide information and accurate pricing on a wide array of sports cards, ranging from main issues by the major card manufacturers to various regional, promotional, and food issues. Also alphabetical checklist books are published to assist the collector in identifying all the cards of any particular player. The seasoned collector will find these tools valuable sources of information that will enable him to pursue his hobby interests.

In addition, abridged editions of the Beckett Price Guides have been published for each of these major sports as part of the House of Collectibles series: *The Official Price Guide to Baseball Cards, The Official Price Guide to Football Cards, The Official Price Guide to Basketball Cards.* Published in a convenient mass-market paperback format, these price guides provide information and accurate pricing on all the main issues by the major card manufacturers.

# Advertising

Within this Price Guide you will find advertisements for sports memorabilia material, mail order, and retail sports collectibles establishments. All advertisements were accepted in good faith based on the reputation of the advertiser; however, neither the author, the publisher, the distributors, nor the other advertisers in this Price Guide accept any responsibility for any particular advertiser not complying with the terms of his or her ad.

Readers also should be aware that prices in advertisements are subject to change over the annual period before a new edition of this volume is issued each spring. When replying to an advertisement late in the baseball year, the reader should take this into account, and contact the dealer by phone or in writing for up-to-date price information. Should you come into contact with any of the advertisers in this guide as a result of their advertisement herein, please mention this source as your contact.

# Prices in This Guide

Prices found in this guide reflect current retail rates just prior to the printing of this book. They do not reflect the FOR SALE prices of the author, the publisher, the distributors, the advertisers, or any card dealers associated with this guide. No one is obligated in any way to buy, sell or trade his or her cards based on these prices. The price listings were compiled by the author from actual buy/sell transactions at sports conventions, sports card shops, buy/sell advertisements in the hobby papers, for-sale prices from dealer catalogs and price lists, and discussions with leading hobbyists in the U.S. and Canada. All prices are in U.S. dollars.

## 1998 Aurora

| | MINT | NRMT |
|---|---|---|
| COMPLETE SET (200) | 50.00 | 22.00 |
| 1 Garret Anderson | .30 | .14 |
| 2 Jim Edmonds | .75 | .35 |
| 3 Darin Erstad | .75 | .35 |
| 4 Cecil Fielder | .30 | .14 |
| 5 Chuck Finley | .30 | .14 |
| 6 Todd Greene | .20 | .09 |
| 7 Ken Hill | .20 | .09 |
| 8 Tim Salmon | .30 | .14 |
| 9 Roberto Alomar | .75 | .35 |
| 10 Brady Anderson | .30 | .14 |
| 11 Joe Carter | .30 | .14 |
| 12 Mike Mussina | .75 | .35 |
| 13 Rafael Palmeiro | .75 | .35 |
| 14 Cal Ripken | 3.00 | 1.35 |
| 15 B.J. Surhoff | .30 | .14 |
| 16 Steve Avery | .20 | .09 |
| 17 Nomar Garciaparra | 2.50 | 1.10 |
| 18 Pedro Martinez | 1.00 | .45 |
| 19 John Valentin | .20 | .09 |
| 20 Jason Varitek | .30 | .14 |
| 21 Mo Vaughn | .30 | .14 |
| 22 Albert Belle | .50 | .23 |
| 23 Ray Durham | .30 | .14 |
| 24 Maggio Ordonez RC | 3.00 | 1.35 |
| 25 Frank Thomas | 1.50 | .70 |
| 26 Robin Ventura | .30 | .14 |
| 27 Sandy Alomar Jr. | .30 | .14 |
| 28 Travis Fryman | .30 | .14 |
| 29 Dwight Gooden | .20 | .09 |
| 30 David Justice | .50 | .23 |
| 31 Kenny Lofton | .30 | .14 |
| 32 Manny Ramirez | 1.00 | .45 |
| 33 Jim Thome | .50 | .23 |
| 34 Omar Vizquel | .30 | .14 |
| 35 Enrique Wilson | .20 | .09 |
| 36 Jaret Wright | .20 | .09 |
| 37 Tony Clark | .20 | .09 |
| 38 Bobby Higginson | .30 | .14 |
| 39 Brian Hunter | .20 | .09 |
| 40 Bip Roberts | .20 | .09 |
| 41 Justin Thompson | .20 | .09 |
| 42 Jeff Conine | .20 | .09 |
| 43 Johnny Damon | .30 | .14 |
| 44 Jermaine Dye | .30 | .14 |
| 45 Jeff King | .20 | .09 |
| 46 Jeff Montgomery | .20 | .09 |
| 47 Hal Morris | .20 | .09 |
| 48 Dean Palmer | .30 | .14 |
| 49 Terry Pendleton | .30 | .14 |
| 50 Rick Aguilera | .20 | .09 |
| 51 Marty Cordova | .20 | .09 |
| 52 Paul Molitor | .75 | .35 |
| 53 Otis Nixon | .20 | .09 |
| 54 Brad Radke | .30 | .14 |
| 55 Terry Steinbach | .20 | .09 |
| 56 Todd Walker | .20 | .09 |
| 57 Chili Davis | .30 | .14 |
| 58 Derek Jeter | 3.00 | 1.35 |
| 59 Chuck Knoblauch | .30 | .14 |
| 60 Tino Martinez | .30 | .14 |
| 61 Paul O'Neill | .30 | .14 |
| 62 Andy Pettitte | .30 | .14 |
| 63 Mariano Rivera | .30 | .14 |
| 64 Bernie Williams | .75 | .35 |
| 65 Jason Giambi | .75 | .35 |
| 66 Ben Grieve | .30 | .14 |
| 67 Rickey Henderson | 1.00 | .45 |
| 68 A.J. Hinch | .20 | .09 |
| 69 Kenny Rogers | .20 | .09 |
| 70 Jay Buhner | .30 | .14 |
| 71 Joey Cora | .20 | .09 |
| 72 Ken Griffey Jr. | 3.00 | 1.35 |
| 73 Randy Johnson | 1.00 | .45 |
| 74 Edgar Martinez | .50 | .23 |
| 75 Jamie Moyer | .20 | .09 |
| 76 Alex Rodriguez | 2.50 | 1.10 |
| 77 David Segui | .20 | .09 |
| 78 Rolando Arrojo RC | .60 | .25 |
| 79 Wade Boggs | 1.00 | .45 |
| 80 Roberto Hernandez | .20 | .09 |
| 81 Dave Martinez | .20 | .09 |
| 82 Fred McGriff | .50 | .23 |
| 83 Paul Sorrento | .20 | .09 |
| 84 Kevin Stocker | .20 | .09 |
| 85 Will Clark | .75 | .35 |
| 86 Juan Gonzalez | .75 | .35 |
| 87 Tom Goodwin | .20 | .09 |
| 88 Rusty Greer | .30 | .14 |
| 89 Ivan Rodriguez | 1.00 | .45 |
| 90 John Wetteland | .30 | .14 |
| 91 Jose Canseco | 1.00 | .45 |
| 92 Roger Clemens | 1.50 | .70 |
| 93 Jose Cruz Jr. | .30 | .14 |
| 94 Carlos Delgado | .75 | .35 |
| 95 Pat Hentgen | .20 | .09 |
| 96 Jay Bell | .30 | .14 |
| 97 Andy Benes | .20 | .09 |
| 98 Karim Garcia | .20 | .09 |
| 99 Travis Lee | .30 | .14 |
| 100 Devon White | .20 | .09 |
| 101 Matt Williams | .50 | .23 |
| 102 Andres Galarraga | .50 | .23 |
| 103 Tom Glavine | .75 | .35 |
| 104 Andruw Jones | .75 | .35 |
| 105 Chipper Jones | 2.00 | .90 |
| 106 Ryan Klesko | .30 | .14 |
| 107 Javy Lopez | .30 | .14 |
| 108 Greg Maddux | 2.00 | .90 |
| 109 Walt Weiss | .30 | .14 |
| 110 Rod Beck | .20 | .09 |
| 111 Jeff Blauser | .20 | .09 |
| 112 Mark Grace | .75 | .35 |
| 113 Lance Johnson | .20 | .09 |
| 114 Mickey Morandini | .20 | .09 |
| 115 Henry Rodriguez | .20 | .09 |
| 116 Sammy Sosa | 1.50 | .70 |
| 117 Kerry Wood | .75 | .35 |
| 118 Lenny Harris | .20 | .09 |
| 119 Damian Jackson | .20 | .09 |
| 120 Barry Larkin | .75 | .35 |
| 121 Reggie Sanders | .20 | .09 |
| 122 Brett Tomko | .20 | .09 |
| 123 Dante Bichette | .30 | .14 |
| 124 Ellis Burks | .30 | .14 |
| 125 Vinny Castilla | .30 | .14 |
| 126 Todd Helton | 1.00 | .45 |
| 127 Darryl Kile | .30 | .14 |
| 128 Larry Walker | .30 | .14 |
| 129 Bobby Bonilla | .30 | .14 |
| 130 Livan Hernandez | .20 | .09 |
| 131 Charles Johnson | .30 | .14 |
| 132 Derrek Lee | .20 | .09 |
| 133 Edgar Renteria | .20 | .09 |
| 134 Gary Sheffield | .75 | .35 |
| 135 Moises Alou | .30 | .14 |
| 136 Jeff Bagwell | 1.00 | .45 |
| 137 Derek Bell | .20 | .09 |
| 138 Craig Biggio | .50 | .23 |
| 139 John Halama RC | .60 | .25 |
| 140 Mike Hampton | .30 | .14 |
| 141 Richard Hidalgo | .30 | .14 |
| 142 Wilton Guerrero | .20 | .09 |
| 143 Todd Hollandsworth | .20 | .09 |
| 144 Eric Karros | .30 | .14 |
| 145 Paul Konerko | .30 | .14 |
| 146 Raul Mondesi | .30 | .14 |
| 147 Hideo Nomo | .75 | .35 |
| 148 Chan Ho Park | .30 | .14 |
| 149 Mike Piazza | 2.50 | 1.10 |
| 150 Jeromy Burnitz | .30 | .14 |
| 151 Todd Dunn | .20 | .09 |
| 152 Marquis Grissom | .20 | .09 |
| 153 John Jaha | .30 | .14 |
| 154 Dave Nilsson | .20 | .09 |
| 155 Fernando Vina | .20 | .09 |
| 156 Mark Grudzielanek | .20 | .09 |
| 157 Vladimir Guerrero | 1.25 | .55 |
| 158 F.P. Santangelo | .20 | .09 |
| 159 Jose Vidro | .20 | .09 |
| 160 Rondell White | .30 | .14 |
| 161 Edgardo Alfonzo | .30 | .14 |
| 162 Carlos Baerga | .20 | .09 |
| 163 John Franco | .30 | .14 |
| 164 Todd Hundley | .20 | .09 |
| 165 Brian McRae | .20 | .09 |
| 166 John Olerud | .30 | .14 |
| 167 Rey Ordonez | .20 | .09 |
| 168 Masato Yoshii RC | .60 | .25 |
| 169 Ricky Bottalico | .20 | .09 |
| 170 Doug Glanville | .20 | .09 |
| 171 Gregg Jefferies | .20 | .09 |
| 172 Desi Relaford | .20 | .09 |
| 173 Scott Rolen | .75 | .35 |
| 174 Curt Schilling | .30 | .14 |
| 175 Jose Guillen | .20 | .09 |
| 176 Jason Kendall | .30 | .14 |
| 177 Al Martin | .20 | .09 |
| 178 Doug Strange | .20 | .09 |
| 179 Kevin Young | .30 | .14 |
| 180 Royce Clayton | .20 | .09 |
| 181 Delino DeShields | .20 | .09 |
| 182 Gary Gaetti | .00 | .14 |
| 183 Hon Gant | .30 | .14 |
| 184 Brian Jordan | .30 | .14 |
| 185 Ray Lankford | .30 | .14 |
| 186 Willie McGee | .30 | .14 |
| 187 Mark McGwire | 3.00 | 1.35 |
| 188 Kevin Brown | .50 | .23 |
| 189 Ken Caminiti | .30 | .14 |
| 190 Steve Finley | .30 | .14 |
| 191 Tony Gwynn | 1.50 | .70 |
| 192 Wally Joyner | .30 | .14 |
| 193 Ruben Rivera | .20 | .09 |
| 194 Quilvio Veras | .20 | .09 |
| 195 Barry Bonds | 1.25 | .55 |
| 196 Shawn Estes | .20 | .09 |
| 197 Orel Hershiser | .30 | .14 |
| 198 Jeff Kent | .50 | .23 |
| 199 Robb Nen | .20 | .09 |
| 200 J.T. Snow | .30 | .14 |
| NNO Tony Gwynn Sample | 3.00 | 1.35 |

## 1999 Aurora

| | MINT | NRMT |
|---|---|---|
| COMPLETE SET (200) | 50.00 | 22.00 |
| 1 Garret Anderson | .30 | .14 |
| 2 Jim Edmonds | .75 | .35 |
| 3 Darin Erstad | .75 | .35 |
| 4 Matt Luke | .20 | .09 |
| 5 Tim Salmon | .30 | .14 |
| 6 Mo Vaughn | .30 | .14 |
| 7 Jay Bell | .30 | .14 |
| 8 David Dellucci | .20 | .09 |
| 9 Steve Finley | .30 | .14 |
| 10 Bernard Gilkey | .20 | .09 |

❑ 11 Randy Johnson 1.00 .45
❑ 12 Travis Lee .20 .09
❑ 13 Matt Williams .50 .23
❑ 14 Andres Galarraga .50 .23
❑ 15 Tom Glavine .75 .35
❑ 16 Andruw Jones .75 .35
❑ 17 Chipper Jones 2.00 .90
❑ 18 Brian Jordan .30 .14
❑ 19 Javy Lopez .30 .14
❑ 20 Greg Maddux 2.00 .90
❑ 21 Albert Belle .50 .23
❑ 22 Will Clark .75 .35
❑ 23 Scott Erickson .20 .09
❑ 24 Mike Mussina .75 .35
❑ 25 Cal Ripken 3.00 1.35
❑ 26 B.J. Surhoff .30 .14
❑ 27 Nomar Garciaparra 2.50 1.10
❑ 28 Reggie Jefferson .20 .09
❑ 29 Darren Lewis .20 .09
❑ 30 Pedro Martinez 1.00 .45
❑ 31 John Valentin .20 .09
❑ 32 Rod Beck .20 .09
❑ 33 Mark Grace .75 .35
❑ 34 Lance Johnson .20 .09
❑ 35 Mickey Morandini .20 .09
❑ 36 Sammy Sosa 1.50 .70
❑ 37 Kerry Wood .30 .14
❑ 38 James Baldwin .20 .09
❑ 39 Mike Caruso .20 .09
❑ 40 Ray Durham .30 .14
❑ 41 Magglio Ordonez .50 .23
❑ 42 Frank Thomas 1.50 .70
❑ 43 Aaron Boone .20 .09
❑ 44 Sean Casey .30 .14
❑ 45 Barry Larkin .75 .35
❑ 46 Hal Morris .20 .09
❑ 47 Denny Neagle .20 .09
❑ 48 Greg Vaughn .30 .14
❑ 49 Pat Watkins .20 .09
❑ 50 Roberto Alomar .75 .35
❑ 51 Sandy Alomar Jr. .30 .14
❑ 52 David Justice .50 .23
❑ 53 Kenny Lofton .30 .14
❑ 54 Manny Ramirez 1.00 .45
❑ 55 Richie Sexson .30 .14
❑ 56 Jim Thome .50 .23
❑ 57 Omar Vizquel .30 .14
❑ 58 Dante Bichette .30 .14
❑ 59 Vinny Castilla .30 .14
❑ 60 Edgard Clemente .20 .09
❑ 61 Derrick Gibson .20 .09
❑ 62 Todd Helton 1.00 .45
❑ 63 Darryl Kile .30 .14
❑ 64 Larry Walker .30 .14
❑ 65 Tony Clark .20 .09
❑ 66 Damion Easley .20 .09
❑ 67 Bob Higginson .30 .14
❑ 68 Brian Hunter .20 .09
❑ 69 Dean Palmer .30 .14
❑ 70 Justin Thompson .20 .09
❑ 71 Craig Counsell .20 .09
❑ 72 Todd Dunwoody .20 .09
❑ 73 Cliff Floyd .30 .14
❑ 74 Alex Gonzalez .20 .09
❑ 75 Livan Hernandez .20 .09
❑ 76 Mark Kotsay .20 .09
❑ 77 Derrek Lee .20 .09
❑ 78 Moises Alou .30 .14
❑ 79 Jeff Bagwell 1.00 .45
❑ 80 Derek Bell .20 .09
❑ 81 Craig Biggio .50 .23
❑ 82 Ken Caminiti .30 .14
❑ 83 Richard Hidalgo .30 .14
❑ 84 Shane Reynolds .20 .09
❑ 85 Jeff Conine .20 .09
❑ 86 Johnny Damon .30 .14
❑ 87 Jermaine Dye .30 .14
❑ 88 Jeff King .20 .09
❑ 89 Jeff Montgomery .20 .09
❑ 90 Mike Sweeney .30 .14
❑ 91 Kevin Brown .50 .23
❑ 92 Mark Grudzielanek .20 .09
❑ 93 Eric Karros .30 .14
❑ 94 Raul Mondesi .30 .14
❑ 95 Chan Ho Park .30 .14
❑ 96 Gary Sheffield .75 .35
❑ 97 Jeromy Burnitz .30 .14
❑ 98 Jeff Cirillo .30 .14
❑ 99 Marquis Grissom .20 .09
❑ 100 Geoff Jenkins .30 .14
❑ 101 Dave Nilsson .20 .09
❑ 102 Jose Valetin .20 .09
❑ 103 Fernando Vina .20 .09
❑ 104 Marty Cordova .20 .09
❑ 105 Matt Lawton .30 .14
❑ 106 David Ortiz .20 .09
❑ 107 Brad Radke .30 .14
❑ 108 Todd Walker .20 .09
❑ 109 Shane Andrews .20 .09
❑ 110 Orlando Cabrera .20 .09
❑ 111 Brad Fullmer .30 .14
❑ 112 Vladimir Guerrero 1.25 .55
❑ 113 Wilton Guerrero .20 .09
❑ 114 Carl Pavano .20 .09
❑ 115 Fernando Seguignol .20 .09
❑ 116 Ugueth Urbina .20 .09
❑ 117 Edgardo Alfonzo .30 .14
❑ 118 Bobby Bonilla .30 .14
❑ 119 Rickey Henderson 1.00 .45
❑ 120 Hideo Nomo .75 .35
❑ 121 John Olerud .30 .14
❑ 122 Rey Ordonez .20 .09
❑ 123 Mike Piazza 2.50 1.10
❑ 124 Masato Yoshii .30 .14
❑ 125 Scott Brosius .30 .14
❑ 126 Orlando Hernandez .30 .14
❑ 127 Hideki Irabu .20 .09
❑ 128 Derek Jeter 3.00 1.35
❑ 129 Chuck Knoblauch .30 .14
❑ 130 Tino Martinez .30 .14
❑ 131 Jorge Posada .30 .14
❑ 132 Bernie Williams .75 .35
❑ 133 Eric Chavez .30 .14
❑ 134 Ryan Christenson .20 .09
❑ 135 Jason Giambi .75 .35
❑ 136 Ben Grieve .30 .14
❑ 137 A.J. Hinch .20 .09
❑ 138 Matt Stairs .20 .09
❑ 139 Miguel Tejada .30 .14
❑ 140 Bob Abreu .30 .14
❑ 141 Gary Bennett RC .20 .09
❑ 142 Desi Relaford .20 .09
❑ 143 Scott Rolen .75 .35
❑ 144 Curt Schilling .30 .14
❑ 145 Kevin Sefcik .20 .09
❑ 146 Brian Giles .30 .14
❑ 147 Jose Guillen .20 .09
❑ 148 Jason Kendall .30 .14
❑ 149 Aramis Ramirez .20 .09
❑ 150 Tony Womack .20 .09
❑ 151 Kevin Young .30 .14
❑ 152 Eric Davis .30 .14
❑ 153 J.D. Drew .75 .35
❑ 154 Ray Lankford .30 .14
❑ 155 Eli Marrero .20 .09
❑ 156 Mark McGwire 3.00 1.35
❑ 157 Luis Ordaz .20 .09
❑ 158 Edgar Renteria .20 .09
❑ 159 Andy Ashby .20 .09
❑ 160 Tony Gwynn 1.50 .70
❑ 161 Trevor Hoffman .30 .14
❑ 162 Wally Joyner .30 .14
❑ 163 Jim Leyritz .20 .09
❑ 164 Ruben Rivera .20 .09
❑ 165 Reggie Sanders .20 .09
❑ 166 Quilvio Veras .20 .09
❑ 167 Rich Aurilia .20 .09
❑ 168 Marvin Benard .20 .09
❑ 169 Barry Bonds 1.25 .55
❑ 170 Ellis Burks .30 .14
❑ 171 Jeff Kent .50 .23
❑ 172 Bill Mueller .20 .09
❑ 173 J.T. Snow .30 .14
❑ 174 Jay Buhner .30 .14
❑ 175 Jeff Fassero .20 .09
❑ 176 Ken Griffey Jr. 3.00 1.35
❑ 177 Carlos Guillen .20 .09
❑ 178 Edgar Martinez .50 .23
❑ 179 Alex Rodriguez 2.50 1.10
❑ 180 David Segui .20 .09
❑ 181 Dan Wilson .20 .09
❑ 182 Rolando Arrojo .20 .09
❑ 183 Wade Boggs 1.00 .45
❑ 184 Jose Canseco 1.00 .45
❑ 185 Aaron Ledesma .20 .09
❑ 186 Dave Martinez .20 .09
❑ 187 Quinton McCracken .20 .09
❑ 188 Fred McGriff .50 .23
❑ 189 Juan Gonzalez .75 .35
❑ 190 Tom Goodwin .20 .09
❑ 191 Rusty Greer .30 .14
❑ 192 Roberto Kelly .20 .09
❑ 193 Rafael Palmeiro .75 .35
❑ 194 Ivan Rodriguez 1.00 .45
❑ 195 Roger Clemens 1.50 .70
❑ 196 Jose Cruz Jr. .30 .14
❑ 197 Carlos Delgado .75 .35
❑ 198 Alex Gonzalez .20 .09
❑ 199 Roy Halladay .20 .09
❑ 200 Pat Hentgen .20 .09

## 2000 Aurora

| | MINT | NRMT |
|---|---|---|
| COMPLETE SET (151) | 50.00 | 22.00 |

❑ 1 Darin Erstad .75 .35
❑ 2 Troy Glaus 1.00 .45
❑ 3 Tim Salmon .30 .14
❑ 4 Mo Vaughn .30 .14
❑ 5 Jay Bell .30 .14
❑ 6 Erubiel Durazo .30 .14
❑ 7 Luis Gonzalez .30 .14
❑ 8 Randy Johnson 1.00 .45
❑ 9 Matt Williams .50 .23
❑ 10 Tom Glavine .75 .35
❑ 11 Andruw Jones .75 .35
❑ 12 Chipper Jones 2.00 .90
❑ 13 Brian Jordan .30 .14
❑ 14 Greg Maddux 2.00 .90
❑ 15 Kevin Millwood .30 .14
❑ 16 Albert Belle .50 .23
❑ 17 Will Clark .75 .35
❑ 18 Mike Mussina .75 .35
❑ 19 Cal Ripken 3.00 1.35
❑ 20 B.J. Surhoff .30 .14
❑ 21 Nomar Garciaparra 2.50 1.10
❑ 22 Pedro Martinez 1.00 .45
❑ 23 Troy O'Leary .20 .09
❑ 24 Wilton Veras .30 .14
❑ 25 Mark Grace .75 .35
❑ 26 Henry Rodriguez .20 .09
❑ 27 Sammy Sosa 1.50 .70
❑ 28 Kerry Wood .30 .14
❑ 29 Ray Durham .30 .14
❑ 30 Paul Konerko .30 .14
❑ 31 Carlos Lee .30 .14
❑ 32 Magglio Ordonez .30 .14
❑ 33 Chris Singleton .30 .14
❑ 34 Frank Thomas 1.50 .70
❑ 35 Mike Cameron .20 .09
❑ 36 Sean Casey .30 .14
❑ 37 Barry Larkin .75 .35
❑ 38 Pokey Reese .30 .14
❑ 39 Eddie Taubensee .20 .09
❑ 40 Roberto Alomar .75 .35
❑ 41 David Justice .50 .23
❑ 42 Kenny Lofton .30 .14
❑ 43 Manny Ramirez 1.00 .45
❑ 44 Richie Sexson .30 .14

| Card | | |
|---|---|---|
| ❑ 45 Jim Thome | .50 | .23 |
| ❑ 46 Omar Vizquel | .30 | .14 |
| ❑ 47 Todd Helton | 1.00 | .45 |
| ❑ 48 Mike Lansing | .20 | .09 |
| ❑ 49 Neifi Perez | .20 | .09 |
| ❑ 50 Ben Petrick | .20 | .09 |
| ❑ 51 Larry Walker | .30 | .14 |
| ❑ 52 Tony Clark | .20 | .09 |
| ❑ 53 Damion Easley | .20 | .09 |
| ❑ 54 Juan Encarnacion | .30 | .14 |
| ❑ 55 Juan Gonzalez | .75 | .35 |
| ❑ 56 Dean Palmer | .30 | .14 |
| ❑ 57 Luis Castillo | .30 | .14 |
| ❑ 58 Cliff Floyd | .30 | .14 |
| ❑ 59 Alex Gonzalez | .20 | .09 |
| ❑ 60 Mike Lowell | .20 | .09 |
| ❑ 61 Preston Wilson | .30 | .14 |
| ❑ 62 Jeff Bagwell | 1.00 | .45 |
| ❑ 63 Craig Biggio | .50 | .23 |
| ❑ 64 Ken Caminiti | .30 | .14 |
| ❑ 65 Jose Lima | .20 | .09 |
| ❑ 66 Billy Wagner | .20 | .09 |
| ❑ 67 Carlos Beltran | .30 | .14 |
| ❑ 68 Johnny Damon | .30 | .14 |
| ❑ 69 Jermaine Dye | .30 | .14 |
| ❑ 70 Mark Quinn | .30 | .14 |
| ❑ 71 Mike Sweeney | .30 | .14 |
| ❑ 72 Kevin Brown | .50 | .23 |
| ❑ 73 Shawn Green | .75 | .35 |
| ❑ 74 Eric Karros | .30 | .14 |
| ❑ 75 Chan Ho Park | .30 | .14 |
| ❑ 76 Gary Sheffield | .75 | .35 |
| ❑ 77 Ron Belliard | .20 | .09 |
| ❑ 78 Jeromy Burnitz | .30 | .14 |
| ❑ 79 Marquis Grissom | .20 | .09 |
| ❑ 80 Geoff Jenkins | .30 | .14 |
| ❑ 81 David Nilsson | .20 | .09 |
| ❑ 82 Ron Coomer | .20 | .09 |
| ❑ 83 Jacque Jones | .30 | .14 |
| ❑ 84 Brad Radke | .30 | .14 |
| ❑ 85 Todd Walker | .20 | .09 |
| ❑ 86 Michael Barrett | .20 | .09 |
| ❑ 87 Peter Bergeron | .20 | .09 |
| ❑ 88 Vladimir Guerrero | 1.25 | .55 |
| ❑ 89 Jose Vidro | .20 | .09 |
| ❑ 90 Rondell White | .30 | .14 |
| ❑ 91 Edgardo Alfonzo | .30 | .14 |
| ❑ 92 Darryl Hamilton | .20 | .09 |
| ❑ 93 Rey Ordonez | .20 | .09 |
| ❑ 94 Mike Piazza | 2.50 | 1.10 |
| ❑ 95 Robin Ventura | .50 | .23 |
| ❑ 96 Roger Clemens | 1.50 | .70 |
| ❑ 97 Orlando Hernandez | .30 | .14 |
| ❑ 98 Derek Jeter | 3.00 | 1.35 |
| ❑ 99 Tino Martinez | .30 | .14 |
| ❑ 100 Mariano Rivera | .30 | .14 |
| ❑ 101 Bernie Williams | .75 | .35 |
| ❑ 102 Eric Chavez | .30 | .14 |
| ❑ 103 Jason Giambi | .75 | .35 |
| ❑ 104 Ben Grieve | .30 | .14 |
| ❑ 105 Tim Hudson | .75 | .35 |
| ❑ 106 John Jaha | .20 | .09 |
| ❑ 107 Matt Stairs | .20 | .09 |
| ❑ 108 Bob Abreu | .30 | .14 |
| ❑ 109 Doug Glanville | .20 | .09 |
| ❑ 110 Mike Lieberthal | .30 | .14 |
| ❑ 111 Scott Rolen | .75 | .35 |
| ❑ 112 Curt Schilling | .30 | .14 |
| ❑ 113 Brian Giles | .30 | .14 |
| ❑ 114 Chad Hermansen | .20 | .09 |
| ❑ 115 Jason Kendall | .30 | .14 |
| ❑ 116 Warren Morris | .20 | .09 |
| ❑ 117 Kevin Young | .20 | .09 |
| ❑ 118 Rick Ankiel | 1.50 | .70 |
| ❑ 119 J.D. Drew | .75 | .35 |
| ❑ 120 Ray Lankford | .30 | .14 |
| ❑ 121 Mark McGwire | 3.00 | 1.35 |
| ❑ 122 Edgar Renteria | .20 | .09 |
| ❑ 123 Fernando Tatis | .30 | .14 |
| ❑ 124 Ben Davis | .20 | .09 |
| ❑ 125 Tony Gwynn | 1.50 | .70 |
| ❑ 126 Trevor Hoffman | .30 | .14 |
| ❑ 127 Phil Nevin | .30 | .14 |
| ❑ 128 Barry Bonds | 1.25 | .55 |
| ❑ 129 Ellis Burks | .30 | .14 |
| ❑ 130 Jeff Kent | .50 | .23 |
| ❑ 131 J.T. Snow | .30 | .14 |
| ❑ 132 Freddy Garcia | .30 | .14 |
| ❑ 133 Ken Griffey Jr. | 3.00 | 1.35 |
| ❑ 133R Ken Griffey Jr. Reds | 3.00 | 1.35 |
| ❑ 134 Edgar Martinez | .50 | .23 |
| ❑ 135 Alex Rodriguez | 2.50 | 1.10 |
| ❑ 136 Dan Wilson | .20 | .09 |
| ❑ 137 Jose Canseco | 1.00 | .45 |
| ❑ 138 Roberto Hernandez | .20 | .09 |
| ❑ 139 Dave Martinez | .20 | .09 |
| ❑ 140 Fred McGriff | .50 | .23 |
| ❑ 141 Rusty Greer | .30 | .14 |
| ❑ 142 Ruben Mateo | .30 | .14 |
| ❑ 143 Rafael Palmeiro | .75 | .35 |
| ❑ 144 Ivan Rodriguez | 1.00 | .45 |
| ❑ 145 Jeff Zimmerman | .20 | .09 |
| ❑ 146 Homer Bush | .20 | .09 |
| ❑ 147 Carlos Delgado | .75 | .35 |
| ❑ 148 Raul Mondesi | .30 | .14 |
| ❑ 149 Shannon Stewart | .30 | .14 |
| ❑ 150 Vernon Wells | .30 | .14 |
| ❑ SAMP Tony Gwynn Sample | 2.00 | .90 |

## 1999 Black Diamond

| | MINT | NRMT |
|---|---|---|
| COMPLETE SET (120) | 100.00 | 45.00 |
| COMP.SET w/o DD's (90) | 30.00 | 13.50 |
| COMMON CARD (1-90) | .20 | .09 |
| COMMON DIAM DEB (91-120) | 2.00 | .90 |

| Card | | |
|---|---|---|
| ❑ 1 Darin Erstad | .75 | .35 |
| ❑ 2 Tim Salmon | .30 | .14 |
| ❑ 3 Jim Edmonds | .75 | .35 |
| ❑ 4 Matt Williams | .50 | .23 |
| ❑ 5 David Dellucci | .20 | .09 |
| ❑ 6 Jay Bell | .30 | .14 |
| ❑ 7 Andres Galarraga | .50 | .23 |
| ❑ 8 Chipper Jones | 2.00 | .90 |
| ❑ 9 Greg Maddux | 2.00 | .90 |
| ❑ 10 Andruw Jones | .75 | .35 |
| ❑ 11 Cal Ripken | 3.00 | 1.35 |
| ❑ 12 Rafael Palmeiro | .75 | .35 |
| ❑ 13 Brady Anderson | .30 | .14 |
| ❑ 14 Mike Mussina | .75 | .35 |
| ❑ 15 Nomar Garciaparra | 2.50 | 1.10 |
| ❑ 16 Mo Vaughn | .30 | .14 |
| ❑ 17 Pedro Martinez | 1.00 | .45 |
| ❑ 18 Sammy Sosa | 1.50 | .70 |
| ❑ 19 Henry Rodriguez | .20 | .09 |
| ❑ 20 Frank Thomas | 1.50 | .70 |
| ❑ 21 Magglio Ordonez | .50 | .23 |
| ❑ 22 Albert Belle | .50 | .23 |
| ❑ 23 Paul Konerko | .30 | .14 |
| ❑ 24 Sean Casey | .30 | .14 |
| ❑ 25 Jim Thome | .50 | .23 |
| ❑ 26 Kenny Lofton | .30 | .14 |
| ❑ 27 Sandy Alomar Jr. | .30 | .14 |
| ❑ 28 Jaret Wright | .20 | .09 |
| ❑ 29 Larry Walker | .30 | .14 |
| ❑ 30 Todd Helton | 1.00 | .45 |
| ❑ 31 Vinny Castilla | .30 | .14 |
| ❑ 32 Tony Clark | .20 | .09 |
| ❑ 33 Damion Easley | .20 | .09 |
| ❑ 34 Mark Kotsay | .20 | .09 |
| ❑ 35 Derrek Lee | .20 | .09 |
| ❑ 36 Moises Alou | .30 | .14 |
| ❑ 37 Jeff Bagwell | 1.00 | .45 |
| ❑ 38 Craig Biggio | .50 | .23 |
| ❑ 39 Randy Johnson | 1.00 | .45 |
| ❑ 40 Dean Palmer | .30 | .14 |
| ❑ 41 Johnny Damon | .30 | .14 |
| ❑ 42 Chan Ho Park | .30 | .14 |
| ❑ 43 Raul Mondesi | .30 | .14 |
| ❑ 44 Gary Sheffield | .75 | .35 |
| ❑ 45 Jeromy Burnitz | .30 | .14 |
| ❑ 46 Marquis Grissom | .20 | .09 |
| ❑ 47 Jeff Cirillo | .30 | .14 |
| ❑ 48 Paul Molitor | .75 | .35 |
| ❑ 49 Todd Walker | .20 | .09 |
| ❑ 50 Vladimir Guerrero | 1.25 | .55 |
| ❑ 51 Brad Fullmer | .30 | .14 |
| ❑ 52 Mike Piazza | 2.50 | 1.10 |
| ❑ 53 Hideo Nomo | .75 | .35 |
| ❑ 54 Carlos Baerga | .20 | .09 |
| ❑ 55 John Olerud | .30 | .14 |
| ❑ 56 Derek Jeter | 3.00 | 1.35 |
| ❑ 57 Hideki Irabu | .20 | .09 |
| ❑ 58 Tino Martinez | .30 | .14 |
| ❑ 59 Bernie Williams | .75 | .35 |
| ❑ 60 Miguel Tejada | .30 | .14 |
| ❑ 61 Ben Grieve | .30 | .14 |
| ❑ 62 Jason Giambi | .75 | .35 |
| ❑ 63 Scott Rolen | .75 | .35 |
| ❑ 64 Doug Glanville | .20 | .09 |
| ❑ 65 Desi Relaford | .20 | .09 |
| ❑ 66 Tony Womack | .20 | .09 |
| ❑ 67 Jason Kendall | .30 | .14 |
| ❑ 68 Jose Guillen | .20 | .09 |
| ❑ 69 Tony Gwynn | 1.50 | .70 |
| ❑ 70 Ken Caminiti | .30 | .14 |
| ❑ 71 Greg Vaughn | .30 | .14 |
| ❑ 72 Kevin Brown | .50 | .23 |
| ❑ 73 Barry Bonds | 1.25 | .55 |
| ❑ 74 J.T. Snow | .30 | .14 |
| ❑ 75 Jeff Kent | .50 | .23 |
| ❑ 76 Ken Griffey Jr. | 3.00 | 1.35 |
| ❑ 77 Alex Rodriguez | 2.50 | 1.10 |
| ❑ 78 Edgar Martinez | .50 | .23 |
| ❑ 79 Jay Buhner | .30 | .14 |
| ❑ 80 Mark McGwire | 3.00 | 1.35 |
| ❑ 81 Delino DeShields | .20 | .09 |
| ❑ 82 Brian Jordan | .30 | .14 |
| ❑ 83 Quinton McCracken | .20 | .09 |
| ❑ 84 Fred McGriff | .50 | .23 |
| ❑ 85 Juan Gonzalez | .75 | .35 |
| ❑ 86 Ivan Rodriguez | 1.00 | .45 |
| ❑ 87 Will Clark | .75 | .35 |
| ❑ 88 Roger Clemens | 1.50 | .70 |
| ❑ 89 Jose Cruz Jr. | .30 | .14 |
| ❑ 90 Babe Ruth | 5.00 | 2.20 |
| ❑ 91 Troy Glaus DD | 10.00 | 4.50 |
| ❑ 92 Jarrod Washburn DD | 2.00 | .90 |
| ❑ 93 Travis Lee DD | 2.00 | .90 |
| ❑ 94 Bruce Chen DD | 2.00 | .90 |
| ❑ 95 Mike Caruso DD | 2.00 | .90 |
| ❑ 96 Jim Parque DD | 2.00 | .90 |
| ❑ 97 Kerry Wood DD | 2.00 | .90 |
| ❑ 98 Jeremy Giambi DD | 2.00 | .90 |
| ❑ 99 Matt Anderson DD | 2.00 | .90 |
| ❑ 100 Seth Greisinger DD | 2.00 | .90 |
| ❑ 101 Gabe Alvarez DD | 2.00 | .90 |
| ❑ 102 Rafael Medina DD | 2.00 | .90 |
| ❑ 103 Daryle Ward DD | 2.00 | .90 |
| ❑ 104 Alex Cora DD | 2.00 | .90 |
| ❑ 105 Adrian Beltre DD | 2.00 | .90 |
| ❑ 106 Geoff Jenkins DD | 2.00 | .90 |
| ❑ 107 Eric Milton DD | 2.00 | .90 |
| ❑ 108 Carl Pavano DD | 2.00 | .90 |
| ❑ 109 Eric Chavez DD | 2.00 | .90 |
| ❑ 110 Orlando Hernandez DD | 2.00 | .90 |
| ❑ 111 A.J. Hinch DD | 2.00 | .90 |
| ❑ 112 Carlton Loewer DD | 2.00 | .90 |
| ❑ 113 Aramis Ramirez DD | 2.00 | .90 |
| ❑ 114 Cliff Politte DD | 2.00 | .90 |
| ❑ 115 Matt Clement DD | 2.00 | .90 |
| ❑ 116 Alex Gonzalez DD | 2.00 | .90 |
| ❑ 117 J.D. Drew DD | 5.00 | 2.20 |
| ❑ 118 Shane Monahan DD | 2.00 | .90 |
| ❑ 119 Rolando Arrojo DD | 2.00 | .90 |
| ❑ 120 George Lombard DD | 2.00 | .90 |

## 2000 Black Diamond

| | MINT | NRMT |
|---|---|---|
| COMPLETE SET (120) | 150.00 | 70.00 |
| COMP.SET w/o SP's (90) | 30.00 | 13.50 |
| COMMON CARD (1-90) | .20 | .09 |
| COMMON DD (91-120) | 2.00 | .90 |

| Card | MINT | NRMT |
|---|---|---|
| ❑ 1 Darin Erstad | .75 | .35 |
| ❑ 2 Tim Salmon | .30 | .14 |
| ❑ 3 Mo Vaughn | .30 | .14 |
| ❑ 4 Matt Williams | .50 | .23 |
| ❑ 5 Travis Lee | .20 | .09 |
| ❑ 6 Randy Johnson | 1.00 | .45 |
| ❑ 7 Tom Glavine | .75 | .35 |
| ❑ 8 Chipper Jones | 2.00 | .90 |
| ❑ 9 Greg Maddux | 2.00 | .90 |
| ❑ 10 Andruw Jones | .75 | .35 |
| ❑ 11 Brian Jordan | .30 | .14 |
| ❑ 12 Cal Ripken | 3.00 | 1.35 |
| ❑ 13 Albert Belle | .50 | .23 |
| ❑ 14 Mike Mussina | .75 | .35 |
| ❑ 15 Nomar Garciaparra | 2.50 | 1.10 |
| ❑ 16 Troy O'Leary | .20 | .09 |
| ❑ 17 Pedro Martinez | 1.00 | .45 |
| ❑ 18 Sammy Sosa | 1.50 | .70 |
| ❑ 19 Henry Rodriguez | .20 | .09 |
| ❑ 20 Frank Thomas | 1.50 | .70 |
| ❑ 21 Maggio Ordonez | .30 | .14 |
| ❑ 22 Greg Vaughn | .30 | .14 |
| ❑ 23 Barry Larkin | .75 | .35 |
| ❑ 24 Sean Casey | .30 | .14 |
| ❑ 25 Jim Thome | .50 | .23 |
| ❑ 26 Kenny Lofton | .30 | .14 |
| ❑ 27 Roberto Alomar | .75 | .35 |
| ❑ 28 Manny Ramirez | 1.00 | .45 |
| ❑ 29 Larry Walker | .30 | .14 |
| ❑ 30 Todd Helton | 1.00 | .45 |
| ❑ 31 Gabe Kapler | .30 | .14 |
| ❑ 32 Tony Clark | .20 | .09 |
| ❑ 33 Dean Palmer | .30 | .14 |
| ❑ 34 Cliff Floyd | .30 | .14 |
| ❑ 35 Alex Gonzalez | .20 | .09 |
| ❑ 36 Moises Alou | .30 | .14 |
| ❑ 37 Jeff Bagwell | 1.00 | .45 |
| ❑ 38 Craig Biggio | .50 | .23 |
| ❑ 39 Richard Hidalgo | .30 | .14 |
| ❑ 40 Carlos Beltran | .30 | .14 |
| ❑ 41 Johnny Damon | .30 | .14 |
| ❑ 42 Adrian Beltre | .30 | .14 |
| ❑ 43 Gary Sheffield | .75 | .35 |
| ❑ 44 Kevin Brown | .50 | .23 |
| ❑ 45 Jeromy Burnitz | .30 | .14 |
| ❑ 46 Jeff Cirillo | .30 | .14 |
| ❑ 47 Joe Mays | .20 | .09 |
| ❑ 48 Todd Walker | .20 | .09 |
| ❑ 49 Vladimir Guerrero | 1.25 | .55 |
| ❑ 50 Michael Barrett | .20 | .09 |
| ❑ 51 Rickey Henderson | 1.00 | .45 |
| ❑ 52 Mike Piazza | 2.50 | 1.10 |
| ❑ 53 Robin Ventura | .50 | .23 |
| ❑ 54 John Olerud | .30 | .14 |
| ❑ 55 Edgardo Alfonzo | .30 | .14 |
| ❑ 56 Derek Jeter | 3.00 | 1.35 |
| ❑ 57 Orlando Hernandez | .30 | .14 |
| ❑ 58 Tino Martinez | .30 | .14 |
| ❑ 59 Bernie Williams | .75 | .35 |
| ❑ 60 Roger Clemens | 1.50 | .70 |
| ❑ 61 Eric Chavez | .30 | .14 |
| ❑ 62 Ben Grieve | .30 | .14 |
| ❑ 63 Jason Giambi | .50 | .23 |
| ❑ 64 Scott Rolen | .75 | .35 |
| ❑ 65 Bob Abreu | .30 | .14 |
| ❑ 66 Curt Schilling | .30 | .14 |
| ❑ 67 Mike Lieberthal | .30 | .14 |
| ❑ 68 Warren Morris | .20 | .09 |
| ❑ 69 Brian Giles | .30 | .14 |
| ❑ 70 Eric Owens | .20 | .09 |
| ❑ 71 Tony Gwynn | 1.50 | .70 |
| ❑ 72 Reggie Sanders | .20 | .09 |
| ❑ 73 Barry Bonds | 1.25 | .55 |
| ❑ 74 J.T. Snow | .30 | .14 |
| ❑ 75 Jeff Kent | .50 | .23 |
| ❑ 76 Ken Griffey Jr. | 3.00 | 1.35 |
| ❑ 77 Alex Rodriguez | 2.50 | 1.10 |
| ❑ 78 Edgar Martinez | .50 | .23 |
| ❑ 79 Jay Buhner | .30 | .14 |
| ❑ 80 Mark McGwire | 3.00 | 1.35 |
| ❑ 81 J.D. Drew | .75 | .35 |
| ❑ 82 Eric Davis | .30 | .14 |
| ❑ 83 Fernando Tatis | .30 | .14 |
| ❑ 84 Wade Boggs | 1.00 | .45 |
| ❑ 85 Fred McGriff | .50 | .23 |
| ❑ 86 Juan Gonzalez | .75 | .35 |
| ❑ 87 Ivan Rodriguez | 1.00 | .45 |
| ❑ 88 Rafael Palmeiro | .75 | .35 |
| ❑ 89 Shawn Green | .75 | .35 |
| ❑ 90 Carlos Delgado | .75 | .35 |
| ❑ 91 Pat Burrell DD | 6.00 | 2.70 |
| ❑ 92 Eric Munson DD | 4.00 | 1.80 |
| ❑ 93 Jorge Toca DD | 2.00 | .90 |
| ❑ 94 Rick Ankiel DD | 8.00 | 3.60 |
| ❑ 95 Tony Armas Jr. DD | 2.00 | .90 |
| ❑ 96 Byung-Hyun Kim DD | 2.00 | .90 |
| ❑ 97 Alfonso Soriano DD | 2.00 | .90 |
| ❑ 98 Mark Quinn DD | 2.00 | .90 |
| ❑ 99 Ryan Rupe DD | 2.00 | .90 |
| ❑ 100 Adam Kennedy DD | 2.00 | .90 |
| ❑ 101 Jeff Weaver DD | 2.00 | .90 |
| ❑ 102 Ramon Ortiz DD | 2.00 | .90 |
| ❑ 103 Eugene Kingsale DD | 2.00 | .90 |
| ❑ 104 Josh Beckett DD | 4.00 | 1.80 |
| ❑ 105 Eric Gagne DD | 2.00 | .90 |
| ❑ 106 Peter Bergeron DD | 2.00 | .90 |
| ❑ 107 Erubiel Durazo DD | 2.00 | .90 |
| ❑ 108 Chad Meyers DD | 2.00 | .90 |
| ❑ 109 Kip Wells DD | 2.00 | .90 |
| ❑ 110 Chad Harville DD | 2.00 | .90 |
| ❑ 111 Matt Riley DD | 2.00 | .90 |
| ❑ 112 Ben Petrick DD | 2.00 | .90 |
| ❑ 113 Ed Yarnall DD | 2.00 | .90 |
| ❑ 114 Calvin Murray DD | 2.00 | .90 |
| ❑ 115 Vernon Wells DD | 2.00 | .90 |
| ❑ 116 A.J. Burnett DD | 2.00 | .90 |
| ❑ 117 Jacque Jones DD | 2.00 | .90 |
| ❑ 118 Francisco Cordero DD | 2.00 | .90 |
| ❑ 119 Tomokazu Ohka DD RC | 4.00 | 1.80 |
| ❑ 120 Julio Ramirez DD | 2.00 | .90 |

## 2000 Black Diamond Rookie Edition

| | MINT | NRMT |
|---|---|---|
| COMPLETE SET (154) | 1200.00 | 550.00 |
| COMP.SET w/o SP's (90) | 25.00 | 11.00 |
| COMMON CARD (1-90) | .20 | .09 |
| COMMON GEMS (91-120) | 10.00 | 4.50 |
| COMMON JERSEY (121-136) | 20.00 | 9.00 |
| COMMON USA (137-154) | 20.00 | 9.00 |

| Card | MINT | NRMT |
|---|---|---|
| ❑ 1 Troy Glaus | 1.00 | .45 |
| ❑ 2 Mo Vaughn | .30 | .14 |
| ❑ 3 Darin Erstad | .75 | .35 |
| ❑ 4 Jason Giambi | .75 | .35 |
| ❑ 5 Tim Hudson | .60 | .25 |
| ❑ 6 Ben Grieve | .30 | .14 |
| ❑ 7 Eric Chavez | .30 | .14 |
| ❑ 8 Tony Batista | .30 | .14 |
| ❑ 9 Carlos Delgado | .75 | .35 |
| ❑ 10 David Wells | .30 | .14 |
| ❑ 11 Greg Vaughn | .30 | .14 |
| ❑ 12 Fred McGriff | .50 | .23 |
| ❑ 13 Manny Ramirez | 1.00 | .45 |
| ❑ 14 Roberto Alomar | .75 | .35 |
| ❑ 15 Jim Thome | .50 | .23 |
| ❑ 16 Alex Rodriguez | 2.50 | 1.10 |
| ❑ 17 Edgar Martinez | .50 | .23 |
| ❑ 18 John Olerud | .30 | .14 |
| ❑ 19 Albert Belle | .50 | .23 |
| ❑ 20 Mike Mussina | .75 | .35 |
| ❑ 21 Cal Ripken | 3.00 | 1.35 |
| ❑ 22 Ivan Rodriguez | 1.00 | .45 |
| ❑ 23 Rafael Palmeiro | .60 | .25 |
| ❑ 24 Pedro Martinez | 1.00 | .45 |
| ❑ 25 Nomar Garciaparra | 2.50 | 1.10 |
| ❑ 26 Carl Everett | .30 | .14 |
| ❑ 27 Jermaine Dye | .30 | .14 |
| ❑ 28 Mike Sweeney | .30 | .14 |
| ❑ 29 Juan Gonzalez | .60 | .25 |
| ❑ 30 Bobby Higginson | .30 | .14 |
| ❑ 31 Dean Palmer | .30 | .14 |
| ❑ 32 Jacque Jones | .30 | .14 |
| ❑ 33 Eric Milton | .20 | .09 |
| ❑ 34 Matt Lawton | .30 | .14 |
| ❑ 35 Maggio Ordonez | .30 | .14 |
| ❑ 36 Paul Konerko | .30 | .14 |
| ❑ 37 Frank Thomas | 1.50 | .70 |
| ❑ 38 Ray Durham | .30 | .14 |
| ❑ 39 Roger Clemens | 1.50 | .70 |
| ❑ 40 Derek Jeter | 3.00 | 1.35 |
| ❑ 41 Bernie Williams | .60 | .25 |
| ❑ 42 Jose Canseco | 1.00 | .45 |
| ❑ 43 Craig Biggio | .50 | .23 |
| ❑ 44 Richard Hidalgo | .30 | .14 |
| ❑ 45 Jeff Bagwell | 1.00 | .45 |
| ❑ 46 Greg Maddux | 2.00 | .90 |
| ❑ 47 Chipper Jones | 2.00 | .90 |
| ❑ 48 Rafael Furcal | 1.25 | .55 |
| ❑ 49 Andruw Jones | .75 | .35 |
| ❑ 50 Geoff Jenkins | .30 | .14 |
| ❑ 51 Jeromy Burnitz | .30 | .14 |
| ❑ 52 Mark McGwire | 3.00 | 1.35 |
| ❑ 53 Rick Ankiel | 1.00 | .45 |
| ❑ 54 Jim Edmonds | .60 | .25 |
| ❑ 55 Kerry Wood | .30 | .14 |
| ❑ 56 Sammy Sosa | 1.50 | .70 |
| ❑ 57 Matt Williams | .50 | .23 |
| ❑ 58 Randy Johnson | 1.00 | .45 |
| ❑ 59 Steve Finley | .30 | .14 |
| ❑ 60 Curt Schilling | .30 | .14 |
| ❑ 61 Kevin Brown | .30 | .14 |
| ❑ 62 Gary Sheffield | .60 | .25 |
| ❑ 63 Shawn Green | .60 | .25 |
| ❑ 64 Jose Vidro | .30 | .14 |
| ❑ 65 Vladimir Guerrero | 1.25 | .55 |
| ❑ 66 Jeff Kent | .50 | .23 |
| ❑ 67 Barry Bonds | 1.25 | .55 |
| ❑ 68 Ryan Dempster | .30 | .14 |
| ❑ 69 Cliff Floyd | .30 | .14 |
| ❑ 70 Preston Wilson | .30 | .14 |
| ❑ 71 Mike Piazza | 2.50 | 1.10 |
| ❑ 72 Al Leiter | .30 | .14 |
| ❑ 73 Edgardo Alfonzo | .30 | .14 |
| ❑ 74 Derek Bell | .20 | .09 |
| ❑ 75 Ryan Klesko | .30 | .14 |
| ❑ 76 Tony Gwynn | 1.50 | .70 |
| ❑ 77 Bob Abreu | .30 | .14 |
| ❑ 78 Pat Burrell | .75 | .35 |
| ❑ 79 Scott Rolen | .60 | .25 |
| ❑ 80 Mike Lieberthal | .30 | .14 |
| ❑ 81 Jason Kendall | .30 | .14 |
| ❑ 82 Brian Giles | .30 | .14 |

| Card | | NRMT | VG-E |
|---|---|---|---|
| 83 | Ken Griffey Jr. | 3.00 | 1.35 |
| 84 | Pokey Reese | .30 | .14 |
| 85 | Dmitri Young | .30 | .14 |
| 86 | Sean Casey | .30 | .14 |
| 87 | Jeff Cirillo | .30 | .14 |
| 88 | Todd Helton | 1.00 | .45 |
| 89 | Jeffrey Hammonds | .30 | .14 |
| 90 | Larry Walker | .30 | .14 |
| 91 | Barry Zito RC | 50.00 | 22.00 |
| 92 | Keith Ginter RC | 15.00 | 6.75 |
| 93 | Dane Sardinha RC | 15.00 | 6.75 |
| 94 | Kenny Kelly RC | 10.00 | 4.50 |
| 95 | Ryan Kohlmeier RC | 10.00 | 4.50 |
| 96 | Leo Estrella RC | 10.00 | 4.50 |
| 97 | Danys Baez RC | 15.00 | 6.75 |
| 98 | Paul Rigdon RC | 10.00 | 4.50 |
| 99 | Mike Lamb RC | 12.00 | 5.50 |
| 100 | Aaron McNeal RC | 15.00 | 6.75 |
| 101 | Juan Pierre RC | 15.00 | 6.75 |
| 102 | Rico Washington RC | 10.00 | 4.50 |
| 103 | Luis Matos RC | 15.00 | 6.75 |
| 104 | Adam Bernero RC | 10.00 | 4.50 |
| 105 | Wascar Serrano RC | 10.00 | 4.50 |
| 106 | Chris Richard RC | 10.00 | 4.50 |
| 107 | Justin Miller RC | 15.00 | 6.75 |
| 108 | Julio Zuleta RC | 10.00 | 4.50 |
| 109 | Alex Cabrera RC | 15.00 | 6.75 |
| 110 | Gene Stechschulte RC | 10.00 | 4.50 |
| 111 | Tony Mota RC | 10.00 | 4.50 |
| 112 | Tomokazu Ohka RC | 15.00 | 6.75 |
| 113 | Geraldo Guzman RC | 10.00 | 4.50 |
| 114 | Scott Downs RC | 10.00 | 4.50 |
| 115 | Timo Perez RC | 20.00 | 9.00 |
| 116 | Chad Durbin RC | 10.00 | 4.50 |
| 117 | Sun-Woo Kim RC | 15.00 | 6.75 |
| 118 | Tomas De la Rosa RC | 10.00 | 4.50 |
| 119 | Javier Cardona RC | 10.00 | 4.50 |
| 120 | Kazuhiro Sasaki RC | 40.00 | 18.00 |
| 121 | Brad Cresse JSY RC | 50.00 | 22.00 |
| 122 | Matt Wheatland JSY RC | 25.00 | 11.00 |
| 123 | Joe Torres JSY RC | 20.00 | 9.00 |
| 124 | Dave Krynzel JSY RC | 25.00 | 11.00 |
| 125 | Ben Diggins JSY RC | 20.00 | 9.00 |
| 126 | Sean Burnett JSY RC | 20.00 | 9.00 |
| 127 | David Espinosa JSY RC | 25.00 | 11.00 |
| 128 | Scott Heard JSY RC | 20.00 | 9.00 |
| 129 | Daylan Holt JSY RC | 20.00 | 9.00 |
| 130 | Koyie Hill JSY RC | 20.00 | 9.00 |
| 131 | Mark Buehrle JSY RC | 20.00 | 9.00 |
| 132 | Xavier Nady JSY RC | 60.00 | 27.00 |
| 133 | Mike Tonis JSY RC | 30.00 | 13.50 |
| 134 | Matt Ginter JSY RC | 20.00 | 9.00 |
| 135 | Lorenzo Barcelo JSY RC | 20.00 | 9.00 |
| 136 | Cory Vance JSY RC | 20.00 | 9.00 |
| 137 | Sean Burroughs USA | 50.00 | 22.00 |
| 138 | Todd Williams USA | 20.00 | 9.00 |
| 139 | Brad Wilkerson USA RC | 25.00 | 11.00 |
| 140 | Ben Sheets USA RC | 60.00 | 27.00 |
| 141 | Kurt Ainsworth USA RC | 25.00 | 11.00 |
| 142 | Anthony Sanders USA | 20.00 | 9.00 |
| 143 | Ryan Franklin USA RC | 20.00 | 9.00 |
| 144 | Shane Heams USA RC | 20.00 | 9.00 |
| 145 | Roy Oswalt USA RC | 20.00 | 9.00 |
| 146 | Jon Rauch USA RC | 40.00 | 18.00 |
| 147 | Brent Abernathy USA RC | 20.00 | 9.00 |
| 148 | Ernie Young USA | 20.00 | 9.00 |
| 149 | Chris George USA | 20.00 | 9.00 |
| 150 | Gookie Dawkins USA | 20.00 | 9.00 |
| 151 | Adam Everett USA | 20.00 | 9.00 |
| 152 | John Cotton USA RC | 20.00 | 9.00 |
| 153 | Pat Borders USA | 20.00 | 9.00 |
| 154 | Doug Mientkiewicz USA | 20.00 | 9.00 |

## 1948 Bowman

| | NRMT | VG-E |
|---|---|---|
| COMPLETE SET (48) | 3400.00 | 1500.00 |
| COMMON CARD (1-36) | 20.00 | 9.00 |
| COMMON CARD (37-48) | 30.00 | 13.50 |
| WRAPPER (5-CENT) | 700.00 | 325.00 |

| Card | | NRMT | VG-E |
|---|---|---|---|
| 1 | Bob Elliott RC ! | 125.00 | 19.00 |
| 2 | Ewell Blackwell RC | 50.00 | 22.00 |
| 3 | Ralph Kiner RC | 150.00 | 70.00 |
| 4 | Johnny Mize | 100.00 | 45.00 |
| 5 | Bob Feller | 250.00 | 110.00 |

| Card | | NRMT | VG-E |
|---|---|---|---|
| 6 | Yogi Berra RC ! | 450.00 | 200.00 |
| 7 | Pete Reiser SP | 120.00 | 55.00 |
| 8 | Phil Rizzuto RC SP | 300.00 | 135.00 |
| 9 | Walker Cooper | 20.00 | 9.00 |
| 10 | Buddy Rosar | 20.00 | 9.00 |
| 11 | Johnny Lindell | 25.00 | 11.00 |
| 12 | Johnny Sain RC | 50.00 | 22.00 |
| 13 | Willard Marshall SP | 40.00 | 18.00 |
| 14 | Allie Reynolds RC | 50.00 | 22.00 |
| 15 | Eddie Joost | 20.00 | 9.00 |
| 16 | Jack Lohrke SP | 40.00 | 18.00 |
| 17 | Enos Slaughter | 100.00 | 45.00 |
| 18 | Warren Spahn RC | 300.00 | 135.00 |
| 19 | Tommy Henrich | 50.00 | 22.00 |
| 20 | Buddy Kerr SP | 40.00 | 18.00 |
| 21 | Ferris Fain RC | 40.00 | 18.00 |
| 22 | Floyd Bevens RC SP | 50.00 | 22.00 |
| 23 | Larry Jansen RC | 25.00 | 11.00 |
| 24 | Dutch Leonard SP | 40.00 | 18.00 |
| 25 | Barney McCosky | 20.00 | 9.00 |
| 26 | Frank Shea RC SP | 50.00 | 22.00 |
| 27 | Sid Gordon | 25.00 | 11.00 |
| 28 | Emil Verban SP | 40.00 | 18.00 |
| 29 | Joe Page RC SP | 75.00 | 34.00 |
| 30 | Whitey Lockman RC SP | 50.00 | 22.00 |
| 31 | Bill McCahan | 20.00 | 9.00 |
| 32 | Bill Rigney | 20.00 | 9.00 |
| 33 | Bill Johnson | 25.00 | 11.00 |
| 34 | Sheldon Jones SP | 40.00 | 18.00 |
| 35 | Snuffy Stirnweiss RC | 40.00 | 18.00 |
| 36 | Stan Musial RC ! | 800.00 | 350.00 |
| 37 | Clint Hartung RC | 30.00 | 13.50 |
| 38 | Red Schoendienst RC | 150.00 | 70.00 |
| 39 | Augie Galan | 30.00 | 13.50 |
| 40 | Marty Marion RC | 80.00 | 36.00 |
| 41 | Rex Barney RC | 60.00 | 27.00 |
| 42 | Ray Poat | 30.00 | 13.50 |
| 43 | Bruce Edwards | 40.00 | 18.00 |
| 44 | Johnny Wyrostek | 30.00 | 13.50 |
| 45 | Hank Sauer RC | 60.00 | 27.00 |
| 46 | Herman Wehmeier | 30.00 | 13.50 |
| 47 | Bobby Thomson RC | 100.00 | 45.00 |
| 48 | Dave Koslo RC ! | 80.00 | 19.50 |

## 1949 Bowman

JOHNNY VANDER MEER

| | NRMT | VG-E |
|---|---|---|
| COMP. MASTER SET (252) | 16000.00 | 7200.00 |
| COMPLETE SET (240) | 13000.00 | 5800.00 |
| COMMON CARD (1-144) | 15.00 | 6.75 |
| COMMON CARD (145-240) | 50.00 | 22.00 |
| WRAPPER (5-CENT, GR.) | 250.00 | 110.00 |
| WRAPPER (5-CENT, BL.) | 200.00 | 90.00 |

| Card | | NRMT | VG-E |
|---|---|---|---|
| 1 | Vern Bickford RC ! | 125.00 | 25.00 |
| 2 | Whitey Lockman | 40.00 | 18.00 |
| 3 | Bob Porterfield | 15.00 | 6.75 |
| 4A | Jerry Priddy NNOF | 15.00 | 6.75 |
| 4B | Jerry Priddy NOF | 50.00 | 22.00 |
| 5 | Hank Sauer | 40.00 | 18.00 |
| 6 | Phil Cavarretta | 40.00 | 18.00 |
| 7 | Joe Dobson | 15.00 | 6.75 |
| 8 | Murry Dickson | 15.00 | 6.75 |
| 9 | Ferris Fain | 40.00 | 18.00 |
| 10 | Ted Gray | 15.00 | 6.75 |
| 11 | Lou Boudreau | 75.00 | 34.00 |
| 12 | Cass Michaels | 15.00 | 6.75 |
| 13 | Bob Chesnes | 15.00 | 6.75 |
| 14 | Curt Simmons RC | 40.00 | 18.00 |
| 15 | Ned Garver | 15.00 | 6.75 |
| 16 | Al Kozar | 15.00 | 6.75 |
| 17 | Earl Torgeson | 15.00 | 6.75 |
| 18 | Bobby Thomson | 40.00 | 18.00 |
| 19 | Bobby Brown RC | 40.00 | 18.00 |
| 20 | Gene Hermanski | 15.00 | 6.75 |
| 21 | Frank Baumholtz | 25.00 | 11.00 |
| 22 | Peanuts Lowrey | 15.00 | 6.75 |
| 23 | Bobby Doerr | 75.00 | 34.00 |
| 24 | Stan Musial | 500.00 | 220.00 |
| 25 | Carl Scheib | 15.00 | 6.75 |
| 26 | George Kell RC | 75.00 | 34.00 |
| 27 | Bob Feller | 200.00 | 90.00 |
| 28 | Don Kolloway | 15.00 | 6.75 |
| 29 | Ralph Kiner | 125.00 | 55.00 |
| 30 | Andy Seminick | 40.00 | 18.00 |
| 31 | Dick Kokos | 15.00 | 6.75 |
| 32 | Eddie Yost RC | 60.00 | 27.00 |
| 33 | Warren Spahn | 200.00 | 90.00 |
| 34 | Dave Koslo | 15.00 | 6.75 |
| 35 | Vic Raschi RC | 60.00 | 27.00 |
| 36 | Pee Wee Reese | 200.00 | 90.00 |
| 37 | Johnny Wyrostek | 15.00 | 6.75 |
| 38 | Emil Verban | 15.00 | 6.75 |
| 39 | Billy Goodman | 25.00 | 11.00 |
| 40 | Red Munger | 15.00 | 6.75 |
| 41 | Lou Brissie | 15.00 | 6.75 |
| 42 | Hoot Evers | 15.00 | 6.75 |
| 43 | Dale Mitchell | 40.00 | 18.00 |
| 44 | Dave Philley | 15.00 | 6.75 |
| 45 | Wally Westlake | 15.00 | 6.75 |
| 46 | Robin Roberts RC | 250.00 | 110.00 |
| 47 | Johnny Sain | 60.00 | 27.00 |
| 48 | Willard Marshall | 15.00 | 6.75 |
| 49 | Frank Shea | 25.00 | 11.00 |
| 50 | Jackie Robinson RC | 1100.00 | 500.00 |
| 51 | Herman Wehmeier | 15.00 | 6.75 |
| 52 | Johnny Schmitz | 15.00 | 6.75 |
| 53 | Jack Kramer | 15.00 | 6.75 |
| 54 | Marty Marion | 60.00 | 27.00 |
| 55 | Eddie Joost | 15.00 | 6.75 |
| 56 | Pat Mullin | 15.00 | 6.75 |
| 57 | Gene Bearden | 40.00 | 18.00 |
| 58 | Bob Elliott | 40.00 | 18.00 |
| 59 | Jack Lohrke | 15.00 | 6.75 |
| 60 | Yogi Berra | 300.00 | 135.00 |
| 61 | Rex Barney | 40.00 | 18.00 |
| 62 | Grady Hatton | 15.00 | 6.75 |
| 63 | Andy Pafko | 40.00 | 18.00 |
| 64 | Dom DiMaggio | 60.00 | 27.00 |
| 65 | Enos Slaughter | 75.00 | 34.00 |
| 66 | Elmer Valo | 15.00 | 6.75 |
| 67 | Alvin Dark | 40.00 | 18.00 |
| 68 | Sheldon Jones | 15.00 | 6.75 |
| 69 | Tommy Henrich | 40.00 | 18.00 |
| 70 | Carl Furillo RC | 100.00 | 45.00 |
| 71 | Vern Stephens | 15.00 | 6.75 |
| 72 | Tommy Holmes | 40.00 | 18.00 |
| 73 | Billy Cox RC | 40.00 | 18.00 |
| 74 | Tom McBride | 15.00 | 6.75 |
| 75 | Eddie Mayo | 15.00 | 6.75 |
| 76 | Bill Nicholson RC | 25.00 | 11.00 |
| 77 | Ernie Bonham | 15.00 | 6.75 |
| 78A | Sam Zoldak NNOF | 15.00 | 6.75 |
| 78B | Sam Zoldak NOF | 50.00 | 22.00 |
| 79 | Ron Northey | 15.00 | 6.75 |
| 80 | Bill McCahan | 15.00 | 6.75 |
| 81 | Virgil Stallcup | 15.00 | 6.75 |
| 82 | Joe Page | 60.00 | 27.00 |
| 83A | Bob Scheffing NNOF | 15.00 | 6.75 |
| 83B | Bob Scheffing NOF | 50.00 | 22.00 |
| 84 | Roy Campanella RC ! | 700.00 | 325.00 |
| 85A | Johnny Mize NNOF | 100.00 | 45.00 |

| Card | NRMT | VG-E |
|---|---|---|
| ❑ 85B Johnny Mize NOF | 150.00 | 70.00 |
| ❑ 86 Johnny Pesky | 60.00 | 27.00 |
| ❑ 87 Randy Gumpert | 15.00 | 6.75 |
| ❑ 88A Bill Salkeld NNOF | 15.00 | 6.75 |
| ❑ 88B Bill Salkeld NOF | 50.00 | 22.00 |
| ❑ 89 Mizell Platt | 15.00 | 6.75 |
| ❑ 90 Gil Coan | 15.00 | 6.75 |
| ❑ 91 Dick Wakefield | 15.00 | 6.75 |
| ❑ 92 Willie Jones | 40.00 | 18.00 |
| ❑ 93 Ed Stevens | 15.00 | 6.75 |
| ❑ 94 Mickey Vernon RC | 40.00 | 18.00 |
| ❑ 95 Howie Pollet RC | 15.00 | 6.75 |
| ❑ 96 Taft Wright | 15.00 | 6.75 |
| ❑ 97 Danny Litwhiler | 15.00 | 6.75 |
| ❑ 98A Phil Rizzuto NNOF | 175.00 | 80.00 |
| ❑ 98B Phil Rizzuto NOF | 250.00 | 110.00 |
| ❑ 99 Frank Gustine | 15.00 | 6.75 |
| ❑ 100 Gil Hodges RC | 250.00 | 110.00 |
| ❑ 101 Sid Gordon | 15.00 | 6.75 |
| ❑ 102 Stan Spence | 15.00 | 6.75 |
| ❑ 103 Joe Tipton | 15.00 | 6.75 |
| ❑ 104 Eddie Stanky RC | 40.00 | 18.00 |
| ❑ 105 Bill Kennedy | 15.00 | 6.75 |
| ❑ 106 Jake Early | 15.00 | 6.75 |
| ❑ 107 Eddie Lake | 15.00 | 6.75 |
| ❑ 108 Ken Heintzelman | 15.00 | 6.75 |
| ❑ 109A Ed Fitzgerald SCR | 15.00 | 6.75 |
| ❑ 109B Ed Fitzgerald PR | 60.00 | 27.00 |
| ❑ 110 Early Wynn RC | 125.00 | 55.00 |
| ❑ 111 Red Schoendienst | 80.00 | 36.00 |
| ❑ 112 Sam Chapman | 40.00 | 18.00 |
| ❑ 113 Ray LaManno | 15.00 | 6.75 |
| ❑ 114 Allie Reynolds | 40.00 | 18.00 |
| ❑ 115 Dutch Leonard | 15.00 | 6.75 |
| ❑ 116 Joe Hatton | 15.00 | 6.75 |
| ❑ 117 Walker Cooper | 15.00 | 6.75 |
| ❑ 118 Sam Mele | 15.00 | 6.75 |
| ❑ 119 Floyd Baker | 15.00 | 6.75 |
| ❑ 120 Cliff Fannin | 15.00 | 6.75 |
| ❑ 121 Mark Christman | 15.00 | 6.75 |
| ❑ 122 George Vico | 15.00 | 6.75 |
| ❑ 123 Johnny Blatnick | 15.00 | 6.75 |
| ❑ 124A Danny Murtaugh RC SCR | 50.00 | 22.00 |
| ❑ 124B Danny Murtaugh RC PR | 70.00 | 32.00 |
| ❑ 125 Ken Keltner | 25.00 | 11.00 |
| ❑ 126A Al Brazle SCR | 15.00 | 6.75 |
| ❑ 126B Al Brazle PR | 60.00 | 27.00 |
| ❑ 127A Hank Majeski SCR | 15.00 | 6.75 |
| ❑ 127B Hank Majeski PR | 60.00 | 27.00 |
| ❑ 128 Johnny VanderMeer | 60.00 | 27.00 |
| ❑ 129 Bill Johnson | 40.00 | 18.00 |
| ❑ 130 Harry Walker | 15.00 | 6.75 |
| ❑ 131 Paul Lehner | 15.00 | 6.75 |
| ❑ 132A Al Evans SCR | 15.00 | 6.75 |
| ❑ 132B Al Evans PR | 60.00 | 27.00 |
| ❑ 133 Aaron Robinson | 15.00 | 6.75 |
| ❑ 134 Hank Borowy | 15.00 | 6.75 |
| ❑ 135 Stan Rojek | 15.00 | 6.75 |
| ❑ 136 Hank Edwards | 15.00 | 6.75 |
| ❑ 137 Ted Wilks | 15.00 | 6.75 |
| ❑ 138 Buddy Rosar | 15.00 | 6.75 |
| ❑ 139 Hank Arft | 15.00 | 6.75 |
| ❑ 140 Ray Scarborough | 15.00 | 6.75 |
| ❑ 141 Tony Lupien | 15.00 | 6.75 |
| ❑ 142 Eddie Waitkus RC | 40.00 | 18.00 |
| ❑ 143A Bob Dillinger RC SCR | 25.00 | 11.00 |
| ❑ 143B Bob Dillinger RC PR | 60.00 | 27.00 |
| ❑ 144 Mickey Haefner | 15.00 | 6.75 |
| ❑ 145 Sylvester Donnelly | 50.00 | 22.00 |
| ❑ 146 Mike McCormick | 50.00 | 22.00 |
| ❑ 147 Bert Singleton | 50.00 | 22.00 |
| ❑ 148 Bob Swift | 50.00 | 22.00 |
| ❑ 149 Roy Partee | 50.00 | 22.00 |
| ❑ 150 Allie Clark | 50.00 | 22.00 |
| ❑ 151 Mickey Harris | 50.00 | 22.00 |
| ❑ 152 Clarence Maddern | 50.00 | 22.00 |
| ❑ 153 Phil Masi | 50.00 | 22.00 |
| ❑ 154 Clint Hartung | 60.00 | 27.00 |
| ❑ 155 Mickey Guerra | 50.00 | 22.00 |
| ❑ 156 Al Zarilla | 50.00 | 22.00 |
| ❑ 157 Walt Masterson | 50.00 | 22.00 |
| ❑ 158 Harry Brecheen | 60.00 | 27.00 |
| ❑ 159 Glen Moulder | 50.00 | 22.00 |
| ❑ 160 Jim Blackburn | 50.00 | 22.00 |
| ❑ 161 Jocko Thompson | 50.00 | 22.00 |
| ❑ 162 Preacher Roe RC | 125.00 | 55.00 |
| ❑ 163 Clyde McCullough | 50.00 | 22.00 |
| ❑ 164 Vic Wertz RC | 75.00 | 34.00 |
| ❑ 165 Snuffy Stirnweiss | 75.00 | 34.00 |
| ❑ 166 Mike Tresh | 50.00 | 22.00 |
| ❑ 167 Babe Martin | 50.00 | 22.00 |
| ❑ 168 Doyle Lade | 50.00 | 22.00 |
| ❑ 169 Jeff Heath | 60.00 | 27.00 |
| ❑ 170 Bill Rigney | 60.00 | 27.00 |
| ❑ 171 Dick Fowler | 50.00 | 22.00 |
| ❑ 172 Eddie Pellagrini | 50.00 | 22.00 |
| ❑ 173 Eddie Stewart | 50.00 | 22.00 |
| ❑ 174 Terry Moore RC | 75.00 | 34.00 |
| ❑ 175 Luke Appling | 125.00 | 55.00 |
| ❑ 176 Ken Raffensberger | 50.00 | 22.00 |
| ❑ 177 Stan Lopata | 60.00 | 27.00 |
| ❑ 178 Tom Brown | 60.00 | 27.00 |
| ❑ 179 Hugh Casey | 75.00 | 34.00 |
| ❑ 180 Connie Berry | 50.00 | 22.00 |
| ❑ 181 Gus Niarhos | 50.00 | 22.00 |
| ❑ 182 Hal Peck | 50.00 | 22.00 |
| ❑ 183 Lou Stringer | 50.00 | 22.00 |
| ❑ 184 Bob Chipman | 50.00 | 22.00 |
| ❑ 185 Pete Reiser | 75.00 | 34.00 |
| ❑ 186 Buddy Kerr | 50.00 | 22.00 |
| ❑ 187 Phil Marchildon | 50.00 | 22.00 |
| ❑ 188 Karl Drews | 50.00 | 22.00 |
| ❑ 189 Earl Wooten | 50.00 | 22.00 |
| ❑ 190 Jim Hearn | 50.00 | 22.00 |
| ❑ 191 Joe Haynes | 50.00 | 22.00 |
| ❑ 192 Harry Gumbert | 50.00 | 22.00 |
| ❑ 193 Ken Trinkle | 50.00 | 22.00 |
| ❑ 194 Ralph Branca RC | 75.00 | 34.00 |
| ❑ 195 Eddie Bockman | 50.00 | 22.00 |
| ❑ 196 Fred Hutchinson | 60.00 | 27.00 |
| ❑ 197 Johnny Lindell | 60.00 | 27.00 |
| ❑ 198 Steve Gromek | 50.00 | 22.00 |
| ❑ 199 Tex Hughson | 50.00 | 22.00 |
| ❑ 200 Jess Dobernic | 50.00 | 22.00 |
| ❑ 201 Sibby Sisti | 50.00 | 22.00 |
| ❑ 202 Larry Jansen | 60.00 | 27.00 |
| ❑ 203 Barney McCosky | 50.00 | 22.00 |
| ❑ 204 Bob Savage | 50.00 | 22.00 |
| ❑ 205 Dick Sisler | 60.00 | 27.00 |
| ❑ 206 Bruce Edwards | 50.00 | 22.00 |
| ❑ 207 Johnny Hopp | 50.00 | 22.00 |
| ❑ 208 Dizzy Trout | 60.00 | 27.00 |
| ❑ 209 Charlie Keller | 75.00 | 34.00 |
| ❑ 210 Joe Gordon | 75.00 | 34.00 |
| ❑ 211 Boo Ferriss | 50.00 | 22.00 |
| ❑ 212 Ralph Hamner | 50.00 | 22.00 |
| ❑ 213 Red Barrett | 50.00 | 22.00 |
| ❑ 214 Richie Ashburn RC | 550.00 | 250.00 |
| ❑ 215 Kirby Higbe | 50.00 | 22.00 |
| ❑ 216 Schoolboy Rowe | 60.00 | 27.00 |
| ❑ 217 Marino Pieretti | 50.00 | 22.00 |
| ❑ 218 Dick Kryhoski | 50.00 | 22.00 |
| ❑ 219 Virgil Fire Trucks | 60.00 | 27.00 |
| ❑ 220 Johnny McCarthy | 50.00 | 22.00 |
| ❑ 221 Bob Muncrief | 50.00 | 22.00 |
| ❑ 222 Alex Kellner | 50.00 | 22.00 |
| ❑ 223 Bobby Hofman | 50.00 | 22.00 |
| ❑ 224 Satchell Paige RC | 1000.00 | 450.00 |
| ❑ 225 Jerry Coleman RC | 75.00 | 34.00 |
| ❑ 226 Duke Snider RC ! | 900.00 | 400.00 |
| ❑ 227 Fritz Ostermueller | 50.00 | 22.00 |
| ❑ 228 Jackie Mayo | 50.00 | 22.00 |
| ❑ 229 Ed Lopat RC | 125.00 | 55.00 |
| ❑ 230 Augie Galan | 60.00 | 27.00 |
| ❑ 231 Earl Johnson | 50.00 | 22.00 |
| ❑ 232 George McQuinn | 60.00 | 27.00 |
| ❑ 233 Larry Doby RC | 200.00 | 90.00 |
| ❑ 234 Rip Sewell | 50.00 | 22.00 |
| ❑ 235 Jim Russell | 50.00 | 22.00 |
| ❑ 236 Fred Sanford | 50.00 | 22.00 |
| ❑ 237 Monte Kennedy | 50.00 | 22.00 |
| ❑ 238 Bob Lemon RC | 200.00 | 90.00 |
| ❑ 239 Frank McCormick | 50.00 | 22.00 |
| ❑ 240 Babe Young UER (Photo actually Bobby Young) | 100.00 | 25.00 |

## 1950 Bowman

| | NRMT | VG-E |
|---|---|---|
| COMPLETE SET (252) | 8500.00 | 3800.00 |
| COMMON CARD (1-72) | 50.00 | 22.00 |
| COMMON CARD (73-252) | 15.00 | 6.75 |
| WRAPPER (1-CENT) | 250.00 | 110.00 |
| WRAPPER (5-CENT) | 250.00 | 110.00 |

| Card | NRMT | VG-E |
|---|---|---|
| ❑ 1 Mel Parnell RC ! | 150.00 | 30.00 |
| ❑ 2 Vern Stephens | 60.00 | 27.00 |
| ❑ 3 Dom DiMaggio | 80.00 | 36.00 |
| ❑ 4 Gus Zernial RC | 60.00 | 27.00 |
| ❑ 5 Bob Kuzava | 50.00 | 22.00 |
| ❑ 6 Bob Feller | 250.00 | 110.00 |
| ❑ 7 Jim Hegan | 60.00 | 27.00 |
| ❑ 8 George Kell | 80.00 | 36.00 |
| ❑ 9 Vic Wertz | 60.00 | 27.00 |
| ❑ 10 Tommy Henrich | 80.00 | 36.00 |
| ❑ 11 Phil Rizzuto | 225.00 | 100.00 |
| ❑ 12 Joe Page | 80.00 | 36.00 |
| ❑ 13 Ferris Fain | 60.00 | 27.00 |
| ❑ 14 Alex Kellner | 50.00 | 22.00 |
| ❑ 15 Al Kozar | 50.00 | 22.00 |
| ❑ 16 Roy Sievers RC | 80.00 | 36.00 |
| ❑ 17 Sid Hudson | 50.00 | 22.00 |
| ❑ 18 Eddie Robinson | 50.00 | 22.00 |
| ❑ 19 Warren Spahn | 250.00 | 110.00 |
| ❑ 20 Bob Elliott | 60.00 | 27.00 |
| ❑ 21 Pee Wee Reese | 300.00 | 135.00 |
| ❑ 22 Jackie Robinson | 800.00 | 350.00 |
| ❑ 23 Don Newcombe RC | 150.00 | 70.00 |
| ❑ 24 Johnny Schmitz | 50.00 | 22.00 |
| ❑ 25 Hank Sauer | 60.00 | 27.00 |
| ❑ 26 Grady Hatton | 50.00 | 22.00 |
| ❑ 27 Herman Wehmeier | 50.00 | 22.00 |
| ❑ 28 Bobby Thomson | 80.00 | 36.00 |
| ❑ 29 Eddie Stanky | 60.00 | 27.00 |
| ❑ 30 Eddie Waitkus | 60.00 | 27.00 |
| ❑ 31 Del Ennis | 80.00 | 36.00 |
| ❑ 32 Robin Roberts | 150.00 | 70.00 |
| ❑ 33 Ralph Kiner | 100.00 | 45.00 |
| ❑ 34 Murry Dickson | 50.00 | 22.00 |
| ❑ 35 Enos Slaughter | 100.00 | 45.00 |
| ❑ 36 Eddie Kazak | 60.00 | 27.00 |
| ❑ 37 Luke Appling | 80.00 | 36.00 |
| ❑ 38 Bill Wight | 50.00 | 22.00 |
| ❑ 39 Larry Doby | 100.00 | 45.00 |
| ❑ 40 Bob Lemon | 80.00 | 36.00 |
| ❑ 41 Hoot Evers | 50.00 | 22.00 |
| ❑ 42 Art Houtteman | 50.00 | 22.00 |
| ❑ 43 Bobby Doerr | 80.00 | 36.00 |
| ❑ 44 Joe Dobson | 50.00 | 22.00 |
| ❑ 45 Al Zarilla | 50.00 | 22.00 |
| ❑ 46 Yogi Berra | 375.00 | 170.00 |
| ❑ 47 Jerry Coleman | 80.00 | 36.00 |
| ❑ 48 Lou Brissie | 50.00 | 22.00 |
| ❑ 49 Elmer Valo | 50.00 | 22.00 |
| ❑ 50 Dick Kokos | 50.00 | 22.00 |
| ❑ 51 Ned Garver | 60.00 | 27.00 |
| ❑ 52 Sam Mele | 50.00 | 22.00 |
| ❑ 53 Clyde Vollmer | 50.00 | 22.00 |
| ❑ 54 Gil Coan | 50.00 | 22.00 |
| ❑ 55 Buddy Kerr | 50.00 | 22.00 |
| ❑ 56 Del Crandall RC | 60.00 | 27.00 |
| ❑ 57 Vern Bickford | 50.00 | 22.00 |
| ❑ 58 Carl Furillo | 80.00 | 36.00 |
| ❑ 59 Ralph Branca | 80.00 | 36.00 |
| ❑ 60 Andy Pafko | 60.00 | 27.00 |
| ❑ 61 Bob Rush | 50.00 | 22.00 |
| ❑ 62 Ted Kluszewski | 125.00 | 55.00 |

❑ 63 Ewell Blackwell ............ 60.00 27.00
❑ 64 Alvin Dark .................... 60.00 27.00
❑ 65 Dave Koslo .................. 50.00 22.00
❑ 66 Larry Jansen ............... 60.00 27.00
❑ 67 Willie Jones ................. 60.00 27.00
❑ 68 Curt Simmons .............. 60.00 27.00
❑ 69 Wally Westlake ............ 50.00 22.00
❑ 70 Bob Chesnes ............... 50.00 22.00
❑ 71 Red Schoendienst ........ 80.00 36.00
❑ 72 Howie Pollet ............... 50.00 22.00
❑ 73 Willard Marshall ............ 15.00 6.75
❑ 74 Johnny Antonelli RC .... 60.00 27.00
❑ 75 Roy Campanella ......... 275.00 125.00
❑ 76 Rex Barney .................. 40.00 18.00
❑ 77 Duke Snider .............. 275.00 125.00
❑ 78 Mickey Owen ............... 25.00 11.00
❑ 79 Johnny VanderMeer .... 40.00 18.00
❑ 80 Howard Fox .................. 15.00 6.75
❑ 81 Ron Northey ................ 15.00 6.75
❑ 82 Whitey Lockman .......... 25.00 11.00
❑ 83 Sheldon Jones ............ 15.00 6.75
❑ 84 Richie Ashburn .......... 100.00 45.00
❑ 85 Ken Heintzelman .......... 15.00 6.75
❑ 86 Stan Rojek ................... 15.00 6.75
❑ 87 Bill Werle ...................... 15.00 6.75
❑ 88 Marty Marion ............... 40.00 18.00
❑ 89 Red Munger .................. 15.00 6.75
❑ 90 Harry Brecheen ............ 40.00 18.00
❑ 91 Cass Michaels .............. 15.00 6.75
❑ 92 Hank Majeski ................ 15.00 6.75
❑ 93 Gene Bearden .............. 40.00 18.00
❑ 94 Lou Boudreau .............. 60.00 27.00
❑ 95 Aaron Robinson .......... 15.00 6.75
❑ 96 Virgil Trucks ............... 25.00 11.00
❑ 97 Maurice McDermott ...... 15.00 6.75
❑ 98 Ted Williams ............ 1000.00 450.00
❑ 99 Billy Goodman .............. 25.00 11.00
❑ 100 Vic Raschi .................. 60.00 27.00
❑ 101 Bobby Brown .............. 60.00 27.00
❑ 102 Billy Johnson .............. 25.00 11.00
❑ 103 Eddie Joost ................ 15.00 6.75
❑ 104 Sam Chapman .......... 15.00 6.75
❑ 105 Bob Dillinger ............. 15.00 6.75
❑ 106 Cliff Fannin ............... 15.00 6.75
❑ 107 Sam Dente ................ 15.00 6.75
❑ 108 Ray Scarborough ...... 15.00 6.75
❑ 109 Sid Gordon ................ 15.00 6.75
❑ 110 Tommy Holmes .......... 25.00 11.00
❑ 111 Walker Cooper .......... 15.00 6.75
❑ 112 Gil Hodges .............. 100.00 45.00
❑ 113 Gene Hermanski ........ 15.00 6.75
❑ 114 Wayne Terwilliger RC 15.00 6.75
❑ 115 Roy Smalley .............. 15.00 6.75
❑ 116 Virgil Stallcup ........... 15.00 6.75
❑ 117 Bill Rigney ................. 15.00 6.75
❑ 118 Clint Hartung ............. 15.00 6.75
❑ 119 Dick Sisler ................. 25.00 11.00
❑ 120 John Thompson ........ 15.00 6.75
❑ 121 Andy Seminick ......... 25.00 11.00
❑ 122 Johnny Hopp ............. 25.00 11.00
❑ 123 Dino Restelli ............. 15.00 6.75
❑ 124 Clyde McCullough ...... 15.00 6.75
❑ 125 Del Rice ..................... 15.00 6.75
❑ 126 Al Brazle .................... 15.00 6.75
❑ 127 Dave Philley .............. 15.00 6.75
❑ 128 Phil Masi .................... 15.00 6.75
❑ 129 Joe Gordon ................ 25.00 11.00
❑ 130 Dale Mitchell ............. 25.00 11.00
❑ 131 Steve Gromek ............ 15.00 6.75
❑ 132 Mickey Vernon .......... 25.00 11.00
❑ 133 Don Kolloway ............ 15.00 6.75
❑ 134 Paul Trout .................. 15.00 6.75
❑ 135 Pat Mullin .................. 15.00 6.75
❑ 136 Warren Rosar ............ 15.00 6.75
❑ 137 Johnny Pesky ............ 25.00 11.00
❑ 138 Allie Reynolds ........... 60.00 27.00
❑ 139 Johnny Mize .............. 80.00 36.00
❑ 140 Pete Suder ................ 15.00 6.75
❑ 141 Joe Coleman .............. 25.00 11.00
❑ 142 Sherman Lollar RC .... 40.00 18.00
❑ 143 Eddie Stewart ............ 15.00 6.75
❑ 144 Al Evans ..................... 15.00 6.75
❑ 145 Jack Graham .............. 15.00 6.75
❑ 146 Floyd Baker ................ 15.00 6.75
❑ 147 Mike Garcia RC .......... 40.00 18.00
❑ 148 Early Wynn ................ 80.00 36.00
❑ 149 Bob Swift .................... 15.00 6.75
❑ 150 George Vico .............. 15.00 6.75
❑ 151 Fred Hutchinson ........ 25.00 11.00
❑ 152 Ellis Kinder RC .......... 15.00 6.75
❑ 153 Walt Masterson .......... 15.00 6.75
❑ 154 Gus Niarhos ............... 15.00 6.75
❑ 155 Frank Shea ................ 25.00 11.00
❑ 156 Fred Sanford .............. 25.00 11.00
❑ 157 Mike Guerra ............... 15.00 6.75
❑ 158 Paul Lehner ................ 15.00 6.75
❑ 159 Joe Tipton .................. 15.00 6.75
❑ 160 Mickey Harris ............. 15.00 6.75
❑ 161 Sherry Robertson ...... 15.00 6.75
❑ 162 Eddie Yost .................. 25.00 11.00
❑ 163 Earl Torgeson ........... 15.00 6.75
❑ 164 Sibby Sisti .................. 15.00 6.75
❑ 165 Bruce Edwards .......... 15.00 6.75
❑ 166 Joe Hatton .................. 15.00 6.75
❑ 167 Preacher Roe ............ 60.00 27.00
❑ 168 Bob Scheffing ............ 15.00 6.75
❑ 169 Hank Edwards ............ 15.00 6.75
❑ 170 Dutch Leonard ............ 15.00 6.75
❑ 171 Harry Gumbert .......... 15.00 6.75
❑ 172 Peanuts Lowrey ........ 15.00 6.75
❑ 173 Lloyd Merriman .......... 15.00 6.75
❑ 174 Hank Thompson RC .. 40.00 18.00
❑ 175 Monte Kennedy .......... 15.00 6.75
❑ 176 Sylvester Donnelly .... 15.00 6.75
❑ 177 Hank Borowy .............. 15.00 6.75
❑ 178 Ed Fitzgerald .............. 15.00 6.75
❑ 179 Chuck Diering ............ 15.00 6.75
❑ 180 Harry Walker .............. 25.00 11.00
❑ 181 Marino Pieretti ............ 15.00 6.75
❑ 182 Sam Zoldak ................ 15.00 6.75
❑ 183 Mickey Haefner .......... 15.00 6.75
❑ 184 Randy Gumpert .......... 15.00 6.75
❑ 185 Howie Judson ............ 15.00 6.75
❑ 186 Ken Keltner ................ 25.00 11.00
❑ 187 Lou Stringer ............... 15.00 6.75
❑ 188 Earl Johnson ............. 15.00 6.75
❑ 189 Owen Friend .............. 15.00 6.75
❑ 190 Ken Wood .................. 15.00 6.75
❑ 191 Dick Starr .................. 15.00 6.75
❑ 192 Bob Chipman ............. 15.00 6.75
❑ 193 Pete Reiser ............... 40.00 18.00
❑ 194 Billy Cox .................... 60.00 27.00
❑ 195 Phil Cavarretta .......... 40.00 18.00
❑ 196 Doyle Lade ................ 15.00 6.75
❑ 197 Johnny Wyrostek ........ 15.00 6.75
❑ 198 Danny Litwhiler .......... 15.00 6.75
❑ 199 Jack Kramer .............. 15.00 6.75
❑ 200 Kirby Higbe ................ 25.00 11.00
❑ 201 Pete Castiglione ........ 15.00 6.75
❑ 202 Cliff Chambers .......... 15.00 6.75
❑ 203 Danny Murtaugh ........ 25.00 11.00
❑ 204 Granny Hamner RC .. 40.00 18.00
❑ 205 Mike Goliat ................. 15.00 6.75
❑ 206 Stan Lopata ............... 25.00 11.00
❑ 207 Max Lanier ................. 15.00 6.75
❑ 208 Jim Hearn .................. 15.00 6.75
❑ 209 Johnny Lindell ........... 15.00 6.75
❑ 210 Ted Gray .................... 15.00 6.75
❑ 211 Charlie Keller ............. 40.00 18.00
❑ 212 Jerry Priddy ............... 15.00 6.75
❑ 213 Carl Scheib ................ 15.00 6.75
❑ 214 Dick Fowler ................ 15.00 6.75
❑ 215 Ed Lopat ..................... 60.00 27.00
❑ 216 Bob Porterfield ........... 25.00 11.00
❑ 217 Casey Stengel MG .. 125.00 55.00
❑ 218 Cliff Mapes ................. 25.00 11.00
❑ 219 Hank Bauer RC ........ 100.00 45.00
❑ 220 Leo Durocher MG ...... 60.00 27.00
❑ 221 Don Mueller RC .......... 40.00 18.00
❑ 222 Bobby Morgan ........... 15.00 6.75
❑ 223 Jim Russell ................ 15.00 6.75
❑ 224 Jack Banta ................. 15.00 6.75
❑ 225 Eddie Sawyer MG ...... 25.00 11.00
❑ 226 Jim Konstanty RC ...... 60.00 27.00
❑ 227 Bob Miller .................. 25.00 11.00
❑ 228 Bill Nicholson ............ 25.00 11.00
❑ 229 Frank Frisch MG ........ 60.00 27.00
❑ 230 Bill Serena ................. 15.00 6.75
❑ 231 Preston Ward ............ 15.00 6.75
❑ 232 Al Rosen RC ............... 60.00 27.00
❑ 233 Allie Clark .................. 15.00 6.75
❑ 234 Bobby Shantz RC ...... 60.00 27.00
❑ 235 Harold Gilbert ............ 15.00 6.75
❑ 236 Bob Cain .................... 15.00 6.75
❑ 237 Bill Salkeld ................. 15.00 6.75
❑ 238 Nippy Jones ............... 15.00 6.75
❑ 239 Bill Howerton ............. 15.00 6.75
❑ 240 Eddie Lake ................ 15.00 6.75
❑ 241 Neil Berry .................. 15.00 6.75
❑ 242 Dick Kryhoski ............ 15.00 6.75
❑ 243 Johnny Groth ............. 15.00 6.75
❑ 244 Dale Coogan .............. 15.00 6.75
❑ 245 Al Papai ...................... 15.00 6.75
❑ 246 Walt Dropo RC .......... 40.00 18.00
❑ 247 Irv Noren RC .............. 25.00 11.00
❑ 248 Sam Jethroe RC ........ 60.00 27.00
❑ 249 Snuffy Stirnweiss ....... 25.00 11.00
❑ 250 Ray Coleman ............. 15.00 6.75
❑ 251 Les Moss .................... 15.00 6.75
❑ 252 Billy DeMars RC ! ...... 60.00 16.50

## 1951 Bowman

| | NRMT | VG-E |
|---|---|---|
| COMPLETE SET (324) | 16000.00 | 7200.00 |
| COMMON CARD (1-252) | 18.00 | 8.00 |
| COMMON CARD (253-324) | 50.00 | 22.00 |
| WRAPPER (1-CENT) | 200.00 | 90.00 |
| WRAPPER (5-CENT) | 250.00 | 110.00 |

❑ 1 Whitey Ford RC ! ........ 1400.00 350.00
❑ 2 Yogi Berra ................... 350.00 160.00
❑ 3 Robin Roberts .............. 75.00 34.00
❑ 4 Del Ennis ...................... 25.00 11.00
❑ 5 Dale Mitchell ................ 25.00 11.00
❑ 6 Don Newcombe ............ 60.00 27.00
❑ 7 Gil Hodges ................. 100.00 45.00
❑ 8 Paul Lehner .................. 18.00 8.00
❑ 9 Sam Chapman .............. 18.00 8.00
❑ 10 Red Schoendienst ....... 60.00 27.00
❑ 11 Red Munger ................ 18.00 8.00
❑ 12 Hank Majeski ............... 18.00 8.00
❑ 13 Eddie Stanky ............... 25.00 11.00
❑ 14 Alvin Dark .................... 40.00 18.00
❑ 15 Johnny Pesky .............. 25.00 11.00
❑ 16 Maurice McDermott ...... 18.00 8.00
❑ 17 Pete Castiglione .......... 18.00 8.00
❑ 18 Gil Coan ...................... 18.00 8.00
❑ 19 Sid Gordon ................... 18.00 8.00
❑ 20 Del Crandall UER ........ 25.00 11.00
(Misspelled Crandell on card)
❑ 21 Snuffy Stirnweiss ......... 25.00 11.00
❑ 22 Hank Sauer .................. 25.00 11.00
❑ 23 Hoot Evers ................... 18.00 8.00
❑ 24 Ewell Blackwell ............ 40.00 18.00
❑ 25 Vic Raschi .................... 60.00 27.00
❑ 26 Phil Rizzuto ................ 125.00 55.00
❑ 27 Jim Konstanty .............. 25.00 11.00
❑ 28 Eddie Waitkus .............. 18.00 8.00
❑ 29 Allie Clark .................... 18.00 8.00
❑ 30 Bob Feller .................. 125.00 55.00
❑ 31 Roy Campanella ......... 250.00 110.00
❑ 32 Duke Snider ............... 250.00 110.00
❑ 33 Bob Hooper .................. 18.00 8.00
❑ 34 Marty Marion ................ 40.00 18.00
❑ 35 Al Zarilla ...................... 18.00 8.00
❑ 36 Joe Dobson .................. 18.00 8.00
❑ 37 Whitey Lockman ........... 40.00 18.00
❑ 38 Al Evans ...................... 18.00 8.00

❑ 39 Ray Scarborough ........ 18.00 8.00
❑ 40 Gus Bell RC ........ 60.00 27.00
❑ 41 Eddie Yost ........ 25.00 11.00
❑ 42 Vern Bickford ........ 18.00 8.00
❑ 43 Billy DeMars ........ 18.00 8.00
❑ 44 Roy Smalley ........ 18.00 8.00
❑ 45 Art Houtteman ........ 18.00 8.00
❑ 46 George Kell 1941 UER 60.00 27.00
❑ 47 Grady Hatton ........ 18.00 8.00
❑ 48 Ken Raffensberger ........ 18.00 8.00
❑ 49 Jerry Coleman ........ 25.00 11.00
❑ 50 Johnny Mize ........ 60.00 27.00
❑ 51 Andy Seminick ........ 18.00 8.00
❑ 52 Dick Sisler ........ 40.00 18.00
❑ 53 Bob Lemon ........ 60.00 27.00
❑ 54 Ray Boone RC ........ 40.00 18.00
❑ 55 Gene Hermanski ........ 18.00 8.00
❑ 56 Ralph Branca ........ 60.00 27.00
❑ 57 Alex Kellner ........ 18.00 8.00
❑ 58 Enos Slaughter ........ 60.00 27.00
❑ 59 Randy Gumpert ........ 18.00 8.00
❑ 60 Chico Carrasquel RC .. 60.00 27.00
❑ 61 Jim Hearn ........ 25.00 11.00
❑ 62 Lou Boudreau ........ 60.00 27.00
❑ 63 Bob Dillinger ........ 18.00 8.00
❑ 64 Bill Werle ........ 18.00 8.00
❑ 65 Mickey Vernon ........ 40.00 18.00
❑ 66 Bob Elliott ........ 25.00 11.00
❑ 67 Roy Sievers ........ 25.00 11.00
❑ 68 Dick Kokos ........ 18.00 8.00
❑ 69 Johnny Schmitz ........ 18.00 8.00
❑ 70 Ron Northey ........ 18.00 8.00
❑ 71 Jerry Priddy ........ 18.00 8.00
❑ 72 Lloyd Merriman ........ 18.00 8.00
❑ 73 Tommy Byrne ........ 18.00 8.00
❑ 74 Billy Johnson ........ 25.00 11.00
❑ 75 Russ Meyer RC ........ 25.00 11.00
❑ 76 Stan Lopata ........ 25.00 11.00
❑ 77 Mike Goliat ........ 18.00 8.00
❑ 78 Early Wynn ........ 60.00 27.00
❑ 79 Jim Hegan ........ 25.00 11.00
❑ 80 Pee Wee Reese ........ 150.00 70.00
❑ 81 Carl Furillo ........ 40.00 18.00
❑ 82 Joe Tipton ........ 18.00 8.00
❑ 83 Carl Scheib ........ 18.00 8.00
❑ 84 Barney McCosky ........ 18.00 8.00
❑ 85 Eddie Kazak ........ 18.00 8.00
❑ 86 Harry Brecheen ........ 25.00 11.00
❑ 87 Floyd Baker ........ 18.00 8.00
❑ 88 Eddie Robinson ........ 18.00 8.00
❑ 89 Hank Thompson ........ 25.00 11.00
❑ 90 Dave Koslo ........ 18.00 8.00
❑ 91 Clyde Vollmer ........ 18.00 8.00
❑ 92 Vern Stephens ........ 25.00 11.00
❑ 93 Danny O'Connell ........ 18.00 8.00
❑ 94 Clyde McCullough ........ 18.00 8.00
❑ 95 Sherry Robertson ........ 18.00 8.00
❑ 96 Sandy Consuegra ........ 18.00 8.00
❑ 97 Bob Kuzava ........ 18.00 8.00
❑ 98 Willard Marshall ........ 18.00 8.00
❑ 99 Earl Torgeson ........ 18.00 8.00
❑ 100 Sherm Lollar ........ 25.00 11.00
❑ 101 Owen Friend ........ 18.00 8.00
❑ 102 Dutch Leonard ........ 18.00 8.00
❑ 103 Andy Pafko ........ 40.00 18.00
❑ 104 Virgil Trucks ........ 25.00 11.00
❑ 105 Don Kolloway ........ 18.00 8.00
❑ 106 Pat Mullin ........ 18.00 8.00
❑ 107 Johnny Wyrostek ........ 18.00 8.00
❑ 108 Virgil Stallcup ........ 18.00 8.00
❑ 109 Allie Reynolds ........ 60.00 27.00
❑ 110 Bobby Brown ........ 40.00 18.00
❑ 111 Curt Simmons ........ 25.00 11.00
❑ 112 Willie Jones ........ 18.00 8.00
❑ 113 Bill Nicholson ........ 18.00 8.00
❑ 114 Sam Zoldak ........ 18.00 8.00
❑ 115 Steve Gromek ........ 18.00 8.00
❑ 116 Bruce Edwards ........ 18.00 8.00
❑ 117 Eddie Miksis ........ 18.00 8.00
❑ 118 Preacher Roe ........ 60.00 27.00
❑ 119 Eddie Joost ........ 18.00 8.00
❑ 120 Joe Coleman ........ 25.00 11.00
❑ 121 Jerry Staley ........ 18.00 8.00
❑ 122 Joe Garagiola RC ........ 80.00 36.00
❑ 123 Howie Judson ........ 18.00 8.00
❑ 124 Gus Niarhos ........ 18.00 8.00
❑ 125 Bill Rigney ........ 25.00 11.00
❑ 126 Bobby Thomson ........ 60.00 27.00
❑ 127 Sal Maglie RC ........ 60.00 27.00
❑ 128 Ellis Kinder ........ 18.00 8.00
❑ 129 Matt Batts ........ 18.00 8.00
❑ 130 Tom Saffell ........ 18.00 8.00
❑ 131 Cliff Chambers ........ 18.00 8.00
❑ 132 Cass Michaels ........ 18.00 8.00
❑ 133 Sam Dente ........ 18.00 8.00
❑ 134 Warren Spahn ........ 125.00 55.00
❑ 135 Walker Cooper ........ 18.00 8.00
❑ 136 Ray Coleman ........ 18.00 8.00
❑ 137 Dick Starr ........ 18.00 8.00
❑ 138 Phil Cavarretta ........ 25.00 11.00
❑ 139 Doyle Lade ........ 18.00 8.00
❑ 140 Eddie Lake ........ 18.00 8.00
❑ 141 Fred Hutchinson ........ 25.00 11.00
❑ 142 Aaron Robinson ........ 18.00 8.00
❑ 143 Ted Kluszewski ........ 60.00 27.00
❑ 144 Herman Wehmeier ........ 18.00 8.00
❑ 145 Fred Sanford ........ 25.00 11.00
❑ 146 Johnny Hopp ........ 25.00 11.00
❑ 147 Ken Heintzelman ........ 18.00 8.00
❑ 148 Granny Hamner ........ 18.00 8.00
❑ 149 Bubba Church ........ 18.00 8.00
❑ 150 Mike Garcia ........ 25.00 11.00
❑ 151 Larry Doby ........ 60.00 27.00
❑ 152 Cal Abrams ........ 18.00 8.00
❑ 153 Rex Barney ........ 25.00 11.00
❑ 154 Pete Suder ........ 18.00 8.00
❑ 155 Lou Brissie ........ 18.00 8.00
❑ 156 Del Rice ........ 18.00 8.00
❑ 157 Al Brazle ........ 18.00 8.00
❑ 158 Chuck Diering ........ 18.00 8.00
❑ 159 Eddie Stewart ........ 18.00 8.00
❑ 160 Phil Masi ........ 18.00 8.00
❑ 161 Wes Westrum RC ........ 18.00 8.00
❑ 162 Larry Jansen ........ 25.00 11.00
❑ 163 Monte Kennedy ........ 18.00 8.00
❑ 164 Bill Wight ........ 18.00 8.00
❑ 165 Ted Williams ........ 750.00 350.00
❑ 166 Stan Rojek ........ 18.00 8.00
❑ 167 Murry Dickson ........ 18.00 8.00
❑ 168 Sam Mele ........ 18.00 8.00
❑ 169 Sid Hudson ........ 18.00 8.00
❑ 170 Sibby Sisti ........ 18.00 8.00
❑ 171 Buddy Kerr ........ 18.00 8.00
❑ 172 Ned Garver ........ 18.00 8.00
❑ 173 Hank Arft ........ 18.00 8.00
❑ 174 Mickey Owen ........ 25.00 11.00
❑ 175 Wayne Terwilliger ........ 18.00 8.00
❑ 176 Vic Wertz ........ 40.00 18.00
❑ 177 Charlie Keller ........ 25.00 11.00
❑ 178 Ted Gray ........ 18.00 8.00
❑ 179 Danny Litwhiler ........ 18.00 8.00
❑ 180 Howie Fox ........ 18.00 8.00
❑ 181 Casey Stengel MG ........ 75.00 34.00
❑ 182 Tom Ferrick ........ 18.00 8.00
❑ 183 Hank Bauer ........ 60.00 27.00
❑ 184 Eddie Sawyer MG ........ 40.00 18.00
❑ 185 Jimmy Bloodworth ........ 18.00 8.00
❑ 186 Richie Ashburn ........ 100.00 45.00
❑ 187 Al Rosen ........ 40.00 18.00
❑ 188 Bobby Avila RC ........ 25.00 11.00
❑ 189 Erv Palica ........ 18.00 8.00
❑ 190 Joe Hatten ........ 18.00 8.00
❑ 191 Billy Hitchcock ........ 18.00 8.00
❑ 192 Hank Wyse ........ 18.00 8.00
❑ 193 Ted Wilks ........ 18.00 8.00
❑ 194 Peanuts Lowrey ........ 18.00 8.00
❑ 195 Paul Richards MG ........ 25.00 11.00
(Caricature)
❑ 196 Billy Pierce RC ........ 60.00 27.00
❑ 197 Bob Cain ........ 18.00 8.00
❑ 198 Monte Irvin RC ........ 100.00 45.00
❑ 199 Sheldon Jones ........ 18.00 8.00
❑ 200 Jack Kramer ........ 18.00 8.00
❑ 201 Steve O'Neill MG ........ 18.00 8.00
❑ 202 Mike Guerra ........ 18.00 8.00
❑ 203 Vernon Law RC ........ 60.00 27.00
❑ 204 Vic Lombardi ........ 18.00 8.00
❑ 205 Mickey Grasso ........ 18.00 8.00
❑ 206 Conrado Marrero ........ 18.00 8.00
❑ 207 Billy Southworth MG .. 18.00 8.00
❑ 208 Blix Donnelly ........ 18.00 8.00
❑ 209 Ken Wood ........ 18.00 8.00
❑ 210 Les Moss ........ 18.00 8.00
❑ 211 Hal Jeffcoat ........ 18.00 8.00
❑ 212 Bob Rush ........ 18.00 8.00
❑ 213 Neil Berry ........ 18.00 8.00
❑ 214 Bob Swift ........ 18.00 8.00
❑ 215 Ken Peterson ........ 18.00 8.00
❑ 216 Connie Ryan ........ 18.00 8.00
❑ 217 Joe Page ........ 25.00 11.00
❑ 218 Ed Lopat ........ 60.00 27.00
❑ 219 Gene Woodling RC ........ 60.00 27.00
❑ 220 Bob Miller ........ 18.00 8.00
❑ 221 Dick Whitman ........ 18.00 8.00
❑ 222 Thurman Tucker ........ 18.00 8.00
❑ 223 Johnny VanderMeer .. 40.00 18.00
❑ 224 Billy Cox ........ 25.00 11.00
❑ 225 Dan Bankhead ........ 40.00 18.00
❑ 226 Jimmy Dykes MG ........ 18.00 8.00
❑ 227 Bobby Shantz UER ........ 25.00 11.00
(Sic, Schantz)
❑ 228 Cloyd Boyer ........ 25.00 11.00
❑ 229 Bill Howerton ........ 18.00 8.00
❑ 230 Max Lanier ........ 18.00 8.00
❑ 231 Luis Aloma ........ 18.00 8.00
❑ 232 Nelson Fox RC ! ........ 250.00 110.00
❑ 233 Leo Durocher MG ........ 60.00 27.00
❑ 234 Clint Hartung ........ 25.00 11.00
❑ 235 Jack Lohrke ........ 18.00 8.00
❑ 236 Warren Rosar ........ 18.00 8.00
❑ 237 Billy Goodman ........ 25.00 11.00
❑ 238 Pete Reiser ........ 40.00 18.00
❑ 239 Bill MacDonald ........ 18.00 8.00
❑ 240 Joe Haynes ........ 18.00 8.00
❑ 241 Irv Noren ........ 25.00 11.00
❑ 242 Sam Jethroe ........ 25.00 11.00
❑ 243 Johnny Antonelli ........ 25.00 11.00
❑ 244 Cliff Fannin ........ 18.00 8.00
❑ 245 John Berardino RC ........ 60.00 27.00
❑ 246 Bill Serena ........ 18.00 8.00
❑ 247 Bob Ramazzotti ........ 18.00 8.00
❑ 248 Johnny Klippstein ........ 18.00 8.00
❑ 249 Johnny Groth ........ 18.00 8.00
❑ 250 Hank Borowy ........ 18.00 8.00
❑ 251 Willard Ramsdell ........ 18.00 8.00
❑ 252 Dixie Howell ........ 18.00 8.00
❑ 253 Mickey Mantle RC ! 8500.00 3800.00
❑ 254 Jackie Jensen RC ........ 100.00 45.00
❑ 255 Milo Candini ........ 50.00 22.00
❑ 256 Ken Sylvestri ........ 50.00 22.00
❑ 257 Birdie Tebbetts RC ........ 60.00 27.00
❑ 258 Luke Easter RC ........ 60.00 27.00
❑ 259 Chuck Dressen MG ........ 60.00 27.00
❑ 260 Carl Erskine RC ........ 100.00 45.00
❑ 261 Wally Moses ........ 60.00 27.00
❑ 262 Gus Zernial ........ 60.00 27.00
❑ 263 Howie Pollet ........ 60.00 27.00
❑ 264 Don Richmond ........ 50.00 22.00
❑ 265 Steve Bilko ........ 50.00 22.00
❑ 266 Harry Dorish ........ 50.00 22.00
❑ 267 Ken Holcombe ........ 50.00 22.00
❑ 268 Don Mueller ........ 60.00 27.00
❑ 269 Ray Noble ........ 50.00 22.00
❑ 270 Willard Nixon ........ 50.00 22.00
❑ 271 Tommy Wright ........ 50.00 22.00
❑ 272 Billy Meyer MG ........ 50.00 22.00
❑ 273 Danny Murtaugh ........ 60.00 27.00
❑ 274 George Metkovich ........ 50.00 22.00
❑ 275 Bucky Harris MG ........ 60.00 27.00
❑ 276 Frank Quinn ........ 50.00 22.00
❑ 277 Roy Hartsfield ........ 50.00 22.00
❑ 278 Norman Roy ........ 50.00 22.00
❑ 279 Jim Delsing ........ 50.00 22.00
❑ 280 Frank Overmire ........ 50.00 22.00
❑ 281 Al Widmar ........ 50.00 22.00
❑ 282 Frank Frisch MG ........ 100.00 45.00
❑ 283 Walt Dubiel ........ 50.00 22.00
❑ 284 Gene Bearden ........ 60.00 27.00
❑ 285 Johnny Lipon ........ 50.00 22.00
❑ 286 Bob Usher ........ 50.00 22.00
❑ 287 Jim Blackburn ........ 50.00 22.00
❑ 288 Bobby Adams ........ 50.00 22.00
❑ 289 Cliff Mapes ........ 60.00 27.00
❑ 290 Bill Dickey CO ........ 100.00 45.00
❑ 291 Tommy Henrich CO .. 80.00 36.00
❑ 292 Eddie Pellegrini ........ 50.00 22.00
❑ 293 Ken Johnson ........ 50.00 22.00
❑ 294 Jocko Thompson ........ 50.00 22.00

| | | | |
|---|---|---|---|
| ❑ 295 | Al Lopez MG | 125.00 | 55.00 |
| ❑ 296 | Bob Kennedy | 60.00 | 27.00 |
| ❑ 297 | Dave Philley | 50.00 | 22.00 |
| ❑ 298 | Joe Astroth | 50.00 | 22.00 |
| ❑ 299 | Clyde King | 50.00 | 22.00 |
| ❑ 300 | Hal Rice | 50.00 | 22.00 |
| ❑ 301 | Tommy Glaviano | 50.00 | 22.00 |
| ❑ 302 | Jim Busby | 50.00 | 22.00 |
| ❑ 303 | Marv Rotblatt | 50.00 | 22.00 |
| ❑ 304 | Al Gettell | 50.00 | 22.00 |
| ❑ 305 | Willie Mays RC ! | 3000.00 | 1350.00 |
| ❑ 306 | Jim Piersall RC | 125.00 | 55.00 |
| ❑ 307 | Walt Masterson | 50.00 | 22.00 |
| ❑ 308 | Ted Beard | 50.00 | 22.00 |
| ❑ 309 | Mel Queen | 50.00 | 22.00 |
| ❑ 310 | Erv Dusak | 50.00 | 22.00 |
| ❑ 311 | Mickey Harris | 50.00 | 22.00 |
| ❑ 312 | Gene Mauch RC | 60.00 | 27.00 |
| ❑ 313 | Ray Mueller | 50.00 | 22.00 |
| ❑ 314 | Johnny Sain | 60.00 | 27.00 |
| ❑ 315 | Zack Taylor MG | 50.00 | 22.00 |
| ❑ 316 | Duane Pillette | 50.00 | 22.00 |
| ❑ 317 | Smoky Burgess RC | 80.00 | 36.00 |
| ❑ 318 | Warren Hacker | 50.00 | 22.00 |
| ❑ 319 | Red Rolfe MG | 60.00 | 27.00 |
| ❑ 320 | Hal White | 50.00 | 22.00 |
| ❑ 321 | Earl Johnson | 50.00 | 22.00 |
| ❑ 322 | Luke Sewell MG | 60.00 | 27.00 |
| ❑ 323 | Joe Adcock RC | 80.00 | 36.00 |
| ❑ 324 | Johnny Pramesa RC ! | 100.00 | 30.00 |

## 1952 Bowman

| | NRMT | VG-E |
|---|---|---|
| COMPLETE SET (252) | 7500.00 | 3400.00 |
| COMMON CARD (1-216) | 15.00 | 6.75 |
| COMMON CARD (217-252) | 60.00 | 27.00 |
| WRAPPER (1-CENT) | 200.00 | 90.00 |
| WRAPPER (5-CENT) | 100.00 | 45.00 |

| | | | |
|---|---|---|---|
| ❑ 1 | Yogi Berra | 600.00 | 190.00 |
| ❑ 2 | Bobby Thomson | 40.00 | 18.00 |
| ❑ 3 | Fred Hutchinson | 25.00 | 11.00 |
| ❑ 4 | Robin Roberts | 60.00 | 27.00 |
| ❑ 5 | Minnie Minoso RC | 125.00 | 55.00 |
| ❑ 6 | Virgil Stallcup | 15.00 | 6.75 |
| ❑ 7 | Mike Garcia | 25.00 | 11.00 |
| ❑ 8 | Pee Wee Reese | 150.00 | 70.00 |
| ❑ 9 | Vern Stephens | 25.00 | 11.00 |
| ❑ 10 | Bob Hooper | 15.00 | 6.75 |
| ❑ 11 | Ralph Kiner | 60.00 | 27.00 |
| ❑ 12 | Max Surkont | 15.00 | 6.75 |
| ❑ 13 | Cliff Mapes | 15.00 | 6.75 |
| ❑ 14 | Cliff Chambers | 15.00 | 6.75 |
| ❑ 15 | Sam Mele | 15.00 | 6.75 |
| ❑ 16 | Turk Lown | 15.00 | 6.75 |
| ❑ 17 | Ed Lopat | 40.00 | 18.00 |
| ❑ 18 | Don Mueller | 25.00 | 11.00 |
| ❑ 19 | Bob Cain | 15.00 | 6.75 |
| ❑ 20 | Willie Jones | 15.00 | 6.75 |
| ❑ 21 | Nellie Fox | 100.00 | 45.00 |
| ❑ 22 | Willard Ramsdell | 15.00 | 6.75 |
| ❑ 23 | Bob Lemon | 60.00 | 27.00 |
| ❑ 24 | Carl Furillo | 40.00 | 18.00 |
| ❑ 25 | Mickey McDermott | 15.00 | 6.75 |
| ❑ 26 | Eddie Joost | 15.00 | 6.75 |
| ❑ 27 | Joe Garagiola | 40.00 | 18.00 |
| ❑ 28 | Roy Hartsfield | 15.00 | 6.75 |
| ❑ 29 | Ned Garver | 15.00 | 6.75 |
| ❑ 30 | Red Schoendienst | 60.00 | 27.00 |
| ❑ 31 | Eddie Yost | 25.00 | 11.00 |
| ❑ 32 | Eddie Miksis | 15.00 | 6.75 |
| ❑ 33 | Gil McDougald RC | 80.00 | 36.00 |
| ❑ 34 | Alvin Dark | 25.00 | 11.00 |
| ❑ 35 | Granny Hamner | 15.00 | 6.75 |
| ❑ 36 | Cass Michaels | 15.00 | 6.75 |
| ❑ 37 | Vic Raschi | 25.00 | 11.00 |
| ❑ 38 | Whitey Lockman | 25.00 | 11.00 |
| ❑ 39 | Vic Wertz | 25.00 | 11.00 |
| ❑ 40 | Bubba Church | 15.00 | 6.75 |
| ❑ 41 | Chico Carrasquel | 25.00 | 11.00 |
| ❑ 42 | Johnny Wyrostek | 15.00 | 6.75 |
| ❑ 43 | Bob Feller | 150.00 | 70.00 |
| ❑ 44 | Roy Campanella | 250.00 | 110.00 |
| ❑ 45 | Johnny Pesky | 25.00 | 11.00 |
| ❑ 46 | Carl Scheib | 15.00 | 6.75 |
| ❑ 47 | Pete Castiglione | 15.00 | 6.75 |
| ❑ 48 | Vern Bickford | 15.00 | 6.75 |
| ❑ 49 | Jim Hearn | 15.00 | 6.75 |
| ❑ 50 | Jerry Staley | 15.00 | 6.75 |
| ❑ 51 | Gil Coan | 15.00 | 6.75 |
| ❑ 52 | Phil Rizzuto | 150.00 | 70.00 |
| ❑ 53 | Richie Ashburn | 100.00 | 45.00 |
| ❑ 54 | Billy Pierce | 25.00 | 11.00 |
| ❑ 55 | Ken Raffensberger | 15.00 | 6.75 |
| ❑ 56 | Clyde King | 25.00 | 11.00 |
| ❑ 57 | Clyde Vollmer | 15.00 | 6.75 |
| ❑ 58 | Hank Majeski | 15.00 | 6.75 |
| ❑ 59 | Murry Dickson | 15.00 | 6.75 |
| ❑ 60 | Sid Gordon | 15.00 | 6.75 |
| ❑ 61 | Tommy Byrne | 15.00 | 6.75 |
| ❑ 62 | Joe Presko | 15.00 | 6.75 |
| ❑ 63 | Irv Noren | 15.00 | 6.75 |
| ❑ 64 | Roy Smalley | 15.00 | 6.75 |
| ❑ 65 | Hank Bauer | 25.00 | 11.00 |
| ❑ 66 | Sal Maglie | 25.00 | 11.00 |
| ❑ 67 | Johnny Groth | 15.00 | 6.75 |
| ❑ 68 | Jim Busby | 15.00 | 6.75 |
| ❑ 69 | Joe Adcock | 25.00 | 11.00 |
| ❑ 70 | Carl Erskine | 40.00 | 18.00 |
| ❑ 71 | Vernon Law | 25.00 | 11.00 |
| ❑ 72 | Earl Torgeson | 15.00 | 6.75 |
| ❑ 73 | Jerry Coleman | 25.00 | 11.00 |
| ❑ 74 | Wes Westrum | 25.00 | 11.00 |
| ❑ 75 | George Kell | 60.00 | 27.00 |
| ❑ 76 | Del Ennis | 25.00 | 11.00 |
| ❑ 77 | Eddie Robinson | 15.00 | 6.75 |
| ❑ 78 | Lloyd Merriman | 15.00 | 6.75 |
| ❑ 79 | Lou Brissie | 15.00 | 6.75 |
| ❑ 80 | Gil Hodges | 90.00 | 40.00 |
| ❑ 81 | Billy Goodman | 25.00 | 11.00 |
| ❑ 82 | Gus Zernial | 25.00 | 11.00 |
| ❑ 83 | Howie Pollet | 15.00 | 6.75 |
| ❑ 84 | Sam Jethroe | 25.00 | 11.00 |
| ❑ 85 | Marty Marion CO | 25.00 | 11.00 |
| ❑ 86 | Cal Abrams | 15.00 | 6.75 |
| ❑ 87 | Mickey Vernon | 25.00 | 11.00 |
| ❑ 88 | Bruce Edwards | 15.00 | 6.75 |
| ❑ 89 | Billy Hitchcock | 15.00 | 6.75 |
| ❑ 90 | Larry Jansen | 25.00 | 11.00 |
| ❑ 91 | Don Kolloway | 15.00 | 6.75 |
| ❑ 92 | Eddie Waitkus | 25.00 | 11.00 |
| ❑ 93 | Paul Richards MG | 25.00 | 11.00 |
| ❑ 94 | Luke Sewell MG | 25.00 | 11.00 |
| ❑ 95 | Luke Easter | 25.00 | 11.00 |
| ❑ 96 | Ralph Branca | 25.00 | 11.00 |
| ❑ 97 | Willard Marshall | 15.00 | 6.75 |
| ❑ 98 | Jimmy Dykes MG | 25.00 | 11.00 |
| ❑ 99 | Clyde McCullough | 15.00 | 6.75 |
| ❑ 100 | Sibby Sisti | 15.00 | 6.75 |
| ❑ 101 | Mickey Mantle | 2500.00 | 1100.00 |
| ❑ 102 | Peanuts Lowrey | 15.00 | 6.75 |
| ❑ 103 | Joe Haynes | 15.00 | 6.75 |
| ❑ 104 | Hal Jeffcoat | 15.00 | 6.75 |
| ❑ 105 | Bobby Brown | 25.00 | 11.00 |
| ❑ 106 | Randy Gumpert | 15.00 | 6.75 |
| ❑ 107 | Del Rice | 15.00 | 6.75 |
| ❑ 108 | George Metkovich | 15.00 | 6.75 |
| ❑ 109 | Tom Morgan | 15.00 | 6.75 |
| ❑ 110 | Max Lanier | 15.00 | 6.75 |
| ❑ 111 | Hoot Evers | 15.00 | 6.75 |
| ❑ 112 | Smoky Burgess | 25.00 | 11.00 |
| ❑ 113 | Al Zarilla | 15.00 | 6.75 |
| ❑ 114 | Frank Hiller | 15.00 | 6.75 |
| ❑ 115 | Larry Doby | 60.00 | 27.00 |
| ❑ 116 | Duke Snider | 200.00 | 90.00 |
| ❑ 117 | Bill Wight | 15.00 | 6.75 |
| ❑ 118 | Ray Murray | 15.00 | 6.75 |
| ❑ 119 | Bill Howerton | 15.00 | 6.75 |
| ❑ 120 | Chet Nichols | 15.00 | 6.75 |
| ❑ 121 | Al Corwin | 15.00 | 6.75 |
| ❑ 122 | Billy Johnson | 15.00 | 6.75 |
| ❑ 123 | Sid Hudson | 15.00 | 6.75 |
| ❑ 124 | Birdie Tebbetts | 15.00 | 6.75 |
| ❑ 125 | Howie Fox | 15.00 | 6.75 |
| ❑ 126 | Phil Cavarretta | 25.00 | 11.00 |
| ❑ 127 | Dick Sisler | 15.00 | 6.75 |
| ❑ 128 | Don Newcombe | 40.00 | 18.00 |
| ❑ 129 | Gus Niarhos | 15.00 | 6.75 |
| ❑ 130 | Allie Clark | 15.00 | 6.75 |
| ❑ 131 | Bob Swift | 15.00 | 6.75 |
| ❑ 132 | Dave Cole | 15.00 | 6.75 |
| ❑ 133 | Dick Kryhoski | 15.00 | 6.75 |
| ❑ 134 | Al Brazle | 15.00 | 6.75 |
| ❑ 135 | Mickey Harris | 15.00 | 6.75 |
| ❑ 136 | Gene Hermanski | 15.00 | 6.75 |
| ❑ 137 | Stan Rojek | 15.00 | 6.75 |
| ❑ 138 | Ted Wilks | 15.00 | 6.75 |
| ❑ 139 | Jerry Priddy | 15.00 | 6.75 |
| ❑ 140 | Ray Scarborough | 15.00 | 6.75 |
| ❑ 141 | Hank Edwards | 15.00 | 6.75 |
| ❑ 142 | Early Wynn | 60.00 | 27.00 |
| ❑ 143 | Sandy Consuegra | 15.00 | 6.75 |
| ❑ 144 | Joe Hatton | 15.00 | 6.75 |
| ❑ 145 | Johnny Mize | 60.00 | 27.00 |
| ❑ 146 | Leo Durocher MG | 60.00 | 27.00 |
| ❑ 147 | Marlin Stuart | 15.00 | 6.75 |
| ❑ 148 | Ken Heintzelman | 15.00 | 6.75 |
| ❑ 149 | Howie Judson | 15.00 | 6.75 |
| ❑ 150 | Herman Wehmeier | 15.00 | 6.75 |
| ❑ 151 | Al Rosen | 25.00 | 11.00 |
| ❑ 152 | Billy Cox | 15.00 | 6.75 |
| ❑ 153 | Fred Hatfield | 15.00 | 6.75 |
| ❑ 154 | Ferris Fain | 25.00 | 11.00 |
| ❑ 155 | Billy Meyer MG | 15.00 | 6.75 |
| ❑ 156 | Warren Spahn | 125.00 | 55.00 |
| ❑ 157 | Jim Delsing | 15.00 | 6.75 |
| ❑ 158 | Bucky Harris MG | 25.00 | 11.00 |
| ❑ 159 | Dutch Leonard | 15.00 | 6.75 |
| ❑ 160 | Eddie Stanky | 25.00 | 11.00 |
| ❑ 161 | Jackie Jensen | 40.00 | 18.00 |
| ❑ 162 | Monte Irvin | 60.00 | 27.00 |
| ❑ 163 | Johnny Lipon | 15.00 | 6.75 |
| ❑ 164 | Connie Ryan | 15.00 | 6.75 |
| ❑ 165 | Saul Rogovin | 15.00 | 6.75 |
| ❑ 166 | Bobby Adams | 15.00 | 6.75 |
| ❑ 167 | Bobby Avila | 25.00 | 11.00 |
| ❑ 168 | Preacher Roe | 25.00 | 11.00 |
| ❑ 169 | Walt Dropo | 25.00 | 11.00 |
| ❑ 170 | Joe Astroth | 15.00 | 6.75 |
| ❑ 171 | Mel Queen | 15.00 | 6.75 |
| ❑ 172 | Ebba St.Claire | 15.00 | 6.75 |
| ❑ 173 | Gene Bearden | 15.00 | 6.75 |
| ❑ 174 | Mickey Grasso | 15.00 | 6.75 |
| ❑ 175 | Randy Jackson | 15.00 | 6.75 |
| ❑ 176 | Harry Brecheen | 25.00 | 11.00 |
| ❑ 177 | Gene Woodling | 25.00 | 11.00 |
| ❑ 178 | Dave Williams RC | 25.00 | 11.00 |
| ❑ 179 | Pete Suder | 15.00 | 6.75 |
| ❑ 180 | Ed Fitzgerald | 15.00 | 6.75 |
| ❑ 181 | Joe Collins RC | 25.00 | 11.00 |
| ❑ 182 | Dave Koslo | 15.00 | 6.75 |
| ❑ 183 | Pat Mullin | 15.00 | 6.75 |
| ❑ 184 | Curt Simmons | 25.00 | 11.00 |
| ❑ 185 | Eddie Stewart | 15.00 | 6.75 |
| ❑ 186 | Frank Smith | 15.00 | 6.75 |
| ❑ 187 | Jim Hegan | 25.00 | 11.00 |
| ❑ 188 | Chuck Dressen MG | 25.00 | 11.00 |
| ❑ 189 | Jimmy Piersall | 25.00 | 11.00 |
| ❑ 190 | Dick Fowler | 15.00 | 6.75 |
| ❑ 191 | Bob Friend RC | 40.00 | 18.00 |
| ❑ 192 | John Cusick | 15.00 | 6.75 |
| ❑ 193 | Bobby Young | 15.00 | 6.75 |
| ❑ 194 | Bob Porterfield | 15.00 | 6.75 |
| ❑ 195 | Frank Baumholtz | 15.00 | 6.75 |
| ❑ 196 | Stan Musial | 600.00 | 275.00 |
| ❑ 197 | Charlie Silvera RC | 15.00 | 6.75 |
| ❑ 198 | Chuck Diering | 15.00 | 6.75 |
| ❑ 199 | Ted Gray | 15.00 | 6.75 |
| ❑ 200 | Ken Silvestri | 15.00 | 6.75 |

|  | | |
|---|---|---|
| ❑ 201 Ray Coleman | 15.00 | 6.75 |
| ❑ 202 Harry Perkowski | 15.00 | 6.75 |
| ❑ 203 Steve Gromek | 15.00 | 6.75 |
| ❑ 204 Andy Pafko | 25.00 | 11.00 |
| ❑ 205 Walt Masterson | 15.00 | 6.75 |
| ❑ 206 Elmer Valo | 15.00 | 6.75 |
| ❑ 207 George Strickland | 15.00 | 6.75 |
| ❑ 208 Walker Cooper | 15.00 | 6.75 |
| ❑ 209 Dick Littlefield | 15.00 | 6.75 |
| ❑ 210 Archie Wilson | 15.00 | 6.75 |
| ❑ 211 Paul Minner | 15.00 | 6.75 |
| ❑ 212 Solly Hemus | 15.00 | 6.75 |
| ❑ 213 Monte Kennedy | 15.00 | 6.75 |
| ❑ 214 Ray Boone | 15.00 | 6.75 |
| ❑ 215 Sheldon Jones | 15.00 | 6.75 |
| ❑ 216 Matt Batts | 15.00 | 6.75 |
| ❑ 217 Casey Stengel MG | 150.00 | 70.00 |
| ❑ 218 Willie Mays | 1200.00 | 550.00 |
| ❑ 219 Neil Berry | 60.00 | 27.00 |
| ❑ 220 Russ Meyer | 60.00 | 27.00 |
| ❑ 221 Lou Kretlow | 60.00 | 27.00 |
| ❑ 222 Dixie Howell | 60.00 | 27.00 |
| ❑ 223 Harry Simpson | 60.00 | 27.00 |
| ❑ 224 Johnny Schmitz | 60.00 | 27.00 |
| ❑ 225 Del Wilber | 60.00 | 27.00 |
| ❑ 226 Alex Kellner | 60.00 | 27.00 |
| ❑ 227 Clyde Sukeforth CO | 60.00 | 27.00 |
| ❑ 228 Bob Chipman | 60.00 | 27.00 |
| ❑ 229 Hank Arft | 60.00 | 27.00 |
| ❑ 230 Frank Shea | 60.00 | 27.00 |
| ❑ 231 Dee Fondy | 60.00 | 27.00 |
| ❑ 232 Enos Slaughter | 90.00 | 40.00 |
| ❑ 233 Bob Kuzava | 60.00 | 27.00 |
| ❑ 234 Fred Fitzsimmons CO | 70.00 | 32.00 |
| ❑ 235 Steve Souchock | 60.00 | 27.00 |
| ❑ 236 Tommy Brown | 60.00 | 27.00 |
| ❑ 237 Sherm Lollar | 70.00 | 32.00 |
| ❑ 238 Roy McMillan RC | 70.00 | 32.00 |
| ❑ 239 Dale Mitchell | 70.00 | 32.00 |
| ❑ 240 Billy Loes RC | 70.00 | 32.00 |
| ❑ 241 Mel Parnell | 70.00 | 32.00 |
| ❑ 242 Everett Kell | 60.00 | 27.00 |
| ❑ 243 Red Munger | 60.00 | 27.00 |
| ❑ 244 Lew Burdette RC | 80.00 | 36.00 |
| ❑ 245 George Schmees | 60.00 | 27.00 |
| ❑ 246 Jerry Snyder | 60.00 | 27.00 |
| ❑ 247 Johnny Pramesa | 60.00 | 27.00 |
| ❑ 248 Bill Werle (Full name in signature) | 60.00 | 27.00 |
| ❑ 248A Bill Werle (Signature on front has no W) | 60.00 | 27.00 |
| ❑ 249 Hank Thompson | 70.00 | 32.00 |
| ❑ 250 Ike Delock | 60.00 | 27.00 |
| ❑ 251 Jack Lohrke | 60.00 | 27.00 |
| ❑ 252 Frank Crosetti CO | 110.00 | 28.00 |

## 1953 Bowman B/W

| | NRMT | VG-E |
|---|---|---|
| COMPLETE SET (64) | 2400.00 | 1100.00 |
| WRAPPER (1-CENT) | 350.00 | 160.00 |

| Card | NRMT | VG-E |
|---|---|---|
| ❑ 1 Gus Bell | 125.00 | 25.00 |
| ❑ 2 Willard Nixon | 40.00 | 18.00 |
| ❑ 3 Bill Rigney | 40.00 | 18.00 |
| ❑ 4 Pat Mullin | 40.00 | 18.00 |
| ❑ 5 Dee Fondy | 40.00 | 18.00 |
| ❑ 6 Ray Murray | 40.00 | 18.00 |
| ❑ 7 Andy Seminick | 40.00 | 18.00 |
| ❑ 8 Pete Suder | 40.00 | 18.00 |
| ❑ 9 Walt Masterson | 40.00 | 18.00 |
| ❑ 10 Dick Sisler | 70.00 | 32.00 |
| ❑ 11 Dick Gernert | 40.00 | 18.00 |
| ❑ 12 Randy Jackson | 40.00 | 18.00 |
| ❑ 13 Joe Tipton | 40.00 | 18.00 |
| ❑ 14 Bill Nicholson | 70.00 | 32.00 |
| ❑ 15 Johnny Mize | 125.00 | 55.00 |
| ❑ 16 Stu Miller RC | 70.00 | 32.00 |
| ❑ 17 Virgil Trucks | 70.00 | 32.00 |
| ❑ 18 Billy Hoeft | 40.00 | 18.00 |
| ❑ 19 Paul LaPalme | 40.00 | 18.00 |
| ❑ 20 Eddie Robinson | 40.00 | 18.00 |
| ❑ 21 Clarence Podbielan | 40.00 | 18.00 |
| ❑ 22 Matt Batts | 40.00 | 18.00 |
| ❑ 23 Wilmer Mizell | 70.00 | 32.00 |
| ❑ 24 Del Wilber | 40.00 | 18.00 |
| ❑ 25 Johnny Sain | 75.00 | 34.00 |
| ❑ 26 Preacher Roe | 75.00 | 34.00 |
| ❑ 27 Bob Lemon | 125.00 | 55.00 |
| ❑ 28 Hoyt Wilhelm | 125.00 | 55.00 |
| ❑ 29 Sid Hudson | 40.00 | 18.00 |
| ❑ 30 Walker Cooper | 40.00 | 18.00 |
| ❑ 31 Gene Woodling | 75.00 | 34.00 |
| ❑ 32 Rocky Bridges | 40.00 | 18.00 |
| ❑ 33 Bob Kuzava | 40.00 | 18.00 |
| ❑ 34 Ebba St.Claire | 40.00 | 18.00 |
| ❑ 35 Johnny Wyrostek | 40.00 | 18.00 |
| ❑ 36 Jimmy Piersall | 75.00 | 34.00 |
| ❑ 37 Hal Jeffcoat | 40.00 | 18.00 |
| ❑ 38 Dave Cole | 40.00 | 18.00 |
| ❑ 39 Casey Stengel MG | 325.00 | 145.00 |
| ❑ 40 Larry Jansen | 70.00 | 32.00 |
| ❑ 41 Bob Ramazzotti | 40.00 | 18.00 |
| ❑ 42 Howie Judson | 40.00 | 18.00 |
| ❑ 43 Hal Bevan | 40.00 | 18.00 |
| ❑ 44 Jim Delsing | 40.00 | 18.00 |
| ❑ 45 Irv Noren | 70.00 | 32.00 |
| ❑ 46 Bucky Harris MG | 75.00 | 34.00 |
| ❑ 47 Jack Lohrke | 40.00 | 18.00 |
| ❑ 48 Steve Ridzik | 40.00 | 18.00 |
| ❑ 49 Floyd Baker | 40.00 | 18.00 |
| ❑ 50 Dutch Leonard | 40.00 | 18.00 |
| ❑ 51 Lou Burdette | 75.00 | 34.00 |
| ❑ 52 Ralph Branca | 75.00 | 34.00 |
| ❑ 53 Morrie Martin | 40.00 | 18.00 |
| ❑ 54 Bill Miller | 40.00 | 18.00 |
| ❑ 55 Don Johnson | 40.00 | 18.00 |
| ❑ 56 Roy Smalley | 40.00 | 18.00 |
| ❑ 57 Andy Pafko | 70.00 | 32.00 |
| ❑ 58 Jim Konstanty | 70.00 | 32.00 |
| ❑ 59 Duane Pillette | 40.00 | 18.00 |
| ❑ 60 Billy Cox | 75.00 | 34.00 |
| ❑ 61 Tom Gorman | 40.00 | 18.00 |
| ❑ 62 Keith Thomas | 40.00 | 18.00 |
| ❑ 63 Steve Gromek | 40.00 | 18.00 |
| ❑ 64 Andy Hansen | 75.00 | 24.00 |

## 1953 Bowman Color

| | NRMT | VG-E |
|---|---|---|
| COMPLETE SET (160) | 12000.00 | 5400.00 |
| COMMON CARD (1-112) | 40.00 | 18.00 |
| COMMON CARD (113-128) | 80.00 | 36.00 |
| COMMON CARD (129-160) | 75.00 | 34.00 |
| WRAPPER (1-CENT) | 400.00 | 180.00 |
| WRAPPER (5-CENT) | 300.00 | 135.00 |

| Card | NRMT | VG-E |
|---|---|---|
| ❑ 1 Dave Williams | 175.00 | 35.00 |
| ❑ 2 Vic Wertz | 50.00 | 22.00 |
| ❑ 3 Sam Jethroe | 50.00 | 22.00 |
| ❑ 4 Art Houtteman | 40.00 | 18.00 |
| ❑ 5 Sid Gordon | 40.00 | 18.00 |
| ❑ 6 Joe Ginsberg | 40.00 | 18.00 |
| ❑ 7 Harry Chiti | 40.00 | 18.00 |
| ❑ 8 Al Rosen | 50.00 | 22.00 |
| ❑ 9 Phil Rizzuto | 225.00 | 100.00 |
| ❑ 10 Richie Ashburn | 150.00 | 70.00 |
| ❑ 11 Bobby Shantz | 50.00 | 22.00 |
| ❑ 12 Carl Erskine | 60.00 | 27.00 |
| ❑ 13 Gus Zernial | 50.00 | 22.00 |
| ❑ 14 Billy Loes | 50.00 | 22.00 |
| ❑ 15 Jim Busby | 40.00 | 18.00 |
| ❑ 16 Bob Friend | 50.00 | 22.00 |
| ❑ 17 Gerry Staley | 40.00 | 18.00 |
| ❑ 18 Nellie Fox | 150.00 | 70.00 |
| ❑ 19 Alvin Dark | 50.00 | 22.00 |
| ❑ 20 Don Lenhardt | 40.00 | 18.00 |
| ❑ 21 Joe Garagiola | 60.00 | 27.00 |
| ❑ 22 Bob Porterfield | 40.00 | 18.00 |
| ❑ 23 Herman Wehmeier | 40.00 | 18.00 |
| ❑ 24 Jackie Jensen | 60.00 | 27.00 |
| ❑ 25 Hoot Evers | 40.00 | 18.00 |
| ❑ 26 Roy McMillan | 50.00 | 22.00 |
| ❑ 27 Vic Raschi | 60.00 | 27.00 |
| ❑ 28 Smoky Burgess | 50.00 | 22.00 |
| ❑ 29 Bobby Avila | 50.00 | 22.00 |
| ❑ 30 Phil Cavarretta | 50.00 | 22.00 |
| ❑ 31 Jimmy Dykes MG | 50.00 | 22.00 |
| ❑ 32 Stan Musial | 700.00 | 325.00 |
| ❑ 33 Pee Wee Reese | 900.00 | 400.00 |
| ❑ 34 Gil Coan | 40.00 | 18.00 |
| ❑ 35 Maurice McDermott | 40.00 | 18.00 |
| ❑ 36 Minnie Minoso | 80.00 | 36.00 |
| ❑ 37 Jim Wilson | 40.00 | 18.00 |
| ❑ 38 Harry Byrd | 40.00 | 18.00 |
| ❑ 39 Paul Richards MG | 50.00 | 22.00 |
| ❑ 40 Larry Doby | 80.00 | 36.00 |
| ❑ 41 Sammy White | 40.00 | 18.00 |
| ❑ 42 Tommy Brown | 40.00 | 18.00 |
| ❑ 43 Mike Garcia | 50.00 | 22.00 |
| ❑ 44 Yogi Berra<br>Hank Bauer<br>Mickey Mantle | 700.00 | 325.00 |
| ❑ 45 Walt Dropo | 50.00 | 22.00 |
| ❑ 46 Roy Campanella | 350.00 | 160.00 |
| ❑ 47 Ned Garver | 40.00 | 18.00 |
| ❑ 48 Hank Sauer | 50.00 | 22.00 |
| ❑ 49 Eddie Stanky MG | 50.00 | 22.00 |
| ❑ 50 Lou Kretlow | 40.00 | 18.00 |
| ❑ 51 Monte Irvin | 80.00 | 36.00 |
| ❑ 52 Marty Marion MG | 50.00 | 22.00 |
| ❑ 53 Del Rice | 40.00 | 18.00 |
| ❑ 54 Chico Carrasquel | 40.00 | 18.00 |
| ❑ 55 Leo Durocher MG | 80.00 | 36.00 |
| ❑ 56 Bob Cain | 40.00 | 18.00 |
| ❑ 57 Lou Boudreau MG | 80.00 | 36.00 |
| ❑ 58 Willard Marshall | 40.00 | 18.00 |
| ❑ 59 Mickey Mantle | 2500.00 | 1100.00 |
| ❑ 60 Granny Hamner | 40.00 | 18.00 |
| ❑ 61 George Kell | 80.00 | 36.00 |
| ❑ 62 Ted Kluszewski | 100.00 | 45.00 |
| ❑ 63 Gil McDougald | 60.00 | 27.00 |
| ❑ 64 Curt Simmons | 50.00 | 22.00 |
| ❑ 65 Robin Roberts | 110.00 | 50.00 |
| ❑ 66 Mel Parnell | 50.00 | 22.00 |
| ❑ 67 Mel Clark | 40.00 | 18.00 |
| ❑ 68 Allie Reynolds | 60.00 | 27.00 |
| ❑ 69 Charlie Grimm MG | 50.00 | 22.00 |
| ❑ 70 Clint Courtney | 40.00 | 18.00 |
| ❑ 71 Paul Minner | 40.00 | 18.00 |
| ❑ 72 Ted Gray | 40.00 | 18.00 |
| ❑ 73 Billy Pierce | 50.00 | 22.00 |
| ❑ 74 Don Mueller | 50.00 | 22.00 |
| ❑ 75 Saul Rogovin | 40.00 | 18.00 |
| ❑ 76 Jim Hearn | 40.00 | 18.00 |
| ❑ 77 Mickey Grasso | 40.00 | 18.00 |
| ❑ 78 Carl Furillo | 60.00 | 27.00 |
| ❑ 79 Ray Boone | 50.00 | 22.00 |
| ❑ 80 Ralph Kiner | 80.00 | 36.00 |
| ❑ 81 Enos Slaughter | 80.00 | 36.00 |
| ❑ 82 Joe Astroth | 40.00 | 18.00 |
| ❑ 83 Jack Daniels | 40.00 | 18.00 |
| ❑ 84 Hank Bauer | 60.00 | 27.00 |

| | Player | NRMT | VG-E |
|---|---|---|---|
| ❑ 85 | Solly Hemus | 40.00 | 18.00 |
| ❑ 86 | Harry Simpson | 40.00 | 18.00 |
| ❑ 87 | Harry Perkowski | 40.00 | 18.00 |
| ❑ 88 | Joe Dobson | 40.00 | 18.00 |
| ❑ 89 | Sandy Consuegra | 40.00 | 18.00 |
| ❑ 90 | Joe Nuxhall | 50.00 | 22.00 |
| ❑ 91 | Steve Souchock | 40.00 | 18.00 |
| ❑ 92 | Gil Hodges | 200.00 | 90.00 |
| ❑ 93 | Phil Rizzuto and Billy Martin | 275.00 | 125.00 |
| ❑ 94 | Bob Addis | 40.00 | 18.00 |
| ❑ 95 | Wally Moses CO | 50.00 | 22.00 |
| ❑ 96 | Sal Maglie | 50.00 | 22.00 |
| ❑ 97 | Eddie Mathews | 300.00 | 135.00 |
| ❑ 98 | Hector Rodriguez | 40.00 | 18.00 |
| ❑ 99 | Warren Spahn | 350.00 | 160.00 |
| ❑ 100 | Bill Wight | 40.00 | 18.00 |
| ❑ 101 | Red Schoendienst | 80.00 | 36.00 |
| ❑ 102 | Jim Hegan | 50.00 | 22.00 |
| ❑ 103 | Del Ennis | 50.00 | 22.00 |
| ❑ 104 | Luke Easter | 50.00 | 22.00 |
| ❑ 105 | Eddie Joost | 40.00 | 18.00 |
| ❑ 106 | Ken Raffensberger | 40.00 | 18.00 |
| ❑ 107 | Alex Kellner | 40.00 | 18.00 |
| ❑ 108 | Bobby Adams | 40.00 | 18.00 |
| ❑ 109 | Ken Wood | 40.00 | 18.00 |
| ❑ 110 | Bob Rush | 40.00 | 18.00 |
| ❑ 111 | Jim Dyck | 40.00 | 18.00 |
| ❑ 112 | Toby Atwell | 40.00 | 18.00 |
| ❑ 113 | Karl Drews | 80.00 | 36.00 |
| ❑ 114 | Bob Feller | 500.00 | 220.00 |
| ❑ 115 | Cloyd Boyer | 80.00 | 36.00 |
| ❑ 116 | Eddie Yost | 100.00 | 45.00 |
| ❑ 117 | Duke Snider | 600.00 | 275.00 |
| ❑ 118 | Billy Martin | 400.00 | 180.00 |
| ❑ 119 | Dale Mitchell | 100.00 | 45.00 |
| ❑ 120 | Marlin Stuart | 80.00 | 36.00 |
| ❑ 121 | Yogi Berra | 700.00 | 325.00 |
| ❑ 122 | Bill Serena | 80.00 | 36.00 |
| ❑ 123 | Johnny Lipon | 80.00 | 36.00 |
| ❑ 124 | Charlie Dressen MG | 100.00 | 45.00 |
| ❑ 125 | Fred Hatfield | 80.00 | 36.00 |
| ❑ 126 | Al Corwin | 80.00 | 36.00 |
| ❑ 127 | Dick Kryhoski | 80.00 | 36.00 |
| ❑ 128 | Whitey Lockman | 100.00 | 45.00 |
| ❑ 129 | Russ Meyer | 75.00 | 34.00 |
| ❑ 130 | Cass Michaels | 75.00 | 34.00 |
| ❑ 131 | Connie Ryan | 75.00 | 34.00 |
| ❑ 132 | Fred Hutchinson | 90.00 | 40.00 |
| ❑ 133 | Willie Jones | 75.00 | 34.00 |
| ❑ 134 | Johnny Pesky | 90.00 | 40.00 |
| ❑ 135 | Bobby Morgan | 75.00 | 34.00 |
| ❑ 136 | Jim Brideweser | 75.00 | 34.00 |
| ❑ 137 | Sam Dente | 75.00 | 34.00 |
| ❑ 138 | Bubba Church | 75.00 | 34.00 |
| ❑ 139 | Pete Runnels | 90.00 | 40.00 |
| ❑ 140 | Al Brazle | 75.00 | 34.00 |
| ❑ 141 | Frank Shea | 75.00 | 34.00 |
| ❑ 142 | Larry Miggins | 75.00 | 34.00 |
| ❑ 143 | Al Lopez MG | 110.00 | 50.00 |
| ❑ 144 | Warren Hacker | 75.00 | 34.00 |
| ❑ 145 | George Shuba | 90.00 | 40.00 |
| ❑ 146 | Early Wynn | 200.00 | 90.00 |
| ❑ 147 | Clem Koshorek | 75.00 | 34.00 |
| ❑ 148 | Billy Goodman | 90.00 | 40.00 |
| ❑ 149 | Al Corwin | 75.00 | 34.00 |
| ❑ 150 | Carl Scheib | 75.00 | 34.00 |
| ❑ 151 | Joe Adcock | 90.00 | 40.00 |
| ❑ 152 | Clyde Vollmer | 75.00 | 34.00 |
| ❑ 153 | Whitey Ford | 600.00 | 275.00 |
| ❑ 154 | Turk Lown | 75.00 | 34.00 |
| ❑ 155 | Allie Clark | 75.00 | 34.00 |
| ❑ 156 | Max Surkont | 75.00 | 34.00 |
| ❑ 157 | Sherm Lollar | 90.00 | 40.00 |
| ❑ 158 | Howard Fox | 75.00 | 34.00 |
| ❑ 159 | Mickey Vernon UER (Photo actually Floyd Baker) | 90.00 | 40.00 |
| ❑ 160 | Cal Abrams | 200.00 | 70.00 |

## 1954 Bowman

| | Player | NRMT | VG-E |
|---|---|---|---|
| | COMPLETE SET (224) | 4000.00 | 1800.00 |
| | WRAP.(1-CENT, DATED) | 150.00 | 70.00 |
| | WRAP.(1-CENT, UNDAT) | 200.00 | 90.00 |
| | WRAP.(5-CENT, DATED) | 150.00 | 70.00 |
| | WRAP.(5-CENT, UNDAT) | 60.00 | 27.00 |
| ❑ 1 | Phil Rizzuto | 160.00 | 47.50 |
| ❑ 2 | Jackie Jensen | 30.00 | 13.50 |
| ❑ 3 | Marion Fricano | 12.00 | 5.50 |
| ❑ 4 | Bob Hooper | 12.00 | 5.50 |
| ❑ 5 | Billy Hunter | 12.00 | 5.50 |
| ❑ 6 | Nellie Fox | 75.00 | 34.00 |
| ❑ 7 | Walt Dropo | 20.00 | 9.00 |
| ❑ 8 | Jim Busby | 12.00 | 5.50 |
| ❑ 9 | Dave Williams | 12.00 | 5.50 |
| ❑ 10 | Carl Erskine | 20.00 | 9.00 |
| ❑ 11 | Sid Gordon | 12.00 | 5.50 |
| ❑ 12 | Roy McMillan | 20.00 | 9.00 |
| ❑ 13 | Paul Minner | 12.00 | 5.50 |
| ❑ 14 | Jerry Staley | 12.00 | 5.50 |
| ❑ 15 | Richie Ashburn | 75.00 | 34.00 |
| ❑ 16 | Jim Wilson | 12.00 | 5.50 |
| ❑ 17 | Tom Gorman | 12.00 | 5.50 |
| ❑ 18 | Hoot Evers | 12.00 | 5.50 |
| ❑ 19 | Bobby Shantz | 20.00 | 9.00 |
| ❑ 20 | Art Houtteman | 12.00 | 5.50 |
| ❑ 21 | Vic Wertz | 20.00 | 9.00 |
| ❑ 22 | Sam Mele | 12.00 | 5.50 |
| ❑ 23 | Harvey Kuenn RC ! | 30.00 | 13.50 |
| ❑ 24 | Bob Porterfield | 12.00 | 5.50 |
| ❑ 25 | Wes Westrum | 20.00 | 9.00 |
| ❑ 26 | Billy Cox | 20.00 | 9.00 |
| ❑ 27 | Dick Cole | 12.00 | 5.50 |
| ❑ 28 | Jim Greengrass | 12.00 | 5.50 |
| ❑ 29 | Johnny Klippstein | 12.00 | 5.50 |
| ❑ 30 | Del Rice | 12.00 | 5.50 |
| ❑ 31 | Smoky Burgess | 20.00 | 9.00 |
| ❑ 32 | Del Crandall | 20.00 | 9.00 |
| ❑ 33A | Vic Raschi (No mention of trade on back) | 20.00 | 9.00 |
| ❑ 33B | Vic Raschi (Traded to St.Louis) | 30.00 | 13.50 |
| ❑ 34 | Sammy White | 12.00 | 5.50 |
| ❑ 35 | Eddie Joost | 12.00 | 5.50 |
| ❑ 36 | George Strickland | 12.00 | 5.50 |
| ❑ 37 | Dick Kokos | 12.00 | 5.50 |
| ❑ 38 | Minnie Minoso | 30.00 | 13.50 |
| ❑ 39 | Ned Garver | 12.00 | 5.50 |
| ❑ 40 | Gil Coan | 12.00 | 5.50 |
| ❑ 41 | Alvin Dark | 20.00 | 9.00 |
| ❑ 42 | Billy Loes | 20.00 | 9.00 |
| ❑ 43 | Bob Friend | 20.00 | 9.00 |
| ❑ 44 | Harry Perkowski | 12.00 | 5.50 |
| ❑ 45 | Ralph Kiner | 50.00 | 22.00 |
| ❑ 46 | Rip Repulski | 12.00 | 5.50 |
| ❑ 47 | Granny Hamner | 12.00 | 5.50 |
| ❑ 48 | Jack Dittmer | 12.00 | 5.50 |
| ❑ 49 | Harry Byrd | 12.00 | 5.50 |
| ❑ 50 | George Kell | 50.00 | 22.00 |
| ❑ 51 | Alex Kellner | 12.00 | 5.50 |
| ❑ 52 | Joe Ginsberg | 12.00 | 5.50 |
| ❑ 53 | Don Lenhardt | 12.00 | 5.50 |
| ❑ 54 | Chico Carrasquel | 12.00 | 5.50 |
| ❑ 55 | Jim Delsing | 12.00 | 5.50 |
| ❑ 56 | Maurice McDermott | 12.00 | 5.50 |
| ❑ 57 | Hoyt Wilhelm | 50.00 | 22.00 |
| ❑ 58 | Pee Wee Reese | 75.00 | 34.00 |
| ❑ 59 | Bob Schultz | 12.00 | 5.50 |
| ❑ 60 | Fred Baczewski | 12.00 | 5.50 |
| ❑ 61 | Eddie Miksis | 12.00 | 5.50 |
| ❑ 62 | Enos Slaughter | 50.00 | 22.00 |
| ❑ 63 | Earl Torgeson | 12.00 | 5.50 |
| ❑ 64 | Eddie Mathews | 75.00 | 34.00 |
| ❑ 65 | Mickey Mantle | 1400.00 | 650.00 |
| ❑ 66A | Ted Williams | 3500.00 | 1600.00 |
| ❑ 66B | Jimmy Piersall | 75.00 | 34.00 |
| ❑ 67 | Carl Scheib | 12.00 | 5.50 |
| ❑ 68 | Bobby Avila | 20.00 | 9.00 |
| ❑ 69 | Clint Courtney | 12.00 | 5.50 |
| ❑ 70 | Willard Marshall | 12.00 | 5.50 |
| ❑ 71 | Ted Gray | 12.00 | 5.50 |
| ❑ 72 | Eddie Yost | 20.00 | 9.00 |
| ❑ 73 | Don Mueller | 20.00 | 9.00 |
| ❑ 74 | Jim Gilliam | 30.00 | 13.50 |
| ❑ 75 | Max Surkont | 12.00 | 5.50 |
| ❑ 76 | Joe Nuxhall | 20.00 | 9.00 |
| ❑ 77 | Bob Rush | 12.00 | 5.50 |
| ❑ 78 | Sal Yvars | 12.00 | 5.50 |
| ❑ 79 | Curt Simmons | 20.00 | 9.00 |
| ❑ 80 | Johnny Logan | 12.00 | 5.50 |
| ❑ 81 | Jerry Coleman | 20.00 | 9.00 |
| ❑ 82 | Billy Goodman | 20.00 | 9.00 |
| ❑ 83 | Ray Murray | 12.00 | 5.50 |
| ❑ 84 | Larry Doby | 50.00 | 22.00 |
| ❑ 85 | Jim Dyck | 12.00 | 5.50 |
| ❑ 86 | Harry Dorish | 12.00 | 5.50 |
| ❑ 87 | Don Lund | 12.00 | 5.50 |
| ❑ 88 | Tom Umphlett | 12.00 | 5.50 |
| ❑ 89 | Willie Mays | 400.00 | 180.00 |
| ❑ 90 | Roy Campanella | 150.00 | 70.00 |
| ❑ 91 | Cal Abrams | 12.00 | 5.50 |
| ❑ 92 | Ken Raffensberger | 12.00 | 5.50 |
| ❑ 93 | Bill Serena | 12.00 | 5.50 |
| ❑ 94 | Solly Hemus | 12.00 | 5.50 |
| ❑ 95 | Robin Roberts | 50.00 | 22.00 |
| ❑ 96 | Joe Adcock | 20.00 | 9.00 |
| ❑ 97 | Gil McDougald | 20.00 | 9.00 |
| ❑ 98 | Ellis Kinder | 12.00 | 5.50 |
| ❑ 99 | Pete Suder | 12.00 | 5.50 |
| ❑ 100 | Mike Garcia | 20.00 | 9.00 |
| ❑ 101 | Don Larsen RC | 75.00 | 34.00 |
| ❑ 102 | Billy Pierce | 20.00 | 9.00 |
| ❑ 103 | Steve Souchock | 12.00 | 5.50 |
| ❑ 104 | Frank Shea | 12.00 | 5.50 |
| ❑ 105 | Sal Maglie | 20.00 | 9.00 |
| ❑ 106 | Clem Labine | 20.00 | 9.00 |
| ❑ 107 | Paul LaPalme | 12.00 | 5.50 |
| ❑ 108 | Bobby Adams | 12.00 | 5.50 |
| ❑ 109 | Roy Smalley | 12.00 | 5.50 |
| ❑ 110 | Red Schoendienst | 50.00 | 22.00 |
| ❑ 111 | Murry Dickson | 12.00 | 5.50 |
| ❑ 112 | Andy Pafko | 20.00 | 9.00 |
| ❑ 113 | Allie Reynolds | 20.00 | 9.00 |
| ❑ 114 | Willard Nixon | 12.00 | 5.50 |
| ❑ 115 | Don Bollweg | 12.00 | 5.50 |
| ❑ 116 | Luke Easter | 20.00 | 9.00 |
| ❑ 117 | Dick Kryhoski | 12.00 | 5.50 |
| ❑ 118 | Bob Boyd | 12.00 | 5.50 |
| ❑ 119 | Fred Hatfield | 12.00 | 5.50 |
| ❑ 120 | Mel Hoderlein | 12.00 | 5.50 |
| ❑ 121 | Ray Katt | 12.00 | 5.50 |
| ❑ 122 | Carl Furillo | 30.00 | 13.50 |
| ❑ 123 | Toby Atwell | 12.00 | 5.50 |
| ❑ 124 | Gus Bell | 20.00 | 9.00 |
| ❑ 125 | Warren Hacker | 12.00 | 5.50 |
| ❑ 126 | Cliff Chambers | 12.00 | 5.50 |
| ❑ 127 | Del Ennis | 20.00 | 9.00 |
| ❑ 128 | Ebba St.Claire | 12.00 | 5.50 |
| ❑ 129 | Hank Bauer | 30.00 | 13.50 |
| ❑ 130 | Milt Bolling | 12.00 | 5.50 |
| ❑ 131 | Joe Astroth | 12.00 | 5.50 |
| ❑ 132 | Bob Feller | 75.00 | 34.00 |
| ❑ 133 | Duane Pillette | 12.00 | 5.50 |
| ❑ 134 | Luis Aloma | 12.00 | 5.50 |
| ❑ 135 | Johnny Pesky | 20.00 | 9.00 |
| ❑ 136 | Clyde Vollmer | 12.00 | 5.50 |
| ❑ 137 | Al Corwin | 12.00 | 5.50 |
| ❑ 138 | Gil Hodges | 75.00 | 34.00 |
| ❑ 139 | Preston Ward | 12.00 | 5.50 |
| ❑ 140 | Saul Rogovin | 12.00 | 5.50 |
| ❑ 141 | Joe Garagiola | 30.00 | 13.50 |
| ❑ 142 | Al Brazle | 12.00 | 5.50 |
| ❑ 143 | Willie Jones | 12.00 | 5.50 |
| ❑ 144 | Ernie Johnson RC | 30.00 | 13.50 |
| ❑ 145 | Billy Martin | 75.00 | 34.00 |
| ❑ 146 | Dick Gernert | 12.00 | 5.50 |

❑ 147 Joe DeMaestri ........ 12.00 5.50
❑ 148 Dale Mitchell ........ 20.00 9.00
❑ 149 Bob Young ........ 12.00 5.50
❑ 150 Cass Michaels ........ 12.00 5.50
❑ 151 Pat Mullin ........ 12.00 5.50
❑ 152 Mickey Vernon ........ 20.00 9.00
❑ 153 Whitey Lockman ........ 20.00 9.00
❑ 154 Don Newcombe ........ 30.00 13.50
❑ 155 Frank Thomas RC ........ 20.00 9.00
❑ 156 Rocky Bridges ........ 12.00 5.50
❑ 157 Turk Lown ........ 12.00 5.50
❑ 158 Stu Miller ........ 20.00 9.00
❑ 159 Johnny Lindell ........ 12.00 5.50
❑ 160 Danny O'Connell ........ 12.00 5.50
❑ 161 Yogi Berra ........ 175.00 80.00
❑ 162 Ted Lepcio ........ 12.00 5.50
❑ 163A Dave Philley ........ 20.00 9.00
(No mention of trade on back)
❑ 163B Dave Philley ........ 30.00 13.50
(Traded to Cleveland)
❑ 164 Early Wynn ........ 50.00 22.00
❑ 165 Johnny Groth ........ 12.00 5.50
❑ 166 Sandy Consuegra ........ 12.00 5.50
❑ 167 Billy Hoeft ........ 12.00 5.50
❑ 168 Ed Fitzgerald ........ 12.00 5.50
❑ 169 Larry Jansen ........ 20.00 9.00
❑ 170 Duke Snider ........ 150.00 70.00
❑ 171 Carlos Bernier ........ 12.00 5.50
❑ 172 Andy Seminick ........ 12.00 5.50
❑ 173 Dee Fondy ........ 12.00 5.50
❑ 174 Pete Castiglione ........ 12.00 5.50
❑ 175 Mel Clark ........ 12.00 5.50
❑ 176 Vern Bickford ........ 12.00 5.50
❑ 177 Whitey Ford ........ 100.00 45.00
❑ 178 Del Wilber ........ 12.00 5.50
❑ 179 Morrie Martin ........ 12.00 5.50
❑ 180 Joe Tipton ........ 12.00 5.50
❑ 181 Les Moss ........ 12.00 5.50
❑ 182 Sherm Lollar ........ 20.00 9.00
❑ 183 Matt Batts ........ 12.00 5.50
❑ 184 Mickey Grasso ........ 12.00 5.50
❑ 185 Daryl Spencer ........ 12.00 5.50
❑ 186 Russ Meyer ........ 12.00 5.50
❑ 187 Vern Law ........ 20.00 9.00
❑ 188 Frank Smith ........ 12.00 5.50
❑ 189 Randy Jackson ........ 12.00 5.50
❑ 190 Joe Presko ........ 12.00 5.50
❑ 191 Karl Drews ........ 12.00 5.50
❑ 192 Lou Burdette ........ 20.00 9.00
❑ 193 Eddie Robinson ........ 12.00 5.50
❑ 194 Sid Hudson ........ 12.00 5.50
❑ 195 Bob Cain ........ 12.00 5.50
❑ 196 Bob Lemon ........ 50.00 22.00
❑ 197 Lou Kretlow ........ 12.00 5.50
❑ 198 Virgil Trucks ........ 12.00 5.50
❑ 199 Steve Gromek ........ 12.00 5.50
❑ 200 Conrado Marrero ........ 12.00 5.50
❑ 201 Bobby Thomson ........ 30.00 13.50
❑ 202 George Shuba ........ 20.00 9.00
❑ 203 Vic Janowicz ........ 20.00 9.00
❑ 204 Jack Collum ........ 12.00 5.50
❑ 205 Hal Jeffcoat ........ 12.00 5.50
❑ 206 Steve Bilko ........ 12.00 5.50
❑ 207 Stan Lopata ........ 12.00 5.50
❑ 208 Johnny Antonelli ........ 20.00 9.00
❑ 209 Gene Woodling ........ 12.00 5.50
❑ 210 Jimmy Piersall ........ 30.00 13.50
❑ 211 Al Robertson ........ 12.00 5.50
❑ 212 Owen Friend ........ 12.00 5.50
❑ 213 Dick Littlefield ........ 12.00 5.50
❑ 214 Ferris Fain ........ 20.00 9.00
❑ 215 Johnny Bucha ........ 12.00 5.50
❑ 216 Jerry Snyder ........ 12.00 5.50
❑ 217 Hank Thompson ........ 20.00 9.00
❑ 218 Preacher Roe ........ 20.00 9.00
❑ 219 Hal Rice ........ 12.00 5.50
❑ 220 Hobie Landrith ........ 12.00 5.50
❑ 221 Frank Baumholtz ........ 12.00 5.50
❑ 222 Memo Luna ........ 12.00 5.50
❑ 223 Steve Ridzik ........ 12.00 5.50
❑ 224 Bill Bruton ........ 50.00 12.50

## 1955 Bowman

| | NRMT | VG-E |
|---|---|---|
| COMPLETE SET (320) | 4600.00 | 2100.00 |
| COM. CARD (97-224) | 10.00 | 4.50 |
| COM. CARD (225-320) | 15.00 | 6.75 |
| COM. UMPIRE (225-320) | 30.00 | 13.50 |
| WRAPPER (1-CENT) | 60.00 | 27.00 |
| WRAPPER (5-CENT) | 60.00 | 27.00 |

❑ 1 Hoyt Wilhelm ........ 100.00 22.00
❑ 2 Alvin Dark ........ 15.00 6.75
❑ 3 Joe Coleman ........ 15.00 6.75
❑ 4 Eddie Waitkus ........ 15.00 6.75
❑ 5 Jim Robertson ........ 12.00 5.50
❑ 6 Pete Suder ........ 12.00 5.50
❑ 7 Gene Baker ........ 12.00 5.50
❑ 8 Warren Hacker ........ 12.00 5.50
❑ 9 Gil McDougald ........ 20.00 9.00
❑ 10 Phil Rizzuto ........ 100.00 45.00
❑ 11 Bill Bruton ........ 15.00 6.75
❑ 12 Andy Pafko ........ 15.00 6.75
❑ 13 Clyde Vollmer ........ 12.00 5.50
❑ 14 Gus Keriazakos ........ 12.00 5.50
❑ 15 Frank Sullivan ........ 12.00 5.50
❑ 16 Jimmy Piersall ........ 20.00 9.00
❑ 17 Del Ennis ........ 15.00 6.75
❑ 18 Stan Lopata ........ 12.00 5.50
❑ 19 Bobby Avila ........ 15.00 6.75
❑ 20 Al Smith ........ 15.00 6.75
❑ 21 Don Hoak ........ 12.00 5.50
❑ 22 Roy Campanella ........ 125.00 55.00
❑ 23 Al Kaline ........ 150.00 70.00
❑ 24 Al Aber ........ 12.00 5.50
❑ 25 Minnie Minoso ........ 30.00 13.50
❑ 26 Virgil Trucks ........ 15.00 6.75
❑ 27 Preston Ward ........ 12.00 5.50
❑ 28 Dick Cole ........ 12.00 5.50
❑ 29 Red Schoendienst ........ 30.00 13.50
❑ 30 Bill Sarni ........ 12.00 5.50
❑ 31 Johnny Temple RC ........ 15.00 6.75
❑ 32 Wally Post ........ 15.00 6.75
❑ 33 Nellie Fox ........ 50.00 22.00
❑ 34 Clint Courtney ........ 12.00 5.50
❑ 35 Bill Tuttle ........ 12.00 5.50
❑ 36 Wayne Belardi ........ 12.00 5.50
❑ 37 Pee Wee Reese ........ 75.00 34.00
❑ 38 Early Wynn ........ 30.00 13.50
❑ 39 Bob Darnell ........ 15.00 6.75
❑ 40 Vic Wertz ........ 15.00 6.75
❑ 41 Mel Clark ........ 12.00 5.50
❑ 42 Bob Greenwood ........ 12.00 5.50
❑ 43 Bob Buhl ........ 15.00 6.75
❑ 44 Danny O'Connell ........ 12.00 5.50
❑ 45 Tom Umphlett ........ 12.00 5.50
❑ 46 Mickey Vernon ........ 15.00 6.75
❑ 47 Sammy White ........ 12.00 5.50
❑ 48A Milt Bolling ERR ........ 30.00 13.50
(Name on back is Frank Bolling)
❑ 48B Milt Bolling COR ........ 15.00 6.75
❑ 49 Jim Greengrass ........ 12.00 5.50
❑ 50 Hobie Landrith ........ 12.00 5.50
❑ 51 Elvin Tappe ........ 12.00 5.50
❑ 52 Hal Rice ........ 12.00 5.50
❑ 53 Alex Kellner ........ 12.00 5.50
❑ 54 Don Bollweg ........ 12.00 5.50
❑ 55 Cal Abrams ........ 12.00 5.50
❑ 56 Billy Cox ........ 15.00 6.75
❑ 57 Bob Friend ........ 15.00 6.75
❑ 58 Frank Thomas ........ 15.00 6.75
❑ 59 Whitey Ford ........ 80.00 36.00
❑ 60 Enos Slaughter ........ 30.00 13.50
❑ 61 Paul LaPalme ........ 12.00 5.50
❑ 62 Royce Lint ........ 12.00 5.50
❑ 63 Irv Noren ........ 15.00 6.75
❑ 64 Curt Simmons ........ 15.00 6.75
❑ 65 Don Zimmer RC ........ 20.00 9.00
❑ 66 George Shuba ........ 20.00 9.00
❑ 67 Don Larsen ........ 20.00 9.00
❑ 68 Elston Howard RC ........ 75.00 34.00
❑ 69 Billy Hunter ........ 12.00 5.50
❑ 70 Lou Burdette ........ 20.00 9.00
❑ 71 Dave Jolly ........ 12.00 5.50
❑ 72 Chet Nichols ........ 12.00 5.50
❑ 73 Eddie Yost ........ 15.00 6.75
❑ 74 Jerry Snyder ........ 12.00 5.50
❑ 75 Brooks Lawrence RC ........ 12.00 5.50
❑ 76 Tom Poholsky ........ 12.00 5.50
❑ 77 Jim McDonald ........ 12.00 5.50
❑ 78 Gil Coan ........ 12.00 5.50
❑ 79 Willie Miranda ........ 12.00 5.50
❑ 80 Lou Limmer ........ 12.00 5.50
❑ 81 Bobby Morgan ........ 12.00 5.50
❑ 82 Lee Walls ........ 12.00 5.50
❑ 83 Max Surkont ........ 12.00 5.50
❑ 84 George Freese ........ 12.00 5.50
❑ 85 Cass Michaels ........ 12.00 5.50
❑ 86 Ted Gray ........ 12.00 5.50
❑ 87 Randy Jackson ........ 12.00 5.50
❑ 88 Steve Bilko ........ 12.00 5.50
❑ 89 Lou Boudreau MG ........ 30.00 13.50
❑ 90 Art Ditmar ........ 12.00 5.50
❑ 91 Dick Marlowe ........ 12.00 5.50
❑ 92 George Zuverink ........ 12.00 5.50
❑ 93 Andy Seminick ........ 12.00 5.50
❑ 94 Hank Thompson ........ 15.00 6.75
❑ 95 Sal Maglie ........ 15.00 6.75
❑ 96 Ray Narleski RC ........ 12.00 5.50
❑ 97 Johnny Podres ........ 30.00 13.50
❑ 98 Jim Gilliam ........ 20.00 9.00
❑ 99 Jerry Coleman ........ 15.00 6.75
❑ 100 Tom Morgan ........ 10.00 4.50
❑ 101A Don Johnson ERR ........ 15.00 6.75
(Photo actually Ernie Johnson)
❑ 101B Don Johnson COR ........ 30.00 13.50
❑ 102 Bobby Thomson ........ 15.00 6.75
❑ 103 Eddie Mathews ........ 60.00 27.00
❑ 104 Bob Porterfield ........ 10.00 4.50
❑ 105 Johnny Schmitz ........ 10.00 4.50
❑ 106 Del Rice ........ 10.00 4.50
❑ 107 Solly Hemus ........ 10.00 4.50
❑ 108 Lou Kretlow ........ 10.00 4.50
❑ 109 Vern Stephens ........ 15.00 6.75
❑ 110 Bob Miller ........ 10.00 4.50
❑ 111 Steve Ridzik ........ 10.00 4.50
❑ 112 Granny Hamner ........ 10.00 4.50
❑ 113 Bob Hall ........ 10.00 4.50
❑ 114 Vic Janowicz ........ 15.00 6.75
❑ 115 Roger Bowman ........ 10.00 4.50
❑ 116 Sandy Consuegra ........ 10.00 4.50
❑ 117 Johnny Groth ........ 10.00 4.50
❑ 118 Bobby Adams ........ 10.00 4.50
❑ 119 Joe Astroth ........ 10.00 4.50
❑ 120 Ed Burtschy ........ 10.00 4.50
❑ 121 Rufus Crawford ........ 10.00 4.50
❑ 122 Al Corwin ........ 10.00 4.50
❑ 123 Marv Grissom ........ 10.00 4.50
❑ 124 Johnny Antonelli ........ 15.00 6.75
❑ 125 Paul Giel ........ 15.00 6.75
❑ 126 Billy Goodman ........ 15.00 6.75
❑ 127 Hank Majeski ........ 10.00 4.50
❑ 128 Mike Garcia ........ 15.00 6.75
❑ 129 Hal Naragon ........ 10.00 4.50
❑ 130 Richie Ashburn ........ 50.00 22.00
❑ 131 Willard Marshall ........ 10.00 4.50
❑ 132A Harvey Kueen ERR ........ 20.00 9.00
(Sic, Kuenn)
❑ 132B Harvey Kuenn COR ........ 30.00 13.50
❑ 133 Charles King ........ 10.00 4.50
❑ 134 Bob Feller ........ 70.00 32.00
❑ 135 Lloyd Merriman ........ 10.00 4.50
❑ 136 Rocky Bridges ........ 10.00 4.50

- ❑ 137 Bob Talbot 10.00 4.50
- ❑ 138 Davey Williams 15.00 6.75
- ❑ 139 Shantz Brothers 15.00 6.75
  Wilmer Shantz
  Bobby Shantz
- ❑ 140 Bobby Shantz 15.00 6.75
- ❑ 141 Wes Westrum 15.00 6.75
- ❑ 142 Rudy Regalado 10.00 4.50
- ❑ 143 Don Newcombe 30.00 13.50
- ❑ 144 Art Houtteman 10.00 4.50
- ❑ 145 Bob Nieman 10.00 4.50
- ❑ 146 Don Liddle 10.00 4.50
- ❑ 147 Sam Mele 10.00 4.50
- ❑ 148 Bob Chakales 10.00 4.50
- ❑ 149 Cloyd Boyer 10.00 4.50
- ❑ 150 Billy Klaus 10.00 4.50
- ❑ 151 Jim Brideweser 10.00 4.50
- ❑ 152 Johnny Klippstein 10.00 4.50
- ❑ 153 Eddie Robinson 10.00 4.50
- ❑ 154 Frank Lary RC 15.00 6.75
- ❑ 155 Gerry Staley 10.00 4.50
- ❑ 156 Jim Hughes 15.00 6.75
- ❑ 157A Ernie Johnson ERR 20.00 9.00
  (Photo actually
  Don Johnson)
- ❑ 157B Ernie Johnson COR 12.00 5.50
- ❑ 158 Gil Hodges 50.00 22.00
- ❑ 159 Harry Byrd 10.00 4.50
- ❑ 160 Bill Skowron 20.00 9.00
- ❑ 161 Matt Batts 10.00 4.50
- ❑ 162 Charlie Maxwell 10.00 4.50
- ❑ 163 Sid Gordon 15.00 6.75
- ❑ 164 Toby Atwell 10.00 4.50
- ❑ 165 Maurice McDermott 10.00 4.50
- ❑ 166 Jim Busby 10.00 4.50
- ❑ 167 Bob Grim RC 20.00 9.00
- ❑ 168 Yogi Berra 100.00 45.00
- ❑ 169 Carl Furillo 30.00 13.50
- ❑ 170 Carl Erskine 20.00 9.00
- ❑ 171 Robin Roberts 40.00 18.00
- ❑ 172 Willie Jones 10.00 4.50
- ❑ 173 Chico Carrasquel 10.00 4.50
- ❑ 174 Sherm Lollar 15.00 6.75
- ❑ 175 Wilmer Shantz 10.00 4.50
- ❑ 176 Joe DeMaestri 10.00 4.50
- ❑ 177 Willard Nixon 10.00 4.50
- ❑ 178 Tom Brewer 10.00 4.50
- ❑ 179 Hank Aaron 225.00 100.00
- ❑ 180 Johnny Logan 15.00 6.75
- ❑ 181 Eddie Miksis 10.00 4.50
- ❑ 182 Bob Rush 10.00 4.50
- ❑ 183 Ray Katt 10.00 4.50
- ❑ 184 Willie Mays 225.00 100.00
- ❑ 185 Vic Raschi 10.00 4.50
- ❑ 186 Alex Grammas 10.00 4.50
- ❑ 187 Fred Hatfield 10.00 4.50
- ❑ 188 Ned Garver 10.00 4.50
- ❑ 189 Jack Collum 10.00 4.50
- ❑ 190 Fred Baczewski 10.00 4.50
- ❑ 191 Bob Lemon 30.00 13.50
- ❑ 192 George Strickland 10.00 4.50
- ❑ 193 Howie Judson 10.00 4.50
- ❑ 194 Joe Nuxhall 15.00 6.75
- ❑ 195A Erv Palica 15.00 6.75
  (Without trade)
- ❑ 195B Erv Palica 30.00 13.50
  (With trade)
- ❑ 196 Russ Meyer 15.00 6.75
- ❑ 197 Ralph Kiner 30.00 13.50
- ❑ 198 Dave Pope 10.00 4.50
- ❑ 199 Vern Law 15.00 6.75
- ❑ 200 Dick Littlefield 10.00 4.50
- ❑ 201 Allie Reynolds 20.00 9.00
- ❑ 202 Mickey Mantle UER 900.00 400.00
  (Birthdate listed as 10/30/31;
  Should be 10/20/31)
- ❑ 203 Steve Gromek 10.00 4.50
- ❑ 204A Frank Bolling ERR 20.00 9.00
  (Name on back is
  Milt Bolling)
- ❑ 204B Frank Bolling COR 20.00 9.00
- ❑ 205 Rip Repulski 10.00 4.50
- ❑ 206 Ralph Beard 10.00 4.50
- ❑ 207 Frank Shea 10.00 4.50
- ❑ 208 Ed Fitzgerald 10.00 4.50
- ❑ 209 Smoky Burgess 15.00 6.75
- ❑ 210 Earl Torgeson 10.00 4.50
- ❑ 211 Sonny Dixon 10.00 4.50
- ❑ 212 Jack Dittmer 10.00 4.50
- ❑ 213 George Kell 30.00 13.50
- ❑ 214 Billy Pierce 15.00 6.75
- ❑ 215 Bob Kuzava 10.00 4.50
- ❑ 216 Preacher Roe 15.00 6.75
- ❑ 217 Del Crandall 15.00 6.75
- ❑ 218 Joe Adcock 15.00 6.75
- ❑ 219 Whitey Lockman 15.00 6.75
- ❑ 220 Jim Hearn 10.00 4.50
- ❑ 221 Hector Brown 10.00 4.50
- ❑ 222 Russ Kemmerer 10.00 4.50
- ❑ 223 Hal Jeffcoat 10.00 4.50
- ❑ 224 Dee Fondy 10.00 4.50
- ❑ 225 Paul Richards MG 15.00 6.75
- ❑ 226 Bill McKinley UMP 30.00 13.50
- ❑ 227 Frank Baumholtz 15.00 6.75
- ❑ 228 John Phillips 15.00 6.75
- ❑ 229 Jim Brosnan RC 20.00 9.00
- ❑ 230 Al Brazle 15.00 6.75
- ❑ 231 Jim Konstanty 20.00 9.00
- ❑ 232 Birdie Tebbetts MG 20.00 9.00
- ❑ 233 Bill Serena 15.00 6.75
- ❑ 234 Dick Bartell CO 20.00 9.00
- ❑ 235 Joe Paparella UMP 30.00 13.50
- ❑ 236 Murry Dickson 15.00 6.75
- ❑ 237 Johnny Wyrostek 15.00 6.75
- ❑ 238 Eddie Stanky MG 20.00 9.00
- ❑ 239 Edwin Rommel UMP 40.00 18.00
- ❑ 240 Billy Loes 20.00 9.00
- ❑ 241 Johnny Pesky CO 20.00 9.00
- ❑ 242 Ernie Banks 350.00 160.00
- ❑ 243 Gus Bell 20.00 9.00
- ❑ 244 Duane Pillette 15.00 6.75
- ❑ 245 Bill Miller 15.00 6.75
- ❑ 246 Hank Bauer 30.00 13.50
- ❑ 247 Dutch Leonard CO 15.00 6.75
- ❑ 248 Harry Dorish 15.00 6.75
- ❑ 249 Billy Gardner 20.00 9.00
- ❑ 250 Larry Napp UMP 30.00 13.50
- ❑ 251 Stan Jok 15.00 6.75
- ❑ 252 Roy Smalley 15.00 6.75
- ❑ 253 Jim Wilson 15.00 6.75
- ❑ 254 Bennett Flowers 15.00 6.75
- ❑ 255 Pete Runnels 20.00 9.00
- ❑ 256 Owen Friend 15.00 6.75
- ❑ 257 Tom Alston 15.00 6.75
- ❑ 258 John Stevens UMP 30.00 13.50
- ❑ 259 Don Mossi RC 30.00 13.50
- ❑ 260 Edwin Hurley UMP 30.00 13.50
- ❑ 261 Walt Moryn 20.00 9.00
- ❑ 262 Jim Lemon 15.00 6.75
- ❑ 263 Eddie Joost 15.00 6.75
- ❑ 264 Bill Henry 15.00 6.75
- ❑ 265 Albert Barlick UMP 75.00 34.00
- ❑ 266 Mike Fornieles 15.00 6.75
- ❑ 267 Jim Honochick UMP 75.00 34.00
- ❑ 268 Roy Lee Hawes 15.00 6.75
- ❑ 269 Joe Amalfitano RC 20.00 9.00
- ❑ 270 Chico Fernandez 20.00 9.00
- ❑ 271 Bob Hooper 15.00 6.75
- ❑ 272 John Flaherty UMP 30.00 13.50
- ❑ 273 Bubba Church 15.00 6.75
- ❑ 274 Jim Delsing 15.00 6.75
- ❑ 275 William Grieve UMP 30.00 13.50
- ❑ 276 Ike Delock 15.00 6.75
- ❑ 277 Ed Runge UMP 30.00 13.50
- ❑ 278 Charlie Neal RC 40.00 18.00
- ❑ 279 Hank Soar UMP 40.00 18.00
- ❑ 280 Clyde McCullough 15.00 6.75
- ❑ 281 Charles Berry UMP 40.00 18.00
- ❑ 282 Phil Cavarretta 20.00 9.00
- ❑ 283 Nestor Chylak UMP 75.00 34.00
- ❑ 284 Bill Jackowski UMP 30.00 13.50
- ❑ 285 Walt Dropo 20.00 9.00
- ❑ 286 Frank Secory UMP 30.00 13.50
- ❑ 287 Ron Mrozinski 15.00 6.75
- ❑ 288 Dick Smith 15.00 6.75
- ❑ 289 Arthur Gore UMP 30.00 13.50
- ❑ 290 Hershell Freeman 15.00 6.75
- ❑ 291 Frank Dascoli UMP 30.00 13.50
- ❑ 292 Marv Blaylock 15.00 6.75
- ❑ 293 Thomas Gorman UMP 40.00 18.00
- ❑ 294 Wally Moses CO 15.00 6.75
- ❑ 295 Lee Ballanfant UMP 30.00 13.50
- ❑ 296 Bill Virdon RC 30.00 13.50
- ❑ 297 Dusty Boggess UMP 30.00 13.50
- ❑ 298 Charlie Grimm MG 20.00 9.00
- ❑ 299 Lon Warneke UMP 40.00 18.00
- ❑ 300 Tommy Byrne 20.00 9.00
- ❑ 301 William Engeln UMP 30.00 13.50
- ❑ 302 Frank Malzone RC 30.00 13.50
- ❑ 303 Jocko Conlan UMP 75.00 34.00
- ❑ 304 Harry Chiti 15.00 6.75
- ❑ 305 Frank Umont UMP 30.00 13.50
- ❑ 306 Bob Cerv 20.00 9.00
- ❑ 307 Babe Pinelli UMP 40.00 18.00
- ❑ 308 Al Lopez MG 50.00 22.00
- ❑ 309 Hal Dixon UMP 30.00 13.50
- ❑ 310 Ken Lehman 15.00 6.75
- ❑ 311 Lawrence Goetz UMP 30.00 13.50
- ❑ 312 Bill Wight 15.00 6.75
- ❑ 313 Augie Donatelli UMP 50.00 22.00
- ❑ 314 Dale Mitchell 20.00 9.00
- ❑ 315 Cal Hubbard UMP 75.00 34.00
- ❑ 316 Marion Fricano 15.00 6.75
- ❑ 317 William Summers UMP 20.00 9.00
- ❑ 318 Sid Hudson 15.00 6.75
- ❑ 319 Al Schroll 15.00 6.75
- ❑ 320 George Susce Jr. RC ! 50.00 10.00

## 1989 Bowman

| | MINT | NRMT |
|---|---|---|
| COMPLETE SET (484) | 30.00 | 13.50 |
| COMP.FACT.SET (484) | 40.00 | 18.00 |

- ❑ 1 Oswald Peraza .05 .02
- ❑ 2 Brian Holton .05 .02
- ❑ 3 Jose Bautista .05 .02
- ❑ 4 Pete Harnisch RC .25 .11
- ❑ 5 Dave Schmidt .05 .02
- ❑ 6 Gregg Olson RC .20 .09
- ❑ 7 Jeff Ballard .05 .02
- ❑ 8 Bob Melvin .05 .02
- ❑ 9 Cal Ripken .75 .35
- ❑ 10 Randy Milligan .05 .02
- ❑ 11 Juan Bell RC .05 .02
- ❑ 12 Billy Ripken .05 .02
- ❑ 13 Jim Traber .05 .02
- ❑ 14 Pete Stanicek .05 .02
- ❑ 15 Steve Finley RC .50 .23
- ❑ 16 Larry Sheets .05 .02
- ❑ 17 Phil Bradley .05 .02
- ❑ 18 Brady Anderson RC .40 .18
- ❑ 19 Lee Smith .10 .05
- ❑ 20 Tom Fischer .05 .02
- ❑ 21 Mike Boddicker .05 .02
- ❑ 22 Rob Murphy .05 .02
- ❑ 23 Wes Gardner .05 .02
- ❑ 24 John Dopson .05 .02
- ❑ 25 Bob Stanley .05 .02
- ❑ 26 Roger Clemens .40 .18
- ❑ 27 Rich Gedman .05 .02
- ❑ 28 Marty Barrett .05 .02
- ❑ 29 Luis Rivera .05 .02
- ❑ 30 Jody Reed .05 .02
- ❑ 31 Nick Esasky .05 .02
- ❑ 32 Wade Boggs .25 .11
- ❑ 33 Jim Rice .10 .05
- ❑ 34 Mike Greenwell .05 .02
- ❑ 35 Dwight Evans .10 .05
- ❑ 36 Ellis Burks .10 .05

❑ 37 Chuck Finley .10 .05
❑ 38 Kirk McCaskill .05 .02
❑ 39 Jim Abbott RC* .20 .09
❑ 40 Bryan Harvey RC* .05 .02
❑ 41 Bert Blyleven .10 .05
❑ 42 Mike Witt .05 .02
❑ 43 Bob McClure .05 .02
❑ 44 Bill Schroeder .05 .02
❑ 45 Lance Parrish .05 .02
❑ 46 Dick Schofield .05 .02
❑ 47 Wally Joyner .10 .05
❑ 48 Jack Howell .05 .02
❑ 49 Johnny Ray .05 .02
❑ 50 Chili Davis .10 .05
❑ 51 Tony Armas .05 .02
❑ 52 Claudell Washington .05 .02
❑ 53 Brian Downing .05 .02
❑ 54 Devon White .10 .05
❑ 55 Bobby Thigpen .05 .02
❑ 56 Bill Long .05 .02
❑ 57 Jerry Reuss .05 .02
❑ 58 Shawn Hillegas .05 .02
❑ 59 Melido Perez .05 .02
❑ 60 Jeff Bittiger .05 .02
❑ 61 Jack McDowell .10 .05
❑ 62 Carlton Fisk .20 .09
❑ 63 Steve Lyons .05 .02
❑ 64 Ozzie Guillen .05 .02
❑ 65 Robin Ventura RC .75 .35
❑ 66 Fred Manrique .05 .02
❑ 67 Dan Pasqua .05 .02
❑ 68 Ivan Calderon .05 .02
❑ 69 Ron Kittle .05 .02
❑ 70 Daryl Boston .05 .02
❑ 71 Dave Gallagher .05 .02
❑ 72 Harold Baines .10 .05
❑ 73 Charles Nagy RC .25 .11
❑ 74 John Farrell .05 .02
❑ 75 Kevin Wickander .05 .02
❑ 76 Greg Swindell .05 .02
❑ 77 Mike Walker .05 .02
❑ 78 Doug Jones .05 .02
❑ 79 Rich Yett .05 .02
❑ 80 Tom Candiotti .05 .02
❑ 81 Jesse Orosco .05 .02
❑ 82 Bud Black .05 .02
❑ 83 Andy Allanson .05 .02
❑ 84 Pete O'Brien .05 .02
❑ 85 Jerry Browne .05 .02
❑ 86 Brook Jacoby .05 .02
❑ 87 Mark Lewis RC .10 .05
❑ 88 Luis Aguayo .05 .02
❑ 89 Cory Snyder .05 .02
❑ 90 Oddibe McDowell .05 .02
❑ 91 Joe Carter .10 .05
❑ 92 Frank Tanana .05 .02
❑ 93 Jack Morris .10 .05
❑ 94 Doyle Alexander .05 .02
❑ 95 Steve Searcy .05 .02
❑ 96 Randy Bockus .05 .02
❑ 97 Jeff M. Robinson .05 .02
❑ 98 Mike Henneman .05 .02
❑ 99 Paul Gibson .05 .02
❑ 100 Frank Williams .05 .02
❑ 101 Matt Nokes .05 .02
❑ 102 Rico Brogna RC UER .25 .11
(Misspelled Ricco on card back)
❑ 103 Lou Whitaker .10 .05
❑ 104 Al Pedrique .05 .02
❑ 105 Alan Trammell .10 .05
❑ 106 Chris Brown .05 .02
❑ 107 Pat Sheridan .05 .02
❑ 108 Chet Lemon .05 .02
❑ 109 Keith Moreland .05 .02
❑ 110 Mel Stottlemyre Jr. .05 .02
❑ 111 Bret Saberhagen .10 .05
❑ 112 Floyd Bannister .05 .02
❑ 113 Jeff Montgomery .10 .05
❑ 114 Steve Farr .05 .02
❑ 115 Tom Gordon RC UER .20 .09
(Front shows autograph of Don Gordon)
❑ 116 Charlie Leibrandt .05 .02
❑ 117 Mark Gubicza .05 .02
❑ 118 Mike Macfarlane RC* .05 .02
❑ 119 Bob Boone .10 .05
❑ 120 Kurt Stillwell .05 .02
❑ 121 George Brett .40 .18
❑ 122 Frank White .10 .05
❑ 123 Kevin Seitzer .05 .02
❑ 124 Willie Wilson .05 .02
❑ 125 Pat Tabler .05 .02
❑ 126 Bo Jackson .10 .05
❑ 127 Hugh Walker RC .05 .02
❑ 128 Danny Tartabull .05 .02
❑ 129 Teddy Higuera .05 .02
❑ 130 Don August .05 .02
❑ 131 Juan Nieves .05 .02
❑ 132 Mike Birkbeck .05 .02
❑ 133 Dan Plesac .05 .02
❑ 134 Chris Bosio .05 .02
❑ 135 Bill Wegman .05 .02
❑ 136 Chuck Crim .05 .02
❑ 137 B.J. Surhoff .10 .05
❑ 138 Joey Meyer .05 .02
❑ 139 Dale Sveum .05 .02
❑ 140 Paul Molitor .20 .09
❑ 141 Jim Gantner .05 .02
❑ 142 Gary Sheffield RC 1.25 .55
❑ 143 Greg Brock .05 .02
❑ 144 Robin Yount .20 .09
❑ 145 Glenn Braggs .05 .02
❑ 146 Rob Deer .05 .02
❑ 147 Fred Toliver .05 .02
❑ 148 Jeff Reardon .10 .05
❑ 149 Allan Anderson .05 .02
❑ 150 Frank Viola .05 .02
❑ 151 Shane Rawley .05 .02
❑ 152 Juan Berenguer .05 .02
❑ 153 Johnny Ard .05 .02
❑ 154 Tim Laudner .05 .02
❑ 155 Brian Harper .05 .02
❑ 156 Al Newman .05 .02
❑ 157 Kent Hrbek .10 .05
❑ 158 Gary Gaetti .10 .05
❑ 159 Wally Backman .05 .02
❑ 160 Gene Larkin .05 .02
❑ 161 Greg Gagne .05 .02
❑ 162 Kirby Puckett .50 .23
❑ 163 Dan Gladden .05 .02
❑ 164 Randy Bush .05 .02
❑ 165 Dave LaPoint .05 .02
❑ 166 Andy Hawkins .05 .02
❑ 167 Dave Righetti .05 .02
❑ 168 Lance McCullers .05 .02
❑ 169 Jimmy Jones .05 .02
❑ 170 Al Leiter .20 .09
❑ 171 John Candelaria .05 .02
❑ 172 Don Slaught .05 .02
❑ 173 Jamie Quirk .05 .02
❑ 174 Rafael Santana .05 .02
❑ 175 Mike Pagliarulo .05 .02
❑ 176 Don Mattingly .50 .23
❑ 177 Ken Phelps .05 .02
❑ 178 Steve Sax .05 .02
❑ 179 Dave Winfield .20 .09
❑ 180 Stan Jefferson .05 .02
❑ 181 Rickey Henderson .25 .11
❑ 182 Bob Brower .05 .02
❑ 183 Roberto Kelly .10 .05
❑ 184 Curt Young .05 .02
❑ 185 Gene Nelson .05 .02
❑ 186 Bob Welch .05 .02
❑ 187 Rick Honeycutt .05 .02
❑ 188 Dave Stewart .10 .05
❑ 189 Mike Moore .05 .02
❑ 190 Dennis Eckersley .10 .05
❑ 191 Eric Plunk .05 .02
❑ 192 Storm Davis .05 .02
❑ 193 Terry Steinbach .10 .05
❑ 194 Ron Hassey .05 .02
❑ 195 Stan Royer RC .05 .02
❑ 196 Walt Weiss .05 .02
❑ 197 Mark McGwire 1.00 .45
❑ 198 Carney Lansford .10 .05
❑ 199 Glenn Hubbard .05 .02
❑ 200 Dave Henderson .05 .02
❑ 201 Jose Canseco .25 .11
❑ 202 Dave Parker .10 .05
❑ 203 Scott Bankhead .05 .02
❑ 204 Tom Niedenfuer .05 .02
❑ 205 Mark Langston .05 .02
❑ 206 Erik Hanson RC .10 .05
❑ 207 Mike Jackson .05 .02
❑ 208 Dave Valle .05 .02
❑ 209 Scott Bradley .05 .02
❑ 210 Harold Reynolds .05 .02
❑ 211 Tino Martinez RC .50 .23
❑ 212 Rich Renteria .05 .02
❑ 213 Rey Quinones .05 .02
❑ 214 Jim Presley .05 .02
❑ 215 Alvin Davis .05 .02
❑ 216 Edgar Martinez .10 .05
❑ 217 Darnell Coles .05 .02
❑ 218 Jeffrey Leonard .05 .02
❑ 219 Jay Buhner .10 .05
❑ 220 Ken Griffey Jr. RC ! 20.00 9.00
❑ 221 Drew Hall .05 .02
❑ 222 Bobby Witt .05 .02
❑ 223 Jamie Moyer .05 .02
❑ 224 Charlie Hough .10 .05
❑ 225 Nolan Ryan 1.00 .45
❑ 226 Jeff Russell .05 .02
❑ 227 Jim Sundberg .05 .02
❑ 228 Julio Franco .05 .02
❑ 229 Buddy Bell .10 .05
❑ 230 Scott Fletcher .05 .02
❑ 231 Jeff Kunkel .05 .02
❑ 232 Steve Buechele .05 .02
❑ 233 Monty Fariss .05 .02
❑ 234 Rick Leach .05 .02
❑ 235 Ruben Sierra .05 .02
❑ 236 Cecil Espy .05 .02
❑ 237 Rafael Palmeiro .25 .11
❑ 238 Pete Incaviglia .05 .02
❑ 239 Dave Stieb .05 .02
❑ 240 Jeff Musselman .05 .02
❑ 241 Mike Flanagan .05 .02
❑ 242 Todd Stottlemyre .10 .05
❑ 243 Jimmy Key .10 .05
❑ 244 Tony Castillo .05 .02
❑ 245 Alex Sanchez .05 .02
❑ 246 Tom Henke .05 .02
❑ 247 John Cerutti .05 .02
❑ 248 Ernie Whitt .05 .02
❑ 249 Bob Brenly .05 .02
❑ 250 Rance Mulliniks .05 .02
❑ 251 Kelly Gruber .05 .02
❑ 252 Ed Sprague RC .25 .11
❑ 253 Fred McGriff .20 .09
❑ 254 Tony Fernandez .05 .02
❑ 255 Tom Lawless .05 .02
❑ 256 George Bell .05 .02
❑ 257 Jesse Barfield .05 .02
❑ 258 Roberto Alomar .20 .09
Sandy Alomar
❑ 259 Ken Griffey Jr. 2.00 .90
Ken Griffey Sr.
❑ 260 Cal Ripken Jr. .25 .11
Cal Ripken Sr.
❑ 261 Mel Stottlemyre Jr. .05 .02
Mel Stottlemyre Sr.
❑ 262 Zane Smith .05 .02
❑ 263 Charlie Puleo .05 .02
❑ 264 Derek Lilliquist RC .05 .02
❑ 265 Paul Assenmacher .05 .02
❑ 266 John Smoltz RC .40 .18
❑ 267 Tom Glavine .20 .09
❑ 268 Steve Avery RC .20 .09
❑ 269 Pete Smith .05 .02
❑ 270 Jody Davis .05 .02
❑ 271 Bruce Benedict .05 .02
❑ 272 Andres Thomas .05 .02
❑ 273 Gerald Perry .05 .02
❑ 274 Ron Gant .10 .05
❑ 275 Darrell Evans .10 .05
❑ 276 Dale Murphy .20 .09
❑ 277 Dion James .05 .02
❑ 278 Lonnie Smith .05 .02
❑ 279 Geronimo Berroa .05 .02
❑ 280 Steve Wilson .05 .02
❑ 281 Rick Sutcliffe .10 .05
❑ 282 Kevin Coffman .05 .02
❑ 283 Mitch Williams .05 .02
❑ 284 Greg Maddux .60 .25
❑ 285 Paul Kilgus .05 .02
❑ 286 Mike Harkey RC .05 .02

❑ 287 Lloyd McClendon .05 .02
❑ 288 Damon Berryhill .05 .02
❑ 289 Ty Griffin .05 .02
❑ 290 Ryne Sandberg .25 .11
❑ 291 Mark Grace .20 .09
❑ 292 Curt Wilkerson .05 .02
❑ 293 Vance Law .05 .02
❑ 294 Shawon Dunston .05 .02
❑ 295 Jerome Walton .20 .09
❑ 296 Mitch Webster .05 .02
❑ 297 Dwight Smith RC .10 .05
❑ 298 Andre Dawson .10 .05
❑ 299 Jeff Sellers .05 .02
❑ 300 Jose Rijo .05 .02
❑ 301 John Franco .10 .05
❑ 302 Rick Mahler .05 .02
❑ 303 Ron Robinson .05 .02
❑ 304 Danny Jackson .05 .02
❑ 305 Rob Dibble RC* .10 .05
❑ 306 Tom Browning .05 .02
❑ 307 Bo Diaz .05 .02
❑ 308 Manny Trillo .05 .02
❑ 309 Chris Sabo RC* .05 .02
❑ 310 Ron Oester .05 .02
❑ 311 Barry Larkin .20 .09
❑ 312 Todd Benzinger .05 .02
❑ 313 Paul O'Neill .10 .05
❑ 314 Kal Daniels .05 .02
❑ 315 Joel Youngblood .05 .02
❑ 316 Eric Davis .10 .05
❑ 317 Dave Smith .05 .02
❑ 318 Mark Portugal .05 .02
❑ 319 Brian Meyer .05 .02
❑ 320 Jim Deshaies .05 .02
❑ 321 Juan Agosto .05 .02
❑ 322 Mike Scott .05 .02
❑ 323 Rick Rhoden .05 .02
❑ 324 Jim Clancy .05 .02
❑ 325 Larry Andersen .05 .02
❑ 326 Alex Trevino .05 .02
❑ 327 Alan Ashby .05 .02
❑ 328 Craig Reynolds .05 .02
❑ 329 Bill Doran .05 .02
❑ 330 Rafael Ramirez .05 .02
❑ 331 Glenn Davis .05 .02
❑ 332 Willie Ansley RC .05 .02
❑ 333 Gerald Young .05 .02
❑ 334 Cameron Drew .05 .02
❑ 335 Jay Howell .05 .02
❑ 336 Tim Belcher .05 .02
❑ 337 Fernando Valenzuela .10 .05
❑ 338 Ricky Horton .05 .02
❑ 339 Tim Leary .05 .02
❑ 340 Bill Bene .05 .02
❑ 341 Orel Hershiser .10 .05
❑ 342 Mike Scioscia .05 .02
❑ 343 Rick Dempsey .05 .02
❑ 344 Willie Randolph .10 .05
❑ 345 Alfredo Griffin .05 .02
❑ 346 Eddie Murray .20 .09
❑ 347 Mickey Hatcher .05 .02
❑ 348 Mike Sharperson .05 .02
❑ 349 John Shelby .05 .02
❑ 350 Mike Marshall .05 .02
❑ 351 Kirk Gibson .10 .05
❑ 352 Mike Davis .05 .02
❑ 353 Bryn Smith .05 .02
❑ 354 Pascual Perez .05 .02
❑ 355 Kevin Gross .05 .02
❑ 356 Andy McGaffigan .05 .02
❑ 357 Brian Holman RC* .05 .02
❑ 358 Dave Wainhouse RC .05 .02
❑ 359 Dennis Martinez .10 .05
❑ 360 Tim Burke .05 .02
❑ 361 Nelson Santovenia .05 .02
❑ 362 Tim Wallach .05 .02
❑ 363 Spike Owen .05 .02
❑ 364 Rex Hudler .05 .02
❑ 365 Andres Galarraga .10 .05
❑ 366 Otis Nixon .05 .02
❑ 367 Hubie Brooks .05 .02
❑ 368 Mike Aldrete .05 .02
❑ 369 Tim Raines .10 .05
❑ 370 Dave Martinez .05 .02
❑ 371 Bob Ojeda .05 .02
❑ 372 Ron Darling .05 .02
❑ 373 Wally Whitehurst RC .05 .02
❑ 374 Randy Myers .10 .05
❑ 375 David Cone .10 .05
❑ 376 Dwight Gooden .10 .05
❑ 377 Sid Fernandez .05 .02
❑ 378 Dave Proctor .05 .02
❑ 379 Gary Carter .10 .05
❑ 380 Keith Miller .05 .02
❑ 381 Gregg Jefferies .10 .05
❑ 382 Tim Teufel .05 .02
❑ 383 Kevin Elster .05 .02
❑ 384 Dave Magadan .05 .02
❑ 385 Keith Hernandez .10 .05
❑ 386 Mookie Wilson .10 .05
❑ 387 Darryl Strawberry .10 .05
❑ 388 Kevin McReynolds .05 .02
❑ 389 Mark Carreon .05 .02
❑ 390 Jeff Parrett .05 .02
❑ 391 Mike Maddux .05 .02
❑ 392 Don Carman .05 .02
❑ 393 Bruce Ruffin .05 .02
❑ 394 Ken Howell .05 .02
❑ 395 Steve Bedrosian .05 .02
❑ 396 Floyd Youmans .05 .02
❑ 397 Larry McWilliams .05 .02
❑ 398 Pat Combs RC* .05 .02
❑ 399 Steve Lake .05 .02
❑ 400 Dickie Thon .05 .02
❑ 401 Ricky Jordan RC* .05 .02
❑ 402 Mike Schmidt .40 .18
❑ 403 Tom Herr .05 .02
❑ 404 Chris James .05 .02
❑ 405 Juan Samuel .05 .02
❑ 406 Von Hayes .05 .02
❑ 407 Ron Jones .05 .02
❑ 408 Curt Ford .05 .02
❑ 409 Bob Walk .05 .02
❑ 410 Jeff D. Robinson .05 .02
❑ 411 Jim Gott .05 .02
❑ 412 Scott Medvin .05 .02
❑ 413 John Smiley .05 .02
❑ 414 Bob Kipper .05 .02
❑ 415 Brian Fisher .05 .02
❑ 416 Doug Drabek .05 .02
❑ 417 Mike LaValliere .05 .02
❑ 418 Ken Oberkfell .05 .02
❑ 419 Sid Bream .05 .02
❑ 420 Austin Manahan .05 .02
❑ 421 Jose Lind .05 .02
❑ 422 Bobby Bonilla .10 .05
❑ 423 Glenn Wilson .05 .02
❑ 424 Andy Van Slyke .10 .05
❑ 425 Gary Redus .05 .02
❑ 426 Barry Bonds .50 .23
❑ 427 Don Heinkel .05 .02
❑ 428 Ken Dayley .05 .02
❑ 429 Todd Worrell .05 .02
❑ 430 Brad DuVall .05 .02
❑ 431 Jose DeLeon .05 .02
❑ 432 Joe Magrane .05 .02
❑ 433 John Ericks .05 .02
❑ 434 Frank DiPino .05 .02
❑ 435 Tony Pena .05 .02
❑ 436 Ozzie Smith .25 .11
❑ 437 Terry Pendleton .10 .05
❑ 438 Jose Oquendo .05 .02
❑ 439 Tim Jones .05 .02
❑ 440 Pedro Guerrero .05 .02
❑ 441 Milt Thompson .05 .02
❑ 442 Willie McGee .10 .05
❑ 443 Vince Coleman .05 .02
❑ 444 Tom Brunansky .05 .02
❑ 445 Walt Terrell .05 .02
❑ 446 Eric Show .05 .02
❑ 447 Mark Davis .05 .02
❑ 448 Andy Benes RC* .10 .05
❑ 449 Ed Whitson .05 .02
❑ 450 Dennis Rasmussen .05 .02
❑ 451 Bruce Hurst .05 .02
❑ 452 Pat Clements .05 .02
❑ 453 Benito Santiago .05 .02
❑ 454 Sandy Alomar Jr. RC .25 .11
❑ 455 Garry Templeton .05 .02
❑ 456 Jack Clark .05 .02
❑ 457 Tim Flannery .05 .02
❑ 458 Roberto Alomar .30 .14
❑ 459 Carmelo Martinez .05 .02
❑ 460 John Kruk .10 .05
❑ 461 Tony Gwynn .40 .18
❑ 462 Jerald Clark RC .05 .02
❑ 463 Don Robinson .05 .02
❑ 464 Craig Lefferts .05 .02
❑ 465 Kelly Downs .05 .02
❑ 466 Rick Reuschel .05 .02
❑ 467 Scott Garrelts .05 .02
❑ 468 Wil Tejada .05 .02
❑ 469 Kirt Manwaring .05 .02
❑ 470 Terry Kennedy .05 .02
❑ 471 Jose Uribe .05 .02
❑ 472 Royce Clayton RC .25 .11
❑ 473 Robby Thompson .05 .02
❑ 474 Kevin Mitchell .10 .05
❑ 475 Ernie Riles .05 .02
❑ 476 Will Clark .20 .09
❑ 477 Donell Nixon .05 .02
❑ 478 Candy Maldonado .05 .02
❑ 479 Tracy Jones .05 .02
❑ 480 Brett Butler .10 .05
❑ 481 Checklist 1-121 .05 .02
❑ 482 Checklist 122-242 .05 .02
❑ 483 Checklist 243-363 .05 .02
❑ 484 Checklist 364-484 .05 .02

## 1990 Bowman

| | MINT | NRMT |
|---|---|---|
| COMPLETE SET (528) | 30.00 | 13.50 |
| COMP.FACT.SET (528) | 40.00 | 18.00 |

❑ 1 Tommy Greene RC .05 .02
❑ 2 Tom Glavine .20 .09
❑ 3 Andy Nezelek .05 .02
❑ 4 Mike Stanton RC .05 .02
❑ 5 Rick Luecken .05 .02
❑ 6 Kent Mercker RC .05 .02
❑ 7 Derek Lilliquist .05 .02
❑ 8 Charlie Leibrandt .05 .02
❑ 9 Steve Avery .05 .02
❑ 10 John Smoltz .10 .05
❑ 11 Mark Lemke .05 .02
❑ 12 Lonnie Smith .05 .02
❑ 13 Oddibe McDowell .05 .02
❑ 14 Tyler Houston RC .10 .05
❑ 15 Jeff Blauser .05 .02
❑ 16 Ernie Whitt .05 .02
❑ 17 Alexis Infante .05 .02
❑ 18 Jim Presley .05 .02
❑ 19 Dale Murphy .20 .09
❑ 20 Nick Esasky .05 .02
❑ 21 Rick Sutcliffe .10 .05
❑ 22 Mike Bielecki .05 .02
❑ 23 Steve Wilson .05 .02
❑ 24 Kevin Blankenship .05 .02
❑ 25 Mitch Williams .05 .02
❑ 26 Dean Wilkins .05 .02
❑ 27 Greg Maddux .50 .23
❑ 28 Mike Harkey .05 .02
❑ 29 Mark Grace .20 .09
❑ 30 Ryne Sandberg .25 .11
❑ 31 Greg Smith .05 .02
❑ 32 Dwight Smith .05 .02
❑ 33 Damon Berryhill .05 .02
❑ 34 Earl Cunningham RC UER .05 .02
(Errant * by the word "in")

| | | | |
|---|---|---|---|
| ❑ 35 | Jerome Walton | .05 | .02 |
| ❑ 36 | Lloyd McClendon | .05 | .02 |
| ❑ 37 | Ty Griffin | .05 | .02 |
| ❑ 38 | Shawon Dunston | .05 | .02 |
| ❑ 39 | Andre Dawson | .10 | .05 |
| ❑ 40 | Luis Salazar | .05 | .02 |
| ❑ 41 | Tim Layana | .05 | .02 |
| ❑ 42 | Rob Dibble | .05 | .02 |
| ❑ 43 | Tom Browning | .05 | .02 |
| ❑ 44 | Danny Jackson | .05 | .02 |
| ❑ 45 | Jose Rijo | .05 | .02 |
| ❑ 46 | Scott Scudder | .05 | .02 |
| ❑ 47 | Randy Myers UER (Career ERA .274, should be 2.74) | .10 | .05 |
| ❑ 48 | Brian Lane RC | .05 | .02 |
| ❑ 49 | Paul O'Neill | .10 | .05 |
| ❑ 50 | Barry Larkin | .20 | .09 |
| ❑ 51 | Reggie Jefferson RC | .20 | .09 |
| ❑ 52 | Jeff Branson RC** | .05 | .02 |
| ❑ 53 | Chris Sabo | .05 | .02 |
| ❑ 54 | Joe Oliver | .05 | .02 |
| ❑ 55 | Todd Benzinger | .05 | .02 |
| ❑ 56 | Rolando Roomes | .05 | .02 |
| ❑ 57 | Hal Morris | .05 | .02 |
| ❑ 58 | Eric Davis | .10 | .05 |
| ❑ 59 | Scott Bryant | .05 | .02 |
| ❑ 60 | Ken Griffey Sr. | .10 | .05 |
| ❑ 61 | Darryl Kile RC | .75 | .35 |
| ❑ 62 | Dave Smith | .05 | .02 |
| ❑ 63 | Mark Portugal | .05 | .02 |
| ❑ 64 | Jeff Juden RC | .05 | .02 |
| ❑ 65 | Bill Gullickson | .05 | .02 |
| ❑ 66 | Danny Darwin | .05 | .02 |
| ❑ 67 | Larry Andersen | .05 | .02 |
| ❑ 68 | Jose Cano | .05 | .02 |
| ❑ 69 | Dan Schatzeder | .05 | .02 |
| ❑ 70 | Jim Deshaies | .05 | .02 |
| ❑ 71 | Mike Scott | .05 | .02 |
| ❑ 72 | Gerald Young | .05 | .02 |
| ❑ 73 | Ken Caminiti | .10 | .05 |
| ❑ 74 | Ken Oberkfell | .05 | .02 |
| ❑ 75 | Dave Rohde | .05 | .02 |
| ❑ 76 | Bill Doran | .05 | .02 |
| ❑ 77 | Andujar Cedeno RC | .05 | .02 |
| ❑ 78 | Craig Biggio | .10 | .05 |
| ❑ 79 | Karl Rhodes RC | .05 | .02 |
| ❑ 80 | Glenn Davis | .05 | .02 |
| ❑ 81 | Eric Anthony RC | .05 | .02 |
| ❑ 82 | John Wetteland | .20 | .09 |
| ❑ 83 | Jay Howell | .05 | .02 |
| ❑ 84 | Orel Hershiser | .10 | .05 |
| ❑ 85 | Tim Belcher | .05 | .02 |
| ❑ 86 | Kiki Jones | .05 | .02 |
| ❑ 87 | Mike Hartley | .05 | .02 |
| ❑ 88 | Ramon Martinez | .05 | .02 |
| ❑ 89 | Mike Scioscia | .05 | .02 |
| ❑ 90 | Willie Randolph | .10 | .05 |
| ❑ 91 | Juan Samuel | .05 | .02 |
| ❑ 92 | Jose Offerman RC | .40 | .18 |
| ❑ 93 | Dave Hansen RC | .05 | .02 |
| ❑ 94 | Jeff Hamilton | .05 | .02 |
| ❑ 95 | Alfredo Griffin | .05 | .02 |
| ❑ 96 | Tom Goodwin RC | .20 | .09 |
| ❑ 97 | Kirk Gibson | .10 | .05 |
| ❑ 98 | Jose Vizcaino RC | .10 | .05 |
| ❑ 99 | Kal Daniels | .05 | .02 |
| ❑ 100 | Hubie Brooks | .05 | .02 |
| ❑ 101 | Eddie Murray | .20 | .09 |
| ❑ 102 | Dennis Boyd | .05 | .02 |
| ❑ 103 | Tim Burke | .05 | .02 |
| ❑ 104 | Bill Sampen | .05 | .02 |
| ❑ 105 | Brett Gideon | .05 | .02 |
| ❑ 106 | Mark Gardner RC | .05 | .02 |
| ❑ 107 | Howard Farmer | .05 | .02 |
| ❑ 108 | Mel Rojas RC | .10 | .05 |
| ❑ 109 | Kevin Gross | .05 | .02 |
| ❑ 110 | Dave Schmidt | .05 | .02 |
| ❑ 111 | Dennis Martinez | .10 | .05 |
| ❑ 112 | Jerry Goff | .05 | .02 |
| ❑ 113 | Andres Galarraga | .10 | .05 |
| ❑ 114 | Tim Wallach | .05 | .02 |
| ❑ 115 | Marquis Grissom RC | .25 | .11 |
| ❑ 116 | Spike Owen | .05 | .02 |
| ❑ 117 | Larry Walker RC | 1.00 | .45 |
| ❑ 118 | Tim Raines | .10 | .05 |
| ❑ 119 | Delino DeShields RC | .20 | .09 |
| ❑ 120 | Tom Foley | .05 | .02 |
| ❑ 121 | Dave Martinez | .05 | .02 |
| ❑ 122 | Frank Viola UER (Career ERA .384 should be 3.84) | .05 | .02 |
| ❑ 123 | Julio Valera RC | .05 | .02 |
| ❑ 124 | Alejandro Pena | .05 | .02 |
| ❑ 125 | David Cone | .10 | .05 |
| ❑ 126 | Dwight Gooden | .10 | .05 |
| ❑ 127 | Kevin D. Brown | .05 | .02 |
| ❑ 128 | John Franco | .10 | .05 |
| ❑ 129 | Terry Bross | .05 | .02 |
| ❑ 130 | Blaine Beatty | .05 | .02 |
| ❑ 131 | Sid Fernandez | .05 | .02 |
| ❑ 132 | Mike Marshall | .05 | .02 |
| ❑ 133 | Howard Johnson | .05 | .02 |
| ❑ 134 | Jaime Roseboro | .05 | .02 |
| ❑ 135 | Alan Zinter RC | .05 | .02 |
| ❑ 136 | Keith Miller | .05 | .02 |
| ❑ 137 | Kevin Elster | .05 | .02 |
| ❑ 138 | Kevin McReynolds | .05 | .02 |
| ❑ 139 | Barry Lyons | .05 | .02 |
| ❑ 140 | Gregg Jefferies | .10 | .05 |
| ❑ 141 | Darryl Strawberry | .10 | .05 |
| ❑ 142 | Todd Hundley RC | .40 | .18 |
| ❑ 143 | Scott Service | .05 | .02 |
| ❑ 144 | Chuck Malone | .05 | .02 |
| ❑ 145 | Steve Ontiveros | .05 | .02 |
| ❑ 146 | Roger McDowell | .05 | .02 |
| ❑ 147 | Ken Howell | .05 | .02 |
| ❑ 148 | Pat Combs | .05 | .02 |
| ❑ 149 | Jeff Parrett | .05 | .02 |
| ❑ 150 | Chuck McElroy RC | .05 | .02 |
| ❑ 151 | Jason Grimsley RC | .05 | .02 |
| ❑ 152 | Len Dykstra | .10 | .05 |
| ❑ 153 | Mickey Morandini RC** | .20 | .09 |
| ❑ 154 | John Kruk | .10 | .05 |
| ❑ 155 | Dickie Thon | .05 | .02 |
| ❑ 156 | Ricky Jordan | .05 | .02 |
| ❑ 157 | Jeff Jackson RC | .05 | .02 |
| ❑ 158 | Darren Daulton | .10 | .05 |
| ❑ 159 | Tom Herr | .05 | .02 |
| ❑ 160 | Von Hayes | .05 | .02 |
| ❑ 161 | Dave Hollins RC | .20 | .09 |
| ❑ 162 | Carmelo Martinez | .05 | .02 |
| ❑ 163 | Bob Walk | .05 | .02 |
| ❑ 164 | Doug Drabek | .05 | .02 |
| ❑ 165 | Walt Terrell | .05 | .02 |
| ❑ 166 | Bill Landrum | .05 | .02 |
| ❑ 167 | Scott Ruskin | .05 | .02 |
| ❑ 168 | Bob Patterson | .05 | .02 |
| ❑ 169 | Bobby Bonilla | .10 | .05 |
| ❑ 170 | Jose Lind | .05 | .02 |
| ❑ 171 | Andy Van Slyke | .10 | .05 |
| ❑ 172 | Mike LaValliere | .05 | .02 |
| ❑ 173 | Willie Greene RC | .10 | .05 |
| ❑ 174 | Jay Bell | .10 | .05 |
| ❑ 175 | Sid Bream | .05 | .02 |
| ❑ 176 | Tom Prince | .05 | .02 |
| ❑ 177 | Wally Backman | .05 | .02 |
| ❑ 178 | Moises Alou RC | .60 | .25 |
| ❑ 179 | Steve Carter | .05 | .02 |
| ❑ 180 | Gary Redus | .05 | .02 |
| ❑ 181 | Barry Bonds | .30 | .14 |
| ❑ 182 | Don Slaught UER (Card back shows headings for a pitcher) | .05 | .02 |
| ❑ 183 | Joe Magrane | .05 | .02 |
| ❑ 184 | Bryn Smith | .05 | .02 |
| ❑ 185 | Todd Worrell | .05 | .02 |
| ❑ 186 | Jose DeLeon | .05 | .02 |
| ❑ 187 | Frank DiPino | .05 | .02 |
| ❑ 188 | John Tudor | .05 | .02 |
| ❑ 189 | Howard Hilton | .05 | .02 |
| ❑ 190 | John Ericks | .05 | .02 |
| ❑ 191 | Ken Dayley | .05 | .02 |
| ❑ 192 | Ray Lankford RC | .50 | .23 |
| ❑ 193 | Todd Zeile | .10 | .05 |
| ❑ 194 | Willie McGee | .10 | .05 |
| ❑ 195 | Ozzie Smith | .25 | .11 |
| ❑ 196 | Milt Thompson | .05 | .02 |
| ❑ 197 | Terry Pendleton | .10 | .05 |
| ❑ 198 | Vince Coleman | .05 | .02 |
| ❑ 199 | Paul Coleman RC | .05 | .02 |
| ❑ 200 | Jose Oquendo | .05 | .02 |
| ❑ 201 | Pedro Guerrero | .05 | .02 |
| ❑ 202 | Tom Brunansky | .05 | .02 |
| ❑ 203 | Roger Smithberg | .05 | .02 |
| ❑ 204 | Eddie Whitson | .05 | .02 |
| ❑ 205 | Dennis Rasmussen | .05 | .02 |
| ❑ 206 | Craig Lefferts | .05 | .02 |
| ❑ 207 | Andy Benes | .05 | .02 |
| ❑ 208 | Bruce Hurst | .05 | .02 |
| ❑ 209 | Eric Show | .05 | .02 |
| ❑ 210 | Rafael Valdez | .05 | .02 |
| ❑ 211 | Joey Cora | .10 | .05 |
| ❑ 212 | Thomas Howard | .05 | .02 |
| ❑ 213 | Rob Nelson | .05 | .02 |
| ❑ 214 | Jack Clark | .10 | .05 |
| ❑ 215 | Garry Templeton | .05 | .02 |
| ❑ 216 | Fred Lynn | .05 | .02 |
| ❑ 217 | Tony Gwynn | .40 | .18 |
| ❑ 218 | Benito Santiago | .05 | .02 |
| ❑ 219 | Mike Pagliarulo | .05 | .02 |
| ❑ 220 | Joe Carter | .10 | .05 |
| ❑ 221 | Roberto Alomar | .20 | .09 |
| ❑ 222 | Bip Roberts | .05 | .02 |
| ❑ 223 | Rick Reuschel | .05 | .02 |
| ❑ 224 | Russ Swan | .05 | .02 |
| ❑ 225 | Eric Gunderson | .05 | .02 |
| ❑ 226 | Steve Bedrosian | .05 | .02 |
| ❑ 227 | Mike Remlinger | .05 | .02 |
| ❑ 228 | Scott Garrelts | .05 | .02 |
| ❑ 229 | Ernie Camacho | .05 | .02 |
| ❑ 230 | Andres Santana RC | .05 | .02 |
| ❑ 231 | Will Clark | .20 | .09 |
| ❑ 232 | Kevin Mitchell | .05 | .02 |
| ❑ 233 | Robby Thompson | .05 | .02 |
| ❑ 234 | Bill Bathe | .05 | .02 |
| ❑ 235 | Tony Perezchica | .05 | .02 |
| ❑ 236 | Gary Carter | .10 | .05 |
| ❑ 237 | Brett Butler | .10 | .05 |
| ❑ 238 | Matt Williams | .10 | .05 |
| ❑ 239 | Earnie Riles | .05 | .02 |
| ❑ 240 | Kevin Bass | .05 | .02 |
| ❑ 241 | Terry Kennedy | .05 | .02 |
| ❑ 242 | Steve Hosey RC | .05 | .02 |
| ❑ 243 | Ben McDonald RC | .10 | .05 |
| ❑ 244 | Jeff Ballard | .05 | .02 |
| ❑ 245 | Joe Price | .05 | .02 |
| ❑ 246 | Curt Schilling | .10 | .05 |
| ❑ 247 | Pete Harnisch | .05 | .02 |
| ❑ 248 | Mark Williamson | .05 | .02 |
| ❑ 249 | Gregg Olson | .10 | .05 |
| ❑ 250 | Chris Myers | .05 | .02 |
| ❑ 251 | David Segui RC ERR (Missing vital stats at top of card back under name) | .40 | .18 |
| ❑ 251B | David Segui COR RC | .20 | .09 |
| ❑ 252 | Joe Orsulak | .05 | .02 |
| ❑ 253 | Craig Worthington | .05 | .02 |
| ❑ 254 | Mickey Tettleton | .05 | .02 |
| ❑ 255 | Cal Ripken | .75 | .35 |
| ❑ 256 | Bill Ripken | .05 | .02 |
| ❑ 257 | Randy Milligan | .05 | .02 |
| ❑ 258 | Brady Anderson | .20 | .09 |
| ❑ 259 | Chris Hoiles RC UER (Baltimore is spelled Balitmore) | .20 | .09 |
| ❑ 260 | Mike Devereaux | .05 | .02 |
| ❑ 261 | Phil Bradley | .05 | .02 |
| ❑ 262 | Leo Gomez RC | .05 | .02 |
| ❑ 263 | Lee Smith | .10 | .05 |
| ❑ 264 | Mike Rochford | .05 | .02 |
| ❑ 265 | Jeff Reardon | .10 | .05 |
| ❑ 266 | Wes Gardner | .05 | .02 |
| ❑ 267 | Mike Boddicker | .05 | .02 |
| ❑ 268 | Roger Clemens | .40 | .18 |
| ❑ 269 | Rob Murphy | .05 | .02 |
| ❑ 270 | Mickey Pina | .05 | .02 |
| ❑ 271 | Tony Pena | .05 | .02 |
| ❑ 272 | Jody Reed | .05 | .02 |
| ❑ 273 | Kevin Romine | .05 | .02 |
| ❑ 274 | Mike Greenwell | .05 | .02 |
| ❑ 275 | Maurice Vaughn RC | 1.00 | .45 |
| ❑ 276 | Danny Heep | .05 | .02 |
| ❑ 277 | Scott Cooper RC | .05 | .02 |
| ❑ 278 | Greg Blosser RC | .05 | .02 |
| ❑ 279 | Dwight Evans UER (* by "1990 Team | .10 | .05 |

Breakdown")
- ❑ 280 Ellis Burks .10 .05
- ❑ 281 Wade Boggs .25 .11
- ❑ 282 Marty Barrett .05 .02
- ❑ 283 Kirk McCaskill .05 .02
- ❑ 284 Mark Langston .05 .02
- ❑ 285 Bert Blyleven .10 .05
- ❑ 286 Mike Fetters RC .05 .02
- ❑ 287 Kyle Abbott .05 .02
- ❑ 288 Jim Abbott .10 .05
- ❑ 289 Chuck Finley .10 .05
- ❑ 290 Gary DiSarcina RC .10 .05
- ❑ 291 Dick Schofield .05 .02
- ❑ 292 Devon White .05 .02
- ❑ 293 Bobby Rose .05 .02
- ❑ 294 Brian Downing .05 .02
- ❑ 295 Lance Parrish .05 .02
- ❑ 296 Jack Howell .05 .02
- ❑ 297 Claudell Washington .05 .02
- ❑ 298 John Orton RC .05 .02
- ❑ 299 Wally Joyner .10 .05
- ❑ 300 Lee Stevens .10 .05
- ❑ 301 Chili Davis .10 .05
- ❑ 302 Johnny Ray .05 .02
- ❑ 303 Greg Hibbard RC .05 .02
- ❑ 304 Eric King .05 .02
- ❑ 305 Jack McDowell .05 .02
- ❑ 306 Bobby Thigpen .05 .02
- ❑ 307 Adam Peterson .05 .02
- ❑ 308 Scott Radinsky RC .05 .02
- ❑ 309 Wayne Edwards .05 .02
- ❑ 310 Melido Perez .05 .02
- ❑ 311 Robin Ventura .20 .09
- ❑ 312 Sammy Sosa RC 6.00 2.70
- ❑ 313 Dan Pasqua .05 .02
- ❑ 314 Carlton Fisk .20 .09
- ❑ 315 Ozzie Guillen .05 .02
- ❑ 316 Ivan Calderon .05 .02
- ❑ 317 Daryl Boston .05 .02
- ❑ 318 Craig Grebeck RC .05 .02
- ❑ 319 Scott Fletcher .05 .02
- ❑ 320 Frank Thomas RC 4.00 1.80
- ❑ 321 Steve Lyons .05 .02
- ❑ 322 Carlos Martinez .05 .02
- ❑ 323 Joe Skalski .05 .02
- ❑ 324 Tom Candiotti .05 .02
- ❑ 325 Greg Swindell .05 .02
- ❑ 326 Steve Olin RC .10 .05
- ❑ 327 Kevin Wickander .05 .02
- ❑ 328 Doug Jones .05 .02
- ❑ 329 Jeff Shaw .05 .02
- ❑ 330 Kevin Bearse .05 .02
- ❑ 331 Dion James .05 .02
- ❑ 332 Jerry Browne .05 .02
- ❑ 333 Joey Belle 1.00 .45
- ❑ 334 Felix Fermin .05 .02
- ❑ 335 Candy Maldonado .05 .02
- ❑ 336 Cory Snyder .05 .02
- ❑ 337 Sandy Alomar Jr. .10 .05
- ❑ 338 Mark Lewis .05 .02
- ❑ 339 Carlos Baerga RC .10 .05
- ❑ 340 Chris James .05 .02
- ❑ 341 Brook Jacoby .05 .02
- ❑ 342 Keith Hernandez .10 .05
- ❑ 343 Frank Tanana .05 .02
- ❑ 344 Scott Aldred .05 .02
- ❑ 345 Mike Henneman .05 .02
- ❑ 346 Steve Wapnick .05 .02
- ❑ 347 Greg Gohr RC .05 .02
- ❑ 348 Eric Stone .05 .02
- ❑ 349 Brian DuBois .05 .02
- ❑ 350 Kevin Ritz .05 .02
- ❑ 351 Rico Brogna .20 .09
- ❑ 352 Mike Heath .05 .02
- ❑ 353 Alan Trammell .10 .05
- ❑ 354 Chet Lemon .05 .02
- ❑ 355 Dave Bergman .05 .02
- ❑ 356 Lou Whitaker .10 .05
- ❑ 357 Cecil Fielder UER .10 .05
  (* by 1990 Team Breakdown)
- ❑ 358 Milt Cuyler RC .05 .02
- ❑ 359 Tony Phillips .05 .02
- ❑ 360 Travis Fryman RC .40 .18
- ❑ 361 Ed Romero .05 .02
- ❑ 362 Lloyd Moseby .05 .02
- ❑ 363 Mark Gubicza .05 .02
- ❑ 364 Bret Saberhagen .10 .05
- ❑ 365 Tom Gordon .10 .05
- ❑ 366 Steve Farr .05 .02
- ❑ 367 Kevin Appier .10 .05
- ❑ 368 Storm Davis .05 .02
- ❑ 369 Mark Davis .05 .02
- ❑ 370 Jeff Montgomery .10 .05
- ❑ 371 Frank White .10 .05
- ❑ 372 Brent Mayne RC .05 .02
- ❑ 373 Bob Boone .10 .05
- ❑ 374 Jim Eisenreich .05 .02
- ❑ 375 Danny Tartabull .05 .02
- ❑ 376 Kurt Stillwell .05 .02
- ❑ 377 Bill Pecota .05 .02
- ❑ 378 Bo Jackson .10 .05
- ❑ 379 Bob Hamelin RC .20 .09
- ❑ 380 Kevin Seitzer .05 .02
- ❑ 381 Rey Palacios .05 .02
- ❑ 382 George Brett .40 .18
- ❑ 383 Gerald Perry .05 .02
- ❑ 384 Teddy Higuera .05 .02
- ❑ 385 Tom Filer .05 .02
- ❑ 386 Dan Plesac .05 .02
- ❑ 387 Cal Eldred RC .25 .11
- ❑ 388 Jaime Navarro .05 .02
- ❑ 389 Chris Bosio .05 .02
- ❑ 390 Randy Veres .05 .02
- ❑ 391 Gary Sheffield .25 .11
- ❑ 392 George Canale .05 .02
- ❑ 393 B.J. Surhoff .10 .05
- ❑ 394 Tim McIntosh .05 .02
- ❑ 395 Greg Brock .05 .02
- ❑ 396 Greg Vaughn .25 .11
- ❑ 397 Darryl Hamilton .05 .02
- ❑ 398 Dave Parker .10 .05
- ❑ 399 Paul Molitor .20 .09
- ❑ 400 Jim Gantner .05 .02
- ❑ 401 Rob Deer .05 .02
- ❑ 402 Billy Spiers .05 .02
- ❑ 403 Glenn Braggs .05 .02
- ❑ 404 Robin Yount .20 .09
- ❑ 405 Rick Aguilera .10 .05
- ❑ 406 Johnny Ard .05 .02
- ❑ 407 Kevin Tapani RC .10 .05
- ❑ 408 Park Pittman .05 .02
- ❑ 409 Allan Anderson .05 .02
- ❑ 410 Juan Berenguer .05 .02
- ❑ 411 Willie Banks RC .05 .02
- ❑ 412 Rich Yett .05 .02
- ❑ 413 Dave West .05 .02
- ❑ 414 Greg Gagne .05 .02
- ❑ 415 Chuck Knoblauch RC .50 .23
- ❑ 416 Randy Bush .05 .02
- ❑ 417 Gary Gaetti .10 .05
- ❑ 418 Kent Hrbek .10 .05
- ❑ 419 Al Newman .05 .02
- ❑ 420 Danny Gladden .05 .02
- ❑ 421 Paul Sorrento RC .10 .05
- ❑ 422 Derek Parks RC .05 .02
- ❑ 423 Scott Leius RC .05 .02
- ❑ 424 Kirby Puckett .50 .23
- ❑ 425 Willie Smith .05 .02
- ❑ 426 Dave Righetti .05 .02
- ❑ 427 Jeff D. Robinson .05 .02
- ❑ 428 Alan Mills RC .05 .02
- ❑ 429 Tim Leary .05 .02
- ❑ 430 Pascual Perez .05 .02
- ❑ 431 Alvaro Espinoza .05 .02
- ❑ 432 Dave Winfield .20 .09
- ❑ 433 Jesse Barfield .05 .02
- ❑ 434 Randy Velarde .05 .02
- ❑ 435 Rick Cerone .05 .02
- ❑ 436 Steve Balboni .05 .02
- ❑ 437 Mel Hall .05 .02
- ❑ 438 Bob Geren .05 .02
- ❑ 439 Bernie Williams RC 2.00 .90
- ❑ 440 Kevin Maas RC .10 .05
- ❑ 441 Mike Blowers RC .10 .05
- ❑ 442 Steve Sax .05 .02
- ❑ 443 Don Mattingly .50 .23
- ❑ 444 Roberto Kelly .05 .02
- ❑ 445 Mike Moore .05 .02
- ❑ 446 Reggie Harris RC .05 .02
- ❑ 447 Scott Sanderson .05 .02
- ❑ 448 Dave Otto .05 .02
- ❑ 449 Dave Stewart .10 .05
- ❑ 450 Rick Honeycutt .05 .02
- ❑ 451 Dennis Eckersley .10 .05
- ❑ 452 Carney Lansford .10 .05
- ❑ 453 Scott Hemond RC .05 .02
- ❑ 454 Mark McGwire .75 .35
- ❑ 455 Felix Jose .05 .02
- ❑ 456 Terry Steinbach .05 .02
- ❑ 457 Rickey Henderson .25 .11
- ❑ 458 Dave Henderson .05 .02
- ❑ 459 Mike Gallego .05 .02
- ❑ 460 Jose Canseco .25 .11
- ❑ 461 Walt Weiss .05 .02
- ❑ 462 Ken Phelps .05 .02
- ❑ 463 Darren Lewis RC .05 .02
- ❑ 464 Ron Hassey .05 .02
- ❑ 465 Roger Salkeld RC .05 .02
- ❑ 466 Scott Bankhead .05 .02
- ❑ 467 Keith Comstock .05 .02
- ❑ 468 Randy Johnson .40 .18
- ❑ 469 Erik Hanson .05 .02
- ❑ 470 Mike Schooler .05 .02
- ❑ 471 Gary Eave .05 .02
- ❑ 472 Jeffrey Leonard .05 .02
- ❑ 473 Dave Valle .05 .02
- ❑ 474 Omar Vizquel .20 .09
- ❑ 475 Pete O'Brien .05 .02
- ❑ 476 Henry Cotto .05 .02
- ❑ 477 Jay Buhner .10 .05
- ❑ 478 Harold Reynolds .05 .02
- ❑ 479 Alvin Davis .05 .02
- ❑ 480 Darnell Coles .05 .02
- ❑ 481 Ken Griffey Jr. 1.50 .70
- ❑ 482 Greg Briley .05 .02
- ❑ 483 Scott Bradley .05 .02
- ❑ 484 Tino Martinez .20 .09
- ❑ 485 Jeff Russell .05 .02
- ❑ 486 Nolan Ryan 1.00 .45
- ❑ 487 Robb Nen RC .25 .11
- ❑ 488 Kevin Brown .20 .09
- ❑ 489 Brian Bohanon RC .05 .02
- ❑ 490 Ruben Sierra .05 .02
- ❑ 491 Pete Incaviglia .05 .02
- ❑ 492 Juan Gonzalez RC 1.50 .70
- ❑ 493 Steve Buechele .05 .02
- ❑ 494 Scott Coolbaugh .05 .02
- ❑ 495 Geno Petralli .05 .02
- ❑ 496 Rafael Palmeiro .20 .09
- ❑ 497 Julio Franco .05 .02
- ❑ 498 Gary Pettis .05 .02
- ❑ 499 Donald Harris .05 .02
- ❑ 500 Monty Fariss .05 .02
- ❑ 501 Harold Baines .10 .05
- ❑ 502 Cecil Espy .05 .02
- ❑ 503 Jack Daugherty .05 .02
- ❑ 504 Willie Blair RC .05 .02
- ❑ 505 Dave Stieb .10 .05
- ❑ 506 Tom Henke .05 .02
- ❑ 507 John Cerutti .05 .02
- ❑ 508 Paul Kilgus .05 .02
- ❑ 509 Jimmy Key .10 .05
- ❑ 510 John Olerud RC .75 .35
- ❑ 511 Ed Sprague .10 .05
- ❑ 512 Manuel Lee .05 .02
- ❑ 513 Fred McGriff .20 .09
- ❑ 514 Glenallen Hill .05 .02
- ❑ 515 George Bell .05 .02
- ❑ 516 Mookie Wilson .10 .05
- ❑ 517 Luis Sojo RC .05 .02
- ❑ 518 Nelson Liriano .05 .02
- ❑ 519 Kelly Gruber .05 .02
- ❑ 520 Greg Myers .05 .02
- ❑ 521 Pat Borders .05 .02
- ❑ 522 Junior Felix .05 .02
- ❑ 523 Eddie Zosky RC .05 .02
- ❑ 524 Tony Fernandez .05 .02
- ❑ 525 Checklist 1-132 UER .05 .02
  (No copyright mark on the back)
- ❑ 526 Checklist 133-264 .05 .02
- ❑ 527 Checklist 265-396 .05 .02
- ❑ 528 Checklist 397-528 .05 .02

## 1991 Bowman

| | MINT | NRMT |
|---|---|---|
| COMPLETE SET (704) | 40.00 | 18.00 |
| COMP.FACT.SET (704) | 50.00 | 22.00 |

| |  |  | | |
|---|---|---|---|---|
| ❑ | 1 | Rod Carew I | .20 | .09 |
| ❑ | 2 | Rod Carew II | .20 | .09 |
| ❑ | 3 | Rod Carew III | .20 | .09 |
| ❑ | 4 | Rod Carew IV | .20 | .09 |
| ❑ | 5 | Rod Carew V | .20 | .09 |
| ❑ | 6 | Willie Fraser | .05 | .02 |
| ❑ | 7 | John Olerud | .10 | .05 |
| ❑ | 8 | William Suero | .05 | .02 |
| ❑ | 9 | Roberto Alomar | .20 | .09 |
| ❑ | 10 | Todd Stottlemyre | .10 | .05 |
| ❑ | 11 | Joe Carter | .10 | .05 |
| ❑ | 12 | Steve Karsay RC | .25 | .11 |
| ❑ | 13 | Mark Whiten | .05 | .02 |
| ❑ | 14 | Pat Borders | .05 | .02 |
| ❑ | 15 | Mike Timlin RC | .05 | .02 |
| ❑ | 16 | Tom Henke | .05 | .02 |
| ❑ | 17 | Eddie Zosky | .05 | .02 |
| ❑ | 18 | Kelly Gruber | .05 | .02 |
| ❑ | 19 | Jimmy Key | .10 | .05 |
| ❑ | 20 | Jerry Schunk | .05 | .02 |
| ❑ | 21 | Manuel Lee | .05 | .02 |
| ❑ | 22 | Dave Stieb | .05 | .02 |
| ❑ | 23 | Pat Hentgen RC | .50 | .23 |
| ❑ | 24 | Glenallen Hill | .05 | .02 |
| ❑ | 25 | Rene Gonzales | .05 | .02 |
| ❑ | 26 | Ed Sprague | .05 | .02 |
| ❑ | 27 | Ken Dayley | .05 | .02 |
| ❑ | 28 | Pat Tabler | .05 | .02 |
| ❑ | 29 | Denis Boucher RC | .05 | .02 |
| ❑ | 30 | Devon White | .05 | .02 |
| ❑ | 31 | Dante Bichette | .20 | .09 |
| ❑ | 32 | Paul Molitor | .20 | .09 |
| ❑ | 33 | Greg Vaughn | .20 | .09 |
| ❑ | 34 | Dan Plesac | .05 | .02 |
| ❑ | 35 | Chris George RC | .05 | .02 |
| ❑ | 36 | Tim McIntosh | .05 | .02 |
| ❑ | 37 | Franklin Stubbs | .05 | .02 |
| ❑ | 38 | Bo Dodson RC | .05 | .02 |
| ❑ | 39 | Ron Robinson | .05 | .02 |
| ❑ | 40 | Ed Nunez | .05 | .02 |
| ❑ | 41 | Greg Brock | .05 | .02 |
| ❑ | 42 | Jaime Navarro | .05 | .02 |
| ❑ | 43 | Chris Bosio | .05 | .02 |
| ❑ | 44 | B.J. Surhoff | .10 | .05 |
| ❑ | 45 | Chris Johnson | .05 | .02 |
| ❑ | 46 | Willie Randolph | .10 | .05 |
| ❑ | 47 | Narciso Elvira | .05 | .02 |
| ❑ | 48 | Jim Gantner | .05 | .02 |
| ❑ | 49 | Kevin Brown | .10 | .05 |
| ❑ | 50 | Julio Machado | .05 | .02 |
| ❑ | 51 | Chuck Crim | .05 | .02 |
| ❑ | 52 | Gary Sheffield | .20 | .09 |
| ❑ | 53 | Angel Miranda RC | .05 | .02 |
| ❑ | 54 | Ted Higuera | .05 | .02 |
| ❑ | 55 | Robin Yount | .20 | .09 |
| ❑ | 56 | Cal Eldred | .05 | .02 |
| ❑ | 57 | Sandy Alomar Jr. | .10 | .05 |
| ❑ | 58 | Greg Swindell | .05 | .02 |
| ❑ | 59 | Brook Jacoby | .05 | .02 |
| ❑ | 60 | Efrain Valdez | .05 | .02 |
| ❑ | 61 | Ever Magallanes | .05 | .02 |
| ❑ | 62 | Tom Candiotti | .05 | .02 |
| ❑ | 63 | Eric King | .05 | .02 |
| ❑ | 64 | Alex Cole | .05 | .02 |
| ❑ | 65 | Charles Nagy | .05 | .02 |
| ❑ | 66 | Mitch Webster | .05 | .02 |
| ❑ | 67 | Chris James | .05 | .02 |
| ❑ | 68 | Jim Thome RC | 1.50 | .70 |
| ❑ | 69 | Carlos Baerga | .05 | .02 |
| ❑ | 70 | Mark Lewis | .05 | .02 |
| ❑ | 71 | Jerry Browne | .05 | .02 |
| ❑ | 72 | Jesse Orosco | .05 | .02 |
| ❑ | 73 | Mike Huff | .05 | .02 |
| ❑ | 74 | Jose Escobar | .05 | .02 |
| ❑ | 75 | Jeff Manto | .05 | .02 |
| ❑ | 76 | Turner Ward RC | .05 | .02 |
| ❑ | 77 | Doug Jones | .05 | .02 |
| ❑ | 78 | Bruce Egloff | .05 | .02 |
| ❑ | 79 | Tim Costo RC | .05 | .02 |
| ❑ | 80 | Beau Allred | .05 | .02 |
| ❑ | 81 | Albert Belle | .20 | .09 |
| ❑ | 82 | John Farrell | .05 | .02 |
| ❑ | 83 | Glenn Davis | .05 | .02 |
| ❑ | 84 | Joe Orsulak | .05 | .02 |
| ❑ | 85 | Mark Williamson | .05 | .02 |
| ❑ | 86 | Ben McDonald | .05 | .02 |
| ❑ | 87 | Billy Ripken | .05 | .02 |
| ❑ | 88 | Leo Gomez UER<br>(Baltimore is spelled Balitmore) | .05 | .02 |
| ❑ | 89 | Bob Melvin | .05 | .02 |
| ❑ | 90 | Jeff M. Robinson | .05 | .02 |
| ❑ | 91 | Jose Mesa | .05 | .02 |
| ❑ | 92 | Gregg Olson | .05 | .02 |
| ❑ | 93 | Mike Devereaux | .05 | .02 |
| ❑ | 94 | Luis Mercedes RC | .05 | .02 |
| ❑ | 95 | Arthur Rhodes RC | .10 | .05 |
| ❑ | 96 | Juan Bell | .05 | .02 |
| ❑ | 97 | Mike Mussina RC | 2.50 | 1.10 |
| ❑ | 98 | Jeff Ballard | .05 | .02 |
| ❑ | 99 | Chris Hoiles | .05 | .02 |
| ❑ | 100 | Brady Anderson | .20 | .09 |
| ❑ | 101 | Bob Milacki | .05 | .02 |
| ❑ | 102 | David Segui | .05 | .02 |
| ❑ | 103 | Dwight Evans | .10 | .05 |
| ❑ | 104 | Cal Ripken | .75 | .35 |
| ❑ | 105 | Mike Linskey | .05 | .02 |
| ❑ | 106 | Jeff Tackett RC | .05 | .02 |
| ❑ | 107 | Jeff Reardon | .10 | .05 |
| ❑ | 108 | Dana Kiecker | .05 | .02 |
| ❑ | 109 | Ellis Burks | .10 | .05 |
| ❑ | 110 | Dave Owen | .05 | .02 |
| ❑ | 111 | Danny Darwin | .05 | .02 |
| ❑ | 112 | Mo Vaughn | .10 | .05 |
| ❑ | 113 | Jeff McNeely RC | .05 | .02 |
| ❑ | 114 | Tom Bolton | .05 | .02 |
| ❑ | 115 | Greg Blosser | .05 | .02 |
| ❑ | 116 | Mike Greenwell | .05 | .02 |
| ❑ | 117 | Phil Plantier RC | .05 | .02 |
| ❑ | 118 | Roger Clemens | .40 | .18 |
| ❑ | 119 | John Marzano | .05 | .02 |
| ❑ | 120 | Jody Reed | .05 | .02 |
| ❑ | 121 | Scott Taylor | .05 | .02 |
| ❑ | 122 | Jack Clark | .10 | .05 |
| ❑ | 123 | Derek Livernois | .05 | .02 |
| ❑ | 124 | Tony Pena | .05 | .02 |
| ❑ | 125 | Tom Brunansky | .05 | .02 |
| ❑ | 126 | Carlos Quintana | .05 | .02 |
| ❑ | 127 | Tim Naehring | .05 | .02 |
| ❑ | 128 | Matt Young | .05 | .02 |
| ❑ | 129 | Wade Boggs | .25 | .11 |
| ❑ | 130 | Kevin Morton | .05 | .02 |
| ❑ | 131 | Pete Incaviglia | .05 | .02 |
| ❑ | 132 | Rob Deer | .05 | .02 |
| ❑ | 133 | Bill Gullickson | .05 | .02 |
| ❑ | 134 | Rico Brogna | .10 | .05 |
| ❑ | 135 | Lloyd Moseby | .05 | .02 |
| ❑ | 136 | Cecil Fielder | .10 | .05 |
| ❑ | 137 | Tony Phillips | .05 | .02 |
| ❑ | 138 | Mark Leiter RC | .05 | .02 |
| ❑ | 139 | John Cerutti | .05 | .02 |
| ❑ | 140 | Mickey Tettleton | .05 | .02 |
| ❑ | 141 | Milt Cuyler | .05 | .02 |
| ❑ | 142 | Greg Gohr | .05 | .02 |
| ❑ | 143 | Tony Bernazard | .05 | .02 |
| ❑ | 144 | Dan Gakeler | .05 | .02 |
| ❑ | 145 | Travis Fryman | .20 | .09 |
| ❑ | 146 | Dan Petry | .05 | .02 |
| ❑ | 147 | Scott Aldred | .05 | .02 |
| ❑ | 148 | John DeSilva | .05 | .02 |
| ❑ | 149 | Rusty Meacham | .05 | .02 |
| ❑ | 150 | Lou Whitaker | .10 | .05 |
| ❑ | 151 | Dave Haas | .05 | .02 |
| ❑ | 152 | Luis de los Santos | .05 | .02 |
| ❑ | 153 | Ivan Cruz | .05 | .02 |
| ❑ | 154 | Alan Trammell | .10 | .05 |
| ❑ | 155 | Pat Kelly RC | .05 | .02 |
| ❑ | 156 | Carl Everett RC | 2.00 | .90 |
| ❑ | 157 | Greg Cadaret | .05 | .02 |
| ❑ | 158 | Kevin Maas | .05 | .02 |
| ❑ | 159 | Jeff Johnson | .05 | .02 |
| ❑ | 160 | Willie Smith | .05 | .02 |
| ❑ | 161 | Gerald Williams RC | .50 | .23 |
| ❑ | 162 | Mike Humphreys RC | .05 | .02 |
| ❑ | 163 | Alvaro Espinoza | .05 | .02 |
| ❑ | 164 | Matt Nokes | .05 | .02 |
| ❑ | 165 | Wade Taylor | .05 | .02 |
| ❑ | 166 | Roberto Kelly | .05 | .02 |
| ❑ | 167 | John Habyan | .05 | .02 |
| ❑ | 168 | Steve Farr | .05 | .02 |
| ❑ | 169 | Jesse Barfield | .05 | .02 |
| ❑ | 170 | Steve Sax | .05 | .02 |
| ❑ | 171 | Jim Leyritz | .05 | .02 |
| ❑ | 172 | Robert Eenhoorn RC | .05 | .02 |
| ❑ | 173 | Bernie Williams | .25 | .11 |
| ❑ | 174 | Scott Lusader | .05 | .02 |
| ❑ | 175 | Torey Lovullo | .05 | .02 |
| ❑ | 176 | Chuck Cary | .05 | .02 |
| ❑ | 177 | Scott Sanderson | .05 | .02 |
| ❑ | 178 | Don Mattingly | .50 | .23 |
| ❑ | 179 | Mel Hall | .05 | .02 |
| ❑ | 180 | Juan Gonzalez | .25 | .11 |
| ❑ | 181 | Hensley Meulens | .05 | .02 |
| ❑ | 182 | Jose Offerman | .05 | .02 |
| ❑ | 183 | Jeff Bagwell RC | 4.00 | 1.80 |
| ❑ | 184 | Jeff Conine RC | .10 | .05 |
| ❑ | 185 | Henry Rodriguez RC | .50 | .23 |
| ❑ | 186 | Jimmie Reese CO | .10 | .05 |
| ❑ | 187 | Kyle Abbott | .05 | .02 |
| ❑ | 188 | Lance Parrish | .05 | .02 |
| ❑ | 189 | Rafael Montalvo | .05 | .02 |
| ❑ | 190 | Floyd Bannister | .05 | .02 |
| ❑ | 191 | Dick Schofield | .05 | .02 |
| ❑ | 192 | Scott Lewis | .05 | .02 |
| ❑ | 193 | Jeff D. Robinson | .05 | .02 |
| ❑ | 194 | Kent Anderson | .05 | .02 |
| ❑ | 195 | Wally Joyner | .10 | .05 |
| ❑ | 196 | Chuck Finley | .10 | .05 |
| ❑ | 197 | Luis Sojo | .05 | .02 |
| ❑ | 198 | Jeff Richardson | .05 | .02 |
| ❑ | 199 | Dave Parker | .10 | .05 |
| ❑ | 200 | Jim Abbott | .10 | .05 |
| ❑ | 201 | Junior Felix | .05 | .02 |
| ❑ | 202 | Mark Langston | .05 | .02 |
| ❑ | 203 | Tim Salmon RC | 1.00 | .45 |
| ❑ | 204 | Cliff Young | .05 | .02 |
| ❑ | 205 | Scott Bailes | .05 | .02 |
| ❑ | 206 | Bobby Rose | .05 | .02 |
| ❑ | 207 | Gary Gaetti | .10 | .05 |
| ❑ | 208 | Ruben Amaro RC | .05 | .02 |
| ❑ | 209 | Luis Polonia | .05 | .02 |
| ❑ | 210 | Dave Winfield | .20 | .09 |
| ❑ | 211 | Bryan Harvey | .05 | .02 |
| ❑ | 212 | Mike Moore | .05 | .02 |
| ❑ | 213 | Rickey Henderson | .25 | .11 |
| ❑ | 214 | Steve Chitren | .05 | .02 |
| ❑ | 215 | Bob Welch | .05 | .02 |
| ❑ | 216 | Terry Steinbach | .10 | .05 |
| ❑ | 217 | Earnest Riles | .05 | .02 |
| ❑ | 218 | Todd Van Poppel RC | .05 | .02 |
| ❑ | 219 | Mike Gallego | .05 | .02 |
| ❑ | 220 | Curt Young | .05 | .02 |
| ❑ | 221 | Todd Burns | .05 | .02 |
| ❑ | 222 | Vance Law | .05 | .02 |
| ❑ | 223 | Eric Show | .05 | .02 |
| ❑ | 224 | Don Peters | .05 | .02 |
| ❑ | 225 | Dave Stewart | .10 | .05 |
| ❑ | 226 | Dave Henderson | .05 | .02 |
| ❑ | 227 | Jose Canseco | .25 | .11 |
| ❑ | 228 | Walt Weiss | .05 | .02 |
| ❑ | 229 | Dann Howitt | .05 | .02 |
| ❑ | 230 | Willie Wilson | .05 | .02 |
| ❑ | 231 | Harold Baines | .10 | .05 |
| ❑ | 232 | Scott Hemond | .05 | .02 |
| ❑ | 233 | Joe Slusarski | .05 | .02 |
| ❑ | 234 | Mark McGwire | .75 | .35 |
| ❑ | 235 | Kirk Dressendorfer RC | .05 | .02 |
| ❑ | 236 | Craig Paquette RC | .05 | .02 |
| ❑ | 237 | Dennis Eckersley | .10 | .05 |
| ❑ | 238 | Dana Allison | .05 | .02 |
| ❑ | 239 | Scott Bradley | .05 | .02 |

- ❑ 240 Brian Holman .05 .02
- ❑ 241 Mike Schooler .05 .02
- ❑ 242 Rich DeLucia .05 .02
- ❑ 243 Edgar Martinez .10 .05
- ❑ 244 Henry Cotto .05 .02
- ❑ 245 Omar Vizquel .20 .09
- ❑ 246 Ken Griffey Jr. 1.00 .45
  (See also 255)
- ❑ 247 Jay Buhner .10 .05
- ❑ 248 Bill Krueger .05 .02
- ❑ 249 Dave Fleming RC .05 .02
- ❑ 250 Patrick Lennon .05 .02
- ❑ 251 Dave Valle .05 .02
- ❑ 252 Harold Reynolds .05 .02
- ❑ 253 Randy Johnson .30 .14
- ❑ 254 Scott Bankhead .05 .02
- ❑ 255 Ken Griffey Sr. UER .05 .02
  (Card number is 246)
- ❑ 256 Greg Briley .05 .02
- ❑ 257 Tino Martinez .10 .05
- ❑ 258 Alvin Davis .05 .02
- ❑ 259 Pete O'Brien .05 .02
- ❑ 260 Erik Hanson .05 .02
- ❑ 261 Bret Boone RC .50 .23
- ❑ 262 Roger Salkeld .05 .02
- ❑ 263 Dave Burba RC .05 .02
- ❑ 264 Kerry Woodson RC .05 .02
- ❑ 265 Julio Franco .05 .02
- ❑ 266 Dan Peltier RC .05 .02
- ❑ 267 Jeff Russell .05 .02
- ❑ 268 Steve Buechele .05 .02
- ❑ 269 Donald Harris .05 .02
- ❑ 270 Robb Nen .20 .09
- ❑ 271 Rich Gossage .10 .05
- ❑ 272 Ivan Rodriguez RC 4.00 1.80
- ❑ 273 Jeff Huson .05 .02
- ❑ 274 Kevin Brown .10 .05
- ❑ 275 Dan Smith RC .05 .02
- ❑ 276 Gary Pettis .05 .02
- ❑ 277 Jack Daugherty .05 .02
- ❑ 278 Mike Jeffcoat .05 .02
- ❑ 279 Brad Arnsberg .05 .02
- ❑ 280 Nolan Ryan 1.00 .45
- ❑ 281 Eric McCray .05 .02
- ❑ 282 Scott Chiamparino .05 .02
- ❑ 283 Ruben Sierra .05 .02
- ❑ 284 Geno Petralli .05 .02
- ❑ 285 Monty Fariss .05 .02
- ❑ 286 Rafael Palmeiro .20 .09
- ❑ 287 Bobby Witt .05 .02
- ❑ 288 Dean Palmer UER .10 .05
  (Photo is Dan Peltier)
- ❑ 289 Tony Scruggs .05 .02
- ❑ 290 Kenny Rogers .05 .02
- ❑ 291 Bret Saberhagen .10 .05
- ❑ 292 Brian McRae RC .10 .05
- ❑ 293 Storm Davis .05 .02
- ❑ 294 Danny Tartabull .05 .02
- ❑ 295 David Howard .05 .02
- ❑ 296 Mike Boddicker .05 .02
- ❑ 297 Joel Johnston RC .05 .02
- ❑ 298 Tim Spehr .05 .02
- ❑ 299 Hector Wagner .05 .02
- ❑ 300 George Brett .40 .18
- ❑ 301 Mike Macfarlane .05 .02
- ❑ 302 Kirk Gibson .10 .05
- ❑ 303 Harvey Pulliam RC .05 .02
- ❑ 304 Jim Eisenreich .05 .02
- ❑ 305 Kevin Seitzer .05 .02
- ❑ 306 Mark Davis .05 .02
- ❑ 307 Kurt Stillwell .05 .02
- ❑ 308 Jeff Montgomery .10 .05
- ❑ 309 Kevin Appier .10 .05
- ❑ 310 Bob Hamelin .05 .02
- ❑ 311 Tom Gordon .05 .02
- ❑ 312 Kerwin Moore RC .05 .02
- ❑ 313 Hugh Walker .05 .02
- ❑ 314 Terry Shumpert .05 .02
- ❑ 315 Warren Cromartie .05 .02
- ❑ 316 Gary Thurman .05 .02
- ❑ 317 Steve Bedrosian .05 .02
- ❑ 318 Danny Gladden .05 .02
- ❑ 319 Jack Morris .10 .05
- ❑ 320 Kirby Puckett .50 .23
- ❑ 321 Kent Hrbek .10 .05
- ❑ 322 Kevin Tapani .05 .02
- ❑ 323 Denny Neagle RC .50 .23
- ❑ 324 Rich Garces RC .05 .02
- ❑ 325 Larry Casian .05 .02
- ❑ 326 Shane Mack .05 .02
- ❑ 327 Allan Anderson .05 .02
- ❑ 328 Junior Ortiz .05 .02
- ❑ 329 Paul Abbott .05 .02
- ❑ 330 Chuck Knoblauch .10 .05
- ❑ 331 Chili Davis .10 .05
- ❑ 332 Todd Ritchie RC .05 .02
- ❑ 333 Brian Harper .05 .02
- ❑ 334 Rick Aguilera .10 .05
- ❑ 335 Scott Erickson .05 .02
- ❑ 336 Pedro Munoz RC .05 .02
- ❑ 337 Scott Leius .05 .02
- ❑ 338 Greg Gagne .05 .02
- ❑ 339 Mike Pagliarulo .05 .02
- ❑ 340 Terry Leach .05 .02
- ❑ 341 Willie Banks .05 .02
- ❑ 342 Bobby Thigpen .05 .02
- ❑ 343 Roberto Hernandez RC .20 .09
- ❑ 344 Melido Perez .05 .02
- ❑ 345 Carlton Fisk .20 .09
- ❑ 346 Norberto Martin .05 .02
- ❑ 347 Johnny Ruffin RC .05 .02
- ❑ 348 Jeff Carter .05 .02
- ❑ 349 Lance Johnson .05 .02
- ❑ 350 Sammy Sosa .50 .23
- ❑ 351 Alex Fernandez .10 .05
- ❑ 352 Jack McDowell .05 .02
- ❑ 353 Bob Wickman RC .05 .02
- ❑ 354 Wilson Alvarez .05 .02
- ❑ 355 Charlie Hough .10 .05
- ❑ 356 Ozzie Guillen .05 .02
- ❑ 357 Cory Snyder .05 .02
- ❑ 358 Robin Ventura .20 .09
- ❑ 359 Scott Fletcher .05 .02
- ❑ 360 Cesar Bernhardt .05 .02
- ❑ 361 Dan Pasqua .05 .02
- ❑ 362 Tim Raines .10 .05
- ❑ 363 Brian Drahman .05 .02
- ❑ 364 Wayne Edwards .05 .02
- ❑ 365 Scott Radinsky .05 .02
- ❑ 366 Frank Thomas .50 .23
- ❑ 367 Cecil Fielder SLUG .05 .02
- ❑ 368 Julio Franco SLUG .05 .02
- ❑ 369 Kelly Gruber SLUG .05 .02
- ❑ 370 Alan Trammell SLUG .05 .02
- ❑ 371 Rickey Henderson SLUG .10 .05
- ❑ 372 Jose Canseco SLUG .10 .05
- ❑ 373 Ellis Burks SLUG .05 .02
- ❑ 374 Lance Parrish SLUG .05 .02
- ❑ 375 Dave Parker SLUG .05 .02
- ❑ 376 Eddie Murray SLUG .10 .05
- ❑ 377 Ryne Sandberg SLUG .20 .09
- ❑ 378 Matt Williams SLUG .10 .05
- ❑ 379 Barry Larkin SLUG .10 .05
- ❑ 380 Barry Bonds SLUG .20 .09
- ❑ 381 Bobby Bonilla SLUG .05 .02
- ❑ 382 Darryl Strawberry SLUG .05 .02
- ❑ 383 Benny Santiago SLUG .05 .02
- ❑ 384 Don Robinson SLUG .05 .02
- ❑ 385 Paul Coleman .05 .02
- ❑ 386 Milt Thompson .05 .02
- ❑ 387 Lee Smith .10 .05
- ❑ 388 Ray Lankford .20 .09
- ❑ 389 Tom Pagnozzi .05 .02
- ❑ 390 Ken Hill .05 .02
- ❑ 391 Jamie Moyer .05 .02
- ❑ 392 Greg Carmona .05 .02
- ❑ 393 John Ericks .05 .02
- ❑ 394 Bob Tewksbury .05 .02
- ❑ 395 Jose Oquendo .05 .02
- ❑ 396 Rheal Cormier RC .05 .02
- ❑ 397 Mike Milchin .05 .02
- ❑ 398 Ozzie Smith .25 .11
- ❑ 399 Aaron Holbert RC .05 .02
- ❑ 400 Jose DeLeon .05 .02
- ❑ 401 Felix Jose .05 .02
- ❑ 402 Juan Agosto .05 .02
- ❑ 403 Pedro Guerrero .05 .02
- ❑ 404 Todd Zeile .10 .05
- ❑ 405 Gerald Perry .05 .02
- ❑ 406 Donovan Osborne RC UER .05 .02
  (Card number is 410)
- ❑ 407 Bryn Smith .05 .02
- ❑ 408 Bernard Gilkey .10 .05
- ❑ 409 Rex Hudler .05 .02
- ❑ 410 Thomson/Branca Shot .20 .09
  Bobby Thomson
  Ralph Branca
  (See also 406)
- ❑ 411 Lance Dickson RC .05 .02
- ❑ 412 Danny Jackson .05 .02
- ❑ 413 Jerome Walton .05 .02
- ❑ 414 Sean Cheetham .05 .02
- ❑ 415 Joe Girardi .10 .05
- ❑ 416 Ryne Sandberg .25 .11
- ❑ 417 Mike Harkey .05 .02
- ❑ 418 George Bell .05 .02
- ❑ 419 Rick Wilkins RC .05 .02
- ❑ 420 Earl Cunningham .05 .02
- ❑ 421 Heathcliff Slocumb RC .05 .02
- ❑ 422 Mike Bielecki .05 .02
- ❑ 423 Jessie Hollins RC .05 .02
- ❑ 424 Shawon Dunston .05 .02
- ❑ 425 Dave Smith .05 .02
- ❑ 426 Greg Maddux .50 .23
- ❑ 427 Jose Vizcaino .05 .02
- ❑ 428 Luis Salazar .05 .02
- ❑ 429 Andre Dawson .10 .05
- ❑ 430 Rick Sutcliffe .10 .05
- ❑ 431 Paul Assenmacher .05 .02
- ❑ 432 Erik Pappas .05 .02
- ❑ 433 Mark Grace .20 .09
- ❑ 434 Dennis Martinez .10 .05
- ❑ 435 Marquis Grissom .05 .02
- ❑ 436 Wil Cordero RC .05 .02
- ❑ 437 Tim Wallach .05 .02
- ❑ 438 Brian Barnes .05 .02
- ❑ 439 Barry Jones .05 .02
- ❑ 440 Ivan Calderon .05 .02
- ❑ 441 Stan Spencer .05 .02
- ❑ 442 Larry Walker .20 .09
- ❑ 443 Chris Haney RC .05 .02
- ❑ 444 Hector Rivera .05 .02
- ❑ 445 Delino DeShields .10 .05
- ❑ 446 Andres Galarraga .10 .05
- ❑ 447 Gilberto Reyes .05 .02
- ❑ 448 Willie Greene .10 .05
- ❑ 449 Greg Colbrunn RC .05 .02
- ❑ 450 Rondell White RC .75 .35
- ❑ 451 Steve Frey .05 .02
- ❑ 452 Shane Andrews RC .25 .11
- ❑ 453 Mike Fitzgerald .05 .02
- ❑ 454 Spike Owen .05 .02
- ❑ 455 Dave Martinez .05 .02
- ❑ 456 Dennis Boyd .05 .02
- ❑ 457 Eric Bullock .05 .02
- ❑ 458 Reid Cornelius RC .05 .02
- ❑ 459 Chris Nabholz .05 .02
- ❑ 460 David Cone .10 .05
- ❑ 461 Hubie Brooks .05 .02
- ❑ 462 Sid Fernandez .05 .02
- ❑ 463 Doug Simons .05 .02
- ❑ 464 Howard Johnson .05 .02
- ❑ 465 Chris Donnels .05 .02
- ❑ 466 Anthony Young RC .05 .02
- ❑ 467 Todd Hundley .05 .02
- ❑ 468 Rick Cerone .05 .02
- ❑ 469 Kevin Elster .05 .02
- ❑ 470 Wally Whitehurst .05 .02
- ❑ 471 Vince Coleman .05 .02
- ❑ 472 Dwight Gooden .10 .05
- ❑ 473 Charlie O'Brien .05 .02
- ❑ 474 Jeromy Burnitz RC 1.00 .45
- ❑ 475 John Franco .10 .05
- ❑ 476 Daryl Boston .05 .02
- ❑ 477 Frank Viola .05 .02
- ❑ 478 D.J. Dozier .05 .02
- ❑ 479 Kevin McReynolds .05 .02
- ❑ 480 Tom Herr .05 .02
- ❑ 481 Gregg Jefferies .05 .02
- ❑ 482 Pete Schourek RC .10 .05
- ❑ 483 Ron Darling .05 .02
- ❑ 484 Dave Magadan .05 .02
- ❑ 485 Andy Ashby RC .50 .23
- ❑ 486 Dale Murphy .20 .09
- ❑ 487 Von Hayes .05 .02
- ❑ 488 Kim Batiste RC .05 .02
- ❑ 489 Tony Longmire RC .05 .02

❑ 490 Wally Backman .05 .02
❑ 491 Jeff Jackson .05 .02
❑ 492 Mickey Morandini .05 .02
❑ 493 Darrel Akerfelds .05 .02
❑ 494 Ricky Jordan .05 .02
❑ 495 Randy Ready .05 .02
❑ 496 Darrin Fletcher .05 .02
❑ 497 Chuck Malone .05 .02
❑ 498 Pat Combs .05 .02
❑ 499 Dickie Thon .05 .02
❑ 500 Roger McDowell .05 .02
❑ 501 Len Dykstra .10 .05
❑ 502 Joe Boever .05 .02
❑ 503 John Kruk .10 .05
❑ 504 Terry Mulholland .05 .02
❑ 505 Wes Chamberlain RC .05 .02
❑ 506 Mike Lieberthal RC 1.00 .45
❑ 507 Darren Daulton .10 .05
❑ 508 Charlie Hayes .05 .02
❑ 509 John Smiley .05 .02
❑ 510 Gary Varsho .05 .02
❑ 511 Curt Wilkerson .05 .02
❑ 512 Orlando Merced RC .05 .02
❑ 513 Barry Bonds .30 .14
❑ 514 Mike LaValliere .05 .02
❑ 515 Doug Drabek .05 .02
❑ 516 Gary Redus .05 .02
❑ 517 William Pennyfeather RC .05 .02
❑ 518 Randy Tomlin RC .05 .02
❑ 519 Mike Zimmerman RC .05 .02
❑ 520 Jeff King .05 .02
❑ 521 Kurt Miller RC .05 .02
❑ 522 Jay Bell .10 .05
❑ 523 Bill Landrum .05 .02
❑ 524 Zane Smith .05 .02
❑ 525 Bobby Bonilla .10 .05
❑ 526 Bob Walk .05 .02
❑ 527 Austin Manahan .05 .02
❑ 528 Joe Ausanio .05 .02
❑ 529 Andy Van Slyke .10 .05
❑ 530 Jose Lind .05 .02
❑ 531 Carlos Garcia RC .05 .02
❑ 532 Don Slaught .05 .02
❑ 533 Gen.Colin Powell .50 .23
❑ 534 Frank Bolick RC .05 .02
❑ 535 Gary Scott .05 .02
❑ 536 Nikco Riesgo .05 .02
❑ 537 Reggie Sanders RC .50 .23
❑ 538 Tim Howard RC .05 .02
❑ 539 Ryan Bowen RC .05 .02
❑ 540 Eric Anthony .05 .02
❑ 541 Jim Deshaies .05 .02
❑ 542 Tom Nevers RC .05 .02
❑ 543 Ken Caminiti .10 .05
❑ 544 Karl Rhodes .05 .02
❑ 545 Xavier Hernandez .05 .02
❑ 546 Mike Scott .05 .02
❑ 547 Jeff Juden .05 .02
❑ 548 Darryl Kile .10 .05
❑ 549 Willie Ansley .05 .02
❑ 550 Luis Gonzalez RC 1.00 .45
❑ 551 Mike Simms .05 .02
❑ 552 Mark Portugal .05 .02
❑ 553 Jimmy Jones .05 .02
❑ 554 Jim Clancy .05 .02
❑ 555 Pete Harnisch .05 .02
❑ 556 Craig Biggio .10 .05
❑ 557 Eric Yelding .05 .02
❑ 558 Dave Rohde .05 .02
❑ 559 Casey Candaele .05 .02
❑ 560 Curt Schilling .10 .05
❑ 561 Steve Finley .10 .05
❑ 562 Javier Ortiz .05 .02
❑ 563 Andujar Cedeno .05 .02
❑ 564 Rafael Ramirez .05 .02
❑ 565 Kenny Lofton RC 1.00 .45
❑ 566 Steve Avery .05 .02
❑ 567 Lonnie Smith .05 .02
❑ 568 Kent Mercker .05 .02
❑ 569 Chipper Jones RC 8.00 3.60
❑ 570 Terry Pendleton .10 .05
❑ 571 Otis Nixon .05 .02
❑ 572 Juan Berenguer .05 .02
❑ 573 Charlie Leibrandt .05 .02
❑ 574 David Justice .20 .09
❑ 575 Keith Mitchell RC .05 .02
❑ 576 Tom Glavine .20 .09
❑ 577 Greg Olson .05 .02
❑ 578 Rafael Belliard .05 .02
❑ 579 Ben Rivera RC .05 .02
❑ 580 John Smoltz .10 .05
❑ 581 Tyler Houston .05 .02
❑ 582 Mark Wohlers RC .10 .05
❑ 583 Ron Gant .10 .05
❑ 584 Ramon Caraballo RC .05 .02
❑ 585 Sid Bream .05 .02
❑ 586 Jeff Treadway .05 .02
❑ 587 Javier Lopez RC 1.00 .45
❑ 588 Deion Sanders .10 .05
❑ 589 Mike Heath .05 .02
❑ 590 Ryan Klesko RC 1.00 .45
❑ 591 Bob Ojeda .05 .02
❑ 592 Alfredo Griffin .05 .02
❑ 593 Raul Mondesi RC 1.50 .70
❑ 594 Greg Smith .05 .02
❑ 595 Orel Hershiser .10 .05
❑ 596 Juan Samuel .05 .02
❑ 597 Brett Butler .10 .05
❑ 598 Gary Carter .10 .05
❑ 599 Stan Javier .05 .02
❑ 600 Kal Daniels .05 .02
❑ 601 Jamie McAndrew RC .05 .02
❑ 602 Mike Sharperson .05 .02
❑ 603 Jay Howell .05 .02
❑ 604 Eric Karros RC 1.00 .45
❑ 605 Tim Belcher .05 .02
❑ 606 Dan Opperman .05 .02
❑ 607 Lenny Harris .05 .02
❑ 608 Tom Goodwin .10 .05
❑ 609 Darryl Strawberry .10 .05
❑ 610 Ramon Martinez .05 .02
❑ 611 Kevin Gross .05 .02
❑ 612 Zakary Shinall .05 .02
❑ 613 Mike Scioscia .05 .02
❑ 614 Eddie Murray .20 .09
❑ 615 Ronnie Walden RC .05 .02
❑ 616 Will Clark .20 .09
❑ 617 Adam Hyzdu RC .05 .02
❑ 618 Matt Williams .10 .05
❑ 619 Don Robinson .05 .02
❑ 620 Jeff Brantley .05 .02
❑ 621 Greg Litton .05 .02
❑ 622 Steve Decker .05 .02
❑ 623 Robby Thompson .05 .02
❑ 624 Mark Leonard .05 .02
❑ 625 Kevin Bass .05 .02
❑ 626 Scott Garrelts .05 .02
❑ 627 Jose Uribe .05 .02
❑ 628 Eric Gunderson .05 .02
❑ 629 Steve Hosey .05 .02
❑ 630 Trevor Wilson .05 .02
❑ 631 Terry Kennedy .05 .02
❑ 632 Dave Righetti .05 .02
❑ 633 Kelly Downs .05 .02
❑ 634 Johnny Ard .05 .02
❑ 635 Eric Christopherson RC .05 .02
❑ 636 Kevin Mitchell .05 .02
❑ 637 John Burkett .05 .02
❑ 638 Kevin Rogers RC .05 .02
❑ 639 Bud Black .05 .02
❑ 640 Willie McGee .10 .05
❑ 641 Royce Clayton .10 .05
❑ 642 Tony Fernandez .05 .02
❑ 643 Ricky Bones RC .05 .02
❑ 644 Thomas Howard .05 .02
❑ 645 Dave Staton RC .05 .02
❑ 646 Jim Presley .05 .02
❑ 647 Tony Gwynn .40 .18
❑ 648 Marty Barrett .05 .02
❑ 649 Scott Coolbaugh .05 .02
❑ 650 Craig Lefferts .05 .02
❑ 651 Eddie Whitson .05 .02
❑ 652 Oscar Azocar .05 .02
❑ 653 Wes Gardner .05 .02
❑ 654 Bip Roberts .05 .02
❑ 655 Robbie Beckett RC .05 .02
❑ 656 Benito Santiago .05 .02
❑ 657 Greg W.Harris .05 .02
❑ 658 Jerald Clark .05 .02
❑ 659 Fred McGriff .20 .09
❑ 660 Larry Andersen .05 .02
❑ 661 Bruce Hurst .05 .02
❑ 662 Steve Martin UER .05 .02
(Card said he pitched at Waterloo; he's an outfielder)
❑ 663 Rafael Valdez .05 .02
❑ 664 Paul Faries .05 .02
❑ 665 Andy Benes .05 .02
❑ 666 Randy Myers .10 .05
❑ 667 Rob Dibble .05 .02
❑ 668 Glenn Sutko .05 .02
❑ 669 Glenn Braggs .05 .02
❑ 670 Billy Hatcher .05 .02
❑ 671 Joe Oliver .05 .02
❑ 672 Freddy Benavides .05 .02
❑ 673 Barry Larkin .20 .09
❑ 674 Chris Sabo .05 .02
❑ 675 Mariano Duncan .05 .02
❑ 676 Chris Jones RC .05 .02
❑ 677 Gino Minutelli .05 .02
❑ 678 Reggie Jefferson .10 .05
❑ 679 Jack Armstrong .05 .02
❑ 680 Chris Hammond .05 .02
❑ 681 Jose Rijo .05 .02
❑ 682 Bill Doran .05 .02
❑ 683 Terry Lee .05 .02
❑ 684 Tom Browning .05 .02
❑ 685 Paul O'Neill .10 .05
❑ 686 Eric Davis .10 .05
❑ 687 Dan Wilson RC .25 .11
❑ 688 Ted Power .05 .02
❑ 689 Tim Layana .05 .02
❑ 690 Norm Charlton .05 .02
❑ 691 Hal Morris .05 .02
❑ 692 Rickey Henderson .20 .09
❑ 693 Sam Militello RC .05 .02
❑ 694 Matt Mieske RC .05 .02
❑ 695 Paul Russo RC .05 .02
❑ 696 Domingo Mota .05 .02
❑ 697 Todd Guggiana RC .05 .02
❑ 698 Marc Newfield RC .05 .02
❑ 699 Checklist 1-122 .05 .02
❑ 700 Checklist 123-244 .05 .02
❑ 701 Checklist 245-366 .05 .02
❑ 702 Checklist 367-471 .05 .02
❑ 703 Checklist 472-593 .05 .02
❑ 704 Checklist 594-704 .05 .02

# 1992 Bowman

| | MINT | NRMT |
|---|---|---|
| COMPLETE SET (705) | 275.00 | 125.00 |

❑ 1 Ivan Rodriguez 3.00 1.35
❑ 2 Kirk McCaskill .25 .11
❑ 3 Scott Livingstone .25 .11
❑ 4 Salomon Torres RC .25 .11
❑ 5 Carlos Hernandez .25 .11
❑ 6 Dave Hollins .25 .11
❑ 7 Scott Fletcher .25 .11
❑ 8 Jorge Fabregas RC .25 .11
❑ 9 Andujar Cedeno .25 .11
❑ 10 Howard Johnson .25 .11
❑ 11 Trevor Hoffman RC 2.00 .90
❑ 12 Roberto Kelly .25 .11
❑ 13 Gregg Jefferies .25 .11
❑ 14 Marquis Grissom .25 .11
❑ 15 Mike Ignasiak .25 .11
❑ 16 Jack Morris .50 .23
❑ 17 William Pennyfeather .25 .11

❑ 18 Todd Stottlemyre .50 .23
❑ 19 Chito Martinez .25 .11
❑ 20 Roberto Alomar 1.50 .70
❑ 21 Sam Militello .25 .11
❑ 22 Hector Fajardo RC .25 .11
❑ 23 Paul Quantrill RC .25 .11
❑ 24 Chuck Knoblauch .50 .23
❑ 25 Reggie Jefferson .50 .23
❑ 26 Jeremy McGarity RC .25 .11
❑ 27 Jerome Walton .25 .11
❑ 28 Chipper Jones 30.00 13.50
❑ 29 Brian Barber RC .25 .11
❑ 30 Ron Darling .25 .11
❑ 31 Roberto Petagine RC .25 .11
❑ 32 Chuck Finley .50 .23
❑ 33 Edgar Martinez 1.00 .45
❑ 34 Napoleon Robinson .25 .11
❑ 35 Andy Van Slyke .50 .23
❑ 36 Bobby Thigpen .25 .11
❑ 37 Travis Fryman .50 .23
❑ 38 Eric Christopherson .25 .11
❑ 39 Terry Mulholland .25 .11
❑ 40 Darryl Strawberry .50 .23
❑ 41 Manny Alexander RC .25 .11
❑ 42 Tracy Sanders RC .25 .11
❑ 43 Pete Incaviglia .25 .11
❑ 44 Kim Batiste .25 .11
❑ 45 Frank Rodriguez .50 .23
❑ 46 Greg Swindell .25 .11
❑ 47 Delino DeShields .50 .23
❑ 48 John Ericks .25 .11
❑ 49 Franklin Stubbs .25 .11
❑ 50 Tony Gwynn 3.00 1.35
❑ 51 Clifton Garrett RC .25 .11
❑ 52 Mike Gardella .25 .11
❑ 53 Scott Erickson .25 .11
❑ 54 Gary Caraballo RC .25 .11
❑ 55 Jose Oliva RC .25 .11
❑ 56 Brook Fordyce .25 .11
❑ 57 Mark Whiten .25 .11
❑ 58 Joe Slusarski .25 .11
❑ 59 J.R. Phillips RC .25 .11
❑ 60 Barry Bonds 2.50 1.10
❑ 61 Bob Milacki .25 .11
❑ 62 Keith Mitchell .25 .11
❑ 63 Angel Miranda .25 .11
❑ 64 Raul Mondesi 6.00 2.70
❑ 65 Brian Koelling RC .25 .11
❑ 66 Brian McRae .25 .11
❑ 67 John Patterson .25 .11
❑ 68 John Wetteland .50 .23
❑ 69 Wilson Alvarez .25 .11
❑ 70 Wade Boggs 2.00 .90
❑ 71 Darryl Ratliff RC .25 .11
❑ 72 Jeff Jackson .25 .11
❑ 73 Jeremy Hernandez RC .25 .11
❑ 74 Darryl Hamilton .25 .11
❑ 75 Rafael Belliard .25 .11
❑ 76 Rick Trlicek RC .25 .11
❑ 77 Felipe Crespo RC .25 .11
❑ 78 Carney Lansford .50 .23
❑ 79 Ryan Long RC .25 .11
❑ 80 Kirby Puckett 4.00 1.80
❑ 81 Earl Cunningham .25 .11
❑ 82 Pedro Martinez 30.00 13.50
❑ 83 Scott Hatteberg RC .25 .11
❑ 84 Juan Gonzalez UER 1.50 .70
(65 doubles vs. Tigers)
❑ 85 Robert Nutting RC .25 .11
❑ 86 Pokey Reese RC 3.00 1.35
❑ 87 Dave Silvestri .25 .11
❑ 88 Scott Ruffcorn RC .25 .11
❑ 89 Rick Aguilera .50 .23
❑ 90 Cecil Fielder .50 .23
❑ 91 Kirk Dressendorfer .25 .11
❑ 92 Jerry DiPoto RC .25 .11
❑ 93 Mike Felder .25 .11
❑ 94 Craig Paquette .25 .11
❑ 95 Elvin Paulino RC .25 .11
❑ 96 Donovan Osborne .25 .11
❑ 97 Hubie Brooks .25 .11
❑ 98 Derek Lowe RC 2.00 .90
❑ 99 David Zancanaro .25 .11
❑ 100 Ken Griffey Jr. 6.00 2.70
❑ 101 Todd Hundley .25 .11
❑ 102 Mike Trombley RC .25 .11
❑ 103 Ricky Gutierrez RC .25 .11
❑ 104 Braulio Castillo .25 .11
❑ 105 Craig Lefferts .25 .11
❑ 106 Rick Sutcliffe .50 .23
❑ 107 Dean Palmer .50 .23
❑ 108 Henry Rodriguez .25 .11
❑ 109 Mark Clark RC .25 .11
❑ 110 Kenny Lofton 3.00 1.35
❑ 111 Mark Carreon .25 .11
❑ 112 J.T. Bruett .25 .11
❑ 113 Gerald Williams .25 .11
❑ 114 Frank Thomas 3.00 1.35
❑ 115 Kevin Reimer .25 .11
❑ 116 Sammy Sosa 3.00 1.35
❑ 117 Mickey Tettleton .25 .11
❑ 118 Reggie Sanders .25 .11
❑ 119 Trevor Wilson .25 .11
❑ 120 Cliff Brantley .25 .11
❑ 121 Spike Owen .25 .11
❑ 122 Jeff Montgomery .50 .23
❑ 123 Alex Sutherland .25 .11
❑ 124 Brien Taylor RC .25 .11
❑ 125 Brian Williams RC .25 .11
❑ 126 Kevin Seitzer .25 .11
❑ 127 Carlos Delgado RC 30.00 13.50
❑ 128 Gary Scott .25 .11
❑ 129 Scott Cooper .25 .11
❑ 130 Domingo Jean RC .25 .11
❑ 131 Pat Mahomes RC .25 .11
❑ 132 Mike Boddicker .25 .11
❑ 133 Roberto Hernandez .25 .11
❑ 134 Dave Valle .25 .11
❑ 135 Kurt Stillwell .25 .11
❑ 136 Brad Pennington RC .25 .11
❑ 137 Jermaine Swinton RC .25 .11
❑ 138 Ryan Hawblitzel RC .25 .11
❑ 139 Tito Navarro RC .25 .11
❑ 140 Sandy Alomar Jr. .50 .23
❑ 141 Todd Benzinger .25 .11
❑ 142 Danny Jackson .25 .11
❑ 143 Melvin Nieves RC .25 .11
❑ 144 Jim Campanis .25 .11
❑ 145 Luis Gonzalez 1.00 .45
❑ 146 Dave Doorneweerd RC .25 .11
❑ 147 Charlie Hayes .25 .11
❑ 148 Greg Maddux 4.00 1.80
❑ 149 Brian Harper .25 .11
❑ 150 Brent Miller RC .25 .11
❑ 151 Shawn Estes RC 2.00 .90
❑ 152 Mike Williams RC .25 .11
❑ 153 Charlie Hough .50 .23
❑ 154 Randy Myers .50 .23
❑ 155 Kevin Young RC 2.00 .90
❑ 156 Rick Wilkins .25 .11
❑ 157 Terry Shumpert .25 .11
❑ 158 Steve Karsay .25 .11
❑ 159 Gary DiSarcina .25 .11
❑ 160 Deion Sanders .50 .23
❑ 161 Tom Browning .25 .11
❑ 162 Dickie Thon .25 .11
❑ 163 Luis Mercedes .25 .11
❑ 164 Riccardo Ingram .25 .11
❑ 165 Tavo Alvarez RC .25 .11
❑ 166 Rickey Henderson 2.00 .90
❑ 167 Jaime Navarro .25 .11
❑ 168 Billy Ashley RC .25 .11
❑ 169 Phil Dauphin RC .25 .11
❑ 170 Ivan Cruz .25 .11
❑ 171 Harold Baines .50 .23
❑ 172 Bryan Harvey .25 .11
❑ 173 Alex Cole .25 .11
❑ 174 Curtis Shaw RC .25 .11
❑ 175 Matt Williams 1.00 .45
❑ 176 Felix Jose .25 .11
❑ 177 Sam Horn .25 .11
❑ 178 Randy Johnson 2.00 .90
❑ 179 Ivan Calderon .25 .11
❑ 180 Steve Avery .25 .11
❑ 181 William Suero .25 .11
❑ 182 Bill Swift .25 .11
❑ 183 Howard Battle RC .25 .11
❑ 184 Ruben Amaro .25 .11
❑ 185 Jim Abbott .50 .23
❑ 186 Mike Fitzgerald .25 .11
❑ 187 Bruce Hurst .25 .11
❑ 188 Jeff Juden .25 .11
❑ 189 Jeromy Burnitz 3.00 1.35
❑ 190 Dave Burba .25 .11
❑ 191 Kevin Brown 1.00 .45
❑ 192 Patrick Lennon .25 .11
❑ 193 Jeff McNeely .25 .11
❑ 194 Wil Cordero .25 .11
❑ 195 Chili Davis .50 .23
❑ 196 Milt Cuyler .25 .11
❑ 197 Von Hayes .25 .11
❑ 198 Todd Revenig RC .25 .11
❑ 199 Joel Johnston .25 .11
❑ 200 Jeff Bagwell 3.00 1.35
❑ 201 Alex Fernandez .50 .23
❑ 202 Todd Jones RC 1.00 .45
❑ 203 Charles Nagy .25 .11
❑ 204 Tim Raines .50 .23
❑ 205 Kevin Maas .25 .11
❑ 206 Julio Franco .25 .11
❑ 207 Randy Velarde .25 .11
❑ 208 Lance Johnson .25 .11
❑ 209 Scott Leius .25 .11
❑ 210 Derek Lee .25 .11
❑ 211 Joe Sondrini RC .25 .11
❑ 212 Royce Clayton .25 .11
❑ 213 Chris George .25 .11
❑ 214 Gary Sheffield 1.50 .70
❑ 215 Mark Gubicza .25 .11
❑ 216 Mike Moore .25 .11
❑ 217 Rick Huisman RC .25 .11
❑ 218 Jeff Russell .25 .11
❑ 219 D.J. Dozier .25 .11
❑ 220 Dave Martinez .25 .11
❑ 221 Alan Newman RC .25 .11
❑ 222 Nolan Ryan 8.00 3.60
❑ 223 Teddy Higuera .25 .11
❑ 224 Damon Buford RC .25 .11
❑ 225 Ruben Sierra .25 .11
❑ 226 Tom Nevers .25 .11
❑ 227 Tommy Greene .25 .11
❑ 228 Nigel Wilson RC .25 .11
❑ 229 John DeSilva .25 .11
❑ 230 Bobby Witt .25 .11
❑ 231 Greg Cadaret .25 .11
❑ 232 John Vander Wal RC .25 .11
❑ 233 Jack Clark .50 .23
❑ 234 Bill Doran .25 .11
❑ 235 Bobby Bonilla .50 .23
❑ 236 Steve Olin .25 .11
❑ 237 Derek Bell .50 .23
❑ 238 David Cone .50 .23
❑ 239 Victor Cole .25 .11
❑ 240 Rod Bolton RC .25 .11
❑ 241 Tom Pagnozzi .25 .11
❑ 242 Rob Dibble .25 .11
❑ 243 Michael Carter RC .25 .11
❑ 244 Don Peters .25 .11
❑ 245 Mike LaValliere .25 .11
❑ 246 Joe Perona RC .25 .11
❑ 247 Mitch Williams .25 .11
❑ 248 Jay Buhner .50 .23
❑ 249 Andy Benes .25 .11
❑ 250 Alex Ochoa RC .50 .23
❑ 251 Greg Blosser .25 .11
❑ 252 Jack Armstrong .25 .11
❑ 253 Juan Samuel .25 .11
❑ 254 Terry Pendleton .50 .23
❑ 255 Ramon Martinez .25 .11
❑ 256 Rico Brogna .50 .23
❑ 257 John Smiley .25 .11
❑ 258 Carl Everett 3.00 1.35
❑ 259 Tim Salmon 3.00 1.35
❑ 260 Will Clark 1.50 .70
❑ 261 Ugueth Urbina RC 1.00 .45
❑ 262 Jason Wood RC .25 .11
❑ 263 Dave Magadan .25 .11
❑ 264 Dante Bichette 1.00 .45
❑ 265 Jose DeLeon .25 .11
❑ 266 Mike Neill RC .25 .11
❑ 267 Paul O'Neill .50 .23
❑ 268 Anthony Young .25 .11
❑ 269 Greg W. Harris .25 .11
❑ 270 Todd Van Poppel .25 .11
❑ 271 Pedro Castellano RC .25 .11
❑ 272 Tony Phillips .25 .11
❑ 273 Mike Gallego .25 .11
❑ 274 Steve Cooke RC .25 .11

❑ 275 Robin Ventura .50 .23
❑ 276 Kevin Mitchell .50 .23
❑ 277 Doug Linton .25 .11
❑ 278 Robert Eenhoorn .25 .11
❑ 279 Gabe White RC .25 .11
❑ 280 Dave Stewart .25 .11
❑ 281 Mo Sanford .25 .11
❑ 282 Greg Perschke .25 .11
❑ 283 Kevin Flora RC .25 .11
❑ 284 Jeff Williams RC .25 .11
❑ 285 Keith Miller .25 .11
❑ 286 Andy Ashby .50 .23
❑ 287 Doug Dascenzo .25 .11
❑ 288 Eric Karros 1.50 .70
❑ 289 Glenn Murray RC .25 .11
❑ 290 Troy Percival RC 2.00 .90
❑ 291 Orlando Merced .25 .11
❑ 292 Peter Hoy .25 .11
❑ 293 Tony Fernandez .25 .11
❑ 294 Juan Guzman .25 .11
❑ 295 Jesse Barfield .25 .11
❑ 296 Sid Fernandez .25 .11
❑ 297 Scott Cepicky .25 .11
❑ 298 Garret Anderson RC 5.00 2.20
❑ 299 Cal Eldred .25 .11
❑ 300 Ryne Sandberg 2.00 .90
❑ 301 Jim Gantner .25 .11
❑ 302 Mariano Rivera RC 10.00 4.50
❑ 303 Ron Lockett RC .25 .11
❑ 304 Jose Offerman .25 .11
❑ 305 Dennis Martinez .50 .23
❑ 306 Luis Ortiz RC .25 .11
❑ 307 David Howard .25 .11
❑ 308 Russ Springer RC .25 .11
❑ 309 Chris Howard .25 .11
❑ 310 Kyle Abbott .25 .11
❑ 311 Aaron Sele RC 3.00 1.35
❑ 312 David Justice 1.00 .45
❑ 313 Pete O'Brien .25 .11
❑ 314 Greg Hansell RC .25 .11
❑ 315 Dave Winfield 1.50 .70
❑ 316 Lance Dickson .25 .11
❑ 317 Eric King .25 .11
❑ 318 Vaughn Eshelman RC .25 .11
❑ 319 Tim Belcher .25 .11
❑ 320 Andres Galarraga 1.00 .45
❑ 321 Scott Bullett RC .25 .11
❑ 322 Doug Strange .25 .11
❑ 323 Jerald Clark .25 .11
❑ 324 Dave Righetti .25 .11
❑ 325 Greg Hibbard .25 .11
❑ 326 Eric Hillman RC .25 .11
❑ 327 Shane Reynolds RC 1.00 .45
❑ 328 Chris Hammond .25 .11
❑ 329 Albert Belle 1.00 .45
❑ 330 Rich Becker RC .50 .23
❑ 331 Eddie Williams RC .25 .11
❑ 332 Donald Harris .25 .11
❑ 333 Dave Smith .25 .11
❑ 334 Steve Fireovid .25 .11
❑ 335 Steve Buechele .25 .11
❑ 336 Mike Schooler .25 .11
❑ 337 Kevin McReynolds .25 .11
❑ 338 Hensley Meulens .25 .11
❑ 339 Benji Gil RC .25 .11
❑ 340 Don Mattingly 4.00 1.80
❑ 341 Alvin Davis .25 .11
❑ 342 Alan Mills .25 .11
❑ 343 Kelly Downs .25 .11
❑ 344 Leo Gomez .25 .11
❑ 345 Tarrik Brock RC .25 .11
❑ 346 Ryan Turner RC .25 .11
❑ 347 John Smoltz .50 .23
❑ 348 Bill Sampen .25 .11
❑ 349 Paul Byrd RC .50 .23
❑ 350 Mike Bordick .25 .11
❑ 351 Jose Lind .25 .11
❑ 352 David Wells .50 .23
❑ 353 Barry Larkin 1.00 .45
❑ 354 Bruce Ruffin .25 .11
❑ 355 Luis Rivera .25 .11
❑ 356 Sid Bream .25 .11
❑ 357 Julian Vasquez RC .25 .11
❑ 358 Jason Bere RC .25 .11
❑ 359 Ben McDonald .25 .11
❑ 360 Scott Stahoviak RC .25 .11
❑ 361 Kirt Manwaring .25 .11
❑ 362 Jeff Johnson .25 .11
❑ 363 Rob Deer .25 .11
❑ 364 Tony Pena .25 .11
❑ 365 Melido Perez .25 .11
❑ 366 Clay Parker .25 .11
❑ 367 Dale Sveum .25 .11
❑ 368 Mike Scioscia .25 .11
❑ 369 Roger Salkeld .25 .11
❑ 370 Mike Stanley .25 .11
❑ 371 Jack McDowell .25 .11
❑ 372 Tim Wallach .25 .11
❑ 373 Billy Ripken .25 .11
❑ 374 Mike Christopher .25 .11
❑ 375 Paul Molitor 1.50 .70
❑ 376 Dave Stieb .25 .11
❑ 377 Pedro Guerrero .25 .11
❑ 378 Russ Swan .25 .11
❑ 379 Bob Ojeda .25 .11
❑ 380 Donn Pall .25 .11
❑ 381 Eddie Zosky .25 .11
❑ 382 Darnell Coles .25 .11
❑ 383 Tom Smith RC .25 .11
❑ 384 Mark McGwire 6.00 2.70
❑ 385 Gary Carter 1.00 .45
❑ 386 Rich Amaral RC .25 .11
❑ 387 Alan Embree RC .25 .11
❑ 388 Jonathan Hurst RC .25 .11
❑ 389 Bobby Jones RC 1.50 .70
❑ 390 Rico Rossy .25 .11
❑ 391 Dan Smith .25 .11
❑ 392 Terry Steinbach .25 .11
❑ 393 Jon Farrell RC .25 .11
❑ 394 Dave Anderson .25 .11
❑ 395 Benny Santiago .25 .11
❑ 396 Mark Wohlers .25 .11
❑ 397 Mo Vaughn .50 .23
❑ 398 Randy Kramer .25 .11
❑ 399 John Jaha RC 1.00 .45
❑ 400 Cal Ripken 6.00 2.70
❑ 401 Ryan Bowen .25 .11
❑ 402 Tim McIntosh .25 .11
❑ 403 Bernard Gilkey .50 .23
❑ 404 Junior Felix .25 .11
❑ 405 Cris Colon RC .25 .11
❑ 406 Marc Newfield .25 .11
❑ 407 Bernie Williams 1.50 .70
❑ 408 Jay Howell .25 .11
❑ 409 Zane Smith .25 .11
❑ 410 Jeff Shaw .25 .11
❑ 411 Kerry Woodson .25 .11
❑ 412 Wes Chamberlain .25 .11
❑ 413 Dave Mlicki RC .25 .11
❑ 414 Benny Distefano .25 .11
❑ 415 Kevin Rogers .25 .11
❑ 416 Tim Naehring .25 .11
❑ 417 Clemente Nunez RC .50 .23
❑ 418 Luis Sojo .25 .11
❑ 419 Kevin Ritz .25 .11
❑ 420 Omar Olivares .25 .11
❑ 421 Manuel Lee .25 .11
❑ 422 Julio Valera .25 .11
❑ 423 Omar Vizquel .50 .23
❑ 424 Darren Burton RC .25 .11
❑ 425 Mel Hall .25 .11
❑ 426 Dennis Powell .25 .11
❑ 427 Lee Stevens .50 .23
❑ 428 Glenn Davis .25 .11
❑ 429 Willie Greene .25 .11
❑ 430 Kevin Wickander .25 .11
❑ 431 Dennis Eckersley .50 .23
❑ 432 Joe Orsulak .25 .11
❑ 433 Eddie Murray 1.50 .70
❑ 434 Matt Stairs RC 1.50 .70
❑ 435 Wally Joyner .50 .23
❑ 436 Rondell White 2.00 .90
❑ 437 Rob Maurer .25 .11
❑ 438 Joe Redfield .25 .11
❑ 439 Mark Lewis .25 .11
❑ 440 Darren Daulton .50 .23
❑ 441 Mike Henneman .25 .11
❑ 442 John Cangelosi .25 .11
❑ 443 Vince Moore RC .25 .11
❑ 444 John Wehner .25 .11
❑ 445 Kent Hrbek .50 .23
❑ 446 Mark McLemore .25 .11
❑ 447 Bill Wegman .25 .11
❑ 448 Robby Thompson .25 .11
❑ 449 Mark Anthony RC .25 .11
❑ 450 Archi Cianfrocco RC .25 .11
❑ 451 Johnny Ruffin .25 .11
❑ 452 Javier Lopez 4.00 1.80
❑ 453 Greg Gohr .25 .11
❑ 454 Tim Scott .25 .11
❑ 455 Stan Belinda .25 .11
❑ 456 Darrin Jackson .25 .11
❑ 457 Chris Gardner .25 .11
❑ 458 Esteban Beltre .25 .11
❑ 459 Phil Plantier .25 .11
❑ 460 Jim Thome 8.00 3.60
❑ 461 Mike Piazza RC 70.00 32.00
❑ 462 Matt Sinatro .25 .11
❑ 463 Scott Servais .25 .11
❑ 464 Brian Jordan RC 5.00 2.20
❑ 465 Doug Drabek .25 .11
❑ 466 Carl Willis .25 .11
❑ 467 Bret Barberie .25 .11
❑ 468 Hal Morris .25 .11
❑ 469 Steve Sax .25 .11
❑ 470 Jerry Willard .25 .11
❑ 471 Dan Wilson .50 .23
❑ 472 Chris Hoiles .25 .11
❑ 473 Rheal Cormier .25 .11
❑ 474 John Morris .25 .11
❑ 475 Jeff Reardon .50 .23
❑ 476 Mark Leiter .25 .11
❑ 477 Tom Gordon .25 .11
❑ 478 Kent Bottenfield RC 1.00 .45
❑ 479 Gene Larkin .25 .11
❑ 480 Dwight Gooden .50 .23
❑ 481 B.J. Surhoff .50 .23
❑ 482 Andy Stankiewicz .25 .11
❑ 483 Tino Martinez .50 .23
❑ 484 Craig Biggio 1.00 .45
❑ 485 Denny Neagle 1.00 .45
❑ 486 Rusty Meacham .25 .11
❑ 487 Kal Daniels .25 .11
❑ 488 Dave Henderson .25 .11
❑ 489 Tim Costo .25 .11
❑ 490 Doug Davis .25 .11
❑ 491 Frank Viola .25 .11
❑ 492 Cory Snyder .25 .11
❑ 493 Chris Martin .25 .11
❑ 494 Dion James .25 .11
❑ 495 Randy Tomlin .25 .11
❑ 496 Greg Vaughn 1.00 .45
❑ 497 Dennis Cook .25 .11
❑ 498 Rosario Rodriguez .25 .11
❑ 499 Dave Staton .25 .11
❑ 500 George Brett 3.00 1.35
❑ 501 Brian Barnes .25 .11
❑ 502 Butch Henry RC .25 .11
❑ 503 Harold Reynolds .25 .11
❑ 504 David Nied RC .25 .11
❑ 505 Lee Smith .50 .23
❑ 506 Steve Chitren .25 .11
❑ 507 Ken Hill .25 .11
❑ 508 Robbie Beckett .25 .11
❑ 509 Troy Afenir .25 .11
❑ 510 Kelly Gruber .25 .11
❑ 511 Bret Boone 1.50 .70
❑ 512 Jeff Branson .25 .11
❑ 513 Mike Jackson .25 .11
❑ 514 Pete Harnisch .25 .11
❑ 515 Chad Kreuter .25 .11
❑ 516 Joe Vitko RC .25 .11
❑ 517 Orel Hershiser .50 .23
❑ 518 John Doherty RC .25 .11
❑ 519 Jay Bell .50 .23
❑ 520 Mark Langston .25 .11
❑ 521 Dann Howitt .25 .11
❑ 522 Bobby Reed RC .25 .11
❑ 523 Bobby Munoz RC .25 .11
❑ 524 Todd Ritchie .25 .11
❑ 525 Bip Roberts .25 .11
❑ 526 Pat Listach RC .25 .11
❑ 527 Scott Brosius RC 3.00 1.35
❑ 528 John Roper RC .25 .11
❑ 529 Phil Hiatt RC .25 .11
❑ 530 Denny Walling .25 .11
❑ 531 Carlos Baerga .25 .11
❑ 532 Manny Ramirez RC 40.00 18.00

- ❑ 533 Pat Clements UER .25 .11
  (Mistakenly numbered 553)
- ❑ 534 Ron Gant .50 .23
- ❑ 535 Pat Kelly .25 .11
- ❑ 536 Bill Spiers .25 .11
- ❑ 537 Darren Reed .25 .11
- ❑ 538 Ken Caminiti .50 .23
- ❑ 539 Butch Huskey RC .50 .23
- ❑ 540 Matt Nokes .25 .11
- ❑ 541 John Kruk .50 .23
- ❑ 542 John Jaha FOIL 1.50 .70
- ❑ 543 Justin Thompson RC .50 .23
- ❑ 544 Steve Hosey .25 .11
- ❑ 545 Joe Kmak .25 .11
- ❑ 546 John Franco .50 .23
- ❑ 547 Devon White .25 .11
- ❑ 548 Elston Hansen FOIL RC .25 .11
- ❑ 549 Ryan Klesko 3.00 1.35
- ❑ 550 Danny Tartabull .25 .11
- ❑ 551 Frank Thomas FOIL 3.00 1.35
- ❑ 552 Kevin Tapani .25 .11
- ❑ 553 Willie Banks .25 .11
  (See also 533)
- ❑ 554 B.J. Wallace RC FOIL .50 .23
- ❑ 555 Orlando Miller RC .25 .11
- ❑ 556 Mark Smith RC .25 .11
- ❑ 557 Tim Wallach FOIL .25 .11
- ❑ 558 Bill Gullickson .25 .11
- ❑ 559 Derek Bell FOIL .50 .23
- ❑ 560 Joe Randa FOIL RC 2.00 .90
- ❑ 561 Frank Seminara RC .25 .11
- ❑ 562 Mark Gardner .25 .11
- ❑ 563 Rick Greene RC FOIL .25 .11
- ❑ 564 Gary Gaetti .50 .23
- ❑ 565 Ozzie Guillen .25 .11
- ❑ 566 Charles Nagy FOIL .25 .11
- ❑ 567 Mike Milchin .25 .11
- ❑ 568 Ben Shelton RC .25 .11
- ❑ 569 Chris Roberts FOIL .25 .11
- ❑ 570 Ellis Burks .50 .23
- ❑ 571 Scott Scudder .25 .11
- ❑ 572 Jim Abbott FOIL .25 .11
- ❑ 573 Joe Carter .50 .23
- ❑ 574 Steve Finley .50 .23
- ❑ 575 Jim Olander FOIL .25 .11
- ❑ 576 Carlos Garcia .25 .11
- ❑ 577 Gregg Olson .25 .11
- ❑ 578 Greg Swindell FOIL .25 .11
- ❑ 579 Matt Williams FOIL 1.00 .45
- ❑ 580 Mark Grace 1.50 .70
- ❑ 581 Howard House RC FOIL .25 .11
- ❑ 582 Luis Polonia .25 .11
- ❑ 583 Erik Hanson .25 .11
- ❑ 584 Salomon Torres FOIL .25 .11
- ❑ 585 Carlton Fisk 1.50 .70
- ❑ 586 Bret Saberhagen .50 .23
- ❑ 587 Chad McConnell RC FOIL .50 .23
- ❑ 588 Jimmy Key .50 .23
- ❑ 589 Mike Macfarlane .25 .11
- ❑ 590 Barry Bonds FOIL 2.50 1.10
- ❑ 591 Jamie McAndrew .25 .11
- ❑ 592 Shane Mack .25 .11
- ❑ 593 Kerwin Moore .25 .11
- ❑ 594 Joe Oliver .25 .11
- ❑ 595 Chris Sabo .25 .11
- ❑ 596 Alex Gonzalez RC 1.00 .45
- ❑ 597 Brett Butler .50 .23
- ❑ 598 Mark Hutton RC .25 .11
- ❑ 599 Andy Benes FOIL .25 .11
- ❑ 600 Jose Canseco 2.00 .90
- ❑ 601 Darryl Kile .50 .23
- ❑ 602 Matt Stairs FOIL 1.00 .45
- ❑ 603 Robert Butler RC FOIL .25 .11
- ❑ 604 Willie McGee .50 .23
- ❑ 605 Jack McDowell FOIL .25 .11
- ❑ 606 Tom Candiotti .25 .11
- ❑ 607 Ed Martel RC .25 .11
- ❑ 608 Matt Mieske FOIL .25 .11
- ❑ 609 Darrin Fletcher .25 .11
- ❑ 610 Rafael Palmeiro 1.50 .70
- ❑ 611 Bill Swift FOIL .25 .11
- ❑ 612 Mike Mussina 2.50 1.10
- ❑ 613 Vince Coleman .25 .11
- ❑ 614 Scott Cepicky FOIL UER .25 .11
  (Bats: LEFLT)
- ❑ 615 Mike Greenwell .25 .11
- ❑ 616 Kevin McGehee RC .25 .11
- ❑ 617 Jeffrey Hammonds FOIL 2.00 .90
- ❑ 618 Scott Taylor .25 .11
- ❑ 619 Dave Otto .25 .11
- ❑ 620 Mark McGwire FOIL 6.00 2.70
- ❑ 621 Kevin Tatar RC .25 .11
- ❑ 622 Steve Farr .25 .11
- ❑ 623 Ryan Klesko FOIL 1.50 .70
- ❑ 624 Dave Fleming .25 .11
- ❑ 625 Andre Dawson 1.00 .45
- ❑ 626 Tino Martinez FOIL .50 .23
- ❑ 627 Chad Curtis RC 1.00 .45
- ❑ 628 Mickey Morandini .25 .11
- ❑ 629 Gregg Olson FOIL .25 .11
- ❑ 630 Lou Whitaker .50 .23
- ❑ 631 Arthur Rhodes .25 .11
- ❑ 632 Brandon Wilson RC .25 .11
- ❑ 633 Lance Jennings RC .25 .11
- ❑ 634 Allen Watson RC .25 .11
- ❑ 635 Len Dykstra .50 .23
- ❑ 636 Joe Girardi .50 .23
- ❑ 637 Kiki Hernandez RC FOIL .25 .11
- ❑ 638 Mike Hampton RC 6.00 2.70
- ❑ 639 Al Osuna .25 .11
- ❑ 640 Kevin Appier .50 .23
- ❑ 641 Rick Helling FOIL .50 .23
- ❑ 642 Jody Reed .25 .11
- ❑ 643 Ray Lankford 1.50 .70
- ❑ 644 John Olerud .50 .23
- ❑ 645 Paul Molitor FOIL 1.50 .70
- ❑ 646 Pat Borders .25 .11
- ❑ 647 Mike Morgan .25 .11
- ❑ 648 Larry Walker 1.00 .45
- ❑ 649 Pedro Castellano FOIL .25 .11
- ❑ 650 Fred McGriff 1.00 .45
- ❑ 651 Walt Weiss .25 .11
- ❑ 652 Calvin Murray RC FOIL .25 .11
- ❑ 653 Dave Nilsson .50 .23
- ❑ 654 Greg Pirkl RC .25 .11
- ❑ 655 Robin Ventura FOIL .50 .23
- ❑ 656 Mark Portugal .25 .11
- ❑ 657 Roger McDowell .25 .11
- ❑ 658 Rick Hirtensteiner RC .25 .11
  FOIL
- ❑ 659 Glenallen Hill .25 .11
- ❑ 660 Greg Gagne .25 .11
- ❑ 661 Charles Johnson FOIL 2.00 .90
- ❑ 662 Brian Hunter .25 .11
- ❑ 663 Mark Lemke .25 .11
- ❑ 664 Tim Belcher FOIL .25 .11
- ❑ 665 Rich DeLucia .25 .11
- ❑ 666 Bob Walk .25 .11
- ❑ 667 Joe Carter FOIL .50 .23
- ❑ 668 Jose Guzman .25 .11
- ❑ 669 Otis Nixon .25 .11
- ❑ 670 Phil Nevin FOIL 2.00 .90
- ❑ 671 Eric Davis .50 .23
- ❑ 672 Damion Easley RC 1.00 .45
- ❑ 673 Will Clark FOIL 1.50 .70
- ❑ 674 Mark Kiefer RC .25 .11
- ❑ 675 Ozzie Smith 2.00 .90
- ❑ 676 Manny Ramirez FOIL 6.00 2.70
- ❑ 677 Gregg Olson .25 .11
- ❑ 678 Cliff Floyd RC 4.00 1.80
- ❑ 679 Duane Singleton RC .25 .11
- ❑ 680 Jose Rijo .25 .11
- ❑ 681 Willie Randolph .50 .23
- ❑ 682 Michael Tucker FOIL RC 1.00 .45
- ❑ 683 Darren Lewis .25 .11
- ❑ 684 Dale Murphy 1.50 .70
- ❑ 685 Mike Pagliarulo .25 .11
- ❑ 686 Paul Miller RC .25 .11
- ❑ 687 Mike Robertson RC .25 .11
- ❑ 688 Mike Devereaux .25 .11
- ❑ 689 Pedro Astacio RC 2.00 .90
- ❑ 690 Alan Trammell 1.00 .45
- ❑ 691 Roger Clemens 3.00 1.35
- ❑ 692 Bud Black .25 .11
- ❑ 693 Turk Wendell RC .50 .23
- ❑ 694 Barry Larkin FOIL 1.00 .45
- ❑ 695 Todd Zeile .25 .11
- ❑ 696 Pat Hentgen .25 .11
- ❑ 697 Eddie Taubensee RC 1.00 .45
- ❑ 698 Guillermo Velasquez RC .25 .11
- ❑ 699 Tom Glavine 1.00 .45
- ❑ 700 Robin Yount 1.50 .70
- ❑ 701 Checklist 1-141 .25 .11
- ❑ 702 Checklist 142-282 .25 .11
- ❑ 703 Checklist 283-423 .25 .11
- ❑ 704 Checklist 424-564 .25 .11
- ❑ 705 Checklist 565-705 .25 .11

# 1993 Bowman

| | MINT | NRMT |
|---|---|---|
| COMPLETE SET (708) | 80.00 | 36.00 |

- ❑ 1 Glenn Davis .15 .07
- ❑ 2 Hector Roa RC .15 .07
- ❑ 3 Ken Ryan RC .15 .07
- ❑ 4 Derek Wallace RC .15 .07
- ❑ 5 Jorge Fabregas .15 .07
- ❑ 6 Joe Oliver .15 .07
- ❑ 7 Brandon Wilson .15 .07
- ❑ 8 Mark Thompson RC .15 .07
- ❑ 9 Tracy Sanders .15 .07
- ❑ 10 Rich Renteria .15 .07
- ❑ 11 Lou Whitaker .30 .14
- ❑ 12 Brian L. Hunter RC .75 .35
- ❑ 13 Joe Vitiello .15 .07
- ❑ 14 Eric Karros .30 .14
- ❑ 15 Joe Kmak .15 .07
- ❑ 16 Tavo Alvarez .15 .07
- ❑ 17 Steve Dunn RC .15 .07
- ❑ 18 Tony Fernandez .15 .07
- ❑ 19 Melido Perez .15 .07
- ❑ 20 Mike Lieberthal .30 .14
- ❑ 21 Terry Steinbach .15 .07
- ❑ 22 Stan Belinda .15 .07
- ❑ 23 Jay Buhner .30 .14
- ❑ 24 Allen Watson .15 .07
- ❑ 25 Daryl Henderson RC .15 .07
- ❑ 26 Ray McDavid RC .15 .07
- ❑ 27 Shawn Green 2.00 .90
- ❑ 28 Bud Black .15 .07
- ❑ 29 Sherman Obando RC .15 .07
- ❑ 30 Mike Hostetler RC .15 .07
- ❑ 31 Nate Minchey RC .15 .07
- ❑ 32 Randy Myers .30 .14
- ❑ 33 Brian Grebeck .15 .07
- ❑ 34 John Roper .15 .07
- ❑ 35 Larry Thomas .15 .07
- ❑ 36 Alex Cole .15 .07
- ❑ 37 Tom Kramer RC .15 .07
- ❑ 38 Matt Whisenant RC .15 .07
- ❑ 39 Chris Gomez RC .30 .14
- ❑ 40 Luis Gonzalez .30 .14
- ❑ 41 Kevin Appier .30 .14
- ❑ 42 Omar Daal RC .30 .14
- ❑ 43 Duane Singleton .15 .07
- ❑ 44 Bill Risley .15 .07
- ❑ 45 Pat Meares RC .15 .07
- ❑ 46 Butch Huskey .15 .07
- ❑ 47 Bobby Munoz .15 .07
- ❑ 48 Juan Bell .15 .07
- ❑ 49 Scott Lydy RC .15 .07
- ❑ 50 Dennis Moeller .15 .07
- ❑ 51 Marc Newfield .15 .07
- ❑ 52 Tripp Cromer RC .15 .07
- ❑ 53 Kurt Miller .15 .07
- ❑ 54 Jim Pena .15 .07
- ❑ 55 Juan Guzman .15 .07
- ❑ 56 Matt Williams .30 .14

| | | | |
|---|---|---|---|
| ❑ 57 | Harold Reynolds | .15 | .07 |
| ❑ 58 | Donnie Elliott RC | .15 | .07 |
| ❑ 59 | Jon Shave RC | .15 | .07 |
| ❑ 60 | Kevin Roberson RC | .15 | .07 |
| ❑ 61 | Hilly Hathaway RC | .15 | .07 |
| ❑ 62 | Jose Rijo | .15 | .07 |
| ❑ 63 | Kerry Taylor RC | .15 | .07 |
| ❑ 64 | Ryan Hawblitzel | .15 | .07 |
| ❑ 65 | Glenallen Hill | .15 | .07 |
| ❑ 66 | Ramon Martinez RC | .30 | .14 |
| ❑ 67 | Travis Fryman | .30 | .14 |
| ❑ 68 | Tom Nevers | .15 | .07 |
| ❑ 69 | Phil Hiatt | .15 | .07 |
| ❑ 70 | Tim Wallach | .15 | .07 |
| ❑ 71 | B.J. Surhoff | .30 | .14 |
| ❑ 72 | Rondell White | .30 | .14 |
| ❑ 73 | Denny Hocking RC | .15 | .07 |
| ❑ 74 | Mike Oquist RC | .15 | .07 |
| ❑ 75 | Paul O'Neill | .30 | .14 |
| ❑ 76 | Willie Banks | .15 | .07 |
| ❑ 77 | Bob Welch | .15 | .07 |
| ❑ 78 | Jose Sandoval RC | .15 | .07 |
| ❑ 79 | Bill Haselman | .15 | .07 |
| ❑ 80 | Rheal Cormier | .15 | .07 |
| ❑ 81 | Dean Palmer | .30 | .14 |
| ❑ 82 | Pat Gomez RC | .15 | .07 |
| ❑ 83 | Steve Karsay | .30 | .14 |
| ❑ 84 | Carl Hanselman RC | .15 | .07 |
| ❑ 85 | T.R. Lewis RC | .15 | .07 |
| ❑ 86 | Chipper Jones | 2.00 | .90 |
| ❑ 87 | Scott Hatteberg | .15 | .07 |
| ❑ 88 | Greg Hibbard | .15 | .07 |
| ❑ 89 | Lance Painter RC | .15 | .07 |
| ❑ 90 | Chad Mottola RC | .15 | .07 |
| ❑ 91 | Jason Bere | .15 | .07 |
| ❑ 92 | Dante Bichette | .30 | .14 |
| ❑ 93 | Sandy Alomar Jr. | .30 | .14 |
| ❑ 94 | Carl Everett | .30 | .14 |
| ❑ 95 | Danny Bautista RC | .15 | .07 |
| ❑ 96 | Steve Finley | .30 | .14 |
| ❑ 97 | David Cone | .30 | .14 |
| ❑ 98 | Todd Hollandsworth | .15 | .07 |
| ❑ 99 | Matt Mieske | .15 | .07 |
| ❑ 100 | Larry Walker | .30 | .14 |
| ❑ 101 | Shane Mack | .15 | .07 |
| ❑ 102 | Aaron Ledesma RC | .15 | .07 |
| ❑ 103 | Andy Pettitte RC | 4.00 | 1.80 |
| ❑ 104 | Kevin Stocker | .15 | .07 |
| ❑ 105 | Mike Mohler RC | .15 | .07 |
| ❑ 106 | Tony Menendez | .15 | .07 |
| ❑ 107 | Derek Lowe | .30 | .14 |
| ❑ 108 | Basil Shabazz | .15 | .07 |
| ❑ 109 | Dan Smith | .15 | .07 |
| ❑ 110 | Scott Sanders RC | .15 | .07 |
| ❑ 111 | Todd Stottlemyre | .15 | .07 |
| ❑ 112 | Benji Simonton RC | .15 | .07 |
| ❑ 113 | Rick Sutcliffe | .30 | .14 |
| ❑ 114 | Lee Heath RC | .15 | .07 |
| ❑ 115 | Jeff Russell | .15 | .07 |
| ❑ 116 | Dave Stevens RC | .15 | .07 |
| ❑ 117 | Mark Holzemer RC | .15 | .07 |
| ❑ 118 | Tim Belcher | .15 | .07 |
| ❑ 119 | Bobby Thigpen | .15 | .07 |
| ❑ 120 | Roger Bailey RC | .15 | .07 |
| ❑ 121 | Tony Mitchell RC | .15 | .07 |
| ❑ 122 | Junior Felix | .15 | .07 |
| ❑ 123 | Rich Robertson RC | .15 | .07 |
| ❑ 124 | Andy Cook RC | .15 | .07 |
| ❑ 125 | Brian Bevil RC | .15 | .07 |
| ❑ 126 | Darryl Strawberry | .30 | .14 |
| ❑ 127 | Cal Eldred | .15 | .07 |
| ❑ 128 | Cliff Floyd | .30 | .14 |
| ❑ 129 | Alan Newman | .15 | .07 |
| ❑ 130 | Howard Johnson | .15 | .07 |
| ❑ 131 | Jim Abbott | .30 | .14 |
| ❑ 132 | Chad McConnell | .15 | .07 |
| ❑ 133 | Miguel Jimenez RC | .15 | .07 |
| ❑ 134 | Brett Backlund RC | .15 | .07 |
| ❑ 135 | John Cummings RC | .15 | .07 |
| ❑ 136 | Brian Barber | .15 | .07 |
| ❑ 137 | Rafael Palmeiro | .60 | .25 |
| ❑ 138 | Tim Worrell RC | .15 | .07 |
| ❑ 139 | Jose Pett RC | .30 | .14 |
| ❑ 140 | Barry Bonds | 1.00 | .25 |
| ❑ 141 | Damon Buford | .15 | .07 |
| ❑ 142 | Jeff Blauser | .15 | .07 |
| ❑ 143 | Frankie Rodriguez | .15 | .07 |
| ❑ 144 | Mike Morgan | .15 | .07 |
| ❑ 145 | Gary DiSarcina | .15 | .07 |
| ❑ 146 | Pokey Reese | .30 | .14 |
| ❑ 147 | Johnny Ruffin | .15 | .07 |
| ❑ 148 | David Nied | .15 | .07 |
| ❑ 149 | Charles Nagy | .15 | .07 |
| ❑ 150 | Mike Myers RC | .15 | .07 |
| ❑ 151 | Kenny Carlyle RC | .15 | .07 |
| ❑ 152 | Eric Anthony | .15 | .07 |
| ❑ 153 | Jose Lind | .15 | .07 |
| ❑ 154 | Pedro Martinez | 1.50 | .70 |
| ❑ 155 | Mark Kiefer | .15 | .07 |
| ❑ 156 | Tim Laker RC | .15 | .07 |
| ❑ 157 | Pat Mahomes | .15 | .07 |
| ❑ 158 | Bobby Bonilla | .30 | .14 |
| ❑ 159 | Domingo Jean | .15 | .07 |
| ❑ 160 | Darren Daulton | .30 | .14 |
| ❑ 161 | Mark McGwire | 2.50 | 1.10 |
| ❑ 162 | Jason Kendall RC | 4.00 | 1.80 |
| ❑ 163 | Desi Relaford | .30 | .14 |
| ❑ 164 | Ozzie Canseco | .15 | .07 |
| ❑ 165 | Rick Helling | .30 | .14 |
| ❑ 166 | Steve Pegues RC | .15 | .07 |
| ❑ 167 | Paul Molitor | .60 | .25 |
| ❑ 168 | Larry Carter | .15 | .07 |
| ❑ 169 | Arthur Rhodes | .15 | .07 |
| ❑ 170 | Damon Hollins RC | .15 | .07 |
| ❑ 171 | Frank Viola | .15 | .07 |
| ❑ 172 | Steve Trachsel RC | .30 | .14 |
| ❑ 173 | J.T. Snow RC | 1.50 | .70 |
| ❑ 174 | Keith Gordon RC | .15 | .07 |
| ❑ 175 | Carlton Fisk | .60 | .25 |
| ❑ 176 | Jason Bates RC | .15 | .07 |
| ❑ 177 | Mike Crosby RC | .15 | .07 |
| ❑ 178 | Benny Santiago | .15 | .07 |
| ❑ 179 | Mike Moore | .15 | .07 |
| ❑ 180 | Jeff Juden | .15 | .07 |
| ❑ 181 | Darren Burton | .15 | .07 |
| ❑ 182 | Todd Williams RC | .15 | .07 |
| ❑ 183 | John Jaha | .15 | .07 |
| ❑ 184 | Mike Lansing RC | .30 | .14 |
| ❑ 185 | Pedro Grifol RC | .15 | .07 |
| ❑ 186 | Vince Coleman | .15 | .07 |
| ❑ 187 | Pat Kelly | .15 | .07 |
| ❑ 188 | Clemente Alvarez RC | .15 | .07 |
| ❑ 189 | Ron Darling | .15 | .07 |
| ❑ 190 | Orlando Merced | .15 | .07 |
| ❑ 191 | Chris Bosio | .15 | .07 |
| ❑ 192 | Steve Dixon RC | .15 | .07 |
| ❑ 193 | Doug Dascenzo | .15 | .07 |
| ❑ 194 | Ray Holbert RC | .15 | .07 |
| ❑ 195 | Howard Battle | .15 | .07 |
| ❑ 196 | Willie McGee | .30 | .14 |
| ❑ 197 | John O'Donoghue RC | .15 | .07 |
| ❑ 198 | Steve Avery | .15 | .07 |
| ❑ 199 | Greg Blosser | .15 | .07 |
| ❑ 200 | Ryne Sandberg | .75 | .35 |
| ❑ 201 | Joe Grahe | .15 | .07 |
| ❑ 202 | Dan Wilson | .30 | .14 |
| ❑ 203 | Domingo Martinez RC | .15 | .07 |
| ❑ 204 | Andres Galarraga | .30 | .14 |
| ❑ 205 | Jamie Taylor RC | .15 | .07 |
| ❑ 206 | Darrell Whitmore RC | .15 | .07 |
| ❑ 207 | Ben Blomdahl RC | .15 | .07 |
| ❑ 208 | Doug Drabek | .15 | .07 |
| ❑ 209 | Keith Miller | .15 | .07 |
| ❑ 210 | Billy Ashley | .15 | .07 |
| ❑ 211 | Mike Farrell RC | .15 | .07 |
| ❑ 212 | John Wetteland | .30 | .14 |
| ❑ 213 | Randy Tomlin | .15 | .07 |
| ❑ 214 | Sid Fernandez | .15 | .07 |
| ❑ 215 | Quilvio Veras RC | .75 | .35 |
| ❑ 216 | Dave Hollins | .15 | .07 |
| ❑ 217 | Mike Neill | .15 | .07 |
| ❑ 218 | Andy Van Slyke | .30 | .14 |
| ❑ 219 | Bret Boone | .30 | .14 |
| ❑ 220 | Tom Pagnozzi | .15 | .07 |
| ❑ 221 | Mike Welch RC | .15 | .07 |
| ❑ 222 | Frank Seminara | .15 | .07 |
| ❑ 223 | Ron Villone | .15 | .07 |
| ❑ 224 | D.J. Thielen RC | .15 | .07 |
| ❑ 225 | Cal Ripken | 2.50 | 1.10 |
| ❑ 226 | Pedro Borbon Jr. RC | .15 | .07 |
| ❑ 227 | Carlos Quintana | .15 | .07 |
| ❑ 228 | Tommy Shields | .15 | .07 |
| ❑ 229 | Tim Salmon | .30 | .14 |
| ❑ 230 | John Smiley | .15 | .07 |
| ❑ 231 | Ellis Burks | .30 | .14 |
| ❑ 232 | Pedro Castellano | .15 | .07 |
| ❑ 233 | Paul Byrd | .15 | .07 |
| ❑ 234 | Bryan Harvey | .15 | .07 |
| ❑ 235 | Scott Livingstone | .15 | .07 |
| ❑ 236 | James Mouton RC | .15 | .07 |
| ❑ 237 | Joe Randa | .15 | .07 |
| ❑ 238 | Pedro Astacio | .30 | .14 |
| ❑ 239 | Darryl Hamilton | .15 | .07 |
| ❑ 240 | Joey Eischen RC | .15 | .07 |
| ❑ 241 | Edgar Herrera RC | .15 | .07 |
| ❑ 242 | Dwight Gooden | .30 | .14 |
| ❑ 243 | Sam Militello | .15 | .07 |
| ❑ 244 | Ron Blazier RC | .15 | .07 |
| ❑ 245 | Ruben Sierra | .15 | .07 |
| ❑ 246 | Al Martin | .15 | .07 |
| ❑ 247 | Mike Felder | .15 | .07 |
| ❑ 248 | Bob Tewksbury | .15 | .07 |
| ❑ 249 | Craig Lefferts | .15 | .07 |
| ❑ 250 | Luis Lopez RC | .15 | .07 |
| ❑ 251 | Devon White | .15 | .07 |
| ❑ 252 | Will Clark | .60 | .25 |
| ❑ 253 | Mark Smith | .15 | .07 |
| ❑ 254 | Terry Pendleton | .30 | .14 |
| ❑ 255 | Aaron Sele | .60 | .25 |
| ❑ 256 | Jose Viera RC | .15 | .07 |
| ❑ 257 | Damion Easley | .15 | .07 |
| ❑ 258 | Rod Lofton RC | .15 | .07 |
| ❑ 259 | Chris Snopek RC | .30 | .14 |
| ❑ 260 | Quinton McCracken RC | .30 | .14 |
| ❑ 261 | Mike Matthews RC | .15 | .07 |
| ❑ 262 | Hector Carrasco RC | .15 | .07 |
| ❑ 263 | Rick Greene | .15 | .07 |
| ❑ 264 | Chris Holt RC | .15 | .07 |
| ❑ 265 | George Brett | 1.25 | .55 |
| ❑ 266 | Rick Gorecki RC | .15 | .07 |
| ❑ 267 | Francisco Gamez RC | .15 | .07 |
| ❑ 268 | Marquis Grissom | .15 | .07 |
| ❑ 269 | Kevin Tapani UER (Misspelled Tapan on card front) | .15 | .07 |
| ❑ 270 | Ryan Thompson | .15 | .07 |
| ❑ 271 | Gerald Williams | .15 | .07 |
| ❑ 272 | Paul Fletcher RC | .15 | .07 |
| ❑ 273 | Lance Blankenship | .15 | .07 |
| ❑ 274 | Marty Neff RC | .15 | .07 |
| ❑ 275 | Shawn Estes | .60 | .25 |
| ❑ 276 | Rene Arocha RC | .15 | .07 |
| ❑ 277 | Scott Eyre RC | .15 | .07 |
| ❑ 278 | Phil Plantier | .15 | .07 |
| ❑ 279 | Paul Spoljaric RC | .15 | .07 |
| ❑ 280 | Chris Gambs | .15 | .07 |
| ❑ 281 | Harold Baines | .30 | .14 |
| ❑ 282 | Jose Oliva | .15 | .07 |
| ❑ 283 | Matt Whiteside RC | .15 | .07 |
| ❑ 284 | Brant Brown RC | .30 | .14 |
| ❑ 285 | Russ Springer | .15 | .07 |
| ❑ 286 | Chris Sabo | .15 | .07 |
| ❑ 287 | Ozzie Guillen | .15 | .07 |
| ❑ 288 | Marcus Moore RC | .15 | .07 |
| ❑ 289 | Chad Ogea | .30 | .14 |
| ❑ 290 | Walt Weiss | .15 | .07 |
| ❑ 291 | Brian Edmondson | .15 | .07 |
| ❑ 292 | Jimmy Gonzalez | .15 | .07 |
| ❑ 293 | Danny Miceli RC | .15 | .07 |
| ❑ 294 | Jose Offerman | .15 | .07 |
| ❑ 295 | Greg Vaughn | .30 | .14 |
| ❑ 296 | Frank Bolick | .15 | .07 |
| ❑ 297 | Mike Maksudian RC | .15 | .07 |
| ❑ 298 | John Franco | .30 | .14 |
| ❑ 299 | Danny Tartabull | .15 | .07 |
| ❑ 300 | Len Dykstra | .30 | .14 |
| ❑ 301 | Bobby Witt | .15 | .07 |
| ❑ 302 | Trey Beamon RC | .15 | .07 |
| ❑ 303 | Tino Martinez | .30 | .14 |
| ❑ 304 | Aaron Holbert | .15 | .07 |
| ❑ 305 | Juan Gonzalez | .60 | .25 |
| ❑ 306 | Billy Hall RC | .15 | .07 |
| ❑ 307 | Duane Ward | .15 | .07 |
| ❑ 308 | Rod Beck | .15 | .07 |
| ❑ 309 | Jose Mercedes RC | .15 | .07 |
| ❑ 310 | Otis Nixon | .15 | .07 |
| ❑ 311 | Gettys Glaze RC | .15 | .07 |
| ❑ 312 | Candy Maldonado | .15 | .07 |

❑ 313 Chad Curtis .15 .07
❑ 314 Tim Costo .15 .07
❑ 315 Mike Robertson .15 .07
❑ 316 Nigel Wilson .15 .07
❑ 317 Greg McMichael RC .15 .07
❑ 318 Scott Pose RC .15 .07
❑ 319 Ivan Cruz .15 .07
❑ 320 Greg Swindell .15 .07
❑ 321 Kevin McReynolds .15 .07
❑ 322 Tom Candiotti .15 .07
❑ 323 Rob Wishnevski RC .15 .07
❑ 324 Ken Hill .15 .07
❑ 325 Kirby Puckett 1.50 .70
❑ 326 Tim Bogar RC .15 .07
❑ 327 Mariano Rivera 1.00 .45
❑ 328 Mitch Williams .15 .07
❑ 329 Craig Paquette .15 .07
❑ 330 Jay Bell .30 .14
❑ 331 Jose Martinez RC .15 .07
❑ 332 Rob Deer .15 .07
❑ 333 Brook Fordyce .15 .07
❑ 334 Matt Nokes .15 .07
❑ 335 Derek Lee .15 .07
❑ 336 Paul Ellis RC .15 .07
❑ 337 Desi Wilson RC .15 .07
❑ 338 Roberto Alomar .60 .25
❑ 339 Jim Tatum FOIL RC .15 .07
❑ 340 J.T. Snow FOIL .60 .25
❑ 341 Tim Salmon FOIL .30 .14
❑ 342 Russ Davis FOIL RC 1.00 .45
❑ 343 Javier Lopez FOIL .30 .14
❑ 344 Troy O'Leary FOIL RC 1.00 .45
❑ 345 Marty Cordova FOIL RC .75 .35
❑ 346 Bubba Smith RC FOIL .15 .07
❑ 347 Chipper Jones FOIL 2.00 .90
❑ 348 Jessie Hollins FOIL .15 .07
❑ 349 Willie Greene FOIL .15 .07
❑ 350 Mark Thompson FOIL .15 .07
❑ 351 Nigel Wilson FOIL .15 .07
❑ 352 Todd Jones FOIL .30 .14
❑ 353 Raul Mondesi FOIL .30 .14
❑ 354 Cliff Floyd FOIL .30 .14
❑ 355 Bobby Jones FOIL .30 .14
❑ 356 Kevin Stocker FOIL .15 .07
❑ 357 Midre Cummings FOIL .15 .07
❑ 358 Allen Watson FOIL .15 .07
❑ 359 Ray McDavid FOIL .15 .07
❑ 360 Steve Hosey FOIL .15 .07
❑ 361 Brad Pennington FOIL .15 .07
❑ 362 Frankie Rodriguez FOIL .15 .07
❑ 363 Troy Percival FOIL .15 .07
❑ 364 Jason Bere FOIL .15 .07
❑ 365 Manny Ramirez FOIL 1.50 .70
❑ 366 Justin Thompson FOIL .15 .07
❑ 367 Joe Vitiello FOIL .15 .07
❑ 368 Tyrone Hill FOIL .15 .07
❑ 369 David McCarty FOIL .15 .07
❑ 370 Brien Taylor FOIL .15 .07
❑ 371 Todd Van Poppel FOIL .15 .07
❑ 372 Marc Newfield FOIL .15 .07
❑ 373 Terrell Lowery RC FOIL .15 .07
❑ 374 Alex Gonzalez FOIL .30 .14
❑ 375 Ken Griffey Jr. 2.50 1.10
❑ 376 Donovan Osborne .15 .07
❑ 377 Ritchie Moody RC .15 .07
❑ 378 Shane Andrews .15 .07
❑ 379 Carlos Delgado 1.25 .55
❑ 380 Bill Swift .15 .07
❑ 381 Leo Gomez .15 .07
❑ 382 Ron Gant .30 .14
❑ 383 Scott Fletcher .15 .07
❑ 384 Matt Walbeck RC .15 .07
❑ 385 Chuck Finley .30 .14
❑ 386 Kevin Mitchell .30 .14
❑ 387 Wilson Alvarez UER .15 .07
(Misspelled Alverez on card front)
❑ 388 John Burke RC .15 .07
❑ 389 Alan Embree .15 .07
❑ 390 Trevor Hoffman .60 .25
❑ 391 Alan Trammell .30 .14
❑ 392 Todd Jones .30 .14
❑ 393 Felix Jose .15 .07
❑ 394 Orel Hershiser .30 .14
❑ 395 Pat Listach .15 .07
❑ 396 Gabe White .15 .07
❑ 397 Dan Serafini RC .15 .07
❑ 398 Todd Hundley .15 .07
❑ 399 Wade Boggs .75 .35
❑ 400 Tyler Green .15 .07
❑ 401 Mike Bordick .15 .07
❑ 402 Scott Bullett .15 .07
❑ 403 LaGrande Russell RC .15 .07
❑ 404 Ray Lankford .30 .14
❑ 405 Nolan Ryan 3.00 1.35
❑ 406 Robbie Beckett .15 .07
❑ 407 Brent Bowers RC .15 .07
❑ 408 Adell Davenport RC .15 .07
❑ 409 Brady Anderson .30 .14
❑ 410 Tom Glavine .30 .14
❑ 411 Doug Hecker RC .15 .07
❑ 412 Jose Guzman .15 .07
❑ 413 Luis Polonia .15 .07
❑ 414 Brian Williams .15 .07
❑ 415 Bo Jackson .30 .14
❑ 416 Eric Young .15 .07
❑ 417 Kenny Lofton .30 .14
❑ 418 Orestes Destrade .15 .07
❑ 419 Tony Phillips .15 .07
❑ 420 Jeff Bagwell .75 .35
❑ 421 Mark Gardner .15 .07
❑ 422 Brett Butler .30 .14
❑ 423 Graeme Lloyd RC .15 .07
❑ 424 Delino DeShields .30 .14
❑ 425 Scott Erickson .15 .07
❑ 426 Jeff Kent .60 .25
❑ 427 Jimmy Key .30 .14
❑ 428 Mickey Morandini .15 .07
❑ 429 Marcos Armas RC .15 .07
❑ 430 Don Slaught .15 .07
❑ 431 Randy Johnson .75 .35
❑ 432 Omar Olivares .15 .07
❑ 433 Charlie Leibrandt .15 .07
❑ 434 Kurt Stillwell .15 .07
❑ 435 Scott Brow RC .15 .07
❑ 436 Robby Thompson .15 .07
❑ 437 Ben McDonald .15 .07
❑ 438 Deion Sanders .30 .14
❑ 439 Tony Pena .15 .07
❑ 440 Mark Grace .60 .25
❑ 441 Eduardo Perez .15 .07
❑ 442 Tim Pugh RC .15 .07
❑ 443 Scott Ruffcorn .15 .07
❑ 444 Jay Gainer RC .15 .07
❑ 445 Albert Belle .30 .14
❑ 446 Bret Barberie .15 .07
❑ 447 Justin Mashore .15 .07
❑ 448 Pete Harnisch .15 .07
❑ 449 Greg Gagne .15 .07
❑ 450 Eric Davis .30 .14
❑ 451 Dave Mlicki .15 .07
❑ 452 Moises Alou .30 .14
❑ 453 Rick Aguilera .15 .07
❑ 454 Eddie Murray .60 .25
❑ 455 Bob Wickman .15 .07
❑ 456 Wes Chamberlain .15 .07
❑ 457 Brent Gates .15 .07
❑ 458 Paul Wagner .15 .07
❑ 459 Mike Hampton .60 .25
❑ 460 Ozzie Smith .75 .35
❑ 461 Tom Henke .15 .07
❑ 462 Ricky Gutierrez .15 .07
❑ 463 Jack Morris .30 .14
❑ 464 Joel Chimelis .15 .07
❑ 465 Gregg Olson .15 .07
❑ 466 Javier Lopez .30 .14
❑ 467 Scott Cooper .15 .07
❑ 468 Willie Wilson .15 .07
❑ 469 Mark Langston .15 .07
❑ 470 Barry Larkin .60 .25
❑ 471 Rod Bolton .15 .07
❑ 472 Freddie Benavides .15 .07
❑ 473 Ken Ramos RC .15 .07
❑ 474 Chuck Carr .15 .07
❑ 475 Cecil Fielder .30 .14
❑ 476 Eddie Taubensee .15 .07
❑ 477 Chris Eddy RC .15 .07
❑ 478 Greg Hansell .15 .07
❑ 479 Kevin Reimer .15 .07
❑ 480 Dennis Martinez .30 .14
❑ 481 Chuck Knoblauch .30 .14
❑ 482 Mike Draper .15 .07
❑ 483 Spike Owen .15 .07
❑ 484 Terry Mulholland .15 .07
❑ 485 Dennis Eckersley .30 .14
❑ 486 Blas Minor .15 .07
❑ 487 Dave Fleming .15 .07
❑ 488 Dan Cholowsky .15 .07
❑ 489 Ivan Rodriguez .75 .35
❑ 490 Gary Sheffield .60 .25
❑ 491 Ed Sprague .15 .07
❑ 492 Steve Hosey .15 .07
❑ 493 Jimmy Haynes RC .30 .14
❑ 494 John Smoltz .30 .14
❑ 495 Andre Dawson .30 .14
❑ 496 Rey Sanchez .15 .07
❑ 497 Ty Van Burkleo .15 .07
❑ 498 Bobby Ayala RC .15 .07
❑ 499 Tim Raines .30 .14
❑ 500 Charlie Hayes .15 .07
❑ 501 Paul Sorrento .15 .07
❑ 502 Richie Lewis RC .15 .07
❑ 503 Jason Pfaff RC .15 .07
❑ 504 Ken Caminiti .30 .14
❑ 505 Mike Macfarlane .15 .07
❑ 506 Jody Reed .15 .07
❑ 507 Bobby Hughes RC .15 .07
❑ 508 Wil Cordero .15 .07
❑ 509 George Tsamis RC .15 .07
❑ 510 Bret Saberhagen .30 .14
❑ 511 Derek Jeter RC 30.00 13.50
❑ 512 Gene Schall .15 .07
❑ 513 Curtis Shaw .15 .07
❑ 514 Steve Cooke .15 .07
❑ 515 Edgar Martinez .30 .14
❑ 516 Mike Milchin .15 .07
❑ 517 Billy Ripken .15 .07
❑ 518 Andy Benes .15 .07
❑ 519 Juan de la Rosa RC .15 .07
❑ 520 John Burkett .15 .07
❑ 521 Alex Ochoa .15 .07
❑ 522 Tony Tarasco RC .15 .07
❑ 523 Luis Ortiz .15 .07
❑ 524 Rick Wilkins .15 .07
❑ 525 Chris Turner RC .15 .07
❑ 526 Rob Dibble .15 .07
❑ 527 Jack McDowell .15 .07
❑ 528 Daryl Boston .15 .07
❑ 529 Bill Wertz RC .15 .07
❑ 530 Charlie Hough .30 .14
❑ 531 Sean Bergman .15 .07
❑ 532 Doug Jones .15 .07
❑ 533 Jeff Montgomery .30 .14
❑ 534 Roger Cedeno RC 1.00 .45
❑ 535 Robin Yount .30 .14
❑ 536 Mo Vaughn .30 .14
❑ 537 Brian Harper .15 .07
❑ 538 Juan Castillo .15 .07
❑ 539 Steve Farr .15 .07
❑ 540 John Kruk .30 .14
❑ 541 Troy Neel .15 .07
❑ 542 Danny Clyburn RC .15 .07
❑ 543 Jim Converse RC .15 .07
❑ 544 Gregg Jefferies .15 .07
❑ 545 Jose Canseco .75 .35
❑ 546 Julio Bruno RC .15 .07
❑ 547 Rob Butler .15 .07
❑ 548 Royce Clayton .15 .07
❑ 549 Chris Hoiles .15 .07
❑ 550 Greg Maddux 1.50 .70
❑ 551 Joe Ciccarella RC .30 .14
❑ 552 Ozzie Timmons .30 .14
❑ 553 Chili Davis .30 .14
❑ 554 Brian Koelling .15 .07
❑ 555 Frank Thomas 1.25 .55
❑ 556 Vinny Castilla 2.00 .90
❑ 557 Reggie Jefferson .30 .14
❑ 558 Rob Natal .15 .07
❑ 559 Mike Henneman .15 .07
❑ 560 Craig Biggio .30 .14
❑ 561 Billy Brewer .15 .07
❑ 562 Dan Melendez .15 .07
❑ 563 Kenny Felder RC .15 .07
❑ 564 Miguel Batista RC .15 .07
❑ 565 Dave Winfield .60 .25
❑ 566 Al Shirley .15 .07
❑ 567 Robert Eenhoorn .15 .07
❑ 568 Mike Williams .15 .07

❑ 569 Tanyon Sturtze RC .15 .07
❑ 570 Tim Wakefield .15 .07
❑ 571 Greg Pirkl .15 .07
❑ 572 Sean Lowe RC .15 .07
❑ 573 Terry Burrows RC .15 .07
❑ 574 Kevin Higgins .15 .07
❑ 575 Joe Carter .30 .14
❑ 576 Kevin Rogers .15 .07
❑ 577 Manny Alexander .15 .07
❑ 578 David Justice .30 .14
❑ 579 Brian Conroy RC .15 .07
❑ 580 Jessie Hollins .15 .07
❑ 581 Ron Watson RC .15 .07
❑ 582 Bip Roberts .15 .07
❑ 583 Tom Urbani RC .15 .07
❑ 584 Jason Hutchins RC .15 .07
❑ 585 Carlos Baerga .15 .07
❑ 586 Jeff Mutis .15 .07
❑ 587 Justin Thompson .15 .07
❑ 588 Orlando Miller .15 .07
❑ 589 Brian McRae .15 .07
❑ 590 Ramon Martinez .15 .07
❑ 591 Dave Nilsson .30 .14
❑ 592 Jose Vidro RC 6.00 2.70
❑ 593 Rich Becker .15 .07
❑ 594 Preston Wilson RC 2.50 1.10
❑ 595 Don Mattingly 1.50 .70
❑ 596 Tony Longmire .15 .07
❑ 597 Kevin Seitzer .15 .07
❑ 598 Midre Cummings RC .15 .07
❑ 599 Omar Vizquel .30 .14
❑ 600 Lee Smith .30 .14
❑ 601 David Hulse RC .15 .07
❑ 602 Darrell Sherman RC .15 .07
❑ 603 Alex Gonzalez .30 .14
❑ 604 Geronimo Pena .15 .07
❑ 605 Mike Devereaux .15 .07
❑ 606 Sterling Hitchcock RC .75 .35
❑ 607 Mike Greenwell .15 .07
❑ 608 Steve Buechele .15 .07
❑ 609 Troy Percival .15 .07
❑ 610 Roberto Kelly .15 .07
❑ 611 James Baldwin RC 3.00 1.35
❑ 612 Jerald Clark .15 .07
❑ 613 Albie Lopez RC .15 .07
❑ 614 Dave Magadan .15 .07
❑ 615 Mickey Tettleton .15 .07
❑ 616 Sean Runyan RC .15 .07
❑ 617 Bob Hamelin .15 .07
❑ 618 Raul Mondesi .30 .14
❑ 619 Tyrone Hill .15 .07
❑ 620 Darrin Fletcher .15 .07
❑ 621 Mike Trombley .15 .07
❑ 622 Jeromy Burnitz .30 .14
❑ 623 Bernie Williams .60 .25
❑ 624 Mike Farmer RC .15 .07
❑ 625 Rickey Henderson .75 .35
❑ 626 Carlos Garcia .15 .07
❑ 627 Jeff Darwin RC .15 .07
❑ 628 Todd Zeile .15 .07
❑ 629 Benji Gil .15 .07
❑ 630 Tony Gwynn 1.25 .55
❑ 631 Aaron Small RC .15 .07
❑ 632 Joe Rosselli RC .15 .07
❑ 633 Mike Mussina .60 .25
❑ 634 Ryan Klesko .60 .25
❑ 635 Roger Clemens 1.25 .55
❑ 636 Sammy Sosa 1.25 .55
❑ 637 Orlando Palmeiro RC .15 .07
❑ 638 Willie Greene .15 .07
❑ 639 George Bell .15 .07
❑ 640 Garvin Alston RC .15 .07
❑ 641 Pete Janicki RC .15 .07
❑ 642 Chris Sheff RC .15 .07
❑ 643 Felipe Lira RC .30 .14
❑ 644 Roberto Petagine .15 .07
❑ 645 Wally Joyner .30 .14
❑ 646 Mike Piazza 3.00 1.35
❑ 647 Jaime Navarro .15 .07
❑ 648 Jeff Hartsock .15 .07
❑ 649 David McCarty .15 .07
❑ 650 Bobby Jones .30 .14
❑ 651 Mark Hutton .15 .07
❑ 652 Kyle Abbott .15 .07
❑ 653 Steve Cox RC .75 .35
❑ 654 Jeff King .15 .07
❑ 655 Norm Charlton .15 .07
❑ 656 Mike Gulan RC .15 .07
❑ 657 Julio Franco .15 .07
❑ 658 Cameron Cairncross RC .15 .07
❑ 659 John Olerud .30 .14
❑ 660 Salomon Torres .15 .07
❑ 661 Brad Pennington .15 .07
❑ 662 Melvin Nieves .15 .07
❑ 663 Ivan Calderon .15 .07
❑ 664 Turk Wendell .15 .07
❑ 665 Chris Pritchett .15 .07
❑ 666 Reggie Sanders .15 .07
❑ 667 Robin Ventura .30 .14
❑ 668 Joe Girardi .30 .14
❑ 669 Manny Ramirez 1.50 .70
❑ 670 Jeff Conine .15 .07
❑ 671 Greg Gohr .15 .07
❑ 672 Andujar Cedeno .15 .07
❑ 673 Les Norman RC .15 .07
❑ 674 Mike James RC .15 .07
❑ 675 Marshall Boze RC .15 .07
❑ 676 B.J. Wallace .15 .07
❑ 677 Kent Hrbek .30 .14
❑ 678 Jack Voigt RC .15 .07
❑ 679 Brien Taylor .15 .07
❑ 680 Curt Schilling .30 .14
❑ 681 Todd Van Poppel .15 .07
❑ 682 Kevin Young .30 .14
❑ 683 Tommy Adams .15 .07
❑ 684 Bernard Gilkey .15 .07
❑ 685 Kevin Brown .30 .14
❑ 686 Fred McGriff .30 .14
❑ 687 Pat Borders .15 .07
❑ 688 Kirt Manwaring .15 .07
❑ 689 Sid Bream .15 .07
❑ 690 John Valentin .15 .07
❑ 691 Steve Olsen RC .15 .07
❑ 692 Roberto Mejia RC .15 .07
❑ 693 Carlos Delgado FOIL 1.25 .55
❑ 694 Steve Gibralter FOIL RC .30 .14
❑ 695 Gary Mota RC FOIL .15 .07
❑ 696 Jose Malave FOIL RC .15 .07
❑ 697 Larry Sutton FOIL RC .15 .07
❑ 698 Dan Frye FOIL RC .15 .07
❑ 699 Tim Clark RC FOIL .15 .07
❑ 700 Brian Rupp RC FOIL .15 .07
❑ 701 Felipe Alou FOIL .30 .14
Moises Alou
❑ 702 Barry Bonds FOIL .60 .25
Bobby Bonds
❑ 703 Ken Griffey Sr. FOIL .75 .35
Ken Griffey Jr.
❑ 704 Brian McRae FOIL .15 .07
Hal McRae
❑ 705 Checklist 1 .15 .07
❑ 706 Checklist 2 .15 .07
❑ 707 Checklist 3 .15 .07
❑ 708 Checklist 4 .15 .07

## 1994 Bowman

| | MINT | NRMT |
|---|---|---|
| COMPLETE SET (682) | 100.00 | 45.00 |

❑ 1 Joe Carter .40 .18
❑ 2 Marcus Moore .20 .09
❑ 3 Doug Creek RC .20 .09
❑ 4 Pedro Martinez 1.00 .45
❑ 5 Ken Griffey Jr. 3.00 1.35
❑ 6 Greg Swindell .20 .09
❑ 7 J.J. Johnson .40 .18
❑ 8 Homer Bush RC 1.00 .45
❑ 9 Arquimedez Pozo RC .40 .18
❑ 10 Bryan Harvey .20 .09
❑ 11 J.T. Snow .40 .18
❑ 12 Alan Benes RC .40 .18
❑ 13 Chad Kreuter .20 .09
❑ 14 Eric Karros .40 .18
❑ 15 Frank Thomas 1.50 .70
❑ 16 Bret Saberhagen .40 .18
❑ 17 Terrell Lowery .20 .09
❑ 18 Rod Bolton .20 .09
❑ 19 Harold Baines .40 .18
❑ 20 Matt Walbeck .20 .09
❑ 21 Tom Glavine .75 .35
❑ 22 Todd Jones .20 .09
❑ 23 Alberto Castillo RC .20 .09
❑ 24 Ruben Sierra .20 .09
❑ 25 Don Mattingly 2.00 .90
❑ 26 Mike Morgan .20 .09
❑ 27 Jim Musselwhite RC .20 .09
❑ 28 Matt Brunson RC .20 .09
❑ 29 Adam Meinershagen RC .20 .09
❑ 30 Joe Girardi .20 .09
❑ 31 Shane Halter .20 .09
❑ 32 Jose Paniagua RC .40 .18
❑ 33 Paul Perkins RC .20 .09
❑ 34 John Hudek RC .20 .09
❑ 35 Frank Viola .20 .09
❑ 36 David Lamb RC .20 .09
❑ 37 Marshall Boze .20 .09
❑ 38 Jorge Posada RC 5.00 2.20
❑ 39 Brian Anderson RC 1.00 .45
❑ 40 Mark Whiten .20 .09
❑ 41 Sean Bergman .40 .18
❑ 42 Jose Parra RC .40 .18
❑ 43 Mike Robertson .20 .09
❑ 44 Pete Walker RC .20 .09
❑ 45 Juan Gonzalez .75 .35
❑ 46 Cleveland Ladell RC .40 .18
❑ 47 Mark Smith .20 .09
❑ 48 Kevin Jarvis UER .20 .09
(Team listed as Yankees on back)
❑ 49 Amaury Telemaco RC .40 .18
❑ 50 Andy Van Slyke .40 .18
❑ 51 Rikkert Faneyte RC .20 .09
❑ 52 Curtis Shaw .20 .09
❑ 53 Matt Drews RC .20 .09
❑ 54 Wilson Alvarez .20 .09
❑ 55 Manny Ramirez 1.25 .55
❑ 56 Bobby Munoz .20 .09
❑ 57 Ed Sprague .20 .09
❑ 58 Jamey Wright RC 1.00 .45
❑ 59 Jeff Montgomery .20 .09
❑ 60 Kirk Rueter .20 .09
❑ 61 Edgar Martinez .40 .18
❑ 62 Luis Gonzalez .40 .18
❑ 63 Tim Vanegmond RC .20 .09
❑ 64 Bip Roberts .20 .09
❑ 65 John Jaha .20 .09
❑ 66 Chuck Carr .20 .09
❑ 67 Chuck Finley .40 .18
❑ 68 Aaron Holbert .20 .09
❑ 69 Cecil Fielder .40 .18
❑ 70 Tom Engle RC .20 .09
❑ 71 Ron Karkovice .20 .09
❑ 72 Joe Orsulak .20 .09
❑ 73 Duff Brumley RC .20 .09
❑ 74 Craig Clayton RC .20 .09
❑ 75 Cal Ripken 3.00 1.35
❑ 76 Brad Fulmer RC 5.00 2.20
❑ 77 Tony Tarasco .20 .09
❑ 78 Terry Farrar RC .20 .09
❑ 79 Matt Williams .40 .18
❑ 80 Rickey Henderson 1.00 .45
❑ 81 Terry Mulholland .20 .09
❑ 82 Sammy Sosa 1.50 .70
❑ 83 Paul Sorrento .20 .09
❑ 84 Pete Incaviglia .20 .09
❑ 85 Darren Hall RC .20 .09
❑ 86 Scott Klingenbeck .20 .09
❑ 87 Dario Perez RC .20 .09
❑ 88 Ugueth Urbina .40 .18
❑ 89 Dave Vanhof RC .20 .09

❑ 90 Domingo Jean .20 .09
❑ 91 Otis Nixon .20 .09
❑ 92 Andres Berumen .20 .09
❑ 93 Jose Valentin .20 .09
❑ 94 Edgar Renteria RC 2.50 1.10
❑ 95 Chris Turner .20 .09
❑ 96 Ray Lankford .40 .18
❑ 97 Danny Bautista .20 .09
❑ 98 Chan Ho Park RC 3.00 1.35
❑ 99 Glenn DiSarcina RC .40 .18
❑ 100 Butch Huskey .20 .09
❑ 101 Ivan Rodriguez 1.00 .45
❑ 102 Johnny Ruffin .20 .09
❑ 103 Alex Ochoa .20 .09
❑ 104 Torii Hunter RC 1.00 .45
❑ 105 Ryan Klesko .40 .18
❑ 106 Jay Bell .40 .18
❑ 107 Kurt Peltzer RC .20 .09
❑ 108 Miguel Jimenez .20 .09
❑ 109 Russ Davis .20 .09
❑ 110 Derek Wallace .20 .09
❑ 111 Keith Lockhart RC .20 .09
❑ 112 Mike Lieberthal .40 .18
❑ 113 Dave Stewart .40 .18
❑ 114 Tom Schmidt .20 .09
❑ 115 Brian McRae .20 .09
❑ 116 Moises Alou .40 .18
❑ 117 Dave Fleming .20 .09
❑ 118 Jeff Bagwell 1.00 .45
❑ 119 Luis Ortiz .20 .09
❑ 120 Tony Gwynn 1.50 .70
❑ 121 Jaime Navarro .20 .09
❑ 122 Benito Santiago .20 .09
❑ 123 Darrell Whitmore .20 .09
❑ 124 John Mabry RC .20 .09
❑ 125 Mickey Tettleton .20 .09
❑ 126 Tom Candiotti .20 .09
❑ 127 Tim Raines .40 .18
❑ 128 Bobby Bonilla .40 .18
❑ 129 John Dettmer .20 .09
❑ 130 Hector Carrasco .20 .09
❑ 131 Chris Hoiles .20 .09
❑ 132 Rick Aguilera .20 .09
❑ 133 David Justice .40 .18
❑ 134 Esteban Loaiza RC 1.00 .45
❑ 135 Barry Bonds 1.25 .55
❑ 136 Bob Welch .20 .09
❑ 137 Mike Stanley .20 .09
❑ 138 Roberto Hernandez .20 .09
❑ 139 Sandy Alomar Jr. .40 .18
❑ 140 Darren Daulton .40 .18
❑ 141 Angel Martinez RC .20 .09
❑ 142 Howard Johnson .20 .09
❑ 143 Bob Hamelin UER .20 .09
(Name and card number colors don't match)
❑ 144 J.J. Thobe RC .20 .09
❑ 145 Roger Salkeld .20 .09
❑ 146 Orlando Miller .20 .09
❑ 147 Dmitri Young .40 .18
❑ 148 Tim Hyers RC .20 .09
❑ 149 Mark Loretta RC 1.00 .45
❑ 150 Chris Hammond .20 .09
❑ 151 Joel Moore RC .20 .09
❑ 152 Todd Zeile .20 .09
❑ 153 Wil Cordero .20 .09
❑ 154 Chris Smith .20 .09
❑ 155 James Baldwin .40 .18
❑ 156 Edgardo Alfonzo RC 10.00 4.50
❑ 157 Kym Ashworth RC .40 .18
❑ 158 Paul Bako RC .20 .09
❑ 159 Rick Krivda RC .20 .09
❑ 160 Pat Mahomes .20 .09
❑ 161 Damon Hollins .40 .18
❑ 162 Felix Martinez RC .75 .35
❑ 163 Jason Myers RC .20 .09
❑ 164 Izzy Molina RC .40 .18
❑ 165 Brien Taylor .20 .09
❑ 166 Kevin Orie RC .20 .09
❑ 167 Casey Whitten RC .40 .18
❑ 168 Tony Longmire .20 .09
❑ 169 John Olerud .40 .18
❑ 170 Mark Thompson .20 .09
❑ 171 Jorge Fabregas .20 .09
❑ 172 John Wetteland .40 .18
❑ 173 Dan Wilson .20 .09
❑ 174 Doug Drabek .20 .09
❑ 175 Jeff McNeely .20 .09
❑ 176 Melvin Nieves .20 .09
❑ 177 Doug Glanville RC 2.00 .90
❑ 178 Javier De La Hoya RC .20 .09
❑ 179 Chad Curtis .20 .09
❑ 180 Brian Barber .20 .09
❑ 181 Mike Henneman .20 .09
❑ 182 Jose Offerman .20 .09
❑ 183 Robert Ellis RC .20 .09
❑ 184 John Franco .40 .18
❑ 185 Benji Gil .20 .09
❑ 186 Hal Morris .20 .09
❑ 187 Chris Sabo .20 .09
❑ 188 Blaise Ilsley RC .20 .09
❑ 189 Steve Avery .20 .09
❑ 190 Rick White RC .20 .09
❑ 191 Rod Beck .20 .09
❑ 192 Mark McGwire UER 3.00 1.35
(No card number on back)
❑ 193 Jim Abbott .40 .18
❑ 194 Randy Myers .20 .09
❑ 195 Kenny Lofton .40 .18
❑ 196 Mariano Duncan .20 .09
❑ 197 Lee Daniels RC .20 .09
❑ 198 Armando Reynoso .20 .09
❑ 199 Joe Randa .40 .18
❑ 200 Cliff Floyd .40 .18
❑ 201 Tim Harkrider RC .20 .09
❑ 202 Kevin Gallaher RC .20 .09
❑ 203 Scott Cooper .20 .09
❑ 204 Phil Stidham RC .20 .09
❑ 205 Jeff D'Amico RC 3.00 1.35
❑ 206 Matt Whisenant .20 .09
❑ 207 De Shawn Warren .20 .09
❑ 208 Rene Arocha .20 .09
❑ 209 Tony Clark RC 2.50 1.10
❑ 210 Jason Jacome RC .20 .09
❑ 211 Scott Christman RC .20 .09
❑ 212 Bill Pulsipher .40 .18
❑ 213 Dean Palmer .40 .18
❑ 214 Chad Mottola .20 .09
❑ 215 Manny Alexander .20 .09
❑ 216 Rich Becker .20 .09
❑ 217 Andre King RC .20 .09
❑ 218 Carlos Garcia .20 .09
❑ 219 Ron Pezzoni RC .20 .09
❑ 220 Steve Karsay .20 .09
❑ 221 Jose Musset RC .20 .09
❑ 222 Karl Rhodes .20 .09
❑ 223 Frank Cimorelli RC .20 .09
❑ 224 Kevin Jordan RC .20 .09
❑ 225 Duane Ward .20 .09
❑ 226 John Burke .20 .09
❑ 227 Mike Macfarlane .20 .09
❑ 228 Mike Lansing .20 .09
❑ 229 Chuck Knoblauch .40 .18
❑ 230 Ken Caminiti .40 .18
❑ 231 Gar Finnvold RC .20 .09
❑ 232 Derrek Lee RC 2.00 .90
❑ 233 Brady Anderson .40 .18
❑ 234 Vic Darensbourg RC .20 .09
❑ 235 Mark Langston .20 .09
❑ 236 T.J. Mathews RC .40 .18
❑ 237 Lou Whitaker .40 .18
❑ 238 Roger Cedeno .40 .18
❑ 239 Alex Fernandez .20 .09
❑ 240 Ryan Thompson .20 .09
❑ 241 Kerry Lacy RC .20 .09
❑ 242 Reggie Sanders .20 .09
❑ 243 Brad Pennington .20 .09
❑ 244 Bryan Eversgerd RC .20 .09
❑ 245 Greg Maddux 2.00 .90
❑ 246 Jason Kendall .40 .18
❑ 247 J.R. Phillips .20 .09
❑ 248 Bobby Witt .20 .09
❑ 249 Paul O'Neill .40 .18
❑ 250 Ryne Sandberg 1.00 .45
❑ 251 Charles Nagy .20 .09
❑ 252 Kevin Stocker .20 .09
❑ 253 Shawn Green 1.00 .45
❑ 254 Charlie Hayes .20 .09
❑ 255 Donnie Elliott .20 .09
❑ 256 Rob Fitzpatrick RC .20 .09
❑ 257 Tim Davis .20 .09
❑ 258 James Mouton .20 .09
❑ 259 Mike Greenwell .20 .09
❑ 260 Ray McDavid .20 .09
❑ 261 Mike Kelly .20 .09
❑ 262 Andy Larkin RC .20 .09
❑ 263 Marquis Riley UER .20 .09
(No card number on back)
❑ 264 Bob Tewksbury .20 .09
❑ 265 Brian Edmondson .20 .09
❑ 266 Eduardo Lantigua RC .40 .18
❑ 267 Brandon Wilson .20 .09
❑ 268 Mike Welch .20 .09
❑ 269 Tom Henke .20 .09
❑ 270 Pokey Reese .40 .18
❑ 271 Greg Zaun RC .20 .09
❑ 272 Todd Ritchie .20 .09
❑ 273 Javier Lopez .40 .18
❑ 274 Kevin Young .20 .09
❑ 275 Kirt Manwaring .20 .09
❑ 276 Bill Taylor RC .20 .09
❑ 277 Robert Eenhoorn .20 .09
❑ 278 Jessie Hollins .20 .09
❑ 279 Julian Tavarez RC .20 .09
❑ 280 Gene Schall .20 .09
❑ 281 Paul Molitor .75 .35
❑ 282 Neifi Perez RC 2.50 1.10
❑ 283 Greg Gagne .20 .09
❑ 284 Marquis Grissom .20 .09
❑ 285 Randy Johnson 1.00 .45
❑ 286 Pete Harnisch .20 .09
❑ 287 Joel Bennett RC .20 .09
❑ 288 Derek Bell .20 .09
❑ 289 Darryl Hamilton .20 .09
❑ 290 Gary Sheffield .75 .35
❑ 291 Eduardo Perez .20 .09
❑ 292 Basil Shabazz .20 .09
❑ 293 Eric Davis .40 .18
❑ 294 Pedro Astacio .20 .09
❑ 295 Robin Ventura .40 .18
❑ 296 Jeff Kent .40 .18
❑ 297 Rick Helling .40 .18
❑ 298 Joe Oliver .20 .09
❑ 299 Lee Smith .40 .18
❑ 300 Dave Winfield .75 .35
❑ 301 Deion Sanders .40 .18
❑ 302 Ravelo Manzanillo RC .20 .09
❑ 303 Mark Portugal .20 .09
❑ 304 Brent Gates .20 .09
❑ 305 Wade Boggs 1.00 .45
❑ 306 Rick Wilkins .20 .09
❑ 307 Carlos Baerga .20 .09
❑ 308 Curt Schilling .40 .18
❑ 309 Shannon Stewart .75 .35
❑ 310 Darren Holmes .20 .09
❑ 311 Robert Toth RC .20 .09
❑ 312 Gabe White .20 .09
❑ 313 Mac Suzuki RC .40 .18
❑ 314 Alvin Morman RC .20 .09
❑ 315 Mo Vaughn .40 .18
❑ 316 Bryce Florie RC .20 .09
❑ 317 Gabby Martinez RC .40 .18
❑ 318 Carl Everett .40 .18
❑ 319 Kerwin Moore .20 .09
❑ 320 Tom Pagnozzi .20 .09
❑ 321 Chris Gomez .20 .09
❑ 322 Todd Williams .20 .09
❑ 323 Pat Hentgen .20 .09
❑ 324 Kirk Presley RC .20 .09
❑ 325 Kevin Brown .40 .18
❑ 326 Jason Isringhausen RC 2.00 .90
❑ 327 Rick Forney RC .20 .09
❑ 328 Carlos Pulido RC .20 .09
❑ 329 Terrell Wade RC .20 .09
❑ 330 Al Martin .20 .09
❑ 331 Dan Carlson RC .20 .09
❑ 332 Mark Acre RC .20 .09
❑ 333 Sterling Hitchcock .20 .09
❑ 334 Jon Ratliff RC .20 .09
❑ 335 Alex Ramirez RC 1.00 .45
❑ 336 Phil Geisler RC .20 .09
❑ 337 Eddie Zambrano FOIL RC .20 .09
❑ 338 Jim Thome FOIL .40 .18
❑ 339 James Mouton FOIL .20 .09
❑ 340 Cliff Floyd FOIL .40 .18
❑ 341 Carlos Delgado FOIL 1.25 .55
❑ 342 Roberto Petagine FOIL .20 .09

343 Tim Clark FOIL .20 .09
344 Bubba Smith FOIL .20 .09
345 Randy Curtis FOIL RC .20 .09
346 Joe Biasucci FOIL RC .20 .09
347 D.J. Boston FOIL RC .20 .09
348 Ruben Rivera FOIL RC 1.00 .45
349 Bryan Link FOIL RC .20 .09
350 Mike Bell FOIL RC .20 .09
351 Marty Watson FOIL RC .20 .09
352 Jason Myers FOIL .20 .09
353 Chipper Jones FOIL 2.00 .90
354 Brooks Kieschnick FOIL .20 .09
355 Pokey Reese FOIL .40 .18
356 John Burke FOIL .20 .09
357 Kurt Miller FOIL .20 .09
358 Orlando Miller FOIL .20 .09
359 Todd Hollandsworth FOIL .20 .09
360 Rondell White FOIL .40 .18
361 Bill Pulsipher FOIL .40 .18
362 Tyler Green FOIL .20 .09
363 Midre Cummings FOIL .20 .09
364 Brian Barber FOIL .20 .09
365 Melvin Nieves FOIL .20 .09
366 Salomon Torres FOIL .20 .09
367 Alex Ochoa FOIL .20 .09
368 Frankie Rodriguez FOIL .20 .09
369 Brian Anderson FOIL 1.00 .45
370 James Baldwin FOIL .40 .18
371 Manny Ramirez FOIL 1.25 .55
372 Justin Thompson FOIL .20 .09
373 Johnny Damon FOIL .75 .35
374 Jeff D'Amico FOIL 3.00 1.35
375 Rich Becker FOIL .20 .09
376 Derek Jeter FOIL 4.00 1.80
377 Steve Karsay FOIL .20 .09
378 Mac Suzuki FOIL .40 .18
379 Benji Gil FOIL .20 .09
380 Alex Gonzalez FOIL .20 .09
381 Jason Bere FOIL .20 .09
382 Brett Butler FOIL .40 .18
383 Jeff Conine FOIL .20 .09
384 Darren Daulton FOIL .40 .18
385 Jeff Kent FOIL .40 .18
386 Don Mattingly FOIL 2.00 .90
387 Mike Piazza FOIL 2.50 1.10
388 Ryne Sandberg FOIL 1.00 .45
389 Rich Amaral .20 .09
390 Craig Biggio .40 .18
391 Jeff Suppan RC 1.00 .45
392 Andy Benes .20 .09
393 Cal Eldred .20 .09
394 Jeff Conine .20 .09
395 Tim Salmon .40 .18
396 Ray Suplee RC .20 .09
397 Tony Phillips .20 .09
398 Ramon Martinez .20 .09
399 Julio Franco .20 .09
400 Dwight Gooden .40 .18
401 Kevin Lomon RC .20 .09
402 Jose Rijo .20 .09
403 Mike Devereaux .20 .09
404 Mike Zolecki RC .20 .09
405 Fred McGriff .40 .18
406 Danny Clyburn .20 .09
407 Robby Thompson .20 .09
408 Terry Steinbach .20 .09
409 Luis Polonia .20 .09
410 Mark Grace .75 .35
411 Albert Belle .40 .18
412 John Kruk .40 .18
413 Scott Spiezio RC .40 .18
414 Ellis Burks UER .40 .18
(Name spelled Elkis on front)
415 Joe Vitiello .20 .09
416 Tim Costo .20 .09
417 Marc Newfield .20 .09
418 Oscar Henriquez RC .20 .09
419 Matt Perisho RC .75 .35
420 Julio Bruno .20 .09
421 Kenny Felder .20 .09
422 Tyler Green .20 .09
423 Jim Edmonds 1.00 .45
424 Ozzie Smith 1.00 .45
425 Rick Greene .20 .09
426 Todd Hollandsworth .20 .09
427 Eddie Pearson RC .40 .18
428 Quilvio Veras .40 .18
429 Kenny Rogers .20 .09
430 Willie Greene .20 .09
431 Vaughn Eshelman .20 .09
432 Pat Meares .20 .09
433 Jermaine Dye RC 12.00 5.50
434 Steve Cooke .20 .09
435 Bill Swift .20 .09
436 Fausto Cruz RC .20 .09
437 Mark Hutton .20 .09
438 Brooks Kieschnick RC .20 .09
439 Yorkis Perez .20 .09
440 Len Dykstra .40 .18
441 Pat Borders .20 .09
442 Doug Walls RC .20 .09
443 Wally Joyner .40 .18
444 Ken Hill .20 .09
445 Eric Anthony .20 .09
446 Mitch Williams .20 .09
447 Cory Bailey RC .20 .09
448 Dave Staton .20 .09
449 Greg Vaughn .40 .18
450 Dave Magadan .20 .09
451 Chili Davis .40 .18
452 Gerald Santos RC .20 .09
453 Joe Perona .20 .09
454 Delino DeShields .20 .09
455 Jack McDowell .20 .09
456 Todd Hundley .20 .09
457 Ritchie Moody .20 .09
458 Bret Boone .40 .18
459 Ben McDonald .20 .09
460 Kirby Puckett 2.00 .90
461 Gregg Olson .20 .09
462 Rich Aude RC .20 .09
463 John Burkett .20 .09
464 Troy Neel .20 .09
465 Jimmy Key .40 .18
466 Ozzie Timmons .20 .09
467 Eddie Murray .75 .35
468 Mark Tranberg RC .20 .09
469 Alex Gonzalez .20 .09
470 David Nied .20 .09
471 Barry Larkin .75 .35
472 Brian Looney RC .20 .09
473 Shawn Estes .40 .18
474 A.J. Sager RC .20 .09
475 Roger Clemens 1.50 .70
476 Vince Moore .20 .09
477 Scott Karl RC .40 .18
478 Kurt Miller .20 .09
479 Garret Anderson .75 .35
480 Allen Watson .20 .09
481 Jose Lima RC 2.00 .90
482 Rick Gorecki .20 .09
483 Jimmy Hurst RC .20 .09
484 Preston Wilson .75 .35
485 Will Clark .75 .35
486 Mike Ferry RC .20 .09
487 Curtis Goodwin RC .40 .18
488 Mike Myers .20 .09
489 Chipper Jones 2.00 .90
490 Jeff King .20 .09
491 William VanLandingham RC .20 .09
492 Carlos Reyes RC .20 .09
493 Andy Pettitte 1.00 .45
494 Brant Brown .20 .09
495 Daron Kirkreit .20 .09
496 Ricky Bottalico RC .40 .18
497 Devon White .20 .09
498 Jason Johnson RC .20 .09
499 Vince Coleman .20 .09
500 Larry Walker .40 .18
501 Bobby Ayala .20 .09
502 Steve Finley .40 .18
503 Scott Fletcher .20 .09
504 Brad Ausmus .20 .09
505 Scott Talanoa RC .20 .09
506 Orestes Destrade .20 .09
507 Gary DiSarcina .20 .09
508 Willie Smith RC .20 .09
509 Alan Trammell .40 .18
510 Mike Piazza 2.50 1.10
511 Ozzie Guillen .20 .09
512 Jeromy Burnitz .40 .18
513 Darren Oliver RC .40 .18
514 Kevin Mitchell .20 .09
515 Rafael Palmeiro .75 .35
516 David McCarty .20 .09
517 Jeff Blauser .20 .09
518 Trey Beamon .20 .09
519 Royce Clayton .20 .09
520 Dennis Eckersley .40 .18
521 Bernie Williams .75 .35
522 Steve Buechele .20 .09
523 Dennis Martinez .40 .18
524 Dave Hollins .20 .09
525 Joey Hamilton .20 .09
526 Andres Galarraga .40 .18
527 Jeff Granger .20 .09
528 Joey Eischen .20 .09
529 Desi Relaford .40 .18
530 Roberto Petagine .20 .09
531 Andre Dawson .40 .18
532 Ray Holbert .20 .09
533 Duane Singleton .20 .09
534 Kurt Abbott RC .20 .09
535 Bo Jackson .40 .18
536 Gregg Jefferies .20 .09
537 David Mysel .20 .09
538 Raul Mondesi .40 .18
539 Chris Snopek .20 .09
540 Brook Fordyce .20 .09
541 Ron Frazier RC .20 .09
542 Brian Koelling .20 .09
543 Jimmy Haynes .40 .18
544 Marty Cordova .20 .09
545 Jason Green RC .20 .09
546 Orlando Merced .20 .09
547 Lou Pote RC .20 .09
548 Todd Van Poppel .20 .09
549 Pat Kelly .20 .09
550 Turk Wendell .20 .09
551 Herbert Perry RC .20 .09
552 Ryan Karp RC .20 .09
553 Juan Guzman .20 .09
554 Bryan Rekar RC .40 .18
555 Kevin Appier .40 .18
556 Chris Schwab RC .20 .09
557 Jay Buhner .40 .18
558 Andujar Cedeno .20 .09
559 Ryan McGuire RC .40 .18
560 Ricky Gutierrez .20 .09
561 Keith Kimsey RC .20 .09
562 Tim Clark .20 .09
563 Damion Easley .20 .09
564 Clint Davis RC .20 .09
565 Mike Moore .20 .09
566 Orel Hershiser .40 .18
567 Jason Bere .20 .09
568 Kevin McReynolds .20 .09
569 Leland Macon RC .20 .09
570 John Courtright RC .20 .09
571 Sid Fernandez .20 .09
572 Chad Roper .20 .09
573 Terry Pendleton .40 .18
574 Danny Miceli .20 .09
575 Joe Rosselli .20 .09
576 Mike Bordick .20 .09
577 Danny Tartabull .20 .09
578 Jose Guzman .20 .09
579 Omar Vizquel .40 .18
580 Tommy Greene .20 .09
581 Paul Spoljaric .20 .09
582 Walt Weiss .20 .09
583 Oscar Jimenez RC .20 .09
584 Rod Henderson .20 .09
585 Derek Lowe .20 .09
586 Richard Hidalgo RC 15.00 6.75
587 Shayne Bennett RC .40 .18
588 Tim Belk RC .20 .09
589 Matt Mieske .20 .09
590 Nigel Wilson .20 .09
591 Jeff Knox RC .20 .09
592 Bernard Gilkey .20 .09
593 David Cone .40 .18
594 Paul LoDuca RC .40 .18
595 Scott Ruffcorn .20 .09
596 Chris Roberts .40 .18
597 Oscar Munoz RC .20 .09
598 Scott Sullivan RC .20 .09

| Card | Mint | NrMt |
|---|---|---|
| ❑ 599 Matt Jarvis RC | .20 | .09 |
| ❑ 600 Jose Canseco | 1.00 | .45 |
| ❑ 601 Tony Graffanino RC | .40 | .18 |
| ❑ 602 Don Slaught | .20 | .09 |
| ❑ 603 Brett King RC | .40 | .18 |
| ❑ 604 Jose Herrera RC | .40 | .18 |
| ❑ 605 Melido Perez | .20 | .09 |
| ❑ 606 Mike Hubbard RC | .20 | .09 |
| ❑ 607 Chad Ogea | .20 | .09 |
| ❑ 608 Wayne Gomes RC | .20 | .09 |
| ❑ 609 Roberto Alomar | .75 | .35 |
| ❑ 610 Angel Echevarria RC | .20 | .09 |
| ❑ 611 Jose Lind | .20 | .09 |
| ❑ 612 Darrin Fletcher | .20 | .09 |
| ❑ 613 Chris Bosio | .20 | .09 |
| ❑ 614 Darryl Kile | .40 | .18 |
| ❑ 615 Frankie Rodriguez | .20 | .09 |
| ❑ 616 Phil Plantier | .20 | .09 |
| ❑ 617 Pat Listach | .20 | .09 |
| ❑ 618 Charlie Hough | .40 | .18 |
| ❑ 619 Ryan Hancock RC | .20 | .09 |
| ❑ 620 Darrel Deak RC | .20 | .09 |
| ❑ 621 Travis Fryman | .40 | .18 |
| ❑ 622 Brett Butler | .40 | .18 |
| ❑ 623 Lance Johnson | .20 | .09 |
| ❑ 624 Pete Smith | .20 | .09 |
| ❑ 625 James Hurst RC | .20 | .09 |
| ❑ 626 Roberto Kelly | .20 | .09 |
| ❑ 627 Mike Mussina | .75 | .35 |
| ❑ 628 Kevin Tapani | .20 | .09 |
| ❑ 629 John Smoltz | .40 | .18 |
| ❑ 630 Midre Cummings | .20 | .09 |
| ❑ 631 Salomon Torres | .20 | .09 |
| ❑ 632 Willie Adams | .20 | .09 |
| ❑ 633 Derek Jeter | 4.00 | 1.80 |
| ❑ 634 Steve Trachsel | .20 | .09 |
| ❑ 635 Albie Lopez | .20 | .09 |
| ❑ 636 Jason Moler | .20 | .09 |
| ❑ 637 Carlos Delgado | 1.25 | .55 |
| ❑ 638 Roberto Mejia | .20 | .09 |
| ❑ 639 Darren Burton | .20 | .09 |
| ❑ 640 B.J. Wallace | .20 | .09 |
| ❑ 641 Brad Clontz RC | .20 | .09 |
| ❑ 642 Billy Wagner RC | 2.00 | .90 |
| ❑ 643 Aaron Sele | .40 | .18 |
| ❑ 644 Cameron Cairncross | .20 | .09 |
| ❑ 645 Brian Harper | .20 | .09 |
| ❑ 646 Marc Valdes UER (No card number on back) | .20 | .09 |
| ❑ 647 Mark Ratekin | .20 | .09 |
| ❑ 648 Terry Bradshaw RC | .20 | .09 |
| ❑ 649 Justin Thompson | .20 | .09 |
| ❑ 650 Mike Busch RC | .40 | .18 |
| ❑ 651 Joe Hall RC | .20 | .09 |
| ❑ 652 Bobby Jones | .20 | .09 |
| ❑ 653 Kelly Stinnott RC | .20 | .09 |
| ❑ 654 Rod Steph RC | .20 | .09 |
| ❑ 655 Jay Powell RC | .40 | .18 |
| ❑ 656 Keith Caragozzo RC UER (No card number on back) | .20 | .09 |
| ❑ 657 Todd Dunn | .20 | .09 |
| ❑ 658 Charles Peterson RC | .40 | .18 |
| ❑ 659 Darren Lewis | .20 | .09 |
| ❑ 660 John Wasdin RC | .40 | .18 |
| ❑ 661 Tate Seefried RC | .20 | .09 |
| ❑ 662 Hector Trinidad RC | .40 | .18 |
| ❑ 663 John Carter RC | .20 | .09 |
| ❑ 664 Larry Mitchell | .20 | .09 |
| ❑ 665 David Catlett RC | .20 | .09 |
| ❑ 666 Dante Bichette | .40 | .18 |
| ❑ 667 Felix Jose | .20 | .09 |
| ❑ 668 Rondell White | .40 | .18 |
| ❑ 669 Tino Martinez | .40 | .18 |
| ❑ 670 Brian L. Hunter | .20 | .09 |
| ❑ 671 Jose Malave | .20 | .09 |
| ❑ 672 Archi Cianfrocco | .20 | .09 |
| ❑ 673 Mike Matheny RC | .20 | .09 |
| ❑ 674 Bret Barberie | .20 | .09 |
| ❑ 675 Andrew Lorraine RC | .20 | .09 |
| ❑ 676 Brian Jordan | .40 | .18 |
| ❑ 677 Tim Belcher | .20 | .09 |
| ❑ 678 Antonio Osuna RC | .20 | .09 |
| ❑ 679 Checklist | .20 | .09 |
| ❑ 680 Checklist | .20 | .09 |
| ❑ 681 Checklist | .20 | .09 |
| ❑ 682 Checklist | .20 | .09 |

## 1995 Bowman

| | MINT | NRMT |
|---|---|---|
| COMPLETE SET (439) | 300.00 | 135.00 |
| COMMON CARD (1-439) | .25 | .11 |
| ❑ 1 Billy Wagner | .50 | .23 |
| ❑ 2 Chris Widger | .25 | .11 |
| ❑ 3 Brent Bowers | .25 | .11 |
| ❑ 4 Bob Abreu RC | 12.00 | 5.50 |
| ❑ 5 Lou Collier RC | .50 | .23 |
| ❑ 6 Juan Acevedo RC | .25 | .11 |
| ❑ 7 Jason Kelley RC | .25 | .11 |
| ❑ 8 Brian Sackinsky | .25 | .11 |
| ❑ 9 Scott Christman | .25 | .11 |
| ❑ 10 Damon Hollins | .25 | .11 |
| ❑ 11 Willie Otanez RC | .25 | .11 |
| ❑ 12 Jason Ryan RC | .50 | .23 |
| ❑ 13 Jason Giambi | 1.00 | .45 |
| ❑ 14 Andy Taulbee RC | .25 | .11 |
| ❑ 15 Mark Thompson | .25 | .11 |
| ❑ 16 Hugo Pivaral RC | .25 | .11 |
| ❑ 17 Brien Taylor | .25 | .11 |
| ❑ 18 Antonio Osuna | .25 | .11 |
| ❑ 19 Edgardo Alfonzo | 1.00 | .45 |
| ❑ 20 Carl Everett | .50 | .23 |
| ❑ 21 Matt Drews | .25 | .11 |
| ❑ 22 Bartolo Colon RC | 8.00 | 3.60 |
| ❑ 23 Andruw Jones RC | 40.00 | 18.00 |
| ❑ 24 Robert Person RC | 2.00 | .90 |
| ❑ 25 Derrek Lee | .25 | .11 |
| ❑ 26 John Ambrose RC | .25 | .11 |
| ❑ 27 Eric Knowles RC | .50 | .23 |
| ❑ 28 Chris Roberts | .25 | .11 |
| ❑ 29 Don Wengert | .25 | .11 |
| ❑ 30 Marcus Jensen RC | .50 | .23 |
| ❑ 31 Brian Barber | .25 | .11 |
| ❑ 32 Kevin Brown C | .50 | .23 |
| ❑ 33 Benji Gil | .25 | .11 |
| ❑ 34 Mike Hubbard | .25 | .11 |
| ❑ 35 Bart Evans RC | .25 | .11 |
| ❑ 36 Enrique Wilson RC | 1.00 | .45 |
| ❑ 37 Brian Buchanan RC | .25 | .11 |
| ❑ 38 Ken Ray RC | .25 | .11 |
| ❑ 39 Micah Franklin RC | .25 | .11 |
| ❑ 40 Ricky Otero RC | .25 | .11 |
| ❑ 41 Jason Kendall | .50 | .23 |
| ❑ 42 Jimmy Hurst | .25 | .11 |
| ❑ 43 Jerry Wolak RC | .25 | .11 |
| ❑ 44 Jayson Peterson RC | .25 | .11 |
| ❑ 45 Allen Battle RC | .25 | .11 |
| ❑ 46 Scott Stahoviak | .25 | .11 |
| ❑ 47 Steve Schrenk RC | .25 | .11 |
| ❑ 48 Travis Miller RC | .25 | .11 |
| ❑ 49 Eddie Rios RC | .25 | .11 |
| ❑ 50 Mike Hampton | .25 | .11 |
| ❑ 51 Chad Frontera RC | .25 | .11 |
| ❑ 52 Tom Evans | .25 | .11 |
| ❑ 53 C.J. Nitkowski | .25 | .11 |
| ❑ 54 Clay Caruthers RC | .25 | .11 |
| ❑ 55 Shannon Stewart | .50 | .23 |
| ❑ 56 Jorge Posada | .50 | .23 |
| ❑ 57 Aaron Holbert | .25 | .11 |
| ❑ 58 Harry Berrios RC | .25 | .11 |
| ❑ 59 Steve Rodriguez | .25 | .11 |
| ❑ 60 Shane Andrews | .25 | .11 |
| ❑ 61 Will Cunnane RC | .25 | .11 |
| ❑ 62 Richard Hidalgo | 1.50 | .70 |
| ❑ 63 Bill Selby RC | .25 | .11 |
| ❑ 64 Jay Cranford RC | .25 | .11 |
| ❑ 65 Jeff Suppan | .25 | .11 |
| ❑ 66 Curtis Goodwin | .25 | .11 |
| ❑ 67 John Thomson RC | .25 | .11 |
| ❑ 68 Justin Thompson | .25 | .11 |
| ❑ 69 Troy Percival | .25 | .11 |
| ❑ 70 Matt Wagner RC | .50 | .23 |
| ❑ 71 Terry Bradshaw | .25 | .11 |
| ❑ 72 Greg Hansell | .25 | .11 |
| ❑ 73 John Burke | .25 | .11 |
| ❑ 74 Jeff D'Amico | .50 | .23 |
| ❑ 75 Ernie Young | .25 | .11 |
| ❑ 76 Jason Bates | .25 | .11 |
| ❑ 77 Chris Stynes | .25 | .11 |
| ❑ 78 Cade Gaspar RC | .25 | .11 |
| ❑ 79 Melvin Nieves | .25 | .11 |
| ❑ 80 Rick Gorecki | .25 | .11 |
| ❑ 81 Felix Rodriguez RC | .25 | .11 |
| ❑ 82 Ryan Hancock | .25 | .11 |
| ❑ 83 Chris Carpenter RC | 3.00 | 1.35 |
| ❑ 84 Ray McDavid | .25 | .11 |
| ❑ 85 Chris Wimmer | .25 | .11 |
| ❑ 86 Doug Glanville | .25 | .11 |
| ❑ 87 DeShawn Warren | .25 | .11 |
| ❑ 88 Damian Moss RC | .25 | .11 |
| ❑ 89 Rafael Orellano RC | .25 | .11 |
| ❑ 90 Vladimir Guerrero RC ! | 60.00 | 27.00 |
| ❑ 91 Raul Casanova RC | .25 | .11 |
| ❑ 92 Karim Garcia RC | 1.00 | .70 |
| ❑ 93 Bryce Florie | .25 | .11 |
| ❑ 94 Kevin Orie | .25 | .11 |
| ❑ 95 Ryan Nye RC | .25 | .11 |
| ❑ 96 Matt Sachse RC | .25 | .11 |
| ❑ 97 Ivan Arteaga RC | .25 | .11 |
| ❑ 98 Glenn Murray | .25 | .11 |
| ❑ 99 Stacy Hollins RC | .25 | .11 |
| ❑ 100 Jim Pittsley | .25 | .11 |
| ❑ 101 Craig Mattson RC | .25 | .11 |
| ❑ 102 Neifi Perez | .50 | .23 |
| ❑ 103 Keith Williams | .25 | .11 |
| ❑ 104 Roger Cedeno | .25 | .11 |
| ❑ 105 Tony Terry RC | .25 | .11 |
| ❑ 106 Jose Malave | .25 | .11 |
| ❑ 107 Joe Rosselli | .25 | .11 |
| ❑ 108 Kevin Jordan | .25 | .11 |
| ❑ 109 Sid Roberson RC | .25 | .11 |
| ❑ 110 Alan Embree | .25 | .11 |
| ❑ 111 Terrell Wade | .25 | .11 |
| ❑ 112 Bob Wolcott | .25 | .11 |
| ❑ 113 Carlos Perez RC | .50 | .23 |
| ❑ 114 Mike Bovee RC | .25 | .11 |
| ❑ 115 Tommy Davis RC | .25 | .11 |
| ❑ 116 Jeremey Kendall RC | .25 | .11 |
| ❑ 117 Rich Aude | .25 | .11 |
| ❑ 118 Rick Huisman | .25 | .11 |
| ❑ 119 Tim Belk | .25 | .11 |
| ❑ 120 Edgar Renteria | .50 | .23 |
| ❑ 121 Calvin Maduro RC | .50 | .23 |
| ❑ 122 Jerry Martin RC | .25 | .11 |
| ❑ 123 Ramon Fermin RC | .25 | .11 |
| ❑ 124 Kimera Bartee RC | .25 | .11 |
| ❑ 125 Mark Farris | .25 | .11 |
| ❑ 126 Frank Rodriguez | .25 | .11 |
| ❑ 127 Bobby Higginson RC | 4.00 | 1.80 |
| ❑ 128 Bret Wagner | .25 | .11 |
| ❑ 129 Edwin Diaz RC | .50 | .23 |
| ❑ 130 Jimmy Haynes | .25 | .11 |
| ❑ 131 Chris Weinke RC | 6.00 | 2.70 |
| ❑ 132 Damian Jackson RC | 1.50 | .70 |
| ❑ 133 Felix Martinez | .25 | .11 |
| ❑ 134 Edwin Hurtado RC | .25 | .11 |
| ❑ 135 Matt Raleigh RC | .25 | .11 |
| ❑ 136 Paul Wilson | .25 | .11 |
| ❑ 137 Ron Villone | .25 | .11 |
| ❑ 138 Eric Stuckenschneider RC | .25 | .11 |
| ❑ 139 Tate Seefried | .25 | .11 |
| ❑ 140 Rey Ordonez RC | 2.50 | 1.10 |
| ❑ 141 Eddie Pearson | .25 | .11 |
| ❑ 142 Kevin Gallaher | .25 | .11 |
| ❑ 143 Torii Hunter | .50 | .23 |
| ❑ 144 Daron Kirkreit | .25 | .11 |
| ❑ 145 Craig Wilson | .25 | .11 |
| ❑ 146 Ugueth Urbina | .25 | .11 |
| ❑ 147 Chris Snopek | .25 | .11 |

❑ 148 Kym Ashworth .25 .11
❑ 149 Wayne Gomes .25 .11
❑ 150 Mark Loretta .25 .11
❑ 151 Ramon Morel RC .25 .11
❑ 152 Trot Nixon .50 .23
❑ 153 Desi Relaford .25 .11
❑ 154 Scott Sullivan .25 .11
❑ 155 Marc Barcelo .25 .11
❑ 156 Willie Adams .25 .11
❑ 157 Derrick Gibson RC 1.00 .45
❑ 158 Brian Meadows RC .50 .23
❑ 159 Julian Tavarez .25 .11
❑ 160 Bryan Rekar .25 .11
❑ 161 Steve Gibralter .25 .11
❑ 162 Esteban Loaiza .25 .11
❑ 163 John Wasdin .25 .11
❑ 164 Kirk Presley .25 .11
❑ 165 Mariano Rivera .50 .23
❑ 166 Andy Larkin .25 .11
❑ 167 Sean Whiteside RC .25 .11
❑ 168 Matt Apana RC .25 .11
❑ 169 Shawn Senior RC .25 .11
❑ 170 Scott Gentile .25 .11
❑ 171 Quilvio Veras .25 .11
❑ 172 Eli Marrero RC .50 .23
❑ 173 Mendy Lopez RC .25 .11
❑ 174 Homer Bush .25 .11
❑ 175 Brian Stephenson RC .25 .11
❑ 176 Jon Nunnally .25 .11
❑ 177 Jose Herrera .25 .11
❑ 178 Corey Avrard RC .50 .23
❑ 179 David Bell .25 .11
❑ 180 Jason Isringhausen .50 .23
❑ 181 Jamey Wright .25 .11
❑ 182 Lonell Roberts RC .25 .11
❑ 183 Marty Cordova .25 .11
❑ 184 Amaury Telemaco .25 .11
❑ 185 John Mabry .25 .11
❑ 186 Andrew Vessel RC .25 .11
❑ 187 Jim Cole RC .25 .11
❑ 188 Marquis Riley .25 .11
❑ 189 Todd Dunn .25 .11
❑ 190 John Carter .25 .11
❑ 191 Donnie Sadler RC 1.00 .45
❑ 192 Mike Bell .50 .23
❑ 193 Chris Cumberland RC .25 .11
❑ 194 Jason Schmidt .25 .11
❑ 195 Matt Brunson .25 .11
❑ 196 James Baldwin .50 .23
❑ 197 Bill Simas RC .25 .11
❑ 198 Gus Gandarillas .25 .11
❑ 199 Mac Suzuki .25 .11
❑ 200 Rick Holifield RC .25 .11
❑ 201 Fernando Lunar RC .25 .11
❑ 202 Kevin Jarvis .25 .11
❑ 203 Everett Stull .25 .11
❑ 204 Steve Wojciechowski .25 .11
❑ 205 Shawn Estes .50 .23
❑ 206 Jermaine Dye 1.50 .70
❑ 207 Marc Kroon .25 .11
❑ 208 Peter Munro RC .25 .11
❑ 209 Pat Watkins .25 .11
❑ 210 Matt Smith .25 .11
❑ 211 Joe Vitiello .25 .11
❑ 212 Gerald Witasick Jr. .25 .11
❑ 213 Freddy Garcia RC .25 .11
❑ 214 Glenn Dishman RC .25 .11
❑ 215 Jay Canizaro RC .25 .11
❑ 216 Angel Martinez .25 .11
❑ 217 Yamil Benitez RC .25 .11
❑ 218 Fausto Macey RC .25 .11
❑ 219 Eric Owens .50 .23
❑ 220 Checklist .25 .11
❑ 221 Dwayne Hosey FOIL RC .25 .11
❑ 222 Brad Woodall FOIL RC .40 .18
❑ 223 Billy Ashley FOIL .40 .18
❑ 224 Mark Grudzielanek FOIL RC 2.00 .90
❑ 225 Mark Johnson FOIL RC .40 .18
❑ 226 Tim Unroe FOIL RC .40 .18
❑ 227 Todd Greene FOIL .25 .11
❑ 228 Larry Sutton FOIL .40 .18
❑ 229 Derek Jeter FOIL 5.00 2.20
❑ 230 Sal Fasano FOIL RC .40 .18
❑ 231 Ruben Rivera FOIL .25 .11
❑ 232 Chris Truby FOIL RC 4.00 1.80
❑ 233 John Donati FOIL .40 .18
❑ 234 Decomba Conner FOIL RC .25 .11
❑ 235 Sergio Nunez FOIL RC .25 .11
❑ 236 Ray Brown RC FOIL .40 .18
❑ 237 Juan Melo FOIL RC .50 .23
❑ 238 Hideo Nomo FOIL RC 6.00 2.70
❑ 239 Jamie Bluma RC FOIL .40 .18
❑ 240 Jay Payton FOIL RC 5.00 2.20
❑ 241 Paul Konerko FOIL 2.50 1.10
❑ 242 Scott Elarton FOIL RC 5.00 2.20
❑ 243 Jeff Abbott FOIL RC .50 .23
❑ 244 Jim Brower RC FOIL .40 .18
❑ 245 Geoff Blum FOIL RC 2.00 .90
❑ 246 Aaron Boone FOIL RC .50 .23
❑ 247 J.R. Phillips FOIL .40 .18
❑ 248 Alex Ochoa FOIL .40 .18
❑ 249 Nomar Garciaparra FOIL 15.00 6.75
❑ 250 Garret Anderson FOIL .50 .23
❑ 251 Ray Durham FOIL .50 .23
❑ 252 Paul Shuey FOIL .40 .18
❑ 253 Tony Clark FOIL .50 .23
❑ 254 Johnny Damon FOIL .50 .23
❑ 255 Duane Singleton FOIL .40 .18
❑ 256 LaTroy Hawkins FOIL .40 .18
❑ 257 Andy Pettitte FOIL .50 .23
❑ 258 Ben Grieve FOIL 4.00 1.80
❑ 259 Marc Newfield FOIL .40 .18
❑ 260 Terrell Lowery FOIL .40 .18
❑ 261 Shawn Green FOIL 1.00 .45
❑ 262 Chipper Jones FOIL 2.50 1.10
❑ 263 Brooks Kieschnick FOIL .25 .11
❑ 264 Pokey Reese FOIL .50 .23
❑ 265 Doug Million FOIL .40 .18
❑ 266 Marc Valdes FOIL .40 .18
❑ 267 Brian L.Hunter FOIL .25 .11
❑ 268 Todd Hollandsworth FOIL .25 .11
❑ 269 Rod Henderson FOIL .40 .18
❑ 270 Bill Pulsipher FOIL .40 .18
❑ 271 Scott Rolen FOIL RC 20.00 9.00
❑ 272 Trey Beamon FOIL .40 .18
❑ 273 Alan Benes FOIL .25 .11
❑ 274 Dustin Hermanson FOIL .40 .18
❑ 275 Ricky Bottalico .25 .11
❑ 276 Albert Belle .50 .23
❑ 277 Deion Sanders .50 .23
❑ 278 Matt Williams .50 .23
❑ 279 Jeff Bagwell 1.25 .55
❑ 280 Kirby Puckett 2.50 1.10
❑ 281 Dave Hollins .25 .11
❑ 282 Don Mattingly 2.50 1.10
❑ 283 Joey Hamilton .25 .11
❑ 284 Bobby Bonilla .50 .23
❑ 285 Moises Alou .50 .23
❑ 286 Tom Glavine 1.00 .45
❑ 287 Brett Butler .50 .23
❑ 288 Chris Hoiles .25 .11
❑ 289 Kenny Rogers .25 .11
❑ 290 Larry Walker .50 .23
❑ 291 Tim Raines .50 .23
❑ 292 Kevin Appier .50 .23
❑ 293 Roger Clemens 2.00 .90
❑ 294 Chuck Carr .25 .11
❑ 295 Randy Myers .25 .11
❑ 296 Dave Nilsson .25 .11
❑ 297 Joe Carter .50 .23
❑ 298 Chuck Finley .50 .23
❑ 299 Ray Lankford .50 .23
❑ 300 Roberto Kelly .25 .11
❑ 301 Jon Lieber .25 .11
❑ 302 Travis Fryman .50 .23
❑ 303 Mark McGwire 4.00 1.80
❑ 304 Tony Gwynn 2.00 .90
❑ 305 Kenny Lofton .50 .23
❑ 306 Mark Whiten .25 .11
❑ 307 Doug Drabek .25 .11
❑ 308 Terry Steinbach .25 .11
❑ 309 Ryan Klesko .50 .23
❑ 310 Mike Piazza 3.00 1.35
❑ 311 Ben McDonald .25 .11
❑ 312 Reggie Sanders .25 .11
❑ 313 Alex Fernandez .25 .11
❑ 314 Aaron Sele .50 .23
❑ 315 Gregg Jefferies .25 .11
❑ 316 Rickey Henderson 1.25 .55
❑ 317 Brian Anderson .25 .11
❑ 318 Jose Valentin .25 .11
❑ 319 Rod Beck .25 .11
❑ 320 Marquis Grissom .25 .11
❑ 321 Ken Griffey Jr. 4.00 1.80
❑ 322 Bret Saberhagen .50 .23
❑ 323 Juan Gonzalez 1.00 .45
❑ 324 Paul Molitor 1.00 .45
❑ 325 Gary Sheffield 1.00 .45
❑ 326 Darren Daulton .50 .23
❑ 327 Bill Swift .25 .11
❑ 328 Brian McRae .25 .11
❑ 329 Robin Ventura .50 .23
❑ 330 Lee Smith .50 .23
❑ 331 Fred McGriff .50 .23
❑ 332 Delino DeShields .25 .11
❑ 333 Edgar Martinez .50 .23
❑ 334 Mike Mussina 1.00 .45
❑ 335 Orlando Merced .25 .11
❑ 336 Carlos Baerga .25 .11
❑ 337 Wil Cordero .25 .11
❑ 338 Tom Pagnozzi .25 .11
❑ 339 Pat Hentgen .25 .11
❑ 340 Chad Curtis .25 .11
❑ 341 Darren Lewis .25 .11
❑ 342 Jeff Kent .50 .23
❑ 343 Bip Roberts .25 .11
❑ 344 Ivan Rodriguez 1.25 .55
❑ 345 Jeff Montgomery .25 .11
❑ 346 Hal Morris .25 .11
❑ 347 Danny Tartabull .25 .11
❑ 348 Raul Mondesi .50 .23
❑ 349 Ken Hill .25 .11
❑ 350 Pedro Martinez 1.25 .55
❑ 351 Frank Thomas 2.00 .90
❑ 352 Manny Ramirez 1.25 .55
❑ 353 Tim Salmon .50 .23
❑ 354 W. VanLandingham .25 .11
❑ 355 Andres Galarraga .50 .23
❑ 356 Paul O'Neill .50 .23
❑ 357 Brady Anderson .50 .23
❑ 358 Ramon Martinez .25 .11
❑ 359 John Olerud .50 .23
❑ 360 Ruben Sierra .25 .11
❑ 361 Cal Eldred .25 .11
❑ 362 Jay Buhner .50 .23
❑ 363 Jay Bell .50 .23
❑ 364 Wally Joyner .50 .23
❑ 365 Chuck Knoblauch .50 .23
❑ 366 Len Dykstra .50 .23
❑ 367 John Wetteland .50 .23
❑ 368 Roberto Alomar 1.00 .45
❑ 369 Craig Biggio .50 .23
❑ 370 Ozzie Smith 1.25 .55
❑ 371 Terry Pendleton .50 .23
❑ 372 Sammy Sosa 2.00 .90
❑ 373 Carlos Garcia .25 .11
❑ 374 Jose Rijo .25 .11
❑ 375 Chris Gomez .25 .11
❑ 376 Barry Bonds 1.50 .70
❑ 377 Steve Avery .25 .11
❑ 378 Rick Wilkins .25 .11
❑ 379 Pete Harnisch .25 .11
❑ 380 Dean Palmer .50 .23
❑ 381 Bob Hamelin .25 .11
❑ 382 Jason Bere .25 .11
❑ 383 Jimmy Key .50 .23
❑ 384 Dante Bichette .50 .23
❑ 385 Rafael Palmeiro 1.00 .45
❑ 386 David Justice .50 .23
❑ 387 Chili Davis .50 .23
❑ 388 Mike Greenwell .25 .11
❑ 389 Todd Zeile .25 .11
❑ 390 Jeff Conine .25 .11
❑ 391 Rick Aguilera .25 .11
❑ 392 Eddie Murray 1.00 .45
❑ 393 Mike Stanley .25 .11
❑ 394 Cliff Floyd UER .50 .23
(Numbered 294)
❑ 395 Randy Johnson 1.25 .55
❑ 396 David Nied .25 .11
❑ 397 Devon White .50 .23
❑ 398 Royce Clayton .25 .11
❑ 399 Andy Benes .25 .11
❑ 400 John Hudek .25 .11
❑ 401 Bobby Jones .25 .11
❑ 402 Eric Karros .50 .23
❑ 403 Will Clark 1.00 .45

❑ 404 Mark Langston .25 .11
❑ 405 Kevin Brown .50 .23
❑ 406 Greg Maddux 2.50 1.10
❑ 407 David Cone .50 .23
❑ 408 Wade Boggs 1.25 .55
❑ 409 Steve Trachsel .25 .11
❑ 410 Greg Vaughn .50 .23
❑ 411 Mo Vaughn .50 .23
❑ 412 Wilson Alvarez .25 .11
❑ 413 Cal Ripken 4.00 1.80
❑ 414 Rico Brogna .25 .11
❑ 415 Barry Larkin 1.00 .45
❑ 416 Cecil Fielder .50 .23
❑ 417 Jose Canseco 1.25 .55
❑ 418 Jack McDowell .25 .11
❑ 419 Mike Lieberthal .50 .23
❑ 420 Andrew Lorraine .25 .11
❑ 421 Rich Becker .25 .11
❑ 422 Tony Phillips .25 .11
❑ 423 Scott Ruffcorn .25 .11
❑ 424 Jeff Granger .25 .11
❑ 425 Greg Pirkl .25 .11
❑ 426 Dennis Eckersley .50 .23
❑ 427 Jose Lima .25 .11
❑ 428 Russ Davis .25 .11
❑ 429 Armando Benitez .50 .23
❑ 430 Alex Gonzalez .25 .11
❑ 431 Carlos Delgado 1.00 .45
❑ 432 Chan Ho Park .50 .23
❑ 433 Mickey Tettleton .25 .11
❑ 434 Dave Winfield 1.00 .45
❑ 435 John Burkett .25 .11
❑ 436 Orlando Miller .25 .11
❑ 437 Rondell White .50 .23
❑ 438 Jose Oliva .25 .11
❑ 439 Checklist .25 .11

## 1996 Bowman

| | MINT | NRMT |
|---|---|---|
| COMPLETE SET (385) | 120.00 | 55.00 |
| COMMON CARD (1-385) | .15 | .07 |

❑ 1 Cal Ripken 2.50 1.10
❑ 2 Ray Durham .25 .11
❑ 3 Ivan Rodriguez .75 .35
❑ 4 Fred McGriff .50 .23
❑ 5 Hideo Nomo .60 .25
❑ 6 Troy Percival .15 .07
❑ 7 Moises Alou .25 .11
❑ 8 Mike Stanley .15 .07
❑ 9 Jay Buhner .25 .11
❑ 10 Shawn Green .60 .25
❑ 11 Ryan Klesko .25 .11
❑ 12 Andres Galarraga .50 .23
❑ 13 Dean Palmer .25 .11
❑ 14 Jeff Conine .15 .07
❑ 15 Brian L.Hunter .15 .07
❑ 16 J.T. Snow .25 .11
❑ 17 Larry Walker .25 .11
❑ 18 Barry Larkin .60 .25
❑ 19 Alex Gonzalez .15 .07
❑ 20 Edgar Martinez .50 .23
❑ 21 Mo Vaughn .25 .11
❑ 22 Mark McGwire 2.50 1.10
❑ 23 Jose Canseco .75 .35
❑ 24 Jack McDowell .15 .07
❑ 25 Dante Bichette .25 .11
❑ 26 Wade Boggs .75 .35
❑ 27 Mike Piazza 2.00 .90
❑ 28 Ray Lankford .25 .11
❑ 29 Craig Biggio .50 .23
❑ 30 Rafael Palmeiro .60 .25
❑ 31 Ron Gant .15 .07
❑ 32 Javy Lopez .25 .11
❑ 33 Brian Jordan .25 .11
❑ 34 Paul O'Neill .25 .11
❑ 35 Mark Grace .60 .25
❑ 36 Matt Williams .50 .23
❑ 37 Pedro Martinez .75 .35
❑ 38 Rickey Henderson .75 .35
❑ 39 Bobby Bonilla .25 .11
❑ 40 Todd Hollandsworth .15 .07
❑ 41 Jim Thome .50 .23
❑ 42 Gary Sheffield .25 .11
❑ 43 Tim Salmon .25 .11
❑ 44 Gregg Jefferies .15 .07
❑ 45 Roberto Alomar .60 .25
❑ 46 Carlos Baerga .15 .07
❑ 47 Mark Grudzielanek .15 .07
❑ 48 Randy Johnson .75 .35
❑ 49 Tino Martinez .25 .11
❑ 50 Robin Ventura .25 .11
❑ 51 Ryne Sandberg .75 .35
❑ 52 Jay Bell .25 .11
❑ 53 Jason Schmidt .15 .07
❑ 54 Frank Thomas 1.25 .55
❑ 55 Kenny Lofton .25 .11
❑ 56 Ariel Prieto .15 .07
❑ 57 David Cone .25 .11
❑ 58 Reggie Sanders .15 .07
❑ 59 Michael Tucker .15 .07
❑ 60 Vinny Castilla .25 .11
❑ 61 Len Dykstra .25 .11
❑ 62 Todd Hundley .15 .07
❑ 63 Brian McRae .15 .07
❑ 64 Dennis Eckersley .25 .11
❑ 65 Rondell White .25 .11
❑ 66 Eric Karros .25 .11
❑ 67 Greg Maddux 1.50 .70
❑ 68 Kevin Appier .25 .11
❑ 69 Eddie Murray .00 .25
❑ 70 John Olerud .25 .11
❑ 71 Tony Gwynn 1.25 .55
❑ 72 David Justice .50 .23
❑ 73 Ken Caminiti .25 .11
❑ 74 Terry Steinbach .15 .07
❑ 75 Alan Benes .15 .07
❑ 76 Chipper Jones 1.50 .70
❑ 77 Jeff Bagwell .75 .35
❑ 78 Barry Bonds 1.00 .45
❑ 79 Ken Griffey Jr. 3.00 1.35
❑ 80 Roger Cedeno .15 .07
❑ 81 Joe Carter .25 .11
❑ 82 Henry Rodriguez .15 .07
❑ 83 Jason Isringhausen .25 .11
❑ 84 Chuck Knoblauch .25 .11
❑ 85 Manny Ramirez .75 .35
❑ 86 Tom Glavine .60 .25
❑ 87 Jeffrey Hammonds .25 .11
❑ 88 Paul Molitor .60 .25
❑ 89 Roger Clemens 1.25 .55
❑ 90 Greg Vaughn .25 .11
❑ 91 Marty Cordova .15 .07
❑ 92 Albert Belle .50 .23
❑ 93 Mike Mussina .60 .25
❑ 94 Garret Anderson .25 .11
❑ 95 Juan Gonzalez .60 .25
❑ 96 John Valentin .15 .07
❑ 97 Jason Giambi .60 .25
❑ 98 Kirby Puckett 1.50 .70
❑ 99 Jim Edmonds .60 .25
❑ 100 Cecil Fielder .25 .11
❑ 101 Mike Aldrete .15 .07
❑ 102 Marquis Grissom .15 .07
❑ 103 Derek Bell .15 .07
❑ 104 Raul Mondesi .25 .11
❑ 105 Sammy Sosa 1.25 .55
❑ 106 Travis Fryman .25 .11
❑ 107 Rico Brogna .15 .07
❑ 108 Will Clark .60 .25
❑ 109 Bernie Williams .60 .25
❑ 110 Brady Anderson .25 .11
❑ 111 Torii Hunter .25 .11
❑ 112 Derek Jeter 2.50 1.10
❑ 113 Mike Kusiewicz RC .50 .23
❑ 114 Scott Rolen 1.50 .70
❑ 115 Ramon Castro .25 .11
❑ 116 Jose Guillen RC 1.25 .55
❑ 117 Wade Walker RC .15 .07
❑ 118 Shawn Senior .15 .07
❑ 119 Onan Masaoka RC 1.00 .55
❑ 120 Marlon Anderson RC 1.00 .45
❑ 121 Katsuhiro Maeda RC .50 .23
❑ 122 Garrett Stephenson RC 2.00 .90
❑ 123 Butch Huskey .15 .07
❑ 124 D'Angelo Jimenez RC 2.00 .90
❑ 125 Tony Mounce RC .15 .07
❑ 126 Jay Canizaro .15 .07
❑ 127 Juan Melo .25 .11
❑ 128 Steve Gibralter .15 .07
❑ 129 Freddy Garcia .15 .07
❑ 130 Julio Santana UER .15 .07
(Card has him born in 1993)
❑ 131 Richard Hidalgo .25 .11
❑ 132 Jermaine Dye .25 .11
❑ 133 Willie Adams .15 .07
❑ 134 Everett Stull .15 .07
❑ 135 Ramon Morel .15 .07
❑ 136 Chan Ho Park .25 .11
❑ 137 Jamey Wright .15 .07
❑ 138 Luis Garcia RC .15 .07
❑ 139 Dan Serafini .15 .07
❑ 140 Ryan Dempster RC 5.00 2.20
❑ 141 Tate Seefried .15 .07
❑ 142 Jimmy Hurst .15 .07
❑ 143 Travis Miller .15 .07
❑ 144 Curtis Goodwin .15 .07
❑ 145 Rocky Coppinger RC .60 .25
❑ 146 Enrique Wilson .15 .07
❑ 147 Jaime Bluma .15 .07
❑ 148 Andrew Vessel .15 .07
❑ 149 Damian Moss .15 .07
❑ 150 Shawn Gallagher RC .50 .23
❑ 151 Pat Watkins .25 .11
❑ 152 Jose Paniagua .15 .07
❑ 153 Danny Graves .50 .23
❑ 154 Bryon Gainey RC .15 .07
❑ 155 Steve Soderstrom .15 .07
❑ 156 Cliff Brumbaugh RC .15 .07
❑ 157 Eugene Kingsale RC .75 .35
❑ 158 Lou Collier .15 .07
❑ 159 Todd Walker .25 .11
❑ 160 Kris Detmers RC .50 .23
❑ 161 Josh Booty RC .75 .35
❑ 162 Greg Whiteman RC .15 .07
❑ 163 Damian Jackson .15 .07
❑ 164 Tony Clark .15 .07
❑ 165 Jeff D'Amico .15 .07
❑ 166 Johnny Damon .50 .23
❑ 167 Rafael Orellano .15 .07
❑ 168 Ruben Rivera .15 .07
❑ 169 Alex Ochoa .15 .07
❑ 170 Jay Powell .15 .07
❑ 171 Tom Evans .15 .07
❑ 172 Ron Villone .15 .07
❑ 173 Shawn Estes .25 .11
❑ 174 John Wasdin .15 .07
❑ 175 Bill Simas .15 .07
❑ 176 Kevin Brown .50 .23
❑ 177 Shannon Stewart .25 .11
❑ 178 Todd Greene .15 .07
❑ 179 Bob Wolcott .15 .07
❑ 180 Chris Snopek .15 .07
❑ 181 Nomar Garciaparra 2.50 1.10
❑ 182 Cameron Smith RC .15 .07
❑ 183 Matt Drews .15 .07
❑ 184 Jimmy Haynes .15 .07
❑ 185 Chris Carpenter .25 .11
❑ 186 Desi Relaford .15 .07
❑ 187 Ben Grieve .25 .11
❑ 188 Mike Bell .15 .07
❑ 189 Luis Castillo RC 3.00 1.35
❑ 190 Ugueth Urbina .25 .11
❑ 191 Paul Wilson .15 .07
❑ 192 Andruw Jones 2.00 .90
❑ 193 Wayne Gomes .15 .07
❑ 194 Craig Counsell RC .15 .07
❑ 195 Jim Cole .15 .07

| | No. | Player | Mint | NRMT |
|---|---|---|---|---|
| ❑ | 196 | Brooks Kieschnick | .15 | .07 |
| ❑ | 197 | Trey Beamon | .15 | .07 |
| ❑ | 198 | Marino Santana RC | .15 | .07 |
| ❑ | 199 | Bob Abreu | 1.00 | .45 |
| ❑ | 200 | Pokey Reese | .25 | .11 |
| ❑ | 201 | Dante Powell | .25 | .11 |
| ❑ | 202 | George Arias | .15 | .07 |
| ❑ | 203 | Jorge Velandia RC | .15 | .07 |
| ❑ | 204 | George Lombard RC | 2.00 | .90 |
| ❑ | 205 | Byron Browne RC | .15 | .07 |
| ❑ | 206 | John Frascatore | .15 | .07 |
| ❑ | 207 | Terry Adams | .15 | .07 |
| ❑ | 208 | Wilson Delgado RC | .50 | .23 |
| ❑ | 209 | Billy McMillon | .15 | .07 |
| ❑ | 210 | Jeff Abbott | .15 | .07 |
| ❑ | 211 | Trot Nixon | .15 | .07 |
| ❑ | 212 | Amaury Telemaco | .15 | .07 |
| ❑ | 213 | Scott Sullivan | .15 | .07 |
| ❑ | 214 | Justin Thompson | .15 | .07 |
| ❑ | 215 | Decomba Conner | .25 | .11 |
| ❑ | 216 | Ryan McGuire | .15 | .07 |
| ❑ | 217 | Matt Luke | .15 | .07 |
| ❑ | 218 | Doug Million | .15 | .07 |
| ❑ | 219 | Jason Dickson RC | .25 | .11 |
| ❑ | 220 | Ramon Hernandez RC | 2.00 | .90 |
| ❑ | 221 | Mark Bellhorn RC | .50 | .23 |
| ❑ | 222 | Eric Ludwick RC | .15 | .07 |
| ❑ | 223 | Luke Wilcox RC | .15 | .07 |
| ❑ | 224 | Marty Malloy RC | .15 | .07 |
| ❑ | 225 | Gary Coffee RC | .25 | .11 |
| ❑ | 226 | Wendell Magee RC | .25 | .11 |
| ❑ | 227 | Brett Tomko RC | .75 | .35 |
| ❑ | 228 | Derek Lowe | .15 | .07 |
| ❑ | 229 | Jose Rosado RC | .75 | .35 |
| ❑ | 230 | Steve Bourgeois RC | .15 | .07 |
| ❑ | 231 | Neil Weber RC | .15 | .07 |
| ❑ | 232 | Jeff Ware | .15 | .07 |
| ❑ | 233 | Edwin Diaz | .25 | .11 |
| ❑ | 234 | Greg Norton | .15 | .07 |
| ❑ | 235 | Aaron Boone | .15 | .07 |
| ❑ | 236 | Jeff Suppan | .15 | .07 |
| ❑ | 237 | Bret Wagner | .15 | .07 |
| ❑ | 238 | Elieser Marrero | .15 | .07 |
| ❑ | 239 | Will Cunnane | .25 | .11 |
| ❑ | 240 | Brian Barkley RC | .15 | .07 |
| ❑ | 241 | Jay Payton | .25 | .11 |
| ❑ | 242 | Marcus Jensen | .15 | .07 |
| ❑ | 243 | Ryan Nye | .15 | .07 |
| ❑ | 244 | Chad Mottola | .15 | .07 |
| ❑ | 245 | Scott McClain RC | .15 | .07 |
| ❑ | 246 | Jessie Ibarra RC | .25 | .11 |
| ❑ | 247 | Mike Darr RC | 1.50 | .70 |
| ❑ | 248 | Bobby Estalella RC | 2.00 | .90 |
| ❑ | 249 | Michael Barrett | .25 | .11 |
| ❑ | 250 | Jamie Lopiccolo RC | .15 | .07 |
| ❑ | 251 | Shane Spencer RC | 2.00 | 1.35 |
| ❑ | 252 | Ben Petrick RC | 2.00 | 1.35 |
| ❑ | 253 | Jason Bell RC | .50 | .23 |
| ❑ | 254 | Arnold Gooch RC | .15 | .07 |
| ❑ | 255 | T.J. Mathews | .15 | .07 |
| ❑ | 256 | Jason Ryan | .15 | .07 |
| ❑ | 257 | Pat Cline RC | .50 | .23 |
| ❑ | 258 | Rafael Carmona RC | .15 | .07 |
| ❑ | 259 | Carl Pavano RC | 2.00 | .90 |
| ❑ | 260 | Ben Davis | .25 | .11 |
| ❑ | 261 | Matt Lawton RC | 2.00 | .90 |
| ❑ | 262 | Kevin Sefcik RC | .15 | .07 |
| ❑ | 263 | Chris Fussell RC | .50 | .23 |
| ❑ | 264 | Mike Cameron RC | 2.50 | 1.10 |
| ❑ | 265 | Marty Janzen RC | .15 | .07 |
| ❑ | 266 | Livan Hernandez RC | 2.00 | .90 |
| ❑ | 267 | Raul Ibanez RC | .15 | .07 |
| ❑ | 268 | Juan Encarnacion | .60 | .25 |
| ❑ | 269 | David Yocum RC | .15 | .07 |
| ❑ | 270 | Jonathan Johnson RC | .15 | .07 |
| ❑ | 271 | Reggie Taylor | .25 | .11 |
| ❑ | 272 | Danny Buxbaum RC | .15 | .07 |
| ❑ | 273 | Jacob Cruz | .15 | .07 |
| ❑ | 274 | Bobby Morris RC | .15 | .07 |
| ❑ | 275 | Andy Fox RC | .15 | .07 |
| ❑ | 276 | Greg Keagle | .15 | .07 |
| ❑ | 277 | Charles Peterson | .15 | .07 |
| ❑ | 278 | Derrek Lee | .15 | .07 |
| ❑ | 279 | Bryant Nelson RC | .15 | .07 |
| ❑ | 280 | Antone Williamson | .15 | .07 |
| ❑ | 281 | Scott Elarton | .60 | .25 |
| ❑ | 282 | Shad Williams RC | .15 | .07 |
| ❑ | 283 | Rich Hunter RC | .15 | .07 |
| ❑ | 284 | Chris Sheff | .15 | .07 |
| ❑ | 285 | Derrick Gibson | .15 | .07 |
| ❑ | 286 | Felix Rodriguez | .15 | .07 |
| ❑ | 287 | Brian Banks RC | .15 | .07 |
| ❑ | 288 | Jason McDonald | .15 | .07 |
| ❑ | 289 | Glendon Rusch RC | 1.00 | .45 |
| ❑ | 290 | Gary Rath | .15 | .07 |
| ❑ | 291 | Peter Munro | .25 | .11 |
| ❑ | 292 | Tom Fordham | .15 | .07 |
| ❑ | 293 | Jason Kendall | .25 | .11 |
| ❑ | 294 | Russ Johnson | .15 | .07 |
| ❑ | 295 | Joe Long | .15 | .07 |
| ❑ | 296 | Robert Smith RC | .75 | .35 |
| ❑ | 297 | Jarrod Washburn RC | .75 | .35 |
| ❑ | 298 | Dave Coggin RC | .50 | .23 |
| ❑ | 299 | Jeff Yoder RC | .50 | .23 |
| ❑ | 300 | Jed Hansen RC | .25 | .11 |
| ❑ | 301 | Matt Morris RC | .75 | .35 |
| ❑ | 302 | Josh Bishop RC | .15 | .07 |
| ❑ | 303 | Dustin Hermanson | .15 | .07 |
| ❑ | 304 | Mike Gulan | .15 | .07 |
| ❑ | 305 | Felipe Crespo | .15 | .07 |
| ❑ | 306 | Quinton McCracken | .15 | .07 |
| ❑ | 307 | Jim Bonnici RC | .15 | .07 |
| ❑ | 308 | Sal Fasano | .15 | .07 |
| ❑ | 309 | Gabe Alvarez RC | .75 | .35 |
| ❑ | 310 | Heath Murray RC | .15 | .07 |
| ❑ | 311 | Jose Valentin RC | .50 | .23 |
| ❑ | 312 | Bartolo Colon | .25 | .11 |
| ❑ | 313 | Olmedo Saenz | .15 | .07 |
| ❑ | 314 | Norm Hutchins RC | .75 | .35 |
| ❑ | 315 | Chris Holt | .15 | .07 |
| ❑ | 316 | David Doster RC | .15 | .07 |
| ❑ | 317 | Robert Person | .15 | .07 |
| ❑ | 318 | Donne Wall RC | .15 | .07 |
| ❑ | 319 | Adam Riggs RC | .15 | .07 |
| ❑ | 320 | Homer Bush | .15 | .07 |
| ❑ | 321 | Brad Rigby RC | .15 | .07 |
| ❑ | 322 | Lou Merloni RC | 1.00 | .45 |
| ❑ | 323 | Neifi Perez | .15 | .07 |
| ❑ | 324 | Chris Cumberland | .15 | .07 |
| ❑ | 325 | Alvie Shepherd RC | .15 | .07 |
| ❑ | 326 | Jarrod Patterson RC | .15 | .07 |
| ❑ | 327 | Ray Ricken RC | .25 | .11 |
| ❑ | 328 | Danny Klassen RC | .50 | .23 |
| ❑ | 329 | David Miller RC | .15 | .07 |
| ❑ | 330 | Chad Alexander RC | .50 | .23 |
| ❑ | 331 | Matt Beaumont | .15 | .07 |
| ❑ | 332 | Damon Hollins | .15 | .07 |
| ❑ | 333 | Todd Dunn | .15 | .07 |
| ❑ | 334 | Mike Sweeney RC | 6.00 | 2.70 |
| ❑ | 335 | Richie Sexson | .60 | .25 |
| ❑ | 336 | Billy Wagner | .15 | .07 |
| ❑ | 337 | Ron Wright RC | .75 | .35 |
| ❑ | 338 | Paul Konerko | .25 | .11 |
| ❑ | 339 | Tommy Phelps RC | .15 | .07 |
| ❑ | 340 | Karim Garcia | .15 | .07 |
| ❑ | 341 | Mike Grace RC | .15 | .07 |
| ❑ | 342 | Russell Branyan RC | 6.00 | 2.70 |
| ❑ | 343 | Randy Winn RC | .75 | .35 |
| ❑ | 344 | A.J. Pierzynski RC | .75 | .35 |
| ❑ | 345 | Mike Busby RC | .15 | .07 |
| ❑ | 346 | Matt Beech RC | .15 | .07 |
| ❑ | 347 | Jose Cepeda RC | .15 | .07 |
| ❑ | 348 | Brian Stephenson | .15 | .07 |
| ❑ | 349 | Rey Ordonez | .25 | .11 |
| ❑ | 350 | Rich Aurilia RC | 1.50 | .70 |
| ❑ | 351 | Edgard Velazquez RC | .50 | .23 |
| ❑ | 352 | Raul Casanova | .15 | .07 |
| ❑ | 353 | Carlos Guillen RC | 2.00 | .90 |
| ❑ | 354 | Bruce Aven RC | .75 | .35 |
| ❑ | 355 | Ryan Jones RC | .15 | .07 |
| ❑ | 356 | Derek Aucoin RC | .15 | .07 |
| ❑ | 357 | Brian Rose RC | .75 | .35 |
| ❑ | 358 | Richard Almanzar RC | .15 | .07 |
| ❑ | 359 | Fletcher Bates RC | .15 | .07 |
| ❑ | 360 | Russ Ortiz RC | 2.00 | .90 |
| ❑ | 361 | Wilton Guerrero RC | .75 | .35 |
| ❑ | 362 | Geoff Jenkins RC | 5.00 | 2.20 |
| ❑ | 363 | Pete Janicki | .15 | .07 |
| ❑ | 364 | Yamil Benitez | .15 | .07 |
| ❑ | 365 | Aaron Holbert | .15 | .07 |
| ❑ | 366 | Tim Belk | .15 | .07 |
| ❑ | 367 | Terrell Wade | .15 | .07 |
| ❑ | 368 | Terrence Long | .60 | .25 |
| ❑ | 369 | Brad Fullmer | .25 | .11 |
| ❑ | 370 | Matt Wagner | .15 | .07 |
| ❑ | 371 | Craig Wilson RC | .15 | .07 |
| ❑ | 372 | Mark Loretta | .15 | .07 |
| ❑ | 373 | Eric Owens | .15 | .07 |
| ❑ | 374 | Vladimir Guerrero | 3.00 | 1.35 |
| ❑ | 375 | Tommy Davis | .15 | .07 |
| ❑ | 376 | Donnie Sadler | .25 | .11 |
| ❑ | 377 | Edgar Renteria | .25 | .11 |
| ❑ | 378 | Todd Helton | 3.00 | 1.35 |
| ❑ | 379 | Ralph Milliard RC | .15 | .07 |
| ❑ | 380 | Darin Blood RC | .15 | .07 |
| ❑ | 381 | Shayne Bennett | .15 | .07 |
| ❑ | 382 | Mark Redman | .15 | .07 |
| ❑ | 383 | Felix Martinez | .15 | .07 |
| ❑ | 384 | Sean Watkins RC | .15 | .07 |
| ❑ | 385 | Oscar Henriquez | .15 | .07 |
| ❑ | M20 | 1952 Bowman Mantle | 8.00 | 3.60 |
| ❑ | NNO | Unnumbered Checklists | .15 | .07 |

## 1997 Bowman

| | MINT | NRMT |
|---|---|---|
| COMPLETE SET (441) | 100.00 | 45.00 |
| COMPLETE SERIES 1 (221) | 50.00 | 22.00 |
| COMPLETE SERIES 2 (220) | 50.00 | 22.00 |
| COMMON CARD (1-441) | .15 | .07 |

| | No. | Player | Mint | NRMT |
|---|---|---|---|---|
| ❑ | 1 | Derek Jeter | 2.50 | 1.10 |
| ❑ | 2 | Edgar Renteria | .25 | .11 |
| ❑ | 3 | Chipper Jones | 1.50 | .70 |
| ❑ | 4 | Hideo Nomo | .60 | .25 |
| ❑ | 5 | Tim Salmon | .25 | .11 |
| ❑ | 6 | Jason Giambi | .60 | .25 |
| ❑ | 7 | Robin Ventura | .25 | .11 |
| ❑ | 8 | Tony Clark | .15 | .07 |
| ❑ | 9 | Barry Larkin | .60 | .25 |
| ❑ | 10 | Paul Molitor | .60 | .25 |
| ❑ | 11 | Bernard Gilkey | .15 | .07 |
| ❑ | 12 | Jack McDowell | .15 | .07 |
| ❑ | 13 | Andy Benes | .15 | .07 |
| ❑ | 14 | Ryan Klesko | .25 | .11 |
| ❑ | 15 | Mark McGwire | 2.50 | 1.10 |
| ❑ | 16 | Ken Griffey Jr. | 2.50 | 1.10 |
| ❑ | 17 | Robb Nen | .15 | .07 |
| ❑ | 18 | Cal Ripken | 2.50 | 1.10 |
| ❑ | 19 | John Valentin | .15 | .07 |
| ❑ | 20 | Ricky Bottalico | .15 | .07 |
| ❑ | 21 | Mike Lansing | .15 | .07 |
| ❑ | 22 | Ryne Sandberg | .75 | .35 |
| ❑ | 23 | Carlos Delgado | .60 | .25 |
| ❑ | 24 | Craig Biggio | .40 | .18 |
| ❑ | 25 | Eric Karros | .25 | .11 |
| ❑ | 26 | Kevin Appier | .25 | .11 |
| ❑ | 27 | Mariano Rivera | .25 | .11 |
| ❑ | 28 | Vinny Castilla | .25 | .11 |
| ❑ | 29 | Juan Gonzalez | .60 | .25 |
| ❑ | 30 | Al Martin | .15 | .07 |
| ❑ | 31 | Jeff Cirillo | .25 | .11 |
| ❑ | 32 | Eddie Murray | .60 | .25 |
| ❑ | 33 | Ray Lankford | .25 | .11 |
| ❑ | 34 | Manny Ramirez | .75 | .35 |
| ❑ | 35 | Roberto Alomar | .60 | .25 |
| ❑ | 36 | Will Clark | .60 | .25 |
| ❑ | 37 | Chuck Knoblauch | .25 | .11 |
| ❑ | 38 | Harold Baines | .25 | .11 |
| ❑ | 39 | Trevor Hoffman | .25 | .11 |

| No. | Player | Price | Price |
|---|---|---|---|
| ❑ 40 | Edgar Martinez | .40 | .18 |
| ❑ 41 | Geronimo Berroa | .15 | .07 |
| ❑ 42 | Rey Ordonez | .15 | .07 |
| ❑ 43 | Mike Stanley | .15 | .07 |
| ❑ 44 | Mike Mussina | .60 | .25 |
| ❑ 45 | Kevin Brown | .40 | .18 |
| ❑ 46 | Dennis Eckersley | .25 | .11 |
| ❑ 47 | Henry Rodriguez | .15 | .07 |
| ❑ 48 | Tino Martinez | .25 | .11 |
| ❑ 49 | Eric Young | .15 | .07 |
| ❑ 50 | Bret Boone | .25 | .11 |
| ❑ 51 | Raul Mondesi | .25 | .11 |
| ❑ 52 | Sammy Sosa | 1.25 | .55 |
| ❑ 53 | John Smoltz | .25 | .11 |
| ❑ 54 | Billy Wagner | .15 | .07 |
| ❑ 55 | Jeff D'Amico | .15 | .07 |
| ❑ 56 | Ken Caminiti | .25 | .11 |
| ❑ 57 | Jason Kendall | .25 | .11 |
| ❑ 58 | Wade Boggs | .75 | .35 |
| ❑ 59 | Andres Galarraga | .40 | .18 |
| ❑ 60 | Jeff Brantley | .15 | .07 |
| ❑ 61 | Mel Rojas | .15 | .07 |
| ❑ 62 | Brian L. Hunter | .15 | .07 |
| ❑ 63 | Bobby Bonilla | .25 | .11 |
| ❑ 64 | Roger Clemens | 1.25 | .55 |
| ❑ 65 | Jeff Kent | .40 | .18 |
| ❑ 66 | Matt Williams | .40 | .18 |
| ❑ 67 | Albert Belle | .40 | .18 |
| ❑ 68 | Jeff King | .15 | .07 |
| ❑ 69 | John Wetteland | .25 | .11 |
| ❑ 70 | Deion Sanders | .25 | .11 |
| ❑ 71 | Bubba Trammell RC | .50 | .23 |
| ❑ 72 | Felix Heredia RC | .50 | .23 |
| ❑ 73 | Billy Koch RC | 2.00 | .90 |
| ❑ 74 | Sidney Ponson RC | .75 | .35 |
| ❑ 75 | Ricky Ledee RC | 1.00 | .45 |
| ❑ 76 | Brett Tomko | .15 | .07 |
| ❑ 77 | Braden Looper RC | .50 | .23 |
| ❑ 78 | Damian Jackson | .15 | .07 |
| ❑ 79 | Jason Dickson | .15 | .07 |
| ❑ 80 | Chad Green RC | .50 | .23 |
| ❑ 81 | R.A. Dickey RC | .15 | .07 |
| ❑ 82 | Jeff Liefer | .25 | .11 |
| ❑ 83 | Matt Wagner | .15 | .07 |
| ❑ 84 | Richard Hidalgo | .25 | .11 |
| ❑ 85 | Adam Riggs | .15 | .07 |
| ❑ 86 | Robert Smith | .15 | .07 |
| ❑ 87 | Chad Hermansen RC | 1.25 | .55 |
| ❑ 88 | Felix Martinez | .15 | .07 |
| ❑ 89 | J.J. Johnson | .15 | .07 |
| ❑ 90 | Todd Dunwoody | .25 | .11 |
| ❑ 91 | Katsuhiro Maeda | .25 | .11 |
| ❑ 92 | Darin Erstad | .75 | .35 |
| ❑ 93 | Elieser Marrero | .15 | .07 |
| ❑ 94 | Bartolo Colon | .25 | .11 |
| ❑ 95 | Chris Fussell | .15 | .07 |
| ❑ 96 | Ugueth Urbina | .25 | .11 |
| ❑ 97 | Josh Paul RC | .50 | .23 |
| ❑ 98 | Jaime Bluma | .15 | .07 |
| ❑ 99 | Seth Greisinger RC | .50 | .23 |
| ❑ 100 | Jose Cruz Jr. RC | 2.50 | 1.10 |
| ❑ 101 | Todd Dunn | .15 | .07 |
| ❑ 102 | Joe Young RC | .15 | .07 |
| ❑ 103 | Jonathan Johnson | .15 | .07 |
| ❑ 104 | Justin Towle RC | .15 | .07 |
| ❑ 105 | Brian Rose | .15 | .07 |
| ❑ 106 | Jose Guillen | .15 | .07 |
| ❑ 107 | Andruw Jones | .75 | .35 |
| ❑ 108 | Mark Kotsay RC | 1.00 | .45 |
| ❑ 109 | Wilton Guerrero | .15 | .07 |
| ❑ 110 | Jacob Cruz | .15 | .07 |
| ❑ 111 | Mike Sweeney | .25 | .11 |
| ❑ 112 | Julio Mosquera | .15 | .07 |
| ❑ 113 | Matt Morris | .15 | .07 |
| ❑ 114 | Wendell Magee | .15 | .07 |
| ❑ 115 | John Thomson | .15 | .07 |
| ❑ 116 | Javier (Jose) Valentin | .25 | .11 |
| ❑ 117 | Tom Fordham | .15 | .07 |
| ❑ 118 | Ruben Rivera | .15 | .07 |
| ❑ 119 | Mike Drumright RC | .15 | .07 |
| ❑ 120 | Chris Holt | .15 | .07 |
| ❑ 121 | Sean Maloney | .15 | .07 |
| ❑ 122 | Michael Barrett | .15 | .07 |
| ❑ 123 | Tony Saunders RC | .25 | .11 |
| ❑ 124 | Kevin Brown C | .15 | .07 |
| ❑ 125 | Richard Almanzar | .15 | .07 |
| ❑ 126 | Mark Redman | .15 | .07 |
| ❑ 127 | Anthony Sanders RC | .15 | .07 |
| ❑ 128 | Jeff Abbott | .15 | .07 |
| ❑ 129 | Eugene Kingsale | .25 | .11 |
| ❑ 130 | Paul Konerko | .25 | .11 |
| ❑ 131 | Randall Simon RC | .50 | .23 |
| ❑ 132 | Andy Larkin | .15 | .07 |
| ❑ 133 | Rafael Medina | .25 | .11 |
| ❑ 134 | Mendy Lopez | .15 | .07 |
| ❑ 135 | Freddy Garcia | .15 | .07 |
| ❑ 136 | Karim Garcia | .15 | .07 |
| ❑ 137 | Larry Rodriguez RC | .15 | .07 |
| ❑ 138 | Carlos Guillen | .15 | .07 |
| ❑ 139 | Aaron Boone | .15 | .07 |
| ❑ 140 | Donnie Sadler | .25 | .11 |
| ❑ 141 | Brooks Kieschnick | .15 | .07 |
| ❑ 142 | Scott Spiezio | .15 | .07 |
| ❑ 143 | Everett Stull | .15 | .07 |
| ❑ 144 | Enrique Wilson | .15 | .07 |
| ❑ 145 | Milton Bradley RC | 3.00 | 1.35 |
| ❑ 146 | Kevin Orie | .15 | .07 |
| ❑ 147 | Derek Wallace | .15 | .07 |
| ❑ 148 | Russ Johnson | .15 | .07 |
| ❑ 149 | Joe Lagarde RC | .15 | .07 |
| ❑ 150 | Luis Castillo | .25 | .11 |
| ❑ 151 | Jay Payton | .25 | .11 |
| ❑ 152 | Joe Long | .25 | .11 |
| ❑ 153 | Livan Hernandez | .25 | .11 |
| ❑ 154 | Vladimir Nunez RC | .50 | .23 |
| ❑ 155 | Pokey Reese UER (Card actually numbered 156) | .25 | .11 |
| ❑ 156 | George Arias | .15 | .07 |
| ❑ 157 | Homer Bush | .15 | .07 |
| ❑ 158 | Chris Carpenter UER (Card numbered 159) | .25 | .11 |
| ❑ 159 | Eric Milton RC | 1.25 | .55 |
| ❑ 160 | Richie Sexson | .40 | .18 |
| ❑ 161 | Carl Pavano | .60 | .25 |
| ❑ 162 | Chris Gissell RC | .50 | .23 |
| ❑ 163 | Mac Suzuki | .15 | .07 |
| ❑ 164 | Pat Cline | .25 | .11 |
| ❑ 165 | Ron Wright | .25 | .11 |
| ❑ 166 | Dante Powell | .25 | .11 |
| ❑ 167 | Mark Bellhorn | .15 | .07 |
| ❑ 168 | George Lombard | .15 | .07 |
| ❑ 169 | Pee Wee Lopez RC | .50 | .23 |
| ❑ 170 | Paul Wilder RC | .15 | .07 |
| ❑ 171 | Brad Fullmer | .25 | .11 |
| ❑ 172 | Willie Martinez RC | .75 | .35 |
| ❑ 173 | Dario Veras RC | .25 | .11 |
| ❑ 174 | Dave Coggin | .15 | .07 |
| ❑ 175 | Kris Benson RC | 3.00 | 1.35 |
| ❑ 176 | Torii Hunter | .15 | .07 |
| ❑ 177 | D.T. Cromer | .15 | .07 |
| ❑ 178 | Nelson Figueroa RC | .50 | .23 |
| ❑ 179 | Hiram Bocachica RC | .75 | .35 |
| ❑ 180 | Shane Monahan | .25 | .11 |
| ❑ 181 | Jimmy Anderson RC | .50 | .23 |
| ❑ 182 | Juan Melo | .25 | .11 |
| ❑ 183 | Pablo Ortega RC | .15 | .07 |
| ❑ 184 | Calvin Pickering RC | .50 | .23 |
| ❑ 185 | Reggie Taylor | .25 | .11 |
| ❑ 186 | Jeff Farnsworth RC | .50 | .23 |
| ❑ 187 | Terrence Long | .60 | .25 |
| ❑ 188 | Geoff Jenkins | .25 | .11 |
| ❑ 189 | Steve Rain RC | .50 | .23 |
| ❑ 190 | Nerio Rodriguez RC | .15 | .07 |
| ❑ 191 | Derrick Gibson | .15 | .07 |
| ❑ 192 | Darin Blood | .15 | .07 |
| ❑ 193 | Ben Davis | .15 | .07 |
| ❑ 194 | Adrian Beltre RC | 4.00 | 1.80 |
| ❑ 195 | Damian Sapp RC UER | .50 | .23 |
| ❑ 196 | Kerry Wood RC | 5.00 | 2.20 |
| ❑ 197 | Nate Rolison RC | .75 | .35 |
| ❑ 198 | Fernando Tatis RC | 2.50 | 1.10 |
| ❑ 199 | Brad Penny RC | 3.00 | 1.35 |
| ❑ 200 | Jake Westbrook RC | .50 | .23 |
| ❑ 201 | Edwin Diaz | .15 | .07 |
| ❑ 202 | Joe Fontenot RC | .50 | .23 |
| ❑ 203 | Matt Halloran RC | .50 | .23 |
| ❑ 204 | Blake Stein RC | .15 | .07 |
| ❑ 205 | Onan Masaoka | .25 | .11 |
| ❑ 206 | Ben Petrick | .25 | .11 |
| ❑ 207 | Matt Clement RC | 1.00 | .45 |
| ❑ 208 | Todd Greene | .15 | .07 |
| ❑ 209 | Ray Ricken | .15 | .07 |
| ❑ 210 | Eric Chavez RC | 4.00 | 1.80 |
| ❑ 211 | Edgard Velazquez | .40 | .18 |
| ❑ 212 | Bruce Chen RC | 1.25 | .55 |
| ❑ 213 | Danny Patterson | .15 | .07 |
| ❑ 214 | Jeff Yoder | .15 | .07 |
| ❑ 215 | Luis Ordaz RC | .50 | .23 |
| ❑ 216 | Chris Widger | .15 | .07 |
| ❑ 217 | Jason Brester | .25 | .11 |
| ❑ 218 | Carlton Loewer | .25 | .11 |
| ❑ 219 | Chris Reitsma RC | .50 | .23 |
| ❑ 220 | Neifi Perez | .15 | .07 |
| ❑ 221 | Hideki Irabu RC | .75 | .35 |
| ❑ 222 | Ellis Burks | .25 | .11 |
| ❑ 223 | Pedro Martinez | .75 | .35 |
| ❑ 224 | Kenny Lofton | .25 | .11 |
| ❑ 225 | Randy Johnson | .75 | .35 |
| ❑ 226 | Terry Steinbach | .15 | .07 |
| ❑ 227 | Bernie Williams | .60 | .25 |
| ❑ 228 | Dean Palmer | .25 | .11 |
| ❑ 229 | Alan Benes | .15 | .07 |
| ❑ 230 | Marquis Grissom | .15 | .07 |
| ❑ 231 | Gary Sheffield | .60 | .25 |
| ❑ 232 | Curt Schilling | .25 | .11 |
| ❑ 233 | Reggie Sanders | .15 | .07 |
| ❑ 234 | Bobby Higginson | .25 | .11 |
| ❑ 235 | Moises Alou | .25 | .11 |
| ❑ 236 | Tom Glavine | .60 | .25 |
| ❑ 237 | Mark Grace | .60 | .25 |
| ❑ 238 | Ramon Martinez | .15 | .07 |
| ❑ 239 | Rafael Palmeiro | .60 | .25 |
| ❑ 240 | John Olerud | .25 | .11 |
| ❑ 241 | Dante Bichette | .25 | .11 |
| ❑ 242 | Greg Vaughn | .25 | .11 |
| ❑ 243 | Jeff Bagwell | .75 | .35 |
| ❑ 244 | Barry Bonds | 1.00 | .45 |
| ❑ 245 | Pat Hentgen | .15 | .07 |
| ❑ 246 | Jim Thome | .40 | .18 |
| ❑ 247 | Jermaine Allensworth | .15 | .07 |
| ❑ 248 | Andy Pettitte | .25 | .11 |
| ❑ 249 | Jay Bell | .25 | .11 |
| ❑ 250 | John Jaha | .15 | .07 |
| ❑ 251 | Jim Edmonds | .60 | .25 |
| ❑ 252 | Ron Gant | .15 | .07 |
| ❑ 253 | David Cone | .25 | .11 |
| ❑ 254 | Jose Canseco | .75 | .35 |
| ❑ 255 | Jay Buhner | .25 | .11 |
| ❑ 256 | Greg Maddux | 1.50 | .70 |
| ❑ 257 | Brian McRae | .15 | .07 |
| ❑ 258 | Lance Johnson | .15 | .07 |
| ❑ 259 | Travis Fryman | .25 | .11 |
| ❑ 260 | Paul O'Neill | .25 | .11 |
| ❑ 261 | Ivan Rodriguez | .75 | .35 |
| ❑ 262 | Gregg Jefferies | .15 | .07 |
| ❑ 263 | Fred McGriff | .40 | .18 |
| ❑ 264 | Derek Bell | .15 | .07 |
| ❑ 265 | Jeff Conine | .15 | .07 |
| ❑ 266 | Mike Piazza | 2.00 | .90 |
| ❑ 267 | Mark Grudzielanek | .15 | .07 |
| ❑ 268 | Brady Anderson | .25 | .11 |
| ❑ 269 | Marty Cordova | .15 | .07 |
| ❑ 270 | Ray Durham | .25 | .11 |
| ❑ 271 | Joe Carter | .25 | .11 |
| ❑ 272 | Brian Jordan | .25 | .11 |
| ❑ 273 | David Justice | .40 | .18 |
| ❑ 274 | Tony Gwynn | 1.25 | .55 |
| ❑ 275 | Larry Walker | .25 | .11 |
| ❑ 276 | Cecil Fielder | .25 | .11 |
| ❑ 277 | Mo Vaughn | .25 | .11 |
| ❑ 278 | Alex Fernandez | .15 | .07 |
| ❑ 279 | Michael Tucker | .15 | .07 |
| ❑ 280 | Jose Valentin | .15 | .07 |
| ❑ 281 | Sandy Alomar Jr. | .25 | .11 |
| ❑ 282 | Todd Hollandsworth | .15 | .07 |
| ❑ 283 | Rico Brogna | .15 | .07 |
| ❑ 284 | Rusty Greer | .25 | .11 |
| ❑ 285 | Roberto Hernandez | .15 | .07 |
| ❑ 286 | Hal Morris | .15 | .07 |
| ❑ 287 | Johnny Damon | .25 | .11 |
| ❑ 288 | Todd Hundley | .15 | .07 |
| ❑ 289 | Rondell White | .25 | .11 |
| ❑ 290 | Frank Thomas | 1.25 | .55 |
| ❑ 291 | Don Denbow RC | .15 | .07 |
| ❑ 292 | Derrek Lee | .15 | .07 |
| ❑ 293 | Todd Walker | .15 | .07 |
| ❑ 294 | Scott Rolen | .60 | .25 |
| ❑ 295 | Wes Helms | .15 | .07 |

| No. | Player | Mint | NrMt |
|---|---|---|---|
| ❑ 296 | Bob Abreu | .25 | .11 |
| ❑ 297 | John Patterson RC | .60 | .25 |
| ❑ 298 | Alex Gonzalez RC | .50 | .23 |
| ❑ 299 | Grant Roberts RC | .75 | .35 |
| ❑ 300 | Jeff Suppan | .15 | .07 |
| ❑ 301 | Luke Wilcox | .15 | .07 |
| ❑ 302 | Marlon Anderson | .15 | .07 |
| ❑ 303 | Ray Brown | .15 | .07 |
| ❑ 304 | Mike Caruso RC | .50 | .23 |
| ❑ 305 | Sam Marsonek RC | .50 | .23 |
| ❑ 306 | Brady Raggio RC | .15 | .07 |
| ❑ 307 | Kevin McGlinchy RC | .50 | .23 |
| ❑ 308 | Roy Halladay RC | .50 | .23 |
| ❑ 309 | Jeremi Gonzalez RC | .15 | .07 |
| ❑ 310 | Aramis Ramirez RC | 1.50 | .70 |
| ❑ 311 | Dermal Brown RC | 2.50 | 1.10 |
| ❑ 312 | Justin Thompson | .15 | .07 |
| ❑ 313 | Jay Tessmer RC | .15 | .07 |
| ❑ 314 | Mike Johnson RC | .50 | .23 |
| ❑ 315 | Danny Clyburn | .15 | .07 |
| ❑ 316 | Bruce Aven | .15 | .07 |
| ❑ 317 | Keith Foulke RC | .15 | .07 |
| ❑ 318 | Jimmy Osting RC | .50 | .23 |
| ❑ 319 | Valerio De Los Santos RC | .50 | .23 |
| ❑ 320 | Shannon Stewart | .25 | .11 |
| ❑ 321 | Willie Adams | .15 | .07 |
| ❑ 322 | Larry Barnes RC | .25 | .11 |
| ❑ 323 | Mark Johnson RC | .50 | .23 |
| ❑ 324 | Chris Stowers RC | .15 | .07 |
| ❑ 325 | Brandon Reed | .25 | .11 |
| ❑ 326 | Randy Winn | .15 | .07 |
| ❑ 327 | Steve Chavez RC | .15 | .07 |
| ❑ 328 | Nomar Garciaparra | 2.00 | .90 |
| ❑ 329 | Jacque Jones RC | 2.00 | .90 |
| ❑ 330 | Chris Clemons | .15 | .07 |
| ❑ 331 | Todd Helton | 1.00 | .46 |
| ❑ 332 | Ryan Brannan RC | .15 | .07 |
| ❑ 333 | Alex Sanchez RC | .50 | .23 |
| ❑ 334 | Arnold Gooch | .60 | .25 |
| ❑ 335 | Russell Branyan | .60 | .25 |
| ❑ 336 | Daryle Ward | 1.25 | .55 |
| ❑ 337 | John LeRoy RC | .50 | .23 |
| ❑ 338 | Steve Cox | .15 | .07 |
| ❑ 339 | Kevin Witt | .25 | .11 |
| ❑ 340 | Norm Hutchins | .15 | .07 |
| ❑ 341 | Gabby Martinez | .15 | .07 |
| ❑ 342 | Kris Detmers | .15 | .07 |
| ❑ 343 | Mike Villano RC | .15 | .07 |
| ❑ 344 | Preston Wilson | .25 | .11 |
| ❑ 345 | James Manias RC | .15 | .07 |
| ❑ 346 | Deivi Cruz RC | 1.25 | .55 |
| ❑ 347 | Donzell McDonald RC | .50 | .23 |
| ❑ 348 | Rod Myers RC | .15 | .07 |
| ❑ 349 | Shawn Chacon RC | .50 | .23 |
| ❑ 350 | Elvin Hernandez RC | .50 | .23 |
| ❑ 351 | Orlando Cabrera RC | .60 | .25 |
| ❑ 352 | Brian Banks | .15 | .07 |
| ❑ 353 | Robbie Bell | .75 | .35 |
| ❑ 354 | Brad Rigby | .15 | .07 |
| ❑ 355 | Scott Elarton | .25 | .11 |
| ❑ 356 | Kevin Sweeney RC | .15 | .07 |
| ❑ 357 | Steve Soderstrom | .15 | .07 |
| ❑ 358 | Ryan Nye | .25 | .11 |
| ❑ 360 | Donny Leon RC | .50 | .23 |
| ❑ 361 | Garrett Neubart RC | .25 | .11 |
| ❑ 362 | Abraham Nunez RC | .50 | .23 |
| ❑ 363 | Adam Eaton RC | 2.50 | 1.10 |
| ❑ 364 | Octavio Dotel RC | 1.00 | .45 |
| ❑ 365 | Dean Crow RC | .15 | .07 |
| ❑ 366 | Jason Baker RC | .15 | .07 |
| ❑ 367 | Sean Casey | 3.00 | 1.35 |
| ❑ 368 | Joe Lawrence RC | .75 | .35 |
| ❑ 369 | Adam Johnson RC | .50 | .23 |
| ❑ 370 | Scott Schoeneweis RC | .75 | .35 |
| ❑ 371 | Gerald Witasick Jr. | .15 | .07 |
| ❑ 372 | Ronnie Belliard RC | .75 | .35 |
| ❑ 373 | Russ Ortiz | .15 | .07 |
| ❑ 374 | Robert Stratton RC | 1.50 | .70 |
| ❑ 375 | Bobby Estalella | .15 | .07 |
| ❑ 376 | Corey Lee RC | .15 | .07 |
| ❑ 377 | Carlos Beltran | .50 | .23 |
| ❑ 378 | Mike Cameron | .25 | .11 |
| ❑ 379 | Scott Randall RC | .50 | .23 |
| ❑ 380 | Corey Erickson RC | .75 | .35 |
| ❑ 381 | Jay Canizaro | .15 | .07 |
| ❑ 382 | Kerry Robinson RC | .60 | .25 |
| ❑ 383 | Todd Noel RC | .75 | .35 |
| ❑ 384 | A.J. Zapp RC | .60 | .25 |
| ❑ 385 | Jarrod Washburn | .25 | .11 |
| ❑ 386 | Ben Grieve | 1.00 | .45 |
| ❑ 387 | Javier Vazquez RC | 1.25 | .55 |
| ❑ 388 | Tony Graffanino | .15 | .07 |
| ❑ 389 | Travis Lee RC | 1.25 | .55 |
| ❑ 390 | DaRond Stovall | .15 | .07 |
| ❑ 391 | Dennis Reyes RC | .50 | .23 |
| ❑ 392 | Danny Buxbaum | .15 | .07 |
| ❑ 393 | Marc Lewis RC | .50 | .23 |
| ❑ 394 | Kelvim Escobar RC | .75 | .35 |
| ❑ 395 | Danny Klassen | .15 | .07 |
| ❑ 396 | Ken Cloude RC | .25 | .11 |
| ❑ 397 | Gabe Alvarez | .25 | .11 |
| ❑ 398 | Jaret Wright RC | 1.00 | .45 |
| ❑ 399 | Raul Casanova | .15 | .07 |
| ❑ 400 | Clayton Bruner RC | .15 | .07 |
| ❑ 401 | Jason Marquis RC | 1.00 | .45 |
| ❑ 402 | Marc Kroon | .15 | .07 |
| ❑ 403 | Jamey Wright | .15 | .07 |
| ❑ 404 | Matt Snyder RC | .25 | .11 |
| ❑ 405 | Josh Garrett RC | .50 | .23 |
| ❑ 406 | Juan Encarnacion | .25 | .11 |
| ❑ 407 | Heath Murray | .15 | .07 |
| ❑ 408 | Brett Herbison RC | .50 | .23 |
| ❑ 409 | Brent Butler RC | .75 | .35 |
| ❑ 410 | Danny Peoples RC | .50 | .23 |
| ❑ 411 | Miguel Tejada RC | 5.00 | 2.20 |
| ❑ 412 | Damian Moss | .15 | .07 |
| ❑ 413 | Jim Pittsley | .15 | .07 |
| ❑ 414 | Dmitri Young | .25 | .11 |
| ❑ 415 | Glendon Rusch | .15 | .07 |
| ❑ 416 | Vladimir Guerrero | 1.25 | .55 |
| ❑ 417 | Cole Liniak RC | .50 | .23 |
| ❑ 418 | Ramon Hernandez UER (Card back says 1st Bowman card is 1997; he had a 1996 Bowman) | .40 | .18 |
| ❑ 419 | Cliff Politte RC | .50 | .23 |
| ❑ 420 | Mel Rosario RC | .15 | .07 |
| ❑ 421 | Jorge Carrion RC | .15 | .07 |
| ❑ 422 | John Barnes RC | .60 | .25 |
| ❑ 423 | Chris Stowe RC | .15 | .07 |
| ❑ 424 | Vernon Wells RC | 2.50 | 1.10 |
| ❑ 425 | Brett Caradonna RC | .50 | .23 |
| ❑ 426 | Scott Hodges RC | .60 | .25 |
| ❑ 427 | Jon Garland RC | 2.00 | .90 |
| ❑ 428 | Nathan Haynes RC | .50 | .23 |
| ❑ 429 | Geoff Goetz RC | .50 | .23 |
| ❑ 430 | Adam Kennedy RC | 1.50 | .70 |
| ❑ 431 | T.J. Tucker RC | .50 | .23 |
| ❑ 432 | Aaron Akin RC | .50 | .23 |
| ❑ 433 | Jayson Werth RC | .75 | .35 |
| ❑ 434 | Glenn Davis RC | .50 | .23 |
| ❑ 435 | Mark Mangum RC | .50 | .23 |
| ❑ 436 | Troy Cameron RC | .50 | .23 |
| ❑ 437 | J.J. Davis RC | 1.25 | .55 |
| ❑ 438 | Lance Berkman RC | 3.00 | 1.35 |
| ❑ 439 | Jason Standridge RC | .60 | .25 |
| ❑ 440 | Jason Dellaero RC | .50 | .23 |
| ❑ 441 | Hideki Irabu | .50 | .23 |

## 1998 Bowman

| | MINT | NRMT |
|---|---|---|
| COMPLETE SET (441) | 120.00 | 55.00 |
| COMPLETE SERIES 1 (221) | 70.00 | 32.00 |
| COMPLETE SERIES 2 (220) | 50.00 | 22.00 |
| COMMON CARD (1-441) | .15 | .07 |

| No. | Player | Mint | NrMt |
|---|---|---|---|
| ❑ 1 | Nomar Garciaparra | 2.00 | .90 |
| ❑ 2 | Scott Rolen | .60 | .25 |
| ❑ 3 | Andy Pettitte | .25 | .11 |
| ❑ 4 | Ivan Rodriguez | .75 | .35 |
| ❑ 5 | Mark McGwire | 2.50 | 1.10 |
| ❑ 6 | Jason Dickson | .15 | .07 |
| ❑ 7 | Jose Cruz Jr. | .25 | .11 |
| ❑ 8 | Jeff Kent | .40 | .18 |
| ❑ 9 | Mike Mussina | .60 | .25 |
| ❑ 10 | Jason Kendall | .25 | .11 |
| ❑ 11 | Brett Tomko | .15 | .07 |
| ❑ 12 | Jeff King | .15 | .07 |
| ❑ 13 | Brad Radke | .25 | .11 |
| ❑ 14 | Robin Ventura | .25 | .11 |
| ❑ 15 | Jeff Bagwell | .75 | .35 |
| ❑ 16 | Greg Maddux | 1.50 | .70 |
| ❑ 17 | John Jaha | .25 | .11 |
| ❑ 18 | Mike Piazza | 2.00 | .90 |
| ❑ 19 | Edgar Martinez | .40 | .18 |
| ❑ 20 | David Justice | .40 | .18 |
| ❑ 21 | Todd Hundley | .15 | .07 |
| ❑ 22 | Tony Gwynn | 1.25 | .55 |
| ❑ 23 | Larry Walker | .25 | .11 |
| ❑ 24 | Bernie Williams | .60 | .25 |
| ❑ 25 | Edgar Renteria | .15 | .07 |
| ❑ 26 | Rafael Palmeiro | .60 | .25 |
| ❑ 27 | Tim Salmon | .25 | .11 |
| ❑ 28 | Matt Morris | .15 | .07 |
| ❑ 29 | Shawn Estes | .15 | .07 |
| ❑ 30 | Vladimir Guerrero | 1.00 | .45 |
| ❑ 31 | Fernando Tatis | .25 | .11 |
| ❑ 32 | Justin Thompson | .15 | .07 |
| ❑ 33 | Ken Griffey Jr. | 2.50 | 1.10 |
| ❑ 34 | Edgardo Alfonzo | .25 | .11 |
| ❑ 35 | Mo Vaughn | .25 | .11 |
| ❑ 36 | Marty Cordova | .15 | .07 |
| ❑ 37 | Craig Biggio | .40 | .18 |
| ❑ 38 | Roger Clemens | 1.25 | .55 |
| ❑ 39 | Mark Grace | .60 | .25 |
| ❑ 40 | Ken Caminiti | .25 | .11 |
| ❑ 41 | Tony Womack | .15 | .07 |
| ❑ 42 | Albert Belle | .40 | .18 |
| ❑ 43 | Tino Martinez | .25 | .11 |
| ❑ 44 | Sandy Alomar Jr. | .25 | .11 |
| ❑ 45 | Jeff Cirillo | .25 | .11 |
| ❑ 46 | Jason Giambi | .60 | .25 |
| ❑ 47 | Darin Erstad | .60 | .25 |
| ❑ 48 | Livan Hernandez | .15 | .07 |
| ❑ 49 | Mark Grudzielanek | .15 | .07 |
| ❑ 50 | Sammy Sosa | 1.25 | .55 |
| ❑ 51 | Curt Schilling | .25 | .11 |
| ❑ 52 | Brian Hunter | .15 | .07 |
| ❑ 53 | Neifi Perez | .15 | .07 |
| ❑ 54 | Todd Walker | .15 | .07 |
| ❑ 55 | Jose Guillen | .15 | .07 |
| ❑ 56 | Jim Thome | .40 | .18 |
| ❑ 57 | Tom Glavine | .60 | .25 |
| ❑ 58 | Todd Greene | .15 | .07 |
| ❑ 59 | Rondell White | .25 | .11 |
| ❑ 60 | Roberto Alomar | .60 | .25 |
| ❑ 61 | Tony Clark | .15 | .07 |
| ❑ 62 | Vinny Castilla | .25 | .11 |
| ❑ 63 | Barry Larkin | .60 | .25 |
| ❑ 64 | Hideki Irabu | .15 | .07 |
| ❑ 65 | Johnny Damon | .25 | .11 |
| ❑ 66 | Juan Gonzalez | .60 | .25 |
| ❑ 67 | John Olerud | .25 | .11 |
| ❑ 68 | Gary Sheffield | .60 | .25 |
| ❑ 69 | Raul Mondesi | .25 | .11 |
| ❑ 70 | Chipper Jones | 1.50 | .70 |
| ❑ 71 | David Ortiz | .15 | .07 |
| ❑ 72 | Warren Morris RC | 1.00 | .45 |
| ❑ 73 | Alex Gonzalez | .25 | .11 |
| ❑ 74 | Nick Bierbrodt | .60 | .25 |
| ❑ 75 | Roy Halladay | .15 | .07 |
| ❑ 76 | Danny Buxbaum | .15 | .07 |
| ❑ 77 | Adam Kennedy | .25 | .11 |
| ❑ 78 | Jared Sandberg | .15 | .07 |
| ❑ 79 | Michael Barrett | .15 | .07 |
| ❑ 80 | Gil Meche | .75 | .35 |
| ❑ 81 | Jayson Werth | .15 | .07 |
| ❑ 82 | Abraham Nunez | .15 | .07 |
| ❑ 83 | Ben Petrick | .15 | .07 |

❑ 84 Brett Caradonna .15 .07
❑ 85 Mike Lowell RC 1.50 .70
❑ 86 Clayton Bruner .25 .11
❑ 87 John Curtice RC .60 .25
❑ 88 Bobby Estalella .15 .07
❑ 89 Juan Melo .15 .07
❑ 90 Arnold Gooch .15 .07
❑ 91 Kevin Millwood RC 2.00 .90
❑ 92 Richie Sexson .40 .18
❑ 93 Orlando Cabrera .15 .07
❑ 94 Pat Cline .15 .07
❑ 95 Anthony Sanders .15 .07
❑ 96 Russ Johnson .15 .07
❑ 97 Ben Grieve .25 .11
❑ 98 Kevin McGlinchy .15 .07
❑ 99 Paul Wilder .15 .07
❑ 100 Russ Ortiz .25 .11
❑ 101 Ryan Jackson RC .15 .07
❑ 102 Heath Murray .15 .07
❑ 103 Brian Rose .15 .07
❑ 104 Ryan Radmanovich RC .15 .07
❑ 105 Ricky Ledee .15 .07
❑ 106 Jeff Wallace RC .50 .23
❑ 107 Ryan Minor RC .50 .23
❑ 108 Dennis Reyes .15 .07
❑ 109 James Manias .15 .07
❑ 110 Chris Carpenter .25 .11
❑ 111 Daryle Ward .25 .11
❑ 112 Vernon Wells .40 .18
❑ 113 Chad Green .15 .07
❑ 114 Mike Stoner RC .15 .07
❑ 115 Brad Fullmer .25 .11
❑ 116 Adam Eaton .25 .11
❑ 117 Jeff Liefer .15 .07
❑ 118 Corey Koskie RC 1.25 .55
❑ 119 Todd Helton .75 .35
❑ 120 Jaime Jones RC .50 .23
❑ 121 Mel Rosario .15 .07
❑ 122 Geoff Goetz .15 .07
❑ 123 Adrian Beltre .25 .11
❑ 124 Jason Dellaero .15 .07
❑ 125 Gabe Kapler RC 4.00 1.80
❑ 126 Scott Schoeneweis .15 .07
❑ 127 Ryan Brannan .15 .07
❑ 128 Aaron Akin .15 .07
❑ 129 Ryan Anderson RC 5.00 2.20
❑ 130 Brad Penny .25 .11
❑ 131 Bruce Chen .15 .07
❑ 132 Eli Marrero .15 .07
❑ 133 Eric Chavez .25 .11
❑ 134 Troy Glaus RC 8.00 3.60
❑ 135 Troy Cameron .15 .07
❑ 136 Brian Sikorski RC .50 .23
❑ 137 Mike Kinkade RC .50 .23
❑ 138 Braden Looper .15 .07
❑ 139 Mark Mangum .15 .07
❑ 140 Danny Peoples .15 .07
❑ 141 J.J. Davis .25 .11
❑ 142 Ben Davis .15 .07
❑ 143 Jacque Jones .25 .11
❑ 144 Derrick Gibson .15 .07
❑ 145 Bronson Arroyo .50 .23
❑ 146 Luis De Los Santos RC UER .50 .23
(has hitting stat line instead of pitching)
❑ 147 Jeff Abbott .15 .07
❑ 148 Mike Cuddyer RC 1.50 .70
❑ 149 Jason Romano .25 .11
❑ 150 Shane Monahan .15 .07
❑ 151 Ntema Ndungidi RC 1.00 .45
❑ 152 Alex Sanchez .15 .07
❑ 153 Jack Cust RC 2.50 1.10
❑ 154 Brent Butler .15 .07
❑ 155 Ramon Hernandez .15 .07
❑ 156 Norm Hutchins .15 .07
❑ 157 Jason Marquis .25 .11
❑ 158 Jacob Cruz .15 .07
❑ 159 Rob Burger RC .50 .23
❑ 160 Dave Coggin .15 .07
❑ 161 Preston Wilson .25 .11
❑ 162 Jason Fitzgerald RC .50 .23
❑ 163 Dan Serafini .15 .07
❑ 164 Peter Munro .15 .07
❑ 165 Trot Nixon .25 .11
❑ 166 Homer Bush .15 .07
❑ 167 Dermal Brown .25 .11
❑ 168 Chad Hermansen .25 .11
❑ 169 Julio Moreno RC .50 .23
❑ 170 John Roskos RC .50 .23
❑ 171 Grant Roberts .15 .07
❑ 172 Ken Cloude .15 .07
❑ 173 Jason Brester .15 .07
❑ 174 Jason Conti .15 .07
❑ 175 Jon Garland .15 .07
❑ 176 Robbie Bell .15 .07
❑ 177 Nathan Haynes .15 .07
❑ 178 Ramon Ortiz RC 1.50 .70
❑ 179 Shannon Stewart .25 .11
❑ 180 Pablo Ortega .15 .07
❑ 181 Jimmy Rollins RC 1.00 .45
❑ 182 Sean Casey .25 .11
❑ 183 Ted Lilly RC .60 .25
❑ 184 Chris Enochs RC .50 .23
❑ 185 Magglio Ordonez RC UER 5.00 2.20
(Front photo is Mario Valdez)
❑ 186 Mike Drumright .15 .07
❑ 187 Aaron Boone .15 .07
❑ 188 Matt Clement .15 .07
❑ 189 Todd Dunwoody .15 .07
❑ 190 Larry Rodriguez .15 .07
❑ 191 Todd Noel .15 .07
❑ 192 Geoff Jenkins .25 .11
❑ 193 George Lombard .15 .07
❑ 194 Lance Berkman .40 .18
❑ 195 Marcus McCain .25 .11
❑ 196 Ryan McGuire .15 .07
❑ 197 Jhensy Sandoval .15 .07
❑ 198 Corey Lee .15 .07
❑ 199 Mario Valdez .15 .07
❑ 200 Robert Fick RC 1.00 .45
❑ 201 Donnie Sadler .15 .07
❑ 202 Marc Kroon .15 .07
❑ 203 David Miller .15 .07
❑ 204 Jarrod Washburn .15 .07
❑ 205 Miguel Tejada .60 .25
❑ 206 Raul Ibanez .15 .07
❑ 207 John Patterson .15 .07
❑ 208 Calvin Pickering .15 .07
❑ 209 Felix Martinez .15 .07
❑ 210 Mark Redman .15 .07
❑ 211 Scott Elarton .25 .11
❑ 212 Jose Amado RC .50 .23
❑ 213 Kerry Wood .60 .25
❑ 214 Dante Powell .15 .07
❑ 215 Aramis Ramirez .25 .11
❑ 216 A.J. Hinch .15 .07
❑ 217 Dustin Carr RC .50 .23
❑ 218 Mark Kotsay .25 .11
❑ 219 Jason Standridge .15 .07
❑ 220 Luis Ordaz .15 .07
❑ 221 Orlando Hernandez RC 2.00 .90
❑ 222 Cal Ripken 2.50 1.10
❑ 223 Paul Molitor .60 .25
❑ 224 Derek Jeter 2.50 1.10
❑ 225 Barry Bonds 1.00 .45
❑ 226 Jim Edmonds .60 .25
❑ 227 John Smoltz .25 .11
❑ 228 Eric Karros .25 .11
❑ 229 Ray Lankford .25 .11
❑ 230 Rey Ordonez .15 .07
❑ 231 Kenny Lofton .25 .11
❑ 232 Alex Rodriguez 2.00 .90
❑ 233 Dante Bichette .25 .11
❑ 234 Pedro Martinez .75 .35
❑ 235 Carlos Delgado .60 .25
❑ 236 Rod Beck .15 .07
❑ 237 Matt Williams .40 .18
❑ 238 Charles Johnson .25 .11
❑ 239 Rico Brogna .15 .07
❑ 240 Frank Thomas 1.25 .55
❑ 241 Paul O'Neill .25 .11
❑ 242 Jaret Wright .15 .07
❑ 243 Brant Brown .15 .07
❑ 244 Ryan Klesko .25 .11
❑ 245 Chuck Finley .25 .11
❑ 246 Derek Bell .15 .07
❑ 247 Delino DeShields .15 .07
❑ 248 Chan Ho Park .25 .11
❑ 249 Wade Boggs .75 .35
❑ 250 Jay Buhner .25 .11
❑ 251 Butch Huskey .15 .07
❑ 252 Steve Finley .25 .11
❑ 253 Will Clark .60 .25
❑ 254 John Valentin .15 .07
❑ 255 Bobby Higginson .25 .11
❑ 256 Darryl Strawberry .25 .11
❑ 257 Randy Johnson .75 .35
❑ 258 Al Martin .15 .07
❑ 259 Travis Fryman .25 .11
❑ 260 Fred McGriff .40 .18
❑ 261 Jose Valentin .15 .07
❑ 262 Andruw Jones .60 .25
❑ 263 Kenny Rogers .15 .07
❑ 264 Moises Alou .25 .11
❑ 265 Denny Neagle .15 .07
❑ 266 Ugueth Urbina .15 .07
❑ 267 Derrek Lee .15 .07
❑ 268 Ellis Burks .25 .11
❑ 269 Mariano Rivera .25 .11
❑ 270 Dean Palmer .25 .11
❑ 271 Eddie Taubensee .15 .07
❑ 272 Brady Anderson .25 .11
❑ 273 Brian Giles .25 .11
❑ 274 Quinton McCracken .15 .07
❑ 275 Henry Rodriguez .15 .07
❑ 276 Andres Galarraga .40 .18
❑ 277 Jose Canseco .75 .35
❑ 278 David Segui .15 .07
❑ 279 Bret Saberhagen .25 .11
❑ 280 Kevin Brown .40 .18
❑ 281 Chuck Knoblauch .25 .11
❑ 282 Jeromy Burnitz .25 .11
❑ 283 Jay Bell .25 .11
❑ 284 Manny Ramirez .75 .35
❑ 285 Rick Helling .25 .11
❑ 286 Francisco Cordova .15 .07
❑ 287 Bob Abreu .25 .11
❑ 288 J.T. Snow .25 .11
❑ 289 Hideo Nomo .60 .25
❑ 290 Brian Jordan .25 .11
❑ 291 Javy Lopez .25 .11
❑ 292 Travis Lee .25 .11
❑ 293 Russell Branyan .25 .11
❑ 294 Paul Konerko .25 .11
❑ 295 Masato Yoshii RC 1.00 .45
❑ 296 Kris Benson .25 .11
❑ 297 Juan Encarnacion .25 .11
❑ 298 Eric Milton .15 .07
❑ 299 Mike Caruso .15 .07
❑ 300 Ricardo Aramboles RC 1.00 .45
❑ 301 Bobby Smith .15 .07
❑ 302 Billy Koch .25 .11
❑ 303 Richard Hidalgo .25 .11
❑ 304 Justin Baughman RC .15 .07
❑ 305 Chris Gissell .15 .07
❑ 306 Donnie Bridges RC 1.00 .45
❑ 307 Nelson Lara RC .50 .23
❑ 308 Randy Wolf RC 1.00 .45
❑ 309 Jason LaRue RC .75 .35
❑ 310 Jason Gooding RC .15 .07
❑ 311 Edgard Clemente .15 .07
❑ 312 Andrew Vessel .15 .07
❑ 313 Chris Reitsma .15 .07
❑ 314 Jesus Sanchez RC .50 .23
❑ 315 Buddy Carlyle RC .60 .25
❑ 316 Randy Winn .15 .07
❑ 317 Luis Rivera RC .60 .25
❑ 318 Marcus Thames RC 1.00 .45
❑ 319 A.J. Pierzynski .15 .07
❑ 320 Scott Randall .15 .07
❑ 321 Damian Sapp .15 .07
❑ 322 Ed Yarnall RC .60 .25
❑ 323 Luke Allen RC .60 .25
❑ 324 J.D. Smart .15 .07
❑ 325 Willie Martinez .25 .11
❑ 326 Alex Ramirez .15 .07
❑ 327 Eric DuBose RC .50 .23
❑ 328 Kevin Witt .15 .07
❑ 329 Dan McKinley RC .50 .23
❑ 330 Cliff Politte .15 .07
❑ 331 Vladimir Nunez .15 .07
❑ 332 John Halama RC 1.00 .45
❑ 333 Nerio Rodriguez .15 .07
❑ 334 Desi Relaford .15 .07
❑ 335 Robinson Checo .15 .07
❑ 336 John Nicholson .40 .18
❑ 337 Tom LaRosa RC .15 .07

| | # | Player | Mint | NrMt |
|---|---|---|---|---|
| ❑ | 338 | Kevin Nicholson RC | .50 | .23 |
| ❑ | 339 | Javier Vazquez | .15 | .07 |
| ❑ | 340 | A.J. Zapp | .15 | .07 |
| ❑ | 341 | Tom Evans | .15 | .07 |
| ❑ | 342 | Kerry Robinson | .15 | .07 |
| ❑ | 343 | Gabe Gonzalez RC | .15 | .07 |
| ❑ | 344 | Ralph Milliard | .15 | .07 |
| ❑ | 345 | Enrique Wilson | .15 | .07 |
| ❑ | 346 | Elvin Hernandez | .15 | .07 |
| ❑ | 347 | Mike Lincoln RC | .50 | .23 |
| ❑ | 348 | Cesar King RC | .50 | .23 |
| ❑ | 349 | Cristian Guzman RC | 1.00 | .45 |
| ❑ | 350 | Donzell McDonald | .15 | .07 |
| ❑ | 351 | Jim Parque RC | 1.00 | .45 |
| ❑ | 352 | Mike Saipe RC | .15 | .07 |
| ❑ | 353 | Carlos Febles RC | 1.00 | .45 |
| ❑ | 354 | Dernell Stenson RC | 1.50 | .70 |
| ❑ | 355 | Mark Osborne RC | .50 | .23 |
| ❑ | 356 | Odalis Perez RC | .60 | .25 |
| ❑ | 357 | Jason Dewey RC | .50 | .23 |
| ❑ | 358 | Joe Fontenot | .15 | .07 |
| ❑ | 359 | Jason Grilli RC | .50 | .23 |
| ❑ | 360 | Kevin Haverbusch RC | .50 | .23 |
| ❑ | 361 | Jay Yennaco RC | .50 | .23 |
| ❑ | 362 | Brian Buchanan | .15 | .07 |
| ❑ | 363 | John Barnes | .15 | .07 |
| ❑ | 364 | Chris Fussell | .15 | .07 |
| ❑ | 365 | Kevin Gibbs RC | .15 | .07 |
| ❑ | 366 | Joe Lawrence | .15 | .07 |
| ❑ | 367 | DaRond Stovall | .15 | .07 |
| ❑ | 368 | Brian Fuentes RC | .50 | .23 |
| ❑ | 369 | Jimmy Anderson | .15 | .07 |
| ❑ | 370 | Lariel Gonzalez RC | .50 | .23 |
| ❑ | 371 | Scott Williamson RC | .60 | .25 |
| ❑ | 372 | Milton Bradley | .25 | .11 |
| ❑ | 373 | Jason Halper RC | .25 | .11 |
| ❑ | 374 | Brent Billingsley RC | .50 | .23 |
| ❑ | 375 | Joe DePastino RC | .15 | .07 |
| ❑ | 376 | Jake Westbrook | .15 | .07 |
| ❑ | 377 | Octavio Dotel | .15 | .07 |
| ❑ | 378 | Jason Williams RC | .15 | .07 |
| ❑ | 379 | Julio Ramirez RC | 1.00 | .45 |
| ❑ | 380 | Seth Greisinger | .15 | .07 |
| ❑ | 381 | Mike Judd RC | .50 | .23 |
| ❑ | 382 | Ben Ford RC | .25 | .11 |
| ❑ | 383 | Tom Bennett RC | .15 | .07 |
| ❑ | 384 | Adam Butler RC | .15 | .07 |
| ❑ | 385 | Wade Miller RC | .60 | .25 |
| ❑ | 386 | Kyle Peterson RC | .50 | .23 |
| ❑ | 387 | Tommy Peterman RC | .50 | .23 |
| ❑ | 388 | Onan Masaoka | .15 | .07 |
| ❑ | 389 | Jason Rakers RC | .15 | .07 |
| ❑ | 390 | Rafael Medina | .15 | .07 |
| ❑ | 391 | Luis Lopez | .15 | .07 |
| ❑ | 392 | Jeff Yoder | .15 | .07 |
| ❑ | 393 | Vance Wilson RC | .15 | .07 |
| ❑ | 394 | Fernando Seguignol RC | .60 | .25 |
| ❑ | 395 | Ron Wright | .15 | .07 |
| ❑ | 396 | Ruben Mateo RC | 3.00 | 1.35 |
| ❑ | 397 | Steve Lomasney RC | .75 | .35 |
| ❑ | 398 | Damian Jackson | .15 | .07 |
| ❑ | 399 | Mike Jerzembeck RC | .25 | .11 |
| ❑ | 400 | Luis Rivas RC | 1.25 | .55 |
| ❑ | 401 | Kevin Burford RC | .75 | .35 |
| ❑ | 402 | Glenn Davis | .15 | .07 |
| ❑ | 403 | Robert Luce RC | .15 | .07 |
| ❑ | 404 | Cole Liniak | .15 | .07 |
| ❑ | 405 | Matt LeCroy RC | 1.00 | .45 |
| ❑ | 406 | Jeremy Giambi RC | .60 | .25 |
| ❑ | 407 | Shawn Chacon | .15 | .07 |
| ❑ | 408 | Dewayne Wise RC | .50 | .23 |
| ❑ | 409 | Steve Woodard | .15 | .07 |
| ❑ | 410 | Francisco Cordero RC | .60 | .25 |
| ❑ | 411 | Damon Minor RC | .60 | .25 |
| ❑ | 412 | Lou Collier | .15 | .07 |
| ❑ | 413 | Justin Towle | .15 | .07 |
| ❑ | 414 | Juan LeBron | .15 | .07 |
| ❑ | 415 | Michael Coleman | .15 | .07 |
| ❑ | 416 | Felix Rodriguez | .15 | .07 |
| ❑ | 417 | Paul Ah Yat RC | .15 | .07 |
| ❑ | 418 | Kevin Barker RC | .50 | .23 |
| ❑ | 419 | Brian Meadows | .15 | .07 |
| ❑ | 420 | Darnell McDonald RC | 1.00 | .45 |
| ❑ | 421 | Matt Kinney RC | .75 | .35 |
| ❑ | 422 | Mike Vavrek RC | .15 | .07 |
| ❑ | 423 | Courtney Duncan RC | .15 | .07 |
| ❑ | 424 | Kevin Millar RC | .50 | .23 |
| ❑ | 425 | Ruben Rivera | .15 | .07 |
| ❑ | 426 | Steve Shoemaker RC | .15 | .07 |
| ❑ | 427 | Dan Reichert RC | 1.00 | .45 |
| ❑ | 428 | Carlos Lee RC | 3.00 | 1.35 |
| ❑ | 429 | Rod Barajas | .25 | .11 |
| ❑ | 430 | Pablo Ozuna RC | 1.25 | .55 |
| ❑ | 431 | Todd Belitz RC | .50 | .23 |
| ❑ | 432 | Sidney Ponson | .15 | .07 |
| ❑ | 433 | Steve Carver RC | .15 | .07 |
| ❑ | 434 | Esteban Yan RC | .50 | .23 |
| ❑ | 435 | Cedrick Bowers | .25 | .11 |
| ❑ | 436 | Marlon Anderson | .15 | .07 |
| ❑ | 437 | Carl Pavano | .15 | .07 |
| ❑ | 438 | Jae Weong Seo RC | .50 | .23 |
| ❑ | 439 | Jose Taveras RC | .50 | .23 |
| ❑ | 440 | Matt Anderson RC | .50 | .23 |
| ❑ | 441 | Darron Ingram RC | .50 | .23 |
| ❑ | NNO | S.Hasegawa '91 BBM | 10.00 | 4.50 |
| ❑ | NNO | H.Irabu '91 BBM | 15.00 | 6.75 |
| ❑ | NNO | H.Nomo '91 BBM | 30.00 | 13.50 |

## 1999 Bowman

| | MINT | NRMT |
|---|---|---|
| COMPLETE SET (440) | 130.00 | 57.50 |
| COMPLETE SERIES 1 (220) | 50.00 | 22.00 |
| COMPLETE SERIES 2 (220) | 80.00 | 36.00 |

| | # | Player | Mint | NrMt |
|---|---|---|---|---|
| ❑ | 1 | Ben Grieve | .25 | .11 |
| ❑ | 2 | Kerry Wood | .25 | .11 |
| ❑ | 3 | Ruben Rivera | .15 | .07 |
| ❑ | 4 | Sandy Alomar Jr. | .25 | .11 |
| ❑ | 5 | Cal Ripken | 2.50 | 1.10 |
| ❑ | 6 | Mark McGwire | 2.50 | 1.10 |
| ❑ | 7 | Vladimir Guerrero | 1.00 | .45 |
| ❑ | 8 | Moises Alou | .25 | .11 |
| ❑ | 9 | Jim Edmonds | .60 | .25 |
| ❑ | 10 | Greg Maddux | 1.50 | .70 |
| ❑ | 11 | Gary Sheffield | .60 | .25 |
| ❑ | 12 | John Valentin | .15 | .07 |
| ❑ | 13 | Chuck Knoblauch | .25 | .11 |
| ❑ | 14 | Tony Clark | .15 | .07 |
| ❑ | 15 | Rusty Greer | .25 | .11 |
| ❑ | 16 | Al Leiter | .25 | .11 |
| ❑ | 17 | Travis Lee | .15 | .07 |
| ❑ | 18 | Jose Cruz Jr. | .25 | .11 |
| ❑ | 19 | Pedro Martinez | .75 | .35 |
| ❑ | 20 | Paul O'Neill | .25 | .11 |
| ❑ | 21 | Todd Walker | .15 | .07 |
| ❑ | 22 | Vinny Castilla | .25 | .11 |
| ❑ | 23 | Barry Larkin | .60 | .25 |
| ❑ | 24 | Curt Schilling | .25 | .11 |
| ❑ | 25 | Jason Kendall | .25 | .11 |
| ❑ | 26 | Scott Erickson | .15 | .07 |
| ❑ | 27 | Andres Galarraga | .40 | .18 |
| ❑ | 28 | Jeff Shaw | .15 | .07 |
| ❑ | 29 | John Olerud | .25 | .11 |
| ❑ | 30 | Orlando Hernandez | .25 | .11 |
| ❑ | 31 | Larry Walker | .25 | .11 |
| ❑ | 32 | Andruw Jones | .60 | .25 |
| ❑ | 33 | Jeff Cirillo | .25 | .11 |
| ❑ | 34 | Barry Bonds | 1.00 | .45 |
| ❑ | 35 | Manny Ramirez | .75 | .35 |
| ❑ | 36 | Mark Kotsay | .15 | .07 |
| ❑ | 37 | Ivan Rodriguez | .75 | .35 |
| ❑ | 38 | Jeff King | .15 | .07 |
| ❑ | 39 | Brian Hunter | .15 | .07 |
| ❑ | 40 | Ray Durham | .25 | .11 |
| ❑ | 41 | Bernie Williams | .60 | .25 |
| ❑ | 42 | Darin Erstad | .60 | .25 |
| ❑ | 43 | Chipper Jones | 1.50 | .70 |
| ❑ | 44 | Pat Hentgen | .15 | .07 |
| ❑ | 45 | Eric Young | .15 | .07 |
| ❑ | 46 | Jaret Wright | .15 | .07 |
| ❑ | 47 | Juan Guzman | .15 | .07 |
| ❑ | 48 | Jorge Posada | .25 | .11 |
| ❑ | 49 | Bobby Higginson | .25 | .11 |
| ❑ | 50 | Jose Guillen | .15 | .07 |
| ❑ | 51 | Trevor Hoffman | .25 | .11 |
| ❑ | 52 | Ken Griffey Jr. | 2.50 | 1.10 |
| ❑ | 53 | David Justice | .40 | .18 |
| ❑ | 54 | Matt Williams | .40 | .18 |
| ❑ | 55 | Eric Karros | .25 | .11 |
| ❑ | 56 | Derek Bell | .15 | .07 |
| ❑ | 57 | Ray Lankford | .25 | .11 |
| ❑ | 58 | Mariano Rivera | .25 | .11 |
| ❑ | 59 | Brett Tomko | .15 | .07 |
| ❑ | 60 | Mike Mussina | .60 | .25 |
| ❑ | 61 | Kenny Lofton | .25 | .11 |
| ❑ | 62 | Chuck Finley | .25 | .11 |
| ❑ | 63 | Alex Gonzalez | .15 | .07 |
| ❑ | 64 | Mark Grace | .60 | .25 |
| ❑ | 65 | Raul Mondesi | .25 | .11 |
| ❑ | 66 | David Cone | .25 | .11 |
| ❑ | 67 | Brad Fullmer | .25 | .11 |
| ❑ | 68 | Andy Benes | .15 | .07 |
| ❑ | 69 | John Smoltz | .25 | .11 |
| ❑ | 70 | Shane Reynolds | .15 | .07 |
| ❑ | 71 | Bruce Chen | .15 | .07 |
| ❑ | 72 | Adam Kennedy | .25 | .11 |
| ❑ | 73 | Jack Cust | .25 | .11 |
| ❑ | 74 | Matt Clement | .15 | .07 |
| ❑ | 75 | Derrick Gibson | .15 | .07 |
| ❑ | 76 | Darnell McDonald | .15 | .07 |
| ❑ | 77 | Adam Everett RC | .75 | .35 |
| ❑ | 78 | Ricardo Aramboles | .15 | .07 |
| ❑ | 79 | Mark Quinn RC | 2.00 | .90 |
| ❑ | 80 | Jason Rakers | .15 | .07 |
| ❑ | 81 | Seth Etherton RC | .60 | .25 |
| ❑ | 82 | Jeff Urban RC | .50 | .23 |
| ❑ | 83 | Manny Aybar | .15 | .07 |
| ❑ | 84 | Mike Nannini RC | .75 | .35 |
| ❑ | 85 | Onan Masaoka | .15 | .07 |
| ❑ | 86 | Rod Barajas | .15 | .07 |
| ❑ | 87 | Mike Frank | .15 | .07 |
| ❑ | 88 | Scott Randall | .15 | .07 |
| ❑ | 89 | Justin Bowles RC | .15 | .07 |
| ❑ | 90 | Chris Haas | .15 | .07 |
| ❑ | 91 | Arturo McDowell RC | .60 | .25 |
| ❑ | 92 | Matt Belisle RC | 1.00 | .45 |
| ❑ | 93 | Scott Elarton | .25 | .11 |
| ❑ | 94 | Vernon Wells | .25 | .11 |
| ❑ | 95 | Pat Cline | .15 | .07 |
| ❑ | 96 | Ryan Anderson | .25 | .11 |
| ❑ | 97 | Kevin Barker | .15 | .07 |
| ❑ | 98 | Ruben Mateo | .25 | .11 |
| ❑ | 99 | Robert Fick | .15 | .07 |
| ❑ | 100 | Corey Koskie | .15 | .07 |
| ❑ | 101 | Ricky Ledee | .15 | .07 |
| ❑ | 102 | Rick Elder RC | .60 | .25 |
| ❑ | 103 | Jack Cressend RC | .50 | .23 |
| ❑ | 104 | Joe Lawrence | .25 | .11 |
| ❑ | 105 | Mike Lincoln | .15 | .07 |
| ❑ | 106 | Kit Pellow RC | .50 | .23 |
| ❑ | 107 | Matt Burch RC | .50 | .23 |
| ❑ | 108 | Cole Liniak | .15 | .07 |
| ❑ | 109 | Jason Dewey | .15 | .07 |
| ❑ | 110 | Cesar King | .15 | .07 |
| ❑ | 111 | Julio Ramirez | .15 | .07 |
| ❑ | 112 | Jake Westbrook | .15 | .07 |
| ❑ | 113 | Eric Valent RC | 1.25 | .55 |
| ❑ | 114 | Roosevelt Brown RC | .60 | .25 |
| ❑ | 115 | Choo Freeman RC | .75 | .35 |
| ❑ | 116 | Juan Melo | .15 | .07 |
| ❑ | 117 | Jason Grilli | .15 | .07 |
| ❑ | 118 | Jared Sandberg | .15 | .07 |
| ❑ | 119 | Glenn Davis | .15 | .07 |
| ❑ | 120 | David Riske RC | .50 | .23 |
| ❑ | 121 | Jacque Jones | .25 | .11 |
| ❑ | 122 | Corey Lee | .15 | .07 |
| ❑ | 123 | Michael Barrett | .15 | .07 |
| ❑ | 124 | Lariel Gonzalez | .15 | .07 |
| ❑ | 125 | Mitch Meluskey | .15 | .07 |

| |  |  | | |
|---|---|---|---|---|
| ❑ | 126 | Freddy Garcia | .15 | .07 |
| ❑ | 127 | Tony Torcato RC | 1.25 | .55 |
| ❑ | 128 | Jeff Liefer | .15 | .07 |
| ❑ | 129 | Ntema Ndungidi | .25 | .11 |
| ❑ | 130 | Andy Brown RC | 1.00 | .45 |
| ❑ | 131 | Ryan Mills RC | .50 | .23 |
| ❑ | 132 | Andy Abad RC | .15 | .07 |
| ❑ | 133 | Carlos Febles | .15 | .07 |
| ❑ | 134 | Jason Tyner RC | 1.00 | .45 |
| ❑ | 135 | Mark Osborne | .15 | .07 |
| ❑ | 136 | Phil Norton RC | .50 | .23 |
| ❑ | 137 | Nathan Haynes | .15 | .07 |
| ❑ | 138 | Roy Halladay | .15 | .07 |
| ❑ | 139 | Juan Encarnacion | .25 | .11 |
| ❑ | 140 | Brad Penny | .25 | .11 |
| ❑ | 141 | Grant Roberts | .15 | .07 |
| ❑ | 142 | Aramis Ramirez | .15 | .07 |
| ❑ | 143 | Cristian Guzman | .15 | .07 |
| ❑ | 144 | Mamon Tucker RC | .60 | .25 |
| ❑ | 145 | Ryan Bradley | .15 | .07 |
| ❑ | 146 | Brian Simmons | .15 | .07 |
| ❑ | 147 | Dan Reichert | .15 | .07 |
| ❑ | 148 | Russ Branyan | .25 | .11 |
| ❑ | 149 | Victor Valencia RC | .50 | .23 |
| ❑ | 150 | Scott Schoeneweis | .15 | .07 |
| ❑ | 151 | Sean Spencer RC | .50 | .23 |
| ❑ | 152 | Odalis Perez | .15 | .07 |
| ❑ | 153 | Joe Fontenot | .15 | .07 |
| ❑ | 154 | Milton Bradley | .25 | .11 |
| ❑ | 155 | Josh McKinley RC | .60 | .25 |
| ❑ | 156 | Terrence Long | .25 | .11 |
| ❑ | 157 | Danny Klassen | .15 | .07 |
| ❑ | 158 | Paul Hoover RC | .50 | .23 |
| ❑ | 159 | Ron Belliard | .15 | .07 |
| ❑ | 160 | Armando Rios | .15 | .07 |
| ❑ | 161 | Ramon Hernandez | .15 | .07 |
| ❑ | 162 | Jason Conti | .15 | .07 |
| ❑ | 163 | Chad Hermansen | .15 | .07 |
| ❑ | 164 | Jason Standridge | .15 | .07 |
| ❑ | 165 | Jason Dellaero | .15 | .07 |
| ❑ | 166 | John Curtice | .15 | .07 |
| ❑ | 167 | Clayton Andrews RC | .50 | .23 |
| ❑ | 168 | Jeremy Giambi | .15 | .07 |
| ❑ | 169 | Alex Ramirez | .15 | .07 |
| ❑ | 170 | Gabe Molina RC | .50 | .23 |
| ❑ | 171 | Mario Encarnacion RC | .75 | .35 |
| ❑ | 172 | Mike Zywica RC | .15 | .07 |
| ❑ | 173 | Chip Ambres RC | .75 | .35 |
| ❑ | 174 | Trot Nixon | .25 | .11 |
| ❑ | 175 | Pat Burrell RC | 6.00 | 2.70 |
| ❑ | 176 | Jeff Yoder | .15 | .07 |
| ❑ | 177 | Chris Jones RC | .60 | .25 |
| ❑ | 178 | Kevin Witt | .15 | .07 |
| ❑ | 179 | Keith Luuloa RC | .15 | .07 |
| ❑ | 180 | Billy Koch | .25 | .11 |
| ❑ | 181 | Damaso Marte RC | .15 | .07 |
| ❑ | 182 | Ryan Glynn RC | .60 | .25 |
| ❑ | 183 | Calvin Pickering | .15 | .07 |
| ❑ | 184 | Michael Cuddyer | .25 | .11 |
| ❑ | 185 | Nick Johnson RC | 2.50 | 1.10 |
| ❑ | 186 | Doug Mientkiewicz RC | .50 | .23 |
| ❑ | 187 | Nate Cornejo RC | .60 | .25 |
| ❑ | 188 | Octavio Dotel | .15 | .07 |
| ❑ | 189 | Wes Helms | .15 | .07 |
| ❑ | 190 | Nelson Lara | .15 | .07 |
| ❑ | 191 | Chuck Abbott RC | .15 | .07 |
| ❑ | 192 | Tony Armas Jr. | .25 | .11 |
| ❑ | 193 | Gil Meche | .25 | .11 |
| ❑ | 194 | Ben Petrick | .15 | .07 |
| ❑ | 195 | Chris George RC | 1.00 | .45 |
| ❑ | 196 | Scott Hunter RC | .50 | .23 |
| ❑ | 197 | Ryan Brannan | .15 | .07 |
| ❑ | 198 | Amaury Garcia RC | .50 | .23 |
| ❑ | 199 | Chris Gissell | .15 | .07 |
| ❑ | 200 | Austin Kearns RC | 2.50 | 1.10 |
| ❑ | 201 | Alex Gonzalez | .15 | .07 |
| ❑ | 202 | Wade Miller | .15 | .07 |
| ❑ | 203 | Scott Williamson | .15 | .07 |
| ❑ | 204 | Chris Enochs | .15 | .07 |
| ❑ | 205 | Fernando Seguignol | .15 | .07 |
| ❑ | 206 | Marlon Anderson | .15 | .07 |
| ❑ | 207 | Todd Sears RC | .60 | .25 |
| ❑ | 208 | Nate Bump RC | .50 | .23 |
| ❑ | 209 | J.M. Gold RC | .60 | .25 |
| ❑ | 210 | Matt LeCroy | .15 | .07 |
| ❑ | 211 | Alex Hernandez | .15 | .07 |
| ❑ | 212 | Luis Rivera | .15 | .07 |
| ❑ | 213 | Troy Cameron | .15 | .07 |
| ❑ | 214 | Alex Escobar RC | 2.50 | 1.10 |
| ❑ | 215 | Jason LaRue | .15 | .07 |
| ❑ | 216 | Kyle Peterson | .15 | .07 |
| ❑ | 217 | Brent Butler | .15 | .07 |
| ❑ | 218 | Dernell Stenson | .25 | .11 |
| ❑ | 219 | Adrian Beltre | .25 | .11 |
| ❑ | 220 | Daryle Ward | .25 | .11 |
| ❑ | 221 | Jim Thome | .40 | .18 |
| ❑ | 222 | Cliff Floyd | .25 | .11 |
| ❑ | 223 | Rickey Henderson | .75 | .35 |
| ❑ | 224 | Garret Anderson | .25 | .11 |
| ❑ | 225 | Ken Caminiti | .25 | .11 |
| ❑ | 226 | Bret Boone | .25 | .11 |
| ❑ | 227 | Jeromy Burnitz | .25 | .11 |
| ❑ | 228 | Steve Finley | .25 | .11 |
| ❑ | 229 | Miguel Tejada | .25 | .11 |
| ❑ | 230 | Greg Vaughn | .25 | .11 |
| ❑ | 231 | Jose Offerman | .15 | .07 |
| ❑ | 232 | Andy Ashby | .15 | .07 |
| ❑ | 233 | Albert Belle | .40 | .18 |
| ❑ | 234 | Fernando Tatis | .25 | .11 |
| ❑ | 235 | Todd Helton | .75 | .35 |
| ❑ | 236 | Sean Casey | .25 | .11 |
| ❑ | 237 | Brian Giles | .25 | .11 |
| ❑ | 238 | Andy Pettitte | .25 | .11 |
| ❑ | 239 | Fred McGriff | .40 | .18 |
| ❑ | 240 | Roberto Alomar | .60 | .25 |
| ❑ | 241 | Edgar Martinez | .40 | .18 |
| ❑ | 242 | Lee Stevens | .15 | .07 |
| ❑ | 243 | Shawn Green | .60 | .25 |
| ❑ | 244 | Ryan Klesko | .25 | .11 |
| ❑ | 245 | Sammy Sosa | 1.25 | .55 |
| ❑ | 246 | Todd Hundley | .15 | .07 |
| ❑ | 247 | Shannon Stewart | .25 | .11 |
| ❑ | 248 | Randy Johnson | .75 | .35 |
| ❑ | 249 | Rondell White | .25 | .11 |
| ❑ | 250 | Mike Piazza | 2.00 | .90 |
| ❑ | 251 | Craig Biggio | .40 | .18 |
| ❑ | 252 | David Wells | .25 | .11 |
| ❑ | 253 | Brian Jordan | .25 | .11 |
| ❑ | 254 | Edgar Renteria | .15 | .07 |
| ❑ | 255 | Bartolo Colon | .25 | .11 |
| ❑ | 256 | Frank Thomas | 1.25 | .55 |
| ❑ | 257 | Will Clark | .60 | .25 |
| ❑ | 258 | Dean Palmer | .25 | .11 |
| ❑ | 259 | Dmitri Young | .25 | .11 |
| ❑ | 260 | Scott Rolen | .60 | .25 |
| ❑ | 261 | Jeff Kent | .40 | .18 |
| ❑ | 262 | Dante Bichette | .25 | .11 |
| ❑ | 263 | Nomar Garciaparra | 2.00 | .90 |
| ❑ | 264 | Tony Gwynn | 1.25 | .55 |
| ❑ | 265 | Alex Rodriguez | 2.00 | .90 |
| ❑ | 266 | Jose Canseco | .75 | .35 |
| ❑ | 267 | Jason Giambi | .60 | .25 |
| ❑ | 268 | Jeff Bagwell | .75 | .35 |
| ❑ | 269 | Carlos Delgado | .60 | .25 |
| ❑ | 270 | Tom Glavine | .60 | .25 |
| ❑ | 271 | Eric Davis | .25 | .11 |
| ❑ | 272 | Edgardo Alfonzo | .25 | .11 |
| ❑ | 273 | Tim Salmon | .25 | .11 |
| ❑ | 274 | Johnny Damon | .25 | .11 |
| ❑ | 275 | Rafael Palmeiro | .60 | .25 |
| ❑ | 276 | Denny Neagle | .15 | .07 |
| ❑ | 277 | Neifi Perez | .15 | .07 |
| ❑ | 278 | Roger Clemens | 1.25 | .55 |
| ❑ | 279 | Brant Brown | .15 | .07 |
| ❑ | 280 | Kevin Brown | .40 | .18 |
| ❑ | 281 | Jay Bell | .25 | .11 |
| ❑ | 282 | Jay Buhner | .25 | .11 |
| ❑ | 283 | Matt Lawton | .25 | .11 |
| ❑ | 284 | Robin Ventura | .25 | .11 |
| ❑ | 285 | Juan Gonzalez | .60 | .25 |
| ❑ | 286 | Mo Vaughn | .25 | .11 |
| ❑ | 287 | Kevin Millwood | .25 | .11 |
| ❑ | 288 | Tino Martinez | .25 | .11 |
| ❑ | 289 | Justin Thompson | .15 | .07 |
| ❑ | 290 | Derek Jeter | 2.50 | 1.10 |
| ❑ | 291 | Ben Davis | .15 | .07 |
| ❑ | 292 | Mike Lowell | .25 | .11 |
| ❑ | 293 | Calvin Murray | .15 | .07 |
| ❑ | 294 | Micah Bowie RC | .15 | .07 |
| ❑ | 295 | Lance Berkman | .25 | .11 |
| ❑ | 296 | Jason Marquis | .25 | .11 |
| ❑ | 297 | Chad Green | .15 | .07 |
| ❑ | 298 | Dee Brown | .25 | .11 |
| ❑ | 299 | Jerry Hairston Jr. | .25 | .11 |
| ❑ | 300 | Gabe Kapler | .25 | .11 |
| ❑ | 301 | Brent Stentz RC | .50 | .23 |
| ❑ | 302 | Scott Mullen RC | .15 | .07 |
| ❑ | 303 | Brandon Reed | .15 | .07 |
| ❑ | 304 | Shea Hillenbrand RC | .50 | .23 |
| ❑ | 305 | J.D. Closser RC | .60 | .25 |
| ❑ | 306 | Gary Matthews Jr. | .15 | .07 |
| ❑ | 307 | Toby Hall RC | .60 | .25 |
| ❑ | 308 | Jason Phillips RC | .50 | .23 |
| ❑ | 309 | Jose Macias RC | .15 | .07 |
| ❑ | 310 | Jung Bong RC | .60 | .25 |
| ❑ | 311 | Ramon Soler RC | .60 | .25 |
| ❑ | 312 | Kelly Dransfeldt RC | .50 | .23 |
| ❑ | 313 | Carlos Hernandez RC | .50 | .23 |
| ❑ | 314 | Kevin Haverbusch | .15 | .07 |
| ❑ | 315 | Aaron Myette RC | 1.00 | .45 |
| ❑ | 316 | Chad Harville RC | .50 | .23 |
| ❑ | 317 | Kyle Farnsworth RC | .50 | .23 |
| ❑ | 318 | Travis Dawkins RC | 1.00 | .45 |
| ❑ | 319 | Willie Martinez | .15 | .07 |
| ❑ | 320 | Carlos Lee | .25 | .11 |
| ❑ | 321 | Carlos Pena RC | 2.50 | 1.10 |
| ❑ | 322 | Peter Bergeron RC | 1.00 | .45 |
| ❑ | 323 | A.J. Burnett RC | 1.00 | .45 |
| ❑ | 324 | Bucky Jacobsen RC | .50 | .23 |
| ❑ | 325 | Mo Bruce RC | .50 | .23 |
| ❑ | 326 | Reggie Taylor | .15 | .07 |
| ❑ | 327 | Jackie Rexrode | .15 | .07 |
| ❑ | 328 | Alvin Morrow RC | .50 | .23 |
| ❑ | 329 | Carlos Beltran | .25 | .11 |
| ❑ | 330 | Eric Chavez | .25 | .11 |
| ❑ | 331 | John Patterson | .15 | .07 |
| ❑ | 332 | Jayson Werth | .15 | .07 |
| ❑ | 333 | Richie Sexson | .25 | .11 |
| ❑ | 334 | Randy Wolf | .15 | .07 |
| ❑ | 335 | Eli Marrero | .15 | .07 |
| ❑ | 336 | Paul LoDuca | .15 | .07 |
| ❑ | 337 | J.D Smart | .15 | .07 |
| ❑ | 338 | Ryan Minor | .15 | .07 |
| ❑ | 339 | Kris Benson | .25 | .11 |
| ❑ | 340 | George Lombard | .15 | .07 |
| ❑ | 341 | Troy Glaus | 1.00 | .45 |
| ❑ | 342 | Eddie Yarnall | .15 | .07 |
| ❑ | 343 | Kip Wells RC | 1.00 | .45 |
| ❑ | 344 | C.C. Sabathia RC | 2.50 | 1.10 |
| ❑ | 345 | Sean Burroughs RC | 4.00 | 1.80 |
| ❑ | 346 | Felipe Lopez RC | 1.25 | .55 |
| ❑ | 347 | Ryan Rupe RC | .60 | .25 |
| ❑ | 348 | Orber Moreno RC | .50 | .23 |
| ❑ | 349 | Rafael Roque RC | .15 | .07 |
| ❑ | 350 | Alfonso Soriano RC | 2.50 | 1.10 |
| ❑ | 351 | Pablo Ozuna | .25 | .11 |
| ❑ | 352 | Corey Patterson RC | 6.00 | 2.70 |
| ❑ | 353 | Braden Looper | .15 | .07 |
| ❑ | 354 | Robbie Bell | .15 | .07 |
| ❑ | 355 | Mark Mulder RC | 1.25 | .55 |
| ❑ | 356 | Angel Pena | .15 | .07 |
| ❑ | 357 | Kevin McGlinchy | .15 | .07 |
| ❑ | 358 | Michael Restovich RC | 1.25 | .55 |
| ❑ | 359 | Eric DuBose | .15 | .07 |
| ❑ | 360 | Geoff Jenkins | .25 | .11 |
| ❑ | 361 | Mark Harriger RC | .50 | .23 |
| ❑ | 362 | Junior Herndon RC | .50 | .23 |
| ❑ | 363 | Tim Raines Jr. RC | 1.00 | .45 |
| ❑ | 364 | Rafael Furcal RC | 10.00 | 4.50 |
| ❑ | 365 | Marcus Giles RC | 2.00 | .90 |
| ❑ | 366 | Ted Lilly | .15 | .07 |
| ❑ | 367 | Jorge Toca RC | .60 | .25 |
| ❑ | 368 | David Kelton RC | 1.25 | .55 |
| ❑ | 369 | Adam Dunn RC | 2.50 | 1.10 |
| ❑ | 370 | Guillermo Mota RC | .15 | .07 |
| ❑ | 371 | Brett Laxton RC | .15 | .07 |
| ❑ | 372 | Travis Harper RC | .50 | .23 |
| ❑ | 373 | Tom Davey RC | .15 | .07 |
| ❑ | 374 | Darren Blakely RC | .60 | .25 |
| ❑ | 375 | Tim Hudson RC | 5.00 | 2.20 |
| ❑ | 376 | Jason Romano | .25 | .11 |
| ❑ | 377 | Dan Reichert | .15 | .07 |
| ❑ | 378 | Julio Lugo RC | .60 | .25 |
| ❑ | 379 | Jose Garcia RC | .50 | .23 |
| ❑ | 380 | Erubiel Durazo RC | 1.50 | .70 |
| ❑ | 381 | Jose Jimenez | .15 | .07 |
| ❑ | 382 | Chris Fussell | .15 | .07 |
| ❑ | 383 | Steve Lomasney | .15 | .07 |

| Card | Mint | NrMt |
|---|---|---|
| ❑ 384 Juan Pena RC | .50 | .23 |
| ❑ 385 Allen Levrault RC | .60 | .25 |
| ❑ 386 Juan Rivera RC | 1.25 | .55 |
| ❑ 387 Steve Colyer RC | .50 | .23 |
| ❑ 388 Joe Nathan RC | .15 | .07 |
| ❑ 389 Ron Walker RC | .50 | .23 |
| ❑ 390 Nick Bierbrodt | .15 | .07 |
| ❑ 391 Luke Prokopec RC | 1.00 | .45 |
| ❑ 392 Dave Roberts RC | .15 | .07 |
| ❑ 393 Mike Darr | .15 | .07 |
| ❑ 394 Abraham Nunez RC | 2.50 | 1.10 |
| ❑ 395 Giuseppe Chiaramonte RC | .75 | .35 |
| ❑ 396 Jermaine Van Buren RC | .60 | .25 |
| ❑ 397 Mike Kusiewicz | .15 | .07 |
| ❑ 398 Matt Wise RC | .50 | .23 |
| ❑ 399 Joe McEwing RC | .50 | .23 |
| ❑ 400 Matt Holliday RC | 1.00 | .45 |
| ❑ 401 Willi Mo Pena RC | 2.50 | 1.10 |
| ❑ 402 Ruben Quevedo RC | .60 | .25 |
| ❑ 403 Rob Ryan RC | .15 | .07 |
| ❑ 404 Freddy Garcia RC | 2.00 | .90 |
| ❑ 405 Kevin Eberwein RC | .60 | .25 |
| ❑ 406 Jesus Colome RC | 1.00 | .45 |
| ❑ 407 Chris Singleton | .25 | .11 |
| ❑ 408 Bubba Crosby RC | .50 | .23 |
| ❑ 409 Jesus Cordero RC | .50 | .23 |
| ❑ 410 Donny Leon | .15 | .07 |
| ❑ 411 Goefrey Tomlinson RC | .50 | .23 |
| ❑ 412 Jeff Winchester RC | 1.00 | .45 |
| ❑ 413 Adam Piatt RC | 3.00 | 1.35 |
| ❑ 414 Robert Stratton | .25 | .11 |
| ❑ 415 T.J. Tucker | .15 | .07 |
| ❑ 416 Ryan Langerhans RC | .60 | .25 |
| ❑ 417 Anthony Shumaker RC | .15 | .07 |
| ❑ 418 Matt Miller RC | .15 | .07 |
| ❑ 419 Doug Clark RC | .50 | .23 |
| ❑ 420 Kory DeHaan RC | .50 | .23 |
| ❑ 421 David Eckstein RC | .50 | .23 |
| ❑ 422 Brian Cooper RC | .50 | .23 |
| ❑ 423 Brady Clark RC | .50 | .23 |
| ❑ 424 Chris Magruder RC | .50 | .23 |
| ❑ 425 Bobby Seay RC | .75 | .35 |
| ❑ 426 Aubrey Huff RC | 1.50 | .70 |
| ❑ 427 Mike Jerzembeck | .15 | .07 |
| ❑ 428 Matt Blank RC | .50 | .23 |
| ❑ 429 Benny Agbayani RC | 2.00 | .90 |
| ❑ 430 Kevin Beirne RC | .15 | .07 |
| ❑ 431 Josh Hamilton RC | 6.00 | 2.70 |
| ❑ 432 Josh Girdley RC | 1.00 | .45 |
| ❑ 433 Kyle Snyder RC | .50 | .23 |
| ❑ 434 Mike Paradis RC | .50 | .23 |
| ❑ 435 Jason Jennings RC | .75 | .35 |
| ❑ 436 David Walling RC | .60 | .25 |
| ❑ 437 Omar Ortiz RC | .50 | .23 |
| ❑ 438 Jay Gehrke RC | .50 | .23 |
| ❑ 439 Casey Burns RC | .50 | .23 |
| ❑ 440 Carl Crawford RC | 1.50 | .70 |

## 2000 Bowman

| | MINT | NRMT |
|---|---|---|
| COMPLETE SET (440) | 150.00 | 70.00 |
| ❑ 1 Vladimir Guerrero | 1.00 | .45 |
| ❑ 2 Chipper Jones | 1.50 | .70 |
| ❑ 3 Todd Walker | .15 | .07 |
| ❑ 4 Barry Larkin | .60 | .25 |
| ❑ 5 Bernie Williams | .60 | .25 |
| ❑ 6 Todd Helton | .75 | .35 |
| ❑ 7 Jermaine Dye | .25 | .11 |
| ❑ 8 Brian Giles | .25 | .11 |
| ❑ 9 Freddy Garcia | .25 | .11 |
| ❑ 10 Greg Vaughn | .25 | .11 |
| ❑ 11 Alex Gonzalez | .15 | .07 |
| ❑ 12 Luis Gonzalez | .25 | .11 |
| ❑ 13 Ron Belliard | .15 | .07 |
| ❑ 14 Ben Grieve | .25 | .11 |
| ❑ 15 Carlos Delgado | .60 | .25 |
| ❑ 16 Brian Jordan | .25 | .11 |
| ❑ 17 Fernando Tatis | .25 | .11 |
| ❑ 18 Ryan Rupe | .15 | .07 |
| ❑ 19 Miguel Tejada | .25 | .11 |
| ❑ 20 Mark Grace | .60 | .25 |
| ❑ 21 Kenny Lofton | .25 | .11 |
| ❑ 22 Eric Karros | .25 | .11 |
| ❑ 23 Cliff Floyd | .25 | .11 |
| ❑ 24 John Halama | .15 | .07 |
| ❑ 25 Cristian Guzman | .15 | .07 |
| ❑ 26 Scott Williamson | .15 | .07 |
| ❑ 27 Mike Lieberthal | .25 | .11 |
| ❑ 28 Tim Hudson | .60 | .25 |
| ❑ 29 Warren Morris | .15 | .07 |
| ❑ 30 Pedro Martinez | .75 | .35 |
| ❑ 31 John Smoltz | .25 | .11 |
| ❑ 32 Ray Durham | .25 | .11 |
| ❑ 33 Chad Allen | .15 | .07 |
| ❑ 34 Tony Clark | .15 | .07 |
| ❑ 35 Tino Martinez | .25 | .11 |
| ❑ 36 J.T. Snow | .25 | .11 |
| ❑ 37 Kevin Brown | .25 | .11 |
| ❑ 38 Bartolo Colon | .25 | .11 |
| ❑ 39 Rey Ordonez | .15 | .07 |
| ❑ 40 Jeff Bagwell | .75 | .35 |
| ❑ 41 Ivan Rodriguez | .75 | .35 |
| ❑ 42 Eric Chavez | .25 | .11 |
| ❑ 43 Eric Milton | .15 | .07 |
| ❑ 44 Jose Canseco | .75 | .35 |
| ❑ 45 Shawn Green | .60 | .25 |
| ❑ 46 Rich Aurilia | .15 | .07 |
| ❑ 47 Roberto Alomar | .60 | .25 |
| ❑ 48 Brian Daubach | .15 | .07 |
| ❑ 49 Magglio Ordonez | .25 | .11 |
| ❑ 50 Derek Jeter | 2.50 | 1.10 |
| ❑ 51 Kris Benson | .25 | .11 |
| ❑ 52 Albert Belle | .40 | .18 |
| ❑ 53 Rondell White | .25 | .11 |
| ❑ 54 Justin Thompson | .15 | .07 |
| ❑ 55 Nomar Garciaparra | 2.00 | .90 |
| ❑ 56 Chuck Finley | .25 | .11 |
| ❑ 57 Omar Vizquel | .25 | .11 |
| ❑ 58 Luis Castillo | .25 | .11 |
| ❑ 59 Richard Hidalgo | .25 | .11 |
| ❑ 60 Barry Bonds | 1.00 | .45 |
| ❑ 61 Craig Biggio | .40 | .18 |
| ❑ 62 Doug Glanville | .15 | .07 |
| ❑ 63 Gabe Kapler | .25 | .11 |
| ❑ 64 Johnny Damon | .25 | .11 |
| ❑ 65 Pokey Reese | .25 | .11 |
| ❑ 66 Andy Pettitte | .25 | .11 |
| ❑ 67 B.J. Surhoff | .25 | .11 |
| ❑ 68 Richie Sexson | .25 | .11 |
| ❑ 69 Javy Lopez | .25 | .11 |
| ❑ 70 Raul Mondesi | .25 | .11 |
| ❑ 71 Darin Erstad | .60 | .25 |
| ❑ 72 Kevin Millwood | .25 | .11 |
| ❑ 73 Ricky Ledee | .15 | .07 |
| ❑ 74 John Olerud | .25 | .11 |
| ❑ 75 Sean Casey | .25 | .11 |
| ❑ 76 Carlos Febles | .15 | .07 |
| ❑ 77 Paul O'Neill | .25 | .11 |
| ❑ 78 Bob Abreu | .25 | .11 |
| ❑ 79 Neifi Perez | .15 | .07 |
| ❑ 80 Tony Gwynn | 1.25 | .55 |
| ❑ 81 Russ Ortiz | .25 | .11 |
| ❑ 82 Matt Williams | .40 | .18 |
| ❑ 83 Chris Carpenter | .15 | .07 |
| ❑ 84 Roger Cedeno | .15 | .07 |
| ❑ 85 Tim Salmon | .25 | .11 |
| ❑ 86 Billy Koch | .25 | .11 |
| ❑ 87 Jeromy Burnitz | .25 | .11 |
| ❑ 88 Edgardo Alfonzo | .25 | .11 |
| ❑ 89 Jay Bell | .25 | .11 |
| ❑ 90 Manny Ramirez | .75 | .35 |
| ❑ 91 Frank Thomas | 1.25 | .55 |
| ❑ 92 Mike Mussina | .60 | .25 |
| ❑ 93 J.D. Drew | .60 | .25 |
| ❑ 94 Adrian Beltre | .25 | .11 |
| ❑ 95 Alex Rodriguez | 2.00 | .90 |
| ❑ 96 Larry Walker | .25 | .11 |
| ❑ 97 Juan Encarnacion | .25 | .11 |
| ❑ 98 Mike Sweeney | .25 | .11 |
| ❑ 99 Rusty Greer | .25 | .11 |
| ❑ 100 Randy Johnson | .75 | .35 |
| ❑ 101 Jose Vidro | .15 | .07 |
| ❑ 102 Preston Wilson | .25 | .11 |
| ❑ 103 Greg Maddux | 1.50 | .70 |
| ❑ 104 Jason Giambi | .60 | .25 |
| ❑ 105 Cal Ripken | 2.50 | 1.10 |
| ❑ 106 Carlos Beltran | .25 | .11 |
| ❑ 107 Vinny Castilla | .25 | .11 |
| ❑ 108 Mariano Rivera | .25 | .11 |
| ❑ 109 Mo Vaughn | .25 | .11 |
| ❑ 110 Rafael Palmeiro | .60 | .25 |
| ❑ 111 Shannon Stewart | .25 | .11 |
| ❑ 112 Mike Hampton | .25 | .11 |
| ❑ 113 Joe Nathan | .15 | .07 |
| ❑ 114 Ben Davis | .15 | .07 |
| ❑ 115 Andruw Jones | .60 | .25 |
| ❑ 116 Robin Ventura | .25 | .11 |
| ❑ 117 Damion Easley | .15 | .07 |
| ❑ 118 Jeff Cirillo | .25 | .11 |
| ❑ 119 Kerry Wood | .25 | .11 |
| ❑ 120 Scott Rolen | .60 | .25 |
| ❑ 121 Sammy Sosa | 1.25 | .55 |
| ❑ 122 Ken Griffey Jr. | 2.50 | 1.10 |
| ❑ 123 Shane Reynolds | .15 | .07 |
| ❑ 124 Troy Glaus | .75 | .35 |
| ❑ 125 Tom Glavine | .60 | .25 |
| ❑ 126 Michael Barrett | .15 | .07 |
| ❑ 127 Al Leiter | .15 | .07 |
| ❑ 128 Jason Kendall | .25 | .11 |
| ❑ 129 Roger Clemens | 1.25 | .55 |
| ❑ 130 Juan Gonzalez | .60 | .25 |
| ❑ 131 Corey Koskie | .15 | .07 |
| ❑ 132 Curt Schilling | .25 | .11 |
| ❑ 133 Mike Piazza | 2.00 | .90 |
| ❑ 134 Gary Sheffield | .60 | .25 |
| ❑ 135 Jim Thome | .40 | .18 |
| ❑ 136 Orlando Hernandez | .25 | .11 |
| ❑ 137 Ray Lankford | .25 | .11 |
| ❑ 138 Geoff Jenkins | .25 | .11 |
| ❑ 139 Jose Lima | .15 | .07 |
| ❑ 140 Mark McGwire | 2.50 | 1.10 |
| ❑ 141 Adam Piatt | .60 | .25 |
| ❑ 142 Pat Manning RC | 1.25 | .55 |
| ❑ 143 Marcos Castillo RC | .50 | .23 |
| ❑ 144 Leslie Brea RC | .60 | .25 |
| ❑ 145 Humberto Cota RC | 1.00 | .45 |
| ❑ 146 Ben Petrick | .15 | .07 |
| ❑ 147 Kip Wells | .25 | .11 |
| ❑ 148 Wily Pena | .25 | .11 |
| ❑ 149 Chris Wakeland RC | .50 | .23 |
| ❑ 150 Brad Baker RC | 1.25 | .55 |
| ❑ 151 Robbie Morrison RC | .50 | .23 |
| ❑ 152 Reggie Taylor | .15 | .07 |
| ❑ 153 Matt Ginter RC | .75 | .35 |
| ❑ 154 Peter Bergeron | .15 | .07 |
| ❑ 155 Roosevelt Brown | .15 | .07 |
| ❑ 156 Matt Cepicky RC | .60 | .25 |
| ❑ 157 Ramon Castro | .15 | .07 |
| ❑ 158 Brad Baisley RC | .75 | .35 |
| ❑ 159 Jeff Goldbach RC | 1.00 | .45 |
| ❑ 160 Mitch Meluskey | .15 | .07 |
| ❑ 161 Chad Harville | .15 | .07 |
| ❑ 162 Brian Cooper | .15 | .07 |
| ❑ 163 Marcus Giles | .25 | .11 |
| ❑ 164 Jim Morris | .15 | .07 |
| ❑ 165 Geoff Goetz | .15 | .07 |
| ❑ 166 Bobby Bradley RC | 2.50 | 1.10 |
| ❑ 167 Rob Bell | .15 | .07 |
| ❑ 168 Joe Crede | .60 | .25 |
| ❑ 169 Michael Restovich | .25 | .11 |
| ❑ 170 Quincy Foster RC | .50 | .23 |
| ❑ 171 Enrique Cruz RC | .75 | .35 |
| ❑ 172 Mark Quinn | .25 | .11 |
| ❑ 173 Nick Johnson | .25 | .11 |
| ❑ 174 Jeff Liefer | .15 | .07 |
| ❑ 175 Kevin Mench RC | 2.50 | 1.10 |
| ❑ 176 Steve Lomasney | .15 | .07 |

❑ 177 Jayson Werth .15 .07
❑ 178 Tim Drew .15 .07
❑ 179 Chip Ambres .25 .11
❑ 180 Ryan Anderson .25 .11
❑ 181 Matt Blank .15 .07
❑ 182 Giuseppe Chiaramonte .15 .07
❑ 183 Corey Myers RC .75 .35
❑ 184 Jeff Yoder .15 .07
❑ 185 Craig Dingman RC .50 .23
❑ 186 Jon Hamilton RC .75 .35
❑ 187 Toby Hall .15 .07
❑ 188 Russell Branyan .25 .11
❑ 189 Brian Falkenborg RC .50 .23
❑ 190 Aaron Harang RC .50 .23
❑ 191 Juan Pena .15 .07
❑ 192 Travis Thompson RC .50 .23
❑ 193 Alfonso Soriano .25 .11
❑ 194 Alejandro Diaz RC .75 .35
❑ 195 Carlos Pena .25 .11
❑ 196 Kevin Nicholson .15 .07
❑ 197 Mo Bruce .15 .07
❑ 198 C.C. Sabathia .25 .11
❑ 199 Carl Crawford .25 .11
❑ 200 Rafael Furcal 1.50 .70
❑ 201 Andrew Beinbrink RC .50 .23
❑ 202 Jimmy Osting .15 .07
❑ 203 Aaron McNeal RC 1.25 .55
❑ 204 Brett Laxton .15 .07
❑ 205 Chris George .25 .11
❑ 206 Felipe Lopez .25 .11
❑ 207 Ben Sheets RC 4.00 1.80
❑ 208 Mike Meyers RC .60 .25
❑ 209 Jason Conti .15 .07
❑ 210 Milton Bradley .25 .11
❑ 211 Chris Mears RC .75 .35
❑ 212 Carlos Hernandez RC .60 .25
❑ 213 Jason Romano .25 .11
❑ 214 Geofrey Tomlinson .15 .07
❑ 215 Jimmy Rollins .15 .07
❑ 216 Pablo Ozuna .15 .07
❑ 217 Steve Cox .15 .07
❑ 218 Terrence Long .25 .11
❑ 219 Jeff DaVanon RC .50 .23
❑ 220 Rick Ankiel 1.25 .55
❑ 221 Jason Standridge .15 .07
❑ 222 Tony Armas Jr. .25 .11
❑ 223 Jason Tyner .15 .07
❑ 224 Ramon Ortiz .25 .11
❑ 225 Daryle Ward .25 .11
❑ 226 Enger Veras RC .50 .23
❑ 227 Chris Jones .15 .07
❑ 228 Eric Cammack RC .50 .23
❑ 229 Ruben Mateo .25 .11
❑ 230 Ken Harvey RC 1.25 .55
❑ 231 Jake Westbrook .15 .07
❑ 232 Rob Purvis RC .60 .25
❑ 233 Choo Freeman .25 .11
❑ 234 Aramis Ramirez .15 .07
❑ 235 A.J. Burnett .25 .11
❑ 236 Kevin Barker .15 .07
❑ 237 Chance Caple RC .75 .35
❑ 238 Jarrod Washburn .15 .07
❑ 239 Lance Berkman .25 .11
❑ 240 Michael Wenner RC .60 .25
❑ 241 Alex Sanchez .15 .07
❑ 242 Pat Daneker .15 .07
❑ 243 Grant Roberts .15 .07
❑ 244 Mark Ellis RC 1.00 .45
❑ 245 Donny Leon .15 .07
❑ 246 David Eckstein .15 .07
❑ 247 Dicky Gonzalez RC .75 .35
❑ 248 John Patterson .15 .07
❑ 249 Chad Green .15 .07
❑ 250 Scot Shields RC .50 .23
❑ 251 Troy Cameron .15 .07
❑ 252 Jose Molina .15 .07
❑ 253 Rob Pugmire RC .60 .25
❑ 254 Rick Elder .15 .07
❑ 255 Sean Burroughs .60 .25
❑ 256 Josh Kalinowski RC .50 .23
❑ 257 Matt LeCroy .15 .07
❑ 258 Alex Graman RC 1.25 .55
❑ 259 Tomokazu Ohka RC 1.25 .55
❑ 260 Brady Clark .15 .07
❑ 261 Rico Washington RC .60 .25
❑ 262 Gary Matthews Jr. .15 .07
❑ 263 Matt Wise .15 .07
❑ 264 Keith Reed RC 1.00 .45
❑ 265 Santiago Ramirez RC .50 .23
❑ 266 Ben Broussard RC 2.50 1.10
❑ 267 Ryan Langerhans .15 .07
❑ 268 Juan Rivera .15 .07
❑ 269 Shawn Gallagher .15 .07
❑ 270 Jorge Toca .15 .07
❑ 271 Brad Lidge .15 .07
❑ 272 Leoncio Estrella RC .50 .23
❑ 273 Ruben Quevedo .15 .07
❑ 274 Jack Cust .25 .11
❑ 275 T.J. Tucker .15 .07
❑ 276 Mike Colangelo .15 .07
❑ 277 Brian Schneider .15 .07
❑ 278 Calvin Murray .15 .07
❑ 279 Josh Girdley .15 .07
❑ 280 Mike Paradis .15 .07
❑ 281 Chad Hermansen .15 .07
❑ 282 Ty Howington RC 1.00 .45
❑ 283 Aaron Myette .25 .11
❑ 284 D'Angelo Jimenez .25 .11
❑ 285 Dernell Stenson .25 .11
❑ 286 Jerry Hairston Jr. .15 .07
❑ 287 Gary Majewski RC .60 .25
❑ 288 Derrin Ebert .15 .07
❑ 289 Steve Fish RC .50 .23
❑ 290 Carlos Hernandez .15 .07
❑ 291 Allen Levrault .15 .07
❑ 292 Sean McNally RC .50 .23
❑ 293 Randey Dorame RC .60 .25
❑ 294 Wes Anderson RC 1.00 .45
❑ 295 B.J. Ryan .15 .07
❑ 296 Alan Webb RC .50 .23
❑ 297 Brandon Inge RC 1.25 .55
❑ 298 David Walling .15 .07
❑ 299 Sun Woo Kim RC 1.25 .55
❑ 300 Pat Burrell 1.00 .45
❑ 301 Rick Guttormson RC .50 .23
❑ 302 Gil Meche .25 .11
❑ 303 Carlos Zambrano RC 1.50 .70
❑ 304 Eric Byrnes UER RC .75 .35
Bo Porter pictured
❑ 305 Robb Quinlan RC .75 .35
❑ 306 Jackie Rexrode .15 .07
❑ 307 Nate Bump .15 .07
❑ 308 Sean DePaula RC .50 .23
❑ 309 Matt Riley .25 .11
❑ 310 Ryan Minor .15 .07
❑ 311 J.J. Davis .25 .11
❑ 312 Randy Wolf .15 .07
❑ 313 Jason Jennings .15 .07
❑ 314 Scott Seabol RC .60 .25
❑ 315 Doug Davis .15 .07
❑ 316 Todd Moser RC .50 .23
❑ 317 Rob Ryan .15 .07
❑ 318 Bubba Crosby .15 .07
❑ 319 Ryan Knox RC 1.50 .70
❑ 320 Mario Encarnacion .15 .07
❑ 321 Francisco Rodriguez RC .75 .35
❑ 322 Michael Cuddyer .25 .11
❑ 323 Ed Yarnall .15 .07
❑ 324 Cesar Saba RC 1.00 .45
❑ 325 Travis Dawkins .25 .11
❑ 326 Alex Escobar .25 .11
❑ 327 Julio Zuleta RC .50 .23
❑ 328 Josh Hamilton 1.00 .45
❑ 329 Nick Neugebauer RC 1.00 .45
❑ 330 Matt Belisle .25 .11
❑ 331 Kurt Ainsworth RC 1.50 .70
❑ 332 Tim Raines Jr. .25 .11
❑ 333 Eric Munson .60 .25
❑ 334 Donzell McDonald .15 .07
❑ 335 Larry Bigbie RC 1.00 .45
❑ 336 Matt Watson RC .50 .23
❑ 337 Aubrey Huff .25 .11
❑ 338 Julio Ramirez .15 .07
❑ 339 Jason Grabowski RC 1.00 .45
❑ 340 Jon Garland .25 .11
❑ 341 Austin Kearns .25 .11
❑ 342 Josh Pressley RC .75 .35
❑ 343 Miguel Olivo RC .75 .35
❑ 344 Julio Lugo .15 .07
❑ 345 Roberto Vaz .15 .07
❑ 346 Ramon Soler .15 .07
❑ 347 Brandon Phillips RC .75 .35
❑ 348 Vince Faison RC 1.25 .55
❑ 349 Mike Venafro .15 .07
❑ 350 Rick Asadoorian RC 3.00 1.35
❑ 351 B.J. Garbe RC 1.50 .70
❑ 352 Dan Reichert .15 .07
❑ 353 Jason Stumm RC 1.00 .45
❑ 354 Ruben Salazar RC 1.25 .55
❑ 355 Francisco Cordero .15 .07
❑ 356 Juan Guzman RC .50 .23
❑ 357 Mike Bacsik RC .50 .23
❑ 358 Jared Sandberg .15 .07
❑ 359 Rod Barajas .15 .07
❑ 360 Junior Brignac RC .60 .25
❑ 361 J.M. Gold .15 .07
❑ 362 Octavio Dotel .15 .07
❑ 363 David Kelton .25 .11
❑ 364 Scott Morgan .15 .07
❑ 365 Wascar Serrano RC .75 .35
❑ 366 Wilton Veras .25 .11
❑ 367 Eugene Kingsale .15 .07
❑ 368 Ted Lilly .15 .07
❑ 369 George Lombard .15 .07
❑ 370 Chris Haas .15 .07
❑ 371 Wilton Pena RC .50 .23
❑ 372 Vernon Wells .25 .11
❑ 373 Jason Royer RC .50 .23
❑ 374 Jeff Heaverlo RC 1.00 .45
❑ 375 Calvin Pickering .15 .07
❑ 376 Mike Lamb RC 1.00 .45
❑ 377 Kyle Snyder .15 .07
❑ 378 Javier Cardona RC .50 .23
❑ 379 Aaron Rowand RC 1.25 .55
❑ 380 Dee Brown .25 .11
❑ 381 Brett Myers RC 1.00 .45
❑ 382 Abraham Nunez .25 .11
❑ 383 Eric Valent .25 .11
❑ 384 Jody Gerut RC .75 .35
❑ 385 Adam Dunn .25 .11
❑ 386 Jay Gehrke .15 .07
❑ 387 Omar Ortiz .15 .07
❑ 388 Darnell McDonald .15 .07
❑ 389 Tony Schrager RC .50 .23
❑ 390 J.D. Closser .15 .07
❑ 391 Ben Christensen RC 1.25 .55
❑ 392 Adam Kennedy .25 .11
❑ 393 Nick Green RC .50 .23
❑ 394 Ramon Hernandez .15 .07
❑ 395 Roy Oswalt RC 1.00 .45
❑ 396 Andy Tracy RC .50 .23
❑ 397 Eric Gagne .15 .07
❑ 398 Michael Tejera RC .50 .23
❑ 399 Adam Everett .25 .11
❑ 400 Corey Patterson 1.00 .45
❑ 401 Gary Knotts RC .50 .23
❑ 402 Ryan Christianson RC 1.25 .55
❑ 403 Eric Ireland RC .75 .35
❑ 404 Andrew Good RC .50 .23
❑ 405 Brad Penny .25 .11
❑ 406 Jason LaRue .15 .07
❑ 407 Kit Pellow .15 .07
❑ 408 Kevin Beirne .15 .07
❑ 409 Kelly Dransfeldt .15 .07
❑ 410 Jason Grilli .15 .07
❑ 411 Scott Downs RC .50 .23
❑ 412 Jesus Colome .25 .11
❑ 413 John Sneed RC .50 .23
❑ 414 Tony McKnight .15 .07
❑ 415 Luis Rivera .15 .07
❑ 416 Adam Eaton .25 .11
❑ 417 Mike MacDougal RC .60 .25
❑ 418 Mike Nannini .15 .07
❑ 419 Barry Zito RC 5.00 2.20
❑ 420 DeWayne Wise .15 .07
❑ 421 Jason Dellaero .15 .07
❑ 422 Chad Moeller .15 .07
❑ 423 Jason Marquis .25 .11
❑ 424 Tim Redding RC .75 .35
❑ 425 Mark Mulder .25 .11
❑ 426 Josh Paul .15 .07
❑ 427 Chris Enochs .15 .07
❑ 428 Wilfredo Rodriguez RC 1.00 .45
❑ 429 Kevin Witt .15 .07
❑ 430 Scott Sobkowiak RC .60 .25
❑ 431 McKay Christensen .15 .07
❑ 432 Jung Bong .15 .07
❑ 433 Keith Evans RC .50 .23

| | | | |
|---|---|---|---|
| ❑ 434 | Garry Maddox Jr. RC | .50 | .23 |
| ❑ 435 | Ramon Santiago RC | 1.00 | .45 |
| ❑ 436 | Alex Cora | .15 | .07 |
| ❑ 437 | Carlos Lee | .25 | .11 |
| ❑ 438 | Jason Repko RC | 1.00 | .45 |
| ❑ 439 | Matt Burch | .15 | .07 |
| ❑ 440 | Shawn Sonnier RC | .50 | .23 |

## 2000 Bowman Draft Picks

| | MINT | NRMT |
|---|---|---|
| COMP.FACT.SET (111) | 40.00 | 18.00 |
| COMPLETE SET (110) | 30.00 | 13.50 |

| | | | |
|---|---|---|---|
| ❑ 1 | Pat Burrell | 1.00 | .45 |
| ❑ 2 | Rafael Furcal | 1.50 | .70 |
| ❑ 3 | Grant Roberts | .15 | .07 |
| ❑ 4 | Barry Zito | 2.00 | .90 |
| ❑ 5 | Julio Zuleta | .25 | .11 |
| ❑ 6 | Mark Mulder | .25 | .11 |
| ❑ 7 | Rob Bell | .15 | .07 |
| ❑ 8 | Adam Piatt | .60 | .25 |
| ❑ 9 | Mike Lamb | .40 | .18 |
| ❑ 10 | Pablo Ozuna | .15 | .07 |
| ❑ 11 | Jason Tyner | .15 | .07 |
| ❑ 12 | Jason Marquis | .15 | .07 |
| ❑ 13 | Eric Munson | .60 | .25 |
| ❑ 14 | Seth Etherton | .15 | .07 |
| ❑ 15 | Milton Bradley | .25 | .11 |
| ❑ 16 | Nick Green | .25 | .11 |
| ❑ 17 | Chin-Feng Chen RC | 4.00 | 1.80 |
| ❑ 18 | Matt Boone RC | .50 | .23 |
| ❑ 19 | Kevin Gregg RC | .40 | .18 |
| ❑ 20 | Eddy Garabito RC | .40 | .18 |
| ❑ 21 | Aaron Capista RC | .40 | .18 |
| ❑ 22 | Esteban German RC | .50 | .23 |
| ❑ 23 | Derek Thompson RC | .40 | .18 |
| ❑ 24 | Phil Merrell RC | .40 | .18 |
| ❑ 25 | Brian O'Connor RC | .50 | .23 |
| ❑ 26 | Yamid Haad | .15 | .07 |
| ❑ 27 | Hector Mercado RC | .40 | .18 |
| ❑ 28 | Jason Woolf RC | .40 | .18 |
| ❑ 29 | Eddy Furniss RC | .40 | .18 |
| ❑ 30 | Cha Sueng Baek RC | 1.00 | .45 |
| ❑ 31 | Colby Lewis RC | .50 | .23 |
| ❑ 32 | Pasqual Coco RC | .40 | .18 |
| ❑ 33 | Jorge Cantu RC | .40 | .18 |
| ❑ 34 | Erasmo Ramirez RC | .40 | .18 |
| ❑ 35 | Bobby Kielty RC | .75 | .35 |
| ❑ 36 | Joaquin Benoit RC | .75 | .35 |
| ❑ 37 | Brian Esposito RC | .50 | .23 |
| ❑ 38 | Michael Wenner | .25 | .11 |
| ❑ 39 | Juan Rincon RC | .40 | .18 |
| ❑ 40 | Yorvit Torrealba RC | .40 | .18 |
| ❑ 41 | Chad Durham RC | .40 | .18 |
| ❑ 42 | Jim Mann RC | .40 | .18 |
| ❑ 43 | Shane Loux RC | .50 | .23 |
| ❑ 44 | Luis Rivas | .25 | .11 |
| ❑ 45 | Ken Chenard RC | .40 | .18 |
| ❑ 46 | Mike Lockwood RC | .40 | .18 |
| ❑ 47 | Yovanny Lara RC | .40 | .18 |
| ❑ 48 | Bubba Carpenter RC | .40 | .18 |
| ❑ 49 | Ryan Dittfurth RC | .40 | .18 |
| ❑ 50 | John Stephens RC | .50 | .23 |
| ❑ 51 | Pedro Feliz RC | 1.25 | .55 |
| ❑ 52 | Kenny Kelly RC | .75 | .35 |
| ❑ 53 | Neil Jenkins RC | .75 | .35 |
| ❑ 54 | Mike Glendenning RC | .40 | .18 |
| ❑ 55 | Bo Porter | .15 | .07 |
| ❑ 56 | Eric Byrnes | .25 | .11 |
| ❑ 57 | Tony Alvarez RC | .75 | .35 |
| ❑ 58 | Kazuhiro Sasaki RC | 2.50 | 1.10 |
| ❑ 59 | Chad Durbin RC | .40 | .18 |
| ❑ 60 | Mike Bynum RC | .75 | .35 |
| ❑ 61 | Travis Wilson RC | .40 | .18 |
| ❑ 62 | Jose Leon RC | .40 | .18 |
| ❑ 63 | Ryan Vogelsong RC | 1.00 | .45 |
| ❑ 64 | Geraldo Guzman RC | .40 | .18 |
| ❑ 65 | Craig Anderson RC | .50 | .23 |
| ❑ 66 | Carlos Silva RC | .40 | .18 |
| ❑ 67 | Brad Thomas RC | .40 | .18 |
| ❑ 68 | Chin-Hui Tsao RC | 3.00 | 1.35 |
| ❑ 69 | Mark Buehrle RC | .75 | .35 |
| ❑ 70 | Juan Salas RC | .50 | .23 |
| ❑ 71 | Denny Abreu RC | .40 | .18 |
| ❑ 72 | Keith McDonald RC | .40 | .18 |
| ❑ 73 | Chris Richard RC | .75 | .35 |
| ❑ 74 | Tomas De la Rosa RC | .40 | .18 |
| ❑ 75 | Vicente Padilla RC | .40 | .18 |
| ❑ 76 | Justin Brunette RC | .40 | .18 |
| ❑ 77 | Scott Linebrink RC | .40 | .18 |
| ❑ 78 | Jeff Sparks RC | .40 | .18 |
| ❑ 79 | Tike Redman RC | .40 | .18 |
| ❑ 80 | John Lackey RC | .50 | .23 |
| ❑ 81 | Joe Strong RC | .40 | .18 |
| ❑ 82 | Brian Tollberg RC | .40 | .18 |
| ❑ 83 | Steve Sisco RC | .40 | .18 |
| ❑ 84 | Chris Clapinski RC | .40 | .18 |
| ❑ 85 | Augie Ojeda RC | .40 | .18 |
| ❑ 86 | Adrian Gonzalez RC | 2.50 | 1.10 |
| ❑ 87 | Mike Stodolka RC | .75 | .35 |
| ❑ 88 | Adam Johnson RC | 1.00 | .45 |
| ❑ 89 | Matt Wheatland RC | 1.25 | .55 |
| ❑ 90 | Corey Smith RC | 1.00 | .45 |
| ❑ 91 | Rocco Baldelli RC | 1.50 | .70 |
| ❑ 92 | Keith Bucktrot RC | .50 | .23 |
| ❑ 93 | Adam Wainwright RC | 1.25 | .55 |
| ❑ 94 | Blaine Boyer RC | .50 | .23 |
| ❑ 95 | Aaron Herr RC | .75 | .35 |
| ❑ 96 | Scott Thorman RC | .75 | .35 |
| ❑ 97 | Bryan Digby RC | .50 | .23 |
| ❑ 98 | Josh Shortslef RC | .50 | .23 |
| ❑ 99 | Sean Smith RC | .50 | .23 |
| ❑ 100 | Alex Cruz RC | .40 | .18 |
| ❑ 101 | Marc Love RC | .50 | .23 |
| ❑ 102 | Kevin Lee RC | .40 | .18 |
| ❑ 103 | Victor Ramos RC | .50 | .23 |
| ❑ 104 | Jason Kaanoi RC | .50 | .23 |
| ❑ 105 | Luis Escobar RC | .50 | .23 |
| ❑ 106 | Tripper Johnson RC | .75 | .35 |
| ❑ 107 | Phil Dumatrait RC | .75 | .35 |
| ❑ 108 | Bryan Edwards RC | .50 | .23 |
| ❑ 109 | Grady Sizemore RC | 1.00 | .45 |
| ❑ 110 | Thomas Mitchell RC | .50 | .23 |

## 1997 Bowman Chrome

| | MINT | NRMT |
|---|---|---|
| COMPLETE SET (300) | 250.00 | 110.00 |

| | | | |
|---|---|---|---|
| ❑ 1 | Derek Jeter | 4.00 | 1.80 |
| ❑ 2 | Chipper Jones | 2.50 | 1.10 |
| ❑ 3 | Hideo Nomo | 1.00 | .45 |
| ❑ 4 | Tim Salmon | .40 | .18 |
| ❑ 5 | Robin Ventura | .40 | .18 |
| ❑ 6 | Tony Clark | .25 | .11 |
| ❑ 7 | Barry Larkin | 1.00 | .45 |
| ❑ 8 | Paul Molitor | 1.00 | .45 |
| ❑ 9 | Andy Benes | .25 | .11 |
| ❑ 10 | Ryan Klesko | .40 | .18 |
| ❑ 11 | Mark McGwire | 4.00 | 1.80 |
| ❑ 12 | Ken Griffey Jr. | 4.00 | 1.80 |
| ❑ 13 | Robb Nen | .25 | .11 |
| ❑ 14 | Cal Ripken | 4.00 | 1.80 |
| ❑ 15 | John Valentin | .25 | .11 |
| ❑ 16 | Ricky Bottalico | .25 | .11 |
| ❑ 17 | Mike Lansing | .25 | .11 |
| ❑ 18 | Ryne Sandberg | 1.25 | .55 |
| ❑ 19 | Carlos Delgado | 1.00 | .45 |
| ❑ 20 | Craig Biggio | .60 | .25 |
| ❑ 21 | Eric Karros | .40 | .18 |
| ❑ 22 | Kevin Appier | .40 | .18 |
| ❑ 23 | Mariano Rivera | .40 | .18 |
| ❑ 24 | Vinny Castilla | .40 | .18 |
| ❑ 25 | Juan Gonzalez | 1.00 | .45 |
| ❑ 26 | Al Martin | .25 | .11 |
| ❑ 27 | Jeff Cirillo | .40 | .18 |
| ❑ 28 | Ray Lankford | .40 | .18 |
| ❑ 29 | Manny Ramirez | 1.25 | .55 |
| ❑ 30 | Roberto Alomar | 1.00 | .45 |
| ❑ 31 | Will Clark | 1.00 | .45 |
| ❑ 32 | Chuck Knoblauch | .40 | .18 |
| ❑ 33 | Harold Baines | .40 | .18 |
| ❑ 34 | Edgar Martinez | .60 | .25 |
| ❑ 35 | Mike Mussina | 1.00 | .45 |
| ❑ 36 | Kevin Brown | .60 | .25 |
| ❑ 37 | Dennis Eckersley | .40 | .18 |
| ❑ 38 | Tino Martinez | .40 | .18 |
| ❑ 39 | Raul Mondesi | .40 | .18 |
| ❑ 40 | Sammy Sosa | 2.00 | .90 |
| ❑ 41 | John Smoltz | .40 | .18 |
| ❑ 42 | Billy Wagner | .25 | .11 |
| ❑ 43 | Ken Caminiti | .40 | .18 |
| ❑ 44 | Wade Boggs | 1.25 | .55 |
| ❑ 45 | Andres Galarraga | .00 | .25 |
| ❑ 46 | Roger Clemens | 2.00 | .90 |
| ❑ 47 | Matt Williams | .60 | .25 |
| ❑ 48 | Albert Belle | .60 | .25 |
| ❑ 49 | Jeff King | .25 | .11 |
| ❑ 50 | John Wetteland | .40 | .18 |
| ❑ 51 | Deion Sanders | .40 | .18 |
| ❑ 52 | Ellis Burks | .40 | .18 |
| ❑ 53 | Pedro Martinez | 1.25 | .55 |
| ❑ 54 | Kenny Lofton | .40 | .18 |
| ❑ 55 | Randy Johnson | 1.25 | .55 |
| ❑ 56 | Bernie Williams | 1.00 | .45 |
| ❑ 57 | Marquis Grissom | .25 | .11 |
| ❑ 58 | Gary Sheffield | 1.00 | .45 |
| ❑ 59 | Curt Schilling | .40 | .18 |
| ❑ 60 | Reggie Sanders | .25 | .11 |
| ❑ 61 | Bobby Higginson | .40 | .18 |
| ❑ 62 | Moises Alou | .40 | .18 |
| ❑ 63 | Tom Glavine | 1.00 | .45 |
| ❑ 64 | Mark Grace | 1.00 | .45 |
| ❑ 65 | Rafael Palmeiro | 1.00 | .45 |
| ❑ 66 | John Olerud | .40 | .18 |
| ❑ 67 | Dante Bichette | .40 | .18 |
| ❑ 68 | Jeff Bagwell | 1.25 | .55 |
| ❑ 69 | Barry Bonds | 1.50 | .70 |
| ❑ 70 | Pat Hentgen | .25 | .11 |
| ❑ 71 | Jim Thome | .60 | .25 |
| ❑ 72 | Andy Pettitte | .40 | .18 |
| ❑ 73 | Jay Bell | .40 | .18 |
| ❑ 74 | Jim Edmonds | 1.00 | .45 |
| ❑ 75 | Ron Gant | .25 | .11 |
| ❑ 76 | David Cone | .40 | .18 |
| ❑ 77 | Jose Canseco | 1.25 | .55 |
| ❑ 78 | Jay Buhner | .40 | .18 |
| ❑ 79 | Greg Maddux | 2.50 | 1.10 |
| ❑ 80 | Lance Johnson | .25 | .11 |
| ❑ 81 | Travis Fryman | .40 | .18 |
| ❑ 82 | Paul O'Neill | .40 | .18 |
| ❑ 83 | Ivan Rodriguez | 1.25 | .55 |
| ❑ 84 | Fred McGriff | .60 | .25 |
| ❑ 85 | Mike Piazza | 3.00 | 1.35 |
| ❑ 86 | Brady Anderson | .40 | .18 |
| ❑ 87 | Marty Cordova | .25 | .11 |
| ❑ 88 | Joe Carter | .40 | .18 |
| ❑ 89 | Brian Jordan | .40 | .18 |
| ❑ 90 | David Justice | .60 | .25 |
| ❑ 91 | Tony Gwynn | 2.00 | .90 |

| | Player | Mint | NrMt |
|---|---|---|---|
| ❑ 92 | Larry Walker | .40 | .18 |
| ❑ 93 | Mo Vaughn | .40 | .18 |
| ❑ 94 | Sandy Alomar Jr. | .40 | .18 |
| ❑ 95 | Rusty Greer | .40 | .18 |
| ❑ 96 | Roberto Hernandez | .25 | .11 |
| ❑ 97 | Hal Morris | .25 | .11 |
| ❑ 98 | Todd Hundley | .25 | .11 |
| ❑ 99 | Rondell White | .40 | .18 |
| ❑ 100 | Frank Thomas | 2.00 | .90 |
| ❑ 101 | Bubba Trammell RC | 1.50 | .70 |
| ❑ 102 | Sidney Ponson RC | 3.00 | 1.35 |
| ❑ 103 | Ricky Ledee RC | 4.00 | 1.80 |
| ❑ 104 | Brett Tomko | .25 | .11 |
| ❑ 105 | Braden Looper RC | 1.50 | .70 |
| ❑ 106 | Jason Dickson | .25 | .11 |
| ❑ 107 | Chad Green RC | 1.50 | .70 |
| ❑ 108 | R.A. Dickey RC | .25 | .11 |
| ❑ 109 | Jeff Liefer | .40 | .18 |
| ❑ 110 | Richard Hidalgo | .40 | .18 |
| ❑ 111 | Chad Hermansen RC | 5.00 | 2.20 |
| ❑ 112 | Felix Martinez | .25 | .11 |
| ❑ 113 | J.J. Johnson | .25 | .11 |
| ❑ 114 | Todd Dunwoody | .25 | .11 |
| ❑ 115 | Katsuhiro Maeda | .25 | .11 |
| ❑ 116 | Darin Erstad | 1.25 | .55 |
| ❑ 117 | Elieser Marrero | .25 | .11 |
| ❑ 118 | Bartolo Colon | .40 | .18 |
| ❑ 119 | Ugueth Urbina | .25 | .11 |
| ❑ 120 | Jaime Bluma | .25 | .11 |
| ❑ 121 | Seth Greisinger RC | 1.50 | .70 |
| ❑ 122 | Jose Cruz Jr. RC | 10.00 | 4.50 |
| ❑ 123 | Todd Dunn | .25 | .11 |
| ❑ 124 | Justin Towle RC | .25 | .11 |
| ❑ 125 | Brian Rose | .25 | .11 |
| ❑ 126 | Jose Guillen | .25 | .11 |
| ❑ 127 | Andruw Jones | 1.50 | .70 |
| ❑ 128 | Mark Kotsay RC | 4.00 | 1.80 |
| ❑ 129 | Wilton Guerrero | .25 | .11 |
| ❑ 130 | Jacob Cruz | .25 | .11 |
| ❑ 131 | Mike Sweeney | .40 | .18 |
| ❑ 132 | Matt Morris | .25 | .11 |
| ❑ 133 | John Thomson | .25 | .11 |
| ❑ 134 | Javier Valentin | .25 | .11 |
| ❑ 135 | Mike Drumright RC | .25 | .11 |
| ❑ 136 | Michael Barrett | .25 | .11 |
| ❑ 137 | Tony Saunders RC | .25 | .11 |
| ❑ 138 | Kevin Brown | .25 | .11 |
| ❑ 139 | Anthony Sanders RC | .25 | .11 |
| ❑ 140 | Jeff Abbott | .25 | .11 |
| ❑ 141 | Eugene Kingsale | .25 | .11 |
| ❑ 142 | Paul Konerko | .40 | .18 |
| ❑ 143 | Randall Simon RC | 1.50 | .70 |
| ❑ 144 | Freddy Garcia | .25 | .11 |
| ❑ 145 | Karim Garcia | .25 | .11 |
| ❑ 146 | Carlos Guillen | .25 | .11 |
| ❑ 147 | Aaron Boone | .25 | .11 |
| ❑ 148 | Donnie Sadler | .25 | .11 |
| ❑ 149 | Brooks Kieschnick | .25 | .11 |
| ❑ 150 | Scott Spiezio | .25 | .11 |
| ❑ 151 | Kevin Orie | .25 | .11 |
| ❑ 152 | Russ Johnson | .25 | .11 |
| ❑ 153 | Livan Hernandez | .40 | .18 |
| ❑ 154 | Vladimir Nunez RC | 1.50 | .70 |
| ❑ 155 | Pokey Reese | .40 | .18 |
| ❑ 156 | Chris Carpenter | .40 | .18 |
| ❑ 157 | Eric Milton RC | 5.00 | 2.20 |
| ❑ 158 | Richie Sexson | .40 | .18 |
| ❑ 159 | Carl Pavano | .40 | .18 |
| ❑ 160 | Pat Cline | .25 | .11 |
| ❑ 161 | Ron Wright | .25 | .11 |
| ❑ 162 | Dante Powell | .25 | .11 |
| ❑ 163 | Mark Bellhorn | .25 | .11 |
| ❑ 164 | George Lombard | .25 | .11 |
| ❑ 165 | Paul Wilder RC | .25 | .11 |
| ❑ 166 | Brad Fullmer | .40 | .18 |
| ❑ 167 | Kris Benson RC | 12.00 | 5.50 |
| ❑ 168 | Torii Hunter | .25 | .11 |
| ❑ 169 | D.T. Cromer RC | .25 | .11 |
| ❑ 170 | Nelson Figueroa RC | 1.50 | .70 |
| ❑ 171 | Hiram Bocachica RC | 3.00 | 1.35 |
| ❑ 172 | Shane Monahan | .25 | .11 |
| ❑ 173 | Juan Melo | .25 | .11 |
| ❑ 174 | Calvin Pickering RC | 1.50 | .70 |
| ❑ 175 | Reggie Taylor | .40 | .18 |
| ❑ 176 | Geoff Jenkins | .40 | .18 |
| ❑ 177 | Steve Rain RC | 1.50 | .70 |
| ❑ 178 | Nerio Rodriguez RC | .25 | .11 |
| ❑ 179 | Derrick Gibson | .25 | .11 |
| ❑ 180 | Darin Blood | .25 | .11 |
| ❑ 181 | Ben Davis | .25 | .11 |
| ❑ 182 | Adrian Beltre RC | 15.00 | 6.75 |
| ❑ 183 | Kerry Wood RC | 20.00 | 9.00 |
| ❑ 184 | Nate Rolison RC | 3.00 | 1.35 |
| ❑ 185 | Fernando Tatis RC | 10.00 | 4.50 |
| ❑ 186 | Jake Westbrook RC | 2.00 | .90 |
| ❑ 187 | Edwin Diaz | .25 | .11 |
| ❑ 188 | Joe Fontenot RC | 1.50 | .70 |
| ❑ 189 | Matt Halloran RC | 1.50 | .70 |
| ❑ 190 | Matt Clement RC | 4.00 | 1.80 |
| ❑ 191 | Todd Greene | .25 | .11 |
| ❑ 192 | Eric Chavez RC | 15.00 | 6.75 |
| ❑ 193 | Edgard Velazquez | .25 | .11 |
| ❑ 194 | Bruce Chen RC | 5.00 | 2.20 |
| ❑ 195 | Jason Brester | .25 | .11 |
| ❑ 196 | Chris Reitsma RC | 1.50 | .70 |
| ❑ 197 | Neifi Perez | .25 | .11 |
| ❑ 198 | Hideki Irabu RC | 3.00 | 1.35 |
| ❑ 199 | Don Denbow RC | .25 | .11 |
| ❑ 200 | Derrek Lee | .25 | .11 |
| ❑ 201 | Todd Walker | .25 | .11 |
| ❑ 202 | Scott Rolen | 1.00 | .45 |
| ❑ 203 | Wes Helms | .25 | .11 |
| ❑ 204 | Bob Abreu | .40 | .18 |
| ❑ 205 | John Patterson RC | 2.50 | 1.10 |
| ❑ 206 | Alex Gonzalez RC | 2.00 | .90 |
| ❑ 207 | Grant Roberts RC | 3.00 | 1.35 |
| ❑ 208 | Jeff Suppan | .25 | .11 |
| ❑ 209 | Luke Wilcox | .25 | .11 |
| ❑ 210 | Marlon Anderson | .25 | .11 |
| ❑ 211 | Mike Caruso RC | 1.50 | .70 |
| ❑ 212 | Roy Halladay RC | 2.00 | .90 |
| ❑ 213 | Jeremi Gonzalez RC | .25 | .11 |
| ❑ 214 | Aramis Ramirez RC | 6.00 | 2.70 |
| ❑ 215 | Dermal Brown RC | 10.00 | 4.50 |
| ❑ 216 | Justin Thompson | .25 | .11 |
| ❑ 217 | Danny Clyburn | .25 | .11 |
| ❑ 218 | Bruce Aven | .25 | .11 |
| ❑ 219 | Keith Foulke RC | .25 | .11 |
| ❑ 220 | Shannon Stewart | .40 | .18 |
| ❑ 221 | Larry Barnes RC | .25 | .11 |
| ❑ 222 | Mark Johnson RC | 1.50 | .70 |
| ❑ 223 | Randy Winn | .25 | .11 |
| ❑ 224 | Nomar Garciaparra | 3.00 | 1.35 |
| ❑ 225 | Jacque Jones RC | 8.00 | 3.60 |
| ❑ 226 | Chris Clemons | .25 | .11 |
| ❑ 227 | Todd Helton | 2.00 | .90 |
| ❑ 228 | Ryan Brannan RC | .25 | .11 |
| ❑ 229 | Alex Sanchez RC | 1.50 | .70 |
| ❑ 230 | Russell Branyan | 1.00 | .45 |
| ❑ 231 | Daryle Ward | 4.00 | 1.80 |
| ❑ 232 | Kevin Witt | .40 | .18 |
| ❑ 233 | Gabby Martinez | .25 | .11 |
| ❑ 234 | Preston Wilson | .40 | .18 |
| ❑ 235 | Donzell McDonald RC | 1.50 | .70 |
| ❑ 236 | Orlando Cabrera RC | 2.50 | 1.10 |
| ❑ 237 | Brian Banks | .25 | .11 |
| ❑ 238 | Robbie Bell | 2.50 | 1.10 |
| ❑ 239 | Brad Rigby | .25 | .11 |
| ❑ 240 | Scott Elarton | .40 | .18 |
| ❑ 241 | Donny Leon RC | 1.50 | .70 |
| ❑ 242 | Abraham Nunez RC | 1.50 | .70 |
| ❑ 243 | Adam Eaton RC | 10.00 | 4.50 |
| ❑ 244 | Octavio Dotel RC | 4.00 | 1.80 |
| ❑ 245 | Sean Casey | 10.00 | 4.50 |
| ❑ 246 | Joe Lawrence RC | 3.00 | 1.35 |
| ❑ 247 | Adam Johnson RC | 1.50 | .70 |
| ❑ 248 | Ronnie Belliard RC | 3.00 | 1.35 |
| ❑ 249 | Bobby Estalella | .40 | .18 |
| ❑ 250 | Corey Lee RC | .25 | .11 |
| ❑ 251 | Mike Cameron | .40 | .18 |
| ❑ 252 | Kerry Robinson RC | .25 | .11 |
| ❑ 253 | A.J. Zapp RC | 2.50 | 1.10 |
| ❑ 254 | Jarrod Washburn | .25 | .11 |
| ❑ 255 | Ben Grieve | .40 | .18 |
| ❑ 256 | Javier Vazquez RC | 5.00 | 2.20 |
| ❑ 257 | Travis Lee RC | 5.00 | 2.20 |
| ❑ 258 | Dennis Reyes RC | 1.50 | .70 |
| ❑ 259 | Danny Buxbaum | .25 | .11 |
| ❑ 260 | Kelvim Escobar RC | 3.00 | 1.35 |
| ❑ 261 | Danny Klassen | .25 | .11 |
| ❑ 262 | Ken Cloude RC | .25 | .11 |
| ❑ 263 | Gabe Alvarez | .25 | .11 |
| ❑ 264 | Clayton Bruner RC | .25 | .11 |
| ❑ 265 | Jason Marquis RC | 4.00 | 1.80 |
| ❑ 266 | Jamey Wright | .25 | .11 |
| ❑ 267 | Matt Snyder RC | .25 | .11 |
| ❑ 268 | Josh Garrett RC | 1.50 | .70 |
| ❑ 269 | Juan Encarnacion | .40 | .18 |
| ❑ 270 | Heath Murray | .25 | .11 |
| ❑ 271 | Brent Butler RC | 3.00 | 1.35 |
| ❑ 272 | Danny Peoples RC | 2.00 | .90 |
| ❑ 273 | Miguel Tejada RC | 20.00 | 9.00 |
| ❑ 274 | Jim Pittsley | .25 | .11 |
| ❑ 275 | Dmitri Young | .40 | .18 |
| ❑ 276 | Vladimir Guerrero | 2.50 | 1.10 |
| ❑ 277 | Cole Liniak RC | 1.50 | .70 |
| ❑ 278 | Ramon Hernandez | .40 | .18 |
| ❑ 279 | Cliff Politte RC | 1.50 | .70 |
| ❑ 280 | Mel Rosario RC | .25 | .11 |
| ❑ 281 | Jorge Carrion RC | .25 | .11 |
| ❑ 282 | John Barnes RC | 2.50 | 1.10 |
| ❑ 283 | Chris Stowe RC | .25 | .11 |
| ❑ 284 | Vernon Wells RC | 10.00 | 4.50 |
| ❑ 285 | Brett Caradonna RC | 1.50 | .70 |
| ❑ 286 | Scott Hodges RC | 2.50 | 1.10 |
| ❑ 287 | Jon Garland RC | 8.00 | 3.60 |
| ❑ 288 | Nathan Haynes RC | 2.00 | .90 |
| ❑ 289 | Geoff Goetz RC | 1.50 | .70 |
| ❑ 290 | Adam Kennedy RC | 6.00 | 2.70 |
| ❑ 291 | T.J. Tucker RC | 1.50 | .70 |
| ❑ 292 | Aaron Akin RC | 1.50 | .70 |
| ❑ 293 | Jayson Werth RC | 3.00 | 1.35 |
| ❑ 294 | Glenn Davis RC | 1.50 | .70 |
| ❑ 295 | Mark Mangum RC | 1.50 | .70 |
| ❑ 296 | Troy Cameron RC | 2.00 | .90 |
| ❑ 297 | J.J. Davis RC | 5.00 | 2.20 |
| ❑ 298 | Lance Berkman RC | 12.00 | 5.50 |
| ❑ 299 | Jason Standridge RC | 2.00 | .90 |
| ❑ 300 | Jason Dellaero RC | 1.50 | .70 |

## 1998 Bowman Chrome

| | MINT | NRMT |
|---|---|---|
| COMPLETE SET (441) | 150.00 | 70.00 |
| COMPLETE SERIES 1 (221) | 120.00 | 55.00 |
| COMPLETE SERIES 2 (220) | 80.00 | 36.00 |

| | Player | Mint | NrMt |
|---|---|---|---|
| ❑ 1 | Nomar Garciaparra | 3.00 | 1.35 |
| ❑ 2 | Scott Rolen | 1.00 | .45 |
| ❑ 3 | Andy Pettitte | .40 | .18 |
| ❑ 4 | Ivan Rodriguez | 1.25 | .55 |
| ❑ 5 | Mark McGwire | 4.00 | 1.80 |
| ❑ 6 | Jason Dickson | .25 | .11 |
| ❑ 7 | Jose Cruz Jr. | .40 | .18 |
| ❑ 8 | Jeff Kent | .60 | .25 |
| ❑ 9 | Mike Mussina | 1.00 | .45 |
| ❑ 10 | Jason Kendall | .40 | .18 |
| ❑ 11 | Brett Tomko | .25 | .11 |
| ❑ 12 | Jeff King | .25 | .11 |
| ❑ 13 | Brad Radke | .40 | .18 |
| ❑ 14 | Robin Ventura | .40 | .18 |
| ❑ 15 | Jeff Bagwell | 1.25 | .55 |
| ❑ 16 | Greg Maddux | 2.50 | 1.10 |
| ❑ 17 | John Jaha | .40 | .18 |
| ❑ 18 | Mike Piazza | 3.00 | 1.35 |
| ❑ 19 | Edgar Martinez | .60 | .25 |
| ❑ 20 | David Justice | .60 | .25 |
| ❑ 21 | Todd Hundley | .25 | .11 |
| ❑ 22 | Tony Gwynn | 2.00 | .90 |
| ❑ 23 | Larry Walker | .40 | .18 |

❑ 24 Bernie Williams 1.00 .45
❑ 25 Edgar Renteria .25 .11
❑ 26 Rafael Palmeiro 1.00 .45
❑ 27 Tim Salmon .40 .18
❑ 28 Matt Morris .25 .11
❑ 29 Shawn Estes .25 .11
❑ 30 Vladimir Guerrero 1.50 .70
❑ 31 Fernando Tatis .40 .18
❑ 32 Justin Thompson .25 .11
❑ 33 Ken Griffey Jr. 4.00 1.80
❑ 34 Edgardo Alfonzo .40 .18
❑ 35 Mo Vaughn .40 .18
❑ 36 Marty Cordova .25 .11
❑ 37 Craig Biggio .60 .25
❑ 38 Roger Clemens 2.00 .90
❑ 39 Mark Grace 1.00 .45
❑ 40 Ken Caminiti .40 .18
❑ 41 Tony Womack .25 .11
❑ 42 Albert Belle .60 .25
❑ 43 Tino Martinez .40 .18
❑ 44 Sandy Alomar Jr. .40 .18
❑ 45 Jeff Cirillo .40 .18
❑ 46 Jason Giambi 1.00 .45
❑ 47 Darin Erstad 1.00 .45
❑ 48 Livan Hernandez .25 .11
❑ 49 Mark Grudzielanek .25 .11
❑ 50 Sammy Sosa 2.00 .90
❑ 51 Curt Schilling .40 .18
❑ 52 Brian Hunter .25 .11
❑ 53 Neifi Perez .25 .11
❑ 54 Todd Walker .25 .11
❑ 55 Jose Guillen .25 .11
❑ 56 Jim Thome .60 .25
❑ 57 Tom Glavine 1.00 .45
❑ 58 Todd Greene .25 .11
❑ 59 Rondell White .40 .18
❑ 60 Roberto Alomar 1.00 .45
❑ 61 Tony Clark .25 .11
❑ 62 Vinny Castilla .40 .18
❑ 63 Barry Larkin 1.00 .45
❑ 64 Hideki Irabu .25 .11
❑ 65 Johnny Damon .40 .18
❑ 66 Juan Gonzalez 1.00 .45
❑ 67 John Olerud .40 .18
❑ 68 Gary Sheffield 1.00 .45
❑ 69 Raul Mondesi .40 .18
❑ 70 Chipper Jones 2.50 1.10
❑ 71 David Ortiz .25 .11
❑ 72 Warren Morris RC 3.00 1.35
❑ 73 Alex Gonzalez .25 .11
❑ 74 Nick Bierbrodt 1.00 .45
❑ 75 Roy Halladay .25 .11
❑ 76 Danny Buxbaum .25 .11
❑ 77 Adam Kennedy .40 .18
❑ 78 Jared Sandberg .25 .11
❑ 79 Michael Barrett .25 .11
❑ 80 Gil Meche 2.00 .90
❑ 81 Jayson Werth .25 .11
❑ 82 Abraham Nunez .25 .11
❑ 83 Ben Petrick .25 .11
❑ 84 Brett Caradonna .25 .11
❑ 85 Mike Lowell RC 5.00 2.20
❑ 86 Clay Bruner .40 .18
❑ 87 John Curtice RC 2.00 .90
❑ 88 Bobby Estalella .25 .11
❑ 89 Juan Melo .25 .11
❑ 90 Arnold Gooch .25 .11
❑ 91 Kevin Millwood RC 6.00 2.70
❑ 92 Richie Sexson .60 .25
❑ 93 Orlando Cabrera .25 .11
❑ 94 Pat Cline .25 .11
❑ 95 Anthony Sanders .25 .11
❑ 96 Russ Johnson .25 .11
❑ 97 Ben Grieve .40 .18
❑ 98 Kevin McGlinchy .25 .11
❑ 99 Paul Wilder .25 .11
❑ 100 Russ Ortiz .40 .18
❑ 101 Ryan Jackson RC .25 .11
❑ 102 Heath Murray .25 .11
❑ 103 Brian Rose .25 .11
❑ 104 Ryan Radmanovich RC .25 .11
❑ 105 Ricky Ledee .25 .11
❑ 106 Jeff Wallace RC 1.50 .70
❑ 107 Ryan Minor RC 1.50 .70
❑ 108 Dennis Reyes .25 .11
❑ 109 James Manias .25 .11
❑ 110 Chris Carpenter .40 .18
❑ 111 Daryle Ward .40 .18
❑ 112 Vernon Wells .60 .25
❑ 113 Chad Green .25 .11
❑ 114 Mike Stoner RC .25 .11
❑ 115 Brad Fullmer .40 .18
❑ 116 Adam Eaton .40 .18
❑ 117 Jeff Liefer .25 .11
❑ 118 Corey Koskie RC 4.00 1.80
❑ 119 Todd Helton 1.25 .55
❑ 120 Jaime Jones RC 1.50 .70
❑ 121 Mel Rosario .25 .11
❑ 122 Geoff Goetz .25 .11
❑ 123 Adrian Beltre .40 .18
❑ 124 Jason Dellaero .25 .11
❑ 125 Gabe Kapler RC 12.00 5.50
❑ 126 Scott Schoeneweis .25 .11
❑ 127 Ryan Brannan .25 .11
❑ 128 Aaron Akin .25 .11
❑ 129 Ryan Anderson RC 15.00 6.75
❑ 130 Brad Penny .40 .18
❑ 131 Bruce Chen .25 .11
❑ 132 Eli Marrero .25 .11
❑ 133 Eric Chavez .40 .18
❑ 134 Troy Glaus RC 25.00 11.00
❑ 135 Troy Cameron .25 .11
❑ 136 Brian Sikorski RC 1.50 .70
❑ 137 Mike Kinkade RC 1.50 .70
❑ 138 Braden Looper .25 .11
❑ 139 Mark Mangum .25 .11
❑ 140 Danny Peoples .25 .11
❑ 141 J.J. Davis .40 .18
❑ 142 Ben Davis .25 .11
❑ 143 Jacque Jones .40 .18
❑ 144 Derrick Gibson .25 .11
❑ 145 Bronson Arroyo 1.50 .70
❑ 146 Luis De Los Santos RC 1.50 .70
❑ 147 Jeff Abbott .25 .11
❑ 148 Mike Cuddyer RC 5.00 2.20
❑ 149 Jason Romano .40 .18
❑ 150 Shane Monahan .25 .11
❑ 151 Ntema Ndungidi RC 3.00 1.35
❑ 152 Alex Sanchez .25 .11
❑ 153 Jack Cust RC 8.00 3.60
❑ 154 Brent Butler .25 .11
❑ 155 Ramon Hernandez .25 .11
❑ 156 Norm Hutchins .25 .11
❑ 157 Jason Marquis .40 .18
❑ 158 Jacob Cruz .25 .11
❑ 159 Rob Burger RC 1.50 .70
❑ 160 Dave Coggin .25 .11
❑ 161 Preston Wilson .40 .18
❑ 162 Jason Fitzgerald RC 1.50 .70
❑ 163 Dan Serafini .25 .11
❑ 164 Pete Munro .25 .11
❑ 165 Trot Nixon .40 .18
❑ 166 Homer Bush .25 .11
❑ 167 Dermal Brown .40 .18
❑ 168 Chad Hermansen .40 .18
❑ 169 Julio Moreno RC 1.50 .70
❑ 170 John Roskos RC 1.50 .70
❑ 171 Grant Roberts .25 .11
❑ 172 Ken Cloude .25 .11
❑ 173 Jason Brester .25 .11
❑ 174 Jason Conti .25 .11
❑ 175 Jon Garland .25 .11
❑ 176 Robbie Bell .25 .11
❑ 177 Nathan Haynes .25 .11
❑ 178 Ramon Ortiz RC 5.00 2.20
❑ 179 Shannon Stewart .40 .18
❑ 180 Pablo Ortega .25 .11
❑ 181 Jimmy Rollins RC 3.00 1.35
❑ 182 Sean Casey .40 .18
❑ 183 Ted Lilly RC 2.00 .90
❑ 184 Chris Enochs RC 1.50 .70
❑ 185 Magglio Ordonez RC UER 15.00 6.75
(Front photo is Mario Valdez)
❑ 186 Mike Drumright .25 .11
❑ 187 Aaron Boone .25 .11
❑ 188 Matt Clement .25 .11
❑ 189 Todd Dunwoody .25 .11
❑ 190 Larry Rodriguez .25 .11
❑ 191 Todd Noel .25 .11
❑ 192 Geoff Jenkins .40 .18
❑ 193 George Lombard .25 .11
❑ 194 Lance Berkman .60 .25
❑ 195 Marcus McCain .40 .18
❑ 196 Ryan McGuire .25 .11
❑ 197 Jhensy Sandoval .25 .11
❑ 198 Corey Lee .25 .11
❑ 199 Mario Valdez .25 .11
❑ 200 Robert Fick RC 3.00 1.35
❑ 201 Donnie Sadler .25 .11
❑ 202 Marc Kroon .25 .11
❑ 203 David Miller .25 .11
❑ 204 Jarrod Washburn .25 .11
❑ 205 Miguel Tejada 1.00 .45
❑ 206 Raul Ibanez .25 .11
❑ 207 John Patterson .25 .11
❑ 208 Calvin Pickering .25 .11
❑ 209 Felix Martinez .25 .11
❑ 210 Mark Redman .25 .11
❑ 211 Scott Elarton .40 .18
❑ 212 Jose Amado RC 1.50 .70
❑ 213 Kerry Wood 1.00 .45
❑ 214 Dante Powell .25 .11
❑ 215 Aramis Ramirez .40 .18
❑ 216 A.J. Hinch .25 .11
❑ 217 Dustin Carr RC 1.50 .70
❑ 218 Mark Kotsay .40 .18
❑ 219 Jason Standridge .25 .11
❑ 220 Luis Ordaz .25 .11
❑ 221 Orlando Hernandez RC 6.00 2.70
❑ 222 Cal Ripken 4.00 1.80
❑ 223 Paul Molitor 1.00 .45
❑ 224 Derek Jeter 4.00 1.80
❑ 225 Barry Bonds 1.50 .70
❑ 226 Jim Edmonds 1.00 .45
❑ 227 John Smoltz .40 .18
❑ 228 Eric Karros .40 .18
❑ 229 Ray Lankford .40 .18
❑ 230 Rey Ordonez .25 .11
❑ 231 Kenny Lofton .40 .18
❑ 232 Alex Rodriguez 3.00 1.35
❑ 233 Dante Bichette .40 .18
❑ 234 Pedro Martinez 1.25 .55
❑ 235 Carlos Delgado 1.00 .45
❑ 236 Rod Beck .25 .11
❑ 237 Matt Williams .60 .25
❑ 238 Charles Johnson .40 .18
❑ 239 Rico Brogna .25 .11
❑ 240 Frank Thomas 2.00 .90
❑ 241 Paul O'Neill .40 .18
❑ 242 Jaret Wright .25 .11
❑ 243 Brant Brown .25 .11
❑ 244 Ryan Klesko .40 .18
❑ 245 Chuck Finley .40 .18
❑ 246 Derek Bell .25 .11
❑ 247 Delino DeShields .25 .11
❑ 248 Chan Ho Park .40 .18
❑ 249 Wade Boggs 1.25 .55
❑ 250 Jay Buhner .40 .18
❑ 251 Butch Huskey .25 .11
❑ 252 Steve Finley .40 .18
❑ 253 Will Clark 1.00 .45
❑ 254 John Valentin .25 .11
❑ 255 Bobby Higginson .40 .18
❑ 256 Darryl Strawberry .40 .18
❑ 257 Randy Johnson 1.25 .55
❑ 258 Al Martin .25 .11
❑ 259 Travis Fryman .40 .18
❑ 260 Fred McGriff .60 .25
❑ 261 Jose Valentin .25 .11
❑ 262 Andruw Jones 1.00 .45
❑ 263 Kenny Rogers .25 .11
❑ 264 Moises Alou .40 .18
❑ 265 Denny Neagle .25 .11
❑ 266 Ugueth Urbina .25 .11
❑ 267 Derrek Lee .25 .11
❑ 268 Ellis Burks .40 .18
❑ 269 Mariano Rivera .40 .18
❑ 270 Dean Palmer .40 .18
❑ 271 Eddie Taubensee .25 .11
❑ 272 Brady Anderson .40 .18
❑ 273 Brian Giles .40 .18
❑ 274 Quinton McCracken .25 .11
❑ 275 Henry Rodriguez .25 .11
❑ 276 Andres Galarraga .60 .25
❑ 277 Jose Canseco 1.25 .55
❑ 278 David Segui .25 .11
❑ 279 Bret Saberhagen .40 .18

| | # | Player | Mint | NrMt |
|---|---|---|---|---|
| ❑ | 280 | Kevin Brown | .60 | .25 |
| ❑ | 281 | Chuck Knoblauch | .40 | .18 |
| ❑ | 282 | Jeromy Burnitz | .40 | .18 |
| ❑ | 283 | Jay Bell | .40 | .18 |
| ❑ | 284 | Manny Ramirez | 1.25 | .55 |
| ❑ | 285 | Rick Helling | .40 | .18 |
| ❑ | 286 | Francisco Cordova | .25 | .11 |
| ❑ | 287 | Bob Abreu | .40 | .18 |
| ❑ | 288 | J.T. Snow | .25 | .11 |
| ❑ | 289 | Hideo Nomo | 1.00 | .45 |
| ❑ | 290 | Brian Jordan | .40 | .18 |
| ❑ | 291 | Javy Lopez | .40 | .18 |
| ❑ | 292 | Travis Lee | .40 | .18 |
| ❑ | 293 | Russell Branyan | .40 | .18 |
| ❑ | 294 | Paul Konerko | .40 | .18 |
| ❑ | 295 | Masato Yoshii RC | 3.00 | 1.35 |
| ❑ | 296 | Kris Benson | .40 | .18 |
| ❑ | 297 | Juan Encarnacion | .40 | .18 |
| ❑ | 298 | Eric Milton | .25 | .11 |
| ❑ | 299 | Mike Caruso | .25 | .11 |
| ❑ | 300 | Ricardo Aramboles RC | 3.00 | 1.35 |
| ❑ | 301 | Bobby Smith | .25 | .11 |
| ❑ | 302 | Billy Koch | .40 | .18 |
| ❑ | 303 | Richard Hidalgo | .40 | .18 |
| ❑ | 304 | Justin Baughman RC | .25 | .11 |
| ❑ | 305 | Chris Gissell | .25 | .11 |
| ❑ | 306 | Donnie Bridges RC | 3.00 | 1.35 |
| ❑ | 307 | Nelson Lara RC | 1.50 | .70 |
| ❑ | 308 | Randy Wolf RC | 3.00 | 1.35 |
| ❑ | 309 | Jason LaRue RC | 2.50 | 1.10 |
| ❑ | 310 | Jason Gooding RC | .25 | .11 |
| ❑ | 311 | Edgard Clemente | .25 | .11 |
| ❑ | 312 | Andrew Vessel | .25 | .11 |
| ❑ | 313 | Chris Reitsma | .25 | .11 |
| ❑ | 314 | Jesus Sanchez RC | 1.50 | .70 |
| ❑ | 315 | Buddy Carlyle RC | 2.00 | .90 |
| ❑ | 316 | Randy Winn | .25 | .11 |
| ❑ | 317 | Luis Rivera RC | 2.00 | .90 |
| ❑ | 318 | Marcus Thames RC | 3.00 | 1.35 |
| ❑ | 319 | A.J. Pierzynski | .25 | .11 |
| ❑ | 320 | Scott Randall | .25 | .11 |
| ❑ | 321 | Damian Sapp | .25 | .11 |
| ❑ | 322 | Ed Yarnall RC | 2.00 | .90 |
| ❑ | 323 | Luke Allen RC | 2.00 | .90 |
| ❑ | 324 | J.D. Smart | .25 | .11 |
| ❑ | 325 | Willie Martinez | .40 | .18 |
| ❑ | 326 | Alex Ramirez | .25 | .11 |
| ❑ | 327 | Eric DuBose RC | 1.50 | .70 |
| ❑ | 328 | Kevin Witt | .25 | .11 |
| ❑ | 329 | Dan McKinley RC | 1.50 | .70 |
| ❑ | 330 | Cliff Politte | .25 | .11 |
| ❑ | 331 | Vladimir Nunez | .25 | .11 |
| ❑ | 332 | John Halama RC | 3.00 | 1.35 |
| ❑ | 333 | Nerio Rodriguez | .25 | .11 |
| ❑ | 334 | Desi Relaford | .25 | .11 |
| ❑ | 335 | Robinson Checo | .25 | .11 |
| ❑ | 336 | John Nicholson | .60 | .25 |
| ❑ | 337 | Tom LaRosa RC | .25 | .11 |
| ❑ | 338 | Kevin Nicholson RC | 1.50 | .70 |
| ❑ | 339 | Javier Vazquez | .25 | .11 |
| ❑ | 340 | A.J. Zapp | .25 | .11 |
| ❑ | 341 | Tom Evans | .25 | .11 |
| ❑ | 342 | Kerry Robinson | .25 | .11 |
| ❑ | 343 | Gabe Gonzalez RC | .25 | .11 |
| ❑ | 344 | Ralph Milliard | .25 | .11 |
| ❑ | 345 | Enrique Wilson | .25 | .11 |
| ❑ | 346 | Elvin Hernandez | .25 | .11 |
| ❑ | 347 | Mike Lincoln RC | 1.50 | .70 |
| ❑ | 348 | Cesar King RC | 1.50 | .70 |
| ❑ | 349 | Cristian Guzman RC | 3.00 | 1.35 |
| ❑ | 350 | Donzell McDonald | .25 | .11 |
| ❑ | 351 | Jim Parque RC | 3.00 | 1.35 |
| ❑ | 352 | Mike Saipe RC | .25 | .11 |
| ❑ | 353 | Carlos Febles RC | 3.00 | 1.35 |
| ❑ | 354 | Dernell Stenson RC | 5.00 | 2.20 |
| ❑ | 355 | Mark Osborne RC | 1.50 | .70 |
| ❑ | 356 | Odalis Perez RC | 2.00 | .90 |
| ❑ | 357 | Jason Dewey RC | 1.50 | .70 |
| ❑ | 358 | Joe Fontenot | .25 | .11 |
| ❑ | 359 | Jason Grilli RC | 1.50 | .70 |
| ❑ | 360 | Kevin Haverbusch RC | 1.50 | .70 |
| ❑ | 361 | Jay Yennaco RC | 1.50 | .70 |
| ❑ | 362 | Brian Buchanan | .25 | .11 |
| ❑ | 363 | John Barnes | .25 | .11 |
| ❑ | 364 | Chris Fussell | .25 | .11 |
| ❑ | 365 | Kevin Gibbs RC | .25 | .11 |

| | # | Player | Mint | NrMt |
|---|---|---|---|---|
| ❑ | 366 | Joe Lawrence | .25 | .11 |
| ❑ | 367 | DaRond Stovall | .25 | .11 |
| ❑ | 368 | Brian Fuentes RC | 1.50 | .70 |
| ❑ | 369 | Jimmy Anderson | .25 | .11 |
| ❑ | 370 | Lariel Gonzalez RC | 1.50 | .70 |
| ❑ | 371 | Scott Williamson RC | 2.00 | .90 |
| ❑ | 372 | Milton Bradley | 1.00 | .45 |
| ❑ | 373 | Jason Halper RC | .40 | .18 |
| ❑ | 374 | Brent Billingsley RC | 1.50 | .70 |
| ❑ | 375 | Joe DePastino RC | .25 | .11 |
| ❑ | 376 | Jake Westbrook | .25 | .11 |
| ❑ | 377 | Octavio Dotel | .25 | .11 |
| ❑ | 378 | Jason Williams RC | .25 | .11 |
| ❑ | 379 | Julio Ramirez RC | 3.00 | 1.35 |
| ❑ | 380 | Seth Greisinger | .25 | .11 |
| ❑ | 381 | Mike Judd RC | 1.50 | .70 |
| ❑ | 382 | Ben Ford RC | .40 | .18 |
| ❑ | 383 | Tom Bennett RC | .25 | .11 |
| ❑ | 384 | Adam Butler RC | .25 | .11 |
| ❑ | 385 | Wade Miller RC | 2.00 | .90 |
| ❑ | 386 | Kyle Peterson RC | 1.50 | .70 |
| ❑ | 387 | Tommy Peterman RC | 1.50 | .70 |
| ❑ | 388 | Onan Masaoka | .25 | .11 |
| ❑ | 389 | Jason Rakers RC | .25 | .11 |
| ❑ | 390 | Rafael Medina | .25 | .11 |
| ❑ | 391 | Luis Lopez | .25 | .11 |
| ❑ | 392 | Jeff Yoder | .25 | .11 |
| ❑ | 393 | Vance Wilson RC | .25 | .11 |
| ❑ | 394 | Fernando Seguignol RC | 2.00 | .90 |
| ❑ | 395 | Ron Wright | .25 | .11 |
| ❑ | 396 | Ruben Mateo RC | 10.00 | 4.50 |
| ❑ | 397 | Steve Lomasney RC | 2.50 | 1.10 |
| ❑ | 398 | Damian Jackson | .25 | .11 |
| ❑ | 399 | Mike Jerzembeck RC | .40 | .18 |
| ❑ | 400 | Luis Rivas RC | 4.00 | 1.80 |
| ❑ | 401 | Kevin Burford RC | 2.50 | 1.10 |
| ❑ | 402 | Glenn Davis | .25 | .11 |
| ❑ | 403 | Robert Luce RC | .25 | .11 |
| ❑ | 404 | Cole Liniak | .25 | .11 |
| ❑ | 405 | Matt LeCroy RC | 3.00 | 1.35 |
| ❑ | 406 | Jeremy Giambi RC | 2.00 | .90 |
| ❑ | 407 | Shawn Chacon | .25 | .11 |
| ❑ | 408 | Dewayne Wise RC | 1.50 | .70 |
| ❑ | 409 | Steve Woodard | .25 | .11 |
| ❑ | 410 | Francisco Cordero RC | 2.00 | .90 |
| ❑ | 411 | Damon Minor RC | 2.00 | .90 |
| ❑ | 412 | Lou Collier | .25 | .11 |
| ❑ | 413 | Justin Towle | .25 | .11 |
| ❑ | 414 | Juan LeBron | .25 | .11 |
| ❑ | 415 | Michael Coleman | .25 | .11 |
| ❑ | 416 | Felix Rodriguez | .25 | .11 |
| ❑ | 417 | Paul Ah Yat RC | .25 | .11 |
| ❑ | 418 | Kevin Barker RC | 1.50 | .70 |
| ❑ | 419 | Brian Meadows | .25 | .11 |
| ❑ | 420 | Darnell McDonald RC | 3.00 | 1.35 |
| ❑ | 421 | Matt Kinney RC | 2.50 | 1.10 |
| ❑ | 422 | Mike Vavrek RC | .25 | .11 |
| ❑ | 423 | Courtney Duncan RC | .25 | .11 |
| ❑ | 424 | Kevin Millar RC | 1.50 | .70 |
| ❑ | 425 | Ruben Rivera | .25 | .11 |
| ❑ | 426 | Steve Shoemaker RC | .25 | .11 |
| ❑ | 427 | Dan Reichert RC | 3.00 | 1.35 |
| ❑ | 428 | Carlos Lee RC | 10.00 | 4.50 |
| ❑ | 429 | Rod Barajas | .40 | .18 |
| ❑ | 430 | Pablo Ozuna RC | 4.00 | 1.80 |
| ❑ | 431 | Todd Belitz RC | 1.50 | .70 |
| ❑ | 432 | Sidney Ponson | .25 | .11 |
| ❑ | 433 | Steve Carver RC | .25 | .11 |
| ❑ | 434 | Esteban Yan RC | 1.50 | .70 |
| ❑ | 435 | Cedrick Bowers | .40 | .18 |
| ❑ | 436 | Marlon Anderson | .25 | .11 |
| ❑ | 437 | Carl Pavano | .25 | .11 |
| ❑ | 438 | Jae Weong Seo RC | 1.50 | .70 |
| ❑ | 439 | Jose Taveras RC | 1.50 | .70 |
| ❑ | 440 | Matt Anderson RC | 1.50 | .70 |
| ❑ | 441 | Darron Ingram RC | 1.50 | .70 |

## 1999 Bowman Chrome

| | MINT | NRMT |
|---|---|---|
| COMPLETE SET (440) | 400.00 | 180.00 |
| COMPLETE SERIES 1 (220) | 150.00 | 70.00 |
| COMPLETE SERIES 2 (220) | 250.00 | 110.00 |

| | # | Player | Mint | NrMt |
|---|---|---|---|---|
| ❑ | 1 | Ben Grieve | .40 | .18 |
| ❑ | 2 | Kerry Wood | .40 | .18 |
| ❑ | 3 | Ruben Rivera | .25 | .11 |
| ❑ | 4 | Sandy Alomar Jr. | .40 | .18 |
| ❑ | 5 | Cal Ripken | 4.00 | 1.80 |
| ❑ | 6 | Mark McGwire | 4.00 | 1.80 |
| ❑ | 7 | Vladimir Guerrero | 1.50 | .70 |
| ❑ | 8 | Moises Alou | .40 | .18 |
| ❑ | 9 | Jim Edmonds | 1.00 | .45 |
| ❑ | 10 | Greg Maddux | 2.50 | 1.10 |
| ❑ | 11 | Gary Sheffield | 1.00 | .45 |
| ❑ | 12 | John Valentin | .25 | .11 |
| ❑ | 13 | Chuck Knoblauch | .40 | .18 |
| ❑ | 14 | Tony Clark | .25 | .11 |
| ❑ | 15 | Rusty Greer | .40 | .18 |
| ❑ | 16 | Al Leiter | .40 | .18 |
| ❑ | 17 | Travis Lee | .25 | .11 |
| ❑ | 18 | Jose Cruz Jr. | .40 | .18 |
| ❑ | 19 | Pedro Martinez | 1.25 | .55 |
| ❑ | 20 | Paul O'Neill | .40 | .18 |
| ❑ | 21 | Todd Walker | .25 | .11 |
| ❑ | 22 | Vinny Castilla | .40 | .18 |
| ❑ | 23 | Barry Larkin | 1.00 | .45 |
| ❑ | 24 | Curt Schilling | .40 | .18 |
| ❑ | 25 | Jason Kendall | .40 | .18 |
| ❑ | 26 | Scott Erickson | .25 | .11 |
| ❑ | 27 | Andres Galarraga | .60 | .25 |
| ❑ | 28 | Jeff Shaw | .25 | .11 |
| ❑ | 29 | John Olerud | .40 | .18 |
| ❑ | 30 | Orlando Hernandez | .40 | .18 |
| ❑ | 31 | Larry Walker | .40 | .18 |
| ❑ | 32 | Andruw Jones | 1.00 | .45 |
| ❑ | 33 | Jeff Cirillo | .40 | .18 |
| ❑ | 34 | Barry Bonds | 1.50 | .70 |
| ❑ | 35 | Manny Ramirez | 1.25 | .55 |
| ❑ | 36 | Mark Kotsay | .25 | .11 |
| ❑ | 37 | Ivan Rodriguez | 1.25 | .55 |
| ❑ | 38 | Jeff King | .25 | .11 |
| ❑ | 39 | Brian Hunter | .25 | .11 |
| ❑ | 40 | Ray Durham | .40 | .18 |
| ❑ | 41 | Bernie Williams | 1.00 | .45 |
| ❑ | 42 | Darin Erstad | 1.00 | .45 |
| ❑ | 43 | Chipper Jones | 2.50 | 1.10 |
| ❑ | 44 | Pat Hentgen | .25 | .11 |
| ❑ | 45 | Eric Young | .25 | .11 |
| ❑ | 46 | Jaret Wright | .25 | .11 |
| ❑ | 47 | Juan Guzman | .25 | .11 |
| ❑ | 48 | Jorge Posada | .40 | .18 |
| ❑ | 49 | Bobby Higginson | .40 | .18 |
| ❑ | 50 | Jose Guillen | .25 | .11 |
| ❑ | 51 | Trevor Hoffman | .40 | .18 |
| ❑ | 52 | Ken Griffey Jr. | 4.00 | 1.80 |
| ❑ | 53 | David Justice | .60 | .25 |
| ❑ | 54 | Matt Williams | .60 | .25 |
| ❑ | 55 | Eric Karros | .40 | .18 |
| ❑ | 56 | Derek Bell | .25 | .11 |
| ❑ | 57 | Ray Lankford | .40 | .18 |
| ❑ | 58 | Mariano Rivera | .40 | .18 |
| ❑ | 59 | Brett Tomko | .25 | .11 |
| ❑ | 60 | Mike Mussina | 1.00 | .45 |
| ❑ | 61 | Kenny Lofton | .40 | .18 |
| ❑ | 62 | Chuck Finley | .40 | .18 |
| ❑ | 63 | Alex Gonzalez | .25 | .11 |
| ❑ | 64 | Mark Grace | 1.00 | .45 |
| ❑ | 65 | Raul Mondesi | .40 | .18 |
| ❑ | 66 | David Cone | .40 | .18 |
| ❑ | 67 | Brad Fullmer | .40 | .18 |
| ❑ | 68 | Andy Benes | .25 | .11 |
| ❑ | 69 | John Smoltz | .40 | .18 |
| ❑ | 70 | Shane Reynolds | .25 | .11 |

| No. | Player | Price 1 | Price 2 |
|---|---|---|---|
| ❑ 71 | Bruce Chen | .25 | .11 |
| ❑ 72 | Adam Kennedy | .40 | .18 |
| ❑ 73 | Jack Cust | .40 | .18 |
| ❑ 74 | Matt Clement | .25 | .11 |
| ❑ 75 | Derrick Gibson | .25 | .11 |
| ❑ 76 | Darnell McDonald | .25 | .11 |
| ❑ 77 | Adam Everett RC | 2.50 | 1.10 |
| ❑ 78 | Ricardo Aramboles | .25 | .11 |
| ❑ 79 | Mark Quinn RC | 6.00 | 2.70 |
| ❑ 80 | Jason Rakers | .25 | .11 |
| ❑ 81 | Seth Etherton RC | 2.00 | .90 |
| ❑ 82 | Jeff Urban RC | 1.50 | .70 |
| ❑ 83 | Manny Aybar | .25 | .11 |
| ❑ 84 | Mike Nannini RC | 2.50 | 1.10 |
| ❑ 85 | Onan Masaoka | .25 | .11 |
| ❑ 86 | Rod Barajas | .25 | .11 |
| ❑ 87 | Mike Frank | .25 | .11 |
| ❑ 88 | Scott Randall | .25 | .11 |
| ❑ 89 | Justin Bowles RC | .25 | .11 |
| ❑ 90 | Chris Haas | .25 | .11 |
| ❑ 91 | Arturo McDowell RC | 2.00 | .90 |
| ❑ 92 | Matt Belisle RC | 3.00 | 1.35 |
| ❑ 93 | Scott Elarton | .40 | .18 |
| ❑ 94 | Vernon Wells | .40 | .18 |
| ❑ 95 | Pat Cline | .25 | .11 |
| ❑ 96 | Ryan Anderson | .40 | .18 |
| ❑ 97 | Kevin Barker | .25 | .11 |
| ❑ 98 | Ruben Mateo | .40 | .18 |
| ❑ 99 | Robert Fick | .25 | .11 |
| ❑ 100 | Corey Koskie | .25 | .11 |
| ❑ 101 | Ricky Ledee | .25 | .11 |
| ❑ 102 | Rick Elder RC | 2.00 | .90 |
| ❑ 103 | Jack Cressend RC | 1.50 | .70 |
| ❑ 104 | Joe Lawrence | .40 | .18 |
| ❑ 105 | Mike Lincoln | .25 | .11 |
| ❑ 106 | Kit Pellow RC | 1.50 | .70 |
| ❑ 107 | Matt Burch RC | 1.50 | .70 |
| ❑ 108 | Cole Liniak | .25 | .11 |
| ❑ 109 | Jason Dewey | .25 | .11 |
| ❑ 110 | Cesar King | .25 | .11 |
| ❑ 111 | Julio Ramirez | .25 | .11 |
| ❑ 112 | Jake Westbrook | .25 | .11 |
| ❑ 113 | Eric Valent RC | 4.00 | 1.80 |
| ❑ 114 | Roosevelt Brown RC | 2.00 | .90 |
| ❑ 115 | Choo Freeman RC | 2.50 | 1.10 |
| ❑ 116 | Juan Melo | .25 | .11 |
| ❑ 117 | Jason Grilli | .25 | .11 |
| ❑ 118 | Jared Sandberg | .25 | .11 |
| ❑ 119 | Glenn Davis | .25 | .11 |
| ❑ 120 | David Riske RC | 1.50 | .70 |
| ❑ 121 | Jacque Jones | .40 | .18 |
| ❑ 122 | Corey Lee | .25 | .11 |
| ❑ 123 | Michael Barrett | .25 | .11 |
| ❑ 124 | Lariel Gonzalez | .25 | .11 |
| ❑ 125 | Mitch Meluskey | .25 | .11 |
| ❑ 126 | Freddy Garcia | .25 | .11 |
| ❑ 127 | Tony Torcato RC | 4.00 | 1.80 |
| ❑ 128 | Jeff Liefer | .25 | .11 |
| ❑ 129 | Ntema Ndungidi | .40 | .18 |
| ❑ 130 | Andy Brown RC | 3.00 | 1.35 |
| ❑ 131 | Ryan Mills RC | 1.50 | .70 |
| ❑ 132 | Andy Abad RC | .25 | .11 |
| ❑ 133 | Carlos Febles | .25 | .11 |
| ❑ 134 | Jason Tyner RC | 3.00 | 1.35 |
| ❑ 135 | Mark Osborne | .25 | .11 |
| ❑ 136 | Phil Norton RC | 1.50 | .70 |
| ❑ 137 | Nathan Haynes | .25 | .11 |
| ❑ 138 | Roy Halladay | .25 | .11 |
| ❑ 139 | Juan Encarnacion | .40 | .18 |
| ❑ 140 | Brad Penny | .40 | .18 |
| ❑ 141 | Grant Roberts | .25 | .11 |
| ❑ 142 | Aramis Ramirez | .25 | .11 |
| ❑ 143 | Cristian Guzman | .25 | .11 |
| ❑ 144 | Mamon Tucker RC | 2.00 | .90 |
| ❑ 145 | Ryan Bradley | .25 | .11 |
| ❑ 146 | Brian Simmons | .25 | .11 |
| ❑ 147 | Dan Reichert | .25 | .11 |
| ❑ 148 | Russell Branyan | .40 | .18 |
| ❑ 149 | Victor Valencia RC | 1.50 | .70 |
| ❑ 150 | Scott Schoeneweis | .25 | .11 |
| ❑ 151 | Sean Spencer RC | 1.50 | .70 |
| ❑ 152 | Odalis Perez | .25 | .11 |
| ❑ 153 | Joe Fontenot | .25 | .11 |
| ❑ 154 | Milton Bradley | .40 | .18 |
| ❑ 155 | Josh McKinley RC | 2.00 | .90 |
| ❑ 156 | Terrence Long | .40 | .18 |
| ❑ 157 | Danny Klassen | .25 | .11 |
| ❑ 158 | Paul Hoover RC | 1.50 | .70 |
| ❑ 159 | Ron Belliard | .25 | .11 |
| ❑ 160 | Armando Rios | .25 | .11 |
| ❑ 161 | Ramon Hernandez | .25 | .11 |
| ❑ 162 | Jason Conti | .25 | .11 |
| ❑ 163 | Chad Hermansen | .25 | .11 |
| ❑ 164 | Jason Standridge | .25 | .11 |
| ❑ 165 | Jason Dellaero | .25 | .11 |
| ❑ 166 | John Curtice | .25 | .11 |
| ❑ 167 | Clayton Andrews RC | 1.50 | .70 |
| ❑ 168 | Jeremy Giambi | .25 | .11 |
| ❑ 169 | Alex Ramirez | .25 | .11 |
| ❑ 170 | Gabe Molina RC | 1.50 | .70 |
| ❑ 171 | Mario Encarnacion RC | 2.50 | 1.10 |
| ❑ 172 | Mike Zywica RC | .25 | .11 |
| ❑ 173 | Chip Ambres RC | 2.50 | 1.10 |
| ❑ 174 | Trot Nixon | .40 | .18 |
| ❑ 175 | Pat Burrell RC | 20.00 | 9.00 |
| ❑ 176 | Jeff Yoder | .25 | .11 |
| ❑ 177 | Chris Jones RC | 2.00 | .90 |
| ❑ 178 | Kevin Witt | .25 | .11 |
| ❑ 179 | Keith Luuloa RC | .25 | .11 |
| ❑ 180 | Billy Koch | .40 | .18 |
| ❑ 181 | Damaso Marte RC | .25 | .11 |
| ❑ 182 | Ryan Glynn RC | 2.00 | .90 |
| ❑ 183 | Calvin Pickering | .25 | .11 |
| ❑ 184 | Michael Cuddyer | .40 | .18 |
| ❑ 185 | Nick Johnson RC | 8.00 | 3.60 |
| ❑ 186 | Doug Mientkiewicz RC | 1.50 | .70 |
| ❑ 187 | Nate Cornejo RC | 2.00 | .90 |
| ❑ 188 | Octavio Dotel | .25 | .11 |
| ❑ 189 | Wes Helms | .25 | .11 |
| ❑ 190 | Nelson Lara | .25 | .11 |
| ❑ 191 | Chuck Abbott RC | .25 | .11 |
| ❑ 192 | Tony Armas Jr. | .40 | .18 |
| ❑ 193 | Gil Meche | .40 | .18 |
| ❑ 194 | Ben Petrick | .25 | .11 |
| ❑ 195 | Chris George RC | 3.00 | 1.35 |
| ❑ 196 | Scott Hunter RC | 1.50 | .70 |
| ❑ 197 | Ryan Brannan | .25 | .11 |
| ❑ 198 | Amaury Garcia RC | 1.50 | .70 |
| ❑ 199 | Chris Gissell | .25 | .11 |
| ❑ 200 | Austin Kearns RC | 8.00 | 3.60 |
| ❑ 201 | Alex Gonzalez | .25 | .11 |
| ❑ 202 | Wade Miller | .25 | .11 |
| ❑ 203 | Scott Williamson | .25 | .11 |
| ❑ 204 | Chris Enochs | .25 | .11 |
| ❑ 205 | Fernando Seguignol | .25 | .11 |
| ❑ 206 | Marlon Anderson | .25 | .11 |
| ❑ 207 | Todd Sears RC | 2.00 | .90 |
| ❑ 208 | Nate Bump RC | 1.50 | .70 |
| ❑ 209 | J.M. Gold RC | 2.00 | .90 |
| ❑ 210 | Matt LeCroy | .25 | .11 |
| ❑ 211 | Alex Hernandez | .25 | .11 |
| ❑ 212 | Luis Rivera | .25 | .11 |
| ❑ 213 | Troy Cameron | .25 | .11 |
| ❑ 214 | Alex Escobar RC | 8.00 | 3.60 |
| ❑ 215 | Jason LaRue | .25 | .11 |
| ❑ 216 | Kyle Peterson | .25 | .11 |
| ❑ 217 | Brent Butler | .25 | .11 |
| ❑ 218 | Dernell Stenson | .40 | .18 |
| ❑ 219 | Adrian Beltre | .40 | .18 |
| ❑ 220 | Daryle Ward | .40 | .18 |
| ❑ 221 | Jim Thome | .60 | .25 |
| ❑ 222 | Cliff Floyd | .40 | .18 |
| ❑ 223 | Rickey Henderson | 1.25 | .55 |
| ❑ 224 | Garret Anderson | .40 | .18 |
| ❑ 225 | Ken Caminiti | .40 | .18 |
| ❑ 226 | Bret Boone | .40 | .18 |
| ❑ 227 | Jeromy Burnitz | .40 | .18 |
| ❑ 228 | Steve Finley | .40 | .18 |
| ❑ 229 | Miguel Tejada | .40 | .18 |
| ❑ 230 | Greg Vaughn | .40 | .18 |
| ❑ 231 | Jose Offerman | .25 | .11 |
| ❑ 232 | Andy Ashby | .25 | .11 |
| ❑ 233 | Albert Belle | .60 | .25 |
| ❑ 234 | Fernando Tatis | .40 | .18 |
| ❑ 235 | Todd Helton | 1.25 | .55 |
| ❑ 236 | Sean Casey | .40 | .18 |
| ❑ 237 | Brian Giles | .40 | .18 |
| ❑ 238 | Andy Pettitte | .40 | .18 |
| ❑ 239 | Fred McGriff | .60 | .25 |
| ❑ 240 | Roberto Alomar | 1.00 | .45 |
| ❑ 241 | Edgar Martinez | .60 | .25 |
| ❑ 242 | Lee Stevens | .25 | .11 |
| ❑ 243 | Shawn Green | 1.00 | .45 |
| ❑ 244 | Ryan Klesko | .40 | .18 |
| ❑ 245 | Sammy Sosa | 2.00 | .90 |
| ❑ 246 | Todd Hundley | .25 | .11 |
| ❑ 247 | Shannon Stewart | .40 | .18 |
| ❑ 248 | Randy Johnson | 1.25 | .55 |
| ❑ 249 | Rondell White | .40 | .18 |
| ❑ 250 | Mike Piazza | 3.00 | 1.35 |
| ❑ 251 | Craig Biggio | .60 | .25 |
| ❑ 252 | David Wells | .40 | .18 |
| ❑ 253 | Brian Jordan | .40 | .18 |
| ❑ 254 | Edgar Renteria | .25 | .11 |
| ❑ 255 | Bartolo Colon | .40 | .18 |
| ❑ 256 | Frank Thomas | 2.00 | .90 |
| ❑ 257 | Will Clark | 1.00 | .45 |
| ❑ 258 | Dean Palmer | .40 | .18 |
| ❑ 259 | Dmitri Young | .40 | .18 |
| ❑ 260 | Scott Rolen | 1.00 | .45 |
| ❑ 261 | Jeff Kent | .60 | .25 |
| ❑ 262 | Dante Bichette | .40 | .18 |
| ❑ 263 | Nomar Garciaparra | 3.00 | 1.35 |
| ❑ 264 | Tony Gwynn | 2.00 | .90 |
| ❑ 265 | Alex Rodriguez | 3.00 | 1.35 |
| ❑ 266 | Jose Canseco | 1.25 | .55 |
| ❑ 267 | Jason Giambi | 1.00 | .45 |
| ❑ 268 | Jeff Bagwell | 1.25 | .55 |
| ❑ 269 | Carlos Delgado | 1.00 | .45 |
| ❑ 270 | Tom Glavine | 1.00 | .45 |
| ❑ 271 | Eric Davis | .40 | .18 |
| ❑ 272 | Edgardo Alfonzo | .40 | .18 |
| ❑ 273 | Tim Salmon | .40 | .18 |
| ❑ 274 | Johnny Damon | .40 | .18 |
| ❑ 275 | Rafael Palmeiro | 1.00 | .45 |
| ❑ 276 | Denny Neagle | .25 | .11 |
| ❑ 277 | Neifi Perez | .25 | .11 |
| ❑ 278 | Roger Clemens | 2.00 | .90 |
| ❑ 279 | Brant Brown | .25 | .11 |
| ❑ 280 | Kevin Brown | .60 | .25 |
| ❑ 281 | Jay Bell | .40 | .18 |
| ❑ 282 | Jay Buhner | .40 | .18 |
| ❑ 283 | Matt Lawton | .40 | .18 |
| ❑ 284 | Robin Ventura | .40 | .18 |
| ❑ 285 | Juan Gonzalez | 1.00 | .45 |
| ❑ 286 | Mo Vaughn | .40 | .18 |
| ❑ 287 | Kevin Millwood | .40 | .18 |
| ❑ 288 | Tino Martinez | .40 | .18 |
| ❑ 289 | Justin Thompson | .25 | .11 |
| ❑ 290 | Derek Jeter | 4.00 | 1.80 |
| ❑ 291 | Ben Davis | .25 | .11 |
| ❑ 292 | Mike Lowell | .40 | .18 |
| ❑ 293 | Calvin Murray | .25 | .11 |
| ❑ 294 | Micah Bowie RC | .25 | .11 |
| ❑ 295 | Lance Berkman | .40 | .18 |
| ❑ 296 | Jason Marquis | .40 | .18 |
| ❑ 297 | Chad Green | .25 | .11 |
| ❑ 298 | Dee Brown | .40 | .18 |
| ❑ 299 | Jerry Hairston Jr. | .40 | .18 |
| ❑ 300 | Gabe Kapler | .40 | .18 |
| ❑ 301 | Brent Stentz RC | 1.50 | .70 |
| ❑ 302 | Scott Mullen RC | .25 | .11 |
| ❑ 303 | Brandon Reed | .25 | .11 |
| ❑ 304 | Shea Hillenbrand RC | 1.50 | .70 |
| ❑ 305 | J.D. Closser RC | 2.00 | .90 |
| ❑ 306 | Gary Matthews Jr. | .25 | .11 |
| ❑ 307 | Toby Hall RC | 2.00 | .90 |
| ❑ 308 | Jason Phillips RC | 1.50 | .70 |
| ❑ 309 | Jose Macias RC | .25 | .11 |
| ❑ 310 | Jung Bong RC | 2.00 | .90 |
| ❑ 311 | Ramon Soler RC | 2.00 | .90 |
| ❑ 312 | Kelly Dransfeldt RC | 1.50 | .70 |
| ❑ 313 | Carlos Hernandez RC | 1.50 | .70 |
| ❑ 314 | Kevin Haverbusch | .25 | .11 |
| ❑ 315 | Aaron Myette RC | 3.00 | 1.35 |
| ❑ 316 | Chad Harville RC | 1.50 | .70 |
| ❑ 317 | Kyle Farnsworth RC | 1.50 | .70 |
| ❑ 318 | Travis Dawkins RC | 3.00 | 1.35 |
| ❑ 319 | Willie Martinez | .25 | .11 |
| ❑ 320 | Carlos Lee | .40 | .18 |
| ❑ 321 | Carlos Pena RC | 8.00 | 3.60 |
| ❑ 322 | Peter Bergeron RC | 3.00 | 1.35 |
| ❑ 323 | A.J. Burnett RC | 3.00 | 1.35 |
| ❑ 324 | Bucky Jacobsen RC | 1.50 | .70 |
| ❑ 325 | Mo Bruce RC | 1.50 | .70 |
| ❑ 326 | Reggie Taylor | .25 | .11 |
| ❑ 327 | Jackie Rexrode | .25 | .11 |
| ❑ 328 | Alvin Morrow RC | 1.50 | .70 |

329 Carlos Beltran .40 .18
330 Eric Chavez .40 .18
331 John Patterson .25 .11
332 Jayson Werth .25 .11
333 Richie Sexson .40 .18
334 Randy Wolf .25 .11
335 Eli Marrero .25 .11
336 Paul LoDuca .25 .11
337 J.D Smart .25 .11
338 Ryan Minor .25 .11
339 Kris Benson .40 .18
340 George Lombard .25 .11
341 Troy Glaus 1.50 .70
342 Eddie Yarnall .25 .11
343 Kip Wells RC 3.00 1.35
344 C.C. Sabathia RC 8.00 3.60
345 Sean Burroughs RC 12.00 5.50
346 Felipe Lopez RC 4.00 1.80
347 Ryan Rupe RC 2.00 .90
348 Orber Moreno RC 1.50 .70
349 Rafael Roque RC .25 .11
350 Alfonso Soriano RC 8.00 3.60
351 Pablo Ozuna .40 .18
352 Corey Patterson RC 20.00 9.00
353 Braden Looper .25 .11
354 Robbie Bell .25 .11
355 Mark Mulder RC 4.00 1.80
356 Angel Pena .25 .11
357 Kevin McGlinchy .25 .11
358 Michael Restovich RC 4.00 1.80
359 Eric DuBose .25 .11
360 Geoff Jenkins .40 .18
361 Mark Harriger RC 1.50 .70
362 Junior Herndon RC 1.50 .70
363 Tim Raines Jr. RC 3.00 1.35
364 Rafael Furcal RC 30.00 13.50
365 Marcus Giles RC 6.00 2.70
366 Ted Lilly .25 .11
367 Jorge Toca RC 2.00 .90
368 David Kelton RC 4.00 1.80
369 Adam Dunn RC 8.00 3.60
370 Guillermo Mota RC .25 .11
371 Brett Laxton RC .25 .11
372 Travis Harper RC 1.50 .70
373 Tom Davey RC .25 .11
374 Darren Blakely RC 2.00 .90
375 Tim Hudson RC 15.00 6.75
376 Jason Romano .40 .18
377 Dan Reichert .25 .11
378 Julio Lugo RC 2.00 .90
379 Jose Garcia RC 1.50 .70
380 Erubiel Durazo RC 5.00 2.20
381 Jose Jimenez .25 .11
382 Chris Fussell .25 .11
383 Steve Lomasney .25 .11
384 Juan Pena RC 1.50 .70
385 Allen Levrault RC 2.00 .90
386 Juan Rivera RC 4.00 1.80
387 Steve Colyer RC 1.50 .70
388 Joe Nathan RC .25 .11
389 Ron Walker RC 1.50 .70
390 Nick Bierbrodt .25 .11
391 Luke Prokopec RC 3.00 1.35
392 Dave Roberts RC .25 .11
393 Mike Darr .25 .11
394 Abraham Nunez RC 8.00 3.60
395 Giuseppe Chiaramonte RC 2.50 1.10
396 Jermaine Van Buren RC 2.00 .90
397 Mike Kusiewicz .25 .11
398 Matt Wise RC 1.50 .70
399 Joe McEwing RC 1.50 .70
400 Matt Holliday RC 3.00 1.35
401 Willi Mo Pena RC 8.00 3.60
402 Ruben Quevedo RC 2.00 .90
403 Rob Ryan RC .25 .11
404 Freddy Garcia RC 6.00 2.70
405 Kevin Eberwein RC 2.00 .90
406 Jesus Colome RC 3.00 1.35
407 Chris Singleton .40 .18
408 Bubba Crosby RC 1.50 .70
409 Jesus Cordero RC 1.50 .70
410 Donny Leon .25 .11
411 Goefrey Tomlinson RC 1.50 .70
412 Jeff Winchester RC 3.00 1.35
413 Adam Piatt RC 10.00 4.50
414 Robert Stratton .40 .18
415 T.J. Tucker .25 .11
416 Ryan Langerhans RC 2.00 .90
417 Anthony Shumaker RC .25 .11
418 Matt Miller RC .25 .11
419 Doug Clark RC 1.50 .70
420 Kory DeHaan RC 1.50 .70
421 David Eckstein RC 1.50 .70
422 Brian Cooper RC 1.50 .70
423 Brady Clark RC 1.50 .70
424 Chris Magruder RC 1.50 .70
425 Bobby Seay RC 2.50 1.10
426 Aubrey Huff RC 5.00 2.20
427 Mike Jerzembeck .25 .11
428 Matt Blank RC 1.50 .70
429 Benny Agbayani RC 6.00 2.70
430 Kevin Beirne RC .25 .11
431 Josh Hamilton RC 20.00 9.00
432 Josh Girdley RC 3.00 1.35
433 Kyle Snyder RC 1.50 .70
434 Mike Paradis RC 1.50 .70
435 Jason Jennings RC 2.50 1.10
436 David Walling RC 2.00 .90
437 Omar Ortiz RC 1.50 .70
438 Jay Gohrke RC 1.50 .70
439 Casey Burns RC 1.50 .70
440 Carl Crawford RC 5.00 2.20

## 2000 Bowman Chrome

| | MINT | NRMT |
|---|---|---|
| COMPLETE SET (440) | 400.00 | 180.00 |

1 Vladimir Guerrero 1.50 .70
2 Chipper Jones 2.50 1.10
3 Todd Walker .25 .11
4 Barry Larkin 1.00 .45
5 Bernie Williams 1.00 .45
6 Todd Helton 1.25 .55
7 Jermaine Dye .40 .18
8 Brian Giles .40 .18
9 Freddy Garcia .40 .18
10 Greg Vaughn .40 .18
11 Alex Gonzalez .25 .11
12 Luis Gonzalez .40 .18
13 Ron Belliard .25 .11
14 Ben Grieve .40 .18
15 Carlos Delgado 1.00 .45
16 Brian Jordan .40 .18
17 Fernando Tatis .40 .18
18 Ryan Rupe .25 .11
19 Miguel Tejada .40 .18
20 Mark Grace 1.00 .45
21 Kenny Lofton .40 .18
22 Eric Karros .40 .18
23 Cliff Floyd .40 .18
24 John Halama .25 .11
25 Cristian Guzman .25 .11
26 Scott Williamson .25 .11
27 Mike Lieberthal .40 .18
28 Tim Hudson 1.00 .45
29 Warren Morris .25 .11
30 Pedro Martinez 1.25 .55
31 John Smoltz .40 .18
32 Ray Durham .40 .18
33 Chad Allen .25 .11
34 Tony Clark .25 .11
35 Tino Martinez .40 .18
36 J.T. Snow .40 .18
37 Kevin Brown .60 .25
38 Bartolo Colon .40 .18
39 Rey Ordonez .25 .11
40 Jeff Bagwell 1.25 .55
41 Ivan Rodriguez 1.25 .55
42 Eric Chavez .40 .18
43 Eric Milton .25 .11
44 Jose Canseco 1.25 .55
45 Shawn Green 1.00 .45
46 Rich Aurilia .25 .11
47 Roberto Alomar 1.00 .45
48 Brian Daubach .25 .11
49 Magglio Ordonez .40 .18
50 Derek Jeter 4.00 1.80
51 Kris Benson .40 .18
52 Albert Belle .60 .25
53 Rondell White .40 .18
54 Justin Thompson .25 .11
55 Nomar Garciaparra 3.00 1.35
56 Chuck Finley .40 .18
57 Omar Vizquel .40 .18
58 Luis Castillo .40 .18
59 Richard Hidalgo .40 .18
60 Barry Bonds 1.50 .70
61 Craig Biggio .60 .25
62 Doug Glanville .25 .11
63 Gabe Kapler .40 .18
64 Johnny Damon .40 .18
65 Pokey Reese .40 .18
66 Andy Pettitte .40 .18
67 B.J. Surhoff .40 .18
68 Richie Sexson .40 .18
69 Javy Lopez .40 .18
70 Raul Mondesi .40 .18
71 Darin Erstad 1.00 .45
72 Kevin Millwood .40 .18
73 Ricky Ledee .25 .11
74 John Olerud .40 .18
75 Sean Casey .40 .18
76 Carlos Febles .25 .11
77 Paul O'Neill .40 .18
78 Bob Abreu .40 .18
79 Neifi Perez .25 .11
80 Tony Gwynn 2.00 .90
81 Russ Ortiz .40 .18
82 Matt Williams .60 .25
83 Chris Carpenter .25 .11
84 Roger Cedeno .25 .11
85 Tim Salmon .40 .18
86 Billy Koch .40 .18
87 Jeromy Burnitz .40 .18
88 Edgardo Alfonzo .60 .25
89 Jay Bell .40 .18
90 Manny Ramirez 1.25 .55
91 Frank Thomas 2.00 .90
92 Mike Mussina 1.00 .45
93 J.D. Drew 1.00 .45
94 Adrian Beltre .40 .18
95 Alex Rodriguez 3.00 1.35
96 Larry Walker .40 .18
97 Juan Encarnacion .40 .18
98 Mike Sweeney .40 .18
99 Rusty Greer .40 .18
100 Randy Johnson 1.25 .55
101 Jose Vidro .40 .18
102 Preston Wilson .40 .18
103 Greg Maddux 2.50 1.10
104 Jason Giambi 1.00 .45
105 Cal Ripken 4.00 1.80
106 Carlos Beltran .40 .18
107 Vinny Castilla .40 .18
108 Mariano Rivera .40 .18
109 Mo Vaughn .40 .18
110 Rafael Palmeiro 1.00 .45
111 Shannon Stewart .40 .18
112 Mike Hampton .40 .18
113 Joe Nathan .25 .11
114 Ben Davis .25 .11
115 Andruw Jones 1.00 .45
116 Robin Ventura .40 .18
117 Damion Easley .25 .11
118 Jeff Cirillo .40 .18
119 Kerry Wood .40 .18
120 Scott Rolen 1.00 .45
121 Sammy Sosa 2.00 .90
122 Ken Griffey Jr. 4.00 1.80

❑ 123 Shane Reynolds .25 .11
❑ 124 Troy Glaus 1.25 .55
❑ 125 Tom Glavine 1.00 .45
❑ 126 Michael Barrett .25 .11
❑ 127 Al Leiter .25 .11
❑ 128 Jason Kendall .40 .18
❑ 129 Roger Clemens 2.00 .90
❑ 130 Juan Gonzalez 1.00 .45
❑ 131 Corey Koskie .25 .11
❑ 132 Curt Schilling .40 .18
❑ 133 Mike Piazza 3.00 1.35
❑ 134 Gary Sheffield 1.00 .45
❑ 135 Jim Thome .60 .25
❑ 136 Orlando Hernandez .40 .18
❑ 137 Ray Lankford .40 .18
❑ 138 Geoff Jenkins .40 .18
❑ 139 Jose Lima .25 .11
❑ 140 Mark McGwire 4.00 1.80
❑ 141 Adam Piatt 1.00 .45
❑ 142 Pat Manning RC 4.00 1.80
❑ 143 Marcos Castillo RC 1.50 .70
❑ 144 Leslie Brea RC 2.00 .90
❑ 145 Humberto Cota RC 3.00 1.35
❑ 146 Ben Petrick .25 .11
❑ 147 Kip Wells .40 .18
❑ 148 Wily Pena .40 .18
❑ 149 Chris Wakeland RC 1.50 .70
❑ 150 Brad Baker RC 4.00 1.80
❑ 151 Robbie Morrison RC 1.50 .70
❑ 152 Reggie Taylor .25 .11
❑ 153 Matt Ginter RC 2.50 1.10
❑ 154 Peter Bergeron .25 .11
❑ 155 Roosevelt Brown .25 .11
❑ 156 Matt Cepicky RC 2.00 .90
❑ 157 Ramon Castro .25 .11
❑ 158 Brad Baisley RC 2.50 1.10
❑ 159 Jason Hart RC 12.00 5.50
❑ 160 Mitch Meluskey .25 .11
❑ 161 Chad Harville .25 .11
❑ 162 Brian Cooper .25 .11
❑ 163 Marcus Giles .40 .18
❑ 164 Jim Morris .25 .11
❑ 165 Geoff Goetz .25 .11
❑ 166 Bobby Bradley RC 8.00 3.60
❑ 167 Rob Bell .25 .11
❑ 168 Joe Crede 1.00 .45
❑ 169 Michael Restovich .40 .18
❑ 170 Quincy Foster RC 1.50 .70
❑ 171 Enrique Cruz RC 2.50 1.10
❑ 172 Mark Quinn .40 .18
❑ 173 Nick Johnson .40 .18
❑ 174 Jeff Liefer .25 .11
❑ 175 Kevin Mench RC 8.00 3.60
❑ 176 Steve Lomasney .25 .11
❑ 177 Jayson Werth .25 .11
❑ 178 Tim Drew .25 .11
❑ 179 Chip Ambres .40 .18
❑ 180 Ryan Anderson .40 .18
❑ 181 Matt Blank .25 .11
❑ 182 Giuseppe Chiaramonte .25 .11
❑ 183 Corey Myers RC 2.50 1.10
❑ 184 Jeff Yoder .25 .11
❑ 185 Craig Dingman RC 1.50 .70
❑ 186 Jon Hamilton RC 2.00 .90
❑ 187 Toby Hall .25 .11
❑ 188 Russell Branyan .40 .18
❑ 189 Brian Falkenborg RC 1.50 .70
❑ 190 Aaron Harang RC 2.00 .90
❑ 191 Juan Pena .25 .11
❑ 192 Chin-Hui Tsao RC 15.00 6.75
❑ 193 Alfonso Soriano .40 .18
❑ 194 Alejandro Diaz RC 2.50 1.10
❑ 195 Carlos Pena .40 .18
❑ 196 Kevin Nicholson .25 .11
❑ 197 Mo Bruce .25 .11
❑ 198 C.C. Sabathia .40 .18
❑ 199 Carl Crawford .40 .18
❑ 200 Rafael Furcal 2.50 1.10
❑ 201 Andrew Beinbrink RC 1.50 .70
❑ 202 Jimmy Osting .25 .11
❑ 203 Aaron McNeal RC 4.00 1.80
❑ 204 Brett Laxton .25 .11
❑ 205 Chris George .40 .18
❑ 206 Felipe Lopez .40 .18
❑ 207 Ben Sheets RC 12.00 5.50
❑ 208 Mike Meyers RC 2.00 .90
❑ 209 Jason Conti .25 .11
❑ 210 Milton Bradley .40 .18
❑ 211 Chris Mears RC 2.00 .90
❑ 212 Carlos Hernandez RC 2.00 .90
❑ 213 Jason Romano .40 .18
❑ 214 Geofrey Tomlinson .25 .11
❑ 215 Jimmy Rollins .25 .11
❑ 216 Pablo Ozuna .25 .11
❑ 217 Steve Cox .25 .11
❑ 218 Terrence Long .40 .18
❑ 219 Jeff DaVanon RC 1.50 .70
❑ 220 Rick Ankiel 2.00 .90
❑ 221 Jason Standridge .25 .11
❑ 222 Tony Armas Jr. .40 .18
❑ 223 Jason Tyner .25 .11
❑ 224 Ramon Ortiz .40 .18
❑ 225 Daryle Ward .40 .18
❑ 226 Enger Veras RC 1.50 .70
❑ 227 Chris Jones .25 .11
❑ 228 Eric Cammack RC 1.50 .70
❑ 229 Ruben Mateo .40 .18
❑ 230 Ken Harvey RC 4.00 1.80
❑ 231 Jake Westbrook .25 .11
❑ 232 Rob Purvis RC 2.00 .90
❑ 233 Choo Freeman .40 .18
❑ 234 Aramis Ramirez .25 .11
❑ 235 A.J. Burnett .40 .18
❑ 236 Kevin Barker .25 .11
❑ 237 Chance Caple RC 2.50 1.10
❑ 238 Jarrod Washburn .25 .11
❑ 239 Lance Berkman .40 .18
❑ 240 Michael Wenner RC 2.00 .90
❑ 241 Alex Sanchez .25 .11
❑ 242 Pat Daneker .25 .11
❑ 243 Grant Roberts .25 .11
❑ 244 Mark Ellis RC 3.00 1.35
❑ 245 Denny Leon .25 .11
❑ 246 David Eckstein .25 .11
❑ 247 Dicky Gonzalez RC 2.00 .90
❑ 248 John Patterson .25 .11
❑ 249 Chad Green .25 .11
❑ 250 Scot Shields RC 1.50 .70
❑ 251 Troy Cameron .25 .11
❑ 252 Jose Molina .25 .11
❑ 253 Rob Pugmire RC 2.00 .90
❑ 254 Rick Elder .25 .11
❑ 255 Sean Burroughs 1.00 .45
❑ 256 Josh Kalinowski RC 1.50 .70
❑ 257 Matt LeCroy .25 .11
❑ 258 Alex Graman RC 4.00 1.80
❑ 259 Juan Silvestre RC 4.00 1.80
❑ 260 Brady Clark .40 .18
❑ 261 Rico Washington RC 2.00 .90
❑ 262 Gary Matthews Jr. .25 .11
❑ 263 Matt Wise .25 .11
❑ 264 Keith Reed RC 3.00 1.35
❑ 265 Santiago Ramirez RC 1.50 .70
❑ 266 Ben Broussard RC 8.00 3.60
❑ 267 Ryan Langerhans .25 .11
❑ 268 Juan Rivera .40 .18
❑ 269 Shawn Gallagher .25 .11
❑ 270 Jorge Toca .25 .11
❑ 271 Brad Lidge .25 .11
❑ 272 Leoncio Estrella RC 1.50 .70
❑ 273 Ruben Quevedo .25 .11
❑ 274 Jack Cust .40 .18
❑ 275 T.J. Tucker .25 .11
❑ 276 Mike Colangelo .25 .11
❑ 277 Brian Schneider .25 .11
❑ 278 Calvin Murray .25 .11
❑ 279 Josh Girdley .25 .11
❑ 280 Mike Paradis .25 .11
❑ 281 Chad Hermansen .25 .11
❑ 282 Ty Howington RC 3.00 1.35
❑ 283 Aaron Myette .40 .18
❑ 284 D'Angelo Jimenez .40 .18
❑ 285 Dernell Stenson .40 .18
❑ 286 Jerry Hairston Jr. .25 .11
❑ 287 Gary Majewski RC 2.00 .90
❑ 288 Derrin Ebert .25 .11
❑ 289 Steve Fish RC 1.50 .70
❑ 290 Carlos Hernandez .25 .11
❑ 291 Allen Levrault .25 .11
❑ 292 Sean McNally RC 1.50 .70
❑ 293 Randey Dorame RC 2.00 .90
❑ 294 Wes Anderson RC 3.00 1.35
❑ 295 B.J. Ryan .25 .11
❑ 296 Alan Webb RC 1.50 .70
❑ 297 Brandon Inge RC 4.00 1.80
❑ 298 David Walling .25 .11
❑ 299 Sun Woo Kim RC 4.00 1.80
❑ 300 Pat Burrell 1.50 .70
❑ 301 Rick Guttormson RC 1.50 .70
❑ 302 Gil Meche .40 .18
❑ 303 Carlos Zambrano RC 4.00 1.80
❑ 304 Eric Byrnes UER RC 2.50 1.10
(Bo Porter pictured)
❑ 305 Robb Quinlan RC 2.00 .90
❑ 306 Jackie Rexrode .25 .11
❑ 307 Nate Bump .25 .11
❑ 308 Sean DePaula RC 1.50 .70
❑ 309 Matt Riley .40 .18
❑ 310 Ryan Minor .25 .11
❑ 311 J.J. Davis .40 .18
❑ 312 Randy Wolf .25 .11
❑ 313 Jason Jennings .25 .11
❑ 314 Scott Seabol RC 2.00 .90
❑ 315 Doug Davis .25 .11
❑ 316 Todd Moser RC 1.50 .70
❑ 317 Rob Ryan .25 .11
❑ 318 Bubba Crosby .25 .11
❑ 319 Ryan Knox RC 5.00 2.20
❑ 320 Mario Encarnacion .25 .11
❑ 321 Francisco Rodriguez RC 2.50 1.10
❑ 322 Michael Cuddyer .40 .18
❑ 323 Ed Yarnall .25 .11
❑ 324 Cesar Saba RC 3.00 1.35
❑ 325 Travis Dawkins .40 .18
❑ 326 Alex Escobar .40 .18
❑ 327 Julio Zuleta RC 2.00 .90
❑ 328 Josh Hamilton 1.50 .70
❑ 329 Carlos Urquiola RC 4.00 1.80
❑ 330 Matt Belisle .40 .18
❑ 331 Kurt Ainsworth RC 5.00 2.20
❑ 332 Tim Raines Jr. .40 .18
❑ 333 Eric Munson 1.00 .45
❑ 334 Donzell McDonald .25 .11
❑ 335 Larry Bigbie RC 3.00 1.35
❑ 336 Matt Watson RC 1.50 .70
❑ 337 Aubrey Huff .40 .18
❑ 338 Julio Ramirez .25 .11
❑ 339 Jason Grabowski RC 3.00 1.35
❑ 340 Jon Garland .40 .18
❑ 341 Austin Kearns .40 .18
❑ 342 Josh Pressley RC 2.50 1.10
❑ 343 Miguel Olivo RC 2.50 1.10
❑ 344 Julio Lugo .25 .11
❑ 345 Roberto Vaz .25 .11
❑ 346 Ramon Soler .25 .11
❑ 347 Brandon Phillips RC 2.50 1.10
❑ 348 Vince Faison RC 4.00 1.80
❑ 349 Mike Venafro .25 .11
❑ 350 Rick Asadoorian RC 10.00 4.50
❑ 351 B.J. Garbe RC 5.00 2.20
❑ 352 Dan Reichert .25 .11
❑ 353 Jason Stumm RC 3.00 1.35
❑ 354 Ruben Salazar RC 4.00 1.80
❑ 355 Francisco Cordero .25 .11
❑ 356 Juan Guzman RC 1.50 .70
❑ 357 Mike Bacsik RC 1.50 .70
❑ 358 Jared Sandberg .25 .11
❑ 359 Rod Barajas .25 .11
❑ 360 Junior Brignac RC 2.00 .90
❑ 361 J.M. Gold .25 .11
❑ 362 Octavio Dotel .25 .11
❑ 363 David Kelton .40 .18
❑ 364 Scott Morgan .25 .11
❑ 365 Wascar Serrano RC 2.50 1.10
❑ 366 Wilton Veras .40 .18
❑ 367 Eugene Kingsale .25 .11
❑ 368 Ted Lilly .25 .11
❑ 369 George Lombard .25 .11
❑ 370 Chris Haas .25 .11
❑ 371 Wilton Pena RC 1.50 .70
❑ 372 Vernon Wells .40 .18
❑ 373 Keith Ginter RC 6.00 2.70
❑ 374 Jeff Heaverlo RC 3.00 1.35
❑ 375 Calvin Pickering .25 .11
❑ 376 Mike Lamb RC 3.00 1.35
❑ 377 Kyle Snyder .25 .11
❑ 378 Javier Cardona RC 1.50 .70
❑ 379 Aaron Rowand RC 4.00 1.80

| | | | |
|---|---|---|---|
| 380 | Dee Brown | .40 | .18 |
| 381 | Brett Myers RC | 3.00 | 1.35 |
| 382 | Abraham Nunez | .40 | .18 |
| 383 | Eric Valent | .40 | .18 |
| 384 | Jody Gerut RC | 2.00 | .90 |
| 385 | Adam Dunn | .40 | .18 |
| 386 | Jay Gehrke | .25 | .11 |
| 387 | Omar Ortiz | .25 | .11 |
| 388 | Darnell McDonald | .25 | .11 |
| 389 | Tony Schrager RC | 1.50 | .70 |
| 390 | J.D. Closser | .25 | .11 |
| 391 | Ben Christensen RC | 4.00 | 1.80 |
| 392 | Adam Kennedy | .40 | .18 |
| 393 | Nick Green RC | 1.50 | .70 |
| 394 | Ramon Hernandez | .25 | .11 |
| 395 | Roy Oswalt RC | 3.00 | 1.35 |
| 396 | Andy Tracy RC | 1.50 | .70 |
| 397 | Eric Gagne | .25 | .11 |
| 398 | Michael Tejera RC | 1.50 | .70 |
| 399 | Adam Everett | .40 | .18 |
| 400 | Corey Patterson | 1.50 | .70 |
| 401 | Gary Knotts RC | 1.50 | .70 |
| 402 | Ryan Christianson RC | 4.00 | 1.80 |
| 403 | Eric Ireland RC | 2.00 | .90 |
| 404 | Andrew Good RC | 1.50 | .70 |
| 405 | Brad Penny | .40 | .18 |
| 406 | Jason LaRue | .25 | .11 |
| 407 | Kit Pellow | .25 | .11 |
| 408 | Kevin Beirne | .25 | .11 |
| 409 | Kelly Dransfeldt | .25 | .11 |
| 410 | Jason Grilli | .25 | .11 |
| 411 | Scott Downs RC | 1.50 | .70 |
| 412 | Jesus Colome | .40 | .18 |
| 413 | John Sneed RC | 1.50 | .70 |
| 414 | Tony McKnight | .25 | .11 |
| 415 | Luis Rivera | .25 | .11 |
| 416 | Adam Eaton | .40 | .18 |
| 417 | Mike MacDougal RC | 2.00 | .90 |
| 418 | Mike Nannini | .25 | .11 |
| 419 | Barry Zito RC | 15.00 | 6.75 |
| 420 | DeWayne Wise | .25 | .11 |
| 421 | Jason Dellaero | .25 | .11 |
| 422 | Chad Moeller | .25 | .11 |
| 423 | Jason Marquis | .40 | .18 |
| 424 | Tim Redding RC | 3.00 | 1.35 |
| 425 | Mark Mulder | .40 | .18 |
| 426 | Josh Paul | .25 | .11 |
| 427 | Chris Enochs | .25 | .11 |
| 428 | Wilfredo Rodriguez RC | 3.00 | 1.35 |
| 429 | Kevin Witt | .25 | .11 |
| 430 | Scott Sobkowiak RC | 2.00 | .90 |
| 431 | McKay Christensen | .25 | .11 |
| 432 | Jung Bong | .25 | .11 |
| 433 | Keith Evans RC | 1.50 | .70 |
| 434 | Garry Maddox Jr. RC | 1.50 | .70 |
| 435 | Ramon Santiago RC | 3.00 | 1.35 |
| 436 | Alex Cora | .25 | .11 |
| 437 | Carlos Lee | .40 | .18 |
| 438 | Jason Repko RC | 3.00 | 1.35 |
| 439 | Matt Burch | .25 | .11 |
| 440 | Shawn Sonnier RC | 1.50 | .70 |

## 2000 Bowman Chrome Draft Picks

| | MINT | NRMT |
|---|---|---|
| COMP.FACT.SET (110) | 100.00 | 45.00 |

| | | | |
|---|---|---|---|
| 1 | Pat Burrell | 1.50 | .70 |
| 2 | Rafael Furcal | 2.50 | 1.10 |
| 3 | Grant Roberts | .25 | .11 |
| 4 | Barry Zito | 5.00 | 2.20 |
| 5 | Julio Zuleta | .40 | .18 |
| 6 | Mark Mulder | .40 | .18 |
| 7 | Rob Bell | .25 | .11 |
| 8 | Adam Piatt | 1.00 | .45 |
| 9 | Mike Lamb | .60 | .25 |
| 10 | Pablo Ozuna | .25 | .11 |
| 11 | Jason Tyner | .25 | .11 |
| 12 | Jason Marquis | .25 | .11 |
| 13 | Eric Munson | 1.00 | .45 |
| 14 | Seth Etherton | .25 | .11 |
| 15 | Milton Bradley | .40 | .18 |
| 16 | Nick Green | .40 | .18 |
| 17 | Chin-Feng Chen RC | 10.00 | 4.50 |
| 18 | Matt Boone RC | 1.50 | .70 |
| 19 | Kevin Gregg RC | 1.00 | .45 |
| 20 | Eddy Garabito RC | 1.00 | .45 |
| 21 | Aaron Capista RC | 1.00 | .45 |
| 22 | Esteban German RC | 1.50 | .70 |
| 23 | Derek Thompson RC | 1.00 | .45 |
| 24 | Phil Merrell RC | 1.00 | .45 |
| 25 | Brian O'Connor RC | 1.50 | .70 |
| 26 | Yamid Haad | .25 | .11 |
| 27 | Hector Mercado RC | 1.00 | .45 |
| 28 | Jason Woolf RC | 1.00 | .45 |
| 29 | Eddy Furniss RC | 1.00 | .45 |
| 30 | Cha Sueng Baek RC | 3.00 | 1.35 |
| 31 | Colby Lewis RC | 1.50 | .70 |
| 32 | Pasqual Coco RC | 1.00 | .45 |
| 33 | Jorge Cantu RC | 1.00 | .45 |
| 34 | Erasmo Ramirez RC | 1.00 | .45 |
| 35 | Bobby Kielty RC | 2.50 | 1.10 |
| 36 | Joaquin Benoit RC | 2.50 | 1.10 |
| 37 | Brian Esposito RC | 1.50 | .70 |
| 38 | Michael Wenner | .40 | .18 |
| 39 | Juan Rincon RC | 1.00 | .45 |
| 40 | Yorvit Torrealba RC | 1.00 | .45 |
| 41 | Chad Durham RC | 1.00 | .45 |
| 42 | Jim Mann RC | 1.00 | .45 |
| 43 | Shane Loux RC | 1.50 | .70 |
| 44 | Luis Rivas | .40 | .18 |
| 45 | Ken Chenard RC | 1.00 | .45 |
| 46 | Mike Lockwood RC | 1.00 | .45 |
| 47 | Yovanny Lara RC | 1.00 | .45 |
| 48 | Bubba Carpenter RC | 1.00 | .45 |
| 49 | Ryan Dittfurth RC | 1.00 | .45 |
| 50 | John Stephens RC | 1.50 | .70 |
| 51 | Pedro Feliz RC | 4.00 | 1.80 |
| 52 | Kenny Kelly RC | 2.50 | 1.10 |
| 53 | Neil Jenkins RC | 2.50 | 1.10 |
| 54 | Mike Glendenning RC | 1.00 | .45 |
| 55 | Bo Porter | .25 | .11 |
| 56 | Eric Byrnes | .40 | .18 |
| 57 | Tony Alvarez RC | 2.50 | 1.10 |
| 58 | Kazuhiro Sasaki RC | 8.00 | 3.60 |
| 59 | Chad Durbin RC | 1.00 | .45 |
| 60 | Mike Bynum RC | 2.50 | 1.10 |
| 61 | Travis Wilson RC | 1.00 | .45 |
| 62 | Jose Leon RC | 1.00 | .45 |
| 63 | Ryan Vogelsong RC | 3.00 | 1.35 |
| 64 | Geraldo Guzman RC | 1.00 | .45 |
| 65 | Craig Anderson RC | 1.50 | .70 |
| 66 | Carlos Silva RC | 1.00 | .45 |
| 67 | Brad Thomas RC | 1.00 | .45 |
| 68 | Chin-Hui Tsao | 4.00 | 1.80 |
| 69 | Mark Buehrle RC | 2.50 | 1.10 |
| 70 | Juan Salas RC | 1.50 | .70 |
| 71 | Denny Abreu RC | 1.00 | .45 |
| 72 | Keith McDonald RC | 1.00 | .45 |
| 73 | Chris Richard RC | 2.50 | 1.10 |
| 74 | Tomas De la Rosa RC | 1.00 | .45 |
| 75 | Vicente Padilla RC | 1.00 | .45 |
| 76 | Justin Brunette RC | 1.00 | .45 |
| 77 | Scott Linebrink RC | 1.00 | .45 |
| 78 | Jeff Sparks RC | 1.00 | .45 |
| 79 | Tike Redman RC | 1.00 | .45 |
| 80 | John Lackey RC | 1.50 | .70 |
| 81 | Joe Strong RC | 1.00 | .45 |
| 82 | Brian Tollberg RC | 1.00 | .45 |
| 83 | Steve Sisco RC | 1.00 | .45 |
| 84 | Chris Clapinski RC | 1.00 | .45 |
| 85 | Augie Ojeda RC | 1.00 | .45 |
| 86 | Adrian Gonzalez RC | 8.00 | 3.60 |
| 87 | Mike Stodolka RC | 2.50 | 1.10 |
| 88 | Adam Johnson RC | 3.00 | 1.35 |
| 89 | Matt Wheatland RC | 4.00 | 1.80 |
| 90 | Corey Smith RC | 3.00 | 1.35 |
| 91 | Rocco Baldelli RC | 5.00 | 2.20 |
| 92 | Keith Bucktrot RC | 1.50 | .70 |
| 93 | Adam Wainwright RC | 4.00 | 1.80 |
| 94 | Blaine Boyer RC | 1.50 | .70 |
| 95 | Aaron Herr RC | 2.50 | 1.10 |
| 96 | Scott Thorman RC | 2.50 | 1.10 |
| 97 | Bryan Digby RC | 1.50 | .70 |
| 98 | Josh Shortslef RC | 1.50 | .70 |
| 99 | Sean Smith RC | 1.50 | .70 |
| 100 | Alex Cruz RC | 1.00 | .45 |
| 101 | Marc Love RC | 1.50 | .70 |
| 102 | Kevin Lee RC | 1.00 | .45 |
| 103 | Timo Perez RC | 5.00 | 2.20 |
| 104 | Alex Cabrera RC | 3.00 | 1.35 |
| 105 | Shane Heams RC | 1.50 | .70 |
| 106 | Tripper Johnson RC | 2.50 | 1.10 |
| 107 | Brent Abernathy RC | 2.00 | .90 |
| 108 | John Cotton RC | 1.00 | .45 |
| 109 | Brad Wilkerson RC | 5.00 | 2.20 |
| 110 | Jon Rauch RC | 15.00 | 6.75 |

## 1994 Bowman's Best

| | MINT | NRMT |
|---|---|---|
| COMPLETE SET (200) | 80.00 | 36.00 |

| | | | |
|---|---|---|---|
| B1 | Chipper Jones | 2.50 | 1.10 |
| B2 | Derek Jeter | 5.00 | 2.20 |
| B3 | Bill Pulsipher | .25 | .11 |
| B4 | James Baldwin | .40 | .18 |
| B5 | Brooks Kieschnick RC | .40 | .18 |
| B6 | Justin Thompson | .25 | .11 |
| B7 | Midre Cummings | .25 | .11 |
| B8 | Joey Hamilton | .25 | .11 |
| B9 | Pokey Reese | .40 | .18 |
| B10 | Brian Barber | .25 | .11 |
| B11 | John Burke | .25 | .11 |
| B12 | DeShawn Warren | .25 | .11 |
| B13 | Edgardo Alfonzo RC | 15.00 | 6.75 |
| B14 | Eddie Pearson RC | .25 | .11 |
| B15 | Jimmy Haynes | .25 | .11 |
| B16 | Danny Bautista | .25 | .11 |
| B17 | Roger Cedeno | .40 | .18 |
| B18 | Jon Lieber | .25 | .11 |
| B19 | Billy Wagner RC | 2.50 | 1.10 |
| B20 | Tate Seefried RC | .25 | .11 |
| B21 | Chad Mottola | .25 | .11 |
| B22 | Jose Malave | .25 | .11 |
| B23 | Terrell Wade RC | .25 | .11 |
| B24 | Shane Andrews | .25 | .11 |
| B25 | Chan Ho Park RC | 4.00 | 1.80 |
| B26 | Kirk Presley RC | .25 | .11 |
| B27 | Robbie Beckett | .25 | .11 |
| B28 | Orlando Miller | .25 | .11 |
| B29 | Jorge Posada RC | 6.00 | 2.70 |
| B30 | Frankie Rodriguez | .25 | .11 |
| B31 | Brian L. Hunter | .25 | .11 |
| B32 | Billy Ashley | .25 | .11 |
| B33 | Rondell White | .40 | .18 |
| B34 | John Roper | .25 | .11 |
| B35 | Marc Valdes | .25 | .11 |
| B36 | Scott Ruffcorn | .25 | .11 |
| B37 | Rod Henderson | .25 | .11 |
| B38 | Curtis Goodwin RC | .25 | .11 |

❑ B39 Russ Davis .25 .11
❑ B40 Rick Gorecki .25 .11
❑ B41 Johnny Damon 1.00 .45
❑ B42 Roberto Petagine .25 .11
❑ B43 Chris Snopek .25 .11
❑ B44 Mark Acre RC .25 .11
❑ B45 Todd Hollandsworth .25 .11
❑ B46 Shawn Green 1.25 .55
❑ B47 John Carter RC .25 .11
❑ B48 Jim Pittsley RC .25 .11
❑ B49 John Wasdin RC .40 .18
❑ B50 D.J. Boston RC .25 .11
❑ B51 Tim Clark .25 .11
❑ B52 Alex Ochoa .25 .11
❑ B53 Chad Roper .25 .11
❑ B54 Mike Kelly .25 .11
❑ B55 Brad Fullmer RC 6.00 2.70
❑ B56 Carl Everett .40 .18
❑ B57 Tim Belk RC .25 .11
❑ B58 Jimmy Hurst RC .25 .11
❑ B59 Mac Suzuki RC .40 .18
❑ B60 Michael Moore .25 .11
❑ B61 Alan Benes RC .40 .18
❑ B62 Tony Clark RC 3.00 1.35
❑ B63 Edgar Renteria RC 3.00 1.35
❑ B64 Trey Beamon .25 .11
❑ B65 LaTroy Hawkins RC .40 .18
❑ B66 Wayne Gomes RC .25 .11
❑ B67 Ray McDavid .25 .11
❑ B68 John Dettmer .25 .11
❑ B69 Willie Greene .25 .11
❑ B70 Dave Stevens .25 .11
❑ B71 Kevin Orie RC .25 .11
❑ B72 Chad Ogea .25 .11
❑ B73 Ben Van Ryn RC .25 .11
❑ B74 Kym Ashworth RC .25 .11
❑ B75 Dmitri Young .40 .18
❑ B76 Herbert Perry RC .25 .11
❑ B77 Joey Eischen .25 .11
❑ B78 Arquimedez Pozo RC .25 .11
❑ B79 Ugueth Urbina .25 .11
❑ B80 Keith Williams RC .25 .11
❑ B81 John Frascatore RC .25 .11
❑ B82 Garey Ingram RC .25 .11
❑ B83 Aaron Small .25 .11
❑ B84 Olmedo Saenz RC .40 .18
❑ B85 Jesus Tavarez RC .25 .11
❑ B86 Jose Silva RC .25 .11
❑ B87 Jay Witasick RC .25 .11
❑ B88 Jay Maldonado RC .25 .11
❑ B89 Keith Heberling RC .25 .11
❑ B90 Rusty Greer RC 3.00 1.35
❑ R1 Paul Molitor 1.00 .45
❑ R2 Eddie Murray 1.00 .45
❑ R3 Ozzie Smith 1.25 .55
❑ R4 Rickey Henderson 1.25 .55
❑ R5 Lee Smith .40 .18
❑ R6 Dave Winfield 1.00 .45
❑ R7 Roberto Alomar 1.00 .45
❑ R8 Matt Williams .60 .25
❑ R9 Mark Grace 1.00 .45
❑ R10 Lance Johnson .25 .11
❑ R11 Darren Daulton .40 .18
❑ R12 Tom Glavine 1.00 .45
❑ R13 Gary Sheffield 1.00 .45
❑ R14 Rod Beck .25 .11
❑ R15 Fred McGriff .60 .25
❑ R16 Joe Carter .40 .18
❑ R17 Dante Bichette .40 .18
❑ R18 Danny Tartabull .25 .11
❑ R19 Juan Gonzalez 1.00 .45
❑ R20 Steve Avery .25 .11
❑ R21 John Wetteland .40 .18
❑ R22 Ben McDonald .25 .11
❑ R23 Jack McDowell .25 .11
❑ R24 Jose Canseco 1.25 .55
❑ R25 Tim Salmon .40 .18
❑ R26 Wilson Alvarez .25 .11
❑ R27 Gregg Jefferies .25 .11
❑ R28 John Burkett .25 .11
❑ R29 Greg Vaughn .40 .18
❑ R30 Robin Ventura .40 .18
❑ R31 Paul O'Neill .40 .18
❑ R32 Cecil Fielder .40 .18
❑ R33 Kevin Mitchell .25 .11
❑ R34 Jeff Conine .25 .11
❑ R35 Carlos Baerga .25 .11
❑ R36 Greg Maddux 2.50 1.10
❑ R37 Roger Clemens 2.00 .90
❑ R38 Deion Sanders .40 .18
❑ R39 Delino DeShields .25 .11
❑ R40 Ken Griffey Jr. 4.00 1.80
❑ R41 Albert Belle .60 .25
❑ R42 Wade Boggs 1.25 .55
❑ R43 Andres Galarraga .60 .25
❑ R44 Aaron Sele .40 .18
❑ R45 Don Mattingly 2.50 1.10
❑ R46 David Cone .40 .18
❑ R47 Len Dykstra .40 .18
❑ R48 Brett Butler .40 .18
❑ R49 Bill Swift .25 .11
❑ R50 Bobby Bonilla .40 .18
❑ R51 Rafael Palmeiro 1.00 .45
❑ R52 Moises Alou .40 .18
❑ R53 Jeff Bagwell 1.25 .55
❑ R54 Mike Mussina 1.00 .45
❑ R55 Frank Thomas 2.00 .90
❑ R56 Jose Rijo .25 .11
❑ R57 Ruben Sierra .25 .11
❑ R58 Randy Myers .25 .11
❑ R59 Barry Bonds 1.50 .70
❑ R60 Jimmy Key .40 .18
❑ R61 Travis Fryman .40 .18
❑ R62 John Olerud .40 .18
❑ R63 David Justice .60 .25
❑ R64 Ray Lankford .40 .18
❑ R65 Bob Tewksbury .25 .11
❑ R66 Chuck Carr .25 .11
❑ R67 Jay Buhner .40 .18
❑ R68 Kenny Lofton .40 .18
❑ R69 Marquis Grissom .25 .11
❑ R70 Sammy Sosa 2.00 .90
❑ R71 Cal Ripken 4.00 1.80
❑ R72 Ellis Burks .40 .18
❑ R73 Jeff Montgomery .25 .11
❑ R74 Julio Franco .25 .11
❑ R75 Kirby Puckett 2.50 1.10
❑ R76 Larry Walker .40 .18
❑ R77 Andy Van Slyke .40 .18
❑ R78 Tony Gwynn 2.00 .90
❑ R79 Will Clark 1.00 .45
❑ R80 Mo Vaughn .40 .18
❑ R81 Mike Piazza 3.00 1.35
❑ R82 James Mouton .25 .11
❑ R83 Carlos Delgado 1.50 .70
❑ R84 Ryan Klesko .40 .18
❑ R85 Javier Lopez .40 .18
❑ R86 Raul Mondesi .40 .18
❑ R87 Cliff Floyd .40 .18
❑ R88 Manny Ramirez 1.50 .70
❑ R89 Hector Carrasco .25 .11
❑ R90 Jeff Granger .25 .11
❑ X91 Frank Thomas 1.00 .45
Dmitri Young
❑ X92 Fred McGriff .40 .18
Brooks Kieschnick
❑ X93 Matt Williams .25 .11
Shane Andrews
❑ X94 Cal Ripken 2.00 .90
Kevin Orie
❑ X95 Barry Larkin 2.50 1.10
Derek Jeter
❑ X96 Ken Griffey Jr. 2.00 .90
Johnny Damon
❑ X97 Barry Bonds 1.00 .45
Rondell White
❑ X98 Albert Belle .40 .18
Jimmy Hurst
❑ X99 Raul Mondesi 1.50 .70
Ruben Rivera RC
❑ X100 Roger Clemens 1.00 .45
Scott Ruffcorn
❑ X101 Greg Maddux 1.25 .55
John Wasdin
❑ X102 Tim Salmon .40 .18
Chad Mottola
❑ X103 Carlos Baerga .25 .11
Arquimedez Pozo
❑ X104 Mike Piazza 1.50 .70
Bobby Hughes
❑ X105 Carlos Delgado .60 .25
Melvin Nieves
❑ X106 Javier Lopez 1.50 .70
Jorge Posada
❑ X107 Manny Ramirez 1.00 .45
Jose Malave
❑ X108 Travis Fryman 1.25 .55
Chipper Jones
❑ X109 Steve Avery .25 .11
Bill Pulsipher
❑ X110 John Olerud 1.00 .45
Shawn Green

## 1995 Bowman's Best

| | MINT | NRMT |
|---|---|---|
| COMPLETE SET (195) | 350.00 | 160.00 |
| COMMON CARD (B1-R90) | .25 | .11 |
| COMMON MIR.IM.(X1-X15) | .50 | .23 |

❑ B1 Derek Jeter 4.00 1.80
❑ B2 Vladimir Guerrero RC ! 150.00 70.00
❑ B3 Bob Abreu RC 20.00 9.00
❑ B4 Chan Ho Park .40 .18
❑ B5 Paul Wilson .25 .11
❑ B6 Chad Ogea .25 .11
❑ B7 Andruw Jones RC 80.00 36.00
❑ B8 Brian Barber .25 .11
❑ B9 Andy Larkin .25 .11
❑ B10 Richie Sexson RC 15.00 6.75
❑ B11 Everett Stull .25 .11
❑ B12 Brooks Kieschnick .25 .11
❑ B13 Matt Murray .25 .11
❑ B14 John Wasdin .25 .11
❑ B15 Shannon Stewart .40 .18
❑ B16 Luis Ortiz .25 .11
❑ B17 Marc Kroon .25 .11
❑ B18 Todd Greene .25 .11
❑ B19 Juan Acevedo RC .25 .11
❑ B20 Tony Clark .40 .18
❑ B21 Jermaine Dye 5.00 2.20
❑ B22 Derrek Lee .25 .11
❑ B23 Pat Watkins .25 .11
❑ B24 Pokey Reese .40 .18
❑ B25 Ben Grieve 5.00 2.20
❑ B26 Julio Santana .25 .11
❑ B27 Felix Rodriguez RC .25 .11
❑ B28 Paul Konerko 3.00 1.35
❑ B29 Nomar Garciaparra 20.00 9.00
❑ B30 Pat Ahearne .25 .11
❑ B31 Jason Schmidt .25 .11
❑ B32 Billy Wagner .40 .18
❑ B33 Rey Ordonez RC 5.00 2.20
❑ B34 Curtis Goodwin .25 .11
❑ B35 Sergio Nunez RC .25 .11
❑ B36 Tim Belk .25 .11
❑ B37 Scott Elarton RC 10.00 4.50
❑ B38 Jason Isringhausen .40 .18
❑ B39 Trot Nixon .40 .18
❑ B40 Sid Roberson RC .25 .11
❑ B41 Ron Villone .25 .11
❑ B42 Ruben Rivera .25 .11
❑ B43 Rick Huisman .25 .11
❑ B44 Todd Hollandsworth .25 .11
❑ B45 Johnny Damon .40 .18
❑ B46 Garret Anderson .40 .18
❑ B47 Jeff D'Amico .40 .18
❑ B48 Dustin Hermanson .25 .11
❑ B49 Juan Encarnacion RC 15.00 6.75
❑ B50 Andy Pettitte .60 .25

❑ B51 Chris Stynes .25 .11
❑ B52 Troy Percival .25 .11
❑ B53 LaTroy Hawkins .25 .11
❑ B54 Roger Cedeno .25 .11
❑ B55 Alan Benes .25 .11
❑ B56 Karim Garcia RC 1.50 .90
❑ B57 Andrew Lorraine .25 .11
❑ B58 Gary Rath RC .25 .11
❑ B59 Bret Wagner .25 .11
❑ B60 Jeff Suppan .25 .11
❑ B61 Bill Pulsipher .25 .11
❑ B62 Jay Payton RC 10.00 4.50
❑ B63 Alex Ochoa .25 .11
❑ B64 Ugueth Urbina .25 .11
❑ B65 Armando Benitez .40 .18
❑ B66 George Arias .25 .11
❑ B67 Raul Casanova RC .25 .11
❑ B68 Matt Drews .25 .11
❑ B69 Jimmy Haynes .25 .11
❑ B70 Jimmy Hurst .25 .11
❑ B71 C.J. Nitkowski .25 .11
❑ B72 Tommy Davis RC .25 .11
❑ B73 Bartolo Colon RC 12.00 5.50
❑ B74 Chris Carpenter RC 5.00 2.20
❑ B75 Trey Beamon .25 .11
❑ B76 Bryan Rekar .25 .11
❑ B77 James Baldwin .40 .18
❑ B78 Marc Valdes .25 .11
❑ B79 Tom Fordham RC .25 .11
❑ B80 Marc Newfield .25 .11
❑ B81 Angel Martinez .25 .11
❑ B82 Brian L. Hunter .25 .11
❑ B83 Jose Herrera .25 .11
❑ B84 Glenn Dishman RC .25 .11
❑ B85 Jacob Cruz RC 2.00 .90
❑ B86 Paul Shuey .25 .11
❑ B87 Scott Rolen RC 30.00 13.50
❑ B88 Doug Million .25 .11
❑ B89 Desi Relaford .25 .11
❑ B90 Michael Tucker .25 .11
❑ R1 Randy Johnson 1.25 .55
❑ R2 Joe Carter .40 .18
❑ R3 Chili Davis .40 .18
❑ R4 Moises Alou .40 .18
❑ R5 Gary Sheffield 1.00 .45
❑ R6 Kevin Appier .40 .18
❑ R7 Denny Neagle .40 .18
❑ R8 Ruben Sierra .25 .11
❑ R9 Darren Daulton .40 .18
❑ R10 Cal Ripken 4.00 1.80
❑ R11 Bobby Bonilla .40 .18
❑ R12 Manny Ramirez 1.25 .55
❑ R13 Barry Bonds 1.50 .70
❑ R14 Eric Karros .40 .18
❑ R15 Greg Maddux 2.50 1.10
❑ R16 Jeff Bagwell 1.25 .55
❑ R17 Paul Molitor 1.00 .45
❑ R18 Ray Lankford .40 .18
❑ R19 Mark Grace 1.00 .45
❑ R20 Kenny Lofton .40 .18
❑ R21 Tony Gwynn 2.00 .90
❑ R22 Will Clark 1.00 .45
❑ R23 Roger Clemens 2.00 .90
❑ R24 Dante Bichette .40 .18
❑ R25 Barry Larkin 1.00 .45
❑ R26 Wade Boggs 1.25 .55
❑ R27 Kirby Puckett 2.50 1.10
❑ R28 Cecil Fielder .40 .18
❑ R29 Jose Canseco 1.25 .55
❑ R30 Juan Gonzalez 1.00 .45
❑ R31 David Cone .40 .18
❑ R32 Craig Biggio .60 .25
❑ R33 Tim Salmon .40 .18
❑ R34 David Justice .60 .25
❑ R35 Sammy Sosa 2.00 .90
❑ R36 Mike Piazza 3.00 1.35
❑ R37 Carlos Baerga .25 .11
❑ R38 Jeff Conine .25 .11
❑ R39 Rafael Palmeiro 1.00 .45
❑ R40 Bret Saberhagen .40 .18
❑ R41 Len Dykstra .40 .18
❑ R42 Mo Vaughn .40 .18
❑ R43 Wally Joyner .40 .18
❑ R44 Chuck Knoblauch .40 .18
❑ R45 Robin Ventura .40 .18
❑ R46 Don Mattingly 2.50 1.10
❑ R47 Dave Hollins .25 .11
❑ R48 Andy Benes .25 .11
❑ R49 Ken Griffey Jr. 4.00 1.80
❑ R50 Albert Belle .60 .25
❑ R51 Matt Williams .60 .25
❑ R52 Rondell White .40 .18
❑ R53 Raul Mondesi .40 .18
❑ R54 Brian Jordan .40 .18
❑ R55 Greg Vaughn .40 .18
❑ R56 Fred McGriff .60 .25
❑ R57 Roberto Alomar 1.00 .45
❑ R58 Dennis Eckersley .40 .18
❑ R59 Lee Smith .40 .18
❑ R60 Eddie Murray 1.00 .45
❑ R61 Kenny Rogers .25 .11
❑ R62 Ron Gant .25 .11
❑ R63 Larry Walker .40 .18
❑ R64 Chad Curtis .25 .11
❑ R65 Frank Thomas 2.00 .90
❑ R66 Paul O'Neill .40 .18
❑ R67 Kevin Seitzer .25 .11
❑ R68 Marquis Grissom .25 .11
❑ R69 Mark McGwire 5.00 2.20
❑ R70 Travis Fryman .40 .18
❑ R71 Andres Galarraga .60 .25
❑ R72 Carlos Perez RC 2.00 .90
❑ R73 Tyler Green .25 .11
❑ R74 Marty Cordova .25 .11
❑ R75 Shawn Green 1.00 .45
❑ R76 Vaughn Eshelman .25 .11
❑ R77 John Mabry .25 .11
❑ R78 Jason Bates .25 .11
❑ R79 Jon Nunnally .25 .11
❑ R80 Ray Durham .40 .18
❑ R81 Edgardo Alfonzo 1.00 .45
❑ R82 Esteban Loaiza .25 .11
❑ R83 Hideo Nomo RC 10.00 4.50
❑ R84 Orlando Miller .25 .11
❑ R85 Alex Gonzalez .25 .11
❑ R86 Mark Grudzielanek RC 2.00 .90
❑ R87 Julian Tavarez .25 .11
❑ R88 Benji Gil .25 .11
❑ R89 Quilvio Veras .25 .11
❑ R90 Ricky Bottalico .25 .11
❑ X1 Ben Davis RC 4.00 1.80
Ivan Rodriguez
❑ X2 Mark Redman RC 2.00 .90
Manny Ramirez
❑ X3 Reggie Taylor RC 1.00 .70
Deion Sanders
❑ X4 Ryan Jaroncyk RC .60 .25
Shawn Green
❑ X5 Juan LeBron RC 2.00 .90
Juan Gonzalez UER
(Card pictures Carlos Beltran instead of Juan LeBron)
❑ X6 Tony McKnight RC .60 .25
Craig Biggio
❑ X7 Michael Barrett RC 4.00 1.80
Travis Fryman
❑ X8 Corey Jenkins RC .40 .18
Mo Vaughn
❑ X9 Ruben Rivera 1.00 .45
Frank Thomas
❑ X10 Curtis Goodwin .50 .23
Kenny Lofton
❑ X11 Brian L. Hunter 1.00 .45
Tony Gwynn
❑ X12 Todd Greene 2.00 .90
Ken Griffey Jr.
❑ X13 Karim Garcia .40 .18
Matt Williams
❑ X14 Billy Wagner .40 .18
Randy Johnson
❑ X15 Pat Watkins .60 .25
Jeff Bagwell

## 1996 Bowman's Best

| | MINT | NRMT |
|---|---|---|
| COMPLETE SET (180) | 60.00 | 27.00 |
| COMMON CARD (1-180) | .20 | .09 |

❑ 1 Hideo Nomo .75 .35
❑ 2 Edgar Martinez .50 .23
❑ 3 Cal Ripken 3.00 1.35

❑ 4 Wade Boggs 1.00 .45
❑ 5 Cecil Fielder .30 .14
❑ 6 Albert Belle .50 .23
❑ 7 Chipper Jones 2.00 .90
❑ 8 Ryne Sandberg 1.00 .45
❑ 9 Tim Salmon .30 .14
❑ 10 Barry Bonds 1.25 .55
❑ 11 Ken Caminiti .30 .14
❑ 12 Ron Gant .20 .09
❑ 13 Frank Thomas 1.50 .70
❑ 14 Dante Bichette .30 .14
❑ 15 Jason Kendall .30 .14
❑ 16 Mo Vaughn .30 .14
❑ 17 Rey Ordonez .30 .14
❑ 18 Henry Rodriguez .20 .09
❑ 19 Ryan Klesko .30 .14
❑ 20 Jeff Bagwell 1.00 .45
❑ 21 Randy Johnson 1.00 .45
❑ 22 Jim Edmonds .75 .35
❑ 23 Kenny Lofton .30 .14
❑ 24 Andy Pettitte .30 .14
❑ 25 Brady Anderson .30 .14
❑ 26 Mike Piazza 2.50 1.10
❑ 27 Greg Vaughn .30 .14
❑ 28 Joe Carter .30 .14
❑ 29 Jason Giambi .75 .35
❑ 30 Ivan Rodriguez 1.00 .45
❑ 31 Jeff Conine .20 .09
❑ 32 Rafael Palmeiro .75 .35
❑ 33 Roger Clemens 1.50 .70
❑ 34 Chuck Knoblauch .30 .14
❑ 35 Reggie Sanders .20 .09
❑ 36 Andres Galarraga .50 .23
❑ 37 Paul O'Neill .30 .14
❑ 38 Tony Gwynn 1.50 .70
❑ 39 Paul Wilson .20 .09
❑ 40 Garret Anderson .30 .14
❑ 41 David Justice .50 .23
❑ 42 Eddie Murray .75 .35
❑ 43 Mike Grace RC .20 .09
❑ 44 Marty Cordova .20 .09
❑ 45 Kevin Appier .30 .14
❑ 46 Raul Mondesi .30 .14
❑ 47 Jim Thome .50 .23
❑ 48 Sammy Sosa 1.50 .70
❑ 49 Craig Biggio .50 .23
❑ 50 Marquis Grissom .20 .09
❑ 51 Alan Benes .20 .09
❑ 52 Manny Ramirez 1.00 .45
❑ 53 Gary Sheffield .75 .35
❑ 54 Mike Mussina .75 .35
❑ 55 Robin Ventura .30 .14
❑ 56 Johnny Damon .50 .23
❑ 57 Jose Canseco 1.00 .45
❑ 58 Juan Gonzalez .75 .35
❑ 59 Tino Martinez .30 .14
❑ 60 Brian Hunter .20 .09
❑ 61 Fred McGriff .50 .23
❑ 62 Jay Buhner .30 .14
❑ 63 Carlos Delgado .75 .35
❑ 64 Moises Alou .30 .14
❑ 65 Roberto Alomar .75 .35
❑ 66 Barry Larkin .75 .35
❑ 67 Vinny Castilla .30 .14
❑ 68 Ray Durham .30 .14
❑ 69 Travis Fryman .30 .14
❑ 70 Jason Isringhausen .30 .14
❑ 71 Ken Griffey Jr. 3.00 1.35

| Card | MINT | NRMT |
|---|---|---|
| 72 John Smoltz | .30 | .14 |
| 73 Matt Williams | .50 | .23 |
| 74 Chan Ho Park | .30 | .14 |
| 75 Mark McGwire | 4.00 | 1.80 |
| 76 Jeffrey Hammonds | .30 | .14 |
| 77 Will Clark | .75 | .35 |
| 78 Kirby Puckett | 2.00 | .90 |
| 79 Derek Jeter | 3.00 | 1.35 |
| 80 Derek Bell | .20 | .09 |
| 81 Eric Karros | .30 | .14 |
| 82 Len Dykstra | .30 | .14 |
| 83 Larry Walker | .30 | .14 |
| 84 Mark Grudzielanek | .20 | .09 |
| 85 Greg Maddux | 2.00 | .90 |
| 86 Carlos Baerga | .20 | .09 |
| 87 Paul Molitor | .75 | .35 |
| 88 John Valentin | .20 | .09 |
| 89 Mark Grace | .75 | .35 |
| 90 Ray Lankford | .30 | .14 |
| 91 Andruw Jones | 2.50 | 1.10 |
| 92 Nomar Garciaparra | 3.00 | 1.35 |
| 93 Alex Ochoa | .20 | .09 |
| 94 Derrick Gibson | .20 | .09 |
| 95 Jeff D'Amico | .20 | .09 |
| 96 Ruben Rivera | .20 | .09 |
| 97 Vladimir Guerrero | 4.00 | 1.80 |
| 98 Pokey Reese | .30 | .14 |
| 99 Richard Hidalgo | .30 | .14 |
| 100 Bartolo Colon | .30 | .14 |
| 101 Karim Garcia | .20 | .09 |
| 102 Ben Davis | .30 | .14 |
| 103 Jay Powell | .20 | .09 |
| 104 Chris Snopek | .20 | .09 |
| 105 Glendon Rusch RC | 1.50 | .70 |
| 106 Enrique Wilson | .20 | .09 |
| 107 Antonio Alfonseca RC | 1.50 | .70 |
| 108 Wilton Guerrero RC | 1.25 | .55 |
| 109 Jose Guillen RC | 2.00 | .90 |
| 110 Miguel Mejia RC | .20 | .09 |
| 111 Jay Payton | .30 | .14 |
| 112 Scott Elarton | .75 | .35 |
| 113 Brooks Kieschnick | .20 | .09 |
| 114 Dustin Hermanson | .20 | .09 |
| 115 Roger Cedeno | .20 | .09 |
| 116 Matt Wagner | .20 | .09 |
| 117 Lee Daniels | .20 | .09 |
| 118 Ben Grieve | .30 | .14 |
| 119 Ugueth Urbina | .30 | .14 |
| 120 Danny Graves | .50 | .23 |
| 121 Dan Donato RC | .20 | .09 |
| 122 Matt Ruebel RC | .20 | .09 |
| 123 Mark Sievert RC | .20 | .09 |
| 124 Chris Stynes | .20 | .09 |
| 125 Jeff Abbott | .20 | .09 |
| 126 Rocky Coppinger RC | .75 | .35 |
| 127 Jermaine Dye | .30 | .14 |
| 128 Todd Greene | .20 | .09 |
| 129 Chris Carpenter | .30 | .14 |
| 130 Edgar Renteria | .30 | .14 |
| 131 Matt Drews | .20 | .09 |
| 132 Edgard Velazquez RC | 1.00 | .45 |
| 133 Casey Whitten | .30 | .14 |
| 134 Ryan Jones RC | .20 | .09 |
| 135 Todd Walker | .30 | .14 |
| 136 Geoff Jenkins RC | 8.00 | 3.60 |
| 137 Matt Morris RC | 1.00 | .45 |
| 138 Richie Sexson | .75 | .35 |
| 139 Todd Dunwoody RC | 1.00 | .45 |
| 140 Gabe Alvarez RC | 1.00 | .45 |
| 141 J.J. Johnson | .20 | .09 |
| 142 Shannon Stewart | .30 | .14 |
| 143 Brad Fullmer | .30 | .14 |
| 144 Julio Santana | .20 | .09 |
| 145 Scott Rolen | 2.00 | .90 |
| 146 Amaury Telemaco | .20 | .09 |
| 147 Trey Beamon | .20 | .09 |
| 148 Billy Wagner | .20 | .09 |
| 149 Todd Hollandsworth | .20 | .09 |
| 150 Doug Million | .20 | .09 |
| 151 Jose Valentin RC | 1.00 | .45 |
| 152 Wes Helms RC | 1.50 | .70 |
| 153 Jeff Suppan | .20 | .09 |
| 154 Luis Castillo RC | 5.00 | 2.20 |
| 155 Bob Abreu | 1.25 | .55 |
| 156 Paul Konerko | .30 | .14 |
| 157 Jamey Wright | .20 | .09 |
| 158 Eddie Pearson | .20 | .09 |
| 159 Jimmy Haynes | .20 | .09 |
| 160 Derrek Lee | .20 | .09 |
| 161 Damian Moss | .20 | .09 |
| 162 Carlos Guillen RC | 3.00 | 1.35 |
| 163 Chris Fussell RC | 1.00 | .45 |
| 164 Mike Sweeney RC | 10.00 | 4.50 |
| 165 Donnie Sadler | .30 | .14 |
| 166 Desi Relaford | .20 | .09 |
| 167 Steve Gibralter | .20 | .09 |
| 168 Neifi Perez | .20 | .09 |
| 169 Antone Williamson | .20 | .09 |
| 170 Marty Janzen RC | .20 | .09 |
| 171 Todd Helton | 5.00 | 2.20 |
| 172 Raul Ibanez RC | .20 | .09 |
| 173 Bill Selby | .20 | .09 |
| 174 Shane Monahan RC | .20 | .09 |
| 175 Robin Jennings | .20 | .09 |
| 176 Bobby Chouinard | .20 | .09 |
| 177 Einar Diaz | .20 | .09 |
| 178 Jason Thompson | .20 | .09 |
| 179 Rafael Medina RC | .20 | .09 |
| 180 Kevin Orie | .20 | .09 |
| NNO 1952 Mantle Chrome | 5.00 | 2.20 |
| NNO 1952 Mantle Refractor | 15.00 | 6.75 |
| NNO 1952 Mantle Atomic Ref. | 30.00 | 13.50 |

# 1997 Bowman's Best

| | MINT | NRMT |
|---|---|---|
| COMPLETE SET (200) | 50.00 | 22.00 |
| 1 Ken Griffey Jr. | 3.00 | 1.35 |
| 2 Cecil Fielder | .30 | .14 |
| 3 Albert Belle | .50 | .23 |
| 4 Todd Hundley | .20 | .09 |
| 5 Mike Piazza | 2.50 | 1.10 |
| 6 Matt Williams | .50 | .23 |
| 7 Mo Vaughn | .30 | .14 |
| 8 Ryne Sandberg | 1.00 | .45 |
| 9 Chipper Jones | 2.00 | .90 |
| 10 Edgar Martinez | .50 | .23 |
| 11 Kenny Lofton | .30 | .14 |
| 12 Ron Gant | .20 | .09 |
| 13 Moises Alou | .30 | .14 |
| 14 Pat Hentgen | .20 | .09 |
| 15 Steve Finley | .30 | .14 |
| 16 Mark Grace | .75 | .35 |
| 17 Jay Buhner | .30 | .14 |
| 18 Jeff Conine | .20 | .09 |
| 19 Jim Edmonds | .75 | .35 |
| 20 Todd Hollandsworth | .20 | .09 |
| 21 Andy Pettitte | .30 | .14 |
| 22 Jim Thome | .50 | .23 |
| 23 Eric Young | .20 | .09 |
| 24 Ray Lankford | .30 | .14 |
| 25 Marquis Grissom | .20 | .09 |
| 26 Tony Clark | .20 | .09 |
| 27 Jermaine Allensworth | .20 | .09 |
| 28 Ellis Burks | .30 | .14 |
| 29 Tony Gwynn | 1.50 | .70 |
| 30 Barry Larkin | .75 | .35 |
| 31 John Olerud | .30 | .14 |
| 32 Mariano Rivera | .30 | .14 |
| 33 Paul Molitor | .75 | .35 |
| 34 Ken Caminiti | .30 | .14 |
| 35 Gary Sheffield | .75 | .35 |
| 36 Al Martin | .20 | .09 |
| 37 John Valentin | .20 | .09 |
| 38 Frank Thomas | 1.50 | .70 |
| 39 John Jaha | .20 | .09 |
| 40 Greg Maddux | 2.00 | .90 |
| 41 Alex Fernandez | .20 | .09 |
| 42 Dean Palmer | .30 | .14 |
| 43 Bernie Williams | .75 | .35 |
| 44 Deion Sanders | .30 | .14 |
| 45 Mark McGwire | 4.00 | 1.80 |
| 46 Brian Jordan | .30 | .14 |
| 47 Bernard Gilkey | .20 | .09 |
| 48 Will Clark | .75 | .35 |
| 49 Kevin Appier | .30 | .14 |
| 50 Tom Glavine | .75 | .35 |
| 51 Chuck Knoblauch | .30 | .14 |
| 52 Rondell White | .30 | .14 |
| 53 Greg Vaughn | .30 | .14 |
| 54 Mike Mussina | .75 | .35 |
| 55 Brian McRae | .20 | .09 |
| 56 Chili Davis | .30 | .14 |
| 57 Wade Boggs | 1.00 | .45 |
| 58 Jeff Bagwell | 1.00 | .45 |
| 59 Roberto Alomar | .75 | .35 |
| 60 Dennis Eckersley | .30 | .14 |
| 61 Ryan Klesko | .30 | .14 |
| 62 Manny Ramirez | 1.00 | .45 |
| 63 John Wetteland | .30 | .14 |
| 64 Cal Ripken | 3.00 | 1.35 |
| 65 Edgar Renteria | .30 | .14 |
| 66 Tino Martinez | .30 | .14 |
| 67 Larry Walker | .30 | .14 |
| 68 Gregg Jefferies | .20 | .09 |
| 69 Lance Johnson | .20 | .09 |
| 70 Carlos Delgado | .75 | .35 |
| 71 Craig Biggio | .50 | .23 |
| 72 Jose Canseco | 1.00 | .45 |
| 73 Barry Bonds | 1.25 | .55 |
| 74 Juan Gonzalez | .75 | .35 |
| 75 Eric Karros | .30 | .14 |
| 76 Reggie Sanders | .20 | .09 |
| 77 Robin Ventura | .30 | .14 |
| 78 Hideo Nomo | .75 | .35 |
| 79 David Justice | .50 | .23 |
| 80 Vinny Castilla | .30 | .14 |
| 81 Travis Fryman | .30 | .14 |
| 82 Derek Jeter | 3.00 | 1.35 |
| 83 Sammy Sosa | 1.50 | .70 |
| 84 Ivan Rodriguez | 1.00 | .45 |
| 85 Rafael Palmeiro | .75 | .35 |
| 86 Roger Clemens | 1.50 | .70 |
| 87 Jason Giambi | .75 | .35 |
| 88 Andres Galarraga | .50 | .23 |
| 89 Jermaine Dye | .30 | .14 |
| 90 Joe Carter | .30 | .14 |
| 91 Brady Anderson | .30 | .14 |
| 92 Derek Bell | .20 | .09 |
| 93 Randy Johnson | 1.00 | .45 |
| 94 Fred McGriff | .50 | .23 |
| 95 John Smoltz | .30 | .14 |
| 96 Harold Baines | .30 | .14 |
| 97 Raul Mondesi | .30 | .14 |
| 98 Tim Salmon | .30 | .14 |
| 99 Carlos Baerga | .20 | .09 |
| 100 Dante Bichette | .30 | .14 |
| 101 Vladimir Guerrero | 1.50 | .70 |
| 102 Richard Hidalgo | .30 | .14 |
| 103 Paul Konerko | .30 | .14 |
| 104 Alex Gonzalez RC | .60 | .25 |
| 105 Jason Dickson | .20 | .09 |
| 106 Jose Rosado | .20 | .09 |
| 107 Todd Walker | .20 | .09 |
| 108 Seth Greisinger RC | .60 | .25 |
| 109 Todd Helton | 1.25 | .55 |
| 110 Ben Davis | .20 | .09 |
| 111 Bartolo Colon | .30 | .14 |
| 112 Elieser Marrero | .20 | .09 |
| 113 Jeff D'Amico | .20 | .09 |
| 114 Miguel Tejada RC | 6.00 | 2.70 |
| 115 Darin Erstad | 1.00 | .45 |
| 116 Kris Benson RC | 4.00 | 1.80 |
| 117 Adrian Beltre RC | 5.00 | 2.20 |
| 118 Neifi Perez | .20 | .09 |
| 119 Pokey Reese | .30 | .14 |
| 120 Carl Pavano | .75 | .35 |
| 121 Juan Melo | .30 | .14 |
| 122 Kevin McGlinchy RC | .60 | .25 |

| | | | |
|---|---|---|---|
| ❑ 123 | Pat Cline | .30 | .14 |
| ❑ 124 | Felix Heredia RC | .60 | .25 |
| ❑ 125 | Aaron Boone | .20 | .09 |
| ❑ 126 | Glendon Rusch | .20 | .09 |
| ❑ 127 | Mike Cameron | .30 | .14 |
| ❑ 128 | Justin Thompson | .20 | .09 |
| ❑ 129 | Chad Hermansen RC | 1.50 | .70 |
| ❑ 130 | Sidney Ponson RC | 1.00 | .45 |
| ❑ 131 | Willie Martinez RC | 1.00 | .45 |
| ❑ 132 | Paul Wilder RC | .20 | .09 |
| ❑ 133 | Geoff Jenkins | .30 | .14 |
| ❑ 134 | Roy Halladay RC | .60 | .25 |
| ❑ 135 | Carlos Guillen | .20 | .09 |
| ❑ 136 | Tony Batista | .75 | .35 |
| ❑ 137 | Todd Greene | .20 | .09 |
| ❑ 138 | Luis Castillo | .30 | .14 |
| ❑ 139 | Jimmy Anderson RC | .60 | .25 |
| ❑ 140 | Edgard Velazquez | .50 | .23 |
| ❑ 141 | Chris Snopek | .20 | .09 |
| ❑ 142 | Ruben Rivera | .20 | .09 |
| ❑ 143 | Javier Valentin | .30 | .14 |
| ❑ 144 | Brian Rose | .20 | .09 |
| ❑ 145 | Fernando Tatis RC | 3.00 | 1.35 |
| ❑ 146 | Dean Crow RC | .20 | .09 |
| ❑ 147 | Karim Garcia | .20 | .09 |
| ❑ 148 | Dante Powell | .30 | .14 |
| ❑ 149 | Hideki Irabu RC | 1.00 | .45 |
| ❑ 150 | Matt Morris | .20 | .09 |
| ❑ 151 | Wes Helms | .20 | .09 |
| ❑ 152 | Russ Johnson | .20 | .09 |
| ❑ 153 | Jarrod Washburn | .30 | .14 |
| ❑ 154 | Kerry Wood RC | 6.00 | 2.70 |
| ❑ 155 | Joe Fontenot RC | .60 | .25 |
| ❑ 156 | Eugene Kingsale | .30 | .14 |
| ❑ 157 | Terrence Long | .30 | .14 |
| ❑ 158 | Calvin Maduro | .20 | .09 |
| ❑ 159 | Jeff Suppan | .20 | .09 |
| ❑ 160 | DaRond Stovall | .20 | .09 |
| ❑ 161 | Mark Redman | .20 | .09 |
| ❑ 162 | Ken Cloude RC | .30 | .14 |
| ❑ 163 | Bobby Estalella | .20 | .09 |
| ❑ 164 | Abraham Nunez RC | .60 | .25 |
| ❑ 165 | Derrick Gibson | .20 | .09 |
| ❑ 166 | Mike Drumright RC | .20 | .09 |
| ❑ 167 | Katsuhiro Maeda | .30 | .14 |
| ❑ 168 | Jeff Liefer | .30 | .14 |
| ❑ 169 | Ben Grieve | 1.25 | .55 |
| ❑ 170 | Bob Abreu | .30 | .14 |
| ❑ 171 | Shannon Stewart | .30 | .14 |
| ❑ 172 | Braden Looper RC | .60 | .25 |
| ❑ 173 | Brant Brown | .20 | .09 |
| ❑ 174 | Marlon Anderson | .20 | .09 |
| ❑ 175 | Brad Fullmer | .30 | .14 |
| ❑ 176 | Carlos Beltran | .75 | .35 |
| ❑ 177 | Nomar Garciaparra | 2.50 | 1.10 |
| ❑ 178 | Derrek Lee | .20 | .09 |
| ❑ 179 | Valerio De Los Santos RC | .60 | .25 |
| ❑ 180 | Dmitri Young | .30 | .14 |
| ❑ 181 | Jamey Wright | .20 | .09 |
| ❑ 182 | Hiram Bocachica RC | 1.00 | .45 |
| ❑ 183 | Wilton Guerrero | .20 | .09 |
| ❑ 184 | Chris Carpenter | .30 | .14 |
| ❑ 185 | Scott Spiezio | .20 | .09 |
| ❑ 186 | Andruw Jones | 1.00 | .45 |
| ❑ 187 | Travis Lee RC | 1.50 | .70 |
| ❑ 188 | Jose Cruz Jr. RC | 3.00 | 1.35 |
| ❑ 189 | Jose Guillen | .20 | .09 |
| ❑ 190 | Jeff Abbott | .20 | .09 |
| ❑ 191 | Ricky Ledee RC | 1.25 | .55 |
| ❑ 192 | Mike Sweeney | .30 | .14 |
| ❑ 193 | Donnie Sadler | .30 | .14 |
| ❑ 194 | Scott Rolen | .75 | .35 |
| ❑ 195 | Kevin Orie | .20 | .09 |
| ❑ 196 | Jason Conti RC | .60 | .25 |
| ❑ 197 | Mark Kotsay RC | 1.25 | .55 |
| ❑ 198 | Eric Milton RC | 1.50 | .70 |
| ❑ 199 | Russell Branyan | .75 | .35 |
| ❑ 200 | Alex Sanchez RC | .60 | .25 |

## 1998 Bowman's Best

| | | MINT | NRMT |
|---|---|---|---|
| COMPLETE SET (200) | | 80.00 | 36.00 |
| ❑ 1 | Mark McGwire | 3.00 | 1.35 |
| ❑ 2 | Jeromy Burnitz | .30 | .14 |
| ❑ 3 | Barry Bonds | 1.25 | .55 |
| ❑ 4 | Dante Bichette | .30 | .14 |
| ❑ 5 | Chipper Jones | 2.00 | .90 |
| ❑ 6 | Frank Thomas | 1.50 | .70 |
| ❑ 7 | Kevin Brown | .50 | .23 |
| ❑ 8 | Juan Gonzalez | .75 | .35 |
| ❑ 9 | Jay Buhner | .30 | .14 |
| ❑ 10 | Chuck Knoblauch | .30 | .14 |
| ❑ 11 | Cal Ripken | 3.00 | 1.35 |
| ❑ 12 | Matt Williams | .50 | .23 |
| ❑ 13 | Jim Edmonds | .75 | .35 |
| ❑ 14 | Manny Ramirez | 1.00 | .45 |
| ❑ 15 | Tony Clark | .20 | .09 |
| ❑ 16 | Mo Vaughn | .30 | .14 |
| ❑ 17 | Bernie Williams | .75 | .35 |
| ❑ 18 | Scott Rolen | .75 | .35 |
| ❑ 19 | Gary Sheffield | .75 | .35 |
| ❑ 20 | Albert Belle | .50 | .23 |
| ❑ 21 | Mike Piazza | 2.50 | 1.10 |
| ❑ 22 | John Olerud | .30 | .14 |
| ❑ 23 | Tony Gwynn | 1.50 | .70 |
| ❑ 24 | Jay Bell | .30 | .14 |
| ❑ 25 | Jose Cruz Jr. | .30 | .14 |
| ❑ 26 | Justin Thompson | .20 | .09 |
| ❑ 27 | Ken Griffey Jr. | 3.00 | 1.35 |
| ❑ 28 | Sandy Alomar Jr. | .30 | .14 |
| ❑ 29 | Mark Grudzielanek | .20 | .09 |
| ❑ 30 | Mark Grace | .75 | .35 |
| ❑ 31 | Ron Gant | .30 | .14 |
| ❑ 32 | Javy Lopez | .30 | .14 |
| ❑ 33 | Jeff Bagwell | 1.00 | .45 |
| ❑ 34 | Fred McGriff | .50 | .23 |
| ❑ 35 | Rafael Palmeiro | .75 | .35 |
| ❑ 36 | Vinny Castilla | .30 | .14 |
| ❑ 37 | Andy Benes | .20 | .09 |
| ❑ 38 | Pedro Martinez | 1.00 | .45 |
| ❑ 39 | Andy Pettitte | .30 | .14 |
| ❑ 40 | Marty Cordova | .20 | .09 |
| ❑ 41 | Rusty Greer | .30 | .14 |
| ❑ 42 | Kevin Orie | .20 | .09 |
| ❑ 43 | Chan Ho Park | .30 | .14 |
| ❑ 44 | Ryan Klesko | .30 | .14 |
| ❑ 45 | Alex Rodriguez | 2.50 | 1.10 |
| ❑ 46 | Travis Fryman | .30 | .14 |
| ❑ 47 | Jeff King | .20 | .09 |
| ❑ 48 | Roger Clemens | 1.50 | .70 |
| ❑ 49 | Darin Erstad | .75 | .35 |
| ❑ 50 | Brady Anderson | .30 | .14 |
| ❑ 51 | Jason Kendall | .30 | .14 |
| ❑ 52 | John Valentin | .20 | .09 |
| ❑ 53 | Ellis Burks | .30 | .14 |
| ❑ 54 | Brian Hunter | .20 | .09 |
| ❑ 55 | Paul O'Neill | .30 | .14 |
| ❑ 56 | Ken Caminiti | .30 | .14 |
| ❑ 57 | David Justice | .50 | .23 |
| ❑ 58 | Eric Karros | .30 | .14 |
| ❑ 59 | Pat Hentgen | .20 | .09 |
| ❑ 60 | Greg Maddux | 2.00 | .90 |
| ❑ 61 | Craig Biggio | .50 | .23 |
| ❑ 62 | Edgar Martinez | .50 | .23 |
| ❑ 63 | Mike Mussina | .75 | .35 |
| ❑ 64 | Larry Walker | .30 | .14 |
| ❑ 65 | Tino Martinez | .30 | .14 |
| ❑ 66 | Jim Thome | .50 | .23 |
| ❑ 67 | Tom Glavine | .75 | .35 |
| ❑ 68 | Raul Mondesi | .30 | .14 |
| ❑ 69 | Marquis Grissom | .20 | .09 |
| ❑ 70 | Randy Johnson | 1.00 | .45 |
| ❑ 71 | Steve Finley | .30 | .14 |
| ❑ 72 | Jose Guillen | .20 | .09 |
| ❑ 73 | Nomar Garciaparra | 2.50 | 1.10 |
| ❑ 74 | Wade Boggs | 1.00 | .45 |
| ❑ 75 | Bobby Higginson | .30 | .14 |
| ❑ 76 | Robin Ventura | .30 | .14 |
| ❑ 77 | Derek Jeter | 3.00 | 1.35 |
| ❑ 78 | Andruw Jones | .75 | .35 |
| ❑ 79 | Ray Lankford | .30 | .14 |
| ❑ 80 | Vladimir Guerrero | 1.25 | .55 |
| ❑ 81 | Kenny Lofton | .30 | .14 |
| ❑ 82 | Ivan Rodriguez | 1.00 | .45 |
| ❑ 83 | Neifi Perez | .20 | .09 |
| ❑ 84 | John Smoltz | .30 | .14 |
| ❑ 85 | Tim Salmon | .30 | .14 |
| ❑ 86 | Carlos Delgado | .75 | .35 |
| ❑ 87 | Sammy Sosa | 1.50 | .70 |
| ❑ 88 | Jaret Wright | .20 | .09 |
| ❑ 89 | Roberto Alomar | .75 | .35 |
| ❑ 90 | Paul Molitor | .75 | .35 |
| ❑ 91 | Dean Palmer | .30 | .14 |
| ❑ 92 | Barry Larkin | .75 | .35 |
| ❑ 93 | Jason Giambi | .75 | .35 |
| ❑ 94 | Curt Schilling | .30 | .14 |
| ❑ 95 | Eric Young | .20 | .09 |
| ❑ 96 | Denny Neagle | .20 | .09 |
| ❑ 97 | Moises Alou | .30 | .14 |
| ❑ 98 | Livan Hernandez | .20 | .09 |
| ❑ 99 | Todd Hundley | .20 | .09 |
| ❑ 100 | Andres Galarraga | .50 | .23 |
| ❑ 101 | Travis Lee | .30 | .14 |
| ❑ 102 | Lance Berkman | .50 | .23 |
| ❑ 103 | Orlando Cabrera | .20 | .09 |
| ❑ 104 | Mike Lowell RC | 2.00 | .90 |
| ❑ 105 | Ben Grieve | .30 | .14 |
| ❑ 106 | Jae Weong Seo RC | .75 | .35 |
| ❑ 107 | Richie Sexson | .50 | .23 |
| ❑ 108 | Eli Marrero | .20 | .09 |
| ❑ 109 | Aramis Ramirez | .30 | .14 |
| ❑ 110 | Paul Konerko | .30 | .14 |
| ❑ 111 | Carl Pavano | .20 | .09 |
| ❑ 112 | Brad Fullmer | .30 | .14 |
| ❑ 113 | Matt Clement | .20 | .09 |
| ❑ 114 | Donzell McDonald | .20 | .09 |
| ❑ 115 | Todd Helton | 1.00 | .45 |
| ❑ 116 | Mike Caruso | .20 | .09 |
| ❑ 117 | Donnie Sadler | .20 | .09 |
| ❑ 118 | Bruce Chen | .20 | .09 |
| ❑ 119 | Jarrod Washburn | .20 | .09 |
| ❑ 120 | Adrian Beltre | .30 | .14 |
| ❑ 121 | Ryan Jackson RC | .20 | .09 |
| ❑ 122 | Kevin Millar RC | .60 | .25 |
| ❑ 123 | Corey Koskie RC | 1.50 | .70 |
| ❑ 124 | Dermal Brown | .30 | .14 |
| ❑ 125 | Kerry Wood | .75 | .35 |
| ❑ 126 | Juan Melo | .20 | .09 |
| ❑ 127 | Ramon Hernandez | .20 | .09 |
| ❑ 128 | Roy Halladay | .20 | .09 |
| ❑ 129 | Ron Wright | .20 | .09 |
| ❑ 130 | Darnell McDonald RC | 1.25 | .55 |
| ❑ 131 | Odalis Perez RC | .75 | .35 |
| ❑ 132 | Alex Cora RC | 1.00 | .45 |
| ❑ 133 | Justin Towle | .20 | .09 |
| ❑ 134 | Juan Encarnacion | .30 | .14 |
| ❑ 135 | Brian Rose | .20 | .09 |
| ❑ 136 | Russell Branyan | .30 | .14 |
| ❑ 137 | Cesar King RC | .60 | .25 |
| ❑ 138 | Ruben Rivera | .20 | .09 |
| ❑ 139 | Ricky Ledee | .20 | .09 |
| ❑ 140 | Vernon Wells | .50 | .23 |
| ❑ 141 | Luis Rivas RC | 1.50 | .70 |
| ❑ 142 | Brent Butler | .20 | .09 |
| ❑ 143 | Karim Garcia | .20 | .09 |
| ❑ 144 | George Lombard | .20 | .09 |
| ❑ 145 | Masato Yoshii RC | 1.25 | .55 |
| ❑ 146 | Braden Looper | .20 | .09 |
| ❑ 147 | Alex Sanchez | .20 | .09 |
| ❑ 148 | Kris Benson | .30 | .14 |
| ❑ 149 | Mark Kotsay | .30 | .14 |
| ❑ 150 | Richard Hidalgo | .30 | .14 |
| ❑ 151 | Scott Elarton | .30 | .14 |
| ❑ 152 | Ryan Minor RC | .60 | .25 |
| ❑ 153 | Troy Glaus RC | 10.00 | 4.50 |
| ❑ 154 | Carlos Lee RC | 4.00 | 1.80 |
| ❑ 155 | Michael Coleman | .20 | .09 |

❑ 156 Jason Grilli RC .60 .25
❑ 157 Julio Ramirez RC 1.25 .55
❑ 158 Randy Wolf RC 1.25 .55
❑ 159 Ryan Brannan .20 .09
❑ 160 Edgard Clemente .20 .09
❑ 161 Miguel Tejada .75 .35
❑ 162 Chad Hermansen .30 .14
❑ 163 Ryan Anderson RC 6.00 2.70
❑ 164 Ben Petrick .20 .09
❑ 165 Alex Gonzalez .20 .09
❑ 166 Ben Davis .20 .09
❑ 167 John Patterson .20 .09
❑ 168 Cliff Politte .20 .09
❑ 169 Randall Simon .20 .09
❑ 170 Javier Vazquez .20 .09
❑ 171 Kevin Witt .20 .09
❑ 172 Geoff Jenkins .30 .14
❑ 173 David Ortiz .20 .09
❑ 174 Derrick Gibson .20 .09
❑ 175 Abraham Nunez .20 .09
❑ 176 A.J. Hinch .20 .09
❑ 177 Ruben Mateo RC 4.00 1.80
❑ 178 Magglio Ordonez RC 6.00 2.70
❑ 179 Todd Dunwoody .20 .09
❑ 180 Daryle Ward .30 .14
❑ 181 Mike Kinkade RC .50 .23
❑ 182 Willie Martinez .30 .14
❑ 183 Orlando Hernandez RC 2.50 1.10
❑ 184 Eric Milton .20 .09
❑ 185 Eric Chavez .30 .14
❑ 186 Damian Jackson .20 .09
❑ 187 Jim Parque RC 1.25 .55
❑ 188 Dan Reichert RC 1.25 .55
❑ 189 Mike Drumright .20 .09
❑ 190 Todd Walker .20 .09
❑ 191 Shane Monahan .20 .09
❑ 192 Derrek Lee .20 .09
❑ 193 Jeremy Giambi RC .75 .35
❑ 194 Dan McKinley RC .60 .25
❑ 195 Tony Armas Jr. RC 4.00 1.80
❑ 196 Matt Anderson RC .60 .25
❑ 197 Jim Chamblee RC .20 .09
❑ 198 Francisco Cordero RC .75 .35
❑ 199 Calvin Pickering .20 .09
❑ 200 Reggie Taylor .20 .09

## 1999 Bowman's Best

| | MINT | NRMT |
|---|---|---|
| COMPLETE SET (200) | 100.00 | 45.00 |
| COMP.SET w/o SP's (150) | 30.00 | 13.50 |
| COMMON CARD (1-150) | .20 | .09 |
| COMMON ROOKIE (151-200) | .75 | .35 |

❑ 1 Chipper Jones 2.00 .90
❑ 2 Brian Jordan .30 .14
❑ 3 David Justice .50 .23
❑ 4 Jason Kendall .30 .14
❑ 5 Mo Vaughn .30 .14
❑ 6 Jim Edmonds .75 .35
❑ 7 Wade Boggs 1.00 .45
❑ 8 Jeromy Burnitz .30 .14
❑ 9 Todd Hundley .20 .09
❑ 10 Rondell White .30 .14
❑ 11 Cliff Floyd .30 .14
❑ 12 Sean Casey .30 .14
❑ 13 Bernie Williams .75 .35
❑ 14 Dante Bichette .30 .14
❑ 15 Greg Vaughn .30 .14
❑ 16 Andres Galarraga .50 .23
❑ 17 Ray Durham .30 .14
❑ 18 Jim Thome .50 .23
❑ 19 Gary Sheffield .75 .35
❑ 20 Frank Thomas 1.50 .70
❑ 21 Orlando Hernandez .30 .14
❑ 22 Ivan Rodriguez 1.00 .45
❑ 23 Jose Cruz Jr. .30 .14
❑ 24 Jason Giambi .75 .35
❑ 25 Craig Biggio .50 .23
❑ 26 Kerry Wood .30 .14
❑ 27 Manny Ramirez 1.00 .45
❑ 28 Curt Schilling .30 .14
❑ 29 Mike Mussina .75 .35
❑ 30 Tim Salmon .30 .14
❑ 31 Mike Piazza 2.50 1.10
❑ 32 Roberto Alomar .75 .35
❑ 33 Larry Walker .30 .14
❑ 34 Barry Larkin .75 .35
❑ 35 Nomar Garciaparra 2.50 1.10
❑ 36 Paul O'Neill .30 .14
❑ 37 Todd Walker .20 .09
❑ 38 Eric Karros .30 .14
❑ 39 Brad Fullmer .30 .14
❑ 40 John Olerud .30 .14
❑ 41 Todd Helton 1.00 .45
❑ 42 Raul Mondesi .30 .14
❑ 43 Jose Canseco 1.00 .45
❑ 44 Matt Williams .50 .23
❑ 45 Ray Lankford .30 .14
❑ 46 Carlos Delgado .75 .35
❑ 47 Darin Erstad .75 .35
❑ 48 Vladimir Guerrero 1.25 .55
❑ 49 Robin Ventura .30 .14
❑ 50 Alex Rodriguez 2.50 1.10
❑ 51 Vinny Castilla .30 .14
❑ 52 Tony Clark .20 .09
❑ 53 Pedro Martinez 1.00 .45
❑ 54 Rafael Palmeiro .75 .35
❑ 55 Scott Rolen .75 .35
❑ 56 Tino Martinez .30 .14
❑ 57 Tony Gwynn 1.50 .70
❑ 58 Barry Bonds 1.25 .55
❑ 59 Kenny Lofton .30 .14
❑ 60 Javy Lopez .30 .14
❑ 61 Mark Grace .75 .35
❑ 62 Travis Lee .20 .09
❑ 63 Kevin Brown .50 .23
❑ 64 Al Leiter .30 .14
❑ 65 Albert Belle .50 .23
❑ 66 Sammy Sosa 1.50 .70
❑ 67 Greg Maddux 2.00 .90
❑ 68 Mark Kotsay .20 .09
❑ 69 Dmitri Young .30 .14
❑ 70 Mark McGwire 3.00 1.35
❑ 71 Juan Gonzalez .75 .35
❑ 72 Andruw Jones .75 .35
❑ 73 Derek Jeter 3.00 1.35
❑ 74 Randy Johnson 1.00 .45
❑ 75 Cal Ripken 3.00 1.35
❑ 76 Shawn Green .75 .35
❑ 77 Moises Alou .30 .14
❑ 78 Tom Glavine .75 .35
❑ 79 Sandy Alomar Jr. .30 .14
❑ 80 Ken Griffey Jr. 3.00 1.35
❑ 81 Ryan Klesko .30 .14
❑ 82 Jeff Bagwell 1.00 .45
❑ 83 Ben Grieve .30 .14
❑ 84 John Smoltz .30 .14
❑ 85 Roger Clemens 1.50 .70
❑ 86 Ken Griffey Jr. BP 1.50 .70
❑ 87 Roger Clemens BP .75 .35
❑ 88 Derek Jeter BP 1.50 .70
❑ 89 Nomar Garciaparra BP 1.25 .55
❑ 90 Mark McGwire BP 1.50 .70
❑ 91 Sammy Sosa BP .75 .35
❑ 92 Alex Rodriguez BP 1.25 .55
❑ 93 Greg Maddux BP 1.00 .45
❑ 94 Vladimir Guerrero BP .50 .23
❑ 95 Chipper Jones BP 1.00 .45
❑ 96 Kerry Wood BP .30 .14
❑ 97 Ben Grieve BP .30 .14
❑ 98 Tony Gwynn BP .75 .35
❑ 99 Juan Gonzalez BP .30 .14
❑ 100 Mike Piazza BP 1.25 .55
❑ 101 Eric Chavez .30 .14
❑ 102 Billy Koch .30 .14
❑ 103 Dernell Stenson .30 .14
❑ 104 Marlon Anderson .20 .09
❑ 105 Ron Belliard .20 .09
❑ 106 Bruce Chen .20 .09
❑ 107 Carlos Beltran .30 .14
❑ 108 Chad Hermansen .20 .09
❑ 109 Ryan Anderson .30 .14
❑ 110 Michael Barrett .20 .09
❑ 111 Matt Clement .20 .09
❑ 112 Ben Davis .20 .09
❑ 113 Calvin Pickering .20 .09
❑ 114 Brad Penny .30 .14
❑ 115 Paul Konerko .30 .14
❑ 116 Alex Gonzalez .20 .09
❑ 117 George Lombard .20 .09
❑ 118 John Patterson .20 .09
❑ 119 Rob Bell .20 .09
❑ 120 Ruben Mateo .30 .14
❑ 121 Troy Glaus 1.25 .55
❑ 122 Ryan Bradley .20 .09
❑ 123 Carlos Lee .30 .14
❑ 124 Gabe Kapler .30 .14
❑ 125 Ramon Hernandez .20 .09
❑ 126 Carlos Febles .20 .09
❑ 127 Mitch Meluskey .20 .09
❑ 128 Michael Cuddyer .30 .14
❑ 129 Pablo Ozuna .30 .14
❑ 130 Jayson Werth .20 .09
❑ 131 Ricky Ledee .20 .09
❑ 132 Jeremy Giambi .20 .09
❑ 133 Danny Klassen .20 .09
❑ 134 Mark DeRosa .20 .09
❑ 135 Randy Wolf .20 .09
❑ 136 Roy Halladay .20 .09
❑ 137 Derrick Gibson .20 .09
❑ 138 Ben Petrick .20 .09
❑ 139 Warren Morris .20 .09
❑ 140 Lance Berkman .30 .14
❑ 141 Russell Branyan .30 .14
❑ 142 Adrian Beltre .30 .14
❑ 143 Juan Encarnacion .30 .14
❑ 144 Fernando Seguignol .20 .09
❑ 145 Corey Koskie .20 .09
❑ 146 Preston Wilson .30 .14
❑ 147 Homer Bush .20 .09
❑ 148 Daryle Ward .30 .14
❑ 149 Joe McEwing RC .75 .35
❑ 150 Peter Bergeron RC 1.50 .70
❑ 151 Pat Burrell RC 10.00 4.50
❑ 152 Choo Freeman RC 1.25 .55
❑ 153 Matt Belisle RC 1.50 .70
❑ 154 Carlos Pena RC 4.00 1.80
❑ 155 A.J. Burnett RC 1.50 .70
❑ 156 Doug Mientkiewicz RC .75 .35
❑ 157 Sean Burroughs RC 6.00 2.70
❑ 158 Mike Zywica RC .20 .09
❑ 159 Corey Patterson RC 10.00 4.50
❑ 160 Austin Kearns RC 4.00 1.80
❑ 161 Chip Ambres RC 1.25 .55
❑ 162 Kelly Dransfeldt RC .75 .35
❑ 163 Mike Nannini RC 1.25 .55
❑ 164 Mark Mulder RC 2.00 .90
❑ 165 Jason Tyner RC 1.50 .70
❑ 166 Bobby Seay RC 1.25 .55
❑ 167 Alex Escobar RC 4.00 1.80
❑ 168 Nick Johnson RC 4.00 1.80
❑ 169 Alfonso Soriano RC 4.00 1.80
❑ 170 Clayton Andrews RC .75 .35
❑ 171 C.C. Sabathia RC 4.00 1.80
❑ 172 Matt Holliday RC 1.50 .70
❑ 173 Brad Lidge RC .75 .35
❑ 174 Kit Pellow RC .75 .35
❑ 175 J.M. Gold RC 1.00 .45
❑ 176 Roosevelt Brown RC 1.00 .45
❑ 177 Eric Valent RC 2.00 .90
❑ 178 Adam Everett RC 1.25 .55
❑ 179 Jorge Toca RC 1.00 .45
❑ 180 Matt Roney RC 1.00 .45
❑ 181 Andy Brown RC 1.50 .70
❑ 182 Phil Norton RC .75 .35
❑ 183 Mickey Lopez RC .20 .09
❑ 184 Chris George RC 1.50 .70
❑ 185 Arturo McDowell RC 1.00 .45
❑ 186 Jose Fernandez RC .20 .09

| Card | MINT | NRMT |
|---|---|---|
| ❑ 187 Seth Etherton RC | 1.00 | .45 |
| ❑ 188 Josh McKinley RC | 1.00 | .45 |
| ❑ 189 Nate Cornejo RC | 1.00 | .45 |
| ❑ 190 Giuseppe Chiaramonte RC | 1.25 | .55 |
| ❑ 191 Mamon Tucker RC | 1.00 | .45 |
| ❑ 192 Ryan Mills RC | .75 | .35 |
| ❑ 193 Chad Moeller RC | .75 | .35 |
| ❑ 194 Tony Torcato RC | 2.00 | .90 |
| ❑ 195 Jeff Winchester RC | 1.50 | .70 |
| ❑ 196 Rick Elder RC | 1.00 | .45 |
| ❑ 197 Matt Burch RC | .75 | .35 |
| ❑ 198 Jeff Urban RC | .75 | .35 |
| ❑ 199 Chris Jones RC | 1.00 | .45 |
| ❑ 200 Masao Kida RC | .75 | .35 |

## 2000 Bowman's Best

| | MINT | NRMT |
|---|---|---|
| COMPLETE SET (200) | 800.00 | 350.00 |
| COMP.SET w/o RC's (150) | 80.00 | 36.00 |
| COMMON CARD (1-150) | .20 | .09 |
| MINOR STARS 1-150 | .30 | .14 |
| COMMON ROOKIE (151-200) | 10.00 | 4.50 |

| Card | MINT | NRMT |
|---|---|---|
| ❑ 1 Nomar Garciaparra | 2.50 | 1.10 |
| ❑ 2 Chipper Jones | 2.00 | .90 |
| ❑ 3 Tony Clark | .20 | .09 |
| ❑ 4 Bernie Williams | .75 | .35 |
| ❑ 5 Barry Bonds | 1.25 | .55 |
| ❑ 6 Jermaine Dye | .30 | .14 |
| ❑ 7 John Olerud | .30 | .14 |
| ❑ 8 Mike Hampton | .30 | .14 |
| ❑ 9 Cal Ripken | 3.00 | 1.35 |
| ❑ 10 Jeff Bagwell | 1.00 | .45 |
| ❑ 11 Troy Glaus | 1.00 | .45 |
| ❑ 12 J.D. Drew | .75 | .35 |
| ❑ 13 Jeromy Burnitz | .30 | .14 |
| ❑ 14 Carlos Delgado | .75 | .35 |
| ❑ 15 Shawn Green | .75 | .35 |
| ❑ 16 Kevin Millwood | .30 | .14 |
| ❑ 17 Rondell White | .30 | .14 |
| ❑ 18 Scott Rolen | .75 | .35 |
| ❑ 19 Jeff Cirillo | .30 | .14 |
| ❑ 20 Barry Larkin | .75 | .35 |
| ❑ 21 Brian Giles | .30 | .14 |
| ❑ 22 Roger Clemens | 1.50 | .70 |
| ❑ 23 Manny Ramirez | 1.00 | .45 |
| ❑ 24 Alex Gonzalez | .20 | .09 |
| ❑ 25 Mark Grace | .75 | .35 |
| ❑ 26 Fernando Tatis | .30 | .14 |
| ❑ 27 Randy Johnson | 1.00 | .45 |
| ❑ 28 Roger Cedeno | .20 | .09 |
| ❑ 29 Brian Jordan | .30 | .14 |
| ❑ 30 Kevin Brown | .30 | .14 |
| ❑ 31 Greg Vaughn | .30 | .14 |
| ❑ 32 Roberto Alomar | .75 | .35 |
| ❑ 33 Larry Walker | .30 | .14 |
| ❑ 34 Rafael Palmeiro | .75 | .35 |
| ❑ 35 Curt Schilling | .30 | .14 |
| ❑ 36 Orlando Hernandez | .30 | .14 |
| ❑ 37 Todd Walker | .20 | .09 |
| ❑ 38 Juan Gonzalez | .75 | .35 |
| ❑ 39 Sean Casey | .30 | .14 |
| ❑ 40 Tony Gwynn | 1.50 | .70 |
| ❑ 41 Albert Belle | .50 | .23 |
| ❑ 42 Gary Sheffield | .75 | .35 |
| ❑ 43 Michael Barrett | .20 | .09 |
| ❑ 44 Preston Wilson | .30 | .14 |
| ❑ 45 Jim Thome | .50 | .23 |
| ❑ 46 Shannon Stewart | .30 | .14 |
| ❑ 47 Mo Vaughn | .30 | .14 |
| ❑ 48 Ben Grieve | .30 | .14 |
| ❑ 49 Adrian Beltre | .30 | .14 |
| ❑ 50 Sammy Sosa | 1.50 | .70 |
| ❑ 51 Bob Abreu | .30 | .14 |
| ❑ 52 Edgardo Alfonzo | .30 | .14 |
| ❑ 53 Carlos Febles | .20 | .09 |
| ❑ 54 Frank Thomas | 1.50 | .70 |
| ❑ 55 Alex Rodriguez | 2.50 | 1.10 |
| ❑ 56 Cliff Floyd | .30 | .14 |
| ❑ 57 Jose Canseco | 1.00 | .45 |
| ❑ 58 Erubiel Durazo | .30 | .14 |
| ❑ 59 Tim Hudson | .75 | .35 |
| ❑ 60 Craig Biggio | .50 | .23 |
| ❑ 61 Eric Karros | .30 | .14 |
| ❑ 62 Mike Mussina | .75 | .35 |
| ❑ 63 Robin Ventura | .30 | .14 |
| ❑ 64 Carlos Beltran | .30 | .14 |
| ❑ 65 Pedro Martinez | 1.00 | .45 |
| ❑ 66 Gabe Kapler | .30 | .14 |
| ❑ 67 Jason Kendall | .30 | .14 |
| ❑ 68 Derek Jeter | 3.00 | 1.35 |
| ❑ 69 Magglio Ordonez | .30 | .14 |
| ❑ 70 Mike Piazza | 2.50 | 1.10 |
| ❑ 71 Mike Lieberthal | .30 | .14 |
| ❑ 72 Andres Galarraga | .50 | .23 |
| ❑ 73 Raul Mondesi | .30 | .14 |
| ❑ 74 Eric Chavez | .30 | .14 |
| ❑ 75 Greg Maddux | 2.00 | .90 |
| ❑ 76 Matt Williams | .50 | .23 |
| ❑ 77 Kris Benson | .30 | .14 |
| ❑ 78 Ivan Rodriguez | 1.00 | .45 |
| ❑ 79 Pokey Reese | .30 | .14 |
| ❑ 80 Vladimir Guerrero | 1.25 | .55 |
| ❑ 81 Mark McGwire | 3.00 | 1.35 |
| ❑ 82 Vinny Castilla | .30 | .14 |
| ❑ 83 Todd Helton | 1.00 | .45 |
| ❑ 84 Andruw Jones | .75 | .35 |
| ❑ 85 Ken Griffey Jr. | 3.00 | 1.35 |
| ❑ 86 Mark McGwire BP | 1.50 | .70 |
| ❑ 87 Derek Jeter BP | 1.50 | .70 |
| ❑ 88 Chipper Jones BP | 1.00 | .45 |
| ❑ 89 Nomar Garciaparra BP | 1.25 | .55 |
| ❑ 90 Sammy Sosa BP | .75 | .35 |
| ❑ 91 Cal Ripken BP | 1.50 | .70 |
| ❑ 92 Juan Gonzalez BP | .30 | .14 |
| ❑ 93 Alex Rodriguez BP | 1.25 | .55 |
| ❑ 94 Barry Bonds BP | .75 | .35 |
| ❑ 95 Sean Casey BP | .30 | .14 |
| ❑ 96 Vladimir Guerrero BP | .75 | .35 |
| ❑ 97 Mike Piazza BP | 1.25 | .55 |
| ❑ 98 Shawn Green BP | .30 | .14 |
| ❑ 99 Jeff Bagwell BP | .50 | .23 |
| ❑ 100 Ken Griffey Jr. BP | 1.50 | .70 |
| ❑ 101 Rick Ankiel | 1.50 | .70 |
| ❑ 102 John Patterson | .20 | .09 |
| ❑ 103 David Walling | .20 | .09 |
| ❑ 104 Michael Restovich | .30 | .14 |
| ❑ 105 A.J. Burnett | .30 | .14 |
| ❑ 106 Pablo Ozuna | .20 | .09 |
| ❑ 107 Chad Hermansen | .20 | .09 |
| ❑ 108 Choo Freeman | .30 | .14 |
| ❑ 109 Mark Quinn | .30 | .14 |
| ❑ 110 Corey Patterson | 1.25 | .55 |
| ❑ 111 Ramon Ortiz | .30 | .14 |
| ❑ 112 Vernon Wells | .30 | .14 |
| ❑ 113 Milton Bradley | .30 | .14 |
| ❑ 114 Travis Dawkins | .30 | .14 |
| ❑ 115 Sean Burroughs | .75 | .35 |
| ❑ 116 Wily Mo Pena | .30 | .14 |
| ❑ 117 Dee Brown | .30 | .14 |
| ❑ 118 C.C. Sabathia | .30 | .14 |
| ❑ 119 Adam Kennedy | .30 | .14 |
| ❑ 120 Octavio Dotel | .20 | .09 |
| ❑ 121 Kip Wells | .30 | .14 |
| ❑ 122 Ben Petrick | .20 | .09 |
| ❑ 123 Mark Mulder | .30 | .14 |
| ❑ 124 Jason Standridge | .20 | .09 |
| ❑ 125 Adam Piatt | .75 | .35 |
| ❑ 126 Steve Lomasney | .20 | .09 |
| ❑ 127 Jayson Werth | .20 | .09 |
| ❑ 128 Alex Escobar | .30 | .14 |
| ❑ 129 Ryan Anderson | .30 | .14 |
| ❑ 130 Adam Dunn | .30 | .14 |
| ❑ 131 Ted Lilly | .20 | .09 |
| ❑ 132 Brad Penny | .30 | .14 |
| ❑ 133 Daryle Ward | .30 | .14 |
| ❑ 134 Eric Munson | .75 | .35 |
| ❑ 135 Nick Johnson | .30 | .14 |
| ❑ 136 Jason Jennings | .20 | .09 |
| ❑ 137 Tim Raines Jr. | .30 | .14 |
| ❑ 138 Ruben Mateo | .30 | .14 |
| ❑ 139 Jack Cust | .30 | .14 |
| ❑ 140 Rafael Furcal | 2.00 | .90 |
| ❑ 141 Eric Gagne | .20 | .09 |
| ❑ 142 Tony Armas Jr. | .30 | .14 |
| ❑ 143 Mike Paradis | .20 | .09 |
| ❑ 144 Peter Bergeron | .20 | .09 |
| ❑ 145 Alfonso Soriano | .30 | .14 |
| ❑ 146 Josh Hamilton | 1.25 | .55 |
| ❑ 147 Michael Cuddyer | .30 | .14 |
| ❑ 148 Jay Gehrke | .20 | .09 |
| ❑ 149 Josh Girdley | .20 | .09 |
| ❑ 150 Pat Burrell | 1.25 | .55 |
| ❑ 151 Brett Myers RC | 12.00 | 5.50 |
| ❑ 152 Scott Seabol RC | 10.00 | 4.50 |
| ❑ 153 Keith Reed RC | 12.00 | 5.50 |
| ❑ 154 Francisco Rodriguez RC | 10.00 | 4.50 |
| ❑ 155 Barry Zito RC | 60.00 | 27.00 |
| ❑ 156 Pat Manning RC | 15.00 | 6.75 |
| ❑ 157 Ben Christensen RC | 15.00 | 6.75 |
| ❑ 158 Corey Myers RC | 10.00 | 4.50 |
| ❑ 159 Wascar Serrano RC | 10.00 | 4.50 |
| ❑ 160 Wes Anderson RC | 12.00 | 5.50 |
| ❑ 161 Andy Tracy RC | 10.00 | 4.50 |
| ❑ 162 Cesar Saba RC | 12.00 | 5.50 |
| ❑ 163 Mike Lamb RC | 12.00 | 5.50 |
| ❑ 164 Bobby Bradley RC | 30.00 | 13.50 |
| ❑ 165 Vince Faison RC | 15.00 | 6.75 |
| ❑ 166 Ty Howington RC | 12.00 | 5.50 |
| ❑ 167 Ken Harvey RC | 15.00 | 6.75 |
| ❑ 168 Josh Kalinowski RC | 10.00 | 4.50 |
| ❑ 169 Ruben Salazar RC | 15.00 | 6.75 |
| ❑ 170 Aaron Rowand RC | 15.00 | 6.75 |
| ❑ 171 Ramon Santiago RC | 12.00 | 5.50 |
| ❑ 172 Scott Sobkowiak RC | 10.00 | 4.50 |
| ❑ 173 Lyle Overbay RC | 20.00 | 9.00 |
| ❑ 174 Rico Washington RC | 10.00 | 4.50 |
| ❑ 175 Rick Asadoorian RC | 40.00 | 18.00 |
| ❑ 176 Matt Ginter RC | 10.00 | 4.50 |
| ❑ 177 Jason Stumm RC | 12.00 | 5.50 |
| ❑ 178 B.J. Garbe RC | 20.00 | 9.00 |
| ❑ 179 Mike MacDougal RC | 10.00 | 4.50 |
| ❑ 180 Ryan Christianson RC | 15.00 | 6.75 |
| ❑ 181 Kurt Ainsworth RC | 20.00 | 9.00 |
| ❑ 182 Brad Baisley RC | 10.00 | 4.50 |
| ❑ 183 Ben Broussard RC | 30.00 | 13.50 |
| ❑ 184 Aaron McNeal RC | 15.00 | 6.75 |
| ❑ 185 John Sneed RC | 10.00 | 4.50 |
| ❑ 186 Junior Brignac RC | 10.00 | 4.50 |
| ❑ 187 Chance Caple RC | 10.00 | 4.50 |
| ❑ 188 Scott Downs RC | 10.00 | 4.50 |
| ❑ 189 Matt Cepicky RC | 10.00 | 4.50 |
| ❑ 190 Chin-Feng Chen RC | 60.00 | 27.00 |
| ❑ 191 Johan Santana RC | 10.00 | 4.50 |
| ❑ 192 Brad Baker RC | 15.00 | 6.75 |
| ❑ 193 Jason Repko RC | 12.00 | 5.50 |
| ❑ 194 Craig Dingman RC | 10.00 | 4.50 |
| ❑ 195 Chris Wakeland RC | 10.00 | 4.50 |
| ❑ 196 Rogelio Arias RC | 10.00 | 4.50 |
| ❑ 197 Luis Matos RC | 15.00 | 6.75 |
| ❑ 198 Robert Ramsay | 10.00 | 4.50 |
| ❑ 199 Willie Bloomquist RC | 30.00 | 13.50 |
| ❑ 200 Tony Pena Jr. RC | 12.00 | 5.50 |

## 1996 Circa

| | MINT | NRMT |
|---|---|---|
| COMPLETE SET (200) | 25.00 | 11.00 |

| Card | MINT | NRMT |
|---|---|---|
| ❑ 1 Roberto Alomar | .40 | .18 |
| ❑ 2 Brady Anderson | .15 | .07 |
| ❑ 3 Rocky Coppinger RC | .40 | .18 |
| ❑ 4 Eddie Murray | .40 | .18 |
| ❑ 5 Mike Mussina | .40 | .18 |
| ❑ 6 Randy Myers | .10 | .05 |
| ❑ 7 Rafael Palmeiro | .40 | .18 |
| ❑ 8 Cal Ripken | 1.50 | .70 |
| ❑ 9 Jose Canseco | .50 | .23 |

| | No. | Player | Price 1 | Price 2 |
|---|---|---|---|---|
| ❑ | 10 | Roger Clemens | .75 | .35 |
| ❑ | 11 | Mike Greenwell | .10 | .05 |
| ❑ | 12 | Tim Naehring | .10 | .05 |
| ❑ | 13 | John Valentin | .10 | .05 |
| ❑ | 14 | Mo Vaughn | .15 | .07 |
| ❑ | 15 | Tim Wakefield | .10 | .05 |
| ❑ | 16 | Jim Abbott | .15 | .07 |
| ❑ | 17 | Garret Anderson | .15 | .07 |
| ❑ | 18 | Jim Edmonds | .40 | .18 |
| ❑ | 19 | Darin Erstad RC | 3.00 | 1.35 |
| ❑ | 20 | Chuck Finley | .15 | .07 |
| ❑ | 21 | Troy Percival | .10 | .05 |
| ❑ | 22 | Tim Salmon | .15 | .07 |
| ❑ | 23 | J.T. Snow | .15 | .07 |
| ❑ | 24 | Wilson Alvarez | .10 | .05 |
| ❑ | 25 | Harold Baines | .15 | .07 |
| ❑ | 26 | Ray Durham | .15 | .07 |
| ❑ | 27 | Alex Fernandez | .10 | .05 |
| ❑ | 28 | Tony Phillips | .10 | .05 |
| ❑ | 29 | Frank Thomas | .75 | .35 |
| ❑ | 30 | Robin Ventura | .15 | .07 |
| ❑ | 31 | Sandy Alomar Jr. | .15 | .07 |
| ❑ | 32 | Albert Belle | .25 | .11 |
| ❑ | 33 | Kenny Lofton | .15 | .07 |
| ❑ | 34 | Dennis Martinez | .15 | .07 |
| ❑ | 35 | Jose Mesa | .10 | .05 |
| ❑ | 36 | Charles Nagy | .10 | .05 |
| ❑ | 37 | Manny Ramirez | .50 | .23 |
| ❑ | 38 | Jim Thome | .25 | .11 |
| ❑ | 39 | Travis Fryman | .15 | .07 |
| ❑ | 40 | Bob Higginson | .15 | .07 |
| ❑ | 41 | Melvin Nieves | .10 | .05 |
| ❑ | 42 | Alan Trammell | .25 | .11 |
| ❑ | 43 | Kevin Appier | .15 | .07 |
| ❑ | 44 | Johnny Damon | .25 | .11 |
| ❑ | 45 | Keith Lockhart | .10 | .05 |
| ❑ | 46 | Jeff Montgomery | .10 | .05 |
| ❑ | 47 | Joe Randa | .10 | .05 |
| ❑ | 48 | Bip Roberts | .10 | .05 |
| ❑ | 49 | Ricky Bones | .10 | .05 |
| ❑ | 50 | Jeff Cirillo | .15 | .07 |
| ❑ | 51 | Marc Newfield | .10 | .05 |
| ❑ | 52 | Dave Nilsson | .10 | .05 |
| ❑ | 53 | Kevin Seitzer | .10 | .05 |
| ❑ | 54 | Ron Coomer | .10 | .05 |
| ❑ | 55 | Marty Cordova | .10 | .05 |
| ❑ | 56 | Roberto Kelly | .10 | .05 |
| ❑ | 57 | Chuck Knoblauch | .15 | .07 |
| ❑ | 58 | Paul Molitor | .40 | .18 |
| ❑ | 59 | Kirby Puckett | 1.00 | .45 |
| ❑ | 60 | Scott Stahoviak | .10 | .05 |
| ❑ | 61 | Wade Boggs | .50 | .23 |
| ❑ | 62 | David Cone | .15 | .07 |
| ❑ | 63 | Cecil Fielder | .15 | .07 |
| ❑ | 64 | Dwight Gooden | .15 | .07 |
| ❑ | 65 | Derek Jeter | 1.50 | .70 |
| ❑ | 66 | Tino Martinez | .15 | .07 |
| ❑ | 67 | Paul O'Neill | .15 | .07 |
| ❑ | 68 | Andy Pettitte | .15 | .07 |
| ❑ | 69 | Ruben Rivera | .10 | .05 |
| ❑ | 70 | Bernie Williams | .40 | .18 |
| ❑ | 71 | Geronimo Berroa | .10 | .05 |
| ❑ | 72 | Jason Giambi | .40 | .18 |
| ❑ | 73 | Mark McGwire | 1.50 | .70 |
| ❑ | 74 | Terry Steinbach | .10 | .05 |
| ❑ | 75 | Todd Van Poppel | .10 | .05 |
| ❑ | 76 | Jay Buhner | .15 | .07 |
| ❑ | 77 | Norm Charlton | .10 | .05 |
| ❑ | 78 | Ken Griffey Jr. | 1.50 | .70 |
| ❑ | 79 | Randy Johnson | .50 | .23 |
| ❑ | 80 | Edgar Martinez | .25 | .11 |
| ❑ | 81 | Alex Rodriguez | 1.25 | .55 |
| ❑ | 82 | Paul Sorrento | .10 | .05 |
| ❑ | 83 | Dan Wilson | .10 | .05 |
| ❑ | 84 | Will Clark | .40 | .18 |
| ❑ | 85 | Kevin Elster | .10 | .05 |
| ❑ | 86 | Juan Gonzalez | .40 | .18 |
| ❑ | 87 | Rusty Greer | .15 | .07 |
| ❑ | 88 | Ken Hill | .10 | .05 |
| ❑ | 89 | Mark McLemore | .10 | .05 |
| ❑ | 90 | Dean Palmer | .15 | .07 |
| ❑ | 91 | Roger Pavlik | .10 | .05 |
| ❑ | 92 | Ivan Rodriguez | .50 | .23 |
| ❑ | 93 | Joe Carter | .15 | .07 |
| ❑ | 94 | Carlos Delgado | .40 | .18 |
| ❑ | 95 | Juan Guzman | .10 | .05 |
| ❑ | 96 | John Olerud | .15 | .07 |
| ❑ | 97 | Ed Sprague | .10 | .05 |
| ❑ | 98 | Jermaine Dye | .15 | .07 |
| ❑ | 99 | Tom Glavine | .40 | .18 |
| ❑ | 100 | Marquis Grissom | .10 | .05 |
| ❑ | 101 | Andruw Jones | 1.00 | .45 |
| ❑ | 102 | Chipper Jones | 1.00 | .45 |
| ❑ | 103 | David Justice | .25 | .11 |
| ❑ | 104 | Ryan Klesko | .15 | .07 |
| ❑ | 105 | Greg Maddux | 1.00 | .45 |
| ❑ | 106 | Fred McGriff | .25 | .11 |
| ❑ | 107 | John Smoltz | .15 | .07 |
| ❑ | 108 | Brant Brown | .10 | .05 |
| ❑ | 109 | Mark Grace | .40 | .18 |
| ❑ | 110 | Brian McRae | .10 | .05 |
| ❑ | 111 | Ryne Sandberg | .50 | .23 |
| ❑ | 112 | Sammy Sosa | .75 | .35 |
| ❑ | 113 | Steve Trachsel | .10 | .05 |
| ❑ | 114 | Bret Boone | .15 | .07 |
| ❑ | 115 | Eric Davis | .15 | .07 |
| ❑ | 116 | Steve Gibralter | .10 | .05 |
| ❑ | 117 | Barry Larkin | .40 | .18 |
| ❑ | 118 | Reggie Sanders | .10 | .05 |
| ❑ | 119 | John Smiley | .10 | .05 |
| ❑ | 120 | Dante Bichette | .15 | .07 |
| ❑ | 121 | Ellis Burks | .15 | .07 |
| ❑ | 122 | Vinny Castilla | .15 | .07 |
| ❑ | 123 | Andres Galarraga | .25 | .11 |
| ❑ | 124 | Larry Walker | .15 | .07 |
| ❑ | 125 | Eric Young | .10 | .05 |
| ❑ | 126 | Kevin Brown | .25 | .11 |
| ❑ | 127 | Greg Colbrunn | .10 | .05 |
| ❑ | 128 | Jeff Conine | .10 | .05 |
| ❑ | 129 | Charles Johnson | .15 | .07 |
| ❑ | 130 | Al Leiter | .15 | .07 |
| ❑ | 131 | Gary Sheffield | .40 | .18 |
| ❑ | 132 | Devon White | .15 | .07 |
| ❑ | 133 | Jeff Bagwell | .50 | .23 |
| ❑ | 134 | Derek Bell | .10 | .05 |
| ❑ | 135 | Craig Biggio | .25 | .11 |
| ❑ | 136 | Doug Drabek | .10 | .05 |
| ❑ | 137 | Brian L.Hunter | .10 | .05 |
| ❑ | 138 | Darryl Kile | .15 | .07 |
| ❑ | 139 | Shane Reynolds | .10 | .05 |
| ❑ | 140 | Brett Butler | .15 | .07 |
| ❑ | 141 | Eric Karros | .15 | .07 |
| ❑ | 142 | Ramon Martinez | .10 | .05 |
| ❑ | 143 | Raul Mondesi | .15 | .07 |
| ❑ | 144 | Hideo Nomo | .40 | .18 |
| ❑ | 145 | Chan Ho Park | .15 | .07 |
| ❑ | 146 | Mike Piazza | 1.25 | .55 |
| ❑ | 147 | Moises Alou | .15 | .07 |
| ❑ | 148 | Yamil Benitez | .10 | .05 |
| ❑ | 149 | Mark Grudzielanek | .10 | .05 |
| ❑ | 150 | Pedro Martinez | .50 | .23 |
| ❑ | 151 | Henry Rodriguez | .10 | .05 |
| ❑ | 152 | David Segui | .10 | .05 |
| ❑ | 153 | Rondell White | .15 | .07 |
| ❑ | 154 | Carlos Baerga | .10 | .05 |
| ❑ | 155 | John Franco | .15 | .07 |
| ❑ | 156 | Bernard Gilkey | .10 | .05 |
| ❑ | 157 | Todd Hundley | .10 | .05 |
| ❑ | 158 | Jason Isringhausen | .15 | .07 |
| ❑ | 159 | Lance Johnson | .10 | .05 |
| ❑ | 160 | Alex Ochoa | .10 | .05 |
| ❑ | 161 | Rey Ordonez | .15 | .07 |
| ❑ | 162 | Paul Wilson | .10 | .05 |
| ❑ | 163 | Ron Blazier | .10 | .05 |
| ❑ | 164 | Ricky Bottalico | .10 | .05 |
| ❑ | 165 | Jim Eisenreich | .10 | .05 |
| ❑ | 166 | Pete Incaviglia | .10 | .05 |
| ❑ | 167 | Mickey Morandini | .10 | .05 |
| ❑ | 168 | Ricky Otero | .10 | .05 |
| ❑ | 169 | Curt Schilling | .15 | .07 |
| ❑ | 170 | Jay Bell | .15 | .07 |
| ❑ | 171 | Charlie Hayes | .10 | .05 |
| ❑ | 172 | Jason Kendall | .15 | .07 |
| ❑ | 173 | Jeff King | .10 | .05 |
| ❑ | 174 | Al Martin | .10 | .05 |
| ❑ | 175 | Alan Benes | .10 | .05 |
| ❑ | 176 | Royce Clayton | .10 | .05 |
| ❑ | 177 | Brian Jordan | .15 | .07 |
| ❑ | 178 | Ray Lankford | .15 | .07 |
| ❑ | 179 | John Mabry | .10 | .05 |
| ❑ | 180 | Willie McGee | .15 | .07 |
| ❑ | 181 | Ozzie Smith | .50 | .23 |
| ❑ | 182 | Todd Stottlemyre | .10 | .05 |
| ❑ | 183 | Andy Ashby | .10 | .05 |
| ❑ | 184 | Ken Caminiti | .15 | .07 |
| ❑ | 185 | Steve Finley | .15 | .07 |
| ❑ | 186 | Tony Gwynn | .75 | .35 |
| ❑ | 187 | Rickey Henderson | .50 | .23 |
| ❑ | 188 | Wally Joyner | .15 | .07 |
| ❑ | 189 | Fernando Valenzuela | .15 | .07 |
| ❑ | 190 | Greg Vaughn | .15 | .07 |
| ❑ | 191 | Rod Beck | .10 | .05 |
| ❑ | 192 | Barry Bonds | .60 | .25 |
| ❑ | 193 | Shawon Dunston | .10 | .05 |
| ❑ | 194 | Chris Singleton RC | .75 | .35 |
| ❑ | 195 | Robby Thompson | .10 | .05 |
| ❑ | 196 | Matt Williams | .25 | .11 |
| ❑ | 197 | Barry Bonds CL | .25 | .11 |
| ❑ | 198 | Ken Griffey Jr. CL | .75 | .35 |
| ❑ | 199 | Cal Ripken CL | .75 | .35 |
| ❑ | 200 | Frank Thomas CL | .50 | .23 |

## 1997 Circa

| | | | MINT | NRMT |
|---|---|---|---|---|
| | | COMPLETE SET (400) | 25.00 | 11.00 |
| ❑ | 1 | Kenny Lofton | .25 | .11 |
| ❑ | 2 | Ray Durham | .25 | .11 |
| ❑ | 3 | Mariano Rivera | .25 | .11 |
| ❑ | 4 | Jon Lieber | .10 | .05 |
| ❑ | 5 | Tim Salmon | .25 | .11 |
| ❑ | 6 | Mark Grudzielanek | .10 | .05 |
| ❑ | 7 | Neifi Perez | .10 | .05 |
| ❑ | 8 | Cal Ripken | 1.50 | .70 |
| ❑ | 9 | John Olerud | .25 | .11 |
| ❑ | 10 | Edgar Renteria | .25 | .11 |
| ❑ | 11 | Jose Rosado | .10 | .05 |
| ❑ | 12 | Mickey Morandini | .10 | .05 |
| ❑ | 13 | Orlando Miller | .10 | .05 |
| ❑ | 14 | Ben McDonald | .10 | .05 |
| ❑ | 15 | Hideo Nomo | .40 | .18 |
| ❑ | 16 | Fred McGriff | .30 | .14 |
| ❑ | 17 | Sean Berry | .10 | .05 |
| ❑ | 18 | Roger Pavlik | .10 | .05 |
| ❑ | 19 | Aaron Sele | .25 | .11 |
| ❑ | 20 | Joey Hamilton | .10 | .05 |
| ❑ | 21 | Roger Clemens | .75 | .35 |
| ❑ | 22 | Jose Herrera | .10 | .05 |
| ❑ | 23 | Ryne Sandberg | .50 | .23 |
| ❑ | 24 | Ken Griffey Jr. | 1.50 | .70 |
| ❑ | 25 | Barry Bonds | .60 | .25 |

| | | | |
|---|---|---|---|
| ❑ 26 | Dan Naulty | .10 | .05 |
| ❑ 27 | Wade Boggs | .50 | .23 |
| ❑ 28 | Ray Lankford | .25 | .11 |
| ❑ 29 | Rico Brogna | .10 | .05 |
| ❑ 30 | Wally Joyner | .25 | .11 |
| ❑ 31 | F.P. Santangelo | .10 | .05 |
| ❑ 32 | Vinny Castilla | .25 | .11 |
| ❑ 33 | Eddie Murray | .40 | .18 |
| ❑ 34 | Kevin Elster | .10 | .05 |
| ❑ 35 | Mike Macfarlane | .10 | .05 |
| ❑ 36 | Jeff Kent | .30 | .14 |
| ❑ 37 | Orlando Merced | .10 | .05 |
| ❑ 38 | Jason Isringhausen | .10 | .05 |
| ❑ 39 | Chad Ogea | .10 | .05 |
| ❑ 40 | Greg Gagne | .10 | .05 |
| ❑ 41 | Curt Lyons | .10 | .05 |
| ❑ 42 | Mo Vaughn | .25 | .11 |
| ❑ 43 | Rusty Greer | .25 | .11 |
| ❑ 44 | Shane Reynolds | .10 | .05 |
| ❑ 45 | Frank Thomas | .75 | .35 |
| ❑ 46 | Chris Hoiles | .10 | .05 |
| ❑ 47 | Scott Sanders | .10 | .05 |
| ❑ 48 | Mark Lemke | .10 | .05 |
| ❑ 49 | Fernando Vina | .10 | .05 |
| ❑ 50 | Mark McGwire | 1.50 | .70 |
| ❑ 51 | Bernie Williams | .40 | .18 |
| ❑ 52 | Bobby Higginson | .25 | .11 |
| ❑ 53 | Kevin Tapani | .10 | .05 |
| ❑ 54 | Rich Becker | .10 | .05 |
| ❑ 55 | Felix Heredia RC | .25 | .11 |
| ❑ 56 | Delino DeShields | .10 | .05 |
| ❑ 57 | Rick Wilkins | .10 | .05 |
| ❑ 58 | Edgardo Alfonzo | .25 | .11 |
| ❑ 59 | Brett Butler | .25 | .11 |
| ❑ 60 | Ed Sprague | .10 | .05 |
| ❑ 61 | Joe Randa | .10 | .05 |
| ❑ 62 | Ugueth Urbina | .25 | .11 |
| ❑ 63 | Todd Greene | .10 | .05 |
| ❑ 64 | Devon White | .25 | .11 |
| ❑ 65 | Bruce Ruffin | .10 | .05 |
| ❑ 66 | Mark Gardner | .10 | .05 |
| ❑ 67 | Omar Vizquel | .25 | .11 |
| ❑ 68 | Luis Gonzalez | .25 | .11 |
| ❑ 69 | Tom Glavine | .40 | .18 |
| ❑ 70 | Cal Eldred | .10 | .05 |
| ❑ 71 | Wm. VanLandingham | .10 | .05 |
| ❑ 72 | Jay Buhner | .25 | .11 |
| ❑ 73 | James Baldwin | .25 | .11 |
| ❑ 74 | Robin Jennings | .10 | .05 |
| ❑ 75 | Terry Steinbach | .10 | .05 |
| ❑ 76 | Billy Taylor | .10 | .05 |
| ❑ 77 | Armando Benitez | .10 | .05 |
| ❑ 78 | Joe Girardi | .10 | .05 |
| ❑ 79 | Jay Bell | .25 | .11 |
| ❑ 80 | Damon Buford | .10 | .05 |
| ❑ 81 | Deion Sanders | .25 | .11 |
| ❑ 82 | Bill Haselman | .10 | .05 |
| ❑ 83 | John Flaherty | .10 | .05 |
| ❑ 84 | Todd Stottlemyre | .10 | .05 |
| ❑ 85 | J.T. Snow | .25 | .11 |
| ❑ 86 | Felipe Lira | .10 | .05 |
| ❑ 87 | Steve Avery | .10 | .05 |
| ❑ 88 | Trey Beamon | .10 | .05 |
| ❑ 89 | Alex Gonzalez | .10 | .05 |
| ❑ 90 | Mark Clark | .10 | .05 |
| ❑ 91 | Shane Andrews | .10 | .05 |
| ❑ 92 | Randy Myers | .10 | .05 |
| ❑ 93 | Gary Gaetti | .25 | .11 |
| ❑ 94 | Jeff Blauser | .10 | .05 |
| ❑ 95 | Tony Batista | .40 | .18 |
| ❑ 96 | Todd Worrell | .10 | .05 |
| ❑ 97 | Jim Edmonds | .40 | .18 |
| ❑ 98 | Eric Young | .10 | .05 |
| ❑ 99 | Roberto Kelly | .10 | .05 |
| ❑ 100 | Alex Rodriguez | 1.25 | .55 |
| ❑ 101 | Julio Franco | .25 | .11 |
| ❑ 102 | Jeff Bagwell | .50 | .23 |
| ❑ 103 | Bobby Witt | .10 | .05 |
| ❑ 104 | Tino Martinez | .25 | .11 |
| ❑ 105 | Shannon Stewart | .25 | .11 |
| ❑ 106 | Brian Banks | .10 | .05 |
| ❑ 107 | Eddie Taubensee | .10 | .05 |
| ❑ 108 | Terry Mulholland | .10 | .05 |
| ❑ 109 | Lyle Mouton | .10 | .05 |
| ❑ 110 | Jeff Conine | .10 | .05 |
| ❑ 111 | Johnny Damon | .25 | .11 |
| ❑ 112 | Quilvio Veras | .10 | .05 |
| ❑ 113 | Wilton Guerrero | .10 | .05 |
| ❑ 114 | Dmitri Young | .25 | .11 |
| ❑ 115 | Garret Anderson | .25 | .11 |
| ❑ 116 | Bill Pulsipher | .10 | .05 |
| ❑ 117 | Jacob Brumfield | .10 | .05 |
| ❑ 118 | Mike Lansing | .10 | .05 |
| ❑ 119 | Jose Canseco | .50 | .23 |
| ❑ 120 | Mike Bordick | .10 | .05 |
| ❑ 121 | Kevin Stocker | .10 | .05 |
| ❑ 122 | Frankie Rodriguez | .10 | .05 |
| ❑ 123 | Mike Cameron | .25 | .11 |
| ❑ 124 | Tony Womack RC | .50 | .23 |
| ❑ 125 | Bret Boone | .25 | .11 |
| ❑ 126 | Moises Alou | .25 | .11 |
| ❑ 127 | Tim Naehring | .10 | .05 |
| ❑ 128 | Brant Brown | .10 | .05 |
| ❑ 129 | Todd Zeile | .10 | .05 |
| ❑ 130 | Dave Nilsson | .10 | .05 |
| ❑ 131 | Donne Wall | .10 | .05 |
| ❑ 132 | Jose Mesa | .10 | .05 |
| ❑ 133 | Mark McLemore | .10 | .05 |
| ❑ 134 | Mike Stanton | .10 | .05 |
| ❑ 135 | Dan Wilson | .10 | .05 |
| ❑ 136 | Jose Offerman | .10 | .05 |
| ❑ 137 | David Justice | .30 | .14 |
| ❑ 138 | Kirt Manwaring | .10 | .05 |
| ❑ 139 | Raul Casanova | .10 | .05 |
| ❑ 140 | Ron Coomer | .10 | .05 |
| ❑ 141 | Dave Hollins | .10 | .05 |
| ❑ 142 | Shawn Estes | .25 | .11 |
| ❑ 143 | Darren Daulton | .25 | .11 |
| ❑ 144 | Turk Wendell | .10 | .05 |
| ❑ 145 | Darrin Fletcher | .10 | .05 |
| ❑ 146 | Marquis Grissom | .10 | .05 |
| ❑ 147 | Andy Benes | .10 | .05 |
| ❑ 148 | Nomar Garciaparra | 1.25 | .55 |
| ❑ 149 | Andy Pettitte | .25 | .11 |
| ❑ 150 | Tony Gwynn | .75 | .35 |
| ❑ 151 | Robb Nen | .10 | .05 |
| ❑ 152 | Kevin Seitzer | .10 | .05 |
| ❑ 153 | Ariel Prieto | .10 | .05 |
| ❑ 154 | Scott Karl | .10 | .05 |
| ❑ 155 | Carlos Baerga | .10 | .05 |
| ❑ 156 | Wilson Alvarez | .10 | .05 |
| ❑ 157 | Thomas Howard | .10 | .05 |
| ❑ 158 | Kevin Appier | .25 | .11 |
| ❑ 159 | Russ Davis | .10 | .05 |
| ❑ 160 | Justin Thompson | .10 | .05 |
| ❑ 161 | Pete Schourek | .10 | .05 |
| ❑ 162 | John Burkett | .10 | .05 |
| ❑ 163 | Roberto Alomar | .40 | .18 |
| ❑ 164 | Darren Holmes | .10 | .05 |
| ❑ 165 | Travis Miller | .10 | .05 |
| ❑ 166 | Mark Langston | .25 | .11 |
| ❑ 167 | Juan Guzman | .10 | .05 |
| ❑ 168 | Pedro Astacio | .10 | .05 |
| ❑ 169 | Mark Johnson | .10 | .05 |
| ❑ 170 | Mark Leiter | .10 | .05 |
| ❑ 171 | Heathcliff Slocumb | .10 | .05 |
| ❑ 172 | Dante Bichette | .25 | .11 |
| ❑ 173 | Brian Giles RC | 1.50 | .70 |
| ❑ 174 | Paul Wilson | .10 | .05 |
| ❑ 175 | Eric Davis | .25 | .11 |
| ❑ 176 | Charles Johnson | .25 | .11 |
| ❑ 177 | Willie Greene | .10 | .05 |
| ❑ 178 | Geronimo Berroa | .10 | .05 |
| ❑ 179 | Mariano Duncan | .10 | .05 |
| ❑ 180 | Robert Person | .10 | .05 |
| ❑ 181 | David Segui | .10 | .05 |
| ❑ 182 | Ozzie Guillen | .10 | .05 |
| ❑ 183 | Osvaldo Fernandez | .10 | .05 |
| ❑ 184 | Dean Palmer | .25 | .11 |
| ❑ 185 | Bob Wickman | .10 | .05 |
| ❑ 186 | Eric Karros | .25 | .11 |
| ❑ 187 | Travis Fryman | .25 | .11 |
| ❑ 188 | Andy Ashby | .10 | .05 |
| ❑ 189 | Scott Stahoviak | .10 | .05 |
| ❑ 190 | Norm Charlton | .10 | .05 |
| ❑ 191 | Craig Paquette | .10 | .05 |
| ❑ 192 | John Smoltz UER | .25 | .11 |
| | (Name spelled "Smotlz" on back) | | |
| ❑ 193 | Orel Hershiser | .25 | .11 |
| ❑ 194 | Glenallen Hill | .10 | .05 |
| ❑ 195 | George Arias | .10 | .05 |
| ❑ 196 | Brian Jordan | .25 | .11 |
| ❑ 197 | Greg Vaughn | .25 | .11 |
| ❑ 198 | Rafael Palmeiro | .40 | .18 |
| ❑ 199 | Darryl Kile | .25 | .11 |
| ❑ 200 | Derek Jeter | 1.50 | .70 |
| ❑ 201 | Jose Vizcaino | .10 | .05 |
| ❑ 202 | Rick Aguilera | .10 | .05 |
| ❑ 203 | Jason Schmidt | .10 | .05 |
| ❑ 204 | Trot Nixon | .25 | .11 |
| ❑ 205 | Tom Pagnozzi | .10 | .05 |
| ❑ 206 | Mark Wohlers | .10 | .05 |
| ❑ 207 | Lance Johnson | .10 | .05 |
| ❑ 208 | Carlos Delgado | .40 | .18 |
| ❑ 209 | Cliff Floyd | .25 | .11 |
| ❑ 210 | Kent Mercker | .10 | .05 |
| ❑ 211 | Matt Mieske | .10 | .05 |
| ❑ 212 | Ismael Valdes | .10 | .05 |
| ❑ 213 | Shawon Dunston | .10 | .05 |
| ❑ 214 | Melvin Nieves | .10 | .05 |
| ❑ 215 | Tony Phillips | .10 | .05 |
| ❑ 216 | Scott Spiezio | .10 | .05 |
| ❑ 217 | Michael Tucker | .10 | .05 |
| ❑ 218 | Matt Williams | .30 | .14 |
| ❑ 219 | Ricky Otero | .10 | .05 |
| ❑ 220 | Kevin Ritz | .10 | .05 |
| ❑ 221 | Darryl Strawberry | .25 | .11 |
| ❑ 222 | Troy Percival | .10 | .05 |
| ❑ 223 | Eugene Kingsale | .25 | .11 |
| ❑ 224 | Julian Tavarez | .10 | .05 |
| ❑ 225 | Jermaine Dye | .25 | .11 |
| ❑ 226 | Jason Kendall | .25 | .11 |
| ❑ 227 | Sterling Hitchcock | .10 | .05 |
| ❑ 228 | Jeff Cirillo | .25 | .11 |
| ❑ 229 | Roberto Hernandez | .10 | .05 |
| ❑ 230 | Ricky Bottalico | .10 | .05 |
| ❑ 231 | Bobby Bonilla | .25 | .11 |
| ❑ 232 | Edgar Martinez | .30 | .14 |
| ❑ 233 | John Valentin | .10 | .05 |
| ❑ 234 | Ellis Burks | .25 | .11 |
| ❑ 235 | Benito Santiago | .10 | .05 |
| ❑ 236 | Terrell Wade | .10 | .05 |
| ❑ 237 | Armando Reynoso | .10 | .05 |
| ❑ 238 | Danny Graves | .10 | .05 |
| ❑ 239 | Ken Hill | .10 | .05 |
| ❑ 240 | Dennis Eckersley | .25 | .11 |
| ❑ 241 | Darin Erstad | .50 | .23 |
| ❑ 242 | Lee Smith UER | .25 | .11 |
| | Position 2b | | |
| ❑ 243 | Cecil Fielder | .25 | .11 |
| ❑ 244 | Tony Clark | .10 | .05 |
| ❑ 245 | Scott Erickson | .10 | .05 |
| ❑ 246 | Bob Abreu | .25 | .11 |
| ❑ 247 | Ruben Sierra | .10 | .05 |
| ❑ 248 | Chili Davis | .25 | .11 |
| ❑ 249 | Darryl Hamilton | .10 | .05 |
| ❑ 250 | Albert Belle | .30 | .14 |
| ❑ 251 | Todd Hollandsworth | .10 | .05 |
| ❑ 252 | Terry Adams | .10 | .05 |
| ❑ 253 | Rey Ordonez | .10 | .05 |
| ❑ 254 | Steve Finley | .25 | .11 |
| ❑ 255 | Jose Valentin | .10 | .05 |
| ❑ 256 | Royce Clayton | .10 | .05 |
| ❑ 257 | Sandy Alomar Jr. | .25 | .11 |
| ❑ 258 | Mike Lieberthal | .25 | .11 |
| ❑ 259 | Ivan Rodriguez | .50 | .23 |
| ❑ 260 | Rod Beck | .10 | .05 |
| ❑ 261 | Ron Karkovice | .10 | .05 |
| ❑ 262 | Mark Gubicza | .10 | .05 |
| ❑ 263 | Chris Holt | .10 | .05 |
| ❑ 264 | Jaime Bluma UER | .10 | .05 |
| | (Name spelled "Jamie" on front and back) | | |
| ❑ 265 | Francisco Cordova | .10 | .05 |
| ❑ 266 | Javy Lopez | .25 | .11 |
| ❑ 267 | Reggie Jefferson | .10 | .05 |
| ❑ 268 | Kevin Brown | .30 | .14 |
| ❑ 269 | Scott Brosius | .25 | .11 |
| ❑ 270 | Dwight Gooden | .25 | .11 |
| ❑ 271 | Marty Cordova | .10 | .05 |
| ❑ 272 | Jeff Brantley | .10 | .05 |
| ❑ 273 | Joe Carter | .25 | .11 |
| ❑ 274 | Todd Jones | .10 | .05 |
| ❑ 275 | Sammy Sosa | .75 | .35 |
| ❑ 276 | Randy Johnson | .50 | .23 |
| ❑ 277 | B.J. Surhoff | .25 | .11 |
| ❑ 278 | Chan Ho Park | .25 | .11 |
| ❑ 279 | Jamey Wright | .10 | .05 |

❑ 280 Manny Ramirez .50 .23
❑ 281 John Franco .25 .11
❑ 282 Tim Worrell .10 .05
❑ 283 Scott Rolen .40 .18
❑ 284 Reggie Sanders .10 .05
❑ 285 Mike Fetters .10 .05
❑ 286 Tim Wakefield .10 .05
❑ 287 Trevor Hoffman .25 .11
❑ 288 Donovan Osborne .10 .05
❑ 289 Phil Nevin .25 .11
❑ 290 Jermaine Allensworth .10 .05
❑ 291 Rocky Coppinger .10 .05
❑ 292 Tim Raines .25 .11
❑ 293 Henry Rodriguez .10 .05
❑ 294 Paul Sorrento .10 .05
❑ 295 Tom Goodwin .10 .05
❑ 296 Raul Mondesi .25 .11
❑ 297 Allen Watson .10 .05
❑ 298 Derek Bell .10 .05
❑ 299 Gary Sheffield .40 .18
❑ 300 Paul Molitor .40 .18
❑ 301 Shawn Green .40 .18
❑ 302 Darren Oliver .10 .05
❑ 303 Jack McDowell .10 .05
❑ 304 Denny Neagle .25 .11
❑ 305 Doug Drabek .10 .05
❑ 306 Mel Rojas .10 .05
❑ 307 Andres Galarraga .30 .14
❑ 308 Alex Ochoa .10 .05
❑ 309 Gary DiSarcina .10 .05
❑ 310 Ron Gant .10 .05
❑ 311 Gregg Jefferies .10 .05
❑ 312 Ruben Rivera .10 .05
❑ 313 Vladimir Guerrero .75 .35
❑ 314 Willie Adams .10 .05
❑ 315 Bip Roberts .10 .05
❑ 316 Mark Grace .40 .18
❑ 317 Bernard Gilkey .10 .05
❑ 318 Marc Newfield .10 .05
❑ 319 Al Leiter .25 .11
❑ 320 Otis Nixon .10 .05
❑ 321 Tom Candiotti .10 .05
❑ 322 Mike Stanley .10 .05
❑ 323 Jeff Fassero .10 .05
❑ 324 Billy Wagner .10 .05
❑ 325 Todd Walker .10 .05
❑ 326 Chad Curtis .10 .05
❑ 327 Quinton McCracken .10 .05
❑ 328 Will Clark .40 .18
❑ 329 Andruw Jones .50 .23
❑ 330 Robin Ventura .25 .11
❑ 331 Curtis Pride .10 .05
❑ 332 Barry Larkin .40 .18
❑ 333 Jimmy Key .25 .11
❑ 334 David Wells .25 .11
❑ 335 Mike Holtz .10 .05
❑ 336 Paul Wagner .10 .05
❑ 337 Greg Maddux 1.00 .45
❑ 338 Curt Schilling .25 .11
❑ 339 Steve Trachsel .10 .05
❑ 340 John Wetteland .25 .11
❑ 341 Rickey Henderson .50 .23
❑ 342 Ernie Young .10 .05
❑ 343 Harold Baines .25 .11
❑ 344 Bobby Jones .10 .05
❑ 345 Jeff D'Amico .10 .05
❑ 346 John Mabry .10 .05
❑ 347 Pedro Martinez .50 .23
❑ 348 Mark Lewis .10 .05
❑ 349 Dan Miceli .10 .05
❑ 350 Chuck Knoblauch .25 .11
❑ 351 John Smiley .10 .05
❑ 352 Brady Anderson .25 .11
❑ 353 Jim Leyritz .10 .05
❑ 354 Al Martin .10 .05
❑ 355 Pat Hentgen .10 .05
❑ 356 Mike Piazza 1.25 .55
❑ 357 Charles Nagy .10 .05
❑ 358 Luis Castillo .25 .11
❑ 359 Paul O'Neill .25 .11
❑ 360 Steve Reed .10 .05
❑ 361 Tom Gordon .10 .05
❑ 362 Craig Biggio .30 .14
❑ 363 Jeff Montgomery .10 .05
❑ 364 Jamie Moyer .10 .05
❑ 365 Ryan Klesko .25 .11
❑ 366 Todd Hundley .10 .05
❑ 367 Bobby Estalella .10 .05
❑ 368 Jason Giambi .40 .18
❑ 369 Brian Hunter .10 .05
❑ 370 Ramon Martinez .10 .05
❑ 371 Carlos Garcia .10 .05
❑ 372 Hal Morris .10 .05
❑ 373 Juan Gonzalez .40 .18
❑ 374 Brian McRae .10 .05
❑ 375 Mike Mussina .40 .18
❑ 376 John Ericks .10 .05
❑ 377 Larry Walker .25 .11
❑ 378 Chris Gomez .10 .05
❑ 379 John Jaha .10 .05
❑ 380 Rondell White .25 .11
❑ 381 Chipper Jones 1.00 .45
❑ 382 David Cone .25 .11
❑ 383 Alan Benes .10 .05
❑ 384 Troy O'Leary .10 .05
❑ 385 Ken Caminiti .25 .11
❑ 386 Jeff King .10 .05
❑ 387 Mike Hampton .25 .11
❑ 388 Jaime Navarro .10 .05
❑ 389 Brad Radke .25 .11
❑ 390 Joey Cora .10 .05
❑ 391 Jim Thome .30 .14
❑ 392 Alex Fernandez .10 .05
❑ 393 Chuck Finley .25 .11
❑ 394 Andruw Jones CL .30 .14
❑ 395 Ken Griffey Jr. CL .75 .35
❑ 396 Frank Thomas CL .60 .25
❑ 397 Alex Rodriguez CL .60 .25
❑ 398 Cal Ripken CL .75 .35
❑ 399 Mike Piazza CL .60 .25
❑ 400 Greg Maddux CL .50 .23
❑ P100 Alex Rodriguez Promo 3.00 1.35

## 1998 Circa Thunder

| | MINT | NRMT |
|---|---|---|
| COMPLETE SET (300) | 20.00 | 9.00 |
| COMMON CARD (1-300) | .10 | .05 |

❑ 1 Ben Grieve .15 .07
❑ 2 Derek Jeter 1.50 .70
❑ 3 Alex Rodriguez 1.25 .55
❑ 4 Paul Molitor .40 .18
❑ 5 Nomar Garciaparra 1.25 .55
❑ 6 Fred McGriff .25 .11
❑ 7 Kenny Lofton .15 .07
❑ 8 Cal Ripken 1.50 .70
❑ 9 Matt Williams .25 .11
❑ 10 Chipper Jones 1.00 .45
❑ 11 Barry Larkin .40 .18
❑ 12 Steve Finley .15 .07
❑ 13 Billy Wagner .10 .05
❑ 14 Rico Brogna .10 .05
❑ 15 Tim Salmon .15 .07
❑ 16 Hideo Nomo .40 .18
❑ 17 Tony Clark .10 .05
❑ 18 Jason Kendall .15 .07
❑ 19 Juan Gonzalez .40 .18
❑ 20 Jeromy Burnitz .15 .07
❑ 21 Roger Clemens .75 .35
❑ 22 Mark Grace .40 .18
❑ 23 Robin Ventura .15 .07
❑ 24 Manny Ramirez .50 .23
❑ 25 Mark McGwire 1.50 .70
❑ 26 Gary Sheffield .40 .18
❑ 27 Vladimir Guerrero .60 .25
❑ 28 Butch Huskey .10 .05
❑ 29 Cecil Fielder .15 .07
❑ 30 Rod Myers .10 .05
❑ 31 Greg Maddux 1.00 .45
❑ 32 Bill Mueller .10 .05
❑ 33 Larry Walker .15 .07
❑ 34 Henry Rodriguez .10 .05
❑ 35 Mike Mussina .40 .18
❑ 36 Ricky Ledee .10 .05
❑ 37 Bobby Bonilla .15 .07
❑ 38 Curt Schilling .15 .07
❑ 39 Luis Gonzalez .15 .07
❑ 40 Troy Percival .10 .05
❑ 41 Eric Milton .10 .05
❑ 42 Mo Vaughn .15 .07
❑ 43 Raul Mondesi .15 .07
❑ 44 Kenny Rogers .10 .05
❑ 45 Frank Thomas .75 .35
❑ 46 Jose Canseco .50 .23
❑ 47 Tom Glavine .40 .18
❑ 48 Rich Butler RC .10 .05
❑ 49 Jay Buhner .15 .07
❑ 50 Jose Cruz Jr. .15 .07
❑ 51 Bernie Williams .40 .18
❑ 52 Doug Glanville .10 .05
❑ 53 Travis Fryman .15 .07
❑ 54 Rey Ordonez .10 .05
❑ 55 Jeff Conine .10 .05
❑ 56 Trevor Hoffman .15 .07
❑ 57 Kirk Rueter .10 .05
(UER back Reuter)
❑ 58 Ron Gant .15 .07
❑ 59 Carl Everett .15 .07
❑ 60 Joe Carter .15 .07
❑ 61 Livan Hernandez .10 .05
❑ 62 John Jaha .15 .07
❑ 63 Ivan Rodriguez .50 .23
❑ 64 Willie Blair .10 .05
❑ 65 Todd Helton .50 .23
❑ 66 Kevin Young .15 .07
❑ 67 Mike Caruso .10 .05
❑ 68 Steve Trachsel .10 .05
❑ 69 Marty Cordova .10 .05
❑ 70 Alex Fernandez .10 .05
❑ 71 Eric Karros .15 .07
❑ 72 Reggie Sanders .10 .05
❑ 73 Russ Davis .10 .05
❑ 74 Roberto Hernandez .10 .05
❑ 75 Barry Bonds .60 .25
❑ 76 Alex Gonzalez .10 .05
❑ 77 Roberto Alomar .40 .18
❑ 78 Troy O'Leary .10 .05
❑ 79 Bernard Gilkey .10 .05
❑ 80 Ismael Valdes .10 .05
❑ 81 Travis Lee .15 .07
❑ 82 Brant Brown .10 .05
❑ 83 Gary DiSarcina .10 .05
❑ 84 Joe Randa .10 .05
❑ 85 Jaret Wright .10 .05
❑ 86 Quilvio Veras .10 .05
❑ 87 Rickey Henderson .50 .23
❑ 88 Randall Simon .10 .05
❑ 89 Mariano Rivera .15 .07
❑ 90 Ugueth Urbina .10 .05
❑ 91 Fernando Vina .10 .05
❑ 92 Alan Benes .10 .05
❑ 93 Dante Bichette .15 .07
❑ 94 Karim Garcia .10 .05
❑ 95 A.J. Hinch .10 .05
❑ 96 Shane Reynolds .10 .05
❑ 97 Kevin Stocker .10 .05
❑ 98 John Wetteland .15 .07
❑ 99 Terry Steinbach .10 .05
❑ 100 Ken Griffey Jr. 1.50 .70
❑ 101 Mike Cameron .15 .07
❑ 102 Damion Easley .10 .05
❑ 103 Randy Myers .15 .07
❑ 104 Jason Schmidt .10 .05
❑ 105 Jeff King .10 .05
❑ 106 Gregg Jefferies .10 .05
❑ 107 Sean Casey .15 .07
❑ 108 Mark Kotsay .15 .07
❑ 109 Brad Fullmer .15 .07
❑ 110 Wilson Alvarez .10 .05

| | # | Player | Mint | NrMt |
|---|---|---|---|---|
| ❑ | 111 | Sandy Alomar Jr. | .15 | .07 |
| ❑ | 112 | Walt Weiss | .15 | .07 |
| ❑ | 113 | Doug Jones | .10 | .05 |
| ❑ | 114 | Andy Benes | .10 | .05 |
| ❑ | 115 | Paul O'Neill | .15 | .07 |
| ❑ | 116 | Dennis Eckersley | .15 | .07 |
| ❑ | 117 | Todd Greene | .10 | .05 |
| ❑ | 118 | Bobby Jones | .10 | .05 |
| ❑ | 119 | Darrin Fletcher | .10 | .05 |
| ❑ | 120 | Eric Young | .10 | .05 |
| ❑ | 121 | Jeffrey Hammonds | .15 | .07 |
| ❑ | 122 | Mickey Morandini | .10 | .05 |
| ❑ | 123 | Chuck Knoblauch | .15 | .07 |
| ❑ | 124 | Moises Alou | .15 | .07 |
| ❑ | 125 | Miguel Tejada | .40 | .18 |
| ❑ | 126 | Brian Anderson | .10 | .05 |
| ❑ | 127 | Edgar Renteria | .10 | .05 |
| ❑ | 128 | Mike Lansing | .10 | .05 |
| ❑ | 129 | Quinton McCracken | .10 | .05 |
| ❑ | 130 | Ray Lankford | .15 | .07 |
| ❑ | 131 | Andy Ashby | .10 | .05 |
| ❑ | 132 | Kelvim Escobar | .10 | .05 |
| ❑ | 133 | Mike Lowell RC | .50 | .23 |
| ❑ | 134 | Randy Johnson | .50 | .23 |
| ❑ | 135 | Andres Galarraga | .25 | .11 |
| ❑ | 136 | Armando Benitez | .10 | .05 |
| ❑ | 137 | Rusty Greer | .15 | .07 |
| ❑ | 138 | Jose Guillen | .10 | .05 |
| ❑ | 139 | Paul Konerko | .15 | .07 |
| ❑ | 140 | Edgardo Alfonzo | .15 | .07 |
| ❑ | 141 | Jim Leyritz | .10 | .05 |
| ❑ | 142 | Mark Clark | .10 | .05 |
| ❑ | 143 | Brian Johnson | .10 | .05 |
| ❑ | 144 | Scott Rolen | .40 | .18 |
| ❑ | 145 | David Cone | .15 | .07 |
| ❑ | 146 | Jeff Shaw | .10 | .05 |
| ❑ | 147 | Shannon Stewart | .15 | .07 |
| ❑ | 148 | Brian Hunter | .10 | .05 |
| ❑ | 149 | Garret Anderson | .15 | .07 |
| ❑ | 150 | Jeff Bagwell | .50 | .23 |
| ❑ | 151 | James Baldwin | .10 | .05 |
| ❑ | 152 | Dovon White | .10 | .05 |
| ❑ | 153 | Jim Thome | .25 | .11 |
| ❑ | 154 | Wally Joyner | .15 | .07 |
| ❑ | 155 | Mark Wohlers | .10 | .05 |
| ❑ | 156 | Jeff Cirillo | .15 | .07 |
| ❑ | 157 | Jason Giambi | .40 | .18 |
| ❑ | 158 | Royce Clayton | .10 | .05 |
| ❑ | 159 | Dennis Reyes | .10 | .05 |
| ❑ | 160 | Raul Casanova | .10 | .05 |
| ❑ | 161 | Pedro Astacio | .10 | .05 |
| ❑ | 162 | Todd Dunwoody | .10 | .05 |
| ❑ | 163 | Sammy Sosa | .75 | .35 |
| ❑ | 164 | Todd Hundley | .10 | .05 |
| ❑ | 165 | Wade Boggs | .50 | .23 |
| ❑ | 166 | Robb Nen | .10 | .05 |
| ❑ | 167 | Dan Wilson | .10 | .05 |
| ❑ | 168 | Hideki Irabu | .10 | .05 |
| ❑ | 169 | B.J. Surhoff | .15 | .07 |
| ❑ | 170 | Carlos Delgado | .40 | .18 |
| ❑ | 171 | Fernando Tatis | .15 | .07 |
| ❑ | 172 | Bob Abreu | .15 | .07 |
| ❑ | 173 | David Ortiz | .10 | .05 |
| ❑ | 174 | Tony Womack | .10 | .05 |
| ❑ | 175 | Magglio Ordonez RC | 1.50 | .70 |
| ❑ | 176 | Aaron Boone | .10 | .05 |
| ❑ | 177 | Brian Giles | .15 | .07 |
| ❑ | 178 | Kevin Appier | .15 | .07 |
| ❑ | 179 | Chuck Finley | .15 | .07 |
| ❑ | 180 | Brian Rose | .10 | .05 |
| ❑ | 181 | Ryan Klesko | .15 | .07 |
| ❑ | 182 | Mike Stanley | .10 | .05 |
| ❑ | 183 | Dave Nilsson | .10 | .05 |
| ❑ | 184 | Carlos Perez | .10 | .05 |
| ❑ | 185 | Jeff Blauser | .10 | .05 |
| ❑ | 186 | Richard Hidalgo | .15 | .07 |
| ❑ | 187 | Charles Johnson | .15 | .07 |
| ❑ | 188 | Vinny Castilla | .15 | .07 |
| ❑ | 189 | Joey Hamilton | .10 | .05 |
| ❑ | 190 | Bubba Trammell | .10 | .05 |
| ❑ | 191 | Eli Marrero | .10 | .05 |
| ❑ | 192 | Scott Erickson | .10 | .05 |
| ❑ | 193 | Pat Hentgen | .10 | .05 |
| ❑ | 194 | Jorge Fabregas | .10 | .05 |
| ❑ | 195 | Tino Martinez | .15 | .07 |
| ❑ | 196 | Bobby Higginson | .15 | .07 |
| ❑ | 197 | Dave Hollins | .10 | .05 |
| ❑ | 198 | Rolando Arrojo RC | .30 | .14 |
| ❑ | 199 | Joey Cora | .10 | .05 |
| ❑ | 200 | Mike Piazza | 1.25 | .55 |
| ❑ | 201 | Reggie Jefferson | .10 | .05 |
| ❑ | 202 | John Smoltz | .15 | .07 |
| ❑ | 203 | Bobby Smith | .10 | .05 |
| ❑ | 204 | Tom Goodwin | .10 | .05 |
| ❑ | 205 | Omar Vizquel | .15 | .07 |
| ❑ | 206 | John Olerud | .15 | .07 |
| ❑ | 207 | Matt Stairs | .10 | .05 |
| ❑ | 208 | Bobby Estalella | .10 | .05 |
| ❑ | 209 | Miguel Cairo | .10 | .05 |
| ❑ | 210 | Shawn Green | .40 | .18 |
| ❑ | 211 | Jon Nunnally | .10 | .05 |
| ❑ | 212 | Al Leiter | .15 | .07 |
| ❑ | 213 | Matt Lawton | .10 | .05 |
| ❑ | 214 | Brady Anderson | .15 | .07 |
| ❑ | 215 | Jeff Kent | .25 | .11 |
| ❑ | 216 | Ray Durham | .15 | .07 |
| ❑ | 217 | Al Martin | .10 | .05 |
| ❑ | 218 | Jeff D'Amico | .10 | .05 |
| ❑ | 219 | Kevin Tapani | .10 | .05 |
| ❑ | 220 | Jim Edmonds | .40 | .18 |
| ❑ | 221 | Jose Vizcaino | .10 | .05 |
| ❑ | 222 | Jay Bell | .15 | .07 |
| ❑ | 223 | Ken Caminiti | .15 | .07 |
| ❑ | 224 | Craig Biggio | .25 | .11 |
| ❑ | 225 | Bartolo Colon | .15 | .07 |
| ❑ | 226 | Neifi Perez | .10 | .05 |
| ❑ | 227 | Delino DeShields | .10 | .05 |
| ❑ | 228 | Javier Lopez | .15 | .07 |
| ❑ | 229 | David Wells | .15 | .07 |
| ❑ | 230 | Brad Rigby | .10 | .05 |
| ❑ | 231 | John Franco | .15 | .07 |
| ❑ | 232 | Michael Coleman | .10 | .05 |
| ❑ | 233 | Edgar Martinez | .25 | .11 |
| ❑ | 234 | Francisco Cordova | .10 | .05 |
| ❑ | 235 | Johnny Damon | .15 | .07 |
| ❑ | 236 | Deivi Cruz | .10 | .05 |
| ❑ | 237 | J.T. Snow | .15 | .07 |
| ❑ | 238 | Enrique Wilson | .10 | .05 |
| ❑ | 239 | Rondell White | .15 | .07 |
| ❑ | 240 | Aaron Sele | .15 | .07 |
| ❑ | 241 | Tony Saunders | .10 | .05 |
| ❑ | 242 | Ricky Bottalico | .10 | .05 |
| ❑ | 243 | Cliff Floyd | .15 | .07 |
| ❑ | 244 | Chili Davis | .15 | .07 |
| ❑ | 245 | Brian McRae | .10 | .05 |
| ❑ | 246 | Brad Radke | .15 | .07 |
| ❑ | 247 | Chan Ho Park | .15 | .07 |
| ❑ | 248 | Lance Johnson | .10 | .05 |
| ❑ | 249 | Rafael Palmeiro | .40 | .18 |
| ❑ | 250 | Tony Gwynn | .75 | .35 |
| ❑ | 251 | Denny Neagle | .10 | .05 |
| ❑ | 252 | Dean Palmer | .15 | .07 |
| ❑ | 253 | Jose Valentin | .10 | .05 |
| ❑ | 254 | Matt Morris | .10 | .05 |
| ❑ | 255 | Ellis Burks | .15 | .07 |
| ❑ | 256 | Jeff Suppan | .10 | .05 |
| ❑ | 257 | Jimmy Key | .15 | .07 |
| ❑ | 258 | Justin Thompson | .10 | .05 |
| ❑ | 259 | Brett Tomko | .10 | .05 |
| ❑ | 260 | Mark Grudzielanek | .10 | .05 |
| ❑ | 261 | Mike Hampton | .15 | .07 |
| ❑ | 262 | Jeff Fassero | .10 | .05 |
| ❑ | 263 | Charles Nagy | .10 | .05 |
| ❑ | 264 | Pedro Martinez | .50 | .23 |
| ❑ | 265 | Todd Zeile | .15 | .07 |
| ❑ | 266 | Will Clark | .40 | .18 |
| ❑ | 267 | Abraham Nunez | .10 | .05 |
| ❑ | 268 | Dave Martinez | .10 | .05 |
| ❑ | 269 | Jason Dickson | .10 | .05 |
| ❑ | 270 | Eric Davis | .15 | .07 |
| ❑ | 271 | Kevin Orie | .10 | .05 |
| ❑ | 272 | Derrek Lee | .10 | .05 |
| ❑ | 273 | Andruw Jones | .40 | .18 |
| ❑ | 274 | Juan Encarnacion | .15 | .07 |
| ❑ | 275 | Carlos Baerga | .10 | .05 |
| ❑ | 276 | Andy Pettitte | .15 | .07 |
| ❑ | 277 | Brent Brede | .10 | .05 |
| ❑ | 278 | Paul Sorrento | .10 | .05 |
| ❑ | 279 | Mike Lieberthal | .15 | .07 |
| ❑ | 280 | Marquis Grissom (UER #'d 8 instead of 280) | .10 | .05 |
| ❑ | 281 | Darin Erstad | .40 | .18 |
| ❑ | 282 | Willie Greene | .10 | .05 |
| ❑ | 283 | Derek Bell | .10 | .05 |
| ❑ | 284 | Scott Spiezio | .10 | .05 |
| ❑ | 285 | David Segui | .10 | .05 |
| ❑ | 286 | Albert Belle | .25 | .11 |
| ❑ | 287 | Ramon Martinez | .10 | .05 |
| ❑ | 288 | Jeremi Gonzalez | .10 | .05 |
| ❑ | 289 | Shawn Estes | .10 | .05 |
| ❑ | 290 | Ron Coomer | .10 | .05 |
| ❑ | 291 | John Valentin | .10 | .05 |
| ❑ | 292 | Kevin Brown | .25 | .11 |
| ❑ | 293 | Michael Tucker | .10 | .05 |
| ❑ | 294 | Brian Jordan | .15 | .07 |
| ❑ | 295 | Darryl Kile | .15 | .07 |
| ❑ | 296 | David Justice | .25 | .11 |
| ❑ | 297 | Frank Thomas CL | .40 | .18 |
| ❑ | 298 | Alex Rodriguez CL | .60 | .25 |
| ❑ | 299 | Ken Griffey Jr. CL | .75 | .35 |
| ❑ | 300 | Jose Cruz Jr. CL | .10 | .05 |
| ❑ | P8 | Cal Ripken Promo | 3.00 | 1.35 |

## 1994 Collector's Choice

| | MINT | NRMT |
|---|---|---|
| COMPLETE SET (670) | 25.00 | 11.00 |
| COMP.FACT.SET (675) | 30.00 | 13.50 |
| COMPLETE SERIES 1 (320) | 10.00 | 4.50 |
| COMPLETE SERIES 2 (350) | 15.00 | 6.75 |
| COMMON CARD (1-670) | .10 | .05 |

| | # | Player | Mint | NrMt |
|---|---|---|---|---|
| ❑ | 1 | Rich Becker | .10 | .05 |
| ❑ | 2 | Greg Blosser | .10 | .05 |
| ❑ | 3 | Midre Cummings | .10 | .05 |
| ❑ | 4 | Carlos Delgado | .60 | .25 |
| ❑ | 5 | Steve Dreyer RC | .10 | .05 |
| ❑ | 6 | Carl Everett | .15 | .07 |
| ❑ | 7 | Cliff Floyd | .15 | .07 |
| ❑ | 8 | Alex Gonzalez | .10 | .05 |
| ❑ | 9 | Shawn Green | .50 | .23 |
| ❑ | 10 | Butch Huskey | .10 | .05 |
| ❑ | 11 | Mark Hutton | .10 | .05 |
| ❑ | 12 | Miguel Jimenez | .10 | .05 |
| ❑ | 13 | Steve Karsay | .10 | .05 |
| ❑ | 14 | Marc Newfield | .10 | .05 |
| ❑ | 15 | Luis Ortiz | .10 | .05 |
| ❑ | 16 | Manny Ramirez | .60 | .25 |
| ❑ | 17 | Johnny Ruffin | .10 | .05 |
| ❑ | 18 | Scott Stahoviak | .10 | .05 |
| ❑ | 19 | Salomon Torres | .10 | .05 |
| ❑ | 20 | Gabe White | .10 | .05 |
| ❑ | 21 | Brian Anderson RC | .15 | .07 |
| ❑ | 22 | Wayne Gomes RC | .10 | .05 |
| ❑ | 23 | Jeff Granger | .10 | .05 |
| ❑ | 24 | Steve Soderstrom RC | .10 | .05 |
| ❑ | 25 | Trot Nixon RC | .75 | .35 |
| ❑ | 26 | Kirk Presley RC | .10 | .05 |
| ❑ | 27 | Matt Brunson RC | .10 | .05 |
| ❑ | 28 | Brooks Kieschnick RC | .15 | .07 |
| ❑ | 29 | Billy Wagner RC | .40 | .18 |
| ❑ | 30 | Matt Drews RC | .10 | .05 |
| ❑ | 31 | Kurt Abbott RC | .10 | .05 |
| ❑ | 32 | Luis Alicea | .10 | .05 |
| ❑ | 33 | Roberto Alomar | .40 | .18 |
| ❑ | 34 | Sandy Alomar Jr. | .15 | .07 |
| ❑ | 35 | Moises Alou | .15 | .07 |
| ❑ | 36 | Wilson Alvarez | .10 | .05 |
| ❑ | 37 | Rich Amaral | .10 | .05 |
| ❑ | 38 | Eric Anthony | .10 | .05 |

❑ 39 Luis Aquino .10 .05
❑ 40 Jack Armstrong .10 .05
❑ 41 Rene Arocha .10 .05
❑ 42 Rich Aude RC .10 .05
❑ 43 Brad Ausmus .10 .05
❑ 44 Steve Avery .10 .05
❑ 45 Bob Ayrault .10 .05
❑ 46 Willie Banks .10 .05
❑ 47 Bret Barberie .10 .05
❑ 48 Kim Batiste .10 .05
❑ 49 Rod Beck .10 .05
❑ 50 Jason Bere .10 .05
❑ 51 Sean Berry .10 .05
❑ 52 Dante Bichette .15 .07
❑ 53 Jeff Blauser .10 .05
❑ 54 Mike Blowers .10 .05
❑ 55 Tim Bogar .10 .05
❑ 56 Tom Bolton .10 .05
❑ 57 Ricky Bones .10 .05
❑ 58 Bobby Bonilla .15 .07
❑ 59 Bret Boone .15 .07
❑ 60 Pat Borders .10 .05
❑ 61 Mike Bordick .10 .05
❑ 62 Daryl Boston .10 .05
❑ 63 Ryan Bowen .10 .05
❑ 64 Jeff Branson .10 .05
❑ 65 George Brett .75 .35
❑ 66 Steve Buechele .10 .05
❑ 67 Dave Burba .10 .05
❑ 68 John Burkett .10 .05
❑ 69 Jeromy Burnitz .15 .07
❑ 70 Brett Butler .15 .07
❑ 71 Rob Butler .10 .05
❑ 72 Ken Caminiti .15 .07
❑ 73 Cris Carpenter .10 .05
❑ 74 Vinny Castilla .15 .07
❑ 75 Andujar Cedeno .10 .05
❑ 76 Wes Chamberlain .10 .05
❑ 77 Archi Cianfrocco .10 .05
❑ 78 Dave Clark .10 .05
❑ 79 Jerald Clark .10 .05
❑ 80 Royce Clayton .10 .05
❑ 81 David Cone .15 .07
❑ 82 Jeff Conine .10 .05
❑ 83 Steve Cooke .10 .05
❑ 84 Scott Cooper .10 .05
❑ 85 Joey Cora .10 .05
❑ 86 Tim Costo .10 .05
❑ 87 Chad Curtis .10 .05
❑ 88 Ron Darling .10 .05
❑ 89 Danny Darwin .10 .05
❑ 90 Rob Deer .10 .05
❑ 91 Jim Deshaies .10 .05
❑ 92 Delino DeShields .10 .05
❑ 93 Rob Dibble .10 .05
❑ 94 Gary DiSarcina .10 .05
❑ 95 Doug Drabek .10 .05
❑ 96 Scott Erickson .10 .05
❑ 97 Rikkert Faneyte RC .10 .05
❑ 98 Jeff Fassero .10 .05
❑ 99 Alex Fernandez .10 .05
❑ 100 Cecil Fielder .15 .07
❑ 101 Dave Fleming .10 .05
❑ 102 Darrin Fletcher .10 .05
❑ 103 Scott Fletcher .10 .05
❑ 104 Mike Gallego .10 .05
❑ 105 Carlos Garcia .10 .05
❑ 106 Jeff Gardner .10 .05
❑ 107 Brent Gates .10 .05
❑ 108 Benji Gil .10 .05
❑ 109 Bernard Gilkey .10 .05
❑ 110 Chris Gomez .10 .05
❑ 111 Luis Gonzalez .15 .07
❑ 112 Tom Gordon .10 .05
❑ 113 Jim Gott .10 .05
❑ 114 Mark Grace .40 .18
❑ 115 Tommy Greene .10 .05
❑ 116 Willie Greene .10 .05
❑ 117 Ken Griffey Jr. 1.50 .70
❑ 118 Bill Gullickson .10 .05
❑ 119 Ricky Gutierrez .10 .05
❑ 120 Juan Guzman .10 .05
❑ 121 Chris Gwynn .10 .05
❑ 122 Tony Gwynn .75 .35
❑ 123 Jeffrey Hammonds .15 .07
❑ 124 Erik Hanson .10 .05
❑ 125 Gene Harris .10 .05
❑ 126 Greg W. Harris .10 .05
❑ 127 Bryan Harvey .10 .05
❑ 128 Billy Hatcher .10 .05
❑ 129 Hilly Hathaway .10 .05
❑ 130 Charlie Hayes .10 .05
❑ 131 Rickey Henderson .50 .23
❑ 132 Mike Henneman .10 .05
❑ 133 Pat Hentgen .10 .05
❑ 134 Roberto Hernandez .10 .05
❑ 135 Orel Hershiser .15 .07
❑ 136 Phil Hiatt .10 .05
❑ 137 Glenallen Hill .10 .05
❑ 138 Ken Hill .10 .05
❑ 139 Eric Hillman .10 .05
❑ 140 Chris Hoiles .10 .05
❑ 141 Dave Hollins .10 .05
❑ 142 David Hulse .10 .05
❑ 143 Todd Hundley .10 .05
❑ 144 Pete Incaviglia .10 .05
❑ 145 Danny Jackson .10 .05
❑ 146 John Jaha .10 .05
❑ 147 Domingo Jean .10 .05
❑ 148 Gregg Jefferies .10 .05
❑ 149 Reggie Jefferson .10 .05
❑ 150 Lance Johnson .10 .05
❑ 151 Bobby Jones .10 .05
❑ 152 Chipper Jones 1.00 .45
❑ 153 Todd Jones .10 .05
❑ 154 Brian Jordan .15 .07
❑ 155 Wally Joyner .15 .07
❑ 156 David Justice .25 .11
❑ 157 Ron Karkovice .10 .05
❑ 158 Eric Karros .15 .07
❑ 159 Jeff Kent .25 .11
❑ 160 Jimmy Key .15 .07
❑ 161 Mark Kiefer .10 .05
❑ 162 Darryl Kile .15 .07
❑ 163 Jeff King .10 .05
❑ 164 Wayne Kirby .10 .05
❑ 165 Ryan Klesko .15 .07
❑ 166 Chuck Knoblauch .15 .07
❑ 167 Chad Kreuter .10 .05
❑ 168 John Kruk .15 .07
❑ 169 Mark Langston .10 .05
❑ 170 Mike Lansing .10 .05
❑ 171 Barry Larkin .40 .18
❑ 172 Manuel Lee .10 .05
❑ 173 Phil Leftwich RC .10 .05
❑ 174 Darren Lewis .10 .05
❑ 175 Derek Lilliquist .10 .05
❑ 176 Jose Lind .10 .05
❑ 177 Albie Lopez .10 .05
❑ 178 Javier Lopez .15 .07
❑ 179 Torey Lovullo .10 .05
❑ 180 Scott Lydy .10 .05
❑ 181 Mike Macfarlane .10 .05
❑ 182 Shane Mack .10 .05
❑ 183 Greg Maddux 1.00 .45
❑ 184 Dave Magadan .10 .05
❑ 185 Joe Magrane .10 .05
❑ 186 Kirk Manwaring .10 .05
❑ 187 Al Martin .10 .05
❑ 188 Pedro A. Martinez RC .10 .05
❑ 189 Pedro Martinez .60 .25
❑ 190 Ramon Martinez .10 .05
❑ 191 Tino Martinez .15 .07
❑ 192 Don Mattingly 1.00 .45
❑ 193 Derrick May .10 .05
❑ 194 David McCarty .10 .05
❑ 195 Ben McDonald .10 .05
❑ 196 Roger McDowell .10 .05
❑ 197 Fred McGriff UER .25 .11
(Stats on back have 73 stolen bases for 1989; should be 7)
❑ 198 Mark McLemore .10 .05
❑ 199 Greg McMichael .10 .05
❑ 200 Jeff McNeely .10 .05
❑ 201 Brian McRae .10 .05
❑ 202 Pat Meares .10 .05
❑ 203 Roberto Mejia .10 .05
❑ 204 Orlando Merced .10 .05
❑ 205 Jose Mesa .10 .05
❑ 206 Blas Minor .10 .05
❑ 207 Angel Miranda .10 .05
❑ 208 Paul Molitor .40 .18
❑ 209 Raul Mondesi .15 .07
❑ 210 Jeff Montgomery .10 .05
❑ 211 Mickey Morandini .10 .05
❑ 212 Mike Morgan .10 .05
❑ 213 Jamie Moyer .10 .05
❑ 214 Bobby Munoz .10 .05
❑ 215 Troy Neel .10 .05
❑ 216 Dave Nilsson .10 .05
❑ 217 John O'Donoghue .10 .05
❑ 218 Paul O'Neill .15 .07
❑ 219 Jose Offerman .10 .05
❑ 220 Joe Oliver .10 .05
❑ 221 Greg Olson .10 .05
❑ 222 Donovan Osborne .10 .05
❑ 223 J. Owens .10 .05
❑ 224 Mike Pagliarulo .10 .05
❑ 225 Craig Paquette .10 .05
❑ 226 Roger Pavlik .10 .05
❑ 227 Brad Pennington .10 .05
❑ 228 Eduardo Perez .10 .05
❑ 229 Mike Perez .10 .05
❑ 230 Tony Phillips .10 .05
❑ 231 Hipolito Pichardo .10 .05
❑ 232 Phil Plantier .10 .05
❑ 233 Curtis Pride RC .10 .05
❑ 234 Tim Pugh .10 .05
❑ 235 Scott Radinsky .10 .05
❑ 236 Pat Rapp .10 .05
❑ 237 Kevin Reimer .10 .05
❑ 238 Armando Reynoso .10 .05
❑ 239 Jose Rijo .10 .05
❑ 240 Cal Ripken 1.50 .70
❑ 241 Kevin Roberson .10 .05
❑ 242 Kenny Rogers .10 .05
❑ 243 Kevin Rogers .10 .05
❑ 244 Mel Rojas .10 .05
❑ 245 John Roper .10 .05
❑ 246 Kirk Rueter .10 .05
❑ 247 Scott Ruffcorn .10 .05
❑ 248 Ken Ryan .10 .05
❑ 249 Nolan Ryan 2.00 .90
❑ 250 Bret Saberhagen .15 .07
❑ 251 Tim Salmon .15 .07
❑ 252 Reggie Sanders .10 .05
❑ 253 Curt Schilling .15 .07
❑ 254 David Segui .10 .05
❑ 255 Aaron Sele .15 .07
❑ 256 Scott Servais .10 .05
❑ 257 Gary Sheffield .40 .18
❑ 258 Ruben Sierra .10 .05
❑ 259 Don Slaught .10 .05
❑ 260 Lee Smith .15 .07
❑ 261 Cory Snyder .10 .05
❑ 262 Paul Sorrento .10 .05
❑ 263 Sammy Sosa .75 .35
❑ 264 Bill Spiers .10 .05
❑ 265 Mike Stanley .10 .05
❑ 266 Dave Staton .10 .05
❑ 267 Terry Steinbach .10 .05
❑ 268 Kevin Stocker .10 .05
❑ 269 Todd Stottlemyre .10 .05
❑ 270 Doug Strange .10 .05
❑ 271 Bill Swift .10 .05
❑ 272 Kevin Tapani .10 .05
❑ 273 Tony Tarasco .10 .05
❑ 274 Julian Tavarez RC .10 .05
❑ 275 Mickey Tettleton .10 .05
❑ 276 Ryan Thompson .10 .05
❑ 277 Chris Turner .10 .05
❑ 278 John Valentin .10 .05
❑ 279 Todd Van Poppel .10 .05
❑ 280 Andy Van Slyke .15 .07
❑ 281 Mo Vaughn .15 .07
❑ 282 Robin Ventura .15 .07
❑ 283 Frank Viola .10 .05
❑ 284 Jose Vizcaino .10 .05
❑ 285 Omar Vizquel .15 .07
❑ 286 Larry Walker .15 .07
❑ 287 Duane Ward .10 .05
❑ 288 Allen Watson .10 .05
❑ 289 Bill Wegman .10 .05
❑ 290 Turk Wendell .10 .05
❑ 291 Lou Whitaker .15 .07
❑ 292 Devon White .10 .05
❑ 293 Rondell White .15 .07

| | | | |
|---|---|---|---|
| ❑ 294 | Mark Whiten | .10 | .05 |
| ❑ 295 | Darrel Whitmore | .10 | .05 |
| ❑ 296 | Bob Wickman | .10 | .05 |
| ❑ 297 | Rick Wilkins | .10 | .05 |
| ❑ 298 | Bernie Williams | .40 | .18 |
| ❑ 299 | Matt Williams | .25 | .11 |
| ❑ 300 | Woody Williams | .10 | .05 |
| ❑ 301 | Nigel Wilson | .10 | .05 |
| ❑ 302 | Dave Winfield | .40 | .18 |
| ❑ 303 | Anthony Young | .10 | .05 |
| ❑ 304 | Eric Young | .10 | .05 |
| ❑ 305 | Todd Zeile | .10 | .05 |
| ❑ 306 | Jack McDowell TP<br>John Burkett<br>Tom Glavine | .10 | .05 |
| ❑ 307 | Randy Johnson TP | .25 | .11 |
| ❑ 308 | Randy Myers TP | .10 | .05 |
| ❑ 309 | Jack McDowell TP | .10 | .05 |
| ❑ 310 | Mike Piazza TP | .60 | .25 |
| ❑ 311 | Barry Bonds TP | .40 | .18 |
| ❑ 312 | Andres Galarraga TP | .10 | .05 |
| ❑ 313 | Juan Gonzalez TP<br>Barry Bonds | .15 | .07 |
| ❑ 314 | Albert Belle TP | .10 | .05 |
| ❑ 315 | Kenny Lofton TP | .10 | .05 |
| ❑ 316 | Barry Bonds CL | .40 | .18 |
| ❑ 317 | Ken Griffey Jr. CL | .40 | .18 |
| ❑ 318 | Mike Piazza CL | .25 | .11 |
| ❑ 319 | Kirby Puckett CL | .50 | .23 |
| ❑ 320 | Nolan Ryan CL | .50 | .23 |
| ❑ 321 | Roberto Alomar CL | .15 | .07 |
| ❑ 322 | Roger Clemens CL | .40 | .18 |
| ❑ 323 | Juan Gonzalez CL | .15 | .07 |
| ❑ 324 | Ken Griffey Jr. CL | .40 | .18 |
| ❑ 325 | David Justice CL | .10 | .05 |
| ❑ 326 | John Kruk CL | .10 | .05 |
| ❑ 327 | Frank Thomas CL | .40 | .18 |
| ❑ 328 | Tim Salmon TC | .10 | .05 |
| ❑ 329 | Jeff Bagwell TC | .40 | .18 |
| ❑ 330 | Mark McGwire TC | .75 | .35 |
| ❑ 331 | Roberto Alomar TC | .15 | .07 |
| ❑ 332 | David Justice TC | .10 | .05 |
| ❑ 333 | Pat Listach TC | .10 | .05 |
| ❑ 334 | Ozzie Smith TC | .40 | .18 |
| ❑ 335 | Ryne Sandberg TC | .25 | .11 |
| ❑ 336 | Mike Piazza TC | .60 | .25 |
| ❑ 337 | Cliff Floyd TC | .10 | .05 |
| ❑ 338 | Barry Bonds TC | .40 | .18 |
| ❑ 339 | Albert Belle TC | .10 | .05 |
| ❑ 340 | Ken Griffey Jr. TC | .75 | .35 |
| ❑ 341 | Gary Sheffield TC | .15 | .07 |
| ❑ 342 | Dwight Gooden TC | .10 | .05 |
| ❑ 343 | Cal Ripken TC | .75 | .35 |
| ❑ 344 | Tony Gwynn TC | .40 | .18 |
| ❑ 345 | Lenny Dykstra TC | .10 | .05 |
| ❑ 346 | Andy Van Slyke TC | .10 | .05 |
| ❑ 347 | Juan Gonzalez TC | .15 | .07 |
| ❑ 348 | Roger Clemens TC | .40 | .18 |
| ❑ 349 | Barry Larkin TC | .15 | .07 |
| ❑ 350 | Andres Galarraga TC | .10 | .05 |
| ❑ 351 | Kevin Appier TC | .10 | .05 |
| ❑ 352 | Cecil Fielder TC | .10 | .05 |
| ❑ 353 | Kirby Puckett TC | .50 | .23 |
| ❑ 354 | Frank Thomas TC | .40 | .18 |
| ❑ 355 | Don Mattingly TC | .50 | .23 |
| ❑ 356 | Bo Jackson | .15 | .07 |
| ❑ 357 | Randy Johnson | .50 | .23 |
| ❑ 358 | Darren Daulton | .15 | .07 |
| ❑ 359 | Charlie Hough | .15 | .07 |
| ❑ 360 | Andres Galarraga | .25 | .11 |
| ❑ 361 | Mike Felder | .10 | .05 |
| ❑ 362 | Chris Hammond | .10 | .05 |
| ❑ 363 | Shawon Dunston | .10 | .05 |
| ❑ 364 | Junior Felix | .10 | .05 |
| ❑ 365 | Ray Lankford | .15 | .07 |
| ❑ 366 | Darryl Strawberry | .15 | .07 |
| ❑ 367 | Dave Magadan | .10 | .05 |
| ❑ 368 | Gregg Olson | .10 | .05 |
| ❑ 369 | Lenny Dykstra | .15 | .07 |
| ❑ 370 | Darrin Jackson | .10 | .05 |
| ❑ 371 | Dave Stewart | .15 | .07 |
| ❑ 372 | Terry Pendleton | .15 | .07 |
| ❑ 373 | Arthur Rhodes | .10 | .05 |
| ❑ 374 | Benito Santiago | .10 | .05 |
| ❑ 375 | Travis Fryman | .15 | .07 |
| ❑ 376 | Scott Brosius | .15 | .07 |
| ❑ 377 | Stan Belinda | .10 | .05 |
| ❑ 378 | Derek Parks | .10 | .05 |
| ❑ 379 | Kevin Seitzer | .10 | .05 |
| ❑ 380 | Wade Boggs | .50 | .23 |
| ❑ 381 | Wally Whitehurst | .10 | .05 |
| ❑ 382 | Scott Leius | .10 | .05 |
| ❑ 383 | Danny Tartabull | .10 | .05 |
| ❑ 384 | Harold Reynolds | .10 | .05 |
| ❑ 385 | Tim Raines | .15 | .07 |
| ❑ 386 | Darryl Hamilton | .10 | .05 |
| ❑ 387 | Felix Fermin | .10 | .05 |
| ❑ 388 | Jim Eisenreich | .10 | .05 |
| ❑ 389 | Kurt Abbott | .10 | .05 |
| ❑ 390 | Kevin Appier | .15 | .07 |
| ❑ 391 | Chris Bosio | .10 | .05 |
| ❑ 392 | Randy Tomlin | .10 | .05 |
| ❑ 393 | Bob Hamelin | .10 | .05 |
| ❑ 394 | Kevin Gross | .10 | .05 |
| ❑ 395 | Wil Cordero | .10 | .05 |
| ❑ 396 | Joe Girardi | .10 | .05 |
| ❑ 397 | Orestes Destrade | .10 | .05 |
| ❑ 398 | Chris Haney | .10 | .05 |
| ❑ 399 | Xavier Hernandez | .10 | .05 |
| ❑ 400 | Mike Piazza | 1.25 | .55 |
| ❑ 401 | Alex Arias | .10 | .05 |
| ❑ 402 | Tom Candiotti | .10 | .05 |
| ❑ 403 | Kirk Gibson | .15 | .07 |
| ❑ 404 | Chuck Carr | .10 | .05 |
| ❑ 405 | Brady Anderson | .15 | .07 |
| ❑ 406 | Greg Gagne | .10 | .05 |
| ❑ 407 | Bruce Ruffin | .10 | .05 |
| ❑ 408 | Scott Hemond | .10 | .05 |
| ❑ 409 | Keith Miller | .10 | .05 |
| ❑ 410 | John Wetteland | .15 | .07 |
| ❑ 411 | Eric Anthony | .10 | .05 |
| ❑ 412 | Andre Dawson | .25 | .11 |
| ❑ 413 | Doug Henry | .10 | .05 |
| ❑ 414 | John Franco | .15 | .07 |
| ❑ 415 | Julio Franco | .10 | .05 |
| ❑ 416 | Dave Hansen | .10 | .05 |
| ❑ 417 | Mike Harkey | .10 | .05 |
| ❑ 418 | Jack Armstrong | .10 | .05 |
| ❑ 419 | Joe Orsulak | .10 | .05 |
| ❑ 420 | John Smoltz | .15 | .07 |
| ❑ 421 | Scott Livingstone | .10 | .05 |
| ❑ 422 | Darren Holmes | .10 | .05 |
| ❑ 423 | Ed Sprague | .10 | .05 |
| ❑ 424 | Jay Buhner | .15 | .07 |
| ❑ 425 | Kirby Puckett | 1.00 | .45 |
| ❑ 426 | Phil Clark | .10 | .05 |
| ❑ 427 | Anthony Young | .10 | .05 |
| ❑ 428 | Reggie Jefferson | .10 | .05 |
| ❑ 429 | Mariano Duncan | .10 | .05 |
| ❑ 430 | Tom Glavine | .40 | .18 |
| ❑ 431 | Dave Henderson | .10 | .05 |
| ❑ 432 | Melido Perez | .10 | .05 |
| ❑ 433 | Paul Wagner | .10 | .05 |
| ❑ 434 | Tim Worrell | .10 | .05 |
| ❑ 435 | Ozzie Guillen | .10 | .05 |
| ❑ 436 | Mike Butcher | .10 | .05 |
| ❑ 437 | Jim Deshaies | .10 | .05 |
| ❑ 438 | Kevin Young | .10 | .05 |
| ❑ 439 | Tom Browning | .10 | .05 |
| ❑ 440 | Mike Greenwell | .10 | .05 |
| ❑ 441 | Mike Stanton | .10 | .05 |
| ❑ 442 | John Doherty | .10 | .05 |
| ❑ 443 | John Dopson | .10 | .05 |
| ❑ 444 | Carlos Baerga | .10 | .05 |
| ❑ 445 | Jack McDowell | .10 | .05 |
| ❑ 446 | Kent Mercker | .10 | .05 |
| ❑ 447 | Ricky Jordan | .10 | .05 |
| ❑ 448 | Jerry Browne | .10 | .05 |
| ❑ 449 | Fernando Vina | .10 | .05 |
| ❑ 450 | Jim Abbott | .15 | .07 |
| ❑ 451 | Teddy Higuera | .10 | .05 |
| ❑ 452 | Tim Naehring | .10 | .05 |
| ❑ 453 | Jim Leyritz | .10 | .05 |
| ❑ 454 | Frank Castillo | .10 | .05 |
| ❑ 455 | Joe Carter | .15 | .07 |
| ❑ 456 | Craig Biggio | .25 | .11 |
| ❑ 457 | Geronimo Pena | .10 | .05 |
| ❑ 458 | Alejandro Pena | .10 | .05 |
| ❑ 459 | Mike Moore | .10 | .05 |
| ❑ 460 | Randy Myers | .10 | .05 |
| ❑ 461 | Greg Myers | .10 | .05 |
| ❑ 462 | Greg Hibbard | .10 | .05 |
| ❑ 463 | Jose Guzman | .10 | .05 |
| ❑ 464 | Tom Pagnozzi | .10 | .05 |
| ❑ 465 | Marquis Grissom | .10 | .05 |
| ❑ 466 | Tim Wallach | .10 | .05 |
| ❑ 467 | Joe Grahe | .10 | .05 |
| ❑ 468 | Bob Tewksbury | .10 | .05 |
| ❑ 469 | B.J. Surhoff | .15 | .07 |
| ❑ 470 | Kevin Mitchell | .10 | .05 |
| ❑ 471 | Bobby Witt | .10 | .05 |
| ❑ 472 | Milt Thompson | .10 | .05 |
| ❑ 473 | John Smiley | .10 | .05 |
| ❑ 474 | Alan Trammell | .25 | .11 |
| ❑ 475 | Mike Mussina | .40 | .18 |
| ❑ 476 | Rick Aguilera | .10 | .05 |
| ❑ 477 | Jose Valentin | .10 | .05 |
| ❑ 478 | Harold Baines | .15 | .07 |
| ❑ 479 | Bip Roberts | .10 | .05 |
| ❑ 480 | Edgar Martinez | .25 | .11 |
| ❑ 481 | Rheal Cormier | .10 | .05 |
| ❑ 482 | Hal Morris | .10 | .05 |
| ❑ 483 | Pat Kelly | .10 | .05 |
| ❑ 484 | Roberto Kelly | .10 | .05 |
| ❑ 485 | Chris Sabo | .10 | .05 |
| ❑ 486 | Kent Hrbek | .15 | .07 |
| ❑ 487 | Scott Kamieniecki | .10 | .05 |
| ❑ 488 | Walt Weiss | .10 | .05 |
| ❑ 489 | Karl Rhodes | .10 | .05 |
| ❑ 490 | Derek Bell | .10 | .05 |
| ❑ 491 | Chili Davis | .15 | .07 |
| ❑ 492 | Brian Harper | .10 | .05 |
| ❑ 493 | Felix Jose | .10 | .05 |
| ❑ 494 | Trevor Hoffman | .15 | .07 |
| ❑ 495 | Dennis Eckersley | .15 | .07 |
| ❑ 496 | Pedro Astacio | .10 | .05 |
| ❑ 497 | Jay Bell | .15 | .07 |
| ❑ 498 | Randy Velarde | .10 | .05 |
| ❑ 499 | David Wells | .15 | .07 |
| ❑ 500 | Frank Thomas | .75 | .35 |
| ❑ 501 | Mark Lemke | .10 | .05 |
| ❑ 502 | Mike Devereaux | .10 | .05 |
| ❑ 503 | Chuck McElroy | .10 | .05 |
| ❑ 504 | Luis Polonia | .10 | .05 |
| ❑ 505 | Damion Easley | .10 | .05 |
| ❑ 506 | Greg A. Harris | .10 | .05 |
| ❑ 507 | Chris James | .10 | .05 |
| ❑ 508 | Terry Mulholland | .10 | .05 |
| ❑ 509 | Pete Smith | .10 | .05 |
| ❑ 510 | Rickey Henderson | .50 | .23 |
| ❑ 511 | Sid Fernandez | .10 | .05 |
| ❑ 512 | Al Leiter | .15 | .07 |
| ❑ 513 | Doug Jones | .10 | .05 |
| ❑ 514 | Steve Farr | .10 | .05 |
| ❑ 515 | Chuck Finley | .15 | .07 |
| ❑ 516 | Bobby Thigpen | .10 | .05 |
| ❑ 517 | Jim Edmonds | .50 | .23 |
| ❑ 518 | Graeme Lloyd | .10 | .05 |
| ❑ 519 | Dwight Gooden | .15 | .07 |
| ❑ 520 | Pat Listach | .10 | .05 |
| ❑ 521 | Kevin Bass | .10 | .05 |
| ❑ 522 | Willie Banks | .10 | .05 |
| ❑ 523 | Steve Finley | .15 | .07 |
| ❑ 524 | Delino DeShields | .10 | .05 |
| ❑ 525 | Mark McGwire | 1.50 | .70 |
| ❑ 526 | Greg Swindell | .10 | .05 |
| ❑ 527 | Chris Nabholz | .10 | .05 |
| ❑ 528 | Scott Sanders | .10 | .05 |
| ❑ 529 | David Segui | .10 | .05 |
| ❑ 530 | Howard Johnson | .10 | .05 |
| ❑ 531 | Jaime Navarro | .10 | .05 |
| ❑ 532 | Jose Vizcaino | .10 | .05 |
| ❑ 533 | Mark Lewis | .10 | .05 |
| ❑ 534 | Pete Harnisch | .10 | .05 |
| ❑ 535 | Robby Thompson | .10 | .05 |
| ❑ 536 | Marcus Moore | .10 | .05 |
| ❑ 537 | Kevin Brown | .15 | .07 |
| ❑ 538 | Mark Clark | .10 | .05 |
| ❑ 539 | Sterling Hitchcock | .10 | .05 |
| ❑ 540 | Will Clark | .40 | .18 |
| ❑ 541 | Denis Boucher | .10 | .05 |
| ❑ 542 | Jack Morris | .15 | .07 |
| ❑ 543 | Pedro Munoz | .10 | .05 |
| ❑ 544 | Bret Boone | .15 | .07 |
| ❑ 545 | Ozzie Smith | .50 | .23 |
| ❑ 546 | Dennis Martinez | .15 | .07 |
| ❑ 547 | Dan Wilson | .10 | .05 |
| ❑ 548 | Rick Sutcliffe | .15 | .07 |

❑ 549 Kevin McReynolds .10 .05
❑ 550 Roger Clemens .75 .35
❑ 551 Todd Benzinger .10 .05
❑ 552 Bill Haselman .10 .05
❑ 553 Bobby Munoz .10 .05
❑ 554 Ellis Burks .15 .07
❑ 555 Ryne Sandberg .50 .23
❑ 556 Lee Smith .15 .07
❑ 557 Danny Bautista .10 .05
❑ 558 Rey Sanchez .10 .05
❑ 559 Norm Charlton .10 .05
❑ 560 Jose Canseco .50 .23
❑ 561 Tim Belcher .10 .05
❑ 562 Denny Neagle .10 .05
❑ 563 Eric Davis .15 .07
❑ 564 Jody Reed .10 .05
❑ 565 Kenny Lofton .15 .07
❑ 566 Gary Gaetti .15 .07
❑ 567 Todd Worrell .10 .05
❑ 568 Mark Portugal .10 .05
❑ 569 Dick Schofield .10 .05
❑ 570 Andy Benes .10 .05
❑ 571 Zane Smith .10 .05
❑ 572 Bobby Ayala .10 .05
❑ 573 Chip Hale .10 .05
❑ 574 Bob Welch .10 .05
❑ 575 Deion Sanders .15 .07
❑ 576 David Nied .10 .05
❑ 577 Pat Mahomes .10 .05
❑ 578 Charles Nagy .10 .05
❑ 579 Otis Nixon .10 .05
❑ 580 Dean Palmer .15 .07
❑ 581 Roberto Petagine .10 .05
❑ 582 Dwight Smith .10 .05
❑ 583 Jeff Russell .10 .05
❑ 584 Mark Dewey .10 .05
❑ 585 Greg Vaughn .15 .07
❑ 586 Brian Hunter .10 .05
❑ 587 Willie McGee .15 .07
❑ 588 Pedro Martinez .60 .25
❑ 589 Roger Salkeld .10 .05
❑ 590 Jeff Bagwell .50 .23
❑ 591 Spike Owen .10 .05
❑ 592 Jeff Reardon .15 .07
❑ 593 Erik Pappas .10 .05
❑ 594 Brian Williams .10 .05
❑ 595 Eddie Murray .40 .18
❑ 596 Henry Rodriguez .10 .05
❑ 597 Erik Hanson .10 .05
❑ 598 Stan Javier .10 .05
❑ 599 Mitch Williams .10 .05
❑ 600 John Olerud .15 .07
❑ 601 Vince Coleman .10 .05
❑ 602 Damon Berryhill .10 .05
❑ 603 Tom Brunansky .10 .05
❑ 604 Robb Nen .10 .05
❑ 605 Rafael Palmeiro .40 .18
❑ 606 Cal Eldred .10 .05
❑ 607 Jeff Brantley .10 .05
❑ 608 Alan Mills .10 .05
❑ 609 Jeff Nelson .10 .05
❑ 610 Barry Bonds .60 .25
❑ 611 Carlos Pulido RC .10 .05
❑ 612 Tim Hyers RC .10 .05
❑ 613 Steve Howe .10 .05
❑ 614 Brian Turang RC .10 .05
❑ 615 Leo Gomez .10 .05
❑ 616 Jesse Orosco .10 .05
❑ 617 Dan Pasqua .10 .05
❑ 618 Marvin Freeman .10 .05
❑ 619 Tony Fernandez .10 .05
❑ 620 Albert Belle .25 .11
❑ 621 Eddie Taubensee .10 .05
❑ 622 Mike Jackson .10 .05
❑ 623 Jose Bautista .10 .05
❑ 624 Jim Thome .25 .11
❑ 625 Ivan Rodriguez .50 .23
❑ 626 Ben Rivera .10 .05
❑ 627 Dave Valle .10 .05
❑ 628 Tom Henke .10 .05
❑ 629 Omar Vizquel .15 .07
❑ 630 Juan Gonzalez .40 .18
❑ 631 Roberto Alomar UP .15 .07
❑ 632 Barry Bonds UP .40 .18
❑ 633 Juan Gonzalez UP .15 .07
❑ 634 Ken Griffey Jr. UP .75 .35
❑ 635 Michael Jordan UP 1.50 .70
❑ 636 David Justice UP .10 .05
❑ 637 Mike Piazza UP .60 .25
❑ 638 Kirby Puckett UP .50 .23
❑ 639 Tim Salmon UP .10 .05
❑ 640 Frank Thomas UP .40 .18
❑ 641 Alan Benes FF RC .15 .07
❑ 642 Johnny Damon FF .40 .18
❑ 643 Brad Fullmer FF RC .75 .35
❑ 644 Derek Jeter FF 2.00 .90
❑ 645 Derrek Lee FF RC .40 .18
❑ 646 Alex Ochoa .10 .05
❑ 647 Alex Rodriguez FF RC 6.00 2.70
❑ 648 Jose Silva FF RC .10 .05
❑ 649 Terrell Wade FF RC .10 .05
❑ 650 Preston Wilson FF .40 .18
❑ 651 Shane Andrews .10 .05
❑ 652 James Baldwin .15 .07
❑ 653 Ricky Bottalico RC .15 .07
❑ 654 Tavo Alvarez .10 .05
❑ 655 Donnie Elliott .10 .05
❑ 656 Joey Eischen .10 .05
❑ 657 Jason Giambi .50 .23
❑ 658 Todd Hollandsworth .10 .05
❑ 659 Brian L. Hunter .10 .05
❑ 660 Charles Johnson .15 .07
❑ 661 Michael Jordan RC 3.00 1.35
❑ 662 Jeff Juden .10 .05
❑ 663 Mike Kelly .10 .05
❑ 664 James Mouton .10 .05
❑ 665 Ray Holbert .10 .05
❑ 666 Pokey Reese .15 .07
❑ 667 Ruben Santana RC .10 .05
❑ 668 Paul Spoljaric .10 .05
❑ 669 Luis Lopez .10 .05
❑ 670 Matt Walbeck .10 .05
❑ P50 Ken Griffey Jr. Promo 2.00 .90

## 1995 Collector's Choice

| | MINT | NRMT |
|---|---|---|
| COMPLETE SET (530) | 20.00 | 9.00 |
| COMP.FACT.SET (545) | 30.00 | 13.50 |
| COMMON CARD (1-530) | .10 | .05 |
| COMP.TRADE SET (55) | 10.00 | 4.50 |
| COMMON TRADE (531-585) | .25 | .07 |

❑ 1 Charles Johnson .20 .09
❑ 2 Scott Ruffcorn .10 .05
❑ 3 Ray Durham .20 .09
❑ 4 Armando Benitez .20 .09
❑ 5 Alex Rodriguez 1.50 .70
❑ 6 Julian Tavarez .10 .05
❑ 7 Chad Ogea .10 .05
❑ 8 Quilvio Veras .10 .05
❑ 9 Phil Nevin .20 .09
❑ 10 Michael Tucker .10 .05
❑ 11 Mark Thompson .10 .05
❑ 12 Rod Henderson .10 .05
❑ 13 Andrew Lorraine .10 .05
❑ 14 Joe Randa .10 .05
❑ 15 Derek Jeter 1.50 .70
❑ 16 Tony Clark .20 .09
❑ 17 Juan Castillo .10 .05
❑ 18 Mark Acre .10 .05
❑ 19 Orlando Miller .10 .05
❑ 20 Paul Wilson .10 .05
❑ 21 John Mabry .10 .05
❑ 22 Garey Ingram .10 .05
❑ 23 Garret Anderson .20 .09
❑ 24 Dave Stevens .10 .05
❑ 25 Dustin Hermanson .10 .05
❑ 26 Paul Shuey .10 .05
❑ 27 J.R. Phillips .10 .05
❑ 28 Ruben Rivera FF .10 .05
❑ 29 Nomar Garciaparra FF 2.50 1.10
❑ 30 John Wasdin FF .10 .05
❑ 31 Jim Pittsley FF .10 .05
❑ 32 Scott Elarton FF RC 1.00 .45
❑ 33 Raul Casanova FF RC .10 .05
❑ 34 Todd Greene FF .10 .05
❑ 35 Bill Pulsipher FF .10 .05
❑ 36 Trey Beamon FF .10 .05
❑ 37 Curtis Goodwin FF .10 .05
❑ 38 Doug Million FF .10 .05
❑ 39 Karim Garcia FF RC .25 .11
❑ 40 Ben Grieve FF .60 .25
❑ 41 Mark Farris FF .10 .05
❑ 42 Juan Acevedo FF RC .10 .05
❑ 43 C.J. Nitkowski FF .10 .05
❑ 44 Travis Miller FF RC .10 .05
❑ 45 Reid Ryan FF .20 .09
❑ 46 Nolan Ryan 2.00 .90
❑ 47 Robin Yount .40 .18
❑ 48 Ryne Sandberg .50 .23
❑ 49 George Brett .75 .35
❑ 50 Mike Schmidt .60 .25
❑ 51 Cecil Fielder B90 .10 .05
❑ 52 Nolan Ryan B90 1.00 .45
❑ 53 Rickey Henderson B90 .20 .09
❑ 54 George Brett B90 .40 .18
Robin Yount
Dave Winfield
❑ 55 Sid Bream B90 .10 .05
❑ 56 Carlos Baerga B90 .10 .05
❑ 57 Lee Smith B90 .10 .05
❑ 58 Mark Whiten B90 .10 .05
❑ 59 Joe Carter B90 .20 .09
❑ 60 Barry Bonds B90 .20 .09
❑ 61 Tony Gwynn B90 .40 .18
❑ 62 Ken Griffey Jr. B90 .75 .35
❑ 63 Greg Maddux B90 .50 .23
❑ 64 Frank Thomas B90 .50 .23
❑ 65 Dennis Martinez B90 .10 .05
Kenny Rogers
❑ 66 David Cone .20 .09
❑ 67 Greg Maddux 1.00 .45
❑ 68 Jimmy Key .20 .09
❑ 69 Fred McGriff .20 .09
❑ 70 Ken Griffey Jr. 1.50 .70
❑ 71 Matt Williams .20 .09
❑ 72 Paul O'Neill .20 .09
❑ 73 Tony Gwynn .75 .35
❑ 74 Randy Johnson .50 .23
❑ 75 Frank Thomas .75 .35
❑ 76 Jeff Bagwell .50 .23
❑ 77 Kirby Puckett 1.00 .45
❑ 78 Bob Hamelin .10 .05
❑ 79 Raul Mondesi .20 .09
❑ 80 Mike Piazza 1.25 .55
❑ 81 Kenny Lofton .20 .09
❑ 82 Barry Bonds .60 .25
❑ 83 Albert Belle .20 .09
❑ 84 Juan Gonzalez .40 .18
❑ 85 Cal Ripken Jr. 1.50 .70
❑ 86 Barry Bonds WC .20 .09
❑ 87 Mike Piazza WC .60 .25
❑ 88 Ken Griffey Jr. WC .75 .35
❑ 89 Frank Thomas WC .40 .18
❑ 90 Juan Gonzalez WC .20 .09
❑ 91 Jorge Fabregas .10 .05
❑ 92 J.T. Snow .20 .09
❑ 93 Spike Owen .10 .05
❑ 94 Eduardo Perez .10 .05
❑ 95 Bo Jackson .20 .09
❑ 96 Damion Easley .10 .05
❑ 97 Gary DiSarcina .10 .05
❑ 98 Jim Edmonds .40 .18
❑ 99 Chad Curtis .10 .05
❑ 100 Tim Salmon .20 .09
❑ 101 Chili Davis .20 .09
❑ 102 Chuck Finley .20 .09
❑ 103 Mark Langston .10 .05
❑ 104 Brian Anderson .10 .05

❑ 105 Lee Smith .20 .09
❑ 106 Phil Leftwich .10 .05
❑ 107 Chris Donnels .10 .05
❑ 108 John Hudek .10 .05
❑ 109 Craig Biggio .20 .09
❑ 110 Luis Gonzalez .10 .05
❑ 111 Brian L. Hunter .10 .05
❑ 112 James Mouton .10 .05
❑ 113 Scott Servais .10 .05
❑ 114 Tony Eusebio .10 .05
❑ 115 Derek Bell .10 .05
❑ 116 Doug Drabek .10 .05
❑ 117 Shane Reynolds .10 .05
❑ 118 Darryl Kile .20 .09
❑ 119 Greg Swindell .10 .05
❑ 120 Phil Plantier .10 .05
❑ 121 Todd Jones .10 .05
❑ 122 Steve Ontiveros .10 .05
❑ 123 Bobby Witt .10 .05
❑ 124 Brent Gates .10 .05
❑ 125 Rickey Henderson .50 .23
❑ 126 Scott Brosius .20 .09
❑ 127 Mike Bordick .10 .05
❑ 128 Fausto Cruz .10 .05
❑ 129 Stan Javier .10 .05
❑ 130 Mark McGwire 1.50 .70
❑ 131 Geronimo Berroa .10 .05
❑ 132 Terry Steinbach .10 .05
❑ 133 Steve Karsay .10 .05
❑ 134 Dennis Eckersley .20 .09
❑ 135 Ruben Sierra .10 .05
❑ 136 Ron Darling .10 .05
❑ 137 Todd Van Poppel .10 .05
❑ 138 Alex Gonzalez .10 .05
❑ 139 John Olerud .20 .09
❑ 140 Roberto Alomar .40 .18
❑ 141 Darren Hall .10 .05
❑ 142 Ed Sprague .10 .05
❑ 143 Devon White .20 .09
❑ 144 Shawn Green .40 .18
❑ 145 Paul Molitor .40 .18
❑ 146 Pat Borders .10 .05
❑ 147 Carlos Delgado .40 .18
❑ 148 Juan Guzman .10 .05
❑ 149 Pat Hentgen .10 .05
❑ 150 Joe Carter .20 .09
❑ 151 Dave Stewart .20 .09
❑ 152 Todd Stottlemyre .10 .05
❑ 153 Dick Schofield .10 .05
❑ 154 Chipper Jones 1.00 .45
❑ 155 Ryan Klesko .20 .09
❑ 156 David Justice .20 .09
❑ 157 Mike Kelly .10 .05
❑ 158 Roberto Kelly .10 .05
❑ 159 Tony Tarasco .10 .05
❑ 160 Javier Lopez .20 .09
❑ 161 Steve Avery .10 .05
❑ 162 Greg McMichael .10 .05
❑ 163 Kent Mercker .10 .05
❑ 164 Mark Lemke .10 .05
❑ 165 Tom Glavine .40 .18
❑ 166 Jose Oliva .10 .05
❑ 167 John Smoltz .20 .09
❑ 168 Jeff Blauser .10 .05
❑ 169 Troy O'Leary .10 .05
❑ 170 Greg Vaughn .20 .09
❑ 171 Jody Reed .10 .05
❑ 172 Kevin Seitzer .10 .05
❑ 173 Jeff Cirillo .20 .09
❑ 174 B.J. Surhoff .20 .09
❑ 175 Cal Eldred .10 .05
❑ 176 Jose Valentin .10 .05
❑ 177 Turner Ward .10 .05
❑ 178 Darryl Hamilton .10 .05
❑ 179 Pat Listach .10 .05
❑ 180 Matt Mieske .10 .05
❑ 181 Brian Harper .10 .05
❑ 182 Dave Nilsson .10 .05
❑ 183 Mike Fetters .10 .05
❑ 184 John Jaha .10 .05
❑ 185 Ricky Bones .10 .05
❑ 186 Geronimo Pena .10 .05
❑ 187 Bob Tewksbury .10 .05
❑ 188 Todd Zeile .10 .05
❑ 189 Danny Jackson .10 .05
❑ 190 Ray Lankford .20 .09
❑ 191 Bernard Gilkey .10 .05
❑ 192 Brian Jordan .20 .09
❑ 193 Tom Pagnozzi .10 .05
❑ 194 Rick Sutcliffe .20 .09
❑ 195 Mark Whiten .10 .05
❑ 196 Tom Henke .10 .05
❑ 197 Rene Arocha .10 .05
❑ 198 Allen Watson .10 .05
❑ 199 Mike Perez .10 .05
❑ 200 Ozzie Smith .50 .23
❑ 201 Anthony Young .10 .05
❑ 202 Rey Sanchez .10 .05
❑ 203 Steve Buechele .10 .05
❑ 204 Shawon Dunston .10 .05
❑ 205 Mark Grace .40 .18
❑ 206 Glenallen Hill .10 .05
❑ 207 Eddie Zambrano .10 .05
❑ 208 Rick Wilkins .10 .05
❑ 209 Derrick May .10 .05
❑ 210 Sammy Sosa .75 .35
❑ 211 Kevin Roberson .10 .05
❑ 212 Steve Trachsel .10 .05
❑ 213 Willie Banks .10 .05
❑ 214 Kevin Foster .10 .05
❑ 215 Randy Myers .10 .05
❑ 216 Mike Morgan .10 .05
❑ 217 Rafael Bournigal .10 .05
❑ 218 Delino DeShields .10 .05
❑ 219 Tim Wallach .10 .05
❑ 220 Eric Karros .20 .09
❑ 221 Jose Offerman .10 .05
❑ 222 Tom Candiotti .10 .05
❑ 223 Ismael Valdes .10 .05
❑ 224 Henry Rodriguez .10 .05
❑ 225 Billy Ashley .10 .05
❑ 226 Darren Dreifort .20 .09
❑ 227 Ramon Martinez .10 .05
❑ 228 Pedro Astacio .10 .05
❑ 229 Orel Hershiser .20 .09
❑ 230 Brett Butler .20 .09
❑ 231 Todd Hollandsworth .10 .05
❑ 232 Chan Ho Park .20 .09
❑ 233 Mike Lansing .10 .05
❑ 234 Sean Berry .10 .05
❑ 235 Rondell White .20 .09
❑ 236 Ken Hill .10 .05
❑ 237 Marquis Grissom .10 .05
❑ 238 Larry Walker .20 .09
❑ 239 John Wetteland .20 .09
❑ 240 Cliff Floyd .20 .09
❑ 241 Joey Eischen .10 .05
❑ 242 Lou Frazier .10 .05
❑ 243 Darrin Fletcher .10 .05
❑ 244 Pedro Martinez .50 .23
❑ 245 Wil Cordero .10 .05
❑ 246 Jeff Fassero .10 .05
❑ 247 Butch Henry .10 .05
❑ 248 Mel Rojas .10 .05
❑ 249 Kirk Rueter .10 .05
❑ 250 Moises Alou .20 .09
❑ 251 Rod Beck .10 .05
❑ 252 John Patterson .10 .05
❑ 253 Robby Thompson .10 .05
❑ 254 Royce Clayton .10 .05
❑ 255 Wm. VanLandingham .10 .05
❑ 256 Darren Lewis .10 .05
❑ 257 Kirt Manwaring .10 .05
❑ 258 Mark Portugal .10 .05
❑ 259 Bill Swift .10 .05
❑ 260 Rikkert Faneyte .10 .05
❑ 261 Mike Jackson .10 .05
❑ 262 Todd Benzinger .10 .05
❑ 263 Bud Black .10 .05
❑ 264 Salomon Torres .10 .05
❑ 265 Eddie Murray .40 .18
❑ 266 Mark Clark .10 .05
❑ 267 Paul Sorrento .10 .05
❑ 268 Jim Thome .20 .09
❑ 269 Omar Vizquel .20 .09
❑ 270 Carlos Baerga .10 .05
❑ 271 Jeff Russell .10 .05
❑ 272 Herbert Perry .10 .05
❑ 273 Sandy Alomar Jr. .20 .09
❑ 274 Dennis Martinez .20 .09
❑ 275 Manny Ramirez .50 .23
❑ 276 Wayne Kirby .10 .05
❑ 277 Charles Nagy .10 .05
❑ 278 Albie Lopez .10 .05
❑ 279 Jeromy Burnitz .20 .09
❑ 280 Dave Winfield .40 .18
❑ 281 Tim Davis .10 .05
❑ 282 Marc Newfield .10 .05
❑ 283 Tino Martinez .20 .09
❑ 284 Mike Blowers .10 .05
❑ 285 Goose Gossage .20 .09
❑ 286 Luis Sojo .10 .05
❑ 287 Edgar Martinez .20 .09
❑ 288 Rich Amaral .10 .05
❑ 289 Felix Fermin .10 .05
❑ 290 Jay Buhner .20 .09
❑ 291 Dan Wilson .10 .05
❑ 292 Bobby Ayala .10 .05
❑ 293 Dave Fleming .10 .05
❑ 294 Greg Pirkl .10 .05
❑ 295 Reggie Jefferson .10 .05
❑ 296 Greg Hibbard .10 .05
❑ 297 Yorkis Perez .10 .05
❑ 298 Kurt Miller .10 .05
❑ 299 Chuck Carr .10 .05
❑ 300 Gary Sheffield .40 .18
❑ 301 Jerry Browne .10 .05
❑ 302 Dave Magadan .10 .05
❑ 303 Kurt Abbott .10 .05
❑ 304 Pat Rapp .10 .05
❑ 305 Jeff Conine .10 .05
❑ 306 Benito Santiago .10 .05
❑ 307 Dave Weathers .10 .05
❑ 308 Robb Nen .10 .05
❑ 309 Chris Hammond .10 .05
❑ 310 Bryan Harvey .10 .05
❑ 311 Charlie Hough .20 .09
❑ 312 Greg Colbrunn .10 .05
❑ 313 David Segui .10 .05
❑ 314 Rico Brogna .10 .05
❑ 315 Jeff Kent .20 .09
❑ 316 Jose Vizcaino .10 .05
❑ 317 Jim Lindeman .10 .05
❑ 318 Carl Everett .20 .09
❑ 319 Ryan Thompson .10 .05
❑ 320 Bobby Bonilla .20 .09
❑ 321 Joe Orsulak .10 .05
❑ 322 Pete Harnisch .10 .05
❑ 323 Doug Linton .10 .05
❑ 324 Todd Hundley .10 .05
❑ 325 Bret Saberhagen .20 .09
❑ 326 Kelly Stinnett .10 .05
❑ 327 Jason Jacome .10 .05
❑ 328 Bobby Jones .10 .05
❑ 329 John Franco .20 .09
❑ 330 Rafael Palmeiro .40 .18
❑ 331 Chris Hoiles .10 .05
❑ 332 Leo Gomez .10 .05
❑ 333 Chris Sabo .10 .05
❑ 334 Brady Anderson .20 .09
❑ 335 Jeffrey Hammonds .20 .09
❑ 336 Dwight Smith .10 .05
❑ 337 Jack Voigt .10 .05
❑ 338 Harold Baines .20 .09
❑ 339 Ben McDonald .10 .05
❑ 340 Mike Mussina .40 .18
❑ 341 Bret Barberie .10 .05
❑ 342 Jamie Moyer .10 .05
❑ 343 Mike Oquist .10 .05
❑ 344 Sid Fernandez .10 .05
❑ 345 Eddie Williams .10 .05
❑ 346 Joey Hamilton .10 .05
❑ 347 Brian Williams .10 .05
❑ 348 Luis Lopez .10 .05
❑ 349 Steve Finley .20 .09
❑ 350 Andy Benes .10 .05
❑ 351 Andujar Cedeno .10 .05
❑ 352 Bip Roberts .10 .05
❑ 353 Ray McDavid .10 .05
❑ 354 Ken Caminiti .20 .09
❑ 355 Trevor Hoffman .20 .09
❑ 356 Mel Nieves .10 .05
❑ 357 Brad Ausmus .10 .05
❑ 358 Andy Ashby .10 .05
❑ 359 Scott Sanders .10 .05
❑ 360 Gregg Jefferies .10 .05
❑ 361 Mariano Duncan .10 .05
❑ 362 Dave Hollins .10 .05

❑ 363 Kevin Stocker .10 .05
❑ 364 Fernando Valenzuela .20 .09
❑ 365 Lenny Dykstra .20 .09
❑ 366 Jim Eisenreich .10 .05
❑ 367 Ricky Bottalico .10 .05
❑ 368 Doug Jones .10 .05
❑ 369 Ricky Jordan .10 .05
❑ 370 Darren Daulton .20 .09
❑ 371 Mike Lieberthal .20 .09
❑ 372 Bobby Munoz .10 .05
❑ 373 John Kruk .20 .09
❑ 374 Curt Schilling .20 .09
❑ 375 Orlando Merced .10 .05
❑ 376 Carlos Garcia .10 .05
❑ 377 Lance Parrish .10 .05
❑ 378 Steve Cooke .10 .05
❑ 379 Jeff King .10 .05
❑ 380 Jay Bell .20 .09
❑ 381 Al Martin .10 .05
❑ 382 Paul Wagner .10 .05
❑ 383 Rick White .10 .05
❑ 384 Midre Cummings .10 .05
❑ 385 Jon Lieber .10 .05
❑ 386 Dave Clark .10 .05
❑ 387 Don Slaught .10 .05
❑ 388 Denny Neagle .20 .09
❑ 389 Zane Smith .10 .05
❑ 390 Andy Van Slyke .20 .09
❑ 391 Ivan Rodriguez .50 .23
❑ 392 David Hulse .10 .05
❑ 393 John Burkett .10 .05
❑ 394 Kevin Brown .20 .09
❑ 395 Dean Palmer .20 .09
❑ 396 Otis Nixon .10 .05
❑ 397 Rick Helling .20 .09
❑ 398 Kenny Rogers .10 .05
❑ 399 Darren Oliver .10 .05
❑ 400 Will Clark .40 .18
❑ 401 Jeff Frye .10 .05
❑ 402 Kevin Gross .10 .05
❑ 403 John Dettmer .10 .05
❑ 404 Manny Lee .10 .05
❑ 405 Rusty Greer .20 .09
❑ 406 Aaron Sele .20 .09
❑ 407 Carlos Rodriguez .10 .05
❑ 408 Scott Cooper .10 .05
❑ 409 John Valentin .10 .05
❑ 410 Roger Clemens .75 .35
❑ 411 Mike Greenwell .10 .05
❑ 412 Tim Vanegmond .10 .05
❑ 413 Tom Brunansky .10 .05
❑ 414 Steve Farr .10 .05
❑ 415 Jose Canseco .50 .23
❑ 416 Joe Hesketh .10 .05
❑ 417 Ken Ryan .10 .05
❑ 418 Tim Naehring .10 .05
❑ 419 Frank Viola .10 .05
❑ 420 Andre Dawson .20 .09
❑ 421 Mo Vaughn .20 .09
❑ 422 Jeff Brantley .10 .05
❑ 423 Pete Schourek .10 .05
❑ 424 Hal Morris .10 .05
❑ 425 Deion Sanders .20 .09
❑ 426 Brian R. Hunter .10 .05
❑ 427 Bret Boone .20 .09
❑ 428 Willie Greene .10 .05
❑ 429 Ron Gant .10 .05
❑ 430 Barry Larkin .40 .18
❑ 431 Reggie Sanders .10 .05
❑ 432 Eddie Taubensee .10 .05
❑ 433 Jack Morris .20 .09
❑ 434 Jose Rijo .10 .05
❑ 435 Johnny Ruffin .10 .05
❑ 436 John Smiley .10 .05
❑ 437 John Roper .10 .05
❑ 438 Dave Nied .10 .05
❑ 439 Roberto Mejia .10 .05
❑ 440 Andres Galarraga .20 .09
❑ 441 Mike Kingery .10 .05
❑ 442 Curt Leskanic .10 .05
❑ 443 Walt Weiss .10 .05
❑ 444 Marvin Freeman .10 .05
❑ 445 Charlie Hayes .10 .05
❑ 446 Eric Young .10 .05
❑ 447 Ellis Burks .20 .09
❑ 448 Joe Girardi .10 .05
❑ 449 Lance Painter .10 .05
❑ 450 Dante Bichette .20 .09
❑ 451 Bruce Ruffin .10 .05
❑ 452 Jeff Granger .10 .05
❑ 453 Wally Joyner .20 .09
❑ 454 Jose Lind .10 .05
❑ 455 Jeff Montgomery .10 .05
❑ 456 Gary Gaetti .20 .09
❑ 457 Greg Gagne .10 .05
❑ 458 Vince Coleman .10 .05
❑ 459 Mike Macfarlane .10 .05
❑ 460 Brian McRae .10 .05
❑ 461 Tom Gordon .10 .05
❑ 462 Kevin Appier .20 .09
❑ 463 Billy Brewer .10 .05
❑ 464 Mark Gubicza .10 .05
❑ 465 Travis Fryman .20 .09
❑ 466 Danny Bautista .10 .05
❑ 467 Sean Bergman .10 .05
❑ 468 Mike Henneman .10 .05
❑ 469 Mike Moore .10 .05
❑ 470 Cecil Fielder .20 .09
❑ 471 Alan Trammell .20 .09
❑ 472 Kirk Gibson .20 .09
❑ 473 Tony Phillips .10 .05
❑ 474 Mickey Tettleton .10 .05
❑ 475 Lou Whitaker .20 .09
❑ 476 Chris Gomez .10 .05
❑ 477 John Doherty .10 .05
❑ 478 Greg Gohr .10 .05
❑ 479 Bill Gullickson .10 .05
❑ 480 Rick Aguilera .10 .05
❑ 481 Matt Walbeck .10 .05
❑ 482 Kevin Tapani .10 .05
❑ 483 Scott Erickson .10 .05
❑ 484 Steve Dunn .10 .05
❑ 485 David McCarty .10 .05
❑ 486 Scott Leius .10 .05
❑ 487 Pat Meares .10 .05
❑ 488 Jeff Reboulet .10 .05
❑ 489 Pedro Munoz .10 .05
❑ 490 Chuck Knoblauch .20 .09
❑ 491 Rich Becker .10 .05
❑ 492 Alex Cole .10 .05
❑ 493 Pat Mahomes .10 .05
❑ 494 Ozzie Guillen .10 .05
❑ 495 Tim Raines .20 .09
❑ 496 Kirk McCaskill .10 .05
❑ 497 Olmedo Saenz .10 .05
❑ 498 Scott Sanderson .10 .05
❑ 499 Lance Johnson .10 .05
❑ 500 Michael Jordan 1.50 .70
❑ 501 Warren Newson .10 .05
❑ 502 Ron Karkovice .10 .05
❑ 503 Wilson Alvarez .10 .05
❑ 504 Jason Bere .10 .05
❑ 505 Robin Ventura .20 .09
❑ 506 Alex Fernandez .10 .05
❑ 507 Roberto Hernandez .10 .05
❑ 508 Norberto Martin .10 .05
❑ 509 Bob Wickman .10 .05
❑ 510 Don Mattingly 1.00 .45
❑ 511 Melido Perez .10 .05
❑ 512 Pat Kelly .10 .05
❑ 513 Randy Velarde .10 .05
❑ 514 Tony Fernandez .10 .05
❑ 515 Jack McDowell .10 .05
❑ 516 Luis Polonia .10 .05
❑ 517 Bernie Williams .40 .18
❑ 518 Danny Tartabull .10 .05
❑ 519 Mike Stanley .10 .05
❑ 520 Wade Boggs .50 .23
❑ 521 Jim Leyritz .10 .05
❑ 522 Steve Howe .10 .05
❑ 523 Scott Kamieniecki .10 .05
❑ 524 Russ Davis .10 .05
❑ 525 Jim Abbott .20 .09
❑ 526 Eddie Murray CL .20 .09
❑ 527 Alex Rodriguez CL .75 .35
❑ 528 Jeff Bagwell CL .40 .18
❑ 529 Joe Carter CL .10 .05
❑ 530 Fred McGriff CL .10 .05
❑ 531T Tony Phillips TRADE .15 .07
❑ 532T Dave Magadan TRADE .15 .07
❑ 533T Mike Gallego TRADE .15 .07
❑ 534T Dave Stewart TRADE .25 .11
❑ 535T T. Stottlemyre TRADE .15 .07
❑ 536T David Cone TRADE .25 .11
❑ 537T M. Grissom TRADE .15 .07
❑ 538T Derrick May TRADE .15 .07
❑ 539T Joe Oliver TRADE .15 .07
❑ 540T Scott Cooper TRADE .15 .07
❑ 541T Ken Hill TRADE .15 .07
❑ 542T H. Johnson TRADE DP .15 .07
❑ 543T B. McRae TRADE DP .15 .07
❑ 544T J. Navarro TRADE DP .15 .07
❑ 545T O. Timmons TRADE DP .15 .07
❑ 546T R. Kelly TRADE DP .15 .07
❑ 547T Hideo Nomo TRADE DP 2.50 1.10
❑ 548T S. Andrews TRADE DP .15 .07
❑ 549T M.Grudzi TRADE DP .75 .35
❑ 550T C. Perez TRADE DP .25 .11
❑ 551T H.RodriguezTRADE DP .15 .07
❑ 552T T. Tarasco TRADE DP .15 .07
❑ 553T Glenallen Hill TRADE .15 .07
❑ 554T T. Mulholland TRADE .15 .07
❑ 555T Orel Hershiser TRADE .25 .11
❑ 556T Darren Bragg TRADE .15 .07
❑ 557T John Burkett TRADE .15 .07
❑ 558T Bobby Witt TRADE .15 .07
❑ 559T Terry Pendleton TRADE .25 .11
❑ 560T Andre Dawson TRADE .40 .18
❑ 561T Brett Butler TRADE .25 .11
❑ 562T Kevin Brown TRADE .40 .18
❑ 563T Doug Jones TRADE .15 .07
❑ 564T Andy Van Slyke TRADE .25 .11
❑ 565T Jody Reed TRADE .15 .07
❑ 566T F. Valenzuela TRADE .25 .11
❑ 567T Charlie Hayes TRADE .15 .07
❑ 568T Benji Gil TRADE .15 .07
❑ 569T Mark McLemore TRADE .15 .07
❑ 570T Mickey Tettleton TRADE .15 .07
❑ 571T Bob Tewksbury TRADE .15 .07
❑ 572T Rheal Cormier TRADE .15 .07
❑ 573T V. Eshelman TRADE .15 .07
❑ 574T M. Macfarlane TRADE .15 .07
❑ 575T Bill Swift TRADE .15 .07
❑ 576T Mark Whiten TRADE .15 .07
❑ 577T Benito Santiago TRADE .15 .07
❑ 578T Jason Bates TRADE .15 .07
❑ 579T Larry Walker TRADE .25 .11
❑ 580T Chad Curtis TRADE .15 .07
❑ 581T Bob Higginson TRADE 2.00 .90
❑ 582T Marty Cordova TRADE .15 .07
❑ 583T Mike Devereaux TRADE .15 .07
❑ 584T John Kruk TRADE .25 .11
❑ 585T John Wetteland TRADE .25 .11
❑ P172 Ken Griffey Jr. Promo 2.00 1.35

## 1996 Collector's Choice

| | MINT | NRMT |
|---|---|---|
| COMPLETE SET (730) | 24.00 | 11.00 |
| COMP.FACT.SET (790) | 30.00 | 13.50 |
| COMPLETE SERIES 1 (365) | 12.00 | 5.50 |
| COMPLETE SERIES 2 (365) | 12.00 | 5.50 |
| COMMON (1-365/396-760) | .10 | .05 |
| COMP.TRADE SET (30) | 15.00 | 6.75 |
| COMMON TRADE (366T-395T) | .20 | .07 |
| COMP.UPDATE SET (30) | 4.00 | 1.80 |
| COMMON UPDATE (761-790) | .20 | .11 |

❑ 1 Cal Ripken 1.50 .70
❑ 2 Edgar Martinez SL .20 .09

| |  |  | | |
|---|---|---|---|---|
| | | Tony Gwynn | | |
| ❑ | 3 | Albert Belle SL | .20 | .09 |
| | | Dante Bichette | | |
| ❑ | 4 | Albert Belle SL | .20 | .09 |
| | | Mo Vaughn | | |
| | | Dante Bichette | | |
| ❑ | 5 | Kenny Lofton SL | .20 | .09 |
| | | Quilvio Veras | | |
| ❑ | 6 | Mike Mussina SL | .50 | .23 |
| | | Greg Maddux | | |
| ❑ | 7 | Randy Johnson SL | .40 | .18 |
| | | Hideo Nomo | | |
| ❑ | 8 | Randy Johnson SL | .50 | .23 |
| | | Greg Maddux | | |
| ❑ | 9 | Jose Mesa SL | .10 | .05 |
| | | Randy Myers | | |
| ❑ | 10 | Johnny Damon | .20 | .09 |
| ❑ | 11 | Rick Krivda | .10 | .05 |
| ❑ | 12 | Roger Cedeno | .10 | .05 |
| ❑ | 13 | Angel Martinez | .10 | .05 |
| ❑ | 14 | Ariel Prieto | .10 | .05 |
| ❑ | 15 | John Wasdin | .10 | .05 |
| ❑ | 16 | Edwin Hurtado | .10 | .05 |
| ❑ | 17 | Lyle Mouton | .10 | .05 |
| ❑ | 18 | Chris Snopek | .10 | .05 |
| ❑ | 19 | Mariano Rivera | .20 | .09 |
| ❑ | 20 | Ruben Rivera | .10 | .05 |
| ❑ | 21 | Juan Castro RC | .10 | .05 |
| ❑ | 22 | Jimmy Haynes | .10 | .05 |
| ❑ | 23 | Bob Wolcott | .10 | .05 |
| ❑ | 24 | Brian Barber | .10 | .05 |
| ❑ | 25 | Frank Rodriguez | .10 | .05 |
| ❑ | 26 | Jesus Tavarez | .10 | .05 |
| ❑ | 27 | Glenn Dishman | .10 | .05 |
| ❑ | 28 | Jose Herrera | .10 | .05 |
| ❑ | 29 | Chan Ho Park | .20 | .09 |
| ❑ | 30 | Jason Isringhausen | .20 | .09 |
| ❑ | 31 | Doug Johns | .10 | .05 |
| ❑ | 32 | Gene Schall | .10 | .05 |
| ❑ | 33 | Kevin Jordan | .10 | .05 |
| ❑ | 34 | Matt Lawton RC | .50 | .23 |
| ❑ | 35 | Karim Garcia | .10 | .05 |
| ❑ | 36 | George Williams | .10 | .05 |
| ❑ | 37 | Orlando Palmeiro | .10 | .05 |
| ❑ | 38 | Jamie Brewington RC | .10 | .05 |
| ❑ | 39 | Robert Person | .10 | .05 |
| ❑ | 40 | Greg Maddux | 1.00 | .45 |
| ❑ | 41 | Marquis Grissom | .10 | .05 |
| ❑ | 42 | Chipper Jones | 1.00 | .45 |
| ❑ | 43 | David Justice | .20 | .09 |
| ❑ | 44 | Mark Lemke | .10 | .05 |
| ❑ | 45 | Fred McGriff | .20 | .09 |
| ❑ | 46 | Javier Lopez | .20 | .09 |
| ❑ | 47 | Mark Wohlers | .10 | .05 |
| ❑ | 48 | Jason Schmidt | .10 | .05 |
| ❑ | 49 | John Smoltz | .20 | .09 |
| ❑ | 50 | Curtis Goodwin | .10 | .05 |
| ❑ | 51 | Greg Zaun | .10 | .05 |
| ❑ | 52 | Armando Benitez | .10 | .05 |
| ❑ | 53 | Manny Alexander | .10 | .05 |
| ❑ | 54 | Chris Hoiles | .10 | .05 |
| ❑ | 55 | Harold Baines | .20 | .09 |
| ❑ | 56 | Ben McDonald | .10 | .05 |
| ❑ | 57 | Scott Erickson | .10 | .05 |
| ❑ | 58 | Jeff Manto | .10 | .05 |
| ❑ | 59 | Luis Alicea | .10 | .05 |
| ❑ | 60 | Roger Clemens | .75 | .35 |
| ❑ | 61 | Rheal Cormier | .10 | .05 |
| ❑ | 62 | Vaughn Eshelman | .10 | .05 |
| ❑ | 63 | Zane Smith | .10 | .05 |
| ❑ | 64 | Mike Macfarlane | .10 | .05 |
| ❑ | 65 | Erik Hanson | .10 | .05 |
| ❑ | 66 | Tim Naehring | .10 | .05 |
| ❑ | 67 | Lee Tinsley | .10 | .05 |
| ❑ | 68 | Troy O'Leary | .10 | .05 |
| ❑ | 69 | Garret Anderson | .20 | .09 |
| ❑ | 70 | Chili Davis | .20 | .09 |
| ❑ | 71 | Jim Edmonds | .40 | .10 |
| ❑ | 72 | Troy Percival | .10 | .05 |
| ❑ | 73 | Mark Langston | .10 | .05 |
| ❑ | 74 | Spike Owen | .10 | .05 |
| ❑ | 75 | Tim Salmon | .20 | .09 |
| ❑ | 76 | Brian Anderson | .10 | .05 |
| ❑ | 77 | Lee Smith | .20 | .09 |
| ❑ | 78 | Jim Abbott | .20 | .09 |
| ❑ | 79 | Jim Bullinger | .10 | .05 |
| ❑ | 80 | Mark Grace | .40 | .18 |
| ❑ | 81 | Todd Zeile | .10 | .05 |
| ❑ | 82 | Kevin Foster | .10 | .05 |
| ❑ | 83 | Howard Johnson | .20 | .09 |
| ❑ | 84 | Brian McRae | .10 | .05 |
| ❑ | 85 | Randy Myers | .10 | .05 |
| ❑ | 86 | Jaime Navarro | .10 | .05 |
| ❑ | 87 | Luis Gonzalez | .20 | .09 |
| ❑ | 88 | Ozzie Timmons | .10 | .05 |
| ❑ | 89 | Wilson Alvarez | .10 | .05 |
| ❑ | 90 | Frank Thomas | .75 | .35 |
| ❑ | 91 | James Baldwin | .10 | .05 |
| ❑ | 92 | Ray Durham | .20 | .09 |
| ❑ | 93 | Alex Fernandez | .10 | .05 |
| ❑ | 94 | Ozzie Guillen | .10 | .05 |
| ❑ | 95 | Tim Raines | .20 | .09 |
| ❑ | 96 | Roberto Hernandez | .10 | .05 |
| ❑ | 97 | Lance Johnson | .10 | .05 |
| ❑ | 98 | John Kruk | .20 | .09 |
| ❑ | 99 | Mark Portugal | .10 | .05 |
| ❑ | 100 | Don Mattingly TT | .50 | .18 |
| ❑ | 101 | Roger Clemens TT | .40 | .18 |
| ❑ | 102 | Raul Mondesi TT | .10 | .05 |
| ❑ | 103 | Cecil Fielder TT | .10 | .05 |
| ❑ | 104 | Ozzie Smith TT | .40 | .18 |
| ❑ | 105 | Frank Thomas TT | .40 | .18 |
| ❑ | 106 | Sammy Sosa TT | .40 | .18 |
| ❑ | 107 | Fred McGriff TT | .10 | .05 |
| ❑ | 108 | Barry Bonds TT | .20 | .09 |
| ❑ | 109 | Thomas Howard | .10 | .05 |
| ❑ | 110 | Ron Gant | .10 | .05 |
| ❑ | 111 | Eddie Taubensee | .10 | .05 |
| ❑ | 112 | Hal Morris | .10 | .05 |
| ❑ | 113 | Jose Rijo | .10 | .05 |
| ❑ | 114 | Pete Schourek | .10 | .05 |
| ❑ | 115 | Reggie Sanders | .10 | .05 |
| ❑ | 116 | Benito Santiago | .10 | .05 |
| ❑ | 117 | Jeff Brantley | .10 | .05 |
| ❑ | 118 | Julian Tavarez | .10 | .05 |
| ❑ | 119 | Carlos Baerga | .10 | .05 |
| ❑ | 120 | Jim Thome | .20 | .09 |
| ❑ | 121 | Jose Mesa | .10 | .05 |
| ❑ | 122 | Dennis Martinez | .20 | .09 |
| ❑ | 123 | Dave Winfield | .40 | .18 |
| ❑ | 124 | Eddie Murray | .40 | .18 |
| ❑ | 125 | Manny Ramirez | .50 | .23 |
| ❑ | 126 | Paul Sorrento | .10 | .05 |
| ❑ | 127 | Kenny Lofton | .20 | .09 |
| ❑ | 128 | Eric Young | .10 | .05 |
| ❑ | 129 | Jason Bates | .10 | .05 |
| ❑ | 130 | Bret Saberhagen | .20 | .09 |
| ❑ | 131 | Andres Galarraga | .20 | .09 |
| ❑ | 132 | Joe Girardi | .10 | .05 |
| ❑ | 133 | John VanderWal | .10 | .05 |
| ❑ | 134 | David Nied | .10 | .05 |
| ❑ | 135 | Dante Bichette | .20 | .09 |
| ❑ | 136 | Vinny Castilla | .20 | .09 |
| ❑ | 137 | Kevin Ritz | .10 | .05 |
| ❑ | 138 | Felipe Lira | .10 | .05 |
| ❑ | 139 | Joe Boever | .10 | .05 |
| ❑ | 140 | Cecil Fielder | .20 | .09 |
| ❑ | 141 | John Flaherty | .10 | .05 |
| ❑ | 142 | Kirk Gibson | .20 | .09 |
| ❑ | 143 | Brian Maxcy | .10 | .05 |
| ❑ | 144 | Lou Whitaker | .20 | .09 |
| ❑ | 145 | Alan Trammell | .20 | .09 |
| ❑ | 146 | Bobby Higginson | .20 | .09 |
| ❑ | 147 | Chad Curtis | .10 | .05 |
| ❑ | 148 | Quilvio Veras | .10 | .05 |
| ❑ | 149 | Jerry Browne | .10 | .05 |
| ❑ | 150 | Andre Dawson | .20 | .09 |
| ❑ | 151 | Robb Nen | .10 | .05 |
| ❑ | 152 | Greg Colbrunn | .10 | .05 |
| ❑ | 153 | Chris Hammond | .10 | .05 |
| ❑ | 154 | Kurt Abbott | .10 | .05 |
| ❑ | 155 | Charles Johnson | .20 | .09 |
| ❑ | 156 | Terry Pendleton | .20 | .09 |
| ❑ | 157 | Dave Weathers | .10 | .05 |
| ❑ | 158 | Mike Hampton | .20 | .09 |
| ❑ | 159 | Craig Biggio | .20 | .09 |
| ❑ | 160 | Jeff Bagwell | .50 | .23 |
| ❑ | 161 | Brian L.Hunter | .10 | .05 |
| ❑ | 162 | Mike Henneman | .10 | .05 |
| ❑ | 163 | Dave Magadan | .10 | .05 |
| ❑ | 164 | Shane Reynolds | .10 | .05 |
| ❑ | 165 | Derek Bell | .10 | .05 |
| ❑ | 166 | Orlando Miller | .10 | .05 |
| ❑ | 167 | James Mouton | .10 | .05 |
| ❑ | 168 | Melvin Bunch | .10 | .05 |
| ❑ | 169 | Tom Gordon | .10 | .05 |
| ❑ | 170 | Kevin Appier | .20 | .09 |
| ❑ | 171 | Tom Goodwin | .10 | .05 |
| ❑ | 172 | Greg Gagne | .10 | .05 |
| ❑ | 173 | Gary Gaetti | .20 | .09 |
| ❑ | 174 | Jeff Montgomery | .10 | .05 |
| ❑ | 175 | Jon Nunnally | .10 | .05 |
| ❑ | 176 | Michael Tucker | .10 | .05 |
| ❑ | 177 | Joe Vitiello | .10 | .05 |
| ❑ | 178 | Billy Ashley | .10 | .05 |
| ❑ | 179 | Tom Candiotti | .10 | .05 |
| ❑ | 180 | Hideo Nomo | .40 | .18 |
| ❑ | 181 | Chad Fonville | .10 | .05 |
| ❑ | 182 | Todd Hollandsworth | .10 | .05 |
| ❑ | 183 | Eric Karros | .20 | .09 |
| ❑ | 184 | Roberto Kelly | .10 | .05 |
| ❑ | 185 | Mike Piazza | 1.25 | .55 |
| ❑ | 186 | Ramon Martinez | .10 | .05 |
| ❑ | 187 | Tim Wallach | .10 | .05 |
| ❑ | 188 | Jeff Cirillo | .20 | .09 |
| ❑ | 189 | Sid Roberson | .10 | .05 |
| ❑ | 190 | Kevin Seitzer | .10 | .05 |
| ❑ | 191 | Mike Fetters | .10 | .05 |
| ❑ | 192 | Steve Sparks | .10 | .05 |
| ❑ | 193 | Matt Mieske | .10 | .05 |
| ❑ | 194 | Joe Oliver | .10 | .05 |
| ❑ | 195 | B.J. Surhoff | .20 | .09 |
| ❑ | 196 | Alberto Reyes | .10 | .05 |
| ❑ | 197 | Fernando Vina | .10 | .05 |
| ❑ | 198 | LaTroy Hawkins | .10 | .05 |
| ❑ | 199 | Marty Cordova | .10 | .05 |
| ❑ | 200 | Kirby Puckett | 1.00 | .45 |
| ❑ | 201 | Brad Radke | .20 | .09 |
| ❑ | 202 | Pedro Munoz | .10 | .05 |
| ❑ | 203 | Scott Klingenbeck | .10 | .05 |
| ❑ | 204 | Pat Meares | .10 | .05 |
| ❑ | 205 | Chuck Knoblauch | .20 | .09 |
| ❑ | 206 | Scott Stahoviak | .10 | .05 |
| ❑ | 207 | Dave Stevens | .10 | .05 |
| ❑ | 208 | Shane Andrews | .10 | .05 |
| ❑ | 209 | Moises Alou | .20 | .09 |
| ❑ | 210 | David Segui | .10 | .05 |
| ❑ | 211 | Cliff Floyd | .20 | .09 |
| ❑ | 212 | Carlos Perez | .10 | .05 |
| ❑ | 213 | Mark Grudzielanek | .10 | .05 |
| ❑ | 214 | Butch Henry | .10 | .05 |
| ❑ | 215 | Rondell White | .20 | .09 |
| ❑ | 216 | Mel Rojas | .10 | .05 |
| ❑ | 217 | Ugueth Urbina | .20 | .09 |
| ❑ | 218 | Edgardo Alfonzo | .20 | .09 |
| ❑ | 219 | Carl Everett | .20 | .09 |
| ❑ | 220 | John Franco | .20 | .09 |
| ❑ | 221 | Todd Hundley | .10 | .05 |
| ❑ | 222 | Bobby Jones | .10 | .05 |
| ❑ | 223 | Bill Pulsipher | .10 | .05 |
| ❑ | 224 | Rico Brogna | .10 | .05 |
| ❑ | 225 | Jeff Kent | .20 | .09 |
| ❑ | 226 | Chris Jones | .10 | .05 |
| ❑ | 227 | Butch Huskey | .10 | .05 |
| ❑ | 228 | Robert Eenhoorn | .10 | .05 |
| ❑ | 229 | Sterling Hitchcock | .10 | .05 |
| ❑ | 230 | Wade Boggs | .50 | .23 |
| ❑ | 231 | Derek Jeter | 1.50 | .70 |
| ❑ | 232 | Tony Fernandez | .10 | .05 |
| ❑ | 233 | Jack McDowell | .10 | .05 |
| ❑ | 234 | Andy Pettitte | .20 | .09 |
| ❑ | 235 | David Cone | .20 | .09 |
| ❑ | 236 | Mike Stanley | .10 | .05 |
| ❑ | 237 | Don Mattingly | 1.00 | .45 |
| ❑ | 238 | Geronimo Berroa | .10 | .05 |
| ❑ | 239 | Scott Brosius | .20 | .09 |
| ❑ | 240 | Rickey Henderson | .50 | .23 |
| ❑ | 241 | Terry Steinbach | .10 | .05 |
| ❑ | 242 | Mike Gallego | .10 | .05 |
| ❑ | 243 | Jason Giambi | .40 | .18 |
| ❑ | 244 | Steve Ontiveros | .10 | .05 |
| ❑ | 245 | Dennis Eckersley | .20 | .09 |
| ❑ | 246 | Dave Stewart | .20 | .09 |
| ❑ | 247 | Don Wengert | .10 | .05 |
| ❑ | 248 | Paul Quantrill | .10 | .05 |
| ❑ | 249 | Ricky Bottalico | .10 | .05 |
| ❑ | 250 | Kevin Stocker | .10 | .05 |
| ❑ | 251 | Lenny Dykstra | .20 | .09 |

❑ 252 Tony Longmire .10 .05
❑ 253 Tyler Green .10 .05
❑ 254 Mike Mimbs .10 .05
❑ 255 Charlie Hayes .10 .05
❑ 256 Mickey Morandini .10 .05
❑ 257 Heathcliff Slocumb .10 .05
❑ 258 Jeff King .10 .05
❑ 259 Midre Cummings .10 .05
❑ 260 Mark Johnson .10 .05
❑ 261 Freddy Garcia .10 .05
❑ 262 Jon Lieber .10 .05
❑ 263 Esteban Loaiza .10 .05
❑ 264 Dan Miceli .10 .05
❑ 265 Orlando Merced .10 .05
❑ 266 Denny Neagle .20 .09
❑ 267 Steve Parris .10 .05
❑ 268 Greg Maddux FT .50 .23
❑ 269 Randy Johnson FT .20 .09
❑ 270 Hideo Nomo FT .20 .09
❑ 271 Jose Mesa FT .10 .05
❑ 272 Mike Piazza FT .60 .25
❑ 273 Mo Vaughn FT .20 .09
❑ 274 Craig Biggio FT .20 .09
❑ 275 Edgar Martinez FT .20 .09
❑ 276 Barry Larkin FT .10 .05
❑ 277 Sammy Sosa FT .40 .18
❑ 278 Dante Bichette FT .10 .05
❑ 279 Albert Belle FT .10 .05
❑ 280 Ozzie Smith .50 .23
❑ 281 Mark Sweeney .10 .05
❑ 282 Terry Bradshaw .10 .05
❑ 283 Allen Battle .10 .05
❑ 284 Danny Jackson .10 .05
❑ 285 Tom Henke .10 .05
❑ 286 Scott Cooper .10 .05
❑ 287 Tripp Cromer .10 .05
❑ 288 Bernard Gilkey .10 .05
❑ 289 Brian Jordan .20 .09
❑ 290 Tony Gwynn .75 .35
❑ 291 Brad Ausmus .10 .05
❑ 292 Bryce Florie .10 .05
❑ 293 Andres Berumen .10 .05
❑ 294 Ken Caminiti .20 .09
❑ 295 Bip Roberts .10 .05
❑ 296 Trevor Hoffman .20 .09
❑ 297 Roberto Petagine .10 .05
❑ 298 Jody Reed .10 .05
❑ 299 Fernando Valenzuela .20 .09
❑ 300 Barry Bonds .60 .25
❑ 301 Mark Leiter .10 .05
❑ 302 Mark Carreon .10 .05
❑ 303 Royce Clayton .10 .05
❑ 304 Kirt Manwaring .10 .05
❑ 305 Glenallen Hill .10 .05
❑ 306 Deion Sanders .20 .09
❑ 307 Joe Rosselli .10 .05
❑ 308 Robby Thompson .10 .05
❑ 309 W. VanLandingham .10 .05
❑ 310 Ken Griffey Jr. 1.50 .70
❑ 311 Bobby Ayala .10 .05
❑ 312 Joey Cora .10 .05
❑ 313 Mike Blowers .10 .05
❑ 314 Darren Bragg .10 .05
❑ 315 Randy Johnson .50 .23
❑ 316 Alex Rodriguez 1.25 .55
❑ 317 Andy Benes .25 .11
❑ 318 Tino Martinez .20 .09
❑ 319 Dan Wilson .10 .05
❑ 320 Will Clark .40 .18
❑ 321 Jeff Frye .10 .05
❑ 322 Benji Gil .10 .05
❑ 323 Rick Helling .20 .09
❑ 324 Mark McLemore .10 .05
❑ 325 Dave Nilsson IF .10 .05
❑ 326 Larry Walker IF .20 .09
❑ 327 Jose Canseco IF .20 .09
❑ 328 Raul Mondesi IF .10 .05
❑ 329 Manny Ramirez IF .40 .18
❑ 330 Robert Eenhoorn IF .10 .05
❑ 331 Chili Davis IF .10 .05
❑ 332 Hideo Nomo IF .20 .09
❑ 333 Benji Gil IF .10 .05
❑ 334 Fernando Valenzuela IF .10 .05
❑ 335 Dennis Martinez IF .10 .05
❑ 336 Roberto Kelly IF .10 .05
❑ 337 Carlos Baerga IF .10 .05
❑ 338 Juan Gonzalez IF .20 .09
❑ 339 Roberto Alomar IF .20 .09
❑ 340 Chan Ho Park IF .10 .05
❑ 341 Andres Galarraga IF .10 .05
❑ 342 Midre Cummings IF .10 .05
❑ 343 Otis Nixon .10 .05
❑ 344 Jeff Russell .10 .05
❑ 345 Ivan Rodriguez .50 .23
❑ 346 Mickey Tettleton .10 .05
❑ 347 Bob Tewksbury .10 .05
❑ 348 Domingo Cedeno .10 .05
❑ 349 Lance Parrish .10 .05
❑ 350 Joe Carter .20 .09
❑ 351 Devon White .20 .09
❑ 352 Carlos Delgado .40 .18
❑ 353 Alex Gonzalez .10 .05
❑ 354 Darren Hall .10 .05
❑ 355 Paul Molitor .40 .18
❑ 356 Al Leiter .20 .09
❑ 357 Randy Knorr .10 .05
❑ 358 Ken Caminiti CL .10 .05
Steve Finley
Brian Williams
Roberto Petagine
Andujar Cedeno
Phil Plantier
Derek Bell
Pedro A. Martinez
Doug Brocail
Craig Shipley
Ricky Gutierrez
❑ 359 Hideo Nomo CL .20 .09
❑ 360 Ramon A.Martinez CL .10 .05
Ramon J.Martinez
❑ 361 Robin Ventura CL .10 .05
❑ 362 Cal Ripken CL .75 .35
❑ 363 Ken Caminiti CL .10 .05
❑ 364 Albert Belle CL .20 .09
Eddie Murray
❑ 365 Randy Johnson CL .20 .09
❑ 366T Tony Pena TRADE .15 .07
❑ 367T Jim Thome TRADE .50 .23
❑ 368T Don Mattingly TRADE 2.00 .90
❑ 369T Jim Leyritz TRADE .15 .07
❑ 370T Ken Griffey Jr. TRADE 3.00 1.35
❑ 371T Edgar Martinez TRADE .50 .23
❑ 372T Pete Schourek TRADE .15 .07
❑ 373T Mark Lewis TRADE .15 .07
❑ 374T Chipper Jones TRADE 2.00 .90
❑ 375T Fred McGriff TRADE .50 .23
❑ 376T Javy Lopez TRADE .30 .14
❑ 377T Fred McGriff TRADE .50 .23
❑ 378T Charlie O'Brien TRADE .15 .07
❑ 379T Mike Devereaux TRADE .15 .07
❑ 380T Mark Wohlers TRADE .15 .07
❑ 381T Bob Wolcott TRADE .15 .07
❑ 382T Manny Ramirez TRADE 1.00 .45
❑ 383T Jay Buhner TRADE .30 .14
❑ 384T Orel Hershiser TRADE .30 .14
❑ 385T Kenny Lofton TRADE .20 .09
❑ 386T Greg Maddux TRADE 2.00 .90
❑ 387T Javier Lopez TRADE .30 .14
❑ 388T Kenny Lofton TRADE .20 .09
❑ 389T Eddie Murray TRADE .75 .35
❑ 390T Luis Polonia TRADE .15 .07
❑ 391T Pedro Borbon TRADE .15 .07
❑ 392T Jim Thome TRADE .50 .23
❑ 393T Orel Hershiser TRADE .30 .14
❑ 394T David Justice TRADE .15 .07
❑ 395T Tom Glavine TRADE .75 .35
❑ 396 Greg Maddux TC .50 .23
❑ 397 Rico Brogna TC .10 .05
❑ 398 Darren Daulton TC .10 .05
❑ 399 Gary Sheffield TC .20 .09
❑ 400 Moises Alou TC .10 .05
❑ 401 Barry Larkin TC .10 .05
❑ 402 Jeff Bagwell TC .40 .18
❑ 403 Sammy Sosa TC .40 .18
❑ 404 Ozzie Smith TC .40 .18
❑ 405 Jay Bell TC .10 .05
❑ 406 Mike Piazza TC .60 .25
❑ 407 Dante Bichette TC .10 .05
❑ 408 Tony Gwynn TC .40 .18
❑ 409 Barry Bonds TC .20 .09
❑ 410 Kenny Lofton TC .10 .05
❑ 411 Johnny Damon TC .10 .05
❑ 412 Frank Thomas TC .40 .18
❑ 413 Greg Vaughn TC .10 .05
❑ 414 Paul Molitor TC .20 .09
❑ 415 Ken Griffey Jr. TC .75 .35
❑ 416 Tim Salmon TC .10 .05
❑ 417 Juan Gonzalez TC .20 .09
❑ 418 Mark McGwire TC .75 .35
❑ 419 Roger Clemens TC .40 .18
❑ 420 Wade Boggs TC .20 .09
❑ 421 Cal Ripken TC .75 .35
❑ 422 Cecil Fielder TC .10 .05
❑ 423 Joe Carter TC .10 .05
❑ 424 Osvaldo Fernandez RC .10 .05
❑ 425 Billy Wagner .10 .05
❑ 426 George Arias .10 .05
❑ 427 Mendy Lopez .10 .05
❑ 428 Jeff Suppan .10 .05
❑ 429 Rey Ordonez .10 .05
❑ 430 Brooks Kieschnick .10 .05
❑ 431 Raul Ibanez RC .10 .05
❑ 432 Livan Hernandez RC .50 .23
❑ 433 Shannon Stewart .20 .09
❑ 434 Steve Cox .10 .05
❑ 435 Trey Beamon .10 .05
❑ 436 Sergio Nunez .10 .05
❑ 437 Jermaine Dye .20 .09
❑ 438 Mike Sweeney RC 1.50 .70
❑ 439 Richard Hidalgo .20 .09
❑ 440 Todd Greene .10 .05
❑ 441 Robert Smith RC .25 .11
❑ 442 Rafael Orellano .10 .05
❑ 443 Wilton Guerrero RC .25 .11
❑ 444 David Doster .10 .05
❑ 445 Jason Kendall .20 .09
❑ 446 Edgar Renteria .20 .09
❑ 447 Scott Spiezio .10 .05
❑ 448 Jay Canizaro .10 .05
❑ 449 Enrique Wilson .10 .05
❑ 450 Bob Abreu .50 .23
❑ 451 Dwight Smith .10 .05
❑ 452 Jeff Blauser .10 .05
❑ 453 Steve Avery .10 .05
❑ 454 Brad Clontz .10 .05
❑ 455 Tom Glavine .40 .18
❑ 456 Mike Mordecai .10 .05
❑ 457 Rafael Belliard .10 .05
❑ 458 Greg McMichael .10 .05
❑ 459 Pedro Borbon .10 .05
❑ 460 Ryan Klesko .20 .09
❑ 461 Terrell Wade .10 .05
❑ 462 Brady Anderson .20 .09
❑ 463 Roberto Alomar .40 .18
❑ 464 Bobby Bonilla .20 .09
❑ 465 Mike Mussina .40 .18
❑ 466 Cesar Devarez .10 .05
❑ 467 Jeffrey Hammonds .20 .09
❑ 468 Mike Devereaux .10 .05
❑ 469 B.J. Surhoff .20 .09
❑ 470 Rafael Palmeiro .40 .18
❑ 471 John Valentin .10 .05
❑ 472 Mike Greenwell .10 .05
❑ 473 Dwayne Hosey .10 .05
❑ 474 Tim Wakefield .10 .05
❑ 475 Jose Canseco .50 .23
❑ 476 Aaron Sele .20 .09
❑ 477 Stan Belinda .10 .05
❑ 478 Mike Stanley .10 .05
❑ 479 Jamie Moyer .10 .05
❑ 480 Mo Vaughn .20 .09
❑ 481 Randy Velarde .10 .05
❑ 482 Gary DiSarcina .10 .05
❑ 483 Jorge Fabregas .10 .05
❑ 484 Rex Hudler .10 .05
❑ 485 Chuck Finley .20 .09
❑ 486 Tim Wallach .10 .05
❑ 487 Eduardo Perez .10 .05
❑ 488 Scott Sanderson .10 .05
❑ 489 J.T. Snow .20 .09
❑ 490 Sammy Sosa .75 .35
❑ 491 Terry Adams .10 .05
❑ 492 Matt Franco .10 .05
❑ 493 Scott Servais .10 .05
❑ 494 Frank Castillo .10 .05
❑ 495 Ryne Sandberg .50 .23
❑ 496 Rey Sanchez .10 .05
❑ 497 Steve Trachsel .10 .05

❑ 498 Jose Hernandez .10 .05
❑ 499 Dave Martinez .10 .05
❑ 500 Babe Ruth FC 1.00 .45
❑ 501 Ty Cobb FC .40 .18
❑ 502 Walter Johnson FC .20 .09
❑ 503 Christy Mathewson FC .20 .09
❑ 504 Honus Wagner FC .20 .09
❑ 505 Robin Ventura .20 .09
❑ 506 Jason Bere .10 .05
❑ 507 Mike Cameron RC .60 .25
❑ 508 Ron Karkovice .10 .05
❑ 509 Matt Karchner .10 .05
❑ 510 Harold Baines .20 .09
❑ 511 Kirk McCaskill .10 .05
❑ 512 Larry Thomas .10 .05
❑ 513 Danny Tartabull .10 .05
❑ 514 Steve Gibralter .10 .05
❑ 515 Bret Boone .20 .09
❑ 516 Jeff Branson .10 .05
❑ 517 Kevin Jarvis .10 .05
❑ 518 Xavier Hernandez .10 .05
❑ 519 Eric Owens .10 .05
❑ 520 Barry Larkin .40 .18
❑ 521 Dave Burba .10 .05
❑ 522 John Smiley .10 .05
❑ 523 Paul Assenmacher .10 .05
❑ 524 Chad Ogea .10 .05
❑ 525 Orel Hershiser .20 .09
❑ 526 Alan Embree .10 .05
❑ 527 Tony Pena .10 .05
❑ 528 Omar Vizquel .20 .09
❑ 529 Mark Clark .10 .05
❑ 530 Albert Belle .20 .09
❑ 531 Charles Nagy .10 .05
❑ 532 Herbert Perry .10 .05
❑ 533 Darren Holmes .10 .05
❑ 534 Ellis Burks .20 .09
❑ 535 Billy Swift .10 .05
❑ 536 Armando Reynoso .10 .05
❑ 537 Curtis Leskanic .10 .05
❑ 538 Quinton McCracken .10 .05
❑ 539 Steve Reed .10 .05
❑ 540 Larry Walker .20 .09
❑ 541 Walt Weiss .10 .05
❑ 542 Bryan Rekar .10 .05
❑ 543 Tony Clark .10 .05
❑ 544 Steve Rodriguez .10 .05
❑ 545 C.J. Nitkowski .10 .05
❑ 546 Todd Steverson .10 .05
❑ 547 Jose Lima .10 .05
❑ 548 Phil Nevin .20 .09
❑ 549 Chris Gomez .10 .05
❑ 550 Travis Fryman .20 .09
❑ 551 Mark Lewis .10 .05
❑ 552 Alex Arias .10 .05
❑ 553 Marc Valdes .10 .05
❑ 554 Kevin Brown .20 .09
❑ 555 Jeff Conine .10 .05
❑ 556 John Burkett .10 .05
❑ 557 Devon White .20 .09
❑ 558 Pat Rapp .10 .05
❑ 559 Jay Powell .10 .05
❑ 560 Gary Sheffield .40 .18
❑ 561 Jim Dougherty .10 .05
❑ 562 Todd Jones .10 .05
❑ 563 Tony Eusebio .10 .05
❑ 564 Darryl Kile .20 .09
❑ 565 Doug Drabek .10 .05
❑ 566 Mike Simms .10 .05
❑ 567 Derrick May .10 .05
❑ 568 Donne Wall .10 .05
❑ 569 Greg Swindell .10 .05
❑ 570 Jim Pittsley .10 .05
❑ 571 Bob Hamelin .10 .05
❑ 572 Mark Gubicza .10 .05
❑ 573 Chris Haney .10 .05
❑ 574 Keith Lockhart .10 .05
❑ 575 Mike Macfarlane .10 .05
❑ 576 Les Norman .10 .05
❑ 577 Joe Randa .10 .05
❑ 578 Chris Stynes .10 .05
❑ 579 Greg Gagne .10 .05
❑ 580 Raul Mondesi .20 .09
❑ 581 Delino DeShields .10 .05
❑ 582 Pedro Astacio .10 .05
❑ 583 Antonio Osuna .10 .05
❑ 584 Brett Butler .20 .09
❑ 585 Todd Worrell .10 .05
❑ 586 Mike Blowers .10 .05
❑ 587 Felix Rodriguez .10 .05
❑ 588 Ismael Valdes .10 .05
❑ 589 Ricky Bones .10 .05
❑ 590 Greg Vaughn .20 .09
❑ 591 Mark Loretta .10 .05
❑ 592 Cal Eldred .10 .05
❑ 593 Chuck Carr .10 .05
❑ 594 Dave Nilsson .10 .05
❑ 595 John Jaha .10 .05
❑ 596 Scott Karl .10 .05
❑ 597 Pat Listach .10 .05
❑ 598 Jose Valentin .10 .05
❑ 599 Mike Trombley .10 .05
❑ 600 Paul Molitor .40 .18
❑ 601 Dave Hollins .10 .05
❑ 602 Ron Coomer .10 .05
❑ 603 Matt Walbeck .10 .05
❑ 604 Roberto Kelly .10 .05
❑ 605 Rick Aguilera .10 .05
❑ 606 Pat Mahomes .10 .05
❑ 607 Jeff Reboulet .10 .05
❑ 608 Rich Becker .10 .05
❑ 609 Tim Scott .10 .05
❑ 610 Pedro Martinez .50 .23
❑ 611 Kirk Rueter .10 .05
❑ 612 Tavo Alvarez .10 .05
❑ 613 Yamil Benitez .10 .05
❑ 614 Darrin Fletcher .10 .05
❑ 615 Mike Lansing .10 .05
❑ 616 Henry Rodriguez .10 .05
❑ 617 Tony Tarasco .10 .05
❑ 618 Alex Ochoa .10 .05
❑ 619 Tim Bogar .10 .05
❑ 620 Bernard Gilkey .10 .05
❑ 621 Dave Mlicki .10 .05
❑ 622 Brent Mayne .10 .05
❑ 623 Ryan Thompson .10 .05
❑ 624 Pete Harnisch .10 .05
❑ 625 Lance Johnson .10 .05
❑ 626 Jose Vizcaino .10 .05
❑ 627 Doug Henry .10 .05
❑ 628 Scott Kamieniecki .10 .05
❑ 629 Jim Leyritz .10 .05
❑ 630 Ruben Sierra .10 .05
❑ 631 Pat Kelly .10 .05
❑ 632 Joe Girardi .10 .05
❑ 633 John Wetteland .20 .09
❑ 634 Melido Perez .10 .05
❑ 635 Paul O'Neill .20 .09
❑ 636 Jorge Posada .20 .09
❑ 637 Bernie Williams .40 .18
❑ 638 Mark Acre .10 .05
❑ 639 Mike Bordick .10 .05
❑ 640 Mark McGwire 1.50 .70
❑ 641 Fausto Cruz .10 .05
❑ 642 Ernie Young .10 .05
❑ 643 Todd Van Poppel .10 .05
❑ 644 Craig Paquette .10 .05
❑ 645 Brent Gates .10 .05
❑ 646 Pedro Munoz .10 .05
❑ 647 Andrew Lorraine .10 .05
❑ 648 Sid Fernandez .10 .05
❑ 649 Jim Eisenreich .10 .05
❑ 650 Johnny Damon AFL .20 .09
❑ 651 Dustin Hermanson AFL .10 .05
❑ 652 Joe Randa AFL .10 .05
❑ 653 Michael Tucker AFL .10 .05
❑ 654 Alan Benes AFL .10 .05
❑ 655 Chad Fonville AFL .10 .05
❑ 656 David Bell AFL .10 .05
❑ 657 Jon Nunnally AFL .10 .05
❑ 658 Chan Ho Park AFL .20 .09
❑ 659 LaTroy Hawkins AFL .10 .05
❑ 660 Jamie Brewington AFL .10 .05
❑ 661 Quinton McCracken AFL .10 .05
❑ 662 Tim Unroe AFL .10 .05
❑ 663 Jeff Ware AFL .10 .05
❑ 664 Todd Greene AFL .10 .05
❑ 665 Andrew Lorraine AFL .10 .05
❑ 666 Ernie Young AFL .10 .05
❑ 667 Toby Borland .10 .05
❑ 668 Lenny Webster .10 .05
❑ 669 Benito Santiago .10 .05
❑ 670 Gregg Jefferies .10 .05
❑ 671 Darren Daulton .20 .09
❑ 672 Curt Schilling .20 .09
❑ 673 Mark Whiten .10 .05
❑ 674 Todd Zeile .10 .05
❑ 675 Jay Bell .20 .09
❑ 676 Paul Wagner .10 .05
❑ 677 Dave Clark .10 .05
❑ 678 Nelson Liriano .10 .05
❑ 679 Ramon Morel .10 .05
❑ 680 Charlie Hayes .10 .05
❑ 681 Angelo Encarnacion .10 .05
❑ 682 Al Martin .10 .05
❑ 683 Jacob Brumfield .10 .05
❑ 684 Mike Kingery .10 .05
❑ 685 Carlos Garcia .10 .05
❑ 686 Tom Pagnozzi .10 .05
❑ 687 David Bell .10 .05
❑ 688 Todd Stottlemyre .10 .05
❑ 689 Jose Oliva .10 .05
❑ 690 Ray Lankford .20 .09
❑ 691 Mike Morgan .10 .05
❑ 692 John Frascatore .10 .05
❑ 693 John Mabry .10 .05
❑ 694 Mark Petkovsek .10 .05
❑ 695 Alan Benes .10 .05
❑ 696 Steve Finley .20 .09
❑ 697 Marc Newfield .10 .05
❑ 698 Andy Ashby .10 .05
❑ 699 Marc Kroon .10 .05
❑ 700 Wally Joyner .20 .09
❑ 701 Joey Hamilton .10 .05
❑ 702 Dustin Hermanson .10 .05
❑ 703 Scott Sanders .10 .05
❑ 704 Marty Cordova ROY .10 .05
❑ 705 Hideo Nomo ROY .20 .09
❑ 706 Mo Vaughn MVP .20 .09
❑ 707 Barry Larkin MVP .10 .05
❑ 708 Randy Johnson CY .20 .09
❑ 709 Greg Maddux CY .50 .23
❑ 710 Mark McGwire CB .75 .35
❑ 711 Ron Gant CB .10 .05
❑ 712 Andujar Cedeno .10 .05
❑ 713 Brian Johnson .10 .05
❑ 714 J.R. Phillips .10 .05
❑ 715 Rod Beck .10 .05
❑ 716 Sergio Valdez .10 .05
❑ 717 Marvin Benard RC .10 .05
❑ 718 Steve Scarsone .10 .05
❑ 719 Rich Aurilia RC .40 .18
❑ 720 Matt Williams .20 .09
❑ 721 John Patterson .10 .05
❑ 722 Shawn Estes .20 .09
❑ 723 Russ Davis .10 .05
❑ 724 Rich Amaral .10 .05
❑ 725 Edgar Martinez .20 .09
❑ 726 Norm Charlton .10 .05
❑ 727 Paul Sorrento .10 .05
❑ 728 Luis Sojo .10 .05
❑ 729 Arquimedez Pozo .10 .05
❑ 730 Jay Buhner .20 .09
❑ 731 Chris Bosio .10 .05
❑ 732 Chris Widger .10 .05
❑ 733 Kevin Gross .10 .05
❑ 734 Darren Oliver .10 .05
❑ 735 Dean Palmer .20 .09
❑ 736 Matt Whiteside .10 .05
❑ 737 Luis Ortiz .10 .05
❑ 738 Roger Pavlik .10 .05
❑ 739 Damon Buford .10 .05
❑ 740 Juan Gonzalez .40 .18
❑ 741 Rusty Greer .20 .09
❑ 742 Lou Frazier .10 .05
❑ 743 Pat Hentgen .10 .05
❑ 744 Tomas Perez .10 .05
❑ 745 Juan Guzman .10 .05
❑ 746 Otis Nixon .10 .05
❑ 747 Robert Perez .10 .05
❑ 748 Ed Sprague .10 .05
❑ 749 Tony Castillo .10 .05
❑ 750 John Olerud .20 .09
❑ 751 Shawn Green .40 .18
❑ 752 Jeff Ware .10 .05
❑ 753 Dante Bichette CL .10 .05
Vinny Castilla
Andres Galarraga

| | | |
|---|---|---|
| Larry Walker | | |
| ❑ 754 Greg Maddux CL | .50 | .23 |
| ❑ 755 Marty Cordova CL | .10 | .05 |
| ❑ 756 Ozzie Smith CL | .40 | .18 |
| ❑ 757 John Vanderwal CL | .10 | .05 |
| ❑ 758 Andres Galarraga CL | .10 | .05 |
| ❑ 759 Frank Thomas CL | .50 | .23 |
| ❑ 760 Tony Gwynn CL | .40 | .18 |
| ❑ 761 Randy Myers UPD | .25 | .11 |
| ❑ 762 Kent Mercker UPD | .40 | .18 |
| ❑ 763 David Wells UPD | .50 | .23 |
| ❑ 764 Tom Gordon UPD | .25 | .11 |
| ❑ 765 Wil Cordero UPD | .25 | .11 |
| ❑ 766 Dave Magadan UPD | .25 | .11 |
| ❑ 767 Doug Jones UPD | .25 | .11 |
| ❑ 768 Kevin Tapani UPD | .25 | .11 |
| ❑ 769 Curtis Goodwin UPD | .25 | .11 |
| ❑ 770 Julio Franco UPD | .25 | .11 |
| ❑ 771 Jack McDowell UPD | .25 | .11 |
| ❑ 772 Al Leiter UPD | .40 | .18 |
| ❑ 773 Sean Berry UPD | .25 | .11 |
| ❑ 774 Bip Roberts UPD | .25 | .11 |
| ❑ 775 Jose Offerman UPD | .25 | .11 |
| ❑ 776 Ben McDonald UPD | .25 | .11 |
| ❑ 777 Dan Serafini UPD | .25 | .11 |
| ❑ 778 Ryan McGuire UPD | .25 | .11 |
| ❑ 779 Tim Raines UPD | .40 | .18 |
| ❑ 780 Tino Martinez UPD | .40 | .18 |
| ❑ 781 Kenny Rogers UPD | .25 | .11 |
| ❑ 782 Bob Tewksbury UPD | .25 | .11 |
| ❑ 783 Rickey Henderson UPD | 1.00 | .45 |
| ❑ 784 Ron Gant UPD | .25 | .11 |
| ❑ 785 Gary Gaetti UPD | .40 | .18 |
| ❑ 786 Andy Benes UPD | .25 | .11 |
| ❑ 787 Royce Clayton UPD | .25 | .11 |
| ❑ 788 Darryl Hamilton UPD | .25 | .11 |
| ❑ 789 Ken Hill UPD | .25 | .11 |
| ❑ 790 Erik Hanson UPD | .25 | .11 |
| ❑ P100 Ken Griffey Jr. Promo | 2.00 | 1.35 |

## 1997 Collector's Choice

| | MINT | NRMT |
|---|---|---|
| COMPLETE SET (506) | 40.00 | 18.00 |
| COMP.FACT.SET (516) | 40.00 | 18.00 |
| COMPLETE SERIES 1 (246) | 20.00 | 9.00 |
| COMPLETE SERIES 2 (260) | 20.00 | 9.00 |
| COMMON CARD (1-506) | .10 | .05 |

| | | |
|---|---|---|
| ❑ 1 Andruw Jones | .50 | .23 |
| ❑ 2 Rocky Coppinger | .10 | .05 |
| ❑ 3 Jeff D'Amico | .10 | .05 |
| ❑ 4 Dmitri Young | .20 | .09 |
| ❑ 5 Darin Erstad | .50 | .23 |
| ❑ 6 Jermaine Allensworth | .10 | .05 |
| ❑ 7 Damian Jackson | .10 | .05 |
| ❑ 8 Bill Mueller RC | .25 | .11 |
| ❑ 9 Jacob Cruz | .10 | .05 |
| ❑ 10 Vladimir Guerrero | .75 | .35 |
| ❑ 11 Marty Janzen | .10 | .05 |
| ❑ 12 Kevin L. Brown | .10 | .05 |
| ❑ 13 Willie Adams | .10 | .05 |
| ❑ 14 Wendell Magee | .10 | .05 |
| ❑ 15 Scott Rolen | .40 | .18 |
| ❑ 16 Matt Beech | .10 | .05 |
| ❑ 17 Neifi Perez | .10 | .05 |
| ❑ 18 Jamey Wright | .10 | .05 |
| ❑ 19 Jose Paniagua | .10 | .05 |
| ❑ 20 Todd Walker | .10 | .05 |
| ❑ 21 Justin Thompson | .10 | .05 |
| ❑ 22 Robin Jennings | .10 | .05 |
| ❑ 23 Dario Veras RC | .20 | .09 |
| ❑ 24 Brian Lesher RC | .10 | .05 |
| ❑ 25 Nomar Garciaparra | 1.25 | .55 |
| ❑ 26 Luis Castillo | .20 | .09 |
| ❑ 27 Brian Giles RC | 1.50 | .70 |
| ❑ 28 Jermaine Dye | .20 | .09 |
| ❑ 29 Terrell Wade | .10 | .05 |
| ❑ 30 Fred McGriff | .30 | .14 |
| ❑ 31 Marquis Grissom | .10 | .05 |
| ❑ 32 Ryan Klesko | .20 | .09 |
| ❑ 33 Javier Lopez | .20 | .09 |
| ❑ 34 Mark Wohlers | .10 | .05 |
| ❑ 35 Tom Glavine | .40 | .18 |
| ❑ 36 Denny Neagle | .20 | .09 |
| ❑ 37 Scott Erickson | .10 | .05 |
| ❑ 38 Chris Hoiles | .10 | .05 |
| ❑ 39 Roberto Alomar | .40 | .18 |
| ❑ 40 Eddie Murray | .40 | .18 |
| ❑ 41 Cal Ripken | 1.50 | .70 |
| ❑ 42 Randy Myers | .10 | .05 |
| ❑ 43 B.J. Surhoff | .20 | .09 |
| ❑ 44 Rick Krivda | .10 | .05 |
| ❑ 45 Jose Canseco | .50 | .23 |
| ❑ 46 Heathcliff Slocumb | .10 | .05 |
| ❑ 47 Jeff Suppan | .10 | .05 |
| ❑ 48 Tom Gordon | .10 | .05 |
| ❑ 49 Aaron Sele | .20 | .09 |
| ❑ 50 Mo Vaughn | .20 | .09 |
| ❑ 51 Darren Bragg | .10 | .05 |
| ❑ 52 Wil Cordero | .10 | .05 |
| ❑ 53 Scott Bullett | .10 | .05 |
| ❑ 54 Terry Adams | .10 | .05 |
| ❑ 55 Jackie Robinson | 1.00 | .45 |
| ❑ 56 Tony Gwynn LL | .50 | .23 |
| Alex Rodriguez | | |
| ❑ 57 Andres Galarraga LL | .30 | .14 |
| Mark McGwire | | |
| ❑ 58 Andres Galarraga LL | .10 | .05 |
| Albert Belle | | |
| ❑ 59 Eric Young LL | .10 | .05 |
| Kenny Lofton | | |
| ❑ 60 John Smoltz LL | .10 | .05 |
| Andy Pettitte | | |
| ❑ 61 John Smoltz LL | .20 | .09 |
| Roger Clemens | | |
| ❑ 62 Kevin Brown LL | .10 | .05 |
| Juan Guzman | | |
| ❑ 63 John Wetteland LL | .10 | .05 |
| Todd Worrell | | |
| Jeff Brantley | | |
| ❑ 64 Scott Servais | .10 | .05 |
| ❑ 65 Sammy Sosa | .75 | .35 |
| ❑ 66 Ryne Sandberg | .50 | .23 |
| ❑ 67 Frank Castillo | .10 | .05 |
| ❑ 68 Rey Sanchez | .10 | .05 |
| ❑ 69 Steve Trachsel | .10 | .05 |
| ❑ 70 Robin Ventura | .20 | .09 |
| ❑ 71 Wilson Alvarez | .10 | .05 |
| ❑ 72 Tony Phillips | .10 | .05 |
| ❑ 73 Lyle Mouton | .10 | .05 |
| ❑ 74 Mike Cameron | .20 | .09 |
| ❑ 75 Harold Baines | .20 | .09 |
| ❑ 76 Albert Belle | .30 | .14 |
| ❑ 77 Chris Snopek | .10 | .05 |
| ❑ 78 Reggie Sanders | .10 | .05 |
| ❑ 79 Jeff Brantley | .10 | .05 |
| ❑ 80 Barry Larkin | .40 | .18 |
| ❑ 81 Kevin Jarvis | .10 | .05 |
| ❑ 82 John Smiley | .10 | .05 |
| ❑ 83 Pete Schourek | .10 | .05 |
| ❑ 84 Thomas Howard | .10 | .05 |
| ❑ 85 Lee Smith | .20 | .09 |
| ❑ 86 Omar Vizquel | .20 | .09 |
| ❑ 87 Julio Franco | .20 | .09 |
| ❑ 88 Orel Hershiser | .20 | .09 |
| ❑ 89 Charles Nagy | .10 | .05 |
| ❑ 90 Matt Williams | .30 | .14 |
| ❑ 91 Dennis Martinez | .20 | .09 |
| ❑ 92 Jose Mesa | .10 | .05 |
| ❑ 93 Sandy Alomar Jr. | .20 | .09 |
| ❑ 94 Jim Thome | .30 | .14 |
| ❑ 95 Vinny Castilla | .20 | .09 |
| ❑ 96 Armando Reynoso | .10 | .05 |
| ❑ 97 Kevin Ritz | .10 | .05 |
| ❑ 98 Larry Walker | .20 | .09 |
| ❑ 99 Eric Young | .10 | .05 |
| ❑ 100 Dante Bichette | .20 | .09 |
| ❑ 101 Quinton McCracken | .10 | .05 |
| ❑ 102 John Vander Wal | .10 | .05 |
| ❑ 103 Phil Nevin | .20 | .09 |
| ❑ 104 Tony Clark | .10 | .05 |
| ❑ 105 Alan Trammell | .20 | .09 |
| ❑ 106 Felipe Lira | .10 | .05 |
| ❑ 107 Curtis Pride | .10 | .05 |
| ❑ 108 Bobby Higginson | .20 | .09 |
| ❑ 109 Mark Lewis | .10 | .05 |
| ❑ 110 Travis Fryman | .20 | .09 |
| ❑ 111 Al Leiter | .20 | .09 |
| ❑ 112 Devon White | .20 | .09 |
| ❑ 113 Jeff Conine | .10 | .05 |
| ❑ 114 Charles Johnson | .20 | .09 |
| ❑ 115 Andre Dawson | .30 | .14 |
| ❑ 116 Edgar Renteria | .20 | .09 |
| ❑ 117 Robb Nen | .10 | .05 |
| ❑ 118 Kevin Brown | .30 | .14 |
| ❑ 119 Derek Bell | .10 | .05 |
| ❑ 120 Bob Abreu | .20 | .09 |
| ❑ 121 Mike Hampton | .20 | .09 |
| ❑ 122 Todd Jones | .10 | .05 |
| ❑ 123 Billy Wagner | .10 | .05 |
| ❑ 124 Shane Reynolds | .10 | .05 |
| ❑ 125 Jeff Bagwell | .50 | .23 |
| ❑ 126 Brian L. Hunter | .10 | .05 |
| ❑ 127 Jeff Montgomery | .10 | .05 |
| ❑ 128 Rod Myers RC | .10 | .05 |
| ❑ 129 Tim Belcher | .10 | .05 |
| ❑ 130 Kevin Appier | .20 | .09 |
| ❑ 131 Mike Sweeney | .20 | .09 |
| ❑ 132 Craig Paquette | .10 | .05 |
| ❑ 133 Joe Randa | .10 | .05 |
| ❑ 134 Michael Tucker | .10 | .05 |
| ❑ 135 Raul Mondesi | .20 | .09 |
| ❑ 136 Tim Wallach | .10 | .05 |
| ❑ 137 Brett Butler | .20 | .09 |
| ❑ 138 Karim Garcia | .10 | .05 |
| ❑ 139 Todd Hollandsworth | .10 | .05 |
| ❑ 140 Eric Karros | .20 | .09 |
| ❑ 141 Hideo Nomo | .40 | .18 |
| ❑ 142 Ismael Valdes | .10 | .05 |
| ❑ 143 Cal Eldred | .10 | .05 |
| ❑ 144 Scott Karl | .10 | .05 |
| ❑ 145 Matt Mieske | .10 | .05 |
| ❑ 146 Mike Fetters | .10 | .05 |
| ❑ 147 Mark Loretta | .10 | .05 |
| ❑ 148 Fernando Vina | .10 | .05 |
| ❑ 149 Jeff Cirillo | .20 | .09 |
| ❑ 150 Dave Nilsson | .10 | .05 |
| ❑ 151 Kirby Puckett | 1.00 | .45 |
| ❑ 152 Rich Becker | .10 | .05 |
| ❑ 153 Chuck Knoblauch | .20 | .09 |
| ❑ 154 Marty Cordova | .10 | .05 |
| ❑ 155 Paul Molitor | .40 | .18 |
| ❑ 156 Rick Aguilera | .10 | .05 |
| ❑ 157 Pat Meares | .10 | .05 |
| ❑ 158 Frank Rodriguez | .10 | .05 |
| ❑ 159 David Segui | .10 | .05 |
| ❑ 160 Henry Rodriguez | .10 | .05 |
| ❑ 161 Shane Andrews | .10 | .05 |
| ❑ 162 Pedro Martinez | .50 | .23 |
| ❑ 163 Mark Grudzielanek | .10 | .05 |
| ❑ 164 Mike Lansing | .10 | .05 |
| ❑ 165 Rondell White | .20 | .09 |
| ❑ 166 Ugueth Urbina | .20 | .09 |
| ❑ 167 Rey Ordonez | .10 | .05 |
| ❑ 168 Robert Person | .10 | .05 |
| ❑ 169 Carlos Baerga | .10 | .05 |
| ❑ 170 Bernard Gilkey | .10 | .05 |
| ❑ 171 John Franco | .20 | .09 |
| ❑ 172 Pete Harnisch | .10 | .05 |
| ❑ 173 Butch Huskey | .10 | .05 |
| ❑ 174 Paul Wilson | .10 | .05 |
| ❑ 175 Bernie Williams | .40 | .18 |
| ❑ 175 Dwight Gooden ERR | .20 | .09 |
| (incorrectly numbered 175) | | |
| ❑ 177 Wade Boggs | .50 | .23 |
| ❑ 178 Ruben Rivera | .10 | .05 |
| ❑ 179 Jim Leyritz | .10 | .05 |
| ❑ 180 Derek Jeter | 1.50 | .70 |
| ❑ 181 Tino Martinez | .20 | .09 |

| # | Player | | |
|---|---|---|---|
| 182 | Tim Raines | .20 | .09 |
| 183 | Scott Brosius | .20 | .09 |
| 184 | Jason Giambi | .40 | .18 |
| 185 | Geronimo Berroa | .10 | .05 |
| 186 | Ariel Prieto | .10 | .05 |
| 187 | Scott Spiezio | .10 | .05 |
| 188 | John Wasdin | .10 | .05 |
| 189 | Ernie Young | .10 | .05 |
| 190 | Mark McGwire | 1.50 | .70 |
| 191 | Jim Eisenreich | .10 | .05 |
| 192 | Ricky Bottalico | .10 | .05 |
| 193 | Darren Daulton | .20 | .09 |
| 194 | David Doster | .10 | .05 |
| 195 | Gregg Jefferies | .10 | .05 |
| 196 | Lenny Dykstra | .20 | .09 |
| 197 | Curt Schilling | .20 | .09 |
| 198 | Todd Stottlemyre | .10 | .05 |
| 199 | Willie McGee | .20 | .09 |
| 200 | Ozzie Smith | .50 | .23 |
| 201 | Dennis Eckersley | .20 | .09 |
| 202 | Ray Lankford | .20 | .09 |
| 203 | John Mabry | .10 | .05 |
| 204 | Alan Benes | .10 | .05 |
| 205 | Ron Gant | .10 | .05 |
| 206 | Archi Cianfrocco | .10 | .05 |
| 207 | Fernando Valenzuela | .20 | .09 |
| 208 | Greg Vaughn | .20 | .09 |
| 209 | Steve Finley | .20 | .09 |
| 210 | Tony Gwynn | .75 | .35 |
| 211 | Rickey Henderson | .50 | .23 |
| 212 | Trevor Hoffman | .20 | .09 |
| 213 | Jason Thompson | .10 | .05 |
| 214 | Osvaldo Fernandez | .10 | .05 |
| 215 | Glenallen Hill | .10 | .05 |
| 216 | William VanLandingham | .10 | .05 |
| 217 | Marvin Benard | .10 | .05 |
| 218 | Juan Gonzalez POST | .20 | .09 |
| 219 | Roberto Alomar POST | .20 | .09 |
| 220 | Brian Jordan POST | .10 | .05 |
| 221 | John Smoltz POST | .20 | .09 |
| 222 | Javy Lopez POST | .10 | .05 |
| 223 | Bernie Williams POST | .20 | .09 |
| 224 | Jim Leyritz POST John Wetteland | .10 | .05 |
| 225 | Barry Bonds | .60 | .25 |
| 226 | Rich Aurilia | .20 | .09 |
| 227 | Jay Canizaro | .10 | .05 |
| 228 | Dan Wilson | .10 | .05 |
| 229 | Bob Wolcott | .10 | .05 |
| 230 | Ken Griffey Jr. | 1.50 | .70 |
| 231 | Sterling Hitchcock | .10 | .05 |
| 232 | Edgar Martinez | .30 | .14 |
| 233 | Joey Cora | .10 | .05 |
| 234 | Norm Charlton | .10 | .05 |
| 235 | Alex Rodriguez | 1.25 | .55 |
| 236 | Bobby Witt | .10 | .05 |
| 237 | Darren Oliver | .10 | .05 |
| 238 | Kevin Elster | .10 | .05 |
| 239 | Rusty Greer | .20 | .09 |
| 240 | Juan Gonzalez | .40 | .18 |
| 241 | Will Clark | .40 | .18 |
| 242 | Dean Palmer | .20 | .09 |
| 243 | Ivan Rodriguez | .50 | .23 |
| 244 | Ken Griffey Jr. CL | .25 | .11 |
| 245 | Ken Griffey Jr. CL | .25 | .11 |
| 246 | Ken Griffey Jr. CL | .25 | .11 |
| 247 | Ken Griffey Jr. CL | .25 | .11 |
| 248 | Ken Griffey Jr. CL | .25 | .11 |
| 249 | Ken Griffey Jr. CL | .25 | .11 |
| 250 | Eddie Murray | .40 | .18 |
| 251 | Troy Percival | .10 | .05 |
| 252 | Garret Anderson | .20 | .09 |
| 253 | Allen Watson | .10 | .05 |
| 254 | Jason Dickson | .10 | .05 |
| 255 | Jim Edmonds | .40 | .18 |
| 256 | Chuck Finley | .20 | .09 |
| 257 | Randy Velarde | .10 | .05 |
| 258 | Shigetoshi Hasegawa RC | .25 | .11 |
| 259 | Todd Greene | .10 | .05 |
| 260 | Tim Salmon | .20 | .09 |
| 261 | Mark Langston | .20 | .09 |
| 262 | Dave Hollins | .10 | .05 |
| 263 | Gary DiSarcina | .10 | .05 |
| 264 | Kenny Lofton | .20 | .09 |
| 265 | John Smoltz | .20 | .09 |
| 266 | Greg Maddux | 1.00 | .45 |
| 267 | Jeff Blauser | .10 | .05 |
| 268 | Alan Embree | .10 | .05 |
| 269 | Mark Lemke | .10 | .05 |
| 270 | Chipper Jones | 1.00 | .45 |
| 271 | Mike Mussina | .40 | .18 |
| 272 | Rafael Palmeiro | .40 | .18 |
| 273 | Jimmy Key | .20 | .09 |
| 274 | Mike Bordick | .10 | .05 |
| 275 | Brady Anderson | .20 | .09 |
| 276 | Eric Davis | .20 | .09 |
| 277 | Jeffrey Hammonds | .20 | .09 |
| 278 | Reggie Jefferson | .10 | .05 |
| 279 | Tim Naehring | .10 | .05 |
| 280 | John Valentin | .10 | .05 |
| 281 | Troy O'Leary | .10 | .05 |
| 282 | Shane Mack | .10 | .05 |
| 283 | Mike Stanley | .10 | .05 |
| 284 | Tim Wakefield | .10 | .05 |
| 285 | Brian McRae | .10 | .05 |
| 286 | Brooks Kieschnick | .10 | .05 |
| 287 | Shawon Dunston | .10 | .05 |
| 288 | Kevin Foster | .10 | .05 |
| 289 | Mel Rojas | .10 | .05 |
| 290 | Mark Grace | .40 | .18 |
| 291 | Brant Brown | .10 | .05 |
| 292 | Amaury Telemaco | .10 | .05 |
| 293 | Dave Martinez | .10 | .05 |
| 294 | Jaime Navarro | .10 | .05 |
| 295 | Ray Durham | .20 | .09 |
| 296 | Ozzie Guillen | .10 | .05 |
| 297 | Roberto Hernandez | .10 | .05 |
| 298 | Ron Karkovice | .10 | .05 |
| 299 | James Baldwin | .20 | .09 |
| 300 | Frank Thomas | .75 | .35 |
| 301 | Eddie Taubensee | .10 | .05 |
| 302 | Bret Boone | .20 | .09 |
| 303 | Willie Greene | .10 | .05 |
| 304 | Dave Burba | .10 | .05 |
| 305 | Deion Sanders | .20 | .09 |
| 306 | Reggie Sanders | .10 | .05 |
| 307 | Hal Morris | .10 | .05 |
| 308 | Pokey Reese | .20 | .09 |
| 309 | Tony Fernandez | .10 | .05 |
| 310 | Manny Ramirez | .50 | .23 |
| 311 | Chad Ogea | .10 | .05 |
| 312 | Jack McDowell | .10 | .05 |
| 313 | Kevin Mitchell | .10 | .05 |
| 314 | Chad Curtis | .10 | .05 |
| 315 | Steve Kline | .10 | .05 |
| 316 | Kevin Seitzer | .10 | .05 |
| 317 | Kirt Manwaring | .10 | .05 |
| 318 | Billy Swift | .10 | .05 |
| 319 | Ellis Burks | .20 | .09 |
| 320 | Andres Galarraga | .30 | .14 |
| 321 | Bruce Ruffin | .10 | .05 |
| 322 | Mark Thompson | .10 | .05 |
| 323 | Walt Weiss | .10 | .05 |
| 324 | Todd Jones | .10 | .05 |
| 325 | Andruw Jones GHL | .30 | .14 |
| 326 | Chipper Jones GHL | .50 | .23 |
| 327 | Mo Vaughn GHL | .20 | .09 |
| 328 | Frank Thomas GHL | .50 | .23 |
| 329 | Albert Belle GHL | .10 | .05 |
| 330 | Mark McGwire GHL | .75 | .35 |
| 331 | Derek Jeter GHL | .75 | .35 |
| 332 | Alex Rodriguez GHL | .60 | .25 |
| 333 | Jay Buhner GHL with Ken Griffey Jr. | .10 | .05 |
| 334 | Ken Griffey Jr. GHL | .75 | .35 |
| 335 | Brian L. Hunter | .10 | .05 |
| 336 | Brian Johnson | .10 | .05 |
| 337 | Omar Olivares | .10 | .05 |
| 338 | Deivi Cruz RC | .50 | .23 |
| 339 | Damion Easley | .10 | .05 |
| 340 | Melvin Nieves | .10 | .05 |
| 341 | Moises Alou | .20 | .09 |
| 342 | Jim Eisenreich | .10 | .05 |
| 343 | Mark Hutton | .10 | .05 |
| 344 | Alex Fernandez | .10 | .05 |
| 345 | Gary Sheffield | .40 | .18 |
| 346 | Pat Rapp | .10 | .05 |
| 347 | Brad Ausmus | .10 | .05 |
| 348 | Sean Berry | .10 | .05 |
| 349 | Darryl Kile | .20 | .09 |
| 350 | Craig Biggio | .30 | .14 |
| 351 | Chris Holt | .10 | .05 |
| 352 | Luis Gonzalez | .20 | .09 |
| 353 | Pat Listach | .10 | .05 |
| 354 | Jose Rosado | .10 | .05 |
| 355 | Mike Macfarlane | .10 | .05 |
| 356 | Tom Goodwin | .10 | .05 |
| 357 | Chris Haney | .10 | .05 |
| 358 | Chili Davis | .20 | .09 |
| 359 | Jose Offerman | .10 | .05 |
| 360 | Johnny Damon | .20 | .09 |
| 361 | Bip Roberts | .10 | .05 |
| 362 | Ramon Martinez | .10 | .05 |
| 363 | Pedro Astacio | .10 | .05 |
| 364 | Todd Zeile | .10 | .05 |
| 365 | Mike Piazza | 1.25 | .55 |
| 366 | Greg Gagne | .10 | .05 |
| 367 | Chan Ho Park | .20 | .09 |
| 368 | Wilton Guerrero | .10 | .05 |
| 369 | Todd Worrell | .10 | .05 |
| 370 | John Jaha | .10 | .05 |
| 371 | Steve Sparks | .10 | .05 |
| 372 | Mike Matheny | .10 | .05 |
| 373 | Marc Newfield | .10 | .05 |
| 374 | Jeromy Burnitz | .20 | .09 |
| 375 | Jose Valentin | .10 | .05 |
| 376 | Ben McDonald | .10 | .05 |
| 377 | Roberto Kelly | .10 | .05 |
| 378 | Bob Tewksbury | .10 | .05 |
| 379 | Ron Coomer | .10 | .05 |
| 380 | Brad Radke | .20 | .09 |
| 381 | Matt Lawton | .20 | .09 |
| 382 | Dan Naulty | .10 | .05 |
| 383 | Scott Stahoviak | .10 | .05 |
| 384 | Matt Wagner | .10 | .05 |
| 385 | Jim Bullinger | .10 | .05 |
| 386 | Carlos Perez | .10 | .05 |
| 387 | Darrin Fletcher | .10 | .05 |
| 388 | Chris Widger | .10 | .05 |
| 389 | F.P. Santangelo | .10 | .05 |
| 390 | Lee Smith | .20 | .09 |
| 391 | Bobby Jones | .10 | .05 |
| 392 | John Olerud | .20 | .09 |
| 393 | Mark Clark | .10 | .05 |
| 394 | Jason Isringhausen | .10 | .05 |
| 395 | Todd Hundley | .10 | .05 |
| 396 | Lance Johnson | .10 | .05 |
| 397 | Edgardo Alfonzo | .20 | .09 |
| 398 | Alex Ochoa | .10 | .05 |
| 399 | Darryl Strawberry | .20 | .09 |
| 400 | David Cone | .20 | .09 |
| 401 | Paul O'Neill | .20 | .09 |
| 402 | Joe Girardi | .10 | .05 |
| 403 | Charlie Hayes | .10 | .05 |
| 404 | Andy Pettitte | .20 | .09 |
| 405 | Mariano Rivera | .20 | .09 |
| 406 | Mariano Duncan | .10 | .05 |
| 407 | Kenny Rogers | .10 | .05 |
| 408 | Cecil Fielder | .20 | .09 |
| 409 | George Williams | .10 | .05 |
| 410 | Jose Canseco | .50 | .23 |
| 411 | Tony Batista | .40 | .18 |
| 412 | Steve Karsay | .10 | .05 |
| 413 | Dave Telgheder | .10 | .05 |
| 414 | Billy Taylor | .10 | .05 |
| 415 | Mickey Morandini | .10 | .05 |
| 416 | Calvin Maduro | .10 | .05 |
| 417 | Mark Leiter | .10 | .05 |
| 418 | Kevin Stocker | .10 | .05 |
| 419 | Mike Lieberthal | .20 | .09 |
| 420 | Rico Brogna | .10 | .05 |
| 421 | Mark Portugal | .10 | .05 |
| 422 | Rex Hudler | .10 | .05 |
| 423 | Mark Johnson | .10 | .05 |
| 424 | Esteban Loaiza | .10 | .05 |
| 425 | Lou Collier | .10 | .05 |
| 426 | Kevin Elster | .10 | .05 |
| 427 | Francisco Cordova | .10 | .05 |
| 428 | Marc Wilkins | .10 | .05 |
| 429 | Joe Randa | .10 | .05 |
| 430 | Jason Kendall | .20 | .09 |
| 431 | Jon Lieber | .10 | .05 |
| 432 | Steve Cooke | .10 | .05 |
| 433 | Emil Brown RC | .20 | .09 |
| 434 | Tony Womack RC | .50 | .23 |
| 435 | Al Martin | .10 | .05 |
| 436 | Jason Schmidt | .10 | .05 |
| 437 | Andy Benes | .10 | .05 |

| | | | |
|---|---|---|---|
| ❑ 438 | Delino DeShields | .10 | .05 |
| ❑ 439 | Royce Clayton | .10 | .05 |
| ❑ 440 | Brian Jordan | .20 | .09 |
| ❑ 441 | Donovan Osborne | .10 | .05 |
| ❑ 442 | Gary Gaetti | .20 | .09 |
| ❑ 443 | Tom Pagnozzi | .10 | .05 |
| ❑ 444 | Joey Hamilton | .10 | .05 |
| ❑ 445 | Wally Joyner | .20 | .09 |
| ❑ 446 | John Flaherty | .10 | .05 |
| ❑ 447 | Chris Gomez | .10 | .05 |
| ❑ 448 | Sterling Hitchcock | .10 | .05 |
| ❑ 449 | Andy Ashby | .10 | .05 |
| ❑ 450 | Ken Caminiti | .20 | .09 |
| ❑ 451 | Tim Worrell | .10 | .05 |
| ❑ 452 | Jose Vizcaino | .10 | .05 |
| ❑ 453 | Rod Beck | .10 | .05 |
| ❑ 454 | Wilson Delgado | .20 | .09 |
| ❑ 455 | Darryl Hamilton | .10 | .05 |
| ❑ 456 | Mark Lewis | .10 | .05 |
| ❑ 457 | Mark Gardner | .10 | .05 |
| ❑ 458 | Rick Wilkins | .10 | .05 |
| ❑ 459 | Scott Sanders | .10 | .05 |
| ❑ 460 | Kevin Orie | .10 | .05 |
| ❑ 461 | Glendon Rusch | .10 | .05 |
| ❑ 462 | Juan Melo | .20 | .09 |
| ❑ 463 | Richie Sexson | .40 | .18 |
| ❑ 464 | Bartolo Colon | .20 | .09 |
| ❑ 465 | Jose Guillen | .10 | .05 |
| ❑ 466 | Heath Murray | .10 | .05 |
| ❑ 467 | Aaron Boone | .10 | .05 |
| ❑ 468 | Bubba Trammell RC | .20 | .09 |
| ❑ 469 | Jeff Abbott | .10 | .05 |
| ❑ 470 | Derrick Gibson | .10 | .05 |
| ❑ 471 | Matt Morris | .10 | .05 |
| ❑ 472 | Ryan Jones | .10 | .05 |
| ❑ 473 | Pat Cline | .20 | .09 |
| ❑ 474 | Adam Riggs | .10 | .05 |
| ❑ 475 | Jay Payton | .20 | .09 |
| ❑ 476 | Derrek Lee | .10 | .05 |
| ❑ 477 | Eli Marrero | .10 | .05 |
| ❑ 478 | Lee Tinsley | .10 | .05 |
| ❑ 479 | Jamie Moyer | .10 | .05 |
| ❑ 480 | Jay Buhner | .20 | .09 |
| ❑ 481 | Bob Wells | .10 | .05 |
| ❑ 482 | Jeff Fassero | .10 | .05 |
| ❑ 483 | Paul Sorrento | .10 | .05 |
| ❑ 484 | Russ Davis | .10 | .05 |
| ❑ 485 | Randy Johnson | .50 | .23 |
| ❑ 486 | Roger Pavlik | .10 | .05 |
| ❑ 487 | Damon Buford | .10 | .05 |
| ❑ 488 | Julio Santana | .10 | .05 |
| ❑ 489 | Mark McLemore | .10 | .05 |
| ❑ 490 | Mickey Tettleton | .10 | .05 |
| ❑ 491 | Ken Hill | .10 | .05 |
| ❑ 492 | Benji Gil | .10 | .05 |
| ❑ 493 | Ed Sprague | .10 | .05 |
| ❑ 494 | Mike Timlin | .10 | .05 |
| ❑ 495 | Pat Hentgen | .10 | .05 |
| ❑ 496 | Orlando Merced | .10 | .05 |
| ❑ 497 | Carlos Garcia | .10 | .05 |
| ❑ 498 | Carlos Delgado | .40 | .18 |
| ❑ 499 | Juan Guzman | .10 | .05 |
| ❑ 500 | Roger Clemens | .75 | .35 |
| ❑ 501 | Erik Hanson | .10 | .05 |
| ❑ 502 | Otis Nixon | .10 | .05 |
| ❑ 503 | Shawn Green | .40 | .18 |
| ❑ 504 | Charlie O'Brien | .10 | .05 |
| ❑ 505 | Joe Carter | .20 | .09 |
| ❑ 506 | Alex Gonzalez | .10 | .05 |

## 1998 Collector's Choice

| | MINT | NRMT |
|---|---|---|
| COMPLETE SET (530) | 40.00 | 18.00 |
| COMPLETE SERIES 1 (265) | 20.00 | 9.00 |
| COMPLETE SERIES 2 (265) | 20.00 | 9.00 |
| COMP.FACT.SET (530) | 40.00 | 18.00 |
| COMMON CARD (1-530) | .10 | .05 |

| | | | |
|---|---|---|---|
| ❑ 1 | Nomar Garciaparra CG | .60 | .25 |
| ❑ 2 | Roger Clemens CG | .40 | .18 |
| ❑ 3 | Larry Walker CG | .15 | .07 |
| ❑ 4 | Mike Piazza CG | .60 | .25 |
| ❑ 5 | Mark McGwire CG | .75 | .35 |
| ❑ 6 | Tony Gwynn CG | .40 | .18 |
| ❑ 7 | Jose Cruz Jr. CG | .10 | .05 |
| ❑ 8 | Frank Thomas CG | .40 | .18 |
| ❑ 9 | Tino Martinez CG | .10 | .05 |
| ❑ 10 | Ken Griffey Jr. CG | .75 | .35 |
| ❑ 11 | Barry Bonds CG | .25 | .11 |
| ❑ 12 | Scott Rolen CG | .40 | .18 |
| ❑ 13 | Randy Johnson CG | .15 | .07 |
| ❑ 14 | Ryne Sandberg CG | .25 | .11 |
| ❑ 15 | Eddie Murray CG | .15 | .07 |
| ❑ 16 | Kevin Brown CG | .15 | .07 |
| ❑ 17 | Mike Mussina CG | .15 | .07 |
| ❑ 18 | Sandy Alomar Jr. CG | .10 | .05 |
| ❑ 19 | Ken Griffey Jr. CL<br>Adam Riggs | .25 | .11 |
| ❑ 20 | Nomar Garciaparra CL<br>Charlie O'Brien | .15 | .07 |
| ❑ 21 | Ben Grieve CL<br>Frank Thomas<br>Tony Gwynn | .15 | .07 |
| ❑ 22 | Mark McGwire CL<br>Cal Ripken | .25 | .11 |
| ❑ 23 | Tino Martinez CL | .10 | .05 |
| ❑ 24 | Jason Dickson | .10 | .05 |
| ❑ 25 | Darin Erstad | .40 | .18 |
| ❑ 26 | Todd Greene | .10 | .05 |
| ❑ 27 | Chuck Finley | .15 | .07 |
| ❑ 28 | Garret Anderson | .15 | .07 |
| ❑ 29 | Dave Hollins | .10 | .05 |
| ❑ 30 | Rickey Henderson | .50 | .23 |
| ❑ 31 | John Smoltz | .15 | .07 |
| ❑ 32 | Michael Tucker | .10 | .05 |
| ❑ 33 | Jeff Blauser | .10 | .05 |
| ❑ 34 | Javier Lopez | .15 | .07 |
| ❑ 35 | Andruw Jones | .40 | .18 |
| ❑ 36 | Denny Neagle | .10 | .05 |
| ❑ 37 | Randall Simon | .10 | .05 |
| ❑ 38 | Mark Wohlers | .10 | .05 |
| ❑ 39 | Harold Baines | .15 | .07 |
| ❑ 40 | Cal Ripken | 1.50 | .70 |
| ❑ 41 | Mike Bordick | .10 | .05 |
| ❑ 42 | Jimmy Key | .15 | .07 |
| ❑ 43 | Armando Benitez | .10 | .05 |
| ❑ 44 | Scott Erickson | .10 | .05 |
| ❑ 45 | Eric Davis | .15 | .07 |
| ❑ 46 | Bret Saberhagen | .15 | .07 |
| ❑ 47 | Darren Bragg | .10 | .05 |
| ❑ 48 | Steve Avery | .10 | .05 |
| ❑ 49 | Jeff Frye | .10 | .05 |
| ❑ 50 | Aaron Sele | .15 | .07 |
| ❑ 51 | Scott Hatteberg | .10 | .05 |
| ❑ 52 | Tom Gordon | .15 | .07 |
| ❑ 53 | Kevin Orie | .10 | .05 |
| ❑ 54 | Kevin Foster | .10 | .05 |
| ❑ 55 | Ryne Sandberg | .50 | .23 |
| ❑ 56 | Doug Glanville | .10 | .05 |
| ❑ 57 | Tyler Houston | .10 | .05 |
| ❑ 58 | Steve Trachsel | .10 | .05 |
| ❑ 59 | Mark Grace | .40 | .18 |
| ❑ 60 | Frank Thomas | .75 | .35 |
| ❑ 61 | Scott Eyre | .10 | .05 |
| ❑ 62 | Jeff Abbott | .10 | .05 |
| ❑ 63 | Chris Clemons | .10 | .05 |
| ❑ 64 | Jorge Fabregas | .10 | .05 |
| ❑ 65 | Robin Ventura | .15 | .07 |
| ❑ 66 | Matt Karchner | .10 | .05 |
| ❑ 67 | Jon Nunnally | .10 | .05 |
| ❑ 68 | Aaron Boone | .10 | .05 |
| ❑ 69 | Pokey Reese | .15 | .07 |
| ❑ 70 | Deion Sanders | .15 | .07 |
| ❑ 71 | Jeff Shaw | .10 | .05 |
| ❑ 72 | Eduardo Perez | .10 | .05 |
| ❑ 73 | Brett Tomko | .10 | .05 |
| ❑ 74 | Bartolo Colon | .15 | .07 |
| ❑ 75 | Manny Ramirez | .50 | .23 |
| ❑ 76 | Jose Mesa | .10 | .05 |
| ❑ 77 | Brian Giles | .15 | .07 |
| ❑ 78 | Richie Sexson | .25 | .11 |
| ❑ 79 | Orel Hershiser | .15 | .07 |
| ❑ 80 | Matt Williams | .25 | .11 |
| ❑ 81 | Walt Weiss | .15 | .07 |
| ❑ 82 | Jerry DiPoto | .10 | .05 |
| ❑ 83 | Quinton McCracken | .10 | .05 |
| ❑ 84 | Neifi Perez | .10 | .05 |
| ❑ 85 | Vinny Castilla | .15 | .07 |
| ❑ 86 | Ellis Burks | .15 | .07 |
| ❑ 87 | John Thomson | .10 | .05 |
| ❑ 88 | Willie Blair | .10 | .05 |
| ❑ 89 | Bob Hamelin | .10 | .05 |
| ❑ 90 | Tony Clark | .10 | .05 |
| ❑ 91 | Todd Jones | .10 | .05 |
| ❑ 92 | Deivi Cruz | .10 | .05 |
| ❑ 93 | Frank Catalanotto RC | .25 | .11 |
| ❑ 94 | Justin Thompson | .10 | .05 |
| ❑ 95 | Gary Sheffield | .40 | .18 |
| ❑ 96 | Kevin Brown | .25 | .11 |
| ❑ 97 | Charles Johnson | .15 | .07 |
| ❑ 98 | Bobby Bonilla | .15 | .07 |
| ❑ 99 | Livan Hernandez | .10 | .05 |
| ❑ 100 | Paul Konerko | .15 | .07 |
| ❑ 101 | Craig Counsell | .10 | .05 |
| ❑ 102 | Magglio Ordonez RC | 1.50 | .70 |
| ❑ 103 | Garrett Stephenson | .10 | .05 |
| ❑ 104 | Ken Cloude | .10 | .05 |
| ❑ 105 | Miguel Tejada | .40 | .18 |
| ❑ 106 | Juan Encarnacion | .15 | .07 |
| ❑ 107 | Dennis Reyes | .10 | .05 |
| ❑ 108 | Orlando Cabrera | .10 | .05 |
| ❑ 109 | Kelvim Escobar | .10 | .05 |
| ❑ 110 | Ben Grieve | .15 | .07 |
| ❑ 111 | Brian Rose | .10 | .05 |
| ❑ 112 | Fernando Tatis | .15 | .07 |
| ❑ 113 | Tom Evans | .10 | .05 |
| ❑ 114 | Tom Fordham | .10 | .05 |
| ❑ 115 | Mark Kotsay | .15 | .07 |
| ❑ 116 | Mario Valdez | .10 | .05 |
| ❑ 117 | Jeremi Gonzalez | .10 | .05 |
| ❑ 118 | Todd Dunwoody | .10 | .05 |
| ❑ 119 | Javier Valentin | .10 | .05 |
| ❑ 120 | Todd Helton | .50 | .23 |
| ❑ 121 | Jason Varitek | .15 | .07 |
| ❑ 122 | Chris Carpenter | .15 | .07 |
| ❑ 123 | Kevin Millwood RC | .60 | .25 |
| ❑ 124 | Brad Fullmer | .15 | .07 |
| ❑ 125 | Jaret Wright | .10 | .05 |
| ❑ 126 | Brad Rigby | .10 | .05 |
| ❑ 127 | Edgar Renteria | .10 | .05 |
| ❑ 128 | Robb Nen | .10 | .05 |
| ❑ 129 | Tony Pena | .10 | .05 |
| ❑ 130 | Craig Biggio | .25 | .11 |
| ❑ 131 | Brad Ausmus | .10 | .05 |
| ❑ 132 | Shane Reynolds | .10 | .05 |
| ❑ 133 | Mike Hampton | .15 | .07 |
| ❑ 134 | Billy Wagner | .10 | .05 |
| ❑ 135 | Richard Hidalgo | .15 | .07 |
| ❑ 136 | Jose Rosado | .10 | .05 |
| ❑ 137 | Yamil Benitez | .10 | .05 |
| ❑ 138 | Felix Martinez | .10 | .05 |
| ❑ 139 | Jeff King | .10 | .05 |
| ❑ 140 | Jose Offerman | .10 | .05 |
| ❑ 141 | Joe Vitiello | .10 | .05 |
| ❑ 142 | Tim Belcher | .10 | .05 |
| ❑ 143 | Brett Butler | .15 | .07 |
| ❑ 144 | Greg Gagne | .10 | .05 |
| ❑ 145 | Mike Piazza | 1.25 | .55 |
| ❑ 146 | Ramon Martinez | .10 | .05 |
| ❑ 147 | Raul Mondesi | .15 | .07 |
| ❑ 148 | Adam Riggs | .10 | .05 |
| ❑ 149 | Eddie Murray | .40 | .18 |
| ❑ 150 | Jeff Cirillo | .15 | .07 |
| ❑ 151 | Scott Karl | .10 | .05 |
| ❑ 152 | Mike Fetters | .10 | .05 |
| ❑ 153 | Dave Nilsson | .10 | .05 |
| ❑ 154 | Antone Williamson | .10 | .05 |
| ❑ 155 | Jeff D'Amico | .10 | .05 |
| ❑ 156 | Jose Valentin | .10 | .05 |

❑ 157 Brad Radke .15 .07
❑ 158 Torii Hunter .10 .05
❑ 159 Chuck Knoblauch .15 .07
❑ 160 Paul Molitor .40 .18
❑ 161 Travis Miller .10 .05
❑ 162 Rich Robertson .10 .05
❑ 163 Ron Coomer .10 .05
❑ 164 Mark Grudzielanek .10 .05
❑ 165 Lee Smith .15 .07
❑ 166 Vladimir Guerrero .60 .25
❑ 167 Dustin Hermanson .10 .05
❑ 168 Ugueth Urbina .10 .05
❑ 169 F.P. Santangelo .10 .05
❑ 170 Rondell White .15 .07
❑ 171 Bobby Jones .10 .05
❑ 172 Edgardo Alfonzo .15 .07
❑ 173 John Franco .15 .07
❑ 174 Carlos Baerga .10 .05
❑ 175 Butch Huskey .10 .05
❑ 176 Rey Ordonez .10 .05
❑ 177 Matt Franco .10 .05
❑ 178 Dwight Gooden .10 .05
❑ 179 Chad Curtis .10 .05
❑ 180 Tino Martinez .15 .07
❑ 181 Charlie O'Brien MM .10 .05
❑ 182 Sandy Alomar Jr. MM .10 .05
❑ 183 Raul Casanova MM .10 .05
❑ 184 Javier Lopez MM .10 .05
❑ 185 Mike Piazza MM .60 .25
❑ 186 Ivan Rodriguez MM .25 .11
❑ 187 Charles Johnson MM .10 .05
❑ 188 Brad Ausmus MM .10 .05
❑ 189 Brian Johnson MM .10 .05
❑ 190 Wade Boggs .50 .23
❑ 191 David Wells .15 .07
❑ 192 Tim Raines .15 .07
❑ 193 Ramiro Mendoza .10 .05
❑ 194 Willie Adams .10 .05
❑ 195 Matt Stairs .10 .05
❑ 196 Jason McDonald .10 .05
❑ 197 Dave Magadan .10 .05
❑ 198 Mark Bellhorn .10 .05
❑ 199 Ariel Prieto .10 .05
❑ 200 Jose Canseco .50 .23
❑ 201 Bobby Estalella .10 .05
❑ 202 Tony Barron RC .10 .05
❑ 203 Midre Cummings .10 .05
❑ 204 Ricky Bottalico .10 .05
❑ 205 Mike Grace .10 .05
❑ 206 Rico Brogna .10 .05
❑ 207 Mickey Morandini .10 .05
❑ 208 Lou Collier .10 .05
❑ 209 Kevin Polcovich .10 .05
❑ 210 Kevin Young .15 .07
❑ 211 Jose Guillen .10 .05
❑ 212 Esteban Loaiza .10 .05
❑ 213 Marc Wilkins .10 .05
❑ 214 Jason Schmidt .10 .05
❑ 215 Gary Gaetti .15 .07
❑ 216 Fernando Valenzuela .15 .07
❑ 217 Willie McGee .15 .07
❑ 218 Alan Benes .10 .05
❑ 219 Eli Marrero .10 .05
❑ 220 Mark McGwire 1.50 .70
❑ 221 Matt Morris .10 .05
❑ 222 Trevor Hoffman .15 .07
❑ 223 Will Cunnane .10 .05
❑ 224 Joey Hamilton .10 .05
❑ 225 Ken Caminiti .15 .07
❑ 226 Derrek Lee .10 .05
❑ 227 Mark Sweeney .10 .05
❑ 228 Carlos Hernandez .10 .05
❑ 229 Brian Johnson .10 .05
❑ 230 Jeff Kent .25 .11
❑ 231 Kirk Rueter .10 .05
❑ 232 Bill Mueller .10 .05
❑ 233 Dante Powell .10 .05
❑ 234 J.T. Snow .15 .07
❑ 235 Shawn Estes .10 .05
❑ 236 Dennis Martinez .15 .07
❑ 237 Jamie Moyer .10 .05
❑ 238 Dan Wilson .10 .05
❑ 239 Joey Cora .10 .05
❑ 240 Ken Griffey Jr. 1.50 .70
❑ 241 Paul Sorrento .10 .05
❑ 242 Jay Buhner .15 .07
❑ 243 Hanley Frias RC .10 .05
❑ 244 John Burkett .10 .05
❑ 245 Juan Gonzalez .40 .18
❑ 246 Rick Helling .15 .07
❑ 247 Darren Oliver .10 .05
❑ 248 Mickey Tettleton .10 .05
❑ 249 Ivan Rodriguez .50 .23
❑ 250 Joe Carter .15 .07
❑ 251 Pat Hentgen .10 .05
❑ 252 Marty Janzen .10 .05
❑ 253 Frank Thomas TOP .40 .18
Tony Gwynn
❑ 254 Mark McGwire TOP .75 .35
Ken Griffey Jr.
Larry Walker
❑ 255 Ken Griffey Jr. TOP .25 .11
Andres Galarraga
❑ 256 Brian L.Hunter TOP .10 .05
Tony Womack
❑ 257 Roger Clemens TOP .15 .07
Denny Neagle
❑ 258 Roger Clemens TOP .15 .07
Curt Schilling
❑ 259 Roger Clemens TOP .25 .11
Pedro Martinez
❑ 260 Randy Myers TOP .10 .05
Jeff Shaw
❑ 261 Nomar Garciaparra TOP .40 .18
Scott Rolen
❑ 262 Charlie O'Brien .10 .05
❑ 263 Shannon Stewart .15 .07
❑ 264 Robert Person .10 .05
❑ 265 Carlos Delgado .40 .18
❑ 266 Matt Williams CL .15 .07
Travis Lee
❑ 267 Nomar Garciaparra CL .25 .11
Cal Ripken
❑ 268 Mark McGwire CL .40 .18
Mike Piazza
❑ 269 Tony Gwynn CL .40 .18
Ken Griffey Jr
❑ 270 Fred McGriff CL .10 .05
Jose Cruz Jr.
❑ 271 Andruw Jones GJ .15 .07
❑ 272 Alex Rodriguez GJ .60 .25
❑ 273 Juan Gonzalez GJ .15 .07
❑ 274 Nomar Garciaparra GJ .60 .25
❑ 275 Ken Griffey Jr. GJ .75 .35
❑ 276 Tino Martinez GJ .10 .05
❑ 277 Roger Clemens GJ .40 .18
❑ 278 Barry Bonds GJ .25 .11
❑ 279 Mike Piazza GJ .60 .25
❑ 280 Tim Salmon .15 .07
❑ 281 Gary DiSarcina .10 .05
❑ 282 Cecil Fielder .15 .07
❑ 283 Ken Hill .10 .05
❑ 284 Troy Percival .10 .05
❑ 285 Jim Edmonds .15 .07
❑ 286 Allen Watson .10 .05
❑ 287 Brian Anderson .10 .05
❑ 288 Jay Bell .15 .07
❑ 289 Jorge Fabregas .10 .05
❑ 290 Devon White .10 .05
❑ 291 Yamil Benitez .10 .05
❑ 292 Jeff Suppan .10 .05
❑ 293 Tony Batista .15 .07
❑ 294 Brent Brede .10 .05
❑ 295 Andy Benes .10 .05
❑ 296 Felix Rodriguez .10 .05
❑ 297 Karim Garcia .10 .05
❑ 298 Omar Daal .10 .05
❑ 299 Andy Stankiewicz .10 .05
❑ 300 Matt Williams .25 .11
❑ 301 Willie Blair .10 .05
❑ 302 Ryan Klesko .15 .07
❑ 303 Tom Glavine .40 .10
❑ 304 Walt Weiss .15 .07
❑ 305 Greg Maddux 1.00 .45
❑ 306 Chipper Jones 1.00 .45
❑ 307 Keith Lockhart .10 .05
❑ 308 Andres Galarraga .25 .11
❑ 309 Chris Hoiles .10 .05
❑ 310 Roberto Alomar .40 .18
❑ 311 Joe Carter .15 .07
❑ 312 Doug Drabek .10 .05
❑ 313 Jeffrey Hammonds .15 .07
❑ 314 Rafael Palmeiro .40 .18
❑ 315 Mike Mussina .40 .18
❑ 316 Brady Anderson .15 .07
❑ 317 B.J. Surhoff .15 .07
❑ 318 Dennis Eckersley .15 .07
❑ 319 Jim Leyritz .10 .05
❑ 320 Mo Vaughn .15 .07
❑ 321 Nomar Garciaparra 1.25 .55
❑ 322 Reggie Jefferson .10 .05
❑ 323 Tim Naehring .10 .05
❑ 324 Troy O'Leary .10 .05
❑ 325 Pedro Martinez .50 .23
❑ 326 John Valentin .10 .05
❑ 327 Mark Clark .10 .05
❑ 328 Rod Beck .10 .05
❑ 329 Mickey Morandini .10 .05
❑ 330 Sammy Sosa .75 .35
❑ 331 Jeff Blauser .10 .05
❑ 332 Lance Johnson .10 .05
❑ 333 Scott Servais .10 .05
❑ 334 Kevin Tapani .10 .05
❑ 335 Henry Rodriguez .10 .05
❑ 336 Jaime Navarro .10 .05
❑ 337 Bonji Gil .10 .05
❑ 338 James Baldwin .10 .05
❑ 339 Mike Cameron .15 .07
❑ 340 Ray Durham .15 .07
❑ 341 Chris Snopek .10 .05
❑ 342 Eddie Taubensee .10 .05
❑ 343 Bret Boone .15 .07
❑ 344 Willie Greene .10 .05
❑ 345 Barry Larkin .40 .18
❑ 346 Chris Stynes .10 .05
❑ 347 Pete Harnisch .10 .05
❑ 348 Dave Burba .10 .05
❑ 349 Sandy Alomar Jr. .15 .07
❑ 350 Kenny Lofton .15 .07
❑ 351 Geronimo Berroa .10 .05
❑ 352 Omar Vizquel .15 .07
❑ 353 Travis Fryman .15 .07
❑ 354 Dwight Gooden .10 .05
❑ 355 Jim Thome .25 .11
❑ 356 David Justice .25 .11
❑ 357 Charles Nagy .10 .05
❑ 358 Chad Ogea .10 .05
❑ 359 Pedro Astacio .10 .05
❑ 360 Larry Walker .15 .07
❑ 361 Mike Lansing .10 .05
❑ 362 Kirt Manwaring .10 .05
❑ 363 Dante Bichette .15 .07
❑ 364 Jamey Wright .10 .05
❑ 365 Darryl Kile .15 .07
❑ 366 Luis Gonzalez .15 .07
❑ 367 Joe Randa .10 .05
❑ 368 Raul Casanova .10 .05
❑ 369 Damion Easley .10 .05
❑ 370 Brian Hunter .10 .05
❑ 371 Bobby Higginson .15 .07
❑ 372 Brian Moehler .10 .05
❑ 373 Scott Sanders .10 .05
❑ 374 Jim Eisenreich .10 .05
❑ 375 Derrek Lee .10 .05
❑ 376 Jay Powell .10 .05
❑ 377 Cliff Floyd .15 .07
❑ 378 Alex Fernandez .10 .05
❑ 379 Felix Heredia .10 .05
❑ 380 Jeff Bagwell .50 .23
❑ 381 Bill Spiers .10 .05
❑ 382 Chris Holt .10 .05
❑ 383 Carl Everett .15 .07
❑ 384 Derek Bell .10 .05
❑ 385 Moises Alou .15 .07
❑ 386 Ramon Garcia .10 .05
❑ 387 Mike Sweeney .15 .07
❑ 388 Glendon Rusch .10 .05
❑ 389 Kevin Appier .15 .07
❑ 390 Dean Palmer .15 .07
❑ 391 Jeff Conine .10 .05
❑ 392 Johnny Damon .15 .07
❑ 393 Jose Vizcaino .10 .05
❑ 394 Todd Hollandsworth .10 .05
❑ 395 Eric Karros .15 .07
❑ 396 Todd Zeile .15 .07
❑ 397 Chan Ho Park .15 .07
❑ 398 Ismael Valdes .10 .05
❑ 399 Eric Young .10 .05

❑ 400 Hideo Nomo .40 .18
❑ 401 Mark Loretta .10 .05
❑ 402 Doug Jones .10 .05
❑ 403 Jeromy Burnitz .15 .07
❑ 404 John Jaha .15 .07
❑ 405 Marquis Grissom .10 .05
❑ 406 Mike Matheny .10 .05
❑ 407 Todd Walker .10 .05
❑ 408 Marty Cordova .10 .05
❑ 409 Matt Lawton .10 .05
❑ 410 Terry Steinbach .10 .05
❑ 411 Pat Meares .10 .05
❑ 412 Rick Aguilera .10 .05
❑ 413 Otis Nixon .10 .05
❑ 414 Derrick May .10 .05
❑ 415 Carl Pavano .10 .05
❑ 416 A.J. Hinch .10 .05
❑ 417 Dave Dellucci RC .10 .05
❑ 418 Bruce Chen .10 .05
❑ 419 Darron Ingram RC .25 .11
❑ 420 Sean Casey .15 .07
❑ 421 Mark L. Johnson .10 .05
❑ 422 Gabe Alvarez .10 .05
❑ 423 Alex Gonzalez .10 .05
❑ 424 Daryle Ward .15 .07
❑ 425 Russell Branyan .15 .07
❑ 426 Mike Caruso .10 .05
❑ 427 Mike Kinkade RC .25 .11
❑ 428 Ramon Hernandez .10 .05
❑ 429 Matt Clement .15 .07
❑ 430 Travis Lee .15 .07
❑ 431 Shane Monahan .10 .05
❑ 432 Rich Butler RC .10 .05
❑ 433 Chris Widger .10 .05
❑ 434 Jose Vidro .10 .05
❑ 435 Carlos Perez .10 .05
❑ 436 Ryan McGuire .10 .05
❑ 437 Brian McRae .10 .05
❑ 438 Al Leiter .15 .07
❑ 439 Rich Becker .10 .05
❑ 440 Todd Hundley .10 .05
❑ 441 Dave Mlicki .10 .05
❑ 442 Bernard Gilkey .10 .05
❑ 443 John Olerud .15 .07
❑ 444 Paul O'Neill .15 .07
❑ 445 Andy Pettitte .15 .07
❑ 446 David Cone .15 .07
❑ 447 Chili Davis .15 .07
❑ 448 Bernie Williams .40 .18
❑ 449 Joe Girardi .10 .05
❑ 450 Derek Jeter 1.50 .70
❑ 451 Mariano Rivera .15 .07
❑ 452 George Williams .10 .05
❑ 453 Kenny Rogers .10 .05
❑ 454 Tom Candiotti .10 .05
❑ 455 Rickey Henderson .50 .23
❑ 456 Jason Giambi .40 .18
❑ 457 Scott Spiezio .10 .05
❑ 458 Doug Glanville .10 .05
❑ 459 Desi Relaford .10 .05
❑ 460 Curt Schilling .15 .07
❑ 461 Bob Abreu .15 .07
❑ 462 Gregg Jefferies .10 .05
❑ 463 Scott Rolen .40 .18
❑ 464 Mike Lieberthal .15 .07
❑ 465 Tony Womack .10 .05
❑ 466 Jermaine Allensworth .10 .05
❑ 467 Francisco Cordova .10 .05
❑ 468 Jon Lieber .10 .05
❑ 469 Al Martin .10 .05
❑ 470 Jason Kendall .15 .07
❑ 471 Todd Stottlemyre .10 .05
❑ 472 Royce Clayton .10 .05
❑ 473 Brian Jordan .15 .07
❑ 474 John Mabry .10 .05
❑ 475 Ray Lankford .15 .07
❑ 476 Delino DeShields .10 .05
❑ 477 Ron Gant .15 .07
❑ 478 Mark Langston .10 .05
❑ 479 Steve Finley .15 .07
❑ 480 Tony Gwynn .75 .35
❑ 481 Andy Ashby .10 .05
❑ 482 Wally Joyner .15 .07
❑ 483 Greg Vaughn .15 .07
❑ 484 Sterling Hitchcock .10 .05
❑ 485 Kevin Brown .25 .11
❑ 486 Orel Hershiser .15 .07
❑ 487 Charlie Hayes .10 .05
❑ 488 Darryl Hamilton .10 .05
❑ 489 Mark Gardner .10 .05
❑ 490 Barry Bonds .60 .25
❑ 491 Robb Nen .10 .05
❑ 492 Kirk Rueter .10 .05
❑ 493 Randy Johnson .50 .23
❑ 494 Jeff Fassero .10 .05
❑ 495 Alex Rodriguez 1.25 .55
❑ 496 David Segui .10 .05
❑ 497 Rich Amaral .10 .05
❑ 498 Russ Davis .10 .05
❑ 499 Bubba Trammell .10 .05
❑ 500 Wade Boggs .50 .23
❑ 501 Roberto Hernandez .10 .05
❑ 502 Dave Martinez .10 .05
❑ 503 Dennis Springer .10 .05
❑ 504 Paul Sorrento .10 .05
❑ 505 Wilson Alvarez .10 .05
❑ 506 Mike Kelly .10 .05
❑ 507 Albie Lopez .10 .05
❑ 508 Tony Saunders .10 .05
❑ 509 John Flaherty .10 .05
❑ 510 Fred McGriff .25 .11
❑ 511 Quinton McCracken .10 .05
❑ 512 Terrell Wade .10 .05
❑ 513 Kevin Stocker .10 .05
❑ 514 Kevin Elster .10 .05
❑ 515 Will Clark .40 .18
❑ 516 Bobby Witt .10 .05
❑ 517 Tom Goodwin .10 .05
❑ 518 Aaron Sele .15 .07
❑ 519 Lee Stevens .10 .05
❑ 520 Rusty Greer .15 .07
❑ 521 John Wetteland .15 .07
❑ 522 Darrin Fletcher .10 .05
❑ 523 Jose Canseco .50 .23
❑ 524 Randy Myers .15 .07
❑ 525 Jose Cruz Jr. .15 .07
❑ 526 Shawn Green .40 .18
❑ 527 Tony Fernandez .10 .05
❑ 528 Alex Gonzalez .10 .05
❑ 529 Ed Sprague .10 .05
❑ 530 Roger Clemens .75 .35

## 1995 Collector's Choice SE

| | MINT | NRMT |
|---|---|---|
| COMPLETE SET (265) | 20.00 | 9.00 |
| COMMON CARD (1-265) | .15 | .07 |

❑ 1 Alex Rodriguez 2.50 1.10
❑ 2 Derek Jeter 2.50 1.10
❑ 3 Dustin Hermanson .15 .07
❑ 4 Bill Pulsipher .15 .07
❑ 5 Terrell Wade .15 .07
❑ 6 Darren Dreifort .30 .14
❑ 7 LaTroy Hawkins .15 .07
❑ 8 Alex Ochoa .15 .07
❑ 9 Paul Wilson .15 .07
❑ 10 Ernie Young .15 .07
❑ 11 Alan Benes .15 .07
❑ 12 Garret Anderson .30 .14
❑ 13 Armando Benitez .30 .14
❑ 14 Mark Thompson .15 .07
❑ 15 Herbert Perry .15 .07
❑ 16 Jose Silva .15 .07
❑ 17 Orlando Miller .15 .07
❑ 18 Russ Davis .15 .07
❑ 19 Jason Isringhausen .30 .14
❑ 20 Ray McDavid .15 .07
❑ 21 Duane Singleton .15 .07
❑ 22 Paul Shuey .15 .07
❑ 23 Steve Dunn .15 .07
❑ 24 Mike Lieberthal .30 .14
❑ 25 Chan Ho Park .30 .14
❑ 26 Ken Griffey Jr. RP 1.25 .55
❑ 27 Tony Gwynn RP .60 .25
❑ 28 Chuck Knoblauch RP .15 .07
❑ 29 Frank Thomas RP .60 .25
❑ 30 Matt Williams RP .30 .14
❑ 31 Chili Davis .30 .14
❑ 32 Chad Curtis .15 .07
❑ 33 Brian Anderson .15 .07
❑ 34 Chuck Finley .30 .14
❑ 35 Tim Salmon .30 .14
❑ 36 Bo Jackson .30 .14
❑ 37 Doug Drabek .15 .07
❑ 38 Craig Biggio .30 .14
❑ 39 Ken Caminiti .30 .14
❑ 40 Jeff Bagwell .75 .35
❑ 41 Darryl Kile .30 .14
❑ 42 John Hudek .15 .07
❑ 43 Brian L. Hunter .15 .07
❑ 44 Dennis Eckersley .30 .14
❑ 45 Mark McGwire 2.50 1.10
❑ 46 Brent Gates .15 .07
❑ 47 Steve Karsay .15 .07
❑ 48 Rickey Henderson .75 .35
❑ 49 Terry Steinbach .15 .07
❑ 50 Ruben Sierra .15 .07
❑ 51 Roberto Alomar .60 .25
❑ 52 Carlos Delgado .60 .25
❑ 53 Alex Gonzalez .15 .07
❑ 54 Joe Carter .30 .14
❑ 55 Paul Molitor .60 .25
❑ 56 Juan Guzman .15 .07
❑ 57 John Olerud .30 .14
❑ 58 Shawn Green .60 .25
❑ 59 Tom Glavine .60 .25
❑ 60 Greg Maddux 1.50 .70
❑ 61 Roberto Kelly .15 .07
❑ 62 Ryan Klesko .30 .14
❑ 63 Javier Lopez .30 .14
❑ 64 Jose Oliva .15 .07
❑ 65 Fred McGriff .30 .14
❑ 66 Steve Avery .15 .07
❑ 67 David Justice .30 .14
❑ 68 Ricky Bones .15 .07
❑ 69 Cal Eldred .15 .07
❑ 70 Greg Vaughn .30 .14
❑ 71 Dave Nilsson .15 .07
❑ 72 Jose Valentin .15 .07
❑ 73 Matt Mieske .15 .07
❑ 74 Todd Zeile .15 .07
❑ 75 Ozzie Smith .75 .35
❑ 76 Bernard Gilkey .15 .07
❑ 77 Ray Lankford .30 .14
❑ 78 Bob Tewksbury .15 .07
❑ 79 Mark Whiten .15 .07
❑ 80 Gregg Jefferies .15 .07
❑ 81 Randy Myers .15 .07
❑ 82 Shawon Dunston .15 .07
❑ 83 Mark Grace .60 .25
❑ 84 Derrick May .15 .07
❑ 85 Sammy Sosa 1.25 .55
❑ 86 Steve Trachsel .15 .07
❑ 87 Brett Butler .30 .14
❑ 88 Delino DeShields .15 .07
❑ 89 Orel Hershiser .30 .14
❑ 90 Mike Piazza 2.00 .90
❑ 91 Todd Hollandsworth .15 .07
❑ 92 Eric Karros .30 .14
❑ 93 Ramon Martinez .15 .07
❑ 94 Tim Wallach .15 .07
❑ 95 Raul Mondesi .30 .14
❑ 96 Larry Walker .30 .14
❑ 97 Wil Cordero .15 .07
❑ 98 Marquis Grissom .15 .07
❑ 99 Ken Hill .15 .07
❑ 100 Cliff Floyd .30 .14
❑ 101 Pedro Martinez .75 .35

❑ 102 John Wetteland .30 .14
❑ 103 Rondell White .30 .14
❑ 104 Moises Alou .30 .14
❑ 105 Barry Bonds 1.00 .45
❑ 106 Darren Lewis .15 .07
❑ 107 Mark Portugal .15 .07
❑ 108 Matt Williams .30 .14
❑ 109 William VanLandingham .15 .07
❑ 110 Bill Swift .15 .07
❑ 111 Robby Thompson .15 .07
❑ 112 Rod Beck .15 .07
❑ 113 Darryl Strawberry .30 .14
❑ 114 Jim Thome .30 .14
❑ 115 Dave Winfield .60 .25
❑ 116 Eddie Murray .60 .25
❑ 117 Manny Ramirez .75 .35
❑ 118 Carlos Baerga .15 .07
❑ 119 Kenny Lofton .30 .14
❑ 120 Albert Belle .30 .14
❑ 121 Mark Clark .15 .07
❑ 122 Dennis Martinez .30 .14
❑ 123 Randy Johnson .75 .35
❑ 124 Jay Buhner .30 .14
❑ 125 Ken Griffey Jr. 2.50 1.10
❑ 126 Goose Gossage .30 .14
❑ 127 Tino Martinez .30 .14
❑ 128 Reggie Jefferson .15 .07
❑ 129 Edgar Martinez .30 .14
❑ 130 Gary Sheffield .60 .25
❑ 131 Pat Rapp .15 .07
❑ 132 Bret Barberie .15 .07
❑ 133 Chuck Carr .15 .07
❑ 134 Jeff Conine .15 .07
❑ 135 Charles Johnson .30 .14
❑ 136 Benito Santiago .15 .07
❑ 137 Matt Williams STL .30 .14
❑ 138 Jeff Bagwell STL .60 .25
❑ 139 Kenny Lofton STL .15 .07
❑ 140 Tony Gwynn STL .60 .25
❑ 141 Jimmy Key STL .30 .14
❑ 142 Greg Maddux STL .75 .35
❑ 143 Randy Johnson STL .30 .14
❑ 144 Lee Smith STL .15 .07
❑ 145 Bobby Bonilla .30 .14
❑ 146 Jason Jacome .15 .07
❑ 147 Jeff Kent .30 .14
❑ 148 Ryan Thompson .15 .07
❑ 149 Bobby Jones .15 .07
❑ 150 Bret Saberhagen .30 .14
❑ 151 John Franco .30 .14
❑ 152 Lee Smith .30 .14
❑ 153 Rafael Palmeiro .60 .25
❑ 154 Brady Anderson .30 .14
❑ 155 Cal Ripken Jr. 2.50 1.10
❑ 156 Jeffrey Hammonds .30 .14
❑ 157 Mike Mussina .60 .25
❑ 158 Chris Hoiles .15 .07
❑ 159 Ben McDonald .15 .07
❑ 160 Tony Gwynn 1.25 .55
❑ 161 Joey Hamilton .15 .07
❑ 162 Andy Benes .15 .07
❑ 163 Trevor Hoffman .30 .14
❑ 164 Phil Plantier .15 .07
❑ 165 Derek Bell .15 .07
❑ 166 Bip Roberts .15 .07
❑ 167 Eddie Williams .15 .07
❑ 168 Fernando Valenzuela .30 .14
❑ 169 Mariano Duncan .15 .07
❑ 170 Lenny Dykstra .30 .14
❑ 171 Darren Daulton .30 .14
❑ 172 Danny Jackson .15 .07
❑ 173 Bobby Munoz .15 .07
❑ 174 Doug Jones .15 .07
❑ 175 Jay Bell .30 .14
❑ 176 Zane Smith .15 .07
❑ 177 Jon Lieber .15 .07
❑ 178 Carlos Garcia .15 .07
❑ 179 Orlando Merced .15 .07
❑ 180 Andy Van Slyke .30 .14
❑ 181 Rick Helling .30 .14
❑ 182 Rusty Greer .30 .14
❑ 183 Kenny Rogers UER .15 .07
(Shows 110 wins in 1990)
❑ 184 Will Clark .60 .25
❑ 185 Jose Canseco .75 .35
❑ 186 Juan Gonzalez .60 .25
❑ 187 Dean Palmer .30 .14
❑ 188 Ivan Rodriguez .75 .35
❑ 189 John Valentin .15 .07
❑ 190 Roger Clemens 1.25 .55
❑ 191 Aaron Sele .30 .14
❑ 192 Scott Cooper .15 .07
❑ 193 Mike Greenwell .15 .07
❑ 194 Mo Vaughn .30 .14
❑ 195 Andre Dawson .30 .14
❑ 196 Ron Gant .15 .07
❑ 197 Jose Rijo .15 .07
❑ 198 Bret Boone .30 .14
❑ 199 Deion Sanders .30 .14
❑ 200 Barry Larkin .60 .25
❑ 201 Hal Morris .15 .07
❑ 202 Reggie Sanders .15 .07
❑ 203 Kevin Mitchell .15 .07
❑ 204 Marvin Freeman .15 .07
❑ 205 Andres Galarraga .30 .14
❑ 206 Walt Weiss .15 .07
❑ 207 Charlie Hayes .15 .07
❑ 208 Dave Nied .15 .07
❑ 209 Dante Bichette .30 .14
❑ 210 David Cone .30 .14
❑ 211 Jeff Montgomery .15 .07
❑ 212 Felix Jose .15 .07
❑ 213 Mike Macfarlane .15 .07
❑ 214 Wally Joyner .30 .14
❑ 215 Bob Hamelin .15 .07
❑ 216 Brian McRae .15 .07
❑ 217 Kirk Gibson .30 .14
❑ 218 Lou Whitaker .30 .14
❑ 219 Chris Gomez .15 .07
❑ 220 Cecil Fielder .30 .14
❑ 221 Mickey Tettleton .15 .07
❑ 222 Travis Fryman .30 .14
❑ 223 Tony Phillips .15 .07
❑ 224 Rick Aguilera .15 .07
❑ 225 Scott Erickson .15 .07
❑ 226 Chuck Knoblauch .30 .14
❑ 227 Kent Hrbek .15 .07
❑ 228 Shane Mack .15 .07
❑ 229 Kevin Tapani .15 .07
❑ 230 Kirby Puckett 1.50 .70
❑ 231 Julio Franco .15 .07
❑ 232 Jack McDowell .15 .07
❑ 233 Jason Bere .15 .07
❑ 234 Alex Fernandez .15 .07
❑ 235 Frank Thomas 1.25 .55
❑ 236 Ozzie Guillen .15 .07
❑ 237 Robin Ventura .30 .14
❑ 238 Michael Jordan 2.50 1.10
❑ 239 Wilson Alvarez .15 .07
❑ 240 Don Mattingly 1.50 .70
❑ 241 Jim Abbott .30 .14
❑ 242 Jim Leyritz .15 .07
❑ 243 Paul O'Neill .30 .14
❑ 244 Melido Perez .15 .07
❑ 245 Wade Boggs .75 .35
❑ 246 Mike Stanley .15 .07
❑ 247 Danny Tartabull .15 .07
❑ 248 Jimmy Key .30 .14
❑ 249 Greg Maddux FT .75 .35
❑ 250 Randy Johnson FT .30 .14
❑ 251 Bret Saberhagen FT .30 .14
❑ 252 John Wetteland FT .30 .14
❑ 253 Mike Piazza FT 1.00 .45
❑ 254 Jeff Bagwell FT .60 .25
❑ 255 Craig Biggio FT .30 .14
❑ 256 Matt Williams FT .30 .14
❑ 257 Wil Cordero FT .15 .07
❑ 258 Kenny Lofton FT .15 .07
❑ 259 Barry Bonds FT .30 .14
❑ 260 Dante Bichette FT .15 .07
❑ 261 Ken Griffey Jr. CL 1.25 .55
❑ 262 Goose Gossage CL .15 .07
❑ 263 Cal Ripken CL 1.25 .55
❑ 264 Kenny Rogers CL .15 .07
❑ 265 John Valentin CL .15 .07
❑ P125 Ken Griffey Jr. Promo 2.00 .90

## 1998 Crown Royale

| | MINT | NRMT |
|---|---|---|
| COMPLETE SET (144) | 150.00 | 70.00 |

❑ 1 Garret Anderson .75 .35
❑ 2 Jim Edmonds 2.00 .90
❑ 3 Darin Erstad 2.00 .90
❑ 4 Tim Salmon .75 .35
❑ 5 Jarrod Washburn .50 .23
❑ 6 Dave Dellucci RC .50 .23
❑ 7 Travis Lee .75 .35
❑ 8 Devon White .50 .23
❑ 9 Matt Williams 1.25 .55
❑ 10 Andres Galarraga 1.25 .55
❑ 11 Tom Glavine 2.00 .90
❑ 12 Andruw Jones 2.00 .90
❑ 13 Chipper Jones 5.00 2.20
❑ 14 Ryan Klesko .75 .35
❑ 15 Javy Lopez .75 .35
❑ 16 Greg Maddux 5.00 2.20
❑ 17 Walt Weiss .75 .35
❑ 18 Roberto Alomar 2.00 .90
❑ 19 Harold Baines .75 .35
❑ 20 Eric Davis .75 .35
❑ 21 Mike Mussina 2.00 .90
❑ 22 Rafael Palmeiro 2.00 .90
❑ 23 Cal Ripken 8.00 3.60
❑ 24 Nomar Garciaparra 6.00 2.70
❑ 25 Pedro Martinez 2.50 1.10
❑ 26 Troy O'Leary .50 .23
❑ 27 Mo Vaughn .75 .35
❑ 28 Tim Wakefield .50 .23
❑ 29 Mark Grace 2.00 .90
❑ 30 Mickey Morandini .50 .23
❑ 31 Sammy Sosa 4.00 1.80
❑ 32 Kerry Wood 2.00 .90
❑ 33 Albert Belle 1.25 .55
❑ 34 Mike Caruso .50 .23
❑ 35 Ray Durham .75 .35
❑ 36 Frank Thomas 4.00 1.80
❑ 37 Robin Ventura .75 .35
❑ 38 Bret Boone .75 .35
❑ 39 Sean Casey .75 .35
❑ 40 Barry Larkin 2.00 .90
❑ 41 Reggie Sanders .50 .23
❑ 42 Sandy Alomar Jr. .75 .35
❑ 43 David Justice 1.25 .55
❑ 44 Kenny Lofton .75 .35
❑ 45 Manny Ramirez 2.50 1.10
❑ 46 Jim Thome 1.25 .55
❑ 47 Omar Vizquel .75 .35
❑ 48 Jaret Wright .50 .23
❑ 49 Dante Bichette .75 .35
❑ 50 Ellis Burks .75 .35
❑ 51 Vinny Castilla .75 .35
❑ 52 Todd Helton 2.50 1.10
❑ 53 Larry Walker .75 .35
❑ 54 Tony Clark .50 .23
❑ 55 Damion Easley .50 .23
❑ 56 Bobby Higginson .75 .35
❑ 57 Cliff Floyd .75 .35
❑ 58 Livan Hernandez .50 .23
❑ 59 Derrek Lee .50 .23
❑ 60 Edgar Renteria .50 .23
❑ 61 Moises Alou .75 .35
❑ 62 Jeff Bagwell 2.50 1.10
❑ 63 Derek Bell .50 .23
❑ 64 Craig Biggio 1.25 .55
❑ 65 Johnny Damon .75 .35
❑ 66 Jeff King .50 .23
❑ 67 Hal Morris .50 .23
❑ 68 Dean Palmer .75 .35

❑ 69 Bobby Bonilla .75 .35
❑ 70 Eric Karros .75 .35
❑ 71 Raul Mondesi .75 .35
❑ 72 Gary Sheffield 2.00 .90
❑ 73 Jeromy Burnitz .75 .35
❑ 74 Jeff Cirillo .75 .35
❑ 75 Marquis Grissom .50 .23
❑ 76 Fernando Vina .50 .23
❑ 77 Marty Cordova .50 .23
❑ 78 Pat Meares .50 .23
❑ 79 Paul Molitor 2.00 .90
❑ 80 Terry Steinbach .50 .23
❑ 81 Todd Walker .50 .23
❑ 82 Brad Fullmer .75 .35
❑ 83 Vladimir Guerrero 3.00 1.35
❑ 84 Carl Pavano .50 .23
❑ 85 Rondell White .75 .35
❑ 86 Carlos Baerga .50 .23
❑ 87 Hideo Nomo 2.00 .90
❑ 88 John Olerud .75 .35
❑ 89 Rey Ordonez .50 .23
❑ 90 Mike Piazza 6.00 2.70
❑ 91 Masato Yoshii RC 1.50 .70
❑ 92 Orlando Hernandez RC 3.00 1.35
❑ 93 Hideki Irabu .50 .23
❑ 94 Derek Jeter 8.00 3.60
❑ 95 Chuck Knoblauch .75 .35
❑ 96 Ricky Ledee .50 .23
❑ 97 Tino Martinez .75 .35
❑ 98 Paul O'Neill .75 .35
❑ 99 Bernie Williams 2.00 .90
❑ 100 Jason Giambi 2.00 .90
❑ 101 Ben Grieve .75 .35
❑ 102 Rickey Henderson 2.50 1.10
❑ 103 Matt Stairs .50 .23
❑ 104 Bob Abreu .75 .35
❑ 105 Doug Glanville .50 .23
❑ 106 Scott Rolen 2.00 .90
❑ 107 Curt Schilling .75 .35
❑ 108 Jose Guillen .50 .23
❑ 109 Jason Kendall .75 .35
❑ 110 Jason Schmidt .50 .23
❑ 111 Kevin Young .75 .35
❑ 112 Delino DeShields .50 .23
❑ 113 Brian Jordan .75 .35
❑ 114 Ray Lankford .75 .35
❑ 115 Mark McGwire 8.00 3.60
❑ 116 Tony Gwynn 4.00 1.80
❑ 117 Wally Joyner .75 .35
❑ 118 Ruben Rivera .50 .23
❑ 119 Greg Vaughn .75 .35
❑ 120 Rich Aurilia .50 .23
❑ 121 Barry Bonds 3.00 1.35
❑ 122 Bill Mueller .50 .23
❑ 123 Robb Nen .50 .23
❑ 124 Jay Buhner .75 .35
❑ 125 Ken Griffey Jr. 8.00 3.60
❑ 126 Edgar Martinez 1.25 .55
❑ 127 Shane Monahan .50 .23
❑ 128 Alex Rodriguez 6.00 2.70
❑ 129 David Segui .50 .23
❑ 130 Rolando Arrojo RC 1.50 .70
❑ 131 Wade Boggs 2.50 1.10
❑ 132 Quinton McCracken .50 .23
❑ 133 Fred McGriff 1.25 .55
❑ 134 Bobby Smith .50 .23
❑ 135 Will Clark 2.00 .90
❑ 136 Juan Gonzalez 2.00 .90
❑ 137 Rusty Greer .75 .35
❑ 138 Ivan Rodriguez 2.50 1.10
❑ 139 Aaron Sele .75 .35
❑ 140 John Wetteland .75 .35
❑ 141 Jose Canseco 2.50 1.10
❑ 142 Roger Clemens 4.00 1.80
❑ 143 Carlos Delgado 2.00 .90
❑ 144 Shawn Green 2.00 .90

## 1999 Crown Royale

| | MINT | NRMT |
|---|---|---|
| COMPLETE SET (144) | 250.00 | 110.00 |
| COMP.SET w/o SP's (126) | 120.00 | 55.00 |
| COMMON CARD (1-144) | .40 | .18 |
| COMMON PROSPECT SP | 5.00 | 2.20 |

❑ 1 Jim Edmonds 1.50 .70

❑ 2 Darin Erstad 1.50 .70
❑ 3 Troy Glaus 2.50 1.10
❑ 4 Tim Salmon .60 .25
❑ 5 Mo Vaughn .60 .25
❑ 6 Jay Bell .60 .25
❑ 7 Steve Finley .60 .25
❑ 8 Randy Johnson 2.00 .90
❑ 9 Travis Lee .40 .18
❑ 10 Matt Williams 1.00 .45
❑ 11 Andruw Jones 1.50 .70
❑ 12 Chipper Jones 4.00 1.80
❑ 13 Brian Jordan .60 .25
❑ 14 Ryan Klesko .60 .25
❑ 15 Javy Lopez .60 .25
❑ 16 Greg Maddux 4.00 1.80
❑ 17 Randall Simon SP 5.00 2.20
❑ 18 Albert Belle 1.00 .45
❑ 19 Will Clark 1.50 .70
❑ 20 Delino DeShields .40 .18
❑ 21 Mike Mussina 1.50 .70
❑ 22 Cal Ripken 6.00 2.70
❑ 23 Nomar Garciaparra 5.00 2.20
❑ 24 Pedro Martinez 2.00 .90
❑ 25 Jose Offerman .40 .18
❑ 26 John Valentin .40 .18
❑ 27 Mark Grace 1.50 .70
❑ 28 Lance Johnson .40 .18
❑ 29 Henry Rodriguez .40 .18
❑ 30 Sammy Sosa 3.00 1.35
❑ 31 Kerry Wood .60 .25
❑ 32 Mike Caruso .40 .18
❑ 33 Ray Durham .60 .25
❑ 34 Magglio Ordonez 1.00 .45
❑ 35 Brian Simmons SP 5.00 2.20
❑ 36 Frank Thomas 3.00 1.35
❑ 37 Mike Cameron .40 .18
❑ 38 Barry Larkin 1.50 .70
❑ 39 Greg Vaughn .60 .25
❑ 40 Dmitri Young .60 .25
❑ 41 Roberto Alomar 1.50 .70
❑ 42 Sandy Alomar Jr. .60 .25
❑ 43 David Justice 1.00 .45
❑ 44 Kenny Lofton .60 .25
❑ 45 Manny Ramirez 2.00 .90
❑ 46 Jim Thome 1.00 .45
❑ 47 Dante Bichette .60 .25
❑ 48 Vinny Castilla .60 .25
❑ 49 Todd Helton 2.00 .90
❑ 50 Larry Walker .60 .25
❑ 51 Tony Clark .40 .18
❑ 52 Damion Easley .40 .18
❑ 53 Bob Higginson .60 .25
❑ 54 Brian Hunter .40 .18
❑ 55 Gabe Kapler SP 5.00 2.20
❑ 56 Jeff Weaver SP RC 12.00 5.50
❑ 57 Cliff Floyd .60 .25
❑ 58 Alex Gonzalez SP 5.00 2.20
❑ 59 Mark Kotsay .40 .18
❑ 60 Derrek Lee .40 .18
❑ 61 Preston Wilson SP 5.00 2.20
❑ 62 Moises Alou .60 .25
❑ 63 Jeff Bagwell 2.00 .90
❑ 64 Derek Bell .40 .18
❑ 65 Craig Biggio 1.00 .45
❑ 66 Ken Caminiti .60 .25
❑ 67 Carlos Beltran SP 5.00 2.20
❑ 68 Johnny Damon .60 .25
❑ 69 Carlos Febles SP 5.00 2.20
❑ 70 Jeff King .40 .18
❑ 71 Kevin Brown 1.00 .45
❑ 72 Todd Hundley .40 .18
❑ 73 Eric Karros .60 .25
❑ 74 Raul Mondesi .60 .25
❑ 75 Gary Sheffield 1.50 .70
❑ 76 Jeromy Burnitz .60 .25
❑ 77 Jeff Cirillo .60 .25
❑ 78 Marquis Grissom .40 .18
❑ 79 Fernando Vina .40 .18
❑ 80 Chad Allen SP RC 5.00 2.20
❑ 81 Matt Lawton .60 .25
❑ 82 Doug Mientkiewicz SP RC 5.00 2.20
❑ 83 Brad Radke .60 .25
❑ 84 Todd Walker .40 .18
❑ 85 Michael Barrett SP 5.00 2.20
❑ 86 Brad Fullmer .60 .25
❑ 87 Vladimir Guerrero 2.50 1.10
❑ 88 Wilton Guerrero .40 .18
❑ 89 Ugueth Urbina .40 .18
❑ 90 Bobby Bonilla .60 .25
❑ 91 Rickey Henderson 2.00 .90
❑ 92 Rey Ordonez .40 .18
❑ 93 Mike Piazza 5.00 2.20
❑ 94 Robin Ventura .60 .25
❑ 95 Roger Clemens 3.00 1.35
❑ 96 Orlando Hernandez .60 .25
❑ 97 Derek Jeter 6.00 2.70
❑ 98 Chuck Knoblauch .60 .25
❑ 99 Tino Martinez .60 .25
❑ 100 Bernie Williams 1.50 .70
❑ 101 Eric Chavez SP 5.00 2.20
❑ 102 Jason Giambi 1.50 .70
❑ 103 Ben Grieve .60 .25
❑ 104 Tim Raines .60 .25
❑ 105 Marlon Anderson SP 5.00 2.20
❑ 106 Doug Glanville .40 .18
❑ 107 Scott Rolen 1.50 .70
❑ 108 Curt Schilling .60 .25
❑ 109 Brian Giles .60 .25
❑ 110 Jose Guillen .40 .18
❑ 111 Jason Kendall .60 .25
❑ 112 Kevin Young .60 .25
❑ 113 J.D. Drew SP 10.00 4.50
❑ 114 Jose Jimenez SP 5.00 2.20
❑ 115 Ray Lankford .60 .25
❑ 116 Mark McGwire 6.00 2.70
❑ 117 Fernando Tatis .60 .25
❑ 118 Matt Clement SP 5.00 2.20
❑ 119 Tony Gwynn 3.00 1.35
❑ 120 Trevor Hoffman .60 .25
❑ 121 Wally Joyner .60 .25
❑ 122 Reggie Sanders .40 .18
❑ 123 Barry Bonds 2.50 1.10
❑ 124 Ellis Burks .60 .25
❑ 125 Jeff Kent 1.00 .45
❑ 126 J.T. Snow .60 .25
❑ 127 Freddy Garcia SP RC 25.00 11.00
❑ 128 Ken Griffey Jr. 6.00 2.70
❑ 129 Edgar Martinez 1.00 .45
❑ 130 Alex Rodriguez 5.00 2.20
❑ 131 David Segui .40 .18
❑ 132 Rolando Arrojo .40 .18
❑ 133 Wade Boggs 2.00 .90
❑ 134 Jose Canseco 2.00 .90
❑ 135 Quinton McCracken .40 .18
❑ 136 Fred McGriff 1.00 .45
❑ 137 Juan Gonzalez 1.50 .70
❑ 138 Rusty Greer .60 .25
❑ 139 Rafael Palmeiro 1.50 .70
❑ 140 Ivan Rodriguez 2.00 .90
❑ 141 Jose Cruz Jr. .60 .25
❑ 142 Carlos Delgado 1.50 .70
❑ 143 Shawn Green 1.50 .70
❑ 144 Roy Halladay SP 5.00 2.20

## 2000 Crown Royale

| | MINT | NRMT |
|---|---|---|
| COMPLETE SET (144) | 150.00 | 70.00 |
| COMMON CARD (1-144) | .40 | .18 |
| COMMON ROOKIE SP | 2.00 | .90 |

❑ 1 Darin Erstad 1.50 .70
❑ 2 Troy Glaus 2.00 .90
❑ 3 Adam Kennedy SP 2.00 .90

- ❑ 4 Derrick Turnbow SP RC .. 2.00 .90
- ❑ 5 Mo Vaughn .60 .25
- ❑ 6 Erubiel Durazo .60 .25
- ❑ 7 Steve Finley .60 .25
- ❑ 8 Randy Johnson 2.00 .90
- ❑ 9 Travis Lee .40 .18
- ❑ 10 Matt Williams 1.00 .45
- ❑ 11 Rafael Furcal SP 6.00 2.70
- ❑ 12 Andres Galarraga 1.00 .45
- ❑ 13 Andruw Jones 1.50 .70
- ❑ 14 Chipper Jones 4.00 1.80
- ❑ 15 Javy Lopez .60 .25
- ❑ 16 Greg Maddux 4.00 1.80
- ❑ 17 Albert Belle 1.00 .45
- ❑ 18 Will Clark 1.50 .70
- ❑ 19 Mike Mussina 1.50 .70
- ❑ 20 Cal Ripken 6.00 2.70
- ❑ 21 Carl Everett .60 .25
- ❑ 22 Nomar Garciaparra 5.00 2.20
- ❑ 23 Pedro Martinez 2.00 .90
- ❑ 24 Jason Varitek .60 .25
- ❑ 25 Scott Downs SP RC 2.00 .90
- ❑ 26 Mark Grace 1.50 .70
- ❑ 27 Sammy Sosa 3.00 1.35
- ❑ 28 Kerry Wood .60 .25
- ❑ 29 Ray Durham .60 .25
- ❑ 30 Paul Konerko .60 .25
- ❑ 31 Carlos Lee .60 .25
- ❑ 32 Magglio Ordonez .60 .25
- ❑ 33 Frank Thomas 3.00 1.35
- ❑ 34 Rob Bell SP 2.00 .90
- ❑ 35 Sean Casey .60 .25
- ❑ 36 Ken Griffey Jr. 6.00 2.70
- ❑ 37 Barry Larkin 1.50 .70
- ❑ 38 Pokey Reese .60 .25
- ❑ 39 Roberto Alomar 1.50 .70
- ❑ 40 David Justice 1.00 .45
- ❑ 41 Kenny Lofton .00 .25
- ❑ 42 Manny Ramirez 2.00 .90
- ❑ 43 Richie Sexson .60 .25
- ❑ 44 Jim Thome 1.00 .45
- ❑ 45 Rolando Arrojo .40 .18
- ❑ 46 Jeff Cirillo .60 .25
- ❑ 47 Tom Goodwin .40 .18
- ❑ 48 Todd Helton 2.00 .90
- ❑ 49 Larry Walker .60 .25
- ❑ 50 Tony Clark .40 .18
- ❑ 51 Juan Encarnacion .60 .25
- ❑ 52 Juan Gonzalez 1.50 .70
- ❑ 53 Hideo Nomo 1.50 .70
- ❑ 54 Dean Palmer .60 .25
- ❑ 55 Cliff Floyd .60 .25
- ❑ 56 Alex Gonzalez .40 .18
- ❑ 57 Mike Lowell .60 .25
- ❑ 58 Brad Penny SP 2.00 .90
- ❑ 59 Preston Wilson .60 .25
- ❑ 60 Moises Alou .60 .25
- ❑ 61 Jeff Bagwell 2.00 .90
- ❑ 62 Craig Biggio 1.00 .45
- ❑ 63 Roger Cedeno .40 .18
- ❑ 64 Julio Lugo SP 2.00 .90
- ❑ 65 Carlos Beltran .60 .25
- ❑ 66 Johnny Damon .60 .25
- ❑ 67 Jermaine Dye .60 .25
- ❑ 68 Carlos Febles .40 .18
- ❑ 69 Mark Quinn SP 2.00 .90
- ❑ 70 Kevin Brown 1.00 .45
- ❑ 71 Shawn Green 1.50 .70
- ❑ 72 Eric Karros .60 .25
- ❑ 73 Gary Sheffield 1.50 .70
- ❑ 74 Kevin Barker SP 2.00 .90
- ❑ 75 Ron Belliard .40 .18
- ❑ 76 Jeromy Burnitz .60 .25
- ❑ 77 Geoff Jenkins .60 .25
- ❑ 78 Jacque Jones .60 .25
- ❑ 79 Corey Koskie .40 .18
- ❑ 80 Matt LeCroy SP 2.00 .90
- ❑ 81 Brad Radke .60 .25
- ❑ 82 Peter Bergeron SP 2.00 .90
- ❑ 83 Matt Blank SP 2.00 .90
- ❑ 84 Vladimir Guerrero 2.50 1.10
- ❑ 85 Hideki Irabu .40 .18
- ❑ 86 Rondell White .60 .25
- ❑ 87 Edgardo Alfonzo .60 .25
- ❑ 88 Mike Hampton .60 .25
- ❑ 89 Rickey Henderson 2.00 .90
- ❑ 90 Rey Ordonez .40 .18
- ❑ 91 Jay Payton SP 2.00 .90
- ❑ 92 Mike Piazza 5.00 2.20
- ❑ 93 Roger Clemens 3.00 1.35
- ❑ 94 Orlando Hernandez .60 .25
- ❑ 95 Derek Jeter 6.00 2.70
- ❑ 96 Tino Martinez .60 .25
- ❑ 97 Alfonso Soriano SP 2.00 .90
- ❑ 98 Bernie Williams 1.50 .70
- ❑ 99 Eric Chavez .60 .25
- ❑ 100 Jason Giambi 1.50 .70
- ❑ 101 Ben Grieve .60 .25
- ❑ 102 Tim Hudson 1.50 .70
- ❑ 103 Terrence Long SP 2.00 .90
- ❑ 104 Mark Mulder SP 2.00 .00
- ❑ 105 Adam Piatt SP 2.50 1.10
- ❑ 106 Bobby Abreu .60 .25
- ❑ 107 Doug Glanville .40 .18
- ❑ 108 Mike Lieberthal .60 .25
- ❑ 109 Scott Rolen 1.50 .70
- ❑ 110 Brian Giles .60 .25
- ❑ 111 Chad Hermansen SP 2.00 .00
- ❑ 112 Jason Kendall .60 .25
- ❑ 113 Warren Morris .40 .18
- ❑ 114 Rick Ankiel SP 5.00 2.20
- ❑ 115 Justin Brunette SP RC 2.00 .90
- ❑ 116 J.D. Drew 1.50 .70
- ❑ 117 Mark McGwire 6.00 2.70
- ❑ 118 Fernando Tatis .60 .25
- ❑ 119 Wiki Gonzalez SP 2.00 .90
- ❑ 120 Tony Gwynn 3.00 1.35
- ❑ 121 Trevor Hoffman .60 .25
- ❑ 122 Ryan Klesko .60 .25
- ❑ 123 Barry Bonds 2.50 1.10
- ❑ 124 Ellis Burks .40 .18
- ❑ 125 Jeff Kent 1.00 .45
- ❑ 126 Calvin Murray SP 2.00 .90
- ❑ 127 J.T. Snow .60 .25
- ❑ 128 Freddy Garcia .60 .25
- ❑ 129 John Olerud .60 .25
- ❑ 130 Alex Rodriguez 5.00 2.20
- ❑ 131 Kazuhiro Sasaki SP RC 12.00 5.50
- ❑ 132 Jose Canseco 2.00 .90
- ❑ 133 Vinny Castilla .60 .25
- ❑ 134 Fred McGriff 1.00 .45
- ❑ 135 Greg Vaughn .60 .25
- ❑ 136 Gabe Kapler .60 .25
- ❑ 137 Mike Lamb SP RC UER 2.00 .90
  (Rusty Greer pictured on front)
- ❑ 138 Ruben Mateo SP 2.00 .90
- ❑ 139 Rafael Palmeiro 1.50 .70
- ❑ 140 Ivan Rodriguez 2.00 .90
- ❑ 141 Tony Batista .60 .25
- ❑ 142 Carlos Delgado 1.50 .70
- ❑ 143 Raul Mondesi .60 .25
- ❑ 144 Shannon Stewart .60 .25

## 1981 Donruss

| | NRMT | VG-E |
|---|---|---|
| COMPLETE SET (605) | 30.00 | 13.50 |

- ❑ 1 Ozzie Smith 3.00 1.35
- ❑ 2 Rollie Fingers 1.00 .45
- ❑ 3 Rick Wise .10 .05
- ❑ 4 Gene Richards .10 .05
- ❑ 5 Alan Trammell .50 .23
- ❑ 6 Tom Brookens .10 .05

- ❑ 7A Duffy Dyer P1 .25 .11
  (1980 batting average has decimal point)
- ❑ 7B Duffy Dyer P2 .10 .05
  (1980 batting average has no decimal point)
- ❑ 8 Mark Fidrych 1.00 .45
- ❑ 9 Dave Rozema .10 .05
- ❑ 10 Ricky Peters .10 .05
- ❑ 11 Mike Schmidt 2.00 .90
- ❑ 12 Willie Stargell 1.00 .45
- ❑ 13 Tim Foli .10 .05
- ❑ 14 Manny Sanguillen .25 .11
- ❑ 15 Grant Jackson .10 .05
- ❑ 16 Eddie Solomon .10 .05
- ❑ 17 Omar Moreno .10 .05
- ❑ 18 Joe Morgan 1.00 .45
- ❑ 19 Rafael Landestoy .10 .05
- ❑ 20 Bruce Bochy .10 .05
- ❑ 21 Joe Sambito .10 .05
- ❑ 22 Manny Trillo .10 .05
- ❑ 23A Dave Smith RC P1 .25 .11
  (Line box around stats is not complete)
- ❑ 23B Dave Smith RC P2 .25 .11
  (Box totally encloses stats at top)
- ❑ 24 Terry Puhl .10 .05
- ❑ 25 Bump Wills .10 .05
- ❑ 26A John Ellis P1 ERR .50 .23
  (Danny Walton photo on front)
- ❑ 26B John Ellis P2 COR .25 .11
- ❑ 27 Jim Kern .10 .05
- ❑ 28 Richie Zisk .10 .05
- ❑ 29 John Mayberry .10 .05
- ❑ 30 Bob Davis .10 .05
- ❑ 31 Jackson Todd .10 .05
- ❑ 32 Alvis Woods .10 .05
- ❑ 33 Steve Carlton 1.00 .45
- ❑ 34 Lee Mazzilli .10 .05
- ❑ 35 John Stearns .10 .05
- ❑ 36 Roy Lee Jackson .10 .05
- ❑ 37 Mike Scott .25 .11
- ❑ 38 Lamar Johnson .10 .05
- ❑ 39 Kevin Bell .10 .05
- ❑ 40 Ed Farmer .10 .05
- ❑ 41 Ross Baumgarten .10 .05
- ❑ 42 Leo Sutherland .10 .05
- ❑ 43 Dan Meyer .10 .05
- ❑ 44 Ron Reed .10 .05
- ❑ 45 Mario Mendoza .10 .05
- ❑ 46 Rick Honeycutt .10 .05
- ❑ 47 Glenn Abbott .10 .05
- ❑ 48 Leon Roberts .10 .05
- ❑ 49 Rod Carew 1.00 .45
- ❑ 50 Bert Campaneris .25 .11
- ❑ 51A Tom Donahue P1 ERR .. .25 .11
  (Name on front misspelled Donahue)
- ❑ 51B Tom Donohue P2 COR .10 .05
- ❑ 52 Dave Frost .10 .05
- ❑ 53 Ed Halicki .10 .05
- ❑ 54 Dan Ford .10 .05
- ❑ 55 Garry Maddox .10 .05
- ❑ 56A Steve Garvey P1 1.00 .45
  (Surpassed 25 HR)
- ❑ 56B Steve Garvey P2 1.00 .45

(Surpassed 21 HR)
❑ 57 Bill Russell .25 .11
❑ 58 Don Sutton 1.00 .45
❑ 59 Reggie Smith .25 .11
❑ 60 Rick Monday .25 .11
❑ 61 Ray Knight .25 .11
❑ 62 Johnny Bench 1.50 .70
❑ 63 Mario Soto .10 .05
❑ 64 Doug Bair .10 .05
❑ 65 George Foster .25 .11
❑ 66 Jeff Burroughs .10 .05
❑ 67 Keith Hernandez .25 .11
❑ 68 Tom Herr .25 .11
❑ 69 Bob Forsch .10 .05
❑ 70 John Fulgham .10 .05
❑ 71A Bobby Bonds P1 ERR 1.00 .45
(986 lifetime HR)
❑ 71B Bobby Bonds P2 COR .50 .23
(326 lifetime HR)
❑ 72A Rennie Stennett P1 .25 .11
(Breaking broke leg)
❑ 72B Rennie Stennett P2 .10 .05
(Word "broke" deleted)
❑ 73 Joe Strain .10 .05
❑ 74 Ed Whitson .10 .05
❑ 75 Tom Griffin .10 .05
❑ 76 Billy North .10 .05
❑ 77 Gene Garber .10 .05
❑ 78 Mike Hargrove .25 .11
❑ 79 Dave Rosello .10 .05
❑ 80 Ron Hassey .10 .05
❑ 81 Sid Monge .10 .05
❑ 82A Joe Charboneau RC P1 1.00 .45
('78 highlights
for some reason)
❑ 82B Joe Charboneau RC P2 1.00 .45
(Phrase "For some reason" deleted)
❑ 83 Cecil Cooper .25 .11
❑ 84 Sal Bando .25 .11
❑ 85 Moose Haas .10 .05
❑ 86 Mike Caldwell .10 .05
❑ 87A Larry Hisle P1 .25 .11
('77 highlights
line ends with "28 RBI")
❑ 87B Larry Hisle P2 .10 .05
(Correct line "28 HR")
❑ 88 Luis Gomez .10 .05
❑ 89 Larry Parrish .10 .05
❑ 90 Gary Carter .50 .23
❑ 91 Bill Gullickson RC .50 .23
❑ 92 Fred Norman .10 .05
❑ 93 Tommy Hutton .10 .05
❑ 94 Carl Yastrzemski 1.00 .45
❑ 95 Glenn Hoffman .10 .05
❑ 96 Dennis Eckersley 1.00 .45
❑ 97A Tom Burgmeier P1 .25 .11
(ERR Throws: Right)
❑ 97B Tom Burgmeier P2 .10 .05
(COR Throws: Left)
❑ 98 Win Remmerswaal .10 .05
❑ 99 Bob Horner .25 .11
❑ 100 George Brett 2.50 1.10
❑ 101 Dave Chalk .10 .05
❑ 102 Dennis Leonard .10 .05
❑ 103 Renie Martin .10 .05
❑ 104 Amos Otis .25 .11
❑ 105 Graig Nettles .25 .11
❑ 106 Eric Soderholm .10 .05
❑ 107 Tommy John .50 .23
❑ 108 Tom Underwood .10 .05
❑ 109 Lou Piniella .25 .11
❑ 110 Mickey Klutts .10 .05
❑ 111 Bobby Murcer .25 .11
❑ 112 Eddie Murray 2.00 .90
❑ 113 Rick Dempsey .25 .11
❑ 114 Scott McGregor .10 .05
❑ 115 Ken Singleton .25 .11
❑ 116 Gary Roenicke .10 .05
❑ 117 Dave Revering .10 .05
❑ 118 Mike Norris .10 .05
❑ 119 Rickey Henderson 5.00 2.20
❑ 120 Mike Heath .10 .05
❑ 121 Dave Cash .10 .05
❑ 122 Randy Jones .10 .05
❑ 123 Eric Rasmussen .10 .05
❑ 124 Jerry Mumphrey .10 .05
❑ 125 Richie Hebner .10 .05
❑ 126 Mark Wagner .10 .05
❑ 127 Jack Morris 1.00 .45
❑ 128 Dan Petry .10 .05
❑ 129 Bruce Robbins .10 .05
❑ 130 Champ Summers .10 .05
❑ 131 Pete Rose P1 3.00 1.35
(Last line ends with
see card 251)
❑ 131B Pete Rose P2 2.00 .90
(Last line corrected
see card 371)
❑ 132 Willie Stargell 1.00 .45
❑ 133 Ed Ott .10 .05
❑ 134 Jim Bibby .10 .05
❑ 135 Bert Blyleven .50 .23
❑ 136 Dave Parker .25 .11
❑ 137 Bill Robinson .25 .11
❑ 138 Enos Cabell .10 .05
❑ 139 Dave Bergman .10 .05
❑ 140 J.R. Richard .25 .11
❑ 141 Ken Forsch .10 .05
❑ 142 Larry Bowa UER .25 .11
(Shortshop on front)
❑ 143 Frank LaCorte UER .10 .05
(Photo actually Randy Niemann)
❑ 144 Denny Walling .10 .05
❑ 145 Buddy Bell .25 .11
❑ 146 Ferguson Jenkins 1.00 .45
❑ 147 Danny Darwin .25 .11
❑ 148 John Grubb .10 .05
❑ 149 Alfredo Griffin .10 .05
❑ 150 Jerry Garvin .10 .05
❑ 151 Paul Mirabella .10 .05
❑ 152 Rick Bosetti .10 .05
❑ 153 Dick Ruthven .10 .05
❑ 154 Frank Taveras .10 .05
❑ 155 Craig Swan .10 .05
❑ 156 Jeff Reardon RC 1.00 .45
❑ 157 Steve Henderson .10 .05
❑ 158 Jim Morrison .10 .05
❑ 159 Glenn Borgmann .10 .05
❑ 160 LaMarr Hoyt RC .25 .11
❑ 161 Rich Wortham .10 .05
❑ 162 Thad Bosley .10 .05
❑ 163 Julio Cruz .10 .05
❑ 164A Del Unser P1 .25 .11
(No "3B" heading)
❑ 164B Del Unser P2 .10 .05
(Batting record on back
corrected "3B")
❑ 165 Jim Anderson .10 .05
❑ 166 Jim Beattie .10 .05
❑ 167 Shane Rawley .10 .05
❑ 168 Joe Simpson .10 .05
❑ 169 Rod Carew 1.00 .45
❑ 170 Fred Patek .10 .05
❑ 171 Frank Tanana .25 .11
❑ 172 Alfredo Martinez .10 .05
❑ 173 Chris Knapp .10 .05
❑ 174 Joe Rudi .25 .11
❑ 175 Greg Luzinski .25 .11
❑ 176 Steve Garvey .50 .23
❑ 177 Joe Ferguson .10 .05
❑ 178 Bob Welch .25 .11
❑ 179 Dusty Baker .50 .23
❑ 180 Rudy Law .10 .05
❑ 181 Dave Concepcion .25 .11
❑ 182 Johnny Bench 1.50 .70
❑ 183 Mike LaCoss .10 .05
❑ 184 Ken Griffey .50 .23
❑ 185 Dave Collins .10 .05
❑ 186 Brian Asselstine .10 .05
❑ 187 Garry Templeton .10 .05
❑ 188 Mike Phillips .10 .05
❑ 189 Pete Vuckovich .25 .11
❑ 190 John Urrea .10 .05
❑ 191 Tony Scott .10 .05
❑ 192 Darrell Evans .25 .11
❑ 193 Milt May .10 .05
❑ 194 Bob Knepper .10 .05
❑ 195 Randy Moffitt .10 .05
❑ 196 Larry Herndon .10 .05
❑ 197 Rick Camp .10 .05
❑ 198 Andre Thornton .25 .11
❑ 199 Tom Veryzer .10 .05
❑ 200 Gary Alexander .10 .05
❑ 201 Rick Waits .10 .05
❑ 202 Rick Manning .10 .05
❑ 203 Paul Molitor 2.00 .90
❑ 204 Jim Gantner .25 .11
❑ 205 Paul Mitchell .10 .05
❑ 206 Reggie Cleveland .10 .05
❑ 207 Sixto Lezcano .10 .05
❑ 208 Bruce Benedict .10 .05
❑ 209 Rodney Scott .10 .05
❑ 210 John Tamargo .10 .05
❑ 211 Bill Lee .25 .11
❑ 212 Andre Dawson UER .50 .23
(Middle name Fernando
should be Nolan)
❑ 213 Rowland Office .10 .05
❑ 214 Carl Yastrzemski 1.00 .45
❑ 215 Jerry Remy .10 .05
❑ 216 Mike Torrez .10 .05
❑ 217 Skip Lockwood .10 .05
❑ 218 Fred Lynn .25 .11
❑ 219 Chris Chambliss .25 .11
❑ 220 Willie Aikens .10 .05
❑ 221 John Wathan .10 .05
❑ 222 Dan Quisenberry .25 .11
❑ 223 Willie Wilson .25 .11
❑ 224 Clint Hurdle .10 .05
❑ 225 Bob Watson .25 .11
❑ 226 Jim Spencer .10 .05
❑ 227 Ron Guidry .25 .11
❑ 228 Reggie Jackson 1.25 .55
❑ 229 Oscar Gamble .10 .05
❑ 230 Jeff Cox .10 .05
❑ 231 Luis Tiant .25 .11
❑ 232 Rich Dauer .10 .05
❑ 233 Dan Graham .10 .05
❑ 234 Mike Flanagan .25 .11
❑ 235 John Lowenstein .10 .05
❑ 236 Benny Ayala .10 .05
❑ 237 Wayne Gross .10 .05
❑ 238 Rick Langford .10 .05
❑ 239 Tony Armas .25 .11
❑ 240A Bob Lacey P1 ERR .50 .23
(Name misspelled Lacy)
❑ 240B Bob Lacey P2 COR .10 .05
❑ 241 Gene Tenace .25 .11
❑ 242 Bob Shirley .10 .05
❑ 243 Gary Lucas .10 .05
❑ 244 Jerry Turner .10 .05
❑ 245 John Wockenfuss .10 .05
❑ 246 Stan Papi .10 .05
❑ 247 Milt Wilcox .10 .05
❑ 248 Dan Schatzeder .10 .05
❑ 249 Steve Kemp .10 .05
❑ 250 Jim Lentine .10 .05
❑ 251 Pete Rose 3.00 1.35
❑ 252 Bill Madlock .25 .11
❑ 253 Dale Berra .10 .05
❑ 254 Kent Tekulve .25 .11
❑ 255 Enrique Romo .10 .05
❑ 256 Mike Easler .10 .05
❑ 257 Chuck Tanner MG .25 .11
❑ 258 Art Howe .25 .11
❑ 259 Alan Ashby .10 .05
❑ 260 Nolan Ryan 5.00 2.20
❑ 261A Vern Ruhle P1 ERR .50 .23
(Ken Forsch photo on front)
❑ 261B Vern Ruhle P2 COR .25 .11
❑ 262 Bob Boone .25 .11
❑ 263 Cesar Cedeno .25 .11
❑ 264 Jeff Leonard .25 .11
❑ 265 Pat Putnam .10 .05
❑ 266 Jon Matlack .10 .05
❑ 267 Dave Rajsich .10 .05
❑ 268 Billy Sample .10 .05
❑ 269 Damaso Garcia .10 .05
❑ 270 Tom Buskey .10 .05
❑ 271 Joey McLaughlin .10 .05
❑ 272 Barry Bonnell .10 .05
❑ 273 Tug McGraw .25 .11
❑ 274 Mike Jorgensen .10 .05
❑ 275 Pat Zachry .10 .05
❑ 276 Neil Allen .10 .05
❑ 277 Joel Youngblood .10 .05
❑ 278 Greg Pryor .10 .05
❑ 279 Britt Burns .10 .05

| Card | Player | Price | Price |
|---|---|---|---|
| ❑ 280 | Rich Dotson | .10 | .05 |
| ❑ 281 | Chet Lemon | .10 | .05 |
| ❑ 282 | Rusty Kuntz | .10 | .05 |
| ❑ 283 | Ted Cox | .10 | .05 |
| ❑ 284 | Sparky Lyle | .25 | .11 |
| ❑ 285 | Larry Cox | .10 | .05 |
| ❑ 286 | Floyd Bannister | .10 | .05 |
| ❑ 287 | Byron McLaughlin | .10 | .05 |
| ❑ 288 | Rodney Craig | .10 | .05 |
| ❑ 289 | Bobby Grich | .25 | .11 |
| ❑ 290 | Dickie Thon | .25 | .11 |
| ❑ 291 | Mark Clear | .10 | .05 |
| ❑ 292 | Dave Lemanczyk | .10 | .05 |
| ❑ 293 | Jason Thompson | .10 | .05 |
| ❑ 294 | Rick Miller | .10 | .05 |
| ❑ 295 | Lonnie Smith | .25 | .11 |
| ❑ 296 | Ron Cey | .25 | .11 |
| ❑ 297 | Steve Yeager | .10 | .05 |
| ❑ 298 | Bobby Castillo | .10 | .05 |
| ❑ 299 | Manny Mota | .25 | .11 |
| ❑ 300 | Jay Johnstone | .25 | .11 |
| ❑ 301 | Dan Driessen | .10 | .05 |
| ❑ 302 | Joe Nolan | .10 | .05 |
| ❑ 303 | Paul Householder | .10 | .05 |
| ❑ 304 | Harry Spilman | .10 | .05 |
| ❑ 305 | Cesar Geronimo | .10 | .05 |
| ❑ 306A | Gary Mathews P1 ERR (Name misspelled) | .50 | .23 |
| ❑ 306B | Gary Matthews P2 COR | .25 | .11 |
| ❑ 307 | Ken Reitz | .10 | .05 |
| ❑ 308 | Ted Simmons | .25 | .11 |
| ❑ 309 | John Littlefield | .10 | .05 |
| ❑ 310 | George Frazier | .10 | .05 |
| ❑ 311 | Dane Iorg | .10 | .05 |
| ❑ 312 | Mike Ivie | .10 | .05 |
| ❑ 313 | Dennis Littlejohn | .10 | .05 |
| ❑ 314 | Gary Lavelle | .10 | .05 |
| ❑ 315 | Jack Clark | .25 | .11 |
| ❑ 316 | Jim Wohlford | .10 | .05 |
| ❑ 317 | Rick Matula | .10 | .05 |
| ❑ 318 | Toby Harrah | .25 | .11 |
| ❑ 319A | Dwane Kuiper P1 ERR (Name misspelled) | .25 | .11 |
| ❑ 319B | Duane Kuiper P2 COR | .10 | .05 |
| ❑ 320 | Len Barker | .10 | .05 |
| ❑ 321 | Victor Cruz | .10 | .05 |
| ❑ 322 | Dell Alston | .10 | .05 |
| ❑ 323 | Robin Yount | 1.00 | .45 |
| ❑ 324 | Charlie Moore | .10 | .05 |
| ❑ 325 | Lary Sorensen | .10 | .05 |
| ❑ 326A | Gorman Thomas P1 (2nd line on back: "30 HR mark 4th") | .50 | .23 |
| ❑ 326B | Gorman Thomas P2 (30 HR mark 3rd) | .25 | .11 |
| ❑ 327 | Bob Rodgers MG | .10 | .05 |
| ❑ 328 | Phil Niekro | 1.00 | .45 |
| ❑ 329 | Chris Speier | .10 | .05 |
| ❑ 330A | Steve Rodgers P1 (ERR Name misspelled) | .25 | .11 |
| ❑ 330B | Steve Rogers P2 COR | .10 | .05 |
| ❑ 331 | Woodie Fryman | .10 | .05 |
| ❑ 332 | Warren Cromartie | .10 | .05 |
| ❑ 333 | Jerry White | .10 | .05 |
| ❑ 334 | Tony Perez | 1.00 | .45 |
| ❑ 335 | Carlton Fisk | 1.00 | .45 |
| ❑ 336 | Dick Drago | .10 | .05 |
| ❑ 337 | Steve Renko | .10 | .05 |
| ❑ 338 | Jim Rice | .25 | .11 |
| ❑ 339 | Jerry Royster | .10 | .05 |
| ❑ 340 | Frank White | .25 | .11 |
| ❑ 341 | Jamie Quirk | .10 | .05 |
| ❑ 342A | Paul Spittorff P1 ERR (Name misspelled) | .25 | .11 |
| ❑ 342B | Paul Splittorff P2 COR | .10 | .05 |
| ❑ 343 | Marty Pattin | .10 | .05 |
| ❑ 344 | Pete LaCock | .10 | .05 |
| ❑ 345 | Willie Randolph | .25 | .11 |
| ❑ 346 | Rick Cerone | .10 | .05 |
| ❑ 347 | Rich Gossage | .50 | .23 |
| ❑ 348 | Reggie Jackson | 1.25 | .55 |
| ❑ 349 | Ruppert Jones | .10 | .05 |
| ❑ 350 | Dave McKay | .10 | .05 |
| ❑ 351 | Yogi Berra CO | .50 | .23 |
| ❑ 352 | Doug DeCinces | .25 | .11 |
| ❑ 353 | Jim Palmer | 1.00 | .45 |
| ❑ 354 | Tippy Martinez | .10 | .05 |
| ❑ 355 | Al Bumbry | .25 | .11 |
| ❑ 356 | Earl Weaver MG | 1.00 | .45 |
| ❑ 357A | Bob Picciolo P1 ERR (Name misspelled) | .25 | .11 |
| ❑ 357B | Rob Picciolo P2 COR | .10 | .05 |
| ❑ 358 | Matt Keough | .10 | .05 |
| ❑ 359 | Dwayne Murphy | .10 | .05 |
| ❑ 360 | Brian Kingman | .10 | .05 |
| ❑ 361 | Bill Fahey | .10 | .05 |
| ❑ 362 | Steve Mura | .10 | .05 |
| ❑ 363 | Dennis Kinney | .10 | .05 |
| ❑ 364 | Dave Winfield | 1.00 | .45 |
| ❑ 365 | Lou Whitaker | 1.00 | .45 |
| ❑ 366 | Lance Parrish | .25 | .11 |
| ❑ 367 | Tim Corcoran | .10 | .05 |
| ❑ 368 | Pat Underwood | .10 | .05 |
| ❑ 369 | Al Cowens | .10 | .05 |
| ❑ 370 | Sparky Anderson MG | .25 | .11 |
| ❑ 371 | Pete Rose | 3.00 | 1.35 |
| ❑ 372 | Phil Garner | .25 | .11 |
| ❑ 373 | Steve Nicosia | .10 | .05 |
| ❑ 374 | John Candelaria | .25 | .11 |
| ❑ 375 | Don Robinson | .10 | .05 |
| ❑ 376 | Lee Lacy | .10 | .05 |
| ❑ 377 | John Milner | .10 | .05 |
| ❑ 378 | Craig Reynolds | .10 | .05 |
| ❑ 379A | Luis Pujols P1 ERR (Name misspelled Pujois) | .25 | .11 |
| ❑ 379B | Luis Pujols P2 COR | .10 | .05 |
| ❑ 380 | Joe Niekro | .25 | .11 |
| ❑ 381 | Joaquin Andujar | .25 | .11 |
| ❑ 382 | Keith Moreland | .25 | .11 |
| ❑ 383 | Jose Cruz | .25 | .11 |
| ❑ 384 | Bill Virdon MG | .10 | .05 |
| ❑ 385 | Jim Sundberg | .25 | .11 |
| ❑ 386 | Doc Medich | .10 | .05 |
| ❑ 387 | Al Oliver | .25 | .11 |
| ❑ 388 | Jim Norris | .10 | .05 |
| ❑ 389 | Bob Bailor | .10 | .05 |
| ❑ 390 | Ernie Whitt | .10 | .05 |
| ❑ 391 | Otto Velez | .10 | .05 |
| ❑ 392 | Roy Howell | .10 | .05 |
| ❑ 393 | Bob Walk RC | .25 | .11 |
| ❑ 394 | Doug Flynn | .10 | .05 |
| ❑ 395 | Pete Falcone | .10 | .05 |
| ❑ 396 | Tom Hausman | .10 | .05 |
| ❑ 397 | Elliott Maddox | .10 | .05 |
| ❑ 398 | Mike Squires | .10 | .05 |
| ❑ 399 | Marvis Foley | .10 | .05 |
| ❑ 400 | Steve Trout | .10 | .05 |
| ❑ 401 | Wayne Nordhagen | .10 | .05 |
| ❑ 402 | Tony LaRussa MG | .25 | .11 |
| ❑ 403 | Bruce Bochte | .10 | .05 |
| ❑ 404 | Bake McBride | .10 | .05 |
| ❑ 405 | Jerry Narron | .10 | .05 |
| ❑ 406 | Rob Dressler | .10 | .05 |
| ❑ 407 | Dave Heaverlo | .10 | .05 |
| ❑ 408 | Tom Paciorek | .25 | .11 |
| ❑ 409 | Carney Lansford | .25 | .11 |
| ❑ 410 | Brian Downing | .25 | .11 |
| ❑ 411 | Don Aase | .10 | .05 |
| ❑ 412 | Jim Barr | .10 | .05 |
| ❑ 413 | Don Baylor | .50 | .23 |
| ❑ 414 | Jim Fregosi MG | .10 | .05 |
| ❑ 415 | Dallas Green MG | .10 | .05 |
| ❑ 416 | Dave Lopes | .25 | .11 |
| ❑ 417 | Jerry Reuss | .25 | .11 |
| ❑ 418 | Rick Sutcliffe | .25 | .11 |
| ❑ 419 | Derrel Thomas | .10 | .05 |
| ❑ 420 | Tom Lasorda MG | 1.00 | .45 |
| ❑ 421 | Charlie Leibrandt RC | .50 | .23 |
| ❑ 422 | Tom Seaver | 1.50 | .70 |
| ❑ 423 | Ron Oester | .10 | .05 |
| ❑ 424 | Junior Kennedy | .10 | .05 |
| ❑ 425 | Tom Seaver | 1.50 | .70 |
| ❑ 426 | Bobby Cox MG | .25 | .11 |
| ❑ 427 | Leon Durham | .25 | .11 |
| ❑ 428 | Terry Kennedy | .10 | .05 |
| ❑ 429 | Silvio Martinez | .10 | .05 |
| ❑ 430 | George Hendrick | .10 | .05 |
| ❑ 431 | Red Schoendienst MG | .50 | .23 |
| ❑ 432 | Johnnie LeMaster | .10 | .05 |
| ❑ 433 | Vida Blue | .25 | .11 |
| ❑ 434 | John Montefusco | .10 | .05 |
| ❑ 435 | Terry Whitfield | .10 | .05 |
| ❑ 436 | Dave Bristol MG | .10 | .05 |
| ❑ 437 | Dale Murphy | 1.00 | .45 |
| ❑ 438 | Jerry Dybzinski | .10 | .05 |
| ❑ 439 | Jorge Orta | .10 | .05 |
| ❑ 440 | Wayne Garland | .10 | .05 |
| ❑ 441 | Miguel Dilone | .10 | .05 |
| ❑ 442 | Dave Garcia MG | .10 | .05 |
| ❑ 443 | Don Money | .10 | .05 |
| ❑ 444A | Buck Martinez P1 ERR (Reverse negative) | .25 | .11 |
| ❑ 444B | Buck Martinez P2 COR | .10 | .05 |
| ❑ 445 | Jerry Augustine | .10 | .05 |
| ❑ 446 | Ben Oglivie | .25 | .11 |
| ❑ 447 | Jim Slaton | .10 | .05 |
| ❑ 448 | Doyle Alexander | .10 | .05 |
| ❑ 449 | Tony Bernazard | .10 | .05 |
| ❑ 450 | Scott Sanderson | .10 | .05 |
| ❑ 451 | David Palmer | .10 | .05 |
| ❑ 452 | Stan Bahnsen | .10 | .05 |
| ❑ 453 | Dick Williams MG | .10 | .05 |
| ❑ 454 | Rick Burleson | .10 | .05 |
| ❑ 455 | Gary Allenson | .10 | .05 |
| ❑ 456 | Bob Stanley | .10 | .05 |
| ❑ 457A | John Tudor RC P1 ERR (Lifetime W-L 9.7) | .25 | .11 |
| ❑ 457B | John Tudor RC P2 COR (Lifetime W-L 9-7) | .25 | .11 |
| ❑ 458 | Dwight Evans | .50 | .23 |
| ❑ 459 | Glenn Hubbard | .10 | .05 |
| ❑ 460 | U.L. Washington | .10 | .05 |
| ❑ 461 | Larry Gura | .10 | .05 |
| ❑ 462 | Rich Gale | .10 | .05 |
| ❑ 463 | Hal McRae | .25 | .11 |
| ❑ 464 | Jim Frey MG | .10 | .05 |
| ❑ 465 | Bucky Dent | .25 | .11 |
| ❑ 466 | Dennis Werth | .10 | .05 |
| ❑ 467 | Ron Davis | .10 | .05 |
| ❑ 468 | Reggie Jackson UER (32 HR in 1970 should be 23) | 1.25 | .55 |
| ❑ 469 | Bobby Brown | .10 | .05 |
| ❑ 470 | Mike Davis | .10 | .05 |
| ❑ 471 | Gaylord Perry | 1.00 | .45 |
| ❑ 472 | Mark Belanger | .25 | .11 |
| ❑ 473 | Jim Palmer | 1.00 | .45 |
| ❑ 474 | Sammy Stewart | .10 | .05 |
| ❑ 475 | Tim Stoddard | .10 | .05 |
| ❑ 476 | Steve Stone | .25 | .11 |
| ❑ 477 | Jeff Newman | .10 | .05 |
| ❑ 478 | Steve McCatty | .10 | .05 |
| ❑ 479 | Billy Martin MG | .50 | .23 |
| ❑ 480 | Mitchell Page | .10 | .05 |
| ❑ 481 | Steve Carlton CY | .50 | .23 |
| ❑ 482 | Bill Buckner | .25 | .11 |
| ❑ 483A | Ivan DeJesus P1 ERR (Lifetime hits 702) | .25 | .11 |
| ❑ 483B | Ivan DeJesus P2 COR (Lifetime hits 642) | .10 | .05 |
| ❑ 484 | Cliff Johnson | .10 | .05 |
| ❑ 485 | Lenny Randle | .10 | .05 |
| ❑ 486 | Larry Milbourne | .10 | .05 |
| ❑ 487 | Roy Smalley | .10 | .05 |
| ❑ 488 | John Castino | .10 | .05 |
| ❑ 489 | Ron Jackson | .10 | .05 |
| ❑ 490A | Dave Roberts P1 (Career Highlights Showed pop in) | .25 | .11 |
| ❑ 490B | Dave Roberts P2 (Declared himself) | .10 | .05 |
| ❑ 491 | George Brett MVP | 1.25 | .55 |
| ❑ 492 | Mike Cubbage | .10 | .05 |
| ❑ 493 | Rob Wilfong | .10 | .05 |
| ❑ 494 | Danny Goodwin | .10 | .05 |
| ❑ 495 | Jose Morales | .10 | .05 |
| ❑ 496 | Mickey Rivers | .25 | .11 |
| ❑ 497 | Mike Edwards | .10 | .05 |
| ❑ 498 | Mike Sadek | .10 | .05 |
| ❑ 499 | Lenn Sakata | .10 | .05 |
| ❑ 500 | Gene Michael MG | .10 | .05 |
| ❑ 501 | Dave Roberts | .10 | .05 |
| ❑ 502 | Steve Dillard | .10 | .05 |
| ❑ 503 | Jim Essian | .10 | .05 |
| ❑ 504 | Rance Mulliniks | .10 | .05 |

|  | | |
|---|---|---|
| ❑ 505 Darrell Porter | .10 | .05 |
| ❑ 506 Joe Torre MG | .25 | .11 |
| ❑ 507 Terry Crowley | .10 | .05 |
| ❑ 508 Bill Travers | .10 | .05 |
| ❑ 509 Nelson Norman | .10 | .05 |
| ❑ 510 Bob McClure | .10 | .05 |
| ❑ 511 Steve Howe | .25 | .11 |
| ❑ 512 Dave Rader | .10 | .05 |
| ❑ 513 Mick Kelleher | .10 | .05 |
| ❑ 514 Kiko Garcia | .10 | .05 |
| ❑ 515 Larry Biittner | .10 | .05 |
| ❑ 516A Willie Norwood P1 | .25 | .11 |
| (Career Highlights Spent most of) | | |
| ❑ 516B Willie Norwood P2 | .10 | .05 |
| (Traded to Seattle) | | |
| ❑ 517 Bo Diaz | .10 | .05 |
| ❑ 518 Juan Beniquez | .10 | .05 |
| ❑ 519 Scot Thompson | .10 | .05 |
| ❑ 520 Jim Tracy | .10 | .05 |
| ❑ 521 Carlos Lezcano | .10 | .05 |
| ❑ 522 Joe Amalfitano MG | .10 | .05 |
| ❑ 523 Preston Hanna | .10 | .05 |
| ❑ 524A Ray Burris P1 | .25 | .11 |
| (Career Highlights Went on ...) | | |
| ❑ 524B Ray Burris P2 | .10 | .05 |
| (Drafted by...) | | |
| ❑ 525 Broderick Perkins | .10 | .05 |
| ❑ 526 Mickey Hatcher | .25 | .11 |
| ❑ 527 John Goryl MG | .10 | .05 |
| ❑ 528 Dick Davis | .10 | .05 |
| ❑ 529 Butch Wynegar | .10 | .05 |
| ❑ 530 Sal Butera | .10 | .05 |
| ❑ 531 Jerry Koosman | .25 | .11 |
| ❑ 532A Geoff Zahn P1 | .25 | .11 |
| (Career Highlights Was 2nd in) | | |
| ❑ 532B Geoff Zahn P2 | .10 | .05 |
| (Signed a 3 year) | | |
| ❑ 533 Dennis Martinez | .50 | .23 |
| ❑ 534 Gary Thomasson | .10 | .05 |
| ❑ 535 Steve Macko | .10 | .05 |
| ❑ 536 Jim Kaat | .25 | .11 |
| ❑ 537 Best Hitters | 1.50 | .70 |
| George Brett | | |
| Rod Carew | | |
| ❑ 538 Tim Raines RC | 2.00 | .90 |
| ❑ 539 Keith Smith | .10 | .05 |
| ❑ 540 Ken Macha | .10 | .05 |
| ❑ 541 Burt Hooton | .10 | .05 |
| ❑ 542 Butch Hobson | .10 | .05 |
| ❑ 543 Bill Stein | .10 | .05 |
| ❑ 544 Dave Stapleton | .10 | .05 |
| ❑ 545 Bob Pate | .10 | .05 |
| ❑ 546 Doug Corbett | .10 | .05 |
| ❑ 547 Darrell Jackson | .10 | .05 |
| ❑ 548 Pete Redfern | .10 | .05 |
| ❑ 549 Roger Erickson | .10 | .05 |
| ❑ 550 Al Hrabosky | .10 | .05 |
| ❑ 551 Dick Tidrow | .10 | .05 |
| ❑ 552 Dave Ford | .10 | .05 |
| ❑ 553 Dave Kingman | .50 | .23 |
| ❑ 554A Mike Vail P1 | .25 | .11 |
| (Career Highlights After two) | | |
| ❑ 554B Mike Vail P2 | .10 | .05 |
| (Traded to) | | |
| ❑ 555A Jerry Martin P1 | .25 | .11 |
| (Career Highlights Overcame a) | | |
| ❑ 555B Jerry Martin P2 | .10 | .05 |
| (Traded to) | | |
| ❑ 556A Jesus Figueroa P1 | .25 | .11 |
| (Career Highlights Had an) | | |
| ❑ 556B Jesus Figueroa P2 | .10 | .05 |
| (Traded to) | | |
| ❑ 557 Don Stanhouse | .10 | .05 |
| ❑ 558 Barry Foote | .10 | .05 |
| ❑ 559 Tim Blackwell | .10 | .05 |
| ❑ 560 Bruce Sutter | .25 | .11 |
| ❑ 561 Rick Reuschel | .25 | .11 |
| ❑ 562 Lynn McGlothen | .10 | .05 |
| ❑ 563A Bob Owchinko P1 | .25 | .11 |
| (Career Highlights Traded to) | | |
| ❑ 563B Bob Owchinko P2 | .10 | .05 |
| (Involved in a) | | |
| ❑ 564 John Verhoeven | .10 | .05 |
| ❑ 565 Ken Landreaux | .10 | .05 |
| ❑ 566A Glen Adams P1 ERR | .25 | .11 |
| (Name misspelled) | | |
| ❑ 566B Glenn Adams P2 COR | .10 | .05 |
| ❑ 567 Hosken Powell | .10 | .05 |
| ❑ 568 Dick Noles | .10 | .05 |
| ❑ 569 Danny Ainge RC | 2.00 | .90 |
| ❑ 570 Bobby Mattick MG | .10 | .05 |
| ❑ 571 Joe Lefebvre | .10 | .05 |
| ❑ 572 Bobby Clark | .10 | .05 |
| ❑ 573 Dennis Lamp | .10 | .05 |
| ❑ 574 Randy Lerch | .10 | .05 |
| ❑ 575 Mookie Wilson RC | .50 | .23 |
| ❑ 576 Ron LeFlore | .25 | .11 |
| ❑ 577 Jim Dwyer | .10 | .05 |
| ❑ 578 Bill Castro | .10 | .05 |
| ❑ 579 Greg Minton | .10 | .05 |
| ❑ 580 Mark Littell | .10 | .05 |
| ❑ 581 Andy Hassler | .10 | .05 |
| ❑ 582 Dave Stieb | .25 | .11 |
| ❑ 583 Ken Oberkfell | .10 | .05 |
| ❑ 584 Larry Bradford | .10 | .05 |
| ❑ 585 Fred Stanley | .10 | .05 |
| ❑ 586 Bill Caudill | .10 | .05 |
| ❑ 587 Doug Capilla | .10 | .05 |
| ❑ 588 George Riley | .10 | .05 |
| ❑ 589 Willie Hernandez | .25 | .11 |
| ❑ 590 Mike Schmidt MVP | 2.00 | .90 |
| ❑ 591 Steve Stone CY | .10 | .05 |
| ❑ 592 Rick Sofield | .10 | .05 |
| ❑ 593 Bombo Rivera | .10 | .05 |
| ❑ 594 Gary Ward | .10 | .05 |
| ❑ 595A Dave Edwards P1 | .25 | .11 |
| (Career Highlights Sidelined the) | | |
| ❑ 595B Dave Edwards P2 | .10 | .05 |
| (Traded to) | | |
| ❑ 596 Mike Proly | .10 | .05 |
| ❑ 597 Tommy Boggs | .10 | .05 |
| ❑ 598 Greg Gross | .10 | .05 |
| ❑ 599 Elias Sosa | .10 | .05 |
| ❑ 600 Pat Kelly | .10 | .05 |
| ❑ 601A Checklist 1-120 P1 | .25 | .11 |
| (ERR Unnumbered 51 Donahue) | | |
| ❑ 601B Checklist 1-120 P2 | .50 | .23 |
| (COR Unnumbered 51 Donohue) | | |
| ❑ 602 Checklist 121-240 | .25 | .11 |
| (Unnumbered) | | |
| ❑ 603A Checklist 241-360 P1 | .25 | .11 |
| (ERR Unnumbered 306 Mathews) | | |
| ❑ 603B Checklist 241-360 P2 | .25 | .11 |
| (COR Unnumbered 306 Matthews) | | |
| ❑ 604A Checklist 361-480 P1 | .25 | .11 |
| (ERR Unnumbered 379 Pujois) | | |
| ❑ 604B Checklist 361-480 P2 | .25 | .11 |
| (COR Unnumbered 379 Pujols) | | |
| ❑ 605A Checklist 481-600 P1 | .25 | .11 |
| (ERR Unnumbered 566 Glen Adams) | | |
| ❑ 605B Checklist 481-600 P2 | .25 | .11 |
| (COR Unnumbered 566 Glenn Adams) | | |

## 1982 Donruss

| | NRMT | VG-E |
|---|---|---|
| COMPLETE SET (660) | 60.00 | 27.00 |
| COMP.FACT.SET (660) | 70.00 | 32.00 |
| COMP.RUTH PUZZLE | 10.00 | 4.50 |
| ❑ 1 Pete Rose DK | 2.50 | 1.10 |
| ❑ 2 Gary Carter DK | .20 | .09 |
| ❑ 3 Steve Garvey DK | .20 | .09 |
| ❑ 4 Vida Blue DK | .10 | .05 |
| ❑ 5 Alan Trammell DK | .10 | .05 |
| COR | | |
| ❑ 5A Alan Trammel DK ERR | .40 | .18 |
| (Name misspelled) | | |
| ❑ 6 Len Barker DK | .10 | .05 |
| ❑ 7 Dwight Evans DK | .40 | .18 |
| ❑ 8 Rod Carew DK | .75 | .35 |
| ❑ 9 George Hendrick DK | .20 | .09 |
| ❑ 10 Phil Niekro DK | .40 | .18 |
| ❑ 11 Richie Zisk DK | .10 | .05 |
| ❑ 12 Dave Parker DK | .20 | .09 |
| ❑ 13 Nolan Ryan DK | 4.00 | 1.80 |
| ❑ 14 Ivan DeJesus DK | .10 | .05 |
| ❑ 15 George Brett DK | .75 | .35 |
| ❑ 16 Tom Seaver DK | 1.25 | .55 |
| ❑ 17 Dave Kingman DK | .20 | .09 |
| ❑ 18 Dave Winfield DK | .20 | .09 |
| ❑ 19 Mike Norris DK | .10 | .05 |
| ❑ 20 Carlton Fisk DK | .40 | .18 |
| ❑ 21 Ozzie Smith DK | 1.50 | .70 |
| ❑ 22 Roy Smalley DK | .20 | .09 |
| ❑ 23 Buddy Bell DK | .20 | .09 |
| ❑ 24 Ken Singleton DK | .10 | .05 |
| ❑ 25 John Mayberry DK | .10 | .05 |
| ❑ 26 Gorman Thomas DK | .20 | .09 |
| ❑ 27 Earl Weaver MG | .40 | .18 |
| ❑ 28 Rollie Fingers | .75 | .35 |
| ❑ 29 Sparky Anderson MG | .20 | .09 |
| ❑ 30 Dennis Eckersley | .75 | .35 |
| ❑ 31 Dave Winfield | .75 | .35 |
| ❑ 32 Burt Hooton | .10 | .05 |
| ❑ 33 Rick Waits | .10 | .05 |
| ❑ 34 George Brett | 1.50 | .70 |
| ❑ 35 Steve McCatty | .10 | .05 |
| ❑ 36 Steve Rogers | .10 | .05 |
| ❑ 37 Bill Stein | .10 | .05 |
| ❑ 38 Steve Renko | .10 | .05 |
| ❑ 39 Mike Squires | .10 | .05 |
| ❑ 40 George Hendrick | .10 | .05 |
| ❑ 41 Bob Knepper | .10 | .05 |
| ❑ 42 Steve Carlton | .75 | .35 |
| ❑ 43 Larry Biittner | .10 | .05 |
| ❑ 44 Chris Welsh | .10 | .05 |
| ❑ 45 Steve Nicosia | .10 | .05 |
| ❑ 46 Jack Clark | .20 | .09 |
| ❑ 47 Chris Chambliss | .20 | .09 |
| ❑ 48 Ivan DeJesus | .10 | .05 |
| ❑ 49 Lee Mazzilli | .10 | .05 |
| ❑ 50 Julio Cruz | .10 | .05 |
| ❑ 51 Pete Redfern | .10 | .05 |
| ❑ 52 Dave Stieb | .20 | .09 |
| ❑ 53 Doug Corbett | .10 | .05 |
| ❑ 54 Jorge Bell RC | .75 | .35 |
| ❑ 55 Joe Simpson | .10 | .05 |
| ❑ 56 Rusty Staub | .20 | .09 |
| ❑ 57 Hector Cruz | .10 | .05 |
| ❑ 58 Claudell Washington | .10 | .05 |
| ❑ 59 Enrique Romo | .10 | .05 |
| ❑ 60 Gary Lavelle | .10 | .05 |
| ❑ 61 Tim Flannery | .10 | .05 |
| ❑ 62 Joe Nolan | .10 | .05 |
| ❑ 63 Larry Bowa | .20 | .09 |
| ❑ 64 Sixto Lezcano | .10 | .05 |
| ❑ 65 Joe Sambito | .10 | .05 |
| ❑ 66 Bruce Kison | .10 | .05 |
| ❑ 67 Wayne Nordhagen | .10 | .05 |
| ❑ 68 Woodie Fryman | .10 | .05 |
| ❑ 69 Billy Sample | .10 | .05 |
| ❑ 70 Amos Otis | .20 | .09 |
| ❑ 71 Matt Keough | .10 | .05 |

❑ 72 Toby Harrah .20 .09
❑ 73 Dave Righetti RC .75 .35
❑ 74 Carl Yastrzemski .75 .35
❑ 75 Bob Welch .20 .09
❑ 76 Alan Trammell COR .40 .18
❑ 76A Alan Trammel ERR .40 .18
(Name misspelled)
❑ 77 Rick Dempsey .20 .09
❑ 78 Paul Molitor 1.00 .45
❑ 79 Dennis Martinez .40 .18
❑ 80 Jim Slaton .10 .05
❑ 81 Champ Summers .10 .05
❑ 82 Carney Lansford .20 .09
❑ 83 Barry Foote .10 .05
❑ 84 Steve Garvey .40 .18
❑ 85 Rick Manning .10 .05
❑ 86 John Wathan .10 .05
❑ 87 Brian Kingman .10 .05
❑ 88 Andre Dawson UER .40 .18
(Middle name Fernando; should be Nolan)
❑ 89 Jim Kern .10 .05
❑ 90 Bobby Grich .20 .09
❑ 91 Bob Forsch .10 .05
❑ 92 Art Howe .20 .09
❑ 93 Marty Bystrom .10 .05
❑ 94 Ozzie Smith 1.50 .70
❑ 95 Dave Parker .20 .09
❑ 96 Doyle Alexander .10 .05
❑ 97 Al Hrabosky .10 .05
❑ 98 Frank Taveras .10 .05
❑ 99 Tim Blackwell .10 .05
❑ 100 Floyd Bannister .10 .05
❑ 101 Alfredo Griffin .10 .05
❑ 102 Dave Engle .10 .05
❑ 103 Mario Soto .10 .05
❑ 104 Ross Baumgarten .10 .05
❑ 105 Ken Singleton .20 .09
❑ 106 Ted Simmons .20 .09
❑ 107 Jack Morris .20 .09
❑ 108 Bob Watson .20 .09
❑ 109 Dwight Evans .40 .18
❑ 110 Tom Lasorda MG .40 .18
❑ 111 Bert Blyleven .40 .18
❑ 112 Dan Quisenberry .20 .09
❑ 113 Rickey Henderson 2.00 .90
❑ 114 Gary Carter .40 .18
❑ 115 Brian Downing .10 .05
❑ 116 Al Oliver .20 .09
❑ 117 LaMarr Hoyt .10 .05
❑ 118 Cesar Cedeno .20 .09
❑ 119 Keith Moreland .10 .05
❑ 120 Bob Shirley .10 .05
❑ 121 Terry Kennedy .10 .05
❑ 122 Frank Pastore .10 .05
❑ 123 Gene Garber .10 .05
❑ 124 Tony Pena .20 .09
❑ 125 Allen Ripley .10 .05
❑ 126 Randy Martz .10 .05
❑ 127 Richie Zisk .10 .05
❑ 128 Mike Scott .20 .09
❑ 129 Lloyd Moseby .10 .05
❑ 130 Rob Wilfong .10 .05
❑ 131 Tim Stoddard .10 .05
❑ 132 Gorman Thomas .20 .09
❑ 133 Dan Petry .10 .05
❑ 134 Bob Stanley .10 .05
❑ 135 Lou Piniella .20 .09
❑ 136 Pedro Guerrero .20 .09
❑ 137 Len Barker .10 .05
❑ 138 Rich Gale .10 .05
❑ 139 Wayne Gross .10 .05
❑ 140 Tim Wallach RC .40 .18
❑ 141 Gene Mauch MG .10 .05
❑ 142 Doc Medich .10 .05
❑ 143 Tony Bernazard .10 .05
❑ 144 Bill Virdon MG .10 .05
❑ 145 John Littlefield .10 .05
❑ 146 Dave Bergman .10 .05
❑ 147 Dick Davis .10 .05
❑ 148 Tom Seaver 1.25 .55
❑ 149 Matt Sinatro .10 .05
❑ 150 Chuck Tanner MG .10 .05
❑ 151 Leon Durham .10 .05
❑ 152 Gene Tenace .20 .09
❑ 153 Al Bumbry .10 .05
❑ 154 Mark Brouhard .10 .05
❑ 155 Rick Peters .10 .05
❑ 156 Jerry Remy .10 .05
❑ 157 Rick Reuschel .20 .09
❑ 158 Steve Howe .10 .05
❑ 159 Alan Bannister .10 .05
❑ 160 U.L. Washington .10 .05
❑ 161 Rick Langford .10 .05
❑ 162 Bill Gullickson .10 .05
❑ 163 Mark Wagner .10 .05
❑ 164 Geoff Zahn .10 .05
❑ 165 Ron LeFlore .20 .09
❑ 166 Dane Iorg .10 .05
❑ 167 Joe Niekro .20 .09
❑ 168 Pete Rose 2.50 1.10
❑ 169 Dave Collins .10 .05
❑ 170 Rick Wise .10 .05
❑ 171 Jim Bibby .10 .05
❑ 172 Larry Herndon .10 .05
❑ 173 Bob Horner .20 .09
❑ 174 Steve Dillard .10 .05
❑ 175 Mookie Wilson .20 .09
❑ 176 Dan Meyer .10 .05
❑ 177 Fernando Arroyo .10 .05
❑ 178 Jackson Todd .10 .05
❑ 179 Darrell Jackson .10 .05
❑ 180 Alvis Woods .10 .05
❑ 181 Jim Anderson .10 .05
❑ 182 Dave Kingman .20 .09
❑ 183 Steve Henderson .10 .05
❑ 184 Brian Asselstine .10 .05
❑ 185 Rod Scurry .10 .05
❑ 186 Fred Breining .10 .05
❑ 187 Danny Boone .10 .05
❑ 188 Junior Kennedy .10 .05
❑ 189 Sparky Lyle .20 .09
❑ 190 Whitey Herzog MG .20 .09
❑ 191 Dave Smith .10 .05
❑ 192 Ed Ott .10 .05
❑ 193 Greg Luzinski .20 .09
❑ 194 Bill Lee .20 .09
❑ 195 Don Zimmer MG .10 .05
❑ 196 Hal McRae .20 .09
❑ 197 Mike Norris .10 .05
❑ 198 Duane Kuiper .10 .05
❑ 199 Rick Cerone .10 .05
❑ 200 Jim Rice .20 .09
❑ 201 Steve Yeager .10 .05
❑ 202 Tom Brookens .10 .05
❑ 203 Jose Morales .10 .05
❑ 204 Roy Howell .10 .05
❑ 205 Tippy Martinez .10 .05
❑ 206 Moose Haas .10 .05
❑ 207 Al Cowens .10 .05
❑ 208 Dave Stapleton .10 .05
❑ 209 Bucky Dent .20 .09
❑ 210 Ron Cey .20 .09
❑ 211 Jorge Orta .10 .05
❑ 212 Jamie Quirk .10 .05
❑ 213 Jeff Jones .10 .05
❑ 214 Tim Raines .75 .35
❑ 215 Jon Matlack .10 .05
❑ 216 Rod Carew .75 .35
❑ 217 Jim Kaat .20 .09
❑ 218 Joe Pittman .10 .05
❑ 219 Larry Christenson .10 .05
❑ 220 Juan Bonilla .10 .05
❑ 221 Mike Easler .10 .05
❑ 222 Vida Blue .20 .09
❑ 223 Rick Camp .10 .05
❑ 224 Mike Jorgensen .10 .05
❑ 225 Jody Davis .10 .05
❑ 226 Mike Parrott .10 .05
❑ 227 Jim Clancy .10 .05
❑ 228 Hosken Powell .10 .05
❑ 229 Tom Hume .10 .05
❑ 230 Britt Burns .10 .05
❑ 231 Jim Palmer .75 .35
❑ 232 Bob Rodgers MG .10 .05
❑ 233 Milt Wilcox .10 .05
❑ 234 Dave Revering .10 .05
❑ 235 Mike Torrez .10 .05
❑ 236 Robert Castillo .10 .05
❑ 237 Von Hayes .20 .09
❑ 238 Renie Martin .10 .05
❑ 239 Dwayne Murphy .10 .05
❑ 240 Rodney Scott .10 .05
❑ 241 Fred Patek .10 .05
❑ 242 Mickey Rivers .10 .05
❑ 243 Steve Trout .10 .05
❑ 244 Jose Cruz .20 .09
❑ 245 Manny Trillo .10 .05
❑ 246 Lary Sorensen .10 .05
❑ 247 Dave Edwards .10 .05
❑ 248 Dan Driessen .10 .05
❑ 249 Tommy Boggs .10 .05
❑ 250 Dale Berra .10 .05
❑ 251 Ed Whitson .10 .05
❑ 252 Lee Smith RC 2.00 .90
❑ 253 Tom Paciorek .20 .09
❑ 254 Pat Zachry .10 .05
❑ 255 Luis Leal .10 .05
❑ 256 John Castino .10 .05
❑ 257 Rich Dauer .10 .05
❑ 258 Cecil Cooper .20 .09
❑ 259 Dave Rozema .10 .05
❑ 260 John Tudor .10 .05
❑ 261 Jerry Mumphrey .10 .05
❑ 262 Jay Johnstone .20 .09
❑ 263 Bo Diaz .10 .05
❑ 264 Dennis Leonard .10 .05
❑ 265 Jim Spencer .10 .05
❑ 266 John Milner .10 .05
❑ 267 Don Aase .10 .05
❑ 268 Jim Sundberg .10 .05
❑ 269 Lamar Johnson .10 .05
❑ 270 Frank LaCorte .10 .05
❑ 271 Barry Evans .10 .05
❑ 272 Enos Cabell .10 .05
❑ 273 Del Unser .10 .05
❑ 274 George Foster .20 .09
❑ 275 Brett Butler RC 1.00 .45
❑ 276 Lee Lacy .10 .05
❑ 277 Ken Reitz .10 .05
❑ 278 Keith Hernandez .20 .09
❑ 279 Doug DeCinces .20 .09
❑ 280 Charlie Moore .10 .05
❑ 281 Lance Parrish .40 .18
❑ 282 Ralph Houk MG .20 .09
❑ 283 Rich Gossage .40 .18
❑ 284 Jerry Reuss .20 .09
❑ 285 Mike Stanton .10 .05
❑ 286 Frank White .20 .09
❑ 287 Bob Owchinko .10 .05
❑ 288 Scott Sanderson .10 .05
❑ 289 Bump Wills .10 .05
❑ 290 Dave Frost .10 .05
❑ 291 Chet Lemon .10 .05
❑ 292 Tito Landrum .10 .05
❑ 293 Vern Ruhle .10 .05
❑ 294 Mike Schmidt 1.50 .70
❑ 295 Sam Mejias .10 .05
❑ 296 Gary Lucas .10 .05
❑ 297 John Candelaria .10 .05
❑ 298 Jerry Martin .10 .05
❑ 299 Dale Murphy .75 .35
❑ 300 Mike Lum .10 .05
❑ 301 Tom Hausman .10 .05
❑ 302 Glenn Abbott .10 .05
❑ 303 Roger Erickson .10 .05
❑ 304 Otto Velez .10 .05
❑ 305 Danny Goodwin .10 .05
❑ 306 John Mayberry .10 .05
❑ 307 Lenny Randle .10 .05
❑ 308 Bob Bailor .10 .05
❑ 309 Jerry Morales .10 .05
❑ 310 Rufino Linares .10 .05
❑ 311 Kent Tekulve .20 .09
❑ 312 Joe Morgan .75 .35
❑ 313 John Urrea .10 .05
❑ 314 Paul Householder .10 .05
❑ 315 Garry Maddox .10 .05
❑ 316 Mike Ramsey .10 .05
❑ 317 Alan Ashby .10 .05
❑ 318 Bob Clark .10 .05
❑ 319 Tony LaRussa MG .20 .09
❑ 320 Charlie Lea .10 .05
❑ 321 Danny Darwin .10 .05
❑ 322 Cesar Geronimo .10 .05
❑ 323 Tom Underwood .10 .05
❑ 324 Andre Thornton .10 .05
❑ 325 Rudy May .10 .05

| | No. | Card | | |
|---|---|---|---|---|
| ❑ | 326 | Frank Tanana | .20 | .09 |
| ❑ | 327 | Dave Lopes | .20 | .09 |
| ❑ | 328 | Richie Hebner | .20 | .09 |
| ❑ | 329 | Mike Flanagan | .20 | .09 |
| ❑ | 330 | Mike Caldwell | .10 | .05 |
| ❑ | 331 | Scott McGregor | .10 | .05 |
| ❑ | 332 | Jerry Augustine | .10 | .05 |
| ❑ | 333 | Stan Papi | .10 | .05 |
| ❑ | 334 | Rick Miller | .10 | .05 |
| ❑ | 335 | Graig Nettles | .20 | .09 |
| ❑ | 336 | Dusty Baker | .40 | .18 |
| ❑ | 337 | Dave Garcia MG | .10 | .05 |
| ❑ | 338 | Larry Gura | .10 | .05 |
| ❑ | 339 | Cliff Johnson | .10 | .05 |
| ❑ | 340 | Warren Cromartie | .10 | .05 |
| ❑ | 341 | Steve Comer | .10 | .05 |
| ❑ | 342 | Rick Burleson | .10 | .05 |
| ❑ | 343 | John Martin | .10 | .05 |
| ❑ | 344 | Craig Reynolds | .10 | .05 |
| ❑ | 345 | Mike Proly | .10 | .05 |
| ❑ | 346 | Ruppert Jones | .10 | .05 |
| ❑ | 347 | Omar Moreno | .10 | .05 |
| ❑ | 348 | Greg Minton | .10 | .05 |
| ❑ | 349 | Rick Mahler | .10 | .05 |
| ❑ | 350 | Alex Trevino | .10 | .05 |
| ❑ | 351 | Mike Krukow | .10 | .05 |
| ❑ | 352A | Shane Rawley ERR (Photo actually Jim Anderson) | .40 | .18 |
| ❑ | 352B | Shane Rawley COR | .10 | .05 |
| ❑ | 353 | Garth Iorg | .10 | .05 |
| ❑ | 354 | Pete Mackanin | .10 | .05 |
| ❑ | 355 | Paul Moskau | .10 | .05 |
| ❑ | 356 | Richard Dotson | .10 | .05 |
| ❑ | 357 | Steve Stone | .20 | .09 |
| ❑ | 358 | Larry Hisle | .10 | .05 |
| ❑ | 359 | Aurelio Lopez | .10 | .05 |
| ❑ | 360 | Oscar Gamble | .10 | .05 |
| ❑ | 361 | Tom Burgmeier | .10 | .05 |
| ❑ | 362 | Terry Forster | .10 | .05 |
| ❑ | 363 | Joe Charboneau | .20 | .09 |
| ❑ | 364 | Ken Brett | .10 | .05 |
| ❑ | 365 | Tony Armas | .10 | .05 |
| ❑ | 366 | Chris Speier | .10 | .05 |
| ❑ | 367 | Fred Lynn | .20 | .09 |
| ❑ | 368 | Buddy Bell | .20 | .09 |
| ❑ | 369 | Jim Essian | .10 | .05 |
| ❑ | 370 | Terry Puhl | .10 | .05 |
| ❑ | 371 | Greg Gross | .10 | .05 |
| ❑ | 372 | Bruce Sutter | .20 | .09 |
| ❑ | 373 | Joe Lefebvre | .10 | .05 |
| ❑ | 374 | Ray Knight | .20 | .09 |
| ❑ | 375 | Bruce Benedict | .10 | .05 |
| ❑ | 376 | Tim Foli | .10 | .05 |
| ❑ | 377 | Al Holland | .10 | .05 |
| ❑ | 378 | Ken Kravec | .10 | .05 |
| ❑ | 379 | Jeff Burroughs | .10 | .05 |
| ❑ | 380 | Pete Falcone | .10 | .05 |
| ❑ | 381 | Ernie Whitt | .10 | .05 |
| ❑ | 382 | Brad Havens | .10 | .05 |
| ❑ | 383 | Terry Crowley | .10 | .05 |
| ❑ | 384 | Don Money | .10 | .05 |
| ❑ | 385 | Dan Schatzeder | .10 | .05 |
| ❑ | 386 | Gary Allenson | .10 | .05 |
| ❑ | 387 | Yogi Berra CO | .40 | .18 |
| ❑ | 388 | Ken Landreaux | .10 | .05 |
| ❑ | 389 | Mike Hargrove | .20 | .09 |
| ❑ | 390 | Darryl Motley | .10 | .05 |
| ❑ | 391 | Dave McKay | .10 | .05 |
| ❑ | 392 | Stan Bahnsen | .10 | .05 |
| ❑ | 393 | Ken Forsch | .10 | .05 |
| ❑ | 394 | Mario Mendoza | .10 | .05 |
| ❑ | 395 | Jim Morrison | .10 | .05 |
| ❑ | 396 | Mike Ivie | .10 | .05 |
| ❑ | 397 | Broderick Perkins | .10 | .05 |
| ❑ | 398 | Darrell Evans | .20 | .09 |
| ❑ | 399 | Ron Reed | .10 | .05 |
| ❑ | 400 | Johnny Bench | 1.25 | .55 |
| ❑ | 401 | Steve Bedrosian RC | .20 | .09 |
| ❑ | 402 | Bill Robinson | .10 | .05 |
| ❑ | 403 | Bill Buckner | .20 | .09 |
| ❑ | 404 | Ken Oberkfell | .10 | .05 |
| ❑ | 405 | Cal Ripken RC ! | 40.00 | 18.00 |
| ❑ | 406 | Jim Gantner | .20 | .09 |
| ❑ | 407 | Kirk Gibson | .75 | .35 |
| ❑ | 408 | Tony Perez | .75 | .35 |
| ❑ | 409 | Tommy John UER (Text says 52-56 as Yankee, should be 52-26) | .40 | .18 |
| ❑ | 410 | Dave Stewart RC | 1.00 | .45 |
| ❑ | 411 | Dan Spillner | .10 | .05 |
| ❑ | 412 | Willie Aikens | .10 | .05 |
| ❑ | 413 | Mike Heath | .10 | .05 |
| ❑ | 414 | Ray Burris | .10 | .05 |
| ❑ | 415 | Leon Roberts | .10 | .05 |
| ❑ | 416 | Mike Witt | .20 | .09 |
| ❑ | 417 | Bob Molinaro | .10 | .05 |
| ❑ | 418 | Steve Braun | .10 | .05 |
| ❑ | 419 | Nolan Ryan UER (Misnumbering of Nolan's no-hitters on card back) | 4.00 | 1.80 |
| ❑ | 420 | Tug McGraw | .20 | .09 |
| ❑ | 421 | Dave Concepcion | .20 | .09 |
| ❑ | 422A | Juan Eichelberger ERR (Photo actually Gary Lucas) | .40 | .18 |
| ❑ | 422B | Juan Eichelberger COR | .10 | .05 |
| ❑ | 423 | Rick Rhoden | .10 | .05 |
| ❑ | 424 | Frank Robinson MG | .40 | .18 |
| ❑ | 425 | Eddie Miller | .10 | .05 |
| ❑ | 426 | Bill Caudill | .10 | .05 |
| ❑ | 427 | Doug Flynn | .10 | .05 |
| ❑ | 428 | Larry Andersen UER (Misspelled Anderson on card front) | .10 | .05 |
| ❑ | 429 | Al Williams | .10 | .05 |
| ❑ | 430 | Jerry Garvin | .10 | .05 |
| ❑ | 431 | Glenn Adams | .10 | .05 |
| ❑ | 432 | Barry Bonnell | .10 | .05 |
| ❑ | 433 | Jerry Narron | .10 | .05 |
| ❑ | 434 | John Stearns | .10 | .05 |
| ❑ | 435 | Mike Tyson | .10 | .05 |
| ❑ | 436 | Glenn Hubbard | .10 | .05 |
| ❑ | 437 | Eddie Solomon | .10 | .05 |
| ❑ | 438 | Jeff Leonard | .10 | .05 |
| ❑ | 439 | Randy Bass RC | .10 | .05 |
| ❑ | 440 | Mike LaCoss | .10 | .05 |
| ❑ | 441 | Gary Matthews | .20 | .09 |
| ❑ | 442 | Mark Littell | .10 | .05 |
| ❑ | 443 | Don Sutton | .75 | .35 |
| ❑ | 444 | John Harris | .10 | .05 |
| ❑ | 445 | Vada Pinson CO | .20 | .09 |
| ❑ | 446 | Elias Sosa | .10 | .05 |
| ❑ | 447 | Charlie Hough | .20 | .09 |
| ❑ | 448 | Willie Wilson | .20 | .09 |
| ❑ | 449 | Fred Stanley | .10 | .05 |
| ❑ | 450 | Tom Veryzer | .10 | .05 |
| ❑ | 451 | Ron Davis | .10 | .05 |
| ❑ | 452 | Mark Clear | .10 | .05 |
| ❑ | 453 | Bill Russell | .10 | .05 |
| ❑ | 454 | Lou Whitaker | .75 | .35 |
| ❑ | 455 | Dan Graham | .10 | .05 |
| ❑ | 456 | Reggie Cleveland | .10 | .05 |
| ❑ | 457 | Sammy Stewart | .10 | .05 |
| ❑ | 458 | Pete Vuckovich | .10 | .05 |
| ❑ | 459 | John Wockenfuss | .10 | .05 |
| ❑ | 460 | Glenn Hoffman | .10 | .05 |
| ❑ | 461 | Willie Randolph | .20 | .09 |
| ❑ | 462 | Fernando Valenzuela | .75 | .35 |
| ❑ | 463 | Ron Hassey | .10 | .05 |
| ❑ | 464 | Paul Splittorff | .10 | .05 |
| ❑ | 465 | Rob Picciolo | .10 | .05 |
| ❑ | 466 | Larry Parrish | .10 | .05 |
| ❑ | 467 | Johnny Grubb | .10 | .05 |
| ❑ | 468 | Dan Ford | .10 | .05 |
| ❑ | 469 | Silvio Martinez | .10 | .05 |
| ❑ | 470 | Kiko Garcia | .10 | .05 |
| ❑ | 471 | Bob Boone | .20 | .09 |
| ❑ | 472 | Luis Salazar | .10 | .05 |
| ❑ | 473 | Randy Niemann | .10 | .05 |
| ❑ | 474 | Tom Griffin | .10 | .05 |
| ❑ | 475 | Phil Niekro | .75 | .35 |
| ❑ | 476 | Hubie Brooks | .20 | .09 |
| ❑ | 477 | Dick Tidrow | .10 | .05 |
| ❑ | 478 | Jim Beattie | .10 | .05 |
| ❑ | 479 | Damaso Garcia | .10 | .05 |
| ❑ | 480 | Mickey Hatcher | .10 | .05 |
| ❑ | 481 | Joe Price | .10 | .05 |
| ❑ | 482 | Ed Farmer | .10 | .05 |
| ❑ | 483 | Eddie Murray | 1.00 | .45 |
| ❑ | 484 | Ben Oglivie | .20 | .09 |
| ❑ | 485 | Kevin Saucier | .10 | .05 |
| ❑ | 486 | Bobby Murcer | .20 | .09 |
| ❑ | 487 | Bill Campbell | .10 | .05 |
| ❑ | 488 | Reggie Smith | .20 | .09 |
| ❑ | 489 | Wayne Garland | .10 | .05 |
| ❑ | 490 | Jim Wright | .10 | .05 |
| ❑ | 491 | Billy Martin MG | .20 | .09 |
| ❑ | 492 | Jim Fanning MG | .10 | .05 |
| ❑ | 493 | Don Baylor | .40 | .18 |
| ❑ | 494 | Rick Honeycutt | .10 | .05 |
| ❑ | 495 | Carlton Fisk | .75 | .35 |
| ❑ | 496 | Denny Walling | .10 | .05 |
| ❑ | 497 | Bake McBride | .10 | .05 |
| ❑ | 498 | Darrell Porter | .20 | .09 |
| ❑ | 499 | Gene Richards | .10 | .05 |
| ❑ | 500 | Ron Oester | .10 | .05 |
| ❑ | 501 | Ken Dayley | .10 | .05 |
| ❑ | 502 | Jason Thompson | .10 | .05 |
| ❑ | 503 | Milt May | .10 | .05 |
| ❑ | 504 | Doug Bird | .10 | .05 |
| ❑ | 505 | Bruce Bochte | .10 | .05 |
| ❑ | 506 | Neil Allen | .10 | .05 |
| ❑ | 507 | Joey McLaughlin | .10 | .05 |
| ❑ | 508 | Butch Wynegar | .10 | .05 |
| ❑ | 509 | Gary Roenicke | .10 | .05 |
| ❑ | 510 | Robin Yount | .75 | .35 |
| ❑ | 511 | Dave Tobik | .10 | .05 |
| ❑ | 512 | Rich Gedman | .20 | .09 |
| ❑ | 513 | Gene Nelson | .10 | .05 |
| ❑ | 514 | Rick Monday | .10 | .05 |
| ❑ | 515 | Miguel Dilone | .10 | .05 |
| ❑ | 516 | Clint Hurdle | .10 | .05 |
| ❑ | 517 | Jeff Newman | .10 | .05 |
| ❑ | 518 | Grant Jackson | .10 | .05 |
| ❑ | 519 | Andy Hassler | .10 | .05 |
| ❑ | 520 | Pat Putnam | .10 | .05 |
| ❑ | 521 | Greg Pryor | .10 | .05 |
| ❑ | 522 | Tony Scott | .10 | .05 |
| ❑ | 523 | Steve Mura | .10 | .05 |
| ❑ | 524 | Johnnie LeMaster | .10 | .05 |
| ❑ | 525 | Dick Ruthven | .10 | .05 |
| ❑ | 526 | John McNamara MG | .10 | .05 |
| ❑ | 527 | Larry McWilliams | .10 | .05 |
| ❑ | 528 | Johnny Ray | .20 | .09 |
| ❑ | 529 | Pat Tabler | .20 | .09 |
| ❑ | 530 | Tom Herr | .20 | .09 |
| ❑ | 531A | San Diego Chicken RC ERR (Without TM) | .75 | .35 |
| ❑ | 531B | San Diego Chicken COR (With TM) | .75 | .35 |
| ❑ | 532 | Sal Butera | .10 | .05 |
| ❑ | 533 | Mike Griffin | .10 | .05 |
| ❑ | 534 | Kelvin Moore | .10 | .05 |
| ❑ | 535 | Reggie Jackson | 1.00 | .45 |
| ❑ | 536 | Ed Romero | .10 | .05 |
| ❑ | 537 | Derrel Thomas | .10 | .05 |
| ❑ | 538 | Mike O'Berry | .10 | .05 |
| ❑ | 539 | Jack O'Connor | .10 | .05 |
| ❑ | 540 | Bob Ojeda RC | .40 | .18 |
| ❑ | 541 | Roy Lee Jackson | .10 | .05 |
| ❑ | 542 | Lynn Jones | .10 | .05 |
| ❑ | 543 | Gaylord Perry | .75 | .35 |
| ❑ | 544A | Phil Garner ERR (Reverse negative) | .40 | .18 |
| ❑ | 544B | Phil Garner COR | .20 | .09 |
| ❑ | 545 | Garry Templeton | .10 | .05 |
| ❑ | 546 | Rafael Ramirez | .10 | .05 |
| ❑ | 547 | Jeff Reardon | .40 | .18 |
| ❑ | 548 | Ron Guidry | .20 | .09 |
| ❑ | 549 | Tim Laudner | .10 | .05 |
| ❑ | 550 | John Henry Johnson | .10 | .05 |
| ❑ | 551 | Chris Bando | .10 | .05 |
| ❑ | 552 | Bobby Brown | .10 | .05 |
| ❑ | 553 | Larry Bradford | .10 | .05 |
| ❑ | 554 | Scott Fletcher RC | .20 | .09 |
| ❑ | 555 | Jerry Royster | .10 | .05 |
| ❑ | 556 | Shooty Babitt UER (Spelled Babbitt on front) | .10 | .05 |
| ❑ | 557 | Kent Hrbek RC | 1.00 | .45 |
| ❑ | 558 | Yankee Winners Ron Guidry Tommy John | .20 | .09 |
| ❑ | 559 | Mark Bomback | .10 | .05 |

| | | | |
|---|---|---|---|
| ❑ 560 | Julio Valdez | .10 | .05 |
| ❑ 561 | Buck Martinez | .10 | .05 |
| ❑ 562 | Mike A. Marshall | .20 | .09 |
| ❑ 563 | Rennie Stennett | .10 | .05 |
| ❑ 564 | Steve Crawford | .10 | .05 |
| ❑ 565 | Bob Babcock | .10 | .05 |
| ❑ 566 | Johnny Podres CO | .20 | .09 |
| ❑ 567 | Paul Serna | .10 | .05 |
| ❑ 568 | Harold Baines | .75 | .35 |
| ❑ 569 | Dave LaRoche | .10 | .05 |
| ❑ 570 | Lee May | .20 | .09 |
| ❑ 571 | Gary Ward | .10 | .05 |
| ❑ 572 | John Denny | .10 | .05 |
| ❑ 573 | Roy Smalley | .10 | .05 |
| ❑ 574 | Bob Brenly | .40 | .18 |
| ❑ 575 | Bronx Bombers | .75 | .35 |
| | Reggie Jackson | | |
| | Dave Winfield | | |
| ❑ 576 | Luis Pujols | .10 | .05 |
| ❑ 577 | Butch Hobson | .10 | .05 |
| ❑ 578 | Harvey Kuenn MG | .20 | .09 |
| ❑ 579 | Cal Ripken Sr. CO | .20 | .09 |
| ❑ 580 | Juan Berenguer | .10 | .05 |
| ❑ 581 | Benny Ayala | .10 | .05 |
| ❑ 582 | Vance Law | .10 | .05 |
| ❑ 583 | Rick Leach | .10 | .05 |
| ❑ 584 | George Frazier | .10 | .05 |
| ❑ 585 | Phillies Finest | 1.00 | .45 |
| | Pete Rose | | |
| | Mike Schmidt | | |
| ❑ 586 | Joe Rudi | .10 | .05 |
| ❑ 587 | Juan Beniquez | .10 | .05 |
| ❑ 588 | Luis DeLeon | .10 | .05 |
| ❑ 589 | Craig Swan | .10 | .05 |
| ❑ 590 | Dave Chalk | .10 | .05 |
| ❑ 591 | Billy Gardner MG | .10 | .05 |
| ❑ 592 | Sal Bando | .20 | .09 |
| ❑ 593 | Bert Campaneris | .20 | .09 |
| ❑ 594 | Steve Kemp | .10 | .05 |
| ❑ 595A | Randy Lerch ERR | .40 | .18 |
| | (Braves) | | |
| ❑ 595B | Randy Lerch COR | .10 | .05 |
| | (Brewers) | | |
| ❑ 596 | Bryan Clark | .10 | .05 |
| ❑ 597 | Dave Ford | .10 | .05 |
| ❑ 598 | Mike Scioscia | .20 | .09 |
| ❑ 599 | John Lowenstein | .10 | .05 |
| ❑ 600 | Rene Lachemann MG | .10 | .05 |
| ❑ 601 | Mick Kelleher | .10 | .05 |
| ❑ 602 | Ron Jackson | .10 | .05 |
| ❑ 603 | Jerry Koosman | .20 | .09 |
| ❑ 604 | Dave Goltz | .10 | .05 |
| ❑ 605 | Ellis Valentine | .10 | .05 |
| ❑ 606 | Lonnie Smith | .20 | .09 |
| ❑ 607 | Joaquin Andujar | .20 | .09 |
| ❑ 608 | Garry Hancock | .10 | .05 |
| ❑ 609 | Jerry Turner | .10 | .05 |
| ❑ 610 | Bob Bonner | .10 | .05 |
| ❑ 611 | Jim Dwyer | .10 | .05 |
| ❑ 612 | Terry Bulling | .10 | .05 |
| ❑ 613 | Joel Youngblood | .10 | .05 |
| ❑ 614 | Larry Milbourne | .10 | .05 |
| ❑ 615 | Gene Roof UER | .10 | .05 |
| | (Name on front | | |
| | is Phil Roof) | | |
| ❑ 616 | Keith Drumwright | .10 | .05 |
| ❑ 617 | Dave Rosello | .10 | .05 |
| ❑ 618 | Rickey Keeton | .10 | .05 |
| ❑ 619 | Dennis Lamp | .10 | .05 |
| ❑ 620 | Sid Monge | .10 | .05 |
| ❑ 621 | Jerry White | .10 | .05 |
| ❑ 622 | Luis Aguayo | .10 | .05 |
| ❑ 623 | Jamie Easterly | .10 | .05 |
| ❑ 624 | Steve Sax RC | .75 | .35 |
| ❑ 625 | Dave Roberts | .10 | .05 |
| ❑ 626 | Rick Bosetti | .10 | .05 |
| ❑ 627 | Terry Francona | .40 | .18 |
| ❑ 628 | Pride of Reds | 1.00 | .45 |
| | Tom Seaver | | |
| | Johnny Bench | | |
| ❑ 629 | Paul Mirabella | .10 | .05 |
| ❑ 630 | Rance Mulliniks | .10 | .05 |
| ❑ 631 | Kevin Hickey | .10 | .05 |
| ❑ 632 | Reid Nichols | .10 | .05 |
| ❑ 633 | Dave Geisel | .10 | .05 |
| ❑ 634 | Ken Griffey | .20 | .09 |
| ❑ 635 | Bob Lemon MG | .75 | .35 |
| ❑ 636 | Orlando Sanchez | .10 | .05 |
| ❑ 637 | Bill Almon | .10 | .05 |
| ❑ 638 | Danny Ainge | 1.00 | .45 |
| ❑ 639 | Willie Stargell | .75 | .35 |
| ❑ 640 | Bob Sykes | .10 | .05 |
| ❑ 641 | Ed Lynch | .10 | .05 |
| ❑ 642 | John Ellis | .10 | .05 |
| ❑ 643 | Ferguson Jenkins | .75 | .35 |
| ❑ 644 | Lenn Sakata | .10 | .05 |
| ❑ 645 | Julio Gonzalez | .10 | .05 |
| ❑ 646 | Jesse Orosco | .10 | .05 |
| ❑ 647 | Jerry Dybzinski | .10 | .05 |
| ❑ 648 | Tommy Davis CO | .20 | .09 |
| ❑ 649 | Ron Gardenhire | .10 | .05 |
| ❑ 650 | Felipe Alou CO | .20 | .09 |
| ❑ 651 | Harvey Haddix CO | .20 | .09 |
| ❑ 652 | Willie Upshaw | .10 | .05 |
| ❑ 653 | Bill Madlock | .20 | .09 |
| ❑ 654A | DK Checklist 1-26 | .75 | .35 |
| | ERR (Unnumbered) | | |
| | (With Trammel) | | |
| ❑ 654B | DK Checklist 1-26 | .20 | .09 |
| | COR (Unnumbered) | | |
| | (With Trammell) | | |
| ❑ 655 | Checklist 27-130 | .20 | .09 |
| | (Unnumbered) | | |
| ❑ 656 | Checklist 131-234 | .20 | .09 |
| | (Unnumbered) | | |
| ❑ 657 | Checklist 235-338 | .20 | .09 |
| | (Unnumbered) | | |
| ❑ 658 | Checklist 339-442 | .20 | .09 |
| | (Unnumbered) | | |
| ❑ 659 | Checklist 443-544 | .20 | .09 |
| | (Unnumbered) | | |
| ❑ 660 | Checklist 545-653 | .20 | .09 |
| | (Unnumbered) | | |

## 1983 Donruss

| | NRMT | VG-E |
|---|---|---|
| COMPLETE SET (660) | 80.00 | 36.00 |
| COMP.FACT.SET (660) | 80.00 | 36.00 |
| COMP.COBB PUZZLE | 5.00 | 2.20 |

| | | | |
|---|---|---|---|
| ❑ 1 | Fernando Valenzuela DK | .40 | .18 |
| ❑ 2 | Rollie Fingers DK | .40 | .18 |
| ❑ 3 | Reggie Jackson DK | 1.00 | .45 |
| ❑ 4 | Jim Palmer DK | .40 | .18 |
| ❑ 5 | Jack Morris DK | .10 | .05 |
| ❑ 6 | George Foster DK | .20 | .09 |
| ❑ 7 | Jim Sundberg DK | .10 | .05 |
| ❑ 8 | Willie Stargell DK | .40 | .18 |
| ❑ 9 | Dave Stieb DK | .20 | .09 |
| ❑ 10 | Joe Niekro DK | .20 | .09 |
| ❑ 11 | Rickey Henderson DK | 1.25 | .55 |
| ❑ 12 | Dale Murphy DK | .40 | .18 |
| ❑ 13 | Toby Harrah DK | .10 | .05 |
| ❑ 14 | Bill Buckner DK | .10 | .05 |
| ❑ 15 | Willie Wilson DK | .10 | .05 |
| ❑ 16 | Steve Carlton DK | .40 | .18 |
| ❑ 17 | Ron Guidry DK | .10 | .05 |
| ❑ 18 | Steve Rogers DK | .10 | .05 |
| ❑ 19 | Kent Hrbek DK | .20 | .09 |
| ❑ 20 | Keith Hernandez DK | .20 | .09 |
| ❑ 21 | Floyd Bannister DK | .10 | .05 |
| ❑ 22 | Johnny Bench DK | 1.25 | .55 |
| ❑ 23 | Britt Burns DK | .10 | .05 |
| ❑ 24 | Joe Morgan DK | .40 | .18 |
| ❑ 25 | Carl Yastrzemski DK | .40 | .18 |
| ❑ 26 | Terry Kennedy DK | .10 | .05 |
| ❑ 27 | Gary Roenicke | .10 | .05 |
| ❑ 28 | Dwight Bernard | .10 | .05 |
| ❑ 29 | Pat Underwood | .10 | .05 |
| ❑ 30 | Gary Allenson | .10 | .05 |
| ❑ 31 | Ron Guidry | .20 | .09 |
| ❑ 32 | Burt Hooton | .10 | .05 |
| ❑ 33 | Chris Bando | .10 | .05 |
| ❑ 34 | Vida Blue | .20 | .09 |
| ❑ 35 | Rickey Henderson | 1.25 | .55 |
| ❑ 36 | Ray Burris | .10 | .05 |
| ❑ 37 | John Butcher | .10 | .05 |
| ❑ 38 | Don Aase | .10 | .05 |
| ❑ 39 | Jerry Koosman | .20 | .09 |
| ❑ 40 | Bruce Sutter | .20 | .09 |
| ❑ 41 | Jose Cruz | .20 | .09 |
| ❑ 42 | Pete Rose | 2.50 | 1.10 |
| ❑ 43 | Cesar Cedeno | .20 | .09 |
| ❑ 44 | Floyd Chiffer | .10 | .05 |
| ❑ 45 | Larry McWilliams | .10 | .05 |
| ❑ 46 | Alan Fowlkes | .10 | .05 |
| ❑ 47 | Dale Murphy | .75 | .35 |
| ❑ 48 | Doug Bird | .10 | .05 |
| ❑ 49 | Hubie Brooks | .20 | .09 |
| ❑ 50 | Floyd Bannister | .10 | .05 |
| ❑ 51 | Jack O'Connor | .10 | .05 |
| ❑ 52 | Steve Senteney | .10 | .05 |
| ❑ 53 | Gary Gaetti RC | .75 | .35 |
| ❑ 54 | Damaso Garcia | .10 | .05 |
| ❑ 55 | Gene Nelson | .10 | .05 |
| ❑ 56 | Mookie Wilson | .20 | .09 |
| ❑ 57 | Allen Ripley | .10 | .05 |
| ❑ 58 | Bob Horner | .10 | .05 |
| ❑ 59 | Tony Pena | .10 | .05 |
| ❑ 60 | Gary Lavelle | .10 | .05 |
| ❑ 61 | Tim Lollar | .10 | .05 |
| ❑ 62 | Frank Pastore | .10 | .05 |
| ❑ 63 | Garry Maddox | .10 | .05 |
| ❑ 64 | Bob Forsch | .10 | .05 |
| ❑ 65 | Harry Spilman | .10 | .05 |
| ❑ 66 | Geoff Zahn | .10 | .05 |
| ❑ 67 | Salome Barojas | .10 | .05 |
| ❑ 68 | David Palmer | .10 | .05 |
| ❑ 69 | Charlie Hough | .20 | .09 |
| ❑ 70 | Dan Quisenberry | .20 | .09 |
| ❑ 71 | Tony Armas | .10 | .05 |
| ❑ 72 | Rick Sutcliffe | .20 | .09 |
| ❑ 73 | Steve Balboni | .10 | .05 |
| ❑ 74 | Jerry Remy | .10 | .05 |
| ❑ 75 | Mike Scioscia | .20 | .09 |
| ❑ 76 | John Wockenfuss | .10 | .05 |
| ❑ 77 | Jim Palmer | .75 | .35 |
| ❑ 78 | Rollie Fingers | .75 | .35 |
| ❑ 79 | Joe Nolan | .10 | .05 |
| ❑ 80 | Pete Vuckovich | .10 | .05 |
| ❑ 81 | Rick Leach | .10 | .05 |
| ❑ 82 | Rick Miller | .10 | .05 |
| ❑ 83 | Graig Nettles | .20 | .09 |
| ❑ 84 | Ron Cey | .20 | .09 |
| ❑ 85 | Miguel Dilone | .10 | .05 |
| ❑ 86 | John Wathan | .10 | .05 |
| ❑ 87 | Kelvin Moore | .10 | .05 |
| ❑ 88A | Bym Smith ERR | .20 | .09 |
| | (Sic, Bryn) | | |
| ❑ 88B | Bryn Smith COR | .40 | .18 |
| ❑ 89 | Dave Hostetler | .10 | .05 |
| ❑ 90 | Rod Carew | .75 | .35 |
| ❑ 91 | Lonnie Smith | .10 | .05 |
| ❑ 92 | Bob Knepper | .10 | .05 |
| ❑ 93 | Marty Bystrom | .10 | .05 |
| ❑ 94 | Chris Welsh | .10 | .05 |
| ❑ 95 | Jason Thompson | .10 | .05 |
| ❑ 96 | Tom O'Malley | .10 | .05 |
| ❑ 97 | Phil Niekro | .75 | .35 |
| ❑ 98 | Neil Allen | .10 | .05 |
| ❑ 99 | Bill Buckner | .20 | .09 |
| ❑ 100 | Ed VandeBerg | .10 | .05 |
| ❑ 101 | Jim Clancy | .10 | .05 |
| ❑ 102 | Robert Castillo | .10 | .05 |
| ❑ 103 | Bruce Berenyi | .10 | .05 |
| ❑ 104 | Carlton Fisk | .75 | .35 |
| ❑ 105 | Mike Flanagan | .20 | .09 |
| ❑ 106 | Cecil Cooper | .20 | .09 |
| ❑ 107 | Jack Morris | .20 | .09 |

- ❑ 108 Mike Morgan .10 .05
- ❑ 109 Luis Aponte .10 .05
- ❑ 110 Pedro Guerrero .20 .09
- ❑ 111 Len Barker .10 .05
- ❑ 112 Willie Wilson .20 .09
- ❑ 113 Dave Beard .10 .05
- ❑ 114 Mike Gates .10 .05
- ❑ 115 Reggie Jackson 1.00 .45
- ❑ 116 George Wright .10 .05
- ❑ 117 Vance Law .10 .05
- ❑ 118 Nolan Ryan 4.00 1.80
- ❑ 119 Mike Krukow .10 .05
- ❑ 120 Ozzie Smith 1.25 .55
- ❑ 121 Broderick Perkins .10 .05
- ❑ 122 Tom Seaver 1.25 .55
- ❑ 123 Chris Chambliss .20 .09
- ❑ 124 Chuck Tanner MG .10 .05
- ❑ 125 Johnnie LeMaster .10 .05
- ❑ 126 Mel Hall RC .20 .09
- ❑ 127 Bruce Bochte .10 .05
- ❑ 128 Charlie Puleo .10 .05
- ❑ 129 Luis Leal .10 .05
- ❑ 130 John Pacella .10 .05
- ❑ 131 Glenn Gulliver .10 .05
- ❑ 132 Don Money .10 .05
- ❑ 133 Dave Rozema .10 .05
- ❑ 134 Bruce Hurst .10 .05
- ❑ 135 Rudy May .10 .05
- ❑ 136 Tom Lasorda MG .40 .18
- ❑ 137 Dan Spillner UER .10 .05
  (Photo actually
  Ed Whitson)
- ❑ 138 Jerry Martin .10 .05
- ❑ 139 Mike Norris .10 .05
- ❑ 140 Al Oliver .20 .09
- ❑ 141 Daryl Sconiers .10 .05
- ❑ 142 Lamar Johnson .10 .05
- ❑ 143 Harold Baines .75 .35
- ❑ 144 Alan Ashby .10 .05
- ❑ 145 Garry Templeton .10 .05
- ❑ 146 Al Holland .10 .05
- ❑ 147 Bo Diaz .10 .05
- ❑ 148 Dave Concepcion .20 .09
- ❑ 149 Rick Camp .10 .05
- ❑ 150 Jim Morrison .10 .05
- ❑ 151 Randy Martz .10 .05
- ❑ 152 Keith Hernandez .20 .09
- ❑ 153 John Lowenstein .10 .05
- ❑ 154 Mike Caldwell .10 .05
- ❑ 155 Milt Wilcox .10 .05
- ❑ 156 Rich Gedman .10 .05
- ❑ 157 Rich Gossage .40 .18
- ❑ 158 Jerry Reuss .20 .09
- ❑ 159 Ron Hassey .10 .05
- ❑ 160 Larry Gura .10 .05
- ❑ 161 Dwayne Murphy .10 .05
- ❑ 162 Woodie Fryman .10 .05
- ❑ 163 Steve Comer .10 .05
- ❑ 164 Ken Forsch .10 .05
- ❑ 165 Dennis Lamp .10 .05
- ❑ 166 David Green .10 .05
- ❑ 167 Terry Puhl .10 .05
- ❑ 168 Mike Schmidt 1.50 .70
  (Wearing 37
  rather than 20)
- ❑ 169 Eddie Milner .10 .05
- ❑ 170 John Curtis .10 .05
- ❑ 171 Don Robinson .10 .05
- ❑ 172 Rich Gale .10 .05
- ❑ 173 Steve Bedrosian .20 .09
- ❑ 174 Willie Hernandez .20 .09
- ❑ 175 Ron Gardenhire .10 .05
- ❑ 176 Jim Beattie .10 .05
- ❑ 177 Tim Laudner .10 .05
- ❑ 178 Buck Martinez .10 .05
- ❑ 179 Kent Hrbek .20 .09
- ❑ 180 Alfredo Griffin .10 .05
- ❑ 181 Larry Andersen .10 .05
- ❑ 182 Pete Falcone .10 .05
- ❑ 183 Jody Davis .10 .05
- ❑ 184 Glenn Hubbard .10 .05
- ❑ 185 Dale Berra .10 .05
- ❑ 186 Greg Minton .10 .05
- ❑ 187 Gary Lucas .10 .05
- ❑ 188 Dave Van Gorder .10 .05
- ❑ 189 Bob Dernier .10 .05
- ❑ 190 Willie McGee RC 1.50 .70
- ❑ 191 Dickie Thon .10 .05
- ❑ 192 Bob Boone .20 .09
- ❑ 193 Britt Burns .10 .05
- ❑ 194 Jeff Reardon .20 .09
- ❑ 195 Jon Matlack .10 .05
- ❑ 196 Don Slaught RC .40 .18
- ❑ 197 Fred Stanley .10 .05
- ❑ 198 Rick Manning .10 .05
- ❑ 199 Dave Righetti .20 .09
- ❑ 200 Dave Stapleton .10 .05
- ❑ 201 Steve Yeager .10 .05
- ❑ 202 Enos Cabell .10 .05
- ❑ 203 Sammy Stewart .10 .05
- ❑ 204 Moose Haas .10 .05
- ❑ 205 Lenn Sakata .10 .05
- ❑ 206 Charlie Moore .10 .05
- ❑ 207 Alan Trammell .40 .18
- ❑ 208 Jim Rice .20 .09
- ❑ 209 Roy Smalley .10 .05
- ❑ 210 Bill Russell .10 .05
- ❑ 211 Andre Thornton .10 .05
- ❑ 212 Willie Aikens .10 .05
- ❑ 213 Dave McKay .10 .05
- ❑ 214 Tim Blackwell .10 .05
- ❑ 215 Buddy Bell .20 .09
- ❑ 216 Doug DeCinces .20 .09
- ❑ 217 Tom Herr .20 .09
- ❑ 218 Frank LaCorte .10 .05
- ❑ 219 Steve Carlton .75 .35
- ❑ 220 Terry Kennedy .10 .05
- ❑ 221 Mike Easler .10 .05
- ❑ 222 Jack Clark .20 .09
- ❑ 223 Gene Garber .10 .05
- ❑ 224 Scott Holman .10 .05
- ❑ 225 Mike Proly .10 .05
- ❑ 226 Terry Bulling .10 .05
- ❑ 227 Jerry Garvin .10 .05
- ❑ 228 Ron Davis .10 .05
- ❑ 229 Tom Hume .10 .05
- ❑ 230 Marc Hill .10 .05
- ❑ 231 Dennis Martinez .20 .09
- ❑ 232 Jim Gantner .10 .05
- ❑ 233 Larry Pashnick .10 .05
- ❑ 234 Dave Collins .10 .05
- ❑ 235 Tom Burgmeier .10 .05
- ❑ 236 Ken Landreaux .10 .05
- ❑ 237 John Denny .10 .05
- ❑ 238 Hal McRae .20 .09
- ❑ 239 Matt Keough .10 .05
- ❑ 240 Doug Flynn .10 .05
- ❑ 241 Fred Lynn .20 .09
- ❑ 242 Billy Sample .10 .05
- ❑ 243 Tom Paciorek .20 .09
- ❑ 244 Joe Sambito .10 .05
- ❑ 245 Sid Monge .10 .05
- ❑ 246 Ken Oberkfell .10 .05
- ❑ 247 Joe Pittman UER .10 .05
  (Photo actually
  Juan Eichelberger)
- ❑ 248 Mario Soto .10 .05
- ❑ 249 Claudell Washington .10 .05
- ❑ 250 Rick Rhoden .10 .05
- ❑ 251 Darrell Evans .20 .09
- ❑ 252 Steve Henderson .10 .05
- ❑ 253 Manny Castillo .10 .05
- ❑ 254 Craig Swan .10 .05
- ❑ 255 Joey McLaughlin .10 .05
- ❑ 256 Pete Redfern .10 .05
- ❑ 257 Ken Singleton .10 .05
- ❑ 258 Robin Yount .75 .35
- ❑ 259 Elias Sosa .10 .05
- ❑ 260 Bob Ojeda .10 .05
- ❑ 261 Bobby Murcer .20 .09
- ❑ 262 Candy Maldonado RC .20 .09
- ❑ 263 Rick Waits .10 .05
- ❑ 264 Greg Pryor .10 .05
- ❑ 265 Bob Owchinko .10 .05
- ❑ 266 Chris Speier .10 .05
- ❑ 267 Bruce Kison .10 .05
- ❑ 268 Mark Wagner .10 .05
- ❑ 269 Steve Kemp .10 .05
- ❑ 270 Phil Garner .20 .09
- ❑ 271 Gene Richards .10 .05
- ❑ 272 Renie Martin .10 .05
- ❑ 273 Dave Roberts .10 .05
- ❑ 274 Dan Driessen .10 .05
- ❑ 275 Rufino Linares .10 .05
- ❑ 276 Lee Lacy .10 .05
- ❑ 277 Ryne Sandberg RC 12.00 5.50
- ❑ 278 Darrell Porter .10 .05
- ❑ 279 Cal Ripken 8.00 3.60
- ❑ 280 Jamie Easterly .10 .05
- ❑ 281 Bill Fahey .10 .05
- ❑ 282 Glenn Hoffman .10 .05
- ❑ 283 Willie Randolph .20 .09
- ❑ 284 Fernando Valenzuela .40 .18
- ❑ 285 Alan Bannister .10 .05
- ❑ 286 Paul Splittorff .10 .05
- ❑ 287 Joe Rudi .10 .05
- ❑ 288 Bill Gullickson .10 .05
- ❑ 289 Danny Darwin .10 .05
- ❑ 290 Andy Hassler .10 .05
- ❑ 291 Ernesto Escarrega .10 .05
- ❑ 292 Steve Mura .10 .05
- ❑ 293 Tony Scott .10 .05
- ❑ 294 Manny Trillo .10 .05
- ❑ 295 Greg Harris .10 .05
- ❑ 296 Luis DeLeon .10 .05
- ❑ 297 Kent Tekulve .20 .09
- ❑ 298 Atlee Hammaker .10 .05
- ❑ 299 Bruce Benedict .10 .05
- ❑ 300 Fergie Jenkins .75 .35
- ❑ 301 Dave Kingman .40 .18
- ❑ 302 Bill Caudill .10 .05
- ❑ 303 John Castino .10 .05
- ❑ 304 Ernie Whitt .10 .05
- ❑ 305 Randy Johnson .10 .05
- ❑ 306 Garth Iorg .10 .05
- ❑ 307 Gaylord Perry .75 .35
- ❑ 308 Ed Lynch .10 .05
- ❑ 309 Keith Moreland .10 .05
- ❑ 310 Rafael Ramirez .10 .05
- ❑ 311 Bill Madlock .20 .00
- ❑ 312 Milt May .10 .05
- ❑ 313 John Montefusco .10 .05
- ❑ 314 Wayne Krenchicki .10 .05
- ❑ 315 George Vukovich .10 .05
- ❑ 316 Joaquin Andujar .10 .05
- ❑ 317 Craig Reynolds .10 .05
- ❑ 318 Rick Burleson .10 .05
- ❑ 319 Richard Dotson .10 .05
- ❑ 320 Steve Rogers .10 .05
- ❑ 321 Dave Schmidt .10 .05
- ❑ 322 Bud Black RC .20 .09
- ❑ 323 Jeff Burroughs .10 .05
- ❑ 324 Von Hayes .20 .09
- ❑ 325 Butch Wynegar .10 .05
- ❑ 326 Carl Yastrzemski .75 .35
- ❑ 327 Ron Roenicke .10 .05
- ❑ 328 Howard Johnson RC .75 .35
- ❑ 329 Rick Dempsey UER .20 .09
  (Posing as a left-
  handed batter)
- ❑ 330A Jim Slaton .10 .05
  (Bio printed
  black on white)
- ❑ 330B Jim Slaton .20 .09
  (Bio printed
  black on yellow)
- ❑ 331 Benny Ayala .10 .05
- ❑ 332 Ted Simmons .20 .09
- ❑ 333 Lou Whitaker .40 .18
- ❑ 334 Chuck Rainey .10 .05
- ❑ 335 Lou Piniella .20 .09
- ❑ 336 Steve Sax .20 .09
- ❑ 337 Toby Harrah .10 .05
- ❑ 338 George Brett 1.50 .70
- ❑ 339 Dave Lopes .20 .09
- ❑ 340 Gary Carter .40 .18
- ❑ 341 John Grubb .10 .05
- ❑ 342 Tim Foli .10 .05
- ❑ 343 Jim Kaat .20 .09
- ❑ 344 Mike LaCoss .10 .05
- ❑ 345 Larry Christenson .10 .05
- ❑ 346 Juan Bonilla .10 .05
- ❑ 347 Omar Moreno .10 .05
- ❑ 348 Chili Davis .75 .35
- ❑ 349 Tommy Boggs .10 .05
- ❑ 350 Rusty Staub .20 .09
- ❑ 351 Bump Wills .10 .05
- ❑ 352 Rick Sweet .10 .05

❑ 353 Jim Gott RC .10 .05
❑ 354 Terry Felton .10 .05
❑ 355 Jim Kern .10 .05
❑ 356 Bill Almon UER .10 .05
(Expos/Mets in 1983, not Padres/Mets)
❑ 357 Tippy Martinez .10 .05
❑ 358 Roy Howell .10 .05
❑ 359 Dan Petry .10 .05
❑ 360 Jerry Mumphrey .10 .05
❑ 361 Mark Clear .10 .05
❑ 362 Mike Marshall .10 .05
❑ 363 Lary Sorensen .10 .05
❑ 364 Amos Otis .20 .09
❑ 365 Rick Langford .10 .05
❑ 366 Brad Mills .10 .05
❑ 367 Brian Downing .10 .05
❑ 368 Mike Richardt .10 .05
❑ 369 Aurelio Rodriguez .10 .05
❑ 370 Dave Smith .10 .05
❑ 371 Tug McGraw .20 .09
❑ 372 Doug Bair .10 .05
❑ 373 Ruppert Jones .10 .05
❑ 374 Alex Trevino .10 .05
❑ 375 Ken Dayley .10 .05
❑ 376 Rod Scurry .10 .05
❑ 377 Bob Brenly .10 .05
❑ 378 Scot Thompson .10 .05
❑ 379 Julio Cruz .10 .05
❑ 380 John Stearns .10 .05
❑ 381 Dale Murray .10 .05
❑ 382 Frank Viola RC .75 .35
❑ 383 Al Bumbry .10 .05
❑ 384 Ben Oglivie .10 .05
❑ 385 Dave Tobik .10 .05
❑ 386 Bob Stanley .10 .05
❑ 387 Andre Robertson .10 .05
❑ 388 Jorge Orta .10 .05
❑ 389 Ed Whitson .10 .05
❑ 390 Don Hood .10 .05
❑ 391 Tom Underwood .10 .05
❑ 392 Tim Wallach .20 .09
❑ 393 Steve Renko .10 .05
❑ 394 Mickey Rivers .10 .05
❑ 395 Greg Luzinski .20 .09
❑ 396 Art Howe .20 .09
❑ 397 Alan Wiggins .10 .05
❑ 398 Jim Barr .10 .05
❑ 399 Ivan DeJesus .10 .05
❑ 400 Tom Lawless .10 .05
❑ 401 Bob Walk .10 .05
❑ 402 Jimmy Smith .10 .05
❑ 403 Lee Smith .75 .35
❑ 404 George Hendrick .10 .05
❑ 405 Eddie Murray 1.00 .45
❑ 406 Marshall Edwards .10 .05
❑ 407 Lance Parrish .20 .09
❑ 408 Carney Lansford .20 .09
❑ 409 Dave Winfield .75 .35
❑ 410 Bob Welch .20 .09
❑ 411 Larry Milbourne .10 .05
❑ 412 Dennis Leonard .10 .05
❑ 413 Dan Meyer .10 .05
❑ 414 Charlie Lea .10 .05
❑ 415 Rick Honeycutt .10 .05
❑ 416 Mike Witt .10 .05
❑ 417 Steve Trout .10 .05
❑ 418 Glenn Brummer .10 .05
❑ 419 Denny Walling .10 .05
❑ 420 Gary Matthews .20 .09
❑ 421 Charlie Leibrandt UER .10 .05
(Liebrandt on front of card)
❑ 422 Juan Eichelberger UER .10 .05
(Photo actually Joe Pittman)
❑ 423 Cecilio Guante UER .10 .05
(Listed as Matt on card)
❑ 424 Bill Laskey .10 .05
❑ 425 Jerry Royster .10 .05
❑ 426 Dickie Noles .10 .05
❑ 427 George Foster .20 .09
❑ 428 Mike Moore RC .20 .09
❑ 429 Gary Ward .10 .05
❑ 430 Barry Bonnell .10 .05
❑ 431 Ron Washington .10 .05
❑ 432 Rance Mulliniks .10 .05
❑ 433 Mike Stanton .10 .05
❑ 434 Jesse Orosco .10 .05
❑ 435 Larry Bowa .20 .09
❑ 436 Biff Pocoroba .10 .05
❑ 437 Johnny Ray .10 .05
❑ 438 Joe Morgan .75 .35
❑ 439 Eric Show .10 .05
❑ 440 Larry Biittner .10 .05
❑ 441 Greg Gross .10 .05
❑ 442 Gene Tenace .20 .09
❑ 443 Danny Heep .10 .05
❑ 444 Bobby Clark .10 .05
❑ 445 Kevin Hickey .10 .05
❑ 446 Scott Sanderson .10 .05
❑ 447 Frank Tanana .20 .09
❑ 448 Cesar Geronimo .10 .05
❑ 449 Jimmy Sexton .10 .05
❑ 450 Mike Hargrove .20 .09
❑ 451 Doyle Alexander .10 .05
❑ 452 Dwight Evans .20 .09
❑ 453 Terry Forster .10 .05
❑ 454 Tom Brookens .10 .05
❑ 455 Rich Dauer .10 .05
❑ 456 Rob Picciolo .10 .05
❑ 457 Terry Crowley .10 .05
❑ 458 Ned Yost .10 .05
❑ 459 Kirk Gibson .75 .35
❑ 460 Reid Nichols .10 .05
❑ 461 Oscar Gamble .10 .05
❑ 462 Dusty Baker .20 .09
❑ 463 Jack Perconte .10 .05
❑ 464 Frank White .20 .09
❑ 465 Mickey Klutts .10 .05
❑ 466 Warren Cromartie .10 .05
❑ 467 Larry Parrish .10 .05
❑ 468 Bobby Grich .20 .09
❑ 469 Dane Iorg .10 .05
❑ 470 Joe Niekro .20 .09
❑ 471 Ed Farmer .10 .05
❑ 472 Tim Flannery .10 .05
❑ 473 Dave Parker .20 .09
❑ 474 Jeff Leonard .10 .05
❑ 475 Al Hrabosky .10 .05
❑ 476 Ron Hodges .10 .05
❑ 477 Leon Durham .10 .05
❑ 478 Jim Essian .10 .05
❑ 479 Roy Lee Jackson .10 .05
❑ 480 Brad Havens .10 .05
❑ 481 Joe Price .10 .05
❑ 482 Tony Bernazard .10 .05
❑ 483 Scott McGregor .10 .05
❑ 484 Paul Molitor 1.00 .45
❑ 485 Mike Ivie .10 .05
❑ 486 Ken Griffey .20 .09
❑ 487 Dennis Eckersley .75 .35
❑ 488 Steve Garvey .40 .18
❑ 489 Mike Fischlin .10 .05
❑ 490 U.L. Washington .10 .05
❑ 491 Steve McCatty .10 .05
❑ 492 Roy Johnson .10 .05
❑ 493 Don Baylor .40 .18
❑ 494 Bobby Johnson .10 .05
❑ 495 Mike Squires .10 .05
❑ 496 Bert Roberge .10 .05
❑ 497 Dick Ruthven .10 .05
❑ 498 Tito Landrum .10 .05
❑ 499 Sixto Lezcano .10 .05
❑ 500 Johnny Bench 1.25 .55
❑ 501 Larry Whisenton .10 .05
❑ 502 Manny Sarmiento .10 .05
❑ 503 Fred Breining .10 .05
❑ 504 Bill Campbell .10 .05
❑ 505 Todd Cruz .10 .05
❑ 506 Bob Bailor .10 .05
❑ 507 Dave Stieb .20 .09
❑ 508 Al Williams .10 .05
❑ 509 Dan Ford .10 .05
❑ 510 Gorman Thomas .10 .05
❑ 511 Chet Lemon .10 .05
❑ 512 Mike Torrez .10 .05
❑ 513 Shane Rawley .10 .05
❑ 514 Mark Belanger .10 .05
❑ 515 Rodney Craig .10 .05
❑ 516 Onix Concepcion .10 .05
❑ 517 Mike Heath .10 .05
❑ 518 Andre Dawson UER .40 .18
(Middle name Fernando, should be Nolan)
❑ 519 Luis Sanchez .10 .05
❑ 520 Terry Bogener .10 .05
❑ 521 Rudy Law .10 .05
❑ 522 Ray Knight .20 .09
❑ 523 Joe Lefebvre .10 .05
❑ 524 Jim Wohlford .10 .05
❑ 525 Julio Franco RC 1.00 .45
❑ 526 Ron Oester .10 .05
❑ 527 Rick Mahler .10 .05
❑ 528 Steve Nicosia .10 .05
❑ 529 Junior Kennedy .10 .05
❑ 530A Whitey Herzog MG .20 .09
(Bio printed black on white)
❑ 530B Whitey Herzog MG .20 .09
(Bio printed black on yellow)
❑ 531A Don Sutton .75 .35
(Blue border on photo)
❑ 531B Don Sutton .75 .35
(Green border on photo)
❑ 532 Mark Brouhard .10 .05
❑ 533A Sparky Anderson MG .. .20 .09
(Bio printed black on white)
❑ 533B Sparky Anderson MG .. .20 .09
(Bio printed black on yellow)
❑ 534 Roger LaFrancois .10 .05
❑ 535 George Frazier .10 .05
❑ 536 Tom Niedenfuer .10 .05
❑ 537 Ed Glynn .10 .05
❑ 538 Lee May .20 .09
❑ 539 Bob Kearney .10 .05
❑ 540 Tim Raines .75 .35
❑ 541 Paul Mirabella .10 .05
❑ 542 Luis Tiant .20 .09
❑ 543 Ron LeFlore .10 .05
❑ 544 Dave LaPoint .10 .05
❑ 545 Randy Moffitt .10 .05
❑ 546 Luis Aguayo .10 .05
❑ 547 Brad Lesley .20 .09
❑ 548 Luis Salazar .10 .05
❑ 549 John Candelaria .10 .05
❑ 550 Dave Bergman .10 .05
❑ 551 Bob Watson .20 .09
❑ 552 Pat Tabler .10 .05
❑ 553 Brent Gaff .10 .05
❑ 554 Al Cowens .10 .05
❑ 555 Tom Brunansky .20 .09
❑ 556 Lloyd Moseby .10 .05
❑ 557A Pascual Perez ERR .. 2.00 .90
(Twins in glove)
❑ 557B Pascual Perez COR .20 .09
(Braves in glove)
❑ 558 Willie Upshaw .10 .05
❑ 559 Richie Zisk .10 .05
❑ 560 Pat Zachry .10 .05
❑ 561 Jay Johnstone .20 .09
❑ 562 Carlos Diaz .10 .05
❑ 563 John Tudor .10 .05
❑ 564 Frank Robinson MG .40 .18
❑ 565 Dave Edwards .10 .05
❑ 566 Paul Householder .10 .05
❑ 567 Ron Reed .10 .05
❑ 568 Mike Ramsey .10 .05
❑ 569 Kiko Garcia .10 .05
❑ 570 Tommy John .40 .18
❑ 571 Tony LaRussa MG .20 .09
❑ 572 Joel Youngblood .10 .05
❑ 573 Wayne Tolleson .10 .05
❑ 574 Keith Creel .10 .05
❑ 575 Billy Martin MG .20 .09
❑ 576 Jerry Dybzinski .10 .05
❑ 577 Rick Cerone .10 .05
❑ 578 Tony Perez .75 .35
❑ 579 Greg Brock .10 .05
❑ 580 Glenn Wilson .10 .05
❑ 581 Tim Stoddard .10 .05
❑ 582 Bob McClure .10 .05

❑ 583 Jim Dwyer .10 .05
❑ 584 Ed Romero .10 .05
❑ 585 Larry Herndon .10 .05
❑ 586 Wade Boggs RC 12.00 5.50
❑ 587 Jay Howell .10 .05
❑ 588 Dave Stewart .20 .09
❑ 589 Bert Blyleven .40 .18
❑ 590 Dick Howser MG .10 .05
❑ 591 Wayne Gross .10 .05
❑ 592 Terry Francona .10 .05
❑ 593 Don Werner .10 .05
❑ 594 Bill Stein .10 .05
❑ 595 Jesse Barfield .20 .09
❑ 596 Bob Molinaro .10 .05
❑ 597 Mike Vail .10 .05
❑ 598 Tony Gwynn RC 25.00 11.00
❑ 599 Gary Rajsich .10 .05
❑ 600 Jerry Ujdur .10 .05
❑ 601 Cliff Johnson .10 .05
❑ 602 Jerry White .10 .05
❑ 603 Bryan Clark .10 .05
❑ 604 Joe Ferguson .10 .05
❑ 605 Guy Sularz .10 .05
❑ 606A Ozzie Virgil .20 .09
(Green border
on photo)
❑ 606B Ozzie Virgil .20 .09
(Orange border
on photo)
❑ 607 Terry Harper .10 .05
❑ 608 Harvey Kuenn MG .10 .05
❑ 609 Jim Sundberg .20 .09
❑ 610 Willie Stargell .75 .35
❑ 611 Reggie Smith .20 .09
❑ 612 Rob Wilfong .10 .05
❑ 613 The Niekro Brothers .40 .18
Joe Niekro
Phil Niekro
❑ 614 Lee Elia MG .10 .05
❑ 615 Mickey Hatcher .10 .05
❑ 616 Jerry Hairston .10 .05
❑ 617 John Martin .10 .05
❑ 618 Wally Backman .10 .05
❑ 619 Storm Davis RC .10 .05
❑ 620 Alan Knicely .10 .05
❑ 621 John Stuper .10 .05
❑ 622 Matt Sinatro .10 .05
❑ 623 Geno Petralli .40 .18
❑ 624 Duane Walker .10 .05
❑ 625 Dick Williams MG .10 .05
❑ 626 Pat Corrales MG .10 .05
❑ 627 Vern Ruhle .10 .05
❑ 628 Joe Torre MG .20 .09
❑ 629 Anthony Johnson .10 .05
❑ 630 Steve Howe .10 .05
❑ 631 Gary Woods .10 .05
❑ 632 LaMarr Hoyt .20 .09
❑ 633 Steve Swisher .10 .05
❑ 634 Terry Leach .10 .05
❑ 635 Jeff Newman .10 .05
❑ 636 Brett Butler .75 .35
❑ 637 Gary Gray .10 .05
❑ 638 Lee Mazzilli .10 .05
❑ 639A Ron Jackson ERR 5.00 2.20
(A's in glove)
❑ 639B Ron Jackson COR .10 .05
(Angels in glove,
red border
on photo)
❑ 639C Ron Jackson COR .75 .35
(Angels in glove,
green border
on photo)
❑ 640 Juan Beniquez .10 .05
❑ 641 Dave Rucker .10 .05
❑ 642 Luis Pujols .10 .05
❑ 643 Rick Monday .10 .05
❑ 644 Hosken Powell .10 .05
❑ 645 The Chicken .75 .35
❑ 646 Dave Engle .10 .05
❑ 647 Dick Davis .10 .05
❑ 648 Frank Robinson .20 .09
Vida Blue
Joe Morgan
❑ 649 Al Chambers .10 .05
❑ 650 Jesus Vega .10 .05
❑ 651 Jeff Jones .10 .05
❑ 652 Marvis Foley .10 .05
❑ 653 Ty Cobb Puzzle Card .75 .35
❑ 654A Dick Perez/Diamond .75 .35
King Checklist 1-26
(Unnumbered) ERR
(Word "checklist"
omitted from back)
❑ 654B Dick Perez/Diamond .75 .35
King Checklist 1-26
(Unnumbered) COR
(Word "checklist"
is on back)
❑ 655 Checklist 27-130 .10 .05
(Unnumbered)
❑ 656 Checklist 131-234 .10 .05
(Unnumbered)
❑ 657 Checklist 235-338 .10 .05
(Unnumbered)
❑ 658 Checklist 339-442 .10 .05
(Unnumbered)
❑ 659 Checklist 443-544 .10 .05
(Unnumbered)
❑ 660 Checklist 545-653 .10 .05
(Unnumbered)

## 1984 Donruss

| | NRMT | VG-E |
|---|---|---|
| COMPLETE SET (660) | 120.00 | 55.00 |
| COMP.FACT.SET (658) | 150.00 | 70.00 |
| COMP.SNIDER PUZZLE | 5.00 | 2.20 |

❑ 1 Robin Yount DK COR 2.00 .90
❑ 1A Robin Yount DK ERR 3.00 1.35
❑ 2 Dave Concepcion DK 1.50 .70
COR
❑ 2A Dave Concepcion DK .75 .35
ERR (Perez Steel)
❑ 3 Dwayne Murphy DK .75 .35
COR
❑ 3A Dwayne Murphy DK .25 .11
ERR (Perez Steel)
❑ 4 John Castino DK COR .75 .35
❑ 4A John Castino DK ERR .25 .11
(Perez Steel)
❑ 5 Leon Durham DK COR .75 .35
❑ 5A Leon Durham DK ERR .25 .11
(Perez Steel)
❑ 6 Rusty Staub DK COR 1.50 .70
❑ 6A Rusty Staub DK ERR .75 .35
(Perez Steel)
❑ 7 Jack Clark DK COR .75 .35
❑ 7A Jack Clark DK ERR .75 .35
(Perez Steel)
❑ 8 Dave Dravecky DK .75 .35
COR
❑ 8A Dave Dravecky DK .75 .35
ERR (Perez Steel)
❑ 9 Al Oliver DK COR 1.50 .70
❑ 9A Al Oliver DK ERR .75 .35
(Perez Steel)
❑ 10 Dave Righetti DK .75 .35
COR
❑ 10A Dave Righetti DK .75 .35
ERR (Perez Steel)
❑ 11 Hal McRae DK COR 1.50 .70
❑ 11A Hal McRae DK ERR .75 .35
(Perez Steel)
❑ 12 Ray Knight DK COR .75 .35
❑ 12A Ray Knight DK ERR .75 .35
(Perez Steel)
❑ 13 Bruce Sutter DK COR 1.50 .70
❑ 13A Bruce Sutter DK ERR .75 .35
(Perez Steel)
❑ 14 Bob Horner DK COR .75 .35
❑ 14A Bob Horner DK ERR .75 .35
(Perez Steel)
❑ 15 Lance Parrish DK 1.50 .70
COR
❑ 15A Lance Parrish DK .75 .35
ERR (Perez Steel)
❑ 16 Matt Young DK COR .75 .35
❑ 16A Matt Young DK ERR .25 .11
(Perez Steel)
❑ 17 Fred Lynn DK COR .75 .35
❑ 17A Fred Lynn DK ERR .25 .11
(Perez Steel)
(A's logo on back
❑ 18 Ron Kittle DK COR .75 .35
❑ 18A Ron Kittle DK ERR .25 .11
(Perez Steel)
❑ 19 Jim Clancy DK COR .75 .35
❑ 19A Jim Clancy DK ERR .25 .11
(Perez Steel)
❑ 20 Bill Madlock DK COR 1.50 .70
❑ 20A Bill Madlock DK ERR .75 .35
(Perez Steel)
❑ 21 Larry Parrish DK .75 .35
COR
❑ 21A Larry Parrish DK .25 .11
ERR (Perez Steel)
❑ 22 Eddie Murray DK COR 3.00 1.35
❑ 22A Eddie Murray DK ERR 2.50 1.10
❑ 23 Mike Schmidt DK COR 4.00 1.80
❑ 23A Mike Schmidt DK ERR 4.00 1.80
❑ 24 Pedro Guerrero DK .75 .35
COR
❑ 24A Pedro Guerrero DK .75 .35
ERR (Perez Steel)
❑ 25 Andre Thornton DK .75 .35
COR
❑ 25A Andre Thornton DK .75 .35
ERR (Perez Steel)
❑ 26 Wade Boggs DK COR 4.00 1.80
❑ 26A Wade Boggs DK ERR 3.00 1.35
❑ 27 Joel Skinner RR RC .25 .11
❑ 28 Tommy Dunbar RR RC .25 .11
❑ 29A Mike Stenhouse RC RR .25 .11
ERR (No number on back)
❑ 29B Mike Stenhouse RR 3.00 1.35
COR (Numbered on back)
❑ 30A Ron Darling RC RR ERR .75 .35
(No number on back)
❑ 30B Ron Darling RR COR 3.00 1.35
(Numbered on back)
❑ 31 Dion James RR RC .25 .11
❑ 32 Tony Fernandez RR RC 3.00 1.35
❑ 33 Angel Salazar RR RC .25 .11
❑ 34 Kevin McReynolds RR RC 1.50 .70
❑ 35 Dick Schofield RR RC .75 .35
❑ 36 Brad Komminsk RR RC .25 .11
❑ 37 Tim Teufel RR RC .25 .11
❑ 38 Doug Frobel RR RC .25 .11
❑ 39 Greg Gagne RR RC .75 .35
❑ 40 Mike Fuentes RR RC .25 .11
❑ 41 Joe Carter RR RC 10.00 4.50
❑ 42 Mike Brown RC RR .25 .11
(Angels OF)
❑ 43 Mike Jeffcoat RR RC .25 .11
❑ 44 Sid Fernandez RR RC 1.50 .70
❑ 45 Brian Dayett RR RC .25 .11
❑ 46 Chris Smith RR RC .25 .11
❑ 47 Eddie Murray 3.00 1.35
❑ 48 Robin Yount 3.00 1.35
❑ 49 Lance Parrish 1.50 .70
❑ 50 Jim Rice .75 .35
❑ 51 Dave Winfield 3.00 1.35
❑ 52 Fernando Valenzuela .75 .35
❑ 53 George Brett 6.00 2.70
❑ 54 Rickey Henderson 5.00 2.20
❑ 55 Gary Carter 1.50 .70
❑ 56 Buddy Bell .75 .35
❑ 57 Reggie Jackson 4.00 1.80

❑ 58 Harold Baines 3.00 1.35
❑ 59 Ozzie Smith 4.00 1.80
❑ 60 Nolan Ryan UER 15.00 6.75
(Text on back refers to 1972 as the year he struck out 383; the year was 1973)
❑ 61 Pete Rose 10.00 4.50
❑ 62 Ron Oester .25 .11
❑ 63 Steve Garvey 1.50 .70
❑ 64 Jason Thompson .25 .11
❑ 65 Jack Clark .75 .35
❑ 66 Dale Murphy 3.00 1.35
❑ 67 Leon Durham .25 .11
❑ 68 Darryl Strawberry RC 5.00 2.20
❑ 69 Richie Zisk .25 .11
❑ 70 Kent Hrbek .75 .35
❑ 71 Dave Stieb .25 .11
❑ 72 Ken Schrom .25 .11
❑ 73 George Bell .75 .35
❑ 74 John Moses .25 .11
❑ 75 Ed Lynch .25 .11
❑ 76 Chuck Rainey .25 .11
❑ 77 Biff Pocoroba .25 .11
❑ 78 Cecilio Guante .25 .11
❑ 79 Jim Barr .25 .11
❑ 80 Kurt Bevacqua .25 .11
❑ 81 Tom Foley .25 .11
❑ 82 Joe Lefebvre .25 .11
❑ 83 Andy Van Slyke RC 3.00 1.35
❑ 84 Bob Lillis MG .25 .11
❑ 85 Ricky Adams .25 .11
❑ 86 Jerry Hairston .25 .11
❑ 87 Bob James .25 .11
❑ 88 Joe Altobelli MG .25 .11
❑ 89 Ed Romero .25 .11
❑ 90 John Grubb .25 .11
❑ 91 John Henry Johnson .25 .11
❑ 92 Juan Espino .25 .11
❑ 93 Candy Maldonado .25 .11
❑ 94 Andre Thornton .25 .11
❑ 95 Onix Concepcion .25 .11
❑ 96 Donnie Hill UER .25 .11
(Listed as P; should be 2B)
❑ 97 Andre Dawson UER 1.50 .70
(Wrong middle name; should be Nolan)
❑ 98 Frank Tanana .75 .35
❑ 99 Curtis Wilkerson .25 .11
❑ 100 Larry Gura .25 .11
❑ 101 Dwayne Murphy .25 .11
❑ 102 Tom Brennan .25 .11
❑ 103 Dave Righetti .75 .35
❑ 104 Steve Sax .75 .35
❑ 105 Dan Petry .75 .35
❑ 106 Cal Ripken 20.00 9.00
❑ 107 Paul Molitor UER 3.00 1.35
('83 stats should say .270 BA, 608 AB, and 164 hits)
❑ 108 Fred Lynn .75 .35
❑ 109 Neil Allen .25 .11
❑ 110 Joe Niekro .75 .35
❑ 111 Steve Carlton 3.00 1.35
❑ 112 Terry Kennedy .25 .11
❑ 113 Bill Madlock .75 .35
❑ 114 Chili Davis 1.50 .70
❑ 115 Jim Gantner .25 .11
❑ 116 Tom Seaver 5.00 2.20
❑ 117 Bill Buckner .75 .35
❑ 118 Bill Caudill .25 .11
❑ 119 Jim Clancy .25 .11
❑ 120 John Castino .25 .11
❑ 121 Dave Concepcion .75 .35
❑ 122 Greg Luzinski .75 .35
❑ 123 Mike Boddicker .25 .11
❑ 124 Pete Ladd .25 .11
❑ 125 Juan Berenguer .25 .11
❑ 126 John Montefusco .25 .11
❑ 127 Ed Jurak .25 .11
❑ 128 Tom Niedenfuer .25 .11
❑ 129 Bert Blyleven .75 .35
❑ 130 Bud Black .25 .11
❑ 131 Gorman Heimueller .25 .11
❑ 132 Dan Schatzeder .25 .11
❑ 133 Ron Jackson .25 .11
❑ 134 Tom Henke RC 1.50 .70
❑ 135 Kevin Hickey .25 .11
❑ 136 Mike Scott .75 .35
❑ 137 Bo Diaz .25 .11
❑ 138 Glenn Brummer .25 .11
❑ 139 Sid Monge .25 .11
❑ 140 Rich Gale .25 .11
❑ 141 Brett Butler 1.50 .70
❑ 142 Brian Harper RC .75 .35
❑ 143 John Rabb .25 .11
❑ 144 Gary Woods .25 .11
❑ 145 Pat Putnam .25 .11
❑ 146 Jim Acker .25 .11
❑ 147 Mickey Hatcher .25 .11
❑ 148 Todd Cruz .25 .11
❑ 149 Tom Tellmann .25 .11
❑ 150 John Wockenfuss .25 .11
❑ 151 Wade Boggs UER 10.00 4.50
(1983 runs 10; should be 100)
❑ 152 Don Baylor 1.50 .70
❑ 153 Bob Welch .25 .11
❑ 154 Alan Bannister .25 .11
❑ 155 Willie Aikens .25 .11
❑ 156 Jeff Burroughs .25 .11
❑ 157 Bryan Little .25 .11
❑ 158 Bob Boone .75 .35
❑ 159 Dave Hostetler .25 .11
❑ 160 Jerry Dybzinski .25 .11
❑ 161 Mike Madden .25 .11
❑ 162 Luis DeLeon .25 .11
❑ 163 Willie Hernandez .75 .35
❑ 164 Frank Pastore .25 .11
❑ 165 Rick Camp .25 .11
❑ 166 Lee Mazzilli .25 .11
❑ 167 Scot Thompson .25 .11
❑ 168 Bob Forsch .25 .11
❑ 169 Mike Flanagan .25 .11
❑ 170 Rick Manning .25 .11
❑ 171 Chet Lemon .25 .11
❑ 172 Jerry Remy .25 .11
❑ 173 Ron Guidry .75 .35
❑ 174 Pedro Guerrero .75 .35
❑ 175 Willie Wilson .25 .11
❑ 176 Carney Lansford .75 .35
❑ 177 Al Oliver .75 .35
❑ 178 Jim Sundberg .75 .35
❑ 179 Bobby Grich .75 .35
❑ 180 Rich Dotson .25 .11
❑ 181 Joaquin Andujar .25 .11
❑ 182 Jose Cruz .75 .35
❑ 183 Mike Schmidt 6.00 2.70
❑ 184 Gary Redus RC* .25 .11
❑ 185 Garry Templeton .25 .11
❑ 186 Tony Pena .25 .11
❑ 187 Greg Minton .25 .11
❑ 188 Phil Niekro 3.00 1.35
❑ 189 Ferguson Jenkins 3.00 1.35
❑ 190 Mookie Wilson .75 .35
❑ 191 Jim Beattie .25 .11
❑ 192 Gary Ward .25 .11
❑ 193 Jesse Barfield .75 .35
❑ 194 Pete Filson .25 .11
❑ 195 Roy Lee Jackson .25 .11
❑ 196 Rick Sweet .25 .11
❑ 197 Jesse Orosco .25 .11
❑ 198 Steve Lake .25 .11
❑ 199 Ken Dayley .25 .11
❑ 200 Manny Sarmiento .25 .11
❑ 201 Mark Davis .25 .11
❑ 202 Tim Flannery .25 .11
❑ 203 Bill Scherrer .25 .11
❑ 204 Al Holland .25 .11
❑ 205 Dave Von Ohlen .25 .11
❑ 206 Mike LaCoss .25 .11
❑ 207 Juan Beniquez .25 .11
❑ 208 Juan Agosto .25 .11
❑ 209 Bobby Ramos .25 .11
❑ 210 Al Bumbry .25 .11
❑ 211 Mark Brouhard .25 .11
❑ 212 Howard Bailey .25 .11
❑ 213 Bruce Hurst .25 .11
❑ 214 Bob Shirley .25 .11
❑ 215 Pat Zachry .25 .11
❑ 216 Julio Franco 1.50 .70
❑ 217 Mike Armstrong .25 .11
❑ 218 Dave Beard .25 .11
❑ 219 Steve Rogers .25 .11
❑ 220 John Butcher .25 .11
❑ 221 Mike Smithson .25 .11
❑ 222 Frank White .75 .35
❑ 223 Mike Heath .25 .11
❑ 224 Chris Bando .25 .11
❑ 225 Roy Smalley .25 .11
❑ 226 Dusty Baker .75 .35
❑ 227 Lou Whitaker 3.00 1.35
❑ 228 John Lowenstein .25 .11
❑ 229 Ben Oglivie .25 .11
❑ 230 Doug DeCinces .25 .11
❑ 231 Lonnie Smith .25 .11
❑ 232 Ray Knight .75 .35
❑ 233 Gary Matthews .75 .35
❑ 234 Juan Bonilla .25 .11
❑ 235 Rod Scurry .25 .11
❑ 236 Atlee Hammaker .25 .11
❑ 237 Mike Caldwell .25 .11
❑ 238 Keith Hernandez .75 .35
❑ 239 Larry Bowa .75 .35
❑ 240 Tony Bernazard .25 .11
❑ 241 Damaso Garcia .25 .11
❑ 242 Tom Brunansky .75 .35
❑ 243 Dan Driessen .25 .11
❑ 244 Ron Kittle .25 .11
❑ 245 Tim Stoddard .25 .11
❑ 246 Bob L. Gibson .25 .11
(Brewers Pitcher)
❑ 247 Marty Castillo .25 .11
❑ 248 Don Mattingly RC UER 30.00 13.50
("Traiing" on back)
❑ 249 Jeff Newman .25 .11
❑ 250 Alejandro Pena RC* .75 .35
❑ 251 Toby Harrah .75 .35
❑ 252 Cesar Geronimo .25 .11
❑ 253 Tom Underwood .25 .11
❑ 254 Doug Flynn .25 .11
❑ 255 Andy Hassler .25 .11
❑ 256 Odell Jones .25 .11
❑ 257 Rudy Law .25 .11
❑ 258 Harry Spilman .25 .11
❑ 259 Marty Bystrom .25 .11
❑ 260 Dave Rucker .25 .11
❑ 261 Ruppert Jones .25 .11
❑ 262 Jeff R. Jones .25 .11
(Reds OF)
❑ 263 Gerald Perry .75 .35
❑ 264 Gene Tenace .75 .35
❑ 265 Brad Wellman .25 .11
❑ 266 Dickie Noles .25 .11
❑ 267 Jamie Allen .25 .11
❑ 268 Jim Gott .25 .11
❑ 269 Ron Davis .25 .11
❑ 270 Benny Ayala .25 .11
❑ 271 Ned Yost .25 .11
❑ 272 Dave Rozema .25 .11
❑ 273 Dave Stapleton .25 .11
❑ 274 Lou Piniella .75 .35
❑ 275 Jose Morales .25 .11
❑ 276 Broderick Perkins .25 .11
❑ 277 Butch Davis RC .25 .11
❑ 278 Tony Phillips RC 3.00 1.35
❑ 279 Jeff Reardon .75 .35
❑ 280 Ken Forsch .25 .11
❑ 281 Pete O'Brien RC* .75 .35
❑ 282 Tom Paciorek .75 .35
❑ 283 Frank LaCorte .25 .11
❑ 284 Tim Lollar .25 .11
❑ 285 Greg Gross .25 .11
❑ 286 Alex Trevino .25 .11
❑ 287 Gene Garber .25 .11
❑ 288 Dave Parker .75 .35
❑ 289 Lee Smith 3.00 1.35
❑ 290 Dave LaPoint .25 .11
❑ 291 John Shelby .25 .11
❑ 292 Charlie Moore .25 .11
❑ 293 Alan Trammell 1.50 .70
❑ 294 Tony Armas .25 .11
❑ 295 Shane Rawley .25 .11
❑ 296 Greg Brock .25 .11
❑ 297 Hal McRae .75 .35
❑ 298 Mike Davis .25 .11
❑ 299 Tim Raines 1.50 .70
❑ 300 Bucky Dent .75 .35
❑ 301 Tommy John 1.50 .70

- ❑ 302 Carlton Fisk 3.00 1.35
- ❑ 303 Darrell Porter .25 .11
- ❑ 304 Dickie Thon .25 .11
- ❑ 305 Garry Maddox .25 .11
- ❑ 306 Cesar Cedeno .75 .35
- ❑ 307 Gary Lucas .25 .11
- ❑ 308 Johnny Ray .25 .11
- ❑ 309 Andy McGaffigan .25 .11
- ❑ 310 Claudell Washington .25 .11
- ❑ 311 Ryne Sandberg 10.00 4.50
- ❑ 312 George Foster .75 .35
- ❑ 313 Spike Owen RC .75 .35
- ❑ 314 Gary Gaetti 1.50 .70
- ❑ 315 Willie Upshaw .25 .11
- ❑ 316 Al Williams .25 .11
- ❑ 317 Jorge Orta .25 .11
- ❑ 318 Orlando Mercado .25 .11
- ❑ 319 Junior Ortiz .25 .11
- ❑ 320 Mike Proly .25 .11
- ❑ 321 Randy Johnson UER .25 .11
  ('72-'82 stats are from Twins' Randy Johnson, '83 stats are from Braves' Randy Johnson)
- ❑ 322 Jim Morrison .25 .11
- ❑ 323 Max Venable .25 .11
- ❑ 324 Tony Gwynn 15.00 6.75
- ❑ 325 Duane Walker .25 .11
- ❑ 326 Ozzie Virgil .25 .11
- ❑ 327 Jeff Lahti .25 .11
- ❑ 328 Bill Dawley .25 .11
- ❑ 329 Rob Wilfong .25 .11
- ❑ 330 Marc Hill .25 .11
- ❑ 331 Ray Burris .25 .11
- ❑ 332 Allan Ramirez .25 .11
- ❑ 333 Chuck Porter .25 .11
- ❑ 334 Wayne Krenchicki .25 .11
- ❑ 335 Gary Allenson .25 .11
- ❑ 336 Bobby Meacham .25 .11
- ❑ 337 Joe Beckwith .25 .11
- ❑ 338 Rick Sutcliffe .75 .35
- ❑ 339 Mark Huismann .25 .11
- ❑ 340 Tim Conroy .25 .11
- ❑ 341 Scott Sanderson .25 .11
- ❑ 342 Larry Biittner .25 .11
- ❑ 343 Dave Stewart .75 .35
- ❑ 344 Darryl Motley .25 .11
- ❑ 345 Chris Codiroli .25 .11
- ❑ 346 Rich Behenna .25 .11
- ❑ 347 Andre Robertson .25 .11
- ❑ 348 Mike Marshall .25 .11
- ❑ 349 Larry Herndon .75 .35
- ❑ 350 Rich Dauer .25 .11
- ❑ 351 Cecil Cooper .75 .35
- ❑ 352 Rod Carew 3.00 1.35
- ❑ 353 Willie McGee 1.50 .70
- ❑ 354 Phil Garner .75 .35
- ❑ 355 Joe Morgan 3.00 1.35
- ❑ 356 Luis Salazar .25 .11
- ❑ 357 John Candelaria .25 .11
- ❑ 358 Bill Laskey .25 .11
- ❑ 359 Bob McClure .25 .11
- ❑ 360 Dave Kingman 1.50 .70
- ❑ 361 Ron Cey .75 .35
- ❑ 362 Matt Young .25 .11
- ❑ 363 Lloyd Moseby .25 .11
- ❑ 364 Frank Viola 1.50 .70
- ❑ 365 Eddie Milner .25 .11
- ❑ 366 Floyd Bannister .25 .11
- ❑ 367 Dan Ford .25 .11
- ❑ 368 Moose Haas .25 .11
- ❑ 369 Doug Bair .25 .11
- ❑ 370 Ray Fontenot .25 .11
- ❑ 371 Luis Aponte .25 .11
- ❑ 372 Jack Fimple .25 .11
- ❑ 373 Neal Heaton .25 .11
- ❑ 374 Greg Pryor .25 .11
- ❑ 375 Wayne Gross .25 .11
- ❑ 376 Charlie Lea .25 .11
- ❑ 377 Steve Lubratich .25 .11
- ❑ 378 Jon Matlack .25 .11
- ❑ 379 Julio Cruz .25 .11
- ❑ 380 John Mizerock .25 .11
- ❑ 381 Kevin Gross RC .25 .11
- ❑ 382 Mike Ramsey .25 .11
- ❑ 383 Doug Gwosdz .25 .11
- ❑ 384 Kelly Paris .25 .11
- ❑ 385 Pete Falcone .25 .11
- ❑ 386 Milt May .25 .11
- ❑ 387 Fred Breining .25 .11
- ❑ 388 Craig Lefferts RC .25 .11
- ❑ 389 Steve Henderson .25 .11
- ❑ 390 Randy Moffitt .25 .11
- ❑ 391 Ron Washington .25 .11
- ❑ 392 Gary Roenicke .25 .11
- ❑ 393 Tom Candiotti RC 3.00 1.35
- ❑ 394 Larry Pashnick .25 .11
- ❑ 395 Dwight Evans .75 .35
- ❑ 396 Rich Gossage 1.50 .70
- ❑ 397 Derrel Thomas .25 .11
- ❑ 398 Juan Eichelberger .25 .11
- ❑ 399 Leon Roberts .25 .11
- ❑ 400 Dave Lopes .75 .35
- ❑ 401 Bill Gullickson .25 .11
- ❑ 402 Geoff Zahn .25 .11
- ❑ 403 Billy Sample .25 .11
- ❑ 404 Mike Squires .25 .11
- ❑ 405 Craig Reynolds .25 .11
- ❑ 406 Eric Show .25 .11
- ❑ 407 John Denny .25 .11
- ❑ 408 Dann Bilardello .25 .11
- ❑ 409 Bruce Benedict .25 .11
- ❑ 410 Kent Tekulve .75 .35
- ❑ 411 Mel Hall .75 .35
- ❑ 412 John Stuper .25 .11
- ❑ 413 Rick Dempsey .25 .11
- ❑ 414 Don Sutton 3.00 1.35
- ❑ 415 Jack Morris 3.00 1.35
- ❑ 416 John Tudor .25 .11
- ❑ 417 Willie Randolph .75 .35
- ❑ 418 Jerry Reuss .25 .11
- ❑ 410 Don Slaught .75 .35
- ❑ 420 Steve McCatty .25 .11
- ❑ 421 Tim Wallach .75 .35
- ❑ 422 Larry Parrish .25 .11
- ❑ 423 Brian Downing .25 .11
- ❑ 424 Britt Burns .25 .11
- ❑ 425 David Green .25 .11
- ❑ 426 Jerry Mumphrey .25 .11
- ❑ 427 Ivan DeJesus .25 .11
- ❑ 428 Mario Soto .25 .11
- ❑ 429 Gene Richards .25 .11
- ❑ 430 Dale Berra .25 .11
- ❑ 431 Darrell Evans .75 .35
- ❑ 432 Glenn Hubbard .25 .11
- ❑ 433 Jody Davis .25 .11
- ❑ 434 Danny Heep .25 .11
- ❑ 435 Ed Nunez RC .25 .11
- ❑ 436 Bobby Castillo .25 .11
- ❑ 437 Ernie Whitt .25 .11
- ❑ 438 Scott Ullger .25 .11
- ❑ 439 Doyle Alexander .25 .11
- ❑ 440 Domingo Ramos .25 .11
- ❑ 441 Craig Swan .25 .11
- ❑ 442 Warren Brusstar .25 .11
- ❑ 443 Len Barker .25 .11
- ❑ 444 Mike Easler .25 .11
- ❑ 445 Renie Martin .25 .11
- ❑ 446 Dennis Rasmussen RC .25 .11
- ❑ 447 Ted Power .25 .11
- ❑ 448 Charles Hudson .25 .11
- ❑ 449 Danny Cox RC .25 .11
- ❑ 450 Kevin Bass .25 .11
- ❑ 451 Daryl Sconiers .25 .11
- ❑ 452 Scott Fletcher .25 .11
- ❑ 453 Bryn Smith .25 .11
- ❑ 454 Jim Dwyer .25 .11
- ❑ 455 Rob Picciolo .25 .11
- ❑ 456 Enos Cabell .25 .11
- ❑ 457 Dennis Boyd .75 .35
- ❑ 458 Butch Wynegar .25 .11
- ❑ 459 Burt Hooton .25 .11
- ❑ 460 Ron Hassey .25 .11
- ❑ 461 Danny Jackson RC 1.50 .70
- ❑ 462 Bob Kearney .25 .11
- ❑ 463 Terry Francona .25 .11
- ❑ 464 Wayne Tolleson .25 .11
- ❑ 465 Mickey Rivers .25 .11
- ❑ 466 John Wathan .25 .11
- ❑ 467 Bill Almon .25 .11
- ❑ 468 George Vukovich .25 .11
- ❑ 469 Steve Kemp .25 .11
- ❑ 470 Ken Landreaux .25 .11
- ❑ 471 Milt Wilcox .25 .11
- ❑ 472 Tippy Martinez .25 .11
- ❑ 473 Ted Simmons .75 .35
- ❑ 474 Tim Foli .25 .11
- ❑ 475 George Hendrick .25 .11
- ❑ 476 Terry Puhl .25 .11
- ❑ 477 Von Hayes .25 .11
- ❑ 478 Bobby Brown .25 .11
- ❑ 479 Lee Lacy .25 .11
- ❑ 480 Joel Youngblood .25 .11
- ❑ 481 Jim Slaton .25 .11
- ❑ 482 Mike Fitzgerald .25 .11
- ❑ 483 Keith Moreland .25 .11
- ❑ 484 Ron Roenicke .25 .11
- ❑ 485 Luis Leal .25 .11
- ❑ 486 Bryan Oelkers .25 .11
- ❑ 487 Bruce Berenyi .25 .11
- ❑ 488 LaMarr Hoyt .25 .11
- ❑ 489 Joe Nolan .25 .11
- ❑ 490 Marshall Edwards .25 .11
- ❑ 491 Mike Laga .75 .35
- ❑ 492 Rick Cerone .25 .11
- ❑ 493 Rick Miller UER .25 .11
  (Listed as Mike on card front)
- ❑ 494 Rick Honeycutt .25 .11
- ❑ 495 Mike Hargrove .75 .35
- ❑ 496 Joe Simpson .25 .11
- ❑ 497 Keith Atherton .25 .11
- ❑ 498 Chris Welsh .25 .11
- ❑ 499 Bruce Kison .25 .11
- ❑ 500 Bobby Johnson .25 .11
- ❑ 501 Jerry Koosman .75 .35
- ❑ 502 Frank DiPino .25 .11
- ❑ 503 Tony Perez 3.00 1.35
- ❑ 504 Ken Oberkfell .25 .11
- ❑ 505 Mark Thurmond .25 .11
- ❑ 506 Joe Price .25 .11
- ❑ 507 Pascual Perez .25 .11
- ❑ 508 Marvell Wynne .25 .11
- ❑ 509 Mike Krukow .25 .11
- ❑ 510 Dick Ruthven .25 .11
- ❑ 511 Al Cowens .25 .11
- ❑ 512 Cliff Johnson .25 .11
- ❑ 513 Randy Bush .25 .11
- ❑ 514 Sammy Stewart .25 .11
- ❑ 515 Bill Schroeder .25 .11
- ❑ 516 Aurelio Lopez .75 .35
- ❑ 517 Mike G. Brown .25 .11
- ❑ 518 Graig Nettles .75 .35
- ❑ 519 Dave Sax .25 .11
- ❑ 520 Jerry Willard .25 .11
- ❑ 521 Paul Splittorff .25 .11
- ❑ 522 Tom Burgmeier .25 .11
- ❑ 523 Chris Speier .25 .11
- ❑ 524 Bobby Clark .25 .11
- ❑ 525 George Wright .25 .11
- ❑ 526 Dennis Lamp .25 .11
- ❑ 527 Tony Scott .25 .11
- ❑ 528 Ed Whitson .25 .11
- ❑ 529 Ron Reed .25 .11
- ❑ 530 Charlie Puleo .25 .11
- ❑ 531 Jerry Royster .25 .11
- ❑ 532 Don Robinson .25 .11
- ❑ 533 Steve Trout .25 .11
- ❑ 534 Bruce Sutter .75 .35
- ❑ 535 Bob Horner .25 .11
- ❑ 536 Pat Tabler .25 .11
- ❑ 537 Chris Chambliss .75 .35
- ❑ 538 Bob Ojeda .25 .11
- ❑ 539 Alan Ashby .25 .11
- ❑ 540 Jay Johnstone .75 .35
- ❑ 541 Bob Dernier .25 .11
- ❑ 542 Brook Jacoby .75 .35
- ❑ 543 U.L. Washington .25 .11
- ❑ 544 Danny Darwin .25 .11
- ❑ 545 Kiko Garcia .25 .11
- ❑ 546 Vance Law UER .25 .11
  (Listed as P on card front)
- ❑ 547 Tug McGraw .75 .35
- ❑ 548 Dave Smith .25 .11
- ❑ 549 Len Matuszek .25 .11
- ❑ 550 Tom Hume .25 .11
- ❑ 551 Dave Dravecky .75 .35

| | No. | Player | NRMT | VG-E |
|---|---|---|---|---|
| ❑ | 552 | Rick Rhoden | .25 | .11 |
| ❑ | 553 | Duane Kuiper | .25 | .11 |
| ❑ | 554 | Rusty Staub | .75 | .35 |
| ❑ | 555 | Bill Campbell | .25 | .11 |
| ❑ | 556 | Mike Torrez | .25 | .11 |
| ❑ | 557 | Dave Henderson | .75 | .35 |
| ❑ | 558 | Len Whitehouse | .25 | .11 |
| ❑ | 559 | Barry Bonnell | .25 | .11 |
| ❑ | 560 | Rick Lysander | .25 | .11 |
| ❑ | 561 | Garth Iorg | .25 | .11 |
| ❑ | 562 | Bryan Clark | .25 | .11 |
| ❑ | 563 | Brian Giles | .25 | .11 |
| ❑ | 564 | Vern Ruhle | .25 | .11 |
| ❑ | 565 | Steve Bedrosian | .25 | .11 |
| ❑ | 566 | Larry McWilliams | .25 | .11 |
| ❑ | 567 | Jeff Leonard UER (Listed as P on card front) | .25 | .11 |
| ❑ | 568 | Alan Wiggins | .25 | .11 |
| ❑ | 569 | Jeff Russell RC | .75 | .35 |
| ❑ | 570 | Salome Barojas | .25 | .11 |
| ❑ | 571 | Dane Iorg | .25 | .11 |
| ❑ | 572 | Bob Knepper | .25 | .11 |
| ❑ | 573 | Gary Lavelle | .25 | .11 |
| ❑ | 574 | Gorman Thomas | .25 | .11 |
| ❑ | 575 | Manny Trillo | .25 | .11 |
| ❑ | 576 | Jim Palmer | 3.00 | 1.35 |
| ❑ | 577 | Dale Murray | .25 | .11 |
| ❑ | 578 | Tom Brookens | .75 | .35 |
| ❑ | 579 | Rich Gedman | .25 | .11 |
| ❑ | 580 | Bill Doran RC* | .75 | .35 |
| ❑ | 581 | Steve Yeager | .25 | .11 |
| ❑ | 582 | Dan Spillner | .25 | .11 |
| ❑ | 583 | Dan Quisenberry | .25 | .11 |
| ❑ | 584 | Rance Mulliniks | .25 | .11 |
| ❑ | 585 | Storm Davis | .25 | .11 |
| ❑ | 586 | Dave Schmidt | .25 | .11 |
| ❑ | 587 | Bill Russell | .25 | .11 |
| ❑ | 588 | Pat Sheridan | .25 | .11 |
| ❑ | 589 | Rafael Ramirez UER (A's on front) | .25 | .11 |
| ❑ | 590 | Bud Anderson | .25 | .11 |
| ❑ | 591 | George Frazier | .25 | .11 |
| ❑ | 592 | Lee Tunnell | .25 | .11 |
| ❑ | 593 | Kirk Gibson | 3.00 | 1.35 |
| ❑ | 594 | Scott McGregor | .25 | .11 |
| ❑ | 595 | Bob Bailor | .25 | .11 |
| ❑ | 596 | Tom Herr | .75 | .35 |
| ❑ | 597 | Luis Sanchez | .25 | .11 |
| ❑ | 598 | Dave Engle | .25 | .11 |
| ❑ | 599 | Craig McMurtry | .25 | .11 |
| ❑ | 600 | Carlos Diaz | .25 | .11 |
| ❑ | 601 | Tom O'Malley | .25 | .11 |
| ❑ | 602 | Nick Esasky | .25 | .11 |
| ❑ | 603 | Ron Hodges | .25 | .11 |
| ❑ | 604 | Ed VandeBerg | .25 | .11 |
| ❑ | 605 | Alfredo Griffin | .25 | .11 |
| ❑ | 606 | Glenn Hoffman | .25 | .11 |
| ❑ | 607 | Hubie Brooks | .25 | .11 |
| ❑ | 608 | Richard Barnes UER (Photo actually Neal Heaton) | .25 | .11 |
| ❑ | 609 | Greg Walker | .75 | .35 |
| ❑ | 610 | Ken Singleton | .25 | .11 |
| ❑ | 611 | Mark Clear | .25 | .11 |
| ❑ | 612 | Buck Martinez | .25 | .11 |
| ❑ | 613 | Ken Griffey | .75 | .35 |
| ❑ | 614 | Reid Nichols | .25 | .11 |
| ❑ | 615 | Doug Sisk | .25 | .11 |
| ❑ | 616 | Bob Brenly | .25 | .11 |
| ❑ | 617 | Joey McLaughlin | .25 | .11 |
| ❑ | 618 | Glenn Wilson | .75 | .35 |
| ❑ | 619 | Bob Stoddard | .25 | .11 |
| ❑ | 620 | Lenn Sakata UER (Listed as Len on card front) | .25 | .11 |
| ❑ | 621 | Mike Young | .25 | .11 |
| ❑ | 622 | John Stefero | .25 | .11 |
| ❑ | 623 | Carmelo Martinez | .25 | .11 |
| ❑ | 624 | Dave Bergman | .25 | .11 |
| ❑ | 625 | Runnin' Reds UER (Sic, Redbirds) David Green Willie McGee Lonnie Smith Ozzie Smith | 3.00 | 1.35 |
| ❑ | 626 | Rudy May | .25 | .11 |
| ❑ | 627 | Matt Keough | .25 | .11 |
| ❑ | 628 | Jose DeLeon | .25 | .11 |
| ❑ | 629 | Jim Essian | .25 | .11 |
| ❑ | 630 | Darnell Coles RC | .25 | .11 |
| ❑ | 631 | Mike Warren | .25 | .11 |
| ❑ | 632 | Del Crandall MG | .25 | .11 |
| ❑ | 633 | Dennis Martinez | .75 | .35 |
| ❑ | 634 | Mike Moore | .75 | .35 |
| ❑ | 635 | Lary Sorensen | .25 | .11 |
| ❑ | 636 | Ricky Nelson | .25 | .11 |
| ❑ | 637 | Omar Moreno | .25 | .11 |
| ❑ | 638 | Charlie Hough | .75 | .35 |
| ❑ | 639 | Dennis Eckersley | 3.00 | 1.35 |
| ❑ | 640 | Walt Terrell | .25 | .11 |
| ❑ | 641 | Denny Walling | .25 | .11 |
| ❑ | 642 | Dave Anderson | .25 | .11 |
| ❑ | 643 | Jose Oquendo RC | .75 | .35 |
| ❑ | 644 | Bob Stanley | .25 | .11 |
| ❑ | 645 | Dave Geisel | .25 | .11 |
| ❑ | 646 | Scott Garrelts | .25 | .11 |
| ❑ | 647 | Gary Pettis | .25 | .11 |
| ❑ | 648 | Duke Snider Puzzle Card | 1.50 | .70 |
| ❑ | 649 | Johnnie LeMaster | .25 | .11 |
| ❑ | 650 | Dave Collins | .25 | .11 |
| ❑ | 651 | The Chicken | 1.50 | .70 |
| ❑ | 652 | DK Checklist 1-26 (Unnumbered) | .75 | .35 |
| ❑ | 653 | Checklist 27-130 (Unnumbered) | .25 | .11 |
| ❑ | 654 | Checklist 131-234 (Unnumbered) | .25 | .11 |
| ❑ | 655 | Checklist 235-338 (Unnumbered) | .25 | .11 |
| ❑ | 656 | Checklist 339-442 (Unnumbered) | .25 | .11 |
| ❑ | 657 | Checklist 443-546 (Unnumbered) | .25 | .11 |
| ❑ | 658 | Checklist 547-651 (Unnumbered) | .25 | .11 |
| ❑ | A | Living Legends A Gaylord Perry Rollie Fingers | 2.50 | 1.10 |
| ❑ | B | Living Legends B Carl Yastrzemski Johnny Bench | 5.00 | 2.20 |

## 1985 Donruss

| | NRMT | VG-E |
|---|---|---|
| COMPLETE SET (660) | 80.00 | 36.00 |
| COMP.FACT.SET (660) | 100.00 | 45.00 |
| COMP.GEHRIG PUZZLE | 4.00 | 1.80 |

| | No. | Player | NRMT | VG-E |
|---|---|---|---|---|
| ❑ | 1 | Ryne Sandberg DK | 2.00 | .90 |
| ❑ | 2 | Doug DeCinces DK | .15 | .07 |
| ❑ | 3 | Richard Dotson DK | .15 | .07 |
| ❑ | 4 | Bert Blyleven DK | .15 | .07 |
| ❑ | 5 | Lou Whitaker DK | .40 | .18 |
| ❑ | 6 | Dan Quisenberry DK | .40 | .18 |
| ❑ | 7 | Don Mattingly DK | 2.00 | .90 |
| ❑ | 8 | Carney Lansford DK | .15 | .07 |
| ❑ | 9 | Frank Tanana DK | .15 | .07 |
| ❑ | 10 | Willie Upshaw DK | .15 | .07 |
| ❑ | 11 | Claudell Washington DK | .15 | .07 |
| ❑ | 12 | Mike Marshall DK | .15 | .07 |
| ❑ | 13 | Joaquin Andujar DK | .15 | .07 |
| ❑ | 14 | Cal Ripken DK | 3.00 | 1.35 |
| ❑ | 15 | Jim Rice DK | .15 | .07 |
| ❑ | 16 | Don Sutton DK | .40 | .18 |
| ❑ | 17 | Frank Viola DK | .15 | .07 |
| ❑ | 18 | Alvin Davis DK | .15 | .07 |
| ❑ | 19 | Mario Soto DK | .15 | .07 |
| ❑ | 20 | Jose Cruz DK | .15 | .07 |
| ❑ | 21 | Charlie Lea DK | .15 | .07 |
| ❑ | 22 | Jesse Orosco DK | .15 | .07 |
| ❑ | 23 | Juan Samuel DK | .15 | .07 |
| ❑ | 24 | Tony Pena DK | .15 | .07 |
| ❑ | 25 | Tony Gwynn DK | 2.00 | .90 |
| ❑ | 26 | Bob Brenly DK | .15 | .07 |
| ❑ | 27 | Danny Tartabull RR RC | 1.25 | .55 |
| ❑ | 28 | Mike Bielecki RR | .15 | .07 |
| ❑ | 29 | Steve Lyons RR RC | .40 | .18 |
| ❑ | 30 | Jeff Reed RR | .15 | .07 |
| ❑ | 31 | Tony Brewer RR | .15 | .07 |
| ❑ | 32 | John Morris RR | .15 | .07 |
| ❑ | 33 | Daryl Boston RR RC | .15 | .07 |
| ❑ | 34 | Al Pulido RR | .15 | .07 |
| ❑ | 35 | Steve Kiefer RR | .15 | .07 |
| ❑ | 36 | Larry Sheets RR | .15 | .07 |
| ❑ | 37 | Scott Bradley RR | .15 | .07 |
| ❑ | 38 | Calvin Schiraldi RR | .15 | .07 |
| ❑ | 39 | Shawon Dunston RR RC | 1.00 | .45 |
| ❑ | 40 | Charlie Mitchell RR | .15 | .07 |
| ❑ | 41 | Billy Hatcher RR RC | .75 | .35 |
| ❑ | 42 | Russ Stephans RR | .15 | .07 |
| ❑ | 43 | Alejandro Sanchez RR | .15 | .07 |
| ❑ | 44 | Steve Jeltz RR | .15 | .07 |
| ❑ | 45 | Jim Traber RR | .15 | .07 |
| ❑ | 46 | Doug Loman RR | .15 | .07 |
| ❑ | 47 | Eddie Murray | 1.25 | .55 |
| ❑ | 48 | Robin Yount | 1.25 | .55 |
| ❑ | 49 | Lance Parrish | .40 | .18 |
| ❑ | 50 | Jim Rice | .40 | .18 |
| ❑ | 51 | Dave Winfield | 1.25 | .55 |
| ❑ | 52 | Fernando Valenzuela | .40 | .18 |
| ❑ | 53 | George Brett | 2.50 | 1.10 |
| ❑ | 54 | Dave Kingman | .40 | .18 |
| ❑ | 55 | Gary Carter | .75 | .35 |
| ❑ | 56 | Buddy Bell | .40 | .18 |
| ❑ | 57 | Reggie Jackson | 1.50 | .70 |
| ❑ | 58 | Harold Baines | .40 | .18 |
| ❑ | 59 | Ozzie Smith | 1.50 | .70 |
| ❑ | 60 | Nolan Ryan UER (Set strikeout record in 1973, not 1972) | 6.00 | 2.70 |
| ❑ | 61 | Mike Schmidt | 2.50 | 1.10 |
| ❑ | 62 | Dave Parker | .40 | .18 |
| ❑ | 63 | Tony Gwynn | 4.00 | 1.80 |
| ❑ | 64 | Tony Pena | .15 | .07 |
| ❑ | 65 | Jack Clark | .40 | .18 |
| ❑ | 66 | Dale Murphy | 1.25 | .55 |
| ❑ | 67 | Ryne Sandberg | 2.50 | 1.10 |
| ❑ | 68 | Keith Hernandez | .40 | .18 |
| ❑ | 69 | Alvin Davis RC* | .40 | .18 |
| ❑ | 70 | Kent Hrbek | .40 | .18 |
| ❑ | 71 | Willie Upshaw | .15 | .07 |
| ❑ | 72 | Dave Engle | .15 | .07 |
| ❑ | 73 | Alfredo Griffin | .15 | .07 |
| ❑ | 74A | Jack Perconte (Career Highlights takes four lines) | .15 | .07 |
| ❑ | 74B | Jack Perconte (Career Highlights takes three lines) | .15 | .07 |
| ❑ | 75 | Jesse Orosco | .15 | .07 |
| ❑ | 76 | Jody Davis | .15 | .07 |
| ❑ | 77 | Bob Horner | .15 | .07 |
| ❑ | 78 | Larry McWilliams | .15 | .07 |
| ❑ | 79 | Joel Youngblood | .15 | .07 |
| ❑ | 80 | Alan Wiggins | .15 | .07 |
| ❑ | 81 | Ron Oester | .15 | .07 |
| ❑ | 82 | Ozzie Virgil | .15 | .07 |
| ❑ | 83 | Ricky Horton | .15 | .07 |
| ❑ | 84 | Bill Doran | .15 | .07 |
| ❑ | 85 | Rod Carew | 1.25 | .55 |
| ❑ | 86 | LaMarr Hoyt | .15 | .07 |
| ❑ | 87 | Tim Wallach | .40 | .18 |
| ❑ | 88 | Mike Flanagan | .15 | .07 |
| ❑ | 89 | Jim Sundberg | .15 | .07 |
| ❑ | 90 | Chet Lemon | .15 | .07 |
| ❑ | 91 | Bob Stanley | .15 | .07 |
| ❑ | 92 | Willie Randolph | .40 | .18 |

❑ 93 Bill Russell .15 .07
❑ 94 Julio Franco .75 .35
❑ 95 Dan Quisenberry .40 .18
❑ 96 Bill Caudill .15 .07
❑ 97 Bill Gullickson .15 .07
❑ 98 Danny Darwin .15 .07
❑ 99 Curtis Wilkerson .15 .07
❑ 100 Bud Black .15 .07
❑ 101 Tony Phillips .15 .07
❑ 102 Tony Bernazard .15 .07
❑ 103 Jay Howell .15 .07
❑ 104 Burt Hooton .15 .07
❑ 105 Milt Wilcox .15 .07
❑ 106 Rich Dauer .15 .07
❑ 107 Don Sutton 1.25 .55
❑ 108 Mike Witt .15 .07
❑ 109 Bruce Sutter .40 .18
❑ 110 Enos Cabell .15 .07
❑ 111 John Denny .15 .07
❑ 112 Dave Dravecky .40 .18
❑ 113 Marvell Wynne .15 .07
❑ 114 Johnnie LeMaster .15 .07
❑ 115 Chuck Porter .15 .07
❑ 116 John Gibbons .15 .07
❑ 117 Keith Moreland .15 .07
❑ 118 Darnell Coles .15 .07
❑ 119 Dennis Lamp .15 .07
❑ 120 Ron Davis .15 .07
❑ 121 Nick Esasky .15 .07
❑ 122 Vance Law .15 .07
❑ 123 Gary Roenicke .15 .07
❑ 124 Bill Schroeder .15 .07
❑ 125 Dave Rozema .15 .07
❑ 126 Bobby Meacham .15 .07
❑ 127 Marty Barrett .15 .07
❑ 128 R.J. Reynolds .15 .07
❑ 129 Ernie Camacho UER .15 .07
(Photo actually Rich Thompson)
❑ 130 Jorge Orta .15 .07
❑ 131 Lary Sorensen .15 .07
❑ 132 Terry Francona .15 .07
❑ 133 Fred Lynn .40 .18
❑ 134 Bob Jones .15 .07
❑ 135 Jerry Hairston .15 .07
❑ 136 Kevin Bass .15 .07
❑ 137 Garry Maddox .15 .07
❑ 138 Dave LaPoint .15 .07
❑ 139 Kevin McReynolds .40 .18
❑ 140 Wayne Krenchicki .15 .07
❑ 141 Rafael Ramirez .15 .07
❑ 142 Rod Scurry .15 .07
❑ 143 Greg Minton .15 .07
❑ 144 Tim Stoddard .15 .07
❑ 145 Steve Henderson .15 .07
❑ 146 George Bell .40 .18
❑ 147 Dave Meier .15 .07
❑ 148 Sammy Stewart .15 .07
❑ 149 Mark Brouhard .15 .07
❑ 150 Larry Herndon .15 .07
❑ 151 Oil Can Boyd .15 .07
❑ 152 Brian Dayett .15 .07
❑ 153 Tom Niedenfuer .15 .07
❑ 154 Brook Jacoby .15 .07
❑ 155 Onix Concepcion .15 .07
❑ 156 Tim Conroy .15 .07
❑ 157 Joe Hesketh .15 .07
❑ 158 Brian Downing .15 .07
❑ 159 Tommy Dunbar .15 .07
❑ 160 Marc Hill .15 .07
❑ 161 Phil Garner .40 .18
❑ 162 Jerry Davis .15 .07
❑ 163 Bill Campbell .15 .07
❑ 164 John Franco RC 1.25 .55
❑ 165 Len Barker .15 .07
❑ 166 Benny Distefano .15 .07
❑ 167 George Frazier .15 .07
❑ 168 Tito Landrum .15 .07
❑ 169 Cal Ripken 6.00 2.70
❑ 170 Cecil Cooper .40 .18
❑ 171 Alan Trammell .75 .35
❑ 172 Wade Boggs 2.00 .90
❑ 173 Don Baylor .40 .18
❑ 174 Pedro Guerrero .40 .18
❑ 175 Frank White .40 .18
❑ 176 Rickey Henderson 1.50 .70
❑ 177 Charlie Lea .15 .07
❑ 178 Pete O'Brien .15 .07
❑ 179 Doug DeCinces .15 .07
❑ 180 Ron Kittle .15 .07
❑ 181 George Hendrick .15 .07
❑ 182 Joe Niekro .15 .07
❑ 183 Juan Samuel .15 .07
❑ 184 Mario Soto .15 .07
❑ 185 Rich Gossage .40 .18
❑ 186 Johnny Ray .15 .07
❑ 187 Bob Brenly .15 .07
❑ 188 Craig McMurtry .15 .07
❑ 189 Leon Durham .15 .07
❑ 190 Dwight Gooden RC 2.00 .90
❑ 191 Barry Bonnell .15 .07
❑ 192 Tim Teufel .15 .07
❑ 193 Dave Stieb .40 .18
❑ 194 Mickey Hatcher .15 .07
❑ 195 Jesse Barfield .15 .07
❑ 196 Al Cowens .15 .07
❑ 197 Hubie Brooks .15 .07
❑ 198 Steve Trout .15 .07
❑ 199 Glenn Hubbard .15 .07
❑ 200 Bill Madlock .40 .18
❑ 201 Jeff D. Robinson .15 .07
❑ 202 Eric Show .15 .07
❑ 203 Dave Concepcion .40 .18
❑ 204 Ivan DeJesus .15 .07
❑ 205 Neil Allen .15 .07
❑ 206 Jerry Mumphrey .15 .07
❑ 207 Mike C. Brown .15 .07
❑ 208 Carlton Fisk 1.25 .55
❑ 209 Bryn Smith .15 .07
❑ 210 Tippy Martinez .15 .07
❑ 211 Dion James .15 .07
❑ 212 Willie Hernandez .15 .07
❑ 213 Mike Easler .15 .07
❑ 214 Ron Guidry .40 .18
❑ 215 Rick Honeycutt .15 .07
❑ 216 Brett Butler .40 .18
❑ 217 Larry Gura .15 .07
❑ 218 Ray Burris .15 .07
❑ 219 Steve Rogers .15 .07
❑ 220 Frank Tanana UER .15 .07
(Bats Left listed twice on card back)
❑ 221 Ned Yost .15 .07
❑ 222 Bret Saberhagen RC UER 1.00 .45
(18 career IP on back)
❑ 223 Mike Davis .15 .07
❑ 224 Bert Blyleven .40 .18
❑ 225 Steve Kemp .15 .07
❑ 226 Jerry Reuss .15 .07
❑ 227 Darrell Evans UER .40 .18
(80 homers in 1980)
❑ 228 Wayne Gross .15 .07
❑ 229 Jim Gantner .15 .07
❑ 230 Bob Boone .40 .18
❑ 231 Lonnie Smith .15 .07
❑ 232 Frank DiPino .15 .07
❑ 233 Jerry Koosman .40 .18
❑ 234 Graig Nettles .40 .18
❑ 235 John Tudor .15 .07
❑ 236 John Rabb .15 .07
❑ 237 Rick Manning .15 .07
❑ 238 Mike Fitzgerald .15 .07
❑ 239 Gary Matthews .15 .07
❑ 240 Jim Presley .40 .18
❑ 241 Dave Collins .15 .07
❑ 242 Gary Gaetti .40 .18
❑ 243 Dann Bilardello .15 .07
❑ 244 Rudy Law .15 .07
❑ 245 John Lowenstein .15 .07
❑ 246 Tom Tellmann .15 .07
❑ 247 Howard Johnson .40 .18
❑ 248 Ray Fontenot .15 .07
❑ 249 Tony Armas .15 .07
❑ 250 Candy Maldonado .15 .07
❑ 251 Mike Jeffcoat .15 .07
❑ 252 Dane Iorg .15 .07
❑ 253 Bruce Bochte .15 .07
❑ 254 Pete Rose 4.00 1.80
❑ 255 Don Aase .15 .07
❑ 256 George Wright .15 .07
❑ 257 Britt Burns .15 .07
❑ 258 Mike Scott .15 .07
❑ 259 Len Matuszek .15 .07
❑ 260 Dave Rucker .15 .07
❑ 261 Craig Lefferts .15 .07
❑ 262 Jay Tibbs .15 .07
❑ 263 Bruce Benedict .15 .07
❑ 264 Don Robinson .15 .07
❑ 265 Gary Lavelle .15 .07
❑ 266 Scott Sanderson .15 .07
❑ 267 Matt Young .15 .07
❑ 268 Ernie Whitt .15 .07
❑ 269 Houston Jimenez .15 .07
❑ 270 Ken Dixon .15 .07
❑ 271 Pete Ladd .15 .07
❑ 272 Juan Berenguer .15 .07
❑ 273 Roger Clemens RC ! 40.00 18.00
❑ 274 Rick Cerone .15 .07
❑ 275 Dave Anderson .15 .07
❑ 276 George Vukovich .15 .07
❑ 277 Greg Pryor .15 .07
❑ 278 Mike Warren .15 .07
❑ 279 Bob James .15 .07
❑ 280 Bobby Grich .40 .18
❑ 281 Mike Mason .15 .07
❑ 282 Ron Reed .15 .07
❑ 283 Alan Ashby .15 .07
❑ 284 Mark Thurmond .15 .07
❑ 285 Joe Lefebvre .15 .07
❑ 286 Ted Power .15 .07
❑ 287 Chris Chambliss .40 .18
❑ 288 Lee Tunnell .15 .07
❑ 289 Rich Bordi .15 .07
❑ 290 Glenn Brummer .15 .07
❑ 291 Mike Boddicker .15 .07
❑ 292 Rollie Fingers 1.25 .55
❑ 293 Lou Whitaker .75 .35
❑ 294 Dwight Evans .40 .18
❑ 295 Don Mattingly 4.00 1.80
❑ 296 Mike Marshall .15 .07
❑ 297 Willie Wilson .15 .07
❑ 298 Mike Heath .15 .07
❑ 299 Tim Raines .40 .18
❑ 300 Larry Parrish .15 .07
❑ 301 Geoff Zahn .15 .07
❑ 302 Rich Dotson .15 .07
❑ 303 David Green .15 .07
❑ 304 Jose Cruz .40 .18
❑ 305 Steve Carlton 1.25 .55
❑ 306 Gary Redus .15 .07
❑ 307 Steve Garvey .75 .35
❑ 308 Jose DeLeon .15 .07
❑ 309 Randy Lerch .15 .07
❑ 310 Claudell Washington .15 .07
❑ 311 Lee Smith .75 .35
❑ 312 Darryl Strawberry 1.25 .55
❑ 313 Jim Beattie .15 .07
❑ 314 John Butcher .15 .07
❑ 315 Damaso Garcia .15 .07
❑ 316 Mike Smithson .15 .07
❑ 317 Luis Leal .15 .07
❑ 318 Ken Phelps .15 .07
❑ 319 Wally Backman .15 .07
❑ 320 Ron Cey .40 .18
❑ 321 Brad Komminsk .15 .07
❑ 322 Jason Thompson .15 .07
❑ 323 Frank Williams .15 .07
❑ 324 Tim Lollar .15 .07
❑ 325 Eric Davis RC 2.00 .90
❑ 326 Von Hayes .15 .07
❑ 327 Andy Van Slyke .75 .35
❑ 328 Craig Reynolds .15 .07
❑ 329 Dick Schofield .15 .07
❑ 330 Scott Fletcher .15 .07
❑ 331 Jeff Reardon .40 .18
❑ 332 Rick Dempsey .15 .07
❑ 333 Ben Oglivie .15 .07
❑ 334 Dan Petry .15 .07
❑ 335 Jackie Gutierrez .15 .07
❑ 336 Dave Righetti .40 .18
❑ 337 Alejandro Pena .15 .07
❑ 338 Mel Hall .15 .07
❑ 339 Pat Sheridan .15 .07
❑ 340 Keith Atherton .15 .07
❑ 341 David Palmer .15 .07
❑ 342 Gary Ward .15 .07
❑ 343 Dave Stewart .40 .18

| |  |  | | |
|---|---|---|---|---|
| ❑ | 344 | Mark Gubicza RC* | .40 | .18 |
| ❑ | 345 | Carney Lansford | .40 | .18 |
| ❑ | 346 | Jerry Willard | .15 | .07 |
| ❑ | 347 | Ken Griffey | .40 | .18 |
| ❑ | 348 | Franklin Stubbs | .15 | .07 |
| ❑ | 349 | Aurelio Lopez | .15 | .07 |
| ❑ | 350 | Al Bumbry | .15 | .07 |
| ❑ | 351 | Charlie Moore | .15 | .07 |
| ❑ | 352 | Luis Sanchez | .15 | .07 |
| ❑ | 353 | Darrell Porter | .15 | .07 |
| ❑ | 354 | Bill Dawley | .15 | .07 |
| ❑ | 355 | Charles Hudson | .15 | .07 |
| ❑ | 356 | Garry Templeton | .15 | .07 |
| ❑ | 357 | Cecilio Guante | .15 | .07 |
| ❑ | 358 | Jeff Leonard | .15 | .07 |
| ❑ | 359 | Paul Molitor | 1.25 | .55 |
| ❑ | 360 | Ron Gardenhire | .15 | .07 |
| ❑ | 361 | Larry Bowa | .40 | .18 |
| ❑ | 362 | Bob Kearney | .15 | .07 |
| ❑ | 363 | Garth Iorg | .15 | .07 |
| ❑ | 364 | Tom Brunansky | .40 | .18 |
| ❑ | 365 | Brad Gulden | .15 | .07 |
| ❑ | 366 | Greg Walker | .15 | .07 |
| ❑ | 367 | Mike Young | .15 | .07 |
| ❑ | 368 | Rick Waits | .15 | .07 |
| ❑ | 369 | Doug Bair | .15 | .07 |
| ❑ | 370 | Bob Shirley | .15 | .07 |
| ❑ | 371 | Bob Ojeda | .15 | .07 |
| ❑ | 372 | Bob Welch | .15 | .07 |
| ❑ | 373 | Neal Heaton | .15 | .07 |
| ❑ | 374 | Danny Jackson UER (Photo actually Frank Wills) | .15 | .07 |
| ❑ | 375 | Donnie Hill | .15 | .07 |
| ❑ | 376 | Mike Stenhouse | .15 | .07 |
| ❑ | 377 | Bruce Kison | .15 | .07 |
| ❑ | 378 | Wayne Tolleson | .15 | .07 |
| ❑ | 379 | Floyd Bannister | .15 | .07 |
| ❑ | 380 | Vern Ruhle | .15 | .07 |
| ❑ | 381 | Tim Corcoran | .15 | .07 |
| ❑ | 382 | Kurt Kepshire | .15 | .07 |
| ❑ | 383 | Bobby Brown | .15 | .07 |
| ❑ | 384 | Dave Van Gorder | .15 | .07 |
| ❑ | 385 | Rick Mahler | .15 | .07 |
| ❑ | 386 | Lee Mazzilli | .15 | .07 |
| ❑ | 387 | Bill Laskey | .15 | .07 |
| ❑ | 388 | Thad Bosley | .15 | .07 |
| ❑ | 389 | Al Chambers | .15 | .07 |
| ❑ | 390 | Tony Fernandez | .40 | .18 |
| ❑ | 391 | Ron Washington | .15 | .07 |
| ❑ | 392 | Bill Swaggerty | .15 | .07 |
| ❑ | 393 | Bob L. Gibson | .15 | .07 |
| ❑ | 394 | Marty Castillo | .15 | .07 |
| ❑ | 395 | Steve Crawford | .15 | .07 |
| ❑ | 396 | Clay Christiansen | .15 | .07 |
| ❑ | 397 | Bob Bailor | .15 | .07 |
| ❑ | 398 | Mike Hargrove | .40 | .18 |
| ❑ | 399 | Charlie Leibrandt | .15 | .07 |
| ❑ | 400 | Tom Burgmeier | .15 | .07 |
| ❑ | 401 | Razor Shines | .15 | .07 |
| ❑ | 402 | Rob Wilfong | .15 | .07 |
| ❑ | 403 | Tom Henke | .40 | .18 |
| ❑ | 404 | Al Jones | .15 | .07 |
| ❑ | 405 | Mike LaCoss | .15 | .07 |
| ❑ | 406 | Luis DeLeon | .15 | .07 |
| ❑ | 407 | Greg Gross | .15 | .07 |
| ❑ | 408 | Tom Hume | .15 | .07 |
| ❑ | 409 | Rick Camp | .15 | .07 |
| ❑ | 410 | Milt May | .15 | .07 |
| ❑ | 411 | Henry Cotto RC | .15 | .07 |
| ❑ | 412 | David Von Ohlen | .15 | .07 |
| ❑ | 413 | Scott McGregor | .15 | .07 |
| ❑ | 414 | Ted Simmons | .40 | .18 |
| ❑ | 415 | Jack Morris | .40 | .18 |
| ❑ | 416 | Bill Buckner | .40 | .18 |
| ❑ | 417 | Butch Wynegar | .15 | .07 |
| ❑ | 418 | Steve Sax | .15 | .07 |
| ❑ | 419 | Steve Balboni | .15 | .07 |
| ❑ | 420 | Dwayne Murphy | .15 | .07 |
| ❑ | 421 | Andre Dawson | .75 | .35 |
| ❑ | 422 | Charlie Hough | .40 | .18 |
| ❑ | 423 | Tommy John | .75 | .35 |
| ❑ | 424A | Tom Seaver ERR (Photo actually Floyd Bannister) | 2.00 | .90 |
| ❑ | 424B | Tom Seaver COR | 15.00 | 6.75 |
| ❑ | 425 | Tom Herr | .40 | .18 |
| ❑ | 426 | Terry Puhl | .15 | .07 |
| ❑ | 427 | Al Holland | .15 | .07 |
| ❑ | 428 | Eddie Milner | .15 | .07 |
| ❑ | 429 | Terry Kennedy | .15 | .07 |
| ❑ | 430 | John Candelaria | .15 | .07 |
| ❑ | 431 | Manny Trillo | .15 | .07 |
| ❑ | 432 | Ken Oberkfell | .15 | .07 |
| ❑ | 433 | Rick Sutcliffe | .40 | .18 |
| ❑ | 434 | Ron Darling | .40 | .18 |
| ❑ | 435 | Spike Owen | .15 | .07 |
| ❑ | 436 | Frank Viola | .40 | .18 |
| ❑ | 437 | Lloyd Moseby | .15 | .07 |
| ❑ | 438 | Kirby Puckett RC ! | 20.00 | 9.00 |
| ❑ | 439 | Jim Clancy | .15 | .07 |
| ❑ | 440 | Mike Moore | .15 | .07 |
| ❑ | 441 | Doug Sisk | .15 | .07 |
| ❑ | 442 | Dennis Eckersley | 1.25 | .55 |
| ❑ | 443 | Gerald Perry | .15 | .07 |
| ❑ | 444 | Dale Berra | .15 | .07 |
| ❑ | 445 | Dusty Baker | .40 | .18 |
| ❑ | 446 | Ed Whitson | .15 | .07 |
| ❑ | 447 | Cesar Cedeno | .40 | .18 |
| ❑ | 448 | Rick Schu | .15 | .07 |
| ❑ | 449 | Joaquin Andujar | .15 | .07 |
| ❑ | 450 | Mark Bailey | .15 | .07 |
| ❑ | 451 | Ron Romanick | .15 | .07 |
| ❑ | 452 | Julio Cruz | .15 | .07 |
| ❑ | 453 | Miguel Dilone | .15 | .07 |
| ❑ | 454 | Storm Davis | .15 | .07 |
| ❑ | 455 | Jaime Cocanower | .15 | .07 |
| ❑ | 456 | Barbaro Garbey | .15 | .07 |
| ❑ | 457 | Rich Gedman | .15 | .07 |
| ❑ | 458 | Phil Niekro | 1.25 | .55 |
| ❑ | 459 | Mike Scioscia | .15 | .07 |
| ❑ | 460 | Pat Tabler | .15 | .07 |
| ❑ | 461 | Darryl Motley | .15 | .07 |
| ❑ | 462 | Chris Codiroli | .15 | .07 |
| ❑ | 463 | Doug Flynn | .15 | .07 |
| ❑ | 464 | Billy Sample | .15 | .07 |
| ❑ | 465 | Mickey Rivers | .15 | .07 |
| ❑ | 466 | John Wathan | .15 | .07 |
| ❑ | 467 | Bill Krueger | .15 | .07 |
| ❑ | 468 | Andre Thornton | .15 | .07 |
| ❑ | 469 | Rex Hudler | .15 | .07 |
| ❑ | 470 | Sid Bream RC | .40 | .18 |
| ❑ | 471 | Kirk Gibson | .40 | .18 |
| ❑ | 472 | John Shelby | .15 | .07 |
| ❑ | 473 | Moose Haas | .15 | .07 |
| ❑ | 474 | Doug Corbett | .15 | .07 |
| ❑ | 475 | Willie McGee | .40 | .18 |
| ❑ | 476 | Bob Knepper | .15 | .07 |
| ❑ | 477 | Kevin Gross | .15 | .07 |
| ❑ | 478 | Carmelo Martinez | .15 | .07 |
| ❑ | 479 | Kent Tekulve | .15 | .07 |
| ❑ | 480 | Chili Davis | .40 | .18 |
| ❑ | 481 | Bobby Clark | .15 | .07 |
| ❑ | 482 | Mookie Wilson | .40 | .18 |
| ❑ | 483 | Dave Owen | .15 | .07 |
| ❑ | 484 | Ed Nunez | .15 | .07 |
| ❑ | 485 | Rance Mulliniks | .15 | .07 |
| ❑ | 486 | Ken Schrom | .15 | .07 |
| ❑ | 487 | Jeff Russell | .15 | .07 |
| ❑ | 488 | Tom Paciorek | .40 | .18 |
| ❑ | 489 | Dan Ford | .15 | .07 |
| ❑ | 490 | Mike Caldwell | .15 | .07 |
| ❑ | 491 | Scottie Earl | .15 | .07 |
| ❑ | 492 | Jose Rijo RC | .75 | .35 |
| ❑ | 493 | Bruce Hurst | .15 | .07 |
| ❑ | 494 | Ken Landreaux | .15 | .07 |
| ❑ | 495 | Mike Fischlin | .15 | .07 |
| ❑ | 496 | Don Slaught | .15 | .07 |
| ❑ | 497 | Steve McCatty | .15 | .07 |
| ❑ | 498 | Gary Lucas | .15 | .07 |
| ❑ | 499 | Gary Pettis | .15 | .07 |
| ❑ | 500 | Marvis Foley | .15 | .07 |
| ❑ | 501 | Mike Squires | .15 | .07 |
| ❑ | 502 | Jim Pankovits | .15 | .07 |
| ❑ | 503 | Luis Aguayo | .15 | .07 |
| ❑ | 504 | Ralph Citarella | .15 | .07 |
| ❑ | 505 | Bruce Bochy | .15 | .07 |
| ❑ | 506 | Bob Owchinko | .15 | .07 |
| ❑ | 507 | Pascual Perez | .15 | .07 |
| ❑ | 508 | Lee Lacy | .15 | .07 |
| ❑ | 509 | Atlee Hammaker | .15 | .07 |
| ❑ | 510 | Bob Dernier | .15 | .07 |
| ❑ | 511 | Ed VandeBerg | .15 | .07 |
| ❑ | 512 | Cliff Johnson | .15 | .07 |
| ❑ | 513 | Len Whitehouse | .15 | .07 |
| ❑ | 514 | Dennis Martinez | .40 | .18 |
| ❑ | 515 | Ed Romero | .15 | .07 |
| ❑ | 516 | Rusty Kuntz | .15 | .07 |
| ❑ | 517 | Rick Miller | .15 | .07 |
| ❑ | 518 | Dennis Rasmussen | .15 | .07 |
| ❑ | 519 | Steve Yeager | .15 | .07 |
| ❑ | 520 | Chris Bando | .15 | .07 |
| ❑ | 521 | U.L. Washington | .15 | .07 |
| ❑ | 522 | Curt Young | .15 | .07 |
| ❑ | 523 | Angel Salazar | .15 | .07 |
| ❑ | 524 | Curt Kaufman | .15 | .07 |
| ❑ | 525 | Odell Jones | .15 | .07 |
| ❑ | 526 | Juan Agosto | .15 | .07 |
| ❑ | 527 | Denny Walling | .15 | .07 |
| ❑ | 528 | Andy Hawkins | .15 | .07 |
| ❑ | 529 | Sixto Lezcano | .15 | .07 |
| ❑ | 530 | Skeeter Barnes RC | .15 | .07 |
| ❑ | 531 | Randy Johnson | .15 | .07 |
| ❑ | 532 | Jim Morrison | .15 | .07 |
| ❑ | 533 | Warren Brusstar | .15 | .07 |
| ❑ | 534A | Jeff Pendleton RC ERR (Wrong first name) | 1.25 | .55 |
| ❑ | 534B | Terry Pendleton RC COR | 2.00 | .90 |
| ❑ | 535 | Vic Rodriguez | .15 | .07 |
| ❑ | 536 | Bob McClure | .15 | .07 |
| ❑ | 537 | Dave Bergman | .15 | .07 |
| ❑ | 538 | Mark Clear | .15 | .07 |
| ❑ | 539 | Mike Pagliarulo | .15 | .07 |
| ❑ | 540 | Terry Whitfield | .15 | .07 |
| ❑ | 541 | Joe Beckwith | .15 | .07 |
| ❑ | 542 | Jeff Burroughs | .15 | .07 |
| ❑ | 543 | Dan Schatzeder | .15 | .07 |
| ❑ | 544 | Donnie Scott | .15 | .07 |
| ❑ | 545 | Jim Slaton | .15 | .07 |
| ❑ | 546 | Greg Luzinski | .40 | .18 |
| ❑ | 547 | Mark Salas | .15 | .07 |
| ❑ | 548 | Dave Smith | .15 | .07 |
| ❑ | 549 | John Wockenfuss | .15 | .07 |
| ❑ | 550 | Frank Pastore | .15 | .07 |
| ❑ | 551 | Tim Flannery | .15 | .07 |
| ❑ | 552 | Rick Rhoden | .15 | .07 |
| ❑ | 553 | Mark Davis | .15 | .07 |
| ❑ | 554 | Jeff Dedmon | .15 | .07 |
| ❑ | 555 | Gary Woods | .15 | .07 |
| ❑ | 556 | Danny Heep | .15 | .07 |
| ❑ | 557 | Mark Langston RC | .75 | .35 |
| ❑ | 558 | Darrell Brown | .15 | .07 |
| ❑ | 559 | Jimmy Key RC | 1.25 | .55 |
| ❑ | 560 | Rick Lysander | .15 | .07 |
| ❑ | 561 | Doyle Alexander | .15 | .07 |
| ❑ | 562 | Mike Stanton | .15 | .07 |
| ❑ | 563 | Sid Fernandez | .40 | .18 |
| ❑ | 564 | Richie Hebner | .15 | .07 |
| ❑ | 565 | Alex Trevino | .15 | .07 |
| ❑ | 566 | Brian Harper | .15 | .07 |
| ❑ | 567 | Dan Gladden RC | .40 | .18 |
| ❑ | 568 | Luis Salazar | .15 | .07 |
| ❑ | 569 | Tom Foley | .15 | .07 |
| ❑ | 570 | Larry Andersen | .15 | .07 |
| ❑ | 571 | Danny Cox | .15 | .07 |
| ❑ | 572 | Joe Sambito | .15 | .07 |
| ❑ | 573 | Juan Beniquez | .15 | .07 |
| ❑ | 574 | Joel Skinner | .15 | .07 |
| ❑ | 575 | Randy St.Claire | .15 | .07 |
| ❑ | 576 | Floyd Rayford | .15 | .07 |
| ❑ | 577 | Roy Howell | .15 | .07 |
| ❑ | 578 | John Grubb | .15 | .07 |
| ❑ | 579 | Ed Jurak | .15 | .07 |
| ❑ | 580 | John Montefusco | .15 | .07 |
| ❑ | 581 | Orel Hershiser RC | 2.00 | .90 |
| ❑ | 582 | Tom Waddell | .15 | .07 |
| ❑ | 583 | Mark Huismann | .15 | .07 |
| ❑ | 584 | Joe Morgan | 1.25 | .55 |
| ❑ | 585 | Jim Wohlford | .15 | .07 |
| ❑ | 586 | Dave Schmidt | .15 | .07 |
| ❑ | 587 | Jeff Kunkel | .15 | .07 |
| ❑ | 588 | Hal McRae | .40 | .18 |
| ❑ | 589 | Bill Almon | .15 | .07 |
| ❑ | 590 | Carmen Castillo | .15 | .07 |
| ❑ | 591 | Omar Moreno | .15 | .07 |
| ❑ | 592 | Ken Howell | .15 | .07 |
| ❑ | 593 | Tom Brookens | .15 | .07 |

| | | | |
|---|---|---|---|
| ❏ 594 | Joe Nolan | .15 | .07 |
| ❏ 595 | Willie Lozado | .15 | .07 |
| ❏ 596 | Tom Nieto | .15 | .07 |
| ❏ 597 | Walt Terrell | .15 | .07 |
| ❏ 598 | Al Oliver | .40 | .18 |
| ❏ 599 | Shane Rawley | .15 | .07 |
| ❏ 600 | Denny Gonzalez | .15 | .07 |
| ❏ 601 | Mark Grant | .15 | .07 |
| ❏ 602 | Mike Armstrong | .15 | .07 |
| ❏ 603 | George Foster | .40 | .18 |
| ❏ 604 | Dave Lopes | .40 | .18 |
| ❏ 605 | Salome Barojas | .15 | .07 |
| ❏ 606 | Roy Lee Jackson | .15 | .07 |
| ❏ 607 | Pete Filson | .15 | .07 |
| ❏ 608 | Duane Walker | .15 | .07 |
| ❏ 609 | Glenn Wilson | .15 | .07 |
| ❏ 610 | Rafael Santana | .15 | .07 |
| ❏ 611 | Roy Smith | .15 | .07 |
| ❏ 612 | Ruppert Jones | .15 | .07 |
| ❏ 613 | Joe Cowley | .15 | .07 |
| ❏ 614 | Al Nipper UER (Photo actually Mike Brown) | .15 | .07 |
| ❏ 615 | Gene Nelson | .15 | .07 |
| ❏ 616 | Joe Carter | 1.25 | .55 |
| ❏ 617 | Ray Knight | .15 | .07 |
| ❏ 618 | Chuck Rainey | .15 | .07 |
| ❏ 619 | Dan Driessen | .15 | .07 |
| ❏ 620 | Daryl Sconiers | .15 | .07 |
| ❏ 621 | Bill Stein | .15 | .07 |
| ❏ 622 | Roy Smalley | .15 | .07 |
| ❏ 623 | Ed Lynch | .15 | .07 |
| ❏ 624 | Jeff Stone | .15 | .07 |
| ❏ 625 | Bruce Berenyi | .15 | .07 |
| ❏ 626 | Kelvin Chapman | .15 | .07 |
| ❏ 627 | Joe Price | .15 | .07 |
| ❏ 628 | Steve Bedrosian | .15 | .07 |
| ❏ 629 | Vic Mata | .15 | .07 |
| ❏ 630 | Mike Krukow | .15 | .07 |
| ❏ 631 | Phil Bradley | .40 | .18 |
| ❏ 632 | Jim Gott | .15 | .07 |
| ❏ 633 | Randy Bush | .15 | .07 |
| ❏ 634 | Tom Browning RC | .40 | .18 |
| ❏ 635 | Lou Gehrig Puzzle Card | 1.25 | .55 |
| ❏ 636 | Reid Nichols | .15 | .07 |
| ❏ 637 | Dan Pasqua RC | .40 | .18 |
| ❏ 638 | German Rivera | .15 | .07 |
| ❏ 639 | Don Schulze | .15 | .07 |
| ❏ 640A | Mike Jones (Career Highlights, takes five lines) | .15 | .07 |
| ❏ 640B | Mike Jones (Career Highlights, takes four lines) | .15 | .07 |
| ❏ 641 | Pete Rose | 4.00 | 1.80 |
| ❏ 642 | Wade Rowdon | .15 | .07 |
| ❏ 643 | Jerry Narron | .15 | .07 |
| ❏ 644 | Darrell Miller | .15 | .07 |
| ❏ 645 | Tim Hulett RC | .15 | .07 |
| ❏ 646 | Andy McGaffigan | .15 | .07 |
| ❏ 647 | Kurt Bevacqua | .15 | .07 |
| ❏ 648 | John Russell | .15 | .07 |
| ❏ 649 | Ron Robinson | .15 | .07 |
| ❏ 650 | Donnie Moore | .15 | .07 |
| ❏ 651A | Two for the Title Dave Winfield Don Mattingly (Yellow letters) | 1.50 | .70 |
| ❏ 651B | Two for the Title Dave Winfield Don Mattingly (White letters) | 4.00 | 1.80 |
| ❏ 652 | Tim Laudner | .15 | .07 |
| ❏ 653 | Steve Farr RC | .40 | .18 |
| ❏ 654 | DK Checklist 1-26 (Unnumbered) | .15 | .07 |
| ❏ 655 | Checklist 27-130 (Unnumbered) | .15 | .07 |
| ❏ 656 | Checklist 131-234 (Unnumbered) | .15 | .07 |
| ❏ 657 | Checklist 235-338 (Unnumbered) | .15 | .07 |
| ❏ 658 | Checklist 339-442 (Unnumbered) | .15 | .07 |
| ❏ 659 | Checklist 443-546 (Unnumbered) | .15 | .07 |
| ❏ 660 | Checklist 547-653 (Unnumbered) | .15 | .07 |

## 1986 Donruss

| | MINT | NRMT |
|---|---|---|
| COMPLETE SET (660) | 50.00 | 22.00 |
| COMP.FACT.SET (660) | 50.00 | 22.00 |
| COMP.AARON PUZZLE | 2.00 | .90 |

| | | | |
|---|---|---|---|
| ❏ 1 | Kirk Gibson DK | .25 | .11 |
| ❏ 2 | Rich Gossage DK | .25 | .11 |
| ❏ 3 | Willie McGee DK | .25 | .11 |
| ❏ 4 | George Bell DK | .15 | .07 |
| ❏ 5 | Tony Armas DK | .15 | .07 |
| ❏ 6 | Chili Davis DK | .50 | .23 |
| ❏ 7 | Cecil Cooper DK | .15 | .07 |
| ❏ 8 | Mike Boddicker DK | .15 | .07 |
| ❏ 9 | Dave Lopes DK | .25 | .11 |
| ❏ 10 | Bill Doran DK | .15 | .07 |
| ❏ 11 | Bret Saberhagen DK | .25 | .11 |
| ❏ 12 | Brett Butler DK | .15 | .07 |
| ❏ 13 | Harold Baines DK | .50 | .23 |
| ❏ 14 | Mike Davis DK | .15 | .07 |
| ❏ 15 | Tony Perez DK | .25 | .11 |
| ❏ 16 | Willie Randolph DK | .15 | .07 |
| ❏ 17 | Bob Boone DK | .15 | .07 |
| ❏ 18 | Orel Hershiser DK | .25 | .11 |
| ❏ 19 | Johnny Ray DK | .15 | .07 |
| ❏ 20 | Gary Ward DK | .15 | .07 |
| ❏ 21 | Rick Mahler DK | .15 | .07 |
| ❏ 22 | Phil Bradley DK | .15 | .07 |
| ❏ 23 | Jerry Koosman DK | .25 | .11 |
| ❏ 24 | Tom Brunansky DK | .15 | .07 |
| ❏ 25 | Andre Dawson DK | .25 | .11 |
| ❏ 26 | Dwight Gooden DK | .75 | .35 |
| ❏ 27 | Kal Daniels RR | .25 | .11 |
| ❏ 28 | Fred McGriff RR RC | 8.00 | 3.60 |
| ❏ 29 | Cory Snyder RR | .15 | .07 |
| ❏ 30 | Jose Guzman RR RC | .15 | .07 |
| ❏ 31 | Ty Gainey RR | .15 | .07 |
| ❏ 32 | Johnny Abrego RR | .15 | .07 |
| ❏ 33 | Andres Galarraga RC RR (No accent) | 6.00 | 2.70 |
| ❏ 33B | Andrés Galarraga RC RR (Accent over e) | 6.00 | 2.70 |
| ❏ 34 | Dave Shipanoff RR | .15 | .07 |
| ❏ 35 | Mark McLemore RR RC | .75 | .35 |
| ❏ 36 | Marty Clary RR | .15 | .07 |
| ❏ 37 | Paul O'Neill RR RC | 5.00 | 2.20 |
| ❏ 38 | Danny Tartabull RR | .25 | .11 |
| ❏ 39 | Jose Canseco RR RC | 30.00 | 13.50 |
| ❏ 40 | Juan Nieves RR | .15 | .07 |
| ❏ 41 | Lance McCullers RR | .15 | .07 |
| ❏ 42 | Rick Surhoff RR | .15 | .07 |
| ❏ 43 | Todd Worrell RR RC | .75 | .35 |
| ❏ 44 | Bob Kipper RR | .15 | .07 |
| ❏ 45 | John Habyan RR RC | .15 | .07 |
| ❏ 46 | Mike Woodard RR | .15 | .07 |
| ❏ 47 | Mike Boddicker | .15 | .07 |
| ❏ 48 | Robin Yount | .75 | .35 |
| ❏ 49 | Lou Whitaker | .25 | .11 |
| ❏ 50 | Oil Can Boyd | .15 | .07 |
| ❏ 51 | Rickey Henderson | 1.00 | .45 |
| ❏ 52 | Mike Marshall | .15 | .07 |
| ❏ 53 | George Brett | 1.50 | .70 |
| ❏ 54 | Dave Kingman | .25 | .11 |
| ❏ 55 | Hubie Brooks | .15 | .07 |
| ❏ 56 | Oddibe McDowell | .15 | .07 |
| ❏ 57 | Doug DeCinces | .15 | .07 |
| ❏ 58 | Britt Burns | .15 | .07 |
| ❏ 59 | Ozzie Smith | 1.00 | .45 |
| ❏ 60 | Jose Cruz | .25 | .11 |
| ❏ 61 | Mike Schmidt | 1.50 | .70 |
| ❏ 62 | Pete Rose | 2.50 | 1.10 |
| ❏ 63 | Steve Garvey | .50 | .23 |
| ❏ 64 | Tony Pena | .15 | .07 |
| ❏ 65 | Chili Davis | .50 | .23 |
| ❏ 66 | Dale Murphy | .75 | .35 |
| ❏ 67 | Ryne Sandberg | 1.00 | .45 |
| ❏ 68 | Gary Carter | .50 | .23 |
| ❏ 69 | Alvin Davis | .15 | .07 |
| ❏ 70 | Kent Hrbek | .25 | .11 |
| ❏ 71 | George Bell | .25 | .11 |
| ❏ 72 | Kirby Puckett | 3.00 | 1.35 |
| ❏ 73 | Lloyd Moseby | .15 | .07 |
| ❏ 74 | Bob Kearney | .15 | .07 |
| ❏ 75 | Dwight Gooden | .75 | .35 |
| ❏ 76 | Gary Matthews | .15 | .07 |
| ❏ 77 | Rick Mahler | .15 | .07 |
| ❏ 78 | Benny Distefano | .15 | .07 |
| ❏ 79 | Jeff Leonard | .15 | .07 |
| ❏ 80 | Kevin McReynolds | .25 | .11 |
| ❏ 81 | Ron Oester | .15 | .07 |
| ❏ 82 | John Russell | .15 | .07 |
| ❏ 83 | Tommy Herr | .15 | .07 |
| ❏ 84 | Jerry Mumphrey | .15 | .07 |
| ❏ 85 | Ron Romanick | .15 | .07 |
| ❏ 86 | Daryl Boston | .15 | .07 |
| ❏ 87 | Andre Dawson | .50 | .23 |
| ❏ 88 | Eddie Murray | .75 | .35 |
| ❏ 89 | Dion James | .15 | .07 |
| ❏ 90 | Chet Lemon | .15 | .07 |
| ❏ 91 | Bob Stanley | .15 | .07 |
| ❏ 92 | Willie Randolph | .25 | .11 |
| ❏ 93 | Mike Scioscia | .15 | .07 |
| ❏ 94 | Tom Waddell | .15 | .07 |
| ❏ 95 | Danny Jackson | .15 | .07 |
| ❏ 96 | Mike Davis | .15 | .07 |
| ❏ 97 | Mike Fitzgerald | .15 | .07 |
| ❏ 98 | Gary Ward | .15 | .07 |
| ❏ 99 | Pete O'Brien | .15 | .07 |
| ❏ 100 | Bret Saberhagen | .25 | .11 |
| ❏ 101 | Alfredo Griffin | .15 | .07 |
| ❏ 102 | Brett Butler | .25 | .11 |
| ❏ 103 | Ron Guidry | .25 | .11 |
| ❏ 104 | Jerry Reuss | .15 | .07 |
| ❏ 105 | Jack Morris | .25 | .11 |
| ❏ 106 | Rick Dempsey | .15 | .07 |
| ❏ 107 | Ray Burris | .15 | .07 |
| ❏ 108 | Brian Downing | .15 | .07 |
| ❏ 109 | Willie McGee | .25 | .11 |
| ❏ 110 | Bill Doran | .15 | .07 |
| ❏ 111 | Kent Tekulve | .15 | .07 |
| ❏ 112 | Tony Gwynn | 1.50 | .70 |
| ❏ 113 | Marvell Wynne | .15 | .07 |
| ❏ 114 | David Green | .15 | .07 |
| ❏ 115 | Jim Gantner | .15 | .07 |
| ❏ 116 | George Foster | .25 | .11 |
| ❏ 117 | Steve Trout | .15 | .07 |
| ❏ 118 | Mark Langston | .15 | .07 |
| ❏ 119 | Tony Fernandez | .15 | .07 |
| ❏ 120 | John Butcher | .15 | .07 |
| ❏ 121 | Ron Robinson | .15 | .07 |
| ❏ 122 | Dan Spillner | .15 | .07 |
| ❏ 123 | Mike Young | .15 | .07 |
| ❏ 124 | Paul Molitor | .75 | .35 |
| ❏ 125 | Kirk Gibson | .25 | .11 |
| ❏ 126 | Ken Griffey | .25 | .11 |
| ❏ 127 | Tony Armas | .15 | .07 |
| ❏ 128 | Mariano Duncan RC* | .75 | .35 |
| ❏ 129 | Pat Tabler | .15 | .07 |
| ❏ 130 | Frank White | .25 | .11 |
| ❏ 131 | Carney Lansford | .25 | .11 |
| ❏ 132 | Vance Law | .15 | .07 |
| ❏ 133 | Dick Schofield | .15 | .07 |
| ❏ 134 | Wayne Tolleson | .15 | .07 |
| ❏ 135 | Greg Walker | .15 | .07 |
| ❏ 136 | Denny Walling | .15 | .07 |
| ❏ 137 | Ozzie Virgil | .15 | .07 |
| ❏ 138 | Ricky Horton | .15 | .07 |
| ❏ 139 | LaMarr Hoyt | .15 | .07 |

❑ 140 Wayne Krenchicki .15 .07
❑ 141 Glenn Hubbard .15 .07
❑ 142 Cecilio Guante .15 .07
❑ 143 Mike Krukow .15 .07
❑ 144 Lee Smith .50 .23
❑ 145 Edwin Nunez .15 .07
❑ 146 Dave Stieb .15 .07
❑ 147 Mike Smithson .15 .07
❑ 148 Ken Dixon .15 .07
❑ 149 Danny Darwin .15 .07
❑ 150 Chris Pittaro .15 .07
❑ 151 Bill Buckner .25 .11
❑ 152 Mike Pagliarulo .15 .07
❑ 153 Bill Russell .15 .07
❑ 154 Brook Jacoby .15 .07
❑ 155 Pat Sheridan .15 .07
❑ 156 Mike Gallego RC .25 .11
❑ 157 Jim Wohlford .15 .07
❑ 158 Gary Pettis .15 .07
❑ 159 Toby Harrah .15 .07
❑ 160 Richard Dotson .15 .07
❑ 161 Bob Knepper .15 .07
❑ 162 Dave Dravecky .25 .11
❑ 163 Greg Gross .15 .07
❑ 164 Eric Davis .50 .23
❑ 165 Gerald Perry .15 .07
❑ 166 Rick Rhoden .15 .07
❑ 167 Keith Moreland .15 .07
❑ 168 Jack Clark .25 .11
❑ 169 Storm Davis .15 .07
❑ 170 Cecil Cooper .25 .11
❑ 171 Alan Trammell .50 .23
❑ 172 Roger Clemens 4.00 1.80
❑ 173 Don Mattingly 2.00 .90
❑ 174 Pedro Guerrero .25 .11
❑ 175 Willie Wilson .15 .07
❑ 176 Dwayne Murphy .15 .07
❑ 177 Tim Raines .25 .11
❑ 178 Larry Parrish .15 .07
❑ 179 Mike Witt .15 .07
❑ 180 Harold Baines .50 .23
❑ 181 Vince Coleman RC* UER .75 .35
(RA 2.67 on back)
❑ 182 Jeff Heathcock .15 .07
❑ 183 Steve Carlton .75 .35
❑ 184 Mario Soto .15 .07
❑ 185 Rich Gossage .25 .11
❑ 186 Johnny Ray .15 .07
❑ 187 Dan Gladden .15 .07
❑ 188 Bob Horner .15 .07
❑ 189 Rick Sutcliffe .25 .11
❑ 190 Keith Hernandez .25 .11
❑ 191 Phil Bradley .15 .07
❑ 192 Tom Brunansky .15 .07
❑ 193 Jesse Barfield .15 .07
❑ 194 Frank Viola .25 .11
❑ 195 Willie Upshaw .15 .07
❑ 196 Jim Beattie .15 .07
❑ 197 Darryl Strawberry .75 .35
❑ 198 Ron Cey .25 .11
❑ 199 Steve Bedrosian .15 .07
❑ 200 Steve Kemp .15 .07
❑ 201 Manny Trillo .15 .07
❑ 202 Garry Templeton .15 .07
❑ 203 Dave Parker .25 .11
❑ 204 John Denny .15 .07
❑ 205 Terry Pendleton .25 .11
❑ 206 Terry Puhl .15 .07
❑ 207 Bobby Grich .25 .11
❑ 208 Ozzie Guillen RC* .50 .23
❑ 209 Jeff Reardon .15 .07
❑ 210 Cal Ripken 3.00 1.35
❑ 211 Bill Schroeder .15 .07
❑ 212 Dan Petry .15 .07
❑ 213 Jim Rice .25 .11
❑ 214 Dave Righetti .15 .07
❑ 215 Fernando Valenzuela .25 .11
❑ 216 Julio Franco .25 .11
❑ 217 Darryl Motley .15 .07
❑ 218 Dave Collins .15 .07
❑ 219 Tim Wallach .15 .07
❑ 220 George Wright .15 .07
❑ 221 Tommy Dunbar .15 .07
❑ 222 Steve Balboni .15 .07
❑ 223 Jay Howell .15 .07
❑ 224 Joe Carter .75 .35
❑ 225 Ed Whitson .15 .07
❑ 226 Orel Hershiser .50 .23
❑ 227 Willie Hernandez .15 .07
❑ 228 Lee Lacy .15 .07
❑ 229 Rollie Fingers .75 .35
❑ 230 Bob Boone .25 .11
❑ 231 Joaquin Andujar .15 .07
❑ 232 Craig Reynolds .15 .07
❑ 233 Shane Rawley .15 .07
❑ 234 Eric Show .15 .07
❑ 235 Jose DeLeon .15 .07
❑ 236 Jose Uribe .15 .07
❑ 237 Moose Haas .15 .07
❑ 238 Wally Backman .15 .07
❑ 239 Dennis Eckersley .75 .35
❑ 240 Mike Moore .15 .07
❑ 241 Damaso Garcia .15 .07
❑ 242 Tim Teufel .15 .07
❑ 243 Dave Concepcion .25 .11
❑ 244 Floyd Bannister .15 .07
❑ 245 Fred Lynn .25 .11
❑ 246 Charlie Moore .15 .07
❑ 247 Walt Terrell .15 .07
❑ 248 Dave Winfield .75 .35
❑ 249 Dwight Evans .25 .11
❑ 250 Dennis Powell .15 .07
❑ 251 Andre Thornton .15 .07
❑ 252 Onix Concepcion .15 .07
❑ 253 Mike Heath .15 .07
❑ 254A David Palmer ERR .15 .07
(Position 2B)
❑ 254B David Palmer COR .75 .35
(Position P)
❑ 255 Donnie Moore .15 .07
❑ 256 Curtis Wilkerson .15 .07
❑ 257 Julio Cruz .15 .07
❑ 258 Nolan Ryan 4.00 1.80
❑ 259 Jeff Stone .15 .07
❑ 260 John Tudor .15 .07
❑ 261 Mark Thurmond .15 .07
❑ 262 Jay Tibbs .15 .07
❑ 263 Rafael Ramirez .15 .07
❑ 264 Larry McWilliams .15 .07
❑ 265 Mark Davis .15 .07
❑ 266 Bob Dernier .15 .07
❑ 267 Matt Young .15 .07
❑ 268 Jim Clancy .15 .07
❑ 269 Mickey Hatcher .15 .07
❑ 270 Sammy Stewart .15 .07
❑ 271 Bob L. Gibson .15 .07
❑ 272 Nelson Simmons .15 .07
❑ 273 Rich Gedman .15 .07
❑ 274 Butch Wynegar .15 .07
❑ 275 Ken Howell .15 .07
❑ 276 Mel Hall .15 .07
❑ 277 Jim Sundberg .15 .07
❑ 278 Chris Codiroli .15 .07
❑ 279 Herm Winningham .15 .07
❑ 280 Rod Carew .75 .35
❑ 281 Don Slaught .15 .07
❑ 282 Scott Fletcher .15 .07
❑ 283 Bill Dawley .15 .07
❑ 284 Andy Hawkins .15 .07
❑ 285 Glenn Wilson .15 .07
❑ 286 Nick Esasky .15 .07
❑ 287 Claudell Washington .15 .07
❑ 288 Lee Mazzilli .15 .07
❑ 289 Jody Davis .15 .07
❑ 290 Darrell Porter .25 .11
❑ 291 Scott McGregor .15 .07
❑ 292 Ted Simmons .25 .11
❑ 293 Aurelio Lopez .15 .07
❑ 294 Marty Barrett .15 .07
❑ 295 Dale Berra .15 .07
❑ 296 Greg Brock .15 .07
❑ 297 Charlie Leibrandt .15 .07
❑ 298 Bill Krueger .15 .07
❑ 299 Bryn Smith .15 .07
❑ 300 Burt Hooton .15 .07
❑ 301 Stu Cliburn .15 .07
❑ 302 Luis Salazar .15 .07
❑ 303 Ken Dayley .15 .07
❑ 304 Frank DiPino .15 .07
❑ 305 Von Hayes .15 .07
❑ 306 Gary Redus .15 .07
❑ 307 Craig Lefferts .15 .07
❑ 308 Sammy Khalifa .15 .07
❑ 309 Scott Garrelts .15 .07
❑ 310 Rick Cerone .15 .07
❑ 311 Shawon Dunston .25 .11
❑ 312 Howard Johnson .25 .11
❑ 313 Jim Presley .15 .07
❑ 314 Gary Gaetti .25 .11
❑ 315 Luis Leal .15 .07
❑ 316 Mark Salas .15 .07
❑ 317 Bill Caudill .15 .07
❑ 318 Dave Henderson .15 .07
❑ 319 Rafael Santana .15 .07
❑ 320 Leon Durham .15 .07
❑ 321 Bruce Sutter .25 .11
❑ 322 Jason Thompson .15 .07
❑ 323 Bob Brenly .15 .07
❑ 324 Carmelo Martinez .15 .07
❑ 325 Eddie Milner .15 .07
❑ 326 Juan Samuel .15 .07
❑ 327 Tom Nieto .15 .07
❑ 328 Dave Smith .15 .07
❑ 329 Urbano Lugo .15 .07
❑ 330 Joel Skinner .15 .07
❑ 331 Bill Gullickson .15 .07
❑ 332 Floyd Rayford .15 .07
❑ 333 Ben Oglivie .15 .07
❑ 334 Lance Parrish .25 .11
❑ 335 Jackie Gutierrez .15 .07
❑ 336 Dennis Rasmussen .15 .07
❑ 337 Terry Whitfield .15 .07
❑ 338 Neal Heaton .15 .07
❑ 339 Jorge Orta .15 .07
❑ 340 Donnie Hill .15 .07
❑ 341 Joe Hesketh .15 .07
❑ 342 Charlie Hough .25 .11
❑ 343 Dave Rozema .15 .07
❑ 344 Greg Pryor .15 .07
❑ 345 Mickey Tettleton RC .25 .11
❑ 346 George Vukovich .15 .07
❑ 347 Don Baylor .50 .23
❑ 348 Carlos Diaz .15 .07
❑ 349 Barbaro Garbey .15 .07
❑ 350 Larry Sheets .15 .07
❑ 351 Ted Higuera RC* .25 .11
❑ 352 Juan Beniquez .15 .07
❑ 353 Bob Forsch .15 .07
❑ 354 Mark Bailey .15 .07
❑ 355 Larry Andersen .15 .07
❑ 356 Terry Kennedy .15 .07
❑ 357 Don Robinson .15 .07
❑ 358 Jim Gott .15 .07
❑ 359 Earnie Riles .15 .07
❑ 360 John Christensen .15 .07
❑ 361 Ray Fontenot .15 .07
❑ 362 Spike Owen .15 .07
❑ 363 Jim Acker .15 .07
❑ 364 Ron Davis .15 .07
❑ 365 Tom Hume .15 .07
❑ 366 Carlton Fisk .75 .35
❑ 367 Nate Snell .15 .07
❑ 368 Rick Manning .15 .07
❑ 369 Darrell Evans .25 .11
❑ 370 Ron Hassey .15 .07
❑ 371 Wade Boggs 1.00 .45
❑ 372 Rick Honeycutt .15 .07
❑ 373 Chris Bando .15 .07
❑ 374 Bud Black .15 .07
❑ 375 Steve Henderson .15 .07
❑ 376 Charlie Lea .15 .07
❑ 377 Reggie Jackson 1.00 .45
❑ 378 Dave Schmidt .15 .07
❑ 379 Bob James .15 .07
❑ 380 Glenn Davis .25 .11
❑ 381 Tim Corcoran .15 .07
❑ 382 Danny Cox .15 .07
❑ 383 Tim Flannery .15 .07
❑ 384 Tom Browning .15 .07
❑ 385 Rick Camp .15 .07
❑ 386 Jim Morrison .15 .07
❑ 387 Dave LaPoint .15 .07
❑ 388 Dave Lopes .25 .11
❑ 389 Al Cowens .15 .07
❑ 390 Doyle Alexander .15 .07
❑ 391 Tim Laudner .15 .07
❑ 392 Don Aase .15 .07
❑ 393 Jaime Cocanower .15 .07

| |  |  | | |
|---|---|---|---|---|
| ❑ | 394 | Randy O'Neal | .15 | .07 |
| ❑ | 395 | Mike Easler | .15 | .07 |
| ❑ | 396 | Scott Bradley | .15 | .07 |
| ❑ | 397 | Tom Niedenfuer | .15 | .07 |
| ❑ | 398 | Jerry Willard | .15 | .07 |
| ❑ | 399 | Lonnie Smith | .15 | .07 |
| ❑ | 400 | Bruce Bochte | .15 | .07 |
| ❑ | 401 | Terry Francona | .15 | .07 |
| ❑ | 402 | Jim Slaton | .15 | .07 |
| ❑ | 403 | Bill Stein | .15 | .07 |
| ❑ | 404 | Tim Hulett | .15 | .07 |
| ❑ | 405 | Alan Ashby | .15 | .07 |
| ❑ | 406 | Tim Stoddard | .15 | .07 |
| ❑ | 407 | Garry Maddox | .15 | .07 |
| ❑ | 408 | Ted Power | .15 | .07 |
| ❑ | 409 | Len Barker | .15 | .07 |
| ❑ | 410 | Denny Gonzalez | .15 | .07 |
| ❑ | 411 | George Frazier | .15 | .07 |
| ❑ | 412 | Andy Van Slyke | .25 | .11 |
| ❑ | 413 | Jim Dwyer | .15 | .07 |
| ❑ | 414 | Paul Householder | .15 | .07 |
| ❑ | 415 | Alejandro Sanchez | .15 | .07 |
| ❑ | 416 | Steve Crawford | .15 | .07 |
| ❑ | 417 | Dan Pasqua | .15 | .07 |
| ❑ | 418 | Enos Cabell | .15 | .07 |
| ❑ | 419 | Mike Jones | .15 | .07 |
| ❑ | 420 | Steve Kiefer | .15 | .07 |
| ❑ | 421 | Tim Burke | .15 | .07 |
| ❑ | 422 | Mike Mason | .15 | .07 |
| ❑ | 423 | Ruppert Jones | .15 | .07 |
| ❑ | 424 | Jerry Hairston | .15 | .07 |
| ❑ | 425 | Tito Landrum | .15 | .07 |
| ❑ | 426 | Jeff Calhoun | .15 | .07 |
| ❑ | 427 | Don Carman | .15 | .07 |
| ❑ | 428 | Tony Perez | .75 | .35 |
| ❑ | 429 | Jerry Davis | .15 | .07 |
| ❑ | 430 | Bob Walk | .15 | .07 |
| ❑ | 431 | Brad Wellman | .15 | .07 |
| ❑ | 432 | Terry Forster | .15 | .07 |
| ❑ | 433 | Billy Hatcher | .15 | .07 |
| ❑ | 434 | Clint Hurdle | .15 | .07 |
| ❑ | 435 | Ivan Calderon RC* | .25 | .11 |
| ❑ | 436 | Pete Filson | .15 | .07 |
| ❑ | 437 | Tom Henke | .25 | .11 |
| ❑ | 438 | Dave Engle | .15 | .07 |
| ❑ | 439 | Tom Filer | .15 | .07 |
| ❑ | 440 | Gorman Thomas | .15 | .07 |
| ❑ | 441 | Rick Aguilera RC | .75 | .35 |
| ❑ | 442 | Scott Sanderson | .15 | .07 |
| ❑ | 443 | Jeff Dedmon | .15 | .07 |
| ❑ | 444 | Joe Orsulak RC* | .15 | .07 |
| ❑ | 445 | Atlee Hammaker | .15 | .07 |
| ❑ | 446 | Jerry Royster | .15 | .07 |
| ❑ | 447 | Buddy Bell | .25 | .11 |
| ❑ | 448 | Dave Rucker | .15 | .07 |
| ❑ | 449 | Ivan DeJesus | .15 | .07 |
| ❑ | 450 | Jim Pankovits | .15 | .07 |
| ❑ | 451 | Jerry Narron | .15 | .07 |
| ❑ | 452 | Bryan Little | .15 | .07 |
| ❑ | 453 | Gary Lucas | .15 | .07 |
| ❑ | 454 | Dennis Martinez | .25 | .11 |
| ❑ | 455 | Ed Romero | .15 | .07 |
| ❑ | 456 | Bob Melvin | .15 | .07 |
| ❑ | 457 | Glenn Hoffman | .15 | .07 |
| ❑ | 458 | Bob Shirley | .15 | .07 |
| ❑ | 459 | Bob Welch | .15 | .07 |
| ❑ | 460 | Carmen Castillo | .15 | .07 |
| ❑ | 461 | Dave Leeper | .15 | .07 |
| ❑ | 462 | Tim Birtsas | .15 | .07 |
| ❑ | 463 | Randy St.Claire | .15 | .07 |
| ❑ | 464 | Chris Welsh | .15 | .07 |
| ❑ | 465 | Greg Harris | .15 | .07 |
| ❑ | 466 | Lynn Jones | .15 | .07 |
| ❑ | 467 | Dusty Baker | .25 | .11 |
| ❑ | 468 | Roy Smith | .15 | .07 |
| ❑ | 469 | Andre Robertson | .15 | .07 |
| ❑ | 470 | Ken Landreaux | .15 | .07 |
| ❑ | 471 | Dave Bergman | .15 | .07 |
| ❑ | 472 | Gary Roenicke | .15 | .07 |
| ❑ | 473 | Pete Vuckovich | .15 | .07 |
| ❑ | 474 | Kirk McCaskill RC | .25 | .11 |
| ❑ | 475 | Jeff Lahti | .15 | .07 |
| ❑ | 476 | Mike Scott | .15 | .07 |
| ❑ | 477 | Darren Daulton RC | 1.50 | .70 |
| ❑ | 478 | Graig Nettles | .25 | .11 |
| ❑ | 479 | Bill Almon | .15 | .07 |
| ❑ | 480 | Greg Minton | .15 | .07 |
| ❑ | 481 | Randy Ready | .15 | .07 |
| ❑ | 482 | Len Dykstra RC | 1.50 | .70 |
| ❑ | 483 | Thad Bosley | .15 | .07 |
| ❑ | 484 | Harold Reynolds RC | .75 | .35 |
| ❑ | 485 | Al Oliver | .25 | .11 |
| ❑ | 486 | Roy Smalley | .15 | .07 |
| ❑ | 487 | John Franco | .75 | .35 |
| ❑ | 488 | Juan Agosto | .15 | .07 |
| ❑ | 489 | Al Pardo | .15 | .07 |
| ❑ | 490 | Bill Wegman RC | .15 | .07 |
| ❑ | 491 | Frank Tanana | .15 | .07 |
| ❑ | 492 | Brian Fisher | .15 | .07 |
| ❑ | 493 | Mark Clear | .15 | .07 |
| ❑ | 494 | Len Matuszek | .15 | .07 |
| ❑ | 495 | Ramon Romero | .15 | .07 |
| ❑ | 496 | John Wathan | .15 | .07 |
| ❑ | 497 | Rob Picciolo | .15 | .07 |
| ❑ | 498 | U.L. Washington | .15 | .07 |
| ❑ | 499 | John Candelaria | .15 | .07 |
| ❑ | 500 | Duane Walker | .15 | .07 |
| ❑ | 501 | Gene Nelson | .15 | .07 |
| ❑ | 502 | John Mizerock | .15 | .07 |
| ❑ | 503 | Luis Aguayo | .15 | .07 |
| ❑ | 504 | Kurt Kepshire | .15 | .07 |
| ❑ | 505 | Ed Wojna | .15 | .07 |
| ❑ | 506 | Joe Price | .15 | .07 |
| ❑ | 507 | Milt Thompson RC | .25 | .11 |
| ❑ | 508 | Junior Ortiz | .15 | .07 |
| ❑ | 509 | Vida Blue | .25 | .11 |
| ❑ | 510 | Steve Engel | .15 | .07 |
| ❑ | 511 | Karl Best | .15 | .07 |
| ❑ | 512 | Cecil Fielder RC | 1.50 | .70 |
| ❑ | 513 | Frank Eufemia | .15 | .07 |
| ❑ | 514 | Tippy Martinez | .15 | .07 |
| ❑ | 515 | Billy Joe Robidoux | .15 | .07 |
| ❑ | 516 | Bill Scherrer | .15 | .07 |
| ❑ | 517 | Bruce Hurst | .15 | .07 |
| ❑ | 518 | Rich Bordi | .15 | .07 |
| ❑ | 519 | Steve Yeager | .15 | .07 |
| ❑ | 520 | Tony Bernazard | .15 | .07 |
| ❑ | 521 | Hal McRae | .25 | .11 |
| ❑ | 522 | Jose Rijo | .15 | .07 |
| ❑ | 523 | Mitch Webster | .15 | .07 |
| ❑ | 524 | Jack Howell | .15 | .07 |
| ❑ | 525 | Alan Bannister | .15 | .07 |
| ❑ | 526 | Ron Kittle | .15 | .07 |
| ❑ | 527 | Phil Garner | .25 | .11 |
| ❑ | 528 | Kurt Bevacqua | .15 | .07 |
| ❑ | 529 | Kevin Gross | .15 | .07 |
| ❑ | 530 | Bo Diaz | .15 | .07 |
| ❑ | 531 | Ken Oberkfell | .15 | .07 |
| ❑ | 532 | Rick Reuschel | .15 | .07 |
| ❑ | 533 | Ron Meridith | .15 | .07 |
| ❑ | 534 | Steve Braun | .15 | .07 |
| ❑ | 535 | Wayne Gross | .15 | .07 |
| ❑ | 536 | Ray Searage | .15 | .07 |
| ❑ | 537 | Tom Brookens | .15 | .07 |
| ❑ | 538 | Al Nipper | .15 | .07 |
| ❑ | 539 | Billy Sample | .15 | .07 |
| ❑ | 540 | Steve Sax | .15 | .07 |
| ❑ | 541 | Dan Quisenberry | .15 | .07 |
| ❑ | 542 | Tony Phillips | .15 | .07 |
| ❑ | 543 | Floyd Youmans | .15 | .07 |
| ❑ | 544 | Steve Buechele RC | .25 | .11 |
| ❑ | 545 | Craig Gerber | .15 | .07 |
| ❑ | 546 | Joe DeSa | .15 | .07 |
| ❑ | 547 | Brian Harper | .15 | .07 |
| ❑ | 548 | Kevin Bass | .15 | .07 |
| ❑ | 549 | Tom Foley | .15 | .07 |
| ❑ | 550 | Dave Van Gorder | .15 | .07 |
| ❑ | 551 | Bruce Bochy | .15 | .07 |
| ❑ | 552 | R.J. Reynolds | .15 | .07 |
| ❑ | 553 | Chris Brown | .15 | .07 |
| ❑ | 554 | Bruce Benedict | .15 | .07 |
| ❑ | 555 | Warren Brusstar | .15 | .07 |
| ❑ | 556 | Danny Heep | .15 | .07 |
| ❑ | 557 | Darnell Coles | .15 | .07 |
| ❑ | 558 | Greg Gagne | .15 | .07 |
| ❑ | 559 | Ernie Whitt | .15 | .07 |
| ❑ | 560 | Ron Washington | .15 | .07 |
| ❑ | 561 | Jimmy Key | .75 | .35 |
| ❑ | 562 | Billy Swift | .15 | .07 |
| ❑ | 563 | Ron Darling | .15 | .07 |
| ❑ | 564 | Dick Ruthven | .15 | .07 |
| ❑ | 565 | Zane Smith | .15 | .07 |
| ❑ | 566 | Sid Bream | .15 | .07 |
| ❑ | 567A | Joel Youngblood ERR (Position P) | .15 | .07 |
| ❑ | 567B | Joel Youngblood COR (Position IF) | .75 | .35 |
| ❑ | 568 | Mario Ramirez | .15 | .07 |
| ❑ | 569 | Tom Runnells | .15 | .07 |
| ❑ | 570 | Rick Schu | .15 | .07 |
| ❑ | 571 | Bill Campbell | .15 | .07 |
| ❑ | 572 | Dickie Thon | .15 | .07 |
| ❑ | 573 | Al Holland | .15 | .07 |
| ❑ | 574 | Reid Nichols | .15 | .07 |
| ❑ | 575 | Bert Roberge | .15 | .07 |
| ❑ | 576 | Mike Flanagan | .15 | .07 |
| ❑ | 577 | Tim Leary | .15 | .07 |
| ❑ | 578 | Mike Laga | .15 | .07 |
| ❑ | 579 | Steve Lyons | .15 | .07 |
| ❑ | 580 | Phil Niekro | .75 | .35 |
| ❑ | 581 | Gilberto Reyes | .15 | .07 |
| ❑ | 582 | Jamie Easterly | .15 | .07 |
| ❑ | 583 | Mark Gubicza | .15 | .07 |
| ❑ | 584 | Stan Javier RC | .25 | .11 |
| ❑ | 585 | Bill Laskey | .15 | .07 |
| ❑ | 586 | Jeff Russell | .15 | .07 |
| ❑ | 587 | Dickie Noles | .15 | .07 |
| ❑ | 588 | Steve Farr | .15 | .07 |
| ❑ | 589 | Steve Ontiveros RC | .25 | .11 |
| ❑ | 590 | Mike Hargrove | .25 | .11 |
| ❑ | 591 | Marty Bystrom | .15 | .07 |
| ❑ | 592 | Franklin Stubbs | .15 | .07 |
| ❑ | 593 | Larry Herndon | .15 | .07 |
| ❑ | 594 | Bill Swaggerty | .15 | .07 |
| ❑ | 595 | Carlos Ponce | .15 | .07 |
| ❑ | 596 | Pat Perry | .15 | .07 |
| ❑ | 597 | Ray Knight | .25 | .11 |
| ❑ | 598 | Steve Lombardozzi | .15 | .07 |
| ❑ | 599 | Brad Havens | .15 | .07 |
| ❑ | 600 | Pat Clements | .15 | .07 |
| ❑ | 601 | Joe Niekro | .15 | .07 |
| ❑ | 602 | Hank Aaron Puzzle Card | .75 | .35 |
| ❑ | 603 | Dwayne Henry | .15 | .07 |
| ❑ | 604 | Mookie Wilson | .25 | .11 |
| ❑ | 605 | Buddy Biancalana | .15 | .07 |
| ❑ | 606 | Rance Mulliniks | .15 | .07 |
| ❑ | 607 | Alan Wiggins | .15 | .07 |
| ❑ | 608 | Joe Cowley | .15 | .07 |
| ❑ | 609 | Tom Seaver (Green borders on name) | 1.25 | .55 |
| ❑ | 609B | Tom Seaver (Yellow borders on name) | 2.00 | .90 |
| ❑ | 610 | Neil Allen | .15 | .07 |
| ❑ | 611 | Don Sutton | .75 | .35 |
| ❑ | 612 | Fred Toliver | .15 | .07 |
| ❑ | 613 | Jay Baller | .15 | .07 |
| ❑ | 614 | Marc Sullivan | .15 | .07 |
| ❑ | 615 | John Grubb | .15 | .07 |
| ❑ | 616 | Bruce Kison | .15 | .07 |
| ❑ | 617 | Bill Madlock | .15 | .07 |
| ❑ | 618 | Chris Chambliss | .25 | .11 |
| ❑ | 619 | Dave Stewart | .25 | .11 |
| ❑ | 620 | Tim Lollar | .15 | .07 |
| ❑ | 621 | Gary Lavelle | .15 | .07 |
| ❑ | 622 | Charles Hudson | .15 | .07 |
| ❑ | 623 | Joel Davis | .15 | .07 |
| ❑ | 624 | Joe Johnson | .15 | .07 |
| ❑ | 625 | Sid Fernandez | .25 | .11 |
| ❑ | 626 | Dennis Lamp | .15 | .07 |
| ❑ | 627 | Terry Harper | .15 | .07 |
| ❑ | 628 | Jack Lazorko | .15 | .07 |
| ❑ | 629 | Roger McDowell RC* | .25 | .11 |
| ❑ | 630 | Mark Funderburk | .15 | .07 |
| ❑ | 631 | Ed Lynch | .15 | .07 |
| ❑ | 632 | Rudy Law | .15 | .07 |
| ❑ | 633 | Roger Mason RC | .15 | .07 |
| ❑ | 634 | Mike Felder RC | .15 | .07 |
| ❑ | 635 | Ken Schrom | .15 | .07 |
| ❑ | 636 | Bob Ojeda | .15 | .07 |
| ❑ | 637 | Ed VandeBerg | .15 | .07 |
| ❑ | 638 | Bobby Meacham | .15 | .07 |
| ❑ | 639 | Cliff Johnson | .15 | .07 |
| ❑ | 640 | Garth Iorg | .15 | .07 |
| ❑ | 641 | Dan Driessen | .15 | .07 |
| ❑ | 642 | Mike Brown OF | .15 | .07 |

| Card | MINT | NRMT |
|---|---|---|
| ❑ 643 John Shelby | .15 | .07 |
| ❑ 644 Pete Rose (Ty-Breaking) | .75 | .35 |
| ❑ 645 The Knuckle Brothers<br>Phil Niekro<br>Joe Niekro | .25 | .11 |
| ❑ 646 Jesse Orosco | .15 | .07 |
| ❑ 647 Billy Beane | .15 | .07 |
| ❑ 648 Cesar Cedeno | .25 | .11 |
| ❑ 649 Bert Blyleven | .25 | .11 |
| ❑ 650 Max Venable | .15 | .07 |
| ❑ 651 Fleet Feet<br>Vince Coleman<br>Willie McGee | .15 | .07 |
| ❑ 652 Calvin Schiraldi | .15 | .07 |
| ❑ 653 King of Kings (Pete Rose) | .75 | .35 |
| ❑ 654 Diamond Kings CL 1-26 (Unnumbered) | .15 | .07 |
| ❑ 655A CL 1: 27-130 (Unnumbered) (45 Beane ERR) | .15 | .07 |
| ❑ 655B CL 1: 27-130 (Unnumbered) (45 Habyan COR) | .15 | .07 |
| ❑ 656 CL 2: 131-234 (Unnumbered) | .15 | .07 |
| ❑ 657 CL 3: 235-338 (Unnumbered) | .15 | .07 |
| ❑ 658 CL 4: 339-442 (Unnumbered) | .15 | .07 |
| ❑ 659 CL 5: 443-546 (Unnumbered) | .15 | .07 |
| ❑ 660 CL 6: 547-653 (Unnumbered) | .15 | .07 |

## 1986 Donruss Rookies

| | MINT | NRMT |
|---|---|---|
| COMP.FACT.SET (56) | 30.00 | 13.50 |
| ❑ 1 Wally Joyner XRC | 1.00 | .45 |
| ❑ 2 Tracy Jones | .10 | .05 |
| ❑ 3 Allan Anderson | .10 | .05 |
| ❑ 4 Ed Correa | .10 | .05 |
| ❑ 5 Reggie Williams | .10 | .05 |
| ❑ 6 Charlie Kerfeld | .10 | .05 |
| ❑ 7 Andres Galarraga | 2.00 | .90 |
| ❑ 8 Bob Tewksbury XRC | .25 | .11 |
| ❑ 9 Al Newman | .25 | .11 |
| ❑ 10 Andres Thomas | .10 | .05 |
| ❑ 11 Barry Bonds XRC ! | 15.00 | 6.75 |
| ❑ 12 Juan Nieves | .10 | .05 |
| ❑ 13 Mark Eichhorn | .10 | .05 |
| ❑ 14 Dan Plesac XRC | .10 | .05 |
| ❑ 15 Cory Snyder | .10 | .05 |
| ❑ 16 Kelly Gruber XRC** | .10 | .05 |
| ❑ 17 Kevin Mitchell XRC | 1.00 | .45 |
| ❑ 18 Steve Lombardozzi | .10 | .05 |
| ❑ 19 Mitch Williams XRC | .25 | .11 |
| ❑ 20 John Cerutti | .10 | .05 |
| ❑ 21 Todd Worrell | 1.00 | .45 |
| ❑ 22 Jose Canseco | 8.00 | 3.60 |
| ❑ 23 Pete Incaviglia XRC | 1.00 | .45 |
| ❑ 24 Jose Guzman | .10 | .05 |
| ❑ 25 Scott Bailes | .10 | .05 |
| ❑ 26 Greg Mathews | .10 | .05 |
| ❑ 27 Eric King | .10 | .05 |
| ❑ 28 Paul Assenmacher | .10 | .05 |
| ❑ 29 Jeff Sellers | .10 | .05 |
| ❑ 30 Bobby Bonilla XRC | 1.50 | .70 |
| ❑ 31 Doug Drabek XRC | 1.00 | .45 |
| ❑ 32 Will Clark UER (Listed as throwing right, should be left) XRC | 3.00 | 1.35 |
| ❑ 33 Bip Roberts XRC | 1.00 | .45 |
| ❑ 34 Jim Deshaies XRC | .10 | .05 |
| ❑ 35 Mike LaValliere XRC | .10 | .05 |
| ❑ 36 Scott Bankhead | .10 | .05 |
| ❑ 37 Dale Sveum | .10 | .05 |
| ❑ 38 Bo Jackson XRC | 2.50 | 1.10 |
| ❑ 39 Robby Thompson XRC | .25 | .11 |
| ❑ 40 Eric Plunk | .10 | .05 |
| ❑ 41 Bill Bathe | .10 | .05 |
| ❑ 42 John Kruk XRC | 1.00 | .45 |
| ❑ 43 Andy Allanson | .10 | .05 |
| ❑ 44 Mark Portugal XRC | .50 | .23 |
| ❑ 45 Danny Tartabull | .25 | .11 |
| ❑ 46 Bob Kipper | .10 | .05 |
| ❑ 47 Gene Walter | .10 | .05 |
| ❑ 48 Rey Quinones UER (Misspelled Quinonez) | .10 | .05 |
| ❑ 49 Bobby Witt XRC | .50 | .23 |
| ❑ 50 Bill Mooneyham | .10 | .05 |
| ❑ 51 John Cangelosi | .10 | .05 |
| ❑ 52 Ruben Sierra XRC | 1.00 | .45 |
| ❑ 53 Rob Woodward | .10 | .05 |
| ❑ 54 Ed Hearn | .10 | .05 |
| ❑ 55 Joel McKeon | .10 | .05 |
| ❑ 56 Checklist 1-56 | .10 | .05 |

## 1987 Donruss

| | MINT | NRMT |
|---|---|---|
| COMPLETE SET (660) | 60.00 | 27.00 |
| COMP.FACT.SET (660) | 80.00 | 36.00 |
| COMP.CLEMENTE PUZZLE | 1.50 | .70 |
| ❑ 1 Wally Joyner DK | .40 | .18 |
| ❑ 2 Roger Clemens DK | .50 | .23 |
| ❑ 3 Dale Murphy DK | .15 | .07 |
| ❑ 4 Darryl Strawberry DK | .15 | .07 |
| ❑ 5 Ozzie Smith DK | .40 | .18 |
| ❑ 6 Jose Canseco DK | .75 | .35 |
| ❑ 7 Charlie Hough DK | .10 | .05 |
| ❑ 8 Brook Jacoby DK | .10 | .05 |
| ❑ 9 Fred Lynn DK | .15 | .07 |
| ❑ 10 Rick Rhoden DK | .10 | .05 |
| ❑ 11 Chris Brown DK | .10 | .05 |
| ❑ 12 Von Hayes DK | .10 | .05 |
| ❑ 13 Jack Morris DK | .15 | .07 |
| ❑ 14A Kevin McReynolds DK ERR (Yellow strip missing on back) | .40 | .18 |
| ❑ 14B Kevin McReynolds DK COR | .10 | .05 |
| ❑ 15 George Brett DK | .40 | .18 |
| ❑ 16 Ted Higuera DK | .10 | .05 |
| ❑ 17 Hubie Brooks DK | .10 | .05 |
| ❑ 18 Mike Scott DK | .10 | .05 |
| ❑ 19 Kirby Puckett DK | .40 | .18 |
| ❑ 20 Dave Winfield DK | .15 | .07 |
| ❑ 21 Lloyd Moseby DK | .10 | .05 |
| ❑ 22A Eric Davis DK ERR (Yellow strip missing on back) | .40 | .18 |
| ❑ 22B Eric Davis DK COR | .15 | .07 |
| ❑ 23 Jim Presley DK | .10 | .05 |
| ❑ 24 Keith Moreland DK | .10 | .05 |
| ❑ 25A Greg Walker DK ERR (Yellow strip missing on back) | .40 | .18 |
| ❑ 25B Greg Walker DK COR | .10 | .05 |
| ❑ 26 Steve Sax DK | .10 | .05 |
| ❑ 27 DK Checklist 1-26 | .10 | .05 |
| ❑ 28 B.J. Surhoff RR RC | 1.00 | .45 |
| ❑ 29 Randy Myers RR RC | .40 | .18 |
| ❑ 30 Ken Gerhart RR | .10 | .05 |
| ❑ 31 Benito Santiago RR | .15 | .07 |
| ❑ 32 Greg Swindell RR RC | .40 | .18 |
| ❑ 33 Mike Birkbeck RR | .10 | .05 |
| ❑ 34 Terry Steinbach RR RC | .40 | .18 |
| ❑ 35 Bo Jackson RR RC | 1.00 | .45 |
| ❑ 36 Greg Maddux UER RC (Middle name misspelled "Allen") | 15.00 | 6.75 |
| ❑ 37 Jim Lindeman RR | .10 | .05 |
| ❑ 38 Devon White RR RC | .50 | .23 |
| ❑ 39 Eric Bell RR | .10 | .05 |
| ❑ 40 Willie Fraser RR | .10 | .05 |
| ❑ 41 Jerry Browne RR RC | .10 | .05 |
| ❑ 42 Chris James RR RC* | .10 | .05 |
| ❑ 43 Rafael Palmeiro RR RC | 8.00 | 3.60 |
| ❑ 44 Pat Dodson RR | .10 | .05 |
| ❑ 45 Duane Ward RR RC* | .15 | .07 |
| ❑ 46 Mark McGwire RR | 30.00 | 13.50 |
| ❑ 47 Bruce Fields RR UER (Photo actually Darnell Coles) | .10 | .05 |
| ❑ 48 Eddie Murray | .40 | .18 |
| ❑ 49 Ted Higuera | .10 | .05 |
| ❑ 50 Kirk Gibson | .15 | .07 |
| ❑ 51 Oil Can Boyd | .10 | .05 |
| ❑ 52 Don Mattingly | 1.00 | .45 |
| ❑ 53 Pedro Guerrero | .10 | .05 |
| ❑ 54 George Brett | .75 | .35 |
| ❑ 55 Jose Rijo | .10 | .05 |
| ❑ 56 Tim Raines | .15 | .07 |
| ❑ 57 Ed Correa | .10 | .05 |
| ❑ 58 Mike Witt | .10 | .05 |
| ❑ 59 Greg Walker | .10 | .05 |
| ❑ 60 Ozzie Smith | .50 | .23 |
| ❑ 61 Glenn Davis | .10 | .05 |
| ❑ 62 Glenn Wilson | .10 | .05 |
| ❑ 63 Tom Browning | .10 | .05 |
| ❑ 64 Tony Gwynn | .75 | .35 |
| ❑ 65 R.J. Reynolds | .10 | .05 |
| ❑ 66 Will Clark RC | 1.50 | .70 |
| ❑ 67 Ozzie Virgil | .10 | .05 |
| ❑ 68 Rick Sutcliffe | .15 | .07 |
| ❑ 69 Gary Carter | .25 | .11 |
| ❑ 70 Mike Moore | .10 | .05 |
| ❑ 71 Bert Blyleven | .15 | .07 |
| ❑ 72 Tony Fernandez | .10 | .05 |
| ❑ 73 Kent Hrbek | .15 | .07 |
| ❑ 74 Lloyd Moseby | .10 | .05 |
| ❑ 75 Alvin Davis | .10 | .05 |
| ❑ 76 Keith Hernandez | .15 | .07 |
| ❑ 77 Ryne Sandberg | .50 | .23 |
| ❑ 78 Dale Murphy | .40 | .18 |
| ❑ 79 Sid Bream | .10 | .05 |
| ❑ 80 Chris Brown | .10 | .05 |
| ❑ 81 Steve Garvey | .25 | .11 |
| ❑ 82 Mario Soto | .10 | .05 |
| ❑ 83 Shane Rawley | .10 | .05 |
| ❑ 84 Willie McGee | .15 | .07 |
| ❑ 85 Jose Cruz | .15 | .07 |
| ❑ 86 Brian Downing | .10 | .05 |
| ❑ 87 Ozzie Guillen | .10 | .05 |
| ❑ 88 Hubie Brooks | .10 | .05 |
| ❑ 89 Cal Ripken | 1.50 | .70 |
| ❑ 90 Juan Nieves | .10 | .05 |
| ❑ 91 Lance Parrish | .15 | .07 |
| ❑ 92 Jim Rice | .15 | .07 |
| ❑ 93 Ron Guidry | .15 | .07 |
| ❑ 94 Fernando Valenzuela | .15 | .07 |
| ❑ 95 Andy Allanson | .10 | .05 |
| ❑ 96 Willie Wilson | .15 | .07 |
| ❑ 97 Jose Canseco | 1.50 | .70 |
| ❑ 98 Jeff Reardon | .15 | .07 |
| ❑ 99 Bobby Witt RC | .15 | .07 |
| ❑ 100 Checklist 28-133 | .10 | .05 |
| ❑ 101 Jose Guzman | .10 | .05 |

| No. | Player | | |
|---|---|---|---|
| ❑ 102 | Steve Balboni | .10 | .05 |
| ❑ 103 | Tony Phillips | .10 | .05 |
| ❑ 104 | Brook Jacoby | .10 | .05 |
| ❑ 105 | Dave Winfield | .40 | .18 |
| ❑ 106 | Orel Hershiser | .15 | .07 |
| ❑ 107 | Lou Whitaker | .15 | .07 |
| ❑ 108 | Fred Lynn | .15 | .07 |
| ❑ 109 | Bill Wegman | .10 | .05 |
| ❑ 110 | Donnie Moore | .10 | .05 |
| ❑ 111 | Jack Clark | .15 | .07 |
| ❑ 112 | Bob Knepper | .10 | .05 |
| ❑ 113 | Von Hayes | .10 | .05 |
| ❑ 114 | Bip Roberts RC* | .40 | .18 |
| ❑ 115 | Tony Pena | .10 | .05 |
| ❑ 116 | Scott Garrelts | .10 | .05 |
| ❑ 117 | Paul Molitor | .40 | .18 |
| ❑ 118 | Darryl Strawberry | .25 | .11 |
| ❑ 119 | Shawon Dunston | .10 | .05 |
| ❑ 120 | Jim Presley | .10 | .05 |
| ❑ 121 | Jesse Barfield | .10 | .05 |
| ❑ 122 | Gary Gaetti | .15 | .07 |
| ❑ 123 | Kurt Stillwell | .10 | .05 |
| ❑ 124 | Joel Davis | .10 | .05 |
| ❑ 125 | Mike Boddicker | .10 | .05 |
| ❑ 126 | Robin Yount | .40 | .18 |
| ❑ 127 | Alan Trammell | .25 | .11 |
| ❑ 128 | Dave Righetti | .10 | .05 |
| ❑ 129 | Dwight Evans | .15 | .07 |
| ❑ 130 | Mike Scioscia | .10 | .05 |
| ❑ 131 | Julio Franco | .10 | .05 |
| ❑ 132 | Bret Saberhagen | .15 | .07 |
| ❑ 133 | Mike Davis | .10 | .05 |
| ❑ 134 | Joe Hesketh | .10 | .05 |
| ❑ 135 | Wally Joyner RC | .40 | .18 |
| ❑ 136 | Don Slaught | .10 | .05 |
| ❑ 137 | Daryl Boston | .10 | .05 |
| ❑ 138 | Nolan Ryan | 2.00 | .90 |
| ❑ 139 | Mike Schmidt | .75 | .35 |
| ❑ 140 | Tommy Herr | .10 | .05 |
| ❑ 141 | Garry Templeton | .10 | .05 |
| ❑ 142 | Kal Daniels | .10 | .05 |
| ❑ 143 | Billy Sample | .10 | .05 |
| ❑ 144 | Johnny Ray | .10 | .05 |
| ❑ 145 | Rob Thompson RC* | .15 | .07 |
| ❑ 146 | Bob Dernier | .10 | .05 |
| ❑ 147 | Danny Tartabull | .10 | .05 |
| ❑ 148 | Ernie Whitt | .10 | .05 |
| ❑ 149 | Kirby Puckett | 1.00 | .45 |
| ❑ 150 | Mike Young | .10 | .05 |
| ❑ 151 | Ernest Riles | .10 | .05 |
| ❑ 152 | Frank Tanana | .10 | .05 |
| ❑ 153 | Rich Gedman | .10 | .05 |
| ❑ 154 | Willie Randolph | .15 | .07 |
| ❑ 155 | Bill Madlock | .15 | .07 |
| ❑ 156 | Joe Carter | .40 | .18 |
| ❑ 157 | Danny Jackson | .10 | .05 |
| ❑ 158 | Carney Lansford | .15 | .07 |
| ❑ 159 | Bryn Smith | .10 | .05 |
| ❑ 160 | Gary Pettis | .10 | .05 |
| ❑ 161 | Oddibe McDowell | .10 | .05 |
| ❑ 162 | John Cangelosi | .10 | .05 |
| ❑ 163 | Mike Scott | .10 | .05 |
| ❑ 164 | Eric Show | .10 | .05 |
| ❑ 165 | Juan Samuel | .10 | .05 |
| ❑ 166 | Nick Esasky | .10 | .05 |
| ❑ 167 | Zane Smith | .10 | .05 |
| ❑ 168 | Mike C. Brown OF | .10 | .05 |
| ❑ 169 | Keith Moreland | .10 | .05 |
| ❑ 170 | John Tudor | .10 | .05 |
| ❑ 171 | Ken Dixon | .10 | .05 |
| ❑ 172 | Jim Gantner | .10 | .05 |
| ❑ 173 | Jack Morris | .15 | .07 |
| ❑ 174 | Bruce Hurst | .10 | .05 |
| ❑ 175 | Dennis Rasmussen | .10 | .05 |
| ❑ 176 | Mike Marshall | .10 | .05 |
| ❑ 177 | Dan Quisenberry | .10 | .05 |
| ❑ 178 | Eric Plunk | .10 | .05 |
| ❑ 179 | Tim Wallach | .10 | .05 |
| ❑ 180 | Steve Buechele | .10 | .05 |
| ❑ 181 | Don Sutton | .40 | .18 |
| ❑ 182 | Dave Schmidt | .10 | .05 |
| ❑ 183 | Terry Pendleton | .15 | .07 |
| ❑ 184 | Jim Deshaies RC* | .10 | .05 |
| ❑ 185 | Steve Bedrosian | .10 | .05 |
| ❑ 186 | Pete Rose | 1.25 | .55 |
| ❑ 187 | Dave Dravecky | .15 | .07 |
| ❑ 188 | Rick Reuschel | .10 | .05 |
| ❑ 189 | Dan Gladden | .10 | .05 |
| ❑ 190 | Rick Mahler | .10 | .05 |
| ❑ 191 | Thad Bosley | .10 | .05 |
| ❑ 192 | Ron Darling | .10 | .05 |
| ❑ 193 | Matt Young | .10 | .05 |
| ❑ 194 | Tom Brunansky | .10 | .05 |
| ❑ 195 | Dave Stieb | .10 | .05 |
| ❑ 196 | Frank Viola | .10 | .05 |
| ❑ 197 | Tom Henke | .10 | .05 |
| ❑ 198 | Karl Best | .10 | .05 |
| ❑ 199 | Dwight Gooden | .25 | .11 |
| ❑ 200 | Checklist 134-239 | .10 | .05 |
| ❑ 201 | Steve Trout | .10 | .05 |
| ❑ 202 | Rafael Ramirez | .10 | .05 |
| ❑ 203 | Bob Walk | .10 | .05 |
| ❑ 204 | Roger Mason | .10 | .05 |
| ❑ 205 | Terry Kennedy | .10 | .05 |
| ❑ 206 | Ron Oester | .10 | .05 |
| ❑ 207 | John Russell | .10 | .05 |
| ❑ 208 | Greg Mathews | .10 | .05 |
| ❑ 209 | Charlie Kerfeld | .10 | .05 |
| ❑ 210 | Reggie Jackson | .50 | .23 |
| ❑ 211 | Floyd Bannister | .10 | .05 |
| ❑ 212 | Vance Law | .10 | .05 |
| ❑ 213 | Rich Bordi | .10 | .05 |
| ❑ 214 | Dan Plesac | .10 | .05 |
| ❑ 215 | Dave Collins | .10 | .05 |
| ❑ 216 | Bob Stanley | .10 | .05 |
| ❑ 217 | Joe Niekro | .10 | .05 |
| ❑ 218 | Tom Niedenfuer | .10 | .05 |
| ❑ 219 | Brett Butler | .15 | .07 |
| ❑ 220 | Charlie Leibrandt | .10 | .05 |
| ❑ 221 | Steve Ontiveros | .10 | .05 |
| ❑ 222 | Tim Burke | .10 | .05 |
| ❑ 223 | Curtis Wilkerson | .10 | .05 |
| ❑ 224 | Pete Incaviglia RC* | .15 | .07 |
| ❑ 225 | Lonnie Smith | .10 | .05 |
| ❑ 226 | Chris Codiroli | .10 | .05 |
| ❑ 227 | Scott Bailes | .10 | .05 |
| ❑ 228 | Rickey Henderson | .50 | .23 |
| ❑ 229 | Ken Howell | .10 | .05 |
| ❑ 230 | Darnell Coles | .10 | .05 |
| ❑ 231 | Don Aase | .10 | .05 |
| ❑ 232 | Tim Leary | .10 | .05 |
| ❑ 233 | Bob Boone | .15 | .07 |
| ❑ 234 | Ricky Horton | .10 | .05 |
| ❑ 235 | Mark Bailey | .10 | .05 |
| ❑ 236 | Kevin Gross | .10 | .05 |
| ❑ 237 | Lance McCullers | .10 | .05 |
| ❑ 238 | Cecilio Guante | .10 | .05 |
| ❑ 239 | Bob Melvin | .10 | .05 |
| ❑ 240 | Billy Joe Robidoux | .10 | .05 |
| ❑ 241 | Roger McDowell | .10 | .05 |
| ❑ 242 | Leon Durham | .10 | .05 |
| ❑ 243 | Ed Nunez | .10 | .05 |
| ❑ 244 | Jimmy Key | .15 | .07 |
| ❑ 245 | Mike Smithson | .10 | .05 |
| ❑ 246 | Bo Diaz | .10 | .05 |
| ❑ 247 | Carlton Fisk | .40 | .18 |
| ❑ 248 | Larry Sheets | .10 | .05 |
| ❑ 249 | Juan Castillo | .10 | .05 |
| ❑ 250 | Eric King | .10 | .05 |
| ❑ 251 | Doug Drabek RC | .40 | .18 |
| ❑ 252 | Wade Boggs | .50 | .23 |
| ❑ 253 | Mariano Duncan | .10 | .05 |
| ❑ 254 | Pat Tabler | .10 | .05 |
| ❑ 255 | Frank White | .15 | .07 |
| ❑ 256 | Alfredo Griffin | .10 | .05 |
| ❑ 257 | Floyd Youmans | .10 | .05 |
| ❑ 258 | Rob Wilfong | .10 | .05 |
| ❑ 259 | Pete O'Brien | .10 | .05 |
| ❑ 260 | Tim Hulett | .10 | .05 |
| ❑ 261 | Dickie Thon | .10 | .05 |
| ❑ 262 | Darren Daulton | .25 | .11 |
| ❑ 263 | Vince Coleman | .10 | .05 |
| ❑ 264 | Andy Hawkins | .10 | .05 |
| ❑ 265 | Eric Davis | .25 | .11 |
| ❑ 266 | Andres Thomas | .10 | .05 |
| ❑ 267 | Mike Diaz | .10 | .05 |
| ❑ 268 | Chili Davis | .25 | .11 |
| ❑ 269 | Jody Davis | .10 | .05 |
| ❑ 270 | Phil Bradley | .10 | .05 |
| ❑ 271 | George Bell | .10 | .05 |
| ❑ 272 | Keith Atherton | .10 | .05 |
| ❑ 273 | Storm Davis | .10 | .05 |
| ❑ 274 | Rob Deer | .10 | .05 |
| ❑ 275 | Walt Terrell | .10 | .05 |
| ❑ 276 | Roger Clemens | 1.00 | .45 |
| ❑ 277 | Mike Easler | .10 | .05 |
| ❑ 278 | Steve Sax | .10 | .05 |
| ❑ 279 | Andre Thornton | .10 | .05 |
| ❑ 280 | Jim Sundberg | .10 | .05 |
| ❑ 281 | Bill Bathe | .10 | .05 |
| ❑ 282 | Jay Tibbs | .10 | .05 |
| ❑ 283 | Dick Schofield | .10 | .05 |
| ❑ 284 | Mike Mason | .10 | .05 |
| ❑ 285 | Jerry Hairston | .10 | .05 |
| ❑ 286 | Bill Doran | .10 | .05 |
| ❑ 287 | Tim Flannery | .10 | .05 |
| ❑ 288 | Gary Redus | .10 | .05 |
| ❑ 289 | John Franco | .15 | .07 |
| ❑ 290 | Paul Assenmacher | .25 | .11 |
| ❑ 291 | Joe Orsulak | .10 | .05 |
| ❑ 292 | Lee Smith | .25 | .11 |
| ❑ 293 | Mike Laga | .10 | .05 |
| ❑ 294 | Rick Dempsey | .15 | .07 |
| ❑ 295 | Mike Felder | .10 | .05 |
| ❑ 296 | Tom Brookens | .10 | .05 |
| ❑ 297 | Al Nipper | .10 | .05 |
| ❑ 298 | Mike Pagliarulo | .10 | .05 |
| ❑ 299 | Franklin Stubbs | .10 | .05 |
| ❑ 300 | Checklist 240-345 | .10 | .05 |
| ❑ 301 | Steve Farr | .10 | .05 |
| ❑ 302 | Bill Mooneyham | .10 | .05 |
| ❑ 303 | Andres Galarraga | .40 | .18 |
| ❑ 304 | Scott Fletcher | .10 | .05 |
| ❑ 305 | Jack Howell | .10 | .05 |
| ❑ 306 | Russ Morman | .10 | .05 |
| ❑ 307 | Todd Worrell | .15 | .07 |
| ❑ 308 | Dave Smith | .10 | .05 |
| ❑ 309 | Jeff Stone | .10 | .05 |
| ❑ 310 | Ron Robinson | .10 | .05 |
| ❑ 311 | Bruce Bochy | .10 | .05 |
| ❑ 312 | Jim Winn | .10 | .05 |
| ❑ 313 | Mark Davis | .10 | .05 |
| ❑ 314 | Jeff Dedmon | .10 | .05 |
| ❑ 315 | Jamie Moyer RC | .25 | .11 |
| ❑ 316 | Wally Backman | .10 | .05 |
| ❑ 317 | Ken Phelps | .10 | .05 |
| ❑ 318 | Steve Lombardozzi | .10 | .05 |
| ❑ 319 | Rance Mulliniks | .10 | .05 |
| ❑ 320 | Tim Laudner | .10 | .05 |
| ❑ 321 | Mark Eichhorn | .10 | .05 |
| ❑ 322 | Lee Guetterman | .10 | .05 |
| ❑ 323 | Sid Fernandez | .10 | .05 |
| ❑ 324 | Jerry Mumphrey | .10 | .05 |
| ❑ 325 | David Palmer | .10 | .05 |
| ❑ 326 | Bill Almon | .10 | .05 |
| ❑ 327 | Candy Maldonado | .10 | .05 |
| ❑ 328 | John Kruk RC | .40 | .18 |
| ❑ 329 | John Denny | .10 | .05 |
| ❑ 330 | Milt Thompson | .10 | .05 |
| ❑ 331 | Mike LaValliere RC* | .10 | .05 |
| ❑ 332 | Alan Ashby | .10 | .05 |
| ❑ 333 | Doug Corbett | .10 | .05 |
| ❑ 334 | Ron Karkovice RC | .15 | .07 |
| ❑ 335 | Mitch Webster | .10 | .05 |
| ❑ 336 | Lee Lacy | .10 | .05 |
| ❑ 337 | Glenn Braggs RC | .10 | .05 |
| ❑ 338 | Dwight Lowry | .10 | .05 |
| ❑ 339 | Don Baylor | .15 | .07 |
| ❑ 340 | Brian Fisher | .10 | .05 |
| ❑ 341 | Reggie Williams | .10 | .05 |
| ❑ 342 | Tom Candiotti | .10 | .05 |
| ❑ 343 | Rudy Law | .10 | .05 |
| ❑ 344 | Curt Young | .10 | .05 |
| ❑ 345 | Mike Fitzgerald | .10 | .05 |
| ❑ 346 | Ruben Sierra RC | .40 | .18 |
| ❑ 347 | Mitch Williams RC* | .15 | .07 |
| ❑ 348 | Jorge Orta | .10 | .05 |
| ❑ 349 | Mickey Tettleton | .10 | .05 |
| ❑ 350 | Ernie Camacho | .10 | .05 |
| ❑ 351 | Ron Kittle | .10 | .05 |
| ❑ 352 | Ken Landreaux | .10 | .05 |
| ❑ 353 | Chet Lemon | .10 | .05 |
| ❑ 354 | John Shelby | .10 | .05 |
| ❑ 355 | Mark Clear | .10 | .05 |
| ❑ 356 | Doug DeCinces | .10 | .05 |
| ❑ 357 | Ken Dayley | .10 | .05 |
| ❑ 358 | Phil Garner | .10 | .05 |
| ❑ 359 | Steve Jeltz | .10 | .05 |

❑ 360 Ed Whitson .10 .05
❑ 361 Barry Bonds RC 8.00 3.60
❑ 362 Vida Blue .15 .07
❑ 363 Cecil Cooper .15 .07
❑ 364 Bob Ojeda .10 .05
❑ 365 Dennis Eckersley .40 .18
❑ 366 Mike Morgan .10 .05
❑ 367 Willie Upshaw .10 .05
❑ 368 Allan Anderson .10 .05
❑ 369 Bill Gullickson .10 .05
❑ 370 Bobby Thigpen RC .15 .07
❑ 371 Juan Beniquez .10 .05
❑ 372 Charlie Moore .10 .05
❑ 373 Dan Petry .10 .05
❑ 374 Rod Scurry .10 .05
❑ 375 Tom Seaver .40 .18
❑ 376 Ed VandeBerg .10 .05
❑ 377 Tony Bernazard .10 .05
❑ 378 Greg Pryor .10 .05
❑ 379 Dwayne Murphy .10 .05
❑ 380 Andy McGaffigan .10 .05
❑ 381 Kirk McCaskill .10 .05
❑ 382 Greg Harris .10 .05
❑ 383 Rich Dotson .10 .05
❑ 384 Craig Reynolds .10 .05
❑ 385 Greg Gross .10 .05
❑ 386 Tito Landrum .10 .05
❑ 387 Craig Lefferts .10 .05
❑ 388 Dave Parker .15 .07
❑ 389 Bob Horner .10 .05
❑ 390 Pat Clements .10 .05
❑ 391 Jeff Leonard .10 .05
❑ 392 Chris Speier .10 .05
❑ 393 John Moses .10 .05
❑ 394 Garth Iorg .10 .05
❑ 395 Greg Gagne .10 .05
❑ 396 Nate Snell .10 .05
❑ 397 Bryan Clutterbuck .10 .05
❑ 398 Darrell Evans .15 .07
❑ 399 Steve Crawford .10 .05
❑ 400 Checklist 346-451 .10 .05
❑ 401 Phil Lombardi .10 .05
❑ 402 Rick Honeycutt .10 .05
❑ 403 Ken Schrom .10 .05
❑ 404 Bud Black .10 .05
❑ 405 Donnie Hill .10 .05
❑ 406 Wayne Krenchicki .10 .05
❑ 407 Chuck Finley RC .75 .35
❑ 408 Toby Harrah .10 .05
❑ 409 Steve Lyons .10 .05
❑ 410 Kevin Bass .10 .05
❑ 411 Marvell Wynne .10 .05
❑ 412 Ron Roenicke .10 .05
❑ 413 Tracy Jones .10 .05
❑ 414 Gene Garber .10 .05
❑ 415 Mike Bielecki .10 .05
❑ 416 Frank DiPino .10 .05
❑ 417 Andy Van Slyke .15 .07
❑ 418 Jim Dwyer .10 .05
❑ 419 Ben Oglivie .10 .05
❑ 420 Dave Bergman .10 .05
❑ 421 Joe Sambito .10 .05
❑ 422 Bob Tewksbury RC* .15 .07
❑ 423 Len Matuszek .10 .05
❑ 424 Mike Kingery RC .10 .05
❑ 425 Dave Kingman .15 .07
❑ 426 Al Newman .10 .05
❑ 427 Gary Ward .10 .05
❑ 428 Ruppert Jones .10 .05
❑ 429 Harold Baines .15 .07
❑ 430 Pat Perry .10 .05
❑ 431 Terry Puhl .10 .05
❑ 432 Don Carman .10 .05
❑ 433 Eddie Milner .10 .05
❑ 434 LaMarr Hoyt .10 .05
❑ 435 Rick Rhoden .10 .05
❑ 436 Jose Uribe .10 .05
❑ 437 Ken Oberkfell .10 .05
❑ 438 Ron Davis .10 .05
❑ 439 Jesse Orosco .10 .05
❑ 440 Scott Bradley .10 .05
❑ 441 Randy Bush .10 .05
❑ 442 John Cerutti .10 .05
❑ 443 Roy Smalley .10 .05
❑ 444 Kelly Gruber .10 .05
❑ 445 Bob Kearney .10 .05
❑ 446 Ed Hearn .10 .05
❑ 447 Scott Sanderson .10 .05
❑ 448 Bruce Benedict .10 .05
❑ 449 Junior Ortiz .10 .05
❑ 450 Mike Aldrete .10 .05
❑ 451 Kevin McReynolds .10 .05
❑ 452 Rob Murphy .10 .05
❑ 453 Kent Tekulve .10 .05
❑ 454 Curt Ford .10 .05
❑ 455 Dave Lopes .15 .07
❑ 456 Bob Grich .15 .07
❑ 457 Jose DeLeon .10 .05
❑ 458 Andre Dawson .25 .11
❑ 459 Mike Flanagan .10 .05
❑ 460 Joey Meyer .10 .05
❑ 461 Chuck Cary .10 .05
❑ 462 Bill Buckner .15 .07
❑ 463 Bob Shirley .10 .05
❑ 464 Jeff Hamilton .10 .05
❑ 465 Phil Niekro .40 .18
❑ 466 Mark Gubicza .10 .05
❑ 467 Jerry Willard .10 .05
❑ 468 Bob Sebra .10 .05
❑ 469 Larry Parrish .10 .05
❑ 470 Charlie Hough .15 .07
❑ 471 Hal McRae .15 .07
❑ 472 Dave Leiper .10 .05
❑ 473 Mel Hall .10 .05
❑ 474 Dan Pasqua .10 .05
❑ 475 Bob Welch .10 .05
❑ 476 Johnny Grubb .10 .05
❑ 477 Jim Traber .10 .05
❑ 478 Chris Bosio RC .15 .07
❑ 479 Mark McLemore .15 .07
❑ 480 John Morris .10 .05
❑ 481 Billy Hatcher .10 .05
❑ 482 Dan Schatzeder .10 .05
❑ 483 Rich Gossage .15 .07
❑ 484 Jim Morrison .10 .05
❑ 485 Bob Brenly .10 .05
❑ 486 Bill Schroeder .10 .05
❑ 487 Mookie Wilson .15 .07
❑ 488 Dave Martinez RC .15 .07
❑ 489 Harold Reynolds .15 .07
❑ 490 Jeff Hearron .10 .05
❑ 491 Mickey Hatcher .10 .05
❑ 492 Barry Larkin RC 2.00 .90
❑ 493 Bob James .10 .05
❑ 494 John Habyan .10 .05
❑ 495 Jim Adduci .10 .05
❑ 496 Mike Heath .10 .05
❑ 497 Tim Stoddard .10 .05
❑ 498 Tony Armas .10 .05
❑ 499 Dennis Powell .10 .05
❑ 500 Checklist 452-557 .10 .05
❑ 501 Chris Bando .10 .05
❑ 502 David Cone RC 2.00 .90
❑ 503 Jay Howell .10 .05
❑ 504 Tom Foley .10 .05
❑ 505 Ray Chadwick .10 .05
❑ 506 Mike Loynd .10 .05
❑ 507 Neil Allen .10 .05
❑ 508 Danny Darwin .10 .05
❑ 509 Rick Schu .10 .05
❑ 510 Jose Oquendo .10 .05
❑ 511 Gene Walter .10 .05
❑ 512 Terry McGriff .10 .05
❑ 513 Ken Griffey .15 .07
❑ 514 Benny Distefano .10 .05
❑ 515 Terry Mulholland RC .15 .07
❑ 516 Ed Lynch .10 .05
❑ 517 Bill Swift .10 .05
❑ 518 Manny Lee .10 .05
❑ 519 Andre David .10 .05
❑ 520 Scott McGregor .10 .05
❑ 521 Rick Manning .10 .05
❑ 522 Willie Hernandez .10 .05
❑ 523 Marty Barrett .10 .05
❑ 524 Wayne Tolleson .10 .05
❑ 525 Jose Gonzalez .10 .05
❑ 526 Cory Snyder .10 .05
❑ 527 Buddy Biancalana .10 .05
❑ 528 Moose Haas .10 .05
❑ 529 Wilfredo Tejada .10 .05
❑ 530 Stu Cliburn .10 .05
❑ 531 Dale Mohorcic .10 .05
❑ 532 Ron Hassey .10 .05
❑ 533 Ty Gainey .10 .05
❑ 534 Jerry Royster .10 .05
❑ 535 Mike Maddux .10 .05
❑ 536 Ted Power .10 .05
❑ 537 Ted Simmons .15 .07
❑ 538 Rafael Belliard RC .10 .05
❑ 539 Chico Walker .10 .05
❑ 540 Bob Forsch .10 .05
❑ 541 John Stefero .10 .05
❑ 542 Dale Sveum .10 .05
❑ 543 Mark Thurmond .10 .05
❑ 544 Jeff Sellers .10 .05
❑ 545 Joel Skinner .10 .05
❑ 546 Alex Trevino .10 .05
❑ 547 Randy Kutcher .10 .05
❑ 548 Joaquin Andujar .10 .05
❑ 549 Casey Candaele .10 .05
❑ 550 Jeff Russell .10 .05
❑ 551 John Candelaria .10 .05
❑ 552 Joe Cowley .10 .05
❑ 553 Danny Cox .10 .05
❑ 554 Denny Walling .10 .05
❑ 555 Bruce Ruffin RC .10 .05
❑ 556 Buddy Bell .15 .07
❑ 557 Jimmy Jones RC .10 .05
❑ 558 Bobby Bonilla RC .50 .23
❑ 559 Jeff D. Robinson .10 .05
❑ 560 Ed Olwine .10 .05
❑ 561 Glenallen Hill RC .50 .23
❑ 562 Lee Mazzilli .10 .05
❑ 563 Mike G. Brown P .10 .05
❑ 564 George Frazier .10 .05
❑ 565 Mike Sharperson RC .10 .05
❑ 566 Mark Portugal RC* .15 .07
❑ 567 Rick Leach .10 .05
❑ 568 Mark Langston .10 .05
❑ 569 Rafael Santana .10 .05
❑ 570 Manny Trillo .10 .05
❑ 571 Cliff Speck .10 .05
❑ 572 Bob Kipper .10 .05
❑ 573 Kelly Downs RC .10 .05
❑ 574 Randy Asadoor .10 .05
❑ 575 Dave Magadan RC .15 .07
❑ 576 Marvin Freeman RC .10 .05
❑ 577 Jeff Lahti .10 .05
❑ 578 Jeff Calhoun .10 .05
❑ 579 Gus Polidor .10 .05
❑ 580 Gene Nelson .10 .05
❑ 581 Tim Teufel .10 .05
❑ 582 Odell Jones .10 .05
❑ 583 Mark Ryal .10 .05
❑ 584 Randy O'Neal .10 .05
❑ 585 Mike Greenwell RC .40 .18
❑ 586 Ray Knight .10 .05
❑ 587 Ralph Bryant .10 .05
❑ 588 Carmen Castillo .10 .05
❑ 589 Ed Wojna .10 .05
❑ 590 Stan Javier .10 .05
❑ 591 Jeff Musselman .10 .05
❑ 592 Mike Stanley RC .40 .18
❑ 593 Darrell Porter .10 .05
❑ 594 Drew Hall .10 .05
❑ 595 Rob Nelson .10 .05
❑ 596 Bryan Oelkers .10 .05
❑ 597 Scott Nielsen .10 .05
❑ 598 Brian Holton .10 .05
❑ 599 Kevin Mitchell RC* .25 .11
❑ 600 Checklist 558-660 .10 .05
❑ 601 Jackie Gutierrez .10 .05
❑ 602 Barry Jones .10 .05
❑ 603 Jerry Narron .10 .05
❑ 604 Steve Lake .10 .05
❑ 605 Jim Pankovits .10 .05
❑ 606 Ed Romero .10 .05
❑ 607 Dave LaPoint .10 .05
❑ 608 Don Robinson .10 .05
❑ 609 Mike Krukow .10 .05
❑ 610 Dave Valle RC** .10 .05
❑ 611 Len Dykstra .25 .11
❑ 612 Roberto Clemente PUZ .50 .23
❑ 613 Mike Trujillo .10 .05
❑ 614 Damaso Garcia .10 .05
❑ 615 Neal Heaton .10 .05
❑ 616 Juan Berenguer .10 .05
❑ 617 Steve Carlton .40 .18

| | MINT | NRMT |
|---|---|---|
| ❑ 618 Gary Lucas | .10 | .05 |
| ❑ 619 Geno Petralli | .10 | .05 |
| ❑ 620 Rick Aguilera | .15 | .07 |
| ❑ 621 Fred McGriff | .50 | .23 |
| ❑ 622 Dave Henderson | .10 | .05 |
| ❑ 623 Dave Clark RC | .15 | .07 |
| ❑ 624 Angel Salazar | .10 | .05 |
| ❑ 625 Randy Hunt | .10 | .05 |
| ❑ 626 John Gibbons | .10 | .05 |
| ❑ 627 Kevin Brown RC | 3.00 | 1.35 |
| ❑ 628 Bill Dawley | .10 | .05 |
| ❑ 629 Aurelio Lopez | .10 | .05 |
| ❑ 630 Charles Hudson | .10 | .05 |
| ❑ 631 Ray Soff | .10 | .05 |
| ❑ 632 Ray Hayward | .10 | .05 |
| ❑ 633 Spike Owen | .10 | .05 |
| ❑ 634 Glenn Hubbard | .10 | .05 |
| ❑ 635 Kevin Elster RC | .15 | .07 |
| ❑ 636 Mike LaCoss | .10 | .05 |
| ❑ 637 Dwayne Henry | .10 | .05 |
| ❑ 638 Rey Quinones | .10 | .05 |
| ❑ 639 Jim Clancy | .10 | .05 |
| ❑ 640 Larry Andersen | .10 | .05 |
| ❑ 641 Calvin Schiraldi | .10 | .05 |
| ❑ 642 Stan Jefferson | .10 | .05 |
| ❑ 643 Marc Sullivan | .10 | .05 |
| ❑ 644 Mark Grant | .10 | .05 |
| ❑ 645 Cliff Johnson | .10 | .05 |
| ❑ 646 Howard Johnson | .10 | .05 |
| ❑ 647 Dave Sax | .10 | .05 |
| ❑ 648 Dave Stewart | .15 | .07 |
| ❑ 649 Danny Heep | .10 | .05 |
| ❑ 650 Joe Johnson | .10 | .05 |
| ❑ 651 Bob Brower | .10 | .05 |
| ❑ 652 Rob Woodward | .10 | .05 |
| ❑ 653 John Mizerock | .10 | .05 |
| ❑ 654 Tim Pyznarski | .10 | .05 |
| ❑ 655 Luis Aquino | .10 | .05 |
| ❑ 656 Mickey Brantley | .10 | .05 |
| ❑ 657 Doyle Alexander | .10 | .05 |
| ❑ 658 Sammy Stewart | .10 | .05 |
| ❑ 659 Jim Acker | .10 | .05 |
| ❑ 660 Pete Ladd | .10 | .05 |

## 1987 Donruss Rookies

| | MINT | NRMT |
|---|---|---|
| COMP.FACT.SET (56) | 40.00 | 18.00 |
| ❑ 1 Mark McGwire | 25.00 | 11.00 |
| ❑ 2 Eric Bell | .10 | .05 |
| ❑ 3 Mark Williamson | .10 | .05 |
| ❑ 4 Mike Greenwell | .75 | .35 |
| ❑ 5 Ellis Burks XRC | 1.50 | .70 |
| ❑ 6 DeWayne Buice | .10 | .05 |
| ❑ 7 Mark McLemore | .25 | .11 |
| ❑ 8 Devon White | .75 | .35 |
| ❑ 9 Willie Fraser | .10 | .05 |
| ❑ 10 Les Lancaster | .10 | .05 |
| ❑ 11 Ken Williams | .10 | .05 |
| ❑ 12 Matt Nokes XRC | .25 | .11 |
| ❑ 13 Jeff M. Robinson | .10 | .05 |
| ❑ 14 Bo Jackson | .75 | .35 |
| ❑ 15 Kevin Seitzer XRC | .75 | .35 |
| ❑ 16 Billy Ripken XRC | .10 | .05 |
| ❑ 17 B.J. Surhoff | .75 | .35 |
| ❑ 18 Chuck Crim | .10 | .05 |
| ❑ 19 Mike Birkbeck | .10 | .05 |
| ❑ 20 Chris Bosio | .25 | .11 |
| ❑ 21 Les Straker | .10 | .05 |
| ❑ 22 Mark Davidson | .10 | .05 |
| ❑ 23 Gene Larkin XRC | .10 | .05 |
| ❑ 24 Ken Gerhart | .10 | .05 |
| ❑ 25 Luis Polonia XRC | .25 | .11 |
| ❑ 26 Terry Steinbach | .75 | .35 |
| ❑ 27 Mickey Brantley | .10 | .05 |
| ❑ 28 Mike Stanley | .75 | .35 |
| ❑ 29 Jerry Browne | .10 | .05 |
| ❑ 30 Todd Benzinger XRC | .10 | .05 |
| ❑ 31 Fred McGriff | 1.00 | .45 |
| ❑ 32 Mike Henneman XRC | .50 | .23 |
| ❑ 33 Casey Candaele | .10 | .05 |
| ❑ 34 Dave Magadan | .25 | .11 |
| ❑ 35 David Cone | 1.50 | .70 |
| ❑ 36 Mike Jackson XRC | .25 | .11 |
| ❑ 37 John Mitchell | .10 | .05 |
| ❑ 38 Mike Dunne | .10 | .05 |
| ❑ 39 John Smiley XRC | .10 | .05 |
| ❑ 40 Joe Magrane XRC | .10 | .05 |
| ❑ 41 Jim Lindeman | .10 | .05 |
| ❑ 42 Shane Mack XRC** | .25 | .11 |
| ❑ 43 Stan Jefferson | .10 | .05 |
| ❑ 44 Benito Santiago | .25 | .11 |
| ❑ 45 Matt Williams XRC | 3.00 | 1.35 |
| ❑ 46 Dave Meads | .10 | .05 |
| ❑ 47 Rafael Palmeiro | 5.00 | 2.20 |
| ❑ 48 Bill Long | .10 | .05 |
| ❑ 49 Bob Brower | .10 | .05 |
| ❑ 50 James Steels | .10 | .05 |
| ❑ 51 Paul Noce | .10 | .05 |
| ❑ 52 Greg Maddux | 10.00 | 4.50 |
| ❑ 53 Jeff Musselman | .10 | .05 |
| ❑ 54 Brian Holton | .10 | .05 |
| ❑ 55 Chuck Jackson | .10 | .05 |
| ❑ 56 Checklist 1-56 | .10 | .05 |

## 1988 Donruss

| | MINT | NRMT |
|---|---|---|
| COMPLETE SET (660) | 12.00 | 5.50 |
| COMP.FACT.SET (660) | 12.00 | 5.50 |
| COMMON CARD (1-660) | .05 | .02 |
| COMMON SP (648-660) | .07 | .03 |
| COMP.MUSIAL PUZZLE | 1.00 | .45 |
| ❑ 1 Mark McGwire DK | 1.00 | .45 |
| ❑ 2 Tim Raines DK | .10 | .05 |
| ❑ 3 Benito Santiago DK | .05 | .02 |
| ❑ 4 Alan Trammell DK | .05 | .02 |
| ❑ 5 Danny Tartabull DK | .05 | .02 |
| ❑ 6 Ron Darling DK | .05 | .02 |
| ❑ 7 Paul Molitor DK | .20 | .09 |
| ❑ 8 Devon White DK | .05 | .02 |
| ❑ 9 Andre Dawson DK | .10 | .05 |
| ❑ 10 Julio Franco DK | .05 | .02 |
| ❑ 11 Scott Fletcher DK | .05 | .02 |
| ❑ 12 Tony Fernandez DK | .05 | .02 |
| ❑ 13 Shane Rawley DK | .05 | .02 |
| ❑ 14 Kal Daniels DK | .05 | .02 |
| ❑ 15 Jack Clark DK | .10 | .05 |
| ❑ 16 Dwight Evans DK | .05 | .02 |
| ❑ 17 Tommy John DK | .05 | .02 |
| ❑ 18 Andy Van Slyke DK | .05 | .02 |
| ❑ 19 Gary Gaetti DK | .05 | .02 |
| ❑ 20 Mark Langston DK | .05 | .02 |
| ❑ 21 Will Clark DK | .20 | .09 |
| ❑ 22 Glenn Hubbard DK | .05 | .02 |
| ❑ 23 Billy Hatcher DK | .05 | .02 |
| ❑ 24 Bob Welch DK | .05 | .02 |
| ❑ 25 Ivan Calderon DK | .05 | .02 |
| ❑ 26 Cal Ripken DK | .40 | .18 |
| ❑ 27 DK Checklist 1-26 | .05 | .02 |
| ❑ 28 Mackey Sasser RR RC | .05 | .02 |
| ❑ 29 Jeff Treadway RR RC | .05 | .02 |
| ❑ 30 Mike Campbell RR | .05 | .02 |
| ❑ 31 Lance Johnson RR RC | .20 | .09 |
| ❑ 32 Nelson Liriano RR | .05 | .02 |
| ❑ 33 Shawn Abner RR | .05 | .02 |
| ❑ 34 Roberto Alomar RR RC | 1.50 | .70 |
| ❑ 35 Shawn Hillegas RR | .05 | .02 |
| ❑ 36 Joey Meyer RR | .05 | .02 |
| ❑ 37 Kevin Elster RR | .05 | .02 |
| ❑ 38 Jose Lind RR RC | .05 | .02 |
| ❑ 39 Kirt Manwaring RR RC | .05 | .02 |
| ❑ 40 Mark Grace RR RC | 1.00 | .45 |
| ❑ 41 Jody Reed RR RC | .10 | .05 |
| ❑ 42 John Farrell RR | .05 | .02 |
| ❑ 43 Al Leiter RR RC | .40 | .18 |
| ❑ 44 Gary Thurman RR | .05 | .02 |
| ❑ 45 Vicente Palacios RR | .05 | .02 |
| ❑ 46 Eddie Williams RR RC | .05 | .02 |
| ❑ 47 Jack McDowell RR RC | .20 | .09 |
| ❑ 48 Ken Dixon | .05 | .02 |
| ❑ 49 Mike Birkbeck | .05 | .02 |
| ❑ 50 Eric King | .05 | .02 |
| ❑ 51 Roger Clemens | .40 | .18 |
| ❑ 52 Pat Clements | .05 | .02 |
| ❑ 53 Fernando Valenzuela | .10 | .05 |
| ❑ 54 Mark Gubicza | .05 | .02 |
| ❑ 55 Jay Howell | .05 | .02 |
| ❑ 56 Floyd Youmans | .05 | .02 |
| ❑ 57 Ed Correa | .05 | .02 |
| ❑ 58 DeWayne Buice | .05 | .02 |
| ❑ 59 Jose DeLeon | .05 | .02 |
| ❑ 60 Danny Cox | .05 | .02 |
| ❑ 61 Nolan Ryan | 1.00 | .45 |
| ❑ 62 Steve Bedrosian | .05 | .02 |
| ❑ 63 Tom Browning | .05 | .02 |
| ❑ 64 Mark Davis | .05 | .02 |
| ❑ 65 R.J. Reynolds | .05 | .02 |
| ❑ 66 Kevin Mitchell | .10 | .05 |
| ❑ 67 Ken Oberkfell | .05 | .02 |
| ❑ 68 Rick Sutcliffe | .10 | .05 |
| ❑ 69 Dwight Gooden | .10 | .05 |
| ❑ 70 Scott Bankhead | .05 | .02 |
| ❑ 71 Bert Blyleven | .10 | .05 |
| ❑ 72 Jimmy Key | .10 | .05 |
| ❑ 73 Les Straker | .05 | .02 |
| ❑ 74 Jim Clancy | .05 | .02 |
| ❑ 75 Mike Moore | .05 | .02 |
| ❑ 76 Ron Darling | .05 | .02 |
| ❑ 77 Ed Lynch | .05 | .02 |
| ❑ 78 Dale Murphy | .20 | .09 |
| ❑ 79 Doug Drabek | .05 | .02 |
| ❑ 80 Scott Garrelts | .05 | .02 |
| ❑ 81 Ed Whitson | .05 | .02 |
| ❑ 82 Rob Murphy | .05 | .02 |
| ❑ 83 Shane Rawley | .05 | .02 |
| ❑ 84 Greg Mathews | .05 | .02 |
| ❑ 85 Jim Deshaies | .05 | .02 |
| ❑ 86 Mike Witt | .05 | .02 |
| ❑ 87 Donnie Hill | .05 | .02 |
| ❑ 88 Jeff Reed | .05 | .02 |
| ❑ 89 Mike Boddicker | .05 | .02 |
| ❑ 90 Ted Higuera | .05 | .02 |
| ❑ 91 Walt Terrell | .05 | .02 |
| ❑ 92 Bob Stanley | .05 | .02 |
| ❑ 93 Dave Righetti | .05 | .02 |
| ❑ 94 Orel Hershiser | .10 | .05 |
| ❑ 95 Chris Bando | .05 | .02 |
| ❑ 96 Bret Saberhagen | .10 | .05 |
| ❑ 97 Curt Young | .05 | .02 |
| ❑ 98 Tim Burke | .05 | .02 |
| ❑ 99 Charlie Hough | .10 | .05 |
| ❑ 100A Checklist 28-137 | .05 | .02 |
| ❑ 100B Checklist 28-133 | .05 | .02 |
| ❑ 101 Bobby Witt | .05 | .02 |
| ❑ 102 George Brett | .40 | .18 |
| ❑ 103 Mickey Tettleton | .05 | .02 |
| ❑ 104 Scott Bailes | .05 | .02 |
| ❑ 105 Mike Pagliarulo | .05 | .02 |
| ❑ 106 Mike Scioscia | .05 | .02 |

| | No. | Player | | |
|---|---|---|---|---|
| ❑ | 107 | Tom Brookens | .05 | .02 |
| ❑ | 108 | Ray Knight | .05 | .02 |
| ❑ | 109 | Dan Plesac | .05 | .02 |
| ❑ | 110 | Wally Joyner | .15 | .07 |
| ❑ | 111 | Bob Forsch | .05 | .02 |
| ❑ | 112 | Mike Scott | .05 | .02 |
| ❑ | 113 | Kevin Gross | .05 | .02 |
| ❑ | 114 | Benito Santiago | .05 | .02 |
| ❑ | 115 | Bob Kipper | .05 | .02 |
| ❑ | 116 | Mike Krukow | .05 | .02 |
| ❑ | 117 | Chris Bosio | .05 | .02 |
| ❑ | 118 | Sid Fernandez | .05 | .02 |
| ❑ | 119 | Jody Davis | .05 | .02 |
| ❑ | 120 | Mike Morgan | .05 | .02 |
| ❑ | 121 | Mark Eichhorn | .05 | .02 |
| ❑ | 122 | Jeff Reardon | .10 | .05 |
| ❑ | 123 | John Franco | .10 | .05 |
| ❑ | 124 | Richard Dotson | .05 | .02 |
| ❑ | 125 | Eric Bell | .05 | .02 |
| ❑ | 126 | Juan Nieves | .05 | .02 |
| ❑ | 127 | Jack Morris | .10 | .05 |
| ❑ | 128 | Rick Rhoden | .05 | .02 |
| ❑ | 129 | Rich Gedman | .05 | .02 |
| ❑ | 130 | Ken Howell | .05 | .02 |
| ❑ | 131 | Brook Jacoby | .05 | .02 |
| ❑ | 132 | Danny Jackson | .05 | .02 |
| ❑ | 133 | Gene Nelson | .05 | .02 |
| ❑ | 134 | Neal Heaton | .05 | .02 |
| ❑ | 135 | Willie Fraser | .05 | .02 |
| ❑ | 136 | Jose Guzman | .05 | .02 |
| ❑ | 137 | Ozzie Guillen | .05 | .02 |
| ❑ | 138 | Bob Knepper | .05 | .02 |
| ❑ | 139 | Mike Jackson RC* | .10 | .05 |
| ❑ | 140 | Joe Magrane RC* | .05 | .02 |
| ❑ | 141 | Jimmy Jones | .05 | .02 |
| ❑ | 142 | Ted Power | .05 | .02 |
| ❑ | 143 | Ozzie Virgil | .05 | .02 |
| ❑ | 144 | Felix Fermin | .05 | .02 |
| ❑ | 145 | Kelly Downs | .05 | .02 |
| ❑ | 146 | Shawon Dunston | .05 | .02 |
| ❑ | 147 | Scott Bradley | .05 | .02 |
| ❑ | 148 | Dave Stieb | .05 | .02 |
| ❑ | 149 | Frank Viola | .05 | .02 |
| ❑ | 150 | Terry Kennedy | .05 | .02 |
| ❑ | 151 | Bill Wegman | .05 | .02 |
| ❑ | 152 | Matt Nokes RC* | .05 | .02 |
| ❑ | 153 | Wade Boggs | .25 | .11 |
| ❑ | 154 | Wayne Tolleson | .05 | .02 |
| ❑ | 155 | Mariano Duncan | .05 | .02 |
| ❑ | 156 | Julio Franco | .05 | .02 |
| ❑ | 157 | Charlie Leibrandt | .05 | .02 |
| ❑ | 158 | Terry Steinbach | .10 | .05 |
| ❑ | 159 | Mike Fitzgerald | .05 | .02 |
| ❑ | 160 | Jack Lazorko | .05 | .02 |
| ❑ | 161 | Mitch Williams | .05 | .02 |
| ❑ | 162 | Greg Walker | .05 | .02 |
| ❑ | 163 | Alan Ashby | .05 | .02 |
| ❑ | 164 | Tony Gwynn | .40 | .18 |
| ❑ | 165 | Bruce Ruffin | .05 | .02 |
| ❑ | 166 | Ron Robinson | .05 | .02 |
| ❑ | 167 | Zane Smith | .05 | .02 |
| ❑ | 168 | Junior Ortiz | .05 | .02 |
| ❑ | 169 | Jamie Moyer | .05 | .02 |
| ❑ | 170 | Tony Pena | .05 | .02 |
| ❑ | 171 | Cal Ripken | .75 | .35 |
| ❑ | 172 | B.J. Surhoff | .10 | .05 |
| ❑ | 173 | Lou Whitaker | .10 | .05 |
| ❑ | 174 | Ellis Burks RC | .25 | .11 |
| ❑ | 175 | Ron Guidry | .05 | .02 |
| ❑ | 176 | Steve Sax | .05 | .02 |
| ❑ | 177 | Danny Tartabull | .05 | .02 |
| ❑ | 178 | Carney Lansford | .10 | .05 |
| ❑ | 179 | Casey Candaele | .05 | .02 |
| ❑ | 180 | Scott Fletcher | .05 | .02 |
| ❑ | 181 | Mark McLemore | .05 | .02 |
| ❑ | 182 | Ivan Calderon | .05 | .02 |
| ❑ | 183 | Jack Clark | .10 | .05 |
| ❑ | 184 | Glenn Davis | .05 | .02 |
| ❑ | 185 | Luis Aguayo | .05 | .02 |
| ❑ | 186 | Bo Diaz | .05 | .02 |
| ❑ | 187 | Stan Jefferson | .05 | .02 |
| ❑ | 188 | Sid Bream | .05 | .02 |
| ❑ | 189 | Bob Brenly | .05 | .02 |
| ❑ | 190 | Dion James | .05 | .02 |
| ❑ | 191 | Leon Durham | .05 | .02 |
| ❑ | 192 | Jesse Orosco | .05 | .02 |
| ❑ | 193 | Alvin Davis | .05 | .02 |
| ❑ | 194 | Gary Gaetti | .10 | .05 |
| ❑ | 195 | Fred McGriff | .20 | .09 |
| ❑ | 196 | Steve Lombardozzi | .05 | .02 |
| ❑ | 197 | Rance Mulliniks | .05 | .02 |
| ❑ | 198 | Rey Quinones | .05 | .02 |
| ❑ | 199 | Gary Carter | .15 | .07 |
| ❑ | 200A | Checklist 138-247 | .05 | .02 |
| ❑ | 200B | Checklist 134-239 | .05 | .02 |
| ❑ | 201 | Keith Moreland | .05 | .02 |
| ❑ | 202 | Ken Griffey | .10 | .05 |
| ❑ | 203 | Tommy Gregg | .05 | .02 |
| ❑ | 204 | Will Clark | .25 | .11 |
| ❑ | 205 | John Kruk | .10 | .05 |
| ❑ | 206 | Buddy Bell | .10 | .05 |
| ❑ | 207 | Von Hayes | .05 | .02 |
| ❑ | 208 | Tommy Herr | .05 | .02 |
| ❑ | 209 | Craig Reynolds | .05 | .02 |
| ❑ | 210 | Gary Pettis | .05 | .02 |
| ❑ | 211 | Harold Baines | .10 | .05 |
| ❑ | 212 | Vance Law | .05 | .02 |
| ❑ | 213 | Ken Gerhart | .05 | .02 |
| ❑ | 214 | Jim Gantner | .05 | .02 |
| ❑ | 215 | Chet Lemon | .05 | .02 |
| ❑ | 216 | Dwight Evans | .10 | .05 |
| ❑ | 217 | Don Mattingly | .50 | .23 |
| ❑ | 218 | Franklin Stubbs | .05 | .02 |
| ❑ | 219 | Pat Tabler | .05 | .02 |
| ❑ | 220 | Bo Jackson | .20 | .09 |
| ❑ | 221 | Tony Phillips | .05 | .02 |
| ❑ | 222 | Tim Wallach | .05 | .02 |
| ❑ | 223 | Ruben Sierra | .05 | .02 |
| ❑ | 224 | Steve Buechele | .05 | .02 |
| ❑ | 225 | Frank White | .10 | .05 |
| ❑ | 226 | Alfredo Griffin | .05 | .02 |
| ❑ | 227 | Greg Swindell | .05 | .02 |
| ❑ | 228 | Willie Randolph | .10 | .05 |
| ❑ | 229 | Mike Marshall | .05 | .02 |
| ❑ | 230 | Alan Trammell | .15 | .07 |
| ❑ | 231 | Eddie Murray | .20 | .09 |
| ❑ | 232 | Dale Sveum | .05 | .02 |
| ❑ | 233 | Dick Schofield | .05 | .02 |
| ❑ | 234 | Jose Oquendo | .05 | .02 |
| ❑ | 235 | Bill Doran | .05 | .02 |
| ❑ | 236 | Milt Thompson | .05 | .02 |
| ❑ | 237 | Marvell Wynne | .05 | .02 |
| ❑ | 238 | Bobby Bonilla | .10 | .05 |
| ❑ | 239 | Chris Speier | .05 | .02 |
| ❑ | 240 | Glenn Braggs | .05 | .02 |
| ❑ | 241 | Wally Backman | .05 | .02 |
| ❑ | 242 | Ryne Sandberg | .25 | .11 |
| ❑ | 243 | Phil Bradley | .05 | .02 |
| ❑ | 244 | Kelly Gruber | .05 | .02 |
| ❑ | 245 | Tom Brunansky | .05 | .02 |
| ❑ | 246 | Ron Oester | .05 | .02 |
| ❑ | 247 | Bobby Thigpen | .05 | .02 |
| ❑ | 248 | Fred Lynn | .05 | .02 |
| ❑ | 249 | Paul Molitor | .20 | .09 |
| ❑ | 250 | Darrell Evans | .10 | .05 |
| ❑ | 251 | Gary Ward | .05 | .02 |
| ❑ | 252 | Bruce Hurst | .05 | .02 |
| ❑ | 253 | Bob Welch | .05 | .02 |
| ❑ | 254 | Joe Carter | .20 | .09 |
| ❑ | 255 | Willie Wilson | .05 | .02 |
| ❑ | 256 | Mark McGwire | 2.00 | .90 |
| ❑ | 257 | Mitch Webster | .05 | .02 |
| ❑ | 258 | Brian Downing | .05 | .02 |
| ❑ | 259 | Mike Stanley | .10 | .05 |
| ❑ | 260 | Carlton Fisk | .20 | .09 |
| ❑ | 261 | Billy Hatcher | .05 | .02 |
| ❑ | 262 | Glenn Wilson | .05 | .02 |
| ❑ | 263 | Ozzie Smith | .25 | .11 |
| ❑ | 264 | Randy Ready | .05 | .02 |
| ❑ | 265 | Kurt Stillwell | .05 | .02 |
| ❑ | 266 | David Palmer | .05 | .02 |
| ❑ | 267 | Mike Diaz | .05 | .02 |
| ❑ | 268 | Robby Thompson | .05 | .02 |
| ❑ | 269 | Andre Dawson | .15 | .07 |
| ❑ | 270 | Lee Guetterman | .05 | .02 |
| ❑ | 271 | Willie Upshaw | .05 | .02 |
| ❑ | 272 | Randy Bush | .05 | .02 |
| ❑ | 273 | Larry Sheets | .05 | .02 |
| ❑ | 274 | Rob Deer | .05 | .02 |
| ❑ | 275 | Kirk Gibson | .10 | .05 |
| ❑ | 276 | Marty Barrett | .05 | .02 |
| ❑ | 277 | Rickey Henderson | .25 | .11 |
| ❑ | 278 | Pedro Guerrero | .05 | .02 |
| ❑ | 279 | Brett Butler | .10 | .05 |
| ❑ | 280 | Kevin Seitzer | .10 | .05 |
| ❑ | 281 | Mike Davis | .05 | .02 |
| ❑ | 282 | Andres Galarraga | .15 | .07 |
| ❑ | 283 | Devon White | .10 | .05 |
| ❑ | 284 | Pete O'Brien | .05 | .02 |
| ❑ | 285 | Jerry Hairston | .05 | .02 |
| ❑ | 286 | Kevin Bass | .05 | .02 |
| ❑ | 287 | Carmelo Martinez | .05 | .02 |
| ❑ | 288 | Juan Samuel | .05 | .02 |
| ❑ | 289 | Kal Daniels | .05 | .02 |
| ❑ | 290 | Albert Hall | .05 | .02 |
| ❑ | 291 | Andy Van Slyke | .10 | .05 |
| ❑ | 292 | Lee Smith | .10 | .05 |
| ❑ | 293 | Vince Coleman | .05 | .02 |
| ❑ | 294 | Tom Niedenfuer | .05 | .02 |
| ❑ | 295 | Robin Yount | .20 | .09 |
| ❑ | 296 | Jeff M. Robinson | .05 | .02 |
| ❑ | 297 | Todd Benzinger RC* | .05 | .02 |
| ❑ | 298 | Dave Winfield | .20 | .09 |
| ❑ | 299 | Mickey Hatcher | .05 | .02 |
| ❑ | 300A | Checklist 248-357 | .05 | .02 |
| ❑ | 300B | Checklist 240-345 | .05 | .02 |
| ❑ | 301 | Bud Black | .05 | .02 |
| ❑ | 302 | Jose Canseco | .40 | .18 |
| ❑ | 303 | Tom Foley | .05 | .02 |
| ❑ | 304 | Pete Incaviglia | .05 | .02 |
| ❑ | 305 | Bob Boone | .10 | .05 |
| ❑ | 306 | Bill Long | .05 | .02 |
| ❑ | 307 | Willie McGee | .10 | .05 |
| ❑ | 308 | Ken Caminiti RC | .50 | .23 |
| ❑ | 309 | Darren Daulton | .10 | .05 |
| ❑ | 310 | Tracy Jones | .05 | .02 |
| ❑ | 311 | Greg Booker | .05 | .02 |
| ❑ | 312 | Mike LaValliere | .05 | .02 |
| ❑ | 313 | Chili Davis | .15 | .07 |
| ❑ | 314 | Glenn Hubbard | .05 | .02 |
| ❑ | 315 | Paul Noce | .05 | .02 |
| ❑ | 316 | Keith Hernandez | .10 | .05 |
| ❑ | 317 | Mark Langston | .05 | .02 |
| ❑ | 318 | Keith Atherton | .05 | .02 |
| ❑ | 319 | Tony Fernandez | .05 | .02 |
| ❑ | 320 | Kent Hrbek | .10 | .05 |
| ❑ | 321 | John Cerutti | .05 | .02 |
| ❑ | 322 | Mike Kingery | .05 | .02 |
| ❑ | 323 | Dave Magadan | .05 | .02 |
| ❑ | 324 | Rafael Palmeiro | .40 | .18 |
| ❑ | 325 | Jeff Dedmon | .05 | .02 |
| ❑ | 326 | Barry Bonds | .60 | .25 |
| ❑ | 327 | Jeffrey Leonard | .05 | .02 |
| ❑ | 328 | Tim Flannery | .05 | .02 |
| ❑ | 329 | Dave Concepcion | .10 | .05 |
| ❑ | 330 | Mike Schmidt | .40 | .18 |
| ❑ | 331 | Bill Dawley | .05 | .02 |
| ❑ | 332 | Larry Andersen | .05 | .02 |
| ❑ | 333 | Jack Howell | .05 | .02 |
| ❑ | 334 | Ken Williams | .05 | .02 |
| ❑ | 335 | Bryn Smith | .05 | .02 |
| ❑ | 336 | Bill Ripken RC* | .05 | .02 |
| ❑ | 337 | Greg Brock | .05 | .02 |
| ❑ | 338 | Mike Heath | .05 | .02 |
| ❑ | 339 | Mike Greenwell | .05 | .02 |
| ❑ | 340 | Claudell Washington | .05 | .02 |
| ❑ | 341 | Jose Gonzalez | .05 | .02 |
| ❑ | 342 | Mel Hall | .05 | .02 |
| ❑ | 343 | Jim Eisenreich | .20 | .09 |
| ❑ | 344 | Tony Bernazard | .05 | .02 |
| ❑ | 345 | Tim Raines | .10 | .05 |
| ❑ | 346 | Bob Brower | .05 | .02 |
| ❑ | 347 | Larry Parrish | .05 | .02 |
| ❑ | 348 | Thad Bosley | .05 | .02 |
| ❑ | 349 | Dennis Eckersley | .10 | .05 |
| ❑ | 350 | Cory Snyder | .05 | .02 |
| ❑ | 351 | Rick Cerone | .05 | .02 |
| ❑ | 352 | John Shelby | .05 | .02 |
| ❑ | 353 | Larry Herndon | .05 | .02 |
| ❑ | 354 | John Habyan | .05 | .02 |
| ❑ | 355 | Chuck Crim | .05 | .02 |
| ❑ | 356 | Gus Polidor | .05 | .02 |
| ❑ | 357 | Ken Dayley | .05 | .02 |
| ❑ | 358 | Danny Darwin | .05 | .02 |
| ❑ | 359 | Lance Parrish | .05 | .02 |
| ❑ | 360 | James Steels | .05 | .02 |
| ❑ | 361 | Al Pedrique | .05 | .02 |
| ❑ | 362 | Mike Aldrete | .05 | .02 |

❑ 363 Juan Castillo .05 .02
❑ 364 Len Dykstra .10 .05
❑ 365 Luis Quinones .05 .02
❑ 366 Jim Presley .05 .02
❑ 367 Lloyd Moseby .05 .02
❑ 368 Kirby Puckett .50 .23
❑ 369 Eric Davis .10 .05
❑ 370 Gary Redus .05 .02
❑ 371 Dave Schmidt .05 .02
❑ 372 Mark Clear .05 .02
❑ 373 Dave Bergman .05 .02
❑ 374 Charles Hudson .05 .02
❑ 375 Calvin Schiraldi .05 .02
❑ 376 Alex Trevino .05 .02
❑ 377 Tom Candiotti .05 .02
❑ 378 Steve Farr .05 .02
❑ 379 Mike Gallego .05 .02
❑ 380 Andy McGaffigan .05 .02
❑ 381 Kirk McCaskill .05 .02
❑ 382 Oddibe McDowell .05 .02
❑ 383 Floyd Bannister .05 .02
❑ 384 Denny Walling .05 .02
❑ 385 Don Carman .05 .02
❑ 386 Todd Worrell .10 .05
❑ 387 Eric Show .05 .02
❑ 388 Dave Parker .10 .05
❑ 389 Rick Mahler .05 .02
❑ 390 Mike Dunne .05 .02
❑ 391 Candy Maldonado .05 .02
❑ 392 Bob Dernier .05 .02
❑ 393 Dave Valle .05 .02
❑ 394 Ernie Whitt .05 .02
❑ 395 Juan Berenguer .05 .02
❑ 396 Mike Young .05 .02
❑ 397 Mike Felder .05 .02
❑ 398 Willie Hernandez .05 .02
❑ 399 Jim Rice .10 .05
❑ 400A Checklist 358-467 .05 .02
❑ 400B Checklist 346-451 .05 .02
❑ 401 Tommy John .10 .05
❑ 402 Brian Holton .05 .02
❑ 403 Carmen Castillo .05 .02
❑ 404 Jamie Quirk .05 .02
❑ 405 Dwayne Murphy .05 .02
❑ 406 Jeff Parrett .05 .02
❑ 407 Don Sutton .20 .09
❑ 408 Jerry Browne .05 .02
❑ 409 Jim Winn .05 .02
❑ 410 Dave Smith .05 .02
❑ 411 Shane Mack .05 .02
❑ 412 Greg Gross .05 .02
❑ 413 Nick Esasky .05 .02
❑ 414 Damaso Garcia .05 .02
❑ 415 Brian Fisher .05 .02
❑ 416 Brian Dayett .05 .02
❑ 417 Curt Ford .05 .02
❑ 418 Mark Williamson .05 .02
❑ 419 Bill Schroeder .05 .02
❑ 420 Mike Henneman RC* .10 .05
❑ 421 John Marzano .05 .02
❑ 422 Ron Kittle .05 .02
❑ 423 Matt Young .05 .02
❑ 424 Steve Balboni .05 .02
❑ 425 Luis Polonia RC* .05 .02
❑ 426 Randy St.Claire .05 .02
❑ 427 Greg Harris .05 .02
❑ 428 Johnny Ray .05 .02
❑ 429 Ray Searage .05 .02
❑ 430 Ricky Horton .05 .02
❑ 431 Gerald Young .05 .02
❑ 432 Rick Schu .05 .02
❑ 433 Paul O'Neill .15 .07
❑ 434 Rich Gossage .10 .05
❑ 435 John Cangelosi .05 .02
❑ 436 Mike LaCoss .05 .02
❑ 437 Gerald Perry .05 .02
❑ 438 Dave Martinez .05 .02
❑ 439 Darryl Strawberry .10 .05
❑ 440 John Moses .05 .02
❑ 441 Greg Gagne .05 .02
❑ 442 Jesse Barfield .05 .02
❑ 443 George Frazier .05 .02
❑ 444 Garth Iorg .05 .02
❑ 445 Ed Nunez .05 .02
❑ 446 Rick Aguilera .10 .05
❑ 447 Jerry Mumphrey .05 .02
❑ 448 Rafael Ramirez .05 .02
❑ 449 John Smiley RC* .10 .05
❑ 450 Atlee Hammaker .05 .02
❑ 451 Lance McCullers .05 .02
❑ 452 Guy Hoffman .05 .02
❑ 453 Chris James .05 .02
❑ 454 Terry Pendleton .10 .05
❑ 455 Dave Meads .05 .02
❑ 456 Bill Buckner .10 .05
❑ 457 John Pawlowski .05 .02
❑ 458 Bob Sebra .05 .02
❑ 459 Jim Dwyer .05 .02
❑ 460 Jay Aldrich .05 .02
❑ 461 Frank Tanana .05 .02
❑ 462 Oil Can Boyd .05 .02
❑ 463 Dan Pasqua .05 .02
❑ 464 Tim Crews RC .05 .02
❑ 465 Andy Allanson .05 .02
❑ 466 Bill Pecota RC* .05 .02
❑ 467 Steve Ontiveros .05 .02
❑ 468 Hubie Brooks .05 .02
❑ 469 Paul Kilgus .05 .02
❑ 470 Dale Mohorcic .05 .02
❑ 471 Dan Quisenberry .05 .02
❑ 472 Dave Stewart .10 .05
❑ 473 Dave Clark .05 .02
❑ 474 Joel Skinner .05 .02
❑ 475 Dave Anderson .05 .02
❑ 476 Dan Petry .05 .02
❑ 477 Carl Nichols .05 .02
❑ 478 Ernest Riles .05 .02
❑ 479 George Hendrick .05 .02
❑ 480 John Morris .05 .02
❑ 481 Manny Hernandez .05 .02
❑ 482 Jeff Stone .05 .02
❑ 483 Chris Brown .05 .02
❑ 484 Mike Bielecki .05 .02
❑ 485 Dave Dravecky .10 .05
❑ 486 Rick Manning .05 .02
❑ 487 Bill Almon .05 .02
❑ 488 Jim Sundberg .05 .02
❑ 489 Ken Phelps .05 .02
❑ 490 Tom Henke .05 .02
❑ 491 Dan Gladden .05 .02
❑ 492 Barry Larkin .20 .09
❑ 493 Fred Manrique .05 .02
❑ 494 Mike Griffin .05 .02
❑ 495 Mark Knudson .05 .02
❑ 496 Bill Madlock .10 .05
❑ 497 Tim Stoddard .05 .02
❑ 498 Sam Horn RC .05 .02
❑ 499 Tracy Woodson RC .05 .02
❑ 500A Checklist 468-577 .05 .02
❑ 500B Checklist 452-557 .05 .02
❑ 501 Ken Schrom .05 .02
❑ 502 Angel Salazar .05 .02
❑ 503 Eric Plunk .05 .02
❑ 504 Joe Hesketh .05 .02
❑ 505 Greg Minton .05 .02
❑ 506 Geno Petralli .05 .02
❑ 507 Bob James .05 .02
❑ 508 Robbie Wine .05 .02
❑ 509 Jeff Calhoun .05 .02
❑ 510 Steve Lake .05 .02
❑ 511 Mark Grant .05 .02
❑ 512 Frank Williams .05 .02
❑ 513 Jeff Blauser RC .20 .09
❑ 514 Bob Walk .05 .02
❑ 515 Craig Lefferts .05 .02
❑ 516 Manny Trillo .05 .02
❑ 517 Jerry Reed .05 .02
❑ 518 Rick Leach .05 .02
❑ 519 Mark Davidson .05 .02
❑ 520 Jeff Ballard .05 .02
❑ 521 Dave Stapleton .05 .02
❑ 522 Pat Sheridan .05 .02
❑ 523 Al Nipper .05 .02
❑ 524 Steve Trout .05 .02
❑ 525 Jeff Hamilton .05 .02
❑ 526 Tommy Hinzo .05 .02
❑ 527 Lonnie Smith .05 .02
❑ 528 Greg Cadaret .05 .02
❑ 529 Bob McClure UER .05 .02
(Rob on front)
❑ 530 Chuck Finley .15 .07
❑ 531 Jeff Russell .05 .02
❑ 532 Steve Lyons .05 .02
❑ 533 Terry Puhl .05 .02
❑ 534 Eric Nolte .05 .02
❑ 535 Kent Tekulve .05 .02
❑ 536 Pat Pacillo .05 .02
❑ 537 Charlie Puleo .05 .02
❑ 538 Tom Prince .05 .02
❑ 539 Greg Maddux 1.00 .45
❑ 540 Jim Lindeman .05 .02
❑ 541 Pete Stanicek .05 .02
❑ 542 Steve Kiefer .05 .02
❑ 543A Jim Morrison ERR .20 .09
(No decimal before lifetime average)
❑ 543B Jim Morrison COR .05 .02
❑ 544 Spike Owen .05 .02
❑ 545 Jay Buhner RC .40 .18
❑ 546 Mike Devereaux RC .10 .05
❑ 547 Jerry Don Gleaton .05 .02
❑ 548 Jose Rijo .05 .02
❑ 549 Dennis Martinez .10 .05
❑ 550 Mike Loynd .05 .02
❑ 551 Darrell Miller .05 .02
❑ 552 Dave LaPoint .05 .02
❑ 553 John Tudor .05 .02
❑ 554 Rocky Childress .05 .02
❑ 555 Wally Ritchie .05 .02
❑ 556 Terry McGriff .05 .02
❑ 557 Dave Leiper .05 .02
❑ 558 Jeff D. Robinson .05 .02
❑ 559 Jose Uribe .05 .02
❑ 560 Ted Simmons .10 .05
❑ 561 Les Lancaster .05 .02
❑ 562 Keith A. Miller RC .05 .02
❑ 563 Harold Reynolds .10 .05
❑ 564 Gene Larkin RC* .05 .02
❑ 565 Cecil Fielder .15 .07
❑ 566 Roy Smalley .05 .02
❑ 567 Duane Ward .05 .02
❑ 568 Bill Wilkinson .05 .02
❑ 569 Howard Johnson .05 .02
❑ 570 Frank DiPino .05 .02
❑ 571 Pete Smith RC .05 .02
❑ 572 Darnell Coles .05 .02
❑ 573 Don Robinson .05 .02
❑ 574 Rob Nelson UER .05 .02
(Career 0 RBI, but 1 RBI in '87)
❑ 575 Dennis Rasmussen .05 .02
❑ 576 Steve Jeltz UER .05 .02
(Photo actually Juan Samuel; Samuel noted for one batting glove and black bat)
❑ 577 Tom Pagnozzi RC .05 .02
❑ 578 Ty Gainey .05 .02
❑ 579 Gary Lucas .05 .02
❑ 580 Ron Hassey .05 .02
❑ 581 Herm Winningham .05 .02
❑ 582 Rene Gonzales RC .05 .02
❑ 583 Brad Komminsk .05 .02
❑ 584 Doyle Alexander .05 .02
❑ 585 Jeff Sellers .05 .02
❑ 586 Bill Gullickson .05 .02
❑ 587 Tim Belcher .10 .05
❑ 588 Doug Jones RC .20 .09
❑ 589 Melido Perez RC .05 .02
❑ 590 Rick Honeycutt .05 .02
❑ 591 Pascual Perez .05 .02
❑ 592 Curt Wilkerson .05 .02
❑ 593 Steve Howe .05 .02
❑ 594 John Davis .05 .02
❑ 595 Storm Davis .05 .02
❑ 596 Sammy Stewart .05 .02
❑ 597 Neil Allen .05 .02
❑ 598 Alejandro Pena .05 .02
❑ 599 Mark Thurmond .05 .02
❑ 600A Checklist 578-660 .05 .02
BC1-BC26
❑ 600B Checklist 558-660 .05 .02
❑ 601 Jose Mesa RC .15 .07
❑ 602 Don August .05 .02
❑ 603 Terry Leach SP .07 .03
❑ 604 Tom Newell .05 .02
❑ 605 Randall Byers SP .07 .03
❑ 606 Jim Gott .05 .02

❑ 607 Harry Spilman .05 .02
❑ 608 John Candelaria .05 .02
❑ 609 Mike Brumley .05 .02
❑ 610 Mickey Brantley .05 .02
❑ 611 Jose Nunez SP .07 .03
❑ 612 Tom Nieto .05 .02
❑ 613 Rick Reuschel .05 .02
❑ 614 Lee Mazzilli SP .07 .03
❑ 615 Scott Lusader .05 .02
❑ 616 Bobby Meacham .05 .02
❑ 617 Kevin McReynolds SP .07 .03
❑ 618 Gene Garber .05 .02
❑ 619 Barry Lyons SP .07 .03
❑ 620 Randy Myers .15 .07
❑ 621 Donnie Moore .05 .02
❑ 622 Domingo Ramos .05 .02
❑ 623 Ed Romero .05 .02
❑ 624 Greg Myers RC .05 .02
❑ 625 Ripken Family .40 .18
Cal Ripken Sr.
Cal Ripken Jr.
Billy Ripken
❑ 626 Pat Perry .05 .02
❑ 627 Andres Thomas SP .07 .03
❑ 628 Matt Williams SP RC .75 .35
❑ 629 Dave Hengel .05 .02
❑ 630 Jeff Musselman SP .07 .03
❑ 631 Tim Laudner .05 .02
❑ 632 Bob Ojeda SP .07 .03
❑ 633 Rafael Santana .05 .02
❑ 634 Wes Gardner .05 .02
❑ 635 Roberto Kelly RC SP .20 .09
❑ 636 Mike Flanagan SP .07 .03
❑ 637 Jay Bell RC .50 .23
❑ 638 Bob Melvin .05 .02
❑ 639 Damon Berryhill RC UER .05 .02
(Bats: Swithch)
❑ 640 David Wells SP RC 1.00 .45
❑ 641 Stan Musial PUZ .20 .09
❑ 642 Doug Sisk .05 .02
❑ 643 Keith Hughes .05 .02
❑ 644 Tom Glavine RC 1.25 .55
❑ 645 Al Newman .05 .02
❑ 646 Scott Sanderson .05 .02
❑ 647 Scott Terry .05 .02
❑ 648 Tim Teufel SP .07 .03
❑ 649 Garry Templeton SP .07 .03
❑ 650 Manny Lee SP .07 .03
❑ 651 Roger McDowell SP .07 .03
❑ 652 Mookie Wilson SP .20 .09
❑ 653 David Cone SP .10 .05
❑ 654 Ron Gant SP RC .25 .11
❑ 655 Joe Price SP .07 .03
❑ 656 George Bell SP .10 .05
❑ 657 Gregg Jefferies SP RC .20 .09
❑ 658 Todd Stottlemyre SP RC .20 .09
❑ 659 Geronimo Berroa SP RC .25 .11
❑ 660 Jerry Royster SP .07 .03
❑ XX Kirby Puckett 2.00 .90
Blister Pack

## 1988 Donruss Rookies

| | MINT | NRMT |
|---|---|---|
| COMP.FACT.SET (56) | 12.00 | 5.50 |

❑ 1 Mark Grace 2.50 1.10
❑ 2 Mike Campbell .15 .07
❑ 3 Todd Frohwirth .15 .07
❑ 4 Dave Stapleton .15 .07
❑ 5 Shawn Abner .15 .07
❑ 6 Jose Cecena .15 .07
❑ 7 Dave Gallagher .15 .07
❑ 8 Mark Parent .15 .07
❑ 9 Cecil Espy .15 .07
❑ 10 Pete Smith .15 .07
❑ 11 Jay Buhner 1.00 .45
❑ 12 Pat Borders XRC .30 .14
❑ 13 Doug Jennings .15 .07
❑ 14 Brady Anderson XRC 1.50 .70
❑ 15 Pete Stanicek .15 .07
❑ 16 Roberto Kelly .30 .14
❑ 17 Jeff Treadway .15 .07
❑ 18 Walt Weiss XRC* 1.00 .45
❑ 19 Paul Gibson .15 .07
❑ 20 Tim Crews .15 .07
❑ 21 Melido Perez .15 .07
❑ 22 Steve Peters .15 .07
❑ 23 Craig Worthington .15 .07
❑ 24 John Trautwein .15 .07
❑ 25 DeWayne Vaughn .15 .07
❑ 26 David Wells 3.00 1.35
❑ 27 Al Leiter 1.50 .70
❑ 28 Tim Belcher .30 .14
❑ 29 Johnny Paredes .15 .07
❑ 30 Chris Sabo XRC .30 .14
❑ 31 Damon Berryhill .15 .07
❑ 32 Randy Milligan XRC* .15 .07
❑ 33 Gary Thurman .15 .07
❑ 34 Kevin Elster .15 .07
❑ 35 Roberto Alomar 5.00 2.20
❑ 36 Edgar Martinez UER XRC 3.00 1.35
(Photo actually
Edwin Nunez)
❑ 37 Todd Stottlemyre .30 .14
❑ 38 Joey Meyer .15 .07
❑ 39 Carl Nichols .15 .07
❑ 40 Jack McDowell .60 .25
❑ 41 Jose Bautista .15 .07
❑ 42 Sil Campusano .15 .07
❑ 43 John Dopson .15 .07
❑ 44 Jody Reed .30 .14
❑ 45 Darrin Jackson XRC* .15 .07
❑ 46 Mike Capel .15 .07
❑ 47 Ron Gant .30 .14
❑ 48 John Davis .15 .07
❑ 49 Kevin Coffman .15 .07
❑ 50 Cris Carpenter XRC .15 .07
❑ 51 Mackey Sasser .15 .07
❑ 52 Luis Alicea XRC .15 .07
❑ 53 Bryan Harvey XRC .30 .14
❑ 54 Steve Ellsworth .15 .07
❑ 55 Mike Macfarlane XRC .15 .07
❑ 56 Checklist 1-56 .15 .07

## 1989 Donruss

| | MINT | NRMT |
|---|---|---|
| COMPLETE SET (660) | 30.00 | 13.50 |
| COMP.FACT.SET (672) | 40.00 | 18.00 |
| COMP.SPAHN PUZZLE | 1.00 | .45 |

❑ 1 Mike Greenwell DK .05 .02
❑ 2 Bobby Bonilla DK DP .10 .05
❑ 3 Pete Incaviglia DK .05 .02
❑ 4 Chris Sabo DK DP .05 .02
❑ 5 Robin Yount DK .10 .05
❑ 6 Tony Gwynn DK DP .20 .09
❑ 7 Carlton Fisk DK UER .10 .05
(OF on back)
❑ 8 Cory Snyder DK .05 .02
❑ 9 David Cone DK UER .05 .02
("Hurdlers")
❑ 10 Kevin Seitzer DK .05 .02
❑ 11 Rick Reuschel DK .05 .02
❑ 12 Johnny Ray DK .05 .02
❑ 13 Dave Schmidt DK .05 .02
❑ 14 Andres Galarraga DK .05 .02
❑ 15 Kirk Gibson DK .05 .02
❑ 16 Fred McGriff DK .10 .05
❑ 17 Mark Grace DK .10 .05
❑ 18 Jeff M. Robinson DK .05 .02
❑ 19 Vince Coleman DK DP .05 .02
❑ 20 Dave Henderson DK .05 .02
❑ 21 Harold Reynolds DK .05 .02
❑ 22 Gerald Perry DK .05 .02
❑ 23 Frank Viola DK .05 .02
❑ 24 Steve Bedrosian DK .05 .02
❑ 25 Glenn Davis DK .05 .02
❑ 26 Don Mattingly DK UER .15 .07
(Doesn't mention Don's
previous DK in 1985)
❑ 27 DK Checklist 1-26 DP .05 .02
❑ 28 Sandy Alomar Jr. RR RC .25 .11
❑ 29 Steve Searcy RR .05 .02
❑ 30 Cameron Drew RR .05 .02
❑ 31 Gary Sheffield RR RC 1.50 .70
❑ 32 Erik Hanson RR RC .10 .05
❑ 33 Ken Griffey Jr. RR RC ! 20.00 9.00
❑ 34 Greg W. Harris RR RC .05 .02
❑ 35 Gregg Jefferies RR .10 .05
❑ 36 Luis Medina RR .05 .02
❑ 37 Carlos Quintana RR RC .05 .02
❑ 38 Felix Jose RR RC .05 .02
❑ 39 Cris Carpenter RR RC* .05 .02
❑ 40 Ron Jones RR .05 .02
❑ 41 Dave West RR RC .05 .02
❑ 42 Randy Johnson RC RR UER 2.50 1.10
(Card says born in 1964
he was born in 1963)
❑ 43 Mike Harkey RR RC .05 .02
❑ 44 Pete Harnisch RR DP RC .25 .11
❑ 45 Tom Gordon RR DP RC .20 .09
❑ 46 Gregg Olson RC RR DP .20 .09
❑ 47 Alex Sanchez RR DP .05 .02
❑ 48 Ruben Sierra .05 .02
❑ 49 Rafael Palmeiro .25 .11
❑ 50 Ron Gant .10 .05
❑ 51 Cal Ripken .75 .35
❑ 52 Wally Joyner .10 .05
❑ 53 Gary Carter .15 .07
❑ 54 Andy Van Slyke .10 .05
❑ 55 Robin Yount .20 .09
❑ 56 Pete Incaviglia .05 .02
❑ 57 Greg Brock .05 .02
❑ 58 Melido Perez .05 .02
❑ 59 Craig Lefferts .05 .02
❑ 60 Gary Pettis .05 .02
❑ 61 Danny Tartabull .05 .02
❑ 62 Guillermo Hernandez .05 .02
❑ 63 Ozzie Smith .25 .11
❑ 64 Gary Gaetti .10 .05
❑ 65 Mark Davis .05 .02
❑ 66 Lee Smith .10 .05
❑ 67 Dennis Eckersley .15 .07
❑ 68 Wade Boggs .25 .11
❑ 69 Mike Scott .05 .02
❑ 70 Fred McGriff .20 .09
❑ 71 Tom Browning .05 .02
❑ 72 Claudell Washington .05 .02
❑ 73 Mel Hall .05 .02
❑ 74 Don Mattingly .50 .23
❑ 75 Steve Bedrosian .05 .02
❑ 76 Juan Samuel .05 .02
❑ 77 Mike Scioscia .05 .02
❑ 78 Dave Righetti .05 .02
❑ 79 Alfredo Griffin .05 .02
❑ 80 Eric Davis UER .10 .05
(165 games in 1988;
should be 135)
❑ 81 Juan Berenguer .05 .02

| | | | |
|---|---|---|---|
| ❑ | 82 Todd Worrell | .05 | .02 |
| ❑ | 83 Joe Carter | .15 | .07 |
| ❑ | 84 Steve Sax | .05 | .02 |
| ❑ | 85 Frank White | .10 | .05 |
| ❑ | 86 John Kruk | .10 | .05 |
| ❑ | 87 Rance Mulliniks | .05 | .02 |
| ❑ | 88 Alan Ashby | .05 | .02 |
| ❑ | 89 Charlie Leibrandt | .05 | .02 |
| ❑ | 90 Frank Tanana | .05 | .02 |
| ❑ | 91 Jose Canseco | .25 | .11 |
| ❑ | 92 Barry Bonds | .50 | .23 |
| ❑ | 93 Harold Reynolds | .05 | .02 |
| ❑ | 94 Mark McLemore | .05 | .02 |
| ❑ | 95 Mark McGwire | 1.00 | .45 |
| ❑ | 96 Eddie Murray | .20 | .09 |
| ❑ | 97 Tim Raines | .10 | .05 |
| ❑ | 98 Robby Thompson | .05 | .02 |
| ❑ | 99 Kevin McReynolds | .05 | .02 |
| ❑ | 100 Checklist 28-137 | .05 | .02 |
| ❑ | 101 Carlton Fisk | .20 | .09 |
| ❑ | 102 Dave Martinez | .05 | .02 |
| ❑ | 103 Glenn Braggs | .05 | .02 |
| ❑ | 104 Dale Murphy | .20 | .09 |
| ❑ | 105 Ryne Sandberg | .25 | .11 |
| ❑ | 106 Dennis Martinez | .10 | .05 |
| ❑ | 107 Pete O'Brien | .05 | .02 |
| ❑ | 108 Dick Schofield | .05 | .02 |
| ❑ | 109 Henry Cotto | .05 | .02 |
| ❑ | 110 Mike Marshall | .05 | .02 |
| ❑ | 111 Keith Moreland | .05 | .02 |
| ❑ | 112 Tom Brunansky | .05 | .02 |
| ❑ | 113 Kelly Gruber UER (Wrong birthdate) | .05 | .02 |
| ❑ | 114 Brook Jacoby | .05 | .02 |
| ❑ | 115 Keith Brown | .05 | .02 |
| ❑ | 116 Matt Nokes | .05 | .02 |
| ❑ | 117 Keith Hernandez | .10 | .05 |
| ❑ | 118 Bob Forsch | .05 | .02 |
| ❑ | 119 Bert Blyleven UER (... 3000 strikeouts in 1987, should be 1986) | .10 | .05 |
| ❑ | 120 Willie Wilson | .05 | .02 |
| ❑ | 121 Tommy Gregg | .05 | .02 |
| ❑ | 122 Jim Rice | .10 | .05 |
| ❑ | 123 Bob Knepper | .05 | .02 |
| ❑ | 124 Danny Jackson | .05 | .02 |
| ❑ | 125 Eric Plunk | .05 | .02 |
| ❑ | 126 Brian Fisher | .05 | .02 |
| ❑ | 127 Mike Pagliarulo | .05 | .02 |
| ❑ | 128 Tony Gwynn | .40 | .18 |
| ❑ | 129 Lance McCullers | .05 | .02 |
| ❑ | 130 Andres Galarraga | .15 | .07 |
| ❑ | 131 Jose Uribe | .05 | .02 |
| ❑ | 132 Kirk Gibson UER (Wrong birthdate) | .10 | .05 |
| ❑ | 133 David Palmer | .05 | .02 |
| ❑ | 134 R.J. Reynolds | .05 | .02 |
| ❑ | 135 Greg Walker | .05 | .02 |
| ❑ | 136 Kirk McCaskill UER (Wrong birthdate) | .05 | .02 |
| ❑ | 137 Shawon Dunston | .05 | .02 |
| ❑ | 138 Andy Allanson | .05 | .02 |
| ❑ | 139 Rob Murphy | .05 | .02 |
| ❑ | 140 Mike Aldrete | .05 | .02 |
| ❑ | 141 Terry Kennedy | .05 | .02 |
| ❑ | 142 Scott Fletcher | .05 | .02 |
| ❑ | 143 Steve Balboni | .05 | .02 |
| ❑ | 144 Bret Saberhagen | .10 | .05 |
| ❑ | 145 Ozzie Virgil | .05 | .02 |
| ❑ | 146 Dale Sveum | .05 | .02 |
| ❑ | 147 Darryl Strawberry | .10 | .05 |
| ❑ | 148 Harold Baines | .10 | .05 |
| ❑ | 149 George Bell | .05 | .02 |
| ❑ | 150 Dave Parker | .10 | .05 |
| ❑ | 151 Bobby Bonilla | .10 | .05 |
| ❑ | 152 Mookie Wilson | .10 | .05 |
| ❑ | 153 Ted Power | .05 | .02 |
| ❑ | 154 Nolan Ryan | 1.00 | .45 |
| ❑ | 155 Jeff Reardon | .10 | .05 |
| ❑ | 156 Tim Wallach | .05 | .02 |
| ❑ | 157 Jamie Moyer | .05 | .02 |
| ❑ | 158 Rich Gossage | .10 | .05 |
| ❑ | 159 Dave Winfield | .20 | .09 |
| ❑ | 160 Von Hayes | .05 | .02 |
| ❑ | 161 Willie McGee | .10 | .05 |
| ❑ | 162 Rich Gedman | .05 | .02 |
| ❑ | 163 Tony Pena | .05 | .02 |
| ❑ | 164 Mike Morgan | .05 | .02 |
| ❑ | 165 Charlie Hough | .10 | .05 |
| ❑ | 166 Mike Stanley | .05 | .02 |
| ❑ | 167 Andre Dawson | .15 | .07 |
| ❑ | 168 Joe Boever | .05 | .02 |
| ❑ | 169 Pete Stanicek | .05 | .02 |
| ❑ | 170 Bob Boone | .10 | .05 |
| ❑ | 171 Ron Darling | .05 | .02 |
| ❑ | 172 Bob Walk | .05 | .02 |
| ❑ | 173 Rob Deer | .05 | .02 |
| ❑ | 174 Steve Buechele | .05 | .02 |
| ❑ | 175 Ted Higuera | .05 | .02 |
| ❑ | 176 Ozzie Guillen | .05 | .02 |
| ❑ | 177 Candy Maldonado | .05 | .02 |
| ❑ | 178 Doyle Alexander | .05 | .02 |
| ❑ | 179 Mark Gubicza | .05 | .02 |
| ❑ | 180 Alan Trammell | .15 | .07 |
| ❑ | 181 Vince Coleman | .05 | .02 |
| ❑ | 182 Kirby Puckett | .50 | .23 |
| ❑ | 183 Chris Brown | .05 | .02 |
| ❑ | 184 Marty Barrett | .05 | .02 |
| ❑ | 185 Stan Javier | .05 | .02 |
| ❑ | 186 Mike Greenwell | .05 | .02 |
| ❑ | 187 Billy Hatcher | .05 | .02 |
| ❑ | 188 Jimmy Key | .10 | .05 |
| ❑ | 189 Nick Esasky | .05 | .02 |
| ❑ | 190 Don Slaught | .05 | .02 |
| ❑ | 191 Cory Snyder | .05 | .02 |
| ❑ | 192 John Candelaria | .05 | .02 |
| ❑ | 193 Mike Schmidt | .40 | .18 |
| ❑ | 194 Kevin Gross | .05 | .02 |
| ❑ | 195 John Tudor | .05 | .02 |
| ❑ | 196 Neil Allen | .05 | .02 |
| ❑ | 197 Orel Hershiser | .10 | .05 |
| ❑ | 198 Kal Daniels | .05 | .02 |
| ❑ | 199 Kent Hrbek | .10 | .05 |
| ❑ | 200 Checklist 138-247 | .05 | .02 |
| ❑ | 201 Joe Magrane | .05 | .02 |
| ❑ | 202 Scott Bailes | .05 | .02 |
| ❑ | 203 Tim Belcher | .05 | .02 |
| ❑ | 204 George Brett | .40 | .18 |
| ❑ | 205 Benito Santiago | .05 | .02 |
| ❑ | 206 Tony Fernandez | .05 | .02 |
| ❑ | 207 Gerald Young | .05 | .02 |
| ❑ | 208 Bo Jackson | .15 | .07 |
| ❑ | 209 Chet Lemon | .05 | .02 |
| ❑ | 210 Storm Davis | .05 | .02 |
| ❑ | 211 Doug Drabek | .05 | .02 |
| ❑ | 212 Mickey Brantley UER (Photo actually Nelson Simmons) | .05 | .02 |
| ❑ | 213 Devon White | .10 | .05 |
| ❑ | 214 Dave Stewart | .10 | .05 |
| ❑ | 215 Dave Schmidt | .05 | .02 |
| ❑ | 216 Bryn Smith | .05 | .02 |
| ❑ | 217 Brett Butler | .10 | .05 |
| ❑ | 218 Bob Ojeda | .05 | .02 |
| ❑ | 219 Steve Rosenberg | .05 | .02 |
| ❑ | 220 Hubie Brooks | .05 | .02 |
| ❑ | 221 B.J. Surhoff | .10 | .05 |
| ❑ | 222 Rick Mahler | .05 | .02 |
| ❑ | 223 Rick Sutcliffe | .10 | .05 |
| ❑ | 224 Neal Heaton | .05 | .02 |
| ❑ | 225 Mitch Williams | .05 | .02 |
| ❑ | 226 Chuck Finley | .10 | .05 |
| ❑ | 227 Mark Langston | .05 | .02 |
| ❑ | 228 Jesse Orosco | .05 | .02 |
| ❑ | 229 Ed Whitson | .05 | .02 |
| ❑ | 230 Terry Pendleton | .10 | .05 |
| ❑ | 231 Lloyd Moseby | .05 | .02 |
| ❑ | 232 Greg Swindell | .05 | .02 |
| ❑ | 233 John Franco | .10 | .05 |
| ❑ | 234 Jack Morris | .10 | .05 |
| ❑ | 235 Howard Johnson | .05 | .02 |
| ❑ | 236 Glenn Davis | .05 | .02 |
| ❑ | 237 Frank Viola | .05 | .02 |
| ❑ | 238 Kevin Seitzer | .05 | .02 |
| ❑ | 239 Gerald Perry | .05 | .02 |
| ❑ | 240 Dwight Evans | .10 | .05 |
| ❑ | 241 Jim Deshaies | .05 | .02 |
| ❑ | 242 Bo Diaz | .05 | .02 |
| ❑ | 243 Carney Lansford | .10 | .05 |
| ❑ | 244 Mike LaValliere | .05 | .02 |
| ❑ | 245 Rickey Henderson | .25 | .11 |
| ❑ | 246 Roberto Alomar | .30 | .14 |
| ❑ | 247 Jimmy Jones | .05 | .02 |
| ❑ | 248 Pascual Perez | .05 | .02 |
| ❑ | 249 Will Clark | .20 | .09 |
| ❑ | 250 Fernando Valenzuela | .10 | .05 |
| ❑ | 251 Shane Rawley | .05 | .02 |
| ❑ | 252 Sid Bream | .05 | .02 |
| ❑ | 253 Steve Lyons | .05 | .02 |
| ❑ | 254 Brian Downing | .05 | .02 |
| ❑ | 255 Mark Grace | .20 | .09 |
| ❑ | 256 Tom Candiotti | .05 | .02 |
| ❑ | 257 Barry Larkin | .20 | .09 |
| ❑ | 258 Mike Krukow | .05 | .02 |
| ❑ | 259 Billy Ripken | .05 | .02 |
| ❑ | 260 Cecilio Guante | .05 | .02 |
| ❑ | 261 Scott Bradley | .05 | .02 |
| ❑ | 262 Floyd Bannister | .05 | .02 |
| ❑ | 263 Pete Smith | .05 | .02 |
| ❑ | 264 Jim Gantner UER (Wrong birthdate) | .05 | .02 |
| ❑ | 265 Roger McDowell | .05 | .02 |
| ❑ | 266 Bobby Thigpen | .05 | .02 |
| ❑ | 267 Jim Clancy | .05 | .02 |
| ❑ | 268 Terry Steinbach | .10 | .05 |
| ❑ | 269 Mike Dunne | .05 | .02 |
| ❑ | 270 Dwight Gooden | .10 | .05 |
| ❑ | 271 Mike Heath | .05 | .02 |
| ❑ | 272 Dave Smith | .05 | .02 |
| ❑ | 273 Keith Atherton | .05 | .02 |
| ❑ | 274 Tim Burke | .05 | .02 |
| ❑ | 275 Damon Berryhill | .05 | .02 |
| ❑ | 276 Vance Law | .05 | .02 |
| ❑ | 277 Rich Dotson | .05 | .02 |
| ❑ | 278 Lance Parrish | .05 | .02 |
| ❑ | 279 Denny Walling | .05 | .02 |
| ❑ | 280 Roger Clemens | .40 | .18 |
| ❑ | 281 Greg Mathews | .05 | .02 |
| ❑ | 282 Tom Niedenfuer | .05 | .02 |
| ❑ | 283 Paul Kilgus | .05 | .02 |
| ❑ | 284 Jose Guzman | .05 | .02 |
| ❑ | 285 Calvin Schiraldi | .05 | .02 |
| ❑ | 286 Charlie Puleo UER (Career ERA 4.24, should be 4.23) | .05 | .02 |
| ❑ | 287 Joe Orsulak | .05 | .02 |
| ❑ | 288 Jack Howell | .05 | .02 |
| ❑ | 289 Kevin Elster | .05 | .02 |
| ❑ | 290 Jose Lind | .05 | .02 |
| ❑ | 291 Paul Molitor | .20 | .09 |
| ❑ | 292 Cecil Espy | .05 | .02 |
| ❑ | 293 Bill Wegman | .05 | .02 |
| ❑ | 294 Dan Pasqua | .05 | .02 |
| ❑ | 295 Scott Garrelts UER (Wrong birthdate) | .05 | .02 |
| ❑ | 296 Walt Terrell | .05 | .02 |
| ❑ | 297 Ed Hearn | .05 | .02 |
| ❑ | 298 Lou Whitaker | .10 | .05 |
| ❑ | 299 Ken Dayley | .05 | .02 |
| ❑ | 300 Checklist 248-357 | .05 | .02 |
| ❑ | 301 Tommy Herr | .05 | .02 |
| ❑ | 302 Mike Brumley | .05 | .02 |
| ❑ | 303 Ellis Burks | .15 | .07 |
| ❑ | 304 Curt Young UER (Wrong birthdate) | .05 | .02 |
| ❑ | 305 Jody Reed | .05 | .02 |
| ❑ | 306 Bill Doran | .05 | .02 |
| ❑ | 307 David Wells | .05 | .02 |
| ❑ | 308 Ron Robinson | .05 | .02 |
| ❑ | 309 Rafael Santana | .05 | .02 |
| ❑ | 310 Julio Franco | .05 | .02 |
| ❑ | 311 Jack Clark | .05 | .02 |
| ❑ | 312 Chris James | .05 | .02 |
| ❑ | 313 Milt Thompson | .05 | .02 |
| ❑ | 314 John Shelby | .05 | .02 |
| ❑ | 315 Al Leiter | .20 | .09 |
| ❑ | 316 Mike Davis | .05 | .02 |
| ❑ | 317 Chris Sabo RC* | .05 | .02 |
| ❑ | 318 Greg Gagne | .05 | .02 |
| ❑ | 319 Jose Oquendo | .05 | .02 |
| ❑ | 320 John Farrell | .05 | .02 |
| ❑ | 321 Franklin Stubbs | .05 | .02 |
| ❑ | 322 Kurt Stillwell | .05 | .02 |
| ❑ | 323 Shawn Abner | .05 | .02 |
| ❑ | 324 Mike Flanagan | .05 | .02 |
| ❑ | 325 Kevin Bass | .05 | .02 |
| ❑ | 326 Pat Tabler | .05 | .02 |
| ❑ | 327 Mike Henneman | .05 | .02 |

| | | | |
|---|---|---|---|
| ❑ 328 | Rick Honeycutt | .05 | .02 |
| ❑ 329 | John Smiley | .05 | .02 |
| ❑ 330 | Rey Quinones | .05 | .02 |
| ❑ 331 | Johnny Ray | .05 | .02 |
| ❑ 332 | Bob Welch | .05 | .02 |
| ❑ 333 | Larry Sheets | .05 | .02 |
| ❑ 334 | Jeff Parrett | .05 | .02 |
| ❑ 335 | Rick Reuschel UER (For Don Robinson; should be Jeff) | .05 | .02 |
| ❑ 336 | Randy Myers | .10 | .05 |
| ❑ 337 | Ken Williams | .05 | .02 |
| ❑ 338 | Andy McGaffigan | .05 | .02 |
| ❑ 339 | Joey Meyer | .05 | .02 |
| ❑ 340 | Dion James | .05 | .02 |
| ❑ 341 | Les Lancaster | .05 | .02 |
| ❑ 342 | Tom Foley | .05 | .02 |
| ❑ 343 | Gene Petralli | .05 | .02 |
| ❑ 344 | Dan Petry | .05 | .02 |
| ❑ 345 | Alvin Davis | .05 | .02 |
| ❑ 346 | Mickey Hatcher | .05 | .02 |
| ❑ 347 | Marvell Wynne | .05 | .02 |
| ❑ 348 | Danny Cox | .05 | .02 |
| ❑ 349 | Dave Stieb | .05 | .02 |
| ❑ 350 | Jay Bell | .15 | .07 |
| ❑ 351 | Jeff Treadway | .05 | .02 |
| ❑ 352 | Luis Salazar | .05 | .02 |
| ❑ 353 | Len Dykstra | .10 | .05 |
| ❑ 354 | Juan Agosto | .05 | .02 |
| ❑ 355 | Gene Larkin | .05 | .02 |
| ❑ 356 | Steve Farr | .05 | .02 |
| ❑ 357 | Paul Assenmacher | .05 | .02 |
| ❑ 358 | Todd Benzinger | .05 | .02 |
| ❑ 359 | Larry Andersen | .05 | .02 |
| ❑ 360 | Paul O'Neill | .10 | .05 |
| ❑ 361 | Ron Hassey | .05 | .02 |
| ❑ 362 | Jim Gott | .05 | .02 |
| ❑ 363 | Ken Phelps | .05 | .02 |
| ❑ 364 | Tim Flannery | .05 | .02 |
| ❑ 365 | Randy Ready | .05 | .02 |
| ❑ 366 | Nelson Santovenia | .05 | .02 |
| ❑ 367 | Kelly Downs | .05 | .02 |
| ❑ 368 | Danny Heep | .05 | .02 |
| ❑ 369 | Phil Bradley | .05 | .02 |
| ❑ 370 | Jeff D. Robinson | .05 | .02 |
| ❑ 371 | Ivan Calderon | .05 | .02 |
| ❑ 372 | Mike Witt | .05 | .02 |
| ❑ 373 | Greg Maddux | .60 | .25 |
| ❑ 374 | Carmen Castillo | .05 | .02 |
| ❑ 375 | Jose Rijo | .05 | .02 |
| ❑ 376 | Joe Price | .05 | .02 |
| ❑ 377 | Rene Gonzales | .05 | .02 |
| ❑ 378 | Oddibe McDowell | .05 | .02 |
| ❑ 379 | Jim Presley | .05 | .02 |
| ❑ 380 | Brad Wellman | .05 | .02 |
| ❑ 381 | Tom Glavine | .20 | .09 |
| ❑ 382 | Dan Plesac | .05 | .02 |
| ❑ 383 | Wally Backman | .05 | .02 |
| ❑ 384 | Dave Gallagher | .05 | .02 |
| ❑ 385 | Tom Henke | .05 | .02 |
| ❑ 386 | Luis Polonia | .05 | .02 |
| ❑ 387 | Junior Ortiz | .05 | .02 |
| ❑ 388 | David Cone | .10 | .05 |
| ❑ 389 | Dave Bergman | .05 | .02 |
| ❑ 390 | Danny Darwin | .05 | .02 |
| ❑ 391 | Dan Gladden | .05 | .02 |
| ❑ 392 | John Dopson | .05 | .02 |
| ❑ 393 | Frank DiPino | .05 | .02 |
| ❑ 394 | Al Nipper | .05 | .02 |
| ❑ 395 | Willie Randolph | .10 | .05 |
| ❑ 396 | Don Carman | .05 | .02 |
| ❑ 397 | Scott Terry | .05 | .02 |
| ❑ 398 | Rick Cerone | .05 | .02 |
| ❑ 399 | Tom Pagnozzi | .05 | .02 |
| ❑ 400 | Checklist 358-467 | .05 | .02 |
| ❑ 401 | Mickey Tettleton | .05 | .02 |
| ❑ 402 | Curtis Wilkerson | .05 | .02 |
| ❑ 403 | Jeff Russell | .05 | .02 |
| ❑ 404 | Pat Perry | .05 | .02 |
| ❑ 405 | Jose Alvarez | .05 | .02 |
| ❑ 406 | Rick Schu | .05 | .02 |
| ❑ 407 | Sherman Corbett | .05 | .02 |
| ❑ 408 | Dave Magadan | .05 | .02 |
| ❑ 409 | Bob Kipper | .05 | .02 |
| ❑ 410 | Don August | .05 | .02 |
| ❑ 411 | Bob Brower | .05 | .02 |
| ❑ 412 | Chris Bosio | .05 | .02 |
| ❑ 413 | Jerry Reuss | .05 | .02 |
| ❑ 414 | Atlee Hammaker | .05 | .02 |
| ❑ 415 | Jim Walewander | .05 | .02 |
| ❑ 416 | Mike Macfarlane RC* | .05 | .02 |
| ❑ 417 | Pat Sheridan | .05 | .02 |
| ❑ 418 | Pedro Guerrero | .05 | .02 |
| ❑ 419 | Allan Anderson | .05 | .02 |
| ❑ 420 | Mark Parent | .05 | .02 |
| ❑ 421 | Bob Stanley | .05 | .02 |
| ❑ 422 | Mike Gallego | .05 | .02 |
| ❑ 423 | Bruce Hurst | .05 | .02 |
| ❑ 424 | Dave Meads | .05 | .02 |
| ❑ 425 | Jesse Barfield | .05 | .02 |
| ❑ 426 | Rob Dibble RC* | .10 | .05 |
| ❑ 427 | Joel Skinner | .05 | .02 |
| ❑ 428 | Ron Kittle | .05 | .02 |
| ❑ 429 | Rick Rhoden | .05 | .02 |
| ❑ 430 | Bob Dernier | .05 | .02 |
| ❑ 431 | Steve Jeltz | .05 | .02 |
| ❑ 432 | Rick Dempsey | .05 | .02 |
| ❑ 433 | Roberto Kelly | .10 | .05 |
| ❑ 434 | Dave Anderson | .05 | .02 |
| ❑ 435 | Herm Winningham | .05 | .02 |
| ❑ 436 | Al Newman | .05 | .02 |
| ❑ 437 | Jose DeLeon | .05 | .02 |
| ❑ 438 | Doug Jones | .05 | .02 |
| ❑ 439 | Brian Holton | .05 | .02 |
| ❑ 440 | Jeff Montgomery | .10 | .05 |
| ❑ 441 | Dickie Thon | .05 | .02 |
| ❑ 442 | Cecil Fielder | .10 | .05 |
| ❑ 443 | John Fishel | .05 | .02 |
| ❑ 444 | Jerry Don Gleaton | .05 | .02 |
| ❑ 445 | Paul Gibson | .05 | .02 |
| ❑ 446 | Walt Weiss | .05 | .02 |
| ❑ 447 | Glenn Wilson | .05 | .02 |
| ❑ 448 | Mike Moore | .05 | .02 |
| ❑ 449 | Chili Davis | .10 | .05 |
| ❑ 450 | Dave Henderson | .05 | .02 |
| ❑ 451 | Jose Bautista | .05 | .02 |
| ❑ 452 | Rex Hudler | .05 | .02 |
| ❑ 453 | Bob Brenly | .05 | .02 |
| ❑ 454 | Mackey Sasser | .05 | .02 |
| ❑ 455 | Daryl Boston | .05 | .02 |
| ❑ 456 | Mike R. Fitzgerald | .05 | .02 |
| ❑ 457 | Jeffrey Leonard | .05 | .02 |
| ❑ 458 | Bruce Sutter | .05 | .02 |
| ❑ 459 | Mitch Webster | .05 | .02 |
| ❑ 460 | Joe Hesketh | .05 | .02 |
| ❑ 461 | Bobby Witt | .05 | .02 |
| ❑ 462 | Stew Cliburn | .05 | .02 |
| ❑ 463 | Scott Bankhead | .05 | .02 |
| ❑ 464 | Ramon Martinez RC | .25 | .11 |
| ❑ 465 | Dave Leiper | .05 | .02 |
| ❑ 466 | Luis Alicea RC* | .05 | .02 |
| ❑ 467 | John Cerutti | .05 | .02 |
| ❑ 468 | Ron Washington | .05 | .02 |
| ❑ 469 | Jeff Reed | .05 | .02 |
| ❑ 470 | Jeff M. Robinson | .05 | .02 |
| ❑ 471 | Sid Fernandez | .05 | .02 |
| ❑ 472 | Terry Puhl | .05 | .02 |
| ❑ 473 | Charlie Lea | .05 | .02 |
| ❑ 474 | Israel Sanchez | .05 | .02 |
| ❑ 475 | Bruce Benedict | .05 | .02 |
| ❑ 476 | Oil Can Boyd | .05 | .02 |
| ❑ 477 | Craig Reynolds | .05 | .02 |
| ❑ 478 | Frank Williams | .05 | .02 |
| ❑ 479 | Greg Cadaret | .05 | .02 |
| ❑ 480 | Randy Kramer | .05 | .02 |
| ❑ 481 | Dave Eiland | .05 | .02 |
| ❑ 482 | Eric Show | .05 | .02 |
| ❑ 483 | Garry Templeton | .05 | .02 |
| ❑ 484 | Wallace Johnson | .05 | .02 |
| ❑ 485 | Kevin Mitchell | .10 | .05 |
| ❑ 486 | Tim Crews | .05 | .02 |
| ❑ 487 | Mike Maddux | .05 | .02 |
| ❑ 488 | Dave LaPoint | .05 | .02 |
| ❑ 489 | Fred Manrique | .05 | .02 |
| ❑ 490 | Greg Minton | .05 | .02 |
| ❑ 491 | Doug Dascenzo UER (Photo actually Damon Berryhill) | .05 | .02 |
| ❑ 492 | Willie Upshaw | .05 | .02 |
| ❑ 493 | Jack Armstrong RC* | .05 | .02 |
| ❑ 494 | Kirt Manwaring | .05 | .02 |
| ❑ 495 | Jeff Ballard | .05 | .02 |
| ❑ 496 | Jeff Kunkel | .05 | .02 |
| ❑ 497 | Mike Campbell | .05 | .02 |
| ❑ 498 | Gary Thurman | .05 | .02 |
| ❑ 499 | Zane Smith | .05 | .02 |
| ❑ 500 | Checklist 468-577 DP | .05 | .02 |
| ❑ 501 | Mike Birkbeck | .05 | .02 |
| ❑ 502 | Terry Leach | .05 | .02 |
| ❑ 503 | Shawn Hillegas | .05 | .02 |
| ❑ 504 | Manny Lee | .05 | .02 |
| ❑ 505 | Doug Jennings | .05 | .02 |
| ❑ 506 | Ken Oberkfell | .05 | .02 |
| ❑ 507 | Tim Teufel | .05 | .02 |
| ❑ 508 | Tom Brookens | .05 | .02 |
| ❑ 509 | Rafael Ramirez | .05 | .02 |
| ❑ 510 | Fred Toliver | .05 | .02 |
| ❑ 511 | Brian Holman RC* | .05 | .02 |
| ❑ 512 | Mike Bielecki | .05 | .02 |
| ❑ 513 | Jeff Pico | .05 | .02 |
| ❑ 514 | Charles Hudson | .05 | .02 |
| ❑ 515 | Bruce Ruffin | .05 | .02 |
| ❑ 516 | Larry McWilliams UER (New Richland; should be North Richland) | .05 | .02 |
| ❑ 517 | Jeff Sellers | .05 | .02 |
| ❑ 518 | John Costello | .05 | .02 |
| ❑ 519 | Brady Anderson RC | .40 | .18 |
| ❑ 520 | Craig McMurtry | .05 | .02 |
| ❑ 521 | Ray Hayward DP | .05 | .02 |
| ❑ 522 | Drew Hall DP | .05 | .02 |
| ❑ 523 | Mark Lemke DP RC | .15 | .07 |
| ❑ 524 | Oswald Peraza DP | .05 | .02 |
| ❑ 525 | Bryan Harvey DP RC* | .05 | .02 |
| ❑ 526 | Rick Aguilera DP | .10 | .05 |
| ❑ 527 | Tom Prince DP | .05 | .02 |
| ❑ 528 | Mark Clear DP | .05 | .02 |
| ❑ 529 | Jerry Browne DP | .05 | .02 |
| ❑ 530 | Juan Castillo DP | .05 | .02 |
| ❑ 531 | Jack McDowell DP | .10 | .05 |
| ❑ 532 | Chris Speier DP | .05 | .02 |
| ❑ 533 | Darrell Evans DP | .10 | .05 |
| ❑ 534 | Luis Aquino DP | .05 | .02 |
| ❑ 535 | Eric King DP | .05 | .02 |
| ❑ 536 | Ken Hill DP RC | .20 | .09 |
| ❑ 537 | Randy Bush DP | .05 | .02 |
| ❑ 538 | Shane Mack DP | .05 | .02 |
| ❑ 539 | Tom Bolton DP | .05 | .02 |
| ❑ 540 | Gene Nelson DP | .05 | .02 |
| ❑ 541 | Wes Gardner DP | .05 | .02 |
| ❑ 542 | Ken Caminiti DP | .10 | .05 |
| ❑ 543 | Duane Ward DP | .05 | .02 |
| ❑ 544 | Norm Charlton DP RC | .10 | .05 |
| ❑ 545 | Hal Morris DP RC | .20 | .09 |
| ❑ 546 | Rich Yett DP | .05 | .02 |
| ❑ 547 | Hensley Meulens DP RC | .05 | .02 |
| ❑ 548 | Greg A. Harris DP | .05 | .02 |
| ❑ 549 | Darren Daulton DP (Posing as right-handed hitter) | .10 | .05 |
| ❑ 550 | Jeff Hamilton DP | .05 | .02 |
| ❑ 551 | Luis Aguayo DP | .05 | .02 |
| ❑ 552 | Tim Leary DP (Resembles M.Marshall) | .05 | .02 |
| ❑ 553 | Ron Oester DP | .05 | .02 |
| ❑ 554 | Steve Lombardozzi DP | .05 | .02 |
| ❑ 555 | Tim Jones DP | .05 | .02 |
| ❑ 556 | Bud Black DP | .05 | .02 |
| ❑ 557 | Alejandro Pena DP | .05 | .02 |
| ❑ 558 | Jose DeJesus DP | .05 | .02 |
| ❑ 559 | Dennis Rasmussen DP | .05 | .02 |
| ❑ 560 | Pat Borders DP RC* | .10 | .05 |
| ❑ 561 | Craig Biggio DP RC | .75 | .35 |
| ❑ 562 | Luis DeLosSantos DP | .05 | .02 |
| ❑ 563 | Fred Lynn DP | .05 | .02 |
| ❑ 564 | Todd Burns DP | .05 | .02 |
| ❑ 565 | Felix Fermin DP | .05 | .02 |
| ❑ 566 | Darnell Coles DP | .05 | .02 |
| ❑ 567 | Willie Fraser DP | .05 | .02 |
| ❑ 568 | Glenn Hubbard DP | .05 | .02 |
| ❑ 569 | Craig Worthington DP | .05 | .02 |
| ❑ 570 | Johnny Paredes DP | .05 | .02 |
| ❑ 571 | Don Robinson DP | .05 | .02 |
| ❑ 572 | Barry Lyons DP | .05 | .02 |
| ❑ 573 | Bill Long DP | .05 | .02 |
| ❑ 574 | Tracy Jones DP | .05 | .02 |
| ❑ 575 | Juan Nieves DP | .05 | .02 |
| ❑ 576 | Andres Thomas DP | .05 | .02 |

| | | |
|---|---|---|
| ❑ 577 Rolando Roomes DP | .05 | .02 |
| ❑ 578 Luis Rivera UER DP (Wrong birthdate) | .05 | .02 |
| ❑ 579 Chad Kreuter DP RC | .05 | .02 |
| ❑ 580 Tony Armas DP | .05 | .02 |
| ❑ 581 Jay Buhner | .10 | .05 |
| ❑ 582 Ricky Horton DP | .05 | .02 |
| ❑ 583 Andy Hawkins DP | .05 | .02 |
| ❑ 584 Sil Campusano | .05 | .02 |
| ❑ 585 Dave Clark | .05 | .02 |
| ❑ 586 Van Snider DP | .05 | .02 |
| ❑ 587 Todd Frohwirth DP | .05 | .02 |
| ❑ 588 Warren Spahn DP PUZ | .20 | .09 |
| ❑ 589 William Brennan | .05 | .02 |
| ❑ 590 German Gonzalez | .05 | .02 |
| ❑ 591 Ernie Whitt DP | .05 | .02 |
| ❑ 592 Jeff Blauser | .10 | .05 |
| ❑ 593 Spike Owen DP | .05 | .02 |
| ❑ 594 Matt Williams | .15 | .07 |
| ❑ 595 Lloyd McClendon DP | .05 | .02 |
| ❑ 596 Steve Ontiveros | .05 | .02 |
| ❑ 597 Scott Medvin | .05 | .02 |
| ❑ 598 Hipolito Pena DP | .05 | .02 |
| ❑ 599 Jerald Clark DP RC | .05 | .02 |
| ❑ 600A Checklist 578-660 DP (635 Kurt Schilling) | .05 | .02 |
| ❑ 600B Checklist 578-660 DP (635 Curt Schilling; MVP's not listed on checklist card) | .05 | .02 |
| ❑ 600C Checklist 578-660 DP (635 Curt Schilling; MVP's listed following 660) | .05 | .02 |
| ❑ 601 Carmelo Martinez DP | .05 | .02 |
| ❑ 602 Mike LaCoss | .05 | .02 |
| ❑ 603 Mike Devereaux | .05 | .02 |
| ❑ 604 Alex Madrid DP | .05 | .02 |
| ❑ 605 Gary Redus DP | .05 | .02 |
| ❑ 606 Lance Johnson | .10 | .05 |
| ❑ 607 Terry Clark DP | .05 | .02 |
| ❑ 608 Manny Trillo DP | .05 | .02 |
| ❑ 609 Scott Jordan RC | .10 | .05 |
| ❑ 610 Jay Howell DP | .05 | .02 |
| ❑ 611 Francisco Melendez | .05 | .02 |
| ❑ 612 Mike Boddicker | .05 | .02 |
| ❑ 613 Kevin Brown DP | .40 | .18 |
| ❑ 614 Dave Valle | .05 | .02 |
| ❑ 615 Tim Laudner DP | .05 | .02 |
| ❑ 616 Andy Nezelek UER (Wrong birthdate) | .05 | .02 |
| ❑ 617 Chuck Crim | .05 | .02 |
| ❑ 618 Jack Savage DP | .05 | .02 |
| ❑ 619 Adam Peterson | .05 | .02 |
| ❑ 620 Todd Stottlemyre | .15 | .07 |
| ❑ 621 Lance Blankenship RC | .05 | .02 |
| ❑ 622 Miguel Garcia DP | .05 | .02 |
| ❑ 623 Keith A. Miller DP | .05 | .02 |
| ❑ 624 Ricky Jordan DP RC* | .10 | .05 |
| ❑ 625 Ernest Riles DP | .05 | .02 |
| ❑ 626 John Moses DP | .05 | .02 |
| ❑ 627 Nelson Liriano DP | .05 | .02 |
| ❑ 628 Mike Smithson DP | .05 | .02 |
| ❑ 629 Scott Sanderson | .05 | .02 |
| ❑ 630 Dale Mohorcic | .05 | .02 |
| ❑ 631 Marvin Freeman DP | .05 | .02 |
| ❑ 632 Mike Young DP | .05 | .02 |
| ❑ 633 Dennis Lamp | .05 | .02 |
| ❑ 634 Dante Bichette DP RC | .40 | .18 |
| ❑ 635 Curt Schilling DP RC | 1.00 | .45 |
| ❑ 636 Scott May DP | .05 | .02 |
| ❑ 637 Mike Schooler | .05 | .02 |
| ❑ 638 Rick Leach | .05 | .02 |
| ❑ 639 Tom Lampkin UER (Throws Left; should be Throws Right) | .05 | .02 |
| ❑ 640 Brian Meyer | .05 | .02 |
| ❑ 641 Brian Harper | .05 | .02 |
| ❑ 642 John Smoltz RC | .40 | .18 |
| ❑ 643 Jose Canseco (40/40 Club) | .10 | .05 |
| ❑ 644 Bill Schroeder | .05 | .02 |
| ❑ 645 Edgar Martinez | .15 | .07 |
| ❑ 646 Dennis Cook RC | .05 | .02 |
| ❑ 647 Barry Jones | .05 | .02 |
| ❑ 648 Orel Hershiser (59 and Counting) | .10 | .05 |
| ❑ 649 Rod Nichols | .05 | .02 |
| ❑ 650 Jody Davis | .05 | .02 |
| ❑ 651 Bob Milacki | .05 | .02 |
| ❑ 652 Mike Jackson | .05 | .02 |
| ❑ 653 Derek Lilliquist RC | .05 | .02 |
| ❑ 654 Paul Mirabella | .05 | .02 |
| ❑ 655 Mike Diaz | .05 | .02 |
| ❑ 656 Jeff Musselman | .05 | .02 |
| ❑ 657 Jerry Reed | .05 | .02 |
| ❑ 658 Kevin Blankenship | .05 | .02 |
| ❑ 659 Wayne Tolleson | .05 | .02 |
| ❑ 660 Eric Hetzel | .05 | .02 |

## 1989 Donruss Rookies

| | MINT | NRMT |
|---|---|---|
| COMP.FACT.SET (56) | 25.00 | 11.00 |
| ❑ 1 Gary Sheffield | 1.50 | .70 |
| ❑ 2 Gregg Jefferies | .10 | .05 |
| ❑ 3 Ken Griffey Jr. | 20.00 | 9.00 |
| ❑ 4 Tom Gordon | .20 | .09 |
| ❑ 5 Billy Spiers RC | .05 | .02 |
| ❑ 6 Deion Sanders RC | .40 | .18 |
| ❑ 7 Donn Pall | .05 | .02 |
| ❑ 8 Steve Carter | .05 | .02 |
| ❑ 9 Francisco Oliveras | .05 | .02 |
| ❑ 10 Steve Wilson | .05 | .02 |
| ❑ 11 Bob Geren | .05 | .02 |
| ❑ 12 Tony Castillo | .05 | .02 |
| ❑ 13 Kenny Rogers RC | .20 | .09 |
| ❑ 14 Carlos Martinez RC | .05 | .02 |
| ❑ 15 Edgar Martinez | .10 | .05 |
| ❑ 16 Jim Abbott RC* | .20 | .09 |
| ❑ 17 Torey Lovullo RC | .05 | .02 |
| ❑ 18 Mark Carreon | .05 | .02 |
| ❑ 19 Geronimo Berroa | .05 | .02 |
| ❑ 20 Luis Medina | .05 | .02 |
| ❑ 21 Sandy Alomar Jr. | .25 | .11 |
| ❑ 22 Bob Milacki | .05 | .02 |
| ❑ 23 Joe Girardi RC | .20 | .09 |
| ❑ 24 German Gonzalez | .05 | .02 |
| ❑ 25 Craig Worthington | .05 | .02 |
| ❑ 26 Jerome Walton | .20 | .09 |
| ❑ 27 Gary Wayne | .05 | .02 |
| ❑ 28 Tim Jones | .05 | .02 |
| ❑ 29 Dante Bichette | .40 | .18 |
| ❑ 30 Alexis Infante | .05 | .02 |
| ❑ 31 Ken Hill | .20 | .09 |
| ❑ 32 Dwight Smith RC | .10 | .05 |
| ❑ 33 Luis de los Santos | .05 | .02 |
| ❑ 34 Eric Yelding | .05 | .02 |
| ❑ 35 Gregg Olson | .20 | .09 |
| ❑ 36 Phil Stephenson | .05 | .02 |
| ❑ 37 Ken Patterson | .05 | .02 |
| ❑ 38 Rick Wrona | .05 | .02 |
| ❑ 39 Mike Brumley | .05 | .02 |
| ❑ 40 Cris Carpenter | .05 | .02 |
| ❑ 41 Jeff Brantley RC | .10 | .05 |
| ❑ 42 Ron Jones | .05 | .02 |
| ❑ 43 Randy Johnson | 2.50 | 1.10 |
| ❑ 44 Kevin Brown | .40 | .18 |
| ❑ 45 Ramon Martinez | .10 | .05 |
| ❑ 46 Greg W.Harris | .05 | .02 |
| ❑ 47 Steve Finley RC | .50 | .23 |
| ❑ 48 Randy Kramer | .05 | .02 |
| ❑ 49 Erik Hanson | .10 | .05 |
| ❑ 50 Matt Merullo | .05 | .02 |
| ❑ 51 Mike Devereaux | .05 | .02 |
| ❑ 52 Clay Parker | .05 | .02 |
| ❑ 53 Omar Vizquel RC | .50 | .23 |
| ❑ 54 Derek Lilliquist | .05 | .02 |
| ❑ 55 Junior Felix RC | .05 | .02 |
| ❑ 56 Checklist 1-56 | .05 | .02 |

## 1990 Donruss

| | MINT | NRMT |
|---|---|---|
| COMPLETE SET (716) | 15.00 | 6.75 |
| COMP.FACT.SET (728) | 20.00 | 9.00 |
| COMP.YAZ PUZZLE | 1.00 | .45 |
| ❑ 1 Bo Jackson DK | .10 | .05 |
| ❑ 2 Steve Sax DK | .05 | .02 |
| ❑ 3A Ruben Sierra DK ERR (No small line on top border on card back) | .05 | .02 |
| ❑ 3B Ruben Sierra DK COR | .05 | .02 |
| ❑ 4 Ken Griffey Jr. DK | .75 | .35 |
| ❑ 5 Mickey Tettleton DK | .05 | .02 |
| ❑ 6 Dave Stewart DK | .05 | .02 |
| ❑ 7 Jim Deshaies DK DP | .05 | .02 |
| ❑ 8 John Smoltz DK | .10 | .05 |
| ❑ 9 Mike Bielecki DK | .05 | .02 |
| ❑ 10A Brian Downing DK ERR (Reverse negative on card front) | .20 | .09 |
| ❑ 10B Brian Downing DK COR | .05 | .02 |
| ❑ 11 Kevin Mitchell DK | .05 | .02 |
| ❑ 12 Kelly Gruber DK | .05 | .02 |
| ❑ 13 Joe Magrane DK | .05 | .02 |
| ❑ 14 John Franco DK | .05 | .02 |
| ❑ 15 Ozzie Guillen DK | .05 | .02 |
| ❑ 16 Lou Whitaker DK | .05 | .02 |
| ❑ 17 John Smiley DK | .05 | .02 |
| ❑ 18 Howard Johnson DK | .05 | .02 |
| ❑ 19 Willie Randolph DK | .10 | .05 |
| ❑ 20 Chris Bosio DK | .05 | .02 |
| ❑ 21 Tommy Herr DK DP | .05 | .02 |
| ❑ 22 Dan Gladden DK | .05 | .02 |
| ❑ 23 Ellis Burks DK | .10 | .05 |
| ❑ 24 Pete O'Brien DK | .05 | .02 |
| ❑ 25 Bryn Smith DK | .05 | .02 |
| ❑ 26 Ed Whitson DK DP | .05 | .02 |
| ❑ 27 DK Checklist 1-27 DP (Comments on Perez-Steele on back) | .05 | .02 |
| ❑ 28 Robin Ventura RR | .20 | .09 |
| ❑ 29 Todd Zeile RR | .10 | .05 |
| ❑ 30 Sandy Alomar Jr. RR | .10 | .05 |
| ❑ 31 Kent Mercker RR RC | .05 | .02 |
| ❑ 32 Ben McDonald RC RR UER (Middle name Benard, not Benjamin) | .10 | .05 |
| ❑ 33A Juan Gonzalez RC ERR (Reverse negative) | 2.00 | .90 |
| ❑ 33B Juan Gonzalez COR RC | 1.00 | .45 |
| ❑ 34 Eric Anthony RR RC | .05 | .02 |
| ❑ 35 Mike Fetters RR RC | .05 | .02 |
| ❑ 36 Marquis Grissom RR RC | .25 | .11 |
| ❑ 37 Greg Vaughn RR | .25 | .11 |

❑ 38 Brian DuBois RR .05 .02
❑ 39 Steve Avery RR UER .05 .02
(Born in MI, not NJ)
❑ 40 Mark Gardner RR RC .05 .02
❑ 41 Andy Benes RR .05 .02
❑ 42 Delino DeShields RR RC .20 .09
❑ 43 Scott Coolbaugh RR .05 .02
❑ 44 Pat Combs RR DP .05 .02
❑ 45 Alex Sanchez RR DP .05 .02
❑ 46 Kelly Mann RR DP .05 .02
❑ 47 Julio Machado RR DP .05 .02
❑ 48 Pete Incaviglia .05 .02
❑ 49 Shawon Dunston .05 .02
❑ 50 Jeff Treadway .05 .02
❑ 51 Jeff Ballard .05 .02
❑ 52 Claudell Washington .05 .02
❑ 53 Juan Samuel .05 .02
❑ 54 John Smiley .05 .02
❑ 55 Rob Deer .05 .02
❑ 56 Geno Petralli .05 .02
❑ 57 Chris Bosio .05 .02
❑ 58 Carlton Fisk .20 .09
❑ 59 Kirt Manwaring .05 .02
❑ 60 Chet Lemon .05 .02
❑ 61 Bo Jackson .10 .05
❑ 62 Doyle Alexander .05 .02
❑ 63 Pedro Guerrero .05 .02
❑ 64 Allan Anderson .05 .02
❑ 65 Greg W. Harris .05 .02
❑ 66 Mike Greenwell .05 .02
❑ 67 Walt Weiss .05 .02
❑ 68 Wade Boggs .25 .11
❑ 69 Jim Clancy .05 .02
❑ 70 Junior Felix .05 .02
❑ 71 Barry Larkin .20 .09
❑ 72 Dave LaPoint .05 .02
❑ 73 Joel Skinner .05 .02
❑ 74 Jesse Barfield .05 .02
❑ 75 Tommy Herr .05 .02
❑ 76 Ricky Jordan .05 .02
❑ 77 Eddie Murray .20 .09
❑ 78 Steve Sax .05 .02
❑ 79 Tim Belcher .05 .02
❑ 80 Danny Jackson .05 .02
❑ 81 Kent Hrbek .10 .05
❑ 82 Milt Thompson .05 .02
❑ 83 Brook Jacoby .05 .02
❑ 84 Mike Marshall .05 .02
❑ 85 Kevin Seitzer .05 .02
❑ 86 Tony Gwynn .40 .18
❑ 87 Dave Stieb .10 .05
❑ 88 Dave Smith .05 .02
❑ 89 Bret Saberhagen .10 .05
❑ 90 Alan Trammell .10 .05
❑ 91 Tony Phillips .05 .02
❑ 92 Doug Drabek .05 .02
❑ 93 Jeffrey Leonard .05 .02
❑ 94 Wally Joyner .10 .05
❑ 95 Carney Lansford .10 .05
❑ 96 Cal Ripken .75 .35
❑ 97 Andres Galarraga .10 .05
❑ 98 Kevin Mitchell .05 .02
❑ 99 Howard Johnson .05 .02
❑ 100A Checklist 28-129 .05 .02
❑ 100B Checklist 28-125 .05 .02
❑ 101 Melido Perez .05 .02
❑ 102 Spike Owen .05 .02
❑ 103 Paul Molitor .20 .09
❑ 104 Geronimo Berroa .05 .02
❑ 105 Ryne Sandberg .25 .11
❑ 106 Bryn Smith .05 .02
❑ 107 Steve Buechele .05 .02
❑ 108 Jim Abbott .10 .05
❑ 109 Alvin Davis .05 .02
❑ 110 Lee Smith .10 .05
❑ 111 Roberto Alomar .20 .09
❑ 112 Rick Reuschel .05 .02
❑ 113A Kelly Gruber ERR .05 .02
(Born 2/22)
❑ 113B Kelly Gruber COR .05 .02
(Born 2/26; corrected in factory sets)
❑ 114 Joe Carter .10 .05
❑ 115 Jose Rijo .05 .02
❑ 116 Greg Minton .05 .02
❑ 117 Bob Ojeda .05 .02
❑ 118 Glenn Davis .05 .02
❑ 119 Jeff Reardon .10 .05
❑ 120 Kurt Stillwell .05 .02
❑ 121 John Smoltz .10 .05
❑ 122 Dwight Evans .10 .05
❑ 123 Eric Yelding .05 .02
❑ 124 John Franco .10 .05
❑ 125 Jose Canseco .25 .11
❑ 126 Barry Bonds .30 .14
❑ 127 Lee Guetterman .05 .02
❑ 128 Jack Clark .10 .05
❑ 129 Dave Valle .05 .02
❑ 130 Hubie Brooks .05 .02
❑ 131 Ernest Riles .05 .02
❑ 132 Mike Morgan .05 .02
❑ 133 Steve Jeltz .05 .02
❑ 134 Jeff D. Robinson .05 .02
❑ 135 Ozzie Guillen .05 .02
❑ 136 Chili Davis .10 .05
❑ 137 Mitch Webster .05 .02
❑ 138 Jerry Browne .05 .02
❑ 139 Bo Diaz .05 .02
❑ 140 Robby Thompson .05 .02
❑ 141 Craig Worthington .05 .02
❑ 142 Julio Franco .05 .02
❑ 143 Brian Holman .05 .02
❑ 144 George Brett .40 .18
❑ 145 Tom Glavine .20 .09
❑ 146 Robin Yount .20 .09
❑ 147 Gary Carter .10 .05
❑ 148 Ron Kittle .05 .02
❑ 149 Tony Fernandez .05 .02
❑ 150 Dave Stewart .10 .05
❑ 151 Gary Gaetti .10 .05
❑ 152 Kevin Elster .05 .02
❑ 153 Gerald Perry .05 .02
❑ 154 Jesse Orosco .05 .02
❑ 155 Wally Backman .05 .02
❑ 156 Dennis Martinez .10 .05
❑ 157 Rick Sutcliffe .10 .05
❑ 158 Greg Maddux .50 .23
❑ 159 Andy Hawkins .05 .02
❑ 160 John Kruk .10 .05
❑ 161 Jose Oquendo .05 .02
❑ 162 John Dopson .05 .02
❑ 163 Joe Magrane .05 .02
❑ 164 Bill Ripken .05 .02
❑ 165 Fred Manrique .05 .02
❑ 166 Nolan Ryan UER 1.00 .45
(Did not lead NL in K's in '89 as he was in AL in '89)
❑ 167 Damon Berryhill .05 .02
❑ 168 Dale Murphy .20 .09
❑ 169 Mickey Tettleton .05 .02
❑ 170A Kirk McCaskill ERR .05 .02
(Born 4/19)
❑ 170B Kirk McCaskill COR .05 .02
(Born 4/9; corrected in factory sets)
❑ 171 Dwight Gooden .10 .05
❑ 172 Jose Lind .05 .02
❑ 173 B.J. Surhoff .10 .05
❑ 174 Ruben Sierra .05 .02
❑ 175 Dan Plesac .05 .02
❑ 176 Dan Pasqua .05 .02
❑ 177 Kelly Downs .05 .02
❑ 178 Matt Nokes .05 .02
❑ 179 Luis Aquino .05 .02
❑ 180 Frank Tanana .05 .02
❑ 181 Tony Pena .05 .02
❑ 182 Dan Gladden .05 .02
❑ 183 Bruce Hurst .05 .02
❑ 184 Roger Clemens .40 .18
❑ 185 Mark McGwire .75 .35
❑ 186 Rob Murphy .05 .02
❑ 187 Jim Deshaies .05 .02
❑ 188 Fred McGriff .20 .09
❑ 189 Rob Dibble .05 .02
❑ 190 Don Mattingly .50 .23
❑ 191 Felix Fermin .05 .02
❑ 192 Roberto Kelly .05 .02
❑ 193 Dennis Cook .05 .02
❑ 194 Darren Daulton .10 .05
❑ 195 Alfredo Griffin .05 .02
❑ 196 Eric Plunk .05 .02
❑ 197 Orel Hershiser .10 .05
❑ 198 Paul O'Neill .10 .05
❑ 199 Randy Bush .05 .02
❑ 200A Checklist 130-231 .05 .02
❑ 200B Checklist 126-223 .05 .02
❑ 201 Ozzie Smith .25 .11
❑ 202 Pete O'Brien .05 .02
❑ 203 Jay Howell .05 .02
❑ 204 Mark Gubicza .05 .02
❑ 205 Ed Whitson .05 .02
❑ 206 George Bell .05 .02
❑ 207 Mike Scott .05 .02
❑ 208 Charlie Leibrandt .05 .02
❑ 209 Mike Heath .05 .02
❑ 210 Dennis Eckersley .10 .05
❑ 211 Mike LaValliere .05 .02
❑ 212 Darnell Coles .05 .02
❑ 213 Lance Parrish .05 .02
❑ 214 Mike Moore .05 .02
❑ 215 Steve Finley .10 .05
❑ 216 Tim Raines .10 .05
❑ 217A Scott Garrelts ERR .05 .02
(Born 10/20)
❑ 217B Scott Garrelts COR .05 .02
(Born 10/30, corrected in factory sets)
❑ 218 Kevin McReynolds .05 .02
❑ 219 Dave Gallagher .05 .02
❑ 220 Tim Wallach .05 .02
❑ 221 Chuck Crim .05 .02
❑ 222 Lonnie Smith .05 .02
❑ 223 Andre Dawson .10 .05
❑ 224 Nelson Santovenia .05 .02
❑ 225 Rafael Palmeiro .20 .09
❑ 226 Devon White .05 .02
❑ 227 Harold Reynolds .05 .02
❑ 228 Ellis Burks .10 .05
❑ 229 Mark Parent .05 .02
❑ 230 Will Clark .20 .09
❑ 231 Jimmy Key .10 .05
❑ 232 John Farrell .05 .02
❑ 233 Eric Davis .10 .05
❑ 234 Johnny Ray .05 .02
❑ 235 Darryl Strawberry .10 .05
❑ 236 Bill Doran .05 .02
❑ 237 Greg Gagne .05 .02
❑ 238 Jim Eisenreich .05 .02
❑ 239 Tommy Gregg .05 .02
❑ 240 Marty Barrett .05 .02
❑ 241 Rafael Ramirez .05 .02
❑ 242 Chris Sabo .05 .02
❑ 243 Dave Henderson .05 .02
❑ 244 Andy Van Slyke .10 .05
❑ 245 Alvaro Espinoza .05 .02
❑ 246 Garry Templeton .05 .02
❑ 247 Gene Harris .05 .02
❑ 248 Kevin Gross .05 .02
❑ 249 Brett Butler .10 .05
❑ 250 Willie Randolph .10 .05
❑ 251 Roger McDowell .05 .02
❑ 252 Rafael Belliard .05 .02
❑ 253 Steve Rosenberg .05 .02
❑ 254 Jack Howell .05 .02
❑ 255 Marvell Wynne .05 .02
❑ 256 Tom Candiotti .05 .02
❑ 257 Todd Benzinger .05 .02
❑ 258 Don Robinson .05 .02
❑ 259 Phil Bradley .05 .02
❑ 260 Cecil Espy .05 .02
❑ 261 Scott Bankhead .05 .02
❑ 262 Frank White .10 .05
❑ 263 Andres Thomas .05 .02
❑ 264 Glenn Braggs .05 .02
❑ 265 David Cone .10 .05
❑ 266 Bobby Thigpen .05 .02
❑ 267 Nelson Liriano .05 .02
❑ 268 Terry Steinbach .05 .02
❑ 269 Kirby Puckett UER .50 .23
(Back doesn't consider Joe Torre's .363 in '71)
❑ 270 Gregg Jefferies .10 .05
❑ 271 Jeff Blauser .05 .02
❑ 272 Cory Snyder .05 .02
❑ 273 Roy Smith .05 .02
❑ 274 Tom Foley .05 .02
❑ 275 Mitch Williams .05 .02

❑ 276 Paul Kilgus .05 .02
❑ 277 Don Slaught .05 .02
❑ 278 Von Hayes .05 .02
❑ 279 Vince Coleman .05 .02
❑ 280 Mike Boddicker .05 .02
❑ 281 Ken Dayley .05 .02
❑ 282 Mike Devereaux .05 .02
❑ 283 Kenny Rogers .10 .05
❑ 284 Jeff Russell .05 .02
❑ 285 Jerome Walton .05 .02
❑ 286 Derek Lilliquist .05 .02
❑ 287 Joe Orsulak .05 .02
❑ 288 Dick Schofield .05 .02
❑ 289 Ron Darling .05 .02
❑ 290 Bobby Bonilla .10 .05
❑ 291 Jim Gantner .05 .02
❑ 292 Bobby Witt .05 .02
❑ 293 Greg Brock .05 .02
❑ 294 Ivan Calderon .05 .02
❑ 295 Steve Bedrosian .05 .02
❑ 296 Mike Henneman .05 .02
❑ 297 Tom Gordon .10 .05
❑ 298 Lou Whitaker .10 .05
❑ 299 Terry Pendleton .10 .05
❑ 300A Checklist 232-333 .05 .02
❑ 300B Checklist 224-321 .05 .02
❑ 301 Juan Berenguer .05 .02
❑ 302 Mark Davis .05 .02
❑ 303 Nick Esasky .05 .02
❑ 304 Rickey Henderson .25 .11
❑ 305 Rick Cerone .05 .02
❑ 306 Craig Biggio .10 .05
❑ 307 Duane Ward .05 .02
❑ 308 Tom Browning .05 .02
❑ 309 Walt Terrell .05 .02
❑ 310 Greg Swindell .05 .02
❑ 311 Dave Righetti .05 .02
❑ 312 Mike Maddux .05 .02
❑ 313 Len Dykstra .10 .05
❑ 314 Jose Gonzalez .05 .02
❑ 315 Steve Balboni .05 .02
❑ 316 Mike Scioscia .05 .02
❑ 317 Ron Oester .05 .02
❑ 318 Gary Wayne .05 .02
❑ 319 Todd Worrell .05 .02
❑ 320 Doug Jones .05 .02
❑ 321 Jeff Hamilton .05 .02
❑ 322 Danny Tartabull .05 .02
❑ 323 Chris James .05 .02
❑ 324 Mike Flanagan .05 .02
❑ 325 Gerald Young .05 .02
❑ 326 Bob Boone .10 .05
❑ 327 Frank Williams .05 .02
❑ 328 Dave Parker .10 .05
❑ 329 Sid Bream .05 .02
❑ 330 Mike Schooler .05 .02
❑ 331 Bert Blyleven .10 .05
❑ 332 Bob Welch .05 .02
❑ 333 Bob Milacki .05 .02
❑ 334 Tim Burke .05 .02
❑ 335 Jose Uribe .05 .02
❑ 336 Randy Myers .10 .05
❑ 337 Eric King .05 .02
❑ 338 Mark Langston .05 .02
❑ 339 Teddy Higuera .05 .02
❑ 340 Oddibe McDowell .05 .02
❑ 341 Lloyd McClendon .05 .02
❑ 342 Pascual Perez .05 .02
❑ 343 Kevin Brown UER .20 .09
(Signed is misspelled as signeed on back)
❑ 344 Chuck Finley .10 .05
❑ 345 Erik Hanson .05 .02
❑ 346 Rich Gedman .05 .02
❑ 347 Bip Roberts .05 .02
❑ 348 Matt Williams .10 .05
❑ 349 Tom Henke .05 .02
❑ 350 Brad Komminsk .05 .02
❑ 351 Jeff Reed .05 .02
❑ 352 Brian Downing .05 .02
❑ 353 Frank Viola .05 .02
❑ 354 Terry Puhl .05 .02
❑ 355 Brian Harper .05 .02
❑ 356 Steve Farr .05 .02
❑ 357 Joe Boever .05 .02
❑ 358 Danny Heep .05 .02
❑ 359 Larry Andersen .05 .02
❑ 360 Rolando Roomes .05 .02
❑ 361 Mike Gallego .05 .02
❑ 362 Bob Kipper .05 .02
❑ 363 Clay Parker .05 .02
❑ 364 Mike Pagliarulo .05 .02
❑ 365 Ken Griffey Jr. UER 1.50 .70
(Signed through 1990, should be 1991)
❑ 366 Rex Hudler .05 .02
❑ 367 Pat Sheridan .05 .02
❑ 368 Kirk Gibson .10 .05
❑ 369 Jeff Parrett .05 .02
❑ 370 Bob Walk .05 .02
❑ 371 Ken Patterson .05 .02
❑ 372 Bryan Harvey .05 .02
❑ 373 Mike Bielecki .05 .02
❑ 374 Tom Magrann .05 .02
❑ 375 Rick Mahler .05 .02
❑ 376 Craig Lefferts .05 .02
❑ 377 Gregg Olson .10 .05
❑ 378 Jamie Moyer .05 .02
❑ 379 Randy Johnson .40 .18
❑ 380 Jeff Montgomery .10 .05
❑ 381 Marty Clary .05 .02
❑ 382 Bill Spiers .05 .02
❑ 383 Dave Magadan .05 .02
❑ 384 Greg Hibbard RC .05 .02
❑ 385 Ernie Whitt .05 .02
❑ 386 Rick Honeycutt .05 .02
❑ 387 Dave West .05 .02
❑ 388 Keith Hernandez .10 .05
❑ 389 Jose Alvarez .05 .02
❑ 390 Joey Belle .75 .35
❑ 391 Rick Aguilera .10 .05
❑ 392 Mike Fitzgerald .05 .02
❑ 393 Dwight Smith .05 .02
❑ 394 Steve Wilson .05 .02
❑ 395 Bob Geren .05 .02
❑ 396 Randy Ready .05 .02
❑ 397 Ken Hill .10 .05
❑ 398 Jody Reed .05 .02
❑ 399 Tom Brunansky .05 .02
❑ 400A Checklist 334-435 .05 .02
❑ 400B Checklist 322-419 .05 .02
❑ 401 Rene Gonzales .05 .02
❑ 402 Harold Baines .10 .05
❑ 403 Cecilio Guante .05 .02
❑ 404 Joe Girardi .10 .05
❑ 405A Sergio Valdez ERR .05 .02
(Card front shows black line crossing S in Sergio)
❑ 405B Sergio Valdez COR .05 .02
❑ 406 Mark Williamson .05 .02
❑ 407 Glenn Hoffman .05 .02
❑ 408 Jeff Innis .05 .02
❑ 409 Randy Kramer .05 .02
❑ 410 Charlie O'Brien .05 .02
❑ 411 Charlie Hough .10 .05
❑ 412 Gus Polidor .05 .02
❑ 413 Ron Karkovice .05 .02
❑ 414 Trevor Wilson .05 .02
❑ 415 Kevin Ritz .05 .02
❑ 416 Gary Thurman .05 .02
❑ 417 Jeff M. Robinson .05 .02
❑ 418 Scott Terry .05 .02
❑ 419 Tim Laudner .05 .02
❑ 420 Dennis Rasmussen .05 .02
❑ 421 Luis Rivera .05 .02
❑ 422 Jim Corsi .05 .02
❑ 423 Dennis Lamp .05 .02
❑ 424 Ken Caminiti .10 .05
❑ 425 David Wells .10 .05
❑ 426 Norm Charlton .05 .02
❑ 427 Deion Sanders .20 .09
❑ 428 Dion James .05 .02
❑ 429 Chuck Cary .05 .02
❑ 430 Ken Howell .05 .02
❑ 431 Steve Lake .05 .02
❑ 432 Kal Daniels .05 .02
❑ 433 Lance McCullers .05 .02
❑ 434 Lenny Harris .05 .02
❑ 435 Scott Scudder .05 .02
❑ 436 Gene Larkin .05 .02
❑ 437 Dan Quisenberry .05 .02
❑ 438 Steve Olin RC .10 .05
❑ 439 Mickey Hatcher .05 .02
❑ 440 Willie Wilson .05 .02
❑ 441 Mark Grant .05 .02
❑ 442 Mookie Wilson .10 .05
❑ 443 Alex Trevino .05 .02
❑ 444 Pat Tabler .05 .02
❑ 445 Dave Bergman .05 .02
❑ 446 Todd Burns .05 .02
❑ 447 R.J. Reynolds .05 .02
❑ 448 Jay Buhner .10 .05
❑ 449 Lee Stevens .10 .05
❑ 450 Ron Hassey .05 .02
❑ 451 Bob Melvin .05 .02
❑ 452 Dave Martinez .05 .02
❑ 453 Greg Litton .05 .02
❑ 454 Mark Carreon .05 .02
❑ 455 Scott Fletcher .05 .02
❑ 456 Otis Nixon .05 .02
❑ 457 Tony Fossas .05 .02
❑ 458 John Russell .05 .02
❑ 459 Paul Assenmacher .05 .02
❑ 460 Zane Smith .05 .02
❑ 461 Jack Daugherty .05 .02
❑ 462 Rich Monteleone .05 .02
❑ 463 Greg Briley .05 .02
❑ 464 Mike Smithson .05 .02
❑ 465 Benito Santiago .05 .02
❑ 466 Jeff Brantley .05 .02
❑ 467 Jose Nunez .05 .02
❑ 468 Scott Bailes .05 .02
❑ 469 Ken Griffey Sr. .10 .05
❑ 470 Bob McClure .05 .02
❑ 471 Mackey Sasser .05 .02
❑ 472 Glenn Wilson .05 .02
❑ 473 Kevin Tapani RC .10 .05
❑ 474 Bill Buckner .05 .02
❑ 475 Ron Gant .10 .05
❑ 476 Kevin Romine .05 .02
❑ 477 Juan Agosto .05 .02
❑ 478 Herm Winningham .05 .02
❑ 479 Storm Davis .05 .02
❑ 480 Jeff King .05 .02
❑ 481 Kevin Mmahat .05 .02
❑ 482 Carmelo Martinez .05 .02
❑ 483 Omar Vizquel .20 .09
❑ 484 Jim Dwyer .05 .02
❑ 485 Bob Knepper .05 .02
❑ 486 Dave Anderson .05 .02
❑ 487 Ron Jones .05 .02
❑ 488 Jay Bell .10 .05
❑ 489 Sammy Sosa RC 5.00 2.20
❑ 490 Kent Anderson .05 .02
❑ 491 Domingo Ramos .05 .02
❑ 492 Dave Clark .05 .02
❑ 493 Tim Birtsas .05 .02
❑ 494 Ken Oberkfell .05 .02
❑ 495 Larry Sheets .05 .02
❑ 496 Jeff Kunkel .05 .02
❑ 497 Jim Presley .05 .02
❑ 498 Mike Macfarlane .05 .02
❑ 499 Pete Smith .05 .02
❑ 500A Checklist 436-537 DP .05 .02
❑ 500B Checklist 420-517 .05 .02
❑ 501 Gary Sheffield .25 .11
❑ 502 Terry Bross .05 .02
❑ 503 Jerry Kutzler .05 .02
❑ 504 Lloyd Moseby .05 .02
❑ 505 Curt Young .05 .02
❑ 506 Al Newman .05 .02
❑ 507 Keith Miller .05 .02
❑ 508 Mike Stanton RC .05 .02
❑ 509 Rich Yett .05 .02
❑ 510 Tim Drummond .05 .02
❑ 511 Joe Hesketh .05 .02
❑ 512 Rick Wrona .05 .02
❑ 513 Luis Salazar .05 .02
❑ 514 Hal Morris .05 .02
❑ 515 Terry Mulholland .05 .02
❑ 516 John Morris .05 .02
❑ 517 Carlos Quintana .05 .02
❑ 518 Frank DiPino .05 .02
❑ 519 Randy Milligan .05 .02
❑ 520 Chad Kreuter .05 .02
❑ 521 Mike Jeffcoat .05 .02
❑ 522 Mike Harkey .05 .02

❑ 523A Andy Nezelek ERR .05 .02
(Wrong birth year)
❑ 523B Andy Nezelek COR .20 .09
(Finally corrected
in factory sets)
❑ 524 Dave Schmidt .05 .02
❑ 525 Tony Armas .05 .02
❑ 526 Barry Lyons .05 .02
❑ 527 Rick Reed RC .25 .11
❑ 528 Jerry Reuss .05 .02
❑ 529 Dean Palmer RC .40 .18
❑ 530 Jeff Peterek .05 .02
❑ 531 Carlos Martinez .05 .02
❑ 532 Atlee Hammaker .05 .02
❑ 533 Mike Brumley .05 .02
❑ 534 Terry Leach .05 .02
❑ 535 Doug Strange .05 .02
❑ 536 Jose DeLeon .05 .02
❑ 537 Shane Rawley .05 .02
❑ 538 Joey Cora .10 .05
❑ 539 Eric Hetzel .05 .02
❑ 540 Gene Nelson .05 .02
❑ 541 Wes Gardner .05 .02
❑ 542 Mark Portugal .05 .02
❑ 543 Al Leiter .20 .09
❑ 544 Jack Armstrong .05 .02
❑ 545 Greg Cadaret .05 .02
❑ 546 Rod Nichols .05 .02
❑ 547 Luis Polonia .05 .02
❑ 548 Charlie Hayes .05 .02
❑ 549 Dickie Thon .05 .02
❑ 550 Tim Crews .05 .02
❑ 551 Dave Winfield .20 .09
❑ 552 Mike Davis .05 .02
❑ 553 Ron Robinson .05 .02
❑ 554 Carmen Castillo .05 .02
❑ 555 John Costello .05 .02
❑ 556 Bud Black .05 .02
❑ 557 Rick Dempsey .05 .02
❑ 558 Jim Acker .05 .02
❑ 559 Eric Show .05 .02
❑ 560 Pat Borders .05 .02
❑ 561 Danny Darwin .05 .02
❑ 562 Rick Luecken .05 .02
❑ 563 Edwin Nunez .05 .02
❑ 564 Felix Jose .05 .02
❑ 565 John Cangelosi .05 .02
❑ 566 Bill Swift .05 .02
❑ 567 Bill Schroeder .05 .02
❑ 568 Stan Javier .05 .02
❑ 569 Jim Traber .05 .02
❑ 570 Wallace Johnson .05 .02
❑ 571 Donell Nixon .05 .02
❑ 572 Sid Fernandez .05 .02
❑ 573 Lance Johnson .05 .02
❑ 574 Andy McGaffigan .05 .02
❑ 575 Mark Knudson .05 .02
❑ 576 Tommy Greene RC .05 .02
❑ 577 Mark Grace .20 .09
❑ 578 Larry Walker RC .60 .25
❑ 579 Mike Stanley .05 .02
❑ 580 Mike Witt DP .05 .02
❑ 581 Scott Bradley .05 .02
❑ 582 Greg A. Harris .05 .02
❑ 583A Kevin Hickey ERR .20 .09
❑ 583B Kevin Hickey COR .05 .02
❑ 584 Lee Mazzilli .05 .02
❑ 585 Jeff Pico .05 .02
❑ 586 Joe Oliver .05 .02
❑ 587 Willie Fraser DP .05 .02
❑ 588 Carl Yastrzemski .20 .09
Puzzle Card DP
❑ 589 Kevin Bass DP .05 .02
❑ 590 John Moses DP .05 .02
❑ 591 Tom Pagnozzi DP .05 .02
❑ 592 Tony Castillo DP .05 .02
❑ 593 Jerald Clark DP .05 .02
❑ 594 Dan Schatzeder .05 .02
❑ 595 Luis Quinones DP .05 .02
❑ 596 Pete Harnisch DP .05 .02
❑ 597 Gary Redus .05 .02
❑ 598 Mel Hall .05 .02
❑ 599 Rick Schu .05 .02
❑ 600A Checklist 538-639 .05 .02
❑ 600B Checklist 518-617 .05 .02
❑ 601 Mike Kingery DP .05 .02
❑ 602 Terry Kennedy DP .05 .02
❑ 603 Mike Sharperson DP .05 .02
❑ 604 Don Carman DP .05 .02
❑ 605 Jim Gott .05 .02
❑ 606 Donn Pall DP .05 .02
❑ 607 Rance Mulliniks .05 .02
❑ 608 Curt Wilkerson DP .05 .02
❑ 609 Mike Felder DP .05 .02
❑ 610 Guillermo Hernandez DP .05 .02
❑ 611 Candy Maldonado DP .05 .02
❑ 612 Mark Thurmond DP .05 .02
❑ 613 Rick Leach DP .05 .02
❑ 614 Jerry Reed DP .05 .02
❑ 615 Franklin Stubbs .05 .02
❑ 616 Billy Hatcher DP .05 .02
❑ 617 Don August DP .05 .02
❑ 618 Tim Teufel .05 .02
❑ 619 Shawn Hillegas DP .05 .02
❑ 620 Manny Lee .05 .02
❑ 621 Gary Ward DP .05 .02
❑ 622 Mark Guthrie DP .05 .02
❑ 623 Jeff Musselman DP .05 .02
❑ 624 Mark Lemke DP .05 .02
❑ 625 Fernando Valenzuela .10 .05
❑ 626 Paul Sorrento DP RC .10 .05
❑ 627 Glenallen Hill DP .05 .02
❑ 628 Les Lancaster DP .05 .02
❑ 629 Vance Law DP .05 .02
❑ 630 Randy Velarde DP .05 .02
❑ 631 Todd Frohwirth DP .05 .02
❑ 632 Willie McGee .10 .05
❑ 633 Dennis Boyd DP .05 .02
❑ 634 Cris Carpenter DP .05 .02
❑ 635 Brian Holton .05 .02
❑ 636 Tracy Jones DP .05 .02
❑ 637A Terry Steinbach AS .05 .02
(Recent Major
League Performance)
❑ 637B Terry Steinbach AS .05 .02
(All-Star Game
Performance)
❑ 638 Brady Anderson .20 .09
❑ 639A Jack Morris ERR .10 .05
(Card front shows
black line crossing
J in Jack)
❑ 639B Jack Morris COR .10 .05
❑ 640 Jaime Navarro .05 .02
❑ 641 Darrin Jackson .05 .02
❑ 642 Mike Dyer .05 .02
❑ 643 Mike Schmidt .40 .18
❑ 644 Henry Cotto .05 .02
❑ 645 John Cerutti .05 .02
❑ 646 Francisco Cabrera .05 .02
❑ 647 Scott Sanderson .05 .02
❑ 648 Brian Meyer .05 .02
❑ 649 Ray Searage .05 .02
❑ 650A Bo Jackson AS .10 .05
(Recent Major
League Performance)
❑ 650B Bo Jackson AS .10 .05
(All-Star Game
Performance)
❑ 651 Steve Lyons .05 .02
❑ 652 Mike LaCoss .05 .02
❑ 653 Ted Power .05 .02
❑ 654A Howard Johnson AS .05 .02
(Recent Major
League Performance)
❑ 654B Howard Johnson AS .05 .02
(All-Star Game
Performance)
❑ 655 Mauro Gozzo .05 .02
❑ 656 Mike Blowers RC .10 .05
❑ 657 Paul Gibson .05 .02
❑ 658 Neal Heaton .05 .02
❑ 659 Nolan Ryan 5000K .40 .18
COR (Still an error as
Ryan did not lead AL
in K's in '75)
❑ 659A Nolan Ryan 5000K 1.50 .70
(665 King of
Kings back) ERR
❑ 660A Harold Baines AS .75 .35
(Black line through
star on front;
Recent Major
League Performance)
❑ 660B Harold Baines AS 1.00 .45
(Black line through
star on front;
All-Star Game
Performance)
❑ 660C Harold Baines AS .20 .09
(Black line behind
star on front;
Recent Major
League Performance)
❑ 660D Harold Baines AS .05 .02
(Black line behind
star on front;
All-Star Game
Performance)
❑ 661 Gary Pettis .05 .02
❑ 662 Clint Zavaras .05 .02
❑ 663A Rick Reuschel AS .05 .02
(Recent Major
League Performance)
❑ 663B Rick Reuschel AS .05 .02
(All-Star Game
Performance)
❑ 664 Alejandro Pena .05 .02
❑ 665 Nolan Ryan KING COR .40 .18
❑ 665A Nolan Ryan KING 1.50 .70
(659 5000 K
back) ERR
❑ 665C Nolan Ryan KING ERR .75 .35
(No number on back;
in factory sets)
❑ 666 Ricky Horton .05 .02
❑ 667 Curt Schilling .10 .05
❑ 668 Bill Landrum .05 .02
❑ 669 Todd Stottlemyre .10 .05
❑ 670 Tim Leary .05 .02
❑ 671 John Wetteland .20 .09
❑ 672 Calvin Schiraldi .05 .02
❑ 673A Ruben Sierra AS .05 .02
(Recent Major
League Performance)
❑ 673B Ruben Sierra AS .05 .02
(All-Star Game
Performance)
❑ 674A Pedro Guerrero AS .05 .02
(Recent Major
League Performance)
❑ 674B Pedro Guerrero AS .05 .02
(All-Star Game
Performance)
❑ 675 Ken Phelps .05 .02
❑ 676A Cal Ripken AS .40 .18
(All-Star Game
Performance)
❑ 676B Cal Ripken AS .75 .35
(Recent Major
League Performance)
❑ 677 Denny Walling .05 .02
❑ 678 Goose Gossage .10 .05
❑ 679 Gary Mielke .05 .02
❑ 680 Bill Bathe .05 .02
❑ 681 Tom Lawless .05 .02
❑ 682 Xavier Hernandez RC .05 .02
❑ 683A Kirby Puckett AS .25 .11
(Recent Major
League Performance)
❑ 683B Kirby Puckett AS .25 .11
(All-Star Game
Performance)
❑ 684 Mariano Duncan .05 .02
❑ 685 Ramon Martinez .05 .02
❑ 686 Tim Jones .05 .02
❑ 687 Tom Filer .05 .02
❑ 688 Steve Lombardozzi .05 .02
❑ 689 Bernie Williams RC 1.50 .70
❑ 690 Chip Hale .05 .02
❑ 691 Beau Allred .05 .02
❑ 692A Ryne Sandberg AS .20 .09
(Recent Major
League Performance)
❑ 692B Ryne Sandberg AS .20 .09
(All-Star Game
Performance)
❑ 693 Jeff Huson RC .05 .02

❑ 694 Curt Ford .05 .02
❑ 695A Eric Davis AS .05 .02
(Recent Major League Performance)
❑ 695B Eric Davis AS .05 .02
(All-Star Game Performance)
❑ 696 Scott Lusader .05 .02
❑ 697A Mark McGwire AS
(Recent Major League Performance)
❑ 697B Mark McGwire AS .20 .09
(All-Star Game Performance)
❑ 698 Steve Cummings .05 .02
❑ 699 George Canale .05 .02
❑ 700A Checklist 640-715 .20 .09
and BC1-BC26
❑ 700B Checklist 640-716 .10 .05
and BC1-BC26
❑ 700C Checklist 618-716 .05 .02
❑ 701A Julio Franco AS .05 .02
(Recent Major League Performance)
❑ 701B Julio Franco AS .05 .02
(All-Star Game Performance)
❑ 702 Dave Johnson (P) .05 .02
❑ 703A Dave Stewart AS .05 .02
(Recent Major League Performance)
❑ 703B Dave Stewart AS .05 .02
(All-Star Game Performance)
❑ 704 Dave Justice RC .75 .35
❑ 705 Tony Gwynn AS .20 .09
(All-Star Game Performance)
❑ 705A Tony Gwynn AS .20 .09
(Recent Major League Performance)
❑ 706 Greg Myers .05 .02
❑ 707A Will Clark AS .20 .09
(Recent Major League Performance)
❑ 707B Will Clark AS .20 .09
(All-Star Game Performance)
❑ 708A Benito Santiago AS .05 .02
(Recent Major League Performance)
❑ 708B Benito Santiago AS .05 .02
(All-Star Game Performance)
❑ 709 Larry McWilliams .05 .02
❑ 710A Ozzie Smith AS .20 .09
(Recent Major League Performance)
❑ 710B Ozzie Smith AS .10 .05
(All-Star Game Performance)
❑ 711 John Olerud RC .50 .23
❑ 712A Wade Boggs AS .10 .05
(Recent Major League Performance)
❑ 712B Wade Boggs AS .10 .05
(All-Star Game Performance)
❑ 713 Gary Eave .05 .02
❑ 714 Bob Tewksbury .05 .02
❑ 715A Kevin Mitchell AS .05 .02
(Recent Major League Performance)
❑ 715B Kevin Mitchell AS .05 .02
(All-Star Game Performance)
❑ 716 Bart Giamatti RC COMM .20 .09
(In Memoriam)

## 1990 Donruss Rookies

| | MINT | NRMT |
|---|---|---|
| COMP.FACT.SET (56) | 2.00 | .90 |

❑ 1 Sandy Alomar Jr. UER .10 .05

(No stitches on baseball on Donruss logo on card front)
❑ 2 John Olerud .20 .09
❑ 3 Pat Combs .05 .02
❑ 4 Brian DuBois .05 .02
❑ 5 Felix Jose .05 .02
❑ 6 Delino DeShields .20 .09
❑ 7 Mike Stanton .05 .02
❑ 8 Mike Munoz .05 .02
❑ 9 Craig Grebeck RC .05 .02
❑ 10 Joe Kraemer .05 .02
❑ 11 Jeff Huson .05 .02
❑ 12 Bill Sampen .05 .02
❑ 13 Brian Bohanon RC .05 .02
❑ 14 Dave Justice .75 .35
❑ 15 Robin Ventura .20 .09
❑ 16 Greg Vaughn .25 .11
❑ 17 Wayne Edwards .05 .02
❑ 18 Shawn Boskie RC .05 .02
❑ 19 Carlos Baerga RC .10 .05
❑ 20 Mark Gardner .05 .02
❑ 21 Kevin Appier .10 .05
❑ 22 Mike Harkey .05 .02
❑ 23 Tim Layana .05 .02
❑ 24 Glenallen Hill .05 .02
❑ 25 Jerry Kutzler .05 .02
❑ 26 Mike Blowers .10 .05
❑ 27 Scott Ruskin .05 .02
❑ 28 Dana Kiecker .05 .02
❑ 29 Willie Blair RC .05 .02
❑ 30 Ben McDonald .05 .02
❑ 31 Todd Zeile .10 .05
❑ 32 Scott Coolbaugh .05 .02
❑ 33 Xavier Hernandez .05 .02
❑ 34 Mike Hartley .05 .02
❑ 35 Kevin Tapani .10 .05
❑ 36 Kevin Wickander .05 .02
❑ 37 Carlos Hernandez RC .20 .09
❑ 38 Brian Traxler RC .05 .02
❑ 39 Marty Brown .05 .02
❑ 40 Scott Radinsky RC .05 .02
❑ 41 Julio Machado .05 .02
❑ 42 Steve Avery .05 .02
❑ 43 Mark Lemke .05 .02
❑ 44 Alan Mills RC .05 .02
❑ 45 Marquis Grissom .10 .05
❑ 46 Greg Olson RC .05 .02
❑ 47 Dave Hollins RC .20 .09
❑ 48 Jerald Clark .05 .02
❑ 49 Eric Anthony .05 .02
❑ 50 Tim Drummond .05 .02
❑ 51 John Burkett .05 .02
❑ 52 Brent Knackert RC .05 .02
❑ 53 Jeff Shaw .05 .02
❑ 54 John Orton RC .05 .02
❑ 55 Terry Shumpert .05 .02
❑ 56 Checklist 1-56 .05 .02

## 1991 Donruss

| | MINT | NRMT |
|---|---|---|
| COMPLETE SET (770) | 8.00 | 3.60 |
| COMP.FACT.w/LEAF PREV | 10.00 | 4.50 |
| COMP.FACT.w/STUDIO PREV | 10.00 | 4.50 |
| COMP.STARGELL PUZZLE | 1.00 | .45 |

❑ 1 Dave Stieb DK .05 .02

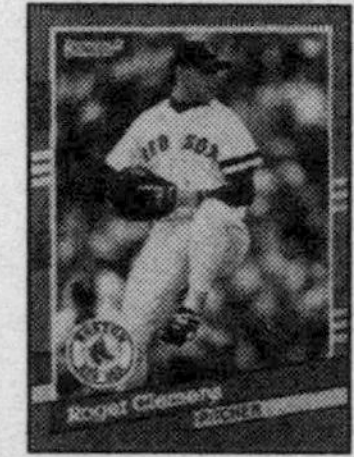


❑ 2 Craig Biggio DK .10 .05
❑ 3 Cecil Fielder DK .05 .02
❑ 4 Barry Bonds DK .20 .09
❑ 5 Barry Larkin DK .10 .05
❑ 6 Dave Parker DK .05 .02
❑ 7 Len Dykstra DK .05 .02
❑ 8 Bobby Thigpen DK .05 .02
❑ 9 Roger Clemens DK .20 .09
❑ 10 Ron Gant DK UER .10 .05
(No trademark on team logo on back)
❑ 11 Delino DeShields DK .05 .02
❑ 12 Roberto Alomar DK UER .10 .05
(No trademark on team logo on back)
❑ 13 Sandy Alomar Jr. DK .05 .02
❑ 14 Ryne Sandberg DK UER .20 .09
(Was DK in '85, not '83 as shown)
❑ 15 Ramon Martinez DK .05 .02
❑ 16 Edgar Martinez DK .10 .05
❑ 17 Dave Magadan DK .05 .02
❑ 18 Matt Williams DK .10 .05
❑ 19 Rafael Palmeiro DK .10 .05
UER (No trademark on team logo on back)
❑ 20 Bob Welch DK .05 .02
❑ 21 Dave Righetti DK .05 .02
❑ 22 Brian Harper DK .05 .02
❑ 23 Gregg Olson DK .05 .02
❑ 24 Kurt Stillwell DK .05 .02
❑ 25 Pedro Guerrero DK UER .05 .02
(No trademark on team logo on back)
❑ 26 Chuck Finley DK UER .05 .02
(No trademark on team logo on back)
❑ 27 DK Checklist 1-27 .05 .02
❑ 28 Tino Martinez RR .10 .05
❑ 29 Mark Lewis RR .05 .02
❑ 30 Bernard Gilkey RR .10 .05
❑ 31 Hensley Meulens RR .05 .02
❑ 32 Derek Bell RR .10 .05
❑ 33 Jose Offerman RR .05 .02
❑ 34 Terry Bross RR .05 .02
❑ 35 Leo Gomez RR .05 .02
❑ 36 Derrick May RR .05 .02
❑ 37 Kevin Morton RR .05 .02
❑ 38 Moises Alou RR .20 .09
❑ 39 Julio Valera RR .05 .02
❑ 40 Milt Cuyler RR .05 .02
❑ 41 Phil Plantier RR RC .05 .02
❑ 42 Scott Chiamparino RR .05 .02
❑ 43 Ray Lankford RR .20 .09
❑ 44 Mickey Morandini RR .05 .02
❑ 45 Dave Hansen RR .05 .02
❑ 46 Kevin Belcher RR .05 .02
❑ 47 Darrin Fletcher RR .05 .02
❑ 48 Steve Sax AS .05 .02
❑ 49 Ken Griffey Jr. AS .75 .35
❑ 50A Jose Canseco AS ERR .10 .05
(Team in stat box should be AL, not A's)
❑ 50B Jose Canseco AS COR .75 .35
❑ 51 Sandy Alomar Jr. AS .05 .02
❑ 52 Cal Ripken AS .40 .18
❑ 53 Rickey Henderson AS .10 .05
❑ 54 Bob Welch AS .05 .02

❑ 55 Wade Boggs AS .10 .05
❑ 56 Mark McGwire AS
❑ 57A Jack McDowell ERR .20 .09
(Career stats do not include 1990)
❑ 57B Jack McDowell COR .50 .23
(Career stats do not include 1990)
❑ 58 Jose Lind .05 .02
❑ 59 Alex Fernandez .10 .05
❑ 60 Pat Combs .05 .02
❑ 61 Mike Walker .05 .02
❑ 62 Juan Samuel .05 .02
❑ 63 Mike Blowers UER .05 .02
(Last line has aseball, not baseball)
❑ 64 Mark Guthrie .05 .02
❑ 65 Mark Salas .05 .02
❑ 66 Tim Jones .05 .02
❑ 67 Tim Leary .05 .02
❑ 68 Andres Galarraga .10 .05
❑ 69 Bob Milacki .05 .02
❑ 70 Tim Belcher .05 .02
❑ 71 Todd Zeile .10 .05
❑ 72 Jerome Walton .05 .02
❑ 73 Kevin Seitzer .05 .02
❑ 74 Jerald Clark .05 .02
❑ 75 John Smoltz UER .10 .05
(Born in Detroit, not Warren)
❑ 76 Mike Henneman .05 .02
❑ 77 Ken Griffey Jr. 1.00 .45
❑ 78 Jim Abbott .10 .05
❑ 79 Gregg Jefferies .05 .02
❑ 80 Kevin Reimer .05 .02
❑ 81 Roger Clemens .40 .18
❑ 82 Mike Fitzgerald .05 .02
❑ 83 Bruce Hurst UER .05 .02
(Middle name is Lee, not Vee)
❑ 84 Eric Davis .10 .05
❑ 85 Paul Molitor .20 .09
❑ 86 Will Clark .20 .09
❑ 87 Mike Bielecki .05 .02
❑ 88 Bret Saberhagen .10 .05
❑ 89 Nolan Ryan 1.00 .45
❑ 90 Bobby Thigpen .05 .02
❑ 91 Dickie Thon .05 .02
❑ 92 Duane Ward .05 .02
❑ 93 Luis Polonia .05 .02
❑ 94 Terry Kennedy .05 .02
❑ 95 Kent Hrbek .10 .05
❑ 96 Danny Jackson .05 .02
❑ 97 Sid Fernandez .05 .02
❑ 98 Jimmy Key .10 .05
❑ 99 Franklin Stubbs .05 .02
❑ 100 Checklist 28-103 .05 .02
❑ 101 R.J. Reynolds .05 .02
❑ 102 Dave Stewart .10 .05
❑ 103 Dan Pasqua .05 .02
❑ 104 Dan Plesac .05 .02
❑ 105 Mark McGwire .75 .35
❑ 106 John Farrell .05 .02
❑ 107 Don Mattingly .50 .23
❑ 108 Carlton Fisk .20 .09
❑ 109 Ken Oberkfell .05 .02
❑ 110 Darrel Akerfelds .05 .02
❑ 111 Gregg Olson .05 .02
❑ 112 Mike Scioscia .05 .02
❑ 113 Bryn Smith .05 .02
❑ 114 Bob Geren .05 .02
❑ 115 Tom Candiotti .05 .02
❑ 116 Kevin Tapani .05 .02
❑ 117 Jeff Treadway .05 .02
❑ 118 Alan Trammell .10 .05
❑ 119 Pete O'Brien .05 .02
(Blue shading goes through stats)
❑ 120 Joel Skinner .05 .02
❑ 121 Mike LaValliere .05 .02
❑ 122 Dwight Evans .10 .05
❑ 123 Jody Reed .05 .02
❑ 124 Lee Guetterman .05 .02
❑ 125 Tim Burke .05 .02
❑ 126 Dave Johnson .05 .02
❑ 127 Fernando Valenzuela .10 .05
(Lower large stripe in yellow instead of blue) UER
❑ 128 Jose DeLeon .05 .02
❑ 129 Andre Dawson .10 .05
❑ 130 Gerald Perry .05 .02
❑ 131 Greg W. Harris .05 .02
❑ 132 Tom Glavine .20 .09
❑ 133 Lance McCullers .05 .02
❑ 134 Randy Johnson .25 .11
❑ 135 Lance Parrish UER .05 .02
(Born in McKeesport, not Clairton)
❑ 136 Mackey Sasser .05 .02
❑ 137 Geno Petralli .05 .02
❑ 138 Dennis Lamp .05 .02
❑ 139 Dennis Martinez .10 .05
❑ 140 Mike Pagliarulo .05 .02
❑ 141 Hal Morris .05 .02
❑ 142 Dave Parker .10 .05
❑ 143 Brett Butler .10 .05
❑ 144 Paul Assenmacher .05 .02
❑ 145 Mark Gubicza .05 .02
❑ 146 Charlie Hough .10 .05
❑ 147 Sammy Sosa .50 .23
❑ 148 Randy Ready .05 .02
❑ 149 Kelly Gruber .05 .02
❑ 150 Devon White .05 .02
❑ 151 Gary Carter .10 .05
❑ 152 Gene Larkin .05 .02
❑ 153 Chris Sabo .05 .02
❑ 154 David Cone .10 .05
❑ 155 Todd Stottlemyre .10 .05
❑ 156 Glenn Wilson .05 .02
❑ 157 Bob Walk .05 .02
❑ 158 Mike Gallego .05 .02
❑ 159 Greg Hibbard .05 .02
❑ 160 Chris Bosio .05 .02
❑ 161 Mike Moore .05 .02
❑ 162 Jerry Browne UER .05 .02
(Born Christiansted, should be St. Croix)
❑ 163 Steve Sax UER .05 .02
(No asterisk next to his 1989 At Bats)
❑ 164 Melido Perez .05 .02
❑ 165 Danny Darwin .05 .02
❑ 166 Roger McDowell .05 .02
❑ 167 Bill Ripken .05 .02
❑ 168 Mike Sharperson .05 .02
❑ 169 Lee Smith .10 .05
❑ 170 Matt Nokes .05 .02
❑ 171 Jesse Orosco .05 .02
❑ 172 Rick Aguilera .10 .05
❑ 173 Jim Presley .05 .02
❑ 174 Lou Whitaker .10 .05
❑ 175 Harold Reynolds .05 .02
❑ 176 Brook Jacoby .05 .02
❑ 177 Wally Backman .05 .02
❑ 178 Wade Boggs .25 .11
❑ 179 Chuck Cary .05 .02
(Comma after DOB, not on other cards)
❑ 180 Tom Foley .05 .02
❑ 181 Pete Harnisch .05 .02
❑ 182 Mike Morgan .05 .02
❑ 183 Bob Tewksbury .05 .02
❑ 184 Joe Girardi .10 .05
❑ 185 Storm Davis .05 .02
❑ 186 Ed Whitson .05 .02
❑ 187 Steve Avery UER .05 .02
(Born in New Jersey, should be Michigan)
❑ 188 Lloyd Moseby .05 .02
❑ 189 Scott Bankhead .05 .02
❑ 190 Mark Langston .05 .02
❑ 191 Kevin McReynolds .05 .02
❑ 192 Julio Franco .05 .02
❑ 193 John Dopson .05 .02
❑ 194 Dennis Boyd .05 .02
❑ 195 Bip Roberts .05 .02
❑ 196 Billy Hatcher .05 .02
❑ 197 Edgar Diaz .05 .02
❑ 198 Greg Litton .05 .02
❑ 199 Mark Grace .20 .09
❑ 200 Checklist 104-179 .05 .02
❑ 201 George Brett .40 .18
❑ 202 Jeff Russell .05 .02
❑ 203 Ivan Calderon .05 .02
❑ 204 Ken Howell .05 .02
❑ 205 Tom Henke .05 .02
❑ 206 Bryan Harvey .05 .02
❑ 207 Steve Bedrosian .05 .02
❑ 208 Al Newman .05 .02
❑ 209 Randy Myers .10 .05
❑ 210 Daryl Boston .05 .02
❑ 211 Manny Lee .05 .02
❑ 212 Dave Smith .05 .02
❑ 213 Don Slaught .05 .02
❑ 214 Walt Weiss .05 .02
❑ 215 Donn Pall .05 .02
❑ 216 Jaime Navarro .05 .02
❑ 217 Willie Randolph .10 .05
❑ 218 Rudy Seanez .05 .02
❑ 219 Jim Leyritz .05 .02
❑ 220 Ron Karkovice .05 .02
❑ 221 Ken Caminiti .10 .05
❑ 222 Von Hayes .05 .02
❑ 223 Cal Ripken .75 .35
❑ 224 Lenny Harris .05 .02
❑ 225 Milt Thompson .05 .02
❑ 226 Alvaro Espinoza .05 .02
❑ 227 Chris James .05 .02
❑ 228 Dan Gladden .05 .02
❑ 229 Jeff Blauser .05 .02
❑ 230 Mike Heath .05 .02
❑ 231 Omar Vizquel .20 .09
❑ 232 Doug Jones .05 .02
❑ 233 Jeff King .05 .02
❑ 234 Luis Rivera .05 .02
❑ 235 Ellis Burks .10 .05
❑ 236 Greg Cadaret .05 .02
❑ 237 Dave Martinez .05 .02
❑ 238 Mark Williamson .05 .02
❑ 239 Stan Javier .05 .02
❑ 240 Ozzie Smith .25 .11
❑ 241 Shawn Boskie .05 .02
❑ 242 Tom Gordon .05 .02
❑ 243 Tony Gwynn .40 .18
❑ 244 Tommy Gregg .05 .02
❑ 245 Jeff M. Robinson .05 .02
❑ 246 Keith Comstock .05 .02
❑ 247 Jack Howell .05 .02
❑ 248 Keith Miller .05 .02
❑ 249 Bobby Witt .05 .02
❑ 250 Rob Murphy UER .05 .02
(Shown as on Reds in '89 in stats; should be Red Sox)
❑ 251 Spike Owen .05 .02
❑ 252 Garry Templeton .05 .02
❑ 253 Glenn Braggs .05 .02
❑ 254 Ron Robinson .05 .02
❑ 255 Kevin Mitchell .05 .02
❑ 256 Les Lancaster .05 .02
❑ 257 Mel Stottlemyre Jr. .05 .02
❑ 258 Kenny Rogers UER .05 .02
(IP listed as 171; should be 172)
❑ 259 Lance Johnson .05 .02
❑ 260 John Kruk .10 .05
❑ 261 Fred McGriff .20 .09
❑ 262 Dick Schofield .05 .02
❑ 263 Trevor Wilson .05 .02
❑ 264 David West .05 .02
❑ 265 Scott Scudder .05 .02
❑ 266 Dwight Gooden .10 .05
❑ 267 Willie Blair .05 .02
❑ 268 Mark Portugal .05 .02
❑ 269 Doug Drabek .05 .02
❑ 270 Dennis Eckersley .10 .05
❑ 271 Eric King .05 .02
❑ 272 Robin Yount .20 .09
❑ 273 Carney Lansford .10 .05
❑ 274 Carlos Baerga .05 .02
❑ 275 Dave Righetti .05 .02
❑ 276 Scott Fletcher .05 .02
❑ 277 Eric Yelding .05 .02
❑ 278 Charlie Hayes .05 .02
❑ 279 Jeff Ballard .05 .02
❑ 280 Orel Hershiser .10 .05
❑ 281 Jose Oquendo .05 .02

| | | | |
|---|---|---|---|
| ❑ 282 | Mike Witt | .05 | .02 |
| ❑ 283 | Mitch Webster | .05 | .02 |
| ❑ 284 | Greg Gagne | .05 | .02 |
| ❑ 285 | Greg Olson | .05 | .02 |
| ❑ 286 | Tony Phillips UER (Born 4/15; should be 4/25) | .05 | .02 |
| ❑ 287 | Scott Bradley | .05 | .02 |
| ❑ 288 | Cory Snyder UER (In text, led is repeated and Inglewood is misspelled as Englewood) | .05 | .02 |
| ❑ 289 | Jay Bell UER (Born in Pensacola, not Eglin AFB) | .10 | .05 |
| ❑ 290 | Kevin Romine | .05 | .02 |
| ❑ 291 | Jeff D. Robinson | .05 | .02 |
| ❑ 292 | Steve Frey UER (Bats left, should be right) | .05 | .02 |
| ❑ 293 | Craig Worthington | .05 | .02 |
| ❑ 294 | Tim Crews | .05 | .02 |
| ❑ 295 | Joe Magrane | .05 | .02 |
| ❑ 296 | Hector Villanueva | .05 | .02 |
| ❑ 297 | Terry Shumpert | .05 | .02 |
| ❑ 298 | Joe Carter | .10 | .05 |
| ❑ 299 | Kent Mercker UER (IP listed as 53, should be 52) | .05 | .02 |
| ❑ 300 | Checklist 180-255 | .05 | .02 |
| ❑ 301 | Chet Lemon | .05 | .02 |
| ❑ 302 | Mike Schooler | .05 | .02 |
| ❑ 303 | Dante Bichette | .20 | .09 |
| ❑ 304 | Kevin Elster | .05 | .02 |
| ❑ 305 | Jeff Huson | .05 | .02 |
| ❑ 306 | Greg A. Harris | .05 | .02 |
| ❑ 307 | Marquis Grissom UER (Middle name Deon, should be Dean) | .05 | .02 |
| ❑ 308 | Calvin Schiraldi | .05 | .02 |
| ❑ 309 | Mariano Duncan | .05 | .02 |
| ❑ 310 | Bill Spiers | .05 | .02 |
| ❑ 311 | Scott Garrelts | .05 | .02 |
| ❑ 312 | Mitch Williams | .05 | .02 |
| ❑ 313 | Mike Macfarlane | .05 | .02 |
| ❑ 314 | Kevin Brown | .10 | .05 |
| ❑ 315 | Robin Ventura | .20 | .09 |
| ❑ 316 | Darren Daulton | .10 | .05 |
| ❑ 317 | Pat Borders | .05 | .02 |
| ❑ 318 | Mark Eichhorn | .05 | .02 |
| ❑ 319 | Jeff Brantley | .05 | .02 |
| ❑ 320 | Shane Mack | .05 | .02 |
| ❑ 321 | Rob Dibble | .05 | .02 |
| ❑ 322 | John Franco | .10 | .05 |
| ❑ 323 | Junior Felix | .05 | .02 |
| ❑ 324 | Casey Candaele | .05 | .02 |
| ❑ 325 | Bobby Bonilla | .10 | .05 |
| ❑ 326 | Dave Henderson | .05 | .02 |
| ❑ 327 | Wayne Edwards | .05 | .02 |
| ❑ 328 | Mark Knudson | .05 | .02 |
| ❑ 329 | Terry Steinbach | .10 | .05 |
| ❑ 330 | Colby Ward UER (No comma between city and state) | .05 | .02 |
| ❑ 331 | Oscar Azocar | .05 | .02 |
| ❑ 332 | Scott Radinsky | .05 | .02 |
| ❑ 333 | Eric Anthony | .05 | .02 |
| ❑ 334 | Steve Lake | .05 | .02 |
| ❑ 335 | Bob Melvin | .05 | .02 |
| ❑ 336 | Kal Daniels | .05 | .02 |
| ❑ 337 | Tom Pagnozzi | .05 | .02 |
| ❑ 338 | Alan Mills | .05 | .02 |
| ❑ 339 | Steve Olin | .05 | .02 |
| ❑ 340 | Juan Berenguer | .05 | .02 |
| ❑ 341 | Francisco Cabrera | .05 | .02 |
| ❑ 342 | Dave Bergman | .05 | .02 |
| ❑ 343 | Henry Cotto | .05 | .02 |
| ❑ 344 | Sergio Valdez | .05 | .02 |
| ❑ 345 | Bob Patterson | .05 | .02 |
| ❑ 346 | John Marzano | .05 | .02 |
| ❑ 347 | Dana Kiecker | .05 | .02 |
| ❑ 348 | Dion James | .05 | .02 |
| ❑ 349 | Hubie Brooks | .05 | .02 |
| ❑ 350 | Bill Landrum | .05 | .02 |
| ❑ 351 | Bill Sampen | .05 | .02 |
| ❑ 352 | Greg Briley | .05 | .02 |
| ❑ 353 | Paul Gibson | .05 | .02 |
| ❑ 354 | Dave Eiland | .05 | .02 |
| ❑ 355 | Steve Finley | .10 | .05 |
| ❑ 356 | Bob Boone | .10 | .05 |
| ❑ 357 | Steve Buechele | .05 | .02 |
| ❑ 358 | Chris Hoiles | .05 | .02 |
| ❑ 359 | Larry Walker | .20 | .09 |
| ❑ 360 | Frank DiPino | .05 | .02 |
| ❑ 361 | Mark Grant | .05 | .02 |
| ❑ 362 | Dave Magadan | .05 | .02 |
| ❑ 363 | Robby Thompson | .05 | .02 |
| ❑ 364 | Lonnie Smith | .05 | .02 |
| ❑ 365 | Steve Farr | .05 | .02 |
| ❑ 366 | Dave Valle | .05 | .02 |
| ❑ 367 | Tim Naehring | .05 | .02 |
| ❑ 368 | Jim Acker | .05 | .02 |
| ❑ 369 | Jeff Reardon UER (Born in Pittsfield, not Dalton) | .10 | .05 |
| ❑ 370 | Tim Teufel | .05 | .02 |
| ❑ 371 | Juan Gonzalez | .25 | .11 |
| ❑ 372 | Luis Salazar | .05 | .02 |
| ❑ 373 | Rick Honeycutt | .05 | .02 |
| ❑ 374 | Greg Maddux | .50 | .23 |
| ❑ 375 | Jose Uribe UER (Middle name Elta, should be Alta) | .05 | .02 |
| ❑ 376 | Donnie Hill | .05 | .02 |
| ❑ 377 | Don Carman | .05 | .02 |
| ❑ 378 | Craig Grebeck | .05 | .02 |
| ❑ 379 | Willie Fraser | .05 | .02 |
| ❑ 380 | Glenallen Hill | .05 | .02 |
| ❑ 381 | Joe Oliver | .05 | .02 |
| ❑ 382 | Randy Bush | .05 | .02 |
| ❑ 383 | Alex Cole | .05 | .02 |
| ❑ 384 | Norm Charlton | .05 | .02 |
| ❑ 385 | Gene Nelson | .05 | .02 |
| ❑ 386 | Checklist 256-331 | .05 | .02 |
| ❑ 387 | Rickey Henderson MVP | .10 | .05 |
| ❑ 388 | Lance Parrish MVP | .05 | .02 |
| ❑ 389 | Fred McGriff MVP | .10 | .05 |
| ❑ 390 | Dave Parker MVP | .05 | .02 |
| ❑ 391 | Candy Maldonado MVP | .05 | .02 |
| ❑ 392 | Ken Griffey Jr. MVP | .75 | .35 |
| ❑ 393 | Gregg Olson MVP | .05 | .02 |
| ❑ 394 | Rafael Palmeiro MVP | .10 | .05 |
| ❑ 395 | Roger Clemens MVP | .20 | .09 |
| ❑ 396 | George Brett MVP | .20 | .09 |
| ❑ 397 | Cecil Fielder MVP | .05 | .02 |
| ❑ 398 | Brian Harper MVP UER (Major League Performance, should be Career) | .05 | .02 |
| ❑ 399 | Bobby Thigpen MVP | .05 | .02 |
| ❑ 400 | Roberto Kelly MVP UER (Second Base on front and OF on back) | .05 | .02 |
| ❑ 401 | Danny Darwin MVP | .05 | .02 |
| ❑ 402 | Dave Justice MVP | .10 | .05 |
| ❑ 403 | Lee Smith MVP | .05 | .02 |
| ❑ 404 | Ryne Sandberg MVP | .20 | .09 |
| ❑ 405 | Eddie Murray MVP | .10 | .05 |
| ❑ 406 | Tim Wallach MVP | .05 | .02 |
| ❑ 407 | Kevin Mitchell MVP | .05 | .02 |
| ❑ 408 | Darryl Strawberry MVP | .05 | .02 |
| ❑ 409 | Joe Carter MVP | .05 | .02 |
| ❑ 410 | Len Dykstra MVP | .05 | .02 |
| ❑ 411 | Doug Drabek MVP | .05 | .02 |
| ❑ 412 | Chris Sabo MVP | .05 | .02 |
| ❑ 413 | Paul Marak RR | .05 | .02 |
| ❑ 414 | Tim McIntosh RR | .05 | .02 |
| ❑ 415 | Brian Barnes RR | .05 | .02 |
| ❑ 416 | Eric Gunderson RR | .05 | .02 |
| ❑ 417 | Mike Gardiner RR | .05 | .02 |
| ❑ 418 | Steve Carter RR | .05 | .02 |
| ❑ 419 | Gerald Alexander RR | .05 | .02 |
| ❑ 420 | Rich Garces RR RC | .05 | .02 |
| ❑ 421 | Chuck Knoblauch RR | .10 | .05 |
| ❑ 422 | Scott Aldred RR | .05 | .02 |
| ❑ 423 | Wes Chamberlain RR RC | .05 | .02 |
| ❑ 424 | Lance Dickson RR RC | .05 | .02 |
| ❑ 425 | Greg Colbrunn RR RC | .05 | .02 |
| ❑ 426 | Rich DeLucia RR UER (Misspelled Delucia on card) | .05 | .02 |
| ❑ 427 | Jeff Conine RR RC | .20 | .09 |
| ❑ 428 | Steve Decker RR | .05 | .02 |
| ❑ 429 | Turner Ward RR RC | .05 | .02 |
| ❑ 430 | Mo Vaughn RR | .10 | .05 |
| ❑ 431 | Steve Chitren RR | .05 | .02 |
| ❑ 432 | Mike Benjamin RR | .05 | .02 |
| ❑ 433 | Ryne Sandberg AS | .20 | .09 |
| ❑ 434 | Len Dykstra AS | .05 | .02 |
| ❑ 435 | Andre Dawson AS | .10 | .05 |
| ❑ 436A | Mike Scioscia AS (White star by name) | .05 | .02 |
| ❑ 436B | Mike Scioscia AS (Yellow star by name) | .05 | .02 |
| ❑ 437 | Ozzie Smith AS | .20 | .09 |
| ❑ 438 | Kevin Mitchell AS | .05 | .02 |
| ❑ 439 | Jack Armstrong AS | .05 | .02 |
| ❑ 440 | Chris Sabo AS | .05 | .02 |
| ❑ 441 | Will Clark AS | .10 | .05 |
| ❑ 442 | Mel Hall | .05 | .02 |
| ❑ 443 | Mark Gardner | .05 | .02 |
| ❑ 444 | Mike Devereaux | .05 | .02 |
| ❑ 445 | Kirk Gibson | .10 | .05 |
| ❑ 446 | Terry Pendleton | .10 | .05 |
| ❑ 447 | Mike Harkey | .05 | .02 |
| ❑ 448 | Jim Eisenreich | .05 | .02 |
| ❑ 449 | Benito Santiago | .05 | .02 |
| ❑ 450 | Oddibe McDowell | .05 | .02 |
| ❑ 451 | Cecil Fielder | .10 | .05 |
| ❑ 452 | Ken Griffey Sr. | .10 | .05 |
| ❑ 453 | Bert Blyleven | .10 | .05 |
| ❑ 454 | Howard Johnson | .05 | .02 |
| ❑ 455 | Monty Fariss UER (Misspelled Farris on card) | .05 | .02 |
| ❑ 456 | Tony Pena | .05 | .02 |
| ❑ 457 | Tim Raines | .10 | .05 |
| ❑ 458 | Dennis Rasmussen | .05 | .02 |
| ❑ 459 | Luis Quinones | .05 | .02 |
| ❑ 460 | B.J. Surhoff | .10 | .05 |
| ❑ 461 | Ernest Riles | .05 | .02 |
| ❑ 462 | Rick Sutcliffe | .10 | .05 |
| ❑ 463 | Danny Tartabull | .05 | .02 |
| ❑ 464 | Pete Incaviglia | .05 | .02 |
| ❑ 465 | Carlos Martinez | .05 | .02 |
| ❑ 466 | Ricky Jordan | .05 | .02 |
| ❑ 467 | John Cerutti | .05 | .02 |
| ❑ 468 | Dave Winfield | .20 | .09 |
| ❑ 469 | Francisco Oliveras | .05 | .02 |
| ❑ 470 | Roy Smith | .05 | .02 |
| ❑ 471 | Barry Larkin | .20 | .09 |
| ❑ 472 | Ron Darling | .05 | .02 |
| ❑ 473 | David Wells | .10 | .05 |
| ❑ 474 | Glenn Davis | .05 | .02 |
| ❑ 475 | Neal Heaton | .05 | .02 |
| ❑ 476 | Ron Hassey | .05 | .02 |
| ❑ 477 | Frank Thomas | .50 | .23 |
| ❑ 478 | Greg Vaughn | .20 | .09 |
| ❑ 479 | Todd Burns | .05 | .02 |
| ❑ 480 | Candy Maldonado | .05 | .02 |
| ❑ 481 | Dave LaPoint | .05 | .02 |
| ❑ 482 | Alvin Davis | .05 | .02 |
| ❑ 483 | Mike Scott | .05 | .02 |
| ❑ 484 | Dale Murphy | .20 | .09 |
| ❑ 485 | Ben McDonald | .05 | .02 |
| ❑ 486 | Jay Howell | .05 | .02 |
| ❑ 487 | Vince Coleman | .05 | .02 |
| ❑ 488 | Alfredo Griffin | .05 | .02 |
| ❑ 489 | Sandy Alomar Jr. | .10 | .05 |
| ❑ 490 | Kirby Puckett | .50 | .23 |
| ❑ 491 | Andres Thomas | .05 | .02 |
| ❑ 492 | Jack Morris | .10 | .05 |
| ❑ 493 | Matt Young | .05 | .02 |
| ❑ 494 | Greg Myers | .05 | .02 |
| ❑ 495 | Barry Bonds | .40 | .18 |
| ❑ 496 | Scott Cooper UER (No BA for 1990 and career) | .05 | .02 |
| ❑ 497 | Dan Schatzeder | .05 | .02 |
| ❑ 498 | Jesse Barfield | .05 | .02 |
| ❑ 499 | Jerry Goff | .05 | .02 |
| ❑ 500 | Checklist 332-408 | .05 | .02 |
| ❑ 501 | Anthony Telford | .05 | .02 |
| ❑ 502 | Eddie Murray | .20 | .09 |
| ❑ 503 | Omar Olivares RC | .05 | .02 |
| ❑ 504 | Ryne Sandberg | .25 | .11 |
| ❑ 505 | Jeff Montgomery | .10 | .05 |
| ❑ 506 | Mark Parent | .05 | .02 |

| |  |  | | |
|---|---|---|---|---|
| ❑ | 507 | Ron Gant | .10 | .05 |
| ❑ | 508 | Frank Tanana | .05 | .02 |
| ❑ | 509 | Jay Buhner | .10 | .05 |
| ❑ | 510 | Max Venable | .05 | .02 |
| ❑ | 511 | Wally Whitehurst | .05 | .02 |
| ❑ | 512 | Gary Pettis | .05 | .02 |
| ❑ | 513 | Tom Brunansky | .05 | .02 |
| ❑ | 514 | Tim Wallach | .05 | .02 |
| ❑ | 515 | Craig Lefferts | .05 | .02 |
| ❑ | 516 | Tim Layana | .05 | .02 |
| ❑ | 517 | Darryl Hamilton | .05 | .02 |
| ❑ | 518 | Rick Reuschel | .05 | .02 |
| ❑ | 519 | Steve Wilson | .05 | .02 |
| ❑ | 520 | Kurt Stillwell | .05 | .02 |
| ❑ | 521 | Rafael Palmeiro | .20 | .09 |
| ❑ | 522 | Ken Patterson | .05 | .02 |
| ❑ | 523 | Len Dykstra | .10 | .05 |
| ❑ | 524 | Tony Fernandez | .05 | .02 |
| ❑ | 525 | Kent Anderson | .05 | .02 |
| ❑ | 526 | Mark Leonard | .05 | .02 |
| ❑ | 527 | Allan Anderson | .05 | .02 |
| ❑ | 528 | Tom Browning | .05 | .02 |
| ❑ | 529 | Frank Viola | .05 | .02 |
| ❑ | 530 | John Olerud | .10 | .05 |
| ❑ | 531 | Juan Agosto | .05 | .02 |
| ❑ | 532 | Zane Smith | .05 | .02 |
| ❑ | 533 | Scott Sanderson | .05 | .02 |
| ❑ | 534 | Barry Jones | .05 | .02 |
| ❑ | 535 | Mike Felder | .05 | .02 |
| ❑ | 536 | Jose Canseco | .25 | .11 |
| ❑ | 537 | Felix Fermin | .05 | .02 |
| ❑ | 538 | Roberto Kelly | .05 | .02 |
| ❑ | 539 | Brian Holman | .05 | .02 |
| ❑ | 540 | Mark Davidson | .05 | .02 |
| ❑ | 541 | Terry Mulholland | .05 | .02 |
| ❑ | 542 | Randy Milligan | .05 | .02 |
| ❑ | 543 | Jose Gonzalez | .05 | .02 |
| ❑ | 544 | Craig Wilson | .05 | .02 |
| ❑ | 545 | Mike Hartley | .05 | .02 |
| ❑ | 546 | Greg Swindell | .05 | .02 |
| ❑ | 547 | Gary Gaetti | .10 | .05 |
| ❑ | 548 | Dave Justice | .20 | .09 |
| ❑ | 549 | Steve Searcy | .05 | .02 |
| ❑ | 550 | Erik Hanson | .05 | .02 |
| ❑ | 551 | Dave Stieb | .05 | .02 |
| ❑ | 552 | Andy Van Slyke | .10 | .05 |
| ❑ | 553 | Mike Greenwell | .05 | .02 |
| ❑ | 554 | Kevin Maas | .05 | .02 |
| ❑ | 555 | Delino DeShields | .10 | .05 |
| ❑ | 556 | Curt Schilling | .10 | .05 |
| ❑ | 557 | Ramon Martinez | .05 | .02 |
| ❑ | 558 | Pedro Guerrero | .05 | .02 |
| ❑ | 559 | Dwight Smith | .05 | .02 |
| ❑ | 560 | Mark Davis | .05 | .02 |
| ❑ | 561 | Shawn Abner | .05 | .02 |
| ❑ | 562 | Charlie Leibrandt | .05 | .02 |
| ❑ | 563 | John Shelby | .05 | .02 |
| ❑ | 564 | Bill Swift | .05 | .02 |
| ❑ | 565 | Mike Fetters | .05 | .02 |
| ❑ | 566 | Alejandro Pena | .05 | .02 |
| ❑ | 567 | Ruben Sierra | .05 | .02 |
| ❑ | 568 | Carlos Quintana | .05 | .02 |
| ❑ | 569 | Kevin Gross | .05 | .02 |
| ❑ | 570 | Derek Lilliquist | .05 | .02 |
| ❑ | 571 | Jack Armstrong | .05 | .02 |
| ❑ | 572 | Greg Brock | .05 | .02 |
| ❑ | 573 | Mike Kingery | .05 | .02 |
| ❑ | 574 | Greg Smith | .05 | .02 |
| ❑ | 575 | Brian McRae RC | .10 | .05 |
| ❑ | 576 | Jack Daugherty | .05 | .02 |
| ❑ | 577 | Ozzie Guillen | .05 | .02 |
| ❑ | 578 | Joe Boever | .05 | .02 |
| ❑ | 579 | Luis Sojo | .05 | .02 |
| ❑ | 580 | Chili Davis | .10 | .05 |
| ❑ | 581 | Don Robinson | .05 | .02 |
| ❑ | 582 | Brian Harper | .05 | .02 |
| ❑ | 583 | Paul O'Neill | .10 | .05 |
| ❑ | 584 | Bob Ojeda | .05 | .02 |
| ❑ | 585 | Mookie Wilson | .10 | .05 |
| ❑ | 586 | Rafael Ramirez | .05 | .02 |
| ❑ | 587 | Gary Redus | .05 | .02 |
| ❑ | 588 | Jamie Quirk | .05 | .02 |
| ❑ | 589 | Shawn Hillegas | .05 | .02 |
| ❑ | 590 | Tom Edens | .05 | .02 |
| ❑ | 591 | Joe Klink | .05 | .02 |
| ❑ | 592 | Charles Nagy | .05 | .02 |
| ❑ | 593 | Eric Plunk | .05 | .02 |
| ❑ | 594 | Tracy Jones | .05 | .02 |
| ❑ | 595 | Craig Biggio | .10 | .05 |
| ❑ | 596 | Jose DeJesus | .05 | .02 |
| ❑ | 597 | Mickey Tettleton | .05 | .02 |
| ❑ | 598 | Chris Gwynn | .05 | .02 |
| ❑ | 599 | Rex Hudler | .05 | .02 |
| ❑ | 600 | Checklist 409-506 | .05 | .02 |
| ❑ | 601 | Jim Gott | .05 | .02 |
| ❑ | 602 | Jeff Manto | .05 | .02 |
| ❑ | 603 | Nelson Liriano | .05 | .02 |
| ❑ | 604 | Mark Lemke | .05 | .02 |
| ❑ | 605 | Clay Parker | .05 | .02 |
| ❑ | 606 | Edgar Martinez | .10 | .05 |
| ❑ | 607 | Mark Whiten | .05 | .02 |
| ❑ | 608 | Ted Power | .05 | .02 |
| ❑ | 609 | Tom Bolton | .05 | .02 |
| ❑ | 610 | Tom Herr | .05 | .02 |
| ❑ | 611 | Andy Hawkins UER (Pitched No-Hitter on 7/1, not 7/2) | .05 | .02 |
| ❑ | 612 | Scott Ruskin | .05 | .02 |
| ❑ | 613 | Ron Kittle | .05 | .02 |
| ❑ | 614 | John Wetteland | .20 | .09 |
| ❑ | 615 | Mike Perez RC | .05 | .02 |
| ❑ | 616 | Dave Clark | .05 | .02 |
| ❑ | 617 | Brent Mayne | .05 | .02 |
| ❑ | 618 | Jack Clark | .10 | .05 |
| ❑ | 619 | Marvin Freeman | .05 | .02 |
| ❑ | 620 | Edwin Nunez | .05 | .02 |
| ❑ | 621 | Russ Swan | .05 | .02 |
| ❑ | 622 | Johnny Ray | .05 | .02 |
| ❑ | 623 | Charlie O'Brien | .05 | .02 |
| ❑ | 624 | Joe Bitker | .05 | .02 |
| ❑ | 625 | Mike Marshall | .05 | .02 |
| ❑ | 626 | Otis Nixon | .05 | .02 |
| ❑ | 627 | Andy Benes | .05 | .02 |
| ❑ | 628 | Ron Oester | .05 | .02 |
| ❑ | 629 | Ted Higuera | .05 | .02 |
| ❑ | 630 | Kevin Bass | .05 | .02 |
| ❑ | 631 | Damon Berryhill | .05 | .02 |
| ❑ | 632 | Bo Jackson | .10 | .05 |
| ❑ | 633 | Brad Arnsberg | .05 | .02 |
| ❑ | 634 | Jerry Willard | .05 | .02 |
| ❑ | 635 | Tommy Greene | .05 | .02 |
| ❑ | 636 | Bob MacDonald | .05 | .02 |
| ❑ | 637 | Kirk McCaskill | .05 | .02 |
| ❑ | 638 | John Burkett | .05 | .02 |
| ❑ | 639 | Paul Abbott | .05 | .02 |
| ❑ | 640 | Todd Benzinger | .05 | .02 |
| ❑ | 641 | Todd Hundley | .05 | .02 |
| ❑ | 642 | George Bell | .05 | .02 |
| ❑ | 643 | Javier Ortiz | .05 | .02 |
| ❑ | 644 | Sid Bream | .05 | .02 |
| ❑ | 645 | Bob Welch | .05 | .02 |
| ❑ | 646 | Phil Bradley | .05 | .02 |
| ❑ | 647 | Bill Krueger | .05 | .02 |
| ❑ | 648 | Rickey Henderson | .25 | .11 |
| ❑ | 649 | Kevin Wickander | .05 | .02 |
| ❑ | 650 | Steve Balboni | .05 | .02 |
| ❑ | 651 | Gene Harris | .05 | .02 |
| ❑ | 652 | Jim Deshaies | .05 | .02 |
| ❑ | 653 | Jason Grimsley | .05 | .02 |
| ❑ | 654 | Joe Orsulak | .05 | .02 |
| ❑ | 655 | Jim Poole | .05 | .02 |
| ❑ | 656 | Felix Jose | .05 | .02 |
| ❑ | 657 | Denis Cook | .05 | .02 |
| ❑ | 658 | Tom Brookens | .05 | .02 |
| ❑ | 659 | Junior Ortiz | .05 | .02 |
| ❑ | 660 | Jeff Parrett | .05 | .02 |
| ❑ | 661 | Jerry Don Gleaton | .05 | .02 |
| ❑ | 662 | Brent Knackert | .05 | .02 |
| ❑ | 663 | Rance Mulliniks | .05 | .02 |
| ❑ | 664 | John Smiley | .05 | .02 |
| ❑ | 665 | Larry Andersen | .05 | .02 |
| ❑ | 666 | Willie McGee | .10 | .05 |
| ❑ | 667 | Chris Nabholz | .05 | .02 |
| ❑ | 668 | Brady Anderson | .20 | .09 |
| ❑ | 669 | Darren Holmes RC UER (19 CG's, should be 0) | .05 | .02 |
| ❑ | 670 | Ken Hill | .05 | .02 |
| ❑ | 671 | Gary Varsho | .05 | .02 |
| ❑ | 672 | Bill Pecota | .05 | .02 |
| ❑ | 673 | Fred Lynn | .05 | .02 |
| ❑ | 674 | Kevin D. Brown | .05 | .02 |
| ❑ | 675 | Dan Petry | .05 | .02 |
| ❑ | 676 | Mike Jackson | .05 | .02 |
| ❑ | 677 | Wally Joyner | .10 | .05 |
| ❑ | 678 | Danny Jackson | .05 | .02 |
| ❑ | 679 | Bill Haselman | .05 | .02 |
| ❑ | 680 | Mike Boddicker | .05 | .02 |
| ❑ | 681 | Mel Rojas | .10 | .05 |
| ❑ | 682 | Roberto Alomar | .20 | .09 |
| ❑ | 683 | Dave Justice ROY | .10 | .05 |
| ❑ | 684 | Chuck Crim | .05 | .02 |
| ❑ | 685 | Matt Williams | .10 | .05 |
| ❑ | 686 | Shawon Dunston | .05 | .02 |
| ❑ | 687 | Jeff Schulz | .05 | .02 |
| ❑ | 688 | John Barfield | .05 | .02 |
| ❑ | 689 | Gerald Young | .05 | .02 |
| ❑ | 690 | Luis Gonzalez RC | .50 | .23 |
| ❑ | 691 | Frank Wills | .05 | .02 |
| ❑ | 692 | Chuck Finley | .10 | .05 |
| ❑ | 693 | Sandy Alomar Jr. ROY | .05 | .02 |
| ❑ | 694 | Tim Drummond | .05 | .02 |
| ❑ | 695 | Herm Winningham | .05 | .02 |
| ❑ | 696 | Darryl Strawberry | .10 | .05 |
| ❑ | 697 | Al Leiter | .10 | .05 |
| ❑ | 698 | Karl Rhodes | .05 | .02 |
| ❑ | 699 | Stan Belinda | .05 | .02 |
| ❑ | 700 | Checklist 507-604 | .05 | .02 |
| ❑ | 701 | Lance Blankenship | .05 | .02 |
| ❑ | 702 | Willie Stargell PUZ | .20 | .09 |
| ❑ | 703 | Jim Gantner | .05 | .02 |
| ❑ | 704 | Reggie Harris | .05 | .02 |
| ❑ | 705 | Rob Ducey | .05 | .02 |
| ❑ | 706 | Tim Hulett | .05 | .02 |
| ❑ | 707 | Atlee Hammaker | .05 | .02 |
| ❑ | 708 | Xavier Hernandez | .05 | .02 |
| ❑ | 709 | Chuck McElroy | .05 | .02 |
| ❑ | 710 | John Mitchell | .05 | .02 |
| ❑ | 711 | Carlos Hernandez | .10 | .05 |
| ❑ | 712 | Geronimo Pena | .05 | .02 |
| ❑ | 713 | Jim Neidlinger | .05 | .02 |
| ❑ | 714 | John Orton | .05 | .02 |
| ❑ | 715 | Terry Leach | .05 | .02 |
| ❑ | 716 | Mike Stanton | .05 | .02 |
| ❑ | 717 | Walt Terrell | .05 | .02 |
| ❑ | 718 | Luis Aquino | .05 | .02 |
| ❑ | 719 | Bud Black (Blue Jays uniform, but Giants logo) | .05 | .02 |
| ❑ | 720 | Bob Kipper | .05 | .02 |
| ❑ | 721 | Jeff Gray | .05 | .02 |
| ❑ | 722 | Jose Rijo | .05 | .02 |
| ❑ | 723 | Curt Young | .05 | .02 |
| ❑ | 724 | Jose Vizcaino | .05 | .02 |
| ❑ | 725 | Randy Tomlin RC | .05 | .02 |
| ❑ | 726 | Junior Noboa | .05 | .02 |
| ❑ | 727 | Bob Welch CY | .05 | .02 |
| ❑ | 728 | Gary Ward | .05 | .02 |
| ❑ | 729 | Rob Deer (Brewers uniform, but Tigers logo) | .05 | .02 |
| ❑ | 730 | David Segui | .05 | .02 |
| ❑ | 731 | Mark Carreon | .05 | .02 |
| ❑ | 732 | Vicente Palacios | .05 | .02 |
| ❑ | 733 | Sam Horn | .05 | .02 |
| ❑ | 734 | Howard Farmer | .05 | .02 |
| ❑ | 735 | Ken Dayley (Cardinals uniform, but Blue Jays logo) | .05 | .02 |
| ❑ | 736 | Kelly Mann | .05 | .02 |
| ❑ | 737 | Joe Grahe RC | .05 | .02 |
| ❑ | 738 | Kelly Downs | .05 | .02 |
| ❑ | 739 | Jimmy Kremers | .05 | .02 |
| ❑ | 740 | Kevin Appier | .10 | .05 |
| ❑ | 741 | Jeff Reed | .05 | .02 |
| ❑ | 742 | Jose Rijo WS | .05 | .02 |
| ❑ | 743 | Dave Rohde | .05 | .02 |
| ❑ | 744 | Dr.Dirt/Mr.Clean Len Dykstra Dale Murphy UER (No '91 Donruss logo on card front) | .10 | .05 |
| ❑ | 745 | Paul Sorrento | .10 | .05 |
| ❑ | 746 | Thomas Howard | .05 | .02 |
| ❑ | 747 | Matt Stark | .05 | .02 |
| ❑ | 748 | Harold Baines | .10 | .05 |
| ❑ | 749 | Doug Dascenzo | .05 | .02 |
| ❑ | 750 | Doug Drabek CY | .05 | .02 |
| ❑ | 751 | Gary Sheffield | .20 | .09 |

| | MINT | NRMT |
|---|---|---|
| ❑ 752 Terry Lee | .05 | .02 |
| ❑ 753 Jim Vatcher | .05 | .02 |
| ❑ 754 Lee Stevens | .10 | .05 |
| ❑ 755 Randy Veres | .05 | .02 |
| ❑ 756 Bill Doran | .05 | .02 |
| ❑ 757 Gary Wayne | .05 | .02 |
| ❑ 758 Pedro Munoz RC | .05 | .02 |
| ❑ 759 Chris Hammond | .05 | .02 |
| ❑ 760 Checklist 605-702 | .05 | .02 |
| ❑ 761 Rickey Henderson MVP | .10 | .05 |
| ❑ 762 Barry Bonds MVP | .20 | .09 |
| ❑ 763 Billy Hatcher WS UER (Line 13, on should be one) | .05 | .02 |
| ❑ 764 Julio Machado | .05 | .02 |
| ❑ 765 Jose Mesa | .05 | .02 |
| ❑ 766 Willie Randolph WS | .05 | .02 |
| ❑ 767 Scott Erickson | .05 | .02 |
| ❑ 768 Travis Fryman | .20 | .09 |
| ❑ 769 Rich Rodriguez | .05 | .02 |
| ❑ 770 Checklist 703-770 and BC1-BC22 | .05 | .02 |

## 1991 Donruss Rookies

| | MINT | NRMT |
|---|---|---|
| COMP.FACT.SET (56) | 6.00 | 2.70 |
| ❑ 1 Pat Kelly RC | .05 | .02 |
| ❑ 2 Rich DeLucia | .05 | .02 |
| ❑ 3 Wes Chamberlain | .05 | .02 |
| ❑ 4 Scott Leius | .05 | .02 |
| ❑ 5 Darryl Kile | .10 | .05 |
| ❑ 6 Milt Cuyler | .05 | .02 |
| ❑ 7 Todd Van Poppel RC | .05 | .02 |
| ❑ 8 Ray Lankford | .20 | .09 |
| ❑ 9 Brian R. Hunter RC | .10 | .05 |
| ❑ 10 Tony Perezchica | .05 | .02 |
| ❑ 11 Ced Landrum | .05 | .02 |
| ❑ 12 Dave Burba RC | .05 | .02 |
| ❑ 13 Ramon Garcia | .05 | .02 |
| ❑ 14 Ed Sprague | .05 | .02 |
| ❑ 15 Warren Newson | .05 | .02 |
| ❑ 16 Paul Faries | .05 | .02 |
| ❑ 17 Luis Gonzalez | .50 | .23 |
| ❑ 18 Charles Nagy | .05 | .02 |
| ❑ 19 Chris Hammond | .05 | .02 |
| ❑ 20 Frank Castillo RC | .25 | .11 |
| ❑ 21 Pedro Munoz | .05 | .02 |
| ❑ 22 Orlando Merced RC | .05 | .02 |
| ❑ 23 Jose Melendez | .05 | .02 |
| ❑ 24 Kirk Dressendorfer RC | .05 | .02 |
| ❑ 25 Heathcliff Slocumb RC | .05 | .02 |
| ❑ 26 Doug Simons | .05 | .02 |
| ❑ 27 Mike Timlin RC | .05 | .02 |
| ❑ 28 Jeff Fassero RC | .10 | .05 |
| ❑ 29 Mark Leiter RC | .05 | .02 |
| ❑ 30 Jeff Bagwell RC | 3.00 | 1.35 |
| ❑ 31 Brian McRae | .10 | .05 |
| ❑ 32 Mark Whiten | .05 | .02 |
| ❑ 33 Ivan Rodriguez RC | 3.00 | 1.35 |
| ❑ 34 Wade Taylor | .05 | .02 |
| ❑ 35 Darren Lewis | .10 | .05 |
| ❑ 36 Mo Vaughn | .10 | .05 |
| ❑ 37 Mike Remlinger | .05 | .02 |
| ❑ 38 Rick Wilkins RC | .05 | .02 |
| ❑ 39 Chuck Knoblauch | .10 | .05 |
| ❑ 40 Kevin Morton | .05 | .02 |
| ❑ 41 Carlos Rodriguez | .05 | .02 |
| ❑ 42 Mark Lewis | .05 | .02 |
| ❑ 43 Brent Mayne | .05 | .02 |
| ❑ 44 Chris Haney RC | .05 | .02 |
| ❑ 45 Denis Boucher RC | .05 | .02 |
| ❑ 46 Mike Gardiner | .05 | .02 |
| ❑ 47 Jeff Johnson | .05 | .02 |
| ❑ 48 Dean Palmer | .10 | .05 |
| ❑ 49 Chuck McElroy | .05 | .02 |
| ❑ 50 Chris Jones RC | .05 | .02 |
| ❑ 51 Scott Kamieniecki RC | .05 | .02 |
| ❑ 52 Al Osuna | .05 | .02 |
| ❑ 53 Rusty Meacham | .05 | .02 |
| ❑ 54 Chito Martinez | .05 | .02 |
| ❑ 55 Reggie Jefferson | .10 | .05 |
| ❑ 56 Checklist 1-56 | .05 | .02 |

## 1992 Donruss

| | MINT | NRMT |
|---|---|---|
| COMPLETE SET (784) | 10.00 | 4.50 |
| COMP.HOBBY SET (788) | 15.00 | 6.75 |
| COMP.RETAIL SET (788) | 10.00 | 4.50 |
| COMPLETE SERIES 1 (396) | 5.00 | 2.20 |
| COMPLETE SERIES 2 (388) | 5.00 | 2.20 |
| COMP.CAREW PUZZLE | 1.00 | .45 |
| ❑ 1 Mark Wohlers RR | .05 | .02 |
| ❑ 2 Wil Cordero RR | .05 | .02 |
| ❑ 3 Kyle Abbott RR | .05 | .02 |
| ❑ 4 Dave Nilsson RR | .10 | .05 |
| ❑ 5 Kenny Lofton RR | .25 | .11 |
| ❑ 6 Luis Mercedes RR | .05 | .02 |
| ❑ 7 Roger Salkeld RR | .05 | .02 |
| ❑ 8 Eddie Zosky RR | .05 | .02 |
| ❑ 9 Todd Van Poppel RR | .05 | .02 |
| ❑ 10 Frank Seminara RR RC | .05 | .02 |
| ❑ 11 Andy Ashby RR | .10 | .05 |
| ❑ 12 Reggie Jefferson RR | .10 | .05 |
| ❑ 13 Ryan Klesko RR | .20 | .09 |
| ❑ 14 Carlos Garcia RR | .05 | .02 |
| ❑ 15 John Ramos RR | .05 | .02 |
| ❑ 16 Eric Karros RR | .20 | .09 |
| ❑ 17 Patrick Lennon RR | .05 | .02 |
| ❑ 18 Eddie Taubensee RR RC | .10 | .05 |
| ❑ 19 Roberto Hernandez RR | .05 | .02 |
| ❑ 20 D.J. Dozier RR | .05 | .02 |
| ❑ 21 Dave Henderson AS | .05 | .02 |
| ❑ 22 Cal Ripken AS | .20 | .09 |
| ❑ 23 Wade Boggs AS | .20 | .09 |
| ❑ 24 Ken Griffey Jr. AS | .60 | .25 |
| ❑ 25 Jack Morris AS | .05 | .02 |
| ❑ 26 Danny Tartabull AS | .05 | .02 |
| ❑ 27 Cecil Fielder AS | .05 | .02 |
| ❑ 28 Roberto Alomar AS | .10 | .05 |
| ❑ 29 Sandy Alomar Jr. AS | .10 | .05 |
| ❑ 30 Rickey Henderson AS | .10 | .05 |
| ❑ 31 Ken Hill | .05 | .02 |
| ❑ 32 John Habyan | .05 | .02 |
| ❑ 33 Otis Nixon HL | .05 | .02 |
| ❑ 34 Tim Wallach | .05 | .02 |
| ❑ 35 Cal Ripken | .75 | .35 |
| ❑ 36 Gary Carter | .10 | .05 |
| ❑ 37 Juan Agosto | .05 | .02 |
| ❑ 38 Doug Dascenzo | .05 | .02 |
| ❑ 39 Kirk Gibson | .10 | .05 |
| ❑ 40 Benito Santiago | .05 | .02 |
| ❑ 41 Otis Nixon | .05 | .02 |
| ❑ 42 Andy Allanson | .05 | .02 |
| ❑ 43 Brian Holman | .05 | .02 |
| ❑ 44 Dick Schofield | .05 | .02 |
| ❑ 45 Dave Magadan | .05 | .02 |
| ❑ 46 Rafael Palmeiro | .20 | .09 |
| ❑ 47 Jody Reed | .05 | .02 |
| ❑ 48 Ivan Calderon | .05 | .02 |
| ❑ 49 Greg W. Harris | .05 | .02 |
| ❑ 50 Chris Sabo | .05 | .02 |
| ❑ 51 Paul Molitor | .20 | .09 |
| ❑ 52 Robby Thompson | .05 | .02 |
| ❑ 53 Dave Smith | .05 | .02 |
| ❑ 54 Mark Davis | .05 | .02 |
| ❑ 55 Kevin Brown | .10 | .05 |
| ❑ 56 Donn Pall | .05 | .02 |
| ❑ 57 Len Dykstra | .10 | .05 |
| ❑ 58 Roberto Alomar | .20 | .09 |
| ❑ 59 Jeff D. Robinson | .05 | .02 |
| ❑ 60 Willie McGee | .10 | .05 |
| ❑ 61 Jay Buhner | .10 | .05 |
| ❑ 62 Mike Pagliarulo | .05 | .02 |
| ❑ 63 Paul O'Neill | .10 | .05 |
| ❑ 64 Hubie Brooks | .05 | .02 |
| ❑ 65 Kelly Gruber | .05 | .02 |
| ❑ 66 Ken Caminiti | .10 | .05 |
| ❑ 67 Gary Redus | .05 | .02 |
| ❑ 68 Harold Baines | .10 | .05 |
| ❑ 69 Charlie Hough | .10 | .05 |
| ❑ 70 B.J. Surhoff | .10 | .05 |
| ❑ 71 Walt Weiss | .05 | .02 |
| ❑ 72 Shawn Hillegas | .05 | .02 |
| ❑ 73 Roberto Kelly | .05 | .02 |
| ❑ 74 Jeff Ballard | .05 | .02 |
| ❑ 75 Craig Biggio | .10 | .05 |
| ❑ 76 Pat Combs | .05 | .02 |
| ❑ 77 Jeff M. Robinson | .05 | .02 |
| ❑ 78 Tim Belcher | .05 | .02 |
| ❑ 79 Cris Carpenter | .05 | .02 |
| ❑ 80 Checklist 1-79 | .05 | .02 |
| ❑ 81 Steve Avery | .05 | .02 |
| ❑ 82 Chris James | .05 | .02 |
| ❑ 83 Brian Harper | .05 | .02 |
| ❑ 84 Charlie Leibrandt | .05 | .02 |
| ❑ 85 Mickey Tettleton | .05 | .02 |
| ❑ 86 Pete O'Brien | .05 | .02 |
| ❑ 87 Danny Darwin | .05 | .02 |
| ❑ 88 Bob Walk | .05 | .02 |
| ❑ 89 Jeff Reardon | .10 | .05 |
| ❑ 90 Bobby Rose | .05 | .02 |
| ❑ 91 Danny Jackson | .05 | .02 |
| ❑ 92 John Morris | .05 | .02 |
| ❑ 93 Bud Black | .05 | .02 |
| ❑ 94 Tommy Greene HL | .05 | .02 |
| ❑ 95 Rick Aguilera | .10 | .05 |
| ❑ 96 Gary Gaetti | .10 | .05 |
| ❑ 97 David Cone | .10 | .05 |
| ❑ 98 John Olerud | .10 | .05 |
| ❑ 99 Joel Skinner | .05 | .02 |
| ❑ 100 Jay Bell | .10 | .05 |
| ❑ 101 Bob Milacki | .05 | .02 |
| ❑ 102 Norm Charlton | .05 | .02 |
| ❑ 103 Chuck Crim | .05 | .02 |
| ❑ 104 Terry Steinbach | .05 | .02 |
| ❑ 105 Juan Samuel | .05 | .02 |
| ❑ 106 Steve Howe | .05 | .02 |
| ❑ 107 Rafael Belliard | .05 | .02 |
| ❑ 108 Joey Cora | .05 | .02 |
| ❑ 109 Tommy Greene | .05 | .02 |
| ❑ 110 Gregg Olson | .05 | .02 |
| ❑ 111 Frank Tanana | .05 | .02 |
| ❑ 112 Lee Smith | .10 | .05 |
| ❑ 113 Greg A. Harris | .05 | .02 |
| ❑ 114 Dwayne Henry | .05 | .02 |
| ❑ 115 Chili Davis | .10 | .05 |
| ❑ 116 Kent Mercker | .05 | .02 |
| ❑ 117 Brian Barnes | .05 | .02 |
| ❑ 118 Rich DeLucia | .05 | .02 |
| ❑ 119 Andre Dawson | .10 | .05 |
| ❑ 120 Carlos Baerga | .05 | .02 |
| ❑ 121 Mike LaValliere | .05 | .02 |
| ❑ 122 Jeff Gray | .05 | .02 |
| ❑ 123 Bruce Hurst | .05 | .02 |
| ❑ 124 Alvin Davis | .05 | .02 |
| ❑ 125 John Candelaria | .05 | .02 |
| ❑ 126 Matt Nokes | .05 | .02 |
| ❑ 127 George Bell | .05 | .02 |

- ❑ 128 Bret Saberhagen .10 .05
- ❑ 129 Jeff Russell .05 .02
- ❑ 130 Jim Abbott .10 .05
- ❑ 131 Bill Gullickson .05 .02
- ❑ 132 Todd Zeile .05 .02
- ❑ 133 Dave Winfield .20 .09
- ❑ 134 Wally Whitehurst .05 .02
- ❑ 135 Matt Williams .10 .05
- ❑ 136 Tom Browning .05 .02
- ❑ 137 Marquis Grissom .05 .02
- ❑ 138 Erik Hanson .05 .02
- ❑ 139 Rob Dibble .05 .02
- ❑ 140 Don August .05 .02
- ❑ 141 Tom Henke .05 .02
- ❑ 142 Dan Pasqua .05 .02
- ❑ 143 George Brett .40 .18
- ❑ 144 Jerald Clark .05 .02
- ❑ 145 Robin Ventura .10 .05
- ❑ 146 Dale Murphy .20 .09
- ❑ 147 Dennis Eckersley .10 .05
- ❑ 148 Eric Yelding .05 .02
- ❑ 149 Mario Diaz .05 .02
- ❑ 150 Casey Candaele .05 .02
- ❑ 151 Steve Olin .05 .02
- ❑ 152 Luis Salazar .05 .02
- ❑ 153 Kevin Maas .05 .02
- ❑ 154 Nolan Ryan HL .40 .18
- ❑ 155 Barry Jones .05 .02
- ❑ 156 Chris Hoiles .05 .02
- ❑ 157 Bob Ojeda .05 .02
- ❑ 158 Pedro Guerrero .05 .02
- ❑ 159 Paul Assenmacher .05 .02
- ❑ 160 Checklist 80-157 .05 .02
- ❑ 161 Mike Macfarlane .05 .02
- ❑ 162 Craig Lefferts .05 .02
- ❑ 163 Brian Hunter .05 .02
- ❑ 164 Alan Trammell .10 .05
- ❑ 165 Ken Griffey Jr. .75 .35
- ❑ 166 Lance Parrish .05 .02
- ❑ 167 Brian Downing .05 .02
- ❑ 168 John Barfield .05 .02
- ❑ 169 Jack Clark .10 .05
- ❑ 170 Chris Nabholz .05 .02
- ❑ 171 Tim Teufel .05 .02
- ❑ 172 Chris Hammond .05 .02
- ❑ 173 Robin Yount .20 .09
- ❑ 174 Dave Righetti .05 .02
- ❑ 175 Joe Girardi .10 .05
- ❑ 176 Mike Boddicker .05 .02
- ❑ 177 Dean Palmer .10 .05
- ❑ 178 Greg Hibbard .05 .02
- ❑ 179 Randy Ready .05 .02
- ❑ 180 Devon White .05 .02
- ❑ 181 Mark Eichhorn .05 .02
- ❑ 182 Mike Felder .05 .02
- ❑ 183 Joe Klink .05 .02
- ❑ 184 Steve Bedrosian .05 .02
- ❑ 185 Barry Larkin .10 .05
- ❑ 186 John Franco .10 .05
- ❑ 187 Ed Sprague .05 .02
- ❑ 188 Mark Portugal .05 .02
- ❑ 189 Jose Lind .05 .02
- ❑ 190 Bob Welch .05 .02
- ❑ 191 Alex Fernandez .10 .05
- ❑ 192 Gary Sheffield .20 .09
- ❑ 193 Rickey Henderson .25 .11
- ❑ 194 Rod Nichols .05 .02
- ❑ 195 Scott Kamieniecki .05 .02
- ❑ 196 Mike Flanagan .05 .02
- ❑ 197 Steve Finley .10 .05
- ❑ 198 Darren Daulton .10 .05
- ❑ 199 Leo Gomez .05 .02
- ❑ 200 Mike Morgan .05 .02
- ❑ 201 Bob Tewksbury .05 .02
- ❑ 202 Sid Bream .05 .02
- ❑ 203 Sandy Alomar Jr. .10 .05
- ❑ 204 Greg Gagne .05 .02
- ❑ 205 Juan Berenguer .05 .02
- ❑ 206 Cecil Fielder .10 .05
- ❑ 207 Randy Johnson .25 .11
- ❑ 208 Tony Pena .05 .02
- ❑ 209 Doug Drabek .05 .02
- ❑ 210 Wade Boggs .25 .11
- ❑ 211 Bryan Harvey .05 .02
- ❑ 212 Jose Vizcaino .05 .02
- ❑ 213 Alonzo Powell .05 .02
- ❑ 214 Will Clark .20 .09
- ❑ 215 Rickey Henderson HL .10 .05
- ❑ 216 Jack Morris .10 .05
- ❑ 217 Junior Felix .05 .02
- ❑ 218 Vince Coleman .05 .02
- ❑ 219 Jimmy Key .10 .05
- ❑ 220 Alex Cole .05 .02
- ❑ 221 Bill Landrum .05 .02
- ❑ 222 Randy Milligan .05 .02
- ❑ 223 Jose Rijo .05 .02
- ❑ 224 Greg Vaughn .10 .05
- ❑ 225 Dave Stewart .10 .05
- ❑ 226 Lenny Harris .05 .02
- ❑ 227 Scott Sanderson .05 .02
- ❑ 228 Jeff Blauser .05 .02
- ❑ 229 Ozzie Guillen .05 .02
- ❑ 230 John Kruk .10 .05
- ❑ 231 Bob Melvin .05 .02
- ❑ 232 Milt Cuyler .05 .02
- ❑ 233 Felix Jose .05 .02
- ❑ 234 Ellis Burks .10 .05
- ❑ 235 Pete Harnisch .05 .02
- ❑ 236 Kevin Tapani .05 .02
- ❑ 237 Terry Pendleton .10 .05
- ❑ 238 Mark Gardner .05 .02
- ❑ 239 Harold Reynolds .05 .02
- ❑ 240 Checklist 158-237 .05 .02
- ❑ 241 Mike Harkey .05 .02
- ❑ 242 Felix Fermin .05 .02
- ❑ 243 Barry Bonds .30 .14
- ❑ 244 Roger Clemens .40 .18
- ❑ 245 Dennis Rasmussen .05 .02
- ❑ 246 Jose DeLeon .05 .02
- ❑ 247 Orel Hershiser .10 .05
- ❑ 248 Mel Hall .05 .02
- ❑ 249 Rick Wilkins .05 .02
- ❑ 250 Tom Gordon .05 .02
- ❑ 251 Kevin Reimer .05 .02
- ❑ 252 Luis Polonia .05 .02
- ❑ 253 Mike Henneman .05 .02
- ❑ 254 Tom Pagnozzi .05 .02
- ❑ 255 Chuck Finley .10 .05
- ❑ 256 Mackey Sasser .05 .02
- ❑ 257 John Burkett .05 .02
- ❑ 258 Hal Morris .05 .02
- ❑ 259 Larry Walker .10 .05
- ❑ 260 Bill Swift .05 .02
- ❑ 261 Joe Oliver .05 .02
- ❑ 262 Julio Machado .05 .02
- ❑ 263 Todd Stottlemyre .10 .05
- ❑ 264 Matt Merullo .05 .02
- ❑ 265 Brent Mayne .05 .02
- ❑ 266 Thomas Howard .05 .02
- ❑ 267 Lance Johnson .05 .02
- ❑ 268 Terry Mulholland .05 .02
- ❑ 269 Rick Honeycutt .05 .02
- ❑ 270 Luis Gonzalez .10 .05
- ❑ 271 Jose Guzman .05 .02
- ❑ 272 Jimmy Jones .05 .02
- ❑ 273 Mark Lewis .05 .02
- ❑ 274 Rene Gonzales .05 .02
- ❑ 275 Jeff Johnson .05 .02
- ❑ 276 Dennis Martinez HL .05 .02
- ❑ 277 Delino DeShields .10 .05
- ❑ 278 Sam Horn .05 .02
- ❑ 279 Kevin Gross .05 .02
- ❑ 280 Jose Oquendo .05 .02
- ❑ 281 Mark Grace .20 .09
- ❑ 282 Mark Gubicza .05 .02
- ❑ 283 Fred McGriff .10 .05
- ❑ 284 Ron Gant .10 .05
- ❑ 285 Lou Whitaker .10 .05
- ❑ 286 Edgar Martinez .10 .05
- ❑ 287 Ron Tingley .05 .02
- ❑ 288 Kevin McReynolds .05 .02
- ❑ 289 Ivan Rodriguez .40 .18
- ❑ 290 Mike Gardiner .05 .02
- ❑ 291 Chris Haney .05 .02
- ❑ 292 Darrin Jackson .05 .02
- ❑ 293 Bill Doran .05 .02
- ❑ 294 Ted Higuera .05 .02
- ❑ 295 Jeff Brantley .05 .02
- ❑ 296 Les Lancaster .05 .02
- ❑ 297 Jim Eisenreich .05 .02
- ❑ 298 Ruben Sierra .05 .02
- ❑ 299 Scott Radinsky .05 .02
- ❑ 300 Jose DeJesus .05 .02
- ❑ 301 Mike Timlin .05 .02
- ❑ 302 Luis Sojo .05 .02
- ❑ 303 Kelly Downs .05 .02
- ❑ 304 Scott Bankhead .05 .02
- ❑ 305 Pedro Munoz .05 .02
- ❑ 306 Scott Scudder .05 .02
- ❑ 307 Kevin Elster .05 .02
- ❑ 308 Duane Ward .05 .02
- ❑ 309 Darryl Kile .10 .05
- ❑ 310 Orlando Merced .05 .02
- ❑ 311 Dave Henderson .05 .02
- ❑ 312 Tim Raines .10 .05
- ❑ 313 Mark Lee .05 .02
- ❑ 314 Mike Gallego .05 .02
- ❑ 315 Charles Nagy .05 .02
- ❑ 316 Jesse Barfield .05 .02
- ❑ 317 Todd Frohwirth .05 .02
- ❑ 318 Al Osuna .05 .02
- ❑ 319 Darrin Fletcher .05 .02
- ❑ 320 Checklist 238-316 .05 .02
- ❑ 321 David Segui .05 .02
- ❑ 322 Stan Javier .05 .02
- ❑ 323 Bryn Smith .05 .02
- ❑ 324 Jeff Treadway .05 .02
- ❑ 325 Mark Whiten .05 .02
- ❑ 326 Kent Hrbek .10 .05
- ❑ 327 Dave Justice .10 .05
- ❑ 328 Tony Phillips .05 .02
- ❑ 329 Rob Murphy .05 .02
- ❑ 330 Kevin Morton .05 .02
- ❑ 331 John Smiley .05 .02
- ❑ 332 Luis Rivera .05 .02
- ❑ 333 Wally Joyner .10 .05
- ❑ 334 Heathcliff Slocumb .05 .02
- ❑ 335 Rick Cerone .05 .02
- ❑ 336 Mike Remlinger .05 .02
- ❑ 337 Mike Moore .05 .02
- ❑ 338 Lloyd McClendon .05 .02
- ❑ 339 Al Newman .05 .02
- ❑ 340 Kirk McCaskill .05 .02
- ❑ 341 Howard Johnson .05 .02
- ❑ 342 Greg Myers .05 .02
- ❑ 343 Kal Daniels .05 .02
- ❑ 344 Bernie Williams .20 .09
- ❑ 345 Shane Mack .05 .02
- ❑ 346 Gary Thurman .05 .02
- ❑ 347 Dante Bichette .10 .05
- ❑ 348 Mark McGwire .75 .35
- ❑ 349 Travis Fryman .10 .05
- ❑ 350 Ray Lankford .20 .09
- ❑ 351 Mike Jeffcoat .05 .02
- ❑ 352 Jack McDowell .05 .02
- ❑ 353 Mitch Williams .05 .02
- ❑ 354 Mike Devereaux .05 .02
- ❑ 355 Andres Galarraga .10 .05
- ❑ 356 Henry Cotto .05 .02
- ❑ 357 Scott Bailes .05 .02
- ❑ 358 Jeff Bagwell .40 .18
- ❑ 359 Scott Leius .05 .02
- ❑ 360 Zane Smith .05 .02
- ❑ 361 Bill Pecota .05 .02
- ❑ 362 Tony Fernandez .05 .02
- ❑ 363 Glenn Braggs .05 .02
- ❑ 364 Bill Spiers .05 .02
- ❑ 365 Vicente Palacios .05 .02
- ❑ 366 Tim Burke .05 .02
- ❑ 367 Randy Tomlin .05 .02
- ❑ 368 Kenny Rogers .05 .02
- ❑ 369 Brett Butler .10 .05
- ❑ 370 Pat Kelly .05 .02
- ❑ 371 Bip Roberts .05 .02
- ❑ 372 Gregg Jefferies .05 .02
- ❑ 373 Kevin Bass .05 .02
- ❑ 374 Ron Karkovice .05 .02
- ❑ 375 Paul Gibson .05 .02
- ❑ 376 Bernard Gilkey .10 .05
- ❑ 377 Dave Gallagher .05 .02
- ❑ 378 Bill Wegman .05 .02
- ❑ 379 Pat Borders .05 .02
- ❑ 380 Ed Whitson .05 .02
- ❑ 381 Gilberto Reyes .05 .02
- ❑ 382 Russ Swan .05 .02
- ❑ 383 Andy Van Slyke .10 .05
- ❑ 384 Wes Chamberlain .05 .02
- ❑ 385 Steve Chitren .05 .02

❑ 386 Greg Olson .05 .02
❑ 387 Brian McRae .05 .02
❑ 388 Rich Rodriguez .05 .02
❑ 389 Steve Decker .05 .02
❑ 390 Chuck Knoblauch .10 .05
❑ 391 Bobby Witt .05 .02
❑ 392 Eddie Murray .20 .09
❑ 393 Juan Gonzalez .20 .09
❑ 394 Scott Ruskin .05 .02
❑ 395 Jay Howell .05 .02
❑ 396 Checklist 317-396 .05 .02
❑ 397 Royce Clayton RR .05 .02
❑ 398 John Jaha RR RC .25 .11
❑ 399 Dan Wilson RR .10 .05
❑ 400 Archie Corbin RR .05 .02
❑ 401 Barry Manuel RR .05 .02
❑ 402 Kim Batiste RR .05 .02
❑ 403 Pat Mahomes RR RC .05 .02
❑ 404 Dave Fleming RR .05 .02
❑ 405 Jeff Juden RR .05 .02
❑ 406 Jim Thome RR .40 .18
❑ 407 Sam Militello RR .05 .02
❑ 408 Jeff Nelson RR RC .05 .02
❑ 409 Anthony Young RR .05 .02
❑ 410 Tino Martinez RR .10 .05
❑ 411 Jeff Mutis RR .05 .02
❑ 412 Rey Sanchez RR RC .05 .02
❑ 413 Chris Gardner RR .05 .02
❑ 414 John Vander Wal RR .05 .02
❑ 415 Reggie Sanders RR .05 .02
❑ 416 Brian Williams RR RC .05 .02
❑ 417 Mo Sanford RR .05 .02
❑ 418 David Weathers RR RC .05 .02
❑ 419 Hector Fajardo RR RC .05 .02
❑ 420 Steve Foster RR .05 .02
❑ 421 Lance Dickson RR .05 .02
❑ 422 Andre Dawson AS .10 .05
❑ 423 Ozzie Smith AS .20 .09
❑ 424 Chris Sabo AS .05 .02
❑ 425 Tony Gwynn AS .20 .09
❑ 426 Tom Glavine AS .10 .05
❑ 427 Bobby Bonilla AS .05 .02
❑ 428 Will Clark AS .10 .05
❑ 429 Ryne Sandberg AS .20 .09
❑ 430 Benito Santiago AS .05 .02
❑ 431 Ivan Calderon AS .05 .02
❑ 432 Ozzie Smith .25 .11
❑ 433 Tim Leary .05 .02
❑ 434 Bret Saberhagen HL .05 .02
❑ 435 Mel Rojas .05 .02
❑ 436 Ben McDonald .05 .02
❑ 437 Tim Crews .05 .02
❑ 438 Rex Hudler .05 .02
❑ 439 Chico Walker .05 .02
❑ 440 Kurt Stillwell .05 .02
❑ 441 Tony Gwynn .40 .18
❑ 442 John Smoltz .10 .05
❑ 443 Lloyd Moseby .05 .02
❑ 444 Mike Schooler .05 .02
❑ 445 Joe Grahe .05 .02
❑ 446 Dwight Gooden .10 .05
❑ 447 Oil Can Boyd .05 .02
❑ 448 John Marzano .05 .02
❑ 449 Bret Barberie .05 .02
❑ 450 Mike Maddux .05 .02
❑ 451 Jeff Reed .05 .02
❑ 452 Dale Sveum .05 .02
❑ 453 Jose Uribe .05 .02
❑ 454 Bob Scanlan .05 .02
❑ 455 Kevin Appier .10 .05
❑ 456 Jeff Huson .05 .02
❑ 457 Ken Patterson .05 .02
❑ 458 Ricky Jordan .05 .02
❑ 459 Tom Candiotti .05 .02
❑ 460 Lee Stevens .10 .05
❑ 461 Rod Beck RC .20 .09
❑ 462 Dave Valle .05 .02
❑ 463 Scott Erickson .05 .02
❑ 464 Chris Jones .05 .02
❑ 465 Mark Carreon .05 .02
❑ 466 Rob Ducey .05 .02
❑ 467 Jim Corsi .05 .02
❑ 468 Jeff King .05 .02
❑ 469 Curt Young .05 .02
❑ 470 Bo Jackson .10 .05
❑ 471 Chris Bosio .05 .02
❑ 472 Jamie Quirk .05 .02
❑ 473 Jesse Orosco .05 .02
❑ 474 Alvaro Espinoza .05 .02
❑ 475 Joe Orsulak .05 .02
❑ 476 Checklist 397-477 .05 .02
❑ 477 Gerald Young .05 .02
❑ 478 Wally Backman .05 .02
❑ 479 Juan Bell .05 .02
❑ 480 Mike Scioscia .05 .02
❑ 481 Omar Olivares .05 .02
❑ 482 Francisco Cabrera .05 .02
❑ 483 Greg Swindell UER .05 .02
(Shown on Indians,
but listed on Reds)
❑ 484 Terry Leach .05 .02
❑ 485 Tommy Gregg .05 .02
❑ 486 Scott Aldred .05 .02
❑ 487 Greg Briley .05 .02
❑ 488 Phil Plantier .05 .02
❑ 489 Curtis Wilkerson .05 .02
❑ 490 Tom Brunansky .05 .02
❑ 491 Mike Fetters .05 .02
❑ 492 Frank Castillo .05 .02
❑ 493 Joe Boever .05 .02
❑ 494 Kirt Manwaring .05 .02
❑ 495 Wilson Alvarez HL .05 .02
❑ 496 Gene Larkin .05 .02
❑ 497 Gary DiSarcina .05 .02
❑ 498 Frank Viola .05 .02
❑ 499 Manuel Lee .05 .02
❑ 500 Albert Belle .10 .05
❑ 501 Stan Belinda .05 .02
❑ 502 Dwight Evans .10 .05
❑ 503 Eric Davis .10 .05
❑ 504 Darren Holmes .05 .02
❑ 505 Mike Bordick .05 .02
❑ 506 Dave Hansen .05 .02
❑ 507 Lee Guetterman .05 .02
❑ 508 Keith Mitchell .05 .02
❑ 509 Melido Perez .05 .02
❑ 510 Dickie Thon .05 .02
❑ 511 Mark Williamson .05 .02
❑ 512 Mark Salas .05 .02
❑ 513 Milt Thompson .05 .02
❑ 514 Mo Vaughn .25 .11
❑ 515 Jim Deshaies .05 .02
❑ 516 Rich Garces .05 .02
❑ 517 Lonnie Smith .05 .02
❑ 518 Spike Owen .05 .02
❑ 519 Tracy Jones .05 .02
❑ 520 Greg Maddux .50 .23
❑ 521 Carlos Martinez .05 .02
❑ 522 Neal Heaton .05 .02
❑ 523 Mike Greenwell .05 .02
❑ 524 Andy Benes .05 .02
❑ 525 Jeff Schaefer UER .05 .02
(Photo actually
Tino Martinez)
❑ 526 Mike Sharperson .05 .02
❑ 527 Wade Taylor .05 .02
❑ 528 Jerome Walton .05 .02
❑ 529 Storm Davis .05 .02
❑ 530 Jose Hernandez RC .05 .02
❑ 531 Mark Langston .05 .02
❑ 532 Rob Deer .05 .02
❑ 533 Geronimo Pena .05 .02
❑ 534 Juan Guzman .05 .02
❑ 535 Pete Schourek .05 .02
❑ 536 Todd Benzinger .05 .02
❑ 537 Billy Hatcher .05 .02
❑ 538 Tom Foley .05 .02
❑ 539 Dave Cochrane .05 .02
❑ 540 Mariano Duncan .05 .02
❑ 541 Edwin Nunez .05 .02
❑ 542 Rance Mulliniks .05 .02
❑ 543 Carlton Fisk .20 .09
❑ 544 Luis Aquino .05 .02
❑ 545 Ricky Bones .05 .02
❑ 546 Craig Grebeck .05 .02
❑ 547 Charlie Hayes .05 .02
❑ 548 Jose Canseco .25 .11
❑ 549 Andujar Cedeno .05 .02
❑ 550 Geno Petralli .05 .02
❑ 551 Javier Ortiz .05 .02
❑ 552 Rudy Seanez .05 .02
❑ 553 Rich Gedman .05 .02
❑ 554 Eric Plunk .05 .02
❑ 555 Nolan Ryan HL .40 .18
(With Rich Gossage)
❑ 556 Checklist 478-555 .05 .02
❑ 557 Greg Colbrunn .05 .02
❑ 558 Chito Martinez .05 .02
❑ 559 Darryl Strawberry .10 .05
❑ 560 Luis Alicea .05 .02
❑ 561 Dwight Smith .05 .02
❑ 562 Terry Shumpert .05 .02
❑ 563 Jim Vatcher .05 .02
❑ 564 Deion Sanders .20 .09
❑ 565 Walt Terrell .05 .02
❑ 566 Dave Burba .05 .02
❑ 567 Dave Howard .05 .02
❑ 568 Todd Hundley .05 .02
❑ 569 Jack Daugherty .05 .02
❑ 570 Scott Cooper .05 .02
❑ 571 Bill Sampen .05 .02
❑ 572 Jose Melendez .05 .02
❑ 573 Freddie Benavides .05 .02
❑ 574 Jim Gantner .05 .02
❑ 575 Trevor Wilson .05 .02
❑ 576 Ryne Sandberg .25 .11
❑ 577 Kevin Seitzer .05 .02
❑ 578 Gerald Alexander .05 .02
❑ 579 Mike Huff .05 .02
❑ 580 Von Hayes .05 .02
❑ 581 Derek Bell .10 .05
❑ 582 Mike Stanley .05 .02
❑ 583 Kevin Mitchell .10 .05
❑ 584 Mike Jackson .05 .02
❑ 585 Dan Gladden .05 .02
❑ 586 Ted Power UER .05 .02
(Wrong year given for
signing with Reds)
❑ 587 Jeff Innis .05 .02
❑ 588 Bob MacDonald .05 .02
❑ 589 Jose Tolentino .05 .02
❑ 590 Bob Patterson .05 .02
❑ 591 Scott Brosius RC .25 .11
❑ 592 Frank Thomas .40 .18
❑ 593 Darryl Hamilton .05 .02
❑ 594 Kirk Dressendorfer .05 .02
❑ 595 Jeff Shaw .05 .02
❑ 596 Don Mattingly .50 .23
❑ 597 Glenn Davis .05 .02
❑ 598 Andy Mota .05 .02
❑ 599 Jason Grimsley .05 .02
❑ 600 Jim Poole .05 .02
❑ 601 Jim Gott .05 .02
❑ 602 Stan Royer .05 .02
❑ 603 Marvin Freeman .05 .02
❑ 604 Denis Boucher .05 .02
❑ 605 Denny Neagle .10 .05
❑ 606 Mark Lemke .05 .02
❑ 607 Jerry Don Gleaton .05 .02
❑ 608 Brent Knackert .05 .02
❑ 609 Carlos Quintana .05 .02
❑ 610 Bobby Bonilla .10 .05
❑ 611 Joe Hesketh .05 .02
❑ 612 Daryl Boston .05 .02
❑ 613 Shawon Dunston .05 .02
❑ 614 Danny Cox .05 .02
❑ 615 Darren Lewis .05 .02
❑ 616 Braves No-Hitter UER .05 .02
Kent Mercker
(Misspelled Merker
on card front)
Alejandro Pena
Mark Wohlers
❑ 617 Kirby Puckett .50 .23
❑ 618 Franklin Stubbs .05 .02
❑ 619 Chris Donnels .05 .02
❑ 620 David Wells UER .10 .05
(Career Highlights
in black not red)
❑ 621 Mike Aldrete .05 .02
❑ 622 Bob Kipper .05 .02
❑ 623 Anthony Telford .05 .02
❑ 624 Randy Myers .10 .05
❑ 625 Willie Randolph .10 .05
❑ 626 Joe Slusarski .05 .02
❑ 627 John Wetteland .10 .05
❑ 628 Greg Cadaret .05 .02
❑ 629 Tom Glavine .10 .05

❑ 630 Wilson Alvarez .05 .02
❑ 631 Wally Ritchie .05 .02
❑ 632 Mike Mussina .30 .14
❑ 633 Mark Leiter .05 .02
❑ 634 Gerald Perry .05 .02
❑ 635 Matt Young .05 .02
❑ 636 Checklist 556-635 .05 .02
❑ 637 Scott Hemond .05 .02
❑ 638 David West .05 .02
❑ 639 Jim Clancy .05 .02
❑ 640 Doug Piatt UER .05 .02
(Not born in 1955 as on card; incorrect info on How Acquired)
❑ 641 Omar Vizquel .10 .05
❑ 642 Rick Sutcliffe .10 .05
❑ 643 Glenallen Hill .05 .02
❑ 644 Gary Varsho .05 .02
❑ 645 Tony Fossas .05 .02
❑ 646 Jack Howell .05 .02
❑ 647 Jim Campanis .05 .02
❑ 648 Chris Gwynn .05 .02
❑ 649 Jim Leyritz .05 .02
❑ 650 Chuck McElroy .05 .02
❑ 651 Sean Berry .05 .02
❑ 652 Donald Harris .05 .02
❑ 653 Don Slaught .05 .02
❑ 654 Rusty Meacham .05 .02
❑ 655 Scott Terry .05 .02
❑ 656 Ramon Martinez .05 .02
❑ 657 Keith Miller .05 .02
❑ 658 Ramon Garcia .05 .02
❑ 659 Milt Hill .05 .02
❑ 660 Steve Frey .05 .02
❑ 661 Bob McClure .05 .02
❑ 662 Cod Landrum .05 .02
❑ 663 Doug Henry RC .05 .02
❑ 664 Candy Maldonado .05 .02
❑ 665 Carl Willis .05 .02
❑ 666 Jeff Montgomery .10 .05
❑ 667 Craig Shipley .05 .02
❑ 668 Warren Newson .05 .02
❑ 669 Mickey Morandini .05 .02
❑ 670 Brook Jacoby .05 .02
❑ 671 Ryan Bowen .05 .02
❑ 672 Bill Krueger .05 .02
❑ 673 Rob Mallicoat .05 .02
❑ 674 Doug Jones .05 .02
❑ 675 Scott Livingstone .05 .02
❑ 676 Danny Tartabull .05 .02
❑ 677 Joe Carter HL .05 .02
❑ 678 Cecil Espy .05 .02
❑ 679 Randy Velarde .05 .02
❑ 680 Bruce Ruffin .05 .02
❑ 681 Ted Wood .05 .02
❑ 682 Dan Plesac .05 .02
❑ 683 Eric Bullock .05 .02
❑ 684 Junior Ortiz .05 .02
❑ 685 Dave Hollins .05 .02
❑ 686 Dennis Martinez .10 .05
❑ 687 Larry Andersen .05 .02
❑ 688 Doug Simons .05 .02
❑ 689 Tim Spehr .05 .02
❑ 690 Calvin Jones .05 .02
❑ 691 Mark Guthrie .05 .02
❑ 692 Alfredo Griffin .05 .02
❑ 693 Joe Carter .10 .05
❑ 694 Terry Mathews .05 .02
❑ 695 Pascual Perez .05 .02
❑ 696 Gene Nelson .05 .02
❑ 697 Gerald Williams .05 .02
❑ 698 Chris Cron .05 .02
❑ 699 Steve Buechele .05 .02
❑ 700 Paul McClellan .05 .02
❑ 701 Jim Lindeman .05 .02
❑ 702 Francisco Oliveras .05 .02
❑ 703 Rob Maurer .05 .02
❑ 704 Pat Hentgen .05 .02
❑ 705 Jaime Navarro .05 .02
❑ 706 Mike Magnante RC .05 .02
❑ 707 Nolan Ryan 1.00 .45
❑ 708 Bobby Thigpen .05 .02
❑ 709 John Cerutti .05 .02
❑ 710 Steve Wilson .05 .02
❑ 711 Hensley Meulens .05 .02
❑ 712 Rheal Cormier .05 .02
❑ 713 Scott Bradley .05 .02
❑ 714 Mitch Webster .05 .02
❑ 715 Roger Mason .05 .02
❑ 716 Checklist 636-716 .05 .02
❑ 717 Jeff Fassero .05 .02
❑ 718 Cal Eldred .05 .02
❑ 719 Sid Fernandez .05 .02
❑ 720 Bob Zupcic RC .05 .02
❑ 721 Jose Offerman .05 .02
❑ 722 Cliff Brantley .05 .02
❑ 723 Ron Darling .05 .02
❑ 724 Dave Stieb .05 .02
❑ 725 Hector Villanueva .05 .02
❑ 726 Mike Hartley .05 .02
❑ 727 Arthur Rhodes .05 .02
❑ 728 Randy Bush .05 .02
❑ 729 Steve Sax .05 .02
❑ 730 Dave Otto .05 .02
❑ 731 John Wehner .05 .02
❑ 732 Dave Martinez .05 .02
❑ 733 Ruben Amaro .05 .02
❑ 734 Billy Ripken .05 .02
❑ 735 Steve Farr .05 .02
❑ 736 Shawn Abner .05 .02
❑ 737 Gil Heredia .05 .02
❑ 738 Ron Jones .05 .02
❑ 739 Tony Castillo .05 .02
❑ 740 Sammy Sosa .40 .18
❑ 741 Julio Franco .05 .02
❑ 742 Tim Naehring .05 .02
❑ 743 Steve Wapnick .05 .02
❑ 744 Craig Wilson .05 .02
❑ 745 Darrin Chapin .05 .02
❑ 746 Chris George .05 .02
❑ 747 Mike Simms .05 .02
❑ 748 Rosario Rodriguez .05 .02
❑ 749 Skeeter Barnes .05 .02
❑ 750 Roger McDowell .05 .02
❑ 751 Dann Howitt .05 .02
❑ 752 Paul Sorrento .05 .02
❑ 753 Braulio Castillo .05 .02
❑ 754 Yorkis Perez .05 .02
❑ 755 Willie Fraser .05 .02
❑ 756 Jeremy Hernandez RC .05 .02
❑ 757 Curt Schilling .10 .05
❑ 758 Steve Lyons .05 .02
❑ 759 Dave Anderson .05 .02
❑ 760 Willie Banks .05 .02
❑ 761 Mark Leonard .05 .02
❑ 762 Jack Armstrong .05 .02
(Listed on Indians, but shown on Reds)
❑ 763 Scott Servais .05 .02
❑ 764 Ray Stephens .05 .02
❑ 765 Junior Noboa .05 .02
❑ 766 Jim Olander .05 .02
❑ 767 Joe Magrane .05 .02
❑ 768 Lance Blankenship .05 .02
❑ 769 Mike Humphreys .05 .02
❑ 770 Jarvis Brown .05 .02
❑ 771 Damon Berryhill .05 .02
❑ 772 Alejandro Pena .05 .02
❑ 773 Jose Mesa .05 .02
❑ 774 Gary Cooper .05 .02
❑ 775 Carney Lansford .10 .05
❑ 776 Mike Bielecki .05 .02
(Shown on Cubs, but listed on Braves)
❑ 777 Charlie O'Brien .05 .02
❑ 778 Carlos Hernandez .05 .02
❑ 779 Howard Farmer .05 .02
❑ 780 Mike Stanton .05 .02
❑ 781 Reggie Harris .05 .02
❑ 782 Xavier Hernandez .05 .02
❑ 783 Bryan Hickerson RC .05 .02
❑ 784 Checklist 717-784 and BC1-BC8 .05 .02

## 1992 Donruss Rookies

| | MINT | NRMT |
|---|---|---|
| COMPLETE SET (132) | 10.00 | 4.50 |

❑ 1 Kyle Abbott .05 .02
❑ 2 Troy Afenir .05 .02
❑ 3 Rich Amaral RC .05 .02

❑ 4 Ruben Amaro .05 .02
❑ 5 Billy Ashley RC .05 .02
❑ 6 Pedro Astacio RC .40 .18
❑ 7 Jim Austin .05 .02
❑ 8 Robert Ayrault .05 .02
❑ 9 Kevin Baez .05 .02
❑ 10 Esteban Beltre .05 .02
❑ 11 Brian Bohanon .05 .02
❑ 12 Kent Bottenfield RC .25 .11
❑ 13 Jeff Branson .05 .02
❑ 14 Brad Brink .05 .02
❑ 15 John Briscoe .05 .02
❑ 16 Doug Brocail RC .05 .02
❑ 17 Rico Brogna .10 .05
❑ 18 J.T. Bruett .05 .02
❑ 19 Jacob Brumfield .05 .02
❑ 20 Jim Bullinger .05 .02
❑ 21 Kevin Campbell .05 .02
❑ 22 Pedro Castellano RC .05 .02
❑ 23 Mike Christopher .05 .02
❑ 24 Archi Cianfrocco RC .05 .02
❑ 25 Mark Clark RC .05 .02
❑ 26 Craig Colbert .05 .02
❑ 27 Victor Cole .05 .02
❑ 28 Steve Cooke RC .05 .02
❑ 29 Tim Costo .05 .02
❑ 30 Chad Curtis RC .25 .11
❑ 31 Doug Davis .05 .02
❑ 32 Gary DiSarcina .05 .02
❑ 33 John Doherty RC .05 .02
❑ 34 Mike Draper .05 .02
❑ 35 Monty Fariss .05 .02
❑ 36 Bien Figueroa .05 .02
❑ 37 John Flaherty .05 .02
❑ 38 Tim Fortugno .05 .02
❑ 39 Eric Fox RC .05 .02
❑ 40 Jeff Frye .05 .02
❑ 41 Ramon Garcia .05 .02
❑ 42 Brent Gates RC .05 .02
❑ 43 Tom Goodwin .10 .05
❑ 44 Buddy Groom .05 .02
❑ 45 Jeff Grotewold .05 .02
❑ 46 Juan Guerrero .05 .02
❑ 47 Johnny Guzman RC .05 .02
❑ 48 Shawn Hare RC .05 .02
❑ 49 Ryan Hawblitzel RC .05 .02
❑ 50 Bert Heffernan .05 .02
❑ 51 Butch Henry .05 .02
❑ 52 Cesar Hernandez RC .05 .02
❑ 53 Vince Horsman .05 .02
❑ 54 Steve Hosey .05 .02
❑ 55 Pat Howell .05 .02
❑ 56 Peter Hoy .05 .02
❑ 57 Jonathan Hurst RC .05 .02
❑ 58 Mark Hutton RC .05 .02
❑ 59 Shawn Jeter RC .05 .02
❑ 60 Joel Johnston .05 .02
❑ 61 Jeff Kent RC 2.00 .90
❑ 62 Kurt Knudsen RC .05 .02
❑ 63 Kevin Koslofski .05 .02
❑ 64 Danny Leon .05 .02
❑ 65 Jesse Levis .05 .02
❑ 66 Tom Marsh .05 .02
❑ 67 Ed Martel .05 .02
❑ 68 Al Martin RC .25 .11
❑ 69 Pedro Martinez 4.00 1.80
❑ 70 Derrick May .05 .02
❑ 71 Matt Maysey .05 .02

❑ 72 Russ McGinnis .05 .02
❑ 73 Tim McIntosh .05 .02
❑ 74 Jim McNamara .05 .02
❑ 75 Jeff McNeely .05 .02
❑ 76 Rusty Meacham .05 .02
❑ 77 Tony Menendez .05 .02
❑ 78 Henry Mercedes .05 .02
❑ 79 Paul Miller .05 .02
❑ 80 Joe Millette .05 .02
❑ 81 Blas Minor .05 .02
❑ 82 Dennis Moeller .05 .02
❑ 83 Raul Mondesi 1.00 .45
❑ 84 Rob Natal .05 .02
❑ 85 Troy Neel RC .05 .02
❑ 86 David Nied RC .05 .02
❑ 87 Jerry Nielson .05 .02
❑ 88 Donovan Osborne .05 .02
❑ 89 John Patterson .05 .02
❑ 90 Roger Pavlik RC .05 .02
❑ 91 Dan Peltier .05 .02
❑ 92 Jim Pena .05 .02
❑ 93 William Pennyfeather .05 .02
❑ 94 Mike Perez .05 .02
❑ 95 Hipolito Pichardo RC .05 .02
❑ 96 Greg Pirkl RC .05 .02
❑ 97 Harvey Pulliam .05 .02
❑ 98 Manny Ramirez RC 3.00 1.35
❑ 99 Pat Rapp RC .05 .02
❑ 100 Jeff Reboulet .05 .02
❑ 101 Darren Reed .05 .02
❑ 102 Shane Reynolds RC .25 .11
❑ 103 Bill Risley .05 .02
❑ 104 Ben Rivera .05 .02
❑ 105 Henry Rodriguez .05 .02
❑ 106 Rico Rossy .05 .02
❑ 107 Johnny Ruffin .05 .02
❑ 108 Steve Scarsone .05 .02
❑ 109 Tim Scott .05 .02
❑ 110 Steve Shifflett .05 .02
❑ 111 Dave Silvestri .05 .02
❑ 112 Matt Stairs RC .40 .18
❑ 113 William Suero .05 .02
❑ 114 Jeff Tackett .05 .02
❑ 115 Eddie Taubensee .10 .05
❑ 116 Rick Trlicek RC .05 .02
❑ 117 Scooter Tucker .05 .02
❑ 118 Shane Turner .05 .02
❑ 119 Julio Valera .05 .02
❑ 120 Paul Wagner RC .05 .02
❑ 121 Tim Wakefield RC .20 .09
❑ 122 Mike Walker .05 .02
❑ 123 Bruce Walton .05 .02
❑ 124 Lenny Webster .05 .02
❑ 125 Bob Wickman .05 .02
❑ 126 Mike Williams RC .05 .02
❑ 127 Kerry Woodson .05 .02
❑ 128 Eric Young RC .05 .02
❑ 129 Kevin Young RC .40 .18
❑ 130 Pete Young .05 .02
❑ 131 Checklist 1-66 .05 .02
❑ 132 Checklist 67-132 .05 .02

## 1993 Donruss

| | MINT | NRMT |
|---|---|---|
| COMPLETE SET (792) | 30.00 | 13.50 |
| COMPLETE SERIES 1 (396) | 15.00 | 6.75 |
| COMPLETE SERIES 2 (396) | 15.00 | 6.75 |

❑ 1 Craig Lefferts .10 .05
❑ 2 Kent Mercker .10 .05
❑ 3 Phil Plantier .10 .05
❑ 4 Alex Arias .10 .05
❑ 5 Julio Valera .10 .05
❑ 6 Dan Wilson .20 .09
❑ 7 Frank Thomas .75 .35
❑ 8 Eric Anthony .10 .05
❑ 9 Derek Lilliquist .10 .05
❑ 10 Rafael Bournigal .10 .05
❑ 11 Manny Alexander RR .10 .05
❑ 12 Bret Barberie .10 .05
❑ 13 Mickey Tettleton .10 .05
❑ 14 Anthony Young .10 .05
❑ 15 Tim Spehr .10 .05
❑ 16 Bob Ayrault .10 .05
❑ 17 Bill Wegman .10 .05
❑ 18 Jay Bell .20 .09
❑ 19 Rick Aguilera .10 .05
❑ 20 Todd Zeile .10 .05
❑ 21 Steve Farr .10 .05
❑ 22 Andy Benes .10 .05
❑ 23 Lance Blankenship .10 .05
❑ 24 Ted Wood .10 .05
❑ 25 Omar Vizquel .20 .09
❑ 26 Steve Avery .10 .05
❑ 27 Brian Bohanon .10 .05
❑ 28 Rick Wilkins .10 .05
❑ 29 Devon White .10 .05
❑ 30 Bobby Ayala RC .10 .05
❑ 31 Leo Gomez .10 .05
❑ 32 Mike Simms .10 .05
❑ 33 Ellis Burks .20 .09
❑ 34 Steve Wilson .10 .05
❑ 35 Jim Abbott .20 .09
❑ 36 Tim Wallach .10 .05
❑ 37 Wilson Alvarez .10 .05
❑ 38 Daryl Boston .10 .05
❑ 39 Sandy Alomar Jr. .20 .09
❑ 40 Mitch Williams .10 .05
❑ 41 Rico Brogna .20 .09
❑ 42 Gary Varsho .10 .05
❑ 43 Kevin Appier .20 .09
❑ 44 Eric Wedge RR RC .10 .05
❑ 45 Dante Bichette .20 .09
❑ 46 Jose Oquendo .10 .05
❑ 47 Mike Trombley .10 .05
❑ 48 Dan Walters .10 .05
❑ 49 Gerald Williams .10 .05
❑ 50 Bud Black .10 .05
❑ 51 Bobby Witt .10 .05
❑ 52 Mark Davis .10 .05
❑ 53 Shawn Barton RC .10 .05
❑ 54 Paul Assenmacher .10 .05
❑ 55 Kevin Reimer .10 .05
❑ 56 Billy Ashley RR .10 .05
❑ 57 Eddie Zosky .10 .05
❑ 58 Chris Sabo .10 .05
❑ 59 Billy Ripken .10 .05
❑ 60 Scooter Tucker .10 .05
❑ 61 Tim Wakefield RR .10 .05
❑ 62 Mitch Webster .10 .05
❑ 63 Jack Clark .10 .05
❑ 64 Mark Gardner .10 .05
❑ 65 Lee Stevens .20 .09
❑ 66 Todd Hundley .10 .05
❑ 67 Bobby Thigpen .10 .05
❑ 68 Dave Hollins .10 .05
❑ 69 Jack Armstrong .10 .05
❑ 70 Alex Cole .10 .05
❑ 71 Mark Carreon .10 .05
❑ 72 Todd Worrell .10 .05
❑ 73 Steve Shifflett .10 .05
❑ 74 Jerald Clark .10 .05
❑ 75 Paul Molitor .40 .18
❑ 76 Larry Carter .10 .05
❑ 77 Rich Rowland RR .10 .05
❑ 78 Damon Berryhill .10 .05
❑ 79 Willie Banks .10 .05
❑ 80 Hector Villanueva .10 .05
❑ 81 Mike Gallego .10 .05
❑ 82 Tim Belcher .10 .05
❑ 83 Mike Bordick .10 .05
❑ 84 Craig Biggio .20 .09
❑ 85 Lance Parrish .10 .05
❑ 86 Brett Butler .20 .09
❑ 87 Mike Timlin .10 .05
❑ 88 Brian Barnes .10 .05
❑ 89 Brady Anderson .20 .09
❑ 90 D.J. Dozier .10 .05
❑ 91 Frank Viola .10 .05
❑ 92 Darren Daulton .20 .09
❑ 93 Chad Curtis .10 .05
❑ 94 Zane Smith .10 .05
❑ 95 George Bell .10 .05
❑ 96 Rex Hudler .10 .05
❑ 97 Mark Whiten .10 .05
❑ 98 Tim Teufel .10 .05
❑ 99 Kevin Ritz .10 .05
❑ 100 Jeff Brantley .10 .05
❑ 101 Jeff Conine .10 .05
❑ 102 Vinny Castilla .50 .23
❑ 103 Greg Vaughn .20 .09
❑ 104 Steve Buechele .10 .05
❑ 105 Darren Reed .10 .05
❑ 106 Bip Roberts .10 .05
❑ 107 John Habyan .10 .05
❑ 108 Scott Servais .10 .05
❑ 109 Walt Weiss .10 .05
❑ 110 J.T. Snow RR RC .50 .23
❑ 111 Jay Buhner .20 .09
❑ 112 Darryl Strawberry .20 .09
❑ 113 Roger Pavlik .10 .05
❑ 114 Chris Nabholz .10 .05
❑ 115 Pat Borders .10 .05
❑ 116 Pat Howell .10 .05
❑ 117 Gregg Olson .10 .05
❑ 118 Curt Schilling .20 .09
❑ 119 Roger Clemens .75 .35
❑ 120 Victor Cole .10 .05
❑ 121 Gary DiSarcina .10 .05
❑ 122 Checklist 1-80 .20 .09
Gary Carter and
Kirt Manwaring
❑ 123 Steve Sax .10 .05
❑ 124 Chuck Carr .10 .05
❑ 125 Mark Lewis .10 .05
❑ 126 Tony Gwynn .75 .35
❑ 127 Travis Fryman .20 .09
❑ 128 Dave Burba .10 .05
❑ 129 Wally Joyner .20 .09
❑ 130 John Smoltz .20 .09
❑ 131 Cal Eldred .10 .05
❑ 132 Checklist 81-159 .20 .09
Roberto Alomar and
Devon White
❑ 133 Arthur Rhodes .10 .05
❑ 134 Jeff Blauser .10 .05
❑ 135 Scott Cooper .10 .05
❑ 136 Doug Strange .10 .05
❑ 137 Luis Sojo .10 .05
❑ 138 Jeff Branson .10 .05
❑ 139 Alex Fernandez .20 .09
❑ 140 Ken Caminiti .20 .09
❑ 141 Charles Nagy .10 .05
❑ 142 Tom Candiotti .10 .05
❑ 143 Willie Greene RR .10 .05
❑ 144 John Vander Wal .10 .05
❑ 145 Kurt Knudsen .10 .05
❑ 146 John Franco .20 .09
❑ 147 Eddie Pierce RC .10 .05
❑ 148 Kim Batiste .10 .05
❑ 149 Darren Holmes .10 .05
❑ 150 Steve Cooke .10 .05
❑ 151 Terry Jorgensen .10 .05
❑ 152 Mark Clark .10 .05
❑ 153 Randy Velarde .10 .05
❑ 154 Greg W. Harris .10 .05
❑ 155 Kevin Campbell .10 .05
❑ 156 John Burkett .10 .05
❑ 157 Kevin Mitchell .20 .09
❑ 158 Deion Sanders .20 .09
❑ 159 Jose Canseco .50 .23
❑ 160 Jeff Hartsock .10 .05
❑ 161 Tom Quinlan RC .10 .05
❑ 162 Tim Pugh RC .10 .05
❑ 163 Glenn Davis .10 .05
❑ 164 Shane Reynolds .10 .05
❑ 165 Jody Reed .10 .05
❑ 166 Mike Sharperson .10 .05
❑ 167 Scott Lewis .10 .05
❑ 168 Dennis Martinez .20 .09

| | No. | Card | | |
|---|---|---|---|---|
| ❑ | 169 | Scott Radinsky | .10 | .05 |
| ❑ | 170 | Dave Gallagher | .10 | .05 |
| ❑ | 171 | Jim Thome | .20 | .09 |
| ❑ | 172 | Terry Mulholland | .10 | .05 |
| ❑ | 173 | Milt Cuyler | .10 | .05 |
| ❑ | 174 | Bob Patterson | .10 | .05 |
| ❑ | 175 | Jeff Montgomery | .20 | .09 |
| ❑ | 176 | Tim Salmon RR | .20 | .09 |
| ❑ | 177 | Franklin Stubbs | .10 | .05 |
| ❑ | 178 | Donovan Osborne | .10 | .05 |
| ❑ | 179 | Jeff Reboulet | .10 | .05 |
| ❑ | 180 | Jeremy Hernandez | .10 | .05 |
| ❑ | 181 | Charlie Hayes | .10 | .05 |
| ❑ | 182 | Matt Williams | .20 | .09 |
| ❑ | 183 | Mike Raczka | .10 | .05 |
| ❑ | 184 | Francisco Cabrera | .10 | .05 |
| ❑ | 185 | Rich DeLucia | .10 | .05 |
| ❑ | 186 | Sammy Sosa | .75 | .35 |
| ❑ | 187 | Ivan Rodriguez | .50 | .23 |
| ❑ | 188 | Bret Boone RR | .20 | .09 |
| ❑ | 189 | Juan Guzman | .10 | .05 |
| ❑ | 190 | Tom Browning | .10 | .05 |
| ❑ | 191 | Randy Milligan | .10 | .05 |
| ❑ | 192 | Steve Finley | .20 | .09 |
| ❑ | 193 | John Patterson RR | .10 | .05 |
| ❑ | 194 | Kip Gross | .10 | .05 |
| ❑ | 195 | Tony Fossas | .10 | .05 |
| ❑ | 196 | Ivan Calderon | .10 | .05 |
| ❑ | 197 | Junior Felix | .10 | .05 |
| ❑ | 198 | Pete Schourek | .10 | .05 |
| ❑ | 199 | Craig Grebeck | .10 | .05 |
| ❑ | 200 | Juan Bell | .10 | .05 |
| ❑ | 201 | Glenallen Hill | .10 | .05 |
| ❑ | 202 | Danny Jackson | .10 | .05 |
| ❑ | 203 | John Kiely | .10 | .05 |
| ❑ | 204 | Bob Tewksbury | .10 | .05 |
| ❑ | 205 | Kevin Koslofski | .10 | .05 |
| ❑ | 206 | Craig Shipley | .10 | .05 |
| ❑ | 207 | John Jaha | .10 | .05 |
| ❑ | 208 | Royce Clayton | .10 | .05 |
| ❑ | 209 | Mike Piazza RR | 2.00 | .90 |
| ❑ | 210 | Ron Gant | .20 | .09 |
| ❑ | 211 | Scott Erickson | .10 | .05 |
| ❑ | 212 | Doug Dascenzo | .10 | .05 |
| ❑ | 213 | Andy Stankiewicz | .10 | .05 |
| ❑ | 214 | Geronimo Berroa | .10 | .05 |
| ❑ | 215 | Dennis Eckersley | .20 | .09 |
| ❑ | 216 | Al Osuna | .10 | .05 |
| ❑ | 217 | Tino Martinez | .20 | .09 |
| ❑ | 218 | Henry Rodriguez | .10 | .05 |
| ❑ | 219 | Ed Sprague | .10 | .05 |
| ❑ | 220 | Ken Hill | .10 | .05 |
| ❑ | 221 | Chito Martinez | .10 | .05 |
| ❑ | 222 | Bret Saberhagen | .20 | .09 |
| ❑ | 223 | Mike Greenwell | .10 | .05 |
| ❑ | 224 | Mickey Morandini | .10 | .05 |
| ❑ | 225 | Chuck Finley | .20 | .09 |
| ❑ | 226 | Denny Neagle | .20 | .09 |
| ❑ | 227 | Kirk McCaskill | .10 | .05 |
| ❑ | 228 | Rheal Cormier | .10 | .05 |
| ❑ | 229 | Paul Sorrento | .10 | .05 |
| ❑ | 230 | Darrin Jackson | .10 | .05 |
| ❑ | 231 | Rob Deer | .10 | .05 |
| ❑ | 232 | Bill Swift | .10 | .05 |
| ❑ | 233 | Kevin McReynolds | .10 | .05 |
| ❑ | 234 | Terry Pendleton | .20 | .09 |
| ❑ | 235 | Dave Nilsson | .20 | .09 |
| ❑ | 236 | Chuck McElroy | .10 | .05 |
| ❑ | 237 | Derek Parks | .10 | .05 |
| ❑ | 238 | Norm Charlton | .10 | .05 |
| ❑ | 239 | Matt Nokes | .10 | .05 |
| ❑ | 240 | Juan Guerrero | .10 | .05 |
| ❑ | 241 | Jeff Parrett | .10 | .05 |
| ❑ | 242 | Ryan Thompson RR | .10 | .05 |
| ❑ | 243 | Dave Fleming | .10 | .05 |
| ❑ | 244 | Dave Hansen | .10 | .05 |
| ❑ | 245 | Monty Fariss | .10 | .05 |
| ❑ | 246 | Archi Cianfrocco | .10 | .05 |
| ❑ | 247 | Pat Hentgen | .10 | .05 |
| ❑ | 248 | Bill Pecota | .10 | .05 |
| ❑ | 249 | Ben McDonald | .10 | .05 |
| ❑ | 250 | Cliff Brantley | .10 | .05 |
| ❑ | 251 | John Valentin | .10 | .05 |
| ❑ | 252 | Jeff King | .10 | .05 |
| ❑ | 253 | Reggie Williams | .10 | .05 |
| ❑ | 254 | Checklist 160-238 | .10 | .05 |
| | | (Damon Berryhill and Alex Arias) | | |
| ❑ | 255 | Ozzie Guillen | .10 | .05 |
| ❑ | 256 | Mike Perez | .10 | .05 |
| ❑ | 257 | Thomas Howard | .10 | .05 |
| ❑ | 258 | Kurt Stillwell | .10 | .05 |
| ❑ | 259 | Mike Henneman | .10 | .05 |
| ❑ | 260 | Steve Decker | .10 | .05 |
| ❑ | 261 | Brent Mayne | .10 | .05 |
| ❑ | 262 | Otis Nixon | .10 | .05 |
| ❑ | 263 | Mark Kiefer | .10 | .05 |
| ❑ | 264 | Checklist 239-317 | .20 | .09 |
| | | (Don Mattingly and Mike Bordick) | | |
| ❑ | 265 | Richie Lewis RC | .10 | .05 |
| ❑ | 266 | Pat Gomez RC | .10 | .05 |
| ❑ | 267 | Scott Taylor | .10 | .05 |
| ❑ | 268 | Shawon Dunston | .10 | .05 |
| ❑ | 269 | Greg Myers | .10 | .05 |
| ❑ | 270 | Tim Costo | .10 | .05 |
| ❑ | 271 | Greg Hibbard | .10 | .05 |
| ❑ | 272 | Pete Harnisch | .10 | .05 |
| ❑ | 273 | Dave Mlicki | .10 | .05 |
| ❑ | 274 | Orel Hershiser | .20 | .09 |
| ❑ | 275 | Sean Berry RR | .10 | .05 |
| ❑ | 276 | Doug Simons | .10 | .05 |
| ❑ | 277 | John Doherty | .10 | .05 |
| ❑ | 278 | Eddie Murray | .40 | .18 |
| ❑ | 279 | Chris Haney | .10 | .05 |
| ❑ | 280 | Stan Javier | .10 | .05 |
| ❑ | 281 | Jaime Navarro | .10 | .05 |
| ❑ | 282 | Orlando Merced | .10 | .05 |
| ❑ | 283 | Kent Hrbek | .20 | .09 |
| ❑ | 284 | Bernard Gilkey | .10 | .05 |
| ❑ | 285 | Russ Springer | .10 | .05 |
| ❑ | 286 | Mike Maddux | .10 | .05 |
| ❑ | 287 | Eric Fox | .10 | .05 |
| ❑ | 288 | Mark Leonard | .10 | .05 |
| ❑ | 289 | Tim Leary | .10 | .05 |
| ❑ | 290 | Brian Hunter | .10 | .05 |
| ❑ | 291 | Donald Harris | .10 | .05 |
| ❑ | 292 | Bob Scanlan | .10 | .05 |
| ❑ | 293 | Turner Ward | .10 | .05 |
| ❑ | 294 | Hal Morris | .10 | .05 |
| ❑ | 295 | Jimmy Poole | .10 | .05 |
| ❑ | 296 | Doug Jones | .10 | .05 |
| ❑ | 297 | Tony Pena | .10 | .05 |
| ❑ | 298 | Ramon Martinez | .10 | .05 |
| ❑ | 299 | Tim Fortugno | .10 | .05 |
| ❑ | 300 | Marquis Grissom | .10 | .05 |
| ❑ | 301 | Lance Johnson | .10 | .05 |
| ❑ | 302 | Jeff Kent | .40 | .18 |
| ❑ | 303 | Reggie Jefferson | .20 | .09 |
| ❑ | 304 | Wes Chamberlain | .10 | .05 |
| ❑ | 305 | Shawn Hare | .10 | .05 |
| ❑ | 306 | Mike LaValliere | .10 | .05 |
| ❑ | 307 | Gregg Jefferies | .10 | .05 |
| ❑ | 308 | Troy Neel RR | .10 | .05 |
| ❑ | 309 | Pat Listach | .10 | .05 |
| ❑ | 310 | Geronimo Pena | .10 | .05 |
| ❑ | 311 | Pedro Munoz | .10 | .05 |
| ❑ | 312 | Guillermo Velasquez | .10 | .05 |
| ❑ | 313 | Roberto Kelly | .10 | .05 |
| ❑ | 314 | Mike Jackson | .10 | .05 |
| ❑ | 315 | Rickey Henderson | .50 | .23 |
| ❑ | 316 | Mark Lemke | .10 | .05 |
| ❑ | 317 | Erik Hanson | .10 | .05 |
| ❑ | 318 | Derrick May | .10 | .05 |
| ❑ | 319 | Geno Petralli | .10 | .05 |
| ❑ | 320 | Melvin Nieves RR | .10 | .05 |
| ❑ | 321 | Doug Linton | .10 | .05 |
| ❑ | 322 | Rob Dibble | .10 | .05 |
| ❑ | 323 | Chris Hoiles | .10 | .05 |
| ❑ | 324 | Jimmy Jones | .10 | .05 |
| ❑ | 325 | Dave Staton RR | .10 | .05 |
| ❑ | 326 | Pedro Martinez | 1.00 | .45 |
| ❑ | 327 | Paul Quantrill | .10 | .05 |
| ❑ | 328 | Greg Colbrunn | .10 | .05 |
| ❑ | 329 | Hilly Hathaway RC | .10 | .05 |
| ❑ | 330 | Jeff Innis | .10 | .05 |
| ❑ | 331 | Ron Karkovice | .10 | .05 |
| ❑ | 332 | Keith Shepherd RC | .10 | .05 |
| ❑ | 333 | Alan Embree | .10 | .05 |
| ❑ | 334 | Paul Wagner | .10 | .05 |
| ❑ | 335 | Dave Haas | .10 | .05 |
| ❑ | 336 | Ozzie Canseco | .10 | .05 |
| ❑ | 337 | Bill Sampen | .10 | .05 |
| ❑ | 338 | Rich Rodriguez | .10 | .05 |
| ❑ | 339 | Dean Palmer | .20 | .09 |
| ❑ | 340 | Greg Litton | .10 | .05 |
| ❑ | 341 | Jim Tatum RR RC | .10 | .05 |
| ❑ | 342 | Todd Haney RC | .10 | .05 |
| ❑ | 343 | Larry Casian | .10 | .05 |
| ❑ | 344 | Ryne Sandberg | .50 | .23 |
| ❑ | 345 | Sterling Hitchcock RC | .25 | .11 |
| ❑ | 346 | Chris Hammond | .10 | .05 |
| ❑ | 347 | Vince Horsman | .10 | .05 |
| ❑ | 348 | Butch Henry | .10 | .05 |
| ❑ | 349 | Dann Howitt | .10 | .05 |
| ❑ | 350 | Roger McDowell | .10 | .05 |
| ❑ | 351 | Jack Morris | .20 | .09 |
| ❑ | 352 | Bill Krueger | .10 | .05 |
| ❑ | 353 | Cris Colon | .10 | .05 |
| ❑ | 354 | Joe Vitko | .10 | .05 |
| ❑ | 355 | Willie McGee | .20 | .09 |
| ❑ | 356 | Jay Baller | .10 | .05 |
| ❑ | 357 | Pat Mahomes | .10 | .05 |
| ❑ | 358 | Roger Mason | .10 | .05 |
| ❑ | 359 | Jerry Nielsen | .10 | .05 |
| ❑ | 360 | Tom Pagnozzi | .10 | .05 |
| ❑ | 361 | Kevin Baez | .10 | .05 |
| ❑ | 362 | Tim Scott | .10 | .05 |
| ❑ | 363 | Domingo Martinez RC | .10 | .05 |
| ❑ | 364 | Kirt Manwaring | .10 | .05 |
| ❑ | 365 | Rafael Palmeiro | .40 | .18 |
| ❑ | 366 | Ray Lankford | .20 | .09 |
| ❑ | 367 | Tim McIntosh | .10 | .05 |
| ❑ | 368 | Jessie Hollins | .10 | .05 |
| ❑ | 369 | Scott Leius | .10 | .05 |
| ❑ | 370 | Bill Doran | .10 | .05 |
| ❑ | 371 | Sam Militello | .10 | .05 |
| ❑ | 372 | Ryan Bowen | .10 | .05 |
| ❑ | 373 | Dave Henderson | .10 | .05 |
| ❑ | 374 | Dan Smith RR | .10 | .05 |
| ❑ | 375 | Steve Reed RR RC | .10 | .05 |
| ❑ | 376 | Jose Offerman | .10 | .05 |
| ❑ | 377 | Kevin Brown | .20 | .09 |
| ❑ | 378 | Darrin Fletcher | .10 | .05 |
| ❑ | 379 | Duane Ward | .10 | .05 |
| ❑ | 380 | Wayne Kirby RR | .10 | .05 |
| ❑ | 381 | Steve Scarsone | .10 | .05 |
| ❑ | 382 | Mariano Duncan | .10 | .05 |
| ❑ | 383 | Ken Ryan RC | .10 | .05 |
| ❑ | 384 | Lloyd McClendon | .10 | .05 |
| ❑ | 385 | Brian Holman | .10 | .05 |
| ❑ | 386 | Braulio Castillo | .10 | .05 |
| ❑ | 387 | Danny Leon | .10 | .05 |
| ❑ | 388 | Omar Olivares | .10 | .05 |
| ❑ | 389 | Kevin Wickander | .10 | .05 |
| ❑ | 390 | Fred McGriff | .20 | .09 |
| ❑ | 391 | Phil Clark | .10 | .05 |
| ❑ | 392 | Darren Lewis | .10 | .05 |
| ❑ | 393 | Phil Hiatt | .10 | .05 |
| ❑ | 394 | Mike Morgan | .10 | .05 |
| ❑ | 395 | Shane Mack | .10 | .05 |
| ❑ | 396 | Checklist 318-396 | .20 | .09 |
| | | (Dennis Eckersley and Art Kusnyer CO) | | |
| ❑ | 397 | David Segui | .10 | .05 |
| ❑ | 398 | Rafael Belliard | .10 | .05 |
| ❑ | 399 | Tim Naehring | .10 | .05 |
| ❑ | 400 | Frank Castillo | .10 | .05 |
| ❑ | 401 | Joe Grahe | .10 | .05 |
| ❑ | 402 | Reggie Sanders | .10 | .05 |
| ❑ | 403 | Roberto Hernandez | .10 | .05 |
| ❑ | 404 | Luis Gonzalez | .20 | .09 |
| ❑ | 405 | Carlos Baerga | .10 | .05 |
| ❑ | 406 | Carlos Hernandez | .10 | .05 |
| ❑ | 407 | Pedro Astacio RR | .20 | .09 |
| ❑ | 408 | Mel Rojas | .10 | .05 |
| ❑ | 409 | Scott Livingstone | .10 | .05 |
| ❑ | 410 | Chico Walker | .10 | .05 |
| ❑ | 411 | Brian McRae | .10 | .05 |
| ❑ | 412 | Ben Rivera | .10 | .05 |
| ❑ | 413 | Ricky Bones | .10 | .05 |
| ❑ | 414 | Andy Van Slyke | .20 | .09 |
| ❑ | 415 | Chuck Knoblauch | .20 | .09 |
| ❑ | 416 | Luis Alicea | .10 | .05 |
| ❑ | 417 | Bob Wickman | .10 | .05 |
| ❑ | 418 | Doug Brocail | .10 | .05 |
| ❑ | 419 | Scott Brosius | .20 | .09 |
| ❑ | 420 | Rod Beck | .10 | .05 |

| |  |  | | |
|---|---|---|---|---|
| ❑ | 421 | Edgar Martinez | .20 | .09 |
| ❑ | 422 | Ryan Klesko | .40 | .18 |
| ❑ | 423 | Nolan Ryan | 2.00 | .90 |
| ❑ | 424 | Rey Sanchez | .10 | .05 |
| ❑ | 425 | Roberto Alomar | .40 | .18 |
| ❑ | 426 | Barry Larkin | .40 | .18 |
| ❑ | 427 | Mike Mussina | .40 | .18 |
| ❑ | 428 | Jeff Bagwell | .50 | .23 |
| ❑ | 429 | Mo Vaughn | .20 | .09 |
| ❑ | 430 | Eric Karros | .20 | .09 |
| ❑ | 431 | John Orton | .10 | .05 |
| ❑ | 432 | Wil Cordero | .10 | .05 |
| ❑ | 433 | Jack McDowell | .10 | .05 |
| ❑ | 434 | Howard Johnson | .10 | .05 |
| ❑ | 435 | Albert Belle | .20 | .09 |
| ❑ | 436 | John Kruk | .20 | .09 |
| ❑ | 437 | Skeeter Barnes | .10 | .05 |
| ❑ | 438 | Don Slaught | .10 | .05 |
| ❑ | 439 | Rusty Meacham | .10 | .05 |
| ❑ | 440 | Tim Laker RR RC | .10 | .05 |
| ❑ | 441 | Robin Yount | .20 | .09 |
| ❑ | 442 | Brian Jordan | .20 | .09 |
| ❑ | 443 | Kevin Tapani | .10 | .05 |
| ❑ | 444 | Gary Sheffield | .40 | .18 |
| ❑ | 445 | Rich Monteleone | .10 | .05 |
| ❑ | 446 | Will Clark | .40 | .18 |
| ❑ | 447 | Jerry Browne | .10 | .05 |
| ❑ | 448 | Jeff Treadway | .10 | .05 |
| ❑ | 449 | Mike Schooler | .10 | .05 |
| ❑ | 450 | Mike Harkey | .10 | .05 |
| ❑ | 451 | Julio Franco | .10 | .05 |
| ❑ | 452 | Kevin Young RR | .20 | .09 |
| ❑ | 453 | Kelly Gruber | .10 | .05 |
| ❑ | 454 | Jose Rijo | .10 | .05 |
| ❑ | 455 | Mike Devereaux | .10 | .05 |
| ❑ | 456 | Andujar Cedeno | .10 | .05 |
| ❑ | 457 | Damion Easley RR | .10 | .05 |
| ❑ | 458 | Kevin Gross | .10 | .05 |
| ❑ | 459 | Matt Young | .10 | .05 |
| ❑ | 460 | Matt Stairs | .10 | .05 |
| ❑ | 461 | Luis Polonia | .10 | .05 |
| ❑ | 462 | Dwight Gooden | .20 | .09 |
| ❑ | 463 | Warren Newson | .10 | .05 |
| ❑ | 464 | Jose DeLeon | .10 | .05 |
| ❑ | 465 | Jose Mesa | .10 | .05 |
| ❑ | 466 | Danny Cox | .10 | .05 |
| ❑ | 467 | Dan Gladden | .10 | .05 |
| ❑ | 468 | Gerald Perry | .10 | .05 |
| ❑ | 469 | Mike Boddicker | .10 | .05 |
| ❑ | 470 | Jeff Gardner | .10 | .05 |
| ❑ | 471 | Doug Henry | .10 | .05 |
| ❑ | 472 | Mike Benjamin | .10 | .05 |
| ❑ | 473 | Dan Peltier RR | .10 | .05 |
| ❑ | 474 | Mike Stanton | .10 | .05 |
| ❑ | 475 | John Smiley | .10 | .05 |
| ❑ | 476 | Dwight Smith | .10 | .05 |
| ❑ | 477 | Jim Leyritz | .10 | .05 |
| ❑ | 478 | Dwayne Henry | .10 | .05 |
| ❑ | 479 | Mark McGwire | 1.50 | .70 |
| ❑ | 480 | Pete Incaviglia | .10 | .05 |
| ❑ | 481 | Dave Cochrane | .10 | .05 |
| ❑ | 482 | Eric Davis | .20 | .09 |
| ❑ | 483 | John Olerud | .20 | .09 |
| ❑ | 484 | Kent Bottenfield | .10 | .05 |
| ❑ | 485 | Mark McLemore | .10 | .05 |
| ❑ | 486 | Dave Magadan | .10 | .05 |
| ❑ | 487 | John Marzano | .10 | .05 |
| ❑ | 488 | Ruben Amaro | .10 | .05 |
| ❑ | 489 | Rob Ducey | .10 | .05 |
| ❑ | 490 | Stan Belinda | .10 | .05 |
| ❑ | 491 | Dan Pasqua | .10 | .05 |
| ❑ | 492 | Joe Magrane | .10 | .05 |
| ❑ | 493 | Brook Jacoby | .10 | .05 |
| ❑ | 494 | Gene Harris | .10 | .05 |
| ❑ | 495 | Mark Leiter | .10 | .05 |
| ❑ | 496 | Bryan Hickerson | .10 | .05 |
| ❑ | 497 | Tom Gordon | .10 | .05 |
| ❑ | 498 | Pete Smith | .10 | .05 |
| ❑ | 499 | Chris Bosio | .10 | .05 |
| ❑ | 500 | Shawn Boskie | .10 | .05 |
| ❑ | 501 | Dave West | .10 | .05 |
| ❑ | 502 | Milt Hill | .10 | .05 |
| ❑ | 503 | Pat Kelly | .10 | .05 |
| ❑ | 504 | Joe Boever | .10 | .05 |
| ❑ | 505 | Terry Steinbach | .10 | .05 |
| ❑ | 506 | Butch Huskey RR | .10 | .05 |
| ❑ | 507 | David Valle | .10 | .05 |
| ❑ | 508 | Mike Scioscia | .10 | .05 |
| ❑ | 509 | Kenny Rogers | .10 | .05 |
| ❑ | 510 | Moises Alou | .20 | .09 |
| ❑ | 511 | David Wells | .20 | .09 |
| ❑ | 512 | Mackey Sasser | .10 | .05 |
| ❑ | 513 | Todd Frohwirth | .10 | .05 |
| ❑ | 514 | Ricky Jordan | .10 | .05 |
| ❑ | 515 | Mike Gardiner | .10 | .05 |
| ❑ | 516 | Gary Redus | .10 | .05 |
| ❑ | 517 | Gary Gaetti | .20 | .09 |
| ❑ | 518 | Checklist | .10 | .05 |
| ❑ | 519 | Carlton Fisk | .40 | .18 |
| ❑ | 520 | Ozzie Smith | .50 | .23 |
| ❑ | 521 | Rod Nichols | .10 | .05 |
| ❑ | 522 | Benito Santiago | .10 | .05 |
| ❑ | 523 | Bill Gullickson | .10 | .05 |
| ❑ | 524 | Robby Thompson | .10 | .05 |
| ❑ | 525 | Mike Macfarlane | .10 | .05 |
| ❑ | 526 | Sid Bream | .10 | .05 |
| ❑ | 527 | Darryl Hamilton | .10 | .05 |
| ❑ | 528 | Checklist | .10 | .05 |
| ❑ | 529 | Jeff Tackett | .10 | .05 |
| ❑ | 530 | Greg Olson | .10 | .05 |
| ❑ | 531 | Bob Zupcic | .10 | .05 |
| ❑ | 532 | Mark Grace | .40 | .18 |
| ❑ | 533 | Steve Frey | .10 | .05 |
| ❑ | 534 | Dave Martinez | .10 | .05 |
| ❑ | 535 | Robin Ventura | .20 | .09 |
| ❑ | 536 | Casey Candaele | .10 | .05 |
| ❑ | 537 | Kenny Lofton | .50 | .23 |
| ❑ | 538 | Jay Howell | .10 | .05 |
| ❑ | 539 | Fernando Ramsey RR RC | .10 | .05 |
| ❑ | 540 | Larry Walker | .20 | .09 |
| ❑ | 541 | Cecil Fielder | .20 | .09 |
| ❑ | 542 | Lee Guetterman | .10 | .05 |
| ❑ | 543 | Keith Miller | .10 | .05 |
| ❑ | 544 | Len Dykstra | .20 | .09 |
| ❑ | 545 | B.J. Surhoff | .20 | .09 |
| ❑ | 546 | Bob Walk | .10 | .05 |
| ❑ | 547 | Brian Harper | .10 | .05 |
| ❑ | 548 | Lee Smith | .20 | .09 |
| ❑ | 549 | Danny Tartabull | .10 | .05 |
| ❑ | 550 | Frank Seminara | .10 | .05 |
| ❑ | 551 | Henry Mercedes | .10 | .05 |
| ❑ | 552 | Dave Righetti | .10 | .05 |
| ❑ | 553 | Ken Griffey Jr. | 1.50 | .70 |
| ❑ | 554 | Tom Glavine | .20 | .09 |
| ❑ | 555 | Juan Gonzalez | .40 | .18 |
| ❑ | 556 | Jim Bullinger | .10 | .05 |
| ❑ | 557 | Derek Bell | .10 | .05 |
| ❑ | 558 | Cesar Hernandez | .10 | .05 |
| ❑ | 559 | Cal Ripken | 1.50 | .70 |
| ❑ | 560 | Eddie Taubensee | .10 | .05 |
| ❑ | 561 | John Flaherty | .10 | .05 |
| ❑ | 562 | Todd Benzinger | .10 | .05 |
| ❑ | 563 | Hubie Brooks | .10 | .05 |
| ❑ | 564 | Delino DeShields | .20 | .09 |
| ❑ | 565 | Tim Raines | .20 | .09 |
| ❑ | 566 | Sid Fernandez | .10 | .05 |
| ❑ | 567 | Steve Olin | .10 | .05 |
| ❑ | 568 | Tommy Greene | .10 | .05 |
| ❑ | 569 | Buddy Groom | .10 | .05 |
| ❑ | 570 | Randy Tomlin | .10 | .05 |
| ❑ | 571 | Hipolito Pichardo | .10 | .05 |
| ❑ | 572 | Rene Arocha RR RC | .10 | .05 |
| ❑ | 573 | Mike Fetters | .10 | .05 |
| ❑ | 574 | Felix Jose | .10 | .05 |
| ❑ | 575 | Gene Larkin | .10 | .05 |
| ❑ | 576 | Bruce Hurst | .10 | .05 |
| ❑ | 577 | Bernie Williams | .40 | .18 |
| ❑ | 578 | Trevor Wilson | .10 | .05 |
| ❑ | 579 | Bob Welch | .10 | .05 |
| ❑ | 580 | David Justice | .20 | .09 |
| ❑ | 581 | Randy Johnson | .50 | .23 |
| ❑ | 582 | Jose Vizcaino | .10 | .05 |
| ❑ | 583 | Jeff Huson | .10 | .05 |
| ❑ | 584 | Rob Maurer RR | .10 | .05 |
| ❑ | 585 | Todd Stottlemyre | .10 | .05 |
| ❑ | 586 | Joe Oliver | .10 | .05 |
| ❑ | 587 | Bob Milacki | .10 | .05 |
| ❑ | 588 | Rob Murphy | .10 | .05 |
| ❑ | 589 | Greg Pirkl RR | .10 | .05 |
| ❑ | 590 | Lenny Harris | .10 | .05 |
| ❑ | 591 | Luis Rivera | .10 | .05 |
| ❑ | 592 | John Wetteland | .20 | .09 |
| ❑ | 593 | Mark Langston | .10 | .05 |
| ❑ | 594 | Bobby Bonilla | .20 | .09 |
| ❑ | 595 | Esteban Beltre | .10 | .05 |
| ❑ | 596 | Mike Hartley | .10 | .05 |
| ❑ | 597 | Felix Fermin | .10 | .05 |
| ❑ | 598 | Carlos Garcia | .10 | .05 |
| ❑ | 599 | Frank Tanana | .10 | .05 |
| ❑ | 600 | Pedro Guerrero | .10 | .05 |
| ❑ | 601 | Terry Shumpert | .10 | .05 |
| ❑ | 602 | Wally Whitehurst | .10 | .05 |
| ❑ | 603 | Kevin Seitzer | .10 | .05 |
| ❑ | 604 | Chris James | .10 | .05 |
| ❑ | 605 | Greg Gohr RR | .10 | .05 |
| ❑ | 606 | Mark Wohlers | .10 | .05 |
| ❑ | 607 | Kirby Puckett | 1.00 | .45 |
| ❑ | 608 | Greg Maddux | 1.00 | .45 |
| ❑ | 609 | Don Mattingly | 1.00 | .45 |
| ❑ | 610 | Greg Cadaret | .10 | .05 |
| ❑ | 611 | Dave Stewart | .20 | .09 |
| ❑ | 612 | Mark Portugal | .10 | .05 |
| ❑ | 613 | Pete O'Brien | .10 | .05 |
| ❑ | 614 | Bob Ojeda | .10 | .05 |
| ❑ | 615 | Joe Carter | .20 | .09 |
| ❑ | 616 | Pete Young | .10 | .05 |
| ❑ | 617 | Sam Horn | .10 | .05 |
| ❑ | 618 | Vince Coleman | .10 | .05 |
| ❑ | 619 | Wade Boggs | .50 | .23 |
| ❑ | 620 | Todd Pratt RC | .25 | .11 |
| ❑ | 621 | Ron Tingley | .10 | .05 |
| ❑ | 622 | Doug Drabek | .10 | .05 |
| ❑ | 623 | Scott Hemond | .10 | .05 |
| ❑ | 624 | Tim Jones | .10 | .05 |
| ❑ | 625 | Dennis Cook | .10 | .05 |
| ❑ | 626 | Jose Melendez | .10 | .05 |
| ❑ | 627 | Mike Munoz | .10 | .05 |
| ❑ | 628 | Jim Pena | .10 | .05 |
| ❑ | 629 | Gary Thurman | .10 | .05 |
| ❑ | 630 | Charlie Leibrandt | .10 | .05 |
| ❑ | 631 | Scott Fletcher | .10 | .05 |
| ❑ | 632 | Andre Dawson | .20 | .09 |
| ❑ | 633 | Greg Gagne | .10 | .05 |
| ❑ | 634 | Greg Swindell | .10 | .05 |
| ❑ | 635 | Kevin Maas | .10 | .05 |
| ❑ | 636 | Xavier Hernandez | .10 | .05 |
| ❑ | 637 | Ruben Sierra | .10 | .05 |
| ❑ | 638 | Dmitri Young RR | .20 | .09 |
| ❑ | 639 | Harold Reynolds | .10 | .05 |
| ❑ | 640 | Tom Goodwin | .10 | .05 |
| ❑ | 641 | Todd Burns | .10 | .05 |
| ❑ | 642 | Jeff Fassero | .10 | .05 |
| ❑ | 643 | Dave Winfield | .40 | .18 |
| ❑ | 644 | Willie Randolph | .20 | .09 |
| ❑ | 645 | Luis Mercedes | .10 | .05 |
| ❑ | 646 | Dale Murphy | .20 | .09 |
| ❑ | 647 | Danny Darwin | .10 | .05 |
| ❑ | 648 | Dennis Moeller | .10 | .05 |
| ❑ | 649 | Chuck Crim | .10 | .05 |
| ❑ | 650 | Checklist | .10 | .05 |
| ❑ | 651 | Shawn Abner | .10 | .05 |
| ❑ | 652 | Tracy Woodson | .10 | .05 |
| ❑ | 653 | Scott Scudder | .10 | .05 |
| ❑ | 654 | Tom Lampkin | .10 | .05 |
| ❑ | 655 | Alan Trammell | .20 | .09 |
| ❑ | 656 | Cory Snyder | .10 | .05 |
| ❑ | 657 | Chris Gwynn | .10 | .05 |
| ❑ | 658 | Lonnie Smith | .10 | .05 |
| ❑ | 659 | Jim Austin | .10 | .05 |
| ❑ | 660 | Checklist | .10 | .05 |
| ❑ | 661 | Tim Hulett | .10 | .05 |
| ❑ | 662 | Marvin Freeman | .10 | .05 |
| ❑ | 663 | Greg A. Harris | .10 | .05 |
| ❑ | 664 | Heathcliff Slocumb | .10 | .05 |
| ❑ | 665 | Mike Butcher | .10 | .05 |
| ❑ | 666 | Steve Foster | .10 | .05 |
| ❑ | 667 | Donn Pall | .10 | .05 |
| ❑ | 668 | Darryl Kile | .20 | .09 |
| ❑ | 669 | Jesse Levis | .10 | .05 |
| ❑ | 670 | Jim Gott | .10 | .05 |
| ❑ | 671 | Mark Hutton RR | .10 | .05 |
| ❑ | 672 | Brian Drahman | .10 | .05 |
| ❑ | 673 | Chad Kreuter | .10 | .05 |
| ❑ | 674 | Tony Fernandez | .10 | .05 |
| ❑ | 675 | Jose Lind | .10 | .05 |
| ❑ | 676 | Kyle Abbott | .10 | .05 |
| ❑ | 677 | Dan Plesac | .10 | .05 |

❑ 678 Barry Bonds .60 .25
❑ 679 Chili Davis .20 .09
❑ 680 Stan Royer .10 .05
❑ 681 Scott Kamieniecki .10 .05
❑ 682 Carlos Martinez .10 .05
❑ 683 Mike Moore .10 .05
❑ 684 Candy Maldonado .10 .05
❑ 685 Jeff Nelson .10 .05
❑ 686 Lou Whitaker .20 .09
❑ 687 Jose Guzman .10 .05
❑ 688 Manuel Lee .10 .05
❑ 689 Bob MacDonald .10 .05
❑ 690 Scott Bankhead .10 .05
❑ 691 Alan Mills .10 .05
❑ 692 Brian Williams .10 .05
❑ 693 Tom Brunansky .10 .05
❑ 694 Lenny Webster .10 .05
❑ 695 Greg Briley .10 .05
❑ 696 Paul O'Neill .20 .09
❑ 697 Joey Cora .10 .05
❑ 698 Charlie O'Brien .10 .05
❑ 699 Junior Ortiz .10 .05
❑ 700 Ron Darling .10 .05
❑ 701 Tony Phillips .10 .05
❑ 702 William Pennyfeather .10 .05
❑ 703 Mark Gubicza .10 .05
❑ 704 Steve Hosey RR .10 .05
❑ 705 Henry Cotto .10 .05
❑ 706 David Hulse RC .10 .05
❑ 707 Mike Pagliarulo .10 .05
❑ 708 Dave Stieb .10 .05
❑ 709 Melido Perez .10 .05
❑ 710 Jimmy Key .20 .09
❑ 711 Jeff Russell .10 .05
❑ 712 David Cone .20 .09
❑ 713 Russ Swan .10 .05
❑ 714 Mark Guthrie .10 .05
❑ 715 Checklist .10 .05
❑ 716 Al Martin RR .10 .05
❑ 717 Randy Knorr .10 .05
❑ 718 Mike Stanley .10 .05
❑ 719 Rick Sutcliffe .20 .09
❑ 720 Terry Leach .10 .05
❑ 721 Chipper Jones RR 1.25 .55
❑ 722 Jim Eisenreich .10 .05
❑ 723 Tom Henke .10 .05
❑ 724 Jeff Frye .10 .05
❑ 725 Harold Baines .20 .09
❑ 726 Scott Sanderson .10 .05
❑ 727 Tom Foley .10 .05
❑ 728 Bryan Harvey .10 .05
❑ 729 Tom Edens .10 .05
❑ 730 Eric Young .10 .05
❑ 731 Dave Weathers .10 .05
❑ 732 Spike Owen .10 .05
❑ 733 Scott Aldred .10 .05
❑ 734 Cris Carpenter .10 .05
❑ 735 Dion James .10 .05
❑ 736 Joe Girardi .20 .09
❑ 737 Nigel Wilson RR .10 .05
❑ 738 Scott Chiamparino .10 .05
❑ 739 Jeff Reardon .20 .09
❑ 740 Willie Blair .10 .05
❑ 741 Jim Corsi .10 .05
❑ 742 Ken Patterson .10 .05
❑ 743 Andy Ashby .20 .09
❑ 744 Rob Natal .10 .05
❑ 745 Kevin Bass .10 .05
❑ 746 Freddie Benavides .10 .05
❑ 747 Chris Donnels .10 .05
❑ 748 Kerry Woodson .10 .05
❑ 749 Calvin Jones .10 .05
❑ 750 Gary Scott .10 .05
❑ 751 Joe Orsulak .10 .05
❑ 752 Armando Reynoso .10 .05
❑ 753 Monty Fariss .10 .05
❑ 754 Billy Hatcher .10 .05
❑ 755 Denis Boucher .10 .05
❑ 756 Walt Weiss .10 .05
❑ 757 Mike Fitzgerald .10 .05
❑ 758 Rudy Seanez .10 .05
❑ 759 Bret Barberie .10 .05
❑ 760 Mo Sanford .10 .05
❑ 761 Pedro Castellano .10 .05
❑ 762 Chuck Carr .10 .05
❑ 763 Steve Howe .10 .05
❑ 764 Andres Galarraga .20 .09
❑ 765 Jeff Conine .10 .05
❑ 766 Ted Power .10 .05
❑ 767 Butch Henry .10 .05
❑ 768 Steve Decker .10 .05
❑ 769 Storm Davis .10 .05
❑ 770 Vinny Castilla .50 .23
❑ 771 Junior Felix .10 .05
❑ 772 Walt Terrell .10 .05
❑ 773 Brad Ausmus .10 .05
❑ 774 Jamie McAndrew .10 .05
❑ 775 Milt Thompson .10 .05
❑ 776 Charlie Hayes .10 .05
❑ 777 Jack Armstrong .10 .05
❑ 778 Dennis Rasmussen .10 .05
❑ 779 Darren Holmes .10 .05
❑ 780 Alex Arias .10 .05
❑ 781 Randy Bush .10 .05
❑ 782 Javier Lopez RR .20 .09
❑ 783 Dante Bichette .20 .09
❑ 784 John Johnstone RC .10 .05
❑ 785 Rene Gonzales .10 .05
❑ 786 Alex Cole .10 .05
❑ 787 Jeromy Burnitz RR .20 .09
❑ 788 Michael Huff .10 .05
❑ 789 Anthony Telford .10 .05
❑ 790 Jerald Clark .10 .05
❑ 791 Joel Johnston .10 .05
❑ 792 David Nied RR .10 .05

## 1994 Donruss

| | MINT | NRMT |
|---|---|---|
| COMPLETE SET (660) | 30.00 | 13.50 |
| COMPLETE SERIES 1 (330) | 15.00 | 6.75 |
| COMPLETE SERIES 2 (330) | 15.00 | 6.75 |
| COMMON CARD (1-660) | .15 | .07 |

❑ 1 Nolan Ryan 4.00 1.80
❑ 2 Mike Piazza 2.00 .90
❑ 3 Moises Alou .30 .14
❑ 4 Ken Griffey Jr. 2.50 1.10
❑ 5 Gary Sheffield .60 .25
❑ 6 Roberto Alomar .60 .25
❑ 7 John Kruk .30 .14
❑ 8 Gregg Olson .15 .07
❑ 9 Gregg Jefferies .15 .07
❑ 10 Tony Gwynn 1.25 .55
❑ 11 Chad Curtis .15 .07
❑ 12 Craig Biggio .30 .14
❑ 13 John Burkett .15 .07
❑ 14 Carlos Baerga .15 .07
❑ 15 Robin Yount .60 .25
❑ 16 Dennis Eckersley .30 .14
❑ 17 Dwight Gooden .30 .14
❑ 18 Ryne Sandberg .75 .35
❑ 19 Rickey Henderson .75 .35
❑ 20 Jack McDowell .15 .07
❑ 21 Jay Bell .30 .14
❑ 22 Kevin Brown .30 .14
❑ 23 Robin Ventura .30 .14
❑ 24 Paul Molitor .60 .25
❑ 25 David Justice .30 .14
❑ 26 Rafael Palmeiro .60 .25
❑ 27 Cecil Fielder .30 .14
❑ 28 Chuck Knoblauch .30 .14
❑ 29 Dave Hollins .15 .07
❑ 30 Jimmy Key .30 .14
❑ 31 Mark Langston .15 .07
❑ 32 Darryl Kile .30 .14
❑ 33 Ruben Sierra .15 .07
❑ 34 Ron Gant .30 .14
❑ 35 Ozzie Smith .75 .35
❑ 36 Wade Boggs .75 .35
❑ 37 Marquis Grissom .15 .07
❑ 38 Will Clark .60 .25
❑ 39 Kenny Lofton .30 .14
❑ 40 Cal Ripken 2.50 1.10
❑ 41 Steve Avery .15 .07
❑ 42 Mo Vaughn .30 .14
❑ 43 Brian McRae .15 .07
❑ 44 Mickey Tettleton .15 .07
❑ 45 Barry Larkin .60 .25
❑ 46 Charlie Hayes .15 .07
❑ 47 Kevin Appier .30 .14
❑ 48 Robby Thompson .15 .07
❑ 49 Juan Gonzalez .60 .25
❑ 50 Paul O'Neill .30 .14
❑ 51 Marcos Armas .15 .07
❑ 52 Mike Butcher .15 .07
❑ 53 Ken Caminiti .30 .14
❑ 54 Pat Borders .15 .07
❑ 55 Pedro Munoz .15 .07
❑ 56 Tim Belcher .15 .07
❑ 57 Paul Assenmacher .15 .07
❑ 58 Damon Berryhill .15 .07
❑ 59 Ricky Bones .15 .07
❑ 60 Rene Arocha .15 .07
❑ 61 Shawn Boskie .15 .07
❑ 62 Pedro Astacio .15 .07
❑ 63 Frank Bolick .15 .07
❑ 64 Bud Black .15 .07
❑ 65 Sandy Alomar Jr. .30 .14
❑ 66 Rich Amaral .15 .07
❑ 67 Luis Aquino .15 .07
❑ 68 Kevin Baez .15 .07
❑ 69 Mike Devereaux .15 .07
❑ 70 Andy Ashby .15 .07
❑ 71 Larry Andersen .15 .07
❑ 72 Steve Cooke .15 .07
❑ 73 Mario Diaz .15 .07
❑ 74 Rob Deer .15 .07
❑ 75 Bobby Ayala .15 .07
❑ 76 Freddie Benavides .15 .07
❑ 77 Stan Belinda .15 .07
❑ 78 John Doherty .15 .07
❑ 79 Willie Banks .15 .07
❑ 80 Spike Owen .15 .07
❑ 81 Mike Bordick .15 .07
❑ 82 Chili Davis .30 .14
❑ 83 Luis Gonzalez .30 .14
❑ 84 Ed Sprague .15 .07
❑ 85 Jeff Reboulet .15 .07
❑ 86 Jason Bere .15 .07
❑ 87 Mark Hutton .15 .07
❑ 88 Jeff Blauser .15 .07
❑ 89 Cal Eldred .15 .07
❑ 90 Bernard Gilkey .15 .07
❑ 91 Frank Castillo .15 .07
❑ 92 Jim Gott .15 .07
❑ 93 Greg Colbrunn .15 .07
❑ 94 Jeff Brantley .15 .07
❑ 95 Jeremy Hernandez .15 .07
❑ 96 Norm Charlton .15 .07
❑ 97 Alex Arias .15 .07
❑ 98 John Franco .30 .14
❑ 99 Chris Hoiles .15 .07
❑ 100 Brad Ausmus .15 .07
❑ 101 Wes Chamberlain .15 .07
❑ 102 Mark Dewey .15 .07
❑ 103 Benji Gil .15 .07
❑ 104 John Dopson .15 .07
❑ 105 John Smiley .15 .07
❑ 106 David Nied .15 .07
❑ 107 George Brett 1.25 .55
❑ 108 Kirk Gibson .30 .14
❑ 109 Larry Casian .15 .07
❑ 110 Ryne Sandberg CL .30 .14
❑ 111 Brent Gates .15 .07
❑ 112 Damion Easley .15 .07
❑ 113 Pete Harnisch .15 .07
❑ 114 Danny Cox .15 .07
❑ 115 Kevin Tapani .15 .07
❑ 116 Roberto Hernandez .15 .07

| |  |  | | |
|---|---|---|---|---|
| ❑ | 117 | Domingo Jean | .15 | .07 |
| ❑ | 118 | Sid Bream | .15 | .07 |
| ❑ | 119 | Doug Henry | .15 | .07 |
| ❑ | 120 | Omar Olivares | .15 | .07 |
| ❑ | 121 | Mike Harkey | .15 | .07 |
| ❑ | 122 | Carlos Hernandez | .15 | .07 |
| ❑ | 123 | Jeff Fassero | .15 | .07 |
| ❑ | 124 | Dave Burba | .15 | .07 |
| ❑ | 125 | Wayne Kirby | .15 | .07 |
| ❑ | 126 | John Cummings | .15 | .07 |
| ❑ | 127 | Bret Barberie | .15 | .07 |
| ❑ | 128 | Todd Hundley | .15 | .07 |
| ❑ | 129 | Tim Hulett | .15 | .07 |
| ❑ | 130 | Phil Clark | .15 | .07 |
| ❑ | 131 | Danny Jackson | .15 | .07 |
| ❑ | 132 | Tom Foley | .15 | .07 |
| ❑ | 133 | Donald Harris | .15 | .07 |
| ❑ | 134 | Scott Fletcher | .15 | .07 |
| ❑ | 135 | Johnny Ruffin | .15 | .07 |
| ❑ | 136 | Jerald Clark | .15 | .07 |
| ❑ | 137 | Billy Brewer | .15 | .07 |
| ❑ | 138 | Dan Gladden | .15 | .07 |
| ❑ | 139 | Eddie Guardado | .15 | .07 |
| ❑ | 140 | Cal Ripken CL | .60 | .25 |
| ❑ | 141 | Scott Hemond | .15 | .07 |
| ❑ | 142 | Steve Frey | .15 | .07 |
| ❑ | 143 | Xavier Hernandez | .15 | .07 |
| ❑ | 144 | Mark Eichhorn | .15 | .07 |
| ❑ | 145 | Ellis Burks | .30 | .14 |
| ❑ | 146 | Jim Leyritz | .15 | .07 |
| ❑ | 147 | Mark Lemke | .15 | .07 |
| ❑ | 148 | Pat Listach | .15 | .07 |
| ❑ | 149 | Donovan Osborne | .15 | .07 |
| ❑ | 150 | Glenallen Hill | .15 | .07 |
| ❑ | 151 | Orel Hershiser | .30 | .14 |
| ❑ | 152 | Darrin Fletcher | .15 | .07 |
| ❑ | 153 | Royce Clayton | .15 | .07 |
| ❑ | 154 | Derek Lilliquist | .15 | .07 |
| ❑ | 155 | Mike Felder | .15 | .07 |
| ❑ | 156 | Jeff Conine | .15 | .07 |
| ❑ | 157 | Ryan Thompson | .15 | .07 |
| ❑ | 158 | Ben McDonald | .15 | .07 |
| ❑ | 159 | Ricky Gutierrez | .15 | .07 |
| ❑ | 160 | Terry Mulholland | .15 | .07 |
| ❑ | 161 | Carlos Garcia | .15 | .07 |
| ❑ | 162 | Tom Henke | .15 | .07 |
| ❑ | 163 | Mike Greenwell | .15 | .07 |
| ❑ | 164 | Thomas Howard | .15 | .07 |
| ❑ | 165 | Joe Girardi | .15 | .07 |
| ❑ | 166 | Hubie Brooks | .15 | .07 |
| ❑ | 167 | Greg Gohr | .15 | .07 |
| ❑ | 168 | Chip Hale | .15 | .07 |
| ❑ | 169 | Rick Honeycutt | .15 | .07 |
| ❑ | 170 | Hilly Hathaway | .15 | .07 |
| ❑ | 171 | Todd Jones | .15 | .07 |
| ❑ | 172 | Tony Fernandez | .15 | .07 |
| ❑ | 173 | Bo Jackson | .30 | .14 |
| ❑ | 174 | Bobby Munoz | .15 | .07 |
| ❑ | 175 | Greg McMichael | .15 | .07 |
| ❑ | 176 | Graeme Lloyd | .15 | .07 |
| ❑ | 177 | Tom Pagnozzi | .15 | .07 |
| ❑ | 178 | Derrick May | .15 | .07 |
| ❑ | 179 | Pedro Martinez | 1.00 | .45 |
| ❑ | 180 | Ken Hill | .15 | .07 |
| ❑ | 181 | Bryan Hickerson | .15 | .07 |
| ❑ | 182 | Jose Mesa | .15 | .07 |
| ❑ | 183 | Dave Fleming | .15 | .07 |
| ❑ | 184 | Henry Cotto | .15 | .07 |
| ❑ | 185 | Jeff Kent | .30 | .14 |
| ❑ | 186 | Mark McLemore | .15 | .07 |
| ❑ | 187 | Trevor Hoffman | .30 | .14 |
| ❑ | 188 | Todd Pratt | .15 | .07 |
| ❑ | 189 | Blas Minor | .15 | .07 |
| ❑ | 190 | Charlie Leibrandt | .15 | .07 |
| ❑ | 191 | Tony Pena | .15 | .07 |
| ❑ | 192 | Larry Luebbers RC | .15 | .07 |
| ❑ | 193 | Greg W. Harris | .15 | .07 |
| ❑ | 194 | David Cone | .30 | .14 |
| ❑ | 195 | Bill Gullickson | .15 | .07 |
| ❑ | 196 | Brian Harper | .15 | .07 |
| ❑ | 197 | Steve Karsay | .15 | .07 |
| ❑ | 198 | Greg Myers | .15 | .07 |
| ❑ | 199 | Mark Portugal | .15 | .07 |
| ❑ | 200 | Pat Hentgen | .15 | .07 |
| ❑ | 201 | Mike LaValliere | .15 | .07 |
| ❑ | 202 | Mike Stanley | .15 | .07 |
| ❑ | 203 | Kent Mercker | .15 | .07 |
| ❑ | 204 | Dave Nilsson | .15 | .07 |
| ❑ | 205 | Erik Pappas | .15 | .07 |
| ❑ | 206 | Mike Morgan | .15 | .07 |
| ❑ | 207 | Roger McDowell | .15 | .07 |
| ❑ | 208 | Mike Lansing | .15 | .07 |
| ❑ | 209 | Kirt Manwaring | .15 | .07 |
| ❑ | 210 | Randy Milligan | .15 | .07 |
| ❑ | 211 | Erik Hanson | .15 | .07 |
| ❑ | 212 | Orestes Destrade | .15 | .07 |
| ❑ | 213 | Mike Maddux | .15 | .07 |
| ❑ | 214 | Alan Mills | .15 | .07 |
| ❑ | 215 | Tim Mauser | .15 | .07 |
| ❑ | 216 | Ben Rivera | .15 | .07 |
| ❑ | 217 | Don Slaught | .15 | .07 |
| ❑ | 218 | Bob Patterson | .15 | .07 |
| ❑ | 219 | Carlos Quintana | .15 | .07 |
| ❑ | 220 | Tim Raines CL | .15 | .07 |
| ❑ | 221 | Hal Morris | .15 | .07 |
| ❑ | 222 | Darren Holmes | .15 | .07 |
| ❑ | 223 | Chris Gwynn | .15 | .07 |
| ❑ | 224 | Chad Kreuter | .15 | .07 |
| ❑ | 225 | Mike Hartley | .15 | .07 |
| ❑ | 226 | Scott Lydy | .15 | .07 |
| ❑ | 227 | Eduardo Perez | .15 | .07 |
| ❑ | 228 | Greg Swindell | .15 | .07 |
| ❑ | 229 | Al Leiter | .30 | .14 |
| ❑ | 230 | Scott Radinsky | .15 | .07 |
| ❑ | 231 | Bob Wickman | .15 | .07 |
| ❑ | 232 | Otis Nixon | .15 | .07 |
| ❑ | 233 | Kevin Reimer | .15 | .07 |
| ❑ | 234 | Geronimo Pena | .15 | .07 |
| ❑ | 235 | Kevin Roberson | .15 | .07 |
| ❑ | 236 | Jody Reed | .15 | .07 |
| ❑ | 237 | Kirk Rueter | .15 | .07 |
| ❑ | 238 | Willie McGee | .30 | .14 |
| ❑ | 239 | Charles Nagy | .15 | .07 |
| ❑ | 240 | Tim Leary | .15 | .07 |
| ❑ | 241 | Carl Everett | .30 | .14 |
| ❑ | 242 | Charlie O'Brien | .15 | .07 |
| ❑ | 243 | Mike Pagliarulo | .15 | .07 |
| ❑ | 244 | Kerry Taylor | .15 | .07 |
| ❑ | 245 | Kevin Stocker | .15 | .07 |
| ❑ | 246 | Joel Johnston | .15 | .07 |
| ❑ | 247 | Geno Petralli | .15 | .07 |
| ❑ | 248 | Jeff Russell | .15 | .07 |
| ❑ | 249 | Joe Oliver | .15 | .07 |
| ❑ | 250 | Roberto Mejia | .15 | .07 |
| ❑ | 251 | Chris Haney | .15 | .07 |
| ❑ | 252 | Bill Krueger | .15 | .07 |
| ❑ | 253 | Shane Mack | .15 | .07 |
| ❑ | 254 | Terry Steinbach | .15 | .07 |
| ❑ | 255 | Luis Polonia | .15 | .07 |
| ❑ | 256 | Eddie Taubensee | .15 | .07 |
| ❑ | 257 | Dave Stewart | .30 | .14 |
| ❑ | 258 | Tim Raines | .30 | .14 |
| ❑ | 259 | Bernie Williams | .60 | .25 |
| ❑ | 260 | John Smoltz | .30 | .14 |
| ❑ | 261 | Kevin Seitzer | .15 | .07 |
| ❑ | 262 | Bob Tewksbury | .15 | .07 |
| ❑ | 263 | Bob Scanlan | .15 | .07 |
| ❑ | 264 | Henry Rodriguez | .15 | .07 |
| ❑ | 265 | Tim Scott | .15 | .07 |
| ❑ | 266 | Scott Sanderson | .15 | .07 |
| ❑ | 267 | Eric Plunk | .15 | .07 |
| ❑ | 268 | Edgar Martinez | .30 | .14 |
| ❑ | 269 | Charlie Hough | .30 | .14 |
| ❑ | 270 | Joe Orsulak | .15 | .07 |
| ❑ | 271 | Harold Reynolds | .15 | .07 |
| ❑ | 272 | Tim Teufel | .15 | .07 |
| ❑ | 273 | Bobby Thigpen | .15 | .07 |
| ❑ | 274 | Randy Tomlin | .15 | .07 |
| ❑ | 275 | Gary Redus | .15 | .07 |
| ❑ | 276 | Ken Ryan | .15 | .07 |
| ❑ | 277 | Tim Pugh | .15 | .07 |
| ❑ | 278 | J. Owens | .15 | .07 |
| ❑ | 279 | Phil Hiatt | .15 | .07 |
| ❑ | 280 | Alan Trammell | .30 | .14 |
| ❑ | 281 | Dave McCarty | .15 | .07 |
| ❑ | 282 | Bob Welch | .15 | .07 |
| ❑ | 283 | J.T. Snow | .30 | .14 |
| ❑ | 284 | Brian Williams | .15 | .07 |
| ❑ | 285 | Devon White | .15 | .07 |
| ❑ | 286 | Steve Sax | .15 | .07 |
| ❑ | 287 | Tony Tarasco | .15 | .07 |
| ❑ | 288 | Bill Spiers | .15 | .07 |
| ❑ | 289 | Allen Watson | .15 | .07 |
| ❑ | 290 | Rickey Henderson CL | .30 | .14 |
| ❑ | 291 | Jose Vizcaino | .15 | .07 |
| ❑ | 292 | Darryl Strawberry | .30 | .14 |
| ❑ | 293 | John Wetteland | .30 | .14 |
| ❑ | 294 | Bill Swift | .15 | .07 |
| ❑ | 295 | Jeff Treadway | .15 | .07 |
| ❑ | 296 | Tino Martinez | .30 | .14 |
| ❑ | 297 | Richie Lewis | .15 | .07 |
| ❑ | 298 | Bret Saberhagen | .30 | .14 |
| ❑ | 299 | Arthur Rhodes | .15 | .07 |
| ❑ | 300 | Guillermo Velasquez | .15 | .07 |
| ❑ | 301 | Milt Thompson | .15 | .07 |
| ❑ | 302 | Doug Strange | .15 | .07 |
| ❑ | 303 | Aaron Sele | .30 | .14 |
| ❑ | 304 | Bip Roberts | .15 | .07 |
| ❑ | 305 | Bruce Ruffin | .15 | .07 |
| ❑ | 306 | Jose Lind | .15 | .07 |
| ❑ | 307 | David Wells | .30 | .14 |
| ❑ | 308 | Bobby Witt | .15 | .07 |
| ❑ | 309 | Mark Wohlers | .15 | .07 |
| ❑ | 310 | B.J. Surhoff | .30 | .14 |
| ❑ | 311 | Mark Whiten | .15 | .07 |
| ❑ | 312 | Turk Wendell | .15 | .07 |
| ❑ | 313 | Raul Mondesi | .30 | .14 |
| ❑ | 314 | Brian Turang RC | .15 | .07 |
| ❑ | 315 | Chris Hammond | .15 | .07 |
| ❑ | 316 | Tim Bogar | .15 | .07 |
| ❑ | 317 | Brad Pennington | .15 | .07 |
| ❑ | 318 | Tim Worrell | .15 | .07 |
| ❑ | 319 | Mitch Williams | .15 | .07 |
| ❑ | 320 | Rondell White | .30 | .14 |
| ❑ | 321 | Frank Viola | .15 | .07 |
| ❑ | 322 | Manny Ramirez | 1.00 | .45 |
| ❑ | 323 | Gary Wayne | .15 | .07 |
| ❑ | 324 | Mike Macfarlane | .15 | .07 |
| ❑ | 325 | Russ Springer | .15 | .07 |
| ❑ | 326 | Tim Wallach | .15 | .07 |
| ❑ | 327 | Salomon Torres | .15 | .07 |
| ❑ | 328 | Omar Vizquel | .30 | .14 |
| ❑ | 329 | Andy Tomberlin RC | .15 | .07 |
| ❑ | 330 | Chris Sabo | .15 | .07 |
| ❑ | 331 | Mike Mussina | .60 | .25 |
| ❑ | 332 | Andy Benes | .15 | .07 |
| ❑ | 333 | Darren Daulton | .30 | .14 |
| ❑ | 334 | Orlando Merced | .15 | .07 |
| ❑ | 335 | Mark McGwire | 2.50 | 1.10 |
| ❑ | 336 | Dave Winfield | .60 | .25 |
| ❑ | 337 | Sammy Sosa | 1.25 | .55 |
| ❑ | 338 | Eric Karros | .30 | .14 |
| ❑ | 339 | Greg Vaughn | .30 | .14 |
| ❑ | 340 | Don Mattingly | 1.50 | .70 |
| ❑ | 341 | Frank Thomas | 1.25 | .55 |
| ❑ | 342 | Fred McGriff | .30 | .14 |
| ❑ | 343 | Kirby Puckett | 1.50 | .70 |
| ❑ | 344 | Roberto Kelly | .15 | .07 |
| ❑ | 345 | Wally Joyner | .30 | .14 |
| ❑ | 346 | Andres Galarraga | .30 | .14 |
| ❑ | 347 | Bobby Bonilla | .30 | .14 |
| ❑ | 348 | Benito Santiago | .15 | .07 |
| ❑ | 349 | Barry Bonds | 1.00 | .45 |
| ❑ | 350 | Delino DeShields | .15 | .07 |
| ❑ | 351 | Albert Belle | .30 | .14 |
| ❑ | 352 | Randy Johnson | .75 | .35 |
| ❑ | 353 | Tim Salmon | .30 | .14 |
| ❑ | 354 | John Olerud | .30 | .14 |
| ❑ | 355 | Dean Palmer | .30 | .14 |
| ❑ | 356 | Roger Clemens | 1.25 | .55 |
| ❑ | 357 | Jim Abbott | .30 | .14 |
| ❑ | 358 | Mark Grace | .60 | .25 |
| ❑ | 359 | Ozzie Guillen | .15 | .07 |
| ❑ | 360 | Lou Whitaker | .30 | .14 |
| ❑ | 361 | Jose Rijo | .15 | .07 |
| ❑ | 362 | Jeff Montgomery | .15 | .07 |
| ❑ | 363 | Chuck Finley | .30 | .14 |
| ❑ | 364 | Tom Glavine | .60 | .25 |
| ❑ | 365 | Jeff Bagwell | .75 | .35 |
| ❑ | 366 | Joe Carter | .30 | .14 |
| ❑ | 367 | Ray Lankford | .30 | .14 |
| ❑ | 368 | Ramon Martinez | .15 | .07 |
| ❑ | 369 | Jay Buhner | .30 | .14 |
| ❑ | 370 | Matt Williams | .30 | .14 |
| ❑ | 371 | Larry Walker | .30 | .14 |
| ❑ | 372 | Jose Canseco | .75 | .35 |
| ❑ | 373 | Lenny Dykstra | .30 | .14 |
| ❑ | 374 | Bryan Harvey | .15 | .07 |

| ❑ | No. | Player | Price | Price |
|---|---|---|---|---|
| ❑ | 375 | Andy Van Slyke | .30 | .14 |
| ❑ | 376 | Ivan Rodriguez | .75 | .35 |
| ❑ | 377 | Kevin Mitchell | .15 | .07 |
| ❑ | 378 | Travis Fryman | .30 | .14 |
| ❑ | 379 | Duane Ward | .15 | .07 |
| ❑ | 380 | Greg Maddux | 1.50 | .70 |
| ❑ | 381 | Scott Servais | .15 | .07 |
| ❑ | 382 | Greg Olson | .15 | .07 |
| ❑ | 383 | Rey Sanchez | .15 | .07 |
| ❑ | 384 | Tom Kramer | .15 | .07 |
| ❑ | 385 | David Valle | .15 | .07 |
| ❑ | 386 | Eddie Murray | .60 | .25 |
| ❑ | 387 | Kevin Higgins | .15 | .07 |
| ❑ | 388 | Dan Wilson | .15 | .07 |
| ❑ | 389 | Todd Frohwirth | .15 | .07 |
| ❑ | 390 | Gerald Williams | .15 | .07 |
| ❑ | 391 | Hipolito Pichardo | .15 | .07 |
| ❑ | 392 | Pat Meares | .15 | .07 |
| ❑ | 393 | Luis Lopez | .15 | .07 |
| ❑ | 394 | Ricky Jordan | .15 | .07 |
| ❑ | 395 | Bob Walk | .15 | .07 |
| ❑ | 396 | Sid Fernandez | .15 | .07 |
| ❑ | 397 | Todd Worrell | .15 | .07 |
| ❑ | 398 | Darryl Hamilton | .15 | .07 |
| ❑ | 399 | Randy Myers | .15 | .07 |
| ❑ | 400 | Rod Brewer | .15 | .07 |
| ❑ | 401 | Lance Blankenship | .15 | .07 |
| ❑ | 402 | Steve Finley | .30 | .14 |
| ❑ | 403 | Phil Leftwich RC | .15 | .07 |
| ❑ | 404 | Juan Guzman | .15 | .07 |
| ❑ | 405 | Anthony Young | .15 | .07 |
| ❑ | 406 | Jeff Gardner | .15 | .07 |
| ❑ | 407 | Ryan Bowen | .15 | .07 |
| ❑ | 408 | Fernando Valenzuela | .30 | .14 |
| ❑ | 409 | David West | .30 | .14 |
| ❑ | 410 | Kenny Rogers | .15 | .07 |
| ❑ | 411 | Bob Zupcic | .15 | .07 |
| ❑ | 412 | Eric Young | .15 | .07 |
| ❑ | 413 | Bret Boone | .30 | .14 |
| ❑ | 414 | Danny Tartabull | .15 | .07 |
| ❑ | 415 | Bob MacDonald | .15 | .07 |
| ❑ | 416 | Ron Karkovice | .15 | .07 |
| ❑ | 417 | Scott Cooper | .15 | .07 |
| ❑ | 418 | Dante Bichette | .30 | .14 |
| ❑ | 419 | Tripp Cromer | .15 | .07 |
| ❑ | 420 | Billy Ashley | .15 | .07 |
| ❑ | 421 | Roger Smithberg | .15 | .07 |
| ❑ | 422 | Dennis Martinez | .30 | .14 |
| ❑ | 423 | Mike Blowers | .15 | .07 |
| ❑ | 424 | Darren Lewis | .15 | .07 |
| ❑ | 425 | Junior Ortiz | .15 | .07 |
| ❑ | 426 | Butch Huskey | .15 | .07 |
| ❑ | 427 | Jimmy Poole | .15 | .07 |
| ❑ | 428 | Walt Weiss | .15 | .07 |
| ❑ | 429 | Scott Bankhead | .15 | .07 |
| ❑ | 430 | Deion Sanders | .30 | .14 |
| ❑ | 431 | Scott Bullett | .15 | .07 |
| ❑ | 432 | Jeff Huson | .15 | .07 |
| ❑ | 433 | Tyler Green | .15 | .07 |
| ❑ | 434 | Billy Hatcher | .15 | .07 |
| ❑ | 435 | Bob Hamelin | .15 | .07 |
| ❑ | 436 | Reggie Sanders | .15 | .07 |
| ❑ | 437 | Scott Erickson | .15 | .07 |
| ❑ | 438 | Steve Reed | .15 | .07 |
| ❑ | 439 | Randy Velarde | .15 | .07 |
| ❑ | 440 | Tony Gwynn CL | .60 | .25 |
| ❑ | 441 | Terry Leach | .15 | .07 |
| ❑ | 442 | Danny Bautista | .15 | .07 |
| ❑ | 443 | Kent Hrbek | .30 | .14 |
| ❑ | 444 | Rick Wilkins | .15 | .07 |
| ❑ | 445 | Tony Phillips | .15 | .07 |
| ❑ | 446 | Dion James | .15 | .07 |
| ❑ | 447 | Joey Cora | .15 | .07 |
| ❑ | 448 | Andre Dawson | .30 | .14 |
| ❑ | 449 | Pedro Castellano | .15 | .07 |
| ❑ | 450 | Tom Gordon | .15 | .07 |
| ❑ | 451 | Rob Dibble | .15 | .07 |
| ❑ | 452 | Ron Darling | .15 | .07 |
| ❑ | 453 | Chipper Jones | 1.50 | .70 |
| ❑ | 454 | Joe Grahe | .15 | .07 |
| ❑ | 455 | Domingo Cedeno | .15 | .07 |
| ❑ | 456 | Tom Edens | .15 | .07 |
| ❑ | 457 | Mitch Webster | .15 | .07 |
| ❑ | 458 | Jose Bautista | .15 | .07 |
| ❑ | 459 | Troy O'Leary | .15 | .07 |
| ❑ | 460 | Todd Zeile | .15 | .07 |
| ❑ | 461 | Sean Berry | .15 | .07 |
| ❑ | 462 | Brad Holman RC | .15 | .07 |
| ❑ | 463 | Dave Martinez | .15 | .07 |
| ❑ | 464 | Mark Lewis | .15 | .07 |
| ❑ | 465 | Paul Carey | .15 | .07 |
| ❑ | 466 | Jack Armstrong | .15 | .07 |
| ❑ | 467 | David Telgheder | .15 | .07 |
| ❑ | 468 | Gene Harris | .15 | .07 |
| ❑ | 469 | Danny Darwin | .15 | .07 |
| ❑ | 470 | Kim Batiste | .15 | .07 |
| ❑ | 471 | Tim Wakefield | .15 | .07 |
| ❑ | 472 | Craig Lefferts | .15 | .07 |
| ❑ | 473 | Jacob Brumfield | .15 | .07 |
| ❑ | 474 | Lance Painter | .15 | .07 |
| ❑ | 475 | Milt Cuyler | .15 | .07 |
| ❑ | 476 | Melido Perez | .15 | .07 |
| ❑ | 477 | Derek Parks | .15 | .07 |
| ❑ | 478 | Gary DiSarcina | .15 | .07 |
| ❑ | 479 | Steve Bedrosian | .15 | .07 |
| ❑ | 480 | Eric Anthony | .15 | .07 |
| ❑ | 481 | Julio Franco | .15 | .07 |
| ❑ | 482 | Tommy Greene | .15 | .07 |
| ❑ | 483 | Pat Kelly | .15 | .07 |
| ❑ | 484 | Nate Minchey | .15 | .07 |
| ❑ | 485 | William Pennyfeather | .15 | .07 |
| ❑ | 486 | Harold Baines | .30 | .14 |
| ❑ | 487 | Howard Johnson | .15 | .07 |
| ❑ | 488 | Angel Miranda | .15 | .07 |
| ❑ | 489 | Scott Sanders | .15 | .07 |
| ❑ | 490 | Shawon Dunston | .15 | .07 |
| ❑ | 491 | Mel Rojas | .15 | .07 |
| ❑ | 492 | Jeff Nelson | .15 | .07 |
| ❑ | 493 | Archi Cianfrocco | .15 | .07 |
| ❑ | 494 | Al Martin | .15 | .07 |
| ❑ | 495 | Mike Gallego | .15 | .07 |
| ❑ | 496 | Mike Henneman | .15 | .07 |
| ❑ | 497 | Armando Reynoso | .15 | .07 |
| ❑ | 498 | Mickey Morandini | .15 | .07 |
| ❑ | 499 | Rick Renteria | .15 | .07 |
| ❑ | 500 | Rick Sutcliffe | .30 | .14 |
| ❑ | 501 | Bobby Jones | .15 | .07 |
| ❑ | 502 | Gary Gaetti | .30 | .14 |
| ❑ | 503 | Rick Aguilera | .15 | .07 |
| ❑ | 504 | Todd Stottlemyre | .15 | .07 |
| ❑ | 505 | Mike Mohler | .15 | .07 |
| ❑ | 506 | Mike Stanton | .15 | .07 |
| ❑ | 507 | Jose Guzman | .15 | .07 |
| ❑ | 508 | Kevin Rogers | .15 | .07 |
| ❑ | 509 | Chuck Carr | .15 | .07 |
| ❑ | 510 | Chris Jones | .15 | .07 |
| ❑ | 511 | Brent Mayne | .15 | .07 |
| ❑ | 512 | Greg Harris | .15 | .07 |
| ❑ | 513 | Dave Henderson | .15 | .07 |
| ❑ | 514 | Eric Hillman | .15 | .07 |
| ❑ | 515 | Dan Peltier | .15 | .07 |
| ❑ | 516 | Craig Shipley | .15 | .07 |
| ❑ | 517 | John Valentin | .15 | .07 |
| ❑ | 518 | Wilson Alvarez | .15 | .07 |
| ❑ | 519 | Andujar Cedeno | .15 | .07 |
| ❑ | 520 | Troy Neel | .15 | .07 |
| ❑ | 521 | Tom Candiotti | .15 | .07 |
| ❑ | 522 | Matt Mieske | .15 | .07 |
| ❑ | 523 | Jim Thome | .30 | .14 |
| ❑ | 524 | Lou Frazier | .15 | .07 |
| ❑ | 525 | Mike Jackson | .15 | .07 |
| ❑ | 526 | Pedro Martinez RC | .15 | .07 |
| ❑ | 527 | Roger Pavlik | .15 | .07 |
| ❑ | 528 | Kent Bottenfield | .15 | .07 |
| ❑ | 529 | Felix Jose | .15 | .07 |
| ❑ | 530 | Mark Guthrie | .15 | .07 |
| ❑ | 531 | Steve Farr | .15 | .07 |
| ❑ | 532 | Craig Paquette | .15 | .07 |
| ❑ | 533 | Doug Jones | .15 | .07 |
| ❑ | 534 | Luis Alicea | .15 | .07 |
| ❑ | 535 | Cory Snyder | .15 | .07 |
| ❑ | 536 | Paul Sorrento | .15 | .07 |
| ❑ | 537 | Nigel Wilson | .15 | .07 |
| ❑ | 538 | Jeff King | .15 | .07 |
| ❑ | 539 | Willie Greene | .15 | .07 |
| ❑ | 540 | Kirk McCaskill | .15 | .07 |
| ❑ | 541 | Al Osuna | .15 | .07 |
| ❑ | 542 | Greg Hibbard | .15 | .07 |
| ❑ | 543 | Brett Butler | .30 | .14 |
| ❑ | 544 | Jose Valentin | .15 | .07 |
| ❑ | 545 | Wil Cordero | .15 | .07 |
| ❑ | 546 | Chris Bosio | .15 | .07 |
| ❑ | 547 | Jamie Moyer | .15 | .07 |
| ❑ | 548 | Jim Eisenreich | .15 | .07 |
| ❑ | 549 | Vinny Castilla | .30 | .14 |
| ❑ | 550 | Dave Winfield CL | .30 | .14 |
| ❑ | 551 | John Roper | .15 | .07 |
| ❑ | 552 | Lance Johnson | .15 | .07 |
| ❑ | 553 | Scott Kamieniecki | .15 | .07 |
| ❑ | 554 | Mike Moore | .15 | .07 |
| ❑ | 555 | Steve Buechele | .15 | .07 |
| ❑ | 556 | Terry Pendleton | .30 | .14 |
| ❑ | 557 | Todd Van Poppel | .15 | .07 |
| ❑ | 558 | Rob Butler | .15 | .07 |
| ❑ | 559 | Zane Smith | .15 | .07 |
| ❑ | 560 | David Hulse | .15 | .07 |
| ❑ | 561 | Tim Costo | .15 | .07 |
| ❑ | 562 | John Habyan | .15 | .07 |
| ❑ | 563 | Terry Jorgensen | .15 | .07 |
| ❑ | 564 | Matt Nokes | .15 | .07 |
| ❑ | 565 | Kevin McReynolds | .15 | .07 |
| ❑ | 566 | Phil Plantier | .15 | .07 |
| ❑ | 567 | Chris Turner | .15 | .07 |
| ❑ | 568 | Carlos Delgado | 1.00 | .45 |
| ❑ | 569 | John Jaha | .15 | .07 |
| ❑ | 570 | Dwight Smith | .15 | .07 |
| ❑ | 571 | John Vander Wal | .15 | .07 |
| ❑ | 572 | Trevor Wilson | .15 | .07 |
| ❑ | 573 | Felix Fermin | .15 | .07 |
| ❑ | 574 | Marc Newfield | .15 | .07 |
| ❑ | 575 | Jeromy Burnitz | .30 | .14 |
| ❑ | 576 | Leo Gomez | .15 | .07 |
| ❑ | 577 | Curt Schilling | .30 | .14 |
| ❑ | 578 | Kevin Young | .15 | .07 |
| ❑ | 579 | Jerry Spradlin RC | .15 | .07 |
| ❑ | 580 | Curt Leskanic | .15 | .07 |
| ❑ | 581 | Carl Willis | .15 | .07 |
| ❑ | 582 | Alex Fernandez | .15 | .07 |
| ❑ | 583 | Mark Holzemer | .15 | .07 |
| ❑ | 584 | Domingo Martinez | .15 | .07 |
| ❑ | 585 | Pete Smith | .15 | .07 |
| ❑ | 586 | Brian Jordan | .30 | .14 |
| ❑ | 587 | Kevin Gross | .15 | .07 |
| ❑ | 588 | J.R. Phillips | .15 | .07 |
| ❑ | 589 | Chris Nabholz | .15 | .07 |
| ❑ | 590 | Bill Wertz | .15 | .07 |
| ❑ | 591 | Derek Bell | .15 | .07 |
| ❑ | 592 | Brady Anderson | .30 | .14 |
| ❑ | 593 | Matt Turner | .15 | .07 |
| ❑ | 594 | Pete Incaviglia | .15 | .07 |
| ❑ | 595 | Greg Gagne | .15 | .07 |
| ❑ | 596 | John Flaherty | .15 | .07 |
| ❑ | 597 | Scott Livingstone | .15 | .07 |
| ❑ | 598 | Rod Bolton | .15 | .07 |
| ❑ | 599 | Mike Perez | .15 | .07 |
| ❑ | 600 | Roger Clemens CL | .60 | .25 |
| ❑ | 601 | Tony Castillo | .15 | .07 |
| ❑ | 602 | Henry Mercedes | .15 | .07 |
| ❑ | 603 | Mike Fetters | .15 | .07 |
| ❑ | 604 | Rod Beck | .15 | .07 |
| ❑ | 605 | Damon Buford | .15 | .07 |
| ❑ | 606 | Matt Whiteside | .15 | .07 |
| ❑ | 607 | Shawn Green | .75 | .35 |
| ❑ | 608 | Midre Cummings | .15 | .07 |
| ❑ | 609 | Jeff McNeely | .15 | .07 |
| ❑ | 610 | Danny Sheaffer | .15 | .07 |
| ❑ | 611 | Paul Wagner | .15 | .07 |
| ❑ | 612 | Torey Lovullo | .15 | .07 |
| ❑ | 613 | Javier Lopez | .30 | .14 |
| ❑ | 614 | Mariano Duncan | .15 | .07 |
| ❑ | 615 | Doug Brocail | .15 | .07 |
| ❑ | 616 | Dave Hansen | .15 | .07 |
| ❑ | 617 | Ryan Klesko | .30 | .14 |
| ❑ | 618 | Eric Davis | .30 | .14 |
| ❑ | 619 | Scott Ruffcorn | .15 | .07 |
| ❑ | 620 | Mike Trombley | .15 | .07 |
| ❑ | 621 | Jaime Navarro | .15 | .07 |
| ❑ | 622 | Rheal Cormier | .15 | .07 |
| ❑ | 623 | Jose Offerman | .15 | .07 |
| ❑ | 624 | David Segui | .15 | .07 |
| ❑ | 625 | Robb Nen | .15 | .07 |
| ❑ | 626 | Dave Gallagher | .15 | .07 |
| ❑ | 627 | Julian Tavarez RC | .15 | .07 |
| ❑ | 628 | Chris Gomez | .15 | .07 |
| ❑ | 629 | Jeffrey Hammonds | .30 | .14 |
| ❑ | 630 | Scott Brosius | .30 | .14 |
| ❑ | 631 | Willie Blair | .15 | .07 |
| ❑ | 632 | Doug Drabek | .15 | .07 |

| | | |
|---|---|---|
| ❑ 633 Bill Wegman | .15 | .07 |
| ❑ 634 Jeff McKnight | .15 | .07 |
| ❑ 635 Rich Rodriguez | .15 | .07 |
| ❑ 636 Steve Trachsel | .15 | .07 |
| ❑ 637 Buddy Groom | .15 | .07 |
| ❑ 638 Sterling Hitchcock | .15 | .07 |
| ❑ 639 Chuck McElroy | .15 | .07 |
| ❑ 640 Rene Gonzales | .15 | .07 |
| ❑ 641 Dan Plesac | .15 | .07 |
| ❑ 642 Jeff Branson | .15 | .07 |
| ❑ 643 Darrell Whitmore | .15 | .07 |
| ❑ 644 Paul Quantrill | .15 | .07 |
| ❑ 645 Rich Rowland | .15 | .07 |
| ❑ 646 Curtis Pride RC | .15 | .07 |
| ❑ 647 Erik Plantenberg RC | .15 | .07 |
| ❑ 648 Albie Lopez | .15 | .07 |
| ❑ 649 Rich Batchelor RC | .15 | .07 |
| ❑ 650 Lee Smith | .30 | .14 |
| ❑ 651 Cliff Floyd | .30 | .14 |
| ❑ 652 Pete Schourek | .15 | .07 |
| ❑ 653 Reggie Jefferson | .15 | .07 |
| ❑ 654 Bill Haselman | .15 | .07 |
| ❑ 655 Steve Hosey | .15 | .07 |
| ❑ 656 Mark Clark | .15 | .07 |
| ❑ 657 Mark Davis | .15 | .07 |
| ❑ 658 Dave Magadan | .15 | .07 |
| ❑ 659 Candy Maldonado | .15 | .07 |
| ❑ 660 Mark Langston CL | .15 | .07 |

## 1995 Donruss

| | MINT | NRMT |
|---|---|---|
| COMPLETE SET (550) | 30.00 | 13.50 |
| COMPLETE SERIES 1 (330) | 20.00 | 9.00 |
| COMPLETE SERIES 2 (220) | 10.00 | 4.50 |
| COMMON CARD (1-550) | .15 | .07 |

| | | |
|---|---|---|
| ❑ 1 David Justice | .40 | .18 |
| ❑ 2 Rene Arocha | .15 | .07 |
| ❑ 3 Sandy Alomar Jr. | .25 | .11 |
| ❑ 4 Luis Lopez | .15 | .07 |
| ❑ 5 Mike Piazza | 2.00 | .90 |
| ❑ 6 Bobby Jones | .15 | .07 |
| ❑ 7 Damion Easley | .15 | .07 |
| ❑ 8 Barry Bonds | 1.00 | .45 |
| ❑ 9 Mike Mussina | .60 | .25 |
| ❑ 10 Kevin Seitzer | .15 | .07 |
| ❑ 11 John Smiley | .15 | .07 |
| ❑ 12 Wm.VanLandingham | .15 | .07 |
| ❑ 13 Ron Darling | .15 | .07 |
| ❑ 14 Walt Weiss | .15 | .07 |
| ❑ 15 Mike Lansing | .15 | .07 |
| ❑ 16 Allen Watson | .15 | .07 |
| ❑ 17 Aaron Sele | .25 | .11 |
| ❑ 18 Randy Johnson | .75 | .35 |
| ❑ 19 Dean Palmer | .25 | .11 |
| ❑ 20 Jeff Bagwell | .75 | .35 |
| ❑ 21 Curt Schilling | .25 | .11 |
| ❑ 22 Darrell Whitmore | .15 | .07 |
| ❑ 23 Steve Trachsel | .15 | .07 |
| ❑ 24 Dan Wilson | .15 | .07 |
| ❑ 25 Steve Finley | .25 | .11 |
| ❑ 26 Bret Boone | .25 | .11 |
| ❑ 27 Charles Johnson | .25 | .11 |
| ❑ 28 Mike Stanton | .15 | .07 |
| ❑ 29 Ismael Valdes | .15 | .07 |
| ❑ 30 Salomon Torres | .15 | .07 |
| ❑ 31 Eric Anthony | .15 | .07 |
| ❑ 32 Spike Owen | .15 | .07 |
| ❑ 33 Joey Cora | .15 | .07 |
| ❑ 34 Robert Eenhoorn | .15 | .07 |
| ❑ 35 Rick White | .15 | .07 |
| ❑ 36 Omar Vizquel | .25 | .11 |
| ❑ 37 Carlos Delgado | .60 | .25 |
| ❑ 38 Eddie Williams | .15 | .07 |
| ❑ 39 Shawon Dunston | .15 | .07 |
| ❑ 40 Darrin Fletcher | .15 | .07 |
| ❑ 41 Leo Gomez | .15 | .07 |
| ❑ 42 Juan Gonzalez | .60 | .25 |
| ❑ 43 Luis Alicea | .15 | .07 |
| ❑ 44 Ken Ryan | .15 | .07 |
| ❑ 45 Lou Whitaker | .25 | .11 |
| ❑ 46 Mike Blowers | .15 | .07 |
| ❑ 47 Willie Blair | .15 | .07 |
| ❑ 48 Todd Van Poppel | .15 | .07 |
| ❑ 49 Roberto Alomar | .60 | .25 |
| ❑ 50 Ozzie Smith | .75 | .35 |
| ❑ 51 Sterling Hitchcock | .15 | .07 |
| ❑ 52 Mo Vaughn | .25 | .11 |
| ❑ 53 Rick Aguilera | .15 | .07 |
| ❑ 54 Kent Mercker | .15 | .07 |
| ❑ 55 Don Mattingly | 1.50 | .70 |
| ❑ 56 Bob Scanlan | .15 | .07 |
| ❑ 57 Wilson Alvarez | .15 | .07 |
| ❑ 58 Jose Mesa | .15 | .07 |
| ❑ 59 Scott Kamieniecki | .15 | .07 |
| ❑ 60 Todd Jones | .15 | .07 |
| ❑ 61 John Kruk | .25 | .11 |
| ❑ 62 Mike Stanley | .15 | .07 |
| ❑ 63 Tino Martinez | .25 | .11 |
| ❑ 64 Eddie Zambrano | .15 | .07 |
| ❑ 65 Todd Hundley | .15 | .07 |
| ❑ 66 Jamie Moyer | .15 | .07 |
| ❑ 67 Rich Amaral | .15 | .07 |
| ❑ 68 Jose Valentin | .15 | .07 |
| ❑ 69 Alex Gonzalez | .15 | .07 |
| ❑ 70 Kurt Abbott | .15 | .07 |
| ❑ 71 Delino DeShields | .15 | .07 |
| ❑ 72 Brian Anderson | .15 | .07 |
| ❑ 73 John Vander Wal | .15 | .07 |
| ❑ 74 Turner Ward | .15 | .07 |
| ❑ 75 Tim Raines | .25 | .11 |
| ❑ 76 Mark Acre | .15 | .07 |
| ❑ 77 Jose Offerman | .15 | .07 |
| ❑ 78 Jimmy Key | .25 | .11 |
| ❑ 79 Mark Whiten | .15 | .07 |
| ❑ 80 Mark Gubicza | .15 | .07 |
| ❑ 81 Darren Hall | .15 | .07 |
| ❑ 82 Travis Fryman | .25 | .11 |
| ❑ 83 Cal Ripken | 2.50 | 1.10 |
| ❑ 84 Geronimo Berroa | .15 | .07 |
| ❑ 85 Bret Barberie | .15 | .07 |
| ❑ 86 Andy Ashby | .15 | .07 |
| ❑ 87 Steve Avery | .15 | .07 |
| ❑ 88 Rich Becker | .15 | .07 |
| ❑ 89 John Valentin | .15 | .07 |
| ❑ 90 Glenallen Hill | .15 | .07 |
| ❑ 91 Carlos Garcia | .15 | .07 |
| ❑ 92 Dennis Martinez | .25 | .11 |
| ❑ 93 Pat Kelly | .15 | .07 |
| ❑ 94 Orlando Miller | .15 | .07 |
| ❑ 95 Felix Jose | .15 | .07 |
| ❑ 96 Mike Kingery | .15 | .07 |
| ❑ 97 Jeff Kent | .40 | .18 |
| ❑ 98 Pete Incaviglia | .15 | .07 |
| ❑ 99 Chad Curtis | .15 | .07 |
| ❑ 100 Thomas Howard | .15 | .07 |
| ❑ 101 Hector Carrasco | .15 | .07 |
| ❑ 102 Tom Pagnozzi | .15 | .07 |
| ❑ 103 Danny Tartabull | .15 | .07 |
| ❑ 104 Donnie Elliott | .15 | .07 |
| ❑ 105 Danny Jackson | .15 | .07 |
| ❑ 106 Steve Dunn | .15 | .07 |
| ❑ 107 Roger Salkeld | .15 | .07 |
| ❑ 108 Jeff King | .15 | .07 |
| ❑ 109 Cecil Fielder | .25 | .11 |
| ❑ 110 Paul Molitor CL | .25 | .11 |
| ❑ 111 Denny Neagle | .25 | .11 |
| ❑ 112 Troy Neel | .15 | .07 |
| ❑ 113 Rod Beck | .15 | .07 |
| ❑ 114 Alex Rodriguez | 2.50 | 1.10 |
| ❑ 115 Joey Eischen | .15 | .07 |
| ❑ 116 Tom Candiotti | .15 | .07 |
| ❑ 117 Ray McDavid | .15 | .07 |

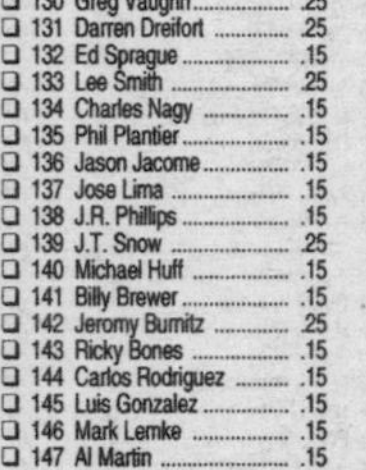

| | | |
|---|---|---|
| ❑ 118 Vince Coleman | .15 | .07 |
| ❑ 119 Pete Harnisch | .15 | .07 |
| ❑ 120 David Nied | .15 | .07 |
| ❑ 121 Pat Rapp | .15 | .07 |
| ❑ 122 Sammy Sosa | 1.25 | .55 |
| ❑ 123 Steve Reed | .15 | .07 |
| ❑ 124 Jose Oliva | .15 | .07 |
| ❑ 125 Ricky Bottalico | .15 | .07 |
| ❑ 126 Jose DeLeon | .15 | .07 |
| ❑ 127 Pat Hentgen | .15 | .07 |
| ❑ 128 Will Clark | .60 | .25 |
| ❑ 129 Mark Dewey | .15 | .07 |
| ❑ 130 Greg Vaughn | .25 | .11 |
| ❑ 131 Darren Dreifort | .25 | .11 |
| ❑ 132 Ed Sprague | .15 | .07 |
| ❑ 133 Lee Smith | .25 | .11 |
| ❑ 134 Charles Nagy | .15 | .07 |
| ❑ 135 Phil Plantier | .15 | .07 |
| ❑ 136 Jason Jacome | .15 | .07 |
| ❑ 137 Jose Lima | .15 | .07 |
| ❑ 138 J.R. Phillips | .15 | .07 |
| ❑ 139 J.T. Snow | .25 | .11 |
| ❑ 140 Michael Huff | .15 | .07 |
| ❑ 141 Billy Brewer | .15 | .07 |
| ❑ 142 Jeromy Burnitz | .25 | .11 |
| ❑ 143 Ricky Bones | .15 | .07 |
| ❑ 144 Carlos Rodriguez | .15 | .07 |
| ❑ 145 Luis Gonzalez | .15 | .07 |
| ❑ 146 Mark Lemke | .15 | .07 |
| ❑ 147 Al Martin | .15 | .07 |
| ❑ 148 Mike Bordick | .15 | .07 |
| ❑ 149 Robb Nen | .15 | .07 |
| ❑ 150 Wil Cordero | .15 | .07 |
| ❑ 151 Edgar Martinez | .40 | .18 |
| ❑ 152 Gerald Williams | .15 | .07 |
| ❑ 153 Esteban Beltre | .15 | .07 |
| ❑ 154 Mike Moore | .15 | .07 |
| ❑ 155 Mark Langston | .15 | .07 |
| ❑ 156 Mark Clark | .15 | .07 |
| ❑ 157 Bobby Ayala | .15 | .07 |
| ❑ 158 Rick Wilkins | .15 | .07 |
| ❑ 159 Bobby Munoz | .15 | .07 |
| ❑ 160 Brett Butler CL | .25 | .11 |
| ❑ 161 Scott Erickson | .15 | .07 |
| ❑ 162 Paul Molitor | .60 | .25 |
| ❑ 163 Jon Lieber | .15 | .07 |
| ❑ 164 Jason Grimsley | .15 | .07 |
| ❑ 165 Norberto Martin | .15 | .07 |
| ❑ 166 Javier Lopez | .25 | .11 |
| ❑ 167 Brian McRae | .15 | .07 |
| ❑ 168 Gary Sheffield | .60 | .25 |
| ❑ 169 Marcus Moore | .15 | .07 |
| ❑ 170 John Hudek | .15 | .07 |
| ❑ 171 Kelly Stinnett | .15 | .07 |
| ❑ 172 Chris Gomez | .15 | .07 |
| ❑ 173 Rey Sanchez | .15 | .07 |
| ❑ 174 Juan Guzman | .15 | .07 |
| ❑ 175 Chan Ho Park | .25 | .11 |
| ❑ 176 Terry Shumpert | .15 | .07 |
| ❑ 177 Steve Ontiveros | .15 | .07 |
| ❑ 178 Brad Ausmus | .15 | .07 |
| ❑ 179 Tim Davis | .15 | .07 |
| ❑ 180 Billy Ashley | .15 | .07 |
| ❑ 181 Vinny Castilla | .25 | .11 |
| ❑ 182 Bill Spiers | .15 | .07 |
| ❑ 183 Randy Knorr | .15 | .07 |
| ❑ 184 Brian Hunter | .15 | .07 |
| ❑ 185 Pat Meares | .15 | .07 |
| ❑ 186 Steve Buechele | .15 | .07 |
| ❑ 187 Kirt Manwaring | .15 | .07 |
| ❑ 188 Tim Naehring | .15 | .07 |
| ❑ 189 Matt Mieske | .15 | .07 |
| ❑ 190 Josias Manzanillo | .15 | .07 |
| ❑ 191 Greg McMichael | .15 | .07 |
| ❑ 192 Chuck Carr | .15 | .07 |
| ❑ 193 Midre Cummings | .15 | .07 |
| ❑ 194 Darryl Strawberry | .25 | .11 |
| ❑ 195 Greg Gagne | .15 | .07 |
| ❑ 196 Steve Cooke | .15 | .07 |
| ❑ 197 Woody Williams | .15 | .07 |
| ❑ 198 Ron Karkovice | .15 | .07 |
| ❑ 199 Phil Leftwich | .15 | .07 |
| ❑ 200 Jim Thome | .40 | .18 |
| ❑ 201 Brady Anderson | .25 | .11 |
| ❑ 202 Pedro A.Martinez | .15 | .07 |
| ❑ 203 Steve Karsay | .15 | .07 |

| |  |  | | |
|---|---|---|---|---|
| ❑ | 204 | Reggie Sanders | .15 | .07 |
| ❑ | 205 | Bill Risley | .15 | .07 |
| ❑ | 206 | Jay Bell | .25 | .11 |
| ❑ | 207 | Kevin Brown | .40 | .18 |
| ❑ | 208 | Tim Scott | .15 | .07 |
| ❑ | 209 | Lenny Dykstra | .25 | .11 |
| ❑ | 210 | Willie Greene | .15 | .07 |
| ❑ | 211 | Jim Eisenreich | .15 | .07 |
| ❑ | 212 | Cliff Floyd | .25 | .11 |
| ❑ | 213 | Otis Nixon | .15 | .07 |
| ❑ | 214 | Eduardo Perez | .15 | .07 |
| ❑ | 215 | Manuel Lee | .15 | .07 |
| ❑ | 216 | Armando Benitez | .25 | .11 |
| ❑ | 217 | Dave McCarty | .15 | .07 |
| ❑ | 218 | Scott Livingstone | .15 | .07 |
| ❑ | 219 | Chad Kreuter | .15 | .07 |
| ❑ | 220 | Don Mattingly CL | .75 | .25 |
| ❑ | 221 | Brian Jordan | .25 | .11 |
| ❑ | 222 | Matt Whiteside | .15 | .07 |
| ❑ | 223 | Jim Edmonds | .60 | .25 |
| ❑ | 224 | Tony Gwynn | 1.25 | .55 |
| ❑ | 225 | Jose Lind | .15 | .07 |
| ❑ | 226 | Marvin Freeman | .15 | .07 |
| ❑ | 227 | Ken Hill | .15 | .07 |
| ❑ | 228 | David Hulse | .15 | .07 |
| ❑ | 229 | Joe Hesketh | .15 | .07 |
| ❑ | 230 | Roberto Petagine | .15 | .07 |
| ❑ | 231 | Jeffrey Hammonds | .25 | .11 |
| ❑ | 232 | John Jaha | .15 | .07 |
| ❑ | 233 | John Burkett | .15 | .07 |
| ❑ | 234 | Hal Morris | .15 | .07 |
| ❑ | 235 | Tony Castillo | .15 | .07 |
| ❑ | 236 | Ryan Bowen | .15 | .07 |
| ❑ | 237 | Wayne Kirby | .15 | .07 |
| ❑ | 238 | Brent Mayne | .15 | .07 |
| ❑ | 239 | Jim Bullinger | .15 | .07 |
| ❑ | 240 | Mike Lieberthal | .25 | .11 |
| ❑ | 241 | Barry Larkin | .60 | .25 |
| ❑ | 242 | David Segui | .15 | .07 |
| ❑ | 243 | Jose Bautista | .15 | .07 |
| ❑ | 244 | Hector Fajardo | .15 | .07 |
| ❑ | 245 | Orel Hershiser | .25 | .11 |
| ❑ | 246 | James Mouton | .15 | .07 |
| ❑ | 247 | Scott Leius | .15 | .07 |
| ❑ | 248 | Tom Glavine | .60 | .25 |
| ❑ | 249 | Danny Bautista | .15 | .07 |
| ❑ | 250 | Jose Mercedes | .15 | .07 |
| ❑ | 251 | Marquis Grissom | .15 | .07 |
| ❑ | 252 | Charlie Hayes | .15 | .07 |
| ❑ | 253 | Ryan Klesko | .25 | .11 |
| ❑ | 254 | Vicente Palacios | .15 | .07 |
| ❑ | 255 | Matias Carrillo | .15 | .07 |
| ❑ | 256 | Gary DiSarcina | .15 | .07 |
| ❑ | 257 | Kirk Gibson | .25 | .11 |
| ❑ | 258 | Garey Ingram | .15 | .07 |
| ❑ | 259 | Alex Fernandez | .15 | .07 |
| ❑ | 260 | John Mabry | .15 | .07 |
| ❑ | 261 | Chris Howard | .15 | .07 |
| ❑ | 262 | Miguel Jimenez | .15 | .07 |
| ❑ | 263 | Heathcliff Slocumb | .15 | .07 |
| ❑ | 264 | Albert Belle | .40 | .18 |
| ❑ | 265 | Dave Clark | .15 | .07 |
| ❑ | 266 | Joe Orsulak | .15 | .07 |
| ❑ | 267 | Joey Hamilton | .15 | .07 |
| ❑ | 268 | Mark Portugal | .15 | .07 |
| ❑ | 269 | Kevin Tapani | .15 | .07 |
| ❑ | 270 | Sid Fernandez | .15 | .07 |
| ❑ | 271 | Steve Dreyer | .15 | .07 |
| ❑ | 272 | Denny Hocking | .15 | .07 |
| ❑ | 273 | Troy O'Leary | .15 | .07 |
| ❑ | 274 | Milt Cuyler | .15 | .07 |
| ❑ | 275 | Frank Thomas | 1.25 | .55 |
| ❑ | 276 | Jorge Fabregas | .15 | .07 |
| ❑ | 277 | Mike Gallego | .15 | .07 |
| ❑ | 278 | Mickey Morandini | .15 | .07 |
| ❑ | 279 | Roberto Hernandez | .15 | .07 |
| ❑ | 280 | Henry Rodriguez | .15 | .07 |
| ❑ | 281 | Garret Anderson | .25 | .11 |
| ❑ | 282 | Bob Wickman | .15 | .07 |
| ❑ | 283 | Gar Finnvold | .15 | .07 |
| ❑ | 284 | Paul O'Neill | .25 | .11 |
| ❑ | 285 | Royce Clayton | .15 | .07 |
| ❑ | 286 | Chuck Knoblauch | .25 | .11 |
| ❑ | 287 | Johnny Ruffin | .15 | .07 |
| ❑ | 288 | Dave Nilsson | .15 | .07 |
| ❑ | 289 | David Cone | .25 | .11 |
| ❑ | 290 | Chuck McElroy | .15 | .07 |
| ❑ | 291 | Kevin Stocker | .15 | .07 |
| ❑ | 292 | Jose Rijo | .15 | .07 |
| ❑ | 293 | Sean Berry | .15 | .07 |
| ❑ | 294 | Ozzie Guillen | .15 | .07 |
| ❑ | 295 | Chris Hoiles | .15 | .07 |
| ❑ | 296 | Kevin Foster | .15 | .07 |
| ❑ | 297 | Jeff Frye | .15 | .07 |
| ❑ | 298 | Lance Johnson | .15 | .07 |
| ❑ | 299 | Mike Kelly | .15 | .07 |
| ❑ | 300 | Ellis Burks | .25 | .11 |
| ❑ | 301 | Roberto Kelly | .15 | .07 |
| ❑ | 302 | Dante Bichette | .25 | .11 |
| ❑ | 303 | Alvaro Ezpinoza | .15 | .07 |
| ❑ | 304 | Alex Cole | .15 | .07 |
| ❑ | 305 | Rickey Henderson | .75 | .35 |
| ❑ | 306 | Dave Weathers | .15 | .07 |
| ❑ | 307 | Shane Reynolds | .15 | .07 |
| ❑ | 308 | Bobby Bonilla | .25 | .11 |
| ❑ | 309 | Junior Felix | .15 | .07 |
| ❑ | 310 | Jeff Fassero | .15 | .07 |
| ❑ | 311 | Darren Lewis | .15 | .07 |
| ❑ | 312 | John Doherty | .15 | .07 |
| ❑ | 313 | Scott Servais | .15 | .07 |
| ❑ | 314 | Rick Helling | .25 | .11 |
| ❑ | 315 | Pedro Martinez | .75 | .35 |
| ❑ | 316 | Wes Chamberlain | .15 | .07 |
| ❑ | 317 | Bryan Eversgerd | .15 | .07 |
| ❑ | 318 | Trevor Hoffman | .25 | .11 |
| ❑ | 319 | John Patterson | .15 | .07 |
| ❑ | 320 | Matt Walbeck | .15 | .07 |
| ❑ | 321 | Jeff Montgomery | .15 | .07 |
| ❑ | 322 | Mel Rojas | .15 | .07 |
| ❑ | 323 | Eddie Taubensee | .15 | .07 |
| ❑ | 324 | Ray Lankford | .25 | .11 |
| ❑ | 325 | Jose Vizcaino | .15 | .07 |
| ❑ | 326 | Carlos Baerga | .15 | .07 |
| ❑ | 327 | Jack Voigt | .15 | .07 |
| ❑ | 328 | Julio Franco | .15 | .07 |
| ❑ | 329 | Brent Gates | .15 | .07 |
| ❑ | 330 | Kirby Puckett CL | .75 | .35 |
| ❑ | 331 | Greg Maddux | 1.50 | .70 |
| ❑ | 332 | Jason Bere | .15 | .07 |
| ❑ | 333 | Bill Wegman | .15 | .07 |
| ❑ | 334 | Tuffy Rhodes | .15 | .07 |
| ❑ | 335 | Kevin Young | .15 | .07 |
| ❑ | 336 | Andy Benes | .15 | .07 |
| ❑ | 337 | Pedro Astacio | .15 | .07 |
| ❑ | 338 | Reggie Jefferson | .15 | .07 |
| ❑ | 339 | Tim Belcher | .15 | .07 |
| ❑ | 340 | Ken Griffey Jr. | 2.50 | 1.10 |
| ❑ | 341 | Mariano Duncan | .15 | .07 |
| ❑ | 342 | Andres Galarraga | .40 | .18 |
| ❑ | 343 | Rondell White | .25 | .11 |
| ❑ | 344 | Cory Bailey | .15 | .07 |
| ❑ | 345 | Bryan Harvey | .15 | .07 |
| ❑ | 346 | John Franco | .25 | .11 |
| ❑ | 347 | Greg Swindell | .15 | .07 |
| ❑ | 348 | David West | .40 | .18 |
| ❑ | 349 | Fred McGriff | .40 | .18 |
| ❑ | 350 | Jose Canseco | .75 | .35 |
| ❑ | 351 | Orlando Merced | .15 | .07 |
| ❑ | 352 | Rheal Cormier | .15 | .07 |
| ❑ | 353 | Carlos Pulido | .15 | .07 |
| ❑ | 354 | Terry Steinbach | .15 | .07 |
| ❑ | 355 | Wade Boggs | .75 | .35 |
| ❑ | 356 | B.J. Surhoff | .25 | .11 |
| ❑ | 357 | Rafael Palmeiro | .60 | .25 |
| ❑ | 358 | Anthony Young | .15 | .07 |
| ❑ | 359 | Tom Brunansky | .15 | .07 |
| ❑ | 360 | Todd Stottlemyre | .15 | .07 |
| ❑ | 361 | Chris Turner | .15 | .07 |
| ❑ | 362 | Joe Boever | .15 | .07 |
| ❑ | 363 | Jeff Blauser | .15 | .07 |
| ❑ | 364 | Derek Bell | .15 | .07 |
| ❑ | 365 | Matt Williams | .40 | .18 |
| ❑ | 366 | Jeremy Hernandez | .15 | .07 |
| ❑ | 367 | Joe Girardi | .15 | .07 |
| ❑ | 368 | Mike Devereaux | .15 | .07 |
| ❑ | 369 | Jim Abbott | .25 | .11 |
| ❑ | 370 | Manny Ramirez | .75 | .35 |
| ❑ | 371 | Kenny Lofton | .25 | .11 |
| ❑ | 372 | Mark Smith | .15 | .07 |
| ❑ | 373 | Dave Fleming | .15 | .07 |
| ❑ | 374 | Dave Stewart | .25 | .11 |
| ❑ | 375 | Roger Pavlik | .15 | .07 |
| ❑ | 376 | Hipolito Pichardo | .15 | .07 |
| ❑ | 377 | Bill Taylor | .15 | .07 |
| ❑ | 378 | Robin Ventura | .25 | .11 |
| ❑ | 379 | Bernard Gilkey | .15 | .07 |
| ❑ | 380 | Kirby Puckett | 1.50 | .70 |
| ❑ | 381 | Steve Howe | .15 | .07 |
| ❑ | 382 | Devon White | .25 | .11 |
| ❑ | 383 | Roberto Mejia | .15 | .07 |
| ❑ | 384 | Darrin Jackson | .15 | .07 |
| ❑ | 385 | Mike Morgan | .15 | .07 |
| ❑ | 386 | Rusty Meacham | .15 | .07 |
| ❑ | 387 | Bill Swift | .15 | .07 |
| ❑ | 388 | Lou Frazier | .15 | .07 |
| ❑ | 389 | Andy Van Slyke | .25 | .11 |
| ❑ | 390 | Brett Butler | .25 | .11 |
| ❑ | 391 | Bobby Witt | .15 | .07 |
| ❑ | 392 | Jeff Conine | .15 | .07 |
| ❑ | 393 | Tim Hyers | .15 | .07 |
| ❑ | 394 | Terry Pendleton | .25 | .11 |
| ❑ | 395 | Ricky Jordan | .15 | .07 |
| ❑ | 396 | Eric Plunk | .15 | .07 |
| ❑ | 397 | Melido Perez | .15 | .07 |
| ❑ | 398 | Darryl Kile | .25 | .11 |
| ❑ | 399 | Mark McLemore | .15 | .07 |
| ❑ | 400 | Greg W.Harris | .15 | .07 |
| ❑ | 401 | Jim Leyritz | .15 | .07 |
| ❑ | 402 | Doug Strange | .15 | .07 |
| ❑ | 403 | Tim Salmon | .25 | .11 |
| ❑ | 404 | Terry Mulholland | .15 | .07 |
| ❑ | 405 | Robby Thompson | .15 | .07 |
| ❑ | 406 | Ruben Sierra | .15 | .07 |
| ❑ | 407 | Tony Phillips | .15 | .07 |
| ❑ | 408 | Moises Alou | .25 | .11 |
| ❑ | 409 | Felix Fermin | .15 | .07 |
| ❑ | 410 | Pat Listach | .15 | .07 |
| ❑ | 411 | Kevin Bass | .15 | .07 |
| ❑ | 412 | Ben McDonald | .15 | .07 |
| ❑ | 413 | Scott Cooper | .15 | .07 |
| ❑ | 414 | Jody Reed | .15 | .07 |
| ❑ | 415 | Deion Sanders | .25 | .11 |
| ❑ | 416 | Ricky Gutierrez | .15 | .07 |
| ❑ | 417 | Gregg Jefferies | .15 | .07 |
| ❑ | 418 | Jack McDowell | .15 | .07 |
| ❑ | 419 | Al Leiter | .25 | .11 |
| ❑ | 420 | Tony Longmire | .15 | .07 |
| ❑ | 421 | Paul Wagner | .15 | .07 |
| ❑ | 422 | Geronimo Pena | .15 | .07 |
| ❑ | 423 | Ivan Rodriguez | .75 | .35 |
| ❑ | 424 | Kevin Gross | .15 | .07 |
| ❑ | 425 | Kirk McCaskill | .15 | .07 |
| ❑ | 426 | Greg Myers | .15 | .07 |
| ❑ | 427 | Roger Clemens | 1.25 | .55 |
| ❑ | 428 | Chris Hammond | .15 | .07 |
| ❑ | 429 | Randy Myers | .15 | .07 |
| ❑ | 430 | Roger Mason | .15 | .07 |
| ❑ | 431 | Bret Saberhagen | .25 | .11 |
| ❑ | 432 | Jeff Reboulet | .15 | .07 |
| ❑ | 433 | John Olerud | .25 | .11 |
| ❑ | 434 | Bill Gullickson | .15 | .07 |
| ❑ | 435 | Eddie Murray | .60 | .25 |
| ❑ | 436 | Pedro Munoz | .15 | .07 |
| ❑ | 437 | Charlie O'Brien | .15 | .07 |
| ❑ | 438 | Jeff Nelson | .15 | .07 |
| ❑ | 439 | Mike Macfarlane | .15 | .07 |
| ❑ | 440 | Don Mattingly CL | .75 | .25 |
| ❑ | 441 | Derrick May | .15 | .07 |
| ❑ | 442 | John Roper | .15 | .07 |
| ❑ | 443 | Darryl Hamilton | .15 | .07 |
| ❑ | 444 | Dan Miceli | .15 | .07 |
| ❑ | 445 | Tony Eusebio | .15 | .07 |
| ❑ | 446 | Jerry Browne | .15 | .07 |
| ❑ | 447 | Wally Joyner | .25 | .11 |
| ❑ | 448 | Brian Harper | .15 | .07 |
| ❑ | 449 | Scott Fletcher | .15 | .07 |
| ❑ | 450 | Bip Roberts | .15 | .07 |
| ❑ | 451 | Pete Smith | .15 | .07 |
| ❑ | 452 | Chili Davis | .25 | .11 |
| ❑ | 453 | Dave Hollins | .15 | .07 |
| ❑ | 454 | Tony Pena | .15 | .07 |
| ❑ | 455 | Butch Henry | .15 | .07 |
| ❑ | 456 | Craig Biggio | .40 | .18 |
| ❑ | 457 | Zane Smith | .15 | .07 |
| ❑ | 458 | Ryan Thompson | .15 | .07 |
| ❑ | 459 | Mike Jackson | .15 | .07 |
| ❑ | 460 | Mark McGwire | 2.50 | 1.10 |
| ❑ | 461 | John Smoltz | .25 | .11 |

❑ 462 Steve Scarsone .15 .07
❑ 463 Greg Colbrunn .15 .07
❑ 464 Shawn Green .60 .25
❑ 465 David Wells .25 .11
❑ 466 Jose Hernandez .15 .07
❑ 467 Chip Hale .15 .07
❑ 468 Tony Tarasco .15 .07
❑ 469 Kevin Mitchell .15 .07
❑ 470 Billy Hatcher .15 .07
❑ 471 Jay Buhner .25 .11
❑ 472 Ken Caminiti .25 .11
❑ 473 Tom Henke .15 .07
❑ 474 Todd Worrell .15 .07
❑ 475 Mark Eichhorn .15 .07
❑ 476 Bruce Ruffin .15 .07
❑ 477 Chuck Finley .25 .11
❑ 478 Marc Newfield .15 .07
❑ 479 Paul Shuey .15 .07
❑ 480 Bob Tewksbury .15 .07
❑ 481 Ramon J.Martinez .15 .07
❑ 482 Melvin Nieves .15 .07
❑ 483 Todd Zeile .15 .07
❑ 484 Benito Santiago .15 .07
❑ 485 Stan Javier .15 .07
❑ 486 Kirk Rueter .15 .07
❑ 487 Andre Dawson .40 .18
❑ 488 Eric Karros .25 .11
❑ 489 Dave Magadan .15 .07
❑ 490 Joe Carter CL .15 .07
❑ 491 Randy Velarde .15 .07
❑ 492 Larry Walker .25 .11
❑ 493 Cris Carpenter .15 .07
❑ 494 Tom Gordon .15 .07
❑ 495 Dave Burba .15 .07
❑ 496 Darren Bragg .15 .07
❑ 497 Darren Daulton .25 .11
❑ 498 Don Slaught .15 .07
❑ 499 Pat Borders .15 .07
❑ 500 Lenny Harris .15 .07
❑ 501 Joe Ausanio .15 .07
❑ 502 Alan Trammell .40 .18
❑ 503 Mike Fetters .15 .07
❑ 504 Scott Ruffcorn .15 .07
❑ 505 Rich Rowland .15 .07
❑ 506 Juan Samuel .15 .07
❑ 507 Bo Jackson .25 .11
❑ 508 Jeff Branson .15 .07
❑ 509 Bernie Williams .60 .25
❑ 510 Paul Sorrento .15 .07
❑ 511 Dennis Eckersley .25 .11
❑ 512 Pat Mahomes .15 .07
❑ 513 Rusty Greer .25 .11
❑ 514 Luis Polonia .15 .07
❑ 515 Willie Banks .15 .07
❑ 516 John Wetteland .25 .11
❑ 517 Mike LaValliere .15 .07
❑ 518 Tommy Greene .15 .07
❑ 519 Mark Grace .60 .25
❑ 520 Bob Hamelin .15 .07
❑ 521 Scott Sanderson .15 .07
❑ 522 Joe Carter .25 .11
❑ 523 Jeff Brantley .15 .07
❑ 524 Andrew Lorraine .15 .07
❑ 525 Rico Brogna .15 .07
❑ 526 Shane Mack .15 .07
❑ 527 Mark Wohlers .15 .07
❑ 528 Scott Sanders .15 .07
❑ 529 Chris Bosio .15 .07
❑ 530 Andujar Cedeno .15 .07
❑ 531 Kenny Rogers .15 .07
❑ 532 Doug Drabek .15 .07
❑ 533 Curt Leskanic .15 .07
❑ 534 Craig Shipley .15 .07
❑ 535 Craig Grebeck .15 .07
❑ 536 Cal Eldred .15 .07
❑ 537 Mickey Tettleton .15 .07
❑ 538 Harold Baines .25 .11
❑ 539 Tim Wallach .15 .07
❑ 540 Damon Buford .15 .07
❑ 541 Lenny Webster .15 .07
❑ 542 Kevin Appier .25 .11
❑ 543 Raul Mondesi .25 .11
❑ 544 Eric Young .15 .07
❑ 545 Russ Davis .15 .07
❑ 546 Mike Benjamin .15 .07
❑ 547 Mike Greenwell .15 .07
❑ 548 Scott Brosius .25 .11
❑ 549 Brian Dorsett .15 .07
❑ 550 Chili Davis CL .15 .07

## 1996 Donruss

| | MINT | NRMT |
|---|---|---|
| COMPLETE SET (550) | 40.00 | 18.00 |
| COMPLETE SERIES 1 (330) | 25.00 | 11.00 |
| COMPLETE SERIES 2 (220) | 15.00 | 6.75 |
| COMMON CARD (1-550) | .15 | .07 |

❑ 1 Frank Thomas 1.25 .55
❑ 2 Jason Bates .15 .07
❑ 3 Steve Sparks .15 .07
❑ 4 Scott Servais .15 .07
❑ 5 Angelo Encarnacion RC .15 .07
❑ 6 Scott Sanders .15 .07
❑ 7 Billy Ashley .15 .07
❑ 8 Alex Rodriguez 2.00 .90
❑ 9 Sean Bergman .15 .07
❑ 10 Brad Radke .30 .14
❑ 11 Andy Van Slyke .30 .14
❑ 12 Joe Girardi .15 .07
❑ 13 Mark Grudzielanek .15 .07
❑ 14 Rick Aguilera .15 .07
❑ 15 Randy Veres .15 .07
❑ 16 Tim Bogar .15 .07
❑ 17 Dave Veres .15 .07
❑ 18 Kevin Stocker .15 .07
❑ 19 Marquis Grissom .15 .07
❑ 20 Will Clark .60 .25
❑ 21 Jay Bell .30 .14
❑ 22 Allen Battle .15 .07
❑ 23 Frank Rodriguez .15 .07
❑ 24 Terry Steinbach .15 .07
❑ 25 Gerald Williams .15 .07
❑ 26 Sid Roberson .15 .07
❑ 27 Greg Zaun .15 .07
❑ 28 Ozzie Timmons .15 .07
❑ 29 Vaughn Eshelman .15 .07
❑ 30 Ed Sprague .15 .07
❑ 31 Gary DiSarcina .15 .07
❑ 32 Joe Boever .15 .07
❑ 33 Steve Avery .15 .07
❑ 34 Brad Ausmus .15 .07
❑ 35 Kirt Manwaring .15 .07
❑ 36 Gary Sheffield .60 .25
❑ 37 Jason Bere .15 .07
❑ 38 Jeff Manto .15 .07
❑ 39 David Cone .30 .14
❑ 40 Manny Ramirez .75 .35
❑ 41 Sandy Alomar Jr. .30 .14
❑ 42 Curtis Goodwin .15 .07
❑ 43 Tino Martinez .30 .14
❑ 44 Woody Williams .15 .07
❑ 45 Dean Palmer .30 .14
❑ 46 Hipolito Pichardo .15 .07
❑ 47 Jason Giambi .60 .25
❑ 48 Lance Johnson .15 .07
❑ 49 Bernard Gilkey .15 .07
❑ 50 Kirby Puckett 1.50 .70
❑ 51 Tony Fernandez .15 .07
❑ 52 Alex Gonzalez .15 .07
❑ 53 Bret Saberhagen .30 .14
❑ 54 Lyle Mouton .15 .07
❑ 55 Brian McRae .15 .07
❑ 56 Mark Gubicza .15 .07
❑ 57 Sergio Valdez .15 .07
❑ 58 Darrin Fletcher .15 .07
❑ 59 Steve Parris .15 .07
❑ 60 Johnny Damon .30 .14
❑ 61 Rickey Henderson .75 .35
❑ 62 Darrell Whitmore .15 .07
❑ 63 Roberto Petagine .15 .07
❑ 64 Trenidad Hubbard .15 .07
❑ 65 Heathcliff Slocumb .15 .07
❑ 66 Steve Finley .30 .14
❑ 67 Mariano Rivera .30 .14
❑ 68 Brian L.Hunter .15 .07
❑ 69 Jamie Moyer .15 .07
❑ 70 Ellis Burks .30 .14
❑ 71 Pat Kelly .15 .07
❑ 72 Mickey Tettleton .15 .07
❑ 73 Garret Anderson .30 .14
❑ 74 Andy Pettitte .30 .14
❑ 75 Glenallen Hill .15 .07
❑ 76 Brent Gates .15 .07
❑ 77 Lou Whitaker .30 .14
❑ 78 David Segui .15 .07
❑ 79 Dan Wilson .15 .07
❑ 80 Pat Listach .15 .07
❑ 81 Jeff Bagwell .75 .35
❑ 82 Ben McDonald .15 .07
❑ 83 John Valentin .15 .07
❑ 84 John Jaha .30 .14
❑ 85 Pete Schourek .15 .07
❑ 86 Bryce Florie .15 .07
❑ 87 Brian Jordan .30 .14
❑ 88 Ron Karkovice .15 .07
❑ 89 Al Leiter .30 .14
❑ 90 Tony Longmire .15 .07
❑ 91 Nelson Liriano .15 .07
❑ 92 David Bell .15 .07
❑ 93 Kevin Gross .15 .07
❑ 94 Tom Candiotti .15 .07
❑ 95 Dave Martinez .15 .07
❑ 96 Greg Myers .15 .07
❑ 97 Rheal Cormier .15 .07
❑ 98 Chris Hammond .15 .07
❑ 99 Randy Myers .15 .07
❑ 100 Bill Pulsipher .15 .07
❑ 101 Jason Isringhausen .30 .14
❑ 102 Dave Stevens .15 .07
❑ 103 Roberto Alomar .60 .25
❑ 104 Bob Higginson .30 .14
❑ 105 Eddie Murray .60 .25
❑ 106 Matt Walbeck .15 .07
❑ 107 Mark Wohlers .15 .07
❑ 108 Jeff Nelson .15 .07
❑ 109 Tom Goodwin .15 .07
❑ 110 Cal Ripken CL 1.25 .55
❑ 111 Rey Sanchez .15 .07
❑ 112 Hector Carrasco .15 .07
❑ 113 B.J. Surhoff .30 .14
❑ 114 Dan Miceli .15 .07
❑ 115 Dean Hartgraves .15 .07
❑ 116 John Burkett .15 .07
❑ 117 Gary Gaetti .30 .14
❑ 118 Ricky Bones .15 .07
❑ 119 Mike Macfarlane .15 .07
❑ 120 Bip Roberts .15 .07
❑ 121 Dave Mlicki .15 .07
❑ 122 Chili Davis .30 .14
❑ 123 Mark Whiten .15 .07
❑ 124 Herbert Perry .15 .07
❑ 125 Butch Henry .15 .07
❑ 126 Derek Bell .15 .07
❑ 127 Al Martin .15 .07
❑ 128 John Franco .30 .14
❑ 129 W. VanLandingham .15 .07
❑ 130 Mike Bordick .15 .07
❑ 131 Mike Mordecai .15 .07
❑ 132 Robby Thompson .15 .07
❑ 133 Greg Colbrunn .15 .07
❑ 134 Domingo Cedeno .15 .07
❑ 135 Chad Curtis .15 .07
❑ 136 Jose Hernandez .15 .07
❑ 137 Scott Klingenbeck .15 .07
❑ 138 Ryan Klesko .30 .14
❑ 139 John Smiley .15 .07
❑ 140 Charlie Hayes .15 .07
❑ 141 Jay Buhner .30 .14
❑ 142 Doug Drabek .15 .07

| |  |  | | |
|---|---|---|---|---|
| ❑ | 143 | Roger Pavlik | .15 | .07 |
| ❑ | 144 | Todd Worrell | .15 | .07 |
| ❑ | 145 | Cal Ripken | 2.50 | 1.10 |
| ❑ | 146 | Steve Reed | .15 | .07 |
| ❑ | 147 | Chuck Finley | .30 | .14 |
| ❑ | 148 | Mike Blowers | .15 | .07 |
| ❑ | 149 | Orel Hershiser | .30 | .14 |
| ❑ | 150 | Allen Watson | .15 | .07 |
| ❑ | 151 | Ramon Martinez | .15 | .07 |
| ❑ | 152 | Melvin Nieves | .15 | .07 |
| ❑ | 153 | Tripp Cromer | .15 | .07 |
| ❑ | 154 | Yorkis Perez | .15 | .07 |
| ❑ | 155 | Stan Javier | .15 | .07 |
| ❑ | 156 | Mel Rojas | .15 | .07 |
| ❑ | 157 | Aaron Sele | .30 | .14 |
| ❑ | 158 | Eric Karros | .30 | .14 |
| ❑ | 159 | Robb Nen | .15 | .07 |
| ❑ | 160 | Raul Mondesi | .30 | .14 |
| ❑ | 161 | John Wetteland | .30 | .14 |
| ❑ | 162 | Tim Scott | .15 | .07 |
| ❑ | 163 | Kenny Rogers | .15 | .07 |
| ❑ | 164 | Melvin Bunch | .15 | .07 |
| ❑ | 165 | Rod Beck | .15 | .07 |
| ❑ | 166 | Andy Benes | .15 | .07 |
| ❑ | 167 | Lenny Dykstra | .30 | .14 |
| ❑ | 168 | Orlando Merced | .15 | .07 |
| ❑ | 169 | Tomas Perez | .15 | .07 |
| ❑ | 170 | Xavier Hernandez | .15 | .07 |
| ❑ | 171 | Ruben Sierra | .15 | .07 |
| ❑ | 172 | Alan Trammell | .30 | .14 |
| ❑ | 173 | Mike Fetters | .15 | .07 |
| ❑ | 174 | Wilson Alvarez | .15 | .07 |
| ❑ | 175 | Erik Hanson | .15 | .07 |
| ❑ | 176 | Travis Fryman | .30 | .14 |
| ❑ | 177 | Jim Abbott | .30 | .14 |
| ❑ | 178 | Bret Boone | .30 | .14 |
| ❑ | 179 | Sterling Hitchcock | .15 | .07 |
| ❑ | 180 | Pat Mahomes | .15 | .07 |
| ❑ | 181 | Mark Acre | .15 | .07 |
| ❑ | 182 | Charles Nagy | .15 | .07 |
| ❑ | 183 | Rusty Greer | .30 | .14 |
| ❑ | 184 | Mike Stanley | .15 | .07 |
| ❑ | 185 | Jim Bullinger | .15 | .07 |
| ❑ | 186 | Shane Andrews | .15 | .07 |
| ❑ | 187 | Brian Keyser | .15 | .07 |
| ❑ | 188 | Tyler Green | .15 | .07 |
| ❑ | 189 | Mark Grace | .60 | .25 |
| ❑ | 190 | Bob Hamelin | .15 | .07 |
| ❑ | 191 | Luis Ortiz | .15 | .07 |
| ❑ | 192 | Joe Carter | .30 | .14 |
| ❑ | 193 | Eddie Taubensee | .15 | .07 |
| ❑ | 194 | Brian Anderson | .15 | .07 |
| ❑ | 195 | Edgardo Alfonzo | .30 | .14 |
| ❑ | 196 | Pedro Munoz | .15 | .07 |
| ❑ | 197 | David Justice | .30 | .14 |
| ❑ | 198 | Trevor Hoffman | .30 | .14 |
| ❑ | 199 | Bobby Ayala | .15 | .07 |
| ❑ | 200 | Tony Eusebio | .15 | .07 |
| ❑ | 201 | Jeff Russell | .15 | .07 |
| ❑ | 202 | Mike Hampton | .30 | .14 |
| ❑ | 203 | Walt Weiss | .15 | .07 |
| ❑ | 204 | Joey Hamilton | .15 | .07 |
| ❑ | 205 | Roberto Hernandez | .15 | .07 |
| ❑ | 206 | Greg Vaughn | .30 | .14 |
| ❑ | 207 | Felipe Lira | .15 | .07 |
| ❑ | 208 | Harold Baines | .30 | .14 |
| ❑ | 209 | Tim Wallach | .15 | .07 |
| ❑ | 210 | Manny Alexander | .15 | .07 |
| ❑ | 211 | Tim Laker | .15 | .07 |
| ❑ | 212 | Chris Haney | .15 | .07 |
| ❑ | 213 | Brian Maxcy | .15 | .07 |
| ❑ | 214 | Eric Young | .15 | .07 |
| ❑ | 215 | Darryl Strawberry | .30 | .14 |
| ❑ | 216 | Barry Bonds | 1.00 | .45 |
| ❑ | 217 | Tim Naehring | .15 | .07 |
| ❑ | 218 | Scott Brosius | .30 | .14 |
| ❑ | 219 | Reggie Sanders | .15 | .07 |
| ❑ | 220 | Eddie Murray CL | .30 | .14 |
| ❑ | 221 | Luis Alicea | .15 | .07 |
| ❑ | 222 | Albert Belle | .30 | .14 |
| ❑ | 223 | Benji Gil | .15 | .07 |
| ❑ | 224 | Dante Bichette | .30 | .14 |
| ❑ | 225 | Bobby Bonilla | .30 | .14 |
| ❑ | 226 | Todd Stottlemyre | .15 | .07 |
| ❑ | 227 | Jim Edmonds | .60 | .25 |
| ❑ | 228 | Todd Jones | .15 | .07 |
| ❑ | 229 | Shawn Green | .60 | .25 |
| ❑ | 230 | Javier Lopez | .30 | .14 |
| ❑ | 231 | Ariel Prieto | .15 | .07 |
| ❑ | 232 | Tony Phillips | .15 | .07 |
| ❑ | 233 | James Mouton | .15 | .07 |
| ❑ | 234 | Jose Oquendo | .15 | .07 |
| ❑ | 235 | Royce Clayton | .15 | .07 |
| ❑ | 236 | Chuck Carr | .15 | .07 |
| ❑ | 237 | Doug Jones | .15 | .07 |
| ❑ | 238 | Mark McLemore | .15 | .07 |
| ❑ | 239 | Bill Swift | .15 | .07 |
| ❑ | 240 | Scott Leius | .15 | .07 |
| ❑ | 241 | Russ Davis | .15 | .07 |
| ❑ | 242 | Ray Durham | .30 | .14 |
| ❑ | 243 | Matt Mieske | .15 | .07 |
| ❑ | 244 | Brent Mayne | .15 | .07 |
| ❑ | 245 | Thomas Howard | .15 | .07 |
| ❑ | 246 | Troy O'Leary | .15 | .07 |
| ❑ | 247 | Jacob Brumfield | .15 | .07 |
| ❑ | 248 | Mickey Morandini | .15 | .07 |
| ❑ | 249 | Todd Hundley | .15 | .07 |
| ❑ | 250 | Chris Bosio | .15 | .07 |
| ❑ | 251 | Omar Vizquel | .30 | .14 |
| ❑ | 252 | Mike Lansing | .15 | .07 |
| ❑ | 253 | John Mabry | .15 | .07 |
| ❑ | 254 | Mike Perez | .15 | .07 |
| ❑ | 255 | Delino DeShields | .15 | .07 |
| ❑ | 256 | Wil Cordero | .15 | .07 |
| ❑ | 257 | Mike James | .15 | .07 |
| ❑ | 258 | Todd Van Poppel | .15 | .07 |
| ❑ | 259 | Joey Cora | .15 | .07 |
| ❑ | 260 | Andre Dawson | .30 | .14 |
| ❑ | 261 | Jerry DiPoto | .15 | .07 |
| ❑ | 262 | Rick Krivda | .15 | .07 |
| ❑ | 263 | Glenn Dishman | .15 | .07 |
| ❑ | 264 | Mike Mimbs | .15 | .07 |
| ❑ | 265 | John Ericks | .15 | .07 |
| ❑ | 266 | Jose Canseco | .75 | .35 |
| ❑ | 267 | Jeff Branson | .15 | .07 |
| ❑ | 268 | Curt Leskanic | .15 | .07 |
| ❑ | 269 | Jon Nunnally | .15 | .07 |
| ❑ | 270 | Scott Stahoviak | .15 | .07 |
| ❑ | 271 | Jeff Montgomery | .15 | .07 |
| ❑ | 272 | Hal Morris | .15 | .07 |
| ❑ | 273 | Esteban Loaiza | .15 | .07 |
| ❑ | 274 | Rico Brogna | .15 | .07 |
| ❑ | 275 | Dave Winfield | .60 | .25 |
| ❑ | 276 | J.R. Phillips | .15 | .07 |
| ❑ | 277 | Todd Zeile | .15 | .07 |
| ❑ | 278 | Tom Pagnozzi | .15 | .07 |
| ❑ | 279 | Mark Lemke | .15 | .07 |
| ❑ | 280 | Dave Magadan | .15 | .07 |
| ❑ | 281 | Greg McMichael | .15 | .07 |
| ❑ | 282 | Mike Morgan | .15 | .07 |
| ❑ | 283 | Moises Alou | .30 | .14 |
| ❑ | 284 | Dennis Martinez | .30 | .14 |
| ❑ | 285 | Jeff Kent | .30 | .14 |
| ❑ | 286 | Mark Johnson | .15 | .07 |
| ❑ | 287 | Darren Lewis | .15 | .07 |
| ❑ | 288 | Brad Clontz | .15 | .07 |
| ❑ | 289 | Chad Fonville | .15 | .07 |
| ❑ | 290 | Paul Sorrento | .15 | .07 |
| ❑ | 291 | Lee Smith | .30 | .14 |
| ❑ | 292 | Tom Glavine | .60 | .25 |
| ❑ | 293 | Antonio Osuna | .15 | .07 |
| ❑ | 294 | Kevin Foster | .15 | .07 |
| ❑ | 295 | Sandy Martinez | .15 | .07 |
| ❑ | 296 | Mark Leiter | .15 | .07 |
| ❑ | 297 | Julian Tavarez | .15 | .07 |
| ❑ | 298 | Mike Kelly | .15 | .07 |
| ❑ | 299 | Joe Oliver | .15 | .07 |
| ❑ | 300 | John Flaherty | .15 | .07 |
| ❑ | 301 | Don Mattingly | 1.50 | .70 |
| ❑ | 302 | Pat Meares | .15 | .07 |
| ❑ | 303 | John Doherty | .15 | .07 |
| ❑ | 304 | Joe Vitiello | .15 | .07 |
| ❑ | 305 | Vinny Castilla | .30 | .14 |
| ❑ | 306 | Jeff Brantley | .15 | .07 |
| ❑ | 307 | Mike Greenwell | .15 | .07 |
| ❑ | 308 | Midre Cummings | .15 | .07 |
| ❑ | 309 | Curt Schilling | .30 | .14 |
| ❑ | 310 | Ken Caminiti | .30 | .14 |
| ❑ | 311 | Scott Erickson | .15 | .07 |
| ❑ | 312 | Carl Everett | .30 | .14 |
| ❑ | 313 | Charles Johnson | .30 | .14 |
| ❑ | 314 | Alex Diaz | .15 | .07 |
| ❑ | 315 | Jose Mesa | .15 | .07 |
| ❑ | 316 | Mark Carreon | .15 | .07 |
| ❑ | 317 | Carlos Perez | .15 | .07 |
| ❑ | 318 | Ismael Valdes | .15 | .07 |
| ❑ | 319 | Frank Castillo | .15 | .07 |
| ❑ | 320 | Tom Henke | .15 | .07 |
| ❑ | 321 | Spike Owen | .15 | .07 |
| ❑ | 322 | Joe Orsulak | .15 | .07 |
| ❑ | 323 | Paul Menhart | .15 | .07 |
| ❑ | 324 | Pedro Borbon | .15 | .07 |
| ❑ | 325 | Paul Molitor CL | .30 | .14 |
| ❑ | 326 | Jeff Cirillo | .30 | .14 |
| ❑ | 327 | Edwin Hurtado | .15 | .07 |
| ❑ | 328 | Orlando Miller | .15 | .07 |
| ❑ | 329 | Steve Ontiveros | .15 | .07 |
| ❑ | 330 | Kirby Puckett CL | .75 | .35 |
| ❑ | 331 | Scott Bullett | .15 | .07 |
| ❑ | 332 | Andres Galarraga | .30 | .14 |
| ❑ | 333 | Cal Eldred | .15 | .07 |
| ❑ | 334 | Sammy Sosa | 1.25 | .55 |
| ❑ | 335 | Don Slaught | .15 | .07 |
| ❑ | 336 | Jody Reed | .15 | .07 |
| ❑ | 337 | Roger Cedeno | .15 | .07 |
| ❑ | 338 | Ken Griffey Jr. | 2.50 | 1.10 |
| ❑ | 339 | Todd Hollandsworth | .15 | .07 |
| ❑ | 340 | Mike Trombley | .15 | .07 |
| ❑ | 341 | Gregg Jefferies | .15 | .07 |
| ❑ | 342 | Larry Walker | .30 | .14 |
| ❑ | 343 | Pedro Martinez | .75 | .35 |
| ❑ | 344 | Dwayne Hosey | .15 | .07 |
| ❑ | 345 | Terry Pendleton | .30 | .14 |
| ❑ | 346 | Pete Harnisch | .15 | .07 |
| ❑ | 347 | Tony Castillo | .15 | .07 |
| ❑ | 348 | Paul Quantrill | .15 | .07 |
| ❑ | 349 | Fred McGriff | .30 | .14 |
| ❑ | 350 | Ivan Rodriguez | .75 | .35 |
| ❑ | 351 | Butch Huskey | .15 | .07 |
| ❑ | 352 | Ozzie Smith | .75 | .35 |
| ❑ | 353 | Marty Cordova | .15 | .07 |
| ❑ | 354 | John Wasdin | .15 | .07 |
| ❑ | 355 | Wade Boggs | .75 | .35 |
| ❑ | 356 | Dave Nilsson | .15 | .07 |
| ❑ | 357 | Rafael Palmeiro | .60 | .25 |
| ❑ | 358 | Luis Gonzalez | .30 | .14 |
| ❑ | 359 | Reggie Jefferson | .15 | .07 |
| ❑ | 360 | Carlos Delgado | .60 | .25 |
| ❑ | 361 | Orlando Palmeiro | .15 | .07 |
| ❑ | 362 | Chris Gomez | .15 | .07 |
| ❑ | 363 | John Smoltz | .30 | .14 |
| ❑ | 364 | Marc Newfield | .15 | .07 |
| ❑ | 365 | Matt Williams | .30 | .14 |
| ❑ | 366 | Jesus Tavarez | .15 | .07 |
| ❑ | 367 | Bruce Ruffin | .15 | .07 |
| ❑ | 368 | Sean Berry | .15 | .07 |
| ❑ | 369 | Randy Velarde | .15 | .07 |
| ❑ | 370 | Tony Pena | .15 | .07 |
| ❑ | 371 | Jim Thome | .30 | .14 |
| ❑ | 372 | Jeffrey Hammonds | .30 | .14 |
| ❑ | 373 | Bob Wolcott | .15 | .07 |
| ❑ | 374 | Juan Guzman | .15 | .07 |
| ❑ | 375 | Juan Gonzalez | .60 | .25 |
| ❑ | 376 | Michael Tucker | .15 | .07 |
| ❑ | 377 | Doug Johns | .15 | .07 |
| ❑ | 378 | Mike Cameron RC | 1.00 | .45 |
| ❑ | 379 | Ray Lankford | .30 | .14 |
| ❑ | 380 | Jose Parra | .15 | .07 |
| ❑ | 381 | Jimmy Key | .30 | .14 |
| ❑ | 382 | John Olerud | .30 | .14 |
| ❑ | 383 | Kevin Ritz | .15 | .07 |
| ❑ | 384 | Tim Raines | .30 | .14 |
| ❑ | 385 | Rich Amaral | .15 | .07 |
| ❑ | 386 | Keith Lockhart | .15 | .07 |
| ❑ | 387 | Steve Scarsone | .15 | .07 |
| ❑ | 388 | Cliff Floyd | .30 | .14 |
| ❑ | 389 | Rich Aude | .15 | .07 |
| ❑ | 390 | Hideo Nomo | .60 | .25 |
| ❑ | 391 | Geronimo Berroa | .15 | .07 |
| ❑ | 392 | Pat Rapp | .15 | .07 |
| ❑ | 393 | Dustin Hermanson | .15 | .07 |
| ❑ | 394 | Greg Maddux | 1.50 | .70 |
| ❑ | 395 | Darren Daulton | .30 | .14 |
| ❑ | 396 | Kenny Lofton | .30 | .14 |
| ❑ | 397 | Ruben Rivera | .15 | .07 |
| ❑ | 398 | Billy Wagner | .15 | .07 |
| ❑ | 399 | Kevin Brown | .30 | .14 |
| ❑ | 400 | Mike Kingery | .15 | .07 |

| | Card | MINT | NRMT |
|---|---|---|---|
| ❑ | 401 Bernie Williams | .60 | .25 |
| ❑ | 402 Otis Nixon | .15 | .07 |
| ❑ | 403 Damion Easley | .15 | .07 |
| ❑ | 404 Paul O'Neill | .30 | .14 |
| ❑ | 405 Deion Sanders | .30 | .14 |
| ❑ | 406 Dennis Eckersley | .30 | .14 |
| ❑ | 407 Tony Clark | .15 | .07 |
| ❑ | 408 Rondell White | .30 | .14 |
| ❑ | 409 Luis Sojo | .15 | .07 |
| ❑ | 410 David Hulse | .15 | .07 |
| ❑ | 411 Shane Reynolds | .15 | .07 |
| ❑ | 412 Chris Hoiles | .15 | .07 |
| ❑ | 413 Lee Tinsley | .15 | .07 |
| ❑ | 414 Scott Karl | .15 | .07 |
| ❑ | 415 Ron Gant | .15 | .07 |
| ❑ | 416 Brian Johnson | .15 | .07 |
| ❑ | 417 Jose Oliva | .15 | .07 |
| ❑ | 418 Jack McDowell | .15 | .07 |
| ❑ | 419 Paul Molitor | .60 | .25 |
| ❑ | 420 Ricky Bottalico | .15 | .07 |
| ❑ | 421 Paul Wagner | .15 | .07 |
| ❑ | 422 Terry Bradshaw | .15 | .07 |
| ❑ | 423 Bob Tewksbury | .15 | .07 |
| ❑ | 424 Mike Piazza | 2.00 | .90 |
| ❑ | 425 Luis Andujar | .15 | .07 |
| ❑ | 426 Mark Langston | .15 | .07 |
| ❑ | 427 Stan Belinda | .15 | .07 |
| ❑ | 428 Kurt Abbott | .15 | .07 |
| ❑ | 429 Shawon Dunston | .15 | .07 |
| ❑ | 430 Bobby Jones | .15 | .07 |
| ❑ | 431 Jose Vizcaino | .15 | .07 |
| ❑ | 432 Matt Lawton RC | .75 | .35 |
| ❑ | 433 Pat Hentgen | .15 | .07 |
| ❑ | 434 Cecil Fielder | .30 | .14 |
| ❑ | 435 Carlos Baerga | .15 | .07 |
| ❑ | 436 Rich Becker | .15 | .07 |
| ❑ | 437 Chipper Jones | 1.50 | .70 |
| ❑ | 438 Bill Risley | .15 | .07 |
| ❑ | 439 Kevin Appier | .30 | .14 |
| ❑ | 440 Wade Boggs CL | .30 | .14 |
| ❑ | 441 Jaime Navarro | .15 | .07 |
| ❑ | 442 Barry Larkin | .60 | .25 |
| ❑ | 443 Jose Valentin | .15 | .07 |
| ❑ | 444 Bryan Rekar | .15 | .07 |
| ❑ | 445 Rick Wilkins | .15 | .07 |
| ❑ | 446 Quilvio Veras | .15 | .07 |
| ❑ | 447 Greg Gagne | .15 | .07 |
| ❑ | 448 Mark Kiefer | .15 | .07 |
| ❑ | 449 Bobby Witt | .15 | .07 |
| ❑ | 450 Andy Ashby | .15 | .07 |
| ❑ | 451 Alex Ochoa | .15 | .07 |
| ❑ | 452 Jorge Fabregas | .15 | .07 |
| ❑ | 453 Gene Schall | .15 | .07 |
| ❑ | 454 Ken Hill | .15 | .07 |
| ❑ | 455 Tony Tarasco | .15 | .07 |
| ❑ | 456 Donnie Wall | .15 | .07 |
| ❑ | 457 Carlos Garcia | .15 | .07 |
| ❑ | 458 Ryan Thompson | .15 | .07 |
| ❑ | 459 Marvin Benard RC | .15 | .07 |
| ❑ | 460 Jose Herrera | .15 | .07 |
| ❑ | 461 Jeff Blauser | .15 | .07 |
| ❑ | 462 Chris Hook | .15 | .07 |
| ❑ | 463 Jeff Conine | .15 | .07 |
| ❑ | 464 Devon White | .30 | .14 |
| ❑ | 465 Danny Bautista | .15 | .07 |
| ❑ | 466 Steve Trachsel | .15 | .07 |
| ❑ | 467 C.J. Nitkowski | .15 | .07 |
| ❑ | 468 Mike Devereaux | .15 | .07 |
| ❑ | 469 David Wells | .30 | .14 |
| ❑ | 470 Jim Eisenreich | .15 | .07 |
| ❑ | 471 Edgar Martinez | .30 | .14 |
| ❑ | 472 Craig Biggio | .30 | .14 |
| ❑ | 473 Jeff Frye | .15 | .07 |
| ❑ | 474 Karim Garcia | .15 | .07 |
| ❑ | 475 Jimmy Haynes | .15 | .07 |
| ❑ | 476 Darren Holmes | .15 | .07 |
| ❑ | 477 Tim Salmon | .30 | .14 |
| ❑ | 478 Randy Johnson | .75 | .35 |
| ❑ | 479 Eric Plunk | .15 | .07 |
| ❑ | 480 Scott Cooper | .15 | .07 |
| ❑ | 481 Chan Ho Park | .30 | .14 |
| ❑ | 482 Ray McDavid | .15 | .07 |
| ❑ | 483 Mark Petkovsek | .15 | .07 |
| ❑ | 484 Greg Swindell | .15 | .07 |
| ❑ | 485 George Williams | .15 | .07 |
| ❑ | 486 Yamil Benitez | .15 | .07 |
| ❑ | 487 Tim Wakefield | .15 | .07 |
| ❑ | 488 Kevin Tapani | .15 | .07 |
| ❑ | 489 Derrick May | .15 | .07 |
| ❑ | 490 Ken Griffey Jr. CL | 1.25 | .55 |
| ❑ | 491 Derek Jeter | 2.50 | 1.10 |
| ❑ | 492 Jeff Fassero | .15 | .07 |
| ❑ | 493 Benito Santiago | .15 | .07 |
| ❑ | 494 Tom Gordon | .15 | .07 |
| ❑ | 495 Jamie Brewington RC | .15 | .07 |
| ❑ | 496 Vince Coleman | .15 | .07 |
| ❑ | 497 Kevin Jordan | .15 | .07 |
| ❑ | 498 Jeff King | .15 | .07 |
| ❑ | 499 Mike Simms | .15 | .07 |
| ❑ | 500 Jose Rijo | .15 | .07 |
| ❑ | 501 Denny Neagle | .30 | .14 |
| ❑ | 502 Jose Lima | .15 | .07 |
| ❑ | 503 Kevin Seitzer | .15 | .07 |
| ❑ | 504 Alex Fernandez | .15 | .07 |
| ❑ | 505 Mo Vaughn | .30 | .14 |
| ❑ | 506 Phil Nevin | .30 | .14 |
| ❑ | 507 J.T. Snow | .30 | .14 |
| ❑ | 508 Andujar Cedeno | .15 | .07 |
| ❑ | 509 Ozzie Guillen | .15 | .07 |
| ❑ | 510 Mark Clark | .15 | .07 |
| ❑ | 511 Mark McGwire | 2.50 | 1.10 |
| ❑ | 512 Jeff Reboulet | .15 | .07 |
| ❑ | 513 Armando Benitez | .15 | .07 |
| ❑ | 514 LaTroy Hawkins | .15 | .07 |
| ❑ | 515 Brett Butler | .30 | .14 |
| ❑ | 516 Tavo Alvarez | .15 | .07 |
| ❑ | 517 Chris Snopek | .15 | .07 |
| ❑ | 518 Mike Mussina | .60 | .25 |
| ❑ | 519 Darryl Kile | .30 | .14 |
| ❑ | 520 Wally Joyner | .30 | .14 |
| ❑ | 521 Willie McGee | .30 | .14 |
| ❑ | 522 Kent Mercker | .15 | .07 |
| ❑ | 523 Mike Jackson | .15 | .07 |
| ❑ | 524 Troy Percival | .15 | .07 |
| ❑ | 525 Tony Gwynn | 1.25 | .55 |
| ❑ | 526 Ron Coomer | .15 | .07 |
| ❑ | 527 Darryl Hamilton | .15 | .07 |
| ❑ | 528 Phil Plantier | .15 | .07 |
| ❑ | 529 Norm Charlton | .15 | .07 |
| ❑ | 530 Craig Paquette | .15 | .07 |
| ❑ | 531 Dave Burba | .15 | .07 |
| ❑ | 532 Mike Henneman | .15 | .07 |
| ❑ | 533 Terrell Wade | .15 | .07 |
| ❑ | 534 Eddie Williams | .15 | .07 |
| ❑ | 535 Robin Ventura | .30 | .14 |
| ❑ | 536 Chuck Knoblauch | .30 | .14 |
| ❑ | 537 Les Norman | .15 | .07 |
| ❑ | 538 Brady Anderson | .30 | .14 |
| ❑ | 539 Roger Clemens | 1.25 | .55 |
| ❑ | 540 Mark Portugal | .15 | .07 |
| ❑ | 541 Mike Matheny | .15 | .07 |
| ❑ | 542 Jeff Parrett | .15 | .07 |
| ❑ | 543 Roberto Kelly | .15 | .07 |
| ❑ | 544 Damon Buford | .15 | .07 |
| ❑ | 545 Chad Ogea | .15 | .07 |
| ❑ | 546 Jose Offerman | .15 | .07 |
| ❑ | 547 Brian Barber | .15 | .07 |
| ❑ | 548 Danny Tartabull | .15 | .07 |
| ❑ | 549 Duane Singleton | .15 | .07 |
| ❑ | 550 Tony Gwynn CL | .60 | .25 |

## 1997 Donruss

| | MINT | NRMT |
|---|---|---|
| COMPLETE SET (450) | 45.00 | 20.00 |
| COMPLETE SERIES 1 (270) | 25.00 | 11.00 |
| COMPLETE UPDATE (180) | 20.00 | 9.00 |
| COMMON CARD (1-450) | .15 | .07 |

| | Card | MINT | NRMT |
|---|---|---|---|
| ❑ | 1 Juan Gonzalez | .60 | .25 |
| ❑ | 2 Jim Edmonds | .60 | .25 |
| ❑ | 3 Tony Gwynn | 1.25 | .55 |
| ❑ | 4 Andres Galarraga | .15 | .07 |
| ❑ | 5 Joe Carter | .30 | .14 |
| ❑ | 6 Raul Mondesi | .30 | .14 |
| ❑ | 7 Greg Maddux | 1.50 | .70 |
| ❑ | 8 Travis Fryman | .30 | .14 |
| ❑ | 9 Brian Jordan | .30 | .14 |
| ❑ | 10 Henry Rodriguez | .15 | .07 |
| ❑ | 11 Manny Ramirez | .75 | .35 |
| ❑ | 12 Mark McGwire | 2.50 | 1.10 |
| ❑ | 13 Marc Newfield | .15 | .07 |
| ❑ | 14 Craig Biggio | .40 | .18 |
| ❑ | 15 Sammy Sosa | 1.25 | .55 |
| ❑ | 16 Brady Anderson | .30 | .14 |
| ❑ | 17 Wade Boggs | .75 | .35 |
| ❑ | 18 Charles Johnson | .30 | .14 |
| ❑ | 19 Matt Williams | .40 | .18 |
| ❑ | 20 Denny Neagle | .30 | .14 |
| ❑ | 21 Ken Griffey Jr. | 2.50 | 1.10 |
| ❑ | 22 Robin Ventura | .30 | .14 |
| ❑ | 23 Barry Larkin | .60 | .25 |
| ❑ | 24 Todd Zeile | .15 | .07 |
| ❑ | 25 Chuck Knoblauch | .30 | .14 |
| ❑ | 26 Todd Hundley | .15 | .07 |
| ❑ | 27 Roger Clemens | 1.25 | .55 |
| ❑ | 28 Michael Tucker | .15 | .07 |
| ❑ | 29 Rondell White | .30 | .14 |
| ❑ | 30 Osvaldo Fernandez | .15 | .07 |
| ❑ | 31 Ivan Rodriguez | .75 | .35 |
| ❑ | 32 Alex Fernandez | .15 | .07 |
| ❑ | 33 Jason Isringhausen | .15 | .07 |
| ❑ | 34 Chipper Jones | 1.50 | .70 |
| ❑ | 35 Paul O'Neill | .30 | .14 |
| ❑ | 36 Hideo Nomo | .60 | .25 |
| ❑ | 37 Roberto Alomar | .60 | .25 |
| ❑ | 38 Derek Bell | .15 | .07 |
| ❑ | 39 Paul Molitor | .60 | .25 |
| ❑ | 40 Andy Benes | .15 | .07 |
| ❑ | 41 Steve Trachsel | .15 | .07 |
| ❑ | 42 J.T. Snow | .30 | .14 |
| ❑ | 43 Jason Kendall | .30 | .14 |
| ❑ | 44 Alex Rodriguez | 2.00 | .90 |
| ❑ | 45 Joey Hamilton | .15 | .07 |
| ❑ | 46 Carlos Delgado | .60 | .25 |
| ❑ | 47 Jason Giambi | .60 | .25 |
| ❑ | 48 Larry Walker | .30 | .14 |
| ❑ | 49 Derek Jeter | 2.50 | 1.10 |
| ❑ | 50 Kenny Lofton | .30 | .14 |
| ❑ | 51 Devon White | .30 | .14 |
| ❑ | 52 Matt Mieske | .15 | .07 |
| ❑ | 53 Melvin Nieves | .15 | .07 |
| ❑ | 54 Jose Canseco | .75 | .35 |
| ❑ | 55 Tino Martinez | .30 | .14 |
| ❑ | 56 Rafael Palmeiro | .60 | .25 |
| ❑ | 57 Edgardo Alfonzo | .30 | .14 |
| ❑ | 58 Jay Buhner | .30 | .14 |
| ❑ | 59 Shane Reynolds | .15 | .07 |
| ❑ | 60 Steve Finley | .30 | .14 |
| ❑ | 61 Bobby Higginson | .30 | .14 |
| ❑ | 62 Dean Palmer | .30 | .14 |
| ❑ | 63 Terry Pendleton | .30 | .14 |
| ❑ | 64 Marquis Grissom | .15 | .07 |
| ❑ | 65 Mike Stanley | .15 | .07 |
| ❑ | 66 Moises Alou | .30 | .14 |
| ❑ | 67 Ray Lankford | .30 | .14 |
| ❑ | 68 Marty Cordova | .15 | .07 |
| ❑ | 69 John Olerud | .30 | .14 |
| ❑ | 70 David Cone | .30 | .14 |
| ❑ | 71 Benito Santiago | .15 | .07 |
| ❑ | 72 Ryne Sandberg | .75 | .35 |
| ❑ | 73 Rickey Henderson | .75 | .35 |
| ❑ | 74 Roger Cedeno | .15 | .07 |
| ❑ | 75 Wilson Alvarez | .15 | .07 |
| ❑ | 76 Tim Salmon | .30 | .14 |
| ❑ | 77 Orlando Merced | .15 | .07 |
| ❑ | 78 Vinny Castilla | .30 | .14 |
| ❑ | 79 Ismael Valdes | .15 | .07 |
| ❑ | 80 Dante Bichette | .30 | .14 |

| | | | |
|---|---|---|---|
| 81 | Kevin Brown | .40 | .18 |
| 82 | Andy Pettitte | .30 | .14 |
| 83 | Scott Stahoviak | .15 | .07 |
| 84 | Mickey Tettleton | .15 | .07 |
| 85 | Jack McDowell | .15 | .07 |
| 86 | Tom Glavine | .60 | .25 |
| 87 | Gregg Jefferies | .15 | .07 |
| 88 | Chili Davis | .30 | .14 |
| 89 | Randy Johnson | .75 | .35 |
| 90 | John Mabry | .15 | .07 |
| 91 | Billy Wagner | .15 | .07 |
| 92 | Jeff Cirillo | .30 | .14 |
| 93 | Trevor Hoffman | .30 | .14 |
| 94 | Juan Guzman | .15 | .07 |
| 95 | Geronimo Berroa | .15 | .07 |
| 96 | Bernard Gilkey | .15 | .07 |
| 97 | Danny Tartabull | .15 | .07 |
| 98 | Johnny Damon | .30 | .14 |
| 99 | Charlie Hayes | .15 | .07 |
| 100 | Reggie Sanders | .15 | .07 |
| 101 | Robby Thompson | .15 | .07 |
| 102 | Bobby Bonilla | .30 | .14 |
| 103 | Reggie Jefferson | .15 | .07 |
| 104 | John Smoltz | .30 | .14 |
| 105 | Jim Thome | .40 | .18 |
| 106 | Ruben Rivera | .15 | .07 |
| 107 | Darren Oliver | .15 | .07 |
| 108 | Mo Vaughn | .30 | .14 |
| 109 | Roger Pavlik | .15 | .07 |
| 110 | Terry Steinbach | .15 | .07 |
| 111 | Jermaine Dye | .30 | .14 |
| 112 | Mark Grudzielanek | .15 | .07 |
| 113 | Rick Aguilera | .15 | .07 |
| 114 | Jamey Wright | .15 | .07 |
| 115 | Eddie Murray | .60 | .25 |
| 116 | Brian L. Hunter | .15 | .07 |
| 117 | Hal Morris | .15 | .07 |
| 118 | Tom Pagnozzi | .15 | .07 |
| 119 | Mike Mussina | .60 | .25 |
| 120 | Mark Grace | .60 | .25 |
| 121 | Cal Ripken | 2.50 | 1.10 |
| 122 | Tom Goodwin | .15 | .07 |
| 123 | Paul Sorrento | .15 | .07 |
| 124 | Jay Bell | .30 | .14 |
| 125 | Todd Hollandsworth | .15 | .07 |
| 126 | Edgar Martinez | .40 | .18 |
| 127 | George Arias | .15 | .07 |
| 128 | Greg Vaughn | .30 | .14 |
| 129 | Roberto Hernandez | .15 | .07 |
| 130 | Delino DeShields | .15 | .07 |
| 131 | Bill Pulsipher | .15 | .07 |
| 132 | Joey Cora | .15 | .07 |
| 133 | Mariano Rivera | .30 | .14 |
| 134 | Mike Piazza | 2.00 | .90 |
| 135 | Carlos Baerga | .15 | .07 |
| 136 | Jose Mesa | .15 | .07 |
| 137 | Will Clark | .60 | .25 |
| 138 | Frank Thomas | 1.25 | .55 |
| 139 | John Wetteland | .30 | .14 |
| 140 | Shawn Estes | .30 | .14 |
| 141 | Garret Anderson | .30 | .14 |
| 142 | Andre Dawson | .40 | .18 |
| 143 | Eddie Taubensee | .15 | .07 |
| 144 | Ryan Klesko | .30 | .14 |
| 145 | Rocky Coppinger | .15 | .07 |
| 146 | Jeff Bagwell | .75 | .35 |
| 147 | Donovan Osborne | .15 | .07 |
| 148 | Greg Myers | .15 | .07 |
| 149 | Brant Brown | .15 | .07 |
| 150 | Kevin Elster | .15 | .07 |
| 151 | Bob Wells | .15 | .07 |
| 152 | Wally Joyner | .30 | .14 |
| 153 | Rico Brogna | .15 | .07 |
| 154 | Dwight Gooden | .30 | .14 |
| 155 | Jermaine Allensworth | .15 | .07 |
| 156 | Ray Durham | .30 | .14 |
| 157 | Cecil Fielder | .30 | .14 |
| 158 | John Burkett | .15 | .07 |
| 159 | Gary Sheffield | .60 | .25 |
| 160 | Albert Belle | .40 | .18 |
| 161 | Tomas Perez | .15 | .07 |
| 162 | David Doster | .15 | .07 |
| 163 | John Valentin | .15 | .07 |
| 164 | Danny Graves | .15 | .07 |
| 165 | Jose Paniagua | .15 | .07 |
| 166 | Brian Giles RC | 2.50 | 1.10 |
| 167 | Barry Bonds | 1.00 | .45 |
| 168 | Sterling Hitchcock | .15 | .07 |
| 169 | Bernie Williams | .60 | .25 |
| 170 | Fred McGriff | .40 | .18 |
| 171 | George Williams | .15 | .07 |
| 172 | Amaury Telemaco | .15 | .07 |
| 173 | Ken Caminiti | .30 | .14 |
| 174 | Ron Gant | .15 | .07 |
| 175 | Dave Justice | .40 | .18 |
| 176 | James Baldwin | .30 | .14 |
| 177 | Pat Hentgen | .15 | .07 |
| 178 | Ben McDonald | .15 | .07 |
| 179 | Tim Naehring | .15 | .07 |
| 180 | Jim Eisenreich | .15 | .07 |
| 181 | Ken Hill | .15 | .07 |
| 182 | Paul Wilson | .15 | .07 |
| 183 | Marvin Benard | .15 | .07 |
| 184 | Alan Benes | .15 | .07 |
| 185 | Ellis Burks | .30 | .14 |
| 186 | Scott Servais | .15 | .07 |
| 187 | David Segui | .15 | .07 |
| 188 | Scott Brosius | .30 | .14 |
| 189 | Jose Offerman | .15 | .07 |
| 190 | Eric Davis | .30 | .14 |
| 191 | Brett Butler | .30 | .14 |
| 192 | Curtis Pride | .15 | .07 |
| 193 | Yamil Benitez | .15 | .07 |
| 194 | Chan Ho Park | .30 | .14 |
| 195 | Bret Boone | .30 | .14 |
| 196 | Omar Vizquel | .30 | .14 |
| 197 | Orlando Miller | .15 | .07 |
| 198 | Ramon Martinez | .15 | .07 |
| 199 | Harold Baines | .30 | .14 |
| 200 | Eric Young | .15 | .07 |
| 201 | Fernando Vina | .15 | .07 |
| 202 | Alex Gonzalez | .15 | .07 |
| 203 | Fernando Valenzuela | .30 | .14 |
| 204 | Steve Avery | .15 | .07 |
| 205 | Ernie Young | .15 | .07 |
| 206 | Kevin Appier | .30 | .14 |
| 207 | Randy Myers | .15 | .07 |
| 208 | Jeff Suppan | .15 | .07 |
| 209 | James Mouton | .15 | .07 |
| 210 | Russ Davis | .15 | .07 |
| 211 | Al Martin | .15 | .07 |
| 212 | Troy Percival | .15 | .07 |
| 213 | Al Leiter | .30 | .14 |
| 214 | Dennis Eckersley | .30 | .14 |
| 215 | Mark Johnson | .15 | .07 |
| 216 | Eric Karros | .30 | .14 |
| 217 | Royce Clayton | .15 | .07 |
| 218 | Tony Phillips | .15 | .07 |
| 219 | Tim Wakefield | .15 | .07 |
| 220 | Alan Trammell | .40 | .18 |
| 221 | Eduardo Perez | .15 | .07 |
| 222 | Butch Huskey | .15 | .07 |
| 223 | Tim Belcher | .15 | .07 |
| 224 | Jamie Moyer | .15 | .07 |
| 225 | F.P. Santangelo | .15 | .07 |
| 226 | Rusty Greer | .30 | .14 |
| 227 | Jeff Brantley | .15 | .07 |
| 228 | Mark Langston | .30 | .14 |
| 229 | Ray Montgomery | .15 | .07 |
| 230 | Rich Becker | .15 | .07 |
| 231 | Ozzie Smith | .75 | .35 |
| 232 | Rey Ordonez | .15 | .07 |
| 233 | Ricky Otero | .15 | .07 |
| 234 | Mike Cameron | .30 | .14 |
| 235 | Mike Sweeney | .30 | .14 |
| 236 | Mark Lewis | .15 | .07 |
| 237 | Luis Gonzalez | .30 | .14 |
| 238 | Marcus Jensen | .15 | .07 |
| 239 | Ed Sprague | .15 | .07 |
| 240 | Jose Valentin | .15 | .07 |
| 241 | Jeff Frye | .15 | .07 |
| 242 | Charles Nagy | .15 | .07 |
| 243 | Carlos Garcia | .15 | .07 |
| 244 | Mike Hampton | .30 | .14 |
| 245 | B.J. Surhoff | .30 | .14 |
| 246 | Wilton Guerrero | .15 | .07 |
| 247 | Frank Rodriguez | .15 | .07 |
| 248 | Gary Gaetti | .30 | .14 |
| 249 | Lance Johnson | .15 | .07 |
| 250 | Darren Bragg | .15 | .07 |
| 251 | Darryl Hamilton | .15 | .07 |
| 252 | John Jaha | .15 | .07 |
| 253 | Craig Paquette | .15 | .07 |
| 254 | Jaime Navarro | .15 | .07 |
| 255 | Shawon Dunston | .15 | .07 |
| 256 | Mark Loretta | .15 | .07 |
| 257 | Tim Belk | .15 | .07 |
| 258 | Jeff Darwin | .15 | .07 |
| 259 | Ruben Sierra | .15 | .07 |
| 260 | Chuck Finley | .30 | .14 |
| 261 | Darryl Strawberry | .30 | .14 |
| 262 | Shannon Stewart | .30 | .14 |
| 263 | Pedro Martinez | .75 | .35 |
| 264 | Neifi Perez | .15 | .07 |
| 265 | Jeff Conine | .15 | .07 |
| 266 | Orel Hershiser | .30 | .14 |
| 267 | Eddie Murray CL | .30 | .14 |
| 268 | Paul Molitor CL | .30 | .14 |
| 269 | Barry Bonds CL | .30 | .14 |
| 270 | Mark McGwire CL | 1.25 | .55 |
| 271 | Matt Williams | .40 | .18 |
| 272 | Todd Zeile | .15 | .07 |
| 273 | Roger Clemens | 1.25 | .55 |
| 274 | Michael Tucker | .15 | .07 |
| 275 | J.T. Snow | .30 | .14 |
| 276 | Kenny Lofton | .30 | .14 |
| 277 | Jose Canseco | .75 | .35 |
| 278 | Marquis Grissom | .15 | .07 |
| 279 | Moises Alou | .30 | .14 |
| 280 | Benito Santiago | .15 | .07 |
| 281 | Willie McGee | .30 | .14 |
| 282 | Chili Davis | .30 | .14 |
| 283 | Ron Coomer | .15 | .07 |
| 284 | Orlando Merced | .15 | .07 |
| 285 | Delino DeShields | .15 | .07 |
| 286 | John Wetteland | .30 | .14 |
| 287 | Darren Daulton | .30 | .14 |
| 288 | Lee Stevens | .30 | .14 |
| 289 | Albert Belle | .15 | .07 |
| 290 | Sterling Hitchcock | .15 | .07 |
| 291 | David Justice | .15 | .07 |
| 292 | Eric Davis | .30 | .14 |
| 293 | Brian Hunter | .15 | .07 |
| 294 | Darryl Hamilton | .15 | .07 |
| 295 | Steve Avery | .15 | .07 |
| 296 | Joe Vitiello | .15 | .07 |
| 297 | Jaime Navarro | .15 | .07 |
| 298 | Eddie Murray | .60 | .25 |
| 299 | Randy Myers | .15 | .07 |
| 300 | Francisco Cordova | .15 | .07 |
| 301 | Javier Lopez | .30 | .14 |
| 302 | Geronimo Berroa | .15 | .07 |
| 303 | Jeffrey Hammonds | .30 | .14 |
| 304 | Deion Sanders | .30 | .14 |
| 305 | Jeff Fassero | .15 | .07 |
| 306 | Curt Schilling | .30 | .14 |
| 307 | Robb Nen | .15 | .07 |
| 308 | Mark McLemore | .15 | .07 |
| 309 | Jimmy Key | .30 | .14 |
| 310 | Quilvio Veras | .15 | .07 |
| 311 | Bip Roberts | .15 | .07 |
| 312 | Esteban Loaiza | .15 | .07 |
| 313 | Andy Ashby | .15 | .07 |
| 314 | Sandy Alomar Jr. | .30 | .14 |
| 315 | Shawn Green | .60 | .25 |
| 316 | Luis Castillo | .30 | .14 |
| 317 | Benji Gil | .15 | .07 |
| 318 | Otis Nixon | .15 | .07 |
| 319 | Aaron Sele | .30 | .14 |
| 320 | Brad Ausmus | .15 | .07 |
| 321 | Troy O'Leary | .15 | .07 |
| 322 | Terrell Wade | .15 | .07 |
| 323 | Jeff King | .15 | .07 |
| 324 | Kevin Seitzer | .15 | .07 |
| 325 | Mark Wohlers | .15 | .07 |
| 326 | Edgar Renteria | .30 | .14 |
| 327 | Dan Wilson | .15 | .07 |
| 328 | Brian McRae | .15 | .07 |
| 329 | Rod Beck | .15 | .07 |
| 330 | Julio Franco | .30 | .14 |
| 331 | Dave Nilsson | .15 | .07 |
| 332 | Glenallen Hill | .15 | .07 |
| 333 | Kevin Elster | .15 | .07 |
| 334 | Joe Girardi | .15 | .07 |
| 335 | David Wells | .30 | .14 |
| 336 | Jeff Blauser | .15 | .07 |
| 337 | Darryl Kile | .30 | .14 |
| 338 | Jeff Kent | .40 | .18 |

| Card | MINT | NRMT |
|---|---|---|
| ❑ 339 Jim Leyritz | .15 | .07 |
| ❑ 340 Todd Stottlemyre | .15 | .07 |
| ❑ 341 Tony Clark | .15 | .07 |
| ❑ 342 Chris Hoiles | .15 | .07 |
| ❑ 343 Mike Lieberthal | .30 | .14 |
| ❑ 344 Matt Lawton | .30 | .14 |
| ❑ 345 Alex Ochoa | .15 | .07 |
| ❑ 346 Chris Snopek | .15 | .07 |
| ❑ 347 Rudy Pemberton | .15 | .07 |
| ❑ 348 Eric Owens | .15 | .07 |
| ❑ 349 Joe Randa | .15 | .07 |
| ❑ 350 John Olerud | .30 | .14 |
| ❑ 351 Steve Karsay | .15 | .07 |
| ❑ 352 Mark Whiten | .15 | .07 |
| ❑ 353 Bob Abreu | .30 | .14 |
| ❑ 354 Bartolo Colon | .30 | .14 |
| ❑ 355 Vladimir Guerrero | 1.25 | .55 |
| ❑ 356 Darin Erstad | .75 | .35 |
| ❑ 357 Scott Rolen | .60 | .25 |
| ❑ 358 Andruw Jones | .75 | .35 |
| ❑ 359 Scott Spiezio | .15 | .07 |
| ❑ 360 Karim Garcia | .15 | .07 |
| ❑ 361 Hideki Irabu RC | .50 | .23 |
| ❑ 362 Nomar Garciaparra | 2.00 | .90 |
| ❑ 363 Dmitri Young | .30 | .14 |
| ❑ 364 Bubba Trammell RC | .30 | .14 |
| ❑ 365 Kevin Orie | .15 | .07 |
| ❑ 366 Jose Rosado | .15 | .07 |
| ❑ 367 Jose Guillen | .15 | .07 |
| ❑ 368 Brooks Kieschnick | .15 | .07 |
| ❑ 369 Pokey Reese | .30 | .14 |
| ❑ 370 Glendon Rusch | .15 | .07 |
| ❑ 371 Jason Dickson | .15 | .07 |
| ❑ 372 Todd Walker | .15 | .07 |
| ❑ 373 Justin Thompson | .15 | .07 |
| ❑ 374 Todd Greene | .15 | .07 |
| ❑ 375 Jeff Suppan | .15 | .07 |
| ❑ 376 Trey Beamon | .15 | .07 |
| ❑ 377 Damon Mashore | .15 | .07 |
| ❑ 378 Wendell Magee | .15 | .07 |
| ❑ 379 Shigetoshi Hasegawa RC | .40 | .18 |
| ❑ 380 Bill Mueller RC | .40 | .18 |
| ❑ 381 Chris Widger | .15 | .07 |
| ❑ 382 Tony Graffanino | .15 | .07 |
| ❑ 383 Derrek Lee | .15 | .07 |
| ❑ 384 Brian Moehler | .15 | .07 |
| ❑ 385 Quinton McCracken | .15 | .07 |
| ❑ 386 Matt Morris | .15 | .07 |
| ❑ 387 Marvin Benard | .15 | .07 |
| ❑ 388 Deivi Cruz RC | .75 | .35 |
| ❑ 389 Javier Valentin | .30 | .14 |
| ❑ 390 Todd Dunwoody | .30 | .14 |
| ❑ 391 Derrick Gibson | .15 | .07 |
| ❑ 392 Raul Casanova | .15 | .07 |
| ❑ 393 George Arias | .15 | .07 |
| ❑ 394 Tony Womack RC | .75 | .35 |
| ❑ 395 Antone Williamson | .15 | .07 |
| ❑ 396 Jose Cruz Jr. RC | 1.50 | .70 |
| ❑ 397 Desi Relaford | .15 | .07 |
| ❑ 398 Frank Thomas HIT | .75 | .35 |
| ❑ 399 Ken Griffey Jr. HIT | 1.25 | .55 |
| ❑ 400 Cal Ripken HIT | 1.25 | .55 |
| ❑ 401 Chipper Jones HIT | .75 | .35 |
| ❑ 402 Mike Piazza HIT | 1.00 | .45 |
| ❑ 403 Gary Sheffield HIT | .30 | .14 |
| ❑ 404 Alex Rodriguez HIT | 1.00 | .45 |
| ❑ 405 Wade Boggs HIT | .30 | .14 |
| ❑ 406 Juan Gonzalez HIT | .60 | .25 |
| ❑ 407 Tony Gwynn HIT | .60 | .25 |
| ❑ 408 Edgar Martinez HIT | .30 | .14 |
| ❑ 409 Jeff Bagwell HIT | .60 | .25 |
| ❑ 410 Larry Walker HIT | .30 | .14 |
| ❑ 411 Kenny Lofton HIT | .30 | .14 |
| ❑ 412 Manny Ramirez HIT | .40 | .18 |
| ❑ 413 Mark McGwire HIT | 1.25 | .55 |
| ❑ 414 Roberto Alomar HIT | .30 | .14 |
| ❑ 415 Derek Jeter HIT | 1.25 | .55 |
| ❑ 416 Brady Anderson HIT | .15 | .07 |
| ❑ 417 Paul Molitor HIT | .30 | .14 |
| ❑ 418 Dante Bichette HIT | .15 | .07 |
| ❑ 419 Jim Edmonds HIT | .30 | .14 |
| ❑ 420 Mo Vaughn HIT | .30 | .14 |
| ❑ 421 Barry Bonds HIT | .30 | .14 |
| ❑ 422 Rusty Greer HIT | .15 | .07 |
| ❑ 423 Greg Maddux KING | .75 | .35 |
| ❑ 424 Andy Pettitte KING | .15 | .07 |
| ❑ 425 John Smoltz KING | .15 | .07 |
| ❑ 426 Randy Johnson KING | .30 | .14 |
| ❑ 427 Hideo Nomo KING | .60 | .25 |
| ❑ 428 Roger Clemens KING | .60 | .25 |
| ❑ 429 Tom Glavine KING | .30 | .14 |
| ❑ 430 Pat Hentgen KING | .15 | .07 |
| ❑ 431 Kevin Brown KING | .15 | .07 |
| ❑ 432 Mike Mussina KING | .30 | .14 |
| ❑ 433 Alex Fernandez KING | .15 | .07 |
| ❑ 434 Kevin Appier KING | .15 | .07 |
| ❑ 435 David Cone KING | .15 | .07 |
| ❑ 436 Jeff Fassero KING | .15 | .07 |
| ❑ 437 John Wetteland KING | .15 | .07 |
| ❑ 438 Barry Bonds IS / Ivan Rodriguez | .60 | .25 |
| ❑ 439 Ken Griffey Jr. IS / Andres Galarraga | 1.00 | .35 |
| ❑ 440 Fred McGriff IS / Rafael Palmeiro | .40 | .18 |
| ❑ 441 Barry Larkin IS / Jim Thome | .25 | .11 |
| ❑ 442 Sammy Sosa IS / Albert Belle | .60 | .25 |
| ❑ 443 Bernie Williams IS / Todd Hundley | .25 | .11 |
| ❑ 444 Chuck Knoblauch IS / Brian Jordan | .15 | .07 |
| ❑ 445 Mo Vaughn IS / Jeff Conine | .30 | .14 |
| ❑ 446 Ken Caminiti IS / Jason Giambi | .25 | .11 |
| ❑ 447 Raul Mondesi IS / Tim Salmon | .15 | .07 |
| ❑ 448 Cal Ripken CL | 1.25 | .55 |
| ❑ 449 Greg Maddux CL | .75 | .35 |
| ❑ 450 Ken Griffey Jr. CL | 1.25 | .55 |

## 1998 Donruss

| | MINT | NRMT |
|---|---|---|
| COMPLETE SET (420) | 60.00 | 27.00 |
| COMPLETE SERIES 1 (170) | 20.00 | 9.00 |
| COMPLETE UPDATE (250) | 40.00 | 18.00 |
| COMMON CARD (1-420) | .10 | .05 |

| Card | MINT | NRMT |
|---|---|---|
| ❑ 1 Paul Molitor | .50 | .23 |
| ❑ 2 Juan Gonzalez | .50 | .23 |
| ❑ 3 Darryl Kile | .20 | .09 |
| ❑ 4 Randy Johnson | .60 | .25 |
| ❑ 5 Tom Glavine | .50 | .23 |
| ❑ 6 Pat Hentgen | .10 | .05 |
| ❑ 7 David Justice | .30 | .14 |
| ❑ 8 Kevin Brown | .30 | .14 |
| ❑ 9 Mike Mussina | .50 | .23 |
| ❑ 10 Ken Caminiti | .20 | .09 |
| ❑ 11 Todd Hundley | .10 | .05 |
| ❑ 12 Frank Thomas | 1.00 | .45 |
| ❑ 13 Ray Lankford | .20 | .09 |
| ❑ 14 Justin Thompson | .10 | .05 |
| ❑ 15 Jason Dickson | .10 | .05 |
| ❑ 16 Kenny Lofton | .20 | .09 |
| ❑ 17 Ivan Rodriguez | .60 | .25 |
| ❑ 18 Pedro Martinez | .60 | .25 |
| ❑ 19 Brady Anderson | .20 | .09 |
| ❑ 20 Barry Larkin | .50 | .23 |
| ❑ 21 Chipper Jones | 1.25 | .55 |
| ❑ 22 Tony Gwynn | 1.00 | .45 |
| ❑ 23 Roger Clemens | 1.00 | .45 |
| ❑ 24 Sandy Alomar Jr. | .20 | .09 |
| ❑ 25 Tino Martinez | .20 | .09 |
| ❑ 26 Jeff Bagwell | .60 | .25 |
| ❑ 27 Shawn Estes | .10 | .05 |
| ❑ 28 Ken Griffey Jr. | 2.00 | .90 |
| ❑ 29 Javier Lopez | .20 | .09 |
| ❑ 30 Denny Neagle | .10 | .05 |
| ❑ 31 Mike Piazza | 1.50 | .70 |
| ❑ 32 Andres Galarraga | .30 | .14 |
| ❑ 33 Larry Walker | .20 | .09 |
| ❑ 34 Alex Rodriguez | 1.50 | .70 |
| ❑ 35 Greg Maddux | 1.25 | .55 |
| ❑ 36 Albert Belle | .30 | .14 |
| ❑ 37 Barry Bonds | .75 | .35 |
| ❑ 38 Mo Vaughn | .20 | .09 |
| ❑ 39 Kevin Appier | .20 | .09 |
| ❑ 40 Wade Boggs | .60 | .25 |
| ❑ 41 Garret Anderson | .20 | .09 |
| ❑ 42 Jeffrey Hammonds | .20 | .09 |
| ❑ 43 Marquis Grissom | .10 | .05 |
| ❑ 44 Jim Edmonds | .50 | .23 |
| ❑ 45 Brian Jordan | .20 | .09 |
| ❑ 46 Raul Mondesi | .20 | .09 |
| ❑ 47 John Valentin | .10 | .05 |
| ❑ 48 Brad Radke | .20 | .09 |
| ❑ 49 Ismael Valdes | .10 | .05 |
| ❑ 50 Matt Stairs | .10 | .05 |
| ❑ 51 Matt Williams | .30 | .14 |
| ❑ 52 Reggie Jefferson | .10 | .05 |
| ❑ 53 Alan Benes | .10 | .05 |
| ❑ 54 Charles Johnson | .20 | .09 |
| ❑ 55 Chuck Knoblauch | .20 | .09 |
| ❑ 56 Edgar Martinez | .30 | .14 |
| ❑ 57 Nomar Garciaparra | 1.50 | .70 |
| ❑ 58 Craig Biggio | .30 | .14 |
| ❑ 59 Bernie Williams | .50 | .23 |
| ❑ 60 David Cone | .20 | .09 |
| ❑ 61 Cal Ripken | 2.00 | .90 |
| ❑ 62 Mark McGwire | 2.00 | .90 |
| ❑ 63 Roberto Alomar | .50 | .23 |
| ❑ 64 Fred McGriff | .30 | .14 |
| ❑ 65 Eric Karros | .20 | .09 |
| ❑ 66 Robin Ventura | .20 | .09 |
| ❑ 67 Darin Erstad | .50 | .23 |
| ❑ 68 Michael Tucker | .10 | .05 |
| ❑ 69 Jim Thome | .30 | .14 |
| ❑ 70 Mark Grace | .50 | .23 |
| ❑ 71 Lou Collier | .10 | .05 |
| ❑ 72 Karim Garcia | .10 | .05 |
| ❑ 73 Alex Fernandez | .10 | .05 |
| ❑ 74 J.T. Snow | .20 | .09 |
| ❑ 75 Reggie Sanders | .10 | .05 |
| ❑ 76 John Smoltz | .20 | .09 |
| ❑ 77 Tim Salmon | .20 | .09 |
| ❑ 78 Paul O'Neill | .20 | .09 |
| ❑ 79 Vinny Castilla | .20 | .09 |
| ❑ 80 Rafael Palmeiro | .50 | .23 |
| ❑ 81 Jaret Wright | .10 | .05 |
| ❑ 82 Jay Buhner | .20 | .09 |
| ❑ 83 Brett Butler | .20 | .09 |
| ❑ 84 Todd Greene | .10 | .05 |
| ❑ 85 Scott Rolen | .50 | .23 |
| ❑ 86 Sammy Sosa | 1.00 | .45 |
| ❑ 87 Jason Giambi | .50 | .23 |
| ❑ 88 Carlos Delgado | .50 | .23 |
| ❑ 89 Deion Sanders | .20 | .09 |
| ❑ 90 Wilton Guerrero | .10 | .05 |
| ❑ 91 Andy Pettitte | .20 | .09 |
| ❑ 92 Brian Giles | .20 | .09 |
| ❑ 93 Dmitri Young | .20 | .09 |
| ❑ 94 Ron Coomer | .10 | .05 |
| ❑ 95 Mike Cameron | .20 | .09 |
| ❑ 96 Edgardo Alfonzo | .20 | .09 |
| ❑ 97 Jimmy Key | .20 | .09 |
| ❑ 98 Ryan Klesko | .20 | .09 |
| ❑ 99 Andy Benes | .10 | .05 |
| ❑ 100 Derek Jeter | 2.00 | .90 |
| ❑ 101 Jeff Fassero | .10 | .05 |
| ❑ 102 Neifi Perez | .10 | .05 |
| ❑ 103 Hideo Nomo | .50 | .23 |
| ❑ 104 Andruw Jones | .50 | .23 |
| ❑ 105 Todd Helton | .60 | .25 |
| ❑ 106 Livan Hernandez | .10 | .05 |
| ❑ 107 Brett Tomko | .10 | .05 |
| ❑ 108 Shannon Stewart | .20 | .09 |
| ❑ 109 Bartolo Colon | .20 | .09 |

| | No. | Player | Price | Price |
|---|---|---|---|---|
| ❑ | 110 | Matt Morris | .10 | .05 |
| ❑ | 111 | Miguel Tejada | .50 | .23 |
| ❑ | 112 | Pokey Reese | .20 | .09 |
| ❑ | 113 | Fernando Tatis | .20 | .09 |
| ❑ | 114 | Todd Dunwoody | .10 | .05 |
| ❑ | 115 | Jose Cruz Jr. | .20 | .09 |
| ❑ | 116 | Chan Ho Park | .20 | .09 |
| ❑ | 117 | Kevin Young | .20 | .09 |
| ❑ | 118 | Rickey Henderson | .60 | .25 |
| ❑ | 119 | Hideki Irabu | .10 | .05 |
| ❑ | 120 | Francisco Cordova | .10 | .05 |
| ❑ | 121 | Al Martin | .10 | .05 |
| ❑ | 122 | Tony Clark | .10 | .05 |
| ❑ | 123 | Curt Schilling | .20 | .09 |
| ❑ | 124 | Rusty Greer | .20 | .09 |
| ❑ | 125 | Jose Canseco | .60 | .25 |
| ❑ | 126 | Edgar Renteria | .10 | .05 |
| ❑ | 127 | Todd Walker | .10 | .05 |
| ❑ | 128 | Wally Joyner | .20 | .09 |
| ❑ | 129 | Bill Mueller | .10 | .05 |
| ❑ | 130 | Jose Guillen | .10 | .05 |
| ❑ | 131 | Manny Ramirez | .60 | .25 |
| ❑ | 132 | Bobby Higginson | .20 | .09 |
| ❑ | 133 | Kevin Orie | .10 | .05 |
| ❑ | 134 | Will Clark | .50 | .23 |
| ❑ | 135 | Dave Nilsson | .10 | .05 |
| ❑ | 136 | Jason Kendall | .20 | .09 |
| ❑ | 137 | Ivan Cruz | .10 | .05 |
| ❑ | 138 | Gary Sheffield | .50 | .23 |
| ❑ | 139 | Bubba Trammell | .10 | .05 |
| ❑ | 140 | Vladimir Guerrero | .75 | .35 |
| ❑ | 141 | Dennis Reyes | .10 | .05 |
| ❑ | 142 | Bobby Bonilla | .20 | .09 |
| ❑ | 143 | Ruben Rivera | .10 | .05 |
| ❑ | 144 | Ben Grieve | .20 | .09 |
| ❑ | 145 | Moises Alou | .20 | .09 |
| ❑ | 146 | Tony Womack | .10 | .05 |
| ❑ | 147 | Eric Young | .10 | .05 |
| ❑ | 148 | Paul Konerko | .20 | .09 |
| ❑ | 149 | Dante Bichette | .20 | .09 |
| ❑ | 150 | Joe Carter | .20 | .09 |
| ❑ | 151 | Rondell White | .20 | .09 |
| ❑ | 152 | Chris Holt | .10 | .05 |
| ❑ | 153 | Shawn Green | .50 | .23 |
| ❑ | 154 | Mark Grudzielanek | .10 | .05 |
| | | UER back rudzielanek | | |
| ❑ | 155 | Jermaine Dye | .20 | .09 |
| ❑ | 156 | Ken Griffey Jr. FC | 1.00 | .45 |
| ❑ | 157 | Frank Thomas FC | .50 | .23 |
| ❑ | 158 | Chipper Jones FC | .60 | .25 |
| ❑ | 159 | Mike Piazza FC | .75 | .35 |
| ❑ | 160 | Cal Ripken FC | 1.00 | .45 |
| ❑ | 161 | Greg Maddux FC | .60 | .25 |
| ❑ | 162 | Juan Gonzalez FC | .20 | .09 |
| ❑ | 163 | Alex Rodriguez FC | .75 | .35 |
| ❑ | 164 | Mark McGwire FC | 1.00 | .45 |
| ❑ | 165 | Derek Jeter FC | 1.00 | .45 |
| ❑ | 166 | Larry Walker CL | .20 | .09 |
| ❑ | 167 | Tony Gwynn CL | .50 | .23 |
| ❑ | 168 | Tino Martinez CL | .10 | .05 |
| ❑ | 169 | Scott Rolen CL | .50 | .23 |
| ❑ | 170 | Nomar Garciaparra CL | .75 | .35 |
| ❑ | 171 | Mike Sweeney | .20 | .09 |
| ❑ | 172 | Dustin Hermanson | .10 | .05 |
| ❑ | 173 | Darren Dreifort | .10 | .05 |
| ❑ | 174 | Ron Gant | .20 | .09 |
| ❑ | 175 | Todd Hollandsworth | .10 | .05 |
| ❑ | 176 | John Jaha | .20 | .09 |
| ❑ | 177 | Kerry Wood | .50 | .23 |
| ❑ | 178 | Chris Stynes | .10 | .05 |
| ❑ | 179 | Kevin Elster | .10 | .05 |
| ❑ | 180 | Derek Bell | .10 | .05 |
| ❑ | 181 | Darryl Strawberry | .20 | .09 |
| ❑ | 182 | Damion Easley | .10 | .05 |
| ❑ | 183 | Jeff Cirillo | .20 | .09 |
| ❑ | 184 | John Thomson | .10 | .05 |
| ❑ | 185 | Dan Wilson | .10 | .05 |
| ❑ | 186 | Jay Bell | .20 | .09 |
| ❑ | 187 | Bernard Gilkey | .10 | .05 |
| ❑ | 188 | Marc Valdes | .10 | .05 |
| ❑ | 189 | Ramon Martinez | .10 | .05 |
| ❑ | 190 | Charles Nagy | .10 | .05 |
| ❑ | 191 | Derek Lowe | .10 | .05 |
| ❑ | 192 | Andy Benes | .10 | .05 |
| ❑ | 193 | Delino DeShields | .10 | .05 |
| ❑ | 194 | Ryan Jackson RC | .10 | .05 |
| ❑ | 195 | Kenny Lofton | .20 | .09 |
| ❑ | 196 | Chuck Knoblauch | .20 | .09 |
| ❑ | 197 | Andres Galarraga | .30 | .14 |
| ❑ | 198 | Jose Canseco | .60 | .25 |
| ❑ | 199 | John Olerud | .20 | .09 |
| ❑ | 200 | Lance Johnson | .10 | .05 |
| ❑ | 201 | Darryl Kile | .20 | .09 |
| ❑ | 202 | Luis Castillo | .20 | .09 |
| ❑ | 203 | Joe Carter | .20 | .09 |
| ❑ | 204 | Dennis Eckersley | .20 | .09 |
| ❑ | 205 | Steve Finley | .20 | .09 |
| ❑ | 206 | Esteban Loaiza | .10 | .05 |
| ❑ | 207 | Ryan Christenson RC UER | .20 | .09 |
| | | (Birthdate says 1988) | | |
| ❑ | 208 | Deivi Cruz | .10 | .05 |
| ❑ | 209 | Mariano Rivera | .20 | .09 |
| ❑ | 210 | Mike Judd RC | .30 | .14 |
| ❑ | 211 | Billy Wagner | .10 | .05 |
| ❑ | 212 | Scott Spiezio | .10 | .05 |
| ❑ | 213 | Russ Davis | .10 | .05 |
| ❑ | 214 | Jeff Suppan | .10 | .05 |
| ❑ | 215 | Doug Glanville | .10 | .05 |
| ❑ | 216 | Dmitri Young | .20 | .09 |
| ❑ | 217 | Rey Ordonez | .10 | .05 |
| ❑ | 218 | Cecil Fielder | .20 | .09 |
| ❑ | 219 | Masato Yoshii RC | .40 | .18 |
| ❑ | 220 | Raul Casanova | .10 | .05 |
| ❑ | 221 | Rolando Arrojo RC | .40 | .18 |
| ❑ | 222 | Ellis Burks | .20 | .09 |
| ❑ | 223 | Butch Huskey | .10 | .05 |
| ❑ | 224 | Brian Hunter | .10 | .05 |
| ❑ | 225 | Marquis Grissom | .10 | .05 |
| ❑ | 226 | Kevin Brown | .30 | .14 |
| ❑ | 227 | Joe Randa | .10 | .05 |
| ❑ | 228 | Henry Rodriguez | .10 | .05 |
| ❑ | 229 | Omar Vizquel | .20 | .09 |
| ❑ | 230 | Fred McGriff | .30 | .14 |
| ❑ | 231 | Matt Williams | .30 | .14 |
| ❑ | 232 | Moises Alou | .20 | .09 |
| ❑ | 233 | Travis Fryman | .20 | .09 |
| ❑ | 234 | Wade Boggs | .60 | .25 |
| ❑ | 235 | Pedro Martinez | .60 | .25 |
| ❑ | 236 | Rickey Henderson | .60 | .25 |
| ❑ | 237 | Bubba Trammell | .10 | .05 |
| ❑ | 238 | Mike Caruso | .10 | .05 |
| ❑ | 239 | Wilson Alvarez | .10 | .05 |
| ❑ | 240 | Geronimo Berroa | .10 | .05 |
| ❑ | 241 | Eric Milton | .10 | .05 |
| ❑ | 242 | Scott Erickson | .10 | .05 |
| ❑ | 243 | Todd Erdos RC | .20 | .09 |
| ❑ | 244 | Bobby Hughes | .10 | .05 |
| ❑ | 245 | Dave Hollins | .10 | .05 |
| ❑ | 246 | Dean Palmer | .20 | .09 |
| ❑ | 247 | Carlos Baerga | .10 | .05 |
| ❑ | 248 | Jose Silva | .10 | .05 |
| ❑ | 249 | Jose Cabrera RC | .10 | .05 |
| ❑ | 250 | Tom Evans | .10 | .05 |
| ❑ | 251 | Marty Cordova | .10 | .05 |
| ❑ | 252 | Hanley Frias RC | .10 | .05 |
| ❑ | 253 | Javier Valentin | .10 | .05 |
| ❑ | 254 | Mario Valdez | .10 | .05 |
| ❑ | 255 | Joey Cora | .10 | .05 |
| ❑ | 256 | Mike Lansing | .10 | .05 |
| ❑ | 257 | Jeff Kent | .30 | .14 |
| ❑ | 258 | Dave Dellucci RC | .10 | .05 |
| ❑ | 259 | Curtis King RC | .10 | .05 |
| ❑ | 260 | David Segui | .10 | .05 |
| ❑ | 261 | Royce Clayton | .10 | .05 |
| ❑ | 262 | Jeff Blauser | .10 | .05 |
| ❑ | 263 | Manny Aybar RC | .20 | .09 |
| ❑ | 264 | Mike Cather RC | .10 | .05 |
| ❑ | 265 | Todd Zeile | .20 | .09 |
| ❑ | 266 | Richard Hidalgo | .20 | .09 |
| ❑ | 267 | Dante Powell | .10 | .05 |
| ❑ | 268 | Mike DeJean RC | .10 | .05 |
| ❑ | 269 | Ken Cloude | .10 | .05 |
| ❑ | 270 | Danny Klassen | .10 | .05 |
| ❑ | 271 | Sean Casey | .20 | .09 |
| ❑ | 272 | A.J. Hinch | .10 | .05 |
| ❑ | 273 | Rich Butler RC | .10 | .05 |
| ❑ | 274 | Ben Ford RC | .20 | .09 |
| ❑ | 275 | Billy McMillon | .10 | .05 |
| ❑ | 276 | Wilson Delgado | .10 | .05 |
| ❑ | 277 | Orlando Cabrera | .10 | .05 |
| ❑ | 278 | Geoff Jenkins | .20 | .09 |
| ❑ | 279 | Enrique Wilson | .10 | .05 |
| ❑ | 280 | Derrek Lee | .10 | .05 |
| ❑ | 281 | Marc Pisciotta RC | .10 | .05 |
| ❑ | 282 | Abraham Nunez | .10 | .05 |
| ❑ | 283 | Aaron Boone | .10 | .05 |
| ❑ | 284 | Brad Fullmer | .20 | .09 |
| ❑ | 285 | Rob Stanifer RC | .10 | .05 |
| ❑ | 286 | Preston Wilson | .20 | .09 |
| ❑ | 287 | Greg Norton | .10 | .05 |
| ❑ | 288 | Bobby Smith | .10 | .05 |
| ❑ | 289 | Josh Booty | .10 | .05 |
| ❑ | 290 | Russell Branyan | .20 | .09 |
| ❑ | 291 | Jeremi Gonzalez | .10 | .05 |
| ❑ | 292 | Michael Coleman | .10 | .05 |
| ❑ | 293 | Cliff Politte | .10 | .05 |
| ❑ | 294 | Eric Ludwick | .10 | .05 |
| ❑ | 295 | Rafael Medina | .10 | .05 |
| ❑ | 296 | Jason Varitek | .20 | .09 |
| ❑ | 297 | Ron Wright | .10 | .05 |
| ❑ | 298 | Mark Kotsay | .20 | .09 |
| ❑ | 299 | David Ortiz | .10 | .05 |
| ❑ | 300 | Frank Catalanotto RC | .30 | .14 |
| ❑ | 301 | Robinson Checo | .10 | .05 |
| ❑ | 302 | Kevin Millwood RC | .75 | .35 |
| ❑ | 303 | Jacob Cruz | .10 | .05 |
| ❑ | 304 | Javier Vazquez | .10 | .05 |
| ❑ | 305 | Magglio Ordonez RC | 2.00 | .90 |
| ❑ | 306 | Kevin Witt | .10 | .05 |
| ❑ | 307 | Derrick Gibson | .10 | .05 |
| ❑ | 308 | Shane Monahan | .10 | .05 |
| ❑ | 309 | Brian Rose | .10 | .05 |
| ❑ | 310 | Bobby Estalella | .10 | .05 |
| ❑ | 311 | Felix Heredia | .10 | .05 |
| ❑ | 312 | Desi Relaford | .10 | .05 |
| ❑ | 313 | Esteban Yan RC | .30 | .14 |
| ❑ | 314 | Ricky Ledee | .10 | .05 |
| ❑ | 315 | Steve Woodard | .10 | .05 |
| ❑ | 316 | Pat Watkins | .10 | .05 |
| ❑ | 317 | Damian Moss | .10 | .05 |
| ❑ | 318 | Bob Abreu | .20 | .09 |
| ❑ | 319 | Jeff Abbott | .10 | .05 |
| ❑ | 320 | Miguel Cairo | .10 | .05 |
| ❑ | 321 | Rigo Beltran RC | .10 | .05 |
| ❑ | 322 | Tony Saunders | .10 | .05 |
| ❑ | 323 | Randall Simon | .10 | .05 |
| ❑ | 324 | Hiram Bocachica | .10 | .05 |
| ❑ | 325 | Richie Sexson | .30 | .14 |
| ❑ | 326 | Karim Garcia | .10 | .05 |
| ❑ | 327 | Mike Lowell RC | .60 | .25 |
| ❑ | 328 | Pat Cline | .10 | .05 |
| ❑ | 329 | Matt Clement | .20 | .09 |
| ❑ | 330 | Scott Elarton | .20 | .09 |
| ❑ | 331 | Manuel Barrios RC | .10 | .05 |
| ❑ | 332 | Bruce Chen | .10 | .05 |
| ❑ | 333 | Juan Encarnacion | .20 | .09 |
| ❑ | 334 | Travis Lee | .20 | .09 |
| ❑ | 335 | Wes Helms | .10 | .05 |
| ❑ | 336 | Chad Fox RC | .10 | .05 |
| ❑ | 337 | Donnie Sadler | .10 | .05 |
| ❑ | 338 | Carlos Mendoza RC | .20 | .09 |
| ❑ | 339 | Damian Jackson | .10 | .05 |
| ❑ | 340 | Julio Ramirez RC | .40 | .18 |
| ❑ | 341 | John Halama RC | .40 | .18 |
| ❑ | 342 | Edwin Diaz | .10 | .05 |
| ❑ | 343 | Felix Martinez | .10 | .05 |
| ❑ | 344 | Eli Marrero | .10 | .05 |
| ❑ | 345 | Carl Pavano | .10 | .05 |
| ❑ | 346 | Vladimir Guerrero HL | .30 | .14 |
| ❑ | 347 | Barry Bonds HL | .30 | .14 |
| ❑ | 348 | Darin Erstad HL | .20 | .09 |
| ❑ | 349 | Albert Belle HL | .10 | .05 |
| ❑ | 350 | Kenny Lofton HL | .10 | .05 |
| ❑ | 351 | Mo Vaughn HL | .20 | .09 |
| ❑ | 352 | Jose Cruz Jr. HL | .10 | .05 |
| ❑ | 353 | Tony Clark HL | .10 | .05 |
| ❑ | 354 | Roberto Alomar HL | .20 | .09 |
| ❑ | 355 | Manny Ramirez HL | .30 | .14 |
| ❑ | 356 | Paul Molitor HL | .20 | .09 |
| ❑ | 357 | Jim Thome HL | .10 | .05 |
| ❑ | 358 | Tino Martinez HL | .10 | .05 |
| ❑ | 359 | Tim Salmon HL | .10 | .05 |
| ❑ | 360 | David Justice HL | .10 | .05 |
| ❑ | 361 | Raul Mondesi HL | .10 | .05 |
| ❑ | 362 | Mark Grace HL | .20 | .09 |
| ❑ | 363 | Craig Biggio HL | .30 | .14 |
| ❑ | 364 | Larry Walker HL | .20 | .09 |
| ❑ | 365 | Mark McGwire HL | 1.00 | .45 |

| | Card | MINT | NRMT |
|---|---|---|---|
| ❑ | 366 Juan Gonzalez HL | .20 | .09 |
| ❑ | 367 Derek Jeter HL | 1.00 | .45 |
| ❑ | 368 Chipper Jones HL | .60 | .25 |
| ❑ | 369 Frank Thomas HL | .50 | .23 |
| ❑ | 370 Alex Rodriguez HL | .75 | .35 |
| ❑ | 371 Mike Piazza HL | .75 | .35 |
| ❑ | 372 Tony Gwynn HL | .50 | .23 |
| ❑ | 373 Jeff Bagwell HL | .30 | .14 |
| ❑ | 374 Nomar Garciaparra HL | .75 | .35 |
| ❑ | 375 Ken Griffey Jr. HL | 1.00 | .45 |
| ❑ | 376 Livan Hernandez UN | .10 | .05 |
| ❑ | 377 Chan Ho Park UN | .10 | .05 |
| ❑ | 378 Mike Mussina UN | .20 | .09 |
| ❑ | 379 Andy Pettitte UN | .10 | .05 |
| ❑ | 380 Greg Maddux UN | .60 | .25 |
| ❑ | 381 Hideo Nomo UN | .20 | .09 |
| ❑ | 382 Roger Clemens UN | .50 | .23 |
| ❑ | 383 Randy Johnson UN | .20 | .09 |
| ❑ | 384 Pedro Martinez UN | .30 | .14 |
| ❑ | 385 Jaret Wright UN | .10 | .05 |
| ❑ | 386 Ken Griffey Jr. SG | 1.00 | .45 |
| ❑ | 387 Todd Helton SG | .50 | .23 |
| ❑ | 388 Paul Konerko SG | .10 | .05 |
| ❑ | 389 Cal Ripken SG | 1.00 | .45 |
| ❑ | 390 Larry Walker SG | .20 | .09 |
| ❑ | 391 Ken Caminiti SG | .10 | .05 |
| ❑ | 392 Jose Guillen SG | .10 | .05 |
| ❑ | 393 Jim Edmonds SG | .50 | .23 |
| ❑ | 394 Barry Larkin SG | .20 | .09 |
| ❑ | 395 Bernie Williams SG | .20 | .09 |
| ❑ | 396 Tony Clark SG | .10 | .05 |
| ❑ | 397 Jose Cruz Jr. SG | .10 | .05 |
| ❑ | 398 Ivan Rodriguez SG | .30 | .14 |
| ❑ | 399 Darin Erstad SG | .20 | .09 |
| ❑ | 400 Scott Rolen SG | .50 | .23 |
| ❑ | 401 Mark McGwire SG | 1.00 | .45 |
| ❑ | 402 Andruw Jones SG | .20 | .09 |
| ❑ | 403 Juan Gonzalez SG | .20 | .09 |
| ❑ | 404 Derek Jeter SG | 1.00 | .45 |
| ❑ | 405 Chipper Jones SG | .60 | .25 |
| ❑ | 406 Greg Maddux SG | .60 | .25 |
| ❑ | 407 Frank Thomas SG | .50 | .23 |
| ❑ | 408 Alex Rodriguez SG | .75 | .35 |
| ❑ | 409 Mike Piazza SG | .75 | .35 |
| ❑ | 410 Tony Gwynn SG | .50 | .23 |
| ❑ | 411 Jeff Bagwell SG | .30 | .14 |
| ❑ | 412 Nomar Garciaparra SG | .75 | .35 |
| ❑ | 413 Hideo Nomo SG | .20 | .09 |
| ❑ | 414 Barry Bonds SG | .30 | .14 |
| ❑ | 415 Ben Grieve SG | .20 | .09 |
| ❑ | 416 Barry Bonds CL | .30 | .14 |
| ❑ | 417 Mark McGwire CL | 1.00 | .45 |
| ❑ | 418 Roger Clemens CL | .50 | .23 |
| ❑ | 419 Livan Hernandez CL | .10 | .05 |
| ❑ | 420 Ken Griffey Jr. CL | 1.00 | .45 |

## 1998 Donruss Collections Donruss

| | MINT | NRMT |
|---|---|---|
| COMPLETE SET (200) | 120.00 | 55.00 |
| COMMON (1-170/176-205) | .30 | .14 |

| | Card | MINT | NRMT |
|---|---|---|---|
| ❑ | 1 Paul Molitor | 1.25 | .55 |
| ❑ | 2 Juan Gonzalez | 1.25 | .55 |
| ❑ | 3 Darryl Kile | .50 | .23 |
| ❑ | 4 Randy Johnson | 1.50 | .70 |
| ❑ | 5 Tom Glavine | 1.25 | .55 |
| ❑ | 6 Pat Hentgen | .30 | .14 |
| ❑ | 7 David Justice | .75 | .35 |
| ❑ | 8 Kevin Brown | .75 | .35 |
| ❑ | 9 Mike Mussina | 1.25 | .55 |
| ❑ | 10 Ken Caminiti | .50 | .23 |
| ❑ | 11 Todd Hundley | .30 | .14 |
| ❑ | 12 Frank Thomas | 2.50 | 1.10 |
| ❑ | 13 Ray Lankford | .50 | .23 |
| ❑ | 14 Justin Thompson | .30 | .14 |
| ❑ | 15 Jason Dickson | .30 | .14 |
| ❑ | 16 Kenny Lofton | .50 | .23 |
| ❑ | 17 Ivan Rodriguez | 1.50 | .70 |
| ❑ | 18 Pedro Martinez | 1.50 | .70 |
| ❑ | 19 Brady Anderson | .50 | .23 |
| ❑ | 20 Barry Larkin | 1.25 | .55 |
| ❑ | 21 Chipper Jones | 3.00 | 1.35 |
| ❑ | 22 Tony Gwynn | 2.50 | 1.10 |
| ❑ | 23 Roger Clemens | 2.50 | 1.10 |
| ❑ | 24 Sandy Alomar Jr. | .50 | .23 |
| ❑ | 25 Tino Martinez | .50 | .23 |
| ❑ | 26 Jeff Bagwell | 1.50 | .70 |
| ❑ | 27 Shawn Estes | .30 | .14 |
| ❑ | 28 Ken Griffey Jr. | 5.00 | 2.20 |
| ❑ | 29 Javier Lopez | .50 | .23 |
| ❑ | 30 Denny Neagle | .30 | .14 |
| ❑ | 31 Mike Piazza | 4.00 | 1.80 |
| ❑ | 32 Andres Galarraga | .75 | .35 |
| ❑ | 33 Larry Walker | .50 | .23 |
| ❑ | 34 Alex Rodriguez | 4.00 | 1.80 |
| ❑ | 35 Greg Maddux | 3.00 | 1.35 |
| ❑ | 36 Albert Belle | .75 | .35 |
| ❑ | 37 Barry Bonds | 2.00 | .90 |
| ❑ | 38 Mo Vaughn | .50 | .23 |
| ❑ | 39 Kevin Appier | .50 | .23 |
| ❑ | 40 Wade Boggs | 1.50 | .70 |
| ❑ | 41 Garret Anderson | .50 | .23 |
| ❑ | 42 Jeffrey Hammonds | .50 | .23 |
| ❑ | 43 Marquis Grissom | .30 | .14 |
| ❑ | 44 Jim Edmonds | 1.25 | .55 |
| ❑ | 45 Brian Jordan | .50 | .23 |
| ❑ | 46 Raul Mondesi | .50 | .23 |
| ❑ | 47 John Valentin | .30 | .14 |
| ❑ | 48 Brad Radke | .50 | .23 |
| ❑ | 49 Ismael Valdes | .30 | .14 |
| ❑ | 50 Matt Stairs | .30 | .14 |
| ❑ | 51 Matt Williams | .75 | .35 |
| ❑ | 52 Reggie Jefferson | .30 | .14 |
| ❑ | 53 Alan Benes | .30 | .14 |
| ❑ | 54 Charles Johnson | .50 | .23 |
| ❑ | 55 Chuck Knoblauch | .50 | .23 |
| ❑ | 56 Edgar Martinez | .75 | .35 |
| ❑ | 57 Nomar Garciaparra | 4.00 | 1.80 |
| ❑ | 58 Craig Biggio | .75 | .35 |
| ❑ | 59 Bernie Williams | 1.25 | .55 |
| ❑ | 60 David Cone | .50 | .23 |
| ❑ | 61 Cal Ripken | 5.00 | 2.20 |
| ❑ | 62 Mark McGwire | 5.00 | 2.20 |
| ❑ | 63 Roberto Alomar | 1.25 | .55 |
| ❑ | 64 Fred McGriff | .75 | .35 |
| ❑ | 65 Eric Karros | .50 | .23 |
| ❑ | 66 Robin Ventura | .50 | .23 |
| ❑ | 67 Darin Erstad | 1.25 | .55 |
| ❑ | 68 Michael Tucker | .30 | .14 |
| ❑ | 69 Jim Thome | .75 | .35 |
| ❑ | 70 Mark Grace | 1.25 | .55 |
| ❑ | 71 Lou Collier | .30 | .14 |
| ❑ | 72 Karim Garcia | .30 | .14 |
| ❑ | 73 Alex Fernandez | .30 | .14 |
| ❑ | 74 J.T. Snow | .50 | .23 |
| ❑ | 75 Reggie Sanders | .30 | .14 |
| ❑ | 76 John Smoltz | .50 | .23 |
| ❑ | 77 Tim Salmon | .50 | .23 |
| ❑ | 78 Paul O'Neill | .50 | .23 |
| ❑ | 79 Vinny Castilla | .50 | .23 |
| ❑ | 80 Rafael Palmeiro | 1.25 | .55 |
| ❑ | 81 Jaret Wright | .30 | .14 |
| ❑ | 82 Jay Buhner | .50 | .23 |
| ❑ | 83 Brett Butler | .50 | .23 |
| ❑ | 84 Todd Greene | .30 | .14 |
| ❑ | 85 Scott Rolen | 1.25 | .55 |
| ❑ | 86 Sammy Sosa | 2.50 | 1.10 |
| ❑ | 87 Jason Giambi | 1.25 | .55 |
| ❑ | 88 Carlos Delgado | 1.25 | .55 |
| ❑ | 89 Deion Sanders | .50 | .23 |
| ❑ | 90 Wilton Guerrero | .30 | .14 |
| ❑ | 91 Andy Pettitte | .50 | .23 |
| ❑ | 92 Brian Giles | .50 | .23 |
| ❑ | 93 Dmitri Young | .50 | .23 |
| ❑ | 94 Ron Coomer | .30 | .14 |
| ❑ | 95 Mike Cameron | .50 | .23 |
| ❑ | 96 Edgardo Alfonzo | .50 | .23 |
| ❑ | 97 Jimmy Key | .50 | .23 |
| ❑ | 98 Ryan Klesko | .50 | .23 |
| ❑ | 99 Andy Benes | .30 | .14 |
| ❑ | 100 Derek Jeter | 5.00 | 2.20 |
| ❑ | 101 Jeff Fassero | .30 | .14 |
| ❑ | 102 Neifi Perez | .30 | .14 |
| ❑ | 103 Hideo Nomo | 1.25 | .55 |
| ❑ | 104 Andruw Jones | 1.25 | .55 |
| ❑ | 105 Todd Helton | 1.50 | .70 |
| ❑ | 106 Livan Hernandez | .30 | .14 |
| ❑ | 107 Brett Tomko | .30 | .14 |
| ❑ | 108 Shannon Stewart | .50 | .23 |
| ❑ | 109 Bartolo Colon | .50 | .23 |
| ❑ | 110 Matt Morris | .30 | .14 |
| ❑ | 111 Miguel Tejada | 1.25 | .55 |
| ❑ | 112 Pokey Reese | .50 | .23 |
| ❑ | 113 Fernando Tatis | .50 | .23 |
| ❑ | 114 Todd Dunwoody | .30 | .14 |
| ❑ | 115 Jose Cruz Jr. | .50 | .23 |
| ❑ | 116 Chan Ho Park | .50 | .23 |
| ❑ | 117 Kevin Young | .50 | .23 |
| ❑ | 118 Rickey Henderson | 1.50 | .70 |
| ❑ | 119 Hideki Irabu | .30 | .14 |
| ❑ | 120 Francisco Cordova | .30 | .14 |
| ❑ | 121 Al Martin | .30 | .14 |
| ❑ | 122 Tony Clark | .30 | .14 |
| ❑ | 123 Curt Schilling | .50 | .23 |
| ❑ | 124 Rusty Greer | .50 | .23 |
| ❑ | 125 Jose Canseco | 1.50 | .70 |
| ❑ | 126 Edgar Renteria | .30 | .14 |
| ❑ | 127 Todd Walker | .30 | .14 |
| ❑ | 128 Wally Joyner | .50 | .23 |
| ❑ | 129 Bill Mueller | .30 | .14 |
| ❑ | 130 Jose Guillen | .30 | .14 |
| ❑ | 131 Manny Ramirez | 1.50 | .70 |
| ❑ | 132 Bobby Higginson | .50 | .23 |
| ❑ | 133 Kevin Orie | .30 | .14 |
| ❑ | 134 Will Clark | 1.25 | .55 |
| ❑ | 135 Dave Nilsson | .30 | .14 |
| ❑ | 136 Jason Kendall | .50 | .23 |
| ❑ | 137 Ivan Cruz | .30 | .14 |
| ❑ | 138 Gary Sheffield | 1.25 | .55 |
| ❑ | 139 Bubba Trammell | .30 | .14 |
| ❑ | 140 Vladimir Guerrero | 2.00 | .90 |
| ❑ | 141 Dennis Reyes | .30 | .14 |
| ❑ | 142 Bobby Bonilla | .50 | .23 |
| ❑ | 143 Ruben Rivera | .30 | .14 |
| ❑ | 144 Ben Grieve | .50 | .23 |
| ❑ | 145 Moises Alou | .50 | .23 |
| ❑ | 146 Tony Womack | .30 | .14 |
| ❑ | 147 Eric Young | .30 | .14 |
| ❑ | 148 Paul Konerko | .50 | .23 |
| ❑ | 149 Dante Bichette | .50 | .23 |
| ❑ | 150 Joe Carter | .50 | .23 |
| ❑ | 151 Rondell White | .50 | .23 |
| ❑ | 152 Chris Holt | .30 | .14 |
| ❑ | 153 Shawn Green | 1.25 | .55 |
| ❑ | 154 Mark Grudzielanek | .30 | .14 |
| ❑ | 155 Jermaine Dye | .50 | .23 |
| ❑ | 156 Ken Griffey Jr. FC | 2.50 | 1.10 |
| ❑ | 157 Frank Thomas FC | 1.25 | .55 |
| ❑ | 158 Chipper Jones FC | 1.50 | .70 |
| ❑ | 159 Mike Piazza FC | 2.00 | .90 |
| ❑ | 160 Cal Ripken FC | 2.50 | 1.10 |
| ❑ | 161 Greg Maddux FC | 1.50 | .70 |
| ❑ | 162 Juan Gonzalez FC | .50 | .23 |
| ❑ | 163 Alex Rodriguez FC | 2.00 | .90 |
| ❑ | 164 Mark McGwire FC | 2.50 | 1.10 |
| ❑ | 165 Derek Jeter FC | 2.50 | 1.10 |
| ❑ | 166 Larry Walker CL | .50 | .23 |
| ❑ | 167 Tony Gwynn CL | 1.25 | .55 |
| ❑ | 168 Tino Martinez CL | .30 | .14 |
| ❑ | 169 Scott Rolen CL | 1.25 | .55 |
| ❑ | 170 Nomar Garciaparra CL | 2.00 | .90 |
| ❑ | 176 Mark Kotsay RR | .50 | .23 |
| ❑ | 177 Neifi Perez RR | .30 | .14 |
| ❑ | 178 Paul Konerko RR | .50 | .23 |
| ❑ | 179 Jose Cruz Jr. RR | .50 | .23 |
| ❑ | 180 Hideki Irabu RR | .30 | .14 |
| ❑ | 181 Mike Cameron RR | .50 | .23 |
| ❑ | 182 Jeff Suppan RR | .30 | .14 |

- ❑ 183 Kevin Orie RR .30 .14
- ❑ 184 Pokey Reese RR .50 .23
- ❑ 185 Todd Dunwoody RR .30 .14
- ❑ 186 Miguel Tejada RR 1.25 .55
- ❑ 187 Jose Guillen RR .30 .14
- ❑ 188 Bartolo Colon RR .50 .23
- ❑ 189 Derrek Lee RR .30 .14
- ❑ 190 Antone Williamson RR .30 .14
- ❑ 191 Wilton Guerrero RR .30 .14
- ❑ 192 Jaret Wright RR .30 .14
- ❑ 193 Todd Helton RR 1.50 .70
- ❑ 194 Shannon Stewart RR .50 .23
- ❑ 195 Nomar Garciaparra RR 4.00 1.80
- ❑ 196 Brett Tomko RR .30 .14
- ❑ 197 Fernando Tatis RR .50 .23
- ❑ 198 Raul Ibanez RR .30 .14
- ❑ 199 Dennis Reyes RR .30 .14
- ❑ 200 Bobby Estalella RR .30 .14
- ❑ 201 Lou Collier RR .30 .14
- ❑ 202 Bubba Trammell RR .30 .14
- ❑ 203 Ben Grieve RR .50 .23
- ❑ 204 Ivan Cruz RR .30 .14
- ❑ 205 Karim Garcia RR .30 .14

## 1997 Donruss Elite

| | MINT | NRMT |
|---|---|---|
| COMPLETE SET (150) | 40.00 | 18.00 |
| COMMON CARD (1-150) | .20 | .09 |

- ❑ 1 Juan Gonzalez .75 .35
- ❑ 2 Alex Rodriguez 2.50 1.10
- ❑ 3 Frank Thomas 1.50 .70
- ❑ 4 Greg Maddux 2.00 .90
- ❑ 5 Ken Griffey Jr. 3.00 1.35
- ❑ 6 Cal Ripken 3.00 1.35
- ❑ 7 Mike Piazza 2.50 1.10
- ❑ 8 Chipper Jones 2.00 .90
- ❑ 9 Albert Belle .50 .23
- ❑ 10 Andruw Jones 1.00 .45
- ❑ 11 Vladimir Guerrero 1.50 .70
- ❑ 12 Mo Vaughn .40 .18 (UER front Gonzales)
- ❑ 13 Ivan Rodriguez 1.00 .45
- ❑ 14 Andy Pettitte .40 .18
- ❑ 15 Tony Gwynn 1.50 .70
- ❑ 16 Barry Bonds 1.25 .55
- ❑ 17 Jeff Bagwell 1.00 .45
- ❑ 18 Manny Ramirez 1.00 .45
- ❑ 19 Kenny Lofton .40 .18
- ❑ 20 Roberto Alomar .75 .35
- ❑ 21 Mark McGwire 3.00 1.35
- ❑ 22 Ryan Klesko .40 .18
- ❑ 23 Tim Salmon .40 .18
- ❑ 24 Derek Jeter 3.00 1.35
- ❑ 25 Eddie Murray .75 .35
- ❑ 26 Jermaine Dye .40 .18
- ❑ 27 Ruben Rivera .20 .09
- ❑ 28 Jim Edmonds .75 .35
- ❑ 29 Mike Mussina .75 .35
- ❑ 30 Randy Johnson 1.00 .45
- ❑ 31 Sammy Sosa 1.50 .70
- ❑ 32 Hideo Nomo .75 .35
- ❑ 33 Chuck Knoblauch .40 .18
- ❑ 34 Paul Molitor .75 .35
- ❑ 35 Rafael Palmeiro .75 .35
- ❑ 36 Brady Anderson .40 .18
- ❑ 37 Will Clark .75 .35
- ❑ 38 Craig Biggio .50 .23
- ❑ 39 Jason Giambi .75 .35
- ❑ 40 Roger Clemens 1.50 .70
- ❑ 41 Jay Buhner .40 .18
- ❑ 42 Edgar Martinez .50 .23
- ❑ 43 Gary Sheffield .75 .35
- ❑ 44 Fred McGriff .50 .23
- ❑ 45 Bobby Bonilla .40 .18
- ❑ 46 Tom Glavine .75 .35
- ❑ 47 Wade Boggs 1.00 .45
- ❑ 48 Jeff Conine .20 .09
- ❑ 49 John Smoltz .40 .18
- ❑ 50 Jim Thome .50 .23
- ❑ 51 Billy Wagner .20 .09
- ❑ 52 Jose Canseco 1.00 .45
- ❑ 53 Javy Lopez .40 .18
- ❑ 54 Cecil Fielder .40 .18
- ❑ 55 Garret Anderson .40 .18
- ❑ 56 Alex Ochoa .20 .09
- ❑ 57 Scott Rolen .75 .35
- ❑ 58 Darin Erstad 1.00 .45
- ❑ 59 Rey Ordonez .20 .09
- ❑ 60 Dante Bichette .40 .18
- ❑ 61 Joe Carter .40 .18
- ❑ 62 Moises Alou .40 .18
- ❑ 63 Jason Isringhausen .20 .09
- ❑ 64 Karim Garcia .20 .09
- ❑ 65 Brian Jordan .40 .18
- ❑ 66 Ruben Sierra .20 .09
- ❑ 67 Todd Hollandsworth .20 .09
- ❑ 68 Paul Wilson .20 .09
- ❑ 69 Ernie Young .20 .09
- ❑ 70 Ryne Sandberg 1.00 .45
- ❑ 71 Raul Mondesi .40 .18
- ❑ 72 George Arias .20 .09
- ❑ 73 Ray Durham .40 .18
- ❑ 74 Dean Palmer .40 .18
- ❑ 75 Shawn Green .75 .35
- ❑ 76 Eric Young .20 .09
- ❑ 77 Jason Kendall .40 .18
- ❑ 78 Greg Vaughn .40 .18
- ❑ 79 Terrell Wade .20 .09
- ❑ 80 Bill Pulsipher .20 .09
- ❑ 81 Bobby Higginson .40 .18
- ❑ 82 Mark Grudzielanek .20 .09
- ❑ 83 Ken Caminiti .40 .18
- ❑ 84 Todd Greene .20 .09
- ❑ 85 Carlos Delgado .75 .35
- ❑ 86 Mark Grace .75 .35
- ❑ 87 Rondell White .40 .18
- ❑ 88 Barry Larkin .75 .35
- ❑ 89 J.T. Snow .40 .18
- ❑ 90 Alex Gonzalez .20 .09
- ❑ 91 Raul Casanova .20 .09
- ❑ 92 Marc Newfield .20 .09
- ❑ 93 Jermaine Allensworth .20 .09
- ❑ 94 John Mabry .20 .09
- ❑ 95 Kirby Puckett 2.00 .90
- ❑ 96 Travis Fryman .40 .18
- ❑ 97 Kevin Brown .50 .23
- ❑ 98 Andres Galarraga .50 .23
- ❑ 99 Marty Cordova .20 .09
- ❑ 100 Henry Rodriguez .20 .09
- ❑ 101 Sterling Hitchcock .20 .09
- ❑ 102 Trey Beamon .20 .09
- ❑ 103 Brett Butler .40 .18
- ❑ 104 Rickey Henderson 1.00 .45
- ❑ 105 Tino Martinez .40 .18
- ❑ 106 Kevin Appier .40 .18
- ❑ 107 Brian Hunter .20 .09
- ❑ 108 Eric Karros .40 .18
- ❑ 109 Andre Dawson .50 .23
- ❑ 110 Darryl Strawberry .40 .18
- ❑ 111 James Baldwin .40 .18
- ❑ 112 Chad Mottola .20 .09
- ❑ 113 Dave Nilsson .20 .09
- ❑ 114 Carlos Baerga .20 .09
- ❑ 115 Chan Ho Park .40 .18
- ❑ 116 John Jaha .20 .09
- ❑ 117 Alan Benes .20 .09
- ❑ 118 Mariano Rivera .40 .18
- ❑ 119 Ellis Burks .40 .18
- ❑ 120 Tony Clark .20 .09
- ❑ 121 Todd Walker .20 .09
- ❑ 122 Dwight Gooden .40 .18
- ❑ 123 Ugueth Urbina .40 .18
- ❑ 124 David Cone .40 .18
- ❑ 125 Ozzie Smith 1.00 .45
- ❑ 126 Kimera Bartee .20 .09
- ❑ 127 Rusty Greer .40 .18
- ❑ 128 Pat Hentgen .20 .09
- ❑ 129 Charles Johnson .40 .18
- ❑ 130 Quinton McCracken .20 .09
- ❑ 131 Troy Percival .20 .09
- ❑ 132 Shane Reynolds .20 .09
- ❑ 133 Charles Nagy .20 .09
- ❑ 134 Tom Goodwin .20 .09
- ❑ 135 Ron Gant .20 .09
- ❑ 136 Dan Wilson .20 .09
- ❑ 137 Matt Williams .50 .23
- ❑ 138 LaTroy Hawkins .20 .09
- ❑ 139 Kevin Seitzer .20 .09
- ❑ 140 Michael Tucker .20 .09
- ❑ 141 Todd Hundley .20 .09
- ❑ 142 Alex Fernandez .20 .09
- ❑ 143 Marquis Grissom .20 .09
- ❑ 144 Steve Finley .40 .18
- ❑ 145 Curtis Pride .20 .09
- ❑ 146 Derek Bell .20 .09
- ❑ 147 Butch Huskey .20 .09
- ❑ 148 Dwight Gooden CL .40 .18
- ❑ 149 Al Leiter CL .40 .18
- ❑ 150 Hideo Nomo CL .40 .18

## 1998 Donruss Elite

| | MINT | NRMT |
|---|---|---|
| COMPLETE SET (150) | 30.00 | 13.50 |

- ❑ 1 Ken Griffey Jr. 2.50 1.10
- ❑ 2 Frank Thomas 1.25 .55
- ❑ 3 Alex Rodriguez 2.00 .90
- ❑ 4 Mike Piazza 2.00 .90
- ❑ 5 Greg Maddux 1.50 .70
- ❑ 6 Cal Ripken 2.50 1.10
- ❑ 7 Chipper Jones 1.50 .70
- ❑ 8 Derek Jeter 2.50 1.10
- ❑ 9 Tony Gwynn 1.25 .55
- ❑ 10 Andruw Jones .60 .25
- ❑ 11 Juan Gonzalez .60 .25
- ❑ 12 Jeff Bagwell .75 .35
- ❑ 13 Mark McGwire 2.50 1.10
- ❑ 14 Roger Clemens 1.25 .55
- ❑ 15 Albert Belle .40 .18
- ❑ 16 Barry Bonds 1.00 .45
- ❑ 17 Kenny Lofton .25 .11
- ❑ 18 Ivan Rodriguez .75 .35
- ❑ 19 Manny Ramirez .75 .35
- ❑ 20 Jim Thome .40 .18
- ❑ 21 Chuck Knoblauch .25 .11
- ❑ 22 Paul Molitor .60 .25
- ❑ 23 Barry Larkin .60 .25
- ❑ 24 Andy Pettitte .25 .11
- ❑ 25 John Smoltz .25 .11
- ❑ 26 Randy Johnson .75 .35
- ❑ 27 Bernie Williams .60 .25
- ❑ 28 Larry Walker .25 .11
- ❑ 29 Mo Vaughn .25 .11
- ❑ 30 Bobby Higginson .25 .11
- ❑ 31 Edgardo Alfonzo .25 .11
- ❑ 32 Justin Thompson .15 .07
- ❑ 33 Jeff Suppan .15 .07
- ❑ 34 Roberto Alomar .60 .25
- ❑ 35 Hideo Nomo .60 .25

❑ 36 Rusty Greer .25 .11
❑ 37 Tim Salmon .25 .11
❑ 38 Jim Edmonds .25 .11
❑ 39 Gary Sheffield .60 .25
❑ 40 Ken Caminiti .25 .11
❑ 41 Sammy Sosa 1.25 .55
❑ 42 Tony Womack .15 .07
❑ 43 Matt Williams .40 .18
❑ 44 Andres Galarraga .40 .18
❑ 45 Garret Anderson .25 .11
❑ 46 Rafael Palmeiro .60 .25
❑ 47 Mike Mussina .60 .25
❑ 48 Craig Biggio .40 .18
❑ 49 Wade Boggs .75 .35
❑ 50 Tom Glavine .60 .25
❑ 51 Jason Giambi .60 .25
❑ 52 Will Clark .60 .25
❑ 53 David Justice .40 .18
❑ 54 Sandy Alomar Jr. .25 .11
❑ 55 Edgar Martinez .40 .18
❑ 56 Brady Anderson .25 .11
❑ 57 Eric Young .15 .07
❑ 58 Ray Lankford .25 .11
❑ 59 Kevin Brown .40 .18
❑ 60 Raul Mondesi .25 .11
❑ 61 Bobby Bonilla .25 .11
❑ 62 Javier Lopez .25 .11
❑ 63 Fred McGriff .40 .18
❑ 64 Rondell White .25 .11
❑ 65 Todd Hundley .15 .07
❑ 66 Mark Grace .60 .25
❑ 67 Alan Benes .15 .07
❑ 68 Jeff Abbott .15 .07
❑ 69 Bob Abreu .25 .11
❑ 70 Deion Sanders .25 .11
❑ 71 Tino Martinez .25 .11
❑ 72 Shannon Stewart .25 .11
❑ 73 Homer Bush .15 .07
❑ 74 Carlos Delgado .60 .25
❑ 75 Raul Ibanez .15 .07
❑ 76 Hideki Irabu .15 .07
❑ 77 Jose Cruz Jr. .25 .11
❑ 78 Tony Clark .15 .07
❑ 79 Wilton Guerrero .15 .07
❑ 80 Vladimir Guerrero 1.00 .45
❑ 81 Scott Rolen .60 .25
❑ 82 Nomar Garciaparra 2.00 .90
❑ 83 Darin Erstad .60 .25
❑ 84 Chan Ho Park .25 .11
❑ 85 Mike Cameron .25 .11
❑ 86 Todd Walker .15 .07
❑ 87 Todd Dunwoody .15 .07
❑ 88 Neifi Perez .15 .07
❑ 89 Brett Tomko .15 .07
❑ 90 Jose Guillen .15 .07
❑ 91 Matt Morris .15 .07
❑ 92 Bartolo Colon .25 .11
❑ 93 Jaret Wright .15 .07
❑ 94 Shawn Estes .15 .07
❑ 95 Livan Hernandez .15 .07
❑ 96 Bobby Estalella .15 .07
❑ 97 Ben Grieve .25 .11
❑ 98 Paul Konerko .25 .11
❑ 99 David Ortiz .15 .07
❑ 100 Todd Helton .75 .35
❑ 101 Juan Encarnacion .25 .11
❑ 102 Bubba Trammell .15 .07
❑ 103 Miguel Tejada .60 .25
❑ 104 Jacob Cruz .15 .07
❑ 105 Todd Greene .15 .07
❑ 106 Kevin Orie .15 .07
❑ 107 Mark Kotsay .25 .11
❑ 108 Fernando Tatis .25 .11
❑ 109 Jay Payton .25 .11
❑ 110 Pokey Reese .25 .11
❑ 111 Derrek Lee .15 .07
❑ 112 Richard Hidalgo .25 .11
❑ 113 Ricky Ledee .15 .07
(UER front Rickey)
❑ 114 Lou Collier .15 .07
❑ 115 Ruben Rivera .15 .07
❑ 116 Shawn Green .60 .25
❑ 117 Moises Alou .25 .11
❑ 118 Ken Griffey Jr. GEN 1.25 .55
❑ 119 Frank Thomas GEN .60 .25
❑ 120 Alex Rodriguez GEN 1.00 .45
❑ 121 Mike Piazza GEN 1.00 .45
❑ 122 Greg Maddux GEN .75 .35
❑ 123 Cal Ripken GEN 1.25 .55
❑ 124 Chipper Jones GEN .75 .35
❑ 125 Derek Jeter GEN 1.25 .55
❑ 126 Tony Gwynn GEN .60 .25
❑ 127 Andruw Jones GEN .25 .11
❑ 128 Juan Gonzalez GEN .25 .11
❑ 129 Jeff Bagwell GEN .40 .18
❑ 130 Mark McGwire GEN 1.25 .55
❑ 131 Roger Clemens GEN .60 .25
❑ 132 Albert Belle GEN .15 .07
❑ 133 Barry Bonds GEN .40 .18
❑ 134 Kenny Lofton GEN .15 .07
❑ 135 Ivan Rodriguez GEN .40 .18
❑ 136 Manny Ramirez GEN .40 .18
❑ 137 Jim Thome GEN .15 .07
❑ 138 Chuck Knoblauch GEN .15 .07
❑ 139 Paul Molitor GEN .25 .11
❑ 140 Barry Larkin GEN .25 .11
❑ 141 Mo Vaughn GEN .25 .11
❑ 142 Hideki Irabu GEN .15 .07
❑ 143 Jose Cruz Jr. GEN .15 .07
❑ 144 Tony Clark GEN .15 .07
❑ 145 Vladimir Guerrero GEN .40 .18
❑ 146 Scott Rolen GEN .60 .25
❑ 147 Nomar Garciaparra GEN 1.00 .45
❑ 148 Nomar Garciaparra CL 1.00 .45
❑ 149 Larry Walker CL .25 .11
❑ 150 Tino Martinez CL .15 .07
❑ AU2 F.Thomas AUTO/100 250.00 110.00

## 1997 Donruss Limited

| | MINT | NRMT |
|---|---|---|
| COMP.COUNTER SET (100) | 25.00 | 11.00 |
| COMMON COUNTERPART | .15 | .07 |
| COUNTERPART UNLISTED | .60 | .25 |
| COMP.DOUBLE SET (40) | 60.00 | 27.00 |
| COMMON DOUBLE TEAM | 1.25 | .55 |
| COMP.STAR FACT.SET (40) | 400.00 | 180.00 |
| COMMON STAR FACTOR | 3.00 | 1.35 |
| COMP.UNLIMITED SET (20) | 250.00 | 110.00 |
| COMMON UNLIMITED | 2.50 | 1.10 |

❑ 1 Ken Griffey Jr. C 2.50 1.10
Rondell White
❑ 2 Greg Maddux C 1.50 .70
David Cone
❑ 3 Gary Sheffield D 3.00 1.35
Moises Alou
❑ 4 Frank Thomas S 15.00 6.75
❑ 5 Cal Ripken C 2.50 1.10
Kevin Orie
❑ 6 Vladimir Guerrero U 10.00 4.50
Barry Bonds
❑ 7 Eddie Murray C .60 .25
Reggie Jefferson
❑ 8 Manny Ramirez D 4.00 1.80
Marquis Grissom
❑ 9 Mike Piazza S 25.00 11.00
❑ 10 Barry Larkin C .60 .25
Rey Ordonez
❑ 11 Jeff Bagwell C .75 .35
Eric Karros
❑ 12 Chuck Knoblauch C .25 .11
Ray Durham
❑ 13 Alex Rodriguez C 2.00 .90
Edgar Renteria
❑ 14 Matt Williams C .40 .18
Vinny Castilla
❑ 15 Todd Hollandsworth C .25 .11
Bob Abreu
❑ 16 John Smoltz C .75 .35
Pedro Martinez
❑ 17 Jose Canseco C .75 .35
Chili Davis
❑ 18 Jose Cruz Jr. U 25.00 11.00
Ken Griffey Jr.
❑ 19 Ken Griffey Jr. S 30.00 13.50
❑ 20 Paul Molitor C .60 .25
John Olerud
❑ 21 Roberto Alomar C .60 .25
Luis Castillo
❑ 22 Derek Jeter C 2.00 .90
Lou Collier
❑ 23 Chipper Jones C 1.50 .70
Robin Ventura
❑ 24 Gary Sheffield C .60 .25
Ron Gant
❑ 25 Ramon Martinez C .15 .07
Bobby Jones
❑ 26 Mike Piazza D 10.00 4.50
Raul Mondesi
❑ 27 Darin Erstad U 8.00 3.60
Jeff Bagwell
❑ 28 Ivan Rodriguez S 10.00 4.50
❑ 29 J.T.Snow C .25 .11
Kevin Young
❑ 30 Ryne Sandberg C .75 .35
Julio Franco
❑ 31 Travis Fryman C .25 .11
Chris Snopek
❑ 32 Wade Boggs C .75 .35
Russ Davis
❑ 33 Brooks Kieschnick C .15 .07
Marty Cordova
❑ 34 Andy Pettitte C .25 .11
Denny Neagle
❑ 35 Paul Molitor D 3.00 1.35
Matt Lawton
❑ 36 Scott Rolen U 25.00 11.00
Cal Ripken
❑ 37 Cal Ripken S 30.00 13.50
❑ 38 Jim Thome C .40 .18
Dave Nilsson
❑ 39 Tony Womack RC C .75 .35
Carlos Baerga
❑ 40 Nomar Garciaparra C 2.00 .90
Mark Grudzielanek
❑ 41 Todd Greene C .15 .07
Chris Widger
❑ 42 Deion Sanders C .25 .11
Bernard Gilkey
❑ 43 Hideo Nomo C 1.00 .45
Charles Nagy
❑ 44 Ivan Rodriguez D 4.00 1.80
Rusty Greer
❑ 45 Todd Walker U 12.00 5.50
Chipper Jones
❑ 46 Greg Maddux S 20.00 9.00
❑ 47 Mo Vaughn C .25 .11
Cecil Fielder
❑ 48 Craig Biggio C .40 .18
Scott Spiezio
❑ 49 Pokey Reese C .25 .11
Jeff Blauser
❑ 50 Ken Caminiti C .25 .11
Joe Randa
❑ 51 Albert Belle C .40 .18
Shawn Green
❑ 52 Randy Johnson C .75 .35
Jason Dickson
❑ 53 Hideo Nomo D 6.00 2.70
Chan Ho Park
❑ 54 Scott Spiezio U 2.50 1.10
Chuck Knoblauch
❑ 55 Chipper Jones S 20.00 9.00
❑ 56 Tino Martinez C .25 .11
Ryan McGuire
❑ 57 Eric Young C .15 .07
Wilton Guerrero
❑ 58 Ron Coomer C .15 .07
Dave Hollins

❑ 59 Sammy Sosa C ............ 1.25 .55
Angel Echevarria
❑ 60 Dennis Reyes RC C ........ .50 .23
Jimmy Key
❑ 61 Barry Larkin D ............... 3.00 1.35
Deion Sanders
❑ 62 Wilton Guerrero U ......... 6.00 2.70
Roberto Alomar
❑ 63 Albert Belle S ............... 5.00 2.20
❑ 64 Mark McGwire C ............ 2.50 1.10
Andre Galarraga
❑ 65 Edgar Martinez C ........... .40 .18
Todd Walker
❑ 66 Steve Finley C................. .25 .11
Rich Becker
❑ 67 Tom Glavine C ............... .60 .25
Andy Ashby
❑ 68 Sammy Sosa D ............. 6.00 2.70
Ryne Sandberg
❑ 69 Nomar Garciaparra U .. 20.00 9.00
Alex Rodriguez
❑ 70 Jeff Bagwell S ............. 10.00 4.50
❑ 71 Darin Erstad C................. .75 .35
Mark Grace
❑ 72 Scott Rolen C ................. .60 .25
Edgardo Alfonzo
❑ 73 Kenny Lofton C ............... .25 .11
Lance Johnson
❑ 74 Joey Hamilton C .............. .15 .07
Brett Tomko
❑ 75 Eddie Murray D .............. 3.00 1.35
Tim Salmon
❑ 76 Dmitri Young U ............... .25 .11
Mo Vaughn
❑ 77 Juan Gonzalez S ............ 8.00 3.60
❑ 78 Frank Thomas C ........... 1.25 .55
Tony Clark
❑ 79 Shannon Stewart C.......... .25 .11
Bip Roberts
❑ 80 Shawn Estes C ............... .15 .07
Alex Fernandez
❑ 81 John Smoltz D................ 1.25 .55
Javier Lopez
❑ 82 Todd Greene U ............ 15.00 6.75
Mike Piazza
❑ 83 Derek Jeter S ............. 30.00 13.50
❑ 84 Dmitri Young C .............. .25 .11
Antone Williamson
❑ 85 Rickey Henderson C ........ .75 .35
Darryl Hamilton
❑ 86 Billy Wagner C ............... .25 .11
Dennis Eckersley
❑ 87 Larry Walker D .............. 1.25 .55
Eric Young
❑ 88 Mark Kotsay RC U ........ 5.00 2.20
Juan Gonzalez
❑ 89 Barry Bonds S............. 12.00 5.50
❑ 90 Will Clark C .................... .60 .25
Jeff Conine
❑ 91 Tony Gwynn C ............... 1.25 .55
Brett Butler
❑ 92 John Wetteland C ............ .25 .11
Rod Beck
❑ 93 Bernie Williams D .......... 3.00 1.35
Tony Martinez
❑ 94 Andruw Jones U ............ 8.00 3.60
Kenny Lofton
❑ 95 Mo Vaughn S ................ 3.00 1.35
❑ 96 Joe Carter C .................... .25 .11
Derrek Lee
❑ 97 John Mabry C .................. .15 .07
F.P. Santangelo
❑ 98 Esteban Loaiza C ............ .15 .07
Wilson Alvarez
❑ 99 Matt Williams D ............. 2.00 .90
David Justice
❑ 100 Derrek Lee U.............. 10.00 4.50
Frank Thomas
❑ 101 Mark McGwire S ........ 30.00 13.50
❑ 102 Fred McGriff C............... .40 .18
Paul Sorrento
❑ 103 Jermaine Allensworth C .60 .25
Bernie Williams
❑ 104 Ismael Valdes C ............ .15 .07
Chris Holt
❑ 105 Fred McGriff D............. 2.00 .90
Ryan Klesko
❑ 106 Tony Clark U ............. 20.00 9.00
Mark McGwire
❑ 107 Tony Gwynn S........... 15.00 6.75
❑ 108 Jeffrey Hammonds C .... .25 .11
Ellis Burks
❑ 109 Shane Reynolds C ........ .15 .07
Andy Benes
❑ 110 Roger Clemens D ....... 6.00 2.70
Carlos Delgado
❑ 111 Karim Garcia U ........... 4.00 1.80
Albert Belle
❑ 112 Paul Molitor S ............. 8.00 3.60
❑ 113 Trey Beamon C............. .15 .07
Eric Owens
❑ 114 Curt Schilling C ............ .25 .11
Darryl Kile
❑ 115 Tom Glavine D ............ 3.00 1.35
Michael Tucker
❑ 116 Pokey Reese U .......... 20.00 9.00
Derek Jeter
❑ 117 Manny Ramirez S ...... 10.00 4.50
❑ 118 Juan Gonzalez C............ .60 .25
Brant Brown
❑ 119 Juan Guzman C ............ .15 .07
Francisco Cordova
❑ 120 Randy Johnson D ....... 4.00 1.80
Edgar Martinez
❑ 121 Hideki Irabu U ........... 12.00 5.50
Greg Maddux
❑ 122 Alex Rodriguez S ...... 30.00 13.50
❑ 123 Barry Bonds C............. 1.00 .45
Quinton McCracken
❑ 124 Roger Clemens C ......... 1.25 .55
Andy Benes
❑ 125 Wade Boggs D ............ 4.00 1.80
Paul O'Neill
❑ 126 Mike Cameron U ......... 2.50 1.10
Larry Walker
❑ 127 Gary Sheffield S .......... 8.00 3.60
❑ 128 Andruw Jones C ............ .75 .35
Raul Mondesi
❑ 129 Brady Anderson C.......... .25 .11
Terrell Wade
❑ 130 Brady Anderson D........ 3.00 1.35
Rafael Palmeiro
❑ 131 Neifi Perez U............... 6.00 2.70
Barry Larkin
❑ 132 Ken Caminiti S ............ 3.00 1.35
❑ 133 Larry Walker C .............. .25 .11
Rusty Greer
❑ 134 Mariano Rivera C .......... .25 .11
Mark Wohlers
❑ 135 Hideki Irabu RC D........ 2.50 1.10
Andy Pettitte
❑ 136 Jose Guillen U........... 10.00 4.50
Tony Gwynn
❑ 137 Hideo Nomo S.............. 8.00 3.60
❑ 138 Vladimir Guerrero C .... 1.25 .55
Jim Edmonds
❑ 139 Justin Thompson C ........ .15 .07
Dwight Gooden
❑ 140 Andres Galarraga D .... 2.00 .90
Dante Bichette
❑ 141 Kenny Lofton S ............ 3.00 1.35
❑ 142 Tim Salmon C ................ .75 .35
Manny Ramirez
❑ 143 Kevin Brown C .............. .25 .11
Matt Morris
❑ 144 Craig Biggio D............. 2.00 .90
Bob Abreu
❑ 145 Roberto Alomar S ........ 8.00 3.60
❑ 146 Jose Guillen C................ .25 .11
Brian Jordan
❑ 147 Bartolo Colon C............. .25 .11
Kevin Appier
❑ 148 Ray Lankford D ........... 1.25 .55
Brian Jordan
❑ 149 Chuck Knoblauch S...... 3.00 1.35
❑ 150 Henry Rodriguez C ........ .25 .11
Ray Lankford
❑ 151 Jaret Wright RC C........ 1.25 .55
Ben McDonald
❑ 152 Bobby Bonilla D............. .25 .11
Kevin Brown
❑ 153 Barry Larkin S ............. 8.00 3.60
❑ 154 David Justice C ............. .40 .18
Reggie Sanders
❑ 155 Mike Mussina C.............. .60 .25
Ken Hill
❑ 156 Mark Grace D .............. 3.00 1.35
Brooks Kieschnick
❑ 157 Jim Thome S................ 5.00 2.20
❑ 158 Michael Tucker C .......... .15 .07
Curtis Goodwin
❑ 159 Jeff Suppan C ................ .15 .07
Jeff Fassero
❑ 160 Mike Mussina D........... 3.00 1.35
Jeffrey Hammonds
❑ 161 John Smoltz S ............. 3.00 1.35
❑ 162 Moises Alou C ............... .25 .11
Eric Davis
❑ 163 Sandy Alomar Jr. C ........ .25 .11
Dan Wilson
❑ 164 Rondell White D .......... 1.25 .55
Henry Rodriguez
❑ 165 Roger Clemens S ...... 15.00 6.75
❑ 166 Brady Anderson C.......... .25 .11
Al Martin
❑ 167 Jason Kendall C ............ .25 .11
Charles Johnson
❑ 168 Jason Giambi D............ 4.00 1.80
Jose Canseco
❑ 169 Larry Walker S ............ 3.00 1.35
❑ 170 Jay Buhner C ................. .25 .11
Geronimo Berroa
❑ 171 Ivan Rodriguez C ........... .75 .35
Mike Sweeney
❑ 172 Kevin Appier D ........... 1.25 .55
Jose Rosado
❑ 173 Bernie Williams S ........ 8.00 3.60
❑ 174 Todd Dunwoody C ...... 2.50 1.10
Brian Giles RC
❑ 175 Javier Lopez C ............... .25 .11
Scott Hatteberg
❑ 176 John Jaha D ................ 1.25 .55
Jeff Cirillo
❑ 177 Andy Pettitte S ............ 3.00 1.35
❑ 178 Dante Bichette C............ .25 .11
Butch Huskey
❑ 179 Raul Casanova C .......... .15 .07
Todd Hundley
❑ 180 Jim Edmonds D............ 3.00 1.35
Garrett Anderson
❑ 181 Deion Sanders S.......... 3.00 1.35
❑ 182 Ryan Klesko C .............. .25 .11
Paul O'Neill
❑ 183 Joe Carter D ............... 1.25 .55
Pat Hentgen
❑ 184 Brady Anderson S ........ 3.00 1.35
❑ 185 Carlos Delgado C .......... .60 .25
Wally Joyner
❑ 186 Jermaine Dye D .......... 1.25 .55
Johnny Damon
❑ 187 Randy Johnson S ...... 10.00 4.50
❑ 188 Todd Hundley D .......... 1.25 .55
Carlos Baerga
❑ 189 Tom Glavine S ............ 8.00 3.60
❑ 190 Damon Mashore D ...... 1.25 .55
Jason McDonald
❑ 191 Wade Boggs S .......... 10.00 4.50
❑ 192 Al Martin D ................. 1.25 .55
Jason Kendall
❑ 193 Matt Williams S .......... 5.00 2.20
❑ 194 Will Clark D ................ 3.00 1.35
Dean Palmer
❑ 195 Sammy Sosa S ......... 15.00 6.75
❑ 196 Jose Cruz Jr. RC D.... 10.00 4.50
Jay Buhner
❑ 197 Eddie Murray S ............ 8.00 3.60
❑ 198 Darin Erstad D............. 4.00 1.80
Jason Dickson
❑ 199 Fred McGriff S............. 5.00 2.20
❑ 200 Bubba Trammell RC D 1.25 .55
Bobby Higginson

## 1997 Donruss Preferred

| | MINT | NRMT |
|---|---|---|
| COMP.BRONZE SET (100) .... | 30.00 | 13.50 |
| COMMON BRONZE.................... | .20 | .09 |
| COMMON SILVER.................... | 1.00 | .45 |

| | MINT | NRMT |
|---|---|---|
| COMMON GOLD | 2.00 | .90 |
| COMMON PLATINUM | 12.00 | 5.50 |
| ❑ 1 Frank Thomas P | 20.00 | 9.00 |
| ❑ 2 Ken Griffey Jr. P | 40.00 | 18.00 |
| ❑ 3 Cecil Fielder B | .40 | .18 |
| ❑ 4 Chuck Knoblauch G | 3.00 | 1.35 |
| ❑ 5 Garret Anderson B | .40 | .18 |
| ❑ 6 Greg Maddux P | 25.00 | 11.00 |
| ❑ 7 Matt Williams S | 2.50 | 1.10 |
| ❑ 8 Marquis Grissom S | 1.00 | .45 |
| ❑ 9 Jason Isringhausen B | .20 | .09 |
| ❑ 10 Larry Walker S | 1.50 | .70 |
| ❑ 11 Charles Nagy B | .20 | .09 |
| ❑ 12 Dan Wilson B | .20 | .09 |
| ❑ 13 Albert Belle G | 5.00 | 2.20 |
| ❑ 14 Javier Lopez B | .40 | .18 |
| ❑ 15 David Cone B | .40 | .18 |
| ❑ 16 Bernard Gilkey B | .20 | .09 |
| ❑ 17 Andres Galarraga S | 2.50 | 1.10 |
| ❑ 18 Bill Pulsipher B | .20 | .09 |
| ❑ 19 Alex Fernandez B | .20 | .09 |
| ❑ 20 Andy Pettitte S | 1.50 | .70 |
| ❑ 21 Mark Grudzielanek B | .20 | .09 |
| ❑ 22 Juan Gonzalez P | 12.00 | 5.50 |
| ❑ 23 Reggie Sanders B | .20 | .09 |
| ❑ 24 Kenny Lofton G | 3.00 | 1.35 |
| ❑ 25 Andy Ashby B | .20 | .09 |
| ❑ 26 John Wetteland B | .40 | .18 |
| ❑ 27 Bobby Bonilla B | .40 | .18 |
| ❑ 28 Hideo Nomo G | 8.00 | 3.60 |
| ❑ 29 Joe Carter B | .40 | .18 |
| ❑ 30 Jose Canseco B | 1.00 | .45 |
| ❑ 31 Ellis Burks B | .40 | .18 |
| ❑ 32 Edgar Martinez S | 2.50 | 1.10 |
| ❑ 33 Chan Ho Park B | .40 | .18 |
| ❑ 34 Dave Justice B | .50 | .23 |
| ❑ 35 Carlos Delgado B | .75 | .35 |
| ❑ 36 Jeff Cirillo S | 1.50 | .70 |
| ❑ 37 Charles Johnson B | .40 | .18 |
| ❑ 38 Manny Ramirez G | 10.00 | 4.50 |
| ❑ 39 Greg Vaughn B | .40 | .18 |
| ❑ 40 Henry Rodriguez B | .20 | .09 |
| ❑ 41 Darryl Strawberry B | .40 | .18 |
| ❑ 42 Jim Thome G | 5.00 | 2.20 |
| ❑ 43 Ryan Klesko S | 1.50 | .70 |
| ❑ 44 Ruben Sierra B | .20 | .09 |
| ❑ 45 Brian Jordan G | 3.00 | 1.35 |
| ❑ 46 Tony Gwynn P | 20.00 | 9.00 |
| ❑ 47 Rafael Palmeiro G | 8.00 | 3.60 |
| ❑ 48 Dante Bichette S | 1.50 | .70 |
| ❑ 49 Ivan Rodriguez G | 10.00 | 4.50 |
| ❑ 50 Mark McGwire G | 30.00 | 13.50 |
| ❑ 51 Tim Salmon S | 1.50 | .70 |
| ❑ 52 Roger Clemens B | 1.50 | .70 |
| ❑ 53 Matt Lawton B | .40 | .18 |
| ❑ 54 Wade Boggs S | 5.00 | 2.20 |
| ❑ 55 Travis Fryman B | .40 | .18 |
| ❑ 56 Bobby Higginson S | 1.50 | .70 |
| ❑ 57 John Jaha S | 1.00 | .45 |
| ❑ 58 Rondell White S | 1.50 | .70 |
| ❑ 59 Tom Glavine S | 4.00 | 1.80 |
| ❑ 60 Eddie Murray S | 4.00 | 1.80 |
| ❑ 61 Vinny Castilla B | .40 | .18 |
| ❑ 62 Todd Hundley B | .20 | .09 |
| ❑ 63 Jay Buhner S | 1.50 | .70 |
| ❑ 64 Paul O'Neill B | .40 | .18 |
| ❑ 65 Steve Finley B | .40 | .18 |
| ❑ 66 Kevin Appier B | .40 | .18 |
| ❑ 67 Ray Durham B | .40 | .18 |
| ❑ 68 Dave Nilsson B | .20 | .09 |
| ❑ 69 Jeff Bagwell G | 10.00 | 4.50 |
| ❑ 70 Al Martin S | 1.00 | .45 |
| ❑ 71 Paul Molitor G | 8.00 | 3.60 |
| ❑ 72 Kevin Brown S | 2.50 | 1.10 |
| ❑ 73 Ron Gant B | .20 | .09 |
| ❑ 74 Dwight Gooden B | .40 | .18 |
| ❑ 75 Quinton McCracken B | .20 | .09 |
| ❑ 76 Rusty Greer S | 1.50 | .70 |
| ❑ 77 Juan Guzman B | .20 | .09 |
| ❑ 78 Fred McGriff S | 2.50 | 1.10 |
| ❑ 79 Tino Martinez B | .40 | .18 |
| ❑ 80 Ray Lankford B | .40 | .18 |
| ❑ 81 Ken Caminiti G | 3.00 | 1.35 |
| ❑ 82 James Baldwin B | .40 | .18 |
| ❑ 83 Jermaine Dye G | 3.00 | 1.35 |
| ❑ 84 Mark Grace S | 4.00 | 1.80 |
| ❑ 85 Pat Hentgen S | 1.00 | .45 |
| ❑ 86 Jason Giambi S | 4.00 | 1.80 |
| ❑ 87 Brian Hunter B | .20 | .09 |
| ❑ 88 Andy Benes B | .20 | .09 |
| ❑ 89 Jose Rosado B | .20 | .09 |
| ❑ 90 Shawn Green B | .75 | .35 |
| ❑ 91 Jason Kendall B | .40 | .18 |
| ❑ 92 Alex Rodriguez P | 30.00 | 13.50 |
| ❑ 93 Chipper Jones P | 25.00 | 11.00 |
| ❑ 94 Barry Bonds G | 12.00 | 5.50 |
| ❑ 95 Brady Anderson G | 3.00 | 1.35 |
| ❑ 96 Ryne Sandberg S | 5.00 | 2.20 |
| ❑ 97 Lance Johnson B | .20 | .09 |
| ❑ 98 Cal Ripken P | 40.00 | 18.00 |
| ❑ 99 Craig Biggio S | 5.00 | 2.20 |
| ❑ 100 Dean Palmer B | .40 | .18 |
| ❑ 101 Gary Sheffield G | 8.00 | 3.60 |
| ❑ 102 Johnny Damon B | .40 | .18 |
| ❑ 103 Mo Vaughn G | 3.00 | 1.35 |
| ❑ 104 Randy Johnson S | 5.00 | 2.20 |
| ❑ 105 Raul Mondesi S | 1.50 | .70 |
| ❑ 106 Roberto Alomar G | 8.00 | 3.60 |
| ❑ 107 Mike Piazza P | 30.00 | 13.50 |
| ❑ 108 Rey Ordonez B | .20 | .09 |
| ❑ 109 Barry Larkin G | 8.00 | 3.60 |
| ❑ 110 Tony Clark S | 1.00 | .45 |
| ❑ 111 Bernie Williams S | 4.00 | 1.80 |
| ❑ 112 John Smoltz G | 3.00 | 1.35 |
| ❑ 113 Moises Alou B | .40 | .18 |
| ❑ 114 Will Clark B | .75 | .35 |
| ❑ 115 Sammy Sosa G | 15.00 | 6.75 |
| ❑ 116 Jim Edmonds S | 4.00 | 1.80 |
| ❑ 117 Jeff Conine B | .20 | .09 |
| ❑ 118 Joey Hamilton B | .20 | .09 |
| ❑ 119 Todd Hollandsworth B | .20 | .09 |
| ❑ 120 Troy Percival B | .20 | .09 |
| ❑ 121 Paul Wilson B | .20 | .09 |
| ❑ 122 Ken Hill B | .20 | .09 |
| ❑ 123 Mariano Rivera S | 1.50 | .70 |
| ❑ 124 Eric Karros B | .40 | .18 |
| ❑ 125 Derek Jeter G | 30.00 | 13.50 |
| ❑ 126 Eric Young S | .20 | .09 |
| ❑ 127 John Mabry B | .20 | .09 |
| ❑ 128 Gregg Jefferies B | .20 | .09 |
| ❑ 129 Ismael Valdes S | 1.00 | .45 |
| ❑ 130 Marty Cordova B | .20 | .09 |
| ❑ 131 Omar Vizquel B | .40 | .18 |
| ❑ 132 Mike Mussina S | 4.00 | 1.80 |
| ❑ 133 Darin Erstad B | 1.00 | .45 |
| ❑ 134 Edgar Renteria S | 1.50 | .70 |
| ❑ 135 Billy Wagner B | .20 | .09 |
| ❑ 136 Alex Ochoa B | .20 | .09 |
| ❑ 137 Luis Castillo B | .40 | .18 |
| ❑ 138 Rocky Coppinger B | .20 | .09 |
| ❑ 139 Mike Sweeney B | .40 | .18 |
| ❑ 140 Michael Tucker B | .20 | .09 |
| ❑ 141 Chris Snopek B | .20 | .09 |
| ❑ 142 Dmitri Young S | 1.50 | .70 |
| ❑ 143 Andruw Jones P | 12.00 | 5.50 |
| ❑ 144 Mike Cameron S | 1.50 | .70 |
| ❑ 145 Brant Brown B | .20 | .09 |
| ❑ 146 Todd Walker G | 2.00 | .90 |
| ❑ 147 Nomar Garciaparra G | 25.00 | 11.00 |
| ❑ 148 Glendon Rusch B | .20 | .09 |
| ❑ 149 Karim Garcia S | 1.00 | .45 |
| ❑ 150 Bubba Trammell S RC | 1.50 | .70 |
| ❑ 151 Todd Greene B | .20 | .09 |
| ❑ 152 Wilton Guerrero G | 2.00 | .90 |
| ❑ 153 Scott Spiezio B | .20 | .09 |
| ❑ 154 Brooks Kieschnick B | .20 | .09 |
| ❑ 155 Vladimir Guerrero G | 15.00 | 6.75 |
| ❑ 156 Brian Giles S RC | 12.00 | 5.50 |
| ❑ 157 Pokey Reese B | .40 | .18 |
| ❑ 158 Jason Dickson G | 2.00 | .90 |
| ❑ 159 Kevin Orie S | 2.00 | .90 |
| ❑ 160 Scott Rolen G | 8.00 | 3.60 |
| ❑ 161 Bartolo Colon S | 1.50 | .70 |
| ❑ 162 Shannon Stewart G | 3.00 | 1.35 |
| ❑ 163 Wendell Magee B | .20 | .09 |
| ❑ 164 Jose Guillen S | 1.00 | .45 |
| ❑ 165 Bob Abreu S | 1.50 | .70 |
| ❑ 166 Deivi Cruz B RC | 1.00 | .45 |
| ❑ 167 Alex Rodriguez NT B | 2.50 | 1.10 |
| ❑ 168 Frank Thomas NT B | 1.50 | .70 |
| ❑ 169 Cal Ripken NT B | 3.00 | 1.35 |
| ❑ 170 Chipper Jones NT B | 2.00 | .90 |
| ❑ 171 Mike Piazza NT B | 2.50 | 1.10 |
| ❑ 172 Tony Gwynn NT S | 8.00 | 3.60 |
| ❑ 173 Juan Gonzalez NT B | .75 | .35 |
| ❑ 174 Kenny Lofton NT S | 1.50 | .70 |
| ❑ 175 Ken Griffey Jr. NT B | 3.00 | 1.35 |
| ❑ 176 Mark McGwire NT B | 3.00 | 1.35 |
| ❑ 177 Jeff Bagwell NT B | 1.00 | .45 |
| ❑ 178 Paul Molitor NT S | 4.00 | 1.80 |
| ❑ 179 Andruw Jones NT B | 1.00 | .45 |
| ❑ 180 Manny Ramirez NT S | 5.00 | 2.20 |
| ❑ 181 Ken Caminiti NT S | 1.50 | .70 |
| ❑ 182 Barry Bonds NT B | 1.25 | .55 |
| ❑ 183 Mo Vaughn NT B | .40 | .18 |
| ❑ 184 Derek Jeter NT B | 3.00 | 1.35 |
| ❑ 185 Barry Larkin NT S | 4.00 | 1.80 |
| ❑ 186 Ivan Rodriguez NT B | 1.00 | .45 |
| ❑ 187 Albert Belle NT S | 1.00 | .45 |
| ❑ 188 John Smoltz NT S | 1.50 | .70 |
| ❑ 189 Chuck Knoblauch NT S | 1.50 | .70 |
| ❑ 190 Brian Jordan NT S | 1.50 | .70 |
| ❑ 191 Gary Sheffield NT S | 4.00 | 1.80 |
| ❑ 192 Jim Thome NT S | 2.50 | 1.10 |
| ❑ 193 Brady Anderson NT S | 1.50 | .70 |
| ❑ 194 Hideo Nomo NT S | .75 | .35 |
| ❑ 195 Sammy Sosa NT S | 8.00 | 3.60 |
| ❑ 196 Greg Maddux NT B | 2.00 | .90 |
| ❑ 197 Vladimir Guerrero CL B | 1.50 | .70 |
| ❑ 198 Scott Rolen CL B | .75 | .35 |
| ❑ 199 Todd Walker CL B | .20 | .09 |
| ❑ 200 Nomar Garciaparra CL B | 2.00 | .90 |

## 1998 Donruss Preferred

| | MINT | NRMT |
|---|---|---|
| COMP.GRAND STAND (100) | 25.00 | 11.00 |
| COMMON GRAND STAND | .15 | .07 |
| COMP.MEZZANINE (40) | 80.00 | 36.00 |
| COMMON MEZZANINE | 1.00 | .45 |
| COMP.CLUB LEVEL (30) | 120.00 | 55.00 |
| COMMON CLUB LEVEL | 1.50 | .70 |
| COMP.FIELD BOX (20) | 200.00 | 90.00 |
| COMMON FIELD BOX | 3.00 | 1.35 |
| COMP.EXEC.SUITE (10) | 200.00 | 90.00 |
| COMMON EXEC.SUITE | 10.00 | 4.50 |
| ❑ 1 Ken Griffey Jr. EX | 30.00 | 13.50 |
| ❑ 2 Frank Thomas EX | 15.00 | 6.75 |
| ❑ 3 Cal Ripken EX | 30.00 | 13.50 |
| ❑ 4 Alex Rodriguez EX | 25.00 | 11.00 |

❑ 5 Greg Maddux EX 20.00 9.00
❑ 6 Mike Piazza EX 25.00 11.00
❑ 7 Chipper Jones EX 20.00 9.00
❑ 8 Tony Gwynn FB 15.00 6.75
❑ 9 Derek Jeter FB 30.00 13.50
❑ 10 Jeff Bagwell EX 10.00 4.50
❑ 11 Juan Gonzalez EX .60 .25
❑ 12 Nomar Garciaparra EX 25.00 11.00
❑ 13 Andruw Jones FB 8.00 3.60
❑ 14 Hideo Nomo FB 8.00 3.60
❑ 15 Roger Clemens FB 15.00 6.75
❑ 16 Mark McGwire FB 30.00 13.50
❑ 17 Scott Rolen FB 8.00 3.60
❑ 18 Vladimir Guerrero FB 12.00 5.50
❑ 19 Barry Bonds FB 12.00 5.50
❑ 20 Darin Erstad FB 8.00 3.60
❑ 21 Albert Belle FB 5.00 2.20
❑ 22 Kenny Lofton FB 5.00 2.20
❑ 23 Mo Vaughn FB 5.00 2.20
❑ 24 Tony Clark FB 3.00 1.35
❑ 25 Ivan Rodriguez FB 10.00 4.50
❑ 26 Larry Walker CB 2.50 1.10
❑ 27 Eddie Murray CB 6.00 2.70
❑ 28 Andy Pettitte CB 2.50 1.10
❑ 29 Roberto Alomar CB 6.00 2.70
❑ 30 Randy Johnson CB 8.00 3.60
❑ 31 Manny Ramirez CB 8.00 3.60
❑ 32 Paul Molitor FB 8.00 3.60
❑ 33 Mike Mussina CB 6.00 2.70
❑ 34 Jim Thome FB 5.00 2.20
❑ 35 Tino Martinez CB 2.50 1.10
❑ 36 Gary Sheffield CB 6.00 2.70
❑ 37 Chuck Knoblauch CB 2.50 1.10
❑ 38 Bernie Williams CB 6.00 2.70
❑ 39 Tim Salmon CB 2.50 1.10
❑ 40 Sammy Sosa CB 12.00 5.50
❑ 41 Wade Boggs ME 5.00 2.20
❑ 42 Will Clark GS .60 .25
❑ 43 Andres Galarraga CB 4.00 1.80
❑ 44 Raul Mondesi CB 2.50 1.10
❑ 45 Rickey Henderson GS .75 .35
❑ 46 Jose Canseco GS .75 .35
❑ 47 Pedro Martinez GS .75 .35
❑ 48 Jay Buhner GS .25 .11
❑ 49 Ryan Klesko GS .25 .11
❑ 50 Barry Larkin CB 6.00 2.70
❑ 51 Charles Johnson GS .25 .11
❑ 52 Tom Glavine GS .60 .25
❑ 53 Edgar Martinez CB 4.00 1.80
❑ 54 Fred McGriff GS .40 .18
❑ 55 Moises Alou ME 1.50 .70
❑ 56 Dante Bichette GS .25 .11
❑ 57 Jim Edmonds CB 6.00 2.70
❑ 58 Mark Grace ME 4.00 1.80
❑ 59 Chan Ho Park ME 1.50 .70
❑ 60 Justin Thompson ME 1.00 .45
❑ 61 John Smoltz ME 1.50 .70
❑ 62 Craig Biggio CB 4.00 1.80
❑ 63 Ken Caminiti ME 1.50 .70
❑ 64 Deion Sanders ME 1.50 .70
❑ 65 Carlos Delgado GS .60 .25
❑ 66 David Justice CB 4.00 1.80
❑ 67 J.T. Snow GS .25 .11
❑ 68 Jason Giambi CB 6.00 2.70
❑ 69 Garret Anderson ME 1.50 .70
❑ 70 Rondell White ME 1.50 .70
❑ 71 Matt Williams ME 2.50 1.10
❑ 72 Brady Anderson ME 1.50 .70
❑ 73 Eric Karros GS .25 .11
❑ 74 Javier Lopez GS .25 .11
❑ 75 Pat Hentgen GS .15 .07
❑ 76 Todd Hundley GS .15 .07
❑ 77 Ray Lankford GS .25 .11
❑ 78 Denny Neagle GS .15 .07
❑ 79 Henry Rodriguez GS .15 .07
❑ 80 Sandy Alomar Jr. ME 1.50 .70
❑ 81 Rafael Palmeiro ME 4.00 1.80
❑ 82 Robin Ventura GS .25 .11
❑ 83 John Olerud GS .25 .11
❑ 84 Omar Vizquel GS .25 .11
❑ 85 Joe Randa GS .15 .07
❑ 86 Lance Johnson GS .15 .07
❑ 87 Kevin Brown GS .40 .18
❑ 88 Curt Schilling GS .25 .11
❑ 89 Ismael Valdes GS .15 .07
❑ 90 Francisco Cordova GS .15 .07
❑ 91 David Cone GS .25 .11
❑ 92 Paul O'Neill GS .25 .11
❑ 93 Jimmy Key GS .25 .11
❑ 94 Brad Radke GS .25 .11
❑ 95 Kevin Appier GS .25 .11
❑ 96 Al Martin GS .15 .07
❑ 97 Rusty Greer ME 1.50 .70
❑ 98 Reggie Jefferson GS .15 .07
❑ 99 Ron Coomer GS .15 .07
❑ 100 Vinny Castilla GS .25 .11
❑ 101 Bobby Bonilla ME 1.50 .70
❑ 102 Eric Young GS .15 .07
❑ 103 Tony Womack GS .15 .07
❑ 104 Jason Kendall GS .25 .11
❑ 105 Jeff Suppan GS .15 .07
❑ 106 Shawn Estes ME 1.00 .45
❑ 107 Shawn Green GS .60 .25
❑ 108 Edgardo Alfonzo ME 1.50 .70
❑ 109 Alan Benes ME 1.00 .45
❑ 110 Bobby Higginson GS .25 .11
❑ 111 Mark Grudzielanek GS .15 .07
❑ 112 Wilton Guerrero GS .15 .07
❑ 113 Todd Greene ME 1.00 .45
❑ 114 Pokey Reese GS .25 .11
❑ 115 Jose Guillen CB 1.50 .70
❑ 116 Neifi Perez ME 1.00 .45
❑ 117 Luis Castillo GS .25 .11
❑ 118 Edgar Renteria GS .15 .07
❑ 119 Karim Garcia GS .15 .07
❑ 120 Butch Huskey GS .15 .07
❑ 121 Michael Tucker GS .15 .07
❑ 122 Jason Dickson GS .15 .07
❑ 123 Todd Walker ME 1.00 .45
❑ 124 Brian Jordan GS .25 .11
❑ 125 Joe Carter GS .25 .11
❑ 126 Matt Morris ME 1.00 .45
❑ 127 Brett Tomko ME 1.00 .45
❑ 128 Mike Cameron CB 2.50 1.10
❑ 129 Russ Davis GS .15 .07
❑ 130 Shannon Stewart ME 1.50 .70
❑ 131 Kevin Orie GS .15 .07
❑ 132 Scott Spiezio GS .15 .07
❑ 133 Brian Giles GS .25 .11
❑ 134 Raul Casanova GS .15 .07
❑ 135 Jose Cruz Jr. CB 2.50 1.10
❑ 136 Hideki Irabu GS .15 .07
❑ 137 Bubba Trammell GS .15 .07
❑ 138 Richard Hidalgo CB 2.50 1.10
❑ 139 Paul Konerko CB 2.50 1.10
❑ 140 Todd Helton FB 10.00 4.50
❑ 141 Miguel Tejada CB 6.00 2.70
❑ 142 Fernando Tatis ME 1.50 .70
❑ 143 Ben Grieve FB 5.00 2.20
❑ 144 Travis Lee FB 5.00 2.20
❑ 145 Mark Kotsay CB 2.50 1.10
❑ 146 Eli Marrero ME 1.00 .45
❑ 147 David Ortiz CB 1.50 .70
❑ 148 Juan Encarnacion ME 1.50 .70
❑ 149 Jaret Wright ME 1.00 .45
❑ 150 Livan Hernandez CB 1.50 .70
❑ 151 Ruben Rivera GS .15 .07
❑ 152 Brad Fullmer ME 1.50 .70
❑ 153 Dennis Reyes GS .15 .07
❑ 154 Enrique Wilson ME 1.00 .45
❑ 155 Todd Dunwoody ME 1.00 .45
❑ 156 Derrick Gibson ME 1.00 .45
❑ 157 Aaron Boone ME 1.00 .45
❑ 158 Ron Wright ME 1.00 .45
❑ 159 Preston Wilson ME 1.50 .70
❑ 160 Abraham Nunez GS .15 .07
❑ 161 Shane Monahan GS .15 .07
❑ 162 Carl Pavano GS .15 .07
❑ 163 Derrek Lee GS .15 .07
❑ 164 Jeff Abbott GS .15 .07
❑ 165 Wes Helms ME 1.00 .45
❑ 166 Brian Rose GS .15 .07
❑ 167 Bobby Estalella GS .15 .07
❑ 168 Ken Griffey Jr. PP GS 2.50 1.10
❑ 169 Frank Thomas PP GS 1.25 .55
❑ 170 Cal Ripken PP GS 2.50 1.10
❑ 171 Alex Rodriguez PP GS 2.00 .90
❑ 172 Greg Maddux PP GS 1.50 .70
❑ 173 Mike Piazza PP GS 2.00 .90
❑ 174 Chipper Jones PP GS 1.50 .70
❑ 175 Tony Gwynn PP GS .60 .25
❑ 176 Derek Jeter PP GS 2.50 1.10
❑ 177 Jeff Bagwell PP GS .75 .35
❑ 178 Juan Gonzalez PP GS .60 .25
❑ 179 N. Garciaparra PP GS 2.00 .90
❑ 180 Andruw Jones PP GS .60 .25
❑ 181 Hideo Nomo PP GS .60 .25
❑ 182 Roger Clemens PP GS 1.25 .55
❑ 183 Mark McGwire PP GS 2.50 1.10
❑ 184 Scott Rolen PP GS .60 .25
❑ 185 Barry Bonds PP GS 1.00 .45
❑ 186 Darin Erstad PP GS .60 .25
❑ 187 Mo Vaughn PP GS .25 .11
❑ 188 Ivan Rodriguez PP GS .75 .35
❑ 189 Larry Walker PP ME 1.50 .70
❑ 190 Andy Pettitte PP GS .25 .11
❑ 191 Randy Johnson PP ME 5.00 2.20
❑ 192 Paul Molitor PP GS .60 .25
❑ 193 Jim Thome PP GS .40 .18
❑ 194 Tino Martinez PP ME 1.50 .70
❑ 195 Gary Sheffield PP GS .60 .25
❑ 196 Albert Belle PP GS .40 .18
❑ 197 Jose Cruz Jr. PP GS .25 .11
❑ 198 Todd Helton CL GS .60 .25
❑ 199 Ben Grieve CL GS .25 .11
❑ 200 Paul Konerko CL GS .15 .07

## 1997 Donruss Signature

| | MINT | NRMT |
|---|---|---|
| COMPLETE SET (100) | 50.00 | 22.00 |
| COMMON CARD (1-100) | .25 | .11 |

❑ 1 Mark McGwire 4.00 2.20
❑ 2 Kenny Lofton .50 .23
❑ 3 Tony Gwynn 2.00 .90
❑ 4 Tony Clark .25 .11
❑ 5 Tim Salmon .50 .23
❑ 6 Ken Griffey Jr 4.00 1.80
❑ 7 Mike Piazza 3.00 1.35
❑ 8 Greg Maddux 2.50 1.10
❑ 9 Roberto Alomar 1.00 .45
❑ 10 Andres Galarraga .60 .25
❑ 11 Roger Clemens 2.00 .90
❑ 12 Bernie Williams 1.00 .45
❑ 13 Rondell White .50 .23
❑ 14 Kevin Appier .50 .23
❑ 15 Ray Lankford .50 .23
❑ 16 Frank Thomas 2.00 .90
❑ 17 Will Clark 1.00 .45
❑ 18 Chipper Jones 2.50 1.10
❑ 19 Jeff Bagwell 1.25 .55
❑ 20 Manny Ramirez 1.25 .55
❑ 21 Ryne Sandberg 1.25 .55
❑ 22 Paul Molitor 1.00 .45
❑ 23 Gary Sheffield 1.00 .45
❑ 24 Jim Edmonds 1.00 .45
❑ 25 Barry Larkin 1.00 .45
❑ 26 Rafael Palmeiro 1.00 .45
❑ 27 Alan Benes .25 .11
❑ 28 Dave Justice .60 .25
❑ 29 Randy Johnson 1.25 .55
❑ 30 Barry Bonds 1.50 .70
❑ 31 Mo Vaughn .50 .23
❑ 32 Michael Tucker .25 .11
❑ 33 Larry Walker .50 .23
❑ 34 Tino Martinez .50 .23
❑ 35 Jose Guillen .25 .11
❑ 36 Carlos Delgado 1.00 .45
❑ 37 Jason Dickson .25 .11

❑ 38 Tom Glavine 1.00 .45
❑ 39 Raul Mondesi .50 .23
❑ 40 Jose Cruz Jr. RC 2.50 1.10
❑ 41 Johnny Damon .50 .23
❑ 42 Mark Grace 1.00 .45
❑ 43 Juan Gonzalez 1.00 .45
❑ 44 Vladimir Guerrero 2.00 .90
❑ 45 Kevin Brown .60 .25
❑ 46 Justin Thompson .25 .11
❑ 47 Eric Young .25 .11
❑ 48 Ron Coomer .25 .11
❑ 49 Mark Kotsay RC .75 .35
❑ 50 Scott Rolen 1.00 .45
❑ 51 Derek Jeter 4.00 1.80
❑ 52 Jim Thome .60 .25
❑ 53 Fred McGriff .60 .25
❑ 54 Albert Belle .60 .25
❑ 55 Garret Anderson .50 .23
❑ 56 Wilton Guerrero .25 .11
❑ 57 Jose Canseco 1.25 .55
❑ 58 Cal Ripken 4.00 1.80
❑ 59 Sammy Sosa 2.00 .90
❑ 60 Dmitri Young .50 .23
❑ 61 Alex Rodriguez 3.00 1.35
❑ 62 Javier Lopez .50 .23
❑ 63 Sandy Alomar Jr. .50 .23
❑ 64 Joe Carter .50 .23
❑ 65 Dante Bichette .50 .23
❑ 66 Al Martin .25 .11
❑ 67 Darin Erstad 1.25 .55
❑ 68 Pokey Reese .50 .23
❑ 69 Brady Anderson .50 .23
❑ 70 Andruw Jones 1.25 .55
❑ 71 Ivan Rodriguez 1.25 .55
❑ 72 Nomar Garciaparra 3.00 1.35
❑ 73 Moises Alou .50 .23
❑ 74 Andy Pettitte .50 .23
❑ 75 Jay Buhner .50 .23
❑ 76 Craig Biggio .60 .25
❑ 77 Wade Boggs 1.25 .55
❑ 78 Shawn Estes .50 .23
❑ 79 Neifi Perez .25 .11
❑ 80 Rusty Greer .50 .23
❑ 81 Pedro Martinez 1.25 .55
❑ 82 Mike Mussina 1.00 .45
❑ 83 Jason Giambi 1.00 .45
❑ 84 Hideo Nomo 1.00 .45
❑ 85 Todd Hundley .25 .11
❑ 86 Deion Sanders .50 .23
❑ 87 Mike Cameron .50 .23
❑ 88 Bobby Bonilla .50 .23
❑ 89 Todd Greene .25 .11
❑ 90 Kevin Orie .25 .11
❑ 91 Ken Caminiti .50 .23
❑ 92 Chuck Knoblauch .50 .23
❑ 93 Matt Morris .25 .11
❑ 94 Matt Williams .60 .25
❑ 95 Pat Hentgen .25 .11
❑ 96 John Smoltz .50 .23
❑ 97 Edgar Martinez .60 .25
❑ 98 Jason Kendall .50 .23
❑ 99 Ken Griffey Jr. CL 2.00 .90
❑ 100 Frank Thomas CL 1.00 .45

## 1998 Donruss Signature

| | MINT | NRMT |
|---|---|---|
| COMPLETE SET (140) | 120.00 | 55.00 |

❑ 1 David Justice .60 .25
❑ 2 Derek Jeter 4.00 1.80
❑ 3 Nomar Garciaparra 3.00 1.35
❑ 4 Ryan Klesko .40 .18
❑ 5 Jeff Bagwell 1.25 .55
❑ 6 Dante Bichette .40 .18
❑ 7 Ivan Rodriguez 1.25 .55
❑ 8 Albert Belle .60 .25
❑ 9 Cal Ripken 4.00 1.80
❑ 10 Craig Biggio .60 .25
❑ 11 Barry Larkin 1.00 .45
❑ 12 Jose Guillen .25 .11
❑ 13 Will Clark 1.00 .45
❑ 14 J.T. Snow .40 .18
❑ 15 Chuck Knoblauch .40 .18
❑ 16 Todd Walker .25 .11
❑ 17 Scott Rolen 1.00 .45
❑ 18 Rickey Henderson 1.25 .55
❑ 19 Juan Gonzalez 1.00 .45
❑ 20 Justin Thompson .25 .11
❑ 21 Roger Clemens 2.00 .90
❑ 22 Ray Lankford .40 .18
❑ 23 Jose Cruz Jr. .40 .18
❑ 24 Ken Griffey Jr. 4.00 1.80
❑ 25 Andruw Jones 1.00 .45
❑ 26 Darin Erstad 1.00 .45
❑ 27 Jim Thome .60 .25
❑ 28 Wade Boggs 1.25 .55
❑ 29 Ken Caminiti .40 .18
❑ 30 Todd Hundley .25 .11
❑ 31 Mike Piazza 3.00 1.35
❑ 32 Sammy Sosa 2.00 .90
❑ 33 Larry Walker .40 .18
❑ 34 Matt Williams .60 .25
❑ 35 Frank Thomas 2.00 .90
❑ 36 Gary Sheffield 1.00 .45
❑ 37 Alex Rodriguez 3.00 1.35
❑ 38 Hideo Nomo 1.00 .45
❑ 39 Kenny Lofton .40 .18
❑ 40 John Smoltz .40 .18
❑ 41 Mo Vaughn .40 .18
❑ 42 Edgar Martinez .60 .25
❑ 43 Paul Molitor 1.00 .45
❑ 44 Rafael Palmeiro 1.00 .45
❑ 45 Barry Bonds 1.50 .70
❑ 46 Vladimir Guerrero 1.50 .70
❑ 47 Carlos Delgado 1.00 .45
❑ 48 Bobby Higginson .40 .18
❑ 49 Greg Maddux 2.50 1.10
❑ 50 Jim Edmonds 1.00 .45
❑ 51 Randy Johnson 1.25 .55
❑ 52 Mark McGwire 4.00 1.80
❑ 53 Rondell White .40 .18
❑ 54 Raul Mondesi .40 .18
❑ 55 Manny Ramirez 1.25 .55
❑ 56 Pedro Martinez 1.25 .55
❑ 57 Tim Salmon .40 .18
❑ 58 Moises Alou .40 .18
❑ 59 Fred McGriff .60 .25
❑ 60 Garret Anderson .40 .18
❑ 61 Sandy Alomar Jr. .40 .18
❑ 62 Chan Ho Park .40 .18
❑ 63 Mark Kotsay .40 .18
❑ 64 Mike Mussina 1.00 .45
❑ 65 Tom Glavine 1.00 .45
❑ 66 Tony Clark .25 .11
❑ 67 Mark Grace 1.00 .45
❑ 68 Tony Gwynn 2.00 .90
❑ 69 Tino Martinez .40 .18
❑ 70 Kevin Brown .60 .25
❑ 71 Todd Greene .25 .11
❑ 72 Andy Pettitte .40 .18
❑ 73 Livan Hernandez .25 .11
❑ 74 Curt Schilling .40 .18
❑ 75 Andres Galarraga .60 .25
❑ 76 Rusty Greer .40 .18
❑ 77 Jay Buhner .40 .18
❑ 78 Bobby Bonilla .40 .18
❑ 79 Chipper Jones 2.50 1.10
❑ 80 Eric Young .25 .11
❑ 81 Jason Giambi 1.00 .45
❑ 82 Javy Lopez .40 .18
❑ 83 Roberto Alomar 1.00 .45
❑ 84 Bernie Williams 1.00 .45
❑ 85 A.J. Hinch .25 .11
❑ 86 Kerry Wood 1.00 .45
❑ 87 Juan Encarnacion .40 .18
❑ 88 Brad Fullmer .40 .18
❑ 89 Ben Grieve .40 .18
❑ 90 Magglio Ordonez RC 10.00 4.50
❑ 91 Todd Helton 1.25 .55
❑ 92 Richard Hidalgo .40 .18
❑ 93 Paul Konerko .40 .18
❑ 94 Aramis Ramirez .40 .18
❑ 95 Ricky Ledee .25 .11
❑ 96 Derrek Lee .25 .11
❑ 97 Travis Lee .40 .18
❑ 98 Matt Anderson RC .75 .35
❑ 99 Jaret Wright .25 .11
❑ 100 David Ortiz .25 .11
❑ 101 Carl Pavano .25 .11
❑ 102 Orlando Hernandez RC 3.00 1.35
❑ 103 Fernando Tatis .40 .18
❑ 104 Miguel Tejada 1.00 .45
❑ 105 Rolando Arrojo RC 1.50 .70
❑ 106 Kevin Millwood RC 3.00 1.35
❑ 107 Ken Griffey Jr. CL 2.00 .90
❑ 108 Frank Thomas CL 1.00 .45
❑ 109 Cal Ripken CL 2.00 .90
❑ 110 Greg Maddux CL 1.25 .55
❑ 111 John Olerud .40 .18
❑ 112 David Cone .40 .18
❑ 113 Vinny Castilla .40 .18
❑ 114 Jason Kendall .40 .18
❑ 115 Brian Jordan .40 .18
❑ 116 Hideki Irabu .25 .11
❑ 117 Bartolo Colon .40 .18
❑ 118 Greg Vaughn .40 .18
❑ 119 David Segui .25 .11
❑ 120 Bruce Chen .25 .11
❑ 121 Julio Ramirez RC 1.50 .70
❑ 122 Troy Glaus RC 12.00 5.50
❑ 123 Jeremy Giambi RC 1.00 .45
❑ 124 Ryan Minor RC .75 .35
❑ 125 Richie Sexson .60 .25
❑ 126 Dermal Brown .40 .18
❑ 127 Adrian Beltre .40 .18
❑ 128 Eric Chavez .40 .18
❑ 129 J.D. Drew RC 15.00 6.75
❑ 130 Gabe Kapler RC 6.00 2.70
❑ 131 Masato Yoshii RC 1.50 .70
❑ 132 Mike Lowell RC 2.50 1.10
❑ 133 Jim Parque RC 1.50 .70
❑ 134 Roy Halladay .25 .11
❑ 135 Carlos Lee RC 5.00 2.20
❑ 136 Jin Ho Cho RC .75 .35
❑ 137 Michael Barrett .25 .11
❑ 138 Fernando Seguignol RC 1.00 .45
❑ 139 Odalis Perez RC UER 1.00 .45
(Back pictures John Rocker)
❑ 140 Mark McGwire CL 2.00 .90

## 1995 Emotion

| | MINT | NRMT |
|---|---|---|
| COMPLETE SET (200) | 40.00 | 18.00 |
| COMMON CARD (1-200) | .20 | .09 |

❑ 1 Brady Anderson .40 .18
❑ 2 Kevin Brown .50 .23
❑ 3 Curtis Goodwin .20 .09
❑ 4 Jeffrey Hammonds .40 .18
❑ 5 Ben McDonald .20 .09

| No. | Player | Mint | NrMt |
|---|---|---|---|
| ❑ 6 | Mike Mussina | .75 | .35 |
| ❑ 7 | Rafael Palmeiro | .75 | .35 |
| ❑ 8 | Cal Ripken Jr. | 3.00 | 1.35 |
| ❑ 9 | Jose Canseco | 1.00 | .45 |
| ❑ 10 | Roger Clemens | 1.50 | .70 |
| ❑ 11 | Vaughn Eshelman | .20 | .09 |
| ❑ 12 | Mike Greenwell | .20 | .09 |
| ❑ 13 | Erik Hanson | .20 | .09 |
| ❑ 14 | Tim Naehring | .20 | .09 |
| ❑ 15 | Aaron Sele | .40 | .18 |
| ❑ 16 | John Valentin | .20 | .09 |
| ❑ 17 | Mo Vaughn | .40 | .18 |
| ❑ 18 | Chili Davis | .40 | .18 |
| ❑ 19 | Gary DiSarcina | .20 | .09 |
| ❑ 20 | Chuck Finley | .40 | .18 |
| ❑ 21 | Tim Salmon | .40 | .18 |
| ❑ 22 | Lee Smith | .40 | .18 |
| ❑ 23 | J.T. Snow | .40 | .18 |
| ❑ 24 | Jim Abbott | .40 | .18 |
| ❑ 25 | Jason Bere | .20 | .09 |
| ❑ 26 | Ray Durham | .40 | .18 |
| ❑ 27 | Ozzie Guillen | .20 | .09 |
| ❑ 28 | Tim Raines | .40 | .18 |
| ❑ 29 | Frank Thomas | 1.50 | .70 |
| ❑ 30 | Robin Ventura | .40 | .18 |
| ❑ 31 | Carlos Baerga | .20 | .09 |
| ❑ 32 | Albert Belle | .50 | .23 |
| ❑ 33 | Orel Hershiser | .40 | .18 |
| ❑ 34 | Kenny Lofton | .40 | .18 |
| ❑ 35 | Dennis Martinez | .40 | .18 |
| ❑ 36 | Eddie Murray | .75 | .35 |
| ❑ 37 | Manny Ramirez | 1.00 | .45 |
| ❑ 38 | Julian Tavarez | .20 | .09 |
| ❑ 39 | Jim Thome | .50 | .23 |
| ❑ 40 | Dave Winfield | .75 | .35 |
| ❑ 41 | Chad Curtis | .20 | .09 |
| ❑ 42 | Cecil Fielder | .40 | .18 |
| ❑ 43 | Travis Fryman | .40 | .18 |
| ❑ 44 | Kirk Gibson | .40 | .18 |
| ❑ 45 | Bobby Higginson RC | 1.25 | .55 |
| ❑ 46 | Alan Trammell | .50 | .23 |
| ❑ 47 | Lou Whitaker | .40 | .18 |
| ❑ 48 | Kevin Appier | .40 | .18 |
| ❑ 49 | Gary Gaetti | .40 | .18 |
| ❑ 50 | Jeff Montgomery | .20 | .09 |
| ❑ 51 | Jon Nunnally | .20 | .09 |
| ❑ 52 | Ricky Bones | .20 | .09 |
| ❑ 53 | Cal Eldred | .20 | .09 |
| ❑ 54 | Joe Oliver | .20 | .09 |
| ❑ 55 | Kevin Seitzer | .20 | .09 |
| ❑ 56 | Marty Cordova | .20 | .09 |
| ❑ 57 | Chuck Knoblauch | .40 | .18 |
| ❑ 58 | Kirby Puckett | 2.00 | .90 |
| ❑ 59 | Wade Boggs | 1.00 | .45 |
| ❑ 60 | Derek Jeter | 3.00 | 1.35 |
| ❑ 61 | Jimmy Key | .40 | .18 |
| ❑ 62 | Don Mattingly | 2.00 | .90 |
| ❑ 63 | Jack McDowell | .20 | .09 |
| ❑ 64 | Paul O'Neill | .40 | .18 |
| ❑ 65 | Andy Pettitte | .50 | .23 |
| ❑ 66 | Ruben Rivera | .20 | .09 |
| ❑ 67 | Mike Stanley | .20 | .09 |
| ❑ 68 | John Wetteland | .40 | .18 |
| ❑ 69 | Geronimo Berroa | .20 | .09 |
| ❑ 70 | Dennis Eckersley | .40 | .18 |
| ❑ 71 | Rickey Henderson | 1.00 | .45 |
| ❑ 72 | Mark McGwire | 3.00 | 1.35 |
| ❑ 73 | Steve Ontiveros | .20 | .09 |
| ❑ 74 | Ruben Sierra | .20 | .09 |
| ❑ 75 | Terry Steinbach | .20 | .09 |
| ❑ 76 | Jay Buhner | .40 | .18 |
| ❑ 77 | Ken Griffey Jr. | 3.00 | 1.35 |
| ❑ 78 | Randy Johnson | 1.00 | .45 |
| ❑ 79 | Edgar Martinez | .50 | .23 |
| ❑ 80 | Tino Martinez | .40 | .18 |
| ❑ 81 | Marc Newfield | .20 | .09 |
| ❑ 82 | Alex Rodriguez | 3.00 | 1.35 |
| ❑ 83 | Will Clark | .75 | .35 |
| ❑ 84 | Benji Gil | .20 | .09 |
| ❑ 85 | Juan Gonzalez | .75 | .35 |
| ❑ 86 | Rusty Greer | .40 | .18 |
| ❑ 87 | Dean Palmer | .40 | .18 |
| ❑ 88 | Ivan Rodriguez | 1.00 | .45 |
| ❑ 89 | Kenny Rogers | .20 | .09 |
| ❑ 90 | Roberto Alomar | .75 | .35 |
| ❑ 91 | Joe Carter | .40 | .18 |
| ❑ 92 | David Cone | .40 | .18 |
| ❑ 93 | Alex Gonzalez | .20 | .09 |
| ❑ 94 | Shawn Green | .75 | .35 |
| ❑ 95 | Pat Hentgen | .20 | .09 |
| ❑ 96 | Paul Molitor | .75 | .35 |
| ❑ 97 | John Olerud | .40 | .18 |
| ❑ 98 | Devon White | .40 | .18 |
| ❑ 99 | Steve Avery | .20 | .09 |
| ❑ 100 | Tom Glavine | .75 | .35 |
| ❑ 101 | Marquis Grissom | .20 | .09 |
| ❑ 102 | Chipper Jones | 2.00 | .90 |
| ❑ 103 | David Justice | .50 | .23 |
| ❑ 104 | Ryan Klesko | .40 | .18 |
| ❑ 105 | Javier Lopez | .40 | .18 |
| ❑ 106 | Greg Maddux | 2.00 | .90 |
| ❑ 107 | Fred McGriff | .50 | .23 |
| ❑ 108 | John Smoltz | .40 | .18 |
| ❑ 109 | Shawon Dunston | .20 | .09 |
| ❑ 110 | Mark Grace | .75 | .35 |
| ❑ 111 | Brian McRae | .20 | .09 |
| ❑ 112 | Randy Myers | .20 | .09 |
| ❑ 113 | Sammy Sosa | 1.50 | .70 |
| ❑ 114 | Steve Trachsel | .20 | .09 |
| ❑ 115 | Bret Boone | .40 | .18 |
| ❑ 116 | Ron Gant | .20 | .09 |
| ❑ 117 | Barry Larkin | .75 | .35 |
| ❑ 118 | Deion Sanders | .40 | .18 |
| ❑ 119 | Reggie Sanders | .20 | .09 |
| ❑ 120 | Pete Schourek | .20 | .09 |
| ❑ 121 | John Smiley | .20 | .09 |
| ❑ 122 | Jason Bates | .20 | .09 |
| ❑ 123 | Dante Bichette | .40 | .18 |
| ❑ 124 | Vinny Castilla | .40 | .18 |
| ❑ 125 | Andres Galarraga | .50 | .23 |
| ❑ 126 | Larry Walker | .40 | .18 |
| ❑ 127 | Greg Colbrunn | .20 | .09 |
| ❑ 128 | Jeff Conine | .20 | .09 |
| ❑ 129 | Andre Dawson | .50 | .23 |
| ❑ 130 | Chris Hammond | .20 | .09 |
| ❑ 131 | Charles Johnson | .40 | .18 |
| ❑ 132 | Gary Sheffield | .75 | .35 |
| ❑ 133 | Quilvio Veras | .20 | .09 |
| ❑ 134 | Jeff Bagwell | 1.00 | .45 |
| ❑ 135 | Derek Bell | .20 | .09 |
| ❑ 136 | Craig Biggio | .50 | .23 |
| ❑ 137 | Jim Dougherty RC | .20 | .09 |
| ❑ 138 | John Hudek | .20 | .09 |
| ❑ 139 | Orlando Miller | .20 | .09 |
| ❑ 140 | Phil Plantier | .20 | .09 |
| ❑ 141 | Eric Karros | .40 | .18 |
| ❑ 142 | Ramon Martinez | .20 | .09 |
| ❑ 143 | Raul Mondesi | .40 | .18 |
| ❑ 144 | Hideo Nomo RC | 2.00 | .90 |
| ❑ 145 | Mike Piazza | 2.50 | 1.10 |
| ❑ 146 | Ismael Valdes | .20 | .09 |
| ❑ 147 | Todd Worrell | .20 | .09 |
| ❑ 148 | Moises Alou | .40 | .18 |
| ❑ 149 | Yamil Benitez RC | .20 | .09 |
| ❑ 150 | Wil Cordero | .20 | .09 |
| ❑ 151 | Jeff Fassero | .20 | .09 |
| ❑ 152 | Cliff Floyd | .40 | .18 |
| ❑ 153 | Pedro Martinez | 1.00 | .45 |
| ❑ 154 | Carlos Perez RC | .40 | .18 |
| ❑ 155 | Tony Tarasco | .20 | .09 |
| ❑ 156 | Rondell White | .40 | .18 |
| ❑ 157 | Edgardo Alfonzo | .75 | .35 |
| ❑ 158 | Bobby Bonilla | .40 | .18 |
| ❑ 159 | Rico Brogna | .20 | .09 |
| ❑ 160 | Bobby Jones | .20 | .09 |
| ❑ 161 | Bill Pulsipher | .20 | .09 |
| ❑ 162 | Bret Saberhagen | .40 | .18 |
| ❑ 163 | Ricky Bottalico | .20 | .09 |
| ❑ 164 | Darren Daulton | .40 | .18 |
| ❑ 165 | Lenny Dykstra | .40 | .18 |
| ❑ 166 | Charlie Hayes | .20 | .09 |
| ❑ 167 | Dave Hollins | .20 | .09 |
| ❑ 168 | Gregg Jefferies | .20 | .09 |
| ❑ 169 | Michael Mimbs RC | .20 | .09 |
| ❑ 170 | Curt Schilling | .40 | .18 |
| ❑ 171 | Heathcliff Slocumb | .20 | .09 |
| ❑ 172 | Jay Bell | .40 | .18 |
| ❑ 173 | Micah Franklin RC | .20 | .09 |
| ❑ 174 | Mark Johnson RC | .20 | .09 |
| ❑ 175 | Jeff King | .20 | .09 |
| ❑ 176 | Al Martin | .20 | .09 |
| ❑ 177 | Dan Miceli | .20 | .09 |
| ❑ 178 | Denny Neagle | .40 | .18 |
| ❑ 179 | Bernard Gilkey | .20 | .09 |
| ❑ 180 | Ken Hill | .20 | .09 |
| ❑ 181 | Brian Jordan | .40 | .18 |
| ❑ 182 | Ray Lankford | .40 | .18 |
| ❑ 183 | Ozzie Smith | 1.00 | .45 |
| ❑ 184 | Andy Benes | .20 | .09 |
| ❑ 185 | Ken Caminiti | .40 | .18 |
| ❑ 186 | Steve Finley | .40 | .18 |
| ❑ 187 | Tony Gwynn | 1.50 | .70 |
| ❑ 188 | Joey Hamilton | .20 | .09 |
| ❑ 189 | Melvin Nieves | .20 | .09 |
| ❑ 190 | Scott Sanders | .20 | .09 |
| ❑ 191 | Rod Beck | .20 | .09 |
| ❑ 192 | Barry Bonds | 1.25 | .55 |
| ❑ 193 | Royce Clayton | .20 | .09 |
| ❑ 194 | Glenallen Hill | .20 | .09 |
| ❑ 195 | Darren Lewis | .20 | .09 |
| ❑ 196 | Mark Portugal | .20 | .09 |
| ❑ 197 | Matt Williams | .50 | .23 |
| ❑ 198 | Checklist 1-82 | .20 | .09 |
| ❑ 199 | Checklist 83-162 | .20 | .09 |
| ❑ 200 | Checklist 163-200/Inserts | .20 | .09 |
| ❑ P8 | Cal Ripken Promo | 3.00 | 1.35 |

## 1996 Emotion-XL

| | | MINT | NRMT |
|---|---|---|---|
| COMPLETE SET (300) | | 80.00 | 36.00 |
| ❑ 1 | Roberto Alomar | 1.50 | .70 |
| ❑ 2 | Brady Anderson | .50 | .23 |
| ❑ 3 | Bobby Bonilla | .50 | .23 |
| ❑ 4 | Jeffrey Hammonds | .50 | .23 |
| ❑ 5 | Chris Hoiles | .40 | .18 |
| ❑ 6 | Mike Mussina | 1.50 | .70 |
| ❑ 7 | Randy Myers | .40 | .18 |
| ❑ 8 | Rafael Palmeiro | 1.50 | .70 |
| ❑ 9 | Cal Ripken | 6.00 | 2.70 |
| ❑ 10 | B.J. Surhoff | .50 | .23 |
| ❑ 11 | Jose Canseco | 2.00 | .90 |
| ❑ 12 | Roger Clemens | 3.00 | 1.35 |
| ❑ 13 | Wil Cordero | .40 | .18 |
| ❑ 14 | Mike Greenwell | .40 | .18 |
| ❑ 15 | Dwayne Hosey | .40 | .18 |
| ❑ 16 | Tim Naehring | .40 | .18 |
| ❑ 17 | Troy O'Leary | .40 | .18 |
| ❑ 18 | Mike Stanley | .40 | .18 |
| ❑ 19 | John Valentin | .40 | .18 |
| ❑ 20 | Mo Vaughn | .50 | .23 |
| ❑ 21 | Jim Abbott | .50 | .23 |
| ❑ 22 | Garret Anderson | .50 | .23 |
| ❑ 23 | George Arias | .40 | .18 |
| ❑ 24 | Chili Davis | .50 | .23 |
| ❑ 25 | Jim Edmonds | 1.50 | .70 |
| ❑ 26 | Chuck Finley | .50 | .23 |
| ❑ 27 | Todd Greene | .40 | .18 |
| ❑ 28 | Mark Langston | .40 | .18 |
| ❑ 29 | Troy Percival | .40 | .18 |
| ❑ 30 | Tim Salmon | .50 | .23 |
| ❑ 31 | Lee Smith | .50 | .23 |
| ❑ 32 | J.T. Snow | .50 | .23 |
| ❑ 33 | Harold Baines | .50 | .23 |
| ❑ 34 | Jason Bere | .40 | .18 |
| ❑ 35 | Ray Durham | .50 | .23 |
| ❑ 36 | Alex Fernandez | .40 | .18 |
| ❑ 37 | Ozzie Guillen | .40 | .18 |
| ❑ 38 | Darren Lewis | .40 | .18 |

| Card | Player | Price 1 | Price 2 |
|---|---|---|---|
| ❑ 39 | Lyle Mouton | .40 | .18 |
| ❑ 40 | Tony Phillips | .40 | .18 |
| ❑ 41 | Danny Tartabull | .40 | .18 |
| ❑ 42 | Frank Thomas | 3.00 | 1.35 |
| ❑ 43 | Robin Ventura | .50 | .23 |
| ❑ 44 | Sandy Alomar Jr. | .50 | .23 |
| ❑ 45 | Carlos Baerga | .40 | .18 |
| ❑ 46 | Albert Belle | .75 | .35 |
| ❑ 47 | Julio Franco | .40 | .18 |
| ❑ 48 | Orel Hershiser | .50 | .23 |
| ❑ 49 | Kenny Lofton | .50 | .23 |
| ❑ 50 | Dennis Martinez | .50 | .23 |
| ❑ 51 | Jack McDowell | .40 | .18 |
| ❑ 52 | Jose Mesa | .40 | .18 |
| ❑ 53 | Eddie Murray | 1.50 | .70 |
| ❑ 54 | Charles Nagy | .40 | .18 |
| ❑ 55 | Manny Ramirez | 2.00 | .90 |
| ❑ 56 | Jim Thome | .75 | .35 |
| ❑ 57 | Omar Vizquel | .50 | .23 |
| ❑ 58 | Chad Curtis | .40 | .18 |
| ❑ 59 | Cecil Fielder | .50 | .23 |
| ❑ 60 | Travis Fryman | .50 | .23 |
| ❑ 61 | Chris Gomez | .40 | .18 |
| ❑ 62 | Felipe Lira | .40 | .18 |
| ❑ 63 | Alan Trammell | .75 | .35 |
| ❑ 64 | Kevin Appier | .50 | .23 |
| ❑ 65 | Johnny Damon | .75 | .35 |
| ❑ 66 | Tom Goodwin | .40 | .18 |
| ❑ 67 | Mark Gubicza | .40 | .18 |
| ❑ 68 | Jeff Montgomery | .40 | .18 |
| ❑ 69 | Jon Nunnally | .40 | .18 |
| ❑ 70 | Bip Roberts | .40 | .18 |
| ❑ 71 | Ricky Bones | .40 | .18 |
| ❑ 72 | Chuck Carr | .40 | .18 |
| ❑ 73 | John Jaha | .40 | .18 |
| ❑ 74 | Ben McDonald | .40 | .18 |
| ❑ 75 | Matt Mieske | .40 | .18 |
| ❑ 76 | Dave Nilsson | .40 | .18 |
| ❑ 77 | Kevin Seitzer | .40 | .18 |
| ❑ 78 | Greg Vaughn | .50 | .23 |
| ❑ 79 | Rick Aguilera | .40 | .18 |
| ❑ 80 | Marty Cordova | .40 | .18 |
| ❑ 81 | Roberto Kelly | .40 | .18 |
| ❑ 82 | Chuck Knoblauch | .50 | .23 |
| ❑ 83 | Pat Meares | .40 | .18 |
| ❑ 84 | Paul Molitor | 1.50 | .70 |
| ❑ 85 | Kirby Puckett | 4.00 | 1.80 |
| ❑ 86 | Brad Radke | .50 | .23 |
| ❑ 87 | Wade Boggs | 2.00 | .90 |
| ❑ 88 | David Cone | .50 | .23 |
| ❑ 89 | Dwight Gooden | .50 | .23 |
| ❑ 90 | Derek Jeter | 6.00 | 2.70 |
| ❑ 91 | Tino Martinez | .50 | .23 |
| ❑ 92 | Paul O'Neill | .50 | .23 |
| ❑ 93 | Andy Pettitte | .50 | .23 |
| ❑ 94 | Tim Raines | .50 | .23 |
| ❑ 95 | Ruben Rivera | .40 | .18 |
| ❑ 96 | Kenny Rogers | .40 | .18 |
| ❑ 97 | Ruben Sierra | .40 | .18 |
| ❑ 98 | John Wetteland | .50 | .23 |
| ❑ 99 | Bernie Williams | 1.50 | .70 |
| ❑ 100 | Allen Battle | .40 | .18 |
| ❑ 101 | Geronimo Berroa | .40 | .18 |
| ❑ 102 | Brent Gates | .40 | .18 |
| ❑ 103 | Doug Johns | .40 | .18 |
| ❑ 104 | Mark McGwire | 6.00 | 2.70 |
| ❑ 105 | Pedro Munoz | .40 | .18 |
| ❑ 106 | Ariel Prieto | .40 | .18 |
| ❑ 107 | Terry Steinbach | .40 | .18 |
| ❑ 108 | Todd Van Poppel | .40 | .18 |
| ❑ 109 | Chris Bosio | .40 | .18 |
| ❑ 110 | Jay Buhner | .50 | .23 |
| ❑ 111 | Joey Cora | .40 | .18 |
| ❑ 112 | Russ Davis | .40 | .18 |
| ❑ 113 | Ken Griffey Jr. | 6.00 | 2.70 |
| ❑ 114 | Sterling Hitchcock | .40 | .18 |
| ❑ 115 | Randy Johnson | 2.00 | .90 |
| ❑ 116 | Edgar Martinez | .75 | .35 |
| ❑ 117 | Alex Rodriguez | 5.00 | 2.20 |
| ❑ 118 | Paul Sorrento | .40 | .18 |
| ❑ 119 | Dan Wilson | .40 | .18 |
| ❑ 120 | Will Clark | 1.50 | .70 |
| ❑ 121 | Juan Gonzalez | 1.50 | .70 |
| ❑ 122 | Rusty Greer | .50 | .23 |
| ❑ 123 | Kevin Gross | .40 | .18 |
| ❑ 124 | Ken Hill | .40 | .18 |
| ❑ 125 | Dean Palmer | .50 | .23 |
| ❑ 126 | Roger Pavlik | .40 | .18 |
| ❑ 127 | Ivan Rodriguez | 2.00 | .90 |
| ❑ 128 | Mickey Tettleton | .40 | .18 |
| ❑ 129 | Joe Carter | .50 | .23 |
| ❑ 130 | Carlos Delgado | 1.50 | .70 |
| ❑ 131 | Alex Gonzalez | .40 | .18 |
| ❑ 132 | Shawn Green | 1.50 | .70 |
| ❑ 133 | Erik Hanson | .40 | .18 |
| ❑ 134 | Pat Hentgen | .40 | .18 |
| ❑ 135 | Otis Nixon | .40 | .18 |
| ❑ 136 | John Olerud | .50 | .23 |
| ❑ 137 | Ed Sprague | .40 | .18 |
| ❑ 138 | Steve Avery | .40 | .18 |
| ❑ 139 | Jermaine Dye | .50 | .23 |
| ❑ 140 | Tom Glavine | 1.50 | .70 |
| ❑ 141 | Marquis Grissom | .40 | .18 |
| ❑ 142 | Chipper Jones | 4.00 | 1.80 |
| ❑ 143 | David Justice | .75 | .35 |
| ❑ 144 | Ryan Klesko | .50 | .23 |
| ❑ 145 | Javier Lopez | .50 | .23 |
| ❑ 146 | Greg Maddux | 4.00 | 1.80 |
| ❑ 147 | Fred McGriff | .75 | .35 |
| ❑ 148 | Jason Schmidt | .40 | .18 |
| ❑ 149 | John Smoltz | .50 | .23 |
| ❑ 150 | Mark Wohlers | .40 | .18 |
| ❑ 151 | Jim Bullinger | .40 | .18 |
| ❑ 152 | Frank Castillo | .40 | .18 |
| ❑ 153 | Kevin Foster | .40 | .18 |
| ❑ 154 | Luis Gonzalez | .50 | .23 |
| ❑ 155 | Mark Grace | 1.50 | .70 |
| ❑ 156 | Brian McRae | .40 | .18 |
| ❑ 157 | Jaime Navarro | .40 | .18 |
| ❑ 158 | Rey Sanchez | .40 | .18 |
| ❑ 159 | Ryne Sandberg | 2.00 | .90 |
| ❑ 160 | Sammy Sosa | 3.00 | 1.35 |
| ❑ 161 | Bret Boone | .50 | .23 |
| ❑ 162 | Jeff Brantley | .40 | .18 |
| ❑ 163 | Vince Coleman | .40 | .18 |
| ❑ 164 | Steve Gibralter | .40 | .18 |
| ❑ 165 | Barry Larkin | 1.50 | .70 |
| ❑ 166 | Hal Morris | .40 | .18 |
| ❑ 167 | Mark Portugal | .40 | .18 |
| ❑ 168 | Reggie Sanders | .40 | .18 |
| ❑ 169 | Pete Schourek | .40 | .18 |
| ❑ 170 | John Smiley | .40 | .18 |
| ❑ 171 | Jason Bates | .40 | .18 |
| ❑ 172 | Dante Bichette | .50 | .23 |
| ❑ 173 | Ellis Burks | .50 | .23 |
| ❑ 174 | Vinny Castilla | .50 | .23 |
| ❑ 175 | Andres Galarraga | .75 | .35 |
| ❑ 176 | Kevin Ritz | .40 | .18 |
| ❑ 177 | Bill Swift | .40 | .18 |
| ❑ 178 | Larry Walker | .50 | .23 |
| ❑ 179 | Walt Weiss | .40 | .18 |
| ❑ 180 | Eric Young | .40 | .18 |
| ❑ 181 | Kurt Abbott | .40 | .18 |
| ❑ 182 | Kevin Brown | .75 | .35 |
| ❑ 183 | John Burkett | .40 | .18 |
| ❑ 184 | Greg Colbrunn | .40 | .18 |
| ❑ 185 | Jeff Conine | .40 | .18 |
| ❑ 186 | Chris Hammond | .40 | .18 |
| ❑ 187 | Charles Johnson | .50 | .23 |
| ❑ 188 | Terry Pendleton | .50 | .23 |
| ❑ 189 | Pat Rapp | .40 | .18 |
| ❑ 190 | Gary Sheffield | 1.50 | .70 |
| ❑ 191 | Quilvio Veras | .40 | .18 |
| ❑ 192 | Devon White | .50 | .23 |
| ❑ 193 | Jeff Bagwell | 2.00 | .90 |
| ❑ 194 | Derek Bell | .40 | .18 |
| ❑ 195 | Sean Berry | .40 | .18 |
| ❑ 196 | Craig Biggio | .75 | .35 |
| ❑ 197 | Doug Drabek | .40 | .18 |
| ❑ 198 | Tony Eusebio | .40 | .18 |
| ❑ 199 | Mike Hampton | .50 | .23 |
| ❑ 200 | Brian L.Hunter | .40 | .18 |
| ❑ 201 | Derrick May | .40 | .18 |
| ❑ 202 | Orlando Miller | .40 | .18 |
| ❑ 203 | Shane Reynolds | .40 | .18 |
| ❑ 204 | Mike Blowers | .40 | .18 |
| ❑ 205 | Tom Candiotti | .40 | .18 |
| ❑ 206 | Delino DeShields | .40 | .18 |
| ❑ 207 | Greg Gagne | .40 | .18 |
| ❑ 208 | Karim Garcia | .40 | .18 |
| ❑ 209 | Todd Hollandsworth | .40 | .18 |
| ❑ 210 | Eric Karros | .50 | .23 |
| ❑ 211 | Ramon Martinez | .40 | .18 |
| ❑ 212 | Raul Mondesi | .50 | .23 |
| ❑ 213 | Hideo Nomo | 1.50 | .70 |
| ❑ 214 | Chan Ho Park | .50 | .23 |
| ❑ 215 | Mike Piazza | 5.00 | 2.20 |
| ❑ 216 | Ismael Valdes | .40 | .18 |
| ❑ 217 | Todd Worrell | .40 | .18 |
| ❑ 218 | Moises Alou | .50 | .23 |
| ❑ 219 | Yamil Benitez | .40 | .18 |
| ❑ 220 | Jeff Fassero | .40 | .18 |
| ❑ 221 | Darrin Fletcher | .40 | .18 |
| ❑ 222 | Cliff Floyd | .50 | .23 |
| ❑ 223 | Pedro Martinez | 2.00 | .90 |
| ❑ 224 | Carlos Perez | .40 | .18 |
| ❑ 225 | Mel Rojas | .40 | .18 |
| ❑ 226 | David Segui | .40 | .18 |
| ❑ 227 | Rondell White | .50 | .23 |
| ❑ 228 | Rico Brogna | .40 | .18 |
| ❑ 229 | Carl Everett | .50 | .23 |
| ❑ 230 | John Franco | .50 | .23 |
| ❑ 231 | Bernard Gilkey | .40 | .18 |
| ❑ 232 | Todd Hundley | .40 | .18 |
| ❑ 233 | Jason Isringhausen | .50 | .23 |
| ❑ 234 | Lance Johnson | .40 | .18 |
| ❑ 235 | Bobby Jones | .40 | .18 |
| ❑ 236 | Jeff Kent | .75 | .35 |
| ❑ 237 | Rey Ordonez | .50 | .23 |
| ❑ 238 | Bill Pulsipher | .40 | .18 |
| ❑ 239 | Jose Vizcaino | .40 | .18 |
| ❑ 240 | Paul Wilson | .40 | .18 |
| ❑ 241 | Ricky Bottalico | .40 | .18 |
| ❑ 242 | Darren Daulton | .50 | .23 |
| ❑ 243 | Lenny Dykstra | .50 | .23 |
| ❑ 244 | Jim Eisenreich | .40 | .18 |
| ❑ 245 | Sid Fernandez | .40 | .18 |
| ❑ 246 | Gregg Jefferies | .40 | .18 |
| ❑ 247 | Mickey Morandini | .40 | .18 |
| ❑ 248 | Benito Santiago | .40 | .18 |
| ❑ 249 | Curt Schilling | .50 | .23 |
| ❑ 250 | Mark Whiten | .40 | .18 |
| ❑ 251 | Todd Zeile | .40 | .18 |
| ❑ 252 | Jay Bell | .50 | .23 |
| ❑ 253 | Carlos Garcia | .40 | .18 |
| ❑ 254 | Charlie Hayes | .40 | .18 |
| ❑ 255 | Jason Kendall | .50 | .23 |
| ❑ 256 | Jeff King | .40 | .18 |
| ❑ 257 | Al Martin | .40 | .18 |
| ❑ 258 | Orlando Merced | .40 | .18 |
| ❑ 259 | Dan Miceli | .40 | .18 |
| ❑ 260 | Denny Neagle | .50 | .23 |
| ❑ 261 | Alan Benes | .40 | .18 |
| ❑ 262 | Andy Benes | .40 | .18 |
| ❑ 263 | Royce Clayton | .40 | .18 |
| ❑ 264 | Dennis Eckersley | .50 | .23 |
| ❑ 265 | Gary Gaetti | .50 | .23 |
| ❑ 266 | Ron Gant | .40 | .18 |
| ❑ 267 | Brian Jordan | .50 | .23 |
| ❑ 268 | Ray Lankford | .50 | .23 |
| ❑ 269 | John Mabry | .40 | .18 |
| ❑ 270 | Tom Pagnozzi | .40 | .18 |
| ❑ 271 | Ozzie Smith | 2.00 | .90 |
| ❑ 272 | Todd Stottlemyre | .40 | .18 |
| ❑ 273 | Andy Ashby | .40 | .18 |
| ❑ 274 | Brad Ausmus | .40 | .18 |
| ❑ 275 | Ken Caminiti | .50 | .23 |
| ❑ 276 | Steve Finley | .50 | .23 |
| ❑ 277 | Tony Gwynn | 3.00 | 1.35 |
| ❑ 278 | Joey Hamilton | .40 | .18 |
| ❑ 279 | Rickey Henderson | 2.00 | .90 |
| ❑ 280 | Trevor Hoffman | .50 | .23 |
| ❑ 281 | Wally Joyner | .50 | .23 |
| ❑ 282 | Jody Reed | .40 | .18 |
| ❑ 283 | Bob Tewksbury | .40 | .18 |
| ❑ 284 | Fernando Valenzuela | .50 | .23 |
| ❑ 285 | Rod Beck | .40 | .18 |
| ❑ 286 | Barry Bonds | 2.50 | 1.10 |
| ❑ 287 | Mark Carreon | .40 | .18 |
| ❑ 288 | Shawon Dunston | .40 | .18 |
| ❑ 289 | Osvaldo Fernandez RC | .40 | .18 |
| ❑ 290 | Glenallen Hill | .40 | .18 |
| ❑ 291 | Stan Javier | .40 | .18 |
| ❑ 292 | Mark Leiter | .40 | .18 |
| ❑ 293 | Kirt Manwaring | .40 | .18 |
| ❑ 294 | Robby Thompson | .40 | .18 |
| ❑ 295 | William VanLandingham | .40 | .18 |
| ❑ 296 | Allen Watson | .40 | .18 |

| | # | Player | MINT | NRMT |
|---|---|---|---|---|
| ❑ | 297 | Matt Williams | .75 | .35 |
| ❑ | 298 | Checklist | .40 | .18 |
| ❑ | 299 | Checklist | .40 | .18 |
| ❑ | 300 | Checklist | .40 | .18 |
| ❑ | P55 | Manny Ramirez Promo | 1.00 | .90 |

## 1997 E-X2000

| | MINT | NRMT |
|---|---|---|
| COMPLETE SET (100) | 80.00 | 36.00 |
| COMMON CARD (1-100) | .40 | .18 |

| | # | Player | MINT | NRMT |
|---|---|---|---|---|
| ❑ | 1 | Jim Edmonds | 1.50 | .70 |
| ❑ | 2 | Darin Erstad | 2.00 | .90 |
| ❑ | 3 | Eddie Murray | 1.50 | .70 |
| ❑ | 4 | Roberto Alomar | 1.50 | .70 |
| ❑ | 5 | Brady Anderson | .60 | .25 |
| ❑ | 6 | Mike Mussina | 1.50 | .70 |
| ❑ | 7 | Rafael Palmeiro | 1.50 | .70 |
| ❑ | 8 | Cal Ripken | 6.00 | 2.70 |
| ❑ | 9 | Steve Avery | .40 | .18 |
| ❑ | 10 | Nomar Garciaparra | 5.00 | 2.20 |
| ❑ | 11 | Mo Vaughn | .60 | .25 |
| ❑ | 12 | Albert Belle | 1.00 | .45 |
| ❑ | 13 | Mike Cameron | .60 | .25 |
| ❑ | 14 | Ray Durham | .60 | .25 |
| ❑ | 15 | Frank Thomas | 3.00 | 1.35 |
| ❑ | 16 | Robin Ventura | .60 | .25 |
| ❑ | 17 | Manny Ramirez | 2.00 | .90 |
| ❑ | 18 | Jim Thome | 1.00 | .45 |
| ❑ | 19 | Matt Williams | 1.00 | .45 |
| ❑ | 20 | Tony Clark | .40 | .18 |
| ❑ | 21 | Travis Fryman | .60 | .25 |
| ❑ | 22 | Bob Higginson | .60 | .25 |
| ❑ | 23 | Kevin Appier | .60 | .25 |
| ❑ | 24 | Johnny Damon | .60 | .25 |
| ❑ | 25 | Jermaine Dye | .60 | .25 |
| ❑ | 26 | Jeff Cirillo | .60 | .25 |
| ❑ | 27 | Ben McDonald | .40 | .18 |
| ❑ | 28 | Chuck Knoblauch | .60 | .25 |
| ❑ | 29 | Paul Molitor | 1.50 | .70 |
| ❑ | 30 | Todd Walker | .40 | .18 |
| ❑ | 31 | Wade Boggs | 2.00 | .90 |
| ❑ | 32 | Cecil Fielder | .60 | .25 |
| ❑ | 33 | Derek Jeter | 6.00 | 2.70 |
| ❑ | 34 | Andy Pettitte | .60 | .25 |
| ❑ | 35 | Ruben Rivera | .40 | .18 |
| ❑ | 36 | Bernie Williams | 1.50 | .70 |
| ❑ | 37 | Jose Canseco | 2.00 | .90 |
| ❑ | 38 | Mark McGwire | 6.00 | 2.70 |
| ❑ | 39 | Jay Buhner | .60 | .25 |
| ❑ | 40 | Ken Griffey Jr. | 6.00 | 2.70 |
| ❑ | 41 | Randy Johnson | 2.00 | .90 |
| ❑ | 42 | Edgar Martinez | 1.00 | .45 |
| ❑ | 43 | Alex Rodriguez | 5.00 | 2.20 |
| ❑ | 44 | Dan Wilson | .40 | .18 |
| ❑ | 45 | Will Clark | 1.50 | .70 |
| ❑ | 46 | Juan Gonzalez | 1.50 | .70 |
| ❑ | 47 | Ivan Rodriguez | 2.00 | .90 |
| ❑ | 48 | Joe Carter | .60 | .25 |
| ❑ | 49 | Roger Clemens | 3.00 | 1.35 |
| ❑ | 50 | Juan Guzman | .40 | .18 |
| ❑ | 51 | Pat Hentgen | .40 | .18 |
| ❑ | 52 | Tom Glavine | 1.50 | .70 |
| ❑ | 53 | Andruw Jones | 2.00 | .90 |
| ❑ | 54 | Chipper Jones | 4.00 | 1.80 |
| ❑ | 55 | Ryan Klesko | .60 | .25 |
| ❑ | 56 | Kenny Lofton | .60 | .25 |
| ❑ | 57 | Greg Maddux | 4.00 | 1.80 |
| ❑ | 58 | Fred McGriff | 1.00 | .45 |
| ❑ | 59 | John Smoltz | .60 | .25 |
| ❑ | 60 | Mark Wohlers | .40 | .18 |
| ❑ | 61 | Mark Grace | 1.50 | .70 |
| ❑ | 62 | Ryne Sandberg | 2.00 | .90 |
| ❑ | 63 | Sammy Sosa | 3.00 | 1.35 |
| ❑ | 64 | Barry Larkin | 1.50 | .70 |
| ❑ | 65 | Deion Sanders | .60 | .25 |
| ❑ | 66 | Reggie Sanders | .40 | .18 |
| ❑ | 67 | Dante Bichette | .60 | .25 |
| ❑ | 68 | Ellis Burks | .60 | .25 |
| ❑ | 69 | Andres Galarraga | 1.00 | .45 |
| ❑ | 70 | Moises Alou | .60 | .25 |
| ❑ | 71 | Kevin Brown | 1.00 | .45 |
| ❑ | 72 | Cliff Floyd | .60 | .25 |
| ❑ | 73 | Edgar Renteria | .60 | .25 |
| ❑ | 74 | Gary Sheffield | 1.50 | .70 |
| ❑ | 75 | Bob Abreu | .60 | .25 |
| ❑ | 76 | Jeff Bagwell | 2.00 | .90 |
| ❑ | 77 | Craig Biggio | 1.00 | .45 |
| ❑ | 78 | Todd Hollandsworth | .40 | .18 |
| ❑ | 79 | Eric Karros | .60 | .25 |
| ❑ | 80 | Raul Mondesi | .60 | .25 |
| ❑ | 81 | Hideo Nomo | 1.50 | .70 |
| ❑ | 82 | Mike Piazza | 5.00 | 2.20 |
| ❑ | 83 | Vladimir Guerrero | 3.00 | 1.35 |
| ❑ | 84 | Henry Rodriguez | .40 | .18 |
| ❑ | 85 | Todd Hundley | .40 | .18 |
| ❑ | 86 | Alex Ochoa | .40 | .18 |
| ❑ | 87 | Rey Ordonez | .60 | .25 |
| ❑ | 88 | Gregg Jefferies | .40 | .18 |
| ❑ | 89 | Scott Rolen | 1.50 | .70 |
| ❑ | 90 | Jermaine Allensworth | .40 | .18 |
| ❑ | 91 | Jason Kendall | .60 | .25 |
| ❑ | 92 | Ken Caminiti | .60 | .25 |
| ❑ | 93 | Tony Gwynn | 3.00 | 1.35 |
| ❑ | 94 | Rickey Henderson | 2.00 | .90 |
| ❑ | 95 | Barry Bonds | 2.50 | 1.10 |
| ❑ | 96 | J.T. Snow | .60 | .25 |
| ❑ | 97 | Dennis Eckersley | .60 | .25 |
| ❑ | 98 | Ron Gant | .40 | .18 |
| ❑ | 99 | Brian Jordan | .60 | .25 |
| ❑ | 100 | Ray Lankford | .60 | .25 |
| ❑ | 101 | Checklist | .40 | .18 |
| ❑ | 102 | Checklist | .40 | .18 |
| ❑ | P43 | Alex Rodriguez<br>Three card promo strip | 3.00 | 1.35 |
| ❑ | S43 | Alex Rodriguez<br>Mailed to Dealers who ordered Cases<br>Card is numbered out of 3,000 | 20.00 | 9.00 |
| ❑ | NNO | Alex Rodriguez<br>Ball Exch 100 produced | 80.00 | 36.00 |

## 1998 E-X2001

| | MINT | NRMT |
|---|---|---|
| COMPLETE SET (100) | 100.00 | 45.00 |

| | # | Player | MINT | NRMT |
|---|---|---|---|---|
| ❑ | 1 | Alex Rodriguez | 5.00 | 2.20 |
| ❑ | 2 | Barry Bonds | 2.50 | 1.10 |
| ❑ | 3 | Greg Maddux | 4.00 | 1.80 |
| ❑ | 4 | Roger Clemens | 3.00 | 1.35 |
| ❑ | 5 | Juan Gonzalez | 1.50 | .70 |
| ❑ | 6 | Chipper Jones | 4.00 | 1.80 |
| ❑ | 7 | Derek Jeter | 6.00 | 2.70 |
| ❑ | 8 | Frank Thomas | 3.00 | 1.35 |
| ❑ | 9 | Cal Ripken | 6.00 | 2.70 |
| ❑ | 10 | Ken Griffey Jr. | 6.00 | 2.70 |
| ❑ | 11 | Mark McGwire | 6.00 | 2.70 |
| ❑ | 12 | Hideo Nomo | 1.50 | .70 |
| ❑ | 13 | Tony Gwynn | 3.00 | 1.35 |
| ❑ | 14 | Ivan Rodriguez | 2.00 | .90 |
| ❑ | 15 | Mike Piazza | 5.00 | 2.20 |
| ❑ | 16 | Roberto Alomar | 1.50 | .70 |
| ❑ | 17 | Jeff Bagwell | 2.00 | .90 |
| ❑ | 18 | Andruw Jones | 1.50 | .70 |
| ❑ | 19 | Albert Belle | 1.00 | .45 |
| ❑ | 20 | Mo Vaughn | .60 | .25 |
| ❑ | 21 | Kenny Lofton | .60 | .25 |
| ❑ | 22 | Gary Sheffield | 1.50 | .70 |
| ❑ | 23 | Tony Clark | .40 | .18 |
| ❑ | 24 | Mike Mussina | 1.50 | .70 |
| ❑ | 25 | Barry Larkin | 1.50 | .70 |
| ❑ | 26 | Moises Alou | .60 | .25 |
| ❑ | 27 | Brady Anderson | .60 | .25 |
| ❑ | 28 | Andy Pettitte | .60 | .25 |
| ❑ | 29 | Sammy Sosa | 3.00 | 1.35 |
| ❑ | 30 | Raul Mondesi | .60 | .25 |
| ❑ | 31 | Andres Galarraga | 1.00 | .45 |
| ❑ | 32 | Chuck Knoblauch | .60 | .25 |
| ❑ | 33 | Jim Thome | 1.00 | .45 |
| ❑ | 34 | Craig Biggio | 1.00 | .45 |
| ❑ | 35 | Jay Buhner | .60 | .25 |
| ❑ | 36 | Rafael Palmeiro | 1.50 | .70 |
| ❑ | 37 | Curt Schilling | .60 | .25 |
| ❑ | 38 | Tino Martinez | .60 | .25 |
| ❑ | 39 | Pedro Martinez | 2.00 | .90 |
| ❑ | 40 | Jose Canseco | 2.00 | .90 |
| ❑ | 41 | Jeff Cirillo | .60 | .25 |
| ❑ | 42 | Dean Palmer | .60 | .25 |
| ❑ | 43 | Tim Salmon | .60 | .25 |
| ❑ | 44 | Jason Giambi | 1.50 | .70 |
| ❑ | 45 | Bobby Higginson | .60 | .25 |
| ❑ | 46 | Jim Edmonds | 1.50 | .70 |
| ❑ | 47 | David Justice | 1.00 | .45 |
| ❑ | 48 | John Olerud | .60 | .25 |
| ❑ | 49 | Ray Lankford | .60 | .25 |
| ❑ | 50 | Al Martin | .40 | .18 |
| ❑ | 51 | Mike Lieberthal | .60 | .25 |
| ❑ | 52 | Henry Rodriguez | .40 | .18 |
| ❑ | 53 | Edgar Renteria | .40 | .18 |
| ❑ | 54 | Eric Karros | .60 | .25 |
| ❑ | 55 | Marquis Grissom | .40 | .18 |
| ❑ | 56 | Wilson Alvarez | .40 | .18 |
| ❑ | 57 | Darryl Kile | .60 | .25 |
| ❑ | 58 | Jeff King | .40 | .18 |
| ❑ | 59 | Shawn Estes | .40 | .18 |
| ❑ | 60 | Tony Womack | .40 | .18 |
| ❑ | 61 | Willie Greene | .40 | .18 |
| ❑ | 62 | Ken Caminiti | .60 | .25 |
| ❑ | 63 | Vinny Castilla | .60 | .25 |
| ❑ | 64 | Mark Grace | 1.50 | .70 |
| ❑ | 65 | Ryan Klesko | .60 | .25 |
| ❑ | 66 | Robin Ventura | .60 | .25 |
| ❑ | 67 | Todd Hundley | .40 | .18 |
| ❑ | 68 | Travis Fryman | .60 | .25 |
| ❑ | 69 | Edgar Martinez | 1.00 | .45 |
| ❑ | 70 | Matt Williams | 1.00 | .45 |
| ❑ | 71 | Paul Molitor | 1.50 | .70 |
| ❑ | 72 | Kevin Brown | 1.00 | .45 |
| ❑ | 73 | Randy Johnson | 2.00 | .90 |
| ❑ | 74 | Bernie Williams | 1.50 | .70 |
| ❑ | 75 | Manny Ramirez | 2.00 | .90 |
| ❑ | 76 | Fred McGriff | 1.00 | .45 |
| ❑ | 77 | Tom Glavine | 1.50 | .70 |
| ❑ | 78 | Carlos Delgado | 1.50 | .70 |
| ❑ | 79 | Larry Walker | .60 | .25 |
| ❑ | 80 | Hideki Irabu | .40 | .18 |
| ❑ | 81 | Ryan McGuire | .40 | .18 |
| ❑ | 82 | Justin Thompson | .40 | .18 |
| ❑ | 83 | Kevin Orie | .40 | .18 |
| ❑ | 84 | Jon Nunnally | .40 | .18 |
| ❑ | 85 | Mark Kotsay | .60 | .25 |
| ❑ | 86 | Todd Walker | .40 | .18 |
| ❑ | 87 | Jason Dickson | .40 | .18 |
| ❑ | 88 | Fernando Tatis | .60 | .25 |
| ❑ | 89 | Karim Garcia | .40 | .18 |
| ❑ | 90 | Ricky Ledee | .40 | .18 |
| ❑ | 91 | Paul Konerko | .60 | .25 |
| ❑ | 92 | Jaret Wright | .40 | .18 |
| ❑ | 93 | Darin Erstad | 1.50 | .70 |
| ❑ | 94 | Livan Hernandez | .40 | .18 |

| | | |
|---|---|---|
| ❑ 95 Nomar Garciaparra | 5.00 | 2.20 |
| ❑ 96 Jose Cruz Jr. | .60 | .25 |
| ❑ 97 Scott Rolen | 1.50 | .70 |
| ❑ 98 Ben Grieve | .60 | .25 |
| ❑ 99 Vladimir Guerrero | 2.50 | 1.10 |
| ❑ 100 Travis Lee | .60 | .25 |
| ❑ 101 Kerry Wood Redemption | 4.00 | 1.80 |
| ❑ NNO Kerry Wood EXCH | 2.00 | .90 |
| ❑ NNO Alex Rodriguez Sample | 3.00 | 1.35 |

## 1999 E-X Century

| | MINT | NRMT |
|---|---|---|
| COMPLETE SET (120) | 80.00 | 36.00 |
| COMP.SET w/o SP's (90) | 40.00 | 18.00 |
| COMMON CARD (1-90) | .40 | .18 |
| COMMON SP (91-120) | .75 | .35 |

| | | |
|---|---|---|
| ❑ 1 Scott Rolen | 1.50 | .70 |
| ❑ 2 Nomar Garciaparra | 5.00 | 2.20 |
| ❑ 3 Mike Piazza | 5.00 | 2.20 |
| ❑ 4 Tony Gwynn | 3.00 | 1.35 |
| ❑ 5 Sammy Sosa | 3.00 | 1.35 |
| ❑ 6 Alex Rodriguez | 5.00 | 2.20 |
| ❑ 7 Vladimir Guerrero | 2.50 | 1.10 |
| ❑ 8 Chipper Jones | 4.00 | 1.80 |
| ❑ 9 Derek Jeter | 6.00 | 2.70 |
| ❑ 10 Kerry Wood | .60 | .25 |
| ❑ 11 Juan Gonzalez | 1.50 | .70 |
| ❑ 12 Frank Thomas | 3.00 | 1.35 |
| ❑ 13 Mo Vaughn | .60 | .25 |
| ❑ 14 Greg Maddux | 4.00 | 1.80 |
| ❑ 15 Jeff Bagwell | 2.00 | .90 |
| ❑ 16 Mark McGwire | 6.00 | 2.70 |
| ❑ 17 Ken Griffey Jr. | 6.00 | 2.70 |
| ❑ 18 Roger Clemens | 3.00 | 1.35 |
| ❑ 19 Cal Ripken | 6.00 | 2.70 |
| ❑ 20 Travis Lee | .40 | .18 |
| ❑ 21 Todd Helton | 2.00 | .90 |
| ❑ 22 Darin Erstad | 1.50 | .70 |
| ❑ 23 Pedro Martinez | 2.00 | .90 |
| ❑ 24 Barry Bonds | 2.50 | 1.10 |
| ❑ 25 Andruw Jones | 1.50 | .70 |
| ❑ 26 Larry Walker | .60 | .25 |
| ❑ 27 Albert Belle | 1.00 | .45 |
| ❑ 28 Ivan Rodriguez | 2.00 | .90 |
| ❑ 29 Magglio Ordonez | 1.00 | .45 |
| ❑ 30 Andres Galarraga | 1.00 | .45 |
| ❑ 31 Mike Mussina | 1.50 | .70 |
| ❑ 32 Randy Johnson | 2.00 | .90 |
| ❑ 33 Tom Glavine | 1.50 | .70 |
| ❑ 34 Barry Larkin | 1.50 | .70 |
| ❑ 35 Jim Thome | 1.00 | .45 |
| ❑ 36 Gary Sheffield | 1.50 | .70 |
| ❑ 37 Bernie Williams | 1.50 | .70 |
| ❑ 38 Carlos Delgado | 1.50 | .70 |
| ❑ 39 Rafael Palmeiro | 1.50 | .70 |
| ❑ 40 Edgar Renteria | .40 | .18 |
| ❑ 41 Brad Fullmer | .60 | .25 |
| ❑ 42 David Wells | .60 | .25 |
| ❑ 43 Dante Bichette | .60 | .25 |
| ❑ 44 Jaret Wright | .40 | .18 |
| ❑ 45 Ricky Ledee | .40 | .18 |
| ❑ 46 Ray Lankford | .60 | .25 |
| ❑ 47 Mark Grace | 1.50 | .70 |
| ❑ 48 Jeff Cirillo | .60 | .25 |
| ❑ 49 Rondell White | .60 | .25 |
| ❑ 50 Jeromy Burnitz | .60 | .25 |
| ❑ 51 Sean Casey | .60 | .25 |
| ❑ 52 Rolando Arrojo | .40 | .18 |
| ❑ 53 Jason Giambi | 1.50 | .70 |
| ❑ 54 John Olerud | .60 | .25 |
| ❑ 55 Will Clark | 1.50 | .70 |
| ❑ 56 Raul Mondesi | .60 | .25 |
| ❑ 57 Scott Brosius | .60 | .25 |
| ❑ 58 Bartolo Colon | .60 | .25 |
| ❑ 59 Steve Finley | .60 | .25 |
| ❑ 60 Javy Lopez | .60 | .25 |
| ❑ 61 Tim Salmon | .60 | .25 |
| ❑ 62 Roberto Alomar | 1.50 | .70 |
| ❑ 63 Vinny Castilla | .60 | .25 |
| ❑ 64 Craig Biggio | 1.00 | .45 |
| ❑ 65 Jose Guillen | .40 | .18 |
| ❑ 66 Greg Vaughn | .60 | .25 |
| ❑ 67 Jose Canseco | 2.00 | .90 |
| ❑ 68 Shawn Green | 1.50 | .70 |
| ❑ 69 Curt Schilling | .60 | .25 |
| ❑ 70 Orlando Hernandez | .60 | .25 |
| ❑ 71 Jose Cruz Jr. | .60 | .25 |
| ❑ 72 Alex Gonzalez | .40 | .18 |
| ❑ 73 Tino Martinez | .60 | .25 |
| ❑ 74 Todd Hundley | .40 | .18 |
| ❑ 75 Brian Giles | .60 | .25 |
| ❑ 76 Cliff Floyd | .60 | .25 |
| ❑ 77 Paul O'Neill | .60 | .25 |
| ❑ 78 Ken Caminiti | .60 | .25 |
| ❑ 79 Ron Gant | .60 | .25 |
| ❑ 80 Juan Encarnacion | .60 | .25 |
| ❑ 81 Ben Grieve | .60 | .25 |
| ❑ 82 Brian Jordan | .60 | .25 |
| ❑ 83 Rickey Henderson | 2.00 | .90 |
| ❑ 84 Tony Clark | .40 | .18 |
| ❑ 85 Shannon Stewart | .60 | .25 |
| ❑ 86 Robin Ventura | .60 | .25 |
| ❑ 87 Todd Walker | .40 | .18 |
| ❑ 88 Kevin Brown | 1.00 | .45 |
| ❑ 89 Moises Alou | .60 | .25 |
| ❑ 90 Manny Ramirez | 2.00 | .90 |
| ❑ 91 Gabe Alvarez SP | .75 | .35 |
| ❑ 92 Jeremy Giambi SP | .75 | .35 |
| ❑ 93 Adrian Beltre SP | 1.25 | .55 |
| ❑ 94 George Lombard SP | .75 | .35 |
| ❑ 95 Ryan Minor SP | .75 | .35 |
| ❑ 96 Kevin Witt SP | .75 | .35 |
| ❑ 97 Scott Hunter SP RC | .75 | .35 |
| ❑ 98 Carlos Guillen SP | .75 | .35 |
| ❑ 99 Derrick Gibson SP | .75 | .35 |
| ❑ 100 Trot Nixon SP | 1.25 | .55 |
| ❑ 101 Troy Glaus SP | 5.00 | 2.20 |
| ❑ 102 Armando Rios SP | .75 | .35 |
| ❑ 103 Preston Wilson SP | 1.25 | .55 |
| ❑ 104 Pat Burrell SP RC | 10.00 | 4.50 |
| ❑ 105 J.D. Drew SP | 3.00 | 1.35 |
| ❑ 106 Bruce Chen SP | .75 | .35 |
| ❑ 107 Matt Clement SP | .75 | .35 |
| ❑ 108 Carlos Beltran SP | 1.25 | .55 |
| ❑ 109 Carlos Febles SP | .75 | .35 |
| ❑ 110 Rob Fick SP | .75 | .35 |
| ❑ 111 Russell Branyan SP | 1.25 | .55 |
| ❑ 112 Roosevelt Brown SP RC | 1.00 | .45 |
| ❑ 113 Corey Koskie SP | .75 | .35 |
| ❑ 114 Mario Encarnacion SP RC | 1.25 | .55 |
| ❑ 115 Peter Tucci SP | .75 | .35 |
| ❑ 116 Eric Chavez SP | 1.25 | .55 |
| ❑ 117 Gabe Kapler SP | 1.25 | .55 |
| ❑ 118 Marlon Anderson SP | .75 | .35 |
| ❑ 119 A.J. Burnett SP RC | 1.50 | .70 |
| ❑ 120 Ryan Bradley SP | .75 | .35 |
| ❑ P81 Ben Grieve Sample | 2.00 | .90 |

## 2000 E-X

| | MINT | NRMT |
|---|---|---|
| COMPLETE SET (90) | 200.00 | 90.00 |
| COMP.SET w/o SP's (60) | 25.00 | 11.00 |
| COMMON CARD (1-60) | .25 | .11 |
| MINOR STARS 1-60 | .40 | .18 |
| SEMISTARS 1-60 | .60 | .25 |
| UNLISTED STARS 1-60 | 1.00 | .45 |
| COMMON PROS (61-90) | 5.00 | 2.20 |
| MINOR STARS 61-90 | 6.00 | 2.70 |
| SEMISTARS 61-90 | 6.00 | 2.70 |
| UNLISTED STARS 61-90 | 8.00 | 3.60 |

| | | |
|---|---|---|
| ❑ 1 Alex Rodriguez | 3.00 | 1.35 |
| ❑ 2 Jeff Bagwell | 1.25 | .55 |
| ❑ 3 Mike Piazza | 3.00 | 1.35 |
| ❑ 4 Tony Gwynn | 2.00 | .90 |
| ❑ 5 Ken Griffey Jr. | 4.00 | 1.80 |
| ❑ 6 Juan Gonzalez | 1.00 | .45 |
| ❑ 7 Vladimir Guerrero | 1.50 | .70 |
| ❑ 8 Cal Ripken | 4.00 | 1.80 |
| ❑ 9 Mo Vaughn | .25 | .11 |
| ❑ 10 Chipper Jones | 2.50 | 1.10 |
| ❑ 11 Derek Jeter | 4.00 | 1.80 |
| ❑ 12 Nomar Garciaparra | 3.00 | 1.35 |
| ❑ 13 Mark McGwire | 4.00 | 1.80 |
| ❑ 14 Sammy Sosa | 2.00 | .90 |
| ❑ 15 Pedro Martinez | 1.25 | .55 |
| ❑ 16 Greg Maddux | 2.50 | 1.10 |
| ❑ 17 Frank Thomas | 2.00 | .90 |
| ❑ 18 Shawn Green | 1.00 | .45 |
| ❑ 19 Carlos Beltran | .40 | .18 |
| ❑ 20 Roger Clemens | 2.00 | .90 |
| ❑ 21 Randy Johnson | 1.25 | .55 |
| ❑ 22 Bernie Williams | 1.00 | .45 |
| ❑ 23 Carlos Delgado | 1.00 | .45 |
| ❑ 24 Manny Ramirez | 1.25 | .55 |
| ❑ 25 Freddy Garcia | .25 | .11 |
| ❑ 26 Barry Bonds | 1.50 | .70 |
| ❑ 27 Tim Hudson | 1.00 | .45 |
| ❑ 28 Larry Walker | .40 | .18 |
| ❑ 29 Raul Mondesi | .25 | .11 |
| ❑ 30 Ivan Rodriguez | 1.25 | .55 |
| ❑ 31 Magglio Ordonez | .25 | .11 |
| ❑ 32 Scott Rolen | 1.00 | .45 |
| ❑ 33 Mike Mussina | 1.00 | .45 |
| ❑ 34 J.D. Drew | 1.00 | .45 |
| ❑ 35 Tom Glavine | 1.00 | .45 |
| ❑ 36 Barry Larkin | 1.00 | .45 |
| ❑ 37 Jim Thome | .25 | .11 |
| ❑ 38 Erubiel Durazo | .40 | .18 |
| ❑ 39 Curt Schilling | .25 | .11 |
| ❑ 40 Orlando Hernandez | .40 | .18 |
| ❑ 41 Rafael Palmeiro | 1.00 | .45 |
| ❑ 42 Gabe Kapler | .25 | .11 |
| ❑ 43 Mark Grace | 1.00 | .45 |
| ❑ 44 Jeff Cirillo | .40 | .18 |
| ❑ 45 Jeromy Burnitz | .25 | .11 |
| ❑ 46 Sean Casey | .40 | .18 |
| ❑ 47 Kevin Millwood | .25 | .11 |
| ❑ 48 Vinny Castilla | .40 | .18 |
| ❑ 49 Jose Canseco | 1.25 | .55 |
| ❑ 50 Roberto Alomar | 1.00 | .45 |
| ❑ 51 Craig Biggio | .60 | .25 |
| ❑ 52 Preston Wilson | .25 | .11 |
| ❑ 53 Jeff Weaver | .25 | .11 |
| ❑ 54 Robin Ventura | .25 | .11 |
| ❑ 55 Ben Grieve | .40 | .18 |
| ❑ 56 Troy Glaus | 1.25 | .55 |
| ❑ 57 Jacque Jones | .25 | .11 |
| ❑ 58 Brian Giles | .25 | .11 |
| ❑ 59 Kevin Brown | .25 | .11 |
| ❑ 60 Todd Helton | 1.25 | .55 |
| ❑ 61 Ben Petrick PROS | 5.00 | 2.20 |
| ❑ 62 Chad Hermansen PROS | 5.00 | 2.20 |
| ❑ 63 Kevin Barker PROS | 5.00 | 2.20 |
| ❑ 64 Matt LeCroy PROS | 5.00 | 2.20 |
| ❑ 65 Brad Penny PROS | 6.00 | 2.70 |
| ❑ 66 D.T. Cromer PROS | 5.00 | 2.20 |
| ❑ 67 Steve Lomasney PROS | 5.00 | 2.20 |
| ❑ 68 Cole Liniak PROS | 5.00 | 2.20 |

| No. | Card | Mint | Nrmt |
|---|---|---|---|
| 69 | B.J. Ryan PROS | 5.00 | 2.20 |
| 70 | Wilton Veras PROS | 6.00 | 2.70 |
| 71 | Aaron McNeal PROS RC | 8.00 | 3.60 |
| 72 | Nick Johnson PROS | 6.00 | 2.70 |
| 73 | Adam Piatt PROS | 8.00 | 3.60 |
| 74 | Adam Kennedy PROS | 6.00 | 2.70 |
| 75 | Cesar King PROS | 5.00 | 2.20 |
| 76 | Peter Bergeron PROS | 5.00 | 2.20 |
| 77 | Rob Bell PROS | 5.00 | 2.20 |
| 78 | Wily Pena PROS | 6.00 | 2.70 |
| 79 | Ruben Mateo PROS | 6.00 | 2.70 |
| 80 | Kip Wells PROS | 6.00 | 2.70 |
| 81 | Alex Escobar PROS | 6.00 | 2.70 |
| 82 | Danys Baez PROS RC | 8.00 | 3.60 |
| 83 | Travis Dawkins PROS | 6.00 | 2.70 |
| 84 | Mark Quinn PROS | 6.00 | 2.70 |
| 85 | Jimmy Anderson PROS | 5.00 | 2.20 |
| 86 | Rick Ankiel PROS | 15.00 | 6.75 |
| 87 | Alfonso Soriano PROS | 6.00 | 2.70 |
| 88 | Pat Burrell PROS | 12.00 | 5.50 |
| 89 | Eric Munson PROS | 8.00 | 3.60 |
| 90 | Josh Beckett PROS | 8.00 | 3.60 |

## 1993 Finest

| | MINT | NRMT |
|---|---|---|
| COMPLETE SET (199) | 150.00 | 70.00 |

| No. | Card | Mint | Nrmt |
|---|---|---|---|
| 1 | David Justice | 3.00 | 1.35 |
| 2 | Lou Whitaker | 1.50 | .70 |
| 3 | Bryan Harvey | 1.00 | .45 |
| 4 | Carlos Garcia | 1.00 | .45 |
| 5 | Sid Fernandez | 1.00 | .45 |
| 6 | Brett Butler | 1.50 | .70 |
| 7 | Scott Cooper | 1.00 | .45 |
| 8 | B.J. Surhoff | 1.50 | .70 |
| 9 | Steve Finley | 1.50 | .70 |
| 10 | Curt Schilling | 1.50 | .70 |
| 11 | Jeff Bagwell | 6.00 | 2.70 |
| 12 | Alex Cole | 1.00 | .45 |
| 13 | John Olerud | 3.00 | 1.35 |
| 14 | John Smiley | 1.00 | .45 |
| 15 | Bip Roberts | 1.00 | .45 |
| 16 | Albert Belle | 3.00 | 1.35 |
| 17 | Duane Ward | 1.00 | .45 |
| 18 | Alan Trammell | 3.00 | 1.35 |
| 19 | Andy Benes | 1.00 | .45 |
| 20 | Reggie Sanders | 1.00 | .45 |
| 21 | Todd Zeile | 1.00 | .45 |
| 22 | Rick Aguilera | 1.00 | .45 |
| 23 | Dave Hollins | 1.00 | .45 |
| 24 | Jose Rijo | 1.00 | .45 |
| 25 | Matt Williams | 3.00 | 1.35 |
| 26 | Sandy Alomar Jr. | 1.50 | .70 |
| 27 | Alex Fernandez | 1.50 | .70 |
| 28 | Ozzie Smith | 6.00 | 2.70 |
| 29 | Ramon Martinez | 1.00 | .45 |
| 30 | Bernie Williams | 5.00 | 2.20 |
| 31 | Gary Sheffield | 5.00 | 2.20 |
| 32 | Eric Karros | 3.00 | 1.35 |
| 33 | Frank Viola | 1.00 | .45 |
| 34 | Kevin Young | 1.50 | .70 |
| 35 | Ken Hill | 1.00 | .45 |
| 36 | Tony Fernandez | 1.00 | .45 |
| 37 | Tim Wakefield | 1.00 | .45 |
| 38 | John Kruk | 1.50 | .70 |
| 39 | Chris Sabo | 1.00 | .45 |
| 40 | Marquis Grissom | 1.00 | .45 |
| 41 | Glenn Davis | 1.00 | .45 |
| 42 | Jeff Montgomery | 1.50 | .70 |
| 43 | Kenny Lofton | 6.00 | 2.70 |
| 44 | John Burkett | 1.00 | .45 |
| 45 | Darryl Hamilton | 1.00 | .45 |
| 46 | Jim Abbott | 1.50 | .70 |
| 47 | Ivan Rodriguez | 6.00 | 2.70 |
| 48 | Eric Young | 1.00 | .45 |
| 49 | Mitch Williams | 1.00 | .45 |
| 50 | Harold Reynolds | 1.00 | .45 |
| 51 | Brian Harper | 1.00 | .45 |
| 52 | Rafael Palmeiro | 5.00 | 2.20 |
| 53 | Bret Saberhagen | 1.50 | .70 |
| 54 | Jeff Conine | 1.00 | .45 |
| 55 | Ivan Calderon | 1.00 | .45 |
| 56 | Juan Guzman | 1.00 | .45 |
| 57 | Carlos Baerga | 1.00 | .45 |
| 58 | Charles Nagy | 1.00 | .45 |
| 59 | Wally Joyner | 1.50 | .70 |
| 60 | Charlie Hayes | 1.00 | .45 |
| 61 | Shane Mack | 1.00 | .45 |
| 62 | Pete Harnisch | 1.00 | .45 |
| 63 | George Brett | 10.00 | 4.50 |
| 64 | Lance Johnson | 1.00 | .45 |
| 65 | Ben McDonald | 1.00 | .45 |
| 66 | Bobby Bonilla | 1.50 | .70 |
| 67 | Terry Steinbach | 1.00 | .45 |
| 68 | Ron Gant | 1.50 | .70 |
| 69 | Doug Jones | 1.00 | .45 |
| 70 | Paul Molitor | 5.00 | 2.20 |
| 71 | Brady Anderson | 1.50 | .70 |
| 72 | Chuck Finley | 1.50 | .70 |
| 73 | Mark Grace | 5.00 | 2.20 |
| 74 | Mike Devereaux | 1.00 | .45 |
| 75 | Tony Phillips | 1.00 | .45 |
| 76 | Chuck Knoblauch | 1.50 | .70 |
| 77 | Tony Gwynn | 10.00 | 4.50 |
| 78 | Kevin Appier | 1.50 | .70 |
| 79 | Sammy Sosa | 10.00 | 4.50 |
| 80 | Mickey Tettleton | 1.00 | .45 |
| 81 | Felix Jose | 1.00 | .45 |
| 82 | Mark Langston | 1.00 | .45 |
| 83 | Gregg Jefferies | 1.00 | .45 |
| 84 | Andre Dawson AS | 3.00 | 1.35 |
| 85 | Greg Maddux AS | 12.00 | 5.50 |
| 86 | Rickey Henderson AS | 6.00 | 2.70 |
| 87 | Tom Glavine AS | 3.00 | 1.35 |
| 88 | Roberto Alomar AS | 5.00 | 2.20 |
| 89 | Darryl Strawberry AS | 1.50 | .70 |
| 90 | Wade Boggs AS | 6.00 | 2.70 |
| 91 | Bo Jackson AS | 1.50 | .70 |
| 92 | Mark McGwire AS | 20.00 | 9.00 |
| 93 | Robin Ventura AS | 1.50 | .70 |
| 94 | Joe Carter AS | 1.50 | .70 |
| 95 | Lee Smith AS | 1.50 | .70 |
| 96 | Cal Ripken AS | 20.00 | 9.00 |
| 97 | Larry Walker AS | 1.50 | .70 |
| 98 | Don Mattingly AS | 12.00 | 5.50 |
| 99 | Jose Canseco AS | 6.00 | 2.70 |
| 100 | Dennis Eckersley AS | 1.00 | .45 |
| 101 | Terry Pendleton AS | 1.50 | .70 |
| 102 | Frank Thomas AS | 10.00 | 4.50 |
| 103 | Barry Bonds AS | 8.00 | 3.60 |
| 104 | Roger Clemens AS | 10.00 | 4.50 |
| 105 | Ryne Sandberg AS | 6.00 | 2.70 |
| 106 | Fred McGriff AS | 3.00 | 1.35 |
| 107 | Nolan Ryan AS | 25.00 | 11.00 |
| 108 | Will Clark AS | 5.00 | 2.20 |
| 109 | Pat Listach AS | 1.00 | .45 |
| 110 | Ken Griffey Jr. AS | 20.00 | 9.00 |
| 111 | Cecil Fielder AS | 1.50 | .70 |
| 112 | Kirby Puckett AS | 12.00 | 5.50 |
| 113 | Dwight Gooden AS | 1.50 | .70 |
| 114 | Barry Larkin AS | 5.00 | 2.20 |
| 115 | David Cone AS | 1.50 | .70 |
| 116 | Juan Gonzalez AS | 5.00 | 2.20 |
| 117 | Kent Hrbek | 1.50 | .70 |
| 118 | Tim Wallach | 1.00 | .45 |
| 119 | Craig Biggio | 3.00 | 1.35 |
| 120 | Roberto Kelly | 1.00 | .45 |
| 121 | Gregg Olson | 1.00 | .45 |
| 122 | Eddie Murray UER | 5.00 | 2.20 |
| | (122 career strikeouts should be 1224) | | |
| 123 | Wil Cordero | 1.00 | .45 |
| 124 | Jay Buhner | 1.50 | .70 |
| 125 | Carlton Fisk | 5.00 | 2.20 |
| 126 | Eric Davis | 1.50 | .70 |
| 127 | Doug Drabek | 1.00 | .45 |
| 128 | Ozzie Guillen | 1.00 | .45 |
| 129 | John Wetteland | 1.50 | .70 |
| 130 | Andres Galarraga | 3.00 | 1.35 |
| 131 | Ken Caminiti | 1.50 | .70 |
| 132 | Tom Candiotti | 1.00 | .45 |
| 133 | Pat Borders | 1.00 | .45 |
| 134 | Kevin Brown | 3.00 | 1.35 |
| 135 | Travis Fryman | 1.50 | .70 |
| 136 | Kevin Mitchell | 1.50 | .70 |
| 137 | Greg Swindell | 1.00 | .45 |
| 138 | Benito Santiago | 1.00 | .45 |
| 139 | Reggie Jefferson | 1.50 | .70 |
| 140 | Chris Bosio | 1.00 | .45 |
| 141 | Deion Sanders | 3.00 | 1.35 |
| 142 | Scott Erickson | 1.00 | .45 |
| 143 | Howard Johnson | 1.00 | .45 |
| 144 | Orestes Destrade | 1.00 | .45 |
| 145 | Jose Guzman | 1.00 | .45 |
| 146 | Chad Curtis | 1.00 | .45 |
| 147 | Cal Eldred | 1.00 | .45 |
| 148 | Willie Greene | 1.00 | .45 |
| 149 | Tommy Greene | 1.00 | .45 |
| 150 | Erik Hanson | 1.00 | .45 |
| 151 | Bob Welch | 1.00 | .45 |
| 152 | John Jaha | 1.00 | .45 |
| 153 | Harold Baines | 1.50 | .70 |
| 154 | Randy Johnson | 6.00 | 2.70 |
| 155 | Al Martin | 1.00 | .45 |
| 156 | J.T. Snow RC | 6.00 | 2.70 |
| 157 | Mike Mussina | 5.00 | 2.20 |
| 158 | Ruben Sierra | 1.00 | .45 |
| 159 | Dean Palmer | 1.50 | .70 |
| 160 | Steve Avery | 1.00 | .45 |
| 161 | Julio Franco | 1.00 | .45 |
| 162 | Dave Winfield | 5.00 | 2.20 |
| 163 | Tim Salmon | 1.50 | .70 |
| 164 | Tom Henke | 1.00 | .45 |
| 165 | Mo Vaughn | 1.50 | .70 |
| 166 | John Smoltz | 1.50 | .70 |
| 167 | Danny Tartabull | 1.00 | .45 |
| 168 | Delino DeShields | 1.50 | .70 |
| 169 | Charlie Hough | 1.50 | .70 |
| 170 | Paul O'Neill | 1.50 | .70 |
| 171 | Darren Daulton | 1.50 | .70 |
| 172 | Jack McDowell | 1.00 | .45 |
| 173 | Junior Felix | 1.00 | .45 |
| 174 | Jimmy Key | 1.50 | .70 |
| 175 | George Bell | 1.00 | .45 |
| 176 | Mike Stanton | 1.00 | .45 |
| 177 | Len Dykstra | 1.50 | .70 |
| 178 | Norm Charlton | 1.00 | .45 |
| 179 | Eric Anthony | 1.00 | .45 |
| 180 | Rob Dibble | 1.00 | .45 |
| 181 | Otis Nixon | 1.00 | .45 |
| 182 | Randy Myers | 1.50 | .70 |
| 183 | Tim Raines | 1.50 | .70 |
| 184 | Orel Hershiser | 1.50 | .70 |
| 185 | Andy Van Slyke | 1.50 | .70 |
| 186 | Mike Lansing RC | 1.50 | .70 |
| 187 | Ray Lankford | 3.00 | 1.35 |
| 188 | Mike Morgan | 1.00 | .45 |
| 189 | Moises Alou | 1.50 | .70 |
| 190 | Edgar Martinez | 3.00 | 1.35 |
| 191 | John Franco | 1.50 | .70 |
| 192 | Robin Yount | 3.00 | 1.35 |
| 193 | Bob Tewksbury | 1.00 | .45 |
| 194 | Jay Bell | 1.50 | .70 |
| 195 | Luis Gonzalez | 1.50 | .70 |
| 196 | Dave Fleming | 1.00 | .45 |
| 197 | Mike Greenwell | 1.00 | .45 |
| 198 | David Nied | 1.00 | .45 |
| 199 | Mike Piazza | 25.00 | 11.00 |

## 1994 Finest

| | MINT | NRMT |
|---|---|---|
| COMPLETE SET (440) | 120.00 | 55.00 |
| COMPLETE SERIES 1 (220) | 60.00 | 27.00 |
| COMPLETE SERIES 2 (220) | 60.00 | 27.00 |
| COMMON CARD (1-440) | .50 | .23 |

| No. | Card | Mint | Nrmt |
|---|---|---|---|
| 1 | Mike Piazza FIN | 8.00 | 3.60 |
| 2 | Kevin Stocker FIN | .50 | .23 |

❑ 3 Greg McMichael FIN .50 .23
❑ 4 Jeff Conine FIN .50 .23
❑ 5 Rene Arocha FIN .50 .23
❑ 6 Aaron Sele FIN 1.00 .45
❑ 7 Brent Gates FIN .50 .23
❑ 8 Chuck Carr FIN .50 .23
❑ 9 Kirk Rueter FIN .50 .23
❑ 10 Mike Lansing FIN .50 .23
❑ 11 Al Martin FIN .50 .23
❑ 12 Jason Bere FIN .50 .23
❑ 13 Troy Neel FIN .50 .23
❑ 14 Armando Reynoso FIN .50 .23
❑ 15 Jeromy Burnitz FIN 1.00 .45
❑ 16 Rich Amaral FIN .50 .23
❑ 17 David McCarty FIN .50 .23
❑ 18 Tim Salmon FIN 1.00 .45
❑ 19 Steve Cooke FIN .50 .23
❑ 20 Wil Cordero FIN .50 .23
❑ 21 Kevin Tapani .50 .23
❑ 22 Deion Sanders 1.00 .45
❑ 23 Jose Offerman .50 .23
❑ 24 Mark Langston .50 .23
❑ 25 Ken Hill .50 .23
❑ 26 Alex Fernandez .50 .23
❑ 27 Jeff Blauser .50 .23
❑ 28 Royce Clayton .50 .23
❑ 29 Brad Ausmus .50 .23
❑ 30 Ryan Bowen .50 .23
❑ 31 Steve Finley 1.00 .45
❑ 32 Charlie Hayes .50 .23
❑ 33 Jeff Kent 1.50 .70
❑ 34 Mike Henneman .50 .23
❑ 35 Andres Galarraga 1.50 .70
❑ 36 Wayne Kirby .50 .23
❑ 37 Joe Oliver .50 .23
❑ 38 Terry Steinbach .50 .23
❑ 39 Ryan Thompson .50 .23
❑ 40 Luis Alicea .50 .23
❑ 41 Randy Velarde .50 .23
❑ 42 Bob Tewksbury .50 .23
❑ 43 Reggie Sanders .50 .23
❑ 44 Brian Williams .50 .23
❑ 45 Joe Orsulak .50 .23
❑ 46 Jose Lind .50 .23
❑ 47 Dave Hollins .50 .23
❑ 48 Graeme Lloyd .50 .23
❑ 49 Jim Gott .50 .23
❑ 50 Andre Dawson 1.50 .70
❑ 51 Steve Buechele .50 .23
❑ 52 David Cone 1.00 .45
❑ 53 Ricky Gutierrez .50 .23
❑ 54 Lance Johnson .50 .23
❑ 55 Tino Martinez 1.00 .45
❑ 56 Phil Hiatt .50 .23
❑ 57 Carlos Garcia .50 .23
❑ 58 Danny Darwin .50 .23
❑ 59 Dante Bichette 1.00 .45
❑ 60 Scott Kamieniecki .50 .23
❑ 61 Orlando Merced .50 .23
❑ 62 Brian McRae .50 .23
❑ 63 Pat Kelly .50 .23
❑ 64 Tom Henke .50 .23
❑ 65 Jeff King .50 .23
❑ 66 Mike Mussina 2.50 1.10
❑ 67 Tim Pugh .50 .23
❑ 68 Robby Thompson .50 .23
❑ 69 Paul O'Neill 1.00 .45
❑ 70 Hal Morris .50 .23
❑ 71 Ron Karkovice .50 .23
❑ 72 Joe Girardi .50 .23
❑ 73 Eduardo Perez .50 .23
❑ 74 Raul Mondesi 1.00 .45
❑ 75 Mike Gallego .50 .23
❑ 76 Mike Stanley .50 .23
❑ 77 Kevin Roberson .50 .23
❑ 78 Mark McGwire 10.00 4.50
❑ 79 Pat Listach .50 .23
❑ 80 Eric Davis 1.00 .45
❑ 81 Mike Bordick .50 .23
❑ 82 Dwight Gooden 1.00 .45
❑ 83 Mike Moore .50 .23
❑ 84 Phil Plantier .50 .23
❑ 85 Darren Lewis .50 .23
❑ 86 Rick Wilkins .50 .23
❑ 87 Darryl Strawberry 1.00 .45
❑ 88 Rob Dibble .50 .23
❑ 89 Greg Vaughn 1.00 .45
❑ 90 Jeff Russell .50 .23
❑ 91 Mark Lewis .50 .23
❑ 92 Gregg Jefferies .50 .23
❑ 93 Jose Guzman .50 .23
❑ 94 Kenny Rogers .50 .23
❑ 95 Mark Lemke .50 .23
❑ 96 Mike Morgan .50 .23
❑ 97 Andujar Cedeno .50 .23
❑ 98 Orel Hershiser 1.00 .45
❑ 99 Greg Swindell .50 .23
❑ 100 John Smoltz 1.00 .45
❑ 101 Pedro A.Martinez RC .50 .23
❑ 102 Jim Thome 1.50 .70
❑ 103 David Segui .50 .23
❑ 104 Charles Nagy .50 .23
❑ 105 Shane Mack .50 .23
❑ 106 John Jaha .50 .23
❑ 107 Tom Candiotti .50 .23
❑ 108 David Wells 1.00 .45
❑ 109 Bobby Jones .50 .23
❑ 110 Bob Hamelin .50 .23
❑ 111 Bernard Gilkey .50 .23
❑ 112 Chili Davis 1.00 .45
❑ 113 Todd Stottlemyre .50 .23
❑ 114 Derek Bell .50 .23
❑ 115 Mark McLemore .50 .23
❑ 116 Mark Whiten .50 .23
❑ 117 Mike Devereaux .50 .23
❑ 118 Terry Pendleton 1.00 .45
❑ 119 Pat Meares .50 .23
❑ 120 Pete Harnisch .50 .23
❑ 121 Moises Alou 1.00 .45
❑ 122 Jay Buhner 1.00 .45
❑ 123 Wes Chamberlain .50 .23
❑ 124 Mike Perez .50 .23
❑ 125 Devon White .50 .23
❑ 126 Ivan Rodriguez 3.00 1.35
❑ 127 Don Slaught .50 .23
❑ 128 John Valentin .50 .23
❑ 129 Jaime Navarro .50 .23
❑ 130 Dave Magadan .50 .23
❑ 131 Brady Anderson 1.00 .45
❑ 132 Juan Guzman .50 .23
❑ 133 John Wetteland 1.00 .45
❑ 134 Dave Stewart 1.00 .45
❑ 135 Scott Servais .50 .23
❑ 136 Ozzie Smith 3.00 1.35
❑ 137 Darrin Fletcher .50 .23
❑ 138 Jose Mesa .50 .23
❑ 139 Wilson Alvarez .50 .23
❑ 140 Pete Incaviglia .50 .23
❑ 141 Chris Hoiles .50 .23
❑ 142 Darryl Hamilton .50 .23
❑ 143 Chuck Finley 1.00 .45
❑ 144 Archi Cianfrocco .50 .23
❑ 145 Bill Wegman .50 .23
❑ 146 Joey Cora .50 .23
❑ 147 Darrell Whitmore .50 .23
❑ 148 David Hulse .50 .23
❑ 149 Jim Abbott 1.00 .45
❑ 150 Curt Schilling 1.00 .45
❑ 151 Bill Swift .50 .23
❑ 152 Tommy Greene .50 .23
❑ 153 Roberto Mejia .50 .23
❑ 154 Edgar Martinez 1.50 .70
❑ 155 Roger Pavlik .50 .23
❑ 156 Randy Tomlin .50 .23
❑ 157 J.T. Snow 1.00 .45
❑ 158 Bob Welch .50 .23
❑ 159 Alan Trammell 1.50 .70
❑ 160 Ed Sprague .50 .23
❑ 161 Ben McDonald .50 .23
❑ 162 Derrick May .50 .23
❑ 163 Roberto Kelly .50 .23
❑ 164 Bryan Harvey .50 .23
❑ 165 Ron Gant 1.00 .45
❑ 166 Scott Erickson .50 .23
❑ 167 Anthony Young .50 .23
❑ 168 Scott Cooper .50 .23
❑ 169 Rod Beck .50 .23
❑ 170 John Franco 1.00 .45
❑ 171 Gary DiSarcina .50 .23
❑ 172 Dave Fleming .50 .23
❑ 173 Wade Boggs 3.00 1.35
❑ 174 Kevin Appier 1.00 .45
❑ 175 Jose Bautista .50 .23
❑ 176 Wally Joyner 1.00 .45
❑ 177 Dean Palmer 1.00 .45
❑ 178 Tony Phillips .50 .23
❑ 179 John Smiley .50 .23
❑ 180 Charlie Hough 1.00 .45
❑ 181 Scott Fletcher .50 .23
❑ 182 Todd Van Poppel .50 .23
❑ 183 Mike Blowers .50 .23
❑ 184 Willie McGee 1.00 .45
❑ 185 Paul Sorrento .50 .23
❑ 186 Eric Young .50 .23
❑ 187 Bret Barberie .50 .23
❑ 188 Manuel Lee .50 .23
❑ 189 Jeff Branson .50 .23
❑ 190 Jim Deshaies .50 .23
❑ 191 Ken Caminiti 1.00 .45
❑ 192 Tim Raines 1.00 .45
❑ 193 Joe Grahe .50 .23
❑ 194 Hipolito Pichardo .50 .23
❑ 195 Denny Neagle .50 .23
❑ 196 Jeff Gardner .50 .23
❑ 197 Mike Benjamin .50 .23
❑ 198 Milt Thompson .50 .23
❑ 199 Bruce Ruffin .50 .23
❑ 200 Chris Hammond UER .50 .23
(Back of card has Mariners; should be Marlins)
❑ 201 Tony Gwynn FIN 5.00 2.20
❑ 202 Robin Ventura FIN 1.00 .45
❑ 203 Frank Thomas FIN 5.00 2.20
❑ 204 Kirby Puckett FIN 6.00 2.70
❑ 205 Roberto Alomar FIN 2.50 1.10
❑ 206 Dennis Eckersley FIN 1.00 .45
❑ 207 Joe Carter FIN 1.00 .45
❑ 208 Albert Belle FIN 1.50 .70
❑ 209 Greg Maddux FIN 6.00 2.70
❑ 210 Ryne Sandberg FIN 3.00 1.35
❑ 211 Juan Gonzalez FIN 2.50 1.10
❑ 212 Jeff Bagwell FIN 3.00 1.35
❑ 213 Randy Johnson FIN 3.00 1.35
❑ 214 Matt Williams FIN 1.50 .70
❑ 215 Dave Winfield FIN 2.50 1.10
❑ 216 Larry Walker FIN 1.00 .45
❑ 217 Roger Clemens FIN 5.00 2.20
❑ 218 Kenny Lofton FIN 1.00 .45
❑ 219 Cecil Fielder FIN 1.00 .45
❑ 220 Darren Daulton FIN 1.00 .45
❑ 221 John Olerud FIN 1.00 .45
❑ 222 Jose Canseco FIN 3.00 1.35
❑ 223 Rickey Henderson FIN 3.00 1.35
❑ 224 Fred McGriff FIN 1.50 .70
❑ 225 Gary Sheffield FIN 2.50 1.10
❑ 226 Jack McDowell FIN .50 .23
❑ 227 Rafael Palmeiro FIN 2.50 1.10
❑ 228 Travis Fryman FIN 1.00 .45
❑ 229 Marquis Grissom FIN .50 .23
❑ 230 Barry Bonds FIN 4.00 1.80
❑ 231 Carlos Baerga FIN .50 .23
❑ 232 Ken Griffey Jr. FIN 10.00 4.50
❑ 233 David Justice FIN 1.50 .70
❑ 234 Bobby Bonilla FIN 1.00 .45
❑ 235 Cal Ripken FIN 10.00 4.50
❑ 236 Sammy Sosa FIN 5.00 2.20
❑ 237 Len Dykstra FIN 1.00 .45
❑ 238 Will Clark FIN 2.50 1.10
❑ 239 Paul Molitor FIN 2.50 1.10
❑ 240 Barry Larkin FIN 2.50 1.10

| | Player | Mint | NrMt |
|---|---|---|---|
| ❑ 241 | Bo Jackson | 1.00 | .45 |
| ❑ 242 | Mitch Williams | .50 | .23 |
| ❑ 243 | Ron Darling | .50 | .23 |
| ❑ 244 | Darryl Kile | 1.00 | .45 |
| ❑ 245 | Geronimo Berroa | .50 | .23 |
| ❑ 246 | Gregg Olson | .50 | .23 |
| ❑ 247 | Brian Harper | .50 | .23 |
| ❑ 248 | Rheal Cormier | .50 | .23 |
| ❑ 249 | Rey Sanchez | .50 | .23 |
| ❑ 250 | Jeff Fassero | .50 | .23 |
| ❑ 251 | Sandy Alomar Jr. | 1.00 | .45 |
| ❑ 252 | Chris Bosio | .50 | .23 |
| ❑ 253 | Andy Stankiewicz | .50 | .23 |
| ❑ 254 | Harold Baines | 1.00 | .45 |
| ❑ 255 | Andy Ashby | .50 | .23 |
| ❑ 256 | Tyler Green | .50 | .23 |
| ❑ 257 | Kevin Brown | 1.00 | .45 |
| ❑ 258 | Mo Vaughn | 1.00 | .45 |
| ❑ 259 | Mike Harkey | .50 | .23 |
| ❑ 260 | Dave Henderson | .50 | .23 |
| ❑ 261 | Kent Hrbek | 1.00 | .45 |
| ❑ 262 | Darrin Jackson | .50 | .23 |
| ❑ 263 | Bob Wickman | .50 | .23 |
| ❑ 264 | Spike Owen | .50 | .23 |
| ❑ 265 | Todd Jones | .50 | .23 |
| ❑ 266 | Pat Borders | .50 | .23 |
| ❑ 267 | Tom Glavine | 2.50 | 1.10 |
| ❑ 268 | Dave Nilsson | .50 | .23 |
| ❑ 269 | Rich Batchelor | .50 | .23 |
| ❑ 270 | Delino DeShields | .50 | .23 |
| ❑ 271 | Felix Fermin | .50 | .23 |
| ❑ 272 | Orestes Destrade | .50 | .23 |
| ❑ 273 | Mickey Morandini | .50 | .23 |
| ❑ 274 | Otis Nixon | .50 | .23 |
| ❑ 275 | Ellis Burks | 1.00 | .45 |
| ❑ 276 | Greg Gagne | .50 | .23 |
| ❑ 277 | John Doherty | .50 | .23 |
| ❑ 278 | Julio Franco | .50 | .23 |
| ❑ 279 | Bernie Williams | 2.50 | 1.10 |
| ❑ 280 | Rick Aguilera | .50 | .23 |
| ❑ 281 | Mickey Tettleton | .50 | .23 |
| ❑ 282 | David Nied | .50 | .23 |
| ❑ 283 | Johnny Ruffin | .50 | .23 |
| ❑ 284 | Dan Wilson | .50 | .23 |
| ❑ 285 | Omar Vizquel | 1.00 | .45 |
| ❑ 286 | Willie Banks | .50 | .23 |
| ❑ 287 | Erik Pappas | .50 | .23 |
| ❑ 288 | Cal Eldred | .50 | .23 |
| ❑ 289 | Bobby Witt | .50 | .23 |
| ❑ 290 | Luis Gonzalez | 1.00 | .45 |
| ❑ 291 | Greg Pirkl | .50 | .23 |
| ❑ 292 | Alex Cole | .50 | .23 |
| ❑ 293 | Ricky Bones | .50 | .23 |
| ❑ 294 | Denis Boucher | .50 | .23 |
| ❑ 295 | John Burkett | .50 | .23 |
| ❑ 296 | Steve Trachsel | .50 | .23 |
| ❑ 297 | Ricky Jordan | .50 | .23 |
| ❑ 298 | Mark Dewey | .50 | .23 |
| ❑ 299 | Jimmy Key | 1.00 | .45 |
| ❑ 300 | Mike Macfarlane | .50 | .23 |
| ❑ 301 | Tim Belcher | .50 | .23 |
| ❑ 302 | Carlos Reyes | .50 | .23 |
| ❑ 303 | Greg A. Harris | .50 | .23 |
| ❑ 304 | Brian Anderson RC | 1.00 | .45 |
| ❑ 305 | Terry Mulholland | .50 | .23 |
| ❑ 306 | Felix Jose | .50 | .23 |
| ❑ 307 | Darren Holmes | .50 | .23 |
| ❑ 308 | Jose Rijo | .50 | .23 |
| ❑ 309 | Paul Wagner | .50 | .23 |
| ❑ 310 | Bob Scanlan | .50 | .23 |
| ❑ 311 | Mike Jackson | .50 | .23 |
| ❑ 312 | Jose Vizcaino | .50 | .23 |
| ❑ 313 | Rob Butler | .50 | .23 |
| ❑ 314 | Kevin Seitzer | .50 | .23 |
| ❑ 315 | Geronimo Pena | .50 | .23 |
| ❑ 316 | Hector Carrasco | .50 | .23 |
| ❑ 317 | Eddie Murray | 2.50 | 1.10 |
| ❑ 318 | Roger Salkeld | .50 | .23 |
| ❑ 319 | Todd Hundley | .50 | .23 |
| ❑ 320 | Danny Jackson | .50 | .23 |
| ❑ 321 | Kevin Young | .50 | .23 |
| ❑ 322 | Mike Greenwell | .50 | .23 |
| ❑ 323 | Kevin Mitchell | .50 | .23 |
| ❑ 324 | Chuck Knoblauch | 1.00 | .45 |
| ❑ 325 | Danny Tartabull | .50 | .23 |
| ❑ 326 | Vince Coleman | .50 | .23 |
| ❑ 327 | Marvin Freeman | .50 | .23 |
| ❑ 328 | Andy Benes | .50 | .23 |
| ❑ 329 | Mike Kelly | .50 | .23 |
| ❑ 330 | Karl Rhodes | .50 | .23 |
| ❑ 331 | Allen Watson | .50 | .23 |
| ❑ 332 | Damion Easley | .50 | .23 |
| ❑ 333 | Reggie Jefferson | .50 | .23 |
| ❑ 334 | Kevin McReynolds | .50 | .23 |
| ❑ 335 | Arthur Rhodes | .50 | .23 |
| ❑ 336 | Brian R. Hunter | .50 | .23 |
| ❑ 337 | Tom Browning | .50 | .23 |
| ❑ 338 | Pedro Munoz | .50 | .23 |
| ❑ 339 | Billy Ripken | .50 | .23 |
| ❑ 340 | Gene Harris | .50 | .23 |
| ❑ 341 | Fernando Vina | .50 | .23 |
| ❑ 342 | Sean Berry | .50 | .23 |
| ❑ 343 | Pedro Astacio | .50 | .23 |
| ❑ 344 | B.J. Surhoff | 1.00 | .45 |
| ❑ 345 | Doug Drabek | .50 | .23 |
| ❑ 346 | Jody Reed | .50 | .23 |
| ❑ 347 | Ray Lankford | 1.00 | .45 |
| ❑ 348 | Steve Farr | .50 | .23 |
| ❑ 349 | Eric Anthony | .50 | .23 |
| ❑ 350 | Pete Smith | .50 | .23 |
| ❑ 351 | Lee Smith | 1.00 | .45 |
| ❑ 352 | Mariano Duncan | .50 | .23 |
| ❑ 353 | Doug Strange | .50 | .23 |
| ❑ 354 | Tim Bogar | .50 | .23 |
| ❑ 355 | Dave Weathers | .50 | .23 |
| ❑ 356 | Eric Karros | 1.00 | .45 |
| ❑ 357 | Randy Myers | .50 | .23 |
| ❑ 358 | Chad Curtis | .50 | .23 |
| ❑ 359 | Steve Avery | .50 | .23 |
| ❑ 360 | Brian Jordan | 1.00 | .45 |
| ❑ 361 | Tim Wallach | .50 | .23 |
| ❑ 362 | Pedro Martinez | 4.00 | 1.80 |
| ❑ 363 | Bip Roberts | .50 | .23 |
| ❑ 364 | Lou Whitaker | 1.00 | .45 |
| ❑ 365 | Luis Polonia | .50 | .23 |
| ❑ 366 | Benito Santiago | .50 | .23 |
| ❑ 367 | Brett Butler | 1.00 | .45 |
| ❑ 368 | Shawon Dunston | .50 | .23 |
| ❑ 369 | Kelly Stinnett RC | .50 | .23 |
| ❑ 370 | Chris Turner | .50 | .23 |
| ❑ 371 | Ruben Sierra | .50 | .23 |
| ❑ 372 | Greg A. Harris | .50 | .23 |
| ❑ 373 | Xavier Hernandez | .50 | .23 |
| ❑ 374 | Howard Johnson | .50 | .23 |
| ❑ 375 | Duane Ward | .50 | .23 |
| ❑ 376 | Roberto Hernandez | .50 | .23 |
| ❑ 377 | Scott Leius | .50 | .23 |
| ❑ 378 | Dave Valle | .50 | .23 |
| ❑ 379 | Sid Fernandez | .50 | .23 |
| ❑ 380 | Doug Jones | .50 | .23 |
| ❑ 381 | Zane Smith | .50 | .23 |
| ❑ 382 | Craig Biggio | 1.50 | .70 |
| ❑ 383 | Rick White RC | .50 | .23 |
| ❑ 384 | Tom Pagnozzi | .50 | .23 |
| ❑ 385 | Chris James | .50 | .23 |
| ❑ 386 | Bret Boone | 1.00 | .45 |
| ❑ 387 | Jeff Montgomery | .50 | .23 |
| ❑ 388 | Chad Kreuter | .50 | .23 |
| ❑ 389 | Greg Hibbard | .50 | .23 |
| ❑ 390 | Mark Grace | 2.50 | 1.10 |
| ❑ 391 | Phil Leftwich RC | .50 | .23 |
| ❑ 392 | Don Mattingly | 6.00 | 2.70 |
| ❑ 393 | Ozzie Guillen | .50 | .23 |
| ❑ 394 | Gary Gaetti | 1.00 | .45 |
| ❑ 395 | Erik Hanson | .50 | .23 |
| ❑ 396 | Scott Brosius | 1.00 | .45 |
| ❑ 397 | Tom Gordon | .50 | .23 |
| ❑ 398 | Bill Gullickson | .50 | .23 |
| ❑ 399 | Matt Mieske | .50 | .23 |
| ❑ 400 | Pat Hentgen | .50 | .23 |
| ❑ 401 | Walt Weiss | .50 | .23 |
| ❑ 402 | Greg Blosser | .50 | .23 |
| ❑ 403 | Stan Javier | .50 | .23 |
| ❑ 404 | Doug Henry | .50 | .23 |
| ❑ 405 | Ramon Martinez | .50 | .23 |
| ❑ 406 | Frank Viola | .50 | .23 |
| ❑ 407 | Mike Hampton | .50 | .23 |
| ❑ 408 | Andy Van Slyke | 1.00 | .45 |
| ❑ 409 | Bobby Ayala | .50 | .23 |
| ❑ 410 | Todd Zeile | .50 | .23 |
| ❑ 411 | Jay Bell | 1.00 | .45 |
| ❑ 412 | Dennis Martinez | 1.00 | .45 |
| ❑ 413 | Mark Portugal | .50 | .23 |
| ❑ 414 | Bobby Munoz | .50 | .23 |
| ❑ 415 | Kirt Manwaring | .50 | .23 |
| ❑ 416 | John Kruk | 1.00 | .45 |
| ❑ 417 | Trevor Hoffman | 1.00 | .45 |
| ❑ 418 | Chris Sabo | .50 | .23 |
| ❑ 419 | Bret Saberhagen | 1.00 | .45 |
| ❑ 420 | Chris Nabholz | .50 | .23 |
| ❑ 421 | James Mouton FIN | .50 | .23 |
| ❑ 422 | Tony Tarasco FIN | .50 | .23 |
| ❑ 423 | Carlos Delgado FIN | 4.00 | 1.80 |
| ❑ 424 | Rondell White FIN | 1.00 | .45 |
| ❑ 425 | Javier Lopez FIN | 1.00 | .45 |
| ❑ 426 | Chan Ho Park FIN RC | 6.00 | 2.70 |
| ❑ 427 | Cliff Floyd FIN | 1.00 | .45 |
| ❑ 428 | Dave Staton FIN | .50 | .23 |
| ❑ 429 | J.R. Phillips FIN | .50 | .23 |
| ❑ 430 | Manny Ramirez FIN | 4.00 | 1.80 |
| ❑ 431 | Kurt Abbott FIN RC | .50 | .23 |
| ❑ 432 | Melvin Nieves FIN | .50 | .23 |
| ❑ 433 | Alex Gonzalez FIN | .50 | .23 |
| ❑ 434 | Rick Helling FIN | 1.00 | .45 |
| ❑ 435 | Danny Bautista FIN | .50 | .23 |
| ❑ 436 | Matt Walbeck FIN | .50 | .23 |
| ❑ 437 | Ryan Klesko FIN | 1.00 | .45 |
| ❑ 438 | Steve Karsay FIN | .50 | .23 |
| ❑ 439 | Salomon Torres FIN | .50 | .23 |
| ❑ 440 | Scott Ruffcorn FIN | .50 | .23 |

## 1995 Finest

| | MINT | NRMT |
|---|---|---|
| COMPLETE SET (330) | 100.00 | 45.00 |
| COMPLETE SERIES 1 (220) | 70.00 | 32.00 |
| COMPLETE SERIES 2 (110) | 30.00 | 13.50 |
| COMMON CARD (1-330) | .50 | .18 |

| | Player | Mint | NrMt |
|---|---|---|---|
| ❑ 1 | Raul Mondesi | .75 | .35 |
| ❑ 2 | Kurt Abbott | .40 | .18 |
| ❑ 3 | Chris Gomez | .40 | .18 |
| ❑ 4 | Manny Ramirez | 2.50 | 1.10 |
| ❑ 5 | Rondell White | .75 | .35 |
| ❑ 6 | William VanLandingham | .40 | .18 |
| ❑ 7 | Jon Lieber | .40 | .18 |
| ❑ 8 | Ryan Klesko | .75 | .35 |
| ❑ 9 | John Hudek | .40 | .18 |
| ❑ 10 | Joey Hamilton | .40 | .18 |
| ❑ 11 | Bob Hamelin | .40 | .18 |
| ❑ 12 | Brian Anderson | .40 | .18 |
| ❑ 13 | Mike Lieberthal | .75 | .35 |
| ❑ 14 | Rico Brogna | .40 | .18 |
| ❑ 15 | Rusty Greer | .75 | .35 |
| ❑ 16 | Carlos Delgado | 2.00 | .90 |
| ❑ 17 | Jim Edmonds | 2.00 | .90 |
| ❑ 18 | Steve Trachsel | .40 | .18 |
| ❑ 19 | Matt Walbeck | .40 | .18 |
| ❑ 20 | Armando Benitez | .75 | .35 |
| ❑ 21 | Steve Karsay | .40 | .18 |
| ❑ 22 | Jose Oliva | .40 | .18 |
| ❑ 23 | Cliff Floyd | .75 | .35 |
| ❑ 24 | Kevin Foster | .40 | .18 |
| ❑ 25 | Javier Lopez | .75 | .35 |
| ❑ 26 | Jose Valentin | .40 | .18 |
| ❑ 27 | James Mouton | .40 | .18 |
| ❑ 28 | Hector Carrasco | .40 | .18 |
| ❑ 29 | Orlando Miller | .40 | .18 |
| ❑ 30 | Garret Anderson | .75 | .35 |
| ❑ 31 | Marvin Freeman | .40 | .18 |

❑ 32 Brett Butler .75 .35
❑ 33 Roberto Kelly .40 .18
❑ 34 Rod Beck .40 .18
❑ 35 Jose Rijo .40 .18
❑ 36 Edgar Martinez 1.25 .55
❑ 37 Jim Thome 1.25 .55
❑ 38 Rick Wilkins .40 .18
❑ 39 Wally Joyner .75 .35
❑ 40 Wil Cordero .40 .18
❑ 41 Tommy Greene .40 .18
❑ 42 Travis Fryman .75 .35
❑ 43 Don Slaught .40 .18
❑ 44 Brady Anderson .75 .35
❑ 45 Matt Williams 1.25 .55
❑ 46 Rene Arocha .40 .18
❑ 47 Rickey Henderson 2.50 1.10
❑ 48 Mike Mussina 2.00 .90
❑ 49 Greg McMichael .40 .18
❑ 50 Jody Reed .40 .18
❑ 51 Tino Martinez .75 .35
❑ 52 Dave Clark .40 .18
❑ 53 John Valentin .40 .18
❑ 54 Bret Boone .75 .35
❑ 55 Walt Weiss .40 .18
❑ 56 Kenny Lofton .75 .35
❑ 57 Scott Leius .40 .18
❑ 58 Eric Karros .75 .35
❑ 59 John Olerud .75 .35
❑ 60 Chris Hoiles .40 .18
❑ 61 Sandy Alomar Jr. .75 .35
❑ 62 Tim Wallach .40 .18
❑ 63 Cal Eldred .40 .18
❑ 64 Tom Glavine 2.00 .90
❑ 65 Mark Grace 2.00 .90
❑ 66 Rey Sanchez .40 .18
❑ 67 Bobby Ayala .40 .18
❑ 68 Dante Bichette .75 .35
❑ 69 Andres Galarraga 1.25 .55
❑ 70 Chuck Carr .40 .18
❑ 71 Bobby Witt .40 .18
❑ 72 Steve Avery .40 .18
❑ 73 Bobby Jones .40 .18
❑ 74 Delino DeShields .40 .18
❑ 75 Kevin Tapani .40 .18
❑ 76 Randy Johnson 2.50 1.10
❑ 77 David Nied .40 .18
❑ 78 Pat Hentgen .40 .18
❑ 79 Tim Salmon .75 .35
❑ 80 Todd Zeile .40 .18
❑ 81 John Wetteland .75 .35
❑ 82 Albert Belle 1.25 .55
❑ 83 Ben McDonald .40 .18
❑ 84 Bobby Munoz .40 .18
❑ 85 Bip Roberts .40 .18
❑ 86 Mo Vaughn .75 .35
❑ 87 Chuck Finley .75 .35
❑ 88 Chuck Knoblauch .75 .35
❑ 89 Frank Thomas 4.00 1.80
❑ 90 Danny Tartabull .40 .18
❑ 91 Dean Palmer .75 .35
❑ 92 Len Dykstra .75 .35
❑ 93 J.R. Phillips .40 .18
❑ 94 Tom Candiotti .40 .18
❑ 95 Marquis Grissom .40 .18
❑ 96 Barry Larkin 2.00 .90
❑ 97 Bryan Harvey .40 .18
❑ 98 David Justice 1.25 .55
❑ 99 David Cone .75 .35
❑ 100 Wade Boggs 2.50 1.10
❑ 101 Jason Bere .40 .18
❑ 102 Hal Morris .40 .18
❑ 103 Fred McGriff 1.25 .55
❑ 104 Bobby Bonilla .75 .35
❑ 105 Jay Buhner .75 .35
❑ 106 Allen Watson .40 .18
❑ 107 Mickey Tettleton .40 .18
❑ 108 Kevin Appier .75 .35
❑ 109 Ivan Rodriguez 2.50 1.10
❑ 110 Carlos Garcia .40 .18
❑ 111 Andy Benes .40 .18
❑ 112 Eddie Murray 2.00 .90
❑ 113 Mike Piazza 6.00 2.70
❑ 114 Greg Vaughn .75 .35
❑ 115 Paul Molitor 2.00 .90
❑ 116 Terry Steinbach .40 .18
❑ 117 Jeff Bagwell 2.50 1.10
❑ 118 Ken Griffey Jr. 8.00 3.60
❑ 119 Gary Sheffield 2.00 .90
❑ 120 Cal Ripken 8.00 3.60
❑ 121 Jeff Kent 1.25 .55
❑ 122 Jay Bell .75 .35
❑ 123 Will Clark 2.00 .90
❑ 124 Cecil Fielder .75 .35
❑ 125 Alex Fernandez .40 .18
❑ 126 Don Mattingly 5.00 2.20
❑ 127 Reggie Sanders .40 .18
❑ 128 Moises Alou .75 .35
❑ 129 Craig Biggio 1.25 .55
❑ 130 Eddie Williams .40 .18
❑ 131 John Franco .75 .35
❑ 132 John Kruk .75 .35
❑ 133 Jeff King .40 .18
❑ 134 Royce Clayton .40 .18
❑ 135 Doug Drabek .40 .18
❑ 136 Ray Lankford .75 .35
❑ 137 Roberto Alomar 2.00 .90
❑ 138 Todd Hundley .40 .18
❑ 139 Alex Cole .40 .18
❑ 140 Shawon Dunston .40 .18
❑ 141 John Roper .40 .18
❑ 142 Mark Langston .40 .18
❑ 143 Tom Pagnozzi .40 .18
❑ 144 Wilson Alvarez .40 .18
❑ 145 Scott Cooper .40 .18
❑ 146 Kevin Mitchell .40 .18
❑ 147 Mark Whiten .40 .18
❑ 148 Jeff Conine .40 .18
❑ 149 Chili Davis .75 .35
❑ 150 Luis Gonzalez .40 .18
❑ 151 Juan Guzman .40 .18
❑ 152 Mike Greenwell .40 .18
❑ 153 Mike Henneman .40 .18
❑ 154 Rick Aguilera .40 .18
❑ 155 Dennis Eckersley .75 .35
❑ 156 Darrin Fletcher .40 .18
❑ 157 Darren Lewis .40 .18
❑ 158 Juan Gonzalez 2.00 .90
❑ 159 Dave Hollins .40 .18
❑ 160 Jimmy Key .75 .35
❑ 161 Roberto Hernandez .40 .18
❑ 162 Randy Myers .40 .18
❑ 163 Joe Carter .75 .35
❑ 164 Darren Daulton .75 .35
❑ 165 Mike Macfarlane .40 .18
❑ 166 Bret Saberhagen .75 .35
❑ 167 Kirby Puckett 5.00 2.20
❑ 168 Lance Johnson .40 .18
❑ 169 Mark McGwire 8.00 3.60
❑ 170 Jose Canseco 2.50 1.10
❑ 171 Mike Stanley .40 .18
❑ 172 Lee Smith .75 .35
❑ 173 Robin Ventura .75 .35
❑ 174 Greg Gagne .40 .18
❑ 175 Brian McRae .40 .18
❑ 176 Mike Bordick .40 .18
❑ 177 Rafael Palmeiro 2.00 .90
❑ 178 Kenny Rogers .40 .18
❑ 179 Chad Curtis .40 .18
❑ 180 Devon White .75 .35
❑ 181 Paul O'Neill .75 .35
❑ 182 Ken Caminiti .75 .35
❑ 183 Dave Nilsson .40 .18
❑ 184 Tim Naehring .40 .18
❑ 185 Roger Clemens 4.00 1.80
❑ 186 Otis Nixon .40 .18
❑ 187 Tim Raines .75 .35
❑ 188 Denny Martinez .75 .35
❑ 189 Pedro Martinez 2.50 1.10
❑ 190 Jim Abbott .75 .35
❑ 191 Ryan Thompson .40 .18
❑ 192 Barry Bonds 3.00 1.35
❑ 193 Joe Girardi .40 .18
❑ 194 Steve Finley .75 .35
❑ 195 John Jaha .40 .18
❑ 196 Tony Gwynn 4.00 1.80
❑ 197 Sammy Sosa 4.00 1.80
❑ 198 John Burkett .40 .18
❑ 199 Carlos Baerga .40 .18
❑ 200 Ramon Martinez .40 .18
❑ 201 Aaron Sele .75 .35
❑ 202 Eduardo Perez .40 .18
❑ 203 Alan Trammell 1.25 .55
❑ 204 Orlando Merced .40 .18
❑ 205 Deion Sanders .75 .35
❑ 206 Robb Nen .40 .18
❑ 207 Jack McDowell .40 .18
❑ 208 Ruben Sierra .40 .18
❑ 209 Bernie Williams 2.00 .90
❑ 210 Kevin Seitzer .40 .18
❑ 211 Charles Nagy .40 .18
❑ 212 Tony Phillips .40 .18
❑ 213 Greg Maddux 5.00 2.20
❑ 214 Jeff Montgomery .40 .18
❑ 215 Larry Walker .75 .35
❑ 216 Andy Van Slyke .75 .35
❑ 217 Ozzie Smith 2.50 1.10
❑ 218 Geronimo Pena .40 .18
❑ 219 Gregg Jefferies .40 .18
❑ 220 Lou Whitaker .75 .35
❑ 221 Chipper Jones 5.00 2.20
❑ 222 Benji Gil .40 .18
❑ 223 Tony Phillips .40 .18
❑ 224 Trevor Wilson .40 .18
❑ 225 Tony Tarasco .40 .18
❑ 226 Roberto Petagine .40 .18
❑ 227 Mike Macfarlane .40 .18
❑ 228 Hideo Nomo RCUER .. 8.00 3.60
(In 3rd line agianst)
❑ 229 Mark McLemore .40 .18
❑ 230 Ron Gant .40 .18
❑ 231 Andujar Cedeno .40 .18
❑ 232 Mike Mimbs RC .40 .18
❑ 233 Jim Abbott .75 .35
❑ 234 Ricky Bones .40 .18
❑ 235 Marty Cordova .40 .18
❑ 236 Mark Johnson RC .40 .18
❑ 237 Marquis Grissom .40 .18
❑ 238 Tom Henke .40 .18
❑ 239 Terry Pendleton .75 .35
❑ 240 John Wetteland .75 .35
❑ 241 Lee Smith .75 .35
❑ 242 Jaime Navarro .40 .18
❑ 243 Luis Alicea .40 .18
❑ 244 Scott Cooper .40 .18
❑ 245 Gary Gaetti .75 .35
❑ 246 Edgardo Alfonzo UER .. 2.00 .90
(Incomplete career BA)
❑ 247 Brad Clontz .40 .18
❑ 248 Dave Mlicki .40 .18
❑ 249 Dave Winfield 2.00 .90
❑ 250 Mark Grudzielanek RC 2.00 .90
❑ 251 Alex Gonzalez .40 .18
❑ 252 Kevin Brown 1.25 .55
❑ 253 Esteban Loaiza .40 .18
❑ 254 Vaughn Eshelman .40 .18
❑ 255 Bill Swift .40 .18
❑ 256 Brian McRae .40 .18
❑ 257 Bobby Higginson RC .... 5.00 2.20
❑ 258 Jack McDowell .40 .18
❑ 259 Scott Stahoviak .40 .18
❑ 260 Jon Nunnally .40 .18
❑ 261 Charlie Hayes .40 .18
❑ 262 Jacob Brumfield .40 .18
❑ 263 Chad Curtis .40 .18
❑ 264 Heathcliff Slocumb .40 .18
❑ 265 Mark Whiten .40 .18
❑ 266 Mickey Tettleton .40 .18
❑ 267 Jose Mesa .40 .18
❑ 268 Doug Jones .40 .18
❑ 269 Trevor Hoffman .75 .35
❑ 270 Paul Sorrento .40 .18
❑ 271 Shane Andrews .40 .18
❑ 272 Brett Butler .75 .35
❑ 273 Curtis Goodwin .40 .18
❑ 274 Larry Walker .75 .35
❑ 275 Phil Plantier .40 .18
❑ 276 Ken Hill .40 .18
❑ 277 Vinny Castilla UER .75 .35
(Rockies spelled Rockie)
❑ 278 Billy Ashley .40 .18
❑ 279 Derek Jeter 8.00 3.60
❑ 280 Bob Tewksbury .40 .18
❑ 281 Jose Offerman .40 .18
❑ 282 Glenallen Hill .40 .18
❑ 283 Tony Fernandez .40 .18
❑ 284 Mike Devereaux .40 .18
❑ 285 John Burkett .40 .18
❑ 286 Geronimo Berroa .40 .18

❑ 287 Quilvio Veras .40 .18
❑ 288 Jason Bates .40 .18
❑ 289 Lee Tinsley .40 .18
❑ 290 Derek Bell .40 .18
❑ 291 Jeff Fassero .40 .18
❑ 292 Ray Durham .75 .35
❑ 293 Chad Ogea .40 .18
❑ 294 Bill Pulsipher .40 .18
❑ 295 Phil Nevin .75 .35
❑ 296 Carlos Perez RC .75 .35
❑ 297 Roberto Kelly .40 .18
❑ 298 Tim Wakefield .40 .18
❑ 299 Jeff Manto .40 .18
❑ 300 Brian Hunter .40 .18
❑ 301 C.J. Nitkowski .40 .18
❑ 302 Dustin Hermanson .40 .18
❑ 303 John Mabry .40 .18
❑ 304 Orel Hershiser .75 .35
❑ 305 Ron Villone .40 .18
❑ 306 Sean Bergman .40 .18
❑ 307 Tom Goodwin .40 .18
❑ 308 Al Reyes .40 .18
❑ 309 Todd Stottlemyre .40 .18
❑ 310 Rich Becker .40 .18
❑ 311 Joey Cora .40 .18
❑ 312 Ed Sprague .40 .18
❑ 313 John Smoltz UER .75 .35
(3rd line; from spelled as form)
❑ 314 Frank Castillo .40 .18
❑ 315 Chris Hammond .40 .18
❑ 316 Ismael Valdes .40 .18
❑ 317 Pete Harnisch .40 .18
❑ 318 Bernard Gilkey .40 .18
❑ 319 John Kruk .75 .35
❑ 320 Marc Newfield .40 .18
❑ 321 Brian Johnson .40 .18
❑ 322 Mark Portugal .40 .18
❑ 323 David Hulse .40 .18
❑ 324 Luis Ortiz UER .40 .18
(Below spelled beloe)
❑ 325 Mike Benjamin .40 .18
❑ 326 Brian Jordan .75 .35
❑ 327 Shawn Green 2.00 .90
❑ 328 Joe Oliver .40 .18
❑ 329 Felipe Lira .40 .18
❑ 330 Andre Dawson 1.25 .55

## 1996 Finest

| | MINT | NRMT |
|---|---|---|
| COMPLETE SET (359) | 1000.00 | 450.00 |
| COMPLETE SERIES 1 (191) | 650.00 | 300.00 |
| COMPLETE SERIES 2 (168) | 350.00 | 160.00 |
| COMP.BRONZE SET (220) | 50.00 | 22.00 |
| COMP.BRONZE SER.1 (110) | 25.00 | 11.00 |
| COMP.BRONZE SER.2 (110) | 30.00 | 13.50 |
| COMMON BRONZE | .25 | .11 |
| COMP.GOLD SET (48) | 750.00 | 350.00 |
| COMP.GOLD SER.1 (26) | 500.00 | 220.00 |
| COMP.GOLD SER.2 (22) | 250.00 | 110.00 |
| COMMON GOLD | 5.00 | 2.20 |
| COMP.SILVER SET (91) | 230.00 | 105.00 |
| COMP.SILVER SER.1 (55) | 150.00 | 70.00 |
| COMP.SILVER SER.2 (36) | 80.00 | 36.00 |
| COMMON SILVER | 1.50 | .70 |

❑ B5 Roberto Hernandez B .25 .11
❑ B8 Terry Pendleton B .50 .23
❑ B12 Ken Caminiti B .50 .23
❑ B15 Dan Miceli B .25 .11
❑ B16 Chipper Jones B 2.50 1.10
❑ B17 John Wetteland B .50 .23
❑ B19 Tim Naehring B .25 .11
❑ B21 Eddie Murray B 1.00 .45
❑ B23 Kevin Appier B .50 .23
❑ B24 Ken Griffey Jr. B 4.00 1.80
❑ B26 Brian McRae B .25 .11
❑ B27 Pedro Martinez B 1.25 .55
❑ B28 Brian Jordan B .50 .23
❑ B29 Mike Fetters B .25 .11
❑ B30 Carlos Delgado B 1.00 .45
❑ B31 Shane Reynolds B .25 .11
❑ B32 Terry Steinbach B .25 .11
❑ B34 Mark Leiter B .25 .11
❑ B36 David Segui B .25 .11
❑ B40 Fred McGriff B .60 .25
❑ B44 Glenallen Hill B .25 .11
❑ B45 Brady Anderson B .50 .23
❑ B47 Jim Thome B .60 .25
❑ B48 Frank Thomas B 2.00 .90
❑ B49 Chuck Knoblauch B .50 .23
❑ B50 Len Dykstra B .50 .23
❑ B53 Tom Pagnozzi B .25 .11
❑ B55 Ricky Bones B .25 .11
❑ B56 David Justice B .60 .25
❑ B57 Steve Avery B .25 .11
❑ B58 Robby Thompson B .25 .11
❑ B61 Tony Gwynn B 2.00 .90
❑ B63 Denny Neagle B .50 .23
❑ B67 Robin Ventura B .50 .23
❑ B70 Kevin Seitzer B .25 .11
❑ B71 Ramon Martinez B .25 .11
❑ B75 Brian L.Hunter B .25 .11
❑ B76 Alan Benes B .25 .11
❑ B80 Ozzie Guillen B .25 .11
❑ B82 Benji Gil B .25 .11
❑ B85 Todd Hundley B .25 .11
❑ B87 Pat Hentgen B .25 .11
❑ B89 Chuck Finley B .50 .23
❑ B92 Derek Jeter B 4.00 1.80
❑ B93 Paul O'Neill B .50 .23
❑ B94 Darrin Fletcher B .25 .11
❑ B96 Delino DeShields B .25 .11
❑ B97 Tim Salmon B .50 .23
❑ B98 John Olerud B .50 .23
❑ B101 Tim Wakefield B .25 .11
❑ B103 Dave Stevens B .25 .11
❑ B104 Orlando Merced B .25 .11
❑ B106 Jay Bell B .50 .23
❑ B107 John Burkett B .25 .11
❑ B108 Chris Hoiles B .25 .11
❑ B110 Dave Nilsson B .25 .11
❑ B111 Rod Beck B .25 .11
❑ B113 Mike Piazza B 3.00 1.35
❑ B114 Mark Langston B .25 .11
❑ B116 Rico Brogna B .25 .11
❑ B118 Tom Goodwin B .25 .11
❑ B119 Bryan Rekar B .25 .11
❑ B120 David Cone B .50 .23
❑ B122 Andy Pettitte B .50 .23
❑ B123 Chili Davis B .50 .23
❑ B124 John Smoltz B .50 .23
❑ B125 Heathcliff Slocumb B .25 .11
❑ B126 Dante Bichette B .50 .23
❑ B128 Alex Gonzalez B .25 .11
❑ B129 Jeff Montgomery B .25 .11
❑ B131 Denny Martinez B .50 .23
❑ B132 Mel Rojas B .25 .11
❑ B133 Derek Bell B .25 .11
❑ B134 Trevor Hoffman B .50 .23
❑ B136 Darren Daulton B .50 .23
❑ B137 Pete Schourek B .25 .11
❑ B138 Phil Nevin B .50 .23
❑ B139 Andres Galarraga B .60 .25
❑ B140 Chad Fonville B .25 .11
❑ B144 J.T. Snow B .50 .23
❑ B146 Barry Bonds B 1.50 .70
❑ B147 Orel Hershiser B .50 .23
❑ B148 Quilvio Veras B .25 .11
❑ B149 Will Clark B 1.00 .45
❑ B150 Jose Rijo B .25 .11
❑ B152 Travis Fryman B .50 .23
❑ B154 Alex Fernandez B .25 .11
❑ B155 Wade Boggs B 1.25 .55
❑ B156 Troy Percival B .25 .11
❑ B157 Moises Alou B .50 .23
❑ B158 Javy Lopez B .50 .23
❑ B159 Jason Giambi B 1.00 .45
❑ B162 Mark McGwire B 4.00 1.80
❑ B163 Eric Karros B .50 .23
❑ B166 Mickey Tettleton B .25 .11
❑ B167 Barry Larkin B 1.00 .45
❑ B169 Ruben Sierra B .25 .11
❑ B170 Bill Swift B .25 .11
❑ B172 Chad Curtis B .25 .11
❑ B173 Dean Palmer B .50 .23
❑ B175 Bobby Bonilla B .50 .23
❑ B176 Greg Colbrunn B .25 .11
❑ B177 Jose Mesa B .25 .11
❑ B178 Mike Greenwell B .25 .11
❑ B181 Doug Drabek B .25 .11
❑ B183 Wilson Alvarez B .25 .11
❑ B184 Marty Cordova B .25 .11
❑ B185 Hal Morris B .25 .11
❑ B187 Carlos Garcia B .25 .11
❑ B190 Marquis Grissom B .25 .11
❑ B193 Will Clark B 1.00 .45
❑ B194 Paul Molitor B 1.00 .45
❑ B195 Kenny Rogers B .25 .11
❑ B196 Reggie Sanders B .25 .11
❑ B199 Raul Mondesi B .50 .23
❑ B200 Lance Johnson B .25 .11
❑ B201 Alvin Morman B .25 .11
❑ B203 Jack McDowell B .25 .11
❑ B204 Randy Myers B .25 .11
❑ B205 Harold Baines B .50 .23
❑ B206 Marty Cordova B .25 .11
❑ B207 Rich Hunter B RC .25 .11
❑ B208 Al Leiter B .50 .23
❑ B209 Greg Gagne B .25 .11
❑ B210 Ben McDonald B .25 .11
❑ B212 Terry Adams B .25 .11
❑ B213 Paul Sorrento B .25 .11
❑ B214 Albert Belle B .60 .25
❑ B215 Mike Blowers B .25 .11
❑ B216 Jim Edmonds B 1.00 .45
❑ B217 Felipe Crespo B .25 .11
❑ B219 Shawon Dunston B .25 .11
❑ B220 Jimmy Haynes B .25 .11
❑ B221 Jose Canseco B 1.25 .55
❑ B222 Eric Davis B .50 .23
❑ B224 Tim Raines B .50 .23
❑ B225 Tony Phillips B .25 .11
❑ B226 Charlie Hayes B .25 .11
❑ B227 Eric Owens B .25 .11
❑ B228 Roberto Alomar B 1.00 .45
❑ B233 Kenny Lofton B .60 .23
❑ B236 Mark McGwire B 4.00 1.80
❑ B237 Jay Buhner B .50 .23
❑ B238 Craig Biggio B .60 .25
❑ B240 Barry Bonds B 1.50 .70
❑ B244 Ron Gant B .25 .11
❑ B245 Paul Wilson B .25 .11
❑ B246 Todd Hollandsworth B .25 .11
❑ B247 Todd Zeile B .25 .11
❑ B248 David Justice B .60 .25
❑ B250 Moises Alou B .50 .23
❑ B251 Bob Wolcott B .25 .11
❑ B252 David Wells B .50 .23
❑ B253 Juan Gonzalez B 1.00 .45
❑ B254 Andres Galarraga B .60 .25
❑ B255 Dave Hollins B .25 .11
❑ B257 Sammy Sosa B 2.00 .90
❑ B258 Ivan Rodriguez B 1.00 .45
❑ B259 Bip Roberts B .25 .11
❑ B260 Tino Martinez B .50 .23
❑ B262 Mike Stanley B .25 .11
❑ B264 Butch Huskey B .25 .11
❑ B265 Jeff Conine B .25 .11
❑ B267 Mark Grace B 1.00 .45
❑ B268 Jason Schmidt B .25 .11
❑ B269 Otis Nixon B .25 .11
❑ B271 Kirby Puckett B 2.50 1.10
❑ B273 Andy Benes B .25 .11
❑ B275 Mike Piazza B 3.00 1.35
❑ B276 Rey Ordonez B .50 .23
❑ B278 Gary Gaetti B .50 .23
❑ B280 Robin Ventura B .50 .23
❑ B281 Cal Ripken B 4.00 1.80
❑ B282 Carlos Baerga B .25 .11

❑ B283 Roger Cedeno B .25 .11
❑ B285 Terrell Wade B .25 .11
❑ B286 Kevin Brown B .60 .25
❑ B287 Rafael Palmeiro B 1.00 .45
❑ B288 Mo Vaughn B .50 .23
❑ B292 Bob Tewksbury B .25 .11
❑ B297 T.J. Mathews B .25 .11
❑ B298 Manny Ramirez B 1.25 .55
❑ B299 Jeff Bagwell B 1.25 .55
❑ B301 Wade Boggs B 1.25 .55
❑ B303 Steve Gibralter B .25 .11
❑ B304 B.J. Surhoff B .50 .23
❑ B306 Royce Clayton B .25 .11
❑ B307 Sal Fasano B .25 .11
❑ B309 Gary Sheffield B 1.00 .45
❑ B310 Ken Hill B .25 .11
❑ B311 Joe Girardi B .25 .11
❑ B312 Matt Lawton B RC 1.50 .70
❑ B314 Julio Franco B .25 .11
❑ B315 Joe Carter B .50 .23
❑ B316 Brooks Kieschnick B .25 .11
❑ B318 Heathcliff Slocumb B .25 .11
❑ B319 Barry Larkin B 1.00 .45
❑ B320 Tony Gwynn B 2.00 .90
❑ B322 Frank Thomas B 2.00 .90
❑ B323 Edgar Martinez B .60 .25
❑ B325 Henry Rodriguez B .25 .11
❑ B326 Marvin Benard B RC .25 .11
❑ B329 Ugueth Urbina B .50 .23
❑ B331 Roger Salkeld B .25 .11
❑ B332 Edgar Renteria B .50 .23
❑ B333 Ryan Klesko B .50 .23
❑ B334 Ray Lankford B .50 .23
❑ B336 Justin Thompson B .25 .11
❑ B339 Mark Clark B .25 .11
❑ B340 Ruben Rivera B .25 .11
❑ B342 Matt Williams B .60 .25
❑ B343 Francisco Cordova B RC .25 .11
❑ B344 Cecil Fielder B .50 .23
❑ B348 Mark Grudzielanek B .25 .11
❑ B349 Ron Coomer B .25 .11
❑ B351 Rich Aurilia B RC .75 .35
❑ B352 Jose Herrera B .25 .11
❑ B356 Tony Clark B .25 .11
❑ B358 Dan Naulty B .25 .11
❑ B359 Checklist B .25 .11
❑ G4 Marty Cordova G 5.00 2.20
❑ G6 Tony Gwynn G 25.00 11.00
❑ G9 Albert Belle G 8.00 3.60
❑ G18 Kirby Puckett G 30.00 13.50
❑ G20 Karim Garcia G 5.00 2.20
❑ G25 Cal Ripken G 50.00 22.00
❑ G33 Hideo Nomo G 12.00 5.50
❑ G39 Ryne Sandberg G 15.00 6.75
❑ G42 Jeff Bagwell G 15.00 6.75
❑ G51 Jason Isringhausen G 6.00 2.70
❑ G64 Mo Vaughn G 6.00 2.70
❑ G66 Dante Bichette G 6.00 2.70
❑ G74 Mark McGwire G 50.00 22.00
❑ G81 Kenny Lofton G 6.00 2.70
❑ G83 Jim Edmonds G 12.00 5.50
❑ G90 Mike Mussina G 12.00 5.50
❑ G100 Jeff Conine G 5.00 2.20
❑ G102 Johnny Damon G 8.00 3.60
❑ G105 Barry Bonds G 20.00 9.00
❑ G117 Jose Canseco G 15.00 6.75
❑ G135 Ken Griffey Jr. G 50.00 22.00
❑ G141 Chipper Jones G 30.00 13.50
❑ G145 Greg Maddux G 30.00 13.50
❑ G164 Jay Buhner G 6.00 2.70
❑ G186 Frank Thomas G 25.00 11.00
❑ G191 Checklist G 5.00 2.20
❑ G192 Chipper Jones G 30.00 13.50
❑ G197 Roberto Alomar G 12.00 5.50
❑ G198 Dennis Eckersley G 6.00 2.70
❑ G202 George Arias G 5.00 2.20
❑ G232 Hideo Nomo G 12.00 5.50
❑ G243 Chris Snopek G 5.00 2.20
❑ G249 Tim Salmon G 6.00 2.70
❑ G266 Matt Williams G 8.00 3.60
❑ G270 Randy Johnson G 15.00 6.75
❑ G279 Paul Molitor G 12.00 5.50
❑ G290 Cecil Fielder G 6.00 2.70
❑ G294 Livan Hernandez G RC 10.00 4.50
❑ G300 Marty Janzen G RC 5.00 2.20
❑ G308 Ron Gant G 5.00 2.20

❑ G321 Ryan Klesko G 6.00 2.70
❑ G324 Jermaine Dye G 6.00 2.70
❑ G330 Jason Giambi G 12.00 5.50
❑ G335 Edgar Martinez G 8.00 3.60
❑ G338 Rey Ordonez G 6.00 2.70
❑ G347 Sammy Sosa G 25.00 11.00
❑ G354 Juan Gonzalez G 1.00 .45
❑ G355 Craig Biggio G 8.00 3.60
❑ S1 Greg Maddux S UER 12.00 5.50
95 stats listed as Mariners
❑ S2 Bernie Williams S 5.00 2.20
❑ S3 Ivan Rodriguez S 6.00 2.70
❑ S7 Barry Larkin S 5.00 2.20
❑ S10 Ray Lankford S 2.50 1.10
❑ S11 Mike Piazza S 15.00 6.75
❑ S13 Larry Walker S 2.50 1.10
❑ S14 Matt Williams S 3.00 1.35
❑ S22 Tim Salmon S 2.50 1.10
❑ S35 Edgar Martinez S 3.00 1.35
❑ S37 Gregg Jefferies S 1.50 .70
❑ S38 Bill Pulsipher S 1.50 .70
❑ S41 Shawn Green S 5.00 2.20
❑ S43 Jim Abbott S 2.50 1.10
❑ S46 Roger Clemens S 10.00 4.50
❑ S52 Rondell White S 2.50 1.10
❑ S54 Dennis Eckersley S 2.50 1.10
❑ S59 Hideo Nomo S 5.00 2.20
❑ S60 Gary Sheffield S 5.00 2.20
❑ S62 Will Clark S 5.00 2.20
❑ S65 Bret Boone S 2.50 1.10
❑ S68 Rafael Palmeiro S 5.00 2.20
❑ S69 Carlos Baerga S 1.50 .70
❑ S72 Tom Glavine S 5.00 2.20
❑ S73 Garret Anderson S 2.50 1.10
❑ S77 Randy Johnson S 6.00 2.70
❑ S78 Jeff King S 1.50 .70
❑ S79 Kirby Puckett S 12.00 5.50
❑ S84 Cecil Fielder S 2.50 1.10
❑ S86 Reggie Sanders S 1.50 .70
❑ S88 Ryan Klesko S 2.50 1.10
❑ S91 John Valentin S 1.50 .70
❑ S95 Manny Ramirez S 6.00 2.70
❑ S99 Vinny Castilla S 2.50 1.10
❑ S109 Carlos Perez S 1.50 .70
❑ S112 Craig Biggio S 3.00 1.35
❑ S115 Juan Gonzalez S 1.00 .45
❑ S121 Ray Durham S 2.50 1.10
❑ S127 C.J. Nitkowski S 1.50 .70
❑ S130 Raul Mondesi S 2.50 1.10
❑ S142 Lee Smith S 2.50 1.10
❑ S143 Joe Carter S 2.50 1.10
❑ S151 Mo Vaughn S 2.50 1.10
❑ S153 Frank Rodriguez S 1.50 .70
❑ S160 Steve Finley S 2.50 1.10
❑ S161 Jeff Bagwell S 6.00 2.70
❑ S165 Cal Ripken S 20.00 9.00
❑ S168 Lyle Mouton S 1.50 .70
❑ S171 Sammy Sosa S 10.00 4.50
❑ S174 John Franco S 2.50 1.10
❑ S179 Greg Vaughn S 2.50 1.10
❑ S180 Mark Wohlers S 1.50 .70
❑ S182 Paul O'Neill S 2.50 1.10
❑ S188 Albert Belle S 3.00 1.35
❑ S189 Mark Grace S 5.00 2.20
❑ S211 Ernie Young S 1.50 .70
❑ S218 Fred McGriff S 3.00 1.35
❑ S223 Kimera Bartee S 1.50 .70
❑ S229 Rickey Henderson S 6.00 2.70
❑ S230 Sterling Hitchcock S 1.50 .70
❑ S231 Bernard Gilkey S 1.50 .70
❑ S234 Ryne Sandberg S 6.00 2.70
❑ S235 Greg Maddux S 12.00 5.50
❑ S239 Todd Stottlemyre S 1.50 .70
❑ S241 Jason Kendall S 2.50 1.10
❑ S242 Paul O'Neill S 2.50 1.10
❑ S256 Devon White S 2.50 1.10
❑ S261 Chuck Knoblauch S 2.50 1.10
❑ S263 Wally Joyner S 2.50 1.10
❑ S272 Andy Fox S 1.50 .70
❑ S274 Sean Berry S 1.50 .70
❑ S277 Benito Santiago S 1.50 .70
❑ S284 Chad Mottola S 1.50 .70
❑ S289 Dante Bichette S 2.50 1.10
❑ S291 Dwight Gooden S 2.50 1.10
❑ S293 Kevin Mitchell S 1.50 .70
❑ S295 Russ Davis S 1.50 .70

❑ S296 Chan Ho Park S 2.50 1.10
❑ S302 Larry Walker S 2.50 1.10
❑ S305 Ken Griffey Jr. S 20.00 9.00
❑ S313 Billy Wagner S 1.50 .70
❑ S317 Mike Grace S RC 1.50 .70
❑ S327 Kenny Lofton S 2.50 1.10
❑ S328 Derek Bell S .25 .11
❑ S337 Gary Sheffield S 5.00 2.20
❑ S341 Mark Grace S 5.00 2.20
❑ S345 Andres Galarraga S 3.00 1.35
❑ S346 Brady Anderson S 2.50 1.10
❑ S350 Derek Jeter S 15.00 6.75
❑ S353 Jay Buhner S 2.50 1.10
❑ S357 Tino Martinez S 2.50 1.10

## 1997 Finest

| | MINT | NRMT |
|---|---|---|
| COMPLETE SET (350) | 1050.00 | 475.00 |
| COMPLETE SERIES 1 (175) | 550.00 | 250.00 |
| COMPLETE SERIES 2 (175) | 500.00 | 220.00 |
| COMP.BRONZE SET (200) | 60.00 | 27.00 |
| COMP.BRONZE SER.1 (100) | 30.00 | 13.50 |
| COMP.BRONZE SER.2 (100) | 30.00 | 13.50 |
| COM.BRON.(1-100/176-275) | .25 | .11 |
| COMP.SILVER SET (100) | 270.00 | 120.00 |
| COMP.SILVER SER.1 (50) | 120.00 | 55.00 |
| COMP.SILVER SER.2 (50) | 150.00 | 70.00 |
| COM.SILV.(101-150/276-325) | 2.00 | .90 |
| COMP.GOLD SET (50) | 550.00 | 250.00 |
| COMP.GOLD SER.1 (25) | 300.00 | 135.00 |
| COMP.GOLD SER.2 (25) | 250.00 | 110.00 |
| COM.GOLD (151-175/326-350) | 5.00 | 2.20 |

❑ 1 Barry Bonds B 1.50 .70
❑ 2 Ryne Sandberg B 1.25 .55
❑ 3 Brian Jordan B .40 .18
❑ 4 Rocky Coppinger B .25 .11
❑ 5 Dante Bichette B UER .40 .18
(Card is erroneously numbered 155)
❑ 6 Al Martin B .25 .11
❑ 7 Charles Nagy B .25 .11
❑ 8 Otis Nixon B .25 .11
❑ 9 Mark Johnson B .25 .11
❑ 10 Jeff Bagwell B 1.25 .55
❑ 11 Ken Hill B .25 .11
❑ 12 Willie Adams B .25 .11
❑ 13 Raul Mondesi B .40 .18
❑ 14 Reggie Sanders B .25 .11
❑ 15 Derek Jeter B 4.00 1.80
❑ 16 Jermaine Dye B .40 .18
❑ 17 Edgar Renteria B .40 .18
❑ 18 Travis Fryman B .40 .18
❑ 19 Roberto Hernandez B .25 .11
❑ 20 Sammy Sosa B 2.00 .90
❑ 21 Garret Anderson B .40 .18
❑ 22 Rey Ordonez B .25 .11
❑ 23 Glenallen Hill B .25 .11
❑ 24 Dave Nilsson B .25 .11
❑ 25 Kevin Brown B .60 .25
❑ 26 Brian McRae B .25 .11
❑ 27 Joey Hamilton B .25 .11
❑ 28 Jamey Wright B .25 .11
❑ 29 Frank Thomas B 2.00 .90
❑ 30 Mark McGwire B 4.00 1.80
❑ 31 Ramon Martinez B .25 .11
❑ 32 Jaime Bluma B .25 .11

❑ 33 Frank Rodriguez B .25 .11
❑ 34 Andy Benes B .25 .11
❑ 35 Jay Buhner B .40 .18
❑ 36 Justin Thompson B .25 .11
❑ 37 Darin Erstad B 1.25 .55
❑ 38 Gregg Jefferies B .25 .11
❑ 39 Jeff D'Amico B .25 .11
❑ 40 Pedro Martinez B 1.25 .55
❑ 41 Nomar Garciaparra B 3.00 1.35
❑ 42 Jose Valentin B .25 .11
❑ 43 Pat Hentgen B .25 .11
❑ 44 Will Clark B 1.00 .45
❑ 45 Bernie Williams B 1.00 .45
❑ 46 Luis Castillo B .40 .18
❑ 47 B.J. Surhoff B .40 .18
❑ 48 Greg Gagne B .25 .11
❑ 49 Pete Schourek B .25 .11
❑ 50 Mike Piazza B 3.00 1.35
❑ 51 Dwight Gooden B .40 .18
❑ 52 Javy Lopez B .40 .18
❑ 53 Chuck Finley B .40 .18
❑ 54 James Baldwin B .40 .18
❑ 55 Jack McDowell B .25 .11
❑ 56 Royce Clayton B .25 .11
❑ 57 Carlos Delgado B 1.00 .45
❑ 58 Neifi Perez B .25 .11
❑ 59 Eddie Taubensee B .25 .11
❑ 60 Rafael Palmeiro B 1.00 .45
❑ 61 Marty Cordova B .25 .11
❑ 62 Wade Boggs B 1.25 .55
❑ 63 Rickey Henderson B 1.25 .55
❑ 64 Mike Hampton B .40 .18
❑ 65 Troy Percival B .25 .11
❑ 66 Barry Larkin B 1.00 .45
❑ 67 Jermaine Allensworth B .25 .11
❑ 68 Mark Clark B .25 .11
❑ 69 Mike Lansing B .25 .11
❑ 70 Mark Grudzielanek B .25 .11
❑ 71 Todd Stottlemyre B .25 .11
❑ 72 Juan Guzman B .25 .11
❑ 73 John Burkett B .25 .11
❑ 74 Wilson Alvarez B .25 .11
❑ 75 Ellis Burks B .40 .18
❑ 76 Bobby Higginson B .40 .18
❑ 77 Ricky Bottalico B .25 .11
❑ 78 Omar Vizquel B .40 .18
❑ 79 Paul Sorrento B .25 .11
❑ 80 Denny Neagle B .40 .18
❑ 81 Roger Pavlik B .25 .11
❑ 82 Mike Lieberthal B .40 .18
❑ 83 Devon White B .40 .18
❑ 84 John Olerud B .40 .18
❑ 85 Kevin Appier B .40 .18
❑ 86 Joe Girardi B .25 .11
❑ 87 Paul O'Neill B .40 .18
❑ 88 Mike Sweeney B .40 .10
❑ 89 John Smiley B .25 .11
❑ 90 Ivan Rodriguez B 1.25 .55
❑ 91 Randy Myers B .25 .11
❑ 92 Bip Roberts B .25 .11
❑ 93 Jose Mesa B .25 .11
❑ 94 Paul Wilson B .25 .11
❑ 95 Mike Mussina B 1.00 .45
❑ 96 Ben McDonald B .25 .11
❑ 97 John Mabry B .25 .11
❑ 98 Tom Goodwin B .25 .11
❑ 99 Edgar Martinez B .60 .25
❑ 100 Andruw Jones B 1.25 .55
❑ 101 Jose Canseco S 5.00 2.20
❑ 102 Billy Wagner S 2.00 .90
❑ 103 Dante Bichette S 2.50 1.10
❑ 104 Curt Schilling S 2.50 1.10
❑ 105 Dean Palmer S 2.50 1.10
❑ 106 Larry Walker S 2.50 1.10
❑ 107 Bernie Williams S 4.00 1.80
❑ 108 Chipper Jones S 10.00 4.50
❑ 109 Gary Sheffield S 4.00 1.80
❑ 110 Randy Johnson S 5.00 2.20
❑ 111 Roberto Alomar S 4.00 1.80
❑ 112 Todd Walker S 2.00 .90
❑ 113 Sandy Alomar Jr. S 2.50 1.10
❑ 114 John Jaha S 2.00 .90
❑ 115 Ken Caminiti S UER 2.50 1.10
(Card is numbered 135)
❑ 116 Ryan Klesko S 2.50 1.10
❑ 117 Mariano Rivera S 2.50 1.10
❑ 118 Jason Giambi S 4.00 1.80
❑ 119 Lance Johnson S 2.00 .90
❑ 120 Robin Ventura S 2.50 1.10
❑ 121 Todd Hollandsworth S 2.00 .90
❑ 122 Johnny Damon S 2.50 1.10
❑ 123 W. VanLandingham S 2.00 .90
❑ 124 Jason Kendall S 2.50 1.10
❑ 125 Vinny Castilla S 2.50 1.10
❑ 126 Harold Baines S 2.50 1.10
❑ 127 Joe Carter S 2.50 1.10
❑ 128 Craig Biggio S 3.00 1.35
❑ 129 Tony Clark S 2.00 .90
❑ 130 Ron Gant S 2.00 .90
❑ 131 David Segui S 2.00 .90
❑ 132 Steve Trachsel S 2.00 .90
❑ 133 Scott Rolen S 4.00 1.80
❑ 134 Mike Stanley S 2.00 .90
❑ 135 Cal Ripken S 15.00 6.75
❑ 136 John Smoltz S 2.50 1.10
❑ 137 Bobby Jones S 2.00 .90
❑ 138 Manny Ramirez S 5.00 2.20
❑ 139 Ken Griffey Jr. S 15.00 6.75
❑ 140 Chuck Knoblauch S 2.50 1.10
❑ 141 Mark Grace S 4.00 1.80
❑ 142 Chris Snopek S 2.00 .90
❑ 143 Hideo Nomo S 4.00 1.80
❑ 144 Tim Salmon S 2.50 1.10
❑ 145 David Cone S 2.50 1.10
❑ 146 Eric Young S 2.00 .90
❑ 147 Jeff Brantley S 2.00 .90
❑ 148 Jim Thome S 3.00 1.35
❑ 149 Trevor Hoffman S 2.50 1.10
❑ 150 Juan Gonzalez S 4.00 1.80
❑ 151 Mike Piazza G 30.00 13.50
❑ 152 Ivan Rodriguez G 12.00 5.50
❑ 153 Mo Vaughn G 6.00 2.70
❑ 154 Brady Anderson G 6.00 2.70
❑ 155 Mark McGwire G 40.00 18.00
❑ 156 Rafael Palmeiro G 10.00 4.50
❑ 157 Barry Larkin G 10.00 4.50
❑ 158 Greg Maddux G 25.00 11.00
❑ 159 Jeff Bagwell G 12.00 5.50
❑ 160 Frank Thomas G 20.00 9.00
❑ 161 Ken Caminiti G 6.00 2.70
❑ 162 Andruw Jones G 12.00 5.50
❑ 163 Dennis Eckersley G 6.00 2.70
❑ 164 Jeff Conine G 5.00 2.20
❑ 165 Jim Edmonds G 10.00 4.50
❑ 166 Derek Jeter G 40.00 18.00
❑ 167 Vladimir Guerrero G 20.00 9.00
❑ 168 Sammy Sosa G 20.00 9.00
❑ 169 Tony Gwynn G 20.00 9.00
❑ 170 Andres Galarraga G 8.00 3.60
❑ 171 Todd Hundley G 5.00 2.20
❑ 172 Jay Buhner G UER 6.00 2.70
(Card is numbered 164)
❑ 173 Paul Molitor G 10.00 4.50
❑ 174 Kenny Lofton G 6.00 2.70
❑ 175 Barry Bonds G 15.00 6.75
❑ 176 Gary Sheffield B 1.00 .45
❑ 177 Dmitri Young B .40 .18
❑ 178 Jay Bell B .40 .18
❑ 179 David Wells B .40 .18
❑ 180 Walt Weiss B .25 .11
❑ 181 Paul Molitor B 1.00 .45
❑ 182 Jose Guillen B .25 .11
❑ 183 Al Leiter B .40 .18
❑ 184 Mike Fetters B .25 .11
❑ 185 Mark Langston B .40 .18
❑ 186 Fred McGriff B .60 .25
❑ 187 Darrin Fletcher B .25 .11
❑ 188 Brant Brown B .25 .11
❑ 189 Geronimo Berroa B .25 .11
❑ 190 Jim Thome B .60 .25
❑ 191 Jose Vizcaino B .25 .11
❑ 192 Andy Ashby B .25 .11
❑ 193 Rusty Greer B .40 .18
❑ 194 Brian Hunter B .25 .11
❑ 195 Chris Hoiles B .25 .11
❑ 196 Orlando Merced B .25 .11
❑ 197 Brett Butler B .40 .18
❑ 198 Derek Bell B .25 .11
❑ 199 Bobby Bonilla B .40 .18
❑ 200 Alex Ochoa B .25 .11
❑ 201 Wally Joyner B .40 .18
❑ 202 Mo Vaughn B .40 .18
❑ 203 Doug Drabek B .25 .11
❑ 204 Tino Martinez B .40 .18
❑ 205 Roberto Alomar B 1.00 .45
❑ 206 Brian Giles B RC 6.00 2.70
❑ 207 Todd Worrell B .25 .11
❑ 208 Alan Benes B .25 .11
❑ 209 Jim Leyritz B .25 .11
❑ 210 Darryl Hamilton B .25 .11
❑ 211 Jimmy Key B .40 .18
❑ 212 Juan Gonzalez B 1.00 .45
❑ 213 Vinny Castilla B .40 .18
❑ 214 Chuck Knoblauch B .40 .18
❑ 215 Tony Phillips B .25 .11
❑ 216 Jeff Cirillo B .40 .18
❑ 217 Carlos Garcia B .25 .11
❑ 218 Brooks Kieschnick B .25 .11
❑ 219 Marquis Grissom B .25 .11
❑ 220 Dan Wilson B .25 .11
❑ 221 Greg Vaughn B .40 .18
❑ 222 John Wetteland B .40 .18
❑ 223 Andres Galarraga B .60 .25
❑ 224 Ozzie Guillen B .25 .11
❑ 225 Kevin Elster B .25 .11
❑ 226 Bernard Gilkey B .25 .11
❑ 227 Mike Macfarlane B .25 .11
❑ 228 Heathcliff Slocumb B .25 .11
❑ 229 Wendell Magee Jr. B .25 .11
❑ 230 Carlos Baerga B .25 .11
❑ 231 Kevin Seitzer B .25 .11
❑ 232 Henry Rodriguez B .25 .11
❑ 233 Roger Clemens B 2.00 .90
❑ 234 Mark Wohlers B .25 .11
❑ 235 Eddie Murray B 1.00 .45
❑ 236 Todd Zeile B .25 .11
❑ 237 J.T. Snow B .40 .18
❑ 238 Ken Griffey Jr. B 4.00 1.80
❑ 239 Sterling Hitchcock B .25 .11
❑ 240 Albert Belle B .60 .25
❑ 241 Terry Steinbach B .25 .11
❑ 242 Robb Nen B .25 .11
❑ 243 Mark McLemore B .25 .11
❑ 244 Jeff King B .25 .11
❑ 245 Tony Clark B .25 .11
❑ 246 Tim Salmon B .40 .18
❑ 247 Benito Santiago B .25 .11
❑ 248 Robin Ventura B .40 .18
❑ 249 Bubba Trammell B RC .40 .18
❑ 250 Chili Davis B .40 .18
❑ 251 John Valentin B .25 .11
❑ 252 Cal Ripken B 4.00 1.80
❑ 253 Matt Williams B .60 .25
❑ 254 Jeff Kent B .60 .25
❑ 255 Eric Karros B .40 .18
❑ 256 Ray Lankford B .40 .18
❑ 257 Ed Sprague B .25 .11
❑ 258 Shane Reynolds B .25 .11
❑ 259 Jaime Navarro B .25 .11
❑ 260 Eric Davis B .40 .18
❑ 261 Orel Hershiser B .40 .18
❑ 262 Mark Grace B 1.00 .45
❑ 263 Rod Beck B .25 .11
❑ 264 Ismael Valdes B .25 .11
❑ 265 Manny Ramirez B 1.25 .55
❑ 266 Ken Caminiti B .40 .18
❑ 267 Tim Naehring B .25 .11
❑ 268 Jose Rosado B .25 .11
❑ 269 Greg Colbrunn B .25 .11
❑ 270 Dean Palmer B .40 .18
❑ 271 David Justice B .60 .25
❑ 272 Scott Spiezio B .25 .11
❑ 273 Chipper Jones B 2.50 1.10
❑ 274 Mel Rojas B .25 .11
❑ 275 Bartolo Colon B .40 .18
❑ 276 Darin Erstad S 5.00 2.20
❑ 277 Sammy Sosa S 8.00 3.60
❑ 278 Rafael Palmeiro S 4.00 1.80
❑ 279 Frank Thomas S 8.00 3.60
❑ 280 Ruben Rivera S 2.00 .90
❑ 281 Hal Morris S 2.00 .90
❑ 282 Jay Buhner S 2.50 1.10
❑ 283 Kenny Lofton S 2.50 1.10
❑ 284 Jose Canseco S 5.00 2.20
❑ 285 Alex Fernandez S 2.00 .90
❑ 286 Todd Helton S 6.00 2.70
❑ 287 Andy Pettitte S 2.50 1.10
❑ 288 John Franco S 2.50 1.10

| | MINT | NRMT |
|---|---|---|
| ❑ 289 Ivan Rodriguez S | 5.00 | 2.20 |
| ❑ 290 Ellis Burks S | 2.50 | 1.10 |
| ❑ 291 Julio Franco S | 2.50 | 1.10 |
| ❑ 292 Mike Piazza S | 12.00 | 5.50 |
| ❑ 293 Brian Jordan S | 2.50 | 1.10 |
| ❑ 294 Greg Maddux S | 10.00 | 4.50 |
| ❑ 295 Bob Abreu S | 2.50 | 1.10 |
| ❑ 296 Rondell White S | 2.50 | 1.10 |
| ❑ 297 Moises Alou S | 2.50 | 1.10 |
| ❑ 298 Tony Gwynn S | 8.00 | 3.60 |
| ❑ 299 Deion Sanders S | 2.50 | 1.10 |
| ❑ 300 Jeff Montgomery S | 2.00 | .90 |
| ❑ 301 Ray Durham S | 2.50 | 1.10 |
| ❑ 302 John Wasdin S | 2.00 | .90 |
| ❑ 303 Ryne Sandberg S | 5.00 | 2.20 |
| ❑ 304 Delino DeShields S | 2.00 | .90 |
| ❑ 305 Mark McGwire S | 15.00 | 6.75 |
| ❑ 306 Andruw Jones S | 5.00 | 2.20 |
| ❑ 307 Kevin Orie S | 2.00 | .90 |
| ❑ 308 Matt Williams S | 3.00 | 1.35 |
| ❑ 309 Karim Garcia S | 2.00 | .90 |
| ❑ 310 Derek Jeter S | 15.00 | 6.75 |
| ❑ 311 Mo Vaughn S | 2.50 | 1.10 |
| ❑ 312 Brady Anderson S | 2.50 | 1.10 |
| ❑ 313 Barry Bonds S | 6.00 | 2.70 |
| ❑ 314 Steve Finley S | 2.50 | 1.10 |
| ❑ 315 Vladimir Guerrero S | 8.00 | 3.60 |
| ❑ 316 Matt Morris S | 2.00 | .90 |
| ❑ 317 Tom Glavine S | 4.00 | 1.80 |
| ❑ 318 Jeff Bagwell S | 5.00 | 2.20 |
| ❑ 319 Albert Belle S | 3.00 | 1.35 |
| ❑ 320 Hideki Irabu S RC | 3.00 | 1.35 |
| ❑ 321 Andres Galarraga S | 3.00 | 1.35 |
| ❑ 322 Cecil Fielder S | 2.50 | 1.10 |
| ❑ 323 Barry Larkin S | 4.00 | 1.80 |
| ❑ 324 Todd Hundley S | 2.00 | .90 |
| ❑ 325 Fred McGriff S | 3.00 | 1.35 |
| ❑ 326 Gary Sheffield G | 10.00 | 4.50 |
| ❑ 327 Craig Biggio G | 8.00 | 3.60 |
| ❑ 328 Raul Mondesi G | 6.00 | 2.70 |
| ❑ 329 Edgar Martinez G | 8.00 | 3.60 |
| ❑ 330 Chipper Jones G | 25.00 | 11.00 |
| ❑ 331 Bernie Williams G | 10.00 | 4.50 |
| ❑ 332 Juan Gonzalez G | 1.00 | .45 |
| ❑ 333 Ron Gant G | 5.00 | 2.20 |
| ❑ 334 Cal Ripken G | 40.00 | 18.00 |
| ❑ 335 Larry Walker G | 6.00 | 2.70 |
| ❑ 336 Matt Williams G | 8.00 | 3.60 |
| ❑ 337 Jose Cruz Jr. G RC | 20.00 | 9.00 |
| ❑ 338 Joe Carter G | 6.00 | 2.70 |
| ❑ 339 Wilton Guerrero G | 5.00 | 2.20 |
| ❑ 340 Cecil Fielder G | 6.00 | 2.70 |
| ❑ 341 Todd Walker G | 5.00 | 2.20 |
| ❑ 342 Ken Griffey Jr. G | 40.00 | 18.00 |
| ❑ 343 Ryan Klesko G | 6.00 | 2.70 |
| ❑ 344 Roger Clemens G | 20.00 | 9.00 |
| ❑ 345 Hideo Nomo G | 10.00 | 4.50 |
| ❑ 346 Dante Bichette G | 6.00 | 2.70 |
| ❑ 347 Albert Belle G | 8.00 | 3.60 |
| ❑ 348 Randy Johnson G | 12.00 | 5.50 |
| ❑ 349 Manny Ramirez G | 12.00 | 5.50 |
| ❑ 350 John Smoltz G | 6.00 | 2.70 |

## 1998 Finest

| | MINT | NRMT |
|---|---|---|
| COMPLETE SET (275) | 70.00 | 32.00 |
| COMPLETE SERIES 1 (150) | 40.00 | 18.00 |
| COMPLETE SERIES 2 (125) | 30.00 | 13.50 |
| COMMON CARD (1-275) | .25 | .11 |
| ❑ 1 Larry Walker | .40 | .18 |
| ❑ 2 Andruw Jones | 1.00 | .45 |
| ❑ 3 Ramon Martinez | .25 | .11 |
| ❑ 4 Geronimo Berroa | .25 | .11 |
| ❑ 5 David Justice | .60 | .25 |
| ❑ 6 Rusty Greer | .40 | .18 |
| ❑ 7 Chad Ogea | .25 | .11 |
| ❑ 8 Tom Goodwin | .25 | .11 |
| ❑ 9 Tino Martinez | .40 | .18 |
| ❑ 10 Jose Guillen | .25 | .11 |
| ❑ 11 Jeffrey Hammonds | .40 | .18 |
| ❑ 12 Brian McRae | .25 | .11 |
| ❑ 13 Jeremi Gonzalez | .25 | .11 |
| ❑ 14 Craig Counsell | .25 | .11 |
| ❑ 15 Mike Piazza | 3.00 | 1.35 |
| ❑ 16 Greg Maddux | 2.50 | 1.10 |
| ❑ 17 Todd Greene | .25 | .11 |
| ❑ 18 Rondell White | .40 | .18 |
| ❑ 19 Kirk Rueter | .25 | .11 |
| ❑ 20 Tony Clark | .25 | .11 |
| ❑ 21 Brad Radke | .40 | .18 |
| ❑ 22 Jaret Wright | .25 | .11 |
| ❑ 23 Carlos Delgado | 1.00 | .45 |
| ❑ 24 Dustin Hermanson | .25 | .11 |
| ❑ 25 Gary Sheffield | 1.00 | .45 |
| ❑ 26 Jose Canseco | 1.25 | .55 |
| ❑ 27 Kevin Young | .40 | .18 |
| ❑ 28 David Wells | .40 | .18 |
| ❑ 29 Mariano Rivera | .40 | .18 |
| ❑ 30 Reggie Sanders | .25 | .11 |
| ❑ 31 Mike Cameron | .40 | .18 |
| ❑ 32 Bobby Witt | .25 | .11 |
| ❑ 33 Kevin Orie | .25 | .11 |
| ❑ 34 Royce Clayton | .25 | .11 |
| ❑ 35 Edgar Martinez | .60 | .25 |
| ❑ 36 Neifi Perez | .25 | .11 |
| ❑ 37 Kevin Appier | .40 | .18 |
| ❑ 38 Darryl Hamilton | .25 | .11 |
| ❑ 39 Michael Tucker | .25 | .11 |
| ❑ 40 Roger Clemens | 2.00 | .90 |
| ❑ 41 Carl Everett | .40 | .18 |
| ❑ 42 Mike Sweeney | .40 | .18 |
| ❑ 43 Pat Meares | .25 | .11 |
| ❑ 44 Brian Giles | .40 | .18 |
| ❑ 45 Matt Morris | .25 | .11 |
| ❑ 46 Jason Dickson | .25 | .11 |
| ❑ 47 Rich Loiselle RC | .40 | .18 |
| ❑ 48 Joe Girardi | .25 | .11 |
| ❑ 49 Steve Trachsel | .25 | .11 |
| ❑ 50 Ben Grieve | .40 | .18 |
| ❑ 51 Brian Johnson | .25 | .11 |
| ❑ 52 Hideki Irabu | .25 | .11 |
| ❑ 53 J.T. Snow | .40 | .18 |
| ❑ 54 Mike Hampton | .40 | .18 |
| ❑ 55 Dave Nilsson | .25 | .11 |
| ❑ 56 Alex Fernandez | .25 | .11 |
| ❑ 57 Brett Tomko | .25 | .11 |
| ❑ 58 Wally Joyner | .40 | .18 |
| ❑ 59 Kelvim Escobar | .25 | .11 |
| ❑ 60 Roberto Alomar | 1.00 | .45 |
| ❑ 61 Todd Jones | .25 | .11 |
| ❑ 62 Paul O'Neill | .40 | .18 |
| ❑ 63 Jamie Moyer | .25 | .11 |
| ❑ 64 Mark Wohlers | .25 | .11 |
| ❑ 65 Jose Cruz Jr. | .40 | .18 |
| ❑ 66 Troy Percival | .25 | .11 |
| ❑ 67 Rick Reed | .25 | .11 |
| ❑ 68 Will Clark | 1.00 | .45 |
| ❑ 69 Jamey Wright | .25 | .11 |
| ❑ 70 Mike Mussina | 1.00 | .45 |
| ❑ 71 David Cone | .40 | .18 |
| ❑ 72 Ryan Klesko | .40 | .18 |
| ❑ 73 Scott Hatteberg | .25 | .11 |
| ❑ 74 James Baldwin | .25 | .11 |
| ❑ 75 Tony Womack | .25 | .11 |
| ❑ 76 Carlos Perez | .25 | .11 |
| ❑ 77 Charles Nagy | .25 | .11 |
| ❑ 78 Jeromy Burnitz | .40 | .18 |
| ❑ 79 Shane Reynolds | .25 | .11 |
| ❑ 80 Cliff Floyd | .40 | .18 |
| ❑ 81 Jason Kendall | .40 | .18 |
| ❑ 82 Chad Curtis | .25 | .11 |
| ❑ 83 Matt Karchner | .25 | .11 |
| ❑ 84 Ricky Bottalico | .25 | .11 |
| ❑ 85 Sammy Sosa | 2.00 | .90 |
| ❑ 86 Javy Lopez | .40 | .18 |
| ❑ 87 Jeff Kent | .60 | .25 |
| ❑ 88 Shawn Green | 1.00 | .45 |
| ❑ 89 Joey Cora | .25 | .11 |
| ❑ 90 Tony Gwynn | 2.00 | .90 |
| ❑ 91 Bob Tewksbury | .25 | .11 |
| ❑ 92 Derek Jeter | 4.00 | 1.80 |
| ❑ 93 Eric Davis | .40 | .18 |
| ❑ 94 Jeff Fassero | .25 | .11 |
| ❑ 95 Denny Neagle | .25 | .11 |
| ❑ 96 Ismael Valdes | .25 | .11 |
| ❑ 97 Tim Salmon | .40 | .18 |
| ❑ 98 Mark Grudzielanek | .25 | .11 |
| ❑ 99 Curt Schilling | .40 | .18 |
| ❑ 100 Ken Griffey Jr. | 4.00 | 1.80 |
| ❑ 101 Edgardo Alfonzo | .40 | .18 |
| ❑ 102 Vinny Castilla | .40 | .18 |
| ❑ 103 Jose Rosado | .25 | .11 |
| ❑ 104 Scott Erickson | .25 | .11 |
| ❑ 105 Alan Benes | .25 | .11 |
| ❑ 106 Shannon Stewart | .40 | .18 |
| ❑ 107 Delino DeShields | .25 | .11 |
| ❑ 108 Mark Loretta | .25 | .11 |
| ❑ 109 Todd Hundley | .25 | .11 |
| ❑ 110 Chuck Knoblauch | .40 | .18 |
| ❑ 111 Todd Helton | 1.25 | .55 |
| ❑ 112 F.P. Santangelo | .25 | .11 |
| ❑ 113 Jeff Cirillo | .40 | .18 |
| ❑ 114 Omar Vizquel | .40 | .18 |
| ❑ 115 John Valentin | .25 | .11 |
| ❑ 116 Damion Easley | .25 | .11 |
| ❑ 117 Matt Lawton | .25 | .11 |
| ❑ 118 Jim Thome | .60 | .25 |
| ❑ 119 Sandy Alomar Jr. | .40 | .18 |
| ❑ 120 Albert Belle | .60 | .25 |
| ❑ 121 Chris Stynes | .25 | .11 |
| ❑ 122 Butch Huskey | .25 | .11 |
| ❑ 123 Shawn Estes | .25 | .11 |
| ❑ 124 Terry Adams | .25 | .11 |
| ❑ 125 Ivan Rodriguez | 1.25 | .55 |
| ❑ 126 Ron Gant | .40 | .18 |
| ❑ 127 John Mabry | .25 | .11 |
| ❑ 128 Jeff Shaw | .25 | .11 |
| ❑ 129 Jeff Montgomery | .25 | .11 |
| ❑ 130 Justin Thompson | .25 | .11 |
| ❑ 131 Livan Hernandez | .25 | .11 |
| ❑ 132 Ugueth Urbina | .25 | .11 |
| ❑ 133 Scott Servais | .25 | .11 |
| ❑ 134 Troy O'Leary | .25 | .11 |
| ❑ 135 Cal Ripken | 4.00 | 1.80 |
| ❑ 136 Quilvio Veras | .25 | .11 |
| ❑ 137 Pedro Astacio | .25 | .11 |
| ❑ 138 Willie Greene | .25 | .11 |
| ❑ 139 Lance Johnson | .25 | .11 |
| ❑ 140 Nomar Garciaparra | 3.00 | 1.35 |
| ❑ 141 Jose Offerman | .25 | .11 |
| ❑ 142 Scott Rolen | 1.00 | .45 |
| ❑ 143 Derek Bell | .25 | .11 |
| ❑ 144 Johnny Damon | .40 | .18 |
| ❑ 145 Mark McGwire | 4.00 | 1.80 |
| ❑ 146 Chan Ho Park | .40 | .18 |
| ❑ 147 Edgar Renteria | .25 | .11 |
| ❑ 148 Eric Young | .25 | .11 |
| ❑ 149 Craig Biggio | .60 | .25 |
| ❑ 150 Checklist (1-150) | .25 | .11 |
| ❑ 151 Frank Thomas | 2.00 | .90 |
| ❑ 152 John Wetteland | .40 | .18 |
| ❑ 153 Mike Lansing | .25 | .11 |
| ❑ 154 Pedro Martinez | 1.25 | .55 |
| ❑ 155 Rico Brogna | .25 | .11 |
| ❑ 156 Kevin Brown | .60 | .25 |
| ❑ 157 Alex Rodriguez | 3.00 | 1.35 |
| ❑ 158 Wade Boggs | 1.25 | .55 |
| ❑ 159 Richard Hidalgo | .40 | .18 |
| ❑ 160 Mark Grace | 1.00 | .45 |
| ❑ 161 Jose Mesa | .25 | .11 |
| ❑ 162 John Olerud | .40 | .18 |
| ❑ 163 Tim Belcher | .25 | .11 |
| ❑ 164 Chuck Finley | .40 | .18 |
| ❑ 165 Brian Hunter | .25 | .11 |
| ❑ 166 Joe Carter | .40 | .18 |
| ❑ 167 Stan Javier | .25 | .11 |
| ❑ 168 Jay Bell | .40 | .18 |
| ❑ 169 Ray Lankford | .40 | .18 |

❑ 170 John Smoltz .40 .18
❑ 171 Ed Sprague .25 .11
❑ 172 Jason Giambi 1.00 .45
❑ 173 Todd Walker .25 .11
❑ 174 Paul Konerko .40 .18
❑ 175 Rey Ordonez .25 .11
❑ 176 Dante Bichette .40 .18
❑ 177 Bernie Williams 1.00 .45
❑ 178 Jon Nunnally .25 .11
❑ 179 Rafael Palmeiro 1.00 .45
❑ 180 Jay Buhner .40 .18
❑ 181 Devon White .25 .11
❑ 182 Jeff D'Amico .25 .11
❑ 183 Walt Weiss .40 .18
❑ 184 Scott Spiezio .25 .11
❑ 185 Moises Alou .40 .18
❑ 186 Carlos Baerga .25 .11
❑ 187 Todd Zeile .40 .18
❑ 188 Gregg Jefferies .25 .11
❑ 189 Mo Vaughn .40 .18
❑ 190 Terry Steinbach .25 .11
❑ 191 Ray Durham .40 .18
❑ 192 Robin Ventura .40 .18
❑ 193 Jeff Reed .25 .11
❑ 194 Ken Caminiti .40 .18
❑ 195 Eric Karros .40 .18
❑ 196 Wilson Alvarez .25 .11
❑ 197 Gary Gaetti .40 .18
❑ 198 Andres Galarraga .60 .25
❑ 199 Alex Gonzalez .25 .11
❑ 200 Garret Anderson .40 .18
❑ 201 Andy Benes .25 .11
❑ 202 Harold Baines .40 .18
❑ 203 Ron Coomer .25 .11
❑ 204 Dean Palmer .40 .18
❑ 205 Reggie Jefferson .25 .11
❑ 206 John Burkett .25 .11
❑ 207 Jermaine Allensworth .25 .11
❑ 208 Bernard Gilkey .25 .11
❑ 209 Jeff Bagwell 1.25 .55
❑ 210 Kenny Lofton .40 .18
❑ 211 Bobby Jones .25 .11
❑ 212 Bartolo Colon .40 .18
❑ 213 Jim Edmonds 1.00 .45
❑ 214 Pat Hentgen .25 .11
❑ 215 Matt Williams .60 .25
❑ 216 Bob Abreu .40 .18
❑ 217 Jorge Posada .25 .11
❑ 218 Marty Cordova .25 .11
❑ 219 Ken Hill .25 .11
❑ 220 Steve Finley .40 .18
❑ 221 Jeff King .25 .11
❑ 222 Quinton McCracken .25 .11
❑ 223 Matt Stairs .25 .11
❑ 224 Darin Erstad 1.00 .45
❑ 225 Fred McGriff .60 .25
❑ 226 Marquis Grissom .25 .11
❑ 227 Doug Glanville .25 .11
❑ 228 Tom Glavine 1.00 .45
❑ 229 John Franco .40 .18
❑ 230 Darren Bragg .25 .11
❑ 231 Barry Larkin 1.00 .45
❑ 232 Trevor Hoffman .40 .18
❑ 233 Brady Anderson .40 .18
❑ 234 Al Martin .25 .11
❑ 235 B.J. Surhoff .40 .18
❑ 236 Ellis Burks .40 .18
❑ 237 Randy Johnson 1.25 .55
❑ 238 Mark Clark .25 .11
❑ 239 Tony Saunders .25 .11
❑ 240 Hideo Nomo 1.00 .45
❑ 241 Brad Fullmer .40 .18
❑ 242 Chipper Jones 2.50 1.10
❑ 243 Jose Valentin .25 .11
❑ 244 Manny Ramirez 1.25 .55
❑ 245 Derrek Lee .25 .11
❑ 246 Jimmy Key .40 .18
❑ 247 Tim Naehring .25 .11
❑ 248 Bobby Higginson .40 .18
❑ 249 Charles Johnson .40 .18
❑ 250 Chili Davis .40 .18
❑ 251 Tom Gordon .40 .18
❑ 252 Mike Lieberthal .40 .18
❑ 253 Billy Wagner .25 .11
❑ 254 Juan Guzman .25 .11
❑ 255 Todd Stottlemyre .25 .11
❑ 256 Brian Jordan .40 .18
❑ 257 Barry Bonds 1.50 .70
❑ 258 Dan Wilson .25 .11
❑ 259 Paul Molitor 1.00 .45
❑ 260 Juan Gonzalez 1.00 .45
❑ 261 Francisco Cordova .25 .11
❑ 262 Cecil Fielder .40 .18
❑ 263 Travis Lee .40 .18
❑ 264 Kevin Tapani .25 .11
❑ 265 Raul Mondesi .40 .18
❑ 266 Travis Fryman .40 .18
❑ 267 Armando Benitez .25 .11
❑ 268 Pokey Reese .40 .18
❑ 269 Rick Aguilera .25 .11
❑ 270 Andy Pettitte .40 .18
❑ 271 Jose Vizcaino .25 .11
❑ 272 Kerry Wood 1.00 .45
❑ 273 Vladimir Guerrero 1.50 .70
❑ 274 John Smiley .25 .11
❑ 275 Checklist (151-275) .25 .11

## 1999 Finest

| | MINT | NRMT |
|---|---|---|
| COMPLETE SET (300) | 200.00 | 90.00 |
| COMPLETE SERIES 1 (150) | 100.00 | 45.00 |
| COMPLETE SERIES 2 (150) | 100.00 | 45.00 |
| COMP.SER.1 w/o SP's (100) | 30.00 | 13.50 |
| COMP.SER.2 w/o SP's (100) | 30.00 | 13.50 |
| COMMON (1-100/151-250) | .20 | .09 |
| COMMON (101-150/251-300) | .50 | .23 |

❑ 1 Darin Erstad .75 .35
❑ 2 Javy Lopez .30 .14
❑ 3 Vinny Castilla .30 .14
❑ 4 Jim Thome .50 .23
❑ 5 Tino Martinez .30 .14
❑ 6 Mark Grace .75 .35
❑ 7 Shawn Green .75 .35
❑ 8 Dustin Hermanson .20 .09
❑ 9 Kevin Young .30 .14
❑ 10 Tony Clark .20 .09
❑ 11 Scott Brosius .30 .14
❑ 12 Craig Biggio .50 .23
❑ 13 Brian McRae .20 .09
❑ 14 Chan Ho Park .30 .14
❑ 15 Manny Ramirez 1.00 .45
❑ 16 Chipper Jones 2.00 .90
❑ 17 Rico Brogna .20 .09
❑ 18 Quinton McCracken .20 .09
❑ 19 J.T. Snow .30 .14
❑ 20 Tony Gwynn 1.50 .70
❑ 21 Juan Guzman .20 .09
❑ 22 John Valentin .20 .09
❑ 23 Rick Helling .30 .14
❑ 24 Sandy Alomar Jr. .30 .14
❑ 25 Frank Thomas 1.50 .70
❑ 26 Jorge Posada .30 .14
❑ 27 Dmitri Young .30 .14
❑ 28 Rick Reed .20 .09
❑ 29 Kevin Tapani .20 .09
❑ 30 Troy Glaus 1.25 .55
❑ 31 Kenny Rogers .20 .09
❑ 32 Jeromy Burnitz .30 .14
❑ 33 Mark Grudzielanek .20 .09
❑ 34 Mike Mussina .75 .35
❑ 35 Scott Rolen .75 .35
❑ 36 Neifi Perez .20 .09
❑ 37 Brad Radke .30 .14
❑ 38 Darryl Strawberry .30 .14
❑ 39 Robb Nen .20 .09
❑ 40 Moises Alou .30 .14
❑ 41 Eric Young .20 .09
❑ 42 Livan Hernandez .20 .09
❑ 43 John Wetteland .30 .14
❑ 44 Matt Lawton .30 .14
❑ 45 Ben Grieve .30 .14
❑ 46 Fernando Tatis .30 .14
❑ 47 Travis Fryman .30 .14
❑ 48 David Segui .20 .09
❑ 49 Bob Abreu .30 .14
❑ 50 Nomar Garciaparra 2.50 1.10
❑ 51 Paul O'Neill .30 .14
❑ 52 Jeff King .20 .09
❑ 53 Francisco Cordova .20 .09
❑ 54 John Olerud .30 .14
❑ 55 Vladimir Guerrero 1.25 .55
❑ 56 Fernando Vina .20 .09
❑ 57 Shane Reynolds .20 .09
❑ 58 Chuck Finley .30 .14
❑ 59 Rondell White .30 .14
❑ 60 Greg Vaughn .30 .14
❑ 61 Ryan Minor .20 .09
❑ 62 Tom Gordon .20 .09
❑ 63 Damion Easley .20 .09
❑ 64 Ray Durham .30 .14
❑ 65 Orlando Hernandez .30 .14
❑ 66 Bartolo Colon .30 .14
❑ 67 Jaret Wright .20 .09
❑ 68 Royce Clayton .20 .09
❑ 69 Tim Salmon .00 .14
❑ 70 Mark McGwire 3.00 1.35
❑ 71 Alex Gonzalez .20 .09
❑ 72 Tom Glavine .75 .35
❑ 73 David Justice .50 .23
❑ 74 Omar Vizquel .30 .14
❑ 75 Juan Gonzalez .75 .35
❑ 76 Bobby Higginson .30 .14
❑ 77 Todd Walker .20 .09
❑ 78 Dante Bichette .30 .14
❑ 79 Kevin Millwood .30 .14
❑ 80 Roger Clemens 1.50 .70
❑ 81 Kerry Wood .30 .14
❑ 82 Cal Ripken 3.00 1.35
❑ 83 Jay Bell .30 .14
❑ 84 Barry Bonds 1.25 .55
❑ 85 Alex Rodriguez 2.50 1.10
❑ 86 Doug Glanville .20 .09
❑ 87 Jason Kendall .30 .14
❑ 88 Sean Casey .30 .14
❑ 89 Aaron Sele .30 .14
❑ 90 Derek Jeter 3.00 1.35
❑ 91 Andy Ashby .20 .09
❑ 92 Rusty Greer .30 .14
❑ 93 Rod Beck .20 .09
❑ 94 Matt Williams .50 .23
❑ 95 Mike Piazza 2.50 1.10
❑ 96 Wally Joyner .30 .14
❑ 97 Barry Larkin .75 .35
❑ 98 Eric Milton .20 .09
❑ 99 Gary Sheffield .75 .35
❑ 100 Greg Maddux 2.00 .90
❑ 101 Ken Griffey Jr. GEM 5.00 2.20
❑ 102 Frank Thomas GEM 2.50 1.10
❑ 103 Nomar Garciaparra GEM 4.00 1.80
❑ 104 Mark McGwire GEM 5.00 2.20
❑ 105 Alex Rodriguez GEM 4.00 1.80
❑ 106 Tony Gwynn GEM 2.50 1.10
❑ 107 Juan Gonzalez GEM .75 .35
❑ 108 Jeff Bagwell GEM 1.50 .70
❑ 109 Sammy Sosa GEM 2.50 1.10
❑ 110 Vladimir Guerrero GEM 2.00 .90
❑ 111 Roger Clemens GEM 2.50 1.10
❑ 112 Barry Bonds GEM 2.00 .90
❑ 113 Darin Erstad GEM 1.25 .55
❑ 114 Mike Piazza GEM 4.00 1.80
❑ 115 Derek Jeter GEM 5.00 2.20
❑ 116 Chipper Jones GEM 3.00 1.35
❑ 117 Larry Walker GEM .50 .23
❑ 118 Scott Rolen GEM 1.25 .55
❑ 119 Cal Ripken GEM 5.00 2.20
❑ 120 Greg Maddux GEM 3.00 1.35
❑ 121 Troy Glaus SENS 2.00 .90
❑ 122 Ben Grieve SENS .50 .23

❑ 123 Ryan Minor SENS .50 .23
❑ 124 Kerry Wood SENS .50 .23
❑ 125 Travis Lee SENS .50 .23
❑ 126 Adrian Beltre SENS .50 .23
❑ 127 Brad Fullmer SENS .50 .23
❑ 128 Aramis Ramirez SENS .50 .23
❑ 129 Eric Chavez SENS .50 .23
❑ 130 Todd Helton SENS 1.50 .70
❑ 131 Pat Burrell RC 12.00 5.50
❑ 132 Ryan Mills RC 1.00 .45
❑ 133 Austin Kearns RC 5.00 2.20
❑ 134 Josh McKinley RC 1.25 .55
❑ 135 Adam Everett RC 1.50 .70
❑ 136 Marlon Anderson .50 .23
❑ 137 Bruce Chen .20 .09
❑ 138 Matt Clement .50 .23
❑ 139 Alex Gonzalez .50 .23
❑ 140 Roy Halladay .50 .23
❑ 141 Calvin Pickering .50 .23
❑ 142 Randy Wolf .50 .23
❑ 143 Ryan Anderson .50 .23
❑ 144 Ruben Mateo .50 .23
❑ 145 Alex Escobar RC 5.00 2.20
❑ 146 Jeremy Giambi .50 .23
❑ 147 Lance Berkman .50 .23
❑ 148 Michael Barrett .50 .23
❑ 149 Preston Wilson .50 .23
❑ 150 Gabe Kapler .50 .23
❑ 151 Roger Clemens 1.50 .70
❑ 152 Jay Buhner .30 .14
❑ 153 Brad Fullmer .30 .14
❑ 154 Ray Lankford .30 .14
❑ 155 Jim Edmonds .75 .35
❑ 156 Jason Giambi .75 .35
❑ 157 Bret Boone .30 .14
❑ 158 Jeff Cirillo .30 .14
❑ 159 Rickey Henderson 1.00 .45
❑ 160 Edgar Martinez .50 .23
❑ 161 Ron Gant .30 .14
❑ 162 Mark Kotsay .20 .09
❑ 163 Trevor Hoffman .30 .14
❑ 164 Jason Schmidt .20 .09
❑ 165 Brett Tomko .20 .09
❑ 166 David Ortiz .20 .09
❑ 167 Dean Palmer .30 .14
❑ 168 Hideki Irabu .20 .09
❑ 169 Mike Cameron .20 .09
❑ 170 Pedro Martinez 1.00 .45
❑ 171 Tom Goodwin .20 .09
❑ 172 Brian Hunter .20 .09
❑ 173 Al Leiter .30 .14
❑ 174 Charles Johnson .30 .14
❑ 175 Curt Schilling .30 .14
❑ 176 Robin Ventura .30 .14
❑ 177 Travis Lee .20 .09
❑ 178 Jeff Shaw .20 .09
❑ 179 Ugueth Urbina .20 .09
❑ 180 Roberto Alomar .75 .35
❑ 181 Cliff Floyd .30 .14
❑ 182 Adrian Beltre .30 .14
❑ 183 Tony Womack .20 .09
❑ 184 Brian Jordan .30 .14
❑ 185 Randy Johnson 1.00 .45
❑ 186 Mickey Morandini .20 .09
❑ 187 Todd Hundley .20 .09
❑ 188 Jose Valentin .20 .09
❑ 189 Eric Davis .30 .14
❑ 190 Ken Caminiti .30 .14
❑ 191 David Wells .30 .14
❑ 192 Ryan Klesko .30 .14
❑ 193 Garret Anderson .30 .14
❑ 194 Eric Karros .30 .14
❑ 195 Ivan Rodriguez 1.00 .45
❑ 196 Aramis Ramirez .20 .09
❑ 197 Mike Lieberthal .30 .14
❑ 198 Will Clark .75 .35
❑ 199 Rey Ordonez .20 .09
❑ 200 Ken Griffey Jr. 3.00 1.35
❑ 201 Jose Guillen .20 .09
❑ 202 Scott Erickson .20 .09
❑ 203 Paul Konerko .30 .14
❑ 204 Johnny Damon .30 .14
❑ 205 Larry Walker .30 .14
❑ 206 Denny Neagle .20 .09
❑ 207 Jose Offerman .20 .09
❑ 208 Andy Pettitte .30 .14
❑ 209 Bobby Jones .20 .09
❑ 210 Kevin Brown .50 .23
❑ 211 John Smoltz .30 .14
❑ 212 Henry Rodriguez .20 .09
❑ 213 Tim Belcher .20 .09
❑ 214 Carlos Delgado .75 .35
❑ 215 Andruw Jones .75 .35
❑ 216 Andy Benes .20 .09
❑ 217 Fred McGriff .50 .23
❑ 218 Edgar Renteria .20 .09
❑ 219 Miguel Tejada .30 .14
❑ 220 Bernie Williams .75 .35
❑ 221 Justin Thompson .20 .09
❑ 222 Marty Cordova .20 .09
❑ 223 Delino DeShields .20 .09
❑ 224 Ellis Burks .30 .14
❑ 225 Kenny Lofton .30 .14
❑ 226 Steve Finley .30 .14
❑ 227 Eric Chavez .30 .14
❑ 228 Jose Cruz Jr. .30 .14
❑ 229 Marquis Grissom .20 .09
❑ 230 Jeff Bagwell 1.00 .45
❑ 231 Jose Canseco 1.00 .45
❑ 232 Edgardo Alfonzo .30 .14
❑ 233 Richie Sexson .30 .14
❑ 234 Jeff Kent .50 .23
❑ 235 Rafael Palmeiro .75 .35
❑ 236 David Cone .30 .14
❑ 237 Gregg Jefferies .20 .09
❑ 238 Mike Lansing .20 .09
❑ 239 Mariano Rivera .30 .14
❑ 240 Albert Belle .50 .23
❑ 241 Chuck Knoblauch .30 .14
❑ 242 Derek Bell .20 .09
❑ 243 Pat Hentgen .20 .09
❑ 244 Andres Galarraga .50 .23
❑ 245 Mo Vaughn .30 .14
❑ 246 Wade Boggs 1.00 .45
❑ 247 Devon White .20 .09
❑ 248 Todd Helton 1.00 .45
❑ 249 Raul Mondesi .30 .14
❑ 250 Sammy Sosa 1.50 .70
❑ 251 Nomar Garciaparra ST 4.00 1.80
❑ 252 Mark McGwire ST 5.00 2.20
❑ 253 Alex Rodriguez ST 4.00 1.80
❑ 254 Juan Gonzalez ST .75 .35
❑ 255 Vladimir Guerrero ST 2.00 .90
❑ 256 Ken Griffey Jr. ST 5.00 2.20
❑ 257 Mike Piazza ST 4.00 1.80
❑ 258 Derek Jeter ST 5.00 2.20
❑ 259 Albert Belle ST .75 .35
❑ 260 Greg Vaughn ST .50 .23
❑ 261 Sammy Sosa ST 2.50 1.10
❑ 262 Greg Maddux ST 3.00 1.35
❑ 263 Frank Thomas ST 2.50 1.10
❑ 264 Mark Grace ST 1.25 .55
❑ 265 Ivan Rodriguez ST 1.50 .70
❑ 266 Roger Clemens GM 2.50 1.10
❑ 267 Mo Vaughn GM .50 .23
❑ 268 Jim Thome GM .75 .35
❑ 269 Darin Erstad GM 1.25 .55
❑ 270 Chipper Jones GM 3.00 1.35
❑ 271 Larry Walker GM .50 .23
❑ 272 Cal Ripken GM 5.00 2.20
❑ 273 Scott Rolen GM 1.25 .55
❑ 274 Randy Johnson GM 1.50 .70
❑ 275 Tony Gwynn GM 2.50 1.10
❑ 276 Barry Bonds GM 2.00 .90
❑ 277 Sean Burroughs RC 8.00 3.60
❑ 278 J.M. Gold RC 1.25 .55
❑ 279 Carlos Lee .50 .23
❑ 280 George Lombard .50 .23
❑ 281 Carlos Beltran .50 .23
❑ 282 Fernando Seguignol .50 .23
❑ 283 Eric Chavez .50 .23
❑ 284 Carlos Pena RC 5.00 2.20
❑ 285 Corey Patterson RC 12.00 5.50
❑ 286 Alfonso Soriano RC 5.00 2.20
❑ 287 Nick Johnson RC 5.00 2.20
❑ 288 Jorge Toca RC 1.25 .55
❑ 289 A.J. Burnett RC 2.00 .90
❑ 290 Andy Brown RC 2.00 .90
❑ 291 Doug Mientkiewicz RC 1.00 .45
❑ 292 Bobby Seay RC 1.50 .70
❑ 293 Chip Ambres RC 1.50 .70
❑ 294 C.C. Sabathia RC 5.00 2.20
❑ 295 Choo Freeman RC 1.50 .70
❑ 296 Eric Valent RC 2.50 1.10
❑ 297 Matt Belisle RC 2.00 .90
❑ 298 Jason Tyner RC 2.00 .90
❑ 299 Masao Kida RC .50 .23
❑ 300 Hank Aaron 4.00 1.80
Mark McGwire

## 2000 Finest

| | MINT | NRMT |
|---|---|---|
| COMPLETE SET (287) | 1200.00 | 550.00 |
| COMPLETE SERIES 1 (147) | 700.00 | 325.00 |
| COMPLETE SERIES 2 (140) | 500.00 | 220.00 |
| COMP.SERIES 1 w/o SP's (100) | 25.00 | 11.00 |
| COMP.SERIES 2 w/o SP's (100) | 25.00 | 11.00 |
| COMMON (1-100/147-246) | .20 | .09 |
| COMMON ROOKIE (101-120) | 12.00 | 5.50 |
| COMMON FEATURES (121-135) | 1.50 | .70 |
| COMM.GEM (136-145/277-286) | 2.50 | 1.10 |
| COMMON ROOKIE (247-266) | 10.00 | 4.50 |
| MINOR STARS 247-266 | 10.00 | 4.50 |
| SEMISTARS 247-266 | 10.00 | 4.50 |
| UNLISTED STARS 247-266 | 10.00 | 4.50 |
| COMMON COUNTER (267-276) | 1.00 | .45 |
| MINOR STARS 267-276 | 1.00 | .45 |
| SEMISTARS 267-276 | 1.25 | .55 |
| UNLISTED STARS 267-276 | 2.00 | .90 |

❑ 1 Nomar Garciaparra 2.50 1.10
❑ 2 Chipper Jones 2.00 .90
❑ 3 Erubiel Durazo .30 .14
❑ 4 Robin Ventura .50 .23
❑ 5 Garret Anderson .30 .14
❑ 6 Dean Palmer .30 .14
❑ 7 Mariano Rivera .30 .14
❑ 8 Rusty Greer .30 .14
❑ 9 Jim Thome .50 .23
❑ 10 Jeff Bagwell 1.00 .45
❑ 11 Jason Giambi .75 .35
❑ 12 Jeromy Burnitz .30 .14
❑ 13 Mark Grace .75 .35
❑ 14 Russ Ortiz .30 .14
❑ 15 Kevin Brown .50 .23
❑ 16 Kevin Millwood .30 .14
❑ 17 Scott Williamson .20 .09
❑ 18 Orlando Hernandez .30 .14
❑ 19 Todd Walker .20 .09
❑ 20 Carlos Beltran .30 .14
❑ 21 Ruben Rivera .20 .09
❑ 22 Curt Schilling .30 .14
❑ 23 Brian Giles .30 .14
❑ 24 Eric Karros .30 .14
❑ 25 Preston Wilson .30 .14
❑ 26 Al Leiter .20 .09
❑ 27 Juan Encarnacion .30 .14
❑ 28 Tim Salmon .30 .14
❑ 29 B.J. Surhoff .30 .14
❑ 30 Bernie Williams .75 .35
❑ 31 Lee Stevens .20 .09
❑ 32 Pokey Reese .30 .14
❑ 33 Mike Sweeney .30 .14
❑ 34 Corey Koskie .20 .09
❑ 35 Roberto Alomar .75 .35
❑ 36 Tim Hudson .75 .35
❑ 37 Tom Glavine .75 .35
❑ 38 Jeff Kent .50 .23
❑ 39 Mike Lieberthal .30 .14

| | No. | Player | Nrmt | Ex |
|---|---|---|---|---|
| ❑ | 40 | Barry Larkin | .75 | .35 |
| ❑ | 41 | Paul O'Neill | .30 | .14 |
| ❑ | 42 | Rico Brogna | .20 | .09 |
| ❑ | 43 | Brian Daubach | .20 | .09 |
| ❑ | 44 | Rich Aurilia | .20 | .09 |
| ❑ | 45 | Vladimir Guerrero | 1.25 | .55 |
| ❑ | 46 | Luis Castillo | .30 | .14 |
| ❑ | 47 | Bartolo Colon | .30 | .14 |
| ❑ | 48 | Kevin Appier | .20 | .09 |
| ❑ | 49 | Mo Vaughn | .30 | .14 |
| ❑ | 50 | Alex Rodriguez | 2.50 | 1.10 |
| ❑ | 51 | Randy Johnson | 1.00 | .45 |
| ❑ | 52 | Kris Benson | .30 | .14 |
| ❑ | 53 | Tony Clark | .20 | .09 |
| ❑ | 54 | Chad Allen | .20 | .09 |
| ❑ | 55 | Larry Walker | .30 | .14 |
| ❑ | 56 | Freddy Garcia | .30 | .14 |
| ❑ | 57 | Paul Konerko | .30 | .14 |
| ❑ | 58 | Edgardo Alfonzo | .30 | .14 |
| ❑ | 59 | Brady Anderson | .30 | .14 |
| ❑ | 60 | Derek Jeter | 3.00 | 1.35 |
| ❑ | 61 | John Smoltz | .30 | .14 |
| ❑ | 62 | Doug Glanville | .20 | .09 |
| ❑ | 63 | Shannon Stewart | .30 | .14 |
| ❑ | 64 | Greg Maddux | 2.00 | .90 |
| ❑ | 65 | Mark McGwire | 3.00 | 1.35 |
| ❑ | 66 | Gary Sheffield | .75 | .35 |
| ❑ | 67 | Kevin Young | .20 | .09 |
| ❑ | 68 | Tony Gwynn | 1.50 | .70 |
| ❑ | 69 | Rey Ordonez | .20 | .09 |
| ❑ | 70 | Cal Ripken | 3.00 | 1.35 |
| ❑ | 71 | Todd Helton | 1.00 | .45 |
| ❑ | 72 | Brian Jordan | .30 | .14 |
| ❑ | 73 | Jose Canseco | 1.00 | .45 |
| ❑ | 74 | Luis Gonzalez | .30 | .14 |
| ❑ | 75 | Barry Bonds | 1.25 | .55 |
| ❑ | 76 | Jermaine Dye | .30 | .14 |
| ❑ | 77 | Jose Offerman | .20 | .09 |
| ❑ | 78 | Maggio Ordonez | .30 | .14 |
| ❑ | 79 | Fred McGriff | .50 | .23 |
| ❑ | 80 | Ivan Rodriguez | 1.00 | .45 |
| ❑ | 81 | Josh Hamilton | 1.25 | .55 |
| ❑ | 82 | Vernon Wells | .30 | .14 |
| ❑ | 83 | Mark Mulder | .30 | .14 |
| ❑ | 84 | John Patterson | .20 | .09 |
| ❑ | 85 | Nick Johnson | .30 | .14 |
| ❑ | 86 | Pablo Ozuna | .20 | .09 |
| ❑ | 87 | A.J. Burnett | .30 | .14 |
| ❑ | 88 | Jack Cust | .30 | .14 |
| ❑ | 89 | Adam Piatt | .75 | .35 |
| ❑ | 90 | Rob Ryan | .20 | .09 |
| ❑ | 91 | Sean Burroughs | .75 | .35 |
| ❑ | 92 | D'Angelo Jimenez | .30 | .14 |
| ❑ | 93 | Chad Hermansen | .20 | .09 |
| ❑ | 94 | Robert Fick | .20 | .09 |
| ❑ | 95 | Ruben Mateo | .30 | .14 |
| ❑ | 96 | Alex Escobar | .30 | .14 |
| ❑ | 97 | Wily Pena | .30 | .14 |
| ❑ | 98 | Corey Patterson | 1.25 | .55 |
| ❑ | 99 | Eric Munson | .75 | .35 |
| ❑ | 100 | Pat Burrell | 1.25 | .55 |
| ❑ | 101 | Michael Tejera RC | 12.00 | 5.50 |
| ❑ | 102 | Bobby Bradley RC | 50.00 | 22.00 |
| ❑ | 103 | Larry Bigbie RC | 20.00 | 9.00 |
| ❑ | 104 | B.J. Garbe RC | 30.00 | 13.50 |
| ❑ | 105 | Josh Kalinowski RC | 12.00 | 5.50 |
| ❑ | 106 | Brett Myers RC | 20.00 | 9.00 |
| ❑ | 107 | Chris Mears RC | 15.00 | 6.75 |
| ❑ | 108 | Aaron Rowand RC | 25.00 | 11.00 |
| ❑ | 109 | Corey Myers RC | 15.00 | 6.75 |
| ❑ | 110 | John Sneed RC | 12.00 | 5.50 |
| ❑ | 111 | Ryan Christianson RC | 25.00 | 11.00 |
| ❑ | 112 | Kyle Snyder | 12.00 | 5.50 |
| ❑ | 113 | Mike Paradis | 12.00 | 5.50 |
| ❑ | 114 | Chance Caple RC | 15.00 | 6.75 |
| ❑ | 115 | Ben Christensen RC | 25.00 | 11.00 |
| ❑ | 116 | Brad Baker RC | 25.00 | 11.00 |
| ❑ | 117 | Rob Purvis RC | 12.00 | 5.50 |
| ❑ | 118 | Rick Asadoorian RC | 60.00 | 27.00 |
| ❑ | 119 | Ruben Salazar RC | 25.00 | 11.00 |
| ❑ | 120 | Julio Zuleta RC | 12.00 | 5.50 |
| ❑ | 121 | Alex Rodriguez | 8.00 | 3.60 |
| | | Ken Griffey Jr. | | |
| ❑ | 122 | Nomar Garciaparra | 8.00 | 3.60 |
| | | Derek Jeter | | |
| ❑ | 123 | Mark Mcgwire | 8.00 | 3.60 |
| | | Sammy Sosa | | |
| ❑ | 124 | Randy Johnson | 2.50 | 1.10 |
| | | Pedro Martinez | | |
| ❑ | 125 | Ivan Rodriguez | 6.00 | 2.70 |
| | | Mike Piazza | | |
| ❑ | 126 | Manny Ramirez | 2.50 | 1.10 |
| | | Roberto Alomar | | |
| ❑ | 127 | Chipper Jones | 5.00 | 2.20 |
| | | Andruw Jones | | |
| ❑ | 128 | Cal Ripken | 8.00 | 3.60 |
| | | Tony Gwynn | | |
| ❑ | 129 | Jeff Bagwell | 2.50 | 1.10 |
| | | Craig Biggio | | |
| ❑ | 130 | Barry Bonds | 3.00 | 1.35 |
| | | Vladimir Guerrero | | |
| ❑ | 131 | Nick Johnson | 1.50 | .70 |
| | | Alfonso Soriano | | |
| ❑ | 132 | Josh Hamilton | 3.00 | 1.35 |
| | | Pat Burrell | | |
| ❑ | 133 | Corey Patterson | 3.00 | 1.35 |
| | | Ruben Mateo | | |
| ❑ | 134 | Larry Walker | 2.50 | 1.10 |
| | | Todd Helton | | |
| ❑ | 135 | Rey Ordonez | 1.50 | .70 |
| | | Edgardo Alfonzo | | |
| ❑ | 136 | Derek Jeter GEM | 15.00 | 6.75 |
| ❑ | 137 | Alex Rodriguez GEM | 12.00 | 5.50 |
| ❑ | 138 | Chipper Jones GEM | 10.00 | 4.50 |
| ❑ | 139 | Mike Piazza GEM | 12.00 | 5.50 |
| ❑ | 140 | Mark McGwire GEM | 15.00 | 6.75 |
| ❑ | 141 | Ivan Rodriguez GEM | 5.00 | 2.20 |
| ❑ | 142 | Cal Ripken GEM | 15.00 | 6.75 |
| ❑ | 143 | Vladimir Guerrero GEM | 6.00 | 2.70 |
| ❑ | 144 | Randy Johnson GEM | 5.00 | 2.20 |
| ❑ | 145 | Jeff Bagwell GEM | 5.00 | 2.20 |
| ❑ | 146 | Ken Griffey Jr. ACTION | 3.00 | 1.35 |
| ❑ | 146A | Ken Griffey Jr. PORT | 3.00 | 1.35 |
| ❑ | 147 | Andruw Jones | .75 | .35 |
| ❑ | 148 | Kerry Wood | .30 | .14 |
| ❑ | 149 | Jim Edmonds | .75 | .35 |
| ❑ | 150 | Pedro Martinez | 1.00 | .45 |
| ❑ | 151 | Warren Morris | .20 | .09 |
| ❑ | 152 | Trevor Hoffman | .30 | .14 |
| ❑ | 153 | Ryan Klesko | .30 | .14 |
| ❑ | 154 | Andy Pettitte | .30 | .14 |
| ❑ | 155 | Frank Thomas | 1.50 | .70 |
| ❑ | 156 | Damion Easley | .20 | .09 |
| ❑ | 157 | Cliff Floyd | .30 | .14 |
| ❑ | 158 | Ben Davis | .20 | .09 |
| ❑ | 159 | John Valentin | .20 | .09 |
| ❑ | 160 | Rafael Palmeiro | .75 | .35 |
| ❑ | 161 | Andy Ashby | .20 | .09 |
| ❑ | 162 | J.D. Drew | .75 | .35 |
| ❑ | 163 | Jay Bell | .30 | .14 |
| ❑ | 164 | Adam Kennedy | .30 | .14 |
| ❑ | 165 | Manny Ramirez | 1.00 | .45 |
| ❑ | 166 | John Halama | .20 | .09 |
| ❑ | 167 | Octavio Dotel | .20 | .09 |
| ❑ | 168 | Darin Erstad | .75 | .35 |
| ❑ | 169 | Jose Lima | .20 | .09 |
| ❑ | 170 | Andres Galarraga | .50 | .23 |
| ❑ | 171 | Scott Rolen | .75 | .35 |
| ❑ | 172 | Delino DeShields | .20 | .09 |
| ❑ | 173 | J.T. Snow | .30 | .14 |
| ❑ | 174 | Tony Womack | .20 | .09 |
| ❑ | 175 | John Olerud | .30 | .14 |
| ❑ | 176 | Jason Kendall | .30 | .14 |
| ❑ | 177 | Carlos Lee | .30 | .14 |
| ❑ | 178 | Eric Milton | .30 | .14 |
| ❑ | 179 | Jeff Cirillo | .30 | .14 |
| ❑ | 180 | Gabe Kapler | .30 | .14 |
| ❑ | 181 | Greg Vaughn | .30 | .14 |
| ❑ | 182 | Denny Neagle | .20 | .09 |
| ❑ | 183 | Tino Martinez | .30 | .14 |
| ❑ | 184 | Doug Mientkiewicz | .20 | .09 |
| ❑ | 185 | Juan Gonzalez | .75 | .35 |
| ❑ | 186 | Ellis Burks | .30 | .14 |
| ❑ | 187 | Mike Hampton | .30 | .14 |
| ❑ | 188 | Royce Clayton | .20 | .09 |
| ❑ | 189 | Mike Mussina | .75 | .35 |
| ❑ | 190 | Carlos Delgado | .75 | .35 |
| ❑ | 191 | Ben Grieve | .30 | .14 |
| ❑ | 192 | Fernando Tatis | .30 | .14 |
| ❑ | 193 | Matt Williams | .50 | .23 |
| ❑ | 194 | Rondell White | .30 | .14 |
| ❑ | 195 | Shawn Green | .75 | .35 |
| ❑ | 196 | Hideki Irabu | .20 | .09 |
| ❑ | 197 | Troy Glaus | 1.00 | .45 |
| ❑ | 198 | Roger Cedeno | .20 | .09 |
| ❑ | 199 | Ray Lankford | .30 | .14 |
| ❑ | 200 | Sammy Sosa | 1.50 | .70 |
| ❑ | 201 | Kenny Lofton | .30 | .14 |
| ❑ | 202 | Edgar Martinez | .50 | .23 |
| ❑ | 203 | Mark Kotsay | .20 | .09 |
| ❑ | 204 | David Wells | .30 | .14 |
| ❑ | 205 | Craig Biggio | .50 | .23 |
| ❑ | 206 | Ray Durham | .30 | .14 |
| ❑ | 207 | Troy O'Leary | .20 | .09 |
| ❑ | 208 | Rickey Henderson | 1.00 | .45 |
| ❑ | 209 | Bob Abreu | .30 | .14 |
| ❑ | 210 | Neifi Perez | .20 | .09 |
| ❑ | 211 | Carlos Febles | .20 | .09 |
| ❑ | 212 | Chuck Knoblauch | .30 | .14 |
| ❑ | 213 | Moises Alou | .30 | .14 |
| ❑ | 214 | Omar Vizquel | .30 | .14 |
| ❑ | 215 | Vinny Castilla | .30 | .14 |
| ❑ | 216 | Javy Lopez | .30 | .14 |
| ❑ | 217 | Johnny Damon | .30 | .14 |
| ❑ | 218 | Roger Clemens | 1.50 | .70 |
| ❑ | 219 | Miguel Tejada | .30 | .14 |
| ❑ | 220 | Carl Everett | .30 | .14 |
| ❑ | 221 | Matt Lawton | .30 | .14 |
| ❑ | 222 | Albert Belle | .50 | .23 |
| ❑ | 223 | Adrian Beltre | .30 | .14 |
| ❑ | 224 | Dante Bichette | .30 | .14 |
| ❑ | 225 | Raul Mondesi | .30 | .14 |
| ❑ | 226 | Mike Piazza | 2.50 | 1.10 |
| ❑ | 227 | Brad Penny | .30 | .14 |
| ❑ | 228 | Kip Wells | .30 | .14 |
| ❑ | 229 | Adam Everett | .20 | .09 |
| ❑ | 230 | Eddie Yarnall | .20 | .09 |
| ❑ | 231 | Matt LeCroy | .20 | .09 |
| ❑ | 232 | Jason Tyner | .20 | .09 |
| ❑ | 233 | Rick Ankiel | 1.50 | .70 |
| ❑ | 234 | Lance Berkman | .30 | .14 |
| ❑ | 235 | Rafael Furcal | 2.00 | .90 |
| ❑ | 236 | Dee Brown | .30 | .14 |
| ❑ | 237 | Gookie Dawkins | .30 | .14 |
| ❑ | 238 | Eric Valent | .30 | .14 |
| ❑ | 239 | Peter Bergeron | .20 | .09 |
| ❑ | 240 | Alfonso Soriano | .30 | .14 |
| ❑ | 241 | Adam Dunn | .30 | .14 |
| ❑ | 242 | Jorge Toca | .20 | .09 |
| ❑ | 243 | Ryan Anderson | .30 | .14 |
| ❑ | 244 | Jason Dellaero | .20 | .09 |
| ❑ | 245 | Jason Grilli | .20 | .09 |
| ❑ | 246 | Milton Bradley | .30 | .14 |
| ❑ | 247 | Scott Downs RC | 10.00 | 4.50 |
| ❑ | 248 | Keith Reed RC | 12.00 | 5.50 |
| ❑ | 249 | Edgar Cruz RC | 10.00 | 4.50 |
| ❑ | 250 | Wes Anderson RC | 12.00 | 5.50 |
| ❑ | 251 | Lyle Overbay RC | 20.00 | 9.00 |
| ❑ | 252 | Mike Lamb RC | 12.00 | 5.50 |
| ❑ | 253 | Vince Faison RC | 15.00 | 6.75 |
| ❑ | 254 | Chad Alexander | 10.00 | 4.50 |
| ❑ | 255 | Chris Wakeland RC | 10.00 | 4.50 |
| ❑ | 256 | Aaron McNeal RC | 15.00 | 6.75 |
| ❑ | 257 | Tomokazu Ohka RC | 15.00 | 6.75 |
| ❑ | 258 | Ty Howington RC | 12.00 | 5.50 |
| ❑ | 259 | Javier Colina RC | 10.00 | 4.50 |
| ❑ | 260 | Jason Jennings | 10.00 | 4.50 |
| ❑ | 261 | Ramon Santiago RC | 10.00 | 4.50 |
| ❑ | 262 | Johan Santana RC | 10.00 | 4.50 |
| ❑ | 263 | Quincy Foster RC | 10.00 | 4.50 |
| ❑ | 264 | Junior Brignac RC | 10.00 | 4.50 |
| ❑ | 265 | Rico Washington RC | 10.00 | 4.50 |
| ❑ | 266 | Scott Sobkowiak RC | 10.00 | 4.50 |
| ❑ | 267 | Pedro Martinez | 5.00 | 2.20 |
| | | Rick Ankiel | | |
| ❑ | 268 | Manny Ramirez | 3.00 | 1.35 |
| | | Vladimir Guerrero | | |
| ❑ | 269 | A.J.Burnett | 1.00 | .45 |
| | | Mark Mulder | | |
| ❑ | 270 | Mike Piazza | 6.00 | 2.70 |
| | | Eric Munson | | |
| ❑ | 271 | Josh Hamilton | 3.00 | 1.35 |
| | | Corey Patterson | | |
| ❑ | 272 | Ken Griffey Jr. | 6.00 | 2.70 |
| | | Sammy Sosa | | |
| ❑ | 273 | Derek Jeter | 8.00 | 3.60 |
| | | Alfonso Soriano | | |
| ❑ | 274 | Mark McGwire | 8.00 | 3.60 |

| # | Card | MINT | NRMT |
|---|---|---|---|
| | Pat Burrell | | |
| ❑ 275 | Chipper Jones | 8.00 | 3.60 |
| | Cal Ripken | | |
| ❑ 276 | Nomar Garciaparra | 6.00 | 2.70 |
| | Alex Rodriguez | | |
| ❑ 277 | Pedro Martinez GEM | 5.00 | 2.20 |
| ❑ 278 | Tony Gwynn GEM | 8.00 | 3.60 |
| ❑ 279 | Barry Bonds GEM | 6.00 | 2.70 |
| ❑ 280 | Juan Gonzalez GEM | 4.00 | 1.80 |
| ❑ 281 | Larry Walker GEM | 2.50 | 1.10 |
| ❑ 282 | Nomar Garciaparra GEM | 12.00 | 5.50 |
| ❑ 283 | Ken Griffey Jr. GEM | 15.00 | 6.75 |
| ❑ 284 | Manny Ramirez GEM | 5.00 | 2.20 |
| ❑ 285 | Shawn Green GEM | .75 | .35 |
| ❑ 286 | Sammy Sosa GEM | 8.00 | 3.60 |
| ❑ NNO | Graded Gems Ser.1 EXCH/10 | | |
| ❑ NNO | Graded Gems Ser.2 EXCH/10 | | |

## 1993 Flair

| | MINT | NRMT |
|---|---|---|
| COMPLETE SET (300) | 50.00 | 22.00 |

| # | Player | MINT | NRMT |
|---|---|---|---|
| ❑ 1 | Steve Avery | .25 | .11 |
| ❑ 2 | Jeff Blauser | .25 | .11 |
| ❑ 3 | Ron Gant | .40 | .18 |
| ❑ 4 | Tom Glavine | .60 | .25 |
| ❑ 5 | David Justice | .60 | .25 |
| ❑ 6 | Mark Lemke | .25 | .11 |
| ❑ 7 | Greg Maddux | 2.50 | 1.10 |
| ❑ 8 | Fred McGriff | .60 | .25 |
| ❑ 9 | Terry Pendleton | .40 | .18 |
| ❑ 10 | Deion Sanders | .60 | .25 |
| ❑ 11 | John Smoltz | .40 | .18 |
| ❑ 12 | Mike Stanton | .25 | .11 |
| ❑ 13 | Steve Buechele | .25 | .11 |
| ❑ 14 | Mark Grace | 1.00 | .45 |
| ❑ 15 | Greg Hibbard | .25 | .11 |
| ❑ 16 | Derrick May | .25 | .11 |
| ❑ 17 | Chuck McElroy | .25 | .11 |
| ❑ 18 | Mike Morgan | .25 | .11 |
| ❑ 19 | Randy Myers | .40 | .18 |
| ❑ 20 | Ryne Sandberg | 1.25 | .55 |
| ❑ 21 | Dwight Smith | .25 | .11 |
| ❑ 22 | Sammy Sosa | 2.00 | .90 |
| ❑ 23 | Jose Vizcaino | .25 | .11 |
| ❑ 24 | Tim Belcher | .25 | .11 |
| ❑ 25 | Rob Dibble | .25 | .11 |
| ❑ 26 | Roberto Kelly | .25 | .11 |
| ❑ 27 | Barry Larkin | 1.00 | .45 |
| ❑ 28 | Kevin Mitchell | .40 | .18 |
| ❑ 29 | Hal Morris | .25 | .11 |
| ❑ 30 | Joe Oliver | .25 | .11 |
| ❑ 31 | Jose Rijo | .25 | .11 |
| ❑ 32 | Bip Roberts | .25 | .11 |
| ❑ 33 | Chris Sabo | .25 | .11 |
| ❑ 34 | Reggie Sanders | .25 | .11 |
| ❑ 35 | Dante Bichette | .40 | .18 |
| ❑ 36 | Willie Blair | .25 | .11 |
| ❑ 37 | Jerald Clark | .25 | .11 |
| ❑ 38 | Alex Cole | .25 | .11 |
| ❑ 39 | Andres Galarraga | .60 | .25 |
| ❑ 40 | Joe Girardi | .40 | .18 |
| ❑ 41 | Charlie Hayes | .25 | .11 |
| ❑ 42 | Chris Jones | .25 | .11 |
| ❑ 43 | David Nied | .25 | .11 |
| ❑ 44 | Eric Young | .25 | .11 |
| ❑ 45 | Alex Arias | .25 | .11 |
| ❑ 46 | Jack Armstrong | .25 | .11 |
| ❑ 47 | Bret Barberie | .25 | .11 |
| ❑ 48 | Chuck Carr | .25 | .11 |
| ❑ 49 | Jeff Conine | .25 | .11 |
| ❑ 50 | Orestes Destrade | .25 | .11 |
| ❑ 51 | Chris Hammond | .25 | .11 |
| ❑ 52 | Bryan Harvey | .25 | .11 |
| ❑ 53 | Benito Santiago | .25 | .11 |
| ❑ 54 | Gary Sheffield | 1.00 | .45 |
| ❑ 55 | Walt Weiss | .25 | .11 |
| ❑ 56 | Eric Anthony | .25 | .11 |
| ❑ 57 | Jeff Bagwell | 1.25 | .55 |
| ❑ 58 | Craig Biggio | .60 | .25 |
| ❑ 59 | Ken Caminiti | .40 | .18 |
| ❑ 60 | Andujar Cedeno | .25 | .11 |
| ❑ 61 | Doug Drabek | .25 | .11 |
| ❑ 62 | Steve Finley | .40 | .18 |
| ❑ 63 | Luis Gonzalez | .40 | .18 |
| ❑ 64 | Pete Harnisch | .25 | .11 |
| ❑ 65 | Doug Jones | .25 | .11 |
| ❑ 66 | Darryl Kile | .40 | .18 |
| ❑ 67 | Greg Swindell | .25 | .11 |
| ❑ 68 | Brett Butler | .40 | .18 |
| ❑ 69 | Jim Gott | .25 | .11 |
| ❑ 70 | Orel Hershiser | .40 | .18 |
| ❑ 71 | Eric Karros | .60 | .25 |
| ❑ 72 | Pedro Martinez | 2.50 | 1.10 |
| ❑ 73 | Ramon Martinez | .25 | .11 |
| ❑ 74 | Roger McDowell | .25 | .11 |
| ❑ 75 | Mike Piazza | 5.00 | 2.20 |
| ❑ 76 | Jody Reed | .25 | .11 |
| ❑ 77 | Tim Wallach | .25 | .11 |
| ❑ 78 | Moises Alou | .40 | .18 |
| ❑ 79 | Greg Colbrunn | .25 | .11 |
| ❑ 80 | Wil Cordero | .25 | .11 |
| ❑ 81 | Delino DeShields | .40 | .18 |
| ❑ 82 | Jeff Fassero | .25 | .11 |
| ❑ 83 | Marquis Grissom | .25 | .11 |
| ❑ 84 | Ken Hill | .25 | .11 |
| ❑ 85 | Mike Lansing RC | .40 | .18 |
| ❑ 86 | Dennis Martinez | .40 | .18 |
| ❑ 87 | Larry Walker | .40 | .18 |
| ❑ 88 | John Wetteland | .40 | .18 |
| ❑ 89 | Bobby Bonilla | .40 | .18 |
| ❑ 90 | Vince Coleman | .25 | .11 |
| ❑ 91 | Dwight Gooden | .40 | .18 |
| ❑ 92 | Todd Hundley | .25 | .11 |
| ❑ 93 | Howard Johnson | .25 | .11 |
| ❑ 94 | Eddie Murray | 1.00 | .45 |
| ❑ 95 | Joe Orsulak | .25 | .11 |
| ❑ 96 | Bret Saberhagen | .40 | .18 |
| ❑ 97 | Darren Daulton | .40 | .18 |
| ❑ 98 | Mariano Duncan | .25 | .11 |
| ❑ 99 | Len Dykstra | .40 | .18 |
| ❑ 100 | Jim Eisenreich | .25 | .11 |
| ❑ 101 | Tommy Greene | .25 | .11 |
| ❑ 102 | Dave Hollins | .25 | .11 |
| ❑ 103 | Pete Incaviglia | .25 | .11 |
| ❑ 104 | Danny Jackson | .25 | .11 |
| ❑ 105 | John Kruk | .40 | .18 |
| ❑ 106 | Terry Mulholland | .25 | .11 |
| ❑ 107 | Curt Schilling | .40 | .18 |
| ❑ 108 | Mitch Williams | .25 | .11 |
| ❑ 109 | Stan Belinda | .25 | .11 |
| ❑ 110 | Jay Bell | .40 | .18 |
| ❑ 111 | Steve Cooke | .25 | .11 |
| ❑ 112 | Carlos Garcia | .25 | .11 |
| ❑ 113 | Jeff King | .25 | .11 |
| ❑ 114 | Al Martin | .25 | .11 |
| ❑ 115 | Orlando Merced | .25 | .11 |
| ❑ 116 | Don Slaught | .25 | .11 |
| ❑ 117 | Andy Van Slyke | .40 | .18 |
| ❑ 118 | Tim Wakefield | .25 | .11 |
| ❑ 119 | Rene Arocha RC | .25 | .11 |
| ❑ 120 | Bernard Gilkey | .25 | .11 |
| ❑ 121 | Gregg Jefferies | .25 | .11 |
| ❑ 122 | Ray Lankford | .60 | .25 |
| ❑ 123 | Donovan Osborne | .25 | .11 |
| ❑ 124 | Tom Pagnozzi | .25 | .11 |
| ❑ 125 | Erik Pappas | .25 | .11 |
| ❑ 126 | Geronimo Pena | .25 | .11 |
| ❑ 127 | Lee Smith | .40 | .18 |
| ❑ 128 | Ozzie Smith | 1.25 | .55 |
| ❑ 129 | Bob Tewksbury | .25 | .11 |
| ❑ 130 | Mark Whiten | .25 | .11 |
| ❑ 131 | Derek Bell | .25 | .11 |
| ❑ 132 | Andy Benes | .25 | .11 |
| ❑ 133 | Tony Gwynn | 2.00 | .90 |
| ❑ 134 | Gene Harris | .25 | .11 |
| ❑ 135 | Trevor Hoffman | 1.00 | .45 |
| ❑ 136 | Phil Plantier | .25 | .11 |
| ❑ 137 | Rod Beck | .25 | .11 |
| ❑ 138 | Barry Bonds | 1.50 | .70 |
| ❑ 139 | John Burkett | .25 | .11 |
| ❑ 140 | Will Clark | 1.00 | .45 |
| ❑ 141 | Royce Clayton | .25 | .11 |
| ❑ 142 | Mike Jackson | .25 | .11 |
| ❑ 143 | Darren Lewis | .25 | .11 |
| ❑ 144 | Kirt Manwaring | .25 | .11 |
| ❑ 145 | Willie McGee | .40 | .18 |
| ❑ 146 | Bill Swift | .25 | .11 |
| ❑ 147 | Robby Thompson | .25 | .11 |
| ❑ 148 | Matt Williams | .60 | .25 |
| ❑ 149 | Brady Anderson | .40 | .18 |
| ❑ 150 | Mike Devereaux | .25 | .11 |
| ❑ 151 | Chris Hoiles | .25 | .11 |
| ❑ 152 | Ben McDonald | .25 | .11 |
| ❑ 153 | Mark McLemore | .25 | .11 |
| ❑ 154 | Mike Mussina | 1.00 | .45 |
| ❑ 155 | Gregg Olson | .25 | .11 |
| ❑ 156 | Harold Reynolds | .25 | .11 |
| ❑ 157 | Cal Ripken UER | 4.00 | 1.80 |
| | (Back refers to his games streak going into 1992; should be 1993. Also streak is spelled steak) | | |
| ❑ 158 | Rick Sutcliffe | .40 | .18 |
| ❑ 159 | Fernando Valenzuela | .40 | .18 |
| ❑ 160 | Roger Clemens | 2.00 | .90 |
| ❑ 161 | Scott Cooper | .25 | .11 |
| ❑ 162 | Andre Dawson | .60 | .25 |
| ❑ 163 | Scott Fletcher | .25 | .11 |
| ❑ 164 | Mike Greenwell | .25 | .11 |
| ❑ 165 | Greg A. Harris | .25 | .11 |
| ❑ 166 | Billy Hatcher | .25 | .11 |
| ❑ 167 | Jeff Russell | .25 | .11 |
| ❑ 168 | Mo Vaughn | .40 | .18 |
| ❑ 169 | Frank Viola | .25 | .11 |
| ❑ 170 | Chad Curtis | .25 | .11 |
| ❑ 171 | Chili Davis | .40 | .18 |
| ❑ 172 | Gary DiSarcina | .25 | .11 |
| ❑ 173 | Damion Easley | .25 | .11 |
| ❑ 174 | Chuck Finley | .40 | .18 |
| ❑ 175 | Mark Langston | .25 | .11 |
| ❑ 176 | Luis Polonia | .25 | .11 |
| ❑ 177 | Tim Salmon | .40 | .18 |
| ❑ 178 | Scott Sanderson | .25 | .11 |
| ❑ 179 | J.T.Snow RC | 1.25 | .55 |
| ❑ 180 | Wilson Alvarez | .25 | .11 |
| ❑ 181 | Ellis Burks | .40 | .18 |
| ❑ 182 | Joey Cora | .25 | .11 |
| ❑ 183 | Alex Fernandez | .40 | .18 |
| ❑ 184 | Ozzie Guillen | .25 | .11 |
| ❑ 185 | Roberto Hernandez | .25 | .11 |
| ❑ 186 | Bo Jackson | .40 | .18 |
| ❑ 187 | Lance Johnson | .25 | .11 |
| ❑ 188 | Jack McDowell | .25 | .11 |
| ❑ 189 | Frank Thomas | 2.00 | .90 |
| ❑ 190 | Robin Ventura | .40 | .18 |
| ❑ 191 | Carlos Baerga | .25 | .11 |
| ❑ 192 | Albert Belle | .60 | .25 |
| ❑ 193 | Wayne Kirby | .25 | .11 |
| ❑ 194 | Derek Lilliquist | .25 | .11 |
| ❑ 195 | Kenny Lofton | .40 | .18 |
| ❑ 196 | Carlos Martinez | .25 | .11 |
| ❑ 197 | Jose Mesa | .25 | .11 |
| ❑ 198 | Eric Plunk | .25 | .11 |
| ❑ 199 | Paul Sorrento | .25 | .11 |
| ❑ 200 | John Doherty | .25 | .11 |
| ❑ 201 | Cecil Fielder | .40 | .18 |
| ❑ 202 | Travis Fryman | .40 | .18 |
| ❑ 203 | Kirk Gibson | .40 | .18 |
| ❑ 204 | Mike Henneman | .25 | .11 |
| ❑ 205 | Chad Kreuter | .25 | .11 |
| ❑ 206 | Scott Livingstone | .25 | .11 |
| ❑ 207 | Tony Phillips | .25 | .11 |
| ❑ 208 | Mickey Tettleton | .25 | .11 |
| ❑ 209 | Alan Trammell | .60 | .25 |
| ❑ 210 | David Wells | .40 | .18 |
| ❑ 211 | Lou Whitaker | .40 | .18 |
| ❑ 212 | Kevin Appier | .40 | .18 |
| ❑ 213 | George Brett | 2.00 | .90 |
| ❑ 214 | David Cone | .40 | .18 |

❑ 215 Tom Gordon .25 .11
❑ 216 Phil Hiatt .25 .11
❑ 217 Felix Jose .25 .11
❑ 218 Wally Joyner .40 .18
❑ 219 Jose Lind .25 .11
❑ 220 Mike Macfarlane .25 .11
❑ 221 Brian McRae .25 .11
❑ 222 Jeff Montgomery .40 .18
❑ 223 Cal Eldred .25 .11
❑ 224 Darryl Hamilton .25 .11
❑ 225 John Jaha .25 .11
❑ 226 Pat Listach .25 .11
❑ 227 Graeme Lloyd RC .25 .11
❑ 228 Kevin Reimer .25 .11
❑ 229 Bill Spiers .25 .11
❑ 230 B.J. Surhoff .40 .18
❑ 231 Greg Vaughn .40 .18
❑ 232 Robin Yount .60 .25
❑ 233 Rick Aguilera .25 .11
❑ 234 Jim Deshaies .25 .11
❑ 235 Brian Harper .25 .11
❑ 236 Kent Hrbek .40 .18
❑ 237 Chuck Knoblauch .40 .18
❑ 238 Shane Mack .25 .11
❑ 239 David McCarty .25 .11
❑ 240 Pedro Munoz .25 .11
❑ 241 Mike Pagliarulo .25 .11
❑ 242 Kirby Puckett 2.50 1.10
❑ 243 Dave Winfield 1.00 .45
❑ 244 Jim Abbott .40 .18
❑ 245 Wade Boggs 1.25 .55
❑ 246 Pat Kelly .25 .11
❑ 247 Jimmy Key .40 .18
❑ 248 Jim Leyritz .25 .11
❑ 249 Don Mattingly 2.50 1.10
❑ 250 Matt Nokes .25 .11
❑ 251 Paul O'Neill .40 .18
❑ 252 Mike Stanley .25 .11
❑ 253 Danny Tartabull .25 .11
❑ 254 Bob Wickman .25 .11
❑ 255 Bernie Williams 1.00 .45
❑ 256 Mike Bordick .25 .11
❑ 257 Dennis Eckersley .40 .18
❑ 258 Brent Gates .25 .11
❑ 259 Rich Gossage .40 .18
❑ 260 Rickey Henderson 1.25 .55
❑ 261 Mark McGwire 4.00 1.80
❑ 262 Ruben Sierra .25 .11
❑ 263 Terry Steinbach .25 .11
❑ 264 Bob Welch .25 .11
❑ 265 Bobby Witt .25 .11
❑ 266 Rich Amaral .25 .11
❑ 267 Chris Bosio .25 .11
❑ 268 Jay Buhner .40 .18
❑ 269 Norm Charlton .25 .11
❑ 270 Ken Griffey Jr. 4.00 1.80
❑ 271 Erik Hanson .25 .11
❑ 272 Randy Johnson 1.25 .55
❑ 273 Edgar Martinez .60 .25
❑ 274 Tino Martinez .40 .18
❑ 275 Dave Valle .25 .11
❑ 276 Omar Vizquel .40 .18
❑ 277 Kevin Brown .60 .25
❑ 278 Jose Canseco 1.25 .55
❑ 279 Julio Franco .25 .11
❑ 280 Juan Gonzalez 1.00 .45
❑ 281 Tom Henke .25 .11
❑ 282 David Hulse RC .25 .11
❑ 283 Rafael Palmeiro 1.00 .45
❑ 284 Dean Palmer .40 .18
❑ 285 Ivan Rodriguez 1.25 .55
❑ 286 Nolan Ryan 5.00 2.20
❑ 287 Roberto Alomar 1.00 .45
❑ 288 Pat Borders .25 .11
❑ 289 Joe Carter .40 .18
❑ 290 Juan Guzman .25 .11
❑ 291 Pat Hentgen .25 .11
❑ 292 Paul Molitor 1.00 .45
❑ 293 John Olerud .60 .25
❑ 294 Ed Sprague .25 .11
❑ 295 Dave Stewart .40 .18
❑ 296 Duane Ward .25 .11
❑ 297 Devon White .25 .11
❑ 298 Checklist 1-100 .25 .11
❑ 299 Checklist 101-200 .25 .11
❑ 300 Checklist 201-300 .25 .11

## 1994 Flair

| | MINT | NRMT |
|---|---|---|
| COMPLETE SET (450) | 100.00 | 45.00 |
| COMPLETE SERIES 1 (250) | 25.00 | 11.00 |
| COMPLETE SERIES 2 (200) | 75.00 | 34.00 |

❑ 1 Harold Baines .50 .23
❑ 2 Jeffrey Hammonds .50 .23
❑ 3 Chris Hoiles .25 .11
❑ 4 Ben McDonald .25 .11
❑ 5 Mark McLemore .25 .11
❑ 6 Jamie Moyer .25 .11
❑ 7 Jim Poole .25 .11
❑ 8 Cal Ripken Jr. 4.00 1.80
❑ 9 Chris Sabo .25 .11
❑ 10 Scott Bankhead .25 .11
❑ 11 Scott Cooper .25 .11
❑ 12 Danny Darwin .25 .11
❑ 13 Andre Dawson .50 .23
❑ 14 Billy Hatcher .25 .11
❑ 15 Aaron Sele .50 .23
❑ 16 John Valentin .25 .11
❑ 17 Dave Valle .25 .11
❑ 18 Mo Vaughn .50 .23
❑ 19 Brian Anderson RC .50 .23
❑ 20 Gary DiSarcina .25 .11
❑ 21 Jim Edmonds 1.25 .55
❑ 22 Chuck Finley .50 .23
❑ 23 Bo Jackson .50 .23
❑ 24 Mark Leiter .25 .11
❑ 25 Greg Myers .25 .11
❑ 26 Eduardo Perez .25 .11
❑ 27 Tim Salmon .50 .23
❑ 28 Wilson Alvarez .25 .11
❑ 29 Jason Bere .25 .11
❑ 30 Alex Fernandez .25 .11
❑ 31 Ozzie Guillen .25 .11
❑ 32 Joe Hall RC .25 .11
❑ 33 Darrin Jackson .25 .11
❑ 34 Kirk McCaskill .25 .11
❑ 35 Tim Raines .50 .23
❑ 36 Frank Thomas 2.00 .90
❑ 37 Carlos Baerga .25 .11
❑ 38 Albert Belle .50 .23
❑ 39 Mark Clark .25 .11
❑ 40 Wayne Kirby .25 .11
❑ 41 Dennis Martinez .50 .23
❑ 42 Charles Nagy .25 .11
❑ 43 Manny Ramirez 1.50 .70
❑ 44 Paul Sorrento .25 .11
❑ 45 Jim Thome .50 .23
❑ 46 Eric Davis .50 .23
❑ 47 John Doherty .25 .11
❑ 48 Junior Felix .25 .11
❑ 49 Cecil Fielder .50 .23
❑ 50 Kirk Gibson .50 .23
❑ 51 Mike Moore .25 .11
❑ 52 Tony Phillips .25 .11
❑ 53 Alan Trammell .50 .23
❑ 54 Kevin Appier .50 .23
❑ 55 Stan Belinda .25 .11
❑ 56 Vince Coleman .25 .11
❑ 57 Greg Gagne .25 .11
❑ 58 Bob Hamelin .25 .11
❑ 59 Dave Henderson .25 .11
❑ 60 Wally Joyner .50 .23
❑ 61 Mike Macfarlane .25 .11
❑ 62 Jeff Montgomery .25 .11
❑ 63 Ricky Bones .25 .11
❑ 64 Jeff Bronkey .25 .11
❑ 65 Alex Diaz RC .25 .11
❑ 66 Cal Eldred .25 .11
❑ 67 Darryl Hamilton .25 .11
❑ 68 John Jaha .25 .11
❑ 69 Mark Kiefer .25 .11
❑ 70 Kevin Seitzer .25 .11
❑ 71 Turner Ward .25 .11
❑ 72 Rich Becker .25 .11
❑ 73 Scott Erickson .25 .11
❑ 74 Keith Garagozzo RC .25 .11
❑ 75 Kent Hrbek .50 .23
❑ 76 Scott Leius .25 .11
❑ 77 Kirby Puckett 2.50 1.10
❑ 78 Matt Walbeck .25 .11
❑ 79 Dave Winfield 1.00 .45
❑ 80 Mike Gallego .25 .11
❑ 81 Xavier Hernandez .25 .11
❑ 82 Jimmy Key .50 .23
❑ 83 Jim Leyritz .25 .11
❑ 84 Don Mattingly 2.50 1.10
❑ 85 Matt Nokes .25 .11
❑ 86 Paul O'Neill .50 .23
❑ 87 Melido Perez .25 .11
❑ 88 Danny Tartabull .25 .11
❑ 89 Mike Bordick .25 .11
❑ 90 Ron Darling .25 .11
❑ 91 Dennis Eckersley .50 .23
❑ 92 Stan Javier .25 .11
❑ 93 Steve Karsay .25 .11
❑ 94 Mark McGwire 4.00 1.80
❑ 95 Troy Neel .25 .11
❑ 96 Terry Steinbach .25 .11
❑ 97 Bill Taylor RC .25 .11
❑ 98 Eric Anthony .25 .11
❑ 99 Chris Bosio .25 .11
❑ 100 Tim Davis .25 .11
❑ 101 Felix Fermin .25 .11
❑ 102 Dave Fleming .25 .11
❑ 103 Ken Griffey Jr. 4.00 1.80
❑ 104 Greg Hibbard .25 .11
❑ 105 Reggie Jefferson .25 .11
❑ 106 Tino Martinez .50 .23
❑ 107 Jack Armstrong .25 .11
❑ 108 Will Clark 1.00 .45
❑ 109 Juan Gonzalez 1.00 .45
❑ 110 Rick Helling .50 .23
❑ 111 Tom Henke .25 .11
❑ 112 David Hulse .25 .11
❑ 113 Manuel Lee .25 .11
❑ 114 Doug Strange .25 .11
❑ 115 Roberto Alomar 1.00 .45
❑ 116 Joe Carter .50 .23
❑ 117 Carlos Delgado 1.50 .70
❑ 118 Pat Hentgen .25 .11
❑ 119 Paul Molitor 1.00 .45
❑ 120 John Olerud .50 .23
❑ 121 Dave Stewart .50 .23
❑ 122 Todd Stottlemyre .25 .11
❑ 123 Mike Timlin .25 .11
❑ 124 Jeff Blauser .25 .11
❑ 125 Tom Glavine 1.00 .45
❑ 126 David Justice .50 .23
❑ 127 Mike Kelly .25 .11
❑ 128 Ryan Klesko .50 .23
❑ 129 Javier Lopez .50 .23
❑ 130 Greg Maddux 2.50 1.10
❑ 131 Fred McGriff .50 .23
❑ 132 Kent Mercker .25 .11
❑ 133 Mark Wohlers .25 .11
❑ 134 Willie Banks .25 .11
❑ 135 Steve Buechele .25 .11
❑ 136 Shawon Dunston .25 .11
❑ 137 Jose Guzman .25 .11
❑ 138 Glenallen Hill .25 .11
❑ 139 Randy Myers .25 .11
❑ 140 Karl Rhodes .25 .11
❑ 141 Ryne Sandberg 1.25 .55
❑ 142 Steve Trachsel .25 .11
❑ 143 Bret Boone .50 .23
❑ 144 Tom Browning .25 .11
❑ 145 Hector Carrasco .25 .11
❑ 146 Barry Larkin 1.00 .45
❑ 147 Hal Morris .25 .11

| No. | Player | | |
|---|---|---|---|
| 148 | Jose Rijo | .25 | .11 |
| 149 | Reggie Sanders | .25 | .11 |
| 150 | John Smiley | .25 | .11 |
| 151 | Dante Bichette | .50 | .23 |
| 152 | Ellis Burks | .50 | .23 |
| 153 | Joe Girardi | .25 | .11 |
| 154 | Mike Harkey | .25 | .11 |
| 155 | Roberto Mejia | .25 | .11 |
| 156 | Marcus Moore | .25 | .11 |
| 157 | Armando Reynoso | .25 | .11 |
| 158 | Bruce Ruffin | .25 | .11 |
| 159 | Eric Young | .25 | .11 |
| 160 | Kurt Abbott RC | .25 | .11 |
| 161 | Jeff Conine | .25 | .11 |
| 162 | Orestes Destrade | .25 | .11 |
| 163 | Chris Hammond | .25 | .11 |
| 164 | Bryan Harvey | .25 | .11 |
| 165 | Dave Magadan | .25 | .11 |
| 166 | Gary Sheffield | 1.00 | .45 |
| 167 | David Weathers | .25 | .11 |
| 168 | Andujar Cedeno | .25 | .11 |
| 169 | Tom Edens | .25 | .11 |
| 170 | Luis Gonzalez | .50 | .23 |
| 171 | Pete Harnisch | .25 | .11 |
| 172 | Todd Jones | .25 | .11 |
| 173 | Darryl Kile | .50 | .23 |
| 174 | James Mouton | .25 | .11 |
| 175 | Scott Servais | .25 | .11 |
| 176 | Mitch Williams | .25 | .11 |
| 177 | Pedro Astacio | .25 | .11 |
| 178 | Orel Hershiser | .50 | .23 |
| 179 | Raul Mondesi | .50 | .23 |
| 180 | Jose Offerman | .25 | .11 |
| 181 | Chan Ho Park RC | 2.00 | .90 |
| 182 | Mike Piazza | 3.00 | 1.35 |
| 183 | Cory Snyder | .25 | .11 |
| 184 | Tim Wallach | .25 | .11 |
| 185 | Todd Worrell | .25 | .11 |
| 186 | Sean Berry | .25 | .11 |
| 187 | Wil Cordero | .25 | .11 |
| 188 | Darrin Fletcher | .25 | .11 |
| 189 | Cliff Floyd | .50 | .23 |
| 190 | Marquis Grissom | .25 | .11 |
| 191 | Rod Henderson | .25 | .11 |
| 192 | Ken Hill | .25 | .11 |
| 193 | Pedro Martinez | 1.50 | .70 |
| 194 | Kirk Rueter | .25 | .11 |
| 195 | Jeromy Burnitz | .50 | .23 |
| 196 | John Franco | .50 | .23 |
| 197 | Dwight Gooden | .50 | .23 |
| 198 | Todd Hundley | .25 | .11 |
| 199 | Bobby Jones | .25 | .11 |
| 200 | Jeff Kent | .50 | .23 |
| 201 | Mike Maddux | .25 | .11 |
| 202 | Ryan Thompson | .25 | .11 |
| 203 | Jose Vizcaino | .25 | .11 |
| 204 | Darren Daulton | .50 | .23 |
| 205 | Lenny Dykstra | .50 | .23 |
| 206 | Jim Eisenreich | .25 | .11 |
| 207 | Dave Hollins | .25 | .11 |
| 208 | Danny Jackson | .25 | .11 |
| 209 | Doug Jones | .25 | .11 |
| 210 | Jeff Juden | .25 | .11 |
| 211 | Ben Rivera | .25 | .11 |
| 212 | Kevin Stocker | .25 | .11 |
| 213 | Milt Thompson | .25 | .11 |
| 214 | Jay Bell | .50 | .23 |
| 215 | Steve Cooke | .25 | .11 |
| 216 | Mark Dewey | .25 | .11 |
| 217 | Al Martin | .25 | .11 |
| 218 | Orlando Merced | .25 | .11 |
| 219 | Don Slaught | .25 | .11 |
| 220 | Zane Smith | .25 | .11 |
| 221 | Rick White RC | .25 | .11 |
| 222 | Kevin Young | .25 | .11 |
| 223 | Rene Arocha | .25 | .11 |
| 224 | Rheal Cormier | .25 | .11 |
| 225 | Brian Jordan | .50 | .23 |
| 226 | Ray Lankford | .50 | .23 |
| 227 | Mike Perez | .25 | .11 |
| 228 | Ozzie Smith | 1.25 | .55 |
| 229 | Mark Whiten | .25 | .11 |
| 230 | Todd Zeile | .25 | .11 |
| 231 | Derek Bell | .25 | .11 |
| 232 | Archi Cianfrocco | .25 | .11 |
| 233 | Ricky Gutierrez | .25 | .11 |
| 234 | Trevor Hoffman | .50 | .23 |
| 235 | Phil Plantier | .25 | .11 |
| 236 | Dave Staton | .25 | .11 |
| 237 | Wally Whitehurst | .25 | .11 |
| 238 | Todd Benzinger | .25 | .11 |
| 239 | Barry Bonds | 1.50 | .70 |
| 240 | John Burkett | .25 | .11 |
| 241 | Royce Clayton | .25 | .11 |
| 242 | Bryan Hickerson | .25 | .11 |
| 243 | Mike Jackson | .25 | .11 |
| 244 | Darren Lewis | .25 | .11 |
| 245 | Kirt Manwaring | .25 | .11 |
| 246 | Mark Portugal | .25 | .11 |
| 247 | Salomon Torres | .25 | .11 |
| 248 | Checklist | .25 | .11 |
| 249 | Checklist | .25 | .11 |
| 250 | Checklist | .25 | .11 |
| 251 | Brady Anderson | .50 | .23 |
| 252 | Mike Devereaux | .25 | .11 |
| 253 | Sid Fernandez | .25 | .11 |
| 254 | Leo Gomez | .25 | .11 |
| 255 | Mike Mussina | 1.00 | .45 |
| 256 | Mike Oquist | .25 | .11 |
| 257 | Rafael Palmeiro | 1.00 | .45 |
| 258 | Lee Smith | .50 | .23 |
| 259 | Damon Berryhill | .25 | .11 |
| 260 | Wes Chamberlain | .25 | .11 |
| 261 | Roger Clemens | 2.00 | .90 |
| 262 | Gar Finnvold RC | .25 | .11 |
| 263 | Mike Greenwell | .25 | .11 |
| 264 | Tim Naehring | .25 | .11 |
| 265 | Otis Nixon | .25 | .11 |
| 266 | Ken Ryan | .25 | .11 |
| 267 | Chad Curtis | .25 | .11 |
| 268 | Chili Davis | .50 | .23 |
| 269 | Damion Easley | .25 | .11 |
| 270 | Jorge Fabregas | .25 | .11 |
| 271 | Mark Langston | .25 | .11 |
| 272 | Phil Leftwich RC | .25 | .11 |
| 273 | Harold Reynolds | .25 | .11 |
| 274 | J.T. Snow | .50 | .23 |
| 275 | Joey Cora | .25 | .11 |
| 276 | Julio Franco | .25 | .11 |
| 277 | Roberto Hernandez | .25 | .11 |
| 278 | Lance Johnson | .25 | .11 |
| 279 | Ron Karkovice | .25 | .11 |
| 280 | Jack McDowell | .25 | .11 |
| 281 | Robin Ventura | .50 | .23 |
| 282 | Sandy Alomar Jr. | .50 | .23 |
| 283 | Kenny Lofton | .50 | .23 |
| 284 | Jose Mesa | .25 | .11 |
| 285 | Jack Morris | .50 | .23 |
| 286 | Eddie Murray | 1.00 | .45 |
| 287 | Chad Ogea | .25 | .11 |
| 288 | Eric Plunk | .25 | .11 |
| 289 | Paul Shuey | .25 | .11 |
| 290 | Omar Vizquel | .50 | .23 |
| 291 | Danny Bautista | .25 | .11 |
| 292 | Travis Fryman | .50 | .23 |
| 293 | Greg Gohr | .25 | .11 |
| 294 | Chris Gomez | .25 | .11 |
| 295 | Mickey Tettleton | .25 | .11 |
| 296 | Lou Whitaker | .50 | .23 |
| 297 | David Cone | .50 | .23 |
| 298 | Gary Gaetti | .50 | .23 |
| 299 | Tom Gordon | .25 | .11 |
| 300 | Felix Jose | .25 | .11 |
| 301 | Jose Lind | .25 | .11 |
| 302 | Brian McRae | .25 | .11 |
| 303 | Mike Fetters | .25 | .11 |
| 304 | Brian Harper | .25 | .11 |
| 305 | Pat Listach | .25 | .11 |
| 306 | Matt Mieske | .25 | .11 |
| 307 | Dave Nilsson | .25 | .11 |
| 308 | Jody Reed | .25 | .11 |
| 309 | Greg Vaughn | .50 | .23 |
| 310 | Bill Wegman | .25 | .11 |
| 311 | Rick Aguilera | .25 | .11 |
| 312 | Alex Cole | .25 | .11 |
| 313 | Denny Hocking | .25 | .11 |
| 314 | Chuck Knoblauch | .50 | .23 |
| 315 | Shane Mack | .25 | .11 |
| 316 | Pat Meares | .25 | .11 |
| 317 | Kevin Tapani | .25 | .11 |
| 318 | Jim Abbott | .50 | .23 |
| 319 | Wade Boggs | 1.25 | .55 |
| 320 | Sterling Hitchcock | .25 | .11 |
| 321 | Pat Kelly | .25 | .11 |
| 322 | Terry Mulholland | .25 | .11 |
| 323 | Luis Polonia | .25 | .11 |
| 324 | Mike Stanley | .25 | .11 |
| 325 | Bob Wickman | .25 | .11 |
| 326 | Bernie Williams | 1.00 | .45 |
| 327 | Mark Acre RC | .25 | .11 |
| 328 | Geronimo Berroa | .25 | .11 |
| 329 | Scott Brosius | .50 | .23 |
| 330 | Brent Gates | .25 | .11 |
| 331 | Rickey Henderson | 1.25 | .55 |
| 332 | Carlos Reyes RC | .25 | .11 |
| 333 | Ruben Sierra | .25 | .11 |
| 334 | Bobby Witt | .25 | .11 |
| 335 | Bobby Ayala | .25 | .11 |
| 336 | Jay Buhner | .50 | .23 |
| 337 | Randy Johnson | 1.25 | .55 |
| 338 | Edgar Martinez | .50 | .23 |
| 339 | Bill Risley | .25 | .11 |
| 340 | Alex Rodriguez RC | 50.00 | 22.00 |
| 341 | Roger Salkeld | .25 | .11 |
| 342 | Dan Wilson | .25 | .11 |
| 343 | Kevin Brown | .50 | .23 |
| 344 | Jose Canseco | 1.25 | .55 |
| 345 | Dean Palmer | .50 | .23 |
| 346 | Ivan Rodriguez | 1.25 | .55 |
| 347 | Kenny Rogers | .25 | .11 |
| 348 | Pat Borders | .25 | .11 |
| 349 | Juan Guzman | .25 | .11 |
| 350 | Ed Sprague | .25 | .11 |
| 351 | Devon White | .25 | .11 |
| 352 | Steve Avery | .25 | .11 |
| 353 | Roberto Kelly | .25 | .11 |
| 354 | Mark Lemke | .25 | .11 |
| 355 | Greg McMichael | .25 | .11 |
| 356 | Terry Pendleton | .50 | .23 |
| 357 | John Smoltz | .50 | .23 |
| 358 | Mike Stanton | .25 | .11 |
| 359 | Tony Tarasco | .25 | .11 |
| 360 | Mark Grace | 1.00 | .45 |
| 361 | Derrick May | .25 | .11 |
| 362 | Rey Sanchez | .25 | .11 |
| 363 | Sammy Sosa | 2.00 | .90 |
| 364 | Rick Wilkins | .25 | .11 |
| 365 | Jeff Brantley | .25 | .11 |
| 366 | Tony Fernandez | .25 | .11 |
| 367 | Chuck McElroy | .25 | .11 |
| 368 | Kevin Mitchell | .25 | .11 |
| 369 | John Roper | .25 | .11 |
| 370 | Johnny Ruffin | .25 | .11 |
| 371 | Deion Sanders | .50 | .23 |
| 372 | Marvin Freeman | .25 | .11 |
| 373 | Andres Galarraga | .50 | .23 |
| 374 | Charlie Hayes | .25 | .11 |
| 375 | Nelson Liriano | .25 | .11 |
| 376 | David Nied | .25 | .11 |
| 377 | Walt Weiss | .25 | .11 |
| 378 | Bret Barberie | .25 | .11 |
| 379 | Jerry Browne | .25 | .11 |
| 380 | Chuck Carr | .25 | .11 |
| 381 | Greg Colbrunn | .25 | .11 |
| 382 | Charlie Hough | .50 | .23 |
| 383 | Kurt Miller | .25 | .11 |
| 384 | Benito Santiago | .25 | .11 |
| 385 | Jeff Bagwell | 1.25 | .55 |
| 386 | Craig Biggio | .50 | .23 |
| 387 | Ken Caminiti | .50 | .23 |
| 388 | Doug Drabek | .25 | .11 |
| 389 | Steve Finley | .50 | .23 |
| 390 | John Hudek RC | .25 | .11 |
| 391 | Orlando Miller | .25 | .11 |
| 392 | Shane Reynolds | .25 | .11 |
| 393 | Brett Butler | .50 | .23 |
| 394 | Tom Candiotti | .25 | .11 |
| 395 | Delino DeShields | .25 | .11 |
| 396 | Kevin Gross | .25 | .11 |
| 397 | Eric Karros | .50 | .23 |
| 398 | Ramon Martinez | .25 | .11 |
| 399 | Henry Rodriguez | .25 | .11 |
| 400 | Moises Alou | .50 | .23 |
| 401 | Jeff Fassero | .25 | .11 |
| 402 | Mike Lansing | .25 | .11 |
| 403 | Mel Rojas | .25 | .11 |
| 404 | Larry Walker | .50 | .23 |
| 405 | John Wetteland | .50 | .23 |

| Card | Mint | NrMt |
|---|---|---|
| ❑ 406 Gabe White | .25 | .11 |
| ❑ 407 Bobby Bonilla | .50 | .23 |
| ❑ 408 Josias Manzanillo | .25 | .11 |
| ❑ 409 Bret Saberhagen | .50 | .23 |
| ❑ 410 David Segui | .25 | .11 |
| ❑ 411 Mariano Duncan | .25 | .11 |
| ❑ 412 Tommy Greene | .25 | .11 |
| ❑ 413 Billy Hatcher | .25 | .11 |
| ❑ 414 Ricky Jordan | .25 | .11 |
| ❑ 415 John Kruk | .50 | .23 |
| ❑ 416 Bobby Munoz | .25 | .11 |
| ❑ 417 Curt Schilling | .50 | .23 |
| ❑ 418 Fernando Valenzuela | .50 | .23 |
| ❑ 419 David West | .50 | .23 |
| ❑ 420 Carlos Garcia | .25 | .11 |
| ❑ 421 Brian Hunter | .25 | .11 |
| ❑ 422 Jeff King | .25 | .11 |
| ❑ 423 Jon Lieber | .25 | .11 |
| ❑ 424 Ravelo Manzanillo | .25 | .11 |
| ❑ 425 Denny Neagle | .25 | .11 |
| ❑ 426 Andy Van Slyke | .50 | .23 |
| ❑ 427 Bryan Eversgerd RC | .25 | .11 |
| ❑ 428 Bernard Gilkey | .25 | .11 |
| ❑ 429 Gregg Jefferies | .25 | .11 |
| ❑ 430 Tom Pagnozzi | .25 | .11 |
| ❑ 431 Bob Tewksbury | .25 | .11 |
| ❑ 432 Allen Watson | .25 | .11 |
| ❑ 433 Andy Ashby | .25 | .11 |
| ❑ 434 Andy Benes | .25 | .11 |
| ❑ 435 Donnie Elliott | .25 | .11 |
| ❑ 436 Tony Gwynn | 2.00 | .90 |
| ❑ 437 Joey Hamilton | .25 | .11 |
| ❑ 438 Tim Hyers RC | .25 | .11 |
| ❑ 439 Luis Lopez | .25 | .11 |
| ❑ 440 Bip Roberts | .25 | .11 |
| ❑ 441 Scott Sanders | .25 | .11 |
| ❑ 442 Rod Beck | .25 | .11 |
| ❑ 443 Dave Burba | .25 | .11 |
| ❑ 444 Darryl Strawberry | .50 | .23 |
| ❑ 445 Bill Swift | .25 | .11 |
| ❑ 446 Robby Thompson | .25 | .11 |
| ❑ 447 Bill VanLandingham RC | .25 | .11 |
| ❑ 448 Matt Williams | .50 | .23 |
| ❑ 449 Checklist | .25 | .11 |
| ❑ 450 Checklist | .25 | .11 |
| ❑ P15 Aaron Sele Promo | 1.00 | .70 |

## 1995 Flair

| | MINT | NRMT |
|---|---|---|
| COMPLETE SET (432) | 60.00 | 27.00 |
| COMPLETE SERIES 1 (216) | 40.00 | 18.00 |
| COMPLETE SERIES 2 (216) | 25.00 | 11.00 |
| COMMON CARD (1-432) | .25 | .11 |

| Card | Mint | NrMt |
|---|---|---|
| ❑ 1 Brady Anderson | .50 | .23 |
| ❑ 2 Harold Baines | .50 | .23 |
| ❑ 3 Leo Gomez | .25 | .11 |
| ❑ 4 Alan Mills | .25 | .11 |
| ❑ 5 Jamie Moyer | .25 | .11 |
| ❑ 6 Mike Mussina | 1.00 | .45 |
| ❑ 7 Mike Oquist | .25 | .11 |
| ❑ 8 Arthur Rhodes | .25 | .11 |
| ❑ 9 Cal Ripken Jr. | 4.00 | 1.80 |
| ❑ 10 Roger Clemens | 2.00 | .90 |
| ❑ 11 Scott Cooper | .25 | .11 |
| ❑ 12 Mike Greenwell | .25 | .11 |
| ❑ 13 Aaron Sele | .50 | .23 |
| ❑ 14 John Valentin | .25 | .11 |
| ❑ 15 Mo Vaughn | .50 | .23 |
| ❑ 16 Chad Curtis | .25 | .11 |
| ❑ 17 Gary DiSarcina | .25 | .11 |
| ❑ 18 Chuck Finley | .50 | .23 |
| ❑ 19 Andrew Lorraine | .25 | .11 |
| ❑ 20 Spike Owen | .25 | .11 |
| ❑ 21 Tim Salmon | .50 | .23 |
| ❑ 22 J.T. Snow | .50 | .23 |
| ❑ 23 Wilson Alvarez | .25 | .11 |
| ❑ 24 Jason Bere | .25 | .11 |
| ❑ 25 Ozzie Guillen | .25 | .11 |
| ❑ 26 Mike LaValliere | .25 | .11 |
| ❑ 27 Frank Thomas | 2.00 | .90 |
| ❑ 28 Robin Ventura | .50 | .23 |
| ❑ 29 Carlos Baerga | .25 | .11 |
| ❑ 30 Albert Belle | .50 | .23 |
| ❑ 31 Jason Grimsley | .25 | .11 |
| ❑ 32 Dennis Martinez | .50 | .23 |
| ❑ 33 Eddie Murray | 1.00 | .45 |
| ❑ 34 Charles Nagy | .25 | .11 |
| ❑ 35 Manny Ramirez | 1.25 | .55 |
| ❑ 36 Paul Sorrento | .25 | .11 |
| ❑ 37 John Doherty | .25 | .11 |
| ❑ 38 Cecil Fielder | .50 | .23 |
| ❑ 39 Travis Fryman | .50 | .23 |
| ❑ 40 Chris Gomez | .25 | .11 |
| ❑ 41 Tony Phillips | .25 | .11 |
| ❑ 42 Lou Whitaker | .50 | .23 |
| ❑ 43 David Cone | .50 | .23 |
| ❑ 44 Gary Gaetti | .50 | .23 |
| ❑ 45 Mark Gubicza | .25 | .11 |
| ❑ 46 Bob Hamelin | .25 | .11 |
| ❑ 47 Wally Joyner | .50 | .23 |
| ❑ 48 Rusty Meacham | .25 | .11 |
| ❑ 49 Jeff Montgomery | .25 | .11 |
| ❑ 50 Ricky Bones | .25 | .11 |
| ❑ 51 Cal Eldred | .25 | .11 |
| ❑ 52 Pat Listach | .25 | .11 |
| ❑ 53 Matt Mieske | .25 | .11 |
| ❑ 54 Dave Nilsson | .25 | .11 |
| ❑ 55 Greg Vaughn | .50 | .23 |
| ❑ 56 Bill Wegman | .25 | .11 |
| ❑ 57 Chuck Knoblauch | .50 | .23 |
| ❑ 58 Scott Leius | .25 | .11 |
| ❑ 59 Pat Mahomes | .25 | .11 |
| ❑ 60 Pat Meares | .25 | .11 |
| ❑ 61 Pedro Munoz | .25 | .11 |
| ❑ 62 Kirby Puckett | 2.50 | 1.10 |
| ❑ 63 Wade Boggs | 1.25 | .55 |
| ❑ 64 Jimmy Key | .50 | .23 |
| ❑ 65 Jim Leyritz | .25 | .11 |
| ❑ 66 Don Mattingly | 2.50 | 1.10 |
| ❑ 67 Paul O'Neill | .50 | .23 |
| ❑ 68 Melido Perez | .25 | .11 |
| ❑ 69 Danny Tartabull | .25 | .11 |
| ❑ 70 John Briscoe | .25 | .11 |
| ❑ 71 Scott Brosius | .50 | .23 |
| ❑ 72 Ron Darling | .25 | .11 |
| ❑ 73 Brent Gates | .25 | .11 |
| ❑ 74 Rickey Henderson | 1.25 | .55 |
| ❑ 75 Stan Javier | .25 | .11 |
| ❑ 76 Mark McGwire | 4.00 | 1.80 |
| ❑ 77 Todd Van Poppel | .25 | .11 |
| ❑ 78 Bobby Ayala | .25 | .11 |
| ❑ 79 Mike Blowers | .25 | .11 |
| ❑ 80 Jay Buhner | .50 | .23 |
| ❑ 81 Ken Griffey Jr. | 4.00 | 1.80 |
| ❑ 82 Randy Johnson | 1.25 | .55 |
| ❑ 83 Tino Martinez | .50 | .23 |
| ❑ 84 Jeff Nelson | .25 | .11 |
| ❑ 85 Alex Rodriguez | 4.00 | 1.80 |
| ❑ 86 Will Clark | 1.00 | .45 |
| ❑ 87 Jeff Frye | .25 | .11 |
| ❑ 88 Juan Gonzalez | 1.00 | .45 |
| ❑ 89 Rusty Greer | .50 | .23 |
| ❑ 90 Darren Oliver | .25 | .11 |
| ❑ 91 Dean Palmer | .50 | .23 |
| ❑ 92 Ivan Rodriguez | 1.25 | .55 |
| ❑ 93 Matt Whiteside | .25 | .11 |
| ❑ 94 Roberto Alomar | 1.00 | .45 |
| ❑ 95 Joe Carter | .50 | .23 |
| ❑ 96 Tony Castillo | .25 | .11 |
| ❑ 97 Juan Guzman | .25 | .11 |
| ❑ 98 Pat Hentgen | .25 | .11 |
| ❑ 99 Mike Huff | .25 | .11 |
| ❑ 100 John Olerud | .50 | .23 |
| ❑ 101 Woody Williams | .25 | .11 |
| ❑ 102 Roberto Kelly | .25 | .11 |
| ❑ 103 Ryan Klesko | .50 | .23 |
| ❑ 104 Javier Lopez | .50 | .23 |
| ❑ 105 Greg Maddux | 2.50 | 1.10 |
| ❑ 106 Fred McGriff | .50 | .23 |
| ❑ 107 Jose Oliva | .25 | .11 |
| ❑ 108 John Smoltz | .50 | .23 |
| ❑ 109 Tony Tarasco | .25 | .11 |
| ❑ 110 Mark Wohlers | .25 | .11 |
| ❑ 111 Jim Bullinger | .25 | .11 |
| ❑ 112 Shawon Dunston | .25 | .11 |
| ❑ 113 Derrick May | .25 | .11 |
| ❑ 114 Randy Myers | .25 | .11 |
| ❑ 115 Karl Rhodes | .25 | .11 |
| ❑ 116 Rey Sanchez | .25 | .11 |
| ❑ 117 Steve Trachsel | .25 | .11 |
| ❑ 118 Eddie Zambrano | .25 | .11 |
| ❑ 119 Bret Boone | .50 | .23 |
| ❑ 120 Brian Dorsett | .25 | .11 |
| ❑ 121 Hal Morris | .25 | .11 |
| ❑ 122 Jose Rijo | .25 | .11 |
| ❑ 123 John Roper | .25 | .11 |
| ❑ 124 Reggie Sanders | .25 | .11 |
| ❑ 125 Pete Schourek | .25 | .11 |
| ❑ 126 John Smiley | .25 | .11 |
| ❑ 127 Ellis Burks | .50 | .23 |
| ❑ 128 Vinny Castilla | .50 | .23 |
| ❑ 129 Marvin Freeman | .25 | .11 |
| ❑ 130 Andres Galarraga | .50 | .23 |
| ❑ 131 Mike Munoz | .25 | .11 |
| ❑ 132 David Nied | .25 | .11 |
| ❑ 133 Bruce Ruffin | .25 | .11 |
| ❑ 134 Walt Weiss | .25 | .11 |
| ❑ 135 Eric Young | .25 | .11 |
| ❑ 136 Greg Colbrunn | .25 | .11 |
| ❑ 137 Jeff Conine | .25 | .11 |
| ❑ 138 Jeremy Hernandez | .25 | .11 |
| ❑ 139 Charles Johnson | .50 | .23 |
| ❑ 140 Robb Nen | .25 | .11 |
| ❑ 141 Gary Sheffield | 1.00 | .45 |
| ❑ 142 Dave Weathers | .25 | .11 |
| ❑ 143 Jeff Bagwell | 1.25 | .55 |
| ❑ 144 Craig Biggio | .50 | .23 |
| ❑ 145 Tony Eusebio | .25 | .11 |
| ❑ 146 Luis Gonzalez | .25 | .11 |
| ❑ 147 John Hudek | .25 | .11 |
| ❑ 148 Darryl Kile | .50 | .23 |
| ❑ 149 Dave Veres | .25 | .11 |
| ❑ 150 Billy Ashley | .25 | .11 |
| ❑ 151 Pedro Astacio | .25 | .11 |
| ❑ 152 Rafael Bournigal | .25 | .11 |
| ❑ 153 Delino DeShields | .25 | .11 |
| ❑ 154 Raul Mondesi | .50 | .23 |
| ❑ 155 Mike Piazza | 3.00 | 1.35 |
| ❑ 156 Rudy Seanez | .25 | .11 |
| ❑ 157 Ismael Valdes | .25 | .11 |
| ❑ 158 Tim Wallach | .25 | .11 |
| ❑ 159 Todd Worrell | .25 | .11 |
| ❑ 160 Moises Alou | .50 | .23 |
| ❑ 161 Cliff Floyd | .50 | .23 |
| ❑ 162 Gil Heredia | .25 | .11 |
| ❑ 163 Mike Lansing | .25 | .11 |
| ❑ 164 Pedro Martinez | 1.25 | .55 |
| ❑ 165 Kirk Rueter | .25 | .11 |
| ❑ 166 Tim Scott | .25 | .11 |
| ❑ 167 Jeff Shaw | .25 | .11 |
| ❑ 168 Rondell White | .50 | .23 |
| ❑ 169 Bobby Bonilla | .50 | .23 |
| ❑ 170 Rico Brogna | .25 | .11 |
| ❑ 171 Todd Hundley | .25 | .11 |
| ❑ 172 Jeff Kent | .50 | .23 |
| ❑ 173 Jim Lindeman | .25 | .11 |
| ❑ 174 Joe Orsulak | .25 | .11 |
| ❑ 175 Bret Saberhagen | .50 | .23 |
| ❑ 176 Toby Borland | .25 | .11 |
| ❑ 177 Darren Daulton | .50 | .23 |
| ❑ 178 Lenny Dykstra | .50 | .23 |
| ❑ 179 Jim Eisenreich | .25 | .11 |
| ❑ 180 Tommy Greene | .25 | .11 |
| ❑ 181 Tony Longmire | .25 | .11 |
| ❑ 182 Bobby Munoz | .25 | .11 |
| ❑ 183 Kevin Stocker | .25 | .11 |
| ❑ 184 Jay Bell | .50 | .23 |
| ❑ 185 Steve Cooke | .25 | .11 |

❑ 186 Ravelo Manzanillo .25 .11
❑ 187 Al Martin .25 .11
❑ 188 Denny Neagle .50 .23
❑ 189 Don Slaught .25 .11
❑ 190 Paul Wagner .25 .11
❑ 191 Rene Arocha .25 .11
❑ 192 Bernard Gilkey .25 .11
❑ 193 Jose Oquendo .25 .11
❑ 194 Tom Pagnozzi .25 .11
❑ 195 Ozzie Smith 1.25 .55
❑ 196 Allen Watson .25 .11
❑ 197 Mark Whiten .25 .11
❑ 198 Andy Ashby .25 .11
❑ 199 Donnie Elliott .25 .11
❑ 200 Bryce Florie .25 .11
❑ 201 Tony Gwynn 2.00 .90
❑ 202 Trevor Hoffman .50 .23
❑ 203 Brian Johnson .25 .11
❑ 204 Tim Mauser .25 .11
❑ 205 Bip Roberts .25 .11
❑ 206 Rod Beck .25 .11
❑ 207 Barry Bonds 1.50 .70
❑ 208 Royce Clayton .25 .11
❑ 209 Darren Lewis .25 .11
❑ 210 Mark Portugal .25 .11
❑ 211 Kevin Rogers .25 .11
❑ 212 Wm. VanLandingham .25 .11
❑ 213 Matt Williams .50 .23
❑ 214 Checklist .25 .11
❑ 215 Checklist .25 .11
❑ 216 Checklist .25 .11
❑ 217 Bret Barberie .25 .11
❑ 218 Armando Benitez .50 .23
❑ 219 Kevin Brown .50 .23
❑ 220 Sid Fernandez .25 .11
❑ 221 Chris Hoiles .25 .11
❑ 222 Doug Jones .25 .11
❑ 223 Ben McDonald .25 .11
❑ 224 Rafael Palmeiro 1.00 .45
❑ 225 Andy Van Slyke .50 .23
❑ 226 Jose Canseco 1.25 .55
❑ 227 Vaughn Eshelman .25 .11
❑ 228 Mike Macfarlane .25 .11
❑ 229 Tim Naehring .25 .11
❑ 230 Frank Rodriguez .25 .11
❑ 231 Lee Tinsley .25 .11
❑ 232 Mark Whiten .25 .11
❑ 233 Garret Anderson .50 .23
❑ 234 Chili Davis .50 .23
❑ 235 Jim Edmonds 1.00 .45
❑ 236 Mark Langston .25 .11
❑ 237 Troy Percival .25 .11
❑ 238 Tony Phillips .25 .11
❑ 239 Lee Smith .50 .23
❑ 240 Jim Abbott .50 .23
❑ 241 James Baldwin .50 .23
❑ 242 Mike Devereaux .25 .11
❑ 243 Ray Durham .50 .23
❑ 244 Alex Fernandez .25 .11
❑ 245 Roberto Hernandez .25 .11
❑ 246 Lance Johnson .25 .11
❑ 247 Ron Karkovice .25 .11
❑ 248 Tim Raines .50 .23
❑ 249 Sandy Alomar Jr. .50 .23
❑ 250 Orel Hershiser .50 .23
❑ 251 Julian Tavarez .25 .11
❑ 252 Jim Thome .50 .23
❑ 253 Omar Vizquel .50 .23
❑ 254 Dave Winfield 1.00 .45
❑ 255 Chad Curtis .25 .11
❑ 256 Kirk Gibson .50 .23
❑ 257 Mike Henneman .25 .11
❑ 258 Bob Higginson RC 1.50 .70
❑ 259 Felipe Lira .25 .11
❑ 260 Rudy Pemberton .25 .11
❑ 261 Alan Trammell .50 .23
❑ 262 Kevin Appier .50 .23
❑ 263 Pat Borders .25 .11
❑ 264 Tom Gordon .25 .11
❑ 265 Jose Lind .25 .11
❑ 266 Jon Nunnally .25 .11
❑ 267 Dilson Torres RC .25 .11
❑ 268 Michael Tucker .25 .11
❑ 269 Jeff Cirillo .50 .23
❑ 270 Darryl Hamilton .25 .11
❑ 271 David Hulse .25 .11
❑ 272 Mark Kiefer .25 .11
❑ 273 Graeme Lloyd .25 .11
❑ 274 Joe Oliver .25 .11
❑ 275 Al Reyes RC .25 .11
❑ 276 Kevin Seitzer .25 .11
❑ 277 Rick Aguilera .25 .11
❑ 278 Marty Cordova .25 .11
❑ 279 Scott Erickson .25 .11
❑ 280 LaTroy Hawkins .25 .11
❑ 281 Brad Radke RC 1.50 .70
❑ 282 Kevin Tapani .25 .11
❑ 283 Tony Fernandez .25 .11
❑ 284 Sterling Hitchcock .25 .11
❑ 285 Pat Kelly .25 .11
❑ 286 Jack McDowell .25 .11
❑ 287 Andy Pettitte .50 .23
❑ 288 Mike Stanley .25 .11
❑ 289 John Wetteland .50 .23
❑ 290 Bernie Williams 1.00 .45
❑ 291 Mark Acre .25 .11
❑ 292 Geronimo Berroa .25 .11
❑ 293 Dennis Eckersley .50 .23
❑ 294 Steve Ontiveros .25 .11
❑ 295 Ruben Sierra .25 .11
❑ 296 Terry Steinbach .25 .11
❑ 297 Dave Stewart .50 .23
❑ 298 Todd Stottlemyre .25 .11
❑ 299 Darren Bragg .25 .11
❑ 300 Joey Cora .25 .11
❑ 301 Edgar Martinez .50 .23
❑ 302 Bill Risley .25 .11
❑ 303 Ron Villone .25 .11
❑ 304 Dan Wilson .25 .11
❑ 305 Benji Gil .25 .11
❑ 306 Wilson Heredia .25 .11
❑ 307 Mark McLemore .25 .11
❑ 308 Otis Nixon .25 .11
❑ 309 Kenny Rogers .25 .11
❑ 310 Jeff Russell .25 .11
❑ 311 Mickey Tettleton .25 .11
❑ 312 Bob Tewksbury .25 .11
❑ 313 David Cone .50 .23
❑ 314 Carlos Delgado 1.00 .45
❑ 315 Alex Gonzalez .25 .11
❑ 316 Shawn Green 1.00 .45
❑ 317 Paul Molitor 1.00 .45
❑ 318 Ed Sprague .25 .11
❑ 319 Devon White .50 .23
❑ 320 Steve Avery .25 .11
❑ 321 Jeff Blauser .25 .11
❑ 322 Brad Clontz .25 .11
❑ 323 Tom Glavine 1.00 .45
❑ 324 Marquis Grissom .25 .11
❑ 325 Chipper Jones 2.50 1.10
❑ 326 David Justice .50 .23
❑ 327 Mark Lemke .25 .11
❑ 328 Kent Mercker .25 .11
❑ 329 Jason Schmidt .25 .11
❑ 330 Steve Buechele .25 .11
❑ 331 Kevin Foster .25 .11
❑ 332 Mark Grace 1.00 .45
❑ 333 Brian McRae .25 .11
❑ 334 Sammy Sosa 2.00 .90
❑ 335 Ozzie Timmons .25 .11
❑ 336 Rick Wilkins .25 .11
❑ 337 Hector Carrasco .25 .11
❑ 338 Ron Gant .25 .11
❑ 339 Barry Larkin 1.00 .45
❑ 340 Deion Sanders .50 .23
❑ 341 Benito Santiago .25 .11
❑ 342 Roger Bailey .25 .11
❑ 343 Jason Bates .25 .11
❑ 344 Dante Bichette .50 .23
❑ 345 Joe Girardi .25 .11
❑ 346 Bill Swift .25 .11
❑ 347 Mark Thompson .25 .11
❑ 348 Larry Walker .50 .23
❑ 349 Kurt Abbott .25 .11
❑ 350 John Burkett .25 .11
❑ 351 Chuck Carr .25 .11
❑ 352 Andre Dawson .50 .23
❑ 353 Chris Hammond .25 .11
❑ 354 Charles Johnson .50 .23
❑ 355 Terry Pendleton .50 .23
❑ 356 Quilvio Veras .25 .11
❑ 357 Derek Bell .25 .11
❑ 358 Jim Dougherty RC .25 .11
❑ 359 Doug Drabek .25 .11
❑ 360 Todd Jones .25 .11
❑ 361 Orlando Miller .25 .11
❑ 362 James Mouton .25 .11
❑ 363 Phil Plantier .25 .11
❑ 364 Shane Reynolds .25 .11
❑ 365 Todd Hollandsworth .25 .11
❑ 366 Eric Karros .50 .23
❑ 367 Ramon Martinez .25 .11
❑ 368 Hideo Nomo RC 2.50 1.10
❑ 369 Jose Offerman .25 .11
❑ 370 Antonio Osuna .25 .11
❑ 371 Todd Williams .25 .11
❑ 372 Shane Andrews .25 .11
❑ 373 Wil Cordero .25 .11
❑ 374 Jeff Fassero .25 .11
❑ 375 Darrin Fletcher .25 .11
❑ 376 Mark Grudzielanek RC .50 .23
❑ 377 Carlos Perez RC .50 .23
❑ 378 Mel Rojas .25 .11
❑ 379 Tony Tarasco .25 .11
❑ 380 Edgardo Alfonzo 1.00 .45
❑ 381 Brett Butler .50 .23
❑ 382 Carl Everett .50 .23
❑ 383 John Franco .50 .23
❑ 384 Pete Harnisch .25 .11
❑ 385 Bobby Jones .25 .11
❑ 386 Dave Mlicki .25 .11
❑ 387 Jose Vizcaino .25 .11
❑ 388 Ricky Bottalico .25 .11
❑ 389 Tyler Green .25 .11
❑ 390 Charlie Hayes .25 .11
❑ 391 Dave Hollins .25 .11
❑ 392 Gregg Jefferies .25 .11
❑ 393 Michael Mimbs RC .25 .11
❑ 394 Mickey Morandini .25 .11
❑ 395 Curt Schilling .50 .23
❑ 396 Heathcliff Slocumb .25 .11
❑ 397 Jason Christiansen RC .25 .11
❑ 398 Midre Cummings .25 .11
❑ 399 Carlos Garcia .25 .11
❑ 400 Mark Johnson RC .25 .11
❑ 401 Jeff King .25 .11
❑ 402 Jon Lieber .25 .11
❑ 403 Esteban Loaiza .25 .11
❑ 404 Orlando Merced .25 .11
❑ 405 Gary Wilson RC .25 .11
❑ 406 Scott Cooper .25 .11
❑ 407 Tom Henke .25 .11
❑ 408 Ken Hill .25 .11
❑ 409 Danny Jackson .25 .11
❑ 410 Brian Jordan .50 .23
❑ 411 Ray Lankford .50 .23
❑ 412 John Mabry .25 .11
❑ 413 Todd Zeile .25 .11
❑ 414 Andy Benes .25 .11
❑ 415 Andres Berumen .25 .11
❑ 416 Ken Caminiti .50 .23
❑ 417 Andujar Cedeno .25 .11
❑ 418 Steve Finley .50 .23
❑ 419 Joey Hamilton .25 .11
❑ 420 Dustin Hermanson .25 .11
❑ 421 Melvin Nieves .25 .11
❑ 422 Roberto Petagine .25 .11
❑ 423 Eddie Williams .25 .11
❑ 424 Glenallen Hill .25 .11
❑ 425 Kirt Manwaring .25 .11
❑ 426 Terry Mulholland .25 .11
❑ 427 J.R. Phillips .25 .11
❑ 428 Joe Rosselli .25 .11
❑ 429 Robby Thompson .25 .11
❑ 430 Checklist .25 .11
❑ 431 Checklist .25 .11
❑ 432 Checklist .25 .11

## 1996 Flair

| | MINT | NRMT |
|---|---|---|
| COMPLETE SET (400) | 200.00 | 90.00 |

❑ 1 Roberto Alomar 2.00 .90
❑ 2 Brady Anderson .75 .35
❑ 3 Bobby Bonilla .75 .35
❑ 4 Scott Erickson .50 .23
❑ 5 Jeffrey Hammonds .75 .35

❑ 6 Jimmy Haynes .50 .23
❑ 7 Chris Hoiles .50 .23
❑ 8 Kent Mercker .50 .23
❑ 9 Mike Mussina 2.00 .90
❑ 10 Randy Myers .50 .23
❑ 11 Rafael Palmeiro 2.00 .90
❑ 12 Cal Ripken 8.00 3.60
❑ 13 B.J. Surhoff .75 .35
❑ 14 David Wells .75 .35
❑ 15 Jose Canseco 2.50 1.10
❑ 16 Roger Clemens 4.00 1.80
❑ 17 Wil Cordero .50 .23
❑ 18 Tom Gordon .50 .23
❑ 19 Mike Greenwell .50 .23
❑ 20 Dwayne Hosey .50 .23
❑ 21 Jose Malave .50 .23
❑ 22 Tim Naehring .50 .23
❑ 23 Troy O'Leary .50 .23
❑ 24 Aaron Sele .75 .35
❑ 25 Heathcliff Slocumb .50 .23
❑ 26 Mike Stanley .50 .23
❑ 27 Jeff Suppan .50 .23
❑ 28 John Valentin .50 .23
❑ 29 Mo Vaughn .75 .35
❑ 30 Tim Wakefield .50 .23
❑ 31 Jim Abbott .75 .35
❑ 32 Garret Anderson .75 .35
❑ 33 George Arias .50 .23
❑ 34 Chili Davis .75 .35
❑ 35 Gary DiSarcina .50 .23
❑ 36 Jim Edmonds 2.00 .90
❑ 37 Chuck Finley .75 .35
❑ 38 Todd Greene .50 .23
❑ 39 Mark Langston .50 .23
❑ 40 Troy Percival .50 .23
❑ 41 Tim Salmon .75 .35
❑ 42 Lee Smith .75 .35
❑ 43 J.T. Snow .75 .35
❑ 44 Randy Velarde .50 .23
❑ 45 Tim Wallach .50 .23
❑ 46 Wilson Alvarez .50 .23
❑ 47 Harold Baines .75 .35
❑ 48 Jason Bere .50 .23
❑ 49 Ray Durham .75 .35
❑ 50 Alex Fernandez .50 .23
❑ 51 Ozzie Guillen .50 .23
❑ 52 Roberto Hernandez .50 .23
❑ 53 Ron Karkovice .50 .23
❑ 54 Darren Lewis .50 .23
❑ 55 Lyle Mouton .50 .23
❑ 56 Tony Phillips .50 .23
❑ 57 Chris Snopek .50 .23
❑ 58 Kevin Tapani .50 .23
❑ 59 Danny Tartabull .50 .23
❑ 60 Frank Thomas 4.00 1.80
❑ 61 Robin Ventura .75 .35
❑ 62 Sandy Alomar Jr. .75 .35
❑ 63 Carlos Baerga .50 .23
❑ 64 Albert Belle 1.25 .55
❑ 65 Julio Franco .50 .23
❑ 66 Orel Hershiser .75 .35
❑ 67 Kenny Lofton .75 .35
❑ 68 Dennis Martinez .75 .35
❑ 69 Jack McDowell .50 .23
❑ 70 Jose Mesa .50 .23
❑ 71 Eddie Murray 2.00 .90
❑ 72 Charles Nagy .50 .23
❑ 73 Tony Pena .50 .23
❑ 74 Manny Ramirez 2.50 1.10
❑ 75 Julian Tavarez .50 .23
❑ 76 Jim Thome 1.25 .55
❑ 77 Omar Vizquel .75 .35
❑ 78 Chad Curtis .50 .23
❑ 79 Cecil Fielder .75 .35
❑ 80 Travis Fryman .75 .35
❑ 81 Chris Gomez .50 .23
❑ 82 Bob Higginson .75 .35
❑ 83 Mark Lewis .50 .23
❑ 84 Felipe Lira .50 .23
❑ 85 Alan Trammell 1.25 .55
❑ 86 Kevin Appier .75 .35
❑ 87 Johnny Damon 1.25 .55
❑ 88 Tom Goodwin .50 .23
❑ 89 Mark Gubicza .50 .23
❑ 90 Bob Hamelin .50 .23
❑ 91 Keith Lockhart .50 .23
❑ 92 Jeff Montgomery .50 .23
❑ 93 Jon Nunnally .50 .23
❑ 94 Bip Roberts .50 .23
❑ 95 Michael Tucker .50 .23
❑ 96 Joe Vitiello .50 .23
❑ 97 Ricky Bones .50 .23
❑ 98 Chuck Carr .50 .23
❑ 99 Jeff Cirillo .75 .35
❑ 100 Mike Fetters .50 .23
❑ 101 John Jaha .50 .23
❑ 102 Mike Matheny .50 .23
❑ 103 Ben McDonald .50 .23
❑ 104 Matt Mieske .50 .23
❑ 105 Dave Nilsson .50 .23
❑ 106 Kevin Seitzer .50 .23
❑ 107 Steve Sparks .50 .23
❑ 108 Jose Valentin .50 .23
❑ 109 Greg Vaughn .75 .35
❑ 110 Rick Aguilera .50 .23
❑ 111 Rich Becker .50 .23
❑ 112 Marty Cordova .50 .23
❑ 113 LaTroy Hawkins .50 .23
❑ 114 Dave Hollins .50 .23
❑ 115 Roberto Kelly .50 .23
❑ 116 Chuck Knoblauch .75 .35
❑ 117 Matt Lawton RC 2.50 1.10
❑ 118 Pat Meares .50 .23
❑ 119 Paul Molitor 2.00 .90
❑ 120 Kirby Puckett 5.00 2.20
❑ 121 Brad Radke .75 .35
❑ 122 Frank Rodriguez .50 .23
❑ 123 Scott Stahoviak .50 .23
❑ 124 Matt Walbeck .50 .23
❑ 125 Wade Boggs 2.50 1.10
❑ 126 David Cone .75 .35
❑ 127 Joe Girardi .50 .23
❑ 128 Dwight Gooden .75 .35
❑ 129 Derek Jeter 8.00 3.60
❑ 130 Jimmy Key .75 .35
❑ 131 Jim Leyritz .50 .23
❑ 132 Tino Martinez .75 .35
❑ 133 Paul O'Neill .75 .35
❑ 134 Andy Pettitte .75 .35
❑ 135 Tim Raines .75 .35
❑ 136 Ruben Rivera .50 .23
❑ 137 Kenny Rogers .50 .23
❑ 138 Ruben Sierra .50 .23
❑ 139 John Wetteland .75 .35
❑ 140 Bernie Williams 2.00 .90
❑ 141 Tony Batista RC 15.00 6.75
❑ 142 Allen Battle .50 .23
❑ 143 Geronimo Berroa .50 .23
❑ 144 Mike Bordick .50 .23
❑ 145 Scott Brosius .75 .35
❑ 146 Steve Cox .50 .23
❑ 147 Brent Gates .50 .23
❑ 148 Jason Giambi 2.00 .90
❑ 149 Doug Johns .50 .23
❑ 150 Mark McGwire 8.00 3.60
❑ 151 Pedro Munoz .50 .23
❑ 152 Ariel Prieto .50 .23
❑ 153 Terry Steinbach .50 .23
❑ 154 Todd Van Poppel .50 .23
❑ 155 Bobby Ayala .50 .23
❑ 156 Chris Bosio .50 .23
❑ 157 Jay Buhner .75 .35
❑ 158 Joey Cora .50 .23
❑ 159 Russ Davis .50 .23
❑ 160 Ken Griffey Jr. 8.00 3.60
❑ 161 Sterling Hitchcock .50 .23
❑ 162 Randy Johnson 2.50 1.10
❑ 163 Edgar Martinez 1.25 .55
❑ 164 Alex Rodriguez 6.00 2.70
❑ 165 Paul Sorrento .50 .23
❑ 166 Dan Wilson .50 .23
❑ 167 Will Clark 2.00 .90
❑ 168 Benji Gil .50 .23
❑ 169 Juan Gonzalez 2.00 .90
❑ 170 Rusty Greer .75 .35
❑ 171 Kevin Gross .50 .23
❑ 172 Darryl Hamilton .50 .23
❑ 173 Mike Henneman .50 .23
❑ 174 Ken Hill .50 .23
❑ 175 Mark McLemore .50 .23
❑ 176 Dean Palmer .75 .35
❑ 177 Roger Pavlik .50 .23
❑ 178 Ivan Rodriguez 2.50 1.10
❑ 179 Mickey Tettleton .50 .23
❑ 180 Bobby Witt .50 .23
❑ 181 Joe Carter .75 .35
❑ 182 Felipe Crespo .50 .23
❑ 183 Alex Gonzalez .50 .23
❑ 184 Shawn Green 2.00 .90
❑ 185 Juan Guzman .50 .23
❑ 186 Erik Hanson .50 .23
❑ 187 Pat Hentgen .50 .23
❑ 188 Sandy Martinez .50 .23
❑ 189 Otis Nixon .50 .23
❑ 190 John Olerud .75 .35
❑ 191 Paul Quantrill .50 .23
❑ 192 Bill Risley .50 .23
❑ 193 Ed Sprague .50 .23
❑ 194 Steve Avery .50 .23
❑ 195 Jeff Blauser .50 .23
❑ 196 Brad Clontz .50 .23
❑ 197 Jermaine Dye .75 .35
❑ 198 Tom Glavine 2.00 .90
❑ 199 Marquis Grissom .50 .23
❑ 200 Chipper Jones 5.00 2.20
❑ 201 David Justice 1.25 .55
❑ 202 Ryan Klesko .75 .35
❑ 203 Mark Lemke .50 .23
❑ 204 Javier Lopez .75 .35
❑ 205 Greg Maddux 5.00 2.20
❑ 206 Fred McGriff 1.25 .55
❑ 207 Greg McMichael .50 .23
❑ 208 Wonderful Monds RC .50 .23
❑ 209 Jason Schmidt .50 .23
❑ 210 John Smoltz .75 .35
❑ 211 Mark Wohlers .50 .23
❑ 212 Jim Bullinger .50 .23
❑ 213 Frank Castillo .50 .23
❑ 214 Kevin Foster .50 .23
❑ 215 Luis Gonzalez .75 .35
❑ 216 Mark Grace 2.00 .90
❑ 217 Robin Jennings .50 .23
❑ 218 Doug Jones .50 .23
❑ 219 Dave Magadan .50 .23
❑ 220 Brian McRae .50 .23
❑ 221 Jaime Navarro .50 .23
❑ 222 Rey Sanchez .50 .23
❑ 223 Ryne Sandberg 2.50 1.10
❑ 224 Scott Servais .50 .23
❑ 225 Sammy Sosa 4.00 1.80
❑ 226 Ozzie Timmons .50 .23
❑ 227 Bret Boone .75 .35
❑ 228 Jeff Branson .50 .23
❑ 229 Jeff Brantley .50 .23
❑ 230 Dave Burba .50 .23
❑ 231 Vince Coleman .50 .23
❑ 232 Steve Gibralter .50 .23
❑ 233 Mike Kelly .50 .23
❑ 234 Barry Larkin 2.00 .90
❑ 235 Hal Morris .50 .23
❑ 236 Mark Portugal .50 .23
❑ 237 Jose Rijo .50 .23
❑ 238 Reggie Sanders .50 .23
❑ 239 Pete Schourek .50 .23
❑ 240 John Smiley .50 .23
❑ 241 Eddie Taubensee .50 .23
❑ 242 Jason Bates .50 .23
❑ 243 Dante Bichette .75 .35
❑ 244 Ellis Burks .75 .35
❑ 245 Vinny Castilla .75 .35

❑ 246 Andres Galarraga 1.25 .55
❑ 247 Darren Holmes .50 .23
❑ 248 Curt Leskanic .50 .23
❑ 249 Steve Reed .50 .23
❑ 250 Kevin Rtiz .50 .23
❑ 251 Bret Saberhagen .75 .35
❑ 252 Bill Swift .50 .23
❑ 253 Larry Walker .75 .35
❑ 254 Walt Weiss .50 .23
❑ 255 Eric Young .50 .23
❑ 256 Kurt Abbott .50 .23
❑ 257 Kevin Brown 1.25 .55
❑ 258 John Burkett .50 .23
❑ 259 Greg Colbrunn .50 .23
❑ 260 Jeff Conine .50 .23
❑ 261 Andre Dawson 1.25 .55
❑ 262 Chris Hammond .50 .23
❑ 263 Charles Johnson .75 .35
❑ 264 Al Leiter .75 .35
❑ 265 Robb Nen .50 .23
❑ 266 Terry Pendleton .75 .35
❑ 267 Pat Rapp .50 .23
❑ 268 Gary Sheffield 2.00 .90
❑ 269 Quilvio Veras .50 .23
❑ 270 Devon White .75 .35
❑ 271 Bob Abreu 2.50 1.10
❑ 272 Jeff Bagwell 2.50 1.10
❑ 273 Derek Bell .50 .23
❑ 274 Sean Berry .50 .23
❑ 275 Craig Biggio 1.25 .55
❑ 276 Doug Drabek .50 .23
❑ 277 Tony Eusebio .50 .23
❑ 278 Richard Hidalgo .75 .35
❑ 279 Brian L.Hunter .50 .23
❑ 280 Todd Jones .50 .23
❑ 281 Derrick May .50 .23
❑ 282 Orlando Miller .50 .23
❑ 283 James Mouton .50 .23
❑ 284 Shane Reynolds .50 .23
❑ 285 Greg Swindell .50 .23
❑ 286 Mike Blowers .50 .23
❑ 287 Brett Butler .75 .35
❑ 288 Tom Candiotti .50 .23
❑ 289 Roger Cedeno .50 .23
❑ 290 Delino DeShields .50 .23
❑ 291 Greg Gagne .50 .23
❑ 292 Karim Garcia .50 .23
❑ 293 Todd Hollandsworth .50 .23
❑ 294 Eric Karros .75 .35
❑ 295 Ramon Martinez .50 .23
❑ 296 Raul Mondesi .75 .35
❑ 297 Hideo Nomo 2.00 .90
❑ 298 Mike Piazza 6.00 2.70
❑ 299 Ismael Valdes .50 .23
❑ 300 Todd Worrell .50 .23
❑ 301 Moises Alou .75 .35
❑ 302 Shane Andrews .50 .23
❑ 303 Yamil Benitez .50 .23
❑ 304 Jeff Fassero .50 .23
❑ 305 Darrin Fletcher .50 .23
❑ 306 Cliff Floyd .75 .35
❑ 307 Mark Grudzielanek .50 .23
❑ 308 Mike Lansing .50 .23
❑ 309 Pedro Martinez 2.50 1.10
❑ 310 Ryan McGuire .50 .23
❑ 311 Carlos Perez .50 .23
❑ 312 Mel Rojas .50 .23
❑ 313 David Segui .50 .23
❑ 314 Rondell White .75 .35
❑ 315 Edgardo Alfonzo .75 .35
❑ 316 Rico Brogna .50 .23
❑ 317 Carl Everett .75 .35
❑ 318 John Franco .75 .35
❑ 319 Bernard Gilkey .50 .23
❑ 320 Todd Hundley .50 .23
❑ 321 Jason Isringhausen .75 .35
❑ 322 Lance Johnson .50 .23
❑ 323 Bobby Jones .50 .23
❑ 324 Jeff Kent 1.25 .55
❑ 325 Rey Ordonez .75 .35
❑ 326 Bill Pulsipher .50 .23
❑ 327 Jose Vizcaino .50 .23
❑ 328 Paul Wilson .50 .23
❑ 329 Ricky Bottalico .50 .23
❑ 330 Darren Daulton .75 .35
❑ 331 David Doster .50 .23
❑ 332 Lenny Dykstra .75 .35
❑ 333 Jim Eisenreich .50 .23
❑ 334 Sid Fernandez .50 .23
❑ 335 Gregg Jefferies .50 .23
❑ 336 Mickey Morandini .50 .23
❑ 337 Benito Santiago .50 .23
❑ 338 Curt Schilling .75 .35
❑ 339 Kevin Stocker .50 .23
❑ 340 David West .50 .23
❑ 341 Mark Whiten .50 .23
❑ 342 Todd Zeile .50 .23
❑ 343 Jay Bell .75 .35
❑ 344 John Ericks .50 .23
❑ 345 Carlos Garcia .50 .23
❑ 346 Charlie Hayes .50 .23
❑ 347 Jason Kendall .75 .35
❑ 348 Jeff King .50 .23
❑ 349 Mike Kingery .50 .23
❑ 350 Al Martin .50 .23
❑ 351 Orlando Merced .50 .23
❑ 352 Dan Miceli .50 .23
❑ 353 Denny Neagle .75 .35
❑ 354 Alan Benes .50 .23
❑ 355 Andy Benes .50 .23
❑ 356 Royce Clayton .50 .23
❑ 357 Dennis Eckersley .75 .35
❑ 358 Gary Gaetti .75 .35
❑ 359 Ron Gant .50 .23
❑ 360 Brian Jordan .75 .35
❑ 361 Ray Lankford .75 .35
❑ 362 John Mabry .50 .23
❑ 363 T.J. Mathews .50 .23
❑ 364 Mike Morgan .50 .23
❑ 365 Donovan Osborne .50 .23
❑ 366 Tom Pagnozzi .50 .23
❑ 367 Ozzie Smith 2.50 1.10
❑ 368 Todd Stottlemyre .50 .23
❑ 369 Andy Ashby .50 .23
❑ 370 Brad Ausmus .50 .23
❑ 371 Ken Caminiti .75 .35
❑ 372 Andujar Cedeno .50 .23
❑ 373 Steve Finley .75 .35
❑ 374 Tony Gwynn 4.00 1.80
❑ 375 Joey Hamilton .50 .23
❑ 376 Rickey Henderson 2.50 1.10
❑ 377 Trevor Hoffman .75 .35
❑ 378 Wally Joyner .75 .35
❑ 379 Marc Newfield .50 .23
❑ 380 Jody Reed .50 .23
❑ 381 Bob Tewksbury .50 .23
❑ 382 Fernando Valenzuela .75 .35
❑ 383 Rod Beck .50 .23
❑ 384 Barry Bonds 3.00 1.35
❑ 385 Mark Carreon .50 .23
❑ 386 Shawon Dunston .50 .23
❑ 387 Osvaldo Fernandez RC .50 .23
❑ 388 Glenallen Hill .50 .23
❑ 389 Stan Javier .50 .23
❑ 390 Mark Leiter .50 .23
❑ 391 Kirt Manwaring .50 .23
❑ 392 Robby Thompson .50 .23
❑ 393 William VanLandingham .50 .23
❑ 394 Allen Watson .50 .23
❑ 395 Matt Williams 1.25 .55
❑ 396 Checklist 1-92 .50 .23
❑ 397 Checklist 93-180 .50 .23
❑ 398 Checklist 181-272 .50 .23
❑ 399 Checklist 273-365 .50 .23
❑ 400 Checklist 366-400/Inserts .50 .23

## 1997 Flair Showcase Row 2

| | MINT | NRMT |
|---|---|---|
| COMPLETE SET (180) | 80.00 | 36.00 |
| COMMON CARD (1-60) | .25 | .11 |
| COMMON CARD (61-120) | .40 | .18 |
| COMMON CARD (121-180) | .30 | .14 |

❑ 1 Andruw Jones 1.25 .55
❑ 2 Derek Jeter 4.00 1.80
❑ 3 Alex Rodriguez 3.00 1.35
❑ 4 Paul Molitor 1.00 .45
❑ 5 Jeff Bagwell 1.25 .55
❑ 6 Scott Rolen 1.00 .45

❑ 7 Kenny Lofton .40 .18
❑ 8 Cal Ripken 4.00 1.80
❑ 9 Brady Anderson .40 .18
❑ 10 Chipper Jones 2.50 1.10
❑ 11 Todd Greene .25 .11
❑ 12 Todd Walker .25 .11
❑ 13 Billy Wagner .25 .11
❑ 14 Craig Biggio .60 .25
❑ 15 Kevin Orie .25 .11
❑ 16 Hideo Nomo 1.00 .45
❑ 17 Kevin Appier .40 .18
❑ 18 Bubba Trammell STY RC .40 .18
❑ 19 Juan Gonzalez 1.00 .45
❑ 20 Randy Johnson 1.25 .55
❑ 21 Roger Clemens 2.00 .90
❑ 22 Johnny Damon .40 .18
❑ 23 Ryne Sandberg 1.25 .55
❑ 24 Ken Griffey Jr. 4.00 1.80
❑ 25 Barry Bonds 1.50 .70
❑ 26 Nomar Garciaparra 3.00 1.35
❑ 27 Vladimir Guerrero 2.00 .90
❑ 28 Ron Gant .25 .11
❑ 29 Joe Carter .40 .18
❑ 30 Tim Salmon .40 .18
❑ 31 Mike Piazza 3.00 1.35
❑ 32 Barry Larkin 1.00 .45
❑ 33 Manny Ramirez 1.25 .55
❑ 34 Sammy Sosa 2.00 .90
❑ 35 Frank Thomas 2.00 .90
❑ 36 Melvin Nieves .25 .11
❑ 37 Tony Gwynn 2.00 .90
❑ 38 Gary Sheffield 1.00 .45
❑ 39 Darin Erstad 1.25 .55
❑ 40 Ken Caminiti .40 .18
❑ 41 Jermaine Dye .40 .18
❑ 42 Mo Vaughn .40 .18
❑ 43 Raul Mondesi .40 .18
❑ 44 Greg Maddux 2.50 1.10
❑ 45 Chuck Knoblauch .40 .18
❑ 46 Andy Pettitte .40 .18
❑ 47 Deion Sanders .40 .18
❑ 48 Albert Belle .60 .25
❑ 49 Jamey Wright .25 .11
❑ 50 Rey Ordonez .25 .11
❑ 51 Bernie Williams 1.00 .45
❑ 52 Mark McGwire 4.00 1.80
❑ 53 Mike Mussina 1.00 .45
❑ 54 Bob Abreu .40 .18
❑ 55 Reggie Sanders .25 .11
❑ 56 Brian Jordan .40 .18
❑ 57 Ivan Rodriguez 1.25 .55
❑ 58 Roberto Alomar 1.00 .45
❑ 59 Tim Naehring .25 .11
❑ 60 Edgar Renteria .40 .18
❑ 61 Dean Palmer .60 .25
❑ 62 Benito Santiago .40 .18
❑ 63 David Cone .60 .25
❑ 64 Carlos Delgado 1.50 .70
❑ 65 Brian Giles RC 3.00 1.35
❑ 66 Alex Ochoa .40 .18
❑ 67 Rondell White .60 .25
❑ 68 Robin Ventura .60 .25
❑ 69 Eric Karros .60 .25
❑ 70 Jose Valentin .40 .18
❑ 71 Rafael Palmeiro 1.50 .70
❑ 72 Chris Snopek .40 .18
❑ 73 David Justice 1.00 .45
❑ 74 Tom Glavine 1.50 .70

| | # | Player | | |
|---|---|---|---|---|
| ❑ | 75 | Rudy Pemberton | .40 | .18 |
| ❑ | 76 | Larry Walker | .60 | .25 |
| ❑ | 77 | Jim Thome | 1.00 | .45 |
| ❑ | 78 | Charles Johnson | .60 | .25 |
| ❑ | 79 | Dante Powell | .60 | .25 |
| ❑ | 80 | Derrek Lee | .40 | .18 |
| ❑ | 81 | Jason Kendall | .60 | .25 |
| ❑ | 82 | Todd Hollandsworth | .40 | .18 |
| ❑ | 83 | Bernard Gilkey | .40 | .18 |
| ❑ | 84 | Mel Rojas | .40 | .18 |
| ❑ | 85 | Dmitri Young | .60 | .25 |
| ❑ | 86 | Bret Boone | .60 | .25 |
| ❑ | 87 | Pat Hentgen | .40 | .18 |
| ❑ | 88 | Bobby Bonilla | .60 | .25 |
| ❑ | 89 | John Wetteland | .60 | .25 |
| ❑ | 90 | Todd Hundley | .40 | .18 |
| ❑ | 91 | Wilton Guerrero | .40 | .18 |
| ❑ | 92 | Geronimo Berroa | .40 | .18 |
| ❑ | 93 | Al Martin | .40 | .18 |
| ❑ | 94 | Danny Tartabull | .40 | .18 |
| ❑ | 95 | Brian McRae | .40 | .18 |
| ❑ | 96 | Steve Finley | .60 | .25 |
| ❑ | 97 | Todd Stottlemyre | .40 | .18 |
| ❑ | 98 | John Smoltz | .60 | .25 |
| ❑ | 99 | Matt Williams | 1.00 | .45 |
| ❑ | 100 | Eddie Murray | 1.50 | .70 |
| ❑ | 101 | Henry Rodriguez | .40 | .18 |
| ❑ | 102 | Marty Cordova | .40 | .18 |
| ❑ | 103 | Juan Guzman | .40 | .18 |
| ❑ | 104 | Chili Davis | .60 | .25 |
| ❑ | 105 | Eric Young | .40 | .18 |
| ❑ | 106 | Jeff Abbott | .40 | .18 |
| ❑ | 107 | Shannon Stewart | .60 | .25 |
| ❑ | 108 | Rocky Coppinger | .40 | .18 |
| ❑ | 109 | Jose Canseco | 2.00 | .90 |
| ❑ | 110 | Dante Bichette | .60 | .25 |
| ❑ | 111 | Dwight Gooden | .60 | .25 |
| ❑ | 112 | Scott Brosius | .60 | .25 |
| ❑ | 113 | Steve Avery | .40 | .18 |
| ❑ | 114 | Andres Galarraga | 1.00 | .45 |
| ❑ | 115 | Sandy Alomar Jr. | .60 | .25 |
| ❑ | 116 | Ray Lankford | .60 | .25 |
| ❑ | 117 | Jorge Posada | .60 | .25 |
| ❑ | 118 | Ryan Klesko | .60 | .25 |
| ❑ | 119 | Jay Buhner | .60 | .25 |
| ❑ | 120 | Jose Guillen | .40 | .10 |
| ❑ | 121 | Paul O'Neill | .50 | .23 |
| ❑ | 122 | Jimmy Key | .50 | .23 |
| ❑ | 123 | Hal Morris | .30 | .14 |
| ❑ | 124 | Travis Fryman | .50 | .23 |
| ❑ | 125 | Jim Edmonds | 1.25 | .55 |
| ❑ | 126 | Jeff Cirillo | .50 | .23 |
| ❑ | 127 | Fred McGriff | .75 | .35 |
| ❑ | 128 | Alan Benes | .30 | .14 |
| ❑ | 129 | Derek Bell | .30 | .14 |
| ❑ | 130 | Tony Graffanino | .30 | .14 |
| ❑ | 131 | Shawn Green | 1.00 | .45 |
| ❑ | 132 | Denny Neagle | .50 | .23 |
| ❑ | 133 | Alex Fernandez | .30 | .14 |
| ❑ | 134 | Mickey Morandini | .30 | .14 |
| ❑ | 135 | Royce Clayton | .30 | .14 |
| ❑ | 136 | Jose Mesa | .30 | .14 |
| ❑ | 137 | Edgar Martinez | .75 | .35 |
| ❑ | 138 | Curt Schilling | .50 | .23 |
| ❑ | 139 | Lance Johnson | .30 | .14 |
| ❑ | 140 | Andy Benes | .30 | .14 |
| ❑ | 141 | Charles Nagy | .30 | .14 |
| ❑ | 142 | Mariano Rivera | .50 | .23 |
| ❑ | 143 | Mark Wohlers | .30 | .14 |
| ❑ | 144 | Ken Hill | .30 | .14 |
| ❑ | 145 | Jay Bell | .50 | .23 |
| ❑ | 146 | Bob Higginson | .50 | .23 |
| ❑ | 147 | Mark Grudzielanek | .30 | .14 |
| ❑ | 148 | Ray Durham | .50 | .23 |
| ❑ | 149 | John Olerud | .50 | .23 |
| ❑ | 150 | Joey Hamilton | .30 | .14 |
| ❑ | 151 | Trevor Hoffman | .50 | .23 |
| ❑ | 152 | Dan Wilson | .30 | .14 |
| ❑ | 153 | J.T. Snow | .50 | .23 |
| ❑ | 154 | Marquis Grissom | .30 | .14 |
| ❑ | 155 | Yamil Benitez | .30 | .14 |
| ❑ | 156 | Rusty Greer | .50 | .23 |
| ❑ | 157 | Darryl Kile | .50 | .23 |
| ❑ | 158 | Ismael Valdes | .30 | .14 |
| ❑ | 159 | Jeff Conine | .30 | .14 |
| ❑ | 160 | Darren Daulton | .50 | .23 |
| ❑ | 161 | Chan Ho Park | .50 | .23 |
| ❑ | 162 | Troy Percival | .30 | .14 |
| ❑ | 163 | Wade Boggs | 1.50 | .70 |
| ❑ | 164 | Dave Nilsson | .30 | .14 |
| ❑ | 165 | Vinny Castilla | .50 | .23 |
| ❑ | 166 | Kevin Brown | .75 | .35 |
| ❑ | 167 | Dennis Eckersley | .50 | .23 |
| ❑ | 168 | Wendell Magee Jr. | .30 | .14 |
| ❑ | 169 | John Jaha | .30 | .14 |
| ❑ | 170 | Garret Anderson | .50 | .23 |
| ❑ | 171 | Jason Giambi | 1.25 | .55 |
| ❑ | 172 | Mark Grace | 1.25 | .55 |
| ❑ | 173 | Tony Clark | .30 | .14 |
| ❑ | 174 | Moises Alou | .50 | .23 |
| ❑ | 175 | Brett Butler | .50 | .23 |
| ❑ | 176 | Cecil Fielder | .50 | .23 |
| ❑ | 177 | Chris Widger | .30 | .14 |
| ❑ | 178 | Doug Drabek | .30 | .14 |
| ❑ | 179 | Ellis Burks | .50 | .23 |
| ❑ | 180 | Shigetoshi Hasegawa RC | 1.00 | .45 |
| ❑ | NNO | A. Rod. Glove EXCH/25 | 200.00 | 90.00 |

## 1998 Flair Showcase Row 3

| | MINT | NRMT |
|---|---|---|
| COMPLETE SET (120) | 80.00 | 36.00 |
| COMMON CARD (1-30) | .40 | .18 |
| COMMON CARD (31-60) | .40 | .18 |
| COMMON CARD (61-90) | .50 | .23 |
| COMMON CARD (91-120) | .60 | .25 |

| | # | Player | MINT | NRMT |
|---|---|---|---|---|
| ❑ | 1 | Ken Griffey Jr. | 4.00 | 1.80 |
| ❑ | 2 | Travis Lee | .40 | .18 |
| ❑ | 3 | Frank Thomas | 2.00 | .90 |
| ❑ | 4 | Ben Grieve | .40 | .18 |
| ❑ | 5 | Nomar Garciaparra | 3.00 | 1.35 |
| ❑ | 6 | Jose Cruz Jr. | .40 | .18 |
| ❑ | 7 | Alex Rodriguez | 3.00 | 1.35 |
| ❑ | 8 | Cal Ripken | 4.00 | 1.80 |
| ❑ | 9 | Mark McGwire | 4.00 | 1.80 |
| ❑ | 10 | Chipper Jones | 2.50 | 1.10 |
| ❑ | 11 | Paul Konerko | .40 | .18 |
| ❑ | 12 | Todd Helton | 1.25 | .55 |
| ❑ | 13 | Greg Maddux | 2.50 | 1.10 |
| ❑ | 14 | Derek Jeter | 4.00 | 1.80 |
| ❑ | 15 | Jaret Wright | .40 | .18 |
| ❑ | 16 | Livan Hernandez | .40 | .18 |
| ❑ | 17 | Mike Piazza | 3.00 | 1.35 |
| ❑ | 18 | Juan Encarnacion | .40 | .18 |
| ❑ | 19 | Tony Gwynn | 2.00 | .90 |
| ❑ | 20 | Scott Rolen | 1.00 | .45 |
| ❑ | 21 | Roger Clemens | 2.00 | .90 |
| ❑ | 22 | Tony Clark | .40 | .18 |
| ❑ | 23 | Albert Belle | .60 | .25 |
| ❑ | 24 | Mo Vaughn | .40 | .18 |
| ❑ | 25 | Andruw Jones | 1.00 | .45 |
| ❑ | 26 | Jason Dickson | .40 | .18 |
| ❑ | 27 | Fernando Tatis | .40 | .18 |
| ❑ | 28 | Ivan Rodriguez | 1.25 | .55 |
| ❑ | 29 | Ricky Ledee | .40 | .18 |
| ❑ | 30 | Darin Erstad | 1.00 | .45 |
| ❑ | 31 | Brian Rose | .40 | .18 |
| ❑ | 32 | Magglio Ordonez RC | 4.00 | 1.80 |
| ❑ | 33 | Larry Walker | .40 | .18 |
| ❑ | 34 | Bobby Higginson | .40 | .18 |
| ❑ | 35 | Chili Davis | .40 | .18 |
| ❑ | 36 | Barry Bonds | 1.50 | .70 |
| ❑ | 37 | Vladimir Guerrero | 1.50 | .70 |
| ❑ | 38 | Jeff Bagwell | 1.25 | .55 |
| ❑ | 39 | Kenny Lofton | .40 | .18 |
| ❑ | 40 | Ryan Klesko | .40 | .18 |
| ❑ | 41 | Mike Cameron | .40 | .18 |
| ❑ | 42 | Charles Johnson | .40 | .18 |
| ❑ | 43 | Andy Pettitte | .40 | .18 |
| ❑ | 44 | Juan Gonzalez | 1.00 | .45 |
| ❑ | 45 | Tim Salmon | .40 | .18 |
| ❑ | 46 | Hideki Irabu | .40 | .18 |
| ❑ | 47 | Paul Molitor | 1.00 | .45 |
| ❑ | 48 | Edgar Renteria | .40 | .18 |
| ❑ | 49 | Manny Ramirez | 1.25 | .55 |
| ❑ | 50 | Jim Edmonds | 1.00 | .45 |
| ❑ | 51 | Bernie Williams | 1.00 | .45 |
| ❑ | 52 | Roberto Alomar | 1.00 | .45 |
| ❑ | 53 | David Justice | .60 | .25 |
| ❑ | 54 | Rey Ordonez | .40 | .18 |
| ❑ | 55 | Ken Caminiti | .40 | .18 |
| ❑ | 56 | Jose Guillen | .40 | .18 |
| ❑ | 57 | Randy Johnson | 1.25 | .55 |
| ❑ | 58 | Brady Anderson | .40 | .18 |
| ❑ | 59 | Hideo Nomo | 1.00 | .45 |
| ❑ | 60 | Tino Martinez | .40 | .18 |
| ❑ | 61 | John Smoltz | .50 | .23 |
| ❑ | 62 | Joe Carter | .50 | .23 |
| ❑ | 63 | Matt Williams | .75 | .35 |
| ❑ | 64 | Robin Ventura | .50 | .23 |
| ❑ | 65 | Barry Larkin | 1.25 | .55 |
| ❑ | 66 | Dante Bichette | .50 | .23 |
| ❑ | 67 | Travis Fryman | .50 | .23 |
| ❑ | 68 | Gary Sheffield | 1.25 | .55 |
| ❑ | 69 | Eric Karros | .50 | .23 |
| ❑ | 70 | Matt Stairs | .50 | .23 |
| ❑ | 71 | Al Martin | .50 | .23 |
| ❑ | 72 | Jay Buhner | .50 | .23 |
| ❑ | 73 | Ray Lankford | .50 | .23 |
| ❑ | 74 | Carlos Delgado | 1.25 | .55 |
| ❑ | 75 | Edgardo Alfonzo | .50 | .23 |
| ❑ | 76 | Rondell White | .50 | .23 |
| ❑ | 77 | Chuck Knoblauch | .50 | .23 |
| ❑ | 78 | Raul Mondesi | .50 | .23 |
| ❑ | 79 | Johnny Damon | .50 | .23 |
| ❑ | 80 | Matt Morris | .50 | .23 |
| ❑ | 81 | Tom Glavine | 1.25 | .55 |
| ❑ | 82 | Kevin Brown | .75 | .35 |
| ❑ | 83 | Garret Anderson | .50 | .23 |
| ❑ | 84 | Mike Mussina | 1.25 | .55 |
| ❑ | 85 | Pedro Martinez | 1.25 | .55 |
| ❑ | 86 | Craig Biggio | .75 | .35 |
| ❑ | 87 | Darryl Kile | .50 | .23 |
| ❑ | 88 | Rafael Palmeiro | 1.25 | .55 |
| ❑ | 89 | Jim Thome | .75 | .35 |
| ❑ | 90 | Andres Galarraga | .75 | .35 |
| ❑ | 91 | Sammy Sosa | 3.00 | 1.35 |
| ❑ | 92 | Willie Greene | .60 | .25 |
| ❑ | 93 | Vinny Castilla | .60 | .25 |
| ❑ | 94 | Justin Thompson | .60 | .25 |
| ❑ | 95 | Jeff King | .60 | .25 |
| ❑ | 96 | Jeff Cirillo | .60 | .25 |
| ❑ | 97 | Mark Grudzielanek | .60 | .25 |
| ❑ | 98 | Brad Radke | .60 | .25 |
| ❑ | 99 | John Olerud | .60 | .25 |
| ❑ | 100 | Curt Schilling | .60 | .25 |
| ❑ | 101 | Steve Finley | .60 | .25 |
| ❑ | 102 | J.T. Snow | .60 | .25 |
| ❑ | 103 | Edgar Martinez | 1.00 | .45 |
| ❑ | 104 | Wilson Alvarez | .60 | .25 |
| ❑ | 105 | Rusty Greer | .60 | .25 |
| ❑ | 106 | Pat Hentgen | .60 | .25 |
| ❑ | 107 | David Cone | .60 | .25 |
| ❑ | 108 | Fred McGriff | 1.00 | .45 |
| ❑ | 109 | Jason Giambi | 1.50 | .70 |
| ❑ | 110 | Tony Womack | .60 | .25 |
| ❑ | 111 | Bernard Gilkey | .60 | .25 |
| ❑ | 112 | Alan Benes | .60 | .25 |
| ❑ | 113 | Mark Grace | 1.50 | .70 |
| ❑ | 114 | Reggie Sanders | .60 | .25 |
| ❑ | 115 | Moises Alou | .60 | .25 |
| ❑ | 116 | John Jaha | .60 | .25 |
| ❑ | 117 | Henry Rodriguez | .60 | .25 |
| ❑ | 118 | Dean Palmer | .60 | .25 |
| ❑ | 119 | Mike Lieberthal | .60 | .25 |
| ❑ | 120 | Shawn Estes | .60 | .25 |

## 1999 Flair Showcase Row 3

| | MINT | NRMT |
|---|---|---|
| COMPLETE SET (144) | 60.00 | 27.00 |
| COMMON CARD (1-48) | .25 | .11 |
| COMMON CARD (49-96) | .25 | .11 |
| COMMON CARD (97-144) | .30 | .14 |
| ❑ 1 Mark McGwire | 4.00 | 1.80 |
| ❑ 2 Sammy Sosa | 2.00 | .90 |
| ❑ 3 Ken Griffey Jr. | 4.00 | 1.80 |
| ❑ 4 Chipper Jones | 2.50 | 1.10 |
| ❑ 5 Ben Grieve | .40 | .18 |
| ❑ 6 J.D. Drew | 1.00 | .45 |
| ❑ 7 Jeff Bagwell | 1.25 | .55 |
| ❑ 8 Cal Ripken | 4.00 | 1.80 |
| ❑ 9 Tony Gwynn | 2.00 | .90 |
| ❑ 10 Nomar Garciaparra | 3.00 | 1.35 |
| ❑ 11 Travis Lee | .25 | .11 |
| ❑ 12 Troy Glaus | 1.50 | .70 |
| ❑ 13 Mike Piazza | 3.00 | 1.35 |
| ❑ 14 Alex Rodriguez | 3.00 | 1.35 |
| ❑ 15 Kevin Brown | .60 | .25 |
| ❑ 16 Darin Erstad | 1.00 | .45 |
| ❑ 17 Scott Rolen | 1.00 | .45 |
| ❑ 18 Micah Bowie RC | .25 | .11 |
| ❑ 19 Juan Gonzalez | 1.00 | .45 |
| ❑ 20 Kerry Wood | .40 | .18 |
| ❑ 21 Roger Clemens | 2.00 | .90 |
| ❑ 22 Derek Jeter | 4.00 | 1.80 |
| ❑ 23 Pat Burrell RC | 5.00 | 2.20 |
| ❑ 24 Tim Salmon | .40 | .18 |
| ❑ 25 Barry Bonds | 1.50 | .70 |
| ❑ 26 Roosevelt Brown RC | .50 | .23 |
| ❑ 27 Vladimir Guerrero | 1.50 | .70 |
| ❑ 28 Randy Johnson | 1.25 | .55 |
| ❑ 29 Mo Vaughn | .40 | .18 |
| ❑ 30 Fernando Seguignol | .25 | .11 |
| ❑ 31 Greg Maddux | 2.50 | 1.10 |
| ❑ 32 Tony Clark | .25 | .11 |
| ❑ 33 Eric Chavez | .40 | .18 |
| ❑ 34 Kris Benson | .40 | .18 |
| ❑ 35 Frank Thomas | 2.00 | .90 |
| ❑ 36 Mario Encarnacion RC | .60 | .25 |
| ❑ 37 Gabe Kapler | .40 | .18 |
| ❑ 38 Jeremy Giambi | .25 | .11 |
| ❑ 39 Peter Tucci | .25 | .11 |
| ❑ 40 Manny Ramirez | 1.25 | .55 |
| ❑ 41 Albert Belle | .60 | .25 |
| ❑ 42 Warren Morris | .25 | .11 |
| ❑ 43 Michael Barrett | .25 | .11 |
| ❑ 44 Andruw Jones | 1.00 | .45 |
| ❑ 45 Carlos Delgado | 1.00 | .45 |
| ❑ 46 Jaret Wright | .25 | .11 |
| ❑ 47 Juan Encarnacion | .40 | .18 |
| ❑ 48 Scott Hunter RC | .50 | .23 |
| ❑ 49 Tino Martinez | .40 | .18 |
| ❑ 50 Craig Biggio | .60 | .25 |
| ❑ 51 Jim Thome | .60 | .25 |
| ❑ 52 Vinny Castilla | .40 | .18 |
| ❑ 53 Tom Glavine | 1.00 | .45 |
| ❑ 54 Bob Higginson | .40 | .18 |
| ❑ 55 Moises Alou | .40 | .18 |
| ❑ 56 Robin Ventura | .40 | .18 |
| ❑ 57 Bernie Williams | 1.00 | .45 |
| ❑ 58 Pedro Martinez | 1.25 | .55 |
| ❑ 59 Greg Vaughn | .40 | .18 |
| ❑ 60 Ray Lankford | .40 | .18 |
| ❑ 61 Jose Canseco | 1.25 | .55 |
| ❑ 62 Ivan Rodriguez | 1.25 | .55 |
| ❑ 63 Shawn Green | 1.00 | .45 |
| ❑ 64 Rafael Palmeiro | 1.00 | .45 |
| ❑ 65 Ellis Burks | .40 | .18 |
| ❑ 66 Jason Kendall | .40 | .18 |
| ❑ 67 David Wells | .40 | .18 |
| ❑ 68 Rondell White | .40 | .18 |
| ❑ 69 Gary Sheffield | 1.00 | .45 |
| ❑ 70 Ken Caminiti | .40 | .18 |
| ❑ 71 Cliff Floyd | .40 | .18 |
| ❑ 72 Larry Walker | .40 | .18 |
| ❑ 73 Bartolo Colon | .40 | .18 |
| ❑ 74 Barry Larkin | 1.00 | .45 |
| ❑ 75 Calvin Pickering | .25 | .11 |
| ❑ 76 Jim Edmonds | 1.00 | .45 |
| ❑ 77 Henry Rodriguez | .25 | .11 |
| ❑ 78 Roberto Alomar | 1.00 | .45 |
| ❑ 79 Andres Galarraga | .60 | .25 |
| ❑ 80 Richie Sexson | .40 | .18 |
| ❑ 81 Todd Helton | 1.25 | .55 |
| ❑ 82 Damion Easley | .25 | .11 |
| ❑ 83 Livan Hernandez | .25 | .11 |
| ❑ 84 Carlos Beltran | .40 | .18 |
| ❑ 85 Todd Hundley | .25 | .11 |
| ❑ 86 Todd Walker | .25 | .11 |
| ❑ 87 Scott Brosius | .40 | .18 |
| ❑ 88 Bob Abreu | .40 | .18 |
| ❑ 89 Corey Koskie | .25 | .11 |
| ❑ 90 Ruben Rivera | .25 | .11 |
| ❑ 91 Edgar Renteria | .25 | .11 |
| ❑ 92 Quinton McCracken | .25 | .11 |
| ❑ 93 Bernard Gilkey | .25 | .11 |
| ❑ 94 Shannon Stewart | .40 | .18 |
| ❑ 95 Dustin Hermanson | .25 | .11 |
| ❑ 96 Mike Caruso | .25 | .11 |
| ❑ 97 Alex Gonzalez | .30 | .14 |
| ❑ 98 Raul Mondesi | .50 | .23 |
| ❑ 99 David Cone | .50 | .23 |
| ❑ 100 Curt Schilling | .50 | .23 |
| ❑ 101 Brian Giles | .50 | .23 |
| ❑ 102 Edgar Martinez | .75 | .35 |
| ❑ 103 Rolando Arrojo | .30 | .14 |
| ❑ 104 Derek Bell | .30 | .14 |
| ❑ 105 Denny Neagle | .30 | .14 |
| ❑ 106 Marquis Grissom | .30 | .14 |
| ❑ 107 Bret Boone | .50 | .23 |
| ❑ 108 Mike Mussina | 1.25 | .55 |
| ❑ 109 John Smoltz | .50 | .23 |
| ❑ 110 Brett Tomko | .30 | .14 |
| ❑ 111 David Justice | .75 | .35 |
| ❑ 112 Andy Pettitte | .50 | .23 |
| ❑ 113 Eric Karros | .50 | .23 |
| ❑ 114 Dante Bichette | .50 | .23 |
| ❑ 115 Jeromy Burnitz | .50 | .23 |
| ❑ 116 Paul Konerko | .50 | .23 |
| ❑ 117 Steve Finley | .50 | .23 |
| ❑ 118 Ricky Ledee | .30 | .14 |
| ❑ 119 Edgardo Alfonzo | .50 | .23 |
| ❑ 120 Dean Palmer | .50 | .23 |
| ❑ 121 Rusty Greer | .50 | .23 |
| ❑ 122 Luis Gonzalez | .50 | .23 |
| ❑ 123 Randy Winn | .30 | .14 |
| ❑ 124 Jeff Kent | .75 | .35 |
| ❑ 125 Doug Glanville | .30 | .14 |
| ❑ 126 Justin Thompson | .30 | .14 |
| ❑ 127 Bret Saberhagen | .50 | .23 |
| ❑ 128 Wade Boggs | 1.50 | .70 |
| ❑ 129 Al Leiter | .50 | .23 |
| ❑ 130 Paul O'Neill | .50 | .23 |
| ❑ 131 Chan Ho Park | .50 | .23 |
| ❑ 132 Johnny Damon | .50 | .23 |
| ❑ 133 Darryl Kile | .50 | .23 |
| ❑ 134 Reggie Sanders | .30 | .14 |
| ❑ 135 Kevin Millwood | .50 | .23 |
| ❑ 136 Charles Johnson | .50 | .23 |
| ❑ 137 Ray Durham | .50 | .23 |
| ❑ 138 Rico Brogna | .30 | .14 |
| ❑ 139 Matt Williams | .50 | .23 |
| ❑ 140 Sandy Alomar Jr. | .50 | .23 |
| ❑ 141 Jeff Cirillo | .50 | .23 |
| ❑ 142 Devon White | .30 | .14 |
| ❑ 143 Andy Benes | .30 | .14 |
| ❑ 144 Mike Stanley | .30 | .14 |

## 1963 Fleer

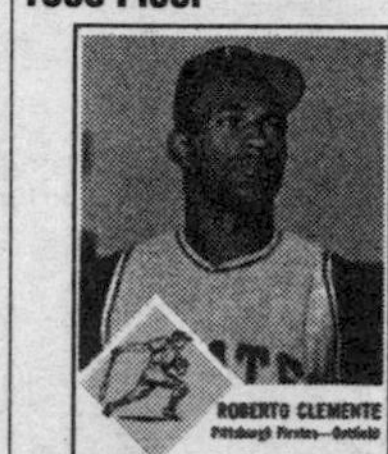


| | NRMT | VG-E |
|---|---|---|
| COMPLETE SET (67) | 2000.00 | 900.00 |
| WRAPPER (5-CENT) | 100.00 | 45.00 |
| ❑ 1 Steve Barber | 25.00 | 7.50 |
| ❑ 2 Ron Hansen | 15.00 | 6.75 |
| ❑ 3 Milt Pappas | 20.00 | 9.00 |
| ❑ 4 Brooks Robinson | 100.00 | 45.00 |
| ❑ 5 Willie Mays | 200.00 | 90.00 |
| ❑ 6 Lou Clinton | 15.00 | 6.75 |
| ❑ 7 Bill Monbouquette | 15.00 | 6.75 |
| ❑ 8 Carl Yastrzemski | 100.00 | 45.00 |
| ❑ 9 Ray Herbert | 15.00 | 6.75 |
| ❑ 10 Jim Landis | 15.00 | 6.75 |
| ❑ 11 Dick Donovan | 15.00 | 6.75 |
| ❑ 12 Tito Francona | 15.00 | 6.75 |
| ❑ 13 Jerry Kindall | 15.00 | 6.75 |
| ❑ 14 Frank Lary | 20.00 | 9.00 |
| ❑ 15 Dick Howser | 20.00 | 9.00 |
| ❑ 16 Jerry Lumpe | 15.00 | 6.75 |
| ❑ 17 Norm Siebern | 15.00 | 6.75 |
| ❑ 18 Don Lee | 15.00 | 6.75 |
| ❑ 19 Albie Pearson | 20.00 | 9.00 |
| ❑ 20 Bob Rodgers | 20.00 | 9.00 |
| ❑ 21 Leon Wagner | 15.00 | 6.75 |
| ❑ 22 Jim Kaat | 25.00 | 11.00 |
| ❑ 23 Vic Power | 20.00 | 9.00 |
| ❑ 24 Rich Rollins | 20.00 | 9.00 |
| ❑ 25 Bobby Richardson | 25.00 | 11.00 |
| ❑ 26 Ralph Terry | 20.00 | 9.00 |
| ❑ 27 Tom Cheney | 15.00 | 6.75 |
| ❑ 28 Chuck Cottier | 15.00 | 6.75 |
| ❑ 29 Jimmy Piersall | 20.00 | 9.00 |
| ❑ 30 Dave Stenhouse | 15.00 | 6.75 |
| ❑ 31 Glen Hobbie | 15.00 | 6.75 |
| ❑ 32 Ron Santo | 25.00 | 11.00 |
| ❑ 33 Gene Freese | 15.00 | 6.75 |
| ❑ 34 Vada Pinson | 25.00 | 11.00 |
| ❑ 35 Bob Purkey | 15.00 | 6.75 |
| ❑ 36 Joe Amalfitano | 15.00 | 6.75 |
| ❑ 37 Bob Aspromonte | 15.00 | 6.75 |
| ❑ 38 Dick Farrell | 15.00 | 6.75 |
| ❑ 39 Al Spangler | 15.00 | 6.75 |
| ❑ 40 Tommy Davis | 20.00 | 9.00 |
| ❑ 41 Don Drysdale | 75.00 | 34.00 |
| ❑ 42 Sandy Koufax | 200.00 | 90.00 |
| ❑ 43 Maury Wills RC | 100.00 | 45.00 |
| ❑ 44 Frank Bolling | 15.00 | 6.75 |
| ❑ 45 Warren Spahn | 75.00 | 34.00 |
| ❑ 46 Joe Adcock SP | 175.00 | 80.00 |
| ❑ 47 Roger Craig | 20.00 | 9.00 |
| ❑ 48 Al Jackson | 20.00 | 9.00 |
| ❑ 49 Rod Kanehl | 20.00 | 9.00 |
| ❑ 50 Ruben Amaro | 15.00 | 6.75 |
| ❑ 51 Johnny Callison | 20.00 | 9.00 |
| ❑ 52 Clay Dalrymple | 15.00 | 6.75 |
| ❑ 53 Don Demeter | 15.00 | 6.75 |
| ❑ 54 Art Mahaffey | 15.00 | 6.75 |
| ❑ 55 Smoky Burgess | 20.00 | 9.00 |
| ❑ 56 Roberto Clemente | 200.00 | 90.00 |
| ❑ 57 Roy Face | 20.00 | 9.00 |
| ❑ 58 Vern Law | 20.00 | 9.00 |
| ❑ 59 Bill Mazeroski | 25.00 | 11.00 |
| ❑ 60 Ken Boyer | 25.00 | 11.00 |
| ❑ 61 Bob Gibson | 75.00 | 34.00 |
| ❑ 62 Gene Oliver | 15.00 | 6.75 |

| Card | NRMT | VG-E |
|---|---|---|
| ❑ 63 Bill White | 20.00 | 9.00 |
| ❑ 64 Orlando Cepeda | 30.00 | 13.50 |
| ❑ 65 Jim Davenport | 15.00 | 6.75 |
| ❑ 66 Billy O'Dell | 25.00 | 7.50 |
| ❑ NNO Checklist card | 500.00 | 160.00 |

## 1981 Fleer

| | NRMT | VG-E |
|---|---|---|
| COMPLETE SET (660) | 30.00 | 13.50 |
| ❑ 1 Pete Rose UER (270 hits in '63; should be 170) | 3.00 | 1.35 |
| ❑ 2 Larry Bowa | .25 | .11 |
| ❑ 3 Manny Trillo | .10 | .05 |
| ❑ 4 Bob Boone | .25 | .11 |
| ❑ 5 Mike Schmidt (See also 640A) | 2.00 | .90 |
| ❑ 6 Steve Carlton P1 Golden Arm (Back "1066 Cardinals"; Number on back 6) | 1.00 | .45 |
| ❑ 6B Steve Carlton P2 Pitcher of Year (Back "1066 Cardinals") | 1.50 | .70 |
| ❑ 6C Steve Carlton P3 (1966 Cardinals) | 2.00 | .90 |
| ❑ 7 Tug McGraw (See 657A) | .25 | .11 |
| ❑ 8 Larry Christenson | .10 | .05 |
| ❑ 9 Bake McBride | .10 | .05 |
| ❑ 10 Greg Luzinski | .25 | .11 |
| ❑ 11 Ron Reed | .10 | .05 |
| ❑ 12 Dickie Noles | .10 | .05 |
| ❑ 13 Keith Moreland | .25 | .11 |
| ❑ 14 Bob Walk RC | .25 | .11 |
| ❑ 15 Lonnie Smith | .25 | .11 |
| ❑ 16 Dick Ruthven | .10 | .05 |
| ❑ 17 Sparky Lyle | .25 | .11 |
| ❑ 18 Greg Gross | .10 | .05 |
| ❑ 19 Garry Maddox | .10 | .05 |
| ❑ 20 Nino Espinosa | .10 | .05 |
| ❑ 21 George Vukovich | .10 | .05 |
| ❑ 22 John Vukovich | .10 | .05 |
| ❑ 23 Ramon Aviles | .10 | .05 |
| ❑ 24A Kevin Saucier P1 (Name on back "Ken") | .10 | .05 |
| ❑ 24B Kevin Saucier P2 (Name on back "Ken") | .10 | .05 |
| ❑ 24C Kevin Saucier P3 (Name on back "Kevin") | 1.00 | .45 |
| ❑ 25 Randy Lerch | .10 | .05 |
| ❑ 26 Del Unser | .10 | .05 |
| ❑ 27 Tim McCarver | .50 | .23 |
| ❑ 28 George Brett (See also 655A) | 2.50 | 1.10 |
| ❑ 29 Willie Wilson (See also 653A) | .25 | .11 |
| ❑ 30 Paul Splittorff | .10 | .05 |
| ❑ 31 Dan Quisenberry | .25 | .11 |
| ❑ 32A Amos Otis P1 (Batting Pose; "Outfield"; 32 on back) | .25 | .11 |
| ❑ 32B Amos Otis P2 Series Starter 483 on back | .25 | .11 |
| ❑ 33 Steve Busby | .10 | .05 |
| ❑ 34 U.L. Washington | .10 | .05 |
| ❑ 35 Dave Chalk | .10 | .05 |
| ❑ 36 Darrell Porter | .10 | .05 |
| ❑ 37 Marty Pattin | .10 | .05 |
| ❑ 38 Larry Gura | .10 | .05 |
| ❑ 39 Renie Martin | .10 | .05 |
| ❑ 40 Rich Gale | .10 | .05 |
| ❑ 41A Hal McRae P1 ("Royals" on front in black letters) | .50 | .23 |
| ❑ 41B Hal McRae P2 ("Royals" on front in blue letters) | .25 | .11 |
| ❑ 42 Dennis Leonard | .10 | .05 |
| ❑ 43 Willie Aikens | .10 | .05 |
| ❑ 44 Frank White | .25 | .11 |
| ❑ 45 Clint Hurdle | .10 | .05 |
| ❑ 46 John Wathan | .10 | .05 |
| ❑ 47 Pete LaCock | .10 | .05 |
| ❑ 48 Rance Mulliniks | .10 | .05 |
| ❑ 49 Jeff Twitty | .10 | .05 |
| ❑ 50 Jamie Quirk | .10 | .05 |
| ❑ 51 Art Howe | .25 | .11 |
| ❑ 52 Ken Forsch | .10 | .05 |
| ❑ 53 Vern Ruhle | .10 | .05 |
| ❑ 54 Joe Niekro | .25 | .11 |
| ❑ 55 Frank LaCorte | .10 | .05 |
| ❑ 56 J.R. Richard | .25 | .11 |
| ❑ 57 Nolan Ryan | 5.00 | 2.20 |
| ❑ 58 Enos Cabell | .10 | .05 |
| ❑ 59 Cesar Cedeno | .25 | .11 |
| ❑ 60 Jose Cruz | .25 | .11 |
| ❑ 61 Bill Virdon MG | .10 | .05 |
| ❑ 62 Terry Puhl | .10 | .05 |
| ❑ 63 Joaquin Andujar | .25 | .11 |
| ❑ 64 Alan Ashby | .10 | .05 |
| ❑ 65 Joe Sambito | .10 | .05 |
| ❑ 66 Denny Walling | .10 | .05 |
| ❑ 67 Jeff Leonard | .25 | .11 |
| ❑ 68 Luis Pujols | .10 | .05 |
| ❑ 69 Bruce Bochy | .10 | .05 |
| ❑ 70 Rafael Landestoy | .10 | .05 |
| ❑ 71 Dave Smith RC | .25 | .11 |
| ❑ 72 Danny Heep | .10 | .05 |
| ❑ 73 Julio Gonzalez | .10 | .05 |
| ❑ 74 Craig Reynolds | .10 | .05 |
| ❑ 75 Gary Woods | .10 | .05 |
| ❑ 76 Dave Bergman | .10 | .05 |
| ❑ 77 Randy Niemann | .10 | .05 |
| ❑ 78 Joe Morgan | 1.00 | .45 |
| ❑ 79 Reggie Jackson (See also 650A) | 1.25 | .55 |
| ❑ 80 Bucky Dent | .25 | .11 |
| ❑ 81 Tommy John | .50 | .23 |
| ❑ 82 Luis Tiant | .25 | .11 |
| ❑ 83 Rick Cerone | .10 | .05 |
| ❑ 84 Dick Howser MG | .25 | .11 |
| ❑ 85 Lou Piniella | .25 | .11 |
| ❑ 86 Ron Davis | .10 | .05 |
| ❑ 87A Graig Nettles P1 ERR (Name on back misspelled "Craig") | 5.00 | 2.20 |
| ❑ 87B Graig Nettles P2 COR ("Graig") | .25 | .11 |
| ❑ 88 Ron Guidry | .25 | .11 |
| ❑ 89 Rich Gossage | .50 | .23 |
| ❑ 90 Rudy May | .10 | .05 |
| ❑ 91 Gaylord Perry | 1.00 | .45 |
| ❑ 92 Eric Soderholm | .10 | .05 |
| ❑ 93 Bob Watson | .25 | .11 |
| ❑ 94 Bobby Murcer | .25 | .11 |
| ❑ 95 Bobby Brown | .10 | .05 |
| ❑ 96 Jim Spencer | .10 | .05 |
| ❑ 97 Tom Underwood | .10 | .05 |
| ❑ 98 Oscar Gamble | .10 | .05 |
| ❑ 99 Johnny Oates | .25 | .11 |
| ❑ 100 Fred Stanley | .10 | .05 |
| ❑ 101 Ruppert Jones | .10 | .05 |
| ❑ 102 Dennis Werth | .10 | .05 |
| ❑ 103 Joe Lefebvre | .10 | .05 |
| ❑ 104 Brian Doyle | .10 | .05 |
| ❑ 105 Aurelio Rodriguez | .10 | .05 |
| ❑ 106 Doug Bird | .10 | .05 |
| ❑ 107 Mike Griffin | .10 | .05 |
| ❑ 108 Tim Lollar | .10 | .05 |
| ❑ 109 Willie Randolph | .25 | .11 |
| ❑ 110 Steve Garvey | .50 | .23 |
| ❑ 111 Reggie Smith | .25 | .11 |
| ❑ 112 Don Sutton | 1.00 | .45 |
| ❑ 113 Burt Hooton | .10 | .05 |
| ❑ 114A Dave Lopes P1 (Small hand on back) | .50 | .23 |
| ❑ 114B Dave Lopes P2 (No hand) | .25 | .11 |
| ❑ 115 Dusty Baker | .50 | .23 |
| ❑ 116 Tom Lasorda MG | .25 | .11 |
| ❑ 117 Bill Russell | .25 | .11 |
| ❑ 118 Jerry Reuss UER ("Home:" omitted) | .25 | .11 |
| ❑ 119 Terry Forster | .10 | .05 |
| ❑ 120A Bob Welch P1 (Name on back is "Bob") | .25 | .11 |
| ❑ 120B Bob Welch P2 (Name on back is "Robert") | .50 | .23 |
| ❑ 121 Don Stanhouse | .10 | .05 |
| ❑ 122 Rick Monday | .25 | .11 |
| ❑ 123 Derrel Thomas | .10 | .05 |
| ❑ 124 Joe Ferguson | .10 | .05 |
| ❑ 125 Rick Sutcliffe | .25 | .11 |
| ❑ 126A Ron Cey P1 (Small hand on back) | .50 | .23 |
| ❑ 126B Ron Cey P2 (No hand) | .25 | .11 |
| ❑ 127 Dave Goltz | .10 | .05 |
| ❑ 128 Jay Johnstone | .25 | .11 |
| ❑ 129 Steve Yeager | .10 | .05 |
| ❑ 130 Gary Weiss | .10 | .05 |
| ❑ 131 Mike Scioscia RC | 1.00 | .45 |
| ❑ 132 Vic Davalillo | .10 | .05 |
| ❑ 133 Doug Rau | .10 | .05 |
| ❑ 134 Pepe Frias | .10 | .05 |
| ❑ 135 Mickey Hatcher | .25 | .11 |
| ❑ 136 Steve Howe | .25 | .11 |
| ❑ 137 Robert Castillo | .10 | .05 |
| ❑ 138 Gary Thomasson | .10 | .05 |
| ❑ 139 Rudy Law | .10 | .05 |
| ❑ 140 Fernando Valenzuela RC UER (Misspelled Fernand on card) | 2.00 | .90 |
| ❑ 141 Manny Mota | .25 | .11 |
| ❑ 142 Gary Carter | .50 | .23 |
| ❑ 143 Steve Rogers | .10 | .05 |
| ❑ 144 Warren Cromartie | .10 | .05 |
| ❑ 145 Andre Dawson | .50 | .23 |
| ❑ 146 Larry Parrish | .10 | .05 |
| ❑ 147 Rowland Office | .10 | .05 |
| ❑ 148 Ellis Valentine | .10 | .05 |
| ❑ 149 Dick Williams MG | .10 | .05 |
| ❑ 150 Bill Gullickson RC | .50 | .23 |
| ❑ 151 Elias Sosa | .10 | .05 |
| ❑ 152 John Tamargo | .10 | .05 |
| ❑ 153 Chris Speier | .10 | .05 |
| ❑ 154 Ron LeFlore | .25 | .11 |
| ❑ 155 Rodney Scott | .10 | .05 |
| ❑ 156 Stan Bahnsen | .10 | .05 |
| ❑ 157 Bill Lee | .25 | .11 |
| ❑ 158 Fred Norman | .10 | .05 |
| ❑ 159 Woodie Fryman | .10 | .05 |
| ❑ 160 David Palmer | .10 | .05 |
| ❑ 161 Jerry White | .10 | .05 |
| ❑ 162 Roberto Ramos | .10 | .05 |
| ❑ 163 John D'Acquisto | .10 | .05 |
| ❑ 164 Tommy Hutton | .10 | .05 |
| ❑ 165 Charlie Lea | .10 | .05 |
| ❑ 166 Scott Sanderson | .10 | .05 |
| ❑ 167 Ken Macha | .10 | .05 |
| ❑ 168 Tony Bernazard | .10 | .05 |
| ❑ 169 Jim Palmer | 1.00 | .45 |
| ❑ 170 Steve Stone | .25 | .11 |
| ❑ 171 Mike Flanagan | .25 | .11 |
| ❑ 172 Al Bumbry | .25 | .11 |
| ❑ 173 Doug DeCinces | .25 | .11 |
| ❑ 174 Scott McGregor | .10 | .05 |
| ❑ 175 Mark Belanger | .25 | .11 |
| ❑ 176 Tim Stoddard | .10 | .05 |
| ❑ 177A Rick Dempsey P1 (Small hand on front) | .50 | .23 |
| ❑ 177B Rick Dempsey P2 (No hand) | .25 | .11 |

❑ 178 Earl Weaver MG 1.00 .45
❑ 179 Tippy Martinez .10 .05
❑ 180 Dennis Martinez .50 .23
❑ 181 Sammy Stewart .10 .05
❑ 182 Rich Dauer .10 .05
❑ 183 Lee May .25 .11
❑ 184 Eddie Murray 2.00 .90
❑ 185 Benny Ayala .10 .05
❑ 186 John Lowenstein .10 .05
❑ 187 Gary Roenicke .10 .05
❑ 188 Ken Singleton .25 .11
❑ 189 Dan Graham .10 .05
❑ 190 Terry Crowley .10 .05
❑ 191 Kiko Garcia .10 .05
❑ 192 Dave Ford .10 .05
❑ 193 Mark Corey .10 .05
❑ 194 Lenn Sakata .10 .05
❑ 195 Doug DeCinces .25 .11
❑ 196 Johnny Bench 1.50 .70
❑ 197 Dave Concepcion .25 .11
❑ 198 Ray Knight .25 .11
❑ 199 Ken Griffey .50 .23
❑ 200 Tom Seaver 1.50 .70
❑ 201 Dave Collins .10 .05
❑ 202A George Foster P1 .50 .23
Slugger
(Number on back 216)
❑ 202B George Foster P2 .50 .23
Slugger
(Number on back 202)
❑ 203 Junior Kennedy .10 .05
❑ 204 Frank Pastore .10 .05
❑ 205 Dan Driessen .10 .05
❑ 206 Hector Cruz .10 .05
❑ 207 Paul Moskau .10 .05
❑ 208 Charlie Leibrandt RC .50 .23
❑ 209 Harry Spilman .10 .05
❑ 210 Joe Price .10 .05
❑ 211 Tom Hume .10 .05
❑ 212 Joe Nolan .10 .05
❑ 213 Doug Bair .10 .05
❑ 214 Mario Soto .10 .05
❑ 215A Bill Bonham P1 .50 .23
(Small hand on back)
❑ 215B Bill Bonham P2 .10 .05
(No hand)
❑ 216 George Foster .25 .11
(See 202)
❑ 217 Paul Householder .10 .05
❑ 218 Ron Oester .10 .05
❑ 219 Sam Mejias .10 .05
❑ 220 Sheldon Burnside .10 .05
❑ 221 Carl Yastrzemski 1.00 .45
❑ 222 Jim Rice .25 .11
❑ 223 Fred Lynn .25 .11
❑ 224 Carlton Fisk 1.00 .45
❑ 225 Rick Burleson .10 .05
❑ 226 Dennis Eckersley 1.00 .45
❑ 227 Butch Hobson .10 .05
❑ 228 Tom Burgmeier .10 .05
❑ 229 Garry Hancock .10 .05
❑ 230 Don Zimmer MG .25 .11
❑ 231 Steve Renko .10 .05
❑ 232 Dwight Evans .50 .23
❑ 233 Mike Torrez .10 .05
❑ 234 Bob Stanley .10 .05
❑ 235 Jim Dwyer .10 .05
❑ 236 Dave Stapleton .10 .05
❑ 237 Glenn Hoffman .10 .05
❑ 238 Jerry Remy .10 .05
❑ 239 Dick Drago .10 .05
❑ 240 Bill Campbell .10 .05
❑ 241 Tony Perez 1.00 .45
❑ 242 Phil Niekro 1.00 .45
❑ 243 Dale Murphy 1.00 .45
❑ 244 Bob Horner .25 .11
❑ 245 Jeff Burroughs .10 .05
❑ 246 Rick Camp .10 .05
❑ 247 Bobby Cox MG .25 .11
❑ 248 Bruce Benedict .10 .05
❑ 249 Gene Garber .10 .05
❑ 250 Jerry Royster .10 .05
❑ 251A Gary Matthews P1 .50 .23
(Small hand on back)
❑ 251B Gary Matthews P2 .25 .11
(No hand)

❑ 252 Chris Chambliss .25 .11
❑ 253 Luis Gomez .10 .05
❑ 254 Bill Nahorodny .10 .05
❑ 255 Doyle Alexander .10 .05
❑ 256 Brian Asselstine .10 .05
❑ 257 Biff Pocoroba .10 .05
❑ 258 Mike Lum .10 .05
❑ 259 Charlie Spikes .10 .05
❑ 260 Glenn Hubbard .10 .05
❑ 261 Tommy Boggs .10 .05
❑ 262 Al Hrabosky .10 .05
❑ 263 Rick Matula .10 .05
❑ 264 Preston Hanna .10 .05
❑ 265 Larry Bradford .10 .05
❑ 266 Rafael Ramirez .10 .05
❑ 267 Larry McWilliams .10 .05
❑ 268 Rod Carew 1.00 .45
❑ 269 Bobby Grich .25 .11
❑ 270 Carney Lansford .25 .11
❑ 271 Don Baylor .50 .23
❑ 272 Joe Rudi .25 .11
❑ 273 Dan Ford .10 .05
❑ 274 Jim Fregosi MG .10 .05
❑ 275 Dave Frost .10 .05
❑ 276 Frank Tanana .25 .11
❑ 277 Dickie Thon .25 .11
❑ 278 Jason Thompson .10 .05
❑ 279 Rick Miller .10 .05
❑ 280 Bert Campaneris .25 .11
❑ 281 Tom Donohue .10 .05
❑ 282 Brian Downing .25 .11
❑ 283 Fred Patek .10 .05
❑ 284 Bruce Kison .10 .05
❑ 285 Dave LaRoche .10 .05
❑ 286 Don Aase .10 .05
❑ 287 Jim Barr .10 .05
❑ 288 Alfredo Martinez .10 .05
❑ 289 Larry Harlow .10 .05
❑ 290 Andy Hassler .10 .05
❑ 291 Dave Kingman .50 .23
❑ 292 Bill Buckner .25 .11
❑ 293 Rick Reuschel .25 .11
❑ 294 Bruce Sutter .25 .11
❑ 295 Jerry Martin .10 .05
❑ 296 Scot Thompson .10 .05
❑ 297 Ivan DeJesus .10 .05
❑ 298 Steve Dillard .10 .05
❑ 299 Dick Tidrow .10 .05
❑ 300 Randy Martz .10 .05
❑ 301 Lenny Randle .10 .05
❑ 302 Lynn McGlothen .10 .05
❑ 303 Cliff Johnson .10 .05
❑ 304 Tim Blackwell .10 .05
❑ 305 Dennis Lamp .10 .05
❑ 306 Bill Caudill .10 .05
❑ 307 Carlos Lezcano .10 .05
❑ 308 Jim Tracy .10 .05
❑ 309 Doug Capilla UER .10 .05
(Cubs on front but
Braves on back)
❑ 310 Willie Hernandez .25 .11
❑ 311 Mike Vail .10 .05
❑ 312 Mike Krukow .10 .05
❑ 313 Barry Foote .10 .05
❑ 314 Larry Biittner .10 .05
❑ 315 Mike Tyson .10 .05
❑ 316 Lee Mazzilli .10 .05
❑ 317 John Stearns .10 .05
❑ 318 Alex Trevino .10 .05
❑ 319 Craig Swan .10 .05
❑ 320 Frank Taveras .10 .05
❑ 321 Steve Henderson .10 .05
❑ 322 Neil Allen .10 .05
❑ 323 Mark Bomback .10 .05
❑ 324 Mike Jorgensen .10 .05
❑ 325 Joe Torre MG .25 .11
❑ 326 Elliott Maddox .10 .05
❑ 327 Pete Falcone .10 .05
❑ 328 Ray Burris .10 .05
❑ 329 Claudell Washington .10 .05
❑ 330 Doug Flynn .10 .05
❑ 331 Joel Youngblood .10 .05
❑ 332 Bill Almon .10 .05
❑ 333 Tom Hausman .10 .05
❑ 334 Pat Zachry .10 .05
❑ 335 Jeff Reardon RC 1.00 .45

❑ 336 Wally Backman .25 .11
❑ 337 Dan Norman .10 .05
❑ 338 Jerry Morales .10 .05
❑ 339 Ed Farmer .10 .05
❑ 340 Bob Molinaro .10 .05
❑ 341 Todd Cruz .10 .05
❑ 342A Britt Burns P1 .50 .23
(Small hand on front)
❑ 342B Britt Burns P2 .25 .11
(No hand)
❑ 343 Kevin Bell .10 .05
❑ 344 Tony LaRussa MG .25 .11
❑ 345 Steve Trout .10 .05
❑ 346 Harold Baines RC 5.00 2.20
❑ 347 Richard Wortham .10 .05
❑ 348 Wayne Nordhagen .10 .05
❑ 349 Mike Squires .10 .05
❑ 350 Lamar Johnson .10 .05
❑ 351 Rickey Henderson 2.50 1.10
(Most Stolen Bases AL)
❑ 352 Francisco Barrios .10 .05
❑ 353 Thad Bosley .10 .05
❑ 354 Chet Lemon .10 .05
❑ 355 Bruce Kimm .10 .05
❑ 356 Richard Dotson .10 .05
❑ 357 Jim Morrison .10 .05
❑ 358 Mike Proly .10 .05
❑ 359 Greg Pryor .10 .05
❑ 360 Dave Parker .25 .11
❑ 361 Omar Moreno .10 .05
❑ 362A Kent Tekulve P1 .25 .11
(Back 1071 Waterbury
and 1078 Pirates)
❑ 362B Kent Tekulve P2 .25 .11
(1971 Waterbury and
1978 Pirates)
❑ 363 Willie Stargell 1.00 .45
❑ 364 Phil Garner .25 .11
❑ 365 Ed Ott .10 .05
❑ 366 Don Robinson .10 .05
❑ 367 Chuck Tanner MG .25 .11
❑ 368 Jim Rooker .10 .05
❑ 369 Dale Berra .10 .05
❑ 370 Jim Bibby .10 .05
❑ 371 Steve Nicosia .10 .05
❑ 372 Mike Easler .10 .05
❑ 373 Bill Robinson .25 .11
❑ 374 Lee Lacy .10 .05
❑ 375 John Candelaria .25 .11
❑ 376 Manny Sanguillen .25 .11
❑ 377 Rick Rhoden .10 .05
❑ 378 Grant Jackson .10 .05
❑ 379 Tim Foli .10 .05
❑ 380 Rod Scurry .10 .05
❑ 381 Bill Madlock .25 .11
❑ 382A Kurt Bevacqua .25 .11
P1 ERR
(P on cap backwards)
❑ 382B Kurt Bevacqua P2 .10 .05
COR
❑ 383 Bert Blyleven .50 .23
❑ 384 Eddie Solomon .10 .05
❑ 385 Enrique Romo .10 .05
❑ 386 John Milner .10 .05
❑ 387 Mike Hargrove .25 .11
❑ 388 Jorge Orta .10 .05
❑ 389 Toby Harrah .25 .11
❑ 390 Tom Veryzer .10 .05
❑ 391 Miguel Dilone .10 .05
❑ 392 Dan Spillner .10 .05
❑ 393 Jack Brohamer .10 .05
❑ 394 Wayne Garland .10 .05
❑ 395 Sid Monge .10 .05
❑ 396 Rick Waits .10 .05
❑ 397 Joe Charboneau RC 1.00 .45
❑ 398 Gary Alexander .10 .05
❑ 399 Jerry Dybzinski .10 .05
❑ 400 Mike Stanton .10 .05
❑ 401 Mike Paxton .10 .05
❑ 402 Gary Gray .10 .05
❑ 403 Rick Manning .10 .05
❑ 404 Bo Diaz .10 .05
❑ 405 Ron Hassey .10 .05
❑ 406 Ross Grimsley .10 .05
❑ 407 Victor Cruz .10 .05
❑ 408 Len Barker .10 .05

❑ 409 Bob Bailor .10 .05
❑ 410 Otto Velez .10 .05
❑ 411 Ernie Whitt .10 .05
❑ 412 Jim Clancy .10 .05
❑ 413 Barry Bonnell .10 .05
❑ 414 Dave Stieb .25 .11
❑ 415 Damaso Garcia .10 .05
❑ 416 John Mayberry .10 .05
❑ 417 Roy Howell .10 .05
❑ 418 Danny Ainge RC 2.00 .90
❑ 419A Jesse Jefferson P1 .10 .05
(Back says Pirates)
❑ 419B Jesse Jefferson P2 .10 .05
(Back says Pirates)
❑ 419C Jesse Jefferson P3 1.00 .45
(Back says Blue Jays)
❑ 420 Joey McLaughlin .10 .05
❑ 421 Lloyd Moseby .25 .11
❑ 422 Alvis Woods .10 .05
❑ 423 Garth Iorg .10 .05
❑ 424 Doug Ault .10 .05
❑ 425 Ken Schrom .10 .05
❑ 426 Mike Willis .10 .05
❑ 427 Steve Braun .10 .05
❑ 428 Bob Davis .10 .05
❑ 429 Jerry Garvin .10 .05
❑ 430 Alfredo Griffin .10 .05
❑ 431 Bob Mattick MG .10 .05
❑ 432 Vida Blue .25 .11
❑ 433 Jack Clark .25 .11
❑ 434 Willie McCovey 1.00 .45
❑ 435 Mike Ivie .10 .05
❑ 436A Darrel Evans P1 ERR .50 .23
(Name on front "Darrel")
❑ 436B Darrell Evans P2 COR .50 .23
(Name on front "Darrell")
❑ 437 Terry Whitfield .10 .05
❑ 438 Rennie Stennett .10 .05
❑ 439 John Montefusco .10 .05
❑ 440 Jim Wohlford .10 .05
❑ 441 Bill North .10 .05
❑ 442 Milt May .10 .05
❑ 443 Max Venable .10 .05
❑ 444 Ed Whitson .10 .05
❑ 445 Al Holland .10 .05
❑ 446 Randy Moffitt .10 .05
❑ 447 Bob Knepper .10 .05
❑ 448 Gary Lavelle .10 .05
❑ 449 Greg Minton .10 .05
❑ 450 Johnnie LeMaster .10 .05
❑ 451 Larry Herndon .10 .05
❑ 452 Rich Murray .10 .05
❑ 453 Joe Pettini .10 .05
❑ 454 Allen Ripley .10 .05
❑ 455 Dennis Littlejohn .10 .05
❑ 456 Tom Griffin .10 .05
❑ 457 Alan Hargesheimer .10 .05
❑ 458 Joe Strain .10 .05
❑ 459 Steve Kemp .10 .05
❑ 460 Sparky Anderson MG .25 .11
❑ 461 Alan Trammell .50 .23
❑ 462 Mark Fidrych 1.00 .45
❑ 463 Lou Whitaker 1.00 .45
❑ 464 Dave Rozema .10 .05
❑ 465 Milt Wilcox .10 .05
❑ 466 Champ Summers .10 .05
❑ 467 Lance Parrish .25 .11
❑ 468 Dan Petry .10 .05
❑ 469 Pat Underwood .10 .05
❑ 470 Rick Peters .10 .05
❑ 471 Al Cowens .10 .05
❑ 472 John Wockenfuss .10 .05
❑ 473 Tom Brookens .10 .05
❑ 474 Richie Hebner .10 .05
❑ 475 Jack Morris 1.00 .45
❑ 476 Jim Lentine .10 .05
❑ 477 Bruce Robbins .10 .05
❑ 478 Mark Wagner .10 .05
❑ 479 Tim Corcoran .10 .05
❑ 480A Stan Papi P1 .25 .11
(Front as Pitcher)
❑ 480B Stan Papi P2 .10 .05
(Front as Shortstop)
❑ 481 Kirk Gibson RC 2.00 .90
❑ 482 Dan Schatzeder .10 .05
❑ 483A Amos Otis P1 .25 .11
(See card 32)
❑ 483B Amos Otis P2 .25 .11
(See card 32)
❑ 484 Dave Winfield 1.00 .45
❑ 485 Rollie Fingers 1.00 .45
❑ 486 Gene Richards .10 .05
❑ 487 Randy Jones .10 .05
❑ 488 Ozzie Smith 3.00 1.35
❑ 489 Gene Tenace .25 .11
❑ 490 Bill Fahey .10 .05
❑ 491 John Curtis .10 .05
❑ 492 Dave Cash .10 .05
❑ 493A Tim Flannery P1 .25 .11
(Batting right)
❑ 493B Tim Flannery P2 .10 .05
(Batting left)
❑ 494 Jerry Mumphrey .10 .05
❑ 495 Bob Shirley .10 .05
❑ 496 Steve Mura .10 .05
❑ 497 Eric Rasmussen .10 .05
❑ 498 Broderick Perkins .10 .05
❑ 499 Barry Evans .10 .05
❑ 500 Chuck Baker .10 .05
❑ 501 Luis Salazar .10 .05
❑ 502 Gary Lucas .10 .05
❑ 503 Mike Armstrong .10 .05
❑ 504 Jerry Turner .10 .05
❑ 505 Dennis Kinney .10 .05
❑ 506 Willie Montanez UER .10 .05
(Misspelled Willy on card front)
❑ 507 Gorman Thomas .25 .11
❑ 508 Ben Oglivie .25 .11
❑ 509 Larry Hisle .10 .05
❑ 510 Sal Bando .25 .11
❑ 511 Robin Yount 1.00 .45
❑ 512 Mike Caldwell .10 .05
❑ 513 Sixto Lezcano .10 .05
❑ 514A Bill Travers P1 ERR .25 .11
("Jerry Augustine" with Augustine back)
❑ 514B Bill Travers P2 COR .10 .05
❑ 515 Paul Molitor 2.00 .90
❑ 516 Moose Haas .10 .05
❑ 517 Bill Castro .10 .05
❑ 518 Jim Slaton .10 .05
❑ 519 Lary Sorensen .10 .05
❑ 520 Bob McClure .10 .05
❑ 521 Charlie Moore .10 .05
❑ 522 Jim Gantner .25 .11
❑ 523 Reggie Cleveland .10 .05
❑ 524 Don Money .10 .05
❑ 525 Bill Travers .10 .05
❑ 526 Buck Martinez .10 .05
❑ 527 Dick Davis .10 .05
❑ 528 Ted Simmons .25 .11
❑ 529 Garry Templeton .10 .05
❑ 530 Ken Reitz .10 .05
❑ 531 Tony Scott .10 .05
❑ 532 Ken Oberkfell .10 .05
❑ 533 Bob Sykes .10 .05
❑ 534 Keith Smith .10 .05
❑ 535 John Littlefield .10 .05
❑ 536 Jim Kaat .25 .11
❑ 537 Bob Forsch .10 .05
❑ 538 Mike Phillips .10 .05
❑ 539 Terry Landrum .10 .05
❑ 540 Leon Durham .25 .11
❑ 541 Terry Kennedy .10 .05
❑ 542 George Hendrick .10 .05
❑ 543 Dane Iorg .10 .05
❑ 544 Mark Littell .10 .05
❑ 545 Keith Hernandez .25 .11
❑ 546 Silvio Martinez .10 .05
❑ 547A Don Hood P1 ERR .25 .11
("Pete Vuckovich" with Vuckovich back)
❑ 547B Don Hood P2 COR .10 .05
❑ 548 Bobby Bonds .25 .11
❑ 549 Mike Ramsey .10 .05
❑ 550 Tom Herr .25 .11
❑ 551 Roy Smalley .10 .05
❑ 552 Jerry Koosman .25 .11
❑ 553 Ken Landreaux .10 .05
❑ 554 John Castino .10 .05
❑ 555 Doug Corbett .10 .05
❑ 556 Bombo Rivera .10 .05
❑ 557 Ron Jackson .10 .05
❑ 558 Butch Wynegar .10 .05
❑ 559 Hosken Powell .10 .05
❑ 560 Pete Redfern .10 .05
❑ 561 Roger Erickson .10 .05
❑ 562 Glenn Adams .10 .05
❑ 563 Rick Sofield .10 .05
❑ 564 Geoff Zahn .10 .05
❑ 565 Pete Mackanin .10 .05
❑ 566 Mike Cubbage .10 .05
❑ 567 Darrell Jackson .10 .05
❑ 568 Dave Edwards .10 .05
❑ 569 Rob Wilfong .10 .05
❑ 570 Sal Butera .10 .05
❑ 571 Jose Morales .10 .05
❑ 572 Rick Langford .10 .05
❑ 573 Mike Norris .10 .05
❑ 574 Rickey Henderson 5.00 2.20
❑ 575 Tony Armas .25 .11
❑ 576 Dave Revering .10 .05
❑ 577 Jeff Newman .10 .05
❑ 578 Bob Lacey .10 .05
❑ 579 Brian Kingman .10 .05
❑ 580 Mitchell Page .10 .05
❑ 581 Billy Martin MG .50 .23
❑ 582 Rob Picciolo .10 .05
❑ 583 Mike Heath .10 .05
❑ 584 Mickey Klutts .10 .05
❑ 585 Orlando Gonzalez .10 .05
❑ 586 Mike Davis .10 .05
❑ 587 Wayne Gross .10 .05
❑ 588 Matt Keough .10 .05
❑ 589 Steve McCatty .10 .05
❑ 590 Dwayne Murphy .10 .05
❑ 591 Mario Guerrero .10 .05
❑ 592 Dave McKay .10 .05
❑ 593 Jim Essian .10 .05
❑ 594 Dave Heaverlo .10 .05
❑ 595 Maury Wills MG .25 .11
❑ 596 Juan Beniquez .10 .05
❑ 597 Rodney Craig .10 .05
❑ 598 Jim Anderson .10 .05
❑ 599 Floyd Bannister .10 .05
❑ 600 Bruce Bochte .10 .05
❑ 601 Julio Cruz .10 .05
❑ 602 Ted Cox .10 .05
❑ 603 Dan Meyer .10 .05
❑ 604 Larry Cox .10 .05
❑ 605 Bill Stein .10 .05
❑ 606 Steve Garvey .50 .23
(Most Hits NL)
❑ 607 Dave Roberts .10 .05
❑ 608 Leon Roberts .10 .05
❑ 609 Reggie Walton .10 .05
❑ 610 Dave Edler .10 .05
❑ 611 Larry Milbourne .10 .05
❑ 612 Kim Allen .10 .05
❑ 613 Mario Mendoza .10 .05
❑ 614 Tom Paciorek .25 .11
❑ 615 Glenn Abbott .10 .05
❑ 616 Joe Simpson .10 .05
❑ 617 Mickey Rivers .25 .11
❑ 618 Jim Kern .10 .05
❑ 619 Jim Sundberg .25 .11
❑ 620 Richie Zisk .10 .05
❑ 621 Jon Matlack .10 .05
❑ 622 Ferguson Jenkins 1.00 .45
❑ 623 Pat Corrales MG .10 .05
❑ 624 Ed Figueroa .10 .05
❑ 625 Buddy Bell .25 .11
❑ 626 Al Oliver .25 .11
❑ 627 Doc Medich .10 .05
❑ 628 Bump Wills .10 .05
❑ 629 Rusty Staub .25 .11
❑ 630 Pat Putnam .10 .05
❑ 631 John Grubb .10 .05
❑ 632 Danny Darwin .10 .05
❑ 633 Ken Clay .10 .05
❑ 634 Jim Norris .10 .05
❑ 635 John Butcher .10 .05
❑ 636 Dave Roberts .10 .05
❑ 637 Billy Sample .10 .05
❑ 638 Carl Yastrzemski 1.00 .45

❑ 639 Cecil Cooper .25 .11
❑ 640 Mike Schmidt P1 2.00 .90
(Portrait; "Third Base"; number on back 5)
❑ 640B Mike Schmidt P2 2.00 .90
("1980 Home Run King"; 640 on back)
❑ 641A CL: Phils/Royals P1 .25 .11
41 is Hal McRae
❑ 641B CL: Phils/Royals P2 .25 .11
(41 is Hal McRae, Double Threat)
❑ 642 CL: Astros/Yankees .10 .05
❑ 643 CL: Expos/Dodgers .10 .05
❑ 644A CL: Reds/Orioles P1 .25 .11
(202 is George Foster; Joe Nolan pitcher, should be catcher)
❑ 644B CL: Reds/Orioles P2 .25 .11
(202 is Foster Slugger; Joe Nolan pitcher, should be catcher)
❑ 645 Pete Rose 1.25 .55
Larry Bowa
Mike Schmidt
Triple Threat P1
(No number on back)
❑ 645B Pete Rose 2.00 .90
Larry Bowa
Mike Schmidt
Triple Threat P2
(Back numbered 645)
❑ 646 CL: Braves/Red Sox .10 .05
❑ 647 CL: Cubs/Angels .10 .05
❑ 648 CL: Mets/White Sox .10 .05
❑ 649 CL: Indians/Pirates .10 .05
❑ 650 Reggie Jackson 1.25 .55
Mr. Baseball P1
(Number on back 79)
❑ 650B Reggie Jackson 1.00 .45
Mr. Baseball P2
(Number on back 650)
❑ 651 CL: Giants/Blue Jays .10 .05
❑ 652A CL: Tigers/Padres P1 .25 .11
(483 is listed)
❑ 652B CL: Tigers/Padres P2 .25 .11
(483 is deleted)
❑ 653A Willie Wilson P1 .25 .11
Most Hits Most Runs
(Number on back 29)
❑ 653B Willie Wilson P2 .25 .11
Most Hits Most Runs
(Number on back 653)
❑ 654A CL:Brewers/Cards P1 .25 .11
(514 Jerry Augustine; 547 Pete Vuckovich)
❑ 654B CL:Brewers/Cards P2 .25 .11
(514 Billy Travers; 547 Don Hood)
❑ 655 George Brett P1 2.50 1.10
.390 Average
(Number on back 28)
❑ 655B George Brett P2 4.00 1.80
.390 Average
(Number on back 655)
❑ 656 CL: Twins/Oakland A's .25 .11
❑ 657A Tug McGraw P1 .25 .11
Game Saver
(Number on back 7)
❑ 657B Tug McGraw P2 .25 .11
Game Saver
(Number on back 657)
❑ 658 CL: Rangers/Mariners .10 .05
❑ 659A Checklist P1 .10 .05
of Special Cards
(Last lines on front, Wilson Most Hits)
❑ 659B Checklist P2 .10 .05
of Special Cards
(Last lines on front, Otis Series Starter)
❑ 660 Steve Carlton P1 1.00 .45
Golden Arm
(Number on back 660 Back 1066 Cardinals)
❑ 660B Steve Carlton P2 2.00 .90
Golden Arm
(1966 Cardinals)

## 1982 Fleer

| | NRMT | VG-E |
|---|---|---|
| COMPLETE SET (660) | 60.00 | 27.00 |

❑ 1 Dusty Baker .40 .18
❑ 2 Robert Castillo .10 .05
❑ 3 Ron Cey .20 .09
❑ 4 Terry Forster .10 .05
❑ 5 Steve Garvey .40 .18
❑ 6 Dave Goltz .10 .05
❑ 7 Pedro Guerrero .20 .09
❑ 8 Burt Hooton .10 .05
❑ 9 Steve Howe .10 .05
❑ 10 Jay Johnstone .20 .09
❑ 11 Ken Landreaux .10 .05
❑ 12 Dave Lopes .20 .09
❑ 13 Mike A. Marshall .20 .09
❑ 14 Bobby Mitchell .10 .05
❑ 15 Rick Monday .10 .05
❑ 16 Tom Niedenfuer .10 .05
❑ 17 Ted Power RC .10 .05
❑ 18 Jerry Reuss UER .20 .09
("Home:" omitted)
❑ 19 Ron Roenicke .10 .05
❑ 20 Bill Russell .10 .05
❑ 21 Steve Sax RC .75 .35
❑ 22 Mike Scioscia .20 .09
❑ 23 Reggie Smith .20 .09
❑ 24 Dave Stewart RC 1.00 .45
❑ 25 Rick Sutcliffe .20 .09
❑ 26 Derrel Thomas .10 .05
❑ 27 Fernando Valenzuela .75 .35
❑ 28 Bob Welch .20 .09
❑ 29 Steve Yeager .10 .05
❑ 30 Bobby Brown .10 .05
❑ 31 Rick Cerone .10 .05
❑ 32 Ron Davis .10 .05
❑ 33 Bucky Dent .20 .09
❑ 34 Barry Foote .10 .05
❑ 35 George Frazier .10 .05
❑ 36 Oscar Gamble .10 .05
❑ 37 Rich Gossage .40 .18
❑ 38 Ron Guidry .20 .09
❑ 39 Reggie Jackson 1.00 .45
❑ 40 Tommy John .40 .18
❑ 41 Rudy May .10 .05
❑ 42 Larry Milbourne .10 .05
❑ 43 Jerry Mumphrey .10 .05
❑ 44 Bobby Murcer .20 .09
❑ 45 Gene Nelson .10 .05
❑ 46 Graig Nettles .20 .09
❑ 47 Johnny Oates .20 .09
❑ 48 Lou Piniella .20 .09
❑ 49 Willie Randolph .20 .09
❑ 50 Rick Reuschel .20 .09
❑ 51 Dave Revering .10 .05
❑ 52 Dave Righetti RC .75 .35
❑ 53 Aurelio Rodriguez .10 .05
❑ 54 Bob Watson .20 .09
❑ 55 Dennis Werth .10 .05
❑ 56 Dave Winfield .75 .35
❑ 57 Johnny Bench 1.25 .55
❑ 58 Bruce Berenyi .10 .05
❑ 59 Larry Biittner .10 .05
❑ 60 Scott Brown .10 .05
❑ 61 Dave Collins .10 .05
❑ 62 Geoff Combe .10 .05
❑ 63 Dave Concepcion .20 .09
❑ 64 Dan Driessen .10 .05
❑ 65 Joe Edelen .10 .05
❑ 66 George Foster .20 .09
❑ 67 Ken Griffey .20 .09
❑ 68 Paul Householder .10 .05
❑ 69 Tom Hume .10 .05
❑ 70 Junior Kennedy .10 .05
❑ 71 Ray Knight .20 .09
❑ 72 Mike LaCoss .10 .05
❑ 73 Rafael Landestoy .10 .05
❑ 74 Charlie Leibrandt .10 .05
❑ 75 Sam Mejias .10 .05
❑ 76 Paul Moskau .10 .05
❑ 77 Joe Nolan .10 .05
❑ 78 Mike O'Berry .10 .05
❑ 79 Ron Oester .10 .05
❑ 80 Frank Pastore .10 .05
❑ 81 Joe Price .10 .05
❑ 82 Tom Seaver 1.25 .55
❑ 83 Mario Soto .10 .05
❑ 84 Mike Vail .10 .05
❑ 85 Tony Armas .10 .05
❑ 86 Shooty Babitt .10 .05
❑ 87 Dave Beard .10 .05
❑ 88 Rick Bosetti .10 .05
❑ 89 Keith Drumwright .10 .05
❑ 90 Wayne Gross .10 .05
❑ 91 Mike Heath .10 .05
❑ 92 Rickey Henderson 2.00 .90
❑ 93 Cliff Johnson .10 .05
❑ 94 Jeff Jones .10 .05
❑ 95 Matt Keough .10 .05
❑ 96 Brian Kingman .10 .05
❑ 97 Mickey Klutts .10 .05
❑ 98 Rick Langford .10 .05
❑ 99 Steve McCatty .10 .05
❑ 100 Dave McKay .10 .05
❑ 101 Dwayne Murphy .10 .05
❑ 102 Jeff Newman .10 .05
❑ 103 Mike Norris .10 .05
❑ 104 Bob Owchinko .10 .05
❑ 105 Mitchell Page .10 .05
❑ 106 Rob Picciolo .10 .05
❑ 107 Jim Spencer .10 .05
❑ 108 Fred Stanley .10 .05
❑ 109 Tom Underwood .10 .05
❑ 110 Joaquin Andujar .20 .09
❑ 111 Steve Braun .10 .05
❑ 112 Bob Forsch .10 .05
❑ 113 George Hendrick .10 .05
❑ 114 Keith Hernandez .20 .09
❑ 115 Tom Herr .20 .09
❑ 116 Dane Iorg .10 .05
❑ 117 Jim Kaat .20 .09
❑ 118 Tito Landrum .10 .05
❑ 119 Sixto Lezcano .10 .05
❑ 120 Mark Littell .10 .05
❑ 121 John Martin .10 .05
❑ 122 Silvio Martinez .10 .05
❑ 123 Ken Oberkfell .10 .05
❑ 124 Darrell Porter .20 .09
❑ 125 Mike Ramsey .10 .05
❑ 126 Orlando Sanchez .10 .05
❑ 127 Bob Shirley .10 .05
❑ 128 Lary Sorensen .10 .05
❑ 129 Bruce Sutter .20 .09
❑ 130 Bob Sykes .10 .05
❑ 131 Garry Templeton .10 .05
❑ 132 Gene Tenace .20 .09
❑ 133 Jerry Augustine .10 .05
❑ 134 Sal Bando .20 .09
❑ 135 Mark Brouhard .10 .05
❑ 136 Mike Caldwell .10 .05
❑ 137 Reggie Cleveland .10 .05
❑ 138 Cecil Cooper .20 .09
❑ 139 Jamie Easterly .10 .05
❑ 140 Marshall Edwards .10 .05
❑ 141 Rollie Fingers .75 .35
❑ 142 Jim Gantner .20 .09
❑ 143 Moose Haas .10 .05
❑ 144 Larry Hisle .10 .05

❑ 145 Roy Howell .10 .05
❑ 146 Rickey Keeton .10 .05
❑ 147 Randy Lerch .10 .05
❑ 148 Paul Molitor 1.00 .45
❑ 149 Don Money .10 .05
❑ 150 Charlie Moore .10 .05
❑ 151 Ben Oglivie .20 .09
❑ 152 Ted Simmons .20 .09
❑ 153 Jim Slaton .10 .05
❑ 154 Gorman Thomas .20 .09
❑ 155 Robin Yount .75 .35
❑ 156 Pete Vuckovich .10 .05
(Should precede Yount
in the team order)
❑ 157 Benny Ayala .10 .05
❑ 158 Mark Belanger .10 .05
❑ 159 Al Bumbry .10 .05
❑ 160 Terry Crowley .10 .05
❑ 161 Rich Dauer .10 .05
❑ 162 Doug DeCinces .20 .09
❑ 163 Rick Dempsey .20 .09
❑ 164 Jim Dwyer .10 .05
❑ 165 Mike Flanagan .20 .09
❑ 166 Dave Ford .10 .05
❑ 167 Dan Graham .10 .05
❑ 168 Wayne Krenchicki .10 .05
❑ 169 John Lowenstein .10 .05
❑ 170 Dennis Martinez .40 .18
❑ 171 Tippy Martinez .10 .05
❑ 172 Scott McGregor .10 .05
❑ 173 Jose Morales .10 .05
❑ 174 Eddie Murray 1.00 .45
❑ 175 Jim Palmer .75 .35
❑ 176 Cal Ripken 40.00 18.00
(Fleer Ripken cards from 1982
through 1993 erroneously have 22
games played in 1981, not 23.) RC !
❑ 177 Gary Roenicke .10 .05
❑ 178 Lenn Sakata .10 .05
❑ 179 Ken Singleton .20 .09
❑ 180 Sammy Stewart .10 .05
❑ 181 Tim Stoddard .10 .05
❑ 182 Steve Stone .20 .09
❑ 183 Stan Bahnsen .10 .05
❑ 184 Ray Burris .10 .05
❑ 185 Gary Carter .40 .18
❑ 186 Warren Cromartie .10 .05
❑ 187 Andre Dawson .40 .18
❑ 188 Terry Francona .40 .18
❑ 189 Woodie Fryman .10 .05
❑ 190 Bill Gullickson .10 .05
❑ 191 Grant Jackson .10 .05
❑ 192 Wallace Johnson .10 .05
❑ 193 Charlie Lea .10 .05
❑ 194 Bill Lee .20 .09
❑ 195 Jerry Manuel .10 .05
❑ 196 Brad Mills .10 .05
❑ 197 John Milner .10 .05
❑ 198 Rowland Office .10 .05
❑ 199 David Palmer .10 .05
❑ 200 Larry Parrish .10 .05
❑ 201 Mike Phillips .10 .05
❑ 202 Tim Raines .75 .35
❑ 203 Bobby Ramos .10 .05
❑ 204 Jeff Reardon .40 .18
❑ 205 Steve Rogers .10 .05
❑ 206 Scott Sanderson .10 .05
❑ 207 Rodney Scott UER .40 .18
(Photo actually
Tim Raines)
❑ 208 Elias Sosa .10 .05
❑ 209 Chris Speier .10 .05
❑ 210 Tim Wallach RC .40 .18
❑ 211 Jerry White .10 .05
❑ 212 Alan Ashby .10 .05
❑ 213 Cesar Cedeno .20 .09
❑ 214 Jose Cruz .20 .09
❑ 215 Kiko Garcia .10 .05
❑ 216 Phil Garner .20 .09
❑ 217 Danny Heep .10 .05
❑ 218 Art Howe .20 .09
❑ 219 Bob Knepper .10 .05
❑ 220 Frank LaCorte .10 .05
❑ 221 Joe Niekro .20 .09
❑ 222 Joe Pittman .10 .05
❑ 223 Terry Puhl .10 .05
❑ 224 Luis Pujols .10 .05
❑ 225 Craig Reynolds .10 .05
❑ 226 J.R. Richard .20 .09
❑ 227 Dave Roberts .10 .05
❑ 228 Vern Ruhle .10 .05
❑ 229 Nolan Ryan 4.00 1.80
❑ 230 Joe Sambito .10 .05
❑ 231 Tony Scott .10 .05
❑ 232 Dave Smith .10 .05
❑ 233 Harry Spilman .10 .05
❑ 234 Don Sutton .75 .35
❑ 235 Dickie Thon .10 .05
❑ 236 Denny Walling .10 .05
❑ 237 Gary Woods .10 .05
❑ 238 Luis Aguayo .10 .05
❑ 239 Ramon Aviles .10 .05
❑ 240 Bob Boone .20 .09
❑ 241 Larry Bowa .20 .09
❑ 242 Warren Brusstar .10 .05
❑ 243 Steve Carlton .75 .35
❑ 244 Larry Christenson .10 .05
❑ 245 Dick Davis .10 .05
❑ 246 Greg Gross .10 .05
❑ 247 Sparky Lyle .20 .09
❑ 248 Garry Maddox .10 .05
❑ 249 Gary Matthews .20 .09
❑ 250 Bake McBride .10 .05
❑ 251 Tug McGraw .20 .09
❑ 252 Keith Moreland .10 .05
❑ 253 Dickie Noles .10 .05
❑ 254 Mike Proly .10 .05
❑ 255 Ron Reed .10 .05
❑ 256 Pete Rose 2.50 1.10
❑ 257 Dick Ruthven .10 .05
❑ 258 Mike Schmidt 1.50 .70
❑ 259 Lonnie Smith .20 .09
❑ 260 Manny Trillo .10 .05
❑ 261 Del Unser .10 .05
❑ 262 George Vukovich .10 .05
❑ 263 Tom Brookens .10 .05
❑ 264 George Cappuzzello .10 .05
❑ 265 Marty Castillo .10 .05
❑ 266 Al Cowens .10 .05
❑ 267 Kirk Gibson .75 .35
❑ 268 Richie Hebner .20 .09
❑ 269 Ron Jackson .10 .05
❑ 270 Lynn Jones .10 .05
❑ 271 Steve Kemp .10 .05
❑ 272 Rick Leach .10 .05
❑ 273 Aurelio Lopez .10 .05
❑ 274 Jack Morris .20 .09
❑ 275 Kevin Saucier .10 .05
❑ 276 Lance Parrish .40 .18
❑ 277 Rick Peters .10 .05
❑ 278 Dan Petry .10 .05
❑ 279 Dave Rozema .10 .05
❑ 280 Stan Papi .10 .05
❑ 281 Dan Schatzeder .10 .05
❑ 282 Champ Summers .10 .05
❑ 283 Alan Trammell .40 .18
❑ 284 Lou Whitaker .75 .35
❑ 285 Milt Wilcox .10 .05
❑ 286 John Wockenfuss .10 .05
❑ 287 Gary Allenson .10 .05
❑ 288 Tom Burgmeier .10 .05
❑ 289 Bill Campbell .10 .05
❑ 290 Mark Clear .10 .05
❑ 291 Steve Crawford .10 .05
❑ 292 Dennis Eckersley .75 .35
❑ 293 Dwight Evans .40 .18
❑ 294 Rich Gedman .20 .09
❑ 295 Garry Hancock .10 .05
❑ 296 Glenn Hoffman .10 .05
❑ 297 Bruce Hurst .10 .05
❑ 298 Carney Lansford .20 .09
❑ 299 Rick Miller .10 .05
❑ 300 Reid Nichols .10 .05
❑ 301 Bob Ojeda RC .40 .18
❑ 302 Tony Perez .75 .35
❑ 303 Chuck Rainey .10 .05
❑ 304 Jerry Remy .10 .05
❑ 305 Jim Rice .20 .09
❑ 306 Joe Rudi .10 .05
❑ 307 Bob Stanley .10 .05
❑ 308 Dave Stapleton .10 .05
❑ 309 Frank Tanana .20 .09
❑ 310 Mike Torrez .10 .05
❑ 311 John Tudor .10 .05
❑ 312 Carl Yastrzemski .75 .35
❑ 313 Buddy Bell .20 .09
❑ 314 Steve Comer .10 .05
❑ 315 Danny Darwin .10 .05
❑ 316 John Ellis .10 .05
❑ 317 John Grubb .10 .05
❑ 318 Rick Honeycutt .10 .05
❑ 319 Charlie Hough .20 .09
❑ 320 Ferguson Jenkins .75 .35
❑ 321 John Henry Johnson .10 .05
❑ 322 Jim Kern .10 .05
❑ 323 Jon Matlack .10 .05
❑ 324 Doc Medich .10 .05
❑ 325 Mario Mendoza .10 .05
❑ 326 Al Oliver .20 .09
❑ 327 Pat Putnam .10 .05
❑ 328 Mickey Rivers .10 .05
❑ 329 Leon Roberts .10 .05
❑ 330 Billy Sample .10 .05
❑ 331 Bill Stein .10 .05
❑ 332 Jim Sundberg .10 .05
❑ 333 Mark Wagner .10 .05
❑ 334 Bump Wills .10 .05
❑ 335 Bill Almon .10 .05
❑ 336 Harold Baines .75 .35
❑ 337 Ross Baumgarten .10 .05
❑ 338 Tony Bernazard .10 .05
❑ 339 Britt Burns .10 .05
❑ 340 Richard Dotson .10 .05
❑ 341 Jim Essian .10 .05
❑ 342 Ed Farmer .10 .05
❑ 343 Carlton Fisk .75 .35
❑ 344 Kevin Hickey .10 .05
❑ 345 LaMarr Hoyt .10 .05
❑ 346 Lamar Johnson .10 .05
❑ 347 Jerry Koosman .20 .09
❑ 348 Rusty Kuntz .10 .05
❑ 349 Dennis Lamp .10 .05
❑ 350 Ron LeFlore .20 .09
❑ 351 Chet Lemon .10 .05
❑ 352 Greg Luzinski .20 .09
❑ 353 Bob Molinaro .10 .05
❑ 354 Jim Morrison .10 .05
❑ 355 Wayne Nordhagen .10 .05
❑ 356 Greg Pryor .10 .05
❑ 357 Mike Squires .10 .05
❑ 358 Steve Trout .10 .05
❑ 359 Alan Bannister .10 .05
❑ 360 Len Barker .10 .05
❑ 361 Bert Blyleven .40 .18
❑ 362 Joe Charboneau .20 .09
❑ 363 John Denny .10 .05
❑ 364 Bo Diaz .10 .05
❑ 365 Miguel Dilone .10 .05
❑ 366 Jerry Dybzinski .10 .05
❑ 367 Wayne Garland .10 .05
❑ 368 Mike Hargrove .20 .09
❑ 369 Toby Harrah .20 .09
❑ 370 Ron Hassey .10 .05
❑ 371 Von Hayes .20 .09
❑ 372 Pat Kelly .10 .05
❑ 373 Duane Kuiper .10 .05
❑ 374 Rick Manning .10 .05
❑ 375 Sid Monge .10 .05
❑ 376 Jorge Orta .10 .05
❑ 377 Dave Rosello .10 .05
❑ 378 Dan Spillner .10 .05
❑ 379 Mike Stanton .10 .05
❑ 380 Andre Thornton .10 .05
❑ 381 Tom Veryzer .10 .05
❑ 382 Rick Waits .10 .05
❑ 383 Doyle Alexander .10 .05
❑ 384 Vida Blue .20 .09
❑ 385 Fred Breining .10 .05
❑ 386 Enos Cabell .10 .05
❑ 387 Jack Clark .20 .09
❑ 388 Darrell Evans .20 .09
❑ 389 Tom Griffin .10 .05
❑ 390 Larry Herndon .10 .05
❑ 391 Al Holland .10 .05
❑ 392 Gary Lavelle .10 .05
❑ 393 Johnnie LeMaster .10 .05
❑ 394 Jerry Martin .10 .05
❑ 395 Milt May .10 .05

- ❑ 396 Greg Minton .10 .05
- ❑ 397 Joe Morgan .75 .35
- ❑ 398 Joe Pettini .10 .05
- ❑ 399 Allen Ripley .10 .05
- ❑ 400 Billy Smith .10 .05
- ❑ 401 Rennie Stennett .10 .05
- ❑ 402 Ed Whitson .10 .05
- ❑ 403 Jim Wohlford .10 .05
- ❑ 404 Willie Aikens .10 .05
- ❑ 405 George Brett 1.50 .70
- ❑ 406 Ken Brett .10 .05
- ❑ 407 Dave Chalk .10 .05
- ❑ 408 Rich Gale .10 .05
- ❑ 409 Cesar Geronimo .10 .05
- ❑ 410 Larry Gura .10 .05
- ❑ 411 Clint Hurdle .10 .05
- ❑ 412 Mike Jones .10 .05
- ❑ 413 Dennis Leonard .10 .05
- ❑ 414 Renie Martin .10 .05
- ❑ 415 Lee May .20 .09
- ❑ 416 Hal McRae .20 .09
- ❑ 417 Darryl Motley .10 .05
- ❑ 418 Rance Mulliniks .10 .05
- ❑ 419 Amos Otis .20 .09
- ❑ 420 Ken Phelps .10 .05
- ❑ 421 Jamie Quirk .10 .05
- ❑ 422 Dan Quisenberry .20 .09
- ❑ 423 Paul Splittorff .10 .05
- ❑ 424 U.L. Washington .10 .05
- ❑ 425 John Wathan .10 .05
- ❑ 426 Frank White .20 .09
- ❑ 427 Willie Wilson .20 .09
- ❑ 428 Brian Asselstine .10 .05
- ❑ 429 Bruce Benedict .10 .05
- ❑ 430 Tommy Boggs .10 .05
- ❑ 431 Larry Bradford .10 .05
- ❑ 432 Rick Camp .10 .05
- ❑ 433 Chris Chambliss .20 .09
- ❑ 434 Gene Garber .10 .05
- ❑ 435 Preston Hanna .10 .05
- ❑ 436 Bob Horner .20 .09
- ❑ 437 Glenn Hubbard .10 .05
- ❑ 438A Al Hrabosky ERR 8.00 3.60
  (Height 5'1"
  All on reverse)
- ❑ 438B Al Hrabosky ERR .40 .18
  (Height 5'1")
- ❑ 438C Al Hrabosky .20 .09
  (Height 5'10")
- ❑ 439 Rufino Linares .10 .05
- ❑ 440 Rick Mahler .10 .05
- ❑ 441 Ed Miller .10 .05
- ❑ 442 John Montefusco .10 .05
- ❑ 443 Dale Murphy .75 .35
- ❑ 444 Phil Niekro .75 .35
- ❑ 445 Gaylord Perry .75 .35
- ❑ 446 Biff Pocoroba .10 .05
- ❑ 447 Rafael Ramirez .10 .05
- ❑ 448 Jerry Royster .10 .05
- ❑ 449 Claudell Washington .10 .05
- ❑ 450 Don Aase .10 .05
- ❑ 451 Don Baylor .40 .18
- ❑ 452 Juan Beniquez .10 .05
- ❑ 453 Rick Burleson .10 .05
- ❑ 454 Bert Campaneris .20 .09
- ❑ 455 Rod Carew .75 .35
- ❑ 456 Bob Clark .10 .05
- ❑ 457 Brian Downing .10 .05
- ❑ 458 Dan Ford .10 .05
- ❑ 459 Ken Forsch .10 .05
- ❑ 460A Dave Frost (5 mm .10 .05
  space before ERA)
- ❑ 460B Dave Frost .10 .05
  (1 mm space)
- ❑ 461 Bobby Grich .20 .09
- ❑ 462 Larry Harlow .10 .05
- ❑ 463 John Harris .10 .05
- ❑ 464 Andy Hassler .10 .05
- ❑ 465 Butch Hobson .10 .05
- ❑ 466 Jesse Jefferson .10 .05
- ❑ 467 Bruce Kison .10 .05
- ❑ 468 Fred Lynn .20 .09
- ❑ 469 Angel Moreno .10 .05
- ❑ 470 Ed Ott .10 .05
- ❑ 471 Fred Patek .10 .05
- ❑ 472 Steve Renko .10 .05
- ❑ 473 Mike Witt .20 .09
- ❑ 474 Geoff Zahn .10 .05
- ❑ 475 Gary Alexander .10 .05
- ❑ 476 Dale Berra .10 .05
- ❑ 477 Kurt Bevacqua .10 .05
- ❑ 478 Jim Bibby .10 .05
- ❑ 479 John Candelaria .10 .05
- ❑ 480 Victor Cruz .10 .05
- ❑ 481 Mike Easler .10 .05
- ❑ 482 Tim Foli .10 .05
- ❑ 483 Lee Lacy .10 .05
- ❑ 484 Vance Law .10 .05
- ❑ 485 Bill Madlock .20 .09
- ❑ 486 Willie Montanez .10 .05
- ❑ 487 Omar Moreno .10 .05
- ❑ 488 Steve Nicosia .10 .05
- ❑ 489 Dave Parker .20 .09
- ❑ 490 Tony Pena .20 .09
- ❑ 491 Pascual Perez .10 .05
- ❑ 492 Johnny Ray .20 .09
- ❑ 493 Rick Rhoden .10 .05
- ❑ 494 Bill Robinson .10 .05
- ❑ 495 Don Robinson .10 .05
- ❑ 496 Enrique Romo .10 .05
- ❑ 497 Rod Scurry .10 .05
- ❑ 498 Eddie Solomon .10 .05
- ❑ 499 Willie Stargell .75 .35
- ❑ 500 Kent Tekulve .20 .09
- ❑ 501 Jason Thompson .10 .05
- ❑ 502 Glenn Abbott .10 .05
- ❑ 503 Jim Anderson .10 .05
- ❑ 504 Floyd Bannister .10 .05
- ❑ 505 Bruce Bochte .10 .05
- ❑ 506 Jeff Burroughs .10 .05
- ❑ 507 Bryan Clark .10 .05
- ❑ 508 Ken Clay .10 .05
- ❑ 509 Julio Cruz .10 .05
- ❑ 510 Dick Drago .10 .05
- ❑ 511 Gary Gray .10 .05
- ❑ 512 Dan Meyer .10 .05
- ❑ 513 Jerry Narron .10 .05
- ❑ 514 Tom Paciorek .20 .09
- ❑ 515 Casey Parsons .10 .05
- ❑ 516 Lenny Randle .10 .05
- ❑ 517 Shane Rawley .10 .05
- ❑ 518 Joe Simpson .10 .05
- ❑ 519 Richie Zisk .10 .05
- ❑ 520 Neil Allen .10 .05
- ❑ 521 Bob Bailor .10 .05
- ❑ 522 Hubie Brooks .20 .09
- ❑ 523 Mike Cubbage .10 .05
- ❑ 524 Pete Falcone .10 .05
- ❑ 525 Doug Flynn .10 .05
- ❑ 526 Tom Hausman .10 .05
- ❑ 527 Ron Hodges .10 .05
- ❑ 528 Randy Jones .10 .05
- ❑ 529 Mike Jorgensen .10 .05
- ❑ 530 Dave Kingman .20 .09
- ❑ 531 Ed Lynch .10 .05
- ❑ 532 Mike G. Marshall .10 .05
- ❑ 533 Lee Mazzilli .10 .05
- ❑ 534 Dyar Miller .10 .05
- ❑ 535 Mike Scott .20 .09
- ❑ 536 Rusty Staub .20 .09
- ❑ 537 John Stearns .10 .05
- ❑ 538 Craig Swan .10 .05
- ❑ 539 Frank Taveras .10 .05
- ❑ 540 Alex Trevino .10 .05
- ❑ 541 Ellis Valentine .10 .05
- ❑ 542 Mookie Wilson .20 .09
- ❑ 543 Joel Youngblood .10 .05
- ❑ 544 Pat Zachry .10 .05
- ❑ 545 Glenn Adams .10 .05
- ❑ 546 Fernando Arroyo .10 .05
- ❑ 547 John Verhoeven .10 .05
- ❑ 548 Sal Butera .10 .05
- ❑ 549 John Castino .10 .05
- ❑ 550 Don Cooper .10 .05
- ❑ 551 Doug Corbett .10 .05
- ❑ 552 Dave Engle .10 .05
- ❑ 553 Roger Erickson .10 .05
- ❑ 554 Danny Goodwin .10 .05
- ❑ 555A Darrell Jackson .40 .18
  (Black cap)
- ❑ 555B Darrell Jackson .20 .09
  (Red cap with T)
- ❑ 555C Darrell Jackson 3.00 1.35
  (Red cap, no emblem)
- ❑ 556 Pete Mackanin .10 .05
- ❑ 557 Jack O'Connor .10 .05
- ❑ 558 Hosken Powell .10 .05
- ❑ 559 Pete Redfern .10 .05
- ❑ 560 Roy Smalley .10 .05
- ❑ 561 Chuck Baker UER .10 .05
  (Shortshop on front)
- ❑ 562 Gary Ward .10 .05
- ❑ 563 Rob Wilfong .10 .05
- ❑ 564 Al Williams .10 .05
- ❑ 565 Butch Wynegar .10 .05
- ❑ 566 Randy Bass RC .10 .05
- ❑ 567 Juan Bonilla .10 .05
- ❑ 568 Danny Boone .10 .05
- ❑ 569 John Curtis .10 .05
- ❑ 570 Juan Eichelberger .10 .05
- ❑ 571 Barry Evans .10 .05
- ❑ 572 Tim Flannery .10 .05
- ❑ 573 Ruppert Jones .10 .05
- ❑ 574 Terry Kennedy .10 .05
- ❑ 575 Joe Lefebvre .10 .05
- ❑ 576A John Littlefield ERR 60.00 27.00
  (Left handed;
  reverse negative)
- ❑ 576B John Littlefield COR .20 .09
  (Right handed)
- ❑ 577 Gary Lucas .10 .05
- ❑ 578 Steve Mura .10 .05
- ❑ 579 Broderick Perkins .10 .05
- ❑ 580 Gene Richards .10 .05
- ❑ 581 Luis Salazar .10 .05
- ❑ 582 Ozzie Smith 1.50 .70
- ❑ 583 John Urrea .10 .05
- ❑ 584 Chris Welsh .10 .05
- ❑ 585 Rick Wise .10 .05
- ❑ 586 Doug Bird .10 .05
- ❑ 587 Tim Blackwell .10 .05
- ❑ 588 Bobby Bonds .20 .09
- ❑ 589 Bill Buckner .20 .09
- ❑ 590 Bill Caudill .10 .05
- ❑ 591 Hector Cruz .10 .05
- ❑ 592 Jody Davis .10 .05
- ❑ 593 Ivan DeJesus .10 .05
- ❑ 594 Steve Dillard .10 .05
- ❑ 595 Leon Durham .10 .05
- ❑ 596 Rawly Eastwick .10 .05
- ❑ 597 Steve Henderson .10 .05
- ❑ 598 Mike Krukow .10 .05
- ❑ 599 Mike Lum .10 .05
- ❑ 600 Randy Martz .10 .05
- ❑ 601 Jerry Morales .10 .05
- ❑ 602 Ken Reitz .10 .05
- ❑ 603 Lee Smith RC ERR 2.00 .90
  (Cubs logo reversed)
- ❑ 603B Lee Smith RC COR 6.00 2.70
- ❑ 604 Dick Tidrow .10 .05
- ❑ 605 Jim Tracy .10 .05
- ❑ 606 Mike Tyson .10 .05
- ❑ 607 Ty Waller .10 .05
- ❑ 608 Danny Ainge 1.00 .45
- ❑ 609 Jorge Bell RC .75 .35
- ❑ 610 Mark Bomback .10 .05
- ❑ 611 Barry Bonnell .10 .05
- ❑ 612 Jim Clancy .10 .05
- ❑ 613 Damaso Garcia .10 .05
- ❑ 614 Jerry Garvin .10 .05
- ❑ 615 Alfredo Griffin .10 .05
- ❑ 616 Garth Iorg .10 .05
- ❑ 617 Luis Leal .10 .05
- ❑ 618 Ken Macha .10 .05
- ❑ 619 John Mayberry .10 .05
- ❑ 620 Joey McLaughlin .10 .05
- ❑ 621 Lloyd Moseby .10 .05
- ❑ 622 Dave Stieb .20 .09
- ❑ 623 Jackson Todd .10 .05
- ❑ 624 Willie Upshaw .10 .05
- ❑ 625 Otto Velez .10 .05
- ❑ 626 Ernie Whitt .10 .05
- ❑ 627 Alvis Woods .10 .05
- ❑ 628 All Star Game .20 .09
  Cleveland, Ohio
- ❑ 629 All Star Infielders .20 .09
  Frank White
  Bucky Dent

❑ 630 Big Red Machine .20 .09
Dan Driessen
Dave Concepcion
George Foster
❑ 631 Bruce Sutter .10 .05
Top NL Relief Pitcher
❑ 632 Steve and Carlton .40 .18
Steve Carlton
Carlton Fisk
❑ 633 Carl Yastrzemski .75 .35
3000th Game
❑ 634 Dynamic Duo 1.00 .45
Johnny Bench
Tom Seaver
❑ 635 West Meets East .20 .09
Fernando Valenzuela
Gary Carter
❑ 636A Fernando Valenzuela .75 .35
NL SO King ("he" NL)
❑ 636B Fernando Valenzuela .75 .35
NL SO King ("the" NL)
❑ 637 Mike Schmidt .40 .18
Home Run King
❑ 638 NL All Stars .20 .09
Gary Carter
Dave Parker
❑ 639 Perfect Game UER .20 .09
Len Barker
Bo Diaz
(Catcher actually
Ron Hassey)
❑ 640 Pete and Re-Pete .75 .35
Pete Rose
Pete Rose Jr.
❑ 641 Phillies Finest .75 .35
Lonnie Smith
Mike Schmidt
Steve Carlton
❑ 642 Red Sox Reunion .20 .09
Fred Lynn
Dwight Evans
❑ 643 Rickey Henderson 1.00 .45
Most Hits and Runs
❑ 644 Rollie Fingers .20 .09
Most Saves AL
❑ 645 Tom Seaver .40 .18
Most 1981 Wins
❑ 646 Yankee Powerhouse .75 .35
Reggie Jackson
Dave Winfield
(Comma on back
after outfielder)
❑ 646B Yankee Powerhouse 2.00 .90
Reggie Jackson
Dave Winfield
(No comma)
❑ 647 CL: Yankees/Dodgers .10 .05
❑ 648 CL: A's/Reds .10 .05
❑ 649 CL: Cards/Brewers .10 .05
❑ 650 CL: Expos/Orioles .10 .05
❑ 651 CL: Astros/Phillies .10 .05
❑ 652 CL: Tigers/Red Sox .10 .05
❑ 653 CL: Rangers/White Sox .10 .05
❑ 654 CL: Giants/Indians .10 .05
❑ 655 CL: Royals/Braves .10 .05
❑ 656 CL: Angels/Pirates .10 .05
❑ 657 CL: Mariners/Mets .10 .05
❑ 658 CL: Padres/Twins .10 .05
❑ 659 CL: Blue Jays/Cubs .10 .05
❑ 660 Specials Checklist .10 .05

## 1983 Fleer

| | NRMT | VG-E |
|---|---|---|
| COMPLETE SET (660) | 80.00 | 36.00 |

❑ 1 Joaquin Andujar .10 .05
❑ 2 Doug Bair .10 .05
❑ 3 Steve Braun .10 .05
❑ 4 Glenn Brummer .10 .05
❑ 5 Bob Forsch .10 .05
❑ 6 David Green .10 .05
❑ 7 George Hendrick .10 .05
❑ 8 Keith Hernandez .20 .09
❑ 9 Tom Herr .20 .09
❑ 10 Dane Iorg .10 .05
❑ 11 Jim Kaat .20 .09
❑ 12 Jeff Lahti .10 .05
❑ 13 Tito Landrum .10 .05
❑ 14 Dave LaPoint .10 .05
❑ 15 Willie McGee RC 1.50 .70
❑ 16 Steve Mura .10 .05
❑ 17 Ken Oberkfell .10 .05
❑ 18 Darrell Porter .10 .05
❑ 19 Mike Ramsey .10 .05
❑ 20 Gene Roof .10 .05
❑ 21 Lonnie Smith .10 .05
❑ 22 Ozzie Smith 1.25 .55
❑ 23 John Stuper .10 .05
❑ 24 Bruce Sutter .20 .09
❑ 25 Gene Tenace .20 .09
❑ 26 Jerry Augustine .10 .05
❑ 27 Dwight Bernard .10 .05
❑ 28 Mark Brouhard .10 .05
❑ 29 Mike Caldwell .10 .05
❑ 30 Cecil Cooper .20 .09
❑ 31 Jamie Easterly .10 .05
❑ 32 Marshall Edwards .10 .05
❑ 33 Rollie Fingers .75 .35
❑ 34 Jim Gantner .10 .05
❑ 35 Moose Haas .10 .05
❑ 36 Roy Howell .10 .05
❑ 37 Pete Ladd .10 .05
❑ 38 Bob McClure .10 .05
❑ 39 Doc Medich .10 .05
❑ 40 Paul Molitor 1.00 .45
❑ 41 Don Money .10 .05
❑ 42 Charlie Moore .10 .05
❑ 43 Ben Oglivie .10 .05
❑ 44 Ed Romero .10 .05
❑ 45 Ted Simmons .20 .09
❑ 46 Jim Slaton .10 .05
❑ 47 Don Sutton .75 .35
❑ 48 Gorman Thomas .10 .05
❑ 49 Pete Vuckovich .10 .05
❑ 50 Ned Yost .10 .05
❑ 51 Robin Yount .75 .35
❑ 52 Benny Ayala .10 .05
❑ 53 Bob Bonner .10 .05
❑ 54 Al Bumbry .10 .05
❑ 55 Terry Crowley .10 .05
❑ 56 Storm Davis RC .10 .05
❑ 57 Rich Dauer .10 .05
❑ 58 Rick Dempsey UER .20 .09
(Posing batting lefty)
❑ 59 Jim Dwyer .10 .05
❑ 60 Mike Flanagan .20 .09
❑ 61 Dan Ford .10 .05
❑ 62 Glenn Gulliver .10 .05
❑ 63 John Lowenstein .10 .05
❑ 64 Dennis Martinez .20 .09
❑ 65 Tippy Martinez .10 .05
❑ 66 Scott McGregor .10 .05
❑ 67 Eddie Murray 1.00 .45
❑ 68 Joe Nolan .10 .05
❑ 69 Jim Palmer .75 .35
❑ 70 Cal Ripken 8.00 3.60
❑ 71 Gary Roenicke .10 .05
❑ 72 Lenn Sakata .10 .05
❑ 73 Ken Singleton .10 .05
❑ 74 Sammy Stewart .10 .05
❑ 75 Tim Stoddard .10 .05
❑ 76 Don Aase .10 .05
❑ 77 Don Baylor .40 .18
❑ 78 Juan Beniquez .10 .05
❑ 79 Bob Boone .20 .09
❑ 80 Rick Burleson .10 .05
❑ 81 Rod Carew .75 .35
❑ 82 Bobby Clark .10 .05
❑ 83 Doug Corbett .10 .05
❑ 84 John Curtis .10 .05
❑ 85 Doug DeCinces .20 .09
❑ 86 Brian Downing .10 .05
❑ 87 Joe Ferguson .10 .05
❑ 88 Tim Foli .10 .05
❑ 89 Ken Forsch .10 .05
❑ 90 Dave Goltz .10 .05
❑ 91 Bobby Grich .20 .09
❑ 92 Andy Hassler .10 .05
❑ 93 Reggie Jackson 1.00 .45
❑ 94 Ron Jackson .10 .05
❑ 95 Tommy John .40 .18
❑ 96 Bruce Kison .10 .05
❑ 97 Fred Lynn .20 .09
❑ 98 Ed Ott .10 .05
❑ 99 Steve Renko .10 .05
❑ 100 Luis Sanchez .10 .05
❑ 101 Rob Wilfong .10 .05
❑ 102 Mike Witt .10 .05
❑ 103 Geoff Zahn .10 .05
❑ 104 Willie Aikens .10 .05
❑ 105 Mike Armstrong .10 .05
❑ 106 Vida Blue .20 .09
❑ 107 Bud Black RC .20 .09
❑ 108 George Brett 1.50 .70
❑ 109 Bill Castro .10 .05
❑ 110 Onix Concepcion .10 .05
❑ 111 Dave Frost .10 .05
❑ 112 Cesar Geronimo .10 .05
❑ 113 Larry Gura .10 .05
❑ 114 Steve Hammond .10 .05
❑ 115 Don Hood .10 .05
❑ 116 Dennis Leonard .10 .05
❑ 117 Jerry Martin .10 .05
❑ 118 Lee May .20 .09
❑ 119 Hal McRae .20 .09
❑ 120 Amos Otis .20 .09
❑ 121 Greg Pryor .10 .05
❑ 122 Dan Quisenberry .20 .09
❑ 123 Don Slaught RC .40 .18
❑ 124 Paul Splittorff .10 .05
❑ 125 U.L. Washington .10 .05
❑ 126 John Wathan .10 .05
❑ 127 Frank White .20 .09
❑ 128 Willie Wilson .20 .09
❑ 129 Steve Bedrosian UER .20 .09
(Height 6'33")
❑ 130 Bruce Benedict .10 .05
❑ 131 Tommy Boggs .10 .05
❑ 132 Brett Butler .75 .35
❑ 133 Rick Camp .10 .05
❑ 134 Chris Chambliss .20 .09
❑ 135 Ken Dayley .10 .05
❑ 136 Gene Garber .10 .05
❑ 137 Terry Harper .10 .05
❑ 138 Bob Horner .10 .05
❑ 139 Glenn Hubbard .10 .05
❑ 140 Rufino Linares .10 .05
❑ 141 Rick Mahler .10 .05
❑ 142 Dale Murphy .75 .35
❑ 143 Phil Niekro .75 .35
❑ 144 Pascual Perez .10 .05
❑ 145 Biff Pocoroba .10 .05
❑ 146 Rafael Ramirez .10 .05
❑ 147 Jerry Royster .10 .05
❑ 148 Ken Smith .10 .05
❑ 149 Bob Walk .10 .05
❑ 150 Claudell Washington .10 .05
❑ 151 Bob Watson .20 .09
❑ 152 Larry Whisenton .10 .05
❑ 153 Porfirio Altamirano .10 .05
❑ 154 Marty Bystrom .10 .05
❑ 155 Steve Carlton .75 .35
❑ 156 Larry Christenson .10 .05
❑ 157 Ivan DeJesus .10 .05
❑ 158 John Denny .10 .05
❑ 159 Bob Dernier .10 .05
❑ 160 Bo Diaz .10 .05
❑ 161 Ed Farmer .10 .05
❑ 162 Greg Gross .10 .05

❑ 163 Mike Krukow .10 .05
❑ 164 Garry Maddox .10 .05
❑ 165 Gary Matthews .20 .09
❑ 166 Tug McGraw .20 .09
❑ 167 Bob Molinaro .10 .05
❑ 168 Sid Monge .10 .05
❑ 169 Ron Reed .10 .05
❑ 170 Bill Robinson .10 .05
❑ 171 Pete Rose 2.50 1.10
❑ 172 Dick Ruthven .10 .05
❑ 173 Mike Schmidt 1.50 .70
❑ 174 Manny Trillo .10 .05
❑ 175 Ozzie Virgil .10 .05
❑ 176 George Vukovich .10 .05
❑ 177 Gary Allenson .10 .05
❑ 178 Luis Aponte .10 .05
❑ 179 Wade Boggs RC 12.00 5.50
❑ 180 Tom Burgmeier .10 .05
❑ 181 Mark Clear .10 .05
❑ 182 Dennis Eckersley .75 .35
❑ 183 Dwight Evans .20 .09
❑ 184 Rich Gedman .10 .05
❑ 185 Glenn Hoffman .10 .05
❑ 186 Bruce Hurst .10 .05
❑ 187 Carney Lansford .20 .09
❑ 188 Rick Miller .10 .05
❑ 189 Reid Nichols .10 .05
❑ 190 Bob Ojeda .10 .05
❑ 191 Tony Perez .75 .35
❑ 192 Chuck Rainey .10 .05
❑ 193 Jerry Remy .10 .05
❑ 194 Jim Rice .20 .09
❑ 195 Bob Stanley .10 .05
❑ 196 Dave Stapleton .10 .05
❑ 197 Mike Torrez .10 .05
❑ 198 John Tudor .10 .05
❑ 199 Julio Valdez .10 .05
❑ 200 Carl Yastrzemski .75 .35
❑ 201 Dusty Baker .20 .09
❑ 202 Joe Beckwith .10 .05
❑ 203 Greg Brock .10 .05
❑ 204 Ron Cey .20 .09
❑ 205 Terry Forster .10 .05
❑ 206 Steve Garvey .40 .18
❑ 207 Pedro Guerrero .20 .09
❑ 208 Burt Hooton .10 .05
❑ 209 Steve Howe .10 .05
❑ 210 Ken Landreaux .10 .05
❑ 211 Mike Marshall .10 .05
❑ 212 Candy Maldonado RC .20 .09
❑ 213 Rick Monday .10 .05
❑ 214 Tom Niedenfuer .10 .05
❑ 215 Jorge Orta .10 .05
❑ 216 Jerry Reuss UER .20 .09
("Home:" omitted)
❑ 217 Ron Roenicke .10 .05
❑ 218 Vicente Romo .10 .05
❑ 219 Bill Russell .10 .05
❑ 220 Steve Sax .20 .09
❑ 221 Mike Scioscia .20 .09
❑ 222 Dave Stewart .20 .09
❑ 223 Derrel Thomas .10 .05
❑ 224 Fernando Valenzuela .40 .18
❑ 225 Bob Welch .20 .09
❑ 226 Ricky Wright .10 .05
❑ 227 Steve Yeager .10 .05
❑ 228 Bill Almon .10 .05
❑ 229 Harold Baines .75 .35
❑ 230 Salome Barojas .10 .05
❑ 231 Tony Bernazard .10 .05
❑ 232 Britt Burns .10 .05
❑ 233 Richard Dotson .10 .05
❑ 234 Ernesto Escarrega .10 .05
❑ 235 Carlton Fisk .75 .35
❑ 236 Jerry Hairston .10 .05
❑ 237 Kevin Hickey .10 .05
❑ 238 LaMarr Hoyt .20 .09
❑ 239 Steve Kemp .10 .05
❑ 240 Jim Kern .10 .05
❑ 241 Ron Kittle RC .40 .18
❑ 242 Jerry Koosman .20 .09
❑ 243 Dennis Lamp .10 .05
❑ 244 Rudy Law .10 .05
❑ 245 Vance Law .10 .05
❑ 246 Ron LeFlore .10 .05
❑ 247 Greg Luzinski .20 .09
❑ 248 Tom Paciorek .20 .09
❑ 249 Aurelio Rodriguez .10 .05
❑ 250 Mike Squires .10 .05
❑ 251 Steve Trout .10 .05
❑ 252 Jim Barr .10 .05
❑ 253 Dave Bergman .10 .05
❑ 254 Fred Breining .10 .05
❑ 255 Bob Brenly .10 .05
❑ 256 Jack Clark .20 .09
❑ 257 Chili Davis .75 .35
❑ 258 Darrell Evans .20 .09
❑ 259 Alan Fowlkes .10 .05
❑ 260 Rich Gale .10 .05
❑ 261 Atlee Hammaker .10 .05
❑ 262 Al Holland .10 .05
❑ 263 Duane Kuiper .10 .05
❑ 264 Bill Laskey .10 .05
❑ 265 Gary Lavelle .10 .05
❑ 266 Johnnie LeMaster .10 .05
❑ 267 Renie Martin .10 .05
❑ 268 Milt May .10 .05
❑ 269 Greg Minton .10 .05
❑ 270 Joe Morgan .75 .35
❑ 271 Tom O'Malley .10 .05
❑ 272 Reggie Smith .20 .09
❑ 273 Guy Sularz .10 .05
❑ 274 Champ Summers .10 .05
❑ 275 Max Venable .10 .05
❑ 276 Jim Wohlford .10 .05
❑ 277 Ray Burris .10 .05
❑ 278 Gary Carter .40 .18
❑ 279 Warren Cromartie .10 .05
❑ 280 Andre Dawson .40 .18
❑ 281 Terry Francona .10 .05
❑ 282 Doug Flynn .10 .05
❑ 283 Woodie Fryman .10 .05
❑ 284 Bill Gullickson .10 .05
❑ 285 Wallace Johnson .10 .05
❑ 286 Charlie Lea .10 .05
❑ 287 Randy Lerch .10 .05
❑ 288 Brad Mills .10 .05
❑ 289 Dan Norman .10 .05
❑ 290 Al Oliver .20 .09
❑ 291 David Palmer .10 .05
❑ 292 Tim Raines .75 .35
❑ 293 Jeff Reardon .20 .09
❑ 294 Steve Rogers .10 .05
❑ 295 Scott Sanderson .10 .05
❑ 296 Dan Schatzeder .10 .05
❑ 297 Bryn Smith .10 .05
❑ 298 Chris Speier .10 .05
❑ 299 Tim Wallach .20 .09
❑ 300 Jerry White .10 .05
❑ 301 Joel Youngblood .10 .05
❑ 302 Ross Baumgarten .10 .05
❑ 303 Dale Berra .10 .05
❑ 304 John Candelaria .10 .05
❑ 305 Dick Davis .10 .05
❑ 306 Mike Easler .10 .05
❑ 307 Richie Hebner .20 .09
❑ 308 Lee Lacy .10 .05
❑ 309 Bill Madlock .20 .09
❑ 310 Larry McWilliams .10 .05
❑ 311 John Milner .10 .05
❑ 312 Omar Moreno .10 .05
❑ 313 Jim Morrison .10 .05
❑ 314 Steve Nicosia .10 .05
❑ 315 Dave Parker .20 .09
❑ 316 Tony Pena .10 .05
❑ 317 Johnny Ray .10 .05
❑ 318 Rick Rhoden .10 .05
❑ 319 Don Robinson .10 .05
❑ 320 Enrique Romo .10 .05
❑ 321 Manny Sarmiento .10 .05
❑ 322 Rod Scurry .10 .05
❑ 323 Jimmy Smith .10 .05
❑ 324 Willie Stargell .75 .35
❑ 325 Jason Thompson .10 .05
❑ 326 Kent Tekulve .20 .09
❑ 327A Tom Brookens .10 .05
(Short .375" brown box shaded in on card back)
❑ 327B Tom Brookens .10 .05
(Longer 1.25" brown box shaded in on card back)
❑ 328 Enos Cabell .10 .05
❑ 329 Kirk Gibson .75 .35
❑ 330 Larry Herndon .10 .05
❑ 331 Mike Ivie .10 .05
❑ 332 Howard Johnson RC .75 .35
❑ 333 Lynn Jones .10 .05
❑ 334 Rick Leach .10 .05
❑ 335 Chet Lemon .10 .05
❑ 336 Jack Morris .20 .09
❑ 337 Lance Parrish .20 .09
❑ 338 Larry Pashnick .10 .05
❑ 339 Dan Petry .10 .05
❑ 340 Dave Rozema .10 .05
❑ 341 Dave Rucker .10 .05
❑ 342 Elias Sosa .10 .05
❑ 343 Dave Tobik .10 .05
❑ 344 Alan Trammell .40 .18
❑ 345 Jerry Turner .10 .05
❑ 346 Jerry Ujdur .10 .05
❑ 347 Pat Underwood .10 .05
❑ 348 Lou Whitaker .40 .18
❑ 349 Milt Wilcox .10 .05
❑ 350 Glenn Wilson .20 .09
❑ 351 John Wockenfuss .10 .05
❑ 352 Kurt Bevacqua .10 .05
❑ 353 Juan Bonilla .10 .05
❑ 354 Floyd Chiffer .10 .05
❑ 355 Luis DeLeon .10 .05
❑ 356 Dave Dravecky RC .75 .35
❑ 357 Dave Edwards .10 .05
❑ 358 Juan Eichelberger .10 .05
❑ 359 Tim Flannery .10 .05
❑ 360 Tony Gwynn RC 25.00 11.00
❑ 361 Ruppert Jones .10 .05
❑ 362 Terry Kennedy .10 .05
❑ 363 Joe Lefebvre .10 .05
❑ 364 Sixto Lezcano .10 .05
❑ 365 Tim Lollar .10 .05
❑ 366 Gary Lucas .10 .05
❑ 367 John Montefusco .10 .05
❑ 368 Broderick Perkins .10 .05
❑ 369 Joe Pittman .10 .05
❑ 370 Gene Richards .10 .05
❑ 371 Luis Salazar .10 .05
❑ 372 Eric Show .10 .05
❑ 373 Garry Templeton .10 .05
❑ 374 Chris Welsh .10 .05
❑ 375 Alan Wiggins .10 .05
❑ 376 Rick Cerone .10 .05
❑ 377 Dave Collins .10 .05
❑ 378 Roger Erickson .10 .05
❑ 379 George Frazier .10 .05
❑ 380 Oscar Gamble .10 .05
❑ 381 Rich Gossage .40 .18
❑ 382 Ken Griffey .20 .09
❑ 383 Ron Guidry .20 .09
❑ 384 Dave LaRoche .10 .05
❑ 385 Rudy May .10 .05
❑ 386 John Mayberry .10 .05
❑ 387 Lee Mazzilli .10 .05
❑ 388 Mike Morgan .10 .05
❑ 389 Jerry Mumphrey .10 .05
❑ 390 Bobby Murcer .20 .09
❑ 391 Graig Nettles .20 .09
❑ 392 Lou Piniella .20 .09
❑ 393 Willie Randolph .20 .09
❑ 394 Shane Rawley .10 .05
❑ 395 Dave Righetti .20 .09
❑ 396 Andre Robertson .10 .05
❑ 397 Roy Smalley .10 .05
❑ 398 Dave Winfield .75 .35
❑ 399 Butch Wynegar .10 .05
❑ 400 Chris Bando .10 .05
❑ 401 Alan Bannister .10 .05
❑ 402 Len Barker .10 .05
❑ 403 Tom Brennan .10 .05
❑ 404 Carmelo Castillo .10 .05
❑ 405 Miguel Dilone .10 .05
❑ 406 Jerry Dybzinski .10 .05
❑ 407 Mike Fischlin .10 .05
❑ 408 Ed Glynn UER .10 .05
(Photo actually Bud Anderson)
❑ 409 Mike Hargrove .20 .09
❑ 410 Toby Harrah .10 .05
❑ 411 Ron Hassey .10 .05
❑ 412 Von Hayes .20 .09

❑ 413 Rick Manning .10 .05
❑ 414 Bake McBride .10 .05
❑ 415 Larry Milbourne .10 .05
❑ 416 Bill Nahorodny .10 .05
❑ 417 Jack Perconte .10 .05
❑ 418 Lary Sorensen .10 .05
❑ 419 Dan Spillner .10 .05
❑ 420 Rick Sutcliffe .20 .09
❑ 421 Andre Thornton .10 .05
❑ 422 Rick Waits .10 .05
❑ 423 Eddie Whitson .10 .05
❑ 424 Jesse Barfield .20 .09
❑ 425 Barry Bonnell .10 .05
❑ 426 Jim Clancy .10 .05
❑ 427 Damaso Garcia .10 .05
❑ 428 Jerry Garvin .10 .05
❑ 429 Alfredo Griffin .10 .05
❑ 430 Garth Iorg .10 .05
❑ 431 Roy Lee Jackson .10 .05
❑ 432 Luis Leal .10 .05
❑ 433 Buck Martinez .10 .05
❑ 434 Joey McLaughlin .10 .05
❑ 435 Lloyd Moseby .10 .05
❑ 436 Rance Mulliniks .10 .05
❑ 437 Dale Murray .10 .05
❑ 438 Wayne Nordhagen .10 .05
❑ 439 Geno Petralli .20 .09
❑ 440 Hosken Powell .10 .05
❑ 441 Dave Stieb .20 .09
❑ 442 Willie Upshaw .10 .05
❑ 443 Ernie Whitt .10 .05
❑ 444 Alvis Woods .10 .05
❑ 445 Alan Ashby .10 .05
❑ 446 Jose Cruz .20 .09
❑ 447 Kiko Garcia .10 .05
❑ 448 Phil Garner .20 .09
❑ 449 Danny Heep .10 .05
❑ 450 Art Howe .20 .09
❑ 451 Bob Knepper .10 .05
❑ 452 Alan Knicely .10 .05
❑ 453 Ray Knight .20 .09
❑ 454 Frank LaCorte .10 .05
❑ 455 Mike LaCoss .10 .05
❑ 456 Randy Moffitt .10 .05
❑ 457 Joe Niekro .20 .09
❑ 458 Terry Puhl .10 .05
❑ 459 Luis Pujols .10 .05
❑ 460 Craig Reynolds .10 .05
❑ 461 Bert Roberge .10 .05
❑ 462 Vern Ruhle .10 .05
❑ 463 Nolan Ryan 4.00 1.80
❑ 464 Joe Sambito .10 .05
❑ 465 Tony Scott .10 .05
❑ 466 Dave Smith .10 .05
❑ 467 Harry Spilman .10 .05
❑ 468 Dickie Thon .10 .05
❑ 469 Denny Walling .10 .05
❑ 470 Larry Andersen .10 .05
❑ 471 Floyd Bannister .10 .05
❑ 472 Jim Beattie .10 .05
❑ 473 Bruce Bochte .10 .05
❑ 474 Manny Castillo .10 .05
❑ 475 Bill Caudill .10 .05
❑ 476 Bryan Clark .10 .05
❑ 477 Al Cowens .10 .05
❑ 478 Julio Cruz .10 .05
❑ 479 Todd Cruz .10 .05
❑ 480 Gary Gray .10 .05
❑ 481 Dave Henderson .10 .05
❑ 482 Mike Moore RC .20 .09
❑ 483 Gaylord Perry .75 .35
❑ 484 Dave Revering .10 .05
❑ 485 Joe Simpson .10 .05
❑ 486 Mike Stanton .10 .05
❑ 487 Rick Sweet .10 .05
❑ 488 Ed VandeBerg .10 .05
❑ 489 Richie Zisk .10 .05
❑ 490 Doug Bird .10 .05
❑ 491 Larry Bowa .20 .09
❑ 492 Bill Buckner .20 .09
❑ 493 Bill Campbell .10 .05
❑ 494 Jody Davis .10 .05
❑ 495 Leon Durham .10 .05
❑ 496 Steve Henderson .10 .05
❑ 497 Willie Hernandez .20 .09
❑ 498 Ferguson Jenkins .75 .35
❑ 499 Jay Johnstone .20 .09
❑ 500 Junior Kennedy .10 .05
❑ 501 Randy Martz .10 .05
❑ 502 Jerry Morales .10 .05
❑ 503 Keith Moreland .10 .05
❑ 504 Dickie Noles .10 .05
❑ 505 Mike Proly .10 .05
❑ 506 Allen Ripley .10 .05
❑ 507 Ryne Sandberg RC UER 12.00 5.50
(Should say High School
in Spokane, Washington)
❑ 508 Lee Smith .75 .35
❑ 509 Pat Tabler .10 .05
❑ 510 Dick Tidrow .10 .05
❑ 511 Bump Wills .10 .05
❑ 512 Gary Woods .10 .05
❑ 513 Tony Armas .10 .05
❑ 514 Dave Beard .10 .05
❑ 515 Jeff Burroughs .10 .05
❑ 516 John D'Acquisto .10 .05
❑ 517 Wayne Gross .10 .05
❑ 518 Mike Heath .10 .05
❑ 519 Rickey Henderson UER 1.25 .55
(Brock record listed
as 120 steals)
❑ 520 Cliff Johnson .10 .05
❑ 521 Matt Keough .10 .05
❑ 522 Brian Kingman .10 .05
❑ 523 Rick Langford .10 .05
❑ 524 Dave Lopes .20 .09
❑ 525 Steve McCatty .10 .05
❑ 526 Dave McKay .10 .05
❑ 527 Dan Meyer .10 .05
❑ 528 Dwayne Murphy .10 .05
❑ 529 Jeff Newman .10 .05
❑ 530 Mike Norris .10 .05
❑ 531 Bob Owchinko .10 .05
❑ 532 Joe Rudi .10 .05
❑ 533 Jimmy Sexton .10 .05
❑ 534 Fred Stanley .10 .05
❑ 535 Tom Underwood .10 .05
❑ 536 Neil Allen .10 .05
❑ 537 Wally Backman .10 .05
❑ 538 Bob Bailor .10 .05
❑ 539 Hubie Brooks .20 .09
❑ 540 Carlos Diaz .10 .05
❑ 541 Pete Falcone .10 .05
❑ 542 George Foster .20 .09
❑ 543 Ron Gardenhire .10 .05
❑ 544 Brian Giles .10 .05
❑ 545 Ron Hodges .10 .05
❑ 546 Randy Jones .10 .05
❑ 547 Mike Jorgensen .10 .05
❑ 548 Dave Kingman .40 .18
❑ 549 Ed Lynch .10 .05
❑ 550 Jesse Orosco .10 .05
❑ 551 Rick Ownbey .10 .05
❑ 552 Charlie Puleo .10 .05
❑ 553 Gary Rajsich .10 .05
❑ 554 Mike Scott .20 .09
❑ 555 Rusty Staub .20 .09
❑ 556 John Stearns .10 .05
❑ 557 Craig Swan .10 .05
❑ 558 Ellis Valentine .10 .05
❑ 559 Tom Veryzer .10 .05
❑ 560 Mookie Wilson .20 .09
❑ 561 Pat Zachry .10 .05
❑ 562 Buddy Bell .20 .09
❑ 563 John Butcher .10 .05
❑ 564 Steve Comer .10 .05
❑ 565 Danny Darwin .10 .05
❑ 566 Bucky Dent .20 .09
❑ 567 John Grubb .10 .05
❑ 568 Rick Honeycutt .10 .05
❑ 569 Dave Hostetler .10 .05
❑ 570 Charlie Hough .20 .09
❑ 571 Lamar Johnson .10 .05
❑ 572 Jon Matlack .10 .05
❑ 573 Paul Mirabella .10 .05
❑ 574 Larry Parrish .10 .05
❑ 575 Mike Richardt .10 .05
❑ 576 Mickey Rivers .10 .05
❑ 577 Billy Sample .10 .05
❑ 578 Dave Schmidt .10 .05
❑ 579 Bill Stein .10 .05
❑ 580 Jim Sundberg .20 .09
❑ 581 Frank Tanana .20 .09
❑ 582 Mark Wagner .10 .05
❑ 583 George Wright .10 .05
❑ 584 Johnny Bench 1.25 .55
❑ 585 Bruce Berenyi .10 .05
❑ 586 Larry Biittner .10 .05
❑ 587 Cesar Cedeno .20 .09
❑ 588 Dave Concepcion .20 .09
❑ 589 Dan Driessen .10 .05
❑ 590 Greg Harris .10 .05
❑ 591 Ben Hayes .10 .05
❑ 592 Paul Householder .10 .05
❑ 593 Tom Hume .10 .05
❑ 594 Wayne Krenchicki .10 .05
❑ 595 Rafael Landestoy .10 .05
❑ 596 Charlie Leibrandt .10 .05
❑ 597 Eddie Milner .10 .05
❑ 598 Ron Oester .10 .05
❑ 599 Frank Pastore .10 .05
❑ 600 Joe Price .10 .05
❑ 601 Tom Seaver 1.25 .55
❑ 602 Bob Shirley .10 .05
❑ 603 Mario Soto .10 .05
❑ 604 Alex Trevino .10 .05
❑ 605 Mike Vail .10 .05
❑ 606 Duane Walker .10 .05
❑ 607 Tom Brunansky .20 .09
❑ 608 Bobby Castillo .10 .05
❑ 609 John Castino .10 .05
❑ 610 Ron Davis .10 .05
❑ 611 Lenny Faedo .10 .05
❑ 612 Terry Felton .10 .05
❑ 613 Gary Gaetti RC .75 .35
❑ 614 Mickey Hatcher .10 .05
❑ 615 Brad Havens .10 .05
❑ 616 Kent Hrbek .20 .09
❑ 617 Randy Johnson .10 .05
❑ 618 Tim Laudner .10 .05
❑ 619 Jeff Little .10 .05
❑ 620 Bobby Mitchell .10 .05
❑ 621 Jack O'Connor .10 .05
❑ 622 John Pacella .10 .05
❑ 623 Pete Redfern .10 .05
❑ 624 Jesus Vega .10 .05
❑ 625 Frank Viola RC .75 .35
❑ 626 Ron Washington .10 .05
❑ 627 Gary Ward .10 .05
❑ 628 Al Williams .10 .05
❑ 629 Red Sox All-Stars .75 .35
Carl Yastrzemski
Dennis Eckersley
Mark Clear
❑ 630 300 Career Wins .20 .09
Gaylord Perry
Terry Bulling 5/6/82
❑ 631 Pride of Venezuela .20 .09
Dave Concepcion and
Manny Trillo
❑ 632 All-Star Infielders .75 .35
Robin Yount and
Buddy Bell
❑ 633 Mr.Vet and Mr.Rookie .20 .09
Dave Winfield and
Kent Hrbek
❑ 634 Fountain of Youth .75 .35
Willie Stargell and
Pete Rose
❑ 635 Big Chiefs .20 .09
Toby Harrah and
Andre Thornton
❑ 636 Smith Brothers .75 .35
Ozzie Smith
Lonnie Smith
❑ 637 Base Stealers' Threat .20 .09
Bo Diaz and
Gary Carter
❑ 638 All-Star Catchers .40 .18
Carlton Fisk and
Gary Carter
❑ 639 The Silver Shoe .40 .18
Rickey Henderson
❑ 640 Home Run Threats .75 .35
Ben Oglivie and
Reggie Jackson
❑ 641 Two Teams Same Day .10 .05
Joel Youngblood

| | | NRMT | VG-E |
|---|---|---|---|
| | August 4, 1982 | | |
| ❑ 642 | Last Perfect Game | .20 | .09 |
| | Ron Hassey and Len Barker | | |
| ❑ 643 | Black and Blue | .20 | .09 |
| | Vida Blue | | |
| ❑ 644 | Black and Blue | .10 | .05 |
| | Bud Black | | |
| ❑ 645 | Speed and Power | .40 | .18 |
| | Reggie Jackson | | |
| ❑ 646 | Speed and Power | .40 | .18 |
| | Rickey Henderson | | |
| ❑ 647 | CL: Cards/Brewers | .10 | .05 |
| ❑ 648 | CL: Orioles/Angels | .10 | .05 |
| ❑ 649 | CL: Royals/Braves | .10 | .05 |
| ❑ 650 | CL: Phillies/Red Sox | .10 | .05 |
| ❑ 651 | CL: Dodgers/White Sox | .10 | .05 |
| ❑ 652 | CL: Giants/Expos | .10 | .05 |
| ❑ 653 | CL: Pirates/Tigers | .10 | .05 |
| ❑ 654 | CL: Padres/Yankees | .10 | .05 |
| ❑ 655 | CL: Indians/Blue Jays | .10 | .05 |
| ❑ 656 | CL: Astros/Mariners | .10 | .05 |
| ❑ 657 | CL: Cubs/A's | .10 | .05 |
| ❑ 658 | CL: Mets/Rangers | .10 | .05 |
| ❑ 659 | CL: Reds/Twins | .10 | .05 |
| ❑ 660 | CL: Specials/Teams | .10 | .05 |

## 1984 Fleer

| | | NRMT | VG-E |
|---|---|---|---|
| COMPLETE SET (660) | | 60.00 | 27.00 |
| ❑ 1 | Mike Boddicker | .15 | .07 |
| ❑ 2 | Al Bumbry | .15 | .07 |
| ❑ 3 | Todd Cruz | .15 | .07 |
| ❑ 4 | Rich Dauer | .15 | .07 |
| ❑ 5 | Storm Davis | .15 | .07 |
| ❑ 6 | Rick Dempsey | .15 | .07 |
| ❑ 7 | Jim Dwyer | .15 | .07 |
| ❑ 8 | Mike Flanagan | .15 | .07 |
| ❑ 9 | Dan Ford | .15 | .07 |
| ❑ 10 | John Lowenstein | .15 | .07 |
| ❑ 11 | Dennis Martinez | .40 | .18 |
| ❑ 12 | Tippy Martinez | .15 | .07 |
| ❑ 13 | Scott McGregor | .15 | .07 |
| ❑ 14 | Eddie Murray | 1.50 | .70 |
| ❑ 15 | Joe Nolan | .15 | .07 |
| ❑ 16 | Jim Palmer | 1.50 | .70 |
| ❑ 17 | Cal Ripken | 10.00 | 4.50 |
| ❑ 18 | Gary Roenicke | .15 | .07 |
| ❑ 19 | Lenn Sakata | .15 | .07 |
| ❑ 20 | John Shelby | .15 | .07 |
| ❑ 21 | Ken Singleton | .15 | .07 |
| ❑ 22 | Sammy Stewart | .15 | .07 |
| ❑ 23 | Tim Stoddard | .15 | .07 |
| ❑ 24 | Marty Bystrom | .15 | .07 |
| ❑ 25 | Steve Carlton | 1.50 | .70 |
| ❑ 26 | Ivan DeJesus | .15 | .07 |
| ❑ 27 | John Denny | .15 | .07 |
| ❑ 28 | Bob Dernier | .15 | .07 |
| ❑ 29 | Bo Diaz | .15 | .07 |
| ❑ 30 | Kiko Garcia | .15 | .07 |
| ❑ 31 | Greg Gross | .15 | .07 |
| ❑ 32 | Kevin Gross RC | .15 | .07 |
| ❑ 33 | Von Hayes | .15 | .07 |
| ❑ 34 | Willie Hernandez | .40 | .18 |
| ❑ 35 | Al Holland | .15 | .07 |
| ❑ 36 | Charles Hudson | .15 | .07 |
| ❑ 37 | Joe Lefebvre | .15 | .07 |
| ❑ 38 | Sixto Lezcano | .15 | .07 |
| ❑ 39 | Garry Maddox | .15 | .07 |
| ❑ 40 | Gary Matthews | .40 | .18 |
| ❑ 41 | Len Matuszek | .15 | .07 |
| ❑ 42 | Tug McGraw | .40 | .18 |
| ❑ 43 | Joe Morgan | 1.50 | .70 |
| ❑ 44 | Tony Perez | 1.50 | .70 |
| ❑ 45 | Ron Reed | .15 | .07 |
| ❑ 46 | Pete Rose | 5.00 | 2.20 |
| ❑ 47 | Juan Samuel RC | .75 | .35 |
| ❑ 48 | Mike Schmidt | 3.00 | 1.35 |
| ❑ 49 | Ozzie Virgil | .15 | .07 |
| ❑ 50 | Juan Agosto | .15 | .07 |
| ❑ 51 | Harold Baines | 1.50 | .70 |
| ❑ 52 | Floyd Bannister | .15 | .07 |
| ❑ 53 | Salome Barojas | .15 | .07 |
| ❑ 54 | Britt Burns | .15 | .07 |
| ❑ 55 | Julio Cruz | .15 | .07 |
| ❑ 56 | Richard Dotson | .15 | .07 |
| ❑ 57 | Jerry Dybzinski | .15 | .07 |
| ❑ 58 | Carlton Fisk | 1.50 | .70 |
| ❑ 59 | Scott Fletcher | .15 | .07 |
| ❑ 60 | Jerry Hairston | .15 | .07 |
| ❑ 61 | Kevin Hickey | .15 | .07 |
| ❑ 62 | Marc Hill | .15 | .07 |
| ❑ 63 | LaMarr Hoyt | .15 | .07 |
| ❑ 64 | Ron Kittle | .15 | .07 |
| ❑ 65 | Jerry Koosman | .40 | .18 |
| ❑ 66 | Dennis Lamp | .15 | .07 |
| ❑ 67 | Rudy Law | .15 | .07 |
| ❑ 68 | Vance Law | .15 | .07 |
| ❑ 69 | Greg Luzinski | .40 | .18 |
| ❑ 70 | Tom Paciorek | .40 | .18 |
| ❑ 71 | Mike Squires | .15 | .07 |
| ❑ 72 | Dick Tidrow | .15 | .07 |
| ❑ 73 | Greg Walker | .40 | .18 |
| ❑ 74 | Glenn Abbott | .15 | .07 |
| ❑ 75 | Howard Bailey | .15 | .07 |
| ❑ 76 | Doug Bair | .15 | .07 |
| ❑ 77 | Juan Berenguer | .15 | .07 |
| ❑ 78 | Tom Brookens | .40 | .18 |
| ❑ 79 | Enos Cabell | .15 | .07 |
| ❑ 80 | Kirk Gibson | 1.50 | .70 |
| ❑ 81 | John Grubb | .15 | .07 |
| ❑ 82 | Larry Herndon | .40 | .18 |
| ❑ 83 | Wayne Krenchicki | .15 | .07 |
| ❑ 84 | Rick Leach | .15 | .07 |
| ❑ 85 | Chet Lemon | .15 | .07 |
| ❑ 86 | Aurelio Lopez | .40 | .18 |
| ❑ 87 | Jack Morris | 1.50 | .70 |
| ❑ 88 | Lance Parrish | .75 | .35 |
| ❑ 89 | Dan Petry | .40 | .18 |
| ❑ 90 | Dave Rozema | .15 | .07 |
| ❑ 91 | Alan Trammell | .75 | .35 |
| ❑ 92 | Lou Whitaker | 1.50 | .70 |
| ❑ 93 | Milt Wilcox | .15 | .07 |
| ❑ 94 | Glenn Wilson | .40 | .18 |
| ❑ 95 | John Wockenfuss | .15 | .07 |
| ❑ 96 | Dusty Baker | .40 | .18 |
| ❑ 97 | Joe Beckwith | .15 | .07 |
| ❑ 98 | Greg Brock | .15 | .07 |
| ❑ 99 | Jack Fimple | .15 | .07 |
| ❑ 100 | Pedro Guerrero | .40 | .18 |
| ❑ 101 | Rick Honeycutt | .15 | .07 |
| ❑ 102 | Burt Hooton | .15 | .07 |
| ❑ 103 | Steve Howe | .15 | .07 |
| ❑ 104 | Ken Landreaux | .15 | .07 |
| ❑ 105 | Mike Marshall | .15 | .07 |
| ❑ 106 | Rick Monday | .15 | .07 |
| ❑ 107 | Jose Morales | .15 | .07 |
| ❑ 108 | Tom Niedenfuer | .15 | .07 |
| ❑ 109 | Alejandro Pena RC* | .40 | .18 |
| ❑ 110 | Jerry Reuss UER | .15 | .07 |
| | ("Home:" omitted) | | |
| ❑ 111 | Bill Russell | .15 | .07 |
| ❑ 112 | Steve Sax | .40 | .18 |
| ❑ 113 | Mike Scioscia | .15 | .07 |
| ❑ 114 | Derrel Thomas | .15 | .07 |
| ❑ 115 | Fernando Valenzuela | .40 | .18 |
| ❑ 116 | Bob Welch | .15 | .07 |
| ❑ 117 | Steve Yeager | .15 | .07 |
| ❑ 118 | Pat Zachry | .15 | .07 |
| ❑ 119 | Don Baylor | .75 | .35 |
| ❑ 120 | Bert Campaneris | .40 | .18 |
| ❑ 121 | Rick Cerone | .15 | .07 |
| ❑ 122 | Ray Fontenot | .15 | .07 |
| ❑ 123 | George Frazier | .15 | .07 |
| ❑ 124 | Oscar Gamble | .15 | .07 |
| ❑ 125 | Rich Gossage | .75 | .35 |
| ❑ 126 | Ken Griffey | .40 | .18 |
| ❑ 127 | Ron Guidry | .40 | .18 |
| ❑ 128 | Jay Howell | .15 | .07 |
| ❑ 129 | Steve Kemp | .15 | .07 |
| ❑ 130 | Matt Keough | .15 | .07 |
| ❑ 131 | Don Mattingly RC | 20.00 | 9.00 |
| ❑ 132 | John Montefusco | .15 | .07 |
| ❑ 133 | Omar Moreno | .15 | .07 |
| ❑ 134 | Dale Murray | .15 | .07 |
| ❑ 135 | Graig Nettles | .40 | .18 |
| ❑ 136 | Lou Piniella | .40 | .18 |
| ❑ 137 | Willie Randolph | .40 | .18 |
| ❑ 138 | Shane Rawley | .15 | .07 |
| ❑ 139 | Dave Righetti | .40 | .18 |
| ❑ 140 | Andre Robertson | .15 | .07 |
| ❑ 141 | Bob Shirley | .15 | .07 |
| ❑ 142 | Roy Smalley | .15 | .07 |
| ❑ 143 | Dave Winfield | 1.50 | .70 |
| ❑ 144 | Butch Wynegar | .15 | .07 |
| ❑ 145 | Jim Acker | .15 | .07 |
| ❑ 146 | Doyle Alexander | .15 | .07 |
| ❑ 147 | Jesse Barfield | .40 | .18 |
| ❑ 148 | Jorge Bell | .40 | .18 |
| ❑ 149 | Barry Bonnell | .15 | .07 |
| ❑ 150 | Jim Clancy | .15 | .07 |
| ❑ 151 | Dave Collins | .15 | .07 |
| ❑ 152 | Tony Fernandez RC | 2.00 | .90 |
| ❑ 153 | Damaso Garcia | .15 | .07 |
| ❑ 154 | Dave Geisel | .15 | .07 |
| ❑ 155 | Jim Gott | .15 | .07 |
| ❑ 156 | Alfredo Griffin | .15 | .07 |
| ❑ 157 | Garth Iorg | .15 | .07 |
| ❑ 158 | Roy Lee Jackson | .15 | .07 |
| ❑ 159 | Cliff Johnson | .15 | .07 |
| ❑ 160 | Luis Leal | .15 | .07 |
| ❑ 161 | Buck Martinez | .15 | .07 |
| ❑ 162 | Joey McLaughlin | .15 | .07 |
| ❑ 163 | Randy Moffitt | .15 | .07 |
| ❑ 164 | Lloyd Moseby | .15 | .07 |
| ❑ 165 | Rance Mulliniks | .15 | .07 |
| ❑ 166 | Jorge Orta | .15 | .07 |
| ❑ 167 | Dave Stieb | .15 | .07 |
| ❑ 168 | Willie Upshaw | .15 | .07 |
| ❑ 169 | Ernie Whitt | .15 | .07 |
| ❑ 170 | Len Barker | .15 | .07 |
| ❑ 171 | Steve Bedrosian | .15 | .07 |
| ❑ 172 | Bruce Benedict | .15 | .07 |
| ❑ 173 | Brett Butler | .75 | .35 |
| ❑ 174 | Rick Camp | .15 | .07 |
| ❑ 175 | Chris Chambliss | .40 | .18 |
| ❑ 176 | Ken Dayley | .15 | .07 |
| ❑ 177 | Pete Falcone | .15 | .07 |
| ❑ 178 | Terry Forster | .15 | .07 |
| ❑ 179 | Gene Garber | .15 | .07 |
| ❑ 180 | Terry Harper | .15 | .07 |
| ❑ 181 | Bob Horner | .15 | .07 |
| ❑ 182 | Glenn Hubbard | .15 | .07 |
| ❑ 183 | Randy Johnson | .15 | .07 |
| ❑ 184 | Craig McMurtry | .15 | .07 |
| ❑ 185 | Donnie Moore | .15 | .07 |
| ❑ 186 | Dale Murphy | 1.50 | .70 |
| ❑ 187 | Phil Niekro | 1.50 | .70 |
| ❑ 188 | Pascual Perez | .15 | .07 |
| ❑ 189 | Biff Pocoroba | .15 | .07 |
| ❑ 190 | Rafael Ramirez | .15 | .07 |
| ❑ 191 | Jerry Royster | .15 | .07 |
| ❑ 192 | Claudell Washington | .15 | .07 |
| ❑ 193 | Bob Watson | .40 | .18 |
| ❑ 194 | Jerry Augustine | .15 | .07 |
| ❑ 195 | Mark Brouhard | .15 | .07 |
| ❑ 196 | Mike Caldwell | .15 | .07 |
| ❑ 197 | Tom Candiotti RC | 1.50 | .70 |
| ❑ 198 | Cecil Cooper | .40 | .18 |
| ❑ 199 | Rollie Fingers | 1.50 | .70 |
| ❑ 200 | Jim Gantner | .15 | .07 |
| ❑ 201 | Bob L. Gibson | .15 | .07 |
| ❑ 202 | Moose Haas | .15 | .07 |
| ❑ 203 | Roy Howell | .15 | .07 |
| ❑ 204 | Pete Ladd | .15 | .07 |
| ❑ 205 | Rick Manning | .15 | .07 |
| ❑ 206 | Bob McClure | .15 | .07 |
| ❑ 207 | Paul Molitor UER | 1.50 | .70 |

| | No. | Player | | |
|---|---|---|---|---|
| | | ('83 stats should say .270 BA and 608 AB) | | |
| ❑ | 208 | Don Money | .15 | .07 |
| ❑ | 209 | Charlie Moore | .15 | .07 |
| ❑ | 210 | Ben Oglivie | .15 | .07 |
| ❑ | 211 | Chuck Porter | .15 | .07 |
| ❑ | 212 | Ed Romero | .15 | .07 |
| ❑ | 213 | Ted Simmons | .40 | .18 |
| ❑ | 214 | Jim Slaton | .15 | .07 |
| ❑ | 215 | Don Sutton | 1.50 | .70 |
| ❑ | 216 | Tom Tellmann | .15 | .07 |
| ❑ | 217 | Pete Vuckovich | .15 | .07 |
| ❑ | 218 | Ned Yost | .15 | .07 |
| ❑ | 219 | Robin Yount | 1.50 | .70 |
| ❑ | 220 | Alan Ashby | .15 | .07 |
| ❑ | 221 | Kevin Bass | .15 | .07 |
| ❑ | 222 | Jose Cruz | .40 | .18 |
| ❑ | 223 | Bill Dawley | .15 | .07 |
| ❑ | 224 | Frank DiPino | .15 | .07 |
| ❑ | 225 | Bill Doran RC* | .40 | .18 |
| ❑ | 226 | Phil Garner | .40 | .18 |
| ❑ | 227 | Art Howe | .40 | .18 |
| ❑ | 228 | Bob Knepper | .15 | .07 |
| ❑ | 229 | Ray Knight | .40 | .18 |
| ❑ | 230 | Frank LaCorte | .15 | .07 |
| ❑ | 231 | Mike LaCoss | .15 | .07 |
| ❑ | 232 | Mike Madden | .15 | .07 |
| ❑ | 233 | Jerry Mumphrey | .15 | .07 |
| ❑ | 234 | Joe Niekro | .40 | .18 |
| ❑ | 235 | Terry Puhl | .15 | .07 |
| ❑ | 236 | Luis Pujols | .15 | .07 |
| ❑ | 237 | Craig Reynolds | .15 | .07 |
| ❑ | 238 | Vern Ruhle | .15 | .07 |
| ❑ | 239 | Nolan Ryan | 8.00 | 3.60 |
| ❑ | 240 | Mike Scott | .40 | .18 |
| ❑ | 241 | Tony Scott | .15 | .07 |
| ❑ | 242 | Dave Smith | .15 | .07 |
| ❑ | 243 | Dickie Thon | .15 | .07 |
| ❑ | 244 | Denny Walling | .15 | .07 |
| ❑ | 245 | Dale Berra | .15 | .07 |
| ❑ | 246 | Jim Bibby | .15 | .07 |
| ❑ | 247 | John Candelaria | .15 | .07 |
| ❑ | 248 | Jose DeLeon | .15 | .07 |
| ❑ | 249 | Mike Easler | .15 | .07 |
| ❑ | 250 | Cecilio Guante | .15 | .07 |
| ❑ | 251 | Richie Hebner | .15 | .07 |
| ❑ | 252 | Lee Lacy | .15 | .07 |
| ❑ | 253 | Bill Madlock | .40 | .18 |
| ❑ | 254 | Milt May | .15 | .07 |
| ❑ | 255 | Lee Mazzilli | .15 | .07 |
| ❑ | 256 | Larry McWilliams | .15 | .07 |
| ❑ | 257 | Jim Morrison | .15 | .07 |
| ❑ | 258 | Dave Parker | .40 | .18 |
| ❑ | 259 | Tony Pena | .15 | .07 |
| ❑ | 260 | Johnny Ray | .15 | .07 |
| ❑ | 261 | Rick Rhoden | .15 | .07 |
| ❑ | 262 | Don Robinson | .15 | .07 |
| ❑ | 263 | Manny Sarmiento | .15 | .07 |
| ❑ | 264 | Rod Scurry | .15 | .07 |
| ❑ | 265 | Kent Tekulve | .40 | .18 |
| ❑ | 266 | Gene Tenace | .40 | .18 |
| ❑ | 267 | Jason Thompson | .15 | .07 |
| ❑ | 268 | Lee Tunnell | .15 | .07 |
| ❑ | 269 | Marvell Wynne | .15 | .07 |
| ❑ | 270 | Ray Burris | .15 | .07 |
| ❑ | 271 | Gary Carter | .75 | .35 |
| ❑ | 272 | Warren Cromartie | .15 | .07 |
| ❑ | 273 | Andre Dawson | .75 | .35 |
| ❑ | 274 | Doug Flynn | .15 | .07 |
| ❑ | 275 | Terry Francona | .15 | .07 |
| ❑ | 276 | Bill Gullickson | .15 | .07 |
| ❑ | 277 | Bob James | .15 | .07 |
| ❑ | 278 | Charlie Lea | .15 | .07 |
| ❑ | 279 | Bryan Little | .15 | .07 |
| ❑ | 280 | Al Oliver | .40 | .18 |
| ❑ | 281 | Tim Raines | .75 | .35 |
| ❑ | 282 | Bobby Ramos | .15 | .07 |
| ❑ | 283 | Jeff Reardon | .40 | .18 |
| ❑ | 284 | Steve Rogers | .15 | .07 |
| ❑ | 285 | Scott Sanderson | .15 | .07 |
| ❑ | 286 | Dan Schatzeder | .15 | .07 |
| ❑ | 287 | Bryn Smith | .15 | .07 |
| ❑ | 288 | Chris Speier | .15 | .07 |
| ❑ | 289 | Manny Trillo | .15 | .07 |
| ❑ | 290 | Mike Vail | .15 | .07 |
| ❑ | 291 | Tim Wallach | .40 | .18 |
| ❑ | 292 | Chris Welsh | .15 | .07 |
| ❑ | 293 | Jim Wohlford | .15 | .07 |
| ❑ | 294 | Kurt Bevacqua | .15 | .07 |
| ❑ | 295 | Juan Bonilla | .15 | .07 |
| ❑ | 296 | Bobby Brown | .15 | .07 |
| ❑ | 297 | Luis DeLeon | .15 | .07 |
| ❑ | 298 | Dave Dravecky | .40 | .18 |
| ❑ | 299 | Tim Flannery | .15 | .07 |
| ❑ | 300 | Steve Garvey | .75 | .35 |
| ❑ | 301 | Tony Gwynn | 8.00 | 3.60 |
| ❑ | 302 | Andy Hawkins | .15 | .07 |
| ❑ | 303 | Ruppert Jones | .15 | .07 |
| ❑ | 304 | Terry Kennedy | .15 | .07 |
| ❑ | 305 | Tim Lollar | .15 | .07 |
| ❑ | 306 | Gary Lucas | .15 | .07 |
| ❑ | 307 | Kevin McReynolds RC | .75 | .35 |
| ❑ | 308 | Sid Monge | .15 | .07 |
| ❑ | 309 | Mario Ramirez | .15 | .07 |
| ❑ | 310 | Gene Richards | .15 | .07 |
| ❑ | 311 | Luis Salazar | .15 | .07 |
| ❑ | 312 | Eric Show | .15 | .07 |
| ❑ | 313 | Elias Sosa | .15 | .07 |
| ❑ | 314 | Garry Templeton | .15 | .07 |
| ❑ | 315 | Mark Thurmond | .15 | .07 |
| ❑ | 316 | Ed Whitson | .15 | .07 |
| ❑ | 317 | Alan Wiggins | .15 | .07 |
| ❑ | 318 | Neil Allen | .15 | .07 |
| ❑ | 319 | Joaquin Andujar | .15 | .07 |
| ❑ | 320 | Steve Braun | .15 | .07 |
| ❑ | 321 | Glenn Brummer | .15 | .07 |
| ❑ | 322 | Bob Forsch | .15 | .07 |
| ❑ | 323 | David Green | .15 | .07 |
| ❑ | 324 | George Hendrick | .15 | .07 |
| ❑ | 325 | Tom Herr | .40 | .18 |
| ❑ | 326 | Dane Iorg | .15 | .07 |
| ❑ | 327 | Jeff Lahti | .15 | .07 |
| ❑ | 328 | Dave LaPoint | .15 | .07 |
| ❑ | 329 | Willie McGee | .75 | .35 |
| ❑ | 330 | Ken Oberkfell | .15 | .07 |
| ❑ | 331 | Darrell Porter | .15 | .07 |
| ❑ | 332 | Jamie Quirk | .15 | .07 |
| ❑ | 333 | Mike Ramsey | .15 | .07 |
| ❑ | 334 | Floyd Rayford | .15 | .07 |
| ❑ | 335 | Lonnie Smith | .15 | .07 |
| ❑ | 336 | Ozzie Smith | 2.00 | .90 |
| ❑ | 337 | John Stuper | .15 | .07 |
| ❑ | 338 | Bruce Sutter | .40 | .18 |
| ❑ | 339 | Andy Van Slyke RC UER | 1.50 | .70 |
| | | (Batting and throwing both wrong on card back) | | |
| ❑ | 340 | Dave Von Ohlen | .15 | .07 |
| ❑ | 341 | Willie Aikens | .15 | .07 |
| ❑ | 342 | Mike Armstrong | .15 | .07 |
| ❑ | 343 | Bud Black | .15 | .07 |
| ❑ | 344 | George Brett | 3.00 | 1.35 |
| ❑ | 345 | Onix Concepcion | .15 | .07 |
| ❑ | 346 | Keith Creel | .15 | .07 |
| ❑ | 347 | Larry Gura | .15 | .07 |
| ❑ | 348 | Don Hood | .15 | .07 |
| ❑ | 349 | Dennis Leonard | .15 | .07 |
| ❑ | 350 | Hal McRae | .40 | .18 |
| ❑ | 351 | Amos Otis | .40 | .18 |
| ❑ | 352 | Gaylord Perry | 1.50 | .70 |
| ❑ | 353 | Greg Pryor | .15 | .07 |
| ❑ | 354 | Dan Quisenberry | .15 | .07 |
| ❑ | 355 | Steve Renko | .15 | .07 |
| ❑ | 356 | Leon Roberts | .15 | .07 |
| ❑ | 357 | Pat Sheridan | .15 | .07 |
| ❑ | 358 | Joe Simpson | .15 | .07 |
| ❑ | 359 | Don Slaught | .40 | .18 |
| ❑ | 360 | Paul Splittorff | .15 | .07 |
| ❑ | 361 | U.L. Washington | .15 | .07 |
| ❑ | 362 | John Wathan | .15 | .07 |
| ❑ | 363 | Frank White | .40 | .18 |
| ❑ | 364 | Willie Wilson | .15 | .07 |
| ❑ | 365 | Jim Barr | .15 | .07 |
| ❑ | 366 | Dave Bergman | .15 | .07 |
| ❑ | 367 | Fred Breining | .15 | .07 |
| ❑ | 368 | Bob Brenly | .15 | .07 |
| ❑ | 369 | Jack Clark | .40 | .18 |
| ❑ | 370 | Chili Davis | .75 | .35 |
| ❑ | 371 | Mark Davis | .15 | .07 |
| ❑ | 372 | Darrell Evans | .40 | .18 |
| ❑ | 373 | Atlee Hammaker | .15 | .07 |
| ❑ | 374 | Mike Krukow | .15 | .07 |
| ❑ | 375 | Duane Kuiper | .15 | .07 |
| ❑ | 376 | Bill Laskey | .15 | .07 |
| ❑ | 377 | Gary Lavelle | .15 | .07 |
| ❑ | 378 | Johnnie LeMaster | .15 | .07 |
| ❑ | 379 | Jeff Leonard | .15 | .07 |
| ❑ | 380 | Randy Lerch | .15 | .07 |
| ❑ | 381 | Renie Martin | .15 | .07 |
| ❑ | 382 | Andy McGaffigan | .15 | .07 |
| ❑ | 383 | Greg Minton | .15 | .07 |
| ❑ | 384 | Tom O'Malley | .15 | .07 |
| ❑ | 385 | Max Venable | .15 | .07 |
| ❑ | 386 | Brad Wellman | .15 | .07 |
| ❑ | 387 | Joel Youngblood | .15 | .07 |
| ❑ | 388 | Gary Allenson | .15 | .07 |
| ❑ | 389 | Luis Aponte | .15 | .07 |
| ❑ | 390 | Tony Armas | .15 | .07 |
| ❑ | 391 | Doug Bird | .15 | .07 |
| ❑ | 392 | Wade Boggs | 5.00 | 2.20 |
| ❑ | 393 | Dennis Boyd | .40 | .18 |
| ❑ | 394 | Mike Brown UER P | .15 | .07 |
| | | (Shown with record of 31-104) | | |
| ❑ | 395 | Mark Clear | .15 | .07 |
| ❑ | 396 | Dennis Eckersley | 1.50 | .70 |
| ❑ | 397 | Dwight Evans | .40 | .18 |
| ❑ | 398 | Rich Gedman | .15 | .07 |
| ❑ | 399 | Glenn Hoffman | .15 | .07 |
| ❑ | 400 | Bruce Hurst | .15 | .07 |
| ❑ | 401 | John Henry Johnson | .15 | .07 |
| ❑ | 402 | Ed Jurak | .15 | .07 |
| ❑ | 403 | Rick Miller | .15 | .07 |
| ❑ | 404 | Jeff Newman | .15 | .07 |
| ❑ | 405 | Reid Nichols | .15 | .07 |
| ❑ | 406 | Bob Ojeda | .15 | .07 |
| ❑ | 407 | Jerry Remy | .15 | .07 |
| ❑ | 408 | Jim Rice | .40 | .18 |
| ❑ | 409 | Bob Stanley | .15 | .07 |
| ❑ | 410 | Dave Stapleton | .15 | .07 |
| ❑ | 411 | John Tudor | .15 | .07 |
| ❑ | 412 | Carl Yastrzemski | 1.50 | .70 |
| ❑ | 413 | Buddy Bell | .40 | .18 |
| ❑ | 414 | Larry Biittner | .15 | .07 |
| ❑ | 415 | John Butcher | .15 | .07 |
| ❑ | 416 | Danny Darwin | .15 | .07 |
| ❑ | 417 | Bucky Dent | .40 | .18 |
| ❑ | 418 | Dave Hostetler | .15 | .07 |
| ❑ | 419 | Charlie Hough | .40 | .18 |
| ❑ | 420 | Bobby Johnson | .15 | .07 |
| ❑ | 421 | Odell Jones | .15 | .07 |
| ❑ | 422 | Jon Matlack | .15 | .07 |
| ❑ | 423 | Pete O'Brien RC* | .40 | .18 |
| ❑ | 424 | Larry Parrish | .15 | .07 |
| ❑ | 425 | Mickey Rivers | .15 | .07 |
| ❑ | 426 | Billy Sample | .15 | .07 |
| ❑ | 427 | Dave Schmidt | .15 | .07 |
| ❑ | 428 | Mike Smithson | .15 | .07 |
| ❑ | 429 | Bill Stein | .15 | .07 |
| ❑ | 430 | Dave Stewart | .40 | .18 |
| ❑ | 431 | Jim Sundberg | .40 | .18 |
| ❑ | 432 | Frank Tanana | .40 | .18 |
| ❑ | 433 | Dave Tobik | .15 | .07 |
| ❑ | 434 | Wayne Tolleson | .15 | .07 |
| ❑ | 435 | George Wright | .15 | .07 |
| ❑ | 436 | Bill Almon | .15 | .07 |
| ❑ | 437 | Keith Atherton | .15 | .07 |
| ❑ | 438 | Dave Beard | .15 | .07 |
| ❑ | 439 | Tom Burgmeier | .15 | .07 |
| ❑ | 440 | Jeff Burroughs | .15 | .07 |
| ❑ | 441 | Chris Codiroli | .15 | .07 |
| ❑ | 442 | Tim Conroy | .15 | .07 |
| ❑ | 443 | Mike Davis | .15 | .07 |
| ❑ | 444 | Wayne Gross | .15 | .07 |
| ❑ | 445 | Garry Hancock | .15 | .07 |
| ❑ | 446 | Mike Heath | .15 | .07 |
| ❑ | 447 | Rickey Henderson | 2.50 | 1.10 |
| ❑ | 448 | Donnie Hill | .15 | .07 |
| ❑ | 449 | Bob Kearney | .15 | .07 |
| ❑ | 450 | Bill Krueger RC | .15 | .07 |
| ❑ | 451 | Rick Langford | .15 | .07 |
| ❑ | 452 | Carney Lansford | .40 | .18 |
| ❑ | 453 | Dave Lopes | .40 | .18 |
| ❑ | 454 | Steve McCatty | .15 | .07 |
| ❑ | 455 | Dan Meyer | .15 | .07 |
| ❑ | 456 | Dwayne Murphy | .15 | .07 |
| ❑ | 457 | Mike Norris | .15 | .07 |
| ❑ | 458 | Ricky Peters | .15 | .07 |
| ❑ | 459 | Tony Phillips RC | 1.50 | .70 |

❑ 460 Tom Underwood .15 .07
❑ 461 Mike Warren .15 .07
❑ 462 Johnny Bench 2.50 1.10
❑ 463 Bruce Berenyi .15 .07
❑ 464 Dann Bilardello .15 .07
❑ 465 Cesar Cedeno .40 .18
❑ 466 Dave Concepcion .40 .18
❑ 467 Dan Driessen .15 .07
❑ 468 Nick Esasky .15 .07
❑ 469 Rich Gale .15 .07
❑ 470 Ben Hayes .15 .07
❑ 471 Paul Householder .15 .07
❑ 472 Tom Hume .15 .07
❑ 473 Alan Knicely .15 .07
❑ 474 Eddie Milner .15 .07
❑ 475 Ron Oester .15 .07
❑ 476 Kelly Paris .15 .07
❑ 477 Frank Pastore .15 .07
❑ 478 Ted Power .15 .07
❑ 479 Joe Price .15 .07
❑ 480 Charlie Puleo .15 .07
❑ 481 Gary Redus RC* .15 .07
❑ 482 Bill Scherrer .15 .07
❑ 483 Mario Soto .15 .07
❑ 484 Alex Trevino .15 .07
❑ 485 Duane Walker .15 .07
❑ 486 Larry Bowa .40 .18
❑ 487 Warren Brusstar .15 .07
❑ 488 Bill Buckner .40 .18
❑ 489 Bill Campbell .15 .07
❑ 490 Ron Cey .40 .18
❑ 491 Jody Davis .15 .07
❑ 492 Leon Durham .15 .07
❑ 493 Mel Hall .40 .18
❑ 494 Ferguson Jenkins 1.50 .70
❑ 495 Jay Johnstone .40 .18
❑ 496 Craig Lefferts RC .15 .07
❑ 497 Carmelo Martinez .15 .07
❑ 498 Jerry Morales .15 .07
❑ 499 Keith Moreland .15 .07
❑ 500 Dickie Noles .15 .07
❑ 501 Mike Proly .15 .07
❑ 502 Chuck Rainey .15 .07
❑ 503 Dick Ruthven .15 .07
❑ 504 Ryne Sandberg 5.00 2.20
❑ 505 Lee Smith 1.50 .70
❑ 506 Steve Trout .15 .07
❑ 507 Gary Woods .15 .07
❑ 508 Juan Beniquez .15 .07
❑ 509 Bob Boone .40 .18
❑ 510 Rick Burleson .15 .07
❑ 511 Rod Carew 1.50 .70
❑ 512 Bobby Clark .15 .07
❑ 513 John Curtis .15 .07
❑ 514 Doug DeCinces .15 .07
❑ 515 Brian Downing .15 .07
❑ 516 Tim Foli .15 .07
❑ 517 Ken Forsch .15 .07
❑ 518 Bobby Grich .40 .18
❑ 519 Andy Hassler .15 .07
❑ 520 Reggie Jackson 2.00 .90
❑ 521 Ron Jackson .15 .07
❑ 522 Tommy John .75 .35
❑ 523 Bruce Kison .15 .07
❑ 524 Steve Lubratich .15 .07
❑ 525 Fred Lynn .40 .18
❑ 526 Gary Pettis .15 .07
❑ 527 Luis Sanchez .15 .07
❑ 528 Daryl Sconiers .15 .07
❑ 529 Ellis Valentine .15 .07
❑ 530 Rob Wilfong .15 .07
❑ 531 Mike Witt .15 .07
❑ 532 Geoff Zahn .15 .07
❑ 533 Bud Anderson .15 .07
❑ 534 Chris Bando .15 .07
❑ 535 Alan Bannister .15 .07
❑ 536 Bert Blyleven .40 .18
❑ 537 Tom Brennan .15 .07
❑ 538 Jamie Easterly .15 .07
❑ 539 Juan Eichelberger .15 .07
❑ 540 Jim Essian .15 .07
❑ 541 Mike Fischlin .15 .07
❑ 542 Julio Franco .75 .35
❑ 543 Mike Hargrove .40 .18
❑ 544 Toby Harrah .40 .18
❑ 545 Ron Hassey .15 .07
❑ 546 Neal Heaton .15 .07
❑ 547 Bake McBride .15 .07
❑ 548 Broderick Perkins .15 .07
❑ 549 Lary Sorensen .15 .07
❑ 550 Dan Spillner .15 .07
❑ 551 Rick Sutcliffe .40 .18
❑ 552 Pat Tabler .15 .07
❑ 553 Gorman Thomas .15 .07
❑ 554 Andre Thornton .15 .07
❑ 555 George Vukovich .15 .07
❑ 556 Darrell Brown .15 .07
❑ 557 Tom Brunansky .40 .18
❑ 558 Randy Bush .15 .07
❑ 559 Bobby Castillo .15 .07
❑ 560 John Castino .15 .07
❑ 561 Ron Davis .15 .07
❑ 562 Dave Engle .15 .07
❑ 563 Lenny Faedo .15 .07
❑ 564 Pete Filson .15 .07
❑ 565 Gary Gaetti .75 .35
❑ 566 Mickey Hatcher .15 .07
❑ 567 Kent Hrbek .40 .18
❑ 568 Rusty Kuntz .15 .07
❑ 569 Tim Laudner .15 .07
❑ 570 Rick Lysander .15 .07
❑ 571 Bobby Mitchell .15 .07
❑ 572 Ken Schrom .15 .07
❑ 573 Ray Smith .15 .07
❑ 574 Tim Teufel RC .15 .07
❑ 575 Frank Viola .75 .35
❑ 576 Gary Ward .15 .07
❑ 577 Ron Washington .15 .07
❑ 578 Len Whitehouse .15 .07
❑ 579 Al Williams .15 .07
❑ 580 Bob Bailor .15 .07
❑ 581 Mark Bradley .15 .07
❑ 582 Hubie Brooks .15 .07
❑ 583 Carlos Diaz .15 .07
❑ 584 George Foster .40 .18
❑ 585 Brian Giles .15 .07
❑ 586 Danny Heep .15 .07
❑ 587 Keith Hernandez .40 .18
❑ 588 Ron Hodges .15 .07
❑ 589 Scott Holman .15 .07
❑ 590 Dave Kingman .75 .35
❑ 591 Ed Lynch .15 .07
❑ 592 Jose Oquendo RC .40 .18
❑ 593 Jesse Orosco .15 .07
❑ 594 Junior Ortiz .15 .07
❑ 595 Tom Seaver 2.50 1.10
❑ 596 Doug Sisk .15 .07
❑ 597 Rusty Staub .40 .18
❑ 598 John Stearns .15 .07
❑ 599 Darryl Strawberry RC 3.00 1.35
❑ 600 Craig Swan .15 .07
❑ 601 Walt Terrell .15 .07
❑ 602 Mike Torrez .15 .07
❑ 603 Mookie Wilson .40 .18
❑ 604 Jamie Allen .15 .07
❑ 605 Jim Beattie .15 .07
❑ 606 Tony Bernazard .15 .07
❑ 607 Manny Castillo .15 .07
❑ 608 Bill Caudill .15 .07
❑ 609 Bryan Clark .15 .07
❑ 610 Al Cowens .15 .07
❑ 611 Dave Henderson .40 .18
❑ 612 Steve Henderson .15 .07
❑ 613 Orlando Mercado .15 .07
❑ 614 Mike Moore .15 .07
❑ 615 Ricky Nelson UER .15 .07
(Jamie Nelson's
stats on back)
❑ 616 Spike Owen RC .40 .18
❑ 617 Pat Putnam .15 .07
❑ 618 Ron Roenicke .15 .07
❑ 619 Mike Stanton .15 .07
❑ 620 Bob Stoddard .15 .07
❑ 621 Rick Sweet .15 .07
❑ 622 Roy Thomas .15 .07
❑ 623 Ed VandeBerg .15 .07
❑ 624 Matt Young .15 .07
❑ 625 Richie Zisk .15 .07
❑ 626 Fred Lynn .40 .18
1982 AS Game RB
❑ 627 Manny Trillo .15 .07
1983 AS Game RB
❑ 628 Steve Garvey .40 .18
NL Iron Man
❑ 629 Rod Carew .75 .35
AL Batting Runner-Up
❑ 630 Wade Boggs 2.00 .90
AL Batting Champion
❑ 631 Tim Raines: Letting .40 .18
Go of the Raines
❑ 632 Al Oliver .40 .18
Double Trouble
❑ 633 Steve Sax .15 .07
AS Second Base
❑ 634 Dickie Thon .15 .07
AS Shortstop
❑ 635 Ace Firemen .15 .07
Dan Quisenberry
and Tippy Martinez
❑ 636 Reds Reunited 1.50 .70
Joe Morgan
Pete Rose
Tony Perez
❑ 637 Backstop Stars .75 .35
Lance Parrish
Bob Boone
❑ 638 George Brett and 2.00 .90
Gaylord Perry
Pine Tar 7/24/83
❑ 639 1983 No Hitters .75 .35
Dave Righetti
Mike Warren
Bob Forsch
❑ 640 Johnny Bench and 2.00 .90
Carl Yastrzemski
Retiring Superstars
❑ 641 Gaylord Perry 1.50 .70
Going Out In Style
❑ 642 Steve Carlton .75 .35
300 Club and
Strikeout Record
❑ 643 Joe Altobelli and .15 .07
Paul Owens
World Series Managers
❑ 644 Rick Dempsey .40 .18
World Series MVP
❑ 645 Mike Boddicker .15 .07
WS Rookie Winner
❑ 646 Scott McGregor .15 .07
WS Clincher
❑ 647 CL: Orioles/Royals .15 .07
Joe Altobelli MG
❑ 648 CL: Phillies/Giants .15 .07
Paul Owens MG
❑ 649 CL: White Sox/Red Sox .75 .35
Tony LaRussa MG
❑ 650 CL: Tigers/Rangers .75 .35
Sparky Anderson MG
❑ 651 CL: Dodgers/A's .75 .35
Tommy Lasorda MG
❑ 652 CL: Yankees/Reds .75 .35
Billy Martin MG
❑ 653 CL: Blue Jays/Cubs .40 .18
Bobby Cox MG
❑ 654 CL: Braves/Angels .75 .35
Joe Torre MG
❑ 655 CL: Brewers/Indians .15 .07
Rene Lachemann MG
❑ 656 CL: Astros/Twins .15 .07
Bob Lillis MG
❑ 657 CL: Pirates/Mets .15 .07
Chuck Tanner MG
❑ 658 CL: Expos/Mariners .15 .07
Bill Virdon MG
❑ 659 CL: Padres/Specials .40 .18
Dick Williams MG
❑ 660 CL: Cardinals/Teams .75 .35
Whitey Herzog MG

## 1984 Fleer Update

| | NRMT | VG-E |
|---|---|---|
| COMP.FACT.SET (132) | 300.00 | 135.00 |

❑ 1 Willie Aikens 1.00 .45
❑ 2 Luis Aponte 1.00 .45
❑ 3 Mark Bailey 1.00 .45
❑ 4 Bob Bailor 1.00 .45

❑ 5 Dusty Baker .......... 1.50 .70
❑ 6 Steve Balboni .......... 1.00 .45
❑ 7 Alan Bannister .......... 1.00 .45
❑ 8 Marty Barrett .......... 1.50 .70
❑ 9 Dave Beard .......... 1.00 .45
❑ 10 Joe Beckwith .......... 1.00 .45
❑ 11 Dave Bergman .......... 1.00 .45
❑ 12 Tony Bernazard .......... 1.00 .45
❑ 13 Bruce Bochte .......... 1.00 .45
❑ 14 Barry Bonnell .......... 1.00 .45
❑ 15 Phil Bradley .......... 1.50 .70
❑ 16 Fred Breining .......... 1.00 .45
❑ 17 Mike C. Brown .......... 1.00 .45
❑ 18 Bill Buckner .......... 1.50 .70
❑ 19 Ray Burris .......... 1.00 .45
❑ 20 John Butcher .......... 1.00 .45
❑ 21 Brett Butler .......... 2.50 1.10
❑ 22 Enos Cabell .......... 1.00 .45
❑ 23 Bill Campbell .......... 1.00 .45
❑ 24 Bill Caudill .......... 1.00 .45
❑ 25 Bobby Clark .......... 1.00 .45
❑ 26 Bryan Clark .......... 1.00 .45
❑ 27 Roger Clemens XRC .. 200.00 90.00
❑ 28 Jaime Cocanower .......... 1.00 .45
❑ 29 Ron Darling XRC* .......... 2.50 1.10
❑ 30 Alvin Davis XRC .......... 1.50 .70
❑ 31 Bob Dernier .......... 1.00 .45
❑ 32 Carlos Diaz .......... 1.00 .45
❑ 33 Mike Easler .......... 1.00 .45
❑ 34 Dennis Eckersley .......... 4.00 1.80
❑ 35 Jim Essian .......... 1.00 .45
❑ 36 Darrell Evans .......... 1.50 .70
❑ 37 Mike Fitzgerald .......... 1.00 .45
❑ 38 Tim Foli .......... 1.00 .45
❑ 39 John Franco XRC .......... 8.00 3.60
❑ 40 George Frazier .......... 1.00 .45
❑ 41 Rich Gale .......... 1.00 .45
❑ 42 Barbaro Garbey .......... 1.00 .45
❑ 43 Dwight Gooden XRC .... 15.00 6.75
❑ 44 Rich Gossage .......... 2.50 1.10
❑ 45 Wayne Gross .......... 1.00 .45
❑ 46 Mark Gubicza XRC .......... 1.50 .70
❑ 47 Jackie Gutierrez .......... 1.00 .45
❑ 48 Toby Harrah .......... 1.50 .70
❑ 49 Ron Hassey .......... 1.00 .45
❑ 50 Richie Hebner .......... 1.00 .45
❑ 51 Willie Hernandez .......... 1.50 .70
❑ 52 Ed Hodge .......... 1.00 .45
❑ 53 Ricky Horton .......... 1.00 .45
❑ 54 Art Howe .......... 1.50 .70
❑ 55 Dane Iorg .......... 1.00 .45
❑ 56 Brook Jacoby .......... 1.50 .70
❑ 57 Dion James XRC* .......... 1.00 .45
❑ 58 Mike Jeffcoat .......... 1.00 .45
❑ 59 Ruppert Jones .......... 1.00 .45
❑ 60 Bob Kearney .......... 1.00 .45
❑ 61 Jimmy Key XRC .......... 2.50 1.10
❑ 62 Dave Kingman .......... 2.50 1.10
❑ 63 Brad Komminsk .......... 1.00 .45
❑ 64 Jerry Koosman .......... 1.50 .70
❑ 65 Wayne Krenchicki .......... 1.00 .45
❑ 66 Rusty Kuntz .......... 1.00 .45
❑ 67 Frank LaCorte .......... 1.00 .45
❑ 68 Dennis Lamp .......... 1.00 .45
❑ 69 Tito Landrum .......... 1.00 .45
❑ 70 Mark Langston XRC .......... 4.00 1.80
❑ 71 Rick Leach .......... 1.00 .45
❑ 72 Craig Lefferts .......... 1.50 .70
❑ 73 Gary Lucas .......... 1.00 .45
❑ 74 Jerry Martin .......... 1.00 .45
❑ 75 Carmelo Martinez .......... 1.00 .45
❑ 76 Mike Mason .......... 1.00 .45
❑ 77 Gary Matthews .......... 1.50 .70
❑ 78 Andy McGaffigan .......... 1.00 .45
❑ 79 Joey McLaughlin .......... 1.00 .45
❑ 80 Joe Morgan .......... 4.00 1.80
❑ 81 Darryl Motley .......... 1.00 .45
❑ 82 Graig Nettles .......... 1.50 .70
❑ 83 Phil Niekro .......... 4.00 1.80
❑ 84 Ken Oberkfell .......... 1.00 .45
❑ 85 Al Oliver .......... 1.50 .70
❑ 86 Jorge Orta .......... 1.00 .45
❑ 87 Amos Otis .......... 1.50 .70
❑ 88 Bob Owchinko .......... 1.00 .45
❑ 89 Dave Parker .......... 1.50 .70
❑ 90 Jack Perconte .......... 1.00 .45
❑ 91 Tony Perez .......... 4.00 1.80
❑ 92 Gerald Perry .......... 1.50 .70
❑ 93 Kirby Puckett XRC .... 100.00 45.00
❑ 94 Shane Rawley .......... 1.00 .45
❑ 95 Floyd Rayford .......... 1.00 .45
❑ 96 Ron Reed .......... 1.00 .45
❑ 97 R.J. Reynolds .......... 1.00 .45
❑ 98 Gene Richards .......... 1.00 .45
❑ 99 Jose Rijo XRC .......... 4.00 1.80
❑ 100 Jeff D. Robinson .......... 1.00 .45
❑ 101 Ron Romanick .......... 1.00 .45
❑ 102 Pete Rose .......... 12.00 5.50
❑ 103 Bret Saberhagen XRC 10.00 4.50
❑ 104 Scott Sanderson .......... 1.00 .45
❑ 105 Dick Schofield XRC* .... 1.50 .70
❑ 106 Tom Seaver .......... 6.00 2.70
❑ 107 Jim Slaton .......... 1.00 .45
❑ 108 Mike Smithson .......... 1.00 .45
❑ 109 Lary Sorensen .......... 1.00 .45
❑ 110 Tim Stoddard .......... 1.00 .45
❑ 111 Jeff Stone .......... 1.00 .45
❑ 112 Champ Summers .......... 1.00 .45
❑ 113 Jim Sundberg .......... 1.50 .70
❑ 114 Rick Sutcliffe .......... 1.50 .70
❑ 115 Craig Swan .......... 1.00 .45
❑ 116 Derrel Thomas .......... 1.00 .45
❑ 117 Gorman Thomas .......... 1.00 .45
❑ 118 Alex Trevino .......... 1.00 .45
❑ 119 Manny Trillo .......... 1.00 .45
❑ 120 John Tudor .......... 1.00 .45
❑ 121 Tom Underwood .......... 1.00 .45
❑ 122 Mike Vail .......... 1.00 .45
❑ 123 Tom Waddell .......... 1.00 .45
❑ 124 Gary Ward .......... 1.00 .45
❑ 125 Terry Whitfield .......... 1.00 .45
❑ 126 Curtis Wilkerson .......... 1.00 .45
❑ 127 Frank Williams .......... 1.00 .45
❑ 128 Glenn Wilson .......... 1.00 .45
❑ 129 John Wockenfuss .......... 1.00 .45
❑ 130 Ned Yost .......... 1.00 .45
❑ 131 Mike Young .......... 1.00 .45
❑ 132 Checklist 1-132 .......... 1.00 .45

## 1985 Fleer

| | NRMT | VG-E |
|---|---|---|
| COMPLETE SET (660) .......... | 80.00 | 36.00 |

❑ 1 Doug Bair .......... .15 .07
❑ 2 Juan Berenguer .......... .15 .07
❑ 3 Dave Bergman .......... .15 .07
❑ 4 Tom Brookens .......... .15 .07
❑ 5 Marty Castillo .......... .15 .07
❑ 6 Darrell Evans .......... .40 .18
❑ 7 Barbaro Garbey .......... .15 .07
❑ 8 Kirk Gibson .......... .40 .18
❑ 9 John Grubb .......... .15 .07
❑ 10 Willie Hernandez .......... .15 .07
❑ 11 Larry Herndon .......... .15 .07
❑ 12 Howard Johnson .......... .40 .18
❑ 13 Ruppert Jones .......... .15 .07
❑ 14 Rusty Kuntz .......... .15 .07
❑ 15 Chet Lemon .......... .15 .07
❑ 16 Aurelio Lopez .......... .15 .07
❑ 17 Sid Monge .......... .15 .07
❑ 18 Jack Morris .......... .40 .18
❑ 19 Lance Parrish .......... .40 .18
❑ 20 Dan Petry .......... .15 .07
❑ 21 Dave Rozema .......... .15 .07
❑ 22 Bill Scherrer .......... .15 .07
❑ 23 Alan Trammell .......... .75 .35
❑ 24 Lou Whitaker .......... .75 .35
❑ 25 Milt Wilcox .......... .15 .07
❑ 26 Kurt Bevacqua .......... .15 .07
❑ 27 Greg Booker .......... .15 .07
❑ 28 Bobby Brown .......... .15 .07
❑ 29 Luis DeLeon .......... .15 .07
❑ 30 Dave Dravecky .......... .40 .18
❑ 31 Tim Flannery .......... .15 .07
❑ 32 Steve Garvey .......... .75 .35
❑ 33 Rich Gossage .......... .40 .18
❑ 34 Tony Gwynn .......... 4.00 1.80
❑ 35 Greg Harris .......... .15 .07
❑ 36 Andy Hawkins .......... .15 .07
❑ 37 Terry Kennedy .......... .15 .07
❑ 38 Craig Lefferts .......... .15 .07
❑ 39 Tim Lollar .......... .15 .07
❑ 40 Carmelo Martinez .......... .15 .07
❑ 41 Kevin McReynolds .......... .40 .18
❑ 42 Graig Nettles .......... .40 .18
❑ 43 Luis Salazar .......... .15 .07
❑ 44 Eric Show .......... .15 .07
❑ 45 Garry Templeton .......... .15 .07
❑ 46 Mark Thurmond .......... .15 .07
❑ 47 Ed Whitson .......... .15 .07
❑ 48 Alan Wiggins .......... .15 .07
❑ 49 Rich Bordi .......... .15 .07
❑ 50 Larry Bowa .......... .40 .18
❑ 51 Warren Brusstar .......... .15 .07
❑ 52 Ron Cey .......... .40 .18
❑ 53 Henry Cotto RC .......... .15 .07
❑ 54 Jody Davis .......... .15 .07
❑ 55 Bob Dernier .......... .15 .07
❑ 56 Leon Durham .......... .15 .07
❑ 57 Dennis Eckersley .......... 1.25 .55
❑ 58 George Frazier .......... .15 .07
❑ 59 Richie Hebner .......... .15 .07
❑ 60 Dave Lopes .......... .40 .18
❑ 61 Gary Matthews .......... .15 .07
❑ 62 Keith Moreland .......... .15 .07
❑ 63 Rick Reuschel .......... .15 .07
❑ 64 Dick Ruthven .......... .15 .07
❑ 65 Ryne Sandberg .......... 2.50 1.10
❑ 66 Scott Sanderson .......... .15 .07
❑ 67 Lee Smith .......... .75 .35
❑ 68 Tim Stoddard .......... .15 .07
❑ 69 Rick Sutcliffe .......... .40 .18
❑ 70 Steve Trout .......... .15 .07
❑ 71 Gary Woods .......... .15 .07
❑ 72 Wally Backman .......... .15 .07
❑ 73 Bruce Berenyi .......... .15 .07
❑ 74 Hubie Brooks UER .......... .15 .07
(Kelvin Chapman's stats on card back)
❑ 75 Kelvin Chapman .......... .15 .07
❑ 76 Ron Darling .......... .40 .18
❑ 77 Sid Fernandez .......... .40 .18
❑ 78 Mike Fitzgerald .......... .15 .07
❑ 79 George Foster .......... .40 .18
❑ 80 Brent Gaff .......... .15 .07
❑ 81 Ron Gardenhire .......... .15 .07
❑ 82 Dwight Gooden RC .......... 2.00 .90
❑ 83 Tom Gorman .......... .15 .07
❑ 84 Danny Heep .......... .15 .07
❑ 85 Keith Hernandez .......... .40 .18
❑ 86 Ray Knight .......... .15 .07

❑ 87 Ed Lynch .15 .07
❑ 88 Jose Oquendo .15 .07
❑ 89 Jesse Orosco .15 .07
❑ 90 Rafael Santana .15 .07
❑ 91 Doug Sisk .15 .07
❑ 92 Rusty Staub .40 .18
❑ 93 Darryl Strawberry 1.25 .55
❑ 94 Walt Terrell .15 .07
❑ 95 Mookie Wilson .40 .18
❑ 96 Jim Acker .15 .07
❑ 97 Willie Aikens .15 .07
❑ 98 Doyle Alexander .15 .07
❑ 99 Jesse Barfield .15 .07
❑ 100 George Bell .40 .18
❑ 101 Jim Clancy .15 .07
❑ 102 Dave Collins .15 .07
❑ 103 Tony Fernandez .40 .18
❑ 104 Damaso Garcia .15 .07
❑ 105 Jim Gott .15 .07
❑ 106 Alfredo Griffin .15 .07
❑ 107 Garth Iorg .15 .07
❑ 108 Roy Lee Jackson .15 .07
❑ 109 Cliff Johnson .15 .07
❑ 110 Jimmy Key RC 1.25 .55
❑ 111 Dennis Lamp .15 .07
❑ 112 Rick Leach .15 .07
❑ 113 Luis Leal .15 .07
❑ 114 Buck Martinez .15 .07
❑ 115 Lloyd Moseby .15 .07
❑ 116 Rance Mulliniks .15 .07
❑ 117 Dave Stieb .40 .18
❑ 118 Willie Upshaw .15 .07
❑ 119 Ernie Whitt .15 .07
❑ 120 Mike Armstrong .15 .07
❑ 121 Don Baylor .40 .18
❑ 122 Marty Bystrom .15 .07
❑ 123 Rick Cerone .15 .07
❑ 124 Joe Cowley .15 .07
❑ 125 Brian Dayett .15 .07
❑ 126 Tim Foli .15 .07
❑ 127 Ray Fontenot .15 .07
❑ 128 Ken Griffey .40 .18
❑ 129 Ron Guidry .40 .18
❑ 130 Toby Harrah .15 .07
❑ 131 Jay Howell .15 .07
❑ 132 Steve Kemp .15 .07
❑ 133 Don Mattingly 4.00 1.80
❑ 134 Bobby Meacham .15 .07
❑ 135 John Montefusco .15 .07
❑ 136 Omar Moreno .15 .07
❑ 137 Dale Murray .15 .07
❑ 138 Phil Niekro 1.25 .55
❑ 139 Mike Pagliarulo .15 .07
❑ 140 Willie Randolph .40 .18
❑ 141 Dennis Rasmussen .15 .07
❑ 142 Dave Righetti .40 .18
❑ 143 Jose Rijo RC .75 .35
❑ 144 Andre Robertson .15 .07
❑ 145 Bob Shirley .15 .07
❑ 146 Dave Winfield 1.25 .55
❑ 147 Butch Wynegar .15 .07
❑ 148 Gary Allenson .15 .07
❑ 149 Tony Armas .15 .07
❑ 150 Marty Barrett .15 .07
❑ 151 Wade Boggs 2.00 .90
❑ 152 Dennis Boyd .15 .07
❑ 153 Bill Buckner .40 .18
❑ 154 Mark Clear .15 .07
❑ 155 Roger Clemens RC ! 40.00 18.00
❑ 156 Steve Crawford .15 .07
❑ 157 Mike Easler .15 .07
❑ 158 Dwight Evans .40 .18
❑ 159 Rich Gedman .15 .07
❑ 160 Jackie Gutierrez .40 .18
(Wade Boggs shown on deck)
❑ 161 Bruce Hurst .15 .07
❑ 162 John Henry Johnson .15 .07
❑ 163 Rick Miller .15 .07
❑ 164 Reid Nichols .15 .07
❑ 165 Al Nipper .15 .07
❑ 166 Bob Ojeda .15 .07
❑ 167 Jerry Remy .15 .07
❑ 168 Jim Rice .40 .18
❑ 169 Bob Stanley .15 .07
❑ 170 Mike Boddicker .15 .07
❑ 171 Al Bumbry .15 .07
❑ 172 Todd Cruz .15 .07
❑ 173 Rich Dauer .15 .07
❑ 174 Storm Davis .15 .07
❑ 175 Rick Dempsey .15 .07
❑ 176 Jim Dwyer .15 .07
❑ 177 Mike Flanagan .15 .07
❑ 178 Dan Ford .15 .07
❑ 179 Wayne Gross .15 .07
❑ 180 John Lowenstein .15 .07
❑ 181 Dennis Martinez .40 .18
❑ 182 Tippy Martinez .15 .07
❑ 183 Scott McGregor .15 .07
❑ 184 Eddie Murray 1.25 .55
❑ 185 Joe Nolan .15 .07
❑ 186 Floyd Rayford .15 .07
❑ 187 Cal Ripken 6.00 2.70
❑ 188 Gary Roenicke .15 .07
❑ 189 Lenn Sakata .15 .07
❑ 190 John Shelby .15 .07
❑ 191 Ken Singleton .15 .07
❑ 192 Sammy Stewart .15 .07
❑ 193 Bill Swaggerty .15 .07
❑ 194 Tom Underwood .15 .07
❑ 195 Mike Young .15 .07
❑ 196 Steve Balboni .15 .07
❑ 197 Joe Beckwith .15 .07
❑ 198 Bud Black .15 .07
❑ 199 George Brett 2.50 1.10
❑ 200 Onix Concepcion .15 .07
❑ 201 Mark Gubicza RC* .40 .18
❑ 202 Larry Gura .15 .07
❑ 203 Mark Huismann .15 .07
❑ 204 Dane Iorg .15 .07
❑ 205 Danny Jackson .15 .07
❑ 206 Charlie Leibrandt .15 .07
❑ 207 Hal McRae .40 .18
❑ 208 Darryl Motley .15 .07
❑ 209 Jorge Orta .15 .07
❑ 210 Greg Pryor .15 .07
❑ 211 Dan Quisenberry .40 .18
❑ 212 Bret Saberhagen RC 1.00 .45
❑ 213 Pat Sheridan .15 .07
❑ 214 Don Slaught .15 .07
❑ 215 U.L. Washington .15 .07
❑ 216 John Wathan .15 .07
❑ 217 Frank White .40 .18
❑ 218 Willie Wilson .15 .07
❑ 219 Neil Allen .15 .07
❑ 220 Joaquin Andujar .15 .07
❑ 221 Steve Braun .15 .07
❑ 222 Danny Cox .15 .07
❑ 223 Bob Forsch .15 .07
❑ 224 David Green .15 .07
❑ 225 George Hendrick .15 .07
❑ 226 Tom Herr .15 .07
❑ 227 Ricky Horton .15 .07
❑ 228 Art Howe .15 .07
❑ 229 Mike Jorgensen .15 .07
❑ 230 Kurt Kepshire .15 .07
❑ 231 Jeff Lahti .15 .07
❑ 232 Tito Landrum .15 .07
❑ 233 Dave LaPoint .15 .07
❑ 234 Willie McGee .40 .18
❑ 235 Tom Nieto .15 .07
❑ 236 Terry Pendleton RC 1.25 .55
❑ 237 Darrell Porter .15 .07
❑ 238 Dave Rucker .15 .07
❑ 239 Lonnie Smith .15 .07
❑ 240 Ozzie Smith 1.50 .70
❑ 241 Bruce Sutter .40 .18
❑ 242 Andy Van Slyke UER .40 .18
(Bats Right, Throws Left)
❑ 243 Dave Von Ohlen .15 .07
❑ 244 Larry Andersen .15 .07
❑ 245 Bill Campbell .15 .07
❑ 246 Steve Carlton 1.25 .55
❑ 247 Tim Corcoran .15 .07
❑ 248 Ivan DeJesus .15 .07
❑ 249 John Denny .15 .07
❑ 250 Bo Diaz .15 .07
❑ 251 Greg Gross .15 .07
❑ 252 Kevin Gross .15 .07
❑ 253 Von Hayes .15 .07
❑ 254 Al Holland .15 .07
❑ 255 Charles Hudson .15 .07
❑ 256 Jerry Koosman .40 .18
❑ 257 Joe Lefebvre .15 .07
❑ 258 Sixto Lezcano .15 .07
❑ 259 Garry Maddox .15 .07
❑ 260 Len Matuszek .15 .07
❑ 261 Tug McGraw .40 .18
❑ 262 Al Oliver .40 .18
❑ 263 Shane Rawley .15 .07
❑ 264 Juan Samuel .15 .07
❑ 265 Mike Schmidt 2.50 1.10
❑ 266 Jeff Stone .15 .07
❑ 267 Ozzie Virgil .15 .07
❑ 268 Glenn Wilson .15 .07
❑ 269 John Wockenfuss .15 .07
❑ 270 Darrell Brown .15 .07
❑ 271 Tom Brunansky .40 .18
❑ 272 Randy Bush .15 .07
❑ 273 John Butcher .15 .07
❑ 274 Bobby Castillo .15 .07
❑ 275 Ron Davis .15 .07
❑ 276 Dave Engle .15 .07
❑ 277 Pete Filson .15 .07
❑ 278 Gary Gaetti .40 .18
❑ 279 Mickey Hatcher .15 .07
❑ 280 Ed Hodge .15 .07
❑ 281 Kent Hrbek .40 .18
❑ 282 Houston Jimenez .15 .07
❑ 283 Tim Laudner .15 .07
❑ 284 Rick Lysander .15 .07
❑ 285 Dave Meier .15 .07
❑ 286 Kirby Puckett RC ! 20.00 9.00
❑ 287 Pat Putnam .15 .07
❑ 288 Ken Schrom .15 .07
❑ 289 Mike Smithson .15 .07
❑ 290 Tim Teufel .15 .07
❑ 291 Frank Viola .40 .18
❑ 292 Ron Washington .15 .07
❑ 293 Don Aase .15 .07
❑ 294 Juan Beniquez .15 .07
❑ 295 Bob Boone .40 .18
❑ 296 Mike C. Brown .15 .07
❑ 297 Rod Carew 1.25 .55
❑ 298 Doug Corbett .15 .07
❑ 299 Doug DeCinces .15 .07
❑ 300 Brian Downing .15 .07
❑ 301 Ken Forsch .15 .07
❑ 302 Bobby Grich .40 .18
❑ 303 Reggie Jackson 1.50 .70
❑ 304 Tommy John .75 .35
❑ 305 Curt Kaufman .15 .07
❑ 306 Bruce Kison .15 .07
❑ 307 Fred Lynn .40 .18
❑ 308 Gary Pettis .15 .07
❑ 309 Ron Romanick .15 .07
❑ 310 Luis Sanchez .15 .07
❑ 311 Dick Schofield .15 .07
❑ 312 Daryl Sconiers .15 .07
❑ 313 Jim Slaton .15 .07
❑ 314 Derrel Thomas .15 .07
❑ 315 Rob Wilfong .15 .07
❑ 316 Mike Witt .15 .07
❑ 317 Geoff Zahn .15 .07
❑ 318 Len Barker .15 .07
❑ 319 Steve Bedrosian .15 .07
❑ 320 Bruce Benedict .15 .07
❑ 321 Rick Camp .15 .07
❑ 322 Chris Chambliss .40 .18
❑ 323 Jeff Dedmon .15 .07
❑ 324 Terry Forster .15 .07
❑ 325 Gene Garber .15 .07
❑ 326 Albert Hall .15 .07
❑ 327 Terry Harper .15 .07
❑ 328 Bob Horner .15 .07
❑ 329 Glenn Hubbard .15 .07
❑ 330 Randy Johnson .15 .07
❑ 331 Brad Komminsk .15 .07
❑ 332 Rick Mahler .15 .07
❑ 333 Craig McMurtry .15 .07
❑ 334 Donnie Moore .15 .07
❑ 335 Dale Murphy 1.25 .55
❑ 336 Ken Oberkfell .15 .07
❑ 337 Pascual Perez .15 .07
❑ 338 Gerald Perry .15 .07
❑ 339 Rafael Ramirez .15 .07
❑ 340 Jerry Royster .15 .07

| | No. | Player | | |
|---|---|---|---|---|
| ❑ | 341 | Alex Trevino | .15 | .07 |
| ❑ | 342 | Claudell Washington | .15 | .07 |
| ❑ | 343 | Alan Ashby | .15 | .07 |
| ❑ | 344 | Mark Bailey | .15 | .07 |
| ❑ | 345 | Kevin Bass | .15 | .07 |
| ❑ | 346 | Enos Cabell | .15 | .07 |
| ❑ | 347 | Jose Cruz | .40 | .18 |
| ❑ | 348 | Bill Dawley | .15 | .07 |
| ❑ | 349 | Frank DiPino | .15 | .07 |
| ❑ | 350 | Bill Doran | .15 | .07 |
| ❑ | 351 | Phil Garner | .40 | .18 |
| ❑ | 352 | Bob Knepper | .15 | .07 |
| ❑ | 353 | Mike LaCoss | .15 | .07 |
| ❑ | 354 | Jerry Mumphrey | .15 | .07 |
| ❑ | 355 | Joe Niekro | .15 | .07 |
| ❑ | 356 | Terry Puhl | .15 | .07 |
| ❑ | 357 | Craig Reynolds | .15 | .07 |
| ❑ | 358 | Vern Ruhle | .15 | .07 |
| ❑ | 359 | Nolan Ryan | 6.00 | 2.70 |
| ❑ | 360 | Joe Sambito | .15 | .07 |
| ❑ | 361 | Mike Scott | .15 | .07 |
| ❑ | 362 | Dave Smith | .15 | .07 |
| ❑ | 363 | Julio Solano | .15 | .07 |
| ❑ | 364 | Dickie Thon | .15 | .07 |
| ❑ | 365 | Donny Walling | .15 | .07 |
| ❑ | 366 | Dave Anderson | .15 | .07 |
| ❑ | 367 | Bob Bailor | .15 | .07 |
| ❑ | 368 | Greg Brock | .15 | .07 |
| ❑ | 369 | Carlos Diaz | .15 | .07 |
| ❑ | 370 | Pedro Guerrero | .40 | .18 |
| ❑ | 371 | Orel Hershiser RC | 2.00 | .90 |
| ❑ | 372 | Rick Honeycutt | .15 | .07 |
| ❑ | 373 | Burt Hooton | .15 | .07 |
| ❑ | 374 | Ken Howell | .15 | .07 |
| ❑ | 375 | Ken Landreaux | .15 | .07 |
| ❑ | 376 | Candy Maldonado | .15 | .07 |
| ❑ | 377 | Mike Marshall | .15 | .07 |
| ❑ | 378 | Tom Niedenfuer | .15 | .07 |
| ❑ | 379 | Alejandro Pena | .15 | .07 |
| ❑ | 380 | Jerry Reuss UER ("Home:" omitted) | .15 | .07 |
| ❑ | 381 | R.J. Reynolds | .15 | .07 |
| ❑ | 382 | German Rivera | .15 | .07 |
| ❑ | 383 | Bill Russell | .15 | .07 |
| ❑ | 384 | Steve Sax | .15 | .07 |
| ❑ | 385 | Mike Scioscia | .15 | .07 |
| ❑ | 386 | Franklin Stubbs | .15 | .07 |
| ❑ | 387 | Fernando Valenzuela | .40 | .18 |
| ❑ | 388 | Bob Welch | .15 | .07 |
| ❑ | 389 | Terry Whitfield | .15 | .07 |
| ❑ | 390 | Steve Yeager | .15 | .07 |
| ❑ | 391 | Pat Zachry | .15 | .07 |
| ❑ | 392 | Fred Breining | .15 | .07 |
| ❑ | 393 | Gary Carter | .75 | .35 |
| ❑ | 394 | Andre Dawson | .75 | .35 |
| ❑ | 395 | Miguel Dilone | .15 | .07 |
| ❑ | 396 | Dan Driessen | .15 | .07 |
| ❑ | 397 | Doug Flynn | .15 | .07 |
| ❑ | 398 | Terry Francona | .15 | .07 |
| ❑ | 399 | Bill Gullickson | .15 | .07 |
| ❑ | 400 | Bob James | .15 | .07 |
| ❑ | 401 | Charlie Lea | .15 | .07 |
| ❑ | 402 | Bryan Little | .15 | .07 |
| ❑ | 403 | Gary Lucas | .15 | .07 |
| ❑ | 404 | David Palmer | .15 | .07 |
| ❑ | 405 | Tim Raines | .40 | .18 |
| ❑ | 406 | Mike Ramsey | .15 | .07 |
| ❑ | 407 | Jeff Reardon | .40 | .18 |
| ❑ | 408 | Steve Rogers | .15 | .07 |
| ❑ | 409 | Dan Schatzeder | .15 | .07 |
| ❑ | 410 | Bryn Smith | .15 | .07 |
| ❑ | 411 | Mike Stenhouse | .15 | .07 |
| ❑ | 412 | Tim Wallach | .40 | .18 |
| ❑ | 413 | Jim Wohlford | .15 | .07 |
| ❑ | 414 | Bill Almon | .15 | .07 |
| ❑ | 415 | Keith Atherton | .15 | .07 |
| ❑ | 416 | Bruce Bochte | .15 | .07 |
| ❑ | 417 | Tom Burgmeier | .15 | .07 |
| ❑ | 418 | Ray Burris | .15 | .07 |
| ❑ | 419 | Bill Caudill | .15 | .07 |
| ❑ | 420 | Chris Codiroli | .15 | .07 |
| ❑ | 421 | Tim Conroy | .15 | .07 |
| ❑ | 422 | Mike Davis | .15 | .07 |
| ❑ | 423 | Jim Esslan | .15 | .07 |
| ❑ | 424 | Mike Heath | .15 | .07 |
| ❑ | 425 | Rickey Henderson | 1.50 | .70 |
| ❑ | 426 | Donnie Hill | .15 | .07 |
| ❑ | 427 | Dave Kingman | .40 | .18 |
| ❑ | 428 | Bill Krueger | .15 | .07 |
| ❑ | 429 | Carney Lansford | .40 | .18 |
| ❑ | 430 | Steve McCatty | .15 | .07 |
| ❑ | 431 | Joe Morgan | 1.25 | .55 |
| ❑ | 432 | Dwayne Murphy | .15 | .07 |
| ❑ | 433 | Tony Phillips | .15 | .07 |
| ❑ | 434 | Lary Sorensen | .15 | .07 |
| ❑ | 435 | Mike Warren | .15 | .07 |
| ❑ | 436 | Curt Young | .15 | .07 |
| ❑ | 437 | Luis Aponte | .15 | .07 |
| ❑ | 438 | Chris Bando | .15 | .07 |
| ❑ | 439 | Tony Bernazard | .15 | .07 |
| ❑ | 440 | Bert Blyleven | .40 | .18 |
| ❑ | 441 | Brett Butler | .40 | .18 |
| ❑ | 442 | Ernie Camacho | .15 | .07 |
| ❑ | 443 | Joe Carter | 1.25 | .55 |
| ❑ | 444 | Carmelo Castillo | .15 | .07 |
| ❑ | 445 | Jamie Easterly | .15 | .07 |
| ❑ | 446 | Steve Farr RC | .40 | .18 |
| ❑ | 447 | Mike Fischlin | .15 | .07 |
| ❑ | 448 | Julio Franco | .75 | .35 |
| ❑ | 449 | Mel Hall | .15 | .07 |
| ❑ | 450 | Mike Hargrove | .40 | .18 |
| ❑ | 451 | Neal Heaton | .15 | .07 |
| ❑ | 452 | Brook Jacoby | .15 | .07 |
| ❑ | 453 | Mike Jeffcoat | .15 | .07 |
| ❑ | 454 | Don Schulze | .15 | .07 |
| ❑ | 455 | Roy Smith | .15 | .07 |
| ❑ | 456 | Pat Tabler | .15 | .07 |
| ❑ | 457 | Andre Thornton | .15 | .07 |
| ❑ | 458 | George Vukovich | .15 | .07 |
| ❑ | 459 | Tom Waddell | .15 | .07 |
| ❑ | 460 | Jerry Willard | .15 | .07 |
| ❑ | 461 | Dale Berra | .15 | .07 |
| ❑ | 462 | John Candelaria | .15 | .07 |
| ❑ | 463 | Jose DeLeon | .15 | .07 |
| ❑ | 464 | Doug Frobel | .15 | .07 |
| ❑ | 465 | Cecilio Guante | .15 | .07 |
| ❑ | 466 | Brian Harper | .15 | .07 |
| ❑ | 467 | Lee Lacy | .15 | .07 |
| ❑ | 468 | Bill Madlock | .40 | .18 |
| ❑ | 469 | Lee Mazzilli | .15 | .07 |
| ❑ | 470 | Larry McWilliams | .15 | .07 |
| ❑ | 471 | Jim Morrison | .15 | .07 |
| ❑ | 472 | Tony Pena | .15 | .07 |
| ❑ | 473 | Johnny Ray | .15 | .07 |
| ❑ | 474 | Rick Rhoden | .15 | .07 |
| ❑ | 475 | Don Robinson | .15 | .07 |
| ❑ | 476 | Rod Scurry | .15 | .07 |
| ❑ | 477 | Kent Tekulve | .15 | .07 |
| ❑ | 478 | Jason Thompson | .15 | .07 |
| ❑ | 479 | John Tudor | .15 | .07 |
| ❑ | 480 | Lee Tunnell | .15 | .07 |
| ❑ | 481 | Marvell Wynne | .15 | .07 |
| ❑ | 482 | Salome Barojas | .15 | .07 |
| ❑ | 483 | Dave Beard | .15 | .07 |
| ❑ | 484 | Jim Beattie | .15 | .07 |
| ❑ | 485 | Barry Bonnell | .15 | .07 |
| ❑ | 486 | Phil Bradley | .40 | .18 |
| ❑ | 487 | Al Cowens | .15 | .07 |
| ❑ | 488 | Alvin Davis RC* | .40 | .18 |
| ❑ | 489 | Dave Henderson | .15 | .07 |
| ❑ | 490 | Steve Henderson | .15 | .07 |
| ❑ | 491 | Bob Kearney | .15 | .07 |
| ❑ | 492 | Mark Langston RC | .75 | .35 |
| ❑ | 493 | Larry Milbourne | .15 | .07 |
| ❑ | 494 | Paul Mirabella | .15 | .07 |
| ❑ | 495 | Mike Moore | .15 | .07 |
| ❑ | 496 | Edwin Nunez | .15 | .07 |
| ❑ | 497 | Spike Owen | .15 | .07 |
| ❑ | 498 | Jack Perconte | .15 | .07 |
| ❑ | 499 | Ken Phelps | .15 | .07 |
| ❑ | 500 | Jim Presley | .40 | .18 |
| ❑ | 501 | Mike Stanton | .15 | .07 |
| ❑ | 502 | Bob Stoddard | .15 | .07 |
| ❑ | 503 | Gorman Thomas | .15 | .07 |
| ❑ | 504 | Ed VandeBerg | .15 | .07 |
| ❑ | 505 | Matt Young | .15 | .07 |
| ❑ | 506 | Juan Agosto | .15 | .07 |
| ❑ | 507 | Harold Baines | .40 | .18 |
| ❑ | 508 | Floyd Bannister | .15 | .07 |
| ❑ | 509 | Britt Burns | .15 | .07 |
| ❑ | 510 | Julio Cruz | .15 | .07 |
| ❑ | 511 | Richard Dotson | .15 | .07 |
| ❑ | 512 | Jerry Dybzinski | .15 | .07 |
| ❑ | 513 | Carlton Fisk | 1.25 | .55 |
| ❑ | 514 | Scott Fletcher | .15 | .07 |
| ❑ | 515 | Jerry Hairston | .15 | .07 |
| ❑ | 516 | Marc Hill | .15 | .07 |
| ❑ | 517 | LaMarr Hoyt | .15 | .07 |
| ❑ | 518 | Ron Kittle | .15 | .07 |
| ❑ | 519 | Rudy Law | .15 | .07 |
| ❑ | 520 | Vance Law | .15 | .07 |
| ❑ | 521 | Greg Luzinski | .40 | .18 |
| ❑ | 522 | Gene Nelson | .15 | .07 |
| ❑ | 523 | Tom Paciorek | .40 | .18 |
| ❑ | 524 | Ron Reed | .15 | .07 |
| ❑ | 525 | Bert Roberge | .15 | .07 |
| ❑ | 526 | Tom Seaver | 2.00 | .90 |
| ❑ | 527 | Roy Smalley | .15 | .07 |
| ❑ | 528 | Dan Spillner | .15 | .07 |
| ❑ | 529 | Mike Squires | .15 | .07 |
| ❑ | 530 | Greg Walker | .15 | .07 |
| ❑ | 531 | Cesar Cedeno | .40 | .18 |
| ❑ | 532 | Dave Concepcion | .40 | .18 |
| ❑ | 533 | Eric Davis RC | 2.00 | .90 |
| ❑ | 534 | Nick Esasky | .15 | .07 |
| ❑ | 535 | Tom Foley | .15 | .07 |
| ❑ | 536 | John Franco RC UER (Koufax misspelled as Kofax on back) | 1.25 | .55 |
| ❑ | 537 | Brad Gulden | .15 | .07 |
| ❑ | 538 | Tom Hume | .15 | .07 |
| ❑ | 539 | Wayne Krenchicki | .15 | .07 |
| ❑ | 540 | Andy McGaffigan | .15 | .07 |
| ❑ | 541 | Eddie Milner | .15 | .07 |
| ❑ | 542 | Ron Oester | .15 | .07 |
| ❑ | 543 | Bob Owchinko | .15 | .07 |
| ❑ | 544 | Dave Parker | .40 | .18 |
| ❑ | 545 | Frank Pastore | .15 | .07 |
| ❑ | 546 | Tony Perez | 1.25 | .55 |
| ❑ | 547 | Ted Power | .15 | .07 |
| ❑ | 548 | Joe Price | .15 | .07 |
| ❑ | 549 | Gary Redus | .15 | .07 |
| ❑ | 550 | Pete Rose | 4.00 | 1.80 |
| ❑ | 551 | Jeff Russell | .15 | .07 |
| ❑ | 552 | Mario Soto | .15 | .07 |
| ❑ | 553 | Jay Tibbs | .15 | .07 |
| ❑ | 554 | Duane Walker | .15 | .07 |
| ❑ | 555 | Alan Bannister | .15 | .07 |
| ❑ | 556 | Buddy Bell | .40 | .18 |
| ❑ | 557 | Danny Darwin | .15 | .07 |
| ❑ | 558 | Charlie Hough | .40 | .18 |
| ❑ | 559 | Bobby Jones | .15 | .07 |
| ❑ | 560 | Odell Jones | .15 | .07 |
| ❑ | 561 | Jeff Kunkel | .15 | .07 |
| ❑ | 562 | Mike Mason | .15 | .07 |
| ❑ | 563 | Pete O'Brien | .15 | .07 |
| ❑ | 564 | Larry Parrish | .15 | .07 |
| ❑ | 565 | Mickey Rivers | .15 | .07 |
| ❑ | 566 | Billy Sample | .15 | .07 |
| ❑ | 567 | Dave Schmidt | .15 | .07 |
| ❑ | 568 | Donnie Scott | .15 | .07 |
| ❑ | 569 | Dave Stewart | .40 | .18 |
| ❑ | 570 | Frank Tanana | .15 | .07 |
| ❑ | 571 | Wayne Tolleson | .15 | .07 |
| ❑ | 572 | Gary Ward | .15 | .07 |
| ❑ | 573 | Curtis Wilkerson | .15 | .07 |
| ❑ | 574 | George Wright | .15 | .07 |
| ❑ | 575 | Ned Yost | .15 | .07 |
| ❑ | 576 | Mark Brouhard | .15 | .07 |
| ❑ | 577 | Mike Caldwell | .15 | .07 |
| ❑ | 578 | Bobby Clark | .15 | .07 |
| ❑ | 579 | Jaime Cocanower | .15 | .07 |
| ❑ | 580 | Cecil Cooper | .40 | .18 |
| ❑ | 581 | Rollie Fingers | 1.25 | .55 |
| ❑ | 582 | Jim Gantner | .15 | .07 |
| ❑ | 583 | Moose Haas | .15 | .07 |
| ❑ | 584 | Dion James | .15 | .07 |
| ❑ | 585 | Pete Ladd | .15 | .07 |
| ❑ | 586 | Rick Manning | .15 | .07 |
| ❑ | 587 | Bob McClure | .15 | .07 |
| ❑ | 588 | Paul Molitor | 1.25 | .55 |
| ❑ | 589 | Charlie Moore | .15 | .07 |
| ❑ | 590 | Ben Oglivie | .15 | .07 |
| ❑ | 591 | Chuck Porter | .15 | .07 |
| ❑ | 592 | Randy Ready RC* | .15 | .07 |
| ❑ | 593 | Ed Romero | .15 | .07 |
| ❑ | 594 | Bill Schroeder | .15 | .07 |
| ❑ | 595 | Ray Searage | .15 | .07 |

❑ 596 Ted Simmons .40 .18
❑ 597 Jim Sundberg .15 .07
❑ 598 Don Sutton 1.25 .55
❑ 599 Tom Tellmann .15 .07
❑ 600 Rick Waits .15 .07
❑ 601 Robin Yount 1.25 .55
❑ 602 Dusty Baker .40 .18
❑ 603 Bob Brenly .15 .07
❑ 604 Jack Clark .40 .18
❑ 605 Chili Davis .40 .18
❑ 606 Mark Davis .15 .07
❑ 607 Dan Gladden RC .40 .18
❑ 608 Atlee Hammaker .15 .07
❑ 609 Mike Krukow .15 .07
❑ 610 Duane Kuiper .15 .07
❑ 611 Bob Lacey .15 .07
❑ 612 Bill Laskey .15 .07
❑ 613 Gary Lavelle .15 .07
❑ 614 Johnnie LeMaster .15 .07
❑ 615 Jeff Leonard .15 .07
❑ 616 Randy Lerch .15 .07
❑ 617 Greg Minton .15 .07
❑ 618 Steve Nicosia .15 .07
❑ 619 Gene Richards .15 .07
❑ 620 Jeff D. Robinson .15 .07
❑ 621 Scot Thompson .15 .07
❑ 622 Manny Trillo .15 .07
❑ 623 Brad Wellman .15 .07
❑ 624 Frank Williams .15 .07
❑ 625 Joel Youngblood .15 .07
❑ 626 Cal Ripken IA 3.00 1.35
❑ 627 Mike Schmidt IA .75 .35
❑ 628 Giving The Signs .40 .18
Sparky Anderson
❑ 629 AL Pitcher's Nightmare 1.25 .55
Dave Winfield
Rickey Henderson
❑ 630 NL Pitcher's Nightmare 2.00 .90
Mike Schmidt
Ryne Sandberg
❑ 631 NL All-Stars 1.25 .55
Darryl Strawberry
Gary Carter
Steve Garvey
Ozzie Smith
❑ 632 A-S Winning Battery .40 .18
Gary Carter
Charlie Lea
❑ 633 NL Pennant Clinchers .75 .35
Steve Garvey
Rich Gossage
❑ 634 NL Rookie Phenoms 1.25 .55
Dwight Gooden
Juan Samuel
❑ 635 Toronto's Big Guns .15 .07
Willie Upshaw
❑ 636 Toronto's Big Guns .15 .07
Lloyd Moseby
❑ 637 HOLLAND: Al Holland .15 .07
❑ 638 TUNNELL: Lee Tunnell .15 .07
❑ 639 Reggie Jackson 1.25 .55
500th Homer
❑ 640 4000th Hit 1.25 .55
Pete Rose
❑ 641 Father and Son 3.00 1.35
Cal Ripken Jr.
Cal Ripken Sr.
❑ 642 Cubs: Division Champs .40 .18
❑ 643 Two Perfect Games .40 .18
and One No-Hitter:
Mike Witt
David Palmer
Jack Morris
❑ 644 Willie Lozado and .15 .07
Vic Mata
❑ 645 Kelly Gruber RC and .40 .18
Randy O'Neal
❑ 646 Jose Roman and .15 .07
Joel Skinner
❑ 647 Steve Kiefer RC and 1.25 .55
Danny Tartabull
❑ 648 Rob Dee RC and .40 .18
Alejandro Sanchez
❑ 649 Billy Hatcher RC and 1.00 .45
Shawon Dunston
❑ 650 Ron Robinson and .15 .07
Mike Bielecki
❑ 651 Zane Smith RC and .40 .18
Paul Zuvella
❑ 652 Joe Hesketh RC and .40 .18
Glenn Davis
❑ 653 John Russell and .15 .07
Steve Jeltz
❑ 654 CL: Tigers/Padres .15 .07
and Cubs/Mets
❑ 655 CL: Blue Jays/Yankees .15 .07
and Red Sox/Orioles
❑ 656 CL: Royals/Cardinals .15 .07
and Phillies/Twins
❑ 657 CL: Angels/Braves .15 .07
and Astros/Dodgers
❑ 658 CL: Expos/A's .15 .07
and Indians/Pirates
❑ 659 CL: Mariners/White Sox .15 .07
and Reds/Rangers
❑ 660 CL: Brewers/Giants .15 .07
and Special Cards

# 1985 Fleer Update

| | NRMT | VG-E |
|---|---|---|
| COMP.FACT.SET (132) | 6.00 | 2.70 |

❑ 1 Don Aase .15 .07
❑ 2 Bill Almon .15 .07
❑ 3 Dusty Baker .40 .18
❑ 4 Dale Berra .15 .07
❑ 5 Karl Best .15 .07
❑ 6 Tim Birtsas .15 .07
❑ 7 Vida Blue .40 .18
❑ 8 Rich Bordi .15 .07
❑ 9 Daryl Boston XRC* .15 .07
❑ 10 Hubie Brooks .15 .07
❑ 11 Chris Brown .15 .07
❑ 12 Tom Browning XRC* .40 .18
❑ 13 Al Bumbry .15 .07
❑ 14 Tim Burke .15 .07
❑ 15 Ray Burris .15 .07
❑ 16 Jeff Burroughs .15 .07
❑ 17 Ivan Calderon XRC .15 .07
❑ 18 Jeff Calhoun .15 .07
❑ 19 Bill Campbell .15 .07
❑ 20 Don Carman .15 .07
❑ 21 Gary Carter .75 .35
❑ 22 Bobby Castillo .15 .07
❑ 23 Bill Caudill .15 .07
❑ 24 Rick Cerone .15 .07
❑ 25 Jack Clark .40 .18
❑ 26 Pat Clements .15 .07
❑ 27 Stewart Cliburn .15 .07
❑ 28 Vince Coleman XRC 1.00 .45
❑ 29 Dave Collins .15 .07
❑ 30 Fritz Connally .15 .07
❑ 31 Henry Cotto .15 .07
❑ 32 Danny Darwin .15 .07
❑ 33 Darren Daulton XRC 2.00 .90
❑ 34 Jerry Davis .15 .07
❑ 35 Brian Dayett .15 .07
❑ 36 Ken Dixon .15 .07
❑ 37 Tommy Dunbar .15 .07
❑ 38 Mariano Duncan XRC 1.00 .45
❑ 39 Bob Fallon .15 .07
❑ 40 Brian Fisher .15 .07
❑ 41 Mike Fitzgerald .15 .07
❑ 42 Ray Fontenot .15 .07
❑ 43 Greg Gagne XRC* .40 .18
❑ 44 Oscar Gamble .15 .07
❑ 45 Jim Gott .15 .07
❑ 46 David Green .15 .07
❑ 47 Alfredo Griffin .15 .07
❑ 48 Ozzie Guillen XRC 1.00 .45
❑ 49 Toby Harrah .15 .07
❑ 50 Ron Hassey .15 .07
❑ 51 Rickey Henderson 2.00 .90
❑ 52 Steve Henderson .15 .07
❑ 53 George Hendrick .15 .07
❑ 54 Teddy Higuera XRC .40 .18
❑ 55 Al Holland .15 .07
❑ 56 Burt Hooton .15 .07
❑ 57 Jay Howell .15 .07
❑ 58 LaMarr Hoyt .15 .07
❑ 59 Tim Hulett XRC* .15 .07
❑ 60 Bob James .15 .07
❑ 61 Cliff Johnson .15 .07
❑ 62 Howard Johnson .40 .18
❑ 63 Ruppert Jones .15 .07
❑ 64 Steve Kemp .15 .07
❑ 65 Bruce Kison .15 .07
❑ 66 Mike LaCoss .15 .07
❑ 67 Lee Lacy .15 .07
❑ 68 Dave LaPoint .15 .07
❑ 69 Gary Lavelle .15 .07
❑ 70 Vance Law .15 .07
❑ 71 Manny Lee XRC .15 .07
❑ 72 Sixto Lezcano .15 .07
❑ 73 Tim Lollar .15 .07
❑ 74 Urbano Lugo .15 .07
❑ 75 Fred Lynn .40 .18
❑ 76 Steve Lyons .40 .18
❑ 77 Mickey Mahler .15 .07
❑ 78 Ron Mathis .15 .07
❑ 79 Len Matuszek .15 .07
❑ 80 Oddibe McDowell XRC* UER .40 .18
(Part of bio
actually Roger's) XRC*
❑ 81 Roger McDowell XRC UER .40 .18
(Part of bio
actually Oddibe's)
❑ 82 Donnie Moore .15 .07
❑ 83 Ron Musselman .15 .07
❑ 84 Al Oliver .40 .18
❑ 85 Joe Orsulak XRC .40 .18
❑ 86 Dan Pasqua XRC* .40 .18
❑ 87 Chris Pittaro .15 .07
❑ 88 Rick Reuschel .15 .07
❑ 89 Earnie Riles .15 .07
❑ 90 Jerry Royster .15 .07
❑ 91 Dave Rozema .15 .07
❑ 92 Dave Rucker .15 .07
❑ 93 Vern Ruhle .15 .07
❑ 94 Mark Salas .15 .07
❑ 95 Luis Salazar .15 .07
❑ 96 Joe Sambito .15 .07
❑ 97 Billy Sample .15 .07
❑ 98 Alejandro Sanchez .15 .07
❑ 99 Calvin Schiraldi .15 .07
❑ 100 Rick Schu .15 .07
❑ 101 Larry Sheets .15 .07
❑ 102 Ron Shephard .15 .07
❑ 103 Nelson Simmons .15 .07
❑ 104 Don Slaught .15 .07
❑ 105 Roy Smalley .15 .07
❑ 106 Lonnie Smith .15 .07
❑ 107 Nate Snell .15 .07
❑ 108 Lary Sorensen .15 .07
❑ 109 Chris Speier .15 .07
❑ 110 Mike Stenhouse .15 .07
❑ 111 Tim Stoddard .15 .07
❑ 112 John Stuper .15 .07
❑ 113 Jim Sundberg .15 .07
❑ 114 Bruce Sutter .40 .18
❑ 115 Don Sutton 1.00 .45
❑ 116 Bruce Tanner .15 .07
❑ 117 Kent Tekulve .15 .07
❑ 118 Walt Terrell .15 .07
❑ 119 Mickey Tettleton XRC 1.00 .45
❑ 120 Rich Thompson .15 .07
❑ 121 Louis Thornton .15 .07
❑ 122 Alex Trevino .15 .07
❑ 123 John Tudor .15 .07

❑ 124 Jose Uribe .15 .07
❑ 125 Dave Valle XRC .15 .07
❑ 126 Dave Von Ohlen .15 .07
❑ 127 Curt Wardle .15 .07
❑ 128 U.L. Washington .15 .07
❑ 129 Ed Whitson .15 .07
❑ 130 Herm Winningham .15 .07
❑ 131 Rich Yett .15 .07
❑ 132 Checklist U1-U132 .15 .07

## 1986 Fleer

| | MINT | NRMT |
|---|---|---|
| COMPLETE SET (660) | 40.00 | 18.00 |
| COMP.FACT.SET (660) | 50.00 | 22.00 |

❑ 1 Steve Balboni .15 .07
❑ 2 Joe Beckwith .15 .07
❑ 3 Buddy Biancalana .15 .07
❑ 4 Bud Black .15 .07
❑ 5 George Brett 1.50 .70
❑ 6 Onix Concepcion .15 .07
❑ 7 Steve Farr .15 .07
❑ 8 Mark Gubicza .15 .07
❑ 9 Dane Iorg .15 .07
❑ 10 Danny Jackson .15 .07
❑ 11 Lynn Jones .15 .07
❑ 12 Mike Jones .15 .07
❑ 13 Charlie Leibrandt .15 .07
❑ 14 Hal McRae .25 .11
❑ 15 Omar Moreno .15 .07
❑ 16 Darryl Motley .15 .07
❑ 17 Jorge Orta .15 .07
❑ 18 Dan Quisenberry .15 .07
❑ 19 Bret Saberhagen .25 .11
❑ 20 Pat Sheridan .15 .07
❑ 21 Lonnie Smith .15 .07
❑ 22 Jim Sundberg .15 .07
❑ 23 John Wathan .15 .07
❑ 24 Frank White .25 .11
❑ 25 Willie Wilson .15 .07
❑ 26 Joaquin Andujar .15 .07
❑ 27 Steve Braun .15 .07
❑ 28 Bill Campbell .15 .07
❑ 29 Cesar Cedeno .25 .11
❑ 30 Jack Clark .25 .11
❑ 31 Vince Coleman RC* .75 .35
❑ 32 Danny Cox .15 .07
❑ 33 Ken Dayley .15 .07
❑ 34 Ivan DeJesus .15 .07
❑ 35 Bob Forsch .15 .07
❑ 36 Brian Harper .15 .07
❑ 37 Tom Herr .15 .07
❑ 38 Ricky Horton .15 .07
❑ 39 Kurt Kepshire .15 .07
❑ 40 Jeff Lahti .15 .07
❑ 41 Tito Landrum .15 .07
❑ 42 Willie McGee .25 .11
❑ 43 Tom Nieto .15 .07
❑ 44 Terry Pendleton .25 .11
❑ 45 Darrell Porter .25 .11
❑ 46 Ozzie Smith 1.00 .45
❑ 47 John Tudor .15 .07
❑ 48 Andy Van Slyke .25 .11
❑ 49 Todd Worrell RC .75 .35
❑ 50 Jim Acker .15 .07
❑ 51 Doyle Alexander .15 .07
❑ 52 Jesse Barfield .15 .07
❑ 53 George Bell .25 .11
❑ 54 Jeff Burroughs .15 .07
❑ 55 Bill Caudill .15 .07
❑ 56 Jim Clancy .15 .07
❑ 57 Tony Fernandez .15 .07
❑ 58 Tom Filer .15 .07
❑ 59 Damaso Garcia .15 .07
❑ 60 Tom Henke .25 .11
❑ 61 Garth Iorg .15 .07
❑ 62 Cliff Johnson .15 .07
❑ 63 Jimmy Key .75 .35
❑ 64 Dennis Lamp .15 .07
❑ 65 Gary Lavelle .15 .07
❑ 66 Buck Martinez .15 .07
❑ 67 Lloyd Moseby .15 .07
❑ 68 Rance Mulliniks .15 .07
❑ 69 Al Oliver .25 .11
❑ 70 Dave Stieb .15 .07
❑ 71 Louis Thornton .15 .07
❑ 72 Willie Upshaw .15 .07
❑ 73 Ernie Whitt .15 .07
❑ 74 Rick Aguilera RC .75 .35
❑ 75 Wally Backman .15 .07
❑ 76 Gary Carter .50 .23
❑ 77 Ron Darling .15 .07
❑ 78 Len Dykstra RC 1.50 .70
❑ 79 Sid Fernandez .25 .11
❑ 80 George Foster .25 .11
❑ 81 Dwight Gooden .75 .35
❑ 82 Tom Gorman .15 .07
❑ 83 Danny Heep .15 .07
❑ 84 Keith Hernandez .25 .11
❑ 85 Howard Johnson .25 .11
❑ 86 Ray Knight .25 .11
❑ 87 Terry Leach .15 .07
❑ 88 Ed Lynch .15 .07
❑ 89 Roger McDowell RC* .25 .11
❑ 90 Jesse Orosco .15 .07
❑ 91 Tom Paciorek .25 .11
❑ 92 Ronn Reynolds .15 .07
❑ 93 Rafael Santana .15 .07
❑ 94 Doug Sisk .15 .07
❑ 95 Rusty Staub .25 .11
❑ 96 Darryl Strawberry .75 .35
❑ 97 Mookie Wilson .25 .11
❑ 98 Neil Allen .15 .07
❑ 99 Don Baylor .50 .23
❑ 100 Dale Berra .15 .07
❑ 101 Rich Bordi .15 .07
❑ 102 Marty Bystrom .15 .07
❑ 103 Joe Cowley .15 .07
❑ 104 Brian Fisher .15 .07
❑ 105 Ken Griffey .25 .11
❑ 106 Ron Guidry .25 .11
❑ 107 Ron Hassey .15 .07
❑ 108 Rickey Henderson UER 1.00 .45
(SB Record of 120, sic)
❑ 109 Don Mattingly 2.00 .90
❑ 110 Bobby Meacham .15 .07
❑ 111 John Montefusco .15 .07
❑ 112 Phil Niekro .75 .35
❑ 113 Mike Pagliarulo .15 .07
❑ 114 Dan Pasqua .15 .07
❑ 115 Willie Randolph .25 .11
❑ 116 Dave Righetti .15 .07
❑ 117 Andre Robertson .15 .07
❑ 118 Billy Sample .15 .07
❑ 119 Bob Shirley .15 .07
❑ 120 Ed Whitson .15 .07
❑ 121 Dave Winfield .75 .35
❑ 122 Butch Wynegar .15 .07
❑ 123 Dave Anderson .15 .07
❑ 124 Bob Bailor .15 .07
❑ 125 Greg Brock .15 .07
❑ 126 Enos Cabell .15 .07
❑ 127 Bobby Castillo .15 .07
❑ 128 Carlos Diaz .15 .07
❑ 129 Mariano Duncan RC* .75 .35
❑ 130 Pedro Guerrero .25 .11
❑ 131 Orel Hershiser .50 .23
❑ 132 Rick Honeycutt .15 .07
❑ 133 Ken Howell .15 .07
❑ 134 Ken Landreaux .15 .07
❑ 135 Bill Madlock .15 .07
❑ 136 Candy Maldonado .15 .07
❑ 137 Mike Marshall .15 .07
❑ 138 Len Matuszek .15 .07
❑ 139 Tom Niedenfuer .15 .07
❑ 140 Alejandro Pena .15 .07
❑ 141 Jerry Reuss .15 .07
❑ 142 Bill Russell .15 .07
❑ 143 Steve Sax .15 .07
❑ 144 Mike Scioscia .15 .07
❑ 145 Fernando Valenzuela .25 .11
❑ 146 Bob Welch .15 .07
❑ 147 Terry Whitfield .15 .07
❑ 148 Juan Beniquez .15 .07
❑ 149 Bob Boone .25 .11
❑ 150 John Candelaria .15 .07
❑ 151 Rod Carew .75 .35
❑ 152 Stewart Cliburn .15 .07
❑ 153 Doug DeCinces .15 .07
❑ 154 Brian Downing .15 .07
❑ 155 Ken Forsch .15 .07
❑ 156 Craig Gerber .15 .07
❑ 157 Bobby Grich .25 .11
❑ 158 George Hendrick .15 .07
❑ 159 Al Holland .15 .07
❑ 160 Reggie Jackson 1.00 .45
❑ 161 Ruppert Jones .15 .07
❑ 162 Urbano Lugo .15 .07
❑ 163 Kirk McCaskill RC .25 .11
❑ 164 Donnie Moore .15 .07
❑ 165 Gary Pettis .15 .07
❑ 166 Ron Romanick .15 .07
❑ 167 Dick Schofield .15 .07
❑ 168 Daryl Sconiers .15 .07
❑ 169 Jim Slaton .15 .07
❑ 170 Don Sutton .75 .35
❑ 171 Mike Witt .15 .07
❑ 172 Buddy Bell .25 .11
❑ 173 Tom Browning .15 .07
❑ 174 Dave Concepcion .25 .11
❑ 175 Eric Davis .50 .23
❑ 176 Bo Diaz .15 .07
❑ 177 Nick Esasky .15 .07
❑ 178 John Franco .75 .35
❑ 179 Tom Hume .15 .07
❑ 180 Wayne Krenchicki .15 .07
❑ 181 Andy McGaffigan .15 .07
❑ 182 Eddie Milner .15 .07
❑ 183 Ron Oester .15 .07
❑ 184 Dave Parker .25 .11
❑ 185 Frank Pastore .15 .07
❑ 186 Tony Perez .75 .35
❑ 187 Ted Power .15 .07
❑ 188 Joe Price .15 .07
❑ 189 Gary Redus .15 .07
❑ 190 Ron Robinson .15 .07
❑ 191 Pete Rose 2.50 1.10
❑ 192 Mario Soto .15 .07
❑ 193 John Stuper .15 .07
❑ 194 Jay Tibbs .15 .07
❑ 195 Dave Van Gorder .15 .07
❑ 196 Max Venable .15 .07
❑ 197 Juan Agosto .15 .07
❑ 198 Harold Baines .50 .23
❑ 199 Floyd Bannister .15 .07
❑ 200 Britt Burns .15 .07
❑ 201 Julio Cruz .15 .07
❑ 202 Joel Davis .15 .07
❑ 203 Richard Dotson .15 .07
❑ 204 Carlton Fisk .75 .35
❑ 205 Scott Fletcher .15 .07
❑ 206 Ozzie Guillen RC* .50 .23
❑ 207 Jerry Hairston .15 .07
❑ 208 Tim Hulett .15 .07
❑ 209 Bob James .15 .07
❑ 210 Ron Kittle .15 .07
❑ 211 Rudy Law .15 .07
❑ 212 Bryan Little .15 .07
❑ 213 Gene Nelson .15 .07
❑ 214 Reid Nichols .15 .07
❑ 215 Luis Salazar .15 .07
❑ 216 Tom Seaver 1.25 .55
❑ 217 Dan Spillner .15 .07
❑ 218 Bruce Tanner .15 .07
❑ 219 Greg Walker .15 .07
❑ 220 Dave Wehrmeister .15 .07
❑ 221 Juan Berenguer .15 .07
❑ 222 Dave Bergman .15 .07
❑ 223 Tom Brookens .15 .07

| | | | |
|---|---|---|---|
| ❑ 224 | Darrell Evans | .25 | .11 |
| ❑ 225 | Barbaro Garbey | .15 | .07 |
| ❑ 226 | Kirk Gibson | .25 | .11 |
| ❑ 227 | John Grubb | .15 | .07 |
| ❑ 228 | Willie Hernandez | .15 | .07 |
| ❑ 229 | Larry Herndon | .15 | .07 |
| ❑ 230 | Chet Lemon | .15 | .07 |
| ❑ 231 | Aurelio Lopez | .15 | .07 |
| ❑ 232 | Jack Morris | .25 | .11 |
| ❑ 233 | Randy O'Neal | .15 | .07 |
| ❑ 234 | Lance Parrish | .25 | .11 |
| ❑ 235 | Dan Petry | .15 | .07 |
| ❑ 236 | Alejandro Sanchez | .15 | .07 |
| ❑ 237 | Bill Scherrer | .15 | .07 |
| ❑ 238 | Nelson Simmons | .15 | .07 |
| ❑ 239 | Frank Tanana | .15 | .07 |
| ❑ 240 | Walt Terrell | .15 | .07 |
| ❑ 241 | Alan Trammell | .50 | .23 |
| ❑ 242 | Lou Whitaker | .25 | .11 |
| ❑ 243 | Milt Wilcox | .15 | .07 |
| ❑ 244 | Hubie Brooks | .15 | .07 |
| ❑ 245 | Tim Burke | .15 | .07 |
| ❑ 246 | Andre Dawson | .50 | .23 |
| ❑ 247 | Mike Fitzgerald | .15 | .07 |
| ❑ 248 | Terry Francona | .15 | .07 |
| ❑ 249 | Bill Gullickson | .15 | .07 |
| ❑ 250 | Joe Hesketh | .15 | .07 |
| ❑ 251 | Bill Laskey | .15 | .07 |
| ❑ 252 | Vance Law | .15 | .07 |
| ❑ 253 | Charlie Lea | .15 | .07 |
| ❑ 254 | Gary Lucas | .15 | .07 |
| ❑ 255 | David Palmer | .15 | .07 |
| ❑ 256 | Tim Raines | .25 | .11 |
| ❑ 257 | Jeff Reardon | .15 | .07 |
| ❑ 258 | Bert Roberge | .15 | .07 |
| ❑ 259 | Dan Schatzeder | .15 | .07 |
| ❑ 260 | Bryn Smith | .15 | .07 |
| ❑ 261 | Randy St.Claire | .15 | .07 |
| ❑ 262 | Scot Thompson | .15 | .07 |
| ❑ 263 | Tim Wallach | .15 | .07 |
| ❑ 264 | U.L. Washington | .15 | .07 |
| ❑ 265 | Mitch Webster | .15 | .07 |
| ❑ 266 | Herm Winningham | .15 | .07 |
| ❑ 267 | Floyd Youmans | .15 | .07 |
| ❑ 268 | Don Aase | .15 | .07 |
| ❑ 269 | Mike Boddicker | .15 | .07 |
| ❑ 270 | Rich Dauer | .15 | .07 |
| ❑ 271 | Storm Davis | .15 | .07 |
| ❑ 272 | Rick Dempsey | .15 | .07 |
| ❑ 273 | Ken Dixon | .15 | .07 |
| ❑ 274 | Jim Dwyer | .15 | .07 |
| ❑ 275 | Mike Flanagan | .15 | .07 |
| ❑ 276 | Wayne Gross | .15 | .07 |
| ❑ 277 | Lee Lacy | .15 | .07 |
| ❑ 278 | Fred Lynn | .25 | .11 |
| ❑ 279 | Tippy Martinez | .15 | .07 |
| ❑ 280 | Dennis Martinez | .25 | .11 |
| ❑ 281 | Scott McGregor | .15 | .07 |
| ❑ 282 | Eddie Murray | .75 | .35 |
| ❑ 283 | Floyd Rayford | .15 | .07 |
| ❑ 284 | Cal Ripken | 3.00 | 1.35 |
| ❑ 285 | Gary Roenicke | .15 | .07 |
| ❑ 286 | Larry Sheets | .15 | .07 |
| ❑ 287 | John Shelby | .15 | .07 |
| ❑ 288 | Nate Snell | .15 | .07 |
| ❑ 289 | Sammy Stewart | .15 | .07 |
| ❑ 290 | Alan Wiggins | .15 | .07 |
| ❑ 291 | Mike Young | .15 | .07 |
| ❑ 292 | Alan Ashby | .15 | .07 |
| ❑ 293 | Mark Bailey | .15 | .07 |
| ❑ 294 | Kevin Bass | .15 | .07 |
| ❑ 295 | Jeff Calhoun | .15 | .07 |
| ❑ 296 | Jose Cruz | .25 | .11 |
| ❑ 297 | Glenn Davis | .25 | .11 |
| ❑ 298 | Bill Dawley | .15 | .07 |
| ❑ 299 | Frank DiPino | .15 | .07 |
| ❑ 300 | Bill Doran | .15 | .07 |
| ❑ 301 | Phil Garner | .25 | .11 |
| ❑ 302 | Jeff Heathcock | .15 | .07 |
| ❑ 303 | Charlie Kerfeld | .15 | .07 |
| ❑ 304 | Bob Knepper | .15 | .07 |
| ❑ 305 | Ron Mathis | .15 | .07 |
| ❑ 306 | Jerry Mumphrey | .15 | .07 |
| ❑ 307 | Jim Pankovits | .15 | .07 |
| ❑ 308 | Terry Puhl | .15 | .07 |
| ❑ 309 | Craig Reynolds | .15 | .07 |
| ❑ 310 | Nolan Ryan | 4.00 | 1.80 |
| ❑ 311 | Mike Scott | .15 | .07 |
| ❑ 312 | Dave Smith | .15 | .07 |
| ❑ 313 | Dickie Thon | .15 | .07 |
| ❑ 314 | Denny Walling | .15 | .07 |
| ❑ 315 | Kurt Bevacqua | .15 | .07 |
| ❑ 316 | Al Bumbry | .15 | .07 |
| ❑ 317 | Jerry Davis | .15 | .07 |
| ❑ 318 | Luis DeLeon | .15 | .07 |
| ❑ 319 | Dave Dravecky | .25 | .11 |
| ❑ 320 | Tim Flannery | .15 | .07 |
| ❑ 321 | Steve Garvey | .50 | .23 |
| ❑ 322 | Rich Gossage | .25 | .11 |
| ❑ 323 | Tony Gwynn | 1.50 | .70 |
| ❑ 324 | Andy Hawkins | .15 | .07 |
| ❑ 325 | LaMarr Hoyt | .15 | .07 |
| ❑ 326 | Roy Lee Jackson | .15 | .07 |
| ❑ 327 | Terry Kennedy | .15 | .07 |
| ❑ 328 | Craig Lefferts | .15 | .07 |
| ❑ 329 | Carmelo Martinez | .15 | .07 |
| ❑ 330 | Lance McCullers | .15 | .07 |
| ❑ 331 | Kevin McReynolds | .15 | .07 |
| ❑ 332 | Graig Nettles | .25 | .11 |
| ❑ 333 | Jerry Royster | .15 | .07 |
| ❑ 334 | Eric Show | .15 | .07 |
| ❑ 335 | Tim Stoddard | .15 | .07 |
| ❑ 336 | Garry Templeton | .15 | .07 |
| ❑ 337 | Mark Thurmond | .15 | .07 |
| ❑ 338 | Ed Wojna | .15 | .07 |
| ❑ 339 | Tony Armas | .15 | .07 |
| ❑ 340 | Marty Barrett | .15 | .07 |
| ❑ 341 | Wade Boggs | 1.00 | .45 |
| ❑ 342 | Dennis Boyd | .15 | .07 |
| ❑ 343 | Bill Buckner | .25 | .11 |
| ❑ 344 | Mark Clear | .15 | .07 |
| ❑ 345 | Roger Clemens | 4.00 | 1.80 |
| ❑ 346 | Steve Crawford | .15 | .07 |
| ❑ 347 | Mike Easler | .15 | .07 |
| ❑ 348 | Dwight Evans | .25 | .11 |
| ❑ 349 | Rich Gedman | .15 | .07 |
| ❑ 350 | Jackie Gutierrez | .15 | .07 |
| ❑ 351 | Glenn Hoffman | .15 | .07 |
| ❑ 352 | Bruce Hurst | .15 | .07 |
| ❑ 353 | Bruce Kison | .15 | .07 |
| ❑ 354 | Tim Lollar | .15 | .07 |
| ❑ 355 | Steve Lyons | .15 | .07 |
| ❑ 356 | Al Nipper | .15 | .07 |
| ❑ 357 | Bob Ojeda | .15 | .07 |
| ❑ 358 | Jim Rice | .25 | .11 |
| ❑ 359 | Bob Stanley | .15 | .07 |
| ❑ 360 | Mike Trujillo | .15 | .07 |
| ❑ 361 | Thad Bosley | .15 | .07 |
| ❑ 362 | Warren Brusstar | .15 | .07 |
| ❑ 363 | Ron Cey | .25 | .11 |
| ❑ 364 | Jody Davis | .15 | .07 |
| ❑ 365 | Bob Dernier | .15 | .07 |
| ❑ 366 | Shawon Dunston | .25 | .11 |
| ❑ 367 | Leon Durham | .15 | .07 |
| ❑ 368 | Dennis Eckersley | .75 | .35 |
| ❑ 369 | Ray Fontenot | .15 | .07 |
| ❑ 370 | George Frazier | .15 | .07 |
| ❑ 371 | Billy Hatcher | .15 | .07 |
| ❑ 372 | Dave Lopes | .25 | .11 |
| ❑ 373 | Gary Matthews | .15 | .07 |
| ❑ 374 | Ron Meridith | .15 | .07 |
| ❑ 375 | Keith Moreland | .15 | .07 |
| ❑ 376 | Reggie Patterson | .15 | .07 |
| ❑ 377 | Dick Ruthven | .15 | .07 |
| ❑ 378 | Ryne Sandberg | 1.00 | .45 |
| ❑ 379 | Scott Sanderson | .15 | .07 |
| ❑ 380 | Lee Smith | .50 | .23 |
| ❑ 381 | Lary Sorensen | .15 | .07 |
| ❑ 382 | Chris Speier | .15 | .07 |
| ❑ 383 | Rick Sutcliffe | .25 | .11 |
| ❑ 384 | Steve Trout | .15 | .07 |
| ❑ 385 | Gary Woods | .15 | .07 |
| ❑ 386 | Bert Blyleven | .25 | .11 |
| ❑ 387 | Tom Brunansky | .15 | .07 |
| ❑ 388 | Randy Bush | .15 | .07 |
| ❑ 389 | John Butcher | .15 | .07 |
| ❑ 390 | Ron Davis | .15 | .07 |
| ❑ 391 | Dave Engle | .15 | .07 |
| ❑ 392 | Frank Eufemia | .15 | .07 |
| ❑ 393 | Pete Filson | .15 | .07 |
| ❑ 394 | Gary Gaetti | .25 | .11 |
| ❑ 395 | Greg Gagne | .15 | .07 |
| ❑ 396 | Mickey Hatcher | .15 | .07 |
| ❑ 397 | Kent Hrbek | .25 | .11 |
| ❑ 398 | Tim Laudner | .15 | .07 |
| ❑ 399 | Rick Lysander | .15 | .07 |
| ❑ 400 | Dave Meier | .15 | .07 |
| ❑ 401 | Kirby Puckett UER (Card has him in NL; should be AL) | 3.00 | 1.35 |
| ❑ 402 | Mark Salas | .15 | .07 |
| ❑ 403 | Ken Schrom | .15 | .07 |
| ❑ 404 | Roy Smalley | .15 | .07 |
| ❑ 405 | Mike Smithson | .15 | .07 |
| ❑ 406 | Mike Stenhouse | .15 | .07 |
| ❑ 407 | Tim Teufel | .15 | .07 |
| ❑ 408 | Frank Viola | .25 | .11 |
| ❑ 409 | Ron Washington | .15 | .07 |
| ❑ 410 | Keith Atherton | .15 | .07 |
| ❑ 411 | Dusty Baker | .25 | .11 |
| ❑ 412 | Tim Birtsas | .15 | .07 |
| ❑ 413 | Bruce Bochte | .15 | .07 |
| ❑ 414 | Chris Codiroli | .15 | .07 |
| ❑ 415 | Dave Collins | .15 | .07 |
| ❑ 416 | Mike Davis | .15 | .07 |
| ❑ 417 | Alfredo Griffin | .15 | .07 |
| ❑ 418 | Mike Heath | .15 | .07 |
| ❑ 419 | Steve Henderson | .15 | .07 |
| ❑ 420 | Donnie Hill | .15 | .07 |
| ❑ 421 | Jay Howell | .15 | .07 |
| ❑ 422 | Tommy John | .75 | .35 |
| ❑ 423 | Dave Kingman | .25 | .11 |
| ❑ 424 | Bill Krueger | .15 | .07 |
| ❑ 425 | Rick Langford | .15 | .07 |
| ❑ 426 | Carney Lansford | .25 | .11 |
| ❑ 427 | Steve McCatty | .15 | .07 |
| ❑ 428 | Dwayne Murphy | .15 | .07 |
| ❑ 429 | Steve Ontiveros RC | .25 | .11 |
| ❑ 430 | Tony Phillips | .15 | .07 |
| ❑ 431 | Jose Rijo | .15 | .07 |
| ❑ 432 | Mickey Tettleton RC | .25 | .11 |
| ❑ 433 | Luis Aguayo | .15 | .07 |
| ❑ 434 | Larry Andersen | .15 | .07 |
| ❑ 435 | Steve Carlton | .75 | .35 |
| ❑ 436 | Don Carman | .15 | .07 |
| ❑ 437 | Tim Corcoran | .15 | .07 |
| ❑ 438 | Darren Daulton RC | 1.50 | .70 |
| ❑ 439 | John Denny | .15 | .07 |
| ❑ 440 | Tom Foley | .15 | .07 |
| ❑ 441 | Greg Gross | .15 | .07 |
| ❑ 442 | Kevin Gross | .15 | .07 |
| ❑ 443 | Von Hayes | .15 | .07 |
| ❑ 444 | Charles Hudson | .15 | .07 |
| ❑ 445 | Garry Maddox | .15 | .07 |
| ❑ 446 | Shane Rawley | .15 | .07 |
| ❑ 447 | Dave Rucker | .15 | .07 |
| ❑ 448 | John Russell | .15 | .07 |
| ❑ 449 | Juan Samuel | .15 | .07 |
| ❑ 450 | Mike Schmidt | 1.50 | .70 |
| ❑ 451 | Rick Schu | .15 | .07 |
| ❑ 452 | Dave Shipanoff | .15 | .07 |
| ❑ 453 | Dave Stewart | .25 | .11 |
| ❑ 454 | Jeff Stone | .15 | .07 |
| ❑ 455 | Kent Tekulve | .15 | .07 |
| ❑ 456 | Ozzie Virgil | .15 | .07 |
| ❑ 457 | Glenn Wilson | .15 | .07 |
| ❑ 458 | Jim Beattie | .15 | .07 |
| ❑ 459 | Karl Best | .15 | .07 |
| ❑ 460 | Barry Bonnell | .15 | .07 |
| ❑ 461 | Phil Bradley | .15 | .07 |
| ❑ 462 | Ivan Calderon RC* | .25 | .11 |
| ❑ 463 | Al Cowens | .15 | .07 |
| ❑ 464 | Alvin Davis | .15 | .07 |
| ❑ 465 | Dave Henderson | .15 | .07 |
| ❑ 466 | Bob Kearney | .15 | .07 |
| ❑ 467 | Mark Langston | .15 | .07 |
| ❑ 468 | Bob Long | .15 | .07 |
| ❑ 469 | Mike Moore | .15 | .07 |
| ❑ 470 | Edwin Nunez | .15 | .07 |
| ❑ 471 | Spike Owen | .15 | .07 |
| ❑ 472 | Jack Perconte | .15 | .07 |
| ❑ 473 | Jim Presley | .15 | .07 |
| ❑ 474 | Donnie Scott | .15 | .07 |
| ❑ 475 | Bill Swift | .15 | .07 |
| ❑ 476 | Danny Tartabull | .25 | .11 |
| ❑ 477 | Gorman Thomas | .15 | .07 |
| ❑ 478 | Roy Thomas | .15 | .07 |
| ❑ 479 | Ed VandeBerg | .15 | .07 |

| No. | Player | Mint | NRMT |
|---|---|---|---|
| 480 | Frank Wills | .15 | .07 |
| 481 | Matt Young | .15 | .07 |
| 482 | Ray Burris | .15 | .07 |
| 483 | Jaime Cocanower | .15 | .07 |
| 484 | Cecil Cooper | .25 | .11 |
| 485 | Danny Darwin | .15 | .07 |
| 486 | Rollie Fingers | .75 | .35 |
| 487 | Jim Gantner | .15 | .07 |
| 488 | Bob L. Gibson | .15 | .07 |
| 489 | Moose Haas | .15 | .07 |
| 490 | Teddy Higuera RC* | .25 | .11 |
| 491 | Paul Householder | .15 | .07 |
| 492 | Pete Ladd | .15 | .07 |
| 493 | Rick Manning | .15 | .07 |
| 494 | Bob McClure | .15 | .07 |
| 495 | Paul Molitor | .75 | .35 |
| 496 | Charlie Moore | .15 | .07 |
| 497 | Ben Oglivie | .15 | .07 |
| 498 | Randy Ready | .15 | .07 |
| 499 | Earnie Riles | .15 | .07 |
| 500 | Ed Romero | .15 | .07 |
| 501 | Bill Schroeder | .15 | .07 |
| 502 | Ray Searage | .15 | .07 |
| 503 | Ted Simmons | .25 | .11 |
| 504 | Pete Vuckovich | .15 | .07 |
| 505 | Rick Waits | .15 | .07 |
| 506 | Robin Yount | .75 | .35 |
| 507 | Len Barker | .15 | .07 |
| 508 | Steve Bedrosian | .15 | .07 |
| 509 | Bruce Benedict | .15 | .07 |
| 510 | Rick Camp | .15 | .07 |
| 511 | Rick Cerone | .15 | .07 |
| 512 | Chris Chambliss | .25 | .11 |
| 513 | Jeff Dedmon | .15 | .07 |
| 514 | Terry Forster | .15 | .07 |
| 515 | Gene Garber | .15 | .07 |
| 516 | Terry Harper | .15 | .07 |
| 517 | Bob Horner | .15 | .07 |
| 518 | Glenn Hubbard | .15 | .07 |
| 519 | Joe Johnson | .15 | .07 |
| 520 | Brad Komminsk | .15 | .07 |
| 521 | Rick Mahler | .15 | .07 |
| 522 | Dale Murphy | .75 | .35 |
| 523 | Ken Oberkfell | .15 | .07 |
| 524 | Pascual Perez | .15 | .07 |
| 525 | Gerald Perry | .15 | .07 |
| 526 | Rafael Ramirez | .15 | .07 |
| 527 | Steve Shields | .15 | .07 |
| 528 | Zane Smith | .15 | .07 |
| 529 | Bruce Sutter | .25 | .11 |
| 530 | Milt Thompson RC | .25 | .11 |
| 531 | Claudell Washington | .15 | .07 |
| 532 | Paul Zuvella | .15 | .07 |
| 533 | Vida Blue | .25 | .11 |
| 534 | Bob Brenly | .15 | .07 |
| 535 | Chris Brown | .15 | .07 |
| 536 | Chili Davis | .50 | [illegible] |
| 537 | Mark Davis | .15 | .07 |
| 538 | Rob Deer | .15 | .07 |
| 539 | Dan Driessen | .15 | .07 |
| 540 | Scott Garrelts | .15 | .07 |
| 541 | Dan Gladden | .15 | .07 |
| 542 | Jim Gott | .15 | .07 |
| 543 | David Green | .15 | .07 |
| 544 | Atlee Hammaker | .15 | .07 |
| 545 | Mike Jeffcoat | .15 | .07 |
| 546 | Mike Krukow | .15 | .07 |
| 547 | Dave LaPoint | .15 | .07 |
| 548 | Jeff Leonard | .15 | .07 |
| 549 | Greg Minton | .15 | .07 |
| 550 | Alex Trevino | .15 | .07 |
| 551 | Manny Trillo | .15 | .07 |
| 552 | Jose Uribe | .15 | .07 |
| 553 | Brad Wellman | .15 | .07 |
| 554 | Frank Williams | .15 | .07 |
| 555 | Joel Youngblood | .15 | .07 |
| 556 | Alan Bannister | .15 | .07 |
| 557 | Glenn Brummer | .15 | .07 |
| 558 | Steve Buechele RC | .25 | .11 |
| 559 | Jose Guzman RC | .15 | .07 |
| 560 | Toby Harrah | .15 | .07 |
| 561 | Greg Harris | .15 | .07 |
| 562 | Dwayne Henry | .15 | .07 |
| 563 | Burt Hooton | .15 | .07 |
| 564 | Charlie Hough | .25 | .11 |
| 565 | Mike Mason | .15 | .07 |
| 566 | Oddibe McDowell | .15 | .07 |
| 567 | Dickie Noles | .15 | .07 |
| 568 | Pete O'Brien | .15 | .07 |
| 569 | Larry Parrish | .15 | .07 |
| 570 | Dave Rozema | .15 | .07 |
| 571 | Dave Schmidt | .15 | .07 |
| 572 | Don Slaught | .15 | .07 |
| 573 | Wayne Tolleson | .15 | .07 |
| 574 | Duane Walker | .15 | .07 |
| 575 | Gary Ward | .15 | .07 |
| 576 | Chris Welsh | .15 | .07 |
| 577 | Curtis Wilkerson | .15 | .07 |
| 578 | George Wright | .15 | .07 |
| 579 | Chris Bando | .15 | .07 |
| 580 | Tony Bernazard | .15 | .07 |
| 581 | Brett Butler | .25 | .11 |
| 582 | Ernie Camacho | .15 | .07 |
| 583 | Joe Carter | .75 | .35 |
| 584 | Carmen Castillo | .15 | .07 |
| 585 | Jamie Easterly | .15 | .07 |
| 586 | Julio Franco | .25 | .11 |
| 587 | Mel Hall | .15 | .07 |
| 588 | Mike Hargrove | .25 | .11 |
| 589 | Neal Heaton | .15 | .07 |
| 590 | Brook Jacoby | .15 | .07 |
| 591 | Otis Nixon RC | .25 | .11 |
| 592 | Jerry Reed | .15 | .07 |
| 593 | Vern Ruhle | .15 | .07 |
| 594 | Pat Tabler | .15 | .07 |
| 595 | Rich Thompson | .15 | .07 |
| 596 | Andre Thornton | .15 | .07 |
| 597 | Dave Von Ohlen | .15 | .07 |
| 598 | George Vukovich | .15 | .07 |
| 599 | Tom Waddell | .15 | .07 |
| 600 | Curt Wardle | .15 | .07 |
| 601 | Jerry Willard | .15 | .07 |
| 602 | Bill Almon | .15 | .07 |
| 603 | Mike Bielecki | .15 | .07 |
| 604 | Sid Bream | .15 | .07 |
| 605 | Mike C. Brown | .15 | .07 |
| 606 | Pat Clements | .15 | .07 |
| 607 | Jose DeLeon | .15 | .07 |
| 608 | Denny Gonzalez | .15 | .07 |
| 609 | Cecilio Guante | .15 | .07 |
| 610 | Steve Kemp | .15 | .07 |
| 611 | Sammy Khalifa | .15 | .07 |
| 612 | Lee Mazzilli | .15 | .07 |
| 613 | Larry McWilliams | .15 | .07 |
| 614 | Jim Morrison | .15 | .07 |
| 615 | Joe Orsulak RC* | .15 | .07 |
| 616 | Tony Pena | .15 | .07 |
| 617 | Johnny Ray | .15 | .07 |
| 618 | Rick Reuschel | .15 | .07 |
| 619 | R.J. Reynolds | .15 | .07 |
| 620 | Rick Rhoden | .15 | .07 |
| 621 | Don Robinson | .15 | .07 |
| 622 | Jason Thompson | .15 | .07 |
| 623 | Lee Tunnell | .15 | .07 |
| 624 | Jim Winn | .15 | .07 |
| 625 | Marvell Wynne | .15 | .07 |
| 626 | Dwight Gooden IA | .25 | .11 |
| 627 | Don Mattingly IA | .75 | .35 |
| 628 | 4192 (Pete Rose) | .50 | .23 |
| 629 | 3000 Career Hits | .75 | .35 |
| | Rod Carew | | |
| 630 | 300 Career Wins | .75 | .35 |
| | Tom Seaver | | |
| | Phil Niekro | | |
| 631 | Ouch (Don Baylor) | .25 | .11 |
| 632 | Instant Offense | .50 | .23 |
| | Darryl Strawberry | | |
| | Tim Raines | | |
| 633 | Shortstops Supreme | 1.50 | .70 |
| | Cal Ripken | | |
| | Alan Trammell | | |
| 634 | Boggs and "Hero" | 1.00 | .45 |
| | Wade Boggs | | |
| | George Brett | | |
| 635 | Braves Dynamic Duo | .25 | .11 |
| | Bob Horner | | |
| | Dale Murphy | | |
| 636 | Cardinal Ignitors | .25 | .11 |
| | Willie McGee | | |
| | Vince Coleman | | |
| 637 | Terror on Basepaths | .25 | .11 |
| | Vince Coleman | | |
| 638 | Charlie Hustle / Dr.K | .75 | .35 |
| | Pete Rose | | |
| | Dwight Gooden | | |
| 639 | 1984 and 1985 AL | 1.00 | .45 |
| | Batting Champs | | |
| | Wade Boggs | | |
| | Don Mattingly | | |
| 640 | NL West Sluggers | .25 | .11 |
| | Dale Murphy | | |
| | Steve Garvey | | |
| | Dave Parker | | |
| 641 | Staff Aces | .25 | .11 |
| | Fernando Valenzuela | | |
| | Dwight Gooden | | |
| 642 | Blue Jay Stoppers | .25 | .11 |
| | Jimmy Key | | |
| | Dave Stieb | | |
| 643 | AL All-Star Backstops | .25 | .11 |
| | Carlton Fisk | | |
| | Rich Gedman | | |
| 644 | Gene Walter RC and | .75 | .35 |
| | Benito Santiago | | |
| 645 | Mike Woodard and | .15 | .07 |
| | Colin Ward | | |
| 646 | Kal Daniels RC and | 4.00 | 1.80 |
| | Paul O'Neill | | |
| 647 | Andres Galarraga RC and | 5.00 | 2.20 |
| | Fred Toliver | | |
| 648 | Bob Kipper and | .15 | .07 |
| | Curt Ford | | |
| 649 | Jose Canseco RC and | 20.00 | 9.00 |
| | Eric Plunk | | |
| 650 | Mark McLemore RC and | .75 | .35 |
| | Gus Polidor | | |
| 651 | Rob Woodward and | .15 | .07 |
| | Mickey Brantley | | |
| 652 | Billy Joe Robidoux and | .15 | .07 |
| | Mark Funderburk | | |
| 653 | Cecil Fielder RC and | 1.50 | .70 |
| | Cory Snyder | | |
| 654 | CL: Royals/Cardinals | .15 | .07 |
| | Blue Jays/Mets | | |
| 655 | CL: Yankees/Dodgers | .15 | .07 |
| | Angels/Reds UER | | |
| | (168 Darly Sconiers) | | |
| 656 | CL: White Sox/Tigers | .15 | .07 |
| | Expos/Orioles | | |
| | (279 Dennis, | | |
| | 280 Tippy) | | |
| 657 | CL: Astros/Padres | .15 | .07 |
| | Red Sox/Cubs | | |
| 658 | CL: Twins/A's | .15 | .07 |
| | Phillies/Mariners | | |
| 659 | CL: Brewers/Braves | .15 | .07 |
| | Giants/Rangers | | |
| 660 | CL: Indians/Pirates | .15 | .07 |
| | Special Cards | | |

## 1986 Fleer Update

| | MINT | NRMT |
|---|---|---|
| COMP.FACT.SET (132) | 30.00 | 13.50 |
| 1 Mike Aldrete | .10 | .05 |
| 2 Andy Allanson | .10 | .05 |
| 3 Neil Allen | .10 | .05 |
| 4 Joaquin Andujar | .10 | .05 |
| 5 Paul Assenmacher | .10 | .05 |

|  | | |
|---|---|---|
| ❑ 6 Scott Bailes | .10 | .05 |
| ❑ 7 Jay Baller | .10 | .05 |
| ❑ 8 Scott Bankhead | .10 | .05 |
| ❑ 9 Bill Bathe | .10 | .05 |
| ❑ 10 Don Baylor | .40 | .18 |
| ❑ 11 Billy Beane | .10 | .05 |
| ❑ 12 Steve Bedrosian | .10 | .05 |
| ❑ 13 Juan Beniquez | .10 | .05 |
| ❑ 14 Barry Bonds XRC ! | 15.00 | 6.75 |
| ❑ 15 Bobby Bonilla UER (Wrong birthday) XRC | 1.25 | .55 |
| ❑ 16 Rich Bordi | .10 | .05 |
| ❑ 17 Bill Campbell | .10 | .05 |
| ❑ 18 Tom Candiotti | .10 | .05 |
| ❑ 19 John Cangelosi | .10 | .05 |
| ❑ 20 Jose Canseco UER (Headings on back for a pitcher) | 6.00 | 2.70 |
| ❑ 21 Chuck Cary | .10 | .05 |
| ❑ 22 Juan Castillo | .10 | .05 |
| ❑ 23 Rick Cerone | .10 | .05 |
| ❑ 24 John Cerutti | .10 | .05 |
| ❑ 25 Will Clark XRC | 2.50 | 1.10 |
| ❑ 26 Mark Clear | .10 | .05 |
| ❑ 27 Darnell Coles | .10 | .05 |
| ❑ 28 Dave Collins | .10 | .05 |
| ❑ 29 Tim Conroy | .10 | .05 |
| ❑ 30 Ed Correa | .10 | .05 |
| ❑ 31 Joe Cowley | .10 | .05 |
| ❑ 32 Bill Dawley | .10 | .05 |
| ❑ 33 Rob Deer | .20 | .09 |
| ❑ 34 John Denny | .10 | .05 |
| ❑ 35 Jim Deshaies XRC | .10 | .05 |
| ❑ 36 Doug Drabek XRC | .75 | .35 |
| ❑ 37 Mike Easler | .10 | .05 |
| ❑ 38 Mark Eichhorn | .10 | .05 |
| ❑ 39 Dave Engle | .10 | .05 |
| ❑ 40 Mike Fischlin | .10 | .05 |
| ❑ 41 Scott Fletcher | .10 | .05 |
| ❑ 42 Terry Forster | .10 | .05 |
| ❑ 43 Terry Francona | .10 | .05 |
| ❑ 44 Andres Galarraga | 1.50 | .70 |
| ❑ 45 Lee Guetterman | .10 | .05 |
| ❑ 46 Bill Gullickson | .10 | .05 |
| ❑ 47 Jackie Gutierrez | .10 | .05 |
| ❑ 48 Moose Haas | .10 | .05 |
| ❑ 49 Billy Hatcher | .10 | .05 |
| ❑ 50 Mike Heath | .10 | .05 |
| ❑ 51 Guy Hoffman | .10 | .05 |
| ❑ 52 Tom Hume | .10 | .05 |
| ❑ 53 Pete Incaviglia XRC | .75 | .35 |
| ❑ 54 Dane Iorg | .10 | .05 |
| ❑ 55 Chris James XRC | .10 | .05 |
| ❑ 56 Stan Javier XRC* | .20 | .09 |
| ❑ 57 Tommy John | .75 | .35 |
| ❑ 58 Tracy Jones | .10 | .05 |
| ❑ 59 Wally Joyner XRC | .75 | .35 |
| ❑ 60 Wayne Krenchicki | .10 | .05 |
| ❑ 61 John Kruk XRC | .75 | .35 |
| ❑ 62 Mike LaCoss | .10 | .05 |
| ❑ 63 Pete Ladd | .10 | .05 |
| ❑ 64 Dave LaPoint | .10 | .05 |
| ❑ 65 Mike LaValliere XRC | .10 | .05 |
| ❑ 66 Rudy Law | .10 | .05 |
| ❑ 67 Dennis Leonard | .10 | .05 |
| ❑ 68 Steve Lombardozzi | .10 | .05 |
| ❑ 69 Aurelio Lopez | .10 | .05 |
| ❑ 70 Mickey Mahler | .10 | .05 |
| ❑ 71 Candy Maldonado | .10 | .05 |
| ❑ 72 Roger Mason XRC* | .10 | .05 |
| ❑ 73 Greg Mathews | .10 | .05 |
| ❑ 74 Andy McGaffigan | .10 | .05 |
| ❑ 75 Joel McKeon | .10 | .05 |
| ❑ 76 Kevin Mitchell XRC | .75 | .35 |
| ❑ 77 Bill Mooneyham | .10 | .05 |
| ❑ 78 Omar Moreno | .10 | .05 |
| ❑ 79 Jerry Mumphrey | .10 | .05 |
| ❑ 80 Al Newman | .20 | .09 |
| ❑ 81 Phil Niekro | .75 | .35 |
| ❑ 82 Randy Niemann | .10 | .05 |
| ❑ 83 Juan Nieves | .10 | .05 |
| ❑ 84 Bob Ojeda | .10 | .05 |
| ❑ 85 Rick Ownbey | .10 | .05 |
| ❑ 86 Tom Paciorek | .20 | .09 |
| ❑ 87 David Palmer | .10 | .05 |
| ❑ 88 Jeff Parrett XRC | .10 | .05 |
| ❑ 89 Pat Perry | .10 | .05 |
| ❑ 90 Dan Plesac | .10 | .05 |
| ❑ 91 Darrell Porter | .20 | .09 |
| ❑ 92 Luis Quinones | .10 | .05 |
| ❑ 93 Rey Quinones UER (Misspelled Quinonez) | .10 | .05 |
| ❑ 94 Gary Redus | .10 | .05 |
| ❑ 95 Jeff Reed | .10 | .05 |
| ❑ 96 Bip Roberts XRC | .75 | .35 |
| ❑ 97 Billy Joe Robidoux | .10 | .05 |
| ❑ 98 Gary Roenicke | .10 | .05 |
| ❑ 99 Ron Roenicke | .10 | .05 |
| ❑ 100 Angel Salazar | .10 | .05 |
| ❑ 101 Joe Sambito | .10 | .05 |
| ❑ 102 Billy Sample | .10 | .05 |
| ❑ 103 Dave Schmidt | .10 | .05 |
| ❑ 104 Ken Schrom | .10 | .05 |
| ❑ 105 Ruben Sierra XRC | .75 | .35 |
| ❑ 106 Ted Simmons | .20 | .09 |
| ❑ 107 Sammy Stewart | .10 | .05 |
| ❑ 108 Kurt Stillwell | .10 | .05 |
| ❑ 109 Dale Sveum | .10 | .05 |
| ❑ 110 Tim Teufel | .10 | .05 |
| ❑ 111 Bob Tewksbury XRC | .20 | .09 |
| ❑ 112 Andres Thomas | .10 | .05 |
| ❑ 113 Jason Thompson | .10 | .05 |
| ❑ 114 Milt Thompson | .20 | .09 |
| ❑ 115 Robby Thompson XRC | .20 | .09 |
| ❑ 116 Jay Tibbs | .10 | .05 |
| ❑ 117 Fred Toliver | .10 | .05 |
| ❑ 118 Wayne Tolleson | .10 | .05 |
| ❑ 119 Alex Trevino | .10 | .05 |
| ❑ 120 Manny Trillo | .10 | .05 |
| ❑ 121 Ed VandeBerg | .10 | .05 |
| ❑ 122 Ozzie Virgil | .10 | .05 |
| ❑ 123 Tony Walker | .10 | .05 |
| ❑ 124 Gene Walter | .10 | .05 |
| ❑ 125 Duane Ward XRC | .20 | .09 |
| ❑ 126 Jerry Willard | .10 | .05 |
| ❑ 127 Mitch Williams XRC | .20 | .09 |
| ❑ 128 Reggie Williams | .10 | .05 |
| ❑ 129 Bobby Witt XRC | .40 | .18 |
| ❑ 130 Marvell Wynne | .10 | .05 |
| ❑ 131 Steve Yeager | .10 | .05 |
| ❑ 132 Checklist 1-132 | .10 | .05 |

## 1987 Fleer

| | MINT | NRMT |
|---|---|---|
| COMPLETE SET (660) | 50.00 | 22.00 |
| COMP.FACT.SET (672) | 60.00 | 27.00 |

|  | | |
|---|---|---|
| ❑ 1 Rick Aguilera | .25 | .11 |
| ❑ 2 Richard Anderson | .15 | .07 |
| ❑ 3 Wally Backman | .15 | .07 |
| ❑ 4 Gary Carter | .40 | .18 |
| ❑ 5 Ron Darling | .15 | .07 |
| ❑ 6 Len Dykstra | .40 | .18 |
| ❑ 7 Kevin Elster RC | .25 | .11 |
| ❑ 8 Sid Fernandez | .15 | .07 |
| ❑ 9 Dwight Gooden | .40 | .18 |
| ❑ 10 Ed Hearn | .15 | .07 |
| ❑ 11 Danny Heep | .15 | .07 |
| ❑ 12 Keith Hernandez | .25 | .11 |
| ❑ 13 Howard Johnson | .15 | .07 |
| ❑ 14 Ray Knight | .15 | .07 |
| ❑ 15 Lee Mazzilli | .15 | .07 |
| ❑ 16 Roger McDowell | .15 | .07 |
| ❑ 17 Kevin Mitchell RC* | .40 | .18 |
| ❑ 18 Randy Niemann | .15 | .07 |
| ❑ 19 Bob Ojeda | .15 | .07 |
| ❑ 20 Jesse Orosco | .15 | .07 |
| ❑ 21 Rafael Santana | .15 | .07 |
| ❑ 22 Doug Sisk | .15 | .07 |
| ❑ 23 Darryl Strawberry | .40 | .18 |
| ❑ 24 Tim Teufel | .15 | .07 |
| ❑ 25 Mookie Wilson | .25 | .11 |
| ❑ 26 Tony Armas | .15 | .07 |
| ❑ 27 Marty Barrett | .15 | .07 |
| ❑ 28 Don Baylor | .25 | .11 |
| ❑ 29 Wade Boggs | .75 | .35 |
| ❑ 30 Oil Can Boyd | .15 | .07 |
| ❑ 31 Bill Buckner | .25 | .11 |
| ❑ 32 Roger Clemens | 1.50 | .70 |
| ❑ 33 Steve Crawford | .15 | .07 |
| ❑ 34 Dwight Evans | .25 | .11 |
| ❑ 35 Rich Gedman | .15 | .07 |
| ❑ 36 Dave Henderson | .15 | .07 |
| ❑ 37 Bruce Hurst | .15 | .07 |
| ❑ 38 Tim Lollar | .15 | .07 |
| ❑ 39 Al Nipper | .15 | .07 |
| ❑ 40 Spike Owen | .15 | .07 |
| ❑ 41 Jim Rice | .25 | .11 |
| ❑ 42 Ed Romero | .15 | .07 |
| ❑ 43 Joe Sambito | .15 | .07 |
| ❑ 44 Calvin Schiraldi | .15 | .07 |
| ❑ 45 Tom Seaver UER (Lifetime saves total 0; should be 1) | .60 | .25 |
| ❑ 46 Jeff Sellers | .15 | .07 |
| ❑ 47 Bob Stanley | .15 | .07 |
| ❑ 48 Sammy Stewart | .15 | .07 |
| ❑ 49 Larry Andersen | .15 | .07 |
| ❑ 50 Alan Ashby | .15 | .07 |
| ❑ 51 Kevin Bass | .15 | .07 |
| ❑ 52 Jeff Calhoun | .15 | .07 |
| ❑ 53 Jose Cruz | .25 | .11 |
| ❑ 54 Danny Darwin | .15 | .07 |
| ❑ 55 Glenn Davis | .15 | .07 |
| ❑ 56 Jim Deshaies RC* | .15 | .07 |
| ❑ 57 Bill Doran | .15 | .07 |
| ❑ 58 Phil Garner | .15 | .07 |
| ❑ 59 Billy Hatcher | .15 | .07 |
| ❑ 60 Charlie Kerfeld | .15 | .07 |
| ❑ 61 Bob Knepper | .15 | .07 |
| ❑ 62 Dave Lopes | .25 | .11 |
| ❑ 63 Aurelio Lopez | .15 | .07 |
| ❑ 64 Jim Pankovits | .15 | .07 |
| ❑ 65 Terry Puhl | .15 | .07 |
| ❑ 66 Craig Reynolds | .15 | .07 |
| ❑ 67 Nolan Ryan | 3.00 | 1.35 |
| ❑ 68 Mike Scott | .15 | .07 |
| ❑ 69 Dave Smith | .15 | .07 |
| ❑ 70 Dickie Thon | .15 | .07 |
| ❑ 71 Tony Walker | .15 | .07 |
| ❑ 72 Denny Walling | .15 | .07 |
| ❑ 73 Bob Boone | .25 | .11 |
| ❑ 74 Rick Burleson | .15 | .07 |
| ❑ 75 John Candelaria | .15 | .07 |
| ❑ 76 Doug Corbett | .15 | .07 |
| ❑ 77 Doug DeCinces | .15 | .07 |
| ❑ 78 Brian Downing | .15 | .07 |
| ❑ 79 Chuck Finley RC | 2.00 | .90 |
| ❑ 80 Terry Forster | .15 | .07 |
| ❑ 81 Bob Grich | .25 | .11 |
| ❑ 82 George Hendrick | .15 | .07 |
| ❑ 83 Jack Howell | .15 | .07 |
| ❑ 84 Reggie Jackson | .75 | .35 |
| ❑ 85 Ruppert Jones | .15 | .07 |
| ❑ 86 Wally Joyner RC | 1.00 | .45 |
| ❑ 87 Gary Lucas | .15 | .07 |
| ❑ 88 Kirk McCaskill | .15 | .07 |
| ❑ 89 Donnie Moore | .15 | .07 |
| ❑ 90 Gary Pettis | .15 | .07 |
| ❑ 91 Vern Ruhle | .15 | .07 |
| ❑ 92 Dick Schofield | .15 | .07 |
| ❑ 93 Don Sutton | .60 | .25 |
| ❑ 94 Rob Wilfong | .15 | .07 |
| ❑ 95 Mike Witt | .15 | .07 |
| ❑ 96 Doug Drabek RC | .60 | .25 |
| ❑ 97 Mike Easler | .15 | .07 |
| ❑ 98 Mike Fischlin | .15 | .07 |
| ❑ 99 Brian Fisher | .15 | .07 |
| ❑ 100 Ron Guidry | .25 | .11 |
| ❑ 101 Rickey Henderson | .75 | .35 |

❑ 102 Tommy John .25 .11
❑ 103 Ron Kittle .15 .07
❑ 104 Don Mattingly 1.50 .70
❑ 105 Bobby Meacham .15 .07
❑ 106 Joe Niekro .15 .07
❑ 107 Mike Pagliarulo .15 .07
❑ 108 Dan Pasqua .15 .07
❑ 109 Willie Randolph .25 .11
❑ 110 Dennis Rasmussen .15 .07
❑ 111 Dave Righetti .15 .07
❑ 112 Gary Roenicke .15 .07
❑ 113 Rod Scurry .15 .07
❑ 114 Bob Shirley .15 .07
❑ 115 Joel Skinner .15 .07
❑ 116 Tim Stoddard .15 .07
❑ 117 Bob Tewksbury RC* .25 .11
❑ 118 Wayne Tolleson .15 .07
❑ 119 Claudell Washington .15 .07
❑ 120 Dave Winfield .60 .25
❑ 121 Steve Buechele .15 .07
❑ 122 Ed Correa .15 .07
❑ 123 Scott Fletcher .15 .07
❑ 124 Jose Guzman .15 .07
❑ 125 Toby Harrah .15 .07
❑ 126 Greg Harris .15 .07
❑ 127 Charlie Hough .25 .11
❑ 128 Pete Incaviglia RC* .25 .11
❑ 129 Mike Mason .15 .07
❑ 130 Oddibe McDowell .15 .07
❑ 131 Dale Mohorcic .15 .07
❑ 132 Pete O'Brien .15 .07
❑ 133 Tom Paciorek .25 .11
❑ 134 Larry Parrish .15 .07
❑ 135 Geno Petralli .15 .07
❑ 136 Darrell Porter .15 .07
❑ 137 Jeff Russell .15 .07
❑ 138 Ruben Sierra RC 1.00 .45
❑ 139 Don Slaught .15 .07
❑ 140 Gary Ward .15 .07
❑ 141 Curtis Wilkerson .15 .07
❑ 142 Mitch Williams RC* .25 .11
❑ 143 Bobby Witt RC UER .25 .11
(Tulsa misspelled as Tusla; ERA should be 6.43, not .643)
❑ 144 Dave Bergman .15 .07
❑ 145 Tom Brookens .15 .07
❑ 146 Bill Campbell .15 .07
❑ 147 Chuck Cary .15 .07
❑ 148 Darnell Coles .15 .07
❑ 149 Dave Collins .15 .07
❑ 150 Darrell Evans .25 .11
❑ 151 Kirk Gibson .25 .11
❑ 152 John Grubb .15 .07
❑ 153 Willie Hernandez .15 .07
❑ 154 Larry Herndon .15 .07
❑ 155 Eric King .15 .07
❑ 156 Chet Lemon .15 .07
❑ 157 Dwight Lowry .15 .07
❑ 158 Jack Morris .25 .11
❑ 159 Randy O'Neal .15 .07
❑ 160 Lance Parrish .25 .11
❑ 161 Dan Petry .15 .07
❑ 162 Pat Sheridan .15 .07
❑ 163 Jim Slaton .15 .07
❑ 164 Frank Tanana .15 .07
❑ 165 Walt Terrell .15 .07
❑ 166 Mark Thurmond .15 .07
❑ 167 Alan Trammell .40 .18
❑ 168 Lou Whitaker .25 .11
❑ 169 Luis Aguayo .15 .07
❑ 170 Steve Bedrosian .15 .07
❑ 171 Don Carman .15 .07
❑ 172 Darren Daulton .40 .18
❑ 173 Greg Gross .15 .07
❑ 174 Kevin Gross .15 .07
❑ 175 Von Hayes .15 .07
❑ 176 Charles Hudson .15 .07
❑ 177 Tom Hume .15 .07
❑ 178 Steve Jeltz .15 .07
❑ 179 Mike Maddux .15 .07
❑ 180 Shane Rawley .15 .07
❑ 181 Gary Redus .15 .07
❑ 182 Ron Roenicke .15 .07
❑ 183 Bruce Ruffin RC .15 .07
❑ 184 John Russell .15 .07
❑ 185 Juan Samuel .15 .07
❑ 186 Dan Schatzeder .15 .07
❑ 187 Mike Schmidt 1.25 .55
❑ 188 Rick Schu .15 .07
❑ 189 Jeff Stone .15 .07
❑ 190 Kent Tekulve .15 .07
❑ 191 Milt Thompson .15 .07
❑ 192 Glenn Wilson .15 .07
❑ 193 Buddy Bell .25 .11
❑ 194 Tom Browning .15 .07
❑ 195 Sal Butera .15 .07
❑ 196 Dave Concepcion .25 .11
❑ 197 Kal Daniels .15 .07
❑ 198 Eric Davis .40 .18
❑ 199 John Denny .15 .07
❑ 200 Bo Diaz .15 .07
❑ 201 Nick Esasky .15 .07
❑ 202 John Franco .25 .11
❑ 203 Bill Gullickson .15 .07
❑ 204 Barry Larkin RC 5.00 2.20
❑ 205 Eddie Milner .15 .07
❑ 206 Rob Murphy .15 .07
❑ 207 Ron Oester .15 .07
❑ 208 Dave Parker .25 .11
❑ 209 Tony Perez .60 .25
❑ 210 Ted Power .15 .07
❑ 211 Joe Price .15 .07
❑ 212 Ron Robinson .15 .07
❑ 213 Pete Rose 2.00 .90
❑ 214 Mario Soto .15 .07
❑ 215 Kurt Stillwell .15 .07
❑ 216 Max Venable .15 .07
❑ 217 Chris Welsh .15 .07
❑ 218 Carl Willis RC .15 .07
❑ 219 Jesse Barfield .15 .07
❑ 220 George Bell .15 .07
❑ 221 Bill Caudill .15 .07
❑ 222 John Cerutti .15 .07
❑ 223 Jim Clancy .15 .07
❑ 224 Mark Eichhorn .15 .07
❑ 225 Tony Fernandez .15 .07
❑ 226 Damaso Garcia .15 .07
❑ 227 Kelly Gruber ERR .15 .07
(Wrong birth year)
❑ 228 Tom Henke .15 .07
❑ 229 Garth Iorg .15 .07
❑ 230 Joe Johnson .15 .07
❑ 231 Cliff Johnson .15 .07
❑ 232 Jimmy Key .25 .11
❑ 233 Dennis Lamp .15 .07
❑ 234 Rick Leach .15 .07
❑ 235 Buck Martinez .15 .07
❑ 236 Lloyd Moseby .15 .07
❑ 237 Rance Mulliniks .15 .07
❑ 238 Dave Stieb .15 .07
❑ 239 Willie Upshaw .15 .07
❑ 240 Ernie Whitt .15 .07
❑ 241 Andy Allanson .15 .07
❑ 242 Scott Bailes .15 .07
❑ 243 Chris Bando .15 .07
❑ 244 Tony Bernazard .15 .07
❑ 245 John Butcher .15 .07
❑ 246 Brett Butler .25 .11
❑ 247 Ernie Camacho .15 .07
❑ 248 Tom Candiotti .15 .07
❑ 249 Joe Carter .60 .25
❑ 250 Carmen Castillo .15 .07
❑ 251 Julio Franco .25 .11
❑ 252 Mel Hall .15 .07
❑ 253 Brook Jacoby .15 .07
❑ 254 Phil Niekro .60 .25
❑ 255 Otis Nixon .15 .07
❑ 256 Dickie Noles .15 .07
❑ 257 Bryan Oelkers .15 .07
❑ 258 Ken Schrom .15 .07
❑ 259 Don Schulze .15 .07
❑ 260 Cory Snyder .15 .07
❑ 261 Pat Tabler .15 .07
❑ 262 Andre Thornton .15 .07
❑ 263 Rich Yett .15 .07
❑ 264 Mike Aldrete .15 .07
❑ 265 Juan Berenguer .15 .07
❑ 266 Vida Blue .25 .11
❑ 267 Bob Brenly .15 .07
❑ 268 Chris Brown .15 .07
❑ 269 Will Clark RC 4.00 1.80
❑ 270 Chili Davis .40 .18
❑ 271 Mark Davis .15 .07
❑ 272 Kelly Downs RC .15 .07
❑ 273 Scott Garrelts .15 .07
❑ 274 Dan Gladden .15 .07
❑ 275 Mike Krukow .15 .07
❑ 276 Randy Kutcher .15 .07
❑ 277 Mike LaCoss .15 .07
❑ 278 Jeff Leonard .15 .07
❑ 279 Candy Maldonado .15 .07
❑ 280 Roger Mason .15 .07
❑ 281 Bob Melvin .15 .07
❑ 282 Greg Minton .15 .07
❑ 283 Jeff D. Robinson .15 .07
❑ 284 Harry Spilman .15 .07
❑ 285 Robby Thompson RC* .25 .11
❑ 286 Jose Uribe .15 .07
❑ 287 Frank Williams .15 .07
❑ 288 Joel Youngblood .15 .07
❑ 289 Jack Clark .25 .11
❑ 290 Vince Coleman .15 .07
❑ 291 Tim Conroy .15 .07
❑ 292 Danny Cox .15 .07
❑ 293 Ken Dayley .15 .07
❑ 294 Curt Ford .15 .07
❑ 295 Bob Forsch .15 .07
❑ 296 Tom Herr .15 .07
❑ 297 Ricky Horton .15 .07
❑ 298 Clint Hurdle .15 .07
❑ 299 Jeff Lahti .15 .07
❑ 300 Steve Lake .15 .07
❑ 301 Tito Landrum .15 .07
❑ 302 Mike LaValliere RC* .15 .07
❑ 303 Greg Mathews .15 .07
❑ 304 Willie McGee .25 .11
❑ 305 Jose Oquendo .15 .07
❑ 306 Terry Pendleton .25 .11
❑ 307 Pat Perry .15 .07
❑ 308 Ozzie Smith .75 .35
❑ 309 Ray Soff .15 .07
❑ 310 John Tudor .15 .07
❑ 311 Andy Van Slyke UER .25 .11
(Bats R, Throws L)
❑ 312 Todd Worrell .25 .11
❑ 313 Dann Bilardello .15 .07
❑ 314 Hubie Brooks .15 .07
❑ 315 Tim Burke .15 .07
❑ 316 Andre Dawson .40 .18
❑ 317 Mike Fitzgerald .15 .07
❑ 318 Tom Foley .15 .07
❑ 319 Andres Galarraga .60 .25
❑ 320 Joe Hesketh .15 .07
❑ 321 Wallace Johnson .15 .07
❑ 322 Wayne Krenchicki .15 .07
❑ 323 Vance Law .15 .07
❑ 324 Dennis Martinez .25 .11
❑ 325 Bob McClure .15 .07
❑ 326 Andy McGaffigan .15 .07
❑ 327 Al Newman .15 .07
❑ 328 Tim Raines .25 .11
❑ 329 Jeff Reardon .25 .11
❑ 330 Luis Rivera .15 .07
❑ 331 Bob Sebra .15 .07
❑ 332 Bryn Smith .15 .07
❑ 333 Jay Tibbs .15 .07
❑ 334 Tim Wallach .15 .07
❑ 335 Mitch Webster .15 .07
❑ 336 Jim Wohlford .15 .07
❑ 337 Floyd Youmans .15 .07
❑ 338 Chris Bosio RC .25 .11
❑ 339 Glenn Braggs RC .15 .07
❑ 340 Rick Cerone .15 .07
❑ 341 Mark Clear .15 .07
❑ 342 Bryan Clutterbuck .15 .07
❑ 343 Cecil Cooper .25 .11
❑ 344 Rob Deer .15 .07
❑ 345 Jim Gantner .15 .07
❑ 346 Ted Higuera .15 .07
❑ 347 John Henry Johnson .15 .07
❑ 348 Tim Leary .15 .07
❑ 349 Rick Manning .15 .07
❑ 350 Paul Molitor .60 .25
❑ 351 Charlie Moore .15 .07
❑ 352 Juan Nieves .15 .07
❑ 353 Ben Oglivie .15 .07
❑ 354 Dan Plesac .15 .07

- ❑ 355 Ernest Riles .15 .07
- ❑ 356 Billy Joe Robidoux .15 .07
- ❑ 357 Bill Schroeder .15 .07
- ❑ 358 Dale Sveum .15 .07
- ❑ 359 Gorman Thomas .15 .07
- ❑ 360 Bill Wegman .15 .07
- ❑ 361 Robin Yount .60 .25
- ❑ 362 Steve Balboni .15 .07
- ❑ 363 Scott Bankhead .15 .07
- ❑ 364 Buddy Biancalana .15 .07
- ❑ 365 Bud Black .15 .07
- ❑ 366 George Brett 1.25 .55
- ❑ 367 Steve Farr .15 .07
- ❑ 368 Mark Gubicza .15 .07
- ❑ 369 Bo Jackson RC 3.00 1.35
- ❑ 370 Danny Jackson .15 .07
- ❑ 371 Mike Kingery RC .15 .07
- ❑ 372 Rudy Law .15 .07
- ❑ 373 Charlie Leibrandt .15 .07
- ❑ 374 Dennis Leonard .15 .07
- ❑ 375 Hal McRae .25 .11
- ❑ 376 Jorge Orta .15 .07
- ❑ 377 Jamie Quirk .15 .07
- ❑ 378 Dan Quisenberry .15 .07
- ❑ 379 Bret Saberhagen .25 .11
- ❑ 380 Angel Salazar .15 .07
- ❑ 381 Lonnie Smith .15 .07
- ❑ 382 Jim Sundberg .15 .07
- ❑ 383 Frank White .25 .11
- ❑ 384 Willie Wilson .25 .11
- ❑ 385 Joaquin Andujar .15 .07
- ❑ 386 Doug Bair .15 .07
- ❑ 387 Dusty Baker .25 .11
- ❑ 388 Bruce Bochte .15 .07
- ❑ 389 Jose Canseco 2.00 .90
- ❑ 390 Chris Codiroli .15 .07
- ❑ 391 Mike Davis .15 .07
- ❑ 392 Alfredo Griffin .15 .07
- ❑ 393 Moose Haas .15 .07
- ❑ 394 Donnie Hill .15 .07
- ❑ 395 Jay Howell .15 .07
- ❑ 396 Dave Kingman .25 .11
- ❑ 397 Carney Lansford .25 .11
- ❑ 398 Dave Leiper .15 .07
- ❑ 399 Bill Mooneyham .15 .07
- ❑ 400 Dwayne Murphy .15 .07
- ❑ 401 Steve Ontiveros .15 .07
- ❑ 402 Tony Phillips .15 .07
- ❑ 403 Eric Plunk .15 .07
- ❑ 404 Jose Rijo .15 .07
- ❑ 405 Terry Steinbach RC 1.00 .45
- ❑ 406 Dave Stewart .25 .11
- ❑ 407 Mickey Tettleton .15 .07
- ❑ 408 Dave Von Ohlen .15 .07
- ❑ 409 Jerry Willard .15 .07
- ❑ 410 Curt Young .15 .07
- ❑ 411 Bruce Bochy .15 .07
- ❑ 412 Dave Dravecky .25 .11
- ❑ 413 Tim Flannery .15 .07
- ❑ 414 Steve Garvey .40 .18
- ❑ 415 Rich Gossage .25 .11
- ❑ 416 Tony Gwynn 1.25 .55
- ❑ 417 Andy Hawkins .15 .07
- ❑ 418 LaMarr Hoyt .15 .07
- ❑ 419 Terry Kennedy .15 .07
- ❑ 420 John Kruk RC 1.00 .45
- ❑ 421 Dave LaPoint .15 .07
- ❑ 422 Craig Lefferts .15 .07
- ❑ 423 Carmelo Martinez .15 .07
- ❑ 424 Lance McCullers .15 .07
- ❑ 425 Kevin McReynolds .15 .07
- ❑ 426 Graig Nettles .25 .11
- ❑ 427 Bip Roberts RC .60 .25
- ❑ 428 Jerry Royster .15 .07
- ❑ 429 Benito Santiago .25 .11
- ❑ 430 Eric Show .15 .07
- ❑ 431 Bob Stoddard .15 .07
- ❑ 432 Garry Templeton .15 .07
- ❑ 433 Gene Walter .15 .07
- ❑ 434 Ed Whitson .15 .07
- ❑ 435 Marvell Wynne .15 .07
- ❑ 436 Dave Anderson .15 .07
- ❑ 437 Greg Brock .15 .07
- ❑ 438 Enos Cabell .15 .07
- ❑ 439 Mariano Duncan .15 .07
- ❑ 440 Pedro Guerrero .15 .07
- ❑ 441 Orel Hershiser .25 .11
- ❑ 442 Rick Honeycutt .15 .07
- ❑ 443 Ken Howell .15 .07
- ❑ 444 Ken Landreaux .15 .07
- ❑ 445 Bill Madlock .25 .11
- ❑ 446 Mike Marshall .15 .07
- ❑ 447 Len Matuszek .15 .07
- ❑ 448 Tom Niedenfuer .15 .07
- ❑ 449 Alejandro Pena .15 .07
- ❑ 450 Dennis Powell .15 .07
- ❑ 451 Jerry Reuss .15 .07
- ❑ 452 Bill Russell .15 .07
- ❑ 453 Steve Sax .15 .07
- ❑ 454 Mike Scioscia .15 .07
- ❑ 455 Franklin Stubbs .15 .07
- ❑ 456 Alex Trevino .15 .07
- ❑ 457 Fernando Valenzuela .25 .11
- ❑ 458 Ed VandeBerg .15 .07
- ❑ 459 Bob Welch .15 .07
- ❑ 460 Reggie Williams .15 .07
- ❑ 461 Don Aase .15 .07
- ❑ 462 Juan Beniquez .15 .07
- ❑ 463 Mike Boddicker .15 .07
- ❑ 464 Juan Bonilla .15 .07
- ❑ 465 Rich Bordi .15 .07
- ❑ 466 Storm Davis .15 .07
- ❑ 467 Rick Dempsey .25 .11
- ❑ 468 Ken Dixon .15 .07
- ❑ 469 Jim Dwyer .15 .07
- ❑ 470 Mike Flanagan .15 .07
- ❑ 471 Jackie Gutierrez .15 .07
- ❑ 472 Brad Havens .15 .07
- ❑ 473 Lee Lacy .15 .07
- ❑ 474 Fred Lynn .25 .11
- ❑ 475 Scott McGregor .15 .07
- ❑ 476 Eddie Murray .60 .25
- ❑ 477 Tom O'Malley .15 .07
- ❑ 478 Cal Ripken Jr. 2.50 1.10
- ❑ 479 Larry Sheets .15 .07
- ❑ 480 John Shelby .15 .07
- ❑ 481 Nate Snell .15 .07
- ❑ 482 Jim Traber .15 .07
- ❑ 483 Mike Young .15 .07
- ❑ 484 Neil Allen .15 .07
- ❑ 485 Harold Baines .25 .11
- ❑ 486 Floyd Bannister .15 .07
- ❑ 487 Daryl Boston .15 .07
- ❑ 488 Ivan Calderon .15 .07
- ❑ 489 John Cangelosi .15 .07
- ❑ 490 Steve Carlton .60 .25
- ❑ 491 Joe Cowley .15 .07
- ❑ 492 Julio Cruz .15 .07
- ❑ 493 Bill Dawley .15 .07
- ❑ 494 Jose DeLeon .15 .07
- ❑ 495 Richard Dotson .15 .07
- ❑ 496 Carlton Fisk .60 .25
- ❑ 497 Ozzie Guillen .15 .07
- ❑ 498 Jerry Hairston .15 .07
- ❑ 499 Ron Hassey .15 .07
- ❑ 500 Tim Hulett .15 .07
- ❑ 501 Bob James .15 .07
- ❑ 502 Steve Lyons .15 .07
- ❑ 503 Joel McKeon .15 .07
- ❑ 504 Gene Nelson .15 .07
- ❑ 505 Dave Schmidt .15 .07
- ❑ 506 Ray Searage .15 .07
- ❑ 507 Bobby Thigpen RC .25 .11
- ❑ 508 Greg Walker .15 .07
- ❑ 509 Jim Acker .15 .07
- ❑ 510 Doyle Alexander .15 .07
- ❑ 511 Paul Assenmacher .40 .18
- ❑ 512 Bruce Benedict .15 .07
- ❑ 513 Chris Chambliss .25 .11
- ❑ 514 Jeff Dedmon .15 .07
- ❑ 515 Gene Garber .15 .07
- ❑ 516 Ken Griffey .25 .11
- ❑ 517 Terry Harper .15 .07
- ❑ 518 Bob Horner .15 .07
- ❑ 519 Glenn Hubbard .15 .07
- ❑ 520 Rick Mahler .15 .07
- ❑ 521 Omar Moreno .15 .07
- ❑ 522 Dale Murphy .60 .25
- ❑ 523 Ken Oberkfell .15 .07
- ❑ 524 Ed Olwine .15 .07
- ❑ 525 David Palmer .15 .07
- ❑ 526 Rafael Ramirez .15 .07
- ❑ 527 Billy Sample .15 .07
- ❑ 528 Ted Simmons .25 .11
- ❑ 529 Zane Smith .15 .07
- ❑ 530 Bruce Sutter .15 .07
- ❑ 531 Andres Thomas .15 .07
- ❑ 532 Ozzie Virgil .15 .07
- ❑ 533 Allan Anderson .15 .07
- ❑ 534 Keith Atherton .15 .07
- ❑ 535 Billy Beane .15 .07
- ❑ 536 Bert Blyleven .25 .11
- ❑ 537 Tom Brunansky .15 .07
- ❑ 538 Randy Bush .15 .07
- ❑ 539 George Frazier .15 .07
- ❑ 540 Gary Gaetti .25 .11
- ❑ 541 Greg Gagne .15 .07
- ❑ 542 Mickey Hatcher .15 .07
- ❑ 543 Neal Heaton .15 .07
- ❑ 544 Kent Hrbek .25 .11
- ❑ 545 Roy Lee Jackson .15 .07
- ❑ 546 Tim Laudner .15 .07
- ❑ 547 Steve Lombardozzi .15 .07
- ❑ 548 Mark Portugal RC* .25 .11
- ❑ 549 Kirby Puckett 1.50 .70
- ❑ 550 Jeff Reed .15 .07
- ❑ 551 Mark Salas .15 .07
- ❑ 552 Roy Smalley .15 .07
- ❑ 553 Mike Smithson .15 .07
- ❑ 554 Frank Viola .15 .07
- ❑ 555 Thad Bosley .15 .07
- ❑ 556 Ron Cey .25 .11
- ❑ 557 Jody Davis .15 .07
- ❑ 558 Ron Davis .15 .07
- ❑ 559 Bob Dernier .15 .07
- ❑ 560 Frank DiPino .15 .07
- ❑ 561 Shawon Dunston UER .15 .07
  (Wrong birth year listed on card back)
- ❑ 562 Leon Durham .15 .07
- ❑ 563 Dennis Eckersley .60 .25
- ❑ 564 Terry Francona .25 .11
- ❑ 565 Dave Gumpert .15 .07
- ❑ 566 Guy Hoffman .15 .07
- ❑ 567 Ed Lynch .15 .07
- ❑ 568 Gary Matthews .15 .07
- ❑ 569 Keith Moreland .15 .07
- ❑ 570 Jamie Moyer RC .40 .18
- ❑ 571 Jerry Mumphrey .15 .07
- ❑ 572 Ryne Sandberg .75 .35
- ❑ 573 Scott Sanderson .15 .07
- ❑ 574 Lee Smith .40 .18
- ❑ 575 Chris Speier .15 .07
- ❑ 576 Rick Sutcliffe .25 .11
- ❑ 577 Manny Trillo .15 .07
- ❑ 578 Steve Trout .15 .07
- ❑ 579 Karl Best .15 .07
- ❑ 580 Scott Bradley .15 .07
- ❑ 581 Phil Bradley .15 .07
- ❑ 582 Mickey Brantley .15 .07
- ❑ 583 Mike G. Brown P .15 .07
- ❑ 584 Alvin Davis .15 .07
- ❑ 585 Lee Guetterman .15 .07
- ❑ 586 Mark Huismann .15 .07
- ❑ 587 Bob Kearney .15 .07
- ❑ 588 Pete Ladd .15 .07
- ❑ 589 Mark Langston .15 .07
- ❑ 590 Mike Moore .15 .07
- ❑ 591 Mike Morgan .15 .07
- ❑ 592 John Moses .15 .07
- ❑ 593 Ken Phelps .15 .07
- ❑ 594 Jim Presley .15 .07
- ❑ 595 Rey Quinones UER .15 .07
  (Quinonez on front)
- ❑ 596 Harold Reynolds .25 .11
- ❑ 597 Billy Swift .15 .07
- ❑ 598 Danny Tartabull .15 .07
- ❑ 599 Steve Yeager .15 .07
- ❑ 600 Matt Young .15 .07
- ❑ 601 Bill Almon .15 .07
- ❑ 602 Rafael Belliard RC .15 .07
- ❑ 603 Mike Bielecki .15 .07
- ❑ 604 Barry Bonds RC ! 30.00 13.50
- ❑ 605 Bobby Bonilla RC 1.50 .70
- ❑ 606 Sid Bream .15 .07
- ❑ 607 Mike C. Brown .15 .07
- ❑ 608 Pat Clements .15 .07
- ❑ 609 Mike Diaz .15 .07

❑ 610 Cecilio Guante .15 .07
❑ 611 Barry Jones .15 .07
❑ 612 Bob Kipper .15 .07
❑ 613 Larry McWilliams .15 .07
❑ 614 Jim Morrison .15 .07
❑ 615 Joe Orsulak .15 .07
❑ 616 Junior Ortiz .15 .07
❑ 617 Tony Pena .15 .07
❑ 618 Johnny Ray .15 .07
❑ 619 Rick Reuschel .15 .07
❑ 620 R.J. Reynolds .15 .07
❑ 621 Rick Rhoden .15 .07
❑ 622 Don Robinson .15 .07
❑ 623 Bob Walk .15 .07
❑ 624 Jim Winn .15 .07
❑ 625 Youthful Power .75 .35
Pete Incaviglia
Jose Canseco
❑ 626 300 Game Winners .40 .18
Don Sutton
Phil Niekro
❑ 627 AL Firemen .15 .07
Dave Righetti
Don Aase
❑ 628 Rookie All-Stars .75 .35
Wally Joyner
Jose Canseco
❑ 629 Magic Mets .40 .18
Gary Carter
Sid Fernandez
Dwight Gooden
Keith Hernandez
Darryl Strawberry
❑ 630 NL Best Righties .15 .07
Mike Scott
Mike Krukow
❑ 631 Sensational Southpaws .15 .07
Fernando Valenzuela
John Franco
❑ 632 Count'Em .15 .07
Bob Horner
❑ 633 AL Pitcher's Nightmare .75 .35
Jose Canseco
Jim Rice
Kirby Puckett
❑ 634 All-Star Battery .75 .35
Gary Carter
Roger Clemens
❑ 635 4000 Strikeouts .25 .11
Steve Carlton
❑ 636 Big Bats at First .60 .25
Glenn Davis
Eddie Murray
❑ 637 On Base .25 .11
Wade Boggs
Keith Hernandez
❑ 638 Sluggers Left Side .60 .25
Don Mattingly
Darryl Strawberry
❑ 639 Former MVP's .25 .11
Dave Parker
Ryne Sandberg
❑ 640 Dr. K and Super K .75 .35
Dwight Gooden
Roger Clemens
❑ 641 AL West Stoppers .15 .07
Mike Witt
Charlie Hough
❑ 642 Doubles and Triples .25 .11
Juan Samuel
Tim Raines
❑ 643 Outfielders with Punch .25 .11
Harold Baines
Jesse Barfield
❑ 644 Dave Clark RC and .60 .25
Greg Swindell
❑ 645 Ron Karkovice RC and .25 .11
Russ Morman
❑ 646 Devon White RC and 1.50 .70
Willie Fraser
❑ 647 Mike Stanley RC and .60 .25
Jerry Browne
❑ 648 Dave Magadan RC and .25 .11
Phil Lombardi
❑ 649 Jose Gonzalez and .15 .07
Ralph Bryant
❑ 650 Jimmy Jones RC and .15 .07
Randy Asadoor
❑ 651 Tracy Jones RC and .15 .07
Marvin Freeman
❑ 652 John Stefero and .60 .25
Kevin Seitzer RC
❑ 653 Rob Nelson and .15 .07
Steve Fireovid
❑ 654 CL: Mets/Red Sox .15 .07
Astros/Angels
❑ 655 CL: Yankees/Rangers .15 .07
Tigers/Phillies
❑ 656 CL: Reds/Blue Jays .15 .07
Indians/Giants
ERR (230/231 wrong)
❑ 657 CL: Cardinals/Expos .15 .07
Brewers/Royals
❑ 658 CL: A's/Padres .15 .07
Dodgers/Orioles
❑ 659 CL: White Sox/Braves .15 .07
Twins/Cubs
❑ 660 CL: Mariners/Pirates .15 .07
Special Cards
ER (580/581 wrong)

## 1987 Fleer Update

| | MINT | NRMT |
|---|---|---|
| COMP.FACT.SET (132) | 30.00 | 13.50 |

❑ 1 Scott Bankhead .10 .05
❑ 2 Eric Bell .10 .05
❑ 3 Juan Beniquez .10 .05
❑ 4 Juan Berenguer .10 .05
❑ 5 Mike Birkbeck .10 .05
❑ 6 Randy Bockus .10 .05
❑ 7 Rod Booker .10 .05
❑ 8 Thad Bosley .10 .05
❑ 9 Greg Brock .10 .05
❑ 10 Bob Brower .10 .05
❑ 11 Chris Brown .10 .05
❑ 12 Jerry Browne .10 .05
❑ 13 Ralph Bryant .10 .05
❑ 14 DeWayne Buice .10 .05
❑ 15 Ellis Burks XRC .75 .35
❑ 16 Casey Candaele .10 .05
❑ 17 Steve Carlton .40 .18
❑ 18 Juan Castillo .10 .05
❑ 19 Chuck Crim .10 .05
❑ 20 Mark Davidson .10 .05
❑ 21 Mark Davis .10 .05
❑ 22 Storm Davis .10 .05
❑ 23 Bill Dawley .10 .05
❑ 24 Andre Dawson .25 .11
❑ 25 Brian Dayett .10 .05
❑ 26 Rick Dempsey .15 .07
❑ 27 Ken Dowell .10 .05
❑ 28 Dave Dravecky .15 .07
❑ 29 Mike Dunne .10 .05
❑ 30 Dennis Eckersley .40 .18
❑ 31 Cecil Fielder .25 .11
❑ 32 Brian Fisher .10 .05
❑ 33 Willie Fraser .10 .05
❑ 34 Ken Gerhart .10 .05
❑ 35 Jim Gott .10 .05
❑ 36 Dan Gladden .10 .05
❑ 37 Mike Greenwell XRC* .40 .18
❑ 38 Cecilio Guante .10 .05
❑ 39 Albert Hall .10 .05
❑ 40 Atlee Hammaker .10 .05
❑ 41 Mickey Hatcher .10 .05
❑ 42 Mike Heath .10 .05
❑ 43 Neal Heaton .10 .05
❑ 44 Mike Henneman XRC .25 .11
❑ 45 Guy Hoffman .10 .05
❑ 46 Charles Hudson .10 .05
❑ 47 Chuck Jackson .10 .05
❑ 48 Mike Jackson XRC .15 .07
❑ 49 Reggie Jackson .50 .23
❑ 50 Chris James .10 .05
❑ 51 Dion James .10 .05
❑ 52 Stan Javier .10 .05
❑ 53 Stan Jefferson .10 .05
❑ 54 Jimmy Jones .10 .05
❑ 55 Tracy Jones .10 .05
❑ 56 Terry Kennedy .10 .05
❑ 57 Mike Kingery .10 .05
❑ 58 Ray Knight .10 .05
❑ 59 Gene Larkin XRC .10 .05
❑ 60 Mike LaValliere .10 .05
❑ 61 Jack Lazorko .10 .05
❑ 62 Terry Leach .10 .05
❑ 63 Rick Leach .10 .05
❑ 64 Craig Lefferts .10 .05
❑ 65 Jim Lindeman .10 .05
❑ 66 Bill Long .10 .05
❑ 67 Mike Loynd .10 .05
❑ 68 Greg Maddux XRC 8.00 3.60
❑ 69 Bill Madlock .15 .07
❑ 70 Dave Magadan .15 .07
❑ 71 Joe Magrane XRC .10 .05
❑ 72 Fred Manrique .10 .05
❑ 73 Mike Mason .10 .05
❑ 74 Lloyd McClendon .10 .05
❑ 75 Fred McGriff .60 .25
❑ 76 Mark McGwire 20.00 9.00
❑ 77 Mark McLemore .15 .07
❑ 78 Kevin McReynolds .10 .05
❑ 79 Dave Meads .10 .05
❑ 80 Greg Minton .10 .05
❑ 81 John Mitchell .10 .05
❑ 82 Kevin Mitchell .25 .11
❑ 83 John Morris .10 .05
❑ 84 Jeff Musselman .10 .05
❑ 85 Randy Myers XRC .40 .18
❑ 86 Gene Nelson .10 .05
❑ 87 Joe Niekro .10 .05
❑ 88 Tom Nieto .10 .05
❑ 89 Reid Nichols .10 .05
❑ 90 Matt Nokes XRC .15 .07
❑ 91 Dickie Noles .10 .05
❑ 92 Edwin Nunez .10 .05
❑ 93 Jose Nunez .10 .05
❑ 94 Paul O'Neill .40 .18
❑ 95 Jim Paciorek .10 .05
❑ 96 Lance Parrish .15 .07
❑ 97 Bill Pecota XRC .10 .05
❑ 98 Tony Pena .10 .05
❑ 99 Luis Polonia XRC .15 .07
❑ 100 Randy Ready .10 .05
❑ 101 Jeff Reardon .15 .07
❑ 102 Gary Redus .10 .05
❑ 103 Rick Rhoden .10 .05
❑ 104 Wally Ritchie .10 .05
❑ 105 Jeff M. Robinson UER .10 .05
(Wrong Jeff's
stats on back)
❑ 106 Mark Salas .10 .05
❑ 107 Dave Schmidt .10 .05
❑ 108 Kevin Seitzer UER .15 .07
(Wrong birth year)
❑ 109 John Shelby .10 .05
❑ 110 John Smiley XRC .10 .05
❑ 111 Lary Sorensen .10 .05
❑ 112 Chris Speier .10 .05
❑ 113 Randy St.Claire .10 .05
❑ 114 Jim Sundberg .10 .05
❑ 115 B.J. Surhoff XRC .75 .35
❑ 116 Greg Swindell .40 .18
❑ 117 Danny Tartabull .10 .05
❑ 118 Dorn Taylor .10 .05
❑ 119 Lee Tunnell .10 .05
❑ 120 Ed VandeBerg .10 .05
❑ 121 Andy Van Slyke .15 .07

❑ 122 Gary Ward .10 .05
❑ 123 Devon White .40 .18
❑ 124 Alan Wiggins .10 .05
❑ 125 Bill Wilkinson .10 .05
❑ 126 Jim Winn .10 .05
❑ 127 Frank Williams .10 .05
❑ 128 Ken Williams .10 .05
❑ 129 Matt Williams XRC 2.00 .90
❑ 130 Herm Willingham .10 .05
❑ 131 Matt Young .10 .05
❑ 132 Checklist 1-132 .10 .05

## 1988 Fleer

| | MINT | NRMT |
|---|---|---|
| COMPLETE SET (660) | 15.00 | 6.75 |
| COMP.RETAIL SET (660) | 15.00 | 6.75 |
| COMP.HOBBY SET (672) | 15.00 | 6.75 |

❑ 1 Keith Atherton .10 .05
❑ 2 Don Baylor .15 .07
❑ 3 Juan Berenguer .10 .05
❑ 4 Bert Blyleven .15 .07
❑ 5 Tom Brunansky .10 .05
❑ 6 Randy Bush .10 .05
❑ 7 Steve Carlton .30 .14
❑ 8 Mark Davidson .10 .05
❑ 9 George Frazier .10 .05
❑ 10 Gary Gaetti .15 .07
❑ 11 Greg Gagne .10 .05
❑ 12 Dan Gladden .10 .05
❑ 13 Kent Hrbek .15 .07
❑ 14 Gene Larkin RC* .10 .05
❑ 15 Tim Laudner .10 .05
❑ 16 Steve Lombardozzi .10 .05
❑ 17 Al Newman .10 .05
❑ 18 Joe Niekro .10 .05
❑ 19 Kirby Puckett .75 .35
❑ 20 Jeff Reardon .15 .07
❑ 21A Dan Schatzeder ERR .15 .07
(Misspelled Schatzader on card front)
❑ 21B Dan Schatzeder COR .10 .05
❑ 22 Roy Smalley .10 .05
❑ 23 Mike Smithson .10 .05
❑ 24 Les Straker .10 .05
❑ 25 Frank Viola .10 .05
❑ 26 Jack Clark .15 .07
❑ 27 Vince Coleman .10 .05
❑ 28 Danny Cox .10 .05
❑ 29 Bill Dawley .10 .05
❑ 30 Ken Dayley .10 .05
❑ 31 Doug DeCinces .10 .05
❑ 32 Curt Ford .10 .05
❑ 33 Bob Forsch .10 .05
❑ 34 David Green .10 .05
❑ 35 Tom Herr .10 .05
❑ 36 Ricky Horton .10 .05
❑ 37 Lance Johnson RC .30 .14
❑ 38 Steve Lake .10 .05
❑ 39 Jim Lindeman .10 .05
❑ 40 Joe Magrane RC* .10 .05
❑ 41 Greg Mathews .10 .05
❑ 42 Willie McGee .15 .07
❑ 43 John Morris .10 .05
❑ 44 Jose Oquendo .10 .05
❑ 45 Tony Pena .10 .05
❑ 46 Terry Pendleton .15 .07
❑ 47 Ozzie Smith .40 .18
❑ 48 John Tudor .10 .05
❑ 49 Lee Tunnell .10 .05
❑ 50 Todd Worrell .15 .07
❑ 51 Doyle Alexander .10 .05
❑ 52 Dave Bergman .10 .05
❑ 53 Tom Brookens .10 .05
❑ 54 Darrell Evans .15 .07
❑ 55 Kirk Gibson .15 .07
❑ 56 Mike Heath .10 .05
❑ 57 Mike Henneman RC* .15 .07
❑ 58 Willie Hernandez .10 .05
❑ 59 Larry Herndon .10 .05
❑ 60 Eric King .10 .05
❑ 61 Chet Lemon .10 .05
❑ 62 Scott Lusader .10 .05
❑ 63 Bill Madlock .15 .07
❑ 64 Jack Morris .15 .07
❑ 65 Jim Morrison .10 .05
❑ 66 Matt Nokes RC* .10 .05
❑ 67 Dan Petry .10 .05
❑ 68A Jeff M. Robinson ERR .30 .14
(Stats for Jeff D. Robinson on card back; born 12-13-60)
❑ 68B Jeff M. Robinson COR .10 .05
(Born 12-14-61)
❑ 69 Pat Sheridan .10 .05
❑ 70 Nate Snell .10 .05
❑ 71 Frank Tanana .10 .05
❑ 72 Walt Terrell .10 .05
❑ 73 Mark Thurmond .10 .05
❑ 74 Alan Trammell .20 .09
❑ 75 Lou Whitaker .15 .07
❑ 76 Mike Aldrete .10 .05
❑ 77 Bob Brenly .10 .05
❑ 78 Will Clark .40 .18
❑ 79 Chili Davis .20 .09
❑ 80 Kelly Downs .10 .05
❑ 81 Dave Dravecky .15 .07
❑ 82 Scott Garrelts .10 .05
❑ 83 Atlee Hammaker .10 .05
❑ 84 Dave Henderson .10 .05
❑ 85 Mike Krukow .10 .05
❑ 86 Mike LaCoss .10 .05
❑ 87 Craig Lefferts .10 .05
❑ 88 Jeff Leonard .10 .05
❑ 89 Candy Maldonado .10 .05
❑ 90 Eddie Milner .10 .05
❑ 91 Bob Melvin .10 .05
❑ 92 Kevin Mitchell .15 .07
❑ 93 Jon Perlman .10 .05
❑ 94 Rick Reuschel .10 .05
❑ 95 Don Robinson .10 .05
❑ 96 Chris Speier .10 .05
❑ 97 Harry Spilman .10 .05
❑ 98 Robby Thompson .10 .05
❑ 99 Jose Uribe .10 .05
❑ 100 Mark Wasinger .10 .05
❑ 101 Matt Williams RC 1.50 .70
❑ 102 Jesse Barfield .10 .05
❑ 103 George Bell .10 .05
❑ 104 Juan Beniquez .10 .05
❑ 105 John Cerutti .10 .05
❑ 106 Jim Clancy .10 .05
❑ 107 Rob Ducey .10 .05
❑ 108 Mark Eichhorn .10 .05
❑ 109 Tony Fernandez .10 .05
❑ 110 Cecil Fielder .20 .09
❑ 111 Kelly Gruber .10 .05
❑ 112 Tom Henke .10 .05
❑ 113A Garth Iorg ERR .30 .14
(Misspelled Iorq on card front)
❑ 113B Garth Iorg COR .10 .05
❑ 114 Jimmy Key .15 .07
❑ 115 Rick Leach .10 .05
❑ 116 Manny Lee .10 .05
❑ 117 Nelson Liriano .10 .05
❑ 118 Fred McGriff .30 .14
❑ 119 Lloyd Moseby .10 .05
❑ 120 Rance Mulliniks .10 .05
❑ 121 Jeff Musselman .10 .05
❑ 122 Jose Nunez .10 .05
❑ 123 Dave Stieb .10 .05
❑ 124 Willie Upshaw .10 .05
❑ 125 Duane Ward .10 .05
❑ 126 Ernie Whitt .10 .05
❑ 127 Rick Aguilera .15 .07
❑ 128 Wally Backman .10 .05
❑ 129 Mark Carreon RC .15 .07
❑ 130 Gary Carter .20 .09
❑ 131 David Cone .15 .07
❑ 132 Ron Darling .10 .05
❑ 133 Len Dykstra .15 .07
❑ 134 Sid Fernandez .10 .05
❑ 135 Dwight Gooden .15 .07
❑ 136 Keith Hernandez .15 .07
❑ 137 Gregg Jefferies RC .30 .14
❑ 138 Howard Johnson .10 .05
❑ 139 Terry Leach .10 .05
❑ 140 Barry Lyons .10 .05
❑ 141 Dave Magadan .10 .05
❑ 142 Roger McDowell .10 .05
❑ 143 Kevin McReynolds .10 .05
❑ 144 Keith A. Miller RC .10 .05
❑ 145 John Mitchell .10 .05
❑ 146 Randy Myers .20 .09
❑ 147 Bob Ojeda .10 .05
❑ 148 Jesse Orosco .10 .05
❑ 149 Rafael Santana .10 .05
❑ 150 Doug Sisk .10 .05
❑ 151 Darryl Strawberry .15 .07
❑ 152 Tim Teufel .10 .05
❑ 153 Gene Walter .10 .05
❑ 154 Mookie Wilson .15 .07
❑ 155 Jay Aldrich .10 .05
❑ 156 Chris Bosio .10 .05
❑ 157 Glenn Braggs .10 .05
❑ 158 Greg Brock .10 .05
❑ 159 Juan Castillo .10 .05
❑ 160 Mark Clear .10 .05
❑ 161 Cecil Cooper .15 .07
❑ 162 Chuck Crim .10 .05
❑ 163 Rob Deer .10 .05
❑ 164 Mike Felder .10 .05
❑ 165 Jim Gantner .10 .05
❑ 166 Ted Higuera .10 .05
❑ 167 Steve Kiefer .10 .05
❑ 168 Rick Manning .10 .05
❑ 169 Paul Molitor .30 .14
❑ 170 Juan Nieves .10 .05
❑ 171 Dan Plesac .10 .05
❑ 172 Earnest Riles .10 .05
❑ 173 Bill Schroeder .10 .05
❑ 174 Steve Stanicek .10 .05
❑ 175 B.J. Surhoff .15 .07
❑ 176 Dale Sveum .10 .05
❑ 177 Bill Wegman .10 .05
❑ 178 Robin Yount .30 .14
❑ 179 Hubie Brooks .10 .05
❑ 180 Tim Burke .10 .05
❑ 181 Casey Candaele .10 .05
❑ 182 Mike Fitzgerald .10 .05
❑ 183 Tom Foley .10 .05
❑ 184 Andres Galarraga .20 .09
❑ 185 Neal Heaton .10 .05
❑ 186 Wallace Johnson .10 .05
❑ 187 Vance Law .10 .05
❑ 188 Dennis Martinez .15 .07
❑ 189 Bob McClure .10 .05
❑ 190 Andy McGaffigan .10 .05
❑ 191 Reid Nichols .10 .05
❑ 192 Pascual Perez .10 .05
❑ 193 Tim Raines .15 .07
❑ 194 Jeff Reed .10 .05
❑ 195 Bob Sebra .10 .05
❑ 196 Bryn Smith .10 .05
❑ 197 Randy St.Claire .10 .05
❑ 198 Tim Wallach .10 .05
❑ 199 Mitch Webster .10 .05
❑ 200 Herm Winningham .10 .05
❑ 201 Floyd Youmans .10 .05
❑ 202 Brad Arnsberg .10 .05
❑ 203 Rick Cerone .10 .05
❑ 204 Pat Clements .10 .05
❑ 205 Henry Cotto .10 .05
❑ 206 Mike Easler .10 .05
❑ 207 Ron Guidry .10 .05
❑ 208 Bill Gullickson .10 .05
❑ 209 Rickey Henderson .40 .18
❑ 210 Charles Hudson .10 .05

- ❑ 211 Tommy John .15 .07
- ❑ 212 Roberto Kelly RC .30 .14
- ❑ 213 Ron Kittle .10 .05
- ❑ 214 Don Mattingly .75 .35
- ❑ 215 Bobby Meacham .10 .05
- ❑ 216 Mike Pagliarulo .10 .05
- ❑ 217 Dan Pasqua .10 .05
- ❑ 218 Willie Randolph .15 .07
- ❑ 219 Rick Rhoden .10 .05
- ❑ 220 Dave Righetti .10 .05
- ❑ 221 Jerry Royster .10 .05
- ❑ 222 Tim Stoddard .10 .05
- ❑ 223 Wayne Tolleson .10 .05
- ❑ 224 Gary Ward .10 .05
- ❑ 225 Claudell Washington .10 .05
- ❑ 226 Dave Winfield .30 .14
- ❑ 227 Buddy Bell .15 .07
- ❑ 228 Tom Browning .10 .05
- ❑ 229 Dave Concepcion .15 .07
- ❑ 230 Kal Daniels .10 .05
- ❑ 231 Eric Davis .15 .07
- ❑ 232 Bo Diaz .10 .05
- ❑ 233 Nick Esasky .10 .05
  (Has a dollar sign before '87 SB totals)
- ❑ 234 John Franco .15 .07
- ❑ 235 Guy Hoffman .10 .05
- ❑ 236 Tom Hume .10 .05
- ❑ 237 Tracy Jones .10 .05
- ❑ 238 Bill Landrum .10 .05
- ❑ 239 Barry Larkin .30 .14
- ❑ 240 Terry McGriff .10 .05
- ❑ 241 Rob Murphy .10 .05
- ❑ 242 Ron Oester .10 .05
- ❑ 243 Dave Parker .15 .07
- ❑ 244 Pat Perry .10 .05
- ❑ 245 Ted Power .10 .05
- ❑ 246 Dennis Rasmussen .10 .05
- ❑ 247 Ron Robinson .10 .05
- ❑ 248 Kurt Stillwell .10 .05
- ❑ 249 Jeff Treadway RC .10 .05
- ❑ 250 Frank Williams .10 .05
- ❑ 251 Steve Balboni .10 .05
- ❑ 252 Bud Black .10 .05
- ❑ 253 Thad Bosley .10 .05
- ❑ 254 George Brett .60 .25
- ❑ 255 John Davis .10 .05
- ❑ 256 Steve Farr .10 .05
- ❑ 257 Gene Garber .10 .05
- ❑ 258 Jerry Don Gleaton .10 .05
- ❑ 259 Mark Gubicza .10 .05
- ❑ 260 Bo Jackson .30 .14
- ❑ 261 Danny Jackson .10 .05
- ❑ 262 Ross Jones .10 .05
- ❑ 263 Charlie Leibrandt .10 .05
- ❑ 264 Bill Pecota RC* .10 .05
- ❑ 265 Melido Perez RC .10 .05
- ❑ 266 Jamie Quirk .10 .05
- ❑ 267 Dan Quisenberry .10 .05
- ❑ 268 Bret Saberhagen .15 .07
- ❑ 269 Angel Salazar .10 .05
- ❑ 270 Kevin Seitzer UER .15 .07
  (Wrong birth year)
- ❑ 271 Danny Tartabull .10 .05
- ❑ 272 Gary Thurman .10 .05
- ❑ 273 Frank White .15 .07
- ❑ 274 Willie Wilson .10 .05
- ❑ 275 Tony Bernazard .10 .05
- ❑ 276 Jose Canseco .60 .25
- ❑ 277 Mike Davis .10 .05
- ❑ 278 Storm Davis .10 .05
- ❑ 279 Dennis Eckersley .15 .07
- ❑ 280 Alfredo Griffin .10 .05
- ❑ 281 Rick Honeycutt .10 .05
- ❑ 282 Jay Howell .10 .05
- ❑ 283 Reggie Jackson .40 .18
- ❑ 284 Dennis Lamp .10 .05
- ❑ 285 Carney Lansford .15 .07
- ❑ 286 Mark McGwire 3.00 1.35
- ❑ 287 Dwayne Murphy .10 .05
- ❑ 288 Gene Nelson .10 .05
- ❑ 289 Steve Ontiveros .10 .05
- ❑ 290 Tony Phillips .10 .05
- ❑ 291 Eric Plunk .10 .05
- ❑ 292 Luis Polonia RC* .10 .05
- ❑ 293 Rick Rodriguez .10 .05
- ❑ 294 Terry Steinbach .15 .07
- ❑ 295 Dave Stewart .15 .07
- ❑ 296 Curt Young .10 .05
- ❑ 297 Luis Aguayo .10 .05
- ❑ 298 Steve Bedrosian .10 .05
- ❑ 299 Jeff Calhoun .10 .05
- ❑ 300 Don Carman .10 .05
- ❑ 301 Todd Frohwirth .10 .05
- ❑ 302 Greg Gross .10 .05
- ❑ 303 Kevin Gross .10 .05
- ❑ 304 Von Hayes .10 .05
- ❑ 305 Keith Hughes .10 .05
- ❑ 306 Mike Jackson RC* .15 .07
- ❑ 307 Chris James .10 .05
- ❑ 308 Steve Jeltz .10 .05
- ❑ 309 Mike Maddux .10 .05
- ❑ 310 Lance Parrish .10 .05
- ❑ 311 Shane Rawley .10 .05
- ❑ 312 Wally Ritchie .10 .05
- ❑ 313 Bruce Ruffin .10 .05
- ❑ 314 Juan Samuel .10 .05
- ❑ 315 Mike Schmidt .60 .25
- ❑ 316 Rick Schu .10 .05
- ❑ 317 Jeff Stone .10 .05
- ❑ 318 Kent Tekulve .10 .05
- ❑ 319 Milt Thompson .10 .05
- ❑ 320 Glenn Wilson .10 .05
- ❑ 321 Rafael Belliard .10 .05
- ❑ 322 Barry Bonds 1.00 .45
- ❑ 323 Bobby Bonilla UER .15 .07
  (Wrong birth year)
- ❑ 324 Sid Bream .10 .05
- ❑ 325 John Cangelosi .10 .05
- ❑ 326 Mike Diaz .10 .05
- ❑ 327 Doug Drabek .10 .05
- ❑ 328 Mike Dunne .10 .05
- ❑ 329 Brian Fisher .10 .05
- ❑ 330 Brett Gideon .10 .05
- ❑ 331 Terry Harper .10 .05
- ❑ 332 Bob Kipper .10 .05
- ❑ 333 Mike LaValliere .10 .05
- ❑ 334 Jose Lind RC .10 .05
- ❑ 335 Junior Ortiz .10 .05
- ❑ 336 Vicente Palacios .10 .05
- ❑ 337 Bob Patterson .10 .05
- ❑ 338 Al Pedrique .10 .05
- ❑ 339 R.J. Reynolds .10 .05
- ❑ 340 John Smiley RC* .15 .07
- ❑ 341 Andy Van Slyke UER .15 .07
  (Wrong batting and throwing listed)
- ❑ 342 Bob Walk .10 .05
- ❑ 343 Marty Barrett .10 .05
- ❑ 344 Todd Benzinger RC* .10 .05
- ❑ 345 Wade Boggs .40 .18
- ❑ 346 Tom Bolton .10 .05
- ❑ 347 Oil Can Boyd .10 .05
- ❑ 348 Ellis Burks RC .50 .23
- ❑ 349 Roger Clemens .60 .25
- ❑ 350 Steve Crawford .10 .05
- ❑ 351 Dwight Evans .15 .07
- ❑ 352 Wes Gardner .10 .05
- ❑ 353 Rich Gedman .10 .05
- ❑ 354 Mike Greenwell .10 .05
- ❑ 355 Sam Horn RC .10 .05
- ❑ 356 Bruce Hurst .10 .05
- ❑ 357 John Marzano .10 .05
- ❑ 358 Al Nipper .10 .05
- ❑ 359 Spike Owen .10 .05
- ❑ 360 Jody Reed RC .15 .07
- ❑ 361 Jim Rice .15 .07
- ❑ 362 Ed Romero .10 .05
- ❑ 363 Kevin Romine .10 .05
- ❑ 364 Joe Sambito .10 .05
- ❑ 365 Calvin Schiraldi .10 .05
- ❑ 366 Jeff Sellers .10 .05
- ❑ 367 Bob Stanley .10 .05
- ❑ 368 Scott Bankhead .10 .05
- ❑ 369 Phil Bradley .10 .05
- ❑ 370 Scott Bradley .10 .05
- ❑ 371 Mickey Brantley .10 .05
- ❑ 372 Mike Campbell .10 .05
- ❑ 373 Alvin Davis .10 .05
- ❑ 374 Lee Guetterman .10 .05
- ❑ 375 Dave Hengel .10 .05
- ❑ 376 Mike Kingery .10 .05
- ❑ 377 Mark Langston .10 .05
- ❑ 378 Edgar Martinez RC 2.50 1.10
- ❑ 379 Mike Moore .10 .05
- ❑ 380 Mike Morgan .10 .05
- ❑ 381 John Moses .10 .05
- ❑ 382 Donell Nixon .10 .05
- ❑ 383 Edwin Nunez .10 .05
- ❑ 384 Ken Phelps .10 .05
- ❑ 385 Jim Presley .10 .05
- ❑ 386 Rey Quinones .10 .05
- ❑ 387 Jerry Reed .10 .05
- ❑ 388 Harold Reynolds .15 .07
- ❑ 389 Dave Valle .10 .05
- ❑ 390 Bill Wilkinson .10 .05
- ❑ 391 Harold Baines .15 .07
- ❑ 392 Floyd Bannister .10 .05
- ❑ 393 Daryl Boston .10 .05
- ❑ 394 Ivan Calderon .10 .05
- ❑ 395 Jose DeLeon .10 .05
- ❑ 396 Richard Dotson .10 .05
- ❑ 397 Carlton Fisk .30 .14
- ❑ 398 Ozzie Guillen .10 .05
- ❑ 399 Ron Hassey .10 .05
- ❑ 400 Donnie Hill .10 .05
- ❑ 401 Bob James .10 .05
- ❑ 402 Dave LaPoint .10 .05
- ❑ 403 Bill Lindsey .10 .05
- ❑ 404 Bill Long .10 .05
- ❑ 405 Steve Lyons .10 .05
- ❑ 406 Fred Manrique .10 .05
- ❑ 407 Jack McDowell RC .30 .14
- ❑ 408 Gary Redus .10 .05
- ❑ 409 Ray Searage .10 .05
- ❑ 410 Bobby Thigpen .10 .05
- ❑ 411 Greg Walker .10 .05
- ❑ 412 Ken Williams .10 .05
- ❑ 413 Jim Winn .10 .05
- ❑ 414 Jody Davis .10 .05
- ❑ 415 Andre Dawson .20 .09
- ❑ 416 Brian Dayett .10 .05
- ❑ 417 Bob Dernier .10 .05
- ❑ 418 Frank DiPino .10 .05
- ❑ 419 Shawon Dunston .10 .05
- ❑ 420 Leon Durham .10 .05
- ❑ 421 Les Lancaster .10 .05
- ❑ 422 Ed Lynch .10 .05
- ❑ 423 Greg Maddux 1.50 .70
- ❑ 424 Dave Martinez .10 .05
- ❑ 425A Keith Moreland ERR 1.50 .70
  (Photo actually Jody Davis)
- ❑ 425B Keith Moreland COR .15 .07
  (Bat on shoulder)
- ❑ 426 Jamie Moyer .10 .05
- ❑ 427 Jerry Mumphrey .10 .05
- ❑ 428 Paul Noce .10 .05
- ❑ 429 Rafael Palmeiro .60 .25
- ❑ 430 Wade Rowdon .10 .05
- ❑ 431 Ryne Sandberg .40 .18
- ❑ 432 Scott Sanderson .10 .05
- ❑ 433 Lee Smith .15 .07
- ❑ 434 Jim Sundberg .10 .05
- ❑ 435 Rick Sutcliffe .15 .07
- ❑ 436 Manny Trillo .10 .05
- ❑ 437 Juan Agosto .10 .05
- ❑ 438 Larry Andersen .10 .05
- ❑ 439 Alan Ashby .10 .05
- ❑ 440 Kevin Bass .10 .05
- ❑ 441 Ken Caminiti RC 1.00 .45
- ❑ 442 Rocky Childress .10 .05
- ❑ 443 Jose Cruz .10 .05
- ❑ 444 Danny Darwin .10 .05
- ❑ 445 Glenn Davis .10 .05
- ❑ 446 Jim Deshaies .10 .05
- ❑ 447 Bill Doran .10 .05
- ❑ 448 Ty Gainey .10 .05
- ❑ 449 Billy Hatcher .10 .05
- ❑ 450 Jeff Heathcock .10 .05
- ❑ 451 Bob Knepper .10 .05
- ❑ 452 Rob Mallicoat .10 .05
- ❑ 453 Dave Meads .10 .05
- ❑ 454 Craig Reynolds .10 .05
- ❑ 455 Nolan Ryan 1.50 .70
- ❑ 456 Mike Scott .10 .05
- ❑ 457 Dave Smith .10 .05
- ❑ 458 Denny Walling .10 .05

❑ 459 Robbie Wine .10 .05
❑ 460 Gerald Young .10 .05
❑ 461 Bob Brower .10 .05
❑ 462A Jerry Browne ERR 1.50 .70
(Photo actually
Bob Brower,
white player)
❑ 462B Jerry Browne COR .15 .07
(Black player)
❑ 463 Steve Buechele .10 .05
❑ 464 Edwin Correa .10 .05
❑ 465 Cecil Espy .10 .05
❑ 466 Scott Fletcher .10 .05
❑ 467 Jose Guzman .10 .05
❑ 468 Greg Harris .10 .05
❑ 469 Charlie Hough .15 .07
❑ 470 Pete Incaviglia .10 .05
❑ 471 Paul Kilgus .10 .05
❑ 472 Mike Loynd .10 .05
❑ 473 Oddibe McDowell .10 .05
❑ 474 Dale Mohorcic .10 .05
❑ 475 Pete O'Brien .10 .05
❑ 476 Larry Parrish .10 .05
❑ 477 Geno Petralli .10 .05
❑ 478 Jeff Russell .10 .05
❑ 479 Ruben Sierra .10 .05
❑ 480 Mike Stanley .15 .07
❑ 481 Curtis Wilkerson .10 .05
❑ 482 Mitch Williams .10 .05
❑ 483 Bobby Witt .10 .05
❑ 484 Tony Armas .10 .05
❑ 485 Bob Boone .15 .07
❑ 486 Bill Buckner .15 .07
❑ 487 DeWayne Buice .10 .05
❑ 488 Brian Downing .10 .05
❑ 489 Chuck Finley .20 .09
❑ 490 Willie Fraser UER .10 .05
(Wrong bio stats,
for George Hendrick)
❑ 491 Jack Howell .10 .05
❑ 492 Ruppert Jones .10 .05
❑ 493 Wally Joyner .20 .09
❑ 494 Jack Lazorko .10 .05
❑ 495 Gary Lucas .10 .05
❑ 496 Kirk McCaskill .10 .05
❑ 497 Mark McLemore .10 .05
❑ 498 Darrell Miller .10 .05
❑ 499 Greg Minton .10 .05
❑ 500 Donnie Moore .10 .05
❑ 501 Gus Polidor .10 .05
❑ 502 Johnny Ray .10 .05
❑ 503 Mark Ryal .10 .05
❑ 504 Dick Schofield .10 .05
❑ 505 Don Sutton .30 .14
❑ 506 Devon White .15 .07
❑ 507 Mike Witt .10 .05
❑ 508 Dave Anderson .10 .05
❑ 509 Tim Belcher .15 .07
❑ 510 Ralph Bryant .10 .05
❑ 511 Tim Crews RC .10 .05
❑ 512 Mike Devereaux RC .15 .07
❑ 513 Mariano Duncan .10 .05
❑ 514 Pedro Guerrero .10 .05
❑ 515 Jeff Hamilton .10 .05
❑ 516 Mickey Hatcher .10 .05
❑ 517 Brad Havens .10 .05
❑ 518 Orel Hershiser .15 .07
❑ 519 Shawn Hillegas .10 .05
❑ 520 Ken Howell .10 .05
❑ 521 Tim Leary .10 .05
❑ 522 Mike Marshall .10 .05
❑ 523 Steve Sax .10 .05
❑ 524 Mike Scioscia .10 .05
❑ 525 Mike Sharperson .10 .05
❑ 526 John Shelby .10 .05
❑ 527 Franklin Stubbs .10 .05
❑ 528 Fernando Valenzuela .15 .07
❑ 529 Bob Welch .10 .05
❑ 530 Matt Young .10 .05
❑ 531 Jim Acker .10 .05
❑ 532 Paul Assenmacher .10 .05
❑ 533 Jeff Blauser RC .30 .14
❑ 534 Joe Boever .10 .05
❑ 535 Martin Clary .10 .05
❑ 536 Kevin Coffman .10 .05
❑ 537 Jeff Dedmon .10 .05
❑ 538 Ron Gant RC .40 .18
❑ 539 Tom Glavine RC 2.50 1.10
❑ 540 Ken Griffey .15 .07
❑ 541 Albert Hall .10 .05
❑ 542 Glenn Hubbard .10 .05
❑ 543 Dion James .10 .05
❑ 544 Dale Murphy .30 .14
❑ 545 Ken Oberkfell .10 .05
❑ 546 David Palmer .10 .05
❑ 547 Gerald Perry .10 .05
❑ 548 Charlie Puleo .10 .05
❑ 549 Ted Simmons .15 .07
❑ 550 Zane Smith .10 .05
❑ 551 Andres Thomas .10 .05
❑ 552 Ozzie Virgil .10 .05
❑ 553 Don Aase .10 .05
❑ 554 Jeff Ballard .10 .05
❑ 555 Eric Bell .10 .05
❑ 556 Mike Boddicker .10 .05
❑ 557 Ken Dixon .10 .05
❑ 558 Jim Dwyer .10 .05
❑ 559 Ken Gerhart .10 .05
❑ 560 Rene Gonzales RC .10 .05
❑ 561 Mike Griffin .10 .05
❑ 562 John Habyan UER .10 .05
(Misspelled Hayban on
both sides of card)
❑ 563 Terry Kennedy .10 .05
❑ 564 Ray Knight .10 .05
❑ 565 Lee Lacy .10 .05
❑ 566 Fred Lynn .10 .05
❑ 567 Eddie Murray .30 .14
❑ 568 Tom Niedenfuer .10 .05
❑ 569 Bill Ripken RC* .10 .05
❑ 570 Cal Ripken 1.25 .55
❑ 571 Dave Schmidt .10 .05
❑ 572 Larry Sheets .10 .05
❑ 573 Pete Stanicek .10 .05
❑ 574 Mark Williamson .10 .05
❑ 575 Mike Young .10 .05
❑ 576 Shawn Abner .10 .05
❑ 577 Greg Booker .10 .05
❑ 578 Chris Brown .10 .05
❑ 579 Keith Comstock .10 .05
❑ 580 Joey Cora RC .30 .14
❑ 581 Mark Davis .10 .05
❑ 582 Tim Flannery .30 .14
(With surfboard)
❑ 583 Goose Gossage .20 .09
❑ 584 Mark Grant .10 .05
❑ 585 Tony Gwynn .60 .25
❑ 586 Andy Hawkins .10 .05
❑ 587 Stan Jefferson .10 .05
❑ 588 Jimmy Jones .10 .05
❑ 589 John Kruk .15 .07
❑ 590 Shane Mack .10 .05
❑ 591 Carmelo Martinez .10 .05
❑ 592 Lance McCullers UER .10 .05
(6'11" tall)
❑ 593 Eric Nolte .10 .05
❑ 594 Randy Ready .10 .05
❑ 595 Luis Salazar .10 .05
❑ 596 Benito Santiago .10 .05
❑ 597 Eric Show .10 .05
❑ 598 Garry Templeton .10 .05
❑ 599 Ed Whitson .10 .05
❑ 600 Scott Bailes .10 .05
❑ 601 Chris Bando .10 .05
❑ 602 Jay Bell RC 1.00 .45
❑ 603 Brett Butler .15 .07
❑ 604 Tom Candiotti .10 .05
❑ 605 Joe Carter .30 .14
❑ 606 Carmen Castillo .10 .05
❑ 607 Brian Dorsett .10 .05
❑ 608 John Farrell .10 .05
❑ 609 Julio Franco .10 .05
❑ 610 Mel Hall .10 .05
❑ 611 Tommy Hinzo .10 .05
❑ 612 Brook Jacoby .10 .05
❑ 613 Doug Jones RC .30 .14
❑ 614 Ken Schrom .10 .05
❑ 615 Cory Snyder .10 .05
❑ 616 Sammy Stewart .10 .05
❑ 617 Greg Swindell .10 .05
❑ 618 Pat Tabler .10 .05
❑ 619 Ed VandeBerg .10 .05
❑ 620 Eddie Williams RC .15 .07
❑ 621 Rich Yett .10 .05
❑ 622 Slugging Sophomores .15 .07
Wally Joyner
Cory Snyder
❑ 623 Dominican Dynamite .10 .05
George Bell
Pedro Guerrero
❑ 624 Oakland's Power Team 1.50 .70
Mark McGwire
Jose Canseco
❑ 625 Classic Relief .10 .05
Dave Righetti
Dan Plesac
❑ 626 All Star Righties .15 .07
Bret Saberhagen
Mike Witt
Jack Morris
❑ 627 Game Closers .10 .05
John Franco
Steve Bedrosian
❑ 628 Masters/Double Play .40 .18
Ozzie Smith
Ryne Sandberg
❑ 629 Rookie Record Setter 1.50 .70
Mark McGwire
❑ 630 Changing the Guard .30 .14
Mike Greenwell
Ellis Burks
Todd Benzinger
❑ 631 NL Batting Champs .30 .14
Tony Gwynn
Tim Raines
❑ 632 Pitching Magic .15 .07
Mike Scott
Orel Hershiser
❑ 633 Big Bats at First 1.50 .70
Pat Tabler
Mark McGwire
❑ 634 Hitting King/Thief .30 .14
Tony Gwynn
Vince Coleman
❑ 635 Slugging Shortstops .40 .18
Tony Fernandez
Cal Ripken
Alan Trammell
❑ 636 Tried/True Sluggers .20 .09
Mike Schmidt
Gary Carter
❑ 637 Crunch Time .15 .07
Darryl Strawberry
Eric Davis
❑ 638 AL All-Stars .20 .09
Matt Nokes
Kirby Puckett
❑ 639 NL All-Stars .15 .07
Keith Hernandez
Dale Murphy
❑ 640 The O's Brothers .60 .25
Billy Ripken
Cal Ripken
❑ 641 Mark Grace RC and 2.00 .90
Darrin Jackson
❑ 642 Damon Berryhill RC and .30 .14
Jeff Montgomery
❑ 643 Felix Fermin and .10 .05
Jesse Reid
❑ 644 Greg Myers RC and .10 .05
Greg Tabor
❑ 645 Joey Meyer and .10 .05
Jim Eppard
❑ 646 Adam Peterson and .15 .07
Randy Velarde
❑ 647 Pete Smith and .15 .07
Chris Gwynn RC
❑ 648 Tom Newell and .10 .05
Greg Jelks
❑ 649 Mario Diaz and .10 .05
Clay Parker
❑ 650 Jack Savage and .10 .05
Todd Simmons
❑ 651 John Burkett RC and .30 .14
Kirt Manwaring
❑ 652 Dave Otto RC and .40 .18
Walt Weiss
❑ 653 Jeff King RC and .15 .07

| Card | Mint | NrMt |
|---|---|---|
| Randell Byers | | |
| ❑ 654 CL: Twins/Cards | .10 | .05 |
| Tigers/Giants UER | | |
| (90 Bob Melvin, | | |
| 91 Eddie Milner) | | |
| ❑ 655 CL: Blue Jays/Mets | .10 | .05 |
| Brewers/Expos UER | | |
| (Mets listed before | | |
| Blue Jays on card) | | |
| ❑ 656 CL: Yankees/Reds | .10 | .05 |
| Royals/A's | | |
| ❑ 657 CL: Phillies/Pirates | .10 | .05 |
| Red Sox/Mariners | | |
| ❑ 658 CL: White Sox/Cubs | .10 | .05 |
| Astros/Rangers | | |
| ❑ 659 CL: Angels/Dodgers | .10 | .05 |
| Braves/Orioles | | |
| ❑ 660 CL: Padres/Indians | .10 | .05 |
| Rookies/Specials | | |

## 1988 Fleer Update

| | MINT | NRMT |
|---|---|---|
| COMP.FACT.SET (132) | 8.00 | 3.60 |
| ❑ 1 Jose Bautista | .10 | .05 |
| ❑ 2 Joe Orsulak | .10 | .05 |
| ❑ 3 Doug Sisk | .10 | .05 |
| ❑ 4 Craig Worthington | .10 | .05 |
| ❑ 5 Mike Boddicker | .10 | .05 |
| ❑ 6 Rick Cerone | .10 | .05 |
| ❑ 7 Larry Parrish | .10 | .05 |
| ❑ 8 Lee Smith | .20 | .09 |
| ❑ 9 Mike Smithson | .10 | .05 |
| ❑ 10 John Trautwein | .10 | .05 |
| ❑ 11 Sherman Corbett | .10 | .05 |
| ❑ 12 Chili Davis | .30 | .14 |
| ❑ 13 Jim Eppard | .10 | .05 |
| ❑ 14 Bryan Harvey XRC | .20 | .09 |
| ❑ 15 John Davis | .10 | .05 |
| ❑ 16 Dave Gallagher | .10 | .05 |
| ❑ 17 Ricky Horton | .10 | .05 |
| ❑ 18 Dan Pasqua | .10 | .05 |
| ❑ 19 Melido Perez | .10 | .05 |
| ❑ 20 Jose Segura | .10 | .05 |
| ❑ 21 Andy Allanson | .10 | .05 |
| ❑ 22 Jon Perlman | .10 | .05 |
| ❑ 23 Domingo Ramos | .10 | .05 |
| ❑ 24 Rick Rodriguez | .10 | .05 |
| ❑ 25 Willie Upshaw | .10 | .05 |
| ❑ 26 Paul Gibson | .10 | .05 |
| ❑ 27 Don Heinkel | .10 | .05 |
| ❑ 28 Ray Knight | .10 | .05 |
| ❑ 29 Gary Pettis | .10 | .05 |
| ❑ 30 Luis Salazar | .10 | .05 |
| ❑ 31 Mike Macfarlane XRC | .10 | .05 |
| ❑ 32 Jeff Montgomery | .50 | .23 |
| ❑ 33 Ted Power | .10 | .05 |
| ❑ 34 Israel Sanchez | .10 | .05 |
| ❑ 35 Kurt Stillwell | .10 | .05 |
| ❑ 36 Pat Tabler | .10 | .05 |
| ❑ 37 Don August | .10 | .05 |
| ❑ 38 Darryl Hamilton XRC | .20 | .09 |
| ❑ 39 Jeff Leonard | .10 | .05 |
| ❑ 40 Joey Meyer | .10 | .05 |
| ❑ 41 Allan Anderson | .10 | .05 |
| ❑ 42 Brian Harper | .10 | .05 |
| ❑ 43 Tom Herr | .10 | .05 |
| ❑ 44 Charlie Lea | .10 | .05 |
| ❑ 45 John Moses | .10 | .05 |
| (Listed as Hohn on | | |
| checklist card) | | |
| ❑ 46 John Candelaria | .10 | .05 |
| ❑ 47 Jack Clark | .20 | .09 |
| ❑ 48 Richard Dotson | .10 | .05 |
| ❑ 49 Al Leiter XRC* | 1.00 | .45 |
| ❑ 50 Rafael Santana | .10 | .05 |
| ❑ 51 Don Slaught | .10 | .05 |
| ❑ 52 Todd Burns | .10 | .05 |
| ❑ 53 Dave Henderson | .10 | .05 |
| ❑ 54 Doug Jennings | .10 | .05 |
| ❑ 55 Dave Parker | .20 | .09 |
| ❑ 56 Walt Weiss | .30 | .14 |
| ❑ 57 Bob Welch | .10 | .05 |
| ❑ 58 Henry Cotto | .10 | .05 |
| ❑ 59 Mario Diaz UER | .10 | .05 |
| (Listed as Marion | | |
| on card front) | | |
| ❑ 60 Mike Jackson | .20 | .09 |
| ❑ 61 Bill Swift | .10 | .05 |
| ❑ 62 Jose Cecena | .10 | .05 |
| ❑ 63 Ray Hayward | .10 | .05 |
| ❑ 64 Jim Steels UER | .10 | .05 |
| (Listed as Jim Steele | | |
| on card back) | | |
| ❑ 65 Pat Borders XRC | .20 | .09 |
| ❑ 66 Sil Campusano | .10 | .05 |
| ❑ 67 Mike Flanagan | .10 | .05 |
| ❑ 68 Todd Stottlemyre XRC | .50 | .23 |
| ❑ 69 David Wells XRC | 2.00 | .90 |
| ❑ 70 Jose Alvarez | .10 | .05 |
| ❑ 71 Paul Runge | .10 | .05 |
| ❑ 72 Cesar Jimenez | .10 | .05 |
| (Card was intended | | |
| for German Jiminez; | | |
| it's his photo) | | |
| ❑ 73 Pete Smith | .10 | .05 |
| ❑ 74 John Smoltz XRC | 1.50 | .70 |
| ❑ 75 Damon Berryhill | .10 | .05 |
| ❑ 76 Goose Gossage | .30 | .14 |
| ❑ 77 Mark Grace | 2.00 | .90 |
| ❑ 78 Darrin Jackson | .10 | .05 |
| ❑ 79 Vance Law | .10 | .05 |
| ❑ 80 Jeff Pico | .10 | .05 |
| ❑ 81 Gary Varsho | .10 | .05 |
| ❑ 82 Tim Birtsas | .10 | .05 |
| ❑ 83 Rob Dibble XRC | .20 | .09 |
| ❑ 84 Danny Jackson | .10 | .05 |
| ❑ 85 Paul O'Neill | .30 | .14 |
| ❑ 86 Jose Rijo | .10 | .05 |
| ❑ 87 Chris Sabo XRC | .20 | .09 |
| ❑ 88 John Fishel | .10 | .05 |
| ❑ 89 Craig Biggio XRC | 2.50 | 1.10 |
| ❑ 90 Terry Puhl | .10 | .05 |
| ❑ 91 Rafael Ramirez | .10 | .05 |
| ❑ 92 Louie Meadows | .10 | .05 |
| ❑ 93 Kirk Gibson | .50 | .23 |
| ❑ 94 Alfredo Griffin | .10 | .05 |
| ❑ 95 Jay Howell | .10 | .05 |
| ❑ 96 Jesse Orosco | .10 | .05 |
| ❑ 97 Alejandro Pena | .10 | .05 |
| ❑ 98 Tracy Woodson XRC* | .10 | .05 |
| ❑ 99 John Dopson | .10 | .05 |
| ❑ 100 Brian Holman XRC | .10 | .05 |
| ❑ 101 Rex Hudler | .10 | .05 |
| ❑ 102 Jeff Parrett | .10 | .05 |
| ❑ 103 Nelson Santovenia | .10 | .05 |
| ❑ 104 Kevin Elster | .10 | .05 |
| ❑ 105 Jeff Innis | .10 | .05 |
| ❑ 106 Mackey Sasser XRC* | .10 | .05 |
| ❑ 107 Phil Bradley | .10 | .05 |
| ❑ 108 Danny Clay | .10 | .05 |
| ❑ 109 Greg A.Harris | .10 | .05 |
| ❑ 110 Ricky Jordan XRC | .20 | .09 |
| ❑ 111 David Palmer | .10 | .05 |
| ❑ 112 Jim Gott | .10 | .05 |
| ❑ 113 Tommy Gregg UER | .10 | .05 |
| (Photo actually | | |
| Randy Milligan) | | |
| ❑ 114 Barry Jones | .10 | .05 |
| ❑ 115 Randy Milligan XRC* | .10 | .05 |
| ❑ 116 Luis Alicea XRC | .20 | .09 |
| ❑ 117 Tom Brunansky | .10 | .05 |
| ❑ 118 John Costello | .10 | .05 |
| ❑ 119 Jose DeLeon | .10 | .05 |
| ❑ 120 Bob Horner | .10 | .05 |
| ❑ 121 Scott Terry | .10 | .05 |
| ❑ 122 Roberto Alomar XRC | 4.00 | 1.80 |
| ❑ 123 Dave Leiper | .10 | .05 |
| ❑ 124 Keith Moreland | .10 | .05 |
| ❑ 125 Mark Parent | .10 | .05 |
| ❑ 126 Dennis Rasmussen | .10 | .05 |
| ❑ 127 Randy Bockus | .10 | .05 |
| ❑ 128 Brett Butler | .20 | .09 |
| ❑ 129 Donell Nixon | .10 | .05 |
| ❑ 130 Earnest Riles | .10 | .05 |
| ❑ 131 Roger Samuels | .10 | .05 |
| ❑ 132 Checklist U1-U132 | .10 | .05 |

## 1989 Fleer

| | MINT | NRMT |
|---|---|---|
| COMPLETE SET (660) | 30.00 | 13.50 |
| COMP.RETAIL SET (660) | 10.00 | 4.50 |
| COMP.FACT.SET (672) | 30.00 | 13.50 |
| ❑ 1 Don Baylor | .10 | .05 |
| ❑ 2 Lance Blankenship RC | .05 | .02 |
| ❑ 3 Todd Burns UER | .05 | .02 |
| (Wrong birthdate; | | |
| before/after All-Star | | |
| stats missing) | | |
| ❑ 4 Greg Cadaret UER | .05 | .02 |
| (All-Star Break stats | | |
| show 3 losses; | | |
| should be 2) | | |
| ❑ 5 Jose Canseco | .25 | .11 |
| ❑ 6 Storm Davis | .05 | .02 |
| ❑ 7 Dennis Eckersley | .15 | .07 |
| ❑ 8 Mike Gallego | .05 | .02 |
| ❑ 9 Ron Hassey | .05 | .02 |
| ❑ 10 Dave Henderson | .05 | .02 |
| ❑ 11 Rick Honeycutt | .05 | .02 |
| ❑ 12 Glenn Hubbard | .05 | .02 |
| ❑ 13 Stan Javier | .05 | .02 |
| ❑ 14 Doug Jennings | .05 | .02 |
| ❑ 15 Felix Jose RC | .05 | .02 |
| ❑ 16 Carney Lansford | .10 | .05 |
| ❑ 17 Mark McGwire | 1.00 | .45 |
| ❑ 18 Gene Nelson | .05 | .02 |
| ❑ 19 Dave Parker | .10 | .05 |
| ❑ 20 Eric Plunk | .05 | .02 |
| ❑ 21 Luis Polonia | .05 | .02 |
| ❑ 22 Terry Steinbach | .10 | .05 |
| ❑ 23 Dave Stewart | .10 | .05 |
| ❑ 24 Walt Weiss | .05 | .02 |
| ❑ 25 Bob Welch | .05 | .02 |
| ❑ 26 Curt Young | .05 | .02 |
| ❑ 27 Rick Aguilera | .10 | .05 |
| ❑ 28 Wally Backman | .05 | .02 |
| ❑ 29 Mark Carreon UER | .05 | .02 |
| (After All-Star Break | | |
| batting 7.14) | | |
| ❑ 30 Gary Carter | .15 | .07 |
| ❑ 31 David Cone | .10 | .05 |
| ❑ 32 Ron Darling | .05 | .02 |
| ❑ 33 Len Dykstra | .10 | .05 |
| ❑ 34 Kevin Elster | .05 | .02 |
| ❑ 35 Sid Fernandez | .05 | .02 |
| ❑ 36 Dwight Gooden | .10 | .05 |
| ❑ 37 Keith Hernandez | .10 | .05 |
| ❑ 38 Gregg Jefferies | .10 | .05 |

- ❑ 39 Howard Johnson .05 .02
- ❑ 40 Terry Leach .05 .02
- ❑ 41 Dave Magadan UER .05 .02 (Bio says 15 doubles; should be 13)
- ❑ 42 Bob McClure .05 .02
- ❑ 43 Roger McDowell UER .05 .02 (Led Mets with 58; should be 62)
- ❑ 44 Kevin McReynolds .05 .02
- ❑ 45 Keith A. Miller .05 .02
- ❑ 46 Randy Myers .10 .05
- ❑ 47 Bob Ojeda .05 .02
- ❑ 48 Mackey Sasser .05 .02
- ❑ 49 Darryl Strawberry .10 .05
- ❑ 50 Tim Teufel .05 .02
- ❑ 51 Dave West RC .05 .02
- ❑ 52 Mookie Wilson .10 .05
- ❑ 53 Dave Anderson .05 .02
- ❑ 54 Tim Belcher .05 .02
- ❑ 55 Mike Davis .05 .02
- ❑ 56 Mike Devereaux .05 .02
- ❑ 57 Kirk Gibson .10 .05
- ❑ 58 Alfredo Griffin .05 .02
- ❑ 59 Chris Gwynn .05 .02
- ❑ 60 Jeff Hamilton .05 .02
- ❑ 61A Danny Heep#ERR Lake Hills .20 .09
- ❑ 61B Danny Heep#COR San Anto .05 .02
- ❑ 62 Orel Hershiser .10 .05
- ❑ 63 Brian Holton .05 .02
- ❑ 64 Jay Howell .05 .02
- ❑ 65 Tim Leary .05 .02
- ❑ 66 Mike Marshall .05 .02
- ❑ 67 Ramon Martinez RC .25 .11
- ❑ 68 Jesse Orosco .05 .02
- ❑ 69 Alejandro Pena .05 .02
- ❑ 70 Steve Sax .05 .02
- ❑ 71 Mike Scioscia .05 .02
- ❑ 72 Mike Sharperson .05 .02
- ❑ 73 John Shelby .05 .02
- ❑ 74 Franklin Stubbs .05 .02
- ❑ 75 John Tudor .05 .02
- ❑ 76 Fernando Valenzuela .10 .05
- ❑ 77 Tracy Woodson .05 .02
- ❑ 78 Marty Barrett .05 .02
- ❑ 79 Todd Benzinger .05 .02
- ❑ 80 Mike Boddicker UER .05 .02 (Rochester in '76; should be '78)
- ❑ 81 Wade Boggs .25 .11
- ❑ 82 Oil Can Boyd .05 .02
- ❑ 83 Ellis Burks .15 .07
- ❑ 84 Rick Cerone .05 .02
- ❑ 85 Roger Clemens .40 .18
- ❑ 86 Steve Curry .05 .02
- ❑ 87 Dwight Evans .10 .05
- ❑ 88 Wes Gardner .05 .02
- ❑ 89 Rich Gedman .05 .02
- ❑ 90 Mike Greenwell .05 .02
- ❑ 91 Bruce Hurst .05 .02
- ❑ 92 Dennis Lamp .05 .02
- ❑ 93 Spike Owen .05 .02
- ❑ 94 Larry Parrish UER .05 .02 (Before All-Star Break batting 1.90)
- ❑ 95 Carlos Quintana RC .05 .02
- ❑ 96 Jody Reed .05 .02
- ❑ 97 Jim Rice .10 .05
- ❑ 98A Kevin Romine ERR .20 .09 (Photo actually Randy Kutcher batting)
- ❑ 98B Kevin Romine COR .05 .02 (Arms folded)
- ❑ 99 Lee Smith .10 .05
- ❑ 100 Mike Smithson .05 .02
- ❑ 101 Bob Stanley .05 .02
- ❑ 102 Allan Anderson .05 .02
- ❑ 103 Keith Atherton .05 .02
- ❑ 104 Juan Berenguer .05 .02
- ❑ 105 Bert Blyleven .10 .05
- ❑ 106 Eric Bullock UER .05 .02 (Bats/Throws Right; should be Left)
- ❑ 107 Randy Bush .05 .02
- ❑ 108 John Christensen .05 .02
- ❑ 109 Mark Davidson .05 .02
- ❑ 110 Gary Gaetti .10 .05
- ❑ 111 Greg Gagne .05 .02
- ❑ 112 Dan Gladden .05 .02
- ❑ 113 German Gonzalez .05 .02
- ❑ 114 Brian Harper .05 .02
- ❑ 115 Tom Herr .05 .02
- ❑ 116 Kent Hrbek .10 .05
- ❑ 117 Gene Larkin .05 .02
- ❑ 118 Tim Laudner .05 .02
- ❑ 119 Charlie Lea .05 .02
- ❑ 120 Steve Lombardozzi .05 .02
- ❑ 121A John Moses#ERR Tempe .20 .09
- ❑ 121B John Moses#COR Phoenix .05 .02
- ❑ 122 Al Newman .05 .02
- ❑ 123 Mark Portugal .05 .02
- ❑ 124 Kirby Puckett .50 .23
- ❑ 125 Jeff Reardon .10 .05
- ❑ 126 Fred Toliver .05 .02
- ❑ 127 Frank Viola .05 .02
- ❑ 128 Doyle Alexander .05 .02
- ❑ 129 Dave Bergman .05 .02
- ❑ 130A Tom Brookens ERR .75 .35 (Mike Heath back)
- ❑ 130B Tom Brookens COR .05 .02
- ❑ 131 Paul Gibson .05 .02
- ❑ 132A Mike Heath ERR .75 .35 (Tom Brookens back)
- ❑ 132B Mike Heath COR .05 .02
- ❑ 133 Don Heinkel .05 .02
- ❑ 134 Mike Henneman .05 .02
- ❑ 135 Guillermo Hernandez .05 .02
- ❑ 136 Eric King .05 .02
- ❑ 137 Chet Lemon .05 .02
- ❑ 138 Fred Lynn UER .05 .02 ('74, '75 stats missing)
- ❑ 139 Jack Morris .10 .05
- ❑ 140 Matt Nokes .05 .02
- ❑ 141 Gary Pettis .05 .02
- ❑ 142 Ted Power .05 .02
- ❑ 143 Jeff M. Robinson .05 .02
- ❑ 144 Luis Salazar .05 .02
- ❑ 145 Steve Searcy .05 .02
- ❑ 146 Pat Sheridan .05 .02
- ❑ 147 Frank Tanana .05 .02
- ❑ 148 Alan Trammell .15 .07
- ❑ 149 Walt Terrell .05 .02
- ❑ 150 Jim Walewander .05 .02
- ❑ 151 Lou Whitaker .10 .05
- ❑ 152 Tim Birtsas .05 .02
- ❑ 153 Tom Browning .05 .02
- ❑ 154 Keith Brown .05 .02
- ❑ 155 Norm Charlton RC .10 .05
- ❑ 156 Dave Concepcion .10 .05
- ❑ 157 Kal Daniels .05 .02
- ❑ 158 Eric Davis .10 .05
- ❑ 159 Bo Diaz .05 .02
- ❑ 160 Rob Dibble RC .10 .05
- ❑ 161 Nick Esasky .05 .02
- ❑ 162 John Franco .10 .05
- ❑ 163 Danny Jackson .05 .02
- ❑ 164 Barry Larkin .20 .09
- ❑ 165 Rob Murphy .05 .02
- ❑ 166 Paul O'Neill .10 .05
- ❑ 167 Jeff Reed .05 .02
- ❑ 168 Jose Rijo .05 .02
- ❑ 169 Ron Robinson .05 .02
- ❑ 170 Chris Sabo RC .05 .02
- ❑ 171 Candy Sierra .05 .02
- ❑ 172 Van Snider .05 .02
- ❑ 173A Jeff Treadway 5.00 2.20 (Target registration mark above head on front in light blue)
- ❑ 173B Jeff Treadway .05 .02 (No target on front)
- ❑ 174 Frank Williams UER .05 .02 (After All-Star Break stats are jumbled)
- ❑ 175 Herm Winningham .05 .02
- ❑ 176 Jim Adduci .05 .02
- ❑ 177 Don August .05 .02
- ❑ 178 Mike Birkbeck .05 .02
- ❑ 179 Chris Bosio .05 .02
- ❑ 180 Glenn Braggs .05 .02
- ❑ 181 Greg Brock .05 .02
- ❑ 182 Mark Clear .05 .02
- ❑ 183 Chuck Crim .05 .02
- ❑ 184 Rob Deer .05 .02
- ❑ 185 Tom Filer .05 .02
- ❑ 186 Jim Gantner .05 .02
- ❑ 187 Darryl Hamilton RC .05 .02
- ❑ 188 Ted Higuera .05 .02
- ❑ 189 Odell Jones .05 .02
- ❑ 190 Jeffrey Leonard .05 .02
- ❑ 191 Joey Meyer .05 .02
- ❑ 192 Paul Mirabella .05 .02
- ❑ 193 Paul Molitor .20 .09
- ❑ 194 Charlie O'Brien .05 .02
- ❑ 195 Dan Plesac .05 .02
- ❑ 196 Gary Sheffield RC 1.25 .55
- ❑ 197 B.J. Surhoff .10 .05
- ❑ 198 Dale Sveum .05 .02
- ❑ 199 Bill Wegman .05 .02
- ❑ 200 Robin Yount .20 .09
- ❑ 201 Rafael Belliard .05 .02
- ❑ 202 Barry Bonds .50 .23
- ❑ 203 Bobby Bonilla .10 .05
- ❑ 204 Sid Bream .05 .02
- ❑ 205 Benny Distefano .05 .02
- ❑ 206 Doug Drabek .05 .02
- ❑ 207 Mike Dunne .05 .02
- ❑ 208 Felix Fermin .05 .02
- ❑ 209 Brian Fisher .05 .02
- ❑ 210 Jim Gott .05 .02
- ❑ 211 Bob Kipper .05 .02
- ❑ 212 Dave LaPoint .05 .02
- ❑ 213 Mike LaValliere .05 .02
- ❑ 214 Jose Lind .05 .02
- ❑ 215 Junior Ortiz .05 .02
- ❑ 216 Vicente Palacios .05 .02
- ❑ 217 Tom Prince .05 .02
- ❑ 218 Gary Redus .05 .02
- ❑ 219 R.J. Reynolds .05 .02
- ❑ 220 Jeff D. Robinson .05 .02
- ❑ 221 John Smiley .05 .02
- ❑ 222 Andy Van Slyke .10 .05
- ❑ 223 Bob Walk .05 .02
- ❑ 224 Glenn Wilson .05 .02
- ❑ 225 Jesse Barfield .05 .02
- ❑ 226 George Bell .05 .02
- ❑ 227 Pat Borders RC .10 .05
- ❑ 228 John Cerutti .05 .02
- ❑ 229 Jim Clancy .05 .02
- ❑ 230 Mark Eichhorn .05 .02
- ❑ 231 Tony Fernandez .05 .02
- ❑ 232 Cecil Fielder .10 .05
- ❑ 233 Mike Flanagan .05 .02
- ❑ 234 Kelly Gruber .05 .02
- ❑ 235 Tom Henke .05 .02
- ❑ 236 Jimmy Key .10 .05
- ❑ 237 Rick Leach .05 .02
- ❑ 238 Manny Lee UER .05 .02 (Bio says regular shortstop, sic, Tony Fernandez)
- ❑ 239 Nelson Liriano .05 .02
- ❑ 240 Fred McGriff .20 .09
- ❑ 241 Lloyd Moseby .05 .02
- ❑ 242 Rance Mulliniks .05 .02
- ❑ 243 Jeff Musselman .05 .02
- ❑ 244 Dave Stieb .05 .02
- ❑ 245 Todd Stottlemyre .15 .07
- ❑ 246 Duane Ward .05 .02
- ❑ 247 David Wells .10 .05
- ❑ 248 Ernie Whitt UER .05 .02 (HR total 21; should be 121)
- ❑ 249 Luis Aguayo .05 .02
- ❑ 250A Neil AllenERR Sarasota, FL .75 .75
- ❑ 250B Neil Allen#COR Syosset,NY .05 .02
- ❑ 251 John Candelaria .05 .02
- ❑ 252 Jack Clark .05 .02
- ❑ 253 Richard Dotson .05 .02
- ❑ 254 Rickey Henderson .25 .11
- ❑ 255 Tommy John .10 .05
- ❑ 256 Roberto Kelly .10 .05
- ❑ 257 Al Leiter .20 .09
- ❑ 258 Don Mattingly .50 .23
- ❑ 259 Dale Mohorcic .05 .02
- ❑ 260 Hal Morris RC .20 .09

❑ 261 Scott Nielsen .05 .02
❑ 262 Mike Pagliarulo UER .05 .02
(Wrong birthdate)
❑ 263 Hipolito Pena .05 .02
❑ 264 Ken Phelps .05 .02
❑ 265 Willie Randolph .10 .05
❑ 266 Rick Rhoden .05 .02
❑ 267 Dave Righetti .05 .02
❑ 268 Rafael Santana .05 .02
❑ 269 Steve Shields .05 .02
❑ 270 Joel Skinner .05 .02
❑ 271 Don Slaught .05 .02
❑ 272 Claudell Washington .05 .02
❑ 273 Gary Ward .05 .02
❑ 274 Dave Winfield .20 .09
❑ 275 Luis Aquino .05 .02
❑ 276 Floyd Bannister .05 .02
❑ 277 George Brett .40 .18
❑ 278 Bill Buckner .10 .05
❑ 279 Nick Capra .05 .02
❑ 280 Jose DeJesus .05 .02
❑ 281 Steve Farr .05 .02
❑ 282 Jerry Don Gleaton .05 .02
❑ 283 Mark Gubicza .05 .02
❑ 284 Tom Gordon RC UER .20 .09
(16.2 innings in '88;
should be 15.2)
❑ 285 Bo Jackson .15 .07
❑ 286 Charlie Leibrandt .05 .02
❑ 287 Mike Macfarlane RC .05 .02
❑ 288 Jeff Montgomery .10 .05
❑ 289 Bill Pecota UER .05 .02
(Photo actually
Brad Wellman)
❑ 290 Jamie Quirk .05 .02
❑ 291 Bret Saberhagen .10 .05
❑ 292 Kevin Seitzer .05 .02
❑ 293 Kurt Stillwell .05 .02
❑ 294 Pat Tabler .05 .02
❑ 295 Danny Tartabull .05 .02
❑ 296 Gary Thurman .05 .02
❑ 297 Frank White .10 .05
❑ 298 Willie Wilson .05 .02
❑ 299 Roberto Alomar .30 .14
❑ 300 Sandy Alomar Jr. RC UER .25 .11
(Wrong birthdate, says
6/16/66, should say
6/18/66)
❑ 301 Chris Brown .05 .02
❑ 302 Mike Brumley UER .05 .02
(133 hits in '88;
should be 134)
❑ 303 Mark Davis .05 .02
❑ 304 Mark Grant .05 .02
❑ 305 Tony Gwynn .40 .18
❑ 306 Greg W. Harris RC .05 .02
❑ 307 Andy Hawkins .05 .02
❑ 308 Jimmy Jones .05 .02
❑ 309 John Kruk .10 .05
❑ 310 Dave Leiper .05 .02
❑ 311 Carmelo Martinez .05 .02
❑ 312 Lance McCullers .05 .02
❑ 313 Keith Moreland .05 .02
❑ 314 Dennis Rasmussen .05 .02
❑ 315 Randy Ready UER .05 .02
(1214 games in '88;
should be 114)
❑ 316 Benito Santiago .05 .02
❑ 317 Eric Show .05 .02
❑ 318 Todd Simmons .05 .02
❑ 319 Garry Templeton .05 .02
❑ 320 Dickie Thon .05 .02
❑ 321 Ed Whitson .05 .02
❑ 322 Marvell Wynne .05 .02
❑ 323 Mike Aldrete .05 .02
❑ 324 Brett Butler .10 .05
❑ 325 Will Clark UER .20 .09
(Three consecutive
100 RBI seasons)
❑ 326 Kelly Downs UER .05 .02
('88 stats missing)
❑ 327 Dave Dravecky .10 .05
❑ 328 Scott Garrelts .05 .02
❑ 329 Atlee Hammaker .05 .02
❑ 330 Charlie Hayes RC .20 .09
❑ 331 Mike Krukow .05 .02
❑ 332 Craig Lefferts .05 .02
❑ 333 Candy Maldonado .05 .02
❑ 334 Kirt Manwaring UER .05 .02
(Bats Rights)
❑ 335 Bob Melvin .05 .02
❑ 336 Kevin Mitchell .10 .05
❑ 337 Donell Nixon .05 .02
❑ 338 Tony Perezchica .05 .02
❑ 339 Joe Price .05 .02
❑ 340 Rick Reuschel .05 .02
❑ 341 Earnest Riles .05 .02
❑ 342 Don Robinson .05 .02
❑ 343 Chris Speier .05 .02
❑ 344 Robby Thompson UER .05 .02
(West Plam Beach)
❑ 345 Jose Uribe .05 .02
❑ 346 Matt Williams .15 .07
❑ 347 Trevor Wilson RC .05 .02
❑ 348 Juan Agosto .05 .02
❑ 349 Larry Andersen .05 .02
❑ 350A Alan Ashby ERR 2.00 .90
(Throws Rig)
❑ 350B Alan Ashby COR .05 .02
❑ 351 Kevin Bass .05 .02
❑ 352 Buddy Bell .10 .05
❑ 353 Craig Biggio RC .75 .35
❑ 354 Danny Darwin .05 .02
❑ 355 Glenn Davis .05 .02
❑ 356 Jim Deshaies .05 .02
❑ 357 Bill Doran .05 .02
❑ 358 John Fishel .05 .02
❑ 359 Billy Hatcher .05 .02
❑ 360 Bob Knepper .05 .02
❑ 361 Louie Meadows UER .05 .02
(Bio says 10 EBH's
and 6 SB's in '88;
should be 3 and 4)
❑ 362 Dave Meads .05 .02
❑ 363 Jim Pankovits .05 .02
❑ 364 Terry Puhl .05 .02
❑ 365 Rafael Ramirez .05 .02
❑ 366 Craig Reynolds .05 .02
❑ 367 Mike Scott .05 .02
(Card number listed
as 368 on Astros CL)
❑ 368 Nolan Ryan 1.00 .45
(Card number listed
as 367 on Astros CL)
❑ 369 Dave Smith .05 .02
❑ 370 Gerald Young .05 .02
❑ 371 Hubie Brooks .05 .02
❑ 372 Tim Burke .05 .02
❑ 373 John Dopson .05 .02
❑ 374 Mike R. Fitzgerald .05 .02
❑ 375 Tom Foley .05 .02
❑ 376 Andres Galarraga UER .15 .07
(Home: Caracus)
❑ 377 Neal Heaton .05 .02
❑ 378 Joe Hesketh .05 .02
❑ 379 Brian Holman RC .05 .02
❑ 380 Rex Hudler .05 .02
❑ 381 Randy Johnson RC UER 2.00 .90
(Innings for '85 and
'86 shown as 27 and
120, should be 27.1
and 119.2)
❑ 382 Wallace Johnson .05 .02
❑ 383 Tracy Jones .05 .02
❑ 384 Dave Martinez .05 .02
❑ 385 Dennis Martinez .10 .05
❑ 386 Andy McGaffigan .05 .02
❑ 387 Otis Nixon .05 .02
❑ 388 Johnny Paredes .05 .02
❑ 389 Jeff Parrett .05 .02
❑ 390 Pascual Perez .05 .02
❑ 391 Tim Raines .10 .05
❑ 392 Luis Rivera .05 .02
❑ 393 Nelson Santovenia .05 .02
❑ 394 Bryn Smith .05 .02
❑ 395 Tim Wallach .05 .02
❑ 396 Andy Allanson UER .05 .02
(1214 hits in '88,
should be 114)
❑ 397 Rod Allen .05 .02
❑ 398 Scott Bailes .05 .02
❑ 399 Tom Candiotti .05 .02
❑ 400 Joe Carter .15 .07
❑ 401 Carmen Castillo UER .05 .02
(After All-Star Break
batting 2.50)
❑ 402 Dave Clark UER .05 .02
(Card front shows
position as Rookie;
after All-Star Break
batting 3.14)
❑ 403 John Farrell UER .05 .02
(Typo in runs
allowed in '88)
❑ 404 Julio Franco .05 .02
❑ 405 Don Gordon .05 .02
❑ 406 Mel Hall .05 .02
❑ 407 Brad Havens .05 .02
❑ 408 Brook Jacoby .05 .02
❑ 409 Doug Jones .05 .02
❑ 410 Jeff Kaiser .05 .02
❑ 411 Luis Medina .05 .02
❑ 412 Cory Snyder .05 .02
❑ 413 Greg Swindell .05 .02
❑ 414 Ron Tingley UER .05 .02
(Hit HR in first ML
at-bat, should be
first AL at-bat)
❑ 415 Willie Upshaw .05 .02
❑ 416 Ron Washington .05 .02
❑ 417 Rich Yett .05 .02
❑ 418 Damon Berryhill .05 .02
❑ 419 Mike Bielecki .05 .02
❑ 420 Doug Dascenzo .05 .02
❑ 421 Jody Davis UER .05 .02
(Braves stats for
'88 missing)
❑ 422 Andre Dawson .15 .07
❑ 423 Frank DiPino .05 .02
❑ 424 Shawon Dunston .05 .02
❑ 425 Rich Gossage .10 .05
❑ 426 Mark Grace UER .20 .09
(Minor League stats
for '88 missing)
❑ 427 Mike Harkey RC .05 .02
❑ 428 Darrin Jackson .05 .02
❑ 429 Les Lancaster .05 .02
❑ 430 Vance Law .05 .02
❑ 431 Greg Maddux .60 .25
❑ 432 Jamie Moyer .05 .02
❑ 433 Al Nipper .05 .02
❑ 434 Rafael Palmeiro UER .25 .11
(170 hits in '88,
should be 178)
❑ 435 Pat Perry .05 .02
❑ 436 Jeff Pico .05 .02
❑ 437 Ryne Sandberg .25 .11
❑ 438 Calvin Schiraldi .05 .02
❑ 439 Rick Sutcliffe .10 .05
❑ 440A Manny Trillo ERR 2.00 .90
(Throws Rig)
❑ 440B Manny Trillo COR .05 .02
❑ 441 Gary Varsho UER .05 .02
(Wrong birthdate;
.303 should be .302;
11/28 should be 9/19)
❑ 442 Mitch Webster .05 .02
❑ 443 Luis Alicea RC .05 .02
❑ 444 Tom Brunansky .05 .02
❑ 445 Vince Coleman UER .05 .02
(Third straight with
83; should be fourth
straight with 81)
❑ 446 John Costello UER .05 .02
(Home California;
should be New York)
❑ 447 Danny Cox .05 .02
❑ 448 Ken Dayley .05 .02
❑ 449 Jose DeLeon .05 .02
❑ 450 Curt Ford .05 .02
❑ 451 Pedro Guerrero .05 .02
❑ 452 Bob Horner .05 .02
❑ 453 Tim Jones .05 .02
❑ 454 Steve Lake .05 .02
❑ 455 Joe Magrane UER .05 .02
(Des Moines, IO)
❑ 456 Greg Mathews .05 .02
❑ 457 Willie McGee .10 .05

❑ 458 Larry McWilliams .05 .02
❑ 459 Jose Oquendo .05 .02
❑ 460 Tony Pena .05 .02
❑ 461 Terry Pendleton .10 .05
❑ 462 Steve Peters UER .05 .02
(Lives in Harrah,
not Harah)
❑ 463 Ozzie Smith .25 .11
❑ 464 Scott Terry .05 .02
❑ 465 Denny Walling .05 .02
❑ 466 Todd Worrell .05 .02
❑ 467 Tony Armas UER .05 .02
(Before All-Star Break
batting 2.39)
❑ 468 Dante Bichette RC .40 .18
❑ 469 Bob Boone .10 .05
❑ 470 Terry Clark .05 .02
❑ 471 Stew Cliburn .05 .02
❑ 472 Mike Cook UER .05 .02
(TM near Angels logo
missing from front)
❑ 473 Sherman Corbett .05 .02
❑ 474 Chili Davis .10 .05
❑ 475 Brian Downing .05 .02
❑ 476 Jim Eppard .05 .02
❑ 477 Chuck Finley .10 .05
❑ 478 Willie Fraser .05 .02
❑ 479 Bryan Harvey UER RC .05 .02
(ML record shows 0-0;
should be 7-5)
❑ 480 Jack Howell .05 .02
❑ 481 Wally Joyner UER .10 .05
(Yorba Linda, GA)
❑ 482 Jack Lazorko .05 .02
❑ 483 Kirk McCaskill .05 .02
❑ 484 Mark McLemore .05 .02
❑ 485 Greg Minton .05 .02
❑ 486 Dan Petry .05 .02
❑ 487 Johnny Ray .05 .02
❑ 488 Dick Schofield .05 .02
❑ 489 Devon White .10 .05
❑ 490 Mike Witt .05 .02
❑ 491 Harold Baines .10 .05
❑ 492 Daryl Boston .05 .02
❑ 493 Ivan Calderon UER .05 .02
('80 stats shifted)
❑ 494 Mike Diaz .05 .02
❑ 495 Carlton Fisk .20 .09
❑ 496 Dave Gallagher .05 .02
❑ 497 Ozzie Guillen .05 .02
❑ 498 Shawn Hillegas .05 .02
❑ 499 Lance Johnson .10 .05
❑ 500 Barry Jones .05 .02
❑ 501 Bill Long .05 .02
❑ 502 Steve Lyons .05 .02
❑ 503 Fred Manrique .05 .02
❑ 504 Jack McDowell .10 .05
❑ 505 Donn Pall .05 .02
❑ 506 Kelly Paris .05 .02
❑ 507 Dan Pasqua .05 .02
❑ 508 Ken Patterson .05 .02
❑ 509 Melido Perez .05 .02
❑ 510 Jerry Reuss .05 .02
❑ 511 Mark Salas .05 .02
❑ 512 Bobby Thigpen UER .05 .02
('86 ERA 4.69,
should be 4.68)
❑ 513 Mike Woodard .05 .02
❑ 514 Bob Brower .05 .02
❑ 515 Steve Buechele .05 .02
❑ 516 Jose Cecena .05 .02
❑ 517 Cecil Espy .05 .02
❑ 518 Scott Fletcher .05 .02
❑ 519 Cecilio Guante .05 .02
('87 Yankee stats
are off-centered)
❑ 520 Jose Guzman .05 .02
❑ 521 Ray Hayward .05 .02
❑ 522 Charlie Hough .10 .05
❑ 523 Pete Incaviglia .05 .02
❑ 524 Mike Jeffcoat .05 .02
❑ 525 Paul Kilgus .05 .02
❑ 526 Chad Kreuter RC .05 .02
❑ 527 Jeff Kunkel .05 .02
❑ 528 Oddibe McDowell .05 .02
❑ 529 Pete O'Brien .05 .02
❑ 530 Geno Petralli .05 .02
❑ 531 Jeff Russell .05 .02
❑ 532 Ruben Sierra .05 .02
❑ 533 Mike Stanley .05 .02
❑ 534A Ed VandeBerg ERR 2.00 .90
(Throws Lef)
❑ 534B Ed VandeBerg COR .05 .02
❑ 535 Curtis Wilkerson ERR .05 .02
(Pitcher headings
at bottom)
❑ 536 Mitch Williams .05 .02
❑ 537 Bobby Witt UER .05 .02
('85 ERA .643;
should be 6.43)
❑ 538 Steve Balboni .05 .02
❑ 539 Scott Bankhead .05 .02
❑ 540 Scott Bradley .05 .02
❑ 541 Mickey Brantley .05 .02
❑ 542 Jay Buhner .10 .05
❑ 543 Mike Campbell .05 .02
❑ 544 Darnell Coles .05 .02
❑ 545 Henry Cotto .05 .02
❑ 546 Alvin Davis .05 .02
❑ 547 Mario Diaz .05 .02
❑ 548 Ken Griffey Jr. RC ! 20.00 9.00
❑ 549 Erik Hanson RC .10 .05
❑ 550 Mike Jackson UER .05 .02
(Lifetime ERA 3.345;
should be 3.45)
❑ 551 Mark Langston .05 .02
❑ 552 Edgar Martinez .15 .07
❑ 553 Bill McGuire .05 .02
❑ 554 Mike Moore .05 .02
❑ 555 Jim Presley .05 .02
❑ 556 Rey Quinones .05 .02
❑ 557 Jerry Reed .05 .02
❑ 558 Harold Reynolds .05 .02
❑ 559 Mike Schooler .05 .02
❑ 560 Bill Swift .05 .02
❑ 561 Dave Valle .05 .02
❑ 562 Steve Bedrosian .05 .02
❑ 563 Phil Bradley .05 .02
❑ 564 Don Carman .05 .02
❑ 565 Bob Dernier .05 .02
❑ 566 Marvin Freeman .05 .02
❑ 567 Todd Frohwirth .05 .02
❑ 568 Greg Gross .05 .02
❑ 569 Kevin Gross .05 .02
❑ 570 Greg A. Harris .05 .02
❑ 571 Von Hayes .05 .02
❑ 572 Chris James .05 .02
❑ 573 Steve Jeltz .05 .02
❑ 574 Ron Jones UER .05 .02
(Led IL in '88 with
85, should be 75)
❑ 575 Ricky Jordan RC .10 .05
❑ 576 Mike Maddux .05 .02
❑ 577 David Palmer .05 .02
❑ 578 Lance Parrish .05 .02
❑ 579 Shane Rawley .05 .02
❑ 580 Bruce Ruffin .05 .02
❑ 581 Juan Samuel .05 .02
❑ 582 Mike Schmidt .40 .18
❑ 583 Kent Tekulve .05 .02
❑ 584 Milt Thompson UER .05 .02
(19 hits in '88,
should be 109)
❑ 585 Jose Alvarez .05 .02
❑ 586 Paul Assenmacher .05 .02
❑ 587 Bruce Benedict .05 .02
❑ 588 Jeff Blauser .10 .05
❑ 589 Terry Blocker .05 .02
❑ 590 Ron Gant .10 .05
❑ 591 Tom Glavine .20 .09
❑ 592 Tommy Gregg .05 .02
❑ 593 Albert Hall .05 .02
❑ 594 Dion James .05 .02
❑ 595 Rick Mahler .05 .02
❑ 596 Dale Murphy .20 .09
❑ 597 Gerald Perry .05 .02
❑ 598 Charlie Puleo .05 .02
❑ 599 Ted Simmons .10 .05
❑ 600 Pete Smith .05 .02
❑ 601 Zane Smith .05 .02
❑ 602 John Smoltz RC .40 .18
❑ 603 Bruce Sutter .05 .02
❑ 604 Andres Thomas .05 .02
❑ 605 Ozzie Virgil .05 .02
❑ 606 Brady Anderson RC .40 .18
❑ 607 Jeff Ballard .05 .02
❑ 608 Jose Bautista .05 .02
❑ 609 Ken Gerhart .05 .02
❑ 610 Terry Kennedy .05 .02
❑ 611 Eddie Murray .20 .09
❑ 612 Carl Nichols UER .05 .02
(Before All-Star Break
batting 1.88)
❑ 613 Tom Niedenfuer .05 .02
❑ 614 Joe Orsulak .05 .02
❑ 615 Oswald Peraza UER .05 .02
(Shown as Oswaldo)
❑ 616A Bill Ripken ERR 15.00 6.75
(Rick Face written
on knob of bat)
❑ 616B Bill Ripken 50.00 22.00
(Bat knob
whited out)
❑ 616C Bill Ripken 6.00 2.70
(Words on bat knob
scribbled out in White)
❑ 616D Bill Ripken
(Words on bat
scribbled out in Black)
❑ 616E Bill Ripken DP .10 .05
(Black box covering
bat knob)
❑ 617 Cal Ripken .75 .35
❑ 618 Dave Schmidt .05 .02
❑ 619 Rick Schu .05 .02
❑ 620 Larry Sheets .05 .02
❑ 621 Doug Sisk .05 .02
❑ 622 Pete Stanicek .05 .02
❑ 623 Mickey Tettleton .05 .02
❑ 624 Jay Tibbs .05 .02
❑ 625 Jim Traber .05 .02
❑ 626 Mark Williamson .05 .02
❑ 627 Craig Worthington .05 .02
❑ 628 Speed/Power .10 .05
Jose Canseco
❑ 629 Pitcher Perfect .05 .02
Tom Browning
❑ 630 Like Father/Like Sons .20 .09
Roberto Alomar
Sandy Alomar Jr.
(Names on card listed
in wrong order) UER
❑ 631 NL All Stars UER .20 .09
Will Clark
Rafael Palmeiro
(Gallaraga, sic;
Clark 3 consecutive
100 RBI seasons;
third with 102 RBI's)
❑ 632 Homeruns - Coast .10 .05
to Coast UER
Darryl Strawberry
Will Clark (Homeruns
should be two words)
❑ 633 Hot Corners - Hot .10 .05
Hitters UER
Wade Boggs
Carney Lansford
(Boggs hit .366 in
'86; should be '88)
❑ 634 Triple A's .50 .23
Jose Canseco
Terry Steinbach
Mark McGwire
❑ 635 Dual Heat .10 .05
Mark Davis
Dwight Gooden
❑ 636 NL Pitching Power UER .05 .02
Danny Jackson
David Cone
(Hersheiser, sic)
❑ 637 Cannon Arms UER .10 .05
Chris Sabo
Bobby Bonilla
(Bobby Bonds, sic)
❑ 638 Double Trouble UER .05 .02
Andres Galarraga
(Misspelled Gallaraga

| | | MINT | NRMT |
|---|---|---|---|
| | on card back) Gerald Perry | | |
| ❑ 639 | Power Center Kirby Puckett Eric Davis | .15 | .07 |
| ❑ 640 | Steve Wilson and Cameron Drew | .05 | .02 |
| ❑ 641 | Kevin Brown and Kevin Reimer | .40 | .18 |
| ❑ 642 | Brad Pounders RC and Jerald Clark | .05 | .02 |
| ❑ 643 | Mike Capel and Drew Hall | .05 | .02 |
| ❑ 644 | Joe Girardi RC and Rolando Roomes | .20 | .09 |
| ❑ 645 | Lenny Harris RC and Marty Brown | .10 | .05 |
| ❑ 646 | Luis DeLosSantos and Jim Campbell | .05 | .02 |
| ❑ 647 | Randy Kramer and Miguel Garcia | .05 | .02 |
| ❑ 648 | Torey Lovullo RC and Robert Palacios | .05 | .02 |
| ❑ 649 | Jim Corsi and Bob Milacki | .05 | .02 |
| ❑ 650 | Grady Hall and Mike Rochford | .05 | .02 |
| ❑ 651 | Terry Taylor and Vance Lovelace | .05 | .02 |
| ❑ 652 | Ken Hill RC and Dennis Cook | .20 | .09 |
| ❑ 653 | Scott Service and Shane Turner | .05 | .02 |
| ❑ 654 | CL: Oakland/Mets Dodgers/Red Sox (10 Henderson; 68 Jess Orosco) | .05 | .02 |
| ❑ 655A | CL: Twins/Tigers ERR Reds/Brewers (179 Boslo and Twins/Tigers positions listed) | .05 | .02 |
| ❑ 655B | CL: Twins/Tigers COR Reds/Brewers (179 Boslo but Twins/Tigers positions not listed) | .05 | .02 |
| ❑ 656 | CL: Pirates/Blue Jays Yankees/Royals (225 Jess Barfield) | .05 | .02 |
| ❑ 657 | CL: Padres/Giants Astros/Expos (367/368 wrong) | .05 | .02 |
| ❑ 658 | CL: Indians/Cubs Cardinals/Angels (449 Dolcon) | .05 | .02 |
| ❑ 659 | CL: White Sox/Rangers Mariners/Phillies | .05 | .02 |
| ❑ 660 | CL: Braves/Orioles Specials/Checklists (632 hyphenated differently and 650 Hali; 595 Rich Mahler; 619 Rich Schu) | .05 | .02 |

## 1989 Fleer Update

| | | MINT | NRMT |
|---|---|---|---|
| | COMP.FACT.SET (132) | 5.00 | 2.20 |
| ❑ 1 | Phil Bradley | .05 | .02 |
| ❑ 2 | Mike Devereaux | .05 | .02 |
| ❑ 3 | Steve Finley RC | .50 | .23 |
| ❑ 4 | Kevin Hickey | .05 | .02 |
| ❑ 5 | Brian Holton | .05 | .02 |
| ❑ 6 | Bob Milacki | .05 | .02 |
| ❑ 7 | Randy Milligan | .05 | .02 |
| ❑ 8 | John Dopson | .05 | .02 |
| ❑ 9 | Nick Esasky | .05 | .02 |
| ❑ 10 | Rob Murphy | .05 | .02 |
| ❑ 11 | Jim Abbott RC* | .20 | .09 |
| ❑ 12 | Bert Blyleven | .10 | .05 |
| ❑ 13 | Jeff Manto RC | .05 | .02 |
| ❑ 14 | Bob McClure | .05 | .02 |
| ❑ 15 | Lance Parrish | .05 | .02 |
| ❑ 16 | Lee Stevens RC | .25 | .11 |
| ❑ 17 | Claudell Washington | .05 | .02 |
| ❑ 18 | Mark Davis | .05 | .02 |
| ❑ 19 | Eric King | .05 | .02 |
| ❑ 20 | Ron Kittle | .05 | .02 |
| ❑ 21 | Matt Merullo | .05 | .02 |
| ❑ 22 | Steve Rosenberg | .05 | .02 |
| ❑ 23 | Robin Ventura RC | .75 | .35 |
| ❑ 24 | Keith Atherton | .05 | .02 |
| ❑ 25 | Joey Belle RC | 2.50 | 1.10 |
| ❑ 26 | Jerry Browne | .05 | .02 |
| ❑ 27 | Felix Fermin | .05 | .02 |
| ❑ 28 | Brad Komminsk | .05 | .02 |
| ❑ 29 | Pete O'Brien | .05 | .02 |
| ❑ 30 | Mike Brumley | .05 | .02 |
| ❑ 31 | Tracy Jones | .05 | .02 |
| ❑ 32 | Mike Schwabe | .05 | .02 |
| ❑ 33 | Gary Ward | .05 | .02 |
| ❑ 34 | Frank Williams | .05 | .02 |
| ❑ 35 | Kevin Appier RC | .25 | .11 |
| ❑ 36 | Bob Boone | .10 | .05 |
| ❑ 37 | Luis DeLosSantos | .05 | .02 |
| ❑ 38 | Jim Eisenreich | .05 | .02 |
| ❑ 39 | Jaime Navarro RC | .05 | .02 |
| ❑ 40 | Bill Spiers RC | .05 | .02 |
| ❑ 41 | Greg Vaughn RC | 1.00 | .45 |
| ❑ 42 | Randy Veres | .05 | .02 |
| ❑ 43 | Wally Backman | .05 | .02 |
| ❑ 44 | Shane Rawley | .05 | .02 |
| ❑ 45 | Steve Balboni | .05 | .02 |
| ❑ 46 | Jesse Barfield | .05 | .02 |
| ❑ 47 | Alvaro Espinoza | .05 | .02 |
| ❑ 48 | Bob Geren | .05 | .02 |
| ❑ 49 | Mel Hall | .05 | .02 |
| ❑ 50 | Andy Hawkins | .05 | .02 |
| ❑ 51 | Hensley Meulens RC | .05 | .02 |
| ❑ 52 | Steve Sax | .05 | .02 |
| ❑ 53 | Deion Sanders RC | .40 | .18 |
| ❑ 54 | Rickey Henderson | .25 | .11 |
| ❑ 55 | Mike Moore | .05 | .02 |
| ❑ 56 | Tony Phillips | .05 | .02 |
| ❑ 57 | Greg Briley | .05 | .02 |
| ❑ 58 | Gene Harris RC | .05 | .02 |
| ❑ 59 | Randy Johnson | 2.00 | .90 |
| ❑ 60 | Jeffrey Leonard | .05 | .02 |
| ❑ 61 | Dennis Powell | .05 | .02 |
| ❑ 62 | Omar Vizquel RC | .50 | .23 |
| ❑ 63 | Kevin Brown | .40 | .18 |
| ❑ 64 | Julio Franco | .05 | .02 |
| ❑ 65 | Jamie Moyer | .05 | .02 |
| ❑ 66 | Rafael Palmeiro | .25 | .11 |
| ❑ 67 | Nolan Ryan | 2.00 | .90 |
| ❑ 68 | Francisco Cabrera RC | .10 | .05 |
| ❑ 69 | Junior Felix RC | .05 | .02 |
| ❑ 70 | Al Leiter | .20 | .09 |
| ❑ 71 | Alex Sanchez | .05 | .02 |
| ❑ 72 | Geronimo Berroa | .05 | .02 |
| ❑ 73 | Derek Lilliquist RC | .05 | .02 |
| ❑ 74 | Lonnie Smith | .05 | .02 |
| ❑ 75 | Jeff Treadway | .05 | .02 |
| ❑ 76 | Paul Kilgus | .05 | .02 |
| ❑ 77 | Lloyd McClendon | .05 | .02 |
| ❑ 78 | Scott Sanderson | .05 | .02 |
| ❑ 79 | Dwight Smith RC | .10 | .05 |
| ❑ 80 | Jerome Walton | .20 | .09 |
| ❑ 81 | Mitch Williams | .05 | .02 |
| ❑ 82 | Steve Wilson | .05 | .02 |
| ❑ 83 | Todd Benzinger | .05 | .02 |
| ❑ 84 | Ken Griffey Sr. | .10 | .05 |
| ❑ 85 | Rick Mahler | .05 | .02 |
| ❑ 86 | Rolando Roomes | .05 | .02 |
| ❑ 87 | Scott Scudder RC | .05 | .02 |
| ❑ 88 | Jim Clancy | .05 | .02 |
| ❑ 89 | Rick Rhoden | .05 | .02 |
| ❑ 90 | Dan Schatzeder | .05 | .02 |
| ❑ 91 | Mike Morgan | .05 | .02 |
| ❑ 92 | Eddie Murray | .20 | .09 |
| ❑ 93 | Willie Randolph | .10 | .05 |
| ❑ 94 | Ray Searage | .05 | .02 |
| ❑ 95 | Mike Aldrete | .05 | .02 |
| ❑ 96 | Kevin Gross | .05 | .02 |
| ❑ 97 | Mark Langston | .05 | .02 |
| ❑ 98 | Spike Owen | .05 | .02 |
| ❑ 99 | Zane Smith | .05 | .02 |
| ❑ 100 | Don Aase | .05 | .02 |
| ❑ 101 | Barry Lyons | .05 | .02 |
| ❑ 102 | Juan Samuel | .05 | .02 |
| ❑ 103 | Wally Whitehurst RC | .05 | .02 |
| ❑ 104 | Dennis Cook | .05 | .02 |
| ❑ 105 | Len Dykstra | .10 | .05 |
| ❑ 106 | Charlie Hayes | .20 | .09 |
| ❑ 107 | Tommy Herr | .05 | .02 |
| ❑ 108 | Ken Howell | .05 | .02 |
| ❑ 109 | John Kruk | .10 | .05 |
| ❑ 110 | Roger McDowell | .05 | .02 |
| ❑ 111 | Terry Mulholland | .05 | .02 |
| ❑ 112 | Jeff Parrett | .05 | .02 |
| ❑ 113 | Neal Heaton | .05 | .02 |
| ❑ 114 | Jeff King | .05 | .02 |
| ❑ 115 | Randy Kramer | .05 | .02 |
| ❑ 116 | Bill Landrum | .05 | .02 |
| ❑ 117 | Cris Carpenter RC* | .05 | .02 |
| ❑ 118 | Frank DiPino | .05 | .02 |
| ❑ 119 | Ken Hill | .20 | .09 |
| ❑ 120 | Dan Quisenberry | .05 | .02 |
| ❑ 121 | Milt Thompson | .05 | .02 |
| ❑ 122 | Todd Zeile RC | .25 | .11 |
| ❑ 123 | Jack Clark | .05 | .02 |
| ❑ 124 | Bruce Hurst | .05 | .02 |
| ❑ 125 | Mark Parent | .05 | .02 |
| ❑ 126 | Bip Roberts | .10 | .05 |
| ❑ 127 | Jeff Brantley RC UER (Photo actually Joe Kmak) | .10 | .05 |
| ❑ 128 | Terry Kennedy | .05 | .02 |
| ❑ 129 | Mike LaCoss | .05 | .02 |
| ❑ 130 | Greg Litton | .05 | .02 |
| ❑ 131 | Mike Schmidt | .60 | .25 |
| ❑ 132 | Checklist 1-132 | .05 | .02 |

## 1990 Fleer

| | | MINT | NRMT |
|---|---|---|---|
| | COMPLETE SET (660) | 12.00 | 5.50 |
| | COMP.RETAIL SET (660) | 8.00 | 3.60 |
| | COMP.HOBBY SET (672) | 15.00 | 6.75 |
| ❑ 1 | Lance Blankenship | .05 | .02 |
| ❑ 2 | Todd Burns | .05 | .02 |
| ❑ 3 | Jose Canseco | .25 | .11 |
| ❑ 4 | Jim Corsi | .05 | .02 |
| ❑ 5 | Storm Davis | .05 | .02 |
| ❑ 6 | Dennis Eckersley | .15 | .07 |
| ❑ 7 | Mike Gallego | .05 | .02 |
| ❑ 8 | Ron Hassey | .05 | .02 |
| ❑ 9 | Dave Henderson | .05 | .02 |
| ❑ 10 | Rickey Henderson | .25 | .11 |

| No. | Player | | |
|---|---|---|---|
| 11 | Rick Honeycutt | .05 | .02 |
| 12 | Stan Javier | .05 | .02 |
| 13 | Felix Jose | .05 | .02 |
| 14 | Carney Lansford | .10 | .05 |
| 15 | Mark McGwire UER (1989 runs listed as 4; should be 74) | .75 | .35 |
| 16 | Mike Moore | .05 | .02 |
| 17 | Gene Nelson | .05 | .02 |
| 18 | Dave Parker | .10 | .05 |
| 19 | Tony Phillips | .05 | .02 |
| 20 | Terry Steinbach | .05 | .02 |
| 21 | Dave Stewart | .10 | .05 |
| 22 | Walt Weiss | .05 | .02 |
| 23 | Bob Welch | .05 | .02 |
| 24 | Curt Young | .05 | .02 |
| 25 | Paul Assenmacher | .05 | .02 |
| 26 | Damon Berryhill | .05 | .02 |
| 27 | Mike Bielecki | .05 | .02 |
| 28 | Kevin Blankenship | .05 | .02 |
| 29 | Andre Dawson | .15 | .07 |
| 30 | Shawon Dunston | .05 | .02 |
| 31 | Joe Girardi | .15 | .07 |
| 32 | Mark Grace | .20 | .09 |
| 33 | Mike Harkey | .05 | .02 |
| 34 | Paul Kilgus | .05 | .02 |
| 35 | Les Lancaster | .05 | .02 |
| 36 | Vance Law | .05 | .02 |
| 37 | Greg Maddux | .50 | .23 |
| 38 | Lloyd McClendon | .05 | .02 |
| 39 | Jeff Pico | .05 | .02 |
| 40 | Ryne Sandberg | .25 | .11 |
| 41 | Scott Sanderson | .05 | .02 |
| 42 | Dwight Smith | .05 | .02 |
| 43 | Rick Sutcliffe | .10 | .05 |
| 44 | Jerome Walton | .05 | .02 |
| 45 | Mitch Webster | .05 | .02 |
| 46 | Curt Wilkerson | .05 | .02 |
| 47 | Dean Wilkins | .05 | .02 |
| 48 | Mitch Williams | .05 | .02 |
| 49 | Steve Wilson | .05 | .02 |
| 50 | Steve Bedrosian | .05 | .02 |
| 51 | Mike Benjamin RC | .05 | .02 |
| 52 | Jeff Brantley | .05 | .02 |
| 53 | Brett Butler | .10 | .05 |
| 54 | Will Clark UER (Did You Know says first in runs; should say tied for first) | .10 | .05 |
| 55 | Kelly Downs | .05 | .02 |
| 56 | Scott Garrelts | .05 | .02 |
| 57 | Atlee Hammaker | .05 | .02 |
| 58 | Terry Kennedy | .05 | .02 |
| 59 | Mike LaCoss | .05 | .02 |
| 60 | Craig Lefferts | .05 | .02 |
| 61 | Greg Litton | .05 | .02 |
| 62 | Candy Maldonado | .05 | .02 |
| 63 | Kirt Manwaring UER (No '88 Phoenix stats as noted in box) | .05 | .02 |
| 64 | Randy McCament | .05 | .02 |
| 65 | Kevin Mitchell | .05 | .02 |
| 66 | Donell Nixon | .05 | .02 |
| 67 | Ken Oberkfell | .05 | .02 |
| 68 | Rick Reuschel | .05 | .02 |
| 69 | Ernest Riles | .05 | .02 |
| 70 | Don Robinson | .05 | .02 |
| 71 | Pat Sheridan | .05 | .02 |
| 72 | Chris Speier | .05 | .02 |
| 73 | Robby Thompson | .05 | .02 |
| 74 | Jose Uribe | .05 | .02 |
| 75 | Matt Williams | .15 | .07 |
| 76 | George Bell | .05 | .02 |
| 77 | Pat Borders | .05 | .02 |
| 78 | John Cerutti | .05 | .02 |
| 79 | Junior Felix | .05 | .02 |
| 80 | Tony Fernandez | .05 | .02 |
| 81 | Mike Flanagan | .05 | .02 |
| 82 | Mauro Gozzo | .05 | .02 |
| 83 | Kelly Gruber | .05 | .02 |
| 84 | Tom Henke | .05 | .02 |
| 85 | Jimmy Key | .10 | .05 |
| 86 | Manny Lee | .05 | .02 |
| 87 | Nelson Liriano UER (Should say "led the IL" instead of "led the TL") | .05 | .02 |
| 88 | Lee Mazzilli | .05 | .02 |
| 89 | Fred McGriff | .20 | .09 |
| 90 | Lloyd Moseby | .05 | .02 |
| 91 | Rance Mulliniks | .05 | .02 |
| 92 | Alex Sanchez | .05 | .02 |
| 93 | Dave Stieb | .10 | .05 |
| 94 | Todd Stottlemyre | .10 | .05 |
| 95 | Duane Ward UER (Double line of '87 Syracuse stats) | .05 | .02 |
| 96 | David Wells | .10 | .05 |
| 97 | Ernie Whitt | .05 | .02 |
| 98 | Frank Wills | .05 | .02 |
| 99 | Mookie Wilson | .10 | .05 |
| 100 | Kevin Appier | .15 | .07 |
| 101 | Luis Aquino | .05 | .02 |
| 102 | Bob Boone | .10 | .05 |
| 103 | George Brett | .40 | .18 |
| 104 | Jose DeJesus | .05 | .02 |
| 105 | Luis De Los Santos | .05 | .02 |
| 106 | Jim Eisenreich | .05 | .02 |
| 107 | Steve Farr | .05 | .02 |
| 108 | Tom Gordon | .10 | .05 |
| 109 | Mark Gubicza | .05 | .02 |
| 110 | Bo Jackson | .10 | .05 |
| 111 | Terry Leach | .05 | .02 |
| 112 | Charlie Leibrandt | .05 | .02 |
| 113 | Rick Luecken | .05 | .02 |
| 114 | Mike Macfarlane | .05 | .02 |
| 115 | Jeff Montgomery | .10 | .05 |
| 116 | Bret Saberhagen | .10 | .05 |
| 117 | Kevin Seitzer | .05 | .02 |
| 118 | Kurt Stillwell | .05 | .02 |
| 119 | Pat Tabler | .05 | .02 |
| 120 | Danny Tartabull | .05 | .02 |
| 121 | Gary Thurman | .05 | .02 |
| 122 | Frank White | .10 | .05 |
| 123 | Willie Wilson | .05 | .02 |
| 124 | Matt Winters | .05 | .02 |
| 125 | Jim Abbott | .15 | .07 |
| 126 | Tony Armas | .05 | .02 |
| 127 | Dante Bichette | .20 | .09 |
| 128 | Bert Blyleven | .10 | .05 |
| 129 | Chili Davis | .10 | .05 |
| 130 | Brian Downing | .05 | .02 |
| 131 | Mike Fetters RC | .05 | .02 |
| 132 | Chuck Finley | .10 | .05 |
| 133 | Willie Fraser | .05 | .02 |
| 134 | Bryan Harvey | .05 | .02 |
| 135 | Jack Howell | .05 | .02 |
| 136 | Wally Joyner | .10 | .05 |
| 137 | Jeff Manto | .05 | .02 |
| 138 | Kirk McCaskill | .05 | .02 |
| 139 | Bob McClure | .05 | .02 |
| 140 | Greg Minton | .05 | .02 |
| 141 | Lance Parrish | .05 | .02 |
| 142 | Dan Petry | .05 | .02 |
| 143 | Johnny Ray | .05 | .02 |
| 144 | Dick Schofield | .05 | .02 |
| 145 | Lee Stevens | .10 | .05 |
| 146 | Claudell Washington | .05 | .02 |
| 147 | Devon White | .05 | .02 |
| 148 | Mike Witt | .05 | .02 |
| 149 | Roberto Alomar | .20 | .09 |
| 150 | Sandy Alomar Jr. | .10 | .05 |
| 151 | Andy Benes | .05 | .02 |
| 152 | Jack Clark | .10 | .05 |
| 153 | Pat Clements | .05 | .02 |
| 154 | Joey Cora | .10 | .05 |
| 155 | Mark Davis | .05 | .02 |
| 156 | Mark Grant | .05 | .02 |
| 157 | Tony Gwynn | .40 | .18 |
| 158 | Greg W. Harris | .05 | .02 |
| 159 | Bruce Hurst | .05 | .02 |
| 160 | Darrin Jackson | .05 | .02 |
| 161 | Chris James | .05 | .02 |
| 162 | Carmelo Martinez | .05 | .02 |
| 163 | Mike Pagliarulo | .05 | .02 |
| 164 | Mark Parent | .05 | .02 |
| 165 | Dennis Rasmussen | .05 | .02 |
| 166 | Bip Roberts | .05 | .02 |
| 167 | Benito Santiago | .05 | .02 |
| 168 | Calvin Schiraldi | .05 | .02 |
| 169 | Eric Show | .05 | .02 |
| 170 | Garry Templeton | .05 | .02 |
| 171 | Ed Whitson | .05 | .02 |
| 172 | Brady Anderson | .20 | .09 |
| 173 | Jeff Ballard | .05 | .02 |
| 174 | Phil Bradley | .05 | .02 |
| 175 | Mike Devereaux | .05 | .02 |
| 176 | Steve Finley | .10 | .05 |
| 177 | Pete Harnisch | .05 | .02 |
| 178 | Kevin Hickey | .05 | .02 |
| 179 | Brian Holton | .05 | .02 |
| 180 | Ben McDonald RC | .10 | .05 |
| 181 | Bob Melvin | .05 | .02 |
| 182 | Bob Milacki | .05 | .02 |
| 183 | Randy Milligan UER (Double line of '87 stats) | .05 | .02 |
| 184 | Gregg Olson | .10 | .05 |
| 185 | Joe Orsulak | .05 | .02 |
| 186 | Bill Ripken | .05 | .02 |
| 187 | Cal Ripken | .75 | .35 |
| 188 | Dave Schmidt | .05 | .02 |
| 189 | Larry Sheets | .05 | .02 |
| 190 | Mickey Tettleton | .05 | .02 |
| 191 | Mark Thurmond | .05 | .02 |
| 192 | Jay Tibbs | .05 | .02 |
| 193 | Jim Traber | .05 | .02 |
| 194 | Mark Williamson | .05 | .02 |
| 195 | Craig Worthington | .05 | .02 |
| 196 | Don Aase | .05 | .02 |
| 197 | Blaine Beatty | .05 | .02 |
| 198 | Mark Carreon | .05 | .02 |
| 199 | Gary Carter | .15 | .07 |
| 200 | David Cone | .10 | .05 |
| 201 | Ron Darling | .05 | .02 |
| 202 | Kevin Elster | .05 | .02 |
| 203 | Sid Fernandez | .05 | .02 |
| 204 | Dwight Gooden | .10 | .05 |
| 205 | Keith Hernandez | .10 | .05 |
| 206 | Jeff Innis | .05 | .02 |
| 207 | Gregg Jefferies | .10 | .05 |
| 208 | Howard Johnson | .05 | .02 |
| 209 | Barry Lyons UER (Double line of '87 stats) | .05 | .02 |
| 210 | Dave Magadan | .05 | .02 |
| 211 | Kevin McReynolds | .05 | .02 |
| 212 | Jeff Musselman | .05 | .02 |
| 213 | Randy Myers | .10 | .05 |
| 214 | Bob Ojeda | .05 | .02 |
| 215 | Juan Samuel | .05 | .02 |
| 216 | Mackey Sasser | .05 | .02 |
| 217 | Darryl Strawberry | .10 | .05 |
| 218 | Tim Teufel | .05 | .02 |
| 219 | Frank Viola | .05 | .02 |
| 220 | Juan Agosto | .05 | .02 |
| 221 | Larry Andersen | .05 | .02 |
| 222 | Eric Anthony RC | .05 | .02 |
| 223 | Kevin Bass | .05 | .02 |
| 224 | Craig Biggio | .15 | .07 |
| 225 | Ken Caminiti | .10 | .05 |
| 226 | Jim Clancy | .05 | .02 |
| 227 | Danny Darwin | .05 | .02 |
| 228 | Glenn Davis | .05 | .02 |
| 229 | Jim Deshaies | .05 | .02 |
| 230 | Bill Doran | .05 | .02 |
| 231 | Bob Forsch | .05 | .02 |
| 232 | Brian Meyer | .05 | .02 |
| 233 | Terry Puhl | .05 | .02 |
| 234 | Rafael Ramirez | .05 | .02 |
| 235 | Rick Rhoden | .05 | .02 |
| 236 | Dan Schatzeder | .05 | .02 |
| 237 | Mike Scott | .05 | .02 |
| 238 | Dave Smith | .05 | .02 |
| 239 | Alex Trevino | .05 | .02 |
| 240 | Glenn Wilson | .05 | .02 |
| 241 | Gerald Young | .05 | .02 |
| 242 | Tom Brunansky | .05 | .02 |
| 243 | Cris Carpenter | .05 | .02 |
| 244 | Alex Cole RC | .05 | .02 |
| 245 | Vince Coleman | .05 | .02 |
| 246 | John Costello | .05 | .02 |
| 247 | Ken Dayley | .05 | .02 |
| 248 | Jose DeLeon | .05 | .02 |
| 249 | Frank DiPino | .05 | .02 |
| 250 | Pedro Guerrero | .05 | .02 |
| 251 | Ken Hill | .10 | .05 |
| 252 | Joe Magrane | .05 | .02 |

❑ 253 Willie McGee UER .10 .05
(No decimal point before 353)
❑ 254 John Morris .05 .02
❑ 255 Jose Oquendo .05 .02
❑ 256 Tony Pena .05 .02
❑ 257 Terry Pendleton .10 .05
❑ 258 Ted Power .05 .02
❑ 259 Dan Quisenberry .05 .02
❑ 260 Ozzie Smith .25 .11
❑ 261 Scott Terry .05 .02
❑ 262 Milt Thompson .05 .02
❑ 263 Denny Walling .05 .02
❑ 264 Todd Worrell .05 .02
❑ 265 Todd Zeile .10 .05
❑ 266 Marty Barrett .05 .02
❑ 267 Mike Boddicker .05 .02
❑ 268 Wade Boggs .25 .11
❑ 269 Ellis Burks .15 .07
❑ 270 Rick Cerone .05 .02
❑ 271 Roger Clemens .40 .18
❑ 272 John Dopson .05 .02
❑ 273 Nick Esasky .05 .02
❑ 274 Dwight Evans .10 .05
❑ 275 Wes Gardner .05 .02
❑ 276 Rich Gedman .05 .02
❑ 277 Mike Greenwell .05 .02
❑ 278 Danny Heep .05 .02
❑ 279 Eric Hetzel .05 .02
❑ 280 Dennis Lamp .05 .02
❑ 281 Rob Murphy UER .05 .02
('89 stats say Reds; should say Red Sox)
❑ 282 Joe Price .05 .02
❑ 283 Carlos Quintana .05 .02
❑ 284 Jody Reed .05 .02
❑ 285 Luis Rivera .05 .02
❑ 286 Kevin Romine .05 .02
❑ 287 Lee Smith .10 .05
❑ 288 Mike Smithson .05 .02
❑ 289 Bob Stanley .05 .02
❑ 290 Harold Baines .10 .05
❑ 291 Kevin Brown .20 .09
❑ 292 Steve Buechele .05 .02
❑ 293 Scott Coolbaugh .05 .02
❑ 294 Jack Daugherty .05 .02
❑ 295 Cecil Espy .05 .02
❑ 296 Julio Franco .05 .02
❑ 297 Juan Gonzalez RC 1.00 .45
❑ 298 Cecilio Guante .05 .02
❑ 299 Drew Hall .05 .02
❑ 300 Charlie Hough .10 .05
❑ 301 Pete Incaviglia .05 .02
❑ 302 Mike Jeffcoat .05 .02
❑ 303 Chad Kreuter .05 .02
❑ 304 Jeff Kunkel .05 .02
❑ 305 Rick Leach .05 .02
❑ 306 Fred Manrique .05 .02
❑ 307 Jamie Moyer .05 .02
❑ 308 Rafael Palmeiro .20 .09
❑ 309 Geno Petralli .05 .02
❑ 310 Kevin Reimer .05 .02
❑ 311 Kenny Rogers .10 .05
❑ 312 Jeff Russell .05 .02
❑ 313 Nolan Ryan 1.00 .45
❑ 314 Ruben Sierra .05 .02
❑ 315 Bobby Witt .05 .02
❑ 316 Chris Bosio .05 .02
❑ 317 Glenn Braggs UER .05 .02
(Stats say 111 K's, but bio says 117 K's)
❑ 318 Greg Brock .05 .02
❑ 319 Chuck Crim .05 .02
❑ 320 Rob Deer .05 .02
❑ 321 Mike Felder .05 .02
❑ 322 Tom Filer .05 .02
❑ 323 Tony Fossas .05 .02
❑ 324 Jim Gantner .05 .02
❑ 325 Darryl Hamilton .05 .02
❑ 326 Teddy Higuera .05 .02
❑ 327 Mark Knudson .05 .02
❑ 328 Bill Krueger UER .05 .02
('86 stats missing)
❑ 329 Tim McIntosh RC .05 .02
❑ 330 Paul Molitor .20 .09
❑ 331 Jaime Navarro .05 .02
❑ 332 Charlie O'Brien .05 .02
❑ 333 Jeff Peterek .05 .02
❑ 334 Dan Plesac .05 .02
❑ 335 Jerry Reuss .05 .02
❑ 336 Gary Sheffield UER .25 .11
(Bio says played for 3 teams in '87, but stats say in '88)
❑ 337 Bill Spiers .05 .02
❑ 338 B.J. Surhoff .10 .05
❑ 339 Greg Vaughn .25 .11
❑ 340 Robin Yount .20 .09
❑ 341 Hubie Brooks .05 .02
❑ 342 Tim Burke .05 .02
❑ 343 Mike Fitzgerald .05 .02
❑ 344 Tom Foley .05 .02
❑ 345 Andres Galarraga .15 .07
❑ 346 Damaso Garcia .05 .02
❑ 347 Marquis Grissom RC .25 .11
❑ 348 Kevin Gross .05 .02
❑ 349 Joe Hesketh .05 .02
❑ 350 Jeff Huson RC .05 .02
❑ 351 Wallace Johnson .05 .02
❑ 352 Mark Langston .05 .02
❑ 353A Dave Martinez 2.00 .90
(Yellow on front)
❑ 353B Dave Martinez .05 .02
(Red on front)
❑ 354 Dennis Martinez UER .10 .05
('87 ERA is 616; should be 6.16)
❑ 355 Andy McGaffigan .05 .02
❑ 356 Otis Nixon .05 .02
❑ 357 Spike Owen .05 .02
❑ 358 Pascual Perez .05 .02
❑ 359 Tim Raines .10 .05
❑ 360 Nelson Santovenia .05 .02
❑ 361 Bryn Smith .05 .02
❑ 362 Zane Smith .05 .02
❑ 363 Larry Walker RC .60 .25
❑ 364 Tim Wallach .05 .02
❑ 365 Rick Aguilera .10 .05
❑ 366 Allan Anderson .05 .02
❑ 367 Wally Backman .05 .02
❑ 368 Doug Baker .05 .02
❑ 369 Juan Berenguer .05 .02
❑ 370 Randy Bush .05 .02
❑ 371 Carmen Castillo .05 .02
❑ 372 Mike Dyer .05 .02
❑ 373 Gary Gaetti .10 .05
❑ 374 Greg Gagne .05 .02
❑ 375 Dan Gladden .05 .02
❑ 376 German Gonzalez UER .05 .02
(Bio says 31 saves in '88, but stats say 30)
❑ 377 Brian Harper .05 .02
❑ 378 Kent Hrbek .10 .05
❑ 379 Gene Larkin .05 .02
❑ 380 Tim Laudner UER .05 .02
(No decimal point before '85 BA of 238)
❑ 381 John Moses .05 .02
❑ 382 Al Newman .05 .02
❑ 383 Kirby Puckett .50 .23
❑ 384 Shane Rawley .05 .02
❑ 385 Jeff Reardon .10 .05
❑ 386 Roy Smith .05 .02
❑ 387 Gary Wayne .05 .02
❑ 388 Dave West .05 .02
❑ 389 Tim Belcher .05 .02
❑ 390 Tim Crews UER .05 .02
(Stats say 163 IP for '83, but bio says 136)
❑ 391 Mike Davis .05 .02
❑ 392 Rick Dempsey .05 .02
❑ 393 Kirk Gibson .10 .05
❑ 394 Jose Gonzalez .05 .02
❑ 395 Alfredo Griffin .05 .02
❑ 396 Jeff Hamilton .05 .02
❑ 397 Lenny Harris .05 .02
❑ 398 Mickey Hatcher .05 .02
❑ 399 Orel Hershiser .10 .05
❑ 400 Jay Howell .05 .02
❑ 401 Mike Marshall .05 .02
❑ 402 Ramon Martinez .05 .02
❑ 403 Mike Morgan .05 .02
❑ 404 Eddie Murray .20 .09
❑ 405 Alejandro Pena .05 .02
❑ 406 Willie Randolph .10 .05
❑ 407 Mike Scioscia .05 .02
❑ 408 Ray Searage .05 .02
❑ 409 Fernando Valenzuela .10 .05
❑ 410 Jose Vizcaino RC .15 .07
❑ 411 John Wetteland .20 .09
❑ 412 Jack Armstrong .05 .02
❑ 413 Todd Benzinger UER .05 .02
(Bio says .323 at Pawtucket, but stats say .321)
❑ 414 Tim Birtsas .05 .02
❑ 415 Tom Browning .05 .02
❑ 416 Norm Charlton .05 .02
❑ 417 Eric Davis .10 .05
❑ 418 Rob Dibble .05 .02
❑ 419 John Franco .10 .05
❑ 420 Ken Griffey Sr. .10 .05
❑ 421 Chris Hammond RC .05 .02
(No 1989 used for "Did Not Play" stat; actually did play for Nashville in 1989)
❑ 422 Danny Jackson .05 .02
❑ 423 Barry Larkin .20 .09
❑ 424 Tim Leary .05 .02
❑ 425 Rick Mahler .05 .02
❑ 426 Joe Oliver .05 .02
❑ 427 Paul O'Neill .10 .05
❑ 428 Luis Quinones UER .05 .02
('86-'88 stats are omitted from card but included in totals)
❑ 429 Jeff Reed .05 .02
❑ 430 Jose Rijo .05 .02
❑ 431 Ron Robinson .05 .02
❑ 432 Rolando Roomes .05 .02
❑ 433 Chris Sabo .05 .02
❑ 434 Scott Scudder .05 .02
❑ 435 Herm Winningham .05 .02
❑ 436 Steve Balboni .05 .02
❑ 437 Jesse Barfield .05 .02
❑ 438 Mike Blowers RC .10 .05
❑ 439 Tom Brookens .05 .02
❑ 440 Greg Cadaret .05 .02
❑ 441 Alvaro Espinoza UER .05 .02
(Career games say 218; should be 219)
❑ 442 Bob Geren .05 .02
❑ 443 Lee Guetterman .05 .02
❑ 444 Mel Hall .05 .02
❑ 445 Andy Hawkins .05 .02
❑ 446 Roberto Kelly .05 .02
❑ 447 Don Mattingly .50 .23
❑ 448 Lance McCullers .05 .02
❑ 449 Hensley Meulens .05 .02
❑ 450 Dale Mohorcic .05 .02
❑ 451 Clay Parker .05 .02
❑ 452 Eric Plunk .05 .02
❑ 453 Dave Righetti .05 .02
❑ 454 Deion Sanders .20 .09
❑ 455 Steve Sax .05 .02
❑ 456 Don Slaught .05 .02
❑ 457 Walt Terrell .05 .02
❑ 458 Dave Winfield .20 .09
❑ 459 Jay Bell .10 .05
❑ 460 Rafael Belliard .05 .02
❑ 461 Barry Bonds .30 .14
❑ 462 Bobby Bonilla .10 .05
❑ 463 Sid Bream .05 .02
❑ 464 Benny Distefano .05 .02
❑ 465 Doug Drabek .05 .02
❑ 466 Jim Gott .05 .02
❑ 467 Billy Hatcher UER .05 .02
(.1 hits for Cubs in 1984)
❑ 468 Neal Heaton .05 .02
❑ 469 Jeff King .05 .02
❑ 470 Bob Kipper .05 .02
❑ 471 Randy Kramer .05 .02
❑ 472 Bill Landrum .05 .02
❑ 473 Mike LaValliere .05 .02
❑ 474 Jose Lind .05 .02
❑ 475 Junior Ortiz .05 .02

❑ 476 Gary Redus .05 .02
❑ 477 Rick Reed RC .25 .11
❑ 478 R.J. Reynolds .05 .02
❑ 479 Jeff D. Robinson .05 .02
❑ 480 John Smiley .05 .02
❑ 481 Andy Van Slyke .10 .05
❑ 482 Bob Walk .05 .02
❑ 483 Andy Allanson .05 .02
❑ 484 Scott Bailes .05 .02
❑ 485 Joey Belle UER .75 .35
(Has Jay Bell "Did You Know")
❑ 486 Bud Black .05 .02
❑ 487 Jerry Browne .05 .02
❑ 488 Tom Candiotti .05 .02
❑ 489 Joe Carter .10 .05
❑ 490 Dave Clark .05 .02
(No '84 stats)
❑ 491 John Farrell .05 .02
❑ 492 Felix Fermin .05 .02
❑ 493 Brook Jacoby .05 .02
❑ 494 Dion James .05 .02
❑ 495 Doug Jones .05 .02
❑ 496 Brad Komminsk .05 .02
❑ 497 Rod Nichols .05 .02
❑ 498 Pete O'Brien .05 .02
❑ 499 Steve Olin RC .10 .05
❑ 500 Jesse Orosco .05 .02
❑ 501 Joel Skinner .05 .02
❑ 502 Cory Snyder .05 .02
❑ 503 Greg Swindell .05 .02
❑ 504 Rich Yett .05 .02
❑ 505 Scott Bankhead .05 .02
❑ 506 Scott Bradley .05 .02
❑ 507 Greg Briley UER .05 .02
(28 SB's in bio, but 27 in stats)
❑ 508 Jay Buhner .10 .05
❑ 509 Darnell Coles .05 .02
❑ 510 Keith Comstock .05 .02
❑ 511 Henry Cotto .05 .02
❑ 512 Alvin Davis .05 .02
❑ 513 Ken Griffey Jr. 1.50 .70
❑ 514 Erik Hanson .05 .02
❑ 515 Gene Harris .05 .02
❑ 516 Brian Holman .05 .02
❑ 517 Mike Jackson .05 .02
❑ 518 Randy Johnson .40 .18
❑ 519 Jeffrey Leonard .05 .02
❑ 520 Edgar Martinez .15 .07
❑ 521 Dennis Powell .05 .02
❑ 522 Jim Presley .05 .02
❑ 523 Jerry Reed .05 .02
❑ 524 Harold Reynolds .05 .02
❑ 525 Mike Schooler .05 .02
❑ 526 Bill Swift .05 .02
❑ 527 Dave Valle .05 .02
❑ 528 Omar Vizquel .20 .09
❑ 529 Ivan Calderon .05 .02
❑ 530 Carlton Fisk UER .20 .09
(Bellow Falls, should be Bellows Falls)
❑ 531 Scott Fletcher .05 .02
❑ 532 Dave Gallagher .05 .02
❑ 533 Ozzie Guillen .05 .02
❑ 534 Greg Hibbard RC .05 .02
❑ 535 Shawn Hillegas .05 .02
❑ 536 Lance Johnson .05 .02
❑ 537 Eric King .05 .02
❑ 538 Ron Kittle .05 .02
❑ 539 Steve Lyons .05 .02
❑ 540 Carlos Martinez .05 .02
❑ 541 Tom McCarthy .05 .02
❑ 542 Matt Merullo .05 .02
(Had 5 ML runs scored entering '90, not 6)
❑ 543 Donn Pall UER .05 .02
(Stats say pro career began in '85; bio says '88)
❑ 544 Dan Pasqua .05 .02
❑ 545 Ken Patterson .05 .02
❑ 546 Melido Perez .05 .02
❑ 547 Steve Rosenberg .05 .02
❑ 548 Sammy Sosa RC 5.00 2.20
❑ 549 Bobby Thigpen .05 .02
❑ 550 Robin Ventura .20 .09
❑ 551 Greg Walker .05 .02
❑ 552 Don Carman .05 .02
❑ 553 Pat Combs .05 .02
(6 walks for Phillies in '89 in stats, brief bio says 4)
❑ 554 Dennis Cook .05 .02
❑ 555 Darren Daulton .10 .05
❑ 556 Len Dykstra .10 .05
❑ 557 Curt Ford .05 .02
❑ 558 Charlie Hayes .05 .02
❑ 559 Von Hayes .05 .02
❑ 560 Tommy Herr .05 .02
❑ 561 Ken Howell .05 .02
❑ 562 Steve Jeltz .05 .02
❑ 563 Ron Jones .05 .02
❑ 564 Ricky Jordan UER .05 .02
(Duplicate line of statistics on back)
❑ 565 John Kruk .10 .05
❑ 566 Steve Lake .05 .02
❑ 567 Roger McDowell .05 .02
❑ 568 Terry Mulholland UER .05 .02
(Did You Know refers to Dave Magadan)
❑ 569 Dwayne Murphy .05 .02
❑ 570 Jeff Parrett .05 .02
❑ 571 Randy Ready .05 .02
❑ 572 Bruce Ruffin .05 .02
❑ 573 Dickie Thon .05 .02
❑ 574 Jose Alvarez UER .05 .02
('78 and '79 stats are reversed)
❑ 575 Geronimo Berroa .05 .02
❑ 576 Jeff Blauser .05 .02
❑ 577 Joe Boever .05 .02
❑ 578 Marty Clary UER .05 .02
(No comma between city and state)
❑ 579 Jody Davis .05 .02
❑ 580 Mark Eichhorn .05 .02
❑ 581 Darrell Evans .10 .05
❑ 582 Ron Gant .10 .05
❑ 583 Tom Glavine .20 .09
❑ 584 Tommy Greene RC .05 .02
❑ 585 Tommy Gregg .05 .02
❑ 586 Dave Justice RC UER .75 .35
(Actually had 16 2B in Sumter in '86)
❑ 587 Mark Lemke .05 .02
❑ 588 Derek Lilliquist .05 .02
❑ 589 Oddibe McDowell .05 .02
❑ 590 Kent Mercker RC ERA .05 .02
(Bio says 2.75 ERA, stats say 2.68 ERA)
❑ 591 Dale Murphy .20 .09
❑ 592 Gerald Perry .05 .02
❑ 593 Lonnie Smith .05 .02
❑ 594 Pete Smith .05 .02
❑ 595 John Smoltz .10 .05
❑ 596 Mike Stanton RC UER .05 .02
(No comma between city and state)
❑ 597 Andres Thomas .05 .02
❑ 598 Jeff Treadway .05 .02
❑ 599 Doyle Alexander .05 .02
❑ 600 Dave Bergman .05 .02
❑ 601 Brian DuBois .05 .02
❑ 602 Paul Gibson .05 .02
❑ 603 Mike Heath .05 .02
❑ 604 Mike Henneman .05 .02
❑ 605 Guillermo Hernandez .05 .02
❑ 606 Shawn Holman .05 .02
❑ 607 Tracy Jones .05 .02
❑ 608 Chet Lemon .05 .02
❑ 609 Fred Lynn .05 .02
❑ 610 Jack Morris .10 .05
❑ 611 Matt Nokes .05 .02
❑ 612 Gary Pettis .05 .02
❑ 613 Kevin Ritz .05 .02
❑ 614 Jeff M. Robinson .05 .02
('88 stats are not in line)
❑ 615 Steve Searcy .05 .02
❑ 616 Frank Tanana .05 .02
❑ 617 Alan Trammell .15 .07
❑ 618 Gary Ward .05 .02
❑ 619 Lou Whitaker .10 .05
❑ 620 Frank Williams .05 .02
❑ 621A George Brett '80 1.50 .70
ERR (Had 10 .390 hitting seasons)
❑ 621B George Brett '80 .20 .09
COR
❑ 622 Fern.Valenzuela '81 .05 .02
❑ 623 Dale Murphy '82 .10 .05
❑ 624A Cal Ripken '83 ERR 5.00 2.20
(Misspelled Ripkin on card back)
❑ 624B Cal Ripken '83 COR .40 .18
❑ 625 Ryne Sandberg '84 .20 .09
❑ 626 Don Mattingly '85 .20 .09
❑ 627 Roger Clemens '86 .20 .09
❑ 628 George Bell '87 .05 .02
❑ 629 Jose Canseco '88 UER .10 .05
(Reggie won MVP in '83; should say '73)
❑ 630A Will Clark '89 ERR 1.00 .45
(32 total bases on card back)
❑ 630B Will Clark '89 COR .20 .09
(321 total bases; technically still an error, listing only 24 runs)
❑ 631 Game Savers .05 .02
Mark Davis
Mitch Williams
❑ 632 Boston Igniters .20 .09
Wade Boggs
Mike Greenwell
❑ 633 Starter and Stopper .05 .02
Mark Gubicza
Jeff Russell
❑ 634 League's Best Shortstops .25 .11
Tony Fernandez
Cal Ripken
❑ 635 Human Dynamos .20 .09
Kirby Puckett
Bo Jackson
❑ 636 300 Strikeout Club .40 .18
Nolan Ryan
Mike Scott
❑ 637 The Dynamic Duo .10 .05
Will Clark
Kevin Mitchell
❑ 638 AL All-Stars .40 .18
Don Mattingly
Mark McGwire
❑ 639 NL East Rivals .20 .09
Howard Johnson
Ryne Sandberg
❑ 640 Rudy Seanez RC .05 .02
Colin Charland
❑ 641 George Canale RC .10 .05
Kevin Maas UER
(Canale listed as INF on front, 1B on back)
❑ 642 Kelly Mann .05 .02
and Dave Hansen RC
❑ 643 Greg Smith .05 .02
and Stu Tate
❑ 644 Tom Drees .05 .02
and Dann Howitt
❑ 645 Mike Roesler RC .20 .09
and Derrick May
❑ 646 Scott Hemond .05 .02
and Mark Gardner RC
❑ 647 John Orton .05 .02
and Scott Leius RC
❑ 648 Rich Monteleone .05 .02
and Dana Williams
❑ 649 Mike Huff .05 .02
and Steve Frey
❑ 650 Chuck McElroy .40 .18
and Moises Alou RC
❑ 651 Bobby Rose .05 .02
and Mike Hartley
❑ 652 Matt Kinzer .05 .02
and Wayne Edwards

| | MINT | NRMT |
|---|---|---|
| ❑ 653 Delino DeShields RC and Jason Grimsley | .20 | .09 |
| ❑ 654 CL: A's/Cubs Giants/Blue Jays | .05 | .02 |
| ❑ 655 CL: Royals/Angels Padres/Orioles | .05 | .02 |
| ❑ 656 CL: Mets/Astros Cards/Red Sox | .05 | .02 |
| ❑ 657 CL: Rangers/Brewers Expos/Twins | .05 | .02 |
| ❑ 658 CL: Dodgers/Reds Yankees/Pirates | .05 | .02 |
| ❑ 659 CL: Indians/Mariners White Sox/Phillies | .05 | .02 |
| ❑ 660A CL: Braves/Tigers Specials/Checklists (Checklist-660 in smaller print on card front) | .05 | .02 |
| ❑ 660B CL: Braves/Tigers Specials/Checklists (Checklist-660 in normal print on card front) | .05 | .02 |

## 1990 Fleer Update

| | MINT | NRMT |
|---|---|---|
| COMP.FACT.SET (132) | 5.00 | 2.20 |
| ❑ 1 Steve Avery | .05 | .02 |
| ❑ 2 Francisco Cabrera | .05 | .02 |
| ❑ 3 Nick Esasky | .05 | .02 |
| ❑ 4 Jim Kremers | .05 | .02 |
| ❑ 5 Greg Olson RC | .05 | .02 |
| ❑ 6 Jim Presley | .05 | .02 |
| ❑ 7 Shawn Boskie RC | .05 | .02 |
| ❑ 8 Joe Kraemer | .05 | .02 |
| ❑ 9 Luis Salazar | .05 | .02 |
| ❑ 10 Hector Villanueva | .05 | .02 |
| ❑ 11 Glenn Braggs | .05 | .02 |
| ❑ 12 Mariano Duncan | .05 | .02 |
| ❑ 13 Billy Hatcher | .05 | .02 |
| ❑ 14 Tim Layana | .05 | .02 |
| ❑ 15 Hal Morris | .05 | .02 |
| ❑ 16 Javier Ortiz | .05 | .02 |
| ❑ 17 Dave Rohde | .05 | .02 |
| ❑ 18 Eric Yelding | .05 | .02 |
| ❑ 19 Hubie Brooks | .05 | .02 |
| ❑ 20 Kal Daniels | .05 | .02 |
| ❑ 21 Dave Hansen | .05 | .02 |
| ❑ 22 Mike Hartley | .05 | .02 |
| ❑ 23 Stan Javier | .05 | .02 |
| ❑ 24 Jose Offerman RC | .25 | .11 |
| ❑ 25 Juan Samuel | .05 | .02 |
| ❑ 26 Dennis Boyd | .05 | .02 |
| ❑ 27 Delino DeShields | .20 | .09 |
| ❑ 28 Steve Frey | .05 | .02 |
| ❑ 29 Mark Gardner | .05 | .02 |
| ❑ 30 Chris Nabholz RC | .05 | .02 |
| ❑ 31 Bill Sampen | .05 | .02 |
| ❑ 32 Dave Schmidt | .05 | .02 |
| ❑ 33 Daryl Boston | .05 | .02 |
| ❑ 34 Chuck Carr RC | .20 | .09 |
| ❑ 35 John Franco | .10 | .05 |
| ❑ 36 Todd Hundley RC | .25 | .11 |
| ❑ 37 Julio Machado | .05 | .02 |
| ❑ 38 Alejandro Pena | .05 | .02 |
| ❑ 39 Darren Reed | .05 | .02 |
| ❑ 40 Kelvin Torve | .05 | .02 |
| ❑ 41 Darrel Akerfelds | .05 | .02 |
| ❑ 42 Jose DeJesus | .05 | .02 |
| ❑ 43 Dave Hollins RC UER (Misspelled Dane on card back) | .20 | .09 |
| ❑ 44 Carmelo Martinez | .05 | .02 |
| ❑ 45 Brad Moore | .05 | .02 |
| ❑ 46 Dale Murphy | .20 | .09 |
| ❑ 47 Wally Backman | .05 | .02 |
| ❑ 48 Stan Belinda RC | .05 | .02 |
| ❑ 49 Bob Patterson | .05 | .02 |
| ❑ 50 Ted Power | .05 | .02 |
| ❑ 51 Don Slaught | .05 | .02 |
| ❑ 52 Geronimo Pena RC | .05 | .02 |
| ❑ 53 Lee Smith | .10 | .05 |
| ❑ 54 John Tudor | .05 | .02 |
| ❑ 55 Joe Carter | .10 | .05 |
| ❑ 56 Thomas Howard | .05 | .02 |
| ❑ 57 Craig Lefferts | .05 | .02 |
| ❑ 58 Rafael Valdez | .05 | .02 |
| ❑ 59 Dave Anderson | .05 | .02 |
| ❑ 60 Kevin Bass | .05 | .02 |
| ❑ 61 John Burkett | .05 | .02 |
| ❑ 62 Gary Carter | .10 | .05 |
| ❑ 63 Rick Parker | .05 | .02 |
| ❑ 64 Trevor Wilson | .05 | .02 |
| ❑ 65 Chris Hoiles RC | .20 | .09 |
| ❑ 66 Tim Hulett | .05 | .02 |
| ❑ 67 Dave Johnson | .05 | .02 |
| ❑ 68 Curt Schilling | .10 | .05 |
| ❑ 69 David Segui RC | .40 | .18 |
| ❑ 70 Tom Brunansky | .05 | .02 |
| ❑ 71 Greg A. Harris | .05 | .02 |
| ❑ 72 Dana Kiecker | .05 | .02 |
| ❑ 73 Tim Naehring RC | .10 | .05 |
| ❑ 74 Tony Pena | .05 | .02 |
| ❑ 75 Jeff Reardon | .10 | .05 |
| ❑ 76 Jerry Reed | .05 | .02 |
| ❑ 77 Mark Eichhorn | .05 | .02 |
| ❑ 78 Mark Langston | .05 | .02 |
| ❑ 79 John Orton | .05 | .02 |
| ❑ 80 Luis Polonia | .05 | .02 |
| ❑ 81 Dave Winfield | .20 | .09 |
| ❑ 82 Cliff Young | .05 | .02 |
| ❑ 83 Wayne Edwards | .05 | .02 |
| ❑ 84 Alex Fernandez RC | .25 | .11 |
| ❑ 85 Craig Grebeck RC | .05 | .02 |
| ❑ 86 Scott Radinsky RC | .05 | .02 |
| ❑ 87 Frank Thomas RC | 2.50 | 1.10 |
| ❑ 88 Beau Allred | .05 | .02 |
| ❑ 89 Sandy Alomar Jr. | .10 | .05 |
| ❑ 90 Carlos Baerga RC | .10 | .05 |
| ❑ 91 Kevin Bearse | .05 | .02 |
| ❑ 92 Chris James | .05 | .02 |
| ❑ 93 Candy Maldonado | .05 | .02 |
| ❑ 94 Jeff Manto | .05 | .02 |
| ❑ 95 Cecil Fielder | .10 | .05 |
| ❑ 96 Travis Fryman RC | .25 | .11 |
| ❑ 97 Lloyd Moseby | .05 | .02 |
| ❑ 98 Edwin Nunez | .05 | .02 |
| ❑ 99 Tony Phillips | .05 | .02 |
| ❑ 100 Larry Sheets | .05 | .02 |
| ❑ 101 Mark Davis | .05 | .02 |
| ❑ 102 Storm Davis | .05 | .02 |
| ❑ 103 Gerald Perry | .05 | .02 |
| ❑ 104 Terry Shumpert | .05 | .02 |
| ❑ 105 Edgar Diaz | .05 | .02 |
| ❑ 106 Dave Parker | .10 | .05 |
| ❑ 107 Tim Drummond | .05 | .02 |
| ❑ 108 Junior Ortiz | .05 | .02 |
| ❑ 109 Park Pittman | .05 | .02 |
| ❑ 110 Kevin Tapani RC | .10 | .05 |
| ❑ 111 Oscar Azocar | .05 | .02 |
| ❑ 112 Jim Leyritz RC | .25 | .11 |
| ❑ 113 Kevin Maas | .10 | .05 |
| ❑ 114 Alan Mills RC | .05 | .02 |
| ❑ 115 Matt Nokes | .05 | .02 |
| ❑ 116 Pascual Perez | .05 | .02 |
| ❑ 117 Ozzie Canseco | .05 | .02 |
| ❑ 118 Scott Sanderson | .05 | .02 |
| ❑ 119 Tino Martinez | .25 | .11 |
| ❑ 120 Jeff Schaefer | .05 | .02 |
| ❑ 121 Matt Young | .05 | .02 |
| ❑ 122 Brian Bohanon RC | .05 | .02 |
| ❑ 123 Jeff Huson | .05 | .02 |
| ❑ 124 Ramon Manon | .05 | .02 |
| ❑ 125 Gary Mielke UER (Shown as Blue Jay on front) | .05 | .02 |
| ❑ 126 Willie Blair RC | .05 | .02 |
| ❑ 127 Glenallen Hill | .05 | .02 |
| ❑ 128 John Olerud RC UER (Listed as throwing right; should be left) | .50 | .23 |
| ❑ 129 Luis Sojo | .05 | .02 |
| ❑ 130 Mark Whiten RC | .05 | .02 |
| ❑ 131 Nolan Ryan | 1.00 | .45 |
| ❑ 132 Checklist U1-U132 | .05 | .02 |

## 1991 Fleer

| | MINT | NRMT |
|---|---|---|
| COMPLETE SET (720) | 8.00 | 3.60 |
| COMP.RETAIL SET (732) | 10.00 | 4.50 |
| COMP.HOBBY SET (732) | 10.00 | 4.50 |
| ❑ 1 Troy Afenir | .05 | .02 |
| ❑ 2 Harold Baines | .10 | .05 |
| ❑ 3 Lance Blankenship | .05 | .02 |
| ❑ 4 Todd Burns | .05 | .02 |
| ❑ 5 Jose Canseco | .25 | .11 |
| ❑ 6 Dennis Eckersley | .10 | .05 |
| ❑ 7 Mike Gallego | .05 | .02 |
| ❑ 8 Ron Hassey | .05 | .02 |
| ❑ 9 Dave Henderson | .05 | .02 |
| ❑ 10 Rickey Henderson | .25 | .11 |
| ❑ 11 Rick Honeycutt | .05 | .02 |
| ❑ 12 Doug Jennings | .05 | .02 |
| ❑ 13 Joe Klink | .05 | .02 |
| ❑ 14 Carney Lansford | .10 | .05 |
| ❑ 15 Darren Lewis | .10 | .05 |
| ❑ 16 Willie McGee UER (Height 6'11") | .10 | .05 |
| ❑ 17 Mark McGwire UER (183 extra base hits in 1987) | .75 | .35 |
| ❑ 18 Mike Moore | .05 | .02 |
| ❑ 19 Gene Nelson | .05 | .02 |
| ❑ 20 Dave Otto | .05 | .02 |
| ❑ 21 Jamie Quirk | .05 | .02 |
| ❑ 22 Willie Randolph | .10 | .05 |
| ❑ 23 Scott Sanderson | .05 | .02 |
| ❑ 24 Terry Steinbach | .10 | .05 |
| ❑ 25 Dave Stewart | .10 | .05 |
| ❑ 26 Walt Weiss | .05 | .02 |
| ❑ 27 Bob Welch | .05 | .02 |
| ❑ 28 Curt Young | .05 | .02 |
| ❑ 29 Wally Backman | .05 | .02 |
| ❑ 30 Stan Belinda UER (Born in Huntington; should be State College) | .05 | .02 |
| ❑ 31 Jay Bell | .10 | .05 |
| ❑ 32 Rafael Belliard | .05 | .02 |
| ❑ 33 Barry Bonds | .30 | .14 |
| ❑ 34 Bobby Bonilla | .10 | .05 |
| ❑ 35 Sid Bream | .05 | .02 |
| ❑ 36 Doug Drabek | .05 | .02 |
| ❑ 37 Carlos Garcia RC | .05 | .02 |
| ❑ 38 Neal Heaton | .05 | .02 |
| ❑ 39 Jeff King | .05 | .02 |
| ❑ 40 Bob Kipper | .05 | .02 |
| ❑ 41 Bill Landrum | .05 | .02 |
| ❑ 42 Mike LaValliere | .05 | .02 |
| ❑ 43 Jose Lind | .05 | .02 |

| | No. | Player | | |
|---|---|---|---|---|
| ❑ | 44 | Carmelo Martinez | .05 | .02 |
| ❑ | 45 | Bob Patterson | .05 | .02 |
| ❑ | 46 | Ted Power | .05 | .02 |
| ❑ | 47 | Gary Redus | .05 | .02 |
| ❑ | 48 | R.J. Reynolds | .05 | .02 |
| ❑ | 49 | Don Slaught | .05 | .02 |
| ❑ | 50 | John Smiley | .05 | .02 |
| ❑ | 51 | Zane Smith | .05 | .02 |
| ❑ | 52 | Randy Tomlin RC | .05 | .02 |
| ❑ | 53 | Andy Van Slyke | .10 | .05 |
| ❑ | 54 | Bob Walk | .05 | .02 |
| ❑ | 55 | Jack Armstrong | .05 | .02 |
| ❑ | 56 | Todd Benzinger | .05 | .02 |
| ❑ | 57 | Glenn Braggs | .05 | .02 |
| ❑ | 58 | Keith Brown | .05 | .02 |
| ❑ | 59 | Tom Browning | .05 | .02 |
| ❑ | 60 | Norm Charlton | .05 | .02 |
| ❑ | 61 | Eric Davis | .10 | .05 |
| ❑ | 62 | Rob Dibble | .05 | .02 |
| ❑ | 63 | Bill Doran | .05 | .02 |
| ❑ | 64 | Mariano Duncan | .05 | .02 |
| ❑ | 65 | Chris Hammond | .05 | .02 |
| ❑ | 66 | Billy Hatcher | .05 | .02 |
| ❑ | 67 | Danny Jackson | .05 | .02 |
| ❑ | 68 | Barry Larkin | .20 | .09 |
| ❑ | 69 | Tim Layana (Black line over made in first text line) | .05 | .02 |
| ❑ | 70 | Terry Lee | .05 | .02 |
| ❑ | 71 | Rick Mahler | .05 | .02 |
| ❑ | 72 | Hal Morris | .05 | .02 |
| ❑ | 73 | Randy Myers | .10 | .05 |
| ❑ | 74 | Ron Oester | .05 | .02 |
| ❑ | 75 | Joe Oliver | .05 | .02 |
| ❑ | 76 | Paul O'Neill | .10 | .05 |
| ❑ | 77 | Luis Quinones | .05 | .02 |
| ❑ | 78 | Jeff Reed | .05 | .02 |
| ❑ | 79 | Jose Rijo | .05 | .02 |
| ❑ | 80 | Chris Sabo | .05 | .02 |
| ❑ | 81 | Scott Scudder | .05 | .02 |
| ❑ | 82 | Herm Winningham | .05 | .02 |
| ❑ | 83 | Larry Andersen | .05 | .02 |
| ❑ | 84 | Marty Barrett | .05 | .02 |
| ❑ | 85 | Mike Boddicker | .05 | .02 |
| ❑ | 86 | Wade Boggs | .25 | .11 |
| ❑ | 87 | Tom Bolton | .05 | .02 |
| ❑ | 88 | Tom Brunansky | .05 | .02 |
| ❑ | 89 | Ellis Burks | .10 | .05 |
| ❑ | 90 | Roger Clemens | .40 | .18 |
| ❑ | 91 | Scott Cooper | .05 | .02 |
| ❑ | 92 | John Dopson | .05 | .02 |
| ❑ | 93 | Dwight Evans | .10 | .05 |
| ❑ | 94 | Wes Gardner | .05 | .02 |
| ❑ | 95 | Jeff Gray | .05 | .02 |
| ❑ | 96 | Mike Greenwell | .05 | .02 |
| ❑ | 97 | Greg A. Harris | .05 | .02 |
| ❑ | 98 | Daryl Irvine | .05 | .02 |
| ❑ | 99 | Dana Kiecker | .05 | .02 |
| ❑ | 100 | Randy Kutcher | .05 | .02 |
| ❑ | 101 | Dennis Lamp | .05 | .02 |
| ❑ | 102 | Mike Marshall | .05 | .02 |
| ❑ | 103 | John Marzano | .05 | .02 |
| ❑ | 104 | Rob Murphy | .05 | .02 |
| ❑ | 105 | Tim Naehring | .05 | .02 |
| ❑ | 106 | Tony Pena | .05 | .02 |
| ❑ | 107 | Phil Plantier RC | .05 | .02 |
| ❑ | 108 | Carlos Quintana | .05 | .02 |
| ❑ | 109 | Jeff Reardon | .10 | .05 |
| ❑ | 110 | Jerry Reed | .05 | .02 |
| ❑ | 111 | Jody Reed | .05 | .02 |
| ❑ | 112 | Luis Rivera UER (Born 1/3/84) | .05 | .02 |
| ❑ | 113 | Kevin Romine | .05 | .02 |
| ❑ | 114 | Phil Bradley | .05 | .02 |
| ❑ | 115 | Ivan Calderon | .05 | .02 |
| ❑ | 116 | Wayne Edwards | .05 | .02 |
| ❑ | 117 | Alex Fernandez | .10 | .05 |
| ❑ | 118 | Carlton Fisk | .20 | .09 |
| ❑ | 119 | Scott Fletcher | .05 | .02 |
| ❑ | 120 | Craig Grebeck | .05 | .02 |
| ❑ | 121 | Ozzie Guillen | .05 | .02 |
| ❑ | 122 | Greg Hibbard | .05 | .02 |
| ❑ | 123 | Lance Johnson UER (Born Cincinnati; should be Lincoln Heights) | .05 | .02 |
| ❑ | 124 | Barry Jones | .05 | .02 |
| ❑ | 125 | Ron Karkovice | .05 | .02 |
| ❑ | 126 | Eric King | .05 | .02 |
| ❑ | 127 | Steve Lyons | .05 | .02 |
| ❑ | 128 | Carlos Martinez | .05 | .02 |
| ❑ | 129 | Jack McDowell UER (Stanford misspelled as Standford on back) | .05 | .02 |
| ❑ | 130 | Donn Pall (No dots over any i's in text) | .05 | .02 |
| ❑ | 131 | Dan Pasqua | .05 | .02 |
| ❑ | 132 | Ken Patterson | .05 | .02 |
| ❑ | 133 | Melido Perez | .05 | .02 |
| ❑ | 134 | Adam Peterson | .05 | .02 |
| ❑ | 135 | Scott Radinsky | .05 | .02 |
| ❑ | 136 | Sammy Sosa | .50 | .23 |
| ❑ | 137 | Bobby Thigpen | .05 | .02 |
| ❑ | 138 | Frank Thomas | .50 | .23 |
| ❑ | 139 | Robin Ventura | .20 | .09 |
| ❑ | 140 | Daryl Boston | .05 | .02 |
| ❑ | 141 | Chuck Carr | .05 | .02 |
| ❑ | 142 | Mark Carreon | .05 | .02 |
| ❑ | 143 | David Cone | .10 | .05 |
| ❑ | 144 | Ron Darling | .05 | .02 |
| ❑ | 145 | Kevin Elster | .05 | .02 |
| ❑ | 146 | Sid Fernandez | .05 | .02 |
| ❑ | 147 | John Franco | .10 | .05 |
| ❑ | 148 | Dwight Gooden | .10 | .05 |
| ❑ | 149 | Tom Herr | .05 | .02 |
| ❑ | 150 | Todd Hundley | .05 | .02 |
| ❑ | 151 | Gregg Jefferies | .05 | .02 |
| ❑ | 152 | Howard Johnson | .05 | .02 |
| ❑ | 153 | Dave Magadan | .05 | .02 |
| ❑ | 154 | Kevin McReynolds | .05 | .02 |
| ❑ | 155 | Keith Miller UER (Text says Rochester in '87; stats say Tidewater, mixed up with other Keith Miller) | .05 | .02 |
| ❑ | 156 | Bob Ojeda | .05 | .02 |
| ❑ | 157 | Tom O'Malley | .05 | .02 |
| ❑ | 158 | Alejandro Pena | .05 | .02 |
| ❑ | 159 | Darren Reed | .05 | .02 |
| ❑ | 160 | Mackey Sasser | .05 | .02 |
| ❑ | 161 | Darryl Strawberry | .10 | .05 |
| ❑ | 162 | Tim Teufel | .05 | .02 |
| ❑ | 163 | Kelvin Torve | .05 | .02 |
| ❑ | 164 | Julio Valera | .05 | .02 |
| ❑ | 165 | Frank Viola | .05 | .02 |
| ❑ | 166 | Wally Whitehurst | .05 | .02 |
| ❑ | 167 | Jim Acker | .05 | .02 |
| ❑ | 168 | Derek Bell | .10 | .05 |
| ❑ | 169 | George Bell | .05 | .02 |
| ❑ | 170 | Willie Blair | .05 | .02 |
| ❑ | 171 | Pat Borders | .05 | .02 |
| ❑ | 172 | John Cerutti | .05 | .02 |
| ❑ | 173 | Junior Felix | .05 | .02 |
| ❑ | 174 | Tony Fernandez | .05 | .02 |
| ❑ | 175 | Kelly Gruber UER (Born in Houston; should be Bellaire) | .05 | .02 |
| ❑ | 176 | Tom Henke | .05 | .02 |
| ❑ | 177 | Glenallen Hill | .05 | .02 |
| ❑ | 178 | Jimmy Key | .10 | .05 |
| ❑ | 179 | Manny Lee | .05 | .02 |
| ❑ | 180 | Fred McGriff | .20 | .09 |
| ❑ | 181 | Rance Mulliniks | .05 | .02 |
| ❑ | 182 | Greg Myers | .05 | .02 |
| ❑ | 183 | John Olerud UER (Listed as throwing right, should be left) | .10 | .05 |
| ❑ | 184 | Luis Sojo | .05 | .02 |
| ❑ | 185 | Dave Stieb | .05 | .02 |
| ❑ | 186 | Todd Stottlemyre | .10 | .05 |
| ❑ | 187 | Duane Ward | .05 | .02 |
| ❑ | 188 | David Wells | .10 | .05 |
| ❑ | 189 | Mark Whiten | .05 | .02 |
| ❑ | 190 | Ken Williams | .05 | .02 |
| ❑ | 191 | Frank Wills | .05 | .02 |
| ❑ | 192 | Mookie Wilson | .10 | .05 |
| ❑ | 193 | Don Aase | .05 | .02 |
| ❑ | 194 | Tim Belcher UER (Born Sparta, Ohio; should say Mt. Gilead) | .05 | .02 |
| ❑ | 195 | Hubie Brooks | .05 | .02 |
| ❑ | 196 | Dennis Cook | .05 | .02 |
| ❑ | 197 | Tim Crews | .05 | .02 |
| ❑ | 198 | Kal Daniels | .05 | .02 |
| ❑ | 199 | Kirk Gibson | .10 | .05 |
| ❑ | 200 | Jim Gott | .05 | .02 |
| ❑ | 201 | Alfredo Griffin | .05 | .02 |
| ❑ | 202 | Chris Gwynn | .05 | .02 |
| ❑ | 203 | Dave Hansen | .05 | .02 |
| ❑ | 204 | Lenny Harris | .05 | .02 |
| ❑ | 205 | Mike Hartley | .05 | .02 |
| ❑ | 206 | Mickey Hatcher | .05 | .02 |
| ❑ | 207 | Carlos Hernandez | .10 | .05 |
| ❑ | 208 | Orel Hershiser | .10 | .05 |
| ❑ | 209 | Jay Howell UER (No 1982 Yankee stats) | .05 | .02 |
| ❑ | 210 | Mike Huff | .05 | .02 |
| ❑ | 211 | Stan Javier | .05 | .02 |
| ❑ | 212 | Ramon Martinez | .05 | .02 |
| ❑ | 213 | Mike Morgan | .05 | .02 |
| ❑ | 214 | Eddie Murray | .20 | .09 |
| ❑ | 215 | Jim Neidlinger | .05 | .02 |
| ❑ | 216 | Jose Offerman | .05 | .02 |
| ❑ | 217 | Jim Poole | .05 | .02 |
| ❑ | 218 | Juan Samuel | .05 | .02 |
| ❑ | 219 | Mike Scioscia | .05 | .02 |
| ❑ | 220 | Ray Searage | .05 | .02 |
| ❑ | 221 | Mike Sharperson | .05 | .02 |
| ❑ | 222 | Fernando Valenzuela | .10 | .05 |
| ❑ | 223 | Jose Vizcaino | .05 | .02 |
| ❑ | 224 | Mike Aldrete | .05 | .02 |
| ❑ | 225 | Scott Anderson | .05 | .02 |
| ❑ | 226 | Dennis Boyd | .05 | .02 |
| ❑ | 227 | Tim Burke | .05 | .02 |
| ❑ | 228 | Delino DeShields | .10 | .05 |
| ❑ | 229 | Mike Fitzgerald | .05 | .02 |
| ❑ | 230 | Tom Foley | .05 | .02 |
| ❑ | 231 | Steve Frey | .05 | .02 |
| ❑ | 232 | Andres Galarraga | .10 | .05 |
| ❑ | 233 | Mark Gardner | .05 | .02 |
| ❑ | 234 | Marquis Grissom | .05 | .02 |
| ❑ | 235 | Kevin Gross (No date given for first Expos win) | .05 | .02 |
| ❑ | 236 | Drew Hall | .05 | .02 |
| ❑ | 237 | Dave Martinez | .05 | .02 |
| ❑ | 238 | Dennis Martinez | .10 | .05 |
| ❑ | 239 | Dale Mohorcic | .05 | .02 |
| ❑ | 240 | Chris Nabholz | .05 | .02 |
| ❑ | 241 | Otis Nixon | .05 | .02 |
| ❑ | 242 | Junior Noboa | .05 | .02 |
| ❑ | 243 | Spike Owen | .05 | .02 |
| ❑ | 244 | Tim Raines | .10 | .05 |
| ❑ | 245 | Mel Rojas UER (Stats show 3.60 ERA, bio says 3.19 ERA) | .10 | .05 |
| ❑ | 246 | Scott Ruskin | .05 | .02 |
| ❑ | 247 | Bill Sampen | .05 | .02 |
| ❑ | 248 | Nelson Santovenia | .05 | .02 |
| ❑ | 249 | Dave Schmidt | .05 | .02 |
| ❑ | 250 | Larry Walker | .20 | .09 |
| ❑ | 251 | Tim Wallach | .05 | .02 |
| ❑ | 252 | Dave Anderson | .05 | .02 |
| ❑ | 253 | Kevin Bass | .05 | .02 |
| ❑ | 254 | Steve Bedrosian | .05 | .02 |
| ❑ | 255 | Jeff Brantley | .05 | .02 |
| ❑ | 256 | John Burkett | .05 | .02 |
| ❑ | 257 | Brett Butler | .10 | .05 |
| ❑ | 258 | Gary Carter | .10 | .05 |
| ❑ | 259 | Will Clark | .20 | .09 |
| ❑ | 260 | Steve Decker RC | .05 | .02 |
| ❑ | 261 | Kelly Downs | .05 | .02 |
| ❑ | 262 | Scott Garrelts | .05 | .02 |
| ❑ | 263 | Terry Kennedy | .05 | .02 |
| ❑ | 264 | Mike LaCoss | .05 | .02 |
| ❑ | 265 | Mark Leonard | .05 | .02 |
| ❑ | 266 | Greg Litton | .05 | .02 |
| ❑ | 267 | Kevin Mitchell | .05 | .02 |
| ❑ | 268 | Randy O'Neal | .05 | .02 |
| ❑ | 269 | Rick Parker | .05 | .02 |
| ❑ | 270 | Rick Reuschel | .05 | .02 |
| ❑ | 271 | Ernest Riles | .05 | .02 |
| ❑ | 272 | Don Robinson | .05 | .02 |
| ❑ | 273 | Robby Thompson | .05 | .02 |
| ❑ | 274 | Mark Thurmond | .05 | .02 |
| ❑ | 275 | Jose Uribe | .05 | .02 |
| ❑ | 276 | Matt Williams | .10 | .05 |
| ❑ | 277 | Trevor Wilson | .05 | .02 |

❑ 278 Gerald Alexander .......... .05 .02
❑ 279 Brad Arnsberg .......... .05 .02
❑ 280 Kevin Belcher .......... .05 .02
❑ 281 Joe Bitker .......... .05 .02
❑ 282 Kevin Brown .......... .10 .05
❑ 283 Steve Buechele .......... .05 .02
❑ 284 Jack Daugherty .......... .05 .02
❑ 285 Julio Franco .......... .05 .02
❑ 286 Juan Gonzalez .......... .25 .11
❑ 287 Bill Haselman .......... .05 .02
❑ 288 Charlie Hough .......... .10 .05
❑ 289 Jeff Huson .......... .05 .02
❑ 290 Pete Incaviglia .......... .05 .02
❑ 291 Mike Jeffcoat .......... .05 .02
❑ 292 Jeff Kunkel .......... .05 .02
❑ 293 Gary Mielke .......... .05 .02
❑ 294 Jamie Moyer .......... .05 .02
❑ 295 Rafael Palmeiro .......... .20 .09
❑ 296 Geno Petralli .......... .05 .02
❑ 297 Gary Pettis .......... .05 .02
❑ 298 Kevin Reimer .......... .05 .02
❑ 299 Kenny Rogers .......... .05 .02
❑ 300 Jeff Russell .......... .05 .02
❑ 301 John Russell .......... .05 .02
❑ 302 Nolan Ryan .......... 1.00 .45
❑ 303 Ruben Sierra .......... .05 .02
❑ 304 Bobby Witt .......... .05 .02
❑ 305 Jim Abbott UER .......... .10 .05
(Text on back states he won Sullivan Award [outstanding amateur athlete] in 1989; should be '88)
❑ 306 Kent Anderson .......... .05 .02
❑ 307 Dante Bichette .......... .20 .09
❑ 308 Bert Blyleven .......... .10 .05
❑ 309 Chili Davis .......... .10 .05
❑ 310 Brian Downing .......... .05 .02
❑ 311 Mark Eichhorn .......... .05 .02
❑ 312 Mike Fetters .......... .05 .02
❑ 313 Chuck Finley .......... .10 .05
❑ 314 Willie Fraser .......... .05 .02
❑ 315 Bryan Harvey .......... .05 .02
❑ 316 Donnie Hill .......... .05 .02
❑ 317 Wally Joyner .......... .10 .05
❑ 318 Mark Langston .......... .05 .02
❑ 319 Kirk McCaskill .......... .05 .02
❑ 320 John Orton .......... .05 .02
❑ 321 Lance Parrish .......... .05 .02
❑ 322 Luis Polonia UER .......... .05 .02
(1984 Madfison; should be Madison)
❑ 323 Johnny Ray .......... .05 .02
❑ 324 Bobby Rose .......... .05 .02
❑ 325 Dick Schofield .......... .05 .02
❑ 326 Rick Schu .......... .05 .02
❑ 327 Lee Stevens .......... .10 .05
❑ 328 Devon White .......... .05 .02
❑ 329 Dave Winfield .......... .20 .09
❑ 330 Cliff Young .......... .05 .02
❑ 331 Dave Bergman .......... .05 .02
❑ 332 Phil Clark RC .......... .05 .02
❑ 333 Darnell Coles .......... .05 .02
❑ 334 Milt Cuyler .......... .05 .02
❑ 335 Cecil Fielder .......... .10 .05
❑ 336 Travis Fryman .......... .20 .09
❑ 337 Paul Gibson .......... .05 .02
❑ 338 Jerry Don Gleaton .......... .05 .02
❑ 339 Mike Heath .......... .05 .02
❑ 340 Mike Henneman .......... .05 .02
❑ 341 Chet Lemon .......... .05 .02
❑ 342 Lance McCullers .......... .05 .02
❑ 343 Jack Morris .......... .10 .05
❑ 344 Lloyd Moseby .......... .05 .02
❑ 345 Edwin Nunez .......... .05 .02
❑ 346 Clay Parker .......... .05 .02
❑ 347 Dan Petry .......... .05 .02
❑ 348 Tony Phillips .......... .05 .02
❑ 349 Jeff M. Robinson .......... .05 .02
❑ 350 Mark Salas .......... .05 .02
❑ 351 Mike Schwabe .......... .05 .02
❑ 352 Larry Sheets .......... .05 .02
❑ 353 John Shelby .......... .05 .02
❑ 354 Frank Tanana .......... .05 .02
❑ 355 Alan Trammell .......... .10 .05
❑ 356 Gary Ward .......... .05 .02
❑ 357 Lou Whitaker .......... .10 .05
❑ 358 Beau Allred .......... .05 .02
❑ 359 Sandy Alomar Jr. .......... .10 .05
❑ 360 Carlos Baerga .......... .05 .02
❑ 361 Kevin Bearse .......... .05 .02
❑ 362 Tom Brookens .......... .05 .02
❑ 363 Jerry Browne UER .......... .05 .02
(No dot over i in first text line)
❑ 364 Tom Candiotti .......... .05 .02
❑ 365 Alex Cole .......... .05 .02
❑ 366 John Farrell UER .......... .05 .02
(Born in Neptune; should be Monmouth)
❑ 367 Felix Fermin .......... .05 .02
❑ 368 Keith Hernandez .......... .10 .05
❑ 369 Brook Jacoby .......... .05 .02
❑ 370 Chris James .......... .05 .02
❑ 371 Dion James .......... .05 .02
❑ 372 Doug Jones .......... .05 .02
❑ 373 Candy Maldonado .......... .05 .02
❑ 374 Steve Olin .......... .05 .02
❑ 375 Jesse Orosco .......... .05 .02
❑ 376 Rudy Seanez .......... .05 .02
❑ 377 Joel Skinner .......... .05 .02
❑ 378 Cory Snyder .......... .05 .02
❑ 379 Greg Swindell .......... .05 .02
❑ 380 Sergio Valdez .......... .05 .02
❑ 381 Mike Walker .......... .05 .02
❑ 382 Colby Ward .......... .05 .02
❑ 383 Turner Ward RC .......... .05 .02
❑ 384 Mitch Webster .......... .05 .02
❑ 385 Kevin Wickander .......... .05 .02
❑ 386 Darrel Akerfelds .......... .05 .02
❑ 387 Joe Boever .......... .05 .02
❑ 388 Rod Booker .......... .05 .02
❑ 389 Sil Campusano .......... .05 .02
❑ 390 Don Carman .......... .05 .02
❑ 391 Wes Chamberlain RC .... .05 .02
❑ 392 Pat Combs .......... .05 .02
❑ 393 Darren Daulton .......... .10 .05
❑ 394 Jose DeJesus .......... .05 .02
❑ 395A Len Dykstra .......... .10 .05
(Name spelled Lenny on back)
❑ 395B Len Dykstra .......... .10 .05
(Name spelled Len on back)
❑ 396 Jason Grimsley .......... .05 .02
❑ 397 Charlie Hayes .......... .05 .02
❑ 398 Von Hayes .......... .05 .02
❑ 399 David Hollins UER .......... .05 .02
(Atl-bats; should say at-bats)
❑ 400 Ken Howell .......... .05 .02
❑ 401 Ricky Jordan .......... .05 .02
❑ 402 John Kruk .......... .10 .05
❑ 403 Steve Lake .......... .05 .02
❑ 404 Chuck Malone .......... .05 .02
❑ 405 Roger McDowell UER .... .05 .02
(Says Phillies is saves; should say in)
❑ 406 Chuck McElroy .......... .05 .02
❑ 407 Mickey Morandini .......... .05 .02
❑ 408 Terry Mulholland .......... .05 .02
❑ 409 Dale Murphy .......... .20 .09
❑ 410A Randy Ready ERR ...... .05 .02
(No Brewers stats listed for 1983)
❑ 410B Randy Ready COR ...... .05 .02
❑ 411 Bruce Ruffin .......... .05 .02
❑ 412 Dickie Thon .......... .05 .02
❑ 413 Paul Assenmacher .......... .05 .02
❑ 414 Damon Berryhill .......... .05 .02
❑ 415 Mike Bielecki .......... .05 .02
❑ 416 Shawn Boskie .......... .05 .02
❑ 417 Dave Clark .......... .05 .02
❑ 418 Doug Dascenzo .......... .05 .02
❑ 419A Andre Dawson ERR .... .10 .05
(No stats for 1976)
❑ 419B Andre Dawson COR .... .10 .05
❑ 420 Shawon Dunston .......... .05 .02
❑ 421 Joe Girardi .......... .10 .05
❑ 422 Mark Grace .......... .20 .09
❑ 423 Mike Harkey .......... .05 .02
❑ 424 Les Lancaster .......... .05 .02
❑ 425 Bill Long .......... .05 .02
❑ 426 Greg Maddux .......... .50 .23
❑ 427 Derrick May .......... .05 .02
❑ 428 Jeff Pico .......... .05 .02
❑ 429 Domingo Ramos .......... .05 .02
❑ 430 Luis Salazar .......... .05 .02
❑ 431 Ryne Sandberg .......... .25 .11
❑ 432 Dwight Smith .......... .05 .02
❑ 433 Greg Smith .......... .05 .02
❑ 434 Rick Sutcliffe .......... .10 .05
❑ 435 Gary Varsho .......... .05 .02
❑ 436 Hector Villanueva .......... .05 .02
❑ 437 Jerome Walton .......... .05 .02
❑ 438 Curtis Wilkerson .......... .05 .02
❑ 439 Mitch Williams .......... .05 .02
❑ 440 Steve Wilson .......... .05 .02
❑ 441 Marvell Wynne .......... .05 .02
❑ 442 Scott Bankhead .......... .05 .02
❑ 443 Scott Bradley .......... .05 .02
❑ 444 Greg Briley .......... .05 .02
❑ 445 Mike Brumley UER .......... .05 .02
(Text 40 SB's in 1988; stats say 41)
❑ 446 Jay Buhner .......... .10 .05
❑ 447 Dave Burba RC .......... .05 .02
❑ 448 Henry Cotto .......... .05 .02
❑ 449 Alvin Davis .......... .05 .02
❑ 450 Ken Griffey Jr. .......... 1.00 .45
(Bat around .300)
❑ 450A Ken Griffey Jr. .......... 1.00 .70
(Bat .300)
❑ 451 Erik Hanson .......... .05 .02
❑ 452 Gene Harris UER .......... .05 .02
(63 career runs, should be 73)
❑ 453 Brian Holman .......... .05 .02
❑ 454 Mike Jackson .......... .05 .02
❑ 455 Randy Johnson .......... .30 .14
❑ 456 Jeffrey Leonard .......... .05 .02
❑ 457 Edgar Martinez .......... .10 .05
❑ 458 Tino Martinez .......... .10 .05
❑ 459 Pete O'Brien UER .......... .05 .02
(1987 BA .266, should be .286)
❑ 460 Harold Reynolds .......... .05 .02
❑ 461 Mike Schooler .......... .05 .02
❑ 462 Bill Swift .......... .05 .02
❑ 463 David Valle .......... .05 .02
❑ 464 Omar Vizquel .......... .20 .09
❑ 465 Matt Young .......... .05 .02
❑ 466 Brady Anderson .......... .20 .09
❑ 467 Jeff Ballard UER .......... .05 .02
(Missing top of right parenthesis after Saberhagen in last text line)
❑ 468 Juan Bell .......... .05 .02
❑ 469A Mike Devereaux .......... .10 .05
(First line of text ends with six)
❑ 469B Mike Devereaux .......... .10 .05
(First line of text ends with runs)
❑ 470 Steve Finley .......... .10 .05
❑ 471 Dave Gallagher .......... .05 .02
❑ 472 Leo Gomez .......... .05 .02
❑ 473 Rene Gonzales .......... .05 .02
❑ 474 Pete Harnisch .......... .05 .02
❑ 475 Kevin Hickey .......... .05 .02
❑ 476 Chris Hoiles .......... .05 .02
❑ 477 Sam Horn .......... .05 .02
❑ 478 Tim Hulett .......... .05 .02
(Photo shows National Leaguer sliding into second base)
❑ 479 Dave Johnson .......... .05 .02
❑ 480 Ron Kittle UER .......... .05 .02
(Edmonton misspelled as Edmundton)
❑ 481 Ben McDonald .......... .05 .02
❑ 482 Bob Melvin .......... .05 .02
❑ 483 Bob Milacki .......... .05 .02
❑ 484 Randy Milligan .......... .05 .02
❑ 485 John Mitchell .......... .05 .02
❑ 486 Gregg Olson .......... .05 .02
❑ 487 Joe Orsulak .......... .05 .02
❑ 488 Joe Price .......... .05 .02
❑ 489 Bill Ripken .......... .05 .02
❑ 490 Cal Ripken .......... .75 .35
❑ 491 Curt Schilling .......... .10 .05

❑ 492 David Segui .05 .02
❑ 493 Anthony Telford .05 .02
❑ 494 Mickey Tettleton .05 .02
❑ 495 Mark Williamson .05 .02
❑ 496 Craig Worthington .05 .02
❑ 497 Juan Agosto .05 .02
❑ 498 Eric Anthony .05 .02
❑ 499 Craig Biggio .10 .05
❑ 500 Ken Caminiti UER .10 .05
(Born 4/4; should be 4/21)
❑ 501 Casey Candaele .05 .02
❑ 502 Andujar Cedeno .05 .02
❑ 503 Danny Darwin .05 .02
❑ 504 Mark Davidson .05 .02
❑ 505 Glenn Davis .05 .02
❑ 506 Jim Deshaies .05 .02
❑ 507 Luis Gonzalez RC .50 .23
❑ 508 Bill Gullickson .05 .02
❑ 509 Xavier Hernandez .05 .02
❑ 510 Brian Meyer .05 .02
❑ 511 Ken Oberkfell .05 .02
❑ 512 Mark Portugal .05 .02
❑ 513 Rafael Ramirez .05 .02
❑ 514 Karl Rhodes .05 .02
❑ 515 Mike Scott .05 .02
❑ 516 Mike Simms .05 .02
❑ 517 Dave Smith .05 .02
❑ 518 Franklin Stubbs .05 .02
❑ 519 Glenn Wilson .05 .02
❑ 520 Eric Yelding UER .05 .02
(Text has 63 steals; stats have 64, which is correct)
❑ 521 Gerald Young .05 .02
❑ 522 Shawn Abner .05 .02
❑ 523 Roberto Alomar .20 .09
❑ 524 Andy Benes .05 .02
❑ 525 Joe Carter .10 .05
❑ 526 Jack Clark .10 .05
❑ 527 Joey Cora .05 .02
❑ 528 Paul Faries .05 .02
❑ 529 Tony Gwynn .40 .18
❑ 530 Atlee Hammaker .05 .02
❑ 531 Greg W. Harris .05 .02
❑ 532 Thomas Howard .05 .02
❑ 533 Bruce Hurst .05 .02
❑ 534 Craig Lefferts .05 .02
❑ 535 Derek Lilliquist .05 .02
❑ 536 Fred Lynn .05 .02
❑ 537 Mike Pagliarulo .05 .02
❑ 538 Mark Parent .05 .02
❑ 539 Dennis Rasmussen .05 .02
❑ 540 Bip Roberts .05 .02
❑ 541 Richard Rodriguez .05 .02
❑ 542 Benito Santiago .05 .02
❑ 543 Calvin Schiraldi .05 .02
❑ 544 Eric Show .05 .02
❑ 545 Phil Stephenson .05 .02
❑ 546 Garry Templeton UER .05 .02
(Born 3/24/57; should be 3/24/56)
❑ 547 Ed Whitson .05 .02
❑ 548 Eddie Williams .05 .02
❑ 549 Kevin Appier .10 .05
❑ 550 Luis Aquino .05 .02
❑ 551 Bob Boone .10 .05
❑ 552 George Brett .40 .18
❑ 553 Jeff Conine RC .20 .09
❑ 554 Steve Crawford .05 .02
❑ 555 Mark Davis .05 .02
❑ 556 Storm Davis .05 .02
❑ 557 Jim Eisenreich .05 .02
❑ 558 Steve Farr .05 .02
❑ 559 Tom Gordon .05 .02
❑ 560 Mark Gubicza .05 .02
❑ 561 Bo Jackson .10 .05
❑ 562 Mike Macfarlane .05 .02
❑ 563 Brian McRae RC .10 .05
❑ 564 Jeff Montgomery .10 .05
❑ 565 Bill Pecota .05 .02
❑ 566 Gerald Perry .05 .02
❑ 567 Bret Saberhagen .10 .05
❑ 568 Jeff Schulz .05 .02
❑ 569 Kevin Seitzer .05 .02
❑ 570 Terry Shumpert .05 .02
❑ 571 Kurt Stillwell .05 .02
❑ 572 Danny Tartabull .05 .02
❑ 573 Gary Thurman .05 .02
❑ 574 Frank White .10 .05
❑ 575 Willie Wilson .05 .02
❑ 576 Chris Bosio .05 .02
❑ 577 Greg Brock .05 .02
❑ 578 George Canale .05 .02
❑ 579 Chuck Crim .05 .02
❑ 580 Rob Deer .05 .02
❑ 581 Edgar Diaz .05 .02
❑ 582 Tom Edens .05 .02
❑ 583 Mike Felder .05 .02
❑ 584 Jim Gantner .05 .02
❑ 585 Darryl Hamilton .05 .02
❑ 586 Ted Higuera .05 .02
❑ 587 Mark Knudson .05 .02
❑ 588 Bill Krueger .05 .02
❑ 589 Tim McIntosh .05 .02
❑ 590 Paul Mirabella .05 .02
❑ 591 Paul Molitor .20 .09
❑ 592 Jaime Navarro .05 .02
❑ 593 Dave Parker .10 .05
❑ 594 Dan Plesac .05 .02
❑ 595 Ron Robinson .05 .02
❑ 596 Gary Sheffield .20 .09
❑ 597 Bill Spiers .05 .02
❑ 598 B.J. Surhoff .10 .05
❑ 599 Greg Vaughn .20 .09
❑ 600 Randy Veres .05 .02
❑ 601 Robin Yount .20 .09
❑ 602 Rick Aguilera .10 .05
❑ 603 Allan Anderson .05 .02
❑ 604 Juan Berenguer .05 .02
❑ 605 Randy Bush .05 .02
❑ 606 Carmen Castillo .05 .02
❑ 607 Tim Drummond .05 .02
❑ 608 Scott Erickson .05 .02
❑ 609 Gary Gaetti .10 .05
❑ 610 Greg Gagne .05 .02
❑ 611 Dan Gladden .05 .02
❑ 612 Mark Guthrie .05 .02
❑ 613 Brian Harper .05 .02
❑ 614 Kent Hrbek .10 .05
❑ 615 Gene Larkin .05 .02
❑ 616 Terry Leach .05 .02
❑ 617 Nelson Liriano .05 .02
❑ 618 Shane Mack .05 .02
❑ 619 John Moses .05 .02
❑ 620 Pedro Munoz RC .05 .02
❑ 621 Al Newman .05 .02
❑ 622 Junior Ortiz .05 .02
❑ 623 Kirby Puckett .50 .23
❑ 624 Roy Smith .05 .02
❑ 625 Kevin Tapani .05 .02
❑ 626 Gary Wayne .05 .02
❑ 627 David West .05 .02
❑ 628 Cris Carpenter .05 .02
❑ 629 Vince Coleman .05 .02
❑ 630 Ken Dayley .05 .02
❑ 631A Jose DeLeon ERR .05 .02
(Missing '79 Bradenton stats)
❑ 631B Jose DeLeon COR .05 .02
(With '79 Bradenton stats)
❑ 632 Frank DiPino .05 .02
❑ 633 Bernard Gilkey .10 .05
❑ 634A Pedro Guerrero ERR .10 .05
(Career SB shown as "$91")
❑ 634B Pedro Guerrero COR .10 .05
❑ 635 Ken Hill .05 .02
❑ 636 Felix Jose .05 .02
❑ 637 Ray Lankford .20 .09
❑ 638 Joe Magrane .05 .02
❑ 639 Tom Niedenfuer .05 .02
❑ 640 Jose Oquendo .05 .02
❑ 641 Tom Pagnozzi .05 .02
❑ 642 Terry Pendleton .10 .05
❑ 643 Mike Perez RC .05 .02
❑ 644 Bryn Smith .05 .02
❑ 645 Lee Smith .10 .05
❑ 646 Ozzie Smith .25 .11
❑ 647 Scott Terry .05 .02
❑ 648 Bob Tewksbury .05 .02
❑ 649 Milt Thompson .05 .02
❑ 650 John Tudor .05 .02
❑ 651 Denny Walling .05 .02
❑ 652 Craig Wilson .05 .02
❑ 653 Todd Worrell .05 .02
❑ 654 Todd Zeile .10 .05
❑ 655 Oscar Azocar .05 .02
❑ 656 Steve Balboni UER .05 .02
(Born 1/5/57; should be 1/16)
❑ 657 Jesse Barfield .05 .02
❑ 658 Greg Cadaret .05 .02
❑ 659 Chuck Cary .05 .02
❑ 660 Rick Cerone .05 .02
❑ 661 Dave Eiland .05 .02
❑ 662 Alvaro Espinoza .05 .02
❑ 663 Bob Geren .05 .02
❑ 664 Lee Guetterman .05 .02
❑ 665 Mel Hall .05 .02
❑ 666 Andy Hawkins .05 .02
❑ 667 Jimmy Jones .05 .02
❑ 668 Roberto Kelly .05 .02
❑ 669 Dave LaPoint UER .05 .02
(No '81 Brewers stats; totals also are wrong)
❑ 670 Tim Leary .05 .02
❑ 671 Jim Leyritz .05 .02
❑ 672 Kevin Maas .05 .02
❑ 673 Don Mattingly .50 .23
❑ 674 Matt Nokes .05 .02
❑ 675 Pascual Perez .05 .02
❑ 676 Eric Plunk .05 .02
❑ 677 Dave Righetti .05 .02
❑ 678 Jeff D. Robinson .05 .02
❑ 679 Steve Sax .05 .02
❑ 680 Mike Witt .05 .02
❑ 681 Steve Avery UER .05 .02
(Born in New Jersey; should say Michigan)
❑ 682 Mike Bell .05 .02
❑ 683 Jeff Blauser .05 .02
❑ 684 Francisco Cabrera UER .05 .02
(Born 10/16; should say 10/10)
❑ 685 Tony Castillo .05 .02
❑ 686 Marty Clary UER .05 .02
(Shown pitching righty, but bio has left)
❑ 687 Nick Esasky .05 .02
❑ 688 Ron Gant .10 .05
❑ 689 Tom Glavine .20 .09
❑ 690 Mark Grant .05 .02
❑ 691 Tommy Gregg .05 .02
❑ 692 Dwayne Henry .05 .02
❑ 693 Dave Justice .20 .09
❑ 694 Jimmy Kremers .05 .02
❑ 695 Charlie Leibrandt .05 .02
❑ 696 Mark Lemke .05 .02
❑ 697 Oddibe McDowell .05 .02
❑ 698 Greg Olson .05 .02
❑ 699 Jeff Parrett .05 .02
❑ 700 Jim Presley .05 .02
❑ 701 Victor Rosario .05 .02
❑ 702 Lonnie Smith .05 .02
❑ 703 Pete Smith .05 .02
❑ 704 John Smoltz .10 .05
❑ 705 Mike Stanton .05 .02
❑ 706 Andres Thomas .05 .02
❑ 707 Jeff Treadway .05 .02
❑ 708 Jim Vatcher .05 .02
❑ 709 Ryne Sandberg .20 .09
Cecil Fielder
Home Run Kings
❑ 710 Barry Bonds .40 .18
Ken Griffey Jr.
2nd Generation Stars
❑ 711 Bobby Bonilla .20 .09
Barry Larkin
NLCS Team Leaders
❑ 712 Bobby Thigpen .05 .02
John Franco
Top Game Savers
❑ 713 Chicago's 100 Club .10 .05
Andre Dawson
Ryne Sandberg UER
(Ryno misspelled Rhino)
❑ 714 CL:A's/Pirates .05 .02
Reds/Red Sox
❑ 715 CL:White Sox/Mets .05 .02

| | | |
|---|---|---|
| Blue Jays/Dodgers | | |
| ❑ 716 CL:Expos/Giants | .05 | .02 |
| Rangers/Angels | | |
| ❑ 717 CL:Tigers/Indians | .05 | .02 |
| Phillies/Cubs | | |
| ❑ 718 CL:Mariners/Orioles | .05 | .02 |
| Astros/Padres | | |
| ❑ 719 CL:Royals/Brewers | .05 | .02 |
| Twins/Cardinals | | |
| ❑ 720 CL:Yankees/Braves | .05 | .02 |
| Superstars/Specials | | |

## 1991 Fleer Update

| | MINT | NRMT |
|---|---|---|
| COMP.FACT.SET (132) | 6.00 | 2.70 |
| ❑ 1 Glenn Davis | .05 | .02 |
| ❑ 2 Dwight Evans | .10 | .05 |
| ❑ 3 Jose Mesa | .05 | .02 |
| ❑ 4 Jack Clark | .10 | .05 |
| ❑ 5 Danny Darwin | .05 | .02 |
| ❑ 6 Steve Lyons | .05 | .02 |
| ❑ 7 Mo Vaughn | .10 | .05 |
| ❑ 8 Floyd Bannister | .05 | .02 |
| ❑ 9 Gary Gaetti | .10 | .05 |
| ❑ 10 Dave Parker | .10 | .05 |
| ❑ 11 Joey Cora | .05 | .02 |
| ❑ 12 Charlie Hough | .10 | .05 |
| ❑ 13 Matt Merullo | .05 | .02 |
| ❑ 14 Warren Newson | .05 | .02 |
| ❑ 15 Tim Raines | .10 | .05 |
| ❑ 16 Albert Belle | .10 | .05 |
| ❑ 17 Glenallen Hill | .05 | .02 |
| ❑ 18 Shawn Hillegas | .05 | .02 |
| ❑ 19 Mark Lewis | .05 | .02 |
| ❑ 20 Charles Nagy | .05 | .02 |
| ❑ 21 Mark Whiten | .05 | .02 |
| ❑ 22 John Cerutti | .05 | .02 |
| ❑ 23 Rob Deer | .05 | .02 |
| ❑ 24 Mickey Tettleton | .05 | .02 |
| ❑ 25 Warren Cromartie | .05 | .02 |
| ❑ 26 Kirk Gibson | .10 | .05 |
| ❑ 27 David Howard | .05 | .02 |
| ❑ 28 Brent Mayne | .05 | .02 |
| ❑ 29 Dante Bichette | .20 | .09 |
| ❑ 30 Mark Lee | .05 | .02 |
| ❑ 31 Julio Machado | .05 | .02 |
| ❑ 32 Edwin Nunez | .05 | .02 |
| ❑ 33 Willie Randolph | .10 | .05 |
| ❑ 34 Franklin Stubbs | .05 | .02 |
| ❑ 35 Bill Wegman | .05 | .02 |
| ❑ 36 Chili Davis | .10 | .05 |
| ❑ 37 Chuck Knoblauch | .10 | .05 |
| ❑ 38 Scott Leius | .05 | .02 |
| ❑ 39 Jack Morris | .10 | .05 |
| ❑ 40 Mike Pagliarulo | .05 | .02 |
| ❑ 41 Lenny Webster | .05 | .02 |
| ❑ 42 John Habyan | .05 | .02 |
| ❑ 43 Steve Howe | .05 | .02 |
| ❑ 44 Jeff Johnson | .05 | .02 |
| ❑ 45 Scott Kamieniecki RC | .05 | .02 |
| ❑ 46 Pat Kelly RC | .05 | .02 |
| ❑ 47 Hensley Meulens | .05 | .02 |
| ❑ 48 Wade Taylor | .05 | .02 |
| ❑ 49 Bernie Williams | .25 | .11 |
| ❑ 50 Kirk Dressendorfer RC | .05 | .02 |
| ❑ 51 Ernest Riles | .05 | .02 |
| ❑ 52 Rich DeLucia | .05 | .02 |
| ❑ 53 Tracy Jones | .05 | .02 |
| ❑ 54 Bill Krueger | .05 | .02 |
| ❑ 55 Alonzo Powell | .05 | .02 |
| ❑ 56 Jeff Schaefer | .05 | .02 |
| ❑ 57 Russ Swan | .05 | .02 |
| ❑ 58 John Barfield | .05 | .02 |
| ❑ 59 Rich Gossage | .10 | .05 |
| ❑ 60 Jose Guzman | .05 | .02 |
| ❑ 61 Dean Palmer | .10 | .05 |
| ❑ 62 Ivan Rodriguez RC | 3.00 | 1.35 |
| ❑ 63 Roberto Alomar | .20 | .09 |
| ❑ 64 Tom Candiotti | .05 | .02 |
| ❑ 65 Joe Carter | .10 | .05 |
| ❑ 66 Ed Sprague | .05 | .02 |
| ❑ 67 Pat Tabler | .05 | .02 |
| ❑ 68 Mike Timlin RC | .05 | .02 |
| ❑ 69 Devon White | .05 | .02 |
| ❑ 70 Rafael Belliard | .05 | .02 |
| ❑ 71 Juan Berenguer | .05 | .02 |
| ❑ 72 Sid Bream | .05 | .02 |
| ❑ 73 Marvin Freeman | .05 | .02 |
| ❑ 74 Kent Mercker | .05 | .02 |
| ❑ 75 Otis Nixon | .05 | .02 |
| ❑ 76 Terry Pendleton | .10 | .05 |
| ❑ 77 George Bell | .05 | .02 |
| ❑ 78 Danny Jackson | .05 | .02 |
| ❑ 79 Chuck McElroy | .05 | .02 |
| ❑ 80 Gary Scott | .05 | .02 |
| ❑ 81 Heathcliff Slocumb RC | .05 | .02 |
| ❑ 82 Dave Smith | .05 | .02 |
| ❑ 83 Rick Wilkins RC | .05 | .02 |
| ❑ 84 Freddie Benavides | .05 | .02 |
| ❑ 85 Ted Power | .05 | .02 |
| ❑ 86 Mo Sanford | .05 | .02 |
| ❑ 87 Jeff Bagwell RC | 3.00 | 1.35 |
| ❑ 88 Steve Finley | .10 | .05 |
| ❑ 89 Pete Harnisch | .05 | .02 |
| ❑ 90 Darryl Kile | .10 | .05 |
| ❑ 91 Brett Butler | .10 | .05 |
| ❑ 92 John Candelaria | .05 | .02 |
| ❑ 93 Gary Carter | .10 | .05 |
| ❑ 94 Kevin Gross | .05 | .02 |
| ❑ 95 Bob Ojeda | .05 | .02 |
| ❑ 96 Darryl Strawberry | .10 | .05 |
| ❑ 97 Ivan Calderon | .05 | .02 |
| ❑ 98 Ron Hassey | .05 | .02 |
| ❑ 99 Gilberto Reyes | .05 | .02 |
| ❑ 100 Hubie Brooks | .05 | .02 |
| ❑ 101 Rick Cerone | .05 | .02 |
| ❑ 102 Vince Coleman | .05 | .02 |
| ❑ 103 Jeff Innis | .05 | .02 |
| ❑ 104 Pete Schourek RC | .10 | .05 |
| ❑ 105 Andy Ashby RC | .25 | .09 |
| ❑ 106 Wally Backman | .05 | .02 |
| ❑ 107 Darrin Fletcher | .05 | .02 |
| ❑ 108 Tommy Greene | .05 | .02 |
| ❑ 109 John Morris | .05 | .02 |
| ❑ 110 Mitch Williams | .05 | .02 |
| ❑ 111 Lloyd McClendon | .05 | .02 |
| ❑ 112 Orlando Merced RC | .05 | .02 |
| ❑ 113 Vicente Palacios | .05 | .02 |
| ❑ 114 Gary Varsho | .05 | .02 |
| ❑ 115 John Wehner | .05 | .02 |
| ❑ 116 Rex Hudler | .05 | .02 |
| ❑ 117 Tim Jones | .05 | .02 |
| ❑ 118 Geronimo Pena | .05 | .02 |
| ❑ 119 Gerald Perry | .05 | .02 |
| ❑ 120 Larry Andersen | .05 | .02 |
| ❑ 121 Jerald Clark | .05 | .02 |
| ❑ 122 Scott Coolbaugh | .05 | .02 |
| ❑ 123 Tony Fernandez | .05 | .02 |
| ❑ 124 Darrin Jackson | .05 | .02 |
| ❑ 125 Fred McGriff | .20 | .09 |
| ❑ 126 Jose Mota | .05 | .02 |
| ❑ 127 Tim Teufel | .05 | .02 |
| ❑ 128 Bud Black | .05 | .02 |
| ❑ 129 Mike Felder | .05 | .02 |
| ❑ 130 Willie McGee | .10 | .05 |
| ❑ 131 Dave Righetti | .05 | .02 |
| ❑ 132 Checklist U1-U132 | .05 | .02 |

## 1992 Fleer

| | MINT | NRMT |
|---|---|---|
| COMPLETE SET (720) | 10.00 | 4.50 |
| COMP.HOBBY SET (732) | 20.00 | 9.00 |
| COMP.RETAIL SET (732) | 20.00 | 9.00 |
| COMMON CARD (1-720) | .05 | .02 |
| ❑ 1 Brady Anderson | .10 | .05 |
| ❑ 2 Jose Bautista | .05 | .02 |
| ❑ 3 Juan Bell | .05 | .02 |
| ❑ 4 Glenn Davis | .05 | .02 |
| ❑ 5 Mike Devereaux | .05 | .02 |
| ❑ 6 Dwight Evans | .10 | .05 |
| ❑ 7 Mike Flanagan | .05 | .02 |
| ❑ 8 Leo Gomez | .05 | .02 |
| ❑ 9 Chris Hoiles | .05 | .02 |
| ❑ 10 Sam Horn | .05 | .02 |
| ❑ 11 Tim Hulett | .05 | .02 |
| ❑ 12 Dave Johnson | .05 | .02 |
| ❑ 13 Chito Martinez | .05 | .02 |
| ❑ 14 Ben McDonald | .05 | .02 |
| ❑ 15 Bob Melvin | .05 | .02 |
| ❑ 16 Luis Mercedes | .05 | .02 |
| ❑ 17 Jose Mesa | .05 | .02 |
| ❑ 18 Bob Milacki | .05 | .02 |
| ❑ 19 Randy Milligan | .05 | .02 |
| ❑ 20 Mike Mussina UER (Card back refers to him as Jeff) | .30 | .14 |
| ❑ 21 Gregg Olson | .05 | .02 |
| ❑ 22 Joe Orsulak | .05 | .02 |
| ❑ 23 Jim Poole | .05 | .02 |
| ❑ 24 Arthur Rhodes | .05 | .02 |
| ❑ 25 Billy Ripken | .05 | .02 |
| ❑ 26 Cal Ripken | .75 | .35 |
| ❑ 27 David Segui | .05 | .02 |
| ❑ 28 Roy Smith | .05 | .02 |
| ❑ 29 Anthony Telford | .05 | .02 |
| ❑ 30 Mark Williamson | .05 | .02 |
| ❑ 31 Craig Worthington | .05 | .02 |
| ❑ 32 Wade Boggs | .25 | .11 |
| ❑ 33 Tom Bolton | .05 | .02 |
| ❑ 34 Tom Brunansky | .05 | .02 |
| ❑ 35 Ellis Burks | .10 | .05 |
| ❑ 36 Jack Clark | .10 | .05 |
| ❑ 37 Roger Clemens | .40 | .18 |
| ❑ 38 Danny Darwin | .05 | .02 |
| ❑ 39 Mike Greenwell | .05 | .02 |
| ❑ 40 Joe Hesketh | .05 | .02 |
| ❑ 41 Daryl Irvine | .05 | .02 |
| ❑ 42 Dennis Lamp | .05 | .02 |
| ❑ 43 Tony Pena | .05 | .02 |
| ❑ 44 Phil Plantier | .05 | .02 |
| ❑ 45 Carlos Quintana | .05 | .02 |
| ❑ 46 Jeff Reardon | .10 | .05 |
| ❑ 47 Jody Reed | .05 | .02 |
| ❑ 48 Luis Rivera | .05 | .02 |
| ❑ 49 Mo Vaughn | .25 | .11 |
| ❑ 50 Jim Abbott | .10 | .05 |
| ❑ 51 Kyle Abbott | .05 | .02 |
| ❑ 52 Ruben Amaro | .05 | .02 |
| ❑ 53 Scott Bailes | .05 | .02 |
| ❑ 54 Chris Beasley | .05 | .02 |
| ❑ 55 Mark Eichhorn | .05 | .02 |
| ❑ 56 Mike Fetters | .05 | .02 |
| ❑ 57 Chuck Finley | .10 | .05 |
| ❑ 58 Gary Gaetti | .10 | .05 |

| No. | Player | Price | Price |
|---|---|---|---|
| 59 | Dave Gallagher | .05 | .02 |
| 60 | Donnie Hill | .05 | .02 |
| 61 | Bryan Harvey UER (Lee Smith led the Majors with 47 saves) | .05 | .02 |
| 62 | Wally Joyner | .10 | .05 |
| 63 | Mark Langston | .05 | .02 |
| 64 | Kirk McCaskill | .05 | .02 |
| 65 | John Orton | .05 | .02 |
| 66 | Lance Parrish | .05 | .02 |
| 67 | Luis Polonia | .05 | .02 |
| 68 | Bobby Rose | .05 | .02 |
| 69 | Dick Schofield | .05 | .02 |
| 70 | Luis Sojo | .05 | .02 |
| 71 | Lee Stevens | .10 | .05 |
| 72 | Dave Winfield | .20 | .09 |
| 73 | Cliff Young | .05 | .02 |
| 74 | Wilson Alvarez | .05 | .02 |
| 75 | Esteban Beltre | .05 | .02 |
| 76 | Joey Cora | .05 | .02 |
| 77 | Brian Drahman | .05 | .02 |
| 78 | Alex Fernandez | .10 | .05 |
| 79 | Carlton Fisk | .20 | .09 |
| 80 | Scott Fletcher | .05 | .02 |
| 81 | Craig Grebeck | .05 | .02 |
| 82 | Ozzie Guillen | .05 | .02 |
| 83 | Greg Hibbard | .05 | .02 |
| 84 | Charlie Hough | .10 | .05 |
| 85 | Mike Huff | .05 | .02 |
| 86 | Bo Jackson | .10 | .05 |
| 87 | Lance Johnson | .05 | .02 |
| 88 | Ron Karkovice | .05 | .02 |
| 89 | Jack McDowell | .05 | .02 |
| 90 | Matt Merullo | .05 | .02 |
| 91 | Warren Newson | .05 | .02 |
| 92 | Donn Pall UER (Called Dunn on card back) | .05 | .02 |
| 93 | Dan Pasqua | .05 | .02 |
| 94 | Ken Patterson | .05 | .02 |
| 95 | Melido Perez | .05 | .02 |
| 96 | Scott Radinsky | .05 | .02 |
| 97 | Tim Raines | .10 | .05 |
| 98 | Sammy Sosa | .40 | .18 |
| 99 | Bobby Thigpen | .05 | .02 |
| 100 | Frank Thomas | .40 | .18 |
| 101 | Robin Ventura | .10 | .05 |
| 102 | Mike Aldrete | .05 | .02 |
| 103 | Sandy Alomar Jr. | .10 | .05 |
| 104 | Carlos Baerga | .05 | .02 |
| 105 | Albert Belle | .10 | .05 |
| 106 | Willie Blair | .05 | .02 |
| 107 | Jerry Browne | .05 | .02 |
| 108 | Alex Cole | .05 | .02 |
| 109 | Felix Fermin | .05 | .02 |
| 110 | Glenallen Hill | .05 | .02 |
| 111 | Shawn Hillegas | .05 | .02 |
| 112 | Chris James | .05 | .02 |
| 113 | Reggie Jefferson | .10 | .05 |
| 114 | Doug Jones | .05 | .02 |
| 115 | Eric King | .05 | .02 |
| 116 | Mark Lewis | .05 | .02 |
| 117 | Carlos Martinez | .05 | .02 |
| 118 | Charles Nagy UER (Throws right, but card says left) | .05 | .02 |
| 119 | Rod Nichols | .05 | .02 |
| 120 | Steve Olin | .05 | .02 |
| 121 | Jesse Orosco | .05 | .02 |
| 122 | Rudy Seanez | .05 | .02 |
| 123 | Joel Skinner | .05 | .02 |
| 124 | Greg Swindell | .05 | .02 |
| 125 | Jim Thome | .40 | .18 |
| 126 | Mark Whiten | .05 | .02 |
| 127 | Scott Aldred | .05 | .02 |
| 128 | Andy Allanson | .05 | .02 |
| 129 | John Cerutti | .05 | .02 |
| 130 | Milt Cuyler | .05 | .02 |
| 131 | Mike Dalton | .05 | .02 |
| 132 | Rob Deer | .05 | .02 |
| 133 | Cecil Fielder | .10 | .05 |
| 134 | Travis Fryman | .10 | .05 |
| 135 | Dan Gakeler | .05 | .02 |
| 136 | Paul Gibson | .05 | .02 |
| 137 | Bill Gullickson | .05 | .02 |
| 138 | Mike Henneman | .05 | .02 |
| 139 | Pete Incaviglia | .05 | .02 |
| 140 | Mark Leiter | .05 | .02 |
| 141 | Scott Livingstone | .05 | .02 |
| 142 | Lloyd Moseby | .05 | .02 |
| 143 | Tony Phillips | .05 | .02 |
| 144 | Mark Salas | .05 | .02 |
| 145 | Frank Tanana | .05 | .02 |
| 146 | Walt Terrell | .05 | .02 |
| 147 | Mickey Tettleton | .05 | .02 |
| 148 | Alan Trammell | .10 | .05 |
| 149 | Lou Whitaker | .10 | .05 |
| 150 | Kevin Appier | .10 | .05 |
| 151 | Luis Aquino | .05 | .02 |
| 152 | Todd Benzinger | .05 | .02 |
| 153 | Mike Boddicker | .05 | .02 |
| 154 | George Brett | .40 | .18 |
| 155 | Storm Davis | .05 | .02 |
| 156 | Jim Eisenreich | .05 | .02 |
| 157 | Kirk Gibson | .10 | .05 |
| 158 | Tom Gordon | .05 | .02 |
| 159 | Mark Gubicza | .05 | .02 |
| 160 | David Howard | .05 | .02 |
| 161 | Mike Macfarlane | .05 | .02 |
| 162 | Brent Mayne | .05 | .02 |
| 163 | Brian McRae | .05 | .02 |
| 164 | Jeff Montgomery | .10 | .05 |
| 165 | Bill Pecota | .05 | .02 |
| 166 | Harvey Pulliam | .05 | .02 |
| 167 | Bret Saberhagen | .10 | .05 |
| 168 | Kevin Seitzer | .05 | .02 |
| 169 | Terry Shumpert | .05 | .02 |
| 170 | Kurt Stillwell | .05 | .02 |
| 171 | Danny Tartabull | .05 | .02 |
| 172 | Gary Thurman | .05 | .02 |
| 173 | Dante Bichette | .10 | .05 |
| 174 | Kevin D. Brown | .05 | .02 |
| 175 | Chuck Crim | .05 | .02 |
| 176 | Jim Gantner | .05 | .02 |
| 177 | Darryl Hamilton | .05 | .02 |
| 178 | Ted Higuera | .05 | .02 |
| 179 | Darren Holmes | .05 | .02 |
| 180 | Mark Lee | .05 | .02 |
| 181 | Julio Machado | .05 | .02 |
| 182 | Paul Molitor | .20 | .09 |
| 183 | Jaime Navarro | .05 | .02 |
| 184 | Edwin Nunez | .05 | .02 |
| 185 | Dan Plesac | .05 | .02 |
| 186 | Willie Randolph | .10 | .05 |
| 187 | Ron Robinson | .05 | .02 |
| 188 | Gary Sheffield | .20 | .09 |
| 189 | Bill Spiers | .05 | .02 |
| 190 | B.J. Surhoff | .10 | .05 |
| 191 | Dale Sveum | .05 | .02 |
| 192 | Greg Vaughn | .10 | .05 |
| 193 | Bill Wegman | .05 | .02 |
| 194 | Robin Yount | .20 | .09 |
| 195 | Rick Aguilera | .10 | .05 |
| 196 | Allan Anderson | .05 | .02 |
| 197 | Steve Bedrosian | .05 | .02 |
| 198 | Randy Bush | .05 | .02 |
| 199 | Larry Casian | .05 | .02 |
| 200 | Chili Davis | .10 | .05 |
| 201 | Scott Erickson | .05 | .02 |
| 202 | Greg Gagne | .05 | .02 |
| 203 | Dan Gladden | .05 | .02 |
| 204 | Brian Harper | .05 | .02 |
| 205 | Kent Hrbek | .10 | .05 |
| 206 | Chuck Knoblauch UER (Career hit total of 59 is wrong) | .10 | .05 |
| 207 | Gene Larkin | .05 | .02 |
| 208 | Terry Leach | .05 | .02 |
| 209 | Scott Leius | .05 | .02 |
| 210 | Shane Mack | .05 | .02 |
| 211 | Jack Morris | .10 | .05 |
| 212 | Pedro Munoz | .05 | .02 |
| 213 | Denny Neagle | .10 | .05 |
| 214 | Al Newman | .05 | .02 |
| 215 | Junior Ortiz | .05 | .02 |
| 216 | Mike Pagliarulo | .05 | .02 |
| 217 | Kirby Puckett | .50 | .23 |
| 218 | Paul Sorrento | .05 | .02 |
| 219 | Kevin Tapani | .05 | .02 |
| 220 | Lenny Webster | .05 | .02 |
| 221 | Jesse Barfield | .05 | .02 |
| 222 | Greg Cadaret | .05 | .02 |
| 223 | Dave Eiland | .05 | .02 |
| 224 | Alvaro Espinoza | .05 | .02 |
| 225 | Steve Farr | .05 | .02 |
| 226 | Bob Geren | .05 | .02 |
| 227 | Lee Guetterman | .05 | .02 |
| 228 | John Habyan | .05 | .02 |
| 229 | Mel Hall | .05 | .02 |
| 230 | Steve Howe | .05 | .02 |
| 231 | Mike Humphreys | .05 | .02 |
| 232 | Scott Kamieniecki | .05 | .02 |
| 233 | Pat Kelly | .05 | .02 |
| 234 | Roberto Kelly | .05 | .02 |
| 235 | Tim Leary | .05 | .02 |
| 236 | Kevin Maas | .05 | .02 |
| 237 | Don Mattingly | .50 | .23 |
| 238 | Hensley Meulens | .05 | .02 |
| 239 | Matt Nokes | .05 | .02 |
| 240 | Pascual Perez | .05 | .02 |
| 241 | Eric Plunk | .05 | .02 |
| 242 | John Ramos | .05 | .02 |
| 243 | Scott Sanderson | .05 | .02 |
| 244 | Steve Sax | .05 | .02 |
| 245 | Wade Taylor | .05 | .02 |
| 246 | Randy Velarde | .05 | .02 |
| 247 | Bernie Williams | .20 | .09 |
| 248 | Troy Afenir | .05 | .02 |
| 249 | Harold Baines | .10 | .05 |
| 250 | Lance Blankenship | .05 | .02 |
| 251 | Mike Bordick | .05 | .02 |
| 252 | Jose Canseco | .25 | .11 |
| 253 | Steve Chitren | .05 | .02 |
| 254 | Ron Darling | .05 | .02 |
| 255 | Dennis Eckersley | .10 | .05 |
| 256 | Mike Gallego | .05 | .02 |
| 257 | Dave Henderson | .05 | .02 |
| 258 | Rickey Henderson UER (Wearing 24 on front and 22 on back) | .25 | .11 |
| 259 | Rick Honeycutt | .05 | .02 |
| 260 | Brook Jacoby | .05 | .02 |
| 261 | Carney Lansford | .10 | .05 |
| 262 | Mark McGwire | .75 | .35 |
| 263 | Mike Moore | .05 | .02 |
| 264 | Gene Nelson | .05 | .02 |
| 265 | Jamie Quirk | .05 | .02 |
| 266 | Joe Slusarski | .05 | .02 |
| 267 | Terry Steinbach | .05 | .02 |
| 268 | Dave Stewart | .10 | .05 |
| 269 | Todd Van Poppel | .05 | .02 |
| 270 | Walt Weiss | .05 | .02 |
| 271 | Bob Welch | .05 | .02 |
| 272 | Curt Young | .05 | .02 |
| 273 | Scott Bradley | .05 | .02 |
| 274 | Greg Briley | .05 | .02 |
| 275 | Jay Buhner | .10 | .05 |
| 276 | Henry Cotto | .05 | .02 |
| 277 | Alvin Davis | .05 | .02 |
| 278 | Rich DeLucia | .05 | .02 |
| 279 | Ken Griffey Jr. | .75 | .35 |
| 280 | Erik Hanson | .05 | .02 |
| 281 | Brian Holman | .05 | .02 |
| 282 | Mike Jackson | .05 | .02 |
| 283 | Randy Johnson | .25 | .11 |
| 284 | Tracy Jones | .05 | .02 |
| 285 | Bill Krueger | .05 | .02 |
| 286 | Edgar Martinez | .10 | .05 |
| 287 | Tino Martinez | .10 | .05 |
| 288 | Rob Murphy | .05 | .02 |
| 289 | Pete O'Brien | .05 | .02 |
| 290 | Alonzo Powell | .05 | .02 |
| 291 | Harold Reynolds | .05 | .02 |
| 292 | Mike Schooler | .05 | .02 |
| 293 | Russ Swan | .05 | .02 |
| 294 | Bill Swift | .05 | .02 |
| 295 | Dave Valle | .05 | .02 |
| 296 | Omar Vizquel | .10 | .05 |
| 297 | Gerald Alexander | .05 | .02 |
| 298 | Brad Arnsberg | .05 | .02 |
| 299 | Kevin Brown | .10 | .05 |
| 300 | Jack Daugherty | .05 | .02 |
| 301 | Mario Diaz | .05 | .02 |
| 302 | Brian Downing | .05 | .02 |
| 303 | Julio Franco | .05 | .02 |
| 304 | Juan Gonzalez | .20 | .09 |
| 305 | Rich Gossage | .10 | .05 |
| 306 | Jose Guzman | .05 | .02 |

| No. | Player | | |
|---|---|---|---|
| ❑ 307 | Jose Hernandez RC | .05 | .02 |
| ❑ 308 | Jeff Huson | .05 | .02 |
| ❑ 309 | Mike Jeffcoat | .05 | .02 |
| ❑ 310 | Terry Mathews | .05 | .02 |
| ❑ 311 | Rafael Palmeiro | .20 | .09 |
| ❑ 312 | Dean Palmer | .10 | .05 |
| ❑ 313 | Geno Petralli | .05 | .02 |
| ❑ 314 | Gary Pettis | .05 | .02 |
| ❑ 315 | Kevin Reimer | .05 | .02 |
| ❑ 316 | Ivan Rodriguez | .40 | .18 |
| ❑ 317 | Kenny Rogers | .05 | .02 |
| ❑ 318 | Wayne Rosenthal | .05 | .02 |
| ❑ 319 | Jeff Russell | .05 | .02 |
| ❑ 320 | Nolan Ryan | 1.00 | .45 |
| ❑ 321 | Ruben Sierra | .05 | .02 |
| ❑ 322 | Jim Acker | .05 | .02 |
| ❑ 323 | Roberto Alomar | .20 | .09 |
| ❑ 324 | Derek Bell | .10 | .05 |
| ❑ 325 | Pat Borders | .05 | .02 |
| ❑ 326 | Tom Candiotti | .05 | .02 |
| ❑ 327 | Joe Carter | .10 | .05 |
| ❑ 328 | Rob Ducey | .05 | .02 |
| ❑ 329 | Kelly Gruber | .05 | .02 |
| ❑ 330 | Juan Guzman | .05 | .02 |
| ❑ 331 | Tom Henke | .05 | .02 |
| ❑ 332 | Jimmy Key | .10 | .05 |
| ❑ 333 | Manny Lee | .05 | .02 |
| ❑ 334 | Al Leiter | .10 | .05 |
| ❑ 335 | Bob MacDonald | .05 | .02 |
| ❑ 336 | Candy Maldonado | .05 | .02 |
| ❑ 337 | Rance Mulliniks | .05 | .02 |
| ❑ 338 | Greg Myers | .05 | .02 |
| ❑ 339 | John Olerud UER (1991 BA has .256, but text says .258) | .10 | .05 |
| ❑ 340 | Ed Sprague | .05 | .02 |
| ❑ 341 | Dave Stieb | .05 | .02 |
| ❑ 342 | Todd Stottlemyre | .10 | .05 |
| ❑ 343 | Mike Timlin | .05 | .02 |
| ❑ 344 | Duane Ward | .05 | .02 |
| ❑ 345 | David Wells | .10 | .05 |
| ❑ 346 | Devon White | .05 | .02 |
| ❑ 347 | Mookie Wilson | .10 | .05 |
| ❑ 348 | Eddie Zosky | .05 | .02 |
| ❑ 349 | Steve Avery | .05 | .02 |
| ❑ 350 | Mike Bell | .05 | .02 |
| ❑ 351 | Rafael Belliard | .05 | .02 |
| ❑ 352 | Juan Berenguer | .05 | .02 |
| ❑ 353 | Jeff Blauser | .05 | .02 |
| ❑ 354 | Sid Bream | .05 | .02 |
| ❑ 355 | Francisco Cabrera | .05 | .02 |
| ❑ 356 | Marvin Freeman | .05 | .02 |
| ❑ 357 | Ron Gant | .10 | .05 |
| ❑ 358 | Tom Glavine | .10 | .05 |
| ❑ 359 | Brian Hunter | .05 | .02 |
| ❑ 360 | Dave Justice | .10 | .05 |
| ❑ 361 | Charlie Leibrandt | .05 | .02 |
| ❑ 362 | Mark Lemke | .05 | .02 |
| ❑ 363 | Kent Mercker | .05 | .02 |
| ❑ 364 | Keith Mitchell | .05 | .02 |
| ❑ 365 | Greg Olson | .05 | .02 |
| ❑ 366 | Terry Pendleton | .10 | .05 |
| ❑ 367 | Armando Reynoso RC | .05 | .02 |
| ❑ 368 | Deion Sanders | .20 | .09 |
| ❑ 369 | Lonnie Smith | .05 | .02 |
| ❑ 370 | Pete Smith | .05 | .02 |
| ❑ 371 | John Smoltz | .10 | .05 |
| ❑ 372 | Mike Stanton | .05 | .02 |
| ❑ 373 | Jeff Treadway | .05 | .02 |
| ❑ 374 | Mark Wohlers | .05 | .02 |
| ❑ 375 | Paul Assenmacher | .05 | .02 |
| ❑ 376 | George Bell | .05 | .02 |
| ❑ 377 | Shawn Boskie | .05 | .02 |
| ❑ 378 | Frank Castillo | .05 | .02 |
| ❑ 379 | Andre Dawson | .10 | .05 |
| ❑ 380 | Shawon Dunston | .05 | .02 |
| ❑ 381 | Mark Grace | .20 | .09 |
| ❑ 382 | Mike Harkey | .05 | .02 |
| ❑ 383 | Danny Jackson | .05 | .02 |
| ❑ 384 | Les Lancaster | .05 | .02 |
| ❑ 385 | Ced Landrum | .05 | .02 |
| ❑ 386 | Greg Maddux | .50 | .23 |
| ❑ 387 | Derrick May | .05 | .02 |
| ❑ 388 | Chuck McElroy | .05 | .02 |
| ❑ 389 | Ryne Sandberg | .25 | .11 |
| ❑ 390 | Heathcliff Slocumb | .05 | .02 |
| ❑ 391 | Dave Smith | .05 | .02 |
| ❑ 392 | Dwight Smith | .05 | .02 |
| ❑ 393 | Rick Sutcliffe | .10 | .05 |
| ❑ 394 | Hector Villanueva | .05 | .02 |
| ❑ 395 | Chico Walker | .05 | .02 |
| ❑ 396 | Jerome Walton | .05 | .02 |
| ❑ 397 | Rick Wilkins | .05 | .02 |
| ❑ 398 | Jack Armstrong | .05 | .02 |
| ❑ 399 | Freddie Benavides | .05 | .02 |
| ❑ 400 | Glenn Braggs | .05 | .02 |
| ❑ 401 | Tom Browning | .05 | .02 |
| ❑ 402 | Norm Charlton | .05 | .02 |
| ❑ 403 | Eric Davis | .10 | .05 |
| ❑ 404 | Rob Dibble | .05 | .02 |
| ❑ 405 | Bill Doran | .05 | .02 |
| ❑ 406 | Mariano Duncan | .05 | .02 |
| ❑ 407 | Kip Gross | .05 | .02 |
| ❑ 408 | Chris Hammond | .05 | .02 |
| ❑ 409 | Billy Hatcher | .05 | .02 |
| ❑ 410 | Chris Jones | .05 | .02 |
| ❑ 411 | Barry Larkin | .10 | .05 |
| ❑ 412 | Hal Morris | .05 | .02 |
| ❑ 413 | Randy Myers | .10 | .05 |
| ❑ 414 | Joe Oliver | .05 | .02 |
| ❑ 415 | Paul O'Neill | .10 | .05 |
| ❑ 416 | Ted Power | .05 | .02 |
| ❑ 417 | Luis Quinones | .05 | .02 |
| ❑ 418 | Jeff Reed | .05 | .02 |
| ❑ 419 | Jose Rijo | .05 | .02 |
| ❑ 420 | Chris Sabo | .05 | .02 |
| ❑ 421 | Reggie Sanders | .05 | .02 |
| ❑ 422 | Scott Scudder | .05 | .02 |
| ❑ 423 | Glenn Sutko | .05 | .02 |
| ❑ 424 | Eric Anthony | .05 | .02 |
| ❑ 425 | Jeff Bagwell | .40 | .18 |
| ❑ 426 | Craig Biggio | .10 | .05 |
| ❑ 427 | Ken Caminiti | .10 | .05 |
| ❑ 428 | Casey Candaele | .05 | .02 |
| ❑ 429 | Mike Capel | .05 | .02 |
| ❑ 430 | Andujar Cedeno | .05 | .02 |
| ❑ 431 | Jim Corsi | .05 | .02 |
| ❑ 432 | Mark Davidson | .05 | .02 |
| ❑ 433 | Steve Finley | .10 | .05 |
| ❑ 434 | Luis Gonzalez | .10 | .05 |
| ❑ 435 | Pete Harnisch | .05 | .02 |
| ❑ 436 | Dwayne Henry | .05 | .02 |
| ❑ 437 | Xavier Hernandez | .05 | .02 |
| ❑ 438 | Jimmy Jones | .05 | .02 |
| ❑ 439 | Darryl Kile | .10 | .05 |
| ❑ 440 | Rob Mallicoat | .05 | .02 |
| ❑ 441 | Andy Mota | .05 | .02 |
| ❑ 442 | Al Osuna | .05 | .02 |
| ❑ 443 | Mark Portugal | .05 | .02 |
| ❑ 444 | Scott Servais | .05 | .02 |
| ❑ 445 | Mike Simms | .05 | .02 |
| ❑ 446 | Gerald Young | .05 | .02 |
| ❑ 447 | Tim Belcher | .05 | .02 |
| ❑ 448 | Brett Butler | .10 | .05 |
| ❑ 449 | John Candelaria | .05 | .02 |
| ❑ 450 | Gary Carter | .10 | .05 |
| ❑ 451 | Dennis Cook | .05 | .02 |
| ❑ 452 | Tim Crews | .05 | .02 |
| ❑ 453 | Kal Daniels | .05 | .02 |
| ❑ 454 | Jim Gott | .05 | .02 |
| ❑ 455 | Alfredo Griffin | .05 | .02 |
| ❑ 456 | Kevin Gross | .05 | .02 |
| ❑ 457 | Chris Gwynn | .05 | .02 |
| ❑ 458 | Lenny Harris | .05 | .02 |
| ❑ 459 | Orel Hershiser | .10 | .05 |
| ❑ 460 | Jay Howell | .05 | .02 |
| ❑ 461 | Stan Javier | .05 | .02 |
| ❑ 462 | Eric Karros | .20 | .09 |
| ❑ 463 | Ramon Martinez UER (Card says bats right; should be left) | .05 | .02 |
| ❑ 464 | Roger McDowell UER (Wins add up to 54; totals have 51) | .05 | .02 |
| ❑ 465 | Mike Morgan | .05 | .02 |
| ❑ 466 | Eddie Murray | .20 | .09 |
| ❑ 467 | Jose Offerman | .05 | .02 |
| ❑ 468 | Bob Ojeda | .05 | .02 |
| ❑ 469 | Juan Samuel | .05 | .02 |
| ❑ 470 | Mike Scioscia | .05 | .02 |
| ❑ 471 | Darryl Strawberry | .10 | .05 |
| ❑ 472 | Bret Barberie | .05 | .02 |
| ❑ 473 | Brian Barnes | .05 | .02 |
| ❑ 474 | Eric Bullock | .05 | .02 |
| ❑ 475 | Ivan Calderon | .05 | .02 |
| ❑ 476 | Delino DeShields | .10 | .05 |
| ❑ 477 | Jeff Fassero | .05 | .02 |
| ❑ 478 | Mike Fitzgerald | .05 | .02 |
| ❑ 479 | Steve Frey | .05 | .02 |
| ❑ 480 | Andres Galarraga | .10 | .05 |
| ❑ 481 | Mark Gardner | .05 | .02 |
| ❑ 482 | Marquis Grissom | .05 | .02 |
| ❑ 483 | Chris Haney | .05 | .02 |
| ❑ 484 | Barry Jones | .05 | .02 |
| ❑ 485 | Dave Martinez | .05 | .02 |
| ❑ 486 | Dennis Martinez | .10 | .05 |
| ❑ 487 | Chris Nabholz | .05 | .02 |
| ❑ 488 | Spike Owen | .05 | .02 |
| ❑ 489 | Gilberto Reyes | .05 | .02 |
| ❑ 490 | Mel Rojas | .05 | .02 |
| ❑ 491 | Scott Ruskin | .05 | .02 |
| ❑ 492 | Bill Sampen | .05 | .02 |
| ❑ 493 | Larry Walker | .10 | .05 |
| ❑ 494 | Tim Wallach | .05 | .02 |
| ❑ 495 | Daryl Boston | .05 | .02 |
| ❑ 496 | Hubie Brooks | .05 | .02 |
| ❑ 497 | Tim Burke | .05 | .02 |
| ❑ 498 | Mark Carreon | .05 | .02 |
| ❑ 499 | Tony Castillo | .05 | .02 |
| ❑ 500 | Vince Coleman | .05 | .02 |
| ❑ 501 | David Cone | .10 | .05 |
| ❑ 502 | Kevin Elster | .05 | .02 |
| ❑ 503 | Sid Fernandez | .05 | .02 |
| ❑ 504 | John Franco | .10 | .05 |
| ❑ 505 | Dwight Gooden | .10 | .05 |
| ❑ 506 | Todd Hundley | .05 | .02 |
| ❑ 507 | Jeff Innis | .05 | .02 |
| ❑ 508 | Gregg Jefferies | .05 | .02 |
| ❑ 509 | Howard Johnson | .05 | .02 |
| ❑ 510 | Dave Magadan | .05 | .02 |
| ❑ 511 | Terry McDaniel | .05 | .02 |
| ❑ 512 | Kevin McReynolds | .05 | .02 |
| ❑ 513 | Keith Miller | .05 | .02 |
| ❑ 514 | Charlie O'Brien | .05 | .02 |
| ❑ 515 | Mackey Sasser | .05 | .02 |
| ❑ 516 | Pete Schourek | .05 | .02 |
| ❑ 517 | Julio Valera | .05 | .02 |
| ❑ 518 | Frank Viola | .05 | .02 |
| ❑ 519 | Wally Whitehurst | .05 | .02 |
| ❑ 520 | Anthony Young | .05 | .02 |
| ❑ 521 | Andy Ashby | .10 | .05 |
| ❑ 522 | Kim Batiste | .05 | .02 |
| ❑ 523 | Joe Boever | .05 | .02 |
| ❑ 524 | Wes Chamberlain | .05 | .02 |
| ❑ 525 | Pat Combs | .05 | .02 |
| ❑ 526 | Danny Cox | .05 | .02 |
| ❑ 527 | Darren Daulton | .10 | .05 |
| ❑ 528 | Jose DeJesus | .05 | .02 |
| ❑ 529 | Len Dykstra | .10 | .05 |
| ❑ 530 | Darrin Fletcher | .05 | .02 |
| ❑ 531 | Tommy Greene | .05 | .02 |
| ❑ 532 | Jason Grimsley | .05 | .02 |
| ❑ 533 | Charlie Hayes | .05 | .02 |
| ❑ 534 | Von Hayes | .05 | .02 |
| ❑ 535 | Dave Hollins | .05 | .02 |
| ❑ 536 | Ricky Jordan | .05 | .02 |
| ❑ 537 | John Kruk | .10 | .05 |
| ❑ 538 | Jim Lindeman | .05 | .02 |
| ❑ 539 | Mickey Morandini | .05 | .02 |
| ❑ 540 | Terry Mulholland | .05 | .02 |
| ❑ 541 | Dale Murphy | .20 | .09 |
| ❑ 542 | Randy Ready | .05 | .02 |
| ❑ 543 | Wally Ritchie UER (Letters in data are cut off on card) | .05 | .02 |
| ❑ 544 | Bruce Ruffin | .05 | .02 |
| ❑ 545 | Steve Searcy | .05 | .02 |
| ❑ 546 | Dickie Thon | .05 | .02 |
| ❑ 547 | Mitch Williams | .05 | .02 |
| ❑ 548 | Stan Belinda | .05 | .02 |
| ❑ 549 | Jay Bell | .10 | .05 |
| ❑ 550 | Barry Bonds | .30 | .14 |
| ❑ 551 | Bobby Bonilla | .10 | .05 |
| ❑ 552 | Steve Buechele | .05 | .02 |
| ❑ 553 | Doug Drabek | .05 | .02 |
| ❑ 554 | Neal Heaton | .05 | .02 |
| ❑ 555 | Jeff King | .05 | .02 |
| ❑ 556 | Bob Kipper | .05 | .02 |

❑ 557 Bill Landrum .05 .02
❑ 558 Mike LaValliere .05 .02
❑ 559 Jose Lind .05 .02
❑ 560 Lloyd McClendon .05 .02
❑ 561 Orlando Merced .05 .02
❑ 562 Bob Patterson .05 .02
❑ 563 Joe Redfield .05 .02
❑ 564 Gary Redus .05 .02
❑ 565 Rosario Rodriguez .05 .02
❑ 566 Don Slaught .05 .02
❑ 567 John Smiley .05 .02
❑ 568 Zane Smith .05 .02
❑ 569 Randy Tomlin .05 .02
❑ 570 Andy Van Slyke .10 .05
❑ 571 Gary Varsho .05 .02
❑ 572 Bob Walk .05 .02
❑ 573 John Wehner UER .05 .02
(Actually played for
Carolina in 1991,
not Cards)
❑ 574 Juan Agosto .05 .02
❑ 575 Cris Carpenter .05 .02
❑ 576 Jose DeLeon .05 .02
❑ 577 Rich Gedman .05 .02
❑ 578 Bernard Gilkey .10 .05
❑ 579 Pedro Guerrero .05 .02
❑ 580 Ken Hill .05 .02
❑ 581 Rex Hudler .05 .02
❑ 582 Felix Jose .05 .02
❑ 583 Ray Lankford .20 .09
❑ 584 Omar Olivares .05 .02
❑ 585 Jose Oquendo .05 .02
❑ 586 Tom Pagnozzi .05 .02
❑ 587 Geronimo Pena .05 .02
❑ 588 Mike Perez .05 .02
❑ 589 Gerald Perry .05 .02
❑ 590 Bryn Smith .05 .02
❑ 591 Lee Smith .10 .05
❑ 592 Ozzie Smith .25 .11
❑ 593 Scott Terry .05 .02
❑ 594 Bob Tewksbury .05 .02
❑ 595 Milt Thompson .05 .02
❑ 596 Todd Zeile .05 .02
❑ 597 Larry Andersen .05 .02
❑ 598 Oscar Azocar .05 .02
❑ 599 Andy Benes .05 .02
❑ 600 Ricky Bones .05 .02
❑ 601 Jerald Clark .05 .02
❑ 602 Pat Clements .05 .02
❑ 603 Paul Faries .05 .02
❑ 604 Tony Fernandez .05 .02
❑ 605 Tony Gwynn .40 .18
❑ 606 Greg W. Harris .05 .02
❑ 607 Thomas Howard .05 .02
❑ 608 Bruce Hurst .05 .02
❑ 609 Darrin Jackson .05 .02
❑ 610 Tom Lampkin .05 .02
❑ 611 Craig Lefferts .05 .02
❑ 612 Jim Lewis .05 .02
❑ 613 Mike Maddux .05 .02
❑ 614 Fred McGriff .10 .05
❑ 615 Jose Melendez .05 .02
❑ 616 Jose Mota .05 .02
❑ 617 Dennis Rasmussen .05 .02
❑ 618 Bip Roberts .05 .02
❑ 619 Rich Rodriguez .05 .02
❑ 620 Benito Santiago .05 .02
❑ 621 Craig Shipley .05 .02
❑ 622 Tim Teufel .05 .02
❑ 623 Kevin Ward .05 .02
❑ 624 Ed Whitson .05 .02
❑ 625 Dave Anderson .05 .02
❑ 626 Kevin Bass .05 .02
❑ 627 Rod Beck RC .20 .09
❑ 628 Bud Black .05 .02
❑ 629 Jeff Brantley .05 .02
❑ 630 John Burkett .05 .02
❑ 631 Will Clark .20 .09
❑ 632 Royce Clayton .05 .02
❑ 633 Steve Decker .05 .02
❑ 634 Kelly Downs .05 .02
❑ 635 Mike Felder .05 .02
❑ 636 Scott Garrelts .05 .02
❑ 637 Eric Gunderson .05 .02
❑ 638 Bryan Hickerson RC .05 .02
❑ 639 Darren Lewis .05 .02
❑ 640 Greg Litton .05 .02
❑ 641 Kirt Manwaring .05 .02
❑ 642 Paul McClellan .05 .02
❑ 643 Willie McGee .10 .05
❑ 644 Kevin Mitchell .10 .05
❑ 645 Francisco Oliveras .05 .02
❑ 646 Mike Remlinger .05 .02
❑ 647 Dave Righetti .05 .02
❑ 648 Robby Thompson .05 .02
❑ 649 Jose Uribe .05 .02
❑ 650 Matt Williams .10 .05
❑ 651 Trevor Wilson .05 .02
❑ 652 Tom Goodwin MLP UER .10 .05
(Timed in 3.5;
should be be timed)
❑ 653 Terry Bross MLP .05 .02
❑ 654 Mike Christopher MLP .05 .02
❑ 655 Kenny Lofton MLP .25 .11
❑ 656 Chris Cron MLP .05 .02
❑ 657 Willie Banks MLP .05 .02
❑ 658 Pat Rice MLP .05 .02
❑ 659A Rob Maurer MLP ERR .75 .35
(Name misspelled as
Mauer on card front)
❑ 659B Rob Maurer MLP COR .10 .05
❑ 660 Don Harris MLP .05 .02
❑ 661 Henry Rodriguez MLP .05 .02
❑ 662 Cliff Brantley MLP .05 .02
❑ 663 Mike Linskey MLP UER .05 .02
(220 pounds in data,
200 in text)
❑ 664 Gary DiSarcina MLP .05 .02
❑ 665 Gil Heredia RC .05 .02
❑ 666 Vinny Castilla MLP RC 1.00 .45
❑ 667 Paul Abbott MLP .05 .02
❑ 668 Monty Fariss MLP UER .05 .02
(Called Paul on back)
❑ 669 Jarvis Brown MLP .05 .02
❑ 670 Wayne Kirby MLP RC .05 .02
❑ 671 Scott Brosius MLP RC .25 .11
❑ 672 Bob Hamelin MLP .05 .02
❑ 673 Joel Johnston MLP .05 .02
❑ 674 Tim Spehr MLP .05 .02
❑ 675A Jeff Gardner MLP ERR .75 .35
(P on front;
should be SS)
❑ 675B Jeff Gardner MLP COR
❑ 676 Rico Rossy MLP .05 .02
❑ 677 Roberto Hernandez MLP .05 .02
❑ 678 Ted Wood MLP .05 .02
❑ 679 Cal Eldred MLP .05 .02
❑ 680 Sean Berry MLP .05 .02
❑ 681 Rickey Henderson RS .10 .05
❑ 682 Nolan Ryan RS .50 .09
❑ 683 Dennis Martinez RS .05 .02
❑ 684 Wilson Alvarez RS .05 .02
❑ 685 Joe Carter RS .05 .02
❑ 686 Dave Winfield RS .10 .05
❑ 687 David Cone RS .05 .02
❑ 688 Jose Canseco LL UER .10 .05
(Text on back has 42 stolen
bases in '88; should be 40)
❑ 689 Howard Johnson LL .05 .02
❑ 690 Julio Franco LL .05 .02
❑ 691 Terry Pendleton LL .05 .02
❑ 692 Cecil Fielder LL .05 .02
❑ 693 Scott Erickson LL .05 .02
❑ 694 Tom Glavine LL .10 .05
❑ 695 Dennis Martinez LL .05 .02
❑ 696 Bryan Harvey LL .05 .02
❑ 697 Lee Smith LL .05 .02
❑ 698 Super Siblings .10 .05
Roberto Alomar
Sandy Alomar Jr.
❑ 699 The Indispensables .10 .05
Bobby Bonilla
Will Clark
❑ 700 Teamwork .05 .02
Mark Wohlers
Kent Mercker
Alejandro Pena
❑ 701 Tiger Tandems .25 .11
Stacy Jones
Bo Jackson
Gregg Olson
Frank Thomas
❑ 702 The Ignitors .20 .09
Paul Molitor
Brett Butler
❑ 703 Indispensables II .40 .18
Cal Ripken
Joe Carter
❑ 704 Power Packs .20 .09
Barry Larkin
Kirby Puckett
❑ 705 Today and Tomorrow .10 .05
Mo Vaughn
Cecil Fielder
❑ 706 Teenage Sensations .05 .02
Ramon Martinez
Ozzie Guillen
❑ 707 Designated Hitters .10 .05
Harold Baines
Wade Boggs
❑ 708 Robin Yount PV .10 .05
❑ 709 Ken Griffey Jr. PV UER .60 .25
(Missing quotations on
back; BA has .322, but
was actually .327)
❑ 710 Nolan Ryan PV .50 .18
❑ 711 Cal Ripken PV .40 .18
❑ 712 Frank Thomas PV .20 .09
❑ 713 Dave Justice PV .05 .02
❑ 714 Checklist 1-101 .05 .02
❑ 715 Checklist 102-194 .05 .02
❑ 716 Checklist 195-296 .05 .02
❑ 717 Checklist 297-397 .05 .02
❑ 718 Checklist 398-494 .05 .02
❑ 719 Checklist 495-596 .05 .02
❑ 720A Checklist 597-720 ERR .05 .02
(659 Rob Mauer)
❑ 720B Checklist 597-720 COR .05 .02
(659 Rob Maurer)

## 1992 Fleer Update

| | MINT | NRMT |
|---|---|---|
| COMP.FACT.SET (136) | 160.00 | 70.00 |
| COMPLETE SET (132) | 140.00 | 65.00 |

❑ 1 Todd Frohwirth .25 .11
❑ 2 Alan Mills .25 .11
❑ 3 Rick Sutcliffe .75 .35
❑ 4 John Valentin RC 1.50 .70
❑ 5 Frank Viola .25 .11
❑ 6 Bob Zupcic RC .25 .11
❑ 7 Mike Butcher .25 .11
❑ 8 Chad Curtis RC 1.50 .70
❑ 9 Damion Easley RC 1.50 .70
❑ 10 Tim Salmon 8.00 3.60
❑ 11 Julio Valera .25 .11
❑ 12 George Bell .25 .11
❑ 13 Roberto Hernandez .25 .11
❑ 14 Shawn Jeter RC .25 .11
❑ 15 Thomas Howard .25 .11
❑ 16 Jesse Levis .25 .11
❑ 17 Kenny Lofton 8.00 3.60
❑ 18 Paul Sorrento .25 .11
❑ 19 Rico Brogna .75 .35
❑ 20 John Doherty RC .25 .11
❑ 21 Dan Gladden .25 .11
❑ 22 Buddy Groom .25 .11
❑ 23 Shawn Hare RC .25 .11
❑ 24 John Kiely .25 .11

| | | |
|---|---|---|
| ❑ 25 Kurt Knudsen | .25 | .11 |
| ❑ 26 Gregg Jefferies | .25 | .11 |
| ❑ 27 Wally Joyner | .75 | .35 |
| ❑ 28 Kevin Koslofski | .25 | .11 |
| ❑ 29 Kevin McReynolds | .25 | .11 |
| ❑ 30 Rusty Meacham | .25 | .11 |
| ❑ 31 Keith Miller | .25 | .11 |
| ❑ 32 Hipolito Pichardo RC | .25 | .11 |
| ❑ 33 James Austin | .25 | .11 |
| ❑ 34 Scott Fletcher | .25 | .11 |
| ❑ 35 John Jaha RC | 2.00 | 1.10 |
| ❑ 36 Pat Listach RC | .25 | .11 |
| ❑ 37 Dave Nilsson | .75 | .35 |
| ❑ 38 Kevin Seitzer | .25 | .11 |
| ❑ 39 Tom Edens | .25 | .11 |
| ❑ 40 Pat Mahomes RC | .25 | .11 |
| ❑ 41 John Smiley | .25 | .11 |
| ❑ 42 Charlie Hayes | .25 | .11 |
| ❑ 43 Sam Militello | .25 | .11 |
| ❑ 44 Andy Stankiewicz | .25 | .11 |
| ❑ 45 Danny Tartabull | .25 | .11 |
| ❑ 46 Bob Wickman | .25 | .11 |
| ❑ 47 Jerry Browne | .25 | .11 |
| ❑ 48 Kevin Campbell | .25 | .11 |
| ❑ 49 Vince Horsman | .25 | .11 |
| ❑ 50 Troy Neel RC | .25 | .11 |
| ❑ 51 Ruben Sierra | .25 | .11 |
| ❑ 52 Bruce Walton | .25 | .11 |
| ❑ 53 Willie Wilson | .25 | .11 |
| ❑ 54 Bret Boone | 1.50 | .70 |
| ❑ 55 Dave Fleming | .25 | .11 |
| ❑ 56 Kevin Mitchell | .75 | .35 |
| ❑ 57 Jeff Nelson RC | .25 | .11 |
| ❑ 58 Shane Turner | .25 | .11 |
| ❑ 59 Jose Canseco | 2.50 | 1.35 |
| ❑ 60 Jeff Frye RC | .25 | .11 |
| ❑ 61 Danny Leon | .25 | .11 |
| ❑ 62 Roger Pavlik RC | .25 | .11 |
| ❑ 63 David Cone | .75 | .35 |
| ❑ 64 Pat Hentgen | .25 | .11 |
| ❑ 65 Randy Knorr | .25 | .11 |
| ❑ 66 Jack Morris | .75 | .35 |
| ❑ 67 Dave Winfield | 1.50 | .70 |
| ❑ 68 David Nied RC | .25 | .11 |
| ❑ 69 Otis Nixon | .25 | .11 |
| ❑ 70 Alejandro Pena | .25 | .11 |
| ❑ 71 Jeff Reardon | .75 | .35 |
| ❑ 72 Alex Arias RC | .25 | .11 |
| ❑ 73 Jim Bullinger | .25 | .11 |
| ❑ 74 Mike Morgan | .25 | .11 |
| ❑ 75 Rey Sanchez RC | .25 | .11 |
| ❑ 76 Bob Scanlan | .25 | .11 |
| ❑ 77 Sammy Sosa | 4.00 | 1.80 |
| ❑ 78 Scott Bankhead | .25 | .11 |
| ❑ 79 Tim Belcher | .25 | .11 |
| ❑ 80 Steve Foster | .25 | .11 |
| ❑ 81 Willie Greene | .25 | .11 |
| ❑ 82 Bip Roberts | .25 | .11 |
| ❑ 83 Scott Ruskin | .25 | .11 |
| ❑ 84 Greg Swindell | .25 | .11 |
| ❑ 85 Juan Guerrero | .25 | .11 |
| ❑ 86 Butch Henry | .25 | .11 |
| ❑ 87 Doug Jones | .25 | .11 |
| ❑ 88 Brian Williams RC | .25 | .11 |
| ❑ 89 Tom Candiotti | .25 | .11 |
| ❑ 90 Eric Davis | .75 | .35 |
| ❑ 91 Carlos Hernandez | .25 | .11 |
| ❑ 92 Mike Piazza RC | 100.00 | 45.00 |
| ❑ 93 Mike Sharperson | .25 | .11 |
| ❑ 94 Eric Young RC | 1.50 | .70 |
| ❑ 95 Moises Alou | 2.00 | 1.10 |
| ❑ 96 Greg Colbrunn | .25 | .11 |
| ❑ 97 Wil Cordero | .25 | .11 |
| ❑ 98 Ken Hill | .25 | .11 |
| ❑ 99 John Vander Wal RC | .25 | .11 |
| ❑ 100 John Wetteland | .75 | .35 |
| ❑ 101 Bobby Bonilla | .75 | .35 |
| ❑ 102 Eric Hillman RC | .25 | .11 |
| ❑ 103 Pat Howell | .25 | .11 |
| ❑ 104 Jeff Kent RC | 20.00 | 9.00 |
| ❑ 105 Dick Schofield | .25 | .11 |
| ❑ 106 Ryan Thompson RC | .25 | .11 |
| ❑ 107 Chico Walker | .25 | .11 |
| ❑ 108 Juan Bell | .25 | .11 |
| ❑ 109 Mariano Duncan | .25 | .11 |
| ❑ 110 Jeff Grotewold | .25 | .11 |
| ❑ 111 Ben Rivera | .25 | .11 |
| ❑ 112 Curt Schilling | 2.00 | .90 |
| ❑ 113 Victor Cole | .25 | .11 |
| ❑ 114 Al Martin RC | 1.50 | .70 |
| ❑ 115 Roger Mason | .25 | .11 |
| ❑ 116 Blas Minor | .25 | .11 |
| ❑ 117 Tim Wakefield RC | 1.50 | .70 |
| ❑ 118 Mark Clark RC | .25 | .11 |
| ❑ 119 Rheal Cormier | .25 | .11 |
| ❑ 120 Donovan Osborne | .25 | .11 |
| ❑ 121 Todd Worrell | .25 | .11 |
| ❑ 122 Jeremy Hernandez RC | .25 | .11 |
| ❑ 123 Randy Myers | .75 | .35 |
| ❑ 124 Frank Seminara RC | .25 | .11 |
| ❑ 125 Gary Sheffield | 1.50 | .70 |
| ❑ 126 Dan Walters | .25 | .11 |
| ❑ 127 Steve Hosey | .25 | .11 |
| ❑ 128 Mike Jackson | .25 | .11 |
| ❑ 129 Jim Pena | .25 | .11 |
| ❑ 130 Cory Snyder | .25 | .11 |
| ❑ 131 Bill Swift | .25 | .11 |
| ❑ 132 Checklist U1-U132 | .25 | .11 |

## 1993 Fleer

| | MINT | NRMT |
|---|---|---|
| COMPLETE SET (720) | 40.00 | 18.00 |
| COMPLETE SERIES 1 (360) | 20.00 | 9.00 |
| COMPLETE SERIES 2 (360) | 20.00 | 9.00 |
| COMMON CARD (1-720) | .10 | .05 |

| | | |
|---|---|---|
| ❑ 1 Steve Avery | .10 | .05 |
| ❑ 2 Sid Bream | .10 | .05 |
| ❑ 3 Ron Gant | .20 | .09 |
| ❑ 4 Tom Glavine | .20 | .09 |
| ❑ 5 Brian Hunter | .10 | .05 |
| ❑ 6 Ryan Klesko | .40 | .18 |
| ❑ 7 Charlie Leibrandt | .10 | .05 |
| ❑ 8 Kent Mercker | .10 | .05 |
| ❑ 9 David Nied | .10 | .05 |
| ❑ 10 Otis Nixon | .10 | .05 |
| ❑ 11 Greg Olson | .10 | .05 |
| ❑ 12 Terry Pendleton | .20 | .09 |
| ❑ 13 Deion Sanders | .20 | .09 |
| ❑ 14 John Smoltz | .20 | .09 |
| ❑ 15 Mike Stanton | .10 | .05 |
| ❑ 16 Mark Wohlers | .10 | .05 |
| ❑ 17 Paul Assenmacher | .10 | .05 |
| ❑ 18 Steve Buechele | .10 | .05 |
| ❑ 19 Shawon Dunston | .10 | .05 |
| ❑ 20 Mark Grace | .40 | .18 |
| ❑ 21 Derrick May | .10 | .05 |
| ❑ 22 Chuck McElroy | .10 | .05 |
| ❑ 23 Mike Morgan | .10 | .05 |
| ❑ 24 Rey Sanchez | .10 | .05 |
| ❑ 25 Ryne Sandberg | .50 | .23 |
| ❑ 26 Bob Scanlan | .10 | .05 |
| ❑ 27 Sammy Sosa | .75 | .35 |
| ❑ 28 Rick Wilkins | .10 | .05 |
| ❑ 29 Bobby Ayala RC | .10 | .05 |
| ❑ 30 Tim Belcher | .10 | .05 |
| ❑ 31 Jeff Branson | .10 | .05 |
| ❑ 32 Norm Charlton | .10 | .05 |
| ❑ 33 Steve Foster | .10 | .05 |
| ❑ 34 Willie Greene | .10 | .05 |
| ❑ 35 Chris Hammond | .10 | .05 |
| ❑ 36 Milt Hill | .10 | .05 |
| ❑ 37 Hal Morris | .10 | .05 |
| ❑ 38 Joe Oliver | .10 | .05 |
| ❑ 39 Paul O'Neill | .20 | .09 |
| ❑ 40 Tim Pugh RC | .10 | .05 |
| ❑ 41 Jose Rijo | .10 | .05 |
| ❑ 42 Bip Roberts | .10 | .05 |
| ❑ 43 Chris Sabo | .10 | .05 |
| ❑ 44 Reggie Sanders | .10 | .05 |
| ❑ 45 Eric Anthony | .10 | .05 |
| ❑ 46 Jeff Bagwell | .50 | .23 |
| ❑ 47 Craig Biggio | .20 | .09 |
| ❑ 48 Joe Boever | .10 | .05 |
| ❑ 49 Casey Candaele | .10 | .05 |
| ❑ 50 Steve Finley | .20 | .09 |
| ❑ 51 Luis Gonzalez | .20 | .09 |
| ❑ 52 Pete Harnisch | .10 | .05 |
| ❑ 53 Xavier Hernandez | .10 | .05 |
| ❑ 54 Doug Jones | .10 | .05 |
| ❑ 55 Eddie Taubensee | .10 | .05 |
| ❑ 56 Brian Williams | .10 | .05 |
| ❑ 57 Pedro Astacio | .20 | .09 |
| ❑ 58 Todd Benzinger | .10 | .05 |
| ❑ 59 Brett Butler | .20 | .09 |
| ❑ 60 Tom Candiotti | .10 | .05 |
| ❑ 61 Lenny Harris | .10 | .05 |
| ❑ 62 Carlos Hernandez | .10 | .05 |
| ❑ 63 Orel Hershiser | .20 | .09 |
| ❑ 64 Eric Karros | .20 | .09 |
| ❑ 65 Ramon Martinez | .10 | .05 |
| ❑ 66 Jose Offerman | .10 | .05 |
| ❑ 67 Mike Scioscia | .10 | .05 |
| ❑ 68 Mike Sharperson | .10 | .05 |
| ❑ 69 Eric Young | .10 | .05 |
| ❑ 70 Moises Alou | .20 | .09 |
| ❑ 71 Ivan Calderon | .10 | .05 |
| ❑ 72 Archi Cianfrocco | .10 | .05 |
| ❑ 73 Wil Cordero | .10 | .05 |
| ❑ 74 Delino DeShields | .20 | .09 |
| ❑ 75 Mark Gardner | .10 | .05 |
| ❑ 76 Ken Hill | .10 | .05 |
| ❑ 77 Tim Laker RC | .10 | .05 |
| ❑ 78 Chris Nabholz | .10 | .05 |
| ❑ 79 Mel Rojas | .10 | .05 |
| ❑ 80 John Vander Wal UER (Misspelled Vander Wall in letters on back) | .10 | .05 |
| ❑ 81 Larry Walker | .20 | .09 |
| ❑ 82 Tim Wallach | .10 | .05 |
| ❑ 83 John Wetteland | .20 | .09 |
| ❑ 84 Bobby Bonilla | .20 | .09 |
| ❑ 85 Daryl Boston | .10 | .05 |
| ❑ 86 Sid Fernandez | .10 | .05 |
| ❑ 87 Eric Hillman | .10 | .05 |
| ❑ 88 Todd Hundley | .10 | .05 |
| ❑ 89 Howard Johnson | .10 | .05 |
| ❑ 90 Jeff Kent | .40 | .18 |
| ❑ 91 Eddie Murray | .40 | .18 |
| ❑ 92 Bill Pecota | .10 | .05 |
| ❑ 93 Bret Saberhagen | .20 | .09 |
| ❑ 94 Dick Schofield | .10 | .05 |
| ❑ 95 Pete Schourek | .10 | .05 |
| ❑ 96 Anthony Young | .10 | .05 |
| ❑ 97 Ruben Amaro | .10 | .05 |
| ❑ 98 Juan Bell | .10 | .05 |
| ❑ 99 Wes Chamberlain | .10 | .05 |
| ❑ 100 Darren Daulton | .20 | .09 |
| ❑ 101 Mariano Duncan | .10 | .05 |
| ❑ 102 Mike Hartley | .10 | .05 |
| ❑ 103 Ricky Jordan | .10 | .05 |
| ❑ 104 John Kruk | .20 | .09 |
| ❑ 105 Mickey Morandini | .10 | .05 |
| ❑ 106 Terry Mulholland | .10 | .05 |
| ❑ 107 Ben Rivera | .10 | .05 |
| ❑ 108 Curt Schilling | .20 | .09 |
| ❑ 109 Keith Shepherd RC | .10 | .05 |
| ❑ 110 Stan Belinda | .10 | .05 |
| ❑ 111 Jay Bell | .20 | .09 |
| ❑ 112 Barry Bonds | .60 | .25 |
| ❑ 113 Jeff King | .10 | .05 |
| ❑ 114 Mike LaValliere | .10 | .05 |
| ❑ 115 Jose Lind | .10 | .05 |
| ❑ 116 Roger Mason | .10 | .05 |
| ❑ 117 Orlando Merced | .10 | .05 |
| ❑ 118 Bob Patterson | .10 | .05 |
| ❑ 119 Don Slaught | .10 | .05 |
| ❑ 120 Zane Smith | .10 | .05 |
| ❑ 121 Randy Tomlin | .10 | .05 |

| | | | |
|---|---|---|---|
| ❑ 122 | Andy Van Slyke | .20 | .09 |
| ❑ 123 | Tim Wakefield | .10 | .05 |
| ❑ 124 | Rheal Cormier | .10 | .05 |
| ❑ 125 | Bernard Gilkey | .10 | .05 |
| ❑ 126 | Felix Jose | .10 | .05 |
| ❑ 127 | Ray Lankford | .20 | .09 |
| ❑ 128 | Bob McClure | .10 | .05 |
| ❑ 129 | Donovan Osborne | .10 | .05 |
| ❑ 130 | Tom Pagnozzi | .10 | .05 |
| ❑ 131 | Geronimo Pena | .10 | .05 |
| ❑ 132 | Mike Perez | .10 | .05 |
| ❑ 133 | Lee Smith | .20 | .09 |
| ❑ 134 | Bob Tewksbury | .10 | .05 |
| ❑ 135 | Todd Worrell | .10 | .05 |
| ❑ 136 | Todd Zeile | .10 | .05 |
| ❑ 137 | Jerald Clark | .10 | .05 |
| ❑ 138 | Tony Gwynn | .75 | .35 |
| ❑ 139 | Greg W. Harris | .10 | .05 |
| ❑ 140 | Jeremy Hernandez | .10 | .05 |
| ❑ 141 | Darrin Jackson | .10 | .05 |
| ❑ 142 | Mike Maddux | .10 | .05 |
| ❑ 143 | Fred McGriff | .20 | .09 |
| ❑ 144 | Jose Melendez | .10 | .05 |
| ❑ 145 | Rich Rodriguez | .10 | .05 |
| ❑ 146 | Frank Seminara | .10 | .05 |
| ❑ 147 | Gary Sheffield | .40 | .18 |
| ❑ 148 | Kurt Stillwell | .10 | .05 |
| ❑ 149 | Dan Walters | .10 | .05 |
| ❑ 150 | Rod Beck | .10 | .05 |
| ❑ 151 | Bud Black | .10 | .05 |
| ❑ 152 | Jeff Brantley | .10 | .05 |
| ❑ 153 | John Burkett | .10 | .05 |
| ❑ 154 | Will Clark | .40 | .18 |
| ❑ 155 | Royce Clayton | .10 | .05 |
| ❑ 156 | Mike Jackson | .10 | .05 |
| ❑ 157 | Darren Lewis | .10 | .05 |
| ❑ 158 | Kirt Manwaring | .10 | .05 |
| ❑ 159 | Willie McGee | .20 | .09 |
| ❑ 160 | Cory Snyder | .10 | .05 |
| ❑ 161 | Bill Swift | .10 | .05 |
| ❑ 162 | Trevor Wilson | .10 | .05 |
| ❑ 163 | Brady Anderson | .20 | .09 |
| ❑ 164 | Glenn Davis | .10 | .05 |
| ❑ 165 | Mike Devereaux | .10 | .05 |
| ❑ 166 | Todd Frohwirth | .10 | .05 |
| ❑ 167 | Leo Gomez | .10 | .05 |
| ❑ 168 | Chris Hoiles | .10 | .05 |
| ❑ 169 | Ben McDonald | .10 | .05 |
| ❑ 170 | Randy Milligan | .10 | .05 |
| ❑ 171 | Alan Mills | .10 | .05 |
| ❑ 172 | Mike Mussina | .40 | .18 |
| ❑ 173 | Gregg Olson | .10 | .05 |
| ❑ 174 | Arthur Rhodes | .10 | .05 |
| ❑ 175 | David Segui | .10 | .05 |
| ❑ 176 | Ellis Burks | .20 | .09 |
| ❑ 177 | Roger Clemens | .75 | .35 |
| ❑ 178 | Scott Cooper | .10 | .05 |
| ❑ 179 | Danny Darwin | .10 | .05 |
| ❑ 180 | Tony Fossas | .10 | .05 |
| ❑ 181 | Paul Quantrill | .10 | .05 |
| ❑ 182 | Jody Reed | .10 | .05 |
| ❑ 183 | John Valentin | .10 | .05 |
| ❑ 184 | Mo Vaughn | .20 | .09 |
| ❑ 185 | Frank Viola | .10 | .05 |
| ❑ 186 | Bob Zupcic | .10 | .05 |
| ❑ 187 | Jim Abbott | .20 | .09 |
| ❑ 188 | Gary DiSarcina | .10 | .05 |
| ❑ 189 | Damion Easley | .10 | .05 |
| ❑ 190 | Junior Felix | .10 | .05 |
| ❑ 191 | Chuck Finley | .20 | .09 |
| ❑ 192 | Joe Grahe | .10 | .05 |
| ❑ 193 | Bryan Harvey | .10 | .05 |
| ❑ 194 | Mark Langston | .10 | .05 |
| ❑ 195 | John Orton | .10 | .05 |
| ❑ 196 | Luis Polonia | .10 | .05 |
| ❑ 197 | Tim Salmon | .20 | .09 |
| ❑ 198 | Luis Sojo | .10 | .05 |
| ❑ 199 | Wilson Alvarez | .10 | .05 |
| ❑ 200 | George Bell | .10 | .05 |
| ❑ 201 | Alex Fernandez | .20 | .09 |
| ❑ 202 | Craig Grebeck | .10 | .05 |
| ❑ 203 | Ozzie Guillen | .10 | .05 |
| ❑ 204 | Lance Johnson | .10 | .05 |
| ❑ 205 | Ron Karkovice | .10 | .05 |
| ❑ 206 | Kirk McCaskill | .10 | .05 |
| ❑ 207 | Jack McDowell | .10 | .05 |
| ❑ 208 | Scott Radinsky | .10 | .05 |
| ❑ 209 | Tim Raines | .20 | .09 |
| ❑ 210 | Frank Thomas | .75 | .35 |
| ❑ 211 | Robin Ventura | .20 | .09 |
| ❑ 212 | Sandy Alomar Jr. | .20 | .09 |
| ❑ 213 | Carlos Baerga | .10 | .05 |
| ❑ 214 | Dennis Cook | .10 | .05 |
| ❑ 215 | Thomas Howard | .10 | .05 |
| ❑ 216 | Mark Lewis | .10 | .05 |
| ❑ 217 | Derek Lilliquist | .10 | .05 |
| ❑ 218 | Kenny Lofton | .20 | .09 |
| ❑ 219 | Charles Nagy | .10 | .05 |
| ❑ 220 | Steve Olin | .10 | .05 |
| ❑ 221 | Paul Sorrento | .10 | .05 |
| ❑ 222 | Jim Thome | .20 | .09 |
| ❑ 223 | Mark Whiten | .10 | .05 |
| ❑ 224 | Milt Cuyler | .10 | .05 |
| ❑ 225 | Rob Deer | .10 | .05 |
| ❑ 226 | John Doherty | .10 | .05 |
| ❑ 227 | Cecil Fielder | .20 | .09 |
| ❑ 228 | Travis Fryman | .20 | .09 |
| ❑ 229 | Mike Henneman | .10 | .05 |
| ❑ 230 | John Kiely UER (Card has batting stats of Pat Kelly) | .10 | .05 |
| ❑ 231 | Kurt Knudsen | .10 | .05 |
| ❑ 232 | Scott Livingstone | .10 | .05 |
| ❑ 233 | Tony Phillips | .10 | .05 |
| ❑ 234 | Mickey Tettleton | .10 | .05 |
| ❑ 235 | Kevin Appier | .20 | .09 |
| ❑ 236 | George Brett | .75 | .35 |
| ❑ 237 | Tom Gordon | .10 | .05 |
| ❑ 238 | Gregg Jefferies | .10 | .05 |
| ❑ 239 | Wally Joyner | .20 | .09 |
| ❑ 240 | Kevin Koslofski | .10 | .05 |
| ❑ 241 | Mike Macfarlane | .10 | .05 |
| ❑ 242 | Brian McRae | .10 | .05 |
| ❑ 243 | Rusty Meacham | .10 | .05 |
| ❑ 244 | Keith Miller | .10 | .05 |
| ❑ 245 | Jeff Montgomery | .20 | .09 |
| ❑ 246 | Hipolito Pichardo | .10 | .05 |
| ❑ 247 | Ricky Bones | .10 | .05 |
| ❑ 248 | Cal Eldred | .10 | .05 |
| ❑ 249 | Mike Fetters | .10 | .05 |
| ❑ 250 | Darryl Hamilton | .10 | .05 |
| ❑ 251 | Doug Henry | .10 | .05 |
| ❑ 252 | John Jaha | .10 | .05 |
| ❑ 253 | Pat Listach | .10 | .05 |
| ❑ 254 | Paul Molitor | .40 | .18 |
| ❑ 255 | Jaime Navarro | .10 | .05 |
| ❑ 256 | Kevin Seitzer | .10 | .05 |
| ❑ 257 | B.J. Surhoff | .20 | .09 |
| ❑ 258 | Greg Vaughn | .20 | .09 |
| ❑ 259 | Bill Wegman | .10 | .05 |
| ❑ 260 | Robin Yount | .20 | .09 |
| ❑ 261 | Rick Aguilera | .10 | .05 |
| ❑ 262 | Chili Davis | .20 | .09 |
| ❑ 263 | Scott Erickson | .10 | .05 |
| ❑ 264 | Greg Gagne | .10 | .05 |
| ❑ 265 | Mark Guthrie | .10 | .05 |
| ❑ 266 | Brian Harper | .10 | .05 |
| ❑ 267 | Kent Hrbek | .20 | .09 |
| ❑ 268 | Terry Jorgensen | .10 | .05 |
| ❑ 269 | Gene Larkin | .10 | .05 |
| ❑ 270 | Scott Leius | .10 | .05 |
| ❑ 271 | Pat Mahomes | .10 | .05 |
| ❑ 272 | Pedro Munoz | .10 | .05 |
| ❑ 273 | Kirby Puckett | 1.00 | .45 |
| ❑ 274 | Kevin Tapani | .10 | .05 |
| ❑ 275 | Carl Willis | .10 | .05 |
| ❑ 276 | Steve Farr | .10 | .05 |
| ❑ 277 | John Habyan | .10 | .05 |
| ❑ 278 | Mel Hall | .10 | .05 |
| ❑ 279 | Charlie Hayes | .10 | .05 |
| ❑ 280 | Pat Kelly | .10 | .05 |
| ❑ 281 | Don Mattingly | 1.00 | .45 |
| ❑ 282 | Sam Militello | .10 | .05 |
| ❑ 283 | Matt Nokes | .10 | .05 |
| ❑ 284 | Melido Perez | .10 | .05 |
| ❑ 285 | Andy Stankiewicz | .10 | .05 |
| ❑ 286 | Danny Tartabull | .10 | .05 |
| ❑ 287 | Randy Velarde | .10 | .05 |
| ❑ 288 | Bob Wickman | .10 | .05 |
| ❑ 289 | Bernie Williams | .40 | .18 |
| ❑ 290 | Lance Blankenship | .10 | .05 |
| ❑ 291 | Mike Bordick | .10 | .05 |
| ❑ 292 | Jerry Browne | .10 | .05 |
| ❑ 293 | Dennis Eckersley | .20 | .09 |
| ❑ 294 | Rickey Henderson | .50 | .23 |
| ❑ 295 | Vince Horsman | .10 | .05 |
| ❑ 296 | Mark McGwire | 1.50 | .70 |
| ❑ 297 | Jeff Parrett | .10 | .05 |
| ❑ 298 | Ruben Sierra | .10 | .05 |
| ❑ 299 | Terry Steinbach | .10 | .05 |
| ❑ 300 | Walt Weiss | .10 | .05 |
| ❑ 301 | Bob Welch | .10 | .05 |
| ❑ 302 | Willie Wilson | .10 | .05 |
| ❑ 303 | Bobby Witt | .10 | .05 |
| ❑ 304 | Bret Boone | .20 | .09 |
| ❑ 305 | Jay Buhner | .20 | .09 |
| ❑ 306 | Dave Fleming | .10 | .05 |
| ❑ 307 | Ken Griffey Jr. | 1.50 | .70 |
| ❑ 308 | Erik Hanson | .10 | .05 |
| ❑ 309 | Edgar Martinez | .20 | .09 |
| ❑ 310 | Tino Martinez | .20 | .09 |
| ❑ 311 | Jeff Nelson | .10 | .05 |
| ❑ 312 | Dennis Powell | .10 | .05 |
| ❑ 313 | Mike Schooler | .10 | .05 |
| ❑ 314 | Russ Swan | .10 | .05 |
| ❑ 315 | Dave Valle | .10 | .05 |
| ❑ 316 | Omar Vizquel | .20 | .09 |
| ❑ 317 | Kevin Brown | .20 | .09 |
| ❑ 318 | Todd Burns | .10 | .05 |
| ❑ 319 | Jose Canseco | .50 | .23 |
| ❑ 320 | Julio Franco | .10 | .05 |
| ❑ 321 | Jeff Frye | .10 | .05 |
| ❑ 322 | Juan Gonzalez | .40 | .18 |
| ❑ 323 | Jose Guzman | .10 | .05 |
| ❑ 324 | Jeff Huson | .10 | .05 |
| ❑ 325 | Dean Palmer | .20 | .09 |
| ❑ 326 | Kevin Reimer | .10 | .05 |
| ❑ 327 | Ivan Rodriguez | .50 | .23 |
| ❑ 328 | Kenny Rogers | .10 | .05 |
| ❑ 329 | Dan Smith | .10 | .05 |
| ❑ 330 | Roberto Alomar | .40 | .18 |
| ❑ 331 | Derek Bell | .20 | .09 |
| ❑ 332 | Pat Borders | .10 | .05 |
| ❑ 333 | Joe Carter | .20 | .09 |
| ❑ 334 | Kelly Gruber | .10 | .05 |
| ❑ 335 | Tom Henke | .10 | .05 |
| ❑ 336 | Jimmy Key | .20 | .09 |
| ❑ 337 | Manuel Lee | .10 | .05 |
| ❑ 338 | Candy Maldonado | .10 | .05 |
| ❑ 339 | John Olerud | .20 | .09 |
| ❑ 340 | Todd Stottlemyre | .10 | .05 |
| ❑ 341 | Duane Ward | .10 | .05 |
| ❑ 342 | Devon White | .10 | .05 |
| ❑ 343 | Dave Winfield | .40 | .18 |
| ❑ 344 | Edgar Martinez LL | .20 | .09 |
| ❑ 345 | Cecil Fielder LL | .10 | .05 |
| ❑ 346 | Kenny Lofton LL | .10 | .05 |
| ❑ 347 | Jack Morris LL | .10 | .05 |
| ❑ 348 | Roger Clemens LL | .40 | .18 |
| ❑ 349 | Fred McGriff RT | .20 | .09 |
| ❑ 350 | Barry Bonds RT | .20 | .09 |
| ❑ 351 | Gary Sheffield RT | .20 | .09 |
| ❑ 352 | Darren Daulton RT | .10 | .05 |
| ❑ 353 | Dave Hollins RT | .10 | .05 |
| ❑ 354 | Brothers in Blue<br>Pedro Martinez<br>Ramon Martinez | .10 | .05 |
| ❑ 355 | Power Packs<br>Ivan Rodriguez<br>Kirby Puckett | .20 | .09 |
| ❑ 356 | Triple Threats<br>Ryne Sandberg<br>Gary Sheffield | .15 | .07 |
| ❑ 357 | Infield Trifecta<br>Roberto Alomar<br>Chuck Knoblauch<br>Carlos Baerga | .20 | .09 |
| ❑ 358 | Checklist 1-120 | .10 | .05 |
| ❑ 359 | Checklist 121-240 | .10 | .05 |
| ❑ 360 | Checklist 241-360 | .10 | .05 |
| ❑ 361 | Rafael Belliard | .10 | .05 |
| ❑ 362 | Damon Berryhill | .10 | .05 |
| ❑ 363 | Mike Bielecki | .10 | .05 |
| ❑ 364 | Jeff Blauser | .10 | .05 |
| ❑ 365 | Francisco Cabrera | .10 | .05 |
| ❑ 366 | Marvin Freeman | .10 | .05 |
| ❑ 367 | David Justice | .20 | .09 |
| ❑ 368 | Mark Lemke | .10 | .05 |

| | No. | Player | | |
|---|---|---|---|---|
| ❑ | 369 | Alejandro Pena | .10 | .05 |
| ❑ | 370 | Jeff Reardon | .20 | .09 |
| ❑ | 371 | Lonnie Smith | .10 | .05 |
| ❑ | 372 | Pete Smith | .10 | .05 |
| ❑ | 373 | Shawn Boskie | .10 | .05 |
| ❑ | 374 | Jim Bullinger | .10 | .05 |
| ❑ | 375 | Frank Castillo | .10 | .05 |
| ❑ | 376 | Doug Dascenzo | .10 | .05 |
| ❑ | 377 | Andre Dawson | .20 | .09 |
| ❑ | 378 | Mike Harkey | .10 | .05 |
| ❑ | 379 | Greg Hibbard | .10 | .05 |
| ❑ | 380 | Greg Maddux | 1.00 | .45 |
| ❑ | 381 | Ken Patterson | .10 | .05 |
| ❑ | 382 | Jeff D. Robinson | .10 | .05 |
| ❑ | 383 | Luis Salazar | .10 | .05 |
| ❑ | 384 | Dwight Smith | .10 | .05 |
| ❑ | 385 | Jose Vizcaino | .10 | .05 |
| ❑ | 386 | Scott Bankhead | .10 | .05 |
| ❑ | 387 | Tom Browning | .10 | .05 |
| ❑ | 388 | Darnell Coles | .10 | .05 |
| ❑ | 389 | Rob Dibble | .10 | .05 |
| ❑ | 390 | Bill Doran | .10 | .05 |
| ❑ | 391 | Dwayne Henry | .10 | .05 |
| ❑ | 392 | Cesar Hernandez | .10 | .05 |
| ❑ | 393 | Roberto Kelly | .10 | .05 |
| ❑ | 394 | Barry Larkin | .40 | .18 |
| ❑ | 395 | Dave Martinez | .10 | .05 |
| ❑ | 396 | Kevin Mitchell | .20 | .09 |
| ❑ | 397 | Jeff Reed | .10 | .05 |
| ❑ | 398 | Scott Ruskin | .10 | .05 |
| ❑ | 399 | Greg Swindell | .10 | .05 |
| ❑ | 400 | Dan Wilson | .20 | .09 |
| ❑ | 401 | Andy Ashby | .20 | .09 |
| ❑ | 402 | Freddie Benavides | .10 | .05 |
| ❑ | 403 | Dante Bichette | .20 | .09 |
| ❑ | 404 | Willie Blair | .10 | .05 |
| ❑ | 405 | Denis Boucher | .10 | .05 |
| ❑ | 406 | Vinny Castilla | .50 | .23 |
| ❑ | 407 | Braulio Castillo | .10 | .05 |
| ❑ | 408 | Alex Cole | .10 | .05 |
| ❑ | 409 | Andres Galarraga | .20 | .09 |
| ❑ | 410 | Joe Girardi | .20 | .09 |
| ❑ | 411 | Butch Henry | .10 | .05 |
| ❑ | 412 | Darren Holmes | .10 | .05 |
| ❑ | 413 | Calvin Jones | .10 | .05 |
| ❑ | 414 | Steve Reed RC | .10 | .05 |
| ❑ | 415 | Kevin Ritz | .10 | .05 |
| ❑ | 416 | Jim Tatum RC | .10 | .05 |
| ❑ | 417 | Jack Armstrong | .10 | .05 |
| ❑ | 418 | Bret Barberie | .10 | .05 |
| ❑ | 419 | Ryan Bowen | .10 | .05 |
| ❑ | 420 | Cris Carpenter | .10 | .05 |
| ❑ | 421 | Chuck Carr | .10 | .05 |
| ❑ | 422 | Scott Chiamparino | .10 | .05 |
| ❑ | 423 | Jeff Conine | .10 | .05 |
| ❑ | 424 | Jim Corsi | .10 | .05 |
| ❑ | 425 | Steve Decker | .10 | .05 |
| ❑ | 426 | Chris Donnels | .10 | .05 |
| ❑ | 427 | Monty Fariss | .10 | .05 |
| ❑ | 428 | Bob Natal | .10 | .05 |
| ❑ | 429 | Pat Rapp | .10 | .05 |
| ❑ | 430 | Dave Weathers | .10 | .05 |
| ❑ | 431 | Nigel Wilson | .10 | .05 |
| ❑ | 432 | Ken Caminiti | .20 | .09 |
| ❑ | 433 | Andujar Cedeno | .10 | .05 |
| ❑ | 434 | Tom Edens | .10 | .05 |
| ❑ | 435 | Juan Guerrero | .10 | .05 |
| ❑ | 436 | Pete Incaviglia | .10 | .05 |
| ❑ | 437 | Jimmy Jones | .10 | .05 |
| ❑ | 438 | Darryl Kile | .20 | .09 |
| ❑ | 439 | Rob Murphy | .10 | .05 |
| ❑ | 440 | Al Osuna | .10 | .05 |
| ❑ | 441 | Mark Portugal | .10 | .05 |
| ❑ | 442 | Scott Servais | .10 | .05 |
| ❑ | 443 | John Candelaria | .10 | .05 |
| ❑ | 444 | Tim Crews | .10 | .05 |
| ❑ | 445 | Eric Davis | .20 | .09 |
| ❑ | 446 | Tom Goodwin | .10 | .05 |
| ❑ | 447 | Jim Gott | .10 | .05 |
| ❑ | 448 | Kevin Gross | .10 | .05 |
| ❑ | 449 | Dave Hansen | .10 | .05 |
| ❑ | 450 | Jay Howell | .10 | .05 |
| ❑ | 451 | Roger McDowell | .10 | .05 |
| ❑ | 452 | Bob Ojeda | .10 | .05 |
| ❑ | 453 | Henry Rodriguez | .10 | .05 |
| ❑ | 454 | Darryl Strawberry | .20 | .09 |
| ❑ | 455 | Mitch Webster | .10 | .05 |
| ❑ | 456 | Steve Wilson | .10 | .05 |
| ❑ | 457 | Brian Barnes | .10 | .05 |
| ❑ | 458 | Sean Berry | .10 | .05 |
| ❑ | 459 | Jeff Fassero | .10 | .05 |
| ❑ | 460 | Darrin Fletcher | .10 | .05 |
| ❑ | 461 | Marquis Grissom | .10 | .05 |
| ❑ | 462 | Dennis Martinez | .20 | .09 |
| ❑ | 463 | Spike Owen | .10 | .05 |
| ❑ | 464 | Matt Stairs | .10 | .05 |
| ❑ | 465 | Sergio Valdez | .10 | .05 |
| ❑ | 466 | Kevin Bass | .10 | .05 |
| ❑ | 467 | Vince Coleman | .10 | .05 |
| ❑ | 468 | Mark Dewey | .10 | .05 |
| ❑ | 469 | Kevin Elster | .10 | .05 |
| ❑ | 470 | Tony Fernandez | .10 | .05 |
| ❑ | 471 | John Franco | .20 | .09 |
| ❑ | 472 | Dave Gallagher | .10 | .05 |
| ❑ | 473 | Paul Gibson | .10 | .05 |
| ❑ | 474 | Dwight Gooden | .20 | .09 |
| ❑ | 475 | Lee Guetterman | .10 | .05 |
| ❑ | 476 | Jeff Innis | .10 | .05 |
| ❑ | 477 | Dave Magadan | .10 | .05 |
| ❑ | 478 | Charlie O'Brien | .10 | .05 |
| ❑ | 479 | Willie Randolph | .20 | .09 |
| ❑ | 480 | Mackey Sasser | .10 | .05 |
| ❑ | 481 | Ryan Thompson | .10 | .05 |
| ❑ | 482 | Chico Walker | .10 | .05 |
| ❑ | 483 | Kyle Abbott | .10 | .05 |
| ❑ | 484 | Bob Ayrault | .10 | .05 |
| ❑ | 485 | Kim Batiste | .10 | .05 |
| ❑ | 486 | Cliff Brantley | .10 | .05 |
| ❑ | 487 | Jose DeLeon | .10 | .05 |
| ❑ | 488 | Len Dykstra | .20 | .09 |
| ❑ | 489 | Tommy Greene | .10 | .05 |
| ❑ | 490 | Jeff Grotewold | .10 | .05 |
| ❑ | 491 | Dave Hollins | .10 | .05 |
| ❑ | 492 | Danny Jackson | .10 | .05 |
| ❑ | 493 | Stan Javier | .10 | .05 |
| ❑ | 494 | Tom Marsh | .10 | .05 |
| ❑ | 495 | Greg Mathews | .10 | .05 |
| ❑ | 496 | Dale Murphy | .20 | .09 |
| ❑ | 497 | Todd Pratt RC | .25 | .11 |
| ❑ | 498 | Mitch Williams | .10 | .05 |
| ❑ | 499 | Danny Cox | .10 | .05 |
| ❑ | 500 | Doug Drabek | .10 | .05 |
| ❑ | 501 | Carlos Garcia | .10 | .05 |
| ❑ | 502 | Lloyd McClendon | .10 | .05 |
| ❑ | 503 | Denny Neagle | .20 | .09 |
| ❑ | 504 | Gary Redus | .10 | .05 |
| ❑ | 505 | Bob Walk | .10 | .05 |
| ❑ | 506 | John Wehner | .10 | .05 |
| ❑ | 507 | Luis Alicea | .10 | .05 |
| ❑ | 508 | Mark Clark | .10 | .05 |
| ❑ | 509 | Pedro Guerrero | .10 | .05 |
| ❑ | 510 | Rex Hudler | .10 | .05 |
| ❑ | 511 | Brian Jordan | .20 | .09 |
| ❑ | 512 | Omar Olivares | .10 | .05 |
| ❑ | 513 | Jose Oquendo | .10 | .05 |
| ❑ | 514 | Gerald Perry | .10 | .05 |
| ❑ | 515 | Bryn Smith | .10 | .05 |
| ❑ | 516 | Craig Wilson | .10 | .05 |
| ❑ | 517 | Tracy Woodson | .10 | .05 |
| ❑ | 518 | Larry Andersen | .10 | .05 |
| ❑ | 519 | Andy Benes | .10 | .05 |
| ❑ | 520 | Jim Deshaies | .10 | .05 |
| ❑ | 521 | Bruce Hurst | .10 | .05 |
| ❑ | 522 | Randy Myers | .20 | .09 |
| ❑ | 523 | Benito Santiago | .10 | .05 |
| ❑ | 524 | Tim Scott | .10 | .05 |
| ❑ | 525 | Tim Teufel | .10 | .05 |
| ❑ | 526 | Mike Benjamin | .10 | .05 |
| ❑ | 527 | Dave Burba | .10 | .05 |
| ❑ | 528 | Craig Colbert | .10 | .05 |
| ❑ | 529 | Mike Felder | .10 | .05 |
| ❑ | 530 | Bryan Hickerson | .10 | .05 |
| ❑ | 531 | Chris James | .10 | .05 |
| ❑ | 532 | Mark Leonard | .10 | .05 |
| ❑ | 533 | Greg Litton | .10 | .05 |
| ❑ | 534 | Francisco Oliveras | .10 | .05 |
| ❑ | 535 | John Patterson | .10 | .05 |
| ❑ | 536 | Jim Pena | .10 | .05 |
| ❑ | 537 | Dave Righetti | .10 | .05 |
| ❑ | 538 | Robby Thompson | .10 | .05 |
| ❑ | 539 | Jose Uribe | .10 | .05 |
| ❑ | 540 | Matt Williams | .20 | .09 |
| ❑ | 541 | Storm Davis | .10 | .05 |
| ❑ | 542 | Sam Horn | .10 | .05 |
| ❑ | 543 | Tim Hulett | .10 | .05 |
| ❑ | 544 | Craig Lefferts | .10 | .05 |
| ❑ | 545 | Chito Martinez | .10 | .05 |
| ❑ | 546 | Mark McLemore | .10 | .05 |
| ❑ | 547 | Luis Mercedes | .10 | .05 |
| ❑ | 548 | Bob Milacki | .10 | .05 |
| ❑ | 549 | Joe Orsulak | .10 | .05 |
| ❑ | 550 | Billy Ripken | .10 | .05 |
| ❑ | 551 | Cal Ripken Jr. | 1.50 | .70 |
| ❑ | 552 | Rick Sutcliffe | .20 | .09 |
| ❑ | 553 | Jeff Tackett | .10 | .05 |
| ❑ | 554 | Wade Boggs | .50 | .23 |
| ❑ | 555 | Tom Brunansky | .10 | .05 |
| ❑ | 556 | Jack Clark | .10 | .05 |
| ❑ | 557 | John Dopson | .10 | .05 |
| ❑ | 558 | Mike Gardiner | .10 | .05 |
| ❑ | 559 | Mike Greenwell | .10 | .05 |
| ❑ | 560 | Greg A. Harris | .10 | .05 |
| ❑ | 561 | Billy Hatcher | .10 | .05 |
| ❑ | 562 | Joe Hesketh | .10 | .05 |
| ❑ | 563 | Tony Pena | .10 | .05 |
| ❑ | 564 | Phil Plantier | .10 | .05 |
| ❑ | 565 | Luis Rivera | .10 | .05 |
| ❑ | 566 | Herm Winningham | .10 | .05 |
| ❑ | 567 | Matt Young | .10 | .05 |
| ❑ | 568 | Bert Blyleven | .20 | .09 |
| ❑ | 569 | Mike Butcher | .10 | .05 |
| ❑ | 570 | Chuck Crim | .10 | .05 |
| ❑ | 571 | Chad Curtis | .10 | .05 |
| ❑ | 572 | Tim Fortugno | .10 | .05 |
| ❑ | 573 | Steve Frey | .10 | .05 |
| ❑ | 574 | Gary Gaetti | .20 | .09 |
| ❑ | 575 | Scott Lewis | .10 | .05 |
| ❑ | 576 | Lee Stevens | .20 | .09 |
| ❑ | 577 | Ron Tingley | .10 | .05 |
| ❑ | 578 | Julio Valera | .10 | .05 |
| ❑ | 579 | Shawn Abner | .10 | .05 |
| ❑ | 580 | Joey Cora | .10 | .05 |
| ❑ | 581 | Chris Cron | .10 | .05 |
| ❑ | 582 | Carlton Fisk | .40 | .18 |
| ❑ | 583 | Roberto Hernandez | .10 | .05 |
| ❑ | 584 | Charlie Hough | .20 | .09 |
| ❑ | 585 | Terry Leach | .10 | .05 |
| ❑ | 586 | Donn Pall | .10 | .05 |
| ❑ | 587 | Dan Pasqua | .10 | .05 |
| ❑ | 588 | Steve Sax | .10 | .05 |
| ❑ | 589 | Bobby Thigpen | .10 | .05 |
| ❑ | 590 | Albert Belle | .20 | .09 |
| ❑ | 591 | Felix Fermin | .10 | .05 |
| ❑ | 592 | Glenallen Hill | .10 | .05 |
| ❑ | 593 | Brook Jacoby | .10 | .05 |
| ❑ | 594 | Reggie Jefferson | .20 | .09 |
| ❑ | 595 | Carlos Martinez | .10 | .05 |
| ❑ | 596 | Jose Mesa | .10 | .05 |
| ❑ | 597 | Rod Nichols | .10 | .05 |
| ❑ | 598 | Junior Ortiz | .10 | .05 |
| ❑ | 599 | Eric Plunk | .10 | .05 |
| ❑ | 600 | Ted Power | .10 | .05 |
| ❑ | 601 | Scott Scudder | .10 | .05 |
| ❑ | 602 | Kevin Wickander | .10 | .05 |
| ❑ | 603 | Skeeter Barnes | .10 | .05 |
| ❑ | 604 | Mark Carreon | .10 | .05 |
| ❑ | 605 | Dan Gladden | .10 | .05 |
| ❑ | 606 | Bill Gullickson | .10 | .05 |
| ❑ | 607 | Chad Kreuter | .10 | .05 |
| ❑ | 608 | Mark Leiter | .10 | .05 |
| ❑ | 609 | Mike Munoz | .10 | .05 |
| ❑ | 610 | Rich Rowland | .10 | .05 |
| ❑ | 611 | Frank Tanana | .10 | .05 |
| ❑ | 612 | Walt Terrell | .10 | .05 |
| ❑ | 613 | Alan Trammell | .20 | .09 |
| ❑ | 614 | Lou Whitaker | .20 | .09 |
| ❑ | 615 | Luis Aquino | .10 | .05 |
| ❑ | 616 | Mike Boddicker | .10 | .05 |
| ❑ | 617 | Jim Eisenreich | .10 | .05 |
| ❑ | 618 | Mark Gubicza | .10 | .05 |
| ❑ | 619 | David Howard | .10 | .05 |
| ❑ | 620 | Mike Magnante | .10 | .05 |
| ❑ | 621 | Brent Mayne | .10 | .05 |
| ❑ | 622 | Kevin McReynolds | .10 | .05 |
| ❑ | 623 | Ed Pierce RC | .10 | .05 |
| ❑ | 624 | Bill Sampen | .10 | .05 |
| ❑ | 625 | Steve Shifflett | .10 | .05 |
| ❑ | 626 | Gary Thurman | .10 | .05 |

❑ 627 Curt Wilkerson .10 .05
❑ 628 Chris Bosio .10 .05
❑ 629 Scott Fletcher .10 .05
❑ 630 Jim Gantner .10 .05
❑ 631 Dave Nilsson .20 .09
❑ 632 Jesse Orosco .10 .05
❑ 633 Dan Plesac .10 .05
❑ 634 Ron Robinson .10 .05
❑ 635 Bill Spiers .10 .05
❑ 636 Franklin Stubbs .10 .05
❑ 637 Willie Banks .10 .05
❑ 638 Randy Bush .10 .05
❑ 639 Chuck Knoblauch .20 .09
❑ 640 Shane Mack .10 .05
❑ 641 Mike Pagliarulo .10 .05
❑ 642 Jeff Reboulet .10 .05
❑ 643 John Smiley .10 .05
❑ 644 Mike Trombley .10 .05
❑ 645 Gary Wayne .10 .05
❑ 646 Lenny Webster .10 .05
❑ 647 Tim Burke .10 .05
❑ 648 Mike Gallego .10 .05
❑ 649 Dion James .10 .05
❑ 650 Jeff Johnson .10 .05
❑ 651 Scott Kamieniecki .10 .05
❑ 652 Kevin Maas .10 .05
❑ 653 Rich Monteleone .10 .05
❑ 654 Jerry Nielsen .10 .05
❑ 655 Scott Sanderson .10 .05
❑ 656 Mike Stanley .10 .05
❑ 657 Gerald Williams .10 .05
❑ 658 Curt Young .10 .05
❑ 659 Harold Baines .20 .09
❑ 660 Kevin Campbell .10 .05
❑ 661 Ron Darling .10 .05
❑ 662 Kelly Downs .10 .05
❑ 663 Eric Fox .10 .05
❑ 664 Dave Henderson .10 .05
❑ 665 Rick Honeycutt .10 .05
❑ 666 Mike Moore .10 .05
❑ 667 Jamie Quirk .10 .05
❑ 668 Jeff Russell .10 .05
❑ 669 Dave Stewart .20 .09
❑ 670 Greg Briley .10 .05
❑ 671 Dave Cochrane .10 .05
❑ 672 Henry Cotto .10 .05
❑ 673 Rich DeLucia .10 .05
❑ 674 Brian Fisher .10 .05
❑ 675 Mark Grant .10 .05
❑ 676 Randy Johnson .50 .23
❑ 677 Tim Leary .10 .05
❑ 678 Pete O'Brien .10 .05
❑ 679 Lance Parrish .10 .05
❑ 680 Harold Reynolds .10 .05
❑ 681 Shane Turner .10 .05
❑ 682 Jack Daugherty .10 .05
❑ 683 David Hulse RC .10 .05
❑ 684 Terry Mathews .10 .05
❑ 685 Al Newman .10 .05
❑ 686 Edwin Nunez .10 .05
❑ 687 Rafael Palmeiro .40 .18
❑ 688 Roger Pavlik .10 .05
❑ 689 Geno Petralli .10 .05
❑ 690 Nolan Ryan 2.00 .90
❑ 691 David Cone .20 .09
❑ 692 Alfredo Griffin .10 .05
❑ 693 Juan Guzman .10 .05
❑ 694 Pat Hentgen .10 .05
❑ 695 Randy Knorr .10 .05
❑ 696 Bob MacDonald .10 .05
❑ 697 Jack Morris .20 .09
❑ 698 Ed Sprague .10 .05
❑ 699 Dave Stieb .10 .05
❑ 700 Pat Tabler .10 .05
❑ 701 Mike Timlin .10 .05
❑ 702 David Wells .20 .09
❑ 703 Eddie Zosky .10 .05
❑ 704 Gary Sheffield LL .40 .18
❑ 705 Darren Daulton LL .10 .05
❑ 706 Marquis Grissom LL .10 .05
❑ 707 Greg Maddux LL .50 .23
❑ 708 Bill Swift LL .10 .05
❑ 709 Juan Gonzalez RT .20 .09
❑ 710 Mark McGwire RT .75 .35
❑ 711 Cecil Fielder RT .10 .05
❑ 712 Albert Belle RT .10 .05
❑ 713 Joe Carter RT .10 .05
❑ 714 Cecil Fielder SS .40 .18
Frank Thomas
Power Brokers
❑ 715 Larry Walker SS .20 .09
Darren Daulton
Unsung Heroes
❑ 716 Edgar Martinez SS .20 .09
Robin Ventura
Hot Corner Hammers
❑ 717 Roger Clemens SS .40 .18
Dennis Eckersley
Start to Finish
❑ 718 Checklist 361-480 .10 .05
❑ 719 Checklist 481-600 .10 .05
❑ 720 Checklist 601-720 .10 .05

## 1993 Fleer Final Edition

| | MINT | NRMT |
|---|---|---|
| COMP.FACT.SET (310) | 12.00 | 5.50 |
| COMPLETE SET (300) | 8.00 | 3.60 |

❑ 1 Steve Bedrosian .10 .05
❑ 2 Jay Howell .10 .05
❑ 3 Greg Maddux 1.00 .45
❑ 4 Greg McMichael RC .10 .05
❑ 5 Tony Tarasco RC .10 .05
❑ 6 Jose Bautista .10 .05
❑ 7 Jose Guzman .10 .05
❑ 8 Greg Hibbard .10 .05
❑ 9 Candy Maldonado .10 .05
❑ 10 Randy Myers .20 .09
❑ 11 Matt Walbeck RC .10 .05
❑ 12 Turk Wendell .10 .05
❑ 13 Willie Wilson .10 .05
❑ 14 Greg Cadaret .10 .05
❑ 15 Roberto Kelly .10 .05
❑ 16 Randy Milligan .10 .05
❑ 17 Kevin Mitchell .20 .09
❑ 18 Jeff Reardon .20 .09
❑ 19 John Roper .10 .05
❑ 20 John Smiley .10 .05
❑ 21 Andy Ashby .20 .09
❑ 22 Dante Bichette .20 .09
❑ 23 Willie Blair .10 .05
❑ 24 Pedro Castellano .10 .05
❑ 25 Vinny Castilla .50 .23
❑ 26 Jerald Clark .10 .05
❑ 27 Alex Cole .10 .05
❑ 28 Scott Fredrickson RC .10 .05
❑ 29 Jay Gainer RC .10 .05
❑ 30 Andres Galarraga .30 .14
❑ 31 Joe Girardi .20 .09
❑ 32 Ryan Hawblitzel .10 .05
❑ 33 Charlie Hayes .10 .05
❑ 34 Darren Holmes .10 .05
❑ 35 Chris Jones .10 .05
❑ 36 David Nied .10 .05
❑ 37 J.Owens RC .10 .05
❑ 38 Lance Painter RC .10 .05
❑ 39 Jeff Parrett .10 .05
❑ 40 Steve Reed .10 .05
❑ 41 Armando Reynoso .10 .05
❑ 42 Bruce Ruffin .10 .05
❑ 43 Danny Sheaffer RC .10 .05
❑ 44 Keith Shepherd .10 .05
❑ 45 Jim Tatum .10 .05
❑ 46 Gary Wayne .10 .05
❑ 47 Eric Young .10 .05
❑ 48 Luis Aquino .10 .05
❑ 49 Alex Arias .10 .05
❑ 50 Jack Armstrong .10 .05
❑ 51 Bret Barberie .10 .05
❑ 52 Geronimo Berroa .10 .05
❑ 53 Ryan Bowen .10 .05
❑ 54 Greg Briley .10 .05
❑ 55 Cris Carpenter .10 .05
❑ 56 Chuck Carr .10 .05
❑ 57 Jeff Conine .10 .05
❑ 58 Jim Corsi .10 .05
❑ 59 Orestes Destrade .10 .05
❑ 60 Junior Felix .10 .05
❑ 61 Chris Hammond .10 .05
❑ 62 Bryan Harvey .10 .05
❑ 63 Charlie Hough .20 .09
❑ 64 Joe Klink .10 .05
❑ 65 Richie Lewis RC UER .10 .05
(Refers to place of birth and residence as Illinois instead of Indiana)
❑ 66 Mitch Lyden RC .10 .05
❑ 67 Bob Natal .10 .05
❑ 68 Scott Pose RC .10 .05
❑ 69 Rich Renteria .10 .05
❑ 70 Benito Santiago .10 .05
❑ 71 Gary Sheffield .40 .18
❑ 72 Matt Turner RC .10 .05
❑ 73 Walt Weiss .10 .05
❑ 74 Darrell Whitmore RC .10 .05
❑ 75 Nigel Wilson .10 .05
❑ 76 Kevin Bass .10 .05
❑ 77 Doug Drabek .10 .05
❑ 78 Tom Edens .10 .05
❑ 79 Chris James .10 .05
❑ 80 Greg Swindell .10 .05
❑ 81 Omar Daal RC .20 .09
❑ 82 Raul Mondesi .20 .09
❑ 83 Jody Reed .10 .05
❑ 84 Cory Snyder .10 .05
❑ 85 Rick Trlicek .10 .05
❑ 86 Tim Wallach .10 .05
❑ 87 Todd Worrell .10 .05
❑ 88 Tavo Alvarez .10 .05
❑ 89 Frank Bolick .10 .05
❑ 90 Kent Bottenfield .10 .05
❑ 91 Greg Colbrunn .10 .05
❑ 92 Cliff Floyd .20 .09
❑ 93 Lou Frazier RC .10 .05
❑ 94 Mike Gardiner .10 .05
❑ 95 Mike Lansing RC .20 .09
❑ 96 Bill Risley .10 .05
❑ 97 Jeff Shaw .10 .05
❑ 98 Kevin Baez .10 .05
❑ 99 Tim Bogar RC .10 .05
❑ 100 Jeromy Burnitz .20 .09
❑ 101 Mike Draper .10 .05
❑ 102 Darrin Jackson .10 .05
❑ 103 Mike Maddux .10 .05
❑ 104 Joe Orsulak .10 .05
❑ 105 Doug Saunders RC .10 .05
❑ 106 Frank Tanana .10 .05
❑ 107 Dave Telgheder RC .10 .05
❑ 108 Larry Andersen .10 .05
❑ 109 Jim Eisenreich .10 .05
❑ 110 Pete Incaviglia .10 .05
❑ 111 Danny Jackson .10 .05
❑ 112 David West .10 .05
❑ 113 Al Martin .10 .05
❑ 114 Blas Minor .10 .05
❑ 115 Dennis Moeller .10 .05
❑ 116 William Pennyfeather .10 .05
❑ 117 Rich Robertson RC .10 .05
❑ 118 Ben Shelton .10 .05
❑ 119 Lonnie Smith .10 .05
❑ 120 Freddie Toliver .10 .05
❑ 121 Paul Wagner .10 .05
❑ 122 Kevin Young .20 .09
❑ 123 Rene Arocha RC .10 .05
❑ 124 Gregg Jefferies .10 .05
❑ 125 Paul Kilgus .10 .05
❑ 126 Les Lancaster .10 .05
❑ 127 Joe Magrane .10 .05
❑ 128 Rob Murphy .10 .05

❑ 129 Erik Pappas .10 .05
❑ 130 Stan Royer .10 .05
❑ 131 Ozzie Smith .50 .23
❑ 132 Tom Urbani RC .10 .05
❑ 133 Mark Whiten .10 .05
❑ 134 Derek Bell .10 .05
❑ 135 Doug Brocail .10 .05
❑ 136 Phil Clark .10 .05
❑ 137 Mark Ettles RC .10 .05
❑ 138 Jeff Gardner .10 .05
❑ 139 Pat Gomez RC .10 .05
❑ 140 Ricky Gutierrez .10 .05
❑ 141 Gene Harris .10 .05
❑ 142 Kevin Higgins .10 .05
❑ 143 Trevor Hoffman .40 .18
❑ 144 Phil Plantier .10 .05
❑ 145 Kerry Taylor RC .10 .05
❑ 146 Guillermo Velasquez .10 .05
❑ 147 Wally Whitehurst .10 .05
❑ 148 Tim Worrell RC .10 .05
❑ 149 Todd Benzinger .10 .05
❑ 150 Barry Bonds .60 .25
❑ 151 Greg Brummett RC .10 .05
❑ 152 Mark Carreon .10 .05
❑ 153 Dave Martinez .10 .05
❑ 154 Jeff Reed .10 .05
❑ 155 Kevin Rogers .10 .05
❑ 156 Harold Baines .20 .09
❑ 157 Damon Buford .10 .05
❑ 158 Paul Carey RC .10 .05
❑ 159 Jeffrey Hammonds .20 .09
❑ 160 Jamie Moyer .10 .05
❑ 161 Sherman Obando RC .10 .05
❑ 162 John O'Donoghue RC .10 .05
❑ 163 Brad Pennington .10 .05
❑ 164 Jim Poole .10 .05
❑ 165 Harold Reynolds .10 .05
❑ 166 Fernando Valenzuela .20 .09
❑ 167 Jack Voigt RC .10 .05
❑ 168 Mark Williamson .10 .05
❑ 169 Scott Bankhead .10 .05
❑ 170 Greg Blosser .10 .05
❑ 171 Jim Byrd RC .10 .05
❑ 172 Ivan Calderon .10 .05
❑ 173 Andre Dawson .30 .14
❑ 174 Scott Fletcher .10 .05
❑ 175 Jose Melendez .10 .05
❑ 176 Carlos Quintana .10 .05
❑ 177 Jeff Russell .10 .05
❑ 178 Aaron Sele .40 .18
❑ 179 Rod Correia RC .10 .05
❑ 180 Chili Davis .20 .09
❑ 181 Jim Edmonds RC 6.00 2.70
❑ 182 Rene Gonzales .10 .05
❑ 183 Hilly Hathaway RC .10 .05
❑ 184 Torey Lovullo .10 .05
❑ 185 Greg Myers .10 .05
❑ 186 Gene Nelson .10 .05
❑ 187 Troy Percival .10 .05
❑ 188 Scott Sanderson .10 .05
❑ 189 Darryl Scott RC .10 .05
❑ 190 J.T. Snow RC .75 .35
❑ 191 Russ Springer .10 .05
❑ 192 Jason Bere .10 .05
❑ 193 Rodney Bolton .10 .05
❑ 194 Ellis Burks .20 .09
❑ 195 Bo Jackson .20 .09
❑ 196 Mike LaValliere .10 .05
❑ 197 Scott Ruffcorn .10 .05
❑ 198 Jeff Schwartz .10 .05
❑ 199 Jerry DiPoto .10 .05
❑ 200 Alvaro Espinoza .10 .05
❑ 201 Wayne Kirby .10 .05
❑ 202 Tom Kramer RC .10 .05
❑ 203 Jesse Levis .10 .05
❑ 204 Manny Ramirez .75 .35
❑ 205 Jeff Treadway .10 .05
❑ 206 Bill Wertz RC .10 .05
❑ 207 Cliff Young .10 .05
❑ 208 Matt Young .10 .05
❑ 209 Kirk Gibson .20 .09
❑ 210 Greg Gohr .10 .05
❑ 211 Bill Krueger .10 .05
❑ 212 Bob MacDonald .10 .05
❑ 213 Mike Moore .10 .05
❑ 214 David Wells .20 .09
❑ 215 Billy Brewer .10 .05
❑ 216 David Cone .20 .09
❑ 217 Greg Gagne .10 .05
❑ 218 Mark Gardner .10 .05
❑ 219 Chris Haney .10 .05
❑ 220 Phil Hiatt .10 .05
❑ 221 Jose Lind .10 .05
❑ 222 Juan Bell .10 .05
❑ 223 Tom Brunansky .10 .05
❑ 224 Mike Ignasiak .10 .05
❑ 225 Joe Kmak .10 .05
❑ 226 Tom Lampkin .10 .05
❑ 227 Graeme Lloyd RC .10 .05
❑ 228 Carlos Maldonado .10 .05
❑ 229 Matt Mieske .10 .05
❑ 230 Angel Miranda .10 .05
❑ 231 Troy O'Leary RC .50 .23
❑ 232 Kevin Reimer .10 .05
❑ 233 Larry Casian .10 .05
❑ 234 Jim Deshaies .10 .05
❑ 235 Eddie Guardado RC .10 .05
❑ 236 Chip Hale .10 .05
❑ 237 Mike Maksudian RC .10 .05
❑ 238 David McCarty .10 .05
❑ 239 Pat Meares RC .10 .05
❑ 240 George Tsamis RC .10 .05
❑ 241 Dave Winfield .40 .18
❑ 242 Jim Abbott .20 .09
❑ 243 Wade Boggs .50 .23
❑ 244 Andy Cook RC .10 .05
❑ 245 Russ Davis RC .20 .09
❑ 246 Mike Humphreys .10 .05
❑ 247 Jimmy Key .20 .09
❑ 248 Jim Leyritz .10 .05
❑ 249 Bobby Munoz .10 .05
❑ 250 Paul O'Neill .20 .09
❑ 251 Spike Owen .10 .05
❑ 252 Dave Silvestri .10 .05
❑ 253 Marcos Armas RC .10 .05
❑ 254 Brent Gates .10 .05
❑ 255 Rich Gossage .20 .09
❑ 256 Scott Lydy RC .10 .05
❑ 257 Henry Mercedes .10 .05
❑ 258 Mike Mohler RC .10 .05
❑ 259 Troy Neel .10 .05
❑ 260 Edwin Nunez .10 .05
❑ 261 Craig Paquette .10 .05
❑ 262 Kevin Seitzer .10 .05
❑ 263 Rich Amaral .10 .05
❑ 264 Mike Blowers .10 .05
❑ 265 Chris Bosio .10 .05
❑ 266 Norm Charlton .10 .05
❑ 267 Jim Converse RC .10 .05
❑ 268 John Cummings RC .10 .05
❑ 269 Mike Felder .10 .05
❑ 270 Mike Hampton .40 .18
❑ 271 Bill Haselman .10 .05
❑ 272 Dwayne Henry .10 .05
❑ 273 Greg Litton .10 .05
❑ 274 Mackey Sasser .10 .05
❑ 275 Lee Tinsley .10 .05
❑ 276 David Wainhouse .10 .05
❑ 277 Jeff Bronkey .10 .05
❑ 278 Benji Gil .10 .05
❑ 279 Tom Henke .10 .05
❑ 280 Charlie Leibrandt .10 .05
❑ 281 Robb Nen .30 .14
❑ 282 Bill Ripken .10 .05
❑ 283 Jon Shave RC .10 .05
❑ 284 Doug Strange .10 .05
❑ 285 Matt Whiteside RC .10 .05
❑ 286 Scott Brow RC .10 .05
❑ 287 Willie Canate RC .10 .05
❑ 288 Tony Castillo .10 .05
❑ 289 Domingo Cedeno RC .10 .05
❑ 290 Darnell Coles .10 .05
❑ 291 Danny Cox .10 .05
❑ 292 Mark Eichhorn .10 .05
❑ 293 Tony Fernandez .10 .05
❑ 294 Al Leiter .20 .09
❑ 295 Paul Molitor .40 .18
❑ 296 Dave Stewart .20 .09
❑ 297 Woody Williams RC .30 .14
❑ 298 Checklist F1-F100 .10 .05
❑ 299 Checklist F101-F200 .10 .05
❑ 300 Checklist F201-F300 .10 .05

## 1994 Fleer

| | MINT | NRMT |
|---|---|---|
| COMPLETE SET (720) | 40.00 | 18.00 |

❑ 1 Brady Anderson .30 .14
❑ 2 Harold Baines .30 .14
❑ 3 Mike Devereaux .15 .07
❑ 4 Todd Frohwirth .15 .07
❑ 5 Jeffrey Hammonds .30 .14
❑ 6 Chris Hoiles .15 .07
❑ 7 Tim Hulett .15 .07
❑ 8 Ben McDonald .15 .07
❑ 9 Mark McLemore .15 .07
❑ 10 Alan Mills .15 .07
❑ 11 Jamie Moyer .15 .07
❑ 12 Mike Mussina .60 .25
❑ 13 Gregg Olson .15 .07
❑ 14 Mike Pagliarulo .15 .07
❑ 15 Brad Pennington .15 .07
❑ 16 Jim Poole .15 .07
❑ 17 Harold Reynolds .15 .07
❑ 18 Arthur Rhodes .15 .07
❑ 19 Cal Ripken Jr. 2.50 1.10
❑ 20 David Segui .15 .07
❑ 21 Rick Sutcliffe .30 .14
❑ 22 Fernando Valenzuela .30 .14
❑ 23 Jack Voigt .15 .07
❑ 24 Mark Williamson .15 .07
❑ 25 Scott Bankhead .15 .07
❑ 26 Roger Clemens 1.25 .55
❑ 27 Scott Cooper .15 .07
❑ 28 Danny Darwin .15 .07
❑ 29 Andre Dawson .30 .14
❑ 30 Rob Deer .15 .07
❑ 31 John Dopson .15 .07
❑ 32 Scott Fletcher .15 .07
❑ 33 Mike Greenwell .15 .07
❑ 34 Greg A. Harris .15 .07
❑ 35 Billy Hatcher .15 .07
❑ 36 Bob Melvin .15 .07
❑ 37 Tony Pena .15 .07
❑ 38 Paul Quantrill .15 .07
❑ 39 Carlos Quintana .15 .07
❑ 40 Ernest Riles .15 .07
❑ 41 Jeff Russell .15 .07
❑ 42 Ken Ryan .15 .07
❑ 43 Aaron Sele .30 .14
❑ 44 John Valentin .15 .07
❑ 45 Mo Vaughn .30 .14
❑ 46 Frank Viola .15 .07
❑ 47 Bob Zupcic .15 .07
❑ 48 Mike Butcher .15 .07
❑ 49 Rod Correia .15 .07
❑ 50 Chad Curtis .15 .07
❑ 51 Chili Davis .30 .14
❑ 52 Gary DiSarcina .15 .07
❑ 53 Damion Easley .15 .07
❑ 54 Jim Edmonds .75 .35
❑ 55 Chuck Finley .30 .14
❑ 56 Steve Frey .15 .07
❑ 57 Rene Gonzales .15 .07
❑ 58 Joe Grahe .15 .07
❑ 59 Hilly Hathaway .15 .07
❑ 60 Stan Javier .15 .07
❑ 61 Mark Langston .15 .07
❑ 62 Phil Leftwich RC .15 .07
❑ 63 Torey Lovullo .15 .07

| No. | Player | | |
|---|---|---|---|
| ❑ 64 | Joe Magrane | .15 | .07 |
| ❑ 65 | Greg Myers | .15 | .07 |
| ❑ 66 | Ken Patterson | .15 | .07 |
| ❑ 67 | Eduardo Perez | .15 | .07 |
| ❑ 68 | Luis Polonia | .15 | .07 |
| ❑ 69 | Tim Salmon | .30 | .14 |
| ❑ 70 | J.T. Snow | .30 | .14 |
| ❑ 71 | Ron Tingley | .15 | .07 |
| ❑ 72 | Julio Valera | .15 | .07 |
| ❑ 73 | Wilson Alvarez | .15 | .07 |
| ❑ 74 | Tim Belcher | .15 | .07 |
| ❑ 75 | George Bell | .15 | .07 |
| ❑ 76 | Jason Bere | .15 | .07 |
| ❑ 77 | Rod Bolton | .15 | .07 |
| ❑ 78 | Ellis Burks | .30 | .14 |
| ❑ 79 | Joey Cora | .15 | .07 |
| ❑ 80 | Alex Fernandez | .15 | .07 |
| ❑ 81 | Craig Grebeck | .15 | .07 |
| ❑ 82 | Ozzie Guillen | .15 | .07 |
| ❑ 83 | Roberto Hernandez | .15 | .07 |
| ❑ 84 | Bo Jackson | .30 | .14 |
| ❑ 85 | Lance Johnson | .15 | .07 |
| ❑ 86 | Ron Karkovice | .15 | .07 |
| ❑ 87 | Mike LaValliere | .15 | .07 |
| ❑ 88 | Kirk McCaskill | .15 | .07 |
| ❑ 89 | Jack McDowell | .15 | .07 |
| ❑ 90 | Warren Newson | .15 | .07 |
| ❑ 91 | Dan Pasqua | .15 | .07 |
| ❑ 92 | Scott Radinsky | .15 | .07 |
| ❑ 93 | Tim Raines | .30 | .14 |
| ❑ 94 | Steve Sax | .15 | .07 |
| ❑ 95 | Jeff Schwarz | .15 | .07 |
| ❑ 96 | Frank Thomas | 1.25 | .55 |
| ❑ 97 | Robin Ventura | .30 | .14 |
| ❑ 98 | Sandy Alomar Jr. | .30 | .14 |
| ❑ 99 | Carlos Baerga | .15 | .07 |
| ❑ 100 | Albert Belle | .30 | .14 |
| ❑ 101 | Mark Clark | .15 | .07 |
| ❑ 102 | Jerry DiPoto | .15 | .07 |
| ❑ 103 | Alvaro Espinoza | .15 | .07 |
| ❑ 104 | Felix Fermin | .15 | .07 |
| ❑ 105 | Jeremy Hernandez | .15 | .07 |
| ❑ 106 | Reggie Jefferson | .15 | .07 |
| ❑ 107 | Wayne Kirby | .15 | .07 |
| ❑ 108 | Tom Kramer | .15 | .07 |
| ❑ 109 | Mark Lewis | .15 | .07 |
| ❑ 110 | Derek Lilliquist | .15 | .07 |
| ❑ 111 | Kenny Lofton | .30 | .14 |
| ❑ 112 | Candy Maldonado | .15 | .07 |
| ❑ 113 | Jose Mesa | .15 | .07 |
| ❑ 114 | Jeff Mutis | .15 | .07 |
| ❑ 115 | Charles Nagy | .15 | .07 |
| ❑ 116 | Bob Ojeda | .15 | .07 |
| ❑ 117 | Junior Ortiz | .15 | .07 |
| ❑ 118 | Eric Plunk | .15 | .07 |
| ❑ 119 | Manny Ramirez | 1.00 | .45 |
| ❑ 120 | Paul Sorrento | .15 | .07 |
| ❑ 121 | Jim Thome | .30 | .14 |
| ❑ 122 | Jeff Treadway | .15 | .07 |
| ❑ 123 | Bill Wertz | .15 | .07 |
| ❑ 124 | Skeeter Barnes | .15 | .07 |
| ❑ 125 | Milt Cuyler | .15 | .07 |
| ❑ 126 | Eric Davis | .30 | .14 |
| ❑ 127 | John Doherty | .15 | .07 |
| ❑ 128 | Cecil Fielder | .30 | .14 |
| ❑ 129 | Travis Fryman | .30 | .14 |
| ❑ 130 | Kirk Gibson | .30 | .14 |
| ❑ 131 | Dan Gladden | .15 | .07 |
| ❑ 132 | Greg Gohr | .15 | .07 |
| ❑ 133 | Chris Gomez | .15 | .07 |
| ❑ 134 | Bill Gullickson | .15 | .07 |
| ❑ 135 | Mike Henneman | .15 | .07 |
| ❑ 136 | Kurt Knudsen | .15 | .07 |
| ❑ 137 | Chad Kreuter | .15 | .07 |
| ❑ 138 | Bill Krueger | .15 | .07 |
| ❑ 139 | Scott Livingstone | .15 | .07 |
| ❑ 140 | Bob MacDonald | .15 | .07 |
| ❑ 141 | Mike Moore | .15 | .07 |
| ❑ 142 | Tony Phillips | .15 | .07 |
| ❑ 143 | Mickey Tettleton | .15 | .07 |
| ❑ 144 | Alan Trammell | .30 | .14 |
| ❑ 145 | David Wells | .30 | .14 |
| ❑ 146 | Lou Whitaker | .30 | .14 |
| ❑ 147 | Kevin Appier | .30 | .14 |
| ❑ 148 | Stan Belinda | .15 | .07 |
| ❑ 149 | George Brett | 1.25 | .55 |
| ❑ 150 | Billy Brewer | .15 | .07 |
| ❑ 151 | Hubie Brooks | .15 | .07 |
| ❑ 152 | David Cone | .30 | .14 |
| ❑ 153 | Gary Gaetti | .30 | .14 |
| ❑ 154 | Greg Gagne | .15 | .07 |
| ❑ 155 | Tom Gordon | .15 | .07 |
| ❑ 156 | Mark Gubicza | .15 | .07 |
| ❑ 157 | Chris Gwynn | .15 | .07 |
| ❑ 158 | John Habyan | .15 | .07 |
| ❑ 159 | Chris Haney | .15 | .07 |
| ❑ 160 | Phil Hiatt | .15 | .07 |
| ❑ 161 | Felix Jose | .15 | .07 |
| ❑ 162 | Wally Joyner | .30 | .14 |
| ❑ 163 | Jose Lind | .15 | .07 |
| ❑ 164 | Mike Macfarlane | .15 | .07 |
| ❑ 165 | Mike Magnante | .15 | .07 |
| ❑ 166 | Brent Mayne | .15 | .07 |
| ❑ 167 | Brian McRae | .15 | .07 |
| ❑ 168 | Kevin McReynolds | .15 | .07 |
| ❑ 169 | Keith Miller | .15 | .07 |
| ❑ 170 | Jeff Montgomery | .15 | .07 |
| ❑ 171 | Hipolito Pichardo | .15 | .07 |
| ❑ 172 | Rico Rossy | .15 | .07 |
| ❑ 173 | Juan Bell | .15 | .07 |
| ❑ 174 | Ricky Bones | .15 | .07 |
| ❑ 175 | Cal Eldred | .15 | .07 |
| ❑ 176 | Mike Fetters | .15 | .07 |
| ❑ 177 | Darryl Hamilton | .15 | .07 |
| ❑ 178 | Doug Henry | .15 | .07 |
| ❑ 179 | Mike Ignasiak | .15 | .07 |
| ❑ 180 | John Jaha | .15 | .07 |
| ❑ 181 | Pat Listach | .15 | .07 |
| ❑ 182 | Graeme Lloyd | .15 | .07 |
| ❑ 183 | Matt Mieske | .15 | .07 |
| ❑ 184 | Angel Miranda | .15 | .07 |
| ❑ 185 | Jaime Navarro | .15 | .07 |
| ❑ 186 | Dave Nilsson | .15 | .07 |
| ❑ 187 | Troy O'Leary | .15 | .07 |
| ❑ 188 | Jesse Orosco | .15 | .07 |
| ❑ 189 | Kevin Reimer | .15 | .07 |
| ❑ 190 | Kevin Seitzer | .15 | .07 |
| ❑ 191 | Bill Spiers | .15 | .07 |
| ❑ 192 | B.J. Surhoff | .30 | .14 |
| ❑ 193 | Dickie Thon | .15 | .07 |
| ❑ 194 | Jose Valentin | .15 | .07 |
| ❑ 195 | Greg Vaughn | .30 | .14 |
| ❑ 196 | Bill Wegman | .15 | .07 |
| ❑ 197 | Robin Yount | .60 | .25 |
| ❑ 198 | Rick Aguilera | .15 | .07 |
| ❑ 199 | Willie Banks | .15 | .07 |
| ❑ 200 | Bernardo Brito | .15 | .07 |
| ❑ 201 | Larry Casian | .15 | .07 |
| ❑ 202 | Scott Erickson | .15 | .07 |
| ❑ 203 | Eddie Guardado | .15 | .07 |
| ❑ 204 | Mark Guthrie | .15 | .07 |
| ❑ 205 | Chip Hale | .15 | .07 |
| ❑ 206 | Brian Harper | .15 | .07 |
| ❑ 207 | Mike Hartley | .15 | .07 |
| ❑ 208 | Kent Hrbek | .30 | .14 |
| ❑ 209 | Terry Jorgensen | .15 | .07 |
| ❑ 210 | Chuck Knoblauch | .30 | .14 |
| ❑ 211 | Gene Larkin | .15 | .07 |
| ❑ 212 | Shane Mack | .15 | .07 |
| ❑ 213 | David McCarty | .15 | .07 |
| ❑ 214 | Pat Meares | .15 | .07 |
| ❑ 215 | Pedro Munoz | .15 | .07 |
| ❑ 216 | Derek Parks | .15 | .07 |
| ❑ 217 | Kirby Puckett | 1.50 | .70 |
| ❑ 218 | Jeff Reboulet | .15 | .07 |
| ❑ 219 | Kevin Tapani | .15 | .07 |
| ❑ 220 | Mike Trombley | .15 | .07 |
| ❑ 221 | George Tsamis | .15 | .07 |
| ❑ 222 | Carl Willis | .15 | .07 |
| ❑ 223 | Dave Winfield | .60 | .25 |
| ❑ 224 | Jim Abbott | .30 | .14 |
| ❑ 225 | Paul Assenmacher | .15 | .07 |
| ❑ 226 | Wade Boggs | .75 | .35 |
| ❑ 227 | Russ Davis | .15 | .07 |
| ❑ 228 | Steve Farr | .15 | .07 |
| ❑ 229 | Mike Gallego | .15 | .07 |
| ❑ 230 | Paul Gibson | .15 | .07 |
| ❑ 231 | Steve Howe | .15 | .07 |
| ❑ 232 | Dion James | .15 | .07 |
| ❑ 233 | Domingo Jean | .15 | .07 |
| ❑ 234 | Scott Kamieniecki | .15 | .07 |
| ❑ 235 | Pat Kelly | .15 | .07 |
| ❑ 236 | Jimmy Key | .30 | .14 |
| ❑ 237 | Jim Leyritz | .15 | .07 |
| ❑ 238 | Kevin Maas | .15 | .07 |
| ❑ 239 | Don Mattingly | 1.50 | .70 |
| ❑ 240 | Rich Monteleone | .15 | .07 |
| ❑ 241 | Bobby Munoz | .15 | .07 |
| ❑ 242 | Matt Nokes | .15 | .07 |
| ❑ 243 | Paul O'Neill | .30 | .14 |
| ❑ 244 | Spike Owen | .15 | .07 |
| ❑ 245 | Melido Perez | .15 | .07 |
| ❑ 246 | Lee Smith | .30 | .14 |
| ❑ 247 | Mike Stanley | .15 | .07 |
| ❑ 248 | Danny Tartabull | .15 | .07 |
| ❑ 249 | Randy Velarde | .15 | .07 |
| ❑ 250 | Bob Wickman | .15 | .07 |
| ❑ 251 | Bernie Williams | .60 | .25 |
| ❑ 252 | Mike Aldrete | .15 | .07 |
| ❑ 253 | Marcos Armas | .15 | .07 |
| ❑ 254 | Lance Blankenship | .15 | .07 |
| ❑ 255 | Mike Bordick | .15 | .07 |
| ❑ 256 | Scott Brosius | .30 | .14 |
| ❑ 257 | Jerry Browne | .15 | .07 |
| ❑ 258 | Ron Darling | .15 | .07 |
| ❑ 259 | Kelly Downs | .15 | .07 |
| ❑ 260 | Dennis Eckersley | .30 | .14 |
| ❑ 261 | Brent Gates | .15 | .07 |
| ❑ 262 | Rich Gossage | .30 | .14 |
| ❑ 263 | Scott Hemond | .15 | .07 |
| ❑ 264 | Dave Henderson | .15 | .07 |
| ❑ 265 | Rick Honeycutt | .15 | .07 |
| ❑ 266 | Vince Horsman | .15 | .07 |
| ❑ 267 | Scott Lydy | .15 | .07 |
| ❑ 268 | Mark McGwire | 2.50 | 1.10 |
| ❑ 269 | Mike Mohler | .15 | .07 |
| ❑ 270 | Troy Neel | .15 | .07 |
| ❑ 271 | Edwin Nunez | .15 | .07 |
| ❑ 272 | Craig Paquette | .15 | .07 |
| ❑ 273 | Ruben Sierra | .15 | .07 |
| ❑ 274 | Terry Steinbach | .15 | .07 |
| ❑ 275 | Todd Van Poppel | .15 | .07 |
| ❑ 276 | Bob Welch | .15 | .07 |
| ❑ 277 | Bobby Witt | .15 | .07 |
| ❑ 278 | Rich Amaral | .15 | .07 |
| ❑ 279 | Mike Blowers | .15 | .07 |
| ❑ 280 | Bret Boone UER (Name spelled Brett on front) | .30 | .14 |
| ❑ 281 | Chris Bosio | .15 | .07 |
| ❑ 282 | Jay Buhner | .30 | .14 |
| ❑ 283 | Norm Charlton | .15 | .07 |
| ❑ 284 | Mike Felder | .15 | .07 |
| ❑ 285 | Dave Fleming | .15 | .07 |
| ❑ 286 | Ken Griffey Jr. | 2.50 | 1.10 |
| ❑ 287 | Erik Hanson | .15 | .07 |
| ❑ 288 | Bill Haselman | .15 | .07 |
| ❑ 289 | Brad Holman RC | .15 | .07 |
| ❑ 290 | Randy Johnson | .75 | .35 |
| ❑ 291 | Tim Leary | .15 | .07 |
| ❑ 292 | Greg Litton | .15 | .07 |
| ❑ 293 | Dave Magadan | .15 | .07 |
| ❑ 294 | Edgar Martinez | .30 | .14 |
| ❑ 295 | Tino Martinez | .30 | .14 |
| ❑ 296 | Jeff Nelson | .15 | .07 |
| ❑ 297 | Erik Plantenberg RC | .15 | .07 |
| ❑ 298 | Mackey Sasser | .15 | .07 |
| ❑ 299 | Brian Turang RC | .15 | .07 |
| ❑ 300 | Dave Valle | .15 | .07 |
| ❑ 301 | Omar Vizquel | .30 | .14 |
| ❑ 302 | Brian Bohanon | .15 | .07 |
| ❑ 303 | Kevin Brown | .30 | .14 |
| ❑ 304 | Jose Canseco UER (Back mentions 1991 as his 40/40 MVP season; should be '88) | .75 | .35 |
| ❑ 305 | Mario Diaz | .15 | .07 |
| ❑ 306 | Julio Franco | .15 | .07 |
| ❑ 307 | Juan Gonzalez | .60 | .25 |
| ❑ 308 | Tom Henke | .15 | .07 |
| ❑ 309 | David Hulse | .15 | .07 |
| ❑ 310 | Manuel Lee | .15 | .07 |
| ❑ 311 | Craig Lefferts | .15 | .07 |
| ❑ 312 | Charlie Leibrandt | .15 | .07 |
| ❑ 313 | Rafael Palmeiro | .60 | .25 |
| ❑ 314 | Dean Palmer | .30 | .14 |
| ❑ 315 | Roger Pavlik | .15 | .07 |
| ❑ 316 | Dan Peltier | .15 | .07 |
| ❑ 317 | Gene Petralli | .15 | .07 |
| ❑ 318 | Gary Redus | .15 | .07 |

❑ 319 Ivan Rodriguez .75 .35
❑ 320 Kenny Rogers .15 .07
❑ 321 Nolan Ryan 3.00 1.35
❑ 322 Doug Strange .15 .07
❑ 323 Matt Whiteside .15 .07
❑ 324 Roberto Alomar .60 .25
❑ 325 Pat Borders .15 .07
❑ 326 Joe Carter .30 .14
❑ 327 Tony Castillo .15 .07
❑ 328 Darnell Coles .15 .07
❑ 329 Danny Cox .15 .07
❑ 330 Mark Eichhorn .15 .07
❑ 331 Tony Fernandez .15 .07
❑ 332 Alfredo Griffin .15 .07
❑ 333 Juan Guzman .15 .07
❑ 334 Rickey Henderson .75 .35
❑ 335 Pat Hentgen .15 .07
❑ 336 Randy Knorr .15 .07
❑ 337 Al Leiter .30 .14
❑ 338 Paul Molitor .60 .25
❑ 339 Jack Morris .30 .14
❑ 340 John Olerud .30 .14
❑ 341 Dick Schofield .15 .07
❑ 342 Ed Sprague .15 .07
❑ 343 Dave Stewart .30 .14
❑ 344 Todd Stottlemyre .15 .07
❑ 345 Mike Timlin .15 .07
❑ 346 Duane Ward .15 .07
❑ 347 Turner Ward .15 .07
❑ 348 Devon White .15 .07
❑ 349 Woody Williams .15 .07
❑ 350 Steve Avery .15 .07
❑ 351 Steve Bedrosian .15 .07
❑ 352 Rafael Belliard .15 .07
❑ 353 Damon Berryhill .15 .07
❑ 354 Jeff Blauser .15 .07
❑ 355 Sid Bream .15 .07
❑ 356 Francisco Cabrera .15 .07
❑ 357 Marvin Freeman .15 .07
❑ 358 Ron Gant .30 .14
❑ 359 Tom Glavine .60 .25
❑ 360 Jay Howell .15 .07
❑ 361 David Justice .30 .14
❑ 362 Ryan Klesko .30 .14
❑ 363 Mark Lemke .15 .07
❑ 364 Javier Lopez .30 .14
❑ 365 Greg Maddux 1.50 .70
❑ 366 Fred McGriff .30 .14
❑ 367 Greg McMichael .15 .07
❑ 368 Kent Mercker .15 .07
❑ 369 Otis Nixon .15 .07
❑ 370 Greg Olson .15 .07
❑ 371 Bill Pecota .15 .07
❑ 372 Terry Pendleton .30 .14
❑ 373 Deion Sanders .30 .14
❑ 374 Pete Smith .15 .07
❑ 375 John Smoltz .30 .14
❑ 376 Mike Stanton .15 .07
❑ 377 Tony Tarasco .15 .07
❑ 378 Mark Wohlers .15 .07
❑ 379 Jose Bautista .15 .07
❑ 380 Shawn Boskie .15 .07
❑ 381 Steve Buechele .15 .07
❑ 382 Frank Castillo .15 .07
❑ 383 Mark Grace .60 .25
❑ 384 Jose Guzman .15 .07
❑ 385 Mike Harkey .15 .07
❑ 386 Greg Hibbard .15 .07
❑ 387 Glenallen Hill .15 .07
❑ 388 Steve Lake .15 .07
❑ 389 Derrick May .15 .07
❑ 390 Chuck McElroy .15 .07
❑ 391 Mike Morgan .15 .07
❑ 392 Randy Myers .15 .07
❑ 393 Dan Plesac .15 .07
❑ 394 Kevin Roberson .15 .07
❑ 395 Rey Sanchez .15 .07
❑ 396 Ryne Sandberg .75 .35
❑ 397 Bob Scanlan .15 .07
❑ 398 Dwight Smith .15 .07
❑ 399 Sammy Sosa 1.25 .55
❑ 400 Jose Vizcaino .15 .07
❑ 401 Rick Wilkins .15 .07
❑ 402 Willie Wilson .15 .07
❑ 403 Eric Yelding .15 .07
❑ 404 Bobby Ayala .15 .07
❑ 405 Jeff Branson .15 .07
❑ 406 Tom Browning .15 .07
❑ 407 Jacob Brumfield .15 .07
❑ 408 Tim Costo .15 .07
❑ 409 Rob Dibble .15 .07
❑ 410 Willie Greene .15 .07
❑ 411 Thomas Howard .15 .07
❑ 412 Roberto Kelly .15 .07
❑ 413 Bill Landrum .15 .07
❑ 414 Barry Larkin .60 .25
❑ 415 Larry Luebbers RC .15 .07
❑ 416 Kevin Mitchell .15 .07
❑ 417 Hal Morris .15 .07
❑ 418 Joe Oliver .15 .07
❑ 419 Tim Pugh .15 .07
❑ 420 Jeff Reardon .30 .14
❑ 421 Jose Rijo .15 .07
❑ 422 Bip Roberts .15 .07
❑ 423 John Roper .15 .07
❑ 424 Johnny Ruffin .15 .07
❑ 425 Chris Sabo .15 .07
❑ 426 Juan Samuel .15 .07
❑ 427 Reggie Sanders .15 .07
❑ 428 Scott Service .15 .07
❑ 429 John Smiley .15 .07
❑ 430 Jerry Spradlin RC .15 .07
❑ 431 Kevin Wickander .15 .07
❑ 432 Freddie Benavides .15 .07
❑ 433 Dante Bichette .30 .14
❑ 434 Willie Blair .15 .07
❑ 435 Daryl Boston .15 .07
❑ 436 Kent Bottenfield .15 .07
❑ 437 Vinny Castilla .30 .14
❑ 438 Jerald Clark .15 .07
❑ 439 Alex Cole .15 .07
❑ 440 Andres Galarraga .30 .14
❑ 441 Joe Girardi .15 .07
❑ 442 Greg W. Harris .15 .07
❑ 443 Charlie Hayes .15 .07
❑ 444 Darren Holmes .15 .07
❑ 445 Chris Jones .15 .07
❑ 446 Roberto Mejia .15 .07
❑ 447 David Nied .15 .07
❑ 448 J. Owens .15 .07
❑ 449 Jeff Parrett .15 .07
❑ 450 Steve Reed .15 .07
❑ 451 Armando Reynoso .15 .07
❑ 452 Bruce Ruffin .15 .07
❑ 453 Mo Sanford .15 .07
❑ 454 Danny Sheaffer .15 .07
❑ 455 Jim Tatum .15 .07
❑ 456 Gary Wayne .15 .07
❑ 457 Eric Young .15 .07
❑ 458 Luis Aquino .15 .07
❑ 459 Alex Arias .15 .07
❑ 460 Jack Armstrong .15 .07
❑ 461 Bret Barberie .15 .07
❑ 462 Ryan Bowen .15 .07
❑ 463 Chuck Carr .15 .07
❑ 464 Jeff Conine .15 .07
❑ 465 Henry Cotto .15 .07
❑ 466 Orestes Destrade .15 .07
❑ 467 Chris Hammond .15 .07
❑ 468 Bryan Harvey .15 .07
❑ 469 Charlie Hough .30 .14
❑ 470 Joe Klink .15 .07
❑ 471 Richie Lewis .15 .07
❑ 472 Bob Natal .15 .07
❑ 473 Pat Rapp .15 .07
❑ 474 Rich Renteria .15 .07
❑ 475 Rich Rodriguez .15 .07
❑ 476 Benito Santiago .15 .07
❑ 477 Gary Sheffield .60 .25
❑ 478 Matt Turner .15 .07
❑ 479 David Weathers .15 .07
❑ 480 Walt Weiss .15 .07
❑ 481 Darrell Whitmore .15 .07
❑ 482 Eric Anthony .15 .07
❑ 483 Jeff Bagwell .75 .35
❑ 484 Kevin Bass .15 .07
❑ 485 Craig Biggio .30 .14
❑ 486 Ken Caminiti .30 .14
❑ 487 Andujar Cedeno .15 .07
❑ 488 Chris Donnels .15 .07
❑ 489 Doug Drabek .15 .07
❑ 490 Steve Finley .30 .14
❑ 491 Luis Gonzalez .30 .14
❑ 492 Pete Harnisch .15 .07
❑ 493 Xavier Hernandez .15 .07
❑ 494 Doug Jones .15 .07
❑ 495 Todd Jones .15 .07
❑ 496 Darryl Kile .30 .14
❑ 497 Al Osuna .15 .07
❑ 498 Mark Portugal .15 .07
❑ 499 Scott Servais .15 .07
❑ 500 Greg Swindell .15 .07
❑ 501 Eddie Taubensee .15 .07
❑ 502 Jose Uribe .15 .07
❑ 503 Brian Williams .15 .07
❑ 504 Billy Ashley .15 .07
❑ 505 Pedro Astacio .15 .07
❑ 506 Brett Butler .30 .14
❑ 507 Tom Candiotti .15 .07
❑ 508 Omar Daal .15 .07
❑ 509 Jim Gott .15 .07
❑ 510 Kevin Gross .15 .07
❑ 511 Dave Hansen .15 .07
❑ 512 Carlos Hernandez .15 .07
❑ 513 Orel Hershiser .30 .14
❑ 514 Eric Karros .30 .14
❑ 515 Pedro Martinez 1.00 .45
❑ 516 Ramon Martinez .15 .07
❑ 517 Roger McDowell .15 .07
❑ 518 Raul Mondesi .30 .14
❑ 519 Jose Offerman .15 .07
❑ 520 Mike Piazza 2.00 .90
❑ 521 Jody Reed .15 .07
❑ 522 Henry Rodriguez .15 .07
❑ 523 Mike Sharperson .15 .07
❑ 524 Cory Snyder .15 .07
❑ 525 Darryl Strawberry .30 .14
❑ 526 Rick Trlicek .15 .07
❑ 527 Tim Wallach .15 .07
❑ 528 Mitch Webster .15 .07
❑ 529 Steve Wilson .15 .07
❑ 530 Todd Worrell .15 .07
❑ 531 Moises Alou .30 .14
❑ 532 Brian Barnes .15 .07
❑ 533 Sean Berry .15 .07
❑ 534 Greg Colbrunn .15 .07
❑ 535 Delino DeShields .15 .07
❑ 536 Jeff Fassero .15 .07
❑ 537 Darrin Fletcher .15 .07
❑ 538 Cliff Floyd .30 .14
❑ 539 Lou Frazier .15 .07
❑ 540 Marquis Grissom .15 .07
❑ 541 Butch Henry .15 .07
❑ 542 Ken Hill .15 .07
❑ 543 Mike Lansing .15 .07
❑ 544 Brian Looney RC .15 .07
❑ 545 Dennis Martinez .30 .14
❑ 546 Chris Nabholz .15 .07
❑ 547 Randy Ready .15 .07
❑ 548 Mel Rojas .15 .07
❑ 549 Kirk Rueter .15 .07
❑ 550 Tim Scott .15 .07
❑ 551 Jeff Shaw .15 .07
❑ 552 Tim Spehr .15 .07
❑ 553 John VanderWal .15 .07
❑ 554 Larry Walker .30 .14
❑ 555 John Wetteland .30 .14
❑ 556 Rondell White .30 .14
❑ 557 Tim Bogar .15 .07
❑ 558 Bobby Bonilla .30 .14
❑ 559 Jeromy Burnitz .30 .14
❑ 560 Sid Fernandez .15 .07
❑ 561 John Franco .30 .14
❑ 562 Dave Gallagher .15 .07
❑ 563 Dwight Gooden .30 .14
❑ 564 Eric Hillman .15 .07
❑ 565 Todd Hundley .15 .07
❑ 566 Jeff Innis .15 .07
❑ 567 Darrin Jackson .15 .07
❑ 568 Howard Johnson .15 .07
❑ 569 Bobby Jones .15 .07
❑ 570 Jeff Kent .30 .14
❑ 571 Mike Maddux .15 .07
❑ 572 Jeff McKnight .15 .07
❑ 573 Eddie Murray .60 .25
❑ 574 Charlie O'Brien .15 .07
❑ 575 Joe Orsulak .15 .07
❑ 576 Bret Saberhagen .30 .14

❑ 577 Pete Schourek .15 .07
❑ 578 Dave Telgheder .15 .07
❑ 579 Ryan Thompson .15 .07
❑ 580 Anthony Young .15 .07
❑ 581 Ruben Amaro .15 .07
❑ 582 Larry Andersen .15 .07
❑ 583 Kim Batiste .15 .07
❑ 584 Wes Chamberlain .15 .07
❑ 585 Darren Daulton .30 .14
❑ 586 Mariano Duncan .15 .07
❑ 587 Lenny Dykstra .30 .14
❑ 588 Jim Eisenreich .15 .07
❑ 589 Tommy Greene .15 .07
❑ 590 Dave Hollins .15 .07
❑ 591 Pete Incaviglia .15 .07
❑ 592 Danny Jackson .15 .07
❑ 593 Ricky Jordan .15 .07
❑ 594 John Kruk .30 .14
❑ 595 Roger Mason .15 .07
❑ 596 Mickey Morandini .15 .07
❑ 597 Terry Mulholland .15 .07
❑ 598 Todd Pratt .15 .07
❑ 599 Ben Rivera .15 .07
❑ 600 Curt Schilling .30 .14
❑ 601 Kevin Stocker .15 .07
❑ 602 Milt Thompson .15 .07
❑ 603 David West .30 .14
❑ 604 Mitch Williams .15 .07
❑ 605 Jay Bell .30 .14
❑ 606 Dave Clark .15 .07
❑ 607 Steve Cooke .15 .07
❑ 608 Tom Foley .15 .07
❑ 609 Carlos Garcia .15 .07
❑ 610 Joel Johnston .15 .07
❑ 611 Jeff King .15 .07
❑ 612 Al Martin .15 .07
❑ 613 Lloyd McClendon .15 .07
❑ 614 Orlando Merced .15 .07
❑ 615 Blas Minor .15 .07
❑ 616 Denny Neagle .15 .07
❑ 617 Mark Petkovsek RC .15 .07
❑ 618 Tom Prince .15 .07
❑ 619 Don Slaught .15 .07
❑ 620 Zane Smith .15 .07
❑ 621 Randy Tomlin .15 .07
❑ 622 Andy Van Slyke .30 .14
❑ 623 Paul Wagner .15 .07
❑ 624 Tim Wakefield .15 .07
❑ 625 Bob Walk .15 .07
❑ 626 Kevin Young .15 .07
❑ 627 Luis Alicea .15 .07
❑ 628 Rene Arocha .15 .07
❑ 629 Rod Brewer .15 .07
❑ 630 Rheal Cormier .15 .07
❑ 631 Bernard Gilkey .15 .07
❑ 632 Lee Guetterman .15 .07
❑ 633 Gregg Jefferies .15 .07
❑ 634 Brian Jordan .30 .14
❑ 635 Les Lancaster .15 .07
❑ 636 Ray Lankford .30 .14
❑ 637 Rob Murphy .15 .07
❑ 638 Omar Olivares .15 .07
❑ 639 Jose Oquendo .15 .07
❑ 640 Donovan Osborne .15 .07
❑ 641 Tom Pagnozzi .15 .07
❑ 642 Erik Pappas .15 .07
❑ 643 Geronimo Pena .15 .07
❑ 644 Mike Perez .15 .07
❑ 645 Gerald Perry .15 .07
❑ 646 Ozzie Smith .75 .35
❑ 647 Bob Tewksbury .15 .07
❑ 648 Allen Watson .15 .07
❑ 649 Mark Whiten .15 .07
❑ 650 Tracy Woodson .15 .07
❑ 651 Todd Zeile .15 .07
❑ 652 Andy Ashby .15 .07
❑ 653 Brad Ausmus .15 .07
❑ 654 Billy Bean .15 .07
❑ 655 Derek Bell .15 .07
❑ 656 Andy Benes .15 .07
❑ 657 Doug Brocail .15 .07
❑ 658 Jarvis Brown .15 .07
❑ 659 Archi Cianfrocco .15 .07
❑ 660 Phil Clark .15 .07
❑ 661 Mark Davis .15 .07
❑ 662 Jeff Gardner .15 .07
❑ 663 Pat Gomez .15 .07
❑ 664 Ricky Gutierrez .15 .07
❑ 665 Tony Gwynn 1.25 .55
❑ 666 Gene Harris .15 .07
❑ 667 Kevin Higgins .15 .07
❑ 668 Trevor Hoffman .30 .14
❑ 669 Pedro Martinez RC .15 .07
❑ 670 Tim Mauser .15 .07
❑ 671 Melvin Nieves .15 .07
❑ 672 Phil Plantier .15 .07
❑ 673 Frank Seminara .15 .07
❑ 674 Craig Shipley .15 .07
❑ 675 Kerry Taylor .15 .07
❑ 676 Tim Teufel .15 .07
❑ 677 Guillermo Velasquez .15 .07
❑ 678 Wally Whitehurst .15 .07
❑ 679 Tim Worrell .15 .07
❑ 680 Rod Beck .15 .07
❑ 681 Mike Benjamin .15 .07
❑ 682 Todd Benzinger .15 .07
❑ 683 Bud Black .15 .07
❑ 684 Barry Bonds 1.00 .45
❑ 685 Jeff Brantley .15 .07
❑ 686 Dave Burba .15 .07
❑ 687 John Burkett .15 .07
❑ 688 Mark Carreon .15 .07
❑ 689 Will Clark .60 .25
❑ 690 Royce Clayton .15 .07
❑ 691 Bryan Hickerson .15 .07
❑ 692 Mike Jackson .15 .07
❑ 693 Darren Lewis .15 .07
❑ 694 Kirt Manwaring .15 .07
❑ 695 Dave Martinez .15 .07
❑ 696 Willie McGee .30 .14
❑ 697 John Patterson .15 .07
❑ 698 Jeff Reed .15 .07
❑ 699 Kevin Rogers .15 .07
❑ 700 Scott Sanderson .15 .07
❑ 701 Steve Scarsone .15 .07
❑ 702 Billy Swift .15 .07
❑ 703 Robby Thompson .15 .07
❑ 704 Matt Williams .30 .14
❑ 705 Trevor Wilson .15 .07
❑ 706 Brave New World .30 .14
Fred McGriff
Ron Gant
David Justice
❑ 707 1-2 Punch .30 .14
John Olerud
Paul Molitor
❑ 708 American Heat .30 .14
Mike Mussina
Jack McDowell
❑ 709 Together Again .30 .14
Lou Whitaker
Alan Trammell
❑ 710 Lone Star Lumber .30 .14
Rafael Palmeiro
Juan Gonzalez
❑ 711 Batmen .30 .14
Brett Butler
Tony Gwynn
❑ 712 Twin Peaks .30 .14
Kirby Puckett
Chuck Knoblauch
❑ 713 Back to Back .75 .35
Mike Piazza
Eric Karros
❑ 714 Checklist 1 .15 .07
❑ 715 Checklist 2 .15 .07
❑ 716 Checklist 3 .15 .07
❑ 717 Checklist 4 .15 .07
❑ 718 Checklist 5 .15 .07
❑ 719 Checklist 6 .15 .07
❑ 720 Checklist 7 .15 .07
❑ P69 Tim Salmon Promo 1.00 .14

## 1994 Fleer Update

| | MINT | NRMT |
|---|---|---|
| COMP.FACT.SET (210) | 80.00 | 36.00 |
| COMPLETE SET (200) | 75.00 | 8.00 |

❑ 1 Mark Eichhorn .15 .07
❑ 2 Sid Fernandez .15 .07
❑ 3 Leo Gomez .15 .07

❑ 4 Mike Oquist .15 .07
❑ 5 Rafael Palmeiro 1.00 .45
❑ 6 Chris Sabo .15 .07
❑ 7 Dwight Smith .15 .07
❑ 8 Lee Smith .25 .11
❑ 9 Damon Berryhill .15 .07
❑ 10 Wes Chamberlain .15 .07
❑ 11 Gar Finnvold .15 .07
❑ 12 Chris Howard .15 .07
❑ 13 Tim Naehring .15 .07
❑ 14 Otis Nixon .15 .07
❑ 15 Brian Anderson RC .25 .11
❑ 16 Jorge Fabregas .15 .07
❑ 17 Rex Hudler .15 .07
❑ 18 Bo Jackson .25 .11
❑ 19 Mark Leiter .15 .07
❑ 20 Spike Owen .15 .07
❑ 21 Harold Reynolds .15 .07
❑ 22 Chris Turner .15 .07
❑ 23 Dennis Cook .15 .07
❑ 24 Jose DeLeon .15 .07
❑ 25 Julio Franco .15 .07
❑ 26 Joe Hall .15 .07
❑ 27 Darrin Jackson .15 .07
❑ 28 Dane Johnson .15 .07
❑ 29 Norberto Martin .15 .07
❑ 30 Scott Sanderson .15 .07
❑ 31 Jason Grimsley .15 .07
❑ 32 Dennis Martinez .25 .11
❑ 33 Jack Morris .25 .11
❑ 34 Eddie Murray 1.00 .45
❑ 35 Chad Ogea .15 .07
❑ 36 Tony Pena .15 .07
❑ 37 Paul Shuey .15 .07
❑ 38 Omar Vizquel .25 .11
❑ 39 Danny Bautista .15 .07
❑ 40 Tim Belcher .15 .07
❑ 41 Joe Boever .15 .07
❑ 42 Storm Davis .15 .07
❑ 43 Junior Felix .15 .07
❑ 44 Mike Gardiner .15 .07
❑ 45 Buddy Groom .15 .07
❑ 46 Juan Samuel .15 .07
❑ 47 Vince Coleman .15 .07
❑ 48 Bob Hamelin .15 .07
❑ 49 Dave Henderson .15 .07
❑ 50 Rusty Meacham .15 .07
❑ 51 Terry Shumpert .15 .07
❑ 52 Jeff Bronkey .15 .07
❑ 53 Alex Diaz .15 .07
❑ 54 Brian Harper .15 .07
❑ 55 Jose Mercedes .15 .07
❑ 56 Jody Reed .15 .07
❑ 57 Bob Scanlan .15 .07
❑ 58 Turner Ward .15 .07
❑ 59 Rich Becker .15 .07
❑ 60 Alex Cole .15 .07
❑ 61 Denny Hocking .15 .07
❑ 62 Scott Leius .15 .07
❑ 63 Pat Mahomes .15 .07
❑ 64 Carlos Pulido .15 .07
❑ 65 Dave Stevens .15 .07
❑ 66 Matt Walbeck .15 .07
❑ 67 Xavier Hernandez .15 .07
❑ 68 Sterling Hitchcock .15 .07
❑ 69 Terry Mulholland .15 .07
❑ 70 Luis Polonia .15 .07
❑ 71 Gerald Williams .15 .07

❑ 72 Mark Acre RC .................. .15 .07
❑ 73 Geronimo Berroa.............. .15 .07
❑ 74 Rickey Henderson.......... 1.25 .55
❑ 75 Stan Javier ..................... .15 .07
❑ 76 Steve Karsay..................... .15 .07
❑ 77 Carlos Reyes..................... .15 .07
❑ 78 Bill Taylor RC .................. .15 .07
❑ 79 Eric Anthony .................... .15 .07
❑ 80 Bobby Ayala ..................... .15 .07
❑ 81 Tim Davis ........................ .15 .07
❑ 82 Felix Fermin ..................... .15 .07
❑ 83 Reggie Jefferson............... .15 .07
❑ 84 Keith Mitchell.................... .15 .07
❑ 85 Bill Risley.......................... .15 .07
❑ 86 Alex Rodriguez RC ! .... 60.00 27.00
❑ 87 Roger Salkeld ................... .15 .07
❑ 88 Dan Wilson ....................... .15 .07
❑ 89 Cris Carpenter.................. .15 .07
❑ 90 Will Clark......................... 1.00 .45
❑ 91 Jeff Frye .......................... .15 .07
❑ 92 Rick Helling ...................... .25 .11
❑ 93 Chris James ..................... .15 .07
❑ 94 Oddibe McDowell ............. .15 .07
❑ 95 Billy Ripken ..................... .15 .07
❑ 96 Carlos Delgado .............. 1.50 .70
❑ 97 Alex Gonzalez.................. .15 .07
❑ 98 Shawn Green ................ 1.25 .55
❑ 99 Darren Hall ...................... .15 .07
❑ 100 Mike Huff....................... .15 .07
❑ 101 Mike Kelly ..................... .15 .07
❑ 102 Roberto Kelly................. .15 .07
❑ 103 Charlie O'Brien .............. .15 .07
❑ 104 Jose Oliva ..................... .15 .07
❑ 105 Gregg Olson .................. .15 .07
❑ 106 Willie Banks................... .15 .07
❑ 107 Jim Bullinger.................. .15 .07
❑ 108 Chuck Crim .................... .15 .07
❑ 109 Shawon Dunston............. .15 .07
❑ 110 Karl Rhodes .................. .15 .07
❑ 111 Steve Trachsel ............... .15 .07
❑ 112 Anthony Young .............. .15 .07
❑ 113 Eddie Zambrano ............ .15 .07
❑ 114 Bret Boone .................... .25 .11
❑ 115 Jeff Brantley .................. .15 .07
❑ 116 Hector Carrasco ............. .15 .07
❑ 117 Tony Fernandez ............. .15 .07
❑ 118 Tim Fortugno.................. .15 .07
❑ 119 Erik Hanson.................... .15 .07
❑ 120 Chuck McElroy .............. .15 .07
❑ 121 Deion Sanders .............. .25 .11
❑ 122 Ellis Burks ..................... .25 .11
❑ 123 Marvin Freeman ............. .15 .07
❑ 124 Mike Harkey .................. .15 .07
❑ 125 Howard Johnson ............. .15 .07
❑ 126 Mike Kingery .................. .15 .07
❑ 127 Nelson Liriano ................ .15 .07
❑ 128 Marcus Moore ................ .15 .07
❑ 129 Mike Munoz.................... .15 .07
❑ 130 Kevin Ritz ...................... .15 .07
❑ 131 Walt Weiss .................... .15 .07
❑ 132 Kurt Abbott RC .............. .15 .07
❑ 133 Jerry Browne.................. .15 .07
❑ 134 Greg Colbrunn................ .15 .07
❑ 135 Jeremy Hernandez ......... .15 .07
❑ 136 Dave Magadan ............... .15 .07
❑ 137 Kurt Miller ..................... .15 .07
❑ 138 Robb Nen ...................... .15 .07
❑ 139 Jesus Tavarez RC.......... .15 .07
❑ 140 Sid Bream ..................... .15 .07
❑ 141 Tom Edens ..................... .15 .07
❑ 142 Tony Eusebio ................ .15 .07
❑ 143 John Hudek RC.............. .15 .07
❑ 144 Brian L. Hunter .............. .15 .07
❑ 145 Orlando Miller ................ .15 .07
❑ 146 James Mouton................ .15 .07
❑ 147 Shane Reynolds ............. .15 .07
❑ 148 Rafael Bournigal ............ .15 .07
❑ 149 Delino DeShields............ .15 .07
❑ 150 Garey Ingram RC ........... .15 .07
❑ 151 Chan Ho Park RC ......... 1.25 .55
❑ 152 Wil Cordero .................... .15 .07
❑ 153 Pedro Martinez ............ 1.50 .70
❑ 154 Randy Milligan................ .15 .07
❑ 155 Lenny Webster ............... .15 .07
❑ 156 Rico Brogna ................... .15 .07
❑ 157 Josias Manzanillo .......... .15 .07
❑ 158 Kevin McReynolds ........ .15 .07
❑ 159 Mike Remlinger ............. .15 .07
❑ 160 David Segui.................... .15 .07
❑ 161 Pete Smith...................... .15 .07
❑ 162 Kelly Stinnett RC ........... .15 .07
❑ 163 Jose Vizcaino ................ .15 .07
❑ 164 Billy Hatcher .................. .15 .07
❑ 165 Doug Jones..................... .15 .07
❑ 166 Mike Lieberthal .............. .25 .11
❑ 167 Tony Longmire ............... .15 .07
❑ 168 Bobby Munoz ................. .15 .07
❑ 169 Paul Quantrill.................. .15 .07
❑ 170 Heathcliff Slocumb ........ .15 .07
❑ 171 Fernando Valenzuela .... .25 .11
❑ 172 Mark Dewey ................... .15 .07
❑ 173 Brian R. Hunter .............. .15 .07
❑ 174 Jon Lieber ...................... .15 .07
❑ 175 Ravelo Manzanillo.......... .15 .07
❑ 176 Dan Miceli ...................... .15 .07
❑ 177 Rick White...................... .15 .07
❑ 178 Bryan Eversgerd ............ .15 .07
❑ 179 John Habyan.................. .15 .07
❑ 180 Terry McGriff .................. .15 .07
❑ 181 Vicente Palacios ............ .15 .07
❑ 182 Rich Rodriguez .............. .15 .07
❑ 183 Rick Sutcliffe .................. .25 .11
❑ 184 Donnie Elliott.................. .15 .07
❑ 185 Joey Hamilton ................ .15 .07
❑ 186 Tim Hyers RC ................ .15 .07
❑ 187 Luis Lopez...................... .15 .07
❑ 188 Ray McDavid.................. .15 .07
❑ 189 Bip Roberts .................... .15 .07
❑ 190 Scott Sanders ................ .15 .07
❑ 191 Eddie Williams ............... .15 .07
❑ 192 Steve Frey...................... .15 .07
❑ 193 Pat Gomez ..................... .15 .07
❑ 194 Rich Monteleone ............ .15 .07
❑ 195 Mark Portugal ................ .15 .07
❑ 196 Darryl Strawberry .......... .25 .11
❑ 197 Salomon Torres.............. .15 .07
❑ 198 W.VanLandingham RC .. .15 .07
❑ 199 Checklist ....................... .15 .07
❑ 200 Checklist ....................... .15 .07

## 1995 Fleer

| | MINT | NRMT |
|---|---|---|
| COMPLETE SET (600) .......... | 50.00 | 22.00 |

❑ 1 Brady Anderson ............... .30 .14
❑ 2 Harold Baines .................. .30 .14
❑ 3 Damon Buford .................. .15 .07
❑ 4 Mike Devereaux ............... .15 .07
❑ 5 Mark Eichhorn .................. .15 .07
❑ 6 Sid Fernandez .................. .15 .07
❑ 7 Leo Gomez ....................... .15 .07
❑ 8 Jeffrey Hammonds .......... .30 .14
❑ 9 Chris Hoiles...................... .15 .07
❑ 10 Rick Krivda .................... .15 .07
❑ 11 Ben McDonald................ .15 .07
❑ 12 Mark McLemore ............. .15 .07
❑ 13 Alan Mills....................... .15 .07
❑ 14 Jamie Moyer .................. .15 .07
❑ 15 Mike Mussina ................. .60 .25
❑ 16 Mike Oquist.................... .15 .07
❑ 17 Rafael Palmeiro.............. .60 .25
❑ 18 Arthur Rhodes................ .15 .07
❑ 19 Cal Ripken Jr. .............. 2.50 1.10
❑ 20 Chris Sabo ..................... .15 .07
❑ 21 Lee Smith ....................... .30 .14
❑ 22 Jack Voigt ...................... .15 .07
❑ 23 Damon Berryhill.............. .15 .07
❑ 24 Tom Brunansky............... .15 .07
❑ 25 Wes Chamberlain ........... .15 .07
❑ 26 Roger Clemens ............ 1.25 .55
❑ 27 Scott Cooper .................. .15 .07
❑ 28 Andre Dawson................ .30 .14
❑ 29 Gar Finnvold .................. .15 .07
❑ 30 Tony Fossas ................... .15 .07
❑ 31 Mike Greenwell .............. .15 .07
❑ 32 Joe Hesketh ................... .15 .07
❑ 33 Chris Howard ................. .15 .07
❑ 34 Chris Nabholz ................ .15 .07
❑ 35 Tim Naehring.................. .15 .07
❑ 36 Otis Nixon ...................... .15 .07
❑ 37 Carlos Rodriguez ........... .15 .07
❑ 38 Rich Rowland ................. .15 .07
❑ 39 Ken Ryan ....................... .15 .07
❑ 40 Aaron Sele ..................... .30 .14
❑ 41 John Valentin ................. .15 .07
❑ 42 Mo Vaughn .................... .30 .14
❑ 43 Frank Viola ..................... .15 .07
❑ 44 Danny Bautista ............... .15 .07
❑ 45 Joe Boever ..................... .15 .07
❑ 46 Milt Cuyler ..................... .15 .07
❑ 47 Storm Davis.................... .15 .07
❑ 48 John Doherty.................. .15 .07
❑ 49 Junior Felix .................... .15 .07
❑ 50 Cecil Fielder ................... .30 .14
❑ 51 Travis Fryman ................ .30 .14
❑ 52 Mike Gardiner ................ .15 .07
❑ 53 Kirk Gibson .................... .30 .14
❑ 54 Chris Gomez .................. .15 .07
❑ 55 Buddy Groom ................. .15 .07
❑ 56 Mike Henneman ............. .15 .07
❑ 57 Chad Kreuter.................. .15 .07
❑ 58 Mike Moore .................... .15 .07
❑ 59 Tony Phillips .................. .15 .07
❑ 60 Juan Samuel .................. .15 .07
❑ 61 Mickey Tettleton ............ .15 .07
❑ 62 Alan Trammell................ .30 .14
❑ 63 David Wells .................... .30 .14
❑ 64 Lou Whitaker .................. .30 .14
❑ 65 Jim Abbott ...................... .30 .14
❑ 66 Joe Ausanio ................... .15 .07
❑ 67 Wade Boggs .................. .75 .35
❑ 68 Mike Gallego .................. .15 .07
❑ 69 Xavier Hernandez .......... .15 .07
❑ 70 Sterling Hitchcock ......... .15 .07
❑ 71 Steve Howe.................... .15 .07
❑ 72 Scott Kamieniecki .......... .15 .07
❑ 73 Pat Kelly ........................ .15 .07
❑ 74 Jimmy Key..................... .30 .14
❑ 75 Jim Leyritz...................... .15 .07
❑ 76 Don Mattingly UER ....... 1.50 .70
(Photo is a reversed negative)
❑ 77 Terry Mulholland ............ .15 .07
❑ 78 Paul O'Neill .................... .30 .14
❑ 79 Melido Perez.................. .15 .07
❑ 80 Luis Polonia................... .15 .07
❑ 81 Mike Stanley .................. .15 .07
❑ 82 Danny Tartabull.............. .15 .07
❑ 83 Randy Velarde ............... .15 .07
❑ 84 Bob Wickman ................ .15 .07
❑ 85 Bernie Williams ............. .60 .25
❑ 86 Gerald Williams ............. .15 .07
❑ 87 Roberto Alomar ............. .60 .25
❑ 88 Pat Borders .................... .15 .07
❑ 89 Joe Carter ...................... .30 .14
❑ 90 Tony Castillo .................. .15 .07
❑ 91 Brad Cornett RC ............ .15 .07
❑ 92 Carlos Delgado .............. .60 .25
❑ 93 Alex Gonzalez................ .15 .07
❑ 94 Shawn Green ................. .60 .25
❑ 95 Juan Guzman ................. .15 .07
❑ 96 Darren Hall .................... .15 .07
❑ 97 Pat Hentgen ................... .15 .07
❑ 98 Mike Huff........................ .15 .07
❑ 99 Randy Knorr .................. .15 .07
❑ 100 Al Leiter........................ .30 .14
❑ 101 Paul Molitor.................. .60 .25
❑ 102 John Olerud.................. .30 .14
❑ 103 Dick Schofield .............. .15 .07
❑ 104 Ed Sprague .................. .15 .07

❑ 105 Dave Stewart .30 .14
❑ 106 Todd Stottlemyre .15 .07
❑ 107 Devon White .30 .14
❑ 108 Woody Williams .15 .07
❑ 109 Wilson Alvarez .15 .07
❑ 110 Paul Assenmacher .15 .07
❑ 111 Jason Bere .15 .07
❑ 112 Dennis Cook .15 .07
❑ 113 Joey Cora .15 .07
❑ 114 Jose DeLeon .15 .07
❑ 115 Alex Fernandez .15 .07
❑ 116 Julio Franco .15 .07
❑ 117 Craig Grebeck .15 .07
❑ 118 Ozzie Guillen .15 .07
❑ 119 Roberto Hernandez .15 .07
❑ 120 Darrin Jackson .15 .07
❑ 121 Lance Johnson .15 .07
❑ 122 Ron Karkovice .15 .07
❑ 123 Mike LaValliere .15 .07
❑ 124 Norberto Martin .15 .07
❑ 125 Kirk McCaskill .15 .07
❑ 126 Jack McDowell .15 .07
❑ 127 Tim Raines .30 .14
❑ 128 Frank Thomas 1.25 .55
❑ 129 Robin Ventura .30 .14
❑ 130 Sandy Alomar Jr. .30 .14
❑ 131 Carlos Baerga .15 .07
❑ 132 Albert Belle .30 .14
❑ 133 Mark Clark .15 .07
❑ 134 Alvaro Espinoza .15 .07
❑ 135 Jason Grimsley .15 .07
❑ 136 Wayne Kirby .15 .07
❑ 137 Kenny Lofton .30 .14
❑ 138 Albie Lopez .15 .07
❑ 139 Dennis Martinez .30 .14
❑ 140 Jose Mesa .15 .07
❑ 141 Eddie Murray .60 .25
❑ 142 Charles Nagy .15 .07
❑ 143 Tony Pena .15 .07
❑ 144 Eric Plunk .15 .07
❑ 145 Manny Ramirez .75 .35
❑ 146 Jeff Russell .15 .07
❑ 147 Paul Shuey .15 .07
❑ 148 Paul Sorrento .15 .07
❑ 149 Jim Thome .30 .14
❑ 150 Omar Vizquel .30 .14
❑ 151 Dave Winfield .60 .25
❑ 152 Kevin Appier .30 .14
❑ 153 Billy Brewer .15 .07
❑ 154 Vince Coleman .15 .07
❑ 155 David Cone .30 .14
❑ 156 Gary Gaetti .30 .14
❑ 157 Greg Gagne .15 .07
❑ 158 Tom Gordon .15 .07
❑ 159 Mark Gubicza .15 .07
❑ 160 Bob Hamelin .15 .07
❑ 161 Dave Henderson .15 .07
❑ 162 Felix Jose .15 .07
❑ 163 Wally Joyner .30 .14
❑ 164 Jose Lind .15 .07
❑ 165 Mike Macfarlane .15 .07
❑ 166 Mike Magnante .15 .07
❑ 167 Brent Mayne .15 .07
❑ 168 Brian McRae .15 .07
❑ 169 Rusty Meacham .15 .07
❑ 170 Jeff Montgomery .15 .07
❑ 171 Hipolito Pichardo .15 .07
❑ 172 Terry Shumpert .15 .07
❑ 173 Michael Tucker .15 .07
❑ 174 Ricky Bones .15 .07
❑ 175 Jeff Cirillo .30 .14
❑ 176 Alex Diaz .15 .07
❑ 177 Cal Eldred .15 .07
❑ 178 Mike Fetters .15 .07
❑ 179 Darryl Hamilton .15 .07
❑ 180 Brian Harper .15 .07
❑ 181 John Jaha .15 .07
❑ 182 Pat Listach .15 .07
❑ 183 Graeme Lloyd .15 .07
❑ 184 Jose Mercedes .15 .07
❑ 185 Matt Mieske .15 .07
❑ 186 Dave Nilsson .15 .07
❑ 187 Jody Reed .15 .07
❑ 188 Bob Scanlan .15 .07
❑ 189 Kevin Seitzer .15 .07
❑ 190 Bill Spiers .15 .07
❑ 191 B.J. Surhoff .30 .14
❑ 192 Jose Valentin .15 .07
❑ 193 Greg Vaughn .30 .14
❑ 194 Turner Ward .15 .07
❑ 195 Bill Wegman .15 .07
❑ 196 Rick Aguilera .15 .07
❑ 197 Rich Becker .15 .07
❑ 198 Alex Cole .15 .07
❑ 199 Marty Cordova .15 .07
❑ 200 Steve Dunn .15 .07
❑ 201 Scott Erickson .15 .07
❑ 202 Mark Guthrie .15 .07
❑ 203 Chip Hale .15 .07
❑ 204 LaTroy Hawkins .15 .07
❑ 205 Denny Hocking .15 .07
❑ 206 Chuck Knoblauch .30 .14
❑ 207 Scott Leius .15 .07
❑ 208 Shane Mack .15 .07
❑ 209 Pat Mahomes .15 .07
❑ 210 Pat Meares .15 .07
❑ 211 Pedro Munoz .15 .07
❑ 212 Kirby Puckett 1.50 .70
❑ 213 Jeff Reboulet .15 .07
❑ 214 Dave Stevens .15 .07
❑ 215 Kevin Tapani .15 .07
❑ 216 Matt Walbeck .15 .07
❑ 217 Carl Willis .15 .07
❑ 218 Brian Anderson .15 .07
❑ 219 Chad Curtis .15 .07
❑ 220 Chili Davis .30 .14
❑ 221 Gary DiSarcina .15 .07
❑ 222 Damion Easley .15 .07
❑ 223 Jim Edmonds .60 .25
❑ 224 Chuck Finley .30 .14
❑ 225 Joe Grahe .15 .07
❑ 226 Rex Hudler .15 .07
❑ 227 Bo Jackson .30 .14
❑ 228 Mark Langston .15 .07
❑ 229 Phil Leftwich .15 .07
❑ 230 Mark Leiter .15 .07
❑ 231 Spike Owen .15 .07
❑ 232 Bob Patterson .15 .07
❑ 233 Troy Percival .15 .07
❑ 234 Eduardo Perez .15 .07
❑ 235 Tim Salmon .30 .14
❑ 236 J.T. Snow .30 .14
❑ 237 Chris Turner .15 .07
❑ 238 Mark Acre .15 .07
❑ 239 Geronimo Berroa .15 .07
❑ 240 Mike Bordick .15 .07
❑ 241 John Briscoe .15 .07
❑ 242 Scott Brosius .30 .14
❑ 243 Ron Darling .15 .07
❑ 244 Dennis Eckersley .30 .14
❑ 245 Brent Gates .15 .07
❑ 246 Rickey Henderson .75 .35
❑ 247 Stan Javier .15 .07
❑ 248 Steve Karsay .15 .07
❑ 249 Mark McGwire 2.50 1.10
❑ 250 Troy Neel .15 .07
❑ 251 Steve Ontiveros .15 .07
❑ 252 Carlos Reyes .15 .07
❑ 253 Ruben Sierra .15 .07
❑ 254 Terry Steinbach .15 .07
❑ 255 Bill Taylor .15 .07
❑ 256 Todd Van Poppel .15 .07
❑ 257 Bobby Witt .15 .07
❑ 258 Rich Amaral .15 .07
❑ 259 Eric Anthony .15 .07
❑ 260 Bobby Ayala .15 .07
❑ 261 Mike Blowers .15 .07
❑ 262 Chris Bosio .15 .07
❑ 263 Jay Buhner .30 .14
❑ 264 John Cummings .15 .07
❑ 265 Tim Davis .15 .07
❑ 266 Felix Fermin .15 .07
❑ 267 Dave Fleming .15 .07
❑ 268 Goose Gossage .30 .14
❑ 269 Ken Griffey Jr. 2.50 1.10
❑ 270 Reggie Jefferson .15 .07
❑ 271 Randy Johnson .75 .35
❑ 272 Edgar Martinez .30 .14
❑ 273 Tino Martinez .30 .14
❑ 274 Greg Pirkl .15 .07
❑ 275 Bill Risley .15 .07
❑ 276 Roger Salkeld .15 .07
❑ 277 Luis Sojo .15 .07
❑ 278 Mac Suzuki .15 .07
❑ 279 Dan Wilson .15 .07
❑ 280 Kevin Brown .30 .14
❑ 281 Jose Canseco .75 .35
❑ 282 Cris Carpenter .15 .07
❑ 283 Will Clark .60 .25
❑ 284 Jeff Frye .15 .07
❑ 285 Juan Gonzalez .60 .25
❑ 286 Rick Helling .30 .14
❑ 287 Tom Henke .15 .07
❑ 288 David Hulse .15 .07
❑ 289 Chris James .15 .07
❑ 290 Manuel Lee .15 .07
❑ 291 Oddibe McDowell .15 .07
❑ 292 Dean Palmer .30 .14
❑ 293 Roger Pavlik .15 .07
❑ 294 Bill Ripken .15 .07
❑ 295 Ivan Rodriguez .75 .35
❑ 296 Kenny Rogers .15 .07
❑ 297 Doug Strange .15 .07
❑ 298 Matt Whiteside .15 .07
❑ 299 Steve Avery .15 .07
❑ 300 Steve Bedrosian .15 .07
❑ 301 Rafael Belliard .15 .07
❑ 302 Jeff Blauser .15 .07
❑ 303 Dave Gallagher .15 .07
❑ 304 Tom Glavine .60 .25
❑ 305 David Justice .30 .14
❑ 306 Mike Kelly .15 .07
❑ 307 Roberto Kelly .15 .07
❑ 308 Ryan Klesko .30 .14
❑ 309 Mark Lemke .15 .07
❑ 310 Javier Lopez .30 .14
❑ 311 Greg Maddux 1.50 .70
❑ 312 Fred McGriff .30 .14
❑ 313 Greg McMichael .15 .07
❑ 314 Kent Mercker .15 .07
❑ 315 Charlie O'Brien .15 .07
❑ 316 Jose Oliva .15 .07
❑ 317 Terry Pendleton .30 .14
❑ 318 John Smoltz .30 .14
❑ 319 Mike Stanton .15 .07
❑ 320 Tony Tarasco .15 .07
❑ 321 Terrell Wade .15 .07
❑ 322 Mark Wohlers .15 .07
❑ 323 Kurt Abbott .15 .07
❑ 324 Luis Aquino .15 .07
❑ 325 Bret Barberie .15 .07
❑ 326 Ryan Bowen .15 .07
❑ 327 Jerry Browne .15 .07
❑ 328 Chuck Carr .15 .07
❑ 329 Matias Carrillo .15 .07
❑ 330 Greg Colbrunn .15 .07
❑ 331 Jeff Conine .15 .07
❑ 332 Mark Gardner .15 .07
❑ 333 Chris Hammond .15 .07
❑ 334 Bryan Harvey .15 .07
❑ 335 Richie Lewis .15 .07
❑ 336 Dave Magadan .15 .07
❑ 337 Terry Mathews .15 .07
❑ 338 Robb Nen .15 .07
❑ 339 Yorkis Perez .15 .07
❑ 340 Pat Rapp .15 .07
❑ 341 Benito Santiago .15 .07
❑ 342 Gary Sheffield .60 .25
❑ 343 Dave Weathers .15 .07
❑ 344 Moises Alou .30 .14
❑ 345 Sean Berry .15 .07
❑ 346 Wil Cordero .15 .07
❑ 347 Joey Eischen .15 .07
❑ 348 Jeff Fassero .15 .07
❑ 349 Darrin Fletcher .15 .07
❑ 350 Cliff Floyd .30 .14
❑ 351 Marquis Grissom .15 .07
❑ 352 Butch Henry .15 .07
❑ 353 Gil Heredia .15 .07
❑ 354 Ken Hill .15 .07
❑ 355 Mike Lansing .15 .07
❑ 356 Pedro Martinez .75 .35
❑ 357 Mel Rojas .15 .07
❑ 358 Kirk Rueter .15 .07
❑ 359 Tim Scott .15 .07
❑ 360 Jeff Shaw .15 .07
❑ 361 Larry Walker .30 .14
❑ 362 Lenny Webster .15 .07

| No. | Player | | |
|---|---|---|---|
| ❑ 363 | John Wetteland | .30 | .14 |
| ❑ 364 | Rondell White | .30 | .14 |
| ❑ 365 | Bobby Bonilla | .30 | .14 |
| ❑ 366 | Rico Brogna | .15 | .07 |
| ❑ 367 | Jeromy Burnitz | .30 | .14 |
| ❑ 368 | John Franco | .30 | .14 |
| ❑ 369 | Dwight Gooden | .30 | .14 |
| ❑ 370 | Todd Hundley | .15 | .07 |
| ❑ 371 | Jason Jacome | .15 | .07 |
| ❑ 372 | Bobby Jones | .15 | .07 |
| ❑ 373 | Jeff Kent | .30 | .14 |
| ❑ 374 | Jim Lindeman | .15 | .07 |
| ❑ 375 | Josias Manzanillo | .15 | .07 |
| ❑ 376 | Roger Mason | .15 | .07 |
| ❑ 377 | Kevin McReynolds | .15 | .07 |
| ❑ 378 | Joe Orsulak | .15 | .07 |
| ❑ 379 | Bill Pulsipher | .15 | .07 |
| ❑ 380 | Bret Saberhagen | .30 | .14 |
| ❑ 381 | David Segui | .15 | .07 |
| ❑ 382 | Pete Smith | .15 | .07 |
| ❑ 383 | Kelly Stinnett | .15 | .07 |
| ❑ 384 | Ryan Thompson | .15 | .07 |
| ❑ 385 | Jose Vizcaino | .15 | .07 |
| ❑ 386 | Toby Borland | .15 | .07 |
| ❑ 387 | Ricky Bottalico | .15 | .07 |
| ❑ 388 | Darren Daulton | .30 | .14 |
| ❑ 389 | Mariano Duncan | .15 | .07 |
| ❑ 390 | Lenny Dykstra | .30 | .14 |
| ❑ 391 | Jim Eisenreich | .15 | .07 |
| ❑ 392 | Tommy Greene | .15 | .07 |
| ❑ 393 | Dave Hollins | .15 | .07 |
| ❑ 394 | Pete Incaviglia | .15 | .07 |
| ❑ 395 | Danny Jackson | .15 | .07 |
| ❑ 396 | Doug Jones | .15 | .07 |
| ❑ 397 | Ricky Jordan | .15 | .07 |
| ❑ 398 | John Kruk | .30 | .14 |
| ❑ 399 | Mike Lieberthal | .30 | .14 |
| ❑ 400 | Tony Longmire | .15 | .07 |
| ❑ 401 | Mickey Morandini | .15 | .07 |
| ❑ 402 | Bobby Munoz | .15 | .07 |
| ❑ 403 | Curt Schilling | .30 | .14 |
| ❑ 404 | Heathcliff Slocumb | .15 | .07 |
| ❑ 405 | Kevin Stocker | .15 | .07 |
| ❑ 406 | Fernando Valenzuela | .30 | .14 |
| ❑ 407 | David West | .30 | .14 |
| ❑ 408 | Willie Banks | .15 | .07 |
| ❑ 409 | Jose Bautista | .15 | .07 |
| ❑ 410 | Steve Buechele | .15 | .07 |
| ❑ 411 | Jim Bullinger | .15 | .07 |
| ❑ 412 | Chuck Crim | .15 | .07 |
| ❑ 413 | Shawon Dunston | .15 | .07 |
| ❑ 414 | Kevin Foster | .15 | .07 |
| ❑ 415 | Mark Grace | .60 | .25 |
| ❑ 416 | Jose Hernandez | .15 | .07 |
| ❑ 417 | Glenallen Hill | .15 | .07 |
| ❑ 418 | Brooks Kieschnick | .15 | .07 |
| ❑ 419 | Derrick May | .15 | .07 |
| ❑ 420 | Randy Myers | .15 | .07 |
| ❑ 421 | Dan Plesac | .15 | .07 |
| ❑ 422 | Karl Rhodes | .15 | .07 |
| ❑ 423 | Rey Sanchez | .15 | .07 |
| ❑ 424 | Sammy Sosa | 1.25 | .55 |
| ❑ 425 | Steve Trachsel | .15 | .07 |
| ❑ 426 | Rick Wilkins | .15 | .07 |
| ❑ 427 | Anthony Young | .15 | .07 |
| ❑ 428 | Eddie Zambrano | .15 | .07 |
| ❑ 429 | Bret Boone | .30 | .14 |
| ❑ 430 | Jeff Branson | .15 | .07 |
| ❑ 431 | Jeff Brantley | .15 | .07 |
| ❑ 432 | Hector Carrasco | .15 | .07 |
| ❑ 433 | Brian Dorsett | .15 | .07 |
| ❑ 434 | Tony Fernandez | .15 | .07 |
| ❑ 435 | Tim Fortugno | .15 | .07 |
| ❑ 436 | Erik Hanson | .15 | .07 |
| ❑ 437 | Thomas Howard | .15 | .07 |
| ❑ 438 | Kevin Jarvis | .15 | .07 |
| ❑ 439 | Barry Larkin | .60 | .25 |
| ❑ 440 | Chuck McElroy | .15 | .07 |
| ❑ 441 | Kevin Mitchell | .15 | .07 |
| ❑ 442 | Hal Morris | .15 | .07 |
| ❑ 443 | Jose Rijo | .15 | .07 |
| ❑ 444 | John Roper | .15 | .07 |
| ❑ 445 | Johnny Ruffin | .15 | .07 |
| ❑ 446 | Deion Sanders | .30 | .14 |
| ❑ 447 | Reggie Sanders | .15 | .07 |
| ❑ 448 | Pete Schourek | .15 | .07 |
| ❑ 449 | John Smiley | .15 | .07 |
| ❑ 450 | Eddie Taubensee | .15 | .07 |
| ❑ 451 | Jeff Bagwell | .75 | .35 |
| ❑ 452 | Kevin Bass | .15 | .07 |
| ❑ 453 | Craig Biggio | .30 | .14 |
| ❑ 454 | Ken Caminiti | .30 | .14 |
| ❑ 455 | Andujar Cedeno | .15 | .07 |
| ❑ 456 | Doug Drabek | .15 | .07 |
| ❑ 457 | Tony Eusebio | .15 | .07 |
| ❑ 458 | Mike Felder | .15 | .07 |
| ❑ 459 | Steve Finley | .30 | .14 |
| ❑ 460 | Luis Gonzalez | .15 | .07 |
| ❑ 461 | Mike Hampton | .15 | .07 |
| ❑ 462 | Pete Harnisch | .15 | .07 |
| ❑ 463 | John Hudek | .15 | .07 |
| ❑ 464 | Todd Jones | .15 | .07 |
| ❑ 465 | Darryl Kile | .30 | .14 |
| ❑ 466 | James Mouton | .15 | .07 |
| ❑ 467 | Shane Reynolds | .15 | .07 |
| ❑ 468 | Scott Servais | .15 | .07 |
| ❑ 469 | Greg Swindell | .15 | .07 |
| ❑ 470 | Dave Veres RC | .15 | .07 |
| ❑ 471 | Brian Williams | .15 | .07 |
| ❑ 472 | Jay Bell | .30 | .14 |
| ❑ 473 | Jacob Brumfield | .15 | .07 |
| ❑ 474 | Dave Clark | .15 | .07 |
| ❑ 475 | Steve Cooke | .15 | .07 |
| ❑ 476 | Midre Cummings | .15 | .07 |
| ❑ 477 | Mark Dewey | .15 | .07 |
| ❑ 478 | Tom Foley | .15 | .07 |
| ❑ 479 | Carlos Garcia | .15 | .07 |
| ❑ 480 | Jeff King | .15 | .07 |
| ❑ 481 | Jon Lieber | .15 | .07 |
| ❑ 482 | Ravelo Manzanillo | .15 | .07 |
| ❑ 483 | Al Martin | .15 | .07 |
| ❑ 484 | Orlando Merced | .15 | .07 |
| ❑ 485 | Danny Miceli | .15 | .07 |
| ❑ 486 | Denny Neagle | .30 | .14 |
| ❑ 487 | Lance Parrish | .15 | .07 |
| ❑ 488 | Don Slaught | .15 | .07 |
| ❑ 489 | Zane Smith | .15 | .07 |
| ❑ 490 | Andy Van Slyke | .30 | .14 |
| ❑ 491 | Paul Wagner | .15 | .07 |
| ❑ 492 | Rick White | .15 | .07 |
| ❑ 493 | Luis Alicea | .15 | .07 |
| ❑ 494 | Rene Arocha | .15 | .07 |
| ❑ 495 | Rheal Cormier | .15 | .07 |
| ❑ 496 | Bryan Eversgerd | .15 | .07 |
| ❑ 497 | Bernard Gilkey | .15 | .07 |
| ❑ 498 | John Habyan | .15 | .07 |
| ❑ 499 | Gregg Jefferies | .15 | .07 |
| ❑ 500 | Brian Jordan | .30 | .14 |
| ❑ 501 | Ray Lankford | .30 | .14 |
| ❑ 502 | John Mabry | .15 | .07 |
| ❑ 503 | Terry McGriff | .15 | .07 |
| ❑ 504 | Tom Pagnozzi | .15 | .07 |
| ❑ 505 | Vicente Palacios | .15 | .07 |
| ❑ 506 | Geronimo Pena | .15 | .07 |
| ❑ 507 | Gerald Perry | .15 | .07 |
| ❑ 508 | Rich Rodriguez | .15 | .07 |
| ❑ 509 | Ozzie Smith | .75 | .35 |
| ❑ 510 | Bob Tewksbury | .15 | .07 |
| ❑ 511 | Allen Watson | .15 | .07 |
| ❑ 512 | Mark Whiten | .15 | .07 |
| ❑ 513 | Todd Zeile | .15 | .07 |
| ❑ 514 | Dante Bichette | .30 | .14 |
| ❑ 515 | Willie Blair | .15 | .07 |
| ❑ 516 | Ellis Burks | .30 | .14 |
| ❑ 517 | Marvin Freeman | .15 | .07 |
| ❑ 518 | Andres Galarraga | .30 | .14 |
| ❑ 519 | Joe Girardi | .15 | .07 |
| ❑ 520 | Greg W. Harris | .15 | .07 |
| ❑ 521 | Charlie Hayes | .15 | .07 |
| ❑ 522 | Mike Kingery | .15 | .07 |
| ❑ 523 | Nelson Liriano | .15 | .07 |
| ❑ 524 | Mike Munoz | .15 | .07 |
| ❑ 525 | David Nied | .15 | .07 |
| ❑ 526 | Steve Reed | .15 | .07 |
| ❑ 527 | Kevin Ritz | .15 | .07 |
| ❑ 528 | Bruce Ruffin | .15 | .07 |
| ❑ 529 | John Vander Wal | .15 | .07 |
| ❑ 530 | Walt Weiss | .15 | .07 |
| ❑ 531 | Eric Young | .15 | .07 |
| ❑ 532 | Billy Ashley | .15 | .07 |
| ❑ 533 | Pedro Astacio | .15 | .07 |
| ❑ 534 | Rafael Bournigal | .15 | .07 |
| ❑ 535 | Brett Butler | .30 | .14 |
| ❑ 536 | Tom Candiotti | .15 | .07 |
| ❑ 537 | Omar Daal | .15 | .07 |
| ❑ 538 | Delino DeShields | .15 | .07 |
| ❑ 539 | Darren Dreifort | .30 | .14 |
| ❑ 540 | Kevin Gross | .15 | .07 |
| ❑ 541 | Orel Hershiser | .30 | .14 |
| ❑ 542 | Garey Ingram | .15 | .07 |
| ❑ 543 | Eric Karros | .30 | .14 |
| ❑ 544 | Ramon Martinez | .15 | .07 |
| ❑ 545 | Raul Mondesi | .30 | .14 |
| ❑ 546 | Chan Ho Park | .30 | .14 |
| ❑ 547 | Mike Piazza | 2.00 | .90 |
| ❑ 548 | Henry Rodriguez | .15 | .07 |
| ❑ 549 | Rudy Seanez | .15 | .07 |
| ❑ 550 | Ismael Valdes | .15 | .07 |
| ❑ 551 | Tim Wallach | .15 | .07 |
| ❑ 552 | Todd Worrell | .15 | .07 |
| ❑ 553 | Andy Ashby | .15 | .07 |
| ❑ 554 | Brad Ausmus | .15 | .07 |
| ❑ 555 | Derek Bell | .15 | .07 |
| ❑ 556 | Andy Benes | .15 | .07 |
| ❑ 557 | Phil Clark | .15 | .07 |
| ❑ 558 | Donnie Elliott | .15 | .07 |
| ❑ 559 | Ricky Gutierrez | .15 | .07 |
| ❑ 560 | Tony Gwynn | 1.25 | .55 |
| ❑ 561 | Joey Hamilton | .15 | .07 |
| ❑ 562 | Trevor Hoffman | .30 | .14 |
| ❑ 563 | Luis Lopez | .15 | .07 |
| ❑ 564 | Pedro A. Martinez | .15 | .07 |
| ❑ 565 | Tim Mauser | .15 | .07 |
| ❑ 566 | Phil Plantier | .15 | .07 |
| ❑ 567 | Bip Roberts | .15 | .07 |
| ❑ 568 | Scott Sanders | .15 | .07 |
| ❑ 569 | Craig Shipley | .15 | .07 |
| ❑ 570 | Jeff Tabaka | .15 | .07 |
| ❑ 571 | Eddie Williams | .15 | .07 |
| ❑ 572 | Rod Beck | .15 | .07 |
| ❑ 573 | Mike Benjamin | .15 | .07 |
| ❑ 574 | Barry Bonds | 1.00 | .45 |
| ❑ 575 | Dave Burba | .15 | .07 |
| ❑ 576 | John Burkett | .15 | .07 |
| ❑ 577 | Mark Carreon | .15 | .07 |
| ❑ 578 | Royce Clayton | .15 | .07 |
| ❑ 579 | Steve Frey | .15 | .07 |
| ❑ 580 | Bryan Hickerson | .15 | .07 |
| ❑ 581 | Mike Jackson | .15 | .07 |
| ❑ 582 | Darren Lewis | .15 | .07 |
| ❑ 583 | Kirt Manwaring | .15 | .07 |
| ❑ 584 | Rich Monteleone | .15 | .07 |
| ❑ 585 | John Patterson | .15 | .07 |
| ❑ 586 | J.R. Phillips | .15 | .07 |
| ❑ 587 | Mark Portugal | .15 | .07 |
| ❑ 588 | Joe Rosselli | .15 | .07 |
| ❑ 589 | Darryl Strawberry | .30 | .14 |
| ❑ 590 | Bill Swift | .15 | .07 |
| ❑ 591 | Robby Thompson | .15 | .07 |
| ❑ 592 | William VanLandingham | .15 | .07 |
| ❑ 593 | Matt Williams | .30 | .14 |
| ❑ 594 | Checklist | .15 | .07 |
| ❑ 595 | Checklist | .15 | .07 |
| ❑ 596 | Checklist | .15 | .07 |
| ❑ 597 | Checklist | .15 | .07 |
| ❑ 598 | Checklist | .15 | .07 |
| ❑ 599 | Checklist | .15 | .07 |
| ❑ 600 | Checklist | .15 | .07 |

## 1995 Fleer Update

| | MINT | NRMT |
|---|---|---|
| COMPLETE SET (200) | 15.00 | 6.75 |
| ❑ 1 Manny Alexander | .10 | .05 |
| ❑ 2 Bret Barberie | .10 | .05 |
| ❑ 3 Armando Benitez | .20 | .09 |
| ❑ 4 Kevin Brown | .20 | .09 |
| ❑ 5 Doug Jones | .10 | .05 |
| ❑ 6 Sherman Obando | .10 | .05 |
| ❑ 7 Andy Van Slyke | .20 | .09 |
| ❑ 8 Stan Belinda | .10 | .05 |
| ❑ 9 Jose Canseco | .50 | .23 |
| ❑ 10 Vaughn Eshelman | .10 | .05 |
| ❑ 11 Mike Macfarlane | .10 | .05 |
| ❑ 12 Troy O'Leary | .10 | .05 |
| ❑ 13 Steve Rodriguez | .10 | .05 |
| ❑ 14 Lee Tinsley | .10 | .05 |
| ❑ 15 Tim Vanegmond | .10 | .05 |
| ❑ 16 Mark Whiten | .10 | .05 |
| ❑ 17 Sean Bergman | .10 | .05 |
| ❑ 18 Chad Curtis | .10 | .05 |
| ❑ 19 John Flaherty | .10 | .05 |
| ❑ 20 Bob Higginson RC | .60 | .25 |
| ❑ 21 Felipe Lira | .10 | .05 |
| ❑ 22 Shannon Penn | .10 | .05 |
| ❑ 23 Todd Steverson | .10 | .05 |
| ❑ 24 Sean Whiteside | .10 | .05 |
| ❑ 25 Tony Fernandez | .10 | .05 |
| ❑ 26 Jack McDowell | .10 | .05 |
| ❑ 27 Andy Pettitte | .20 | .09 |
| ❑ 28 John Wetteland | .20 | .09 |
| ❑ 29 David Cone | .20 | .09 |
| ❑ 30 Mike Timlin | .10 | .05 |
| ❑ 31 Duane Ward | .10 | .05 |
| ❑ 32 Jim Abbott | .20 | .09 |
| ❑ 33 James Baldwin | .20 | .09 |
| ❑ 34 Mike Devereaux | .10 | .05 |
| ❑ 35 Ray Durham | .20 | .09 |
| ❑ 36 Tim Fortugno | .10 | .05 |
| ❑ 37 Scott Ruffcorn | .10 | .05 |
| ❑ 38 Chris Sabo | .10 | .05 |
| ❑ 39 Paul Assenmacher | .10 | .05 |
| ❑ 40 Bud Black | .10 | .05 |
| ❑ 41 Orel Hershiser | .20 | .09 |
| ❑ 42 Julian Tavarez | .10 | .05 |
| ❑ 43 Dave Winfield | .40 | .18 |
| ❑ 44 Pat Borders | .10 | .05 |
| ❑ 45 Melvin Bunch RC | .10 | .05 |
| ❑ 46 Tom Goodwin | .10 | .05 |
| ❑ 47 Jon Nunnally | .10 | .05 |
| ❑ 48 Joe Randa | .10 | .05 |
| ❑ 49 Dilson Torres RC | .10 | .05 |
| ❑ 50 Joe Vitiello | .10 | .05 |
| ❑ 51 David Hulse | .10 | .05 |
| ❑ 52 Scott Karl | .10 | .05 |
| ❑ 53 Mark Kiefer | .10 | .05 |
| ❑ 54 Derrick May | .10 | .05 |
| ❑ 55 Joe Oliver | .10 | .05 |
| ❑ 56 Al Reyes RC | .10 | .05 |
| ❑ 57 Steve Sparks RC | .10 | .05 |
| ❑ 58 Jerald Clark | .10 | .05 |
| ❑ 59 Eddie Guardado | .10 | .05 |
| ❑ 60 Kevin Maas | .10 | .05 |
| ❑ 61 David McCarty | .10 | .05 |
| ❑ 62 Brad Radke RC | .60 | .25 |
| ❑ 63 Scott Stahoviak | .10 | .05 |
| ❑ 64 Garret Anderson | .20 | .09 |
| ❑ 65 Shawn Boskie | .10 | .05 |
| ❑ 66 Mike James | .10 | .05 |
| ❑ 67 Tony Phillips | .10 | .05 |
| ❑ 68 Lee Smith | .20 | .09 |
| ❑ 69 Mitch Williams | .10 | .05 |
| ❑ 70 Jim Corsi | .10 | .05 |
| ❑ 71 Mark Harkey | .10 | .05 |
| ❑ 72 Dave Stewart | .20 | .09 |
| ❑ 73 Todd Stottlemyre | .10 | .05 |
| ❑ 74 Joey Cora | .10 | .05 |
| ❑ 75 Chad Kreuter | .10 | .05 |
| ❑ 76 Jeff Nelson | .10 | .05 |
| ❑ 77 Alex Rodriguez | 1.50 | .70 |
| ❑ 78 Ron Villone | .10 | .05 |
| ❑ 79 Bob Wells RC | .10 | .05 |
| ❑ 80 Jose Alberro RC | .10 | .05 |
| ❑ 81 Terry Burrows | .10 | .05 |
| ❑ 82 Kevin Gross | .10 | .05 |
| ❑ 83 Wilson Heredia | .10 | .05 |
| ❑ 84 Mark McLemore | .10 | .05 |
| ❑ 85 Otis Nixon | .10 | .05 |
| ❑ 86 Jeff Russell | .10 | .05 |
| ❑ 87 Mickey Tettleton | .10 | .05 |
| ❑ 88 Bob Tewksbury | .10 | .05 |
| ❑ 89 Pedro Borbon | .10 | .05 |
| ❑ 90 Marquis Grissom | .10 | .05 |
| ❑ 91 Chipper Jones | 1.00 | .45 |
| ❑ 92 Mike Mordecai | .10 | .05 |
| ❑ 93 Jason Schmidt | .10 | .05 |
| ❑ 94 John Burkett | .10 | .05 |
| ❑ 95 Andre Dawson | .20 | .09 |
| ❑ 96 Matt Dunbar RC | .10 | .05 |
| ❑ 97 Charles Johnson | .20 | .09 |
| ❑ 98 Terry Pendleton | .20 | .09 |
| ❑ 99 Rich Scheid | .10 | .05 |
| ❑ 100 Quilvio Veras | .10 | .05 |
| ❑ 101 Bobby Witt | .10 | .05 |
| ❑ 102 Eddie Zosky | .10 | .05 |
| ❑ 103 Shane Andrews | .10 | .05 |
| ❑ 104 Reid Cornelius | .10 | .05 |
| ❑ 105 Chad Fonville RC | .10 | .05 |
| ❑ 106 Mark Grudzielanek RC | .20 | .09 |
| ❑ 107 Roberto Kelly | .10 | .05 |
| ❑ 108 Carlos Perez RC | .20 | .09 |
| ❑ 109 Tony Tarasco | .10 | .05 |
| ❑ 110 Brett Butler | .20 | .09 |
| ❑ 111 Carl Everett | .20 | .09 |
| ❑ 112 Pete Harnisch | .10 | .05 |
| ❑ 113 Doug Henry | .10 | .05 |
| ❑ 114 Kevin Lomon RC | .10 | .05 |
| ❑ 115 Blas Minor | .10 | .05 |
| ❑ 116 Dave Mlicki | .10 | .05 |
| ❑ 117 Ricky Otero RC | .10 | .05 |
| ❑ 118 Norm Charlton | .10 | .05 |
| ❑ 119 Tyler Green | .10 | .05 |
| ❑ 120 Gene Harris | .10 | .05 |
| ❑ 121 Charlie Hayes | .10 | .05 |
| ❑ 122 Gregg Jefferies | .10 | .05 |
| ❑ 123 Michael Mimbs RC | .10 | .05 |
| ❑ 124 Paul Quantrill | .10 | .05 |
| ❑ 125 Frank Castillo | .10 | .05 |
| ❑ 126 Brian McRae | .10 | .05 |
| ❑ 127 Jaime Navarro | .10 | .05 |
| ❑ 128 Mike Perez | .10 | .05 |
| ❑ 129 Tanyon Sturtze | .10 | .05 |
| ❑ 130 Ozzie Timmons | .10 | .05 |
| ❑ 131 John Courtright | .10 | .05 |
| ❑ 132 Ron Gant | .10 | .05 |
| ❑ 133 Xavier Hernandez | .10 | .05 |
| ❑ 134 Brian Hunter | .10 | .05 |
| ❑ 135 Benito Santiago | .10 | .05 |
| ❑ 136 Pete Smith | .10 | .05 |
| ❑ 137 Scott Sullivan | .10 | .05 |
| ❑ 138 Derek Bell | .10 | .05 |
| ❑ 139 Doug Brocail | .10 | .05 |
| ❑ 140 Ricky Gutierrez | .10 | .05 |
| ❑ 141 Pedro A.Martinez | .10 | .05 |
| ❑ 142 Orlando Miller | .10 | .05 |
| ❑ 143 Phil Plantier | .10 | .05 |
| ❑ 144 Craig Shipley | .10 | .05 |
| ❑ 145 Rich Aude | .10 | .05 |
| ❑ 146 Jason Christiansen RC | .10 | .05 |
| ❑ 147 Freddy Garcia RC | .10 | .05 |
| ❑ 148 Jim Gott | .10 | .05 |
| ❑ 149 Mark Johnson RC | .10 | .05 |
| ❑ 150 Esteban Loaiza | .10 | .05 |
| ❑ 151 Dan Plesac | .10 | .05 |
| ❑ 152 Gary Wilson RC | .10 | .05 |
| ❑ 153 Allen Battle | .10 | .05 |
| ❑ 154 Terry Bradshaw | .10 | .05 |
| ❑ 155 Scott Cooper | .10 | .05 |
| ❑ 156 Tripp Cromer | .10 | .05 |
| ❑ 157 John Frascatore RC | .10 | .05 |
| ❑ 158 John Habyan | .10 | .05 |
| ❑ 159 Tom Henke | .10 | .05 |
| ❑ 160 Ken Hill | .10 | .05 |
| ❑ 161 Danny Jackson | .10 | .05 |
| ❑ 162 Donovan Osborne | .10 | .05 |
| ❑ 163 Tom Urbani | .10 | .05 |
| ❑ 164 Roger Bailey | .10 | .05 |
| ❑ 165 Jorge Brito RC | .10 | .05 |
| ❑ 166 Vinny Castilla | .20 | .09 |
| ❑ 167 Darren Holmes | .10 | .05 |
| ❑ 168 Roberto Mejia | .10 | .05 |
| ❑ 169 Bill Swift | .10 | .05 |
| ❑ 170 Mark Thompson | .10 | .05 |
| ❑ 171 Larry Walker | .20 | .09 |
| ❑ 172 Greg Hansell | .10 | .05 |
| ❑ 173 Dave Hansen | .10 | .05 |
| ❑ 174 Carlos Hernandez | .10 | .05 |
| ❑ 175 Hideo Nomo RC | 1.00 | .45 |
| ❑ 176 Jose Offerman | .10 | .05 |
| ❑ 177 Antonio Osuna | .10 | .05 |
| ❑ 178 Reggie Williams | .10 | .05 |
| ❑ 179 Todd Williams | .10 | .05 |
| ❑ 180 Andres Berumen | .10 | .05 |
| ❑ 181 Ken Caminiti | .20 | .09 |
| ❑ 182 Andujar Cedeno | .10 | .05 |
| ❑ 183 Steve Finley | .20 | .09 |
| ❑ 184 Bryce Florie | .10 | .05 |
| ❑ 185 Dustin Hermanson | .10 | .05 |
| ❑ 186 Ray Holbert | .10 | .05 |
| ❑ 187 Melvin Nieves | .10 | .05 |
| ❑ 188 Roberto Petagine | .10 | .05 |
| ❑ 189 Jody Reed | .10 | .05 |
| ❑ 190 Fernando Valenzuela | .20 | .09 |
| ❑ 191 Brian Williams | .10 | .05 |
| ❑ 192 Mark Dewey | .10 | .05 |
| ❑ 193 Glenallen Hill | .10 | .05 |
| ❑ 194 Chris Hook RC | .10 | .05 |
| ❑ 195 Terry Mulholland | .10 | .05 |
| ❑ 196 Steve Scarsone | .10 | .05 |
| ❑ 197 Trevor Wilson | .10 | .05 |
| ❑ 198 Checklist | .10 | .05 |
| ❑ 199 Checklist | .10 | .05 |
| ❑ 200 Checklist | .10 | .05 |

## 1996 Fleer

| | MINT | NRMT |
|---|---|---|
| COMPLETE SET (600) | 80.00 | 36.00 |
| COMMON CARD (1-600) | .15 | .07 |
| ❑ 1 Manny Alexander | .15 | .07 |
| ❑ 2 Brady Anderson | .25 | .11 |
| ❑ 3 Harold Baines | .25 | .11 |
| ❑ 4 Armando Benitez | .15 | .07 |
| ❑ 5 Bobby Bonilla | .25 | .11 |
| ❑ 6 Kevin Brown | .40 | .18 |
| ❑ 7 Scott Erickson | .15 | .07 |
| ❑ 8 Curtis Goodwin | .15 | .07 |
| ❑ 9 Jeffrey Hammonds | .25 | .11 |
| ❑ 10 Jimmy Haynes | .15 | .07 |
| ❑ 11 Chris Hoiles | .15 | .07 |
| ❑ 12 Doug Jones | .15 | .07 |
| ❑ 13 Rick Krivda | .15 | .07 |
| ❑ 14 Jeff Manto | .15 | .07 |
| ❑ 15 Ben McDonald | .15 | .07 |
| ❑ 16 Jamie Moyer | .15 | .07 |
| ❑ 17 Mike Mussina | .60 | .25 |
| ❑ 18 Jesse Orosco | .15 | .07 |
| ❑ 19 Rafael Palmeiro | .60 | .25 |
| ❑ 20 Cal Ripken | 2.50 | 1.10 |
| ❑ 21 Rick Aguilera | .15 | .07 |
| ❑ 22 Luis Alicea | .15 | .07 |
| ❑ 23 Stan Belinda | .15 | .07 |
| ❑ 24 Jose Canseco | .75 | .35 |
| ❑ 25 Roger Clemens | 1.25 | .55 |
| ❑ 26 Vaughn Eshelman | .15 | .07 |
| ❑ 27 Mike Greenwell | .15 | .07 |
| ❑ 28 Erik Hanson | .15 | .07 |
| ❑ 29 Dwayne Hosey | .15 | .07 |
| ❑ 30 Mike Macfarlane UER | .15 | .07 |

❑ 31 Tim Naehring .15 .07
❑ 32 Troy O'Leary .15 .07
❑ 33 Aaron Sele .25 .11
❑ 34 Zane Smith .15 .07
❑ 35 Jeff Suppan .15 .07
❑ 36 Lee Tinsley .15 .07
❑ 37 John Valentin .15 .07
❑ 38 Mo Vaughn .25 .11
❑ 39 Tim Wakefield .15 .07
❑ 40 Jim Abbott .25 .11
❑ 41 Brian Anderson .15 .07
❑ 42 Garret Anderson .25 .11
❑ 43 Chili Davis .25 .11
❑ 44 Gary DiSarcina .15 .07
❑ 45 Damion Easley .15 .07
❑ 46 Jim Edmonds .60 .25
❑ 47 Chuck Finley .25 .11
❑ 48 Todd Greene .15 .07
❑ 49 Mike Harkey .15 .07
❑ 50 Mike James .15 .07
❑ 51 Mark Langston .15 .07
❑ 52 Greg Myers .15 .07
❑ 53 Orlando Palmeiro .15 .07
❑ 54 Bob Patterson .15 .07
❑ 55 Troy Percival .15 .07
❑ 56 Tony Phillips .15 .07
❑ 57 Tim Salmon .25 .11
❑ 58 Lee Smith .25 .11
❑ 59 J.T. Snow .25 .11
❑ 60 Randy Velarde .15 .07
❑ 61 Wilson Alvarez .15 .07
❑ 62 Luis Andujar .15 .07
❑ 63 Jason Bere .15 .07
❑ 64 Ray Durham .25 .11
❑ 65 Alex Fernandez .15 .07
❑ 66 Ozzie Guillen .15 .07
❑ 67 Roberto Hernandez .15 .07
❑ 68 Lance Johnson .15 .07
❑ 69 Matt Karchner .15 .07
❑ 70 Ron Karkovice .15 .07
❑ 71 Norberto Martin .15 .07
❑ 72 Dave Martinez .15 .07
❑ 73 Kirk McCaskill .15 .07
❑ 74 Lyle Mouton .15 .07
❑ 75 Tim Raines .25 .11
❑ 76 Mike Sirotka RC .75 .35
❑ 77 Frank Thomas 1.25 .55
❑ 78 Larry Thomas .15 .07
❑ 79 Robin Ventura .25 .11
❑ 80 Sandy Alomar Jr. .25 .11
❑ 81 Paul Assenmacher .15 .07
❑ 82 Carlos Baerga .15 .07
❑ 83 Albert Belle .40 .18
❑ 84 Mark Clark .15 .07
❑ 85 Alan Embree .15 .07
❑ 86 Alvaro Espinoza .15 .07
❑ 87 Orel Hershiser .25 .11
❑ 88 Ken Hill .15 .07
❑ 89 Kenny Lofton .25 .11
❑ 90 Dennis Martinez .25 .11
❑ 91 Jose Mesa .15 .07
❑ 92 Eddie Murray .60 .25
❑ 93 Charles Nagy .15 .07
❑ 94 Chad Ogea .15 .07
❑ 95 Tony Pena .15 .07
❑ 96 Herb Perry .15 .07
❑ 97 Eric Plunk .15 .07
❑ 98 Jim Poole .15 .07
❑ 99 Manny Ramirez .75 .35
❑ 100 Paul Sorrento .15 .07
❑ 101 Julian Tavarez .15 .07
❑ 102 Jim Thome .40 .18
❑ 103 Omar Vizquel .25 .11
❑ 104 Dave Winfield .60 .25
❑ 105 Danny Bautista .15 .07
❑ 106 Joe Boever .15 .07
❑ 107 Chad Curtis .15 .07
❑ 108 John Doherty .15 .07
❑ 109 Cecil Fielder .25 .11
❑ 110 John Flaherty .15 .07
❑ 111 Travis Fryman .25 .11
❑ 112 Chris Gomez .15 .07
❑ 113 Bob Higginson .25 .11
❑ 114 Mark Lewis .15 .07
❑ 115 Jose Lima .15 .07
❑ 116 Felipe Lira .15 .07
❑ 117 Brian Maxcy .15 .07
❑ 118 C.J. Nitkowski .15 .07
❑ 119 Phil Plantier .15 .07
❑ 120 Clint Sodowsky .15 .07
❑ 121 Alan Trammell .40 .18
❑ 122 Lou Whitaker .25 .11
❑ 123 Kevin Appier .25 .11
❑ 124 Johnny Damon .40 .18
❑ 125 Gary Gaetti .25 .11
❑ 126 Tom Goodwin .15 .07
❑ 127 Tom Gordon .15 .07
❑ 128 Mark Gubicza .15 .07
❑ 129 Bob Hamelin .15 .07
❑ 130 David Howard .15 .07
❑ 131 Jason Jacome .15 .07
❑ 132 Wally Joyner .25 .11
❑ 133 Keith Lockhart .15 .07
❑ 134 Brent Mayne .15 .07
❑ 135 Jeff Montgomery .15 .07
❑ 136 Jon Nunnally .15 .07
❑ 137 Juan Samuel .15 .07
❑ 138 Mike Sweeney RC 2.50 1.10
❑ 139 Michael Tucker .15 .07
❑ 140 Joe Vitiello .15 .07
❑ 141 Ricky Bones .15 .07
❑ 142 Chuck Carr .15 .07
❑ 143 Jeff Cirillo .25 .11
❑ 144 Mike Fetters .15 .07
❑ 145 Darryl Hamilton .15 .07
❑ 146 David Hulse .15 .07
❑ 147 John Jaha .15 .07
❑ 148 Scott Karl .15 .07
❑ 149 Mark Kiefer .15 .07
❑ 150 Pat Listach .15 .07
❑ 151 Mark Loretta .15 .07
❑ 152 Mike Matheny .15 .07
❑ 153 Matt Mieske .15 .07
❑ 154 Dave Nilsson .15 .07
❑ 155 Joe Oliver .15 .07
❑ 156 Al Reyes .15 .07
❑ 157 Kevin Seltzer .15 .07
❑ 158 Steve Sparks .15 .07
❑ 159 B.J. Surhoff .25 .11
❑ 160 Jose Valentin .15 .07
❑ 161 Greg Vaughn .25 .11
❑ 162 Fernando Vina .15 .07
❑ 163 Rich Becker .15 .07
❑ 164 Ron Coomer .15 .07
❑ 165 Marty Cordova .15 .07
❑ 166 Chuck Knoblauch .25 .11
❑ 167 Matt Lawton RC .75 .35
❑ 168 Pat Meares .15 .07
❑ 169 Paul Molitor .60 .25
❑ 170 Pedro Munoz .15 .07
❑ 171 Jose Parra .15 .07
❑ 172 Kirby Puckett 1.50 .70
❑ 173 Brad Radke .25 .11
❑ 174 Jeff Reboulet .15 .07
❑ 175 Rich Robertson .15 .07
❑ 176 Frank Rodriguez .15 .07
❑ 177 Scott Stahoviak .15 .07
❑ 178 Dave Stevens .15 .07
❑ 179 Matt Walbeck .15 .07
❑ 180 Wade Boggs .75 .35
❑ 181 David Cone .25 .11
❑ 182 Tony Fernandez .15 .07
❑ 183 Joe Girardi .15 .07
❑ 184 Derek Jeter 2.50 1.10
❑ 185 Scott Kamieniecki .15 .07
❑ 186 Pat Kelly .15 .07
❑ 187 Jim Leyritz .15 .07
❑ 188 Tino Martinez .25 .11
❑ 189 Don Mattingly 1.50 .70
❑ 190 Jack McDowell .15 .07
❑ 191 Jeff Nelson .15 .07
❑ 192 Paul O'Neill .25 .11
❑ 193 Melido Perez .15 .07
❑ 194 Andy Pettitte .25 .11
❑ 195 Mariano Rivera .25 .11
❑ 196 Ruben Sierra .15 .07
❑ 197 Mike Stanley .15 .07
❑ 198 Darryl Strawberry .25 .11
❑ 199 John Wetteland .25 .11
❑ 200 Bob Wickman .15 .07
❑ 201 Bernie Williams .60 .25
❑ 202 Mark Acre .15 .07
❑ 203 Geronimo Berroa .15 .07
❑ 204 Mike Bordick .15 .07
❑ 205 Scott Brosius .25 .11
❑ 206 Dennis Eckersley .25 .11
❑ 207 Brent Gates .15 .07
❑ 208 Jason Giambi .60 .25
❑ 209 Rickey Henderson .75 .35
❑ 210 Jose Herrera .15 .07
❑ 211 Stan Javier .15 .07
❑ 212 Doug Johns .15 .07
❑ 213 Mark McGwire 2.50 1.10
❑ 214 Steve Ontiveros .15 .07
❑ 215 Craig Paquette .15 .07
❑ 216 Ariel Prieto .15 .07
❑ 217 Carlos Reyes .15 .07
❑ 218 Terry Steinbach .15 .07
❑ 219 Todd Stottlemyre .15 .07
❑ 220 Danny Tartabull .15 .07
❑ 221 Todd Van Poppel .15 .07
❑ 222 John Wasdin .15 .07
❑ 223 George Williams .15 .07
❑ 224 Steve Wojciechowski .15 .07
❑ 225 Rich Amaral .15 .07
❑ 226 Bobby Ayala .15 .07
❑ 227 Tim Belcher .15 .07
❑ 228 Andy Benes .15 .07
❑ 229 Chris Bosio .15 .07
❑ 230 Darren Bragg .15 .07
❑ 231 Jay Buhner .25 .11
❑ 232 Norm Charlton .15 .07
❑ 233 Vince Coleman .15 .07
❑ 234 Joey Cora .15 .07
❑ 235 Russ Davis .15 .07
❑ 236 Alex Diaz .15 .07
❑ 237 Felix Fermin .15 .07
❑ 238 Ken Griffey Jr. 2.50 1.10
❑ 239 Sterling Hitchcock .15 .07
❑ 240 Randy Johnson .75 .35
❑ 241 Edgar Martinez .40 .18
❑ 242 Bill Risley .15 .07
❑ 243 Alex Rodriguez 2.00 .90
❑ 244 Luis Sojo .15 .07
❑ 245 Dan Wilson .15 .07
❑ 246 Bob Wolcott .15 .07
❑ 247 Will Clark .60 .25
❑ 248 Jeff Frye .15 .07
❑ 249 Benji Gil .15 .07
❑ 250 Juan Gonzalez .60 .25
❑ 251 Rusty Greer .25 .11
❑ 252 Kevin Gross .15 .07
❑ 253 Roger McDowell .15 .07
❑ 254 Mark McLemore .15 .07
❑ 255 Otis Nixon .15 .07
❑ 256 Luis Ortiz .15 .07
❑ 257 Mike Pagliarulo .15 .07
❑ 258 Dean Palmer .25 .11
❑ 259 Roger Pavlik .15 .07
❑ 260 Ivan Rodriguez .75 .35
❑ 261 Kenny Rogers .15 .07
❑ 262 Jeff Russell .15 .07
❑ 263 Mickey Tettleton .15 .07
❑ 264 Bob Tewksbury .15 .07
❑ 265 Dave Valle .15 .07
❑ 266 Matt Whiteside .15 .07
❑ 267 Roberto Alomar .60 .25
❑ 268 Joe Carter .25 .11
❑ 269 Tony Castillo .15 .07
❑ 270 Domingo Cedeno .15 .07
❑ 271 Tim Crabtree UER .15 .07
❑ 272 Carlos Delgado .60 .25
❑ 273 Alex Gonzalez .15 .07
❑ 274 Shawn Green .60 .25
❑ 275 Juan Guzman .15 .07
❑ 276 Pat Hentgen .15 .07
❑ 277 Al Leiter .25 .11
❑ 278 Sandy Martinez .15 .07
❑ 279 Paul Menhart .15 .07
❑ 280 John Olerud .25 .11
❑ 281 Paul Quantrill .15 .07
❑ 282 Ken Robinson .15 .07
❑ 283 Ed Sprague .15 .07
❑ 284 Mike Timlin .15 .07
❑ 285 Steve Avery .15 .07
❑ 286 Rafael Belliard .15 .07
❑ 287 Jeff Blauser .15 .07
❑ 288 Pedro Borbon .15 .07

❑ 289 Brad Clontz .15 .07
❑ 290 Mike Devereaux .15 .07
❑ 291 Tom Glavine .60 .25
❑ 292 Marquis Grissom .15 .07
❑ 293 Chipper Jones 1.50 .70
❑ 294 David Justice .40 .18
❑ 295 Mike Kelly .15 .07
❑ 296 Ryan Klesko .25 .11
❑ 297 Mark Lemke .15 .07
❑ 298 Javier Lopez .25 .11
❑ 299 Greg Maddux 1.50 .70
❑ 300 Fred McGriff .40 .18
❑ 301 Greg McMichael .15 .07
❑ 302 Kent Mercker .15 .07
❑ 303 Mike Mordecai .15 .07
❑ 304 Charlie O'Brien .15 .07
❑ 305 Eduardo Perez .15 .07
❑ 306 Luis Polonia .15 .07
❑ 307 Jason Schmidt .15 .07
❑ 308 John Smoltz .25 .11
❑ 309 Terrell Wade .15 .07
❑ 310 Mark Wohlers .15 .07
❑ 311 Scott Bullett .15 .07
❑ 312 Jim Bullinger .15 .07
❑ 313 Larry Casian .15 .07
❑ 314 Frank Castillo .15 .07
❑ 315 Shawon Dunston .15 .07
❑ 316 Kevin Foster .15 .07
❑ 317 Matt Franco .15 .07
❑ 318 Luis Gonzalez .25 .11
❑ 319 Mark Grace .60 .25
❑ 320 Jose Hernandez .15 .07
❑ 321 Mike Hubbard .15 .07
❑ 322 Brian McRae .15 .07
❑ 323 Randy Myers .15 .07
❑ 324 Jaime Navarro .15 .07
❑ 325 Mark Parent .15 .07
❑ 326 Mike Perez .15 .07
❑ 327 Rey Sanchez .15 .07
❑ 328 Ryne Sandberg .75 .35
❑ 329 Scott Servais .15 .07
❑ 330 Sammy Sosa 1.25 .55
❑ 331 Ozzie Timmons .15 .07
❑ 332 Steve Trachsel .15 .07
❑ 333 Todd Zeile .15 .07
❑ 334 Bret Boone .25 .11
❑ 335 Jeff Branson .15 .07
❑ 336 Jeff Brantley .15 .07
❑ 337 Dave Burba .15 .07
❑ 338 Hector Carrasco .15 .07
❑ 339 Mariano Duncan .15 .07
❑ 340 Ron Gant .15 .07
❑ 341 Lenny Harris .15 .07
❑ 342 Xavier Hernandez .15 .07
❑ 343 Thomas Howard .15 .07
❑ 344 Mike Jackson .15 .07
❑ 345 Barry Larkin .60 .25
❑ 346 Darren Lewis .15 .07
❑ 347 Hal Morris .15 .07
❑ 348 Eric Owens .15 .07
❑ 349 Mark Portugal .15 .07
❑ 350 Jose Rijo .15 .07
❑ 351 Reggie Sanders .15 .07
❑ 352 Benito Santiago .15 .07
❑ 353 Pete Schourek .15 .07
❑ 354 John Smiley .15 .07
❑ 355 Eddie Taubensee .15 .07
❑ 356 Jerome Walton .15 .07
❑ 357 David Wells .25 .11
❑ 358 Roger Bailey .15 .07
❑ 359 Jason Bates .15 .07
❑ 360 Dante Bichette .25 .11
❑ 361 Ellis Burks .25 .11
❑ 362 Vinny Castilla .25 .11
❑ 363 Andres Galarraga .40 .18
❑ 364 Darren Holmes .15 .07
❑ 365 Mike Kingery .15 .07
❑ 366 Curt Leskanic .15 .07
❑ 367 Quinton McCracken .15 .07
❑ 368 Mike Munoz .15 .07
❑ 369 David Nied .15 .07
❑ 370 Steve Reed .15 .07
❑ 371 Bryan Rekar .15 .07
❑ 372 Kevin Ritz .15 .07
❑ 373 Bruce Ruffin .15 .07
❑ 374 Bret Saberhagen .25 .11
❑ 375 Bill Swift .15 .07
❑ 376 John Vander Wal .15 .07
❑ 377 Larry Walker .25 .11
❑ 378 Walt Weiss .15 .07
❑ 379 Eric Young .15 .07
❑ 380 Kurt Abbott .15 .07
❑ 381 Alex Arias .15 .07
❑ 382 Jerry Browne .15 .07
❑ 383 John Burkett .15 .07
❑ 384 Greg Colbrunn .15 .07
❑ 385 Jeff Conine .15 .07
❑ 386 Andre Dawson .40 .18
❑ 387 Chris Hammond .15 .07
❑ 388 Charles Johnson .25 .11
❑ 389 Terry Mathews .15 .07
❑ 390 Robb Nen .15 .07
❑ 391 Joe Orsulak .15 .07
❑ 392 Terry Pendleton .25 .11
❑ 393 Pat Rapp .15 .07
❑ 394 Gary Sheffield .60 .25
❑ 395 Jesus Tavarez .15 .07
❑ 396 Marc Valdes .15 .07
❑ 397 Quilvio Veras .15 .07
❑ 398 Randy Veres .15 .07
❑ 399 Devon White .25 .11
❑ 400 Jeff Bagwell .75 .35
❑ 401 Derek Bell .15 .07
❑ 402 Craig Biggio .40 .18
❑ 403 John Cangelosi .15 .07
❑ 404 Jim Dougherty .15 .07
❑ 405 Doug Drabek .15 .07
❑ 406 Tony Eusebio .15 .07
❑ 407 Ricky Gutierrez .15 .07
❑ 408 Mike Hampton .25 .11
❑ 409 Dean Hartgraves .15 .07
❑ 410 John Hudek .15 .07
❑ 411 Brian L. Hunter .15 .07
❑ 412 Todd Jones .15 .07
❑ 413 Darryl Kile .25 .11
❑ 414 Dave Magadan .15 .07
❑ 415 Derrick May .15 .07
❑ 416 Orlando Miller .15 .07
❑ 417 James Mouton .15 .07
❑ 418 Shane Reynolds .15 .07
❑ 419 Greg Swindell .15 .07
❑ 420 Jeff Tabaka .15 .07
❑ 421 Dave Veres .15 .07
❑ 422 Billy Wagner .15 .07
❑ 423 Donne Wall .15 .07
❑ 424 Rick Wilkins .15 .07
❑ 425 Billy Ashley .15 .07
❑ 426 Mike Blowers .15 .07
❑ 427 Brett Butler .25 .11
❑ 428 Tom Candiotti .15 .07
❑ 429 Juan Castro .15 .07
❑ 430 John Cummings .15 .07
❑ 431 Delino DeShields .15 .07
❑ 432 Joey Eischen .15 .07
❑ 433 Chad Fonville .15 .07
❑ 434 Greg Gagne .15 .07
❑ 435 Dave Hansen .15 .07
❑ 436 Carlos Hernandez .15 .07
❑ 437 Todd Hollandsworth .15 .07
❑ 438 Eric Karros .25 .11
❑ 439 Roberto Kelly .15 .07
❑ 440 Ramon Martinez .15 .07
❑ 441 Raul Mondesi .25 .11
❑ 442 Hideo Nomo .60 .25
❑ 443 Antonio Osuna .15 .07
❑ 444 Chan Ho Park .25 .11
❑ 445 Mike Piazza 2.00 .90
❑ 446 Felix Rodriguez .15 .07
❑ 447 Kevin Tapani .15 .07
❑ 448 Ismael Valdes .15 .07
❑ 449 Todd Worrell .15 .07
❑ 450 Moises Alou .25 .11
❑ 451 Shane Andrews .15 .07
❑ 452 Yamil Benitez .15 .07
❑ 453 Sean Berry .15 .07
❑ 454 Wil Cordero .15 .07
❑ 455 Jeff Fassero .15 .07
❑ 456 Darrin Fletcher .15 .07
❑ 457 Cliff Floyd .25 .11
❑ 458 Mark Grudzielanek .15 .07
❑ 459 Gil Heredia .15 .07
❑ 460 Tim Laker .15 .07
❑ 461 Mike Lansing .15 .07
❑ 462 Pedro J.Martinez .75 .35
❑ 463 Carlos Perez .15 .07
❑ 464 Curtis Pride .15 .07
❑ 465 Mel Rojas .15 .07
❑ 466 Kirk Rueter .15 .07
❑ 467 F.P. Santangelo .15 .07
❑ 468 Tim Scott .15 .07
❑ 469 David Segui .15 .07
❑ 470 Tony Tarasco .15 .07
❑ 471 Rondell White .25 .11
❑ 472 Edgardo Alfonzo .25 .11
❑ 473 Tim Bogar .15 .07
❑ 474 Rico Brogna .15 .07
❑ 475 Damon Buford .15 .07
❑ 476 Paul Byrd .15 .07
❑ 477 Carl Everett .25 .11
❑ 478 John Franco .25 .11
❑ 479 Todd Hundley .15 .07
❑ 480 Butch Huskey .15 .07
❑ 481 Jason Isringhausen .25 .11
❑ 482 Bobby Jones .15 .07
❑ 483 Chris Jones .15 .07
❑ 484 Jeff Kent .40 .18
❑ 485 Dave Mlicki .15 .07
❑ 486 Robert Person .15 .07
❑ 487 Bill Pulsipher .15 .07
❑ 488 Kelly Stinnett .15 .07
❑ 489 Ryan Thompson .15 .07
❑ 490 Jose Vizcaino .15 .07
❑ 491 Howard Battle .15 .07
❑ 492 Toby Borland .15 .07
❑ 493 Ricky Bottalico .15 .07
❑ 494 Darren Daulton .25 .11
❑ 495 Lenny Dykstra .25 .11
❑ 496 Jim Eisenreich .15 .07
❑ 497 Sid Fernandez .15 .07
❑ 498 Tyler Green .15 .07
❑ 499 Charlie Hayes .15 .07
❑ 500 Gregg Jefferies .15 .07
❑ 501 Kevin Jordan .15 .07
❑ 502 Tony Longmire .15 .07
❑ 503 Tom Marsh .15 .07
❑ 504 Michael Mimbs .15 .07
❑ 505 Mickey Morandini .15 .07
❑ 506 Gene Schall .15 .07
❑ 507 Curt Schilling .25 .11
❑ 508 Heathcliff Slocumb .15 .07
❑ 509 Kevin Stocker .15 .07
❑ 510 Andy Van Slyke .25 .11
❑ 511 Lenny Webster .15 .07
❑ 512 Mark Whiten .15 .07
❑ 513 Mike Williams .15 .07
❑ 514 Jay Bell .25 .11
❑ 515 Jacob Brumfield .15 .07
❑ 516 Jason Christiansen .15 .07
❑ 517 Dave Clark .15 .07
❑ 518 Midre Cummings .15 .07
❑ 519 Angelo Encarnacion .15 .07
❑ 520 John Ericks .15 .07
❑ 521 Carlos Garcia .15 .07
❑ 522 Mark Johnson .15 .07
❑ 523 Jeff King .15 .07
❑ 524 Nelson Liriano .15 .07
❑ 525 Esteban Loaiza .15 .07
❑ 526 Al Martin .15 .07
❑ 527 Orlando Merced .15 .07
❑ 528 Dan Miceli .15 .07
❑ 529 Ramon Morel .15 .07
❑ 530 Denny Neagle .25 .11
❑ 531 Steve Parris .15 .07
❑ 532 Dan Plesac .15 .07
❑ 533 Don Slaught .15 .07
❑ 534 Paul Wagner .15 .07
❑ 535 John Wehner .15 .07
❑ 536 Kevin Young .15 .07
❑ 537 Allen Battle .15 .07
❑ 538 David Bell .15 .07
❑ 539 Alan Benes .15 .07
❑ 540 Scott Cooper .15 .07
❑ 541 Tripp Cromer .15 .07
❑ 542 Tony Fossas .15 .07
❑ 543 Bernard Gilkey .15 .07
❑ 544 Tom Henke .15 .07
❑ 545 Brian Jordan .25 .11
❑ 546 Ray Lankford .25 .11

| | | |
|---|---|---|
| ❑ 547 John Mabry | .15 | .07 |
| ❑ 548 T.J. Mathews | .15 | .07 |
| ❑ 549 Mike Morgan | .15 | .07 |
| ❑ 550 Jose Oliva | .15 | .07 |
| ❑ 551 Jose Oquendo | .15 | .07 |
| ❑ 552 Donovan Osborne | .15 | .07 |
| ❑ 553 Tom Pagnozzi | .15 | .07 |
| ❑ 554 Mark Petkovsek | .15 | .07 |
| ❑ 555 Danny Sheaffer | .15 | .07 |
| ❑ 556 Ozzie Smith | .75 | .35 |
| ❑ 557 Mark Sweeney | .15 | .07 |
| ❑ 558 Allen Watson | .15 | .07 |
| ❑ 559 Andy Ashby | .15 | .07 |
| ❑ 560 Brad Ausmus | .15 | .07 |
| ❑ 561 Willie Blair | .15 | .07 |
| ❑ 562 Ken Caminiti | .25 | .11 |
| ❑ 563 Andujar Cedeno | .15 | .07 |
| ❑ 564 Glenn Dishman | .15 | .07 |
| ❑ 565 Steve Finley | .25 | .11 |
| ❑ 566 Bryce Florie | .15 | .07 |
| ❑ 567 Tony Gwynn | 1.25 | .55 |
| ❑ 568 Joey Hamilton | .15 | .07 |
| ❑ 569 Dustin Hermanson UER | .15 | .07 |
| ❑ 570 Trevor Hoffman | .25 | .11 |
| ❑ 571 Brian Johnson | .15 | .07 |
| ❑ 572 Marc Kroon | .15 | .07 |
| ❑ 573 Scott Livingstone | .15 | .07 |
| ❑ 574 Marc Newfield | .15 | .07 |
| ❑ 575 Melvin Nieves | .15 | .07 |
| ❑ 576 Jody Reed | .15 | .07 |
| ❑ 577 Bip Roberts | .15 | .07 |
| ❑ 578 Scott Sanders | .15 | .07 |
| ❑ 579 Fernando Valenzuela | .25 | .11 |
| ❑ 580 Eddie Williams | .15 | .07 |
| ❑ 581 Rod Beck | .15 | .07 |
| ❑ 582 Marvin Benard UER RC | .15 | .07 |
| ❑ 583 Barry Bonds | 1.00 | .45 |
| ❑ 584 Jamie Brewington RC | .15 | .07 |
| ❑ 585 Mark Carreon | .15 | .07 |
| ❑ 586 Royce Clayton | .15 | .07 |
| ❑ 587 Shawn Estes | .25 | .11 |
| ❑ 588 Glenallen Hill | .15 | .07 |
| ❑ 589 Mark Leiter | .15 | .07 |
| ❑ 590 Kirt Manwaring | .15 | .07 |
| ❑ 591 David McCarty | .15 | .07 |
| ❑ 592 Terry Mulholland | .15 | .07 |
| ❑ 593 John Patterson | .15 | .07 |
| ❑ 594 J.R. Phillips | .15 | .07 |
| ❑ 595 Deion Sanders | .25 | .11 |
| ❑ 596 Steve Scarsone | .15 | .07 |
| ❑ 597 Robby Thompson | .15 | .07 |
| ❑ 598 Sergio Valdez | .15 | .07 |
| ❑ 599 William Van Landingham | .15 | .07 |
| ❑ 600 Matt Williams | .40 | .18 |
| ❑ P20 Cal Ripken Promo | 3.00 | 1.35 |

## 1996 Fleer Update

| | MINT | NRMT |
|---|---|---|
| COMPLETE SET (250) | 30.00 | 13.50 |
| ❑ U1 Roberto Alomar | .60 | .25 |
| ❑ U2 Mike Devereaux | .15 | .07 |
| ❑ U3 Scott McClain RC | .15 | .07 |
| ❑ U4 Roger McDowell | .15 | .07 |
| ❑ U5 Kent Mercker | .15 | .07 |
| ❑ U6 Jimmy Myers RC | .15 | .07 |
| ❑ U7 Randy Myers | .15 | .07 |
| ❑ U8 B.J. Surhoff | .30 | .14 |
| ❑ U9 Tony Tarasco | .15 | .07 |
| ❑ U10 David Wells | .30 | .14 |
| ❑ U11 Wil Cordero | .15 | .07 |
| ❑ U12 Tom Gordon | .15 | .07 |
| ❑ U13 Reggie Jefferson | .15 | .07 |
| ❑ U14 Jose Malave | .15 | .07 |
| ❑ U15 Kevin Mitchell | .15 | .07 |
| ❑ U16 Jamie Moyer | .15 | .07 |
| ❑ U17 Heathcliff Slocumb | .15 | .07 |
| ❑ U18 Mike Stanley | .15 | .07 |
| ❑ U19 George Arias | .15 | .07 |
| ❑ U20 Jorge Fabregas | .15 | .07 |
| ❑ U21 Don Slaught | .15 | .07 |
| ❑ U22 Randy Velarde | .15 | .07 |
| ❑ U23 Harold Baines | .30 | .14 |
| ❑ U24 Mike Cameron RC | 2.50 | 1.10 |
| ❑ U25 Darren Lewis | .15 | .07 |
| ❑ U26 Tony Phillips | .15 | .07 |
| ❑ U27 Bill Simas | .15 | .07 |
| ❑ U28 Chris Snopek | .15 | .07 |
| ❑ U29 Kevin Tapani | .15 | .07 |
| ❑ U30 Danny Tartabull | .15 | .07 |
| ❑ U31 Julio Franco | .15 | .07 |
| ❑ U32 Jack McDowell | .15 | .07 |
| ❑ U33 Kimera Bartee | .15 | .07 |
| ❑ U34 Mark Lewis | .15 | .07 |
| ❑ U35 Melvin Nieves | .15 | .07 |
| ❑ U36 Mark Parent | .15 | .07 |
| ❑ U37 Eddie Williams | .15 | .07 |
| ❑ U38 Tim Belcher | .15 | .07 |
| ❑ U39 Sal Fasano | .15 | .07 |
| ❑ U40 Chris Haney | .15 | .07 |
| ❑ U41 Mike Macfarlane | .15 | .07 |
| ❑ U42 Jose Offerman | .15 | .07 |
| ❑ U43 Joe Randa | .15 | .07 |
| ❑ U44 Bip Roberts | .15 | .07 |
| ❑ U45 Chuck Carr | .15 | .07 |
| ❑ U46 Bobby Hughes | .15 | .07 |
| ❑ U47 Graeme Lloyd | .15 | .07 |
| ❑ U48 Ben McDonald | .15 | .07 |
| ❑ U49 Kevin Wickander | .15 | .07 |
| ❑ U50 Rick Aguilera | .15 | .07 |
| ❑ U51 Mike Durant | .15 | .07 |
| ❑ U52 Chip Hale | .15 | .07 |
| ❑ U53 LaTroy Hawkins | .15 | .07 |
| ❑ U54 Dave Hollins | .15 | .07 |
| ❑ U55 Roberto Kelly | .15 | .07 |
| ❑ U56 Paul Molitor | .60 | .25 |
| ❑ U57 Dan Naulty | .15 | .07 |
| ❑ U58 Mariano Duncan | .15 | .07 |
| ❑ U59 Andy Fox | .15 | .07 |
| ❑ U60 Joe Girardi | .15 | .07 |
| ❑ U61 Dwight Gooden | .30 | .14 |
| ❑ U62 Jimmy Key | .30 | .14 |
| ❑ U63 Matt Luke | .15 | .07 |
| ❑ U64 Tino Martinez | .30 | .14 |
| ❑ U65 Jeff Nelson | .15 | .07 |
| ❑ U66 Tim Raines | .30 | .14 |
| ❑ U67 Ruben Rivera | .15 | .07 |
| ❑ U68 Kenny Rogers | .15 | .07 |
| ❑ U69 Gerald Williams | .15 | .07 |
| ❑ U70 Tony Batista RC | 8.00 | 3.60 |
| ❑ U71 Allen Battle | .15 | .07 |
| ❑ U72 Jim Corsi | .15 | .07 |
| ❑ U73 Steve Cox | .15 | .07 |
| ❑ U74 Pedro Munoz | .15 | .07 |
| ❑ U75 Phil Plantier | .15 | .07 |
| ❑ U76 Scott Spiezio | .15 | .07 |
| ❑ U77 Ernie Young | .15 | .07 |
| ❑ U78 Russ Davis | .15 | .07 |
| ❑ U79 Sterling Hitchcock | .15 | .07 |
| ❑ U80 Edwin Hurtado | .15 | .07 |
| ❑ U81 Raul Ibanez RC | .15 | .07 |
| ❑ U82 Mike Jackson | .15 | .07 |
| ❑ U83 Ricky Jordan | .15 | .07 |
| ❑ U84 Paul Sorrento | .15 | .07 |
| ❑ U85 Doug Strange | .15 | .07 |
| ❑ U86 Mark Brandenburg RC | .15 | .07 |
| ❑ U87 Damon Buford | .15 | .07 |
| ❑ U88 Kevin Elster | .15 | .07 |
| ❑ U89 Darryl Hamilton | .15 | .07 |
| ❑ U90 Ken Hill | .15 | .07 |
| ❑ U91 Ed Vosberg | .15 | .07 |
| ❑ U92 Craig Worthington | .15 | .07 |
| ❑ U93 Tilson Brito RC | .15 | .07 |
| ❑ U94 Giovanni Carrara RC | .15 | .07 |
| ❑ U95 Felipe Crespo | .15 | .07 |
| ❑ U96 Erik Hanson | .15 | .07 |
| ❑ U97 Marty Janzen RC | .15 | .07 |
| ❑ U98 Otis Nixon | .15 | .07 |
| ❑ U99 Charlie O'Brien | .15 | .07 |
| ❑ U100 Robert Perez | .15 | .07 |
| ❑ U101 Paul Quantrill | .15 | .07 |
| ❑ U102 Bill Risley | .15 | .07 |
| ❑ U103 Juan Samuel | .15 | .07 |
| ❑ U104 Jermaine Dye | .30 | .14 |
| ❑ U105 Wonderful Monds RC | .15 | .07 |
| ❑ U106 Dwight Smith | .15 | .07 |
| ❑ U107 Jerome Walton | .15 | .07 |
| ❑ U108 Terry Adams | .15 | .07 |
| ❑ U109 Leo Gomez | .15 | .07 |
| ❑ U110 Robin Jennings | .15 | .07 |
| ❑ U111 Doug Jones | .15 | .07 |
| ❑ U112 Brooks Kieschnick | .15 | .07 |
| ❑ U113 Dave Magadan | .15 | .07 |
| ❑ U114 Jason Maxwell RC | .15 | .07 |
| ❑ U115 Rodney Myers RC | .15 | .07 |
| ❑ U116 Eric Anthony | .15 | .07 |
| ❑ U117 Vince Coleman | .15 | .07 |
| ❑ U118 Eric Davis | .30 | .14 |
| ❑ U119 Steve Gibralter | .15 | .07 |
| ❑ U120 Curtis Goodwin | .15 | .07 |
| ❑ U121 Willie Greene | .30 | .14 |
| ❑ U122 Mike Kelly | .15 | .07 |
| ❑ U123 Marcus Moore | .15 | .07 |
| ❑ U124 Chad Mottola | .15 | .07 |
| ❑ U125 Chris Sabo | .15 | .07 |
| ❑ U126 Roger Salkeld | .15 | .07 |
| ❑ U127 Pedro Castellano | .15 | .07 |
| ❑ U128 Trenidad Hubbard | .15 | .07 |
| ❑ U129 Jayhawk Owens | .15 | .07 |
| ❑ U130 Jeff Reed | .15 | .07 |
| ❑ U131 Kevin Brown | .30 | .14 |
| ❑ U132 Al Leiter | .30 | .14 |
| ❑ U133 Matt Mantei RC | 1.00 | .45 |
| ❑ U134 Dave Weathers | .15 | .07 |
| ❑ U135 Devon White | .30 | .14 |
| ❑ U136 Bob Abreu | .75 | .35 |
| ❑ U137 Sean Berry | .15 | .07 |
| ❑ U138 Doug Brocail | .15 | .07 |
| ❑ U139 Richard Hidalgo | .30 | .14 |
| ❑ U140 Alvin Morman | .15 | .07 |
| ❑ U141 Mike Blowers | .15 | .07 |
| ❑ U142 Roger Cedeno | .15 | .07 |
| ❑ U143 Greg Gagne | .15 | .07 |
| ❑ U144 Karim Garcia | .15 | .07 |
| ❑ U145 Wilton Guerrero RC | .75 | .35 |
| ❑ U146 Israel Alcantara RC | .15 | .07 |
| ❑ U147 Omar Daal | .15 | .07 |
| ❑ U148 Ryan McGuire | .15 | .07 |
| ❑ U149 Sherman Obando | .15 | .07 |
| ❑ U150 Jose Paniagua | .15 | .07 |
| ❑ U151 Henry Rodriguez | .15 | .07 |
| ❑ U152 Andy Stankiewicz | .15 | .07 |
| ❑ U153 Dave Veres | .15 | .07 |
| ❑ U154 Juan Acevedo | .15 | .07 |
| ❑ U155 Mark Clark | .15 | .07 |
| ❑ U156 Bernard Gilkey | .15 | .07 |
| ❑ U157 Pete Harnisch | .15 | .07 |
| ❑ U158 Lance Johnson | .15 | .07 |
| ❑ U159 Brent Mayne | .15 | .07 |
| ❑ U160 Rey Ordonez | .30 | .14 |
| ❑ U161 Kevin Roberson | .15 | .07 |
| ❑ U162 Paul Wilson | .15 | .07 |
| ❑ U163 David Doster RC | .15 | .07 |
| ❑ U164 Mike Grace RC | .15 | .07 |
| ❑ U165 Rich Hunter RC | .15 | .07 |
| ❑ U166 Pete Incaviglia | .15 | .07 |
| ❑ U167 Mike Lieberthal | .30 | .14 |
| ❑ U168 Terry Mulholland | .15 | .07 |
| ❑ U169 Ken Ryan | .15 | .07 |
| ❑ U170 Benito Santiago | .15 | .07 |
| ❑ U171 Kevin Sefcik RC | .15 | .07 |
| ❑ U172 Lee Tinsley | .15 | .07 |
| ❑ U173 Todd Zeile | .15 | .07 |
| ❑ U174 Francisco Cordova RC | .15 | .07 |
| ❑ U175 Danny Darwin | .15 | .07 |
| ❑ U176 Charlie Hayes | .15 | .07 |
| ❑ U177 Jason Kendall | .30 | .14 |
| ❑ U178 Mike Kingery | .15 | .07 |

❑ U179 Jon Lieber .15 .07
❑ U180 Zane Smith .15 .07
❑ U181 Luis Alicea .15 .07
❑ U182 Cory Bailey .15 .07
❑ U183 Andy Benes .15 .07
❑ U184 Pat Borders .15 .07
❑ U185 Mike Busby RC .15 .07
❑ U186 Royce Clayton .15 .07
❑ U187 Dennis Eckersley .30 .14
❑ U188 Gary Gaetti .30 .14
❑ U189 Ron Gant .15 .07
❑ U190 Aaron Holbert .15 .07
❑ U191 Willie McGee .30 .14
❑ U192 Miguel Mejia RC .15 .07
❑ U193 Jeff Parrett .15 .07
❑ U194 Todd Stottlemyre .15 .07
❑ U195 Sean Bergman .15 .07
❑ U196 Archi Cianfrocco .15 .07
❑ U197 Rickey Henderson .75 .35
❑ U198 Wally Joyner .30 .14
❑ U199 Craig Shipley .15 .07
❑ U200 Bob Tewksbury .15 .07
❑ U201 Tim Worrell .15 .07
❑ U202 Rich Aurilia RC .75 .35
❑ U203 Doug Creek .15 .07
❑ U204 Shawon Dunston .15 .07
❑ U205 Osvaldo Fernandez RC .15 .07
❑ U206 Mark Gardner .15 .07
❑ U207 Stan Javier .15 .07
❑ U208 Marcus Jensen .15 .07
❑ U209 Chris Singleton RC 3.00 1.35
❑ U210 Allen Watson .15 .07
❑ U211 Jeff Bagwell ENC .75 .35
❑ U212 Derek Bell ENC .15 .07
❑ U213 Albert Belle ENC .30 .14
❑ U214 Wade Boggs ENC .75 .35
❑ U215 Barry Bonds ENC 1.00 .45
❑ U216 Jose Canseco ENC .75 .35
❑ U217 Marty Cordova ENC .15 .07
❑ U218 Jim Edmonds ENC .60 .25
❑ U219 Cecil Fielder ENC .15 .07
❑ U220 Andres Galarraga ENC .30 .14
❑ U221 Juan Gonzalez ENC .60 .25
❑ U222 Mark Grace ENC .30 .14
❑ U223 Ken Griffey Jr. ENC 2.50 1.10
❑ U224 Tony Gwynn ENC 1.25 .55
❑ U225 J. Isringhausen ENC .15 .07
❑ U226 Derek Jeter ENC 2.50 1.10
❑ U227 Randy Johnson ENC .75 .35
❑ U228 Chipper Jones ENC 1.50 .70
❑ U229 Ryan Klesko ENC .15 .07
❑ U230 Barry Larkin ENC .15 .07
❑ U231 Kenny Lofton ENC .15 .07
❑ U232 Greg Maddux ENC 1.50 .70
❑ U233 Raul Mondesi ENC .15 .07
❑ U234 Hideo Nomo ENC .30 .14
❑ U235 Mike Piazza ENC 2.00 .90
❑ U236 Manny Ramirez ENC .75 .35
❑ U237 Cal Ripken ENC 1.50 .70
❑ U238 Tim Salmon ENC .30 .14
❑ U239 Ryne Sandberg ENC .75 .35
❑ U240 Reggie Sanders ENC .15 .07
❑ U241 Gary Sheffield ENC .60 .25
❑ U242 Sammy Sosa ENC 1.25 .55
❑ U243 Frank Thomas ENC 1.25 .55
❑ U244 Mo Vaughn ENC .30 .14
❑ U245 Matt Williams ENC .30 .14
❑ U246 Barry Bonds CL .30 .14
❑ U247 Ken Griffey Jr. CL 1.25 .55
❑ U248 Rey Ordonez CL .30 .14
❑ U249 Ryne Sandberg CL .60 .25
❑ U250 Frank Thomas CL .60 .25

## 1997 Fleer

| | MINT | NRMT |
|---|---|---|
| COMPLETE SET (761) | 90.00 | 40.00 |
| COMPLETE SERIES 1 (500) | 50.00 | 22.00 |
| COMPLETE SERIES 2 (261) | 40.00 | 18.00 |
| COMMON CARD (1-750) | .15 | .07 |
| COMMON CARD (751-761) | .25 | .11 |

❑ 1 Roberto Alomar .60 .25
❑ 2 Brady Anderson .30 .14
❑ 3 Bobby Bonilla .30 .14
❑ 4 Rocky Coppinger .15 .07

❑ 5 Cesar Devarez .15 .07
❑ 6 Scott Erickson .15 .07
❑ 7 Jeffrey Hammonds .30 .14
❑ 8 Chris Hoiles .15 .07
❑ 9 Eddie Murray .60 .25
❑ 10 Mike Mussina .60 .25
❑ 11 Randy Myers .15 .07
❑ 12 Rafael Palmeiro .60 .25
❑ 13 Cal Ripken 2.50 1.10
❑ 14 B.J. Surhoff .30 .14
❑ 15 David Wells .30 .14
❑ 16 Todd Zeile .15 .07
❑ 17 Darren Bragg .15 .07
❑ 18 Jose Canseco .75 .35
❑ 19 Roger Clemens 1.25 .55
❑ 20 Wil Cordero .15 .07
❑ 21 Jeff Frye .15 .07
❑ 22 Nomar Garciaparra 2.00 .90
❑ 23 Tom Gordon .15 .07
❑ 24 Mike Greenwell .15 .07
❑ 25 Reggie Jefferson .15 .07
❑ 26 Jose Malave .15 .07
❑ 27 Tim Naehring .15 .07
❑ 28 Troy O'Leary .15 .07
❑ 29 Heathcliff Slocumb .15 .07
❑ 30 Mike Stanley .15 .07
❑ 31 John Valentin .15 .07
❑ 32 Mo Vaughn .30 .14
❑ 33 Tim Wakefield .15 .07
❑ 34 Garret Anderson .30 .14
❑ 35 George Arias .15 .07
❑ 36 Shawn Boskie .15 .07
❑ 37 Chili Davis .30 .14
❑ 38 Jason Dickson .15 .07
❑ 39 Gary DiSarcina .15 .07
❑ 40 Jim Edmonds .60 .25
❑ 41 Darin Erstad .75 .35
❑ 42 Jorge Fabregas .15 .07
❑ 43 Chuck Finley .30 .14
❑ 44 Todd Greene .15 .07
❑ 45 Mike Holtz .15 .07
❑ 46 Rex Hudler .15 .07
❑ 47 Mike James .15 .07
❑ 48 Mark Langston .30 .14
❑ 49 Troy Percival .15 .07
❑ 50 Tim Salmon .30 .14
❑ 51 Jeff Schmidt .15 .07
❑ 52 J.T. Snow .30 .14
❑ 53 Randy Velarde .15 .07
❑ 54 Wilson Alvarez .15 .07
❑ 55 Harold Baines .30 .14
❑ 56 James Baldwin .30 .14
❑ 57 Jason Bere .15 .07
❑ 58 Mike Cameron .30 .14
❑ 59 Ray Durham .30 .14
❑ 60 Alex Fernandez .15 .07
❑ 61 Ozzie Guillen .15 .07
❑ 62 Roberto Hernandez .15 .07
❑ 63 Ron Karkovice .15 .07
❑ 64 Darren Lewis .15 .07
❑ 65 Dave Martinez .15 .07
❑ 66 Lyle Mouton .15 .07
❑ 67 Greg Norton .15 .07
❑ 68 Tony Phillips .15 .07
❑ 69 Chris Snopek .15 .07
❑ 70 Kevin Tapani .15 .07
❑ 71 Danny Tartabull .15 .07
❑ 72 Frank Thomas 1.25 .55
❑ 73 Robin Ventura .30 .14
❑ 74 Sandy Alomar Jr. .30 .14
❑ 75 Albert Belle .40 .18
❑ 76 Mark Carreon .15 .07
❑ 77 Julio Franco .30 .14
❑ 78 Brian Giles RC 2.50 1.10
❑ 79 Orel Hershiser .30 .14
❑ 80 Kenny Lofton .30 .14
❑ 81 Dennis Martinez .30 .14
❑ 82 Jack McDowell .15 .07
❑ 83 Jose Mesa .15 .07
❑ 84 Charles Nagy .15 .07
❑ 85 Chad Ogea .15 .07
❑ 86 Eric Plunk .15 .07
❑ 87 Manny Ramirez .75 .35
❑ 88 Kevin Seitzer .15 .07
❑ 89 Julian Tavarez .15 .07
❑ 90 Jim Thome .40 .18
❑ 91 Jose Vizcaino .15 .07
❑ 92 Omar Vizquel .30 .14
❑ 93 Brad Ausmus .15 .07
❑ 94 Kimera Bartee .15 .07
❑ 95 Raul Casanova .15 .07
❑ 96 Tony Clark .15 .07
❑ 97 John Cummings .15 .07
❑ 98 Travis Fryman .30 .14
❑ 99 Bob Higginson .30 .14
❑ 100 Mark Lewis .15 .07
❑ 101 Felipe Lira .15 .07
❑ 102 Phil Nevin .30 .14
❑ 103 Melvin Nieves .15 .07
❑ 104 Curtis Pride .15 .07
❑ 105 A.J. Sager .15 .07
❑ 106 Ruben Sierra .15 .07
❑ 107 Justin Thompson .15 .07
❑ 108 Alan Trammell .40 .18
❑ 109 Kevin Appier .30 .14
❑ 110 Tim Belcher .15 .07
❑ 111 Jaime Bluma .15 .07
❑ 112 Johnny Damon .30 .14
❑ 113 Tom Goodwin .15 .07
❑ 114 Chris Haney .15 .07
❑ 115 Keith Lockhart .15 .07
❑ 116 Mike Macfarlane .15 .07
❑ 117 Jeff Montgomery .15 .07
❑ 118 Jose Offerman .15 .07
❑ 119 Craig Paquette .15 .07
❑ 120 Joe Randa .15 .07
❑ 121 Bip Roberts .15 .07
❑ 122 Jose Rosado .15 .07
❑ 123 Mike Sweeney .30 .14
❑ 124 Michael Tucker .15 .07
❑ 125 Jeromy Burnitz .30 .14
❑ 126 Jeff Cirillo .30 .14
❑ 127 Jeff D'Amico .15 .07
❑ 128 Mike Fetters .15 .07
❑ 129 John Jaha .15 .07
❑ 130 Scott Karl .15 .07
❑ 131 Jesse Levis .15 .07
❑ 132 Mark Loretta .15 .07
❑ 133 Mike Matheny .15 .07
❑ 134 Ben McDonald .15 .07
❑ 135 Matt Mieske .15 .07
❑ 136 Marc Newfield .15 .07
❑ 137 Dave Nilsson .15 .07
❑ 138 Jose Valentin .15 .07
❑ 139 Fernando Vina .15 .07
❑ 140 Bob Wickman .15 .07
❑ 141 Gerald Williams .15 .07
❑ 142 Rick Aguilera .15 .07
❑ 143 Rich Becker .15 .07
❑ 144 Ron Coomer .15 .07
❑ 145 Marty Cordova .15 .07
❑ 146 Roberto Kelly .15 .07
❑ 147 Chuck Knoblauch .30 .14
❑ 148 Matt Lawton .30 .14
❑ 149 Pat Meares .15 .07
❑ 150 Travis Miller .15 .07
❑ 151 Paul Molitor .60 .25
❑ 152 Greg Myers .15 .07
❑ 153 Dan Naulty .15 .07
❑ 154 Kirby Puckett 1.50 .70
❑ 155 Brad Radke .30 .14
❑ 156 Frank Rodriguez .15 .07
❑ 157 Scott Stahoviak .15 .07
❑ 158 Dave Stevens .15 .07

| | No. | Player | | |
|---|---|---|---|---|
| ❑ | 159 | Matt Walbeck | .15 | .07 |
| ❑ | 160 | Todd Walker | .15 | .07 |
| ❑ | 161 | Wade Boggs | .75 | .35 |
| ❑ | 162 | David Cone | .30 | .14 |
| ❑ | 163 | Mariano Duncan | .15 | .07 |
| ❑ | 164 | Cecil Fielder | .30 | .14 |
| ❑ | 165 | Joe Girardi | .15 | .07 |
| ❑ | 166 | Dwight Gooden | .30 | .14 |
| ❑ | 167 | Charlie Hayes | .15 | .07 |
| ❑ | 168 | Derek Jeter | 2.50 | 1.10 |
| ❑ | 169 | Jimmy Key | .30 | .14 |
| ❑ | 170 | Jim Leyritz | .15 | .07 |
| ❑ | 171 | Tino Martinez | .30 | .14 |
| ❑ | 172 | Ramiro Mendoza RC | .50 | .23 |
| ❑ | 173 | Jeff Nelson | .15 | .07 |
| ❑ | 174 | Paul O'Neill | .30 | .14 |
| ❑ | 175 | Andy Pettitte | .30 | .14 |
| ❑ | 176 | Mariano Rivera | .30 | .14 |
| ❑ | 177 | Ruben Rivera | .15 | .07 |
| ❑ | 178 | Kenny Rogers | .15 | .07 |
| ❑ | 179 | Darryl Strawberry | .30 | .14 |
| ❑ | 180 | John Wetteland | .30 | .14 |
| ❑ | 181 | Bernie Williams | .60 | .25 |
| ❑ | 182 | Willie Adams | .15 | .07 |
| ❑ | 183 | Tony Batista | .60 | .25 |
| ❑ | 184 | Geronimo Berroa | .15 | .07 |
| ❑ | 185 | Mike Bordick | .15 | .07 |
| ❑ | 186 | Scott Brosius | .30 | .14 |
| ❑ | 187 | Bobby Chouinard | .15 | .07 |
| ❑ | 188 | Jim Corsi | .15 | .07 |
| ❑ | 189 | Brent Gates | .15 | .07 |
| ❑ | 190 | Jason Giambi | .60 | .25 |
| ❑ | 191 | Jose Herrera | .15 | .07 |
| ❑ | 192 | Damon Mashore | .15 | .07 |
| ❑ | 193 | Mark McGwire | 2.50 | 1.10 |
| ❑ | 194 | Mike Mohler | .15 | .07 |
| ❑ | 195 | Scott Spiezio | .15 | .07 |
| ❑ | 196 | Terry Steinbach | .15 | .07 |
| ❑ | 197 | Bill Taylor | .15 | .07 |
| ❑ | 198 | John Wasdin | .15 | .07 |
| ❑ | 199 | Steve Wojciechowski | .15 | .07 |
| ❑ | 200 | Ernie Young | .15 | .07 |
| ❑ | 201 | Rich Amaral | .15 | .07 |
| ❑ | 202 | Jay Buhner | .30 | .14 |
| ❑ | 203 | Norm Charlton | .15 | .07 |
| ❑ | 204 | Joey Cora | .15 | .07 |
| ❑ | 205 | Russ Davis | .15 | .07 |
| ❑ | 206 | Ken Griffey Jr. | 2.50 | 1.10 |
| ❑ | 207 | Sterling Hitchcock | .15 | .07 |
| ❑ | 208 | Brian Hunter | .15 | .07 |
| ❑ | 209 | Raul Ibanez | .15 | .07 |
| ❑ | 210 | Randy Johnson | .75 | .35 |
| ❑ | 211 | Edgar Martinez | .40 | .18 |
| ❑ | 212 | Jamie Moyer | .15 | .07 |
| ❑ | 213 | Alex Rodriguez | 2.00 | .90 |
| ❑ | 214 | Paul Sorrento | .15 | .07 |
| ❑ | 215 | Matt Wagner | .15 | .07 |
| ❑ | 216 | Bob Wells | .15 | .07 |
| ❑ | 217 | Dan Wilson | .15 | .07 |
| ❑ | 218 | Damon Buford | .15 | .07 |
| ❑ | 219 | Will Clark | .60 | .25 |
| ❑ | 220 | Kevin Elster | .15 | .07 |
| ❑ | 221 | Juan Gonzalez | .60 | .25 |
| ❑ | 222 | Rusty Greer | .30 | .14 |
| ❑ | 223 | Kevin Gross | .15 | .07 |
| ❑ | 224 | Darryl Hamilton | .15 | .07 |
| ❑ | 225 | Mike Henneman | .15 | .07 |
| ❑ | 226 | Ken Hill | .15 | .07 |
| ❑ | 227 | Mark McLemore | .15 | .07 |
| ❑ | 228 | Darren Oliver | .15 | .07 |
| ❑ | 229 | Dean Palmer | .30 | .14 |
| ❑ | 230 | Roger Pavlik | .15 | .07 |
| ❑ | 231 | Ivan Rodriguez | .75 | .35 |
| ❑ | 232 | Mickey Tettleton | .15 | .07 |
| ❑ | 233 | Bobby Witt | .15 | .07 |
| ❑ | 234 | Jacob Brumfield | .15 | .07 |
| ❑ | 235 | Joe Carter | .30 | .14 |
| ❑ | 236 | Tim Crabtree | .15 | .07 |
| ❑ | 237 | Carlos Delgado | .60 | .25 |
| ❑ | 238 | Huck Flener | .15 | .07 |
| ❑ | 239 | Alex Gonzalez | .15 | .07 |
| ❑ | 240 | Shawn Green | .60 | .25 |
| ❑ | 241 | Juan Guzman | .15 | .07 |
| ❑ | 242 | Pat Hentgen | .15 | .07 |
| ❑ | 243 | Marty Janzen | .15 | .07 |
| ❑ | 244 | Sandy Martinez | .15 | .07 |
| ❑ | 245 | Otis Nixon | .15 | .07 |
| ❑ | 246 | Charlie O'Brien | .15 | .07 |
| ❑ | 247 | John Olerud | .30 | .14 |
| ❑ | 248 | Robert Perez | .15 | .07 |
| ❑ | 249 | Ed Sprague | .15 | .07 |
| ❑ | 250 | Mike Timlin | .15 | .07 |
| ❑ | 251 | Steve Avery | .15 | .07 |
| ❑ | 252 | Jeff Blauser | .15 | .07 |
| ❑ | 253 | Brad Clontz | .15 | .07 |
| ❑ | 254 | Jermaine Dye | .30 | .14 |
| ❑ | 255 | Tom Glavine | .60 | .25 |
| ❑ | 256 | Marquis Grissom | .15 | .07 |
| ❑ | 257 | Andruw Jones | .75 | .35 |
| ❑ | 258 | Chipper Jones | 1.50 | .70 |
| ❑ | 259 | David Justice | .40 | .18 |
| ❑ | 260 | Ryan Klesko | .30 | .14 |
| ❑ | 261 | Mark Lemke | 15 | .07 |
| ❑ | 262 | Javier Lopez | .30 | .14 |
| ❑ | 263 | Greg Maddux | 1.50 | .70 |
| ❑ | 264 | Fred McGriff | .40 | .18 |
| ❑ | 265 | Greg McMichael | .15 | .07 |
| ❑ | 266 | Denny Neagle | .30 | .14 |
| ❑ | 267 | Terry Pendleton | .30 | .14 |
| ❑ | 268 | Eddie Perez | .15 | .07 |
| ❑ | 269 | John Smoltz | .30 | .14 |
| ❑ | 270 | Terrell Wade | .15 | .07 |
| ❑ | 271 | Mark Wohlers | .15 | .07 |
| ❑ | 272 | Terry Adams | .15 | .07 |
| ❑ | 273 | Brant Brown | .15 | .07 |
| ❑ | 274 | Leo Gomez | .15 | .07 |
| ❑ | 275 | Luis Gonzalez | .30 | .14 |
| ❑ | 276 | Mark Grace | .60 | .25 |
| ❑ | 277 | Tyler Houston | .15 | .07 |
| ❑ | 278 | Robin Jennings | .15 | .07 |
| ❑ | 279 | Brooks Kieschnick | .15 | .07 |
| ❑ | 280 | Brian McRae | .15 | .07 |
| ❑ | 281 | Jaime Navarro | .15 | .07 |
| ❑ | 282 | Ryne Sandberg | .75 | .35 |
| ❑ | 283 | Scott Servais | .15 | .07 |
| ❑ | 284 | Sammy Sosa | 1.25 | .55 |
| ❑ | 285 | Dave Swartzbaugh | .15 | .07 |
| ❑ | 286 | Amaury Telemaco | .15 | .07 |
| ❑ | 287 | Steve Trachsel | .15 | .07 |
| ❑ | 288 | Pedro Valdes | .15 | .07 |
| ❑ | 289 | Turk Wendell | .15 | .07 |
| ❑ | 290 | Bret Boone | .30 | .14 |
| ❑ | 291 | Jeff Branson | .15 | .07 |
| ❑ | 292 | Jeff Brantley | .15 | .07 |
| ❑ | 293 | Eric Davis | .30 | .14 |
| ❑ | 294 | Willie Greene | .15 | .07 |
| ❑ | 295 | Thomas Howard | .15 | .07 |
| ❑ | 296 | Barry Larkin | .60 | .25 |
| ❑ | 297 | Kevin Mitchell | .15 | .07 |
| ❑ | 298 | Hal Morris | .15 | .07 |
| ❑ | 299 | Chad Mottola | .15 | .07 |
| ❑ | 300 | Joe Oliver | .15 | .07 |
| ❑ | 301 | Mark Portugal | .15 | .07 |
| ❑ | 302 | Roger Salkeld | .15 | .07 |
| ❑ | 303 | Reggie Sanders | .15 | .07 |
| ❑ | 304 | Pete Schourek | .15 | .07 |
| ❑ | 305 | John Smiley | .15 | .07 |
| ❑ | 306 | Eddie Taubensee | .15 | .07 |
| ❑ | 307 | Dante Bichette | .30 | .14 |
| ❑ | 308 | Ellis Burks | .30 | .14 |
| ❑ | 309 | Vinny Castilla | .30 | .14 |
| ❑ | 310 | Andres Galarraga | .40 | .18 |
| ❑ | 311 | Curt Leskanic | .15 | .07 |
| ❑ | 312 | Quinton McCracken | .15 | .07 |
| ❑ | 313 | Neifi Perez | .15 | .07 |
| ❑ | 314 | Jeff Reed | .15 | .07 |
| ❑ | 315 | Steve Reed | .15 | .07 |
| ❑ | 316 | Armando Reynoso | .15 | .07 |
| ❑ | 317 | Kevin Ritz | .15 | .07 |
| ❑ | 318 | Bruce Ruffin | .15 | .07 |
| ❑ | 319 | Larry Walker | .30 | .14 |
| ❑ | 320 | Walt Weiss | .15 | .07 |
| ❑ | 321 | Jamey Wright | .15 | .07 |
| ❑ | 322 | Eric Young | .15 | .07 |
| ❑ | 323 | Kurt Abbott | .15 | .07 |
| ❑ | 324 | Alex Arias | .15 | .07 |
| ❑ | 325 | Kevin Brown | .40 | .18 |
| ❑ | 326 | Luis Castillo | .30 | .14 |
| ❑ | 327 | Greg Colbrunn | .15 | .07 |
| ❑ | 328 | Jeff Conine | .15 | .07 |
| ❑ | 329 | Andre Dawson | .40 | .18 |
| ❑ | 330 | Charles Johnson | .30 | .14 |
| ❑ | 331 | Al Leiter | .30 | .14 |
| ❑ | 332 | Ralph Milliard | .15 | .07 |
| ❑ | 333 | Robb Nen | .15 | .07 |
| ❑ | 334 | Pat Rapp | .15 | .07 |
| ❑ | 335 | Edgar Renteria | .30 | .14 |
| ❑ | 336 | Gary Sheffield | .60 | .25 |
| ❑ | 337 | Devon White | .30 | .14 |
| ❑ | 338 | Bob Abreu | .30 | .14 |
| ❑ | 339 | Jeff Bagwell | .75 | .35 |
| ❑ | 340 | Derek Bell | .15 | .07 |
| ❑ | 341 | Sean Berry | .15 | .07 |
| ❑ | 342 | Craig Biggio | .40 | .18 |
| ❑ | 343 | Doug Drabek | .15 | .07 |
| ❑ | 344 | Tony Eusebio | .15 | .07 |
| ❑ | 345 | Ricky Gutierrez | .15 | .07 |
| ❑ | 346 | Mike Hampton | .30 | .14 |
| ❑ | 347 | Brian Hunter | .15 | .07 |
| ❑ | 348 | Todd Jones | .15 | .07 |
| ❑ | 349 | Darryl Kile | .30 | .14 |
| ❑ | 350 | Derrick May | .15 | .07 |
| ❑ | 351 | Orlando Miller | .15 | .07 |
| ❑ | 352 | James Mouton | .15 | .07 |
| ❑ | 353 | Shane Reynolds | .15 | .07 |
| ❑ | 354 | Billy Wagner | .15 | .07 |
| ❑ | 355 | Donne Wall | .15 | .07 |
| ❑ | 356 | Mike Blowers | .15 | .07 |
| ❑ | 357 | Brett Butler | .30 | .14 |
| ❑ | 358 | Roger Cedeno | .15 | .07 |
| ❑ | 359 | Chad Curtis | .15 | .07 |
| ❑ | 360 | Delino DeShields | .15 | .07 |
| ❑ | 361 | Greg Gagne | .15 | .07 |
| ❑ | 362 | Karim Garcia | .15 | .07 |
| ❑ | 363 | Wilton Guerrero | .15 | .07 |
| ❑ | 364 | Todd Hollandsworth | .15 | .07 |
| ❑ | 365 | Eric Karros | .30 | .14 |
| ❑ | 366 | Ramon Martinez | .15 | .07 |
| ❑ | 367 | Raul Mondesi | .30 | .14 |
| ❑ | 368 | Hideo Nomo | .60 | .25 |
| ❑ | 369 | Antonio Osuna | .15 | .07 |
| ❑ | 370 | Chan Ho Park | .30 | .14 |
| ❑ | 371 | Mike Piazza | 2.00 | .90 |
| ❑ | 372 | Ismael Valdes | .15 | .07 |
| ❑ | 373 | Todd Worrell | .15 | .07 |
| ❑ | 374 | Moises Alou | .30 | .14 |
| ❑ | 375 | Shane Andrews | .15 | .07 |
| ❑ | 376 | Yamil Benitez | .15 | .07 |
| ❑ | 377 | Jeff Fassero | .15 | .07 |
| ❑ | 378 | Darrin Fletcher | .15 | .07 |
| ❑ | 379 | Cliff Floyd | .30 | .14 |
| ❑ | 380 | Mark Grudzielanek | .15 | .07 |
| ❑ | 381 | Mike Lansing | .15 | .07 |
| ❑ | 382 | Barry Manuel | .15 | .07 |
| ❑ | 383 | Pedro Martinez | .75 | .35 |
| ❑ | 384 | Henry Rodriguez | .15 | .07 |
| ❑ | 385 | Mel Rojas | .15 | .07 |
| ❑ | 386 | F.P. Santangelo | .15 | .07 |
| ❑ | 387 | David Segui | .15 | .07 |
| ❑ | 388 | Ugueth Urbina | .30 | .14 |
| ❑ | 389 | Rondell White | .30 | .14 |
| ❑ | 390 | Edgardo Alfonzo | .30 | .14 |
| ❑ | 391 | Carlos Baerga | .15 | .07 |
| ❑ | 392 | Mark Clark | .15 | .07 |
| ❑ | 393 | Alvaro Espinoza | .15 | .07 |
| ❑ | 394 | John Franco | .30 | .14 |
| ❑ | 395 | Bernard Gilkey | .15 | .07 |
| ❑ | 396 | Pete Harnisch | .15 | .07 |
| ❑ | 397 | Todd Hundley | .15 | .07 |
| ❑ | 398 | Butch Huskey | .15 | .07 |
| ❑ | 399 | Jason Isringhausen | .15 | .07 |
| ❑ | 400 | Lance Johnson | .15 | .07 |
| ❑ | 401 | Bobby Jones | .15 | .07 |
| ❑ | 402 | Alex Ochoa | .15 | .07 |
| ❑ | 403 | Rey Ordonez | .15 | .07 |
| ❑ | 404 | Robert Person | .15 | .07 |
| ❑ | 405 | Paul Wilson | .15 | .07 |
| ❑ | 406 | Matt Beech | .15 | .07 |
| ❑ | 407 | Ron Blazier | .15 | .07 |
| ❑ | 408 | Ricky Bottalico | .15 | .07 |
| ❑ | 409 | Lenny Dykstra | .30 | .14 |
| ❑ | 410 | Jim Eisenreich | .15 | .07 |
| ❑ | 411 | Bobby Estalella | .15 | .07 |
| ❑ | 412 | Mike Grace | .15 | .07 |
| ❑ | 413 | Gregg Jefferies | .15 | .07 |
| ❑ | 414 | Mike Lieberthal | .30 | .14 |
| ❑ | 415 | Wendell Magee | .15 | .07 |
| ❑ | 416 | Mickey Morandini | .15 | .07 |

| | No. | Player | | |
|---|---|---|---|---|
| ❑ | 417 | Ricky Otero | .15 | .07 |
| ❑ | 418 | Scott Rolen | .60 | .25 |
| ❑ | 419 | Ken Ryan | .15 | .07 |
| ❑ | 420 | Benito Santiago | .15 | .07 |
| ❑ | 421 | Curt Schilling | .30 | .14 |
| ❑ | 422 | Kevin Sefcik | .15 | .07 |
| ❑ | 423 | Jermaine Allensworth | .15 | .07 |
| ❑ | 424 | Trey Beamon | .15 | .07 |
| ❑ | 425 | Jay Bell | .30 | .14 |
| ❑ | 426 | Francisco Cordova | .15 | .07 |
| ❑ | 427 | Carlos Garcia | .15 | .07 |
| ❑ | 428 | Mark Johnson | .15 | .07 |
| ❑ | 429 | Jason Kendall | .30 | .14 |
| ❑ | 430 | Jeff King | .15 | .07 |
| ❑ | 431 | Jon Lieber | .15 | .07 |
| ❑ | 432 | Al Martin | .15 | .07 |
| ❑ | 433 | Orlando Merced | .15 | .07 |
| ❑ | 434 | Ramon Morel | .15 | .07 |
| ❑ | 435 | Matt Ruebel | .15 | .07 |
| ❑ | 436 | Jason Schmidt | .15 | .07 |
| ❑ | 437 | Marc Wilkins | .15 | .07 |
| ❑ | 438 | Alan Benes | .15 | .07 |
| ❑ | 439 | Andy Benes | .15 | .07 |
| ❑ | 440 | Royce Clayton | .15 | .07 |
| ❑ | 441 | Dennis Eckersley | .30 | .14 |
| ❑ | 442 | Gary Gaetti | .30 | .14 |
| ❑ | 443 | Ron Gant | .15 | .07 |
| ❑ | 444 | Aaron Holbert | .15 | .07 |
| ❑ | 445 | Brian Jordan | .30 | .14 |
| ❑ | 446 | Ray Lankford | .30 | .14 |
| ❑ | 447 | John Mabry | .15 | .07 |
| ❑ | 448 | T.J. Mathews | .15 | .07 |
| ❑ | 449 | Willie McGee | .30 | .14 |
| ❑ | 450 | Donovan Osborne | .15 | .07 |
| ❑ | 451 | Tom Pagnozzi | .15 | .07 |
| ❑ | 452 | Ozzie Smith | .75 | .35 |
| ❑ | 453 | Todd Stottlemyre | .15 | .07 |
| ❑ | 454 | Mark Sweeney | .15 | .07 |
| ❑ | 455 | Dmitri Young | .30 | .14 |
| ❑ | 456 | Andy Ashby | .15 | .07 |
| ❑ | 457 | Ken Caminiti | .30 | .14 |
| ❑ | 458 | Archi Cianfrocco | .15 | .07 |
| ❑ | 459 | Steve Finley | .30 | .14 |
| ❑ | 460 | John Flaherty | .15 | .07 |
| ❑ | 461 | Chris Gomez | .15 | .07 |
| ❑ | 462 | Tony Gwynn | 1.25 | .55 |
| ❑ | 463 | Joey Hamilton | .15 | .07 |
| ❑ | 464 | Rickey Henderson | .75 | .35 |
| ❑ | 465 | Trevor Hoffman | .30 | .14 |
| ❑ | 466 | Brian Johnson | .15 | .07 |
| ❑ | 467 | Wally Joyner | .30 | .14 |
| ❑ | 468 | Jody Reed | .15 | .07 |
| ❑ | 469 | Scott Sanders | .15 | .07 |
| ❑ | 470 | Bob Tewksbury | .15 | .07 |
| ❑ | 471 | Fernando Valenzuela | .30 | .14 |
| ❑ | 472 | Greg Vaughn | .30 | .14 |
| ❑ | 473 | Tim Worrell | .15 | .07 |
| ❑ | 474 | Rich Aurilia | .30 | .14 |
| ❑ | 475 | Rod Beck | .15 | .07 |
| ❑ | 476 | Marvin Benard | .15 | .07 |
| ❑ | 477 | Barry Bonds | 1.00 | .45 |
| ❑ | 478 | Jay Canizaro | .15 | .07 |
| ❑ | 479 | Shawon Dunston | .15 | .07 |
| ❑ | 480 | Shawn Estes | .30 | .14 |
| ❑ | 481 | Mark Gardner | .15 | .07 |
| ❑ | 482 | Glenallen Hill | .15 | .07 |
| ❑ | 483 | Stan Javier | .15 | .07 |
| ❑ | 484 | Marcus Jensen | .15 | .07 |
| ❑ | 485 | Bill Mueller RC | .40 | .18 |
| ❑ | 486 | Wm. VanLandingham | .15 | .07 |
| ❑ | 487 | Allen Watson | .15 | .07 |
| ❑ | 488 | Rick Wilkins | .15 | .07 |
| ❑ | 489 | Matt Williams | .40 | .18 |
| ❑ | 490 | Desi Wilson | .15 | .07 |
| ❑ | 491 | Albert Belle CL | .15 | .07 |
| ❑ | 492 | Ken Griffey Jr. CL | 1.25 | .55 |
| ❑ | 493 | Andruw Jones CL | .40 | .18 |
| ❑ | 494 | Chipper Jones CL | .75 | .35 |
| ❑ | 495 | Mark McGwire CL | 1.25 | .55 |
| ❑ | 496 | Paul Molitor CL | .30 | .14 |
| ❑ | 497 | Mike Piazza CL | 1.00 | .45 |
| ❑ | 498 | Cal Ripken CL | 1.25 | .55 |
| ❑ | 499 | Alex Rodriguez CL | 1.00 | .45 |
| ❑ | 500 | Frank Thomas CL | .75 | .35 |
| ❑ | 501 | Kenny Lofton | .30 | .14 |
| ❑ | 502 | Carlos Perez | .15 | .07 |
| ❑ | 503 | Tim Raines | .30 | .14 |
| ❑ | 504 | Danny Patterson | .15 | .07 |
| ❑ | 505 | Derrick May | .15 | .07 |
| ❑ | 506 | Dave Hollins | .15 | .07 |
| ❑ | 507 | Felipe Crespo | .15 | .07 |
| ❑ | 508 | Brian Banks | .15 | .07 |
| ❑ | 509 | Jeff Kent | .40 | .18 |
| ❑ | 510 | Bubba Trammell RC | .30 | .14 |
| ❑ | 511 | Robert Person | .15 | .07 |
| ❑ | 512 | David Arias-Ortiz RC | .75 | .35 |
| ❑ | 513 | Ryan Jones | .15 | .07 |
| ❑ | 514 | David Justice | .40 | .18 |
| ❑ | 515 | Will Cunnane | .15 | .07 |
| ❑ | 516 | Russ Johnson | .15 | .07 |
| ❑ | 517 | John Burkett | .15 | .07 |
| ❑ | 518 | Robinson Checo RC | .15 | .07 |
| ❑ | 519 | Ricardo Rincon RC | .15 | .07 |
| ❑ | 520 | Woody Williams | .15 | .07 |
| ❑ | 521 | Rick Helling | .30 | .14 |
| ❑ | 522 | Jorge Posada | .30 | .14 |
| ❑ | 523 | Kevin Orie | .15 | .07 |
| ❑ | 524 | Fernando Tatis RC | 1.50 | .70 |
| ❑ | 525 | Jermaine Dye | .30 | .14 |
| ❑ | 526 | Brian Hunter | .15 | .07 |
| ❑ | 527 | Greg McMichael | .15 | .07 |
| ❑ | 528 | Matt Wagner | .15 | .07 |
| ❑ | 529 | Richie Sexson | .60 | .25 |
| ❑ | 530 | Scott Ruffcorn | .15 | .07 |
| ❑ | 531 | Luis Gonzalez | .30 | .14 |
| ❑ | 532 | Mike Johnson RC | .40 | .18 |
| ❑ | 533 | Mark Petkovsek | .15 | .07 |
| ❑ | 534 | Doug Drabek | .15 | .07 |
| ❑ | 535 | Jose Canseco | .75 | .35 |
| ❑ | 536 | Bobby Bonilla | .30 | .14 |
| ❑ | 537 | J.T. Snow | .30 | .14 |
| ❑ | 538 | Shawon Dunston | .15 | .07 |
| ❑ | 539 | John Ericks | .15 | .07 |
| ❑ | 540 | Terry Steinbach | .15 | .07 |
| ❑ | 541 | Jay Bell | .30 | .14 |
| ❑ | 542 | Joe Borowski RC | .15 | .07 |
| ❑ | 543 | David Wells | .30 | .14 |
| ❑ | 544 | Justin Towle RC | .15 | .07 |
| ❑ | 545 | Mike Blowers | .15 | .07 |
| ❑ | 546 | Shannon Stewart | .30 | .14 |
| ❑ | 547 | Rudy Pemberton | .15 | .07 |
| ❑ | 548 | Bill Swift | .15 | .07 |
| ❑ | 549 | Osvaldo Fernandez | .15 | .07 |
| ❑ | 550 | Eddie Murray | .60 | .25 |
| ❑ | 551 | Don Wengert | .15 | .07 |
| ❑ | 552 | Brad Ausmus | .15 | .07 |
| ❑ | 553 | Carlos Garcia | .15 | .07 |
| ❑ | 554 | Jose Guillen | .15 | .07 |
| ❑ | 555 | Rheal Cormier | .15 | .07 |
| ❑ | 556 | Doug Brocail | .15 | .07 |
| ❑ | 557 | Rex Hudler | .15 | .07 |
| ❑ | 558 | Armando Benitez | .15 | .07 |
| ❑ | 559 | Eli Marrero | .15 | .07 |
| ❑ | 560 | Ricky Ledee RC | .60 | .25 |
| ❑ | 561 | Bartolo Colon | .30 | .14 |
| ❑ | 562 | Quilvio Veras | .15 | .07 |
| ❑ | 563 | Alex Fernandez | .15 | .07 |
| ❑ | 564 | Darren Dreifort | .30 | .14 |
| ❑ | 565 | Benji Gil | .15 | .07 |
| ❑ | 566 | Kent Mercker | .15 | .07 |
| ❑ | 567 | Glendon Rusch | .15 | .07 |
| ❑ | 568 | Ramon Tatis RC | .15 | .07 |
| ❑ | 569 | Roger Clemens | 1.25 | .55 |
| ❑ | 570 | Mark Lewis | .15 | .07 |
| ❑ | 571 | Emil Brown RC | .15 | .07 |
| ❑ | 572 | Jaime Navarro | .15 | .07 |
| ❑ | 573 | Sherman Obando | .15 | .07 |
| ❑ | 574 | John Wasdin | .15 | .07 |
| ❑ | 575 | Calvin Maduro | .15 | .07 |
| ❑ | 576 | Todd Jones | .15 | .07 |
| ❑ | 577 | Orlando Merced | .15 | .07 |
| ❑ | 578 | Cal Eldred | .15 | .07 |
| ❑ | 579 | Mark Gubicza | .15 | .07 |
| ❑ | 580 | Michael Tucker | .15 | .07 |
| ❑ | 581 | Tony Saunders RC | .15 | .07 |
| ❑ | 582 | Garvin Alston | .15 | .07 |
| ❑ | 583 | Joe Roa | .15 | .07 |
| ❑ | 584 | Brady Raggio RC | .15 | .07 |
| ❑ | 585 | Jimmy Key | .30 | .14 |
| ❑ | 586 | Marc Sagmoen RC | .15 | .07 |
| ❑ | 587 | Jim Bullinger | .15 | .07 |
| ❑ | 588 | Yorkis Perez | .15 | .07 |
| ❑ | 589 | Jose Cruz Jr. RC | 1.50 | .70 |
| ❑ | 590 | Mike Stanton | .15 | .07 |
| ❑ | 591 | Deivi Cruz RC | .75 | .35 |
| ❑ | 592 | Steve Karsay | .15 | .07 |
| ❑ | 593 | Mike Trombley | .15 | .07 |
| ❑ | 594 | Doug Glanville | .15 | .07 |
| ❑ | 595 | Scott Sanders | .15 | .07 |
| ❑ | 596 | Thomas Howard | .15 | .07 |
| ❑ | 597 | T.J. Staton RC | .30 | .14 |
| ❑ | 598 | Garrett Stephenson | .15 | .07 |
| ❑ | 599 | Rico Brogna | .15 | .07 |
| ❑ | 600 | Albert Belle | .40 | .18 |
| ❑ | 601 | Jose Vizcaino | .15 | .07 |
| ❑ | 602 | Chili Davis | .30 | .14 |
| ❑ | 603 | Shane Mack | .15 | .07 |
| ❑ | 604 | Jim Eisenreich | .15 | .07 |
| ❑ | 605 | Todd Zeile | .15 | .07 |
| ❑ | 606 | Brian Boehringer RC | .15 | .07 |
| ❑ | 607 | Paul Shuey | .15 | .07 |
| ❑ | 608 | Kevin Tapani | .15 | .07 |
| ❑ | 609 | John Wetteland | .30 | .14 |
| ❑ | 610 | Jim Leyritz | .15 | .07 |
| ❑ | 611 | Ray Montgomery RC | .15 | .07 |
| ❑ | 612 | Doug Bochtler | .15 | .07 |
| ❑ | 613 | Wady Almonte RC | .40 | .18 |
| ❑ | 614 | Danny Tartabull | .15 | .07 |
| ❑ | 615 | Orlando Miller | .15 | .07 |
| ❑ | 616 | Bobby Ayala | .15 | .07 |
| ❑ | 617 | Tony Graffanino | .15 | .07 |
| ❑ | 618 | Marc Valdes | .15 | .07 |
| ❑ | 619 | Ron Villone | .15 | .07 |
| ❑ | 620 | Derrek Lee | .15 | .07 |
| ❑ | 621 | Greg Colbrunn | .15 | .07 |
| ❑ | 622 | Felix Heredia RC | .30 | .14 |
| ❑ | 623 | Carl Everett | .30 | .14 |
| ❑ | 624 | Mark Thompson | .15 | .07 |
| ❑ | 625 | Jeff Granger | .15 | .07 |
| ❑ | 626 | Damian Jackson | .15 | .07 |
| ❑ | 627 | Mark Leiter | .15 | .07 |
| ❑ | 628 | Chris Holt | .15 | .07 |
| ❑ | 629 | Dario Veras RC | .30 | .14 |
| ❑ | 630 | Dave Burba | .15 | .07 |
| ❑ | 631 | Darryl Hamilton | .15 | .07 |
| ❑ | 632 | Mark Acre | .15 | .07 |
| ❑ | 633 | Fernando Hernandez RC | .15 | .07 |
| ❑ | 634 | Terry Mulholland | .15 | .07 |
| ❑ | 635 | Dustin Hermanson | .15 | .07 |
| ❑ | 636 | Delino DeShields | .15 | .07 |
| ❑ | 637 | Steve Avery | .15 | .07 |
| ❑ | 638 | Tony Womack RC | .75 | .35 |
| ❑ | 639 | Mark Whiten | .15 | .07 |
| ❑ | 640 | Marquis Grissom | .15 | .07 |
| ❑ | 641 | Xavier Hernandez | .15 | .07 |
| ❑ | 642 | Eric Davis | .30 | .14 |
| ❑ | 643 | Bob Tewksbury | .15 | .07 |
| ❑ | 644 | Dante Powell | .30 | .14 |
| ❑ | 645 | Carlos Castillo RC | .15 | .07 |
| ❑ | 646 | Chris Widger | .15 | .07 |
| ❑ | 647 | Moises Alou | .30 | .14 |
| ❑ | 648 | Pat Listach | .15 | .07 |
| ❑ | 649 | Edgar Ramos RC | .15 | .07 |
| ❑ | 650 | Deion Sanders | .30 | .14 |
| ❑ | 651 | John Olerud | .30 | .14 |
| ❑ | 652 | Todd Dunwoody | .30 | .14 |
| ❑ | 653 | Randall Simon RC | .40 | .18 |
| ❑ | 654 | Dan Carlson | .15 | .07 |
| ❑ | 655 | Matt Williams | .40 | .18 |
| ❑ | 656 | Jeff King | .15 | .07 |
| ❑ | 657 | Luis Alicea | .15 | .07 |
| ❑ | 658 | Brian Moehler RC | .15 | .07 |
| ❑ | 659 | Ariel Prieto | .15 | .07 |
| ❑ | 660 | Kevin Elster | .15 | .07 |
| ❑ | 661 | Mark Hutton | .15 | .07 |
| ❑ | 662 | Aaron Sele | .30 | .14 |
| ❑ | 663 | Graeme Lloyd | .15 | .07 |
| ❑ | 664 | John Burke | .15 | .07 |
| ❑ | 665 | Mel Rojas | .15 | .07 |
| ❑ | 666 | Sid Fernandez | .15 | .07 |
| ❑ | 667 | Pedro Astacio | .15 | .07 |
| ❑ | 668 | Jeff Abbott | .15 | .07 |
| ❑ | 669 | Darren Daulton | .30 | .14 |
| ❑ | 670 | Mike Bordick | .15 | .07 |
| ❑ | 671 | Sterling Hitchcock | .15 | .07 |
| ❑ | 672 | Damion Easley | .15 | .07 |
| ❑ | 673 | Armando Reynoso | .15 | .07 |
| ❑ | 674 | Pat Cline | .30 | .14 |

| | No. | Player | | |
|---|---|---|---|---|
| ❑ | 675 | Orlando Cabrera RC | .40 | .18 |
| ❑ | 676 | Alan Embree | .15 | .07 |
| ❑ | 677 | Brian Bevil | .15 | .07 |
| ❑ | 678 | David Weathers | .15 | .07 |
| ❑ | 679 | Cliff Floyd | .30 | .14 |
| ❑ | 680 | Joe Randa | .15 | .07 |
| ❑ | 681 | Bill Haselman | .15 | .07 |
| ❑ | 682 | Jeff Fassero | .15 | .07 |
| ❑ | 683 | Matt Morris | .15 | .07 |
| ❑ | 684 | Mark Portugal | .15 | .07 |
| ❑ | 685 | Lee Smith | .30 | .14 |
| ❑ | 686 | Pokey Reese | .30 | .14 |
| ❑ | 687 | Benito Santiago | .15 | .07 |
| ❑ | 688 | Brian Johnson | .15 | .07 |
| ❑ | 689 | Brent Brede RC | .15 | .07 |
| ❑ | 690 | Shigetoshi Hasegawa RC | .40 | .18 |
| ❑ | 691 | Julio Santana | .15 | .07 |
| ❑ | 692 | Steve Kline | .15 | .07 |
| ❑ | 693 | Julian Tavarez | .15 | .07 |
| ❑ | 694 | John Hudek | .15 | .07 |
| ❑ | 695 | Manny Alexander | .15 | .07 |
| ❑ | 696 | Roberto Alomar ENC | .30 | .14 |
| ❑ | 697 | Jeff Bagwell ENC | .30 | .14 |
| ❑ | 698 | Barry Bonds ENC | .30 | .14 |
| ❑ | 699 | Ken Caminiti ENC | .15 | .07 |
| ❑ | 700 | Juan Gonzalez ENC | .30 | .14 |
| ❑ | 701 | Ken Griffey Jr. ENC | 1.25 | .55 |
| ❑ | 702 | Tony Gwynn ENC | .60 | .25 |
| ❑ | 703 | Derek Jeter ENC | 1.25 | .55 |
| ❑ | 704 | Andruw Jones ENC | .40 | .18 |
| ❑ | 705 | Chipper Jones ENC | .75 | .35 |
| ❑ | 706 | Barry Larkin ENC | .30 | .14 |
| ❑ | 707 | Greg Maddux ENC | .75 | .35 |
| ❑ | 708 | Mark McGwire ENC | 1.25 | .55 |
| ❑ | 709 | Paul Molitor ENC | .30 | .14 |
| ❑ | 710 | Hideo Nomo ENC | .30 | .14 |
| ❑ | 711 | Andy Pettitte ENC | .15 | .07 |
| ❑ | 712 | Mike Piazza ENC | 1.00 | .45 |
| ❑ | 713 | Manny Ramirez ENC | .40 | .18 |
| ❑ | 714 | Cal Ripken ENC | 1.25 | .55 |
| ❑ | 715 | Alex Rodriguez ENC | 1.00 | .45 |
| ❑ | 716 | Ryne Sandberg ENC | .60 | .25 |
| ❑ | 717 | John Smoltz ENC | .15 | .07 |
| ❑ | 718 | Frank Thomas ENC | .75 | .35 |
| ❑ | 719 | Mo Vaughn ENC | .30 | .14 |
| ❑ | 720 | Bernie Williams ENC | .30 | .14 |
| ❑ | 721 | Tim Salmon CL | .15 | .07 |
| ❑ | 722 | Greg Maddux CL | .75 | .35 |
| ❑ | 723 | Cal Ripken CL | 1.25 | .55 |
| ❑ | 724 | Mo Vaughn CL | .30 | .14 |
| ❑ | 725 | Ryne Sandberg CL | .60 | .25 |
| ❑ | 726 | Frank Thomas CL | .75 | .35 |
| ❑ | 727 | Barry Larkin CL | .30 | .14 |
| ❑ | 728 | Manny Ramirez CL | .40 | .18 |
| ❑ | 729 | Andres Galarraga CL | .15 | .07 |
| ❑ | 730 | Tony Clark CL | .15 | .07 |
| ❑ | 731 | Gary Sheffield CL | .30 | .14 |
| ❑ | 732 | Jeff Bagwell CL | .30 | .14 |
| ❑ | 733 | Kevin Appier CL | .15 | .07 |
| ❑ | 734 | Mike Piazza CL | 1.00 | .45 |
| ❑ | 735 | Jeff Cirillo CL | .30 | .14 |
| ❑ | 736 | Paul Molitor CL | .30 | .14 |
| ❑ | 737 | Henry Rodriguez CL | .15 | .07 |
| ❑ | 738 | Todd Hundley CL | .15 | .07 |
| ❑ | 739 | Derek Jeter CL | 1.25 | .55 |
| ❑ | 740 | Mark McGwire CL | 1.25 | .55 |
| ❑ | 741 | Curt Schilling CL | .30 | .14 |
| ❑ | 742 | Jason Kendall CL | .15 | .07 |
| ❑ | 743 | Tony Gwynn CL | .60 | .25 |
| ❑ | 744 | Barry Bonds CL | .30 | .14 |
| ❑ | 745 | Ken Griffey Jr. CL | 1.25 | .55 |
| ❑ | 746 | Brian Jordan CL | .15 | .07 |
| ❑ | 747 | Juan Gonzalez CL | .30 | .14 |
| ❑ | 748 | Joe Carter CL | .15 | .07 |
| ❑ | 749 | Arizona Diamondbacks CL (Inserts) | .30 | .14 |
| ❑ | 750 | Tampa Bay Devil Rays CL (Inserts) | .30 | .14 |
| ❑ | 751 | Hideki Irabu RC | .75 | .35 |
| ❑ | 752 | Jeremi Gonzalez RC | .25 | .11 |
| ❑ | 753 | Mario Valdez RC | .50 | .23 |
| ❑ | 754 | Aaron Boone | .25 | .11 |
| ❑ | 755 | Brett Tomko | .15 | .07 |
| ❑ | 756 | Jaret Wright RC | .75 | .35 |
| ❑ | 757 | Ryan McGuire | .25 | .11 |
| ❑ | 758 | Jason McDonald | .25 | .11 |
| ❑ | 759 | Adrian Brown RC | .25 | .11 |
| ❑ | 760 | Keith Foulke RC | .25 | .11 |
| ❑ | 761 | Bonus Checklist | .25 | .11 |
| ❑ | P489 | Matt Williams Promo | 1.00 | .90 |
| ❑ | NNO | Andruw Jones Circa AU/200 | 60.00 | 27.00 |

## 1998 Fleer

| | MINT | NRMT |
|---|---|---|
| COMPLETE SET (600) | 170.00 | 75.00 |
| COMPLETE SERIES 1 (350) | 100.00 | 45.00 |
| COMPLETE SERIES 2 (250) | 70.00 | 32.00 |
| COMMON CARD (1-600) | .15 | .07 |
| COMMON GM (311-320) | .40 | .18 |
| COMMON TT (321-340) | .50 | .23 |
| COMMON UM (576-600) | .60 | .25 |

| | No. | Player | | |
|---|---|---|---|---|
| ❑ | 1 | Ken Griffey Jr. | 2.50 | 1.10 |
| ❑ | 2 | Derek Jeter | 2.50 | 1.10 |
| ❑ | 3 | Gerald Williams | .15 | .07 |
| ❑ | 4 | Carlos Delgado | .60 | .25 |
| ❑ | 5 | Nomar Garciaparra | 2.00 | .90 |
| ❑ | 6 | Gary Sheffield | .60 | .25 |
| ❑ | 7 | Jeff King | .15 | .07 |
| ❑ | 8 | Cal Ripken | 2.50 | 1.10 |
| ❑ | 9 | Matt Williams | .40 | .18 |
| ❑ | 10 | Chipper Jones | 1.50 | .70 |
| ❑ | 11 | Chuck Knoblauch | .25 | .11 |
| ❑ | 12 | Mark Grudzielanek | .15 | .07 |
| ❑ | 13 | Edgardo Alfonzo | .25 | .11 |
| ❑ | 14 | Andres Galarraga | .40 | .18 |
| ❑ | 15 | Tim Salmon | .25 | .11 |
| ❑ | 16 | Reggie Sanders | .15 | .07 |
| ❑ | 17 | Tony Clark | .15 | .07 |
| ❑ | 18 | Jason Kendall | .25 | .11 |
| ❑ | 19 | Juan Gonzalez | .60 | .25 |
| ❑ | 20 | Ben Grieve | .25 | .11 |
| ❑ | 21 | Roger Clemens | 1.25 | .55 |
| ❑ | 22 | Raul Mondesi | .25 | .11 |
| ❑ | 23 | Robin Ventura | .25 | .11 |
| ❑ | 24 | Derrek Lee | .15 | .07 |
| ❑ | 25 | Mark McGwire | 2.50 | 1.10 |
| ❑ | 26 | Luis Gonzalez | .25 | .11 |
| ❑ | 27 | Kevin Brown | .40 | .18 |
| ❑ | 28 | Kirk Rueter | .15 | .07 |
| ❑ | 29 | Bobby Estalella | .15 | .07 |
| ❑ | 30 | Shawn Green | .60 | .25 |
| ❑ | 31 | Greg Maddux | 1.50 | .70 |
| ❑ | 32 | Jorge Velandia | .15 | .07 |
| ❑ | 33 | Larry Walker | .25 | .11 |
| ❑ | 34 | Joey Cora | .15 | .07 |
| ❑ | 35 | Frank Thomas | 1.25 | .55 |
| ❑ | 36 | Curtis King RC | .15 | .07 |
| ❑ | 37 | Aaron Boone | .15 | .07 |
| ❑ | 38 | Curt Schilling | .25 | .11 |
| ❑ | 39 | Bruce Aven | .15 | .07 |
| ❑ | 40 | Ben McDonald | .15 | .07 |
| ❑ | 41 | Andy Ashby | .15 | .07 |
| ❑ | 42 | Jason McDonald | .15 | .07 |
| ❑ | 43 | Eric Davis | .25 | .11 |
| ❑ | 44 | Mark Grace | .60 | .25 |
| ❑ | 45 | Pedro Martinez | .75 | .35 |
| ❑ | 46 | Lou Collier | .15 | .07 |
| ❑ | 47 | Chan Ho Park | .25 | .11 |
| ❑ | 48 | Shane Halter | .15 | .07 |
| ❑ | 49 | Brian Hunter | .15 | .07 |
| ❑ | 50 | Jeff Bagwell | .75 | .35 |
| ❑ | 51 | Bernie Williams | .60 | .25 |
| ❑ | 52 | J.T. Snow | .25 | .11 |
| ❑ | 53 | Todd Greene | .15 | .07 |
| ❑ | 54 | Shannon Stewart | .25 | .11 |
| ❑ | 55 | Darren Bragg | .15 | .07 |
| ❑ | 56 | Fernando Tatis | .25 | .11 |
| ❑ | 57 | Darryl Kile | .25 | .11 |
| ❑ | 58 | Chris Stynes | .15 | .07 |
| ❑ | 59 | Javier Valentin | .15 | .07 |
| ❑ | 60 | Brian McRae | .15 | .07 |
| ❑ | 61 | Tom Evans | .15 | .07 |
| ❑ | 62 | Randall Simon | .15 | .07 |
| ❑ | 63 | Darrin Fletcher | .15 | .07 |
| ❑ | 64 | Jaret Wright | .15 | .07 |
| ❑ | 65 | Luis Ordaz | .15 | .07 |
| ❑ | 66 | Jose Canseco | .75 | .35 |
| ❑ | 67 | Edgar Renteria | .15 | .07 |
| ❑ | 68 | Jay Buhner | .25 | .11 |
| ❑ | 69 | Paul Konerko | .25 | .11 |
| ❑ | 70 | Adrian Brown | .15 | .07 |
| ❑ | 71 | Chris Carpenter | .25 | .11 |
| ❑ | 72 | Mike Lieberthal | .25 | .11 |
| ❑ | 73 | Dean Palmer | .25 | .11 |
| ❑ | 74 | Jorge Fabregas | .15 | .07 |
| ❑ | 75 | Stan Javier | .15 | .07 |
| ❑ | 76 | Damion Easley | .15 | .07 |
| ❑ | 77 | David Cone | .25 | .11 |
| ❑ | 78 | Aaron Sele | .25 | .11 |
| ❑ | 79 | Antonio Alfonseca | .15 | .07 |
| ❑ | 80 | Bobby Jones | .15 | .07 |
| ❑ | 81 | David Justice | .40 | .18 |
| ❑ | 82 | Jeffrey Hammonds | .25 | .11 |
| ❑ | 83 | Doug Glanville | .15 | .07 |
| ❑ | 84 | Jason Dickson | .15 | .07 |
| ❑ | 85 | Brad Radke | .25 | .11 |
| ❑ | 86 | David Segui | .15 | .07 |
| ❑ | 87 | Greg Vaughn | .25 | .11 |
| ❑ | 88 | Mike Cather RC | .15 | .07 |
| ❑ | 89 | Alex Fernandez | .15 | .07 |
| ❑ | 90 | Billy Taylor | .15 | .07 |
| ❑ | 91 | Jason Schmidt | .15 | .07 |
| ❑ | 92 | Mike DeJean RC | .15 | .07 |
| ❑ | 93 | Domingo Cedeno | .15 | .07 |
| ❑ | 94 | Jeff Cirillo | .25 | .11 |
| ❑ | 95 | Manny Aybar RC | .25 | .11 |
| ❑ | 96 | Jaime Navarro | .15 | .07 |
| ❑ | 97 | Dennis Reyes | .15 | .07 |
| ❑ | 98 | Barry Larkin | .60 | .25 |
| ❑ | 99 | Troy O'Leary | .15 | .07 |
| ❑ | 100 | Alex Rodriguez | 2.00 | .90 |
| ❑ | 101 | Pat Hentgen | .15 | .07 |
| ❑ | 102 | Bubba Trammell | .15 | .07 |
| ❑ | 103 | Glendon Rusch | .15 | .07 |
| ❑ | 104 | Kenny Lofton | .25 | .11 |
| ❑ | 105 | Craig Biggio | .40 | .18 |
| ❑ | 106 | Kelvim Escobar | .15 | .07 |
| ❑ | 107 | Mark Kotsay | .25 | .11 |
| ❑ | 108 | Rondell White | .25 | .11 |
| ❑ | 109 | Darren Oliver | .15 | .07 |
| ❑ | 110 | Jim Thome | .40 | .18 |
| ❑ | 111 | Rich Becker | .15 | .07 |
| ❑ | 112 | Chad Curtis | .15 | .07 |
| ❑ | 113 | Dave Hollins | .15 | .07 |
| ❑ | 114 | Bill Mueller | .15 | .07 |
| ❑ | 115 | Antone Williamson | .15 | .07 |
| ❑ | 116 | Tony Womack | .15 | .07 |
| ❑ | 117 | Randy Myers | .25 | .11 |
| ❑ | 118 | Rico Brogna | .15 | .07 |
| ❑ | 119 | Pat Watkins | .15 | .07 |
| ❑ | 120 | Eli Marrero | .15 | .07 |
| ❑ | 121 | Jay Bell | .25 | .11 |
| ❑ | 122 | Kevin Tapani | .15 | .07 |
| ❑ | 123 | Todd Erdos RC | .25 | .11 |
| ❑ | 124 | Neifi Perez | .15 | .07 |
| ❑ | 125 | Todd Hundley | .15 | .07 |
| ❑ | 126 | Jeff Abbott | .15 | .07 |
| ❑ | 127 | Todd Zeile | .25 | .11 |
| ❑ | 128 | Travis Fryman | .25 | .11 |
| ❑ | 129 | Sandy Alomar Jr. | .25 | .11 |
| ❑ | 130 | Fred McGriff | .40 | .18 |
| ❑ | 131 | Richard Hidalgo | .25 | .11 |
| ❑ | 132 | Scott Spiezio | .15 | .07 |
| ❑ | 133 | John Valentin | .15 | .07 |
| ❑ | 134 | Quilvio Veras | .15 | .07 |
| ❑ | 135 | Mike Lansing | .15 | .07 |
| ❑ | 136 | Paul Molitor | .60 | .25 |

| | | | |
|---|---|---|---|
| 137 | Randy Johnson | .75 | .35 |
| 138 | Harold Baines | .25 | .11 |
| 139 | Doug Jones | .15 | .07 |
| 140 | Abraham Nunez | .15 | .07 |
| 141 | Alan Benes | .15 | .07 |
| 142 | Matt Perisho | .15 | .07 |
| 143 | Chris Clemons | .15 | .07 |
| 144 | Andy Pettitte | .25 | .11 |
| 145 | Jason Giambi | .60 | .25 |
| 146 | Moises Alou | .25 | .11 |
| 147 | Chad Fox RC | .15 | .07 |
| 148 | Felix Martinez | .15 | .07 |
| 149 | Carlos Mendoza RC | .25 | .11 |
| 150 | Scott Rolen | .60 | .25 |
| 151 | Jose Cabrera RC | .15 | .07 |
| 152 | Justin Thompson | .15 | .07 |
| 153 | Ellis Burks | .25 | .11 |
| 154 | Pokey Reese | .25 | .11 |
| 155 | Bartolo Colon | .25 | .11 |
| 156 | Ray Durham | .25 | .11 |
| 157 | Ugueth Urbina | .15 | .07 |
| 158 | Tom Goodwin | .15 | .07 |
| 159 | Dave Dellucci RC | .15 | .07 |
| 160 | Rod Beck | .15 | .07 |
| 161 | Ramon Martinez | .15 | .07 |
| 162 | Joe Carter | .25 | .11 |
| 163 | Kevin Orie | .15 | .07 |
| 164 | Trevor Hoffman | .25 | .11 |
| 165 | Emil Brown | .15 | .07 |
| 166 | Robb Nen | .15 | .07 |
| 167 | Paul O'Neill | .25 | .11 |
| 168 | Ryan Long | .15 | .07 |
| 169 | Ray Lankford | .25 | .11 |
| 170 | Ivan Rodriguez | .75 | .35 |
| 171 | Rick Aguilera | .15 | .07 |
| 172 | Deivi Cruz | .15 | .07 |
| 173 | Ricky Bottalico | .15 | .07 |
| 174 | Garret Anderson | .25 | .11 |
| 175 | Jose Vizcaino | .15 | .07 |
| 176 | Omar Vizquel | .25 | .11 |
| 177 | Jeff Blauser | .15 | .07 |
| 178 | Orlando Cabrera | .15 | .07 |
| 179 | Russ Johnson | .15 | .07 |
| 180 | Matt Stairs | .15 | .07 |
| 181 | Will Cunnane | .15 | .07 |
| 182 | Adam Riggs | .15 | .07 |
| 183 | Matt Morris | .15 | .07 |
| 184 | Mario Valdez | .15 | .07 |
| 185 | Larry Sutton | .15 | .07 |
| 186 | Marc Pisciotta RC | .15 | .07 |
| 187 | Dan Wilson | .15 | .07 |
| 188 | John Franco | .25 | .11 |
| 189 | Darren Daulton | .25 | .11 |
| 190 | Todd Helton | .75 | .35 |
| 191 | Brady Anderson | .25 | .11 |
| 192 | Ricardo Rincon | .15 | .07 |
| 193 | Kevin Stocker | .15 | .07 |
| 194 | Jose Valentin | .15 | .07 |
| 195 | Ed Sprague | .15 | .07 |
| 196 | Ryan McGuire | .15 | .07 |
| 197 | Scott Eyre | .15 | .07 |
| 198 | Steve Finley | .25 | .11 |
| 199 | T.J. Mathews | .15 | .07 |
| 200 | Mike Piazza | 2.00 | .90 |
| 201 | Mark Wohlers | .15 | .07 |
| 202 | Brian Giles | .25 | .11 |
| 203 | Eduardo Perez | .15 | .07 |
| 204 | Shigetoshi Hasegawa | .25 | .11 |
| 205 | Mariano Rivera | .25 | .11 |
| 206 | Jose Rosado | .15 | .07 |
| 207 | Michael Coleman | .15 | .07 |
| 208 | James Baldwin | .15 | .07 |
| 209 | Russ Davis | .15 | .07 |
| 210 | Billy Wagner | .15 | .07 |
| 211 | Sammy Sosa | 1.25 | .55 |
| 212 | Frank Catalanotto RC | .40 | .18 |
| 213 | Delino DeShields | .15 | .07 |
| 214 | John Olerud | .25 | .11 |
| 215 | Heath Murray | .15 | .07 |
| 216 | Jose Vidro | .15 | .07 |
| 217 | Jim Edmonds | .60 | .25 |
| 218 | Shawon Dunston | .15 | .07 |
| 219 | Homer Bush | .15 | .07 |
| 220 | Midre Cummings | .15 | .07 |
| 221 | Tony Saunders | .15 | .07 |
| 222 | Jeromy Burnitz | .25 | .11 |
| 223 | Enrique Wilson | .15 | .07 |
| 224 | Chili Davis | .25 | .11 |
| 225 | Jerry DiPoto | .15 | .07 |
| 226 | Dante Powell | .15 | .07 |
| 227 | Javier Lopez | .25 | .11 |
| 228 | Kevin Polcovich | .15 | .07 |
| 229 | Deion Sanders | .25 | .11 |
| 230 | Jimmy Key | .25 | .11 |
| 231 | Rusty Greer | .25 | .11 |
| 232 | Reggie Jefferson | .15 | .07 |
| 233 | Ron Coomer | .15 | .07 |
| 234 | Bobby Higginson | .25 | .11 |
| 235 | Maggio Ordonez RC | 2.50 | 1.10 |
| 236 | Miguel Tejada | .60 | .25 |
| 237 | Rick Gorecki | .15 | .07 |
| 238 | Charles Johnson | .25 | .11 |
| 239 | Lance Johnson | .15 | .07 |
| 240 | Derek Bell | .15 | .07 |
| 241 | Will Clark | .60 | .25 |
| 242 | Brady Raggio | .15 | .07 |
| 243 | Orel Hershiser | .25 | .11 |
| 244 | Vladimir Guerrero | 1.00 | .45 |
| 245 | John LeRoy | .15 | .07 |
| 246 | Shawn Estes | .15 | .07 |
| 247 | Brett Tomko | .15 | .07 |
| 248 | Dave Nilsson | .15 | .07 |
| 249 | Edgar Martinez | .40 | .18 |
| 250 | Tony Gwynn | 1.25 | .55 |
| 251 | Mark Bellhorn | .15 | .07 |
| 252 | Jed Hansen | .15 | .07 |
| 253 | Butch Huskey | .15 | .07 |
| 254 | Eric Young | .15 | .07 |
| 255 | Vinny Castilla | .25 | .11 |
| 256 | Hideki Irabu | .15 | .07 |
| 257 | Mike Cameron | .25 | .11 |
| 258 | Juan Encarnacion | .25 | .11 |
| 259 | Brian Rose | .15 | .07 |
| 260 | Brad Ausmus | .15 | .07 |
| 261 | Dan Serafini | .15 | .07 |
| 262 | Willie Greene | .15 | .07 |
| 263 | Troy Percival | .15 | .07 |
| 264 | Jeff Wallace | .25 | .11 |
| 265 | Richie Sexson | .40 | .18 |
| 266 | Rafael Palmeiro | .60 | .25 |
| 267 | Brad Fullmer | .25 | .11 |
| 268 | Jeremi Gonzalez | .15 | .07 |
| 269 | Rob Stanifer RC | .15 | .07 |
| 270 | Mickey Morandini | .15 | .07 |
| 271 | Andruw Jones | .60 | .25 |
| 272 | Royce Clayton | .15 | .07 |
| 273 | Takashi Kashiwada RC | .15 | .07 |
| 274 | Steve Woodard | .15 | .07 |
| 275 | Jose Cruz Jr. | .25 | .11 |
| 276 | Keith Foulke | .15 | .07 |
| 277 | Brad Rigby | .15 | .07 |
| 278 | Tino Martinez | .25 | .11 |
| 279 | Todd Jones | .15 | .07 |
| 280 | John Wetteland | .25 | .11 |
| 281 | Alex Gonzalez | .15 | .07 |
| 282 | Ken Cloude | .15 | .07 |
| 283 | Jose Guillen | .15 | .07 |
| 284 | Danny Clyburn | .15 | .07 |
| 285 | David Ortiz | .15 | .07 |
| 286 | John Thomson | .15 | .07 |
| 287 | Kevin Appier | .25 | .11 |
| 288 | Ismael Valdes | .15 | .07 |
| 289 | Gary DiSarcina | .15 | .07 |
| 290 | Todd Dunwoody | .15 | .07 |
| 291 | Wally Joyner | .25 | .11 |
| 292 | Charles Nagy | .15 | .07 |
| 293 | Jeff Shaw | .15 | .07 |
| 294 | Kevin Millwood RC | 1.00 | .45 |
| 295 | Rigo Beltran RC | .15 | .07 |
| 296 | Jeff Frye | .15 | .07 |
| 297 | Oscar Henriquez | .15 | .07 |
| 298 | Mike Thurman | .15 | .07 |
| 299 | Garrett Stephenson | .15 | .07 |
| 300 | Barry Bonds | 1.00 | .45 |
| 301 | Roger Clemens SH | .60 | .25 |
| 302 | David Cone SH | .15 | .07 |
| 303 | Hideki Irabu SH | .15 | .07 |
| 304 | Randy Johnson SH | .25 | .11 |
| 305 | Greg Maddux SH | .75 | .35 |
| 306 | Pedro Martinez SH | .40 | .18 |
| 307 | Mike Mussina SH | .25 | .11 |
| 308 | Andy Pettitte SH | .15 | .07 |
| 309 | Curt Schilling SH | .15 | .07 |
| 310 | John Smoltz SH | .15 | .07 |
| 311 | Roger Clemens GM | 2.00 | .90 |
| 312 | Jose Cruz JR. GM | .50 | .23 |
| 313 | Nomar Garciaparra GM | 3.00 | 1.35 |
| 314 | Ken Griffey Jr. GM | 4.00 | 1.80 |
| 315 | Tony Gwynn GM | 2.00 | .90 |
| 316 | Hideki Irabu GM | .40 | .18 |
| 317 | Randy Johnson GM | 1.25 | .55 |
| 318 | Mark McGwire GM | 4.00 | 1.80 |
| 319 | Curt Schilling GM | .50 | .23 |
| 320 | Larry Walker GM | .50 | .23 |
| 321 | Jeff Bagwell TT | 1.50 | .70 |
| 322 | Albert Belle TT | .75 | .35 |
| 323 | Barry Bonds TT | 2.00 | .90 |
| 324 | Jay Buhner TT | .60 | .25 |
| 325 | Tony Clark TT | .50 | .23 |
| 326 | Jose Cruz Jr. TT | .60 | .25 |
| 327 | Andres Galarraga TT | .75 | .35 |
| 328 | Juan Gonzalez TT | 1.25 | .55 |
| 329 | Ken Griffey Jr. TT | 5.00 | 2.20 |
| 330 | Andruw Jones TT | 1.25 | .55 |
| 331 | Tino Martinez TT | .60 | .25 |
| 332 | Mark McGwire TT | 5.00 | 2.20 |
| 333 | Rafael Palmeiro TT | 1.25 | .55 |
| 334 | Mike Piazza TT | 4.00 | 1.80 |
| 335 | Manny Ramirez TT | 1.50 | .70 |
| 336 | Alex Rodriguez TT | 4.00 | 1.80 |
| 337 | Frank Thomas TT | 2.50 | 1.10 |
| 338 | Jim Thome TT | .75 | .35 |
| 339 | Mo Vaughn TT | .60 | .25 |
| 340 | Larry Walker TT | .60 | .25 |
| 341 | Jose Cruz Jr. CL | .15 | .07 |
| 342 | Ken Griffey Jr. CL | 1.25 | .55 |
| 343 | Derek Jeter CL | 1.25 | .55 |
| 344 | Andruw Jones CL | .25 | .11 |
| 345 | Chipper Jones CL | .75 | .35 |
| 346 | Greg Maddux CL | .75 | .35 |
| 347 | Mike Piazza CL | 1.00 | .45 |
| 348 | Cal Ripken CL | 1.25 | .55 |
| 349 | Alex Rodriguez CL | 1.00 | .45 |
| 350 | Frank Thomas CL | .60 | .25 |
| 351 | Mo Vaughn | .25 | .11 |
| 352 | Andres Galarraga | .40 | .18 |
| 353 | Roberto Alomar | .60 | .25 |
| 354 | Darin Erstad | .60 | .25 |
| 355 | Albert Belle | .40 | .18 |
| 356 | Matt Williams | .40 | .18 |
| 357 | Darryl Kile | .25 | .11 |
| 358 | Kenny Lofton | .25 | .11 |
| 359 | Orel Hershiser | .25 | .11 |
| 360 | Bob Abreu | .25 | .11 |
| 361 | Chris Widger | .15 | .07 |
| 362 | Glenallen Hill | .15 | .07 |
| 363 | Chili Davis | .25 | .11 |
| 364 | Kevin Brown | .40 | .18 |
| 365 | Marquis Grissom | .15 | .07 |
| 366 | Livan Hernandez | .15 | .07 |
| 367 | Moises Alou | .25 | .11 |
| 368 | Matt Lawton | .15 | .07 |
| 369 | Rey Ordonez | .15 | .07 |
| 370 | Kenny Rogers | .15 | .07 |
| 371 | Lee Stevens | .15 | .07 |
| 372 | Wade Boggs | .75 | .35 |
| 373 | Luis Gonzalez | .25 | .11 |
| 374 | Jeff Conine | .15 | .07 |
| 375 | Esteban Loaiza | .15 | .07 |
| 376 | Jose Canseco | .75 | .35 |
| 377 | Henry Rodriguez | .15 | .07 |
| 378 | Dave Burba | .15 | .07 |
| 379 | Todd Hollandsworth | .15 | .07 |
| 380 | Ron Gant | .25 | .11 |
| 381 | Pedro Martinez | .75 | .35 |
| 382 | Ryan Klesko | .25 | .11 |
| 383 | Derrek Lee | .15 | .07 |
| 384 | Doug Glanville | .15 | .07 |
| 385 | David Wells | .25 | .11 |
| 386 | Ken Caminiti | .25 | .11 |
| 387 | Damon Hollins | .15 | .07 |
| 388 | Manny Ramirez | .75 | .35 |
| 389 | Mike Mussina | .60 | .25 |
| 390 | Jay Bell | .25 | .11 |
| 391 | Mike Piazza | 2.00 | .90 |
| 392 | Mike Lansing | .15 | .07 |
| 393 | Mike Hampton | .25 | .11 |
| 394 | Geoff Jenkins | .25 | .11 |

- ❑ 395 Jimmy Haynes .15 .07
- ❑ 396 Scott Servais .15 .07
- ❑ 397 Kent Mercker .15 .07
- ❑ 398 Jeff Kent .40 .18
- ❑ 399 Kevin Elster .15 .07
- ❑ 400 Masato Yoshii RC .50 .23
- ❑ 401 Jose Vizcaino .15 .07
- ❑ 402 Javier Martinez RC .40 .18
- ❑ 403 David Segui .15 .07
- ❑ 404 Tony Saunders .15 .07
- ❑ 405 Karim Garcia .15 .07
- ❑ 406 Armando Benitez .15 .07
- ❑ 407 Joe Randa .15 .07
- ❑ 408 Vic Darensbourg .15 .07
- ❑ 409 Sean Casey .25 .11
- ❑ 410 Eric Milton .15 .07
- ❑ 411 Trey Moore .15 .07
- ❑ 412 Mike Stanley .15 .07
- ❑ 413 Tom Gordon .25 .11
- ❑ 414 Hal Morris .15 .07
- ❑ 415 Braden Looper .15 .07
- ❑ 416 Mike Kelly .15 .07
- ❑ 417 John Smoltz .25 .11
- ❑ 418 Roger Cedeno .15 .07
- ❑ 419 Al Leiter .25 .11
- ❑ 420 Chuck Knoblauch .25 .11
- ❑ 421 Felix Rodriguez .15 .07
- ❑ 422 Bip Roberts .15 .07
- ❑ 423 Ken Hill .15 .07
- ❑ 424 Jermaine Allensworth .15 .07
- ❑ 425 Esteban Yan RC .40 .18
- ❑ 426 Scott Karl .15 .07
- ❑ 427 Sean Berry .15 .07
- ❑ 428 Rafael Medina .15 .07
- ❑ 429 Javier Vazquez .15 .07
- ❑ 430 Rickey Henderson .75 .35
- ❑ 431 Adam Butler .25 .11
- ❑ 432 Todd Stottlemyre .15 .07
- ❑ 433 Yamil Benitez .15 .07
- ❑ 434 Sterling Hitchcock .15 .07
- ❑ 435 Paul Sorrento .15 .07
- ❑ 436 Bobby Ayala .15 .07
- ❑ 437 Tim Raines .25 .11
- ❑ 438 Chris Hoiles .15 .07
- ❑ 439 Rod Beck .15 .07
- ❑ 440 Donnie Sadler .15 .07
- ❑ 441 Charles Johnson .25 .11
- ❑ 442 Russ Ortiz .25 .11
- ❑ 443 Pedro Astacio .15 .07
- ❑ 444 Wilson Alvarez .15 .07
- ❑ 445 Mike Blowers .15 .07
- ❑ 446 Todd Zeile .25 .11
- ❑ 447 Mel Rojas .15 .07
- ❑ 448 F.P. Santangelo .15 .07
- ❑ 449 Dmitri Young .25 .11
- ❑ 450 Brian Anderson .15 .07
- ❑ 451 Cecil Fielder .25 .11
- ❑ 452 Roberto Hernandez .15 .07
- ❑ 453 Todd Walker .15 .07
- ❑ 454 Tyler Green .15 .07
- ❑ 455 Jorge Posada .15 .07
- ❑ 456 Geronimo Berroa .15 .07
- ❑ 457 Jose Silva .15 .07
- ❑ 458 Bobby Bonilla .25 .11
- ❑ 459 Walt Weiss .25 .11
- ❑ 460 Darren Dreifort .15 .07
- ❑ 461 B.J. Surhoff .25 .11
- ❑ 462 Quinton McCracken .15 .07
- ❑ 463 Derek Lowe .15 .07
- ❑ 464 Jorge Fabregas .15 .07
- ❑ 465 Joey Hamilton .15 .07
- ❑ 466 Brian Jordan .25 .11
- ❑ 467 Allen Watson .15 .07
- ❑ 468 John Jaha .25 .11
- ❑ 469 Heathcliff Slocumb .15 .07
- ❑ 470 Gregg Jefferies .15 .07
- ❑ 471 Scott Brosius .25 .11
- ❑ 472 Chad Ogea .15 .07
- ❑ 473 A.J. Hinch .15 .07
- ❑ 474 Bobby Smith .15 .07
- ❑ 475 Brian Moehler .15 .07
- ❑ 476 DaRond Stovall .15 .07
- ❑ 477 Kevin Young .25 .11
- ❑ 478 Jeff Suppan .15 .07
- ❑ 479 Marty Cordova .15 .07
- ❑ 480 John Halama RC .50 .23
- ❑ 481 Bubba Trammell .15 .07
- ❑ 482 Mike Caruso .15 .07
- ❑ 483 Eric Karros .25 .11
- ❑ 484 Jamey Wright .15 .07
- ❑ 485 Mike Sweeney .25 .11
- ❑ 486 Aaron Sele .25 .11
- ❑ 487 Cliff Floyd .25 .11
- ❑ 488 Jeff Brantley .15 .07
- ❑ 489 Jim Leyritz .15 .07
- ❑ 490 Denny Neagle .15 .07
- ❑ 491 Travis Fryman .25 .11
- ❑ 492 Carlos Baerga .15 .07
- ❑ 493 Eddie Taubensee .15 .07
- ❑ 494 Darryl Strawberry .25 .11
- ❑ 495 Brian Johnson .15 .07
- ❑ 496 Randy Myers .25 .11
- ❑ 497 Jeff Blauser .15 .07
- ❑ 498 Jason Wood .15 .07
- ❑ 499 Rolando Arrojo RC .50 .23
- ❑ 500 Johnny Damon .25 .11
- ❑ 501 Jose Mercedes .15 .07
- ❑ 502 Tony Batista .25 .11
- ❑ 503 Mike Piazza Mets 2.00 .90
- ❑ 504 Hideo Nomo .60 .25
- ❑ 505 Chris Gomez .15 .07
- ❑ 506 Jesus Sanchez RC .40 .18
- ❑ 507 Al Martin .15 .07
- ❑ 508 Brian Edmondson .15 .07
- ❑ 509 Joe Girardi .15 .07
- ❑ 510 Shayne Bennett .15 .07
- ❑ 511 Joe Carter .25 .11
- ❑ 512 Dave Mlicki .15 .07
- ❑ 513 Rich Butler RC .15 .07
- ❑ 514 Dennis Eckersley .25 .11
- ❑ 515 Travis Lee .25 .11
- ❑ 516 John Mabry .15 .07
- ❑ 517 Jose Mesa .15 .07
- ❑ 518 Phil Nevin .25 .11
- ❑ 519 Raul Casanova .15 .07
- ❑ 520 Mike Fetters .15 .07
- ❑ 521 Gary Sheffield .60 .25
- ❑ 522 Terry Steinbach .15 .07
- ❑ 523 Steve Trachsel .15 .07
- ❑ 524 Josh Booty .15 .07
- ❑ 525 Darryl Hamilton .15 .07
- ❑ 526 Mark McLemore .15 .07
- ❑ 527 Kevin Stocker .15 .07
- ❑ 528 Bret Boone .25 .11
- ❑ 529 Shane Andrews .15 .07
- ❑ 530 Robb Nen .15 .07
- ❑ 531 Carl Everett .25 .11
- ❑ 532 LaTroy Hawkins .15 .07
- ❑ 533 Fernando Vina .15 .07
- ❑ 534 Michael Tucker .15 .07
- ❑ 535 Mark Langston .15 .07
- ❑ 536 Mickey Mantle 5.00 2.20
- ❑ 537 Bernard Gilkey .15 .07
- ❑ 538 Francisco Cordova .15 .07
- ❑ 539 Mike Bordick .15 .07
- ❑ 540 Fred McGriff .40 .18
- ❑ 541 Cliff Politte .15 .07
- ❑ 542 Jason Varitek .25 .11
- ❑ 543 Shawon Dunston .15 .07
- ❑ 544 Brian Meadows .15 .07
- ❑ 545 Pat Meares .15 .07
- ❑ 546 Carlos Perez .15 .07
- ❑ 547 Desi Relaford .15 .07
- ❑ 548 Antonio Osuna .15 .07
- ❑ 549 Devon White .15 .07
- ❑ 550 Sean Runyan .15 .07
- ❑ 551 Mickey Morandini .15 .07
- ❑ 552 Dave Martinez .15 .07
- ❑ 553 Jeff Fassero .15 .07
- ❑ 554 Ryan Jackson RC .15 .07
- ❑ 555 Stan Javier .15 .07
- ❑ 556 Jaime Navarro .15 .07
- ❑ 557 Jose Offerman .15 .07
- ❑ 558 Mike Lowell RC .75 .35
- ❑ 559 Darrin Fletcher .15 .07
- ❑ 560 Mark Lewis .15 .07
- ❑ 561 Dante Bichette .25 .11
- ❑ 562 Chuck Finley .25 .11
- ❑ 563 Kerry Wood .60 .25
- ❑ 564 Andy Benes .15 .07
- ❑ 565 Freddy Garcia .15 .07
- ❑ 566 Tom Glavine .60 .25
- ❑ 567 Jon Nunnally .15 .07
- ❑ 568 Miguel Cairo .15 .07
- ❑ 569 Shane Reynolds .15 .07
- ❑ 570 Roberto Kelly .15 .07
- ❑ 571 Jose Cruz Jr. CL .15 .07
- ❑ 572 Ken Griffey Jr. CL 1.25 .55
- ❑ 573 Mark McGwire CL 1.25 .55
- ❑ 574 Cal Ripken CL 1.25 .55
- ❑ 575 Frank Thomas CL .60 .25
- ❑ 576 Jeff Bagwell UM 2.00 .90
- ❑ 577 Barry Bonds UM 2.50 1.10
- ❑ 578 Tony Clark UM .60 .25
- ❑ 579 Roger Clemens UM 3.00 1.35
- ❑ 580 Jose Cruz Jr. UM .75 .35
- ❑ 581 Nomar Garciaparra UM 5.00 2.20
- ❑ 582 Juan Gonzalez UM 1.50 .70
- ❑ 583 Ben Grieve UM .75 .35
- ❑ 584 Ken Griffey Jr. UM 6.00 2.70
- ❑ 585 Tony Gwynn UM 3.00 1.35
- ❑ 586 Derek Jeter UM 6.00 2.70
- ❑ 587 Randy Johnson UM 2.00 .90
- ❑ 588 Chipper Jones UM 4.00 1.80
- ❑ 589 Greg Maddux UM 4.00 1.80
- ❑ 590 Mark McGwire UM 6.00 2.70
- ❑ 591 Paul Molitor UM 1.50 .70
- ❑ 592 Andy Pettitte UM .75 .35
- ❑ 593 Cal Ripken UM 6.00 2.70
- ❑ 594 Alex Rodriguez UM 5.00 2.20
- ❑ 595 Scott Rolen UM 1.50 .70
- ❑ 596 Curt Schilling UM .75 .35
- ❑ 597 Frank Thomas UM 3.00 1.35
- ❑ 598 Jim Thome UM 1.00 .45
- ❑ 599 Larry Walker UM .75 .35
- ❑ 600 Bernie Williams UM 1.50 .70
- ❑ P100 Alex Rodriguez Promo 3.00 1.35

## 1998 Fleer Update

| | MINT | NRMT |
|---|---|---|
| COMP.FACT.SET (100) | 40.00 | 18.00 |

- ❑ U1 Mark McGwire HL 1.50 .70
- ❑ U2 Sammy Sosa HL .75 .35
- ❑ U3 Roger Clemens HL .75 .35
- ❑ U4 Barry Bonds HL .60 .25
- ❑ U5 Kerry Wood HL .40 .18
- ❑ U6 Paul Molitor HL .15 .07
- ❑ U7 Ken Griffey Jr. HL 1.50 .70
- ❑ U8 Cal Ripken HL 1.50 .70
- ❑ U9 David Wells HL .15 .07
- ❑ U10 Alex Rodriguez HL 1.25 .55
- ❑ U11 Angel Pena RC .40 .18
- ❑ U12 Bruce Chen .10 .05
- ❑ U13 Craig Wilson .10 .05
- ❑ U14 Orlando Hernandez RC 1.50 .70
- ❑ U15 Aramis Ramirez .15 .07
- ❑ U16 Aaron Boone .10 .05
- ❑ U17 Bob Henley .10 .05
- ❑ U18 Juan Guzman .10 .05
- ❑ U19 Darryl Hamilton .10 .05
- ❑ U20 Jay Payton .15 .07
- ❑ U21 Jeremy Powell .10 .05
- ❑ U22 Ben Davis .10 .05
- ❑ U23 Preston Wilson .15 .07
- ❑ U24 Jim Parque RC .75 .35
- ❑ U25 Odalis Perez RC .50 .23
- ❑ U26 Ronnie Belliard .10 .05
- ❑ U27 Royce Clayton .10 .05

| | | |
|---|---|---|
| ❑ U28 George Lombard | .10 | .05 |
| ❑ U29 Tony Phillips | .10 | .05 |
| ❑ U30 Fernando Seguignol RC | .50 | .23 |
| ❑ U31 Armando Rios RC | .40 | .18 |
| ❑ U32 Jerry Hairston Jr. RC | .75 | .35 |
| ❑ U33 Justin Baughman RC | .10 | .05 |
| ❑ U34 Seth Greisinger | .10 | .05 |
| ❑ U35 Alex Gonzalez | .10 | .05 |
| ❑ U36 Michael Barrett | .10 | .05 |
| ❑ U37 Carlos Beltran | .15 | .07 |
| ❑ U38 Ellis Burks | .15 | .07 |
| ❑ U39 Jose Jimenez RC | .10 | .05 |
| ❑ U40 Carlos Guillen | .10 | .05 |
| ❑ U41 Marlon Anderson | .10 | .05 |
| ❑ U42 Scott Elarton | .15 | .07 |
| ❑ U43 Glenallen Hill | .10 | .05 |
| ❑ U44 Shane Monahan | .10 | .05 |
| ❑ U45 Dennis Martinez | .15 | .07 |
| ❑ U46 Carlos Febles RC | .75 | .35 |
| ❑ U47 Carlos Perez | .10 | .05 |
| ❑ U48 Wilton Guerrero | .10 | .05 |
| ❑ U49 Randy Johnson | .50 | .23 |
| ❑ U50 Brian Simmons RC | .10 | .05 |
| ❑ U51 Carlton Loewer | .10 | .05 |
| ❑ U52 Mark DeRosa RC | .10 | .05 |
| ❑ U53 Tim Young RC | .15 | .07 |
| ❑ U54 Gary Gaetti | .15 | .07 |
| ❑ U55 Eric Chavez | .15 | .07 |
| ❑ U56 Carl Pavano | .10 | .05 |
| ❑ U57 Mike Stanley | .10 | .05 |
| ❑ U58 Todd Stottlemyre | .10 | .05 |
| ❑ U59 Gabe Kapler RC | 3.00 | 1.35 |
| ❑ U60 Mike Jerzembeck RC | .15 | .07 |
| ❑ U61 Mitch Meluskey RC | .75 | .35 |
| ❑ U62 Bill Pulsipher | .10 | .05 |
| ❑ U63 Derrick Gibson | .10 | .05 |
| ❑ U64 John Rocker RC | 4.00 | 1.80 |
| ❑ U65 Calvin Pickering | .10 | .05 |
| ❑ U66 Blake Stein | .10 | .05 |
| ❑ U67 Fernando Tatis | .15 | .07 |
| ❑ U68 Gabe Alvarez | .10 | .05 |
| ❑ U69 Jeffrey Hammonds | .15 | .07 |
| ❑ U70 Adrian Beltre | .15 | .07 |
| ❑ U71 Ryan Bradley RC | .40 | .18 |
| ❑ U72 Edgard Clemente | .10 | .05 |
| ❑ U73 Rick Croushore RC | .10 | .05 |
| ❑ U74 Matt Clement | .15 | .07 |
| ❑ U75 Dermal Brown | .15 | .07 |
| ❑ U76 Paul Bako | .10 | .05 |
| ❑ U77 Placido Polanco RC | .40 | .18 |
| ❑ U78 Jay Tessmer | .10 | .05 |
| ❑ U79 Jarrod Washburn | .10 | .05 |
| ❑ U80 Kevin Witt | .10 | .05 |
| ❑ U81 Mike Metcalfe | .10 | .05 |
| ❑ U82 Daryle Ward | .15 | .07 |
| ❑ U83 Benj Sampson RC | .40 | .18 |
| ❑ U84 Mike Kinkade RC | .40 | .18 |
| ❑ U85 Randy Winn | .10 | .05 |
| ❑ U86 Jeff Shaw | .10 | .05 |
| ❑ U87 Troy Glaus RC | 6.00 | 2.70 |
| ❑ U88 Hideo Nomo | .40 | .18 |
| ❑ U89 Mark Grudzielanek | .10 | .05 |
| ❑ U90 Mike Frank RC | .10 | .05 |
| ❑ U91 Bobby Howry RC | .40 | .18 |
| ❑ U92 Ryan Minor RC | .40 | .18 |
| ❑ U93 Corey Koskie RC | 1.00 | .45 |
| ❑ U94 Matt Anderson RC | .40 | .18 |
| ❑ U95 Joe Carter | .15 | .07 |
| ❑ U96 Paul Konerko | .15 | .07 |
| ❑ U97 Sidney Ponson | .10 | .05 |
| ❑ U98 Jeremy Giambi RC | .50 | .23 |
| ❑ U99 Jeff Kubenka RC | .10 | .05 |
| ❑ U100 J.D. Drew RC | 10.00 | 4.50 |

## 1999 Fleer

| | MINT | NRMT |
|---|---|---|
| COMPLETE SET (600) | 75.00 | 34.00 |
| ❑ 1 Mark McGwire | 2.50 | 1.10 |
| ❑ 2 Sammy Sosa | 1.25 | .55 |
| ❑ 3 Ken Griffey Jr. | 2.50 | 1.10 |
| ❑ 4 Kerry Wood | .25 | .11 |
| ❑ 5 Derek Jeter | 2.50 | 1.10 |
| ❑ 6 Stan Musial | 2.00 | .90 |
| ❑ 7 J.D. Drew | .60 | .25 |
| ❑ 8 Cal Ripken | 2.50 | 1.10 |
| ❑ 9 Alex Rodriguez | 2.00 | .90 |
| ❑ 10 Travis Lee | .15 | .07 |
| ❑ 11 Andres Galarraga | .40 | .18 |
| ❑ 12 Nomar Garciaparra | 2.00 | .90 |
| ❑ 13 Albert Belle | .40 | .18 |
| ❑ 14 Barry Larkin | .60 | .25 |
| ❑ 15 Dante Bichette | .25 | .11 |
| ❑ 16 Tony Clark | .15 | .07 |
| ❑ 17 Moises Alou | .25 | .11 |
| ❑ 18 Rafael Palmeiro | .60 | .25 |
| ❑ 19 Raul Mondesi | .25 | .11 |
| ❑ 20 Vladimir Guerrero | 1.00 | .45 |
| ❑ 21 John Olerud | .25 | .11 |
| ❑ 22 Bernie Williams | .60 | .25 |
| ❑ 23 Ben Grieve | .25 | .11 |
| ❑ 24 Scott Rolen | .60 | .25 |
| ❑ 25 Jeromy Burnitz | .25 | .11 |
| ❑ 26 Ken Caminiti | .25 | .11 |
| ❑ 27 Barry Bonds | 1.00 | .45 |
| ❑ 28 Todd Helton | .75 | .35 |
| ❑ 29 Juan Gonzalez | .60 | .25 |
| ❑ 30 Roger Clemens | 1.25 | .55 |
| ❑ 31 Andruw Jones | .60 | .25 |
| ❑ 32 Mo Vaughn | .25 | .11 |
| ❑ 33 Larry Walker | .25 | .11 |
| ❑ 34 Frank Thomas | 1.25 | .55 |
| ❑ 35 Manny Ramirez | .75 | .35 |
| ❑ 36 Randy Johnson | .75 | .35 |
| ❑ 37 Vinny Castilla | .25 | .11 |
| ❑ 38 Juan Encarnacion | .25 | .11 |
| ❑ 39 Jeff Bagwell | .75 | .35 |
| ❑ 40 Gary Sheffield | .60 | .25 |
| ❑ 41 Mike Piazza | 2.00 | .90 |
| ❑ 42 Richie Sexson | .25 | .11 |
| ❑ 43 Tony Gwynn | 1.25 | .55 |
| ❑ 44 Chipper Jones | 1.50 | .70 |
| ❑ 45 Jim Thome | .40 | .18 |
| ❑ 46 Craig Biggio | .40 | .18 |
| ❑ 47 Carlos Delgado | .60 | .25 |
| ❑ 48 Greg Vaughn | .25 | .11 |
| ❑ 49 Greg Maddux | 1.50 | .70 |
| ❑ 50 Troy Glaus | 1.00 | .45 |
| ❑ 51 Roberto Alomar | .60 | .25 |
| ❑ 52 Dennis Eckersley | .25 | .11 |
| ❑ 53 Mike Caruso | .15 | .07 |
| ❑ 54 Bruce Chen | .15 | .07 |
| ❑ 55 Aaron Boone | .15 | .07 |
| ❑ 56 Bartolo Colon | .25 | .11 |
| ❑ 57 Derrick Gibson | .15 | .07 |
| ❑ 58 Brian Anderson | .15 | .07 |
| ❑ 59 Gabe Alvarez | .15 | .07 |
| ❑ 60 Todd Dunwoody | .15 | .07 |
| ❑ 61 Rod Beck | .15 | .07 |
| ❑ 62 Derek Bell | .15 | .07 |
| ❑ 63 Francisco Cordova | .15 | .07 |
| ❑ 64 Johnny Damon | .25 | .11 |
| ❑ 65 Adrian Beltre | .25 | .11 |
| ❑ 66 Garret Anderson | .25 | .11 |
| ❑ 67 Armando Benitez | .15 | .07 |
| ❑ 68 Edgardo Alfonzo | .25 | .11 |
| ❑ 69 Ryan Bradley | .15 | .07 |
| ❑ 70 Eric Chavez | .25 | .11 |
| ❑ 71 Bobby Abreu | .25 | .11 |
| ❑ 72 Andy Ashby | .15 | .07 |
| ❑ 73 Ellis Burks | .25 | .11 |
| ❑ 74 Jeff Cirillo | .25 | .11 |
| ❑ 75 Jay Buhner | .25 | .11 |
| ❑ 76 Ron Gant | .25 | .11 |
| ❑ 77 Rolando Arrojo | .15 | .07 |
| ❑ 78 Will Clark | .60 | .25 |
| ❑ 79 Chris Carpenter | .15 | .07 |
| ❑ 80 Jim Edmonds | .60 | .25 |
| ❑ 81 Tony Batista | .25 | .11 |
| ❑ 82 Shane Andrews | .15 | .07 |
| ❑ 83 Mark DeRosa | .15 | .07 |
| ❑ 84 Brady Anderson | .25 | .11 |
| ❑ 85 Tom Gordon | .15 | .07 |
| ❑ 86 Brant Brown | .15 | .07 |
| ❑ 87 Ray Durham | .25 | .11 |
| ❑ 88 Ron Coomer | .15 | .07 |
| ❑ 89 Bret Boone | .25 | .11 |
| ❑ 90 Travis Fryman | .25 | .11 |
| ❑ 91 Darryl Kile | .25 | .11 |
| ❑ 92 Paul Bako | .15 | .07 |
| ❑ 93 Cliff Floyd | .25 | .11 |
| ❑ 94 Scott Elarton | .25 | .11 |
| ❑ 95 Jeremy Giambi | .15 | .07 |
| ❑ 96 Darren Dreifort | .15 | .07 |
| ❑ 97 Marquis Grissom | .15 | .07 |
| ❑ 98 Marty Cordova | .15 | .07 |
| ❑ 99 Fernando Seguignol | .15 | .07 |
| ❑ 100 Orlando Hernandez | .25 | .11 |
| ❑ 101 Jose Cruz Jr. | .25 | .11 |
| ❑ 102 Jason Giambi | .60 | .25 |
| ❑ 103 Damion Easley | .15 | .07 |
| ❑ 104 Freddy Garcia | .15 | .07 |
| ❑ 105 Marlon Anderson | .15 | .07 |
| ❑ 106 Kevin Brown | .40 | .18 |
| ❑ 107 Joe Carter | .25 | .11 |
| ❑ 108 Russ Davis | .15 | .07 |
| ❑ 109 Brian Jordan | .25 | .11 |
| ❑ 110 Wade Boggs | .75 | .35 |
| ❑ 111 Tom Goodwin | .15 | .07 |
| ❑ 112 Scott Brosius | .25 | .11 |
| ❑ 113 Darin Erstad | .60 | .25 |
| ❑ 114 Jay Bell | .25 | .11 |
| ❑ 115 Tom Glavine | .60 | .25 |
| ❑ 116 Pedro Martinez | .75 | .35 |
| ❑ 117 Mark Grace | .60 | .25 |
| ❑ 118 Russ Ortiz | .15 | .07 |
| ❑ 119 Magglio Ordonez | .40 | .18 |
| ❑ 120 Sean Casey | .25 | .11 |
| ❑ 121 Rafael Roque RC | .25 | .11 |
| ❑ 122 Brian Giles | .25 | .11 |
| ❑ 123 Mike Lansing | .15 | .07 |
| ❑ 124 David Cone | .25 | .11 |
| ❑ 125 Alex Gonzalez | .15 | .07 |
| ❑ 126 Carl Everett | .25 | .11 |
| ❑ 127 Jeff King | .15 | .07 |
| ❑ 128 Charles Johnson | .25 | .11 |
| ❑ 129 Geoff Jenkins | .25 | .11 |
| ❑ 130 Corey Koskie | .15 | .07 |
| ❑ 131 Brad Fullmer | .25 | .11 |
| ❑ 132 Al Leiter | .25 | .11 |
| ❑ 133 Rickey Henderson | .75 | .35 |
| ❑ 134 Rico Brogna | .15 | .07 |
| ❑ 135 Jose Guillen | .15 | .07 |
| ❑ 136 Matt Clement | .15 | .07 |
| ❑ 137 Carlos Guillen | .15 | .07 |
| ❑ 138 Orel Hershiser | .25 | .11 |
| ❑ 139 Ray Lankford | .25 | .11 |
| ❑ 140 Miguel Cairo | .15 | .07 |
| ❑ 141 Chuck Finley | .25 | .11 |
| ❑ 142 Rusty Greer | .25 | .11 |
| ❑ 143 Kelvim Escobar | .15 | .07 |
| ❑ 144 Ryan Klesko | .25 | .11 |
| ❑ 145 Andy Benes | .15 | .07 |
| ❑ 146 Eric Davis | .25 | .11 |
| ❑ 147 David Wells | .25 | .11 |
| ❑ 148 Trot Nixon | .25 | .11 |
| ❑ 149 Jose Hernandez | .15 | .07 |
| ❑ 150 Mark Johnson | .15 | .07 |
| ❑ 151 Mike Frank | .15 | .07 |
| ❑ 152 Joey Hamilton | .15 | .07 |
| ❑ 153 David Justice | .40 | .18 |
| ❑ 154 Mike Mussina | .60 | .25 |
| ❑ 155 Neifi Perez | .15 | .07 |
| ❑ 156 Luis Gonzalez | .25 | .11 |
| ❑ 157 Livan Hernandez | .15 | .07 |
| ❑ 158 Dermal Brown | .25 | .11 |
| ❑ 159 Jose Lima | .15 | .07 |
| ❑ 160 Eric Karros | .25 | .11 |
| ❑ 161 Ronnie Belliard | .15 | .07 |

❑ 162 Matt Lawton .25 .11
❑ 163 Dustin Hermanson .15 .07
❑ 164 Brian McRae .15 .07
❑ 165 Mike Kinkade .15 .07
❑ 166 A.J. Hinch .15 .07
❑ 167 Doug Glanville .15 .07
❑ 168 Hideo Nomo .60 .25
❑ 169 Jason Kendall .25 .11
❑ 170 Steve Finley .25 .11
❑ 171 Jeff Kent .40 .18
❑ 172 Ben Davis .15 .07
❑ 173 Edgar Martinez .40 .18
❑ 174 Eli Marrero .15 .07
❑ 175 Quinton McCracken .15 .07
❑ 176 Rick Helling .25 .11
❑ 177 Tom Evans .15 .07
❑ 178 Carl Pavano .15 .07
❑ 179 Todd Greene .15 .07
❑ 180 Omar Daal .15 .07
❑ 181 George Lombard .15 .07
❑ 182 Ryan Minor .15 .07
❑ 183 Troy O'Leary .15 .07
❑ 184 Robb Nen .15 .07
❑ 185 Mickey Morandini .15 .07
❑ 186 Robin Ventura .25 .11
❑ 187 Pete Harnisch .15 .07
❑ 188 Kenny Lofton .25 .11
❑ 189 Eric Milton .15 .07
❑ 190 Bobby Higginson .25 .11
❑ 191 Jamie Moyer .15 .07
❑ 192 Mark Kotsay .15 .07
❑ 193 Shane Reynolds .15 .07
❑ 194 Carlos Febles .15 .07
❑ 195 Jeff Kubenka .15 .07
❑ 196 Chuck Knoblauch .25 .11
❑ 197 Kenny Rogers .15 .07
❑ 198 Bill Mueller .15 .07
❑ 199 Shane Monahan .15 .07
❑ 200 Matt Morris .15 .07
❑ 201 Fred McGriff .40 .18
❑ 202 Ivan Rodriguez .75 .35
❑ 203 Kevin Witt .15 .07
❑ 204 Troy Percival .15 .07
❑ 205 David Dellucci .15 .07
❑ 206 Kevin Millwood .25 .11
❑ 207 Jerry Hairston Jr. .25 .11
❑ 208 Mike Stanley .15 .07
❑ 209 Henry Rodriguez .15 .07
❑ 210 Trevor Hoffman .25 .11
❑ 211 Craig Wilson .15 .07
❑ 212 Reggie Sanders .15 .07
❑ 213 Carlton Loewer .15 .07
❑ 214 Omar Vizquel .25 .11
❑ 215 Gabe Kapler .25 .11
❑ 216 Derrek Lee .15 .07
❑ 217 Billy Wagner .15 .07
❑ 218 Dean Palmer .25 .11
❑ 219 Chan Ho Park .25 .11
❑ 220 Fernando Vina .15 .07
❑ 221 Roy Halladay .15 .07
❑ 222 Paul Molitor .60 .25
❑ 223 Ugueth Urbina .15 .07
❑ 224 Rey Ordonez .15 .07
❑ 225 Ricky Ledee .15 .07
❑ 226 Scott Spiezio .15 .07
❑ 227 Wendell Magee .15 .07
❑ 228 Aramis Ramirez .15 .07
❑ 229 Brian Simmons .15 .07
❑ 230 Fernando Tatis .25 .11
❑ 231 Bobby Smith .15 .07
❑ 232 Aaron Sele .25 .11
❑ 233 Shawn Green .60 .25
❑ 234 Mariano Rivera .25 .11
❑ 235 Tim Salmon .25 .11
❑ 236 Andy Fox .15 .07
❑ 237 Denny Neagle .15 .07
❑ 238 John Valentin .15 .07
❑ 239 Kevin Tapani .15 .07
❑ 240 Paul Konerko .25 .11
❑ 241 Robert Fick .15 .07
❑ 242 Edgar Renteria .15 .07
❑ 243 Brett Tomko .15 .07
❑ 244 Daryle Ward .25 .11
❑ 245 Carlos Beltran .25 .11
❑ 246 Angel Pena .15 .07
❑ 247 Steve Woodard .15 .07
❑ 248 David Ortiz .15 .07
❑ 249 Justin Thompson .15 .07
❑ 250 Rondell White .25 .11
❑ 251 Jaret Wright .15 .07
❑ 252 Ed Sprague .15 .07
❑ 253 Jay Payton .25 .11
❑ 254 Mike Lowell .25 .11
❑ 255 Orlando Cabrera .15 .07
❑ 256 Jason Schmidt .15 .07
❑ 257 David Segui .15 .07
❑ 258 Paul Sorrento .15 .07
❑ 259 John Wetteland .25 .11
❑ 260 Devon White .15 .07
❑ 261 Odalis Perez .15 .07
❑ 262 Calvin Pickering .15 .07
❑ 263 Tyler Green .15 .07
❑ 264 Preston Wilson .25 .11
❑ 265 Brad Radke .25 .11
❑ 266 Walt Weiss .15 .07
❑ 267 Tim Young .15 .07
❑ 268 Tino Martinez .25 .11
❑ 269 Matt Stairs .15 .07
❑ 270 Curt Schilling .25 .11
❑ 271 Tony Womack .15 .07
❑ 272 Ismael Valdes .15 .07
❑ 273 Wally Joyner .25 .11
❑ 274 Armando Rios .15 .07
❑ 275 Andy Pettitte .25 .11
❑ 276 Bubba Trammell .15 .07
❑ 277 Todd Zeile .25 .11
❑ 278 Shannon Stewart .25 .11
❑ 279 Matt Williams .40 .18
❑ 280 John Rocker .25 .11
❑ 281 B.J. Surhoff .25 .11
❑ 282 Eric Young .15 .07
❑ 283 Dmitri Young .25 .11
❑ 284 John Smoltz .25 .11
❑ 285 Todd Walker .15 .07
❑ 286 Paul O'Neill .25 .11
❑ 287 Blake Stein .15 .07
❑ 288 Kevin Young .25 .11
❑ 289 Quilvio Veras .15 .07
❑ 290 Kirk Rueter .15 .07
❑ 291 Randy Winn .15 .07
❑ 292 Miguel Tejada .25 .11
❑ 293 J.T. Snow .25 .11
❑ 294 Michael Tucker .15 .07
❑ 295 Jay Tessmer .15 .07
❑ 296 Scott Erickson .15 .07
❑ 297 Tim Wakefield .15 .07
❑ 298 Jeff Abbott .15 .07
❑ 299 Eddie Taubensee .15 .07
❑ 300 Darryl Hamilton .15 .07
❑ 301 Kevin Orie .15 .07
❑ 302 Jose Offerman .15 .07
❑ 303 Scott Karl .15 .07
❑ 304 Chris Widger .15 .07
❑ 305 Todd Hundley .15 .07
❑ 306 Desi Relaford .15 .07
❑ 307 Sterling Hitchcock .15 .07
❑ 308 Delino DeShields .15 .07
❑ 309 Alex Gonzalez .15 .07
❑ 310 Justin Baughman .15 .07
❑ 311 Jamey Wright .15 .07
❑ 312 Wes Helms .15 .07
❑ 313 Dante Powell .15 .07
❑ 314 Jim Abbott .25 .11
❑ 315 Manny Alexander .15 .07
❑ 316 Harold Baines .25 .11
❑ 317 Danny Graves .15 .07
❑ 318 Sandy Alomar Jr. .25 .11
❑ 319 Pedro Astacio .15 .07
❑ 320 Jermaine Allensworth .15 .07
❑ 321 Matt Anderson .15 .07
❑ 322 Chad Curtis .15 .07
❑ 323 Antonio Osuna .15 .07
❑ 324 Brad Ausmus .15 .07
❑ 325 Steve Trachsel .15 .07
❑ 326 Mike Blowers .15 .07
❑ 327 Brian Bohanon .15 .07
❑ 328 Chris Gomez .15 .07
❑ 329 Valerio De Los Santos .15 .07
❑ 330 Rich Aurilia .15 .07
❑ 331 Michael Barrett .15 .07
❑ 332 Rick Aguilera .15 .07
❑ 333 Adrian Brown .15 .07
❑ 334 Bill Spiers .15 .07
❑ 335 Matt Beech .15 .07
❑ 336 David Bell .15 .07
❑ 337 Juan Acevedo .15 .07
❑ 338 Jose Canseco .75 .35
❑ 339 Wilson Alvarez .15 .07
❑ 340 Luis Alicea .15 .07
❑ 341 Jason Dickson .15 .07
❑ 342 Mike Bordick .15 .07
❑ 343 Ben Ford .15 .07
❑ 344 Javy Lopez .25 .11
❑ 345 Jason Christiansen .15 .07
❑ 346 Darren Bragg .15 .07
❑ 347 Doug Brocail .15 .07
❑ 348 Jeff Blauser .15 .07
❑ 349 James Baldwin .15 .07
❑ 350 Jeffrey Hammonds .25 .11
❑ 351 Ricky Bottalico .15 .07
❑ 352 Russ Branyan .25 .11
❑ 353 Mark Brownson RC .25 .11
❑ 354 Dave Berg .15 .07
❑ 355 Sean Bergman .15 .07
❑ 356 Jeff Conine .15 .07
❑ 357 Shayne Bennett .15 .07
❑ 358 Bobby Bonilla .25 .11
❑ 359 Bob Wickman .15 .07
❑ 360 Carlos Baerga .15 .07
❑ 361 Chris Fussell .15 .07
❑ 362 Chili Davis .25 .11
❑ 363 Jerry Spradlin .15 .07
❑ 364 Carlos Hernandez .15 .07
❑ 365 Roberto Hernandez .15 .07
❑ 366 Marvin Benard .15 .07
❑ 367 Ken Cloude .15 .07
❑ 368 Tony Fernandez .15 .07
❑ 369 John Burkett .15 .07
❑ 370 Gary DiSarcina .15 .07
❑ 371 Alan Benes .15 .07
❑ 372 Karim Garcia .15 .07
❑ 373 Carlos Perez .15 .07
❑ 374 Damon Buford .15 .07
❑ 375 Mark Clark .15 .07
❑ 376 Edgard Clemente .15 .07
❑ 377 Chad Bradford RC .15 .07
❑ 378 Frank Catalanotto .15 .07
❑ 379 Vic Darensbourg .15 .07
❑ 380 Sean Berry .15 .07
❑ 381 Dave Burba .15 .07
❑ 382 Sal Fasano .15 .07
❑ 383 Steve Parris .15 .07
❑ 384 Roger Cedeno .15 .07
❑ 385 Chad Fox .15 .07
❑ 386 Wilton Guerrero .15 .07
❑ 387 Dennis Cook .15 .07
❑ 388 Joe Girardi .15 .07
❑ 389 LaTroy Hawkins .15 .07
❑ 390 Ryan Christenson .15 .07
❑ 391 Paul Byrd .15 .07
❑ 392 Lou Collier .15 .07
❑ 393 Jeff Fassero .15 .07
❑ 394 Jim Leyritz .15 .07
❑ 395 Shawn Estes .15 .07
❑ 396 Mike Kelly .15 .07
❑ 397 Rich Croushore .15 .07
❑ 398 Royce Clayton .15 .07
❑ 399 Rudy Seanez .15 .07
❑ 400 Darrin Fletcher .15 .07
❑ 401 Shigetoshi Hasegawa .15 .07
❑ 402 Bernard Gilkey .15 .07
❑ 403 Juan Guzman .15 .07
❑ 404 Jeff Frye .15 .07
❑ 405 Donovan Osborne .15 .07
❑ 406 Alex Fernandez .15 .07
❑ 407 Gary Gaetti .15 .07
❑ 408 Dan Miceli .15 .07
❑ 409 Mike Cameron .15 .07
❑ 410 Mike Remlinger .15 .07
❑ 411 Joey Cora .15 .07
❑ 412 Mark Gardner .15 .07
❑ 413 Aaron Ledesma .15 .07
❑ 414 Jerry Dipoto .15 .07
❑ 415 Ricky Gutierrez .15 .07
❑ 416 John Franco .25 .11
❑ 417 Mendy Lopez .15 .07
❑ 418 Hideki Irabu .15 .07
❑ 419 Mark Grudzielanek .15 .07

| | | |
|---|---|---|
| ❑ 420 Bobby Hughes | .15 | .07 |
| ❑ 421 Pat Meares | .15 | .07 |
| ❑ 422 Jimmy Haynes | .15 | .07 |
| ❑ 423 Bob Henley | .15 | .07 |
| ❑ 424 Bobby Estalella | .15 | .07 |
| ❑ 425 Jon Lieber | .15 | .07 |
| ❑ 426 Giomar Guevara RC | .25 | .11 |
| ❑ 427 Jose Jimenez | .15 | .07 |
| ❑ 428 Deivi Cruz | .15 | .07 |
| ❑ 429 Jonathan Johnson | .15 | .07 |
| ❑ 430 Ken Hill | .15 | .07 |
| ❑ 431 Craig Grebeck | .15 | .07 |
| ❑ 432 Jose Rosado | .15 | .07 |
| ❑ 433 Danny Klassen | .15 | .07 |
| ❑ 434 Bobby Howry | .15 | .07 |
| ❑ 435 Gerald Williams | .15 | .07 |
| ❑ 436 Omar Olivares | .15 | .07 |
| ❑ 437 Chris Hoiles | .15 | .07 |
| ❑ 438 Seth Greisinger | .15 | .07 |
| ❑ 439 Scott Hatteberg | .15 | .07 |
| ❑ 440 Jeremi Gonzalez | .15 | .07 |
| ❑ 441 Wil Cordero | .15 | .07 |
| ❑ 442 Jeff Montgomery | .15 | .07 |
| ❑ 443 Chris Stynes | .15 | .07 |
| ❑ 444 Tony Saunders | .15 | .07 |
| ❑ 445 Einar Diaz | .15 | .07 |
| ❑ 446 Lariel Gonzalez | .15 | .07 |
| ❑ 447 Ryan Jackson | .15 | .07 |
| ❑ 448 Mike Hampton | .25 | .11 |
| ❑ 449 Todd Hollandsworth | .15 | .07 |
| ❑ 450 Gabe White | .15 | .07 |
| ❑ 451 John Jaha | .15 | .07 |
| ❑ 452 Bret Saberhagen | .25 | .11 |
| ❑ 453 Otis Nixon | .15 | .07 |
| ❑ 454 Steve Kline | .15 | .07 |
| ❑ 455 Butch Huskey | .15 | .07 |
| ❑ 456 Mike Jerzembeck | .15 | .07 |
| ❑ 457 Wayne Gomes | .15 | .07 |
| ❑ 458 Mike Macfarlane | .15 | .07 |
| ❑ 459 Jesus Sanchez | .15 | .07 |
| ❑ 460 Al Martin | .15 | .07 |
| ❑ 461 Dwight Gooden | .25 | .11 |
| ❑ 462 Ruben Rivera | .15 | .07 |
| ❑ 463 Pat Hentgen | .15 | .07 |
| ❑ 464 Jose Valentin | .15 | .07 |
| ❑ 465 Vladimir Nunez | .15 | .07 |
| ❑ 466 Charlie Hayes | .15 | .07 |
| ❑ 467 Jay Powell | .15 | .07 |
| ❑ 468 Raul Ibanez | .15 | .07 |
| ❑ 469 Kent Mercker | .15 | .07 |
| ❑ 470 John Mabry | .15 | .07 |
| ❑ 471 Woody Williams | .15 | .07 |
| ❑ 472 Roberto Kelly | .15 | .07 |
| ❑ 473 Jim Mecir | .15 | .07 |
| ❑ 474 Dave Hollins | .15 | .07 |
| ❑ 475 Rafael Medina | .15 | .07 |
| ❑ 476 Darren Lewis | .15 | .07 |
| ❑ 477 Felix Heredia | .15 | .07 |
| ❑ 478 Brian Hunter | .15 | .07 |
| ❑ 479 Matt Mantei | .15 | .07 |
| ❑ 480 Richard Hidalgo | .25 | .11 |
| ❑ 481 Bobby Jones | .15 | .07 |
| ❑ 482 Hal Morris | .15 | .07 |
| ❑ 483 Ramiro Mendoza | .15 | .07 |
| ❑ 484 Matt Luke | .15 | .07 |
| ❑ 485 Esteban Loaiza | .15 | .07 |
| ❑ 486 Mark Loretta | .15 | .07 |
| ❑ 487 A.J. Pierzynski | .15 | .07 |
| ❑ 488 Charles Nagy | .15 | .07 |
| ❑ 489 Kevin Sefcik | .15 | .07 |
| ❑ 490 Jason McDonald | .15 | .07 |
| ❑ 491 Jeremy Powell | .15 | .07 |
| ❑ 492 Scott Servais | .15 | .07 |
| ❑ 493 Abraham Nunez | .15 | .07 |
| ❑ 494 Stan Spencer | .15 | .07 |
| ❑ 495 Stan Javier | .15 | .07 |
| ❑ 496 Jose Paniagua | .15 | .07 |
| ❑ 497 Gregg Jefferies | .15 | .07 |
| ❑ 498 Gregg Olson | .15 | .07 |
| ❑ 499 Derek Lowe | .15 | .07 |
| ❑ 500 Willis Otanez | .15 | .07 |
| ❑ 501 Brian Moehler | .15 | .07 |
| ❑ 502 Glenallen Hill | .15 | .07 |
| ❑ 503 Bobby M. Jones | .15 | .07 |
| ❑ 504 Greg Norton | .15 | .07 |
| ❑ 505 Mike Jackson | .15 | .07 |
| ❑ 506 Kirt Manwaring | .15 | .07 |
| ❑ 507 Eric Weaver RC | .15 | .07 |
| ❑ 508 Mitch Meluskey | .15 | .07 |
| ❑ 509 Todd Jones | .15 | .07 |
| ❑ 510 Mike Matheny | .15 | .07 |
| ❑ 511 Benj Sampson | .15 | .07 |
| ❑ 512 Tony Phillips | .15 | .07 |
| ❑ 513 Mike Thurman | .15 | .07 |
| ❑ 514 Jorge Posada | .25 | .11 |
| ❑ 515 Bill Taylor | .15 | .07 |
| ❑ 516 Mike Sweeney | .25 | .11 |
| ❑ 517 Jose Silva | .15 | .07 |
| ❑ 518 Mark Lewis | .15 | .07 |
| ❑ 519 Chris Peters | .15 | .07 |
| ❑ 520 Brian Johnson | .15 | .07 |
| ❑ 521 Mike Timlin | .15 | .07 |
| ❑ 522 Mark McLemore | .15 | .07 |
| ❑ 523 Dan Plesac | .15 | .07 |
| ❑ 524 Kelly Stinnett | .15 | .07 |
| ❑ 525 Sidney Ponson | .15 | .07 |
| ❑ 526 Jim Parque | .15 | .07 |
| ❑ 527 Tyler Houston | .15 | .07 |
| ❑ 528 John Thomson | .15 | .07 |
| ❑ 529 Reggie Jefferson | .15 | .07 |
| ❑ 530 Robert Person | .15 | .07 |
| ❑ 531 Marc Newfield | .15 | .07 |
| ❑ 532 Javier Vazquez | .15 | .07 |
| ❑ 533 Terry Steinbach | .15 | .07 |
| ❑ 534 Turk Wendell | .15 | .07 |
| ❑ 535 Tim Raines | .25 | .11 |
| ❑ 536 Brian Meadows | .15 | .07 |
| ❑ 537 Mike Lieberthal | .25 | .11 |
| ❑ 538 Ricardo Rincon | .15 | .07 |
| ❑ 539 Dan Wilson | .15 | .07 |
| ❑ 540 John Johnstone | .15 | .07 |
| ❑ 541 Todd Stottlemyre | .15 | .07 |
| ❑ 542 Kevin Stocker | .15 | .07 |
| ❑ 543 Ramon Martinez | .15 | .07 |
| ❑ 544 Mike Simms | .15 | .07 |
| ❑ 545 Paul Quantrill | .15 | .07 |
| ❑ 546 Matt Walbeck | .15 | .07 |
| ❑ 547 Turner Ward | .15 | .07 |
| ❑ 548 Bill Pulsipher | .15 | .07 |
| ❑ 549 Donnie Sadler | .15 | .07 |
| ❑ 550 Lance Johnson | .15 | .07 |
| ❑ 551 Bill Simas | .15 | .07 |
| ❑ 552 Jeff Reed | .15 | .07 |
| ❑ 553 Jeff Shaw | .15 | .07 |
| ❑ 554 Joe Randa | .15 | .07 |
| ❑ 555 Paul Shuey | .15 | .07 |
| ❑ 556 Mike Redmond RC | .15 | .07 |
| ❑ 557 Sean Runyan | .15 | .07 |
| ❑ 558 Enrique Wilson | .15 | .07 |
| ❑ 559 Scott Radinsky | .15 | .07 |
| ❑ 560 Larry Sutton | .15 | .07 |
| ❑ 561 Masato Yoshii | .25 | .11 |
| ❑ 562 David Nilsson | .15 | .07 |
| ❑ 563 Mike Trombley | .15 | .07 |
| ❑ 564 Darryl Strawberry | .25 | .11 |
| ❑ 565 Dave Mlicki | .15 | .07 |
| ❑ 566 Placido Polanco | .15 | .07 |
| ❑ 567 Yorkis Perez | .15 | .07 |
| ❑ 568 Esteban Yan | .15 | .07 |
| ❑ 569 Lee Stevens | .15 | .07 |
| ❑ 570 Steve Sinclair | .15 | .07 |
| ❑ 571 Jarrod Washburn | .15 | .07 |
| ❑ 572 Lenny Webster | .15 | .07 |
| ❑ 573 Mike Sirotka | .15 | .07 |
| ❑ 574 Jason Varitek | .25 | .11 |
| ❑ 575 Terry Mulholland | .15 | .07 |
| ❑ 576 Adrian Beltre FF | .25 | .11 |
| ❑ 577 Eric Chavez FF | .25 | .11 |
| ❑ 578 J.D. Drew FF | .60 | .25 |
| ❑ 579 Juan Encarnacion FF | .15 | .07 |
| ❑ 580 Nomar Garciaparra FF | 1.00 | .45 |
| ❑ 581 Troy Glaus FF | .60 | .25 |
| ❑ 582 Ben Grieve FF | .25 | .11 |
| ❑ 583 Vladimir Guerrero FF | .40 | .18 |
| ❑ 584 Todd Helton FF | .60 | .25 |
| ❑ 585 Derek Jeter FF | 1.25 | .55 |
| ❑ 586 Travis Lee FF | .15 | .07 |
| ❑ 587 Alex Rodriguez FF | 1.00 | .45 |
| ❑ 588 Scott Rolen FF | .60 | .25 |
| ❑ 589 Richie Sexson FF | .25 | .11 |
| ❑ 590 Kerry Wood FF | .25 | .11 |
| ❑ 591 Ken Griffey Jr. CL | 1.25 | .55 |
| ❑ 592 Chipper Jones CL | .75 | .35 |
| ❑ 593 Alex Rodriguez CL | 1.00 | .45 |
| ❑ 594 Sammy Sosa CL | .60 | .25 |
| ❑ 595 Mark McGwire CL | 1.25 | .55 |
| ❑ 596 Cal Ripken CL | 1.25 | .55 |
| ❑ 597 Nomar Garciaparra CL | 1.00 | .45 |
| ❑ 598 Derek Jeter CL | 1.25 | .55 |
| ❑ 599 Kerry Wood CL | .25 | .11 |
| ❑ 600 J.D. Drew CL | .60 | .25 |
| ❑ P7 J.D. Drew Promo | 1.50 | .70 |

## 1999 Fleer Update

| | MINT | NRMT |
|---|---|---|
| COMP.FACT.SET (150) | 30.00 | 13.50 |
| ❑ U1 Rick Ankiel RC | 12.00 | 5.50 |
| ❑ U2 Peter Bergeron RC | .60 | .25 |
| ❑ U3 Pat Burrell RC | 4.00 | 1.80 |
| ❑ U4 Eric Munson RC | 2.00 | .90 |
| ❑ U5 Alfonso Soriano RC | 1.50 | .70 |
| ❑ U6 Tim Hudson RC | 3.00 | 1.35 |
| ❑ U7 Erubiel Durazo RC | 1.00 | .45 |
| ❑ U8 Chad Hermansen | .10 | .05 |
| ❑ U9 Jeff Zimmerman RC | .25 | .11 |
| ❑ U10 Jesus Pena RC | .10 | .05 |
| ❑ U11 Ramon Hernandez | .10 | .05 |
| ❑ U12 Trent Durrington RC | .25 | .11 |
| ❑ U13 Tony Armas Jr. | .15 | .07 |
| ❑ U14 Mike Fyhrie RC | .10 | .05 |
| ❑ U15 Danny Kolb RC | .25 | .11 |
| ❑ U16 Mike Porzio RC | .10 | .05 |
| ❑ U17 Will Brunson RC | .10 | .05 |
| ❑ U18 Mike Duvall RC | .10 | .05 |
| ❑ U19 Doug Mientkiewicz RC | .25 | .11 |
| ❑ U20 Gabe Molina RC | .25 | .11 |
| ❑ U21 Luis Vizcaino RC | .25 | .11 |
| ❑ U22 Robinson Cancel RC | .25 | .11 |
| ❑ U23 Brett Laxton RC | .10 | .05 |
| ❑ U24 Joe McEwing RC | .25 | .11 |
| ❑ U25 Justin Speier RC | .10 | .05 |
| ❑ U26 Kip Wells RC | .60 | .25 |
| ❑ U27 Armando Almanza RC | .10 | .05 |
| ❑ U28 Joe Davenport RC | .25 | .11 |
| ❑ U29 Yamid Haad RC | .25 | .11 |
| ❑ U30 John Halama | .10 | .05 |
| ❑ U31 Adam Kennedy | .15 | .07 |
| ❑ U32 Micah Bowie RC | .10 | .05 |
| ❑ U33 Travis Dawkins RC | .60 | .25 |
| ❑ U34 Ryan Rupe RC | .40 | .18 |
| ❑ U35 B.J. Ryan RC | .25 | .11 |
| ❑ U36 Chance Sanford RC | .10 | .05 |
| ❑ U37 Anthony Shumaker RC | .10 | .05 |
| ❑ U38 Ryan Glynn RC | .40 | .18 |
| ❑ U39 Roosevelt Brown RC | .40 | .18 |
| ❑ U40 Ben Molina RC | 1.00 | .45 |
| ❑ U41 Scott Williamson | .10 | .05 |
| ❑ U42 Eric Gagne RC | .60 | .25 |
| ❑ U43 John McDonald RC | .10 | .05 |
| ❑ U44 Scott Sauerbeck RC | .10 | .05 |
| ❑ U45 Mike Venafro RC | .10 | .05 |
| ❑ U46 Edwards Guzman RC | .25 | .11 |
| ❑ U47 Richard Barker RC | .10 | .05 |
| ❑ U48 Braden Looper | .10 | .05 |
| ❑ U49 Chad Meyers RC | .10 | .05 |
| ❑ U50 Scott Strickland RC | .25 | .11 |
| ❑ U51 Billy Koch | .15 | .07 |
| ❑ U52 David Newhan RC | .10 | .05 |

❑ U53 David Riske RC .25 .11
❑ U54 Jose Santiago RC .10 .05
❑ U55 Miguel Del Toro RC .10 .05
❑ U56 Orber Moreno RC .25 .11
❑ U57 Dave Roberts RC .10 .05
❑ U58 Tim Byrdak RC .10 .05
❑ U59 David Lee RC .10 .05
❑ U60 Guillermo Mota RC .10 .05
❑ U61 Wilton Veras RC .60 .25
❑ U62 Joe Mays RC .40 .18
❑ U63 Jose Fernandez RC .10 .05
❑ U64 Ray King RC .10 .05
❑ U65 Chris Petersen RC .10 .05
❑ U66 Vernon Wells .15 .07
❑ U67 Ruben Mateo .15 .07
❑ U68 Ben Petrick .10 .05
❑ U69 Chris Tremie RC .10 .05
❑ U70 Lance Berkman .15 .07
❑ U71 Dan Smith RC .25 .11
❑ U72 Carlos Hernandez RC .25 .11
❑ U73 Chad Harville RC .25 .11
❑ U74 Damaso Marte RC .10 .05
❑ U75 Aaron Myette RC .60 .25
❑ U76 Willis Roberts RC .25 .11
❑ U77 Erik Sabel RC .10 .05
❑ U78 Hector Almonte RC .25 .11
❑ U79 Kris Benson .15 .07
❑ U80 Pat Daneker RC .25 .11
❑ U81 Freddy Garcia RC 1.25 .55
❑ U82 Byung-Hyun Kim RC 1.00 .45
❑ U83 Wily Pena RC 1.50 .70
❑ U84 Dan Wheeler RC .40 .18
❑ U85 Tim Harikkala RC .10 .05
❑ U86 Derrin Ebert RC .25 .11
❑ U87 Horacio Estrada RC .25 .11
❑ U88 Liu Rodriguez RC .25 .11
❑ U89 Jordan Zimmerman RC .10 .05
❑ U90 A.J. Burnett RC .60 .25
❑ U91 Doug Davis RC .50 .23
❑ U92 Robert Ramsay RC .10 .05
❑ U93 Clay Bellinger RC .10 .05
❑ U94 Charlie Greene RC .10 .05
❑ U95 Bo Porter RC .10 .05
❑ U96 Jorge Toca RC .40 .18
❑ U97 Casey Blake RC .10 .05
❑ U98 Amaury Garcia RC .25 .11
❑ U99 Jose Molina RC .25 .11
❑ U100 Melvin Mora RC .40 .18
❑ U101 Joe Nathan RC .10 .05
❑ U102 Juan Pena RC .25 .11
❑ U103 Dave Borkowski RC .25 .11
❑ U104 Eddie Gaillard RC .10 .05
❑ U105 Glen Barker RC .10 .05
❑ U106 Brett Hinchliffe RC .10 .05
❑ U107 Carlos Lee .15 .07
❑ U108 Rob Ryan RC .10 .05
❑ U109 Jeff Weaver RC .60 .25
❑ U110 Ed Yarnall .10 .05
❑ U111 Nelson Cruz RC .10 .05
❑ U112 Cleatus Davidson RC .25 .11
❑ U113 Tim Kubinski RC .10 .05
❑ U114 Sean Spencer RC .25 .11
❑ U115 Joe Winkelsas RC .10 .05
❑ U116 Mike Colangelo RC .25 .11
❑ U117 Tom Davey RC .10 .05
❑ U118 Warren Morris .10 .05
❑ U119 Dan Murray RC .10 .05
❑ U120 Jose Nieves RC .25 .11
❑ U121 Mark Quinn RC 1.25 .55
❑ U122 Josh Beckett RC 2.50 1.10
❑ U123 Chad Allen RC .25 .11
❑ U124 Mike Figga .10 .05
❑ U125 Beiker Graterol RC .10 .05
❑ U126 Aaron Scheffer RC .10 .05
❑ U127 Wiki Gonzalez RC .25 .11
❑ U128 Ramon E.Martinez RC .10 .05
❑ U129 Matt Riley RC .60 .25
❑ U130 Chris Woodward RC .25 .11
❑ U131 Albert Belle .25 .11
❑ U132 Roger Cedeno .10 .05
❑ U133 Roger Clemens .75 .35
❑ U134 Brian Giles .15 .07
❑ U135 Rickey Henderson .50 .23
❑ U136 Randy Johnson .50 .23
❑ U137 Brian Jordan .15 .07
❑ U138 Paul Konerko .15 .07
❑ U139 Hideo Nomo .40 .18
❑ U140 Kenny Rogers .10 .05
❑ U141 Wade Boggs HL .50 .23
❑ U142 Jose Canseco HL .25 .11
❑ U143 Roger Clemens HL .75 .35
❑ U144 David Cone HL .10 .05
❑ U145 Tony Gwynn HL .75 .35
❑ U146 Mark McGwire HL 1.50 .70
❑ U147 Cal Ripken HL 1.50 .70
❑ U148 Alex Rodriguez HL 1.25 .55
❑ U149 Fernando Tatis HL .15 .07
❑ U150 Robin Ventura HL .15 .07

## 2000 Fleer

| | MINT | NRMT |
|---|---|---|
| COMPLETE SET (450) | 120.00 | 55.00 |
| COMMON CARD (1-450) | .15 | .07 |

❑ 1 AL Home Run LL 1.50 .70
Ken Griffey Jr
Rafael Palmeiro
Carlos Delgado
❑ 2 NL Home Run LL 1.50 .70
Mark McGwire
Sammy Sosa
Chipper Jones
❑ 3 AL RBI LL .75 .35
Manny Ramirez
Rafael Palmeiro
Ken Griffey Jr.
❑ 4 NL RBI LL .75 .35
Mark McGwire
Matt Williams
Sammy Sosa
❑ 5 AL Avg LL 1.00 .45
Nomar Garciaparra
Derek Jeter
Bernie Williams
❑ 6 NL Avg LL .25 .11
Larry Walker
Luis Gonzalez
Bob Abreu
❑ 7 AL Wins LL .25 .11
Pedro Martinez
Bartolo Colon
Mike Mussina
❑ 8 NL Wins LL .15 .07
Mike Hampton
Jose Lima
Greg Maddux
❑ 9 AL ERA LL .25 .11
Pedro Martinez
David Cone
Mike Mussina
❑ 10 NL ERA LL .25 .11
Randy Johnson
Kevin Millwood
Mike Hampton
❑ 11 Matt Mantei .15 .07
❑ 12 John Rocker .25 .11
❑ 13 Kyle Farnsworth .15 .07
❑ 14 Juan Guzman .15 .07
❑ 15 Manny Ramirez .75 .35
❑ 16 Matt Riley .25 .11
Calvin Pickering
❑ 17 Tony Clark .15 .07
❑ 18 Brian Meadows .15 .07
❑ 19 Orber Moreno .15 .07
❑ 20 Eric Karros .25 .11
❑ 21 Steve Woodard .15 .07
❑ 22 Scott Brosius .25 .11
❑ 23 Gary Bennett .15 .07
❑ 24 Jason Wood .15 .07
Dave Borkowski
❑ 25 Joe McEwing .15 .07
❑ 26 Juan Gonzalez .60 .25
❑ 27 Roy Halladay .15 .07
❑ 28 Trevor Hoffman .25 .11
❑ 29 Arizona Diamondbacks .25 .11
❑ 30 Domingo Guzman RC .40 .18
Wiki Gonzalez
❑ 31 Bret Boone .15 .07
❑ 32 Nomar Garciaparra 2.00 .90
❑ 33 Bo Porter .15 .07
❑ 34 Eddie Taubensee .15 .07
❑ 35 Pedro Astacio .15 .07
❑ 36 Derek Bell .15 .07
❑ 37 Jacque Jones .25 .11
❑ 38 Ricky Ledee .15 .07
❑ 39 Jeff Kent .40 .18
❑ 40 Matt Williams .40 .18
❑ 41 Alfonso Soriano .25 .11
D'Angelo Jimenez
❑ 42 B.J. Surhoff .25 .11
❑ 43 Denny Neagle .15 .07
❑ 44 Omar Vizquel .25 .11
❑ 45 Jeff Bagwell .75 .35
❑ 46 Mark Grudzielanek .15 .07
❑ 47 LaTroy Hawkins .15 .07
❑ 48 Orlando Hernandez .25 .11
❑ 49 Ken Griffey Jr. CL .60 .25
❑ 50 Fernando Tatis .25 .11
❑ 51 Quilvio Veras .15 .07
❑ 52 Wayne Gomes .15 .07
❑ 53 Rick Helling .25 .11
❑ 54 Shannon Stewart .25 .11
❑ 55 Dermal Brown .25 .11
Mark Quinn
❑ 56 Randy Johnson .75 .35
❑ 57 Greg Maddux 1.50 .70
❑ 58 Mike Cameron .15 .07
❑ 59 Matt Anderson .15 .07
❑ 60 Milwaukee Brewers .25 .11
❑ 61 Derrek Lee .15 .07
❑ 62 Mike Sweeney .25 .11
❑ 63 Fernando Vina .15 .07
❑ 64 Orlando Cabrera .15 .07
❑ 65 Doug Glanville .15 .07
❑ 66 Stan Spencer .15 .07
❑ 67 Ray Lankford .25 .11
❑ 68 Kelly Dransfeldt .15 .07
❑ 69 Alex Gonzalez .15 .07
❑ 70 Russ Branyan .15 .07
Danny Peoples
❑ 71 Jim Edmonds .60 .25
❑ 72 Brady Anderson .25 .11
❑ 73 Mike Stanley .15 .07
❑ 74 Travis Fryman .25 .11
❑ 75 Carlos Febles .15 .07
❑ 76 Bobby Higginson .15 .07
❑ 77 Carlos Perez .15 .07
❑ 78 Steve Cox .15 .07
Alex Sanchez
❑ 79 Dustin Hermanson .15 .07
❑ 80 Kenny Rogers .15 .07
❑ 81 Miguel Tejada .25 .11
❑ 82 Ben Davis .15 .07
❑ 83 Reggie Sanders .15 .07
❑ 84 Eric Davis .25 .11
❑ 85 J.D. Drew .60 .25
❑ 86 Ryan Rupe .15 .07
❑ 87 Bobby Smith .15 .07
❑ 88 Jose Cruz Jr. .25 .11
❑ 89 Carlos Delgado .60 .25
❑ 90 Toronto Blue Jays .25 .11
❑ 91 Denny Stark RC .40 .18
Gil Meche
❑ 92 Randy Velarde .15 .07
❑ 93 Aaron Boone .15 .07
❑ 94 Javy Lopez .25 .11
❑ 95 Johnny Damon .25 .11
❑ 96 Jon Lieber .15 .07
❑ 97 Montreal Expos .25 .11

| No. | Card | | |
|---|---|---|---|
| 98 | Mark Kotsay | .15 | .07 |
| 99 | Luis Gonzalez | .25 | .11 |
| 100 | Larry Walker | .25 | .11 |
| 101 | Adrian Beltre | .25 | .11 |
| 102 | Alex Ochoa | .15 | .07 |
| 103 | Michael Barrett | .15 | .07 |
| 104 | Tampa Bay Devil Rays | .25 | .11 |
| 105 | Rey Ordonez | .15 | .07 |
| 106 | Derek Jeter | 2.00 | .90 |
| 107 | Mike Lieberthal | .25 | .11 |
| 108 | Ellis Burks | .25 | .11 |
| 109 | Steve Finley | .25 | .11 |
| 110 | Ryan Klesko | .25 | .11 |
| 111 | Steve Avery | .15 | .07 |
| 112 | Dave Veres | .15 | .07 |
| 113 | Cliff Floyd | .25 | .11 |
| 114 | Shane Reynolds | .15 | .07 |
| 115 | Kevin Brown | .40 | .18 |
| 116 | Dave Nilsson | .15 | .07 |
| 117 | Mike Trombley | .15 | .07 |
| 118 | Todd Walker | .15 | .07 |
| 119 | John Olerud | .25 | .11 |
| 120 | Chuck Knoblauch | .25 | .11 |
| 121 | Nomar Garciaparra CL | .60 | .25 |
| 122 | Trot Nixon | .25 | .11 |
| 123 | Erubiel Durazo | .25 | .11 |
| 124 | Edwards Guzman | .15 | .07 |
| 125 | Curt Schilling | .25 | .11 |
| 126 | Brian Jordan | .25 | .11 |
| 127 | Cleveland Indians | .25 | .11 |
| 128 | Benito Santiago | .15 | .07 |
| 129 | Frank Thomas | 1.25 | .55 |
| 130 | Neifi Perez | .15 | .07 |
| 131 | Alex Fernandez | .15 | .07 |
| 132 | Jose Lima | .15 | .07 |
| 133 | Jorge Toca<br>Melvin Mora | .15 | .07 |
| 134 | Scott Karl | .15 | .07 |
| 135 | Brad Radke | .25 | .11 |
| 136 | Paul O'Neill | .25 | .11 |
| 137 | Kris Benson | .25 | .11 |
| 138 | Colorado Rockies | .25 | .11 |
| 139 | Jason Phillips | .15 | .07 |
| 140 | Robb Nen | .15 | .07 |
| 141 | Ken Hill | .15 | .07 |
| 142 | Charles Johnson | .25 | .11 |
| 143 | Paul Konerko | .25 | .11 |
| 144 | Dmitri Young | .25 | .11 |
| 145 | Justin Thompson | .15 | .07 |
| 146 | Mark Loretta | .15 | .07 |
| 147 | Edgardo Alfonzo | .25 | .11 |
| 148 | Armando Benitez | .25 | .11 |
| 149 | Octavio Dotel | .15 | .07 |
| 150 | Wade Boggs | .75 | .35 |
| 151 | Ramon Hernandez | .15 | .07 |
| 152 | Freddy Garcia | .25 | .11 |
| 153 | Edgar Martinez | .40 | .18 |
| 154 | Ivan Rodriguez | .75 | .35 |
| 155 | Kansas City Royals | .25 | .11 |
| 156 | Cleatus Davidson<br>Cristian Guzman | .15 | .07 |
| 157 | Andy Benes | .15 | .07 |
| 158 | Todd Dunwoody | .15 | .07 |
| 159 | Pedro Martinez | .75 | .35 |
| 160 | Mike Caruso | .15 | .07 |
| 161 | Mike Sirotka | .15 | .07 |
| 162 | Houston Astros | .25 | .11 |
| 163 | Darryl Kile | .25 | .11 |
| 164 | Chipper Jones | 1.50 | .70 |
| 165 | Carl Everett | .25 | .11 |
| 166 | Geoff Jenkins | .25 | .11 |
| 167 | Dan Perkins | .15 | .07 |
| 168 | Andy Pettitte | .25 | .11 |
| 169 | Francisco Cordova | .15 | .07 |
| 170 | Jay Buhner | .25 | .11 |
| 171 | Jay Bell | .25 | .11 |
| 172 | Andruw Jones | .60 | .25 |
| 173 | Bobby Howry | .15 | .07 |
| 174 | Chris Singleton | .25 | .11 |
| 175 | Todd Helton | .75 | .35 |
| 176 | A.J. Burnett | .25 | .11 |
| 177 | Marquis Grissom | .15 | .07 |
| 178 | Eric Milton | .15 | .07 |
| 179 | Los Angeles Dodgers | .25 | .11 |
| 180 | Kevin Appier | .15 | .07 |
| 181 | Brian Giles | .25 | .11 |
| 182 | Tom Davey | .15 | .07 |
| 183 | Mo Vaughn | .25 | .11 |
| 184 | Jose Hernandez | .15 | .07 |
| 185 | Jim Parque | .15 | .07 |
| 186 | Derrick Gibson | .15 | .07 |
| 187 | Bruce Aven | .15 | .07 |
| 188 | Jeff Cirillo | .25 | .11 |
| 189 | Doug Mientkiewicz | .15 | .07 |
| 190 | Eric Chavez | .25 | .11 |
| 191 | Al Martin | .15 | .07 |
| 192 | Tom Glavine | .60 | .25 |
| 193 | Butch Huskey | .15 | .07 |
| 194 | Ray Durham | .25 | .11 |
| 195 | Greg Vaughn | .25 | .11 |
| 196 | Vinny Castilla | .25 | .11 |
| 197 | Ken Caminiti | .25 | .11 |
| 198 | Joe Mays | .15 | .07 |
| 199 | Chicago White Sox | .25 | .11 |
| 200 | Mariano Rivera | .25 | .11 |
| 201 | Mark McGwire CL | .60 | .25 |
| 202 | Pat Meares | .15 | .07 |
| 203 | Andres Galarraga | .40 | .18 |
| 204 | Tom Gordon | .15 | .07 |
| 205 | Henry Rodriguez | .15 | .07 |
| 206 | Brett Tomko | .15 | .07 |
| 207 | Dante Bichette | .25 | .11 |
| 208 | Craig Biggio | .40 | .18 |
| 209 | Matt Lawton | .15 | .07 |
| 210 | Tino Martinez | .25 | .11 |
| 211 | Aaron Myette<br>Josh Paul | .25 | .11 |
| 212 | Warren Morris | .15 | .07 |
| 213 | San Diego Padres | .25 | .11 |
| 214 | Ramon E. Martinez | .15 | .07 |
| 215 | Troy Percival | .15 | .07 |
| 216 | Jason Johnson | .15 | .07 |
| 217 | Carlos Lee | .25 | .11 |
| 218 | Scott Williamson | .15 | .07 |
| 219 | Jeff Weaver | .15 | .07 |
| 220 | Ronnie Belliard | .15 | .07 |
| 221 | Jason Giambi | .60 | .25 |
| 222 | Ken Griffey Jr. | 2.50 | 1.10 |
| 223 | John Halama | .15 | .07 |
| 224 | Brett Hinchliffe | .15 | .07 |
| 225 | Wilson Alvarez | .15 | .07 |
| 226 | Rolando Arrojo | .15 | .07 |
| 227 | Ruben Mateo | .25 | .11 |
| 228 | Rafael Palmeiro | .60 | .25 |
| 229 | David Wells | .25 | .11 |
| 230 | Eric Gagne<br>Jeff Williams RC | .40 | .18 |
| 231 | Tim Salmon | .25 | .11 |
| 232 | Mike Mussina | .60 | .25 |
| 233 | Magglio Ordonez | .25 | .11 |
| 234 | Ron Villone | .15 | .07 |
| 235 | Antonio Alfonseca | .15 | .07 |
| 236 | Jeromy Burnitz | .25 | .11 |
| 237 | Ben Grieve | .25 | .11 |
| 238 | Giomar Guevara | .15 | .07 |
| 239 | Garret Anderson | .25 | .11 |
| 240 | John Smoltz | .25 | .11 |
| 241 | Mark Grace | .60 | .25 |
| 242 | Cole Liniak<br>Jose Molina | .15 | .07 |
| 243 | Damion Easley | .15 | .07 |
| 244 | Jeff Montgomery | .15 | .07 |
| 245 | Kenny Lofton | .25 | .11 |
| 246 | Masato Yoshii | .15 | .07 |
| 247 | Philadelphia Phillies | .25 | .11 |
| 248 | Raul Mondesi | .25 | .11 |
| 249 | Marlon Anderson | .15 | .07 |
| 250 | Shawn Green | .60 | .25 |
| 251 | Sterling Hitchcock | .15 | .07 |
| 252 | Randy Wolf<br>Anthony Shumaker | .15 | .07 |
| 253 | Jeff Fassero | .15 | .07 |
| 254 | Eli Marrero | .15 | .07 |
| 255 | Cincinnati Reds | .25 | .11 |
| 256 | Rick Ankiel<br>Adam Kennedy | 1.25 | .55 |
| 257 | Darin Erstad | .60 | .25 |
| 258 | Albert Belle | .40 | .18 |
| 259 | Bartolo Colon | .25 | .11 |
| 260 | Bret Saberhagen | .25 | .11 |
| 261 | Carlos Beltran | .25 | .11 |
| 262 | Glenallen Hill | .15 | .07 |
| 263 | Gregg Jefferies | .15 | .07 |
| 264 | Matt Clement | .15 | .07 |
| 265 | Miguel Del Toro | .15 | .07 |
| 266 | Robinson Cancel<br>Kevin Barker | .15 | .07 |
| 267 | San Francisco Giants | .25 | .11 |
| 268 | Kent Bottenfield | .15 | .07 |
| 269 | Fred McGriff | .40 | .18 |
| 270 | Chris Carpenter | .15 | .07 |
| 271 | Atlanta Braves | .25 | .11 |
| 272 | Wilton Veras<br>Tomokazu Ohka RC | .60 | .25 |
| 273 | Will Clark | .60 | .25 |
| 274 | Troy O'Leary | .15 | .07 |
| 275 | Sammy Sosa CL | .60 | .25 |
| 276 | Travis Lee | .15 | .07 |
| 277 | Sean Casey | .25 | .11 |
| 278 | Ron Gant | .25 | .11 |
| 279 | Roger Clemens | 1.25 | .55 |
| 280 | Phil Nevin | .25 | .11 |
| 281 | Mike Piazza | 2.00 | .90 |
| 282 | Mike Lowell | .15 | .07 |
| 283 | Kevin Millwood | .25 | .11 |
| 284 | Joe Randa | .15 | .07 |
| 285 | Jeff Shaw | .15 | .07 |
| 286 | Jason Varitek | .25 | .11 |
| 287 | Harold Baines | .25 | .11 |
| 288 | Gabe Kapler | .25 | .11 |
| 289 | Chuck Finley | .25 | .11 |
| 290 | Carl Pavano | .15 | .07 |
| 291 | Brad Ausmus | .15 | .07 |
| 292 | Brad Fullmer | .25 | .11 |
| 293 | Boston Red Sox | .25 | .11 |
| 294 | Bob Wickman | .15 | .07 |
| 295 | Billy Wagner | .15 | .07 |
| 296 | Shawn Estes | .15 | .07 |
| 297 | Gary Sheffield | .60 | .25 |
| 298 | Fernando Seguignol | .15 | .07 |
| 299 | Omar Olivares | .15 | .07 |
| 300 | Baltimore Orioles | .25 | .11 |
| 301 | Matt Stairs | .15 | .07 |
| 302 | Andy Ashby | .15 | .07 |
| 303 | Todd Greene | .15 | .07 |
| 304 | Jesse Garcia | .15 | .07 |
| 305 | Kerry Wood | .25 | .11 |
| 306 | Roberto Alomar | .60 | .25 |
| 307 | New York Mets | .25 | .11 |
| 308 | Dean Palmer | .25 | .11 |
| 309 | Mike Hampton | .25 | .11 |
| 310 | Devon White | .15 | .07 |
| 311 | Chad Hermansen<br>Mike Garcia RC | .40 | .18 |
| 312 | Tim Hudson | .60 | .25 |
| 313 | John Franco | .25 | .11 |
| 314 | Jason Schmidt | .15 | .07 |
| 315 | J.T. Snow | .25 | .11 |
| 316 | Ed Sprague | .15 | .07 |
| 317 | Chris Widger | .15 | .07 |
| 318 | Ben Petrick<br>Luther Hackman RC | .40 | .18 |
| 319 | Jose Mesa | .15 | .07 |
| 320 | Jose Canseco | .75 | .35 |
| 321 | John Wetteland | .25 | .11 |
| 322 | Minnesota Twins | .25 | .11 |
| 323 | Jeff DaVanon RC<br>Brian Cooper | .25 | .11 |
| 324 | Tony Womack | .15 | .07 |
| 325 | Rod Beck | .15 | .07 |
| 326 | Mickey Morandini | .15 | .07 |
| 327 | Pokey Reese | .25 | .11 |
| 328 | Jaret Wright | .15 | .07 |
| 329 | Glen Barker | .15 | .07 |
| 330 | Darren Dreifort | .15 | .07 |
| 331 | Torii Hunter | .15 | .07 |
| 332 | Tony Armas<br>Peter Bergeron | .25 | .11 |
| 333 | Hideki Irabu | .15 | .07 |
| 334 | Desi Relaford | .15 | .07 |
| 335 | Barry Bonds | 1.00 | .45 |
| 336 | Gary DiSarcina | .15 | .07 |
| 337 | Gerald Williams | .15 | .07 |
| 338 | John Valentin | .15 | .07 |
| 339 | David Justice | .40 | .18 |
| 340 | Juan Encarnacion | .25 | .11 |
| 341 | Jeremy Giambi | .15 | .07 |
| 342 | Chan Ho Park | .25 | .11 |

❑ 343 Vladimir Guerrero ........ 1.00 .45
❑ 344 Robin Ventura ........ .40 .18
❑ 345 Bob Abreu ........ .25 .11
❑ 346 Tony Gwynn ........ 1.25 .55
❑ 347 Jose Jimenez ........ .15 .07
❑ 348 Royce Clayton ........ .15 .07
❑ 349 Kelvim Escobar ........ .15 .07
❑ 350 Chicago Cubs ........ .25 .11
❑ 351 Travis Dawkins ........ .15 .07
Jason LaRue
❑ 352 Barry Larkin ........ .60 .25
❑ 353 Cal Ripken ........ 2.50 1.10
❑ 354 Alex Rodriguez CL ........ .60 .25
❑ 355 Todd Stottlemyre ........ .15 .07
❑ 356 Terry Adams ........ .15 .07
❑ 357 Pittsburgh Pirates ........ .25 .11
❑ 358 Jim Thome ........ .40 .18
❑ 359 Corey Lee ........ .15 .07
Doug Davis
❑ 360 Moises Alou ........ .25 .11
❑ 361 Todd Hollandsworth ........ .15 .07
❑ 362 Marty Cordova ........ .15 .07
❑ 363 David Cone ........ .25 .11
❑ 364 Joe Nathan ........ .15 .07
Wilson Delgado
❑ 365 Paul Byrd ........ .15 .07
❑ 366 Edgar Renteria ........ .15 .07
❑ 367 Rusty Greer ........ .25 .11
❑ 368 David Segui ........ .15 .07
❑ 369 New York Yankees ........ .40 .18
❑ 370 Daryle Ward ........ .25 .11
Carlos Hernandez
❑ 371 Troy Glaus ........ .75 .35
❑ 372 Delino DeShields ........ .15 .07
❑ 373 Jose Offerman ........ .15 .07
❑ 374 Sammy Sosa ........ 1.25 .55
❑ 375 Sandy Alomar Jr. ........ .15 .07
❑ 376 Masao Kida ........ .15 .07
❑ 377 Richard Hidalgo ........ .25 .11
❑ 378 Ismael Valdes ........ .15 .07
❑ 379 Ugueth Urbina ........ .15 .07
❑ 380 Darryl Hamilton ........ .15 .07
❑ 381 John Jaha ........ .15 .07
❑ 382 St. Louis Cardinals ........ .25 .11
❑ 383 Scott Sauerbeck ........ .15 .07
❑ 384 Russ Ortiz ........ .25 .11
❑ 385 Jamie Moyer ........ .15 .07
❑ 386 Dave Martinez ........ .15 .07
❑ 387 Todd Zeile ........ .25 .11
❑ 388 Anaheim Angels ........ .25 .11
❑ 389 Rob Ryan ........ .15 .07
Nick Bierbrodt
❑ 390 Rickey Henderson ........ .75 .35
❑ 391 Alex Rodriguez ........ 2.00 .90
❑ 392 Texas Rangers ........ .25 .11
❑ 393 Roberto Hernandez ........ .15 .07
❑ 394 Tony Batista ........ .25 .11
❑ 395 Oakland Athletics ........ .25 .11
❑ 396 Randall Simon ........ .40 .18
Dave Cortes RC
❑ 397 Gregg Olson ........ .15 .07
❑ 398 Sidney Ponson ........ .15 .07
❑ 399 Micah Bowie ........ .15 .07
❑ 400 Mark McGwire ........ 2.50 1.10
❑ 401 Florida Marlins ........ .25 .11
❑ 402 Chad Allen ........ .15 .07
❑ 403 Casey Blake ........ .25 .11
Vernon Wells
❑ 404 Pete Harnisch ........ .15 .07
❑ 405 Preston Wilson ........ .25 .11
❑ 406 Richie Sexson ........ .25 .11
❑ 407 Rico Brogna ........ .15 .07
❑ 408 Todd Hundley ........ .15 .07
❑ 409 Wally Joyner ........ .25 .11
❑ 410 Tom Goodwin ........ .15 .07
❑ 411 Joey Hamilton ........ .15 .07
❑ 412 Detroit Tigers ........ .25 .11
❑ 413 Michael Tejera RC ........ .40 .18
Ramon Castro
❑ 414 Alex Gonzalez ........ .15 .07
❑ 415 Jermaine Dye ........ .25 .11
❑ 416 Jose Rosado ........ .15 .07
❑ 417 Wilton Guerrero ........ .15 .07
❑ 418 Rondell White ........ .25 .11
❑ 419 Al Leiter ........ .15 .07
❑ 420 Bernie Williams ........ .60 .25
❑ 421 A.J. Hinch ........ .15 .07
❑ 422 Pat Burrell ........ 1.00 .45
❑ 423 Scott Rolen ........ .60 .25
❑ 424 Jason Kendall ........ .25 .11
❑ 425 Kevin Young ........ .15 .07
❑ 426 Eric Owens ........ .15 .07
❑ 427 Derek Jeter CL ........ .60 .25
❑ 428 Livan Hernandez ........ .15 .07
❑ 429 Russ Davis ........ .15 .07
❑ 430 Dan Wilson ........ .15 .07
❑ 431 Quinton McCracken ........ .15 .07
❑ 432 Homer Bush ........ .15 .07
❑ 433 Seattle Mariners ........ .25 .11
❑ 434 Chad Harville ........ .15 .07
Luis Vizcaino
❑ 435 Carlos Beltran AW ........ .25 .11
❑ 436 Scott Williamson AW ........ .15 .07
❑ 437 Pedro Martinez AW ........ .40 .18
❑ 438 Randy Johnson AW ........ .40 .18
❑ 439 Ivan Rodriguez AW ........ .40 .18
❑ 440 Chipper Jones AW ........ .75 .35
❑ 441 Bernie Williams DIV ........ .25 .11
❑ 442 Pedro Martinez DIV ........ .40 .18
❑ 443 Derek Jeter DIV ........ 1.25 .55
❑ 444 Brian Jordan DIV ........ .15 .07
❑ 445 Todd Pratt DIV ........ .15 .07
❑ 446 Kevin Millwood DIV ........ .15 .07
❑ 447 Orlando Hernandez WS ........ .15 .07
❑ 448 Derek Jeter WS ........ 1.25 .55
❑ 449 Chad Curtis WS ........ .15 .07
❑ 450 Roger Clemens WS ........ .60 .25
❑ P353 Cal Ripken Promo ........ 3.00 1.35

## 2000 Fleer Glossy

| | MINT | NRMT |
|---|---|---|
| COMPLETE SET (500) | 900.00 | 400.00 |
| COMP.FACT.SET (455) | 110.00 | 50.00 |
| COMMON CARD (1-450) | .30 | .14 |
| *STARS 1-450: .75X TO 2X BASIC | | |
| *YNG.STARS 1-450: .75X TO 2X BASIC | | |
| *ROOKIES 1-450: .75X TO 2X BASIC | | |
| COMMON CARD (451-500) | 10.00 | 4.50 |
| MINOR STARS 451-500 | 10.00 | 4.50 |
| SEMISTARS 451-500 | 10.00 | 4.50 |
| UNLISTED STARS 451-500 | 10.00 | 4.50 |

❑ 451 Carlos Casimiro RC ........ 10.00 4.50
❑ 452 Adam Melhuse RC ........ 10.00 4.50
❑ 453 Adam Bernero RC ........ 10.00 4.50
❑ 454 Dusty Allen RC ........ 10.00 4.50
❑ 455 Chan Perry RC ........ 10.00 4.50
❑ 456 Damian Rolls RC ........ 10.00 4.50
❑ 457 Josh Phelps RC ........ 10.00 4.50
❑ 458 Barry Zito ........ 60.00 27.00
❑ 459 Hector Ortiz RC ........ 10.00 4.50
❑ 460 Juan Pierre RC ........ 15.00 6.75
❑ 461 Jose Ortiz RC ........ 50.00 22.00
❑ 462 Chad Zerbe RC ........ 10.00 4.50
❑ 463 Julio Zuleta RC ........ 15.00 6.75
❑ 464 Eric Byrnes ........ 12.00 5.50
❑ 465 Wilfredo Rodriguez RC 15.00 6.75
❑ 466 Wascar Serrano RC ........ 12.00 5.50
❑ 467 Aaron McNeal RC ........ 20.00 9.00
❑ 468 Paul Rigdon RC ........ 15.00 6.75
❑ 469 John Snyder RC ........ 10.00 4.50
❑ 470 J.C. Romero RC ........ 10.00 4.50
❑ 471 Talmadge Nunnari RC 10.00 4.50
❑ 472 Mike Lamb ........ 15.00 6.75
❑ 473 Ryan Kohlmeier RC ........ 10.00 4.50
❑ 474 Rodney Lindsey RC ........ 10.00 4.50
❑ 475 Elvis Pena RC ........ 10.00 4.50
❑ 476 Alex Cabrera ........ 15.00 6.75
❑ 477 Chris Richard ........ 15.00 6.75
❑ 478 Pedro Feliz RC ........ 25.00 11.00
❑ 479 Ross Gload RC ........ 10.00 4.50
❑ 480 Timo Perez RC ........ 25.00 11.00
❑ 481 Jason Woolf RC ........ 10.00 4.50
❑ 482 Kenny Kelly RC ........ 15.00 6.75
❑ 483 Sang-Hoon Lee ........ 10.00 4.50
❑ 484 John Riedling RC ........ 10.00 4.50
❑ 485 Chris Wakeland RC ........ 10.00 4.50
❑ 486 Britt Reames RC ........ 20.00 9.00
❑ 487 Greg LaRocca RC ........ 10.00 4.50
❑ 488 Randy Keisler RC ........ 12.00 5.50
❑ 489 Xavier Nady RC ........ 60.00 27.00
❑ 490 Keith Ginter RC ........ 20.00 9.00
❑ 491 Joey Nation RC ........ 10.00 4.50
❑ 492 Kazuhiro Sasaki ........ 50.00 22.00
❑ 493 Lesli Brea RC ........ 10.00 4.50
❑ 494 Jace Brewer ........ 10.00 4.50
❑ 495 Yohanny Valera RC ........ 10.00 4.50
❑ 496 Adam Piatt ........ 15.00 6.75
❑ 497 Nate Rolison ........ 10.00 4.50
❑ 498 Aubrey Huff ........ 10.00 4.50
❑ 499 Jason Tyner ........ 10.00 4.50
❑ 500 Corey Patterson ........ 20.00 9.00

## 2000 Fleer Update

| | MINT | NRMT |
|---|---|---|
| COMP.FACT.SET (149) | 25.00 | 11.00 |

❑ 1 Ken Griffey Jr. SH ........ 1.00 .45
❑ 2 Cal Ripken SH ........ 1.00 .45
❑ 3 Randy Velarde SH ........ .15 .07
❑ 4 Fred McGriff SH ........ .25 .11
❑ 5 Derek Jeter SH ........ 1.00 .45
❑ 6 Tom Glavine SH ........ .25 .11
❑ 7 Brent Mayne SH ........ .15 .07
❑ 8 Alex Ochoa SH ........ .15 .07
❑ 9 Scott Sheldon SH ........ .15 .07
❑ 10 Randy Johnson SH ........ .40 .18
❑ 11 Daniel Garibay RC ........ .25 .11
❑ 12 Brad Fullmer ........ .25 .11
❑ 13 Kazuhiro Sasaki RC ........ 3.00 1.35
❑ 14 Andy Tracy RC ........ .25 .11
❑ 15 Bret Boone ........ .25 .11
❑ 16 Chad Durbin RC ........ .40 .18
❑ 17 Mark Buehrle RC ........ .50 .23
❑ 18 Julio Zuleta RC ........ .40 .18
❑ 19 Jeremy Giambi ........ .15 .07
❑ 20 Gene Stechschulte RC ........ .25 .11
❑ 21 Lou Pote ........ .25 .11
Bengie Molina
❑ 22 Darrell Einertson RC ........ .25 .11
❑ 23 Ken Griffey Jr. ........ 2.50 1.10
❑ 24 Jeff Sparks RC ........ .25 .11
Dan Wheeler
❑ 25 Aaron Fultz RC ........ .25 .11
❑ 26 Derek Bell ........ .15 .07
❑ 27 Rob Bell ........ .15 .07
D.T. Cromer
❑ 28 Robert Fick ........ .15 .07
❑ 29 Darryl Kile ........ .25 .11
❑ 30 Clayton Andrews ........ .25 .11

| No. | Player | Mint | NrMt |
|---|---|---|---|
| | John Bale RC | | |
| 31 | Dave Veres | .15 | .07 |
| 32 | Hector Mercado RC | .25 | .11 |
| 33 | Willie Morales RC | .25 | .11 |
| 34 | Kelly Wunsch | .25 | .11 |
| | Kip Wells | | |
| 35 | Hideki Irabu | .15 | .07 |
| 36 | Sean DePaula RC | .25 | .11 |
| 37 | DeWayne Wise | .15 | .07 |
| | Chris Woodward | | |
| 38 | Curt Schilling | .25 | .11 |
| 39 | Mark Johnson | .15 | .07 |
| 40 | Mike Cameron | .25 | .11 |
| 41 | Scott Sheldon | .15 | .07 |
| | Tom Evans | | |
| 42 | Brett Tomko | .15 | .07 |
| 43 | Johan Santana RC | .40 | .18 |
| 44 | Andy Benes | .15 | .07 |
| 45 | Matt LeCroy | .15 | .07 |
| | Mark Redman | | |
| 46 | Ryan Klesko | .25 | .11 |
| 47 | Andy Ashby | .15 | .07 |
| 48 | Octavio Dotel | .15 | .07 |
| 49 | Eric Byrnes RC | .40 | .18 |
| 50 | Does Not Exist | | |
| 51 | Kenny Rogers | .15 | .07 |
| 52 | Ben Weber RC | .25 | .11 |
| 53 | Matt Blank | .15 | .07 |
| | Scott Strickland | | |
| 54 | Tom Goodwin | .15 | .07 |
| 55 | Jim Edmonds Cardinals | .75 | .35 |
| 56 | Derrick Turnbow RC | .40 | .18 |
| 57 | Mark Mulder | .25 | .11 |
| 58 | Tarrick Brock | .15 | .07 |
| | Ruben Quevedo | | |
| 59 | Danny Young RC | .25 | .11 |
| 60 | Fernando Vina | .15 | .07 |
| 61 | Justin Brunette RC | .25 | .11 |
| 62 | Jimmy Anderson | .15 | .07 |
| 63 | Reggie Sanders | .15 | .07 |
| 64 | Adam Kennedy | .25 | .11 |
| 65 | Jesse Garcia | .15 | .07 |
| | B.J. Ryan | | |
| 66 | Al Martin | .15 | .07 |
| 67 | Kevin Walker RC | .40 | .18 |
| 68 | Brad Penny | .25 | .11 |
| 69 | B.J. Surhoff | .25 | .11 |
| 70 | Geoff Blum | .25 | .11 |
| | Trace Coquillette RC | | |
| 71 | Jose Jimenez | .15 | .07 |
| 72 | Chuck Finley | .25 | .11 |
| 73 | Valerio De Los Santos | .15 | .07 |
| | Everett Stull | | |
| 74 | Terry Adams | .15 | .07 |
| 75 | Rafael Furcal | 1.50 | .70 |
| 76 | John Roskos | .25 | .11 |
| | Mike Darr | | |
| 77 | Quilvio Veras | .15 | .07 |
| 78 | Armando Almanza | .15 | .07 |
| | Nate Rolison | | |
| 79 | Greg Vaughn | .25 | .11 |
| 80 | Keith McDonald RC | .25 | .11 |
| 81 | Eric Cammack RC | .25 | .11 |
| 82 | Horacio Estrada | .15 | .07 |
| | Ray King | | |
| 83 | Kory DeHaan | .15 | .07 |
| 84 | Kevin Hodges RC | .25 | .11 |
| 85 | Mike Lamb RC | .50 | .23 |
| 86 | Shawn Green | .60 | .25 |
| 87 | Dan Reichert | .15 | .07 |
| | Jason Rakers | | |
| 88 | Adam Piatt | .60 | .25 |
| 89 | Mike Garcia | .15 | .07 |
| 90 | Rodrigo Lopez RC | .40 | .18 |
| 91 | John Olerud | .25 | .11 |
| 92 | Barry Zito RC | 3.00 | 1.35 |
| | Terrence Long | | |
| 93 | Jimmy Rollins | .15 | .07 |
| 94 | Denny Neagle | .25 | .11 |
| 95 | Rickey Henderson | .75 | .35 |
| 96 | Adam Eaton | .25 | .11 |
| | Buddy Carlyle | | |
| 97 | Brian O'Connor RC | .25 | .11 |
| 98 | Andy Thompson RC | .40 | .18 |
| 99 | Jason Boyd RC | .25 | .11 |
| 100 | Joel Pineiro RC | .40 | .18 |
| | Carlos Guillen | | |
| 101 | Raul Gonzalez RC | .25 | .11 |
| 102 | Brandon Kolb RC | .25 | .11 |
| 103 | Jason Maxwell | .15 | .07 |
| | Mike Lincoln | | |
| 104 | Luis Matos RC | .60 | .25 |
| 105 | Morgan Burkhart RC | .40 | .18 |
| 106 | Ismael Villegas RC | .25 | .11 |
| | Steve Sisco RC | | |
| 107 | David Justice Yankees | .75 | .35 |
| 108 | Pablo Ozuna | .15 | .07 |
| 109 | Jose Canseco Yankees | 1.00 | .45 |
| 110 | Alex Cora | .15 | .07 |
| | Shawn Gilbert | | |
| 111 | Will Clark Cardinals | .75 | .35 |
| 112 | Keith Luuloa | .15 | .07 |
| | Eric Weaver | | |
| 113 | Bruce Chen | .25 | .11 |
| 114 | Adam Hyzdu | .15 | .07 |
| 115 | Scott Forster RC | .25 | .11 |
| | Yovanny Lara RC | | |
| 116 | Allen McDill RC | .25 | .11 |
| | Jose Macias | | |
| 117 | Kevin Nicholson | .15 | .07 |
| 118 | Israel Alcantara | .15 | .07 |
| | Tim Young | | |
| 119 | Juan Alvarez RC | .25 | .11 |
| 120 | Julio Lugo | .15 | .07 |
| | Mitch Meluskey | | |
| 121 | B.J. Waszgis RC | .25 | .11 |
| 122 | Jeff M. D'Amico RC | .25 | .11 |
| | Brett Laxton | | |
| 123 | Ricky Ledee | .15 | .07 |
| 124 | Mark DeRosa | .15 | .07 |
| | Jason Marquis | | |
| 125 | Alex Cabrera RC | .50 | .23 |
| 126 | Augie Ojeda RC | .25 | .11 |
| | Gary Matthews Jr. | | |
| 127 | Richie Sexson | .25 | .11 |
| 128 | Santiago Perez RC | .25 | .11 |
| | Hector Ramirez RC | | |
| 129 | Rondell White | .25 | .11 |
| 130 | Craig House RC | .40 | .18 |
| 131 | Kevin Beirne | .25 | .11 |
| | Jon Garland | | |
| 132 | Wayne Franklin RC | .25 | .11 |
| 133 | Henry Rodriguez | .15 | .07 |
| 134 | Jay Payton | .25 | .11 |
| | Jim Mann | | |
| 135 | Ron Gant | .15 | .07 |
| 136 | Paxton Crawford RC | .40 | .18 |
| | Sang-Hoon Lee RC | | |
| 137 | Kent Bottenfield | .15 | .07 |
| 138 | Rocky Biddle RC | .40 | .18 |
| 139 | Travis Lee | .15 | .07 |
| 140 | Ryan Vogelsong RC | .75 | .35 |
| 141 | Jason Conti | .25 | .11 |
| | Geraldo Guzman RC | | |
| 142 | Tim Drew | .25 | .11 |
| | Mark Watson RC | | |
| 143 | John Parrish RC | .40 | .18 |
| | Chris Richard RC | | |
| 144 | Javier Cardona RC | .40 | .18 |
| | Brandon Villafuerte RC | | |
| 145 | Tike Redman RC | .40 | .18 |
| | Steve Sparks RC | | |
| 146 | Brian Schneider | .25 | .11 |
| | Matt Skrmetta RC | | |
| 147 | Pasqual Coco RC | .40 | .18 |
| 148 | Lorenzo Barcelo RC | .40 | .18 |
| | Joe Crede | | |
| 149 | Jace Brewer RC | .40 | .18 |
| 150 | Milton Bradley | .25 | .11 |
| | Tomas De La Rosa RC | | |
| MP1 | Mickey Mantle | 400.00 | 180.00 |

## 1999 Fleer Brilliants

| | MINT | NRMT |
|---|---|---|
| COMPLETE SET (175) | 120.00 | 55.00 |
| COMP.SET w/o SP's (125) | 50.00 | 22.00 |
| COMMON CARD (1-125) | .25 | .11 |
| COMMON CARD (126-175) | 1.00 | .45 |

| No. | Player | Mint | NrMt |
|---|---|---|---|
| 1 | Mark McGwire | 4.00 | 1.80 |
| 2 | Derek Jeter | 4.00 | 1.80 |
| 3 | Nomar Garciaparra | 3.00 | 1.35 |
| 4 | Travis Lee | .25 | .11 |
| 5 | Jeff Bagwell | 1.25 | .55 |
| 6 | Andres Galarraga | .60 | .25 |
| 7 | Pedro Martinez | 1.25 | .55 |
| 8 | Cal Ripken | 4.00 | 1.80 |
| 9 | Vladimir Guerrero | 1.50 | .70 |
| 10 | Chipper Jones | 2.50 | 1.10 |
| 11 | Rusty Greer | .40 | .18 |
| 12 | Omar Vizquel | .40 | .18 |
| 13 | Quinton McCracken | .25 | .11 |
| 14 | Jaret Wright | .25 | .11 |
| 15 | Mike Mussina | 1.00 | .45 |
| 16 | Jason Giambi | 1.00 | .45 |
| 17 | Tony Clark | .25 | .11 |
| 18 | Troy O'Leary | .25 | .11 |
| 19 | Troy Percival | .25 | .11 |
| 20 | Kerry Wood | .40 | .18 |
| 21 | Vinny Castilla | .40 | .18 |
| 22 | Chris Carpenter | .25 | .11 |
| 23 | Richie Sexson | .40 | .18 |
| 24 | Ken Griffey Jr. | 4.00 | 1.80 |
| 25 | Barry Bonds | 1.50 | .70 |
| 26 | Carlos Delgado | 1.00 | .45 |
| 27 | Frank Thomas | 2.00 | .90 |
| 28 | Manny Ramirez | 1.25 | .55 |
| 29 | Shawn Green | 1.00 | .45 |
| 30 | Mike Piazza | 3.00 | 1.35 |
| 31 | Tino Martinez | .40 | .18 |
| 32 | Dante Bichette | .40 | .18 |
| 33 | Scott Rolen | 1.00 | .45 |
| 34 | Gabe Alvarez | .25 | .11 |
| 35 | Raul Mondesi | .40 | .18 |
| 36 | Damion Easley | .25 | .11 |
| 37 | Jeff Kent | .60 | .25 |
| 38 | Al Leiter | .40 | .18 |
| 39 | Alex Rodriguez | 3.00 | 1.35 |
| 40 | Jeff King | .25 | .11 |
| 41 | Mark Grace | 1.00 | .45 |
| 42 | Larry Walker | .40 | .18 |
| 43 | Moises Alou | .40 | .18 |
| 44 | Juan Gonzalez | 1.00 | .45 |
| 45 | Rolando Arrojo | .25 | .11 |
| 46 | Tom Glavine | 1.00 | .45 |
| 47 | Johnny Damon | .40 | .18 |
| 48 | Livan Hernandez | .25 | .11 |
| 49 | Craig Biggio | .60 | .25 |
| 50 | Dmitri Young | .40 | .18 |
| 51 | Chan Ho Park | .40 | .18 |
| 52 | Todd Walker | .25 | .11 |
| 53 | Derrek Lee | .25 | .11 |
| 54 | Todd Helton | 1.25 | .55 |
| 55 | Ray Lankford | .40 | .18 |
| 56 | Jim Thome | .60 | .25 |
| 57 | Matt Lawton | .40 | .18 |
| 58 | Matt Anderson | .25 | .11 |
| 59 | Jose Offerman | .25 | .11 |
| 60 | Eric Karros | .40 | .18 |
| 61 | Orlando Hernandez | .40 | .18 |
| 62 | Ben Grieve | .40 | .18 |
| 63 | Bobby Abreu | .40 | .18 |
| 64 | Kevin Young | .40 | .18 |
| 65 | John Olerud | .40 | .18 |
| 66 | Sammy Sosa | 2.00 | .90 |
| 67 | Andy Ashby | .25 | .11 |
| 68 | Juan Encarnacion | .40 | .18 |
| 69 | Shane Reynolds | .25 | .11 |
| 70 | Bernie Williams | 1.00 | .45 |

| | | | |
|---|---|---|---|
| ❑ 71 | Mike Cameron | .25 | .11 |
| ❑ 72 | Troy Glaus | 1.50 | .70 |
| ❑ 73 | Gary Sheffield | 1.00 | .45 |
| ❑ 74 | Jeromy Burnitz | .40 | .18 |
| ❑ 75 | Mike Caruso | .25 | .11 |
| ❑ 76 | Chuck Knoblauch | .40 | .18 |
| ❑ 77 | Kenny Rogers | .25 | .11 |
| ❑ 78 | David Cone | .40 | .18 |
| ❑ 79 | Tony Gwynn | 2.00 | .90 |
| ❑ 80 | Jay Buhner | .40 | .18 |
| ❑ 81 | Paul O'Neill | .40 | .18 |
| ❑ 82 | Charles Nagy | .25 | .11 |
| ❑ 83 | Javy Lopez | .40 | .18 |
| ❑ 84 | Scott Erickson | .25 | .11 |
| ❑ 85 | Trevor Hoffman | .40 | .18 |
| ❑ 86 | Andruw Jones | 1.00 | .45 |
| ❑ 87 | Ray Durham | .40 | .18 |
| ❑ 88 | Jorge Posada | .40 | .18 |
| ❑ 89 | Edgar Martinez | .60 | .25 |
| ❑ 90 | Tim Salmon | .40 | .18 |
| ❑ 91 | Bobby Higginson | .40 | .18 |
| ❑ 92 | Adrian Beltre | .40 | .18 |
| ❑ 93 | Jason Kendall | .40 | .18 |
| ❑ 94 | Henry Rodriguez | .25 | .11 |
| ❑ 95 | Greg Maddux | 2.50 | 1.10 |
| ❑ 96 | David Justice | .60 | .25 |
| ❑ 97 | Ivan Rodriguez | 1.25 | .55 |
| ❑ 98 | Curt Schilling | .40 | .18 |
| ❑ 99 | Matt Williams | .60 | .25 |
| ❑ 100 | Darin Erstad | 1.00 | .45 |
| ❑ 101 | Rafael Palmeiro | 1.00 | .45 |
| ❑ 102 | David Wells | .40 | .18 |
| ❑ 103 | Barry Larkin | 1.00 | .45 |
| ❑ 104 | Robin Ventura | .40 | .18 |
| ❑ 105 | Edgar Renteria | .25 | .11 |
| ❑ 106 | Andy Pettitte | .40 | .18 |
| ❑ 107 | Albert Belle | .60 | .25 |
| ❑ 108 | Steve Finley | .40 | .18 |
| ❑ 109 | Fernando Vina | .25 | .11 |
| ❑ 110 | Rondell White | .40 | .18 |
| ❑ 111 | Kevin Brown | .60 | .25 |
| ❑ 112 | Jose Canseco | 1.25 | .55 |
| ❑ 113 | Roger Clemens | 2.00 | .90 |
| ❑ 114 | Todd Hundley | .25 | .11 |
| ❑ 115 | Will Clark | 1.00 | .45 |
| ❑ 116 | Jim Edmonds | 1.00 | .45 |
| ❑ 117 | Randy Johnson | 1.25 | .55 |
| ❑ 118 | Denny Neagle | .25 | .11 |
| ❑ 119 | Brian Jordan | .40 | .18 |
| ❑ 120 | Dean Palmer | .40 | .18 |
| ❑ 121 | Roberto Alomar | 1.00 | .45 |
| ❑ 122 | Ken Caminiti | .40 | .18 |
| ❑ 123 | Brian Giles | .40 | .18 |
| ❑ 124 | Todd Stottlemyre | .25 | .11 |
| ❑ 125 | Mo Vaughn | .40 | .18 |
| ❑ 126 | J.D. Drew | 3.00 | 1.35 |
| ❑ 127 | Ryan Minor | 1.00 | .45 |
| ❑ 128 | Gabe Kapler | 1.25 | .55 |
| ❑ 129 | Jeremy Giambi | 1.00 | .45 |
| ❑ 130 | Eric Chavez | 1.25 | .55 |
| ❑ 131 | Ben Davis | 1.00 | .45 |
| ❑ 132 | Rob Fick | 1.00 | .45 |
| ❑ 133 | George Lombard | 1.00 | .45 |
| ❑ 134 | Calvin Pickering | 1.00 | .45 |
| ❑ 135 | Preston Wilson | 1.25 | .55 |
| ❑ 136 | Corey Koskie | 1.00 | .45 |
| ❑ 137 | Russell Branyan | 1.25 | .55 |
| ❑ 138 | Bruce Chen | 1.00 | .45 |
| ❑ 139 | Matt Clement | 1.00 | .45 |
| ❑ 140 | Pat Burrell RC | 10.00 | 4.50 |
| ❑ 141 | Freddy Garcia RC | 3.00 | 1.35 |
| ❑ 142 | Brian Simmons | 1.00 | .45 |
| ❑ 143 | Carlos Febles | 1.00 | .45 |
| ❑ 144 | Carlos Guillen | 1.00 | .45 |
| ❑ 145 | Fernando Seguignol | 1.00 | .45 |
| ❑ 146 | Carlos Beltran | 1.25 | .55 |
| ❑ 147 | Edgard Clemente | 1.00 | .45 |
| ❑ 148 | Mitch Meluskey | 1.00 | .45 |
| ❑ 149 | Ryan Bradley | 1.00 | .45 |
| ❑ 150 | Marlon Anderson | 1.00 | .45 |
| ❑ 151 | A.J. Burnett RC | 1.50 | .70 |
| ❑ 152 | Scott Hunter RC | 1.00 | .45 |
| ❑ 153 | Mark Johnson | 1.00 | .45 |
| ❑ 154 | Angel Pena | 1.00 | .45 |
| ❑ 155 | Roy Halladay | 1.00 | .45 |
| ❑ 156 | Chad Allen RC | 1.00 | .45 |
| ❑ 157 | Trot Nixon | 1.25 | .55 |
| ❑ 158 | Ricky Ledee | 1.00 | .45 |
| ❑ 159 | Gary Bennett RC | 1.00 | .45 |
| ❑ 160 | Micah Bowie RC | 1.00 | .45 |
| ❑ 161 | Doug Mientkiewicz RC | 1.00 | .45 |
| ❑ 162 | Danny Klassen | 1.00 | .45 |
| ❑ 163 | Willis Otanez | 1.00 | .45 |
| ❑ 164 | Jin Ho Cho | 1.00 | .45 |
| ❑ 165 | Mike Lowell | 1.25 | .55 |
| ❑ 166 | Armando Rios | 1.00 | .45 |
| ❑ 167 | Warren Morris | 1.00 | .45 |
| ❑ 168 | Michael Barrett | 1.00 | .45 |
| ❑ 169 | Alex Gonzalez | 1.00 | .45 |
| ❑ 170 | Masao Kida RC | 1.25 | .55 |
| ❑ 171 | Peter Tucci | 1.00 | .45 |
| ❑ 172 | Luis Saturria RC | 1.00 | .45 |
| ❑ 173 | Kris Benson | 1.25 | .55 |
| ❑ 174 | Mario Encarnacion RC | 1.25 | .55 |
| ❑ 175 | Roosevelt Brown RC | 1.00 | .45 |
| ❑ NNO | J.D. Drew Sample | 1.00 | .45 |

## 2000 Fleer Focus

| | MINT | NRMT |
|---|---|---|
| COMP.MASTER SET (275) | 600.00 | 275.00 |
| COMP.SET w/o SP's (225) | 25.00 | 11.00 |
| COMMON CARD (1-225) | .15 | .07 |
| COMMON ROOKIE (226-250) | 6.00 | 2.70 |
| COMMON PORT (226P-250P) | 12.00 | 5.50 |

| | | | |
|---|---|---|---|
| ❑ 1 | Nomar Garciaparra | 2.00 | .90 |
| ❑ 2 | Adrian Beltre | .25 | .11 |
| ❑ 3 | Miguel Tejada | .25 | .11 |
| ❑ 4 | Joe Randa | .15 | .07 |
| ❑ 5 | Larry Walker | .25 | .11 |
| ❑ 6 | Jeff Weaver | .15 | .07 |
| ❑ 7 | Jay Bell | .25 | .11 |
| ❑ 8 | Ivan Rodriguez | .75 | .35 |
| ❑ 9 | Edgar Martinez | .40 | .18 |
| ❑ 10 | Desi Relaford | .15 | .07 |
| ❑ 11 | Derek Jeter | 2.50 | 1.10 |
| ❑ 12 | Delino DeShields | .15 | .07 |
| ❑ 13 | Craig Biggio | .40 | .18 |
| ❑ 14 | Chuck Knoblauch | .25 | .11 |
| ❑ 15 | Chuck Finley | .25 | .11 |
| ❑ 16 | Brett Tomko | .15 | .07 |
| ❑ 17 | Bobby Higginson | .15 | .07 |
| ❑ 18 | Pedro Martinez | .75 | .35 |
| ❑ 19 | Troy O'Leary | .15 | .07 |
| ❑ 20 | Rickey Henderson | .75 | .35 |
| ❑ 21 | Robb Nen | .15 | .07 |
| ❑ 22 | Rolando Arrojo | .15 | .07 |
| ❑ 23 | Rondell White | .25 | .11 |
| ❑ 24 | Royce Clayton | .15 | .07 |
| ❑ 25 | Rusty Greer | .25 | .11 |
| ❑ 26 | Stan Spencer | .15 | .07 |
| ❑ 27 | Steve Finley | .25 | .11 |
| ❑ 28 | Tom Goodwin | .15 | .07 |
| ❑ 29 | Troy Percival | .15 | .07 |
| ❑ 30 | Wilton Guerrero | .15 | .07 |
| ❑ 31 | Roberto Alomar | .60 | .25 |
| ❑ 32 | Mike Hampton | .25 | .11 |
| ❑ 33 | Michael Barrett | .15 | .07 |
| ❑ 34 | Curt Schilling | .25 | .11 |
| ❑ 35 | Bill Mueller | .15 | .07 |
| ❑ 36 | Bernie Williams | .60 | .25 |
| ❑ 37 | John Smoltz | .25 | .11 |
| ❑ 38 | B.J. Surhoff | .25 | .11 |

| | | | |
|---|---|---|---|
| ❑ 39 | Pete Harnisch | .15 | .07 |
| ❑ 40 | Juan Encarnacion | .25 | .11 |
| ❑ 41 | Derrek Lee | .15 | .07 |
| ❑ 42 | Jeff Shaw | .15 | .07 |
| ❑ 43 | David Cone | .25 | .11 |
| ❑ 44 | Jason Christiansen | .15 | .07 |
| ❑ 45 | Jeff Kent | .40 | .18 |
| ❑ 46 | Randy Johnson | .75 | .35 |
| ❑ 47 | Todd Walker | .15 | .07 |
| ❑ 48 | Jose Lima | .15 | .07 |
| ❑ 49 | Jason Giambi | .60 | .25 |
| ❑ 50 | Ken Griffey Jr. Reds | 2.50 | 1.10 |
| ❑ 51 | Bartolo Colon | .25 | .11 |
| ❑ 52 | Mike Lieberthal | .25 | .11 |
| ❑ 53 | Shane Reynolds | .15 | .07 |
| ❑ 54 | Travis Lee | .15 | .07 |
| ❑ 55 | Travis Fryman | .25 | .11 |
| ❑ 56 | John Valentin | .15 | .07 |
| ❑ 57 | Joey Hamilton | .15 | .07 |
| ❑ 58 | Jay Buhner | .25 | .11 |
| ❑ 59 | Brad Radke | .25 | .11 |
| ❑ 60 | A.J. Burnett | .25 | .11 |
| ❑ 61 | Roy Halladay | .15 | .07 |
| ❑ 62 | Raul Mondesi | .25 | .11 |
| ❑ 63 | Matt Mantei | .15 | .07 |
| ❑ 64 | Mark Grace | .60 | .25 |
| ❑ 65 | David Justice | .40 | .18 |
| ❑ 66 | Billy Wagner | .15 | .07 |
| ❑ 67 | Eric Milton | .15 | .07 |
| ❑ 68 | Eric Chavez | .25 | .11 |
| ❑ 69 | Doug Glanville | .15 | .07 |
| ❑ 70 | Ray Durham | .25 | .11 |
| ❑ 71 | Mike Sirotka | .15 | .07 |
| ❑ 72 | Greg Vaughn | .25 | .11 |
| ❑ 73 | Brian Jordan | .25 | .11 |
| ❑ 74 | Alex Gonzalez | .15 | .07 |
| ❑ 75 | Alex Rodriguez | 2.00 | .90 |
| ❑ 76 | David Nilsson | .15 | .07 |
| ❑ 77 | Robin Ventura | .40 | .18 |
| ❑ 78 | Kevin Young | .15 | .07 |
| ❑ 79 | Wilson Alvarez | .15 | .07 |
| ❑ 80 | Matt Williams | .40 | .18 |
| ❑ 81 | Ismael Valdes | .15 | .07 |
| ❑ 82 | Kenny Lofton | .25 | .11 |
| ❑ 83 | Carlos Beltran | .25 | .11 |
| ❑ 84 | Doug Mientkiewicz | .15 | .07 |
| ❑ 85 | Wally Joyner | .25 | .11 |
| ❑ 86 | J.D. Drew | .60 | .25 |
| ❑ 87 | Carlos Delgado | .60 | .25 |
| ❑ 88 | Tony Womack | .15 | .07 |
| ❑ 89 | Eric Young | .15 | .07 |
| ❑ 90 | Manny Ramirez | .75 | .35 |
| ❑ 91 | Johnny Damon | .25 | .11 |
| ❑ 92 | Torii Hunter | .15 | .07 |
| ❑ 93 | Kenny Rogers | .15 | .07 |
| ❑ 94 | Trevor Hoffman | .25 | .11 |
| ❑ 95 | John Wetteland | .25 | .11 |
| ❑ 96 | Ray Lankford | .25 | .11 |
| ❑ 97 | Tom Glavine | .60 | .25 |
| ❑ 98 | Carlos Lee | .25 | .11 |
| ❑ 99 | Richie Sexson | .25 | .11 |
| ❑ 100 | Carlos Febles | .15 | .07 |
| ❑ 101 | Chad Allen | .15 | .07 |
| ❑ 102 | Sterling Hitchcock | .15 | .07 |
| ❑ 103 | Joe McEwing | .15 | .07 |
| ❑ 104 | Justin Thompson | .15 | .07 |
| ❑ 105 | Jim Edmonds | .60 | .25 |
| ❑ 106 | Kerry Wood | .25 | .11 |
| ❑ 107 | Jim Thome | .40 | .18 |
| ❑ 108 | Jeremy Giambi | .15 | .07 |
| ❑ 109 | Mike Piazza | 2.00 | .90 |
| ❑ 110 | Darryl Kile | .25 | .11 |
| ❑ 111 | Darin Erstad | .60 | .25 |
| ❑ 112 | Kyle Farnsworth | .15 | .07 |
| ❑ 113 | Omar Vizquel | .25 | .11 |
| ❑ 114 | Orber Moreno | .15 | .07 |
| ❑ 115 | Al Leiter | .15 | .07 |
| ❑ 116 | John Olerud | .25 | .11 |
| ❑ 117 | Aaron Sele | .15 | .07 |
| ❑ 118 | Chipper Jones | 1.50 | .70 |
| ❑ 119 | Paul Konerko | .25 | .11 |
| ❑ 120 | Chris Singleton | .25 | .11 |
| ❑ 121 | Fernando Vina | .15 | .07 |
| ❑ 122 | Andy Ashby | .15 | .07 |
| ❑ 123 | Eli Marrero | .15 | .07 |
| ❑ 124 | Edgar Renteria | .15 | .07 |

| No. | Player | | |
|---|---|---|---|
| ❑ 125 | Roberto Hernandez | .15 | .07 |
| ❑ 126 | Andruw Jones | .60 | .25 |
| ❑ 127 | Magglio Ordonez | .25 | .11 |
| ❑ 128 | Bob Wickman | .15 | .07 |
| ❑ 129 | Tony Gwynn | 1.25 | .55 |
| ❑ 130 | Mark McGwire | 2.50 | 1.10 |
| ❑ 131 | Albert Belle | .40 | .18 |
| ❑ 132 | Pokey Reese | .25 | .11 |
| ❑ 133 | Tony Clark | .15 | .07 |
| ❑ 134 | Jeff Bagwell | .75 | .35 |
| ❑ 135 | Mark Grudzielanek | .15 | .07 |
| ❑ 136 | Dustin Hermanson | .15 | .07 |
| ❑ 137 | Reggie Sanders | .15 | .07 |
| ❑ 138 | Ryan Rupe | .15 | .07 |
| ❑ 139 | Kevin Millwood | .25 | .11 |
| ❑ 140 | Bret Saberhagen | .25 | .11 |
| ❑ 141 | Juan Guzman | .15 | .07 |
| ❑ 142 | Alex Gonzalez | .15 | .07 |
| ❑ 143 | Gary Sheffield | .60 | .25 |
| ❑ 144 | Roger Clemens | 1.25 | .55 |
| ❑ 145 | Ben Grieve | .25 | .11 |
| ❑ 146 | Bobby Abreu | .25 | .11 |
| ❑ 147 | Brian Giles | .25 | .11 |
| ❑ 148 | Quinton McCracken | .15 | .07 |
| ❑ 149 | Freddy Garcia | .25 | .11 |
| ❑ 150 | Erubiel Durazo | .25 | .11 |
| ❑ 151 | Sidney Ponson | .15 | .07 |
| ❑ 152 | Scott Williamson | .15 | .07 |
| ❑ 153 | Ken Caminiti | .25 | .11 |
| ❑ 154 | Vladimir Guerrero | 1.00 | .45 |
| ❑ 155 | Andy Pettitte | .25 | .11 |
| ❑ 156 | Edwards Guzman | .15 | .07 |
| ❑ 157 | Shannon Stewart | .25 | .11 |
| ❑ 158 | Greg Maddux | 1.50 | .70 |
| ❑ 159 | Mike Stanley | .15 | .07 |
| ❑ 160 | Sean Casey | .25 | .11 |
| ❑ 161 | Cliff Floyd | .25 | .11 |
| ❑ 162 | Devon White | .15 | .07 |
| ❑ 163 | Scott Brosius | .25 | .11 |
| ❑ 164 | Marlon Anderson | .15 | .07 |
| ❑ 165 | Jason Kendall | .25 | .11 |
| ❑ 166 | Ryan Klesko | .25 | .11 |
| ❑ 167 | Sammy Sosa | 1.25 | .55 |
| ❑ 168 | Frank Thomas | 1.25 | .55 |
| ❑ 169 | Geoff Jenkins | .25 | .11 |
| ❑ 170 | Jason Schmidt | .15 | .07 |
| ❑ 171 | Dan Wilson | .15 | .07 |
| ❑ 172 | Jose Canseco | .75 | .35 |
| ❑ 173 | Troy Glaus | .75 | .35 |
| ❑ 174 | Mariano Rivera | .25 | .11 |
| ❑ 175 | Scott Rolen | .60 | .25 |
| ❑ 176 | J.T. Snow | .25 | .11 |
| ❑ 177 | Rafael Palmeiro | .60 | .25 |
| ❑ 178 | A.J. Hinch | .15 | .07 |
| ❑ 179 | Jose Offerman | .15 | .07 |
| ❑ 180 | Jeff Cirillo | .25 | .11 |
| ❑ 181 | Dean Palmer | .25 | .11 |
| ❑ 182 | Jose Rosado | .15 | .07 |
| ❑ 183 | Armando Benitez | .25 | .11 |
| ❑ 184 | Brady Anderson | .25 | .11 |
| ❑ 185 | Cal Ripken | 2.50 | 1.10 |
| ❑ 186 | Barry Larkin | .60 | .25 |
| ❑ 187 | Damion Easley | .15 | .07 |
| ❑ 188 | Moises Alou | .25 | .11 |
| ❑ 189 | Todd Hundley | .15 | .07 |
| ❑ 190 | Tim Hudson | .60 | .25 |
| ❑ 191 | Livan Hernandez | .15 | .07 |
| ❑ 192 | Fred McGriff | .40 | .18 |
| ❑ 193 | Orlando Hernandez | .25 | .11 |
| ❑ 194 | Tim Salmon | .25 | .11 |
| ❑ 195 | Mike Mussina | .60 | .25 |
| ❑ 196 | Todd Helton | .75 | .35 |
| ❑ 197 | Juan Gonzalez | .60 | .25 |
| ❑ 198 | Kevin Brown | .40 | .18 |
| ❑ 199 | Ugueth Urbina | .15 | .07 |
| ❑ 200 | Matt Stairs | .15 | .07 |
| ❑ 201 | Shawn Estes | .15 | .07 |
| ❑ 202 | Gabe Kapler | .25 | .11 |
| ❑ 203 | Javy Lopez | .25 | .11 |
| ❑ 204 | Henry Rodriguez | .15 | .07 |
| ❑ 205 | Dante Bichette | .25 | .11 |
| ❑ 206 | Jeromy Burnitz | .25 | .11 |
| ❑ 207 | Todd Zeile | .25 | .11 |
| ❑ 208 | Rico Brogna | .15 | .07 |
| ❑ 209 | Warren Morris | .15 | .07 |
| ❑ 210 | David Segui | .15 | .07 |
| ❑ 211 | Vinny Castilla | .25 | .11 |
| ❑ 212 | Mo Vaughn | .25 | .11 |
| ❑ 213 | Charles Johnson | .25 | .11 |
| ❑ 214 | Neifi Perez | .15 | .07 |
| ❑ 215 | Shawn Green | .60 | .25 |
| ❑ 216 | Carl Pavano | .15 | .07 |
| ❑ 217 | Tino Martinez | .25 | .11 |
| ❑ 218 | Barry Bonds | 1.00 | .45 |
| ❑ 219 | David Wells | .25 | .11 |
| ❑ 220 | Paul O'Neill | .25 | .11 |
| ❑ 221 | Masato Yoshii | .15 | .07 |
| ❑ 222 | Kris Benson | .25 | .11 |
| ❑ 223 | Fernando Tatis | .25 | .11 |
| ❑ 224 | Lee Stevens | .15 | .07 |
| ❑ 225 | Jose Cruz Jr. | .25 | .11 |
| ❑ 226 | Rick Ankiel | 20.00 | 9.00 |
| ❑ 226P | Rick Ankiel PORT | 40.00 | 18.00 |
| ❑ 227 | Matt Riley | 6.00 | 2.70 |
| ❑ 227P | Matt Riley PORT | 12.00 | 5.50 |
| ❑ 228 | Norm Hutchins | 6.00 | 2.70 |
| ❑ 228P | Norm Hutchins PORT | 12.00 | 5.50 |
| ❑ 229 | Ruben Mateo | 6.00 | 2.70 |
| ❑ 229P | Ruben Mateo PORT | 12.00 | 5.50 |
| ❑ 230 | Ben Petrick | 6.00 | 2.70 |
| ❑ 230P | Ben Petrick PORT | 12.00 | 5.50 |
| ❑ 231 | Mario Encarnacion | 6.00 | 2.70 |
| ❑ 231P | Mario Encarnacion PORT | 12.00 | 5.50 |
| ❑ 232 | Nick Johnson | 6.00 | 2.70 |
| ❑ 232P | Nick Johnson PORT | 12.00 | 5.50 |
| ❑ 233 | Adam Piatt | 10.00 | 4.50 |
| ❑ 233P | Adam Piatt PORT | 20.00 | 9.00 |
| ❑ 234 | Mike Darr | 6.00 | 2.70 |
| ❑ 234P | Mike Darr PORT | 12.00 | 5.50 |
| ❑ 235 | Chad Hermansen | 6.00 | 2.70 |
| ❑ 235P | Chad Hermansen PORT | 12.00 | 5.50 |
| ❑ 236 | Wily Pena | 6.00 | 2.70 |
| ❑ 236P | Wily Pena PORT | 12.00 | 5.50 |
| ❑ 237 | Octavio Dotel | 6.00 | 2.70 |
| ❑ 237P | Octavio Dotel PORT | 12.00 | 5.50 |
| ❑ 238 | Vernon Wells | 6.00 | 2.70 |
| ❑ 238P | Vernon Wells PORT | 12.00 | 5.50 |
| ❑ 239 | Daryle Ward | 6.00 | 2.70 |
| ❑ 239P | Daryle Ward PORT | 12.00 | 5.50 |
| ❑ 240 | Adam Kennedy | 6.00 | 2.70 |
| ❑ 240P | Adam Kennedy PORT | 12.00 | 5.50 |
| ❑ 241 | Angel Pena | 6.00 | 2.70 |
| ❑ 241P | Angel Pena PORT | 12.00 | 5.50 |
| ❑ 242 | Lance Berkman | 6.00 | 2.70 |
| ❑ 242P | Lance Berkman PORT | 12.00 | 5.50 |
| ❑ 243 | Gabe Molina | 6.00 | 2.70 |
| ❑ 243P | Gabe Molina PORT | 12.00 | 5.50 |
| ❑ 244 | Steve Lomasney | 6.00 | 2.70 |
| ❑ 244P | Steve Lomasney PORT | 12.00 | 5.50 |
| ❑ 245 | Jacob Cruz | 6.00 | 2.70 |
| ❑ 245P | Jacob Cruz PORT | 12.00 | 5.50 |
| ❑ 246 | Mark Quinn | 6.00 | 2.70 |
| ❑ 246P | Mark Quinn PORT | 12.00 | 5.50 |
| ❑ 247 | Eric Munson | 10.00 | 4.50 |
| ❑ 247P | Eric Munson PORT | 20.00 | 9.00 |
| ❑ 248 | Alfonso Soriano | 6.00 | 2.70 |
| ❑ 248P | Alfonso Soriano PORT | 12.00 | 5.50 |
| ❑ 249 | Kip Wells | 6.00 | 2.70 |
| ❑ 249P | Kip Wells PORT | 12.00 | 5.50 |
| ❑ 250 | Josh Beckett | 10.00 | 4.50 |
| ❑ 250P | Josh Beckett PORT | 20.00 | 9.00 |

## 2000 Fleer Gamers

| | MINT | NRMT |
|---|---|---|
| COMPLETE SET (120) | 120.00 | 55.00 |
| COMP.SET w/o SP's (90) | 30.00 | 13.50 |
| COMMON CARD (1-90) | .15 | .07 |
| COMMON NG (91-110) | 2.00 | .90 |
| COMMON FG (111-120) | 4.00 | 1.80 |

| No. | Player | MINT | NRMT |
|---|---|---|---|
| ❑ 1 | Cal Ripken | 2.50 | 1.10 |
| ❑ 2 | Derek Jeter | 2.50 | 1.10 |
| ❑ 3 | Alex Rodriguez | 2.00 | .90 |
| ❑ 4 | Alex Gonzalez | .15 | .07 |
| ❑ 5 | Nomar Garciaparra | 2.00 | .90 |
| ❑ 6 | Brian Giles | .25 | .11 |
| ❑ 7 | Chris Singleton | .25 | .11 |
| ❑ 8 | Kevin Brown | .40 | .18 |
| ❑ 9 | J.D. Drew | .60 | .25 |
| ❑ 10 | Raul Mondesi | .25 | .11 |
| ❑ 11 | Sammy Sosa | 1.25 | .55 |
| ❑ 12 | Carlos Beltran | .25 | .11 |
| ❑ 13 | Eric Chavez | .25 | .11 |
| ❑ 14 | Gabe Kapler | .25 | .11 |
| ❑ 15 | Tim Salmon | .25 | .11 |
| ❑ 16 | Manny Ramirez | .75 | .35 |
| ❑ 17 | Orlando Hernandez | .25 | .11 |
| ❑ 18 | Jeff Kent | .40 | .18 |
| ❑ 19 | Juan Gonzalez | .60 | .25 |
| ❑ 20 | Moises Alou | .25 | .11 |
| ❑ 21 | Jason Giambi | .60 | .25 |
| ❑ 22 | Ivan Rodriguez | .75 | .35 |
| ❑ 23 | Geoff Jenkins | .25 | .11 |
| ❑ 24 | Ken Griffey Jr. | 2.50 | 1.10 |
| ❑ 25 | Mark McGwire | 2.50 | 1.10 |
| ❑ 26 | Jose Canseco | .75 | .35 |
| ❑ 27 | Roberto Alomar | .60 | .25 |
| ❑ 28 | Craig Biggio | .40 | .18 |
| ❑ 29 | Scott Rolen | .60 | .25 |
| ❑ 30 | Vinny Castilla | .25 | .11 |
| ❑ 31 | Greg Maddux | 1.50 | .70 |
| ❑ 32 | Pedro Martinez | .75 | .35 |
| ❑ 33 | Mike Piazza | 2.00 | .90 |
| ❑ 34 | Albert Belle | .40 | .18 |
| ❑ 35 | Frank Thomas | 1.25 | .55 |
| ❑ 36 | Bobby Abreu | .25 | .11 |
| ❑ 37 | Edgar Martinez | .40 | .18 |
| ❑ 38 | Pokey Reese | .25 | .11 |
| ❑ 39 | Preston Wilson | .25 | .11 |
| ❑ 40 | Mike Lieberthal | .25 | .11 |
| ❑ 41 | Andruw Jones | .60 | .25 |
| ❑ 42 | Damion Easley | .15 | .07 |
| ❑ 43 | Mike Cameron | .15 | .07 |
| ❑ 44 | Todd Walker | .15 | .07 |
| ❑ 45 | Jason Kendall | .25 | .11 |
| ❑ 46 | Sean Casey | .25 | .11 |
| ❑ 47 | Corey Koskie | .15 | .07 |
| ❑ 48 | Warren Morris | .15 | .07 |
| ❑ 49 | Andres Galarraga | .40 | .18 |
| ❑ 50 | Dean Palmer | .25 | .11 |
| ❑ 51 | Jose Vidro | .15 | .07 |
| ❑ 52 | Brian Jordan | .25 | .11 |
| ❑ 53 | Tony Clark | .15 | .07 |
| ❑ 54 | Vladimir Guerrero | 1.00 | .45 |
| ❑ 55 | Mo Vaughn | .25 | .11 |
| ❑ 56 | Richie Sexson | .25 | .11 |
| ❑ 57 | Tino Martinez | .25 | .11 |
| ❑ 58 | Eric Owens | .15 | .07 |
| ❑ 59 | Matt Williams | .40 | .18 |
| ❑ 60 | Omar Vizquel | .25 | .11 |
| ❑ 61 | Rickey Henderson | .75 | .35 |
| ❑ 62 | J.T. Snow | .25 | .11 |
| ❑ 63 | Mark Grace | .60 | .25 |
| ❑ 64 | Carlos Febles | .15 | .07 |
| ❑ 65 | Paul O'Neill | .25 | .11 |
| ❑ 66 | Randy Johnson | .75 | .35 |
| ❑ 67 | Kenny Lofton | .25 | .11 |
| ❑ 68 | Roger Cedeno | .15 | .07 |
| ❑ 69 | Shawn Green | .60 | .25 |
| ❑ 70 | Chipper Jones | 1.50 | .70 |
| ❑ 71 | Jeff Cirillo | .25 | .11 |
| ❑ 72 | Robin Ventura | .40 | .18 |
| ❑ 73 | Paul Konerko | .25 | .11 |
| ❑ 74 | Jeromy Burnitz | .25 | .11 |
| ❑ 75 | Ben Grieve | .25 | .11 |
| ❑ 76 | Troy Glaus | .75 | .35 |
| ❑ 77 | Jim Thome | .40 | .18 |
| ❑ 78 | Bernie Williams | .60 | .25 |
| ❑ 79 | Barry Bonds | 1.00 | .45 |

| # | Player | MINT | NRMT |
|---|---|---|---|
| ❑ 80 | Ray Durham | .25 | .11 |
| ❑ 81 | Adrian Beltre | .25 | .11 |
| ❑ 82 | Ray Lankford | .25 | .11 |
| ❑ 83 | Carlos Delgado | .60 | .25 |
| ❑ 84 | Erubiel Durazo | .25 | .11 |
| ❑ 85 | Larry Walker | .25 | .11 |
| ❑ 86 | Edgardo Alfonzo | .25 | .11 |
| ❑ 87 | Rafael Palmeiro | .60 | .25 |
| ❑ 88 | Maggio Ordonez | .25 | .11 |
| ❑ 89 | Jeff Bagwell | .75 | .35 |
| ❑ 90 | Tony Gwynn | 1.25 | .55 |
| ❑ 91 | Norm Hutchins NG | 2.00 | .90 |
| ❑ 92 | Derrick Turnbow NG RC | 2.00 | .90 |
| ❑ 93 | Matt Riley NG | 2.00 | .90 |
| ❑ 94 | David Eckstein NG | 2.00 | .90 |
| ❑ 95 | Dernell Stenson NG | 2.00 | .90 |
| ❑ 96 | Joe Crede NG | 4.00 | 1.80 |
| ❑ 97 | Ben Petrick NG | 2.00 | .90 |
| ❑ 98 | Eric Munson NG | 4.00 | 1.80 |
| ❑ 99 | Pablo Ozuna NG | 2.00 | .90 |
| ❑ 100 | Josh Beckett NG | 4.00 | 1.80 |
| ❑ 101 | Aaron McNeal NG RC | 4.00 | 1.80 |
| ❑ 102 | Milton Bradley NG | 2.00 | .90 |
| ❑ 103 | Alex Escobar NG | 2.00 | .90 |
| ❑ 104 | Alfonso Soriano NG | 2.00 | .90 |
| ❑ 105 | Wily Pena NG | 2.00 | .90 |
| ❑ 106 | Nick Johnson NG | 2.00 | .90 |
| ❑ 107 | Adam Piatt NG | 4.00 | 1.80 |
| ❑ 108 | Pat Burrell NG | 6.00 | 2.70 |
| ❑ 109 | Rick Ankiel NG | 8.00 | 3.60 |
| ❑ 110 | Vernon Wells NG | 2.00 | .90 |
| ❑ 111 | Alex Rodriguez FG | 6.00 | 2.70 |
| ❑ 112 | Cal Ripken FG | 8.00 | 3.60 |
| ❑ 113 | Mark McGwire FG | 8.00 | 3.60 |
| ❑ 114 | Ken Griffey Jr. FG | 8.00 | 3.60 |
| ❑ 115 | Mike Piazza FG | 6.00 | 2.70 |
| ❑ 116 | Nomar Garciaparra FG | 6.00 | 2.70 |
| ❑ 117 | Derek Jeter FG | 8.00 | 3.60 |
| ❑ 118 | Chipper Jones FG | 5.00 | 2.20 |
| ❑ 119 | Sammy Sosa FG | 4.00 | 1.80 |
| ❑ 120 | Tony Gwynn FG | 4.00 | 1.80 |

## 2000 Fleer Greats of the Game

| | MINT | NRMT |
|---|---|---|
| COMPLETE SET (107) | 80.00 | 36.00 |

| # | Player | MINT | NRMT |
|---|---|---|---|
| ❑ 1 | Mickey Mantle | 15.00 | 6.75 |
| ❑ 2 | Gil Hodges | 2.00 | .90 |
| ❑ 3 | Monte Irvin | 1.25 | .55 |
| ❑ 4 | Satchel Paige | 2.50 | 1.10 |
| ❑ 5 | Roy Campanella | 2.50 | 1.10 |
| ❑ 6 | Richie Ashburn | 2.00 | .90 |
| ❑ 7 | Roger Maris | 2.50 | 1.10 |
| ❑ 8 | Ozzie Smith | 2.50 | 1.10 |
| ❑ 9 | Reggie Jackson | 2.50 | 1.10 |
| ❑ 10 | Eddie Mathews | 2.00 | .90 |
| ❑ 11 | Dave Righetti | .50 | .23 |
| ❑ 12 | Dave Winfield | 2.00 | .90 |
| ❑ 13 | Lou Whitaker | .75 | .35 |
| ❑ 14 | Phil Garner | .50 | .23 |
| ❑ 15 | Ron Cey | .75 | .35 |
| ❑ 16 | Brooks Robinson | 2.50 | 1.10 |
| ❑ 17 | Bruce Sutter | .75 | .35 |
| ❑ 18 | Dave Parker | .75 | .35 |
| ❑ 19 | Johnny Bench | 2.50 | 1.10 |
| ❑ 20 | Fernando Valenzuela | .75 | .35 |
| ❑ 21 | George Brett | 4.00 | 1.80 |
| ❑ 22 | Paul Molitor | 2.00 | .90 |
| ❑ 23 | Hoyt Wilhelm | 1.25 | .55 |
| ❑ 24 | Luis Aparicio | 2.00 | .90 |
| ❑ 25 | Frank White | .50 | .23 |
| ❑ 26 | Herb Score | .75 | .35 |
| ❑ 27 | Kirk Gibson | .75 | .35 |
| ❑ 28 | Mike Schmidt | 3.00 | 1.35 |
| ❑ 29 | Don Baylor | .50 | .23 |
| ❑ 30 | Joe Pepitone | .50 | .23 |
| ❑ 31 | Hal McRae | .50 | .23 |
| ❑ 32 | Lee Smith | .50 | .23 |
| ❑ 33 | Nolan Ryan | 10.00 | 4.50 |
| ❑ 34 | Bill Mazeroski | 1.25 | .55 |
| ❑ 35 | Bobby Doerr | 1.25 | .55 |
| ❑ 36 | Duke Snider | 2.50 | 1.10 |
| ❑ 37 | Dick Groat | .75 | .35 |
| ❑ 38 | Larry Doby | 1.25 | .55 |
| ❑ 39 | Kirby Puckett | 5.00 | 2.20 |
| ❑ 40 | Steve Carlton | 2.50 | 1.10 |
| ❑ 41 | Dennis Eckersley | .75 | .35 |
| ❑ 42 | Jim Bunning | 1.25 | .55 |
| ❑ 43 | Ron Guidry | .75 | .35 |
| ❑ 44 | Alan Trammell | 1.25 | .55 |
| ❑ 45 | Bob Feller | 2.00 | .90 |
| ❑ 46 | Dave Concepcion | .75 | .35 |
| ❑ 47 | Dwight Evans | .75 | .35 |
| ❑ 48 | Enos Slaughter | 1.25 | .55 |
| ❑ 49 | Tom Seaver | 2.50 | 1.10 |
| ❑ 50 | Tony Oliva | .75 | .35 |
| ❑ 51 | Mel Stottlemyre | .50 | .23 |
| ❑ 52 | Tommy John | .75 | .35 |
| ❑ 53 | Willie McCovey | 2.00 | .90 |
| ❑ 54 | Red Schoendienst | .75 | .35 |
| ❑ 55 | Gorman Thomas | .50 | .23 |
| ❑ 56 | Ralph Kiner | .75 | .35 |
| ❑ 57 | Robin Yount | 2.00 | .90 |
| ❑ 58 | Andre Dawson | 1.25 | .55 |
| ❑ 59 | Al Kaline | 2.00 | .90 |
| ❑ 60 | Dom DiMaggio | 1.25 | .55 |
| ❑ 61 | Juan Marichal | 2.00 | .90 |
| ❑ 62 | Jack Morris | .75 | .35 |
| ❑ 63 | Warren Spahn | 2.00 | .90 |
| ❑ 64 | Preacher Roe | .75 | .35 |
| ❑ 65 | Darrell Evans | .50 | .23 |
| ❑ 66 | Jim Bouton | .75 | .35 |
| ❑ 67 | Rocky Colavito | 2.00 | .90 |
| ❑ 68 | Bob Gibson | 2.00 | .90 |
| ❑ 69 | Whitey Ford | 2.00 | .90 |
| ❑ 70 | Moose Skowron | .75 | .35 |
| ❑ 71 | Boog Powell | .75 | .35 |
| ❑ 72 | Al Lopez | 1.25 | .55 |
| ❑ 73 | Lou Brock | 2.00 | .90 |
| ❑ 74 | Mickey Lolich | .50 | .23 |
| ❑ 75 | Rod Carew | 2.00 | .00 |
| ❑ 76 | Bob Lemon | 1.25 | .55 |
| ❑ 77 | Frank Howard | .75 | .35 |
| ❑ 78 | Phil Rizzuto | 2.00 | .90 |
| ❑ 79 | Carl Yastrzemski | 2.50 | 1.10 |
| ❑ 80 | Rico Carty | .50 | .23 |
| ❑ 81 | Jim Kaat | .75 | .35 |
| ❑ 82 | Bert Blyleven | .75 | .35 |
| ❑ 83 | George Kell | 1.25 | .55 |
| ❑ 84 | Jim Palmer | 2.00 | .90 |
| ❑ 85 | Maury Wills | .75 | .35 |
| ❑ 86 | Jim Rice | .75 | .35 |
| ❑ 87 | Joe Carter | .75 | .35 |
| ❑ 88 | Clete Boyer | .75 | .35 |
| ❑ 89 | Yogi Berra | 2.50 | 1.10 |
| ❑ 90 | Cecil Cooper | .50 | .23 |
| ❑ 91 | Davey Johnson | .75 | .35 |
| ❑ 92 | Lou Boudreau | 1.25 | .55 |
| ❑ 93 | Orlando Cepeda | 2.00 | .90 |
| ❑ 94 | Tommy Henrich | .75 | .35 |
| ❑ 95 | Hank Bauer | .75 | .35 |
| ❑ 96 | Don Larsen | .75 | .35 |
| ❑ 97 | Vida Blue | .50 | .23 |
| ❑ 98 | Ben Oglivie | .50 | .23 |
| ❑ 99 | Don Mattingly | 5.00 | 2.20 |
| ❑ 100 | Dale Murphy | 2.00 | .90 |
| ❑ 101 | Ferguson Jenkins | 2.00 | .90 |
| ❑ 102 | Bobby Bonds | .75 | .35 |
| ❑ 103 | Dick Allen | 1.25 | .55 |
| ❑ 104 | Stan Musial | 2.50 | 1.10 |
| ❑ 105 | Gaylord Perry | 2.00 | .90 |
| ❑ 106 | Willie Randolph | .75 | .35 |
| ❑ 107 | Willie Stargell | 1.25 | .55 |
| ❑ P33 | Nolan Ryan Promo | 4.00 | 1.80 |

## 1999 Fleer Mystique

| | MINT | NRMT |
|---|---|---|
| COMPLETE SET (160) | 400.00 | 180.00 |
| COMP.SHORT SET (100) | 40.00 | 18.00 |
| COMMON CARD (1-100) | .20 | .09 |
| COMMON SP (1-100) | .75 | .35 |
| COMMON CARD (101-150) | 5.00 | 2.20 |
| COMMON CARD (151-160) | 5.00 | 2.20 |

| # | Player | MINT | NRMT |
|---|---|---|---|
| ❑ 1 | Ken Griffey Jr. SP | 5.00 | 2.20 |
| ❑ 2 | Livan Hernandez | .20 | .09 |
| ❑ 3 | Jeff Kent | .50 | .23 |
| ❑ 4 | Brian Jordan | .30 | .14 |
| ❑ 5 | Kevin Young | .30 | .14 |
| ❑ 6 | Vinny Castilla | .30 | .14 |
| ❑ 7 | Orlando Hernandez SP | 1.00 | .45 |
| ❑ 8 | Bobby Abreu | .30 | .14 |
| ❑ 9 | Vladimir Guerrero SP | 2.00 | .90 |
| ❑ 10 | Chuck Knoblauch | .30 | .14 |
| ❑ 11 | Nomar Garciaparra SP | 4.00 | 1.80 |
| ❑ 12 | Jeff Bagwell | 1.00 | .45 |
| ❑ 13 | Todd Walker | .20 | .09 |
| ❑ 14 | Johnny Damon | .30 | .14 |
| ❑ 15 | Mike Caruso | .20 | .09 |
| ❑ 16 | Cliff Floyd | .30 | .14 |
| ❑ 17 | Andy Pettitte | .30 | .14 |
| ❑ 18 | Cal Ripken SP | 5.00 | 2.20 |
| ❑ 19 | Brian Giles | .30 | .14 |
| ❑ 20 | Robin Ventura | .30 | .14 |
| ❑ 21 | Alex Gonzalez | .20 | .09 |
| ❑ 22 | Randy Johnson | 1.00 | .45 |
| ❑ 23 | Raul Mondesi | .30 | .14 |
| ❑ 24 | Ken Caminiti | .30 | .14 |
| ❑ 25 | Tom Glavine | .75 | .35 |
| ❑ 26 | Derek Jeter SP | 5.00 | 2.20 |
| ❑ 27 | Carlos Delgado | .75 | .35 |
| ❑ 28 | Adrian Beltre | .30 | .14 |
| ❑ 29 | Tino Martinez | .30 | .14 |
| ❑ 30 | Todd Helton | 1.00 | .45 |
| ❑ 31 | Juan Gonzalez SP | 1.25 | .55 |
| ❑ 32 | Henry Rodriguez | .20 | .09 |
| ❑ 33 | Jim Thome | .50 | .23 |
| ❑ 34 | Paul O'Neill | .30 | .14 |
| ❑ 35 | Scott Rolen SP | 1.25 | .55 |
| ❑ 36 | Rafael Palmeiro | .75 | .35 |
| ❑ 37 | Will Clark | .75 | .35 |
| ❑ 38 | Todd Hundley | .20 | .09 |
| ❑ 39 | Andruw Jones SP | 1.25 | .55 |
| ❑ 40 | Rolando Arrojo | .20 | .09 |
| ❑ 41 | Barry Larkin | .75 | .35 |
| ❑ 42 | Tim Salmon | .30 | .14 |
| ❑ 43 | Rondell White | .30 | .14 |
| ❑ 44 | Curt Schilling | .30 | .14 |
| ❑ 45 | Chipper Jones SP | 3.00 | 1.35 |
| ❑ 46 | Jeromy Burnitz | .30 | .14 |
| ❑ 47 | Mo Vaughn | .30 | .14 |
| ❑ 48 | Tony Clark | .20 | .09 |
| ❑ 49 | Fernando Tatis | .30 | .14 |
| ❑ 50 | Dmitri Young | .30 | .14 |
| ❑ 51 | Wade Boggs | 1.00 | .45 |
| ❑ 52 | Rickey Henderson | 1.00 | .45 |
| ❑ 53 | Manny Ramirez SP | 1.50 | .70 |
| ❑ 54 | Edgar Martinez | .50 | .23 |
| ❑ 55 | Jason Giambi | .75 | .35 |

| | Card | MINT | NRMT |
|---|---|---|---|
| ❑ 56 | Jason Kendall | .30 | .14 |
| ❑ 57 | Eric Karros | .30 | .14 |
| ❑ 58 | Jose Canseco SP | 1.50 | .70 |
| ❑ 59 | Shawn Green | .75 | .35 |
| ❑ 60 | Ellis Burks | .30 | .14 |
| ❑ 61 | Derek Bell | .20 | .09 |
| ❑ 62 | Shannon Stewart | .30 | .14 |
| ❑ 63 | Roger Clemens SP | 2.50 | 1.10 |
| ❑ 64 | Sean Casey SP | 1.00 | .45 |
| ❑ 65 | Jose Offerman | .20 | .09 |
| ❑ 66 | Sammy Sosa SP | 2.50 | 1.10 |
| ❑ 67 | Frank Thomas SP | 2.50 | 1.10 |
| ❑ 68 | Tony Gwynn SP | 2.00 | .90 |
| ❑ 69 | Roberto Alomar | .75 | .35 |
| ❑ 70 | Mark McGwire SP | 5.00 | 2.20 |
| ❑ 71 | Troy Glaus | 1.25 | .55 |
| ❑ 72 | Ray Durham | .30 | .14 |
| ❑ 73 | Jeff Cirillo | .30 | .14 |
| ❑ 74 | Alex Rodriguez SP | 4.00 | 1.80 |
| ❑ 75 | Jose Cruz Jr. | .30 | .14 |
| ❑ 76 | Juan Encarnacion | .30 | .14 |
| ❑ 77 | Mark Grace | .75 | .35 |
| ❑ 78 | Barry Bonds SP | 2.00 | .90 |
| ❑ 79 | Ivan Rodriguez SP | 1.50 | .70 |
| ❑ 80 | Greg Vaughn | .30 | .14 |
| ❑ 81 | Greg Maddux SP | 3.00 | 1.35 |
| ❑ 82 | Albert Belle | .50 | .23 |
| ❑ 83 | John Olerud | .30 | .14 |
| ❑ 84 | Kenny Lofton | .30 | .14 |
| ❑ 85 | Bernie Williams | .75 | .35 |
| ❑ 86 | Matt Williams | .50 | .23 |
| ❑ 87 | Ray Lankford | .30 | .14 |
| ❑ 88 | Darin Erstad | .75 | .35 |
| ❑ 89 | Ben Grieve | .30 | .14 |
| ❑ 90 | Craig Biggio | .50 | .23 |
| ❑ 91 | Dean Palmer | .30 | .14 |
| ❑ 92 | Reggie Sanders | .20 | .09 |
| ❑ 93 | Dante Bichette | .30 | .14 |
| ❑ 94 | Pedro Martinez SP | 1.50 | .70 |
| ❑ 95 | Larry Walker | .30 | .14 |
| ❑ 96 | David Wells | .30 | .14 |
| ❑ 97 | Travis Lee SP | .75 | .35 |
| ❑ 98 | Mike Piazza SP | 4.00 | 1.80 |
| ❑ 99 | Mike Mussina | .75 | .35 |
| ❑ 100 | Kevin Brown | .50 | .23 |
| ❑ 101 | Ruben Mateo PROS | 5.00 | 2.20 |
| ❑ 102 | Roberto Ramirez PROS RC | 5.00 | 2.20 |
| ❑ 103 | Glen Barker PROS RC | 5.00 | 2.20 |
| ❑ 104 | Clay Bellinger PROS RC | 5.00 | 2.20 |
| ❑ 105 | Carlos Guillen PROS | 5.00 | 2.20 |
| ❑ 106 | S.Schoeneweis PROS | 5.00 | 2.20 |
| ❑ 107 | C.Gubanich PROS RC | 5.00 | 2.20 |
| ❑ 108 | Scott Williamson PROS | 5.00 | 2.20 |
| ❑ 109 | Edwards Guzman PROS RC | 5.00 | 2.20 |
| ❑ 110 | A.J. Burnett PROS RC | 10.00 | 4.50 |
| ❑ 111 | Jeremy Giambi PROS | 5.00 | 2.20 |
| ❑ 112 | Trot Nixon PROS | 5.00 | 2.20 |
| ❑ 113 | J.D. Drew PROS | 10.00 | 4.50 |
| ❑ 114 | Roy Halladay PROS | 5.00 | 2.20 |
| ❑ 115 | Jose Macias PROS RC | 5.00 | 2.20 |
| ❑ 116 | Corey Koskie PROS | 5.00 | 2.20 |
| ❑ 117 | Ryan Rupe PROS RC | 6.00 | 2.70 |
| ❑ 118 | Scott Hunter PROS RC | 5.00 | 2.20 |
| ❑ 119 | Rob Fick PROS | 5.00 | 2.20 |
| ❑ 120 | M.Christensen PROS | 5.00 | 2.20 |
| ❑ 121 | Carlos Febles PROS | 5.00 | 2.20 |
| ❑ 122 | Gabe Kapler PROS | 5.00 | 2.20 |
| ❑ 123 | Jeff Liefer PROS | 5.00 | 2.20 |
| ❑ 124 | Warren Morris PROS | 5.00 | 2.20 |
| ❑ 125 | Chris Pritchett PROS | 5.00 | 2.20 |
| ❑ 126 | Torii Hunter PROS | 5.00 | 2.20 |
| ❑ 127 | Armando Rios PROS | 5.00 | 2.20 |
| ❑ 128 | Ricky Ledee PROS | 5.00 | 2.20 |
| ❑ 129 | Kelly Dransfeldt PROS RC | 5.00 | 2.20 |
| ❑ 130 | Jeff Zimmerman PROS RC | 5.00 | 2.20 |
| ❑ 131 | Eric Chavez PROS | 5.00 | 2.20 |
| ❑ 132 | Freddy Garcia PROS RC | 20.00 | 9.00 |
| ❑ 133 | Jose Jimenez PROS | 5.00 | 2.20 |
| ❑ 134 | Pat Burrell PROS RC | 100.00 | 45.00 |
| ❑ 135 | Joe McEwing PROS RC | 5.00 | 2.20 |
| ❑ 136 | Kris Benson PROS | 5.00 | 2.20 |
| ❑ 137 | Joe Mays PROS RC | 6.00 | 2.70 |
| ❑ 138 | Rafael Roque PROS RC | 5.00 | 2.20 |
| ❑ 139 | Cristian Guzman PROS | 5.00 | 2.20 |
| ❑ 140 | Michael Barrett PROS | 5.00 | 2.20 |
| ❑ 141 | Doug Mientkiewicz PROS RC | 5.00 | 2.20 |
| ❑ 142 | Jeff Weaver PROS RC | 10.00 | 4.50 |
| ❑ 143 | Mike Lowell PROS | 5.00 | 2.20 |
| ❑ 144 | Jason Phillips PROS RC | 5.00 | 2.20 |
| ❑ 145 | Marlon Anderson PROS | 5.00 | 2.20 |
| ❑ 146 | Brett Hinchliffe PROS RC | 5.00 | 2.20 |
| ❑ 147 | Matt Clement PROS | 5.00 | 2.20 |
| ❑ 148 | Terrence Long PROS | 5.00 | 2.20 |
| ❑ 149 | Carlos Beltran PROS | 5.00 | 2.20 |
| ❑ 150 | Preston Wilson PROS | 5.00 | 2.20 |
| ❑ 151 | Ken Griffey Jr. STAR | 15.00 | 6.75 |
| ❑ 152 | Mark McGwire STAR | 15.00 | 6.75 |
| ❑ 153 | Sammy Sosa STAR | 8.00 | 3.60 |
| ❑ 154 | Mike Piazza STAR | 12.00 | 5.50 |
| ❑ 155 | Alex Rodriguez STAR | 12.00 | 5.50 |
| ❑ 156 | Nomar Garciaparra STAR | 12.00 | 5.50 |
| ❑ 157 | Cal Ripken STAR | 15.00 | 6.75 |
| ❑ 158 | Greg Maddux STAR | 10.00 | 4.50 |
| ❑ 159 | Derek Jeter STAR | 15.00 | 6.75 |
| ❑ 160 | Juan Gonzalez STAR | .75 | .35 |
| ❑ P113 | J.D. Drew Promo | 1.00 | .45 |

## 2000 Fleer Mystique

| | MINT | NRMT |
|---|---|---|
| COMPLETE SET (175) | 700.00 | 325.00 |
| COMP.SHORT SET (125) | 40.00 | 18.00 |
| COMMON CARD (1-125) | .30 | .14 |
| MINOR STARS 1-125 | .50 | .23 |
| SEMISTARS 1-125 | .75 | .35 |
| UNLISTED STARS 1-125 | 1.25 | .55 |
| COMMON CARD (126-175) | 10.00 | 4.50 |
| MINOR STARS 126-175 | 10.00 | 4.50 |
| SEMISTARS 126-175 | 10.00 | 4.50 |
| UNLISTED STARS 126-175 | 12.00 | 5.50 |

| | Card | MINT | NRMT |
|---|---|---|---|
| ❑ 1 | Derek Jeter | 5.00 | 2.20 |
| ❑ 2 | David Justice | .75 | .35 |
| ❑ 3 | Kevin Brown | .75 | .35 |
| ❑ 4 | Jason Giambi | 1.25 | .55 |
| ❑ 5 | Jose Canseco | 1.50 | .70 |
| ❑ 6 | Mark Grace | 1.25 | .55 |
| ❑ 7 | Hideo Nomo | 1.25 | .55 |
| ❑ 8 | Edgardo Alfonzo | .50 | .23 |
| ❑ 9 | Barry Bonds | 2.00 | .90 |
| ❑ 10 | Pedro Martinez | 1.50 | .70 |
| ❑ 11 | Juan Gonzalez | 1.25 | .55 |
| ❑ 12 | Vladimir Guerrero | 2.00 | .90 |
| ❑ 13 | Chuck Finley | .50 | .23 |
| ❑ 14 | Brian Jordan | .50 | .23 |
| ❑ 15 | Richie Sexson | .50 | .23 |
| ❑ 16 | Chan Ho Park | .50 | .23 |
| ❑ 17 | Tim Hudson | 1.25 | .55 |
| ❑ 18 | Fred McGriff | .75 | .35 |
| ❑ 19 | Darin Erstad | 1.25 | .55 |
| ❑ 20 | Chris Singleton | .50 | .23 |
| ❑ 21 | Jeff Bagwell | 1.50 | .70 |
| ❑ 22 | David Cone | .50 | .23 |
| ❑ 23 | Edgar Martinez | .75 | .35 |
| ❑ 24 | Greg Maddux | 3.00 | 1.35 |
| ❑ 25 | Jim Thome | .75 | .35 |
| ❑ 26 | Eric Karros | .50 | .23 |
| ❑ 27 | Bob Abreu | .50 | .23 |
| ❑ 28 | Greg Vaughn | .50 | .23 |
| ❑ 29 | Kevin Millwood | .50 | .23 |
| ❑ 30 | Omar Vizquel | .50 | .23 |
| ❑ 31 | Marquis Grissom | .30 | .14 |
| ❑ 32 | Mike Lieberthal | .50 | .23 |
| ❑ 33 | Gabe Kapler | .50 | .23 |
| ❑ 34 | Brady Anderson | .50 | .23 |
| ❑ 35 | Jeff Cirillo | .50 | .23 |
| ❑ 36 | Geoff Jenkins | .50 | .23 |
| ❑ 37 | Scott Rolen | 1.25 | .55 |
| ❑ 38 | Rafael Palmeiro | 1.25 | .55 |
| ❑ 39 | Randy Johnson | 1.50 | .70 |
| ❑ 40 | Barry Larkin | 1.25 | .55 |
| ❑ 41 | Johnny Damon | .50 | .23 |
| ❑ 42 | Andy Pettitte | .50 | .23 |
| ❑ 43 | Mark McGwire | 5.00 | 2.20 |
| ❑ 44 | Albert Belle | .75 | .35 |
| ❑ 45 | Derrick Gibson | .30 | .14 |
| ❑ 46 | Corey Koskie | .30 | .14 |
| ❑ 47 | Curt Schilling | .50 | .23 |
| ❑ 48 | Ivan Rodriguez | 1.50 | .70 |
| ❑ 49 | Mike Mussina | 1.25 | .55 |
| ❑ 50 | Todd Helton | 1.50 | .70 |
| ❑ 51 | Matt Lawton | .50 | .23 |
| ❑ 52 | Jason Kendall | .50 | .23 |
| ❑ 53 | Kenny Rogers | .30 | .14 |
| ❑ 54 | Cal Ripken | 5.00 | 2.20 |
| ❑ 55 | Larry Walker | .50 | .23 |
| ❑ 56 | Eric Milton | .50 | .23 |
| ❑ 57 | Warren Morris | .30 | .14 |
| ❑ 58 | Carlos Delgado | 1.25 | .55 |
| ❑ 59 | Kerry Wood | .50 | .23 |
| ❑ 60 | Cliff Floyd | .50 | .23 |
| ❑ 61 | Mike Piazza | 4.00 | 1.80 |
| ❑ 62 | Jeff Kent | .75 | .35 |
| ❑ 63 | Sammy Sosa | 2.50 | 1.10 |
| ❑ 64 | Alex Fernandez | .30 | .14 |
| ❑ 65 | Mike Hampton | .50 | .23 |
| ❑ 66 | Livan Hernandez | .30 | .14 |
| ❑ 67 | Matt Williams | .75 | .35 |
| ❑ 68 | Roberto Alomar | 1.25 | .55 |
| ❑ 69 | Jermaine Dye | .50 | .23 |
| ❑ 70 | Bernie Williams | 1.25 | .55 |
| ❑ 71 | Edgar Martinez | .75 | .35 |
| ❑ 72 | Tom Glavine | 1.25 | .55 |
| ❑ 73 | Bartolo Colon | .50 | .23 |
| ❑ 74 | Jason Varitek | .50 | .23 |
| ❑ 75 | Eric Chavez | .50 | .23 |
| ❑ 76 | Fernando Tatis | .50 | .23 |
| ❑ 77 | Adrian Beltre | .50 | .23 |
| ❑ 78 | Paul Konerko | .50 | .23 |
| ❑ 79 | Mike Lowell | .50 | .23 |
| ❑ 80 | Robin Ventura | .50 | .23 |
| ❑ 81 | Russ Ortiz | .30 | .14 |
| ❑ 82 | Troy Glaus | 1.50 | .70 |
| ❑ 83 | Frank Thomas | 2.50 | 1.10 |
| ❑ 84 | Craig Biggio | 1.25 | .55 |
| ❑ 85 | Orlando Hernandez | .50 | .23 |
| ❑ 86 | John Olerud | .50 | .23 |
| ❑ 87 | Chipper Jones | 3.00 | 1.35 |
| ❑ 88 | Manny Ramirez | 1.50 | .70 |
| ❑ 89 | Shawn Green | 1.25 | .55 |
| ❑ 90 | Ben Grieve | .50 | .23 |
| ❑ 91 | Vinny Castilla | .50 | .23 |
| ❑ 92 | Tim Salmon | .50 | .23 |
| ❑ 93 | Dante Bichette | .50 | .23 |
| ❑ 94 | Ken Caminiti | .50 | .23 |
| ❑ 95 | Andruw Jones | 1.25 | .55 |
| ❑ 96 | Alex Rodriguez | 4.00 | 1.80 |
| ❑ 97 | Erubiel Durazo | .50 | .23 |
| ❑ 98 | Sean Casey | .50 | .23 |
| ❑ 99 | Carlos Beltran | .50 | .23 |
| ❑ 100 | Paul O'Neill | .50 | .23 |
| ❑ 101 | Ray Lankford | .50 | .23 |
| ❑ 102 | Troy O'Leary | .30 | .14 |
| ❑ 103 | Bobby Higginson | .30 | .14 |
| ❑ 104 | Rondell White | .50 | .23 |
| ❑ 105 | Tony Gwynn | 2.50 | 1.10 |
| ❑ 106 | Jim Edmonds | 1.25 | .55 |
| ❑ 107 | Magglio Ordonez | .50 | .23 |
| ❑ 108 | Preston Wilson | .50 | .23 |
| ❑ 109 | Roger Clemens | 2.50 | 1.10 |
| ❑ 110 | Ken Griffey Jr. | 5.00 | 2.20 |
| ❑ 111 | Nomar Garciaparra | 4.00 | 1.80 |
| ❑ 112 | Juan Encarnacion | .50 | .23 |
| ❑ 113 | Michael Barrett | .30 | .14 |
| ❑ 114 | Matt Clement | .30 | .14 |
| ❑ 115 | David Wells | .50 | .23 |
| ❑ 116 | Mo Vaughn | .50 | .23 |
| ❑ 117 | Mike Cameron | .30 | .14 |
| ❑ 118 | Jose Lima | .30 | .14 |
| ❑ 119 | Tino Martinez | .50 | .23 |

| | Card | Mint | NrMt |
|---|---|---|---|
| ❑ 120 | J.D. Drew | 1.25 | .55 |
| ❑ 121 | Carl Everett | .50 | .23 |
| ❑ 122 | Tony Clark | .30 | .14 |
| ❑ 123 | Brad Radke | .30 | .14 |
| ❑ 124 | Kevin Young | .30 | .14 |
| ❑ 125 | Raul Mondesi | .50 | .23 |
| ❑ 126 | Cole Liniak PROS | 10.00 | 4.50 |
| ❑ 127 | Alfonso Soriano PROS | 10.00 | 4.50 |
| ❑ 128 | Lance Berkman PROS | 10.00 | 4.50 |
| ❑ 129 | Danny Young PROS RC | 10.00 | 4.50 |
| ❑ 130 | Francisco Cordero PROS | 10.00 | 4.50 |
| ❑ 131 | Robert Fick PROS | 10.00 | 4.50 |
| ❑ 132 | Matt LeCroy PROS | 10.00 | 4.50 |
| ❑ 133 | Adam Piatt PROS | 12.00 | 5.50 |
| ❑ 134 | Derrick Turnbow PROS RC | 10.00 | 4.50 |
| ❑ 135 | Mark Quinn PROS | 10.00 | 4.50 |
| ❑ 136 | Kip Wells PROS | 10.00 | 4.50 |
| ❑ 137 | Rob Bell PROS | 10.00 | 4.50 |
| ❑ 138 | Brad Penny PROS | 10.00 | 4.50 |
| ❑ 139 | Pat Burrell PROS | 20.00 | 9.00 |
| ❑ 140 | Danys Baez PROS RC | 12.00 | 5.50 |
| ❑ 141 | Chad Hermansen PROS | 10.00 | 4.50 |
| ❑ 142 | Steve Lomasney PROS | 10.00 | 4.50 |
| ❑ 143 | Peter Bergeron PROS | 10.00 | 4.50 |
| ❑ 144 | Jimmy Anderson PROS | 10.00 | 4.50 |
| ❑ 145 | Mike Darr PROS | 10.00 | 4.50 |
| ❑ 146 | Jacob Cruz PROS | 10.00 | 4.50 |
| ❑ 147 | Kazuhiro Sasaki PROS RC | 40.00 | 18.00 |
| ❑ 148 | Ben Petrick PROS | 10.00 | 4.50 |
| ❑ 149 | Rick Ankiel PROS | 25.00 | 11.00 |
| ❑ 150 | Aaron McNeal PROS RC | 12.00 | 5.50 |
| ❑ 151 | Octavio Dotel PROS | 10.00 | 4.50 |
| ❑ 152 | Juan Pena PROS | 10.00 | 4.50 |
| ❑ 153 | Nick Johnson PROS | 10.00 | 4.50 |
| ❑ 154 | Wilton Veras PROS | 10.00 | 4.50 |
| ❑ 155 | Wily Pena PROS | 10.00 | 4.50 |
| ❑ 156 | Mark Mulder PROS | 10.00 | 4.50 |
| ❑ 157 | Daryle Ward PROS | 10.00 | 4.50 |
| ❑ 158 | Chad Durbin PROS RC | 10.00 | 4.50 |
| ❑ 159 | Angel Pena PROS | 10.00 | 4.50 |
| ❑ 160 | DeWayne Wise PROS | 10.00 | 4.50 |
| ❑ 161 | Tarrik Brock PROS | 10.00 | 4.50 |
| ❑ 162 | Marcus Jensen PROS | 10.00 | 4.50 |
| ❑ 163 | Kevin Barker PROS | 10.00 | 4.50 |
| ❑ 164 | B.J. Ryan PROS | 10.00 | 4.50 |
| ❑ 165 | Cesar King PROS | 10.00 | 4.50 |
| ❑ 166 | Geoff Blum PROS | 10.00 | 4.50 |
| ❑ 167 | Ruben Mateo PROS | 10.00 | 4.50 |
| ❑ 168 | Ramon Ortiz PROS | 10.00 | 4.50 |
| ❑ 169 | Eric Munson PROS | 12.00 | 5.50 |
| ❑ 170 | Josh Beckett PROS | 12.00 | 5.50 |
| ❑ 171 | Rafael Furcal PROS | 30.00 | 13.50 |
| ❑ 172 | Matt Riley PROS | 10.00 | 4.50 |
| ❑ 173 | Johan Santana PROS RC | 10.00 | 4.50 |
| ❑ 174 | Mark Johnson PROS | 10.00 | 4.50 |
| ❑ 175 | Adam Kennedy PROS | 10.00 | 4.50 |
| ❑ P54 | Cal Ripken PROMO | 3.00 | 1.35 |
| ❑ DW1 | D.Winfield Ball/20 | | |
| ❑ DW2 | D.Winfield Helmet/40 | 150.00 | 70.00 |

## 2000 Fleer Showcase

| | MINT | NRMT |
|---|---|---|
| COMPLETE SET (140) | 600.00 | 275.00 |
| COMP.SET w/o SP's (100) | 30.00 | 13.50 |
| COMMON CARD (1-100) | .25 | .11 |
| MINOR STARS 1-100 | .40 | .18 |
| SEMISTARS 1-100 | .60 | .25 |
| UNLISTED STARS 1-100 | 1.00 | .45 |
| COMMON CARD (101-115) | 15.00 | 6.75 |
| MINOR STARS 101-115 | 15.00 | 6.75 |
| SEMISTARS 101-115 | 15.00 | 6.75 |
| UNLISTED STARS 101-115 | 20.00 | 9.00 |
| COMMON CARD (116-140) | 10.00 | 4.50 |
| MINOR STARS 116-140 | 10.00 | 4.50 |
| SEMISTARS 116-140 | 10.00 | 4.50 |
| UNLISTED STARS 116-140 | 15.00 | 6.75 |

| | Card | Mint | NrMt |
|---|---|---|---|
| ❑ 1 | Alex Rodriguez | 3.00 | 1.35 |
| ❑ 2 | Derek Jeter | 4.00 | 1.80 |
| ❑ 3 | Jeromy Burnitz | .40 | .18 |
| ❑ 4 | John Olerud | .40 | .18 |
| ❑ 5 | Paul Konerko | .40 | .18 |
| ❑ 6 | Johnny Damon | .40 | .18 |
| ❑ 7 | Curt Schilling | .40 | .18 |
| ❑ 8 | Barry Larkin | 1.00 | .45 |
| ❑ 9 | Adrian Beltre | .40 | .18 |
| ❑ 10 | Scott Rolen | .60 | .25 |
| ❑ 11 | Carlos Delgado | 1.00 | .45 |
| ❑ 12 | Pedro Martinez | 1.25 | .55 |
| ❑ 13 | Todd Helton | 1.25 | .55 |
| ❑ 14 | Jacque Jones | .40 | .18 |
| ❑ 15 | Jeff Kent | .60 | .25 |
| ❑ 16 | Darin Erstad | 1.00 | .45 |
| ❑ 17 | Juan Encarnacion | .40 | .18 |
| ❑ 18 | Roger Clemens | 2.00 | .90 |
| ❑ 19 | Tony Gwynn | 2.00 | .90 |
| ❑ 20 | Nomar Garciaparra | 3.00 | 1.35 |
| ❑ 21 | Roberto Alomar | 1.00 | .45 |
| ❑ 22 | Matt Lawton | .40 | .18 |
| ❑ 23 | Rich Aurilia | .25 | .11 |
| ❑ 24 | Charles Johnson | .40 | .18 |
| ❑ 25 | Jim Thome | .60 | .25 |
| ❑ 26 | Eric Milton | .40 | .18 |
| ❑ 27 | Barry Bonds | 1.50 | .70 |
| ❑ 28 | Albert Belle | .60 | .25 |
| ❑ 29 | Travis Fryman | .40 | .18 |
| ❑ 30 | Ken Griffey Jr. | 4.00 | 1.80 |
| ❑ 31 | Phil Nevin | .40 | .18 |
| ❑ 32 | Chipper Jones | 2.50 | 1.10 |
| ❑ 33 | Craig Biggio | .60 | .25 |
| ❑ 34 | Mike Hampton | .40 | .18 |
| ❑ 35 | Fred McGriff | .60 | .25 |
| ❑ 36 | Cal Ripken | 4.00 | 1.80 |
| ❑ 37 | Manny Ramirez | 1.25 | .55 |
| ❑ 38 | Jose Vidro | .40 | .18 |
| ❑ 39 | Trevor Hoffman | .40 | .18 |
| ❑ 40 | Tom Glavine | 1.00 | .45 |
| ❑ 41 | Frank Thomas | 2.00 | .90 |
| ❑ 42 | Chris Widger | .25 | .11 |
| ❑ 43 | J.D. Drew | 1.00 | .45 |
| ❑ 44 | Andres Galarraga | .60 | .25 |
| ❑ 45 | Pokey Reese | .40 | .18 |
| ❑ 46 | Mike Piazza | 3.00 | 1.35 |
| ❑ 47 | Kevin Young | .25 | .11 |
| ❑ 48 | Sean Casey | .40 | .18 |
| ❑ 49 | Carlos Beltran | .40 | .18 |
| ❑ 50 | Jason Kendall | .40 | .18 |
| ❑ 51 | Vladimir Guerrero | 1.50 | .70 |
| ❑ 52 | Jermaine Dye | .40 | .18 |
| ❑ 53 | Brian Giles | .40 | .18 |
| ❑ 54 | Andruw Jones | 1.00 | .45 |
| ❑ 55 | Richard Hidalgo | .40 | .18 |
| ❑ 56 | Robin Ventura | .40 | .18 |
| ❑ 57 | Ivan Rodriguez | 1.25 | .55 |
| ❑ 58 | Greg Maddux | 2.50 | 1.10 |
| ❑ 59 | Billy Wagner | .25 | .11 |
| ❑ 60 | Ruben Mateo | .40 | .18 |
| ❑ 61 | Troy Glaus | 1.25 | .55 |
| ❑ 62 | Dean Palmer | .40 | .18 |
| ❑ 63 | Eric Chavez | .40 | .18 |
| ❑ 64 | Edgar Martinez | .40 | .18 |
| ❑ 65 | Randy Johnson | 1.25 | .55 |
| ❑ 66 | Preston Wilson | .40 | .18 |
| ❑ 67 | Orlando Hernandez | .40 | .18 |
| ❑ 68 | Jim Edmonds | 1.00 | .45 |
| ❑ 69 | Carl Everett | .40 | .18 |
| ❑ 70 | Larry Walker | .40 | .18 |
| ❑ 71 | Ron Belliard | .25 | .11 |
| ❑ 72 | Sammy Sosa | 2.00 | .90 |
| ❑ 73 | Matt Williams | .40 | .18 |
| ❑ 74 | Cliff Floyd | .40 | .18 |
| ❑ 75 | Bernie Williams | 1.00 | .45 |
| ❑ 76 | Fernando Tatis | .40 | .18 |
| ❑ 77 | Steve Finley | .40 | .18 |
| ❑ 78 | Jeff Bagwell | 1.25 | .55 |
| ❑ 79 | Edgardo Alfonzo | .40 | .18 |
| ❑ 80 | Jose Canseco | 1.25 | .55 |
| ❑ 81 | Magglio Ordonez | .40 | .18 |
| ❑ 82 | Shawn Green | 1.00 | .45 |
| ❑ 83 | Bobby Abreu | .40 | .18 |
| ❑ 84 | Tony Batista | .40 | .18 |
| ❑ 85 | Mo Vaughn | .40 | .18 |
| ❑ 86 | Juan Gonzalez | 1.00 | .45 |
| ❑ 87 | Paul O'Neill | .40 | .18 |
| ❑ 88 | Mark McGwire | 4.00 | 1.80 |
| ❑ 89 | Mark Grace | 1.00 | .45 |
| ❑ 90 | Kevin Brown | .40 | .18 |
| ❑ 91 | Ben Grieve | .40 | .18 |
| ❑ 92 | Shannon Stewart | .40 | .18 |
| ❑ 93 | Erubiel Durazo | .40 | .18 |
| ❑ 94 | Antonio Alfonseca | .25 | .11 |
| ❑ 95 | Jeff Cirillo | .40 | .18 |
| ❑ 96 | Greg Vaughn | .40 | .18 |
| ❑ 97 | Kerry Wood | .40 | .18 |
| ❑ 98 | Geoff Jenkins | .40 | .18 |
| ❑ 99 | Jason Giambi | 1.00 | .45 |
| ❑ 100 | Rafael Palmeiro | 1.00 | .45 |
| ❑ 101 | Rafael Furcal PROS | 40.00 | 18.00 |
| ❑ 102 | Pablo Ozuna PROS | 15.00 | 6.75 |
| ❑ 103 | Brad Penny PROS | 15.00 | 6.75 |
| ❑ 104 | Mark Mulder PROS | 15.00 | 6.75 |
| ❑ 105 | Adam Piatt PROS | 20.00 | 9.00 |
| ❑ 106 | Mike Lamb PROS RC | 15.00 | 6.75 |
| ❑ 107 | Kazuhiro Sasaki PROS RC | 60.00 | 27.00 |
| ❑ 108 | Aaron McNeal PROS RC | 20.00 | 9.00 |
| ❑ 109 | Pat Burrell PROS | 30.00 | 13.50 |
| ❑ 110 | Rick Ankiel PROS | 40.00 | 18.00 |
| ❑ 111 | Eric Munson PROS | 20.00 | 9.00 |
| ❑ 112 | Josh Beckett PROS | 20.00 | 9.00 |
| ❑ 113 | Adam Kennedy PROS | 15.00 | 6.75 |
| ❑ 114 | Alex Escobar PROS | 15.00 | 6.75 |
| ❑ 115 | Chad Hermansen PROS | 15.00 | 6.75 |
| ❑ 116 | Kip Wells PROS | 10.00 | 4.50 |
| ❑ 117 | Matt LeCroy PROS | 10.00 | 4.50 |
| ❑ 118 | Julio Ramirez PROS | 10.00 | 4.50 |
| ❑ 119 | Ben Petrick PROS | 10.00 | 4.50 |
| ❑ 120 | Nick Johnson PROS | 10.00 | 4.50 |
| ❑ 121 | Gookie Dawkins PROS | 10.00 | 4.50 |
| ❑ 122 | Julio Zuleta PROS RC | 10.00 | 4.50 |
| ❑ 123 | Alfonso Soriano PROS | 10.00 | 4.50 |
| ❑ 124 | Keith McDonald PROS RC | 10.00 | 4.50 |
| ❑ 125 | Kory DeHaan PROS | 10.00 | 4.50 |
| ❑ 126 | Vernon Wells PROS | 10.00 | 4.50 |
| ❑ 127 | Dernell Stenson PROS | 10.00 | 4.50 |
| ❑ 128 | David Eckstein PROS | 10.00 | 4.50 |
| ❑ 129 | Robert Fick PROS | 10.00 | 4.50 |
| ❑ 130 | Cole Liniak PROS | 10.00 | 4.50 |
| ❑ 131 | Mark Quinn PROS | 10.00 | 4.50 |
| ❑ 132 | Eric Gagne PROS | 10.00 | 4.50 |
| ❑ 133 | Wily Mo Pena PROS | 10.00 | 4.50 |
| ❑ 134 | Andy Thompson PROS RC | 10.00 | 4.50 |
| ❑ 135 | Steve Sisco PROS RC | 10.00 | 4.50 |
| ❑ 136 | Paul Rigdon PROS RC | 10.00 | 4.50 |
| ❑ 137 | Rob Bell PROS | 10.00 | 4.50 |
| ❑ 138 | Carlos Guillen PROS | 10.00 | 4.50 |
| ❑ 139 | Jimmy Rollins PROS | 10.00 | 4.50 |
| ❑ 140 | Jason Conti PROS | 10.00 | 4.50 |

## 2000 Impact

| | MINT | NRMT |
|---|---|---|
| COMPLETE SET (200) | 15.00 | 6.75 |
| ❑ 1 Cal Ripken | 1.50 | .70 |
| ❑ 2 Jose Canseco | .50 | .23 |
| ❑ 3 Manny Ramirez | .50 | .23 |
| ❑ 4 Bernie Williams | .40 | .18 |
| ❑ 5 Troy Glaus | .50 | .23 |
| ❑ 6 Jeff Bagwell | .50 | .23 |
| ❑ 7 Corey Koskie | .10 | .05 |
| ❑ 8 Barry Larkin | .40 | .18 |
| ❑ 9 Mark Quinn | .15 | .07 |
| ❑ 10 Russ Ortiz | .10 | .05 |
| ❑ 11 Tim Salmon | .15 | .07 |
| ❑ 12 Preston Wilson | .15 | .07 |
| ❑ 13 Mo Vaughn | .15 | .07 |
| ❑ 14 Ray Lankford | .10 | .05 |
| ❑ 15 Sterling Hitchcock | .10 | .05 |
| ❑ 16 Al Leiter | .10 | .05 |
| ❑ 17 Jim Morris | .10 | .05 |
| ❑ 18 Freddy Garcia | .15 | .07 |
| ❑ 19 Adrian Beltre | .15 | .07 |
| ❑ 20 Eric Chavez | .15 | .07 |
| ❑ 21 Robinson Cancel | .10 | .05 |
| ❑ 22 Edgar Renteria | .10 | .05 |
| ❑ 23 John Jaha | .10 | .05 |
| ❑ 24 Chuck Finley | .15 | .07 |
| ❑ 25 Andres Galarraga | .25 | .11 |
| ❑ 26 Paul Byrd | .10 | .05 |
| ❑ 27 John Halama | .10 | .05 |
| ❑ 28 Eric Karros | .15 | .07 |
| ❑ 29 Mike Piazza | 1.25 | .55 |
| ❑ 30 Ryan Rupe | .10 | .05 |
| ❑ 31 Frank Thomas | .75 | .35 |
| ❑ 32 Randy Velarde | .10 | .05 |
| ❑ 33 Bobby Abreu | .15 | .07 |
| ❑ 34 Randy Johnson | .50 | .23 |
| ❑ 35 Matt Williams | .25 | .11 |
| ❑ 36 Tony Gwynn | .75 | .35 |
| ❑ 37 Dean Palmer | .15 | .07 |
| ❑ 38 Aaron Sele | .10 | .05 |
| ❑ 39 Rondell White | .15 | .07 |
| ❑ 40 Erubiel Durazo | .15 | .07 |
| ❑ 41 Curt Schilling | .15 | .07 |
| ❑ 42 Kip Wells | .10 | .05 |
| ❑ 43 Craig Biggio | .25 | .11 |
| ❑ 44 Tom Glavine | .40 | .18 |
| ❑ 45 Trevor Hoffman | .15 | .07 |
| ❑ 46 Greg Vaughn | .15 | .07 |
| ❑ 47 Edgar Martinez | .25 | .11 |
| ❑ 48 Magglio Ordonez | .25 | .11 |
| ❑ 49 Mark Mulder | .10 | .05 |
| ❑ 50 John Rocker | .15 | .07 |
| ❑ 51 Kenny Rogers | .10 | .05 |
| ❑ 52 Gary Sheffield | .40 | .18 |
| ❑ 53 Brian Simmons | .10 | .05 |
| ❑ 54 Tony Womack | .10 | .05 |
| ❑ 55 Ken Caminiti | .15 | .07 |
| ❑ 56 Jeff Cirillo | .15 | .07 |
| ❑ 57 Ray Durham | .15 | .07 |
| ❑ 58 Mike Lieberthal | .15 | .07 |
| ❑ 59 Ruben Mateo | .15 | .07 |
| ❑ 60 Mike Cameron | .10 | .05 |
| ❑ 61 Rusty Greer | .15 | .07 |
| ❑ 62 Alex Rodriguez | 1.25 | .55 |
| ❑ 63 Robin Ventura | .15 | .07 |
| ❑ 64 Pokey Reese | .15 | .07 |
| ❑ 65 Jose Lima | .10 | .05 |
| ❑ 66 Neifi Perez | .10 | .05 |
| ❑ 67 Rafael Palmeiro | .40 | .18 |
| ❑ 68 Scott Rolen | .40 | .18 |
| ❑ 69 Mike Hampton | .15 | .07 |
| ❑ 70 Sammy Sosa | .75 | .35 |
| ❑ 71 Mike Stanley | .10 | .05 |
| ❑ 72 Dan Wilson | .10 | .05 |
| ❑ 73 Kerry Wood | .15 | .07 |
| ❑ 74 Mike Mussina | .40 | .18 |
| ❑ 75 Masato Yoshii | .10 | .05 |
| ❑ 76 Peter Bergeron | .10 | .05 |
| ❑ 77 Carlos Delgado | .40 | .18 |
| ❑ 78 Juan Encarnacion | .15 | .07 |
| ❑ 79 Nomar Garciaparra | 1.25 | .55 |
| ❑ 80 Jason Kendall | .15 | .07 |
| ❑ 81 Pedro Martinez | .50 | .23 |
| ❑ 82 Darin Erstad | .40 | .18 |
| ❑ 83 Larry Walker | .15 | .07 |
| ❑ 84 Rick Ankiel | .75 | .35 |
| ❑ 85 Scott Erickson | .10 | .05 |
| ❑ 86 Roger Clemens | .75 | .35 |
| ❑ 87 Matt Lawton | .15 | .07 |
| ❑ 88 Jon Lieber | .10 | .05 |
| ❑ 89 Shane Reynolds | .10 | .05 |
| ❑ 90 Ivan Rodriguez | .50 | .23 |
| ❑ 91 Pat Burrell | .60 | .25 |
| ❑ 92 Kent Bottenfield | .10 | .05 |
| ❑ 93 David Cone | .15 | .07 |
| ❑ 94 Mark Grace | .40 | .18 |
| ❑ 95 Paul Konerko | .15 | .07 |
| ❑ 96 Eric Milton | .10 | .05 |
| ❑ 97 Lee Stevens | .10 | .05 |
| ❑ 98 B.J. Surhoff | .15 | .07 |
| ❑ 99 Billy Wagner | .10 | .05 |
| ❑ 100 Ken Griffey Jr. | 1.50 | .70 |
| ❑ 101 Randy Wolf | .10 | .05 |
| ❑ 102 Henry Rodriguez | .10 | .05 |
| ❑ 103 Carlos Beltran | .15 | .07 |
| ❑ 104 Rich Aurilia | .10 | .05 |
| ❑ 105 Chipper Jones | 1.00 | .45 |
| ❑ 106 Homer Bush | .10 | .05 |
| ❑ 107 Johnny Damon | .15 | .07 |
| ❑ 108 J.D. Drew | .40 | .18 |
| ❑ 109 Orlando Hernandez | .15 | .07 |
| ❑ 110 Brad Radke | .10 | .05 |
| ❑ 111 Wilton Veras | .10 | .05 |
| ❑ 112 Dmitri Young | .10 | .05 |
| ❑ 113 Jermaine Dye | .15 | .07 |
| ❑ 114 Kris Benson | .15 | .07 |
| ❑ 115 Derek Jeter | 1.50 | .70 |
| ❑ 116 Cole Liniak | .10 | .05 |
| ❑ 117 Jim Thome | .25 | .11 |
| ❑ 118 Pedro Astacio | .10 | .05 |
| ❑ 119 Carlos Febles | .10 | .05 |
| ❑ 120 Darryl Kile | .10 | .05 |
| ❑ 121 Alfonso Soriano | .15 | .07 |
| ❑ 122 Michael Barrett | .10 | .05 |
| ❑ 123 Ellis Burks | .15 | .07 |
| ❑ 124 Chad Hermansen | .10 | .05 |
| ❑ 125 Trot Nixon | .15 | .07 |
| ❑ 126 Bobby Higginson | .10 | .05 |
| ❑ 127 Rick Helling | .10 | .05 |
| ❑ 128 Chris Carpenter | .10 | .05 |
| ❑ 129 Vinny Castilla | .15 | .07 |
| ❑ 130 Brian Giles | .15 | .07 |
| ❑ 131 Todd Helton | .50 | .23 |
| ❑ 132 Jason Varitek | .10 | .05 |
| ❑ 133 Rob Ducey | .10 | .05 |
| ❑ 134 Octavio Dotel | .10 | .05 |
| ❑ 135 Adam Kennedy | .10 | .05 |
| ❑ 136 Jeff Kent | .25 | .11 |
| ❑ 137 Aaron Boone | .10 | .05 |
| ❑ 138 Todd Walker | .15 | .07 |
| ❑ 139 Jeromy Burnitz | .15 | .07 |
| ❑ 140 Roberto Hernandez | .15 | .07 |
| ❑ 141 Matt LeCroy | .10 | .05 |
| ❑ 142 Ugueth Urbina | .10 | .05 |
| ❑ 143 David Wells | .15 | .07 |
| ❑ 144 Luis Gonzalez | .15 | .07 |
| ❑ 145 Andruw Jones | .40 | .18 |
| ❑ 146 Juan Gonzalez | .40 | .18 |
| ❑ 147 Moises Alou | .15 | .07 |
| ❑ 148 Michael Tejera | .10 | .05 |
| ❑ 149 Brian Jordan | .15 | .07 |
| ❑ 150 Mark McGwire | 1.50 | .70 |
| ❑ 151 Shawn Green | .40 | .18 |
| ❑ 152 Jay Bell | .15 | .07 |
| ❑ 153 Fred McGriff | .25 | .11 |
| ❑ 154 Rey Ordonez | .10 | .05 |
| ❑ 155 Matt Stairs | .10 | .05 |
| ❑ 156 A.J. Burnett | .10 | .05 |
| ❑ 157 Omar Vizquel | .15 | .07 |
| ❑ 158 Damion Easley | .10 | .05 |
| ❑ 159 Dante Bichette | .15 | .07 |
| ❑ 160 Javy Lopez | .15 | .07 |
| ❑ 161 Fernando Seguignol | .10 | .05 |
| ❑ 162 Richie Sexson | .15 | .07 |
| ❑ 163 Vladimir Guerrero | .60 | .25 |
| ❑ 164 Kevin Young | .10 | .05 |
| ❑ 165 Josh Beckett | .40 | .18 |
| ❑ 166 Albert Belle | .25 | .11 |
| ❑ 167 Cliff Floyd | .15 | .07 |
| ❑ 168 Gabe Kapler | .15 | .07 |
| ❑ 169 Nick Johnson | .15 | .07 |
| ❑ 170 Raul Mondesi | .15 | .07 |
| ❑ 171 Warren Morris | .10 | .05 |
| ❑ 172 Kenny Lofton | .15 | .07 |
| ❑ 173 Reggie Sanders | .10 | .05 |
| ❑ 174 Mike Sweeney | .15 | .07 |
| ❑ 175 Robert Fick | .10 | .05 |
| ❑ 176 Barry Bonds | .60 | .25 |
| ❑ 177 Luis Castillo | .15 | .07 |
| ❑ 178 Roger Cedeno | .10 | .05 |
| ❑ 179 Jim Edmonds | .40 | .18 |
| ❑ 180 Geoff Jenkins | .15 | .07 |
| ❑ 181 Adam Piatt | .40 | .18 |
| ❑ 182 Phil Nevin | .15 | .07 |
| ❑ 183 Roberto Alomar | .40 | .18 |
| ❑ 184 Kevin Brown | .15 | .07 |
| ❑ 185 D.T. Cromer | .10 | .05 |
| ❑ 186 Jason Giambi | .40 | .18 |
| ❑ 187 Fernando Tatis | .15 | .07 |
| ❑ 188 Brady Anderson | .15 | .07 |
| ❑ 189 Tony Clark | .10 | .05 |
| ❑ 190 Alex Fernandez | .10 | .05 |
| ❑ 191 Matt Blank | .10 | .05 |
| ❑ 192 Greg Maddux | 1.00 | .45 |
| ❑ 193 Kevin Millwood | .15 | .07 |
| ❑ 194 Jason Schmidt | .10 | .05 |
| ❑ 195 Shannon Stewart | .15 | .07 |
| ❑ 196 Rolando Arrojo | .10 | .05 |
| ❑ 197 Darren Dreifort | .10 | .05 |
| ❑ 198 Ben Grieve | .15 | .07 |
| ❑ 199 Bartolo Colon | .15 | .07 |
| ❑ 200 Sean Casey | .15 | .07 |

## 1949 Leaf

| | NRMT | VG-E |
|---|---|---|
| COMPLETE SET (98) | 25000.00 | 11200.00 |
| COMMON CARD (1-168) | 25.00 | 11.00 |
| COMMON SP's | 300.00 | 135.00 |
| WRAPPER (1-CENT) | 160.00 | 70.00 |
| ❑ 1 Joe DiMaggio | 3000.00 | 1200.00 |
| ❑ 3 Babe Ruth | 2500.00 | 1100.00 |
| ❑ 4 Stan Musial | 850.00 | 375.00 |
| ❑ 5 Virgil Trucks RC SP | 400.00 | 180.00 |
| ❑ 8 Satchel Paige SP RC ! | 4000.00 | 1800.00 |
| ❑ 10 Dizzy Trout | 40.00 | 18.00 |
| ❑ 11 Phil Rizzuto | 300.00 | 135.00 |
| ❑ 13 Cass Michaels SP | 300.00 | 135.00 |
| ❑ 14 Billy Johnson | 40.00 | 18.00 |
| ❑ 17 Frank Overmire | 25.00 | 11.00 |
| ❑ 19 Johnny Wyrostek SP | 300.00 | 135.00 |
| ❑ 20 Hank Sauer SP | 400.00 | 180.00 |
| ❑ 22 Al Evans | 25.00 | 11.00 |
| ❑ 26 Sam Chapman | 40.00 | 18.00 |
| ❑ 27 Mickey Harris | 25.00 | 11.00 |
| ❑ 28 Jim Hegan RC | 40.00 | 18.00 |
| ❑ 29 Elmer Valo RC | 40.00 | 18.00 |
| ❑ 30 Billy Goodman RC SP | 400.00 | 180.00 |
| ❑ 31 Lou Brissie | 25.00 | 11.00 |
| ❑ 32 Warren Spahn | 275.00 | 125.00 |
| ❑ 33 Peanuts Lowrey SP | 300.00 | 135.00 |
| ❑ 36 Al Zarilla SP | 300.00 | 135.00 |
| ❑ 38 Ted Kluszewski RC | 150.00 | 70.00 |
| ❑ 39 Ewell Blackwell | 60.00 | 27.00 |
| ❑ 42 Kent Peterson | 25.00 | 11.00 |
| ❑ 43 Ed Stevens SP | 300.00 | 135.00 |
| ❑ 45 Ken Keltner SP | 300.00 | 135.00 |
| ❑ 46 Johnny Mize | 100.00 | 45.00 |
| ❑ 47 George Vico | 25.00 | 11.00 |
| ❑ 48 Johnny Schmitz SP | 300.00 | 135.00 |

❑ 49 Del Ennis RC ........ 60.00 27.00
❑ 50 Dick Wakefield ........ 25.00 11.00
❑ 51 Al Dark RC SP ........ 500.00 220.00
❑ 53 Johnny VanderMeer .. 100.00 45.00
❑ 54 Bobby Adams SP ...... 300.00 135.00
❑ 55 Tommy Henrich SP .... 500.00 220.00
❑ 56 Larry Jansen RC UER.. 40.00 18.00
(Misspelled Jensen)
❑ 57 Bob McCall ........ 25.00 11.00
❑ 59 Luke Appling ........ 100.00 45.00
❑ 61 Jake Early ........ 25.00 11.00
❑ 62 Eddie Joost SP ........ 300.00 135.00
❑ 63 Barney McCosky SP .. 300.00 135.00
❑ 65 Robert Elliott RC UER 100.00 45.00
(Misspelled Elliot
on card front)
❑ 66 Orval Grove SP ........ 300.00 135.00
❑ 68 Eddie Miller SP ........ 300.00 135.00
❑ 70 Honus Wagner CO .... 300.00 135.00
❑ 72 Hank Edwards ........ 25.00 11.00
❑ 73 Pat Seerey ........ 25.00 11.00
❑ 75 Dom DiMaggio SP ...... 550.00 250.00
❑ 76 Ted Williams ........ 1200.00 550.00
❑ 77 Roy Smalley RC ........ 25.00 11.00
❑ 78 Hoot Evers SP ........ 300.00 135.00
❑ 79 Jackie Robinson RC ! 1300.00 575.00
❑ 81 Whitey Kurowski SP .. 300.00 135.00
❑ 82 Johnny Lindell ........ 40.00 18.00
❑ 83 Bobby Doerr ........ 100.00 45.00
❑ 84 Sid Hudson ........ 25.00 11.00
❑ 85 Dave Philley RC SP .. 400.00 180.00
❑ 86 Ralph Weigel ........ 25.00 11.00
❑ 88 Frank Gustine SP ...... 300.00 135.00
❑ 91 Ralph Kiner ........ 200.00 90.00
❑ 93 Bob Feller SP ........ 1500.00 700.00
❑ 95 George Stirnweiss RC.. 40.00 18.00
❑ 97 Marty Marion ........ 60.00 27.00
❑ 98 Hal Newhouser RC SP 600.00 275.00
❑ 102A Gene Hermansk ERR 250.00 110.00
❑ 102B Gene Hermanski COR 40.00 18.00
❑ 104 Eddie Stewart SP .... 300.00 135.00
❑ 106 Lou Boudreau ........ 100.00 45.00
❑ 108 Matt Batts SP ........ 300.00 135.00
❑ 111 Jerry Priddy ........ 25.00 11.00
❑ 113 Dutch Leonard SP .... 300.00 135.00
❑ 117 Joe Gordon ........ 40.00 18.00
❑ 120 George Kell RC SP .. 600.00 275.00
❑ 121 Johnny Pesky RC SP 400.00 180.00
❑ 123 Cliff Fannin SP ........ 300.00 135.00
❑ 125 Andy Pafko RC ........ 25.00 11.00
❑ 127 Enos Slaughter SP .. 750.00 350.00
❑ 128 Buddy Rosar ........ 25.00 11.00
❑ 129 Kirby Higbe SP ........ 300.00 135.00
❑ 131 Sid Gordon SP ........ 300.00 135.00
❑ 133 Tommy Holmes SP .. 500.00 220.00
❑ 136A Cliff Aberson ........ 25.00 11.00
(Full sleeve)
❑ 136B Cliff Aberson ........ 250.00 110.00
(Short sleeve)
❑ 137 Harry Walker SP ...... 400.00 180.00
❑ 138 Larry Doby RC SP .... 650.00 300.00
❑ 139 Johnny Hopp RC ........ 25.00 11.00
❑ 142 Danny Murtaugh RC SP 400.00 180.00
❑ 143 Dick Sisler SP ........ 300.00 135.00
❑ 144 Bob Dillinger SP ...... 300.00 135.00
❑ 146 Pete Reiser SP ........ 500.00 220.00
❑ 149 Hank Majeski SP ...... 300.00 135.00
❑ 153 Floyd Baker SP ........ 300.00 135.00
❑ 158 Harry Brecheen RC SP 400.00 180.00
❑ 159 Mizell Platt ........ 25.00 11.00
❑ 160 Bob Scheffing SP .... 300.00 135.00
❑ 161 Vern Stephens RC SP 400.00 180.00
❑ 163 Fred Hutchinson RC SP 400.00 180.00
❑ 165 Dale Mitchell RC SP 400.00 180.00
❑ 168 Phil Cavarretta SP UER 500.00 200.00
(Name spelled Cavaretta)
❑ XX Album ........

## 1990 Leaf

| | MINT | NRMT |
|---|---|---|
| COMPLETE SET (528) ........ | 250.00 | 110.00 |
| COMPLETE SERIES 1 (264) | 150.00 | 70.00 |
| COMPLETE SERIES 2 (264) | 100.00 | 45.00 |
| COMP. BERRA PUZZLE ........ | 1.00 | .45 |

❑ 1 Introductory Card ........ .25 .11
❑ 2 Mike Henneman ........ .25 .11
❑ 3 Steve Bedrosian ........ .25 .11
❑ 4 Mike Scott ........ .25 .11
❑ 5 Allan Anderson ........ .25 .11
❑ 6 Rick Sutcliffe ........ .50 .23
❑ 7 Gregg Olson ........ .50 .23
❑ 8 Kevin Elster ........ .25 .11
❑ 9 Pete O'Brien ........ .25 .11
❑ 10 Carlton Fisk ........ 1.50 .70
❑ 11 Joe Magrane ........ .25 .11
❑ 12 Roger Clemens ........ 3.00 1.35
❑ 13 Tom Glavine ........ 4.00 1.80
❑ 14 Tom Gordon ........ .50 .23
❑ 15 Todd Benzinger ........ .25 .11
❑ 16 Hubie Brooks ........ .25 .11
❑ 17 Roberto Kelly ........ .25 .11
❑ 18 Barry Larkin ........ 1.50 .70
❑ 19 Mike Boddicker ........ .25 .11
❑ 20 Roger McDowell ........ .25 .11
❑ 21 Nolan Ryan ........ 8.00 3.60
❑ 22 John Farrell ........ .25 .11
❑ 23 Bruce Hurst ........ .25 .11
❑ 24 Wally Joyner ........ .50 .23
❑ 25 Greg Maddux ........ 8.00 3.60
❑ 26 Chris Bosio ........ .25 .11
❑ 27 John Cerutti ........ .25 .11
❑ 28 Tim Burke ........ .25 .11
❑ 29 Dennis Eckersley ........ 1.00 .45
❑ 30 Glenn Davis ........ .25 .11
❑ 31 Jim Abbott ........ 1.00 .45
❑ 32 Mike LaValliere ........ .25 .11
❑ 33 Andres Thomas ........ .25 .11
❑ 34 Lou Whitaker ........ .50 .23
❑ 35 Alvin Davis ........ .25 .11
❑ 36 Melido Perez ........ .25 .11
❑ 37 Craig Biggio ........ 1.00 .45
❑ 38 Rick Aguilera ........ .50 .23
❑ 39 Pete Harnisch ........ .25 .11
❑ 40 David Cone ........ .50 .23
❑ 41 Scott Garrelts ........ .25 .11
❑ 42 Jay Howell ........ .25 .11
❑ 43 Eric King ........ .25 .11
❑ 44 Pedro Guerrero ........ .25 .11
❑ 45 Mike Bielecki ........ .25 .11
❑ 46 Bob Boone ........ .50 .23
❑ 47 Kevin Brown ........ 2.00 .90
❑ 48 Jerry Browne ........ .25 .11
❑ 49 Mike Scioscia ........ .25 .11
❑ 50 Chuck Cary ........ .25 .11
❑ 51 Wade Boggs ........ 2.00 .90
❑ 52 Von Hayes ........ .25 .11
❑ 53 Tony Fernandez ........ .25 .11
❑ 54 Dennis Martinez ........ .50 .23
❑ 55 Tom Candiotti ........ .25 .11
❑ 56 Andy Benes ........ .25 .11
❑ 57 Rob Dibble ........ .25 .11
❑ 58 Chuck Crim ........ .25 .11
❑ 59 John Smoltz ........ .50 .23
❑ 60 Mike Heath ........ .25 .11
❑ 61 Kevin Gross ........ .25 .11
❑ 62 Mark McGwire ........ 6.00 2.70
❑ 63 Bert Blyleven ........ .50 .23
❑ 64 Bob Walk ........ .25 .11
❑ 65 Mickey Tettleton ........ .25 .11
❑ 66 Sid Fernandez ........ .25 .11
❑ 67 Terry Kennedy ........ .25 .11
❑ 68 Fernando Valenzuela ...... .50 .23
❑ 69 Don Mattingly ........ 4.00 1.80
❑ 70 Paul O'Neill ........ .50 .23
❑ 71 Robin Yount ........ 1.50 .70
❑ 72 Bret Saberhagen ........ .50 .23
❑ 73 Geno Petralli ........ .25 .11
❑ 74 Brook Jacoby ........ .25 .11
❑ 75 Roberto Alomar ........ 1.50 .70
❑ 76 Devon White ........ .25 .11
❑ 77 Jose Lind ........ .25 .11
❑ 78 Pat Combs ........ .25 .11
❑ 79 Dave Stieb ........ .50 .23
❑ 80 Tim Wallach ........ .25 .11
❑ 81 Dave Stewart ........ .50 .23
❑ 82 Eric Anthony RC ........ .25 .11
❑ 83 Randy Bush ........ .25 .11
❑ 84 Rickey Henderson CL ...... .50 .23
❑ 85 Jaime Navarro ........ .25 .11
❑ 86 Tommy Gregg ........ .25 .11
❑ 87 Frank Tanana ........ .25 .11
❑ 88 Omar Vizquel ........ 2.00 .90
❑ 89 Ivan Calderon ........ .25 .11
❑ 90 Vince Coleman ........ .25 .11
❑ 91 Barry Bonds ........ 2.50 1.10
❑ 92 Randy Milligan ........ .25 .11
❑ 93 Frank Viola ........ .25 .11
❑ 94 Matt Williams ........ 1.00 .45
❑ 95 Alfredo Griffin ........ .25 .11
❑ 96 Steve Sax ........ .25 .11
❑ 97 Gary Gaetti ........ .50 .23
❑ 98 Ryne Sandberg ........ 2.00 .90
❑ 99 Danny Tartabull ........ .25 .11
❑ 100 Rafael Palmeiro ........ 2.00 .90
❑ 101 Jesse Orosco ........ .25 .11
❑ 102 Garry Templeton ........ .25 .11
❑ 103 Frank DiPino ........ .25 .11
❑ 104 Tony Pena ........ .25 .11
❑ 105 Dickie Thon ........ .25 .11
❑ 106 Kelly Gruber ........ .25 .11
❑ 107 Marquis Grissom RC .... 2.00 .90
❑ 108 Jose Canseco ........ 2.00 .90
❑ 109 Mike Blowers RC ........ .50 .23
❑ 110 Tom Browning ........ .25 .11
❑ 111 Greg Vaughn ........ 3.00 1.35
❑ 112 Oddibe McDowell ........ .25 .11
❑ 113 Gary Ward ........ .25 .11
❑ 114 Jay Buhner ........ .50 .23
❑ 115 Eric Show ........ .25 .11
❑ 116 Bryan Harvey ........ .25 .11
❑ 117 Andy Van Slyke ........ .50 .23
❑ 118 Jeff Ballard ........ .25 .11
❑ 119 Barry Lyons ........ .25 .11
❑ 120 Kevin Mitchell ........ .25 .11
❑ 121 Mike Gallego ........ .25 .11
❑ 122 Dave Smith ........ .25 .11
❑ 123 Kirby Puckett ........ 4.00 1.80
❑ 124 Jerome Walton ........ .25 .11
❑ 125 Bo Jackson ........ .50 .23
❑ 126 Harold Baines ........ .50 .23
❑ 127 Scott Bankhead ........ .25 .11
❑ 128 Ozzie Guillen ........ .25 .11
❑ 129 Jose Oquendo UER ........ .25 .11
(League misspelled
as Logue)
❑ 130 John Dopson ........ .25 .11
❑ 131 Charlie Hayes ........ .25 .11
❑ 132 Fred McGriff ........ 1.50 .70
❑ 133 Chet Lemon ........ .25 .11
❑ 134 Gary Carter ........ 1.00 .45
❑ 135 Rafael Ramirez ........ .25 .11
❑ 136 Shane Mack ........ .25 .11
❑ 137 Mark Grace UER ........ 1.50 .70
(Card back has OB:L;
should be B:L)
❑ 138 Phil Bradley ........ .25 .11
❑ 139 Dwight Gooden ........ .50 .23
❑ 140 Harold Reynolds ........ .25 .11
❑ 141 Scott Fletcher ........ .25 .11
❑ 142 Ozzie Smith ........ 2.00 .90
❑ 143 Mike Greenwell ........ .25 .11
❑ 144 Pete Smith ........ .25 .11
❑ 145 Mark Gubicza ........ .25 .11
❑ 146 Chris Sabo ........ .25 .11
❑ 147 Ramon Martinez ........ .25 .11
❑ 148 Tim Leary ........ .25 .11
❑ 149 Randy Myers ........ .50 .23
❑ 150 Jody Reed ........ .25 .11

❑ 151 Bruce Ruffin .25 .11
❑ 152 Jeff Russell .25 .11
❑ 153 Doug Jones .25 .11
❑ 154 Tony Gwynn 3.00 1.35
❑ 155 Mark Langston .25 .11
❑ 156 Mitch Williams .25 .11
❑ 157 Gary Sheffield 3.00 1.35
❑ 158 Tom Henke .25 .11
❑ 159 Oil Can Boyd .25 .11
❑ 160 Rickey Henderson 2.00 .90
❑ 161 Bill Doran .25 .11
❑ 162 Chuck Finley .50 .23
❑ 163 Jeff King .25 .11
❑ 164 Nick Esasky .25 .11
❑ 165 Cecil Fielder .50 .23
❑ 166 Dave Valle .25 .11
❑ 167 Robin Ventura 2.00 .90
❑ 168 Jim Deshaies .25 .11
❑ 169 Juan Berenguer .25 .11
❑ 170 Craig Worthington .25 .11
❑ 171 Gregg Jefferies .50 .23
❑ 172 Will Clark 1.50 .70
❑ 173 Kirk Gibson .50 .23
❑ 174 Carlton Fisk CL 1.00 .45
❑ 175 Bobby Thigpen .25 .11
❑ 176 John Tudor .25 .11
❑ 177 Andre Dawson 1.00 .45
❑ 178 George Brett 3.00 1.35
❑ 179 Steve Buechele .25 .11
❑ 180 Joey Belle 8.00 3.60
❑ 181 Eddie Murray 1.50 .70
❑ 182 Bob Geren .25 .11
❑ 183 Rob Murphy .25 .11
❑ 184 Tom Herr .25 .11
❑ 185 George Bell .25 .11
❑ 186 Spike Owen .25 .11
❑ 187 Cory Snyder .25 .11
❑ 188 Fred Lynn .25 .11
❑ 189 Eric Davis .50 .23
❑ 190 Dave Parker .50 .23
❑ 191 Jeff Blauser .25 .11
❑ 192 Matt Nokes .25 .11
❑ 193 Delino DeShields RC 1.50 .70
❑ 194 Scott Sanderson .25 .11
❑ 195 Lance Parrish .25 .11
❑ 196 Bobby Bonilla .50 .23
❑ 197 Cal Ripken UER 6.00 2.70
(Reistertown, should be Reisterstown)
❑ 198 Kevin McReynolds .25 .11
❑ 199 Robby Thompson .25 .11
❑ 200 Tim Belcher .25 .11
❑ 201 Jesse Barfield .25 .11
❑ 202 Mariano Duncan .25 .11
❑ 203 Bill Spiers .25 .11
❑ 204 Frank White .50 .23
❑ 205 Julio Franco .25 .11
❑ 206 Greg Swindell .25 .11
❑ 207 Benito Santiago .25 .11
❑ 208 Johnny Ray .25 .11
❑ 209 Gary Redus .25 .11
❑ 210 Jeff Parrett .25 .11
❑ 211 Jimmy Key .50 .23
❑ 212 Tim Raines .50 .23
❑ 213 Carney Lansford .50 .23
❑ 214 Gerald Young .25 .11
❑ 215 Gene Larkin .25 .11
❑ 216 Dan Plesac .25 .11
❑ 217 Lonnie Smith .25 .11
❑ 218 Alan Trammell 1.00 .45
❑ 219 Jeffrey Leonard .25 .11
❑ 220 Sammy Sosa RC 50.00 22.00
❑ 221 Todd Zeile .50 .23
❑ 222 Bill Landrum .25 .11
❑ 223 Mike Devereaux .25 .11
❑ 224 Mike Marshall .25 .11
❑ 225 Jose Uribe .25 .11
❑ 226 Juan Samuel .25 .11
❑ 227 Mel Hall .25 .11
❑ 228 Kent Hrbek .50 .23
❑ 229 Shawon Dunston .25 .11
❑ 230 Kevin Seitzer .25 .11
❑ 231 Pete Incaviglia .25 .11
❑ 232 Sandy Alomar Jr. .50 .23
❑ 233 Bip Roberts .25 .11
❑ 234 Scott Terry .25 .11
❑ 235 Dwight Evans .50 .23
❑ 236 Ricky Jordan .25 .11
❑ 237 John Olerud RC 5.00 2.20
❑ 238 Zane Smith .25 .11
❑ 239 Walt Weiss .25 .11
❑ 240 Alvaro Espinoza .25 .11
❑ 241 Billy Hatcher .25 .11
❑ 242 Paul Molitor 1.50 .70
❑ 243 Dale Murphy 1.50 .70
❑ 244 Dave Bergman .25 .11
❑ 245 Ken Griffey Jr. 20.00 9.00
❑ 246 Ed Whitson .25 .11
❑ 247 Kirk McCaskill .25 .11
❑ 248 Jay Bell .50 .23
❑ 249 Ben McDonald RC .50 .23
❑ 250 Darryl Strawberry .50 .23
❑ 251 Brett Butler .50 .23
❑ 252 Terry Steinbach .25 .11
❑ 253 Ken Caminiti 2.50 1.10
❑ 254 Dan Gladden .25 .11
❑ 255 Dwight Smith .25 .11
❑ 256 Kurt Stillwell .25 .11
❑ 257 Ruben Sierra .25 .11
❑ 258 Mike Schooler .25 .11
❑ 259 Lance Johnson .25 .11
❑ 260 Terry Pendleton .50 .23
❑ 261 Ellis Burks 1.00 .45
❑ 262 Len Dykstra .50 .23
❑ 263 Mookie Wilson .50 .23
❑ 264 Nolan Ryan CL UER 1.50 .70
(No TM after Ranger logo)
❑ 265 Nolan Ryan 4.00 1.80
No Hit King
❑ 266 Brian DuBois .25 .11
❑ 267 Don Robinson .25 .11
❑ 268 Glenn Wilson .25 .11
❑ 269 Kevin Tapani RC .50 .23
❑ 270 Marvell Wynne .25 .11
❑ 271 Bill Ripken .25 .11
❑ 272 Howard Johnson .25 .11
❑ 273 Brian Holman .25 .11
❑ 274 Dan Pasqua .25 .11
❑ 275 Ken Dayley .25 .11
❑ 276 Jeff Reardon .50 .23
❑ 277 Jim Presley .25 .11
❑ 278 Jim Eisenreich .25 .11
❑ 279 Danny Jackson .25 .11
❑ 280 Orel Hershiser .50 .23
❑ 281 Andy Hawkins .25 .11
❑ 282 Jose Rijo .25 .11
❑ 283 Luis Rivera .25 .11
❑ 284 John Kruk .50 .23
❑ 285 Jeff Huson RC .25 .11
❑ 286 Joel Skinner .25 .11
❑ 287 Jack Clark .50 .23
❑ 288 Chili Davis .50 .23
❑ 289 Joe Girardi 1.00 .45
❑ 290 B.J. Surhoff .50 .23
❑ 291 Luis Sojo .25 .11
❑ 292 Tom Foley .25 .11
❑ 293 Mike Moore .25 .11
❑ 294 Ken Oberkfell .25 .11
❑ 295 Luis Polonia .25 .11
❑ 296 Doug Drabek .25 .11
❑ 297 Dave Justice RC 8.00 3.60
❑ 298 Paul Gibson .25 .11
❑ 299 Edgar Martinez 1.00 .45
❑ 300 Frank Thomas RC UER 40.00 18.00
(No B in front of birthdate)
❑ 301 Eric Yelding .25 .11
❑ 302 Greg Gagne .25 .11
❑ 303 Brad Komminsk .25 .11
❑ 304 Ron Darling .25 .11
❑ 305 Kevin Bass .25 .11
❑ 306 Jeff Hamilton .25 .11
❑ 307 Ron Karkovice .25 .11
❑ 308 Milt Thompson UER 1.50 .70
(Ray Lankford pictured on card back)
❑ 309 Mike Harkey .25 .11
❑ 310 Mel Stottlemyre Jr. .25 .11
❑ 311 Kenny Rogers .50 .23
❑ 312 Mitch Webster .25 .11
❑ 313 Kal Daniels .25 .11
❑ 314 Matt Nokes .25 .11
❑ 315 Dennis Lamp .25 .11
❑ 316 Ken Howell .25 .11
❑ 317 Glenallen Hill .25 .11
❑ 318 Dave Martinez .25 .11
❑ 319 Chris James .25 .11
❑ 320 Mike Pagliarulo .25 .11
❑ 321 Hal Morris .25 .11
❑ 322 Rob Deer .25 .11
❑ 323 Greg Olson .25 .11
❑ 324 Tony Phillips .25 .11
❑ 325 Larry Walker RC 6.00 2.70
❑ 326 Ron Hassey .25 .11
❑ 327 Jack Howell .25 .11
❑ 328 John Smiley .25 .11
❑ 329 Steve Finley .50 .23
❑ 330 Dave Magadan .25 .11
❑ 331 Greg Litton .25 .11
❑ 332 Mickey Hatcher .25 .11
❑ 333 Lee Guetterman .25 .11
❑ 334 Norm Charlton .25 .11
❑ 335 Edgar Diaz .25 .11
❑ 336 Willie Wilson .25 .11
❑ 337 Bobby Witt .25 .11
❑ 338 Candy Maldonado .25 .11
❑ 339 Craig Lefferts .25 .11
❑ 340 Dante Bichette 2.00 .90
❑ 341 Wally Backman .25 .11
❑ 342 Dennis Cook .25 .11
❑ 343 Pat Borders .25 .11
❑ 344 Wallace Johnson .25 .11
❑ 345 Willie Randolph .50 .23
❑ 346 Danny Darwin .25 .11
❑ 347 Al Newman .25 .11
❑ 348 Mark Knudson .25 .11
❑ 349 Joe Boever .25 .11
❑ 350 Larry Sheets .25 .11
❑ 351 Mike Jackson .25 .11
❑ 352 Wayne Edwards .25 .11
❑ 353 Bernard Gilkey RC .50 .23
❑ 354 Don Slaught .25 .11
❑ 355 Joe Orsulak .25 .11
❑ 356 John Franco .50 .23
❑ 357 Jeff Brantley .25 .11
❑ 358 Mike Morgan .25 .11
❑ 359 Deion Sanders 2.00 .90
❑ 360 Terry Leach .25 .11
❑ 361 Les Lancaster .25 .11
❑ 362 Storm Davis .25 .11
❑ 363 Scott Coolbaugh .25 .11
❑ 364 Ozzie Smith CL 1.00 .45
❑ 365 Cecilio Guante .25 .11
❑ 366 Joey Cora .50 .23
❑ 367 Willie McGee .50 .23
❑ 368 Jerry Reed .25 .11
❑ 369 Darren Daulton .50 .23
❑ 370 Manny Lee .25 .11
❑ 371 Mark Gardner .25 .11
❑ 372 Rick Honeycutt .25 .11
❑ 373 Steve Balboni .25 .11
❑ 374 Jack Armstrong .25 .11
❑ 375 Charlie O'Brien .25 .11
❑ 376 Ron Gant .50 .23
❑ 377 Lloyd Moseby .25 .11
❑ 378 Gene Harris .25 .11
❑ 379 Joe Carter .50 .23
❑ 380 Scott Bailes .25 .11
❑ 381 R.J. Reynolds .25 .11
❑ 382 Bob Melvin .25 .11
❑ 383 Tim Teufel .25 .11
❑ 384 John Burkett .25 .11
❑ 385 Felix Jose .25 .11
❑ 386 Larry Andersen .25 .11
❑ 387 David West .25 .11
❑ 388 Luis Salazar .25 .11
❑ 389 Mike Macfarlane .25 .11
❑ 390 Charlie Hough .50 .23
❑ 391 Greg Briley .25 .11
❑ 392 Donn Pall .25 .11
❑ 393 Bryn Smith .25 .11
❑ 394 Carlos Quintana .25 .11
❑ 395 Steve Lake .25 .11
❑ 396 Mark Whiten RC .25 .11
❑ 397 Edwin Nunez .25 .11
❑ 398 Rick Parker .25 .11
❑ 399 Mark Portugal .25 .11
❑ 400 Roy Smith .25 .11

| Card | Mint | NrMt |
|---|---|---|
| ❑ 401 Hector Villanueva | .25 | .11 |
| ❑ 402 Bob Milacki | .25 | .11 |
| ❑ 403 Alejandro Pena | .25 | .11 |
| ❑ 404 Scott Bradley | .25 | .11 |
| ❑ 405 Ron Kittle | .25 | .11 |
| ❑ 406 Bob Tewksbury | .25 | .11 |
| ❑ 407 Wes Gardner | .25 | .11 |
| ❑ 408 Ernie Whitt | .25 | .11 |
| ❑ 409 Terry Shumpert | .25 | .11 |
| ❑ 410 Tim Layana | .25 | .11 |
| ❑ 411 Chris Gwynn | .25 | .11 |
| ❑ 412 Jeff D. Robinson | .25 | .11 |
| ❑ 413 Scott Scudder | .25 | .11 |
| ❑ 414 Kevin Romine | .25 | .11 |
| ❑ 415 Jose DeJesus | .25 | .11 |
| ❑ 416 Mike Jeffcoat | .25 | .11 |
| ❑ 417 Rudy Seanez | .25 | .11 |
| ❑ 418 Mike Dunne | .25 | .11 |
| ❑ 419 Dick Schofield | .25 | .11 |
| ❑ 420 Steve Wilson | .25 | .11 |
| ❑ 421 Bill Krueger | .25 | .11 |
| ❑ 422 Junior Felix | .25 | .11 |
| ❑ 423 Drew Hall | .25 | .11 |
| ❑ 424 Curt Young | .25 | .11 |
| ❑ 425 Franklin Stubbs | .25 | .11 |
| ❑ 426 Dave Winfield | 1.50 | .70 |
| ❑ 427 Rick Reed RC | 2.00 | .90 |
| ❑ 428 Charlie Leibrandt | .25 | .11 |
| ❑ 429 Jeff M. Robinson | .25 | .11 |
| ❑ 430 Erik Hanson | .25 | .11 |
| ❑ 431 Barry Jones | .25 | .11 |
| ❑ 432 Alex Trevino | .25 | .11 |
| ❑ 433 John Moses | .25 | .11 |
| ❑ 434 Dave Johnson | .25 | .11 |
| ❑ 435 Mackey Sasser | .25 | .11 |
| ❑ 436 Rick Leach | .25 | .11 |
| ❑ 437 Lenny Harris | .25 | .11 |
| ❑ 438 Carlos Martinez | .25 | .11 |
| ❑ 439 Rex Hudler | .25 | .11 |
| ❑ 440 Domingo Ramos | .25 | .11 |
| ❑ 441 Gerald Perry | .25 | .11 |
| ❑ 442 Jeff Russell | .25 | .11 |
| ❑ 443 Carlos Baerga RC | .50 | .23 |
| ❑ 444 Will Clark CL | .50 | .23 |
| ❑ 445 Stan Javier | .25 | .11 |
| ❑ 446 Kevin Maas RC | .50 | .23 |
| ❑ 447 Tom Brunansky | .25 | .11 |
| ❑ 448 Carmelo Martinez | .25 | .11 |
| ❑ 449 Willie Blair RC | .50 | .23 |
| ❑ 450 Andres Galarraga | 1.00 | .45 |
| ❑ 451 Bud Black | .25 | .11 |
| ❑ 452 Greg W. Harris | .25 | .11 |
| ❑ 453 Joe Oliver | .25 | .11 |
| ❑ 454 Greg Brock | .25 | .11 |
| ❑ 455 Jeff Treadway | .25 | .11 |
| ❑ 456 Lance McCullers | .25 | .11 |
| ❑ 457 Dave Schmidt | .25 | .11 |
| ❑ 458 Todd Burns | .25 | .11 |
| ❑ 459 Max Venable | .25 | .11 |
| ❑ 460 Neal Heaton | .25 | .11 |
| ❑ 461 Mark Williamson | .25 | .11 |
| ❑ 462 Keith Miller | .25 | .11 |
| ❑ 463 Mike LaCoss | .25 | .11 |
| ❑ 464 Jose Offerman RC | 2.00 | .90 |
| ❑ 465 Jim Leyritz RC | .50 | .23 |
| ❑ 466 Glenn Braggs | .25 | .11 |
| ❑ 467 Ron Robinson | .25 | .11 |
| ❑ 468 Mark Davis | .25 | .11 |
| ❑ 469 Gary Pettis | .25 | .11 |
| ❑ 470 Keith Hernandez | .50 | .23 |
| ❑ 471 Dennis Rasmussen | .25 | .11 |
| ❑ 472 Mark Eichhorn | .25 | .11 |
| ❑ 473 Ted Power | .25 | .11 |
| ❑ 474 Terry Mulholland | .25 | .11 |
| ❑ 475 Todd Stottlemyre | .50 | .23 |
| ❑ 476 Jerry Goff | .25 | .11 |
| ❑ 477 Gene Nelson | .25 | .11 |
| ❑ 478 Rich Gedman | .25 | .11 |
| ❑ 479 Brian Harper | .25 | .11 |
| ❑ 480 Mike Felder | .25 | .11 |
| ❑ 481 Steve Avery | 1.50 | .70 |
| ❑ 482 Jack Morris | .50 | .23 |
| ❑ 483 Randy Johnson | 5.00 | 2.20 |
| ❑ 484 Scott Radinsky RC | .25 | .11 |
| ❑ 485 Jose DeLeon | .25 | .11 |
| ❑ 486 Stan Belinda RC | .25 | .11 |
| ❑ 487 Brian Holton | .25 | .11 |
| ❑ 488 Mark Carreon | .25 | .11 |
| ❑ 489 Trevor Wilson | .25 | .11 |
| ❑ 490 Mike Sharperson | .25 | .11 |
| ❑ 491 Alan Mills RC | .25 | .11 |
| ❑ 492 John Candelaria | .25 | .11 |
| ❑ 493 Paul Assenmacher | .25 | .11 |
| ❑ 494 Steve Crawford | .25 | .11 |
| ❑ 495 Brad Arnsberg | .25 | .11 |
| ❑ 496 Sergio Valdez | .25 | .11 |
| ❑ 497 Mark Parent | .25 | .11 |
| ❑ 498 Tom Pagnozzi | .25 | .11 |
| ❑ 499 Greg A. Harris | .25 | .11 |
| ❑ 500 Randy Ready | .25 | .11 |
| ❑ 501 Duane Ward | .25 | .11 |
| ❑ 502 Nelson Santovenia | .25 | .11 |
| ❑ 503 Joe Klink | .25 | .11 |
| ❑ 504 Eric Plunk | .25 | .11 |
| ❑ 505 Jeff Reed | .25 | .11 |
| ❑ 506 Ted Higuera | .25 | .11 |
| ❑ 507 Joe Hesketh | .25 | .11 |
| ❑ 508 Dan Petry | .25 | .11 |
| ❑ 509 Matt Young | .25 | .11 |
| ❑ 510 Jerald Clark | .25 | .11 |
| ❑ 511 John Orton | .25 | .11 |
| ❑ 512 Scott Ruskin | .25 | .11 |
| ❑ 513 Chris Hoiles RC | 1.50 | .70 |
| ❑ 514 Daryl Boston | .25 | .11 |
| ❑ 515 Francisco Oliveras | .25 | .11 |
| ❑ 516 Ozzie Canseco | .25 | .11 |
| ❑ 517 Xavier Hernandez RC | .25 | .11 |
| ❑ 518 Fred Manrique | .25 | .11 |
| ❑ 519 Shawn Boskie RC | .25 | .11 |
| ❑ 520 Jeff Montgomery | .50 | .23 |
| ❑ 521 Jack Daugherty | .25 | .11 |
| ❑ 522 Keith Comstock | .25 | .11 |
| ❑ 523 Greg Hibbard RC | .25 | .11 |
| ❑ 524 Lee Smith | .50 | .23 |
| ❑ 525 Dana Kiecker | .25 | .11 |
| ❑ 526 Darrel Akerfelds | .25 | .11 |
| ❑ 527 Greg Myers | .25 | .11 |
| ❑ 528 Ryne Sandberg CL | 1.50 | .70 |

## 1991 Leaf

| | MINT | NRMT |
|---|---|---|
| COMPLETE SET (528) | 15.00 | 6.75 |
| COMPLETE SERIES 1 (264) | 5.00 | 2.20 |
| COMPLETE SERIES 2 (264) | 10.00 | 4.50 |
| COMP. KILLEBREW PUZZLE | | |

| Card | Mint | NrMt |
|---|---|---|
| ❑ 1 The Leaf Card | .10 | .05 |
| ❑ 2 Kurt Stillwell | .10 | .05 |
| ❑ 3 Bobby Witt | .10 | .05 |
| ❑ 4 Tony Phillips | .10 | .05 |
| ❑ 5 Scott Garrelts | .10 | .05 |
| ❑ 6 Greg Swindell | .10 | .05 |
| ❑ 7 Billy Ripken | .10 | .05 |
| ❑ 8 Dave Martinez | .10 | .05 |
| ❑ 9 Kelly Gruber | .10 | .05 |
| ❑ 10 Juan Samuel | .10 | .05 |
| ❑ 11 Brian Holman | .10 | .05 |
| ❑ 12 Craig Biggio | .30 | .14 |
| ❑ 13 Lonnie Smith | .10 | .05 |
| ❑ 14 Ron Robinson | .10 | .05 |
| ❑ 15 Mike LaValliere | .10 | .05 |
| ❑ 16 Mark Davis | .10 | .05 |
| ❑ 17 Jack Daugherty | .10 | .05 |
| ❑ 18 Mike Henneman | .10 | .05 |
| ❑ 19 Mike Greenwell | .10 | .05 |
| ❑ 20 Dave Magadan | .10 | .05 |
| ❑ 21 Mark Williamson | .10 | .05 |
| ❑ 22 Marquis Grissom | .10 | .05 |
| ❑ 23 Pat Borders | .10 | .05 |
| ❑ 24 Mike Scioscia | .10 | .05 |
| ❑ 25 Shawon Dunston | .10 | .05 |
| ❑ 26 Randy Bush | .10 | .05 |
| ❑ 27 John Smoltz | .20 | .09 |
| ❑ 28 Chuck Crim | .10 | .05 |
| ❑ 29 Don Slaught | .10 | .05 |
| ❑ 30 Mike Macfarlane | .10 | .05 |
| ❑ 31 Wally Joyner | .20 | .09 |
| ❑ 32 Pat Combs | .10 | .05 |
| ❑ 33 Tony Pena | .10 | .05 |
| ❑ 34 Howard Johnson | .10 | .05 |
| ❑ 35 Leo Gomez | .10 | .05 |
| ❑ 36 Spike Owen | .10 | .05 |
| ❑ 37 Eric Davis | .20 | .09 |
| ❑ 38 Roberto Kelly | .10 | .05 |
| ❑ 39 Jerome Walton | .10 | .05 |
| ❑ 40 Shane Mack | .10 | .05 |
| ❑ 41 Kent Mercker | .10 | .05 |
| ❑ 42 B.J. Surhoff | .20 | .09 |
| ❑ 43 Jerry Browne | .10 | .05 |
| ❑ 44 Lee Smith | .20 | .09 |
| ❑ 45 Chuck Finley | .20 | .09 |
| ❑ 46 Terry Mulholland | .10 | .05 |
| ❑ 47 Tom Bolton | .10 | .05 |
| ❑ 48 Tom Herr | .10 | .05 |
| ❑ 49 Jim Deshaies | .10 | .05 |
| ❑ 50 Walt Weiss | .10 | .05 |
| ❑ 51 Hal Morris | .10 | .05 |
| ❑ 52 Lee Guetterman | .10 | .05 |
| ❑ 53 Paul Assenmacher | .10 | .05 |
| ❑ 54 Brian Harper | .10 | .05 |
| ❑ 55 Paul Gibson | .10 | .05 |
| ❑ 56 John Burkett | .10 | .05 |
| ❑ 57 Doug Jones | .10 | .05 |
| ❑ 58 Jose Oquendo | .10 | .05 |
| ❑ 59 Dick Schofield | .10 | .05 |
| ❑ 60 Dickie Thon | .10 | .05 |
| ❑ 61 Ramon Martinez | .10 | .05 |
| ❑ 62 Jay Buhner | .20 | .09 |
| ❑ 63 Mark Portugal | .10 | .05 |
| ❑ 64 Bob Welch | .10 | .05 |
| ❑ 65 Chris Sabo | .10 | .05 |
| ❑ 66 Chuck Cary | .10 | .05 |
| ❑ 67 Mark Langston | .10 | .05 |
| ❑ 68 Joe Boever | .10 | .05 |
| ❑ 69 Jody Reed | .10 | .05 |
| ❑ 70 Alejandro Pena | .10 | .05 |
| ❑ 71 Jeff King | .10 | .05 |
| ❑ 72 Tom Pagnozzi | .10 | .05 |
| ❑ 73 Joe Oliver | .10 | .05 |
| ❑ 74 Mike Witt | .10 | .05 |
| ❑ 75 Hector Villanueva | .10 | .05 |
| ❑ 76 Dan Gladden | .10 | .05 |
| ❑ 77 Dave Justice | .40 | .18 |
| ❑ 78 Mike Gallego | .10 | .05 |
| ❑ 79 Tom Candiotti | .10 | .05 |
| ❑ 80 Ozzie Smith | .50 | .23 |
| ❑ 81 Luis Polonia | .10 | .05 |
| ❑ 82 Randy Ready | .10 | .05 |
| ❑ 83 Greg A. Harris | .10 | .05 |
| ❑ 84 David Justice CL | .20 | .09 |
| ❑ 85 Kevin Mitchell | .10 | .05 |
| ❑ 86 Mark McLemore | .10 | .05 |
| ❑ 87 Terry Steinbach | .20 | .09 |
| ❑ 88 Tom Browning | .10 | .05 |
| ❑ 89 Matt Nokes | .10 | .05 |
| ❑ 90 Mike Harkey | .10 | .05 |
| ❑ 91 Omar Vizquel | .40 | .18 |
| ❑ 92 Dave Bergman | .10 | .05 |
| ❑ 93 Matt Williams | .30 | .14 |
| ❑ 94 Steve Olin | .10 | .05 |
| ❑ 95 Craig Wilson | .10 | .05 |
| ❑ 96 Dave Stieb | .10 | .05 |
| ❑ 97 Ruben Sierra | .10 | .05 |
| ❑ 98 Jay Howell | .10 | .05 |
| ❑ 99 Scott Bradley | .10 | .05 |
| ❑ 100 Eric Yelding | .10 | .05 |
| ❑ 101 Rickey Henderson | .50 | .23 |
| ❑ 102 Jeff Reed | .10 | .05 |
| ❑ 103 Jimmy Key | .20 | .09 |
| ❑ 104 Terry Shumpert | .10 | .05 |

❑ 105 Kenny Rogers .10 .05
❑ 106 Cecil Fielder .20 .09
❑ 107 Robby Thompson .10 .05
❑ 108 Alex Cole .10 .05
❑ 109 Randy Milligan .10 .05
❑ 110 Andres Galarraga .30 .14
❑ 111 Bill Spiers .10 .05
❑ 112 Kal Daniels .10 .05
❑ 113 Henry Cotto .10 .05
❑ 114 Casey Candaele .10 .05
❑ 115 Jeff Blauser .10 .05
❑ 116 Robin Yount .40 .18
❑ 117 Ben McDonald .10 .05
❑ 118 Bret Saberhagen .20 .09
❑ 119 Juan Gonzalez .50 .23
❑ 120 Lou Whitaker .20 .09
❑ 121 Ellis Burks .20 .09
❑ 122 Charlie O'Brien .10 .05
❑ 123 John Smiley .10 .05
❑ 124 Tim Burke .10 .05
❑ 125 John Olerud .30 .14
❑ 126 Eddie Murray .40 .18
❑ 127 Greg Maddux 1.00 .45
❑ 128 Kevin Tapani .10 .05
❑ 129 Ron Gant .20 .09
❑ 130 Jay Bell .20 .09
❑ 131 Chris Hoiles .10 .05
❑ 132 Tom Gordon .10 .05
❑ 133 Kevin Seitzer .10 .05
❑ 134 Jeff Huson .10 .05
❑ 135 Jerry Don Gleaton .10 .05
❑ 136 Jeff Brantley UER .10 .05
(Photo actually Rick Leach on back)
❑ 137 Felix Fermin .10 .05
❑ 138 Mike Devereaux .10 .05
❑ 139 Delino DeShields .20 .09
❑ 140 David Wells .20 .09
❑ 141 Tim Crews .10 .05
❑ 142 Erik Hanson .10 .05
❑ 143 Mark Davidson .10 .05
❑ 144 Tommy Gregg .10 .05
❑ 145 Jim Gantner .10 .05
❑ 146 Jose Lind .10 .05
❑ 147 Danny Tartabull .10 .05
❑ 148 Geno Petralli .10 .05
❑ 149 Travis Fryman .40 .18
❑ 150 Tim Naehring .10 .05
❑ 151 Kevin McReynolds .10 .05
❑ 152 Joe Orsulak .10 .05
❑ 153 Steve Frey .10 .05
❑ 154 Duane Ward .10 .05
❑ 155 Stan Javier .10 .05
❑ 156 Damon Berryhill .10 .05
❑ 157 Gene Larkin .10 .05
❑ 158 Greg Olson .10 .05
❑ 159 Mark Knudson .10 .05
❑ 160 Carmelo Martinez .10 .05
❑ 161 Storm Davis .10 .05
❑ 162 Jim Abbott .20 .09
❑ 163 Len Dykstra .20 .09
❑ 164 Tom Brunansky .10 .05
❑ 165 Dwight Gooden .20 .09
❑ 166 Jose Mesa .10 .05
❑ 167 Oil Can Boyd .10 .05
❑ 168 Barry Larkin .40 .18
❑ 169 Scott Sanderson .10 .05
❑ 170 Mark Grace .40 .18
❑ 171 Mark Guthrie .10 .05
❑ 172 Tom Glavine .40 .18
❑ 173 Gary Sheffield .40 .18
❑ 174 Roger Clemens CL .40 .18
❑ 175 Chris James .10 .05
❑ 176 Milt Thompson .10 .05
❑ 177 Donnie Hill .10 .05
❑ 178 Wes Chamberlain RC .10 .05
❑ 179 John Marzano .10 .05
❑ 180 Frank Viola .10 .05
❑ 181 Eric Anthony .10 .05
❑ 182 Jose Canseco .50 .23
❑ 183 Scott Scudder .10 .05
❑ 184 Dave Eiland .10 .05
❑ 185 Luis Salazar .10 .05
❑ 186 Pedro Munoz RC .10 .05
❑ 187 Steve Searcy .10 .05
❑ 188 Don Robinson .10 .05
❑ 189 Sandy Alomar Jr. .20 .09
❑ 190 Jose DeLeon .10 .05
❑ 191 John Orton .10 .05
❑ 192 Darren Daulton .20 .09
❑ 193 Mike Morgan .10 .05
❑ 194 Greg Briley .10 .05
❑ 195 Karl Rhodes .10 .05
❑ 196 Harold Baines .20 .09
❑ 197 Bill Doran .10 .05
❑ 198 Alvaro Espinoza .10 .05
❑ 199 Kirk McCaskill .10 .05
❑ 200 Jose DeJesus .10 .05
❑ 201 Jack Clark .20 .09
❑ 202 Daryl Boston .10 .05
❑ 203 Randy Tomlin RC .10 .05
❑ 204 Pedro Guerrero .10 .05
❑ 205 Billy Hatcher .10 .05
❑ 206 Tim Leary .10 .05
❑ 207 Ryne Sandberg .50 .23
❑ 208 Kirby Puckett 1.00 .45
❑ 209 Charlie Leibrandt .10 .05
❑ 210 Rick Honeycutt .10 .05
❑ 211 Joel Skinner .10 .05
❑ 212 Rex Hudler .10 .05
❑ 213 Bryan Harvey .10 .05
❑ 214 Charlie Hayes .10 .05
❑ 215 Matt Young .10 .05
❑ 216 Terry Kennedy .10 .05
❑ 217 Carl Nichols .10 .05
❑ 218 Mike Moore .10 .05
❑ 219 Paul O'Neill .20 .09
❑ 220 Steve Sax .10 .05
❑ 221 Shawn Boskie .10 .05
❑ 222 Rich DeLucia .10 .05
❑ 223 Lloyd Moseby .10 .05
❑ 224 Mike Kingery .10 .05
❑ 225 Carlos Baerga .10 .05
❑ 226 Bryn Smith .10 .05
❑ 227 Todd Stottlemyre .20 .09
❑ 228 Julio Franco .10 .05
❑ 229 Jim Gott .10 .05
❑ 230 Mike Schooler .10 .05
❑ 231 Steve Finley .20 .09
❑ 232 Dave Henderson .10 .05
❑ 233 Luis Quinones .10 .05
❑ 234 Mark Whiten .10 .05
❑ 235 Brian McRae RC .20 .09
❑ 236 Rich Gossage .20 .09
❑ 237 Rob Deer .10 .05
❑ 238 Will Clark .40 .18
❑ 239 Albert Belle .40 .18
❑ 240 Bob Melvin .10 .05
❑ 241 Larry Walker .40 .18
❑ 242 Dante Bichette .40 .18
❑ 243 Orel Hershiser .20 .09
❑ 244 Pete O'Brien .10 .05
❑ 245 Pete Harnisch .10 .05
❑ 246 Jeff Treadway .10 .05
❑ 247 Julio Machado .10 .05
❑ 248 Dave Johnson .10 .05
❑ 249 Kirk Gibson .20 .09
❑ 250 Kevin Brown .30 .14
❑ 251 Milt Cuyler .10 .05
❑ 252 Jeff Reardon .20 .09
❑ 253 David Cone .20 .09
❑ 254 Gary Redus .10 .05
❑ 255 Junior Noboa .10 .05
❑ 256 Greg Myers .10 .05
❑ 257 Dennis Cook .10 .05
❑ 258 Joe Girardi .20 .09
❑ 259 Allan Anderson .10 .05
❑ 260 Paul Marak .10 .05
❑ 261 Barry Bonds .60 .25
❑ 262 Juan Bell .10 .05
❑ 263 Russ Morman .10 .05
❑ 264 George Brett CL .40 .18
❑ 265 Jerald Clark .10 .05
❑ 266 Dwight Evans .20 .09
❑ 267 Roberto Alomar .40 .18
❑ 268 Danny Jackson .10 .05
❑ 269 Brian Downing .10 .05
❑ 270 John Cerutti .10 .05
❑ 271 Robin Ventura .40 .18
❑ 272 Gerald Perry .10 .05
❑ 273 Wade Boggs .50 .23
❑ 274 Dennis Martinez .20 .09
❑ 275 Andy Benes .10 .05
❑ 276 Tony Fossas .10 .05
❑ 277 Franklin Stubbs .10 .05
❑ 278 John Kruk .20 .09
❑ 279 Kevin Gross .10 .05
❑ 280 Von Hayes .10 .05
❑ 281 Frank Thomas 1.00 .45
❑ 282 Rob Dibble .10 .05
❑ 283 Mel Hall .10 .05
❑ 284 Rick Mahler .10 .05
❑ 285 Dennis Eckersley .20 .09
❑ 286 Bernard Gilkey .20 .09
❑ 287 Dan Plesac .10 .05
❑ 288 Jason Grimsley .10 .05
❑ 289 Mark Lewis .10 .05
❑ 290 Tony Gwynn .75 .35
❑ 291 Jeff Russell .10 .05
❑ 292 Curt Schilling .20 .09
❑ 293 Pascual Perez .10 .05
❑ 294 Jack Morris .20 .09
❑ 295 Hubie Brooks .10 .05
❑ 296 Alex Fernandez .20 .09
❑ 297 Harold Reynolds .10 .05
❑ 298 Craig Worthington .10 .05
❑ 299 Willie Wilson .10 .05
❑ 300 Mike Maddux .10 .05
❑ 301 Dave Righetti .10 .05
❑ 302 Paul Molitor .40 .18
❑ 303 Gary Gaetti .20 .09
❑ 304 Terry Pendleton .20 .09
❑ 305 Kevin Elster .10 .05
❑ 306 Scott Fletcher .10 .05
❑ 307 Jeff Robinson .10 .05
❑ 308 Jesse Barfield .10 .05
❑ 309 Mike LaCoss .10 .05
❑ 310 Andy Van Slyke .20 .09
❑ 311 Glenallen Hill .10 .05
❑ 312 Bud Black .10 .05
❑ 313 Kent Hrbek .20 .09
❑ 314 Tim Teufel .10 .05
❑ 315 Tony Fernandez .10 .05
❑ 316 Beau Allred .10 .05
❑ 317 Curtis Wilkerson .10 .05
❑ 318 Bill Sampen .10 .05
❑ 319 Randy Johnson .60 .25
❑ 320 Mike Heath .10 .05
❑ 321 Sammy Sosa 1.00 .45
❑ 322 Mickey Tettleton .10 .05
❑ 323 Jose Vizcaino .10 .05
❑ 324 John Candelaria .10 .05
❑ 325 Dave Howard .10 .05
❑ 326 Jose Rijo .10 .05
❑ 327 Todd Zeile .20 .09
❑ 328 Gene Nelson .10 .05
❑ 329 Dwayne Henry .10 .05
❑ 330 Mike Boddicker .10 .05
❑ 331 Ozzie Guillen .10 .05
❑ 332 Sam Horn .10 .05
❑ 333 Wally Whitehurst .10 .05
❑ 334 Dave Parker .20 .09
❑ 335 George Brett .75 .35
❑ 336 Bobby Thigpen .10 .05
❑ 337 Ed Whitson .10 .05
❑ 338 Ivan Calderon .10 .05
❑ 339 Mike Pagliarulo .10 .05
❑ 340 Jack McDowell .10 .05
❑ 341 Dana Kiecker .10 .05
❑ 342 Fred McGriff .40 .18
❑ 343 Mark Lee .10 .05
❑ 344 Alfredo Griffin .10 .05
❑ 345 Scott Bankhead .10 .05
❑ 346 Darrin Jackson .10 .05
❑ 347 Rafael Palmeiro .40 .18
❑ 348 Steve Farr .10 .05
❑ 349 Hensley Meulens .10 .05
❑ 350 Danny Cox .10 .05
❑ 351 Alan Trammell .30 .14
❑ 352 Edwin Nunez .10 .05
❑ 353 Joe Carter .20 .09
❑ 354 Eric Show .10 .05
❑ 355 Vance Law .10 .05
❑ 356 Jeff Gray .10 .05
❑ 357 Bobby Bonilla .20 .09
❑ 358 Ernest Riles .10 .05
❑ 359 Ron Hassey .10 .05
❑ 360 Willie McGee .20 .09

❑ 361 Mackey Sasser .10 .05
❑ 362 Glenn Braggs .10 .05
❑ 363 Mario Diaz .10 .05
❑ 364 Barry Bonds CL .40 .18
❑ 365 Kevin Bass .10 .05
❑ 366 Pete Incaviglia .10 .05
❑ 367 Luis Sojo UER .10 .05
(1989 stats interspersed with 1990s)
❑ 368 Lance Parrish .10 .05
❑ 369 Mark Leonard .10 .05
❑ 370 Heathcliff Slocumb RC .10 .05
❑ 371 Jimmy Jones .10 .05
❑ 372 Ken Griffey Jr. 2.00 .90
❑ 373 Chris Hammond .10 .05
❑ 374 Chili Davis .20 .09
❑ 375 Joey Cora .10 .05
❑ 376 Ken Hill .10 .05
❑ 377 Darryl Strawberry .20 .09
❑ 378 Ron Darling .10 .05
❑ 379 Sid Bream .10 .05
❑ 380 Bill Swift .10 .05
❑ 381 Shawn Abner .10 .05
❑ 382 Eric King .10 .05
❑ 383 Mickey Morandini .10 .05
❑ 384 Carlton Fisk .40 .18
❑ 385 Steve Lake .10 .05
❑ 386 Mike Jeffcoat .10 .05
❑ 387 Darren Holmes RC .10 .05
❑ 388 Tim Wallach .10 .05
❑ 389 George Bell .10 .05
❑ 390 Craig Lefferts .10 .05
❑ 391 Ernie Whitt .10 .05
❑ 392 Felix Jose .10 .05
❑ 393 Kevin Maas .10 .05
❑ 394 Devon White .10 .05
❑ 395 Otis Nixon .10 .05
❑ 396 Chuck Knoblauch .20 .09
❑ 397 Scott Coolbaugh .10 .05
❑ 398 Glenn Davis .10 .05
❑ 399 Manny Lee .10 .05
❑ 400 Andre Dawson .30 .14
❑ 401 Scott Chiamparino .10 .05
❑ 402 Bill Gullickson .10 .05
❑ 403 Lance Johnson .10 .05
❑ 404 Juan Agosto .10 .05
❑ 405 Danny Darwin .10 .05
❑ 406 Barry Jones .10 .05
❑ 407 Larry Andersen .10 .05
❑ 408 Luis Rivera .10 .05
❑ 409 Jaime Navarro .10 .05
❑ 410 Roger McDowell .10 .05
❑ 411 Brett Butler .20 .09
❑ 412 Dale Murphy .40 .18
❑ 413 Tim Raines UER .20 .09
(Listed as hitting .500 in 1980; should be .050)
❑ 414 Norm Charlton .10 .05
❑ 415 Greg Cadaret .10 .05
❑ 416 Chris Nabholz .10 .05
❑ 417 Dave Stewart .20 .09
❑ 418 Rich Gedman .10 .05
❑ 419 Willie Randolph .20 .09
❑ 420 Mitch Williams .10 .05
❑ 421 Brook Jacoby .10 .05
❑ 422 Greg W. Harris .10 .05
❑ 423 Nolan Ryan 2.00 .90
❑ 424 Dave Rohde .10 .05
❑ 425 Don Mattingly 1.00 .45
❑ 426 Greg Gagne .10 .05
❑ 427 Vince Coleman .10 .05
❑ 428 Dan Pasqua .10 .05
❑ 429 Alvin Davis .10 .05
❑ 430 Cal Ripken 1.50 .70
❑ 431 Jamie Quirk .10 .05
❑ 432 Benito Santiago .10 .05
❑ 433 Jose Uribe .10 .05
❑ 434 Candy Maldonado .10 .05
❑ 435 Junior Felix .10 .05
❑ 436 Deion Sanders .20 .09
❑ 437 John Franco .20 .09
❑ 438 Greg Hibbard .10 .05
❑ 439 Floyd Bannister .10 .05
❑ 440 Steve Howe .10 .05
❑ 441 Steve Decker .10 .05
❑ 442 Vicente Palacios .10 .05
❑ 443 Pat Tabler .10 .05
❑ 444 Darryl Strawberry CL .20 .09
❑ 445 Mike Felder .10 .05
❑ 446 Al Newman .10 .05
❑ 447 Chris Donnels .10 .05
❑ 448 Rich Rodriguez .10 .05
❑ 449 Turner Ward RC .10 .05
❑ 450 Bob Walk .10 .05
❑ 451 Gilberto Reyes .10 .05
❑ 452 Mike Jackson .10 .05
❑ 453 Rafael Belliard .10 .05
❑ 454 Wayne Edwards .10 .05
❑ 455 Andy Allanson .10 .05
❑ 456 Dave Smith .10 .05
❑ 457 Gary Carter .30 .14
❑ 458 Warren Cromartie .10 .05
❑ 459 Jack Armstrong .10 .05
❑ 460 Bob Tewksbury .10 .05
❑ 461 Joe Klink .10 .05
❑ 462 Xavier Hernandez .10 .05
❑ 463 Scott Radinsky .10 .05
❑ 464 Jeff Robinson .10 .05
❑ 465 Gregg Jefferies .10 .05
❑ 466 Denny Neagle RC .50 .23
❑ 467 Carmelo Martinez .10 .05
❑ 468 Donn Pall .10 .05
❑ 469 Bruce Hurst .10 .05
❑ 470 Eric Bullock .10 .05
❑ 471 Rick Aguilera .20 .09
❑ 472 Charlie Hough .20 .09
❑ 473 Carlos Quintana .10 .05
❑ 474 Marty Barrett .10 .05
❑ 475 Kevin D. Brown .10 .05
❑ 476 Bobby Ojeda .10 .05
❑ 477 Edgar Martinez .30 .14
❑ 478 Bip Roberts .10 .05
❑ 479 Mike Flanagan .10 .05
❑ 480 John Habyan .10 .05
❑ 481 Larry Casian .10 .05
❑ 482 Wally Backman .10 .05
❑ 483 Doug Dascenzo .10 .05
❑ 484 Rick Dempsey .10 .05
❑ 485 Ed Sprague .10 .05
❑ 486 Steve Chitren .10 .05
❑ 487 Mark McGwire 1.50 .70
❑ 488 Roger Clemens .75 .35
❑ 489 Orlando Merced RC .10 .05
❑ 490 Rene Gonzales .10 .05
❑ 491 Mike Stanton .10 .05
❑ 492 Al Osuna RC .10 .05
❑ 493 Rick Cerone .10 .05
❑ 494 Mariano Duncan .10 .05
❑ 495 Zane Smith .10 .05
❑ 496 John Morris .10 .05
❑ 497 Frank Tanana .10 .05
❑ 498 Junior Ortiz .10 .05
❑ 499 Dave Winfield .40 .18
❑ 500 Gary Varsho .10 .05
❑ 501 Chico Walker .10 .05
❑ 502 Ken Caminiti .20 .09
❑ 503 Ken Griffey Sr. .20 .09
❑ 504 Randy Myers .20 .09
❑ 505 Steve Bedrosian .10 .05
❑ 506 Cory Snyder .10 .05
❑ 507 Cris Carpenter .10 .05
❑ 508 Tim Belcher .10 .05
❑ 509 Jeff Hamilton .10 .05
❑ 510 Steve Avery .10 .05
❑ 511 Dave Valle .10 .05
❑ 512 Tom Lampkin .10 .05
❑ 513 Shawn Hillegas .10 .05
❑ 514 Reggie Jefferson .30 .14
❑ 515 Ron Karkovice .10 .05
❑ 516 Doug Drabek .10 .05
❑ 517 Tom Henke .10 .05
❑ 518 Chris Bosio .10 .05
❑ 519 Gregg Olson .10 .05
❑ 520 Bob Scanlan .10 .05
❑ 521 Alonzo Powell .10 .05
❑ 522 Jeff Ballard .10 .05
❑ 523 Ray Lankford .40 .18
❑ 524 Tommy Greene .10 .05
❑ 525 Mike Timlin RC .10 .05
❑ 526 Juan Berenguer .10 .05
❑ 527 Scott Erickson .10 .05
❑ 528 Sandy Alomar Jr. CL .10 .05

## 1992 Leaf

| | MINT | NRMT |
|---|---|---|
| COMPLETE SET (528) | 15.00 | 6.75 |
| COMPLETE SERIES 1 (264) | 5.00 | 2.20 |
| COMPLETE SERIES 2 (264) | 10.00 | 4.50 |
| COMMON CARD (1-528) | .05 | .02 |

❑ 1 Jim Abbott .15 .07
❑ 2 Cal Eldred .05 .02
❑ 3 Bud Black .05 .02
❑ 4 Dave Howard .05 .02
❑ 5 Luis Sojo .05 .02
❑ 6 Gary Scott .05 .02
❑ 7 Joe Oliver .05 .02
❑ 8 Chris Gardner .05 .02
❑ 9 Sandy Alomar Jr. .15 .07
❑ 10 Greg W. Harris .05 .02
❑ 11 Doug Drabek .05 .02
❑ 12 Darryl Hamilton .05 .02
❑ 13 Mike Mussina .50 .23
❑ 14 Kevin Tapani .05 .02
❑ 15 Ron Gant .15 .07
❑ 16 Mark McGwire 1.25 .55
❑ 17 Robin Ventura .15 .07
❑ 18 Pedro Guerrero .05 .02
❑ 19 Roger Clemens .60 .25
❑ 20 Steve Farr .05 .02
❑ 21 Frank Tanana .05 .02
❑ 22 Joe Hesketh .05 .02
❑ 23 Erik Hanson .05 .02
❑ 24 Greg Cadaret .05 .02
❑ 25 Rex Hudler .05 .02
❑ 26 Mark Grace .30 .14
❑ 27 Kelly Gruber .05 .02
❑ 28 Jeff Bagwell .60 .25
❑ 29 Darryl Strawberry .15 .07
❑ 30 Dave Smith .05 .02
❑ 31 Kevin Appier .15 .07
❑ 32 Steve Chitren .05 .02
❑ 33 Kevin Gross .05 .02
❑ 34 Rick Aguilera .15 .07
❑ 35 Juan Guzman .05 .02
❑ 36 Joe Orsulak .05 .02
❑ 37 Tim Raines .15 .07
❑ 38 Harold Reynolds .05 .02
❑ 39 Charlie Hough .15 .07
❑ 40 Tony Phillips .05 .02
❑ 41 Nolan Ryan 1.50 .70
❑ 42 Vince Coleman .05 .02
❑ 43 Andy Van Slyke .15 .07
❑ 44 Tim Burke .05 .02
❑ 45 Luis Polonia .05 .02
❑ 46 Tom Browning .05 .02
❑ 47 Willie McGee .15 .07
❑ 48 Gary DiSarcina .05 .02
❑ 49 Mark Lewis .05 .02
❑ 50 Phil Plantier .05 .02
❑ 51 Doug Dascenzo .05 .02
❑ 52 Cal Ripken 1.25 .55
❑ 53 Pedro Munoz .05 .02
❑ 54 Carlos Hernandez .05 .02
❑ 55 Jerald Clark .05 .02
❑ 56 Jeff Brantley .05 .02
❑ 57 Don Mattingly .75 .35
❑ 58 Roger McDowell .05 .02
❑ 59 Steve Avery .05 .02
❑ 60 John Olerud .15 .07

❑ 61 Bill Gullickson .05 .02
❑ 62 Juan Gonzalez .30 .14
❑ 63 Felix Jose .05 .02
❑ 64 Robin Yount .30 .14
❑ 65 Greg Briley .05 .02
❑ 66 Steve Finley .15 .07
❑ 67 Frank Thomas CL .30 .14
❑ 68 Tom Gordon .05 .02
❑ 69 Rob Dibble .05 .02
❑ 70 Glenallen Hill .05 .02
❑ 71 Calvin Jones .05 .02
❑ 72 Joe Girardi .15 .07
❑ 73 Barry Larkin .20 .09
❑ 74 Andy Benes .05 .02
❑ 75 Milt Cuyler .05 .02
❑ 76 Kevin Bass .05 .02
❑ 77 Pete Harnisch .05 .02
❑ 78 Wilson Alvarez .05 .02
❑ 79 Mike Devereaux .05 .02
❑ 80 Doug Henry RC .05 .02
❑ 81 Orel Hershiser .15 .07
❑ 82 Shane Mack .05 .02
❑ 83 Mike Macfarlane .05 .02
❑ 84 Thomas Howard .05 .02
❑ 85 Alex Fernandez .15 .07
❑ 86 Reggie Jefferson .15 .07
❑ 87 Leo Gomez .05 .02
❑ 88 Mel Hall .05 .02
❑ 89 Mike Greenwell .05 .02
❑ 90 Jeff Russell .05 .02
❑ 91 Steve Buechele .05 .02
❑ 92 David Cone .15 .07
❑ 93 Kevin Reimer .05 .02
❑ 94 Mark Lemke .05 .02
❑ 95 Bob Tewksbury .05 .02
❑ 96 Zane Smith .05 .02
❑ 97 Mark Eichhorn .05 .02
❑ 98 Kirby Puckett .75 .35
❑ 99 Paul O'Neill .15 .07
❑ 100 Dennis Eckersley .15 .07
❑ 101 Duane Ward .05 .02
❑ 102 Matt Nokes .05 .02
❑ 103 Mo Vaughn .15 .07
❑ 104 Pat Kelly .05 .02
❑ 105 Ron Karkovice .05 .02
❑ 106 Bill Spiers .05 .02
❑ 107 Gary Gaetti .15 .07
❑ 108 Mackey Sasser .05 .02
❑ 109 Robby Thompson .05 .02
❑ 110 Marvin Freeman .05 .02
❑ 111 Jimmy Key .15 .07
❑ 112 Dwight Gooden .15 .07
❑ 113 Charlie Leibrandt .05 .02
❑ 114 Devon White .05 .02
❑ 115 Charles Nagy .05 .02
❑ 116 Rickey Henderson .40 .18
❑ 117 Paul Assenmacher .05 .02
❑ 118 Junior Felix .05 .02
❑ 119 Julio Franco .05 .02
❑ 120 Norm Charlton .05 .02
❑ 121 Scott Servais .05 .02
❑ 122 Gerald Perry .05 .02
❑ 123 Brian McRae .05 .02
❑ 124 Don Slaught .05 .02
❑ 125 Juan Samuel .05 .02
❑ 126 Harold Baines .15 .07
❑ 127 Scott Livingstone .05 .02
❑ 128 Jay Buhner .15 .07
❑ 129 Darrin Jackson .05 .02
❑ 130 Luis Mercedes .05 .02
❑ 131 Brian Harper .05 .02
❑ 132 Howard Johnson .05 .02
❑ 133 Nolan Ryan CL .30 .14
❑ 134 Dante Bichette .20 .09
❑ 135 Dave Righetti .05 .02
❑ 136 Jeff Montgomery .15 .07
❑ 137 Joe Grahe .05 .02
❑ 138 Delino DeShields .15 .07
❑ 139 Jose Rijo .05 .02
❑ 140 Ken Caminiti .15 .07
❑ 141 Steve Olin .05 .02
❑ 142 Kurt Stillwell .05 .02
❑ 143 Jay Bell .15 .07
❑ 144 Jaime Navarro .05 .02
❑ 145 Ben McDonald .05 .02
❑ 146 Greg Gagne .05 .02
❑ 147 Jeff Blauser .05 .02
❑ 148 Carney Lansford .15 .07
❑ 149 Ozzie Guillen .05 .02
❑ 150 Milt Thompson .05 .02
❑ 151 Jeff Reardon .15 .07
❑ 152 Scott Sanderson .05 .02
❑ 153 Cecil Fielder .15 .07
❑ 154 Greg A. Harris .05 .02
❑ 155 Rich DeLucia .05 .02
❑ 156 Roberto Kelly .05 .02
❑ 157 Bryn Smith .05 .02
❑ 158 Chuck McElroy .05 .02
❑ 159 Tom Henke .05 .02
❑ 160 Luis Gonzalez .20 .09
❑ 161 Steve Wilson .05 .02
❑ 162 Shawn Boskie .05 .02
❑ 163 Mark Davis .05 .02
❑ 164 Mike Moore .05 .02
❑ 165 Mike Scioscia .05 .02
❑ 166 Scott Erickson .05 .02
❑ 167 Todd Stottlemyre .15 .07
❑ 168 Alvin Davis .05 .02
❑ 169 Greg Hibbard .05 .02
❑ 170 David Valle .05 .02
❑ 171 Dave Winfield .30 .14
❑ 172 Alan Trammell .20 .09
❑ 173 Kenny Rogers .05 .02
❑ 174 John Franco .15 .07
❑ 175 Jose Lind .05 .02
❑ 176 Pete Schourek .05 .02
❑ 177 Von Hayes .05 .02
❑ 178 Chris Hammond .05 .02
❑ 179 John Burkett .05 .02
❑ 180 Dickie Thon .05 .02
❑ 181 Joel Skinner .05 .02
❑ 182 Scott Cooper .05 .02
❑ 183 Andre Dawson .20 .09
❑ 184 Billy Ripken .05 .02
❑ 185 Kevin Mitchell .15 .07
❑ 186 Brett Butler .15 .07
❑ 187 Tony Fernandez .05 .02
❑ 188 Cory Snyder .05 .02
❑ 189 John Habyan .05 .02
❑ 190 Dennis Martinez .15 .07
❑ 191 John Smoltz .15 .07
❑ 192 Greg Myers .05 .02
❑ 193 Rob Deer .05 .02
❑ 194 Ivan Rodriguez .60 .25
❑ 195 Ray Lankford .30 .14
❑ 196 Bill Wegman .05 .02
❑ 197 Edgar Martinez .20 .09
❑ 198 Darryl Kile .15 .07
❑ 199 Cal Ripken CL .30 .14
❑ 200 Brent Mayne .05 .02
❑ 201 Larry Walker .20 .09
❑ 202 Carlos Baerga .05 .02
❑ 203 Russ Swan .05 .02
❑ 204 Mike Morgan .05 .02
❑ 205 Hal Morris .05 .02
❑ 206 Tony Gwynn .60 .25
❑ 207 Mark Leiter .05 .02
❑ 208 Kirt Manwaring .05 .02
❑ 209 Al Osuna .05 .02
❑ 210 Bobby Thigpen .05 .02
❑ 211 Chris Hoiles .05 .02
❑ 212 B.J. Surhoff .15 .07
❑ 213 Lenny Harris .05 .02
❑ 214 Scott Leius .05 .02
❑ 215 Gregg Jefferies .05 .02
❑ 216 Bruce Hurst .05 .02
❑ 217 Steve Sax .05 .02
❑ 218 Dave Otto .05 .02
❑ 219 Sam Horn .05 .02
❑ 220 Charlie Hayes .05 .02
❑ 221 Frank Viola .05 .02
❑ 222 Jose Guzman .05 .02
❑ 223 Gary Redus .05 .02
❑ 224 Dave Gallagher .05 .02
❑ 225 Dean Palmer .15 .07
❑ 226 Greg Olson .05 .02
❑ 227 Jose DeLeon .05 .02
❑ 228 Mike LaValliere .05 .02
❑ 229 Mark Langston .05 .02
❑ 230 Chuck Knoblauch .15 .07
❑ 231 Bill Doran .05 .02
❑ 232 Dave Henderson .05 .02
❑ 233 Roberto Alomar .30 .14
❑ 234 Scott Fletcher .05 .02
❑ 235 Tim Naehring .05 .02
❑ 236 Mike Gallego .05 .02
❑ 237 Lance Johnson .05 .02
❑ 238 Paul Molitor .30 .14
❑ 239 Dan Gladden .05 .02
❑ 240 Willie Randolph .15 .07
❑ 241 Will Clark .30 .14
❑ 242 Sid Bream .05 .02
❑ 243 Derek Bell .15 .07
❑ 244 Bill Pecota .05 .02
❑ 245 Terry Pendleton .15 .07
❑ 246 Randy Ready .05 .02
❑ 247 Jack Armstrong .05 .02
❑ 248 Todd Van Poppel .05 .02
❑ 249 Shawon Dunston .05 .02
❑ 250 Bobby Rose .05 .02
❑ 251 Jeff Huson .05 .02
❑ 252 Bip Roberts .05 .02
❑ 253 Doug Jones .05 .02
❑ 254 Lee Smith .15 .07
❑ 255 George Brett .60 .25
❑ 256 Randy Tomlin .05 .02
❑ 257 Todd Benzinger .05 .02
❑ 258 Dave Stewart .15 .07
❑ 259 Mark Carreon .05 .02
❑ 260 Pete O'Brien .05 .02
❑ 261 Tim Teufel .05 .02
❑ 262 Bob Milacki .05 .02
❑ 263 Mark Guthrie .05 .02
❑ 264 Darrin Fletcher .05 .02
❑ 265 Omar Vizquel .15 .07
❑ 266 Chris Bosio .05 .02
❑ 267 Jose Canseco .40 .18
❑ 268 Mike Boddicker .05 .02
❑ 269 Lance Parrish .05 .02
❑ 270 Jose Vizcaino .05 .02
❑ 271 Chris Sabo .05 .02
❑ 272 Royce Clayton .05 .02
❑ 273 Marquis Grissom .05 .02
❑ 274 Fred McGriff .20 .09
❑ 275 Barry Bonds .50 .23
❑ 276 Greg Vaughn .20 .09
❑ 277 Gregg Olson .05 .02
❑ 278 Dave Hollins .05 .02
❑ 279 Tom Glavine .20 .09
❑ 280 Bryan Hickerson UER .05 .02
(Name spelled Brian on front)
❑ 281 Scott Radinsky .05 .02
❑ 282 Omar Olivares .05 .02
❑ 283 Ivan Calderon .05 .02
❑ 284 Kevin Maas .05 .02
❑ 285 Mickey Tettleton .05 .02
❑ 286 Wade Boggs .40 .18
❑ 287 Stan Belinda .05 .02
❑ 288 Bret Barberie .05 .02
❑ 289 Jose Oquendo .05 .02
❑ 290 Frank Castillo .05 .02
❑ 291 Dave Stieb .05 .02
❑ 292 Tommy Greene .05 .02
❑ 293 Eric Karros .30 .14
❑ 294 Greg Maddux .75 .35
❑ 295 Jim Eisenreich .05 .02
❑ 296 Rafael Palmeiro .30 .14
❑ 297 Ramon Martinez .05 .02
❑ 298 Tim Wallach .05 .02
❑ 299 Jim Thome .60 .25
❑ 300 Chito Martinez .05 .02
❑ 301 Mitch Williams .05 .02
❑ 302 Randy Johnson .40 .18
❑ 303 Carlton Fisk .30 .14
❑ 304 Travis Fryman .15 .07
❑ 305 Bobby Witt .05 .02
❑ 306 Dave Magadan .05 .02
❑ 307 Alex Cole .05 .02
❑ 308 Bobby Bonilla .15 .07
❑ 309 Bryan Harvey .05 .02
❑ 310 Rafael Belliard .05 .02
❑ 311 Mariano Duncan .05 .02
❑ 312 Chuck Crim .05 .02
❑ 313 John Kruk .15 .07
❑ 314 Ellis Burks .15 .07
❑ 315 Craig Biggio .20 .09
❑ 316 Glenn Davis .05 .02
❑ 317 Ryne Sandberg .40 .18

❑ 318 Mike Sharperson .05 .02
❑ 319 Rich Rodriguez .05 .02
❑ 320 Lee Guetterman .05 .02
❑ 321 Benito Santiago .05 .02
❑ 322 Jose Offerman .05 .02
❑ 323 Tony Pena .05 .02
❑ 324 Pat Borders .05 .02
❑ 325 Mike Henneman .05 .02
❑ 326 Kevin Brown .20 .09
❑ 327 Chris Nabholz .05 .02
❑ 328 Franklin Stubbs .05 .02
❑ 329 Tino Martinez .15 .07
❑ 330 Mickey Morandini .05 .02
❑ 331 Ryne Sandberg CL .30 .14
❑ 332 Mark Gubicza .05 .02
❑ 333 Bill Landrum .05 .02
❑ 334 Mark Whiten .05 .02
❑ 335 Darren Daulton .15 .07
❑ 336 Rick Wilkins .05 .02
❑ 337 Brian Jordan RC .75 .35
❑ 338 Kevin Ward .05 .02
❑ 339 Ruben Amaro .05 .02
❑ 340 Trevor Wilson .05 .02
❑ 341 Andujar Cedeno .05 .02
❑ 342 Michael Huff .05 .02
❑ 343 Brady Anderson .20 .09
❑ 344 Craig Grebeck .05 .02
❑ 345 Bob Ojeda .05 .02
❑ 346 Mike Pagliarulo .05 .02
❑ 347 Terry Shumpert .05 .02
❑ 348 Dann Bilardello .05 .02
❑ 349 Frank Thomas .60 .25
❑ 350 Albert Belle .20 .09
❑ 351 Jose Mesa .05 .02
❑ 352 Rich Monteleone .05 .02
❑ 353 Bob Walk .05 .02
❑ 354 Monty Fariss .05 .02
❑ 355 Luis Rivera .05 .02
❑ 356 Anthony Young .05 .02
❑ 357 Geno Petralli .05 .02
❑ 358 Otis Nixon .05 .02
❑ 359 Tom Pagnozzi .05 .02
❑ 360 Reggie Sanders .05 .02
❑ 361 Lee Stevens .15 .07
❑ 362 Kent Hrbek .15 .07
❑ 363 Orlando Merced .05 .02
❑ 364 Mike Bordick .05 .02
❑ 365 Dion James UER .05 .02
(Blue Jays logo on card back)
❑ 366 Jack Clark .15 .07
❑ 367 Mike Stanley .05 .02
❑ 368 Randy Velarde .05 .02
❑ 369 Dan Pasqua .05 .02
❑ 370 Pat Listach RC .05 .02
❑ 371 Mike Fitzgerald .05 .02
❑ 372 Tom Foley .05 .02
❑ 373 Matt Williams .20 .09
❑ 374 Brian Hunter .05 .02
❑ 375 Joe Carter .15 .07
❑ 376 Bret Saberhagen .15 .07
❑ 377 Mike Stanton .05 .02
❑ 378 Hubie Brooks .05 .02
❑ 379 Eric Bell .05 .02
❑ 380 Walt Weiss .05 .02
❑ 381 Danny Jackson .05 .02
❑ 382 Manuel Lee .05 .02
❑ 383 Ruben Sierra .05 .02
❑ 384 Greg Swindell .05 .02
❑ 385 Ryan Bowen .05 .02
❑ 386 Kevin Ritz .05 .02
❑ 387 Curtis Wilkerson .05 .02
❑ 388 Gary Varsho .05 .02
❑ 389 Dave Hansen .05 .02
❑ 390 Bob Welch .05 .02
❑ 391 Lou Whitaker .15 .07
❑ 392 Ken Griffey Jr. 1.25 .55
❑ 393 Mike Maddux .05 .02
❑ 394 Arthur Rhodes .05 .02
❑ 395 Chili Davis .15 .07
❑ 396 Eddie Murray .30 .14
❑ 397 Robin Yount CL .20 .09
❑ 398 Dave Cochrane .05 .02
❑ 399 Kevin Seitzer .05 .02
❑ 400 Ozzie Smith .40 .18
❑ 401 Paul Sorrento .05 .02
❑ 402 Les Lancaster .05 .02
❑ 403 Junior Noboa .05 .02
❑ 404 David Justice .20 .09
❑ 405 Andy Ashby .15 .07
❑ 406 Danny Tartabull .05 .02
❑ 407 Bill Swift .05 .02
❑ 408 Craig Lefferts .05 .02
❑ 409 Tom Candiotti .05 .02
❑ 410 Lance Blankenship .05 .02
❑ 411 Jeff Tackett .05 .02
❑ 412 Sammy Sosa .60 .25
❑ 413 Jody Reed .05 .02
❑ 414 Bruce Ruffin .05 .02
❑ 415 Gene Larkin .05 .02
❑ 416 John Vander Wal RC .05 .02
❑ 417 Tim Belcher .05 .02
❑ 418 Steve Frey .05 .02
❑ 419 Dick Schofield .05 .02
❑ 420 Jeff King .05 .02
❑ 421 Kim Batiste .05 .02
❑ 422 Jack McDowell .05 .02
❑ 423 Damon Berryhill .05 .02
❑ 424 Gary Wayne .05 .02
❑ 425 Jack Morris .15 .07
❑ 426 Moises Alou .30 .14
❑ 427 Mark McLemore .05 .02
❑ 428 Juan Guerrero .05 .02
❑ 429 Scott Scudder .05 .02
❑ 430 Eric Davis .15 .07
❑ 431 Joe Slusarski .05 .02
❑ 432 Todd Zeile .05 .02
❑ 433 Dwayne Henry .05 .02
❑ 434 Cliff Brantley .05 .02
❑ 435 Butch Henry RC .05 .02
❑ 436 Todd Worrell .05 .02
❑ 437 Bob Scanlan .05 .02
❑ 438 Wally Joyner .15 .07
❑ 439 John Flaherty .05 .02
❑ 440 Brian Downing .05 .02
❑ 441 Darren Lewis .05 .02
❑ 442 Gary Carter .20 .09
❑ 443 Wally Ritchie .05 .02
❑ 444 Chris Jones .05 .02
❑ 445 Jeff Kent RC 2.00 .90
❑ 446 Gary Sheffield .30 .14
❑ 447 Ron Darling .05 .02
❑ 448 Deion Sanders .30 .14
❑ 449 Andres Galarraga .20 .09
❑ 450 Chuck Finley .15 .07
❑ 451 Derek Lilliquist .05 .02
❑ 452 Carl Willis .05 .02
❑ 453 Wes Chamberlain .05 .02
❑ 454 Roger Mason .05 .02
❑ 455 Spike Owen .05 .02
❑ 456 Thomas Howard .05 .02
❑ 457 Dave Martinez .05 .02
❑ 458 Pete Incaviglia .05 .02
❑ 459 Keith A. Miller .05 .02
❑ 460 Mike Fetters .05 .02
❑ 461 Paul Gibson .05 .02
❑ 462 George Bell .05 .02
❑ 463 Bobby Bonilla CL .05 .02
❑ 464 Terry Mulholland .05 .02
❑ 465 Storm Davis .05 .02
❑ 466 Gary Pettis .05 .02
❑ 467 Randy Bush .05 .02
❑ 468 Ken Hill .05 .02
❑ 469 Rheal Cormier .05 .02
❑ 470 Andy Stankiewicz .05 .02
❑ 471 Dave Burba .05 .02
❑ 472 Henry Cotto .05 .02
❑ 473 Dale Sveum .05 .02
❑ 474 Rich Gossage .15 .07
❑ 475 William Suero .05 .02
❑ 476 Doug Strange .05 .02
❑ 477 Bill Krueger .05 .02
❑ 478 John Wetteland .15 .07
❑ 479 Melido Perez .05 .02
❑ 480 Lonnie Smith .05 .02
❑ 481 Mike Jackson .05 .02
❑ 482 Mike Gardiner .05 .02
❑ 483 David Wells .15 .07
❑ 484 Barry Jones .05 .02
❑ 485 Scott Bankhead .05 .02
❑ 486 Terry Leach .05 .02
❑ 487 Vince Horsman .05 .02
❑ 488 Dave Eiland .05 .02
❑ 489 Alejandro Pena .05 .02
❑ 490 Julio Valera .05 .02
❑ 491 Joe Boever .05 .02
❑ 492 Paul Miller RC .05 .02
❑ 493 Archi Cianfrocco RC .05 .02
❑ 494 Dave Fleming .05 .02
❑ 495 Kyle Abbott .05 .02
❑ 496 Chad Kreuter .05 .02
❑ 497 Chris James .05 .02
❑ 498 Donnie Hill .05 .02
❑ 499 Jacob Brumfield .05 .02
❑ 500 Ricky Bones .05 .02
❑ 501 Terry Steinbach .05 .02
❑ 502 Bernard Gilkey .15 .07
❑ 503 Dennis Cook .05 .02
❑ 504 Len Dykstra .15 .07
❑ 505 Mike Bielecki .05 .02
❑ 506 Bob Kipper .05 .02
❑ 507 Jose Melendez .05 .02
❑ 508 Rick Sutcliffe .15 .07
❑ 509 Ken Patterson .05 .02
❑ 510 Andy Allanson .05 .02
❑ 511 Al Newman .05 .02
❑ 512 Mark Gardner .05 .02
❑ 513 Jeff Schaefer .05 .02
❑ 514 Jim McNamara .05 .02
❑ 515 Peter Hoy .05 .02
❑ 516 Curt Schilling .15 .07
❑ 517 Kirk McCaskill .05 .02
❑ 518 Chris Gwynn .05 .02
❑ 519 Sid Fernandez .05 .02
❑ 520 Jeff Parrett .05 .02
❑ 521 Scott Ruskin .05 .02
❑ 522 Kevin McReynolds .05 .02
❑ 523 Rick Cerone .05 .02
❑ 524 Jesse Orosco .05 .02
❑ 525 Troy Afenir .05 .02
❑ 526 John Smiley .05 .02
❑ 527 Dale Murphy .30 .14
❑ 528 Leaf Set Card .05 .02

## 1993 Leaf

| | MINT | NRMT |
|---|---|---|
| COMPLETE SET (550) | 35.00 | 16.00 |
| COMPLETE SERIES 1 (220) | 15.00 | 6.75 |
| COMPLETE SERIES 2 (220) | 15.00 | 6.75 |
| COMPLETE UPDATE (110) | 5.00 | 2.20 |
| COMMON CARD (1-550) | .15 | .07 |

❑ 1 Ben McDonald .15 .07
❑ 2 Sid Fernandez .15 .07
❑ 3 Juan Guzman .15 .07
❑ 4 Curt Schilling .30 .14
❑ 5 Ivan Rodriguez .75 .35
❑ 6 Don Slaught .15 .07
❑ 7 Terry Steinbach .15 .07
❑ 8 Todd Zeile .15 .07
❑ 9 Andy Stankiewicz .15 .07
❑ 10 Tim Teufel .15 .07
❑ 11 Marvin Freeman .15 .07
❑ 12 Jim Austin .15 .07
❑ 13 Bob Scanlan .15 .07
❑ 14 Rusty Meacham .15 .07
❑ 15 Casey Candaele .15 .07
❑ 16 Travis Fryman .30 .14
❑ 17 Jose Offerman .15 .07

❑ 18 Albert Belle .40 .18
❑ 19 John Vander Wal .15 .07
❑ 20 Dan Pasqua .15 .07
❑ 21 Frank Viola .15 .07
❑ 22 Terry Mulholland .15 .07
❑ 23 Gregg Olson .15 .07
❑ 24 Randy Tomlin .15 .07
❑ 25 Todd Stottlemyre .15 .07
❑ 26 Jose Oquendo .15 .07
❑ 27 Julio Franco .15 .07
❑ 28 Tony Gwynn 1.25 .55
❑ 29 Ruben Sierra .15 .07
❑ 30 Robby Thompson .15 .07
❑ 31 Jim Bullinger .15 .07
❑ 32 Rick Aguilera .15 .07
❑ 33 Scott Servais .15 .07
❑ 34 Cal Eldred .15 .07
❑ 35 Mike Piazza 3.00 1.35
❑ 36 Brent Mayne .15 .07
❑ 37 Wil Cordero .15 .07
❑ 38 Milt Cuyler .15 .07
❑ 39 Howard Johnson .15 .07
❑ 40 Kenny Lofton .30 .14
❑ 41 Alex Fernandez .30 .14
❑ 42 Denny Neagle .30 .14
❑ 43 Tony Pena .15 .07
❑ 44 Bob Tewksbury .15 .07
❑ 45 Glenn Davis .15 .07
❑ 46 Fred McGriff .40 .18
❑ 47 John Olerud .40 .18
❑ 48 Steve Hosey .15 .07
❑ 49 Rafael Palmeiro .60 .25
❑ 50 David Justice .40 .18
❑ 51 Pete Harnisch .15 .07
❑ 52 Sam Militello .15 .07
❑ 53 Orel Hershiser .30 .14
❑ 54 Pat Mahomes .15 .07
❑ 55 Greg Colbrunn .15 .07
❑ 56 Greg Vaughn .30 .14
❑ 57 Vince Coleman .15 .07
❑ 58 Brian McRae .15 .07
❑ 59 Len Dykstra .30 .14
❑ 60 Dan Gladden .15 .07
❑ 61 Ted Power .15 .07
❑ 62 Donovan Osborne .15 .07
❑ 63 Ron Karkovice .15 .07
❑ 64 Frank Seminara .15 .07
❑ 65 Bob Zupcic .15 .07
❑ 66 Kirt Manwaring .15 .07
❑ 67 Mike Devereaux .15 .07
❑ 68 Mark Lemke .15 .07
❑ 69 Devon White .15 .07
❑ 70 Sammy Sosa 1.25 .55
❑ 71 Pedro Astacio .30 .14
❑ 72 Dennis Eckersley .30 .14
❑ 73 Chris Nabholz .15 .07
❑ 74 Melido Perez .15 .07
❑ 75 Todd Hundley .15 .07
❑ 76 Kent Hrbek .30 .14
❑ 77 Mickey Morandini .15 .07
❑ 78 Tim McIntosh .15 .07
❑ 79 Andy Van Slyke .30 .14
❑ 80 Kevin McReynolds .15 .07
❑ 81 Mike Henneman .15 .07
❑ 82 Greg W. Harris .15 .07
❑ 83 Sandy Alomar Jr. .30 .14
❑ 84 Mike Jackson .15 .07
❑ 85 Ozzie Guillen .15 .07
❑ 86 Jeff Blauser .15 .07
❑ 87 John Valentin .15 .07
❑ 88 Rey Sanchez .15 .07
❑ 89 Rick Sutcliffe .30 .14
❑ 90 Luis Gonzalez .30 .14
❑ 91 Jeff Fassero .15 .07
❑ 92 Kenny Rogers .15 .07
❑ 93 Bret Saberhagen .30 .14
❑ 94 Bob Welch .15 .07
❑ 95 Darren Daulton .30 .14
❑ 96 Mike Gallego .15 .07
❑ 97 Orlando Merced .15 .07
❑ 98 Chuck Knoblauch .30 .14
❑ 99 Bernard Gilkey .15 .07
❑ 100 Billy Ashley .15 .07
❑ 101 Kevin Appier .30 .14
❑ 102 Jeff Brantley .15 .07
❑ 103 Bill Gullickson .15 .07
❑ 104 John Smoltz .30 .14
❑ 105 Paul Sorrento .15 .07
❑ 106 Steve Buechele .15 .07
❑ 107 Steve Sax .15 .07
❑ 108 Andujar Cedeno .15 .07
❑ 109 Billy Hatcher .15 .07
❑ 110 Checklist .15 .07
❑ 111 Alan Mills .15 .07
❑ 112 John Franco .30 .14
❑ 113 Jack Morris .30 .14
❑ 114 Mitch Williams .15 .07
❑ 115 Nolan Ryan 3.00 1.35
❑ 116 Jay Bell .30 .14
❑ 117 Mike Bordick .15 .07
❑ 118 Geronimo Pena .15 .07
❑ 119 Danny Tartabull .15 .07
❑ 120 Checklist .15 .07
❑ 121 Steve Avery .15 .07
❑ 122 Ricky Bones .15 .07
❑ 123 Mike Morgan .15 .07
❑ 124 Jeff Montgomery .30 .14
❑ 125 Jeff Bagwell .75 .35
❑ 126 Tony Phillips .15 .07
❑ 127 Lenny Harris .15 .07
❑ 128 Glenallen Hill .15 .07
❑ 129 Marquis Grissom .15 .07
❑ 130 Gerald Williams UER .15 .07
(Bernie Williams
picture and stats)
❑ 131 Greg A. Harris .15 .07
❑ 132 Tommy Greene .15 .07
❑ 133 Chris Hoiles .15 .07
❑ 134 Bob Walk .15 .07
❑ 135 Duane Ward .15 .07
❑ 136 Tom Pagnozzi .15 .07
❑ 137 Jeff Huson .15 .07
❑ 138 Kurt Stillwell .15 .07
❑ 139 Dave Henderson .15 .07
❑ 140 Darrin Jackson .15 .07
❑ 141 Frank Castillo .15 .07
❑ 142 Scott Erickson .15 .07
❑ 143 Darryl Kile .30 .14
❑ 144 Bill Wegman .15 .07
❑ 145 Steve Wilson .15 .07
❑ 146 George Brett 1.25 .55
❑ 147 Moises Alou .30 .14
❑ 148 Lou Whitaker .30 .14
❑ 149 Chico Walker .15 .07
❑ 150 Jerry Browne .15 .07
❑ 151 Kirk McCaskill .15 .07
❑ 152 Zane Smith .15 .07
❑ 153 Matt Young .15 .07
❑ 154 Lee Smith .30 .14
❑ 155 Leo Gomez .15 .07
❑ 156 Dan Walters .15 .07
❑ 157 Pat Borders .15 .07
❑ 158 Matt Williams .40 .18
❑ 159 Dean Palmer .30 .14
❑ 160 John Patterson .15 .07
❑ 161 Doug Jones .15 .07
❑ 162 John Habyan .15 .07
❑ 163 Pedro Martinez 1.50 .70
❑ 164 Carl Willis .15 .07
❑ 165 Darrin Fletcher .15 .07
❑ 166 B.J. Surhoff .30 .14
❑ 167 Eddie Murray .60 .25
❑ 168 Keith Miller .15 .07
❑ 169 Ricky Jordan .15 .07
❑ 170 Juan Gonzalez .60 .25
❑ 171 Charles Nagy .15 .07
❑ 172 Mark Clark .15 .07
❑ 173 Bobby Thigpen .15 .07
❑ 174 Tim Scott .15 .07
❑ 175 Scott Cooper .15 .07
❑ 176 Royce Clayton .15 .07
❑ 177 Brady Anderson .30 .14
❑ 178 Sid Bream .15 .07
❑ 179 Derek Bell .15 .07
❑ 180 Otis Nixon .15 .07
❑ 181 Kevin Gross .15 .07
❑ 182 Ron Darling .15 .07
❑ 183 John Wetteland .30 .14
❑ 184 Mike Stanley .15 .07
❑ 185 Jeff Kent .60 .25
❑ 186 Brian Harper .15 .07
❑ 187 Mariano Duncan .15 .07
❑ 188 Robin Yount .40 .18
❑ 189 Al Martin .15 .07
❑ 190 Eddie Zosky .15 .07
❑ 191 Mike Munoz .15 .07
❑ 192 Andy Benes .15 .07
❑ 193 Dennis Cook .15 .07
❑ 194 Bill Swift .15 .07
❑ 195 Frank Thomas 1.25 .55
❑ 195A Frank Thomas
(Franklin visible on batting glove)
❑ 196 Damon Berryhill .15 .07
❑ 197 Mike Greenwell .15 .07
❑ 198 Mark Grace .60 .25
❑ 199 Darryl Hamilton .15 .07
❑ 200 Derrick May .15 .07
❑ 201 Ken Hill .15 .07
❑ 202 Kevin Brown .40 .18
❑ 203 Dwight Gooden .30 .14
❑ 204 Bobby Witt .15 .07
❑ 205 Juan Bell .15 .07
❑ 206 Kevin Maas .15 .07
❑ 207 Jeff King .15 .07
❑ 208 Scott Leius .15 .07
❑ 209 Rheal Cormier .15 .07
❑ 210 Darryl Strawberry .30 .14
❑ 211 Tom Gordon .15 .07
❑ 212 Bud Black .15 .07
❑ 213 Mickey Tettleton .15 .07
❑ 214 Pete Smith .15 .07
❑ 215 Felix Fermin .15 .07
❑ 216 Rick Wilkins .15 .07
❑ 217 George Bell .15 .07
❑ 218 Eric Anthony .15 .07
❑ 219 Pedro Munoz .15 .07
❑ 220 Checklist .15 .07
❑ 221 Lance Blankenship .15 .07
❑ 222 Deion Sanders .40 .18
❑ 223 Craig Biggio .40 .18
❑ 224 Ryne Sandberg .75 .35
❑ 225 Ron Gant .30 .14
❑ 226 Tom Brunansky .15 .07
❑ 227 Chad Curtis .15 .07
❑ 228 Joe Carter .30 .14
❑ 229 Brian Jordan .30 .14
❑ 230 Brett Butler .30 .14
❑ 231 Frank Bolick .15 .07
❑ 232 Rod Beck .15 .07
❑ 233 Carlos Baerga .15 .07
❑ 234 Eric Karros .40 .18
❑ 235 Jack Armstrong .15 .07
❑ 236 Bobby Bonilla .30 .14
❑ 237 Don Mattingly 1.50 .70
❑ 238 Jeff Gardner .15 .07
❑ 239 Dave Hollins .15 .07
❑ 240 Steve Cooke .15 .07
❑ 241 Jose Canseco .75 .35
❑ 242 Ivan Calderon .15 .07
❑ 243 Tim Belcher .15 .07
❑ 244 Freddie Benavides .15 .07
❑ 245 Roberto Alomar .60 .25
❑ 246 Rob Deer .15 .07
❑ 247 Will Clark .60 .25
❑ 248 Mike Felder .15 .07
❑ 249 Harold Baines .30 .14
❑ 250 David Cone .30 .14
❑ 251 Mark Guthrie .15 .07
❑ 252 Ellis Burks .30 .14
❑ 253 Jim Abbott .30 .14
❑ 254 Chili Davis .30 .14
❑ 255 Chris Bosio .15 .07
❑ 256 Bret Barberie .15 .07
❑ 257 Hal Morris .15 .07
❑ 258 Dante Bichette .30 .14
❑ 259 Storm Davis .15 .07
❑ 260 Gary DiSarcina .15 .07
❑ 261 Ken Caminiti .30 .14
❑ 262 Paul Molitor .60 .25
❑ 263 Joe Oliver .15 .07
❑ 264 Pat Listach .15 .07
❑ 265 Gregg Jefferies .15 .07
❑ 266 Jose Guzman .15 .07
❑ 267 Eric Davis .30 .14
❑ 268 Delino DeShields .30 .14
❑ 269 Barry Bonds 1.00 .45
❑ 270 Mike Bielecki .15 .07
❑ 271 Jay Buhner .30 .14

❑ 272 Scott Pose RC .15 .07
❑ 273 Tony Fernandez .15 .07
❑ 274 Chito Martinez .15 .07
❑ 275 Phil Plantier .15 .07
❑ 276 Pete Incaviglia .15 .07
❑ 277 Carlos Garcia .15 .07
❑ 278 Tom Henke .15 .07
❑ 279 Roger Clemens 1.25 .55
❑ 280 Rob Dibble .15 .07
❑ 281 Daryl Boston .15 .07
❑ 282 Greg Gagne .15 .07
❑ 283 Cecil Fielder .30 .14
❑ 284 Carlton Fisk .60 .25
❑ 285 Wade Boggs .75 .35
❑ 286 Damion Easley .15 .07
❑ 287 Norm Charlton .15 .07
❑ 288 Jeff Conine .15 .07
❑ 289 Roberto Kelly .15 .07
❑ 290 Jerald Clark .15 .07
❑ 291 Rickey Henderson .75 .35
❑ 292 Chuck Finley .30 .14
❑ 293 Doug Drabek .15 .07
❑ 294 Dave Stewart .30 .14
❑ 295 Tom Glavine .40 .18
❑ 296 Jaime Navarro .15 .07
❑ 297 Ray Lankford .40 .18
❑ 298 Greg Hibbard .15 .07
❑ 299 Jody Reed .15 .07
❑ 300 Dennis Martinez .30 .14
❑ 301 Dave Martinez .15 .07
❑ 302 Reggie Jefferson .30 .14
❑ 303 John Cummings RC .15 .07
❑ 304 Orestes Destrade .15 .07
❑ 305 Mike Maddux .15 .07
❑ 306 David Segui .15 .07
❑ 307 Gary Sheffield .60 .25
❑ 308 Danny Jackson .15 .07
❑ 309 Craig Lefferts .15 .07
❑ 310 Andre Dawson .40 .18
❑ 311 Barry Larkin .60 .25
❑ 312 Alex Cole .15 .07
❑ 313 Mark Gardner .15 .07
❑ 314 Kirk Gibson .30 .14
❑ 315 Shane Mack .15 .07
❑ 316 Bo Jackson .30 .14
❑ 317 Jimmy Key .30 .14
❑ 318 Greg Myers .15 .07
❑ 319 Ken Griffey Jr. 2.50 1.10
❑ 320 Monty Fariss .15 .07
❑ 321 Kevin Mitchell .30 .14
❑ 322 Andres Galarraga .40 .18
❑ 323 Mark McGwire 2.50 1.10
❑ 324 Mark Langston .15 .07
❑ 325 Steve Finley .30 .14
❑ 326 Greg Maddux 1.50 .70
❑ 327 Dave Nilsson .30 .14
❑ 328 Ozzie Smith .75 .35
❑ 329 Candy Maldonado .15 .07
❑ 330 Checklist .15 .07
❑ 331 Tim Pugh RC .15 .07
❑ 332 Joe Girardi .30 .14
❑ 333 Junior Felix .15 .07
❑ 334 Greg Swindell .15 .07
❑ 335 Ramon Martinez .15 .07
❑ 336 Sean Berry .15 .07
❑ 337 Joe Orsulak .15 .07
❑ 338 Wes Chamberlain .15 .07
❑ 339 Stan Belinda .15 .07
❑ 340 Checklist UER .15 .07
(306 Luis Mercedes)
❑ 341 Bruce Hurst .15 .07
❑ 342 John Burkett .15 .07
❑ 343 Mike Mussina .60 .25
❑ 344 Scott Fletcher .15 .07
❑ 345 Rene Gonzales .15 .07
❑ 346 Roberto Hernandez .15 .07
❑ 347 Carlos Martinez .15 .07
❑ 348 Bill Krueger .15 .07
❑ 349 Felix Jose .15 .07
❑ 350 John Jaha .15 .07
❑ 351 Willie Banks .15 .07
❑ 352 Matt Nokes .15 .07
❑ 353 Kevin Seitzer .15 .07
❑ 354 Erik Hanson .15 .07
❑ 355 David Hulse RC .15 .07
❑ 356 Domingo Martinez RC .15 .07
❑ 357 Greg Olson .15 .07
❑ 358 Randy Myers .30 .14
❑ 359 Tom Browning .15 .07
❑ 360 Charlie Hayes .15 .07
❑ 361 Bryan Harvey .15 .07
❑ 362 Eddie Taubensee .15 .07
❑ 363 Tim Wallach .15 .07
❑ 364 Mel Rojas .15 .07
❑ 365 Frank Tanana .15 .07
❑ 366 John Kruk .30 .14
❑ 367 Tim Laker RC .15 .07
❑ 368 Rich Rodriguez .15 .07
❑ 369 Darren Lewis .15 .07
❑ 370 Harold Reynolds .15 .07
❑ 371 Jose Melendez .15 .07
❑ 372 Joe Grahe .15 .07
❑ 373 Lance Johnson .15 .07
❑ 374 Jose Mesa .15 .07
❑ 375 Scott Livingstone .15 .07
❑ 376 Wally Joyner .30 .14
❑ 377 Kevin Reimer .15 .07
❑ 378 Kirby Puckett 1.50 .70
❑ 379 Paul O'Neill .30 .14
❑ 380 Randy Johnson .75 .35
❑ 381 Manuel Lee .15 .07
❑ 382 Dick Schofield .15 .07
❑ 383 Darren Holmes .15 .07
❑ 384 Charlie Hough .30 .14
❑ 385 John Orton .15 .07
❑ 386 Edgar Martinez .40 .18
❑ 387 Terry Pendleton .30 .14
❑ 388 Dan Plesac .15 .07
❑ 389 Jeff Reardon .30 .14
❑ 390 David Nied .15 .07
❑ 391 Dave Magadan .15 .07
❑ 392 Larry Walker .30 .14
❑ 393 Ben Rivera .15 .07
❑ 394 Lonnie Smith .15 .07
❑ 395 Craig Shipley .15 .07
❑ 396 Willie McGee .30 .14
❑ 397 Arthur Rhodes .15 .07
❑ 398 Mike Stanton .15 .07
❑ 399 Luis Polonia .15 .07
❑ 400 Jack McDowell .15 .07
❑ 401 Mike Moore .15 .07
❑ 402 Jose Lind .15 .07
❑ 403 Bill Spiers .15 .07
❑ 404 Kevin Tapani .15 .07
❑ 405 Spike Owen .15 .07
❑ 406 Tino Martinez .30 .14
❑ 407 Charlie Leibrandt .15 .07
❑ 408 Ed Sprague .15 .07
❑ 409 Bryn Smith .15 .07
❑ 410 Benito Santiago .15 .07
❑ 411 Jose Rijo .15 .07
❑ 412 Pete O'Brien .15 .07
❑ 413 Willie Wilson .15 .07
❑ 414 Bip Roberts .15 .07
❑ 415 Eric Young .15 .07
❑ 416 Walt Weiss .15 .07
❑ 417 Milt Thompson .15 .07
❑ 418 Chris Sabo .15 .07
❑ 419 Scott Sanderson .15 .07
❑ 420 Tim Raines .30 .14
❑ 421 Alan Trammell .40 .18
❑ 422 Mike Macfarlane .15 .07
❑ 423 Dave Winfield .60 .25
❑ 424 Bob Wickman .15 .07
❑ 425 David Valle .15 .07
❑ 426 Gary Redus .15 .07
❑ 427 Turner Ward .15 .07
❑ 428 Reggie Sanders .15 .07
❑ 429 Todd Worrell .15 .07
❑ 430 Julio Valera .15 .07
❑ 431 Cal Ripken Jr. 2.50 1.10
❑ 432 Mo Vaughn .30 .14
❑ 433 John Smiley .15 .07
❑ 434 Omar Vizquel .30 .14
❑ 435 Billy Ripken .15 .07
❑ 436 Cory Snyder .15 .07
❑ 437 Carlos Quintana .15 .07
❑ 438 Omar Olivares .15 .07
❑ 439 Robin Ventura .30 .14
❑ 440 Checklist .15 .07
❑ 441 Kevin Higgins .15 .07
❑ 442 Carlos Hernandez .15 .07
❑ 443 Dan Peltier .15 .07
❑ 444 Derek Lilliquist .15 .07
❑ 445 Tim Salmon .30 .14
❑ 446 Sherman Obando RC .15 .07
❑ 447 Pat Kelly .15 .07
❑ 448 Todd Van Poppel .15 .07
❑ 449 Mark Whiten .15 .07
❑ 450 Checklist .15 .07
❑ 451 Pat Meares RC .15 .07
❑ 452 Tony Tarasco RC .15 .07
❑ 453 Chris Gwynn .15 .07
❑ 454 Armando Reynoso .15 .07
❑ 455 Danny Darwin .15 .07
❑ 456 Willie Greene .15 .07
❑ 457 Mike Blowers .15 .07
❑ 458 Kevin Roberson RC .15 .07
❑ 459 Graeme Lloyd RC .15 .07
❑ 460 David West .15 .07
❑ 461 Joey Cora .15 .07
❑ 462 Alex Arias .15 .07
❑ 463 Chad Kreuter .15 .07
❑ 464 Mike Lansing RC .30 .14
❑ 465 Mike Timlin .15 .07
❑ 466 Paul Wagner .15 .07
❑ 467 Mark Portugal .15 .07
❑ 468 Jim Leyritz .15 .07
❑ 469 Ryan Klesko .60 .25
❑ 470 Mario Diaz .15 .07
❑ 471 Guillermo Velasquez .15 .07
❑ 472 Fernando Valenzuela .30 .14
❑ 473 Raul Mondesi .30 .14
❑ 474 Mike Pagliarulo .15 .07
❑ 475 Chris Hammond .15 .07
❑ 476 Torey Lovullo .15 .07
❑ 477 Trevor Wilson .15 .07
❑ 478 Marcos Armas RC .15 .07
❑ 479 Dave Gallagher .15 .07
❑ 480 Jeff Treadway .15 .07
❑ 481 Jeff Branson .15 .07
❑ 482 Dickie Thon .15 .07
❑ 483 Eduardo Perez .15 .07
❑ 484 David Wells .30 .14
❑ 485 Brian Williams .15 .07
❑ 486 Domingo Cedeno RC .15 .07
❑ 487 Tom Candiotti .15 .07
❑ 488 Steve Frey .15 .07
❑ 489 Greg McMichael RC .15 .07
❑ 490 Marc Newfield .15 .07
❑ 491 Larry Andersen .15 .07
❑ 492 Damon Buford .15 .07
❑ 493 Ricky Gutierrez .15 .07
❑ 494 Jeff Russell .15 .07
❑ 495 Vinny Castilla .75 .35
❑ 496 Wilson Alvarez .15 .07
❑ 497 Scott Bullett .15 .07
❑ 498 Larry Casian .15 .07
❑ 499 Jose Vizcaino .15 .07
❑ 500 J.T. Snow RC .75 .35
❑ 501 Bryan Hickerson .15 .07
❑ 502 Jeremy Hernandez .15 .07
❑ 503 Jeromy Burnitz .30 .14
❑ 504 Steve Farr .15 .07
❑ 505 J. Owens RC .15 .07
❑ 506 Craig Paquette .15 .07
❑ 507 Jim Eisenreich .15 .07
❑ 508 Matt Whiteside RC .15 .07
❑ 509 Luis Aquino .15 .07
❑ 510 Mike LaValliere .15 .07
❑ 511 Jim Gott .15 .07
❑ 512 Mark McLemore .15 .07
❑ 513 Randy Milligan .15 .07
❑ 514 Gary Gaetti .30 .14
❑ 515 Lou Frazier RC .15 .07
❑ 516 Rich Amaral .15 .07
❑ 517 Gene Harris .15 .07
❑ 518 Aaron Sele .60 .25
❑ 519 Mark Wohlers .15 .07
❑ 520 Scott Kamieniecki .15 .07
❑ 521 Kent Mercker .15 .07
❑ 522 Jim Deshaies .15 .07
❑ 523 Kevin Stocker .15 .07
❑ 524 Jason Bere .15 .07
❑ 525 Tim Bogar RC .15 .07
❑ 526 Brad Pennington .15 .07
❑ 527 Curt Leskanic RC .15 .07
❑ 528 Wayne Kirby .15 .07

| | No. | Player | MINT | NRMT |
|---|---|---|---|---|
| ❑ | 529 | Tim Costo | .15 | .07 |
| ❑ | 530 | Doug Henry | .15 | .07 |
| ❑ | 531 | Trevor Hoffman | .60 | .25 |
| ❑ | 532 | Kelly Gruber | .15 | .07 |
| ❑ | 533 | Mike Harkey | .15 | .07 |
| ❑ | 534 | John Doherty | .15 | .07 |
| ❑ | 535 | Erik Pappas | .15 | .07 |
| ❑ | 536 | Brent Gates | .15 | .07 |
| ❑ | 537 | Roger McDowell | .15 | .07 |
| ❑ | 538 | Chris Haney | .15 | .07 |
| ❑ | 539 | Blas Minor | .15 | .07 |
| ❑ | 540 | Pat Hentgen | .15 | .07 |
| ❑ | 541 | Chuck Carr | .15 | .07 |
| ❑ | 542 | Doug Strange | .15 | .07 |
| ❑ | 543 | Xavier Hernandez | .15 | .07 |
| ❑ | 544 | Paul Quantrill | .15 | .07 |
| ❑ | 545 | Anthony Young | .15 | .07 |
| ❑ | 546 | Bret Boone | .30 | .14 |
| ❑ | 547 | Dwight Smith | .15 | .07 |
| ❑ | 548 | Bobby Munoz | .15 | .07 |
| ❑ | 549 | Russ Springer | .15 | .07 |
| ❑ | 550 | Roger Pavlik | .15 | .07 |
| ❑ | DW | Dave Winfield 3000 Hits | 1.00 | .45 |
| ❑ | FT | Frank Thomas AU/3500 (Certified autograph) | 80.00 | 36.00 |

## 1994 Leaf

| | MINT | NRMT |
|---|---|---|
| COMPLETE SET (440) | 24.00 | 11.00 |
| COMPLETE SERIES 1 (220) | 12.00 | 5.50 |
| COMPLETE SERIES 2 (220) | 12.00 | 5.50 |

| | No. | Player | MINT | NRMT |
|---|---|---|---|---|
| ❑ | 1 | Cal Ripken Jr. | 2.50 | 1.10 |
| ❑ | 2 | Tony Tarasco | .15 | .07 |
| ❑ | 3 | Joe Girardi | .15 | .07 |
| ❑ | 4 | Bernie Williams | .60 | .25 |
| ❑ | 5 | Chad Kreuter | .15 | .07 |
| ❑ | 6 | Troy Neel | .15 | .07 |
| ❑ | 7 | Tom Pagnozzi | .15 | .07 |
| ❑ | 8 | Kirk Rueter | .15 | .07 |
| ❑ | 9 | Chris Bosio | .15 | .07 |
| ❑ | 10 | Dwight Gooden | .30 | .14 |
| ❑ | 11 | Mariano Duncan | .15 | .07 |
| ❑ | 12 | Jay Bell | .30 | .14 |
| ❑ | 13 | Lance Johnson | .15 | .07 |
| ❑ | 14 | Richie Lewis | .15 | .07 |
| ❑ | 15 | Dave Martinez | .15 | .07 |
| ❑ | 16 | Orel Hershiser | .30 | .14 |
| ❑ | 17 | Rob Butler | .15 | .07 |
| ❑ | 18 | Glenallen Hill | .15 | .07 |
| ❑ | 19 | Chad Curtis | .15 | .07 |
| ❑ | 20 | Mike Stanton | .15 | .07 |
| ❑ | 21 | Tim Wallach | .15 | .07 |
| ❑ | 22 | Milt Thompson | .15 | .07 |
| ❑ | 23 | Kevin Young | .15 | .07 |
| ❑ | 24 | John Smiley | .15 | .07 |
| ❑ | 25 | Jeff Montgomery | .15 | .07 |
| ❑ | 26 | Robin Ventura | .30 | .14 |
| ❑ | 27 | Scott Lydy | .15 | .07 |
| ❑ | 28 | Todd Stottlemyre | .15 | .07 |
| ❑ | 29 | Mark Whiten | .15 | .07 |
| ❑ | 30 | Robby Thompson | .15 | .07 |
| ❑ | 31 | Bobby Bonilla | .30 | .14 |
| ❑ | 32 | Andy Ashby | .15 | .07 |
| ❑ | 33 | Greg Myers | .15 | .07 |
| ❑ | 34 | Billy Hatcher | .15 | .07 |
| ❑ | 35 | Brad Holman | .15 | .07 |
| ❑ | 36 | Mark McLemore | .15 | .07 |
| ❑ | 37 | Scott Sanders | .15 | .07 |
| ❑ | 38 | Jim Abbott | .30 | .14 |
| ❑ | 39 | David Wells | .30 | .14 |
| ❑ | 40 | Roberto Kelly | .15 | .07 |
| ❑ | 41 | Jeff Conine | .15 | .07 |
| ❑ | 42 | Sean Berry | .15 | .07 |
| ❑ | 43 | Mark Grace | .60 | .25 |
| ❑ | 44 | Eric Young | .15 | .07 |
| ❑ | 45 | Rick Aguilera | .15 | .07 |
| ❑ | 46 | Chipper Jones | 1.50 | .70 |
| ❑ | 47 | Mel Rojas | .15 | .07 |
| ❑ | 48 | Ryan Thompson | .15 | .07 |
| ❑ | 49 | Al Martin | .15 | .07 |
| ❑ | 50 | Cecil Fielder | .30 | .14 |
| ❑ | 51 | Pat Kelly | .15 | .07 |
| ❑ | 52 | Kevin Tapani | .15 | .07 |
| ❑ | 53 | Tim Costo | .15 | .07 |
| ❑ | 54 | Dave Hollins | .15 | .07 |
| ❑ | 55 | Kirt Manwaring | .15 | .07 |
| ❑ | 56 | Gregg Jefferies | .15 | .07 |
| ❑ | 57 | Ron Darling | .15 | .07 |
| ❑ | 58 | Bill Haselman | .15 | .07 |
| ❑ | 59 | Phil Plantier | .15 | .07 |
| ❑ | 60 | Frank Viola | .15 | .07 |
| ❑ | 61 | Todd Zeile | .15 | .07 |
| ❑ | 62 | Bret Barberie | .15 | .07 |
| ❑ | 63 | Roberto Mejia | .15 | .07 |
| ❑ | 64 | Chuck Knoblauch | .30 | .14 |
| ❑ | 65 | Jose Lind | .15 | .07 |
| ❑ | 66 | Brady Anderson | .30 | .14 |
| ❑ | 67 | Ruben Sierra | .15 | .07 |
| ❑ | 68 | Jose Vizcaino | .15 | .07 |
| ❑ | 69 | Joe Grahe | .15 | .07 |
| ❑ | 70 | Kevin Appier | .30 | .14 |
| ❑ | 71 | Wilson Alvarez | .15 | .07 |
| ❑ | 72 | Tom Candiotti | .15 | .07 |
| ❑ | 73 | John Burkett | .15 | .07 |
| ❑ | 74 | Anthony Young | .15 | .07 |
| ❑ | 75 | Scott Cooper | .15 | .07 |
| ❑ | 76 | Nigel Wilson | .15 | .07 |
| ❑ | 77 | John Valentin | .15 | .07 |
| ❑ | 78 | David McCarty | .15 | .07 |
| ❑ | 79 | Archi Cianfrocco | .15 | .07 |
| ❑ | 80 | Lou Whitaker | .30 | .14 |
| ❑ | 81 | Dante Bichette | .30 | .14 |
| ❑ | 82 | Mark Dewey | .15 | .07 |
| ❑ | 83 | Danny Jackson | .15 | .07 |
| ❑ | 84 | Harold Baines | .30 | .14 |
| ❑ | 85 | Todd Benzinger | .15 | .07 |
| ❑ | 86 | Damion Easley | .15 | .07 |
| ❑ | 87 | Danny Cox | .15 | .07 |
| ❑ | 88 | Jose Bautista | .15 | .07 |
| ❑ | 89 | Mike Lansing | .15 | .07 |
| ❑ | 90 | Phil Hiatt | .15 | .07 |
| ❑ | 91 | Tim Pugh | .15 | .07 |
| ❑ | 92 | Tino Martinez | .30 | .14 |
| ❑ | 93 | Raul Mondesi | .30 | .14 |
| ❑ | 94 | Greg Maddux | 1.50 | .70 |
| ❑ | 95 | Al Leiter | .30 | .14 |
| ❑ | 96 | Benito Santiago | .15 | .07 |
| ❑ | 97 | Lenny Dykstra | .30 | .14 |
| ❑ | 98 | Sammy Sosa | 1.50 | .70 |
| ❑ | 99 | Tim Bogar | .15 | .07 |
| ❑ | 100 | Checklist | .15 | .07 |
| ❑ | 101 | Deion Sanders | .30 | .14 |
| ❑ | 102 | Bobby Witt | .15 | .07 |
| ❑ | 103 | Wil Cordero | .15 | .07 |
| ❑ | 104 | Rich Amaral | .15 | .07 |
| ❑ | 105 | Mike Mussina | .60 | .25 |
| ❑ | 106 | Reggie Sanders | .15 | .07 |
| ❑ | 107 | Ozzie Guillen | .15 | .07 |
| ❑ | 108 | Paul O'Neill | .30 | .14 |
| ❑ | 109 | Tim Salmon | .30 | .14 |
| ❑ | 110 | Rheal Cormier | .15 | .07 |
| ❑ | 111 | Billy Ashley | .15 | .07 |
| ❑ | 112 | Jeff Kent | .40 | .18 |
| ❑ | 113 | Derek Bell | .15 | .07 |
| ❑ | 114 | Danny Darwin | .15 | .07 |
| ❑ | 115 | Chip Hale | .15 | .07 |
| ❑ | 116 | Tim Raines | .30 | .14 |
| ❑ | 117 | Ed Sprague | .15 | .07 |
| ❑ | 118 | Darrin Fletcher | .15 | .07 |
| ❑ | 119 | Darren Holmes | .15 | .07 |
| ❑ | 120 | Alan Trammell | .40 | .18 |
| ❑ | 121 | Don Mattingly | 1.50 | .70 |
| ❑ | 122 | Greg Gagne | .15 | .07 |
| ❑ | 123 | Jose Offerman | .15 | .07 |
| ❑ | 124 | Joe Orsulak | .15 | .07 |
| ❑ | 125 | Jack McDowell | .15 | .07 |
| ❑ | 126 | Barry Larkin | .60 | .25 |
| ❑ | 127 | Ben McDonald | .15 | .07 |
| ❑ | 128 | Mike Bordick | .15 | .07 |
| ❑ | 129 | Devon White | .15 | .07 |
| ❑ | 130 | Mike Perez | .15 | .07 |
| ❑ | 131 | Jay Buhner | .30 | .14 |
| ❑ | 132 | Phil Leftwich RC | .15 | .07 |
| ❑ | 133 | Tommy Greene | .15 | .07 |
| ❑ | 134 | Charlie Hayes | .15 | .07 |
| ❑ | 135 | Don Slaught | .15 | .07 |
| ❑ | 136 | Mike Gallego | .15 | .07 |
| ❑ | 137 | Dave Winfield | .60 | .25 |
| ❑ | 138 | Steve Avery | .15 | .07 |
| ❑ | 139 | Derrick May | .15 | .07 |
| ❑ | 140 | Bryan Harvey | .15 | .07 |
| ❑ | 141 | Wally Joyner | .30 | .14 |
| ❑ | 142 | Andre Dawson | .40 | .18 |
| ❑ | 143 | Andy Benes | .15 | .07 |
| ❑ | 144 | John Franco | .30 | .14 |
| ❑ | 145 | Jeff King | .15 | .07 |
| ❑ | 146 | Joe Oliver | .15 | .07 |
| ❑ | 147 | Bill Gullickson | .15 | .07 |
| ❑ | 148 | Armando Reynoso | .15 | .07 |
| ❑ | 149 | Dave Fleming | .15 | .07 |
| ❑ | 150 | Checklist | .15 | .07 |
| ❑ | 151 | Todd Van Poppel | .15 | .07 |
| ❑ | 152 | Bernard Gilkey | .15 | .07 |
| ❑ | 153 | Kevin Gross | .15 | .07 |
| ❑ | 154 | Mike Devereaux | .15 | .07 |
| ❑ | 155 | Tim Wakefield | .15 | .07 |
| ❑ | 156 | Andres Galarraga | .40 | .18 |
| ❑ | 157 | Pat Meares | .15 | .07 |
| ❑ | 158 | Jim Leyritz | .15 | .07 |
| ❑ | 159 | Mike Macfarlane | .15 | .07 |
| ❑ | 160 | Tony Phillips | .15 | .07 |
| ❑ | 161 | Brent Gates | .15 | .07 |
| ❑ | 162 | Mark Langston | .15 | .07 |
| ❑ | 163 | Allen Watson | .15 | .07 |
| ❑ | 164 | Randy Johnson | .75 | .35 |
| ❑ | 165 | Doug Brocail | .15 | .07 |
| ❑ | 166 | Rob Dibble | .15 | .07 |
| ❑ | 167 | Roberto Hernandez | .15 | .07 |
| ❑ | 168 | Felix Jose | .15 | .07 |
| ❑ | 169 | Steve Cooke | .15 | .07 |
| ❑ | 170 | Darren Daulton | .30 | .14 |
| ❑ | 171 | Eric Karros | .30 | .14 |
| ❑ | 172 | Geronimo Pena | .15 | .07 |
| ❑ | 173 | Gary DiSarcina | .15 | .07 |
| ❑ | 174 | Marquis Grissom | .15 | .07 |
| ❑ | 175 | Joey Cora | .15 | .07 |
| ❑ | 176 | Jim Eisenreich | .15 | .07 |
| ❑ | 177 | Brad Pennington | .15 | .07 |
| ❑ | 178 | Terry Steinbach | .15 | .07 |
| ❑ | 179 | Pat Borders | .15 | .07 |
| ❑ | 180 | Steve Buechele | .15 | .07 |
| ❑ | 181 | Jeff Fassero | .15 | .07 |
| ❑ | 182 | Mike Greenwell | .15 | .07 |
| ❑ | 183 | Mike Henneman | .15 | .07 |
| ❑ | 184 | Ron Karkovice | .15 | .07 |
| ❑ | 185 | Pat Hentgen | .15 | .07 |
| ❑ | 186 | Jose Guzman | .15 | .07 |
| ❑ | 187 | Brett Butler | .30 | .14 |
| ❑ | 188 | Charlie Hough | .30 | .14 |
| ❑ | 189 | Terry Pendleton | .30 | .14 |
| ❑ | 190 | Melido Perez | .15 | .07 |
| ❑ | 191 | Orestes Destrade | .15 | .07 |
| ❑ | 192 | Mike Morgan | .15 | .07 |
| ❑ | 193 | Joe Carter | .30 | .14 |
| ❑ | 194 | Jeff Blauser | .15 | .07 |
| ❑ | 195 | Chris Hoiles | .15 | .07 |
| ❑ | 196 | Ricky Gutierrez | .15 | .07 |
| ❑ | 197 | Mike Moore | .15 | .07 |
| ❑ | 198 | Carl Willis | .15 | .07 |
| ❑ | 199 | Aaron Sele | .30 | .14 |
| ❑ | 200 | Checklist | .15 | .07 |
| ❑ | 201 | Tim Naehring | .15 | .07 |
| ❑ | 202 | Scott Livingstone | .15 | .07 |
| ❑ | 203 | Luis Alicea | .15 | .07 |
| ❑ | 204 | Torey Lovullo | .15 | .07 |
| ❑ | 205 | Jim Gott | .15 | .07 |
| ❑ | 206 | Bob Wickman | .15 | .07 |

❑ 207 Greg McMichael .15 .07
❑ 208 Scott Brosius .30 .14
❑ 209 Chris Gwynn .15 .07
❑ 210 Steve Sax .15 .07
❑ 211 Dick Schofield .15 .07
❑ 212 Robb Nen .15 .07
❑ 213 Ben Rivera .15 .07
❑ 214 Vinny Castilla .30 .14
❑ 215 Jamie Moyer .15 .07
❑ 216 Wally Whitehurst .15 .07
❑ 217 Frank Castillo .15 .07
❑ 218 Mike Blowers .15 .07
❑ 219 Tim Scott .15 .07
❑ 220 Paul Wagner .15 .07
❑ 221 Jeff Bagwell .75 .35
❑ 222 Ricky Bones .15 .07
❑ 223 Sandy Alomar Jr. .30 .14
❑ 224 Rod Beck .15 .07
❑ 225 Roberto Alomar .60 .25
❑ 226 Jack Armstrong .15 .07
❑ 227 Scott Erickson .15 .07
❑ 228 Rene Arocha .15 .07
❑ 229 Eric Anthony .15 .07
❑ 230 Jeromy Burnitz .30 .14
❑ 231 Kevin Brown .30 .14
❑ 232 Tim Belcher .15 .07
❑ 233 Bret Boone .30 .14
❑ 234 Dennis Eckersley .30 .14
❑ 235 Tom Glavine .60 .25
❑ 236 Craig Biggio .40 .18
❑ 237 Pedro Astacio .15 .07
❑ 238 Ryan Bowen .15 .07
❑ 239 Brad Ausmus .15 .07
❑ 240 Vince Coleman .15 .07
❑ 241 Jason Bere .15 .07
❑ 242 Ellis Burks .30 .14
❑ 243 Wes Chamberlain .15 .07
❑ 244 Ken Caminiti .30 .14
❑ 245 Willie Banks .15 .07
❑ 246 Sid Fernandez .15 .07
❑ 247 Carlos Baerga .15 .07
❑ 248 Carlos Garcia .15 .07
❑ 249 Jose Canseco .75 .35
❑ 250 Alex Diaz .15 .07
❑ 251 Albert Belle .40 .18
❑ 252 Moises Alou .30 .14
❑ 253 Bobby Ayala .15 .07
❑ 254 Tony Gwynn 1.25 .55
❑ 255 Roger Clemens 1.25 .55
❑ 256 Eric Davis .30 .14
❑ 257 Wade Boggs .75 .35
❑ 258 Chili Davis .30 .14
❑ 259 Rickey Henderson .75 .35
❑ 260 Andujar Cedeno .15 .07
❑ 261 Cris Carpenter .15 .07
❑ 262 Juan Guzman .15 .07
❑ 263 David Justice .40 .18
❑ 264 Barry Bonds 1.00 .45
❑ 265 Pete Incaviglia .15 .07
❑ 266 Tony Fernandez .15 .07
❑ 267 Cal Eldred .15 .07
❑ 268 Alex Fernandez .15 .07
❑ 269 Kent Hrbek .30 .14
❑ 270 Steve Farr .15 .07
❑ 271 Doug Drabek .15 .07
❑ 272 Brian Jordan .30 .14
❑ 273 Xavier Hernandez .15 .07
❑ 274 David Cone .30 .14
❑ 275 Brian Hunter .15 .07
❑ 276 Mike Harkey .15 .07
❑ 277 Delino DeShields .15 .07
❑ 278 David Hulse .15 .07
❑ 279 Mickey Tettleton .15 .07
❑ 280 Kevin McReynolds .15 .07
❑ 281 Darryl Hamilton .15 .07
❑ 282 Ken Hill .15 .07
❑ 283 Wayne Kirby .15 .07
❑ 284 Chris Hammond .15 .07
❑ 285 Mo Vaughn .30 .14
❑ 286 Ryan Klesko .30 .14
❑ 287 Rick Wilkins .15 .07
❑ 288 Bill Swift .15 .07
❑ 289 Rafael Palmeiro .60 .25
❑ 290 Brian Harper .15 .07
❑ 291 Chris Turner .15 .07
❑ 292 Luis Gonzalez .30 .14
❑ 293 Kenny Rogers .15 .07
❑ 294 Kirby Puckett 1.50 .70
❑ 295 Mike Stanley .15 .07
❑ 296 Carlos Reyes RC .15 .07
❑ 297 Charles Nagy .15 .07
❑ 298 Reggie Jefferson .15 .07
❑ 299 Bip Roberts .15 .07
❑ 300 Darrin Jackson .15 .07
❑ 301 Mike Jackson .15 .07
❑ 302 Dave Nilsson .15 .07
❑ 303 Ramon Martinez .15 .07
❑ 304 Bobby Jones .15 .07
❑ 305 Johnny Ruffin .15 .07
❑ 306 Brian McRae .15 .07
❑ 307 Bo Jackson .30 .14
❑ 308 Dave Stewart .30 .14
❑ 309 John Smoltz .30 .14
❑ 310 Dennis Martinez .30 .14
❑ 311 Dean Palmer .30 .14
❑ 312 David Nied .15 .07
❑ 313 Eddie Murray .60 .25
❑ 314 Darryl Kile .30 .14
❑ 315 Rick Sutcliffe .30 .14
❑ 316 Shawon Dunston .15 .07
❑ 317 John Jaha .15 .07
❑ 318 Salomon Torres .15 .07
❑ 319 Gary Sheffield .60 .25
❑ 320 Curt Schilling .30 .14
❑ 321 Greg Vaughn .30 .14
❑ 322 Jay Howell .15 .07
❑ 323 Todd Hundley .15 .07
❑ 324 Chris Sabo .15 .07
❑ 325 Stan Javier .15 .07
❑ 326 Willie Greene .15 .07
❑ 327 Hipolito Pichardo .15 .07
❑ 328 Doug Strange .15 .07
❑ 329 Dan Wilson .15 .07
❑ 330 Checklist .15 .07
❑ 331 Omar Vizquel .30 .14
❑ 332 Scott Servais .15 .07
❑ 333 Bob Tewksbury .15 .07
❑ 334 Matt Williams .40 .18
❑ 335 Tom Foley .15 .07
❑ 336 Jeff Russell .15 .07
❑ 337 Scott Leius .15 .07
❑ 338 Ivan Rodriguez .75 .35
❑ 339 Kevin Seitzer .15 .07
❑ 340 Jose Rijo .15 .07
❑ 341 Eduardo Perez .15 .07
❑ 342 Kirk Gibson .30 .14
❑ 343 Randy Milligan .15 .07
❑ 344 Edgar Martinez .40 .18
❑ 345 Fred McGriff .40 .18
❑ 346 Kurt Abbott RC .15 .07
❑ 347 John Kruk .30 .14
❑ 348 Mike Felder .15 .07
❑ 349 Dave Staton .15 .07
❑ 350 Kenny Lofton .30 .14
❑ 351 Graeme Lloyd .15 .07
❑ 352 David Segui .15 .07
❑ 353 Danny Tartabull .15 .07
❑ 354 Bob Welch .15 .07
❑ 355 Duane Ward .15 .07
❑ 356 Karl Rhodes .15 .07
❑ 357 Lee Smith .30 .14
❑ 358 Chris James .15 .07
❑ 359 Walt Weiss .15 .07
❑ 360 Pedro Munoz .15 .07
❑ 361 Paul Sorrento .15 .07
❑ 362 Todd Worrell .15 .07
❑ 363 Bob Hamelin .15 .07
❑ 364 Julio Franco .15 .07
❑ 365 Roberto Petagine .15 .07
❑ 366 Willie McGee .30 .14
❑ 367 Pedro Martinez 1.00 .45
❑ 368 Ken Griffey Jr. 2.50 1.10
❑ 369 B.J. Surhoff .30 .14
❑ 370 Kevin Mitchell .15 .07
❑ 371 John Doherty .15 .07
❑ 372 Manuel Lee .15 .07
❑ 373 Terry Mulholland .15 .07
❑ 374 Zane Smith .15 .07
❑ 375 Otis Nixon .15 .07
❑ 376 Jody Reed .15 .07
❑ 377 Doug Jones .15 .07
❑ 378 John Olerud .30 .14
❑ 379 Greg Swindell .15 .07
❑ 380 Checklist .15 .07
❑ 381 Royce Clayton .15 .07
❑ 382 Jim Thome .40 .18
❑ 383 Steve Finley .30 .14
❑ 384 Ray Lankford .30 .14
❑ 385 Henry Rodriguez .15 .07
❑ 386 Dave Magadan .15 .07
❑ 387 Gary Redus .15 .07
❑ 388 Orlando Merced .15 .07
❑ 389 Tom Gordon .15 .07
❑ 390 Luis Polonia .15 .07
❑ 391 Mark McGwire 2.50 1.10
❑ 392 Mark Lemke .15 .07
❑ 393 Doug Henry .15 .07
❑ 394 Chuck Finley .30 .14
❑ 395 Paul Molitor .60 .25
❑ 396 Randy Myers .15 .07
❑ 397 Larry Walker .30 .14
❑ 398 Pete Harnisch .15 .07
❑ 399 Darren Lewis .15 .07
❑ 400 Frank Thomas 1.25 .55
❑ 401 Jack Morris .30 .14
❑ 402 Greg Hibbard .15 .07
❑ 403 Jeffrey Hammonds .30 .14
❑ 404 Will Clark .60 .25
❑ 405 Travis Fryman .30 .14
❑ 406 Scott Sanderson .15 .07
❑ 407 Gene Harris .15 .07
❑ 408 Chuck Carr .15 .07
❑ 409 Ozzie Smith .75 .35
❑ 410 Kent Mercker .15 .07
❑ 411 Andy Van Slyke .30 .14
❑ 412 Jimmy Key .30 .14
❑ 413 Pat Mahomes .15 .07
❑ 414 John Wetteland .30 .14
❑ 415 Todd Jones .15 .07
❑ 416 Greg Harris .15 .07
❑ 417 Kevin Stocker .15 .07
❑ 418 Juan Gonzalez .60 .25
❑ 419 Pete Smith .15 .07
❑ 420 Pat Listach .15 .07
❑ 421 Trevor Hoffman .30 .14
❑ 422 Scott Fletcher .15 .07
❑ 423 Mark Lewis .15 .07
❑ 424 Mickey Morandini .15 .07
❑ 425 Ryne Sandberg .75 .35
❑ 426 Erik Hanson .15 .07
❑ 427 Gary Gaetti .30 .14
❑ 428 Harold Reynolds .15 .07
❑ 429 Mark Portugal .15 .07
❑ 430 David Valle .15 .07
❑ 431 Mitch Williams .15 .07
❑ 432 Howard Johnson .15 .07
❑ 433 Hal Morris .15 .07
❑ 434 Tom Henke .15 .07
❑ 435 Shane Mack .15 .07
❑ 436 Mike Piazza 2.00 .90
❑ 437 Bret Saberhagen .30 .14
❑ 438 Jose Mesa .15 .07
❑ 439 Jaime Navarro .15 .07
❑ 440 Checklist .15 .07
❑ A300 Frank Thomas 1.50 .70
Leaf 5th Anniversary

## 1995 Leaf

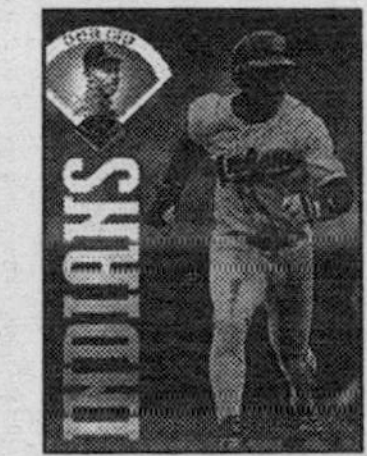

| | MINT | NRMT |
|---|---|---|
| COMPLETE SET (400) | 40.00 | 18.00 |
| COMPLETE SERIES 1 (200) | 15.00 | 6.75 |
| COMPLETE SERIES 2 (200) | 25.00 | 11.00 |
| COMMON CARD (1-400) | .15 | .07 |

| Card | MINT | NRMT |
|---|---|---|
| ❑ 1 Frank Thomas | 1.25 | .55 |
| ❑ 2 Carlos Garcia | .15 | .07 |
| ❑ 3 Todd Hundley | .15 | .07 |
| ❑ 4 Damion Easley | .15 | .07 |
| ❑ 5 Roberto Mejia | .15 | .07 |
| ❑ 6 John Mabry | .15 | .07 |
| ❑ 7 Aaron Sele | .30 | .14 |
| ❑ 8 Kenny Lofton | .30 | .14 |
| ❑ 9 John Doherty | .15 | .07 |
| ❑ 10 Joe Carter | .30 | .14 |
| ❑ 11 Mike Lansing | .15 | .07 |
| ❑ 12 John Valentin | .15 | .07 |
| ❑ 13 Ismael Valdes | .15 | .07 |
| ❑ 14 Dave McCarty | .15 | .07 |
| ❑ 15 Melvin Nieves | .15 | .07 |
| ❑ 16 Bobby Jones | .15 | .07 |
| ❑ 17 Trevor Hoffman | .30 | .14 |
| ❑ 18 John Smoltz | .30 | .14 |
| ❑ 19 Leo Gomez | .15 | .07 |
| ❑ 20 Roger Pavlik | .15 | .07 |
| ❑ 21 Dean Palmer | .30 | .14 |
| ❑ 22 Rickey Henderson | .75 | .35 |
| ❑ 23 Eddie Taubensee | .15 | .07 |
| ❑ 24 Damon Buford | .15 | .07 |
| ❑ 25 Mark Wohlers | .15 | .07 |
| ❑ 26 Jim Edmonds | .60 | .25 |
| ❑ 27 Wilson Alvarez | .15 | .07 |
| ❑ 28 Matt Williams | .40 | .18 |
| ❑ 29 Jeff Montgomery | .15 | .07 |
| ❑ 30 Shawon Dunston | .15 | .07 |
| ❑ 31 Tom Pagnozzi | .15 | .07 |
| ❑ 32 Jose Lind | .15 | .07 |
| ❑ 33 Royce Clayton | .15 | .07 |
| ❑ 34 Cal Eldred | .15 | .07 |
| ❑ 35 Chris Gomez | .15 | .07 |
| ❑ 36 Henry Rodriguez | .15 | .07 |
| ❑ 37 Dave Fleming | .15 | .07 |
| ❑ 38 Jon Lieber | .15 | .07 |
| ❑ 39 Scott Servais | .15 | .07 |
| ❑ 40 Wade Boggs | .75 | .35 |
| ❑ 41 John Olerud | .30 | .14 |
| ❑ 42 Eddie Williams | .15 | .07 |
| ❑ 43 Paul Sorrento | .15 | .07 |
| ❑ 44 Ron Karkovice | .15 | .07 |
| ❑ 45 Kevin Foster | .15 | .07 |
| ❑ 46 Miguel Jimenez | .15 | .07 |
| ❑ 47 Reggie Sanders | .15 | .07 |
| ❑ 48 Rondell White | .30 | .14 |
| ❑ 49 Scott Leius | .15 | .07 |
| ❑ 50 Jose Valentin | .15 | .07 |
| ❑ 51 Wm. VanLandingham | .15 | .07 |
| ❑ 52 Denny Hocking | .15 | .07 |
| ❑ 53 Jeff Fassero | .15 | .07 |
| ❑ 54 Chris Hoiles | .15 | .07 |
| ❑ 55 Walt Weiss | .15 | .07 |
| ❑ 56 Geronimo Berroa | .15 | .07 |
| ❑ 57 Rich Rowland | .15 | .07 |
| ❑ 58 Dave Weathers | .15 | .07 |
| ❑ 59 Sterling Hitchcock | .15 | .07 |
| ❑ 60 Raul Mondesi | .30 | .14 |
| ❑ 61 Rusty Greer | .30 | .14 |
| ❑ 62 David Justice | .40 | .18 |
| ❑ 63 Cecil Fielder | .30 | .14 |
| ❑ 64 Brian Jordan | .30 | .14 |
| ❑ 65 Mike Lieberthal | .30 | .14 |
| ❑ 66 Rick Aguilera | .15 | .07 |
| ❑ 67 Chuck Finley | .30 | .14 |
| ❑ 68 Andy Ashby | .15 | .07 |
| ❑ 69 Alex Fernandez | .15 | .07 |
| ❑ 70 Ed Sprague | .15 | .07 |
| ❑ 71 Steve Buechele | .15 | .07 |
| ❑ 72 Willie Greene | .15 | .07 |
| ❑ 73 Dave Nilsson | .15 | .07 |
| ❑ 74 Bret Saberhagen | .30 | .14 |
| ❑ 75 Jimmy Key | .30 | .14 |
| ❑ 76 Darren Lewis | .15 | .07 |
| ❑ 77 Steve Cooke | .15 | .07 |
| ❑ 78 Kirk Gibson | .30 | .14 |
| ❑ 79 Ray Lankford | .30 | .14 |
| ❑ 80 Paul O'Neill | .30 | .14 |
| ❑ 81 Mike Bordick | .15 | .07 |
| ❑ 82 Wes Chamberlain | .15 | .07 |
| ❑ 83 Rico Brogna | .15 | .07 |
| ❑ 84 Kevin Appier | .30 | .14 |
| ❑ 85 Juan Guzman | .15 | .07 |
| ❑ 86 Kevin Seitzer | .15 | .07 |
| ❑ 87 Mickey Morandini | .15 | .07 |
| ❑ 88 Pedro Martinez | .75 | .35 |
| ❑ 89 Matt Mieske | .15 | .07 |
| ❑ 90 Tino Martinez | .30 | .14 |
| ❑ 91 Paul Shuey | .15 | .07 |
| ❑ 92 Bip Roberts | .15 | .07 |
| ❑ 93 Chili Davis | .30 | .14 |
| ❑ 94 Deion Sanders | .30 | .14 |
| ❑ 95 Darrell Whitmore | .15 | .07 |
| ❑ 96 Joe Orsulak | .15 | .07 |
| ❑ 97 Bret Boone | .30 | .14 |
| ❑ 98 Kent Mercker | .15 | .07 |
| ❑ 99 Scott Livingstone | .15 | .07 |
| ❑ 100 Brady Anderson | .30 | .14 |
| ❑ 101 James Mouton | .15 | .07 |
| ❑ 102 Jose Rijo | .15 | .07 |
| ❑ 103 Bobby Munoz | .15 | .07 |
| ❑ 104 Ramon Martinez | .15 | .07 |
| ❑ 105 Bernie Williams | .60 | .25 |
| ❑ 106 Troy Neel | .15 | .07 |
| ❑ 107 Ivan Rodriguez | .75 | .35 |
| ❑ 108 Salomon Torres | .15 | .07 |
| ❑ 109 Johnny Ruffin | .15 | .07 |
| ❑ 110 Darryl Kile | .30 | .14 |
| ❑ 111 Bobby Ayala | .15 | .07 |
| ❑ 112 Ron Darling | .15 | .07 |
| ❑ 113 Jose Lima | .15 | .07 |
| ❑ 114 Joey Hamilton | .15 | .07 |
| ❑ 115 Greg Maddux | 1.50 | .70 |
| ❑ 116 Greg Colbrunn | .15 | .07 |
| ❑ 117 Ozzie Guillen | .15 | .07 |
| ❑ 118 Brian Anderson | .15 | .07 |
| ❑ 119 Jeff Bagwell | .75 | .35 |
| ❑ 120 Pat Listach | .15 | .07 |
| ❑ 121 Sandy Alomar Jr. | .30 | .14 |
| ❑ 122 Jose Vizcaino | .15 | .07 |
| ❑ 123 Rick Helling | .30 | .14 |
| ❑ 124 Allen Watson | .15 | .07 |
| ❑ 125 Pedro Munoz | .15 | .07 |
| ❑ 126 Craig Biggio | .40 | .18 |
| ❑ 127 Kevin Stocker | .15 | .07 |
| ❑ 128 Wil Cordero | .15 | .07 |
| ❑ 129 Rafael Palmeiro | .60 | .25 |
| ❑ 130 Gar Finnvold | .15 | .07 |
| ❑ 131 Darren Hall | .15 | .07 |
| ❑ 132 Heathcliff Slocumb | .15 | .07 |
| ❑ 133 Darrin Fletcher | .15 | .07 |
| ❑ 134 Cal Ripken | 2.50 | 1.10 |
| ❑ 135 Dante Bichette | .30 | .14 |
| ❑ 136 Don Slaught | .15 | .07 |
| ❑ 137 Pedro Astacio | .15 | .07 |
| ❑ 138 Ryan Thompson | .15 | .07 |
| ❑ 139 Greg Gohr | .15 | .07 |
| ❑ 140 Javier Lopez | .30 | .14 |
| ❑ 141 Lenny Dykstra | .30 | .14 |
| ❑ 142 Pat Rapp | .15 | .07 |
| ❑ 143 Mark Kiefer | .15 | .07 |
| ❑ 144 Greg Gagne | .15 | .07 |
| ❑ 145 Eduardo Perez | .15 | .07 |
| ❑ 146 Felix Fermin | .15 | .07 |
| ❑ 147 Jeff Frye | .15 | .07 |
| ❑ 148 Terry Steinbach | .15 | .07 |
| ❑ 149 Jim Eisenreich | .15 | .07 |
| ❑ 150 Brad Ausmus | .15 | .07 |
| ❑ 151 Randy Myers | .15 | .07 |
| ❑ 152 Rick White | .15 | .07 |
| ❑ 153 Mark Portugal | .15 | .07 |
| ❑ 154 Delino DeShields | .15 | .07 |
| ❑ 155 Scott Cooper | .15 | .07 |
| ❑ 156 Pat Hentgen | .15 | .07 |
| ❑ 157 Mark Gubicza | .15 | .07 |
| ❑ 158 Carlos Baerga | .15 | .07 |
| ❑ 159 Joe Girardi | .15 | .07 |
| ❑ 160 Rey Sanchez | .15 | .07 |
| ❑ 161 Todd Jones | .15 | .07 |
| ❑ 162 Luis Polonia | .15 | .07 |
| ❑ 163 Steve Trachsel | .15 | .07 |
| ❑ 164 Roberto Hernandez | .15 | .07 |
| ❑ 165 John Patterson | .15 | .07 |
| ❑ 166 Rene Arocha | .15 | .07 |
| ❑ 167 Will Clark | .60 | .25 |
| ❑ 168 Jim Leyritz | .15 | .07 |
| ❑ 169 Todd Van Poppel | .15 | .07 |
| ❑ 170 Robb Nen | .15 | .07 |
| ❑ 171 Midre Cummings | .15 | .07 |
| ❑ 172 Jay Buhner | .30 | .14 |
| ❑ 173 Kevin Tapani | .15 | .07 |
| ❑ 174 Mark Lemke | .15 | .07 |
| ❑ 175 Marcus Moore | .15 | .07 |
| ❑ 176 Wayne Kirby | .15 | .07 |
| ❑ 177 Rich Amaral | .15 | .07 |
| ❑ 178 Lou Whitaker | .30 | .14 |
| ❑ 179 Jay Bell | .30 | .14 |
| ❑ 180 Rick Wilkins | .15 | .07 |
| ❑ 181 Paul Molitor | .60 | .25 |
| ❑ 182 Gary Sheffield | .60 | .25 |
| ❑ 183 Kirby Puckett | 1.50 | .70 |
| ❑ 184 Cliff Floyd | .30 | .14 |
| ❑ 185 Darren Oliver | .15 | .07 |
| ❑ 186 Tim Naehring | .15 | .07 |
| ❑ 187 John Hudek | .15 | .07 |
| ❑ 188 Eric Young | .15 | .07 |
| ❑ 189 Roger Salkeld | .15 | .07 |
| ❑ 190 Kirt Manwaring | .15 | .07 |
| ❑ 191 Kurt Abbott | .15 | .07 |
| ❑ 192 David Nied | .15 | .07 |
| ❑ 193 Todd Zeile | .15 | .07 |
| ❑ 194 Wally Joyner | .30 | .14 |
| ❑ 195 Dennis Martinez | .30 | .14 |
| ❑ 196 Billy Ashley | .15 | .07 |
| ❑ 197 Ben McDonald | .15 | .07 |
| ❑ 198 Bob Hamelin | .15 | .07 |
| ❑ 199 Chris Turner | .15 | .07 |
| ❑ 200 Lance Johnson | .15 | .07 |
| ❑ 201 Willie Banks | .15 | .07 |
| ❑ 202 Juan Gonzalez | .60 | .25 |
| ❑ 203 Scott Sanders | .15 | .07 |
| ❑ 204 Scott Brosius | .30 | .14 |
| ❑ 205 Curt Schilling | .30 | .14 |
| ❑ 206 Alex Gonzalez | .15 | .07 |
| ❑ 207 Travis Fryman | .30 | .14 |
| ❑ 208 Tim Raines | .30 | .14 |
| ❑ 209 Steve Avery | .15 | .07 |
| ❑ 210 Hal Morris | .15 | .07 |
| ❑ 211 Ken Griffey Jr. | 2.50 | 1.10 |
| ❑ 212 Ozzie Smith | .75 | .35 |
| ❑ 213 Chuck Carr | .15 | .07 |
| ❑ 214 Ryan Klesko | .30 | .14 |
| ❑ 215 Robin Ventura | .30 | .14 |
| ❑ 216 Luis Gonzalez | .15 | .07 |
| ❑ 217 Ken Ryan | .15 | .07 |
| ❑ 218 Mike Piazza | 2.00 | .90 |
| ❑ 219 Matt Walbeck | .15 | .07 |
| ❑ 220 Jeff Kent | .40 | .18 |
| ❑ 221 Orlando Miller | .15 | .07 |
| ❑ 222 Kenny Rogers | .15 | .07 |
| ❑ 223 J.T. Snow | .30 | .14 |
| ❑ 224 Alan Trammell | .40 | .18 |
| ❑ 225 John Franco | .30 | .14 |
| ❑ 226 Gerald Williams | .15 | .07 |
| ❑ 227 Andy Benes | .15 | .07 |
| ❑ 228 Dan Wilson | .15 | .07 |
| ❑ 229 Dave Hollins | .15 | .07 |
| ❑ 230 Vinny Castilla | .30 | .14 |
| ❑ 231 Devon White | .30 | .14 |
| ❑ 232 Fred McGriff | .40 | .18 |
| ❑ 233 Quilvio Veras | .15 | .07 |
| ❑ 234 Tom Candiotti | .15 | .07 |
| ❑ 235 Jason Bere | .15 | .07 |
| ❑ 236 Mark Langston | .15 | .07 |
| ❑ 237 Mel Rojas | .15 | .07 |
| ❑ 238 Chuck Knoblauch | .30 | .14 |
| ❑ 239 Bernard Gilkey | .15 | .07 |
| ❑ 240 Mark McGwire | 2.50 | 1.10 |
| ❑ 241 Kirk Rueter | .15 | .07 |
| ❑ 242 Pat Kelly | .15 | .07 |
| ❑ 243 Ruben Sierra | .15 | .07 |
| ❑ 244 Randy Johnson | .75 | .35 |
| ❑ 245 Shane Reynolds | .15 | .07 |
| ❑ 246 Danny Tartabull | .15 | .07 |
| ❑ 247 Darryl Hamilton | .15 | .07 |
| ❑ 248 Danny Bautista | .15 | .07 |
| ❑ 249 Tom Gordon | .15 | .07 |
| ❑ 250 Tom Glavine | .60 | .25 |
| ❑ 251 Orlando Merced | .15 | .07 |
| ❑ 252 Eric Karros | .30 | .14 |

|  | | |
|---|---|---|
| ❑ 253 Benji Gil | .15 | .07 |
| ❑ 254 Sean Bergman | .15 | .07 |
| ❑ 255 Roger Clemens | 1.25 | .55 |
| ❑ 256 Roberto Alomar | .60 | .25 |
| ❑ 257 Benito Santiago | .15 | .07 |
| ❑ 258 Robby Thompson | .15 | .07 |
| ❑ 259 Marvin Freeman | .15 | .07 |
| ❑ 260 Jose Offerman | .15 | .07 |
| ❑ 261 Greg Vaughn | .30 | .14 |
| ❑ 262 David Segui | .15 | .07 |
| ❑ 263 Geronimo Pena | .15 | .07 |
| ❑ 264 Tim Salmon | .30 | .14 |
| ❑ 265 Eddie Murray | .60 | .25 |
| ❑ 266 Mariano Duncan | .15 | .07 |
| ❑ 267 Hideo Nomo RC | 1.50 | .70 |
| ❑ 268 Derek Bell | .15 | .07 |
| ❑ 269 Mo Vaughn | .30 | .14 |
| ❑ 270 Jeff King | .15 | .07 |
| ❑ 271 Edgar Martinez | .40 | .18 |
| ❑ 272 Sammy Sosa | 1.25 | .55 |
| ❑ 273 Scott Ruffcorn | .15 | .07 |
| ❑ 274 Darren Daulton | .30 | .14 |
| ❑ 275 John Jaha | .15 | .07 |
| ❑ 276 Andres Galarraga | .40 | .18 |
| ❑ 277 Mark Grace | .60 | .25 |
| ❑ 278 Mike Moore | .15 | .07 |
| ❑ 279 Barry Bonds | 1.00 | .45 |
| ❑ 280 Manny Ramirez | .75 | .35 |
| ❑ 281 Ellis Burks | .30 | .14 |
| ❑ 282 Greg Swindell | .15 | .07 |
| ❑ 283 Barry Larkin | .60 | .25 |
| ❑ 284 Albert Belle | .40 | .18 |
| ❑ 285 Shawn Green | .60 | .25 |
| ❑ 286 John Hoper | .15 | .07 |
| ❑ 287 Scott Erickson | .15 | .07 |
| ❑ 288 Moises Alou | .30 | .14 |
| ❑ 289 Mike Blowers | .15 | .07 |
| ❑ 290 Brent Gates | .15 | .07 |
| ❑ 291 Sean Berry | .15 | .07 |
| ❑ 292 Mike Stanley | .15 | .07 |
| ❑ 293 Jeff Conine | .15 | .07 |
| ❑ 294 Tim Wallach | .15 | .07 |
| ❑ 295 Bobby Bonilla | .30 | .14 |
| ❑ 296 Bruce Ruffin | .15 | .07 |
| ❑ 297 Chad Curtis | .15 | .07 |
| ❑ 298 Mike Greenwell | .15 | .07 |
| ❑ 299 Tony Gwynn | 1.25 | .55 |
| ❑ 300 Russ Davis | .15 | .07 |
| ❑ 301 Danny Jackson | .15 | .07 |
| ❑ 302 Pete Harnisch | .15 | .07 |
| ❑ 303 Don Mattingly | 1.50 | .70 |
| ❑ 304 Rheal Cormier | .15 | .07 |
| ❑ 305 Larry Walker | .30 | .14 |
| ❑ 306 Hector Carrasco | .15 | .07 |
| ❑ 307 Jason Jacome | .15 | .07 |
| ❑ 308 Phil Plantier | .15 | .07 |
| ❑ 309 Harold Baines | .30 | .14 |
| ❑ 310 Mitch Williams | .15 | .07 |
| ❑ 311 Charles Nagy | .15 | .07 |
| ❑ 312 Ken Caminiti | .30 | .14 |
| ❑ 313 Alex Rodriguez | 2.50 | 1.10 |
| ❑ 314 Chris Sabo | .15 | .07 |
| ❑ 315 Gary Gaetti | .30 | .14 |
| ❑ 316 Andre Dawson | .40 | .18 |
| ❑ 317 Mark Clark | .15 | .07 |
| ❑ 318 Vince Coleman | .15 | .07 |
| ❑ 319 Brad Clontz | .15 | .07 |
| ❑ 320 Steve Finley | .30 | .14 |
| ❑ 321 Doug Drabek | .15 | .07 |
| ❑ 322 Mark McLemore | .15 | .07 |
| ❑ 323 Stan Javier | .15 | .07 |
| ❑ 324 Ron Gant | .15 | .07 |
| ❑ 325 Charlie Hayes | .15 | .07 |
| ❑ 326 Carlos Delgado | .60 | .25 |
| ❑ 327 Ricky Bottalico | .15 | .07 |
| ❑ 328 Rod Beck | .15 | .07 |
| ❑ 329 Mark Acre | .15 | .07 |
| ❑ 330 Chris Bosio | .15 | .07 |
| ❑ 331 Tony Phillips | .15 | .07 |
| ❑ 332 Garret Anderson | .30 | .14 |
| ❑ 333 Pat Meares | .15 | .07 |
| ❑ 334 Todd Worrell | .15 | .07 |
| ❑ 335 Marquis Grissom | .15 | .07 |
| ❑ 336 Brent Mayne | .15 | .07 |
| ❑ 337 Lee Tinsley | .15 | .07 |
| ❑ 338 Terry Pendleton | .30 | .14 |
| ❑ 339 David Cone | .30 | .14 |
| ❑ 340 Tony Fernandez | .15 | .07 |
| ❑ 341 Jim Bullinger | .15 | .07 |
| ❑ 342 Armando Benitez | .30 | .14 |
| ❑ 343 John Smiley | .15 | .07 |
| ❑ 344 Dan Miceli | .15 | .07 |
| ❑ 345 Charles Johnson | .30 | .14 |
| ❑ 346 Lee Smith | .30 | .14 |
| ❑ 347 Brian McRae | .15 | .07 |
| ❑ 348 Jim Thome | .40 | .18 |
| ❑ 349 Jose Oliva | .15 | .07 |
| ❑ 350 Terry Mulholland | .15 | .07 |
| ❑ 351 Tom Henke | .15 | .07 |
| ❑ 352 Dennis Eckersley | .30 | .14 |
| ❑ 353 Sid Fernandez | .15 | .07 |
| ❑ 354 Paul Wagner | .15 | .07 |
| ❑ 355 John Dettmer | .15 | .07 |
| ❑ 356 John Wetteland | .30 | .14 |
| ❑ 357 John Burkett | .15 | .07 |
| ❑ 358 Marty Cordova | .15 | .07 |
| ❑ 359 Norm Charlton | .15 | .07 |
| ❑ 360 Mike Devereaux | .15 | .07 |
| ❑ 361 Alex Cole | .15 | .07 |
| ❑ 362 Brett Butler | .30 | .14 |
| ❑ 363 Mickey Tettleton | .15 | .07 |
| ❑ 364 Al Martin | .15 | .07 |
| ❑ 365 Tony Tarasco | .15 | .07 |
| ❑ 366 Pat Mahomes | .15 | .07 |
| ❑ 367 Gary DiSarcina | .15 | .07 |
| ❑ 368 Bill Swift | .15 | .07 |
| ❑ 369 Chipper Jones | 1.50 | .70 |
| ❑ 370 Orel Hershiser | .30 | .14 |
| ❑ 371 Kevin Gross | .15 | .07 |
| ❑ 372 Dave Winfield | .60 | .25 |
| ❑ 373 Andujar Cedeno | .15 | .07 |
| ❑ 374 Jim Abbott | .30 | .14 |
| ❑ 375 Glenallen Hill | .15 | .07 |
| ❑ 376 Otis Nixon | .15 | .07 |
| ❑ 377 Roberto Kelly | .15 | .07 |
| ❑ 378 Chris Hammond | .15 | .07 |
| ❑ 379 Mike Macfarlane | .15 | .07 |
| ❑ 380 J.R. Phillips | .15 | .07 |
| ❑ 381 Luis Alicea | .15 | .07 |
| ❑ 382 Bret Barberie | .15 | .07 |
| ❑ 383 Tom Goodwin | .15 | .07 |
| ❑ 384 Mark Whiten | .15 | .07 |
| ❑ 385 Jeffrey Hammonds | .30 | .14 |
| ❑ 386 Omar Vizquel | .30 | .14 |
| ❑ 387 Mike Mussina | .60 | .25 |
| ❑ 388 Ricky Bones | .15 | .07 |
| ❑ 389 Steve Ontiveros | .15 | .07 |
| ❑ 390 Jeff Blauser | .15 | .07 |
| ❑ 391 Jose Canseco | .75 | .35 |
| ❑ 392 Bob Tewksbury | .15 | .07 |
| ❑ 393 Jacob Brumfield | .15 | .07 |
| ❑ 394 Doug Jones | .15 | .07 |
| ❑ 395 Ken Hill | .15 | .07 |
| ❑ 396 Pat Borders | .15 | .07 |
| ❑ 397 Carl Everett | .30 | .14 |
| ❑ 398 Gregg Jefferies | .15 | .07 |
| ❑ 399 Jack McDowell | .15 | .07 |
| ❑ 400 Denny Neagle | .30 | .14 |

## 1996 Leaf

| | MINT | NRMT |
|---|---|---|
| COMPLETE SET (220) | 20.00 | 9.00 |
| COMMON CARD (1-220) | .15 | .07 |
| ❑ 1 John Smoltz | .30 | .14 |
| ❑ 2 Dennis Eckersley | .30 | .14 |
| ❑ 3 Delino DeShields | .15 | .07 |
| ❑ 4 Cliff Floyd | .30 | .14 |
| ❑ 5 Chuck Finley | .30 | .14 |
| ❑ 6 Cecil Fielder | .30 | .14 |
| ❑ 7 Tim Naehring | .15 | .07 |
| ❑ 8 Carlos Perez | .15 | .07 |
| ❑ 9 Brad Ausmus | .15 | .07 |
| ❑ 10 Matt Lawton RC | .75 | .35 |
| ❑ 11 Alan Trammell | .40 | .18 |
| ❑ 12 Steve Finley | .30 | .14 |
| ❑ 13 Paul O'Neill | .30 | .14 |
| ❑ 14 Gary Sheffield | .60 | .25 |
| ❑ 15 Mark McGwire | 2.50 | 1.10 |
| ❑ 16 Bernie Williams | .60 | .25 |
| ❑ 17 Jeff Montgomery | .15 | .07 |
| ❑ 18 Chan Ho Park | .30 | .14 |
| ❑ 19 Greg Vaughn | .30 | .14 |
| ❑ 20 Jeff Kent | .40 | .18 |
| ❑ 21 Cal Ripken | 2.50 | 1.10 |
| ❑ 22 Charles Johnson | .30 | .14 |
| ❑ 23 Eric Karros | .30 | .14 |
| ❑ 24 Alex Rodriguez | 2.00 | .90 |
| ❑ 25 Chris Snopek | .15 | .07 |
| ❑ 26 Jason Isringhausen | .30 | .14 |
| ❑ 27 Chili Davis | .30 | .14 |
| ❑ 28 Chipper Jones | 1.50 | .70 |
| ❑ 29 Bret Saberhagen | .30 | .14 |
| ❑ 30 Tony Clark | .15 | .07 |
| ❑ 31 Marty Cordova | .15 | .07 |
| ❑ 32 Dwayne Hosey | .15 | .07 |
| ❑ 33 Fred McGriff | .40 | .18 |
| ❑ 34 Deion Sanders | .30 | .14 |
| ❑ 35 Orlando Merced | .15 | .07 |
| ❑ 36 Brady Anderson | .30 | .14 |
| ❑ 37 Ray Lankford | .30 | .14 |
| ❑ 38 Manny Ramirez | .75 | .35 |
| ❑ 39 Alex Fernandez | .15 | .07 |
| ❑ 40 Greg Colbrunn | .15 | .07 |
| ❑ 41 Ken Griffey, Jr. | 2.50 | 1.10 |
| ❑ 42 Mickey Morandini | .15 | .07 |
| ❑ 43 Chuck Knoblauch | .30 | .14 |
| ❑ 44 Quinton McCracken | .15 | .07 |
| ❑ 45 Tim Salmon | .30 | .14 |
| ❑ 46 Jose Mesa | .15 | .07 |
| ❑ 47 Marquis Grissom | .15 | .07 |
| ❑ 48 Checklist | .15 | .07 |
| ❑ 49 Raul Mondesi | .30 | .14 |
| ❑ 50 Mark Grudzielanek | .15 | .07 |
| ❑ 51 Ray Durham | .30 | .14 |
| ❑ 52 Matt Williams | .40 | .18 |
| ❑ 53 Bob Hamelin | .15 | .07 |
| ❑ 54 Lenny Dykstra | .30 | .14 |
| ❑ 55 Jeff King | .15 | .07 |
| ❑ 56 LaTroy Hawkins | .15 | .07 |
| ❑ 57 Terry Pendleton | .30 | .14 |
| ❑ 58 Kevin Stocker | .15 | .07 |
| ❑ 59 Ozzie Timmons | .15 | .07 |
| ❑ 60 David Justice | .40 | .18 |
| ❑ 61 Ricky Bottalico | .15 | .07 |
| ❑ 62 Andy Ashby | .15 | .07 |
| ❑ 63 Larry Walker | .30 | .14 |
| ❑ 64 Jose Canseco | .75 | .35 |
| ❑ 65 Bret Boone | .30 | .14 |
| ❑ 66 Shawn Green | .60 | .25 |
| ❑ 67 Chad Curtis | .15 | .07 |
| ❑ 68 Travis Fryman | .30 | .14 |
| ❑ 69 Roger Clemens | 1.25 | .55 |
| ❑ 70 David Bell | .15 | .07 |
| ❑ 71 Rusty Greer | .30 | .14 |
| ❑ 72 Bob Higginson | .30 | .14 |
| ❑ 73 Joey Hamilton | .15 | .07 |
| ❑ 74 Kevin Seitzer | .15 | .07 |
| ❑ 75 Julian Tavarez | .15 | .07 |
| ❑ 76 Troy Percival | .15 | .07 |
| ❑ 77 Kirby Puckett | 1.50 | .70 |
| ❑ 78 Barry Bonds | 1.00 | .45 |
| ❑ 79 Michael Tucker | .15 | .07 |
| ❑ 80 Paul Molitor | .60 | .25 |
| ❑ 81 Carlos Garcia | .15 | .07 |
| ❑ 82 Johnny Damon | .40 | .18 |
| ❑ 83 Mike Hampton | .30 | .14 |
| ❑ 84 Ariel Prieto | .15 | .07 |
| ❑ 85 Tony Tarasco | .15 | .07 |
| ❑ 86 Pete Schourek | .15 | .07 |

| | No. | Player | MINT | NRMT |
|---|---|---|---|---|
| ❑ | 87 | Tom Glavine | .60 | .25 |
| ❑ | 88 | Rondell White | .30 | .14 |
| ❑ | 89 | Jim Edmonds | .60 | .25 |
| ❑ | 90 | Robby Thompson | .15 | .07 |
| ❑ | 91 | Wade Boggs | .75 | .35 |
| ❑ | 92 | Pedro Martinez | .75 | .35 |
| ❑ | 93 | Gregg Jefferies | .15 | .07 |
| ❑ | 94 | Albert Belle | .40 | .18 |
| ❑ | 95 | Benji Gil | .15 | .07 |
| ❑ | 96 | Denny Neagle | .30 | .14 |
| ❑ | 97 | Mark Langston | .15 | .07 |
| ❑ | 98 | Sandy Alomar Jr. | .30 | .14 |
| ❑ | 99 | Tony Gwynn | 1.25 | .55 |
| ❑ | 100 | Todd Hundley | .15 | .07 |
| ❑ | 101 | Dante Bichette | .30 | .14 |
| ❑ | 102 | Eddie Murray | .60 | .25 |
| ❑ | 103 | Lyle Mouton | .15 | .07 |
| ❑ | 104 | John Jaha | .15 | .07 |
| ❑ | 105 | Checklist | .15 | .07 |
| ❑ | 106 | Jon Nunnally | .15 | .07 |
| ❑ | 107 | Juan Gonzalez | .60 | .25 |
| ❑ | 108 | Kevin Appier | .30 | .14 |
| ❑ | 109 | Brian McRae | .15 | .07 |
| ❑ | 110 | Lee Smith | .30 | .14 |
| ❑ | 111 | Tim Wakefield | .15 | .07 |
| ❑ | 112 | Sammy Sosa | 1.25 | .55 |
| ❑ | 113 | Jay Buhner | .30 | .14 |
| ❑ | 114 | Garret Anderson | .30 | .14 |
| ❑ | 115 | Edgar Martinez | .40 | .18 |
| ❑ | 116 | Edgardo Alfonzo | .30 | .14 |
| ❑ | 117 | Billy Ashley | .15 | .07 |
| ❑ | 118 | Joe Carter | .30 | .14 |
| ❑ | 119 | Javy Lopez | .30 | .14 |
| ❑ | 120 | Bobby Bonilla | .30 | .14 |
| ❑ | 121 | Ken Caminiti | .30 | .14 |
| ❑ | 122 | Barry Larkin | .60 | .25 |
| ❑ | 123 | Shannon Stewart | .30 | .14 |
| ❑ | 124 | Orel Hershiser | .30 | .14 |
| ❑ | 125 | Jeff Conine | .15 | .07 |
| ❑ | 126 | Mark Grace | .60 | .25 |
| ❑ | 127 | Kenny Lofton | .30 | .14 |
| ❑ | 128 | Luis Gonzalez | .30 | .14 |
| ❑ | 129 | Rico Brogna | .15 | .07 |
| ❑ | 130 | Mo Vaughn | .30 | .14 |
| ❑ | 131 | Brad Radke | .30 | .14 |
| ❑ | 132 | Jose Herrera | .15 | .07 |
| ❑ | 133 | Rick Aguilera | .15 | .07 |
| ❑ | 134 | Gary DiSarcina | .15 | .07 |
| ❑ | 135 | Andres Galarraga | .40 | .18 |
| ❑ | 136 | Carl Everett | .30 | .14 |
| ❑ | 137 | Steve Avery | .15 | .07 |
| ❑ | 138 | Vinny Castilla | .30 | .14 |
| ❑ | 139 | Dennis Martinez | .30 | .14 |
| ❑ | 140 | John Wetteland | .30 | .14 |
| ❑ | 141 | Alex Gonzalez | .15 | .07 |
| ❑ | 142 | Brian Jordan | .30 | .14 |
| ❑ | 143 | Todd Hollandsworth | .15 | .07 |
| ❑ | 144 | Terrell Wade | .15 | .07 |
| ❑ | 145 | Wilson Alvarez | .15 | .07 |
| ❑ | 146 | Reggie Sanders | .15 | .07 |
| ❑ | 147 | Will Clark | .60 | .25 |
| ❑ | 148 | Hideo Nomo | .60 | .25 |
| ❑ | 149 | J.T.Snow | .30 | .14 |
| ❑ | 150 | Frank Thomas | 1.25 | .55 |
| ❑ | 151 | Ivan Rodriguez | .75 | .35 |
| ❑ | 152 | Jay Bell | .30 | .14 |
| ❑ | 153 | Checklist | .15 | .07 |
| ❑ | 154 | David Cone | .30 | .14 |
| ❑ | 155 | Roberto Alomar | .60 | .25 |
| ❑ | 156 | Carlos Delgado | .60 | .25 |
| ❑ | 157 | Carlos Baerga | .15 | .07 |
| ❑ | 158 | Geronimo Berroa | .15 | .07 |
| ❑ | 159 | Joe Vitiello | .15 | .07 |
| ❑ | 160 | Terry Steinbach | .15 | .07 |
| ❑ | 161 | Doug Drabek | .15 | .07 |
| ❑ | 162 | David Segui | .15 | .07 |
| ❑ | 163 | Ozzie Smith | .75 | .35 |
| ❑ | 164 | Kurt Abbott | .15 | .07 |
| ❑ | 165 | Randy Johnson | .75 | .35 |
| ❑ | 166 | John Valentin | .15 | .07 |
| ❑ | 167 | Mickey Tettleton | .15 | .07 |
| ❑ | 168 | Ruben Sierra | .15 | .07 |
| ❑ | 169 | Jim Thome | .40 | .18 |
| ❑ | 170 | Mike Greenwell | .15 | .07 |
| ❑ | 171 | Quilvio Veras | .15 | .07 |
| ❑ | 172 | Robin Ventura | .30 | .14 |
| ❑ | 173 | Bill Pulsipher | .15 | .07 |
| ❑ | 174 | Rafael Palmeiro | .60 | .25 |
| ❑ | 175 | Hal Morris | .15 | .07 |
| ❑ | 176 | Ryan Klesko | .30 | .14 |
| ❑ | 177 | Eric Young | .15 | .07 |
| ❑ | 178 | Shane Andrews | .15 | .07 |
| ❑ | 179 | Brian L.Hunter | .15 | .07 |
| ❑ | 180 | Brett Butler | .30 | .14 |
| ❑ | 181 | John Olerud | .30 | .14 |
| ❑ | 182 | Moises Alou | .30 | .14 |
| ❑ | 183 | Glenallen Hill | .15 | .07 |
| ❑ | 184 | Ismael Valdes | .15 | .07 |
| ❑ | 185 | Andy Pettitte | .30 | .14 |
| ❑ | 186 | Yamil Benitez | .15 | .07 |
| ❑ | 187 | Jason Bere | .15 | .07 |
| ❑ | 188 | Dean Palmer | .30 | .14 |
| ❑ | 189 | Jimmy Haynes | .15 | .07 |
| ❑ | 190 | Trevor Hoffman | .30 | .14 |
| ❑ | 191 | Mike Mussina | .60 | .25 |
| ❑ | 192 | Greg Maddux | 1.50 | .70 |
| ❑ | 193 | Ozzie Guillen | .15 | .07 |
| ❑ | 194 | Pat Listach | .15 | .07 |
| ❑ | 195 | Derek Bell | .15 | .07 |
| ❑ | 196 | Darren Daulton | .30 | .14 |
| ❑ | 197 | John Mabry | .15 | .07 |
| ❑ | 198 | Ramon Martinez | .15 | .07 |
| ❑ | 199 | Jeff Bagwell | .75 | .35 |
| ❑ | 200 | Mike Piazza | 2.00 | .90 |
| ❑ | 201 | Al Martin | .15 | .07 |
| ❑ | 202 | Aaron Sele | .30 | .14 |
| ❑ | 203 | Ed Sprague | .15 | .07 |
| ❑ | 204 | Rod Beck | .15 | .07 |
| ❑ | 205 | Checklist | .15 | .07 |
| ❑ | 206 | Mike Lansing | .15 | .07 |
| ❑ | 207 | Craig Biggio | .40 | .18 |
| ❑ | 208 | Jeffrey Hammonds | .30 | .14 |
| ❑ | 209 | Dave Nilsson | .15 | .07 |
| ❑ | 210 | Checklist | .15 | .07 |
| ❑ | 211 | Derek Jeter | 2.50 | 1.10 |
| ❑ | 212 | Alan Benes | .15 | .07 |
| ❑ | 213 | Jason Schmidt | .15 | .07 |
| ❑ | 214 | Alex Ochoa | .15 | .07 |
| ❑ | 215 | Ruben Rivera | .15 | .07 |
| ❑ | 216 | Roger Cedeno | .15 | .07 |
| ❑ | 217 | Jeff Suppan | .15 | .07 |
| ❑ | 218 | Billy Wagner | .15 | .07 |
| ❑ | 219 | Mark Loretta | .15 | .07 |
| ❑ | 220 | Karim Garcia | .15 | .07 |

## 1997 Leaf

| | MINT | NRMT |
|---|---|---|
| COMPLETE SET (400) | 40.00 | 18.00 |
| COMPLETE SERIES 1 (200) | 20.00 | 9.00 |
| COMPLETE SERIES 2 (200) | 20.00 | 9.00 |

| | No. | Player | MINT | NRMT |
|---|---|---|---|---|
| ❑ | 1 | Wade Boggs | .75 | .35 |
| ❑ | 2 | Brian McRae | .15 | .07 |
| ❑ | 3 | Jeff D'Amico | .15 | .07 |
| ❑ | 4 | George Arias | .15 | .07 |
| ❑ | 5 | Billy Wagner | .15 | .07 |
| ❑ | 6 | Ray Lankford | .30 | .14 |
| ❑ | 7 | Will Clark | .60 | .25 |
| ❑ | 8 | Edgar Renteria | .30 | .14 |
| ❑ | 9 | Alex Ochoa | .15 | .07 |
| ❑ | 10 | Roberto Hernandez | .15 | .07 |
| ❑ | 11 | Joe Carter | .30 | .14 |
| ❑ | 12 | Gregg Jefferies | .15 | .07 |
| ❑ | 13 | Mark Grace | .60 | .25 |
| ❑ | 14 | Roberto Alomar | .60 | .25 |
| ❑ | 15 | Joe Randa | .15 | .07 |
| ❑ | 16 | Alex Rodriguez | 2.00 | .90 |
| ❑ | 17 | Tony Gwynn | 1.25 | .55 |
| ❑ | 18 | Steve Gibralter | .15 | .07 |
| ❑ | 19 | Scott Stahoviak | .15 | .07 |
| ❑ | 20 | Matt Williams | .40 | .18 |
| ❑ | 21 | Quinton McCracken | .15 | .07 |
| ❑ | 22 | Ugueth Urbina | .30 | .14 |
| ❑ | 23 | Jermaine Allensworth | .15 | .07 |
| ❑ | 24 | Paul Molitor | .60 | .25 |
| ❑ | 25 | Carlos Delgado | .60 | .25 |
| ❑ | 26 | Bob Abreu | .30 | .14 |
| ❑ | 27 | John Jaha | .15 | .07 |
| ❑ | 28 | Rusty Greer | .30 | .14 |
| ❑ | 29 | Kimera Bartee | .15 | .07 |
| ❑ | 30 | Ruben Rivera | .15 | .07 |
| ❑ | 31 | Jason Kendall | .30 | .14 |
| ❑ | 32 | Lance Johnson | .15 | .07 |
| ❑ | 33 | Robin Ventura | .30 | .14 |
| ❑ | 34 | Kevin Appier | .30 | .14 |
| ❑ | 35 | John Mabry | .15 | .07 |
| ❑ | 36 | Ricky Otero | .15 | .07 |
| ❑ | 37 | Mike Lansing | .15 | .07 |
| ❑ | 38 | Mark McGwire | 2.50 | 1.10 |
| ❑ | 39 | Tim Naehring | .15 | .07 |
| ❑ | 40 | Tom Glavine | .60 | .25 |
| ❑ | 41 | Rey Ordonez | .15 | .07 |
| ❑ | 42 | Tony Clark | .15 | .07 |
| ❑ | 43 | Rafael Palmeiro | .60 | .25 |
| ❑ | 44 | Pedro Martinez | .75 | .35 |
| ❑ | 45 | Keith Lockhart | .15 | .07 |
| ❑ | 46 | Dan Wilson | .15 | .07 |
| ❑ | 47 | John Wetteland | .30 | .14 |
| ❑ | 48 | Chan Ho Park | .30 | .14 |
| ❑ | 49 | Gary Sheffield | .60 | .25 |
| ❑ | 50 | Shawn Estes | .30 | .14 |
| ❑ | 51 | Royce Clayton | .15 | .07 |
| ❑ | 52 | Jaime Navarro | .15 | .07 |
| ❑ | 53 | Raul Casanova | .15 | .07 |
| ❑ | 54 | Jeff Bagwell | .75 | .35 |
| ❑ | 55 | Barry Larkin | .60 | .25 |
| ❑ | 56 | Charles Nagy | .15 | .07 |
| ❑ | 57 | Ken Caminiti | .30 | .14 |
| ❑ | 58 | Todd Hollandsworth | .15 | .07 |
| ❑ | 59 | Pat Hentgen | .15 | .07 |
| ❑ | 60 | Jose Valentin | .15 | .07 |
| ❑ | 61 | Frank Rodriguez | .15 | .07 |
| ❑ | 62 | Mickey Tettleton | .15 | .07 |
| ❑ | 63 | Marty Cordova | .15 | .07 |
| ❑ | 64 | Cecil Fielder | .30 | .14 |
| ❑ | 65 | Barry Bonds | 1.00 | .45 |
| ❑ | 66 | Scott Servais | .15 | .07 |
| ❑ | 67 | Ernie Young | .15 | .07 |
| ❑ | 68 | Wilson Alvarez | .15 | .07 |
| ❑ | 69 | Mike Grace | .15 | .07 |
| ❑ | 70 | Shane Reynolds | .15 | .07 |
| ❑ | 71 | Henry Rodriguez | .15 | .07 |
| ❑ | 72 | Eric Karros | .30 | .14 |
| ❑ | 73 | Mark Langston | .30 | .14 |
| ❑ | 74 | Scott Karl | .15 | .07 |
| ❑ | 75 | Trevor Hoffman | .30 | .14 |
| ❑ | 76 | Orel Hershiser | .30 | .14 |
| ❑ | 77 | John Smoltz | .30 | .14 |
| ❑ | 78 | Raul Mondesi | .30 | .14 |
| ❑ | 79 | Jeff Brantley | .15 | .07 |
| ❑ | 80 | Donne Wall | .15 | .07 |
| ❑ | 81 | Joey Cora | .15 | .07 |
| ❑ | 82 | Mel Rojas | .15 | .07 |
| ❑ | 83 | Chad Mottola | .15 | .07 |
| ❑ | 84 | Omar Vizquel | .30 | .14 |
| ❑ | 85 | Greg Maddux | 1.50 | .70 |
| ❑ | 86 | Jamey Wright | .15 | .07 |
| ❑ | 87 | Chuck Finley | .30 | .14 |
| ❑ | 88 | Brady Anderson | .30 | .14 |
| ❑ | 89 | Alex Gonzalez | .15 | .07 |
| ❑ | 90 | Andy Benes | .15 | .07 |
| ❑ | 91 | Reggie Jefferson | .15 | .07 |
| ❑ | 92 | Paul O'Neill | .30 | .14 |
| ❑ | 93 | Javier Lopez | .30 | .14 |
| ❑ | 94 | Mark Grudzielanek | .15 | .07 |
| ❑ | 95 | Marc Newfield | .15 | .07 |
| ❑ | 96 | Kevin Ritz | .15 | .07 |
| ❑ | 97 | Fred McGriff | .40 | .18 |
| ❑ | 98 | Dwight Gooden | .30 | .14 |

| |  |  | | |
|---|---|---|---|---|
| ❑ | 99 | Hideo Nomo | .60 | .25 |
| ❑ | 100 | Steve Finley | .30 | .14 |
| ❑ | 101 | Juan Gonzalez | .60 | .25 |
| ❑ | 102 | Jay Buhner | .30 | .14 |
| ❑ | 103 | Paul Wilson | .15 | .07 |
| ❑ | 104 | Alan Benes | .15 | .07 |
| ❑ | 105 | Manny Ramirez | .75 | .35 |
| ❑ | 106 | Kevin Elster | .15 | .07 |
| ❑ | 107 | Frank Thomas | 1.25 | .55 |
| ❑ | 108 | Orlando Miller | .15 | .07 |
| ❑ | 109 | Ramon Martinez | .15 | .07 |
| ❑ | 110 | Kenny Lofton | .30 | .14 |
| ❑ | 111 | Bernie Williams | .60 | .25 |
| ❑ | 112 | Robby Thompson | .15 | .07 |
| ❑ | 113 | Bernard Gilkey | .15 | .07 |
| ❑ | 114 | Ray Durham | .30 | .14 |
| ❑ | 115 | Jeff Cirillo | .30 | .14 |
| ❑ | 116 | Brian Jordan | .30 | .14 |
| ❑ | 117 | Rich Becker | .15 | .07 |
| ❑ | 118 | Al Leiter | .30 | .14 |
| ❑ | 119 | Mark Johnson | .15 | .07 |
| ❑ | 120 | Ellis Burks | .30 | .14 |
| ❑ | 121 | Sammy Sosa | 1.25 | .55 |
| ❑ | 122 | Willie Greene | .15 | .07 |
| ❑ | 123 | Michael Tucker | .15 | .07 |
| ❑ | 124 | Eddie Murray | .60 | .25 |
| ❑ | 125 | Joey Hamilton | .15 | .07 |
| ❑ | 126 | Antonio Osuna | .15 | .07 |
| ❑ | 127 | Bobby Higginson | .30 | .14 |
| ❑ | 128 | Tomas Perez | .15 | .07 |
| ❑ | 129 | Tim Salmon | .30 | .14 |
| ❑ | 130 | Mark Wohlers | .15 | .07 |
| ❑ | 131 | Charles Johnson | .30 | .14 |
| ❑ | 132 | Randy Johnson | .75 | .35 |
| ❑ | 133 | Brooks Kieschnick | .15 | .07 |
| ❑ | 134 | Al Martin | .15 | .07 |
| ❑ | 135 | Dante Bichette | .30 | .14 |
| ❑ | 136 | Andy Pettitte | .30 | .14 |
| ❑ | 137 | Jason Giambi | .60 | .25 |
| ❑ | 138 | James Baldwin | .30 | .14 |
| ❑ | 139 | Ben McDonald | .15 | .07 |
| ❑ | 140 | Shawn Green | .60 | .25 |
| ❑ | 141 | Geronimo Berroa | .15 | .07 |
| ❑ | 142 | Jose Offerman | .15 | .07 |
| ❑ | 143 | Curtis Pride | .15 | .07 |
| ❑ | 144 | Terrell Wade | .15 | .07 |
| ❑ | 145 | Ismael Valdes | .15 | .07 |
| ❑ | 146 | Mike Mussina | .60 | .25 |
| ❑ | 147 | Mariano Rivera | .30 | .14 |
| ❑ | 148 | Ken Hill | .15 | .07 |
| ❑ | 149 | Darin Erstad | .75 | .35 |
| ❑ | 150 | Jay Bell | .30 | .14 |
| ❑ | 151 | Mo Vaughn | .30 | .14 |
| ❑ | 152 | Ozzie Smith | .75 | .35 |
| ❑ | 153 | Jose Mesa | .15 | .07 |
| ❑ | 154 | Osvaldo Fernandez | .15 | .07 |
| ❑ | 155 | Vinny Castilla | .30 | .14 |
| ❑ | 156 | Jason Isringhausen | .15 | .07 |
| ❑ | 157 | D.J. Surhoff | .30 | .14 |
| ❑ | 158 | Robert Perez | .15 | .07 |
| ❑ | 159 | Ron Coomer | .15 | .07 |
| ❑ | 160 | Darren Oliver | .15 | .07 |
| ❑ | 161 | Mike Mohler | .15 | .07 |
| ❑ | 162 | Russ Davis | .15 | .07 |
| ❑ | 163 | Bret Boone | .30 | .14 |
| ❑ | 164 | Ricky Bottalico | .15 | .07 |
| ❑ | 165 | Derek Jeter | 2.50 | 1.10 |
| ❑ | 166 | Orlando Merced | .15 | .07 |
| ❑ | 167 | John Valentin | .15 | .07 |
| ❑ | 168 | Andruw Jones | .75 | .35 |
| ❑ | 169 | Angel Echevarria | .15 | .07 |
| ❑ | 170 | Todd Walker | .15 | .07 |
| ❑ | 171 | Desi Relaford | .15 | .07 |
| ❑ | 172 | Trey Beamon | .15 | .07 |
| ❑ | 173 | Brian Giles RC | 2.50 | 1.10 |
| ❑ | 174 | Scott Rolen | .60 | .25 |
| ❑ | 175 | Shannon Stewart | .30 | .14 |
| ❑ | 176 | Dmitri Young | .30 | .14 |
| ❑ | 177 | Justin Thompson | .15 | .07 |
| ❑ | 178 | Trot Nixon | .30 | .14 |
| ❑ | 179 | Josh Booty | .15 | .07 |
| ❑ | 180 | Robin Jennings | .15 | .07 |
| ❑ | 181 | Marvin Benard | .15 | .07 |
| ❑ | 182 | Luis Castillo | .30 | .14 |
| ❑ | 183 | Wendell Magee | .15 | .07 |
| ❑ | 184 | Vladimir Guerrero | 1.25 | .55 |
| ❑ | 185 | Nomar Garciaparra | 2.00 | .90 |
| ❑ | 186 | Ryan Hancock | .15 | .07 |
| ❑ | 187 | Mike Cameron | .30 | .14 |
| ❑ | 188 | Cal Ripken LG | 1.25 | .55 |
| ❑ | 189 | Chipper Jones LG | .75 | .35 |
| ❑ | 190 | Albert Belle LG | .15 | .07 |
| ❑ | 191 | Mike Piazza LG | 1.00 | .45 |
| ❑ | 192 | Chuck Knoblauch LG | .15 | .07 |
| ❑ | 193 | Ken Griffey Jr. LG | 1.25 | .55 |
| ❑ | 194 | Ivan Rodriguez LG | .40 | .18 |
| ❑ | 195 | Jose Canseco LG | .60 | .25 |
| ❑ | 196 | Ryne Sandberg LG | .60 | .25 |
| ❑ | 197 | Jim Thome LG | .15 | .07 |
| ❑ | 198 | Andy Pettitte CL | .15 | .07 |
| ❑ | 199 | Andruw Jones CL | .40 | .18 |
| ❑ | 200 | Derek Jeter CL | 1.25 | .55 |
| ❑ | 201 | Chipper Jones | 1.50 | .70 |
| ❑ | 202 | Albert Belle | .40 | .18 |
| ❑ | 203 | Mike Piazza | 2.00 | .90 |
| ❑ | 204 | Ken Griffey Jr. | 2.50 | 1.10 |
| ❑ | 205 | Ryne Sandberg | .75 | .35 |
| ❑ | 206 | Jose Canseco | .75 | .35 |
| ❑ | 207 | Chili Davis | .30 | .14 |
| ❑ | 208 | Roger Clemens | 1.25 | .55 |
| ❑ | 209 | Deion Sanders | .30 | .14 |
| ❑ | 210 | Darryl Hamilton | .15 | .07 |
| ❑ | 211 | Jermaine Dye | .30 | .14 |
| ❑ | 212 | Matt Williams | .40 | .18 |
| ❑ | 213 | Kevin Elster | .15 | .07 |
| ❑ | 214 | John Wetteland | .30 | .14 |
| ❑ | 215 | Garret Anderson | .30 | .14 |
| ❑ | 216 | Kevin Brown | .40 | .18 |
| ❑ | 217 | Matt Lawton | .30 | .14 |
| ❑ | 218 | Cal Ripken | 2.50 | 1.10 |
| ❑ | 219 | Moises Alou | .30 | .14 |
| ❑ | 220 | Chuck Knoblauch | .30 | .14 |
| ❑ | 221 | Ivan Rodriguez | .75 | .35 |
| ❑ | 222 | Travis Fryman | .30 | .14 |
| ❑ | 223 | Jim Thome | .40 | .18 |
| ❑ | 224 | Eddie Murray | .60 | .25 |
| ❑ | 225 | Eric Young | .15 | .07 |
| ❑ | 226 | Ron Gant | .15 | .07 |
| ❑ | 227 | Tony Phillips | .15 | .07 |
| ❑ | 228 | Reggie Sanders | .15 | .07 |
| ❑ | 229 | Johnny Damon | .30 | .14 |
| ❑ | 230 | Bill Pulsipher | .15 | .07 |
| ❑ | 231 | Jim Edmonds | .60 | .25 |
| ❑ | 232 | Melvin Nieves | .15 | .07 |
| ❑ | 233 | Ryan Klesko | .30 | .14 |
| ❑ | 234 | David Cone | .30 | .14 |
| ❑ | 235 | Derek Bell | .15 | .07 |
| ❑ | 236 | Julio Franco | .30 | .14 |
| ❑ | 237 | Juan Guzman | .15 | .07 |
| ❑ | 238 | Larry Walker | .30 | .14 |
| ❑ | 239 | Delino DeShields | .15 | .07 |
| ❑ | 240 | Troy Percival | .15 | .07 |
| ❑ | 241 | Andres Galarraga | .40 | .18 |
| ❑ | 242 | Rondell White | .30 | .14 |
| ❑ | 243 | John Burkett | .15 | .07 |
| ❑ | 244 | J.T. Snow | .30 | .14 |
| ❑ | 245 | Alex Fernandez | .15 | .07 |
| ❑ | 246 | Edgar Martinez | .40 | .18 |
| ❑ | 247 | Craig Biggio | .40 | .18 |
| ❑ | 248 | Todd Hundley | .15 | .07 |
| ❑ | 249 | Jimmy Key | .30 | .14 |
| ❑ | 250 | Cliff Floyd | .30 | .14 |
| ❑ | 251 | Jeff Conine | .15 | .07 |
| ❑ | 252 | Curt Schilling | .30 | .14 |
| ❑ | 253 | Jeff King | .15 | .07 |
| ❑ | 254 | Tino Martinez | .30 | .14 |
| ❑ | 255 | Carlos Baerga | .15 | .07 |
| ❑ | 256 | Jeff Fassero | .15 | .07 |
| ❑ | 257 | Dean Palmer | .30 | .14 |
| ❑ | 258 | Robb Nen | .15 | .07 |
| ❑ | 259 | Sandy Alomar Jr. | .30 | .14 |
| ❑ | 260 | Carlos Perez | .15 | .07 |
| ❑ | 261 | Rickey Henderson | .75 | .35 |
| ❑ | 262 | Bobby Bonilla | .30 | .14 |
| ❑ | 263 | Darren Daulton | .30 | .14 |
| ❑ | 264 | Jim Leyritz | .15 | .07 |
| ❑ | 265 | Dennis Martinez | .30 | .14 |
| ❑ | 266 | Butch Huskey | .15 | .07 |
| ❑ | 267 | Joe Vitiello | .15 | .07 |
| ❑ | 268 | Steve Trachsel | .15 | .07 |
| ❑ | 269 | Glenallen Hill | .15 | .07 |
| ❑ | 270 | Terry Steinbach | .15 | .07 |
| ❑ | 271 | Mark McLemore | .15 | .07 |
| ❑ | 272 | Devon White | .30 | .14 |
| ❑ | 273 | Jeff Kent | .40 | .18 |
| ❑ | 274 | Tim Raines | .30 | .14 |
| ❑ | 275 | Carlos Garcia | .15 | .07 |
| ❑ | 276 | Hal Morris | .15 | .07 |
| ❑ | 277 | Gary Gaetti | .30 | .14 |
| ❑ | 278 | John Olerud | .30 | .14 |
| ❑ | 279 | Wally Joyner | .30 | .14 |
| ❑ | 280 | Brian Hunter | .15 | .07 |
| ❑ | 281 | Steve Karsay | .15 | .07 |
| ❑ | 282 | Denny Neagle | .30 | .14 |
| ❑ | 283 | Jose Herrera | .15 | .07 |
| ❑ | 284 | Todd Stottlemyre | .15 | .07 |
| ❑ | 285 | Bip Roberts | .15 | .07 |
| ❑ | 286 | Kevin Seitzer | .15 | .07 |
| ❑ | 287 | Benji Gil | .15 | .07 |
| ❑ | 288 | Dennis Eckersley | .30 | .14 |
| ❑ | 289 | Brad Ausmus | .15 | .07 |
| ❑ | 290 | Otis Nixon | .15 | .07 |
| ❑ | 291 | Darryl Strawberry | .30 | .14 |
| ❑ | 292 | Marquis Grissom | .15 | .07 |
| ❑ | 293 | Darryl Kile | .30 | .14 |
| ❑ | 294 | Quilvio Veras | .15 | .07 |
| ❑ | 295 | Tom Goodwin | .15 | .07 |
| ❑ | 296 | Benito Santiago | .15 | .07 |
| ❑ | 297 | Mike Bordick | .15 | .07 |
| ❑ | 298 | Roberto Kelly | .15 | .07 |
| ❑ | 299 | David Justice | .40 | .18 |
| ❑ | 300 | Carl Everett | .30 | .14 |
| ❑ | 301 | Mark Whiten | .15 | .07 |
| ❑ | 302 | Aaron Sele | .30 | .14 |
| ❑ | 303 | Darren Dreifort | .30 | .14 |
| ❑ | 304 | Bobby Jones | .15 | .07 |
| ❑ | 305 | Fernando Vina | .15 | .07 |
| ❑ | 306 | Ed Sprague | .15 | .07 |
| ❑ | 307 | Andy Ashby | .15 | .07 |
| ❑ | 308 | Tony Fernandez | .15 | .07 |
| ❑ | 309 | Roger Pavlik | .15 | .07 |
| ❑ | 310 | Mark Clark | .15 | .07 |
| ❑ | 311 | Mariano Duncan | .15 | .07 |
| ❑ | 312 | Tyler Houston | .15 | .07 |
| ❑ | 313 | Eric Davis | .30 | .14 |
| ❑ | 314 | Greg Vaughn | .30 | .14 |
| ❑ | 315 | David Segui | .15 | .07 |
| ❑ | 316 | Dave Nilsson | .15 | .07 |
| ❑ | 317 | F.P. Santangelo | .15 | .07 |
| ❑ | 318 | Wilton Guerrero | .15 | .07 |
| ❑ | 319 | Jose Guillen | .15 | .07 |
| ❑ | 320 | Kevin Orie | .15 | .07 |
| ❑ | 321 | Derrek Lee | .15 | .07 |
| ❑ | 322 | Bubba Trammell RC | .30 | .14 |
| ❑ | 323 | Pokey Reese | .30 | .14 |
| ❑ | 324 | Hideki Irabu RC | .50 | .23 |
| ❑ | 325 | Scott Spiezio | .15 | .07 |
| ❑ | 326 | Bartolo Colon | .30 | .14 |
| ❑ | 327 | Damon Mashore | .15 | .07 |
| ❑ | 329 | Chris Carpenter | .30 | .14 |
| ❑ | 330 | Jose Cruz Jr. RC | 1.50 | .70 |
| ❑ | 331 | Todd Greene | .15 | .07 |
| ❑ | 332 | Brian Moehler | .15 | .07 |
| ❑ | 333 | Mike Sweeney | .30 | .14 |
| ❑ | 334 | Neifi Perez | .15 | .07 |
| ❑ | 335 | Matt Morris | .15 | .07 |
| ❑ | 336 | Marvin Benard | .15 | .07 |
| ❑ | 337 | Karim Garcia | .15 | .07 |
| ❑ | 338 | Jason Dickson | .15 | .07 |
| ❑ | 339 | Brant Brown | .15 | .07 |
| ❑ | 340 | Jeff Suppan | .15 | .07 |
| ❑ | 341 | Deivi Cruz RC | .75 | .35 |
| ❑ | 342 | Antone Williamson | .15 | .07 |
| ❑ | 343 | Curtis Goodwin | .15 | .07 |
| ❑ | 344 | Brooks Kieschnick | .15 | .07 |
| ❑ | 345 | Tony Womack RC | .75 | .35 |
| ❑ | 346 | Rudy Pemberton | .15 | .07 |
| ❑ | 347 | Todd Dunwoody | .30 | .14 |
| ❑ | 348 | Frank Thomas LG | .60 | .25 |
| ❑ | 349 | Andruw Jones LG | .40 | .18 |
| ❑ | 350 | Alex Rodriguez LG | 1.00 | .45 |
| ❑ | 351 | Greg Maddux LG | .75 | .35 |
| ❑ | 352 | Jeff Bagwell LG | .60 | .25 |
| ❑ | 353 | Juan Gonzalez LG | .30 | .14 |
| ❑ | 354 | Barry Bonds LG | .30 | .14 |
| ❑ | 355 | Mark McGwire LG | 1.25 | .55 |
| ❑ | 356 | Tony Gwynn LG | .60 | .25 |
| ❑ | 357 | Gary Sheffield LG | .30 | .14 |

| Card | | |
|---|---|---|
| ❑ 358 Derek Jeter LG | 1.25 | .55 |
| ❑ 359 Manny Ramirez LG | .40 | .18 |
| ❑ 360 Hideo Nomo LG | .60 | .25 |
| ❑ 361 Sammy Sosa LG | .60 | .25 |
| ❑ 362 Paul Molitor LG | .30 | .14 |
| ❑ 363 Kenny Lofton LG | .15 | .07 |
| ❑ 364 Eddie Murray LG | .30 | .14 |
| ❑ 365 Barry Larkin LG | .30 | .14 |
| ❑ 366 Roger Clemens LG | .60 | .25 |
| ❑ 367 John Smoltz LG | .15 | .07 |
| ❑ 368 Alex Rodriguez GM | 1.00 | .45 |
| ❑ 369 Frank Thomas GM | .60 | .25 |
| ❑ 370 Cal Ripken GM | 1.25 | .55 |
| ❑ 371 Ken Griffey Jr. GM | 1.25 | .55 |
| ❑ 372 Greg Maddux GM | .75 | .35 |
| ❑ 373 Mike Piazza GM | 1.00 | .45 |
| ❑ 374 Chipper Jones GM | .75 | .35 |
| ❑ 375 Albert Belle GM | .15 | .07 |
| ❑ 376 Chuck Knoblauch GM | .15 | .07 |
| ❑ 377 Brady Anderson GM | .15 | .07 |
| ❑ 378 David Justice GM | .15 | .07 |
| ❑ 379 Randy Johnson GM | .30 | .14 |
| ❑ 380 Wade Boggs GM | .30 | .14 |
| ❑ 381 Kevin Brown GM | .15 | .07 |
| ❑ 382 Tom Glavine GM | .30 | .14 |
| ❑ 383 Raul Mondesi GM | .15 | .07 |
| ❑ 384 Ivan Rodriguez GM | .40 | .18 |
| ❑ 385 Larry Walker GM | .30 | .14 |
| ❑ 386 Bernie Williams GM | .30 | .14 |
| ❑ 387 Rusty Greer GM | .30 | .14 |
| ❑ 388 Rafael Palmeiro GM | .30 | .14 |
| ❑ 389 Matt Williams GM | .40 | .18 |
| ❑ 390 Eric Young GM | .15 | .07 |
| ❑ 391 Fred McGriff GM | .30 | .14 |
| ❑ 392 Ken Caminiti GM | .15 | .07 |
| ❑ 393 Roberto Alomar GM | .30 | .14 |
| ❑ 394 Brian Jordan GM | .15 | .07 |
| ❑ 395 Mark Grace GM | .30 | .14 |
| ❑ 396 Jim Edmonds GM | .30 | .14 |
| ❑ 397 Deion Sanders GM | .30 | .14 |
| ❑ 398 Vladimir Guerrero CL | .60 | .25 |
| ❑ 399 Darin Erstad CL | .40 | .18 |
| ❑ 400 N. Garciaparra CL | 1.00 | .45 |
| ❑ NNO J.Robinson Reprint | 30.00 | 13.50 |

## 1998 Leaf

| | MINT | NRMT |
|---|---|---|
| COMPLETE SET (200) | 150.00 | 70.00 |
| COMP.SET w/o SP's (147) | 15.00 | 6.75 |
| COMMON CARD (1-201) | .15 | .07 |
| COMMON SP (148-197) | 1.00 | .45 |

| Card | | |
|---|---|---|
| ❑ 1 Rusty Greer | .25 | .11 |
| ❑ 2 Tino Martinez | .25 | .11 |
| ❑ 3 Bobby Bonilla | .25 | .11 |
| ❑ 4 Jason Giambi | .60 | .25 |
| ❑ 5 Matt Morris | .15 | .07 |
| ❑ 6 Craig Counsell | .15 | .07 |
| ❑ 7 Reggie Jefferson | .15 | .07 |
| ❑ 8 Brian Rose | .15 | .07 |
| ❑ 9 Ruben Rivera | .15 | .07 |
| ❑ 10 Shawn Estes | .15 | .07 |
| ❑ 11 Tony Gwynn | 1.25 | .55 |
| ❑ 12 Jeff Abbott | .15 | .07 |
| ❑ 13 Jose Cruz Jr. | .25 | .11 |
| ❑ 14 Francisco Cordova | .15 | .07 |
| ❑ 15 Ryan Klesko | .25 | .11 |
| ❑ 16 Tim Salmon | .25 | .11 |
| ❑ 17 Brett Tomko | .15 | .07 |
| ❑ 18 Matt Williams | .40 | .18 |
| ❑ 19 Joe Carter | .25 | .11 |
| ❑ 20 Harold Baines | .25 | .11 |
| ❑ 21 Gary Sheffield | .60 | .25 |
| ❑ 22 Charles Johnson | .25 | .11 |
| ❑ 23 Aaron Boone | .15 | .07 |
| ❑ 24 Eddie Murray | .60 | .25 |
| ❑ 25 Matt Stairs | .15 | .07 |
| ❑ 26 David Cone | .25 | .11 |
| ❑ 27 Jon Nunnally | .15 | .07 |
| ❑ 28 Chris Stynes | .15 | .07 |
| ❑ 29 Enrique Wilson | .15 | .07 |
| ❑ 30 Randy Johnson | .75 | .35 |
| ❑ 31 Garret Anderson | .25 | .11 |
| ❑ 32 Manny Ramirez | .75 | .35 |
| ❑ 33 Jeff Suppan | .15 | .07 |
| ❑ 34 Rickey Henderson | .75 | .35 |
| ❑ 35 Scott Spiezio | .15 | .07 |
| ❑ 36 Rondell White | .25 | .11 |
| ❑ 37 Todd Greene | .15 | .07 |
| ❑ 38 Delino DeShields | .15 | .07 |
| ❑ 39 Kevin Brown | .40 | .18 |
| ❑ 40 Chili Davis | .25 | .11 |
| ❑ 41 Jimmy Key | .25 | .11 |
| ❑ 43 Mike Mussina | .60 | .25 |
| ❑ 44 Joe Randa | .15 | .07 |
| ❑ 45 Chan Ho Park | .25 | .11 |
| ❑ 46 Brad Radke | .25 | .11 |
| ❑ 47 Geronimo Berroa | .15 | .07 |
| ❑ 48 Wade Boggs | .75 | .35 |
| ❑ 49 Kevin Appier | .25 | .11 |
| ❑ 50 Moises Alou | .25 | .11 |
| ❑ 51 David Justice | .40 | .18 |
| ❑ 52 Ivan Rodriguez | .75 | .35 |
| ❑ 53 J.T. Snow | .25 | .11 |
| ❑ 54 Brian Giles | .25 | .11 |
| ❑ 55 Will Clark | .60 | .25 |
| ❑ 56 Justin Thompson | .15 | .07 |
| ❑ 57 Javier Lopez | .25 | .11 |
| ❑ 58 Hideki Irabu | .15 | .07 |
| ❑ 59 Mark Grudzielanek | .15 | .07 |
| ❑ 60 Abraham Nunez | .15 | .07 |
| ❑ 61 Todd Hollandsworth | .15 | .07 |
| ❑ 62 Jay Bell | .25 | .11 |
| ❑ 63 Nomar Garciaparra | 2.00 | .90 |
| ❑ 64 Vinny Castilla | .25 | .11 |
| ❑ 65 Lou Collier | .15 | .07 |
| ❑ 66 Kevin Orie | .15 | .07 |
| ❑ 67 John Valentin | .15 | .07 |
| ❑ 68 Robin Ventura | .25 | .11 |
| ❑ 69 Denny Neagle | .15 | .07 |
| ❑ 70 Tony Womack | .15 | .07 |
| ❑ 71 Dennis Reyes | .15 | .07 |
| ❑ 72 Wally Joyner | .25 | .11 |
| ❑ 73 Kevin Brown | .40 | .18 |
| ❑ 74 Ray Durham | .25 | .11 |
| ❑ 75 Mike Cameron | .25 | .11 |
| ❑ 76 Dante Bichette | .25 | .11 |
| ❑ 77 Jose Guillen | .15 | .07 |
| ❑ 78 Carlos Delgado | .60 | .25 |
| ❑ 79 Paul Molitor | .60 | .25 |
| ❑ 80 Jason Kendall | .25 | .11 |
| ❑ 81 Mark Bellhorn | .15 | .07 |
| ❑ 82 Damian Jackson | .15 | .07 |
| ❑ 83 Bill Mueller | .15 | .07 |
| ❑ 84 Kevin Young | .25 | .11 |
| ❑ 85 Curt Schilling | .25 | .11 |
| ❑ 86 Jeffrey Hammonds | .25 | .11 |
| ❑ 87 Sandy Alomar Jr. | .25 | .11 |
| ❑ 88 Bartolo Colon | .25 | .11 |
| ❑ 89 Wilton Guerrero | .15 | .07 |
| ❑ 90 Bernie Williams | .60 | .25 |
| ❑ 91 Deion Sanders | .25 | .11 |
| ❑ 92 Mike Piazza | 2.00 | .90 |
| ❑ 93 Butch Huskey | .15 | .07 |
| ❑ 94 Edgardo Alfonzo | .25 | .11 |
| ❑ 95 Alan Benes | .15 | .07 |
| ❑ 96 Craig Biggio | .40 | .18 |
| ❑ 97 Mark Grace | .60 | .25 |
| ❑ 98 Shawn Green | .60 | .25 |
| ❑ 99 Derrek Lee | .15 | .07 |
| ❑ 100 Ken Griffey Jr. | 2.50 | 1.10 |
| ❑ 101 Tim Raines | .25 | .11 |
| ❑ 102 Pokey Reese | .25 | .11 |
| ❑ 103 Lee Stevens | .15 | .07 |
| ❑ 104 Shannon Stewart | .25 | .11 |
| ❑ 105 John Smoltz | .25 | .11 |
| ❑ 106 Frank Thomas | 1.25 | .55 |
| ❑ 107 Jeff Fassero | .15 | .07 |
| ❑ 108 Jay Buhner | .25 | .11 |
| ❑ 109 Jose Canseco | .75 | .35 |
| ❑ 110 Omar Vizquel | .25 | .11 |
| ❑ 111 Travis Fryman | .25 | .11 |
| ❑ 112 Dave Nilsson | .15 | .07 |
| ❑ 113 John Olerud | .25 | .11 |
| ❑ 114 Larry Walker | .25 | .11 |
| ❑ 115 Jim Edmonds | .60 | .25 |
| ❑ 116 Bobby Higginson | .25 | .11 |
| ❑ 117 Todd Hundley | .15 | .07 |
| ❑ 118 Paul O'Neill | .25 | .11 |
| ❑ 119 Bip Roberts | .15 | .07 |
| ❑ 120 Ismael Valdes | .15 | .07 |
| ❑ 121 Pedro Martinez | .75 | .35 |
| ❑ 122 Jeff Cirillo | .25 | .11 |
| ❑ 123 Andy Benes | .15 | .07 |
| ❑ 124 Bobby Jones | .15 | .07 |
| ❑ 125 Brian Hunter | .15 | .07 |
| ❑ 126 Darryl Kile | .25 | .11 |
| ❑ 127 Pat Hentgen | .15 | .07 |
| ❑ 128 Marquis Grissom | .15 | .07 |
| ❑ 129 Eric Davis | .25 | .11 |
| ❑ 130 Chipper Jones | 1.50 | .70 |
| ❑ 131 Edgar Martinez | .40 | .18 |
| ❑ 132 Andy Pettitte | .25 | .11 |
| ❑ 133 Cal Ripken | 2.50 | 1.10 |
| ❑ 134 Scott Rolen | .60 | .25 |
| ❑ 135 Ron Coomer | .15 | .07 |
| ❑ 136 Luis Castillo | .25 | .11 |
| ❑ 137 Fred McGriff | .40 | .18 |
| ❑ 138 Neifi Perez | .15 | .07 |
| ❑ 139 Eric Karros | .25 | .11 |
| ❑ 140 Alex Fernandez | .15 | .07 |
| ❑ 141 Jason Dickson | .15 | .07 |
| ❑ 142 Lance Johnson | .15 | .07 |
| ❑ 143 Ray Lankford | .25 | .11 |
| ❑ 144 Sammy Sosa | 1.25 | .55 |
| ❑ 145 Eric Young | .15 | .07 |
| ❑ 146 Bubba Trammell | .15 | .07 |
| ❑ 147 Todd Walker | .15 | .07 |
| ❑ 148 Mo Vaughn CC | 1.50 | .70 |
| ❑ 149 Jeff Bagwell CC | 4.00 | 1.80 |
| ❑ 150 Kenny Lofton CC | 1.50 | .70 |
| ❑ 151 Raul Mondesi CC | 1.50 | .70 |
| ❑ 152 Mike Piazza CC | 10.00 | 4.50 |
| ❑ 153 Chipper Jones CC | 8.00 | 3.60 |
| ❑ 154 Larry Walker CC | 1.50 | .70 |
| ❑ 155 Greg Maddux CC | 8.00 | 3.60 |
| ❑ 156 Ken Griffey Jr. CC | 12.00 | 5.50 |
| ❑ 157 Frank Thomas CC | 6.00 | 2.70 |
| ❑ 158 Darin Erstad GLS | 3.00 | 1.35 |
| ❑ 159 Roberto Alomar GLS | 3.00 | 1.35 |
| ❑ 160 Albert Belle GLS | 2.00 | .90 |
| ❑ 161 Jim Thome GLS | 2.00 | .90 |
| ❑ 162 Tony Clark GLS | 1.00 | .45 |
| ❑ 163 Chuck Knoblauch GLS | 1.50 | .70 |
| ❑ 164 Derek Jeter GLS | 12.00 | 5.50 |
| ❑ 165 Alex Rodriguez GLS | 10.00 | 4.50 |
| ❑ 166 Tony Gwynn GLS | 6.00 | 2.70 |
| ❑ 167 Roger Clemens GLS | 6.00 | 2.70 |
| ❑ 168 Barry Larkin GLS | 3.00 | 1.35 |
| ❑ 169 Andres Galarraga GLS | 2.00 | .90 |
| ❑ 170 Vladimir Guerrero GLS | 5.00 | 2.20 |
| ❑ 171 Mark McGwire GLS | 12.00 | 5.50 |
| ❑ 172 Barry Bonds GLS | 5.00 | 2.20 |
| ❑ 173 Juan Gonzalez GLS | 3.00 | 1.35 |
| ❑ 174 Andruw Jones GLS | 3.00 | 1.35 |
| ❑ 175 Paul Molitor GLS | 3.00 | 1.35 |
| ❑ 176 Hideo Nomo GLS | 3.00 | 1.35 |
| ❑ 177 Cal Ripken GLS | 12.00 | 5.50 |
| ❑ 178 Brad Fullmer GLR | 1.50 | .70 |
| ❑ 179 Jaret Wright GLR | 1.00 | .45 |
| ❑ 180 Bobby Estalella GLR | 1.00 | .45 |
| ❑ 181 Ben Grieve GLR | 1.50 | .70 |
| ❑ 182 Paul Konerko GLR | 1.50 | .70 |
| ❑ 183 David Ortiz GLR | 1.00 | .45 |
| ❑ 184 Todd Helton GLR | 4.00 | 1.80 |
| ❑ 185 Juan Encarnacion GLR | 1.50 | .70 |
| ❑ 186 Miguel Tejada GLR | 3.00 | 1.35 |
| ❑ 187 Jacob Cruz GLR | 1.00 | .45 |
| ❑ 188 Mark Kotsay GLR | 1.50 | .70 |

| | | |
|---|---|---|
| ❑ 189 Fernando Tatis GLR | 1.50 | .70 |
| ❑ 190 Ricky Ledee GLR | 1.00 | .45 |
| ❑ 191 Richard Hidalgo GLR | 1.50 | .70 |
| ❑ 192 Richie Sexson GLR | 2.00 | .90 |
| ❑ 193 Luis Ordaz GLR | 1.00 | .45 |
| ❑ 194 Eli Marrero GLR | 1.00 | .45 |
| ❑ 195 Livan Hernandez GLR | 1.00 | .45 |
| ❑ 196 Homer Bush GLR | 1.00 | .45 |
| ❑ 197 Raul Ibanez GLR | 1.00 | .45 |
| ❑ 198 Nomar Garciaparra CL | 1.00 | .45 |
| ❑ 199 Scott Rolen CL | .60 | .25 |
| ❑ 200 Jose Cruz Jr. CL | .15 | .07 |
| ❑ 201 Al Martin | .15 | .07 |

## 1994 Leaf Limited

| | MINT | NRMT |
|---|---|---|
| COMPLETE SET (160) | 80.00 | 36.00 |
| ❑ 1 Jeffrey Hammonds | .75 | .35 |
| ❑ 2 Ben McDonald | .50 | .23 |
| ❑ 3 Mike Mussina | 2.00 | .90 |
| ❑ 4 Rafael Palmeiro | 2.00 | .90 |
| ❑ 5 Cal Ripken Jr. | 8.00 | 3.60 |
| ❑ 6 Lee Smith | .75 | .35 |
| ❑ 7 Roger Clemens | 4.00 | 1.80 |
| ❑ 8 Scott Cooper | .50 | .23 |
| ❑ 9 Andre Dawson | 1.25 | .55 |
| ❑ 10 Mike Greenwell | .50 | .23 |
| ❑ 11 Aaron Sele | .75 | .35 |
| ❑ 12 Mo Vaughn | .75 | .35 |
| ❑ 13 Brian Anderson RC | .75 | .35 |
| ❑ 14 Chad Curtis | .50 | .23 |
| ❑ 15 Chili Davis | .75 | .35 |
| ❑ 16 Gary DiSarcina | .50 | .23 |
| ❑ 17 Mark Langston | .50 | .23 |
| ❑ 18 Tim Salmon | .75 | .35 |
| ❑ 19 Wilson Alvarez | .50 | .23 |
| ❑ 20 Jason Bere | .50 | .23 |
| ❑ 21 Julio Franco | .50 | .23 |
| ❑ 22 Jack McDowell | .50 | .23 |
| ❑ 23 Tim Raines | .75 | .35 |
| ❑ 24 Frank Thomas | 4.00 | 1.80 |
| ❑ 25 Robin Ventura | .75 | .35 |
| ❑ 26 Carlos Baerga | .50 | .23 |
| ❑ 27 Albert Belle | 1.25 | .55 |
| ❑ 28 Kenny Lofton | .75 | .35 |
| ❑ 29 Eddie Murray | 2.00 | .90 |
| ❑ 30 Manny Ramirez | 3.00 | 1.35 |
| ❑ 31 Cecil Fielder | .75 | .35 |
| ❑ 32 Travis Fryman | .75 | .35 |
| ❑ 33 Mickey Tettleton | .50 | .23 |
| ❑ 34 Alan Trammell | 1.25 | .55 |
| ❑ 35 Lou Whitaker | .75 | .35 |
| ❑ 36 David Cone | .75 | .35 |
| ❑ 37 Gary Gaetti | .75 | .35 |
| ❑ 38 Greg Gagne | .50 | .23 |
| ❑ 39 Bob Hamelin | .50 | .23 |
| ❑ 40 Wally Joyner | .75 | .35 |
| ❑ 41 Brian McRae | .50 | .23 |
| ❑ 42 Ricky Bones | .50 | .23 |
| ❑ 43 Brian Harper | .50 | .23 |
| ❑ 44 John Jaha | .50 | .23 |
| ❑ 45 Pat Listach | .50 | .23 |
| ❑ 46 Dave Nilsson | .50 | .23 |
| ❑ 47 Greg Vaughn | .75 | .35 |
| ❑ 48 Kent Hrbek | .75 | .35 |
| ❑ 49 Chuck Knoblauch | .75 | .35 |
| ❑ 50 Shane Mack | .50 | .23 |
| ❑ 51 Kirby Puckett | 5.00 | 2.20 |
| ❑ 52 Dave Winfield | 2.00 | .90 |
| ❑ 53 Jim Abbott | .75 | .35 |
| ❑ 54 Wade Boggs | 2.50 | 1.10 |
| ❑ 55 Jimmy Key | .75 | .35 |
| ❑ 56 Don Mattingly | 5.00 | 2.20 |
| ❑ 57 Paul O'Neill | .75 | .35 |
| ❑ 58 Danny Tartabull | .50 | .23 |
| ❑ 59 Dennis Eckersley | .75 | .35 |
| ❑ 60 Rickey Henderson | 2.50 | 1.10 |
| ❑ 61 Mark McGwire | 8.00 | 3.60 |
| ❑ 62 Troy Neel | .50 | .23 |
| ❑ 63 Ruben Sierra | .50 | .23 |
| ❑ 64 Eric Anthony | .50 | .23 |
| ❑ 65 Jay Buhner | .75 | .35 |
| ❑ 66 Ken Griffey Jr. | 8.00 | 3.60 |
| ❑ 67 Randy Johnson | 2.50 | 1.10 |
| ❑ 68 Edgar Martinez | 1.25 | .55 |
| ❑ 69 Tino Martinez | .75 | .35 |
| ❑ 70 Jose Canseco | 2.50 | 1.10 |
| ❑ 71 Will Clark | 2.00 | .90 |
| ❑ 72 Juan Gonzalez | 2.00 | .90 |
| ❑ 73 Dean Palmer | .75 | .35 |
| ❑ 74 Ivan Rodriguez | 2.50 | 1.10 |
| ❑ 75 Roberto Alomar | 2.00 | .90 |
| ❑ 76 Joe Carter | .75 | .35 |
| ❑ 77 Carlos Delgado | 3.00 | 1.35 |
| ❑ 78 Paul Molitor | 2.00 | .90 |
| ❑ 79 John Olerud | .75 | .35 |
| ❑ 80 Devon White | .50 | .23 |
| ❑ 81 Steve Avery | .50 | .23 |
| ❑ 82 Tom Glavine | 2.00 | .90 |
| ❑ 83 David Justice | 1.25 | .55 |
| ❑ 84 Roberto Kelly | .50 | .23 |
| ❑ 85 Ryan Klesko | .75 | .35 |
| ❑ 86 Javier Lopez | .75 | .35 |
| ❑ 87 Greg Maddux | 5.00 | 2.20 |
| ❑ 88 Fred McGriff | 1.25 | .55 |
| ❑ 89 Shawon Dunston | .50 | .23 |
| ❑ 90 Mark Grace | 2.00 | .90 |
| ❑ 91 Derrick May | .50 | .23 |
| ❑ 92 Sammy Sosa | 4.00 | 1.80 |
| ❑ 93 Rick Wilkins | .50 | .23 |
| ❑ 94 Bret Boone | .75 | .35 |
| ❑ 95 Barry Larkin | 2.00 | .90 |
| ❑ 96 Kevin Mitchell | .50 | .23 |
| ❑ 97 Hal Morris | .50 | .23 |
| ❑ 98 Deion Sanders | .75 | .35 |
| ❑ 99 Reggie Sanders | .50 | .23 |
| ❑ 100 Dante Bichette | .75 | .35 |
| ❑ 101 Ellis Burks | .75 | .35 |
| ❑ 102 Andres Galarraga | 1.25 | .55 |
| ❑ 103 Joe Girardi | .50 | .23 |
| ❑ 104 Charlie Hayes | .50 | .23 |
| ❑ 105 Chuck Carr | .50 | .23 |
| ❑ 106 Jeff Conine | .50 | .23 |
| ❑ 107 Bryan Harvey | .50 | .23 |
| ❑ 108 Benito Santiago | .50 | .23 |
| ❑ 109 Gary Sheffield | 2.00 | .90 |
| ❑ 110 Jeff Bagwell | 2.50 | 1.10 |
| ❑ 111 Craig Biggio | 1.25 | .55 |
| ❑ 112 Ken Caminiti | .75 | .35 |
| ❑ 113 Andujar Cedeno | .50 | .23 |
| ❑ 114 Doug Drabek | .50 | .23 |
| ❑ 115 Luis Gonzalez | .75 | .35 |
| ❑ 116 Brett Butler | .75 | .35 |
| ❑ 117 Delino DeShields | .50 | .23 |
| ❑ 118 Eric Karros | .75 | .35 |
| ❑ 119 Raul Mondesi | .75 | .35 |
| ❑ 120 Mike Piazza | 6.00 | 2.70 |
| ❑ 121 Henry Rodriguez | .50 | .23 |
| ❑ 122 Tim Wallach | .50 | .23 |
| ❑ 123 Moises Alou | .75 | .35 |
| ❑ 124 Cliff Floyd | .75 | .35 |
| ❑ 125 Marquis Grissom | .50 | .23 |
| ❑ 126 Ken Hill | .50 | .23 |
| ❑ 127 Larry Walker | .75 | .35 |
| ❑ 128 John Wetteland | .75 | .35 |
| ❑ 129 Bobby Bonilla | .75 | .35 |
| ❑ 130 John Franco | .75 | .35 |
| ❑ 131 Jeff Kent | 1.25 | .55 |
| ❑ 132 Bret Saberhagen | .75 | .35 |
| ❑ 133 Ryan Thompson | .50 | .23 |
| ❑ 134 Darren Daulton | .75 | .35 |
| ❑ 135 Mariano Duncan | .50 | .23 |
| ❑ 136 Lenny Dykstra | .75 | .35 |
| ❑ 137 Danny Jackson | .50 | .23 |
| ❑ 138 John Kruk | .75 | .35 |
| ❑ 139 Jay Bell | .75 | .35 |
| ❑ 140 Jeff King | .50 | .23 |
| ❑ 141 Al Martin | .50 | .23 |
| ❑ 142 Orlando Merced | .50 | .23 |
| ❑ 143 Andy Van Slyke | .75 | .35 |
| ❑ 144 Bernard Gilkey | .50 | .23 |
| ❑ 145 Gregg Jefferies | .50 | .23 |
| ❑ 146 Ray Lankford | .75 | .35 |
| ❑ 147 Ozzie Smith | 2.50 | 1.10 |
| ❑ 148 Mark Whiten | .50 | .23 |
| ❑ 149 Todd Zeile | .50 | .23 |
| ❑ 150 Derek Bell | .50 | .23 |
| ❑ 151 Andy Benes | .50 | .23 |
| ❑ 152 Tony Gwynn | 4.00 | 1.80 |
| ❑ 153 Phil Plantier | .50 | .23 |
| ❑ 154 Bip Roberts | .50 | .23 |
| ❑ 155 Rod Beck | .50 | .23 |
| ❑ 156 Barry Bonds | 3.00 | 1.35 |
| ❑ 157 John Burkett | .50 | .23 |
| ❑ 158 Royce Clayton | .50 | .23 |
| ❑ 159 Bill Swift | .50 | .23 |
| ❑ 160 Matt Williams | 1.25 | .55 |

## 1994 Leaf Limited Rookies

| | MINT | NRMT |
|---|---|---|
| COMPLETE SET (80) | 25.00 | 11.00 |
| ❑ 1 Charles Johnson | .75 | .35 |
| ❑ 2 Rico Brogna | .40 | .18 |
| ❑ 3 Melvin Nieves | .40 | .18 |
| ❑ 4 Rich Becker | .40 | .18 |
| ❑ 5 Russ Davis | .40 | .18 |
| ❑ 6 Matt Mieske | .40 | .18 |
| ❑ 7 Paul Shuey | .40 | .18 |
| ❑ 8 Hector Carrasco | .40 | .18 |
| ❑ 9 J.R. Phillips | .40 | .18 |
| ❑ 10 Scott Ruffcorn | .40 | .18 |
| ❑ 11 Kurt Abbott RC | .40 | .18 |
| ❑ 12 Danny Bautista | .40 | .18 |
| ❑ 13 Rick White | .40 | .18 |
| ❑ 14 Steve Dunn | .40 | .18 |
| ❑ 15 Joe Ausanio | .40 | .18 |
| ❑ 16 Salomon Torres | .40 | .18 |
| ❑ 17 Ricky Bottalico RC | .40 | .18 |
| ❑ 18 Johnny Ruffin | .40 | .18 |
| ❑ 19 Kevin Foster RC | .40 | .18 |
| ❑ 20 W.VanLandingham RC | .40 | .18 |
| ❑ 21 Troy O'Leary | .40 | .18 |
| ❑ 22 Mark Acre RC | .40 | .18 |
| ❑ 23 Norberto Martin | .40 | .18 |
| ❑ 24 Jason Jacome RC | .40 | .18 |
| ❑ 25 Steve Trachsel | .40 | .18 |
| ❑ 26 Denny Hocking | .40 | .18 |
| ❑ 27 Mike Lieberthal | .75 | .35 |
| ❑ 28 Gerald Williams | .40 | .18 |
| ❑ 29 John Mabry RC | .40 | .18 |
| ❑ 30 Greg Blosser | .40 | .18 |
| ❑ 31 Carl Everett | .75 | .35 |
| ❑ 32 Steve Karsay | .40 | .18 |
| ❑ 33 Jose Valentin | .40 | .18 |
| ❑ 34 Jon Lieber | .40 | .18 |
| ❑ 35 Chris Gomez | .40 | .18 |
| ❑ 36 Jesus Tavarez RC | .40 | .18 |
| ❑ 37 Tony Longmire | .40 | .18 |

| # | Player | | |
|---|---|---|---|
| ❑ 38 | Luis Lopez | .40 | .18 |
| ❑ 39 | Matt Walbeck | .40 | .18 |
| ❑ 40 | Rikkert Faneyte RC | .40 | .18 |
| ❑ 41 | Shane Reynolds | .40 | .18 |
| ❑ 42 | Joey Hamilton | .40 | .18 |
| ❑ 43 | Ismael Valdes RC | 1.00 | .45 |
| ❑ 44 | Danny Miceli | .40 | .18 |
| ❑ 45 | Darren Bragg RC | .40 | .18 |
| ❑ 46 | Alex Gonzalez | .40 | .18 |
| ❑ 47 | Rick Helling | .75 | .35 |
| ❑ 48 | Jose Oliva | .40 | .18 |
| ❑ 49 | Jim Edmonds | 2.00 | .90 |
| ❑ 50 | Miguel Jimenez | .40 | .18 |
| ❑ 51 | Tony Eusebio | .40 | .18 |
| ❑ 52 | Shawn Green | 2.50 | 1.10 |
| ❑ 53 | Billy Ashley | .40 | .18 |
| ❑ 54 | Rondell White | .75 | .35 |
| ❑ 55 | Cory Bailey RC | .40 | .18 |
| ❑ 56 | Tim Davis | .40 | .18 |
| ❑ 57 | John Hudek RC | .40 | .18 |
| ❑ 58 | Darren Hall | .40 | .18 |
| ❑ 59 | Darren Dreifort | .75 | .35 |
| ❑ 60 | Mike Kelly | .40 | .18 |
| ❑ 61 | Marcus Moore | .40 | .18 |
| ❑ 62 | Garret Anderson | 1.50 | .70 |
| ❑ 63 | Brian L. Hunter | .40 | .18 |
| ❑ 64 | Mark Smith | .40 | .18 |
| ❑ 65 | Garey Ingram RC | .40 | .18 |
| ❑ 66 | Rusty Greer RC | 3.00 | 1.35 |
| ❑ 67 | Marc Newfield | .40 | .18 |
| ❑ 68 | Gar Finnvold | .40 | .18 |
| ❑ 69 | Paul Spoljaric | .40 | .18 |
| ❑ 70 | Ray McDavid | .40 | .18 |
| ❑ 71 | Orlando Miller | .40 | .18 |
| ❑ 72 | Jorge Fabregas | .40 | .18 |
| ❑ 73 | Ray Holbert | .40 | .18 |
| ❑ 74 | Armando Benitez RC | 2.00 | .90 |
| ❑ 75 | Ernie Young RC | .40 | .18 |
| ❑ 76 | James Mouton | .40 | .18 |
| ❑ 77 | Robert Perez RC | .40 | .18 |
| ❑ 78 | Chan Ho Park RC | 3.00 | 1.35 |
| ❑ 79 | Roger Salkeld | .40 | .18 |
| ❑ 80 | Tony Tarasco | .40 | .18 |

## 1995 Leaf Limited

| | MINT | NRMT |
|---|---|---|
| COMPLETE SET (192) | 50.00 | 22.00 |
| COMPLETE SERIES 1 (96) | 25.00 | 11.00 |
| COMPLETE SERIES 2 (96) | 25.00 | 11.00 |
| COMP.GOLD SET (24) | 30.00 | 13.50 |

*GOLD: .4X TO 1X HI COLUMN ..
ONE GOLD PER SERIES 1 PACK

| # | Player | MINT | NRMT |
|---|---|---|---|
| ❑ 1 | Frank Thomas | 2.50 | 1.10 |
| ❑ 2 | Geronimo Berroa | .25 | .11 |
| ❑ 3 | Tony Phillips | .25 | .11 |
| ❑ 4 | Roberto Alomar | 1.25 | .55 |
| ❑ 5 | Steve Avery | .25 | .11 |
| ❑ 6 | Darryl Hamilton | .25 | .11 |
| ❑ 7 | Scott Cooper | .25 | .11 |
| ❑ 8 | Mark Grace | 1.25 | .55 |
| ❑ 9 | Billy Ashley | .25 | .11 |
| ❑ 10 | Wil Cordero | .25 | .11 |
| ❑ 11 | Barry Bonds | 2.00 | .90 |
| ❑ 12 | Kenny Lofton | .50 | .23 |
| ❑ 13 | Jay Buhner | .50 | .23 |
| ❑ 14 | Alex Rodriguez | 5.00 | 2.20 |
| ❑ 15 | Bobby Bonilla | .50 | .23 |
| ❑ 16 | Brady Anderson | .50 | .23 |
| ❑ 17 | Ken Caminiti | .50 | .23 |
| ❑ 18 | Charlie Hayes | .25 | .11 |
| ❑ 19 | Jay Bell | .50 | .23 |
| ❑ 20 | Will Clark | 1.25 | .55 |
| ❑ 21 | Jose Canseco | 1.50 | .70 |
| ❑ 22 | Bret Boone | .50 | .23 |
| ❑ 23 | Dante Bichette | .50 | .23 |
| ❑ 24 | Kevin Appier | .50 | .23 |
| ❑ 25 | Chad Curtis | .25 | .11 |
| ❑ 26 | Marty Cordova | .25 | .11 |
| ❑ 27 | Jason Bere | .25 | .11 |
| ❑ 28 | Jimmy Key | .50 | .23 |
| ❑ 29 | Rickey Henderson | 1.50 | .70 |
| ❑ 30 | Tim Salmon | .50 | .23 |
| ❑ 31 | Joe Carter | .50 | .23 |
| ❑ 32 | Tom Glavine | 1.25 | .55 |
| ❑ 33 | Pat Listach | .25 | .11 |
| ❑ 34 | Brian Jordan | .50 | .23 |
| ❑ 35 | Brian McRae | .25 | .11 |
| ❑ 36 | Eric Karros | .50 | .23 |
| ❑ 37 | Pedro Martinez | 1.50 | .70 |
| ❑ 38 | Royce Clayton | .25 | .11 |
| ❑ 39 | Eddie Murray | 1.25 | .55 |
| ❑ 40 | Randy Johnson | 1.50 | .70 |
| ❑ 41 | Jeff Conine | .25 | .11 |
| ❑ 42 | Brett Butler | .50 | .23 |
| ❑ 43 | Jeffrey Hammonds | .50 | .23 |
| ❑ 44 | Andujar Cedeno | .25 | .11 |
| ❑ 45 | Dave Hollins | .25 | .11 |
| ❑ 46 | Jeff King | .25 | .11 |
| ❑ 47 | Benji Gil | .25 | .11 |
| ❑ 48 | Roger Clemens | 2.50 | 1.10 |
| ❑ 49 | Barry Larkin | 1.25 | .55 |
| ❑ 50 | Joe Girardi | .25 | .11 |
| ❑ 51 | Bob Hamelin | .25 | .11 |
| ❑ 52 | Travis Fryman | .50 | .23 |
| ❑ 53 | Chuck Knoblauch | .50 | .23 |
| ❑ 54 | Ray Durham | .50 | .23 |
| ❑ 55 | Don Mattingly | 3.00 | 1.35 |
| ❑ 56 | Ruben Sierra | .25 | .11 |
| ❑ 57 | J.T. Snow | .50 | .23 |
| ❑ 58 | Derek Bell | .25 | .11 |
| ❑ 59 | David Cone | .50 | .23 |
| ❑ 60 | Marquis Grissom | .25 | .11 |
| ❑ 61 | Kevin Seitzer | .25 | .11 |
| ❑ 62 | Ozzie Smith | 1.50 | .70 |
| ❑ 63 | Rick Wilkins | .25 | .11 |
| ❑ 64 | Hideo Nomo RC | 3.00 | 1.35 |
| ❑ 65 | Tony Tarasco | .25 | .11 |
| ❑ 66 | Manny Ramirez | 1.50 | .70 |
| ❑ 67 | Charles Johnson | .50 | .23 |
| ❑ 68 | Craig Biggio | .75 | .35 |
| ❑ 69 | Bobby Jones | .25 | .11 |
| ❑ 70 | Mike Mussina | 1.25 | .55 |
| ❑ 71 | Alex Gonzalez | .25 | .11 |
| ❑ 72 | Gregg Jefferies | .25 | .11 |
| ❑ 73 | Rusty Greer | .50 | .23 |
| ❑ 74 | Mike Greenwell | .25 | .11 |
| ❑ 75 | Hal Morris | .25 | .11 |
| ❑ 76 | Paul O'Neill | .50 | .23 |
| ❑ 77 | Luis Gonzalez | .25 | .11 |
| ❑ 78 | Chipper Jones | 3.00 | 1.35 |
| ❑ 79 | Mike Piazza | 4.00 | 1.80 |
| ❑ 80 | Rondell White | .50 | .23 |
| ❑ 81 | Glenallen Hill | .25 | .11 |
| ❑ 82 | Shawn Green | 1.25 | .55 |
| ❑ 83 | Bernie Williams | 1.25 | .55 |
| ❑ 84 | Jim Thome | .75 | .35 |
| ❑ 85 | Terry Pendleton | .50 | .23 |
| ❑ 86 | Rafael Palmeiro | 1.25 | .55 |
| ❑ 87 | Tony Gwynn | 2.50 | 1.10 |
| ❑ 88 | Mickey Tettleton | .25 | .11 |
| ❑ 89 | John Valentin | .25 | .11 |
| ❑ 90 | Deion Sanders | .50 | .23 |
| ❑ 91 | Larry Walker | .50 | .23 |
| ❑ 92 | Michael Tucker | .25 | .11 |
| ❑ 93 | Alan Trammell | .75 | .35 |
| ❑ 94 | Tim Raines | .50 | .23 |
| ❑ 95 | David Justice | .75 | .35 |
| ❑ 96 | Tino Martinez | .50 | .23 |
| ❑ 97 | Cal Ripken Jr. | 5.00 | 2.20 |
| ❑ 98 | Deion Sanders | .50 | .23 |
| ❑ 99 | Darren Daulton | .50 | .23 |
| ❑ 100 | Paul Molitor | 1.25 | .55 |
| ❑ 101 | Randy Myers | .25 | .11 |
| ❑ 102 | Wally Joyner | .50 | .23 |
| ❑ 103 | Carlos Perez RC | .50 | .23 |
| ❑ 104 | Brian Hunter | .25 | .11 |
| ❑ 105 | Wade Boggs | 1.50 | .70 |
| ❑ 106 | Bob Higginson RC | 2.00 | .90 |
| ❑ 107 | Jeff Kent | .75 | .35 |
| ❑ 108 | Jose Offerman | .25 | .11 |
| ❑ 109 | Dennis Eckersley | .50 | .23 |
| ❑ 110 | Dave Nilsson | .25 | .11 |
| ❑ 111 | Chuck Finley | .50 | .23 |
| ❑ 112 | Devon White | .50 | .23 |
| ❑ 113 | Bip Roberts | .25 | .11 |
| ❑ 114 | Ramon Martinez | .25 | .11 |
| ❑ 115 | Greg Maddux | 3.00 | 1.35 |
| ❑ 116 | Curtis Goodwin | .25 | .11 |
| ❑ 117 | John Jaha | .25 | .11 |
| ❑ 118 | Ken Griffey Jr. | 5.00 | 2.20 |
| ❑ 119 | Geronimo Pena | .25 | .11 |
| ❑ 120 | Shawon Dunston | .25 | .11 |
| ❑ 121 | Ariel Prieto RC | .25 | .11 |
| ❑ 122 | Kirby Puckett | 3.00 | 1.35 |
| ❑ 123 | Carlos Baerga | .25 | .11 |
| ❑ 124 | Todd Hundley | .25 | .11 |
| ❑ 125 | Tim Naehring | .25 | .11 |
| ❑ 126 | Gary Sheffield | 1.25 | .55 |
| ❑ 127 | Dean Palmer | .50 | .23 |
| ❑ 128 | Rondell White | .50 | .23 |
| ❑ 129 | Greg Gagne | .25 | .11 |
| ❑ 130 | Jose Rijo | .25 | .11 |
| ❑ 131 | Ivan Rodriguez | 1.50 | .70 |
| ❑ 132 | Jeff Bagwell | 1.50 | .70 |
| ❑ 133 | Greg Vaughn | .50 | .23 |
| ❑ 134 | Chili Davis | .50 | .23 |
| ❑ 135 | Al Martin | .25 | .11 |
| ❑ 136 | Kenny Rogers | .25 | .11 |
| ❑ 137 | Aaron Sele | .50 | .23 |
| ❑ 138 | Raul Mondesi | .50 | .23 |
| ❑ 139 | Cecil Fielder | .50 | .23 |
| ❑ 140 | Tim Wallach | .25 | .11 |
| ❑ 141 | Andres Galarraga | .75 | .35 |
| ❑ 142 | Lou Whitaker | .50 | .23 |
| ❑ 143 | Jack McDowell | .25 | .11 |
| ❑ 144 | Matt Williams | .75 | .35 |
| ❑ 145 | Ryan Klesko | .50 | .23 |
| ❑ 146 | Carlos Garcia | .25 | .11 |
| ❑ 147 | Albert Belle | .75 | .35 |
| ❑ 148 | Ryan Thompson | .25 | .11 |
| ❑ 149 | Roberto Kelly | .25 | .11 |
| ❑ 150 | Edgar Martinez | .75 | .35 |
| ❑ 151 | Robby Thompson | .25 | .11 |
| ❑ 152 | Mo Vaughn | .50 | .23 |
| ❑ 153 | Todd Zeile | .25 | .11 |
| ❑ 154 | Harold Baines | .50 | .23 |
| ❑ 155 | Phil Plantier | .25 | .11 |
| ❑ 156 | Mike Stanley | .25 | .11 |
| ❑ 157 | Ed Sprague | .25 | .11 |
| ❑ 158 | Moises Alou | .50 | .23 |
| ❑ 159 | Quilvio Veras | .25 | .11 |
| ❑ 160 | Reggie Sanders | .25 | .11 |
| ❑ 161 | Delino DeShields | .25 | .11 |
| ❑ 162 | Rico Brogna | .25 | .11 |
| ❑ 163 | Greg Colbrunn | .25 | .11 |
| ❑ 164 | Steve Finley | .50 | .23 |
| ❑ 165 | Orlando Merced | .25 | .11 |
| ❑ 166 | Mark McGwire | 5.00 | 2.20 |
| ❑ 167 | Garret Anderson | .50 | .23 |
| ❑ 168 | Paul Sorrento | .25 | .11 |
| ❑ 169 | Mark Langston | .25 | .11 |
| ❑ 170 | Danny Tartabull | .25 | .11 |
| ❑ 171 | Vinny Castilla | .50 | .23 |
| ❑ 172 | Javier Lopez | .50 | .23 |
| ❑ 173 | Bret Saberhagen | .50 | .23 |
| ❑ 174 | Eddie Williams | .25 | .11 |
| ❑ 175 | Scott Leius | .25 | .11 |
| ❑ 176 | Juan Gonzalez | 1.25 | .55 |
| ❑ 177 | Gary Gaetti | .50 | .23 |
| ❑ 178 | Jim Edmonds | 1.25 | .55 |
| ❑ 179 | John Olerud | .50 | .23 |
| ❑ 180 | Lenny Dykstra | .50 | .23 |
| ❑ 181 | Ray Lankford | .50 | .23 |
| ❑ 182 | Ron Gant | .25 | .11 |
| ❑ 183 | Doug Drabek | .25 | .11 |
| ❑ 184 | Fred McGriff | .75 | .35 |
| ❑ 185 | Andy Benes | .25 | .11 |
| ❑ 186 | Kurt Abbott | .25 | .11 |

| | | MINT | NRMT |
|---|---|---|---|
| ❑ 187 | Bernard Gilkey | .25 | .11 |
| ❑ 188 | Sammy Sosa | 2.50 | 1.10 |
| ❑ 189 | Lee Smith | .50 | .23 |
| ❑ 190 | Dennis Martinez | .50 | .23 |
| ❑ 191 | Ozzie Guillen | .25 | .11 |
| ❑ 192 | Robin Ventura | .50 | .23 |

## 1996 Leaf Limited

| | MINT | NRMT |
|---|---|---|
| COMPLETE SET (90) | 50.00 | 22.00 |
| COMMON CARD (1-90) | .30 | .14 |

| | | MINT | NRMT |
|---|---|---|---|
| ❑ 1 | Ivan Rodriguez | 1.50 | .70 |
| ❑ 2 | Roger Clemens | 2.50 | 1.10 |
| ❑ 3 | Gary Sheffield | 1.25 | .55 |
| ❑ 4 | Tino Martinez | .50 | .23 |
| ❑ 5 | Sammy Sosa | 2.50 | 1.10 |
| ❑ 6 | Reggie Sanders | .30 | .14 |
| ❑ 7 | Ray Lankford | .50 | .23 |
| ❑ 8 | Manny Ramirez | 1.50 | .70 |
| ❑ 9 | Jeff Bagwell | 1.50 | .70 |
| ❑ 10 | Greg Maddux | 3.00 | 1.35 |
| ❑ 11 | Ken Griffey Jr. | 5.00 | 2.20 |
| ❑ 12 | Rondell White | .50 | .23 |
| ❑ 13 | Mike Piazza | 4.00 | 1.00 |
| ❑ 14 | Marc Newfield | .30 | .14 |
| ❑ 15 | Cal Ripken | 5.00 | 2.20 |
| ❑ 16 | Carlos Delgado | 1.25 | .55 |
| ❑ 17 | Tim Salmon | .50 | .23 |
| ❑ 18 | Andres Galarraga | .75 | .35 |
| ❑ 19 | Chuck Knoblauch | .50 | .23 |
| ❑ 20 | Matt Williams | .75 | .35 |
| ❑ 21 | Mark McGwire | 5.00 | 2.20 |
| ❑ 22 | Ben McDonald | .30 | .14 |
| ❑ 23 | Frank Thomas | 2.50 | 1.10 |
| ❑ 24 | Johnny Damon | .75 | .35 |
| ❑ 25 | Gregg Jefferies | .30 | .14 |
| ❑ 26 | Travis Fryman | .50 | .23 |
| ❑ 27 | Chipper Jones | 3.00 | 1.35 |
| ❑ 28 | David Cone | .50 | .23 |
| ❑ 29 | Kenny Lofton | .50 | .23 |
| ❑ 30 | Mike Mussina | 1.25 | .55 |
| ❑ 31 | Alex Rodriguez | 4.00 | 1.80 |
| ❑ 32 | Carlos Baerga | .30 | .14 |
| ❑ 33 | Brian Hunter | .30 | .14 |
| ❑ 34 | Juan Gonzalez | 1.25 | .55 |
| ❑ 35 | Bernie Williams | 1.25 | .55 |
| ❑ 36 | Wally Joyner | .50 | .23 |
| ❑ 37 | Fred McGriff | .75 | .35 |
| ❑ 38 | Randy Johnson | 1.50 | .70 |
| ❑ 39 | Marty Cordova | .30 | .14 |
| ❑ 40 | Garret Anderson | .50 | .23 |
| ❑ 41 | Albert Belle | .75 | .35 |
| ❑ 42 | Edgar Martinez | .75 | .35 |
| ❑ 43 | Barry Larkin | 1.25 | .55 |
| ❑ 44 | Paul O'Neill | .50 | .23 |
| ❑ 45 | Cecil Fielder | .50 | .23 |
| ❑ 46 | Rusty Greer | .50 | .23 |
| ❑ 47 | Mo Vaughn | .50 | .23 |
| ❑ 48 | Dante Bichette | .50 | .23 |
| ❑ 49 | Ryan Klesko | .50 | .23 |
| ❑ 50 | Roberto Alomar | 1.25 | .55 |
| ❑ 51 | Raul Mondesi | .50 | .23 |
| ❑ 52 | Robin Ventura | .50 | .23 |
| ❑ 53 | Tony Gwynn | 2.50 | 1.10 |
| ❑ 54 | Mark Grace | 1.25 | .55 |
| ❑ 55 | Jim Thome | .75 | .35 |
| ❑ 56 | Jason Giambi | 1.25 | .55 |
| ❑ 57 | Tom Glavine | 1.25 | .55 |
| ❑ 58 | Jim Edmonds | 1.25 | .55 |
| ❑ 59 | Pedro Martinez | 1.50 | .70 |
| ❑ 60 | Charles Johnson | .50 | .23 |
| ❑ 61 | Wade Boggs | 1.50 | .70 |
| ❑ 62 | Orlando Merced | .30 | .14 |
| ❑ 63 | Craig Biggio | .75 | .35 |
| ❑ 64 | Brady Anderson | .50 | .23 |
| ❑ 65 | Hideo Nomo | 1.25 | .55 |
| ❑ 66 | Ozzie Smith | 1.50 | .70 |
| ❑ 67 | Eddie Murray | 1.25 | .55 |
| ❑ 68 | Will Clark | 1.25 | .55 |
| ❑ 69 | Jay Buhner | .50 | .23 |
| ❑ 70 | Kirby Puckett | 3.00 | 1.35 |
| ❑ 71 | Barry Bonds | 2.00 | .90 |
| ❑ 72 | Ray Durham | .50 | .23 |
| ❑ 73 | Sterling Hitchcock | .30 | .14 |
| ❑ 74 | John Smoltz | .50 | .23 |
| ❑ 75 | Andre Dawson | .75 | .35 |
| ❑ 76 | Joe Carter | .50 | .23 |
| ❑ 77 | Ryne Sandberg | 1.50 | .70 |
| ❑ 78 | Rickey Henderson | 1.50 | .70 |
| ❑ 79 | Brian Jordan | .50 | .23 |
| ❑ 80 | Greg Vaughn | .50 | .23 |
| ❑ 81 | Andy Pettitte | .50 | .23 |
| ❑ 82 | Dean Palmer | .50 | .23 |
| ❑ 83 | Paul Molitor | 1.25 | .55 |
| ❑ 84 | Rafael Palmeiro | 1.25 | .55 |
| ❑ 85 | Henry Rodriguez | .30 | .14 |
| ❑ 86 | Larry Walker | .50 | .23 |
| ❑ 87 | Ismael Valdes | .30 | .14 |
| ❑ 88 | Derek Bell | .30 | .14 |
| ❑ 89 | J.T. Snow | .50 | .23 |
| ❑ 90 | Jack McDowell | .30 | .14 |

## 1998 Leaf Rookies and Stars

| | MINT | NRMT |
|---|---|---|
| COMPLETE SET (339) | 600.00 | 275.00 |
| COMP.SET w/o SP's (200) | 30.00 | 13.50 |
| COMMON (1-130/231-300) | .15 | .07 |
| COMMON CARD (131-190) | .50 | .23 |
| COMMON CARD (191-230) | 1.00 | .45 |
| COMMON RC (191-230) | 2.50 | 1.10 |
| COMMON CARD (301-339) | 1.25 | .55 |
| COMMON RC (301-339) | 3.00 | 1.35 |

| | | MINT | NRMT |
|---|---|---|---|
| ❑ 2 | Roberto Alomar | .60 | .25 |
| ❑ 3 | Randy Johnson | .75 | .35 |
| ❑ 4 | Manny Ramirez | .75 | .35 |
| ❑ 5 | Paul Molitor | .60 | .25 |
| ❑ 6 | Mike Mussina | .60 | .25 |
| ❑ 7 | Jim Thome | .40 | .18 |
| ❑ 8 | Tino Martinez | .25 | .11 |
| ❑ 9 | Gary Sheffield | .60 | .25 |
| ❑ 10 | Chuck Knoblauch | .25 | .11 |
| ❑ 11 | Bernie Williams | .60 | .25 |
| ❑ 12 | Tim Salmon | .25 | .11 |
| ❑ 13 | Sammy Sosa | 1.25 | .55 |
| ❑ 14 | Wade Boggs | .75 | .35 |
| ❑ 15 | Andres Galarraga | .40 | .18 |
| ❑ 16 | Pedro Martinez | .75 | .35 |
| ❑ 17 | David Justice | .40 | .18 |
| ❑ 18 | Chan Ho Park | .25 | .11 |
| ❑ 19 | Jay Buhner | .25 | .11 |
| ❑ 20 | Ryan Klesko | .25 | .11 |
| ❑ 21 | Barry Larkin | .60 | .25 |
| ❑ 22 | Will Clark | .60 | .25 |
| ❑ 23 | Raul Mondesi | .25 | .11 |
| ❑ 24 | Rickey Henderson | .75 | .35 |
| ❑ 25 | Jim Edmonds | .60 | .25 |
| ❑ 26 | Ken Griffey Jr. | 2.50 | 1.10 |
| ❑ 27 | Frank Thomas | 1.25 | .55 |
| ❑ 28 | Cal Ripken | 2.50 | 1.10 |
| ❑ 29 | Alex Rodriguez | 2.00 | .90 |
| ❑ 30 | Mike Piazza | 2.00 | .90 |
| ❑ 31 | Greg Maddux | 1.50 | .70 |
| ❑ 32 | Chipper Jones | 1.50 | .70 |
| ❑ 33 | Tony Gwynn | 1.25 | .55 |
| ❑ 34 | Derek Jeter | 2.50 | 1.10 |
| ❑ 35 | Jeff Bagwell | .75 | .35 |
| ❑ 36 | Juan Gonzalez | .60 | .25 |
| ❑ 37 | Nomar Garciaparra | 2.00 | .90 |
| ❑ 38 | Andruw Jones | .60 | .25 |
| ❑ 39 | Hideo Nomo | .60 | .25 |
| ❑ 40 | Roger Clemens | 1.25 | .55 |
| ❑ 41 | Mark McGwire | 2.50 | 1.10 |
| ❑ 42 | Scott Rolen | .60 | .25 |
| ❑ 43 | Vladimir Guerrero | 1.00 | .45 |
| ❑ 44 | Barry Bonds | 1.00 | .45 |
| ❑ 45 | Darin Erstad | .60 | .25 |
| ❑ 46 | Albert Belle | .40 | .18 |
| ❑ 47 | Kenny Lofton | .25 | .11 |
| ❑ 48 | Mo Vaughn | .25 | .11 |
| ❑ 49 | Ivan Rodriguez | .75 | .35 |
| ❑ 50 | Jose Cruz Jr. | .25 | .11 |
| ❑ 51 | Tony Clark | .15 | .07 |
| ❑ 52 | Larry Walker | .25 | .11 |
| ❑ 53 | Mark Grace | .60 | .25 |
| ❑ 54 | Edgar Martinez | .40 | .18 |
| ❑ 55 | Fred McGriff | .40 | .18 |
| ❑ 56 | Rafael Palmeiro | .60 | .25 |
| ❑ 57 | Matt Williams | .40 | .18 |
| ❑ 58 | Craig Biggio | .40 | .18 |
| ❑ 59 | Ken Caminiti | .25 | .11 |
| ❑ 60 | Jose Canseco | .75 | .35 |
| ❑ 61 | Brady Anderson | .25 | .11 |
| ❑ 62 | Moises Alou | .25 | .11 |
| ❑ 63 | Justin Thompson | .15 | .07 |
| ❑ 64 | John Smoltz | .25 | .11 |
| ❑ 65 | Carlos Delgado | .60 | .25 |
| ❑ 66 | J.T. Snow | .25 | .11 |
| ❑ 67 | Jason Giambi | .60 | .25 |
| ❑ 68 | Garret Anderson | .25 | .11 |
| ❑ 69 | Rondell White | .25 | .11 |
| ❑ 70 | Eric Karros | .25 | .11 |
| ❑ 71 | Javier Lopez | .25 | .11 |
| ❑ 72 | Pat Hentgen | .15 | .07 |
| ❑ 73 | Dante Bichette | .25 | .11 |
| ❑ 74 | Charles Johnson | .25 | .11 |
| ❑ 75 | Tom Glavine | .60 | .25 |
| ❑ 76 | Rusty Greer | .25 | .11 |
| ❑ 77 | Travis Fryman | .25 | .11 |
| ❑ 78 | Todd Hundley | .15 | .07 |
| ❑ 79 | Ray Lankford | .25 | .11 |
| ❑ 80 | Denny Neagle | .15 | .07 |
| ❑ 81 | Henry Rodriguez | .15 | .07 |
| ❑ 82 | Sandy Alomar Jr. | .25 | .11 |
| ❑ 83 | Robin Ventura | .25 | .11 |
| ❑ 84 | John Olerud | .25 | .11 |
| ❑ 85 | Omar Vizquel | .25 | .11 |
| ❑ 86 | Darren Dreifort | .15 | .07 |
| ❑ 87 | Kevin Brown | .25 | .11 |
| ❑ 88 | Curt Schilling | .25 | .11 |
| ❑ 89 | Francisco Cordova | .15 | .07 |
| ❑ 90 | Brad Radke | .25 | .11 |
| ❑ 91 | David Cone | .25 | .11 |
| ❑ 92 | Paul O'Neill | .25 | .11 |
| ❑ 93 | Vinny Castilla | .25 | .11 |
| ❑ 94 | Marquis Grissom | .15 | .07 |
| ❑ 95 | Brian L.Hunter | .15 | .07 |
| ❑ 96 | Kevin Appier | .25 | .11 |
| ❑ 97 | Bobby Bonilla | .25 | .11 |
| ❑ 98 | Eric Young | .15 | .07 |
| ❑ 99 | Jason Kendall | .25 | .11 |
| ❑ 100 | Shawn Green | .60 | .25 |
| ❑ 101 | Edgardo Alfonzo | .25 | .11 |
| ❑ 102 | Alan Benes | .15 | .07 |
| ❑ 103 | Bobby Higginson | .25 | .11 |
| ❑ 104 | Todd Greene | .15 | .07 |
| ❑ 105 | Jose Guillen | .15 | .07 |
| ❑ 106 | Neifi Perez | .15 | .07 |

| Card | Mint | NrMt |
|---|---|---|
| ❑ 107 Edgar Renteria | .15 | .07 |
| ❑ 108 Chris Stynes | .15 | .07 |
| ❑ 109 Todd Walker | .15 | .07 |
| ❑ 110 Brian Jordan | .25 | .11 |
| ❑ 111 Joe Carter | .25 | .11 |
| ❑ 112 Ellis Burks | .25 | .11 |
| ❑ 113 Brett Tomko | .15 | .07 |
| ❑ 114 Mike Cameron | .25 | .11 |
| ❑ 115 Shannon Stewart | .25 | .11 |
| ❑ 116 Kevin Orie | .15 | .07 |
| ❑ 117 Brian Giles | .25 | .11 |
| ❑ 118 Hideki Irabu | .15 | .07 |
| ❑ 119 Delino DeShields | .15 | .07 |
| ❑ 120 David Segui | .15 | .07 |
| ❑ 121 Dustin Hermanson | .15 | .07 |
| ❑ 122 Kevin Young | .15 | .07 |
| ❑ 123 Jay Bell | .25 | .11 |
| ❑ 124 Doug Glanville | .15 | .07 |
| ❑ 125 John Roskos RC | .40 | .18 |
| ❑ 126 Damon Hollins | .15 | .07 |
| ❑ 127 Matt Stairs | .15 | .07 |
| ❑ 128 Cliff Floyd | .25 | .11 |
| ❑ 129 Derek Bell | .15 | .07 |
| ❑ 130 Darryl Strawberry | .25 | .11 |
| ❑ 131 Ken Griffey Jr. PT SP | 8.00 | 3.60 |
| ❑ 132 Tim Salmon PT SP | .75 | .35 |
| ❑ 133 Manny Ramirez PT SP | 2.50 | 1.10 |
| ❑ 134 Paul Konerko PT SP | .75 | .35 |
| ❑ 135 Frank Thomas PT SP | 4.00 | 1.80 |
| ❑ 136 Todd Helton PT SP | 2.50 | 1.10 |
| ❑ 137 Larry Walker PT SP | .75 | .35 |
| ❑ 138 Mo Vaughn PT SP | .75 | .35 |
| ❑ 139 Travis Lee PT SP | .75 | .35 |
| ❑ 140 Ivan Rodriguez PT SP | 2.50 | 1.10 |
| ❑ 141 Ben Grieve PT SP | .75 | .35 |
| ❑ 142 Brad Fullmer PT SP | .75 | .35 |
| ❑ 143 Alex Rodriguez PT SP | 6.00 | 2.70 |
| ❑ 144 Mike Piazza PT SP | 6.00 | 2.70 |
| ❑ 145 Greg Maddux PT SP | 5.00 | 2.20 |
| ❑ 146 Chipper Jones PT SP | 5.00 | 2.20 |
| ❑ 147 Kenny Lofton PT SP | .75 | .35 |
| ❑ 148 Albert Belle PT SP | 1.25 | .55 |
| ❑ 149 Barry Bonds PT SP | 3.00 | 1.35 |
| ❑ 150 Vladimir Guerrero PT SP | 3.00 | 1.35 |
| ❑ 151 Tony Gwynn PT SP | 4.00 | 1.80 |
| ❑ 152 Derek Jeter PT SP | 8.00 | 3.60 |
| ❑ 153 Jeff Bagwell PT SP | 2.50 | 1.10 |
| ❑ 154 Juan Gonzalez PT SP | 2.00 | .90 |
| ❑ 155 N.Garciaparra PT SP | 6.00 | 2.70 |
| ❑ 156 Andruw Jones PT SP | 2.00 | .90 |
| ❑ 157 Hideo Nomo PT SP | 2.00 | .90 |
| ❑ 158 Roger Clemens PT SP | 4.00 | 1.80 |
| ❑ 159 Mark McGwire PT SP | 8.00 | 3.60 |
| ❑ 160 Scott Rolen PT SP | 2.00 | .90 |
| ❑ 161 Travis Lee TLU SP | .75 | .35 |
| ❑ 162 Ben Grieve TLU SP | .75 | .35 |
| ❑ 163 Jose Guillen TLU SP | .50 | .23 |
| ❑ 164 Mike Piazza TLU SP | 6.00 | 2.70 |
| ❑ 165 Kevin Appier TLU SP | .75 | .35 |
| ❑ 166 Marquis Grissom TLU SP | .50 | .23 |
| ❑ 167 Rusty Greer TLU SP | .75 | .35 |
| ❑ 168 Ken Caminiti TLU SP | .75 | .35 |
| ❑ 169 Craig Biggio TLU SP | 1.25 | .55 |
| ❑ 170 Ken Griffey Jr. TLU SP | 8.00 | 3.60 |
| ❑ 171 Larry Walker TLU SP | .75 | .35 |
| ❑ 172 Barry Larkin TLU SP | 2.00 | .90 |
| ❑ 173 A.Galarraga TLU SP | 1.25 | .55 |
| ❑ 174 Wade Boggs TLU SP | 2.50 | 1.10 |
| ❑ 175 Sammy Sosa TLU SP | 4.00 | 1.80 |
| ❑ 176 Todd Dunwoody TLU SP | .50 | .23 |
| ❑ 177 Jim Thome TLU SP | 1.25 | .55 |
| ❑ 178 Paul Molitor TLU SP | 2.00 | .90 |
| ❑ 179 Tony Clark TLU SP | .50 | .23 |
| ❑ 180 Jose Cruz Jr. TLU SP | .75 | .35 |
| ❑ 181 Darin Erstad TLU SP | 2.00 | .90 |
| ❑ 182 Barry Bonds TLU SP | 3.00 | 1.35 |
| ❑ 183 Vlad.Guerrero TLU SP | 3.00 | 1.35 |
| ❑ 184 Scott Rolen TLU SP | 2.00 | .90 |
| ❑ 185 Mark McGwire TLU SP | 8.00 | 3.60 |
| ❑ 186 N.Garciaparra TLU SP | 6.00 | 2.70 |
| ❑ 187 Gary Sheffield TLU SP | 2.00 | .90 |
| ❑ 188 Cal Ripken TLU SP | 8.00 | 3.60 |
| ❑ 189 Frank Thomas TLU SP | 4.00 | 1.80 |
| ❑ 190 Andy Pettitte TLU SP | .75 | .35 |
| ❑ 191 Paul Konerko SP | 1.50 | .70 |
| ❑ 192 Todd Helton SP | 5.00 | 2.20 |
| ❑ 193 Mark Kotsay SP | 1.50 | .70 |
| ❑ 194 Brad Fullmer SP | 1.50 | .70 |
| ❑ 195 Kevin Millwood SP RC | 20.00 | 9.00 |
| ❑ 196 David Ortiz SP | 1.00 | .45 |
| ❑ 197 Kerry Wood SP | 4.00 | 1.80 |
| ❑ 198 Miguel Tejada SP | 4.00 | 1.80 |
| ❑ 199 Fernando Tatis SP | 1.50 | .70 |
| ❑ 200 Jaret Wright SP | 1.00 | .45 |
| ❑ 201 Ben Grieve SP | 1.50 | .70 |
| ❑ 202 Travis Lee SP | 1.50 | .70 |
| ❑ 203 Wes Helms SP | 1.00 | .45 |
| ❑ 204 Geoff Jenkins SP | 1.50 | .70 |
| ❑ 205 Russell Branyan SP | 1.50 | .70 |
| ❑ 206 Esteban Yan SP RC | 4.00 | 1.80 |
| ❑ 207 Ben Ford SP RC | 2.50 | 1.10 |
| ❑ 208 Rich Butler SP RC | 2.50 | 1.10 |
| ❑ 209 Ryan Jackson SP RC | 2.50 | 1.10 |
| ❑ 210 A.J. Hinch SP | 1.00 | .45 |
| ❑ 211 Magglio Ordonez SP RC | 50.00 | 22.00 |
| ❑ 212 Dave Dellucci SP RC | 2.50 | 1.10 |
| ❑ 213 Billy McMillon SP | 1.00 | .45 |
| ❑ 214 Mike Lowell SP RC | 12.00 | 5.50 |
| ❑ 215 Todd Erdos SP RC | 2.50 | 1.10 |
| ❑ 216 Carlos Mendoza SP RC | 2.50 | 1.10 |
| ❑ 217 Frank Catalanotto SP RC | 4.00 | 1.80 |
| ❑ 218 Julio Ramirez SP RC | 8.00 | 3.60 |
| ❑ 219 John Halama SP RC | 8.00 | 3.60 |
| ❑ 220 Wilson Delgado SP | 1.00 | .45 |
| ❑ 221 Mike Judd SP RC | 4.00 | 1.80 |
| ❑ 222 Rolando Arrojo SP RC | 8.00 | 3.60 |
| ❑ 223 Jason LaRue SP RC | 6.00 | 2.70 |
| ❑ 224 Manny Aybar SP RC | 4.00 | 1.80 |
| ❑ 225 Jorge Velandia SP | 1.00 | .45 |
| ❑ 226 Mike Kinkade SP RC | 4.00 | 1.80 |
| ❑ 227 Carlos Lee SP RC | 25.00 | 11.00 |
| ❑ 228 Bobby Hughes SP | 1.00 | .45 |
| ❑ 229 Ryan Christenson SP RC | 2.50 | 1.10 |
| ❑ 230 Masato Yoshii SP RC | 8.00 | 3.60 |
| ❑ 231 Richard Hidalgo | .25 | .11 |
| ❑ 232 Rafael Medina | .15 | .07 |
| ❑ 233 Damian Jackson | .15 | .07 |
| ❑ 234 Derek Lowe | .15 | .07 |
| ❑ 235 Mario Valdez | .15 | .07 |
| ❑ 236 Eli Marrero | .15 | .07 |
| ❑ 237 Juan Encarnacion | .25 | .11 |
| ❑ 238 Livan Hernandez | .15 | .07 |
| ❑ 239 Bruce Chen | .15 | .07 |
| ❑ 240 Eric Milton | .25 | .11 |
| ❑ 241 Jason Varitek | .25 | .11 |
| ❑ 242 Scott Elarton | .25 | .11 |
| ❑ 243 Manuel Barrios RC | .15 | .07 |
| ❑ 244 Mike Caruso | .15 | .07 |
| ❑ 245 Tom Evans | .15 | .07 |
| ❑ 246 Pat Cline | .15 | .07 |
| ❑ 247 Matt Clement | .25 | .11 |
| ❑ 248 Karim Garcia | .15 | .07 |
| ❑ 249 Richie Sexson | .25 | .11 |
| ❑ 250 Sidney Ponson | .15 | .07 |
| ❑ 251 Randall Simon | .15 | .07 |
| ❑ 252 Tony Saunders | .15 | .07 |
| ❑ 253 Javier Valentin | .15 | .07 |
| ❑ 254 Danny Clyburn | .15 | .07 |
| ❑ 255 Michael Coleman | .15 | .07 |
| ❑ 256 Hanley Frias RC | .15 | .07 |
| ❑ 257 Miguel Cairo | .15 | .07 |
| ❑ 258 Rob Stanifer RC | .15 | .07 |
| ❑ 259 Lou Collier | .15 | .07 |
| ❑ 260 Abraham Nunez | .15 | .07 |
| ❑ 261 Ricky Ledee | .15 | .07 |
| ❑ 262 Carl Pavano | .15 | .07 |
| ❑ 263 Derrek Lee | .15 | .07 |
| ❑ 264 Jeff Abbott | .15 | .07 |
| ❑ 265 Bob Abreu | .25 | .11 |
| ❑ 266 Bartolo Colon | .25 | .11 |
| ❑ 267 Mike Drumright | .15 | .07 |
| ❑ 268 Daryle Ward | .25 | .11 |
| ❑ 269 Gabe Alvarez | .15 | .07 |
| ❑ 270 Josh Booty | .15 | .07 |
| ❑ 271 Damian Moss | .15 | .07 |
| ❑ 272 Brian Rose | .15 | .07 |
| ❑ 273 Jarrod Washburn | .15 | .07 |
| ❑ 274 Bobby Estalella | .15 | .07 |
| ❑ 275 Enrique Wilson | .15 | .07 |
| ❑ 276 Derrick Gibson | .15 | .07 |
| ❑ 277 Ken Cloude | .15 | .07 |
| ❑ 278 Kevin Witt | .15 | .07 |
| ❑ 279 Donnie Sadler | .15 | .07 |
| ❑ 280 Sean Casey | .25 | .11 |
| ❑ 281 Jacob Cruz | .15 | .07 |
| ❑ 282 Ron Wright | .15 | .07 |
| ❑ 283 Jeremi Gonzalez | .15 | .07 |
| ❑ 284 Desi Relaford | .15 | .07 |
| ❑ 285 Bobby Smith | .15 | .07 |
| ❑ 286 Javier Vazquez | .15 | .07 |
| ❑ 287 Steve Woodard | .15 | .07 |
| ❑ 288 Greg Norton | .15 | .07 |
| ❑ 289 Cliff Politte | .15 | .07 |
| ❑ 290 Felix Heredia | .15 | .07 |
| ❑ 291 Braden Looper | .15 | .07 |
| ❑ 292 Felix Martinez | .15 | .07 |
| ❑ 293 Brian Meadows | .15 | .07 |
| ❑ 294 Edwin Diaz | .15 | .07 |
| ❑ 295 Pat Watkins | .15 | .07 |
| ❑ 296 Marc Pisciotta RC | .15 | .07 |
| ❑ 297 Rick Gorecki | .15 | .07 |
| ❑ 298 DaRond Stovall | .15 | .07 |
| ❑ 299 Andy Larkin | .15 | .07 |
| ❑ 300 Felix Rodriguez | .15 | .07 |
| ❑ 301 Blake Stein SP | 1.25 | .55 |
| ❑ 302 John Rocker SP RC | 25.00 | 11.00 |
| ❑ 303 Justin Baughman SP RC | 3.00 | 1.35 |
| ❑ 304 Jesus Sanchez SP RC | 5.00 | 2.20 |
| ❑ 305 Randy Winn SP | 1.25 | .55 |
| ❑ 306 Lou Merloni SP | 1.25 | .55 |
| ❑ 307 Jim Parque SP RC | 10.00 | 4.50 |
| ❑ 308 Dennis Reyes SP | 1.25 | .55 |
| ❑ 309 Orlando Hernandez SP RC | 20.00 | 9.00 |
| ❑ 310 Jason Johnson SP | 1.25 | .55 |
| ❑ 311 Torii Hunter SP | 1.25 | .55 |
| ❑ 312 Mike Piazza Marlins SP | 15.00 | 6.75 |
| ❑ 313 Mike Frank SP RC | 3.00 | 1.35 |
| ❑ 314 Troy Glaus SP RC | 200.00 | 90.00 |
| ❑ 315 Jin Ho Cho SP RC | 5.00 | 2.20 |
| ❑ 316 Ruben Mateo SP RC | 30.00 | 13.50 |
| ❑ 317 Ryan Minor SP RC | 40.00 | 18.00 |
| ❑ 318 Aramis Ramirez SP | 2.00 | .90 |
| ❑ 319 Adrian Beltre SP | 2.00 | .90 |
| ❑ 320 Matt Anderson SP RC | 5.00 | 2.20 |
| ❑ 321 Gabe Kapler SP RC | 40.00 | 18.00 |
| ❑ 322 Jeremy Giambi SP RC | 5.00 | 2.20 |
| ❑ 323 Carlos Beltran SP | 2.00 | .90 |
| ❑ 324 Dermal Brown SP | 2.00 | .90 |
| ❑ 325 Ben Davis SP | 1.25 | .55 |
| ❑ 326 Eric Chavez SP | 2.00 | .90 |
| ❑ 327 Bobby Howry SP RC | 5.00 | 2.20 |
| ❑ 328 Roy Halladay SP | 1.25 | .55 |
| ❑ 329 George Lombard SP | 1.25 | .55 |
| ❑ 330 Michael Barrett SP | 1.25 | .55 |
| ❑ 331 Fernando Seguignol SP RC | 6.00 | 2.70 |
| ❑ 332 J.D. Drew SP RC | 80.00 | 36.00 |
| ❑ 333 Odalis Perez SP RC | 5.00 | 2.20 |
| ❑ 334 Alex Cora SP RC | 5.00 | 2.20 |
| ❑ 335 Placido Polanco SP RC | 5.00 | 2.20 |
| ❑ 336 Armando Rios SP RC | 5.00 | 2.20 |
| ❑ 337 Sammy Sosa HR SP | 10.00 | 4.50 |
| ❑ 338 Mark McGwire HR SP | 20.00 | 9.00 |
| ❑ 339 Sammy Sosa / Mark McGwire CL SP | 15.00 | 6.75 |

## 1996 Leaf Signature

| | MINT | NRMT |
|---|---|---|
| COMPLETE SET (150) | 100.00 | 45.00 |
| COMPLETE SERIES 1 (100) | 60.00 | 27.00 |

| | | |
|---|---|---|
| COMPLETE SERIES 2 (50) | 40.00 | 18.00 |
| COMMON CARD (1-100) | .25 | .11 |
| COMMON CARD (101-150) | .30 | .14 |

| | | |
|---|---|---|
| ❑ 1 Mike Piazza | 3.00 | 1.35 |
| ❑ 2 Juan Gonzalez | 1.00 | .45 |
| ❑ 3 Greg Maddux | 2.50 | 1.10 |
| ❑ 4 Marc Newfield | .25 | .11 |
| ❑ 5 Wade Boggs | 1.25 | .55 |
| ❑ 6 Ray Lankford | .40 | .18 |
| ❑ 7 Frank Thomas | 2.00 | .90 |
| ❑ 8 Rico Brogna | .25 | .11 |
| ❑ 9 Tim Salmon | .40 | .18 |
| ❑ 10 Ken Griffey Jr. | 4.00 | 1.80 |
| ❑ 11 Manny Ramirez | 1.25 | .55 |
| ❑ 12 Cecil Fielder | .40 | .18 |
| ❑ 13 Gregg Jefferies | .25 | .11 |
| ❑ 14 Rondell White | .40 | .18 |
| ❑ 15 Cal Ripken | 4.00 | 1.80 |
| ❑ 16 Alex Rodriguez | 3.00 | 1.35 |
| ❑ 17 Bernie Williams | 1.00 | .45 |
| ❑ 18 Andres Galarraga | .60 | .25 |
| ❑ 19 Mike Mussina | 1.00 | .45 |
| ❑ 20 Chuck Knoblauch | .40 | .18 |
| ❑ 21 Joe Carter | .40 | .18 |
| ❑ 22 Jeff Bagwell | 1.25 | .55 |
| ❑ 23 Mark McGwire | 4.00 | 1.80 |
| ❑ 24 Sammy Sosa | 2.00 | .90 |
| ❑ 25 Reggie Sanders | .25 | .11 |
| ❑ 26 Chipper Jones | 2.50 | 1.10 |
| ❑ 27 Jeff Cirillo | .40 | .18 |
| ❑ 28 Roger Clemens | 2.00 | .90 |
| ❑ 29 Craig Biggio | .60 | .25 |
| ❑ 30 Gary Sheffield | 1.00 | .45 |
| ❑ 31 Paul O'Neill | .40 | .18 |
| ❑ 32 Johnny Damon | .60 | .25 |
| ❑ 33 Jason Isringhausen | .40 | .18 |
| ❑ 34 Jay Bell | .40 | .18 |
| ❑ 35 Henry Rodriguez | .25 | .11 |
| ❑ 36 Matt Williams | .60 | .25 |
| ❑ 37 Randy Johnson | 1.25 | .55 |
| ❑ 38 Fred McGriff | .60 | .25 |
| ❑ 39 Jason Giambi | 1.00 | .45 |
| ❑ 40 Ivan Rodriguez | 1.25 | .55 |
| ❑ 41 Raul Mondesi | .40 | .18 |
| ❑ 42 Barry Larkin | 1.00 | .45 |
| ❑ 43 Ryan Klesko | .40 | .18 |
| ❑ 44 Joey Hamilton | .25 | .11 |
| ❑ 45 Todd Hundley | .25 | .11 |
| ❑ 46 Jim Edmonds | 1.00 | .45 |
| ❑ 47 Dante Bichette | .40 | .18 |
| ❑ 48 Roberto Alomar | 1.00 | .45 |
| ❑ 49 Mark Grace | 1.00 | .45 |
| ❑ 50 Brady Anderson | .40 | .18 |
| ❑ 51 Hideo Nomo | 1.00 | .45 |
| ❑ 52 Ozzie Smith | 1.25 | .55 |
| ❑ 53 Robin Ventura | .40 | .18 |
| ❑ 54 Andy Pettitte | .40 | .18 |
| ❑ 55 Kenny Lofton | .40 | .18 |
| ❑ 56 John Mabry | .25 | .11 |
| ❑ 57 Paul Molitor | 1.00 | .45 |
| ❑ 58 Rey Ordonez | .40 | .18 |
| ❑ 59 Albert Belle | .60 | .25 |
| ❑ 60 Charles Johnson | .40 | .18 |
| ❑ 61 Edgar Martinez | .60 | .25 |
| ❑ 62 Derek Bell | .25 | .11 |
| ❑ 63 Carlos Delgado | 1.00 | .45 |
| ❑ 64 Raul Casanova | .25 | .11 |
| ❑ 65 Ismael Valdes | .25 | .11 |
| ❑ 66 J.T. Snow | .40 | .18 |
| ❑ 67 Derek Jeter | 4.00 | 1.80 |
| ❑ 68 Jason Kendall | .40 | .18 |
| ❑ 69 John Smoltz | .40 | .18 |
| ❑ 70 Chad Mottola | .25 | .11 |
| ❑ 71 Jim Thome | .60 | .25 |
| ❑ 72 Will Clark | 1.00 | .45 |
| ❑ 73 Mo Vaughn | .40 | .18 |
| ❑ 74 John Wasdin | .25 | .11 |
| ❑ 75 Rafael Palmeiro | 1.00 | .45 |
| ❑ 76 Mark Grudzielanek | .25 | .11 |
| ❑ 77 Larry Walker | .40 | .18 |
| ❑ 78 Alan Benes | .25 | .11 |
| ❑ 79 Michael Tucker | .25 | .11 |
| ❑ 80 Billy Wagner | .25 | .11 |
| ❑ 81 Paul Wilson | .25 | .11 |
| ❑ 82 Greg Vaughn | .40 | .18 |
| ❑ 83 Dean Palmer | .40 | .18 |
| ❑ 84 Ryne Sandberg | 1.25 | .55 |
| ❑ 85 Eric Young | .25 | .11 |
| ❑ 86 Jay Buhner | .40 | .18 |
| ❑ 87 Tony Clark | .25 | .11 |
| ❑ 88 Jermaine Dye | .40 | .18 |
| ❑ 89 Barry Bonds | 1.50 | .70 |
| ❑ 90 Ugueth Urbina | .40 | .18 |
| ❑ 91 Charles Nagy | .25 | .11 |
| ❑ 92 Ruben Rivera | .25 | .11 |
| ❑ 93 Todd Hollandsworth | .25 | .11 |
| ❑ 94 Darin Erstad RC | 10.00 | 4.50 |
| ❑ 95 Brooks Kieschnick | .25 | .11 |
| ❑ 96 Edgar Renteria | .40 | .18 |
| ❑ 97 Lenny Dykstra | .40 | .18 |
| ❑ 98 Tony Gwynn | 2.00 | .90 |
| ❑ 99 Kirby Puckett | 2.50 | 1.10 |
| ❑ 100 Checklist | .25 | .11 |
| ❑ 101 Andruw Jones | 3.00 | 1.35 |
| ❑ 102 Alex Ochoa | .30 | .14 |
| ❑ 103 David Cone | .50 | .23 |
| ❑ 104 Rusty Greer | .50 | .23 |
| ❑ 105 Jose Canseco | 1.50 | .70 |
| ❑ 106 Ken Caminiti | .50 | .23 |
| ❑ 107 Mariano Rivera | .50 | .23 |
| ❑ 108 Ron Gant | .30 | .14 |
| ❑ 109 Darryl Strawberry | .50 | .23 |
| ❑ 110 Vladimir Guerrero | 5.00 | 2.20 |
| ❑ 111 George Arias | .30 | .14 |
| ❑ 112 Jeff Conine | .30 | .14 |
| ❑ 113 Bobby Higginson | .50 | .23 |
| ❑ 114 Eric Karros | .50 | .23 |
| ❑ 115 Brian Hunter | .30 | .14 |
| ❑ 116 Eddie Murray | 1.25 | .55 |
| ❑ 117 Todd Walker | .50 | .23 |
| ❑ 118 Chan Ho Park | .50 | .23 |
| ❑ 119 John Jaha | .30 | .14 |
| ❑ 120 Dave Justice | .75 | .35 |
| ❑ 121 Makoto Suzuki | .50 | .23 |
| ❑ 122 Scott Rolen | 2.50 | 1.10 |
| ❑ 123 Tino Martinez | .50 | .23 |
| ❑ 124 Kimera Bartee | .30 | .14 |
| ❑ 125 Garret Anderson | .50 | .23 |
| ❑ 126 Brian Jordan | .50 | .23 |
| ❑ 127 Andre Dawson | .75 | .35 |
| ❑ 128 Javier Lopez | .50 | .23 |
| ❑ 129 Bill Pulsipher | .30 | .14 |
| ❑ 130 Dwight Gooden | .50 | .23 |
| ❑ 131 Al Martin | .30 | .14 |
| ❑ 132 Terrell Wade | .30 | .14 |
| ❑ 133 Steve Gibralter | .30 | .14 |
| ❑ 134 Tom Glavine | 1.25 | .55 |
| ❑ 135 Kevin Appier | .50 | .23 |
| ❑ 136 Tim Raines | .50 | .23 |
| ❑ 137 Curtis Pride | .30 | .14 |
| ❑ 138 Todd Greene | .30 | .14 |
| ❑ 139 Bobby Bonilla | .40 | .18 |
| ❑ 140 Trey Beamon | .30 | .14 |
| ❑ 141 Marty Cordova | .30 | .14 |
| ❑ 142 Rickey Henderson | 1.50 | .70 |
| ❑ 143 Ellis Burks | .50 | .23 |
| ❑ 144 Dennis Eckersley | .50 | .23 |
| ❑ 145 Kevin Brown | .75 | .35 |
| ❑ 146 Carlos Baerga | .30 | .14 |
| ❑ 147 Brett Butler | .50 | .23 |
| ❑ 148 Marquis Grissom | .30 | .14 |
| ❑ 149 Karim Garcia | .30 | .14 |
| ❑ 150 Frank Thomas CL | 1.25 | .55 |

## 1996 Metal Universe

| | MINT | NRMT |
|---|---|---|
| COMPLETE SET (250) | 40.00 | 18.00 |
| COMMON CARD (1-250) | .15 | .07 |

| | | |
|---|---|---|
| ❑ 1 Roberto Alomar | .60 | .25 |
| ❑ 2 Brady Anderson | .30 | .14 |
| ❑ 3 Bobby Bonilla | .30 | .14 |
| ❑ 4 Chris Hoiles | .15 | .07 |
| ❑ 5 Ben McDonald | .15 | .07 |
| ❑ 6 Mike Mussina | .60 | .25 |
| ❑ 7 Randy Myers | .15 | .07 |
| ❑ 8 Rafael Palmeiro | .60 | .25 |
| ❑ 9 Cal Ripken | 2.50 | 1.10 |
| ❑ 10 B.J. Surhoff | .30 | .14 |
| ❑ 11 Luis Alicea | .15 | .07 |

| | | |
|---|---|---|
| ❑ 12 Jose Canseco | .75 | .35 |
| ❑ 13 Roger Clemens | 1.25 | .55 |
| ❑ 14 Wil Cordero | .15 | .07 |
| ❑ 15 Tom Gordon | .15 | .07 |
| ❑ 16 Mike Greenwell | .15 | .07 |
| ❑ 17 Tim Naehring | .15 | .07 |
| ❑ 18 Troy O'Leary | .15 | .07 |
| ❑ 19 Mike Stanley | .15 | .07 |
| ❑ 20 John Valentin | .15 | .07 |
| ❑ 21 Mo Vaughn | .30 | .14 |
| ❑ 22 Tim Wakefield | .15 | .07 |
| ❑ 23 Garret Anderson | .30 | .14 |
| ❑ 24 Chili Davis | .30 | .14 |
| ❑ 25 Gary DiSarcina | .15 | .07 |
| ❑ 26 Jim Edmonds | .60 | .25 |
| ❑ 27 Chuck Finley | .30 | .14 |
| ❑ 28 Todd Greene | .15 | .07 |
| ❑ 29 Mark Langston | .15 | .07 |
| ❑ 30 Troy Percival | .15 | .07 |
| ❑ 31 Tony Phillips | .15 | .07 |
| ❑ 32 Tim Salmon | .30 | .14 |
| ❑ 33 Lee Smith | .30 | .14 |
| ❑ 34 J.T. Snow | .30 | .14 |
| ❑ 35 Ray Durham | .30 | .14 |
| ❑ 36 Alex Fernandez | .15 | .07 |
| ❑ 37 Ozzie Guillen | .15 | .07 |
| ❑ 38 Roberto Hernandez | .15 | .07 |
| ❑ 39 Lyle Mouton | .15 | .07 |
| ❑ 40 Frank Thomas | 1.25 | .55 |
| ❑ 41 Robin Ventura | .30 | .14 |
| ❑ 42 Sandy Alomar Jr. | .30 | .14 |
| ❑ 43 Carlos Baerga | .15 | .07 |
| ❑ 44 Albert Belle | .40 | .18 |
| ❑ 45 Orel Hershiser | .30 | .14 |
| ❑ 46 Kenny Lofton | .30 | .14 |
| ❑ 47 Dennis Martinez | .30 | .14 |
| ❑ 48 Jack McDowell | .15 | .07 |
| ❑ 49 Jose Mesa | .15 | .07 |
| ❑ 50 Eddie Murray | .60 | .25 |
| ❑ 51 Charles Nagy | .15 | .07 |
| ❑ 52 Manny Ramirez | .75 | .35 |
| ❑ 53 Julian Tavarez | .15 | .07 |
| ❑ 54 Jim Thome | .40 | .18 |
| ❑ 55 Omar Vizquel | .30 | .14 |
| ❑ 56 Chad Curtis | .15 | .07 |
| ❑ 57 Cecil Fielder | .30 | .14 |
| ❑ 58 John Flaherty | .15 | .07 |
| ❑ 59 Travis Fryman | .30 | .14 |
| ❑ 60 Chris Gomez | .15 | .07 |
| ❑ 61 Felipe Lira | .15 | .07 |
| ❑ 62 Kevin Appier | .30 | .14 |
| ❑ 63 Johnny Damon | .40 | .18 |
| ❑ 64 Tom Goodwin | .15 | .07 |
| ❑ 65 Mark Gubicza | .15 | .07 |
| ❑ 66 Jeff Montgomery | .15 | .07 |
| ❑ 67 Jon Nunnally | .15 | .07 |
| ❑ 68 Ricky Bones | .15 | .07 |
| ❑ 69 Jeff Cirillo | .30 | .14 |
| ❑ 70 John Jaha | .15 | .07 |
| ❑ 71 Dave Nilsson | .15 | .07 |
| ❑ 72 Joe Oliver | .15 | .07 |
| ❑ 73 Kevin Seitzer | .15 | .07 |
| ❑ 74 Greg Vaughn | .30 | .14 |
| ❑ 75 Marty Cordova | .15 | .07 |
| ❑ 76 Chuck Knoblauch | .30 | .14 |
| ❑ 77 Pat Meares | .15 | .07 |
| ❑ 78 Paul Molitor | .60 | .25 |
| ❑ 79 Pedro Munoz | .15 | .07 |

| | MINT | NRMT |
|---|---|---|
| ❑ 80 Kirby Puckett | 1.50 | .70 |
| ❑ 81 Brad Radke | .30 | .14 |
| ❑ 82 Scott Stahoviak | .15 | .07 |
| ❑ 83 Matt Walbeck | .15 | .07 |
| ❑ 84 Wade Boggs | .75 | .35 |
| ❑ 85 David Cone | .30 | .14 |
| ❑ 86 Joe Girardi | .15 | .07 |
| ❑ 87 Derek Jeter | 2.50 | 1.10 |
| ❑ 88 Jim Leyritz | .15 | .07 |
| ❑ 89 Tino Martinez | .30 | .14 |
| ❑ 90 Don Mattingly | 1.50 | .70 |
| ❑ 91 Paul O'Neill | .30 | .14 |
| ❑ 92 Andy Pettitte | .30 | .14 |
| ❑ 93 Tim Raines | .30 | .14 |
| ❑ 94 Kenny Rogers | .15 | .07 |
| ❑ 95 Ruben Sierra | .15 | .07 |
| ❑ 96 John Wetteland | .30 | .14 |
| ❑ 97 Bernie Williams | .60 | .25 |
| ❑ 98 Geronimo Berroa | .15 | .07 |
| ❑ 99 Dennis Eckersley | .30 | .14 |
| ❑ 100 Brent Gates | .15 | .07 |
| ❑ 101 Mark McGwire | 2.50 | 1.10 |
| ❑ 102 Steve Ontiveros | .15 | .07 |
| ❑ 103 Terry Steinbach | .15 | .07 |
| ❑ 104 Jay Buhner | .30 | .14 |
| ❑ 105 Vince Coleman | .15 | .07 |
| ❑ 106 Joey Cora | .15 | .07 |
| ❑ 107 Ken Griffey, Jr. | 2.50 | 1.10 |
| ❑ 108 Randy Johnson | .75 | .35 |
| ❑ 109 Edgar Martinez | .40 | .18 |
| ❑ 110 Alex Rodriguez | 2.00 | .90 |
| ❑ 111 Paul Sorrento | .15 | .07 |
| ❑ 112 Will Clark | .60 | .25 |
| ❑ 113 Juan Gonzalez | .60 | .25 |
| ❑ 114 Rusty Greer | .30 | .14 |
| ❑ 115 Dean Palmer | .30 | .14 |
| ❑ 116 Ivan Rodriguez | .75 | .35 |
| ❑ 117 Mickey Tettleton | .15 | .07 |
| ❑ 118 Joe Carter | .30 | .14 |
| ❑ 119 Alex Gonzalez | .15 | .07 |
| ❑ 120 Shawn Green | .60 | .25 |
| ❑ 121 Erik Hanson | .15 | .07 |
| ❑ 122 Pat Hentgen | .15 | .07 |
| ❑ 123 Sandy Martinez | .15 | .07 |
| ❑ 124 Otis Nixon | .15 | .07 |
| ❑ 125 John Olerud | .30 | .14 |
| ❑ 126 Steve Avery | .15 | .07 |
| ❑ 127 Tom Glavine | .60 | .25 |
| ❑ 128 Marquis Grissom | .15 | .07 |
| ❑ 129 Chipper Jones | 1.50 | .70 |
| ❑ 130 David Justice | .40 | .18 |
| ❑ 131 Ryan Klesko | .30 | .14 |
| ❑ 132 Mark Lemke | .15 | .07 |
| ❑ 133 Javier Lopez | .30 | .14 |
| ❑ 134 Greg Maddux | 1.50 | .70 |
| ❑ 135 Fred McGriff | .40 | .18 |
| ❑ 136 John Smoltz | .30 | .14 |
| ❑ 137 Mark Wohlers | .15 | .07 |
| ❑ 138 Frank Castillo | .15 | .07 |
| ❑ 139 Shawon Dunston | .15 | .07 |
| ❑ 140 Luis Gonzalez | .30 | .14 |
| ❑ 141 Mark Grace | .60 | .25 |
| ❑ 142 Brian McRae | .15 | .07 |
| ❑ 143 Jaime Navarro | .15 | .07 |
| ❑ 144 Rey Sanchez | .15 | .07 |
| ❑ 145 Ryne Sandberg | .75 | .35 |
| ❑ 146 Sammy Sosa | 1.25 | .55 |
| ❑ 147 Bret Boone | .30 | .14 |
| ❑ 148 Curtis Goodwin | .15 | .07 |
| ❑ 149 Barry Larkin | .60 | .25 |
| ❑ 150 Hal Morris | .15 | .07 |
| ❑ 151 Reggie Sanders | .15 | .07 |
| ❑ 152 Pete Schourek | .15 | .07 |
| ❑ 153 John Smiley | .15 | .07 |
| ❑ 154 Dante Bichette | .30 | .14 |
| ❑ 155 Vinny Castilla | .30 | .14 |
| ❑ 156 Andres Galarraga | .40 | .18 |
| ❑ 157 Bret Saberhagen | .30 | .14 |
| ❑ 158 Bill Swift | .15 | .07 |
| ❑ 159 Larry Walker | .30 | .14 |
| ❑ 160 Walt Weiss | .15 | .07 |
| ❑ 161 Kurt Abbott | .15 | .07 |
| ❑ 162 John Burkett | .15 | .07 |
| ❑ 163 Greg Colbrunn | .15 | .07 |
| ❑ 164 Jeff Conine | .15 | .07 |
| ❑ 165 Chris Hammond | .15 | .07 |
| ❑ 166 Charles Johnson | .30 | .14 |
| ❑ 167 Al Leiter | .30 | .14 |
| ❑ 168 Pat Rapp | .15 | .07 |
| ❑ 169 Gary Sheffield | .60 | .25 |
| ❑ 170 Quilvio Veras | .15 | .07 |
| ❑ 171 Devon White | .30 | .14 |
| ❑ 172 Jeff Bagwell | .75 | .35 |
| ❑ 173 Derek Bell | .15 | .07 |
| ❑ 174 Sean Berry | .15 | .07 |
| ❑ 175 Craig Biggio | .40 | .18 |
| ❑ 176 Doug Drabek | .15 | .07 |
| ❑ 177 Tony Eusebio | .15 | .07 |
| ❑ 178 Brian L.Hunter | .15 | .07 |
| ❑ 179 Orlando Miller | .15 | .07 |
| ❑ 180 Shane Reynolds | .15 | .07 |
| ❑ 181 Mike Blowers | .15 | .07 |
| ❑ 182 Roger Cedeno | .15 | .07 |
| ❑ 183 Eric Karros | .30 | .14 |
| ❑ 184 Ramon Martinez | .15 | .07 |
| ❑ 185 Raul Mondesi | .30 | .14 |
| ❑ 186 Hideo Nomo | .60 | .25 |
| ❑ 187 Mike Piazza | 2.00 | .90 |
| ❑ 188 Moises Alou | .30 | .14 |
| ❑ 189 Yamil Benitez | .15 | .07 |
| ❑ 190 Darrin Fletcher | .15 | .07 |
| ❑ 191 Cliff Floyd | .30 | .14 |
| ❑ 192 Pedro Martinez | .75 | .35 |
| ❑ 193 Carlos Perez | .15 | .07 |
| ❑ 194 David Segui | .15 | .07 |
| ❑ 195 Tony Tarasco | .15 | .07 |
| ❑ 196 Rondell White | .30 | .14 |
| ❑ 197 Edgardo Alfonzo | .30 | .14 |
| ❑ 198 Rico Brogna | .15 | .07 |
| ❑ 199 Carl Everett | .30 | .14 |
| ❑ 200 Todd Hundley | .15 | .07 |
| ❑ 201 Jason Isringhausen | .30 | .14 |
| ❑ 202 Lance Johnson | .15 | .07 |
| ❑ 203 Bobby Jones | .15 | .07 |
| ❑ 204 Jeff Kent | .40 | .18 |
| ❑ 205 Bill Pulsipher | .15 | .07 |
| ❑ 206 Jose Vizcaino | .15 | .07 |
| ❑ 207 Ricky Bottalico | .15 | .07 |
| ❑ 208 Darren Daulton | .30 | .14 |
| ❑ 209 Lenny Dykstra | .30 | .14 |
| ❑ 210 Jim Eisenreich | .15 | .07 |
| ❑ 211 Gregg Jefferies | .15 | .07 |
| ❑ 212 Mickey Morandini | .15 | .07 |
| ❑ 213 Heathcliff Slocumb | .15 | .07 |
| ❑ 214 Jay Bell | .30 | .14 |
| ❑ 215 Carlos Garcia | .15 | .07 |
| ❑ 216 Jeff King | .15 | .07 |
| ❑ 217 Al Martin | .15 | .07 |
| ❑ 218 Orlando Merced | .15 | .07 |
| ❑ 219 Dan Miceli | .15 | .07 |
| ❑ 220 Denny Neagle | .30 | .14 |
| ❑ 221 Andy Benes | .15 | .07 |
| ❑ 222 Royce Clayton | .15 | .07 |
| ❑ 223 Gary Gaetti | .30 | .14 |
| ❑ 224 Ron Gant | .15 | .07 |
| ❑ 225 Bernard Gilkey | .15 | .07 |
| ❑ 226 Brian Jordan | .30 | .14 |
| ❑ 227 Ray Lankford | .30 | .14 |
| ❑ 228 John Mabry | .15 | .07 |
| ❑ 229 Ozzie Smith | .75 | .35 |
| ❑ 230 Todd Stottlemyre | .15 | .07 |
| ❑ 231 Andy Ashby | .15 | .07 |
| ❑ 232 Brad Ausmus | .15 | .07 |
| ❑ 233 Ken Caminiti | .30 | .14 |
| ❑ 234 Steve Finley | .30 | .14 |
| ❑ 235 Tony Gwynn | 1.25 | .55 |
| ❑ 236 Joey Hamilton | .15 | .07 |
| ❑ 237 Rickey Henderson | .75 | .35 |
| ❑ 238 Trevor Hoffman | .30 | .14 |
| ❑ 239 Wally Joyner | .30 | .14 |
| ❑ 240 Rod Beck | .15 | .07 |
| ❑ 241 Barry Bonds | 1.00 | .45 |
| ❑ 242 Glenallen Hill | .15 | .07 |
| ❑ 243 Stan Javier | .15 | .07 |
| ❑ 244 Mark Leiter | .15 | .07 |
| ❑ 245 Deion Sanders | .30 | .14 |
| ❑ 246 William Van Landingham | .15 | .07 |
| ❑ 247 Matt Williams | .40 | .18 |
| ❑ 248 Checklist | .15 | .07 |
| ❑ 249 Checklist | .15 | .07 |
| ❑ 250 Checklist | .15 | .07 |

## 1997 Metal Universe

| | MINT | NRMT |
|---|---|---|
| COMPLETE SET (250) | 40.00 | 18.00 |
| ❑ 1 Roberto Alomar | .60 | .25 |
| ❑ 2 Brady Anderson | .30 | .14 |
| ❑ 3 Rocky Coppinger | .15 | .07 |
| ❑ 4 Chris Hoiles | .15 | .07 |
| ❑ 5 Eddie Murray | .60 | .25 |
| ❑ 6 Mike Mussina | .60 | .25 |
| ❑ 7 Rafael Palmeiro | .60 | .25 |
| ❑ 8 Cal Ripken | 2.50 | 1.10 |
| ❑ 9 B.J. Surhoff | .30 | .14 |
| ❑ 10 Brant Brown | .15 | .07 |
| ❑ 11 Mark Grace | .60 | .25 |
| ❑ 12 Brian McRae | .15 | .07 |
| ❑ 13 Jaime Navarro | .15 | .07 |
| ❑ 14 Ryne Sandberg | .75 | .35 |
| ❑ 15 Sammy Sosa | 1.25 | .55 |
| ❑ 16 Amaury Telemaco | .15 | .07 |
| ❑ 17 Steve Trachsel | .15 | .07 |
| ❑ 18 Darren Bragg | .15 | .07 |
| ❑ 19 Jose Canseco | .75 | .35 |
| ❑ 20 Roger Clemens | 1.25 | .55 |
| ❑ 21 Nomar Garciaparra | 2.00 | .90 |
| ❑ 22 Tom Gordon | .15 | .07 |
| ❑ 23 Tim Naehring | .15 | .07 |
| ❑ 24 Mike Stanley | .15 | .07 |
| ❑ 25 John Valentin | .15 | .07 |
| ❑ 26 Mo Vaughn | .30 | .14 |
| ❑ 27 Jermaine Dye | .30 | .14 |
| ❑ 28 Tom Glavine | .60 | .25 |
| ❑ 29 Marquis Grissom | .15 | .07 |
| ❑ 30 Andruw Jones | .75 | .35 |
| ❑ 31 Chipper Jones | 1.50 | .70 |
| ❑ 32 Ryan Klesko | .30 | .14 |
| ❑ 33 Greg Maddux | 1.50 | .70 |
| ❑ 34 Fred McGriff | .40 | .18 |
| ❑ 35 John Smoltz | .30 | .14 |
| ❑ 36 Garret Anderson | .30 | .14 |
| ❑ 37 George Arias | .15 | .07 |
| ❑ 38 Gary DiSarcina | .15 | .07 |
| ❑ 39 Jim Edmonds | .60 | .25 |
| ❑ 40 Darin Erstad | .75 | .35 |
| ❑ 41 Chuck Finley | .30 | .14 |
| ❑ 42 Troy Percival | .15 | .07 |
| ❑ 43 Tim Salmon | .30 | .14 |
| ❑ 44 Bret Boone | .30 | .14 |
| ❑ 45 Jeff Brantley | .15 | .07 |
| ❑ 46 Eric Davis | .30 | .14 |
| ❑ 47 Barry Larkin | .60 | .25 |
| ❑ 48 Hal Morris | .15 | .07 |
| ❑ 49 Mark Portugal | .15 | .07 |
| ❑ 50 Reggie Sanders | .15 | .07 |
| ❑ 51 John Smiley | .15 | .07 |
| ❑ 52 Wilson Alvarez | .15 | .07 |
| ❑ 53 Harold Baines | .30 | .14 |
| ❑ 54 James Baldwin | .30 | .14 |
| ❑ 55 Albert Belle | .40 | .18 |
| ❑ 56 Mike Cameron | .30 | .14 |
| ❑ 57 Ray Durham | .30 | .14 |
| ❑ 58 Alex Fernandez | .15 | .07 |
| ❑ 59 Roberto Hernandez | .15 | .07 |
| ❑ 60 Tony Phillips | .15 | .07 |
| ❑ 61 Frank Thomas | 1.25 | .55 |
| ❑ 62 Robin Ventura | .30 | .14 |
| ❑ 63 Jeff Cirillo | .30 | .14 |

❑ 64 Jeff D'Amico .15 .07
❑ 65 John Jaha .15 .07
❑ 66 Scott Karl .15 .07
❑ 67 Ben McDonald .15 .07
❑ 68 Marc Newfield .15 .07
❑ 69 Dave Nilsson .15 .07
❑ 70 Jose Valentin .15 .07
❑ 71 Dante Bichette .30 .14
❑ 72 Ellis Burks .30 .14
❑ 73 Vinny Castilla .30 .14
❑ 74 Andres Galarraga .40 .18
❑ 75 Kevin Ritz .15 .07
❑ 76 Larry Walker .30 .14
❑ 77 Walt Weiss .15 .07
❑ 78 Jamey Wright .15 .07
❑ 79 Eric Young .15 .07
❑ 80 Julio Franco .30 .14
❑ 81 Orel Hershiser .30 .14
❑ 82 Kenny Lofton .30 .14
❑ 83 Jack McDowell .15 .07
❑ 84 Jose Mesa .15 .07
❑ 85 Charles Nagy .15 .07
❑ 86 Manny Ramirez .75 .35
❑ 87 Jim Thome .40 .18
❑ 88 Omar Vizquel .30 .14
❑ 89 Matt Williams .40 .18
❑ 90 Kevin Appier .30 .14
❑ 91 Johnny Damon .30 .14
❑ 92 Chili Davis .30 .14
❑ 93 Tom Goodwin .15 .07
❑ 94 Keith Lockhart .15 .07
❑ 95 Jeff Montgomery .15 .07
❑ 96 Craig Paquette .15 .07
❑ 97 Jose Rosado .15 .07
❑ 98 Michael Tucker .15 .07
❑ 99 Wilton Guerrero .15 .07
❑ 100 Todd Hollandsworth .15 .07
❑ 101 Eric Karros .30 .14
❑ 102 Ramon Martinez .15 .07
❑ 103 Raul Mondesi .30 .14
❑ 104 Hideo Nomo .60 .25
❑ 105 Mike Piazza 2.00 .90
❑ 106 Ismael Valdes .15 .07
❑ 107 Todd Worrell .15 .07
❑ 108 Tony Clark .15 .07
❑ 109 Travis Fryman .30 .14
❑ 110 Bob Higginson .30 .14
❑ 111 Mark Lewis .15 .07
❑ 112 Melvin Nieves .15 .07
❑ 113 Justin Thompson .15 .07
❑ 114 Wade Boggs .75 .35
❑ 115 David Cone .30 .14
❑ 116 Cecil Fielder .30 .14
❑ 117 Dwight Gooden .30 .14
❑ 118 Derek Jeter 2.50 1.10
❑ 119 Tino Martinez .30 .14
❑ 120 Paul O'Neill .30 .14
❑ 121 Andy Pettitte .30 .14
❑ 122 Mariano Rivera .30 .14
❑ 123 Darryl Strawberry .30 .14
❑ 124 John Wetteland .30 .14
❑ 125 Bernie Williams .60 .25
❑ 126 Tony Batista .60 .25
❑ 127 Geronimo Berroa .15 .07
❑ 128 Scott Brosius .30 .14
❑ 129 Jason Giambi .60 .25
❑ 130 Jose Herrera .15 .07
❑ 131 Mark McGwire 2.50 1.10
❑ 132 John Wasdin .15 .07
❑ 133 Bob Abreu .30 .14
❑ 134 Jeff Bagwell .75 .35
❑ 135 Derek Bell .15 .07
❑ 136 Craig Biggio .40 .18
❑ 137 Brian Hunter .15 .07
❑ 138 Darryl Kile .30 .14
❑ 139 Orlando Miller .15 .07
❑ 140 Shane Reynolds .15 .07
❑ 141 Billy Wagner .15 .07
❑ 142 Donne Wall .15 .07
❑ 143 Jay Buhner .30 .14
❑ 144 Jeff Fassero .15 .07
❑ 145 Ken Griffey Jr. 2.50 1.10
❑ 146 Sterling Hitchcock .15 .07
❑ 147 Randy Johnson .75 .35
❑ 148 Edgar Martinez .40 .18
❑ 149 Alex Rodriguez 2.00 .90
❑ 150 Paul Sorrento .15 .07
❑ 151 Dan Wilson .15 .07
❑ 152 Moises Alou .30 .14
❑ 153 Darrin Fletcher .15 .07
❑ 154 Cliff Floyd .30 .14
❑ 155 Mark Grudzielanek .15 .07
❑ 156 Vladimir Guerrero 1.25 .55
❑ 157 Mike Lansing .15 .07
❑ 158 Pedro Martinez .75 .35
❑ 159 Henry Rodriguez .15 .07
❑ 160 Rondell White .30 .14
❑ 161 Will Clark .60 .25
❑ 162 Juan Gonzalez .60 .25
❑ 163 Rusty Greer .30 .14
❑ 164 Ken Hill .15 .07
❑ 165 Mark McLemore .15 .07
❑ 166 Dean Palmer .30 .14
❑ 167 Roger Pavlik .15 .07
❑ 168 Ivan Rodriguez .75 .35
❑ 169 Mickey Tettleton .15 .07
❑ 170 Bobby Bonilla .30 .14
❑ 171 Kevin Brown .40 .18
❑ 172 Greg Colbrunn .15 .07
❑ 173 Jeff Conine .15 .07
❑ 174 Jim Eisenreich .15 .07
❑ 175 Charles Johnson .30 .14
❑ 176 Al Leiter .30 .14
❑ 177 Robb Nen .15 .07
❑ 178 Edgar Renteria .30 .14
❑ 179 Gary Sheffield .60 .25
❑ 180 Devon White .30 .14
❑ 181 Joe Carter .30 .14
❑ 182 Carlos Delgado .60 .25
❑ 183 Alex Gonzalez .15 .07
❑ 184 Shawn Green .60 .25
❑ 185 Juan Guzman .15 .07
❑ 186 Pat Hentgen .15 .07
❑ 187 Orlando Merced .15 .07
❑ 188 John Olerud .30 .14
❑ 189 Robert Perez .15 .07
❑ 190 Ed Sprague .15 .07
❑ 191 Mark Clark .15 .07
❑ 192 John Franco .30 .14
❑ 193 Bernard Gilkey .15 .07
❑ 194 Todd Hundley .15 .07
❑ 195 Lance Johnson .15 .07
❑ 196 Bobby Jones .15 .07
❑ 197 Alex Ochoa .15 .07
❑ 198 Rey Ordonez .15 .07
❑ 199 Paul Wilson .15 .07
❑ 200 Ricky Bottalico .15 .07
❑ 201 Gregg Jefferies .15 .07
❑ 202 Wendell Magee .15 .07
❑ 203 Mickey Morandini .15 .07
❑ 204 Ricky Otero .15 .07
❑ 205 Scott Rolen .60 .25
❑ 206 Benito Santiago .15 .07
❑ 207 Curt Schilling .30 .14
❑ 208 Rich Becker .15 .07
❑ 209 Marty Cordova .15 .07
❑ 210 Chuck Knoblauch .30 .14
❑ 211 Pat Meares .15 .07
❑ 212 Paul Molitor .60 .25
❑ 213 Frank Rodriguez .15 .07
❑ 214 Terry Steinbach .15 .07
❑ 215 Todd Walker .15 .07
❑ 216 Andy Ashby .15 .07
❑ 217 Ken Caminiti .30 .14
❑ 218 Steve Finley .30 .14
❑ 219 Tony Gwynn 1.25 .55
❑ 220 Joey Hamilton .15 .07
❑ 221 Rickey Henderson .75 .35
❑ 222 Trevor Hoffman .30 .14
❑ 223 Wally Joyner .30 .14
❑ 224 Scott Sanders .15 .07
❑ 225 Fernando Valenzuela .30 .14
❑ 226 Greg Vaughn .30 .14
❑ 227 Alan Benes .15 .07
❑ 228 Andy Benes .15 .07
❑ 229 Dennis Eckersley .30 .14
❑ 230 Ron Gant .15 .07
❑ 231 Brian Jordan .30 .14
❑ 232 Ray Lankford .30 .14
❑ 233 John Mabry .15 .07
❑ 234 Tom Pagnozzi .15 .07
❑ 235 Todd Stottlemyre .15 .07
❑ 236 Jermaine Allensworth .15 .07
❑ 237 Francisco Cordova .15 .07
❑ 238 Jason Kendall .30 .14
❑ 239 Jeff King .15 .07
❑ 240 Al Martin .15 .07
❑ 241 Rod Beck .15 .07
❑ 242 Barry Bonds 1.00 .45
❑ 243 Shawn Estes .30 .14
❑ 244 Mark Gardner .15 .07
❑ 245 Glenallen Hill .15 .07
❑ 246 Bill Mueller RC .40 .18
❑ 247 J.T. Snow .30 .14
❑ 248 Checklist 1-107 .15 .07
❑ 249 Checklist 108-207 .15 .07
❑ 250 Checklist 208-250/inserts .15 .07
❑ P149 Alex Rodriguez Promo 2.00 .90

## 1998 Metal Universe

| | MINT | NRMT |
|---|---|---|
| COMPLETE SET (220) | 40.00 | 18.00 |

❑ 1 Jose Cruz Jr. .25 .11
❑ 2 Jeff Abbott .15 .07
❑ 3 Rafael Palmeiro .60 .25
❑ 4 Ivan Rodriguez .75 .35
❑ 5 Jaret Wright .15 .07
❑ 6 Derek Bell .15 .07
❑ 7 Chuck Finley .25 .11
❑ 8 Travis Fryman .25 .11
❑ 9 Randy Johnson .75 .35
❑ 10 Derrek Lee .15 .07
❑ 11 Bernie Williams .60 .25
❑ 12 Carlos Baerga .15 .07
❑ 13 Ricky Bottalico .15 .07
❑ 14 Ellis Burks .25 .11
❑ 15 Russ Davis .15 .07
❑ 16 Nomar Garciaparra 2.00 .90
❑ 17 Joey Hamilton .15 .07
❑ 18 Jason Kendall .25 .11
❑ 19 Darryl Kile .25 .11
❑ 20 Edgardo Alfonzo .25 .11
❑ 21 Moises Alou .25 .11
❑ 22 Bobby Bonilla .25 .11
❑ 23 Jim Edmonds .25 .11
❑ 24 Jose Guillen .15 .07
❑ 25 Chuck Knoblauch .25 .11
❑ 26 Javy Lopez .25 .11
❑ 27 Billy Wagner .15 .07
❑ 28 Kevin Appier .25 .11
❑ 29 Joe Carter .25 .11
❑ 30 Todd Dunwoody .15 .07
❑ 31 Gary Gaetti .25 .11
❑ 32 Juan Gonzalez .60 .25
❑ 33 Jeffrey Hammonds .25 .11
❑ 34 Roberto Hernandez .15 .07
❑ 35 Dave Nilsson .15 .07
❑ 36 Manny Ramirez .75 .35
❑ 37 Robin Ventura .25 .11
❑ 38 Rondell White .25 .11
❑ 39 Vinny Castilla .25 .11
❑ 40 Will Clark .60 .25
❑ 41 Scott Hatteberg .15 .07
❑ 42 Russ Johnson .15 .07
❑ 43 Ricky Ledee .15 .07
❑ 44 Kenny Lofton .25 .11
❑ 45 Paul Molitor .60 .25
❑ 46 Justin Thompson .15 .07

| No. | Player | MINT | NRMT |
|---|---|---|---|
| 47 | Craig Biggio | .40 | .18 |
| 48 | Damion Easley | .15 | .07 |
| 49 | Brad Radke | .25 | .11 |
| 50 | Ben Grieve | .25 | .11 |
| 51 | Mark Bellhorn | .15 | .07 |
| 52 | Henry Blanco | .15 | .07 |
| 53 | Mariano Rivera | .25 | .11 |
| 54 | Reggie Sanders | .15 | .07 |
| 55 | Paul Sorrento | .15 | .07 |
| 56 | Terry Steinbach | .15 | .07 |
| 57 | Mo Vaughn | .25 | .11 |
| 58 | Brady Anderson | .25 | .11 |
| 59 | Tom Glavine | .60 | .25 |
| 60 | Sammy Sosa | 1.25 | .55 |
| 61 | Larry Walker | .25 | .11 |
| 62 | Rod Beck | .15 | .07 |
| 63 | Jose Canseco | .75 | .35 |
| 64 | Steve Finley | .25 | .11 |
| 65 | Pedro Martinez | .75 | .35 |
| 66 | John Olerud | .25 | .11 |
| 67 | Scott Rolen | .60 | .25 |
| 68 | Ismael Valdes | .15 | .07 |
| 69 | Andrew Vessel | .15 | .07 |
| 70 | Mark Grudzielanek | .15 | .07 |
| 71 | Eric Karros | .25 | .11 |
| 72 | Jeff Shaw | .15 | .07 |
| 73 | Lou Collier | .15 | .07 |
| 74 | Edgar Martinez | .40 | .18 |
| 75 | Vladimir Guerrero | 1.00 | .45 |
| 76 | Paul Konerko | .25 | .11 |
| 77 | Kevin Orie | .15 | .07 |
| 78 | Kevin Polcovich | .15 | .07 |
| 79 | Brett Tomko | .15 | .07 |
| 80 | Jeff Bagwell | .75 | .35 |
| 81 | Barry Bonds | 1.00 | .45 |
| 82 | David Justice | .40 | .18 |
| 83 | Hideo Nomo | .60 | .25 |
| 84 | Ryne Sandberg | .75 | .35 |
| 85 | Shannon Stewart | .25 | .11 |
| 86 | Derek Wallace | .15 | .07 |
| 87 | Tony Womack | .15 | .07 |
| 88 | Jason Giambi | .60 | .25 |
| 89 | Mark Grace | .60 | .25 |
| 90 | Pat Hentgen | .15 | .07 |
| 91 | Raul Mondesi | .25 | .11 |
| 92 | Matt Morris | .15 | .07 |
| 93 | Matt Perisho | .15 | .07 |
| 94 | Tim Salmon | .25 | .11 |
| 95 | Jeremi Gonzalez | .15 | .07 |
| 96 | Shawn Green | .60 | .25 |
| 97 | Todd Greene | .15 | .07 |
| 98 | Ruben Rivera | .15 | .07 |
| 99 | Deion Sanders | .25 | .11 |
| 100 | Alex Rodriguez | 2.00 | .90 |
| 101 | Will Cunnane | .15 | .07 |
| 102 | Ray Lankford | .25 | .11 |
| 103 | Ryan McGuire | .15 | .07 |
| 104 | Charles Nagy | .15 | .07 |
| 105 | Rey Ordonez | .15 | .07 |
| 106 | Mike Piazza | 2.00 | .90 |
| 107 | Tony Saunders | .15 | .07 |
| 108 | Curt Schilling | .25 | .11 |
| 109 | Fernando Tatis | .25 | .11 |
| 110 | Mark McGwire | 2.50 | 1.10 |
| 111 | Dave Dellucci RC | .15 | .07 |
| 112 | Garret Anderson | .25 | .11 |
| 113 | Shane Bowers RC | .15 | .07 |
| 114 | David Cone | .25 | .11 |
| 115 | Jeff King | .15 | .07 |
| 116 | Matt Williams | .40 | .18 |
| 117 | Aaron Boone | .15 | .07 |
| 118 | Dennis Eckersley | .25 | .11 |
| 119 | Livan Hernandez | .15 | .07 |
| 120 | Richard Hidalgo | .25 | .11 |
| 121 | Bobby Higginson | .25 | .11 |
| 122 | Tino Martinez | .25 | .11 |
| 123 | Tim Naehring | .15 | .07 |
| 124 | Jose Vidro | .15 | .07 |
| 125 | John Wetteland | .25 | .11 |
| 126 | Jay Bell | .25 | .11 |
| 127 | Albert Belle | .40 | .18 |
| 128 | Marty Cordova | .15 | .07 |
| 129 | Chili Davis | .25 | .11 |
| 130 | Jason Dickson | .15 | .07 |
| 131 | Rusty Greer | .25 | .11 |
| 132 | Hideki Irabu | .15 | .07 |
| 133 | Greg Maddux | 1.50 | .70 |
| 134 | Billy Taylor | .15 | .07 |
| 135 | Jim Thome | .40 | .18 |
| 136 | Gerald Williams | .15 | .07 |
| 137 | Jeff Cirillo | .25 | .11 |
| 138 | Delino DeShields | .15 | .07 |
| 139 | Andres Galarraga | .40 | .18 |
| 140 | Willie Greene | .15 | .07 |
| 141 | John Jaha | .25 | .11 |
| 142 | Charles Johnson | .25 | .11 |
| 143 | Ryan Klesko | .25 | .11 |
| 144 | Paul O'Neill | .25 | .11 |
| 145 | Robinson Checo | .15 | .07 |
| 146 | Roberto Alomar | .60 | .25 |
| 147 | Wilson Alvarez | .15 | .07 |
| 148 | Bobby Jones | .15 | .07 |
| 149 | Raul Casanova | .15 | .07 |
| 150 | Andruw Jones | .60 | .25 |
| 151 | Mike Lansing | .15 | .07 |
| 152 | Mickey Morandini | .15 | .07 |
| 153 | Neifi Perez | .15 | .07 |
| 154 | Pokey Reese | .25 | .11 |
| 155 | Edgar Renteria | .15 | .07 |
| 156 | Eric Young | .15 | .07 |
| 157 | Darin Erstad | .60 | .25 |
| 158 | Kelvim Escobar | .15 | .07 |
| 159 | Carl Everett | .25 | .11 |
| 160 | Tom Gordon | .25 | .11 |
| 161 | Ken Griffey Jr. | 2.50 | 1.10 |
| 162 | Al Martin | .15 | .07 |
| 163 | Bubba Trammell | .15 | .07 |
| 164 | Carlos Delgado | .60 | .25 |
| 165 | Kevin Brown | .40 | .18 |
| 166 | Ken Caminiti | .25 | .11 |
| 167 | Roger Clemens | 1.25 | .55 |
| 168 | Ron Gant | .25 | .11 |
| 169 | Jeff Kent | .40 | .18 |
| 170 | Mike Mussina | .60 | .25 |
| 171 | Dean Palmer | .25 | .11 |
| 172 | Henry Rodriguez | .15 | .07 |
| 173 | Matt Stairs | .15 | .07 |
| 174 | Jay Buhner | .25 | .11 |
| 175 | Frank Thomas | 1.25 | .55 |
| 176 | Mike Cameron | .25 | .11 |
| 177 | Johnny Damon | .25 | .11 |
| 178 | Tony Gwynn | 1.25 | .55 |
| 179 | John Smoltz | .25 | .11 |
| 180 | B.J. Surhoff | .25 | .11 |
| 181 | Antone Williamson | .15 | .07 |
| 182 | Alan Benes | .15 | .07 |
| 183 | Jeromy Burnitz | .25 | .11 |
| 184 | Tony Clark | .15 | .07 |
| 185 | Shawn Estes | .15 | .07 |
| 186 | Todd Helton | .75 | .35 |
| 187 | Todd Hundley | .15 | .07 |
| 188 | Chipper Jones | 1.50 | .70 |
| 189 | Mark Kotsay | .25 | .11 |
| 190 | Barry Larkin | .60 | .25 |
| 191 | Mike Lieberthal | .25 | .11 |
| 192 | Andy Pettitte | .25 | .11 |
| 193 | Gary Sheffield | .60 | .25 |
| 194 | Jeff Suppan | .15 | .07 |
| 195 | Mark Wohlers | .15 | .07 |
| 196 | Dante Bichette | .25 | .11 |
| 197 | Trevor Hoffman | .25 | .11 |
| 198 | J.T. Snow | .25 | .11 |
| 199 | Derek Jeter | 2.50 | 1.10 |
| 200 | Cal Ripken | 2.50 | 1.10 |
| 201 | Steve Woodard | .15 | .07 |
| 202 | Ray Durham | .25 | .11 |
| 203 | Barry Bonds HG | .40 | .18 |
| 204 | Tony Clark HG | .15 | .07 |
| 205 | Roger Clemens HG | .60 | .25 |
| 206 | Ken Griffey Jr. HG | 1.25 | .55 |
| 207 | Deion Sanders HG | .25 | .11 |
| 208 | Derek Jeter HG | 1.25 | .55 |
| 209 | Randy Johnson HG | .25 | .11 |
| 210 | Brady Anderson HG | .15 | .07 |
| 211 | Hideo Nomo HG | .25 | .11 |
| 212 | Mike Piazza HG | 1.00 | .45 |
| 213 | Cal Ripken HG | 1.25 | .55 |
| 214 | Alex Rodriguez HG | 1.00 | .45 |
| 215 | Frank Thomas HG | .60 | .25 |
| 216 | Mo Vaughn HG | .25 | .11 |
| 217 | Larry Walker HG | .25 | .11 |
| 218 | Ken Griffey Jr. CL | 1.25 | .55 |
| 219 | Alex Rodriguez CL | 1.00 | .45 |
| 220 | Frank Thomas CL | .60 | .25 |
| P100 | Alex Rodriguez Promo | 3.00 | 1.35 |

## 1999 Metal Universe

| | MINT | NRMT |
|---|---|---|
| COMPLETE SET (300) | 50.00 | 22.00 |

| No. | Player | MINT | NRMT |
|---|---|---|---|
| 1 | Mark McGwire | 2.50 | 1.10 |
| 2 | Jim Edmonds | .60 | .25 |
| 3 | Travis Fryman | .25 | .11 |
| 4 | Tom Gordon | .15 | .07 |
| 5 | Jeff Bagwell | .75 | .35 |
| 6 | Rico Brogna | .15 | .07 |
| 7 | Tom Evans | .15 | .07 |
| 8 | John Franco | .25 | .11 |
| 9 | Juan Gonzalez | .60 | .25 |
| 10 | Paul Molitor | .60 | .25 |
| 11 | Roberto Alomar | .60 | .25 |
| 12 | Mike Hampton | .25 | .11 |
| 13 | Orel Hershiser | .25 | .11 |
| 14 | Todd Stottlemyre | .15 | .07 |
| 15 | Robin Ventura | .25 | .11 |
| 16 | Todd Walker | .15 | .07 |
| 17 | Bernie Williams | .60 | .25 |
| 18 | Shawn Estes | .15 | .07 |
| 19 | Richie Sexson | .25 | .11 |
| 20 | Kevin Millwood | .25 | .11 |
| 21 | David Ortiz | .15 | .07 |
| 22 | Mariano Rivera | .25 | .11 |
| 23 | Ivan Rodriguez | .75 | .35 |
| 24 | Mike Sirotka | .15 | .07 |
| 25 | David Justice | .40 | .18 |
| 26 | Carl Pavano | .15 | .07 |
| 27 | Albert Belle | .40 | .18 |
| 28 | Will Clark | .60 | .25 |
| 29 | Jose Cruz Jr. | .25 | .11 |
| 30 | Trevor Hoffman | .25 | .11 |
| 31 | Dean Palmer | .25 | .11 |
| 32 | Edgar Renteria | .15 | .07 |
| 33 | David Segui | .15 | .07 |
| 34 | B.J. Surhoff | .25 | .11 |
| 35 | Miguel Tejada | .25 | .11 |
| 36 | Bob Wickman | .15 | .07 |
| 37 | Charles Johnson | .25 | .11 |
| 38 | Andruw Jones | .60 | .25 |
| 39 | Mike Lieberthal | .25 | .11 |
| 40 | Eli Marrero | .15 | .07 |
| 41 | Neifi Perez | .15 | .07 |
| 42 | Jim Thome | .40 | .18 |
| 43 | Barry Bonds | 1.00 | .45 |
| 44 | Carlos Delgado | .60 | .25 |
| 45 | Chuck Finley | .25 | .11 |
| 46 | Brian Meadows | .15 | .07 |
| 47 | Tony Gwynn | 1.25 | .55 |
| 48 | Jose Offerman | .15 | .07 |
| 49 | Cal Ripken | 2.50 | 1.10 |
| 50 | Alex Rodriguez | 2.00 | .90 |
| 51 | Esteban Yan | .15 | .07 |
| 52 | Matt Stairs | .15 | .07 |
| 53 | Fernando Vina | .15 | .07 |
| 54 | Rondell White | .25 | .11 |
| 55 | Kerry Wood | .25 | .11 |
| 56 | Dmitri Young | .25 | .11 |
| 57 | Ken Caminiti | .25 | .11 |
| 58 | Alex Gonzalez | .15 | .07 |
| 59 | Matt Mantei | .15 | .07 |

| | Card | Mint | NRMT |
|---|---|---|---|
| ❑ | 60 Tino Martinez | .25 | .11 |
| ❑ | 61 Hal Morris | .15 | .07 |
| ❑ | 62 Rafael Palmeiro | .60 | .25 |
| ❑ | 63 Troy Percival | .15 | .07 |
| ❑ | 64 Bobby Smith | .15 | .07 |
| ❑ | 65 Ed Sprague | .15 | .07 |
| ❑ | 66 Brett Tomko | .15 | .07 |
| ❑ | 67 Steve Trachsel | .15 | .07 |
| ❑ | 68 Ugueth Urbina | .15 | .07 |
| ❑ | 69 Jose Valentin | .15 | .07 |
| ❑ | 70 Kevin Brown | .40 | .18 |
| ❑ | 71 Shawn Green | .60 | .25 |
| ❑ | 72 Dustin Hermanson | .15 | .07 |
| ❑ | 73 Livan Hernandez | .15 | .07 |
| ❑ | 74 Geoff Jenkins | .25 | .11 |
| ❑ | 75 Jeff King | .15 | .07 |
| ❑ | 76 Chuck Knoblauch | .25 | .11 |
| ❑ | 77 Edgar Martinez | .40 | .18 |
| ❑ | 78 Fred McGriff | .40 | .18 |
| ❑ | 79 Mike Mussina | .60 | .25 |
| ❑ | 80 Dave Nilsson | .15 | .07 |
| ❑ | 81 Kenny Rogers | .15 | .07 |
| ❑ | 82 Tim Salmon | .25 | .11 |
| ❑ | 83 Reggie Sanders | .15 | .07 |
| ❑ | 84 Wilson Alvarez | .15 | .07 |
| ❑ | 85 Rod Beck | .15 | .07 |
| ❑ | 86 Jose Guillen | .15 | .07 |
| ❑ | 87 Bob Higginson | .25 | .11 |
| ❑ | 88 Gregg Olson | .15 | .07 |
| ❑ | 89 Jeff Shaw | .15 | .07 |
| ❑ | 90 Masato Yoshii | .25 | .11 |
| ❑ | 91 Todd Helton | .75 | .35 |
| ❑ | 92 David Dellucci | .15 | .07 |
| ❑ | 93 Johnny Damon | .25 | .11 |
| ❑ | 94 Cliff Floyd | .25 | .11 |
| ❑ | 95 Ken Griffey Jr. | 2.50 | 1.10 |
| ❑ | 96 Juan Guzman | .15 | .07 |
| ❑ | 97 Derek Jeter | 2.50 | 1.10 |
| ❑ | 98 Barry Larkin | .60 | .25 |
| ❑ | 99 Quinton McCracken | .15 | .07 |
| ❑ | 100 Sammy Sosa | 1.25 | .55 |
| ❑ | 101 Kevin Young | .25 | .11 |
| ❑ | 102 Jay Bell | .25 | .11 |
| ❑ | 103 Jay Buhner | .25 | .11 |
| ❑ | 104 Jeff Conine | .15 | .07 |
| ❑ | 105 Ryan Jackson | .15 | .07 |
| ❑ | 106 Sidney Ponson | .15 | .07 |
| ❑ | 107 Jeromy Burnitz | .25 | .11 |
| ❑ | 108 Roberto Hernandez | .15 | .07 |
| ❑ | 109 A.J. Hinch | .15 | .07 |
| ❑ | 110 Hideki Irabu | .15 | .07 |
| ❑ | 111 Paul Konerko | .25 | .11 |
| ❑ | 112 Henry Rodriguez | .15 | .07 |
| ❑ | 113 Shannon Stewart | .25 | .11 |
| ❑ | 114 Tony Womack | .15 | .07 |
| ❑ | 115 Wilton Guerrero | .15 | .07 |
| ❑ | 116 Andy Benes | .15 | .07 |
| ❑ | 117 Jeff Cirillo | .25 | .11 |
| ❑ | 118 Chili Davis | .25 | .11 |
| ❑ | 119 Eric Davis | .25 | .11 |
| ❑ | 120 Vladimir Guerrero | 1.00 | .45 |
| ❑ | 121 Dennis Reyes | .15 | .07 |
| ❑ | 122 Rickey Henderson | .75 | .35 |
| ❑ | 123 Mickey Morandini | .15 | .07 |
| ❑ | 124 Jason Schmidt | .15 | .07 |
| ❑ | 125 J.T. Snow | .25 | .11 |
| ❑ | 126 Justin Thompson | .15 | .07 |
| ❑ | 127 Billy Wagner | .15 | .07 |
| ❑ | 128 Armando Benitez | .15 | .07 |
| ❑ | 129 Sean Casey | .25 | .11 |
| ❑ | 130 Brad Fullmer | .25 | .11 |
| ❑ | 131 Ben Grieve | .25 | .11 |
| ❑ | 132 Robb Nen | .15 | .07 |
| ❑ | 133 Shane Reynolds | .15 | .07 |
| ❑ | 134 Todd Zeile | .25 | .11 |
| ❑ | 135 Brady Anderson | .25 | .11 |
| ❑ | 136 Aaron Boone | .15 | .07 |
| ❑ | 137 Orlando Cabrera | .15 | .07 |
| ❑ | 138 Jason Giambi | .60 | .25 |
| ❑ | 139 Randy Johnson | .75 | .35 |
| ❑ | 140 Jeff Kent | .40 | .18 |
| ❑ | 141 John Wetteland | .25 | .11 |
| ❑ | 142 Rolando Arrojo | .15 | .07 |
| ❑ | 143 Scott Brosius | .25 | .11 |
| ❑ | 144 Mark Grace | .60 | .25 |
| ❑ | 145 Jason Kendall | .25 | .11 |
| ❑ | 146 Travis Lee | .15 | .07 |
| ❑ | 147 Gary Sheffield | .60 | .25 |
| ❑ | 148 David Cone | .25 | .11 |
| ❑ | 149 Jose Hernandez | .15 | .07 |
| ❑ | 150 Todd Jones | .15 | .07 |
| ❑ | 151 Al Martin | .15 | .07 |
| ❑ | 152 Ismael Valdes | .15 | .07 |
| ❑ | 153 Wade Boggs | .75 | .35 |
| ❑ | 154 Garret Anderson | .25 | .11 |
| ❑ | 155 Bobby Bonilla | .25 | .11 |
| ❑ | 156 Darryl Kile | .25 | .11 |
| ❑ | 157 Ryan Klesko | .25 | .11 |
| ❑ | 158 Tim Wakefield | .15 | .07 |
| ❑ | 159 Kenny Lofton | .25 | .11 |
| ❑ | 160 Jose Canseco | .75 | .35 |
| ❑ | 161 Doug Glanville | .15 | .07 |
| ❑ | 162 Todd Hundley | .15 | .07 |
| ❑ | 163 Brian Jordan | .25 | .11 |
| ❑ | 164 Steve Finley | .25 | .11 |
| ❑ | 165 Tom Glavine | .60 | .25 |
| ❑ | 166 Al Leiter | .25 | .11 |
| ❑ | 167 Raul Mondesi | .25 | .11 |
| ❑ | 168 Desi Relaford | .15 | .07 |
| ❑ | 169 Bret Saberhagen | .25 | .11 |
| ❑ | 170 Omar Vizquel | .25 | .11 |
| ❑ | 171 Larry Walker | .25 | .11 |
| ❑ | 172 Bobby Abreu | .25 | .11 |
| ❑ | 173 Moises Alou | .25 | .11 |
| ❑ | 174 Mike Caruso | .15 | .07 |
| ❑ | 175 Royce Clayton | .15 | .07 |
| ❑ | 176 Bartolo Colon | .25 | .11 |
| ❑ | 177 Marty Cordova | .15 | .07 |
| ❑ | 178 Darin Erstad | .60 | .25 |
| ❑ | 179 Nomar Garciaparra | 2.00 | .90 |
| ❑ | 180 Andy Ashby | .15 | .07 |
| ❑ | 181 Dan Wilson | .15 | .07 |
| ❑ | 182 Larry Sutton | .15 | .07 |
| ❑ | 183 Tony Clark | .15 | .07 |
| ❑ | 184 Andres Galarraga | .40 | .18 |
| ❑ | 185 Ray Durham | .25 | .11 |
| ❑ | 186 Hideo Nomo | .60 | .25 |
| ❑ | 187 Steve Woodard | .15 | .07 |
| ❑ | 188 Scott Rolen | .60 | .25 |
| ❑ | 189 Mike Stanley | .15 | .07 |
| ❑ | 190 Jaret Wright | .15 | .07 |
| ❑ | 191 Vinny Castilla | .25 | .11 |
| ❑ | 192 Jason Christiansen | .15 | .07 |
| ❑ | 193 Paul Bako | .15 | .07 |
| ❑ | 194 Carlos Perez | .15 | .07 |
| ❑ | 195 Mike Piazza | 2.00 | .90 |
| ❑ | 196 Fernando Tatis | .25 | .11 |
| ❑ | 197 Mo Vaughn | .25 | .11 |
| ❑ | 198 Devon White | .15 | .07 |
| ❑ | 199 Ricky Gutierrez | .15 | .07 |
| ❑ | 200 Charlie Hayes | .15 | .07 |
| ❑ | 201 Brad Radke | .25 | .11 |
| ❑ | 202 Rick Helling | .25 | .11 |
| ❑ | 203 John Smoltz | .25 | .11 |
| ❑ | 204 Frank Thomas | 1.25 | .55 |
| ❑ | 205 David Wells | .25 | .11 |
| ❑ | 206 Roger Clemens | 1.25 | .55 |
| ❑ | 207 Mark Grudzielanek | .15 | .07 |
| ❑ | 208 Chipper Jones | 1.50 | .70 |
| ❑ | 209 Ray Lankford | .25 | .11 |
| ❑ | 210 Pedro Martinez | .75 | .35 |
| ❑ | 211 Manny Ramirez | .75 | .35 |
| ❑ | 212 Greg Vaughn | .25 | .11 |
| ❑ | 213 Craig Biggio | .40 | .18 |
| ❑ | 214 Rusty Greer | .25 | .11 |
| ❑ | 215 Greg Maddux | 1.50 | .70 |
| ❑ | 216 Rick Aguilera | .15 | .07 |
| ❑ | 217 Andy Pettitte | .25 | .11 |
| ❑ | 218 Dante Bichette | .25 | .11 |
| ❑ | 219 Damion Easley | .15 | .07 |
| ❑ | 220 Matt Morris | .15 | .07 |
| ❑ | 221 John Olerud | .25 | .11 |
| ❑ | 222 Chan Ho Park | .25 | .11 |
| ❑ | 223 Curt Schilling | .25 | .11 |
| ❑ | 224 John Valentin | .15 | .07 |
| ❑ | 225 Matt Williams | .40 | .18 |
| ❑ | 226 Ellis Burks | .25 | .11 |
| ❑ | 227 Tom Goodwin | .15 | .07 |
| ❑ | 228 Javy Lopez | .25 | .11 |
| ❑ | 229 Eric Milton | .15 | .07 |
| ❑ | 230 Paul O'Neill | .25 | .11 |
| ❑ | 231 Maggio Ordonez | .40 | .18 |
| ❑ | 232 Derrek Lee | .15 | .07 |
| ❑ | 233 Ken Griffey Jr. FLY | 1.25 | .55 |
| ❑ | 234 Randy Johnson FLY | .25 | .11 |
| ❑ | 235 Alex Rodriguez FLY | 1.00 | .45 |
| ❑ | 236 Darin Erstad FLY | .60 | .25 |
| ❑ | 237 Juan Gonzalez FLY | .40 | .18 |
| ❑ | 238 Derek Jeter FLY | 1.25 | .55 |
| ❑ | 239 Tony Gwynn FLY | .60 | .25 |
| ❑ | 240 Kerry Wood FLY | .25 | .11 |
| ❑ | 241 Cal Ripken FLY | 1.25 | .55 |
| ❑ | 242 Sammy Sosa FLY | .60 | .25 |
| ❑ | 243 Greg Maddux FLY | .75 | .35 |
| ❑ | 244 Mark McGwire FLY | 1.25 | .55 |
| ❑ | 245 Chipper Jones FLY | .75 | .35 |
| ❑ | 246 Barry Bonds FLY | .40 | .18 |
| ❑ | 247 Ben Grieve FLY | .25 | .11 |
| ❑ | 248 Ben Davis BB | .15 | .07 |
| ❑ | 249 Robert Fick BB | .15 | .07 |
| ❑ | 250 Carlos Guillen BB | .15 | .07 |
| ❑ | 251 Mike Frank BB | .15 | .07 |
| ❑ | 252 Ryan Minor BB | .15 | .07 |
| ❑ | 253 Troy Glaus BB | 1.00 | .45 |
| ❑ | 254 Matt Anderson BB | .15 | .07 |
| ❑ | 255 Josh Booty BB | .15 | .07 |
| ❑ | 256 Gabe Alvarez BB | .15 | .07 |
| ❑ | 257 Gabe Kapler BB | .25 | .11 |
| ❑ | 258 Enrique Wilson BB | .15 | .07 |
| ❑ | 259 Alex Gonzalez BB | .15 | .07 |
| ❑ | 260 Preston Wilson BB | .25 | .11 |
| ❑ | 261 Eric Chavez BB | .25 | .11 |
| ❑ | 262 Adrian Beltre BB | .25 | .11 |
| ❑ | 263 Corey Koskie BB | .15 | .07 |
| ❑ | 264 Robert Machado BB | .15 | .07 |
| ❑ | 265 Orlando Hernandez BB | .25 | .11 |
| ❑ | 266 Matt Clement BB | .15 | .07 |
| ❑ | 267 Luis Ordaz BB | .15 | .07 |
| ❑ | 268 Jeremy Giambi BB | .15 | .07 |
| ❑ | 269 J.D. Drew BB | .60 | .25 |
| ❑ | 270 Cliff Politte BB | .15 | .07 |
| ❑ | 271 Carlton Loewer BB | .15 | .07 |
| ❑ | 272 Aramis Ramirez BB | .15 | .07 |
| ❑ | 273 Ken Griffey Jr. MLPD | 1.25 | .55 |
| ❑ | 274 Randy Johnson MLPD | .25 | .11 |
| ❑ | 275 Alex Rodriguez MLPD | 1.00 | .45 |
| ❑ | 276 Darin Erstad MLPD | .60 | .25 |
| ❑ | 277 Scott Rolen MLPD | .60 | .25 |
| ❑ | 278 Juan Gonzalez MLPD | .40 | .18 |
| ❑ | 279 Jeff Bagwell MLPD | .40 | .18 |
| ❑ | 280 Mike Piazza MLPD | 1.00 | .45 |
| ❑ | 281 Derek Jeter MLPD | 1.25 | .55 |
| ❑ | 282 Travis Lee MLPD | .15 | .07 |
| ❑ | 283 Tony Gwynn MLPD | .60 | .25 |
| ❑ | 284 Kerry Wood MLPD | .25 | .11 |
| ❑ | 285 Albert Belle MLPD | .15 | .07 |
| ❑ | 286 Sammy Sosa MLPD | .60 | .25 |
| ❑ | 287 Mo Vaughn MLPD | .25 | .11 |
| ❑ | 288 Nomar Garciaparra MLPD | 1.00 | .45 |
| ❑ | 289 FrankThomas MLPD | .60 | .25 |
| ❑ | 290 Cal Ripken MLPD | 1.25 | .55 |
| ❑ | 291 Greg Maddux MLPD | .75 | .35 |
| ❑ | 292 Chipper Jones MLPD | .75 | .35 |
| ❑ | 293 Ben Grieve MLPD | .25 | .11 |
| ❑ | 294 Andruw Jones MLPD | .25 | .11 |
| ❑ | 295 Mark McGwire MLPD | 1.25 | .55 |
| ❑ | 296 Roger Clemens MLPD | .60 | .25 |
| ❑ | 297 Barry Bonds MLPD | .40 | .18 |
| ❑ | 298 Ken Griffey Jr. CL | 1.25 | .55 |
| ❑ | 299 Kerry Wood CL | .25 | .11 |
| ❑ | 300 Alex Rodriguez CL | 1.00 | .45 |
| ❑ | SAMP J.D. Drew AU/35 | | |

## 2000 Metal

| | MINT | NRMT |
|---|---|---|
| COMPLETE SET (250) | 60.00 | 27.00 |
| COMP.SET w/o SP's (200) | 20.00 | 9.00 |
| COMMON CARD (1-200) | .15 | .07 |
| COMMON PROS (201-250) | .75 | .35 |

| | Card | Mint | NRMT |
|---|---|---|---|
| ❑ | 1 Tony Gwynn | 1.25 | .55 |
| ❑ | 2 Derek Jeter | 2.50 | 1.10 |
| ❑ | 3 Johnny Damon | .25 | .11 |
| ❑ | 4 Javy Lopez | .25 | .11 |
| ❑ | 5 Preston Wilson | .25 | .11 |
| ❑ | 6 Derek Bell | .15 | .07 |
| ❑ | 7 Richie Sexson | .25 | .11 |

❑ 8 Vinny Castilla .25 .11
❑ 9 Billy Wagner .15 .07
❑ 10 Carlos Beltran .25 .11
❑ 11 Chris Singleton .25 .11
❑ 12 Nomar Garciaparra 2.00 .90
❑ 13 Carlos Febles .15 .07
❑ 14 Jason Varitek .25 .11
❑ 15 Luis Gonzalez .25 .11
❑ 16 Jon Lieber .15 .07
❑ 17 Mo Vaughn .25 .11
❑ 18 Dave Burba .15 .07
❑ 19 Brady Anderson .25 .11
❑ 20 Carlos Lee .25 .11
❑ 21 Chuck Finley .25 .11
❑ 22 Alex Gonzalez .15 .07
❑ 23 Matt Williams .40 .18
❑ 24 Chipper Jones 1.50 .70
❑ 25 Pokey Reese .25 .11
❑ 26 Todd Helton .75 .35
❑ 27 Mike Mussina .60 .25
❑ 28 Butch Huskey .15 .07
❑ 29 Jeff Bagwell .75 .35
❑ 30 Juan Encarnacion .25 .11
❑ 31 A.J. Burnett .25 .11
❑ 32 Micah Bowie .15 .07
❑ 33 Brian Jordan .25 .11
❑ 34 Scott Erickson .15 .07
❑ 35 Sean Casey .25 .11
❑ 36 John Smoltz .25 .11
❑ 37 Edgard Clemente .15 .07
❑ 38 Mike Hampton .25 .11
❑ 39 Tom Glavine .60 .25
❑ 40 Albert Belle .40 .18
❑ 41 Jim Thome .40 .18
❑ 42 Jermaine Dye .25 .11
❑ 43 Sammy Sosa 1.25 .55
❑ 44 Pedro Martinez .75 .35
❑ 45 Paul Konerko .25 .11
❑ 46 Damion Easley .15 .07
❑ 47 Cal Ripken 2.50 1.10
❑ 48 Jose Lima .15 .07
❑ 49 Mike Lowell .15 .07
❑ 50 Randy Johnson .75 .35
❑ 51 Dean Palmer .25 .11
❑ 52 Tim Salmon .25 .11
❑ 53 Kevin Millwood .25 .11
❑ 54 Mark Grace .60 .25
❑ 55 Aaron Boone .15 .07
❑ 56 Omar Vizquel .25 .11
❑ 57 Moises Alou .25 .11
❑ 58 Travis Fryman .25 .11
❑ 59 Erubiel Durazo .25 .11
❑ 60 Carl Everett .25 .11
❑ 61 Charles Johnson .25 .11
❑ 62 Trot Nixon .25 .11
❑ 63 Andres Galarraga .40 .18
❑ 64 Magglio Ordonez .25 .11
❑ 65 Pedro Astacio .15 .07
❑ 66 Roberto Alomar .60 .25
❑ 67 Pete Harnisch .15 .07
❑ 68 Scott Williamson .15 .07
❑ 69 Alex Fernandez .15 .07
❑ 70 Robin Ventura .40 .18
❑ 71 Chad Allen .15 .07
❑ 72 Darin Erstad .60 .25
❑ 73 Ron Coomer .15 .07
❑ 74 Ellis Burks .25 .11
❑ 75 Kent Bottenfield .15 .07
❑ 76 Ken Griffey Jr. 2.50 1.10
❑ 77 Mike Piazza 2.00 .90
❑ 78 Jorge Posada .25 .11
❑ 79 Dante Bichette .25 .11
❑ 80 Adrian Beltre .25 .11
❑ 81 Andruw Jones .60 .25
❑ 82 Wilson Alvarez .15 .07
❑ 83 Edgardo Alfonzo .25 .11
❑ 84 Brian Giles .25 .11
❑ 85 Gary Sheffield .60 .25
❑ 86 Matt Stairs .15 .07
❑ 87 Bret Boone .15 .07
❑ 88 Kenny Rogers .15 .07
❑ 89 Barry Bonds 1.00 .45
❑ 90 Scott Rolen .60 .25
❑ 91 Edgar Renteria .15 .07
❑ 92 Larry Walker .25 .11
❑ 93 Roger Cedeno .15 .07
❑ 94 Kevin Brown .40 .18
❑ 95 Lee Stevens .15 .07
❑ 96 Brad Radke .25 .11
❑ 97 Andy Pettitte .25 .11
❑ 98 Bobby Higginson .15 .07
❑ 99 Eric Chavez .25 .11
❑ 100 Alex Rodriguez 2.00 .90
❑ 101 Shannon Stewart .25 .11
❑ 102 Ryan Rupe .15 .07
❑ 103 Freddy Garcia .25 .11
❑ 104 John Jaha .15 .07
❑ 105 Greg Maddux 1.50 .70
❑ 106 Hideki Irabu .15 .07
❑ 107 Rey Ordonez .15 .07
❑ 108 Troy O'Leary .15 .07
❑ 109 Frank Thomas 1.25 .55
❑ 110 Corey Koskie .15 .07
❑ 111 Bernie Williams .60 .25
❑ 112 Barry Larkin .60 .25
❑ 113 Kevin Appier .15 .07
❑ 114 Curt Schilling .25 .11
❑ 115 Bartolo Colon .25 .11
❑ 116 Edgar Martinez .40 .18
❑ 117 Ray Lankford .25 .11
❑ 118 Todd Walker .15 .07
❑ 119 John Wetteland .25 .11
❑ 120 David Nilsson .15 .07
❑ 121 Tino Martinez .25 .11
❑ 122 Phil Nevin .25 .11
❑ 123 Ben Grieve .25 .11
❑ 124 Ron Gant .25 .11
❑ 125 Jeff Kent .40 .18
❑ 126 Rick Helling .25 .11
❑ 127 Russ Ortiz .25 .11
❑ 128 Troy Glaus .75 .35
❑ 129 Chan Ho Park .25 .11
❑ 130 Jeromy Burnitz .25 .11
❑ 131 Aaron Sele .15 .07
❑ 132 Mike Sirotka .15 .07
❑ 133 Brad Ausmus .15 .07
❑ 134 Jose Rosado .15 .07
❑ 135 Mariano Rivera .25 .11
❑ 136 Jason Giambi .60 .25
❑ 137 Mike Lieberthal .25 .11
❑ 138 Chris Carpenter .15 .07
❑ 139 Henry Rodriguez .15 .07
❑ 140 Mike Sweeney .25 .11
❑ 141 Vladimir Guerrero 1.00 .45
❑ 142 Charles Nagy .15 .07
❑ 143 Jason Kendall .25 .11
❑ 144 Matt Lawton .15 .07
❑ 145 Michael Barrett .15 .07
❑ 146 David Cone .25 .11
❑ 147 Bobby Abreu .25 .11
❑ 148 Fernando Tatis .25 .11
❑ 149 Jose Canseco .75 .35
❑ 150 Craig Biggio .40 .18
❑ 151 Matt Mantei .15 .07
❑ 152 Jacque Jones .25 .11
❑ 153 John Halama .15 .07
❑ 154 Trevor Hoffman .25 .11
❑ 155 Rondell White .25 .11
❑ 156 Reggie Sanders .15 .07
❑ 157 Steve Finley .25 .11
❑ 158 Roberto Hernandez .15 .07
❑ 159 Geoff Jenkins .25 .11
❑ 160 Chris Widger .15 .07
❑ 161 Orel Hershiser .25 .11
❑ 162 Tim Hudson .60 .25
❑ 163 Kris Benson .25 .11
❑ 164 Kevin Young .15 .07
❑ 165 Rafael Palmeiro .60 .25
❑ 166 David Wells .25 .11
❑ 167 Ben Davis .15 .07
❑ 168 Jamie Moyer .15 .07
❑ 169 Randy Wolf .15 .07
❑ 170 Jeff Cirillo .25 .11
❑ 171 Warren Morris .15 .07
❑ 172 Billy Koch .25 .11
❑ 173 Marquis Grissom .15 .07
❑ 174 Geoff Blum .15 .07
❑ 175 Octavio Dotel .15 .07
❑ 176 Orlando Hernandez .25 .11
❑ 177 J.D. Drew .60 .25
❑ 178 Carlos Delgado .60 .25
❑ 179 Sterling Hitchcock .15 .07
❑ 180 Shawn Green .60 .25
❑ 181 Tony Clark .15 .07
❑ 182 Joe McEwing .15 .07
❑ 183 Fred McGriff .40 .18
❑ 184 Tony Batista .25 .11
❑ 185 Al Leiter .15 .07
❑ 186 Roger Clemens 1.25 .55
❑ 187 Al Martin .15 .07
❑ 188 Eric Milton .15 .07
❑ 189 Bobby Smith .15 .07
❑ 190 Rusty Greer .25 .11
❑ 191 Shawn Estes .15 .07
❑ 192 Ken Caminiti .25 .11
❑ 193 Eric Karros .25 .11
❑ 194 Manny Ramirez .75 .35
❑ 195 Jim Edmonds .60 .25
❑ 196 Paul O'Neill .25 .11
❑ 197 Rico Brogna .15 .07
❑ 198 Ivan Rodriguez .75 .35
❑ 199 Doug Glanville .15 .07
❑ 200 Mark McGwire 2.50 1.10
❑ 201 Mark Quinn PROS .75 .35
❑ 202 Norm Hutchins PROS .75 .35
❑ 203 Ramon Ortiz PROS .75 .35
❑ 204 Brett Laxton PROS .75 .35
❑ 205 Jimmy Anderson PROS .75 .35
❑ 206 Calvin Murray PROS .75 .35
❑ 207 Wilton Veras PROS .75 .35
❑ 208 Chad Hermansen PROS .75 .35
❑ 209 Nick Johnson PROS .75 .35
❑ 210 Kevin Barker PROS .75 .35
❑ 211 Casey Blake PROS .75 .35
❑ 212 Chad Meyers PROS .75 .35
❑ 213 Kip Wells PROS .75 .35
❑ 214 Eric Munson PROS 1.50 .70
❑ 215 Lance Berkman PROS .75 .35
❑ 216 Wily Pena PROS .75 .35
❑ 217 Gary Matthews Jr. PROS .75 .35
❑ 218 Travis Dawkins PROS .75 .35
❑ 219 Josh Beckett PROS 1.50 .70
❑ 220 Tony Armas Jr. PROS .75 .35
❑ 221 Alfonso Soriano PROS .75 .35
❑ 222 Pat Burrell PROS 2.50 1.10
❑ 223 Danys Baez PROS RC 1.50 .70
❑ 224 Adam Kennedy PROS .75 .35
❑ 225 Ruben Mateo PROS .75 .35
❑ 226 Vernon Wells PROS .75 .35
❑ 227 Brian Cooper PROS .75 .35
❑ 228 Jeff DaVanon PROS .75 .35
❑ 229 Glen Barker PROS .75 .35
❑ 230 Robinson Cancel PROS .75 .35
❑ 231 D'Angelo Jimenez PROS .75 .35
❑ 232 Adam Piatt PROS 1.50 .70
❑ 233 Buddy Carlyle PROS .75 .35
❑ 234 Chad Hutchinson PROS .75 .35
❑ 235 Matt Riley PROS .75 .35
❑ 236 Cole Liniak PROS .75 .35
❑ 237 Ben Petrick PROS .75 .35
❑ 238 Peter Bergeron PROS .75 .35
❑ 239 Cesar King PROS .75 .35
❑ 240 Aaron Myette PROS .75 .35
❑ 241 Eric Gagne PROS .75 .35
❑ 242 Joe Nathan PROS .75 .35
❑ 243 Bruce Chen PROS .75 .35
❑ 244 Rob Bell PROS .75 .35
❑ 245 Juan Sosa PROS RC .75 .35
❑ 246 Julio Ramirez PROS .75 .35
❑ 247 Wade Miller PROS .75 .35

❑ 248 Trace Coquillette PROS RC .75 .35
❑ 249 Robert Ramsay PROS .. .75 .35
❑ 250 Rick Ankiel PROS ........ 3.00 1.35
❑ P100 Alex Rodriguez Promo 3.00 1.35

## 2000 MLB Showdown 1st Edition

| | MINT | NRMT |
|---|---|---|
| COMPLETE SET (462) ........ | 500.00 | 220.00 |
| COMP.SET w/o FOIL (400) .. | 100.00 | 45.00 |
| COMMON CARD (1-462) ........... | .25 | .11 |
| MINOR STARS ........................ | .75 | .35 |
| SEMISTARS ............................ | 1.25 | .55 |
| UNLISTED STARS .................... | 2.00 | .90 |
| COMMON FOIL ........................ | 5.00 | 2.20 |
| FOIL MINOR STARS ............. | 10.00 | 4.50 |
| FOIL SEMISTARS ................. | 10.00 | 4.50 |
| FOIL UNLISTED STARS ........ | 10.00 | 4.50 |

❑ 1 Garret Anderson .................. .75 .35
❑ 2 Tim Belcher ........................ .25 .11
❑ 3 Gary DiSarcina UER .......... .25 .11
(Tim Salmon incorrectly pictured)
❑ 4 Darin Erstad ...................... 2.00 .90
❑ 5 Chuck Finley FOIL ........ 10.00 4.50
❑ 6 Troy Glaus ......................... 2.50 1.10
❑ 7 Todd Greene ....................... .25 .11
❑ 8 Jeff Huson ........................... .25 .11
❑ 9 Orlando Palmeiro .................. .25 .11
❑ 10 Troy Percival ..................... .25 .11
❑ 11 Mark Petkovsek ................... .25 .11
❑ 12 Tim Salmon ........................ .75 .35
❑ 13 Steve Sparks ...................... .25 .11
❑ 14 Mo Vaughn ......................... .75 .35
❑ 15 Matt Walbeck ...................... .25 .11
❑ 16 Jay Bell FOIL .................. 10.00 4.50
❑ 17 Andy Benes ........................ .25 .11
❑ 18 Omar Daal ........................... .25 .11
❑ 19 Steve Finley ........................ .75 .35
❑ 20 Andy Fox ............................. .25 .11
❑ 21 Hanley Frias ........................ .25 .11
❑ 22 Bernard Gilkey ..................... .25 .11
❑ 23 Luis Gonzalez FOIL .... 10.00 4.50
❑ 24 Randy Johnson FOIL .. 30.00 13.50
❑ 25 Travis Lee ............................ .25 .11
❑ 26 Matt Mantei .......................... .25 .11
❑ 27 Dan Plesac ........................... .25 .11
❑ 28 Kelly Stinnett ........................ .25 .11
❑ 29 Greg Swindell ....................... .25 .11
❑ 30 Matt Williams FOIL ...... 10.00 4.50
❑ 31 Tony Womack ....................... .25 .11
❑ 32 Bret Boone ........................... .25 .11
❑ 33 Tom Glavine ....................... 2.00 .90
❑ 34 Jose Hernandez .................... .25 .11
❑ 35 Brian Hunter ......................... .25 .11
❑ 36 Andruw Jones .................... 2.00 .90
❑ 37 Chipper Jones FOIL .... 15.00 6.75
❑ 38 Brian Jordan ......................... .25 .11
❑ 39 Ryan Klesko ......................... .25 .11
❑ 40 Keith Lockhart ....................... .25 .11
❑ 41 Greg Maddux FOIL ........ 5.00 2.20
❑ 42 Kevin Millwood FOIL ..... 10.00 4.50
❑ 43 Eddie Perez ........................... .25 .11
❑ 44 Mike Remlinger ..................... .25 .11
❑ 45 John Rocker ......................... .75 .35
❑ 46 John Smoltz ......................... .75 .35
❑ 47 Walt Weiss ........................... .25 .11
❑ 48 Gerald Williams ..................... .25 .11
❑ 49 Rich Amaral ........................... .25 .11
❑ 50 Brady Anderson ..................... .75 .35
❑ 51 Albert Belle ......................... 1.25 .55
❑ 52 Mike Bordick .......................... .25 .11
❑ 53 Jeff Conine ............................ .25 .11
❑ 54 Delino DeShields ................... .75 .35
❑ 55 Scott Erickson ........................ .25 .11
❑ 56 Charles Johnson .................... .75 .35
❑ 57 Mike Mussina ...................... 2.00 .90
❑ 58 Jesse Orosco ......................... .25 .11
❑ 59 Sidney Ponson ....................... .25 .11
❑ 60 Jeff Reboulet .......................... .25 .11
❑ 61 Cal Ripken FOIL .......... 25.00 11.00
❑ 62 B.J. Surhoff ............................ .75 .35
❑ 63 Mike Timlin ............................ .25 .11
❑ 64 Rod Beck ................................ .25 .11
❑ 65 Damon Buford ........................ .25 .11
❑ 66 Rheal Cormier ........................ .25 .11
❑ 67 Nomar Garciaparra FOIL 20.00 9.00
❑ 68 Butch Huskey ......................... .25 .11
❑ 69 Darren Lewis .......................... .25 .11
❑ 70 Derek Lowe ............................ .25 .11
❑ 71 Pedro Martinez FOIL .... 30.00 13.50
❑ 72 Trot Nixon .............................. .75 .35
❑ 73 Jose Offerman ....................... .25 .11
❑ 74 Troy O'Leary .......................... .25 .11
❑ 75 Mark Portugal ......................... .25 .11
❑ 76 Pat Rapp ................................. .25 .11
❑ 77 Mike Stanley .......................... .25 .11
❑ 78 John Valentin ......................... .25 .11
❑ 79 Jason Varitek ......................... .25 .11
❑ 80 Tim Wakefield ........................ .25 .11
❑ 81 Rick Aguilera .......................... .75 .35
❑ 82 Jeff Blauser ............................ .25 .11
❑ 83 Kyle Farnsworth ..................... .25 .11
❑ 84 Gary Gaetti ............................. .75 .35
❑ 85 Mark Grace .......................... 2.00 .90
❑ 86 Lance Johnson ....................... .25 .11
❑ 87 Jon Lieber ............................... .25 .11
❑ 88 Mickey Morandini ................... .25 .11
❑ 89 Jose Nieves ............................ .25 .11
❑ 90 Jeff Reed ................................ .25 .11
❑ 91 Henry Rodriguez ..................... .25 .11
❑ 92 Scott Sanders ......................... .25 .11
❑ 93 Benito Santiago ....................... .25 .11
❑ 94 Sammy Sosa FOIL ...... 25.00 11.00
❑ 95 Steve Trachsel ........................ .25 .11
❑ 96 James Baldwin ........................ .75 .35
❑ 97 Mike Caruso ............................ .25 .11
❑ 98 Ray Durham ............................ .75 .35
❑ 99 Brook Fordyce ......................... .25 .11
❑ 100 Bob Howry ............................ .25 .11
❑ 101 Paul Konerko ......................... .75 .35
❑ 102 Carlos Lee ............................. .25 .11
❑ 103 Greg Norton ........................... .25 .11
❑ 104 Magglio Ordonez .................... .75 .35
❑ 105 Jim Parque ............................ .25 .11
❑ 106 Bill Simas .............................. .25 .11
❑ 107 Chris Singleton ....................... .75 .35
❑ 108 Mike Sirotka ........................... .25 .11
❑ 109 Frank Thomas FOIL .. 15.00 6.75
❑ 110 Craig Wilson .......................... .25 .11
❑ 111 Aaron Boone .......................... .25 .11
❑ 112 Mike Cameron ....................... .25 .11
❑ 113 Sean Casey FOIL ...... 10.00 4.50
❑ 114 Danny Graves ........................ .25 .11
❑ 115 Pete Harnisch ........................ .25 .11
❑ 116 Barry Larkin FOIL ...... 10.00 4.50
❑ 117 Pokey Reese ......................... .75 .35
❑ 118 Scott Sullivan ........................ .25 .11
❑ 119 Eddie Taubensee .................. .25 .11
❑ 120 Brett Tomko ........................... .25 .11
❑ 121 Michael Tucker ...................... .25 .11
❑ 122 Greg Vaughn ......................... .75 .35
❑ 123 Ron Villone ............................ .25 .11
❑ 124 Scott Williamson FOIL .. 5.00 2.20
❑ 125 Dmitri Young .......................... .75 .35
❑ 126 Roberto Alomar FOIL 10.00 4.50
❑ 127 Harold Baines ........................ .75 .35
❑ 128 Dave Burba ............................ .25 .11
❑ 129 Bartolo Colon ......................... .25 .11
❑ 130 Einar Diaz .............................. .25 .11
❑ 131 Travis Fryman ........................ .75 .35
❑ 132 Mike Jackson ......................... .25 .11
❑ 133 David Justice ...................... 1.25 .55
❑ 134 Kenny Lofton FOIL .... 10.00 4.50
❑ 135 Charles Nagy ......................... .25 .11
❑ 136 Manny Ramirez FOIL 10.00 4.50
❑ 137 Richie Sexson ........................ .25 .11
❑ 138 Paul Shuey ............................ .25 .11
❑ 139 Jim Thome FOIL ........ 10.00 4.50
❑ 140 Omar Vizquel ......................... .75 .35
❑ 141 Enrique Wilson ....................... .25 .11
❑ 142 Kurt Abbott ............................. .25 .11
❑ 143 Pedro Astacio ........................ .25 .11
❑ 144 Jeff Barry ............................... .25 .11
❑ 145 Dante Bichette ....................... .75 .35
❑ 146 Henry Blanco ......................... .25 .11
❑ 147 Brian Bohanon ....................... .25 .11
❑ 148 Vinny Castilla ......................... .75 .35
❑ 149 Jerry Dipoto ........................... .25 .11
❑ 150 Todd Helton ........................ 2.50 1.10
❑ 151 Darryl Kile .............................. .75 .35
❑ 152 Curtis Leskanic ...................... .25 .11
❑ 153 Neifi Perez ............................. .25 .11
❑ 154 Terry Shumpert ...................... .25 .11
❑ 155 Dave Veres ............................ .25 .11
❑ 156 Larry Walker FOIL ...... 10.00 4.50
❑ 157 Brad Ausmus ......................... .25 .11
❑ 158 Frank Catalanotto .................. .25 .11
❑ 159 Tony Clark ............................. .25 .11
❑ 160 Deivi Cruz .............................. .25 .11
❑ 161 Damion Easley ....................... .25 .11
❑ 162 Juan Encarnacion .................. .75 .35
❑ 163 Karim Garcia ......................... .25 .11
❑ 164 Bobby Higginson .................... .25 .11
❑ 165 Todd Jones ............................ .25 .11
❑ 166 Gabe Kapler .......................... .75 .35
❑ 167 Dave Mlicki ............................ .25 .11
❑ 168 Brian Moehler ........................ .25 .11
❑ 169 C.J. Nitkowski ........................ .25 .11
❑ 170 Dean Palmer FOIL .... 10.00 4.50
❑ 171 Jeff Weaver ............................ .25 .11
❑ 172 Antonio Alfonseca .................. .25 .11
❑ 173 Bruce Aven ............................ .25 .11
❑ 174 Dave Berg .............................. .25 .11
❑ 175 Luis Castillo FOIL ...... 10.00 4.50
❑ 176 Ryan Dempster ....................... .75 .35
❑ 177 Brian Edmondson .................. .25 .11
❑ 178 Alex Gonzalez ........................ .25 .11
❑ 179 Mark Kotsay ........................... .25 .11
❑ 180 Derrek Lee ............................. .25 .11
❑ 181 Braden Looper ....................... .25 .11
❑ 182 Mike Lowell ............................ .25 .11
❑ 183 Brian Meadows ...................... .25 .11
❑ 184 Mike Redmond ....................... .25 .11
❑ 185 Dennis Springer ..................... .25 .11
❑ 186 Preston Wilson ....................... .75 .35
❑ 187 Jeff Bagwell FOIL ...... 15.00 6.75
❑ 188 Derek Bell .............................. .25 .11
❑ 189 Craig Biggio ........................ 1.25 .55
❑ 190 Tim Bogar .............................. .25 .11
❑ 191 Ken Caminiti ........................... .75 .35
❑ 192 Scott Elarton .......................... .75 .35
❑ 193 Tony Eusebio ......................... .25 .11
❑ 194 Carl Everett FOIL ...... 10.00 4.50
❑ 195 Mike Hampton FOIL .. 10.00 4.50
❑ 196 Richard Hidalgo ..................... .75 .35
❑ 197 Stan Javier ............................. .25 .11
❑ 198 Jose Lima .............................. .25 .11
❑ 199 Jay Powell .............................. .25 .11
❑ 200 Shane Reynolds ..................... .25 .11
❑ 201 Bill Spiers ............................... .25 .11
❑ 202 Billy Wagner FOIL ........ 5.00 2.20
❑ 203 Carlos Beltran FOIL .. 10.00 4.50
❑ 204 Johnny Damon ....................... .75 .35
❑ 205 Jermaine Dye ......................... .25 .11
❑ 206 Carlos Febles ......................... .25 .11
❑ 207 Jeremy Giambi ....................... .25 .11
❑ 208 Chad Kreuter ......................... .25 .11
❑ 209 Jeff Montgomery .................... .25 .11
❑ 210 Joe Randa ............................. .75 .35
❑ 211 Jose Rosado .......................... .25 .11
❑ 212 Rey Sanchez .......................... .25 .11
❑ 213 Scott Service .......................... .25 .11
❑ 214 Tim Spehr ............................... .25 .11
❑ 215 Jeff Suppan ............................ .25 .11
❑ 216 Mike Sweeney ........................ .75 .35
❑ 217 Jay Witasick ........................... .25 .11
❑ 218 Adrian Beltre .......................... .25 .11
❑ 219 Pedro Borbon ......................... .25 .11

❑ 220 Kevin Brown FOIL 10.00 4.50
❑ 221 Mark Grudzielanek .25 .11
❑ 222 Dave Hansen .25 .11
❑ 223 Todd Hundley .25 .11
❑ 224 Eric Karros .75 .35
❑ 225 Raul Mondesi .75 .35
❑ 226 Chan Ho Park .75 .35
❑ 227 Jeff Shaw .25 .11
❑ 228 Gary Sheffield FOIL 10.00 4.50
❑ 229 Ismael Valdes .25 .11
❑ 230 Jose Vizcaino .25 .11
❑ 231 Devon White .25 .11
❑ 232 Eric Young .25 .11
❑ 233 Ron Belliard .25 .11
❑ 234 Sean Berry .25 .11
❑ 235 Jeromy Burnitz FOIL 10.00 4.50
❑ 236 Jeff Cirillo .75 .35
❑ 237 Marquis Grissom .25 .11
❑ 238 Geoff Jenkins .75 .35
❑ 239 Scott Karl .25 .11
❑ 240 Mark Loretta .25 .11
❑ 241 Mike Myers .25 .11
❑ 242 David Nilsson FOIL 5.00 2.20
❑ 243 Hideo Nomo 2.00 .90
❑ 244 Alex Ochoa .25 .11
❑ 245 Jose Valentin .25 .11
❑ 246 Bob Wickman .25 .11
❑ 247 Steve Woodard .25 .11
❑ 248 Chad Allen .25 .11
❑ 249 Ron Coomer .25 .11
❑ 250 Cristian Guzman .25 .11
❑ 251 Denny Hocking .25 .11
❑ 252 Torii Hunter .25 .11
❑ 253 Corey Koskie .25 .11
❑ 254 Matt Lawton .75 .35
❑ 255 Joe Mays .25 .11
❑ 256 Doug Mientkiewicz .25 .11
❑ 257 Eric Milton .25 .11
❑ 258 Brad Radke FOIL 10.00 4.50
❑ 259 Terry Steinbach .25 .11
❑ 260 Mike Trombley .25 .11
❑ 261 Todd Walker .25 .11
❑ 262 Bob Wells .25 .11
❑ 263 Shane Andrews .25 .11
❑ 264 Michael Barrett .25 .11
❑ 265 Orlando Cabrera .25 .11
❑ 266 Brad Fullmer .75 .35
❑ 267 Vladimir Guerrero FOIL 15.00 6.75
❑ 268 Wilton Guerrero .25 .11
❑ 269 Dustin Hermanson .25 .11
❑ 270 Steve Kline .25 .11
❑ 271 Manny Martinez .25 .11
❑ 272 Mike Thurman .25 .11
❑ 273 Ugueth Urbina .25 .11
❑ 274 Javier Vazquez .25 .11
❑ 275 Jose Vidro .75 .35
❑ 276 Rondell White .75 .35
❑ 277 Chris Widger .25 .11
❑ 278 Edgardo Alfonzo FOIL 10.00 4.50
❑ 279 Armando Benitez .75 .35
❑ 280 Roger Cedeno .25 .11
❑ 281 Dennis Cook .25 .11
❑ 282 Shawon Dunston .25 .11
❑ 283 Matt Franco .25 .11
❑ 284 Darryl Hamilton .25 .11
❑ 285 Rickey Henderson FOIL 15.00 6.75
❑ 286 Orel Hershiser .75 .35
❑ 287 Al Leiter .75 .35
❑ 288 John Olerud .75 .35
❑ 289 Rey Ordonez .25 .11
❑ 290 Mike Piazza FOIL 15.00 6.75
❑ 291 Kenny Rogers .25 .11
❑ 292 Robin Ventura 1.25 .55
❑ 293 Turk Wendell .25 .11
❑ 294 Masato Yoshii .25 .11
❑ 295 Scott Brosius .25 .11
❑ 296 Roger Clemens FOIL 12.00 5.50
❑ 297 David Cone FOIL 3.00 1.35
❑ 298 Chad Curtis .25 .11
❑ 299 Chili Davis .75 .35
❑ 300 Orlando Hernandez .75 .35
❑ 301 Derek Jeter FOIL 20.00 9.00
❑ 302 Chuck Knoblauch .75 .35
❑ 303 Ricky Ledee .25 .11
❑ 304 Tino Martinez .75 .35
❑ 305 Ramiro Mendoza .25 .11
❑ 306 Paul O'Neill .75 .35
❑ 307 Andy Pettitte .75 .35
❑ 308 Jorge Posada .75 .35
❑ 309 Mariano Rivera FOIL 10.00 4.50
❑ 310 Mike Stanton .25 .11
❑ 311 Bernie Williams FOIL 10.00 4.50
❑ 312 Kevin Appier .25 .11
❑ 313 Eric Chavez .75 .35
❑ 314 Ryan Christenson .25 .11
❑ 315 Jason Giambi FOIL 10.00 4.50
❑ 316 Ben Grieve .75 .35
❑ 317 Buddy Groom .25 .11
❑ 318 Gil Heredia .25 .11
❑ 319 A.J. Hinch .25 .11
❑ 320 John Jaha .25 .11
❑ 321 Doug Jones .25 .11
❑ 322 Omar Olivares .25 .11
❑ 323 Tony Phillips .25 .11
❑ 324 Matt Stairs .25 .11
❑ 325 Miguel Tejada .75 .35
❑ 326 Randy Velarde FOIL 5.00 2.20
❑ 327 Bobby Abreu FOIL 10.00 4.50
❑ 328 Marlon Anderson .25 .11
❑ 329 Alex Arias .25 .11
❑ 330 Rico Brogna .25 .11
❑ 331 Paul Byrd .25 .11
❑ 332 Ron Gant .25 .11
❑ 333 Doug Glanville .25 .11
❑ 334 Wayne Gomes .25 .11
❑ 335 Kevin Jordan .25 .11
❑ 336 Mike Lieberthal .75 .35
❑ 337 Steve Montgomery .25 .11
❑ 338 Chad Ogea .25 .11
❑ 339 Scott Rolen 2.00 .90
❑ 340 Curt Schilling FOIL 10.00 4.50
❑ 341 Kevin Sefcik .25 .11
❑ 342 Mike Benjamin .25 .11
❑ 343 Kris Benson .75 .35
❑ 344 Adrian Brown .25 .11
❑ 345 Brant Brown .25 .11
❑ 345 Tom Goodwin .25 .11
❑ 346 Brad Clontz .25 .11
❑ 347 Brian Giles FOIL 10.00 4.50
❑ 348 Jason Kendall FOIL 10.00 4.50
❑ 349 Al Martin .25 .11
❑ 350 Warren Morris .25 .11
❑ 351 Todd Ritchie .25 .11
❑ 352 Scott Sauerbeck .25 .11
❑ 353 Jason Schmidt .25 .11
❑ 354 Ed Sprague .25 .11
❑ 355 Mike Williams .25 .11
❑ 356 Kevin Young .25 .11
❑ 357 Andy Ashby .25 .11
❑ 358 Ben Davis .25 .11
❑ 359 Tony Gwynn FOIL 12.00 5.50
❑ 360 Sterling Hitchcock .25 .11
❑ 361 Trevor Hoffman FOIL 10.00 4.50
❑ 362 Damian Jackson .25 .11
❑ 363 Wally Joyner .75 .35
❑ 364 Phil Nevin .75 .35
❑ 365 Eric Owens .25 .11
❑ 366 Ruben Rivera .25 .11
❑ 367 Reggie Sanders .25 .11
❑ 368 John VanderWal .25 .11
❑ 369 Quilvio Veras .25 .11
❑ 370 Matt Whisenant .25 .11
❑ 371 Woody Williams .25 .11
❑ 372 Rich Aurilia .75 .35
❑ 373 Marvin Benard .25 .11
❑ 374 Barry Bonds FOIL 15.00 6.75
❑ 375 Ellis Burks .25 .11
❑ 376 Alan Embree .25 .11
❑ 377 Shawn Estes .25 .11
❑ 378 John Johnstone .25 .11
❑ 379 Jeff Kent .25 .11
❑ 380 Brent Mayne .25 .11
❑ 381 Bill Mueller .25 .11
❑ 382 Robb Nen .25 .11
❑ 383 Russ Ortiz .25 .11
❑ 384 Kirk Rueter .25 .11
❑ 385 F.P. Santangelo .25 .11
❑ 386 J.T. Snow .75 .35
❑ 387 David Bell .25 .11
❑ 388 Jay Buhner .75 .35
❑ 389 Russ Davis .25 .11
❑ 390 Freddy Garcia .25 .11
❑ 391 Ken Griffey Jr. FOIL 30.00 13.50
❑ 392 John Halama .25 .11
❑ 393 Brian Hunter .25 .11
❑ 394 Raul Ibanez .25 .11
❑ 395 Tom Lampkin .25 .11
❑ 396 Edgar Martinez FOIL 10.00 4.50
❑ 397 Jose Mesa .25 .11
❑ 398 Jamie Moyer .25 .11
❑ 399 Jose Paniagua .25 .11
❑ 400 Alex Rodriguez FOIL 25.00 11.00
❑ 401 Dan Wilson .25 .11
❑ 402 Manny Aybar .25 .11
❑ 403 Ricky Bottalico .25 .11
❑ 404 Kent Bottenfield .25 .11
❑ 405 Darren Bragg .25 .11
❑ 406 Alberto Castillo .25 .11
❑ 407 J.D. Drew 2.00 .90
❑ 408 Jose Jimenez .25 .11
❑ 409 Ray Lankford .75 .35
❑ 410 Joe McEwing .25 .11
❑ 411 Willie McGee .75 .35
❑ 412 Mark McGwire FOIL 40.00 18.00
❑ 413 Darren Oliver .25 .11
❑ 414 Lance Painter .25 .11
❑ 415 Edgar Renteria .25 .11
❑ 416 Fernando Tatis FOIL 10.00 4.50
❑ 417 Wilson Alvarez .25 .11
❑ 418 Rolando Arrojo .25 .11
❑ 419 Wade Boggs 2.50 1.10
❑ 420 Miguel Cairo .25 .11
❑ 421 Jose Canseco FOIL 10.00 4.50
❑ 422 John Flaherty .25 .11
❑ 423 Roberto Hernandez .25 .11
❑ 424 Dave Martinez .25 .11
❑ 425 Fred McGriff 1.25 .55
❑ 426 Paul Sorrento .25 .11
❑ 427 Kevin Stocker .25 .11
❑ 428 Bubba Trammell .25 .11
❑ 429 Rick White .25 .11
❑ 430 Randy Winn .25 .11
❑ 431 Bobby Witt .25 .11
❑ 432 Royce Clayton .25 .11
❑ 433 Tim Crabtree .25 .11
❑ 434 Juan Gonzalez 2.00 .90
❑ 436 Rusty Greer .25 .11
❑ 437 Rick Helling .75 .35
❑ 438 Mark McLemore .25 .11
❑ 439 Mike Morgan .25 .11
❑ 440 Rafael Palmeiro FOIL 10.00 4.50
❑ 441 Ivan Rodriguez FOIL 15.00 6.75
❑ 442 Aaron Sele .25 .11
❑ 443 Lee Stevens .25 .11
❑ 444 Mike Venafro .25 .11
❑ 445 John Wetteland .25 .11
❑ 446 Todd Zeile .75 .35
❑ 447 Jeff Zimmerman FOIL 5.00 2.20
❑ 448 Tony Batista .75 .35
❑ 449 Homer Bush .25 .11
❑ 450 Jose Cruz Jr. .25 .11
❑ 451 Carlos Delgado 2.00 .90
❑ 452 Kelvim Escobar .25 .11
❑ 453 Tony Fernandez FOIL 5.00 2.20
❑ 454 Darrin Fletcher .25 .11
❑ 455 Shawn Green FOIL 10.00 4.50
❑ 456 Pat Hentgen .25 .11
❑ 457 Billy Koch .25 .11
❑ 458 Graeme Lloyd .25 .11
❑ 459 Brian McRae .25 .11
❑ 460 David Segui .25 .11
❑ 461 Shannon Stewart .75 .35
❑ 462 David Wells .25 .11

## 2000 MLB Showdown Pennant Run 1st Edition

| | MINT | NRMT |
|---|---|---|
| COMPLETE SET (150) | 150.00 | 70.00 |
| COMP.SET w/o FOIL (130) | 30.00 | 13.50 |
| COMMON CARD (1-150) | .25 | .11 |
| COMMON FOIL | 5.00 | 2.20 |

❑ 1 Kent Bottenfield .25 .11
❑ 2 Ken Hill .25 .11
❑ 3 Adam Kennedy .75 .35
❑ 4 Ben Molina .75 .35

❑ 5 Scott Spiezio .25 .11
❑ 6 Brian Anderson .25 .11
❑ 7 Erubiel Durazo FOIL 5.00 2.20
❑ 8 Armando Reynoso .25 .11
❑ 9 Russ Springer .25 .11
❑ 10 Todd Stottlemyre .25 .11
❑ 11 Tony Womack .25 .11
❑ 12 Andres Galarraga FOIL 8.00 3.60
❑ 13 Javy Lopez FOIL 5.00 2.20
❑ 14 Kevin McGlinchy .25 .11
❑ 15 Terry Mulholland .25 .11
❑ 16 Reggie Sanders .25 .11
❑ 17 Harold Baines .75 .35
❑ 18 Will Clark 2.00 .90
❑ 19 Mike Trombley .25 .11
❑ 20 Manny Alexander .25 .11
❑ 21 Carl Everett FOIL 5.00 2.20
❑ 22 Ramon Martinez FOIL 5.00 2.20
❑ 23 Bret Saberhagen .75 .35
❑ 24 John Wasdin .25 .11
❑ 25 Joe Girardi .25 .11
❑ 26 Ricky Gutierrez .25 .11
❑ 27 Glenallen Hill .25 .11
❑ 28 Kevin Tapani .25 .11
❑ 29 Kerry Wood FOIL 5.00 2.20
❑ 30 Eric Young .25 .11
❑ 31 Keith Foulke FOIL 5.00 2.20
❑ 32 Mark Johnson .25 .11
❑ 33 Sean Lowe .25 .11
❑ 34 Jose Valentin .25 .11
❑ 35 Dante Bichette .75 .35
❑ 36 Ken Griffey Jr. FOIL 30.00 13.50
❑ 37 Denny Neagle .25 .11
❑ 38 Steve Parris .25 .11
❑ 39 Dennys Reyes .25 .11
❑ 40 Sandy Alomar Jr. .25 .11
❑ 41 Chuck Finley FOIL 5.00 2.20
❑ 42 Steve Karsay .25 .11
❑ 43 Steve Reed .25 .11
❑ 44 Jaret Wright .25 .11
❑ 45 Jeff Cirillo .75 .35
❑ 46 Tom Goodwin .25 .11
❑ 47 Jeffrey Hammonds .75 .35
❑ 48 Mike Lansing .25 .11
❑ 49 Aaron Ledesma .25 .11
❑ 50 Brent Mayne .25 .11
❑ 51 Doug Brocail .25 .11
❑ 52 Robert Fick .25 .11
❑ 53 Juan Gonzalez 2.00 .90
❑ 54 Hideo Nomo 2.00 .90
❑ 55 Luis Polonia .25 .11
❑ 56 Brant Brown .25 .11
❑ 57 Alex Fernandez .25 .11
❑ 58 Cliff Floyd .75 .35
❑ 59 Dan Miceli .25 .11
❑ 60 Vladimir Nunez .25 .11
❑ 61 Moises Alou FOIL 5.00 2.20
❑ 62 Roger Cedeno FOIL 5.00 2.20
❑ 63 Octavio Dotel .25 .11
❑ 64 Mitch Meluskey .25 .11
❑ 65 Daryle Ward .75 .35
❑ 66 Mark Quinn FOIL 5.00 2.20
❑ 67 Brad Rigby .25 .11
❑ 68 Blake Stein .25 .11
❑ 69 Mac Suzuki .25 .11
❑ 70 Terry Adams .25 .11
❑ 71 Darren Dreifort .25 .11
❑ 72 Kevin Elster .25 .11
❑ 73 Shawn Green FOIL 10.00 4.50
❑ 74 Todd Hollandsworth .25 .11
❑ 75 Gregg Olson .25 .11
❑ 76 Kevin Barker .25 .11
❑ 77 Jose Hernandez .25 .11
❑ 78 Dave Weathers .25 .11
❑ 79 Hector Carrasco .25 .11
❑ 80 Eddie Guardado .25 .11
❑ 81 Jacque Jones .75 .35
❑ 82 David Ortiz .25 .11
❑ 83 Peter Bergeron .25 .11
❑ 84 Hideki Irabu .25 .11
❑ 85 Lee Stevens .25 .11
❑ 86 Anthony Telford .25 .11
❑ 87 Derek Bell .25 .11
❑ 88 John Franco .75 .35
❑ 89 Mike Hampton FOIL 5.00 2.20
❑ 90 Bobby Jones .25 .11
❑ 91 Todd Pratt .25 .11
❑ 92 Todd Zeile .75 .35
❑ 93 Jason Grimsley .25 .11
❑ 94 Roberto Kelly .25 .11
❑ 95 Jim Leyritz .25 .11
❑ 96 Ramiro Mendoza .25 .11
❑ 97 Rich Becker .25 .11
❑ 98 Ramon Hernandez .25 .11
❑ 99 Tim Hudson FOIL 10.00 4.50
❑ 100 Jason Isringhausen .25 .11
❑ 101 Mike Magnante .25 .11
❑ 102 Olmedo Saenz .25 .11
❑ 103 Mickey Morandini .25 .11
❑ 104 Robert Person .25 .11
❑ 105 Desi Relaford .25 .11
❑ 106 Jason Christiansen .25 .11
❑ 107 Wil Cordero .25 .11
❑ 108 Francisco Cordova .25 .11
❑ 109 Chad Hermansen .25 .11
❑ 110 Pat Meares .25 .11
❑ 111 Aramis Ramirez .25 .11
❑ 112 Bret Boone .75 .35
❑ 113 Matt Clement .25 .11
❑ 114 Carlos Hernandez .25 .11
❑ 115 Ryan Klesko .75 .35
❑ 116 Dave Magadan .25 .11
❑ 117 Al Martin .25 .11
❑ 118 Bobby Estalella .25 .11
❑ 119 Livan Hernandez .25 .11
❑ 120 Doug Mirabelli .25 .11
❑ 121 Joe Nathan .25 .11
❑ 122 Mike Cameron .25 .11
❑ 123 Mark McLemore .25 .11
❑ 124 Gil Meche .75 .35
❑ 125 John Olerud .75 .35
❑ 126 Arthur Rhodes .25 .11
❑ 127 Aaron Sele FOIL 5.00 2.20
❑ 128 Jim Edmonds FOIL 10.00 4.50
❑ 129 Pat Hentgen .25 .11
❑ 130 Darryl Kile .75 .35
❑ 131 Eli Marrero .25 .11
❑ 132 Dave Veres .25 .11
❑ 133 Fernando Vina .25 .11
❑ 134 Vinny Castilla .75 .35
❑ 135 Juan Guzman .25 .11
❑ 136 Ryan Rupe .25 .11
❑ 137 Greg Vaughn FOIL 5.00 2.20
❑ 138 Gerald Williams .25 .11
❑ 139 Esteban Yan .25 .11
❑ 140 Tom Evans .25 .11
❑ 141 Gabe Kapler .75 .35
❑ 142 Ruben Mateo FOIL 5.00 2.20
❑ 143 Kenny Rogers .25 .11
❑ 144 David Segui .25 .11
❑ 145 Tony Batista .75 .35
❑ 146 Chris Carpenter .25 .11
❑ 147 Brad Fullmer .75 .35
❑ 148 Alex Gonzalez .25 .11
❑ 149 Roy Halladay .25 .11
❑ 150 Raul Mondesi FOIL 5.00 2.20

## 1994 Pacific

| | MINT | NRMT |
|---|---|---|
| COMPLETE SET (660) | 40.00 | 18.00 |
| COMMON CARD (1-660) | .10 | .05 |
| COMP.CHECKLIST SET (6) | 2.00 | .90 |
| COMMON CHECKLIST | .40 | .18 |

CL: RANDOM INSERTS IN PACKS

❑ 1 Steve Avery .10 .05
❑ 2 Steve Bedrosian .10 .05
❑ 3 Damon Berryhill .10 .05
❑ 4 Jeff Blauser .10 .05
❑ 5 Sid Bream .10 .05
❑ 6 Francisco Cabrera .10 .05
❑ 7 Ramon Caraballo .10 .05
❑ 8 Ron Gant .20 .09
❑ 9 Tom Glavine .40 .18
❑ 10 Chipper Jones 1.00 .45
❑ 11 Dave Justice .20 .09
❑ 12 Ryan Klesko .20 .09
❑ 13 Mark Lemke .10 .05
❑ 14 Javier Lopez .20 .09
❑ 15 Greg Maddux 1.00 .45
❑ 16 Fred McGriff .20 .09
❑ 17 Greg McMichael .10 .05
❑ 18 Kent Mercker .10 .05
❑ 19 Otis Nixon .10 .05
❑ 20 Terry Pendleton .20 .09
❑ 21 Deion Sanders .20 .09
❑ 22 John Smoltz .20 .09
❑ 23 Tony Tarasco .10 .05
❑ 24 Manny Alexander .10 .05
❑ 25 Brady Anderson .20 .09
❑ 26 Harold Baines .20 .09
❑ 27 Damon Buford .10 .05
❑ 28 Paul Carey .10 .05
❑ 29 Mike Devereaux .10 .05
❑ 30 Todd Frohwirth .10 .05
❑ 31 Leo Gomez .10 .05
❑ 32 Jeffrey Hammonds .20 .09
❑ 33 Chris Hoiles .10 .05
❑ 34 Tim Hulett .10 .05
❑ 35 Ben McDonald .10 .05
❑ 36 Mark McLemore .10 .05
❑ 37 Alan Mills .10 .05
❑ 38 Mike Mussina .40 .18
❑ 39 Sherman Obando .10 .05
❑ 40 Gregg Olson .10 .05
❑ 41 Mike Pagliarulo .10 .05
❑ 42 Jim Poole .10 .05
❑ 43 Harold Reynolds .10 .05
❑ 44 Cal Ripken 1.50 .70
❑ 45 David Segui .10 .05
❑ 46 Fernando Valenzuela .20 .09
❑ 47 Jack Voigt .10 .05
❑ 48 Scott Bankhead .10 .05
❑ 49 Roger Clemens .75 .35
❑ 50 Scott Cooper .10 .05
❑ 51 Danny Darwin .10 .05
❑ 52 Andre Dawson .20 .09
❑ 53 John Dopson .10 .05
❑ 54 Scott Fletcher .10 .05
❑ 55 Tony Fossas .10 .05
❑ 56 Mike Greenwell .10 .05
❑ 57 Billy Hatcher .10 .05
❑ 58 Jeff McNeely .10 .05
❑ 59 Jose Melendez .10 .05
❑ 60 Tim Naehring .10 .05
❑ 61 Tony Pena .10 .05
❑ 62 Paul Quantrill .10 .05
❑ 63 Carlos Quintana .10 .05
❑ 64 Luis Rivera .10 .05
❑ 65 Jeff Russell .10 .05
❑ 66 Aaron Sele .20 .09

| |  |  | | |
|---|---|---|---|---|
| ❑ | 67 | John Valentin | .10 | .05 |
| ❑ | 68 | Mo Vaughn | .20 | .09 |
| ❑ | 69 | Frank Viola | .10 | .05 |
| ❑ | 70 | Bob Zupcic | .10 | .05 |
| ❑ | 71 | Mike Butcher | .10 | .05 |
| ❑ | 72 | Rod Correia | .10 | .05 |
| ❑ | 73 | Chad Curtis | .10 | .05 |
| ❑ | 74 | Chili Davis | .20 | .09 |
| ❑ | 75 | Gary DiSarcina | .10 | .05 |
| ❑ | 76 | Damion Easley | .10 | .05 |
| ❑ | 77 | John Farrell | .10 | .05 |
| ❑ | 78 | Chuck Finley | .20 | .09 |
| ❑ | 79 | Joe Grahe | .10 | .05 |
| ❑ | 80 | Stan Javier | .10 | .05 |
| ❑ | 81 | Mark Langston | .10 | .05 |
| ❑ | 82 | Phil Leftwich RC | .10 | .05 |
| ❑ | 83 | Torey Lovullo | .10 | .05 |
| ❑ | 84 | Joe Magrane | .10 | .05 |
| ❑ | 85 | Greg Myers | .10 | .05 |
| ❑ | 86 | Eduardo Perez | .10 | .05 |
| ❑ | 87 | Luis Polonia | .10 | .05 |
| ❑ | 88 | Tim Salmon | .20 | .09 |
| ❑ | 89 | J.T. Snow | .20 | .09 |
| ❑ | 90 | Kurt Stillwell | .10 | .05 |
| ❑ | 91 | Ron Tingley | .10 | .05 |
| ❑ | 92 | Chris Turner | .10 | .05 |
| ❑ | 93 | Julio Valera | .10 | .05 |
| ❑ | 94 | Jose Bautista | .10 | .05 |
| ❑ | 95 | Shawn Boskie | .10 | .05 |
| ❑ | 96 | Steve Buechele | .10 | .05 |
| ❑ | 97 | Frank Castillo | .10 | .05 |
| ❑ | 98 | Mark Grace UER | .40 | .18 |
| | | (Stats have 98 home runs in 1993; should be 14) | | |
| ❑ | 99 | Jose Guzman | .10 | .05 |
| ❑ | 100 | Mike Harkey | .10 | .05 |
| ❑ | 101 | Greg Hibbard | .10 | .05 |
| ❑ | 102 | Doug Jennings | .10 | .05 |
| ❑ | 103 | Derrick May | .10 | .05 |
| ❑ | 104 | Mike Morgan | .10 | .05 |
| ❑ | 105 | Randy Myers | .10 | .05 |
| ❑ | 106 | Karl Rhodes | .10 | .05 |
| ❑ | 107 | Kevin Roberson | .10 | .05 |
| ❑ | 108 | Rey Sanchez | .10 | .05 |
| ❑ | 109 | Ryne Sandberg | .50 | .23 |
| ❑ | 110 | Tommy Shields | .10 | .05 |
| ❑ | 111 | Dwight Smith | .10 | .05 |
| ❑ | 112 | Sammy Sosa | .75 | .35 |
| ❑ | 113 | Jose Vizcaino | .10 | .05 |
| ❑ | 114 | Turk Wendell | .10 | .05 |
| ❑ | 115 | Rick Wilkins | .10 | .05 |
| ❑ | 116 | Willie Wilson | .10 | .05 |
| ❑ | 117 | Eduardo Zambrano RC | .10 | .05 |
| ❑ | 118 | Wilson Alvarez | .10 | .05 |
| ❑ | 119 | Tim Belcher | .10 | .05 |
| ❑ | 120 | Jason Bere | .10 | .05 |
| ❑ | 121 | Rodney Bolton | .10 | .05 |
| ❑ | 122 | Ellis Burks | .20 | .09 |
| ❑ | 123 | Joey Cora | .10 | .05 |
| ❑ | 124 | Alex Fernandez | .10 | .05 |
| ❑ | 125 | Ozzie Guillen | .10 | .05 |
| ❑ | 126 | Craig Grebeck | .10 | .05 |
| ❑ | 127 | Roberto Hernandez | .10 | .05 |
| ❑ | 128 | Bo Jackson | .20 | .09 |
| ❑ | 129 | Lance Johnson | .10 | .05 |
| ❑ | 130 | Ron Karkovice | .10 | .05 |
| ❑ | 131 | Mike LaValliere | .10 | .05 |
| ❑ | 132 | Norberto Martin | .10 | .05 |
| ❑ | 133 | Kirk McCaskill | .10 | .05 |
| ❑ | 134 | Jack McDowell | .10 | .05 |
| ❑ | 135 | Scott Radinsky | .10 | .05 |
| ❑ | 136 | Tim Raines | .20 | .09 |
| ❑ | 137 | Steve Sax | .10 | .05 |
| ❑ | 138 | Frank Thomas | .75 | .35 |
| ❑ | 139 | Dan Pasqua | .10 | .05 |
| ❑ | 140 | Robin Ventura | .20 | .09 |
| ❑ | 141 | Jeff Branson | .10 | .05 |
| ❑ | 142 | Tom Browning | .10 | .05 |
| ❑ | 143 | Jacob Brumfield | .10 | .05 |
| ❑ | 144 | Tim Costo | .10 | .05 |
| ❑ | 145 | Rob Dibble | .10 | .05 |
| ❑ | 146 | Brian Dorsett | .10 | .05 |
| ❑ | 147 | Steve Foster | .10 | .05 |
| ❑ | 148 | Cesar Hernandez | .10 | .05 |
| ❑ | 149 | Roberto Kelly | .10 | .05 |
| ❑ | 150 | Barry Larkin | .40 | .18 |
| ❑ | 151 | Larry Luebbers | .10 | .05 |
| ❑ | 152 | Kevin Mitchell | .10 | .05 |
| ❑ | 153 | Joe Oliver | .10 | .05 |
| ❑ | 154 | Tim Pugh | .10 | .05 |
| ❑ | 155 | Jeff Reardon | .20 | .09 |
| ❑ | 156 | Jose Rijo | .10 | .05 |
| ❑ | 157 | Bip Roberts | .10 | .05 |
| ❑ | 158 | Chris Sabo | .10 | .05 |
| ❑ | 159 | Juan Samuel | .10 | .05 |
| ❑ | 160 | Reggie Sanders | .10 | .05 |
| ❑ | 161 | John Smiley | .10 | .05 |
| ❑ | 162 | Jerry Spradlin | .10 | .05 |
| ❑ | 163 | Gary Varsho | .10 | .05 |
| ❑ | 164 | Sandy Alomar Jr. | .20 | .09 |
| ❑ | 165 | Albert Belle | .20 | .09 |
| ❑ | 166 | Carlos Baerga | .10 | .05 |
| ❑ | 167 | Mark Clark | .10 | .05 |
| ❑ | 168 | Alvaro Espinoza | .10 | .05 |
| ❑ | 169 | Felix Fermin | .10 | .05 |
| ❑ | 170 | Reggie Jefferson | .10 | .05 |
| ❑ | 171 | Wayne Kirby | .10 | .05 |
| ❑ | 172 | Tom Kramer | .10 | .05 |
| ❑ | 173 | Kenny Lofton | .20 | .09 |
| ❑ | 174 | Jesse Levis | .10 | .05 |
| ❑ | 175 | Candy Maldonado | .10 | .05 |
| ❑ | 176 | Carlos Martinez | .10 | .05 |
| ❑ | 177 | Jose Mesa | .10 | .05 |
| ❑ | 178 | Jeff Mutis | .10 | .05 |
| ❑ | 179 | Charles Nagy | .10 | .05 |
| ❑ | 180 | Bob Ojeda | .10 | .05 |
| ❑ | 181 | Junior Ortiz | .10 | .05 |
| ❑ | 182 | Eric Plunk | .10 | .05 |
| ❑ | 183 | Manny Ramirez | .60 | .25 |
| ❑ | 184 | Paul Sorrento | .10 | .05 |
| ❑ | 185 | Jeff Treadway | .10 | .05 |
| ❑ | 186 | Bill Wertz | .10 | .05 |
| ❑ | 187 | Freddie Benavides | .10 | .05 |
| ❑ | 188 | Dante Bichette | .20 | .09 |
| ❑ | 189 | Willie Blair | .10 | .05 |
| ❑ | 190 | Daryl Boston | .10 | .05 |
| ❑ | 191 | Pedro Castellano | .10 | .05 |
| ❑ | 192 | Vinny Castilla | .20 | .09 |
| ❑ | 193 | Jerald Clark | .10 | .05 |
| ❑ | 194 | Alex Cole | .10 | .05 |
| ❑ | 195 | Andres Galarraga | .20 | .09 |
| ❑ | 196 | Joe Girardi | .10 | .05 |
| ❑ | 197 | Charlie Hayes | .10 | .05 |
| ❑ | 198 | Darren Holmes | .10 | .05 |
| ❑ | 199 | Chris Jones | .10 | .05 |
| ❑ | 200 | Curt Leskanic | .10 | .05 |
| ❑ | 201 | Roberto Mejia | .10 | .05 |
| ❑ | 202 | David Nied | .10 | .05 |
| ❑ | 203 | J. Owens | .10 | .05 |
| ❑ | 204 | Steve Reed | .10 | .05 |
| ❑ | 205 | Armando Reynoso | .10 | .05 |
| ❑ | 206 | Bruce Ruffin | .10 | .05 |
| ❑ | 207 | Keith Shepherd | .10 | .05 |
| ❑ | 208 | Jim Tatum | .10 | .05 |
| ❑ | 209 | Eric Young | .10 | .05 |
| ❑ | 210 | Skeeter Barnes | .10 | .05 |
| ❑ | 211 | Danny Bautista | .10 | .05 |
| ❑ | 212 | Tom Bolton | .10 | .05 |
| ❑ | 213 | Eric Davis | .20 | .09 |
| ❑ | 214 | Storm Davis | .10 | .05 |
| ❑ | 215 | Cecil Fielder | .20 | .09 |
| ❑ | 216 | Travis Fryman | .20 | .09 |
| ❑ | 217 | Kirk Gibson | .20 | .09 |
| ❑ | 218 | Dan Gladden | .10 | .05 |
| ❑ | 219 | John Doherty | .10 | .05 |
| ❑ | 220 | Chris Gomez | .10 | .05 |
| ❑ | 221 | David Haas | .10 | .05 |
| ❑ | 222 | Bill Krueger | .10 | .05 |
| ❑ | 223 | Chad Kreuter | .10 | .05 |
| ❑ | 224 | Mark Leiter | .10 | .05 |
| ❑ | 225 | Bob MacDonald | .10 | .05 |
| ❑ | 226 | Mike Moore | .10 | .05 |
| ❑ | 227 | Tony Phillips | .10 | .05 |
| ❑ | 228 | Rich Rowland | .10 | .05 |
| ❑ | 229 | Mickey Tettleton | .10 | .05 |
| ❑ | 230 | Alan Trammell | .20 | .09 |
| ❑ | 231 | Lou Whitaker | .20 | .09 |
| ❑ | 232 | David Wells | .20 | .09 |
| ❑ | 233 | Luis Aquino | .10 | .05 |
| ❑ | 234 | Alex Arias | .10 | .05 |
| ❑ | 235 | Jack Armstrong | .10 | .05 |
| ❑ | 236 | Ryan Bowen | .10 | .05 |
| ❑ | 237 | Chuck Carr | .10 | .05 |
| ❑ | 238 | Matias Carrillo | .10 | .05 |
| ❑ | 239 | Jeff Conine | .10 | .05 |
| ❑ | 240 | Henry Cotto | .10 | .05 |
| ❑ | 241 | Orestes Destrade | .10 | .05 |
| ❑ | 242 | Chris Hammond | .10 | .05 |
| ❑ | 243 | Bryan Harvey | .10 | .05 |
| ❑ | 244 | Charlie Hough | .20 | .09 |
| ❑ | 245 | Richie Lewis | .10 | .05 |
| ❑ | 246 | Mitch Lyden | .10 | .05 |
| ❑ | 247 | Dave Magadan | .10 | .05 |
| ❑ | 248 | Bob Natal | .10 | .05 |
| ❑ | 249 | Benito Santiago | .10 | .05 |
| ❑ | 250 | Gary Sheffield | .40 | .18 |
| ❑ | 251 | Matt Turner | .10 | .05 |
| ❑ | 252 | David Weathers | .10 | .05 |
| ❑ | 253 | Walt Weiss | .10 | .05 |
| ❑ | 254 | Darrell Whitmore | .10 | .05 |
| ❑ | 255 | Nigel Wilson | .10 | .05 |
| ❑ | 256 | Eric Anthony | .10 | .05 |
| ❑ | 257 | Jeff Bagwell | .50 | .23 |
| ❑ | 258 | Kevin Bass | .10 | .05 |
| ❑ | 259 | Craig Biggio | .20 | .09 |
| ❑ | 260 | Ken Caminiti | .20 | .09 |
| ❑ | 261 | Andujar Cedeno | .10 | .05 |
| ❑ | 262 | Chris Donnels | .10 | .05 |
| ❑ | 263 | Doug Drabek | .10 | .05 |
| ❑ | 264 | Tom Edens | .10 | .05 |
| ❑ | 265 | Steve Finley | .20 | .09 |
| ❑ | 266 | Luis Gonzalez | .20 | .09 |
| ❑ | 267 | Pete Harnisch | .10 | .05 |
| ❑ | 268 | Xavier Hernandez | .10 | .05 |
| ❑ | 269 | Todd Jones | .10 | .05 |
| ❑ | 270 | Darryl Kile | .20 | .09 |
| ❑ | 271 | Al Osuna | .10 | .05 |
| ❑ | 272 | Rick Parker | .10 | .05 |
| ❑ | 273 | Mark Portugal | .10 | .05 |
| ❑ | 274 | Scott Servais | .10 | .05 |
| ❑ | 275 | Greg Swindell | .10 | .05 |
| ❑ | 276 | Eddie Taubensee | .10 | .05 |
| ❑ | 277 | Jose Uribe | .10 | .05 |
| ❑ | 278 | Brian Williams | .10 | .05 |
| ❑ | 279 | Kevin Appier | .20 | .09 |
| ❑ | 280 | Billy Brewer | .10 | .05 |
| ❑ | 281 | David Cone | .20 | .09 |
| ❑ | 282 | Greg Gagne | .10 | .05 |
| ❑ | 283 | Tom Gordon | .10 | .05 |
| ❑ | 284 | Chris Gwynn | .10 | .05 |
| ❑ | 285 | John Habyan | .10 | .05 |
| ❑ | 286 | Chris Haney | .10 | .05 |
| ❑ | 287 | Phil Hiatt | .10 | .05 |
| ❑ | 288 | David Howard | .10 | .05 |
| ❑ | 289 | Felix Jose | .10 | .05 |
| ❑ | 290 | Wally Joyner | .20 | .09 |
| ❑ | 291 | Kevin Koslofski | .10 | .05 |
| ❑ | 292 | Jose Lind | .10 | .05 |
| ❑ | 293 | Brent Mayne | .10 | .05 |
| ❑ | 294 | Mike Macfarlane | .10 | .05 |
| ❑ | 295 | Brian McRae | .10 | .05 |
| ❑ | 296 | Kevin McReynolds | .10 | .05 |
| ❑ | 297 | Keith Miller | .10 | .05 |
| ❑ | 298 | Jeff Montgomery | .10 | .05 |
| ❑ | 299 | Hipolito Pichardo | .10 | .05 |
| ❑ | 300 | Rico Rossy | .10 | .05 |
| ❑ | 301 | Curtis Wilkerson | .10 | .05 |
| ❑ | 302 | Pedro Astacio | .10 | .05 |
| ❑ | 303 | Rafael Bournigal | .10 | .05 |
| ❑ | 304 | Brett Butler | .20 | .09 |
| ❑ | 305 | Tom Candiotti | .10 | .05 |
| ❑ | 306 | Omar Daal | .10 | .05 |
| ❑ | 307 | Jim Gott | .10 | .05 |
| ❑ | 308 | Kevin Gross | .10 | .05 |
| ❑ | 309 | Dave Hansen | .10 | .05 |
| ❑ | 310 | Carlos Hernandez | .10 | .05 |
| ❑ | 311 | Orel Hershiser | .20 | .09 |
| ❑ | 312 | Eric Karros | .20 | .09 |
| ❑ | 313 | Pedro Martinez | .60 | .25 |
| ❑ | 314 | Ramon Martinez | .10 | .05 |
| ❑ | 315 | Roger McDowell | .10 | .05 |
| ❑ | 316 | Raul Mondesi | .20 | .09 |
| ❑ | 317 | Jose Offerman | .10 | .05 |
| ❑ | 318 | Mike Piazza | 1.25 | .55 |
| ❑ | 319 | Jody Reed | .10 | .05 |
| ❑ | 320 | Henry Rodriguez | .10 | .05 |
| ❑ | 321 | Cory Snyder | .10 | .05 |
| ❑ | 322 | Darryl Strawberry | .20 | .09 |

| Card | Player | | |
|---|---|---|---|
| ❑ 323 | Tim Wallach | .10 | .05 |
| ❑ 324 | Steve Wilson | .10 | .05 |
| ❑ 325 | Juan Bell | .10 | .05 |
| ❑ 326 | Ricky Bones | .10 | .05 |
| ❑ 327 | Alex Diaz RC | .10 | .05 |
| ❑ 328 | Cal Eldred | .10 | .05 |
| ❑ 329 | Darryl Hamilton | .10 | .05 |
| ❑ 330 | Doug Henry | .10 | .05 |
| ❑ 331 | John Jaha | .10 | .05 |
| ❑ 332 | Pat Listach | .10 | .05 |
| ❑ 333 | Graeme Lloyd | .10 | .05 |
| ❑ 334 | Carlos Maldonado | .10 | .05 |
| ❑ 335 | Angel Miranda | .10 | .05 |
| ❑ 336 | Jaime Navarro | .10 | .05 |
| ❑ 337 | Dave Nilsson | .10 | .05 |
| ❑ 338 | Rafael Novoa | .10 | .05 |
| ❑ 339 | Troy O'Leary | .10 | .05 |
| ❑ 340 | Jesse Orosco | .10 | .05 |
| ❑ 341 | Kevin Seitzer | .10 | .05 |
| ❑ 342 | Bill Spiers | .10 | .05 |
| ❑ 343 | William Suero | .10 | .05 |
| ❑ 344 | B.J. Surhoff | .20 | .09 |
| ❑ 345 | Dickie Thon | .10 | .05 |
| ❑ 346 | Jose Valentin | .10 | .05 |
| ❑ 347 | Greg Vaughn | .20 | .09 |
| ❑ 348 | Robin Yount | .40 | .18 |
| ❑ 349 | Willie Banks | .10 | .05 |
| ❑ 350 | Bernardo Brito | .10 | .05 |
| ❑ 351 | Scott Erickson | .10 | .05 |
| ❑ 352 | Mark Guthrie | .10 | .05 |
| ❑ 353 | Chip Hale | .10 | .05 |
| ❑ 354 | Brian Harper | .10 | .05 |
| ❑ 355 | Kent Hrbek | .20 | .09 |
| ❑ 356 | Terry Jorgensen | .10 | .05 |
| ❑ 357 | Chuck Knoblauch | .20 | .09 |
| ❑ 358 | Gene Larkin | .10 | .05 |
| ❑ 359 | Scott Leius | .10 | .05 |
| ❑ 360 | Shane Mack | .10 | .05 |
| ❑ 361 | David McCarty | .10 | .05 |
| ❑ 362 | Pat Meares | .10 | .05 |
| ❑ 363 | Pedro Munoz | .10 | .05 |
| ❑ 364 | Derek Parks | .10 | .05 |
| ❑ 365 | Kirby Puckett | 1.00 | .45 |
| ❑ 366 | Jeff Reboulet | .10 | .05 |
| ❑ 367 | Kevin Tapani | .10 | .05 |
| ❑ 368 | Mike Trombley | .10 | .05 |
| ❑ 369 | George Tsamis | .10 | .05 |
| ❑ 370 | Carl Willis | .10 | .05 |
| ❑ 371 | Dave Winfield | .40 | .18 |
| ❑ 372 | Moises Alou | .20 | .09 |
| ❑ 373 | Brian Barnes | .10 | .05 |
| ❑ 374 | Sean Berry | .10 | .05 |
| ❑ 375 | Frank Bolick | .10 | .05 |
| ❑ 376 | Wil Cordero | .10 | .05 |
| ❑ 377 | Delino DeShields | .10 | .05 |
| ❑ 378 | Jeff Fassero | .10 | .05 |
| ❑ 379 | Darrin Fletcher | .10 | .05 |
| ❑ 380 | Cliff Floyd | .20 | .09 |
| ❑ 381 | Lou Frazier | .10 | .05 |
| ❑ 382 | Marquis Grissom | .10 | .05 |
| ❑ 383 | Gil Heredia | .10 | .05 |
| ❑ 384 | Mike Lansing | .10 | .05 |
| ❑ 385 | Oreste Marrero RC | .10 | .05 |
| ❑ 386 | Dennis Martinez | .20 | .09 |
| ❑ 387 | Curtis Pride RC | .10 | .05 |
| ❑ 388 | Mel Rojas | .10 | .05 |
| ❑ 389 | Kirk Rueter | .10 | .05 |
| ❑ 390 | Joe Siddall | .10 | .05 |
| ❑ 391 | John Vander Wal | .10 | .05 |
| ❑ 392 | Larry Walker | .20 | .09 |
| ❑ 393 | John Wetteland | .20 | .09 |
| ❑ 394 | Rondell White | .20 | .09 |
| ❑ 395 | Tim Bogar | .10 | .05 |
| ❑ 396 | Bobby Bonilla | .20 | .09 |
| ❑ 397 | Jeromy Burnitz | .20 | .09 |
| ❑ 398 | Mike Draper | .10 | .05 |
| ❑ 399 | Sid Fernandez | .10 | .05 |
| ❑ 400 | John Franco | .20 | .09 |
| ❑ 401 | Dave Gallagher | .10 | .05 |
| ❑ 402 | Dwight Gooden | .20 | .09 |
| ❑ 403 | Eric Hillman | .10 | .05 |
| ❑ 404 | Todd Hundley | .10 | .05 |
| ❑ 405 | Butch Huskey | .10 | .05 |
| ❑ 406 | Jeff Innis | .10 | .05 |
| ❑ 407 | Howard Johnson | .10 | .05 |
| ❑ 408 | Jeff Kent | .20 | .09 |
| ❑ 409 | Ced Landrum | .10 | .05 |
| ❑ 410 | Mike Maddux | .10 | .05 |
| ❑ 411 | Josias Manzanillo | .10 | .05 |
| ❑ 412 | Jeff McKnight | .10 | .05 |
| ❑ 413 | Eddie Murray | .40 | .18 |
| ❑ 414 | Tito Navarro | .10 | .05 |
| ❑ 415 | Joe Orsulak | .10 | .05 |
| ❑ 416 | Bret Saberhagen | .20 | .09 |
| ❑ 417 | Dave Telgheder | .10 | .05 |
| ❑ 418 | Ryan Thompson | .10 | .05 |
| ❑ 419 | Chico Walker | .10 | .05 |
| ❑ 420 | Jim Abbott | .20 | .09 |
| ❑ 421 | Wade Boggs | .50 | .23 |
| ❑ 422 | Mike Gallego | .10 | .05 |
| ❑ 423 | Mark Hutton | .10 | .05 |
| ❑ 424 | Dion James | .10 | .05 |
| ❑ 425 | Domingo Jean | .10 | .05 |
| ❑ 426 | Pat Kelly | .10 | .05 |
| ❑ 427 | Jimmy Key | .20 | .09 |
| ❑ 428 | Jim Leyritz | .10 | .05 |
| ❑ 429 | Kevin Maas | .10 | .05 |
| ❑ 430 | Don Mattingly | 1.00 | .45 |
| ❑ 431 | Bobby Munoz | .10 | .05 |
| ❑ 432 | Matt Nokes | .10 | .05 |
| ❑ 433 | Paul O'Neill | .20 | .09 |
| ❑ 434 | Spike Owen | .10 | .05 |
| ❑ 435 | Melido Perez | .10 | .05 |
| ❑ 436 | Lee Smith | .20 | .09 |
| ❑ 437 | Andy Stankiewicz | .10 | .05 |
| ❑ 438 | Mike Stanley | .10 | .05 |
| ❑ 439 | Danny Tartabull | .10 | .05 |
| ❑ 440 | Randy Velarde | .10 | .05 |
| ❑ 441 | Bernie Williams | .40 | .18 |
| ❑ 442 | Gerald Williams | .10 | .05 |
| ❑ 443 | Mike Witt | .10 | .05 |
| ❑ 444 | Marcos Armas | .10 | .05 |
| ❑ 445 | Lance Blankenship | .10 | .05 |
| ❑ 446 | Mike Bordick | .10 | .05 |
| ❑ 447 | Ron Darling UER<br>(Reversed negative on front) | .10 | .05 |
| ❑ 448 | Dennis Eckersley | .20 | .09 |
| ❑ 449 | Brent Gates | .10 | .05 |
| ❑ 450 | Rich Gossage | .20 | .09 |
| ❑ 451 | Scott Hemond | .10 | .05 |
| ❑ 452 | Dave Henderson | .10 | .05 |
| ❑ 453 | Shawn Hillegas | .10 | .05 |
| ❑ 454 | Rick Honeycutt | .10 | .05 |
| ❑ 455 | Scott Lydy | .10 | .05 |
| ❑ 456 | Mark McGwire | 1.50 | .70 |
| ❑ 457 | Henry Mercedes | .10 | .05 |
| ❑ 458 | Mike Mohler | .10 | .05 |
| ❑ 459 | Troy Neel | .10 | .05 |
| ❑ 460 | Edwin Nunez | .10 | .05 |
| ❑ 461 | Craig Paquette | .10 | .05 |
| ❑ 462 | Ruben Sierra | .10 | .05 |
| ❑ 463 | Terry Steinbach | .10 | .05 |
| ❑ 464 | Todd Van Poppel | .10 | .05 |
| ❑ 465 | Bob Welch | .10 | .05 |
| ❑ 466 | Bobby Witt | .10 | .05 |
| ❑ 467 | Ruben Amaro | .10 | .05 |
| ❑ 468 | Larry Andersen | .10 | .05 |
| ❑ 469 | Kim Batiste | .10 | .05 |
| ❑ 470 | Wes Chamberlain | .10 | .05 |
| ❑ 471 | Darren Daulton | .20 | .09 |
| ❑ 472 | Mariano Duncan | .10 | .05 |
| ❑ 473 | Len Dykstra | .20 | .09 |
| ❑ 474 | Jim Eisenreich | .10 | .05 |
| ❑ 475 | Tommy Greene | .10 | .05 |
| ❑ 476 | Dave Hollins | .10 | .05 |
| ❑ 477 | Pete Incaviglia | .10 | .05 |
| ❑ 478 | Danny Jackson | .10 | .05 |
| ❑ 479 | John Kruk | .20 | .09 |
| ❑ 480 | Tony Longmire | .10 | .05 |
| ❑ 481 | Jeff Manto | .10 | .05 |
| ❑ 482 | Mickey Morandini | .10 | .05 |
| ❑ 483 | Terry Mulholland | .10 | .05 |
| ❑ 484 | Todd Pratt | .10 | .05 |
| ❑ 485 | Ben Rivera | .10 | .05 |
| ❑ 486 | Curt Schilling | .20 | .09 |
| ❑ 487 | Kevin Stocker | .10 | .05 |
| ❑ 488 | Milt Thompson | .10 | .05 |
| ❑ 489 | David West | .20 | .09 |
| ❑ 490 | Mitch Williams | .10 | .05 |
| ❑ 491 | Jeff Ballard | .10 | .05 |
| ❑ 492 | Jay Bell | .20 | .09 |
| ❑ 493 | Scott Bullett | .10 | .05 |
| ❑ 494 | Dave Clark | .10 | .05 |
| ❑ 495 | Steve Cooke | .10 | .05 |
| ❑ 496 | Midre Cummings | .10 | .05 |
| ❑ 497 | Mark Dewey | .10 | .05 |
| ❑ 498 | Carlos Garcia | .10 | .05 |
| ❑ 499 | Jeff King | .10 | .05 |
| ❑ 500 | Al Martin | .10 | .05 |
| ❑ 501 | Lloyd McClendon | .10 | .05 |
| ❑ 502 | Orlando Merced | .10 | .05 |
| ❑ 503 | Blas Minor | .10 | .05 |
| ❑ 504 | Denny Neagle | .10 | .05 |
| ❑ 505 | Tom Prince | .10 | .05 |
| ❑ 506 | Don Slaught | .10 | .05 |
| ❑ 507 | Zane Smith | .10 | .05 |
| ❑ 508 | Randy Tomlin | .10 | .05 |
| ❑ 509 | Andy Van Slyke | .20 | .09 |
| ❑ 510 | Paul Wagner | .10 | .05 |
| ❑ 511 | Tim Wakefield | .10 | .05 |
| ❑ 512 | Bob Walk | .10 | .05 |
| ❑ 513 | John Wehner | .10 | .05 |
| ❑ 514 | Kevin Young | .10 | .05 |
| ❑ 515 | Billy Bean | .10 | .05 |
| ❑ 516 | Andy Benes | .10 | .05 |
| ❑ 517 | Derek Bell | .10 | .05 |
| ❑ 518 | Doug Brocail | .10 | .05 |
| ❑ 519 | Jarvis Brown | .10 | .05 |
| ❑ 520 | Phil Clark | .10 | .05 |
| ❑ 521 | Mark Davis | .10 | .05 |
| ❑ 522 | Jeff Gardner | .10 | .05 |
| ❑ 523 | Pat Gomez | .10 | .05 |
| ❑ 524 | Ricky Gutierrez | .10 | .05 |
| ❑ 525 | Tony Gwynn | .75 | .35 |
| ❑ 526 | Gene Harris | .10 | .05 |
| ❑ 527 | Kevin Higgins | .10 | .05 |
| ❑ 528 | Trevor Hoffman | .20 | .09 |
| ❑ 529 | Luis Lopez | .10 | .05 |
| ❑ 530 | Pedro A.Martinez RC | .10 | .05 |
| ❑ 531 | Melvin Nieves | .10 | .05 |
| ❑ 532 | Phil Plantier | .10 | .05 |
| ❑ 533 | Frank Seminara | .10 | .05 |
| ❑ 534 | Craig Shipley | .10 | .05 |
| ❑ 535 | Tim Teufel | .10 | .05 |
| ❑ 536 | Guillermo Velasquez | .10 | .05 |
| ❑ 537 | Wally Whitehurst | .10 | .05 |
| ❑ 538 | Rod Beck | .10 | .05 |
| ❑ 539 | Todd Benzinger | .10 | .05 |
| ❑ 540 | Barry Bonds | .60 | .25 |
| ❑ 541 | Jeff Brantley | .10 | .05 |
| ❑ 542 | Dave Burba | .10 | .05 |
| ❑ 543 | John Burkett | .10 | .05 |
| ❑ 544 | Will Clark | .40 | .18 |
| ❑ 545 | Royce Clayton | .10 | .05 |
| ❑ 546 | Bryan Hickerson | .10 | .05 |
| ❑ 547 | Mike Jackson | .10 | .05 |
| ❑ 548 | Darren Lewis | .10 | .05 |
| ❑ 549 | Kirt Manwaring | .10 | .05 |
| ❑ 550 | Dave Martinez | .10 | .05 |
| ❑ 551 | Willie McGee | .20 | .09 |
| ❑ 552 | Jeff Reed | .10 | .05 |
| ❑ 553 | Dave Righetti | .10 | .05 |
| ❑ 554 | Kevin Rogers | .10 | .05 |
| ❑ 555 | Steve Scarsone | .10 | .05 |
| ❑ 556 | Bill Swift | .10 | .05 |
| ❑ 557 | Robby Thompson | .10 | .05 |
| ❑ 558 | Salomon Torres | .10 | .05 |
| ❑ 559 | Matt Williams | .20 | .09 |
| ❑ 560 | Trevor Wilson | .10 | .05 |
| ❑ 561 | Rich Amaral | .10 | .05 |
| ❑ 562 | Mike Blowers | .10 | .05 |
| ❑ 563 | Chris Bosio | .10 | .05 |
| ❑ 564 | Jay Buhner | .20 | .09 |
| ❑ 565 | Norm Charlton | .10 | .05 |
| ❑ 566 | Jim Converse | .10 | .05 |
| ❑ 567 | Rich DeLucia | .10 | .05 |
| ❑ 568 | Mike Felder | .10 | .05 |
| ❑ 569 | Dave Fleming | .10 | .05 |
| ❑ 570 | Ken Griffey Jr. | 1.50 | .70 |
| ❑ 571 | Bill Haselman | .10 | .05 |
| ❑ 572 | Dwayne Henry | .10 | .05 |
| ❑ 573 | Brad Holman | .10 | .05 |
| ❑ 574 | Randy Johnson | .50 | .23 |
| ❑ 575 | Greg Litton | .10 | .05 |
| ❑ 576 | Edgar Martinez | .20 | .09 |
| ❑ 577 | Tino Martinez | .20 | .09 |
| ❑ 578 | Jeff Nelson | .10 | .05 |
| ❑ 579 | Marc Newfield | .10 | .05 |

❑ 580 Roger Salkeld .10 .05
❑ 581 Mackey Sasser .10 .05
❑ 582 Brian Turang RC .10 .05
❑ 583 Omar Vizquel .20 .09
❑ 584 Dave Valle .10 .05
❑ 585 Luis Alicea .10 .05
❑ 586 Rene Arocha .10 .05
❑ 587 Rheal Cormier .10 .05
❑ 588 Tripp Cromer .10 .05
❑ 589 Bernard Gilkey .10 .05
❑ 590 Lee Guetterman .10 .05
❑ 591 Gregg Jefferies .10 .05
❑ 592 Tim Jones .10 .05
❑ 593 Paul Kilgus .10 .05
❑ 594 Les Lancaster .10 .05
❑ 595 Omar Olivares .10 .05
❑ 596 Jose Oquendo .10 .05
❑ 597 Donovan Osborne .10 .05
❑ 598 Tom Pagnozzi .10 .05
❑ 599 Erik Pappas .10 .05
❑ 600 Geronimo Pena .10 .05
❑ 601 Mike Perez .10 .05
❑ 602 Gerald Perry .10 .05
❑ 603 Stan Royer .10 .05
❑ 604 Ozzie Smith .50 .23
❑ 605 Bob Tewksbury .10 .05
❑ 606 Allen Watson .10 .05
❑ 607 Mark Whiten .10 .05
❑ 608 Todd Zeile .10 .05
❑ 609 Jeff Bronkey .10 .05
❑ 610 Kevin Brown .20 .09
❑ 611 Jose Canseco .50 .23
❑ 612 Doug Dascenzo .10 .05
❑ 613 Butch Davis .10 .05
❑ 614 Mario Diaz .10 .05
❑ 615 Julio Franco .10 .05
❑ 616 Benji Gil .10 .05
❑ 617 Juan Gonzalez .40 .18
❑ 618 Tom Henke .10 .05
❑ 619 Jeff Huson .10 .05
❑ 620 David Hulse .10 .05
❑ 621 Craig Lefferts .10 .05
❑ 622 Rafael Palmeiro .40 .18
❑ 623 Dean Palmer .20 .09
❑ 624 Bob Patterson .10 .05
❑ 625 Roger Pavlik .10 .05
❑ 626 Gary Redus .10 .05
❑ 627 Ivan Rodriguez .50 .23
❑ 628 Kenny Rogers .10 .05
❑ 629 Jon Shave .10 .05
❑ 630 Doug Strange .10 .05
❑ 631 Matt Whiteside .10 .05
❑ 632 Roberto Alomar .40 .18
❑ 633 Pat Borders .10 .05
❑ 634 Scott Brow .10 .05
❑ 635 Rob Butler .10 .05
❑ 636 Joe Carter .20 .09
❑ 637 Tony Castillo .10 .05
❑ 638 Mark Eichhorn .10 .05
❑ 639 Tony Fernandez .10 .05
❑ 640 Huck Flener RC .10 .05
❑ 641 Alfredo Griffin .10 .05
❑ 642 Juan Guzman .10 .05
❑ 643 Rickey Henderson .50 .23
❑ 644 Pat Hentgen .10 .05
❑ 645 Randy Knorr .10 .05
❑ 646 Al Leiter .20 .09
❑ 647 Domingo Martinez .10 .05
❑ 648 Paul Molitor .40 .18
❑ 649 Jack Morris .20 .09
❑ 650 John Olerud .20 .09
❑ 651 Ed Sprague .10 .05
❑ 652 Dave Stewart .20 .09
❑ 653 Devon White .10 .05
❑ 654 Woody Williams .10 .05
❑ 655 Barry Bonds MVP .40 .18
❑ 656 Greg Maddux CY .50 .23
❑ 657 Jack McDowell CY .10 .05
❑ 658 Mike Piazza ROY .60 .25
❑ 659 Tim Salmon ROY .20 .09
❑ 660 Frank Thomas MVP .40 .18

## 1995 Pacific

| | MINT | NRMT |
|---|---|---|
| COMPLETE SET (450) | 40.00 | 18.00 |

❑ 1 Steve Avery .10 .05
❑ 2 Rafael Belliard .10 .05
❑ 3 Jeff Blauser .10 .05
❑ 4 Tom Glavine .40 .18
❑ 5 David Justice .20 .09
❑ 6 Mike Kelly .10 .05
❑ 7 Roberto Kelly .10 .05
❑ 8 Ryan Klesko .20 .09
❑ 9 Mark Lemke .10 .05
❑ 10 Javier Lopez .20 .09
❑ 11 Greg Maddux 1.00 .45
❑ 12 Fred McGriff .20 .09
❑ 13 Greg McMichael .10 .05
❑ 14 Jose Oliva .10 .05
❑ 15 John Smoltz .20 .09
❑ 16 Tony Tarasco .10 .05
❑ 17 Brady Anderson .20 .09
❑ 18 Harold Baines .20 .09
❑ 19 Armando Benitez .20 .09
❑ 20 Mike Devereaux .10 .05
❑ 21 Leo Gomez .10 .05
❑ 22 Jeffrey Hammonds .20 .09
❑ 23 Chris Hoiles .10 .05
❑ 24 Ben McDonald .10 .05
❑ 25 Mark McLemore .10 .05
❑ 26 Jamie Moyer .10 .05
❑ 27 Mike Mussina .40 .18
❑ 28 Rafael Palmeiro .40 .18
❑ 29 Jim Poole .10 .05
❑ 30 Cal Ripken Jr. 1.50 .70
❑ 31 Lee Smith .20 .09
❑ 32 Mark Smith .10 .05
❑ 33 Jose Canseco .50 .23
❑ 34 Roger Clemens .75 .35
❑ 35 Scott Cooper .10 .05
❑ 36 Andre Dawson .20 .09
❑ 37 Tony Fossas .10 .05
❑ 38 Mike Greenwell .10 .05
❑ 39 Chris Howard .10 .05
❑ 40 Jose Melendez .10 .05
❑ 41 Nate Minchey .10 .05
❑ 42 Tim Naehring .10 .05
❑ 43 Otis Nixon .10 .05
❑ 44 Carlos Rodriguez .10 .05
❑ 45 Aaron Sele .20 .09
❑ 46 Lee Tinsley .10 .05
❑ 47 Sergio Valdez .10 .05
❑ 48 John Valentin .10 .05
❑ 49 Mo Vaughn .20 .09
❑ 50 Brian Anderson .10 .05
❑ 51 Garret Anderson .20 .09
❑ 52 Rod Correia .10 .05
❑ 53 Chad Curtis .10 .05
❑ 54 Mark Dalesandro .10 .05
❑ 55 Chili Davis .20 .09
❑ 56 Gary DiSarcina .10 .05
❑ 57 Damion Easley .10 .05
❑ 58 Jim Edmonds .40 .18
❑ 59 Jorge Fabregas .10 .05
❑ 60 Chuck Finley .20 .09
❑ 61 Bo Jackson .20 .09
❑ 62 Mark Langston .10 .05
❑ 63 Eduardo Perez .10 .05
❑ 64 Tim Salmon .20 .09
❑ 65 J.T. Snow .20 .09
❑ 66 Willie Banks .10 .05
❑ 67 Jose Bautista .10 .05
❑ 68 Shawon Dunston .10 .05
❑ 69 Kevin Foster .10 .05
❑ 70 Mark Grace .40 .18
❑ 71 Jose Guzman .10 .05
❑ 72 Jose Hernandez .10 .05
❑ 73 Blaise Ilsley .10 .05
❑ 74 Derrick May .10 .05
❑ 75 Randy Myers .10 .05
❑ 76 Karl Rhodes .10 .05
❑ 77 Kevin Roberson .10 .05
❑ 78 Rey Sanchez .10 .05
❑ 79 Sammy Sosa .75 .35
❑ 80 Steve Trachsel .10 .05
❑ 81 Eddie Zambrano .10 .05
❑ 82 Wilson Alvarez .10 .05
❑ 83 Jason Bere .10 .05
❑ 84 Joey Cora .10 .05
❑ 85 Jose DeLeon .10 .05
❑ 86 Alex Fernandez .10 .05
❑ 87 Julio Franco .10 .05
❑ 88 Ozzie Guillen .10 .05
❑ 89 Joe Hall .10 .05
❑ 90 Roberto Hernandez .10 .05
❑ 91 Darrin Jackson .10 .05
❑ 92 Lance Johnson .10 .05
❑ 93 Norberto Martin .10 .05
❑ 94 Jack McDowell .10 .05
❑ 95 Tim Raines .20 .09
❑ 96 Olmedo Saenz .10 .05
❑ 97 Frank Thomas .75 .35
❑ 98 Robin Ventura .20 .09
❑ 99 Bret Boone .20 .09
❑ 100 Jeff Brantley .10 .05
❑ 101 Jacob Brumfield .10 .05
❑ 102 Hector Carrasco .10 .05
❑ 103 Brian Dorsett .10 .05
❑ 104 Tony Fernandez .10 .05
❑ 105 Willie Greene .10 .05
❑ 106 Erik Hanson .10 .05
❑ 107 Kevin Jarvis .10 .05
❑ 108 Barry Larkin .40 .18
❑ 109 Kevin Mitchell .10 .05
❑ 110 Hal Morris .10 .05
❑ 111 Jose Rijo .10 .05
❑ 112 Johnny Ruffin .10 .05
❑ 113 Deion Sanders .20 .09
❑ 114 Reggie Sanders .10 .05
❑ 115 Sandy Alomar Jr. .20 .09
❑ 116 Ruben Amaro .10 .05
❑ 117 Carlos Baerga .10 .05
❑ 118 Albert Belle .20 .09
❑ 119 Alvaro Espinoza .10 .05
❑ 120 Rene Gonzales .10 .05
❑ 121 Wayne Kirby .10 .05
❑ 122 Kenny Lofton .20 .09
❑ 123 Candy Maldonado .10 .05
❑ 124 Dennis Martinez .20 .09
❑ 125 Eddie Murray .40 .18
❑ 126 Charles Nagy .10 .05
❑ 127 Tony Pena .10 .05
❑ 128 Manny Ramirez .50 .23
❑ 129 Paul Sorrento .10 .05
❑ 130 Jim Thome .20 .09
❑ 131 Omar Vizquel .20 .09
❑ 132 Dante Bichette .20 .09
❑ 133 Ellis Burks .20 .09
❑ 134 Vinny Castilla .20 .09
❑ 135 Marvin Freeman .10 .05
❑ 136 Andres Galarraga .20 .09
❑ 137 Joe Girardi .10 .05
❑ 138 Charlie Hayes .10 .05
❑ 139 Mike Kingery .10 .05
❑ 140 Nelson Liriano .10 .05
❑ 141 Roberto Mejia .10 .05
❑ 142 David Nied .10 .05
❑ 143 Steve Reed .10 .05
❑ 144 Armando Reynoso .10 .05
❑ 145 Bruce Ruffin .10 .05
❑ 146 John Vander Wal .10 .05
❑ 147 Walt Weiss .10 .05
❑ 148 Skeeter Barnes .10 .05
❑ 149 Tim Belcher .10 .05
❑ 150 Junior Felix .10 .05
❑ 151 Cecil Fielder .20 .09
❑ 152 Travis Fryman .20 .09
❑ 153 Kirk Gibson .20 .09
❑ 154 Chris Gomez .10 .05

| No. | Player | | |
|---|---|---|---|
| ❑ 155 | Buddy Groom | .10 | .05 |
| ❑ 156 | Chad Kreuter | .10 | .05 |
| ❑ 157 | Mike Moore | .10 | .05 |
| ❑ 158 | Tony Phillips | .10 | .05 |
| ❑ 159 | Juan Samuel | .10 | .05 |
| ❑ 160 | Mickey Tettleton | .10 | .05 |
| ❑ 161 | Alan Trammell | .20 | .09 |
| ❑ 162 | David Wells | .20 | .09 |
| ❑ 163 | Lou Whitaker | .20 | .09 |
| ❑ 164 | Kurt Abbott | .10 | .05 |
| ❑ 165 | Luis Aquino | .10 | .05 |
| ❑ 166 | Alex Arias | .10 | .05 |
| ❑ 167 | Bret Barberie | .10 | .05 |
| ❑ 168 | Jerry Browne | .10 | .05 |
| ❑ 169 | Chuck Carr | .10 | .05 |
| ❑ 170 | Matias Carrillo | .10 | .05 |
| ❑ 171 | Greg Colbrunn | .10 | .05 |
| ❑ 172 | Jeff Conine | .10 | .05 |
| ❑ 173 | Carl Everett | .20 | .09 |
| ❑ 174 | Robb Nen | .10 | .05 |
| ❑ 175 | Yorkis Perez | .10 | .05 |
| ❑ 176 | Pat Rapp | .10 | .05 |
| ❑ 177 | Benito Santiago | .10 | .05 |
| ❑ 178 | Gary Sheffield | .40 | .18 |
| ❑ 179 | Darrell Whitmore | .10 | .05 |
| ❑ 180 | Jeff Bagwell | .50 | .23 |
| ❑ 181 | Kevin Bass | .10 | .05 |
| ❑ 182 | Craig Biggio | .20 | .09 |
| ❑ 183 | Andujar Cedeno | .10 | .05 |
| ❑ 184 | Doug Drabek | .10 | .05 |
| ❑ 185 | Tony Eusebio | .10 | .05 |
| ❑ 186 | Steve Finley | .20 | .09 |
| ❑ 187 | Luis Gonzalez | .10 | .05 |
| ❑ 188 | Pete Harnisch | .10 | .05 |
| ❑ 189 | John Hudek | .10 | .05 |
| ❑ 190 | Orlando Miller | .10 | .05 |
| ❑ 191 | James Mouton | .10 | .05 |
| ❑ 192 | Roberto Petagine | .10 | .05 |
| ❑ 193 | Shane Reynolds | .10 | .05 |
| ❑ 194 | Greg Swindell | .10 | .05 |
| ❑ 195 | Dave Veres | .10 | .05 |
| ❑ 196 | Kevin Appier | .20 | .09 |
| ❑ 197 | Stan Belinda | .10 | .05 |
| ❑ 198 | Vince Coleman | .10 | .05 |
| ❑ 199 | David Cone | .20 | .09 |
| ❑ 200 | Gary Gaetti | .20 | .09 |
| ❑ 201 | Greg Gagne | .10 | .05 |
| ❑ 202 | Mark Gubicza | .10 | .05 |
| ❑ 203 | Bob Hamelin | .10 | .05 |
| ❑ 204 | Dave Henderson | .10 | .05 |
| ❑ 205 | Felix Jose | .10 | .05 |
| ❑ 206 | Wally Joyner | .20 | .09 |
| ❑ 207 | Jose Lind | .10 | .05 |
| ❑ 208 | Mike Macfarlane | .10 | .05 |
| ❑ 209 | Brian McRae | .10 | .05 |
| ❑ 210 | Jeff Montgomery | .10 | .05 |
| ❑ 211 | Hipolito Pichardo | .10 | .05 |
| ❑ 212 | Pedro Astacio | .10 | .05 |
| ❑ 213 | Brett Butler | .20 | .09 |
| ❑ 214 | Omar Daal | .10 | .05 |
| ❑ 215 | Delino DeShields | .10 | .05 |
| ❑ 216 | Darren Dreifort | .20 | .09 |
| ❑ 217 | Carlos Hernandez | .10 | .05 |
| ❑ 218 | Orel Hershiser | .20 | .09 |
| ❑ 219 | Garey Ingram | .10 | .05 |
| ❑ 220 | Eric Karros | .20 | .09 |
| ❑ 221 | Ramon Martinez | .10 | .05 |
| ❑ 222 | Raul Mondesi | .20 | .09 |
| ❑ 223 | Jose Offerman | .10 | .05 |
| ❑ 224 | Mike Piazza | 1.25 | .55 |
| ❑ 225 | Henry Rodriguez | .10 | .05 |
| ❑ 226 | Ismael Valdes | .10 | .05 |
| ❑ 227 | Tim Wallach | .10 | .05 |
| ❑ 228 | Jeff Cirillo | .20 | .09 |
| ❑ 229 | Alex Diaz | .10 | .05 |
| ❑ 230 | Cal Eldred | .10 | .05 |
| ❑ 231 | Mike Fetters | .10 | .05 |
| ❑ 232 | Brian Harper | .10 | .05 |
| ❑ 233 | Ted Higuera | .10 | .05 |
| ❑ 234 | John Jaha | .10 | .05 |
| ❑ 235 | Graeme Lloyd | .10 | .05 |
| ❑ 236 | Jose Mercedes | .10 | .05 |
| ❑ 237 | Jaime Navarro | .10 | .05 |
| ❑ 238 | Dave Nilsson | .10 | .05 |
| ❑ 239 | Jesse Orosco | .10 | .05 |
| ❑ 240 | Jody Reed | .10 | .05 |
| ❑ 241 | Jose Valentin | .10 | .05 |
| ❑ 242 | Greg Vaughn | .20 | .09 |
| ❑ 243 | Turner Ward | .10 | .05 |
| ❑ 244 | Rick Aguilera | .10 | .05 |
| ❑ 245 | Rich Becker | .10 | .05 |
| ❑ 246 | Jim Deshaies | .10 | .05 |
| ❑ 247 | Steve Dunn | .10 | .05 |
| ❑ 248 | Scott Erickson | .10 | .05 |
| ❑ 249 | Kent Hrbek | .10 | .05 |
| ❑ 250 | Chuck Knoblauch | .20 | .09 |
| ❑ 251 | Scott Leius | .10 | .05 |
| ❑ 252 | David McCarty | .10 | .05 |
| ❑ 253 | Pat Meares | .10 | .05 |
| ❑ 254 | Pedro Munoz | .10 | .05 |
| ❑ 255 | Kirby Puckett | 1.00 | .45 |
| ❑ 256 | Carlos Pulido | .10 | .05 |
| ❑ 257 | Kevin Tapani | .10 | .05 |
| ❑ 258 | Matt Walbeck | .10 | .05 |
| ❑ 259 | Dave Winfield | .40 | .18 |
| ❑ 260 | Moises Alou | .20 | .09 |
| ❑ 261 | Juan Bell | .10 | .05 |
| ❑ 262 | Freddie Benavides | .10 | .05 |
| ❑ 263 | Sean Berry | .10 | .05 |
| ❑ 264 | Wil Cordero | .10 | .05 |
| ❑ 265 | Jeff Fassero | .10 | .05 |
| ❑ 266 | Darrin Fletcher | .10 | .05 |
| ❑ 267 | Cliff Floyd | .20 | .09 |
| ❑ 268 | Marquis Grissom | .10 | .05 |
| ❑ 269 | Gil Heredia | .10 | .05 |
| ❑ 270 | Ken Hill | .10 | .05 |
| ❑ 271 | Pedro Martinez | .50 | .23 |
| ❑ 272 | Mel Rojas | .10 | .05 |
| ❑ 273 | Larry Walker | .20 | .09 |
| ❑ 274 | John Wetteland | .20 | .09 |
| ❑ 275 | Rondell White | .20 | .09 |
| ❑ 276 | Tim Bogar | .10 | .05 |
| ❑ 277 | Bobby Bonilla | .20 | .09 |
| ❑ 278 | Rico Brogna | .10 | .05 |
| ❑ 279 | Jeromy Burnitz | .20 | .09 |
| ❑ 280 | John Franco | .20 | .09 |
| ❑ 281 | Eric Hillman | .10 | .05 |
| ❑ 282 | Todd Hundley | .10 | .05 |
| ❑ 283 | Jeff Kent | .20 | .09 |
| ❑ 284 | Mike Maddux | .10 | .05 |
| ❑ 285 | Joe Orsulak | .10 | .05 |
| ❑ 286 | Luis Rivera | .10 | .05 |
| ❑ 287 | Bret Saberhagen | .20 | .09 |
| ❑ 288 | David Segui | .10 | .05 |
| ❑ 289 | Ryan Thompson | .10 | .05 |
| ❑ 290 | Fernando Vina | .10 | .05 |
| ❑ 291 | Jose Vizcaino | .10 | .05 |
| ❑ 292 | Jim Abbott | .20 | .09 |
| ❑ 293 | Wade Boggs | .50 | .23 |
| ❑ 294 | Russ Davis | .10 | .05 |
| ❑ 295 | Mike Gallego | .10 | .05 |
| ❑ 296 | Xavier Hernandez | .10 | .05 |
| ❑ 297 | Steve Howe | .10 | .05 |
| ❑ 298 | Jimmy Key | .20 | .09 |
| ❑ 299 | Don Mattingly | 1.00 | .45 |
| ❑ 300 | Terry Mulholland | .10 | .05 |
| ❑ 301 | Paul O'Neill | .20 | .09 |
| ❑ 302 | Luis Polonia | .10 | .05 |
| ❑ 303 | Mike Stanley | .10 | .05 |
| ❑ 304 | Danny Tartabull | .10 | .05 |
| ❑ 305 | Randy Velarde | .10 | .05 |
| ❑ 306 | Bob Wickman | .10 | .05 |
| ❑ 307 | Bernie Williams | .40 | .18 |
| ❑ 308 | Mark Acre | .10 | .05 |
| ❑ 309 | Geronimo Berroa | .10 | .05 |
| ❑ 310 | Mike Bordick | .10 | .05 |
| ❑ 311 | Dennis Eckersley | .20 | .09 |
| ❑ 312 | Rickey Henderson | .50 | .23 |
| ❑ 313 | Stan Javier | .10 | .05 |
| ❑ 314 | Miguel Jimenez | .10 | .05 |
| ❑ 315 | Francisco Matos RC | .10 | .05 |
| ❑ 316 | Mark McGwire | 1.50 | .70 |
| ❑ 317 | Troy Neel | .10 | .05 |
| ❑ 318 | Steve Ontiveros | .10 | .05 |
| ❑ 319 | Carlos Reyes | .10 | .05 |
| ❑ 320 | Ruben Sierra | .10 | .05 |
| ❑ 321 | Terry Steinbach | .10 | .05 |
| ❑ 322 | Bob Welch | .10 | .05 |
| ❑ 323 | Bobby Witt | .10 | .05 |
| ❑ 324 | Larry Andersen | .10 | .05 |
| ❑ 325 | Kim Batiste | .10 | .05 |
| ❑ 326 | Darren Daulton | .20 | .09 |
| ❑ 327 | Mariano Duncan | .10 | .05 |
| ❑ 328 | Lenny Dykstra | .20 | .09 |
| ❑ 329 | Jim Eisenreich | .10 | .05 |
| ❑ 330 | Danny Jackson | .10 | .05 |
| ❑ 331 | John Kruk | .20 | .09 |
| ❑ 332 | Tony Longmire | .10 | .05 |
| ❑ 333 | Tom Marsh | .10 | .05 |
| ❑ 334 | Mickey Morandini | .10 | .05 |
| ❑ 335 | Bobby Munoz | .10 | .05 |
| ❑ 336 | Todd Pratt | .10 | .05 |
| ❑ 337 | Tom Quinlan | .10 | .05 |
| ❑ 338 | Kevin Stocker | .10 | .05 |
| ❑ 339 | Fernando Valenzuela | .20 | .09 |
| ❑ 340 | Jay Bell | .20 | .09 |
| ❑ 341 | Dave Clark | .10 | .05 |
| ❑ 342 | Steve Cooke | .10 | .05 |
| ❑ 343 | Carlos Garcia | .10 | .05 |
| ❑ 344 | Jeff King | .10 | .05 |
| ❑ 345 | Jon Lieber | .10 | .05 |
| ❑ 346 | Ravelo Manzanillo | .10 | .05 |
| ❑ 347 | Al Martin | .10 | .05 |
| ❑ 348 | Orlando Merced | .10 | .05 |
| ❑ 349 | Denny Neagle | .20 | .09 |
| ❑ 350 | Alejandro Pena | .10 | .05 |
| ❑ 351 | Don Slaught | .10 | .05 |
| ❑ 352 | Zane Smith | .10 | .05 |
| ❑ 353 | Andy Van Slyke | .20 | .09 |
| ❑ 354 | Rick White | .10 | .05 |
| ❑ 355 | Kevin Young | .10 | .05 |
| ❑ 356 | Andy Ashby | .10 | .05 |
| ❑ 357 | Derek Bell | .10 | .05 |
| ❑ 358 | Andy Benes | .10 | .05 |
| ❑ 359 | Phil Clark | .10 | .05 |
| ❑ 360 | Donnie Elliott | .10 | .05 |
| ❑ 361 | Ricky Gutierrez | .10 | .05 |
| ❑ 362 | Tony Gwynn | .75 | .35 |
| ❑ 363 | Trevor Hoffman | .20 | .09 |
| ❑ 364 | Tim Hyers | .10 | .05 |
| ❑ 365 | Luis Lopez | .10 | .05 |
| ❑ 366 | Jose Martinez | .10 | .05 |
| ❑ 367 | Pedro A. Martinez | .10 | .05 |
| ❑ 368 | Phil Plantier | .10 | .05 |
| ❑ 369 | Bip Roberts | .10 | .05 |
| ❑ 370 | A.J. Sager | .10 | .05 |
| ❑ 371 | Jeff Tabaka | .10 | .05 |
| ❑ 372 | Todd Benzinger | .10 | .05 |
| ❑ 373 | Barry Bonds | .60 | .25 |
| ❑ 374 | John Burkett | .10 | .05 |
| ❑ 375 | Mark Carreon | .10 | .05 |
| ❑ 376 | Royce Clayton | .10 | .05 |
| ❑ 377 | Pat Gomez | .10 | .05 |
| ❑ 378 | Erik Johnson | .10 | .05 |
| ❑ 379 | Darren Lewis | .10 | .05 |
| ❑ 380 | Kirt Manwaring | .10 | .05 |
| ❑ 381 | Dave Martinez | .10 | .05 |
| ❑ 382 | John Patterson | .10 | .05 |
| ❑ 383 | Mark Portugal | .10 | .05 |
| ❑ 384 | Darryl Strawberry | .20 | .09 |
| ❑ 385 | Salomon Torres | .10 | .05 |
| ❑ 386 | Wm. VanLandingham | .10 | .05 |
| ❑ 387 | Matt Williams | .20 | .09 |
| ❑ 388 | Rich Amaral | .10 | .05 |
| ❑ 389 | Bobby Ayala | .10 | .05 |
| ❑ 390 | Mike Blowers | .10 | .05 |
| ❑ 391 | Chris Bosio | .10 | .05 |
| ❑ 392 | Jay Buhner | .20 | .09 |
| ❑ 393 | Jim Converse | .10 | .05 |
| ❑ 394 | Tim Davis | .10 | .05 |
| ❑ 395 | Felix Fermin | .10 | .05 |
| ❑ 396 | Dave Fleming | .10 | .05 |
| ❑ 397 | Goose Gossage | .20 | .09 |
| ❑ 398 | Ken Griffey Jr. | 1.50 | .70 |
| ❑ 399 | Randy Johnson | .50 | .23 |
| ❑ 400 | Edgar Martinez | .20 | .09 |
| ❑ 401 | Tino Martinez | .20 | .09 |
| ❑ 402 | Alex Rodriguez | 1.50 | .70 |
| ❑ 403 | Dan Wilson | .10 | .05 |
| ❑ 404 | Luis Alicea | .10 | .05 |
| ❑ 405 | Rene Arocha | .10 | .05 |
| ❑ 406 | Bernard Gilkey | .10 | .05 |
| ❑ 407 | Gregg Jefferies | .10 | .05 |
| ❑ 408 | Ray Lankford | .20 | .09 |
| ❑ 409 | Terry McGriff | .10 | .05 |
| ❑ 410 | Omar Olivares | .10 | .05 |
| ❑ 411 | Jose Oquendo | .10 | .05 |
| ❑ 412 | Vicente Palacios | .10 | .05 |

| | | MINT | NRMT |
|---|---|---|---|
| ❑ 413 | Geronimo Pena | .10 | .05 |
| ❑ 414 | Mike Perez | .10 | .05 |
| ❑ 415 | Gerald Perry | .10 | .05 |
| ❑ 416 | Ozzie Smith | .50 | .23 |
| ❑ 417 | Bob Tewksbury | .10 | .05 |
| ❑ 418 | Mark Whiten | .10 | .05 |
| ❑ 419 | Todd Zeile | .10 | .05 |
| ❑ 420 | Esteban Beltre | .10 | .05 |
| ❑ 421 | Kevin Brown | .20 | .09 |
| ❑ 422 | Cris Carpenter | .10 | .05 |
| ❑ 423 | Will Clark | .40 | .18 |
| ❑ 424 | Hector Fajardo | .10 | .05 |
| ❑ 425 | Jeff Frye | .10 | .05 |
| ❑ 426 | Juan Gonzalez | .40 | .18 |
| ❑ 427 | Rusty Greer | .20 | .09 |
| ❑ 428 | Rick Honeycutt | .10 | .05 |
| ❑ 429 | David Hulse | .10 | .05 |
| ❑ 430 | Manny Lee | .10 | .05 |
| ❑ 431 | Junior Ortiz | .10 | .05 |
| ❑ 432 | Dean Palmer | .20 | .09 |
| ❑ 433 | Ivan Rodriguez | .50 | .23 |
| ❑ 434 | Dan Smith | .10 | .05 |
| ❑ 435 | Roberto Alomar | .40 | .18 |
| ❑ 436 | Pat Borders | .10 | .05 |
| ❑ 437 | Scott Brow | .10 | .05 |
| ❑ 438 | Rob Butler | .10 | .05 |
| ❑ 439 | Joe Carter | .20 | .09 |
| ❑ 440 | Tony Castillo | .10 | .05 |
| ❑ 441 | Domingo Cedeno | .10 | .05 |
| ❑ 442 | Brad Cornett | .10 | .05 |
| ❑ 443 | Carlos Delgado | .40 | .18 |
| ❑ 444 | Alex Gonzalez | .10 | .05 |
| ❑ 445 | Juan Guzman | .10 | .05 |
| ❑ 446 | Darren Hall | .10 | .05 |
| ❑ 447 | Paul Molitor | .40 | .18 |
| ❑ 448 | John Olerud | .20 | .09 |
| ❑ 449 | Robert Perez | .10 | .05 |
| ❑ 450 | Devon White | .20 | .09 |

## 1996 Pacific

| | MINT | NRMT |
|---|---|---|
| COMPLETE SET (450) | 40.00 | 18.00 |

| | | MINT | NRMT |
|---|---|---|---|
| ❑ 1 | Steve Avery | .10 | .05 |
| ❑ 2 | Ryan Klesko | .20 | .09 |
| ❑ 3 | Pedro Borbon | .10 | .05 |
| ❑ 4 | Chipper Jones | 1.00 | .45 |
| ❑ 5 | Kent Mercker | .10 | .05 |
| ❑ 6 | Greg Maddux | 1.00 | .45 |
| ❑ 7 | Greg McMichael | .10 | .05 |
| ❑ 8 | Mark Wohlers | .10 | .05 |
| ❑ 9 | Fred McGriff | .20 | .09 |
| ❑ 10 | John Smoltz | .20 | .09 |
| ❑ 11 | Rafael Belliard | .10 | .05 |
| ❑ 12 | Mark Lemke | .10 | .05 |
| ❑ 13 | Tom Glavine | .40 | .18 |
| ❑ 14 | Javier Lopez | .20 | .09 |
| ❑ 15 | Jeff Blauser | .10 | .05 |
| ❑ 16 | David Justice | .20 | .09 |
| ❑ 17 | Marquis Grissom | .10 | .05 |
| ❑ 18 | Greg Maddux CY | .50 | .23 |
| ❑ 19 | Randy Myers | .10 | .05 |
| ❑ 20 | Scott Servais | .10 | .05 |
| ❑ 21 | Sammy Sosa | .75 | .35 |
| ❑ 22 | Kevin Foster | .10 | .05 |
| ❑ 23 | Jose Hernandez | .10 | .05 |
| ❑ 24 | Jim Bullinger | .10 | .05 |
| ❑ 25 | Mike Perez | .10 | .05 |
| ❑ 26 | Shawon Dunston | .10 | .05 |
| ❑ 27 | Rey Sanchez | .10 | .05 |
| ❑ 28 | Frank Castillo | .10 | .05 |
| ❑ 29 | Jaime Navarro | .10 | .05 |
| ❑ 30 | Brian McRae | .10 | .05 |
| ❑ 31 | Mark Grace | .40 | .18 |
| ❑ 32 | Roberto Rivera | .10 | .05 |
| ❑ 33 | Luis Gonzalez | .20 | .09 |
| ❑ 34 | Hector Carrasco | .10 | .05 |
| ❑ 35 | Bret Boone | .20 | .09 |
| ❑ 36 | Thomas Howard | .10 | .05 |
| ❑ 37 | Hal Morris | .10 | .05 |
| ❑ 38 | John Smiley | .10 | .05 |
| ❑ 39 | Jeff Brantley | .10 | .05 |
| ❑ 40 | Barry Larkin | .40 | .18 |
| ❑ 41 | Mariano Duncan | .10 | .05 |
| ❑ 42 | Xavier Hernandez | .10 | .05 |
| ❑ 43 | Pete Schourek | .10 | .05 |
| ❑ 44 | Reggie Sanders | .10 | .05 |
| ❑ 45 | Dave Burba | .10 | .05 |
| ❑ 46 | Jeff Branson | .10 | .05 |
| ❑ 47 | Mark Portugal | .10 | .05 |
| ❑ 48 | Ron Gant | .10 | .05 |
| ❑ 49 | Benito Santiago | .10 | .05 |
| ❑ 50 | Barry Larkin MVP | .10 | .05 |
| ❑ 51 | Steve Reed | .10 | .05 |
| ❑ 52 | Kevin Ritz | .10 | .05 |
| ❑ 53 | Dante Bichette | .20 | .09 |
| ❑ 54 | Darren Holmes | .10 | .05 |
| ❑ 55 | Ellis Burks | .20 | .09 |
| ❑ 56 | Walt Weiss | .10 | .05 |
| ❑ 57 | Armando Reynoso | .10 | .05 |
| ❑ 58 | Vinny Castilla | .20 | .09 |
| ❑ 59 | Jason Bates | .10 | .05 |
| ❑ 60 | Mike Kingery | .10 | .05 |
| ❑ 61 | Bryan Rekar | .10 | .05 |
| ❑ 62 | Curtis Leskanic | .10 | .05 |
| ❑ 63 | Bret Saberhagen | .20 | .09 |
| ❑ 64 | Andres Galarraga | .20 | .09 |
| ❑ 65 | Larry Walker | .20 | .09 |
| ❑ 66 | Joe Girardi | .10 | .05 |
| ❑ 67 | Quilvio Veras | .10 | .05 |
| ❑ 68 | Robb Nen | .10 | .05 |
| ❑ 69 | Mario Diaz | .10 | .05 |
| ❑ 70 | Chuck Carr | .10 | .05 |
| ❑ 71 | Alex Arias | .10 | .05 |
| ❑ 72 | Pat Rapp | .10 | .05 |
| ❑ 73 | Rich Garces | .10 | .05 |
| ❑ 74 | Kurt Abbott | .10 | .05 |
| ❑ 75 | Andre Dawson | .20 | .09 |
| ❑ 76 | Greg Colbrunn | .10 | .05 |
| ❑ 77 | John Burkett | .10 | .05 |
| ❑ 78 | Terry Pendleton | .20 | .09 |
| ❑ 79 | Jesus Tavarez | .10 | .05 |
| ❑ 80 | Charles Johnson | .20 | .09 |
| ❑ 81 | Yorkis Perez | .10 | .05 |
| ❑ 82 | Jeff Conine | .10 | .05 |
| ❑ 83 | Gary Sheffield | .40 | .18 |
| ❑ 84 | Brian L. Hunter | .10 | .05 |
| ❑ 85 | Derrick May | .10 | .05 |
| ❑ 86 | Greg Swindell | .10 | .05 |
| ❑ 87 | Derek Bell | .10 | .05 |
| ❑ 88 | Dave Veres | .10 | .05 |
| ❑ 89 | Jeff Bagwell | .50 | .23 |
| ❑ 90 | Todd Jones | .10 | .05 |
| ❑ 91 | Orlando Miller | .10 | .05 |
| ❑ 92 | Pedro A. Martinez | .10 | .05 |
| ❑ 93 | Tony Eusebio | .10 | .05 |
| ❑ 94 | Craig Biggio | .20 | .09 |
| ❑ 95 | Shane Reynolds | .10 | .05 |
| ❑ 96 | James Mouton | .10 | .05 |
| ❑ 97 | Doug Drabek | .10 | .05 |
| ❑ 98 | Dave Magadan | .10 | .05 |
| ❑ 99 | Ricky Gutierrez | .10 | .05 |
| ❑ 100 | Hideo Nomo | .40 | .18 |
| ❑ 101 | Delino DeShields | .10 | .05 |
| ❑ 102 | Tom Candiotti | .10 | .05 |
| ❑ 103 | Mike Piazza | 1.25 | .55 |
| ❑ 104 | Ramon Martinez | .10 | .05 |
| ❑ 105 | Pedro Astacio | .10 | .05 |
| ❑ 106 | Chad Fonville | .10 | .05 |
| ❑ 107 | Raul Mondesi | .20 | .09 |
| ❑ 108 | Ismael Valdes | .10 | .05 |
| ❑ 109 | Jose Offerman | .10 | .05 |
| ❑ 110 | Todd Worrell | .10 | .05 |
| ❑ 111 | Eric Karros | .20 | .09 |
| ❑ 112 | Brett Butler | .20 | .09 |
| ❑ 113 | Juan Castro | .10 | .05 |
| ❑ 114 | Roberto Kelly | .10 | .05 |
| ❑ 115 | Omar Daal | .10 | .05 |
| ❑ 116 | Antonio Osuna | .10 | .05 |
| ❑ 117 | Hideo Nomo ROY | .20 | .09 |
| ❑ 118 | Mike Lansing | .10 | .05 |
| ❑ 119 | Mel Rojas | .10 | .05 |
| ❑ 120 | Sean Berry | .10 | .05 |
| ❑ 121 | David Segui | .10 | .05 |
| ❑ 122 | Tavo Alvarez | .10 | .05 |
| ❑ 123 | Pedro J.Martinez | .50 | .23 |
| ❑ 124 | F.P. Santangelo | .10 | .05 |
| ❑ 125 | Rondell White | .20 | .09 |
| ❑ 126 | Cliff Floyd | .20 | .09 |
| ❑ 127 | Henry Rodriguez | .10 | .05 |
| ❑ 128 | Tony Tarasco | .10 | .05 |
| ❑ 129 | Yamil Benitez | .10 | .05 |
| ❑ 130 | Carlos Perez | .10 | .05 |
| ❑ 131 | Wil Cordero | .10 | .05 |
| ❑ 132 | Jeff Fassero | .10 | .05 |
| ❑ 133 | Moises Alou | .20 | .09 |
| ❑ 134 | John Franco | .20 | .09 |
| ❑ 135 | Rico Brogna | .10 | .05 |
| ❑ 136 | Dave Mlicki | .10 | .05 |
| ❑ 137 | Bill Pulsipher | .10 | .05 |
| ❑ 138 | Jose Vizcaino | .10 | .05 |
| ❑ 139 | Carl Everett | .20 | .09 |
| ❑ 140 | Edgardo Alfonzo | .20 | .09 |
| ❑ 141 | Bobby Jones | .10 | .05 |
| ❑ 142 | Alberto Castillo | .10 | .05 |
| ❑ 143 | Joe Orsulak | .10 | .05 |
| ❑ 144 | Jeff Kent | .20 | .09 |
| ❑ 145 | Ryan Thompson | .10 | .05 |
| ❑ 146 | Jason Isringhausen | .20 | .09 |
| ❑ 147 | Todd Hundley | .10 | .05 |
| ❑ 148 | Alex Ochoa | .10 | .05 |
| ❑ 149 | Charlie Hayes | .10 | .05 |
| ❑ 150 | Michael Mimbs | .10 | .05 |
| ❑ 151 | Darren Daulton | .20 | .09 |
| ❑ 152 | Toby Borland | .10 | .05 |
| ❑ 153 | Andy Van Slyke | .20 | .09 |
| ❑ 154 | Mickey Morandini | .10 | .05 |
| ❑ 155 | Sid Fernandez | .10 | .05 |
| ❑ 156 | Tom Marsh | .10 | .05 |
| ❑ 157 | Kevin Stocker | .10 | .05 |
| ❑ 158 | Paul Quantrill | .10 | .05 |
| ❑ 159 | Gregg Jefferies | .10 | .05 |
| ❑ 160 | Ricky Bottalico | .10 | .05 |
| ❑ 161 | Lenny Dykstra | .20 | .09 |
| ❑ 162 | Mark Whiten | .10 | .05 |
| ❑ 163 | Tyler Green | .10 | .05 |
| ❑ 164 | Jim Eisenreich | .10 | .05 |
| ❑ 165 | Heathcliff Slocumb | .10 | .05 |
| ❑ 166 | Esteban Loaiza | .10 | .05 |
| ❑ 167 | Rich Aude | .10 | .05 |
| ❑ 168 | Jason Christiansen | .10 | .05 |
| ❑ 169 | Ramon Morel | .10 | .05 |
| ❑ 170 | Orlando Merced | .10 | .05 |
| ❑ 171 | Paul Wagner | .10 | .05 |
| ❑ 172 | Jeff King | .10 | .05 |
| ❑ 173 | Jay Bell | .20 | .09 |
| ❑ 174 | Jacob Brumfield | .10 | .05 |
| ❑ 175 | Nelson Liriano | .10 | .05 |
| ❑ 176 | Dan Miceli | .10 | .05 |
| ❑ 177 | Carlos Garcia | .10 | .05 |
| ❑ 178 | Denny Neagle | .20 | .09 |
| ❑ 179 | Angelo Encarnacion | .10 | .05 |
| ❑ 180 | Al Martin | .10 | .05 |
| ❑ 181 | Midre Cummings | .10 | .05 |
| ❑ 182 | Eddie Williams | .10 | .05 |
| ❑ 183 | Roberto Petagine | .10 | .05 |
| ❑ 184 | Tony Gwynn | .75 | .35 |
| ❑ 185 | Andy Ashby | .10 | .05 |
| ❑ 186 | Melvin Nieves | .10 | .05 |
| ❑ 187 | Phil Clark | .10 | .05 |
| ❑ 188 | Brad Ausmus | .10 | .05 |
| ❑ 189 | Bip Roberts | .10 | .05 |
| ❑ 190 | Fernando Valenzuela | .20 | .09 |
| ❑ 191 | Marc Newfield | .10 | .05 |
| ❑ 192 | Steve Finley | .20 | .09 |
| ❑ 193 | Trevor Hoffman | .20 | .09 |
| ❑ 194 | Andujar Cedeno | .10 | .05 |
| ❑ 195 | Jody Reed | .10 | .05 |
| ❑ 196 | Ken Caminiti | .20 | .09 |

| | No. | Player | | |
|---|---|---|---|---|
| ❑ | 197 | Joey Hamilton | .10 | .05 |
| ❑ | 198 | Tony Gwynn BAC | .40 | .18 |
| ❑ | 199 | Shawn Barton | .10 | .05 |
| ❑ | 200 | Deion Sanders | .20 | .09 |
| ❑ | 201 | Rikkert Faneyte | .10 | .05 |
| ❑ | 202 | Barry Bonds | .60 | .25 |
| ❑ | 203 | Matt Williams | .20 | .09 |
| ❑ | 204 | Jose Bautista | .10 | .05 |
| ❑ | 205 | Mark Leiter | .10 | .05 |
| ❑ | 206 | Mark Carreon | .10 | .05 |
| ❑ | 207 | Robby Thompson | .10 | .05 |
| ❑ | 208 | Terry Mulholland | .10 | .05 |
| ❑ | 209 | Rod Beck | .10 | .05 |
| ❑ | 210 | Royce Clayton | .10 | .05 |
| ❑ | 211 | J.R. Phillips | .10 | .05 |
| ❑ | 212 | Kirt Manwaring | .10 | .05 |
| ❑ | 213 | Glenallen Hill | .10 | .05 |
| ❑ | 214 | William VanLandingham | .10 | .05 |
| ❑ | 215 | Scott Cooper | .10 | .05 |
| ❑ | 216 | Bernard Gilkey | .10 | .05 |
| ❑ | 217 | Allen Watson | .10 | .05 |
| ❑ | 218 | Donovan Osborne | .10 | .05 |
| ❑ | 219 | Ray Lankford | .20 | .09 |
| ❑ | 220 | Tony Fossas | .10 | .05 |
| ❑ | 221 | Tom Pagnozzi | .10 | .05 |
| ❑ | 222 | John Mabry | .10 | .05 |
| ❑ | 223 | Tripp Cromer | .10 | .05 |
| ❑ | 224 | Mark Petkovsek | .10 | .05 |
| ❑ | 225 | Mike Morgan | .10 | .05 |
| ❑ | 226 | Ozzie Smith | .50 | .23 |
| ❑ | 227 | Tom Henke | .10 | .05 |
| ❑ | 228 | Jose Oquendo | .10 | .05 |
| ❑ | 229 | Brian Jordan | .20 | .09 |
| ❑ | 230 | Cal Ripken | 1.50 | .70 |
| ❑ | 231 | Scott Erickson | .10 | .05 |
| ❑ | 232 | Harold Baines | .20 | .09 |
| ❑ | 233 | Jeff Manto | .10 | .05 |
| ❑ | 234 | Jesse Orosco | .10 | .05 |
| ❑ | 235 | Jeffrey Hammonds | .20 | .09 |
| ❑ | 236 | Brady Anderson | .20 | .09 |
| ❑ | 237 | Manny Alexander | .10 | .05 |
| ❑ | 238 | Chris Hoiles | .10 | .05 |
| ❑ | 239 | Rafael Palmeiro | .40 | .18 |
| ❑ | 240 | Ben McDonald | .10 | .05 |
| ❑ | 241 | Curtis Goodwin | .10 | .05 |
| ❑ | 242 | Bobby Bonilla | .20 | .09 |
| ❑ | 243 | Mike Mussina | .40 | .18 |
| ❑ | 244 | Kevin Brown | .20 | .09 |
| ❑ | 245 | Armando Benitez | .10 | .05 |
| ❑ | 246 | Jose Canseco | .50 | .23 |
| ❑ | 247 | Erik Hanson | .10 | .05 |
| ❑ | 248 | Mo Vaughn | .20 | .09 |
| ❑ | 249 | Tim Naehring | .10 | .05 |
| ❑ | 250 | Vaughn Eshelman | .10 | .05 |
| ❑ | 251 | Mike Greenwell | .10 | .05 |
| ❑ | 252 | Troy O'Leary | .10 | .05 |
| ❑ | 253 | Tim Wakefield | .10 | .05 |
| ❑ | 254 | Dwayne Hosey | .10 | .05 |
| ❑ | 255 | John Valentin | .10 | .05 |
| ❑ | 256 | Rick Aguilera | .10 | .05 |
| ❑ | 257 | Mike Macfarlane | .10 | .05 |
| ❑ | 258 | Roger Clemens | .75 | .35 |
| ❑ | 259 | Luis Alicea | .10 | .05 |
| ❑ | 260 | Mo Vaughn MVP | .20 | .09 |
| ❑ | 261 | Mark Langston | .10 | .05 |
| ❑ | 262 | Jim Edmonds | .40 | .18 |
| ❑ | 263 | Rod Correia | .10 | .05 |
| ❑ | 264 | Tim Salmon | .20 | .09 |
| ❑ | 265 | J.T. Snow | .20 | .09 |
| ❑ | 266 | Orlando Palmeiro | .10 | .05 |
| ❑ | 267 | Jorge Fabregas | .10 | .05 |
| ❑ | 268 | Jim Abbott | .20 | .09 |
| ❑ | 269 | Eduardo Perez | .10 | .05 |
| ❑ | 270 | Lee Smith | .20 | .09 |
| ❑ | 271 | Gary DiSarcina | .10 | .05 |
| ❑ | 272 | Damion Easley | .10 | .05 |
| ❑ | 273 | Tony Phillips | .10 | .05 |
| ❑ | 274 | Garret Anderson | .20 | .09 |
| ❑ | 275 | Chuck Finley | .20 | .09 |
| ❑ | 276 | Chili Davis | .20 | .09 |
| ❑ | 277 | Lance Johnson | .10 | .05 |
| ❑ | 278 | Alex Fernandez | .10 | .05 |
| ❑ | 279 | Robin Ventura | .20 | .09 |
| ❑ | 280 | Chris Snopek | .10 | .05 |
| ❑ | 281 | Brian Keyser | .10 | .05 |
| ❑ | 282 | Lyle Mouton | .10 | .05 |
| ❑ | 283 | Luis Andujar | .10 | .05 |
| ❑ | 284 | Tim Raines | .20 | .09 |
| ❑ | 285 | Larry Thomas | .10 | .05 |
| ❑ | 286 | Ozzie Guillen | .10 | .05 |
| ❑ | 287 | Frank Thomas | .75 | .35 |
| ❑ | 288 | Roberto Hernandez | .10 | .05 |
| ❑ | 289 | Dave Martinez | .10 | .05 |
| ❑ | 290 | Ray Durham | .20 | .09 |
| ❑ | 291 | Ron Karkovice | .10 | .05 |
| ❑ | 292 | Wilson Alvarez | .10 | .05 |
| ❑ | 293 | Omar Vizquel | .20 | .09 |
| ❑ | 294 | Eddie Murray | .40 | .18 |
| ❑ | 295 | Sandy Alomar Jr. | .20 | .09 |
| ❑ | 296 | Orel Hershiser | .20 | .09 |
| ❑ | 297 | Jose Mesa | .10 | .05 |
| ❑ | 298 | Julian Tavarez | .10 | .05 |
| ❑ | 299 | Dennis Martinez | .20 | .09 |
| ❑ | 300 | Carlos Baerga | .10 | .05 |
| ❑ | 301 | Manny Ramirez | .50 | .23 |
| ❑ | 302 | Jim Thome | .20 | .09 |
| ❑ | 303 | Kenny Lofton | .20 | .09 |
| ❑ | 304 | Tony Pena | .10 | .05 |
| ❑ | 305 | Alvaro Espinoza | .10 | .05 |
| ❑ | 306 | Paul Sorrento | .10 | .05 |
| ❑ | 307 | Albert Belle | .20 | .09 |
| ❑ | 308 | Danny Bautista | .10 | .05 |
| ❑ | 309 | Chris Gomez | .10 | .05 |
| ❑ | 310 | Jose Lima | .10 | .05 |
| ❑ | 311 | Phil Nevin | .20 | .09 |
| ❑ | 312 | Alan Trammell | .20 | .09 |
| ❑ | 313 | Chad Curtis | .10 | .05 |
| ❑ | 314 | John Flaherty | .10 | .05 |
| ❑ | 315 | Travis Fryman | .20 | .09 |
| ❑ | 316 | Todd Steverson | .10 | .05 |
| ❑ | 317 | Brian Bohanon | .10 | .05 |
| ❑ | 318 | Lou Whitaker | .20 | .09 |
| ❑ | 319 | Bobby Higginson | .20 | .09 |
| ❑ | 320 | Steve Rodriguez | .10 | .05 |
| ❑ | 321 | Cecil Fielder | .20 | .09 |
| ❑ | 322 | Felipe Lira | .10 | .05 |
| ❑ | 323 | Juan Samuel | .10 | .05 |
| ❑ | 324 | Bob Hamelin | .10 | .05 |
| ❑ | 325 | Tom Goodwin | .10 | .05 |
| ❑ | 326 | Johnny Damon | .20 | .09 |
| ❑ | 327 | Hipolito Pichardo | .10 | .05 |
| ❑ | 328 | Dilson Torres | .10 | .05 |
| ❑ | 329 | Kevin Appier | .20 | .09 |
| ❑ | 330 | Mark Gubicza | .10 | .05 |
| ❑ | 331 | Jon Nunnally | .10 | .05 |
| ❑ | 332 | Gary Gaetti | .20 | .09 |
| ❑ | 333 | Brent Mayne | .10 | .05 |
| ❑ | 334 | Brent Cookson | .10 | .05 |
| ❑ | 335 | Tom Gordon | .10 | .05 |
| ❑ | 336 | Wally Joyner | .20 | .09 |
| ❑ | 337 | Greg Gagne | .10 | .05 |
| ❑ | 338 | Fernando Vina | .10 | .05 |
| ❑ | 339 | Joe Oliver | .10 | .05 |
| ❑ | 340 | John Jaha | .10 | .05 |
| ❑ | 341 | Jeff Cirillo | .20 | .09 |
| ❑ | 342 | Pat Listach | .10 | .05 |
| ❑ | 343 | Dave Nilsson | .10 | .05 |
| ❑ | 344 | Steve Sparks | .10 | .05 |
| ❑ | 345 | Ricky Bones | .10 | .05 |
| ❑ | 346 | David Hulse | .10 | .05 |
| ❑ | 347 | Scott Karl | .10 | .05 |
| ❑ | 348 | Darryl Hamilton | .10 | .05 |
| ❑ | 349 | B.J. Surhoff | .20 | .09 |
| ❑ | 350 | Angel Miranda | .10 | .05 |
| ❑ | 351 | Sid Roberson | .10 | .05 |
| ❑ | 352 | Matt Mieske | .10 | .05 |
| ❑ | 353 | Jose Valentin | .10 | .05 |
| ❑ | 354 | Matt Lawton RC | .50 | .23 |
| ❑ | 355 | Eddie Guardado | .10 | .05 |
| ❑ | 356 | Brad Radke | .20 | .09 |
| ❑ | 357 | Pedro Munoz | .10 | .05 |
| ❑ | 358 | Scott Stahoviak | .10 | .05 |
| ❑ | 359 | Erik Schullstrom | .10 | .05 |
| ❑ | 360 | Pat Meares | .10 | .05 |
| ❑ | 361 | Marty Cordova | .10 | .05 |
| ❑ | 362 | Scott Leius | .10 | .05 |
| ❑ | 363 | Matt Walbeck | .10 | .05 |
| ❑ | 364 | Rich Becker | .10 | .05 |
| ❑ | 365 | Kirby Puckett | 1.00 | .45 |
| ❑ | 366 | Oscar Munoz | .10 | .05 |
| ❑ | 367 | Chuck Knoblauch | .20 | .09 |
| ❑ | 368 | Marty Cordova ROY | .10 | .05 |
| ❑ | 369 | Bernie Williams | .40 | .18 |
| ❑ | 370 | Mike Stanley | .10 | .05 |
| ❑ | 371 | Andy Pettitte | .20 | .09 |
| ❑ | 372 | Jack McDowell | .10 | .05 |
| ❑ | 373 | Sterling Hitchcock | .10 | .05 |
| ❑ | 374 | David Cone | .20 | .09 |
| ❑ | 375 | Randy Velarde | .10 | .05 |
| ❑ | 376 | Don Mattingly | 1.00 | .45 |
| ❑ | 377 | Melido Perez | .10 | .05 |
| ❑ | 378 | Wade Boggs | .50 | .23 |
| ❑ | 379 | Ruben Sierra | .10 | .05 |
| ❑ | 380 | Tony Fernandez | .10 | .05 |
| ❑ | 381 | John Wetteland | .20 | .09 |
| ❑ | 382 | Mariano Rivera | .20 | .09 |
| ❑ | 383 | Derek Jeter | 1.50 | .70 |
| ❑ | 384 | Paul O'Neill | .20 | .09 |
| ❑ | 385 | Mark McGwire | 1.50 | .70 |
| ❑ | 386 | Scott Brosius | .20 | .09 |
| ❑ | 387 | Don Wengert | .10 | .05 |
| ❑ | 388 | Terry Steinbach | .10 | .05 |
| ❑ | 389 | Brent Gates | .10 | .05 |
| ❑ | 390 | Craig Paquette | .10 | .05 |
| ❑ | 391 | Mike Bordick | .10 | .05 |
| ❑ | 392 | Ariel Prieto | .10 | .05 |
| ❑ | 393 | Dennis Eckersley | .20 | .09 |
| ❑ | 394 | Carlos Reyes | .10 | .05 |
| ❑ | 395 | Todd Stottlemyre | .10 | .05 |
| ❑ | 396 | Rickey Henderson | .50 | .23 |
| ❑ | 397 | Geronimo Berroa | .10 | .05 |
| ❑ | 398 | Steve Ontiveros | .10 | .05 |
| ❑ | 399 | Mike Gallego | .10 | .05 |
| ❑ | 400 | Stan Javier | .10 | .05 |
| ❑ | 401 | Randy Johnson | .50 | .23 |
| ❑ | 402 | Norm Charlton | .10 | .05 |
| ❑ | 403 | Mike Blowers | .10 | .05 |
| ❑ | 404 | Tino Martinez | .20 | .09 |
| ❑ | 405 | Dan Wilson | .10 | .05 |
| ❑ | 406 | Andy Benes | .10 | .05 |
| ❑ | 407 | Alex Diaz | .10 | .05 |
| ❑ | 408 | Edgar Martinez | .20 | .09 |
| ❑ | 409 | Chris Bosio | .10 | .05 |
| ❑ | 410 | Ken Griffey, Jr. | 1.50 | .70 |
| ❑ | 411 | Luis Sojo | .10 | .05 |
| ❑ | 412 | Bob Wolcott | .10 | .05 |
| ❑ | 413 | Vince Coleman | .10 | .05 |
| ❑ | 414 | Rich Amaral | .10 | .05 |
| ❑ | 415 | Jay Buhner | .20 | .09 |
| ❑ | 416 | Alex Rodriguez | 1.25 | .55 |
| ❑ | 417 | Joey Cora | .10 | .05 |
| ❑ | 418 | Randy Johnson CY | .20 | .09 |
| ❑ | 419 | Edgar Martinez BAC | .20 | .09 |
| ❑ | 420 | Ivan Rodriguez | .50 | .23 |
| ❑ | 421 | Mark McLemore | .10 | .05 |
| ❑ | 422 | Mickey Tettleton | .10 | .05 |
| ❑ | 423 | Juan Gonzalez | .40 | .18 |
| ❑ | 424 | Will Clark | .40 | .18 |
| ❑ | 425 | Kevin Gross | .10 | .05 |
| ❑ | 426 | Dean Palmer | .20 | .09 |
| ❑ | 427 | Kenny Rogers | .10 | .05 |
| ❑ | 428 | Bob Tewksbury | .10 | .05 |
| ❑ | 429 | Benji Gil | .10 | .05 |
| ❑ | 430 | Jeff Russell | .10 | .05 |
| ❑ | 431 | Rusty Greer | .20 | .09 |
| ❑ | 432 | Roger Pavlik | .10 | .05 |
| ❑ | 433 | Esteban Beltre | .10 | .05 |
| ❑ | 434 | Otis Nixon | .10 | .05 |
| ❑ | 435 | Paul Molitor | .40 | .18 |
| ❑ | 436 | Carlos Delgado | .40 | .18 |
| ❑ | 437 | Ed Sprague | .10 | .05 |
| ❑ | 438 | Juan Guzman | .10 | .05 |
| ❑ | 439 | Domingo Cedeno | .10 | .05 |
| ❑ | 440 | Pat Hentgen | .10 | .05 |
| ❑ | 441 | Tomas Perez | .10 | .05 |
| ❑ | 442 | John Olerud | .20 | .09 |
| ❑ | 443 | Shawn Green | .40 | .18 |
| ❑ | 444 | Al Leiter | .20 | .09 |
| ❑ | 445 | Joe Carter | .20 | .09 |
| ❑ | 446 | Robert Perez | .10 | .05 |
| ❑ | 447 | Devon White | .20 | .09 |
| ❑ | 448 | Tony Castillo | .10 | .05 |
| ❑ | 449 | Alex Gonzalez | .10 | .05 |
| ❑ | 450 | Roberto Alomar | .40 | .18 |

## 1997 Pacific

| | MINT | NRMT |
|---|---|---|
| COMPLETE SET (450) | 40.00 | 18.00 |
| COMMON CARD (1-450) | .15 | .07 |

| Card | MINT | NRMT |
|---|---|---|
| ❑ 1 Garret Anderson | .30 | .14 |
| ❑ 2 George Arias | .15 | .07 |
| ❑ 3 Chili Davis | .30 | .14 |
| ❑ 4 Gary DiSarcina | .15 | .07 |
| ❑ 5 Jim Edmonds | .60 | .25 |
| ❑ 6 Darin Erstad | .75 | .35 |
| ❑ 7 Jorge Fabregas | .15 | .07 |
| ❑ 8 Chuck Finley | .30 | .14 |
| ❑ 9 Rex Hudler | .15 | .07 |
| ❑ 10 Mark Langston | .30 | .14 |
| ❑ 11 Orlando Palmeiro | .15 | .07 |
| ❑ 12 Troy Percival | .15 | .07 |
| ❑ 13 Tim Salmon | .30 | .14 |
| ❑ 14 J.T. Snow | .30 | .14 |
| ❑ 15 Randy Velarde | .15 | .07 |
| ❑ 16 Manny Alexander | .15 | .07 |
| ❑ 17 Roberto Alomar | .60 | .25 |
| ❑ 18 Brady Anderson | .30 | .14 |
| ❑ 19 Armando Benitez | .15 | .07 |
| ❑ 20 Bobby Bonilla | .30 | .14 |
| ❑ 21 Rocky Coppinger | .15 | .07 |
| ❑ 22 Scott Erickson | .15 | .07 |
| ❑ 23 Jeffrey Hammonds | .30 | .14 |
| ❑ 24 Chris Hoiles | .15 | .07 |
| ❑ 25 Eddie Murray | .60 | .25 |
| ❑ 26 Mike Mussina | .60 | .25 |
| ❑ 27 Randy Myers | .15 | .07 |
| ❑ 28 Rafael Palmeiro | .60 | .25 |
| ❑ 29 Cal Ripken | 2.50 | 1.10 |
| ❑ 30 B.J. Surhoff | .30 | .14 |
| ❑ 31 Tony Tarasco | .15 | .07 |
| ❑ 32 Esteban Beltre | .15 | .07 |
| ❑ 33 Darren Bragg | .15 | .07 |
| ❑ 34 Jose Canseco | .75 | .35 |
| ❑ 35 Roger Clemens | 1.25 | .55 |
| ❑ 36 Wil Cordero | .15 | .07 |
| ❑ 37 Alex Delgado | .15 | .07 |
| ❑ 38 Jeff Frye | .15 | .07 |
| ❑ 39 Nomar Garciaparra | 2.00 | .90 |
| ❑ 40 Tom Gordon | .15 | .07 |
| ❑ 41 Mike Greenwell | .15 | .07 |
| ❑ 42 Reggie Jefferson | .15 | .07 |
| ❑ 43 Tim Naehring | .15 | .07 |
| ❑ 44 Troy O'Leary | .15 | .07 |
| ❑ 45 Heathcliff Slocumb | .15 | .07 |
| ❑ 46 Lee Tinsley | .15 | .07 |
| ❑ 47 John Valentin | .15 | .07 |
| ❑ 48 Mo Vaughn | .30 | .14 |
| ❑ 49 Wilson Alvarez | .15 | .07 |
| ❑ 50 Harold Baines | .30 | .14 |
| ❑ 51 Ray Durham | .30 | .14 |
| ❑ 52 Alex Fernandez | .15 | .07 |
| ❑ 53 Ozzie Guillen | .15 | .07 |
| ❑ 54 Roberto Hernandez | .15 | .07 |
| ❑ 55 Ron Karkovice | .15 | .07 |
| ❑ 56 Darren Lewis | .15 | .07 |
| ❑ 57 Norberto Martin | .15 | .07 |
| ❑ 58 Dave Martinez | .15 | .07 |
| ❑ 59 Lyle Mouton | .15 | .07 |
| ❑ 60 Jose Munoz | .15 | .07 |
| ❑ 61 Tony Phillips | .15 | .07 |
| ❑ 62 Kevin Tapani | .15 | .07 |
| ❑ 63 Danny Tartabull | .15 | .07 |
| ❑ 64 Frank Thomas | 1.25 | .55 |
| ❑ 65 Robin Ventura | .30 | .14 |
| ❑ 66 Sandy Alomar Jr. | .30 | .14 |
| ❑ 67 Albert Belle | .40 | .18 |
| ❑ 68 Julio Franco | .30 | .14 |
| ❑ 69 Brian Giles RC | 2.50 | 1.10 |
| ❑ 70 Danny Graves | .15 | .07 |
| ❑ 71 Orel Hershiser | .30 | .14 |
| ❑ 72 Jeff Kent | .40 | .18 |
| ❑ 73 Kenny Lofton | .30 | .14 |
| ❑ 74 Dennis Martinez | .30 | .14 |
| ❑ 75 Jack McDowell | .15 | .07 |
| ❑ 76 Jose Mesa | .15 | .07 |
| ❑ 77 Charles Nagy | .15 | .07 |
| ❑ 78 Manny Ramirez | .75 | .35 |
| ❑ 79 Julian Tavarez | .15 | .07 |
| ❑ 80 Jim Thome | .40 | .18 |
| ❑ 81 Jose Vizcaino | .15 | .07 |
| ❑ 82 Omar Vizquel | .30 | .14 |
| ❑ 83 Brad Ausmus | .15 | .07 |
| ❑ 84 Kimera Bartee | .15 | .07 |
| ❑ 85 Raul Casanova | .15 | .07 |
| ❑ 86 Tony Clark | .15 | .07 |
| ❑ 87 Travis Fryman | .30 | .14 |
| ❑ 88 Bobby Higginson | .30 | .14 |
| ❑ 89 Mark Lewis | .15 | .07 |
| ❑ 90 Jose Lima | .15 | .07 |
| ❑ 91 Felipe Lira | .15 | .07 |
| ❑ 92 Phil Nevin | .30 | .14 |
| ❑ 93 Melvin Nieves | .15 | .07 |
| ❑ 94 Curtis Pride | .15 | .07 |
| ❑ 95 Ruben Sierra | .15 | .07 |
| ❑ 96 Alan Trammell | .40 | .18 |
| ❑ 97 Kevin Appier | .30 | .14 |
| ❑ 98 Tim Belcher | .15 | .07 |
| ❑ 99 Johnny Damon | .30 | .14 |
| ❑ 100 Tom Goodwin | .15 | .07 |
| ❑ 101 Bob Hamelin | .15 | .07 |
| ❑ 102 David Howard | .15 | .07 |
| ❑ 103 Jason Jacome | .15 | .07 |
| ❑ 104 Keith Lockhart | .15 | .07 |
| ❑ 105 Mike Macfarlane | .15 | .07 |
| ❑ 106 Jeff Montgomery | .15 | .07 |
| ❑ 107 Jose Offerman | .15 | .07 |
| ❑ 108 Hipolito Pichardo | .15 | .07 |
| ❑ 109 Joe Randa | .15 | .07 |
| ❑ 110 Bip Roberts | .15 | .07 |
| ❑ 111 Chris Stynes | .15 | .07 |
| ❑ 112 Mike Sweeney | .30 | .14 |
| ❑ 113 Joe Vitiello | .15 | .07 |
| ❑ 114 Jeromy Burnitz | .30 | .14 |
| ❑ 115 Chuck Carr | .15 | .07 |
| ❑ 116 Jeff Cirillo | .30 | .14 |
| ❑ 117 Mike Fetters | .15 | .07 |
| ❑ 118 David Hulse | .15 | .07 |
| ❑ 119 John Jaha | .15 | .07 |
| ❑ 120 Scott Karl | .15 | .07 |
| ❑ 121 Jesse Levis | .15 | .07 |
| ❑ 122 Mark Loretta | .15 | .07 |
| ❑ 123 Mike Matheny | .15 | .07 |
| ❑ 124 Ben McDonald | .15 | .07 |
| ❑ 125 Matt Mieske | .15 | .07 |
| ❑ 126 Angel Miranda | .15 | .07 |
| ❑ 127 Dave Nilsson | .15 | .07 |
| ❑ 128 Jose Valentin | .15 | .07 |
| ❑ 129 Fernando Vina | .15 | .07 |
| ❑ 130 Ron Villone | .15 | .07 |
| ❑ 131 Gerald Williams | .15 | .07 |
| ❑ 132 Rick Aguilera | .15 | .07 |
| ❑ 133 Rich Becker | .15 | .07 |
| ❑ 134 Ron Coomer | .15 | .07 |
| ❑ 135 Marty Cordova | .15 | .07 |
| ❑ 136 Eddie Guardado | .15 | .07 |
| ❑ 137 Denny Hocking | .15 | .07 |
| ❑ 138 Roberto Kelly | .15 | .07 |
| ❑ 139 Chuck Knoblauch | .30 | .14 |
| ❑ 140 Matt Lawton | .30 | .14 |
| ❑ 141 Pat Meares | .15 | .07 |
| ❑ 142 Paul Molitor | .60 | .25 |
| ❑ 143 Greg Myers | .15 | .07 |
| ❑ 144 Jeff Reboulet | .15 | .07 |
| ❑ 145 Scott Stahoviak | .15 | .07 |
| ❑ 146 Todd Walker | .15 | .07 |
| ❑ 147 Wade Boggs | .75 | .35 |
| ❑ 148 David Cone | .30 | .14 |
| ❑ 149 Mariano Duncan | .15 | .07 |
| ❑ 150 Cecil Fielder | .30 | .14 |
| ❑ 151 Dwight Gooden | .30 | .14 |
| ❑ 152 Derek Jeter | 2.50 | 1.10 |
| ❑ 153 Jim Leyritz | .15 | .07 |
| ❑ 154 Tino Martinez | .30 | .14 |
| ❑ 155 Paul O'Neill | .30 | .14 |
| ❑ 156 Andy Pettitte | .30 | .14 |
| ❑ 157 Tim Raines | .30 | .14 |
| ❑ 158 Mariano Rivera | .30 | .14 |
| ❑ 159 Ruben Rivera | .15 | .07 |
| ❑ 160 Kenny Rogers | .15 | .07 |
| ❑ 161 Darryl Strawberry | .30 | .14 |
| ❑ 162 John Wetteland | .30 | .14 |
| ❑ 163 Bernie Williams | .60 | .25 |
| ❑ 164 Tony Batista | .60 | .25 |
| ❑ 165 Geronimo Berroa | .15 | .07 |
| ❑ 166 Mike Bordick | .15 | .07 |
| ❑ 167 Scott Brosius | .30 | .14 |
| ❑ 168 Brent Gates | .15 | .07 |
| ❑ 169 Jason Giambi | .60 | .25 |
| ❑ 170 Jose Herrera | .15 | .07 |
| ❑ 171 Brian Lesher RC | .15 | .07 |
| ❑ 172 Damon Mashore | .15 | .07 |
| ❑ 173 Mark McGwire | 2.50 | 1.10 |
| ❑ 174 Ariel Prieto | .15 | .07 |
| ❑ 175 Carlos Reyes | .15 | .07 |
| ❑ 176 Matt Stairs | .15 | .07 |
| ❑ 177 Terry Steinbach | .15 | .07 |
| ❑ 178 John Wasdin | .15 | .07 |
| ❑ 179 Ernie Young | .15 | .07 |
| ❑ 180 Rich Amaral | .15 | .07 |
| ❑ 181 Bobby Ayala | .15 | .07 |
| ❑ 182 Jay Buhner | .30 | .14 |
| ❑ 183 Rafael Carmona | .15 | .07 |
| ❑ 184 Norm Charlton | .15 | .07 |
| ❑ 185 Joey Cora | .15 | .07 |
| ❑ 186 Ken Griffey Jr. | 2.50 | 1.10 |
| ❑ 187 Sterling Hitchcock | .15 | .07 |
| ❑ 188 Dave Hollins | .15 | .07 |
| ❑ 189 Randy Johnson | .75 | .35 |
| ❑ 190 Edgar Martinez | .40 | .18 |
| ❑ 191 Jamie Moyer | .15 | .07 |
| ❑ 192 Alex Rodriguez | 2.00 | .90 |
| ❑ 193 Paul Sorrento | .15 | .07 |
| ❑ 194 Salomon Torres | .15 | .07 |
| ❑ 195 Bob Wells | .15 | .07 |
| ❑ 196 Dan Wilson | .15 | .07 |
| ❑ 197 Will Clark | .60 | .25 |
| ❑ 198 Kevin Elster | .15 | .07 |
| ❑ 199 Rene Gonzales | .15 | .07 |
| ❑ 200 Juan Gonzalez | .60 | .25 |
| ❑ 201 Rusty Greer | .30 | .14 |
| ❑ 202 Darryl Hamilton | .15 | .07 |
| ❑ 203 Mike Henneman | .15 | .07 |
| ❑ 204 Ken Hill | .15 | .07 |
| ❑ 205 Mark McLemore | .15 | .07 |
| ❑ 206 Darren Oliver | .15 | .07 |
| ❑ 207 Dean Palmer | .30 | .14 |
| ❑ 208 Roger Pavlik | .15 | .07 |
| ❑ 209 Ivan Rodriguez | .75 | .35 |
| ❑ 210 Kurt Stillwell | .15 | .07 |
| ❑ 211 Mickey Tettleton | .15 | .07 |
| ❑ 212 Bobby Witt | .15 | .07 |
| ❑ 213 Tilson Brito | .15 | .07 |
| ❑ 214 Jacob Brumfield | .15 | .07 |
| ❑ 215 Miguel Cairo | .30 | .14 |
| ❑ 216 Joe Carter | .30 | .14 |
| ❑ 217 Felipe Crespo | .15 | .07 |
| ❑ 218 Carlos Delgado | .60 | .25 |
| ❑ 219 Alex Gonzalez | .15 | .07 |
| ❑ 220 Shawn Green | .60 | .25 |
| ❑ 221 Juan Guzman | .15 | .07 |
| ❑ 222 Pat Hentgen | .15 | .07 |
| ❑ 223 Charlie O'Brien | .15 | .07 |
| ❑ 224 John Olerud | .30 | .14 |
| ❑ 225 Robert Perez | .15 | .07 |
| ❑ 226 Tomas Perez | .15 | .07 |
| ❑ 227 Juan Samuel | .15 | .07 |
| ❑ 228 Ed Sprague | .15 | .07 |
| ❑ 229 Mike Timlin | .15 | .07 |
| ❑ 230 Rafael Belliard | .15 | .07 |
| ❑ 231 Jermaine Dye | .30 | .14 |
| ❑ 232 Tom Glavine | .60 | .25 |
| ❑ 233 Marquis Grissom | .15 | .07 |
| ❑ 234 Andruw Jones | .75 | .35 |

❑ 235 Chipper Jones 1.50 .70
❑ 236 David Justice .40 .18
❑ 237 Ryan Klesko .30 .14
❑ 238 Mark Lemke .15 .07
❑ 239 Javier Lopez .30 .14
❑ 240 Greg Maddux 1.50 .70
❑ 241 Fred McGriff .40 .18
❑ 242 Denny Neagle .30 .14
❑ 243 Eddie Perez .15 .07
❑ 244 John Smoltz .30 .14
❑ 245 Mark Wohlers .15 .07
❑ 246 Brant Brown .15 .07
❑ 247 Scott Bullett .15 .07
❑ 248 Leo Gomez .15 .07
❑ 249 Luis Gonzalez .30 .14
❑ 250 Mark Grace .60 .25
❑ 251 Jose Hernandez .15 .07
❑ 252 Brooks Kieschnick .15 .07
❑ 253 Brian McRae .15 .07
❑ 254 Jaime Navarro .15 .07
❑ 255 Mike Perez .15 .07
❑ 256 Rey Sanchez .15 .07
❑ 257 Ryne Sandberg .75 .35
❑ 258 Scott Servais .15 .07
❑ 259 Sammy Sosa 1.25 .55
❑ 260 Pedro Valdes .15 .07
❑ 261 Turk Wendell .15 .07
❑ 262 Bret Boone .30 .14
❑ 263 Jeff Branson .15 .07
❑ 264 Jeff Brantley .15 .07
❑ 265 Dave Burba .15 .07
❑ 266 Hector Carrasco .15 .07
❑ 267 Eric Davis .30 .14
❑ 268 Willie Greene .15 .07
❑ 269 Lenny Harris .15 .07
❑ 270 Thomas Howard .15 .07
❑ 271 Barry Larkin .60 .25
❑ 272 Hal Morris .15 .07
❑ 273 Joe Oliver .15 .07
❑ 274 Eric Owens .15 .07
❑ 275 Jose Rijo .15 .07
❑ 276 Reggie Sanders .15 .07
❑ 277 Eddie Taubensee .15 .07
❑ 278 Jason Bates .15 .07
❑ 279 Dante Bichette .30 .14
❑ 280 Ellis Burks .30 .14
❑ 281 Vinny Castilla .30 .14
❑ 282 Andres Galarraga .40 .18
❑ 283 Quinton McCracken .15 .07
❑ 284 Jayhawk Owens .15 .07
❑ 285 Jeff Reed .15 .07
❑ 286 Bryan Rekar .15 .07
❑ 287 Armando Reynoso .15 .07
❑ 288 Kevin Ritz .15 .07
❑ 289 Bruce Ruffin .15 .07
❑ 290 John Vander Wal .15 .07
❑ 291 Larry Walker .30 .14
❑ 292 Walt Weiss .15 .07
❑ 293 Eric Young .15 .07
❑ 294 Kurt Abbott .15 .07
❑ 295 Alex Arias .15 .07
❑ 296 Miguel Batista .15 .07
❑ 297 Kevin Brown .40 .18
❑ 298 Luis Castillo .30 .14
❑ 299 Greg Colbrunn .15 .07
❑ 300 Jeff Conine .15 .07
❑ 301 Charles Johnson .30 .14
❑ 302 Al Leiter .30 .14
❑ 303 Robb Nen .15 .07
❑ 304 Joe Orsulak .15 .07
❑ 305 Yorkis Perez .15 .07
❑ 306 Edgar Renteria .30 .14
❑ 307 Gary Sheffield .60 .25
❑ 308 Jesus Tavarez .15 .07
❑ 309 Quilvio Veras .15 .07
❑ 310 Devon White .30 .14
❑ 311 Jeff Bagwell .75 .35
❑ 312 Derek Bell .15 .07
❑ 313 Sean Berry .15 .07
❑ 314 Craig Biggio .40 .18
❑ 315 Doug Drabek .15 .07
❑ 316 Tony Eusebio .15 .07
❑ 317 Ricky Gutierrez .15 .07
❑ 318 Xavier Hernandez .15 .07
❑ 319 Brian L. Hunter .15 .07
❑ 320 Darryl Kile .30 .14
❑ 321 Derrick May .15 .07
❑ 322 Orlando Miller .15 .07
❑ 323 James Mouton .15 .07
❑ 324 Bill Spiers .15 .07
❑ 325 Pedro Astacio .15 .07
❑ 326 Brett Butler .30 .14
❑ 327 Juan Castro .15 .07
❑ 328 Roger Cedeno .15 .07
❑ 329 Delino DeShields .15 .07
❑ 330 Karim Garcia .15 .07
❑ 331 Todd Hollandsworth .15 .07
❑ 332 Eric Karros .30 .14
❑ 333 Oreste Marrero .15 .07
❑ 334 Ramon Martinez .15 .07
❑ 335 Raul Mondesi .30 .14
❑ 336 Hideo Nomo .60 .25
❑ 337 Antonio Osuna .15 .07
❑ 338 Chan Ho Park .30 .14
❑ 339 Mike Piazza 2.00 .90
❑ 340 Ismael Valdes .15 .07
❑ 341 Moises Alou .30 .14
❑ 342 Omar Daal .15 .07
❑ 343 Jeff Fassero .15 .07
❑ 344 Cliff Floyd .30 .14
❑ 345 Mark Grudzielanek .15 .07
❑ 346 Mike Lansing .15 .07
❑ 347 Pedro Martinez .75 .35
❑ 348 Sherman Obando .15 .07
❑ 349 Jose Paniagua .15 .07
❑ 350 Henry Rodriguez .15 .07
❑ 351 Mel Rojas .15 .07
❑ 352 F.P. Santangelo .15 .07
❑ 353 David Segui .15 .07
❑ 354 Dave Silvestri .15 .07
❑ 355 Ugueth Urbina .30 .14
❑ 356 Rondell White .30 .14
❑ 357 Edgardo Alfonzo .30 .14
❑ 358 Carlos Baerga .15 .07
❑ 359 Tim Bogar .15 .07
❑ 360 Rico Brogna .15 .07
❑ 361 Alvaro Espinoza .15 .07
❑ 362 Carl Everett .30 .14
❑ 363 John Franco .30 .14
❑ 364 Bernard Gilkey .15 .07
❑ 365 Todd Hundley .15 .07
❑ 366 Butch Huskey .15 .07
❑ 367 Jason Isringhausen .15 .07
❑ 368 Bobby Jones .15 .07
❑ 369 Lance Johnson .15 .07
❑ 370 Brent Mayne .15 .07
❑ 371 Alex Ochoa .15 .07
❑ 372 Rey Ordonez .15 .07
❑ 373 Ron Blazier .15 .07
❑ 374 Ricky Bottalico .15 .07
❑ 375 David Doster .15 .07
❑ 376 Lenny Dykstra .30 .14
❑ 377 Jim Eisenreich .15 .07
❑ 378 Bobby Estalella .15 .07
❑ 379 Gregg Jefferies .15 .07
❑ 380 Kevin Jordan .15 .07
❑ 381 Ricardo Jordan .15 .07
❑ 382 Mickey Morandini .15 .07
❑ 383 Ricky Otero .15 .07
❑ 384 Benito Santiago .15 .07
❑ 385 Gene Schall .15 .07
❑ 386 Curt Schilling .30 .14
❑ 387 Kevin Sefcik .15 .07
❑ 388 Kevin Stocker .15 .07
❑ 389 Jermaine Allensworth .15 .07
❑ 390 Jay Bell .30 .14
❑ 391 Jason Christiansen .15 .07
❑ 392 Francisco Cordova .15 .07
❑ 393 Mark Johnson .15 .07
❑ 394 Jason Kendall .30 .14
❑ 395 Jeff King .15 .07
❑ 396 Jon Lieber .15 .07
❑ 397 Nelson Liriano .15 .07
❑ 398 Esteban Loaiza .15 .07
❑ 399 Al Martin .15 .07
❑ 400 Orlando Merced .15 .07
❑ 401 Ramon Morel .15 .07
❑ 402 Luis Alicea .15 .07
❑ 403 Alan Benes .15 .07
❑ 404 Andy Benes .15 .07
❑ 405 Terry Bradshaw .15 .07
❑ 406 Royce Clayton .15 .07
❑ 407 Dennis Eckersley .30 .14
❑ 408 Gary Gaetti .30 .14
❑ 409 Mike Gallego .15 .07
❑ 410 Ron Gant .15 .07
❑ 411 Brian Jordan .30 .14
❑ 412 Ray Lankford .30 .14
❑ 413 John Mabry .15 .07
❑ 414 Willie McGee .30 .14
❑ 415 Tom Pagnozzi .15 .07
❑ 416 Ozzie Smith .75 .35
❑ 417 Todd Stottlemyre .15 .07
❑ 418 Mark Sweeney .15 .07
❑ 419 Andy Ashby .15 .07
❑ 420 Ken Caminiti .30 .14
❑ 421 Archi Cianfrocco .15 .07
❑ 422 Steve Finley .30 .14
❑ 423 Chris Gomez .15 .07
❑ 424 Tony Gwynn 1.25 .55
❑ 425 Joey Hamilton .15 .07
❑ 426 Rickey Henderson .75 .35
❑ 427 Trevor Hoffman .30 .14
❑ 428 Brian Johnson .15 .07
❑ 429 Wally Joyner .30 .14
❑ 430 Scott Livingstone .15 .07
❑ 431 Jody Reed .15 .07
❑ 432 Craig Shipley .15 .07
❑ 433 Fernando Valenzuela .30 .14
❑ 434 Greg Vaughn .30 .14
❑ 435 Rich Aurilia .30 .14
❑ 436 Kim Batiste .15 .07
❑ 437 Jose Bautista .15 .07
❑ 438 Rod Beck .15 .07
❑ 439 Marvin Benard .15 .07
❑ 440 Barry Bonds 1.00 .45
❑ 441 Shawon Dunston .15 .07
❑ 442 Shawn Estes .30 .14
❑ 443 Osvaldo Fernandez .15 .07
❑ 444 Stan Javier .15 .07
❑ 445 David McCarty .15 .07
❑ 446 Bill Mueller RC .40 .18
❑ 447 Steve Scarsone .15 .07
❑ 448 Robby Thompson .15 .07
❑ 449 Rick Wilkins .15 .07
❑ 450 Matt Williams .40 .18

## 1998 Pacific

| | MINT | NRMT |
|---|---|---|
| COMPLETE SET (450) | 60.00 | 27.00 |
| COMMON CARD (1-450) | .15 | .07 |

❑ 1 Luis Alicea .15 .07
❑ 2 Garret Anderson .25 .11
❑ 3 Jason Dickson .15 .07
❑ 4 Gary DiSarcina .15 .07
❑ 5 Jim Edmonds .25 .11
❑ 6 Darin Erstad .60 .25
❑ 7 Chuck Finley .25 .11
❑ 8 Shigetoshi Hasegawa .25 .11
❑ 9 Rickey Henderson .75 .35
❑ 10 Dave Hollins .15 .07
❑ 11 Mark Langston .15 .07
❑ 12 Orlando Palmeiro .15 .07
❑ 13 Troy Percival .15 .07
❑ 14 Tony Phillips .15 .07
❑ 15 Tim Salmon .25 .11
❑ 16 Allen Watson .15 .07
❑ 17 Roberto Alomar .60 .25

| | # | Player | | |
|---|---|---|---|---|
| ❑ | 18 | Brady Anderson | .25 | .11 |
| ❑ | 19 | Harold Baines | .25 | .11 |
| ❑ | 20 | Armando Benitez | .15 | .07 |
| ❑ | 21 | Geronimo Berroa | .15 | .07 |
| ❑ | 22 | Mike Bordick | .15 | .07 |
| ❑ | 23 | Eric Davis | .25 | .11 |
| ❑ | 24 | Scott Erickson | .15 | .07 |
| ❑ | 25 | Chris Hoiles | .15 | .07 |
| ❑ | 26 | Jimmy Key | .25 | .11 |
| ❑ | 27 | Aaron Ledesma | .15 | .07 |
| ❑ | 28 | Mike Mussina | .60 | .25 |
| ❑ | 29 | Randy Myers | .25 | .11 |
| ❑ | 30 | Jesse Orosco | .15 | .07 |
| ❑ | 31 | Rafael Palmeiro | .60 | .25 |
| ❑ | 32 | Jeff Reboulet | .15 | .07 |
| ❑ | 33 | Cal Ripken | 2.50 | 1.10 |
| ❑ | 34 | B.J. Surhoff | .25 | .11 |
| ❑ | 35 | Steve Avery | .15 | .07 |
| ❑ | 36 | Darren Bragg | .15 | .07 |
| ❑ | 37 | Wil Cordero | .15 | .07 |
| ❑ | 38 | Jeff Frye | .15 | .07 |
| ❑ | 39 | Nomar Garciaparra | 2.00 | .90 |
| ❑ | 40 | Tom Gordon | .25 | .11 |
| ❑ | 41 | Bill Haselman | .15 | .07 |
| ❑ | 42 | Scott Hatteberg | .15 | .07 |
| ❑ | 43 | Butch Henry | .15 | .07 |
| ❑ | 44 | Reggie Jefferson | .15 | .07 |
| ❑ | 45 | Tim Naehring | .15 | .07 |
| ❑ | 46 | Troy O'Leary | .15 | .07 |
| ❑ | 47 | Jeff Suppan | .15 | .07 |
| ❑ | 48 | John Valentin | .15 | .07 |
| ❑ | 49 | Mo Vaughn | .25 | .11 |
| ❑ | 50 | Tim Wakefield | .15 | .07 |
| ❑ | 51 | James Baldwin | .15 | .07 |
| ❑ | 52 | Albert Belle | .40 | .18 |
| ❑ | 53 | Tony Castillo | .15 | .07 |
| ❑ | 54 | Doug Drabek | .15 | .07 |
| ❑ | 55 | Ray Durham | .25 | .11 |
| ❑ | 56 | Jorge Fabregas | .15 | .07 |
| ❑ | 57 | Ozzie Guillen | .15 | .07 |
| ❑ | 58 | Matt Karchner | .15 | .07 |
| ❑ | 59 | Norberto Martin | .15 | .07 |
| ❑ | 60 | Dave Martinez | .15 | .07 |
| ❑ | 61 | Lyle Mouton | .15 | .07 |
| ❑ | 62 | Jaime Navarro | .15 | .07 |
| ❑ | 63 | Frank Thomas | 1.25 | .55 |
| ❑ | 64 | Mario Valdez | .15 | .07 |
| ❑ | 65 | Robin Ventura | .25 | .11 |
| ❑ | 66 | Sandy Alomar Jr. | .25 | .11 |
| ❑ | 67 | Paul Assenmacher | .15 | .07 |
| ❑ | 68 | Tony Fernandez | .15 | .07 |
| ❑ | 69 | Brian Giles | .25 | .11 |
| ❑ | 70 | Marquis Grissom | .15 | .07 |
| ❑ | 71 | Orel Hershiser | .25 | .11 |
| ❑ | 72 | Mike Jackson | .15 | .07 |
| ❑ | 73 | David Justice | .40 | .18 |
| ❑ | 74 | Albie Lopez | .15 | .07 |
| ❑ | 75 | Jose Mesa | .15 | .07 |
| ❑ | 76 | Charles Nagy | .15 | .07 |
| ❑ | 77 | Chad Ogea | .15 | .07 |
| ❑ | 78 | Manny Ramirez | .75 | .35 |
| ❑ | 79 | Jim Thome | .40 | .18 |
| ❑ | 80 | Omar Vizquel | .25 | .11 |
| ❑ | 81 | Matt Williams | .40 | .18 |
| ❑ | 82 | Jaret Wright | .15 | .07 |
| ❑ | 83 | Willie Blair | .15 | .07 |
| ❑ | 84 | Raul Casanova | .15 | .07 |
| ❑ | 85 | Tony Clark | .15 | .07 |
| ❑ | 86 | Deivi Cruz | .15 | .07 |
| ❑ | 87 | Damion Easley | .15 | .07 |
| ❑ | 88 | Travis Fryman | .25 | .11 |
| ❑ | 89 | Bobby Higginson | .25 | .11 |
| ❑ | 90 | Brian L. Hunter | .15 | .07 |
| ❑ | 91 | Todd Jones | .15 | .07 |
| ❑ | 92 | Dan Miceli | .15 | .07 |
| ❑ | 93 | Brian Moehler | .15 | .07 |
| ❑ | 94 | Mel Nieves | .15 | .07 |
| ❑ | 95 | Jody Reed | .15 | .07 |
| ❑ | 96 | Justin Thompson | .15 | .07 |
| ❑ | 97 | Bubba Trammell | .15 | .07 |
| ❑ | 98 | Kevin Appier | .25 | .11 |
| ❑ | 99 | Jay Bell | .25 | .11 |
| ❑ | 100 | Yamil Benitez | .15 | .07 |
| ❑ | 101 | Johnny Damon | .25 | .11 |
| ❑ | 102 | Chili Davis | .25 | .11 |
| ❑ | 103 | Jermaine Dye | .25 | .11 |
| ❑ | 104 | Jed Hansen | .15 | .07 |
| ❑ | 105 | Jeff King | .15 | .07 |
| ❑ | 106 | Mike Macfarlane | .15 | .07 |
| ❑ | 107 | Felix Martinez | .15 | .07 |
| ❑ | 108 | Jeff Montgomery | .15 | .07 |
| ❑ | 109 | Jose Offerman | .15 | .07 |
| ❑ | 110 | Dean Palmer | .25 | .11 |
| ❑ | 111 | Hipolito Pichardo | .15 | .07 |
| ❑ | 112 | Jose Rosado | .15 | .07 |
| ❑ | 113 | Jeromy Burnitz | .25 | .11 |
| ❑ | 114 | Jeff Cirillo | .25 | .11 |
| ❑ | 115 | Cal Eldred | .15 | .07 |
| ❑ | 116 | John Jaha | .25 | .11 |
| ❑ | 117 | Doug Jones | .15 | .07 |
| ❑ | 118 | Scott Karl | .15 | .07 |
| ❑ | 119 | Jesse Levis | .15 | .07 |
| ❑ | 120 | Mark Loretta | .15 | .07 |
| ❑ | 121 | Ben McDonald | .15 | .07 |
| ❑ | 122 | Jose Mercedes | .15 | .07 |
| ❑ | 123 | Matt Mieske | .15 | .07 |
| ❑ | 124 | Dave Nilsson | .15 | .07 |
| ❑ | 125 | Jose Valentin | .15 | .07 |
| ❑ | 126 | Fernando Vina | .15 | .07 |
| ❑ | 127 | Gerald Williams | .15 | .07 |
| ❑ | 128 | Rick Aguilera | .15 | .07 |
| ❑ | 129 | Rich Becker | .15 | .07 |
| ❑ | 130 | Ron Coomer | .15 | .07 |
| ❑ | 131 | Marty Cordova | .15 | .07 |
| ❑ | 132 | Eddie Guardado | .15 | .07 |
| ❑ | 133 | LaTroy Hawkins | .15 | .07 |
| ❑ | 134 | Denny Hocking | .15 | .07 |
| ❑ | 135 | Chuck Knoblauch | .25 | .11 |
| ❑ | 136 | Matt Lawton | .15 | .07 |
| ❑ | 137 | Pat Meares | .15 | .07 |
| ❑ | 138 | Paul Molitor | .60 | .25 |
| ❑ | 139 | David Ortiz | .15 | .07 |
| ❑ | 140 | Brad Radke | .25 | .11 |
| ❑ | 141 | Terry Steinbach | .15 | .07 |
| ❑ | 142 | Bob Tewksbury | .15 | .07 |
| ❑ | 143 | Javier Valentin | .15 | .07 |
| ❑ | 144 | Wade Boggs | .75 | .35 |
| ❑ | 145 | David Cone | .25 | .11 |
| ❑ | 146 | Chad Curtis | .15 | .07 |
| ❑ | 147 | Cecil Fielder | .25 | .11 |
| ❑ | 148 | Joe Girardi | .15 | .07 |
| ❑ | 149 | Dwight Gooden | .15 | .07 |
| ❑ | 150 | Hideki Irabu | .15 | .07 |
| ❑ | 151 | Derek Jeter | 2.50 | 1.10 |
| ❑ | 152 | Tino Martinez | .25 | .11 |
| ❑ | 153 | Ramiro Mendoza | .15 | .07 |
| ❑ | 154 | Paul O'Neill | .25 | .11 |
| ❑ | 155 | Andy Pettitte | .25 | .11 |
| ❑ | 156 | Jorge Posada | .15 | .07 |
| ❑ | 157 | Mariano Rivera | .25 | .11 |
| ❑ | 158 | Rey Sanchez | .15 | .07 |
| ❑ | 159 | Luis Sojo | .15 | .07 |
| ❑ | 160 | David Wells | .25 | .11 |
| ❑ | 161 | Bernie Williams | .60 | .25 |
| ❑ | 162 | Rafael Bournigal | .15 | .07 |
| ❑ | 163 | Scott Brosius | .25 | .11 |
| ❑ | 164 | Jose Canseco | .75 | .35 |
| ❑ | 165 | Jason Giambi | .60 | .25 |
| ❑ | 166 | Ben Grieve | .25 | .11 |
| ❑ | 167 | Dave Magadan | .15 | .07 |
| ❑ | 168 | Brent Mayne | .15 | .07 |
| ❑ | 169 | Jason McDonald | .15 | .07 |
| ❑ | 170 | Izzy Molina | .15 | .07 |
| ❑ | 171 | Ariel Prieto | .15 | .07 |
| ❑ | 172 | Carlos Reyes | .15 | .07 |
| ❑ | 173 | Scott Spiezio | .15 | .07 |
| ❑ | 174 | Matt Stairs | .15 | .07 |
| ❑ | 175 | Bill Taylor | .15 | .07 |
| ❑ | 176 | Dave Telgheder | .15 | .07 |
| ❑ | 177 | Steve Wojciechowski | .15 | .07 |
| ❑ | 178 | Rich Amaral | .15 | .07 |
| ❑ | 179 | Bobby Ayala | .15 | .07 |
| ❑ | 180 | Jay Buhner | .25 | .11 |
| ❑ | 181 | Rafael Carmona | .15 | .07 |
| ❑ | 182 | Ken Cloude | .15 | .07 |
| ❑ | 183 | Joey Cora | .15 | .07 |
| ❑ | 184 | Russ Davis | .15 | .07 |
| ❑ | 185 | Jeff Fassero | .15 | .07 |
| ❑ | 186 | Ken Griffey Jr. | 2.50 | 1.10 |
| ❑ | 187 | Raul Ibanez | .15 | .07 |
| ❑ | 188 | Randy Johnson | .75 | .35 |
| ❑ | 189 | Roberto Kelly | .15 | .07 |
| ❑ | 190 | Edgar Martinez | .40 | .18 |
| ❑ | 191 | Jamie Moyer | .15 | .07 |
| ❑ | 192 | Omar Olivares | .15 | .07 |
| ❑ | 193 | Alex Rodriguez | 2.00 | .90 |
| ❑ | 194 | Heathcliff Slocumb | .15 | .07 |
| ❑ | 195 | Paul Sorrento | .15 | .07 |
| ❑ | 196 | Dan Wilson | .15 | .07 |
| ❑ | 197 | Scott Bailes | .15 | .07 |
| ❑ | 198 | John Burkett | .15 | .07 |
| ❑ | 199 | Domingo Cedeno | .15 | .07 |
| ❑ | 200 | Will Clark | .60 | .25 |
| ❑ | 201 | Hanley Frias RC | .15 | .07 |
| ❑ | 202 | Juan Gonzalez | .60 | .25 |
| ❑ | 203 | Tom Goodwin | .15 | .07 |
| ❑ | 204 | Rusty Greer | .25 | .11 |
| ❑ | 205 | Wilson Heredia | .15 | .07 |
| ❑ | 206 | Darren Oliver | .15 | .07 |
| ❑ | 207 | Bill Ripken | .15 | .07 |
| ❑ | 208 | Ivan Rodriguez | .60 | .25 |
| ❑ | 209 | Lee Stevens | .15 | .07 |
| ❑ | 210 | Fernando Tatis | .25 | .11 |
| ❑ | 211 | John Wetteland | .25 | .11 |
| ❑ | 212 | Bobby Witt | .15 | .07 |
| ❑ | 213 | Jacob Brumfield | .15 | .07 |
| ❑ | 214 | Joe Carter | .25 | .11 |
| ❑ | 215 | Roger Clemens | 1.25 | .55 |
| ❑ | 216 | Felipe Crespo | .15 | .07 |
| ❑ | 217 | Jose Cruz Jr. | .25 | .11 |
| ❑ | 218 | Carlos Delgado | .60 | .25 |
| ❑ | 219 | Mariano Duncan | .15 | .07 |
| ❑ | 220 | Carlos Garcia | .15 | .07 |
| ❑ | 221 | Alex Gonzalez | .15 | .07 |
| ❑ | 222 | Juan Guzman | .15 | .07 |
| ❑ | 223 | Pat Hentgen | .15 | .07 |
| ❑ | 224 | Orlando Merced | .15 | .07 |
| ❑ | 225 | Tomas Perez | .15 | .07 |
| ❑ | 226 | Paul Quantrill | .15 | .07 |
| ❑ | 227 | Benito Santiago | .15 | .07 |
| ❑ | 228 | Woody Williams | .15 | .07 |
| ❑ | 229 | Rafael Belliard | .15 | .07 |
| ❑ | 230 | Jeff Blauser | .15 | .07 |
| ❑ | 231 | Pedro Borbon | .15 | .07 |
| ❑ | 232 | Tom Glavine | .60 | .25 |
| ❑ | 233 | Tony Graffanino | .15 | .07 |
| ❑ | 234 | Andruw Jones | .60 | .25 |
| ❑ | 235 | Chipper Jones | 1.50 | .70 |
| ❑ | 236 | Ryan Klesko | .25 | .11 |
| ❑ | 237 | Mark Lemke | .15 | .07 |
| ❑ | 238 | Kenny Lofton | .25 | .11 |
| ❑ | 239 | Javier Lopez | .25 | .11 |
| ❑ | 240 | Fred McGriff | .40 | .18 |
| ❑ | 241 | Greg Maddux | 1.50 | .70 |
| ❑ | 242 | Denny Neagle | .15 | .07 |
| ❑ | 243 | John Smoltz | .25 | .11 |
| ❑ | 244 | Michael Tucker | .15 | .07 |
| ❑ | 245 | Mark Wohlers | .15 | .07 |
| ❑ | 246 | Manny Alexander | .15 | .07 |
| ❑ | 247 | Miguel Batista | .15 | .07 |
| ❑ | 248 | Mark Clark | .15 | .07 |
| ❑ | 249 | Doug Glanville | .15 | .07 |
| ❑ | 250 | Jeremi Gonzalez | .15 | .07 |
| ❑ | 251 | Mark Grace | .60 | .25 |
| ❑ | 252 | Jose Hernandez | .15 | .07 |
| ❑ | 253 | Lance Johnson | .15 | .07 |
| ❑ | 254 | Brooks Kieschnick | .15 | .07 |
| ❑ | 255 | Kevin Orie | .15 | .07 |
| ❑ | 256 | Ryne Sandberg | .75 | .35 |
| ❑ | 257 | Scott Servais | .15 | .07 |
| ❑ | 258 | Sammy Sosa | 1.25 | .55 |
| ❑ | 259 | Kevin Tapani | .15 | .07 |
| ❑ | 260 | Ramon Tatis | .15 | .07 |
| ❑ | 261 | Bret Boone | .25 | .11 |
| ❑ | 262 | Dave Burba | .15 | .07 |
| ❑ | 263 | Brook Fordyce | .15 | .07 |
| ❑ | 264 | Willie Greene | .15 | .07 |
| ❑ | 265 | Barry Larkin | .60 | .25 |
| ❑ | 266 | Pedro A. Martinez | .15 | .07 |
| ❑ | 267 | Hal Morris | .15 | .07 |
| ❑ | 268 | Joe Oliver | .15 | .07 |
| ❑ | 269 | Eduardo Perez | .15 | .07 |
| ❑ | 270 | Pokey Reese | .25 | .11 |
| ❑ | 271 | Felix Rodriguez | .15 | .07 |
| ❑ | 272 | Deion Sanders | .25 | .11 |
| ❑ | 273 | Reggie Sanders | .15 | .07 |
| ❑ | 274 | Jeff Shaw | .15 | .07 |
| ❑ | 275 | Scott Sullivan | .15 | .07 |

| No. | Player | MINT | NRMT |
|---|---|---|---|
| ❑ 276 | Brett Tomko | .15 | .07 |
| ❑ 277 | Roger Bailey | .15 | .07 |
| ❑ 278 | Dante Bichette | .25 | .11 |
| ❑ 279 | Ellis Burks | .25 | .11 |
| ❑ 280 | Vinny Castilla | .25 | .11 |
| ❑ 281 | Frank Castillo | .15 | .07 |
| ❑ 282 | Mike DeJean RC | .15 | .07 |
| ❑ 283 | Andres Galarraga | .40 | .18 |
| ❑ 284 | Darren Holmes | .15 | .07 |
| ❑ 285 | Kirt Manwaring | .15 | .07 |
| ❑ 286 | Quinton McCracken | .15 | .07 |
| ❑ 287 | Neifi Perez | .15 | .07 |
| ❑ 288 | Steve Reed | .15 | .07 |
| ❑ 289 | John Thomson | .15 | .07 |
| ❑ 290 | Larry Walker | .25 | .11 |
| ❑ 291 | Walt Weiss | .25 | .11 |
| ❑ 292 | Kurt Abbott | .15 | .07 |
| ❑ 293 | Antonio Alfonseca | .15 | .07 |
| ❑ 294 | Moises Alou | .25 | .11 |
| ❑ 295 | Alex Arias | .15 | .07 |
| ❑ 296 | Bobby Bonilla | .25 | .11 |
| ❑ 297 | Kevin Brown | .40 | .18 |
| ❑ 298 | Craig Counsell | .15 | .07 |
| ❑ 299 | Darren Daulton | .25 | .11 |
| ❑ 300 | Jim Eisenreich | .15 | .07 |
| ❑ 301 | Alex Fernandez | .15 | .07 |
| ❑ 302 | Felix Heredia | .15 | .07 |
| ❑ 303 | Livan Hernandez | .15 | .07 |
| ❑ 304 | Charles Johnson | .25 | .11 |
| ❑ 305 | Al Leiter | .25 | .11 |
| ❑ 306 | Robb Nen | .15 | .07 |
| ❑ 307 | Edgar Renteria | .15 | .07 |
| ❑ 308 | Gary Sheffield | .60 | .25 |
| ❑ 309 | Devon White | .15 | .07 |
| ❑ 310 | Bob Abreu | .25 | .11 |
| ❑ 311 | Brad Ausmus | .15 | .07 |
| ❑ 312 | Jeff Bagwell | .75 | .35 |
| ❑ 313 | Derek Bell | .15 | .07 |
| ❑ 314 | Sean Berry | .15 | .07 |
| ❑ 315 | Craig Biggio | .40 | .18 |
| ❑ 316 | Ramon Garcia | .15 | .07 |
| ❑ 317 | Luis Gonzalez | .25 | .11 |
| ❑ 318 | Ricky Gutierrez | .15 | .07 |
| ❑ 319 | Mike Hampton | .25 | .11 |
| ❑ 320 | Richard Hidalgo | .25 | .11 |
| ❑ 321 | Thomas Howard | .15 | .07 |
| ❑ 322 | Darryl Kile | .25 | .11 |
| ❑ 323 | Jose Lima | .15 | .07 |
| ❑ 324 | Shane Reynolds | .15 | .07 |
| ❑ 325 | Bill Spiers | .15 | .07 |
| ❑ 326 | Tom Candiotti | .15 | .07 |
| ❑ 327 | Roger Cedeno | .15 | .07 |
| ❑ 328 | Greg Gagne | .15 | .07 |
| ❑ 329 | Karim Garcia | .15 | .07 |
| ❑ 330 | Wilton Guerrero | .15 | .07 |
| ❑ 331 | Todd Hollandsworth | .15 | .07 |
| ❑ 332 | Eric Karros | .25 | .11 |
| ❑ 333 | Ramon Martinez | .15 | .07 |
| ❑ 334 | Raul Mondesi | .25 | .11 |
| ❑ 335 | Otis Nixon | .15 | .07 |
| ❑ 336 | Hideo Nomo | .60 | .25 |
| ❑ 337 | Antonio Osuna | .15 | .07 |
| ❑ 338 | Chan Ho Park | .25 | .11 |
| ❑ 339 | Mike Piazza | 2.00 | .90 |
| ❑ 340 | Dennis Reyes | .15 | .07 |
| ❑ 341 | Ismael Valdes | .15 | .07 |
| ❑ 342 | Todd Worrell | .15 | .07 |
| ❑ 343 | Todd Zeile | .25 | .11 |
| ❑ 344 | Darrin Fletcher | .15 | .07 |
| ❑ 345 | Mark Grudzielanek | .15 | .07 |
| ❑ 346 | Vladimir Guerrero | 1.00 | .45 |
| ❑ 347 | Dustin Hermanson | .15 | .07 |
| ❑ 348 | Mike Lansing | .15 | .07 |
| ❑ 349 | Pedro Martinez | .75 | .35 |
| ❑ 350 | Ryan McGuire | .15 | .07 |
| ❑ 351 | Jose Paniagua | .15 | .07 |
| ❑ 352 | Carlos Perez | .15 | .07 |
| ❑ 353 | Henry Rodriguez | .15 | .07 |
| ❑ 354 | F.P. Santangelo | .15 | .07 |
| ❑ 355 | David Segui | .15 | .07 |
| ❑ 356 | Ugueth Urbina | .15 | .07 |
| ❑ 357 | Marc Valdes | .15 | .07 |
| ❑ 358 | Jose Vidro | .15 | .07 |
| ❑ 359 | Rondell White | .25 | .11 |
| ❑ 360 | Juan Acevedo | .15 | .07 |
| ❑ 361 | Edgardo Alfonzo | .25 | .11 |
| ❑ 362 | Carlos Baerga | .15 | .07 |
| ❑ 363 | Carl Everett | .25 | .11 |
| ❑ 364 | John Franco | .25 | .11 |
| ❑ 365 | Bernard Gilkey | .15 | .07 |
| ❑ 366 | Todd Hundley | .15 | .07 |
| ❑ 367 | Butch Huskey | .15 | .07 |
| ❑ 368 | Bobby Jones | .15 | .07 |
| ❑ 369 | Takashi Kashiwada RC | .15 | .07 |
| ❑ 370 | Greg McMichael | .15 | .07 |
| ❑ 371 | Brian McRae | .15 | .07 |
| ❑ 372 | Alex Ochoa | .15 | .07 |
| ❑ 373 | John Olerud | .25 | .11 |
| ❑ 374 | Rey Ordonez | .15 | .07 |
| ❑ 375 | Turk Wendell | .15 | .07 |
| ❑ 376 | Ricky Bottalico | .15 | .07 |
| ❑ 377 | Rico Brogna | .15 | .07 |
| ❑ 378 | Len Dykstra | .25 | .11 |
| ❑ 379 | Bobby Estalella | .15 | .07 |
| ❑ 380 | Wayne Gomes | .15 | .07 |
| ❑ 381 | Tyler Green | .15 | .07 |
| ❑ 382 | Gregg Jefferies | .15 | .07 |
| ❑ 383 | Mark Leiter | .15 | .07 |
| ❑ 384 | Mike Lieberthal | .25 | .11 |
| ❑ 385 | Mickey Morandini | .15 | .07 |
| ❑ 386 | Scott Rolen | .60 | .25 |
| ❑ 387 | Curt Schilling | .25 | .11 |
| ❑ 388 | Kevin Stocker | .15 | .07 |
| ❑ 389 | Danny Tartabull | .15 | .07 |
| ❑ 390 | Jermaine Allensworth | .15 | .07 |
| ❑ 391 | Adrian Brown | .15 | .07 |
| ❑ 392 | Jason Christiansen | .15 | .07 |
| ❑ 393 | Steve Cooke | .15 | .07 |
| ❑ 394 | Francisco Cordova | .15 | .07 |
| ❑ 395 | Jose Guillen | .15 | .07 |
| ❑ 396 | Jason Kendall | .25 | .11 |
| ❑ 397 | Jon Lieber | .15 | .07 |
| ❑ 398 | Esteban Loaiza | .15 | .07 |
| ❑ 399 | Al Martin | .15 | .07 |
| ❑ 400 | Kevin Polcovich | .15 | .07 |
| ❑ 401 | Joe Randa | .15 | .07 |
| ❑ 402 | Ricardo Rincon | .15 | .07 |
| ❑ 403 | Tony Womack | .15 | .07 |
| ❑ 404 | Kevin Young | .25 | .11 |
| ❑ 405 | Andy Benes | .15 | .07 |
| ❑ 406 | Royce Clayton | .15 | .07 |
| ❑ 407 | Delino DeShields | .15 | .07 |
| ❑ 408 | Mike Difelice RC | .15 | .07 |
| ❑ 409 | Dennis Eckersley | .25 | .11 |
| ❑ 410 | John Frascatore | .15 | .07 |
| ❑ 411 | Gary Gaetti | .25 | .11 |
| ❑ 412 | Ron Gant | .25 | .11 |
| ❑ 413 | Brian Jordan | .25 | .11 |
| ❑ 414 | Ray Lankford | .25 | .11 |
| ❑ 415 | Willie McGee | .25 | .11 |
| ❑ 416 | Mark McGwire | 2.50 | 1.10 |
| ❑ 417 | Matt Morris | .15 | .07 |
| ❑ 418 | Luis Ordaz | .15 | .07 |
| ❑ 419 | Todd Stottlemyre | .15 | .07 |
| ❑ 420 | Andy Ashby | .15 | .07 |
| ❑ 421 | Jim Bruske | .15 | .07 |
| ❑ 422 | Ken Caminiti | .25 | .11 |
| ❑ 423 | Will Cunnane | .15 | .07 |
| ❑ 424 | Steve Finley | .25 | .11 |
| ❑ 425 | John Flaherty | .15 | .07 |
| ❑ 426 | Chris Gomez | .15 | .07 |
| ❑ 427 | Tony Gwynn | 1.25 | .55 |
| ❑ 428 | Joey Hamilton | .15 | .07 |
| ❑ 429 | Carlos Hernandez | .15 | .07 |
| ❑ 430 | Sterling Hitchcock | .15 | .07 |
| ❑ 431 | Trevor Hoffman | .25 | .11 |
| ❑ 432 | Wally Joyner | .25 | .11 |
| ❑ 433 | Greg Vaughn | .25 | .11 |
| ❑ 434 | Quilvio Veras | .15 | .07 |
| ❑ 435 | Wilson Alvarez | .15 | .07 |
| ❑ 436 | Rod Beck | .15 | .07 |
| ❑ 437 | Barry Bonds | 1.00 | .45 |
| ❑ 438 | Jacob Cruz | .15 | .07 |
| ❑ 439 | Shawn Estes | .15 | .07 |
| ❑ 440 | Darryl Hamilton | .15 | .07 |
| ❑ 441 | Roberto Hernandez | .15 | .07 |
| ❑ 442 | Glenallen Hill | .15 | .07 |
| ❑ 443 | Stan Javier | .15 | .07 |
| ❑ 444 | Brian Johnson | .15 | .07 |
| ❑ 445 | Jeff Kent | .40 | .18 |
| ❑ 446 | Bill Mueller | .15 | .07 |
| ❑ 447 | Kirk Rueter | .15 | .07 |
| ❑ 448 | J.T. Snow | .25 | .11 |
| ❑ 449 | Julian Tavarez | .15 | .07 |
| ❑ 450 | Jose Vizcaino | .15 | .07 |

## 1999 Pacific

| No. | Player | MINT | NRMT |
|---|---|---|---|
| | COMPLETE SET (500) | 80.00 | 36.00 |
| ❑ 1 | Garret Anderson | .25 | .11 |
| ❑ 2 | Jason Dickson | .15 | .07 |
| ❑ 3 | Gary DiSarcina | .15 | .07 |
| ❑ 4 | Jim Edmonds | .60 | .25 |
| ❑ 5 | Darin Erstad | .60 | .25 |
| ❑ 6 | Chuck Finley | .25 | .11 |
| ❑ 7 | Shigetoshi Hasegawa | .15 | .07 |
| ❑ 8 | Ken Hill | .15 | .07 |
| ❑ 9 | Dave Hollins | .15 | .07 |
| ❑ 10 | Phil Nevin | .25 | .11 |
| ❑ 11 | Troy Percival | .15 | .07 |
| ❑ 12 | Tim Salmon * | .25 | .11 |
| ❑ 12A | Tim Salmon Headshot | .25 | .11 |
| ❑ 13 | Brian Anderson | .15 | .07 |
| ❑ 14 | Tony Batista | .25 | .11 |
| ❑ 15 | Jay Bell | .25 | .11 |
| ❑ 16 | Andy Benes | .15 | .07 |
| ❑ 17 | Yamil Benitez | .15 | .07 |
| ❑ 18 | Omar Daal | .15 | .07 |
| ❑ 19 | David Dellucci | .15 | .07 |
| ❑ 20 | Karim Garcia | .15 | .07 |
| ❑ 21 | Bernard Gilkey | .15 | .07 |
| ❑ 22 | Travis Lee * | .15 | .07 |
| ❑ 22A | Travis Lee Headshot | .15 | .07 |
| ❑ 23 | Aaron Small | .15 | .07 |
| ❑ 24 | Kelly Stinnett | .15 | .07 |
| ❑ 25 | Devon White | .15 | .07 |
| ❑ 26 | Matt Williams | .40 | .18 |
| ❑ 27 | Bruce Chen * | .15 | .07 |
| ❑ 27A | Bruce Chen Headshot | .15 | .07 |
| ❑ 28 | Andres Galarraga * | .40 | .18 |
| ❑ 28A | A. Galarraga Headshot | .40 | .18 |
| ❑ 29 | Tom Glavine | .60 | .25 |
| ❑ 30 | Ozzie Guillen | .15 | .07 |
| ❑ 31 | Andruw Jones | .60 | .25 |
| ❑ 32 | Chipper Jones * | 1.50 | .70 |
| ❑ 32A | Chipper Jones Headshot | 1.50 | .70 |
| ❑ 33 | Ryan Klesko | .25 | .11 |
| ❑ 34 | George Lombard | .15 | .07 |
| ❑ 35 | Javy Lopez | .25 | .11 |
| ❑ 36 | Greg Maddux * | 1.50 | .70 |
| ❑ 36A | Greg Maddux Headshot | 1.50 | .70 |
| ❑ 37 | Marty Malloy * | .15 | .07 |
| ❑ 37A | Marty Malloy Headshot | .15 | .07 |
| ❑ 38 | Dennis Martinez | .25 | .11 |
| ❑ 39 | Kevin Millwood | .25 | .11 |
| ❑ 40 | Alex Rodriguez * | 2.00 | .90 |
| ❑ 40A | Alex Rodriguez Headshot | 2.00 | .90 |
| ❑ 41 | Denny Neagle | .15 | .07 |
| ❑ 42 | John Smoltz | .25 | .11 |
| ❑ 43 | Michael Tucker | .15 | .07 |
| ❑ 44 | Walt Weiss | .15 | .07 |
| ❑ 45 | Roberto Alomar * | .60 | .25 |
| ❑ 45A | R.Alomar Headshot | .60 | .25 |
| ❑ 46 | Brady Anderson | .25 | .11 |
| ❑ 47 | Harold Baines | .25 | .11 |
| ❑ 48 | Mike Bordick | .15 | .07 |
| ❑ 49 | Danny Clyburn * | .15 | .07 |
| ❑ 49A | Danny Clyburn Headshot | .15 | .07 |

- ❑ 50 Eric Davis .25 .11
- ❑ 51 Scott Erickson .15 .07
- ❑ 52 Chris Hoiles .15 .07
- ❑ 53 Jimmy Key .15 .07
- ❑ 54 Ryan Minor * .15 .07
- ❑ 54A Ryan Minor Headshot .15 .07
- ❑ 55 Mike Mussina .60 .25
- ❑ 56 Jesse Orosco .15 .07
- ❑ 57 Rafael Palmeiro * .60 .25
- ❑ 57A R.Palmeiro Headshot .60 .25
- ❑ 58 Sidney Ponson .15 .07
- ❑ 59 Arthur Rhodes .15 .07
- ❑ 60 Cal Ripken * 2.50 1.10
- ❑ 60A Cal Ripken Headshot 2.50 1.10
- ❑ 61 B.J. Surhoff .25 .11
- ❑ 62 Steve Avery .15 .07
- ❑ 63 Darren Bragg .15 .07
- ❑ 64 Dennis Eckersley .25 .11
- ❑ 65 Nomar Garciaparra * 2.00 .90
- ❑ 65A N.Garciaparra Headshot 2.00 .90
- ❑ 66 Sammy Sosa * 1.25 .55
- ❑ 66A Sammy Sosa Headshot 1.25 .55
- ❑ 67 Tom Gordon .15 .07
- ❑ 68 Reggie Jefferson .15 .07
- ❑ 69 Darren Lewis .15 .07
- ❑ 70 Mark McGwire * 2.50 1.10
- ❑ 70A Mark McGwire Headshot 2.50 1.10
- ❑ 71 Pedro Martinez .75 .35
- ❑ 72 Troy O'Leary .15 .07
- ❑ 73 Bret Saberhagen .25 .11
- ❑ 74 Mike Stanley .15 .07
- ❑ 75 John Valentin .15 .07
- ❑ 76 Jason Varitek .25 .11
- ❑ 77 Mo Vaughn .25 .11
- ❑ 78 Tim Wakefield .15 .07
- ❑ 79 Manny Alexander .15 .07
- ❑ 80 Rod Beck .15 .07
- ❑ 81 Brant Brown .15 .07
- ❑ 82 Mark Clark .15 .07
- ❑ 83 Gary Gaetti .15 .07
- ❑ 84 Mark Grace .60 .25
- ❑ 85 Jose Hernandez .15 .07
- ❑ 86 Lance Johnson .15 .07
- ❑ 87 Jason Maxwell * .15 .07
- ❑ 87A Jason Maxwell Headshot .15 .07
- ❑ 88 Mickey Morandini .15 .07
- ❑ 89 Terry Mulholland .15 .07
- ❑ 90 Henry Rodriguez .15 .07
- ❑ 91 Scott Servais .15 .07
- ❑ 92 Kevin Tapani .15 .07
- ❑ 93 Pedro Valdes .15 .07
- ❑ 94 Kerry Wood .25 .11
- ❑ 95 Jeff Abbott .15 .07
- ❑ 96 James Baldwin .15 .07
- ❑ 97 Albert Belle .40 .18
- ❑ 98 Mike Cameron .15 .07
- ❑ 99 Mike Caruso .15 .07
- ❑ 100 Wil Cordero .15 .07
- ❑ 101 Ray Durham .25 .11
- ❑ 102 Jaime Navarro .15 .07
- ❑ 103 Greg Norton .15 .07
- ❑ 104 Magglio Ordonez .40 .18
- ❑ 105 Mike Sirotka .15 .07
- ❑ 106 Frank Thomas * 1.25 .55
- ❑ 106A F.Thomas Headshot 1.25 .55
- ❑ 107 Robin Ventura .25 .11
- ❑ 108 Craig Wilson .15 .07
- ❑ 109 Aaron Boone .15 .07
- ❑ 110 Bret Boone .25 .11
- ❑ 111 Sean Casey .25 .11
- ❑ 112 Pete Harnisch .15 .07
- ❑ 113 John Hudek .15 .07
- ❑ 114 Barry Larkin .60 .25
- ❑ 115 Eduardo Perez .15 .07
- ❑ 116 Mike Remlinger .15 .07
- ❑ 117 Reggie Sanders .15 .07
- ❑ 118 Chris Stynes .15 .07
- ❑ 119 Eddie Taubensee .15 .07
- ❑ 120 Brett Tomko .15 .07
- ❑ 121 Pat Watkins .15 .07
- ❑ 122 Dmitri Young .25 .11
- ❑ 123 Sandy Alomar Jr. .25 .11
- ❑ 124 Dave Burba .15 .07
- ❑ 125 Bartolo Colon .25 .11
- ❑ 126 Joey Cora .15 .07
- ❑ 127 Brian Giles .25 .11
- ❑ 128 Dwight Gooden .25 .11
- ❑ 129 Mike Jackson .15 .07
- ❑ 130 David Justice .40 .18
- ❑ 131 Kenny Lofton .25 .11
- ❑ 132 Charles Nagy .15 .07
- ❑ 133 Chad Ogea .15 .07
- ❑ 134 Manny Ramirez * .75 .35
- ❑ 134A M.Ramirez Headshot .75 .35
- ❑ 135 Richie Sexson .25 .11
- ❑ 136 Jim Thome * .40 .18
- ❑ 136A Jim Thome Headshot .40 .18
- ❑ 137 Omar Vizquel .25 .11
- ❑ 138 Jaret Wright .15 .07
- ❑ 139 Pedro Astacio .15 .07
- ❑ 140 Jason Bates .15 .07
- ❑ 141 Dante Bichette * .25 .11
- ❑ 141A D. Bichette Headshot .25 .11
- ❑ 142 Vinny Castilla * .25 .11
- ❑ 142A Vinny Castilla Headshot .25 .11
- ❑ 143 Edgard Clemente * .15 .07
- ❑ 143A E. Clemente Headshot .15 .07
- ❑ 144 Derrick Gibson * .15 .07
- ❑ 144A D. Gibson Headshot .15 .07
- ❑ 145 Curtis Goodwin .15 .07
- ❑ 146 Todd Helton * .75 .35
- ❑ 146A Todd Helton Headshot .75 .35
- ❑ 147 Bobby Jones .15 .07
- ❑ 148 Darryl Kile .25 .11
- ❑ 149 Mike Lansing .15 .07
- ❑ 150 Chuck McElroy .15 .07
- ❑ 151 Neifi Perez .15 .07
- ❑ 152 Jeff Reed .15 .07
- ❑ 153 John Thomson .15 .07
- ❑ 154 Larry Walker * .25 .11
- ❑ 154A Larry Walker Headshot .25 .11
- ❑ 155 Jamey Wright .15 .07
- ❑ 156 Kimera Bartee .15 .07
- ❑ 157 Geronimo Berroa .15 .07
- ❑ 158 Raul Casanova .15 .07
- ❑ 159 Frank Catalanotto .15 .07
- ❑ 160 Tony Clark .15 .07
- ❑ 161 Deivi Cruz .15 .07
- ❑ 162 Damion Easley .15 .07
- ❑ 163 Juan Encarnacion .25 .11
- ❑ 164 Luis Gonzalez .25 .11
- ❑ 165 Seth Greisinger .15 .07
- ❑ 166 Bob Higginson .25 .11
- ❑ 167 Brian L.Hunter .15 .07
- ❑ 168 Todd Jones .15 .07
- ❑ 169 Justin Thompson .15 .07
- ❑ 170 Antonio Alfonseca .15 .07
- ❑ 171 Dave Berg .15 .07
- ❑ 172 John Cangelosi .15 .07
- ❑ 173 Craig Counsell .15 .07
- ❑ 174 Todd Dunwoody .15 .07
- ❑ 175 Cliff Floyd .25 .11
- ❑ 176 Alex Gonzalez .15 .07
- ❑ 177 Livan Hernandez .15 .07
- ❑ 178 Ryan Jackson .15 .07
- ❑ 179 Mark Kotsay .15 .07
- ❑ 180 Derrek Lee .15 .07
- ❑ 181 Matt Mantei .15 .07
- ❑ 182 Brian Meadows .15 .07
- ❑ 183 Edgar Renteria .15 .07
- ❑ 184 Moises Alou * .25 .11
- ❑ 184A Moises Alou Headshot .25 .11
- ❑ 185 Brad Ausmus .15 .07
- ❑ 186 Jeff Bagwell * .75 .35
- ❑ 186A Jeff Bagwell Headshot .75 .35
- ❑ 187 Derek Bell .15 .07
- ❑ 188 Sean Berry .15 .07
- ❑ 189 Craig Biggio .40 .18
- ❑ 190 Carl Everett .25 .11
- ❑ 191 Ricky Gutierrez .15 .07
- ❑ 192 Mike Hampton .25 .11
- ❑ 193 Doug Henry .15 .07
- ❑ 194 Richard Hidalgo .25 .11
- ❑ 195 Randy Johnson .75 .35
- ❑ 196 Russ Johnson * .15 .07
- ❑ 196A Russ Johnson Headshot .15 .07
- ❑ 197 Shane Reynolds .15 .07
- ❑ 198 Bill Spiers .15 .07
- ❑ 199 Kevin Appier .25 .11
- ❑ 200 Tim Belcher .15 .07
- ❑ 201 Jeff Conine .15 .07
- ❑ 202 Johnny Damon .25 .11
- ❑ 203 Jermaine Dye .25 .11
- ❑ 204 Jeremy Giambi * .15 .07
- ❑ 204A Je. Giambi Headshot .15 .07
- ❑ 205 Jeff King .15 .07
- ❑ 206 Shane Mack .15 .07
- ❑ 207 Jeff Montgomery .15 .07
- ❑ 208 Hal Morris .15 .07
- ❑ 209 Jose Offerman .15 .07
- ❑ 210 Dean Palmer .25 .11
- ❑ 211 Jose Rosado .15 .07
- ❑ 212 Glendon Rusch .15 .07
- ❑ 213 Larry Sutton .15 .07
- ❑ 214 Mike Sweeney .25 .11
- ❑ 215 Bobby Bonilla .25 .11
- ❑ 216 Alex Cora .15 .07
- ❑ 217 Darren Dreifort .15 .07
- ❑ 218 Mark Grudzielanek .15 .07
- ❑ 219 Todd Hollandsworth .15 .07
- ❑ 220 Trenidad Hubbard .15 .07
- ❑ 221 Charles Johnson .25 .11
- ❑ 222 Eric Karros .25 .11
- ❑ 223 Matt Luke .15 .07
- ❑ 224 Ramon Martinez .15 .07
- ❑ 225 Raul Mondesi .25 .11
- ❑ 226 Chan Ho Park .25 .11
- ❑ 227 Jeff Shaw .15 .07
- ❑ 228 Gary Sheffield .60 .25
- ❑ 229 Eric Young .15 .07
- ❑ 230 Jeromy Burnitz .25 .11
- ❑ 231 Jeff Cirillo .25 .11
- ❑ 232 Marquis Grissom .15 .07
- ❑ 233 Bobby Hughes .15 .07
- ❑ 234 John Jaha .15 .07
- ❑ 235 Geoff Jenkins .25 .11
- ❑ 236 Scott Karl .15 .07
- ❑ 237 Mark Loretta .15 .07
- ❑ 238 Mike Matheny .15 .07
- ❑ 239 Mike Myers .15 .07
- ❑ 240 Dave Nilsson .15 .07
- ❑ 241 Bob Wickman .15 .07
- ❑ 242 Jose Valentin .15 .07
- ❑ 243 Fernando Vina .15 .07
- ❑ 244 Rick Aguilera .15 .07
- ❑ 245 Ron Coomer .15 .07
- ❑ 246 Marty Cordova .15 .07
- ❑ 247 Denny Hocking .15 .07
- ❑ 248 Matt Lawton .25 .11
- ❑ 249 Pat Meares .15 .07
- ❑ 250 Paul Molitor * .60 .25
- ❑ 250A Paul Molitor Headshot .60 .25
- ❑ 251 Otis Nixon .15 .07
- ❑ 252 Alex Ochoa .15 .07
- ❑ 253 David Ortiz .15 .07
- ❑ 254 A.J. Pierzynski .15 .07
- ❑ 255 Brad Radke .25 .11
- ❑ 256 Terry Steinbach .15 .07
- ❑ 257 Bob Tewksbury .15 .07
- ❑ 258 Todd Walker .15 .07
- ❑ 259 Shane Andrews .15 .07
- ❑ 260 Shayne Bennett .15 .07
- ❑ 261 Orlando Cabrera .15 .07
- ❑ 262 Brad Fullmer .25 .11
- ❑ 263 Vladimir Guerrero 1.00 .45
- ❑ 264 Wilton Guerrero .15 .07
- ❑ 265 Dustin Hermanson .15 .07
- ❑ 266 Terry Jones RC .15 .07
- ❑ 267 Steve Kline .15 .07
- ❑ 268 Carl Pavano .15 .07
- ❑ 269 F.P. Santangelo .15 .07
- ❑ 270 Fernando Seguignol * .15 .07
- ❑ 270A F.Seguignol Headshot .15 .07
- ❑ 271 Ugueth Urbina .15 .07
- ❑ 272 Jose Vidro .15 .07
- ❑ 273 Chris Widger .15 .07
- ❑ 274 Edgardo Alfonzo .25 .11
- ❑ 275 Carlos Baerga .15 .07
- ❑ 276 John Franco .25 .11
- ❑ 277 Todd Hundley .15 .07
- ❑ 278 Butch Huskey .15 .07
- ❑ 279 Bobby Jones .15 .07
- ❑ 280 Al Leiter .25 .11
- ❑ 281 Greg McMichael .15 .07
- ❑ 282 Brian McRae .15 .07
- ❑ 283 Hideo Nomo .60 .25
- ❑ 284 John Olerud .25 .11
- ❑ 285 Rey Ordonez .15 .07

❑ 286 Mike Piazza * 2.00 .90
❑ 286A Mike Piazza Headshot 2.00 .90
❑ 287 Turk Wendell .15 .07
❑ 288 Masato Yoshii .25 .11
❑ 289 David Cone .25 .11
❑ 290 Chad Curtis .15 .07
❑ 291 Joe Girardi .15 .07
❑ 292 Orlando Hernandez .25 .11
❑ 293 Hideki Irabu * .15 .07
❑ 293A Hideki Irabu Headshot .15 .07
❑ 294 Derek Jeter * 2.50 1.10
❑ 294A Derek Jeter Headshot 2.50 1.10
❑ 295 Chuck Knoblauch .25 .11
❑ 296 Mike Lowell * .25 .11
❑ 296A Mike Lowell Headshot .25 .11
❑ 297 Tino Martinez .25 .11
❑ 298 Ramiro Mendoza .15 .07
❑ 299 Paul O'Neill .25 .11
❑ 300 Andy Pettitte .25 .11
❑ 301 Jorge Posada .25 .11
❑ 302 Tim Raines .25 .11
❑ 303 Mariano Rivera .25 .11
❑ 304 David Wells .25 .11
❑ 305 Bernie Williams * .60 .25
❑ 305A B. Williams Headshot .60 .25
❑ 306 Mike Blowers .15 .07
❑ 307 Tom Candiotti .15 .07
❑ 308 Eric Chavez * .25 .11
❑ 308A Eric Chavez Headshot .25 .11
❑ 309 Ryan Christenson .15 .07
❑ 310 Jason Giambi .60 .25
❑ 311 Ben Grieve * .25 .11
❑ 311A Ben Grieve Headshot .25 .11
❑ 312 Rickey Henderson .75 .35
❑ 313 A.J. Hinch .15 .07
❑ 314 Jason McDonald .15 .07
❑ 315 Bip Roberts .15 .07
❑ 316 Kenny Rogers .15 .07
❑ 317 Scott Spiezio .15 .07
❑ 318 Matt Stairs .15 .07
❑ 319 Miguel Tejada .25 .11
❑ 320 Bob Abreu .25 .11
❑ 321 Alex Arias .15 .07
❑ 322 Gary Bennett RC* .15 .07
❑ 322A Gary Bennett RC* Headshot .15 .07
❑ 323 Ricky Bottalico .15 .07
❑ 324 Rico Brogna .15 .07
❑ 325 Bobby Estalella .15 .07
❑ 326 Doug Glanville .15 .07
❑ 327 Kevin Jordan .15 .07
❑ 328 Mark Leiter .15 .07
❑ 329 Wendell Magee .15 .07
❑ 330 Mark Portugal .15 .07
❑ 331 Desi Relaford .15 .07
❑ 332 Scott Rolen .60 .25
❑ 333 Curt Schilling .25 .11
❑ 334 Kevin Sefcik .15 .07
❑ 335 Adrian Brown .15 .07
❑ 336 Emil Brown .15 .07
❑ 337 Lou Collier .15 .07
❑ 338 Francisco Cordova .15 .07
❑ 339 Freddy Garcia .15 .07
❑ 340 Jose Guillen .15 .07
❑ 341 Jason Kendall .25 .11
❑ 342 Al Martin .15 .07
❑ 343 Abraham Nunez .15 .07
❑ 344 Aramis Ramirez .15 .07
❑ 345 Ricardo Rincon .15 .07
❑ 346 Jason Schmidt .15 .07
❑ 347 Turner Ward .15 .07
❑ 348 Tony Womack .15 .07
❑ 349 Kevin Young .25 .11
❑ 350 Juan Acevedo .15 .07
❑ 351 Delino DeShields .15 .07
❑ 352 J.D. Drew * .60 .25
❑ 352A J.D. Drew Headshot .60 .25
❑ 353 Ron Gant .25 .11
❑ 354 Brian Jordan .25 .11
❑ 355 Ray Lankford .25 .11
❑ 356 Eli Marrero .15 .07
❑ 357 Kent Mercker .15 .07
❑ 358 Matt Morris .15 .07
❑ 359 Luis Ordaz .15 .07
❑ 360 Donovan Osborne .15 .07
❑ 361 Placido Polanco .15 .07
❑ 362 Fernando Tatis .25 .11
❑ 363 Andy Ashby .15 .07
❑ 364 Kevin Brown .40 .18
❑ 365 Ken Caminiti .25 .11
❑ 366 Steve Finley .25 .11
❑ 367 Chris Gomez .15 .07
❑ 368 Tony Gwynn * 1.25 .55
❑ 368A Tony Gwynn Headshot 1.25 .55
❑ 369 Joey Hamilton .15 .07
❑ 370 Carlos Hernandez .15 .07
❑ 371 Trevor Hoffman .25 .11
❑ 372 Wally Joyner .25 .11
❑ 373 Jim Leyritz .15 .07
❑ 374 Ruben Rivera .15 .07
❑ 375 Greg Vaughn .25 .11
❑ 376 Quilvio Veras .15 .07
❑ 377 Rich Aurilia .15 .07
❑ 378 Barry Bonds * 1.00 .45
❑ 378A Barry Bonds Headshot 1.00 .45
❑ 379 Ellis Burks .25 .11
❑ 380 Joe Carter .25 .11
❑ 381 Stan Javier .15 .07
❑ 382 Brian Johnson .15 .07
❑ 383 Jeff Kent .40 .18
❑ 384 Jose Mesa .15 .07
❑ 385 Bill Mueller .15 .07
❑ 386 Robb Nen .15 .07
❑ 387 Armando Rios * .15 .07
❑ 387A Armando Rios Headshot .15 .07
❑ 388 Kirk Rueter .15 .07
❑ 389 Rey Sanchez .15 .07
❑ 390 J.T. Snow .25 .11
❑ 391 David Bell .15 .07
❑ 392 Jay Buhner .25 .11
❑ 393 Ken Cloude .15 .07
❑ 394 Russ Davis .15 .07
❑ 395 Jeff Fassero .15 .07
❑ 396 Ken Griffey Jr. * 2.50 1.10
❑ 396A Ken Griffey Jr. Headshot 2.50 1.10
❑ 397 Giomar Guevara RC .15 .07
❑ 398 Carlos Guillen .15 .07
❑ 399 Edgar Martinez .40 .18
❑ 400 Shane Monahan .15 .07
❑ 401 Jamie Moyer .15 .07
❑ 402 David Segui .15 .07
❑ 403 Makoto Suzuki .15 .07
❑ 404 Mike Timlin .15 .07
❑ 405 Dan Wilson .15 .07
❑ 406 Wilson Alvarez .15 .07
❑ 407 Rolando Arrojo .15 .07
❑ 408 Wade Boggs .75 .35
❑ 409 Miguel Cairo .15 .07
❑ 410 Roberto Hernandez .15 .07
❑ 411 Mike Kelly .15 .07
❑ 412 Aaron Ledesma .15 .07
❑ 413 Albie Lopez .15 .07
❑ 414 Dave Martinez .15 .07
❑ 415 Quinton McCracken .15 .07
❑ 416 Fred McGriff .40 .18
❑ 417 Bryan Rekar .15 .07
❑ 418 Paul Sorrento .15 .07
❑ 419 Randy Winn .15 .07
❑ 420 John Burkett .15 .07
❑ 421 Will Clark .60 .25
❑ 422 Royce Clayton .15 .07
❑ 423 Juan Gonzalez * .60 .25
❑ 423A J. Gonzalez Headshot .60 .25
❑ 424 Tom Goodwin .15 .07
❑ 425 Rusty Greer .25 .11
❑ 426 Rick Helling .25 .11
❑ 427 Roberto Kelly .15 .07
❑ 428 Mark McLemore .15 .07
❑ 429 Ivan Rodriguez * .75 .35
❑ 429A Ivan Rodriguez Headshot .75 .35
❑ 430 Aaron Sele .25 .11
❑ 431 Lee Stevens .15 .07
❑ 432 Todd Stottlemyre .15 .07
❑ 433 John Wetteland .25 .11
❑ 434 Todd Zeile .25 .11
❑ 435 Jose Canseco * .75 .35
❑ 435A Jose Canseco Headshot .60 .25
❑ 436 Roger Clemens * 1.25 .55
❑ 436A R.Clemens Headshot 1.25 .55
❑ 437 Felipe Crespo .15 .07
❑ 438 Jose Cruz Jr. .25 .11
❑ 439 Carlos Delgado .60 .25
❑ 440 Tom Evans * .15 .07
❑ 440A Tom Evans Headshot .15 .07
❑ 441 Tony Fernandez .15 .07
❑ 442 Darrin Fletcher .15 .07
❑ 443 Alex Gonzalez .15 .07
❑ 444 Shawn Green .60 .25
❑ 445 Roy Halladay .15 .07
❑ 446 Pat Hentgen .15 .07
❑ 447 Juan Samuel .15 .07
❑ 448 Benito Santiago .15 .07
❑ 449 Shannon Stewart .25 .11
❑ 450 Woody Williams .15 .07
❑ NNO Tony Gwynn Sample 2.00 .90

## 2000 Pacific

| | MINT | NRMT |
|---|---|---|
| COMPLETE SET (500) | 100.00 | 45.00 |

❑ 1 Garret Anderson .25 .11
❑ 2 Tim Belcher .15 .07
❑ 3 Gary DiSarcina .15 .07
❑ 4 Trent Durrington .15 .07
❑ 5 Jim Edmonds .60 .25
❑ 6 Darin Erstad ACTION .60 .25
❑ 6A Darin Erstad POR .60 .25
❑ 7 Chuck Finley .25 .11
❑ 8 Troy Glaus .75 .35
❑ 9 Todd Greene .15 .07
❑ 10 Bret Hemphill .15 .07
❑ 11 Ken Hill .15 .07
❑ 12 Ramon Ortiz .25 .11
❑ 13 Troy Percival .15 .07
❑ 14 Mark Petkovsek .15 .07
❑ 15 Tim Salmon .25 .11
❑ 16 Mo Vaughn ACTION .25 .11
❑ 16A Mo Vaughn POR .25 .11
❑ 17 Jay Bell .25 .11
❑ 18 Omar Daal .15 .07
❑ 19 Erubiel Durazo .25 .11
❑ 20 Steve Finley .25 .11
❑ 21 Bernard Gilkey .15 .07
❑ 22 Luis Gonzalez .25 .11
❑ 23 Randy Johnson .75 .35
❑ 24 Byung-Hyun Kim .25 .11
❑ 25 Travis Lee .15 .07
❑ 26 Matt Mantei .15 .07
❑ 27 Armando Reynoso .15 .07
❑ 28 Rob Ryan .15 .07
❑ 29 Kelly Stinnett .15 .07
❑ 30 Todd Stottlemyre .15 .07
❑ 31 Matt Williams ACTION .40 .18
❑ 31A Matt Williams POR .40 .18
❑ 32 Tony Womack .15 .07
❑ 33 Bret Boone .15 .07
❑ 34 Andres Galarraga .40 .18
❑ 35 Tom Glavine .60 .25
❑ 36 Ozzie Guillen .15 .07
❑ 37 Andruw Jones ACTION .60 .25
❑ 37A Andruw Jones POR .60 .25
❑ 38 Chipper Jones ACTION 1.50 .70
❑ 38A Chipper Jones POR 1.50 .70
❑ 39 Brian Jordan .25 .11
❑ 40 Ryan Klesko .25 .11
❑ 41 Javy Lopez .25 .11
❑ 42 Greg Maddux ACTION 1.50 .70
❑ 42A Greg Maddux POR 1.50 .70
❑ 43 Kevin Millwood .25 .11
❑ 44 John Rocker .25 .11

❑ 45 Randall Simon .15 .07
❑ 46 John Smoltz .25 .11
❑ 47 Gerald Williams .15 .07
❑ 48 Brady Anderson .25 .11
❑ 49 Albert Belle ACTION .40 .18
❑ 49A Albert Belle POR .40 .18
❑ 50 Mike Bordick .15 .07
❑ 51 Will Clark .60 .25
❑ 52 Jeff Conine .15 .07
❑ 53 Delino DeShields .15 .07
❑ 54 Jerry Hairston Jr. .15 .07
❑ 55 Charles Johnson .25 .11
❑ 56 Eugene Kingsale .15 .07
❑ 57 Ryan Minor .15 .07
❑ 58 Mike Mussina .60 .25
❑ 59 Sidney Ponson .15 .07
❑ 60 Cal Ripken ACTION 2.50 1.10
❑ 60A Cal Ripken POR 2.50 1.10
❑ 61 B.J. Surhoff .25 .11
❑ 62 Mike Timlin .15 .07
❑ 63 Rod Beck .15 .07
❑ 64 N.Garciaparra ACTION 2.00 .90
❑ 64A Nomar Garciaparra POR 2.00 .90
❑ 65 Tom Gordon .15 .07
❑ 66 Butch Huskey .15 .07
❑ 67 Derek Lowe .15 .07
❑ 68 Pedro Martinez ACTION .75 .35
❑ 68A Pedro Martinez POR .75 .35
❑ 69 Trot Nixon .25 .11
❑ 70 Jose Offerman .15 .07
❑ 71 Troy O'Leary .15 .07
❑ 72 Pat Rapp .15 .07
❑ 73 Donnie Sadler .15 .07
❑ 74 Mike Stanley .15 .07
❑ 75 John Valentin .15 .07
❑ 76 Jason Varitek .25 .11
❑ 77 Wilton Veras .25 .11
❑ 78 Tim Wakefield .15 .07
❑ 79 Rick Aguilera .25 .11
❑ 80 Manny Alexander .15 .07
❑ 81 Roosevelt Brown .15 .07
❑ 82 Mark Grace .60 .25
❑ 83 Glenallen Hill .15 .07
❑ 84 Lance Johnson .15 .07
❑ 85 Jon Lieber .15 .07
❑ 86 Cole Liniak .15 .07
❑ 87 Chad Meyers .15 .07
❑ 88 Mickey Morandini .15 .07
❑ 89 Jose Nieves .15 .07
❑ 90 Henry Rodriguez .15 .07
❑ 91 Sammy Sosa ACTION 1.25 .55
❑ 91A Sammy Sosa POR 1.25 .55
❑ 92 Kevin Tapani .15 .07
❑ 93 Kerry Wood .25 .11
❑ 94 Mike Caruso .15 .07
❑ 95 Ray Durham .25 .11
❑ 96 Brook Fordyce .15 .07
❑ 97 Bobby Howry .15 .07
❑ 98 Paul Konerko .25 .11
❑ 99 Carlos Lee .25 .11
❑ 100 Aaron Myette .25 .11
❑ 101 Greg Norton .15 .07
❑ 102 Magglio Ordonez .25 .11
❑ 103 Jim Parque .15 .07
❑ 104 Liu Rodriguez .15 .07
❑ 105 Chris Singleton .25 .11
❑ 106 Mike Sirotka .15 .07
❑ 107 Frank Thomas ACTION 1.25 .55
❑ 107A Frank Thomas POR 1.25 .55
❑ 108 Kip Wells .25 .11
❑ 109 Aaron Boone .15 .07
❑ 110 Mike Cameron .15 .07
❑ 111 Sean Casey ACTION .25 .11
❑ 111A Sean Casey POR .25 .11
❑ 112 Jeffrey Hammonds .25 .11
❑ 113 Pete Harnisch .15 .07
❑ 114 Barry Larkin ACTION .60 .25
❑ 114A Barry Larkin POR .60 .25
❑ 115 Jason LaRue .15 .07
❑ 116 Denny Neagle .15 .07
❑ 117 Pokey Reese .25 .11
❑ 118 Scott Sullivan .15 .07
❑ 119 Eddie Taubensee .15 .07
❑ 120 Greg Vaughn .25 .11
❑ 121 Scott Williamson .15 .07
❑ 122 Dmitri Young .25 .11
❑ 123 Roberto Alomar ACTION .60 .25
❑ 123A Roberto Alomar POR .60 .25
❑ 124 Sandy Alomar Jr. .15 .07
❑ 125 Harold Baines .25 .11
❑ 126 Russell Branyan .25 .11
❑ 127 Dave Burba .15 .07
❑ 128 Bartolo Colon .25 .11
❑ 129 Travis Fryman .25 .11
❑ 130 Mike Jackson .15 .07
❑ 131 David Justice .40 .18
❑ 132 Kenny Lofton ACTION .25 .11
❑ 132A Kenny Lofton POR .25 .11
❑ 133 Charles Nagy .15 .07
❑ 134 Manny Ramirez ACTION .75 .35
❑ 134A Manny Ramirez POR .75 .35
❑ 135 Dave Roberts .15 .07
❑ 136 Richie Sexson .25 .11
❑ 137 Jim Thome .40 .18
❑ 138 Omar Vizquel .25 .11
❑ 139 Jaret Wright .15 .07
❑ 140 Pedro Astacio .15 .07
❑ 141 Dante Bichette .25 .11
❑ 142 Brian Bohanon .15 .07
❑ 143 Vinny Castilla ACTION .25 .11
❑ 143A Vinny Castilla POR .25 .11
❑ 144 Edgard Clemente .15 .07
❑ 145 Derrick Gibson .15 .07
❑ 146 Todd Helton .75 .35
❑ 147 Darryl Kile .25 .11
❑ 148 Mike Lansing .15 .07
❑ 149 Kirt Manwaring .15 .07
❑ 150 Neifi Perez .15 .07
❑ 151 Ben Petrick .15 .07
❑ 152 Juan Sosa RC .25 .11
❑ 153 Dave Veres .15 .07
❑ 154 Larry Walker ACTION .25 .11
❑ 154A Larry Walker POR .25 .11
❑ 155 Brad Ausmus .15 .07
❑ 156 Dave Borkowski .15 .07
❑ 157 Tony Clark .15 .07
❑ 158 Francisco Cordero .15 .07
❑ 159 Deivi Cruz .15 .07
❑ 160 Damion Easley .15 .07
❑ 161 Juan Encarnacion .25 .11
❑ 162 Robert Fick .15 .07
❑ 163 Bobby Higginson .15 .07
❑ 164 Gabe Kapler .25 .11
❑ 165 Brian Moehler .15 .07
❑ 166 Dean Palmer .25 .11
❑ 167 Luis Polonia .15 .07
❑ 168 Justin Thompson .15 .07
❑ 169 Jeff Weaver .15 .07
❑ 170 Antonio Alfonseca .15 .07
❑ 171 Bruce Aven .15 .07
❑ 172 A.J. Burnett .25 .11
❑ 173 Luis Castillo .25 .11
❑ 174 Ramon Castro .15 .07
❑ 175 Ryan Dempster .25 .11
❑ 176 Alex Fernandez .15 .07
❑ 177 Cliff Floyd .25 .11
❑ 178 Amaury Garcia .15 .07
❑ 179 Alex Gonzalez .15 .07
❑ 180 Mark Kotsay .15 .07
❑ 181 Mike Lowell .15 .07
❑ 182 Brian Meadows .15 .07
❑ 183 Kevin Orie .15 .07
❑ 184 Julio Ramirez .15 .07
❑ 185 Preston Wilson .25 .11
❑ 186 Moises Alou .25 .11
❑ 187 Jeff Bagwell ACTION .75 .35
❑ 187A Jeff Bagwell POR .75 .35
❑ 188 Glen Barker .15 .07
❑ 189 Derek Bell .15 .07
❑ 190 Craig Biggio ACTION .40 .18
❑ 190A Craig Biggio POR .40 .18
❑ 191 Ken Caminiti .25 .11
❑ 192 Scott Elarton .25 .11
❑ 193 Carl Everett .25 .11
❑ 194 Mike Hampton .25 .11
❑ 195 Carlos Hernandez .15 .07
❑ 196 Richard Hidalgo .25 .11
❑ 197 Jose Lima .15 .07
❑ 198 Shane Reynolds .15 .07
❑ 199 Bill Spiers .15 .07
❑ 200 Billy Wagner .15 .07
❑ 201 Carlos Beltran ACTION .25 .11
❑ 201A Carlos Beltran POR .25 .11
❑ 202 Dermal Brown .25 .11
❑ 203 Johnny Damon .25 .11
❑ 204 Jermaine Dye .25 .11
❑ 205 Carlos Febles .15 .07
❑ 206 Jeremy Giambi .15 .07
❑ 207 Mark Quinn .25 .11
❑ 208 Joe Randa .15 .07
❑ 209 Dan Reichert .15 .07
❑ 210 Jose Rosado .15 .07
❑ 211 Rey Sanchez .15 .07
❑ 212 Jeff Suppan .15 .07
❑ 213 Mike Sweeney .25 .11
❑ 214 Kevin Brown ACTION .25 .11
❑ 214A Kevin Brown POR .25 .11
❑ 215 Darren Dreifort .15 .07
❑ 216 Eric Gagne .15 .07
❑ 217 Mark Grudzielanek .15 .07
❑ 218 Todd Hollandsworth .15 .07
❑ 219 Todd Hundley .15 .07
❑ 220 Eric Karros .25 .11
❑ 221 Raul Mondesi .25 .11
❑ 222 Chan Ho Park .25 .11
❑ 223 Jeff Shaw .15 .07
❑ 224 Gary Sheffield ACTION .60 .25
❑ 224A Gary Sheffield POR .60 .25
❑ 225 Ismael Valdes .15 .07
❑ 226 Devon White .15 .07
❑ 227 Eric Young .15 .07
❑ 228 Kevin Barker .15 .07
❑ 229 Ron Belliard .15 .07
❑ 230 Jeromy Burnitz ACTION .25 .11
❑ 230A Jeromy Burnitz POR .25 .11
❑ 231 Jeff Cirillo .25 .11
❑ 232 Marquis Grissom .15 .07
❑ 233 Geoff Jenkins .25 .11
❑ 234 Mark Loretta .15 .07
❑ 235 David Nilsson .15 .07
❑ 236 Hideo Nomo .60 .25
❑ 237 Alex Ochoa .15 .07
❑ 238 Kyle Peterson .15 .07
❑ 239 Fernando Vina .15 .07
❑ 240 Bob Wickman .15 .07
❑ 241 Steve Woodard .15 .07
❑ 242 Chad Allen .15 .07
❑ 243 Ron Coomer .15 .07
❑ 244 Marty Cordova .15 .07
❑ 245 Cristian Guzman .15 .07
❑ 246 Denny Hocking .15 .07
❑ 247 Jacque Jones .25 .11
❑ 248 Corey Koskie .15 .07
❑ 249 Matt Lawton .15 .07
❑ 250 Joe Mays .15 .07
❑ 251 Eric Milton .15 .07
❑ 252 Brad Radke .25 .11
❑ 253 Mark Redman .15 .07
❑ 254 Terry Steinbach .15 .07
❑ 255 Todd Walker .15 .07
❑ 256 Tony Armas Jr. .25 .11
❑ 257 Michael Barrett .15 .07
❑ 258 Peter Bergeron .15 .07
❑ 259 Geoff Blum .15 .07
❑ 260 Orlando Cabrera .15 .07
❑ 261 Trace Coquillette RC .25 .11
❑ 262 Brad Fullmer .25 .11
❑ 263 V.Guerrero ACTION 1.00 .45
❑ 263A Vladimir Guerrero POR 1.00 .45
❑ 264 Wilton Guerrero .15 .07
❑ 265 Dustin Hermanson .15 .07
❑ 266 Manny Martinez RC .25 .11
❑ 267 Ryan McGuire .15 .07
❑ 268 Ugueth Urbina .15 .07
❑ 269 Jose Vidro .15 .07
❑ 270 Rondell White .25 .11
❑ 271 Chris Widger .15 .07
❑ 272 Edgardo Alfonzo .25 .11
❑ 273 Armando Benitez .25 .11
❑ 274 Roger Cedeno .15 .07
❑ 275 Dennis Cook .15 .07
❑ 276 Octavio Dotel .15 .07
❑ 277 John Franco .25 .11
❑ 278 Darryl Hamilton .15 .07
❑ 279 Rickey Henderson .75 .35
❑ 280 Orel Hershiser .25 .11
❑ 281 Al Leiter .15 .07
❑ 282 John Olerud ACTION .25 .11

| No. | Player | MINT | NRMT |
|---|---|---|---|
| ❑ 282A | John Olerud POR | .25 | .11 |
| ❑ 283 | Rey Ordonez | .15 | .07 |
| ❑ 284 | Mike Piazza ACTION | 2.00 | .90 |
| ❑ 284A | Mike Piazza POR | 2.00 | .90 |
| ❑ 285 | Kenny Rogers | .15 | .07 |
| ❑ 286 | Jorge Toca | .15 | .07 |
| ❑ 287 | Robin Ventura | .40 | .18 |
| ❑ 288 | Scott Brosius | .25 | .11 |
| ❑ 289 | Roger Clemens ACTION | 1.25 | .55 |
| ❑ 289A | Roger Clemens POR | 1.25 | .55 |
| ❑ 290 | David Cone | .25 | .11 |
| ❑ 291 | Chili Davis | .25 | .11 |
| ❑ 292 | Orlando Hernandez | .25 | .11 |
| ❑ 293 | Hideki Irabu | .15 | .07 |
| ❑ 294 | Derek Jeter ACTION | 2.50 | 1.10 |
| ❑ 294A | Derek Jeter POR | 2.50 | 1.10 |
| ❑ 295 | Chuck Knoblauch | .25 | .11 |
| ❑ 296 | Ricky Ledee | .15 | .07 |
| ❑ 297 | Jim Leyritz | .15 | .07 |
| ❑ 298 | Tino Martinez | .25 | .11 |
| ❑ 299 | Paul O'Neill | .25 | .11 |
| ❑ 300 | Andy Pettitte | .25 | .11 |
| ❑ 301 | Jorge Posada | .25 | .11 |
| ❑ 302 | Mariano Rivera | .25 | .11 |
| ❑ 303 | Alfonso Soriano | .25 | .11 |
| ❑ 304 | Bernie Williams ACTION | .60 | .25 |
| ❑ 304A | Bernie Williams POR | .60 | .25 |
| ❑ 305 | Ed Yarnall | .15 | .07 |
| ❑ 306 | Kevin Appier | .15 | .07 |
| ❑ 307 | Rich Becker | .15 | .07 |
| ❑ 308 | Eric Chavez | .25 | .11 |
| ❑ 309 | Jason Giambi | .60 | .25 |
| ❑ 310 | Ben Grieve | .25 | .11 |
| ❑ 311 | Ramon Hernandez | .15 | .07 |
| ❑ 312 | Tim Hudson | .60 | .25 |
| ❑ 313 | John Jaha | .15 | .07 |
| ❑ 314 | Doug Jones | .15 | .07 |
| ❑ 315 | Omar Olivares | .15 | .07 |
| ❑ 316 | Mike Oquist | .15 | .07 |
| ❑ 317 | Matt Stairs | .15 | .07 |
| ❑ 318 | Miguel Tejada | .25 | .11 |
| ❑ 319 | Randy Velarde | .15 | .07 |
| ❑ 320 | Bob Abreu | .25 | .11 |
| ❑ 321 | Marlon Anderson | .15 | .07 |
| ❑ 322 | Alex Arias | .15 | .07 |
| ❑ 323 | Rico Brogna | .15 | .07 |
| ❑ 324 | Paul Byrd | .15 | .07 |
| ❑ 325 | Ron Gant | .25 | .11 |
| ❑ 326 | Doug Glanville | .15 | .07 |
| ❑ 327 | Wayne Gomes | .15 | .07 |
| ❑ 328 | Mike Lieberthal | .25 | .11 |
| ❑ 329 | Robert Person | .15 | .07 |
| ❑ 330 | Desi Relaford | .15 | .07 |
| ❑ 331 | Scott Rolen ACTION | .60 | .25 |
| ❑ 331A | Scott Rolen POR | .60 | .25 |
| ❑ 332 | Curt Schilling ACTION | .25 | .11 |
| ❑ 332A | Curt Schilling POR | .25 | .11 |
| ❑ 333 | Kris Benson | .25 | .11 |
| ❑ 334 | Adrian Brown | .15 | .07 |
| ❑ 335 | Brant Brown | .15 | .07 |
| ❑ 336 | Brian Giles | .25 | .11 |
| ❑ 337 | Chad Hermansen | .15 | .07 |
| ❑ 338 | Jason Kendall | .25 | .11 |
| ❑ 339 | Al Martin | .15 | .07 |
| ❑ 340 | Pat Meares | .15 | .07 |
| ❑ 341 | Warren Morris ACTION | .15 | .07 |
| ❑ 341A | Warren Morris POR | .15 | .07 |
| ❑ 342 | Todd Ritchie | .15 | .07 |
| ❑ 343 | Jason Schmidt | .15 | .07 |
| ❑ 344 | Ed Sprague | .15 | .07 |
| ❑ 345 | Mike Williams | .15 | .07 |
| ❑ 346 | Kevin Young | .15 | .07 |
| ❑ 347 | Rick Ankiel | 1.25 | .55 |
| ❑ 348 | Ricky Bottalico | .15 | .07 |
| ❑ 349 | Kent Bottenfield | .15 | .07 |
| ❑ 350 | Darren Bragg | .15 | .07 |
| ❑ 351 | Eric Davis | .25 | .11 |
| ❑ 352 | J.D. Drew ACTION | .60 | .25 |
| ❑ 352A | J.D. Drew POR | .60 | .25 |
| ❑ 353 | Adam Kennedy | .25 | .11 |
| ❑ 354 | Ray Lankford | .25 | .11 |
| ❑ 355 | Joe McEwing | .15 | .07 |
| ❑ 356 | Mark McGwire ACTION | 2.50 | 1.10 |
| ❑ 356A | Mark McGwire POR | 2.50 | 1.10 |
| ❑ 357 | Matt Morris | .15 | .07 |
| ❑ 358 | Darren Oliver | .15 | .07 |
| ❑ 359 | Edgar Renteria | .15 | .07 |
| ❑ 360 | Fernando Tatis | .25 | .11 |
| ❑ 361 | Andy Ashby | .15 | .07 |
| ❑ 362 | Ben Davis | .15 | .07 |
| ❑ 363 | Tony Gwynn ACTION | 1.25 | .55 |
| ❑ 363A | Tony Gwynn POR | 1.25 | .55 |
| ❑ 364 | Sterling Hitchcock | .15 | .07 |
| ❑ 365 | Trevor Hoffman | .25 | .11 |
| ❑ 366 | Damian Jackson | .15 | .07 |
| ❑ 367 | Wally Joyner | .25 | .11 |
| ❑ 368 | Dave Magadan | .15 | .07 |
| ❑ 369 | Gary Matthews Jr. | .15 | .07 |
| ❑ 370 | Phil Nevin | .25 | .11 |
| ❑ 371 | Eric Owens | .15 | .07 |
| ❑ 372 | Ruben Rivera | .15 | .07 |
| ❑ 373 | Reggie Sanders ACTION | .15 | .07 |
| ❑ 373A | Reggie Sanders POR | .15 | .07 |
| ❑ 374 | Quilvio Veras | .15 | .07 |
| ❑ 375 | Rich Aurilia | .15 | .07 |
| ❑ 376 | Marvin Benard | .15 | .07 |
| ❑ 377 | Barry Bonds ACTION | 1.00 | .45 |
| ❑ 377A | Barry Bonds POR | 1.00 | .45 |
| ❑ 378 | Ellis Burks | .25 | .11 |
| ❑ 379 | Shawn Estes | .15 | .07 |
| ❑ 380 | Livan Hernandez | .15 | .07 |
| ❑ 381 | Jeff Kent ACTION | .40 | .18 |
| ❑ 381A | Jeff Kent POR | .40 | .18 |
| ❑ 382 | Brent Mayne | .15 | .07 |
| ❑ 383 | Bill Mueller | .15 | .07 |
| ❑ 384 | Calvin Murray | .15 | .07 |
| ❑ 385 | Robb Nen | .15 | .07 |
| ❑ 386 | Russ Ortiz | .25 | .11 |
| ❑ 387 | Kirk Rueter | .15 | .07 |
| ❑ 388 | J.T. Snow | .25 | .11 |
| ❑ 389 | David Bell | .15 | .07 |
| ❑ 390 | Jay Buhner | .25 | .11 |
| ❑ 391 | Russ Davis | .15 | .07 |
| ❑ 392 | Freddy Garcia ACTION | .25 | .11 |
| ❑ 392A | Freddy Garcia POR | .25 | .11 |
| ❑ 393 | Ken Griffey Jr. ACTION | 2.50 | 1.10 |
| ❑ 393A | Ken Griffey Jr. POR | 2.50 | 1.10 |
| ❑ 394 | Carlos Guillen | .15 | .07 |
| ❑ 395 | John Halama | .15 | .07 |
| ❑ 396 | Brian L.Hunter | .15 | .07 |
| ❑ 397 | Ryan Jackson | .15 | .07 |
| ❑ 398 | Edgar Martinez | .40 | .18 |
| ❑ 399 | Gil Meche | .25 | .11 |
| ❑ 400 | Jose Mesa | .15 | .07 |
| ❑ 401 | Jamie Moyer | .15 | .07 |
| ❑ 402 | Alex Rodriguez ACTION | 2.00 | .90 |
| ❑ 402A | Alex Rodriguez POR | 2.00 | .90 |
| ❑ 403 | Dan Wilson | .15 | .07 |
| ❑ 404 | Wilson Alvarez | .15 | .07 |
| ❑ 405 | Rolando Arrojo | .15 | .07 |
| ❑ 406 | Wade Boggs ACTION | .75 | .35 |
| ❑ 406A | Wade Boggs POR | .75 | .35 |
| ❑ 407 | Miguel Cairo | .15 | .07 |
| ❑ 408 | Jose Canseco ACTION | .75 | .35 |
| ❑ 408A | Jose Canseco POR | .75 | .35 |
| ❑ 409 | John Flaherty | .15 | .07 |
| ❑ 410 | Jose Guillen | .15 | .07 |
| ❑ 411 | Roberto Hernandez | .15 | .07 |
| ❑ 412 | Terrell Lowery | .15 | .07 |
| ❑ 413 | Dave Martinez | .15 | .07 |
| ❑ 414 | Quinton McCracken | .15 | .07 |
| ❑ 415 | Fred McGriff ACTION | .40 | .18 |
| ❑ 415A | Fred McGriff POR | .40 | .18 |
| ❑ 416 | Ryan Rupe | .15 | .07 |
| ❑ 417 | Kevin Stocker | .15 | .07 |
| ❑ 418 | Bubba Trammell | .15 | .07 |
| ❑ 419 | Royce Clayton | .15 | .07 |
| ❑ 420 | Juan Gonzalez ACTION | .60 | .25 |
| ❑ 420A | Juan Gonzalez POR | .60 | .25 |
| ❑ 421 | Tom Goodwin | .15 | .07 |
| ❑ 422 | Rusty Greer | .25 | .11 |
| ❑ 423 | Rick Helling | .25 | .11 |
| ❑ 424 | Roberto Kelly | .15 | .07 |
| ❑ 425 | Ruben Mateo | .25 | .11 |
| ❑ 426 | Mark McLemore | .15 | .07 |
| ❑ 427 | Mike Morgan | .15 | .07 |
| ❑ 428 | Rafael Palmeiro | .60 | .25 |
| ❑ 429 | Ivan Rodriguez ACTION | .75 | .35 |
| ❑ 429A | Ivan Rodriguez POR | .75 | .35 |
| ❑ 430 | Aaron Sele | .15 | .07 |
| ❑ 431 | Lee Stevens | .15 | .07 |
| ❑ 432 | John Wetteland | .25 | .11 |
| ❑ 433 | Todd Zeile | .25 | .11 |
| ❑ 434 | Jeff Zimmerman | .15 | .07 |
| ❑ 435 | Tony Batista | .25 | .11 |
| ❑ 436 | Casey Blake | .15 | .07 |
| ❑ 437 | Homer Bush | .15 | .07 |
| ❑ 438 | Chris Carpenter | .15 | .07 |
| ❑ 439 | Jose Cruz Jr. | .25 | .11 |
| ❑ 440 | Carlos Delgado ACTION | .60 | .25 |
| ❑ 440A | Carlos Delgado POR | .60 | .25 |
| ❑ 441 | Tony Fernandez | .15 | .07 |
| ❑ 442 | Darrin Fletcher | .15 | .07 |
| ❑ 443 | Alex Gonzalez | .15 | .07 |
| ❑ 444 | Shawn Green ACTION | .60 | .25 |
| ❑ 444A | Shawn Green POR | .60 | .25 |
| ❑ 445 | Roy Halladay | .15 | .07 |
| ❑ 446 | Billy Koch | .25 | .11 |
| ❑ 447 | David Segui | .15 | .07 |
| ❑ 448 | Shannon Stewart | .25 | .11 |
| ❑ 449 | David Wells | .25 | .11 |
| ❑ 450 | Vernon Wells | .25 | .11 |
| ❑ SAMP | Tony Gwynn Sample | 2.00 | .90 |

## 2001 Pacific

| | MINT | NRMT |
|---|---|---|
| COMPLETE SET (500) | 100.00 | 45.00 |
| MINOR STARS | .25 | .11 |
| SEMISTARS | .40 | .18 |
| UNLISTED STARS | .60 | .25 |

| No. | Player | MINT | NRMT |
|---|---|---|---|
| ❑ 1 | Garret Anderson | .25 | .11 |
| ❑ 2 | Gary DiSarcina | .15 | .07 |
| ❑ 3 | Darin Erstad | .60 | .25 |
| ❑ 4 | Seth Etherton | .15 | .07 |
| ❑ 5 | Ron Gant | .15 | .07 |
| ❑ 6 | Troy Glaus | .75 | .35 |
| ❑ 7 | Shigetoshi Hasegawa | .25 | .11 |
| ❑ 8 | Adam Kennedy | .25 | .11 |
| ❑ 9 | Ben Molina | .25 | .11 |
| ❑ 10 | Ramon Ortiz | .25 | .11 |
| ❑ 11 | Troy Percival | .15 | .07 |
| ❑ 12 | Tim Salmon | .25 | .11 |
| ❑ 13 | Scott Schoeneweis | .15 | .07 |
| ❑ 14 | Mo Vaughn | .25 | .11 |
| ❑ 15 | Jarrod Washburn | .15 | .07 |
| ❑ 16 | Brian Anderson | .15 | .07 |
| ❑ 17 | Danny Bautista | .15 | .07 |
| ❑ 18 | Jay Bell | .25 | .11 |
| ❑ 19 | Greg Colbrunn | .15 | .07 |
| ❑ 20 | Erubiel Durazo | .15 | .07 |
| ❑ 21 | Steve Finley | .25 | .11 |
| ❑ 22 | Luis Gonzalez | .25 | .11 |
| ❑ 23 | Randy Johnson | .75 | .35 |
| ❑ 24 | Byung-Hyun Kim | .25 | .11 |
| ❑ 25 | Matt Mantei | .15 | .07 |
| ❑ 26 | Armando Reynoso | .15 | .07 |
| ❑ 27 | Todd Stottlemyre | .15 | .07 |
| ❑ 28 | Matt Williams | .40 | .18 |
| ❑ 29 | Tony Womack | .15 | .07 |
| ❑ 30 | Andy Ashby | .15 | .07 |
| ❑ 31 | Bobby Bonilla | .25 | .11 |
| ❑ 32 | Rafael Furcal | 1.00 | .45 |
| ❑ 33 | Andres Galarraga | .40 | .18 |
| ❑ 34 | Tom Glavine | .50 | .23 |
| ❑ 35 | Andruw Jones | .60 | .25 |
| ❑ 36 | Chipper Jones | 1.50 | .70 |
| ❑ 37 | Brian Jordan | .25 | .11 |
| ❑ 38 | Wally Joyner | .25 | .11 |

| |  |  | | |
|---|---|---|---|---|
| ❑ | 39 | Keith Lockhart | .15 | .07 |
| ❑ | 40 | Javy Lopez | .25 | .11 |
| ❑ | 41 | Greg Maddux | 1.50 | .70 |
| ❑ | 42 | Kevin Millwood | .25 | .11 |
| ❑ | 43 | John Rocker | .25 | .11 |
| ❑ | 44 | Reggie Sanders | .15 | .07 |
| ❑ | 45 | John Smoltz | .25 | .11 |
| ❑ | 46 | B.J. Surhoff | .25 | .11 |
| ❑ | 47 | Quilvio Veras | .15 | .07 |
| ❑ | 48 | Walt Weiss | .15 | .07 |
| ❑ | 49 | Brady Anderson | .25 | .11 |
| ❑ | 50 | Albert Belle | .25 | .11 |
| ❑ | 51 | Jeff Conine | .15 | .07 |
| ❑ | 52 | Delino DeShields | .15 | .07 |
| ❑ | 53 | Brook Fordyce | .15 | .07 |
| ❑ | 54 | Jerry Hairston Jr. | .15 | .07 |
| ❑ | 55 | Mark Lewis | .15 | .07 |
| ❑ | 56 | Luis Matos | .25 | .11 |
| ❑ | 57 | Melvin Mora | .15 | .07 |
| ❑ | 58 | Mike Mussina | .60 | .25 |
| ❑ | 59 | Chris Richard | .15 | .07 |
| ❑ | 60 | Cal Ripken | 2.50 | 1.10 |
| ❑ | 61 | Manny Alexander | .15 | .07 |
| ❑ | 62 | Rolando Arrojo | .15 | .07 |
| ❑ | 63 | Midre Cummings | .15 | .07 |
| ❑ | 64 | Carl Everett | .25 | .11 |
| ❑ | 65 | Nomar Garciaparra | 2.00 | .90 |
| ❑ | 66 | Mike Lansing | .15 | .07 |
| ❑ | 67 | Darren Lewis | .15 | .07 |
| ❑ | 68 | Derek Lowe | .15 | .07 |
| ❑ | 69 | Pedro Martinez | .75 | .35 |
| ❑ | 70 | Ramon Martinez | .15 | .07 |
| ❑ | 71 | Trot Nixon | .25 | .11 |
| ❑ | 72 | Troy O'Leary | .15 | .07 |
| ❑ | 73 | Jose Offerman | .15 | .07 |
| ❑ | 74 | Tomo Ohka | .25 | .11 |
| ❑ | 75 | Jason Varitek | .25 | .11 |
| ❑ | 76 | Rick Aguilera | .15 | .07 |
| ❑ | 77 | Shane Andrews | .15 | .07 |
| ❑ | 78 | Brant Brown | .15 | .07 |
| ❑ | 79 | Damon Buford | .15 | .07 |
| ❑ | 80 | Joe Girardi | .15 | .07 |
| ❑ | 81 | Mark Grace | .60 | .25 |
| ❑ | 82 | Willie Greene | .15 | .07 |
| ❑ | 83 | Ricky Gutierrez | .15 | .07 |
| ❑ | 84 | Jon Lieber | .15 | .07 |
| ❑ | 85 | Sammy Sosa | 1.25 | .55 |
| ❑ | 86 | Kevin Tapani | .15 | .07 |
| ❑ | 87 | Rondell White | .25 | .11 |
| ❑ | 88 | Kerry Wood | .25 | .11 |
| ❑ | 89 | Eric Young | .15 | .07 |
| ❑ | 90 | Harold Baines | .25 | .11 |
| ❑ | 91 | James Baldwin | .25 | .11 |
| ❑ | 92 | Ray Durham | .25 | .11 |
| ❑ | 93 | Cal Eldred | .15 | .07 |
| ❑ | 94 | Keith Foulke | .15 | .07 |
| ❑ | 95 | Charles Johnson | .25 | .11 |
| ❑ | 96 | Paul Konerko | .25 | .11 |
| ❑ | 97 | Carlos Lee | .25 | .11 |
| ❑ | 98 | Magglio Ordonez | .25 | .11 |
| ❑ | 99 | Jim Parque | .15 | .07 |
| ❑ | 100 | Herbert Perry | .15 | .07 |
| ❑ | 101 | Chris Singleton | .25 | .11 |
| ❑ | 102 | Mike Sirotka | .15 | .07 |
| ❑ | 103 | Frank Thomas | 1.25 | .55 |
| ❑ | 104 | Jose Valentin | .15 | .07 |
| ❑ | 105 | Rob Bell | .15 | .07 |
| ❑ | 106 | Aaron Boone | .15 | .07 |
| ❑ | 107 | Sean Casey | .25 | .11 |
| ❑ | 108 | Danny Graves | .15 | .07 |
| ❑ | 109 | Ken Griffey Jr. | 2.50 | 1.10 |
| ❑ | 110 | Pete Harnisch | .15 | .07 |
| ❑ | 111 | Brian Hunter | .15 | .07 |
| ❑ | 112 | Barry Larkin | .50 | .23 |
| ❑ | 113 | Pokey Reese | .25 | .11 |
| ❑ | 114 | Benito Santiago | .15 | .07 |
| ❑ | 115 | Chris Stynes | .15 | .07 |
| ❑ | 116 | Michael Tucker | .15 | .07 |
| ❑ | 117 | Ron Villone | .15 | .07 |
| ❑ | 118 | Scott Williamson | .15 | .07 |
| ❑ | 119 | Dmitri Young | .25 | .11 |
| ❑ | 120 | Roberto Alomar | .60 | .25 |
| ❑ | 121 | Sandy Alomar Jr. | .25 | .11 |
| ❑ | 122 | Russell Branyan | .25 | .11 |
| ❑ | 123 | Dave Burba | .15 | .07 |
| ❑ | 124 | Bartolo Colon | .25 | .11 |
| ❑ | 125 | Wil Cordero | .15 | .07 |
| ❑ | 126 | Einar Diaz | .15 | .07 |
| ❑ | 127 | Chuck Finley | .25 | .11 |
| ❑ | 128 | Travis Fryman | .25 | .11 |
| ❑ | 129 | Kenny Lofton | .25 | .11 |
| ❑ | 130 | Charles Nagy | .15 | .07 |
| ❑ | 131 | Manny Ramirez | .75 | .35 |
| ❑ | 132 | David Segui | .15 | .07 |
| ❑ | 133 | Jim Thome | .40 | .18 |
| ❑ | 134 | Omar Vizquel | .25 | .11 |
| ❑ | 135 | Brian Bohanon | .15 | .07 |
| ❑ | 136 | Jeff Cirillo | .25 | .11 |
| ❑ | 137 | Jeff Frye | .15 | .07 |
| ❑ | 138 | Jeffrey Hammonds | .25 | .11 |
| ❑ | 139 | Todd Helton | .75 | .35 |
| ❑ | 140 | Todd Hollandsworth | .15 | .07 |
| ❑ | 141 | Jose Jimenez | .15 | .07 |
| ❑ | 142 | Brent Mayne | .15 | .07 |
| ❑ | 143 | Neifi Perez | .15 | .07 |
| ❑ | 144 | Ben Petrick | .15 | .07 |
| ❑ | 145 | Juan Pierre | .25 | .11 |
| ❑ | 146 | Larry Walker | .25 | .11 |
| ❑ | 147 | Todd Walker | .15 | .07 |
| ❑ | 148 | Masato Yoshii | .15 | .07 |
| ❑ | 149 | Brad Ausmus | .15 | .07 |
| ❑ | 150 | Rich Becker | .15 | .07 |
| ❑ | 151 | Tony Clark | .15 | .07 |
| ❑ | 152 | Deivi Cruz | .15 | .07 |
| ❑ | 153 | Damion Easley | .15 | .07 |
| ❑ | 154 | Juan Encarnacion | .25 | .11 |
| ❑ | 155 | Robert Fick | .15 | .07 |
| ❑ | 156 | Juan Gonzalez | .50 | .23 |
| ❑ | 157 | Bobby Higginson | .25 | .11 |
| ❑ | 158 | Todd Jones | .15 | .07 |
| ❑ | 159 | Wendell Magee Jr. | .15 | .07 |
| ❑ | 160 | Brian Moehler | .15 | .07 |
| ❑ | 161 | Hideo Nomo | .60 | .25 |
| ❑ | 162 | Dean Palmer | .25 | .11 |
| ❑ | 163 | Jeff Weaver | .15 | .07 |
| ❑ | 164 | Antonio Alfonseca | .15 | .07 |
| ❑ | 165 | Dave Berg | .15 | .07 |
| ❑ | 166 | A.J. Burnett | .15 | .07 |
| ❑ | 167 | Luis Castillo | .25 | .11 |
| ❑ | 168 | Ryan Dempster | .25 | .11 |
| ❑ | 169 | Cliff Floyd | .25 | .11 |
| ❑ | 170 | Alex Gonzalez | .15 | .07 |
| ❑ | 171 | Mark Kotsay | .15 | .07 |
| ❑ | 172 | Derrek Lee | .25 | .11 |
| ❑ | 173 | Mike Lowell | .25 | .11 |
| ❑ | 174 | Mike Redmond | .15 | .07 |
| ❑ | 175 | Henry Rodriguez | .15 | .07 |
| ❑ | 176 | Jesus Sanchez | .15 | .07 |
| ❑ | 177 | Preston Wilson | .25 | .11 |
| ❑ | 178 | Moises Alou | .25 | .11 |
| ❑ | 179 | Jeff Bagwell | .75 | .35 |
| ❑ | 180 | Glen Barker | .15 | .07 |
| ❑ | 181 | Lance Berkman | .25 | .11 |
| ❑ | 182 | Craig Biggio | .40 | .18 |
| ❑ | 183 | Tim Bogar | .15 | .07 |
| ❑ | 184 | Ken Caminiti | .25 | .11 |
| ❑ | 185 | Roger Cedeno | .15 | .07 |
| ❑ | 186 | Scott Elarton | .25 | .11 |
| ❑ | 187 | Tony Eusebio | .15 | .07 |
| ❑ | 188 | Richard Hidalgo | .25 | .11 |
| ❑ | 189 | Jose Lima | .15 | .07 |
| ❑ | 190 | Mitch Meluskey | .15 | .07 |
| ❑ | 191 | Shane Reynolds | .15 | .07 |
| ❑ | 192 | Bill Spiers | .15 | .07 |
| ❑ | 193 | Billy Wagner | .15 | .07 |
| ❑ | 194 | Daryle Ward | .15 | .07 |
| ❑ | 195 | Carlos Beltran | .25 | .11 |
| ❑ | 196 | Ricky Bottalico | .15 | .07 |
| ❑ | 197 | Johnny Damon | .25 | .11 |
| ❑ | 198 | Jermaine Dye | .25 | .11 |
| ❑ | 199 | Jorge Fabregas | .15 | .07 |
| ❑ | 200 | David McCarty | .15 | .07 |
| ❑ | 201 | Mark Quinn | .25 | .11 |
| ❑ | 202 | Joe Randa | .15 | .07 |
| ❑ | 203 | Jeff Reboulet | .15 | .07 |
| ❑ | 204 | Rey Sanchez | .15 | .07 |
| ❑ | 205 | Blake Stein | .15 | .07 |
| ❑ | 206 | Jeff Suppan | .15 | .07 |
| ❑ | 207 | Mac Suzuki | .15 | .07 |
| ❑ | 208 | Mike Sweeney | .25 | .11 |
| ❑ | 209 | Greg Zaun | .15 | .07 |
| ❑ | 210 | Adrian Beltre | .25 | .11 |
| ❑ | 211 | Kevin Brown | .25 | .11 |
| ❑ | 212 | Alex Cora | .15 | .07 |
| ❑ | 213 | Darren Dreifort | .15 | .07 |
| ❑ | 214 | Tom Goodwin | .15 | .07 |
| ❑ | 215 | Shawn Green | .50 | .23 |
| ❑ | 216 | Mark Grudzielanek | .15 | .07 |
| ❑ | 217 | Todd Hundley | .15 | .07 |
| ❑ | 218 | Eric Karros | .25 | .11 |
| ❑ | 219 | Chad Kreuter | .15 | .07 |
| ❑ | 220 | Jim Leyritz | .15 | .07 |
| ❑ | 221 | Chan Ho Park | .25 | .11 |
| ❑ | 222 | Jeff Shaw | .15 | .07 |
| ❑ | 223 | Gary Sheffield | .50 | .23 |
| ❑ | 224 | Devon White | .15 | .07 |
| ❑ | 225 | Ron Belliard | .15 | .07 |
| ❑ | 226 | Henry Blanco | .15 | .07 |
| ❑ | 227 | Jeromy Burnitz | .25 | .11 |
| ❑ | 228 | Jeff D'Amico | .15 | .07 |
| ❑ | 229 | Marquis Grissom | .15 | .07 |
| ❑ | 230 | Charlie Hayes | .15 | .07 |
| ❑ | 231 | Jimmy Haynes | .15 | .07 |
| ❑ | 232 | Tyler Houston | .15 | .07 |
| ❑ | 233 | Geoff Jenkins | .25 | .11 |
| ❑ | 234 | Mark Loretta | .15 | .07 |
| ❑ | 235 | James Mouton | .15 | .07 |
| ❑ | 236 | Richie Sexson | .25 | .11 |
| ❑ | 237 | Jamey Wright | .15 | .07 |
| ❑ | 238 | Jay Canizaro | .15 | .07 |
| ❑ | 239 | Ron Coomer | .15 | .07 |
| ❑ | 240 | Cristian Guzman | .15 | .07 |
| ❑ | 241 | Denny Hocking | .15 | .07 |
| ❑ | 242 | Torii Hunter | .15 | .07 |
| ❑ | 243 | Jacque Jones | .25 | .11 |
| ❑ | 244 | Corey Koskie | .15 | .07 |
| ❑ | 245 | Matt Lawton | .25 | .11 |
| ❑ | 246 | Matt LeCroy | .15 | .07 |
| ❑ | 247 | Eric Milton | .15 | .07 |
| ❑ | 248 | David Ortiz | .15 | .07 |
| ❑ | 249 | Brad Radke | .25 | .11 |
| ❑ | 250 | Mark Redman | .15 | .07 |
| ❑ | 251 | Michael Barrett | .15 | .07 |
| ❑ | 252 | Peter Bergeron | .15 | .07 |
| ❑ | 253 | Milton Bradley | .25 | .11 |
| ❑ | 254 | Orlando Cabrera | .15 | .07 |
| ❑ | 255 | Vladimir Guerrero | 1.00 | .45 |
| ❑ | 256 | Wilton Guerrero | .15 | .07 |
| ❑ | 257 | Dustin Hermanson | .15 | .07 |
| ❑ | 258 | Hideki Irabu | .15 | .07 |
| ❑ | 259 | Fernando Seguignol | .15 | .07 |
| ❑ | 260 | Lee Stevens | .15 | .07 |
| ❑ | 261 | Andy Tracy | .15 | .07 |
| ❑ | 262 | Javier Vazquez | .15 | .07 |
| ❑ | 263 | Jose Vidro | .25 | .11 |
| ❑ | 264 | Edgardo Alfonzo | .25 | .11 |
| ❑ | 265 | Derek Bell | .15 | .07 |
| ❑ | 266 | Armando Benitez | .15 | .07 |
| ❑ | 267 | Mike Bordick | .15 | .07 |
| ❑ | 268 | John Franco | .25 | .11 |
| ❑ | 269 | Darryl Hamilton | .15 | .07 |
| ❑ | 270 | Mike Hampton | .25 | .11 |
| ❑ | 271 | Lenny Harris | .15 | .07 |
| ❑ | 272 | Al Leiter | .25 | .11 |
| ❑ | 273 | Joe McEwing | .15 | .07 |
| ❑ | 274 | Rey Ordonez | .15 | .07 |
| ❑ | 275 | Jay Payton | .25 | .11 |
| ❑ | 276 | Mike Piazza | 2.00 | .90 |
| ❑ | 277 | Glendon Rusch | .15 | .07 |
| ❑ | 278 | Bubba Trammell | .15 | .07 |
| ❑ | 279 | Robin Ventura | .25 | .11 |
| ❑ | 280 | Todd Zeile | .25 | .11 |
| ❑ | 281 | Scott Brosius | .25 | .11 |
| ❑ | 282 | Jose Canseco | .75 | .35 |
| ❑ | 283 | Roger Clemens | 1.25 | .55 |
| ❑ | 284 | David Cone | .25 | .11 |
| ❑ | 285 | Dwight Gooden | .25 | .11 |
| ❑ | 286 | Orlando Hernandez | .25 | .11 |
| ❑ | 287 | Glenallen Hill | .15 | .07 |
| ❑ | 288 | Derek Jeter | 2.50 | 1.10 |
| ❑ | 289 | David Justice | .40 | .18 |
| ❑ | 290 | Chuck Knoblauch | .25 | .11 |
| ❑ | 291 | Tino Martinez | .25 | .11 |
| ❑ | 292 | Denny Neagle | .15 | .07 |
| ❑ | 293 | Paul O'Neill | .25 | .11 |
| ❑ | 294 | Andy Pettitte | .25 | .11 |
| ❑ | 295 | Jorge Posada | .25 | .11 |
| ❑ | 296 | Mariano Rivera | .25 | .11 |

❑ 297 Luis Sojo .15 .07
❑ 298 Jose Vizcaino .15 .07
❑ 299 Bernie Williams .50 .23
❑ 300 Kevin Appier .25 .11
❑ 301 Eric Chavez .25 .11
❑ 302 Ryan Christenson .15 .07
❑ 303 Jason Giambi .60 .25
❑ 304 Jeremy Giambi .15 .07
❑ 305 Ben Grieve .25 .11
❑ 306 Gil Heredia .15 .07
❑ 307 Ramon Hernandez .15 .07
❑ 308 Tim Hudson .25 .11
❑ 309 Jason Isringhausen .15 .07
❑ 310 Terrence Long .25 .11
❑ 311 Mark Mulder .25 .11
❑ 312 Adam Piatt .25 .11
❑ 313 Matt Stairs .15 .07
❑ 314 Miguel Tejada .25 .11
❑ 315 Randy Velarde .15 .07
❑ 316 Alex Arias .15 .07
❑ 317 Pat Burrell .60 .25
❑ 318 Omar Daal .15 .07
❑ 319 Travis Lee .15 .07
❑ 320 Mike Lieberthal .25 .11
❑ 321 Randy Wolf .15 .07
❑ 322 Bobby Abreu .25 .11
❑ 323 Jeff Brantley .15 .07
❑ 324 Bruce Chen .15 .07
❑ 325 Doug Glanville .15 .07
❑ 326 Kevin Jordan .15 .07
❑ 327 Robert Person .15 .07
❑ 328 Scott Rolen .50 .23
❑ 329 Jimmy Anderson .15 .07
❑ 330 Mike Benjamin .15 .07
❑ 331 Kris Benson .25 .11
❑ 332 Adrian Brown .15 .07
❑ 333 Brian Giles .25 .11
❑ 334 Jason Kendall .25 .11
❑ 335 Pat Meares .15 .07
❑ 336 Warren Morris .15 .07
❑ 337 Aramis Ramirez .15 .07
❑ 338 Todd Ritchie .15 .07
❑ 339 Jason Schmidt .15 .07
❑ 340 John VanderWal .15 .07
❑ 341 Mike Williams .15 .07
❑ 342 Enrique Wilson .15 .07
❑ 343 Kevin Young .15 .07
❑ 344 Rick Ankiel .75 .35
❑ 345 Andy Benes .15 .07
❑ 346 Will Clark .60 .25
❑ 347 Eric Davis .25 .11
❑ 348 J.D. Drew .50 .23
❑ 349 Shawon Dunston .15 .07
❑ 350 Jim Edmonds .50 .23
❑ 351 Pat Hentgen .15 .07
❑ 352 Darryl Kile .25 .11
❑ 353 Ray Lankford .25 .11
❑ 354 Mike Matheny .15 .07
❑ 355 Mark McGwire 2.50 1.10
❑ 356 Craig Paquette .15 .07
❑ 357 Edgar Renteria .25 .11
❑ 358 Garrett Stephenson .15 .07
❑ 359 Fernando Tatis .25 .11
❑ 360 Dave Veres .15 .07
❑ 361 Fernando Vina .15 .07
❑ 362 Bret Boone .15 .07
❑ 363 Matt Clement .15 .07
❑ 364 Ben Davis .15 .07
❑ 365 Adam Eaton .25 .11
❑ 366 Wiki Gonzalez .15 .07
❑ 367 Tony Gwynn 1.25 .55
❑ 368 Damian Jackson .15 .07
❑ 369 Ryan Klesko .25 .11
❑ 370 John Mabry .15 .07
❑ 371 Dave Magadan .15 .07
❑ 372 Phil Nevin .25 .11
❑ 373 Eric Owens .15 .07
❑ 374 Desi Relaford .15 .07
❑ 375 Ruben Rivera .15 .07
❑ 376 Woody Williams .15 .07
❑ 377 Rich Aurilia .15 .07
❑ 378 Marvin Benard .15 .07
❑ 379 Barry Bonds 1.00 .45
❑ 380 Ellis Burks .25 .11
❑ 381 Bobby Estalella .15 .07
❑ 382 Shawn Estes .15 .07
❑ 383 Mark Gardner .15 .07
❑ 384 Livan Hernandez .15 .07
❑ 385 Jeff Kent .40 .18
❑ 386 Bill Mueller .15 .07
❑ 387 Robb Nen .15 .07
❑ 388 Russ Ortiz .15 .07
❑ 389 Armando Rios .15 .07
❑ 390 Kirk Rueter .15 .07
❑ 391 J.T. Snow .25 .11
❑ 392 David Bell .15 .07
❑ 393 Jay Buhner .25 .11
❑ 394 Mike Cameron .15 .07
❑ 395 Freddy Garcia .25 .11
❑ 396 Carlos Guillen .15 .07
❑ 397 John Halama .15 .07
❑ 398 Rickey Henderson .75 .35
❑ 399 Al Martin .15 .07
❑ 400 Edgar Martinez .40 .18
❑ 401 Mark McLemore .15 .07
❑ 402 Jamie Moyer .15 .07
❑ 403 John Olerud .25 .11
❑ 404 Joe Oliver .15 .07
❑ 405 Alex Rodriguez 2.00 .90
❑ 406 Kazuhiro Sasaki .75 .35
❑ 407 Aaron Sele .25 .11
❑ 408 Dan Wilson .15 .07
❑ 409 Miguel Cairo .15 .07
❑ 410 Vinny Castilla .25 .11
❑ 411 Steve Cox .15 .07
❑ 412 John Flaherty .15 .07
❑ 413 Jose Guillen .15 .07
❑ 414 Roberto Hernandez .15 .07
❑ 415 Russ Johnson .15 .07
❑ 416 Felix Martinez .15 .07
❑ 417 Fred McGriff .40 .18
❑ 418 Greg Vaughn .25 .11
❑ 419 Gerald Williams .15 .07
❑ 420 Luis Alicea .15 .07
❑ 421 Frank Catalanotto .15 .07
❑ 422 Royce Clayton .15 .07
❑ 423 Chad Curtis .15 .07
❑ 424 Rusty Greer .25 .11
❑ 425 Bill Haselman .15 .07
❑ 426 Rick Helling .25 .11
❑ 427 Gabe Kapler .25 .11
❑ 428 Mike Lamb .15 .07
❑ 429 Ricky Ledee .15 .07
❑ 430 Ruben Mateo .25 .11
❑ 431 Rafael Palmeiro .50 .23
❑ 432 Ivan Rodriguez .75 .35
❑ 433 Kenny Rogers .15 .07
❑ 434 John Wetteland .25 .11
❑ 435 Jeff Zimmerman .15 .07
❑ 436 Tony Batista .25 .11
❑ 437 Homer Bush .15 .07
❑ 438 Chris Carpenter .15 .07
❑ 439 Marty Cordova .15 .07
❑ 440 Jose Cruz Jr. .25 .11
❑ 441 Carlos Delgado .60 .25
❑ 442 Darrin Fletcher .15 .07
❑ 443 Brad Fullmer .25 .11
❑ 444 Alex Gonzalez .15 .07
❑ 445 Billy Koch .25 .11
❑ 446 Raul Mondesi .25 .11
❑ 447 Mickey Morandini .15 .07
❑ 448 Shannon Stewart .25 .11
❑ 449 Steve Trachsel .15 .07
❑ 450 David Wells .25 .11
❑ 451 Juan Alvarez .15 .07
❑ 452 Shawn Wooten .15 .07
❑ 453 Ismael Villegas .15 .07
❑ 454 Carlos Casimiro .15 .07
❑ 455 Morgan Burkhart .15 .07
❑ 456 Paxton Crawford .15 .07
❑ 457 Dernell Stenson .25 .11
❑ 458 Ross Gload .15 .07
❑ 459 Raul Gonzalez .15 .07
❑ 460 Corey Patterson .60 .25
❑ 461 Julio Zuleta .15 .07
❑ 462 Rocky Biddle .15 .07
❑ 463 Joe Crede .25 .11
❑ 464 Matt Ginter .25 .11
❑ 465 Aaron Myette .15 .07
❑ 466 Mike Bell .15 .07
❑ 467 Travis Dawkins .15 .07
❑ 468 Mark Watson .15 .07
❑ 469 Elvis Pena .15 .07
❑ 470 Eric Munson .25 .11
❑ 471 Pablo Ozuna .15 .07
❑ 472 Frank Charles .15 .07
❑ 473 Mike Judd .15 .07
❑ 474 Hector Ramirez .15 .07
❑ 475 Jack Cressend .15 .07
❑ 476 Talmadge Nunnari .15 .07
❑ 477 Jorge Toca .15 .07
❑ 478 Alfonso Soriano .25 .11
❑ 479 Jay Tessmer .15 .07
❑ 480 Jake Westbrook .15 .07
❑ 481 Eric Byrnes .25 .11
❑ 482 Jose Ortiz .75 .35
❑ 483 Tike Redman .15 .07
❑ 484 Domingo Guzman .15 .07
❑ 485 Rodrigo Lopez .15 .07
❑ 486 Xavier Nady 1.00 .45
❑ 487 Pedro Feliz .25 .11
❑ 488 Damon Minor .15 .07
❑ 489 Ryan Vogelsong .25 .11
❑ 490 Joel Pineiro .25 .11
❑ 491 Justin Brunette .15 .07
❑ 492 Keith McDonald .15 .07
❑ 493 Aubrey Huff .25 .11
❑ 494 Kenny Kelly .25 .11
❑ 495 Damian Rolls .15 .07
❑ 496 John Bale .15 .07
❑ 497 Pasqual Coco .15 .07
❑ 498 Matt DeWitt .15 .07
❑ 499 Leo Estrella .15 .07
❑ 500 Josh Phelps .15 .07

## 1999 Pacific Crown Collection

| | MINT | NRMT |
|---|---|---|
| COMPLETE SET (300) | 50.00 | 22.00 |

❑ 1 Garret Anderson .25 .11
❑ 2 Gary DiSarcina .15 .07
❑ 3 Jim Edmonds .60 .25
❑ 4 Darin Erstad .60 .25
❑ 5 Shigetoshi Hasegawa .15 .07
❑ 6 Norberto Martin .15 .07
❑ 7 Omar Olivares .15 .07
❑ 8 Orlando Palmeiro .15 .07
❑ 9 Tim Salmon .25 .11
❑ 10 Randy Velarde .15 .07
❑ 11 Tony Batista .25 .11
❑ 12 Jay Bell .25 .11
❑ 13 Yamil Benitez .15 .07
❑ 14 Omar Daal .15 .07
❑ 15 David Dellucci .15 .07
❑ 16 Karim Garcia .15 .07
❑ 17 Travis Lee .15 .07
❑ 18 Felix Rodriguez .15 .07
❑ 19 Devon White .15 .07
❑ 20 Matt Williams .40 .18
❑ 21 Andres Galarraga .40 .18
❑ 22 Tom Glavine .60 .25
❑ 23 Ozzie Guillen .15 .07
❑ 24 Andruw Jones .60 .25
❑ 25 Chipper Jones 1.50 .70
❑ 26 Ryan Klesko .25 .11
❑ 27 Javy Lopez .25 .11
❑ 28 Greg Maddux 1.50 .70
❑ 29 Dennis Martinez .25 .11

❑ 30 Odalis Perez .15 .07
❑ 31 Rudy Seanez .15 .07
❑ 32 John Smoltz .25 .11
❑ 33 Roberto Alomar .60 .25
❑ 34 Armando Benitez .15 .07
❑ 35 Scott Erickson .15 .07
❑ 36 Juan Guzman .15 .07
❑ 37 Mike Mussina .60 .25
❑ 38 Jesse Orosco .15 .07
❑ 39 Rafael Palmeiro .60 .25
❑ 40 Sidney Ponson .15 .07
❑ 41 Cal Ripken 2.50 1.10
❑ 42 B.J. Surhoff .25 .11
❑ 43 Lenny Webster .15 .07
❑ 44 Dennis Eckersley .25 .11
❑ 45 Nomar Garciaparra 2.00 .90
❑ 46 Darren Lewis .15 .07
❑ 47 Pedro Martinez .75 .35
❑ 48 Troy O'Leary .15 .07
❑ 49 Bret Saberhagen .25 .11
❑ 50 John Valentin .15 .07
❑ 51 Mo Vaughn .25 .11
❑ 52 Tim Wakefield .15 .07
❑ 53 Manny Alexander .15 .07
❑ 54 Rod Beck .15 .07
❑ 55 Gary Gaetti .15 .07
❑ 56 Mark Grace .60 .25
❑ 57 Felix Heredia .15 .07
❑ 58 Jose Hernandez .15 .07
❑ 59 Henry Rodriguez .15 .07
❑ 60 Sammy Sosa 1.25 .55
❑ 61 Kevin Tapani .15 .07
❑ 62 Kerry Wood .25 .11
❑ 63 James Baldwin .15 .07
❑ 64 Albert Belle .40 .18
❑ 65 Mike Caruso .15 .07
❑ 66 Carlos Castillo .15 .07
❑ 67 Wil Cordero .15 .07
❑ 68 Jaime Navarro .15 .07
❑ 69 Magglio Ordonez .40 .18
❑ 70 Frank Thomas 1.25 .55
❑ 71 Robin Ventura .25 .11
❑ 72 Bret Boone .25 .11
❑ 73 Sean Casey .25 .11
❑ 74 Guillermo Garcia RC .15 .07
❑ 75 Barry Larkin .60 .25
❑ 76 Melvin Nieves .15 .07
❑ 77 Eduardo Perez .15 .07
❑ 78 Roberto Petagine .15 .07
❑ 79 Reggie Sanders .15 .07
❑ 80 Eddie Taubensee .15 .07
❑ 81 Brett Tomko .15 .07
❑ 82 Sandy Alomar Jr. .25 .11
❑ 83 Bartolo Colon .25 .11
❑ 84 Joey Cora .15 .07
❑ 85 Einar Diaz .15 .07
❑ 86 David Justice .40 .18
❑ 87 Kenny Lofton .25 .11
❑ 88 Manny Ramirez .75 .35
❑ 89 Jim Thome .40 .18
❑ 90 Omar Vizquel .25 .11
❑ 91 Enrique Wilson .15 .07
❑ 92 Pedro Astacio .15 .07
❑ 93 Dante Bichette .25 .11
❑ 94 Vinny Castilla .25 .11
❑ 95 Edgard Clemente .15 .07
❑ 96 Todd Helton .75 .35
❑ 97 Darryl Kile .25 .11
❑ 98 Mike Munoz .15 .07
❑ 99 Neifi Perez .15 .07
❑ 100 Jeff Reed .15 .07
❑ 101 Larry Walker .25 .11
❑ 102 Gabe Alvarez .15 .07
❑ 103 Kimera Bartee .15 .07
❑ 104 Frank Castillo .15 .07
❑ 105 Tony Clark .15 .07
❑ 106 Deivi Cruz .15 .07
❑ 107 Damion Easley .15 .07
❑ 108 Luis Gonzalez .25 .11
❑ 109 Marino Santana .15 .07
❑ 110 Justin Thompson .15 .07
❑ 111 Antonio Alfonseca .15 .07
❑ 112 Alex Fernandez .15 .07
❑ 113 Cliff Floyd .25 .11
❑ 114 Alex Gonzalez .15 .07
❑ 115 Livan Hernandez .15 .07
❑ 116 Mark Kotsay .15 .07
❑ 117 Derrek Lee .15 .07
❑ 118 Edgar Renteria .15 .07
❑ 119 Jesus Sanchez .15 .07
❑ 120 Moises Alou .25 .11
❑ 121 Jeff Bagwell .75 .35
❑ 122 Derek Bell .15 .07
❑ 123 Craig Biggio .40 .18
❑ 124 Tony Eusebio .15 .07
❑ 125 Ricky Gutierrez .15 .07
❑ 126 Richard Hidalgo .25 .11
❑ 127 Randy Johnson .75 .35
❑ 128 Jose Lima .15 .07
❑ 129 Shane Reynolds .15 .07
❑ 130 Johnny Damon .25 .11
❑ 131 Carlos Febles .15 .07
❑ 132 Jeff King .15 .07
❑ 133 Mendy Lopez .15 .07
❑ 134 Hal Morris .15 .07
❑ 135 Jose Offerman .15 .07
❑ 136 Jose Rosado .15 .07
❑ 137 Jose Santiago RC .15 .07
❑ 138 Bobby Bonilla .25 .11
❑ 139 Roger Cedeno .15 .07
❑ 140 Alex Cora .15 .07
❑ 141 Eric Karros .25 .11
❑ 142 Raul Mondesi .25 .11
❑ 143 Antonio Osuna .15 .07
❑ 144 Chan Ho Park .25 .11
❑ 145 Gary Sheffield .60 .25
❑ 146 Ismael Valdes .15 .07
❑ 147 Jeromy Burnitz .25 .11
❑ 148 Jeff Cirillo .25 .11
❑ 149 Valerio De Los Santos .15 .07
❑ 150 Marquis Grissom .15 .07
❑ 151 Scott Karl .15 .07
❑ 152 Dave Nilsson .15 .07
❑ 153 Al Reyes .15 .07
❑ 154 Rafael Roque RC .25 .11
❑ 155 Jose Valentin .15 .07
❑ 156 Fernando Vina .15 .07
❑ 157 Rick Aguilera .15 .07
❑ 158 Hector Carrasco .15 .07
❑ 159 Marty Cordova .15 .07
❑ 160 Eddie Guardado .15 .07
❑ 161 Paul Molitor .60 .25
❑ 162 Otis Nixon .15 .07
❑ 163 Alex Ochoa .15 .07
❑ 164 David Ortiz .15 .07
❑ 165 Frank Rodriguez .15 .07
❑ 166 Todd Walker .15 .07
❑ 167 Miguel Batista .15 .07
❑ 168 Orlando Cabrera .15 .07
❑ 169 Vladimir Guerrero 1.00 .45
❑ 170 Wilton Guerrero .15 .07
❑ 171 Carl Pavano .15 .07
❑ 172 Robert Perez .15 .07
❑ 173 F.P. Santangelo .15 .07
❑ 174 Fernando Seguignol .15 .07
❑ 175 Ugueth Urbina .15 .07
❑ 176 Javier Vazquez .15 .07
❑ 177 Edgardo Alfonzo .25 .11
❑ 178 Carlos Baerga .15 .07
❑ 179 John Franco .25 .11
❑ 180 Luis Lopez .15 .07
❑ 181 Hideo Nomo .60 .25
❑ 182 John Olerud .25 .11
❑ 183 Rey Ordonez .15 .07
❑ 184 Mike Piazza 2.00 .90
❑ 185 Armando Reynoso .15 .07
❑ 186 Masato Yoshii .25 .11
❑ 187 David Cone .25 .11
❑ 188 Orlando Hernandez .25 .11
❑ 189 Hideki Irabu .15 .07
❑ 190 Derek Jeter 2.50 1.10
❑ 191 Ricky Ledee .15 .07
❑ 192 Tino Martinez .25 .11
❑ 193 Ramiro Mendoza .15 .07
❑ 194 Paul O'Neill .25 .11
❑ 195 Jorge Posada .25 .11
❑ 196 Mariano Rivera .25 .11
❑ 197 Luis Sojo .15 .07
❑ 198 Bernie Williams .60 .25
❑ 199 Rafael Bournigal .15 .07
❑ 200 Eric Chavez .25 .11
❑ 201 Ryan Christenson .15 .07
❑ 202 Jason Giambi .60 .25
❑ 203 Ben Grieve .25 .11
❑ 204 Rickey Henderson .75 .35
❑ 205 A.J. Hinch .15 .07
❑ 206 Kenny Rogers .15 .07
❑ 207 Miguel Tejada .25 .11
❑ 208 Jorge Velandia .15 .07
❑ 209 Bobby Abreu .25 .11
❑ 210 Marlon Anderson .15 .07
❑ 211 Alex Arias .15 .07
❑ 212 Bobby Estalella .15 .07
❑ 213 Doug Glanville .15 .07
❑ 214 Scott Rolen .60 .25
❑ 215 Curt Schilling .25 .11
❑ 216 Kevin Sefcik .15 .07
❑ 217 Adrian Brown .15 .07
❑ 218 Francisco Cordova .15 .07
❑ 219 Freddy Garcia .15 .07
❑ 220 Jose Guillen .15 .07
❑ 221 Jason Kendall .25 .11
❑ 222 Al Martin .15 .07
❑ 223 Abraham Nunez .15 .07
❑ 224 Aramis Ramirez .15 .07
❑ 225 Ricardo Rincon .15 .07
❑ 226 Kevin Young .25 .11
❑ 227 J.D. Drew .60 .25
❑ 228 Ron Gant .25 .11
❑ 229 Jose Jimenez .15 .07
❑ 230 Brian Jordan .25 .11
❑ 231 Ray Lankford .25 .11
❑ 232 Eli Marrero .15 .07
❑ 233 Mark McGwire 2.50 1.10
❑ 234 Luis Ordaz .15 .07
❑ 235 Placido Polanco .15 .07
❑ 236 Fernando Tatis .25 .11
❑ 237 Andy Ashby .15 .07
❑ 238 Kevin Brown .40 .18
❑ 239 Ken Caminiti .25 .11
❑ 240 Steve Finley .25 .11
❑ 241 Chris Gomez .15 .07
❑ 242 Tony Gwynn 1.25 .55
❑ 243 Carlos Hernandez .15 .07
❑ 244 Trevor Hoffman .25 .11
❑ 245 Wally Joyner .25 .11
❑ 246 Ruben Rivera .15 .07
❑ 247 Greg Vaughn .25 .11
❑ 248 Quilvio Veras .15 .07
❑ 249 Rich Aurilia .15 .07
❑ 250 Barry Bonds 1.00 .45
❑ 251 Stan Javier .15 .07
❑ 252 Jeff Kent .40 .18
❑ 253 Ramon E.Martinez RC .15 .07
❑ 254 Jose Mesa .15 .07
❑ 255 Armando Rios .15 .07
❑ 256 Rich Rodriguez .15 .07
❑ 257 Rey Sanchez .15 .07
❑ 258 J.T. Snow .25 .11
❑ 259 Julian Tavarez .15 .07
❑ 260 Jeff Fassero .15 .07
❑ 261 Ken Griffey Jr. 2.50 1.10
❑ 262 Giomar Guevara RC .15 .07
❑ 263 Carlos Guillen .15 .07
❑ 264 Raul Ibanez .15 .07
❑ 265 Edgar Martinez .40 .18
❑ 266 Jamie Moyer .15 .07
❑ 267 Alex Rodriguez 2.00 .90
❑ 268 David Segui .15 .07
❑ 269 Makato Suzuki .15 .07
❑ 270 Wilson Alvarez .15 .07
❑ 271 Rolando Arrojo .15 .07
❑ 272 Wade Boggs .75 .35
❑ 273 Miguel Cairo .15 .07
❑ 274 Roberto Hernandez .15 .07
❑ 275 Aaron Ledesma .15 .07
❑ 276 Albie Lopez .15 .07
❑ 277 Quinton McCracken .15 .07
❑ 278 Fred McGriff .40 .18
❑ 279 Esteban Yan .15 .07
❑ 280 Luis Alicea .15 .07
❑ 281 Will Clark .60 .25
❑ 282 Juan Gonzalez .60 .25
❑ 283 Rusty Greer .25 .11
❑ 284 Rick Helling .25 .11
❑ 285 Xavier Hernandez .15 .07
❑ 286 Roberto Kelly .15 .07
❑ 287 Esteban Loaiza .15 .07

| | | | |
|---|---|---|---|
| ❑ | 288 Ivan Rodriguez | .75 | .35 |
| ❑ | 289 Aaron Sele | .25 | .11 |
| ❑ | 290 John Wetteland | .25 | .11 |
| ❑ | 291 Jose Canseco | .75 | .35 |
| ❑ | 292 Roger Clemens | 1.25 | .55 |
| ❑ | 293 Felipe Crespo | .15 | .07 |
| ❑ | 294 Jose Cruz Jr. | .25 | .11 |
| ❑ | 295 Carlos Delgado | .60 | .25 |
| ❑ | 296 Kelvim Escobar | .15 | .07 |
| ❑ | 297 Tony Fernandez | .15 | .07 |
| ❑ | 298 Alex Gonzalez | .15 | .07 |
| ❑ | 299 Tomas Perez | .15 | .07 |
| ❑ | 300 Juan Samuel | .15 | .07 |
| ❑ | NNO Tony Gwynn Sample | 2.00 | .90 |

## 2000 Pacific Crown Collection

| | MINT | NRMT |
|---|---|---|
| COMPLETE SET (300) | 50.00 | 22.00 |

| | | MINT | NRMT |
|---|---|---|---|
| ❑ | 1 Garret Anderson | .25 | .11 |
| ❑ | 2 Darin Erstad | .60 | .25 |
| ❑ | 3 Ben Molina | .25 | .11 |
| ❑ | 4 Ramon Ortiz | .25 | .11 |
| ❑ | 5 Orlando Palmeiro | .15 | .07 |
| ❑ | 6 Troy Percival | .15 | .07 |
| ❑ | 7 Tim Salmon | .25 | .11 |
| ❑ | 8 Mo Vaughn | .25 | .11 |
| ❑ | 9 Mo Vaughn TC | .25 | .11 |
| ❑ | 10 Jay Bell | .25 | .11 |
| ❑ | 11 Omar Daal | .15 | .07 |
| ❑ | 12 Erubiel Durazo | .25 | .11 |
| ❑ | 13 Steve Finley | .25 | .11 |
| ❑ | 14 Hanley Frias | .15 | .07 |
| ❑ | 15 Luis Gonzalez | .25 | .11 |
| ❑ | 16 Randy Johnson | .75 | .35 |
| ❑ | 17 Matt Williams | .40 | .18 |
| ❑ | 18 Matt Williams TC | .25 | .11 |
| ❑ | 19 Andres Galarraga | .40 | .18 |
| ❑ | 20 Tom Glavine | .60 | .25 |
| ❑ | 21 Andruw Jones | .60 | .25 |
| ❑ | 22 Chipper Jones | 1.50 | .70 |
| ❑ | 23 Brian Jordan | .25 | .11 |
| ❑ | 24 Javy Lopez | .25 | .11 |
| ❑ | 25 Greg Maddux | 1.50 | .70 |
| ❑ | 26 Kevin Millwood | .25 | .11 |
| ❑ | 27 Eddie Perez | .15 | .07 |
| ❑ | 28 John Smoltz | .25 | .11 |
| ❑ | 29 Chipper Jones TC | .75 | .35 |
| ❑ | 30 Albert Belle | .40 | .18 |
| ❑ | 31 Jesse Garcia | .15 | .07 |
| ❑ | 32 Jerry Hairston Jr. | .15 | .07 |
| ❑ | 33 Charles Johnson | .25 | .11 |
| ❑ | 34 Mike Mussina | .60 | .25 |
| ❑ | 35 Sidney Ponson | .15 | .07 |
| ❑ | 36 Cal Ripken | 2.50 | 1.10 |
| ❑ | 37 B.J. Surhoff | .25 | .11 |
| ❑ | 38 Cal Ripken TC | 1.25 | .55 |
| ❑ | 39 Nomar Garciaparra | 2.00 | .90 |
| ❑ | 40 Pedro Martinez | .75 | .35 |
| ❑ | 41 Ramon Martinez | .15 | .07 |
| ❑ | 42 Trot Nixon | .25 | .11 |
| ❑ | 43 Jose Offerman | .15 | .07 |
| ❑ | 44 Troy O'Leary | .15 | .07 |
| ❑ | 45 John Valentin | .15 | .07 |
| ❑ | 46 Wilton Veras | .25 | .11 |
| ❑ | 47 Nomar Garciaparra TC | 1.00 | .45 |
| ❑ | 48 Mark Grace | .60 | .25 |
| ❑ | 49 Felix Heredia | .15 | .07 |
| ❑ | 50 Jose Molina | .15 | .07 |
| ❑ | 51 Jose Nieves | .15 | .07 |
| ❑ | 52 Henry Rodriguez | .15 | .07 |
| ❑ | 53 Sammy Sosa | 1.25 | .55 |
| ❑ | 54 Kerry Wood | .25 | .11 |
| ❑ | 55 Sammy Sosa TC | .60 | .25 |
| ❑ | 56 Mike Caruso | .15 | .07 |
| ❑ | 57 Carlos Castillo | .15 | .07 |
| ❑ | 58 Jason Dellaero | .15 | .07 |
| ❑ | 59 Carlos Lee | .25 | .11 |
| ❑ | 60 Magglio Ordonez | .25 | .11 |
| ❑ | 61 Jesus Pena | .15 | .07 |
| ❑ | 62 Liu Rodriguez | .15 | .07 |
| ❑ | 63 Frank Thomas | 1.25 | .55 |
| ❑ | 64 Magglio Ordonez TC | .25 | .11 |
| ❑ | 65 Aaron Boone | .15 | .07 |
| ❑ | 66 Mike Cameron | .15 | .07 |
| ❑ | 67 Sean Casey | .25 | .11 |
| ❑ | 68 Juan Guzman | .15 | .07 |
| ❑ | 69 Barry Larkin | .60 | .25 |
| ❑ | 70 Pokey Reese | .25 | .11 |
| ❑ | 71 Eddie Taubensee | .15 | .07 |
| ❑ | 72 Greg Vaughn | .25 | .11 |
| ❑ | 73 Sean Casey TC | .25 | .11 |
| ❑ | 74 Roberto Alomar | .60 | .25 |
| ❑ | 75 Sandy Alomar Jr. | .15 | .07 |
| ❑ | 76 Bartolo Colon | .25 | .11 |
| ❑ | 77 Jacob Cruz | .15 | .07 |
| ❑ | 78 Einar Diaz | .15 | .07 |
| ❑ | 79 David Justice | .40 | .18 |
| ❑ | 80 Kenny Lofton | .25 | .11 |
| ❑ | 81 Manny Ramirez | .75 | .35 |
| ❑ | 82 Richie Sexson | .25 | .11 |
| ❑ | 83 Jim Thome | .40 | .18 |
| ❑ | 84 Omar Vizquel | .25 | .11 |
| ❑ | 85 Enrique Wilson | .15 | .07 |
| ❑ | 86 Manny Ramirez TC | .25 | .11 |
| ❑ | 87 Pedro Astacio | .15 | .07 |
| ❑ | 88 Henry Blanco | .15 | .07 |
| ❑ | 89 Vinny Castilla | .25 | .11 |
| ❑ | 90 Edgard Clemente | .15 | .07 |
| ❑ | 91 Todd Helton | .75 | .35 |
| ❑ | 92 Neifi Perez | .15 | .07 |
| ❑ | 93 Terry Shumpert | .15 | .07 |
| ❑ | 94 Juan Sosa RC | .25 | .11 |
| ❑ | 95 Larry Walker | .25 | .11 |
| ❑ | 96 Larry Walker TC | .25 | .11 |
| ❑ | 97 Tony Clark | .15 | .07 |
| ❑ | 98 Deivi Cruz | .15 | .07 |
| ❑ | 99 Damion Easley | .15 | .07 |
| ❑ | 100 Juan Encarnacion | .25 | .11 |
| ❑ | 101 Karim Garcia | .15 | .07 |
| ❑ | 102 Luis Garcia | .15 | .07 |
| ❑ | 103 Juan Gonzalez | .60 | .25 |
| ❑ | 104 Jose Macias | .15 | .07 |
| ❑ | 105 Dean Palmer | .25 | .11 |
| ❑ | 106 Juan Encarnacion TC | .15 | .07 |
| ❑ | 107 Antonio Alfonseca | .15 | .07 |
| ❑ | 108 Armando Almanza | .15 | .07 |
| ❑ | 109 Bruce Aven | .15 | .07 |
| ❑ | 110 Luis Castillo | .25 | .11 |
| ❑ | 111 Ramon Castro | .15 | .07 |
| ❑ | 112 Alex Fernandez | .15 | .07 |
| ❑ | 113 Cliff Floyd | .25 | .11 |
| ❑ | 114 Alex Gonzalez | .15 | .07 |
| ❑ | 115 Michael Tejera RC | .25 | .11 |
| ❑ | 116 Preston Wilson | .25 | .11 |
| ❑ | 117 Luis Castillo TC | .25 | .11 |
| ❑ | 118 Jeff Bagwell | .75 | .35 |
| ❑ | 119 Craig Biggio | .40 | .18 |
| ❑ | 120 Jose Cabrera | .15 | .07 |
| ❑ | 121 Tony Eusebio | .15 | .07 |
| ❑ | 122 Carl Everett | .25 | .11 |
| ❑ | 123 Ricky Gutierrez | .15 | .07 |
| ❑ | 124 Mike Hampton | .25 | .11 |
| ❑ | 125 Richard Hidalgo | .25 | .11 |
| ❑ | 126 Jose Lima | .15 | .07 |
| ❑ | 127 Billy Wagner | .15 | .07 |
| ❑ | 128 Jeff Bagwell TC | .40 | .18 |
| ❑ | 129 Carlos Beltran | .25 | .11 |
| ❑ | 130 Johnny Damon | .25 | .11 |
| ❑ | 131 Jermaine Dye | .25 | .11 |
| ❑ | 132 Carlos Febles | .15 | .07 |
| ❑ | 133 Jeremy Giambi | .15 | .07 |
| ❑ | 134 Jose Rosado | .15 | .07 |
| ❑ | 135 Rey Sanchez | .15 | .07 |
| ❑ | 136 Jose Santiago | .15 | .07 |
| ❑ | 137 Carlos Beltran TC | .25 | .11 |
| ❑ | 138 Kevin Brown | .40 | .18 |
| ❑ | 139 Craig Counsell | .15 | .07 |
| ❑ | 140 Shawn Green | .60 | .25 |
| ❑ | 141 Eric Karros | .25 | .11 |
| ❑ | 142 Chan Ho Park | .25 | .11 |
| ❑ | 143 Angel Pena | .15 | .07 |
| ❑ | 144 Gary Sheffield | .60 | .25 |
| ❑ | 145 Jose Vizcaino | .15 | .07 |
| ❑ | 146 Devon White | .15 | .07 |
| ❑ | 147 Eric Karros TC | .15 | .07 |
| ❑ | 148 Ron Belliard | .15 | .07 |
| ❑ | 149 Jason Bere | .15 | .07 |
| ❑ | 150 Jeromy Burnitz | .25 | .11 |
| ❑ | 151 Marquis Grissom | .15 | .07 |
| ❑ | 152 Geoff Jenkins | .25 | .11 |
| ❑ | 153 Dave Nilsson | .15 | .07 |
| ❑ | 154 Rafael Roque | .15 | .07 |
| ❑ | 155 Jose Valentin | .15 | .07 |
| ❑ | 156 Fernando Vina | .15 | .07 |
| ❑ | 157 Jeromy Burnitz TC | .15 | .07 |
| ❑ | 158 Chad Allen | .15 | .07 |
| ❑ | 159 Ron Coomer | .15 | .07 |
| ❑ | 160 Eddie Guardado | .15 | .07 |
| ❑ | 161 Cristian Guzman | .15 | .07 |
| ❑ | 162 Jacque Jones | .25 | .11 |
| ❑ | 163 Javier Valentin | .15 | .07 |
| ❑ | 164 Todd Walker | .15 | .07 |
| ❑ | 165 Ron Coomer TC | .15 | .07 |
| ❑ | 166 Michael Barrett | .15 | .07 |
| ❑ | 167 Miguel Batista | .15 | .07 |
| ❑ | 168 Vladimir Guerrero | 1.00 | .45 |
| ❑ | 169 Wilton Guerrero | .15 | .07 |
| ❑ | 170 Fernando Seguignol | .15 | .07 |
| ❑ | 171 Ugueth Urbina | .15 | .07 |
| ❑ | 172 Javier Vazquez | .15 | .07 |
| ❑ | 173 Jose Vidro | .15 | .07 |
| ❑ | 174 Rondell White | .25 | .11 |
| ❑ | 175 Vladimir Guerrero TC | .40 | .18 |
| ❑ | 176 Edgardo Alfonzo | .25 | .11 |
| ❑ | 177 Armando Benitez | .25 | .11 |
| ❑ | 178 Roger Cedeno | .15 | .07 |
| ❑ | 179 Octavio Dotel | .15 | .07 |
| ❑ | 180 Melvin Mora | .15 | .07 |
| ❑ | 181 Rey Ordonez | .15 | .07 |
| ❑ | 182 Mike Piazza | 2.00 | .90 |
| ❑ | 183 Jorge Toca | .15 | .07 |
| ❑ | 184 Robin Ventura | .40 | .18 |
| ❑ | 185 Edgardo Alfonzo TC | .25 | .11 |
| ❑ | 186 Roger Clemens | 1.25 | .55 |
| ❑ | 187 David Cone | .25 | .11 |
| ❑ | 188 Orlando Hernandez | .25 | .11 |
| ❑ | 189 Derek Jeter | 2.50 | 1.10 |
| ❑ | 190 Ricky Ledee | .15 | .07 |
| ❑ | 191 Tino Martinez | .25 | .11 |
| ❑ | 192 Ramiro Mendoza | .15 | .07 |
| ❑ | 193 Jorge Posada | .25 | .11 |
| ❑ | 194 Mariano Rivera | .25 | .11 |
| ❑ | 195 Alfonso Soriano | .25 | .11 |
| ❑ | 196 Bernie Williams | .60 | .25 |
| ❑ | 197 Derek Jeter TC | 1.25 | .55 |
| ❑ | 198 Eric Chavez | .25 | .11 |
| ❑ | 199 Jason Giambi | .60 | .25 |
| ❑ | 200 Ben Grieve | .25 | .11 |
| ❑ | 201 Ramon Hernandez | .15 | .07 |
| ❑ | 202 Tim Hudson | .60 | .25 |
| ❑ | 203 John Jaha | .15 | .07 |
| ❑ | 204 Omar Olivares | .15 | .07 |
| ❑ | 205 Olmedo Saenz | .15 | .07 |
| ❑ | 206 Matt Stairs | .15 | .07 |
| ❑ | 207 Miguel Tejada | .25 | .11 |
| ❑ | 208 Tim Hudson TC | .25 | .11 |
| ❑ | 209 Rico Brogna | .15 | .07 |
| ❑ | 210 Bob Abreu | .25 | .11 |
| ❑ | 211 Marlon Anderson | .15 | .07 |
| ❑ | 212 Alex Arias | .15 | .07 |
| ❑ | 213 Doug Glanville | .15 | .07 |
| ❑ | 214 Robert Person | .15 | .07 |
| ❑ | 215 Scott Rolen | .60 | .25 |
| ❑ | 216 Curt Schilling | .25 | .11 |
| ❑ | 217 Scott Rolen TC | .40 | .18 |
| ❑ | 218 Francisco Cordova | .15 | .07 |
| ❑ | 219 Brian Giles | .25 | .11 |

| Card | Mint | NrMt |
|---|---|---|
| ❑ 220 Jason Kendall | .25 | .11 |
| ❑ 221 Warren Morris | .15 | .07 |
| ❑ 222 Abraham Nunez | .15 | .07 |
| ❑ 223 Aramis Ramirez | .15 | .07 |
| ❑ 224 Jose Silva | .15 | .07 |
| ❑ 225 Kevin Young | .15 | .07 |
| ❑ 226 Brian Giles TC | .15 | .07 |
| ❑ 227 Rick Ankiel | 1.25 | .55 |
| ❑ 228 Ricky Bottalico | .15 | .07 |
| ❑ 229 J.D. Drew | .60 | .25 |
| ❑ 230 Ray Lankford | .25 | .11 |
| ❑ 231 Mark McGwire | 2.50 | 1.10 |
| ❑ 232 Eduardo Perez | .15 | .07 |
| ❑ 233 Placido Polanco | .15 | .07 |
| ❑ 234 Edgar Renteria | .15 | .07 |
| ❑ 235 Fernando Tatis | .25 | .11 |
| ❑ 236 Mark McGwire TC | 1.25 | .55 |
| ❑ 237 Carlos Almanzar | .15 | .07 |
| ❑ 238 Wiki Gonzalez | .15 | .07 |
| ❑ 239 Tony Gwynn | 1.25 | .55 |
| ❑ 240 Trevor Hoffman | .25 | .11 |
| ❑ 241 Damian Jackson | .15 | .07 |
| ❑ 242 Wally Joyner | .25 | .11 |
| ❑ 243 Ruben Rivera | .15 | .07 |
| ❑ 244 Reggie Sanders | .15 | .07 |
| ❑ 245 Quilvio Veras | .15 | .07 |
| ❑ 246 Tony Gwynn TC | .60 | .25 |
| ❑ 247 Rich Aurilia | .15 | .07 |
| ❑ 248 Marvin Benard | .15 | .07 |
| ❑ 249 Barry Bonds | 1.00 | .45 |
| ❑ 250 Ellis Burks | .25 | .11 |
| ❑ 251 Miguel Del Toro | .15 | .07 |
| ❑ 252 Edwards Guzman | .15 | .07 |
| ❑ 253 Livan Hernandez | .15 | .07 |
| ❑ 254 Jeff Kent | .40 | .18 |
| ❑ 255 Russ Ortiz | .25 | .11 |
| ❑ 256 Armando Rios | .15 | .07 |
| ❑ 257 Barry Bonds TC | .40 | .18 |
| ❑ 258 Rafael Bournigal | .15 | .07 |
| ❑ 259 Freddy Garcia | .25 | .11 |
| ❑ 260 Ken Griffey Jr. | 2.50 | 1.10 |
| ❑ 261 Carlos Guillen | .15 | .07 |
| ❑ 262 Raul Ibanez | .15 | .07 |
| ❑ 263 Edgar Martinez | .40 | .18 |
| ❑ 264 Jose Mesa | .15 | .07 |
| ❑ 265 Jamie Moyer | .15 | .07 |
| ❑ 266 John Olerud | .25 | .11 |
| ❑ 267 Jose Paniagua | .15 | .07 |
| ❑ 268 Alex Rodriguez | 2.00 | .90 |
| ❑ 269 Alex Rodriguez TC | 1.00 | .45 |
| ❑ 270 Wilson Alvarez | .15 | .07 |
| ❑ 271 Wade Boggs | .75 | .35 |
| ❑ 272 Miguel Cairo | .15 | .07 |
| ❑ 273 Jose Canseco | .75 | .35 |
| ❑ 274 Jose Guillen | .15 | .07 |
| ❑ 275 Roberto Hernandez | .15 | .07 |
| ❑ 276 Albie Lopez | .15 | .07 |
| ❑ 277 Quinton McCracken | .15 | .07 |
| ❑ 278 Fred McGriff | .40 | .18 |
| ❑ 279 Esteban Yan | .15 | .07 |
| ❑ 280 Jose Canseco TC | .40 | .18 |
| ❑ 281 Rusty Greer | .25 | .11 |
| ❑ 282 Roberto Kelly | .15 | .07 |
| ❑ 283 Esteban Loaiza | .15 | .07 |
| ❑ 284 Ruben Mateo | .25 | .11 |
| ❑ 285 Rafael Palmeiro | .60 | .25 |
| ❑ 286 Ivan Rodriguez | .75 | .35 |
| ❑ 287 Aaron Sele | .15 | .07 |
| ❑ 288 John Wetteland | .25 | .11 |
| ❑ 289 Ivan Rodriguez TC | .40 | .18 |
| ❑ 290 Tony Batista | .25 | .11 |
| ❑ 291 Jose Cruz Jr. | .25 | .11 |
| ❑ 292 Carlos Delgado | .60 | .25 |
| ❑ 293 Kelvim Escobar | .15 | .07 |
| ❑ 294 Tony Fernandez | .15 | .07 |
| ❑ 295 Billy Koch | .25 | .11 |
| ❑ 296 Raul Mondesi | .25 | .11 |
| ❑ 297 Willis Otanez | .15 | .07 |
| ❑ 298 David Segui | .15 | .07 |
| ❑ 299 David Wells | .25 | .11 |
| ❑ 300 Carlos Delgado TC | .25 | .11 |
| ❑ SAMP Tony Gwynn Sample | 2.00 | .90 |

## 1998 Pacific Invincible

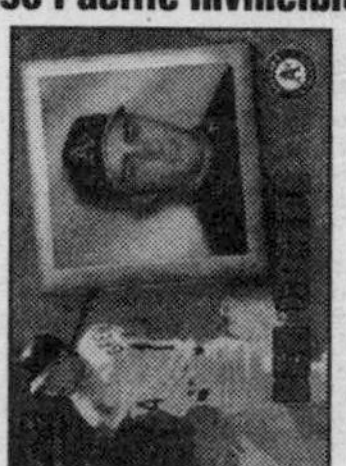

| | MINT | NRMT |
|---|---|---|
| COMPLETE SET (150) | 180.00 | 80.00 |
| COMMON CARD (1-150) | .75 | .35 |
| ❑ 1 Garret Anderson | 1.25 | .55 |
| ❑ 2 Jim Edmonds | 3.00 | 1.35 |
| ❑ 3 Darin Erstad | 3.00 | 1.35 |
| ❑ 4 Chuck Finley | 1.25 | .55 |
| ❑ 5 Tim Salmon | 1.25 | .55 |
| ❑ 6 Roberto Alomar | 3.00 | 1.35 |
| ❑ 7 Brady Anderson | 1.25 | .55 |
| ❑ 8 Geronimo Berroa | .75 | .35 |
| ❑ 9 Eric Davis | 1.25 | .55 |
| ❑ 10 Mike Mussina | 3.00 | 1.35 |
| ❑ 11 Rafael Palmeiro | 3.00 | 1.35 |
| ❑ 12 Cal Ripken | 12.00 | 5.50 |
| ❑ 13 Steve Avery | .75 | .35 |
| ❑ 14 Nomar Garciaparra | 10.00 | 4.50 |
| ❑ 15 John Valentin | .75 | .35 |
| ❑ 16 Mo Vaughn | 1.25 | .55 |
| ❑ 17 Albert Belle | 2.00 | .90 |
| ❑ 18 Ozzie Guillen | .75 | .35 |
| ❑ 19 Norberto Martin | .75 | .35 |
| ❑ 20 Frank Thomas | 6.00 | 2.70 |
| ❑ 21 Robin Ventura | 1.25 | .55 |
| ❑ 22 Sandy Alomar Jr. | 1.25 | .55 |
| ❑ 23 David Justice | 2.00 | .90 |
| ❑ 24 Kenny Lofton | 1.25 | .55 |
| ❑ 25 Manny Ramirez | 4.00 | 1.80 |
| ❑ 26 Jim Thome | 2.00 | .90 |
| ❑ 27 Omar Vizquel | 1.25 | .55 |
| ❑ 28 Matt Williams | 2.00 | .90 |
| ❑ 29 Jaret Wright | .75 | .35 |
| ❑ 30 Raul Casanova | .75 | .35 |
| ❑ 31 Tony Clark | .75 | .35 |
| ❑ 32 Deivi Cruz | .75 | .35 |
| ❑ 33 Bobby Higginson | 1.25 | .55 |
| ❑ 34 Justin Thompson | .75 | .35 |
| ❑ 35 Yamil Benitez | .75 | .35 |
| ❑ 36 Johnny Damon | 1.25 | .55 |
| ❑ 37 Jermaine Dye | 1.25 | .55 |
| ❑ 38 Jed Hansen | .75 | .35 |
| ❑ 39 Larry Sutton | .75 | .35 |
| ❑ 40 Jeromy Burnitz | 1.25 | .55 |
| ❑ 41 Jeff Cirillo | 1.25 | .55 |
| ❑ 42 Dave Nilsson | .75 | .35 |
| ❑ 43 Jose Valentin | .75 | .35 |
| ❑ 44 Fernando Vina | .75 | .35 |
| ❑ 45 Marty Cordova | .75 | .35 |
| ❑ 46 Chuck Knoblauch | 1.25 | .55 |
| ❑ 47 Paul Molitor | 3.00 | 1.35 |
| ❑ 48 Brad Radke | 1.25 | .55 |
| ❑ 49 Terry Steinbach | .75 | .35 |
| ❑ 50 Wade Boggs | 4.00 | 1.80 |
| ❑ 51 Hideki Irabu | .75 | .35 |
| ❑ 52 Derek Jeter | 12.00 | 5.50 |
| ❑ 53 Tino Martinez | 1.25 | .55 |
| ❑ 54 Andy Pettitte | 1.25 | .55 |
| ❑ 55 Mariano Rivera | 1.25 | .55 |
| ❑ 56 Bernie Williams | 3.00 | 1.35 |
| ❑ 57 Jose Canseco | 4.00 | 1.80 |
| ❑ 58 Jason Giambi | 3.00 | 1.35 |
| ❑ 59 Ben Grieve | 1.25 | .55 |
| ❑ 60 Aaron Small | .75 | .35 |
| ❑ 61 Jay Buhner | 1.25 | .55 |
| ❑ 62 Ken Cloude | .75 | .35 |

| Card | Mint | NrMt |
|---|---|---|
| ❑ 63 Joey Cora | .75 | .35 |
| ❑ 64 Ken Griffey Jr. | 12.00 | 5.50 |
| ❑ 65 Randy Johnson | 4.00 | 1.80 |
| ❑ 66 Edgar Martinez | 2.00 | .90 |
| ❑ 67 Alex Rodriguez | 10.00 | 4.50 |
| ❑ 68 Will Clark | 3.00 | 1.35 |
| ❑ 69 Juan Gonzalez | 3.00 | 1.35 |
| ❑ 70 Rusty Greer | 1.25 | .55 |
| ❑ 71 Ivan Rodriguez | 4.00 | 1.80 |
| ❑ 72 Joe Carter | 1.25 | .55 |
| ❑ 73 Roger Clemens | 6.00 | 2.70 |
| ❑ 74 Jose Cruz Jr. | 1.25 | .55 |
| ❑ 75 Carlos Delgado | 3.00 | 1.35 |
| ❑ 76 Andruw Jones | 3.00 | 1.35 |
| ❑ 77 Chipper Jones | 8.00 | 3.60 |
| ❑ 78 Ryan Klesko | 1.25 | .55 |
| ❑ 79 Javier Lopez | 1.25 | .55 |
| ❑ 80 Greg Maddux | 8.00 | 3.60 |
| ❑ 81 Miguel Batista | .75 | .35 |
| ❑ 82 Jeremi Gonzalez | .75 | .35 |
| ❑ 83 Mark Grace | 3.00 | 1.35 |
| ❑ 84 Kevin Orie | .75 | .35 |
| ❑ 85 Sammy Sosa | 6.00 | 2.70 |
| ❑ 86 Barry Larkin | 3.00 | 1.35 |
| ❑ 87 Deion Sanders | 1.25 | .55 |
| ❑ 88 Reggie Sanders | .75 | .35 |
| ❑ 89 Chris Stynes | .75 | .35 |
| ❑ 90 Dante Bichette | 1.25 | .55 |
| ❑ 91 Vinny Castilla | 1.25 | .55 |
| ❑ 92 Andres Galarraga | 2.00 | .90 |
| ❑ 93 Neifi Perez | .75 | .35 |
| ❑ 94 Larry Walker | 1.25 | .55 |
| ❑ 95 Moises Alou | 1.25 | .55 |
| ❑ 96 Bobby Bonilla | 1.25 | .55 |
| ❑ 97 Kevin Brown | 2.00 | .90 |
| ❑ 98 Craig Counsell | .75 | .35 |
| ❑ 99 Livan Hernandez | .75 | .35 |
| ❑ 100 Edgar Renteria | .75 | .35 |
| ❑ 101 Gary Sheffield | 3.00 | 1.35 |
| ❑ 102 Jeff Bagwell | 4.00 | 1.80 |
| ❑ 103 Craig Biggio | 2.00 | .90 |
| ❑ 104 Luis Gonzalez | 1.25 | .55 |
| ❑ 105 Darryl Kile | 1.25 | .55 |
| ❑ 106 Wilton Guerrero | .75 | .35 |
| ❑ 107 Eric Karros | 1.25 | .55 |
| ❑ 108 Ramon Martinez | .75 | .35 |
| ❑ 109 Raul Mondesi | 1.25 | .55 |
| ❑ 110 Hideo Nomo | 3.00 | 1.35 |
| ❑ 111 Chan Ho Park | 1.25 | .55 |
| ❑ 112 Mike Piazza | 10.00 | 4.50 |
| ❑ 113 Mark Grudzielanek | .75 | .35 |
| ❑ 114 Vladimir Guerrero | 5.00 | 2.20 |
| ❑ 115 Pedro Martinez | 4.00 | 1.80 |
| ❑ 116 Henry Rodriguez | .75 | .35 |
| ❑ 117 David Segui | .75 | .35 |
| ❑ 118 Edgardo Alfonzo | 1.25 | .55 |
| ❑ 119 Carlos Baerga | .75 | .35 |
| ❑ 120 John Franco | 1.25 | .55 |
| ❑ 121 John Olerud | 1.25 | .55 |
| ❑ 122 Rey Ordonez | .75 | .35 |
| ❑ 123 Ricky Bottalico | .75 | .35 |
| ❑ 124 Gregg Jefferies | .75 | .35 |
| ❑ 125 Mickey Morandini | .75 | .35 |
| ❑ 126 Scott Rolen | 3.00 | 1.35 |
| ❑ 127 Curt Schilling | 1.25 | .55 |
| ❑ 128 Jose Guillen | .75 | .35 |
| ❑ 129 Esteban Loaiza | .75 | .35 |
| ❑ 130 Al Martin | .75 | .35 |
| ❑ 131 Tony Womack | .75 | .35 |
| ❑ 132 Dennis Eckersley | 1.25 | .55 |
| ❑ 133 Gary Gaetti | 1.25 | .55 |
| ❑ 134 Curtis King | .75 | .35 |
| ❑ 135 Ray Lankford | 1.25 | .55 |
| ❑ 136 Mark McGwire | 12.00 | 5.50 |
| ❑ 137 Ken Caminiti | 1.25 | .55 |
| ❑ 138 Steve Finley | 1.25 | .55 |
| ❑ 139 Tony Gwynn | 6.00 | 2.70 |
| ❑ 140 Carlos Hernandez | .75 | .35 |
| ❑ 141 Wally Joyner | 1.25 | .55 |
| ❑ 142 Barry Bonds | 5.00 | 2.20 |
| ❑ 143 Jacob Cruz | .75 | .35 |
| ❑ 144 Shawn Estes | .75 | .35 |
| ❑ 145 Stan Javier | .75 | .35 |
| ❑ 146 J.T. Snow | 1.25 | .55 |
| ❑ 147 Nomar Garciaparra ROY | 5.00 | 2.20 |
| ❑ 148 Scott Rolen ROY | 3.00 | 1.35 |

| # | Player | MINT | NRMT |
|---|---|---|---|
| ❑ 149 | Ken Griffey Jr. MVP | 6.00 | 2.70 |
| ❑ 150 | Larry Walker MVP | 1.25 | .55 |

## 1999 Pacific Invincible

| | | MINT | NRMT |
|---|---|---|---|
| COMPLETE SET (150) | | 180.00 | 80.00 |
| ❑ 1 | Jim Edmonds | 2.50 | 1.10 |
| ❑ 2 | Darin Erstad | 2.50 | 1.10 |
| ❑ 3 | Troy Glaus | 4.00 | 1.80 |
| ❑ 4 | Tim Salmon | 1.00 | .45 |
| ❑ 5 | Mo Vaughn | 1.00 | .45 |
| ❑ 6 | Steve Finley | 1.00 | .45 |
| ❑ 7 | Randy Johnson | 3.00 | 1.35 |
| ❑ 8 | Travis Lee | .60 | .25 |
| ❑ 9 | Dante Powell | .60 | .25 |
| ❑ 10 | Matt Williams | 1.50 | .70 |
| ❑ 11 | Bret Boone | 1.00 | .45 |
| ❑ 12 | Andruw Jones | 2.50 | 1.10 |
| ❑ 13 | Chipper Jones | 6.00 | 2.70 |
| ❑ 14 | Brian Jordan | 1.00 | .45 |
| ❑ 15 | Ryan Klesko | 1.00 | .45 |
| ❑ 16 | Javy Lopez | 1.00 | .45 |
| ❑ 17 | Greg Maddux | 6.00 | 2.70 |
| ❑ 18 | Brady Anderson | 1.00 | .45 |
| ❑ 19 | Albert Belle | 1.50 | .70 |
| ❑ 20 | Will Clark | 2.50 | 1.10 |
| ❑ 21 | Mike Mussina | 2.50 | 1.10 |
| ❑ 22 | Cal Ripken | 10.00 | 4.50 |
| ❑ 23 | Nomar Garciaparra | 8.00 | 3.60 |
| ❑ 24 | Pedro Martinez | 3.00 | 1.35 |
| ❑ 25 | Trot Nixon | 1.00 | .45 |
| ❑ 26 | Jose Offerman | .60 | .25 |
| ❑ 27 | Donnie Sadler | .60 | .25 |
| ❑ 28 | John Valentin | .60 | .25 |
| ❑ 29 | Mark Grace | 2.50 | 1.10 |
| ❑ 30 | Lance Johnson | .60 | .25 |
| ❑ 31 | Henry Rodriguez | .60 | .25 |
| ❑ 32 | Sammy Sosa | 5.00 | 2.20 |
| ❑ 33 | Kerry Wood | 1.00 | .45 |
| ❑ 34 | McKay Christenson | .60 | .25 |
| ❑ 35 | Ray Durham | 1.00 | .45 |
| ❑ 36 | Jeff Liefer | .60 | .25 |
| ❑ 37 | Frank Thomas | 5.00 | 2.20 |
| ❑ 38 | Mike Cameron | .60 | .25 |
| ❑ 39 | Barry Larkin | 2.50 | 1.10 |
| ❑ 40 | Greg Vaughn | 1.00 | .45 |
| ❑ 41 | Dmitri Young | 1.00 | .45 |
| ❑ 42 | Roberto Alomar | 2.50 | 1.10 |
| ❑ 43 | Sandy Alomar Jr. | 1.00 | .45 |
| ❑ 44 | David Justice | 1.50 | .70 |
| ❑ 45 | Kenny Lofton | 1.00 | .45 |
| ❑ 46 | Manny Ramirez | 3.00 | 1.35 |
| ❑ 47 | Jim Thome | 1.50 | .70 |
| ❑ 48 | Dante Bichette | 1.00 | .45 |
| ❑ 49 | Vinny Castilla | 1.00 | .45 |
| ❑ 50 | Darryl Hamilton | .60 | .25 |
| ❑ 51 | Todd Helton | 3.00 | 1.35 |
| ❑ 52 | Neifi Perez | .60 | .25 |
| ❑ 53 | Larry Walker | 1.00 | .45 |
| ❑ 54 | Tony Clark | .60 | .25 |
| ❑ 55 | Damion Easley | .60 | .25 |
| ❑ 56 | Bob Higginson | 1.00 | .45 |
| ❑ 57 | Brian L.Hunter | .60 | .25 |
| ❑ 58 | Gabe Kapler | 1.00 | .45 |
| ❑ 59 | Cliff Floyd | 1.00 | .45 |
| ❑ 60 | Alex Gonzalez | .60 | .25 |
| ❑ 61 | Mark Kotsay | .60 | .25 |
| ❑ 62 | Derrek Lee | .60 | .25 |
| ❑ 63 | Braden Looper | .60 | .25 |
| ❑ 64 | Moises Alou | 1.00 | .45 |
| ❑ 65 | Jeff Bagwell | 3.00 | 1.35 |
| ❑ 66 | Craig Biggio | 1.50 | .70 |
| ❑ 67 | Ken Caminiti | 1.00 | .45 |
| ❑ 68 | Scott Elarton | 1.00 | .45 |
| ❑ 69 | Mitch Meluskey | .60 | .25 |
| ❑ 70 | Carlos Beltran | 1.00 | .45 |
| ❑ 71 | Johnny Damon | 1.00 | .45 |
| ❑ 72 | Carlos Febles | .60 | .25 |
| ❑ 73 | Jeremy Giambi | .60 | .25 |
| ❑ 74 | Kevin Brown | 1.50 | .70 |
| ❑ 75 | Todd Hundley | .60 | .25 |
| ❑ 76 | Paul LoDuca | .60 | .25 |
| ❑ 77 | Raul Mondesi | 1.00 | .45 |
| ❑ 78 | Gary Sheffield | 2.50 | 1.10 |
| ❑ 79 | Geoff Jenkins | 1.00 | .45 |
| ❑ 80 | Jeromy Burnitz | 1.00 | .45 |
| ❑ 81 | Marquis Grissom | .60 | .25 |
| ❑ 82 | Jose Valentin | .00 | .25 |
| ❑ 83 | Fernando Vina | .60 | .25 |
| ❑ 84 | Corey Koskie | .60 | .25 |
| ❑ 85 | Matt Lawton | 1.00 | .45 |
| ❑ 86 | Christian Guzman | .60 | .25 |
| ❑ 87 | Torii Hunter | .60 | .25 |
| ❑ 88 | Doug Mientkiewicz RC | 1.25 | .55 |
| ❑ 89 | Michael Barrett | .60 | .25 |
| ❑ 90 | Brad Fullmer | 1.00 | .45 |
| ❑ 91 | Vladimir Guerrero | 4.00 | 1.80 |
| ❑ 92 | Fernando Seguignol | .60 | .25 |
| ❑ 93 | Ugueth Urbina | .60 | .25 |
| ❑ 94 | Bobby Bonilla | 1.00 | .45 |
| ❑ 95 | Rickey Henderson | 3.00 | 1.35 |
| ❑ 96 | Rey Ordonez | .60 | .25 |
| ❑ 97 | Mike Piazza | 8.00 | 3.60 |
| ❑ 98 | Robin Ventura | 1.00 | .45 |
| ❑ 99 | Roger Clemens | 5.00 | 2.20 |
| ❑ 100 | Derek Jeter | 10.00 | 4.50 |
| ❑ 101 | Chuck Knoblauch | 1.00 | .45 |
| ❑ 102 | Tino Martinez | 1.00 | .45 |
| ❑ 103 | Paul O'Neill | 1.00 | .45 |
| ❑ 104 | Bernie Williams | 2.50 | 1.10 |
| ❑ 105 | Eric Chavez | 1.00 | .45 |
| ❑ 106 | Ryan Christenson | .60 | .25 |
| ❑ 107 | Jason Giambi | 2.50 | 1.10 |
| ❑ 108 | Ben Grieve | 1.00 | .45 |
| ❑ 109 | Miguel Tejada | 1.00 | .45 |
| ❑ 110 | Marlon Anderson | .60 | .25 |
| ❑ 111 | Doug Glanville | .60 | .25 |
| ❑ 112 | Scott Rolen | 2.50 | 1.10 |
| ❑ 113 | Curt Schilling | 1.00 | .45 |
| ❑ 114 | Brian Giles | 1.00 | .45 |
| ❑ 115 | Warren Morris | .60 | .25 |
| ❑ 116 | Jason Kendall | 1.00 | .45 |
| ❑ 117 | Kris Benson | 1.00 | .45 |
| ❑ 118 | J.D. Drew | 2.50 | 1.10 |
| ❑ 119 | Ray Lankford | 1.00 | .45 |
| ❑ 120 | Mark McGwire | 10.00 | 4.50 |
| ❑ 121 | Matt Clement | .60 | .25 |
| ❑ 122 | Tony Gwynn | 5.00 | 2.20 |
| ❑ 123 | Trevor Hoffman | 1.00 | .45 |
| ❑ 124 | Wally Joyner | 1.00 | .45 |
| ❑ 125 | Reggie Sanders | .60 | .25 |
| ❑ 126 | Barry Bonds | 4.00 | 1.80 |
| ❑ 127 | Ellis Burks | 1.00 | .45 |
| ❑ 128 | Jeff Kent | 1.50 | .70 |
| ❑ 129 | Stan Javier | .60 | .25 |
| ❑ 130 | J.T. Snow | 1.00 | .45 |
| ❑ 131 | Jay Buhner | 1.00 | .45 |
| ❑ 132 | Freddy Garcia RC | 5.00 | 2.20 |
| ❑ 133 | Ken Griffey Jr. | 10.00 | 4.50 |
| ❑ 134 | Russ Davis | .60 | .25 |
| ❑ 135 | Edgar Martinez | 1.50 | .70 |
| ❑ 136 | Alex Rodriguez | 8.00 | 3.60 |
| ❑ 137 | David Segui | .60 | .25 |
| ❑ 138 | Rolando Arrojo | .60 | .25 |
| ❑ 139 | Wade Boggs | 3.00 | 1.35 |
| ❑ 140 | Jose Canseco | 3.00 | 1.35 |
| ❑ 141 | Quinton McCracken | .60 | .25 |
| ❑ 142 | Fred McGriff | 1.50 | .70 |
| ❑ 143 | Juan Gonzalez | 2.50 | 1.10 |
| ❑ 144 | Tom Goodwin | .60 | .25 |
| ❑ 145 | Rusty Greer | 1.00 | .45 |
| ❑ 146 | Ivan Rodriguez | 3.00 | 1.35 |
| ❑ 147 | Jose Cruz Jr. | 1.00 | .45 |
| ❑ 148 | Carlos Delgado | 2.50 | 1.10 |
| ❑ 149 | Shawn Green | 2.50 | 1.10 |
| ❑ 150 | Roy Halladay | .60 | .25 |

## 2000 Pacific Invincible

| | | MINT | NRMT |
|---|---|---|---|
| COMPLETE SET (150) | | 250.00 | 110.00 |
| MINOR STARS | | 1.00 | .45 |
| SEMISTARS | | 1.50 | .70 |
| ❑ 1 | Darin Erstad | 2.50 | 1.10 |
| ❑ 2 | Troy Glaus | 3.00 | 1.35 |
| ❑ 3 | Ramon Ortiz | 1.00 | .45 |
| ❑ 4 | Tim Salmon | 1.00 | .45 |
| ❑ 5 | Mo Vaughn | 1.00 | .45 |
| ❑ 6 | Erubiel Durazo | 1.00 | .45 |
| ❑ 7 | Luis Gonzalez | 1.00 | .45 |
| ❑ 8 | Randy Johnson | 3.00 | 1.35 |
| ❑ 9 | Matt Williams | 1.00 | .45 |
| ❑ 10 | Rafael Furcal | 6.00 | 2.70 |
| ❑ 11 | Andres Galarraga | 1.50 | .70 |
| ❑ 12 | Tom Glavine | 2.50 | 1.10 |
| ❑ 13 | Andruw Jones | 2.50 | 1.10 |
| ❑ 14 | Chipper Jones | 6.00 | 2.70 |
| ❑ 15 | Greg Maddux | 6.00 | 2.70 |
| ❑ 16 | Kevin Millwood | 1.00 | .45 |
| ❑ 17 | Albert Belle | 1.50 | .70 |
| ❑ 18 | Will Clark | 2.50 | 1.10 |
| ❑ 19 | Mike Mussina | 2.50 | 1.10 |
| ❑ 20 | Matt Riley | 1.00 | .45 |
| ❑ 21 | Cal Ripken | 10.00 | 4.50 |
| ❑ 22 | Carl Everett | 1.00 | .45 |
| ❑ 23 | Nomar Garciaparra | 8.00 | 3.60 |
| ❑ 24 | Steve Lomasney | .60 | .25 |
| ❑ 25 | Pedro Martinez | 3.00 | 1.35 |
| ❑ 26 | Tomo Ohka RC | 2.50 | 1.10 |
| ❑ 27 | Wilton Veras | 1.00 | .45 |
| ❑ 28 | Mark Grace | 2.50 | 1.10 |
| ❑ 29 | Sammy Sosa | 5.00 | 2.20 |
| ❑ 30 | Kerry Wood | 1.00 | .45 |
| ❑ 31 | Eric Young | .60 | .25 |
| ❑ 32 | Julio Zuleta RC | 1.50 | .70 |
| ❑ 33 | Paul Konerko | 1.00 | .45 |
| ❑ 34 | Carlos Lee | 1.00 | .45 |
| ❑ 35 | Magglio Ordonez | 1.00 | .45 |
| ❑ 36 | Josh Paul | .60 | .25 |
| ❑ 37 | Frank Thomas | 5.00 | 2.20 |
| ❑ 38 | Rob Bell | .60 | .25 |
| ❑ 39 | Dante Bichette | 1.00 | .45 |
| ❑ 40 | Sean Casey | 1.00 | .45 |
| ❑ 41 | Ken Griffey Jr. | 10.00 | 4.50 |
| ❑ 42 | Barry Larkin | 2.50 | 1.10 |
| ❑ 43 | Pokey Reese | 1.00 | .45 |
| ❑ 44 | Roberto Alomar | 2.50 | 1.10 |
| ❑ 45 | Manny Ramirez | 3.00 | 1.35 |
| ❑ 46 | Richie Sexson | 1.00 | .45 |
| ❑ 47 | Jim Thome | 1.50 | .70 |
| ❑ 48 | Omar Vizquel | 1.00 | .45 |
| ❑ 49 | Jeff Cirillo | 1.00 | .45 |
| ❑ 50 | Todd Helton | 3.00 | 1.35 |
| ❑ 51 | Neifi Perez | .60 | .25 |
| ❑ 52 | Larry Walker | 1.00 | .45 |
| ❑ 53 | Tony Clark | .60 | .25 |
| ❑ 54 | Juan Encarnacion | 1.00 | .45 |
| ❑ 55 | Juan Gonzalez | 2.50 | 1.10 |
| ❑ 56 | Hideo Nomo | 2.50 | 1.10 |

❑ 57 Luis Castillo 1.00 .45
❑ 58 Alex Gonzalez .60 .25
❑ 59 Brad Penny 1.00 .45
❑ 60 Preston Wilson 1.00 .45
❑ 61 Moises Alou 1.00 .45
❑ 62 Jeff Bagwell 3.00 1.35
❑ 63 Lance Berkman 1.00 .45
❑ 64 Craig Biggio 1.50 .70
❑ 65 Roger Cedeno .60 .25
❑ 66 Jose Lima .60 .25
❑ 67 Carlos Beltran 1.00 .45
❑ 68 Johnny Damon 1.00 .45
❑ 69 Chad Durbin RC 1.50 .70
❑ 70 Jermaine Dye 1.00 .45
❑ 71 Carlos Febles .60 .25
❑ 72 Mark Quinn 1.00 .45
❑ 73 Kevin Brown 1.00 .45
❑ 74 Eric Gagne .60 .25
❑ 75 Shawn Green 2.50 1.10
❑ 76 Eric Karros 1.00 .45
❑ 77 Gary Sheffield 2.50 1.10
❑ 78 Kevin Barker .60 .25
❑ 79 Ron Belliard .60 .25
❑ 80 Jeromy Burnitz 1.00 .45
❑ 81 Geoff Jenkins 1.00 .45
❑ 82 Jacque Jones 1.00 .45
❑ 83 Corey Koskie .60 .25
❑ 84 Matt LeCroy .60 .25
❑ 85 David Ortiz .60 .25
❑ 86 Johan Santana RC 1.50 .70
❑ 87 Todd Walker .60 .25
❑ 88 Peter Bergeron .60 .25
❑ 89 Vladimir Guerrero 4.00 1.80
❑ 90 Jose Vidro 1.00 .45
❑ 91 Rondell White 1.00 .45
❑ 92 Edgardo Alfonzo 1.00 .45
❑ 93 Derek Bell .60 .25
❑ 94 Mike Hampton 1.00 .45
❑ 95 Rey Ordonez .60 .25
❑ 96 Mike Piazza 8.00 3.60
❑ 97 Robin Ventura 1.00 .45
❑ 98 Roger Clemens 5.00 2.20
❑ 99 Orlando Hernandez 1.00 .45
❑ 100 Derek Jeter 10.00 4.50
❑ 101 Alfonso Soriano 1.00 .45
❑ 102 Bernie Williams 2.50 1.10
❑ 103 Eric Chavez 1.00 .45
❑ 104 Jason Giambi 2.50 1.10
❑ 105 Ben Grieve 1.00 .45
❑ 106 Tim Hudson 2.50 1.10
❑ 107 Miguel Tejada 1.00 .45
❑ 108 Bob Abreu 1.00 .45
❑ 109 Doug Glanville .60 .25
❑ 110 Mike Lieberthal 1.00 .45
❑ 111 Scott Rolen 1.50 .70
❑ 112 Brian Giles 1.00 .45
❑ 113 Chad Hermansen .60 .25
❑ 114 Jason Kendall 1.00 .45
❑ 115 Warren Morris .60 .25
❑ 116 Aramis Ramirez .60 .25
❑ 117 Rick Ankiel 5.00 2.20
❑ 118 J.D. Drew 2.50 1.10
❑ 119 Mark McGwire 10.00 4.50
❑ 120 Fernando Tatis 1.00 .45
❑ 121 Fernando Vina .60 .25
❑ 122 Bret Boone .60 .25
❑ 123 Ben Davis .60 .25
❑ 124 Tony Gwynn 5.00 2.20
❑ 125 Trevor Hoffman 1.00 .45
❑ 126 Ryan Klesko 1.00 .45
❑ 127 Rich Aurilia .60 .25
❑ 128 Barry Bonds 4.00 1.80
❑ 129 Ellis Burks 1.00 .45
❑ 130 Jeff Kent 1.50 .70
❑ 131 Freddy Garcia 1.00 .45
❑ 132 Carlos Guillen .60 .25
❑ 133 Edgar Martinez 1.00 .45
❑ 134 John Olerud 1.00 .45
❑ 135 Robert Ramsay .60 .25
❑ 136 Alex Rodriguez 8.00 3.60
❑ 137 Kazuhiro Sasaki RC 10.00 4.50
❑ 138 Jose Canseco 3.00 1.35
❑ 139 Vinny Castilla 1.00 .45
❑ 140 Fred McGriff 1.50 .70
❑ 141 Greg Vaughn 1.00 .45
❑ 142 Dan Wheeler .60 .25
❑ 143 Gabe Kapler 1.00 .45
❑ 144 Ruben Mateo 1.00 .45
❑ 145 Rafael Palmeiro 2.50 1.10
❑ 146 Ivan Rodriguez 3.00 1.35
❑ 147 Tony Batista 1.00 .45
❑ 148 Carlos Delgado 2.50 1.10
❑ 149 Raul Mondesi 1.00 .45
❑ 150 Vernon Wells 1.00 .45

## 1998 Pacific Omega

| | MINT | NRMT |
|---|---|---|
| COMPLETE SET (250) | 40.00 | 18.00 |
| COMMON CARD (1-250) | .15 | .07 |

❑ 1 Garret Anderson .25 .11
❑ 2 Gary DiSarcina .15 .07
❑ 3 Jim Edmonds .60 .25
❑ 4 Darin Erstad .60 .25
❑ 5 Cecil Fielder .25 .11
❑ 6 Chuck Finley .25 .11
❑ 7 Shigetoshi Hasegawa .25 .11
❑ 8 Tim Salmon .25 .11
❑ 9 Brian Anderson .15 .07
❑ 10 Jay Bell .25 .11
❑ 11 Andy Benes .15 .07
❑ 12 Yamil Benitez .15 .07
❑ 13 Jorge Fabregas .15 .07
❑ 14 Travis Lee .25 .11
❑ 15 Devon White .15 .07
❑ 16 Matt Williams .40 .18
❑ 17 Andres Galarraga .40 .18
❑ 18 Tom Glavine .60 .25
❑ 19 Andruw Jones .60 .25
❑ 20 Chipper Jones 1.50 .70
❑ 21 Ryan Klesko .25 .11
❑ 22 Javy Lopez .25 .11
❑ 23 Greg Maddux 1.50 .70
❑ 24 Kevin Millwood RC 1.00 .45
❑ 25 Denny Neagle .15 .07
❑ 26 John Smoltz .25 .11
❑ 27 Roberto Alomar .60 .25
❑ 28 Brady Anderson .25 .11
❑ 29 Joe Carter .25 .11
❑ 30 Eric Davis .25 .11
❑ 31 Jimmy Key .25 .11
❑ 32 Mike Mussina .60 .25
❑ 33 Rafael Palmeiro .60 .25
❑ 34 Cal Ripken 2.50 1.10
❑ 35 B.J. Surhoff .25 .11
❑ 36 Dennis Eckersley .25 .11
❑ 37 Nomar Garciaparra 2.00 .90
❑ 38 Reggie Jefferson .15 .07
❑ 39 Derek Lowe .15 .07
❑ 40 Pedro Martinez .75 .35
❑ 41 Brian Rose .15 .07
❑ 42 John Valentin .15 .07
❑ 43 Jason Varitek .25 .11
❑ 44 Mo Vaughn .25 .11
❑ 45 Jeff Blauser .15 .07
❑ 46 Jeremi Gonzalez .15 .07
❑ 47 Mark Grace .60 .25
❑ 48 Lance Johnson .15 .07
❑ 49 Kevin Orie .15 .07
❑ 50 Henry Rodriguez .15 .07
❑ 51 Sammy Sosa 1.25 .55
❑ 52 Kerry Wood .60 .25
❑ 53 Albert Belle .40 .18
❑ 54 Mike Cameron .25 .11
❑ 55 Mike Caruso .15 .07
❑ 56 Ray Durham .25 .11
❑ 57 Jaime Navarro .15 .07
❑ 58 Greg Norton .15 .07
❑ 59 Maggio Ordonez RC 2.50 1.10
❑ 60 Frank Thomas 1.25 .55
❑ 61 Robin Ventura .25 .11
❑ 62 Bret Boone .25 .11
❑ 63 Willie Greene .15 .07
❑ 64 Barry Larkin .60 .25
❑ 65 Jon Nunnally .15 .07
❑ 66 Eduardo Perez .15 .07
❑ 67 Reggie Sanders .15 .07
❑ 68 Brett Tomko .15 .07
❑ 69 Sandy Alomar Jr. .25 .11
❑ 70 Travis Fryman .25 .11
❑ 71 David Justice .40 .18
❑ 72 Kenny Lofton .25 .11
❑ 73 Charles Nagy .15 .07
❑ 74 Manny Ramirez .75 .35
❑ 75 Jim Thome .40 .18
❑ 76 Omar Vizquel .25 .11
❑ 77 Enrique Wilson .15 .07
❑ 78 Jaret Wright .15 .07
❑ 79 Dante Bichette .25 .11
❑ 80 Ellis Burks .25 .11
❑ 81 Vinny Castilla .25 .11
❑ 82 Todd Helton .75 .35
❑ 83 Darryl Kile .25 .11
❑ 84 Mike Lansing .15 .07
❑ 85 Neifi Perez .15 .07
❑ 86 Larry Walker .25 .11
❑ 87 Raul Casanova .15 .07
❑ 88 Tony Clark .15 .07
❑ 89 Luis Gonzalez .25 .11
❑ 90 Bobby Higginson .25 .11
❑ 91 Brian Hunter .15 .07
❑ 92 Bip Roberts .15 .07
❑ 93 Justin Thompson .15 .07
❑ 94 Josh Booty .15 .07
❑ 95 Craig Counsell .15 .07
❑ 96 Livan Hernandez .15 .07
❑ 97 Ryan Jackson RC .15 .07
❑ 98 Mark Kotsay .25 .11
❑ 99 Derrek Lee .15 .07
❑ 100 Mike Piazza 2.00 .90
❑ 101 Edgar Renteria .15 .07
❑ 102 Cliff Floyd .25 .11
❑ 103 Moises Alou .25 .11
❑ 104 Jeff Bagwell .75 .35
❑ 105 Derek Bell .15 .07
❑ 106 Sean Berry .15 .07
❑ 107 Craig Biggio .40 .18
❑ 108 John Halama RC .50 .23
❑ 109 Richard Hidalgo .25 .11
❑ 110 Shane Reynolds .15 .07
❑ 111 Tim Belcher .15 .07
❑ 112 Brian Bevil .15 .07
❑ 113 Jeff Conine .15 .07
❑ 114 Johnny Damon .25 .11
❑ 115 Jeff King .15 .07
❑ 116 Jeff Montgomery .15 .07
❑ 117 Dean Palmer .25 .11
❑ 118 Terry Pendleton .25 .11
❑ 119 Bobby Bonilla .25 .11
❑ 120 Wilton Guerrero .15 .07
❑ 121 Todd Hollandsworth .15 .07
❑ 122 Charles Johnson .25 .11
❑ 123 Eric Karros .25 .11
❑ 124 Paul Konerko .25 .11
❑ 125 Ramon Martinez .15 .07
❑ 126 Raul Mondesi .25 .11
❑ 127 Hideo Nomo .60 .25
❑ 128 Gary Sheffield .60 .25
❑ 129 Ismael Valdes .15 .07
❑ 130 Jeromy Burnitz .25 .11
❑ 131 Jeff Cirillo .25 .11
❑ 132 Todd Dunn .15 .07
❑ 133 Marquis Grissom .15 .07
❑ 134 John Jaha .25 .11
❑ 135 Scott Karl .15 .07
❑ 136 Dave Nilsson .15 .07
❑ 137 Jose Valentin .15 .07
❑ 138 Fernando Vina .15 .07
❑ 139 Rick Aguilera .15 .07

- ❑ 140 Marty Cordova .15 .07
- ❑ 141 Pat Meares .15 .07
- ❑ 142 Paul Molitor .60 .25
- ❑ 143 David Ortiz .15 .07
- ❑ 144 Brad Radke .25 .11
- ❑ 145 Terry Steinbach .15 .07
- ❑ 146 Todd Walker .15 .07
- ❑ 147 Shane Andrews .15 .07
- ❑ 148 Brad Fullmer .25 .11
- ❑ 149 Mark Grudzielanek .15 .07
- ❑ 150 Vladimir Guerrero 1.00 .45
- ❑ 151 F.P. Santangelo .15 .07
- ❑ 152 Jose Vidro .15 .07
- ❑ 153 Rondell White .25 .11
- ❑ 154 Carlos Baerga .15 .07
- ❑ 155 Bernard Gilkey .15 .07
- ❑ 156 Todd Hundley .15 .07
- ❑ 157 Butch Huskey .15 .07
- ❑ 158 Bobby Jones .15 .07
- ❑ 159 Brian McRae .15 .07
- ❑ 160 John Olerud .25 .11
- ❑ 161 Rey Ordonez .15 .07
- ❑ 162 Masato Yoshii RC .50 .23
- ❑ 163 David Cone .25 .11
- ❑ 164 Hideki Irabu .15 .07
- ❑ 165 Derek Jeter 2.50 1.10
- ❑ 166 Chuck Knoblauch .25 .11
- ❑ 167 Tino Martinez .25 .11
- ❑ 168 Paul O'Neill .25 .11
- ❑ 169 Andy Pettitte .25 .11
- ❑ 170 Mariano Rivera .25 .11
- ❑ 171 Darryl Strawberry .25 .11
- ❑ 172 David Wells .25 .11
- ❑ 173 Bernie Williams .60 .25
- ❑ 174 Ryan Christenson RC .25 .11
- ❑ 175 Jason Giambi .60 .25
- ❑ 176 Ben Grieve .25 .11
- ❑ 177 Rickey Henderson .75 .35
- ❑ 178 A.J. Hinch .15 .07
- ❑ 179 Kenny Rogers .15 .07
- ❑ 180 Ricky Bottalico .15 .07
- ❑ 181 Rico Brogna .15 .07
- ❑ 182 Doug Glanville .15 .07
- ❑ 183 Gregg Jefferies .15 .07
- ❑ 184 Mike Lieberthal .25 .11
- ❑ 185 Scott Rolen .60 .25
- ❑ 186 Curt Schilling .25 .11
- ❑ 187 Jermaine Allensworth .15 .07
- ❑ 188 Lou Collier .15 .07
- ❑ 189 Jose Guillen .15 .07
- ❑ 190 Jason Kendall .25 .11
- ❑ 191 Al Martin .15 .07
- ❑ 192 Tony Womack .15 .07
- ❑ 193 Kevin Young .25 .11
- ❑ 194 Royce Clayton .15 .07
- ❑ 195 Delino DeShields .15 .07
- ❑ 196 Gary Gaetti .25 .11
- ❑ 197 Ron Gant .25 .11
- ❑ 198 Brian Jordan .25 .11
- ❑ 199 Ray Lankford .25 .11
- ❑ 200 Mark McGwire 2.50 1.10
- ❑ 201 Todd Stottlemyre .15 .07
- ❑ 202 Kevin Brown .40 .18
- ❑ 203 Ken Caminiti .25 .11
- ❑ 204 Steve Finley .25 .11
- ❑ 205 Tony Gwynn 1.25 .55
- ❑ 206 Carlos Hernandez .15 .07
- ❑ 207 Wally Joyner .25 .11
- ❑ 208 Greg Vaughn .25 .11
- ❑ 209 Barry Bonds 1.00 .45
- ❑ 210 Shawn Estes .15 .07
- ❑ 211 Orel Hershiser .25 .11
- ❑ 212 Stan Javier .15 .07
- ❑ 213 Jeff Kent .40 .18
- ❑ 214 Bill Mueller .15 .07
- ❑ 215 Robb Nen .15 .07
- ❑ 216 J.T. Snow .25 .11
- ❑ 217 Jay Buhner .25 .11
- ❑ 218 Ken Cloude .15 .07
- ❑ 219 Joey Cora .15 .07
- ❑ 220 Ken Griffey Jr. 2.50 1.10
- ❑ 221 Glenallen Hill .15 .07
- ❑ 222 Randy Johnson .75 .35
- ❑ 223 Edgar Martinez .40 .18
- ❑ 224 Jamie Moyer .15 .07
- ❑ 225 Alex Rodriguez 2.00 .90
- ❑ 226 David Segui .15 .07
- ❑ 227 Dan Wilson .15 .07
- ❑ 228 Rolando Arrojo RC .50 .23
- ❑ 229 Wade Boggs .75 .35
- ❑ 230 Miguel Cairo .15 .07
- ❑ 231 Roberto Hernandez .15 .07
- ❑ 232 Quinton McCracken .15 .07
- ❑ 233 Fred McGriff .40 .18
- ❑ 234 Paul Sorrento .15 .07
- ❑ 235 Kevin Stocker .15 .07
- ❑ 236 Will Clark .60 .25
- ❑ 237 Juan Gonzalez .60 .25
- ❑ 238 Rusty Greer .25 .11
- ❑ 239 Rick Helling .25 .11
- ❑ 240 Roberto Kelly .15 .07
- ❑ 241 Ivan Rodriguez .75 .35
- ❑ 242 Aaron Sele .25 .11
- ❑ 243 John Wetteland .25 .11
- ❑ 244 Jose Canseco .75 .35
- ❑ 245 Roger Clemens 1.25 .55
- ❑ 246 Jose Cruz Jr. .25 .11
- ❑ 247 Carlos Delgado .60 .25
- ❑ 248 Alex Gonzalez .15 .07
- ❑ 249 Ed Sprague .15 .07
- ❑ 250 Shannon Stewart .25 .11
- ❑ NNO Tony Gwynn Sample .. 2.00 .90

## 1999 Pacific Omega

| | MINT | NRMT |
|---|---|---|
| COMPLETE SET (250) | 40.00 | 18.00 |
| COMMON CARD (1-250) | .15 | .07 |
| COMMON DUAL-PLAYER | .25 | .11 |

- ❑ 1 Garret Anderson .25 .11
- ❑ 2 Jim Edmonds .60 .25
- ❑ 3 Darin Erstad .60 .25
- ❑ 4 Chuck Finley .25 .11
- ❑ 5 Troy Glaus 1.00 .45
- ❑ 6 Troy Percival .15 .07
- ❑ 7 Chris Pritchett .15 .07
- ❑ 8 Tim Salmon .25 .11
- ❑ 9 Mo Vaughn .25 .11
- ❑ 10 Jay Bell .25 .11
- ❑ 11 Steve Finley .25 .11
- ❑ 12 Luis Gonzalez .25 .11
- ❑ 13 Randy Johnson .75 .35
- ❑ 14 Byung-Hyun Kim RC 1.25 .55
- ❑ 15 Travis Lee .15 .07
- ❑ 16 Matt Williams .40 .18
- ❑ 17 Tony Womack .15 .07
- ❑ 18 Bret Boone .25 .11
- ❑ 19 Mark DeRosa .15 .07
- ❑ 20 Tom Glavine .60 .25
- ❑ 21 Andruw Jones .60 .25
- ❑ 22 Chipper Jones 1.50 .70
- ❑ 23 Brian Jordan .25 .11
- ❑ 24 Ryan Klesko .25 .11
- ❑ 25 Javy Lopez .25 .11
- ❑ 26 Greg Maddux 1.50 .70
- ❑ 27 John Smoltz .25 .11
- ❑ 28 Bruce Chen .25 .11
  Odalis Perez
- ❑ 29 Brady Anderson .25 .11
- ❑ 30 Harold Baines .25 .11
- ❑ 31 Albert Belle .40 .18
- ❑ 32 Will Clark .60 .25
- ❑ 33 Delino DeShields .15 .07
- ❑ 34 Jerry Hairston Jr. .25 .11
- ❑ 35 Charles Johnson .25 .11
- ❑ 36 Mike Mussina .60 .25
- ❑ 37 Cal Ripken 2.50 1.10
- ❑ 38 B.J. Surhoff .25 .11
- ❑ 39 Jin Ho Cho .15 .07
- ❑ 40 Nomar Garciaparra 2.00 .90
- ❑ 41 Pedro Martinez .75 .35
- ❑ 42 Jose Offerman .15 .07
- ❑ 43 Troy O'Leary .15 .07
- ❑ 44 John Valentin .15 .07
- ❑ 45 Jason Varitek .25 .11
- ❑ 46 Juan Pena RC .40 .18
  Brian Rose
- ❑ 47 Mark Grace .60 .25
- ❑ 48 Glenallen Hill .15 .07
- ❑ 49 Tyler Houston .15 .07
- ❑ 50 Mickey Morandini .15 .07
- ❑ 51 Henry Rodriguez .15 .07
- ❑ 52 Sammy Sosa 1.25 .55
- ❑ 53 Kevin Tapani .15 .07
- ❑ 54 Mike Caruso .15 .07
- ❑ 55 Ray Durham .25 .11
- ❑ 56 Paul Konerko .25 .11
- ❑ 57 Carlos Lee .25 .11
- ❑ 58 Magglio Ordonez .40 .18
- ❑ 59 Mike Sirotka .15 .07
- ❑ 60 Frank Thomas 1.25 .55
- ❑ 61 Mark Johnson .40 .18
  Chris Singleton
- ❑ 62 Mike Cameron .15 .07
- ❑ 63 Sean Casey .25 .11
- ❑ 64 Pete Harnisch .15 .07
- ❑ 65 Barry Larkin .60 .25
- ❑ 66 Pokey Reese .25 .11
- ❑ 67 Greg Vaughn .25 .11
- ❑ 68 Scott Williamson .15 .07
- ❑ 69 Dmitri Young .25 .11
- ❑ 70 Roberto Alomar .60 .25
- ❑ 71 Sandy Alomar Jr. .25 .11
- ❑ 72 Travis Fryman .25 .11
- ❑ 73 David Justice .40 .18
- ❑ 74 Kenny Lofton .25 .11
- ❑ 75 Manny Ramirez .75 .35
- ❑ 76 Richie Sexson .25 .11
- ❑ 77 Jim Thome .40 .18
- ❑ 78 Omar Vizquel .25 .11
- ❑ 79 Jaret Wright .15 .07
- ❑ 80 Dante Bichette .25 .11
- ❑ 81 Vinny Castilla .25 .11
- ❑ 82 Todd Helton .75 .35
- ❑ 83 Darryl Hamilton .15 .07
- ❑ 84 Darryl Kile .25 .11
- ❑ 85 Neifi Perez .15 .07
- ❑ 86 Larry Walker .25 .11
- ❑ 87 Tony Clark .15 .07
- ❑ 88 Damion Easley .15 .07
- ❑ 89 Juan Encarnacion .25 .11
- ❑ 90 Bobby Higginson .25 .11
- ❑ 91 Gabe Kapler .25 .11
- ❑ 92 Dean Palmer .25 .11
- ❑ 93 Justin Thompson .15 .07
- ❑ 94 Jeff Weaver 1.00 .45
  Masao Kida RC
- ❑ 95 Bruce Aven .15 .07
- ❑ 96 Luis Castillo .25 .11
- ❑ 97 Alex Fernandez .15 .07
- ❑ 98 Cliff Floyd .25 .11
- ❑ 99 Alex Gonzalez .15 .07
- ❑ 100 Mark Kotsay .15 .07
- ❑ 101 Preston Wilson .25 .11
- ❑ 102 Moises Alou .25 .11
- ❑ 103 Jeff Bagwell .75 .35
- ❑ 104 Craig Biggio .40 .18
- ❑ 105 Derek Bell .15 .07
- ❑ 106 Mike Hampton .25 .11
- ❑ 107 Richard Hidalgo .25 .11
- ❑ 108 Jose Lima .15 .07
- ❑ 109 Billy Wagner .15 .07
- ❑ 110 Russ Johnson .40 .18
  Daryle Ward
- ❑ 111 Carlos Beltran .25 .11
- ❑ 112 Johnny Damon .25 .11
- ❑ 113 Jermaine Dye .25 .11
- ❑ 114 Carlos Febles .15 .07
- ❑ 115 Jeremy Giambi .15 .07

| | Card | Mint | NrMt |
|---|---|---|---|
| ❑ | 116 Joe Randa | .15 | .07 |
| ❑ | 117 Mike Sweeney | .25 | .11 |
| ❑ | 118 Orber Moreno | .40 | .18 |
| | Jose Santiago RC | | |
| ❑ | 119 Kevin Brown | .40 | .18 |
| ❑ | 120 Todd Hundley | .15 | .07 |
| ❑ | 121 Eric Karros | .25 | .11 |
| ❑ | 122 Raul Mondesi | .25 | .11 |
| ❑ | 123 Chan Ho Park | .25 | .11 |
| ❑ | 124 Angel Pena | .15 | .07 |
| ❑ | 125 Gary Sheffield | .60 | .25 |
| ❑ | 126 Devon White | .15 | .07 |
| ❑ | 127 Eric Young | .15 | .07 |
| ❑ | 128 Ron Belliard | .15 | .07 |
| ❑ | 129 Jeromy Burnitz | .25 | .11 |
| ❑ | 130 Jeff Cirillo | .25 | .11 |
| ❑ | 131 Marquis Grissom | .15 | .07 |
| ❑ | 132 Geoff Jenkins | .25 | .11 |
| ❑ | 133 David Nilsson | .15 | .07 |
| ❑ | 134 Hideo Nomo | .60 | .25 |
| ❑ | 135 Fernando Vina | .15 | .07 |
| ❑ | 136 Ron Coomer | .15 | .07 |
| ❑ | 137 Marty Cordova | .15 | .07 |
| ❑ | 138 Corey Koskie | .15 | .07 |
| ❑ | 139 Brad Radke | .25 | .11 |
| ❑ | 140 Todd Walker | .15 | .07 |
| ❑ | 141 Chad Allen RC | .40 | .18 |
| | Torii Hunter | | |
| ❑ | 142 Cristian Guzman | .40 | .18 |
| | Jacque Jones | | |
| ❑ | 143 Michael Barrett | .15 | .07 |
| ❑ | 144 Orlando Cabrera | .15 | .07 |
| ❑ | 145 Vladimir Guerrero | 1.00 | .45 |
| ❑ | 146 Wilton Guerrero | .15 | .07 |
| ❑ | 147 Ugueth Urbina | .15 | .07 |
| ❑ | 148 Rondell White | .25 | .11 |
| ❑ | 149 Chris Widger | .15 | .07 |
| ❑ | 150 Edgardo Alfonzo | .25 | .11 |
| ❑ | 151 Roger Cedeno | .15 | .07 |
| ❑ | 152 Octavio Dotel | .15 | .07 |
| ❑ | 153 Rickey Henderson | .75 | .35 |
| ❑ | 154 John Olerud | .25 | .11 |
| ❑ | 155 Rey Ordonez | .15 | .07 |
| ❑ | 156 Mike Piazza | 2.00 | .90 |
| ❑ | 157 Robin Ventura | .25 | .11 |
| ❑ | 158 Scott Brosius | .25 | .11 |
| ❑ | 159 Roger Clemens | 1.25 | .55 |
| ❑ | 160 David Cone | .25 | .11 |
| ❑ | 161 Chili Davis | .25 | .11 |
| ❑ | 162 Orlando Hernandez | .25 | .11 |
| ❑ | 163 Derek Jeter | 2.50 | 1.10 |
| ❑ | 164 Chuck Knoblauch | .25 | .11 |
| ❑ | 165 Tino Martinez | .25 | .11 |
| ❑ | 166 Paul O'Neill | .25 | .11 |
| ❑ | 167 Bernie Williams | .60 | .25 |
| ❑ | 168 Jason Giambi | .60 | .25 |
| ❑ | 169 Ben Grieve | .25 | .11 |
| ❑ | 170 Chad Harville RC | .40 | .18 |
| ❑ | 171 Tim Hudson RC | 4.00 | 1.80 |
| ❑ | 172 Tony Phillips | .15 | .07 |
| ❑ | 173 Kenny Rogers | .15 | .07 |
| ❑ | 174 Matt Stairs | .15 | .07 |
| ❑ | 175 Miguel Tejada | .25 | .11 |
| ❑ | 176 Eric Chavez | .60 | .25 |
| | Olmedo Saenz | | |
| ❑ | 177 Bobby Abreu | .25 | .11 |
| ❑ | 178 Ron Gant | .25 | .11 |
| ❑ | 179 Doug Glanville | .15 | .07 |
| ❑ | 180 Mike Lieberthal | .25 | .11 |
| ❑ | 181 Desi Relaford | .15 | .07 |
| ❑ | 182 Scott Rolen | .60 | .25 |
| ❑ | 183 Curt Schilling | .25 | .11 |
| ❑ | 184 Marlon Anderson | .25 | .11 |
| | Randy Wolf | | |
| ❑ | 185 Brant Brown | .15 | .07 |
| ❑ | 186 Brian Giles | .25 | .11 |
| ❑ | 187 Jason Kendall | .25 | .11 |
| ❑ | 188 Al Martin | .15 | .07 |
| ❑ | 189 Ed Sprague | .15 | .07 |
| ❑ | 190 Kevin Young | .25 | .11 |
| ❑ | 191 Kris Benson | .25 | .11 |
| | Warren Morris | | |
| ❑ | 192 Kent Bottenfield | .15 | .07 |
| ❑ | 193 Eric Davis | .25 | .11 |
| ❑ | 194 J.D. Drew | .60 | .25 |
| ❑ | 195 Ray Lankford | .25 | .11 |
| ❑ | 196 Joe McEwing RC | .40 | .18 |
| ❑ | 197 Mark McGwire | 2.50 | 1.10 |
| ❑ | 198 Edgar Renteria | .15 | .07 |
| ❑ | 199 Fernando Tatis | .25 | .11 |
| ❑ | 200 Andy Ashby | .15 | .07 |
| ❑ | 201 Ben Davis | .15 | .07 |
| ❑ | 202 Tony Gwynn | 1.25 | .55 |
| ❑ | 203 Trevor Hoffman | .25 | .11 |
| ❑ | 204 Wally Joyner | .25 | .11 |
| ❑ | 205 Gary Matthews Jr. | .15 | .07 |
| ❑ | 206 Ruben Rivera | .15 | .07 |
| ❑ | 207 Reggie Sanders | .15 | .07 |
| ❑ | 208 Rich Aurilia | .15 | .07 |
| ❑ | 209 Marvin Benard | .15 | .07 |
| ❑ | 210 Barry Bonds | 1.00 | .45 |
| ❑ | 211 Ellis Burks | .25 | .11 |
| ❑ | 212 Stan Javier | .15 | .07 |
| ❑ | 213 Jeff Kent | .40 | .18 |
| ❑ | 214 Robb Nen | .15 | .07 |
| ❑ | 215 J.T. Snow | .25 | .11 |
| ❑ | 216 Gil Meche | .25 | .11 |
| ❑ | 217 David Bell | .15 | .07 |
| ❑ | 218 Freddy Garcia RC | 1.50 | .70 |
| ❑ | 219 Ken Griffey Jr. | 2.50 | 1.10 |
| ❑ | 220 Brian L.Hunter | .15 | .07 |
| ❑ | 221 John Halama | .15 | .07 |
| ❑ | 222 Edgar Martinez | .40 | .18 |
| ❑ | 223 Jamie Moyer | .15 | .07 |
| ❑ | 224 Alex Rodriguez | 2.00 | .90 |
| ❑ | 225 Jay Buhner | .25 | .11 |
| ❑ | 226 Rolando Arrojo | .15 | .07 |
| ❑ | 227 Wade Boggs | .75 | .35 |
| ❑ | 228 Miguel Cairo | .15 | .07 |
| ❑ | 229 Jose Canseco | .75 | .35 |
| ❑ | 230 Dave Martinez | .15 | .07 |
| ❑ | 231 Fred McGriff | .40 | .18 |
| ❑ | 232 Kevin Stocker | .15 | .07 |
| ❑ | 233 Michael Duvall RC | .40 | .18 |
| | David Lamb | | |
| ❑ | 234 Royce Clayton | .15 | .07 |
| ❑ | 235 Juan Gonzalez | .60 | .25 |
| ❑ | 236 Rusty Greer | .25 | .11 |
| ❑ | 237 Ruben Mateo | .25 | .11 |
| ❑ | 238 Rafael Palmeiro | .60 | .25 |
| ❑ | 239 Ivan Rodriguez | .75 | .35 |
| ❑ | 240 John Wetteland | .25 | .11 |
| ❑ | 241 Todd Zeile | .25 | .11 |
| ❑ | 242 Jeff Zimmerman RC | .40 | .18 |
| ❑ | 243 Homer Bush | .15 | .07 |
| ❑ | 244 Jose Cruz Jr. | .25 | .11 |
| ❑ | 245 Carlos Delgado | .60 | .25 |
| ❑ | 246 Tony Fernandez | .15 | .07 |
| ❑ | 247 Shawn Green | .60 | .25 |
| ❑ | 248 Shannon Stewart | .25 | .11 |
| ❑ | 249 David Wells | .25 | .11 |
| ❑ | 250 Roy Halladay | .25 | .11 |
| | Billy Koch | | |
| ❑ | S1 Tony Gwynn Sample | 2.00 | .90 |
| ❑ | S1A T.Gwynn Samp. Stamp | 5.00 | 2.20 |

## 2000 Pacific Omega

| | MINT | NRMT |
|---|---|---|
| COMPLETE SET (255) | 1200.00 | 550.00 |
| COMP.SET w/o SP's (150) | 25.00 | 11.00 |
| COMMON CARD (1-150) | .15 | .07 |
| COMMON CARD (151-255) | 10.00 | 4.50 |

| | Card | Mint | NrMt |
|---|---|---|---|
| ❑ | 1 Garret Anderson | .25 | .11 |
| ❑ | 2 Darin Erstad | .60 | .25 |
| ❑ | 3 Troy Glaus | .75 | .35 |
| ❑ | 4 Tim Salmon | .25 | .11 |
| ❑ | 5 Mo Vaughn | .25 | .11 |
| ❑ | 6 Jay Bell | .25 | .11 |
| ❑ | 7 Steve Finley | .25 | .11 |
| ❑ | 8 Luis Gonzalez | .25 | .11 |
| ❑ | 9 Randy Johnson | .75 | .35 |
| ❑ | 10 Matt Williams | .25 | .11 |
| ❑ | 11 Andres Galarraga | .40 | .18 |
| ❑ | 12 Andruw Jones | .60 | .25 |
| ❑ | 13 Chipper Jones | 1.50 | .70 |
| ❑ | 14 Brian Jordan | .25 | .11 |
| ❑ | 15 Greg Maddux | 1.50 | .70 |
| ❑ | 16 B.J. Surhoff | .25 | .11 |
| ❑ | 17 Brady Anderson | .25 | .11 |
| ❑ | 18 Albert Belle | .40 | .18 |
| ❑ | 19 Mike Mussina | .60 | .25 |
| ❑ | 20 Cal Ripken | 2.50 | 1.10 |
| ❑ | 21 Carl Everett | .25 | .11 |
| ❑ | 22 Nomar Garciaparra | 2.00 | .90 |
| ❑ | 23 Pedro Martinez | .75 | .35 |
| ❑ | 24 Jason Varitek | .25 | .11 |
| ❑ | 25 Mark Grace | .60 | .25 |
| ❑ | 26 Sammy Sosa | 1.25 | .55 |
| ❑ | 27 Rondell White | .25 | .11 |
| ❑ | 28 Kerry Wood | .25 | .11 |
| ❑ | 29 Eric Young | .15 | .07 |
| ❑ | 30 Ray Durham | .25 | .11 |
| ❑ | 31 Carlos Lee | .25 | .11 |
| ❑ | 32 Magglio Ordonez | .25 | .11 |
| ❑ | 33 Frank Thomas | 1.25 | .55 |
| ❑ | 34 Sean Casey | .25 | .11 |
| ❑ | 35 Ken Griffey Jr. | 2.50 | 1.10 |
| ❑ | 36 Barry Larkin | .60 | .25 |
| ❑ | 37 Pokey Reese | .25 | .11 |
| ❑ | 38 Roberto Alomar | .60 | .25 |
| ❑ | 39 Kenny Lofton | .25 | .11 |
| ❑ | 40 Manny Ramirez | .75 | .35 |
| ❑ | 41 David Segui | .15 | .07 |
| ❑ | 42 Jim Thome | .40 | .18 |
| ❑ | 43 Omar Vizquel | .25 | .11 |
| ❑ | 44 Jeff Cirillo | .25 | .11 |
| ❑ | 45 Jeffrey Hammonds | .25 | .11 |
| ❑ | 46 Todd Helton | .75 | .35 |
| ❑ | 47 Todd Hollandsworth | .15 | .07 |
| ❑ | 48 Larry Walker | .25 | .11 |
| ❑ | 49 Tony Clark | .15 | .07 |
| ❑ | 50 Juan Encarnacion | .25 | .11 |
| ❑ | 51 Juan Gonzalez | .60 | .25 |
| ❑ | 52 Bobby Higginson | .25 | .11 |
| ❑ | 53 Hideo Nomo | .60 | .25 |
| ❑ | 54 Dean Palmer | .25 | .11 |
| ❑ | 55 Luis Castillo | .25 | .11 |
| ❑ | 56 Cliff Floyd | .25 | .11 |
| ❑ | 57 Derrek Lee | .25 | .11 |
| ❑ | 58 Mike Lowell | .25 | .11 |
| ❑ | 59 Henry Rodriguez | .15 | .07 |
| ❑ | 60 Preston Wilson | .25 | .11 |
| ❑ | 61 Moises Alou | .25 | .11 |
| ❑ | 62 Jeff Bagwell | .75 | .35 |
| ❑ | 63 Craig Biggio | .40 | .18 |
| ❑ | 64 Ken Caminiti | .25 | .11 |
| ❑ | 65 Richard Hidalgo | .25 | .11 |
| ❑ | 66 Carlos Beltran | .25 | .11 |
| ❑ | 67 Johnny Damon | .25 | .11 |
| ❑ | 68 Jermaine Dye | .25 | .11 |
| ❑ | 69 Joe Randa | .15 | .07 |
| ❑ | 70 Mike Sweeney | .25 | .11 |
| ❑ | 71 Adrian Beltre | .25 | .11 |
| ❑ | 72 Kevin Brown | .25 | .11 |
| ❑ | 73 Shawn Green | .60 | .25 |
| ❑ | 74 Eric Karros | .25 | .11 |
| ❑ | 75 Chan Ho Park | .25 | .11 |
| ❑ | 76 Gary Sheffield | .60 | .25 |
| ❑ | 77 Ron Belliard | .15 | .07 |
| ❑ | 78 Jeromy Burnitz | .25 | .11 |
| ❑ | 79 Geoff Jenkins | .25 | .11 |
| ❑ | 80 Richie Sexson | .25 | .11 |
| ❑ | 81 Ron Coomer | .15 | .07 |
| ❑ | 82 Jacque Jones | .25 | .11 |
| ❑ | 83 Corey Koskie | .15 | .07 |
| ❑ | 84 Matt Lawton | .25 | .11 |
| ❑ | 85 Vladimir Guerrero | 1.00 | .45 |
| ❑ | 86 Lee Stevens | .15 | .07 |

❑ 87 Jose Vidro .25 .11
❑ 88 Edgardo Alfonzo .25 .11
❑ 89 Derek Bell .15 .07
❑ 90 Mike Bordick .15 .07
❑ 91 Mike Piazza 2.00 .90
❑ 92 Robin Ventura .25 .11
❑ 93 Jose Canseco .75 .35
❑ 94 Roger Clemens 1.25 .55
❑ 95 Orlando Hernandez .25 .11
❑ 96 Derek Jeter 2.50 1.10
❑ 97 David Justice .40 .18
❑ 98 Tino Martinez .25 .11
❑ 99 Jorge Posada .25 .11
❑ 100 Bernie Williams .60 .25
❑ 101 Eric Chavez .25 .11
❑ 102 Jason Giambi .60 .25
❑ 103 Ben Grieve .25 .11
❑ 104 Miguel Tejada .25 .11
❑ 105 Bobby Abreu .25 .11
❑ 106 Doug Glanville .15 .07
❑ 107 Travis Lee .15 .07
❑ 108 Mike Lieberthal .25 .11
❑ 109 Scott Rolen .60 .25
❑ 110 Brian Giles .25 .11
❑ 111 Jason Kendall .25 .11
❑ 112 Warren Morris .15 .07
❑ 113 Kevin Young .15 .07
❑ 114 Will Clark .60 .25
❑ 115 J.D. Drew .60 .25
❑ 116 Jim Edmonds .60 .25
❑ 117 Mark McGwire 2.50 1.10
❑ 118 Edgar Renteria .15 .07
❑ 119 Fernando Tatis .25 .11
❑ 120 Fernando Vina .15 .07
❑ 121 Bret Boone .25 .11
❑ 122 Tony Gwynn 1.25 .55
❑ 123 Trevor Hoffman .25 .11
❑ 124 Phil Nevin .25 .11
❑ 125 Eric Owens .15 .07
❑ 126 Barry Bonds 1.00 .45
❑ 127 Ellis Burks .25 .11
❑ 128 Jeff Kent .40 .18
❑ 129 J.T. Snow .25 .11
❑ 130 Jay Buhner .25 .11
❑ 131 Mike Cameron .15 .07
❑ 132 Rickey Henderson .75 .35
❑ 133 Edgar Martinez .25 .11
❑ 134 John Olerud .25 .11
❑ 135 Alex Rodriguez 2.00 .90
❑ 136 Kazuhiro Sasaki RC 3.00 1.35
❑ 137 Fred McGriff .40 .18
❑ 138 Greg Vaughn .25 .11
❑ 139 Gerald Williams .15 .07
❑ 140 Rusty Greer .25 .11
❑ 141 Gabe Kapler .25 .11
❑ 142 Ricky Ledee .15 .07
❑ 143 Rafael Palmeiro .60 .25
❑ 144 Ivan Rodriguez .75 .35
❑ 145 Tony Batista .25 .11
❑ 146 Jose Cruz Jr. .25 .11
❑ 147 Carlos Delgado .60 .25
❑ 148 Brad Fullmer .25 .11
❑ 149 Shannon Stewart .25 .11
❑ 150 David Wells .25 .11
❑ 151 Juan Alvarez RC 10.00 4.50
Jeff DaVanon RC
❑ 152 Seth Etherton 10.00 4.50
Adam Kennedy
❑ 153 Ramon Ortiz 10.00 4.50
Lou Pote
❑ 154 Derrick Turnbow RC 10.00 4.50
Eric Weaver
❑ 155 Rod Barajas 10.00 4.50
Jason Conti
❑ 156 Byung-Hyun Kim 10.00 4.50
Rob Ryan
❑ 157 David Cortes RC 10.00 4.50
George Lombard
❑ 158 Ivanon Coffie 10.00 4.50
Melvin Mora
❑ 159 Ryan Kohlmeier RC 15.00 6.75
Luis Matos RC
❑ 160 Willie Morales RC 10.00 4.50
John Parrish RC
❑ 161 Chris Richard RC 15.00 6.75
Jay Spurgeon RC
❑ 162 Israel Alcantara 15.00 6.75
Tomokazu Ohka RC
❑ 163 Paxton Crawford RC 10.00 4.50
Sang-Hoon Lee RC
❑ 164 Mike Mahoney RC 10.00 4.50
Wilton Veras
❑ 165 Daniel Garibay RC 10.00 4.50
Ross Gload RC
❑ 166 Gary Matthews Jr./ 10.00 4.50
Phil Norton
❑ 167 Roosevelt Brown 10.00 4.50
Ruben Quevedo
❑ 168 Lorenzo Barcelo RC 10.00 4.50
Rocky Biddle RC
❑ 169 Mark Buehrle 10.00 4.50
John Garland
❑ 170 Aaron Myette 10.00 4.50
Josh Paul
❑ 171 Kip Wells 10.00 4.50
Kelly Wunsch
❑ 172 Rob Bell 10.00 4.50
Travis Dawkins
❑ 173 Hector Mercado RC 10.00 4.50
John Riedling RC
❑ 174 Russell Branyan 10.00 4.50
Sean DePaula RC
❑ 175 Tim Drew 10.00 4.50
Mark Watson RC
❑ 176 Craig House RC 10.00 4.50
Ben Petrick
❑ 177 Robert Fick 10.00 4.50
Jose Macias
❑ 178 Javier Cardona RC 10.00 4.50
Brandon Villafuerte RC
❑ 179 Armando Almanza 10.00 4.50
A.J. Burnett
❑ 180 Ramon Castro 10.00 4.50
Pablo Ozuna
❑ 181 Lance Berkman 10.00 4.50
Jason Green
❑ 182 Julio Lugo 10.00 4.50
Tony McKnight
❑ 183 Mitch Meluskey 10.00 4.50
Wade Miller
❑ 184 Chad Durbin RC 10.00 4.50
Hector Ortiz RC
❑ 185 Dermal Brown 10.00 4.50
Mark Quinn
❑ 186 Eric Gagne 10.00 4.50
Mike Judd
❑ 187 Kane Davis RC 10.00 4.50
Valerio De Los Santos
❑ 188 Santiago Perez RC 10.00 4.50
Paul Rigdon RC
❑ 189 Matt Kinney 10.00 4.50
Matt LeCroy
❑ 190 Jason Maxwell 10.00 4.50
A.J. Pierzynski
❑ 191 J.C. Romero RC 10.00 4.50
Johan Santana RC
❑ 192 Tony Armas Jr. 10.00 4.50
Peter Bergeron
❑ 193 Matt Blank 10.00 4.50
Milton Bradley
❑ 194 Tomas De La Rosa RC 10.00 4.50
Scott Forster RC
❑ 195 Yovanny Lara RC 10.00 4.50
Talmadge Nunnari RC
❑ 196 Brian Schneider 10.00 4.50
Andy Tracy RC
❑ 197 Scott Strickland 10.00 4.50
T.J. Tucker
❑ 198 Eric Cammack RC 10.00 4.50
Jim Mann RC
❑ 199 Grant Roberts 10.00 4.50
Jorge Toca
❑ 200 Alfonso Soriano 10.00 4.50
Jay Tessmer
❑ 201 Terrence Long 15.00 6.75
Mark Mulder
❑ 202 Pat Burrell 20.00 9.00
Cliff Politte
❑ 203 Jimmy Anderson 10.00 4.50
Bronson Arroyo
❑ 204 Mike Darr 10.00 4.50
Kory DeHaan
❑ 205 Adam Eaton 10.00 4.50
Wiki Gonzalez
❑ 206 Brandon Kolb RC 10.00 4.50
Kevin Walker RC
❑ 207 Damon Minor 10.00 4.50
Calvin Murray
❑ 208 Kevin Hodges RC 15.00 6.75
Joel Pineiro RC
❑ 209 Rob Ramsay 40.00 18.00
Kazuhiro Sasaki
❑ 210 Rick Ankiel 25.00 11.00
Mike Matthews
❑ 211 Steve Cox 10.00 4.50
Travis Harper
❑ 212 Kenny Kelly RC 15.00 6.75
Damian Rolls RC
❑ 213 Doug Davis 10.00 4.50
Scott Sheldon
❑ 214 Brian Sikorski 10.00 4.50
Pedro Valdes
❑ 215 Francisco Cordero 10.00 4.50
B.J. Waszgis RC
❑ 216 Matt DeWitt RC 10.00 4.50
Josh Phelps RC
❑ 217 Vernon Wells 10.00 4.50
Dewayne Wise
❑ 218 Geraldo Guzman RC 10.00 4.50
Jason Marquis
❑ 219 Rafael Furcal 30.00 13.50
Steve Sisco RC
❑ 220 B.J. Ryan 10.00 4.50
Kevin Beirne
❑ 221 Matt Ginter RC 10.00 4.50
Brad Penny
❑ 222 Julio Zuleta RC 15.00 6.75
Eric Munson
❑ 223 Dan Reichert 10.00 4.50
Jeff Williams RC
❑ 224 Jason LaRue 10.00 4.50
Danny Ardoin RC
❑ 225 Ray King 10.00 4.50
Mark Redman
❑ 226 Joe Crede 15.00 6.75
Mike Bell
❑ 227 Juan Pierre RC 20.00 9.00
Jay Payton
❑ 228 Wayne Franklin RC 10.00 4.50
Randy Choate RC
❑ 229 Chris Truby 15.00 6.75
Adam Piatt
❑ 230 Kevin Nicholson 10.00 4.50
Chris Woodward
❑ 231 Barry Zito RC 50.00 22.00
Jason Boyd RC
❑ 232 Brian O'Connor RC 10.00 4.50
Miguel Del Toro
❑ 233 Carlos Guillen 10.00 4.50
Aubrey Huff
❑ 234 Chad Hermansen 10.00 4.50
Jason Tyner
❑ 235 Aaron Fultz RC 15.00 6.75
Ryan Vogelsong RC
❑ 236 Shawn Wooten 10.00 4.50
Vance Wilson
❑ 237 Danny Klassen 15.00 6.75
Mike Lamb RC
❑ 238 Chad Bradford 10.00 4.50
Gene Stechshulte RC
❑ 239 Ismael Villegas RC 10.00 4.50
Hector Ramirez RC
Matt T.Williams RC
Luis Vizcaino
❑ 240 Mike Garcia RC 10.00 4.50
Domingo Guzman RC
Justin Brunette RC
Pasqual Coco RC
❑ 241 Frank Charles RC 10.00 4.50
Keith McDonald RC
❑ 242 Carlos Casimiro RC 10.00 4.50
Morgan Burkhart RC
❑ 243 Raul Gonzalez RC 10.00 4.50
Shawn Gilbert
❑ 244 Darrell Einertson RC 10.00 4.50
Jeff Sparks RC
❑ 245 Augie Ojeda RC 10.00 4.50
Brady Clark

| | | MINT | NRMT |
|---|---|---|---|
| | Todd Belitz<br>Eric Byrnes RC | | |
| ❑ 246 | Leo Estrella RC<br>Charlie Greene | 10.00 | 4.50 |
| ❑ 247 | Trace Coquillette RC<br>Pedro Feliz RC | 15.00 | 6.75 |
| ❑ 248 | Tike Redman RC<br>David Newhan | 10.00 | 4.50 |
| ❑ 249 | Rodrigo Lopez RC<br>John Bale RC | 10.00 | 4.50 |
| ❑ 250 | Corey Patterson<br>Jose Ortiz RC | 40.00 | 18.00 |
| ❑ 251 | Britt Reames RC<br>Oswaldo Mairena RC | 10.00 | 4.50 |
| ❑ 252 | Xavier Nady RC<br>Timo Perez RC | 60.00 | 27.00 |
| ❑ 253 | Tom Jacquez RC<br>Vicente Padilla RC | 10.00 | 4.50 |
| ❑ 254 | Elvis Pena RC<br>Adam Melhuse RC | 10.00 | 4.50 |
| ❑ 255 | Ben Weber RC<br>Alex Cabrera RC | 15.00 | 6.75 |

## 1998 Pacific Online

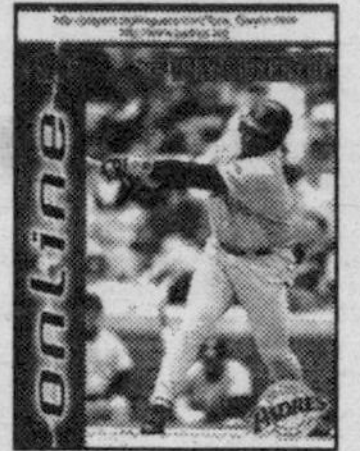


| | MINT | NRMT |
|---|---|---|
| COMPLETE SET (800) | 180.00 | 80.00 |
| COMMON CARD (1-780) | .20 | .09 |

| | | MINT | NRMT |
|---|---|---|---|
| ❑ 1 | Garret Anderson | .30 | .14 |
| ❑ 2 | Rich DeLucia | .20 | .09 |
| ❑ 3 | Jason Dickson | .20 | .09 |
| ❑ 4 | Gary DiSarcina | .20 | .09 |
| ❑ 5 | Jim Edmonds | .75 | .35 |
| ❑ 6 | Darin Erstad | .75 | .35 |
| ❑ 7 | Cecil Fielder | .30 | .14 |
| ❑ 8 | Chuck Finley | .30 | .14 |
| ❑ 9 | Carlos Garcia | .20 | .09 |
| ❑ 10 | Shigetoshi Hasegawa | .30 | .14 |
| ❑ 11 | Ken Hill | .20 | .09 |
| ❑ 12 | Dave Hollins | .20 | .09 |
| ❑ 13 | Mike Holtz | .20 | .09 |
| ❑ 14 | Mike James | .20 | .09 |
| ❑ 15 | Norberto Martin | .20 | .09 |
| ❑ 16 | Damon Mashore | .20 | .09 |
| ❑ 17 | Jack McDowell | .20 | .09 |
| ❑ 18 | Phil Nevin | .30 | .14 |
| ❑ 19 | Omar Olivares | .20 | .09 |
| ❑ 20 | Troy Percival | .20 | .09 |
| ❑ 21 | Rich Robertson | .20 | .09 |
| ❑ 22 | Tim Salmon | .30 | .14 |
| ❑ 23 | Craig Shipley | .20 | .09 |
| ❑ 24 | Matt Walbeck | .20 | .09 |
| ❑ 25 | Allen Watson | .20 | .09 |
| ❑ 26 | Jim Edmonds TC | .75 | .35 |
| ❑ 27 | Brian Anderson | .20 | .09 |
| ❑ 28 | Tony Batista | .30 | .14 |
| ❑ 29 | Jay Bell | .30 | .14 |
| ❑ 30 | Andy Benes | .20 | .09 |
| ❑ 31 | Yamil Benitez | .20 | .09 |
| ❑ 32 | Willie Blair | .20 | .09 |
| ❑ 33 | Brent Brede | .20 | .09 |
| ❑ 34 | Scott Brow | .20 | .09 |
| ❑ 35 | Omar Daal | .20 | .09 |
| ❑ 36 | Dave Dellucci RC | .20 | .09 |
| ❑ 37 | Edwin Diaz | .20 | .09 |
| ❑ 38 | Jorge Fabregas | .20 | .09 |
| ❑ 39 | Andy Fox | .20 | .09 |
| ❑ 40 | Karim Garcia | .20 | .09 |
| ❑ 41 | T.Lee Fielding | .30 | .14 |
| ❑ 41A | T.Lee Hitting | .30 | .14 |
| ❑ 42 | Barry Manuel | .20 | .09 |
| ❑ 43 | Gregg Olson | .20 | .09 |
| ❑ 44 | Felix Rodriguez | .20 | .09 |
| ❑ 45 | Clint Sodowsky | .20 | .09 |
| ❑ 46 | Russ Springer | .20 | .09 |
| ❑ 47 | Andy Stankiewicz | .20 | .09 |
| ❑ 48 | Kelly Stinnett | .20 | .09 |
| ❑ 49 | Jeff Suppan | .20 | .09 |
| ❑ 50 | Devon White | .20 | .09 |
| ❑ 51 | Matt Williams | .50 | .23 |
| ❑ 52 | Travis Lee TC | .30 | .14 |
| ❑ 53 | Danny Bautista | .20 | .09 |
| ❑ 54 | Rafael Belliard | .20 | .09 |
| ❑ 55 | Adam Butler RC | .30 | .14 |
| ❑ 56 | Mike Cather RC | .20 | .09 |
| ❑ 57 | Brian Edmondson | .20 | .09 |
| ❑ 58 | Alan Embree | .20 | .09 |
| ❑ 59 | Andres Galarraga | .50 | .23 |
| ❑ 60 | Tom Glavine | .75 | .35 |
| ❑ 61 | Tony Graffanino | .20 | .09 |
| ❑ 62 | Andruw Jones | .75 | .35 |
| ❑ 63 | C.Jones Fielding | 2.00 | .90 |
| ❑ 63A | C.Jones Hitting | 2.00 | .90 |
| ❑ 64 | Ryan Klesko | .30 | .14 |
| ❑ 65 | Keith Lockhart | .20 | .09 |
| ❑ 66 | Javy Lopez | .30 | .14 |
| ❑ 67 | G.Maddux Hitting | 2.00 | .90 |
| ❑ 67A | G.Maddux Pitching | 2.00 | .90 |
| ❑ 68 | Dennis Martinez | .30 | .14 |
| ❑ 69 | Kevin Millwood RC | 1.25 | .55 |
| ❑ 70 | Denny Neagle | .20 | .09 |
| ❑ 71 | Eddie Perez | .20 | .09 |
| ❑ 72 | Curtis Pride | .20 | .09 |
| ❑ 73 | John Smoltz | .30 | .14 |
| ❑ 74 | Michael Tucker | .20 | .09 |
| ❑ 75 | Walt Weiss | .30 | .14 |
| ❑ 76 | Gerald Williams | .20 | .09 |
| ❑ 77 | Mark Wohlers | .20 | .09 |
| ❑ 78 | Chipper Jones TC | 1.00 | .45 |
| ❑ 79 | Roberto Alomar | .75 | .35 |
| ❑ 80 | Brady Anderson | .30 | .14 |
| ❑ 81 | Harold Baines | .30 | .14 |
| ❑ 82 | Armando Benitez | .20 | .09 |
| ❑ 83 | Mike Bordick | .20 | .09 |
| ❑ 84 | Joe Carter | .30 | .14 |
| ❑ 85 | Norm Charlton | .20 | .09 |
| ❑ 86 | Eric Davis | .30 | .14 |
| ❑ 87 | Doug Drabek | .20 | .09 |
| ❑ 88 | Scott Erickson | .20 | .09 |
| ❑ 89 | Jeffrey Hammonds | .30 | .14 |
| ❑ 90 | Chris Hoiles | .20 | .09 |
| ❑ 91 | Scott Kamieniecki | .20 | .09 |
| ❑ 92 | Jimmy Key | .30 | .14 |
| ❑ 93 | Terry Mathews | .20 | .09 |
| ❑ 94 | Alan Mills | .20 | .09 |
| ❑ 95 | Mike Mussina | .75 | .35 |
| ❑ 96 | Jesse Orosco | .20 | .09 |
| ❑ 97 | Rafael Palmeiro | .75 | .35 |
| ❑ 98 | Sidney Ponson | .20 | .09 |
| ❑ 99 | Jeff Reboulet | .20 | .09 |
| ❑ 100 | Arthur Rhodes | .20 | .09 |
| ❑ 101 | C.Ripken Hitting | 3.00 | 1.35 |
| ❑ 101A | C.Ripken<br>Hitting Close-Up | 3.00 | 1.35 |
| ❑ 102 | Nerio Rodriguez | .20 | .09 |
| ❑ 103 | B.J. Surhoff | .30 | .14 |
| ❑ 104 | Lenny Webster | .20 | .09 |
| ❑ 105 | Cal Ripken TC | 1.50 | .70 |
| ❑ 106 | Steve Avery | .20 | .09 |
| ❑ 107 | Mike Benjamin | .20 | .09 |
| ❑ 108 | Darren Bragg | .20 | .09 |
| ❑ 109 | Damon Buford | .20 | .09 |
| ❑ 110 | Jim Corsi | .20 | .09 |
| ❑ 111 | Dennis Eckersley | .30 | .14 |
| ❑ 112 | Rich Garces | .20 | .09 |
| ❑ 113 | N.Garciaparra Fielding | 2.50 | 1.10 |
| ❑ 113A | N.Garciaparra Hitting | 2.50 | 1.10 |
| ❑ 114 | Tom Gordon | .30 | .14 |
| ❑ 115 | Scott Hatteberg | .20 | .09 |
| ❑ 116 | Butch Henry | .20 | .09 |
| ❑ 117 | Reggie Jefferson | .20 | .09 |
| ❑ 118 | Mark Lemke | .20 | .09 |
| ❑ 119 | Darren Lewis | .20 | .09 |
| ❑ 120 | Jim Leyritz | .20 | .09 |
| ❑ 121 | Derek Lowe | .20 | .09 |
| ❑ 122 | Pedro Martinez | 1.00 | .45 |
| ❑ 123 | Troy O'Leary | .20 | .09 |
| ❑ 124 | Brian Rose | .20 | .09 |
| ❑ 125 | Bret Saberhagen | .30 | .14 |
| ❑ 126 | Donnie Sadler | .20 | .09 |
| ❑ 127 | Brian Shouse RC | .30 | .14 |
| ❑ 128 | John Valentin | .20 | .09 |
| ❑ 129 | Jason Varitek | .30 | .14 |
| ❑ 130 | Mo Vaughn | .30 | .14 |
| ❑ 131 | Tim Wakefield | .20 | .09 |
| ❑ 132 | John Wasdin | .20 | .09 |
| ❑ 133 | Nomar Garciaparra TC | 1.25 | .55 |
| ❑ 134 | Terry Adams | .20 | .09 |
| ❑ 135 | Manny Alexander | .20 | .09 |
| ❑ 136 | Rod Beck | .20 | .09 |
| ❑ 137 | Jeff Blauser | .20 | .09 |
| ❑ 138 | Brant Brown | .20 | .09 |
| ❑ 139 | Mark Clark | .20 | .09 |
| ❑ 140 | Jeremi Gonzalez | .20 | .09 |
| ❑ 141 | Mark Grace | .75 | .35 |
| ❑ 142 | Jose Hernandez | .20 | .09 |
| ❑ 143 | Tyler Houston | .20 | .09 |
| ❑ 144 | Lance Johnson | .20 | .09 |
| ❑ 145 | Sandy Martinez | .20 | .09 |
| ❑ 146 | Matt Mieske | .20 | .09 |
| ❑ 147 | Mickey Morandini | .20 | .09 |
| ❑ 148 | Terry Mulholland | .20 | .09 |
| ❑ 149 | Kevin Orie | .20 | .09 |
| ❑ 150 | Bob Patterson | .20 | .09 |
| ❑ 151 | Marc Pisciotta RC | .20 | .09 |
| ❑ 152 | Henry Rodriguez | .20 | .09 |
| ❑ 153 | Scott Servais | .20 | .09 |
| ❑ 154 | Sammy Sosa | 1.50 | .70 |
| ❑ 155 | Kevin Tapani | .20 | .09 |
| ❑ 156 | Steve Trachsel | .20 | .09 |
| ❑ 157 | K.Wood Pitching | .75 | .35 |
| ❑ 157A | K.Wood<br>Pitching Close-Up | .75 | .35 |
| ❑ 158 | Kerry Wood TC | .75 | .35 |
| ❑ 159 | Jeff Abbott | .20 | .09 |
| ❑ 160 | James Baldwin | .20 | .09 |
| ❑ 161 | Albert Belle | .50 | .23 |
| ❑ 162 | Jason Bere | .20 | .09 |
| ❑ 163 | Mike Cameron | .30 | .14 |
| ❑ 164 | Mike Caruso | .20 | .09 |
| ❑ 165 | Carlos Castillo | .20 | .09 |
| ❑ 166 | Tony Castillo | .20 | .09 |
| ❑ 167 | Ray Durham | .30 | .14 |
| ❑ 168 | Scott Eyre | .20 | .09 |
| ❑ 169 | Tom Fordham | .20 | .09 |
| ❑ 170 | Keith Foulke | .20 | .09 |
| ❑ 171 | Lou Frazier | .20 | .09 |
| ❑ 172 | Matt Karchner | .20 | .09 |
| ❑ 173 | Chad Kreuter | .20 | .09 |
| ❑ 174 | Jaime Navarro | .20 | .09 |
| ❑ 175 | Greg Norton | .20 | .09 |
| ❑ 176 | Charlie O'Brien | .20 | .09 |
| ❑ 177 | Maggio Ordonez RC | 3.00 | 1.35 |
| ❑ 178 | Ruben Sierra | .20 | .09 |
| ❑ 179 | Bill Simas | .20 | .09 |
| ❑ 180 | Mike Sirotka | .20 | .09 |
| ❑ 181 | Chris Snopek | .20 | .09 |
| ❑ 182 | F.Thomas Batter's Box | 1.50 | .70 |
| ❑ 182A | F.Thomas Swing | 1.50 | .70 |
| ❑ 183 | Robin Ventura | .30 | .14 |
| ❑ 184 | Frank Thomas TC | .75 | .35 |
| ❑ 185 | Stan Belinda | .20 | .09 |
| ❑ 186 | Aaron Boone | .20 | .09 |
| ❑ 187 | Bret Boone | .30 | .14 |
| ❑ 188 | Brook Fordyce | .20 | .09 |
| ❑ 189 | Willie Greene | .20 | .09 |
| ❑ 190 | Pete Harnisch | .20 | .09 |
| ❑ 191 | Lenny Harris | .20 | .09 |
| ❑ 192 | Mark Hutton | .20 | .09 |
| ❑ 193 | Damian Jackson | .20 | .09 |
| ❑ 194 | Ricardo Jordan | .20 | .09 |
| ❑ 195 | Barry Larkin | .75 | .35 |
| ❑ 196 | Eduardo Perez | .20 | .09 |
| ❑ 197 | Pokey Reese | .30 | .14 |
| ❑ 198 | Mike Remlinger | .20 | .09 |
| ❑ 199 | Reggie Sanders | .20 | .09 |
| ❑ 200 | Jeff Shaw | .20 | .09 |
| ❑ 201 | Chris Stynes | .20 | .09 |
| ❑ 202 | Scott Sullivan | .20 | .09 |

| | # | Player | | |
|---|---|---|---|---|
| ☐ | 203 | Eddie Taubensee | .20 | .09 |
| ☐ | 204 | Brett Tomko | .20 | .09 |
| ☐ | 205 | Pat Watkins | .20 | .09 |
| ☐ | 206 | David Weathers | .20 | .09 |
| ☐ | 207 | Gabe White | .20 | .09 |
| ☐ | 208 | Scott Winchester | .20 | .09 |
| ☐ | 209 | Barry Larkin TC | .30 | .14 |
| ☐ | 210 | Sandy Alomar Jr. | .30 | .14 |
| ☐ | 211 | Paul Assenmacher | .20 | .09 |
| ☐ | 212 | Geronimo Berroa | .20 | .09 |
| ☐ | 213 | Pat Borders | .20 | .09 |
| ☐ | 214 | Jeff Branson | .20 | .09 |
| ☐ | 215 | Dave Burba | .20 | .09 |
| ☐ | 216 | Bartolo Colon | .30 | .14 |
| ☐ | 217 | Shawon Dunston | .20 | .09 |
| ☐ | 218 | Travis Fryman | .30 | .14 |
| ☐ | 219 | Brian Giles | .30 | .14 |
| ☐ | 220 | Dwight Gooden | .20 | .09 |
| ☐ | 221 | Mike Jackson | .20 | .09 |
| ☐ | 222 | David Justice | .50 | .23 |
| ☐ | 223 | Kenny Lofton | .30 | .14 |
| ☐ | 224 | Jose Mesa | .20 | .09 |
| ☐ | 225 | Alvin Morman | .20 | .09 |
| ☐ | 226 | Charles Nagy | .20 | .09 |
| ☐ | 227 | Chad Ogea | .20 | .09 |
| ☐ | 228 | Eric Plunk | .20 | .09 |
| ☐ | 229 | Manny Ramirez | 1.00 | .45 |
| ☐ | 230 | Paul Shuey | .20 | .09 |
| ☐ | 231 | Jim Thome | .50 | .23 |
| ☐ | 232 | Ron Villone | .20 | .09 |
| ☐ | 233 | Omar Vizquel | .30 | .14 |
| ☐ | 234 | Enrique Wilson | .20 | .09 |
| ☐ | 235 | Jaret Wright | .20 | .09 |
| ☐ | 236 | Manny Ramirez TC | .50 | .23 |
| ☐ | 237 | Pedro Astacio | .20 | .09 |
| ☐ | 238 | Jason Bates | .20 | .09 |
| ☐ | 239 | Dante Bichette | .30 | .14 |
| ☐ | 240 | Ellis Burks | .30 | .14 |
| ☐ | 241 | Vinny Castilla | .30 | .14 |
| ☐ | 242 | Greg Colbrunn | .20 | .09 |
| ☐ | 243 | Mike DeJean RC | .20 | .09 |
| ☐ | 244 | Jerry Dipoto | .20 | .09 |
| ☐ | 245 | Curtis Goodwin | .20 | .09 |
| ☐ | 246 | Todd Helton | 1.00 | .45 |
| ☐ | 247 | Bobby Jones RC | .20 | .09 |
| ☐ | 248 | Darryl Kile | .30 | .14 |
| ☐ | 249 | Mike Lansing | .20 | .09 |
| ☐ | 250 | Curtis Leskanic | .20 | .09 |
| ☐ | 251 | Nelson Liriano | .20 | .09 |
| ☐ | 252 | Kirt Manwaring | .20 | .09 |
| ☐ | 253 | Chuck McElroy | .20 | .09 |
| ☐ | 254 | Mike Munoz | .20 | .09 |
| ☐ | 255 | Neifi Perez | .20 | .09 |
| ☐ | 256 | Jeff Reed | .20 | .09 |
| ☐ | 257 | Mark Thompson | .20 | .09 |
| ☐ | 258 | John Vander Wal | .20 | .09 |
| ☐ | 259 | Dave Veres | .20 | .09 |
| ☐ | 260 | L.Walker Hitting | .30 | .14 |
| ☐ | 260A | L.Walker Hitting Close Up | .30 | .14 |
| ☐ | 261 | Jamey Wright | .20 | .09 |
| ☐ | 262 | Larry Walker TC | .30 | .14 |
| ☐ | 263 | Kimera Bartee | .20 | .09 |
| ☐ | 264 | Doug Brocail | .20 | .09 |
| ☐ | 265 | Raul Casanova | .20 | .09 |
| ☐ | 266 | Frank Castillo | .20 | .09 |
| ☐ | 267 | Frank Catalanotto RC | .50 | .23 |
| ☐ | 268 | Tony Clark | .20 | .09 |
| ☐ | 269 | Deivi Cruz | .20 | .09 |
| ☐ | 270 | Roberto Duran RC | .30 | .14 |
| ☐ | 271 | Damion Easley | .20 | .09 |
| ☐ | 272 | Bryce Florie | .20 | .09 |
| ☐ | 273 | Luis Gonzalez | .30 | .14 |
| ☐ | 274 | Bobby Higginson | .30 | .14 |
| ☐ | 275 | Brian Hunter | .20 | .09 |
| ☐ | 276 | Todd Jones | .20 | .09 |
| ☐ | 277 | Greg Keagle | .20 | .09 |
| ☐ | 278 | Jeff Manto | .20 | .09 |
| ☐ | 279 | Brian Moehler | .20 | .09 |
| ☐ | 280 | Joe Oliver | .20 | .09 |
| ☐ | 281 | Joe Randa | .20 | .09 |
| ☐ | 282 | Bill Ripken | .20 | .09 |
| ☐ | 283 | Bip Roberts | .20 | .09 |
| ☐ | 284 | Sean Runyan | .20 | .09 |
| ☐ | 285 | A.J. Sager | .20 | .09 |
| ☐ | 286 | Justin Thompson | .20 | .09 |
| ☐ | 287 | Tony Clark TC | .20 | .09 |
| ☐ | 288 | Antonio Alfonseca | .20 | .09 |
| ☐ | 289 | Dave Berg RC | .20 | .09 |
| ☐ | 290 | Josh Booty | .20 | .09 |
| ☐ | 291 | John Cangelosi | .20 | .09 |
| ☐ | 292 | Craig Counsell | .20 | .09 |
| ☐ | 293 | Vic Darensbourg | .20 | .09 |
| ☐ | 294 | Cliff Floyd | .30 | .14 |
| ☐ | 295 | Oscar Henriquez | .20 | .09 |
| ☐ | 296 | Felix Heredia | .20 | .09 |
| ☐ | 297 | Ryan Jackson RC | .20 | .09 |
| ☐ | 298 | Mark Kotsay | .30 | .14 |
| ☐ | 299 | Andy Larkin | .20 | .09 |
| ☐ | 300 | Derrek Lee | .20 | .09 |
| ☐ | 301 | Brian Meadows | .20 | .09 |
| ☐ | 302 | Rafael Medina | .20 | .09 |
| ☐ | 303 | Jay Powell | .20 | .09 |
| ☐ | 304 | Edgar Renteria | .20 | .09 |
| ☐ | 305 | Jesus Sanchez RC | .50 | .23 |
| ☐ | 306 | Rob Stanifer RC | .20 | .09 |
| ☐ | 307 | Gregg Zaun | .20 | .09 |
| ☐ | 308 | Derrek Lee TC | .20 | .09 |
| ☐ | 309 | Moises Alou | .30 | .14 |
| ☐ | 310 | Brad Ausmus | .20 | .09 |
| ☐ | 311 | J.Bagwell Fielding | 1.00 | .45 |
| ☐ | 311A | J.Bagwell Hitting | 1.00 | .45 |
| ☐ | 312 | Derek Bell | .20 | .09 |
| ☐ | 313 | Sean Bergman | .20 | .09 |
| ☐ | 314 | Sean Berry | .20 | .09 |
| ☐ | 315 | Craig Biggio | .50 | .23 |
| ☐ | 316 | Tim Bogar | .20 | .09 |
| ☐ | 317 | Jose Cabrera RC | .20 | .09 |
| ☐ | 318 | Dave Clark | .20 | .09 |
| ☐ | 319 | Tony Eusebio | .20 | .09 |
| ☐ | 320 | Carl Everett | .30 | .14 |
| ☐ | 321 | Ricky Gutierrez | .20 | .09 |
| ☐ | 322 | John Halama RC | .60 | .25 |
| ☐ | 323 | Mike Hampton | .30 | .14 |
| ☐ | 324 | Doug Henry | .20 | .09 |
| ☐ | 325 | Richard Hidalgo | .30 | .14 |
| ☐ | 326 | Jack Howell | .20 | .09 |
| ☐ | 327 | Jose Lima | .20 | .09 |
| ☐ | 328 | Mike Magnante | .20 | .09 |
| ☐ | 329 | Trever Miller | .20 | .09 |
| ☐ | 330 | C.J. Nitkowski | .20 | .09 |
| ☐ | 331 | Shane Reynolds | .20 | .09 |
| ☐ | 332 | Bill Spiers | .20 | .09 |
| ☐ | 333 | Billy Wagner | .20 | .09 |
| ☐ | 334 | Jeff Bagwell TC | .50 | .23 |
| ☐ | 335 | Tim Belcher | .20 | .09 |
| ☐ | 336 | Brian Bevil | .20 | .09 |
| ☐ | 337 | Johnny Damon | .30 | .14 |
| ☐ | 338 | Jermaine Dye | .30 | .14 |
| ☐ | 339 | Sal Fasano | .20 | .09 |
| ☐ | 340 | Shane Halter | .20 | .09 |
| ☐ | 341 | Chris Haney | .20 | .09 |
| ☐ | 342 | Jed Hansen | .20 | .09 |
| ☐ | 343 | Jeff King | .20 | .09 |
| ☐ | 344 | Jeff Montgomery | .20 | .09 |
| ☐ | 345 | Hal Morris | .20 | .09 |
| ☐ | 346 | Jose Offerman | .20 | .09 |
| ☐ | 347 | Dean Palmer | .30 | .14 |
| ☐ | 348 | Terry Pendleton | .30 | .14 |
| ☐ | 349 | Hipolito Pichardo | .20 | .09 |
| ☐ | 350 | Jim Pittsley | .20 | .09 |
| ☐ | 351 | Pat Rapp | .20 | .09 |
| ☐ | 352 | Jose Rosado | .20 | .09 |
| ☐ | 353 | Glendon Rusch | .20 | .09 |
| ☐ | 354 | Scott Service | .20 | .09 |
| ☐ | 355 | Larry Sutton | .20 | .09 |
| ☐ | 356 | Mike Sweeney | .30 | .14 |
| ☐ | 357 | Joe Vitiello | .20 | .09 |
| ☐ | 358 | Matt Whisenant | .20 | .09 |
| ☐ | 359 | Ernie Young | .20 | .09 |
| ☐ | 360 | Jeff King TC | .20 | .09 |
| ☐ | 361 | Bobby Bonilla | .30 | .14 |
| ☐ | 362 | Jim Bruske | .20 | .09 |
| ☐ | 363 | Juan Castro | .20 | .09 |
| ☐ | 364 | Roger Cedeno | .20 | .09 |
| ☐ | 365 | Mike Devereaux | .20 | .09 |
| ☐ | 366 | Darren Dreifort | .20 | .09 |
| ☐ | 367 | Jim Eisenreich | .20 | .09 |
| ☐ | 368 | Wilton Guerrero | .20 | .09 |
| ☐ | 369 | Mark Guthrie | .20 | .09 |
| ☐ | 370 | Darren Hall | .20 | .09 |
| ☐ | 371 | Todd Hollandsworth | .20 | .09 |
| ☐ | 372 | Thomas Howard | .20 | .09 |
| ☐ | 373 | Trenidad Hubbard | .20 | .09 |
| ☐ | 374 | Charles Johnson | .30 | .14 |
| ☐ | 375 | Eric Karros | .30 | .14 |
| ☐ | 376 | Paul Konerko | .30 | .14 |
| ☐ | 377 | Matt Luke | .20 | .09 |
| ☐ | 378 | Ramon Martinez | .20 | .09 |
| ☐ | 379 | Raul Mondesi | .30 | .14 |
| ☐ | 380 | Hideo Nomo | .75 | .35 |
| ☐ | 381 | Antonio Osuna | .20 | .09 |
| ☐ | 382 | Chan Ho Park | .30 | .14 |
| ☐ | 383 | Tom Prince | .20 | .09 |
| ☐ | 384 | Scott Radinsky | .20 | .09 |
| ☐ | 385 | Gary Sheffield | .75 | .35 |
| ☐ | 386 | Ismael Valdes | .20 | .09 |
| ☐ | 387 | Jose Vizcaino | .20 | .09 |
| ☐ | 388 | Eric Young | .20 | .09 |
| ☐ | 389 | Gary Sheffield TC | .30 | .14 |
| ☐ | 390 | Jeromy Burnitz | .30 | .14 |
| ☐ | 391 | Jeff Cirillo | .30 | .14 |
| ☐ | 392 | Cal Eldred | .20 | .09 |
| ☐ | 393 | Chad Fox RC | .20 | .09 |
| ☐ | 394 | Marquis Grissom | .20 | .09 |
| ☐ | 395 | Bob Hamelin | .20 | .09 |
| ☐ | 396 | Bobby Hughes | .20 | .09 |
| ☐ | 397 | Darrin Jackson | .20 | .09 |
| ☐ | 398 | John Jaha | .30 | .14 |
| ☐ | 399 | Geoff Jenkins | .30 | .14 |
| ☐ | 400 | Doug Jones | .20 | .09 |
| ☐ | 401 | Jeff Juden | .20 | .09 |
| ☐ | 402 | Scott Karl | .20 | .09 |
| ☐ | 403 | Jesse Levis | .20 | .09 |
| ☐ | 404 | Mark Loretta | .20 | .09 |
| ☐ | 405 | Mike Matheny | .20 | .09 |
| ☐ | 406 | Jose Mercedes | .20 | .09 |
| ☐ | 407 | Mike Myers | .20 | .09 |
| ☐ | 408 | Marc Newfield | .20 | .09 |
| ☐ | 409 | Dave Nilsson | .20 | .09 |
| ☐ | 410 | Al Reyes | .20 | .09 |
| ☐ | 411 | Jose Valentin | .20 | .09 |
| ☐ | 412 | Fernando Vina | .20 | .09 |
| ☐ | 413 | Paul Wagner | .20 | .09 |
| ☐ | 414 | Bob Wickman | .20 | .09 |
| ☐ | 415 | Steve Woodard | .20 | .09 |
| ☐ | 416 | Marquis Grissom TC | .20 | .09 |
| ☐ | 417 | Rick Aguilera | .20 | .09 |
| ☐ | 418 | Ron Coomer | .20 | .09 |
| ☐ | 419 | Marty Cordova | .20 | .09 |
| ☐ | 420 | Brent Gates | .20 | .09 |
| ☐ | 421 | Eddie Guardado | .20 | .09 |
| ☐ | 422 | Denny Hocking | .20 | .09 |
| ☐ | 423 | Matt Lawton | .20 | .09 |
| ☐ | 424 | Pat Meares | .20 | .09 |
| ☐ | 425 | Orlando Merced | .20 | .09 |
| ☐ | 426 | Eric Milton | .20 | .09 |
| ☐ | 427 | Paul Molitor | .75 | .35 |
| ☐ | 428 | Mike Morgan | .20 | .09 |
| ☐ | 429 | Dan Naulty | .20 | .09 |
| ☐ | 430 | Otis Nixon | .20 | .09 |
| ☐ | 431 | Alex Ochoa | .20 | .09 |
| ☐ | 432 | David Ortiz | .20 | .09 |
| ☐ | 433 | Brad Radke | .30 | .14 |
| ☐ | 434 | Todd Ritchie | .20 | .09 |
| ☐ | 435 | Frank Rodriguez | .20 | .09 |
| ☐ | 436 | Terry Steinbach | .20 | .09 |
| ☐ | 437 | Greg Swindell | .20 | .09 |
| ☐ | 438 | Bob Tewksbury | .20 | .09 |
| ☐ | 439 | Mike Trombley | .20 | .09 |
| ☐ | 440 | Javier Valentin | .20 | .09 |
| ☐ | 441 | Todd Walker | .20 | .09 |
| ☐ | 442 | Paul Molitor TC | .30 | .14 |
| ☐ | 443 | Shane Andrews | .20 | .09 |
| ☐ | 444 | Miguel Batista | .20 | .09 |
| ☐ | 445 | Shayne Bennett | .20 | .09 |
| ☐ | 446 | Rick DeHart RC | .20 | .09 |
| ☐ | 447 | Brad Fullmer | .30 | .14 |
| ☐ | 448 | Mark Grudzielanek | .20 | .09 |
| ☐ | 449 | Vladimir Guerrero | 1.25 | .55 |
| ☐ | 450 | Dustin Hermanson | .20 | .09 |
| ☐ | 451 | Steve Kline | .20 | .09 |
| ☐ | 452 | Scott Livingstone | .20 | .09 |
| ☐ | 453 | Mike Maddux | .20 | .09 |
| ☐ | 454 | Derrick May | .20 | .09 |
| ☐ | 455 | Ryan McGuire | .20 | .09 |
| ☐ | 456 | Trey Moore | .20 | .09 |
| ☐ | 457 | Mike Mordecai | .20 | .09 |
| ☐ | 458 | Carl Pavano | .20 | .09 |

| |  |  | | |
|---|---|---|---|---|
| ❑ | 459 | Carlos Perez | .20 | .09 |
| ❑ | 460 | F.P. Santangelo | .20 | .09 |
| ❑ | 461 | DaRond Stovall | .20 | .09 |
| ❑ | 462 | Anthony Telford | .20 | .09 |
| ❑ | 463 | Ugueth Urbina | .20 | .09 |
| ❑ | 464 | Marc Valdes | .20 | .09 |
| ❑ | 465 | Jose Vidro | .20 | .09 |
| ❑ | 466 | Rondell White | .30 | .14 |
| ❑ | 467 | Chris Widger | .20 | .09 |
| ❑ | 468 | Vladimir Guerrero TC | .50 | .23 |
| ❑ | 469 | Edgardo Alfonzo | .30 | .14 |
| ❑ | 470 | Carlos Baerga | .20 | .09 |
| ❑ | 471 | Rich Becker | .20 | .09 |
| ❑ | 472 | Brian Bohanon | .20 | .09 |
| ❑ | 473 | Alberto Castillo | .20 | .09 |
| ❑ | 474 | Dennis Cook | .20 | .09 |
| ❑ | 475 | John Franco | .30 | .14 |
| ❑ | 476 | Matt Franco | .20 | .09 |
| ❑ | 477 | Bernard Gilkey | .20 | .09 |
| ❑ | 478 | John Hudek | .20 | .09 |
| ❑ | 479 | Butch Huskey | .20 | .09 |
| ❑ | 480 | Bobby Jones | .20 | .09 |
| ❑ | 481 | Al Leiter | .30 | .14 |
| ❑ | 482 | Luis Lopez | .20 | .09 |
| ❑ | 483 | Brian McRae | .20 | .09 |
| ❑ | 484 | Dave Mlicki | .20 | .09 |
| ❑ | 485 | John Olerud | .30 | .14 |
| ❑ | 486 | Rey Ordonez | .20 | .09 |
| ❑ | 487 | Craig Paquette | .20 | .09 |
| ❑ | 488 | M.Piazza Hitting | 2.50 | 1.10 |
| ❑ | 488A | M.Piazza Close-Up | 2.50 | 1.10 |
| ❑ | 489 | Todd Pratt | .20 | .09 |
| ❑ | 490 | Mel Rojas | .20 | .09 |
| ❑ | 491 | Tim Spehr | .20 | .09 |
| ❑ | 492 | Turk Wendell | .20 | .09 |
| ❑ | 493 | Masato Yoshii RC | .60 | .25 |
| ❑ | 494 | Mike Piazza TC | 1.25 | .55 |
| ❑ | 495 | Willie Banks | .20 | .09 |
| ❑ | 496 | Scott Brosius | .30 | .14 |
| ❑ | 497 | Mike Buddie RC | .20 | .09 |
| ❑ | 498 | Homer Bush | .20 | .09 |
| ❑ | 499 | David Cone | .30 | .14 |
| ❑ | 500 | Chad Curtis | .20 | .09 |
| ❑ | 501 | Chili Davis | .30 | .14 |
| ❑ | 502 | Joe Girardi | .20 | .09 |
| ❑ | 503 | Darren Holmes | .20 | .09 |
| ❑ | 504 | Hideki Irabu | .20 | .09 |
| ❑ | 505 | D.Jeter Fielding | 3.00 | 1.35 |
| ❑ | 505A | D.Jeter Hitting | 3.00 | 1.35 |
| ❑ | 506 | Chuck Knoblauch | .30 | .14 |
| ❑ | 507 | Graeme Lloyd | .20 | .09 |
| ❑ | 508 | Tino Martinez | .30 | .14 |
| ❑ | 509 | Ramiro Mendoza | .20 | .09 |
| ❑ | 510 | Jeff Nelson | .20 | .09 |
| ❑ | 511 | Paul O'Neill | .30 | .14 |
| ❑ | 512 | Andy Pettitte | .30 | .14 |
| ❑ | 513 | Jorge Posada | .20 | .09 |
| ❑ | 514 | Tim Raines | .30 | .14 |
| ❑ | 515 | Mariano Rivera | .30 | .14 |
| ❑ | 516 | Luis Sojo | .20 | .09 |
| ❑ | 517 | Mike Stanton | .20 | .09 |
| ❑ | 518 | Darryl Strawberry | .30 | .14 |
| ❑ | 519 | Dale Sveum | .20 | .09 |
| ❑ | 520 | David Wells | .30 | .14 |
| ❑ | 521 | Bernie Williams | .75 | .35 |
| ❑ | 522 | Bernie Williams TC | .30 | .14 |
| ❑ | 523 | Kurt Abbott | .20 | .09 |
| ❑ | 524 | Mike Blowers | .20 | .09 |
| ❑ | 525 | Rafael Bournigal | .20 | .09 |
| ❑ | 526 | Tom Candiotti | .20 | .09 |
| ❑ | 527 | Ryan Christenson RC | .30 | .14 |
| ❑ | 528 | Mike Fetters | .20 | .09 |
| ❑ | 529 | Jason Giambi | .75 | .35 |
| ❑ | 530 | B.Grieve Running | .30 | .14 |
| ❑ | 530A | B.Grieve Swinging | .30 | .14 |
| ❑ | 531 | Buddy Groom | .20 | .09 |
| ❑ | 532 | Jimmy Haynes | .20 | .09 |
| ❑ | 533 | Rickey Henderson | 1.00 | .45 |
| ❑ | 534 | A.J. Hinch | .20 | .09 |
| ❑ | 535 | Mike Macfarlane | .20 | .09 |
| ❑ | 536 | Dave Magadan | .20 | .09 |
| ❑ | 537 | T.J. Mathews | .20 | .09 |
| ❑ | 538 | Jason McDonald | .20 | .09 |
| ❑ | 539 | Kevin Mitchell | .20 | .09 |
| ❑ | 540 | Mike Mohler | .20 | .09 |
| ❑ | 541 | Mike Oquist | .20 | .09 |
| ❑ | 542 | Ariel Prieto | .20 | .09 |
| ❑ | 543 | Kenny Rogers | .20 | .09 |
| ❑ | 544 | Aaron Small | .20 | .09 |
| ❑ | 545 | Scott Spiezio | .20 | .09 |
| ❑ | 546 | Matt Stairs | .20 | .09 |
| ❑ | 547 | Bill Taylor | .20 | .09 |
| ❑ | 548 | Dave Telgheder | .20 | .09 |
| ❑ | 549 | Jack Voigt | .20 | .09 |
| ❑ | 550 | Ben Grieve TC | .30 | .14 |
| ❑ | 551 | Bob Abreu | .30 | .14 |
| ❑ | 552 | Ruben Amaro | .20 | .09 |
| ❑ | 553 | Alex Arias | .20 | .09 |
| ❑ | 554 | Matt Beech | .20 | .09 |
| ❑ | 555 | Ricky Bottalico | .20 | .09 |
| ❑ | 556 | Billy Brewer | .20 | .09 |
| ❑ | 557 | Rico Brogna | .20 | .09 |
| ❑ | 558 | Doug Glanville | .20 | .09 |
| ❑ | 559 | Wayne Gomes | .20 | .09 |
| ❑ | 560 | Mike Grace | .20 | .09 |
| ❑ | 561 | Tyler Green | .20 | .09 |
| ❑ | 562 | Rex Hudler | .20 | .09 |
| ❑ | 563 | Gregg Jefferies | .20 | .09 |
| ❑ | 564 | Kevin Jordan | .20 | .09 |
| ❑ | 565 | Mark Leiter | .20 | .09 |
| ❑ | 566 | Mark Lewis | .20 | .09 |
| ❑ | 567 | Mike Lieberthal | .30 | .14 |
| ❑ | 568 | Mark Parent | .20 | .09 |
| ❑ | 569 | Yorkis Perez | .20 | .09 |
| ❑ | 570 | Desi Relaford | .20 | .09 |
| ❑ | 571 | Scott Rolen | .75 | .35 |
| ❑ | 572 | Curt Schilling | .30 | .14 |
| ❑ | 573 | Kevin Sefcik | .20 | .09 |
| ❑ | 574 | Jerry Spradlin | .20 | .09 |
| ❑ | 575 | Garrett Stephenson | .20 | .09 |
| ❑ | 576 | Darrin Winston RC | .20 | .09 |
| ❑ | 577 | Scott Rolen TC | .75 | .35 |
| ❑ | 578 | Jermaine Allensworth | .20 | .09 |
| ❑ | 579 | Jason Christiansen | .20 | .09 |
| ❑ | 580 | Lou Collier | .20 | .09 |
| ❑ | 581 | Francisco Cordova | .20 | .09 |
| ❑ | 582 | Elmer Dessens | .20 | .09 |
| ❑ | 583 | Freddy Garcia | .20 | .09 |
| ❑ | 584 | Jose Guillen | .20 | .09 |
| ❑ | 585 | Jason Kendall | .30 | .14 |
| ❑ | 586 | Jon Lieber | .20 | .09 |
| ❑ | 587 | Esteban Loaiza | .20 | .09 |
| ❑ | 588 | Al Martin | .20 | .09 |
| ❑ | 589 | Javier Martinez RC | .50 | .23 |
| ❑ | 590 | Chris Peters | .20 | .09 |
| ❑ | 591 | Kevin Polcovich | .20 | .09 |
| ❑ | 592 | Ricardo Rincon | .20 | .09 |
| ❑ | 593 | Jason Schmidt | .20 | .09 |
| ❑ | 594 | Jose Silva | .20 | .09 |
| ❑ | 595 | Mark Smith | .20 | .09 |
| ❑ | 596 | Doug Strange | .20 | .09 |
| ❑ | 597 | Turner Ward | .20 | .09 |
| ❑ | 598 | Marc Wilkins | .20 | .09 |
| ❑ | 599 | Mike Williams | .20 | .09 |
| ❑ | 600 | Tony Womack | .20 | .09 |
| ❑ | 601 | Kevin Young | .30 | .14 |
| ❑ | 602 | Tony Womack TC | .20 | .09 |
| ❑ | 603 | Manny Aybar RC | .30 | .14 |
| ❑ | 604 | Kent Bottenfield | .20 | .09 |
| ❑ | 605 | Jeff Brantley | .20 | .09 |
| ❑ | 606 | Mike Busby | .20 | .09 |
| ❑ | 607 | Royce Clayton | .20 | .09 |
| ❑ | 608 | Delino DeShields | .20 | .09 |
| ❑ | 609 | John Frascatore | .20 | .09 |
| ❑ | 610 | Gary Gaetti | .30 | .14 |
| ❑ | 611 | Ron Gant | .30 | .14 |
| ❑ | 612 | David Howard | .20 | .09 |
| ❑ | 613 | Brian Hunter | .20 | .09 |
| ❑ | 614 | Brian Jordan | .30 | .14 |
| ❑ | 615 | Tom Lampkin | .20 | .09 |
| ❑ | 616 | Ray Lankford | .30 | .14 |
| ❑ | 617 | Braden Looper | .20 | .09 |
| ❑ | 618 | John Mabry | .20 | .09 |
| ❑ | 619 | Eli Marrero | .20 | .09 |
| ❑ | 620 | Willie McGee | .30 | .14 |
| ❑ | 621 | M.McGwire Fielding | 3.00 | 1.35 |
| ❑ | 621A | M.McGwire Hitting | 3.00 | 1.35 |
| ❑ | 622 | Kent Mercker | .20 | .09 |
| ❑ | 623 | Matt Morris | .20 | .09 |
| ❑ | 624 | Donovan Osborne | .20 | .09 |
| ❑ | 625 | Tom Pagnozzi | .20 | .09 |
| ❑ | 626 | Lance Painter | .20 | .09 |
| ❑ | 627 | Mark Petkovsek | .20 | .09 |
| ❑ | 628 | Todd Stottlemyre | .20 | .09 |
| ❑ | 629 | Mark McGwire TC | 1.50 | .70 |
| ❑ | 630 | Andy Ashby | .20 | .09 |
| ❑ | 631 | Brian Boehringer | .20 | .09 |
| ❑ | 632 | Kevin Brown | .50 | .23 |
| ❑ | 633 | Ken Caminiti | .30 | .14 |
| ❑ | 634 | Steve Finley | .30 | .14 |
| ❑ | 635 | Ed Giovanola | .20 | .09 |
| ❑ | 636 | Chris Gomez | .20 | .09 |
| ❑ | 637 | T.Gwynn Blue Jersey | 1.50 | .70 |
| ❑ | 637A | T.Gwynn White Jersey | 1.50 | .70 |
| ❑ | 638 | Joey Hamilton | .20 | .09 |
| ❑ | 639 | Carlos Hernandez | .20 | .09 |
| ❑ | 640 | Sterling Hitchcock | .20 | .09 |
| ❑ | 641 | Trevor Hoffman | .30 | .14 |
| ❑ | 642 | Wally Joyner | .30 | .14 |
| ❑ | 643 | Dan Miceli | .20 | .09 |
| ❑ | 644 | James Mouton | .20 | .09 |
| ❑ | 645 | Greg Myers | .20 | .09 |
| ❑ | 646 | Carlos Reyes | .20 | .09 |
| ❑ | 647 | Andy Sheets | .20 | .09 |
| ❑ | 648 | Pete Smith | .20 | .09 |
| ❑ | 649 | Mark Sweeney | .20 | .09 |
| ❑ | 650 | Greg Vaughn | .30 | .14 |
| ❑ | 651 | Quilvio Veras | .20 | .09 |
| ❑ | 652 | Tony Gwynn TC | .75 | .35 |
| ❑ | 653 | Rich Aurilia | .20 | .09 |
| ❑ | 654 | Marvin Benard | .20 | .09 |
| ❑ | 655 | B.Bonds Hitting | 1.25 | .55 |
| ❑ | 655A | B.Bonds Close-Up | 1.25 | .55 |
| ❑ | 656 | Danny Darwin | .20 | .09 |
| ❑ | 657 | Shawn Estes | .20 | .09 |
| ❑ | 658 | Mark Gardner | .20 | .09 |
| ❑ | 659 | Darryl Hamilton | .20 | .09 |
| ❑ | 660 | Charlie Hayes | .20 | .09 |
| ❑ | 661 | Orel Hershiser | .30 | .14 |
| ❑ | 662 | Stan Javier | .20 | .09 |
| ❑ | 663 | Brian Johnson | .20 | .09 |
| ❑ | 664 | John Johnstone | .20 | .09 |
| ❑ | 665 | Jeff Kent | .50 | .23 |
| ❑ | 666 | Brent Mayne | .20 | .09 |
| ❑ | 667 | Bill Mueller | .20 | .09 |
| ❑ | 668 | Robb Nen | .20 | .09 |
| ❑ | 669 | Jim Poole | .20 | .09 |
| ❑ | 670 | Steve Reed | .20 | .09 |
| ❑ | 671 | Rich Rodriguez | .20 | .09 |
| ❑ | 672 | Kirk Rueter | .20 | .09 |
| ❑ | 673 | Rey Sanchez | .20 | .09 |
| ❑ | 674 | J.T. Snow | .30 | .14 |
| ❑ | 675 | Julian Tavarez | .20 | .09 |
| ❑ | 676 | Barry Bonds TC | .50 | .23 |
| ❑ | 677 | Rich Amaral | .20 | .09 |
| ❑ | 678 | Bobby Ayala | .20 | .09 |
| ❑ | 679 | Jay Buhner | .30 | .14 |
| ❑ | 680 | Ken Cloude | .20 | .09 |
| ❑ | 681 | Joey Cora | .20 | .09 |
| ❑ | 682 | Russ Davis | .20 | .09 |
| ❑ | 683 | Rob Ducey | .20 | .09 |
| ❑ | 684 | Jeff Fassero | .20 | .09 |
| ❑ | 685 | Tony Fossas | .20 | .09 |
| ❑ | 686 | K.Griffey Jr. Fielding | 3.00 | 1.35 |
| ❑ | 686A | K.Griffey Jr. Hitting | 3.00 | 1.35 |
| ❑ | 687 | Glenallen Hill | .20 | .09 |
| ❑ | 688 | Jeff Huson | .20 | .09 |
| ❑ | 689 | Randy Johnson | 1.00 | .45 |
| ❑ | 690 | Edgar Martinez | .50 | .23 |
| ❑ | 691 | John Marzano | .20 | .09 |
| ❑ | 692 | Jamie Moyer | .20 | .09 |
| ❑ | 693 | A.Rodriguez Fielding | 2.50 | 1.10 |
| ❑ | 693A | A.Rodriguez Hitting | 2.50 | 1.10 |
| ❑ | 694 | David Segui | .20 | .09 |
| ❑ | 695 | Heathcliff Slocumb | .20 | .09 |
| ❑ | 696 | Paul Spoljaric | .20 | .09 |
| ❑ | 697 | Bill Swift | .20 | .09 |
| ❑ | 698 | Mike Timlin | .20 | .09 |
| ❑ | 699 | Bob Wells | .20 | .09 |
| ❑ | 700 | Dan Wilson | .20 | .09 |
| ❑ | 701 | Ken Griffey Jr. TC | 1.50 | .70 |
| ❑ | 702 | Wilson Alvarez | .20 | .09 |
| ❑ | 703 | Rolando Arrojo RC | .60 | .25 |
| ❑ | 704 | W.Boggs Fielding | 1.00 | .45 |
| ❑ | 704A | W.Boggs Hitting | 1.00 | .45 |
| ❑ | 705 | Rich Butler RC | .20 | .09 |
| ❑ | 706 | Miguel Cairo | .20 | .09 |
| ❑ | 707 | Mike Difelice RC | .20 | .09 |

- ❑ 708 John Flaherty .20 .09
- ❑ 709 Roberto Hernandez .20 .09
- ❑ 710 Mike Kelly .20 .09
- ❑ 711 Aaron Ledesma .20 .09
- ❑ 712 Albie Lopez .20 .09
- ❑ 713 Dave Martinez .20 .09
- ❑ 714 Quinton McCracken .20 .09
- ❑ 715 Fred McGriff .50 .23
- ❑ 716 Jim Mecir .20 .09
- ❑ 717 Tony Saunders .20 .09
- ❑ 718 Bobby Smith .20 .09
- ❑ 719 Paul Sorrento .20 .09
- ❑ 720 Dennis Springer .20 .09
- ❑ 721 Kevin Stocker .20 .09
- ❑ 722 Ramon Tatis .20 .09
- ❑ 723 Bubba Trammell .20 .09
- ❑ 724 Esteban Yan RC .50 .23
- ❑ 725 Wade Boggs TC .30 .14
- ❑ 726 Luis Alicea .20 .09
- ❑ 727 Scott Bailes .20 .09
- ❑ 728 John Burkett .20 .09
- ❑ 729 Domingo Cedeno .20 .09
- ❑ 730 Will Clark .75 .35
- ❑ 731 Kevin Elster .20 .09
- ❑ 732 J.Gonzalez With Bat .75 .35
- ❑ 732A J.Gonzalez Without Bat .75 .35
- ❑ 733 Tom Goodwin .20 .09
- ❑ 734 Rusty Greer .30 .14
- ❑ 735 Eric Gunderson .20 .09
- ❑ 736 Bill Haselman .20 .09
- ❑ 737 Rick Helling .30 .14
- ❑ 738 Roberto Kelly .20 .09
- ❑ 739 Mark McLemore .20 .09
- ❑ 740 Darren Oliver .20 .09
- ❑ 741 Danny Patterson .20 .09
- ❑ 742 Roger Pavlik .20 .09
- ❑ 743 I.Rodriguez Fielding 1.00 .45
- ❑ 743A I.Rodriguez Hitting 1.00 .45
- ❑ 744 Aaron Sele .30 .14
- ❑ 745 Mike Simms .20 .09
- ❑ 746 Lee Stevens .20 .09
- ❑ 747 Fernando Tatis .30 .14
- ❑ 748 John Wetteland .30 .14
- ❑ 749 Bobby Witt .20 .09
- ❑ 750 Juan Gonzalez TC .30 .14
- ❑ 751 Carlos Almanzar RC .30 .14
- ❑ 752 Kevin Brown .50 .23
- ❑ 753 Jose Canseco 1.00 .45
- ❑ 754 Chris Carpenter .30 .14
- ❑ 755 Roger Clemens 1.50 .70
- ❑ 756 Felipe Crespo .20 .09
- ❑ 757 Jose Cruz Jr. .30 .14
- ❑ 758 Mark Dalesandro .20 .09
- ❑ 759 Carlos Delgado .75 .35
- ❑ 760 Kelvim Escobar .20 .09
- ❑ 761 Tony Fernandez .20 .09
- ❑ 762 Darrin Fletcher .20 .09
- ❑ 763 Alex Gonzalez .20 .09
- ❑ 764 Craig Grebeck .20 .09
- ❑ 765 Shawn Green .75 .35
- ❑ 766 Juan Guzman .20 .09
- ❑ 767 Erik Hanson .20 .09
- ❑ 768 Pat Hentgen .20 .09
- ❑ 769 Randy Myers .30 .14
- ❑ 770 Robert Person .20 .09
- ❑ 771 Dan Plesac .20 .09
- ❑ 772 Paul Quantrill .20 .09
- ❑ 773 Bill Risley .20 .09
- ❑ 774 Juan Samuel .20 .09
- ❑ 775 Steve Sinclair RC .20 .09
- ❑ 776 Ed Sprague .20 .09
- ❑ 777 Mike Stanley .20 .09
- ❑ 778 Shannon Stewart .30 .14
- ❑ 779 Woody Williams .20 .09
- ❑ 780 Roger Clemens TC .75 .35
- ❑ SAMP Tony Gwynn Sample 2.00 .90

## 1995 Pacific Prisms

| | MINT | NRMT |
|---|---|---|
| COMPLETE SET (144) | 180.00 | 80.00 |
| COMMON CARD (1-144) | .75 | .45 |
| COMP.TEAM LOGO SET (28) | 5.00 | 2.20 |
| COMMON TEAM LOGO | .10 | .05 |

- ❑ 1 David Justice 2.00 .90
- ❑ 2 Ryan Klesko 1.50 .70
- ❑ 3 Javier Lopez 1.50 .70
- ❑ 4 Greg Maddux 8.00 3.60
- ❑ 5 Fred McGriff 2.00 .90
- ❑ 6 Tony Tarasco 1.00 .45
- ❑ 7 Jeffrey Hammonds 1.50 .70
- ❑ 8 Mike Mussina 3.00 1.35
- ❑ 9 Rafael Palmeiro 3.00 1.35
- ❑ 10 Cal Ripken 12.00 5.50
- ❑ 11 Lee Smith 1.50 .70
- ❑ 12 Roger Clemens 6.00 2.70
- ❑ 13 Scott Cooper 1.00 .45
- ❑ 14 Mike Greenwell 1.00 .45
- ❑ 15 Carlos Rodriguez 1.00 .45
- ❑ 16 Mo Vaughn 1.50 .70
- ❑ 17 Chili Davis 1.50 .70
- ❑ 18 Jim Edmonds UER 3.00 1.35
  (Card incorrectly numbered 21)
- ❑ 19 Jorge Fabregas 1.00 .45
- ❑ 20 Bo Jackson 1.50 .70
- ❑ 21 Tim Salmon 1.50 .70
- ❑ 22 Mark Grace 3.00 1.35
- ❑ 23 Jose Guzman 1.00 .45
- ❑ 24 Randy Myers 1.00 .45
- ❑ 25 Rey Sanchez 1.00 .45
- ❑ 26 Sammy Sosa 6.00 2.70
- ❑ 27 Wilson Alvarez 1.00 .45
- ❑ 28 Julio Franco 1.00 .45
- ❑ 29 Ozzie Guillen 1.00 .45
- ❑ 30 Jack McDowell 1.00 .45
- ❑ 31 Frank Thomas 6.00 2.70
- ❑ 32 Bret Boone 1.50 .70
- ❑ 33 Barry Larkin 3.00 1.35
- ❑ 34 Hal Morris 1.00 .45
- ❑ 35 Jose Rijo 1.00 .45
- ❑ 36 Deion Sanders 1.50 .70
- ❑ 37 Carlos Baerga 1.00 .45
- ❑ 38 Albert Belle 2.00 .90
- ❑ 39 Kenny Lofton 1.50 .70
- ❑ 40 Dennis Martinez 1.50 .70
- ❑ 41 Manny Ramirez 4.00 1.80
- ❑ 42 Omar Vizquel 1.50 .70
- ❑ 43 Dante Bichette 1.50 .70
- ❑ 44 Marvin Freeman 1.00 .45
- ❑ 45 Andres Galarraga 2.00 .90
- ❑ 46 Mike Kingery 1.00 .45
- ❑ 47 Danny Bautista 1.00 .45
- ❑ 48 Cecil Fielder 1.50 .70
- ❑ 49 Travis Fryman 1.50 .70
- ❑ 50 Tony Phillips 1.00 .45
- ❑ 51 Alan Trammell 2.00 .90
- ❑ 52 Lou Whitaker 1.50 .70
- ❑ 53 Alex Arias 1.00 .45
- ❑ 54 Bret Barberie 1.00 .45
- ❑ 55 Jeff Conine 1.00 .45
- ❑ 56 Charles Johnson 1.50 .70
- ❑ 57 Gary Sheffield 3.00 1.35
- ❑ 58 Jeff Bagwell 4.00 1.80
- ❑ 59 Craig Biggio 2.00 .90
- ❑ 60 Doug Drabek 1.00 .45
- ❑ 61 Tony Eusebio 1.00 .45
- ❑ 62 Luis Gonzalez 1.00 .45
- ❑ 63 David Cone 1.50 .70
- ❑ 64 Bob Hamelin 1.00 .45
- ❑ 65 Felix Jose 1.00 .45
- ❑ 66 Wally Joyner 1.50 .70
- ❑ 67 Brian McRae 1.00 .45
- ❑ 68 Brett Butler 1.50 .70
- ❑ 69 Garey Ingram 1.00 .45
- ❑ 70 Ramon Martinez 1.00 .45
- ❑ 71 Raul Mondesi 1.50 .70
- ❑ 72 Mike Piazza 10.00 4.50
- ❑ 73 Henry Rodriguez 1.00 .45
- ❑ 74 Ricky Bones 1.00 .45
- ❑ 75 Pat Listach 1.00 .45
- ❑ 76 Dave Nilsson 1.00 .45
- ❑ 77 Jose Valentin 1.00 .45
- ❑ 78 Rick Aguilera 1.00 .45
- ❑ 79 Denny Hocking 1.00 .45
- ❑ 80 Shane Mack 1.00 .45
- ❑ 81 Pedro Munoz 1.00 .45
- ❑ 82 Kirby Puckett 8.00 3.60
- ❑ 83 Dave Winfield 3.00 1.35
- ❑ 84 Moises Alou 1.50 .70
- ❑ 85 Wil Cordero 1.00 .45
- ❑ 86 Cliff Floyd 1.50 .70
- ❑ 87 Marquis Grissom 1.00 .45
- ❑ 88 Pedro Martinez 4.00 1.80
- ❑ 89 Larry Walker 1.50 .70
- ❑ 90 Bobby Bonilla 1.50 .70
- ❑ 91 Jeromy Burnitz 1.50 .70
- ❑ 92 John Franco 1.50 .70
- ❑ 93 Jeff Kent 2.00 .90
- ❑ 94 Jose Vizcaino 1.00 .45
- ❑ 95 Wade Boggs 4.00 1.80
- ❑ 96 Jimmy Key 1.50 .70
- ❑ 97 Don Mattingly 10.00 4.50
- ❑ 98 Paul O'Neill 1.50 .70
- ❑ 99 Luis Polonia 1.00 .45
- ❑ 100 Danny Tartabull 1.00 .45
- ❑ 101 Geronimo Berroa 1.00 .45
- ❑ 102 Rickey Henderson 4.00 1.80
- ❑ 103 Ruben Sierra 1.00 .45
- ❑ 104 Terry Steinbach 1.00 .45
- ❑ 105 Darren Daulton 1.50 .70
- ❑ 106 Mariano Duncan 1.00 .45
- ❑ 107 Lenny Dykstra 1.50 .70
- ❑ 108 Mike Lieberthal 1.50 .70
- ❑ 109 Tony Longmire 1.00 .45
- ❑ 110 Tom Marsh 1.00 .45
- ❑ 111 Jay Bell 1.50 .70
- ❑ 112 Carlos Garcia 1.00 .45
- ❑ 113 Orlando Merced 1.00 .45
- ❑ 114 Andy Van Slyke 1.50 .70
- ❑ 115 Derek Bell 1.00 .45
- ❑ 116 Tony Gwynn 6.00 2.70
- ❑ 117 Luis Lopez 1.00 .45
- ❑ 118 Bip Roberts 1.00 .45
- ❑ 119 Rod Beck 1.00 .45
- ❑ 120 Barry Bonds 5.00 2.20
- ❑ 121 Darryl Strawberry 1.50 .70
- ❑ 122 Wm. Van Landingham 1.00 .45
- ❑ 123 Matt Williams 2.00 .90
- ❑ 124 Jay Buhner 1.50 .70
- ❑ 125 Felix Fermin 1.00 .45
- ❑ 126 Ken Griffey Jr. 12.00 5.50
- ❑ 127 Randy Johnson 4.00 1.80
- ❑ 128 Edgar Martinez 2.00 .90
- ❑ 129 Alex Rodriguez 12.00 5.50
- ❑ 130 Rene Arocha 1.00 .45
- ❑ 131 Gregg Jefferies 1.00 .45
- ❑ 132 Mike Perez 1.00 .45
- ❑ 133 Ozzie Smith 4.00 1.80
- ❑ 134 Jose Canseco 4.00 1.80
- ❑ 135 Will Clark 3.00 1.35
- ❑ 136 Juan Gonzalez 3.00 1.35
- ❑ 137 Ivan Rodriguez 4.00 1.80
- ❑ 138 Roberto Alomar 3.00 1.35
- ❑ 139 Joe Carter 1.50 .70
- ❑ 140 Carlos Delgado 3.00 1.35
- ❑ 141 Alex Gonzalez 1.00 .45
- ❑ 142 Juan Guzman 1.00 .45
- ❑ 143 Paul Molitor 3.00 1.35
- ❑ 144 John Olerud 1.50 .70

## 1996 Pacific Prisms

| | MINT | NRMT |
|---|---|---|
| COMPLETE SET (144) | 180.00 | 80.00 |
| COMMON CARD (1-144) | .75 | .35 |

- ❑ P1 Tom Glavine 3.00 1.35
- ❑ P2 Chipper Jones 8.00 3.60
- ❑ P3 David Justice 2.00 .90

❑ P4 Ryan Klesko 1.25 .55
❑ P5 Javy Lopez 1.25 .55
❑ P6 Greg Maddux 8.00 3.60
❑ P7 Fred McGriff 2.00 .90
❑ P8 Frank Castillo .75 .35
❑ P9 Luis Gonzalez 1.25 .55
❑ P10 Mark Grace 3.00 1.35
❑ P11 Brian McRae .75 .35
❑ P12 Jaime Navarro .75 .35
❑ P13 Sammy Sosa 6.00 2.70
❑ P14 Bret Boone 1.25 .55
❑ P15 Ron Gant .75 .35
❑ P16 Barry Larkin 3.00 1.35
❑ P17 Reggie Sanders .75 .35
❑ P18 Benito Santiago .75 .35
❑ P19 Dante Bichette 1.25 .55
❑ P20 Vinny Castilla 1.25 .55
❑ P21 Andres Galarraga 2.00 .90
❑ P22 Bryan Rekar .75 .35
❑ P23 Roberto Alomar 3.00 1.35
❑ P24 Jeff Conine .75 .35
❑ P25 Andre Dawson 2.00 .90
❑ P26 Charles Johnson 1.25 .55
❑ P27 Gary Sheffield 3.00 1.35
❑ P28 Quilvio Veras .75 .35
❑ P29 Jeff Bagwell 4.00 1.80
❑ P30 Derek Bell .75 .35
❑ P31 Craig Biggio 2.00 .90
❑ P32 Tony Eusebio .75 .35
❑ P33 Karim Garcia .75 .35
❑ P34 Eric Karros 1.25 .55
❑ P35 Ramon Martinez .75 .35
❑ P36 Raul Mondesi 1.25 .55
❑ P37 Hideo Nomo 3.00 1.35
❑ P38 Mike Piazza 10.00 4.50
❑ P39 Ismael Valdes .75 .35
❑ P40 Moises Alou 1.25 .55
❑ P41 Wil Cordero .75 .35
❑ P42 Pedro Martinez 4.00 1.80
❑ P43 Mel Rojas .75 .35
❑ P44 David Segui .75 .35
❑ P45 Edgardo Alfonzo 1.25 .55
❑ P46 Rico Brogna .75 .35
❑ P47 John Franco 1.25 .55
❑ P48 Jason Isringhausen 1.25 .55
❑ P49 Jose Vizcaino .75 .35
❑ P50 Ricky Bottalico .75 .35
❑ P51 Darren Daulton 1.25 .55
❑ P52 Lenny Dykstra 1.25 .55
❑ P53 Tyler Green .75 .35
❑ P54 Gregg Jefferies .75 .35
❑ P55 Jay Bell 1.25 .55
❑ P56 Jason Christiansen .75 .35
❑ P57 Carlos Garcia .75 .35
❑ P58 Esteban Loaiza .75 .35
❑ P59 Orlando Merced .75 .35
❑ P60 Andujar Cedeno .75 .35
❑ P61 Tony Gwynn 6.00 2.70
❑ P62 Melvin Nieves .75 .35
❑ P63 Phil Plantier .75 .35
❑ P64 Fernando Valenzuela 1.25 .55
❑ P65 Barry Bonds 5.00 2.20
❑ P66 J.R. Phillips .75 .35
❑ P67 Deion Sanders 1.25 .55
❑ P68 Matt Williams 2.00 .90
❑ P69 Bernard Gilkey .75 .35
❑ P70 Tom Henke .75 .35
❑ P71 Brian Jordan 1.25 .55
❑ P72 Ozzie Smith 4.00 1.80
❑ P73 Manny Alexander .75 .35
❑ P74 Bobby Bonilla 1.25 .55
❑ P75 Mike Mussina 3.00 1.35
❑ P76 Rafael Palmeiro 3.00 1.35
❑ P77 Cal Ripken 12.00 5.50
❑ P78 Jose Canseco 4.00 1.80
❑ P79 Roger Clemens 6.00 2.70
❑ P80 John Valentin .75 .35
❑ P81 Mo Vaughn 1.25 .55
❑ P82 Tim Wakefield .75 .35
❑ P83 Garret Anderson 1.25 .55
❑ P84 Damion Easley .75 .35
❑ P85 Jim Edmonds 3.00 1.35
❑ P86 Tim Salmon 1.25 .55
❑ P87 Wilson Alvarez .75 .35
❑ P88 Alex Fernandez .75 .35
❑ P89 Ozzie Guillen .75 .35
❑ P90 Roberto Hernandez .75 .35
❑ P91 Frank Thomas 6.00 2.70
❑ P92 Robin Ventura 1.25 .55
❑ P93 Carlos Baerga .75 .35
❑ P94 Albert Belle 2.00 .90
❑ P95 Kenny Lofton 1.25 .55
❑ P96 Dennis Martinez 1.25 .55
❑ P97 Eddie Murray 3.00 1.35
❑ P98 Manny Ramirez 4.00 1.80
❑ P99 Omar Vizquel 1.25 .55
❑ P100 Chad Curtis .75 .35
❑ P101 Cecil Fielder 1.25 .55
❑ P102 Felipe Lira .75 .35
❑ P103 Alan Trammell 2.00 .90
❑ P104 Kevin Appier 1.25 .55
❑ P105 Johnny Damon 2.00 .90
❑ P106 Gary Gaetti 1.25 .55
❑ P107 Wally Joyner 1.25 .55
❑ P108 Ricky Bones .75 .35
❑ P109 John Jaha .75 .35
❑ P110 B.J. Surhoff 1.25 .55
❑ P111 Jose Valentin .75 .35
❑ P112 Fernando Vina .75 .35
❑ P113 Marty Cordova .75 .35
❑ P114 Chuck Knoblauch 1.25 .55
❑ P115 Scott Leius .75 .35
❑ P116 Pedro Munoz .75 .35
❑ P117 Kirby Puckett 8.00 3.60
❑ P118 Wade Boggs 4.00 1.80
❑ P119 Don Mattingly 8.00 3.60
❑ P120 Jack McDowell .75 .35
❑ P121 Paul O'Neill 1.25 .55
❑ P122 Ruben Rivera .75 .35
❑ P123 Bernie Williams 3.00 1.35
❑ P124 Geronimo Berroa .75 .35
❑ P125 Rickey Henderson 4.00 1.80
❑ P126 Mark McGwire 12.00 5.50
❑ P127 Terry Steinbach .75 .35
❑ P128 Danny Tartabull .75 .35
❑ P129 Jay Buhner 1.25 .55
❑ P130 Joey Cora .75 .35
❑ P131 Ken Griffey Jr. 12.00 5.50
❑ P132 Randy Johnson 4.00 1.80
❑ P133 Edgar Martinez 2.00 .90
❑ P134 Tino Martinez 1.25 .55
❑ P135 Will Clark 3.00 1.35
❑ P136 Juan Gonzalez 3.00 1.35
❑ P137 Dean Palmer 1.25 .55
❑ P138 Ivan Rodriguez 4.00 1.80
❑ P139 Mickey Tettleton .75 .35
❑ P140 Larry Walker 1.25 .55
❑ P141 Joe Carter 1.25 .55
❑ P142 Carlos Delgado 3.00 1.35
❑ P143 Alex Gonzalez .75 .35
❑ P144 Paul Molitor 3.00 1.35

## 1997 Pacific Prisms

| | MINT | NRMT |
|---|---|---|
| COMPLETE SET (150) | 180.00 | 80.00 |
| COMMON CARD (1-150) | .75 | .45 |

❑ 1 Chili Davis 1.50 .70
❑ 2 Jim Edmonds 3.00 1.35
❑ 3 Darin Erstad 4.00 1.80
❑ 4 Orlando Palmeiro 1.00 .45
❑ 5 Tim Salmon 1.50 .70
❑ 6 J.T. Snow 1.50 .70

❑ 7 Roberto Alomar 3.00 1.35
❑ 8 Brady Anderson 1.50 .70
❑ 9 Eddie Murray 3.00 1.35
❑ 10 Mike Mussina 3.00 1.35
❑ 11 Rafael Palmeiro 3.00 1.35
❑ 12 Cal Ripken 12.00 5.50
❑ 13 Jose Canseco 4.00 1.80
❑ 14 Roger Clemens 6.00 2.70
❑ 15 Nomar Garciaparra 10.00 4.50
❑ 16 Reggie Jefferson 1.00 .45
❑ 17 Mo Vaughn 1.50 .70
❑ 18 Wilson Alvarez 1.00 .45
❑ 19 Harold Baines 1.50 .70
❑ 20 Alex Fernandez 1.00 .45
❑ 21 Danny Tartabull 1.00 .45
❑ 22 Frank Thomas 6.00 2.70
❑ 23 Robin Ventura 1.50 .70
❑ 24 Sandy Alomar Jr. 1.50 .70
❑ 25 Albert Belle 2.00 .90
❑ 26 Kenny Lofton 1.50 .70
❑ 27 Jim Thome 2.00 .90
❑ 28 Omar Vizquel 1.50 .70
❑ 29 Raul Casanova 1.00 .45
❑ 30 Tony Clark 1.00 .45
❑ 31 Travis Fryman 1.50 .70
❑ 32 Bobby Higginson 1.50 .70
❑ 33 Melvin Nieves 1.00 .45
❑ 34 Justin Thompson 1.00 .45
❑ 35 Johnny Damon 1.50 .70
❑ 36 Tom Goodwin 1.00 .45
❑ 37 Jeff Montgomery 1.00 .45
❑ 38 Jose Offerman 1.00 .45
❑ 39 John Jaha 1.00 .45
❑ 40 Jeff Cirillo 1.50 .70
❑ 41 Dave Nilsson 1.00 .45
❑ 42 Jose Valentin 1.00 .45
❑ 43 Fernando Vina 1.00 .45
❑ 44 Marty Cordova 1.00 .45
❑ 45 Roberto Kelly 1.00 .45
❑ 46 Chuck Knoblauch 1.50 .70
❑ 47 Paul Molitor 3.00 1.35
❑ 48 Todd Walker 1.00 .45
❑ 49 Wade Boggs 4.00 1.80
❑ 50 Cecil Fielder 1.50 .70
❑ 51 Derek Jeter 10.00 4.50
❑ 52 Tino Martinez 1.50 .70
❑ 53 Andy Pettitte 1.50 .70
❑ 54 Mariano Rivera 1.50 .70
❑ 55 Bernie Williams 3.00 1.35
❑ 56 Tony Batista 3.00 1.35
❑ 57 Geronimo Berroa 1.00 .45
❑ 58 Jason Giambi 3.00 1.35
❑ 59 Mark McGwire 12.00 5.50
❑ 60 Terry Steinbach 1.00 .45
❑ 61 Jay Buhner 1.50 .70
❑ 62 Joey Cora 1.00 .45
❑ 63 Ken Griffey Jr. 12.00 5.50
❑ 64 Edgar Martinez 2.00 .90
❑ 65 Alex Rodriguez 10.00 4.50
❑ 66 Paul Sorrento 1.00 .45
❑ 67 Will Clark 3.00 1.35
❑ 68 Juan Gonzalez 3.00 1.35
❑ 69 Rusty Greer 1.50 .70
❑ 70 Dean Palmer 1.50 .70
❑ 71 Ivan Rodriguez 4.00 1.80
❑ 72 Joe Carter 1.50 .70
❑ 73 Carlos Delgado 3.00 1.35
❑ 74 Juan Guzman 1.00 .45

| | MINT | NRMT |
|---|---|---|
| ❑ 75 Pat Hentgen | 1.00 | .45 |
| ❑ 76 Ed Sprague | 1.00 | .45 |
| ❑ 77 Jermaine Dye | 1.50 | .70 |
| ❑ 78 Andruw Jones | 4.00 | 1.80 |
| ❑ 79 Chipper Jones | 8.00 | 3.60 |
| ❑ 80 Ryan Klesko | 1.50 | .70 |
| ❑ 81 Javier Lopez | 1.50 | .70 |
| ❑ 82 Greg Maddux | 10.00 | 4.50 |
| ❑ 83 John Smoltz | 1.50 | .70 |
| ❑ 84 Mark Grace | 3.00 | 1.35 |
| ❑ 85 Luis Gonzalez | 1.50 | .70 |
| ❑ 86 Brooks Kieschnick | 1.00 | .45 |
| ❑ 87 Jaime Navarro | 1.00 | .45 |
| ❑ 88 Ryne Sandberg | 4.00 | 1.80 |
| ❑ 89 Sammy Sosa | 6.00 | 2.70 |
| ❑ 90 Bret Boone | 1.50 | .70 |
| ❑ 91 Jeff Brantley | 1.00 | .45 |
| ❑ 92 Eric Davis | 1.50 | .70 |
| ❑ 93 Barry Larkin | 3.00 | 1.35 |
| ❑ 94 Reggie Sanders | 1.00 | .45 |
| ❑ 95 Ellis Burks | 1.50 | .70 |
| ❑ 96 Dante Bichette | 1.50 | .70 |
| ❑ 97 Vinny Castilla | 1.50 | .70 |
| ❑ 98 Andres Galarraga | 2.00 | .90 |
| ❑ 99 Eric Young | 1.00 | .45 |
| ❑ 100 Kevin Brown | 2.00 | .90 |
| ❑ 101 Jeff Conine | 1.00 | .45 |
| ❑ 102 Charles Johnson | 1.50 | .70 |
| ❑ 103 Edgar Renteria | 1.50 | .70 |
| ❑ 104 Gary Sheffield | 3.00 | 1.35 |
| ❑ 105 Jeff Bagwell | 4.00 | 1.80 |
| ❑ 106 Derek Bell | 1.00 | .45 |
| ❑ 107 Sean Berry | 1.00 | .45 |
| ❑ 108 Craig Biggio | 2.00 | .90 |
| ❑ 109 Shane Reynolds | 1.00 | .45 |
| ❑ 110 Karim Garcia | 1.00 | .45 |
| ❑ 111 Todd Hollandsworth | 1.00 | .45 |
| ❑ 112 Ramon Martinez | 1.00 | .45 |
| ❑ 113 Raul Mondesi | 1.50 | .70 |
| ❑ 114 Hideo Nomo | 3.00 | 1.35 |
| ❑ 115 Mike Piazza | 10.00 | 4.50 |
| ❑ 116 Ismael Valdes | 1.00 | .45 |
| ❑ 117 Moises Alou | 1.50 | .70 |
| ❑ 118 Mark Grudzielanek | 1.00 | .45 |
| ❑ 119 Pedro Martinez | 4.00 | 1.80 |
| ❑ 120 Henry Rodriguez | 1.00 | .45 |
| ❑ 121 F.P. Santangelo | 1.00 | .45 |
| ❑ 122 Carlos Baerga | 1.00 | .45 |
| ❑ 123 Bernard Gilkey | 1.00 | .45 |
| ❑ 124 Todd Hundley | 1.00 | .45 |
| ❑ 125 Lance Johnson | 1.00 | .45 |
| ❑ 126 Alex Ochoa | 1.00 | .45 |
| ❑ 127 Rey Ordonez | 1.00 | .45 |
| ❑ 128 Lenny Dykstra | 1.50 | .70 |
| ❑ 129 Gregg Jefferies | 1.00 | .45 |
| ❑ 130 Ricky Otero | 1.00 | .45 |
| ❑ 131 Benito Santiago | 1.00 | .45 |
| ❑ 132 Jermaine Allensworth | 1.00 | .45 |
| ❑ 133 Francisco Cordova | 1.00 | .45 |
| ❑ 134 Carlos Garcia | 1.00 | .45 |
| ❑ 135 Jason Kendall | 1.50 | .70 |
| ❑ 136 Al Martin | 1.00 | .45 |
| ❑ 137 Dennis Eckersley | 1.50 | .70 |
| ❑ 138 Ron Gant | 1.00 | .45 |
| ❑ 139 Brian Jordan | 1.50 | .70 |
| ❑ 140 John Mabry | 1.00 | .45 |
| ❑ 141 Ozzie Smith | 4.00 | 1.80 |
| ❑ 142 Ken Caminiti | 1.50 | .70 |
| ❑ 143 Steve Finley | 1.50 | .70 |
| ❑ 144 Tony Gwynn | 6.00 | 2.70 |
| ❑ 145 Wally Joyner | 1.50 | .70 |
| ❑ 146 Fernando Valenzuela | 1.50 | .70 |
| ❑ 147 Barry Bonds | 5.00 | 2.20 |
| ❑ 148 Jacob Cruz | 1.00 | .45 |
| ❑ 149 Osvaldo Fernandez | 1.00 | .45 |
| ❑ 150 Matt Williams | 2.00 | .90 |

## 1999 Pacific Prism

| | MINT | NRMT |
|---|---|---|
| COMPLETE SET (150) | 60.00 | 27.00 |
| ❑ 1 Garret Anderson | .50 | .23 |
| ❑ 2 Jim Edmonds | 1.25 | .55 |
| ❑ 3 Darin Erstad | 1.25 | .55 |
| ❑ 4 Chuck Finley | .50 | .23 |
| ❑ 5 Tim Salmon | .50 | .23 |
| ❑ 6 Jay Bell | .50 | .23 |
| ❑ 7 David Dellucci | .30 | .14 |
| ❑ 8 Travis Lee | .30 | .14 |
| ❑ 9 Matt Williams | .75 | .35 |
| ❑ 10 Andres Galarraga | .75 | .35 |
| ❑ 11 Tom Glavine | 1.25 | .55 |
| ❑ 12 Andruw Jones | 1.25 | .55 |
| ❑ 13 Chipper Jones | 3.00 | 1.35 |
| ❑ 14 Ryan Klesko | .50 | .23 |
| ❑ 15 Javy Lopez | .50 | .23 |
| ❑ 16 Greg Maddux | 3.00 | 1.35 |
| ❑ 17 Roberto Alomar | 1.25 | .55 |
| ❑ 18 Ryan Minor | .30 | .14 |
| ❑ 19 Mike Mussina | 1.25 | .55 |
| ❑ 20 Rafael Palmeiro | 1.25 | .55 |
| ❑ 21 Cal Ripken | 5.00 | 2.20 |
| ❑ 22 Nomar Garciaparra | 4.00 | 1.80 |
| ❑ 23 Pedro Martinez | 1.50 | .70 |
| ❑ 24 John Valentin | .30 | .14 |
| ❑ 25 Mo Vaughn | .50 | .23 |
| ❑ 26 Tim Wakefield | .30 | .14 |
| ❑ 27 Rod Beck | .30 | .14 |
| ❑ 28 Mark Grace | 1.25 | .55 |
| ❑ 29 Lance Johnson | .30 | .14 |
| ❑ 30 Sammy Sosa | 2.50 | 1.10 |
| ❑ 31 Kerry Wood | .50 | .23 |
| ❑ 32 Albert Belle | .75 | .35 |
| ❑ 33 Mike Caruso | .30 | .14 |
| ❑ 34 Magglio Ordonez | .75 | .35 |
| ❑ 35 Frank Thomas | 2.50 | 1.10 |
| ❑ 36 Robin Ventura | .50 | .23 |
| ❑ 37 Aaron Boone | .30 | .14 |
| ❑ 38 Barry Larkin | 1.25 | .55 |
| ❑ 39 Reggie Sanders | .30 | .14 |
| ❑ 40 Brett Tomko | .30 | .14 |
| ❑ 41 Sandy Alomar Jr. | .50 | .23 |
| ❑ 42 Bartolo Colon | .50 | .23 |
| ❑ 43 David Justice | .75 | .35 |
| ❑ 44 Kenny Lofton | .50 | .20 |
| ❑ 45 Manny Ramirez | 1.50 | .70 |
| ❑ 46 Richie Sexson | .50 | .23 |
| ❑ 47 Jim Thome | .75 | .35 |
| ❑ 48 Omar Vizquel | .50 | .23 |
| ❑ 49 Dante Bichette | .50 | .23 |
| ❑ 50 Vinny Castilla | .50 | .23 |
| ❑ 51 Edgard Clemente | .30 | .14 |
| ❑ 52 Todd Helton | 1.50 | .70 |
| ❑ 53 Quinton McCracken | .30 | .14 |
| ❑ 54 Larry Walker | .50 | .23 |
| ❑ 55 Tony Clark | .30 | .14 |
| ❑ 56 Damion Easley | .30 | .14 |
| ❑ 57 Luis Gonzalez | .50 | .23 |
| ❑ 58 Bob Higginson | .50 | .23 |
| ❑ 59 Brian Hunter | .30 | .14 |
| ❑ 60 Cliff Floyd | .50 | .23 |
| ❑ 61 Alex Gonzalez | .30 | .14 |
| ❑ 62 Livan Hernandez | .30 | .14 |
| ❑ 63 Derrek Lee | .30 | .14 |
| ❑ 64 Edgar Renteria | .30 | .14 |
| ❑ 65 Moises Alou | .50 | .23 |
| ❑ 66 Jeff Bagwell | 1.50 | .70 |
| ❑ 67 Derek Bell | .30 | .14 |
| ❑ 68 Craig Biggio | .75 | .35 |
| ❑ 69 Randy Johnson | 1.50 | .70 |
| ❑ 70 Johnny Damon | .50 | .23 |
| ❑ 71 Jeff King | .30 | .14 |
| ❑ 72 Hal Morris | .30 | .14 |
| ❑ 73 Dean Palmer | .50 | .23 |
| ❑ 74 Eric Karros | .50 | .23 |
| ❑ 75 Raul Mondesi | .50 | .23 |
| ❑ 76 Chan Ho Park | .50 | .23 |
| ❑ 77 Gary Sheffield | 1.25 | .55 |
| ❑ 78 Jeromy Burnitz | .50 | .23 |
| ❑ 79 Jeff Cirillo | .50 | .23 |
| ❑ 80 Marquis Grissom | .30 | .14 |
| ❑ 81 Jose Valentin | .30 | .14 |
| ❑ 82 Fernando Vina | .30 | .14 |
| ❑ 83 Paul Molitor | 1.25 | .55 |
| ❑ 84 Otis Nixon | .30 | .14 |
| ❑ 85 David Ortiz | .30 | .14 |
| ❑ 86 Todd Walker | .30 | .14 |
| ❑ 87 Vladimir Guerrero | 2.00 | .90 |
| ❑ 88 Carl Pavano | .30 | .14 |
| ❑ 89 Fernando Seguignol | .30 | .14 |
| ❑ 90 Ugueth Urbina | .30 | .14 |
| ❑ 91 Carlos Baerga | .30 | .14 |
| ❑ 92 Bobby Bonilla | .50 | .23 |
| ❑ 93 Hideo Nomo | 1.25 | .55 |
| ❑ 94 John Olerud | .50 | .23 |
| ❑ 95 Rey Ordonez | .30 | .14 |
| ❑ 96 Mike Piazza | 4.00 | 1.80 |
| ❑ 97 David Cone | .50 | .23 |
| ❑ 98 Orlando Hernandez | .50 | .23 |
| ❑ 99 Hideki Irabu | .30 | .14 |
| ❑ 100 Derek Jeter | 5.00 | 2.20 |
| ❑ 101 Tino Martinez | .50 | .23 |
| ❑ 102 Bernie Williams | 1.25 | .55 |
| ❑ 103 Eric Chavez | .50 | .23 |
| ❑ 104 Jason Giambi | 1.25 | .55 |
| ❑ 105 Ben Grieve | .50 | .23 |
| ❑ 106 Rickey Henderson | 1.50 | .70 |
| ❑ 107 Bob Abreu | .50 | .23 |
| ❑ 108 Doug Glanville | .30 | .14 |
| ❑ 109 Scott Rolen | 1.25 | .55 |
| ❑ 110 Curt Schilling | .50 | .23 |
| ❑ 111 Emil Brown | .30 | .14 |
| ❑ 112 Jose Guillen | .30 | .14 |
| ❑ 113 Jason Kendall | .50 | .23 |
| ❑ 114 Al Martin | .30 | .14 |
| ❑ 115 Aramis Ramirez | .30 | .14 |
| ❑ 116 Kevin Young | .50 | .23 |
| ❑ 117 J.D. Drew | 1.25 | .55 |
| ❑ 118 Ron Gant | .50 | .23 |
| ❑ 119 Brian Jordan | .50 | .23 |
| ❑ 120 Eli Marrero | .30 | .14 |
| ❑ 121 Mark McGwire | 5.00 | 2.20 |
| ❑ 122 Kevin Brown | .75 | .35 |
| ❑ 123 Tony Gwynn | 2.50 | 1.10 |
| ❑ 124 Trevor Hoffman | .50 | .23 |
| ❑ 125 Wally Joyner | .50 | .23 |
| ❑ 126 Greg Vaughn | .50 | .23 |
| ❑ 127 Barry Bonds | 2.00 | .90 |
| ❑ 128 Ellis Burks | .50 | .23 |
| ❑ 129 Jeff Kent | .75 | .35 |
| ❑ 130 Robb Nen | .30 | .14 |
| ❑ 131 J.T. Snow | .50 | .23 |
| ❑ 132 Jay Buhner | .50 | .23 |
| ❑ 133 Ken Griffey Jr. | 5.00 | 2.20 |
| ❑ 134 Edgar Martinez | .75 | .35 |
| ❑ 135 Alex Rodriguez | 4.00 | 1.80 |
| ❑ 136 David Segui | .30 | .14 |
| ❑ 137 Rolando Arrojo | .30 | .14 |
| ❑ 138 Wade Boggs | 1.50 | .70 |
| ❑ 139 Aaron Ledesma | .30 | .14 |
| ❑ 140 Fred McGriff | .75 | .35 |
| ❑ 141 Will Clark | 1.25 | .55 |
| ❑ 142 Juan Gonzalez | 1.25 | .55 |
| ❑ 143 Rusty Greer | .50 | .23 |
| ❑ 144 Ivan Rodriguez | 1.50 | .70 |
| ❑ 145 Aaron Sele | .50 | .23 |
| ❑ 146 Jose Canseco | 1.50 | .70 |
| ❑ 147 Roger Clemens | 2.50 | 1.10 |
| ❑ 148 Jose Cruz Jr. | .50 | .23 |
| ❑ 149 Carlos Delgado | 1.25 | .55 |
| ❑ 150 Alex Gonzalez | .30 | .14 |
| ❑ SA Tony Gwynn Sample | 2.00 | .90 |
| ❑ SAH Tony Gwynn Sample Hawaii/200 | 20.00 | 9.00 |

## 2000 Pacific Prism

| | MINT | NRMT |
|---|---|---|
| COMPLETE SET (150) | 60.00 | 27.00 |

| # | Player | MINT | NRMT |
|---|---|---|---|
| ❑ 1 | Jeff DaVanon RC | .50 | .23 |
| ❑ 2 | Troy Glaus | 1.50 | .70 |
| ❑ 3 | Tim Salmon | .50 | .23 |
| ❑ 4 | Mo Vaughn | .50 | .23 |
| ❑ 5 | Jay Bell | .50 | .23 |
| ❑ 6 | Erubiel Durazo | .50 | .23 |
| ❑ 7 | Luis Gonzalez | .50 | .23 |
| ❑ 8 | Randy Johnson | 1.50 | .70 |
| ❑ 9 | Matt Williams | .75 | .35 |
| ❑ 10 | Andres Galarraga | .75 | .35 |
| ❑ 11 | Andruw Jones | 1.25 | .55 |
| ❑ 12 | Chipper Jones | 3.00 | 1.35 |
| ❑ 13 | Brian Jordan | .50 | .23 |
| ❑ 14 | Greg Maddux | 3.00 | 1.35 |
| ❑ 15 | Kevin Millwood | .50 | .23 |
| ❑ 16 | John Smoltz | .50 | .23 |
| ❑ 17 | Albert Belle | .75 | .35 |
| ❑ 18 | Mike Mussina | 1.25 | .55 |
| ❑ 19 | Calvin Pickering | .30 | .14 |
| ❑ 20 | Cal Ripken | 5.00 | 2.20 |
| ❑ 21 | B.J. Surhoff | .50 | .23 |
| ❑ 22 | Nomar Garciaparra | 4.00 | 1.80 |
| ❑ 23 | Pedro Martinez | 1.50 | .70 |
| ❑ 24 | Troy O'Leary | .30 | .14 |
| ❑ 25 | John Valentin | .30 | .14 |
| ❑ 26 | Jason Varitek | .50 | .23 |
| ❑ 27 | Mark Grace | 1.25 | .55 |
| ❑ 28 | Henry Rodriguez | .30 | .14 |
| ❑ 29 | Sammy Sosa | 2.50 | 1.10 |
| ❑ 30 | Kerry Wood | .50 | .23 |
| ❑ 31 | Ray Durham | .50 | .23 |
| ❑ 32 | Carlos Lee | .50 | .23 |
| ❑ 33 | Magglio Ordonez | .50 | .23 |
| ❑ 34 | Chris Singleton | .50 | .23 |
| ❑ 35 | Frank Thomas | 2.50 | 1.10 |
| ❑ 36 | Sean Casey | .50 | .23 |
| ❑ 37 | Travis Dawkins | .50 | .23 |
| ❑ 38 | Barry Larkin | 1.25 | .55 |
| ❑ 39 | Pokey Reese | .50 | .23 |
| ❑ 40 | Scott Williamson | .30 | .14 |
| ❑ 41 | Roberto Alomar | 1.25 | .55 |
| ❑ 42 | Bartolo Colon | .50 | .23 |
| ❑ 43 | David Justice | .75 | .35 |
| ❑ 44 | Manny Ramirez | 1.50 | .70 |
| ❑ 45 | Richie Sexson | .50 | .23 |
| ❑ 46 | Jim Thome | .75 | .35 |
| ❑ 47 | Omar Vizquel | .50 | .23 |
| ❑ 48 | Pedro Astacio | .30 | .14 |
| ❑ 49 | Todd Helton | 1.50 | .70 |
| ❑ 50 | Neifi Perez | .30 | .14 |
| ❑ 51 | Ben Petrick | .30 | .14 |
| ❑ 52 | Larry Walker | .50 | .23 |
| ❑ 53 | Tony Clark | .30 | .14 |
| ❑ 54 | Damion Easley | .30 | .14 |
| ❑ 55 | Juan Gonzalez | 1.25 | .55 |
| ❑ 56 | Dean Palmer | .50 | .23 |
| ❑ 57 | A.J. Burnett | .50 | .23 |
| ❑ 58 | Luis Castillo | .50 | .23 |
| ❑ 59 | Cliff Floyd | .50 | .23 |
| ❑ 60 | Alex Gonzalez | .30 | .14 |
| ❑ 61 | Preston Wilson | .50 | .23 |
| ❑ 62 | Jeff Bagwell | 1.50 | .70 |
| ❑ 63 | Craig Biggio | .75 | .35 |
| ❑ 64 | Ken Caminiti | .50 | .23 |
| ❑ 65 | Jose Lima | .30 | .14 |
| ❑ 66 | Billy Wagner | .30 | .14 |
| ❑ 67 | Carlos Beltran | .50 | .23 |
| ❑ 68 | Johnny Damon | .50 | .23 |
| ❑ 69 | Jermaine Dye | .50 | .23 |
| ❑ 70 | Carlos Febles | .30 | .14 |
| ❑ 71 | Mike Sweeney | .50 | .23 |
| ❑ 72 | Kevin Brown | .75 | .35 |
| ❑ 73 | Shawn Green | 1.25 | .55 |
| ❑ 74 | Eric Karros | .50 | .23 |
| ❑ 75 | Chan Ho Park | .50 | .23 |
| ❑ 76 | Gary Sheffield | 1.25 | .55 |
| ❑ 77 | Ron Belliard | .30 | .14 |
| ❑ 78 | Jeromy Burnitz | .50 | .23 |
| ❑ 79 | Marquis Grissom | .30 | .14 |
| ❑ 80 | Geoff Jenkins | .50 | .23 |
| ❑ 81 | Mark Loretta | .30 | .14 |
| ❑ 82 | Ron Coomer | .30 | .14 |
| ❑ 83 | Jacque Jones | .50 | .23 |
| ❑ 84 | Corey Koskie | .30 | .14 |
| ❑ 85 | Brad Radke | .50 | .23 |
| ❑ 86 | Todd Walker | .30 | .14 |
| ❑ 87 | Michael Barrett | .30 | .14 |
| ❑ 88 | Peter Bergeron | .30 | .14 |
| ❑ 89 | Vladimir Guerrero | 2.00 | .90 |
| ❑ 90 | Jose Vidro | .30 | .14 |
| ❑ 91 | Rondell White | .50 | .23 |
| ❑ 92 | Edgardo Alfonzo | .50 | .23 |
| ❑ 93 | Rickey Henderson | 1.50 | .70 |
| ❑ 94 | Rey Ordonez | .30 | .14 |
| ❑ 95 | Mike Piazza | 4.00 | 1.80 |
| ❑ 96 | Robin Ventura | .75 | .35 |
| ❑ 97 | Roger Clemens | 2.50 | 1.10 |
| ❑ 98 | Orlando Hernandez | .50 | .23 |
| ❑ 99 | Derek Jeter | 5.00 | 2.20 |
| ❑ 100 | Tino Martinez | .50 | .23 |
| ❑ 101 | Mariano Rivera | .50 | .23 |
| ❑ 102 | Alfonso Soriano | .50 | .23 |
| ❑ 103 | Bernie Williams | 1.25 | .55 |
| ❑ 104 | Eric Chavez | .50 | .23 |
| ❑ 105 | Jason Giambi | 1.25 | .55 |
| ❑ 106 | Ben Grieve | .50 | .23 |
| ❑ 107 | Tim Hudson | 1.25 | .55 |
| ❑ 108 | John Jaha | .30 | .14 |
| ❑ 109 | Bobby Abreu | .50 | .23 |
| ❑ 110 | Doug Glanville | .30 | .14 |
| ❑ 111 | Mike Lieberthal | .50 | .23 |
| ❑ 112 | Scott Rolen | 1.25 | .55 |
| ❑ 113 | Curt Schilling | .50 | .23 |
| ❑ 114 | Brian Giles | .50 | .23 |
| ❑ 115 | Jason Kendall | .50 | .23 |
| ❑ 116 | Warren Morris | .30 | .14 |
| ❑ 117 | Kevin Young | .30 | .14 |
| ❑ 118 | Rick Ankiel | 2.50 | 1.10 |
| ❑ 119 | J.D. Drew | 1.25 | .55 |
| ❑ 120 | Chad Hutchinson | .30 | .14 |
| ❑ 121 | Ray Lankford | .50 | .23 |
| ❑ 122 | Mark McGwire | 5.00 | 2.20 |
| ❑ 123 | Fernando Tatis | .50 | .23 |
| ❑ 124 | Bret Boone | .30 | .14 |
| ❑ 125 | Ben Davis | .30 | .14 |
| ❑ 126 | Tony Gwynn | 2.50 | 1.10 |
| ❑ 127 | Trevor Hoffman | .50 | .23 |
| ❑ 128 | Barry Bonds | 2.00 | .90 |
| ❑ 129 | Ellis Burks | .50 | .23 |
| ❑ 130 | Jeff Kent | .75 | .35 |
| ❑ 131 | J.T. Snow | .50 | .23 |
| ❑ 132 | Freddy Garcia | .50 | .23 |
| ❑ 133 | Ken Griffey Jr. | 5.00 | 2.20 |
| ❑ 134 | Edgar Martinez | .75 | .35 |
| ❑ 135 | John Olerud | .50 | .23 |
| ❑ 136 | Alex Rodriguez | 4.00 | 1.80 |
| ❑ 137 | Jose Canseco | 1.50 | .70 |
| ❑ 138 | Vinny Castilla | .50 | .23 |
| ❑ 139 | Roberto Hernandez | .30 | .14 |
| ❑ 140 | Fred McGriff | .75 | .35 |
| ❑ 141 | Rusty Greer | .50 | .23 |
| ❑ 142 | Ruben Mateo | .50 | .23 |
| ❑ 143 | Rafael Palmeiro | 1.25 | .55 |
| ❑ 144 | Ivan Rodriguez | 1.50 | .70 |
| ❑ 145 | Lee Stevens | .30 | .14 |
| ❑ 146 | Tony Batista | .50 | .23 |
| ❑ 147 | Carlos Delgado | 1.25 | .55 |
| ❑ 148 | Shannon Stewart | .50 | .23 |
| ❑ 149 | David Wells | .50 | .23 |
| ❑ 150 | Vernon Wells | .50 | .23 |

## 1999 Pacific Private Stock

| | | MINT | NRMT |
|---|---|---|---|
| | COMPLETE SET (150) | 80.00 | 36.00 |
| ❑ 1 | Jeff Bagwell | 1.25 | .55 |
| ❑ 2 | Roger Clemens | 2.00 | .90 |
| ❑ 3 | J.D. Drew | 1.00 | .45 |
| ❑ 4 | Nomar Garciaparra | 3.00 | 1.35 |
| ❑ 5 | Juan Gonzalez | 1.00 | .45 |
| ❑ 6 | Ken Griffey Jr. | 4.00 | 1.80 |
| ❑ 7 | Tony Gwynn | 2.00 | .90 |
| ❑ 8 | Derek Jeter | 4.00 | 1.80 |
| ❑ 9 | Chipper Jones | 2.50 | 1.10 |
| ❑ 10 | Travis Lee | .25 | .11 |
| ❑ 11 | Greg Maddux | 2.50 | 1.10 |
| ❑ 12 | Mark McGwire | 4.00 | 1.80 |
| ❑ 13 | Mike Piazza | 3.00 | 1.35 |
| ❑ 14 | Manny Ramirez | 1.25 | .55 |
| ❑ 15 | Cal Ripken | 4.00 | 1.80 |
| ❑ 16 | Alex Rodriguez | 3.00 | 1.35 |
| ❑ 17 | Ivan Rodriguez | 1.25 | .55 |
| ❑ 18 | Sammy Sosa | 2.00 | .90 |
| ❑ 19 | Frank Thomas | 2.00 | .90 |
| ❑ 20 | Kerry Wood | .40 | .18 |
| ❑ 21 | Roberto Alomar | 1.00 | .45 |
| ❑ 22 | Moises Alou | .40 | .18 |
| ❑ 23 | Albert Belle | .60 | .25 |
| ❑ 24 | Craig Biggio | .60 | .25 |
| ❑ 25 | Wade Boggs | 1.25 | .55 |
| ❑ 26 | Barry Bonds | 1.50 | .70 |
| ❑ 27 | Jose Canseco | 1.25 | .55 |
| ❑ 28 | Jim Edmonds | 1.00 | .45 |
| ❑ 29 | Darin Erstad | 1.00 | .45 |
| ❑ 30 | Andres Galarraga | .60 | .25 |
| ❑ 31 | Tom Glavine | 1.00 | .45 |
| ❑ 32 | Ben Grieve | .40 | .18 |
| ❑ 33 | Vladimir Guerrero | 1.50 | .70 |
| ❑ 34 | Wilton Guerrero | .25 | .11 |
| ❑ 35 | Todd Helton | 1.25 | .55 |
| ❑ 36 | Andruw Jones | 1.00 | .45 |
| ❑ 37 | Ryan Klesko | .40 | .18 |
| ❑ 38 | Kenny Lofton | .40 | .18 |
| ❑ 39 | Javy Lopez | .40 | .18 |
| ❑ 40 | Pedro Martinez | 1.25 | .55 |
| ❑ 41 | Paul Molitor | 1.00 | .45 |
| ❑ 42 | Raul Mondesi | .40 | .18 |
| ❑ 43 | Rafael Palmeiro | 1.00 | .45 |
| ❑ 44 | Tim Salmon | .40 | .18 |
| ❑ 45 | Jim Thome | .60 | .25 |
| ❑ 46 | Mo Vaughn | .40 | .18 |
| ❑ 47 | Larry Walker | .40 | .18 |
| ❑ 48 | David Wells | .40 | .18 |
| ❑ 49 | Bernie Williams | 1.00 | .45 |
| ❑ 50 | Jaret Wright | .25 | .11 |
| ❑ 51 | Bob Abreu | .40 | .18 |
| ❑ 52 | Garret Anderson | .40 | .18 |
| ❑ 53 | Rolando Arrojo | .25 | .11 |
| ❑ 54 | Tony Batista | .40 | .18 |
| ❑ 55 | Rod Beck | .25 | .11 |
| ❑ 56 | Derek Bell | .25 | .11 |
| ❑ 57 | Marvin Benard | .25 | .11 |
| ❑ 58 | Dave Berg | .25 | .11 |
| ❑ 59 | Dante Bichette | .40 | .18 |
| ❑ 60 | Aaron Boone | .25 | .11 |
| ❑ 61 | Bret Boone | .40 | .18 |
| ❑ 62 | Scott Brosius | .40 | .18 |

| | | |
|---|---|---|
| ❑ 63 Brant Brown | .25 | .11 |
| ❑ 64 Kevin Brown | .60 | .25 |
| ❑ 65 Jeromy Burnitz | .40 | .18 |
| ❑ 66 Ken Caminiti | .40 | .18 |
| ❑ 67 Mike Caruso | .25 | .11 |
| ❑ 68 Sean Casey | .40 | .18 |
| ❑ 69 Vinny Castilla | .40 | .18 |
| ❑ 70 Eric Chavez | .40 | .18 |
| ❑ 71 Ryan Christenson | .25 | .11 |
| ❑ 72 Jeff Cirillo | .40 | .18 |
| ❑ 73 Tony Clark | .25 | .11 |
| ❑ 74 Will Clark | 1.00 | .45 |
| ❑ 75 Edgard Clemente | .25 | .11 |
| ❑ 76 David Cone | .40 | .18 |
| ❑ 77 Marty Cordova | .25 | .11 |
| ❑ 78 Jose Cruz Jr. | .40 | .18 |
| ❑ 79 Eric Davis | .40 | .18 |
| ❑ 80 Carlos Delgado | 1.00 | .45 |
| ❑ 81 David Dellucci | .25 | .11 |
| ❑ 82 Delino DeShields | .25 | .11 |
| ❑ 83 Gary DiSarcina | .25 | .11 |
| ❑ 84 Damion Easley | .25 | .11 |
| ❑ 85 Dennis Eckersley | .40 | .18 |
| ❑ 86 Cliff Floyd | .40 | .18 |
| ❑ 87 Jason Giambi | 1.00 | .45 |
| ❑ 88 Doug Glanville | .25 | .11 |
| ❑ 89 Alex Gonzalez | .25 | .11 |
| ❑ 90 Mark Grace | 1.00 | .45 |
| ❑ 91 Rusty Greer | .40 | .18 |
| ❑ 92 Jose Guillen | .25 | .11 |
| ❑ 93 Carlos Guillen | .25 | .11 |
| ❑ 94 Jeffrey Hammonds | .40 | .18 |
| ❑ 95 Rick Helling | .40 | .18 |
| ❑ 96 Bob Henley | .25 | .11 |
| ❑ 97 Livan Hernandez | .25 | .11 |
| ❑ 98 Orlando Hernandez | .40 | .18 |
| ❑ 99 Bob Higginson | .40 | .18 |
| ❑ 100 Trevor Hoffman | .40 | .18 |
| ❑ 101 Randy Johnson | 1.25 | .55 |
| ❑ 102 Brian Jordan | .40 | .18 |
| ❑ 103 Wally Joyner | .40 | .18 |
| ❑ 104 Eric Karros | .40 | .18 |
| ❑ 105 Jason Kendall | .40 | .18 |
| ❑ 106 Jeff Kent | .60 | .25 |
| ❑ 107 Jeff King | .25 | .11 |
| ❑ 108 Mark Kotsay | .25 | .11 |
| ❑ 109 Ray Lankford | .40 | .18 |
| ❑ 110 Barry Larkin | 1.00 | .45 |
| ❑ 111 Mark Loretta | .25 | .11 |
| ❑ 112 Edgar Martinez | .60 | .25 |
| ❑ 113 Tino Martinez | .40 | .18 |
| ❑ 114 Quinton McCracken | .25 | .11 |
| ❑ 115 Fred McGriff | .60 | .25 |
| ❑ 116 Ryan Minor | .25 | .11 |
| ❑ 117 Hal Morris | .25 | .11 |
| ❑ 118 Bill Mueller | .25 | .11 |
| ❑ 119 Mike Mussina | 1.00 | .45 |
| ❑ 120 Dave Nilsson | .25 | .11 |
| ❑ 121 Otis Nixon | .25 | .11 |
| ❑ 122 Hideo Nomo | 1.00 | .45 |
| ❑ 123 Paul O'Neill | .40 | .18 |
| ❑ 124 Jose Offerman | .25 | .11 |
| ❑ 125 John Olerud | .40 | .18 |
| ❑ 126 Rey Ordonez | .25 | .11 |
| ❑ 127 David Ortiz | .25 | .11 |
| ❑ 128 Dean Palmer | .40 | .18 |
| ❑ 129 Chan Ho Park | .40 | .18 |
| ❑ 130 Aramis Ramirez | .25 | .11 |
| ❑ 131 Edgar Renteria | .25 | .11 |
| ❑ 132 Armando Rios | .25 | .11 |
| ❑ 133 Henry Rodriguez | .25 | .11 |
| ❑ 134 Scott Rolen | 1.00 | .45 |
| ❑ 135 Curt Schilling | .40 | .18 |
| ❑ 136 David Segui | .25 | .11 |
| ❑ 137 Richie Sexson | .40 | .18 |
| ❑ 138 Gary Sheffield | 1.00 | .45 |
| ❑ 139 John Smoltz | .40 | .18 |
| ❑ 140 Matt Stairs | .25 | .11 |
| ❑ 141 Justin Thompson | .25 | .11 |
| ❑ 142 Greg Vaughn | .40 | .18 |
| ❑ 143 Omar Vizquel | .40 | .18 |
| ❑ 144 Tim Wakefield | .25 | .11 |
| ❑ 145 Todd Walker | .25 | .11 |
| ❑ 146 Devon White | .25 | .11 |
| ❑ 147 Rondell White | .40 | .18 |
| ❑ 148 Matt Williams | .60 | .25 |
| ❑ 149 Enrique Wilson | .25 | .11 |
| ❑ 150 Kevin Young | .40 | .18 |

## 2000 Pacific Private Stock

| | MINT | NRMT |
|---|---|---|
| COMPLETE SET (150) | 200.00 | 90.00 |
| COMP.SET w/o SP's (125) | 50.00 | 22.00 |
| COMMON CARD (1-150) | .25 | .11 |
| COMMON SP PROSPECT | 5.00 | 2.20 |

| | | |
|---|---|---|
| ❑ 1 Darin Erstad | 1.00 | .45 |
| ❑ 2 Troy Glaus | 1.25 | .55 |
| ❑ 3 Tim Salmon | .40 | .18 |
| ❑ 4 Mo Vaughn | .40 | .18 |
| ❑ 5 Jay Bell | .40 | .18 |
| ❑ 6 Luis Gonzalez | .40 | .18 |
| ❑ 7 Randy Johnson | 1.25 | .55 |
| ❑ 8 Matt Williams | .60 | .25 |
| ❑ 9 Andruw Jones | 1.00 | .45 |
| ❑ 10 Chipper Jones | 2.50 | 1.10 |
| ❑ 11 Brian Jordan | .40 | .18 |
| ❑ 12 Greg Maddux | 2.50 | 1.10 |
| ❑ 13 Kevin Millwood | .40 | .18 |
| ❑ 14 Albert Belle | .60 | .25 |
| ❑ 15 Mike Mussina | 1.00 | .45 |
| ❑ 16 Cal Ripken | 4.00 | 1.80 |
| ❑ 17 B.J. Surhoff | .40 | .18 |
| ❑ 18 Nomar Garciaparra | 3.00 | 1.35 |
| ❑ 19 Butch Huskey | .25 | .11 |
| ❑ 20 Pedro Martinez | 1.25 | .55 |
| ❑ 21 Troy O'Leary | .25 | .11 |
| ❑ 22 Mark Grace | 1.00 | .45 |
| ❑ 23 Bo Porter SP | 5.00 | 2.20 |
| ❑ 24 Henry Rodriguez | .25 | .11 |
| ❑ 25 Sammy Sosa | 2.00 | .90 |
| ❑ 26 Kerry Wood | .40 | .18 |
| ❑ 27 Jason Dellaero SP | 5.00 | 2.20 |
| ❑ 28 Ray Durham | .40 | .18 |
| ❑ 29 Paul Konerko | .40 | .18 |
| ❑ 30 Carlos Lee | .40 | .18 |
| ❑ 31 Magglio Ordonez | .40 | .18 |
| ❑ 32 Frank Thomas | 2.00 | .90 |
| ❑ 33 Mike Cameron | .25 | .11 |
| ❑ 34 Sean Casey | .40 | .18 |
| ❑ 35 Barry Larkin | 1.00 | .45 |
| ❑ 36 Greg Vaughn | .40 | .18 |
| ❑ 37 Roberto Alomar | 1.00 | .45 |
| ❑ 38 Russell Branyan SP | 5.00 | 2.20 |
| ❑ 39 Kenny Lofton | .40 | .18 |
| ❑ 40 Manny Ramirez | 1.25 | .55 |
| ❑ 41 Richie Sexson | .40 | .18 |
| ❑ 42 Jim Thome | .60 | .25 |
| ❑ 43 Omar Vizquel | .40 | .18 |
| ❑ 44 Pedro Astacio | .25 | .11 |
| ❑ 45 Vinny Castilla | .40 | .18 |
| ❑ 46 Todd Helton | 1.25 | .55 |
| ❑ 47 Ben Petrick SP | 5.00 | 2.20 |
| ❑ 48 Juan Sosa SP RC | 5.00 | 2.20 |
| ❑ 49 Larry Walker | .40 | .18 |
| ❑ 50 Tony Clark | .25 | .11 |
| ❑ 51 Damion Easley | .25 | .11 |
| ❑ 52 Juan Encarnacion | .40 | .18 |
| ❑ 53 Robert Fick SP | 5.00 | 2.20 |
| ❑ 54 Dean Palmer | .40 | .18 |
| ❑ 55 A.J. Burnett SP | 5.00 | 2.20 |
| ❑ 56 Luis Castillo | .40 | .18 |
| ❑ 57 Alex Gonzalez | .25 | .11 |
| ❑ 58 Julio Ramirez SP | 5.00 | 2.20 |
| ❑ 59 Preston Wilson | .40 | .18 |
| ❑ 60 Jeff Bagwell | 1.25 | .55 |
| ❑ 61 Craig Biggio | .60 | .25 |
| ❑ 62 Ken Caminiti | .40 | .18 |
| ❑ 63 Carl Everett | .40 | .18 |
| ❑ 64 Mike Hampton | .40 | .18 |
| ❑ 65 Billy Wagner | .25 | .11 |
| ❑ 66 Carlos Beltran | .40 | .18 |
| ❑ 67 Dermal Brown SP | 5.00 | 2.20 |
| ❑ 68 Jermaine Dye | .40 | .18 |
| ❑ 69 Carlos Febles | .25 | .11 |
| ❑ 70 Mark Quinn SP | 5.00 | 2.20 |
| ❑ 71 Mike Sweeney | .40 | .18 |
| ❑ 72 Kevin Brown | .60 | .25 |
| ❑ 73 Eric Gagne SP | 5.00 | 2.20 |
| ❑ 74 Eric Karros | .40 | .18 |
| ❑ 75 Raul Mondesi | .40 | .18 |
| ❑ 76 Gary Sheffield | 1.00 | .45 |
| ❑ 77 Jeromy Burnitz | .40 | .18 |
| ❑ 78 Jeff Cirillo | .40 | .18 |
| ❑ 79 Geoff Jenkins | .40 | .18 |
| ❑ 80 David Nilsson | .25 | .11 |
| ❑ 81 Ron Coomer | .25 | .11 |
| ❑ 82 Jacque Jones | .40 | .18 |
| ❑ 83 Corey Koskie | .25 | .11 |
| ❑ 84 Brad Radke | .40 | .18 |
| ❑ 85 Tony Armas Jr. SP | 5.00 | 2.20 |
| ❑ 86 Peter Bergeron SP | 5.00 | 2.20 |
| ❑ 87 Vladimir Guerrero | 1.50 | .70 |
| ❑ 88 Jose Vidro | .25 | .11 |
| ❑ 89 Rondell White | .40 | .18 |
| ❑ 90 Edgardo Alfonzo | .40 | .18 |
| ❑ 91 Roger Cedeno | .25 | .11 |
| ❑ 92 Rickey Henderson | 1.25 | .55 |
| ❑ 93 Jay Payton SP | 5.00 | 2.20 |
| ❑ 94 Mike Piazza | 3.00 | 1.35 |
| ❑ 95 Jorge Toca SP | 5.00 | 2.20 |
| ❑ 96 Robin Ventura | .60 | .25 |
| ❑ 97 Roger Clemens | 2.00 | .90 |
| ❑ 98 David Cone | .40 | .18 |
| ❑ 99 Derek Jeter | 4.00 | 1.80 |
| ❑ 100 D'Angelo Jimenez SP | 5.00 | 2.20 |
| ❑ 101 Tino Martinez | .40 | .18 |
| ❑ 102 Alfonso Soriano SP | 6.00 | 2.70 |
| ❑ 103 Bernie Williams | 1.00 | .45 |
| ❑ 104 Jason Giambi | 1.00 | .45 |
| ❑ 105 Ben Grieve | .40 | .18 |
| ❑ 106 Tim Hudson | 1.00 | .45 |
| ❑ 107 Matt Stairs | .25 | .11 |
| ❑ 108 Bob Abreu | .40 | .18 |
| ❑ 109 Doug Glanville | .25 | .11 |
| ❑ 110 Scott Rolen | 1.00 | .45 |
| ❑ 111 Curt Schilling | .40 | .18 |
| ❑ 112 Brian Giles | .40 | .18 |
| ❑ 113 Chad Hermansen SP | 5.00 | 2.20 |
| ❑ 114 Jason Kendall | .40 | .18 |
| ❑ 115 Warren Morris | .25 | .11 |
| ❑ 116 Rick Ankiel SP | 20.00 | 9.00 |
| ❑ 117 J.D. Drew | 1.00 | .45 |
| ❑ 118 Adam Kennedy SP | 5.00 | 2.20 |
| ❑ 119 Ray Lankford | .40 | .18 |
| ❑ 120 Mark McGwire | 4.00 | 1.80 |
| ❑ 121 Fernando Tatis | .40 | .18 |
| ❑ 122 Mike Darr SP | 5.00 | 2.20 |
| ❑ 123 Ben Davis | .25 | .11 |
| ❑ 124 Tony Gwynn | 2.00 | .90 |
| ❑ 125 Trevor Hoffman | .40 | .18 |
| ❑ 126 Reggie Sanders | .25 | .11 |
| ❑ 127 Barry Bonds | 1.50 | .70 |
| ❑ 128 Ellis Burks | .40 | .18 |
| ❑ 129 Jeff Kent | .60 | .25 |
| ❑ 130 J.T. Snow | .40 | .18 |
| ❑ 131 Freddy Garcia | .40 | .18 |
| ❑ 132 Ken Griffey Jr. | 4.00 | 1.80 |
| ❑ 133 Carlos Guillen SP | 5.00 | 2.20 |
| ❑ 134 Edgar Martinez | .60 | .25 |
| ❑ 135 Alex Rodriguez | 3.00 | 1.35 |
| ❑ 136 Miguel Cairo | .25 | .11 |
| ❑ 137 Jose Canseco | 1.25 | .55 |
| ❑ 138 Steve Cox SP | 5.00 | 2.20 |
| ❑ 139 Roberto Hernandez | .25 | .11 |
| ❑ 140 Fred McGriff | .60 | .25 |
| ❑ 141 Juan Gonzalez | 1.00 | .45 |
| ❑ 142 Rusty Greer | .40 | .18 |

| | | MINT | NRMT |
|---|---|---|---|
| ❑ 143 | Ruben Mateo SP | 5.00 | 2.20 |
| ❑ 144 | Rafael Palmeiro | 1.00 | .45 |
| ❑ 145 | Ivan Rodriguez | 1.25 | .55 |
| ❑ 146 | Carlos Delgado | 1.00 | .45 |
| ❑ 147 | Tony Fernandez | .25 | .11 |
| ❑ 148 | Shawn Green | 1.00 | .45 |
| ❑ 149 | Shannon Stewart | .40 | .18 |
| ❑ 150 | Vernon Wells SP | 5.00 | 2.20 |

## 2001 Pacific Private Stock

| | MINT | NRMT |
|---|---|---|
| COMPLETE SET (150) | 200.00 | 90.00 |
| COMP.SET w/o SP's (125) | 50.00 | 22.00 |

| | | MINT | NRMT |
|---|---|---|---|
| ❑ 1 | Darin Erstad | 1.00 | .45 |
| ❑ 2 | Troy Glaus | 1.25 | .55 |
| ❑ 3 | Tim Salmon | .40 | .18 |
| ❑ 4 | Mo Vaughn | .40 | .18 |
| ❑ 5 | Steve Finley | .40 | .18 |
| ❑ 6 | Luis Gonzalez | .40 | .18 |
| ❑ 7 | Randy Johnson | 1.25 | .55 |
| ❑ 8 | Matt Williams | .60 | .25 |
| ❑ 9 | Rafael Furcal | 1.50 | .70 |
| ❑ 10 | Andres Galarraga | .60 | .25 |
| ❑ 11 | Tom Glavine | .75 | .35 |
| ❑ 12 | Andruw Jones | 1.00 | .45 |
| ❑ 13 | Chipper Jones | 2.50 | 1.10 |
| ❑ 14 | Greg Maddux | 2.50 | 1.10 |
| ❑ 15 | B.J. Surhoff | .40 | .18 |
| ❑ 16 | Brady Anderson | .40 | .18 |
| ❑ 17 | Albert Belle | .60 | .25 |
| ❑ 18 | Mike Mussina | 1.00 | .45 |
| ❑ 19 | Cal Ripken | 4.00 | 1.80 |
| ❑ 20 | Carl Everett | .40 | .18 |
| ❑ 21 | Nomar Garciaparra | 3.00 | 1.35 |
| ❑ 22 | Pedro Martinez | 1.25 | .55 |
| ❑ 23 | Mark Grace | 1.00 | .45 |
| ❑ 24 | Sammy Sosa | 2.00 | .90 |
| ❑ 25 | Kerry Wood | .40 | .18 |
| ❑ 26 | Carlos Lee | .40 | .18 |
| ❑ 27 | Magglio Ordonez | .40 | .18 |
| ❑ 28 | Frank Thomas | 2.00 | .90 |
| ❑ 29 | Sean Casey | .40 | .18 |
| ❑ 30 | Ken Griffey Jr. | 4.00 | 1.80 |
| ❑ 31 | Barry Larkin | .75 | .35 |
| ❑ 32 | Pokey Reese | .40 | .18 |
| ❑ 33 | Roberto Alomar | 1.00 | .45 |
| ❑ 34 | Kenny Lofton | .40 | .18 |
| ❑ 35 | Manny Ramirez | 1.25 | .55 |
| ❑ 36 | Jim Thome | .40 | .18 |
| ❑ 37 | Omar Vizquel | .40 | .18 |
| ❑ 38 | Jeff Cirillo | .40 | .18 |
| ❑ 39 | Jeffrey Hammonds | .40 | .18 |
| ❑ 40 | Todd Helton | 1.25 | .55 |
| ❑ 41 | Larry Walker | .40 | .18 |
| ❑ 42 | Tony Clark | .25 | .11 |
| ❑ 43 | Juan Encarnacion | .40 | .18 |
| ❑ 44 | Juan Gonzalez | .75 | .35 |
| ❑ 45 | Hideo Nomo | 1.00 | .45 |
| ❑ 46 | Cliff Floyd | .40 | .18 |
| ❑ 47 | Derek Lee | .25 | .11 |
| ❑ 48 | Henry Rodriguez | .25 | .11 |
| ❑ 49 | Preston Wilson | .40 | .18 |
| ❑ 50 | Jeff Bagwell | 1.25 | .55 |
| ❑ 51 | Craig Biggio | .60 | .25 |
| ❑ 52 | Richard Hidalgo | .40 | .18 |
| ❑ 53 | Moises Alou | .40 | .18 |
| ❑ 54 | Carlos Beltran | .25 | .11 |
| ❑ 55 | Johnny Damon | .40 | .18 |
| ❑ 56 | Jermaine Dye | .40 | .18 |
| ❑ 57 | Mac Suzuki | .25 | .11 |
| ❑ 58 | Mike Sweeney | .40 | .18 |
| ❑ 59 | Adrian Beltre | .40 | .18 |
| ❑ 60 | Kevin Brown | .40 | .18 |
| ❑ 61 | Shawn Green | .75 | .35 |
| ❑ 62 | Eric Karros | .40 | .18 |
| ❑ 63 | Chan Ho Park | .40 | .18 |
| ❑ 64 | Gary Sheffield | .75 | .35 |
| ❑ 65 | Jeromy Burnitz | .40 | .18 |
| ❑ 66 | Geoff Jenkins | .40 | .18 |
| ❑ 67 | Richie Sexson | .40 | .18 |
| ❑ 68 | Jacque Jones | .40 | .18 |
| ❑ 69 | Matt Lawton | .40 | .18 |
| ❑ 70 | Eric Milton | .40 | .18 |
| ❑ 71 | Vladimir Guerrero | 1.50 | .70 |
| ❑ 72 | Jose Vidro | .40 | .18 |
| ❑ 73 | Edgardo Alfonzo | .40 | .18 |
| ❑ 74 | Mike Hampton | .40 | .18 |
| ❑ 75 | Mike Piazza | 3.00 | 1.35 |
| ❑ 76 | Robin Ventura | .40 | .18 |
| ❑ 77 | Jose Canseco | 1.25 | .55 |
| ❑ 78 | Roger Clemens | 2.00 | .90 |
| ❑ 79 | Derek Jeter | 4.00 | 1.80 |
| ❑ 80 | David Justice | .60 | .25 |
| ❑ 81 | Jorge Posada | .40 | .18 |
| ❑ 82 | Bernie Williams | .75 | .35 |
| ❑ 83 | Jason Giambi | 1.00 | .45 |
| ❑ 84 | Ben Grieve | .40 | .18 |
| ❑ 85 | Tim Hudson | .75 | .35 |
| ❑ 86 | Terrence Long | .40 | .18 |
| ❑ 87 | Miguel Tejada | .60 | .25 |
| ❑ 88 | Bob Abreu | .40 | .18 |
| ❑ 89 | Pat Burrell | 1.00 | .45 |
| ❑ 90 | Mike Lieberthal | .40 | .18 |
| ❑ 91 | Scott Rolen | .75 | .35 |
| ❑ 92 | Kris Benson | .40 | .18 |
| ❑ 93 | Brian Giles | .40 | .18 |
| ❑ 94 | Jason Kendall | .40 | .18 |
| ❑ 95 | Aramis Ramirez | .25 | .11 |
| ❑ 96 | Rick Ankiel | 1.25 | .55 |
| ❑ 97 | Will Clark | 1.00 | .45 |
| ❑ 98 | J.D. Drew | .75 | .35 |
| ❑ 99 | Jim Edmonds | 1.00 | .45 |
| ❑ 100 | Mark McGwire | 4.00 | 1.80 |
| ❑ 101 | Fernando Tatis | .40 | .18 |
| ❑ 102 | Adam Eaton | .40 | .18 |
| ❑ 103 | Tony Gwynn | 2.00 | .90 |
| ❑ 104 | Phil Nevin | .40 | .18 |
| ❑ 105 | Eric Owens | .25 | .11 |
| ❑ 106 | Barry Bonds | 1.50 | .70 |
| ❑ 107 | Jeff Kent | .60 | .25 |
| ❑ 108 | J.T. Snow | .40 | .18 |
| ❑ 109 | Rickey Henderson | 1.25 | .55 |
| ❑ 110 | Edgar Martinez | .60 | .25 |
| ❑ 111 | John Olerud | .40 | .18 |
| ❑ 112 | Alex Rodriguez | 3.00 | 1.35 |
| ❑ 113 | Kazuhiro Sasaki | 1.25 | .55 |
| ❑ 114 | Vinny Castilla | .40 | .18 |
| ❑ 115 | Fred McGriff | .60 | .25 |
| ❑ 116 | Greg Vaughn | .40 | .18 |
| ❑ 117 | Gabe Kapler | .40 | .18 |
| ❑ 118 | Ruben Mateo | .40 | .18 |
| ❑ 119 | Rafael Palmeiro | .75 | .35 |
| ❑ 120 | Ivan Rodriguez | 1.25 | .55 |
| ❑ 121 | Tony Batista | .40 | .18 |
| ❑ 122 | Jose Cruz Jr. | .40 | .18 |
| ❑ 123 | Carlos Delgado | 1.00 | .45 |
| ❑ 124 | Shannon Stewart | .40 | .18 |
| ❑ 125 | David Wells | .40 | .18 |
| ❑ 126 | Shawn Wooten SP | 5.00 | 2.20 |
| ❑ 127 | George Lombard SP | 5.00 | 2.20 |
| ❑ 128 | Morgan Burkhart SP | 5.00 | 2.20 |
| ❑ 129 | Ross Gload SP | 5.00 | 2.20 |
| ❑ 130 | Corey Patterson SP | 10.00 | 4.50 |
| ❑ 131 | Julio Zuleta SP | 5.00 | 2.20 |
| ❑ 132 | Joe Crede SP | 8.00 | 3.60 |
| ❑ 133 | Matt Ginter SP | 5.00 | 2.20 |
| ❑ 134 | Travis Dawkins SP | 5.00 | 2.20 |
| ❑ 135 | Eric Munson SP | 8.00 | 3.60 |
| ❑ 136 | Dee Brown SP | 5.00 | 2.20 |
| ❑ 137 | Luke Prokopec SP | 5.00 | 2.20 |
| ❑ 138 | Timo Perez SP | 8.00 | 3.60 |
| ❑ 139 | Alfonso Soriano SP | 5.00 | 2.20 |
| ❑ 140 | Jake Westbrook SP | 5.00 | 2.20 |
| ❑ 141 | Eric Byrnes SP | 5.00 | 2.20 |
| ❑ 142 | Adam Hyzdu SP | 5.00 | 2.20 |
| ❑ 143 | Jimmy Rollins SP | 5.00 | 2.20 |
| ❑ 144 | Xavier Nady SP | 15.00 | 6.75 |
| ❑ 145 | Ryan Vogelsong SP | 5.00 | 2.20 |
| ❑ 146 | Joel Pineiro SP | 8.00 | 3.60 |
| ❑ 147 | Aubrey Huff SP | 5.00 | 2.20 |
| ❑ 148 | Kenny Kelly SP | 5.00 | 2.20 |
| ❑ 149 | Josh Phelps SP | 5.00 | 2.20 |
| ❑ 150 | Vernon Wells SP | 8.00 | 3.60 |

## 2000 Pacific Vanguard

| | MINT | NRMT |
|---|---|---|
| COMPLETE SET (100) | 80.00 | 36.00 |

| | | MINT | NRMT |
|---|---|---|---|
| ❑ 1 | Troy Glaus | 1.50 | .70 |
| ❑ 2 | Tim Salmon | .50 | .23 |
| ❑ 3 | Mo Vaughn | .50 | .23 |
| ❑ 4 | Albert Belle | .75 | .35 |
| ❑ 5 | Mike Mussina | 1.25 | .55 |
| ❑ 6 | Cal Ripken | 5.00 | 2.20 |
| ❑ 7 | Nomar Garciaparra | 4.00 | 1.80 |
| ❑ 8 | Pedro Martinez | 1.50 | .70 |
| ❑ 9 | Troy O'Leary | .30 | .14 |
| ❑ 10 | Wilton Veras | .50 | .23 |
| ❑ 11 | Magglio Ordonez | .50 | .23 |
| ❑ 12 | Chris Singleton | .50 | .23 |
| ❑ 13 | Frank Thomas | 2.50 | 1.10 |
| ❑ 14 | Roberto Alomar | 1.25 | .55 |
| ❑ 15 | Russell Branyan | .50 | .23 |
| ❑ 16 | Manny Ramirez | 1.50 | .70 |
| ❑ 17 | Jim Thome | .75 | .35 |
| ❑ 18 | Omar Vizquel | .50 | .23 |
| ❑ 19 | Tony Clark | .30 | .14 |
| ❑ 20 | Juan Gonzalez | 1.25 | .55 |
| ❑ 21 | Dean Palmer | .50 | .23 |
| ❑ 22 | Carlos Beltran | .50 | .23 |
| ❑ 23 | Johnny Damon | .50 | .23 |
| ❑ 24 | Jermaine Dye | .50 | .23 |
| ❑ 25 | Mark Quinn | .50 | .23 |
| ❑ 26 | Jacque Jones | .50 | .23 |
| ❑ 27 | Corey Koskie | .30 | .14 |
| ❑ 28 | Brad Radke | .50 | .23 |
| ❑ 29 | Roger Clemens | 2.50 | 1.10 |
| ❑ 30 | Derek Jeter | 5.00 | 2.20 |
| ❑ 31 | Alfonso Soriano | .50 | .23 |
| ❑ 32 | Bernie Williams | 1.25 | .55 |
| ❑ 33 | Eric Chavez | .50 | .23 |
| ❑ 34 | Jason Giambi | 1.25 | .55 |
| ❑ 35 | Ben Grieve | .50 | .23 |
| ❑ 36 | Tim Hudson | 1.25 | .55 |
| ❑ 37 | Mike Cameron | .30 | .14 |
| ❑ 38 | Freddy Garcia | .50 | .23 |
| ❑ 39 | Edgar Martinez | .75 | .35 |
| ❑ 40 | Alex Rodriguez | 4.00 | 1.80 |
| ❑ 41 | Jose Canseco | 1.50 | .70 |
| ❑ 42 | Vinny Castilla | .50 | .23 |
| ❑ 43 | Fred McGriff | .75 | .35 |
| ❑ 44 | Rusty Greer | .50 | .23 |
| ❑ 45 | Ruben Mateo | .50 | .23 |
| ❑ 46 | Rafael Palmeiro | 1.25 | .55 |
| ❑ 47 | Ivan Rodriguez | 1.50 | .70 |
| ❑ 48 | Carlos Delgado | 1.25 | .55 |
| ❑ 49 | Shannon Stewart | .50 | .23 |
| ❑ 50 | Vernon Wells | .50 | .23 |
| ❑ 51 | Erubiel Durazo | .50 | .23 |
| ❑ 52 | Randy Johnson | 1.50 | .70 |
| ❑ 53 | Matt Williams | .75 | .35 |
| ❑ 54 | Andruw Jones | 1.25 | .55 |
| ❑ 55 | Chipper Jones | 3.00 | 1.35 |
| ❑ 56 | Greg Maddux | 3.00 | 1.35 |
| ❑ 57 | Mark Grace | 1.25 | .55 |
| ❑ 58 | Sammy Sosa | 2.50 | 1.10 |
| ❑ 59 | Kerry Wood | .50 | .23 |
| ❑ 60 | Sean Casey | .50 | .23 |
| ❑ 61 | Ken Griffey Jr. | 5.00 | 2.20 |
| ❑ 62 | Barry Larkin | 1.25 | .55 |
| ❑ 63 | Todd Helton | 1.50 | .70 |

|  | | |
|---|---|---|
| ❑ 64 Ben Petrick | .30 | .14 |
| ❑ 65 Larry Walker | .50 | .23 |
| ❑ 66 Luis Castillo | .50 | .23 |
| ❑ 67 Alex Gonzalez | .30 | .14 |
| ❑ 68 Preston Wilson | .50 | .23 |
| ❑ 69 Jeff Bagwell | 1.50 | .70 |
| ❑ 70 Craig Biggio | .75 | .35 |
| ❑ 71 Billy Wagner | .30 | .14 |
| ❑ 72 Kevin Brown | .75 | .35 |
| ❑ 73 Shawn Green | 1.25 | .55 |
| ❑ 74 Gary Sheffield | 1.25 | .55 |
| ❑ 75 Kevin Barker | .30 | .14 |
| ❑ 76 Ron Belliard | .30 | .14 |
| ❑ 77 Jeromy Burnitz | .50 | .23 |
| ❑ 78 Michael Barrett | .30 | .14 |
| ❑ 79 Peter Bergeron | .30 | .14 |
| ❑ 80 Vladimir Guerrero | 2.00 | .90 |
| ❑ 81 Edgardo Alfonzo | .50 | .23 |
| ❑ 82 Rey Ordonez | .30 | .14 |
| ❑ 83 Mike Piazza | 4.00 | 1.80 |
| ❑ 84 Robin Ventura | .75 | .35 |
| ❑ 85 Bobby Abreu | .50 | .23 |
| ❑ 86 Mike Lieberthal | .50 | .23 |
| ❑ 87 Scott Rolen | 1.25 | .55 |
| ❑ 88 Brian Giles | .50 | .23 |
| ❑ 89 Chad Hermansen | .30 | .14 |
| ❑ 90 Jason Kendall | .50 | .23 |
| ❑ 91 Rick Ankiel | 2.50 | 1.10 |
| ❑ 92 J.D. Drew | 1.25 | .55 |
| ❑ 93 Mark McGwire | 5.00 | 2.20 |
| ❑ 94 Fernando Tatis | .50 | .23 |
| ❑ 95 Ben Davis | .30 | .14 |
| ❑ 96 Tony Gwynn | 2.50 | 1.10 |
| ❑ 97 Trevor Hoffman | .50 | .23 |
| ❑ 98 Barry Bonds | 2.00 | .90 |
| ❑ 99 Ellis Burks | .50 | .23 |
| ❑ 100 Jeff Kent | .75 | .35 |
| ❑ SAMP Tony Gwynn | 2.00 | .90 |

## 1998 Paramount

| | MINT | NRMT |
|---|---|---|
| COMPLETE SET (250) | 30.00 | 13.50 |
| COMMON CARD (1-250) | .10 | .05 |
| ❑ 1 Garret Anderson | .15 | .07 |
| ❑ 2 Gary DiSarcina | .10 | .05 |
| ❑ 3 Jim Edmonds | .40 | .18 |
| ❑ 4 Darin Erstad | .40 | .18 |
| ❑ 5 Cecil Fielder | .15 | .07 |
| ❑ 6 Chuck Finley | .15 | .07 |
| ❑ 7 Todd Greene | .10 | .05 |
| ❑ 8 Shigetoshi Hasegawa | .15 | .07 |
| ❑ 9 Tim Salmon | .15 | .07 |
| ❑ 10 Roberto Alomar | .40 | .18 |
| ❑ 11 Brady Anderson | .15 | .07 |
| ❑ 12 Joe Carter | .15 | .07 |
| ❑ 13 Eric Davis | .15 | .07 |
| ❑ 14 Ozzie Guillen | .10 | .05 |
| ❑ 15 Mike Mussina | .40 | .18 |
| ❑ 16 Rafael Palmeiro | .40 | .18 |
| ❑ 17 Cal Ripken | 1.50 | .70 |
| ❑ 18 B.J. Surhoff | .15 | .07 |
| ❑ 19 Steve Avery | .10 | .05 |
| ❑ 20 Nomar Garciaparra | 1.25 | .55 |
| ❑ 21 Reggie Jefferson | .10 | .05 |
| ❑ 22 Pedro Martinez | .50 | .23 |
| ❑ 23 Tim Naehring | .10 | .05 |
| ❑ 24 John Valentin | .10 | .05 |
| ❑ 25 Mo Vaughn | .15 | .07 |
| ❑ 26 James Baldwin | .10 | .05 |
| ❑ 27 Albert Belle | .25 | .11 |
| ❑ 28 Ray Durham | .15 | .07 |
| ❑ 29 Benji Gil | .10 | .05 |
| ❑ 30 Jaime Navarro | .10 | .05 |
| ❑ 31 Magglio Ordonez RC | 1.50 | .70 |
| ❑ 32 Frank Thomas | .75 | .35 |
| ❑ 33 Robin Ventura | .15 | .07 |
| ❑ 34 Sandy Alomar Jr. | .15 | .07 |
| ❑ 35 Geronimo Berroa | .10 | .05 |
| ❑ 36 Travis Fryman | .15 | .07 |
| ❑ 37 David Justice | .25 | .11 |
| ❑ 38 Kenny Lofton | .15 | .07 |
| ❑ 39 Charles Nagy | .10 | .05 |
| ❑ 40 Manny Ramirez | .50 | .23 |
| ❑ 41 Jim Thome | .25 | .11 |
| ❑ 42 Omar Vizquel | .15 | .07 |
| ❑ 43 Jaret Wright | .10 | .05 |
| ❑ 44 Raul Casanova | .10 | .05 |
| ❑ 45 Frank Catalanotto RC | .25 | .11 |
| ❑ 46 Tony Clark | .10 | .05 |
| ❑ 47 Bobby Higginson | .15 | .07 |
| ❑ 48 Brian Hunter | .10 | .05 |
| ❑ 49 Todd Jones | .10 | .05 |
| ❑ 50 Bip Roberts | .10 | .05 |
| ❑ 51 Justin Thompson | .10 | .05 |
| ❑ 52 Kevin Appier | .15 | .07 |
| ❑ 53 Johnny Damon | .15 | .07 |
| ❑ 54 Jermaine Dye | .15 | .07 |
| ❑ 55 Jeff King | .10 | .05 |
| ❑ 56 Jeff Montgomery | .10 | .05 |
| ❑ 57 Dean Palmer | .15 | .07 |
| ❑ 58 Jose Rosado | .10 | .05 |
| ❑ 59 Larry Sutton | .10 | .05 |
| ❑ 60 Rick Aguilera | .10 | .05 |
| ❑ 61 Marty Cordova | .10 | .05 |
| ❑ 62 Pat Meares | .10 | .05 |
| ❑ 63 Paul Molitor | .40 | .18 |
| ❑ 64 Otis Nixon | .10 | .05 |
| ❑ 65 Brad Radke | .15 | .07 |
| ❑ 66 Terry Steinbach | .10 | .05 |
| ❑ 67 Todd Walker | .10 | .05 |
| ❑ 68 Hideki Irabu | .10 | .05 |
| ❑ 69 Derek Jeter | 1.50 | .70 |
| ❑ 70 Chuck Knoblauch | .15 | .07 |
| ❑ 71 Tino Martinez | .15 | .07 |
| ❑ 72 Paul O'Neill | .15 | .07 |
| ❑ 73 Andy Pettitte | .15 | .07 |
| ❑ 74 Mariano Rivera | .15 | .07 |
| ❑ 75 Bernie Williams | .40 | .18 |
| ❑ 76 Mark Bellhorn | .10 | .05 |
| ❑ 77 Tom Candiotti | .10 | .05 |
| ❑ 78 Jason Giambi | .40 | .18 |
| ❑ 79 Ben Grieve | .15 | .07 |
| ❑ 80 Rickey Henderson | .50 | .23 |
| ❑ 81 Jason McDonald | .10 | .05 |
| ❑ 82 Aaron Small | .10 | .05 |
| ❑ 83 Miguel Tejada | .40 | .18 |
| ❑ 84 Jay Buhner | .15 | .07 |
| ❑ 85 Joey Cora | .10 | .05 |
| ❑ 86 Jeff Fassero | .10 | .05 |
| ❑ 87 Ken Griffey Jr. | 1.50 | .70 |
| ❑ 88 Randy Johnson | .50 | .23 |
| ❑ 89 Edgar Martinez | .25 | .11 |
| ❑ 90 Alex Rodriguez | 1.25 | .55 |
| ❑ 91 David Segui | .10 | .05 |
| ❑ 92 Dan Wilson | .10 | .05 |
| ❑ 93 Wilson Alvarez | .10 | .05 |
| ❑ 94 Wade Boggs | .50 | .23 |
| ❑ 95 Miguel Cairo | .10 | .05 |
| ❑ 96 John Flaherty | .10 | .05 |
| ❑ 97 Dave Martinez | .10 | .05 |
| ❑ 98 Quinton McCracken | .10 | .05 |
| ❑ 99 Fred McGriff | .25 | .11 |
| ❑ 100 Paul Sorrento | .10 | .05 |
| ❑ 101 Kevin Stocker | .10 | .05 |
| ❑ 102 John Burkett | .10 | .05 |
| ❑ 103 Will Clark | .40 | .18 |
| ❑ 104 Juan Gonzalez | .40 | .18 |
| ❑ 105 Rusty Greer | .15 | .07 |
| ❑ 106 Roberto Kelly | .10 | .05 |
| ❑ 107 Ivan Rodriguez | .50 | .23 |
| ❑ 108 Fernando Tatis | .15 | .07 |
| ❑ 109 John Wetteland | .15 | .07 |
| ❑ 110 Jose Canseco | .50 | .23 |
| ❑ 111 Roger Clemens | .75 | .35 |
| ❑ 112 Jose Cruz Jr. | .15 | .07 |
| ❑ 113 Carlos Delgado | .40 | .18 |
| ❑ 114 Alex Gonzalez | .10 | .05 |
| ❑ 115 Pat Hentgen | .10 | .05 |
| ❑ 116 Ed Sprague | .10 | .05 |
| ❑ 117 Shannon Stewart | .15 | .07 |
| ❑ 118 Brian Anderson | .10 | .05 |
| ❑ 119 Jay Bell | .15 | .07 |
| ❑ 120 Andy Benes | .10 | .05 |
| ❑ 121 Yamil Benitez | .10 | .05 |
| ❑ 122 Jorge Fabregas | .10 | .05 |
| ❑ 123 Travis Lee | .15 | .07 |
| ❑ 124 Devon White | .10 | .05 |
| ❑ 125 Matt Williams | .25 | .11 |
| ❑ 126 Bob Wolcott | .10 | .05 |
| ❑ 127 Andres Galarraga | .25 | .11 |
| ❑ 128 Tom Glavine | .40 | .18 |
| ❑ 129 Andruw Jones | .40 | .18 |
| ❑ 130 Chipper Jones | 1.00 | .45 |
| ❑ 131 Ryan Klesko | .15 | .07 |
| ❑ 132 Javy Lopez | .15 | .07 |
| ❑ 133 Greg Maddux | 1.00 | .45 |
| ❑ 134 Denny Neagle | .10 | .05 |
| ❑ 135 John Smoltz | .15 | .07 |
| ❑ 136 Rod Beck | .10 | .05 |
| ❑ 137 Jeff Blauser | .10 | .05 |
| ❑ 138 Mark Grace | .40 | .18 |
| ❑ 139 Lance Johnson | .10 | .05 |
| ❑ 140 Mickey Morandini | .10 | .05 |
| ❑ 141 Kevin Orie | .10 | .05 |
| ❑ 142 Sammy Sosa | .75 | .35 |
| ❑ 143 Aaron Boone | .10 | .05 |
| ❑ 144 Bret Boone | .15 | .07 |
| ❑ 145 Dave Burba | .10 | .05 |
| ❑ 146 Lenny Harris | .10 | .05 |
| ❑ 147 Barry Larkin | .40 | .18 |
| ❑ 148 Reggie Sanders | .10 | .05 |
| ❑ 149 Brett Tomko | .10 | .05 |
| ❑ 150 Pedro Astacio | .10 | .05 |
| ❑ 151 Dante Bichette | .15 | .07 |
| ❑ 152 Ellis Burks | .15 | .07 |
| ❑ 153 Vinny Castilla | .15 | .07 |
| ❑ 154 Todd Helton | .50 | .23 |
| ❑ 155 Darryl Kile | .15 | .07 |
| ❑ 156 Jeff Reed | .10 | .05 |
| ❑ 157 Larry Walker | .15 | .07 |
| ❑ 158 Bobby Bonilla | .15 | .07 |
| ❑ 159 Todd Dunwoody | .10 | .05 |
| ❑ 160 Livan Hernandez | .10 | .05 |
| ❑ 161 Charles Johnson | .15 | .07 |
| ❑ 162 Mark Kotsay | .15 | .07 |
| ❑ 163 Derrek Lee | .10 | .05 |
| ❑ 164 Edgar Renteria | .10 | .05 |
| ❑ 165 Gary Sheffield | .40 | .18 |
| ❑ 166 Moises Alou | .15 | .07 |
| ❑ 167 Jeff Bagwell | .50 | .23 |
| ❑ 168 Derek Bell | .10 | .05 |
| ❑ 169 Craig Biggio | .25 | .11 |
| ❑ 170 Mike Hampton | .15 | .07 |
| ❑ 171 Richard Hidalgo | .15 | .07 |
| ❑ 172 Chris Holt | .10 | .05 |
| ❑ 173 Shane Reynolds | .10 | .05 |
| ❑ 174 Wilton Guerrero | .10 | .05 |
| ❑ 175 Eric Karros | .15 | .07 |
| ❑ 176 Paul Konerko | .15 | .07 |
| ❑ 177 Ramon Martinez | .10 | .05 |
| ❑ 178 Raul Mondesi | .15 | .07 |
| ❑ 179 Hideo Nomo | .40 | .18 |
| ❑ 180 Chan Ho Park | .15 | .07 |
| ❑ 181 Mike Piazza | 1.25 | .55 |
| ❑ 182 Ismael Valdes | .10 | .05 |
| ❑ 183 Jeromy Burnitz | .15 | .07 |
| ❑ 184 Jeff Cirillo | .15 | .07 |
| ❑ 185 Todd Dunn | .10 | .05 |
| ❑ 186 Marquis Grissom | .10 | .05 |
| ❑ 187 John Jaha | .15 | .07 |
| ❑ 188 Doug Jones | .10 | .05 |
| ❑ 189 Dave Nilsson | .10 | .05 |
| ❑ 190 Jose Valentin | .10 | .05 |
| ❑ 191 Fernando Vina | .10 | .05 |
| ❑ 192 Orlando Cabrera | .10 | .05 |
| ❑ 193 Steve Falteisek RC | .10 | .05 |
| ❑ 194 Mark Grudzielanek | .10 | .05 |
| ❑ 195 Vladimir Guerrero | .60 | .25 |

| | MINT | NRMT |
|---|---|---|
| ❑ 196 Carlos Perez | .10 | .05 |
| ❑ 197 F.P. Santangelo | .10 | .05 |
| ❑ 198 Jose Vidro | .10 | .05 |
| ❑ 199 Rondell White | .15 | .07 |
| ❑ 200 Edgardo Alfonzo | .15 | .07 |
| ❑ 201 Carlos Baerga | .10 | .05 |
| ❑ 202 John Franco | .15 | .07 |
| ❑ 203 Bernard Gilkey | .10 | .05 |
| ❑ 204 Todd Hundley | .10 | .05 |
| ❑ 205 Butch Huskey | .10 | .05 |
| ❑ 206 Bobby Jones | .10 | .05 |
| ❑ 207 Brian McRae | .10 | .05 |
| ❑ 208 John Olerud | .15 | .07 |
| ❑ 209 Rey Ordonez | .10 | .05 |
| ❑ 210 Ricky Bottalico | .10 | .05 |
| ❑ 211 Bobby Estalella | .10 | .05 |
| ❑ 212 Doug Glanville | .10 | .05 |
| ❑ 213 Gregg Jefferies | .10 | .05 |
| ❑ 214 Mike Lieberthal | .15 | .07 |
| ❑ 215 Desi Relaford | .10 | .05 |
| ❑ 216 Scott Rolen | .40 | .18 |
| ❑ 217 Curt Schilling | .15 | .07 |
| ❑ 218 Adrian Brown | .10 | .05 |
| ❑ 219 Emil Brown | .10 | .05 |
| ❑ 220 Francisco Cordova | .10 | .05 |
| ❑ 221 Jose Guillen | .10 | .05 |
| ❑ 222 Al Martin | .10 | .05 |
| ❑ 223 Abraham Nunez | .10 | .05 |
| ❑ 224 Tony Womack | .10 | .05 |
| ❑ 225 Kevin Young | .15 | .07 |
| ❑ 226 Alan Benes | .10 | .05 |
| ❑ 227 Royce Clayton | .10 | .05 |
| ❑ 228 Gary Gaetti | .15 | .07 |
| ❑ 229 Ron Gant | .15 | .07 |
| ❑ 230 Brian Jordan | .15 | .07 |
| ❑ 231 Ray Lankford | .15 | .07 |
| ❑ 232 Mark McGwire | 1.50 | .70 |
| ❑ 233 Todd Stottlemyre | .10 | .05 |
| ❑ 234 Kevin Brown | .25 | .11 |
| ❑ 235 Ken Caminiti | .15 | .07 |
| ❑ 236 Steve Finley | .15 | .07 |
| ❑ 237 Tony Gwynn | .75 | .35 |
| ❑ 238 Wally Joyner | .15 | .07 |
| ❑ 239 Ruben Rivera | .10 | .05 |
| ❑ 240 Greg Vaughn | .15 | .07 |
| ❑ 241 Quilvio Veras | .10 | .05 |
| ❑ 242 Barry Bonds | .60 | .25 |
| ❑ 243 Jacob Cruz | .10 | .05 |
| ❑ 244 Shawn Estes | .10 | .05 |
| ❑ 245 Orel Hershiser | .15 | .07 |
| ❑ 246 Stan Javier | .10 | .05 |
| ❑ 247 Brian Johnson | .10 | .05 |
| ❑ 248 Jeff Kent | .25 | .11 |
| ❑ 249 Robb Nen | .10 | .05 |
| ❑ 250 J.T. Snow | .15 | .07 |

## 1999 Paramount

| | MINT | NRMT |
|---|---|---|
| COMPLETE SET (250) | 40.00 | 18.00 |
| ❑ 1 Garret Anderson | .15 | .07 |
| ❑ 2 Gary DiSarcina | .10 | .05 |
| ❑ 3 Jim Edmonds | .40 | .18 |
| ❑ 4 Darin Erstad | .40 | .18 |
| ❑ 5 Chuck Finley | .15 | .07 |
| ❑ 6 Troy Glaus | .60 | .25 |
| ❑ 7 Troy Percival | .10 | .05 |
| ❑ 8 Tim Salmon | .15 | .07 |
| ❑ 9 Mo Vaughn | .15 | .07 |
| ❑ 10 Tony Batista | .15 | .07 |
| ❑ 11 Jay Bell | .15 | .07 |
| ❑ 12 Andy Benes | .10 | .05 |
| ❑ 13 Steve Finley | .15 | .07 |
| ❑ 14 Luis Gonzalez | .15 | .07 |
| ❑ 15 Randy Johnson | .50 | .23 |
| ❑ 16 Travis Lee | .10 | .05 |
| ❑ 17 Todd Stottlemyre | .10 | .05 |
| ❑ 18 Matt Williams | .25 | .11 |
| ❑ 19 David Dellucci | .10 | .05 |
| ❑ 20 Bret Boone | .15 | .07 |
| ❑ 21 Andres Galarraga | .25 | .11 |
| ❑ 22 Tom Glavine | .40 | .18 |
| ❑ 23 Andruw Jones | .40 | .18 |
| ❑ 24 Chipper Jones | 1.00 | .45 |
| ❑ 25 Brian Jordan | .15 | .07 |
| ❑ 26 Ryan Klesko | .15 | .07 |
| ❑ 27 Javy Lopez | .15 | .07 |
| ❑ 28 Greg Maddux | 1.00 | .45 |
| ❑ 29 John Smoltz | .15 | .07 |
| ❑ 30 Brady Anderson | .15 | .07 |
| ❑ 31 Albert Belle | .25 | .11 |
| ❑ 32 Will Clark | .40 | .18 |
| ❑ 33 Delino DeShields | .10 | .05 |
| ❑ 34 Charles Johnson | .15 | .07 |
| ❑ 35 Mike Mussina | .40 | .18 |
| ❑ 36 Cal Ripken | 1.50 | .70 |
| ❑ 37 B.J. Surhoff | .15 | .07 |
| ❑ 38 Nomar Garciaparra | 1.25 | .55 |
| ❑ 39 Reggie Jefferson | .10 | .05 |
| ❑ 40 Darren Lewis | .10 | .05 |
| ❑ 41 Pedro Martinez | .50 | .23 |
| ❑ 42 Troy O'Leary | .10 | .05 |
| ❑ 43 Jose Offerman | .10 | .05 |
| ❑ 44 Donnie Sadler | .10 | .05 |
| ❑ 45 John Valentin | .10 | .05 |
| ❑ 46 Rod Beck | .10 | .05 |
| ❑ 47 Gary Gaetti | .10 | .05 |
| ❑ 48 Mark Grace | .40 | .18 |
| ❑ 49 Lance Johnson | .10 | .05 |
| ❑ 50 Mickey Morandini | .10 | .05 |
| ❑ 51 Henry Rodriguez | .10 | .05 |
| ❑ 52 Sammy Sosa | .75 | .35 |
| ❑ 53 Kerry Wood | .15 | .07 |
| ❑ 54 Mike Caruso | .10 | .05 |
| ❑ 55 Ray Durham | .15 | .07 |
| ❑ 56 Paul Konerko | .15 | .07 |
| ❑ 57 Jaime Navarro | .10 | .05 |
| ❑ 58 Greg Norton | .10 | .05 |
| ❑ 59 Magglio Ordonez | .25 | .11 |
| ❑ 60 Frank Thomas | .75 | .35 |
| ❑ 61 Aaron Boone | .10 | .05 |
| ❑ 62 Mike Cameron | .10 | .05 |
| ❑ 63 Barry Larkin | .40 | .18 |
| ❑ 64 Hal Morris | .10 | .05 |
| ❑ 65 Pokey Reese | .15 | .07 |
| ❑ 66 Brett Tomko | .10 | .05 |
| ❑ 67 Greg Vaughn | .15 | .07 |
| ❑ 68 Dmitri Young | .15 | .07 |
| ❑ 69 Roberto Alomar | .40 | .18 |
| ❑ 70 Sandy Alomar Jr. | .15 | .07 |
| ❑ 71 Bartolo Colon | .15 | .07 |
| ❑ 72 Travis Fryman | .15 | .07 |
| ❑ 73 David Justice | .25 | .11 |
| ❑ 74 Kenny Lofton | .15 | .07 |
| ❑ 75 Manny Ramirez | .50 | .23 |
| ❑ 76 Richie Sexson | .15 | .07 |
| ❑ 77 Jim Thome | .25 | .11 |
| ❑ 78 Omar Vizquel | .15 | .07 |
| ❑ 79 Dante Bichette | .15 | .07 |
| ❑ 80 Vinny Castilla | .15 | .07 |
| ❑ 81 Darryl Hamilton | .10 | .05 |
| ❑ 82 Todd Helton | .50 | .23 |
| ❑ 83 Darryl Kile | .15 | .07 |
| ❑ 84 Mike Lansing | .10 | .05 |
| ❑ 85 Neifi Perez | .10 | .05 |
| ❑ 86 Larry Walker | .15 | .07 |
| ❑ 87 Tony Clark | .10 | .05 |
| ❑ 88 Damion Easley | .10 | .05 |
| ❑ 89 Bob Higginson | .15 | .07 |
| ❑ 90 Brian Hunter | .10 | .05 |
| ❑ 91 Dean Palmer | .15 | .07 |
| ❑ 92 Justin Thompson | .10 | .05 |
| ❑ 93 Todd Dunwoody | .10 | .05 |
| ❑ 94 Cliff Floyd | .15 | .07 |
| ❑ 95 Alex Gonzalez | .10 | .05 |
| ❑ 96 Livan Hernandez | .10 | .05 |
| ❑ 97 Mark Kotsay | .10 | .05 |
| ❑ 98 Derrek Lee | .10 | .05 |
| ❑ 99 Kevin Orie | .10 | .05 |
| ❑ 100 Moises Alou | .15 | .07 |
| ❑ 101 Jeff Bagwell | .50 | .23 |
| ❑ 102 Derek Bell | .10 | .05 |
| ❑ 103 Craig Biggio | .25 | .11 |
| ❑ 104 Ken Caminiti | .15 | .07 |
| ❑ 105 Ricky Gutierrez | .10 | .05 |
| ❑ 106 Richard Hidalgo | .15 | .07 |
| ❑ 107 Billy Wagner | .10 | .05 |
| ❑ 108 Jeff Conine | .10 | .05 |
| ❑ 109 Johnny Damon | .15 | .07 |
| ❑ 110 Carlos Febles | .10 | .05 |
| ❑ 111 Jeremy Giambi | .10 | .05 |
| ❑ 112 Jeff King | .10 | .05 |
| ❑ 113 Jeff Montgomery | .10 | .05 |
| ❑ 114 Joe Randa | .10 | .05 |
| ❑ 115 Kevin Brown | .25 | .11 |
| ❑ 116 Mark Grudzielanek | .10 | .05 |
| ❑ 117 Todd Hundley | .10 | .05 |
| ❑ 118 Eric Karros | .15 | .07 |
| ❑ 119 Raul Mondesi | .15 | .07 |
| ❑ 120 Chan Ho Park | .15 | .07 |
| ❑ 121 Gary Sheffield | .40 | .18 |
| ❑ 122 Devon White | .10 | .05 |
| ❑ 123 Eric Young | .10 | .05 |
| ❑ 124 Jeromy Burnitz | .15 | .07 |
| ❑ 125 Jeff Cirillo | .15 | .07 |
| ❑ 126 Marquis Grissom | .10 | .05 |
| ❑ 127 Geoff Jenkins | .15 | .07 |
| ❑ 128 Dave Nilsson | .10 | .05 |
| ❑ 129 Jose Valentin | .10 | .05 |
| ❑ 130 Fernando Vina | .10 | .05 |
| ❑ 131 Rick Aguilera | .10 | .05 |
| ❑ 132 Ron Coomer | .10 | .05 |
| ❑ 133 Marty Cordova | .10 | .05 |
| ❑ 134 Matt Lawton | .15 | .07 |
| ❑ 135 David Ortiz | .10 | .05 |
| ❑ 136 Brad Radke | .15 | .07 |
| ❑ 137 Terry Steinbach | .10 | .05 |
| ❑ 138 Javier Valentin | .10 | .05 |
| ❑ 139 Todd Walker | .10 | .05 |
| ❑ 140 Orlando Cabrera | .10 | .05 |
| ❑ 141 Brad Fullmer | .15 | .07 |
| ❑ 142 Vladimir Guerrero | .60 | .25 |
| ❑ 143 Wilton Guerrero | .10 | .05 |
| ❑ 144 Carl Pavano | .10 | .05 |
| ❑ 145 Ugueth Urbina | .10 | .05 |
| ❑ 146 Rondell White | .15 | .07 |
| ❑ 147 Chris Widger | .10 | .05 |
| ❑ 148 Edgardo Alfonzo | .15 | .07 |
| ❑ 149 Bobby Bonilla | .15 | .07 |
| ❑ 150 Rickey Henderson | .50 | .23 |
| ❑ 151 Brian McRae | .10 | .05 |
| ❑ 152 Hideo Nomo | .40 | .18 |
| ❑ 153 John Olerud | .15 | .07 |
| ❑ 154 Rey Ordonez | .10 | .05 |
| ❑ 155 Mike Piazza | 1.25 | .55 |
| ❑ 156 Robin Ventura | .15 | .07 |
| ❑ 157 Masato Yoshii | .15 | .07 |
| ❑ 158 Roger Clemens | .75 | .35 |
| ❑ 159 David Cone | .15 | .07 |
| ❑ 160 Orlando Hernandez | .15 | .07 |
| ❑ 161 Hideki Irabu | .10 | .05 |
| ❑ 162 Derek Jeter | 1.50 | .70 |
| ❑ 163 Chuck Knoblauch | .15 | .07 |
| ❑ 164 Tino Martinez | .15 | .07 |
| ❑ 165 Paul O'Neill | .15 | .07 |
| ❑ 166 Darryl Strawberry | .15 | .07 |
| ❑ 167 Bernie Williams | .40 | .18 |
| ❑ 168 Eric Chavez | .15 | .07 |
| ❑ 169 Ryan Christenson | .10 | .05 |
| ❑ 170 Jason Giambi | .40 | .18 |
| ❑ 171 Ben Grieve | .15 | .07 |
| ❑ 172 Tony Phillips | .10 | .05 |
| ❑ 173 Tim Raines | .15 | .07 |
| ❑ 174 Scott Spiezio | .10 | .05 |
| ❑ 175 Miguel Tejada | .15 | .07 |
| ❑ 176 Bobby Abreu | .15 | .07 |
| ❑ 177 Rico Brogna | .10 | .05 |
| ❑ 178 Ron Gant | .15 | .07 |
| ❑ 179 Doug Glanville | .10 | .05 |

| | MINT | NRMT |
|---|---|---|
| ❑ 180 Desi Relaford | .10 | .05 |
| ❑ 181 Scott Rolen | .40 | .18 |
| ❑ 182 Curt Schilling | .15 | .07 |
| ❑ 183 Brant Brown | .10 | .05 |
| ❑ 184 Brian Giles | .15 | .07 |
| ❑ 185 Jose Guillen | .10 | .05 |
| ❑ 186 Jason Kendall | .15 | .07 |
| ❑ 187 Al Martin | .10 | .05 |
| ❑ 188 Ed Sprague | .10 | .05 |
| ❑ 189 Kevin Young | .15 | .07 |
| ❑ 190 Eric Davis | .15 | .07 |
| ❑ 191 J.D. Drew | .40 | .18 |
| ❑ 192 Ray Lankford | .15 | .07 |
| ❑ 193 Eli Marrero | .10 | .05 |
| ❑ 194 Mark McGwire | 1.50 | .70 |
| ❑ 195 Edgar Renteria | .10 | .05 |
| ❑ 196 Fernando Tatis | .15 | .07 |
| ❑ 197 Andy Ashby | .10 | .05 |
| ❑ 198 Tony Gwynn | .75 | .35 |
| ❑ 199 Carlos Hernandez | .10 | .05 |
| ❑ 200 Trevor Hoffman | .15 | .07 |
| ❑ 201 Wally Joyner | .15 | .07 |
| ❑ 202 Jim Leyritz | .10 | .05 |
| ❑ 203 Ruben Rivera | .10 | .05 |
| ❑ 204 Matt Clement | .10 | .05 |
| ❑ 205 Quilvio Veras | .10 | .05 |
| ❑ 206 Rich Aurilia | .10 | .05 |
| ❑ 207 Marvin Benard | .10 | .05 |
| ❑ 208 Barry Bonds | .60 | .25 |
| ❑ 209 Ellis Burks | .15 | .07 |
| ❑ 210 Jeff Kent | .25 | .11 |
| ❑ 211 Bill Mueller | .10 | .05 |
| ❑ 212 Robb Nen | .10 | .05 |
| ❑ 213 J.T. Snow | .15 | .07 |
| ❑ 214 Jay Buhner | .15 | .07 |
| ❑ 215 Jeff Fassero | .10 | .05 |
| ❑ 216 Ken Griffey Jr. | 1.50 | .70 |
| ❑ 217 Carlos Guillen | .10 | .05 |
| ❑ 218 Butch Huskey | .10 | .05 |
| ❑ 219 Edgar Martinez | .25 | .11 |
| ❑ 220 Alex Rodriguez | 1.25 | .55 |
| ❑ 221 David Segui | .10 | .05 |
| ❑ 222 Dan Wilson | .10 | .05 |
| ❑ 223 Rolando Arrojo | .10 | .05 |
| ❑ 224 Wade Boggs | .50 | .23 |
| ❑ 225 Jose Canseco | .50 | .23 |
| ❑ 226 Roberto Hernandez | .10 | .05 |
| ❑ 227 Dave Martinez | .10 | .05 |
| ❑ 228 Quinton McCracken | .10 | .05 |
| ❑ 229 Fred McGriff | .25 | .11 |
| ❑ 230 Kevin Stocker | .10 | .05 |
| ❑ 231 Randy Winn | .10 | .05 |
| ❑ 232 Royce Clayton | .10 | .05 |
| ❑ 233 Juan Gonzalez | .40 | .18 |
| ❑ 234 Tom Goodwin | .10 | .05 |
| ❑ 235 Rusty Greer | .15 | .07 |
| ❑ 236 Rick Helling | .15 | .07 |
| ❑ 237 Rafael Palmeiro | .40 | .18 |
| ❑ 238 Ivan Rodriguez | .50 | .23 |
| ❑ 239 Aaron Sele | .15 | .07 |
| ❑ 240 John Wetteland | .15 | .07 |
| ❑ 241 Todd Zeile | .15 | .07 |
| ❑ 242 Jose Cruz Jr. | .15 | .07 |
| ❑ 243 Carlos Delgado | .40 | .18 |
| ❑ 244 Tony Fernandez | .10 | .05 |
| ❑ 245 Cecil Fielder | .15 | .07 |
| ❑ 246 Alex Gonzalez | .10 | .05 |
| ❑ 247 Shawn Green | .40 | .18 |
| ❑ 248 Roy Halladay | .10 | .05 |
| ❑ 249 Shannon Stewart | .15 | .07 |
| ❑ 250 David Wells | .15 | .07 |
| ❑ NNO Tony Gwynn Sample | 2.00 | .90 |

## 2000 Paramount

| | MINT | NRMT |
|---|---|---|
| COMPLETE SET (250) | 40.00 | 18.00 |
| ❑ 1 Garret Anderson | .15 | .07 |
| ❑ 2 Jim Edmonds | .40 | .18 |
| ❑ 3 Darin Erstad | .40 | .18 |
| ❑ 4 Chuck Finley | .15 | .07 |
| ❑ 5 Troy Glaus | .50 | .23 |
| ❑ 6 Troy Percival | .10 | .05 |
| ❑ 7 Tim Salmon | .15 | .07 |
| ❑ 8 Mo Vaughn | .15 | .07 |

| | MINT | NRMT |
|---|---|---|
| ❑ 9 Jay Bell | .15 | .07 |
| ❑ 10 Erubiel Durazo | .15 | .07 |
| ❑ 11 Steve Finley | .15 | .07 |
| ❑ 12 Luis Gonzalez | .15 | .07 |
| ❑ 13 Randy Johnson | .50 | .23 |
| ❑ 14 Travis Lee | .10 | .05 |
| ❑ 15 Matt Mantei | .10 | .05 |
| ❑ 16 Matt Williams | .25 | .11 |
| ❑ 17 Tony Womack | .10 | .05 |
| ❑ 18 Bret Boone | .10 | .05 |
| ❑ 19 Tom Glavine | .40 | .18 |
| ❑ 20 Andruw Jones | .40 | .18 |
| ❑ 21 Chipper Jones | 1.00 | .45 |
| ❑ 22 Brian Jordan | .15 | .07 |
| ❑ 23 Javy Lopez | .15 | .07 |
| ❑ 24 Greg Maddux | 1.00 | .45 |
| ❑ 25 Kevin Millwood | .15 | .07 |
| ❑ 26 John Rocker | .15 | .07 |
| ❑ 27 John Smoltz | .15 | .07 |
| ❑ 28 Brady Anderson | .15 | .07 |
| ❑ 29 Albert Belle | .25 | .11 |
| ❑ 30 Will Clark | .40 | .18 |
| ❑ 31 Charles Johnson | .15 | .07 |
| ❑ 32 Mike Mussina | .40 | .18 |
| ❑ 33 Cal Ripken | 1.50 | .70 |
| ❑ 34 B.J. Surhoff | .15 | .07 |
| ❑ 35 Nomar Garciaparra | 1.25 | .55 |
| ❑ 36 Derek Lowe | .10 | .05 |
| ❑ 37 Pedro Martinez | .50 | .23 |
| ❑ 38 Trot Nixon | .15 | .07 |
| ❑ 39 Troy O'Leary | .10 | .05 |
| ❑ 40 Jose Offerman | .10 | .05 |
| ❑ 41 John Valentin | .10 | .05 |
| ❑ 42 Jason Varitek | .15 | .07 |
| ❑ 43 Mark Grace | .40 | .18 |
| ❑ 44 Glenallen Hill | .10 | .05 |
| ❑ 45 Jon Lieber | .10 | .05 |
| ❑ 46 Cole Liniak | .10 | .05 |
| ❑ 47 Jose Nieves | .10 | .05 |
| ❑ 48 Henry Rodriguez | .10 | .05 |
| ❑ 49 Sammy Sosa | .75 | .35 |
| ❑ 50 Kerry Wood | .15 | .07 |
| ❑ 51 Jason Dellaero | .10 | .05 |
| ❑ 52 Ray Durham | .15 | .07 |
| ❑ 53 Paul Konerko | .15 | .07 |
| ❑ 54 Carlos Lee | .15 | .07 |
| ❑ 55 Greg Norton | .10 | .05 |
| ❑ 56 Magglio Ordonez | .15 | .07 |
| ❑ 57 Chris Singleton | .15 | .07 |
| ❑ 58 Frank Thomas | .75 | .35 |
| ❑ 59 Aaron Boone | .10 | .05 |
| ❑ 60 Mike Cameron | .10 | .05 |
| ❑ 61 Sean Casey | .15 | .07 |
| ❑ 62 Pete Harnisch | .10 | .05 |
| ❑ 63 Barry Larkin | .40 | .18 |
| ❑ 64 Pokey Reese | .15 | .07 |
| ❑ 65 Greg Vaughn | .15 | .07 |
| ❑ 66 Scott Williamson | .10 | .05 |
| ❑ 67 Roberto Alomar | .40 | .18 |
| ❑ 68 Sean DePaula RC | .25 | .11 |
| ❑ 69 Travis Fryman | .15 | .07 |
| ❑ 70 David Justice | .25 | .11 |
| ❑ 71 Kenny Lofton | .15 | .07 |
| ❑ 72 Manny Ramirez | .50 | .23 |
| ❑ 73 Richie Sexson | .15 | .07 |
| ❑ 74 Jim Thome | .25 | .11 |
| ❑ 75 Omar Vizquel | .15 | .07 |
| ❑ 76 Pedro Astacio | .10 | .05 |
| ❑ 77 Vinny Castilla | .15 | .07 |
| ❑ 78 Derrick Gibson | .10 | .05 |
| ❑ 79 Todd Helton | .50 | .23 |
| ❑ 80 Neifi Perez | .10 | .05 |
| ❑ 81 Ben Petrick | .10 | .05 |
| ❑ 82 Larry Walker | .15 | .07 |
| ❑ 83 Brad Ausmus | .10 | .05 |
| ❑ 84 Tony Clark | .10 | .05 |
| ❑ 85 Deivi Cruz | .10 | .05 |
| ❑ 86 Damion Easley | .10 | .05 |
| ❑ 87 Juan Encarnacion | .15 | .07 |
| ❑ 88 Juan Gonzalez | .40 | .18 |
| ❑ 89 Bobby Higginson | .10 | .05 |
| ❑ 90 Dave Mlicki | .10 | .05 |
| ❑ 91 Dean Palmer | .15 | .07 |
| ❑ 92 Bruce Aven | .10 | .05 |
| ❑ 93 Luis Castillo | .15 | .07 |
| ❑ 94 Ramon Castro | .10 | .05 |
| ❑ 95 Cliff Floyd | .15 | .07 |
| ❑ 96 Alex Gonzalez | .10 | .05 |
| ❑ 97 Mike Lowell | .10 | .05 |
| ❑ 98 Preston Wilson | .15 | .07 |
| ❑ 99 Jeff Bagwell | .50 | .23 |
| ❑ 100 Derek Bell | .10 | .05 |
| ❑ 101 Craig Biggio | .25 | .11 |
| ❑ 102 Ken Caminiti | .15 | .07 |
| ❑ 103 Carl Everett | .15 | .07 |
| ❑ 104 Mike Hampton | .15 | .07 |
| ❑ 105 Jose Lima | .10 | .05 |
| ❑ 106 Billy Wagner | .10 | .05 |
| ❑ 107 Daryle Ward | .15 | .07 |
| ❑ 108 Carlos Beltran | .15 | .07 |
| ❑ 109 Johnny Damon | .15 | .07 |
| ❑ 110 Jermaine Dye | .15 | .07 |
| ❑ 111 Carlos Febles | .10 | .05 |
| ❑ 112 Mark Quinn | .15 | .07 |
| ❑ 113 Joe Randa | .10 | .05 |
| ❑ 114 Jose Rosado | .10 | .05 |
| ❑ 115 Mike Sweeney | .15 | .07 |
| ❑ 116 Kevin Brown | .25 | .11 |
| ❑ 117 Shawn Green | .40 | .18 |
| ❑ 118 Mark Grudzielanek | .10 | .05 |
| ❑ 119 Todd Hollandsworth | .10 | .05 |
| ❑ 120 Eric Karros | .15 | .07 |
| ❑ 121 Chan Ho Park | .15 | .07 |
| ❑ 122 Gary Sheffield | .40 | .18 |
| ❑ 123 Devon White | .10 | .05 |
| ❑ 124 Eric Young | .10 | .05 |
| ❑ 125 Kevin Barker | .10 | .05 |
| ❑ 126 Ron Belliard | .10 | .05 |
| ❑ 127 Jeromy Burnitz | .15 | .07 |
| ❑ 128 Jeff Cirillo | .15 | .07 |
| ❑ 129 Marquis Grissom | .10 | .05 |
| ❑ 130 Geoff Jenkins | .15 | .07 |
| ❑ 131 David Nilsson | .10 | .05 |
| ❑ 132 Chad Allen | .10 | .05 |
| ❑ 133 Ron Coomer | .10 | .05 |
| ❑ 134 Jacque Jones | .15 | .07 |
| ❑ 135 Corey Koskie | .10 | .05 |
| ❑ 136 Matt Lawton | .10 | .05 |
| ❑ 137 Brad Radke | .15 | .07 |
| ❑ 138 Todd Walker | .10 | .05 |
| ❑ 139 Michael Barrett | .10 | .05 |
| ❑ 140 Peter Bergeron | .10 | .05 |
| ❑ 141 Brad Fullmer | .15 | .07 |
| ❑ 142 Vladimir Guerrero | .60 | .25 |
| ❑ 143 Ugueth Urbina | .10 | .05 |
| ❑ 144 Jose Vidro | .10 | .05 |
| ❑ 145 Rondell White | .15 | .07 |
| ❑ 146 Edgardo Alfonzo | .15 | .07 |
| ❑ 147 Armando Benitez | .15 | .07 |
| ❑ 148 Roger Cedeno | .10 | .05 |
| ❑ 149 Rickey Henderson | .50 | .23 |
| ❑ 150 Melvin Mora | .10 | .05 |
| ❑ 151 John Olerud | .15 | .07 |
| ❑ 152 Rey Ordonez | .10 | .05 |
| ❑ 153 Mike Piazza | 1.25 | .55 |
| ❑ 154 Jorge Toca | .10 | .05 |
| ❑ 155 Robin Ventura | .25 | .11 |
| ❑ 156 Roger Clemens | .75 | .35 |
| ❑ 157 David Cone | .15 | .07 |
| ❑ 158 Orlando Hernandez | .15 | .07 |
| ❑ 159 Derek Jeter | 1.50 | .70 |
| ❑ 160 Chuck Knoblauch | .15 | .07 |
| ❑ 161 Ricky Ledee | .10 | .05 |
| ❑ 162 Tino Martinez | .15 | .07 |

❑ 163 Paul O'Neill .15 .07
❑ 164 Mariano Rivera .15 .07
❑ 165 Alfonso Soriano .15 .07
❑ 166 Bernie Williams .40 .18
❑ 167 Eric Chavez .15 .07
❑ 168 Jason Giambi .40 .18
❑ 169 Ben Grieve .15 .07
❑ 170 Tim Hudson .40 .18
❑ 171 John Jaha .10 .05
❑ 172 Matt Stairs .10 .05
❑ 173 Miguel Tejada .15 .07
❑ 174 Randy Velarde .10 .05
❑ 175 Bobby Abreu .15 .07
❑ 176 Marlon Anderson .10 .05
❑ 177 Rico Brogna .10 .05
❑ 178 Ron Gant .15 .07
❑ 179 Doug Glanville .10 .05
❑ 180 Mike Lieberthal .15 .07
❑ 181 Scott Rolen .40 .18
❑ 182 Curt Schilling .15 .07
❑ 183 Brian Giles .15 .07
❑ 184 Chad Hermansen .10 .05
❑ 185 Jason Kendall .15 .07
❑ 186 Al Martin .10 .05
❑ 187 Pat Meares .10 .05
❑ 188 Warren Morris .10 .05
❑ 189 Ed Sprague .10 .05
❑ 190 Kevin Young .10 .05
❑ 191 Rick Ankiel .75 .35
❑ 192 Kent Bottenfield .10 .05
❑ 193 Eric Davis .15 .07
❑ 194 J.D. Drew .40 .18
❑ 195 Adam Kennedy .15 .07
❑ 196 Ray Lankford .15 .07
❑ 197 Joe McEwing .10 .05
❑ 198 Mark McGwire 1.50 .70
❑ 199 Edgar Renteria .10 .05
❑ 200 Fernando Tatis .15 .07
❑ 201 Mike Darr .15 .07
❑ 202 Ben Davis .10 .05
❑ 203 Tony Gwynn .75 .35
❑ 204 Trevor Hoffman .15 .07
❑ 205 Damian Jackson .10 .05
❑ 206 Phil Nevin .15 .07
❑ 207 Reggie Sanders .10 .05
❑ 208 Quilvio Veras .10 .05
❑ 209 Rich Aurilia .10 .05
❑ 210 Marvin Benard .10 .05
❑ 211 Barry Bonds .60 .25
❑ 212 Ellis Burks .15 .07
❑ 213 Livan Hernandez .10 .05
❑ 214 Jeff Kent .25 .11
❑ 215 Russ Ortiz .15 .07
❑ 216 J.T. Snow .15 .07
❑ 217 Paul Abbott .10 .05
❑ 218 David Bell .10 .05
❑ 219 Freddy Garcia .15 .07
❑ 220 Ken Griffey Jr. 1.50 .70
❑ 221 Carlos Guillen .10 .05
❑ 222 Brian Hunter .10 .05
❑ 223 Edgar Martinez .25 .11
❑ 224 Jamie Moyer .10 .05
❑ 225 Alex Rodriguez 1.25 .55
❑ 226 Wade Boggs .50 .23
❑ 227 Miguel Cairo .10 .05
❑ 228 Jose Canseco .50 .23
❑ 229 Roberto Hernandez .10 .05
❑ 230 Dave Martinez .10 .05
❑ 231 Quinton McCracken .10 .05
❑ 232 Fred McGriff .25 .11
❑ 233 Kevin Stocker .10 .05
❑ 234 Royce Clayton .10 .05
❑ 235 Rusty Greer .15 .07
❑ 236 Ruben Mateo .15 .07
❑ 237 Rafael Palmeiro .40 .18
❑ 238 Ivan Rodriguez .50 .23
❑ 239 Aaron Sele .10 .05
❑ 240 John Wetteland .15 .07
❑ 241 Todd Zeile .15 .07
❑ 242 Tony Batista .15 .07
❑ 243 Homer Bush .10 .05
❑ 244 Carlos Delgado .40 .18
❑ 245 Tony Fernandez .10 .05
❑ 246 Billy Koch .15 .07
❑ 247 Raul Mondesi .15 .07
❑ 248 Shannon Stewart .15 .07
❑ 249 David Wells .15 .07
❑ 250 Vernon Wells .15 .07

## 2000 Paramount Update

| | MINT | NRMT |
|---|---|---|
| COMP.FACT.SET (100) | 30.00 | 13.50 |
| MINOR STARS | .25 | .11 |
| SEMISTARS | .40 | .18 |
| UNLISTED STARS | .60 | .25 |

❑ U1 Adam Kennedy .25 .11
❑ U2 Bengie Molina .25 .11
❑ U3 Derrick Turnbow RC .75 .35
❑ U4 Randy Johnson .75 .35
❑ U5 Danny Klassen .15 .07
❑ U6 Vicente Padilla RC .75 .35
❑ U7 Rafael Furcal 1.50 .70
❑ U8 Andres Galarraga .40 .18
❑ U9 Chipper Jones 1.50 .70
❑ U10 Fernando Lunar .15 .07
❑ U11 Willie Morales RC .50 .23
❑ U12 Cal Ripken 2.50 1.10
❑ U13 B.J. Ryan .15 .07
❑ U14 Carl Everett .25 .11
❑ U15 Nomar Garciaparra 2.00 .90
❑ U16 Pedro Martinez .75 .35
❑ U17 Wilton Veras .25 .11
❑ U18 Scott Downs RC .75 .35
❑ U19 Daniel Garibay RC .50 .23
❑ U20 Sammy Sosa 1.25 .55
❑ U21 Julio Zuleta RC 1.00 .45
❑ U22 Josh Paul .15 .07
❑ U23 Frank Thomas 1.25 .55
❑ U24 Rob Bell .15 .07
❑ U25 Dante Bichette .25 .11
❑ U26 Travis Dawkins .25 .11
❑ U27 Ken Griffey Jr. 2.50 1.10
❑ U28 Chuck Finley .25 .11
❑ U29 Manny Ramirez .75 .35
❑ U30 Paul Rigdon RC 1.50 .70
❑ U31 Jeff Cirillo .25 .11
❑ U32 Larry Walker .25 .11
❑ U33 Masato Yoshii .15 .07
❑ U34 Robert Fick .15 .07
❑ U35 Jose Macias .15 .07
❑ U36 Juan Gonzalez .60 .25
❑ U37 Hideo Nomo .60 .25
❑ U38 Jason Grilli .15 .07
❑ U39 Pablo Ozuna .15 .07
❑ U40 Brad Penny .25 .11
❑ U41 Jeff Bagwell .75 .35
❑ U42 Lance Berkman .25 .11
❑ U43 Roger Cedeno .15 .07
❑ U44 Octavio Dotel .15 .07
❑ U45 Chad Durbin RC .75 .35
❑ U46 Eric Gagne .25 .11
❑ U47 Shawn Green .60 .25
❑ U48 Jose Hernandez .15 .07
❑ U49 Matt LeCroy .15 .07
❑ U50 Johan Santana RC 1.00 .45
❑ U51 Vladimir Guerrero 1.00 .45
❑ U52 Hideki Irabu .15 .07
❑ U53 Andy Tracy RC .50 .23
❑ U54 Derek Bell .15 .07
❑ U55 Eric Cammack RC .75 .35
❑ U56 Mike Hampton .25 .11
❑ U57 Jay Payton .25 .11
❑ U58 Mike Piazza 2.00 .90
❑ U59 Todd Zeile .25 .11
❑ U60 Roger Clemens 1.25 .55
❑ U61 Darrell Einertson RC .50 .23
❑ U62 Derek Jeter 2.50 1.10
❑ U63 Jeremy Giambi .15 .07
❑ U64 Terrence Long .25 .11
❑ U65 Mark Mulder .25 .11
❑ U66 Adam Piatt .60 .25
❑ U67 Luis Vizcaino .15 .07
❑ U68 Pat Burrell 1.00 .45
❑ U69 Scott Rolen .40 .18
❑ U70 Chad Hermansen .15 .07
❑ U71 Rick Ankiel 1.25 .55
❑ U72 Jim Edmonds Cardinals .60 .25
❑ U73 Mark McGwire 2.50 1.10
❑ U74 Gene Stechschulte RC .50 .23
❑ U75 Fernando Vina .15 .07
❑ U76 Bret Boone .25 .11
❑ U77 Tony Gwynn 1.25 .55
❑ U78 Ryan Klesko .25 .11
❑ U79 David Newhan .15 .07
❑ U80 Kevin Walker RC .75 .35
❑ U81 Barry Bonds 1.00 .45
❑ U82 Aaron Fultz RC .50 .23
❑ U83 Ben Weber RC .50 .23
❑ U84 Rickey Henderson .75 .35
❑ U85 Kevin Hodges RC .50 .23
❑ U86 John Olerud .25 .11
❑ U87 Robert Ramsay .15 .07
❑ U88 Alex Rodriguez 2.00 .90
❑ U89 Kazuhiro Sasaki RC 6.00 2.70
❑ U90 Vinny Castilla .25 .11
❑ U91 Jeff Sparks RC .50 .23
❑ U92 Greg Vaughn .25 .11
❑ U93 Francisco Cordero .15 .07
❑ U94 Gabe Kapler .25 .11
❑ U95 Mike Lamb RC 1.50 .70
❑ U96 Ivan Rodriguez .75 .35
❑ U97 Clayton Andrews .15 .07
❑ U98 Brad Fullmer .25 .11
❑ U99 Raul Mondesi .25 .11
❑ U100 Dewayne Wise .15 .07

## 1992 Pinnacle

| | MINT | NRMT |
|---|---|---|
| COMPLETE SET (620) | 40.00 | 18.00 |
| COMPLETE SERIES 1 (310) | 25.00 | 11.00 |
| COMPLETE SERIES 2 (310) | 15.00 | 6.75 |

❑ 1 Frank Thomas .75 .35
❑ 2 Benito Santiago .10 .05
❑ 3 Carlos Baerga .10 .05
❑ 4 Cecil Fielder .20 .09
❑ 5 Barry Larkin .20 .09
❑ 6 Ozzie Smith .50 .23
❑ 7 Willie McGee .20 .09
❑ 8 Paul Molitor .40 .18
❑ 9 Andy Van Slyke .20 .09
❑ 10 Ryne Sandberg .50 .23
❑ 11 Kevin Seitzer .10 .05
❑ 12 Len Dykstra .20 .09
❑ 13 Edgar Martinez .20 .09
❑ 14 Ruben Sierra .10 .05
❑ 15 Howard Johnson .10 .05
❑ 16 Dave Henderson .10 .05
❑ 17 Devon White .10 .05

| | | |
|---|---|---|
| ❑ 18 Terry Pendleton | .20 | .09 |
| ❑ 19 Steve Finley | .20 | .09 |
| ❑ 20 Kirby Puckett | 1.00 | .45 |
| ❑ 21 Orel Hershiser | .20 | .09 |
| ❑ 22 Hal Morris | .10 | .05 |
| ❑ 23 Don Mattingly | 1.00 | .45 |
| ❑ 24 Delino DeShields | .20 | .09 |
| ❑ 25 Dennis Eckersley | .20 | .09 |
| ❑ 26 Ellis Burks | .20 | .09 |
| ❑ 27 Jay Buhner | .20 | .09 |
| ❑ 28 Matt Williams | .20 | .09 |
| ❑ 29 Lou Whitaker | .20 | .09 |
| ❑ 30 Alex Fernandez | .20 | .09 |
| ❑ 31 Albert Belle | .20 | .09 |
| ❑ 32 Todd Zeile | .10 | .05 |
| ❑ 33 Tony Pena | .10 | .05 |
| ❑ 34 Jay Bell | .20 | .09 |
| ❑ 35 Rafael Palmeiro | .40 | .18 |
| ❑ 36 Wes Chamberlain | .10 | .05 |
| ❑ 37 George Bell | .10 | .05 |
| ❑ 38 Robin Yount | .40 | .18 |
| ❑ 39 Vince Coleman | .10 | .05 |
| ❑ 40 Bruce Hurst | .10 | .05 |
| ❑ 41 Harold Baines | .20 | .09 |
| ❑ 42 Chuck Finley | .20 | .09 |
| ❑ 43 Ken Caminiti | .20 | .09 |
| ❑ 44 Ben McDonald | .10 | .05 |
| ❑ 45 Roberto Alomar | .40 | .18 |
| ❑ 46 Chili Davis | .20 | .09 |
| ❑ 47 Bill Doran | .10 | .05 |
| ❑ 48 Jerald Clark | .10 | .05 |
| ❑ 49 Jose Lind | .10 | .05 |
| ❑ 50 Nolan Ryan | 2.00 | .90 |
| ❑ 51 Phil Plantier | .10 | .05 |
| ❑ 52 Gary DiSarcina | .10 | .05 |
| ❑ 53 Kevin Bass | .10 | .05 |
| ❑ 54 Pat Kelly | .10 | .05 |
| ❑ 55 Mark Wohlers | .10 | .05 |
| ❑ 56 Walt Weiss | .10 | .05 |
| ❑ 57 Lenny Harris | .10 | .05 |
| ❑ 58 Ivan Calderon | .10 | .05 |
| ❑ 59 Harold Reynolds | .10 | .05 |
| ❑ 60 George Brett | .75 | .35 |
| ❑ 61 Gregg Olson | .10 | .05 |
| ❑ 62 Orlando Merced | .10 | .05 |
| ❑ 63 Steve Decker | .10 | .05 |
| ❑ 64 John Franco | .20 | .09 |
| ❑ 65 Greg Maddux | 1.00 | .45 |
| ❑ 66 Alex Cole | .10 | .05 |
| ❑ 67 Dave Hollins | .10 | .05 |
| ❑ 68 Kent Hrbek | .20 | .09 |
| ❑ 69 Tom Pagnozzi | .10 | .05 |
| ❑ 70 Jeff Bagwell | .75 | .35 |
| ❑ 71 Jim Gantner | .10 | .05 |
| ❑ 72 Matt Nokes | .10 | .05 |
| ❑ 73 Brian Harper | .10 | .05 |
| ❑ 74 Andy Benes | .10 | .05 |
| ❑ 75 Tom Glavine | .20 | .09 |
| ❑ 76 Terry Steinbach | .10 | .05 |
| ❑ 77 Dennis Martinez | .20 | .09 |
| ❑ 78 John Olerud | .20 | .09 |
| ❑ 79 Ozzie Guillen | .10 | .05 |
| ❑ 80 Darryl Strawberry | .20 | .09 |
| ❑ 81 Gary Gaetti | .20 | .09 |
| ❑ 82 Dave Righetti | .10 | .05 |
| ❑ 83 Chris Hoiles | .10 | .05 |
| ❑ 84 Andujar Cedeno | .10 | .05 |
| ❑ 85 Jack Clark | .20 | .09 |
| ❑ 86 David Howard | .10 | .05 |
| ❑ 87 Bill Gullickson | .10 | .05 |
| ❑ 88 Bernard Gilkey | .20 | .09 |
| ❑ 89 Kevin Elster | .10 | .05 |
| ❑ 90 Kevin Maas | .10 | .05 |
| ❑ 91 Mark Lewis | .10 | .05 |
| ❑ 92 Greg Vaughn | .20 | .09 |
| ❑ 93 Bret Barberie | .10 | .05 |
| ❑ 94 Dave Smith | .10 | .05 |
| ❑ 95 Roger Clemens | .75 | .35 |
| ❑ 96 Doug Drabek | .10 | .05 |
| ❑ 97 Omar Vizquel | .20 | .09 |
| ❑ 98 Jose Guzman | .10 | .05 |
| ❑ 99 Juan Samuel | .10 | .05 |
| ❑ 100 Dave Justice | .20 | .09 |
| ❑ 101 Tom Browning | .10 | .05 |
| ❑ 102 Mark Gubicza | .10 | .05 |
| ❑ 103 Mickey Morandini | .10 | .05 |
| ❑ 104 Ed Whitson | .10 | .05 |
| ❑ 105 Lance Parrish | .10 | .05 |
| ❑ 106 Scott Erickson | .10 | .05 |
| ❑ 107 Jack McDowell | .10 | .05 |
| ❑ 108 Dave Stieb | .10 | .05 |
| ❑ 109 Mike Moore | .10 | .05 |
| ❑ 110 Travis Fryman | .20 | .09 |
| ❑ 111 Dwight Gooden | .20 | .09 |
| ❑ 112 Fred McGriff | .20 | .09 |
| ❑ 113 Alan Trammell | .20 | .09 |
| ❑ 114 Roberto Kelly | .10 | .05 |
| ❑ 115 Andre Dawson | .20 | .09 |
| ❑ 116 Bill Landrum | .10 | .05 |
| ❑ 117 Brian McRae | .10 | .05 |
| ❑ 118 B.J. Surhoff | .20 | .09 |
| ❑ 119 Chuck Knoblauch | .20 | .09 |
| ❑ 120 Steve Olin | .10 | .05 |
| ❑ 121 Robin Ventura | .20 | .09 |
| ❑ 122 Will Clark | .40 | .18 |
| ❑ 123 Tino Martinez | .20 | .09 |
| ❑ 124 Dale Murphy | .40 | .18 |
| ❑ 125 Pete O'Brien | .10 | .05 |
| ❑ 126 Ray Lankford | .40 | .18 |
| ❑ 127 Juan Gonzalez | .40 | .18 |
| ❑ 128 Ron Gant | .20 | .09 |
| ❑ 129 Marquis Grissom | .10 | .05 |
| ❑ 130 Jose Canseco | .50 | .23 |
| ❑ 131 Mike Greenwell | .10 | .05 |
| ❑ 132 Mark Langston | .10 | .05 |
| ❑ 133 Brett Butler | .20 | .09 |
| ❑ 134 Kelly Gruber | .10 | .05 |
| ❑ 135 Chris Sabo | .10 | .05 |
| ❑ 136 Mark Grace | .40 | .18 |
| ❑ 137 Tony Fernandez | .10 | .05 |
| ❑ 138 Glenn Davis | .10 | .05 |
| ❑ 139 Pedro Munoz | .10 | .05 |
| ❑ 140 Craig Biggio | .20 | .09 |
| ❑ 141 Pete Schourek | .10 | .05 |
| ❑ 142 Mike Boddicker | .10 | .05 |
| ❑ 143 Robby Thompson | .10 | .05 |
| ❑ 144 Mel Hall | .10 | .05 |
| ❑ 145 Bryan Harvey | .10 | .05 |
| ❑ 146 Mike LaValliere | .10 | .05 |
| ❑ 147 John Kruk | .20 | .09 |
| ❑ 148 Joe Carter | .20 | .09 |
| ❑ 149 Greg Olson | .10 | .05 |
| ❑ 150 Julio Franco | .10 | .05 |
| ❑ 151 Darryl Hamilton | .10 | .05 |
| ❑ 152 Felix Fermin | .10 | .05 |
| ❑ 153 Jose Offerman | .10 | .05 |
| ❑ 154 Paul O'Neill | .20 | .09 |
| ❑ 155 Tommy Greene | .10 | .05 |
| ❑ 156 Ivan Rodriguez | .75 | .35 |
| ❑ 157 Dave Stewart | .20 | .09 |
| ❑ 158 Jeff Reardon | .20 | .09 |
| ❑ 159 Felix Jose | .10 | .05 |
| ❑ 160 Doug Dascenzo | .10 | .05 |
| ❑ 161 Tim Wallach | .10 | .05 |
| ❑ 162 Dan Plesac | .10 | .05 |
| ❑ 163 Luis Gonzalez | .20 | .09 |
| ❑ 164 Mike Henneman | .10 | .05 |
| ❑ 165 Mike Devereaux | .10 | .05 |
| ❑ 166 Luis Polonia | .10 | .05 |
| ❑ 167 Mike Sharperson | .10 | .05 |
| ❑ 168 Chris Donnels | .10 | .05 |
| ❑ 169 Greg W. Harris | .10 | .05 |
| ❑ 170 Deion Sanders | .40 | .18 |
| ❑ 171 Mike Schooler | .10 | .05 |
| ❑ 172 Jose DeJesus | .10 | .05 |
| ❑ 173 Jeff Montgomery | .20 | .09 |
| ❑ 174 Milt Cuyler | .10 | .05 |
| ❑ 175 Wade Boggs | .50 | .23 |
| ❑ 176 Kevin Tapani | .10 | .05 |
| ❑ 177 Bill Spiers | .10 | .05 |
| ❑ 178 Tim Raines | .20 | .09 |
| ❑ 179 Randy Milligan | .10 | .05 |
| ❑ 180 Rob Dibble | .10 | .05 |
| ❑ 181 Kirt Manwaring | .10 | .05 |
| ❑ 182 Pascual Perez | .10 | .05 |
| ❑ 183 Juan Guzman | .10 | .05 |
| ❑ 184 John Smiley | .10 | .05 |
| ❑ 185 David Segui | .10 | .05 |
| ❑ 186 Omar Olivares | .10 | .05 |
| ❑ 187 Joe Slusarski | .10 | .05 |
| ❑ 188 Erik Hanson | .10 | .05 |
| ❑ 189 Mark Portugal | .10 | .05 |
| ❑ 190 Walt Terrell | .10 | .05 |
| ❑ 191 John Smoltz | .20 | .09 |
| ❑ 192 Wilson Alvarez | .10 | .05 |
| ❑ 193 Jimmy Key | .20 | .09 |
| ❑ 194 Larry Walker | .20 | .09 |
| ❑ 195 Lee Smith | .20 | .09 |
| ❑ 196 Pete Harnisch | .10 | .05 |
| ❑ 197 Mike Harkey | .10 | .05 |
| ❑ 198 Frank Tanana | .10 | .05 |
| ❑ 199 Terry Mulholland | .10 | .05 |
| ❑ 200 Cal Ripken | 1.50 | .70 |
| ❑ 201 Dave Magadan | .10 | .05 |
| ❑ 202 Bud Black | .10 | .05 |
| ❑ 203 Terry Shumpert | .10 | .05 |
| ❑ 204 Mike Mussina | .60 | .25 |
| ❑ 205 Mo Vaughn | .20 | .09 |
| ❑ 206 Steve Farr | .10 | .05 |
| ❑ 207 Darrin Jackson | .10 | .05 |
| ❑ 208 Jerry Browne | .10 | .05 |
| ❑ 209 Jeff Russell | .10 | .05 |
| ❑ 210 Mike Scioscia | .10 | .05 |
| ❑ 211 Rick Aguilera | .20 | .09 |
| ❑ 212 Jaime Navarro | .10 | .05 |
| ❑ 213 Randy Tomlin | .10 | .05 |
| ❑ 214 Bobby Thigpen | .10 | .05 |
| ❑ 215 Mark Gardner | .10 | .05 |
| ❑ 216 Norm Charlton | .10 | .05 |
| ❑ 217 Mark McGwire | 1.50 | .70 |
| ❑ 218 Skeeter Barnes | .10 | .05 |
| ❑ 219 Bob Tewksbury | .10 | .05 |
| ❑ 220 Junior Felix | .10 | .05 |
| ❑ 221 Sam Horn | .10 | .05 |
| ❑ 222 Jody Reed | .10 | .05 |
| ❑ 223 Luis Sojo | .10 | .05 |
| ❑ 224 Jerome Walton | .10 | .05 |
| ❑ 225 Darryl Kile | .20 | .09 |
| ❑ 226 Mickey Tettleton | .10 | .05 |
| ❑ 227 Dan Pasqua | .10 | .05 |
| ❑ 228 Jim Gott | .10 | .05 |
| ❑ 229 Bernie Williams | .40 | .18 |
| ❑ 230 Shane Mack | .10 | .05 |
| ❑ 231 Steve Avery | .10 | .05 |
| ❑ 232 Dave Valle | .10 | .05 |
| ❑ 233 Mark Leonard | .10 | .05 |
| ❑ 234 Spike Owen | .10 | .05 |
| ❑ 235 Gary Sheffield | .40 | .18 |
| ❑ 236 Steve Chitren | .10 | .05 |
| ❑ 237 Zane Smith | .10 | .05 |
| ❑ 238 Tom Gordon | .10 | .05 |
| ❑ 239 Jose Oquendo | .10 | .05 |
| ❑ 240 Todd Stottlemyre | .20 | .09 |
| ❑ 241 Darren Daulton | .20 | .09 |
| ❑ 242 Tim Naehring | .10 | .05 |
| ❑ 243 Tony Phillips | .10 | .05 |
| ❑ 244 Shawon Dunston | .10 | .05 |
| ❑ 245 Manuel Lee | .10 | .05 |
| ❑ 246 Mike Pagliarulo | .10 | .05 |
| ❑ 247 Jim Thome | .75 | .35 |
| ❑ 248 Luis Mercedes | .10 | .05 |
| ❑ 249 Cal Eldred | .10 | .05 |
| ❑ 250 Derek Bell | .20 | .09 |
| ❑ 251 Arthur Rhodes | .10 | .05 |
| ❑ 252 Scott Cooper | .10 | .05 |
| ❑ 253 Roberto Hernandez | .10 | .05 |
| ❑ 254 Mo Sanford | .10 | .05 |
| ❑ 255 Scott Servais | .10 | .05 |
| ❑ 256 Eric Karros | .40 | .18 |
| ❑ 257 Andy Mota | .10 | .05 |
| ❑ 258 Keith Mitchell | .10 | .05 |
| ❑ 259 Joel Johnston | .10 | .05 |
| ❑ 260 John Wehner | .10 | .05 |
| ❑ 261 Gino Minutelli | .10 | .05 |
| ❑ 262 Greg Gagne | .10 | .05 |
| ❑ 263 Stan Royer | .10 | .05 |
| ❑ 264 Carlos Garcia | .10 | .05 |
| ❑ 265 Andy Ashby | .20 | .09 |
| ❑ 266 Kim Batiste | .10 | .05 |
| ❑ 267 Julio Valera | .10 | .05 |
| ❑ 268 Royce Clayton | .10 | .05 |
| ❑ 269 Gary Scott | .10 | .05 |
| ❑ 270 Kirk Dressendorfer | .10 | .05 |
| ❑ 271 Sean Berry | .10 | .05 |
| ❑ 272 Lance Dickson | .10 | .05 |
| ❑ 273 Rob Maurer | .10 | .05 |
| ❑ 274 Scott Brosius RC | .50 | .23 |
| ❑ 275 Dave Fleming | .10 | .05 |

❑ 276 Lenny Webster .10 .05
❑ 277 Mike Humphreys .10 .05
❑ 278 Freddie Benavides .10 .05
❑ 279 Harvey Pulliam .10 .05
❑ 280 Jeff Carter .10 .05
❑ 281 Jim Abbott I .40 .18
Nolan Ryan
❑ 282 Wade Boggs I .50 .23
George Brett
❑ 283 Ken Griffey Jr. I .75 .35
Rickey Henderson
❑ 284 Wally Joyner .20 .09
Dale Murphy
❑ 285 Chuck Knoblauch I .20 .09
Ozzie Smith
❑ 286 Robin Ventura I .50 .23
Lou Gehrig
❑ 287 Robin Yount SIDE .20 .09
❑ 288 Bob Tewksbury SIDE .10 .05
❑ 289 Kirby Puckett SIDE .50 .23
❑ 290 Kenny Lofton SIDE .20 .09
❑ 291 Jack McDowell SIDE .10 .05
❑ 292 John Burkett SIDE .10 .05
❑ 293 Dwight Smith SIDE .10 .05
❑ 294 Nolan Ryan SIDE 1.00 .35
❑ 295 Manny Ramirez DP RC 3.00 1.35
❑ 296 Cliff Floyd RC DP UER .75 .35
(Throws right, not left as indicated on back)
❑ 297 Al Shirley DP RC .10 .05
❑ 298 Brian Barber DP RC .10 .05
❑ 299 Jon Farrell DP RC .10 .05
❑ 300 Scott Ruffcorn DP RC .10 .05
❑ 301 Tyrone Hill DP RC .10 .05
❑ 302 Benji Gil DP RC .10 .05
❑ 303 Tyler Green DP RC .10 .05
❑ 304 Allen Watson DP RC .10 .05
❑ 305 Jay Buhner SH .10 .05
❑ 306 Roberto Alomar SH .20 .09
❑ 307 Chuck Knoblauch SH .10 .05
❑ 308 Darryl Strawberry SH .10 .05
❑ 309 Danny Tartabull SH .10 .05
❑ 310 Bobby Bonilla SH .10 .05
❑ 311 Mike Felder .10 .05
❑ 312 Storm Davis .10 .05
❑ 313 Tim Teufel .10 .05
❑ 314 Tom Brunansky .10 .05
❑ 315 Rex Hudler .10 .05
❑ 316 Dave Otto .10 .05
❑ 317 Jeff King .10 .05
❑ 318 Dan Gladden .10 .05
❑ 319 Bill Pecota .10 .05
❑ 320 Franklin Stubbs .10 .05
❑ 321 Gary Carter .20 .09
❑ 322 Melido Perez .10 .05
❑ 323 Eric Davis .20 .09
❑ 324 Greg Myers .10 .05
❑ 325 Pete Incaviglia .10 .05
❑ 326 Von Hayes .10 .05
❑ 327 Greg Swindell .10 .05
❑ 328 Steve Sax .10 .05
❑ 329 Chuck McElroy .10 .05
❑ 330 Gregg Jefferies .10 .05
❑ 331 Joe Oliver .10 .05
❑ 332 Paul Faries .10 .05
❑ 333 David West .10 .05
❑ 334 Craig Grebeck .10 .05
❑ 335 Chris Hammond .10 .05
❑ 336 Billy Ripken .10 .05
❑ 337 Scott Sanderson .10 .05
❑ 338 Dick Schofield .10 .05
❑ 339 Bob Milacki .10 .05
❑ 340 Kevin Reimer .10 .05
❑ 341 Jose DeLeon .10 .05
❑ 342 Henry Cotto .10 .05
❑ 343 Daryl Boston .10 .05
❑ 344 Kevin Gross .10 .05
❑ 345 Milt Thompson .10 .05
❑ 346 Luis Rivera .10 .05
❑ 347 Al Osuna .10 .05
❑ 348 Rob Deer .10 .05
❑ 349 Tim Leary .10 .05
❑ 350 Mike Stanton .10 .05
❑ 351 Dean Palmer .20 .09
❑ 352 Trevor Wilson .10 .05
❑ 353 Mark Eichhorn .10 .05
❑ 354 Scott Aldred .10 .05
❑ 355 Mark Whiten .10 .05
❑ 356 Leo Gomez .10 .05
❑ 357 Rafael Belliard .10 .05
❑ 358 Carlos Quintana .10 .05
❑ 359 Mark Davis .10 .05
❑ 360 Chris Nabholz .10 .05
❑ 361 Carlton Fisk .40 .18
❑ 362 Joe Orsulak .10 .05
❑ 363 Eric Anthony .10 .05
❑ 364 Greg Hibbard .10 .05
❑ 365 Scott Leius .10 .05
❑ 366 Hensley Meulens .10 .05
❑ 367 Chris Bosio .10 .05
❑ 368 Brian Downing .10 .05
❑ 369 Sammy Sosa .75 .35
❑ 370 Stan Belinda .10 .05
❑ 371 Joe Grahe .10 .05
❑ 372 Luis Salazar .10 .05
❑ 373 Lance Johnson .10 .05
❑ 374 Kal Daniels .10 .05
❑ 375 Dave Winfield .40 .18
❑ 376 Brook Jacoby .10 .05
❑ 377 Mariano Duncan .10 .05
❑ 378 Ron Darling .10 .05
❑ 379 Randy Johnson .50 .23
❑ 380 Chito Martinez .10 .05
❑ 381 Andres Galarraga .20 .09
❑ 382 Willie Randolph .20 .09
❑ 383 Charles Nagy .10 .05
❑ 384 Tim Belcher .10 .05
❑ 385 Duane Ward .10 .05
❑ 386 Vicente Palacios .10 .05
❑ 387 Mike Gallego .10 .05
❑ 388 Rich DeLucia .10 .05
❑ 389 Scott Radinsky .10 .05
❑ 390 Damon Berryhill .10 .05
❑ 391 Kirk McCaskill .10 .05
❑ 392 Pedro Guerrero .10 .05
❑ 393 Kevin Mitchell .20 .09
❑ 394 Dickie Thon .10 .05
❑ 395 Bobby Bonilla .20 .09
❑ 396 Bill Wegman .10 .05
❑ 397 Dave Martinez .10 .05
❑ 398 Rick Sutcliffe .20 .09
❑ 399 Larry Andersen .10 .05
❑ 400 Tony Gwynn .75 .35
❑ 401 Rickey Henderson .50 .23
❑ 402 Greg Cadaret .10 .05
❑ 403 Keith Miller .10 .05
❑ 404 Bip Roberts .10 .05
❑ 405 Kevin Brown .20 .09
❑ 406 Mitch Williams .10 .05
❑ 407 Frank Viola .10 .05
❑ 408 Darren Lewis .10 .05
❑ 409 Bob Welch .10 .05
❑ 410 Bob Walk .10 .05
❑ 411 Todd Frohwirth .10 .05
❑ 412 Brian Hunter .10 .05
❑ 413 Ron Karkovice .10 .05
❑ 414 Mike Morgan .10 .05
❑ 415 Joe Hesketh .10 .05
❑ 416 Don Slaught .10 .05
❑ 417 Tom Henke .10 .05
❑ 418 Kurt Stillwell .10 .05
❑ 419 Hector Villaneuva .10 .05
❑ 420 Glenallen Hill .10 .05
❑ 421 Pat Borders .10 .05
❑ 422 Charlie Hough .20 .09
❑ 423 Charlie Leibrandt .10 .05
❑ 424 Eddie Murray .40 .18
❑ 425 Jesse Barfield .10 .05
❑ 426 Mark Lemke .10 .05
❑ 427 Kevin McReynolds .10 .05
❑ 428 Gilberto Reyes .10 .05
❑ 429 Ramon Martinez .10 .05
❑ 430 Steve Buechele .10 .05
❑ 431 David Wells .20 .09
❑ 432 Kyle Abbott .10 .05
❑ 433 John Habyan .10 .05
❑ 434 Kevin Appier .20 .09
❑ 435 Gene Larkin .10 .05
❑ 436 Sandy Alomar Jr. .20 .09
❑ 437 Mike Jackson .10 .05
❑ 438 Todd Benzinger .10 .05
❑ 439 Teddy Higuera .10 .05
❑ 440 Reggie Sanders .10 .05
❑ 441 Mark Carreon .10 .05
❑ 442 Bret Saberhagen .20 .09
❑ 443 Gene Nelson .10 .05
❑ 444 Jay Howell .10 .05
❑ 445 Roger McDowell .10 .05
❑ 446 Sid Bream .10 .05
❑ 447 Mackey Sasser .10 .05
❑ 448 Bill Swift .10 .05
❑ 449 Hubie Brooks .10 .05
❑ 450 David Cone .20 .09
❑ 451 Bobby Witt .10 .05
❑ 452 Brady Anderson .20 .09
❑ 453 Lee Stevens .20 .09
❑ 454 Luis Aquino .10 .05
❑ 455 Carney Lansford .20 .09
❑ 456 Carlos Hernandez .10 .05
❑ 457 Danny Jackson .10 .05
❑ 458 Gerald Young .10 .05
❑ 459 Tom Candiotti .10 .05
❑ 460 Billy Hatcher .10 .05
❑ 461 John Wetteland .20 .09
❑ 462 Mike Bordick .10 .05
❑ 463 Don Robinson .10 .05
❑ 464 Jeff Johnson .10 .05
❑ 465 Lonnie Smith .10 .05
❑ 466 Paul Assenmacher .10 .05
❑ 467 Alvin Davis .10 .05
❑ 468 Jim Eisenreich .10 .05
❑ 469 Brent Mayne .10 .05
❑ 470 Jeff Brantley .10 .05
❑ 471 Tim Burke .10 .05
❑ 472 Pat Mahomes RC .10 .05
❑ 473 Ryan Bowen .10 .05
❑ 474 Bryn Smith .10 .05
❑ 475 Mike Flanagan .10 .05
❑ 476 Reggie Jefferson .20 .09
❑ 477 Jeff Blauser .10 .05
❑ 478 Craig Lefferts .10 .05
❑ 479 Todd Worrell .10 .05
❑ 480 Scott Scudder .10 .05
❑ 481 Kirk Gibson .20 .09
❑ 482 Kenny Rogers .10 .05
❑ 483 Jack Morris .20 .09
❑ 484 Russ Swan .10 .05
❑ 485 Mike Huff .10 .05
❑ 486 Ken Hill .10 .05
❑ 487 Geronimo Pena .10 .05
❑ 488 Charlie O'Brien .10 .05
❑ 489 Mike Maddux .10 .05
❑ 490 Scott Livingstone .10 .05
❑ 491 Carl Willis .10 .05
❑ 492 Kelly Downs .10 .05
❑ 493 Dennis Cook .10 .05
❑ 494 Joe Magrane .10 .05
❑ 495 Bob Kipper .10 .05
❑ 496 Jose Mesa .10 .05
❑ 497 Charlie Hayes .10 .05
❑ 498 Joe Girardi .20 .09
❑ 499 Doug Jones .10 .05
❑ 500 Barry Bonds .60 .25
❑ 501 Bill Krueger .10 .05
❑ 502 Glenn Braggs .10 .05
❑ 503 Eric King .10 .05
❑ 504 Frank Castillo .10 .05
❑ 505 Mike Gardiner .10 .05
❑ 506 Cory Snyder .10 .05
❑ 507 Steve Howe .10 .05
❑ 508 Jose Rijo .10 .05
❑ 509 Sid Fernandez .10 .05
❑ 510 Archi Cianfrocco RC .10 .05
❑ 511 Mark Guthrie .10 .05
❑ 512 Bob Ojeda .10 .05
❑ 513 John Doherty RC .10 .05
❑ 514 Dante Bichette .20 .09
❑ 515 Juan Berenguer .10 .05
❑ 516 Jeff M. Robinson .10 .05
❑ 517 Mike Macfarlane .10 .05
❑ 518 Matt Young .10 .05
❑ 519 Otis Nixon .10 .05
❑ 520 Brian Holman .10 .05
❑ 521 Chris Haney .10 .05
❑ 522 Jeff Kent RC 3.00 1.35
❑ 523 Chad Curtis RC .40 .18
❑ 524 Vince Horsman .10 .05
❑ 525 Rod Nichols .10 .05

| | No. | Player | Mint | NrMt |
|---|---|---|---|---|
| ❑ | 526 | Peter Hoy | .10 | .05 |
| ❑ | 527 | Shawn Boskie | .10 | .05 |
| ❑ | 528 | Alejandro Pena | .10 | .05 |
| ❑ | 529 | Dave Burba | .10 | .05 |
| ❑ | 530 | Ricky Jordan | .10 | .05 |
| ❑ | 531 | Dave Silvestri | .10 | .05 |
| ❑ | 532 | John Patterson UER (Listed as being born in 1960; should be 1967) | .10 | .05 |
| ❑ | 533 | Jeff Branson | .10 | .05 |
| ❑ | 534 | Derrick May | .10 | .05 |
| ❑ | 535 | Esteban Beltre | .10 | .05 |
| ❑ | 536 | Jose Melendez | .10 | .05 |
| ❑ | 537 | Wally Joyner | .20 | .09 |
| ❑ | 538 | Eddie Taubensee RC | .20 | .09 |
| ❑ | 539 | Jim Abbott | .20 | .09 |
| ❑ | 540 | Brian Williams RC | .10 | .05 |
| ❑ | 541 | Donovan Osborne | .10 | .05 |
| ❑ | 542 | Patrick Lennon | .10 | .05 |
| ❑ | 543 | Mike Groppuso RC | .10 | .05 |
| ❑ | 544 | Jarvis Brown | .10 | .05 |
| ❑ | 545 | Shawn Livsey RC | .10 | .05 |
| ❑ | 546 | Jeff Ware | .10 | .05 |
| ❑ | 547 | Danny Tartabull | .10 | .05 |
| ❑ | 548 | Bobby Jones RC | .40 | .18 |
| ❑ | 549 | Ken Griffey Jr. | 1.50 | .70 |
| ❑ | 550 | Rey Sanchez RC | .10 | .05 |
| ❑ | 551 | Pedro Astacio RC | .50 | .23 |
| ❑ | 552 | Juan Guerrero | .10 | .05 |
| ❑ | 553 | Jacob Brumfield | .10 | .05 |
| ❑ | 554 | Ben Rivera | .10 | .05 |
| ❑ | 555 | Brian Jordan RC | 1.00 | .45 |
| ❑ | 556 | Denny Neagle | .20 | .09 |
| ❑ | 557 | Cliff Brantley | .10 | .05 |
| ❑ | 558 | Anthony Young | .10 | .05 |
| ❑ | 559 | John Vander Wal | .10 | .05 |
| ❑ | 560 | Monty Fariss | .10 | .05 |
| ❑ | 561 | Russ Springer RC | .10 | .05 |
| ❑ | 562 | Pat Listach RC | .10 | .05 |
| ❑ | 563 | Pat Hentgen | .10 | .05 |
| ❑ | 564 | Andy Stankiewicz | .10 | .05 |
| ❑ | 565 | Mike Perez | .10 | .05 |
| ❑ | 566 | Mike Bielecki | .10 | .05 |
| ❑ | 567 | Butch Henry RC | .10 | .05 |
| ❑ | 568 | Dave Nilsson | .20 | .09 |
| ❑ | 569 | Scott Hatteberg RC | .10 | .05 |
| ❑ | 570 | Ruben Amaro | .10 | .05 |
| ❑ | 571 | Todd Hundley | .10 | .05 |
| ❑ | 572 | Moises Alou | .40 | .18 |
| ❑ | 573 | Hector Fajardo RC | .10 | .05 |
| ❑ | 574 | Todd Van Poppel | .10 | .05 |
| ❑ | 575 | Willie Banks | .10 | .05 |
| ❑ | 576 | Bob Zupcic RC | .10 | .05 |
| ❑ | 577 | J.J. Johnson RC | .20 | .09 |
| ❑ | 578 | John Burkett | .10 | .05 |
| ❑ | 579 | Trever Miller RC | .10 | .05 |
| ❑ | 580 | Scott Bankhead | .10 | .05 |
| ❑ | 581 | Rich Amaral | .10 | .05 |
| ❑ | 582 | Kenny Lofton | .50 | .23 |
| ❑ | 583 | Matt Stairs RC | .25 | .11 |
| ❑ | 584 | Don Mattingly Rod Carew IDOLS | .40 | .18 |
| ❑ | 585 | Steve Avery Jack Morris IDOLS | .10 | .05 |
| ❑ | 586 | Roberto Alomar Sandy Alomar SR. IDOLS | .20 | .09 |
| ❑ | 587 | Scott Sanderson Catfish Hunter IDOLS | .20 | .09 |
| ❑ | 588 | Dave Justice Willie Stargell IDOLS | .20 | .09 |
| ❑ | 589 | Rex Hudler Roger Staubach IDOLS | .40 | .18 |
| ❑ | 590 | David Cone Jackie Gleason IDOLS | .20 | .09 |
| ❑ | 591 | Tony Gwynn Willie Davis IDOLS | .40 | .18 |
| ❑ | 592 | Orel Hershiser SIDE | .10 | .05 |
| ❑ | 593 | John Wetteland SIDE | .10 | .05 |
| ❑ | 594 | Tom Glavine SIDE | .20 | .09 |
| ❑ | 595 | Randy Johnson SIDE | .20 | .09 |
| ❑ | 596 | Jim Gott SIDE | .10 | .05 |
| ❑ | 597 | Donald Harris | .10 | .05 |
| ❑ | 598 | Shawn Hare RC | .10 | .05 |
| ❑ | 599 | Chris Gardner | .10 | .05 |
| ❑ | 600 | Rusty Meacham | .10 | .05 |
| ❑ | 601 | Benito Santiago | .10 | .05 |
| ❑ | 602 | Eric Davis SHADE | .10 | .05 |
| ❑ | 603 | Jose Lind SHADE | .10 | .05 |
| ❑ | 604 | Dave Justice SHADE | .10 | .05 |
| ❑ | 605 | Tim Raines SHADE | .20 | .09 |
| ❑ | 606 | Randy Tomlin GRIP | .10 | .05 |
| ❑ | 607 | Jack McDowell GRIP | .10 | .05 |
| ❑ | 608 | Greg Maddux GRIP | .40 | .18 |
| ❑ | 609 | Charles Nagy GRIP | .10 | .05 |
| ❑ | 610 | Tom Candiotti GRIP | .10 | .05 |
| ❑ | 611 | David Cone GRIP | .10 | .05 |
| ❑ | 612 | Steve Avery GRIP | .10 | .05 |
| ❑ | 613 | Rod Beck GRIP RC | .20 | .09 |
| ❑ | 614 | Rickey Henderson TECH | .20 | .09 |
| ❑ | 615 | Benito Santiago TECH | .10 | .05 |
| ❑ | 616 | Ruben Sierra TECH | .10 | .05 |
| ❑ | 617 | Ryne Sandberg TECH | .40 | .18 |
| ❑ | 618 | Nolan Ryan TECH | 1.00 | .35 |
| ❑ | 619 | Brett Butler TECH | .10 | .05 |
| ❑ | 620 | Dave Justice TECH | .10 | .05 |

## 1993 Pinnacle

Carlos Baerga

| | MINT | NRMT |
|---|---|---|
| COMPLETE SET (620) | 45.00 | 20.00 |
| COMPLETE SERIES 1 (310) | 15.00 | 6.75 |
| COMPLETE SERIES 2 (310) | 30.00 | 13.50 |
| COMMON CARD (1-620) | .15 | .07 |

| | No. | Player | Mint | NrMt |
|---|---|---|---|---|
| ❑ | 1 | Gary Sheffield | .60 | .25 |
| ❑ | 2 | Cal Eldred | .15 | .07 |
| ❑ | 3 | Larry Walker | .30 | .14 |
| ❑ | 4 | Deion Sanders | .30 | .14 |
| ❑ | 5 | Dave Fleming | .15 | .07 |
| ❑ | 6 | Carlos Baerga | .15 | .07 |
| ❑ | 7 | Bernie Williams | .60 | .25 |
| ❑ | 8 | John Kruk | .30 | .14 |
| ❑ | 9 | Jimmy Key | .30 | .14 |
| ❑ | 10 | Jeff Bagwell | .75 | .35 |
| ❑ | 11 | Jim Abbott | .30 | .14 |
| ❑ | 12 | Terry Steinbach | .15 | .07 |
| ❑ | 13 | Bob Tewksbury | .15 | .07 |
| ❑ | 14 | Eric Karros | .30 | .14 |
| ❑ | 15 | Ryne Sandberg | .75 | .35 |
| ❑ | 16 | Will Clark | .60 | .25 |
| ❑ | 17 | Edgar Martinez | .30 | .14 |
| ❑ | 18 | Eddie Murray | .60 | .25 |
| ❑ | 19 | Andy Van Slyke | .30 | .14 |
| ❑ | 20 | Cal Ripken Jr. | 2.50 | 1.10 |
| ❑ | 21 | Ivan Rodriguez | .75 | .35 |
| ❑ | 22 | Barry Larkin | .60 | .25 |
| ❑ | 23 | Don Mattingly | 1.50 | .70 |
| ❑ | 24 | Gregg Jefferies | .15 | .07 |
| ❑ | 25 | Roger Clemens | 1.25 | .55 |
| ❑ | 26 | Cecil Fielder | .30 | .14 |
| ❑ | 27 | Kent Hrbek | .30 | .14 |
| ❑ | 28 | Robin Ventura | .30 | .14 |
| ❑ | 29 | Rickey Henderson | .75 | .35 |
| ❑ | 30 | Roberto Alomar | .60 | .25 |
| ❑ | 31 | Luis Polonia | .15 | .07 |
| ❑ | 32 | Andujar Cedeno | .15 | .07 |
| ❑ | 33 | Pat Listach | .15 | .07 |
| ❑ | 34 | Mark Grace | .60 | .25 |
| ❑ | 35 | Otis Nixon | .15 | .07 |
| ❑ | 36 | Felix Jose | .15 | .07 |
| ❑ | 37 | Mike Sharperson | .15 | .07 |
| ❑ | 38 | Dennis Martinez | .30 | .14 |
| ❑ | 39 | Willie McGee | .30 | .14 |
| ❑ | 40 | Kenny Lofton | .30 | .14 |
| ❑ | 41 | Randy Johnson | .75 | .35 |
| ❑ | 42 | Andy Benes | .15 | .07 |
| ❑ | 43 | Bobby Bonilla | .30 | .14 |
| ❑ | 44 | Mike Mussina | .60 | .25 |
| ❑ | 45 | Len Dykstra | .30 | .14 |
| ❑ | 46 | Ellis Burks | .30 | .14 |
| ❑ | 47 | Chris Sabo | .15 | .07 |
| ❑ | 48 | Jay Bell | .30 | .14 |
| ❑ | 49 | Jose Canseco | .75 | .35 |
| ❑ | 50 | Craig Biggio | .30 | .14 |
| ❑ | 51 | Wally Joyner | .30 | .14 |
| ❑ | 52 | Mickey Tettleton | .15 | .07 |
| ❑ | 53 | Tim Raines | .30 | .14 |
| ❑ | 54 | Brian Harper | .15 | .07 |
| ❑ | 55 | Rene Gonzales | .15 | .07 |
| ❑ | 56 | Mark Langston | .15 | .07 |
| ❑ | 57 | Jack Morris | .30 | .14 |
| ❑ | 58 | Mark McGwire | 2.50 | 1.10 |
| ❑ | 59 | Ken Caminiti | .30 | .14 |
| ❑ | 60 | Terry Pendleton | .30 | .14 |
| ❑ | 61 | Dave Nilsson | .30 | .14 |
| ❑ | 62 | Tom Pagnozzi | .15 | .07 |
| ❑ | 63 | Mike Morgan | .15 | .07 |
| ❑ | 64 | Darryl Strawberry | .30 | .14 |
| ❑ | 65 | Charles Nagy | .15 | .07 |
| ❑ | 66 | Ken Hill | .15 | .07 |
| ❑ | 67 | Matt Williams | .30 | .14 |
| ❑ | 68 | Jay Buhner | .30 | .14 |
| ❑ | 69 | Vince Coleman | .15 | .07 |
| ❑ | 70 | Brady Anderson | .30 | .14 |
| ❑ | 71 | Fred McGriff | .30 | .14 |
| ❑ | 72 | Ben McDonald | .15 | .07 |
| ❑ | 73 | Terry Mulholland | .15 | .07 |
| ❑ | 74 | Randy Tomlin | .15 | .07 |
| ❑ | 75 | Nolan Ryan | 3.00 | 1.35 |
| ❑ | 76 | Frank Viola UER (Card incorrectly states he has a surgically repaired elbow) | .15 | .07 |
| ❑ | 77 | Jose Rijo | .15 | .07 |
| ❑ | 78 | Shane Mack | .15 | .07 |
| ❑ | 79 | Travis Fryman | .30 | .14 |
| ❑ | 80 | Jack McDowell | .15 | .07 |
| ❑ | 81 | Mark Gubicza | .15 | .07 |
| ❑ | 82 | Matt Nokes | .15 | .07 |
| ❑ | 83 | Bert Blyleven | .30 | .14 |
| ❑ | 84 | Eric Anthony | .15 | .07 |
| ❑ | 85 | Mike Bordick | .15 | .07 |
| ❑ | 86 | John Olerud | .30 | .14 |
| ❑ | 87 | B.J. Surhoff | .30 | .14 |
| ❑ | 88 | Bernard Gilkey | .15 | .07 |
| ❑ | 89 | Shawon Dunston | .15 | .07 |
| ❑ | 90 | Tom Glavine | .30 | .14 |
| ❑ | 91 | Brett Butler | .30 | .14 |
| ❑ | 92 | Moises Alou | .30 | .14 |
| ❑ | 93 | Albert Belle | .30 | .14 |
| ❑ | 94 | Darren Lewis | .15 | .07 |
| ❑ | 95 | Omar Vizquel | .30 | .14 |
| ❑ | 96 | Dwight Gooden | .30 | .14 |
| ❑ | 97 | Gregg Olson | .15 | .07 |
| ❑ | 98 | Tony Gwynn | 1.25 | .55 |
| ❑ | 99 | Darren Daulton | .30 | .14 |
| ❑ | 100 | Dennis Eckersley | .30 | .14 |
| ❑ | 101 | Rob Dibble | .15 | .07 |
| ❑ | 102 | Mike Greenwell | .15 | .07 |
| ❑ | 103 | Jose Lind | .15 | .07 |
| ❑ | 104 | Julio Franco | .15 | .07 |
| ❑ | 105 | Tom Gordon | .15 | .07 |
| ❑ | 106 | Scott Livingstone | .15 | .07 |
| ❑ | 107 | Chuck Knoblauch | .30 | .14 |
| ❑ | 108 | Frank Thomas | 1.25 | .55 |
| ❑ | 109 | Melido Perez | .15 | .07 |
| ❑ | 110 | Ken Griffey Jr. | 2.50 | 1.10 |
| ❑ | 111 | Harold Baines | .30 | .14 |
| ❑ | 112 | Gary Gaetti | .30 | .14 |
| ❑ | 113 | Pete Harnisch | .15 | .07 |
| ❑ | 114 | David Wells | .30 | .14 |
| ❑ | 115 | Charlie Leibrandt | .15 | .07 |
| ❑ | 116 | Ray Lankford | .30 | .14 |
| ❑ | 117 | Kevin Seitzer | .15 | .07 |
| ❑ | 118 | Robin Yount | .30 | .14 |
| ❑ | 119 | Lenny Harris | .15 | .07 |
| ❑ | 120 | Chris James | .15 | .07 |
| ❑ | 121 | Delino DeShields | .30 | .14 |
| ❑ | 122 | Kirt Manwaring | .15 | .07 |
| ❑ | 123 | Glenallen Hill | .15 | .07 |

- ❑ 124 Hensley Meulens .15 .07
- ❑ 125 Darrin Jackson .15 .07
- ❑ 126 Todd Hundley .15 .07
- ❑ 127 Dave Hollins .15 .07
- ❑ 128 Sam Horn .15 .07
- ❑ 129 Roberto Hernandez .15 .07
- ❑ 130 Vicente Palacios .15 .07
- ❑ 131 George Brett 1.25 .55
- ❑ 132 Dave Martinez .15 .07
- ❑ 133 Kevin Appier .30 .14
- ❑ 134 Pat Kelly .15 .07
- ❑ 135 Pedro Munoz .15 .07
- ❑ 136 Mark Carreon .15 .07
- ❑ 137 Lance Johnson .15 .07
- ❑ 138 Devon White .15 .07
- ❑ 139 Julio Valera .15 .07
- ❑ 140 Eddie Taubensee .15 .07
- ❑ 141 Willie Wilson .15 .07
- ❑ 142 Stan Belinda .15 .07
- ❑ 143 John Smoltz .30 .14
- ❑ 144 Darryl Hamilton .15 .07
- ❑ 145 Sammy Sosa 1.25 .55
- ❑ 146 Carlos Hernandez .15 .07
- ❑ 147 Tom Candiotti .15 .07
- ❑ 148 Mike Felder .15 .07
- ❑ 149 Rusty Meacham .15 .07
- ❑ 150 Ivan Calderon .15 .07
- ❑ 151 Pete O'Brien .15 .07
- ❑ 152 Erik Hanson .15 .07
- ❑ 153 Billy Ripken .15 .07
- ❑ 154 Kurt Stillwell .15 .07
- ❑ 155 Jeff Kent .60 .25
- ❑ 156 Mickey Morandini .15 .07
- ❑ 157 Randy Milligan .15 .07
- ❑ 158 Reggie Sanders .15 .07
- ❑ 159 Luis Rivera .15 .07
- ❑ 160 Orlando Merced .15 .07
- ❑ 161 Dean Palmer .30 .14
- ❑ 162 Mike Perez .15 .07
- ❑ 163 Scott Erickson .15 .07
- ❑ 164 Kevin McReynolds .15 .07
- ❑ 165 Kevin Maas .15 .07
- ❑ 166 Ozzie Guillen .15 .07
- ❑ 167 Rob Deer .15 .07
- ❑ 168 Danny Tartabull .15 .07
- ❑ 169 Lee Stevens .30 .14
- ❑ 170 Dave Henderson .15 .07
- ❑ 171 Derek Bell .15 .07
- ❑ 172 Steve Finley .30 .14
- ❑ 173 Greg Olson .15 .07
- ❑ 174 Geronimo Pena .15 .07
- ❑ 175 Paul Quantrill .15 .07
- ❑ 176 Steve Buechele .15 .07
- ❑ 177 Kevin Gross .15 .07
- ❑ 178 Tim Wallach .15 .07
- ❑ 179 Dave Valle .15 .07
- ❑ 180 Dave Silvestri .15 .07
- ❑ 181 Bud Black .15 .07
- ❑ 182 Henry Rodriguez .15 .07
- ❑ 183 Tim Teufel .15 .07
- ❑ 184 Mark McLemore .15 .07
- ❑ 185 Bret Saberhagen .30 .14
- ❑ 186 Chris Hoiles .15 .07
- ❑ 187 Ricky Jordan .15 .07
- ❑ 188 Don Slaught .15 .07
- ❑ 189 Mo Vaughn .30 .14
- ❑ 190 Joe Oliver .15 .07
- ❑ 191 Juan Gonzalez .60 .25
- ❑ 192 Scott Leius .15 .07
- ❑ 193 Milt Cuyler .15 .07
- ❑ 194 Chris Haney .15 .07
- ❑ 195 Ron Karkovice .15 .07
- ❑ 196 Steve Farr .15 .07
- ❑ 197 John Orton .15 .07
- ❑ 198 Kelly Gruber .15 .07
- ❑ 199 Ron Darling .15 .07
- ❑ 200 Ruben Sierra .15 .07
- ❑ 201 Chuck Finley .30 .14
- ❑ 202 Mike Moore .15 .07
- ❑ 203 Pat Borders .15 .07
- ❑ 204 Sid Bream .15 .07
- ❑ 205 Todd Zeile .15 .07
- ❑ 206 Rick Wilkins .15 .07
- ❑ 207 Jim Gantner .15 .07
- ❑ 208 Frank Castillo .15 .07
- ❑ 209 Dave Hansen .15 .07
- ❑ 210 Trevor Wilson .15 .07
- ❑ 211 Sandy Alomar Jr. .30 .14
- ❑ 212 Sean Berry .15 .07
- ❑ 213 Tino Martinez .30 .14
- ❑ 214 Chito Martinez .15 .07
- ❑ 215 Dan Walters .15 .07
- ❑ 216 John Franco .30 .14
- ❑ 217 Glenn Davis .15 .07
- ❑ 218 Mariano Duncan .15 .07
- ❑ 219 Mike LaValliere .15 .07
- ❑ 220 Rafael Palmeiro .60 .25
- ❑ 221 Jack Clark .15 .07
- ❑ 222 Hal Morris .15 .07
- ❑ 223 Ed Sprague .15 .07
- ❑ 224 John Valentin .15 .07
- ❑ 225 Sam Militello .15 .07
- ❑ 226 Bob Wickman .15 .07
- ❑ 227 Damion Easley .15 .07
- ❑ 228 John Jaha .15 .07
- ❑ 229 Bob Ayrault .15 .07
- ❑ 230 Mo Sanford .15 .07
- ❑ 231 Walt Weiss .15 .07
- ❑ 232 Dante Bichette .30 .14
- ❑ 233 Steve Decker .15 .07
- ❑ 234 Jerald Clark .15 .07
- ❑ 235 Bryan Harvey .15 .07
- ❑ 236 Joe Girardi .30 .14
- ❑ 237 Dave Magadan .15 .07
- ❑ 238 David Nied .15 .07
- ❑ 239 Eric Wedge RC .15 .07
- ❑ 240 Rico Brogna .30 .14
- ❑ 241 J.T. Bruett .15 .07
- ❑ 242 Jonathan Hurst .15 .07
- ❑ 243 Bret Boone .30 .14
- ❑ 244 Manny Alexander .15 .07
- ❑ 245 Scooter Tucker .15 .07
- ❑ 246 Troy Neel .15 .07
- ❑ 247 Eddie Zosky .15 .07
- ❑ 248 Melvin Nieves .15 .07
- ❑ 249 Ryan Thompson .15 .07
- ❑ 250 Shawn Barton RC .15 .07
- ❑ 251 Ryan Klesko .60 .25
- ❑ 252 Mike Piazza 3.00 1.35
- ❑ 253 Steve Hosey .15 .07
- ❑ 254 Shane Reynolds .15 .07
- ❑ 255 Dan Wilson .30 .14
- ❑ 256 Tom Marsh .15 .07
- ❑ 257 Barry Manuel .15 .07
- ❑ 258 Paul Miller .15 .07
- ❑ 259 Pedro Martinez 1.50 .70
- ❑ 260 Steve Cooke .15 .07
- ❑ 261 Johnny Guzman .15 .07
- ❑ 262 Mike Butcher .15 .07
- ❑ 263 Bien Figueroa .15 .07
- ❑ 264 Rich Rowland .15 .07
- ❑ 265 Shawn Jeter .15 .07
- ❑ 266 Gerald Williams .15 .07
- ❑ 267 Derek Parks .15 .07
- ❑ 268 Henry Mercedes .15 .07
- ❑ 269 David Hulse RC .15 .07
- ❑ 270 Tim Pugh RC .15 .07
- ❑ 271 William Suero .15 .07
- ❑ 272 Ozzie Canseco .15 .07
- ❑ 273 Fernando Ramsey RC .15 .07
- ❑ 274 Bernardo Brito .15 .07
- ❑ 275 Dave Mlicki .15 .07
- ❑ 276 Tim Salmon .30 .14
- ❑ 277 Mike Raczka .15 .07
- ❑ 278 Ken Ryan RC .15 .07
- ❑ 279 Rafael Bournigal .15 .07
- ❑ 280 Wil Cordero .15 .07
- ❑ 281 Billy Ashley .15 .07
- ❑ 282 Paul Wagner .15 .07
- ❑ 283 Blas Minor .15 .07
- ❑ 284 Rick Trlicek .15 .07
- ❑ 285 Willie Greene .15 .07
- ❑ 286 Ted Wood .15 .07
- ❑ 287 Phil Clark .15 .07
- ❑ 288 Jesse Levis .15 .07
- ❑ 289 Tony Gwynn NT .60 .25
- ❑ 290 Nolan Ryan NT 1.50 .70
- ❑ 291 Dennis Martinez NT .15 .07
- ❑ 292 Eddie Murray NT .30 .14
- ❑ 293 Robin Yount NT .30 .14
- ❑ 294 George Brett NT .60 .25
- ❑ 295 Dave Winfield NT .30 .14
- ❑ 296 Bert Blyleven NT .15 .07
- ❑ 297 Jeff Bagwell .60 .25
  Carl Yastrzemski
- ❑ 298 John Smoltz .30 .14
  Jack Morris
- ❑ 299 Larry Walker .30 .14
  Mike Bossy
- ❑ 300 Gary Sheffield .30 .14
  Barry Larkin
- ❑ 301 Ivan Rodriguez .30 .14
  Carlton Fisk
- ❑ 302 Delino DeShields .60 .25
  Malcolm X
- ❑ 303 Tim Salmon .30 .14
  Dwight Evans
- ❑ 304 Bernard Gilkey HH .15 .07
- ❑ 305 Cal Ripken Jr. HH 1.25 .55
- ❑ 306 Barry Larkin HH .30 .14
- ❑ 307 Kent Hrbek HH .15 .07
- ❑ 308 Rickey Henderson HH .30 .14
- ❑ 309 Darryl Strawberry HH .15 .07
- ❑ 310 John Franco HH .15 .07
- ❑ 311 Todd Stottlemyre .15 .07
- ❑ 312 Luis Gonzalez .30 .14
- ❑ 313 Tommy Greene .15 .07
- ❑ 314 Randy Velarde .15 .07
- ❑ 315 Steve Avery .15 .07
- ❑ 316 Jose Oquendo .15 .07
- ❑ 317 Rey Sanchez .15 .07
- ❑ 318 Greg Vaughn .30 .14
- ❑ 319 Orel Hershiser .30 .14
- ❑ 320 Paul Sorrento .15 .07
- ❑ 321 Royce Clayton .15 .07
- ❑ 322 John Vander Wal .15 .07
- ❑ 323 Henry Cotto .15 .07
- ❑ 324 Pete Schourek .15 .07
- ❑ 325 David Segui .15 .07
- ❑ 326 Arthur Rhodes .15 .07
- ❑ 327 Bruce Hurst .15 .07
- ❑ 328 Wes Chamberlain .15 .07
- ❑ 329 Ozzie Smith .75 .35
- ❑ 330 Scott Cooper .15 .07
- ❑ 331 Felix Fermin .15 .07
- ❑ 332 Mike Macfarlane .15 .07
- ❑ 333 Dan Gladden .15 .07
- ❑ 334 Kevin Tapani .15 .07
- ❑ 335 Steve Sax .15 .07
- ❑ 336 Jeff Montgomery .30 .14
- ❑ 337 Gary DiSarcina .15 .07
- ❑ 338 Lance Blankenship .15 .07
- ❑ 339 Brian Williams .15 .07
- ❑ 340 Duane Ward .15 .07
- ❑ 341 Chuck McElroy .15 .07
- ❑ 342 Joe Magrane .15 .07
- ❑ 343 Jaime Navarro .15 .07
- ❑ 344 Dave Justice .30 .14
- ❑ 345 Jose Offerman .15 .07
- ❑ 346 Marquis Grissom .15 .07
- ❑ 347 Bill Swift .15 .07
- ❑ 348 Jim Thome .30 .14
- ❑ 349 Archi Cianfrocco .15 .07
- ❑ 350 Anthony Young .15 .07
- ❑ 351 Leo Gomez .15 .07
- ❑ 352 Bill Gullickson .15 .07
- ❑ 353 Alan Trammell .30 .14
- ❑ 354 Dan Pasqua .15 .07
- ❑ 355 Jeff King .15 .07
- ❑ 356 Kevin Brown .30 .14
- ❑ 357 Tim Belcher .15 .07
- ❑ 358 Bip Roberts .15 .07
- ❑ 359 Brent Mayne .15 .07
- ❑ 360 Rheal Cormier .15 .07
- ❑ 361 Mark Guthrie .15 .07
- ❑ 362 Craig Grebeck .15 .07
- ❑ 363 Andy Stankiewicz .15 .07
- ❑ 364 Juan Guzman .15 .07
- ❑ 365 Bobby Witt .15 .07
- ❑ 366 Mark Portugal .15 .07
- ❑ 367 Brian McRae .15 .07
- ❑ 368 Mark Lemke .15 .07
- ❑ 369 Bill Wegman .15 .07
- ❑ 370 Donovan Osborne .15 .07
- ❑ 371 Derrick May .15 .07
- ❑ 372 Carl Willis .15 .07
- ❑ 373 Chris Nabholz .15 .07
- ❑ 374 Mark Lewis .15 .07

| | No. | Player | Mint | Nrmt |
|---|---|---|---|---|
| ❑ | 375 | John Burkett | .15 | .07 |
| ❑ | 376 | Luis Mercedes | .15 | .07 |
| ❑ | 377 | Ramon Martinez | .15 | .07 |
| ❑ | 378 | Kyle Abbott | .15 | .07 |
| ❑ | 379 | Mark Wohlers | .15 | .07 |
| ❑ | 380 | Bob Walk | .15 | .07 |
| ❑ | 381 | Kenny Rogers | .15 | .07 |
| ❑ | 382 | Tim Naehring | .15 | .07 |
| ❑ | 383 | Alex Fernandez | .30 | .14 |
| ❑ | 384 | Keith Miller | .15 | .07 |
| ❑ | 385 | Mike Henneman | .15 | .07 |
| ❑ | 386 | Rick Aguilera | .15 | .07 |
| ❑ | 387 | George Bell | .15 | .07 |
| ❑ | 388 | Mike Gallego | .15 | .07 |
| ❑ | 389 | Howard Johnson | .15 | .07 |
| ❑ | 390 | Kim Batiste | .15 | .07 |
| ❑ | 391 | Jerry Browne | .15 | .07 |
| ❑ | 392 | Damon Berryhill | .15 | .07 |
| ❑ | 393 | Ricky Bones | .15 | .07 |
| ❑ | 394 | Omar Olivares | .15 | .07 |
| ❑ | 395 | Mike Harkey | .15 | .07 |
| ❑ | 396 | Pedro Astacio | .30 | .14 |
| ❑ | 397 | John Wetteland | .30 | .14 |
| ❑ | 398 | Rod Beck | .15 | .07 |
| ❑ | 399 | Thomas Howard | .15 | .07 |
| ❑ | 400 | Mike Devereaux | .15 | .07 |
| ❑ | 401 | Tim Wakefield | .15 | .07 |
| ❑ | 402 | Curt Schilling | .30 | .14 |
| ❑ | 403 | Zane Smith | .15 | .07 |
| ❑ | 404 | Bob Zupcic | .15 | .07 |
| ❑ | 405 | Tom Browning | .15 | .07 |
| ❑ | 406 | Tony Phillips | .15 | .07 |
| ❑ | 407 | John Doherty | .15 | .07 |
| ❑ | 408 | Pat Mahomes | .15 | .07 |
| ❑ | 409 | John Habyan | .15 | .07 |
| ❑ | 410 | Steve Olin | .15 | .07 |
| ❑ | 411 | Chad Curtis | .15 | .07 |
| ❑ | 412 | Joe Grahe | .15 | .07 |
| ❑ | 413 | John Patterson | .15 | .07 |
| ❑ | 414 | Brian Hunter | .15 | .07 |
| ❑ | 415 | Doug Henry | .15 | .07 |
| ❑ | 416 | Lee Smith | .30 | .14 |
| ❑ | 417 | Bob Scanlan | .15 | .07 |
| ❑ | 418 | Kent Mercker | .15 | .07 |
| ❑ | 419 | Mel Rojas | .15 | .07 |
| ❑ | 420 | Mark Whiten | .15 | .07 |
| ❑ | 421 | Carlton Fisk | .60 | .25 |
| ❑ | 422 | Candy Maldonado | .15 | .07 |
| ❑ | 423 | Doug Drabek | .15 | .07 |
| ❑ | 424 | Wade Boggs | .75 | .35 |
| ❑ | 425 | Mark Davis | .15 | .07 |
| ❑ | 426 | Kirby Puckett | 1.50 | .70 |
| ❑ | 427 | Joe Carter | .30 | .14 |
| ❑ | 428 | Paul Molitor | .60 | .25 |
| ❑ | 429 | Eric Davis | .30 | .14 |
| ❑ | 430 | Darryl Kile | .30 | .14 |
| ❑ | 431 | Jeff Parrett | .15 | .07 |
| ❑ | 432 | Jeff Blauser | .15 | .07 |
| ❑ | 433 | Dan Plesac | .15 | .07 |
| ❑ | 434 | Andres Galarraga | .30 | .14 |
| ❑ | 435 | Jim Gott | .15 | .07 |
| ❑ | 436 | Jose Mesa | .15 | .07 |
| ❑ | 437 | Ben Rivera | .15 | .07 |
| ❑ | 438 | Dave Winfield | .60 | .25 |
| ❑ | 439 | Norm Charlton | .15 | .07 |
| ❑ | 440 | Chris Bosio | .15 | .07 |
| ❑ | 441 | Wilson Alvarez | .15 | .07 |
| ❑ | 442 | Dave Stewart | .30 | .14 |
| ❑ | 443 | Doug Jones | .15 | .07 |
| ❑ | 444 | Jeff Russell | .15 | .07 |
| ❑ | 445 | Ron Gant | .30 | .14 |
| ❑ | 446 | Paul O'Neill | .30 | .14 |
| ❑ | 447 | Charlie Hayes | .15 | .07 |
| ❑ | 448 | Joe Hesketh | .15 | .07 |
| ❑ | 449 | Chris Hammond | .15 | .07 |
| ❑ | 450 | Hipolito Pichardo | .15 | .07 |
| ❑ | 451 | Scott Radinsky | .15 | .07 |
| ❑ | 452 | Bobby Thigpen | .15 | .07 |
| ❑ | 453 | Xavier Hernandez | .15 | .07 |
| ❑ | 454 | Lonnie Smith | .15 | .07 |
| ❑ | 455 | Jamie Arnold DP RC | .15 | .07 |
| ❑ | 456 | B.J. Wallace DP | .15 | .07 |
| ❑ | 457 | Derek Jeter DP RC | 20.00 | 9.00 |
| ❑ | 458 | Jason Kendall DP RC | 2.00 | .90 |
| ❑ | 459 | Rick Helling DP | .30 | .14 |
| ❑ | 460 | Derek Wallace DP RC | .15 | .07 |
| ❑ | 461 | Sean Lowe DP RC | .15 | .07 |
| ❑ | 462 | Shannon Stewart DP RC | 1.50 | .70 |
| ❑ | 463 | Benji Grigsby DP RC | .15 | .07 |
| ❑ | 464 | Todd Steverson DP RC | .15 | .07 |
| ❑ | 465 | Dan Serafini DP RC | .15 | .07 |
| ❑ | 466 | Michael Tucker DP | .60 | .25 |
| ❑ | 467 | Chris Roberts DP | .15 | .07 |
| ❑ | 468 | Pete Janicki DP RC | .15 | .07 |
| ❑ | 469 | Jeff Schmidt DP RC | .15 | .07 |
| ❑ | 470 | Don Mattingly NT | .75 | .25 |
| ❑ | 471 | Cal Ripken Jr. NT | 1.25 | .55 |
| ❑ | 472 | Jack Morris NT | .15 | .07 |
| ❑ | 473 | Terry Pendleton NT | .30 | .14 |
| ❑ | 474 | Dennis Eckersley NT | .15 | .07 |
| ❑ | 475 | Carlton Fisk NT | .30 | .14 |
| ❑ | 476 | Wade Boggs NT | .60 | .25 |
| ❑ | 477 | Len Dykstra<br>Ken Stabler | .30 | .14 |
| ❑ | 478 | Danny Tartabull<br>Jose Tartabull | .15 | .07 |
| ❑ | 479 | Jeff Conine<br>Dale Murphy | .30 | .14 |
| ❑ | 480 | Gregg Jefferies<br>Ron Cey | .15 | .07 |
| ❑ | 481 | Paul Molitor<br>Harmon Killebrew | .30 | .14 |
| ❑ | 482 | John Valentin<br>Dave Concepcion | .15 | .07 |
| ❑ | 483 | Alex Arias<br>Dave Winfield | .30 | .14 |
| ❑ | 484 | Barry Bonds HH | .30 | .14 |
| ❑ | 485 | Doug Drabek HH | .15 | .07 |
| ❑ | 486 | Dave Winfield HH | .30 | .14 |
| ❑ | 487 | Brett Butler HH | .15 | .07 |
| ❑ | 488 | Harold Baines HH | .15 | .07 |
| ❑ | 489 | David Cone HH | .30 | .14 |
| ❑ | 490 | Willie McGee HH | .15 | .07 |
| ❑ | 491 | Robby Thompson | .15 | .07 |
| ❑ | 492 | Pete Incaviglia | .15 | .07 |
| ❑ | 493 | Manuel Lee | .15 | .07 |
| ❑ | 494 | Rafael Belliard | .15 | .07 |
| ❑ | 495 | Scott Fletcher | .15 | .07 |
| ❑ | 496 | Jeff Frye | .15 | .07 |
| ❑ | 497 | Andre Dawson | .30 | .14 |
| ❑ | 498 | Mike Scioscia | .15 | .07 |
| ❑ | 499 | Spike Owen | .15 | .07 |
| ❑ | 500 | Sid Fernandez | .15 | .07 |
| ❑ | 501 | Joe Orsulak | .15 | .07 |
| ❑ | 502 | Benito Santiago | .15 | .07 |
| ❑ | 503 | Dale Murphy | .30 | .14 |
| ❑ | 504 | Barry Bonds | 1.00 | .45 |
| ❑ | 505 | Jose Guzman | .15 | .07 |
| ❑ | 506 | Tony Pena | .15 | .07 |
| ❑ | 507 | Greg Swindell | .15 | .07 |
| ❑ | 508 | Mike Pagliarulo | .15 | .07 |
| ❑ | 509 | Lou Whitaker | .30 | .14 |
| ❑ | 510 | Greg Gagne | .15 | .07 |
| ❑ | 511 | Butch Henry | .15 | .07 |
| ❑ | 512 | Jeff Brantley | .15 | .07 |
| ❑ | 513 | Jack Armstrong | .15 | .07 |
| ❑ | 514 | Danny Jackson | .15 | .07 |
| ❑ | 515 | Junior Felix | .15 | .07 |
| ❑ | 516 | Milt Thompson | .15 | .07 |
| ❑ | 517 | Greg Maddux | 1.50 | .70 |
| ❑ | 518 | Eric Young | .15 | .07 |
| ❑ | 519 | Jody Reed | .15 | .07 |
| ❑ | 520 | Roberto Kelly | .15 | .07 |
| ❑ | 521 | Darren Holmes | .15 | .07 |
| ❑ | 522 | Craig Lefferts | .15 | .07 |
| ❑ | 523 | Charlie Hough | .30 | .14 |
| ❑ | 524 | Bo Jackson | .30 | .14 |
| ❑ | 525 | Bill Spiers | .15 | .07 |
| ❑ | 526 | Orestes Destrade | .15 | .07 |
| ❑ | 527 | Greg Hibbard | .15 | .07 |
| ❑ | 528 | Roger McDowell | .15 | .07 |
| ❑ | 529 | Cory Snyder | .15 | .07 |
| ❑ | 530 | Harold Reynolds | .15 | .07 |
| ❑ | 531 | Kevin Reimer | .15 | .07 |
| ❑ | 532 | Rick Sutcliffe | .30 | .14 |
| ❑ | 533 | Tony Fernandez | .15 | .07 |
| ❑ | 534 | Tom Brunansky | .15 | .07 |
| ❑ | 535 | Jeff Reardon | .30 | .14 |
| ❑ | 536 | Chili Davis | .30 | .14 |
| ❑ | 537 | Bob Ojeda | .15 | .07 |
| ❑ | 538 | Greg Colbrunn | .15 | .07 |
| ❑ | 539 | Phil Plantier | .15 | .07 |
| ❑ | 540 | Brian Jordan | .30 | .14 |
| ❑ | 541 | Pete Smith | .15 | .07 |
| ❑ | 542 | Frank Tanana | .15 | .07 |
| ❑ | 543 | John Smiley | .15 | .07 |
| ❑ | 544 | David Cone | .30 | .14 |
| ❑ | 545 | Daryl Boston | .15 | .07 |
| ❑ | 546 | Tom Henke | .15 | .07 |
| ❑ | 547 | Bill Krueger | .15 | .07 |
| ❑ | 548 | Freddie Benavides | .15 | .07 |
| ❑ | 549 | Randy Myers | .30 | .14 |
| ❑ | 550 | Reggie Jefferson | .30 | .14 |
| ❑ | 551 | Kevin Mitchell | .30 | .14 |
| ❑ | 552 | Dave Stieb | .15 | .07 |
| ❑ | 553 | Bret Barberie | .15 | .07 |
| ❑ | 554 | Tim Crews | .15 | .07 |
| ❑ | 555 | Doug Dascenzo | .15 | .07 |
| ❑ | 556 | Alex Cole | .15 | .07 |
| ❑ | 557 | Jeff Innis | .15 | .07 |
| ❑ | 558 | Carlos Garcia | .15 | .07 |
| ❑ | 559 | Steve Howe | .15 | .07 |
| ❑ | 560 | Kirk McCaskill | .15 | .07 |
| ❑ | 561 | Frank Seminara | .15 | .07 |
| ❑ | 562 | Cris Carpenter | .15 | .07 |
| ❑ | 563 | Mike Stanley | .15 | .07 |
| ❑ | 564 | Carlos Quintana | .15 | .07 |
| ❑ | 565 | Mitch Williams | .15 | .07 |
| ❑ | 566 | Juan Bell | .15 | .07 |
| ❑ | 567 | Eric Fox | .15 | .07 |
| ❑ | 568 | Al Leiter | .30 | .14 |
| ❑ | 569 | Mike Stanton | .15 | .07 |
| ❑ | 570 | Scott Kamieniecki | .15 | .07 |
| ❑ | 571 | Ryan Bowen | .15 | .07 |
| ❑ | 572 | Andy Ashby | .30 | .14 |
| ❑ | 573 | Bob Welch | .15 | .07 |
| ❑ | 574 | Scott Sanderson | .15 | .07 |
| ❑ | 575 | Joe Kmak | .15 | .07 |
| ❑ | 576 | Scott Pose RC | .15 | .07 |
| ❑ | 577 | Ricky Gutierrez | .15 | .07 |
| ❑ | 578 | Mike Trombley | .15 | .07 |
| ❑ | 579 | Sterling Hitchcock RC | .50 | .23 |
| ❑ | 580 | Rodney Bolton | .15 | .07 |
| ❑ | 581 | Tyler Green | .15 | .07 |
| ❑ | 582 | Tim Costo | .15 | .07 |
| ❑ | 583 | Tim Laker RC | .15 | .07 |
| ❑ | 584 | Steve Reed RC | .15 | .07 |
| ❑ | 585 | Tom Kramer RC | .15 | .07 |
| ❑ | 586 | Robb Nen | .30 | .14 |
| ❑ | 587 | Jim Tatum RC | .15 | .07 |
| ❑ | 588 | Frank Bolick | .15 | .07 |
| ❑ | 589 | Kevin Young | .30 | .14 |
| ❑ | 590 | Matt Whiteside RC | .15 | .07 |
| ❑ | 591 | Cesar Hernandez | .15 | .07 |
| ❑ | 592 | Mike Mohler RC | .15 | .07 |
| ❑ | 593 | Alan Embree | .15 | .07 |
| ❑ | 594 | Terry Jorgensen | .15 | .07 |
| ❑ | 595 | John Cummings RC | .15 | .07 |
| ❑ | 596 | Domingo Martinez RC | .15 | .07 |
| ❑ | 597 | Benji Gil | .15 | .07 |
| ❑ | 598 | Todd Pratt RC | .40 | .18 |
| ❑ | 599 | Rene Arocha RC | .15 | .07 |
| ❑ | 600 | Dennis Moeller | .15 | .07 |
| ❑ | 601 | Jeff Conine | .15 | .07 |
| ❑ | 602 | Trevor Hoffman | .60 | .25 |
| ❑ | 603 | Daniel Smith | .15 | .07 |
| ❑ | 604 | Lee Tinsley | .15 | .07 |
| ❑ | 605 | Dan Peltier | .15 | .07 |
| ❑ | 606 | Billy Brewer | .15 | .07 |
| ❑ | 607 | Matt Walbeck RC | .15 | .07 |
| ❑ | 608 | Richie Lewis RC | .15 | .07 |
| ❑ | 609 | J.T. Snow RC | .75 | .35 |
| ❑ | 610 | Pat Gomez RC | .15 | .07 |
| ❑ | 611 | Phil Hiatt | .15 | .07 |
| ❑ | 612 | Alex Arias | .15 | .07 |
| ❑ | 613 | Kevin Rogers | .15 | .07 |
| ❑ | 614 | Al Martin | .15 | .07 |
| ❑ | 615 | Greg Gohr | .15 | .07 |
| ❑ | 616 | Graeme Lloyd RC | .15 | .07 |
| ❑ | 617 | Kent Bottenfield | .30 | .14 |
| ❑ | 618 | Chuck Carr | .15 | .07 |
| ❑ | 619 | Darrell Sherman RC | .15 | .07 |
| ❑ | 620 | Mike Lansing RC | .30 | .14 |

## 1994 Pinnacle

| | MINT | NRMT |
|---|---|---|
| COMPLETE SET (540) | 20.00 | 9.00 |

| | | |
|---|---|---|
| COMPLETE SERIES 1 (270) | 10.00 | 4.50 |
| COMPLETE SERIES 2 (270) | 10.00 | 4.50 |
| COMMON CARD (1-540) | .12 | .05 |

| Card | Player | NRMT | EX-MT |
|---|---|---|---|
| ❑ 1 | Frank Thomas | 1.00 | .45 |
| ❑ 2 | Carlos Baerga | .10 | .05 |
| ❑ 3 | Sammy Sosa | 1.00 | .45 |
| ❑ 4 | Tony Gwynn | 1.00 | .45 |
| ❑ 5 | John Olerud | .20 | .09 |
| ❑ 6 | Ryne Sandberg | .60 | .25 |
| ❑ 7 | Moises Alou | .20 | .09 |
| ❑ 8 | Steve Avery | .10 | .05 |
| ❑ 9 | Tim Salmon | .20 | .09 |
| ❑ 10 | Cecil Fielder | .20 | .09 |
| ❑ 11 | Greg Maddux | 1.25 | .55 |
| ❑ 12 | Barry Larkin | .50 | .23 |
| ❑ 13 | Mike Devereaux | .10 | .05 |
| ❑ 14 | Charlie Hayes | .10 | .05 |
| ❑ 15 | Albert Belle | .30 | .14 |
| ❑ 16 | Andy Van Slyke | .20 | .09 |
| ❑ 17 | Mo Vaughn | .20 | .09 |
| ❑ 18 | Brian McRae | .10 | .05 |
| ❑ 19 | Cal Eldred | .10 | .05 |
| ❑ 20 | Craig Biggio | .30 | .14 |
| ❑ 21 | Kirby Puckett | 1.25 | .55 |
| ❑ 22 | Derek Bell | .10 | .05 |
| ❑ 23 | Don Mattingly | 1.25 | .55 |
| ❑ 24 | John Burkett | .10 | .05 |
| ❑ 25 | Roger Clemens | 1.00 | .45 |
| ❑ 26 | Barry Bonds | .75 | .35 |
| ❑ 27 | Paul Molitor | .50 | .23 |
| ❑ 28 | Mike Piazza | 1.50 | .70 |
| ❑ 29 | Robin Ventura | .20 | .09 |
| ❑ 30 | Jeff Conine | .10 | .05 |
| ❑ 31 | Wade Boggs | .60 | .25 |
| ❑ 32 | Dennis Eckersley | .20 | .09 |
| ❑ 33 | Bobby Bonilla | .20 | .09 |
| ❑ 34 | Lenny Dykstra | .20 | .09 |
| ❑ 35 | Manny Alexander | .10 | .05 |
| ❑ 36 | Ray Lankford | .20 | .09 |
| ❑ 37 | Greg Vaughn | .20 | .09 |
| ❑ 38 | Chuck Finley | .20 | .09 |
| ❑ 39 | Todd Benzinger | .10 | .05 |
| ❑ 40 | Dave Justice | .30 | .14 |
| ❑ 41 | Rob Dibble | .10 | .05 |
| ❑ 42 | Tom Henke | .10 | .05 |
| ❑ 43 | David Nied | .10 | .05 |
| ❑ 44 | Sandy Alomar Jr. | .20 | .09 |
| ❑ 45 | Pete Harnisch | .10 | .05 |
| ❑ 46 | Jeff Russell | .10 | .05 |
| ❑ 47 | Terry Mulholland | .10 | .05 |
| ❑ 48 | Kevin Appier | .20 | .09 |
| ❑ 49 | Randy Tomlin | .10 | .05 |
| ❑ 50 | Cal Ripken Jr. | 2.00 | .90 |
| ❑ 51 | Andy Benes | .10 | .05 |
| ❑ 52 | Jimmy Key | .20 | .09 |
| ❑ 53 | Kirt Manwaring | .10 | .05 |
| ❑ 54 | Kevin Tapani | .10 | .05 |
| ❑ 55 | Jose Guzman | .10 | .05 |
| ❑ 56 | Todd Stottlemyre | .10 | .05 |
| ❑ 57 | Jack McDowell | .10 | .05 |
| ❑ 58 | Orel Hershiser | .20 | .09 |
| ❑ 59 | Chris Hammond | .10 | .05 |
| ❑ 60 | Chris Nabholz | .10 | .05 |
| ❑ 61 | Ruben Sierra | .10 | .05 |
| ❑ 62 | Dwight Gooden | .20 | .09 |
| ❑ 63 | John Kruk | .20 | .09 |
| ❑ 64 | Omar Vizquel | .20 | .09 |
| ❑ 65 | Tim Naehring | .10 | .05 |
| ❑ 66 | Dwight Smith | .10 | .05 |
| ❑ 67 | Mickey Tettleton | .10 | .05 |
| ❑ 68 | J.T. Snow | .20 | .09 |
| ❑ 69 | Greg McMichael | .10 | .05 |
| ❑ 70 | Kevin Mitchell | .10 | .05 |
| ❑ 71 | Kevin Brown | .20 | .09 |
| ❑ 72 | Scott Cooper | .10 | .05 |
| ❑ 73 | Jim Thome | .30 | .14 |
| ❑ 74 | Joe Girardi | .10 | .05 |
| ❑ 75 | Eric Anthony | .10 | .05 |
| ❑ 76 | Orlando Merced | .10 | .05 |
| ❑ 77 | Felix Jose | .10 | .05 |
| ❑ 78 | Tommy Greene | .10 | .05 |
| ❑ 79 | Bernard Gilkey | .10 | .05 |
| ❑ 80 | Phil Plantier | .10 | .05 |
| ❑ 81 | Danny Tartabull | .10 | .05 |
| ❑ 82 | Trevor Wilson | .10 | .05 |
| ❑ 83 | Chuck Knoblauch | .20 | .09 |
| ❑ 84 | Rick Wilkins | .10 | .05 |
| ❑ 85 | Devon White | .10 | .05 |
| ❑ 86 | Lance Johnson | .10 | .05 |
| ❑ 87 | Eric Karros | .20 | .09 |
| ❑ 88 | Gary Sheffield | .50 | .23 |
| ❑ 89 | Wil Cordero | .10 | .05 |
| ❑ 90 | Ron Darling | .10 | .05 |
| ❑ 91 | Darren Daulton | .20 | .09 |
| ❑ 92 | Joe Orsulak | .10 | .05 |
| ❑ 93 | Steve Cooke | .10 | .05 |
| ❑ 94 | Darryl Hamilton | .10 | .05 |
| ❑ 95 | Aaron Sele | .20 | .09 |
| ❑ 96 | John Doherty | .10 | .05 |
| ❑ 97 | Gary DiSarcina | .10 | .05 |
| ❑ 98 | Jeff Blauser | .10 | .05 |
| ❑ 99 | John Smiley | .10 | .05 |
| ❑ 100 | Ken Griffey Jr. | 2.00 | .90 |
| ❑ 101 | Dean Palmer | .20 | .09 |
| ❑ 102 | Felix Fermin | .10 | .05 |
| ❑ 103 | Jerald Clark | .10 | .05 |
| ❑ 104 | Doug Drabek | .10 | .05 |
| ❑ 105 | Curt Schilling | .20 | .09 |
| ❑ 106 | Jeff Montgomery | .10 | .05 |
| ❑ 107 | Rene Arocha | .10 | .05 |
| ❑ 108 | Carlos Garcia | .10 | .05 |
| ❑ 109 | Wally Whitehurst | .10 | .05 |
| ❑ 110 | Jim Abbott | .20 | .09 |
| ❑ 111 | Royce Clayton | .10 | .05 |
| ❑ 112 | Chris Hoiles | .10 | .05 |
| ❑ 113 | Mike Morgan | .10 | .05 |
| ❑ 114 | Joe Magrane | .10 | .05 |
| ❑ 115 | Tom Candiotti | .10 | .05 |
| ❑ 116 | Ron Karkovice | .10 | .05 |
| ❑ 117 | Ryan Bowen | .10 | .05 |
| ❑ 118 | Rod Beck | .10 | .05 |
| ❑ 119 | John Wetteland | .20 | .09 |
| ❑ 120 | Terry Steinbach | .10 | .05 |
| ❑ 121 | Dave Hollins | .10 | .05 |
| ❑ 122 | Jeff Kent | .30 | .14 |
| ❑ 123 | Ricky Bones | .10 | .05 |
| ❑ 124 | Brian Jordan | .20 | .09 |
| ❑ 125 | Chad Kreuter | .10 | .05 |
| ❑ 126 | John Valentin | .10 | .05 |
| ❑ 127 | Hilly Hathaway | .10 | .05 |
| ❑ 128 | Wilson Alvarez | .10 | .05 |
| ❑ 129 | Tino Martinez | .20 | .09 |
| ❑ 130 | Rodney Bolton | .10 | .05 |
| ❑ 131 | David Segui | .10 | .05 |
| ❑ 132 | Wayne Kirby | .10 | .05 |
| ❑ 133 | Eric Young | .10 | .05 |
| ❑ 134 | Scott Servais | .10 | .05 |
| ❑ 135 | Scott Radinsky | .10 | .05 |
| ❑ 136 | Bret Barberie | .10 | .05 |
| ❑ 137 | John Roper | .10 | .05 |
| ❑ 138 | Ricky Gutierrez | .10 | .05 |
| ❑ 139 | Bernie Williams | .50 | .23 |
| ❑ 140 | Bud Black | .10 | .05 |
| ❑ 141 | Jose Vizcaino | .10 | .05 |
| ❑ 142 | Gerald Williams | .10 | .05 |
| ❑ 143 | Duane Ward | .10 | .05 |
| ❑ 144 | Danny Jackson | .10 | .05 |
| ❑ 145 | Allen Watson | .10 | .05 |
| ❑ 146 | Scott Fletcher | .10 | .05 |
| ❑ 147 | Delino DeShields | .10 | .05 |
| ❑ 148 | Shane Mack | .10 | .05 |
| ❑ 149 | Jim Eisenreich | .10 | .05 |
| ❑ 150 | Troy Neel | .10 | .05 |
| ❑ 151 | Jay Bell | .20 | .09 |
| ❑ 152 | B.J. Surhoff | .20 | .09 |
| ❑ 153 | Mark Whiten | .10 | .05 |
| ❑ 154 | Mike Henneman | .10 | .05 |
| ❑ 155 | Todd Hundley | .10 | .05 |
| ❑ 156 | Greg Myers | .10 | .05 |
| ❑ 157 | Ryan Klesko | .20 | .09 |
| ❑ 158 | Dave Fleming | .10 | .05 |
| ❑ 159 | Mickey Morandini | .10 | .05 |
| ❑ 160 | Blas Minor | .10 | .05 |
| ❑ 161 | Reggie Jefferson | .10 | .05 |
| ❑ 162 | David Hulse | .10 | .05 |
| ❑ 163 | Greg Swindell | .10 | .05 |
| ❑ 164 | Roberto Hernandez | .10 | .05 |
| ❑ 165 | Brady Anderson | .20 | .09 |
| ❑ 166 | Jack Armstrong | .10 | .05 |
| ❑ 167 | Phil Clark | .10 | .05 |
| ❑ 168 | Melido Perez | .10 | .05 |
| ❑ 169 | Darren Lewis | .10 | .05 |
| ❑ 170 | Sam Horn | .10 | .05 |
| ❑ 171 | Mike Harkey | .10 | .05 |
| ❑ 172 | Juan Guzman | .10 | .05 |
| ❑ 173 | Bob Natal | .10 | .05 |
| ❑ 174 | Deion Sanders | .20 | .09 |
| ❑ 175 | Carlos Quintana | .10 | .05 |
| ❑ 176 | Mel Rojas | .10 | .05 |
| ❑ 177 | Willie Banks | .10 | .05 |
| ❑ 178 | Ben Rivera | .10 | .05 |
| ❑ 179 | Kenny Lofton | .20 | .09 |
| ❑ 180 | Leo Gomez | .10 | .05 |
| ❑ 181 | Roberto Mejia | .10 | .05 |
| ❑ 182 | Mike Perez | .10 | .05 |
| ❑ 183 | Travis Fryman | .20 | .09 |
| ❑ 184 | Ben McDonald | .10 | .05 |
| ❑ 185 | Steve Frey | .10 | .05 |
| ❑ 186 | Kevin Young | .10 | .05 |
| ❑ 187 | Dave Magadan | .10 | .05 |
| ❑ 188 | Bobby Munoz | .10 | .05 |
| ❑ 189 | Pat Rapp | .10 | .05 |
| ❑ 190 | Jose Offerman | .10 | .05 |
| ❑ 191 | Vinny Castilla | .20 | .09 |
| ❑ 192 | Ivan Calderon | .10 | .05 |
| ❑ 193 | Ken Caminiti | .20 | .09 |
| ❑ 194 | Benji Gil | .10 | .05 |
| ❑ 195 | Chuck Carr | .10 | .05 |
| ❑ 196 | Derrick May | .10 | .05 |
| ❑ 197 | Pat Kelly | .10 | .05 |
| ❑ 198 | Jeff Brantley | .10 | .05 |
| ❑ 199 | Jose Lind | .10 | .05 |
| ❑ 200 | Steve Buechele | .10 | .05 |
| ❑ 201 | Wes Chamberlain | .10 | .05 |
| ❑ 202 | Eduardo Perez | .10 | .05 |
| ❑ 203 | Bret Saberhagen | .20 | .09 |
| ❑ 204 | Gregg Jefferies | .10 | .05 |
| ❑ 205 | Darrin Fletcher | .10 | .05 |
| ❑ 206 | Kent Hrbek | .20 | .09 |
| ❑ 207 | Kim Batiste | .10 | .05 |
| ❑ 208 | Jeff King | .10 | .05 |
| ❑ 209 | Donovan Osborne | .10 | .05 |
| ❑ 210 | Dave Nilsson | .10 | .05 |
| ❑ 211 | Al Martin | .10 | .05 |
| ❑ 212 | Mike Moore | .10 | .05 |
| ❑ 213 | Sterling Hitchcock | .10 | .05 |
| ❑ 214 | Geronimo Pena | .10 | .05 |
| ❑ 215 | Kevin Higgins | .10 | .05 |
| ❑ 216 | Norm Charlton | .10 | .05 |
| ❑ 217 | Don Slaught | .10 | .05 |
| ❑ 218 | Mitch Williams | .10 | .05 |
| ❑ 219 | Derek Lilliquist | .10 | .05 |
| ❑ 220 | Armando Reynoso | .10 | .05 |
| ❑ 221 | Kenny Rogers | .10 | .05 |
| ❑ 222 | Doug Jones | .10 | .05 |
| ❑ 223 | Luis Aquino | .10 | .05 |
| ❑ 224 | Mike Oquist | .10 | .05 |
| ❑ 225 | Darryl Scott | .10 | .05 |
| ❑ 226 | Kurt Abbott RC | .10 | .05 |
| ❑ 227 | Andy Tomberlin | .10 | .05 |
| ❑ 228 | Norberto Martin | .10 | .05 |
| ❑ 229 | Pedro Castellano | .10 | .05 |
| ❑ 230 | Curtis Pride RC | .10 | .05 |
| ❑ 231 | Jeff McNeely | .10 | .05 |
| ❑ 232 | Scott Lydy | .10 | .05 |
| ❑ 233 | Darren Oliver RC | .20 | .09 |
| ❑ 234 | Danny Bautista | .10 | .05 |
| ❑ 235 | Butch Huskey | .10 | .05 |
| ❑ 236 | Chipper Jones | 1.25 | .55 |

❑ 237 Eddie Zambrano RC .10 .05
❑ 238 Domingo Jean .10 .05
❑ 239 Javier Lopez .20 .09
❑ 240 Nigel Wilson .10 .05
❑ 241 Drew Denson .10 .05
❑ 242 Raul Mondesi .20 .09
❑ 243 Luis Ortiz .10 .05
❑ 244 Manny Ramirez .75 .35
❑ 245 Greg Blosser .10 .05
❑ 246 Rondell White .20 .09
❑ 247 Steve Karsay .10 .05
❑ 248 Scott Stahoviak .10 .05
❑ 249 Jose Valentin .10 .05
❑ 250 Marc Newfield .10 .05
❑ 251 Keith Kessinger .10 .05
❑ 252 Carl Everett .20 .09
❑ 253 John O'Donoghue .10 .05
❑ 254 Turk Wendell .10 .05
❑ 255 Scott Ruffcorn .10 .05
❑ 256 Tony Tarasco .10 .05
❑ 257 Andy Cook .10 .05
❑ 258 Matt Mieske .10 .05
❑ 259 Luis Lopez .10 .05
❑ 260 Ramon Caraballo .10 .05
❑ 261 Salomon Torres .10 .05
❑ 262 Brooks Kieschnick RC .10 .05
❑ 263 Daron Kirkreit .10 .05
❑ 264 Bill Wagner RC .40 .18
❑ 265 Matt Drews RC .10 .05
❑ 266 Scott Christman RC .10 .05
❑ 267 Torii Hunter RC .10 .05
❑ 268 Jamey Wright RC .20 .09
❑ 269 Jeff Granger .10 .05
❑ 270 Trot Nixon RC 1.00 .45
❑ 271 Randy Myers .10 .05
❑ 272 Trevor Hoffman .20 .09
❑ 273 Bob Wickman .10 .05
❑ 274 Willie McGee .20 .09
❑ 275 Hipolito Pichardo .10 .05
❑ 276 Bobby Witt .10 .05
❑ 277 Gregg Olson .10 .05
❑ 278 Randy Johnson .60 .25
❑ 279 Robb Nen .10 .05
❑ 280 Paul O'Neill .20 .09
❑ 281 Lou Whitaker .20 .09
❑ 282 Chad Curtis .10 .05
❑ 283 Doug Henry .10 .05
❑ 284 Tom Glavine .50 .23
❑ 285 Mike Greenwell .10 .05
❑ 286 Roberto Kelly .10 .05
❑ 287 Roberto Alomar .50 .23
❑ 288 Charlie Hough .20 .09
❑ 289 Alex Fernandez .10 .05
❑ 290 Jeff Bagwell .60 .25
❑ 291 Wally Joyner .20 .09
❑ 292 Andujar Cedeno .10 .05
❑ 293 Rick Aguilera .10 .05
❑ 294 Darryl Strawberry .20 .09
❑ 295 Mike Mussina .50 .23
❑ 296 Jeff Gardner .10 .05
❑ 297 Chris Gwynn .10 .05
❑ 298 Matt Williams .30 .14
❑ 299 Brent Gates .10 .05
❑ 300 Mark McGwire 2.00 .90
❑ 301 Jim Deshaies .10 .05
❑ 302 Edgar Martinez .30 .14
❑ 303 Danny Darwin .10 .05
❑ 304 Pat Meares .10 .05
❑ 305 Benito Santiago .10 .05
❑ 306 Jose Canseco .60 .25
❑ 307 Jim Gott .10 .05
❑ 308 Paul Sorrento .10 .05
❑ 309 Scott Kamieniecki .10 .05
❑ 310 Larry Walker .20 .09
❑ 311 Mark Langston .10 .05
❑ 312 John Jaha .10 .05
❑ 313 Stan Javier .10 .05
❑ 314 Hal Morris .10 .05
❑ 315 Robby Thompson .10 .05
❑ 316 Pat Hentgen .10 .05
❑ 317 Tom Gordon .10 .05
❑ 318 Joey Cora .10 .05
❑ 319 Luis Alicea .10 .05
❑ 320 Andre Dawson .30 .14
❑ 321 Darryl Kile .20 .09
❑ 322 Jose Rijo .10 .05
❑ 323 Luis Gonzalez .20 .09
❑ 324 Billy Ashley .10 .05
❑ 325 David Cone .20 .09
❑ 326 Bill Swift .10 .05
❑ 327 Phil Hiatt .10 .05
❑ 328 Craig Paquette .10 .05
❑ 329 Bob Welch .10 .05
❑ 330 Tony Phillips .10 .05
❑ 331 Archi Cianfrocco .10 .05
❑ 332 Dave Winfield .50 .23
❑ 333 David McCarty .10 .05
❑ 334 Al Leiter .20 .09
❑ 335 Tom Browning .10 .05
❑ 336 Mark Grace .50 .23
❑ 337 Jose Mesa .10 .05
❑ 338 Mike Stanley .10 .05
❑ 339 Roger McDowell .10 .05
❑ 340 Damion Easley .10 .05
❑ 341 Angel Miranda .10 .05
❑ 342 John Smoltz .20 .09
❑ 343 Jay Buhner .20 .09
❑ 344 Bryan Harvey .10 .05
❑ 345 Joe Carter .20 .09
❑ 346 Dante Bichette .20 .09
❑ 347 Jason Bere .10 .05
❑ 348 Frank Viola .10 .05
❑ 349 Ivan Rodriguez .60 .25
❑ 350 Juan Gonzalez .50 .23
❑ 351 Steve Finley .20 .09
❑ 352 Mike Felder .10 .05
❑ 353 Ramon Martinez .10 .05
❑ 354 Greg Gagne .10 .05
❑ 355 Ken Hill .10 .05
❑ 356 Pedro Munoz .10 .05
❑ 357 Todd Van Poppel .10 .05
❑ 358 Marquis Grissom .10 .05
❑ 359 Milt Cuyler .10 .05
❑ 360 Reggie Sanders .10 .05
❑ 361 Scott Erickson .10 .05
❑ 362 Billy Hatcher .10 .05
❑ 363 Gene Harris .10 .05
❑ 364 Rene Gonzales .10 .05
❑ 365 Kevin Rogers .10 .05
❑ 366 Eric Plunk .10 .05
❑ 367 Todd Zeile .10 .05
❑ 368 John Franco .20 .09
❑ 369 Brett Butler .20 .09
❑ 370 Bill Spiers .10 .05
❑ 371 Terry Pendleton .20 .09
❑ 372 Chris Bosio .10 .05
❑ 373 Orestes Destrade .10 .05
❑ 374 Dave Stewart .20 .09
❑ 375 Darren Holmes .10 .05
❑ 376 Doug Strange .10 .05
❑ 377 Brian Turang .10 .05
❑ 378 Carl Willis .10 .05
❑ 379 Mark McLemore .10 .05
❑ 380 Bobby Jones .10 .05
❑ 381 Scott Sanders .10 .05
❑ 382 Kirk Rueter .10 .05
❑ 383 Randy Velarde .10 .05
❑ 384 Fred McGriff .30 .14
❑ 385 Charles Nagy .10 .05
❑ 386 Rich Amaral .10 .05
❑ 387 Geronimo Berroa .10 .05
❑ 388 Eric Davis .20 .09
❑ 389 Ozzie Smith .60 .25
❑ 390 Alex Arias .10 .05
❑ 391 Brad Ausmus .10 .05
❑ 392 Cliff Floyd .20 .09
❑ 393 Roger Salkeld .10 .05
❑ 394 Jim Edmonds .60 .25
❑ 395 Jeromy Burnitz .20 .09
❑ 396 Dave Staton .10 .05
❑ 397 Rob Butler .10 .05
❑ 398 Marcos Armas .10 .05
❑ 399 Darrell Whitmore .10 .05
❑ 400 Ryan Thompson .10 .05
❑ 401 Ross Powell RC .10 .05
❑ 402 Joe Oliver .10 .05
❑ 403 Paul Carey .10 .05
❑ 404 Bob Hamelin .10 .05
❑ 405 Chris Turner .10 .05
❑ 406 Nate Minchey .10 .05
❑ 407 Lonnie Maclin RC .10 .05
❑ 408 Harold Baines .20 .09
❑ 409 Brian Williams .10 .05
❑ 410 Johnny Ruffin .10 .05
❑ 411 Julian Tavarez RC .10 .05
❑ 412 Mark Hutton .10 .05
❑ 413 Carlos Delgado .75 .35
❑ 414 Chris Gomez .10 .05
❑ 415 Mike Hampton .10 .05
❑ 416 Alex Diaz RC .10 .05
❑ 417 Jeffrey Hammonds .20 .09
❑ 418 Jayhawk Owens .10 .05
❑ 419 J.R. Phillips .10 .05
❑ 420 Cory Bailey RC .10 .05
❑ 421 Denny Hocking .10 .05
❑ 422 Jon Shave .10 .05
❑ 423 Damon Buford .10 .05
❑ 424 Troy O'Leary .10 .05
❑ 425 Tripp Cromer .10 .05
❑ 426 Albie Lopez .10 .05
❑ 427 Tony Fernandez .10 .05
❑ 428 Ozzie Guillen .10 .05
❑ 429 Alan Trammell .30 .14
❑ 430 John Wasdin RC .20 .09
❑ 431 Marc Valdes .10 .05
❑ 432 Brian Anderson RC .20 .09
❑ 433 Matt Brunson RC .10 .05
❑ 434 Wayne Gomes RC .10 .05
❑ 435 Jay Powell RC .30 .14
❑ 436 Kirk Presley RC .10 .05
❑ 437 Jon Ratliff RC .10 .05
❑ 438 Derrek Lee RC .40 .18
❑ 439 Tom Pagnozzi .10 .05
❑ 440 Kent Mercker .10 .05
❑ 441 Phil Leftwich RC .10 .05
❑ 442 Jamie Moyer .10 .05
❑ 443 John Flaherty .10 .05
❑ 444 Mark Wohlers .10 .05
❑ 445 Jose Bautista .10 .05
❑ 446 Andres Galarraga .30 .14
❑ 447 Mark Lemke .10 .05
❑ 448 Tim Wakefield .10 .05
❑ 449 Pat Listach .10 .05
❑ 450 Rickey Henderson .60 .25
❑ 451 Mike Gallego .10 .05
❑ 452 Bob Tewksbury .10 .05
❑ 453 Kirk Gibson .20 .09
❑ 454 Pedro Astacio .10 .05
❑ 455 Mike Lansing .10 .05
❑ 456 Sean Berry .10 .05
❑ 457 Bob Walk .10 .05
❑ 458 Chili Davis .20 .09
❑ 459 Ed Sprague .10 .05
❑ 460 Kevin Stocker .10 .05
❑ 461 Mike Stanton .10 .05
❑ 462 Tim Raines .20 .09
❑ 463 Mike Bordick .10 .05
❑ 464 David Wells .20 .09
❑ 465 Tim Laker .10 .05
❑ 466 Cory Snyder .10 .05
❑ 467 Alex Cole .10 .05
❑ 468 Pete Incaviglia .10 .05
❑ 469 Roger Pavlik .10 .05
❑ 470 Greg W. Harris .10 .05
❑ 471 Xavier Hernandez .10 .05
❑ 472 Erik Hanson .10 .05
❑ 473 Jesse Orosco .10 .05
❑ 474 Greg Colbrunn .10 .05
❑ 475 Harold Reynolds .10 .05
❑ 476 Greg A. Harris .10 .05
❑ 477 Pat Borders .10 .05
❑ 478 Melvin Nieves .10 .05
❑ 479 Mariano Duncan .10 .05
❑ 480 Greg Hibbard .10 .05
❑ 481 Tim Pugh .10 .05
❑ 482 Bobby Ayala .10 .05
❑ 483 Sid Fernandez .10 .05
❑ 484 Tim Wallach .10 .05
❑ 485 Randy Milligan .10 .05
❑ 486 Walt Weiss .10 .05
❑ 487 Matt Walbeck .10 .05
❑ 488 Mike Macfarlane .10 .05
❑ 489 Jerry Browne .10 .05
❑ 490 Chris Sabo .10 .05
❑ 491 Tim Belcher .10 .05
❑ 492 Spike Owen .10 .05
❑ 493 Rafael Palmeiro .50 .23
❑ 494 Brian Harper .10 .05

| | No. | Player | MINT | NRMT |
|---|---|---|---|---|
| ❑ | 495 | Eddie Murray | .50 | .23 |
| ❑ | 496 | Ellis Burks | .20 | .09 |
| ❑ | 497 | Karl Rhodes | .10 | .05 |
| ❑ | 498 | Otis Nixon | .10 | .05 |
| ❑ | 499 | Lee Smith | .20 | .09 |
| ❑ | 500 | Bip Roberts | .10 | .05 |
| ❑ | 501 | Pedro Martinez | .75 | .35 |
| ❑ | 502 | Brian Hunter | .10 | .05 |
| ❑ | 503 | Tyler Green | .10 | .05 |
| ❑ | 504 | Bruce Hurst | .10 | .05 |
| ❑ | 505 | Alex Gonzalez | .10 | .05 |
| ❑ | 506 | Mark Portugal | .10 | .05 |
| ❑ | 507 | Bob Ojeda | .10 | .05 |
| ❑ | 508 | Dave Henderson | .10 | .05 |
| ❑ | 509 | Bo Jackson | .20 | .09 |
| ❑ | 510 | Bret Boone | .20 | .09 |
| ❑ | 511 | Mark Eichhorn | .10 | .05 |
| ❑ | 512 | Luis Polonia | .10 | .05 |
| ❑ | 513 | Will Clark | .50 | .23 |
| ❑ | 514 | Dave Valle | .10 | .05 |
| ❑ | 515 | Dan Wilson | .10 | .05 |
| ❑ | 516 | Dennis Martinez | .20 | .09 |
| ❑ | 517 | Jim Leyritz | .10 | .05 |
| ❑ | 518 | Howard Johnson | .10 | .05 |
| ❑ | 519 | Jody Reed | .10 | .05 |
| ❑ | 520 | Julio Franco | .10 | .05 |
| ❑ | 521 | Jeff Reardon | .20 | .09 |
| ❑ | 522 | Willie Greene | .10 | .05 |
| ❑ | 523 | Shawon Dunston | .10 | .05 |
| ❑ | 524 | Keith Mitchell | .10 | .05 |
| ❑ | 525 | Rick Helling | .20 | .09 |
| ❑ | 526 | Mark Kiefer | .10 | .05 |
| ❑ | 527 | Chan Ho Park RC | .60 | .25 |
| ❑ | 528 | Tony Longmire | .10 | .05 |
| ❑ | 529 | Rich Becker | .10 | .05 |
| ❑ | 530 | Tim Hyers RC | .10 | .05 |
| ❑ | 531 | Darrin Jackson | .10 | .05 |
| ❑ | 532 | Jack Morris | .20 | .09 |
| ❑ | 533 | Rick White | .10 | .05 |
| ❑ | 534 | Mike Kelly | .10 | .05 |
| ❑ | 535 | James Mouton | .10 | .05 |
| ❑ | 536 | Steve Trachsel | .10 | .05 |
| ❑ | 537 | Tony Eusebio | .10 | .05 |
| ❑ | 538 | Kelly Stinnett RC | .10 | .05 |
| ❑ | 539 | Paul Spoljaric | .10 | .05 |
| ❑ | 540 | Darren Dreifort | .20 | .09 |
| ❑ | SR1 | Carlos Delgado Super Rookie | 6.00 | 2.70 |

## 1995 Pinnacle

| | MINT | NRMT |
|---|---|---|
| COMPLETE SET (450) | 30.00 | 13.50 |
| COMPLETE SERIES 1 (225) | 15.00 | 6.75 |
| COMPLETE SERIES 2 (225) | 15.00 | 6.75 |
| COMMON CARD (1-450) | .12 | .07 |

| | No. | Player | MINT | NRMT |
|---|---|---|---|---|
| ❑ | 1 | Jeff Bagwell | .60 | .25 |
| ❑ | 2 | Roger Clemens | 1.00 | .45 |
| ❑ | 3 | Mark Whiten | .15 | .07 |
| ❑ | 4 | Shawon Dunston | .15 | .07 |
| ❑ | 5 | Bobby Bonilla | .25 | .11 |
| ❑ | 6 | Kevin Tapani | .15 | .07 |
| ❑ | 7 | Eric Karros | .25 | .11 |
| ❑ | 8 | Cliff Floyd | .25 | .11 |
| ❑ | 9 | Pat Kelly | .15 | .07 |
| ❑ | 10 | Jeffrey Hammonds | .25 | .11 |
| ❑ | 11 | Jeff Conine | .15 | .07 |
| ❑ | 12 | Fred McGriff | .30 | .14 |
| ❑ | 13 | Chris Bosio | .15 | .07 |
| ❑ | 14 | Mike Mussina | .50 | .23 |
| ❑ | 15 | Danny Bautista | .15 | .07 |
| ❑ | 16 | Mickey Morandini | .15 | .07 |
| ❑ | 17 | Chuck Finley | .25 | .11 |
| ❑ | 18 | Jim Thome | .30 | .14 |
| ❑ | 19 | Luis Ortiz | .15 | .07 |
| ❑ | 20 | Walt Weiss | .15 | .07 |
| ❑ | 21 | Don Mattingly | 1.25 | .55 |
| ❑ | 22 | Bob Hamelin | .15 | .07 |
| ❑ | 23 | Melido Perez | .15 | .07 |
| ❑ | 24 | Keith Mitchell | .15 | .07 |
| ❑ | 25 | John Smoltz | .25 | .11 |
| ❑ | 26 | Hector Carrasco | .15 | .07 |
| ❑ | 27 | Pat Hentgen | .15 | .07 |
| ❑ | 28 | Derrick May | .15 | .07 |
| ❑ | 29 | Mike Kingery | .15 | .07 |
| ❑ | 30 | Chuck Carr | .15 | .07 |
| ❑ | 31 | Billy Ashley | .15 | .07 |
| ❑ | 32 | Todd Hundley | .15 | .07 |
| ❑ | 33 | Luis Gonzalez | .15 | .07 |
| ❑ | 34 | Marquis Grissom | .15 | .07 |
| ❑ | 35 | Jeff King | .15 | .07 |
| ❑ | 36 | Eddie Williams | .15 | .07 |
| ❑ | 37 | Tom Pagnozzi | .15 | .07 |
| ❑ | 38 | Chris Hoiles | .15 | .07 |
| ❑ | 39 | Sandy Alomar Jr. | .25 | .11 |
| ❑ | 40 | Mike Greenwell | .15 | .07 |
| ❑ | 41 | Lance Johnson | .15 | .07 |
| ❑ | 42 | Junior Felix | .15 | .07 |
| ❑ | 43 | Felix Jose | .15 | .07 |
| ❑ | 44 | Scott Leius | .15 | .07 |
| ❑ | 45 | Ruben Sierra | .15 | .07 |
| ❑ | 46 | Kevin Seitzer | .15 | .07 |
| ❑ | 47 | Wade Boggs | .60 | .25 |
| ❑ | 48 | Reggie Jefferson | .15 | .07 |
| ❑ | 49 | Jose Canseco | .60 | .25 |
| ❑ | 50 | David Justice | .30 | .14 |
| ❑ | 51 | John Smiley | .15 | .07 |
| ❑ | 52 | Joe Carter | .25 | .11 |
| ❑ | 53 | Rick Wilkins | .15 | .07 |
| ❑ | 54 | Ellis Burks | .25 | .11 |
| ❑ | 55 | Dave Weathers | .15 | .07 |
| ❑ | 56 | Pedro Astacio | .15 | .07 |
| ❑ | 57 | Ryan Thompson | .15 | .07 |
| ❑ | 58 | James Mouton | .15 | .07 |
| ❑ | 59 | Mel Rojas | .15 | .07 |
| ❑ | 60 | Orlando Merced | .15 | .07 |
| ❑ | 61 | Matt Williams | .30 | .14 |
| ❑ | 62 | Bernard Gilkey | .15 | .07 |
| ❑ | 63 | J.R. Phillips | .15 | .07 |
| ❑ | 64 | Lee Smith | .25 | .11 |
| ❑ | 65 | Jim Edmonds | .50 | .23 |
| ❑ | 66 | Darrin Jackson | .15 | .07 |
| ❑ | 67 | Scott Cooper | .15 | .07 |
| ❑ | 68 | Ron Karkovice | .15 | .07 |
| ❑ | 69 | Chris Gomez | .15 | .07 |
| ❑ | 70 | Kevin Appier | .25 | .11 |
| ❑ | 71 | Bobby Jones | .15 | .07 |
| ❑ | 72 | Doug Drabek | .15 | .07 |
| ❑ | 73 | Matt Mieske | .15 | .07 |
| ❑ | 74 | Sterling Hitchcock | .15 | .07 |
| ❑ | 75 | John Valentin | .15 | .07 |
| ❑ | 76 | Reggie Sanders | .15 | .07 |
| ❑ | 77 | Wally Joyner | .25 | .11 |
| ❑ | 78 | Turk Wendell | .15 | .07 |
| ❑ | 79 | Charlie Hayes | .15 | .07 |
| ❑ | 80 | Bret Barberie | .15 | .07 |
| ❑ | 81 | Troy Neel | .15 | .07 |
| ❑ | 82 | Ken Caminiti | .25 | .11 |
| ❑ | 83 | Milt Thompson | .15 | .07 |
| ❑ | 84 | Paul Sorrento | .15 | .07 |
| ❑ | 85 | Trevor Hoffman | .25 | .11 |
| ❑ | 86 | Jay Bell | .25 | .11 |
| ❑ | 87 | Mark Portugal | .15 | .07 |
| ❑ | 88 | Sid Fernandez | .15 | .07 |
| ❑ | 89 | Charles Nagy | .15 | .07 |
| ❑ | 90 | Jeff Montgomery | .15 | .07 |
| ❑ | 91 | Chuck Knoblauch | .25 | .11 |
| ❑ | 92 | Jeff Frye | .15 | .07 |
| ❑ | 93 | Tony Gwynn | 1.00 | .45 |
| ❑ | 94 | John Olerud | .25 | .11 |
| ❑ | 95 | David Nied | .15 | .07 |
| ❑ | 96 | Chris Hammond | .15 | .07 |
| ❑ | 97 | Edgar Martinez | .30 | .14 |
| ❑ | 98 | Kevin Stocker | .15 | .07 |
| ❑ | 99 | Jeff Fassero | .15 | .07 |
| ❑ | 100 | Curt Schilling | .25 | .11 |
| ❑ | 101 | Dave Clark | .15 | .07 |
| ❑ | 102 | Delino DeShields | .15 | .07 |
| ❑ | 103 | Leo Gomez | .15 | .07 |
| ❑ | 104 | Dave Hollins | .15 | .07 |
| ❑ | 105 | Tim Naehring | .15 | .07 |
| ❑ | 106 | Otis Nixon | .15 | .07 |
| ❑ | 107 | Ozzie Guillen | .15 | .07 |
| ❑ | 108 | Jose Lind | .15 | .07 |
| ❑ | 109 | Stan Javier | .15 | .07 |
| ❑ | 110 | Greg Vaughn | .25 | .11 |
| ❑ | 111 | Chipper Jones | 1.25 | .55 |
| ❑ | 112 | Ed Sprague | .15 | .07 |
| ❑ | 113 | Mike Macfarlane | .15 | .07 |
| ❑ | 114 | Steve Finley | .25 | .11 |
| ❑ | 115 | Ken Hill | .15 | .07 |
| ❑ | 116 | Carlos Garcia | .15 | .07 |
| ❑ | 117 | Lou Whitaker | .25 | .11 |
| ❑ | 118 | Todd Zeile | .15 | .07 |
| ❑ | 119 | Gary Sheffield | .50 | .23 |
| ❑ | 120 | Ben McDonald | .15 | .07 |
| ❑ | 121 | Pete Harnisch | .15 | .07 |
| ❑ | 122 | Ivan Rodriguez | .60 | .25 |
| ❑ | 123 | Wilson Alvarez | .15 | .07 |
| ❑ | 124 | Travis Fryman | .25 | .11 |
| ❑ | 125 | Pedro Munoz | .15 | .07 |
| ❑ | 126 | Mark Lemke | .15 | .07 |
| ❑ | 127 | Jose Valentin | .15 | .07 |
| ❑ | 128 | Ken Griffey Jr. | 2.00 | .90 |
| ❑ | 129 | Omar Vizquel | .25 | .11 |
| ❑ | 130 | Milt Cuyler | .15 | .07 |
| ❑ | 131 | Steve Trachsel | .15 | .07 |
| ❑ | 132 | Alex Rodriguez | 2.00 | .90 |
| ❑ | 133 | Garret Anderson | .25 | .11 |
| ❑ | 134 | Armando Benitez | .25 | .11 |
| ❑ | 135 | Shawn Green | .50 | .23 |
| ❑ | 136 | Jorge Fabregas | .15 | .07 |
| ❑ | 137 | Orlando Miller | .15 | .07 |
| ❑ | 138 | Rikkert Faneyte | .15 | .07 |
| ❑ | 139 | Ismael Valdes | .15 | .07 |
| ❑ | 140 | Jose Oliva | .15 | .07 |
| ❑ | 141 | Aaron Small | .15 | .07 |
| ❑ | 142 | Tim Davis | .15 | .07 |
| ❑ | 143 | Ricky Bottalico | .15 | .07 |
| ❑ | 144 | Mike Matheny | .15 | .07 |
| ❑ | 145 | Roberto Petagine | .15 | .07 |
| ❑ | 146 | Fausto Cruz | .15 | .07 |
| ❑ | 147 | Bryce Florie | .15 | .07 |
| ❑ | 148 | Jose Lima | .15 | .07 |
| ❑ | 149 | John Hudek | .15 | .07 |
| ❑ | 150 | Duane Singleton | .15 | .07 |
| ❑ | 151 | John Mabry | .15 | .07 |
| ❑ | 152 | Robert Eenhoorn | .15 | .07 |
| ❑ | 153 | Jon Lieber | .15 | .07 |
| ❑ | 154 | Garey Ingram | .15 | .07 |
| ❑ | 155 | Paul Shuey | .15 | .07 |
| ❑ | 156 | Mike Lieberthal | .25 | .11 |
| ❑ | 157 | Steve Dunn | .15 | .07 |
| ❑ | 158 | Charles Johnson | .25 | .11 |
| ❑ | 159 | Ernie Young | .15 | .07 |
| ❑ | 160 | Jose Martinez | .15 | .07 |
| ❑ | 161 | Kurt Miller | .15 | .07 |
| ❑ | 162 | Joey Eischen | .15 | .07 |
| ❑ | 163 | Dave Stevens | .15 | .07 |
| ❑ | 164 | Brian L.Hunter | .15 | .07 |
| ❑ | 165 | Jeff Cirillo | .25 | .11 |
| ❑ | 166 | Mark Smith | .15 | .07 |
| ❑ | 167 | McKay Christensen RC | .15 | .07 |
| ❑ | 168 | C.J. Nitkowski | .15 | .07 |
| ❑ | 169 | Antone Williamson RC | .15 | .07 |
| ❑ | 170 | Paul Konerko | .50 | .23 |
| ❑ | 171 | Scott Elarton RC | 1.25 | .55 |
| ❑ | 172 | Jacob Shumate | .15 | .07 |
| ❑ | 173 | Terrence Long | .50 | .23 |
| ❑ | 174 | Mark Johnson RC | .15 | .07 |
| ❑ | 175 | Ben Grieve | .75 | .35 |
| ❑ | 176 | Jayson Peterson RC | .15 | .07 |
| ❑ | 177 | Checklist | .15 | .07 |
| ❑ | 178 | Checklist | .15 | .07 |
| ❑ | 179 | Checklist | .15 | .07 |
| ❑ | 180 | Checklist | .15 | .07 |
| ❑ | 181 | Brian Anderson | .15 | .07 |
| ❑ | 182 | Steve Buechele | .15 | .07 |
| ❑ | 183 | Mark Clark | .15 | .07 |

| |  |  | | |
|---|---|---|---|---|
| ❑ | 184 | Cecil Fielder | .25 | .11 |
| ❑ | 185 | Steve Avery | .15 | .07 |
| ❑ | 186 | Devon White | .25 | .11 |
| ❑ | 187 | Craig Shipley | .15 | .07 |
| ❑ | 188 | Brady Anderson | .25 | .11 |
| ❑ | 189 | Kenny Lofton | .25 | .11 |
| ❑ | 190 | Alex Cole | .15 | .07 |
| ❑ | 191 | Brent Gates | .15 | .07 |
| ❑ | 192 | Dean Palmer | .25 | .11 |
| ❑ | 193 | Alex Gonzalez | .15 | .07 |
| ❑ | 194 | Steve Cooke | .15 | .07 |
| ❑ | 195 | Ray Lankford | .25 | .11 |
| ❑ | 196 | Mark McGwire | 2.00 | .90 |
| ❑ | 197 | Marc Newfield | .15 | .07 |
| ❑ | 198 | Pat Rapp | .15 | .07 |
| ❑ | 199 | Darren Lewis | .15 | .07 |
| ❑ | 200 | Carlos Baerga | .15 | .07 |
| ❑ | 201 | Rickey Henderson | .60 | .25 |
| ❑ | 202 | Kurt Abbott | .15 | .07 |
| ❑ | 203 | Kirt Manwaring | .15 | .07 |
| ❑ | 204 | Cal Ripken | 2.00 | .90 |
| ❑ | 205 | Darren Daulton | .25 | .11 |
| ❑ | 206 | Greg Colbrunn | .15 | .07 |
| ❑ | 207 | Darryl Hamilton | .15 | .07 |
| ❑ | 208 | Bo Jackson | .25 | .11 |
| ❑ | 209 | Tony Phillips | .15 | .07 |
| ❑ | 210 | Geronimo Berroa | .15 | .07 |
| ❑ | 211 | Rich Becker | .15 | .07 |
| ❑ | 212 | Tony Tarasco | .15 | .07 |
| ❑ | 213 | Karl Rhodes | .15 | .07 |
| ❑ | 214 | Phil Plantier | .15 | .07 |
| ❑ | 215 | J.T. Snow | .25 | .11 |
| ❑ | 216 | Mo Vaughn | .25 | .11 |
| ❑ | 217 | Greg Gagne | .15 | .07 |
| ❑ | 218 | Ricky Bones | .15 | .07 |
| ❑ | 219 | Mike Bordick | .15 | .07 |
| ❑ | 220 | Chad Curtis | .15 | .07 |
| ❑ | 221 | Royce Clayton | .15 | .07 |
| ❑ | 222 | Roberto Alomar | .50 | .23 |
| ❑ | 223 | Jose Rijo | .15 | .07 |
| ❑ | 224 | Ryan Klesko | .25 | .11 |
| ❑ | 225 | Mark Langston | .15 | .07 |
| ❑ | 226 | Frank Thomas | 1.00 | .45 |
| ❑ | 227 | Juan Gonzalez | .50 | .23 |
| ❑ | 228 | Ron Gant | .15 | .07 |
| ❑ | 229 | Javier Lopez | .25 | .11 |
| ❑ | 230 | Sammy Sosa | 1.00 | .45 |
| ❑ | 231 | Kevin Brown | .30 | .14 |
| ❑ | 232 | Gary DiSarcina | .15 | .07 |
| ❑ | 233 | Albert Belle | .30 | .14 |
| ❑ | 234 | Jay Buhner | .25 | .11 |
| ❑ | 235 | Pedro Martinez | .60 | .25 |
| ❑ | 236 | Bob Tewksbury | .15 | .07 |
| ❑ | 237 | Mike Piazza | 1.50 | .70 |
| ❑ | 238 | Darryl Kile | .25 | .11 |
| ❑ | 239 | Bryan Harvey | .15 | .07 |
| ❑ | 240 | Andres Galarraga | .30 | .14 |
| ❑ | 241 | Jeff Blauser | .15 | .07 |
| ❑ | 242 | Jeff Kent | .30 | .14 |
| ❑ | 243 | Bobby Munoz | .15 | .07 |
| ❑ | 244 | Greg Maddux | 1.25 | .55 |
| ❑ | 245 | Paul O'Neill | .25 | .11 |
| ❑ | 246 | Lenny Dykstra | .25 | .11 |
| ❑ | 247 | Todd Van Poppel | .15 | .07 |
| ❑ | 248 | Bernie Williams | .50 | .23 |
| ❑ | 249 | Glenallen Hill | .15 | .07 |
| ❑ | 250 | Duane Ward | .15 | .07 |
| ❑ | 251 | Dennis Eckersley | .25 | .11 |
| ❑ | 252 | Pat Mahomes | .15 | .07 |
| ❑ | 253 | Rusty Greer | .25 | .11 |
| ❑ | 254 | Roberto Kelly | .15 | .07 |
| ❑ | 255 | Randy Myers | .15 | .07 |
| ❑ | 256 | Scott Ruffcorn | .15 | .07 |
| ❑ | 257 | Robin Ventura | .25 | .11 |
| ❑ | 258 | Eduardo Perez | .15 | .07 |
| ❑ | 259 | Aaron Sele | .25 | .11 |
| ❑ | 260 | Paul Molitor | .50 | .23 |
| ❑ | 261 | Juan Guzman | .15 | .07 |
| ❑ | 262 | Darren Oliver | .15 | .07 |
| ❑ | 263 | Mike Stanley | .15 | .07 |
| ❑ | 264 | Tom Glavine | .50 | .23 |
| ❑ | 265 | Rico Brogna | .15 | .07 |
| ❑ | 266 | Craig Biggio | .30 | .14 |
| ❑ | 267 | Darrell Whitmore | .15 | .07 |
| ❑ | 268 | Jimmy Key | .25 | .11 |
| ❑ | 269 | Will Clark | .50 | .23 |
| ❑ | 270 | David Cone | .25 | .11 |
| ❑ | 271 | Brian Jordan | .25 | .11 |
| ❑ | 272 | Barry Bonds | .75 | .35 |
| ❑ | 273 | Danny Tartabull | .15 | .07 |
| ❑ | 274 | Ramon J.Martinez | .15 | .07 |
| ❑ | 275 | Al Martin | .15 | .07 |
| ❑ | 276 | Fred McGriff SM | .15 | .07 |
| ❑ | 277 | Carlos Delgado SM | .25 | .11 |
| ❑ | 278 | Juan Gonzalez SM | .25 | .11 |
| ❑ | 279 | Shawn Green SM | .25 | .11 |
| ❑ | 280 | Carlos Baerga SM | .15 | .07 |
| ❑ | 281 | Cliff Floyd SM | .15 | .07 |
| ❑ | 282 | Ozzie Smith SM | .30 | .14 |
| ❑ | 283 | Alex Rodriguez SM | 1.00 | .45 |
| ❑ | 284 | Kenny Lofton SM | .15 | .07 |
| ❑ | 285 | Dave Justice SM | .15 | .07 |
| ❑ | 286 | Tim Salmon SM | .25 | .11 |
| ❑ | 287 | Manny Ramirez SM | .30 | .14 |
| ❑ | 288 | Will Clark SM | .25 | .11 |
| ❑ | 289 | Garret Anderson SM | .15 | .07 |
| ❑ | 290 | Billy Ashley SM | .15 | .07 |
| ❑ | 291 | Tony Gwynn SM | .50 | .23 |
| ❑ | 292 | Raul Mondesi SM | .15 | .07 |
| ❑ | 293 | Rafael Palmeiro SM | .25 | .11 |
| ❑ | 294 | Matt Williams SM | .25 | .11 |
| ❑ | 295 | Don Mattingly SM | .60 | .23 |
| ❑ | 296 | Kirby Puckett SM | .60 | .25 |
| ❑ | 297 | Paul Molitor SM | .25 | .11 |
| ❑ | 298 | Albert Belle SM | .15 | .07 |
| ❑ | 299 | Barry Bonds SM | .30 | .14 |
| ❑ | 300 | Mike Piazza SM | .75 | .35 |
| ❑ | 301 | Jeff Bagwell SM | .50 | .23 |
| ❑ | 302 | Frank Thomas SM | .50 | .23 |
| ❑ | 303 | Chipper Jones SM | .60 | .25 |
| ❑ | 304 | Ken Griffey Jr. SM | 1.00 | .45 |
| ❑ | 305 | Cal Ripken Jr. SM | 1.00 | .45 |
| ❑ | 306 | Eric Anthony | .15 | .07 |
| ❑ | 307 | Todd Benzinger | .15 | .07 |
| ❑ | 308 | Jacob Brumfield | .15 | .07 |
| ❑ | 309 | Wes Chamberlain | .15 | .07 |
| ❑ | 310 | Tino Martinez | .25 | .11 |
| ❑ | 311 | Roberto Mejia | .15 | .07 |
| ❑ | 312 | Jose Offerman | .15 | .07 |
| ❑ | 313 | David Segui | .15 | .07 |
| ❑ | 314 | Eric Young | .15 | .07 |
| ❑ | 315 | Rey Sanchez | .15 | .07 |
| ❑ | 316 | Raul Mondesi | .25 | .11 |
| ❑ | 317 | Bret Boone | .25 | .11 |
| ❑ | 318 | Andre Dawson | .30 | .14 |
| ❑ | 319 | Brian McRae | .15 | .07 |
| ❑ | 320 | Dave Nilsson | .15 | .07 |
| ❑ | 321 | Moises Alou | .25 | .11 |
| ❑ | 322 | Don Slaught | .15 | .07 |
| ❑ | 323 | Dave McCarty | .15 | .07 |
| ❑ | 324 | Mike Huff | .15 | .07 |
| ❑ | 325 | Rick Aguilera | .15 | .07 |
| ❑ | 326 | Rod Beck | .15 | .07 |
| ❑ | 327 | Kenny Rogers | .15 | .07 |
| ❑ | 328 | Andy Benes | .15 | .07 |
| ❑ | 329 | Allen Watson | .15 | .07 |
| ❑ | 330 | Randy Johnson | .60 | .25 |
| ❑ | 331 | Willie Greene | .15 | .07 |
| ❑ | 332 | Hal Morris | .15 | .07 |
| ❑ | 333 | Ozzie Smith | .60 | .25 |
| ❑ | 334 | Jason Bere | .15 | .07 |
| ❑ | 335 | Scott Erickson | .15 | .07 |
| ❑ | 336 | Dante Bichette | .25 | .11 |
| ❑ | 337 | Willie Banks | .15 | .07 |
| ❑ | 338 | Eric Davis | .25 | .11 |
| ❑ | 339 | Rondell White | .25 | .11 |
| ❑ | 340 | Kirby Puckett | 1.25 | .55 |
| ❑ | 341 | Deion Sanders | .25 | .11 |
| ❑ | 342 | Eddie Murray | .50 | .23 |
| ❑ | 343 | Mike Harkey | .15 | .07 |
| ❑ | 344 | Joey Hamilton | .15 | .07 |
| ❑ | 345 | Roger Salkeld | .15 | .07 |
| ❑ | 346 | Wil Cordero | .15 | .07 |
| ❑ | 347 | John Wetteland | .25 | .11 |
| ❑ | 348 | Geronimo Pena | .15 | .07 |
| ❑ | 349 | Kirk Gibson | .25 | .11 |
| ❑ | 350 | Manny Ramirez | .60 | .25 |
| ❑ | 351 | Wm.VanLandingham | .15 | .07 |
| ❑ | 352 | B.J. Surhoff | .25 | .11 |
| ❑ | 353 | Ken Ryan | .15 | .07 |
| ❑ | 354 | Terry Steinbach | .15 | .07 |
| ❑ | 355 | Bret Saberhagen | .25 | .11 |
| ❑ | 356 | John Jaha | .15 | .07 |
| ❑ | 357 | Joe Girardi | .15 | .07 |
| ❑ | 358 | Steve Karsay | .15 | .07 |
| ❑ | 359 | Alex Fernandez | .15 | .07 |
| ❑ | 360 | Salomon Torres | .15 | .07 |
| ❑ | 361 | John Burkett | .15 | .07 |
| ❑ | 362 | Derek Bell | .15 | .07 |
| ❑ | 363 | Tom Henke | .15 | .07 |
| ❑ | 364 | Gregg Jefferies | .15 | .07 |
| ❑ | 365 | Jack McDowell | .15 | .07 |
| ❑ | 366 | Andujar Cedeno | .15 | .07 |
| ❑ | 367 | Dave Winfield | .50 | .23 |
| ❑ | 368 | Carl Everett | .25 | .11 |
| ❑ | 369 | Danny Jackson | .15 | .07 |
| ❑ | 370 | Jeromy Burnitz | .25 | .11 |
| ❑ | 371 | Mark Grace | .50 | .23 |
| ❑ | 372 | Larry Walker | .25 | .11 |
| ❑ | 373 | Bill Swift | .15 | .07 |
| ❑ | 374 | Dennis Martinez | .25 | .11 |
| ❑ | 375 | Mickey Tettleton | .15 | .07 |
| ❑ | 376 | Mel Nieves | .15 | .07 |
| ❑ | 377 | Cal Eldred | .15 | .07 |
| ❑ | 378 | Orel Hershiser | .25 | .11 |
| ❑ | 379 | David Wells | .25 | .11 |
| ❑ | 380 | Gary Gaetti | .25 | .11 |
| ❑ | 381 | Jeromy Burnitz | .25 | .11 |
| ❑ | 382 | Barry Larkin | .50 | .23 |
| ❑ | 383 | Jason Jacome | .15 | .07 |
| ❑ | 384 | Tim Wallach | .15 | .07 |
| ❑ | 385 | Robby Thompson | .15 | .07 |
| ❑ | 386 | Frank Viola | .15 | .07 |
| ❑ | 387 | Dave Stewart | .25 | .11 |
| ❑ | 388 | Bip Roberts | .15 | .07 |
| ❑ | 389 | Ron Darling | .15 | .07 |
| ❑ | 390 | Carlos Delgado | .50 | .23 |
| ❑ | 391 | Tim Salmon | .25 | .11 |
| ❑ | 392 | Alan Trammell | .30 | .14 |
| ❑ | 393 | Kevin Foster | .15 | .07 |
| ❑ | 394 | Jim Abbott | .25 | .11 |
| ❑ | 395 | John Kruk | .25 | .11 |
| ❑ | 396 | Andy Van Slyke | .25 | .11 |
| ❑ | 397 | Dave Magadan | .15 | .07 |
| ❑ | 398 | Rafael Palmeiro | .50 | .23 |
| ❑ | 399 | Mike Devereaux | .15 | .07 |
| ❑ | 400 | Benito Santiago | .15 | .07 |
| ❑ | 401 | Brett Butler | .25 | .11 |
| ❑ | 402 | John Franco | .25 | .11 |
| ❑ | 403 | Matt Walbeck | .15 | .07 |
| ❑ | 404 | Terry Pendleton | .25 | .11 |
| ❑ | 405 | Chris Sabo | .15 | .07 |
| ❑ | 406 | Andrew Lorraine | .15 | .07 |
| ❑ | 407 | Dan Wilson | .15 | .07 |
| ❑ | 408 | Mike Lansing | .15 | .07 |
| ❑ | 409 | Ray McDavid | .15 | .07 |
| ❑ | 410 | Shane Andrews | .15 | .07 |
| ❑ | 411 | Tom Gordon | .15 | .07 |
| ❑ | 412 | Chad Ogea | .15 | .07 |
| ❑ | 413 | James Baldwin | .25 | .11 |
| ❑ | 414 | Russ Davis | .15 | .07 |
| ❑ | 415 | Ray Holbert | .15 | .07 |
| ❑ | 416 | Ray Durham | .25 | .11 |
| ❑ | 417 | Matt Nokes | .15 | .07 |
| ❑ | 418 | Rod Henderson | .15 | .07 |
| ❑ | 419 | Gabe White | .15 | .07 |
| ❑ | 420 | Todd Hollandsworth | .15 | .07 |
| ❑ | 421 | Midre Cummings | .15 | .07 |
| ❑ | 422 | Harold Baines | .25 | .11 |
| ❑ | 423 | Troy Percival | .15 | .07 |
| ❑ | 424 | Joe Vitiello | .15 | .07 |
| ❑ | 425 | Andy Ashby | .15 | .07 |
| ❑ | 426 | Michael Tucker | .15 | .07 |
| ❑ | 427 | Mark Gubicza | .15 | .07 |
| ❑ | 428 | Jim Bullinger | .15 | .07 |
| ❑ | 429 | Jose Malave | .15 | .07 |
| ❑ | 430 | Pete Schourek | .15 | .07 |
| ❑ | 431 | Bobby Ayala | .15 | .07 |
| ❑ | 432 | Marvin Freeman | .15 | .07 |
| ❑ | 433 | Pat Listach | .15 | .07 |
| ❑ | 434 | Eddie Taubensee | .15 | .07 |
| ❑ | 435 | Steve Howe | .15 | .07 |
| ❑ | 436 | Kent Mercker | .15 | .07 |
| ❑ | 437 | Hector Fajardo | .15 | .07 |
| ❑ | 438 | Scott Kamieniecki | .15 | .07 |
| ❑ | 439 | Robb Nen | .15 | .07 |
| ❑ | 440 | Mike Kelly | .15 | .07 |
| ❑ | 441 | Tom Candiotti | .15 | .07 |

❑ 442 Albie Lopez .15 .07
❑ 443 Jeff Granger .15 .07
❑ 444 Rich Aude .15 .07
❑ 445 Luis Polonia .15 .07
❑ 446 Frank Thomas CL .50 .23
❑ 447 Ken Griffey Jr. CL 1.00 .45
❑ 448 Mike Piazza CL .75 .35
❑ 449 Jeff Bagwell CL .50 .23
❑ 450 Jeff Bagwell CL .75 .35
Frank Thomas
Ken Griffey Jr.
Mike Piazza

## 1996 Pinnacle

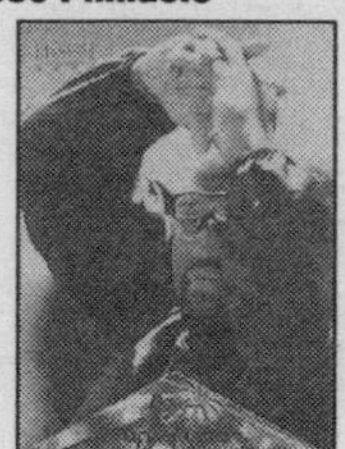

| | MINT | NRMT |
|---|---|---|
| COMPLETE SET (400) | 30.00 | 13.50 |
| COMPLETE SERIES 1 (200) | 15.00 | 6.75 |
| COMPLETE SERIES 2 (200) | 15.00 | 6.75 |
| COMMON CARD (1-399) | .10 | .05 |

❑ 1 Greg Maddux 1.00 .45
❑ 2 Bill Pulsipher .10 .05
❑ 3 Dante Bichette .15 .07
❑ 4 Mike Piazza 1.25 .55
❑ 5 Garret Anderson .15 .07
❑ 6 Steve Finley .15 .07
❑ 7 Andy Benes .10 .05
❑ 8 Chuck Knoblauch .15 .07
❑ 9 Tom Gordon .10 .05
❑ 10 Jeff Bagwell .50 .23
❑ 11 Wil Cordero .10 .05
❑ 12 John Mabry .10 .05
❑ 13 Jeff Frye .10 .05
❑ 14 Travis Fryman .15 .07
❑ 15 John Wetteland .15 .07
❑ 16 Jason Bates .10 .05
❑ 17 Danny Tartabull .10 .05
❑ 18 Charles Nagy .10 .05
❑ 19 Robin Ventura .15 .07
❑ 20 Reggie Sanders .10 .05
❑ 21 Dave Clark .10 .05
❑ 22 Jaime Navarro .10 .05
❑ 23 Joey Hamilton .10 .05
❑ 24 Al Leiter .15 .07
❑ 25 Deion Sanders .15 .07
❑ 26 Tim Salmon .15 .07
❑ 27 Tino Martinez .15 .07
❑ 28 Mike Greenwell .10 .05
❑ 29 Phil Plantier .10 .05
❑ 30 Bobby Bonilla .15 .07
❑ 31 Kenny Rogers .10 .05
❑ 32 Chili Davis .15 .07
❑ 33 Joe Carter .15 .07
❑ 34 Mike Mussina .40 .18
❑ 35 Matt Mieske .10 .05
❑ 36 Jose Canseco .50 .23
❑ 37 Brad Radke .15 .07
❑ 38 Juan Gonzalez .40 .18
❑ 39 David Segui .10 .05
❑ 40 Alex Fernandez .10 .05
❑ 41 Jeff Kent .30 .14
❑ 42 Todd Zeile .10 .05
❑ 43 Darryl Strawberry .15 .07
❑ 44 Jose Rijo .10 .05
❑ 45 Ramon Martinez .10 .05
❑ 46 Manny Ramirez .50 .23
❑ 47 Gregg Jefferies .10 .05
❑ 48 Bryan Rekar .10 .05
❑ 49 Jeff King .10 .05
❑ 50 John Olerud .15 .07
❑ 51 Marc Newfield .10 .05
❑ 52 Charles Johnson .15 .07
❑ 53 Robby Thompson .10 .05
❑ 54 Brian L. Hunter .10 .05
❑ 55 Mike Blowers .10 .05
❑ 56 Keith Lockhart .10 .05
❑ 57 Ray Lankford .15 .07
❑ 58 Tim Wallach .10 .05
❑ 59 Ivan Rodriguez .50 .23
❑ 60 Ed Sprague .10 .05
❑ 61 Paul Molitor .40 .18
❑ 62 Eric Karros .15 .07
❑ 63 Glenallen Hill .10 .05
❑ 64 Jay Bell .15 .07
❑ 65 Tom Pagnozzi .10 .05
❑ 66 Greg Colbrunn .10 .05
❑ 67 Edgar Martinez .30 .14
❑ 68 Paul Sorrento .10 .05
❑ 69 Kirt Manwaring .10 .05
❑ 70 Pete Schourek .10 .05
❑ 71 Orlando Merced .10 .05
❑ 72 Shawon Dunston .10 .05
❑ 73 Ricky Bottalico .10 .05
❑ 74 Brady Anderson .15 .07
❑ 75 Steve Ontiveros .10 .05
❑ 76 Jim Abbott .15 .07
❑ 77 Carl Everett .15 .07
❑ 78 Mo Vaughn .15 .07
❑ 79 Pedro Martinez .50 .23
❑ 80 Harold Baines .15 .07
❑ 81 Alan Trammell .30 .14
❑ 82 Steve Avery .10 .05
❑ 83 Jeff Cirillo .15 .07
❑ 84 John Valentin .10 .05
❑ 85 Bernie Williams .40 .18
❑ 86 Andre Dawson .30 .14
❑ 87 Dave Winfield .40 .18
❑ 88 B.J. Surhoff .15 .07
❑ 89 Jeff Blauser .10 .05
❑ 90 Barry Larkin .40 .18
❑ 91 Cliff Floyd .15 .07
❑ 92 Sammy Sosa .75 .35
❑ 93 Andres Galarraga .30 .14
❑ 94 Dave Nilsson .10 .05
❑ 95 James Mouton .10 .05
❑ 96 Marquis Grissom .10 .05
❑ 97 Matt Williams .30 .14
❑ 98 John Jaha .10 .05
❑ 99 Don Mattingly 1.00 .45
❑ 100 Tim Naehring .10 .05
❑ 101 Kevin Appier .15 .07
❑ 102 Bobby Higginson .15 .07
❑ 103 Andy Pettitte .15 .07
❑ 104 Ozzie Smith .50 .23
❑ 105 Kenny Lofton .15 .07
❑ 106 Ken Caminiti .15 .07
❑ 107 Walt Weiss .10 .05
❑ 108 Jack McDowell .10 .05
❑ 109 Brian McRae .10 .05
❑ 110 Gary Gaetti .15 .07
❑ 111 Curtis Goodwin .10 .05
❑ 112 Dennis Martinez .15 .07
❑ 113 Omar Vizquel .15 .07
❑ 114 Chipper Jones 1.00 .45
❑ 115 Mark Gubicza .10 .05
❑ 116 Ruben Sierra .10 .05
❑ 117 Eddie Murray .40 .18
❑ 118 Chad Curtis .10 .05
❑ 119 Hal Morris .10 .05
❑ 120 Ben McDonald .10 .05
❑ 121 Marty Cordova .10 .05
❑ 122 Ken Griffey Jr. UER 1.50 .70
(Card says Ken homered from both sides; He is only a left hitter)
❑ 123 Gary Sheffield .40 .18
❑ 124 Charlie Hayes .10 .05
❑ 125 Shawn Green .40 .18
❑ 126 Jason Giambi .15 .07
❑ 127 Mark Langston .10 .05
❑ 128 Mark Whiten .10 .05
❑ 129 Greg Vaughn .15 .07
❑ 130 Mark McGwire 1.50 .70
❑ 131 Hideo Nomo .40 .18
❑ 132 Eric Karros .40 .18
Mike Piazza
Raul Mondesi
Hideo Nomo
❑ 133 Jason Bere .10 .05
❑ 134 Ken Griffey Jr. NAT .75 .35
❑ 135 Frank Thomas NAT .40 .18
❑ 136 Cal Ripken NAT .75 .35
❑ 137 Albert Belle NAT .10 .05
❑ 138 Mike Piazza NAT .60 .25
❑ 139 Dante Bichette NAT .10 .05
❑ 140 Sammy Sosa NAT .40 .18
❑ 141 Mo Vaughn NAT .15 .07
❑ 142 Tim Salmon NAT .10 .05
❑ 143 Reggie Sanders NAT .10 .05
❑ 144 Cecil Fielder NAT .10 .05
❑ 145 Jim Edmonds NAT .40 .18
❑ 146 Rafael Palmeiro NAT .15 .07
❑ 147 Edgar Martinez NAT .15 .07
❑ 148 Barry Bonds NAT .30 .14
❑ 149 Manny Ramirez NAT .40 .18
❑ 150 Larry Walker NAT .15 .07
❑ 151 Jeff Bagwell NAT .40 .18
❑ 152 Ron Gant NAT .10 .05
❑ 153 Andres Galarraga NAT .10 .05
❑ 154 Eddie Murray NAT .15 .07
❑ 155 Kirby Puckett NAT .50 .23
❑ 156 Will Clark NAT .15 .07
❑ 157 Don Mattingly NAT .50 .18
❑ 158 Mark McGwire NAT .75 .35
❑ 159 Dean Palmer NAT .10 .05
❑ 160 Matt Williams NAT .30 .14
❑ 161 Fred McGriff NAT .10 .05
❑ 162 Joe Carter NAT .10 .05
❑ 163 Juan Gonzalez NAT .15 .07
❑ 164 Alex Ochoa .10 .05
❑ 165 Ruben Rivera .10 .05
❑ 166 Tony Clark .10 .05
❑ 167 Brian Barber .10 .05
❑ 168 Matt Lawton RC .50 .23
❑ 169 Terrell Wade .10 .05
❑ 170 Johnny Damon .30 .14
❑ 171 Derek Jeter 1.50 .70
❑ 172 Phil Nevin .15 .07
❑ 173 Robert Perez .10 .05
❑ 174 C.J. Nitkowski .10 .05
❑ 175 Joe Vitiello .10 .05
❑ 176 Roger Cedeno .10 .05
❑ 177 Ron Coomer .10 .05
❑ 178 Chris Widger .10 .05
❑ 179 Jimmy Haynes .10 .05
❑ 180 Mike Sweeney RC 1.50 .70
❑ 181 Howard Battle .10 .05
❑ 182 John Wasdin .10 .05
❑ 183 Jim Pittsley .10 .05
❑ 184 Bob Wolcott .10 .05
❑ 185 LaTroy Hawkins .10 .05
❑ 186 Nigel Wilson .10 .05
❑ 187 Dustin Hermanson .10 .05
❑ 188 Chris Snopek .10 .05
❑ 189 Mariano Rivera .15 .07
❑ 190 Jose Herrera .10 .05
❑ 191 Chris Stynes .10 .05
❑ 192 Larry Thomas .10 .05
❑ 193 David Bell .10 .05
❑ 194 Frank Thomas CL .40 .18
❑ 195 Ken Griffey Jr. CL .75 .35
❑ 196 Cal Ripken CL .75 .35
❑ 197 Jeff Bagwell CL .40 .18
❑ 198 Mike Piazza CL .60 .25
❑ 199 Barry Bonds CL .30 .14
❑ 200 Garret Anderson CL .40 .18
Chipper Jones
❑ 201 Frank Thomas .75 .35
❑ 202 Michael Tucker .10 .05
❑ 203 Kirby Puckett 1.00 .45
❑ 204 Alex Gonzalez .10 .05
❑ 205 Tony Gwynn .75 .35
❑ 206 Moises Alou .15 .07
❑ 207 Albert Belle .30 .14
❑ 208 Barry Bonds .60 .25
❑ 209 Fred McGriff .30 .14
❑ 210 Dennis Eckersley .15 .07
❑ 211 Craig Biggio .30 .14
❑ 212 David Cone .15 .07
❑ 213 Will Clark .40 .18

❑ 214 Cal Ripken 1.50 .70
❑ 215 Wade Boggs .50 .23
❑ 216 Pete Schourek .10 .05
❑ 217 Darren Daulton .15 .07
❑ 218 Carlos Baerga .10 .05
❑ 219 Larry Walker .15 .07
❑ 220 Denny Neagle .15 .07
❑ 221 Jim Edmonds .40 .18
❑ 222 Lee Smith .15 .07
❑ 223 Jason Isringhausen .15 .07
❑ 224 Jay Buhner .15 .07
❑ 225 John Olerud .15 .07
❑ 226 Jeff Conine .10 .05
❑ 227 Dean Palmer .15 .07
❑ 228 Jim Abbott .15 .07
❑ 229 Raul Mondesi .15 .07
❑ 230 Tom Glavine .40 .18
❑ 231 Kevin Seltzer .10 .05
❑ 232 Lenny Dykstra .15 .07
❑ 233 Brian Jordan .15 .07
❑ 234 Rondell White .15 .07
❑ 235 Bret Boone .15 .07
❑ 236 Randy Johnson .50 .23
❑ 237 Paul O'Neill .15 .07
❑ 238 Jim Thome .30 .14
❑ 239 Edgardo Alfonzo .15 .07
❑ 240 Terry Pendleton .15 .07
❑ 241 Harold Baines .15 .07
❑ 242 Roberto Alomar .40 .18
❑ 243 Mark Grace .40 .18
❑ 244 Derek Bell .10 .05
❑ 245 Vinny Castilla .15 .07
❑ 246 Cecil Fielder .15 .07
❑ 247 Roger Clemens .75 .35
❑ 248 Orel Hershiser .15 .07
❑ 249 J.T. Snow .15 .07
❑ 250 Rafael Palmeiro .40 .18
❑ 251 Bret Saberhagen .15 .07
❑ 252 Todd Hollandsworth .10 .05
❑ 253 Ryan Klesko .15 .07
❑ 254 Greg Maddux HH .50 .23
❑ 255 Ken Griffey Jr. HH .75 .35
❑ 256 Hideo Nomo HH .15 .07
❑ 257 Frank Thomas HH .40 .18
❑ 258 Cal Ripken HH .75 .35
❑ 259 Jeff Bagwell HH .40 .18
❑ 260 Barry Bonds HH .30 .14
❑ 261 Mo Vaughn HH .15 .07
❑ 262 Albert Belle HH .10 .05
❑ 263 Sammy Sosa HH .40 .18
❑ 264 Reggie Sanders HH .10 .05
❑ 265 Mike Piazza HH .60 .25
❑ 266 Chipper Jones HH .50 .23
❑ 267 Tony Gwynn HH .40 .18
❑ 268 Kirby Puckett HH .50 .23
❑ 269 Wade Boggs HH .15 .07
❑ 270 Will Clark HH .15 .07
❑ 271 Gary Sheffield HH .15 .07
❑ 272 Dante Bichette HH .10 .05
❑ 273 Randy Johnson HH .15 .07
❑ 274 Matt Williams HH .30 .14
❑ 275 Alex Rodriguez HH .60 .25
❑ 276 Tim Salmon HH .10 .05
❑ 277 Johnny Damon HH .10 .05
❑ 278 Manny Ramirez HH .40 .18
❑ 279 Derek Jeter HH .75 .35
❑ 280 Eddie Murray HH .15 .07
❑ 281 Ozzie Smith HH .40 .18
❑ 282 Garret Anderson HH .10 .05
❑ 283 Raul Mondesi HH .10 .05
❑ 284 Terry Steinbach .10 .05
❑ 285 Carlos Garcia .10 .05
❑ 286 Dave Justice .30 .14
❑ 287 Eric Anthony .10 .05
❑ 288 Benji Gil .10 .05
❑ 289 Bob Hamelin .10 .05
❑ 290 Dwayne Hosey .10 .05
❑ 291 Andy Pettitte HH .10 .05
❑ 292 Rod Beck .10 .05
❑ 293 Shane Andrews .10 .05
❑ 294 Julian Tavarez .10 .05
❑ 295 Willie Greene .15 .07
❑ 296 Ismael Valdes .10 .05
❑ 297 Glenallen Hill .10 .05
❑ 298 Troy Percival .10 .05
❑ 299 Ray Durham .15 .07
❑ 300 Jeff Conine 300 .10 .05
❑ 301 Ken Griffey Jr. 300 .75 .35
❑ 302 Will Clark 300 .15 .07
❑ 303 Mike Greenwell 300 .10 .05
❑ 304 Carlos Baerga 300 .10 .05
❑ 305A Paul Molitor 300 .15 .07
❑ 305B Jeff Bagwell 300 .40 .18
❑ 306 Mark Grace 300 .15 .07
❑ 307 Don Mattingly 300 .50 .18
❑ 308 Hal Morris 300 .10 .05
❑ 309 Butch Huskey .10 .05
❑ 310 Ozzie Guillen .10 .05
❑ 311 Erik Hanson .10 .05
❑ 312 Kenny Lofton 300 .10 .05
❑ 313 Edgar Martinez 300 .15 .07
❑ 314 Kurt Abbott .10 .05
❑ 315 John Smoltz .15 .07
❑ 316 Ariel Prieto .10 .05
❑ 317 Mark Carreon .10 .05
❑ 318 Kirby Puckett 300 .50 .23
❑ 319 Carlos Perez .10 .05
❑ 320 Gary DiSarcina .10 .05
❑ 321 Trevor Hoffman .15 .07
❑ 322 Mike Piazza 300 .60 .25
❑ 323 Frank Thomas 300 .40 .18
❑ 324 Juan Acevedo .10 .05
❑ 325 Bip Roberts .10 .05
❑ 326 Javier Lopez .15 .07
❑ 327 Benito Santiago .10 .05
❑ 328 Mark Lewis .10 .05
❑ 329 Royce Clayton .10 .05
❑ 330 Tom Gordon .10 .05
❑ 331 Ben McDonald .10 .05
❑ 332 Dan Wilson .10 .05
❑ 333 Ron Gant .10 .05
❑ 334 Wade Boggs 300 .15 .07
❑ 335 Paul Molitor .40 .18
❑ 336 Tony Gwynn 300 .40 .18
❑ 337 Sean Berry .10 .05
❑ 338 Rickey Henderson .50 .23
❑ 339 Wil Cordero .10 .05
❑ 340 Kent Mercker .10 .05
❑ 341 Kenny Rogers .10 .05
❑ 342 Ryne Sandberg .50 .23
❑ 343 Charlie Hayes .10 .05
❑ 344 Andy Benes .10 .05
❑ 345 Sterling Hitchcock .10 .05
❑ 346 Bernard Gilkey .10 .05
❑ 347 Julio Franco .10 .05
❑ 348 Ken Hill .10 .05
❑ 349 Russ Davis .10 .05
❑ 350 Mike Blowers .10 .05
❑ 351 B.J. Surhoff .15 .07
❑ 352 Lance Johnson .10 .05
❑ 353 Darryl Hamilton .10 .05
❑ 354 Shawon Dunston .10 .05
❑ 355 Rick Aguilera .10 .05
❑ 356 Danny Tartabull .10 .05
❑ 357 Todd Stottlemyre .10 .05
❑ 358 Mike Bordick .10 .05
❑ 359 Jack McDowell .10 .05
❑ 360 Todd Zeile .10 .05
❑ 361 Tino Martinez .15 .07
❑ 362 Greg Gagne .10 .05
❑ 363 Mike Kelly .10 .05
❑ 364 Tim Raines .15 .07
❑ 365 Ernie Young .10 .05
❑ 366 Mike Stanley .10 .05
❑ 367 Wally Joyner .15 .07
❑ 368 Karim Garcia .10 .05
❑ 369 Paul Wilson .10 .05
❑ 370 Sal Fasano .10 .05
❑ 371 Jason Schmidt .10 .05
❑ 372 Livan Hernandez RC .50 .23
❑ 373 George Arias .10 .05
❑ 374 Steve Gibralter .10 .05
❑ 375 Jermaine Dye .15 .07
❑ 376 Jason Kendall .15 .07
❑ 377 Brooks Kieschnick .10 .05
❑ 378 Jeff Ware .10 .05
❑ 379 Alan Benes .10 .05
❑ 380 Rey Ordonez .10 .05
❑ 381 Jay Powell .10 .05
❑ 382 Osvaldo Fernandez RC .10 .05
❑ 383 Wilton Guerrero RC .25 .11
❑ 384 Eric Owens .10 .05
❑ 385 George Williams RC .10 .05
❑ 386 Chan Ho Park .15 .07
❑ 387 Jeff Suppan .10 .05
❑ 388 F.P. Santangelo RC .10 .05
❑ 389 Terry Adams .10 .05
❑ 390 Bob Abreu .50 .23
❑ 391 Quinton McCracken .10 .05
❑ 392 Mike Busby RC .10 .05
❑ 393 Cal Ripken CL .75 .35
❑ 394 Ken Griffey Jr. CL .75 .35
❑ 395 Frank Thomas CL .40 .18
❑ 396 Chipper Jones CL .50 .23
❑ 397 Greg Maddux CL .50 .23
❑ 398 Mike Piazza CL .60 .25
❑ 399 Ken Griffey Jr CL .60 .25
Cal Ripken Jr.
Chipper Jones
Frank Thomas
Greg Maddux
Mike Piazza
❑ CR1 Cal Ripken Tribute 15.00 6.75

## 1997 Pinnacle

MINT NRMT
COMPLETE SET (200) 20.00 9.00

❑ 1 Cecil Fielder .30 .14
❑ 2 Garret Anderson .30 .14
❑ 3 Charles Nagy .15 .07
❑ 4 Darryl Hamilton .15 .07
❑ 5 Greg Myers .15 .07
❑ 6 Eric Davis .30 .14
❑ 7 Jeff Frye .15 .07
❑ 8 Marquis Grissom .15 .07
❑ 9 Curt Schilling .30 .14
❑ 10 Jeff Fassero .15 .07
❑ 11 Alan Benes .15 .07
❑ 12 Orlando Miller .15 .07
❑ 13 Alex Fernandez .15 .07
❑ 14 Andy Pettitte .30 .14
❑ 15 Andre Dawson .50 .23
❑ 16 Mark Grudzielanek .15 .07
❑ 17 Joe Vitiello .15 .07
❑ 18 Juan Gonzalez .60 .25
❑ 19 Mark Whiten .15 .07
❑ 20 Lance Johnson .15 .07
❑ 21 Trevor Hoffman .30 .14
❑ 22 Marc Newfield .15 .07
❑ 23 Jim Eisenreich .15 .07
❑ 24 Joe Carter .30 .14
❑ 25 Jose Canseco .75 .35
❑ 26 Bill Swift .15 .07
❑ 27 Ellis Burks .30 .14
❑ 28 Ben McDonald .15 .07
❑ 29 Edgar Martinez .50 .23
❑ 30 Jamie Moyer .15 .07
❑ 31 Chan Ho Park .30 .14
❑ 32 Carlos Delgado .60 .25
❑ 33 Kevin Mitchell .15 .07
❑ 34 Carlos Garcia .15 .07
❑ 35 Darryl Strawberry .30 .14
❑ 36 Jim Thome .50 .23
❑ 37 Jose Offerman .15 .07
❑ 38 Ryan Klesko .30 .14
❑ 39 Ruben Sierra .15 .07
❑ 40 Devon White .30 .14
❑ 41 Brian Jordan .30 .14
❑ 42 Tony Gwynn 1.25 .55

❑ 43 Rafael Palmeiro .60 .25
❑ 44 Dante Bichette .30 .14
❑ 45 Scott Stahoviak .15 .07
❑ 46 Roger Cedeno .15 .07
❑ 47 Ivan Rodriguez .75 .35
❑ 48 Bob Abreu .30 .14
❑ 49 Darryl Kile .30 .14
❑ 50 Darren Dreifort .30 .14
❑ 51 Shawon Dunston .15 .07
❑ 52 Mark McGwire 2.50 1.10
❑ 53 Tim Salmon .30 .14
❑ 54 Gene Schall .15 .07
❑ 55 Roger Clemens 1.25 .55
❑ 56 Rondell White .30 .14
❑ 57 Ed Sprague .15 .07
❑ 58 Craig Paquette .15 .07
❑ 59 David Segui .15 .07
❑ 60 Jaime Navarro .15 .07
❑ 61 Tom Glavine .60 .25
❑ 62 Jeff Brantley .15 .07
❑ 63 Kimera Bartee .15 .07
❑ 64 Fernando Vina .15 .07
❑ 65 Eddie Murray .60 .25
❑ 66 Lenny Dykstra .30 .14
❑ 67 Kevin Elster .15 .07
❑ 68 Vinny Castilla .30 .14
❑ 69 Mike Fetters .15 .07
❑ 70 Brett Butler .30 .14
❑ 71 Robby Thompson .15 .07
❑ 72 Reggie Jefferson .15 .07
❑ 73 Todd Hundley .15 .07
❑ 74 Jeff King .15 .07
❑ 75 Ernie Young .15 .07
❑ 76 Jeff Bagwell .75 .35
❑ 77 Dan Wilson .15 .07
❑ 78 Paul Molitor .60 .25
❑ 79 Kevin Seitzer .15 .07
❑ 80 Kevin Brown .50 .23
❑ 81 Ron Gant .15 .07
❑ 82 Dwight Gooden .30 .14
❑ 83 Todd Stottlemyre .15 .07
❑ 84 Ken Caminiti .30 .14
❑ 85 James Baldwin .30 .14
❑ 86 Jermaine Dye .30 .14
❑ 87 Harold Baines .30 .14
❑ 88 Pat Hentgen .15 .07
❑ 89 Frank Rodriguez .15 .07
❑ 90 Mark Johnson .15 .07
❑ 91 Jason Kendall .30 .14
❑ 92 Alex Rodriguez 2.00 .90
❑ 93 Alan Trammell .50 .23
❑ 94 Scott Brosius .30 .14
❑ 95 Delino DeShields .15 .07
❑ 96 Chipper Jones 1.50 .70
❑ 97 Barry Bonds 1.00 .45
❑ 98 Brady Anderson .30 .14
❑ 99 Ryne Sandberg .75 .35
❑ 100 Albert Belle .50 .23
❑ 101 Jeff Cirillo .30 .14
❑ 102 Frank Thomas 1.25 .55
❑ 103 Mike Piazza 2.00 .90
❑ 104 Rickey Henderson .75 .35
❑ 105 Rey Ordonez .15 .07
❑ 106 Mark Grace .60 .25
❑ 107 Terry Steinbach .15 .07
❑ 108 Ray Durham .30 .14
❑ 109 Barry Larkin .60 .25
❑ 110 Tony Clark .15 .07
❑ 111 Bernie Williams .60 .25
❑ 112 John Smoltz .30 .14
❑ 113 Moises Alou .30 .14
❑ 114 Alex Gonzalez .15 .07
❑ 115 Rico Brogna .15 .07
❑ 116 Eric Karros .30 .14
❑ 117 Jeff Conine .15 .07
❑ 118 Todd Hollandsworth .15 .07
❑ 119 Troy Percival .15 .07
❑ 120 Paul Wilson .15 .07
❑ 121 Orel Hershiser .30 .14
❑ 122 Ozzie Smith .75 .35
❑ 123 Dave Hollins .15 .07
❑ 124 Ken Hill .15 .07
❑ 125 Rick Wilkins .15 .07
❑ 126 Scott Servais .15 .07
❑ 127 Fernando Valenzuela .30 .14
❑ 128 Mariano Rivera .30 .14
❑ 129 Mark Loretta .15 .07
❑ 130 Shane Reynolds .15 .07
❑ 131 Darren Oliver .15 .07
❑ 132 Steve Trachsel .15 .07
❑ 133 Darren Bragg .15 .07
❑ 134 Jason Dickson .15 .07
❑ 135 Darrin Fletcher .15 .07
❑ 136 Gary Gaetti .30 .14
❑ 137 Joey Cora .15 .07
❑ 138 Terry Pendleton .30 .14
❑ 139 Derek Jeter 2.50 1.10
❑ 140 Danny Tartabull .15 .07
❑ 141 John Flaherty .15 .07
❑ 142 B.J. Surhoff .30 .14
❑ 143 Mike Sweeney .30 .14
❑ 144 Chad Mottola .15 .07
❑ 145 Andujar Cedeno .15 .07
❑ 146 Tim Belcher .15 .07
❑ 147 Mark Thompson .15 .07
❑ 148 Rafael Bournigal .15 .07
❑ 149 Marty Cordova .15 .07
❑ 150 Osvaldo Fernandez .15 .07
❑ 151 Mike Stanley .15 .07
❑ 152 Ricky Bottalico .15 .07
❑ 153 Donne Wall .15 .07
❑ 154 Omar Vizquel .30 .14
❑ 155 Mike Mussina .60 .25
❑ 156 Brant Brown .15 .07
❑ 157 F.P. Santangelo .15 .07
❑ 158 Ryan Hancock .15 .07
❑ 159 Jeff D'Amico .15 .07
❑ 160 Luis Castillo .30 .14
❑ 161 Darin Erstad .75 .35
❑ 162 Ugueth Urbina .30 .14
❑ 163 Andruw Jones .75 .35
❑ 164 Steve Gibralter .15 .07
❑ 165 Robin Jennings .15 .07
❑ 166 Mike Cameron .30 .14
❑ 167 George Arias .15 .07
❑ 168 Chris Stynes .15 .07
❑ 169 Justin Thompson .15 .07
❑ 170 Jamey Wright .15 .07
❑ 171 Todd Walker .15 .07
❑ 172 Nomar Garciaparra 2.00 .90
❑ 173 Jose Paniagua .15 .07
❑ 174 Marvin Benard .15 .07
❑ 175 Rocky Coppinger .15 .07
❑ 176 Quinton McCracken .15 .07
❑ 177 Amaury Telemaco .15 .07
❑ 178 Neifi Perez .15 .07
❑ 179 Todd Greene .15 .07
❑ 180 Jason Thompson .15 .07
❑ 181 Wilton Guerrero .15 .07
❑ 182 Edgar Renteria .30 .14
❑ 183 Billy Wagner .15 .07
❑ 184 Alex Ochoa .15 .07
❑ 185 Dmitri Young .30 .14
❑ 186 Kenny Lofton CT .30 .14
❑ 187 Andres Galarraga CT .50 .23
❑ 188 Chuck Knoblauch CT .30 .14
❑ 189 Greg Maddux CT 1.50 .70
❑ 190 Mo Vaughn CT .30 .14
❑ 191 Cal Ripken CT 2.50 1.10
❑ 192 Hideo Nomo CT .30 .14
❑ 193 Ken Griffey Jr. CT 2.50 1.10
❑ 194 Sammy Sosa CT 1.25 .55
❑ 195 Jay Buhner CT .15 .07
❑ 196 Manny Ramirez CT .75 .23
❑ 197 Matt Williams CT .50 .23
❑ 198 Andruw Jones CL .75 .23
❑ 199 Darin Erstad CL .75 .23
❑ 200 Trey Beamon CL .15 .07

## 1998 Pinnacle

| | MINT | NRMT |
|---|---|---|
| COMPLETE SET (200) | 25.00 | 11.00 |
| COMMON CARD (1-200) | .15 | .07 |

❑ 1 Tony Gwynn 1.25 .55
❑ 2 Pedro Martinez .75 .35
❑ 3 Kenny Lofton .25 .11
❑ 4 Curt Schilling .25 .11
❑ 5 Shawn Estes .15 .07
❑ 6 Tom Glavine .60 .25

❑ 7 Mike Piazza 2.00 .90
❑ 8 Ray Lankford .25 .11
❑ 9 Barry Larkin .60 .25
❑ 10 Tony Womack .15 .07
❑ 11 Jeff Blauser .15 .07
❑ 12 Rod Beck .15 .07
❑ 13 Larry Walker .25 .11
❑ 14 Greg Maddux 1.50 .70
❑ 15 Mark Grace .60 .25
❑ 16 Ken Caminiti .25 .11
❑ 17 Bobby Jones .15 .07
❑ 18 Chipper Jones 1.50 .70
❑ 19 Javier Lopez .25 .11
❑ 20 Moises Alou .25 .11
❑ 21 Royce Clayton .15 .07
❑ 22 Darryl Kile .25 .11
❑ 23 Barry Bonds 1.00 .45
❑ 24 Steve Finley .25 .11
❑ 25 Andres Galarraga .40 .18
❑ 26 Denny Neagle .15 .07
❑ 27 Todd Hundley .15 .07
❑ 28 Jeff Bagwell .75 .35
❑ 29 Andy Pettitte .25 .11
❑ 30 Darin Erstad .60 .25
❑ 31 Carlos Delgado .60 .25
❑ 32 Matt Williams .40 .18
❑ 33 Will Clark .60 .25
❑ 34 Vinny Castilla .25 .11
❑ 35 Brad Radke .25 .11
❑ 36 John Olerud .25 .11
❑ 37 Andruw Jones .60 .25
❑ 38 Jason Giambi .60 .25
❑ 39 Scott Rolen .60 .25
❑ 40 Gary Sheffield .60 .25
❑ 41 Jimmy Key .25 .11
❑ 42 Kevin Appier .25 .11
❑ 43 Wade Boggs .75 .35
❑ 44 Hideo Nomo .60 .25
❑ 45 Manny Ramirez .75 .35
❑ 46 Wilton Guerrero .15 .07
❑ 47 Travis Fryman .25 .11
❑ 48 Chili Davis .25 .11
❑ 49 Jeromy Burnitz .25 .11
❑ 50 Craig Biggio .40 .18
❑ 51 Tim Salmon .25 .11
❑ 52 Jose Cruz Jr. .25 .11
❑ 53 Sammy Sosa 1.25 .55
❑ 54 Hideki Irabu .15 .07
❑ 55 Chan Ho Park .25 .11
❑ 56 Robin Ventura .25 .11
❑ 57 Jose Guillen .15 .07
❑ 58 Deion Sanders .25 .11
❑ 59 Jose Canseco .75 .35
❑ 60 Jay Buhner .25 .11
❑ 61 Rafael Palmeiro .60 .25
❑ 62 Vladimir Guerrero 1.00 .45
❑ 63 Mark McGwire 2.50 1.10
❑ 64 Derek Jeter 2.50 1.10
❑ 65 Bobby Bonilla .25 .11
❑ 66 Raul Mondesi .25 .11
❑ 67 Paul Molitor .60 .25
❑ 68 Joe Carter .25 .11
❑ 69 Marquis Grissom .15 .07
❑ 70 Juan Gonzalez .60 .25
❑ 71 Kevin Orie .15 .07
❑ 72 Rusty Greer .25 .11
❑ 73 Henry Rodriguez .15 .07
❑ 74 Fernando Tatis .25 .11

|  | | |
|---|---|---|
| ❑ 75 John Valentin | .15 | .07 |
| ❑ 76 Matt Morris | .15 | .07 |
| ❑ 77 Ray Durham | .25 | .11 |
| ❑ 78 Geronimo Berroa | .15 | .07 |
| ❑ 79 Scott Brosius | .25 | .11 |
| ❑ 80 Willie Greene | .15 | .07 |
| ❑ 81 Rondell White | .25 | .11 |
| ❑ 82 Doug Drabek | .15 | .07 |
| ❑ 83 Derek Bell | .15 | .07 |
| ❑ 84 Butch Huskey | .15 | .07 |
| ❑ 85 Doug Jones | .15 | .07 |
| ❑ 86 Jeff Kent | .40 | .18 |
| ❑ 87 Jim Edmonds | .60 | .25 |
| ❑ 88 Mark McLemore | .15 | .07 |
| ❑ 89 Todd Zeile | .25 | .11 |
| ❑ 90 Edgardo Alfonzo | .25 | .11 |
| ❑ 91 Carlos Baerga | .15 | .07 |
| ❑ 92 Jorge Fabregas | .15 | .07 |
| ❑ 93 Alan Benes | .15 | .07 |
| ❑ 94 Troy Percival | .15 | .07 |
| ❑ 95 Edgar Renteria | .15 | .07 |
| ❑ 96 Jeff Fassero | .15 | .07 |
| ❑ 97 Reggie Sanders | .15 | .07 |
| ❑ 98 Dean Palmer | .25 | .11 |
| ❑ 99 J.T. Snow | .25 | .11 |
| ❑ 100 Dave Nilsson | .15 | .07 |
| ❑ 101 Dan Wilson | .15 | .07 |
| ❑ 102 Robb Nen | .15 | .07 |
| ❑ 103 Damion Easley | .15 | .07 |
| ❑ 104 Kevin Foster | .15 | .07 |
| ❑ 105 Jose Offerman | .15 | .07 |
| ❑ 106 Steve Cooke | .15 | .07 |
| ❑ 107 Matt Stairs | .15 | .07 |
| ❑ 108 Darryl Hamilton | .15 | .07 |
| ❑ 109 Steve Karsay | .15 | .07 |
| ❑ 110 Gary DiSarcina | .15 | .07 |
| ❑ 111 Dante Bichette | .25 | .11 |
| ❑ 112 Billy Wagner | .15 | .07 |
| ❑ 113 David Segui | .15 | .07 |
| ❑ 114 Bobby Higginson | .25 | .11 |
| ❑ 115 Jeffrey Hammonds | .25 | .11 |
| ❑ 116 Kevin Brown | .25 | .11 |
| ❑ 117 Paul Sorrento | .15 | .07 |
| ❑ 118 Mark Leiter | .15 | .07 |
| ❑ 119 Charles Nagy | .15 | .07 |
| ❑ 120 Danny Patterson | .15 | .07 |
| ❑ 121 Brian McRae | .15 | .07 |
| ❑ 122 Jay Bell | .25 | .11 |
| ❑ 123 Jamie Moyer | .15 | .07 |
| ❑ 124 Carl Everett | .25 | .11 |
| ❑ 125 Greg Colbrunn | .15 | .07 |
| ❑ 126 Jason Kendall | .25 | .11 |
| ❑ 127 Luis Sojo | .15 | .07 |
| ❑ 128 Mike Lieberthal | .25 | .11 |
| ❑ 129 Reggie Jefferson | .15 | .07 |
| ❑ 130 Cal Eldred | .15 | .07 |
| ❑ 131 Orel Hershiser | .25 | .11 |
| ❑ 132 Doug Glanville | .15 | .07 |
| ❑ 133 Willie Blair | .15 | .07 |
| ❑ 134 Neifi Perez | .15 | .07 |
| ❑ 135 Sean Berry | .15 | .07 |
| ❑ 136 Chuck Finley | .25 | .11 |
| ❑ 137 Alex Gonzalez | .15 | .07 |
| ❑ 138 Dennis Eckersley | .25 | .11 |
| ❑ 139 Kenny Rogers | .15 | .07 |
| ❑ 140 Troy O'Leary | .15 | .07 |
| ❑ 141 Roger Bailey | .15 | .07 |
| ❑ 142 Yamil Benitez | .15 | .07 |
| ❑ 143 Wally Joyner | .25 | .11 |
| ❑ 144 Bobby Witt | .15 | .07 |
| ❑ 145 Pete Schourek | .15 | .07 |
| ❑ 146 Terry Steinbach | .15 | .07 |
| ❑ 147 B.J. Surhoff | .25 | .11 |
| ❑ 148 Esteban Loaiza | .15 | .07 |
| ❑ 149 Heathcliff Slocumb | .15 | .07 |
| ❑ 150 Ed Sprague | .15 | .07 |
| ❑ 151 Gregg Jefferies | .15 | .07 |
| ❑ 152 Scott Erickson | .15 | .07 |
| ❑ 153 Jaime Navarro | .15 | .07 |
| ❑ 154 David Wells | .25 | .11 |
| ❑ 155 Alex Fernandez | .15 | .07 |
| ❑ 156 Tim Belcher | .15 | .07 |
| ❑ 157 Mark Grudzielanek | .15 | .07 |
| ❑ 158 Scott Hatteberg | .15 | .07 |
| ❑ 159 Paul Konerko | .25 | .11 |
| ❑ 160 Ben Grieve | .25 | .11 |
| ❑ 161 Abraham Nunez | .15 | .07 |
| ❑ 162 Shannon Stewart | .25 | .11 |
| ❑ 163 Jaret Wright | .15 | .07 |
| ❑ 164 Derrek Lee | .15 | .07 |
| ❑ 165 Todd Dunwoody | .15 | .07 |
| ❑ 166 Steve Woodard | .15 | .07 |
| ❑ 167 Ryan McGuire | .15 | .07 |
| ❑ 168 Jeremi Gonzalez | .15 | .07 |
| ❑ 169 Mark Kotsay | .25 | .11 |
| ❑ 170 Brett Tomko | .15 | .07 |
| ❑ 171 Bobby Estalella | .15 | .07 |
| ❑ 172 Livan Hernandez | .15 | .07 |
| ❑ 173 Todd Helton | .75 | .35 |
| ❑ 174 Garrett Stephenson | .15 | .07 |
| ❑ 175 Pokey Reese | .25 | .11 |
| ❑ 176 Tony Saunders | .15 | .07 |
| ❑ 177 Antone Williamson | .15 | .07 |
| ❑ 178 Bartolo Colon | .25 | .11 |
| ❑ 179 Karim Garcia | .15 | .07 |
| ❑ 180 Juan Encarnacion | .25 | .11 |
| ❑ 181 Jacob Cruz | .15 | .07 |
| ❑ 182 Alex Rodriguez FV | 2.00 | .90 |
| ❑ 183 Cal Ripken FV<br>Roberto Alomar | 2.00 | .90 |
| ❑ 184 Roger Clemens FV | 1.25 | .55 |
| ❑ 185 Derek Jeter FV | 2.50 | 1.10 |
| ❑ 186 Frank Thomas FV | .60 | .25 |
| ❑ 187 Ken Griffey Jr. FV | 2.50 | 1.10 |
| ❑ 188 Mark McGwire GJ | 2.50 | 1.10 |
| ❑ 189 Tino Martinez GJ | .15 | .07 |
| ❑ 190 Larry Walker GJ | .25 | .11 |
| ❑ 191 Brady Anderson GJ | .15 | .07 |
| ❑ 192 Jeff Bagwell GJ | .40 | .18 |
| ❑ 193 Ken Griffey Jr. GJ | 2.50 | 1.10 |
| ❑ 194 Chipper Jones GJ | 1.50 | .70 |
| ❑ 195 Ray Lankford GJ | .15 | .07 |
| ❑ 196 Jim Thome GJ | .40 | .18 |
| ❑ 197 Nomar Garciaparra GJ | 2.00 | .90 |
| ❑ 198 AS HR Contestants<br>Brady Anderson<br>Jeff Bagwell<br>Nomar Garciaparra<br>Ken Griffey Jr.<br>Chipper Jones<br>Ray Lankford<br>Tino Martinez<br>Mark McGwire<br>Jim Thome<br>Larry Walker | .75 | .35 |
| ❑ 199 Tino Martinez CL | .15 | .07 |
| ❑ 200 Jacobs Field CL | .15 | .07 |

## 1998 Revolution

| | MINT | NRMT |
|---|---|---|
| COMPLETE SET (150) | 125.00 | 55.00 |
| ❑ 1 Garret Anderson | .75 | .35 |
| ❑ 2 Jim Edmonds | 2.00 | .90 |
| ❑ 3 Darin Erstad | 2.00 | .90 |
| ❑ 4 Chuck Finley | .75 | .35 |
| ❑ 5 Tim Salmon | .75 | .35 |
| ❑ 6 Jay Bell | .75 | .35 |
| ❑ 7 Travis Lee | .75 | .35 |
| ❑ 8 Devon White | .50 | .23 |
| ❑ 9 Matt Williams | 1.25 | .55 |
| ❑ 10 Andres Galarraga | 1.25 | .55 |
| ❑ 11 Tom Glavine | 2.00 | .90 |
| ❑ 12 Andruw Jones | 2.00 | .90 |
| ❑ 13 Chipper Jones | 5.00 | 2.20 |
| ❑ 14 Ryan Klesko | .75 | .35 |
| ❑ 15 Javy Lopez | .75 | .35 |
| ❑ 16 Greg Maddux | 5.00 | 2.20 |
| ❑ 17 Walt Weiss | .75 | .35 |
| ❑ 18 Roberto Alomar | 2.00 | .90 |
| ❑ 19 Joe Carter | .75 | .35 |
| ❑ 20 Mike Mussina | 2.00 | .90 |
| ❑ 21 Rafael Palmeiro | 2.00 | .90 |
| ❑ 22 Cal Ripken | 8.00 | 3.60 |
| ❑ 23 B.J. Surhoff | .75 | .35 |
| ❑ 24 Nomar Garciaparra | 6.00 | 2.70 |
| ❑ 25 Reggie Jefferson | .50 | .23 |
| ❑ 26 Pedro Martinez | 2.50 | 1.10 |
| ❑ 27 Troy O'Leary | .50 | .23 |
| ❑ 28 Mo Vaughn | .75 | .35 |
| ❑ 29 Mark Grace | 2.00 | .90 |
| ❑ 30 Mickey Morandini | .50 | .23 |
| ❑ 31 Henry Rodriguez | .50 | .23 |
| ❑ 32 Sammy Sosa | 4.00 | 1.80 |
| ❑ 33 Kerry Wood | 2.00 | .90 |
| ❑ 34 Albert Belle | 1.25 | .55 |
| ❑ 35 Ray Durham | .75 | .35 |
| ❑ 36 Magglio Ordonez RC | 8.00 | 3.60 |
| ❑ 37 Frank Thomas | 4.00 | 1.80 |
| ❑ 38 Robin Ventura | .75 | .35 |
| ❑ 39 Bret Boone | .75 | .35 |
| ❑ 40 Barry Larkin | 2.00 | .90 |
| ❑ 41 Reggie Sanders | .50 | .23 |
| ❑ 42 Brett Tomko | .50 | .23 |
| ❑ 43 Sandy Alomar Jr. | .75 | .35 |
| ❑ 44 David Justice | 1.25 | .55 |
| ❑ 45 Kenny Lofton | .75 | .35 |
| ❑ 46 Manny Ramirez | 2.50 | 1.10 |
| ❑ 47 Jim Thome | 1.25 | .55 |
| ❑ 48 Omar Vizquel | .75 | .35 |
| ❑ 49 Jaret Wright | .50 | .23 |
| ❑ 50 Dante Bichette | .75 | .35 |
| ❑ 51 Ellis Burks | .75 | .35 |
| ❑ 52 Vinny Castilla | .75 | .35 |
| ❑ 53 Todd Helton | 2.50 | 1.10 |
| ❑ 54 Larry Walker | .75 | .35 |
| ❑ 55 Tony Clark | .50 | .23 |
| ❑ 56 Deivi Cruz | .50 | .23 |
| ❑ 57 Damion Easley | .50 | .23 |
| ❑ 58 Bobby Higginson | .75 | .35 |
| ❑ 59 Brian Hunter | .50 | .23 |
| ❑ 60 Cliff Floyd | .75 | .35 |
| ❑ 61 Livan Hernandez | .50 | .23 |
| ❑ 62 Derrek Lee | .50 | .23 |
| ❑ 63 Edgar Renteria | .50 | .23 |
| ❑ 64 Moises Alou | .75 | .35 |
| ❑ 65 Jeff Bagwell | 2.50 | 1.10 |
| ❑ 66 Derek Bell | .50 | .23 |
| ❑ 67 Craig Biggio | 1.25 | .55 |
| ❑ 68 Richard Hidalgo | .75 | .35 |
| ❑ 69 Johnny Damon | .75 | .35 |
| ❑ 70 Jeff King | .50 | .23 |
| ❑ 71 Hal Morris | .50 | .23 |
| ❑ 72 Dean Palmer | .75 | .35 |
| ❑ 73 Bobby Bonilla | .75 | .35 |
| ❑ 74 Charles Johnson | .75 | .35 |
| ❑ 75 Eric Karros | .75 | .35 |
| ❑ 76 Raul Mondesi | .75 | .35 |
| ❑ 77 Gary Sheffield | 2.00 | .90 |
| ❑ 78 Jeromy Burnitz | .75 | .35 |
| ❑ 79 Marquis Grissom | .50 | .23 |
| ❑ 80 Dave Nilsson | .50 | .23 |
| ❑ 81 Fernando Vina | .50 | .23 |
| ❑ 82 Marty Cordova | .50 | .23 |
| ❑ 83 Pat Meares | .50 | .23 |
| ❑ 84 Paul Molitor | 2.00 | .90 |
| ❑ 85 Brad Radke | .75 | .35 |
| ❑ 86 Terry Steinbach | .50 | .23 |
| ❑ 87 Todd Walker | .50 | .23 |
| ❑ 88 Brad Fullmer | .75 | .35 |
| ❑ 89 Vladimir Guerrero | 3.00 | 1.35 |
| ❑ 90 Carl Pavano | .50 | .23 |
| ❑ 91 Rondell White | .75 | .35 |
| ❑ 92 Bernard Gilkey | .50 | .23 |
| ❑ 93 Hideo Nomo | 2.00 | .90 |
| ❑ 94 John Olerud | .75 | .35 |
| ❑ 95 Rey Ordonez | .50 | .23 |
| ❑ 96 Mike Piazza | 6.00 | 2.70 |
| ❑ 97 Masato Yoshii RC | 1.50 | .70 |
| ❑ 98 Hideki Irabu | .50 | .23 |

| | MINT | NRMT |
|---|---|---|
| ❑ 99 Derek Jeter | 8.00 | 3.60 |
| ❑ 100 Chuck Knoblauch | .75 | .35 |
| ❑ 101 Tino Martinez | .75 | .35 |
| ❑ 102 Paul O'Neill | .75 | .35 |
| ❑ 103 Darryl Strawberry | .75 | .35 |
| ❑ 104 Bernie Williams | 2.00 | .90 |
| ❑ 105 Jason Giambi | 2.00 | .90 |
| ❑ 106 Ben Grieve | .75 | .35 |
| ❑ 107 Rickey Henderson | 2.50 | 1.10 |
| ❑ 108 Matt Stairs | .50 | .23 |
| ❑ 109 Doug Glanville | .50 | .23 |
| ❑ 110 Desi Relaford | .50 | .23 |
| ❑ 111 Scott Rolen | 2.00 | .90 |
| ❑ 112 Curt Schilling | .75 | .35 |
| ❑ 113 Jason Kendall | .75 | .35 |
| ❑ 114 Al Martin | .50 | .23 |
| ❑ 115 Jason Schmidt | .50 | .23 |
| ❑ 116 Kevin Young | .75 | .35 |
| ❑ 117 Delino DeShields | .50 | .23 |
| ❑ 118 Gary Gaetti | .75 | .35 |
| ❑ 119 Brian Jordan | .75 | .35 |
| ❑ 120 Ray Lankford | .75 | .35 |
| ❑ 121 Mark McGwire | 8.00 | 3.60 |
| ❑ 122 Kevin Brown | 1.25 | .55 |
| ❑ 123 Steve Finley | .75 | .35 |
| ❑ 124 Tony Gwynn | 4.00 | 1.80 |
| ❑ 125 Wally Joyner | .75 | .35 |
| ❑ 126 Greg Vaughn | .75 | .35 |
| ❑ 127 Barry Bonds | 3.00 | 1.35 |
| ❑ 128 Orel Hershiser | .75 | .35 |
| ❑ 129 Jeff Kent | 1.25 | .55 |
| ❑ 130 Bill Mueller | .50 | .23 |
| ❑ 131 Jay Buhner | .75 | .35 |
| ❑ 132 Ken Griffey Jr. | 8.00 | 3.60 |
| ❑ 133 Randy Johnson | 2.50 | 1.10 |
| ❑ 134 Edgar Martinez | 1.25 | .55 |
| ❑ 135 Alex Rodriguez | 6.00 | 2.70 |
| ❑ 136 David Segui | .50 | .23 |
| ❑ 137 Rolando Arrojo RC | 1.50 | .70 |
| ❑ 138 Wade Boggs | 2.50 | 1.10 |
| ❑ 139 Quinton McCracken | .50 | .23 |
| ❑ 140 Fred McGriff | 1.25 | .55 |
| ❑ 141 Will Clark | 2.00 | .90 |
| ❑ 142 Juan Gonzalez | 2.00 | .90 |
| ❑ 143 Tom Goodwin | .50 | .23 |
| ❑ 144 Ivan Rodriguez | 2.50 | 1.10 |
| ❑ 145 Aaron Sele | .75 | .35 |
| ❑ 146 John Wetteland | .75 | .35 |
| ❑ 147 Jose Canseco | 2.50 | 1.10 |
| ❑ 148 Roger Clemens | 4.00 | 1.80 |
| ❑ 149 Jose Cruz Jr. | .75 | .35 |
| ❑ 150 Carlos Delgado | 2.00 | .90 |

## 1999 Revolution

| | MINT | NRMT |
|---|---|---|
| COMPLETE SET (150) | 150.00 | 70.00 |
| COMMON CARD (1-150) | .50 | .23 |
| COMMON SP | 2.00 | .90 |

| | MINT | NRMT |
|---|---|---|
| ❑ 1 Jim Edmonds | 2.00 | .90 |
| ❑ 2 Darin Erstad | 2.00 | .90 |
| ❑ 3 Troy Glaus | 3.00 | 1.35 |
| ❑ 4 Tim Salmon | .75 | .35 |
| ❑ 5 Mo Vaughn | .75 | .35 |
| ❑ 6 Steve Finley | .75 | .35 |
| ❑ 7 Luis Gonzalez | .75 | .35 |
| ❑ 8 Randy Johnson | 2.50 | 1.10 |
| ❑ 9 Travis Lee | .50 | .23 |
| ❑ 10 Matt Williams | 1.25 | .55 |
| ❑ 11 Andruw Jones | 2.00 | .90 |
| ❑ 12 Chipper Jones | 5.00 | 2.20 |
| ❑ 13 Brian Jordan | .75 | .35 |
| ❑ 14 Javy Lopez | .75 | .35 |
| ❑ 15 Greg Maddux | 5.00 | 2.20 |
| ❑ 16 Kevin McGlinchy SP | 2.00 | .90 |
| ❑ 17 John Smoltz | .75 | .35 |
| ❑ 18 Brady Anderson | .75 | .35 |
| ❑ 19 Albert Belle | 1.25 | .55 |
| ❑ 20 Will Clark | 2.00 | .90 |
| ❑ 21 Willis Otanez SP | 2.00 | .90 |
| ❑ 22 Calvin Pickering SP | 2.00 | .90 |
| ❑ 23 Cal Ripken | 8.00 | 3.60 |
| ❑ 24 Nomar Garciaparra | 6.00 | 2.70 |
| ❑ 25 Pedro Martinez | 2.50 | 1.10 |
| ❑ 26 Troy O'Leary | .50 | .23 |
| ❑ 27 Jose Offerman | .50 | .23 |
| ❑ 28 Mark Grace | 2.00 | .90 |
| ❑ 29 Mickey Morandini | .50 | .23 |
| ❑ 30 Henry Rodriguez | .50 | .23 |
| ❑ 31 Sammy Sosa | 4.00 | 1.80 |
| ❑ 32 Ray Durham | .75 | .35 |
| ❑ 33 Carlos Lee SP | 2.00 | .90 |
| ❑ 34 Jeff Liefer SP | 2.00 | .90 |
| ❑ 35 Magglio Ordonez | 1.25 | .55 |
| ❑ 36 Frank Thomas | 4.00 | 1.80 |
| ❑ 37 Mike Cameron | .50 | .23 |
| ❑ 38 Sean Casey | .75 | .35 |
| ❑ 39 Barry Larkin | 2.00 | .90 |
| ❑ 40 Greg Vaughn | .75 | .35 |
| ❑ 41 Roberto Alomar | 2.00 | .90 |
| ❑ 42 Sandy Alomar Jr. | .75 | .35 |
| ❑ 43 David Justice | 1.25 | .55 |
| ❑ 44 Kenny Lofton | .75 | .35 |
| ❑ 45 Manny Ramirez | 2.50 | 1.10 |
| ❑ 46 Richie Sexson | .75 | .35 |
| ❑ 47 Jim Thome | 1.25 | .55 |
| ❑ 48 Dante Bichette | .75 | .35 |
| ❑ 49 Vinny Castilla | .75 | .35 |
| ❑ 50 Darryl Hamilton | .50 | .23 |
| ❑ 51 Todd Helton | 2.50 | 1.10 |
| ❑ 52 Larry Walker | .75 | .35 |
| ❑ 53 Tony Clark | .50 | .23 |
| ❑ 54 Damion Easley | .50 | .23 |
| ❑ 55 Bob Higginson | .75 | .35 |
| ❑ 56 Gabe Kapler SP | 2.00 | .90 |
| ❑ 57 Alex Gonzalez SP | 2.00 | .90 |
| ❑ 58 Mark Kotsay | .50 | .23 |
| ❑ 59 Kevin Orie | .50 | .23 |
| ❑ 60 Preston Wilson SP | 2.00 | .90 |
| ❑ 61 Jeff Bagwell | 2.50 | 1.10 |
| ❑ 62 Derek Bell | .50 | .23 |
| ❑ 63 Craig Biggio | 1.25 | .55 |
| ❑ 64 Ken Caminiti | .75 | .35 |
| ❑ 65 Carlos Beltran SP | 2.00 | .90 |
| ❑ 66 Johnny Damon | .75 | .35 |
| ❑ 67 Jermaine Dye | .75 | .35 |
| ❑ 68 Carlos Febles SP | 2.00 | .90 |
| ❑ 69 Kevin Brown | 1.25 | .55 |
| ❑ 70 Todd Hundley | .50 | .23 |
| ❑ 71 Eric Karros | .75 | .35 |
| ❑ 72 Raul Mondesi | .75 | .35 |
| ❑ 73 Gary Sheffield | 2.00 | .90 |
| ❑ 74 Jeromy Burnitz | .75 | .35 |
| ❑ 75 Jeff Cirillo | .75 | .35 |
| ❑ 76 Marquis Grissom | .50 | .23 |
| ❑ 77 Fernando Vina | .50 | .23 |
| ❑ 78 Chad Allen SP RC | 2.00 | .90 |
| ❑ 79 Corey Koskie SP | 2.00 | .90 |
| ❑ 80 Doug Mientkiewicz SP RC | 2.00 | .90 |
| ❑ 81 Brad Radke | .75 | .35 |
| ❑ 82 Todd Walker | .50 | .23 |
| ❑ 83 Michael Barrett SP | 2.00 | .90 |
| ❑ 84 Vladimir Guerrero | 3.00 | 1.35 |
| ❑ 85 Wilton Guerrero | .50 | .23 |
| ❑ 86 Guillermo Mota SP RC | .50 | .23 |
| ❑ 87 Rondell White | .75 | .35 |
| ❑ 88 Edgardo Alfonzo | .75 | .35 |
| ❑ 89 Rickey Henderson | 2.50 | 1.10 |
| ❑ 90 John Olerud | .75 | .35 |
| ❑ 91 Mike Piazza | 6.00 | 2.70 |
| ❑ 92 Robin Ventura | .75 | .35 |
| ❑ 93 Roger Clemens | 4.00 | 1.80 |
| ❑ 94 Chili Davis | .75 | .35 |
| ❑ 95 Derek Jeter | 8.00 | 3.60 |
| ❑ 96 Chuck Knoblauch | .75 | .35 |
| ❑ 97 Tino Martinez | .75 | .35 |
| ❑ 98 Paul O'Neill | .75 | .35 |
| ❑ 99 Bernie Williams | 2.00 | .90 |
| ❑ 100 Eric Chavez SP | 2.00 | .90 |
| ❑ 101 Jason Giambi | 2.00 | .90 |
| ❑ 102 Ben Grieve | .75 | .35 |
| ❑ 103 John Jaha | .50 | .23 |
| ❑ 104 Olmedo Saenz SP | 2.00 | .90 |
| ❑ 105 Bobby Abreu | .75 | .35 |
| ❑ 106 Doug Glanville | .50 | .23 |
| ❑ 107 Desi Relaford | .50 | .23 |
| ❑ 108 Scott Rolen | 2.00 | .90 |
| ❑ 109 Curt Schilling | .75 | .35 |
| ❑ 110 Brian Giles | .75 | .35 |
| ❑ 111 Jason Kendall | .75 | .35 |
| ❑ 112 Pat Meares | .50 | .23 |
| ❑ 113 Kevin Young | .75 | .35 |
| ❑ 114 J.D. Drew SP | 4.00 | 1.80 |
| ❑ 115 Ray Lankford | .75 | .35 |
| ❑ 116 Eli Marrero | .50 | .23 |
| ❑ 117 Joe McEwing SP RC | 2.00 | .90 |
| ❑ 118 Mark McGwire | 8.00 | 3.60 |
| ❑ 119 Fernando Tatis | .75 | .35 |
| ❑ 120 Tony Gwynn | 4.00 | 1.80 |
| ❑ 121 Trevor Hoffman | .75 | .35 |
| ❑ 122 Wally Joyner | .75 | .35 |
| ❑ 123 Reggie Sanders | .50 | .23 |
| ❑ 124 Barry Bonds | 3.00 | 1.35 |
| ❑ 125 Ellis Burks | .75 | .35 |
| ❑ 126 Jeff Kent | 1.25 | .55 |
| ❑ 127 Ramon E.Martinez SP RC | 2.00 | .90 |
| ❑ 128 Joe Nathan SP RC | .50 | .23 |
| ❑ 129 Freddy Garcia SP RC | 8.00 | 3.60 |
| ❑ 130 Ken Griffey Jr. | 8.00 | 3.60 |
| ❑ 131 Brian Hunter | .50 | .23 |
| ❑ 132 Edgar Martinez | 1.25 | .55 |
| ❑ 133 Alex Rodriguez | 6.00 | 2.70 |
| ❑ 134 David Segui | .50 | .23 |
| ❑ 135 Wade Boggs | 2.50 | 1.10 |
| ❑ 136 Jose Canseco | 2.50 | 1.10 |
| ❑ 137 Quinton McCracken | .50 | .23 |
| ❑ 138 Fred McGriff | 1.25 | .55 |
| ❑ 139 Kelly Dransfeldt SP RC | 2.00 | .90 |
| ❑ 140 Juan Gonzalez | 2.00 | .90 |
| ❑ 141 Rusty Greer | .75 | .35 |
| ❑ 142 Rafael Palmeiro | 2.00 | .90 |
| ❑ 143 Ivan Rodriguez | 2.50 | 1.10 |
| ❑ 144 Lee Stevens | .50 | .23 |
| ❑ 145 Jose Cruz Jr. | .75 | .35 |
| ❑ 146 Carlos Delgado | 2.00 | .90 |
| ❑ 147 Shawn Green | 2.00 | .90 |
| ❑ 148 Roy Halladay SP | 2.00 | .90 |
| ❑ 149 Shannon Stewart | .75 | .35 |
| ❑ 150 Kevin Witt SP | 2.00 | .90 |

## 2000 Revolution

| | MINT | NRMT |
|---|---|---|
| COMPLETE SET (150) | 150.00 | 70.00 |
| COMMON CARD (1-150) | .50 | .23 |
| COMMON SP | 2.50 | 1.10 |

| | MINT | NRMT |
|---|---|---|
| ❑ 1 Darin Erstad | 2.00 | .90 |
| ❑ 2 Troy Glaus | 2.50 | 1.10 |
| ❑ 3 Adam Kennedy SP | 2.50 | 1.10 |
| ❑ 4 Mo Vaughn | .75 | .35 |

- ❑ 5 Erubiel Durazo .75 .35
- ❑ 6 Steve Finley .75 .35
- ❑ 7 Luis Gonzalez .75 .35
- ❑ 8 Randy Johnson 2.50 1.10
- ❑ 9 Travis Lee .50 .23
- ❑ 10 Vicente Padilla SP RC 2.50 1.10
- ❑ 11 Matt Williams 1.25 .55
- ❑ 12 Rafael Furcal SP 12.00 5.50
- ❑ 13 Andres Galarraga 1.25 .55
- ❑ 14 Andruw Jones 2.00 .90
- ❑ 15 Chipper Jones 5.00 2.20
- ❑ 16 Greg Maddux 5.00 2.20
- ❑ 17 Luis Rivera SP 2.50 1.10
- ❑ 18 Albert Belle 1.25 .55
- ❑ 19 Mike Bordick .50 .23
- ❑ 20 Will Clark 2.00 .90
- ❑ 21 Mike Mussina 2.00 .90
- ❑ 22 Cal Ripken 8.00 3.60
- ❑ 23 B.J. Surhoff .75 .35
- ❑ 24 Carl Everett .75 .35
- ❑ 25 Nomar Garciaparra 6.00 2.70
- ❑ 26 Pedro Martinez 2.50 1.10
- ❑ 27 Jason Varitek .75 .35
- ❑ 28 Wilton Veras SP 2.50 1.10
- ❑ 29 Shane Andrews .50 .23
- ❑ 30 Scott Downs SP RC 2.50 1.10
- ❑ 31 Mark Grace 2.00 .90
- ❑ 32 Sammy Sosa 4.00 1.80
- ❑ 33 Kerry Wood .75 .35
- ❑ 34 Ray Durham .75 .35
- ❑ 35 Paul Konerko .75 .35
- ❑ 36 Carlos Lee .75 .35
- ❑ 37 Magglio Ordonez .75 .35
- ❑ 38 Frank Thomas 4.00 1.80
- ❑ 39 Rob Bell SP 2.50 1.10
- ❑ 40 Sean Casey .75 .35
- ❑ 41 Ken Griffey Jr. 8.00 3.60
- ❑ 42 Barry Larkin 2.00 .90
- ❑ 43 Pokey Reese .75 .35
- ❑ 44 Roberto Alomar 2.00 .90
- ❑ 45 David Justice 1.25 .55
- ❑ 46 Kenny Lofton .75 .35
- ❑ 47 Manny Ramirez 2.50 1.10
- ❑ 48 Richie Sexson .75 .35
- ❑ 49 Jim Thome 1.25 .55
- ❑ 50 Jeff Cirillo .75 .35
- ❑ 51 Jeffrey Hammonds .75 .35
- ❑ 52 Todd Helton 2.50 1.10
- ❑ 53 Larry Walker .75 .35
- ❑ 54 Tony Clark .50 .23
- ❑ 55 Juan Gonzalez 2.00 .90
- ❑ 56 Hideo Nomo 2.00 .90
- ❑ 57 Dean Palmer .75 .35
- ❑ 58 Alex Gonzalez .50 .23
- ❑ 59 Mike Lowell .75 .35
- ❑ 60 Pablo Ozuna SP 2.50 1.10
- ❑ 61 Brad Penny SP 2.50 1.10
- ❑ 62 Preston Wilson .75 .35
- ❑ 63 Moises Alou .75 .35
- ❑ 64 Jeff Bagwell 2.50 1.10
- ❑ 65 Craig Biggio 1.25 .55
- ❑ 66 Ken Caminiti .75 .35
- ❑ 67 Julio Lugo SP 2.50 1.10
- ❑ 68 Carlos Beltran .75 .35
- ❑ 69 Johnny Damon UER .75 .35 (Carlos Beltran pictured on front)
- ❑ 70 Jermaine Dye .75 .35
- ❑ 71 Carlos Febles .50 .23
- ❑ 72 Mark Quinn SP 2.50 1.10
- ❑ 73 Kevin Brown .75 .35
- ❑ 74 Shawn Green 2.00 .90
- ❑ 75 Chan Ho Park .75 .35
- ❑ 76 Gary Sheffield 2.00 .90
- ❑ 77 Kevin Barker SP 2.50 1.10
- ❑ 78 Ron Belliard .50 .23
- ❑ 79 Jeromy Burnitz .75 .35
- ❑ 80 Geoff Jenkins .75 .35
- ❑ 81 Cristian Guzman .50 .23
- ❑ 82 Jacque Jones .75 .35
- ❑ 83 Corey Koskie .50 .23
- ❑ 84 Matt Lawton .75 .35
- ❑ 85 Peter Bergeron SP 2.50 1.10
- ❑ 86 Vladimir Guerrero 3.00 1.35
- ❑ 87 Andy Tracy SP RC 2.50 1.10
- ❑ 88 Jose Vidro .75 .35
- ❑ 89 Rondell White .75 .35
- ❑ 90 Edgardo Alfonzo .75 .35
- ❑ 91 Derek Bell .50 .23
- ❑ 92 Eric Cammack SP RC 2.50 1.10
- ❑ 93 Mike Piazza 6.00 2.70
- ❑ 94 Robin Ventura .75 .35
- ❑ 95 Roger Clemens 4.00 1.80
- ❑ 96 Orlando Hernandez .75 .35
- ❑ 97 Derek Jeter 8.00 3.60
- ❑ 98 Tino Martinez .75 .35
- ❑ 99 Alfonso Soriano SP 2.50 1.10
- ❑ 100 Bernie Williams 2.00 .90
- ❑ 101 Eric Chavez .75 .35
- ❑ 102 Jason Giambi 2.00 .90
- ❑ 103 Ben Grieve .75 .35
- ❑ 104 Terrence Long SP 2.50 1.10
- ❑ 105 Mark Mulder SP 2.50 1.10
- ❑ 106 Adam Piatt SP 5.00 2.20
- ❑ 107 Bobby Abreu .75 .35
- ❑ 108 Pat Burrell SP 8.00 3.60
- ❑ 109 Rico Brogna .50 .23
- ❑ 110 Doug Glanville .50 .23
- ❑ 111 Mike Lieberthal .75 .35
- ❑ 112 Scott Rolen 2.00 .90
- ❑ 113 Brian Giles .75 .35
- ❑ 114 Jason Kendall .75 .35
- ❑ 115 Warren Morris .50 .23
- ❑ 116 Rick Ankiel SP 10.00 4.50
- ❑ 117 J.D. Drew 2.00 .90
- ❑ 118 Jim Edmonds 2.00 .90
- ❑ 119 Mark McGwire 8.00 3.60
- ❑ 120 Fernando Tatis .75 .35
- ❑ 121 Fernando Vina .50 .23
- ❑ 122 Tony Gwynn 4.00 1.80
- ❑ 123 Trevor Hoffman .75 .35
- ❑ 124 Ryan Klesko .75 .35
- ❑ 125 Eric Owens .50 .23
- ❑ 126 Barry Bonds 3.00 1.35
- ❑ 127 Ellis Burks .75 .35
- ❑ 128 Bobby Estalella .50 .23
- ❑ 129 Jeff Kent 1.25 .55
- ❑ 130 Scott Linebrink SP RC 2.50 1.10
- ❑ 131 Jay Buhner .75 .35
- ❑ 132 Stan Javier .50 .23
- ❑ 133 Edgar Martinez 1.25 .55
- ❑ 134 John Olerud .75 .35
- ❑ 135 Alex Rodriguez 6.00 2.70
- ❑ 136 Kazuhiro Sasaki SP RC 10.00 4.50
- ❑ 137 Jose Canseco 2.50 1.10
- ❑ 138 Vinny Castilla .75 .35
- ❑ 139 Fred McGriff 1.25 .55
- ❑ 140 Greg Vaughn .75 .35
- ❑ 141 Gabe Kapler .75 .35
- ❑ 142 Mike Lamb SP RC 2.00 .90
- ❑ 143 Ruben Mateo SP 2.50 1.10
- ❑ 144 Rafael Palmeiro 2.00 .90
- ❑ 145 Ivan Rodriguez 2.50 1.10
- ❑ 146 Tony Batista .75 .35
- ❑ 147 Jose Cruz Jr. .75 .35
- ❑ 148 Carlos Delgado 2.00 .90
- ❑ 149 Brad Fullmer .75 .35
- ❑ 150 Raul Mondesi .75 .35

## 1988 Score

| | MINT | NRMT |
|---|---|---|
| COMPLETE SET (660) | 10.00 | 4.50 |
| COMP.FACT.SET (660) | 12.00 | 5.50 |

- ❑ 1 Don Mattingly .50 .23
- ❑ 2 Wade Boggs .25 .11
- ❑ 3 Tim Raines .10 .05
- ❑ 4 Andre Dawson .15 .07
- ❑ 5 Mark McGwire 2.00 .90
- ❑ 6 Kevin Seitzer .10 .05
- ❑ 7 Wally Joyner .15 .07
- ❑ 8 Jesse Barfield .05 .02
- ❑ 9 Pedro Guerrero .05 .02
- ❑ 10 Eric Davis .10 .05
- ❑ 11 George Brett .40 .18
- ❑ 12 Ozzie Smith .25 .11
- ❑ 13 Rickey Henderson .25 .11
- ❑ 14 Jim Rice .10 .05
- ❑ 15 Matt Nokes RC* .05 .02
- ❑ 16 Mike Schmidt .40 .18
- ❑ 17 Dave Parker .10 .05
- ❑ 18 Eddie Murray .20 .09
- ❑ 19 Andres Galarraga .15 .07
- ❑ 20 Tony Fernandez .05 .02
- ❑ 21 Kevin McReynolds .05 .02
- ❑ 22 B.J. Surhoff .10 .05
- ❑ 23 Pat Tabler .05 .02
- ❑ 24 Kirby Puckett .50 .23
- ❑ 25 Benny Santiago .05 .02
- ❑ 26 Ryne Sandberg .25 .11
- ❑ 27 Kelly Downs .10 .05 (Will Clark in background, out of focus)
- ❑ 28 Jose Cruz .05 .02
- ❑ 29 Pete O'Brien .05 .02
- ❑ 30 Mark Langston .05 .02
- ❑ 31 Lee Smith .10 .05
- ❑ 32 Juan Samuel .05 .02
- ❑ 33 Kevin Bass .05 .02
- ❑ 34 R.J. Reynolds .05 .02
- ❑ 35 Steve Sax .05 .02
- ❑ 36 John Kruk .10 .05
- ❑ 37 Alan Trammell .15 .07
- ❑ 38 Chris Bosio .05 .02
- ❑ 39 Brook Jacoby .05 .02
- ❑ 40 Willie McGee UER .10 .05 (Excited misspelled as excitd)
- ❑ 41 Dave Magadan .05 .02
- ❑ 42 Fred Lynn .05 .02
- ❑ 43 Kent Hrbek .10 .05
- ❑ 44 Brian Downing .05 .02
- ❑ 45 Jose Canseco .40 .18
- ❑ 46 Jim Presley .05 .02
- ❑ 47 Mike Stanley .10 .05
- ❑ 48 Tony Pena .05 .02
- ❑ 49 David Cone .10 .05
- ❑ 50 Rick Sutcliffe .10 .05
- ❑ 51 Doug Drabek .05 .02
- ❑ 52 Bill Doran .05 .02
- ❑ 53 Mike Scioscia .05 .02
- ❑ 54 Candy Maldonado .05 .02
- ❑ 55 Dave Winfield .20 .09
- ❑ 56 Lou Whitaker .10 .05
- ❑ 57 Tom Henke .05 .02
- ❑ 58 Ken Gerhart .05 .02
- ❑ 59 Glenn Braggs .05 .02
- ❑ 60 Julio Franco .05 .02
- ❑ 61 Charlie Leibrandt .05 .02
- ❑ 62 Gary Gaetti .10 .05
- ❑ 63 Bob Boone .10 .05
- ❑ 64 Luis Polonia RC* .05 .02
- ❑ 65 Dwight Evans .10 .05
- ❑ 66 Phil Bradley .05 .02
- ❑ 67 Mike Boddicker .05 .02
- ❑ 68 Vince Coleman .05 .02
- ❑ 69 Howard Johnson .05 .02
- ❑ 70 Tim Wallach .05 .02
- ❑ 71 Keith Moreland .05 .02
- ❑ 72 Barry Larkin .20 .09
- ❑ 73 Alan Ashby .05 .02
- ❑ 74 Rick Rhoden .05 .02
- ❑ 75 Darrell Evans .10 .05
- ❑ 76 Dave Stieb .05 .02
- ❑ 77 Dan Plesac .05 .02
- ❑ 78 Will Clark UER .25 .11 (Born 3/17/64; should be 3/13/64)
- ❑ 79 Frank White .10 .05
- ❑ 80 Joe Carter .20 .09

❑ 81 Mike Witt .05 .02
❑ 82 Terry Steinbach .10 .05
❑ 83 Alvin Davis .05 .02
❑ 84 Tommy Herr .10 .05
(Will Clark shown sliding into second)
❑ 85 Vance Law .05 .02
❑ 86 Kal Daniels .05 .02
❑ 87 Rick Honeycutt UER .05 .02
(Wrong years for stats on back)
❑ 88 Alfredo Griffin .05 .02
❑ 89 Bret Saberhagen .10 .05
❑ 90 Bert Blyleven .10 .05
❑ 91 Jeff Reardon .10 .05
❑ 92 Cory Snyder .05 .02
❑ 93A Greg Walker ERR 2.00 .90
(93 of 66)
❑ 93B Greg Walker COR .05 .02
(93 of 660)
❑ 94 Joe Magrane RC* .05 .02
❑ 95 Rob Deer .05 .02
❑ 96 Ray Knight .05 .02
❑ 97 Casey Candaele .05 .02
❑ 98 John Cerutti .05 .02
❑ 99 Buddy Bell .10 .05
❑ 100 Jack Clark .10 .05
❑ 101 Eric Bell .05 .02
❑ 102 Willie Wilson .05 .02
❑ 103 Dave Schmidt .05 .02
❑ 104 Dennis Eckersley UER .10 .05
(Complete games stats are wrong)
❑ 105 Don Sutton .20 .09
❑ 106 Danny Tartabull .05 .02
❑ 107 Fred McGriff .20 .09
❑ 108 Les Straker .05 .02
❑ 109 Lloyd Moseby .05 .02
❑ 110 Roger Clemens .40 .18
❑ 111 Glenn Hubbard .05 .02
❑ 112 Ken Williams .05 .02
❑ 113 Ruben Sierra .05 .02
❑ 114 Stan Jefferson .05 .02
❑ 115 Milt Thompson .05 .02
❑ 116 Bobby Bonilla .10 .05
❑ 117 Wayne Tolleson .05 .02
❑ 118 Matt Williams RC .75 .35
❑ 119 Chet Lemon .05 .02
❑ 120 Dale Sveum .05 .02
❑ 121 Dennis Boyd .05 .02
❑ 122 Brett Butler .10 .05
❑ 123 Terry Kennedy .05 .02
❑ 124 Jack Howell .05 .02
❑ 125 Curt Young .05 .02
❑ 126A Dave Valle ERR .10 .05
(Misspelled Dale on card front)
❑ 126B Dave Valle COR .05 .02
❑ 127 Curt Wilkerson .05 .02
❑ 128 Tim Teufel .05 .02
❑ 129 Ozzie Virgil .05 .02
❑ 130 Brian Fisher .05 .02
❑ 131 Lance Parrish .05 .02
❑ 132 Tom Browning .05 .02
❑ 133A Larry Andersen ERR .10 .05
(Misspelled Anderson on card front)
❑ 133B Larry Andersen COR .05 .02
❑ 134A Bob Brenly ERR .10 .05
(Misspelled Brenley on card front)
❑ 134B Bob Brenly COR .05 .02
❑ 135 Mike Marshall .05 .02
❑ 136 Gerald Perry .05 .02
❑ 137 Bobby Meacham .05 .02
❑ 138 Larry Herndon .05 .02
❑ 139 Fred Manrique .05 .02
❑ 140 Charlie Hough .10 .05
❑ 141 Ron Darling .05 .02
❑ 142 Herm Winningham .05 .02
❑ 143 Mike Diaz .05 .02
❑ 144 Mike Jackson RC* .10 .05
❑ 145 Denny Walling .05 .02
❑ 146 Robby Thompson .05 .02
❑ 147 Franklin Stubbs .05 .02
❑ 148 Albert Hall .05 .02
❑ 149 Bobby Witt .05 .02
❑ 150 Lance McCullers .05 .02
❑ 151 Scott Bradley .05 .02
❑ 152 Mark McLemore .05 .02
❑ 153 Tim Laudner .05 .02
❑ 154 Greg Swindell .05 .02
❑ 155 Marty Barrett .05 .02
❑ 156 Mike Heath .05 .02
❑ 157 Gary Ward .05 .02
❑ 158A Lee Mazzilli ERR .10 .05
(Misspelled Mazilli on card front)
❑ 158B Lee Mazzilli COR .05 .02
❑ 159 Tom Foley .05 .02
❑ 160 Robin Yount .20 .09
❑ 161 Steve Bedrosian .05 .02
❑ 162 Bob Walk .05 .02
❑ 163 Nick Esasky .05 .02
❑ 164 Ken Caminiti RC .50 .23
❑ 165 Jose Uribe .05 .02
❑ 166 Dave Anderson .05 .02
❑ 167 Ed Whitson .05 .02
❑ 168 Ernie Whitt .05 .02
❑ 169 Cecil Cooper .10 .05
❑ 170 Mike Pagliarulo .05 .02
❑ 171 Pat Sheridan .05 .02
❑ 172 Chris Bando .05 .02
❑ 173 Lee Lacy .05 .02
❑ 174 Steve Lombardozzi .05 .02
❑ 175 Mike Greenwell .05 .02
❑ 176 Greg Minton .05 .02
❑ 177 Moose Haas .05 .02
❑ 178 Mike Kingery .05 .02
❑ 179 Greg A. Harris .05 .02
❑ 180 Bo Jackson .20 .09
❑ 181 Carmelo Martinez .05 .02
❑ 182 Alex Trevino .05 .02
❑ 183 Ron Oester .05 .02
❑ 184 Danny Darwin .05 .02
❑ 185 Mike Krukow .05 .02
❑ 186 Rafael Palmeiro .40 .18
❑ 187 Tim Burke .05 .02
❑ 188 Roger McDowell .05 .02
❑ 189 Garry Templeton .05 .02
❑ 190 Terry Pendleton .10 .05
❑ 191 Larry Parrish .05 .02
❑ 192 Rey Quinones .05 .02
❑ 193 Joaquin Andujar .05 .02
❑ 194 Tom Brunansky .05 .02
❑ 195 Donnie Moore .05 .02
❑ 196 Dan Pasqua .05 .02
❑ 197 Jim Gantner .05 .02
❑ 198 Mark Eichhorn .05 .02
❑ 199 John Grubb .05 .02
❑ 200 Bill Ripken RC* .05 .02
❑ 201 Sam Horn RC .05 .02
❑ 202 Todd Worrell .10 .05
❑ 203 Terry Leach .05 .02
❑ 204 Garth Iorg .05 .02
❑ 205 Brian Dayett .05 .02
❑ 206 Bo Diaz .05 .02
❑ 207 Craig Reynolds .05 .02
❑ 208 Brian Holton .05 .02
❑ 209 Marvell Wynne UER .05 .02
(Misspelled Marvelle on card front)
❑ 210 Dave Concepcion .10 .05
❑ 211 Mike Davis .05 .02
❑ 212 Devon White .10 .05
❑ 213 Mickey Brantley .05 .02
❑ 214 Greg Gagne .05 .02
❑ 215 Oddibe McDowell .05 .02
❑ 216 Jimmy Key .10 .05
❑ 217 Dave Bergman .05 .02
❑ 218 Calvin Schiraldi .05 .02
❑ 219 Larry Sheets .05 .02
❑ 220 Mike Easler .05 .02
❑ 221 Kurt Stillwell .05 .02
❑ 222 Chuck Jackson .05 .02
❑ 223 Dave Martinez .05 .02
❑ 224 Tim Leary .05 .02
❑ 225 Steve Garvey .15 .07
❑ 226 Greg Mathews .05 .02
❑ 227 Doug Sisk .05 .02
❑ 228 Dave Henderson .05 .02
(Wearing Red Sox uniform; Red Sox logo on back)
❑ 229 Jimmy Dwyer .05 .02
❑ 230 Larry Owen .05 .02
❑ 231 Andre Thornton .10 .05
❑ 232 Mark Salas .05 .02
❑ 233 Tom Brookens .05 .02
❑ 234 Greg Brock .05 .02
❑ 235 Rance Mulliniks .05 .02
❑ 236 Bob Brower .05 .02
❑ 237 Joe Niekro .05 .02
❑ 238 Scott Bankhead .05 .02
❑ 239 Doug DeCinces .05 .02
❑ 240 Tommy John .10 .05
❑ 241 Rich Gedman .05 .02
❑ 242 Ted Power .05 .02
❑ 243 Dave Meads .05 .02
❑ 244 Jim Sundberg .05 .02
❑ 245 Ken Oberkfell .05 .02
❑ 246 Jimmy Jones .05 .02
❑ 247 Ken Landreaux .05 .02
❑ 248 Jose Oquendo .05 .02
❑ 249 John Mitchell .05 .02
❑ 250 Don Baylor .10 .05
❑ 251 Scott Fletcher .05 .02
❑ 252 Al Newman .05 .02
❑ 253 Carney Lansford .10 .05
❑ 254 Johnny Ray .05 .02
❑ 255 Gary Pettis .05 .02
❑ 256 Ken Phelps .05 .02
❑ 257 Rick Leach .05 .02
❑ 258 Tim Stoddard .05 .02
❑ 259 Ed Romero .05 .02
❑ 260 Sid Bream .05 .02
❑ 261A Tom Niedenfuer ERR .10 .05
(Misspelled Neidenfuer on card front)
❑ 261B Tom Niedenfuer COR .05 .02
❑ 262 Rick Dempsey .05 .02
❑ 263 Lonnie Smith .05 .02
❑ 264 Bob Forsch .05 .02
❑ 265 Barry Bonds .60 .25
❑ 266 Willie Randolph .10 .05
❑ 267 Mike Ramsey .05 .02
❑ 268 Don Slaught .05 .02
❑ 269 Mickey Tettleton .05 .02
❑ 270 Jerry Reuss .05 .02
❑ 271 Marc Sullivan .05 .02
❑ 272 Jim Morrison .05 .02
❑ 273 Steve Balboni .05 .02
❑ 274 Dick Schofield .05 .02
❑ 275 John Tudor .05 .02
❑ 276 Gene Larkin RC* .05 .02
❑ 277 Harold Reynolds .10 .05
❑ 278 Jerry Browne .05 .02
❑ 279 Willie Upshaw .05 .02
❑ 280 Ted Higuera .05 .02
❑ 281 Terry McGriff .05 .02
❑ 282 Terry Puhl .05 .02
❑ 283 Mark Wasinger .05 .02
❑ 284 Luis Salazar .05 .02
❑ 285 Ted Simmons .10 .05
❑ 286 John Shelby .05 .02
❑ 287 John Smiley RC* .10 .05
❑ 288 Curt Ford .05 .02
❑ 289 Steve Crawford .05 .02
❑ 290 Dan Quisenberry .05 .02
❑ 291 Alan Wiggins .05 .02
❑ 292 Randy Bush .05 .02
❑ 293 John Candelaria .05 .02
❑ 294 Tony Phillips .05 .02
❑ 295 Mike Morgan .05 .02
❑ 296 Bill Wegman .05 .02
❑ 297A Terry Francona ERR .10 .05
(Misspelled Franconia on card front)
❑ 297B Terry Francona COR .05 .02
❑ 298 Mickey Hatcher .05 .02
❑ 299 Andres Thomas .05 .02
❑ 300 Bob Stanley .05 .02
❑ 301 Al Pedrique .05 .02
❑ 302 Jim Lindeman .05 .02
❑ 303 Wally Backman .05 .02
❑ 304 Paul O'Neill .15 .07
❑ 305 Hubie Brooks .05 .02
❑ 306 Steve Buechele .05 .02
❑ 307 Bobby Thigpen .05 .02

❑ 308 George Hendrick .05 .02
❑ 309 John Moses .05 .02
❑ 310 Ron Guidry .05 .02
❑ 311 Bill Schroeder .05 .02
❑ 312 Jose Nunez .05 .02
❑ 313 Bud Black .05 .02
❑ 314 Joe Sambito .05 .02
❑ 315 Scott McGregor .05 .02
❑ 316 Rafael Santana .05 .02
❑ 317 Frank Williams .05 .02
❑ 318 Mike Fitzgerald .05 .02
❑ 319 Rick Mahler .05 .02
❑ 320 Jim Gott .05 .02
❑ 321 Mariano Duncan .05 .02
❑ 322 Jose Guzman .05 .02
❑ 323 Lee Guetterman .05 .02
❑ 324 Dan Gladden .05 .02
❑ 325 Gary Carter .15 .07
❑ 326 Tracy Jones .05 .02
❑ 327 Floyd Youmans .05 .02
❑ 328 Bill Dawley .05 .02
❑ 329 Paul Noce .05 .02
❑ 330 Angel Salazar .05 .02
❑ 331 Goose Gossage .15 .07
❑ 332 George Frazier .05 .02
❑ 333 Ruppert Jones .05 .02
❑ 334 Billy Joe Robidoux .05 .02
❑ 335 Mike Scott .05 .02
❑ 336 Randy Myers .15 .07
❑ 337 Bob Sebra .05 .02
❑ 338 Eric Show .05 .02
❑ 339 Mitch Williams .05 .02
❑ 340 Paul Molitor .20 .09
❑ 341 Gus Polidor .05 .02
❑ 342 Steve Trout .05 .02
❑ 343 Jerry Don Gleaton .05 .02
❑ 344 Bob Knepper .05 .02
❑ 345 Mitch Webster .05 .02
❑ 346 John Morris .05 .02
❑ 347 Andy Hawkins .05 .02
❑ 348 Dave Leiper .05 .02
❑ 349 Ernest Riles .05 .02
❑ 350 Dwight Gooden .10 .05
❑ 351 Dave Righetti .05 .02
❑ 352 Pat Dodson .05 .02
❑ 353 John Habyan .05 .02
❑ 354 Jim Deshaies .05 .02
❑ 355 Butch Wynegar .05 .02
❑ 356 Bryn Smith .05 .02
❑ 357 Matt Young .05 .02
❑ 358 Tom Pagnozzi RC .05 .02
❑ 359 Floyd Rayford .05 .02
❑ 360 Darryl Strawberry .10 .05
❑ 361 Sal Butera .05 .02
❑ 362 Domingo Ramos .05 .02
❑ 363 Chris Brown .05 .02
❑ 364 Jose Gonzalez .05 .02
❑ 365 Dave Smith .05 .02
❑ 366 Andy McGaffigan .05 .02
❑ 367 Stan Javier .05 .02
❑ 368 Henry Cotto .05 .02
❑ 369 Mike Birkbeck .05 .02
❑ 370 Len Dykstra .10 .05
❑ 371 Dave Collins .05 .02
❑ 372 Spike Owen .05 .02
❑ 373 Geno Petralli .05 .02
❑ 374 Ron Karkovice .05 .02
❑ 375 Shane Rawley .05 .02
❑ 376 DeWayne Buice .05 .02
❑ 377 Bill Pecota RC* .05 .02
❑ 378 Leon Durham .05 .02
❑ 379 Ed Olwine .05 .02
❑ 380 Bruce Hurst .05 .02
❑ 381 Bob McClure .05 .02
❑ 382 Mark Thurmond .05 .02
❑ 383 Buddy Biancalana .05 .02
❑ 384 Tim Conroy .05 .02
❑ 385 Tony Gwynn .40 .18
❑ 386 Greg Gross .05 .02
❑ 387 Barry Lyons .05 .02
❑ 388 Mike Felder .05 .02
❑ 389 Pat Clements .05 .02
❑ 390 Ken Griffey .10 .05
❑ 391 Mark Davis .05 .02
❑ 392 Jose Rijo .05 .02
❑ 393 Mike Young .05 .02
❑ 394 Willie Fraser .05 .02
❑ 395 Dion James .05 .02
❑ 396 Steve Shields .05 .02
❑ 397 Randy St.Claire .05 .02
❑ 398 Danny Jackson .05 .02
❑ 399 Cecil Fielder .15 .07
❑ 400 Keith Hernandez .10 .05
❑ 401 Don Carman .05 .02
❑ 402 Chuck Crim .05 .02
❑ 403 Rob Woodward .05 .02
❑ 404 Junior Ortiz .05 .02
❑ 405 Glenn Wilson .05 .02
❑ 406 Ken Howell .05 .02
❑ 407 Jeff Kunkel .05 .02
❑ 408 Jeff Reed .05 .02
❑ 409 Chris James .05 .02
❑ 410 Zane Smith .05 .02
❑ 411 Ken Dixon .05 .02
❑ 412 Ricky Horton .05 .02
❑ 413 Frank DiPino .05 .02
❑ 414 Shane Mack .05 .02
❑ 415 Danny Cox .05 .02
❑ 416 Andy Van Slyke .10 .05
❑ 417 Danny Heep .05 .02
❑ 418 John Cangelosi .05 .02
❑ 419A John Christensen ERR .10 .05
(Christiansen
on card front)
❑ 419B John Christensen COR .05 .02
❑ 420 Joey Cora RC .20 .09
❑ 421 Mike LaValliere .05 .02
❑ 422 Kelly Gruber .05 .02
❑ 423 Bruce Benedict .05 .02
❑ 424 Len Matuszek .05 .02
❑ 425 Kent Tekulve .05 .02
❑ 426 Rafael Ramirez .05 .02
❑ 427 Mike Flanagan .05 .02
❑ 428 Mike Gallego .05 .02
❑ 429 Juan Castillo .05 .02
❑ 430 Neal Heaton .05 .02
❑ 431 Phil Garner .05 .02
❑ 432 Mike Dunne .05 .02
❑ 433 Wallace Johnson .05 .02
❑ 434 Jack O'Connor .05 .02
❑ 435 Steve Jeltz .05 .02
❑ 436 Donell Nixon .05 .02
❑ 437 Jack Lazorko .05 .02
❑ 438 Keith Comstock .05 .02
❑ 439 Jeff D. Robinson .05 .02
❑ 440 Graig Nettles .10 .05
❑ 441 Mel Hall .05 .02
❑ 442 Gerald Young .05 .02
❑ 443 Gary Redus .05 .02
❑ 444 Charlie Moore .05 .02
❑ 445 Bill Madlock .10 .05
❑ 446 Mark Clear .05 .02
❑ 447 Greg Booker .05 .02
❑ 448 Rick Schu .05 .02
❑ 449 Ron Kittle .05 .02
❑ 450 Dale Murphy .20 .09
❑ 451 Bob Dernier .05 .02
❑ 452 Dale Mohorcic .05 .02
❑ 453 Rafael Belliard .05 .02
❑ 454 Charlie Puleo .05 .02
❑ 455 Dwayne Murphy .05 .02
❑ 456 Jim Eisenreich .20 .09
❑ 457 David Palmer .05 .02
❑ 458 Dave Stewart .10 .05
❑ 459 Pascual Perez .05 .02
❑ 460 Glenn Davis .05 .02
❑ 461 Dan Petry .05 .02
❑ 462 Jim Winn .05 .02
❑ 463 Darrell Miller .05 .02
❑ 464 Mike Moore .05 .02
❑ 465 Mike LaCoss .05 .02
❑ 466 Steve Farr .05 .02
❑ 467 Jerry Mumphrey .05 .02
❑ 468 Kevin Gross .05 .02
❑ 469 Bruce Bochy .05 .02
❑ 470 Orel Hershiser .10 .05
❑ 471 Eric King .05 .02
❑ 472 Ellis Burks RC .25 .11
❑ 473 Darren Daulton .10 .05
❑ 474 Mookie Wilson .10 .05
❑ 475 Frank Viola .05 .02
❑ 476 Ron Robinson .05 .02
❑ 477 Bob Melvin .05 .02
❑ 478 Jeff Musselman .05 .02
❑ 479 Charlie Kerfeld .05 .02
❑ 480 Richard Dotson .05 .02
❑ 481 Kevin Mitchell .10 .05
❑ 482 Gary Roenicke .05 .02
❑ 483 Tim Flannery .05 .02
❑ 484 Rich Yett .05 .02
❑ 485 Pete Incaviglia .05 .02
❑ 486 Rick Cerone .05 .02
❑ 487 Tony Armas .05 .02
❑ 488 Jerry Reed .05 .02
❑ 489 Dave Lopes .10 .05
❑ 490 Frank Tanana .05 .02
❑ 491 Mike Loynd .05 .02
❑ 492 Bruce Ruffin .05 .02
❑ 493 Chris Speier .05 .02
❑ 494 Tom Hume .05 .02
❑ 495 Jesse Orosco .05 .02
❑ 496 Robbie Wine UER .05 .02
(Misspelled Robby
on card front)
❑ 497 Jeff Montgomery RC .20 .09
❑ 498 Jeff Dedmon .05 .02
❑ 499 Luis Aguayo .05 .02
❑ 500 Reggie Jackson .20 .09
(Oakland A's)
❑ 501 Reggie Jackson .20 .09
(Baltimore Orioles)
❑ 502 Reggie Jackson .20 .09
(New York Yankees)
❑ 503 Reggie Jackson .20 .09
(California Angels)
❑ 504 Reggie Jackson .20 .09
(Oakland A's)
❑ 505 Billy Hatcher .05 .02
❑ 506 Ed Lynch .05 .02
❑ 507 Willie Hernandez .05 .02
❑ 508 Jose DeLeon .05 .02
❑ 509 Joel Youngblood .05 .02
❑ 510 Bob Welch .05 .02
❑ 511 Steve Ontiveros .05 .02
❑ 512 Randy Ready .05 .02
❑ 513 Juan Nieves .05 .02
❑ 514 Jeff Russell .05 .02
❑ 515 Von Hayes .05 .02
❑ 516 Mark Gubicza .05 .02
❑ 517 Ken Dayley .05 .02
❑ 518 Don Aase .05 .02
❑ 519 Rick Reuschel .05 .02
❑ 520 Mike Henneman RC* .10 .05
❑ 521 Rick Aguilera .10 .05
❑ 522 Jay Howell .05 .02
❑ 523 Ed Correa .05 .02
❑ 524 Manny Trillo .05 .02
❑ 525 Kirk Gibson .10 .05
❑ 526 Wally Ritchie .05 .02
❑ 527 Al Nipper .05 .02
❑ 528 Atlee Hammaker .05 .02
❑ 529 Shawon Dunston .05 .02
❑ 530 Jim Clancy .05 .02
❑ 531 Tom Paciorek .10 .05
❑ 532 Joel Skinner .05 .02
❑ 533 Scott Garrelts .05 .02
❑ 534 Tom O'Malley .05 .02
❑ 535 John Franco .10 .05
❑ 536 Paul Kilgus .05 .02
❑ 537 Darrell Porter .05 .02
❑ 538 Walt Terrell .05 .02
❑ 539 Bill Long .05 .02
❑ 540 George Bell .05 .02
❑ 541 Jeff Sellers .05 .02
❑ 542 Joe Boever .05 .02
❑ 543 Steve Howe .05 .02
❑ 544 Scott Sanderson .05 .02
❑ 545 Jack Morris .10 .05
❑ 546 Todd Benzinger RC* .05 .02
❑ 547 Steve Henderson .05 .02
❑ 548 Eddie Milner .05 .02
❑ 549 Jeff M. Robinson .05 .02
❑ 550 Cal Ripken .75 .35
❑ 551 Jody Davis .05 .02
❑ 552 Kirk McCaskill .05 .02
❑ 553 Craig Lefferts .05 .02
❑ 554 Darnell Coles .05 .02
❑ 555 Phil Niekro .20 .09

❑ 556 Mike Aldrete .05 .02
❑ 557 Pat Perry .05 .02
❑ 558 Juan Agosto .05 .02
❑ 559 Rob Murphy .05 .02
❑ 560 Dennis Rasmussen .05 .02
❑ 561 Manny Lee .05 .02
❑ 562 Jeff Blauser RC .20 .09
❑ 563 Bob Ojeda .05 .02
❑ 564 Dave Dravecky .10 .05
❑ 565 Gene Garber .05 .02
❑ 566 Ron Roenicke .05 .02
❑ 567 Tommy Hinzo .05 .02
❑ 568 Eric Nolte .05 .02
❑ 569 Ed Hearn .05 .02
❑ 570 Mark Davidson .05 .02
❑ 571 Jim Walewander .05 .02
❑ 572 Donnie Hill UER .05 .02
(84 Stolen Base
total listed as 7)
❑ 573 Jamie Moyer .05 .02
❑ 574 Ken Schrom .05 .02
❑ 575 Nolan Ryan 1.00 .45
❑ 576 Jim Acker .05 .02
❑ 577 Jamie Quirk .05 .02
❑ 578 Jay Aldrich .05 .02
❑ 579 Claudell Washington .05 .02
❑ 580 Jeff Leonard .05 .02
❑ 581 Carmen Castillo .05 .02
❑ 582 Daryl Boston .05 .02
❑ 583 Jeff DeWillis .05 .02
❑ 584 John Marzano .05 .02
❑ 585 Bill Gullickson .05 .02
❑ 586 Andy Allanson .05 .02
❑ 587 Lee Tunnell UER .05 .02
(1987 stat line
reads .4.84 ERA)
❑ 588 Gene Nelson .05 .02
❑ 589 Dave LaPoint .05 .02
❑ 590 Harold Baines .10 .05
❑ 591 Bill Buckner .10 .05
❑ 592 Carlton Fisk .20 .09
❑ 593 Rick Manning .05 .02
❑ 594 Doug Jones RC .20 .09
❑ 595 Tom Candiotti .05 .02
❑ 596 Steve Lake .05 .02
❑ 597 Jose Lind RC .05 .02
❑ 598 Ross Jones .05 .02
❑ 599 Gary Matthews .05 .02
❑ 600 Fernando Valenzuela .10 .05
❑ 601 Dennis Martinez .10 .05
❑ 602 Les Lancaster .05 .02
❑ 603 Ozzie Guillen .05 .02
❑ 604 Tony Bernazard .05 .02
❑ 605 Chili Davis .15 .07
❑ 606 Roy Smalley .05 .02
❑ 607 Ivan Calderon .05 .02
❑ 608 Jay Tibbs .05 .02
❑ 609 Guy Hoffman .05 .02
❑ 610 Doyle Alexander .05 .02
❑ 611 Mike Bielecki .05 .02
❑ 612 Shawn Hillegas .05 .02
❑ 613 Keith Atherton .05 .02
❑ 614 Eric Plunk .05 .02
❑ 615 Sid Fernandez .05 .02
❑ 616 Dennis Lamp .05 .02
❑ 617 Dave Engle .05 .02
❑ 618 Harry Spilman .05 .02
❑ 619 Don Robinson .05 .02
❑ 620 John Farrell .05 .02
❑ 621 Nelson Liriano .05 .02
❑ 622 Floyd Bannister .05 .02
❑ 623 Randy Milligan RC .05 .02
❑ 624 Kevin Elster .05 .02
❑ 625 Jody Reed RC .10 .05
❑ 626 Shawn Abner .05 .02
❑ 627 Kirt Manwaring RC .05 .02
❑ 628 Pete Stanicek .05 .02
❑ 629 Rob Ducey .05 .02
❑ 630 Steve Kiefer .05 .02
❑ 631 Gary Thurman .05 .02
❑ 632 Darrel Akerfelds .05 .02
❑ 633 Dave Clark .05 .02
❑ 634 Roberto Kelly RC .20 .09
❑ 635 Keith Hughes .05 .02
❑ 636 John Davis .05 .02
❑ 637 Mike Devereaux RC .10 .05
❑ 638 Tom Glavine RC 1.25 .55
❑ 639 Keith A. Miller RC .05 .02
❑ 640 Chris Gwynn RC UER .10 .05
(Wrong batting and
throwing on back)
❑ 641 Tim Crews RC .05 .02
❑ 642 Mackey Sasser RC .05 .02
❑ 643 Vicente Palacios .05 .02
❑ 644 Kevin Romine .05 .02
❑ 645 Gregg Jefferies RC .20 .09
❑ 646 Jeff Treadway RC .05 .02
❑ 647 Ron Gant RC .25 .11
❑ 648 Mark McGwire 1.00 .45
Matt Nokes
Rookie Sluggers
❑ 649 Eric Davis .10 .05
Tim Raines
Speed and Power
❑ 650 Don Mattingly .15 .07
Jack Clark
❑ 651 Tony Fernandez .25 .11
Alan Trammell
Cal Ripken
❑ 652 Vince Coleman HL .05 .02
100 Stolen Bases
❑ 653 Kirby Puckett HL .25 .11
10 Hits in a Row
❑ 654 Benito Santiago HL .05 .02
Hitting Streak
❑ 655 Juan Nieves HL .05 .02
No Hitter
❑ 656 Steve Bedrosian HL .05 .02
Saves Record
❑ 657 Mike Schmidt HL .15 .07
500 Homers
❑ 658 Don Mattingly HL .15 .07
Home Run Streak
❑ 659 Mark McGwire HL 1.00 .45
Rookie HR Record
❑ 660 Paul Molitor HL .15 .07
Hitting Streak

## 1988 Score Rookie/Traded

| | MINT | NRMT |
|---|---|---|
| COMP.FACT.SET (110) | 40.00 | 18.00 |

❑ 1T Jack Clark .75 .35
❑ 2T Danny Jackson .25 .11
❑ 3T Brett Butler .75 .35
❑ 4T Kurt Stillwell .25 .11
❑ 5T Tom Brunansky .25 .11
❑ 6T Dennis Lamp .25 .11
❑ 7T Jose DeLeon .25 .11
❑ 8T Tom Herr .25 .11
❑ 9T Keith Moreland .25 .11
❑ 10T Kirk Gibson 2.00 .90
❑ 11T Bud Black .25 .11
❑ 12T Rafael Ramirez .25 .11
❑ 13T Luis Salazar .25 .11
❑ 14T Goose Gossage 1.25 .55
❑ 15T Bob Welch .25 .11
❑ 16T Vance Law .25 .11
❑ 17T Ray Knight .25 .11
❑ 18T Dan Quisenberry .25 .11
❑ 19T Don Slaught .25 .11
❑ 20T Lee Smith .75 .35
❑ 21T Rick Cerone .25 .11
❑ 22T Pat Tabler .25 .11
❑ 23T Larry McWilliams .25 .11
❑ 24T Ricky Horton .25 .11
❑ 25T Graig Nettles .75 .35
❑ 26T Dan Petry .25 .11
❑ 27T Jose Rijo .25 .11
❑ 28T Chili Davis 1.25 .55
❑ 29T Dickie Thon .25 .11
❑ 30T Mackey Sasser .25 .11
❑ 31T Mickey Tettleton .25 .11
❑ 32T Rick Dempsey .25 .11
❑ 33T Ron Hassey .25 .11
❑ 34T Phil Bradley .25 .11
❑ 35T Jay Howell .25 .11
❑ 36T Bill Buckner .75 .35
❑ 37T Alfredo Griffin .25 .11
❑ 38T Gary Pettis .25 .11
❑ 39T Calvin Schiraldi .25 .11
❑ 40T John Candelaria .25 .11
❑ 41T Joe Orsulak .25 .11
❑ 42T Willie Upshaw .25 .11
❑ 43T Herm Winningham .25 .11
❑ 44T Ron Kittle .25 .11
❑ 45T Bob Dernier .25 .11
❑ 46T Steve Balboni .25 .11
❑ 47T Steve Shields .25 .11
❑ 48T Henry Cotto .25 .11
❑ 49T Dave Henderson .25 .11
❑ 50T Dave Parker .75 .35
❑ 51T Mike Young .25 .11
❑ 52T Mark Salas .25 .11
❑ 53T Mike Davis .25 .11
❑ 54T Rafael Santana .25 .11
❑ 55T Don Baylor .75 .35
❑ 56T Dan Pasqua .25 .11
❑ 57T Ernest Riles .25 .11
❑ 58T Glenn Hubbard .25 .11
❑ 59T Mike Smithson .25 .11
❑ 60T Richard Dotson .25 .11
❑ 61T Jerry Reuss .25 .11
❑ 62T Mike Jackson .75 .35
❑ 63T Floyd Bannister .25 .11
❑ 64T Jesse Orosco .25 .11
❑ 65T Larry Parrish .25 .11
❑ 66T Jeff Bittiger .25 .11
❑ 67T Ray Hayward .25 .11
❑ 68T Ricky Jordan XRC .75 .35
❑ 69T Tommy Gregg .25 .11
❑ 70T Brady Anderson XRC 3.00 1.35
❑ 71T Jeff Montgomery 2.00 .90
❑ 72T Darryl Hamilton XRC .75 .35
❑ 73T Cecil Espy .25 .11
❑ 74T Greg Briley XRC .25 .11
❑ 75T Joey Meyer .25 .11
❑ 76T Mike Macfarlane XRC .25 .11
❑ 77T Oswald Peraza .25 .11
❑ 78T Jack Armstrong XRC .25 .11
❑ 79T Don Heinkel .25 .11
❑ 80T Mark Grace XRC 10.00 4.50
❑ 81T Steve Curry .25 .11
❑ 82T Damon Berryhill XRC* .25 .11
❑ 83T Steve Ellsworth .25 .11
❑ 84T Pete Smith XRC* .25 .11
❑ 85T Jack McDowell XRC 2.00 .90
❑ 86T Rob Dibble XRC .75 .35
❑ 87T Bryan Harvey UER .75 .35
(Games Pitched 47,
Innings 5) XRC
❑ 88T John Dopson .25 .11
❑ 89T Dave Gallagher .25 .11
❑ 90T Todd Stottlemyre XRC 2.00 .90
❑ 91T Mike Schooler .25 .11
❑ 92T Don Gordon .25 .11
❑ 93T Sil Campusano .25 .11
❑ 94T Jeff Pico .25 .11
❑ 95T Jay Buhner XRC 3.00 1.35
❑ 96T Nelson Santovenia .25 .11
❑ 97T Al Leiter XRC* 3.00 1.35
❑ 98T Luis Alicea XRC .75 .35
❑ 99T Pat Borders XRC .75 .35
❑ 100T Chris Sabo XRC .75 .35
❑ 101T Tim Belcher .75 .35
❑ 102T Walt Weiss XRC* 2.00 .90
❑ 103T Craig Biggio XRC 12.00 5.50
❑ 104T Don August .25 .11

| | MINT | NRMT |
|---|---|---|
| ❑ 105T Roberto Alomar XRC | 20.00 | 9.00 |
| ❑ 106T Todd Burns | .25 | .11 |
| ❑ 107T John Costello | .25 | .11 |
| ❑ 108T Melido Perez XRC* | .25 | .11 |
| ❑ 109T Darrin Jackson XRC* | .25 | .11 |
| ❑ 110T Orestes Destrade XRC | .75 | .35 |

## 1989 Score

| | MINT | NRMT |
|---|---|---|
| COMPLETE SET (660) | 8.00 | 3.60 |
| COMP.FACT.SET (660) | 10.00 | 4.50 |
| ❑ 1 Jose Canseco | .25 | .11 |
| ❑ 2 Andre Dawson | .15 | .07 |
| ❑ 3 Mark McGwire UER | 1.00 | .45 |
| ❑ 4 Benito Santiago | .05 | .02 |
| ❑ 5 Rick Reuschel | .05 | .02 |
| ❑ 6 Fred McGriff | .20 | .09 |
| ❑ 7 Kal Daniels | .05 | .02 |
| ❑ 8 Gary Gaetti | .10 | .05 |
| ❑ 9 Ellis Burks | .15 | .07 |
| ❑ 10 Darryl Strawberry | .10 | .05 |
| ❑ 11 Julio Franco | .05 | .02 |
| ❑ 12 Lloyd Moseby | .05 | .02 |
| ❑ 13 Jeff Pico | .05 | .02 |
| ❑ 14 Johnny Ray | .05 | .02 |
| ❑ 15 Cal Ripken | .75 | .35 |
| ❑ 16 Dick Schofield | .05 | .02 |
| ❑ 17 Mel Hall | .05 | .02 |
| ❑ 18 Bill Ripken | .05 | .02 |
| ❑ 19 Brook Jacoby | .05 | .02 |
| ❑ 20 Kirby Puckett | .50 | .23 |
| ❑ 21 Bill Doran | .05 | .02 |
| ❑ 22 Pete O'Brien | .05 | .02 |
| ❑ 23 Matt Nokes | .05 | .02 |
| ❑ 24 Brian Fisher | .05 | .02 |
| ❑ 25 Jack Clark | .05 | .02 |
| ❑ 26 Gary Pettis | .05 | .02 |
| ❑ 27 Dave Valle | .05 | .02 |
| ❑ 28 Willie Wilson | .05 | .02 |
| ❑ 29 Curt Young | .05 | .02 |
| ❑ 30 Dale Murphy | .20 | .09 |
| ❑ 31 Barry Larkin | .20 | .09 |
| ❑ 32 Dave Stewart | .10 | .05 |
| ❑ 33 Mike LaValliere | .05 | .02 |
| ❑ 34 Glenn Hubbard | .05 | .02 |
| ❑ 35 Ryne Sandberg | .25 | .11 |
| ❑ 36 Tony Pena | .05 | .02 |
| ❑ 37 Greg Walker | .05 | .02 |
| ❑ 38 Von Hayes | .05 | .02 |
| ❑ 39 Kevin Mitchell | .10 | .05 |
| ❑ 40 Tim Raines | .10 | .05 |
| ❑ 41 Keith Hernandez | .10 | .05 |
| ❑ 42 Keith Moreland | .05 | .02 |
| ❑ 43 Ruben Sierra | .05 | .02 |
| ❑ 44 Chet Lemon | .05 | .02 |
| ❑ 45 Willie Randolph | .10 | .05 |
| ❑ 46 Andy Allanson | .05 | .02 |
| ❑ 47 Candy Maldonado | .05 | .02 |
| ❑ 48 Sid Bream | .05 | .02 |
| ❑ 49 Denny Walling | .05 | .02 |
| ❑ 50 Dave Winfield | .20 | .09 |
| ❑ 51 Alvin Davis | .05 | .02 |
| ❑ 52 Cory Snyder | .05 | .02 |
| ❑ 53 Hubie Brooks | .05 | .02 |
| ❑ 54 Chili Davis | .10 | .05 |
| ❑ 55 Kevin Seitzer | .05 | .02 |
| ❑ 56 Jose Uribe | .05 | .02 |
| ❑ 57 Tony Fernandez | .05 | .02 |
| ❑ 58 Tim Teufel | .05 | .02 |
| ❑ 59 Oddibe McDowell | .05 | .02 |
| ❑ 60 Les Lancaster | .05 | .02 |
| ❑ 61 Billy Hatcher | .05 | .02 |
| ❑ 62 Dan Gladden | .05 | .02 |
| ❑ 63 Marty Barrett | .05 | .02 |
| ❑ 64 Nick Esasky | .05 | .02 |
| ❑ 65 Wally Joyner | .10 | .05 |
| ❑ 66 Mike Greenwell | .05 | .02 |
| ❑ 67 Ken Williams | .05 | .02 |
| ❑ 68 Bob Horner | .05 | .02 |
| ❑ 69 Steve Sax | .05 | .02 |
| ❑ 70 Rickey Henderson | .25 | .11 |
| ❑ 71 Mitch Webster | .05 | .02 |
| ❑ 72 Rob Deer | .05 | .02 |
| ❑ 73 Jim Presley | .05 | .02 |
| ❑ 74 Albert Hall | .05 | .02 |
| ❑ 75 George Brett COR (At age 35) | .40 | .18 |
| ❑ 75A George Brett ERR (At age 33) | .75 | .35 |
| ❑ 76 Brian Downing | .05 | .02 |
| ❑ 77 Dave Martinez | .05 | .02 |
| ❑ 78 Scott Fletcher | .05 | .02 |
| ❑ 79 Phil Bradley | .05 | .02 |
| ❑ 80 Ozzie Smith | .25 | .11 |
| ❑ 81 Larry Sheets | .05 | .02 |
| ❑ 82 Mike Aldrete | .05 | .02 |
| ❑ 83 Darnell Coles | .05 | .02 |
| ❑ 84 Len Dykstra | .10 | .05 |
| ❑ 85 Jim Rice | .10 | .05 |
| ❑ 86 Jeff Treadway | .05 | .02 |
| ❑ 87 Jose Lind | .05 | .02 |
| ❑ 88 Willie McGee | .10 | .05 |
| ❑ 89 Mickey Brantley | .05 | .02 |
| ❑ 90 Tony Gwynn | .40 | .18 |
| ❑ 91 R.J. Reynolds | .05 | .02 |
| ❑ 92 Milt Thompson | .05 | .02 |
| ❑ 93 Kevin McReynolds | .05 | .02 |
| ❑ 94 Eddie Murray UER ('86 batting .205; should be .305) | .20 | .09 |
| ❑ 95 Lance Parrish | .05 | .02 |
| ❑ 96 Ron Kittle | .05 | .02 |
| ❑ 97 Gerald Young | .05 | .02 |
| ❑ 98 Ernie Whitt | .05 | .02 |
| ❑ 99 Jeff Reed | .05 | .02 |
| ❑ 100 Don Mattingly | .50 | .23 |
| ❑ 101 Gerald Perry | .05 | .02 |
| ❑ 102 Vance Law | .05 | .02 |
| ❑ 103 John Shelby | .05 | .02 |
| ❑ 104 Chris Sabo RC* | .05 | .02 |
| ❑ 105 Danny Tartabull | .05 | .02 |
| ❑ 106 Glenn Wilson | .05 | .02 |
| ❑ 107 Mark Davidson | .05 | .02 |
| ❑ 108 Dave Parker | .10 | .05 |
| ❑ 109 Eric Davis | .10 | .05 |
| ❑ 110 Alan Trammell | .15 | .07 |
| ❑ 111 Ozzie Virgil | .05 | .02 |
| ❑ 112 Frank Tanana | .05 | .02 |
| ❑ 113 Rafael Ramirez | .05 | .02 |
| ❑ 114 Dennis Martinez | .10 | .05 |
| ❑ 115 Jose DeLeon | .05 | .02 |
| ❑ 116 Bob Ojeda | .05 | .02 |
| ❑ 117 Doug Drabek | .05 | .02 |
| ❑ 118 Andy Hawkins | .05 | .02 |
| ❑ 119 Greg Maddux | .60 | .25 |
| ❑ 120 Cecil Fielder UER (Reversed photo on back) | .10 | .05 |
| ❑ 121 Mike Scioscia | .05 | .02 |
| ❑ 122 Dan Petry | .05 | .02 |
| ❑ 123 Terry Kennedy | .05 | .02 |
| ❑ 124 Kelly Downs | .05 | .02 |
| ❑ 125 Greg Gross UER (Gregg on back) | .05 | .02 |
| ❑ 126 Fred Lynn | .05 | .02 |
| ❑ 127 Barry Bonds | .50 | .23 |
| ❑ 128 Harold Baines | .10 | .05 |
| ❑ 129 Doyle Alexander | .05 | .02 |
| ❑ 130 Kevin Elster | .05 | .02 |
| ❑ 131 Mike Heath | .05 | .02 |
| ❑ 132 Teddy Higuera | .05 | .02 |
| ❑ 133 Charlie Leibrandt | .05 | .02 |
| ❑ 134 Tim Laudner | .05 | .02 |
| ❑ 135A Ray Knight ERR (Reverse negative) | .20 | .09 |
| ❑ 135B Ray Knight COR | .05 | .02 |
| ❑ 136 Howard Johnson | .05 | .02 |
| ❑ 137 Terry Pendleton | .10 | .05 |
| ❑ 138 Andy McGaffigan | .05 | .02 |
| ❑ 139 Ken Oberkfell | .05 | .02 |
| ❑ 140 Butch Wynegar | .05 | .02 |
| ❑ 141 Rob Murphy | .05 | .02 |
| ❑ 142 Rich Renteria | .05 | .02 |
| ❑ 143 Jose Guzman | .05 | .02 |
| ❑ 144 Andres Galarraga | .15 | .07 |
| ❑ 145 Ricky Horton | .05 | .02 |
| ❑ 146 Frank DiPino | .05 | .02 |
| ❑ 147 Glenn Braggs | .05 | .02 |
| ❑ 148 John Kruk | .10 | .05 |
| ❑ 149 Mike Schmidt | .40 | .18 |
| ❑ 150 Lee Smith | .10 | .05 |
| ❑ 151 Robin Yount | .20 | .09 |
| ❑ 152 Mark Eichhorn | .05 | .02 |
| ❑ 153 DeWayne Buice | .05 | .02 |
| ❑ 154 B.J. Surhoff | .10 | .05 |
| ❑ 155 Vince Coleman | .05 | .02 |
| ❑ 156 Tony Phillips | .05 | .02 |
| ❑ 157 Willie Fraser | .05 | .02 |
| ❑ 158 Lance McCullers | .05 | .02 |
| ❑ 159 Greg Gagne | .05 | .02 |
| ❑ 160 Jesse Barfield | .05 | .02 |
| ❑ 161 Mark Langston | .05 | .02 |
| ❑ 162 Kurt Stillwell | .05 | .02 |
| ❑ 163 Dion James | .05 | .02 |
| ❑ 164 Glenn Davis | .05 | .02 |
| ❑ 165 Walt Weiss | .05 | .02 |
| ❑ 166 Dave Concepcion | .10 | .05 |
| ❑ 167 Alfredo Griffin | .05 | .02 |
| ❑ 168 Don Heinkel | .05 | .02 |
| ❑ 169 Luis Rivera | .05 | .02 |
| ❑ 170 Shane Rawley | .05 | .02 |
| ❑ 171 Darrell Evans | .10 | .05 |
| ❑ 172 Robby Thompson | .05 | .02 |
| ❑ 173 Jody Davis | .05 | .02 |
| ❑ 174 Andy Van Slyke | .10 | .05 |
| ❑ 175 Wade Boggs UER (Bio says .364; should be .356) | .25 | .11 |
| ❑ 176 Garry Templeton ('85 stats off-centered) | .05 | .02 |
| ❑ 177 Gary Redus | .05 | .02 |
| ❑ 178 Craig Lefferts | .05 | .02 |
| ❑ 179 Carney Lansford | .10 | .05 |
| ❑ 180 Ron Darling | .05 | .02 |
| ❑ 181 Kirk McCaskill | .05 | .02 |
| ❑ 182 Tony Armas | .05 | .02 |
| ❑ 183 Steve Farr | .05 | .02 |
| ❑ 184 Tom Brunansky | .05 | .02 |
| ❑ 185 Bryan Harvey RC* UER ('87 games 47; should be 3) | .05 | .02 |
| ❑ 186 Mike Marshall | .05 | .02 |
| ❑ 187 Bo Diaz | .05 | .02 |
| ❑ 188 Willie Upshaw | .05 | .02 |
| ❑ 189 Mike Pagliarulo | .05 | .02 |
| ❑ 190 Mike Krukow | .05 | .02 |
| ❑ 191 Tommy Herr | .05 | .02 |
| ❑ 192 Jim Pankovits | .05 | .02 |
| ❑ 193 Dwight Evans | .10 | .05 |
| ❑ 194 Kelly Gruber | .05 | .02 |
| ❑ 195 Bobby Bonilla | .10 | .05 |
| ❑ 196 Wallace Johnson | .05 | .02 |
| ❑ 197 Dave Stieb | .05 | .02 |
| ❑ 198 Pat Borders RC* | .10 | .05 |
| ❑ 199 Rafael Palmeiro | .25 | .11 |
| ❑ 200 Dwight Gooden | .10 | .05 |
| ❑ 201 Pete Incaviglia | .05 | .02 |
| ❑ 202 Chris James | .05 | .02 |
| ❑ 203 Marvell Wynne | .05 | .02 |
| ❑ 204 Pat Sheridan | .05 | .02 |
| ❑ 205 Don Baylor | .10 | .05 |
| ❑ 206 Paul O'Neill | .10 | .05 |
| ❑ 207 Pete Smith | .05 | .02 |
| ❑ 208 Mark McLemore | .05 | .02 |
| ❑ 209 Henry Cotto | .05 | .02 |
| ❑ 210 Kirk Gibson | .10 | .05 |
| ❑ 211 Claudell Washington | .05 | .02 |

❑ 212 Randy Bush .05 .02
❑ 213 Joe Carter .15 .07
❑ 214 Bill Buckner .10 .05
❑ 215 Bert Blyleven UER .10 .05
(Wrong birth year)
❑ 216 Brett Butler .10 .05
❑ 217 Lee Mazzilli .05 .02
❑ 218 Spike Owen .05 .02
❑ 219 Bill Swift .05 .02
❑ 220 Tim Wallach .05 .02
❑ 221 David Cone .10 .05
❑ 222 Don Carman .05 .02
❑ 223 Rich Gossage .10 .05
❑ 224 Bob Walk .05 .02
❑ 225 Dave Righetti .05 .02
❑ 226 Kevin Bass .05 .02
❑ 227 Kevin Gross .05 .02
❑ 228 Tim Burke .05 .02
❑ 229 Rick Mahler .05 .02
❑ 230 Lou Whitaker UER .10 .05
(252 games in '85;
should be 152)
❑ 231 Luis Alicea RC* .05 .02
❑ 232 Roberto Alomar .30 .14
❑ 233 Bob Boone .10 .05
❑ 234 Dickie Thon .05 .02
❑ 235 Shawon Dunston .05 .02
❑ 236 Pete Stanicek .05 .02
❑ 237 Craig Biggio RC .75 .35
(Inconsistent design,
portrait on front)
❑ 238 Dennis Boyd .05 .02
❑ 239 Tom Candiotti .05 .02
❑ 240 Gary Carter .15 .07
❑ 241 Mike Stanley .05 .02
❑ 242 Ken Phelps .05 .02
❑ 243 Chris Bosio .05 .02
❑ 244 Les Straker .05 .02
❑ 245 Dave Smith .05 .02
❑ 246 John Candelaria .05 .02
❑ 247 Joe Orsulak .05 .02
❑ 248 Storm Davis .05 .02
❑ 249 Floyd Bannister UER .05 .02
(ML Batting Record)
❑ 250 Jack Morris .10 .05
❑ 251 Bret Saberhagen .10 .05
❑ 252 Tom Niedenfuer .05 .02
❑ 253 Neal Heaton .05 .02
❑ 254 Eric Show .05 .02
❑ 255 Juan Samuel .05 .02
❑ 256 Dale Sveum .05 .02
❑ 257 Jim Gott .05 .02
❑ 258 Scott Garrelts .05 .02
❑ 259 Larry McWilliams .05 .02
❑ 260 Steve Bedrosian .05 .02
❑ 261 Jack Howell .05 .02
❑ 262 Jay Tibbs .05 .02
❑ 263 Jamie Moyer .05 .02
❑ 264 Doug Sisk .05 .02
❑ 265 Todd Worrell .05 .02
❑ 266 John Farrell .05 .02
❑ 267 Dave Collins .05 .02
❑ 268 Sid Fernandez .05 .02
❑ 269 Tom Brookens .05 .02
❑ 270 Shane Mack .05 .02
❑ 271 Paul Kilgus .05 .02
❑ 272 Chuck Crim .05 .02
❑ 273 Bob Knepper .05 .02
❑ 274 Mike Moore .05 .02
❑ 275 Guillermo Hernandez .05 .02
❑ 276 Dennis Eckersley .15 .07
❑ 277 Graig Nettles .10 .05
❑ 278 Rich Dotson .05 .02
❑ 279 Larry Herndon .05 .02
❑ 280 Gene Larkin .05 .02
❑ 281 Roger McDowell .05 .02
❑ 282 Greg Swindell .05 .02
❑ 283 Juan Agosto .05 .02
❑ 284 Jeff M. Robinson .05 .02
❑ 285 Mike Dunne .05 .02
❑ 286 Greg Mathews .05 .02
❑ 287 Kent Tekulve .05 .02
❑ 288 Jerry Mumphrey .05 .02
❑ 289 Jack McDowell .10 .05
❑ 290 Frank Viola .05 .02
❑ 291 Mark Gubicza .05 .02
❑ 292 Dave Schmidt .05 .02
❑ 293 Mike Henneman .05 .02
❑ 294 Jimmy Jones .05 .02
❑ 295 Charlie Hough .10 .05
❑ 296 Rafael Santana .05 .02
❑ 297 Chris Speier .05 .02
❑ 298 Mike Witt .05 .02
❑ 299 Pascual Perez .05 .02
❑ 300 Nolan Ryan 1.00 .45
❑ 301 Mitch Williams .05 .02
❑ 302 Mookie Wilson .10 .05
❑ 303 Mackey Sasser .05 .02
❑ 304 John Cerutti .05 .02
❑ 305 Jeff Reardon .10 .05
❑ 306 Randy Myers UER .10 .05
(6 hits in '87;
should be 61)
❑ 307 Greg Brock .05 .02
❑ 308 Bob Welch .05 .02
❑ 309 Jeff D. Robinson .05 .02
❑ 310 Harold Reynolds .05 .02
❑ 311 Jim Walewander .05 .02
❑ 312 Dave Magadan .05 .02
❑ 313 Jim Gantner .05 .02
❑ 314 Walt Terrell .05 .02
❑ 315 Wally Backman .05 .02
❑ 316 Luis Salazar .05 .02
❑ 317 Rick Rhoden .05 .02
❑ 318 Tom Henke .05 .02
❑ 319 Mike Macfarlane RC* .05 .02
❑ 320 Dan Plesac .05 .02
❑ 321 Calvin Schiraldi .05 .02
❑ 322 Stan Javier .05 .02
❑ 323 Devon White .10 .05
❑ 324 Scott Bradley .05 .02
❑ 325 Bruce Hurst .05 .02
❑ 326 Manny Lee .05 .02
❑ 327 Rick Aguilera .10 .05
❑ 328 Bruce Ruffin .05 .02
❑ 329 Ed Whitson .05 .02
❑ 330 Bo Jackson .15 .07
❑ 331 Ivan Calderon .05 .02
❑ 332 Mickey Hatcher .05 .02
❑ 333 Barry Jones .05 .02
❑ 334 Ron Hassey .05 .02
❑ 335 Bill Wegman .05 .02
❑ 336 Damon Berryhill .05 .02
❑ 337 Steve Ontiveros .05 .02
❑ 338 Dan Pasqua .05 .02
❑ 339 Bill Pecota .05 .02
❑ 340 Greg Cadaret .05 .02
❑ 341 Scott Bankhead .05 .02
❑ 342 Ron Guidry .10 .05
❑ 343 Danny Heep .05 .02
❑ 344 Bob Brower .05 .02
❑ 345 Rich Gedman .05 .02
❑ 346 Nelson Santovenia .05 .02
❑ 347 George Bell .05 .02
❑ 348 Ted Power .05 .02
❑ 349 Mark Grant .05 .02
❑ 350 Roger Clemens COR .40 .18
(78 career wins)
❑ 350A Roger Clemens ERR 1.00 .45
(778 career wins)
❑ 351 Bill Long .05 .02
❑ 352 Jay Bell .15 .07
❑ 353 Steve Balboni .05 .02
❑ 354 Bob Kipper .05 .02
❑ 355 Steve Jeltz .05 .02
❑ 356 Jesse Orosco .05 .02
❑ 357 Bob Dernier .05 .02
❑ 358 Mickey Tettleton .05 .02
❑ 359 Duane Ward .05 .02
❑ 360 Darrin Jackson .05 .02
❑ 361 Rey Quinones .05 .02
❑ 362 Mark Grace .20 .09
❑ 363 Steve Lake .05 .02
❑ 364 Pat Perry .05 .02
❑ 365 Terry Steinbach .10 .05
❑ 366 Alan Ashby .05 .02
❑ 367 Jeff Montgomery .10 .05
❑ 368 Steve Buechele .05 .02
❑ 369 Chris Brown .05 .02
❑ 370 Orel Hershiser .10 .05
❑ 371 Todd Benzinger .05 .02
❑ 372 Ron Gant .10 .05
❑ 373 Paul Assenmacher .05 .02
❑ 374 Joey Meyer .05 .02
❑ 375 Neil Allen .05 .02
❑ 376 Mike Davis .05 .02
❑ 377 Jeff Parrett .05 .02
❑ 378 Jay Howell .05 .02
❑ 379 Rafael Belliard .05 .02
❑ 380 Luis Polonia UER .05 .02
(2 triples in '87;
should be 10)
❑ 381 Keith Atherton .05 .02
❑ 382 Kent Hrbek .10 .05
❑ 383 Bob Stanley .05 .02
❑ 384 Dave LaPoint .05 .02
❑ 385 Rance Mulliniks .05 .02
❑ 386 Melido Perez .05 .02
❑ 387 Doug Jones .05 .02
❑ 388 Steve Lyons .05 .02
❑ 389 Alejandro Pena .05 .02
❑ 390 Frank White .10 .05
❑ 391 Pat Tabler .05 .02
❑ 392 Eric Plunk .05 .02
❑ 393 Mike Maddux .05 .02
❑ 394 Allan Anderson .05 .02
❑ 395 Bob Brenly .05 .02
❑ 396 Rick Cerone .05 .02
❑ 397 Scott Terry .05 .02
❑ 398 Mike Jackson .05 .02
❑ 399 Bobby Thigpen UER .05 .02
(Bio says 37 saves in
'88; should be 34)
❑ 400 Don Sutton .20 .09
❑ 401 Cecil Espy .05 .02
❑ 402 Junior Ortiz .05 .02
❑ 403 Mike Smithson .05 .02
❑ 404 Bud Black .05 .02
❑ 405 Tom Foley .05 .02
❑ 406 Andres Thomas .05 .02
❑ 407 Rick Sutcliffe .10 .05
❑ 408 Brian Harper .05 .02
❑ 409 John Smiley .05 .02
❑ 410 Juan Nieves .05 .02
❑ 411 Shawn Abner .05 .02
❑ 412 Wes Gardner .05 .02
❑ 413 Darren Daulton .10 .05
❑ 414 Juan Berenguer .05 .02
❑ 415 Charles Hudson .05 .02
❑ 416 Rick Honeycutt .05 .02
❑ 417 Greg Booker .05 .02
❑ 418 Tim Belcher .05 .02
❑ 419 Don August .05 .02
❑ 420 Dale Mohorcic .05 .02
❑ 421 Steve Lombardozzi .05 .02
❑ 422 Atlee Hammaker .05 .02
❑ 423 Jerry Don Gleaton .05 .02
❑ 424 Scott Bailes .05 .02
❑ 425 Bruce Sutter .05 .02
❑ 426 Randy Ready .05 .02
❑ 427 Jerry Reed .05 .02
❑ 428 Bryn Smith .05 .02
❑ 429 Tim Leary .05 .02
❑ 430 Mark Clear .05 .02
❑ 431 Terry Leach .05 .02
❑ 432 John Moses .05 .02
❑ 433 Ozzie Guillen .05 .02
❑ 434 Gene Nelson .05 .02
❑ 435 Gary Ward .05 .02
❑ 436 Luis Aguayo .05 .02
❑ 437 Fernando Valenzuela .10 .05
❑ 438 Jeff Russell UER .05 .02
(Saves total does
not add up correctly)
❑ 439 Cecilio Guante .05 .02
❑ 440 Don Robinson .05 .02
❑ 441 Rick Anderson .05 .02
❑ 442 Tom Glavine .20 .09
❑ 443 Daryl Boston .05 .02
❑ 444 Joe Price .05 .02
❑ 445 Stewart Cliburn .05 .02
❑ 446 Manny Trillo .05 .02
❑ 447 Joel Skinner .05 .02
❑ 448 Charlie Puleo .05 .02
❑ 449 Carlton Fisk .20 .09
❑ 450 Will Clark .20 .09
❑ 451 Otis Nixon .05 .02
❑ 452 Rick Schu .05 .02

❑ 453 Todd Stottlemyre UER .. .15 .07
(ML Batting Record)
❑ 454 Tim Birtsas .05 .02
❑ 455 Dave Gallagher .05 .02
❑ 456 Barry Lyons .05 .02
❑ 457 Fred Manrique .05 .02
❑ 458 Ernest Riles .05 .02
❑ 459 Doug Jennings .05 .02
❑ 460 Joe Magrane .05 .02
❑ 461 Jamie Quirk .05 .02
❑ 462 Jack Armstrong RC* .05 .02
❑ 463 Bobby Witt .05 .02
❑ 464 Keith A. Miller .05 .02
❑ 465 Todd Burns .05 .02
❑ 466 John Dopson .05 .02
❑ 467 Rich Yett .05 .02
❑ 468 Craig Reynolds .05 .02
❑ 469 Dave Bergman .05 .02
❑ 470 Rex Hudler .05 .02
❑ 471 Eric King .05 .02
❑ 472 Joaquin Andujar .05 .02
❑ 473 Sil Campusano .05 .02
❑ 474 Terry Mulholland .05 .02
❑ 475 Mike Flanagan .05 .02
❑ 476 Greg A. Harris .05 .02
❑ 477 Tommy John .10 .05
❑ 478 Dave Anderson .05 .02
❑ 479 Fred Toliver .05 .02
❑ 480 Jimmy Key .10 .05
❑ 481 Donell Nixon .05 .02
❑ 482 Mark Portugal .05 .02
❑ 483 Tom Pagnozzi .05 .02
❑ 484 Jeff Kunkel .05 .02
❑ 485 Frank Williams .05 .02
❑ 486 Jody Reed .05 .02
❑ 487 Roberto Kelly .10 .05
❑ 488 Shawn Hillegas UER .05 .02
(165 innings in '87;
should be 165.2)
❑ 489 Jerry Reuss .05 .02
❑ 490 Mark Davis .05 .02
❑ 491 Jeff Sellers .05 .02
❑ 492 Zane Smith .05 .02
❑ 493 Al Newman .05 .02
❑ 494 Mike Young .05 .02
❑ 495 Larry Parrish .05 .02
❑ 496 Herm Winningham .05 .02
❑ 497 Carmen Castillo .05 .02
❑ 498 Joe Hesketh .05 .02
❑ 499 Darrell Miller .05 .02
❑ 500 Mike LaCoss .05 .02
❑ 501 Charlie Lea .05 .02
❑ 502 Bruce Benedict .05 .02
❑ 503 Chuck Finley .10 .05
❑ 504 Brad Wellman .05 .02
❑ 505 Tim Crews .05 .02
❑ 506 Ken Gerhart .05 .02
❑ 507A Brian Holton ERR .05 .02
(Born 1/25/65 Denver;
should be 11/29/59
in McKeesport)
❑ 507B Brian Holton COR 2.00 .90
❑ 508 Dennis Lamp .05 .02
❑ 509 Bobby Meacham UER .05 .02
('84 games 099)
❑ 510 Tracy Jones .05 .02
❑ 511 Mike R. Fitzgerald .05 .02
❑ 512 Jeff Bittiger .05 .02
❑ 513 Tim Flannery .05 .02
❑ 514 Ray Hayward .05 .02
❑ 515 Dave Leiper .05 .02
❑ 516 Rod Scurry .05 .02
❑ 517 Carmelo Martinez .05 .02
❑ 518 Curtis Wilkerson .05 .02
❑ 519 Stan Jefferson .05 .02
❑ 520 Dan Quisenberry .05 .02
❑ 521 Lloyd McClendon .05 .02
❑ 522 Steve Trout .05 .02
❑ 523 Larry Andersen .05 .02
❑ 524 Don Aase .05 .02
❑ 525 Bob Forsch .05 .02
❑ 526 Geno Petralli .05 .02
❑ 527 Angel Salazar .05 .02
❑ 528 Mike Schooler .05 .02
❑ 529 Jose Oquendo .05 .02
❑ 530 Jay Buhner UER .10 .05
(Wearing 43 on front,
listed as 34 on back)
❑ 531 Tom Bolton .05 .02
❑ 532 Al Nipper .05 .02
❑ 533 Dave Henderson .05 .02
❑ 534 John Costello .05 .02
❑ 535 Donnie Moore .05 .02
❑ 536 Mike Laga .05 .02
❑ 537 Mike Gallego .05 .02
❑ 538 Jim Clancy .05 .02
❑ 539 Joel Youngblood .05 .02
❑ 540 Rick Leach .05 .02
❑ 541 Kevin Romine .05 .02
❑ 542 Mark Salas .05 .02
❑ 543 Greg Minton .05 .02
❑ 544 Dave Palmer .05 .02
❑ 545 Dwayne Murphy UER .05 .02
(Game-sinning)
❑ 546 Jim Deshaies .05 .02
❑ 547 Don Gordon .05 .02
❑ 548 Ricky Jordan RC* .10 .05
❑ 549 Mike Boddicker .05 .02
❑ 550 Mike Scott .05 .02
❑ 551 Jeff Ballard .05 .02
❑ 552A Jose Rijo ERR .20 .09
(Uniform listed as
27 on back)
❑ 552B Jose Rijo COR .20 .09
(Uniform listed as
24 on back)
❑ 553 Danny Darwin .05 .02
❑ 554 Tom Browning .05 .02
❑ 555 Danny Jackson .05 .02
❑ 556 Rick Dempsey .05 .02
❑ 557 Jeffrey Leonard .05 .02
❑ 558 Jeff Musselman .05 .02
❑ 559 Ron Robinson .05 .02
❑ 560 John Tudor .05 .02
❑ 561 Don Slaught UER .05 .02
(237 games in 1987)
❑ 562 Dennis Rasmussen .05 .02
❑ 563 Brady Anderson RC .40 .18
❑ 564 Pedro Guerrero .05 .02
❑ 565 Paul Molitor .20 .09
❑ 566 Terry Clark .05 .02
❑ 567 Terry Puhl .05 .02
❑ 568 Mike Campbell .05 .02
❑ 569 Paul Mirabella .05 .02
❑ 570 Jeff Hamilton .05 .02
❑ 571 Oswald Peraza .05 .02
❑ 572 Bob McClure .05 .02
❑ 573 Jose Bautista .05 .02
❑ 574 Alex Trevino .05 .02
❑ 575 John Franco .10 .05
❑ 576 Mark Parent .05 .02
❑ 577 Nelson Liriano .05 .02
❑ 578 Steve Shields .05 .02
❑ 579 Odell Jones .05 .02
❑ 580 Al Leiter .20 .09
❑ 581 Dave Stapleton .05 .02
❑ 582 World Series '88 .10 .05
Orel Hershiser
Jose Canseco
Kirk Gibson
Dave Stewart
❑ 583 Donnie Hill .05 .02
❑ 584 Chuck Jackson .05 .02
❑ 585 Rene Gonzales .05 .02
❑ 586 Tracy Woodson .05 .02
❑ 587 Jim Adduci .05 .02
❑ 588 Mario Soto .05 .02
❑ 589 Jeff Blauser .10 .05
❑ 590 Jim Traber .05 .02
❑ 591 Jon Perlman .05 .02
❑ 592 Mark Williamson .05 .02
❑ 593 Dave Meads .05 .02
❑ 594 Jim Eisenreich .05 .02
❑ 595A Paul Gibson P1 1.00 .45
❑ 595B Paul Gibson P2 .05 .02
(Airbrushed leg on
player in background)
❑ 596 Mike Birkbeck .05 .02
❑ 597 Terry Francona .10 .05
❑ 598 Paul Zuvella .05 .02
❑ 599 Franklin Stubbs .05 .02
❑ 600 Gregg Jefferies .10 .05
❑ 601 John Cangelosi .05 .02
❑ 602 Mike Sharperson .05 .02
❑ 603 Mike Diaz .05 .02
❑ 604 Gary Varsho .05 .02
❑ 605 Terry Blocker .05 .02
❑ 606 Charlie O'Brien .05 .02
❑ 607 Jim Eppard .05 .02
❑ 608 John Davis .05 .02
❑ 609 Ken Griffey Sr. .10 .05
❑ 610 Buddy Bell .10 .05
❑ 611 Ted Simmons UER .10 .05
('78 stats Cardinal)
❑ 612 Matt Williams .15 .07
❑ 613 Danny Cox .05 .02
❑ 614 Al Pedrique .05 .02
❑ 615 Ron Oester .05 .02
❑ 616 John Smoltz RC .40 .18
❑ 617 Bob Melvin .05 .02
❑ 618 Rob Dibble RC* .10 .05
❑ 619 Kirt Manwaring .05 .02
❑ 620 Felix Fermin .05 .02
❑ 621 Doug Dascenzo .05 .02
❑ 622 Bill Brennan .05 .02
❑ 623 Carlos Quintana RC .05 .02
❑ 624 Mike Harkey RC UER .05 .02
(13 and 31 walks
in '88; should
be 35 and 33)
❑ 625 Gary Sheffield RC 1.50 .70
❑ 626 Tom Prince .05 .02
❑ 627 Steve Searcy .05 .02
❑ 628 Charlie Hayes RC .20 .09
(Listed as outfielder)
❑ 629 Felix Jose RC UER .05 .02
(Modesto misspelled
as Modesta)
❑ 630 Sandy Alomar Jr. RC .25 .11
(Inconsistent design;
portrait on front)
❑ 631 Derek Lilliquist RC .05 .02
❑ 632 Geronimo Berroa .05 .02
❑ 633 Luis Medina .05 .02
❑ 634 Tom Gordon RC UER .20 .09
(Height 6'0")
❑ 635 Ramon Martinez RC .25 .11
❑ 636 Craig Worthington .05 .02
❑ 637 Edgar Martinez .15 .07
❑ 638 Chad Kreuter RC .05 .02
❑ 639 Ron Jones .05 .02
❑ 640 Van Snider .05 .02
❑ 641 Lance Blankenship RC .. .05 .02
❑ 642 Dwight Smith RC UER .. .10 .05
(10 HR's in '87;
should be 18)
❑ 643 Cameron Drew .05 .02
❑ 644 Jerald Clark RC .05 .02
❑ 645 Randy Johnson RC 2.00 .90
❑ 646 Norm Charlton RC .10 .05
❑ 647 Todd Frohwirth UER .05 .02
(Southpaw on back)
❑ 648 Luis De Los Santos .05 .02
❑ 649 Tim Jones .05 .02
❑ 650 Dave West RC UER .05 .02
(ML hits 3;
should be 6)
❑ 651 Bob Milacki .05 .02
❑ 652 Wrigley Field HL .10 .05
(Let There Be Lights)
❑ 653 Orel Hershiser HL .10 .05
(The Streak)
❑ 654A Wade Boggs HL ERR 1.50 .70
(Wade Whacks 'Em)
("seaason" on back)
❑ 654B Wade Boggs HL COR.. .10 .05
(Wade Whacks 'Em)
❑ 655 Jose Canseco HL .10 .05
(One of a Kind)
❑ 656 Doug Jones HL .05 .02
(Doug Sets Saves)
❑ 657 Rickey Henderson HL .10 .05
(Rickey Rocks 'Em)
❑ 658 Tom Browning HL .05 .02
(Tom Perfect Pitches)
❑ 659 Mike Greenwell HL .05 .02
(Greenwell Gamers)
❑ 660 Boston Red Sox HL .05 .02

(Joe Morgan MG, Sox Sock 'Em)

## 1989 Score Rookie/Traded

| | MINT | NRMT |
|---|---|---|
| COMP.FACT.SET (110) | 30.00 | 13.50 |
| ❑ 1T Rafael Palmeiro | .50 | .23 |
| ❑ 2T Nolan Ryan | 4.00 | 1.80 |
| ❑ 3T Jack Clark | .10 | .05 |
| ❑ 4T Dave LaPoint | .10 | .05 |
| ❑ 5T Mike Moore | .10 | .05 |
| ❑ 6T Pete O'Brien | .10 | .05 |
| ❑ 7T Jeffrey Leonard | .10 | .05 |
| ❑ 8T Rob Murphy | .10 | .05 |
| ❑ 9T Tom Herr | .10 | .05 |
| ❑ 10T Claudell Washington | .10 | .05 |
| ❑ 11T Mike Pagliarulo | .10 | .05 |
| ❑ 12T Steve Lake | .10 | .05 |
| ❑ 13T Spike Owen | .10 | .05 |
| ❑ 14T Andy Hawkins | .10 | .05 |
| ❑ 15T Todd Benzinger | .10 | .05 |
| ❑ 16T Mookie Wilson | .20 | .09 |
| ❑ 17T Bert Blyleven | .20 | .09 |
| ❑ 18T Jeff Treadway | .10 | .05 |
| ❑ 19T Bruce Hurst | .10 | .05 |
| ❑ 20T Steve Sax | .10 | .05 |
| ❑ 21T Juan Samuel | .10 | .05 |
| ❑ 22T Jesse Barfield | .10 | .05 |
| ❑ 23T Carmen Castillo | .10 | .05 |
| ❑ 24T Terry Leach | .10 | .05 |
| ❑ 25T Mark Langston | .10 | .05 |
| ❑ 26T Eric King | .10 | .05 |
| ❑ 27T Steve Balboni | .10 | .05 |
| ❑ 28T Len Dykstra | .20 | .09 |
| ❑ 29T Keith Moreland | .10 | .05 |
| ❑ 30T Terry Kennedy | .10 | .05 |
| ❑ 31T Eddie Murray | .40 | .18 |
| ❑ 32T Mitch Williams | .10 | .05 |
| ❑ 33T Jeff Parrett | .10 | .05 |
| ❑ 34T Wally Backman | .10 | .05 |
| ❑ 35T Julio Franco | .10 | .05 |
| ❑ 36T Lance Parrish | .10 | .05 |
| ❑ 37T Nick Esasky | .10 | .05 |
| ❑ 38T Luis Polonia | .10 | .05 |
| ❑ 39T Kevin Gross | .10 | .05 |
| ❑ 40T John Dopson | .10 | .05 |
| ❑ 41T Willie Randolph | .20 | .09 |
| ❑ 42T Jim Clancy | .10 | .05 |
| ❑ 43T Tracy Jones | .10 | .05 |
| ❑ 44T Phil Bradley | .10 | .05 |
| ❑ 45T Milt Thompson | .10 | .05 |
| ❑ 46T Chris James | .10 | .05 |
| ❑ 47T Scott Fletcher | .10 | .05 |
| ❑ 48T Kal Daniels | .10 | .05 |
| ❑ 49T Steve Bedrosian | .10 | .05 |
| ❑ 50T Rickey Henderson | .50 | .23 |
| ❑ 51T Dion James | .10 | .05 |
| ❑ 52T Tim Leary | .10 | .05 |
| ❑ 53T Roger McDowell | .10 | .05 |
| ❑ 54T Mel Hall | .10 | .05 |
| ❑ 55T Dickie Thon | .10 | .05 |
| ❑ 56T Zane Smith | .10 | .05 |
| ❑ 57T Danny Heep | .10 | .05 |
| ❑ 58T Bob McClure | .10 | .05 |
| ❑ 59T Brian Holton | .10 | .05 |
| ❑ 60T Randy Ready | .10 | .05 |
| ❑ 61T Bob Melvin | .10 | .05 |
| ❑ 62T Harold Baines | .20 | .09 |
| ❑ 63T Lance McCullers | .10 | .05 |
| ❑ 64T Jody Davis | .10 | .05 |
| ❑ 65T Darrell Evans | .20 | .09 |
| ❑ 66T Joel Youngblood | .10 | .05 |
| ❑ 67T Frank Viola | .10 | .05 |
| ❑ 68T Mike Aldrete | .10 | .05 |
| ❑ 69T Greg Cadaret | .10 | .05 |
| ❑ 70T John Kruk | .20 | .09 |
| ❑ 71T Pat Sheridan | .10 | .05 |
| ❑ 72T Oddibe McDowell | .10 | .05 |
| ❑ 73T Tom Brookens | .10 | .05 |
| ❑ 74T Bob Boone | .20 | .09 |
| ❑ 75T Walt Terrell | .10 | .05 |
| ❑ 76T Joel Skinner | .10 | .05 |
| ❑ 77T Randy Johnson | 2.50 | 1.10 |
| ❑ 78T Felix Fermin | .10 | .05 |
| ❑ 79T Rick Mahler | .10 | .05 |
| ❑ 80T Richard Dotson | .10 | .05 |
| ❑ 81T Cris Carpenter RC* | .10 | .05 |
| ❑ 82T Bill Spiers RC | .10 | .05 |
| ❑ 83T Junior Felix RC | .10 | .05 |
| ❑ 84T Joe Girardi RC | .40 | .18 |
| ❑ 85T Jerome Walton | .40 | .18 |
| ❑ 86T Greg Litton | .10 | .05 |
| ❑ 87T Greg W.Harris RC | .10 | .05 |
| ❑ 88T Jim Abbott RC* | .40 | .18 |
| ❑ 89T Kevin Brown | 1.00 | .45 |
| ❑ 90T John Wetteland RC | .50 | .23 |
| ❑ 91T Gary Wayne | .10 | .05 |
| ❑ 92T Rich Monteleone | .10 | .05 |
| ❑ 93T Bob Geren | .10 | .05 |
| ❑ 94T Clay Parker | .10 | .05 |
| ❑ 95T Steve Finley RC | 1.25 | .55 |
| ❑ 96T Gregg Olson RC | .40 | .18 |
| ❑ 97T Ken Patterson | .10 | .05 |
| ❑ 98T Ken Hill RC | .40 | .18 |
| ❑ 99T Scott Scudder RC | .10 | .05 |
| ❑ 100T Ken Griffey Jr. RC ! | 20.00 | 9.00 |
| ❑ 101T Jeff Brantley RC | .30 | .14 |
| ❑ 102T Donn Pall | .10 | .05 |
| ❑ 103T Carlos Martinez RC | .10 | .05 |
| ❑ 104T Joe Oliver RC | .20 | .09 |
| ❑ 105T Omar Vizquel RC | 1.25 | .55 |
| ❑ 106T Joey Belle RC | 5.00 | 2.20 |
| ❑ 107T Kenny Rogers RC | .40 | .18 |
| ❑ 108T Mark Carreon | .10 | .05 |
| ❑ 109T Rolando Roomes | .10 | .05 |
| ❑ 110T Pete Harnisch RC | .50 | .23 |

## 1990 Score

| | MINT | NRMT |
|---|---|---|
| COMPLETE SET (704) | 12.00 | 5.50 |
| COMP.RETAIL SET (704) | 15.00 | 6.75 |
| COMP.HOBBY SET (714) | 20.00 | 9.00 |
| ❑ 1 Don Mattingly | .50 | .23 |
| ❑ 2 Cal Ripken | .75 | .35 |
| ❑ 3 Dwight Evans | .10 | .05 |
| ❑ 4 Barry Bonds | .30 | .14 |
| ❑ 5 Kevin McReynolds | .05 | .02 |
| ❑ 6 Ozzie Guillen | .05 | .02 |
| ❑ 7 Terry Kennedy | .05 | .02 |
| ❑ 8 Bryan Harvey | .05 | .02 |
| ❑ 9 Alan Trammell | .15 | .07 |
| ❑ 10 Cory Snyder | .05 | .02 |
| ❑ 11 Jody Reed | .05 | .02 |
| ❑ 12 Roberto Alomar | .20 | .09 |
| ❑ 13 Pedro Guerrero | .05 | .02 |
| ❑ 14 Gary Redus | .05 | .02 |
| ❑ 15 Marty Barrett | .05 | .02 |
| ❑ 16 Ricky Jordan | .05 | .02 |
| ❑ 17 Joe Magrane | .05 | .02 |
| ❑ 18 Sid Fernandez | .05 | .02 |
| ❑ 19 Richard Dotson | .05 | .02 |
| ❑ 20 Jack Clark | .10 | .05 |
| ❑ 21 Bob Walk | .05 | .02 |
| ❑ 22 Ron Karkovice | .05 | .02 |
| ❑ 23 Lenny Harris | .05 | .02 |
| ❑ 24 Phil Bradley | .05 | .02 |
| ❑ 25 Andres Galarraga | .15 | .07 |
| ❑ 26 Brian Downing | .05 | .02 |
| ❑ 27 Dave Martinez | .05 | .02 |
| ❑ 28 Eric King | .05 | .02 |
| ❑ 29 Barry Lyons | .05 | .02 |
| ❑ 30 Dave Schmidt | .05 | .02 |
| ❑ 31 Mike Boddicker | .05 | .02 |
| ❑ 32 Tom Foley | .05 | .02 |
| ❑ 33 Brady Anderson | .20 | .09 |
| ❑ 34 Jim Presley | .05 | .02 |
| ❑ 35 Lance Parrish | .05 | .02 |
| ❑ 36 Von Hayes | .05 | .02 |
| ❑ 37 Lee Smith | .10 | .05 |
| ❑ 38 Herm Winningham | .05 | .02 |
| ❑ 39 Alejandro Pena | .05 | .02 |
| ❑ 40 Mike Scott | .05 | .02 |
| ❑ 41 Joe Orsulak | .05 | .02 |
| ❑ 42 Rafael Ramirez | .05 | .02 |
| ❑ 43 Gerald Young | .05 | .02 |
| ❑ 44 Dick Schofield | .05 | .02 |
| ❑ 45 Dave Smith | .05 | .02 |
| ❑ 46 Dave Magadan | .05 | .02 |
| ❑ 47 Dennis Martinez | .10 | .05 |
| ❑ 48 Greg Minton | .05 | .02 |
| ❑ 49 Milt Thompson | .05 | .02 |
| ❑ 50 Orel Hershiser | .10 | .05 |
| ❑ 51 Bip Roberts | .05 | .02 |
| ❑ 52 Jerry Browne | .05 | .02 |
| ❑ 53 Bob Ojeda | .05 | .02 |
| ❑ 54 Fernando Valenzuela | .10 | .05 |
| ❑ 55 Matt Nokes | .05 | .02 |
| ❑ 56 Brook Jacoby | .05 | .02 |
| ❑ 57 Frank Tanana | .05 | .02 |
| ❑ 58 Scott Fletcher | .05 | .02 |
| ❑ 59 Ron Oester | .05 | .02 |
| ❑ 60 Bob Boone | .10 | .05 |
| ❑ 61 Dan Gladden | .05 | .02 |
| ❑ 62 Darnell Coles | .05 | .02 |
| ❑ 63 Gregg Olson | .10 | .05 |
| ❑ 64 Todd Burns | .05 | .02 |
| ❑ 65 Todd Benzinger | .05 | .02 |
| ❑ 66 Dale Murphy | .20 | .09 |
| ❑ 67 Mike Flanagan | .05 | .02 |
| ❑ 68 Jose Oquendo | .05 | .02 |
| ❑ 69 Cecil Espy | .05 | .02 |
| ❑ 70 Chris Sabo | .05 | .02 |
| ❑ 71 Shane Rawley | .05 | .02 |
| ❑ 72 Tom Brunansky | .05 | .02 |
| ❑ 73 Vance Law | .05 | .02 |
| ❑ 74 B.J. Surhoff | .10 | .05 |
| ❑ 75 Lou Whitaker | .10 | .05 |
| ❑ 76 Ken Caminiti UER (Euclid and Ohio should be Hanford and California) | .10 | .05 |
| ❑ 77 Nelson Liriano | .05 | .02 |
| ❑ 78 Tommy Gregg | .05 | .02 |
| ❑ 79 Don Slaught | .05 | .02 |
| ❑ 80 Eddie Murray | .20 | .09 |
| ❑ 81 Joe Boever | .05 | .02 |
| ❑ 82 Charlie Leibrandt | .05 | .02 |
| ❑ 83 Jose Lind | .05 | .02 |
| ❑ 84 Tony Phillips | .05 | .02 |
| ❑ 85 Mitch Webster | .05 | .02 |
| ❑ 86 Dan Plesac | .05 | .02 |
| ❑ 87 Rick Mahler | .05 | .02 |
| ❑ 88 Steve Lyons | .05 | .02 |
| ❑ 89 Tony Fernandez | .05 | .02 |
| ❑ 90 Ryne Sandberg | .25 | .11 |
| ❑ 91 Nick Esasky | .05 | .02 |
| ❑ 92 Luis Salazar | .05 | .02 |
| ❑ 93 Pete Incaviglia | .05 | .02 |

❑ 94 Ivan Calderon .05 .02
❑ 95 Jeff Treadway .05 .02
❑ 96 Kurt Stillwell .05 .02
❑ 97 Gary Sheffield .25 .11
❑ 98 Jeffrey Leonard .05 .02
❑ 99 Andres Thomas .05 .02
❑ 100 Roberto Kelly .05 .02
❑ 101 Alvaro Espinoza .05 .02
❑ 102 Greg Gagne .05 .02
❑ 103 John Farrell .05 .02
❑ 104 Willie Wilson .05 .02
❑ 105 Glenn Braggs .05 .02
❑ 106 Chet Lemon .05 .02
❑ 107A Jamie Moyer ERR .05 .02
(Scintilating)
❑ 107B Jamie Moyer COR .10 .05
(Scintillating)
❑ 108 Chuck Crim .05 .02
❑ 109 Dave Valle .05 .02
❑ 110 Walt Weiss .05 .02
❑ 111 Larry Sheets .05 .02
❑ 112 Don Robinson .05 .02
❑ 113 Danny Heep .05 .02
❑ 114 Carmelo Martinez .05 .02
❑ 115 Dave Gallagher .05 .02
❑ 116 Mike LaValliere .05 .02
❑ 117 Bob McClure .05 .02
❑ 118 Rene Gonzales .05 .02
❑ 119 Mark Parent .05 .02
❑ 120 Wally Joyner .10 .05
❑ 121 Mark Gubicza .05 .02
❑ 122 Tony Pena .05 .02
❑ 123 Carmen Castillo .05 .02
❑ 124 Howard Johnson .05 .02
❑ 125 Steve Sax .05 .02
❑ 126 Tim Belcher .05 .02
❑ 127 Tim Burke .05 .02
❑ 128 Al Newman .05 .02
❑ 129 Dennis Rasmussen .05 .02
❑ 130 Doug Jones .05 .02
❑ 131 Fred Lynn .05 .02
❑ 132 Jeff Hamilton .05 .02
❑ 133 German Gonzalez .05 .02
❑ 134 John Morris .05 .02
❑ 135 Dave Parker .10 .05
❑ 136 Gary Pettis .05 .02
❑ 137 Dennis Boyd .05 .02
❑ 138 Candy Maldonado .05 .02
❑ 139 Rick Cerone .05 .02
❑ 140 George Brett .40 .18
❑ 141 Dave Clark .05 .02
❑ 142 Dickie Thon .05 .02
❑ 143 Junior Ortiz .05 .02
❑ 144 Don August .05 .02
❑ 145 Gary Gaetti .10 .05
❑ 146 Kirt Manwaring .05 .02
❑ 147 Jeff Reed .05 .02
❑ 148 Jose Alvarez .05 .02
❑ 149 Mike Schooler .05 .02
❑ 150 Mark Grace .20 .09
❑ 151 Geronimo Berroa .05 .02
❑ 152 Barry Jones .05 .02
❑ 153 Geno Petralli .05 .02
❑ 154 Jim Deshaies .05 .02
❑ 155 Barry Larkin .20 .09
❑ 156 Alfredo Griffin .05 .02
❑ 157 Tom Henke .05 .02
❑ 158 Mike Jeffcoat .05 .02
❑ 159 Bob Welch .05 .02
❑ 160 Julio Franco .05 .02
❑ 161 Henry Cotto .05 .02
❑ 162 Terry Steinbach .05 .02
❑ 163 Damon Berryhill .05 .02
❑ 164 Tim Crews .05 .02
❑ 165 Tom Browning .05 .02
❑ 166 Fred Manrique .05 .02
❑ 167 Harold Reynolds .05 .02
❑ 168A Ron Hassey ERR .05 .02
(27 on back)
❑ 168B Ron Hassey COR .50 .23
(24 on back)
❑ 169 Shawon Dunston .05 .02
❑ 170 Bobby Bonilla .10 .05
❑ 171 Tommy Herr .05 .02
❑ 172 Mike Heath .05 .02
❑ 173 Rich Gedman .05 .02
❑ 174 Bill Ripken .05 .02
❑ 175 Pete O'Brien .05 .02
❑ 176A Lloyd McClendon ERR ..
(Uniform number on back listed as 1)
❑ 176B Lloyd McClendon COR .05 .02
(Uniform number on back listed as 10)
❑ 177 Brian Holton .05 .02
❑ 178 Jeff Blauser .05 .02
❑ 179 Jim Eisenreich .05 .02
❑ 180 Bert Blyleven .10 .05
❑ 181 Rob Murphy .05 .02
❑ 182 Bill Doran .05 .02
❑ 183 Curt Ford .05 .02
❑ 184 Mike Henneman .05 .02
❑ 185 Eric Davis .10 .05
❑ 186 Lance McCullers .05 .02
❑ 187 Steve Davis .05 .02
❑ 188 Bill Wegman .05 .02
❑ 189 Brian Harper .05 .02
❑ 190 Mike Moore .05 .02
❑ 191 Dale Mohorcic .05 .02
❑ 192 Tim Wallach .05 .02
❑ 193 Keith Hernandez .10 .05
❑ 194 Dave Righetti .05 .02
❑ 195A Bret Saberhagen ERR .10 .05
(Joke)
❑ 195B Bret Saberhagen COR .10 .05
(Joker)
❑ 196 Paul Kilgus .05 .02
❑ 197 Bud Black .05 .02
❑ 198 Juan Samuel .05 .02
❑ 199 Kevin Seitzer .05 .02
❑ 200 Darryl Strawberry .10 .05
❑ 201 Dave Stieb .10 .05
❑ 202 Charlie Hough .10 .05
❑ 203 Jack Morris .10 .05
❑ 204 Rance Mulliniks .05 .02
❑ 205 Alvin Davis .05 .02
❑ 206 Jack Howell .05 .02
❑ 207 Ken Patterson .05 .02
❑ 208 Terry Pendleton .10 .05
❑ 209 Craig Lefferts .05 .02
❑ 210 Kevin Brown UER .20 .09
(First mention of '89 Rangers should be '88)
❑ 211 Dan Petry .05 .02
❑ 212 Dave Leiper .05 .02
❑ 213 Daryl Boston .05 .02
❑ 214 Kevin Hickey .05 .02
❑ 215 Mike Krukow .05 .02
❑ 216 Terry Francona .10 .05
❑ 217 Kirk McCaskill .05 .02
❑ 218 Scott Bailes .05 .02
❑ 219 Bob Forsch .05 .02
❑ 220A Mike Aldrete ERR .05 .02
(25 on back)
❑ 220B Mike Aldrete COR .10 .05
(24 on back)
❑ 221 Steve Buechele .05 .02
❑ 222 Jesse Barfield .05 .02
❑ 223 Juan Berenguer .05 .02
❑ 224 Andy McGaffigan .05 .02
❑ 225 Pete Smith .05 .02
❑ 226 Mike Witt .05 .02
❑ 227 Jay Howell .05 .02
❑ 228 Scott Bradley .05 .02
❑ 229 Jerome Walton .05 .02
❑ 230 Greg Swindell .05 .02
❑ 231 Atlee Hammaker .05 .02
❑ 232A Mike Devereaux ERR .. .05 .02
(RF on front)
❑ 232B Mike Devereaux COR .. .50 .23
(CF on front)
❑ 233 Ken Hill .10 .05
❑ 234 Craig Worthington .05 .02
❑ 235 Scott Terry .05 .02
❑ 236 Brett Butler .10 .05
❑ 237 Doyle Alexander .05 .02
❑ 238 Dave Anderson .05 .02
❑ 239 Bob Milacki .05 .02
❑ 240 Dwight Smith .05 .02
❑ 241 Otis Nixon .05 .02
❑ 242 Pat Tabler .05 .02
❑ 243 Derek Lilliquist .05 .02
❑ 244 Danny Tartabull .05 .02
❑ 245 Wade Boggs .25 .11
❑ 246 Scott Garrelts .05 .02
(Should say Relief Pitcher on front)
❑ 247 Spike Owen .05 .02
❑ 248 Norm Charlton .05 .02
❑ 249 Gerald Perry .05 .02
❑ 250 Nolan Ryan 1.00 .45
❑ 251 Kevin Gross .05 .02
❑ 252 Randy Milligan .05 .02
❑ 253 Mike LaCoss .05 .02
❑ 254 Dave Bergman .05 .02
❑ 255 Tony Gwynn .40 .18
❑ 256 Felix Fermin .05 .02
❑ 257 Greg W. Harris .05 .02
❑ 258 Junior Felix .05 .02
❑ 259 Mark Davis .05 .02
❑ 260 Vince Coleman .05 .02
❑ 261 Paul Gibson .05 .02
❑ 262 Mitch Williams .05 .02
❑ 263 Jeff Russell .05 .02
❑ 264 Omar Vizquel .20 .09
❑ 265 Andre Dawson .15 .07
❑ 266 Storm Davis .05 .02
❑ 267 Guillermo Hernandez .05 .02
❑ 268 Mike Felder .05 .02
❑ 269 Tom Candiotti .05 .02
❑ 270 Bruce Hurst .05 .02
❑ 271 Fred McGriff .20 .09
❑ 272 Glenn Davis .05 .02
❑ 273 John Franco .10 .05
❑ 274 Rich Yett .05 .02
❑ 275 Craig Biggio .15 .07
❑ 276 Gene Larkin .05 .02
❑ 277 Rob Dibble .05 .02
❑ 278 Randy Bush .05 .02
❑ 279 Kevin Bass .05 .02
❑ 280A Bo Jackson ERR .20 .09
(Watham)
❑ 280B Bo Jackson COR .10 .05
(Wathan)
❑ 281 Wally Backman .05 .02
❑ 282 Larry Andersen .05 .02
❑ 283 Chris Bosio .05 .02
❑ 284 Juan Agosto .05 .02
❑ 285 Ozzie Smith .25 .11
❑ 286 George Bell .05 .02
❑ 287 Rex Hudler .05 .02
❑ 288 Pat Borders .05 .02
❑ 289 Danny Jackson .05 .02
❑ 290 Carlton Fisk .20 .09
❑ 291 Tracy Jones .05 .02
❑ 292 Allan Anderson .05 .02
❑ 293 Johnny Ray .05 .02
❑ 294 Lee Guetterman .05 .02
❑ 295 Paul O'Neill .10 .05
❑ 296 Carney Lansford .10 .05
❑ 297 Tom Brookens .05 .02
❑ 298 Claudell Washington .05 .02
❑ 299 Hubie Brooks .05 .02
❑ 300 Will Clark .20 .09
❑ 301 Kenny Rogers .10 .05
❑ 302 Darrell Evans .10 .05
❑ 303 Greg Briley .05 .02
❑ 304 Donn Pall .05 .02
❑ 305 Teddy Higuera .05 .02
❑ 306 Dan Pasqua .05 .02
❑ 307 Dave Winfield .20 .09
❑ 308 Dennis Powell .05 .02
❑ 309 Jose DeLeon .05 .02
❑ 310 Roger Clemens UER .40 .18
(Dominate, should say dominant)
❑ 311 Melido Perez .05 .02
❑ 312 Devon White .05 .02
❑ 313 Dwight Gooden .10 .05
❑ 314 Carlos Martinez .05 .02
❑ 315 Dennis Eckersley .15 .07
❑ 316 Clay Parker UER .05 .02
(Height 6'11")
❑ 317 Rick Honeycutt .05 .02
❑ 318 Tim Laudner .05 .02
❑ 319 Joe Carter .10 .05
❑ 320 Robin Yount .20 .09
❑ 321 Felix Jose .05 .02

| |  |  | | |
|---|---|---|---|---|
| ❑ | 322 | Mickey Tettleton | .05 | .02 |
| ❑ | 323 | Mike Gallego | .05 | .02 |
| ❑ | 324 | Edgar Martinez | .15 | .07 |
| ❑ | 325 | Dave Henderson | .05 | .02 |
| ❑ | 326 | Chili Davis | .10 | .05 |
| ❑ | 327 | Steve Balboni | .05 | .02 |
| ❑ | 328 | Jody Davis | .05 | .02 |
| ❑ | 329 | Shawn Hillegas | .05 | .02 |
| ❑ | 330 | Jim Abbott | .15 | .07 |
| ❑ | 331 | John Dopson | .05 | .02 |
| ❑ | 332 | Mark Williamson | .05 | .02 |
| ❑ | 333 | Jeff D. Robinson | .05 | .02 |
| ❑ | 334 | John Smiley | .05 | .02 |
| ❑ | 335 | Bobby Thigpen | .05 | .02 |
| ❑ | 336 | Garry Templeton | .05 | .02 |
| ❑ | 337 | Marvell Wynne | .05 | .02 |
| ❑ | 338A | Ken Griffey Sr. ERR (Uniform number on back listed as 25) | .10 | .05 |
| ❑ | 338B | Ken Griffey Sr. COR (Uniform number on back listed as 30) | .50 | .23 |
| ❑ | 339 | Steve Finley | .10 | .05 |
| ❑ | 340 | Ellis Burks | .15 | .07 |
| ❑ | 341 | Frank Williams | .05 | .02 |
| ❑ | 342 | Mike Morgan | .05 | .02 |
| ❑ | 343 | Kevin Mitchell | .05 | .02 |
| ❑ | 344 | Joel Youngblood | .05 | .02 |
| ❑ | 345 | Mike Greenwell | .05 | .02 |
| ❑ | 346 | Glenn Wilson | .05 | .02 |
| ❑ | 347 | John Costello | .05 | .02 |
| ❑ | 348 | Wes Gardner | .05 | .02 |
| ❑ | 349 | Jeff Ballard | .05 | .02 |
| ❑ | 350 | Mark Thurmond UER (ERA is 192; should be 1.92) | .05 | .02 |
| ❑ | 351 | Randy Myers | .10 | .05 |
| ❑ | 352 | Shawn Abner | .05 | .02 |
| ❑ | 353 | Jesse Orosco | .05 | .02 |
| ❑ | 354 | Greg Walker | .05 | .02 |
| ❑ | 355 | Pete Harnisch | .05 | .02 |
| ❑ | 356 | Steve Farr | .05 | .02 |
| ❑ | 357 | Dave LaPoint | .05 | .02 |
| ❑ | 358 | Willie Fraser | .05 | .02 |
| ❑ | 359 | Mickey Hatcher | .05 | .02 |
| ❑ | 360 | Rickey Henderson | .25 | .11 |
| ❑ | 361 | Mike Fitzgerald | .05 | .02 |
| ❑ | 362 | Bill Schroeder | .05 | .02 |
| ❑ | 363 | Mark Carreon | .05 | .02 |
| ❑ | 364 | Ron Jones | .05 | .02 |
| ❑ | 365 | Jeff Montgomery | .10 | .05 |
| ❑ | 366 | Bill Krueger | .05 | .02 |
| ❑ | 367 | John Cangelosi | .05 | .02 |
| ❑ | 368 | Jose Gonzalez | .05 | .02 |
| ❑ | 369 | Greg Hibbard RC | .05 | .02 |
| ❑ | 370 | John Smoltz | .10 | .05 |
| ❑ | 371 | Jeff Brantley | .05 | .02 |
| ❑ | 372 | Frank White | .10 | .05 |
| ❑ | 373 | Ed Whitson | .05 | 02 |
| ❑ | 374 | Willie McGee | .10 | .05 |
| ❑ | 375 | Jose Canseco | .25 | .11 |
| ❑ | 376 | Randy Ready | .05 | .02 |
| ❑ | 377 | Don Aase | .05 | .02 |
| ❑ | 378 | Tony Armas | .05 | .02 |
| ❑ | 379 | Steve Bedrosian | .05 | .02 |
| ❑ | 380 | Chuck Finley | .10 | .05 |
| ❑ | 381 | Kent Hrbek | .10 | .05 |
| ❑ | 382 | Jim Gantner | .05 | .02 |
| ❑ | 383 | Mel Hall | .05 | .02 |
| ❑ | 384 | Mike Marshall | .05 | .02 |
| ❑ | 385 | Mark McGwire | .75 | .35 |
| ❑ | 386 | Wayne Tolleson | .05 | .02 |
| ❑ | 387 | Brian Holman | .05 | .02 |
| ❑ | 388 | John Wetteland | .20 | .09 |
| ❑ | 389 | Darren Daulton | .10 | .05 |
| ❑ | 390 | Rob Deer | .05 | .02 |
| ❑ | 391 | John Moses | .05 | .02 |
| ❑ | 392 | Todd Worrell | .05 | .02 |
| ❑ | 393 | Chuck Cary | .05 | .02 |
| ❑ | 394 | Stan Javier | .05 | .02 |
| ❑ | 395 | Willie Randolph | .10 | .05 |
| ❑ | 396 | Bill Buckner | .05 | .02 |
| ❑ | 397 | Robby Thompson | .05 | .02 |
| ❑ | 398 | Mike Scioscia | .05 | .02 |
| ❑ | 399 | Lonnie Smith | .05 | .02 |
| ❑ | 400 | Kirby Puckett | .50 | .23 |
| ❑ | 401 | Mark Langston | .05 | .02 |
| ❑ | 402 | Danny Darwin | .05 | .02 |
| ❑ | 403 | Greg Maddux | .50 | .23 |
| ❑ | 404 | Lloyd Moseby | .05 | .02 |
| ❑ | 405 | Rafael Palmeiro | .20 | .09 |
| ❑ | 406 | Chad Kreuter | .05 | .02 |
| ❑ | 407 | Jimmy Key | .10 | .05 |
| ❑ | 408 | Tim Birtsas | .05 | .02 |
| ❑ | 409 | Tim Raines | .10 | .05 |
| ❑ | 410 | Dave Stewart | .10 | .05 |
| ❑ | 411 | Eric Yelding | .05 | .02 |
| ❑ | 412 | Kent Anderson | .05 | .02 |
| ❑ | 413 | Les Lancaster | .05 | .02 |
| ❑ | 414 | Rick Dempsey | .05 | .02 |
| ❑ | 415 | Randy Johnson | .40 | .18 |
| ❑ | 416 | Gary Carter | .15 | .07 |
| ❑ | 417 | Rolando Roomes | .05 | .02 |
| ❑ | 418 | Dan Schatzeder | .05 | .02 |
| ❑ | 419 | Bryn Smith | .05 | .02 |
| ❑ | 420 | Ruben Sierra | .05 | .02 |
| ❑ | 421 | Steve Jeltz | .05 | .02 |
| ❑ | 422 | Ken Oberkfell | .05 | .02 |
| ❑ | 423 | Sid Bream | .05 | .02 |
| ❑ | 424 | Jim Clancy | .05 | .02 |
| ❑ | 425 | Kelly Gruber | .05 | .02 |
| ❑ | 426 | Rick Leach | .05 | .02 |
| ❑ | 427 | Len Dykstra | .10 | .05 |
| ❑ | 428 | Jeff Pico | .05 | .02 |
| ❑ | 429 | John Cerutti | .05 | .02 |
| ❑ | 430 | David Cone | .10 | .05 |
| ❑ | 431 | Jeff Kunkel | .05 | .02 |
| ❑ | 432 | Luis Aquino | .05 | .02 |
| ❑ | 433 | Ernie Whitt | .05 | .02 |
| ❑ | 434 | Bo Diaz | .05 | .02 |
| ❑ | 435 | Steve Lake | .05 | .02 |
| ❑ | 436 | Pat Perry | .05 | .02 |
| ❑ | 437 | Mike Davis | .05 | .02 |
| ❑ | 438 | Cecilio Guante | .05 | .02 |
| ❑ | 439 | Duane Ward | .05 | .02 |
| ❑ | 440 | Andy Van Slyke | .10 | .05 |
| ❑ | 441 | Gene Nelson | .05 | .02 |
| ❑ | 442 | Luis Polonia | .05 | .02 |
| ❑ | 443 | Kevin Elster | .05 | .02 |
| ❑ | 444 | Keith Moreland | .05 | .02 |
| ❑ | 445 | Roger McDowell | .05 | .02 |
| ❑ | 446 | Ron Darling | .05 | .02 |
| ❑ | 447 | Ernest Riles | .05 | .02 |
| ❑ | 448 | Mookie Wilson | .10 | .05 |
| ❑ | 449A | Billy Spiers ERR (No birth year) | .20 | .09 |
| ❑ | 449B | Billy Spiers COR (Born in 1966) | .05 | .02 |
| ❑ | 450 | Rick Sutcliffe | .10 | .05 |
| ❑ | 451 | Nelson Santovenia | .05 | .02 |
| ❑ | 452 | Andy Allanson | .05 | .02 |
| ❑ | 453 | Bob Melvin | .05 | .02 |
| ❑ | 454 | Benito Santiago | .05 | .02 |
| ❑ | 455 | Jose Uribe | .05 | .02 |
| ❑ | 456 | Bill Landrum | .05 | .02 |
| ❑ | 457 | Bobby Witt | .05 | .02 |
| ❑ | 458 | Kevin Romine | .05 | .02 |
| ❑ | 459 | Lee Mazzilli | .05 | .02 |
| ❑ | 460 | Paul Molitor | .20 | .09 |
| ❑ | 461 | Ramon Martinez | .05 | .02 |
| ❑ | 462 | Frank DiPino | .05 | .02 |
| ❑ | 463 | Walt Terrell | .05 | .02 |
| ❑ | 464 | Bob Geren | .05 | .02 |
| ❑ | 465 | Rick Reuschel | .05 | .02 |
| ❑ | 466 | Mark Grant | .05 | .02 |
| ❑ | 467 | John Kruk | .10 | .05 |
| ❑ | 468 | Gregg Jefferies | .10 | .05 |
| ❑ | 469 | R.J. Reynolds | .05 | .02 |
| ❑ | 470 | Harold Baines | .10 | .05 |
| ❑ | 471 | Dennis Lamp | .05 | .02 |
| ❑ | 472 | Tom Gordon | .10 | .05 |
| ❑ | 473 | Terry Puhl | .05 | .02 |
| ❑ | 474 | Curt Wilkerson | .05 | .02 |
| ❑ | 475 | Dan Quisenberry | .05 | .02 |
| ❑ | 476 | Oddibe McDowell | .05 | .02 |
| ❑ | 477A | Zane Smith ERR (Career ERA .393) | .05 | .02 |
| ❑ | 477B | Zane Smith COR (Career ERA 3.93) | .05 | .02 |
| ❑ | 478 | Franklin Stubbs | .05 | .02 |
| ❑ | 479 | Wallace Johnson | .05 | .02 |
| ❑ | 480 | Jay Tibbs | .05 | .02 |
| ❑ | 481 | Tom Glavine | .20 | .09 |
| ❑ | 482 | Manny Lee | .05 | .02 |
| ❑ | 483 | Joe Hesketh UER (Says Rookiess on back, should say Rookies) | .05 | .02 |
| ❑ | 484 | Mike Bielecki | .05 | .02 |
| ❑ | 485 | Greg Brock | .05 | .02 |
| ❑ | 486 | Pascual Perez | .05 | .02 |
| ❑ | 487 | Kirk Gibson | .10 | .05 |
| ❑ | 488 | Scott Sanderson | .05 | .02 |
| ❑ | 489 | Domingo Ramos | .05 | .02 |
| ❑ | 490 | Kal Daniels | .05 | .02 |
| ❑ | 491A | David Wells ERR (Reverse negative photo on card back) | .50 | .23 |
| ❑ | 491B | David Wells COR | .10 | .05 |
| ❑ | 492 | Jerry Reed | .05 | .02 |
| ❑ | 493 | Eric Show | .05 | .02 |
| ❑ | 494 | Mike Pagliarulo | .05 | .02 |
| ❑ | 495 | Ron Robinson | .05 | .02 |
| ❑ | 496 | Brad Komminsk | .05 | .02 |
| ❑ | 497 | Greg Litton | .05 | .02 |
| ❑ | 498 | Chris James | .05 | .02 |
| ❑ | 499 | Luis Quinones | .05 | .02 |
| ❑ | 500 | Frank Viola | .05 | .02 |
| ❑ | 501 | Tim Teufel UER (Twins '85, the s is lower case; should be upper case) | .05 | .02 |
| ❑ | 502 | Terry Leach | .05 | .02 |
| ❑ | 503 | Matt Williams UER (Wearing 10 on front; listed as 9 on back) | .15 | .07 |
| ❑ | 504 | Tim Leary | .05 | .02 |
| ❑ | 505 | Doug Drabek | .05 | .02 |
| ❑ | 506 | Mariano Duncan | .05 | .02 |
| ❑ | 507 | Charlie Hayes | .05 | .02 |
| ❑ | 508 | Joey Belle | .75 | .35 |
| ❑ | 509 | Pat Sheridan | .05 | .02 |
| ❑ | 510 | Mackey Sasser | .05 | .02 |
| ❑ | 511 | Jose Rijo | .05 | .02 |
| ❑ | 512 | Mike Smithson | .05 | .02 |
| ❑ | 513 | Gary Ward | .05 | .02 |
| ❑ | 514 | Dion James | .05 | .02 |
| ❑ | 515 | Jim Gott | .05 | .02 |
| ❑ | 516 | Drew Hall | .05 | .02 |
| ❑ | 517 | Doug Bair | .05 | .02 |
| ❑ | 518 | Scott Scudder | .05 | .02 |
| ❑ | 519 | Rick Aguilera | .10 | .05 |
| ❑ | 520 | Rafael Belliard | .05 | .02 |
| ❑ | 521 | Jay Buhner | .10 | .05 |
| ❑ | 522 | Jeff Reardon | .10 | .05 |
| ❑ | 523 | Steve Rosenberg | .05 | .02 |
| ❑ | 524 | Randy Velarde | .05 | .02 |
| ❑ | 525 | Jeff Musselman | .05 | .02 |
| ❑ | 526 | Bill Long | .05 | .02 |
| ❑ | 527 | Gary Wayne | .05 | .02 |
| ❑ | 528 | Dave Johnson (P) | .05 | .02 |
| ❑ | 529 | Ron Kittle | .05 | .02 |
| ❑ | 530 | Erik Hanson UER (5th line on back says seson; should say season) | .05 | .02 |
| ❑ | 531 | Steve Wilson | .05 | .02 |
| ❑ | 532 | Joey Meyer | .05 | .02 |
| ❑ | 533 | Curt Young | .05 | .02 |
| ❑ | 534 | Kelly Downs | .05 | .02 |
| ❑ | 535 | Joe Girardi | .15 | .07 |
| ❑ | 536 | Lance Blankenship | .05 | .02 |
| ❑ | 537 | Greg Mathews | .05 | .02 |
| ❑ | 538 | Donell Nixon | .05 | .02 |
| ❑ | 539 | Mark Knudson | .05 | .02 |
| ❑ | 540 | Jeff Wetherby | .05 | .02 |
| ❑ | 541 | Darrin Jackson | .05 | .02 |
| ❑ | 542 | Terry Mulholland | .05 | .02 |
| ❑ | 543 | Eric Hetzel | .05 | .02 |
| ❑ | 544 | Rick Reed RC | .25 | .11 |
| ❑ | 545 | Dennis Cook | .05 | .02 |
| ❑ | 546 | Mike Jackson | .05 | .02 |
| ❑ | 547 | Brian Fisher | .05 | .02 |
| ❑ | 548 | Gene Harris | .05 | .02 |
| ❑ | 549 | Jeff King | .05 | .02 |
| ❑ | 550 | Dave Dravecky | .20 | .09 |
| ❑ | 551 | Randy Kutcher | .05 | .02 |
| ❑ | 552 | Mark Portugal | .05 | .02 |
| ❑ | 553 | Jim Corsi | .05 | .02 |

- ❑ 554 Todd Stottlemyre .10 .05
- ❑ 555 Scott Bankhead .05 .02
- ❑ 556 Ken Dayley .05 .02
- ❑ 557 Rick Wrona .05 .02
- ❑ 558 Sammy Sosa RC 5.00 2.20
- ❑ 559 Keith Miller .05 .02
- ❑ 560 Ken Griffey Jr. 1.50 .70
- ❑ 561A Ryne Sandberg HL ERR 5.00 2.20 (Position on front listed as 3B)
- ❑ 561B Ryne Sandberg HL COR .20 .09
- ❑ 562 Billy Hatcher .05 .02
- ❑ 563 Jay Bell .10 .05
- ❑ 564 Jack Daugherty .05 .02
- ❑ 565 Rich Monteleone .05 .02
- ❑ 566 Bo Jackson AS-MVP .10 .05
- ❑ 567 Tony Fossas .05 .02
- ❑ 568 Roy Smith .05 .02
- ❑ 569 Jaime Navarro .05 .02
- ❑ 570 Lance Johnson .05 .02
- ❑ 571 Mike Dyer .05 .02
- ❑ 572 Kevin Ritz .05 .02
- ❑ 573 Dave West .05 .02
- ❑ 574 Gary Mielke .05 .02
- ❑ 575 Scott Lusader .05 .02
- ❑ 576 Joe Oliver .05 .02
- ❑ 577 Sandy Alomar Jr. .10 .05
- ❑ 578 Andy Benes UER .05 .02 (Extra comma between day and year)
- ❑ 579 Tim Jones .05 .02
- ❑ 580 Randy McCament .05 .02
- ❑ 581 Curt Schilling .10 .05
- ❑ 582 John Orton RC .05 .02
- ❑ 583A Milt Cuyler RC ERR ...... (998 games)
- ❑ 583B Milt Cuyler RC COR .05 .02 (98 games; the extra 9 was ghosted out and may still be visible)
- ❑ 584 Eric Anthony RC .05 .02
- ❑ 585 Greg Vaughn .25 .11
- ❑ 586 Deion Sanders .20 .09
- ❑ 587 Jose DeJesus .05 .02
- ❑ 588 Chip Hale .05 .02
- ❑ 589 John Olerud RC .50 .23
- ❑ 590 Steve Olin RC .10 .05
- ❑ 591 Marquis Grissom RC .25 .11
- ❑ 592 Moises Alou RC .40 .18
- ❑ 593 Mark Lemke .05 .02
- ❑ 594 Dean Palmer RC .40 .18
- ❑ 595 Robin Ventura .20 .09
- ❑ 596 Tino Martinez .25 .11
- ❑ 597 Mike Huff .05 .02
- ❑ 598 Scott Hemond RC .05 .02
- ❑ 599 Wally Whitehurst .05 .02
- ❑ 600 Todd Zeile .10 .05
- ❑ 601 Glenallen Hill .05 .02
- ❑ 602 Hal Morris .05 .02
- ❑ 603 Juan Bell .05 .02
- ❑ 604 Bobby Rose .05 .02
- ❑ 605 Matt Merullo .05 .02
- ❑ 606 Kevin Maas RC .10 .05
- ❑ 607 Randy Nosek .05 .02
- ❑ 608A Billy Bates .05 .02 (Text mentions 12 triples in tenth line)
- ❑ 608B Billy Bates .05 .02 (Text has no mention of triples)
- ❑ 609 Mike Stanton RC .05 .02
- ❑ 610 Mauro Gozzo .05 .02
- ❑ 611 Charles Nagy .05 .02
- ❑ 612 Scott Coolbaugh .05 .02
- ❑ 613 Jose Vizcaino RC .15 .07
- ❑ 614 Greg Smith .05 .02
- ❑ 615 Jeff Huson RC .05 .02
- ❑ 616 Mickey Weston .05 .02
- ❑ 617 John Pawlowski .05 .02
- ❑ 618A Joe Skalski ERR .05 .02 (27 on back)
- ❑ 618B Joe Skalski COR .50 .23 (67 on back)
- ❑ 619 Bernie Williams RC 1.50 .70
- ❑ 620 Shawn Holman .05 .02
- ❑ 621 Gary Eave .05 .02
- ❑ 622 Darrin Fletcher UER .10 .05 (Elmherst, should be Elmhurst)
- ❑ 623 Pat Combs .05 .02
- ❑ 624 Mike Blowers RC .10 .05
- ❑ 625 Kevin Appier .15 .07
- ❑ 626 Pat Austin .05 .02
- ❑ 627 Kelly Mann .05 .02
- ❑ 628 Matt Kinzer .05 .02
- ❑ 629 Chris Hammond RC .05 .02
- ❑ 630 Dean Wilkins .05 .02
- ❑ 631 Larry Walker RC UER .60 .25 (Uniform number 55 on front and 33 on back; home is Maple Ridge, not Maple River)
- ❑ 632 Blaine Beatty .05 .02
- ❑ 633A Tommy Barrett ERR .05 .02 (29 on back)
- ❑ 633B Tommy Barrett COR .50 .23 (14 on back)
- ❑ 634 Stan Belinda RC .05 .02
- ❑ 635 Mike (Tex) Smith .05 .02
- ❑ 636 Hensley Meulens .05 .02
- ❑ 637 Juan Gonzalez RC UER 1.00 .45 (Sarasots on back, should be Sarasota)
- ❑ 638 Lenny Webster RC .05 .02
- ❑ 639 Mark Gardner RC .05 .02
- ❑ 640 Tommy Greene RC .05 .02
- ❑ 641 Mike Hartley .05 .02
- ❑ 642 Phil Stephenson .05 .02
- ❑ 643 Kevin Mmahat .05 .02
- ❑ 644 Ed Whited .05 .02
- ❑ 645 Delino DeShields RC .20 .09
- ❑ 646 Kevin Blankenship .05 .02
- ❑ 647 Paul Sorrento RC .15 .07
- ❑ 648 Mike Roesler .05 .02
- ❑ 649 Jason Grimsley RC .05 .02
- ❑ 650 Dave Justice RC .75 .35
- ❑ 651 Scott Cooper RC .05 .02
- ❑ 652 Dave Eiland .05 .02
- ❑ 653 Mike Munoz .05 .02
- ❑ 654 Jeff Fischer .05 .02
- ❑ 655 Terry Jorgensen .05 .02
- ❑ 656 George Canale .05 .02
- ❑ 657 Brian DuBois UER .05 .02 (Misspelled Dubois on card)
- ❑ 658 Carlos Quintana .05 .02
- ❑ 659 Luis de los Santos .05 .02
- ❑ 660 Jerald Clark .05 .02
- ❑ 661 Donald Harris DC .05 .02
- ❑ 662 Paul Coleman DC RC .05 .02
- ❑ 663 Frank Thomas DC RC 2.50 1.10
- ❑ 664 Brent Mayne DC RC .05 .02
- ❑ 665 Eddie Zosky DC RC .05 .02
- ❑ 666 Steve Hosey DC RC .05 .02
- ❑ 667 Scott Bryant DC .05 .02
- ❑ 668 Tom Goodwin DC RC .20 .09
- ❑ 669 Cal Eldred DC RC .25 .11
- ❑ 670 Earl Cunningham DC RC .05 .02
- ❑ 671 Alan Zinter DC RC .05 .02
- ❑ 672 Chuck Knoblauch DC RC .50 .23
- ❑ 673 Kyle Abbott DC .05 .02
- ❑ 674 Roger Salkeld DC RC .05 .02
- ❑ 675 Maurice Vaughn DC RC .60 .25
- ❑ 676 Keith(Kiki) Jones DC .05 .02
- ❑ 677 Tyler Houston DC RC .15 .07
- ❑ 678 Jeff Jackson DC RC .05 .02
- ❑ 679 Greg Gohr DC RC .05 .02
- ❑ 680 Ben McDonald DC RC .10 .05
- ❑ 681 Greg Blosser DC RC .05 .02
- ❑ 682 Willie Greene RC DC UER .10 .05 (Name spelled as Green)
- ❑ 683A Wade Boggs DT ERR .10 .05 (Text says 215 hits in '89; should be 205)
- ❑ 683B Wade Boggs DT COR .10 .05 (Text says 205 hits in '89)
- ❑ 684 Will Clark DT .10 .05
- ❑ 685 Tony Gwynn DT UER .20 .09 (Text reads battling instead of batting)
- ❑ 686 Rickey Henderson DT .10 .05
- ❑ 687 Bo Jackson DT .10 .05
- ❑ 688 Mark Langston DT .05 .02
- ❑ 689 Barry Larkin DT .10 .05
- ❑ 690 Kirby Puckett DT .25 .11
- ❑ 691 Ryne Sandberg DT .20 .09
- ❑ 692 Mike Scott DT .05 .02
- ❑ 693A Terry Steinbach DT .05 .02 ERR (cathers)
- ❑ 693B Terry Steinbach DT .05 .02 COR (catchers)
- ❑ 694 Bobby Thigpen DT .05 .02
- ❑ 695 Mitch Williams DT .05 .02
- ❑ 696 Nolan Ryan HL .20 .09
- ❑ 697 Bo Jackson FB/BB .50 .23
- ❑ 698 Rickey Henderson .10 .05 ALCS-MVP
- ❑ 699 Will Clark .10 .05 NLCS-MVP
- ❑ 700 WS Games 1/2 .10 .05 (Dave Stewart Mike Moore)
- ❑ 701 Lights Out: .20 .09 Candlestick 5:04pm (10/17/89)
- ❑ 702 WS Game 3 .20 .09 Bashers Blast Giants (Carney Lansford, Rickey Henderson, Jose Canseco, Dave Henderson)
- ❑ 703 WS Game 4/Wrap-up .05 .02 A's Sweep Battle of of the Bay (A's Celebrate)
- ❑ 704 Wade Boggs HL .10 .05 Wade Raps 200

## 1990 Score Rookie/Traded

| | MINT | NRMT |
|---|---|---|
| COMP.FACT.SET (110) | 5.00 | 2.20 |
| ❑ 1T Dave Winfield | .20 | .09 |
| ❑ 2T Kevin Bass | .05 | .02 |
| ❑ 3T Nick Esasky | .05 | .02 |
| ❑ 4T Mitch Webster | .05 | .02 |
| ❑ 5T Pascual Perez | .05 | .02 |
| ❑ 6T Gary Pettis | .05 | .02 |
| ❑ 7T Tony Pena | .05 | .02 |
| ❑ 8T Candy Maldonado | .05 | .02 |
| ❑ 9T Cecil Fielder | .10 | .05 |
| ❑ 10T Carmelo Martinez | .05 | .02 |
| ❑ 11T Mark Langston | .05 | .02 |
| ❑ 12T Dave Parker | .10 | .05 |
| ❑ 13T Don Slaught | .05 | .02 |
| ❑ 14T Tony Phillips | .05 | .02 |
| ❑ 15T John Franco | .10 | .05 |
| ❑ 16T Randy Myers | .10 | .05 |
| ❑ 17T Jeff Reardon | .10 | .05 |
| ❑ 18T Sandy Alomar Jr. | .10 | .05 |
| ❑ 19T Joe Carter | .10 | .05 |
| ❑ 20T Fred Lynn | .05 | .02 |
| ❑ 21T Storm Davis | .05 | .02 |
| ❑ 22T Craig Lefferts | .05 | .02 |
| ❑ 23T Pete O'Brien | .05 | .02 |
| ❑ 24T Dennis Boyd | .05 | .02 |
| ❑ 25T Lloyd Moseby | .05 | .02 |
| ❑ 26T Mark Davis | .05 | .02 |

| | Card | Player | MINT | NRMT |
|---|---|---|---|---|
| ❑ | 27T | Tim Leary | .05 | .02 |
| ❑ | 28T | Gerald Perry | .05 | .02 |
| ❑ | 29T | Don Aase | .05 | .02 |
| ❑ | 30T | Ernie Whitt | .05 | .02 |
| ❑ | 31T | Dale Murphy | .20 | .09 |
| ❑ | 32T | Alejandro Pena | .05 | .02 |
| ❑ | 33T | Juan Samuel | .05 | .02 |
| ❑ | 34T | Hubie Brooks | .05 | .02 |
| ❑ | 35T | Gary Carter | .15 | .07 |
| ❑ | 36T | Jim Presley | .05 | .02 |
| ❑ | 37T | Wally Backman | .05 | .02 |
| ❑ | 38T | Matt Nokes | .05 | .02 |
| ❑ | 39T | Dan Petry | .05 | .02 |
| ❑ | 40T | Franklin Stubbs | .05 | .02 |
| ❑ | 41T | Jeff Huson | .05 | .02 |
| ❑ | 42T | Billy Hatcher | .05 | .02 |
| ❑ | 43T | Terry Leach | .05 | .02 |
| ❑ | 44T | Phil Bradley | .05 | .02 |
| ❑ | 45T | Claudell Washington | .05 | .02 |
| ❑ | 46T | Luis Polonia | .05 | .02 |
| ❑ | 47T | Daryl Boston | .05 | .02 |
| ❑ | 48T | Lee Smith | .10 | .05 |
| ❑ | 49T | Tom Brunansky | .05 | .02 |
| ❑ | 50T | Mike Witt | .05 | .02 |
| ❑ | 51T | Willie Randolph | .10 | .05 |
| ❑ | 52T | Stan Javier | .05 | .02 |
| ❑ | 53T | Brad Komminsk | .05 | .02 |
| ❑ | 54T | John Candelaria | .05 | .02 |
| ❑ | 55T | Bryn Smith | .05 | .02 |
| ❑ | 56T | Glenn Braggs | .05 | .02 |
| ❑ | 57T | Keith Hernandez | .10 | .05 |
| ❑ | 58T | Ken Oberkfell | .05 | .02 |
| ❑ | 59T | Steve Jeltz | .05 | .02 |
| ❑ | 60T | Chris James | .05 | .02 |
| ❑ | 61T | Scott Sanderson | .05 | .02 |
| ❑ | 62T | Bill Long | .05 | .02 |
| ❑ | 63T | Rick Cerone | .05 | .02 |
| ❑ | 64T | Scott Bailes | .05 | .02 |
| ❑ | 65T | Larry Sheets | .05 | .02 |
| ❑ | 66T | Junior Ortiz | .05 | .02 |
| ❑ | 67T | Francisco Cabrera | .05 | .02 |
| ❑ | 68T | Gary DiSarcina RC | .15 | .07 |
| ❑ | 69T | Greg Olson | .05 | .02 |
| ❑ | 70T | Beau Allred | .05 | .02 |
| ❑ | 71T | Oscar Azocar | .05 | .02 |
| ❑ | 72T | Kent Mercker RC | .05 | .02 |
| ❑ | 73T | John Burkett | .05 | .02 |
| ❑ | 74T | Carlos Baerga RC | .10 | .05 |
| ❑ | 75T | Dave Hollins RC | .20 | .09 |
| ❑ | 76T | Todd Hundley RC | .25 | .11 |
| ❑ | 77T | Rick Parker | .05 | .02 |
| ❑ | 78T | Steve Cummings | .05 | .02 |
| ❑ | 79T | Bill Sampen | .05 | .02 |
| ❑ | 80T | Jerry Kutzler | .05 | .02 |
| ❑ | 81T | Derek Bell RC | .50 | .23 |
| ❑ | 82T | Kevin Tapani RC | .10 | .05 |
| ❑ | 83T | Jim Leyritz RC | .25 | .11 |
| ❑ | 84T | Ray Lankford RC | .40 | .18 |
| ❑ | 85T | Wayne Edwards | .05 | .02 |
| ❑ | 86T | Frank Thomas | 2.50 | 1.10 |
| ❑ | 87T | Tim Naehring RC | .10 | .05 |
| ❑ | 88T | Willie Blair RC | .05 | .02 |
| ❑ | 89T | Alan Mills RC | .05 | .02 |
| ❑ | 90T | Scott Radinsky RC | .05 | .02 |
| ❑ | 91T | Howard Farmer | .05 | .02 |
| ❑ | 92T | Julio Machado | .05 | .02 |
| ❑ | 93T | Rafael Valdez | .05 | .02 |
| ❑ | 94T | Shawn Boskie RC | .05 | .02 |
| ❑ | 95T | David Segui RC | .40 | .18 |
| ❑ | 96T | Chris Hoiles RC | .20 | .09 |
| ❑ | 97T | D.J. Dozier RC | .10 | .05 |
| ❑ | 98T | Hector Villanueva | .05 | .02 |
| ❑ | 99T | Eric Gunderson | .05 | .02 |
| ❑ | 100T | Eric Lindros | 1.00 | .45 |
| ❑ | 101T | Dave Otto | .05 | .02 |
| ❑ | 102T | Dana Kiecker | .05 | .02 |
| ❑ | 103T | Tim Drummond | .05 | .02 |
| ❑ | 104T | Mickey Pina | .05 | .02 |
| ❑ | 105T | Craig Grebeck RC | .05 | .02 |
| ❑ | 106T | Bernard Gilkey RC | .25 | .11 |
| ❑ | 107T | Tim Layana | .05 | .02 |
| ❑ | 108T | Scott Chiamparino | .05 | .02 |
| ❑ | 109T | Steve Avery | .05 | .02 |
| ❑ | 110T | Terry Shumpert | .05 | .02 |

# 1991 Score

| | MINT | NRMT |
|---|---|---|
| COMPLETE SET (893) | 10.00 | 4.50 |
| COMP.FACT.SET (900) | 20.00 | 9.00 |
| COMMON CARD (1-893) | .05 | .02 |

| | Card | Player | MINT | NRMT |
|---|---|---|---|---|
| ❑ | 1 | Jose Canseco | .25 | .11 |
| ❑ | 2 | Ken Griffey Jr. | 1.00 | .45 |
| ❑ | 3 | Ryne Sandberg | .25 | .11 |
| ❑ | 4 | Nolan Ryan | 1.00 | .45 |
| ❑ | 5 | Bo Jackson | .10 | .05 |
| ❑ | 6 | Bret Saberhagen UER (In bio, missed misspelled as mised) | .05 | .02 |
| ❑ | 7 | Will Clark | .20 | .09 |
| ❑ | 8 | Ellis Burks | .10 | .05 |
| ❑ | 9 | Joe Carter | .10 | .05 |
| ❑ | 10 | Rickey Henderson | .25 | .11 |
| ❑ | 11 | Ozzie Guillen | .05 | .02 |
| ❑ | 12 | Wade Boggs | .25 | .11 |
| ❑ | 13 | Jerome Walton | .05 | .02 |
| ❑ | 14 | John Franco | .10 | .05 |
| ❑ | 15 | Ricky Jordan UER (League misspelled as legue) | .05 | .02 |
| ❑ | 16 | Wally Backman | .05 | .02 |
| ❑ | 17 | Rob Dibble | .05 | .02 |
| ❑ | 18 | Glenn Braggs | .05 | .02 |
| ❑ | 19 | Cory Snyder | .05 | .02 |
| ❑ | 20 | Kal Daniels | .05 | .02 |
| ❑ | 21 | Mark Langston | .05 | .02 |
| ❑ | 22 | Kevin Gross | .05 | .02 |
| ❑ | 23 | Don Mattingly UER (First line, ' is missing from Yankee) | .50 | .23 |
| ❑ | 24 | Dave Righetti | .05 | .02 |
| ❑ | 25 | Roberto Alomar | .20 | .09 |
| ❑ | 26 | Robby Thompson | .05 | .02 |
| ❑ | 27 | Jack McDowell | .05 | .02 |
| ❑ | 28 | Bip Roberts UER (Bio reads playd) | .05 | .02 |
| ❑ | 29 | Jay Howell | .05 | .02 |
| ❑ | 30 | Dave Stieb UER (17 wins in bio, 18 in stats) | .05 | .02 |
| ❑ | 31 | Johnny Ray | .05 | .02 |
| ❑ | 32 | Steve Sax | .05 | .02 |
| ❑ | 33 | Terry Mulholland | .05 | .02 |
| ❑ | 34 | Lee Guetterman | .05 | .02 |
| ❑ | 35 | Tim Raines | .10 | .05 |
| ❑ | 36 | Scott Fletcher | .05 | .02 |
| ❑ | 37 | Lance Parrish | .05 | .02 |
| ❑ | 38 | Tony Phillips UER (Born 4/15; should be 4/25) | .05 | .02 |
| ❑ | 39 | Todd Stottlemyre | .10 | .05 |
| ❑ | 40 | Alan Trammell | .15 | .07 |
| ❑ | 41 | Todd Burns | .05 | .02 |
| ❑ | 42 | Mookie Wilson | .10 | .05 |
| ❑ | 43 | Chris Bosio | .05 | .02 |
| ❑ | 44 | Jeffrey Leonard | .05 | .02 |
| ❑ | 45 | Doug Jones | .05 | .02 |
| ❑ | 46 | Mike Scott UER (In first line, dominate should read dominating) | .05 | .02 |
| ❑ | 47 | Andy Hawkins | .05 | .02 |
| ❑ | 48 | Harold Reynolds | .05 | .02 |
| ❑ | 49 | Paul Molitor | .20 | .09 |
| ❑ | 50 | John Farrell | .05 | .02 |
| ❑ | 51 | Danny Darwin | .05 | .02 |
| ❑ | 52 | Jeff Blauser | .05 | .02 |
| ❑ | 53 | John Tudor UER (41 wins in '81) | .05 | .02 |
| ❑ | 54 | Milt Thompson | .05 | .02 |
| ❑ | 55 | Dave Justice | .20 | .09 |
| ❑ | 56 | Greg Olson | .05 | .02 |
| ❑ | 57 | Willie Blair | .05 | .02 |
| ❑ | 58 | Rick Parker | .05 | .02 |
| ❑ | 59 | Shawn Boskie | .05 | .02 |
| ❑ | 60 | Kevin Tapani | .05 | .02 |
| ❑ | 61 | Dave Hollins | .05 | .02 |
| ❑ | 62 | Scott Radinsky | .05 | .02 |
| ❑ | 63 | Francisco Cabrera | .05 | .02 |
| ❑ | 64 | Tim Layana | .05 | .02 |
| ❑ | 65 | Jim Leyritz | .05 | .02 |
| ❑ | 66 | Wayne Edwards | .05 | .02 |
| ❑ | 67 | Lee Stevens | .10 | .05 |
| ❑ | 68 | Bill Sampen UER (Fourth line, long is spelled along) | .05 | .02 |
| ❑ | 69 | Craig Grebeck UER (Born in Cerritos, not Johnstown) | .05 | .02 |
| ❑ | 70 | John Burkett | .05 | .02 |
| ❑ | 71 | Hector Villanueva | .05 | .02 |
| ❑ | 72 | Oscar Azocar | .05 | .02 |
| ❑ | 73 | Alan Mills | .05 | .02 |
| ❑ | 74 | Carlos Baerga | .05 | .02 |
| ❑ | 75 | Charles Nagy | .05 | .02 |
| ❑ | 76 | Tim Drummond | .05 | .02 |
| ❑ | 77 | Dana Kiecker | .05 | .02 |
| ❑ | 78 | Tom Edens | .05 | .02 |
| ❑ | 79 | Kent Mercker | .05 | .02 |
| ❑ | 80 | Steve Avery | .05 | .02 |
| ❑ | 81 | Lee Smith | .10 | .05 |
| ❑ | 82 | Dave Martinez | .05 | .02 |
| ❑ | 83 | Dave Winfield | .20 | .09 |
| ❑ | 84 | Bill Spiers | .05 | .02 |
| ❑ | 85 | Dan Pasqua | .05 | .02 |
| ❑ | 86 | Randy Milligan | .05 | .02 |
| ❑ | 87 | Tracy Jones | .05 | .02 |
| ❑ | 88 | Greg Myers | .05 | .02 |
| ❑ | 89 | Keith Hernandez | .10 | .05 |
| ❑ | 90 | Todd Benzinger | .05 | .02 |
| ❑ | 91 | Mike Jackson | .05 | .02 |
| ❑ | 92 | Mike Stanley | .05 | .02 |
| ❑ | 93 | Candy Maldonado | .05 | .02 |
| ❑ | 94 | John Kruk UER (No decimal point before 1990 BA) | .10 | .05 |
| ❑ | 95 | Cal Ripken UER (Genius spelled genuis) | .75 | .35 |
| ❑ | 96 | Willie Fraser | .05 | .02 |
| ❑ | 97 | Mike Felder | .05 | .02 |
| ❑ | 98 | Bill Landrum | .05 | .02 |
| ❑ | 99 | Chuck Crim | .05 | .02 |
| ❑ | 100 | Chuck Finley | .10 | .05 |
| ❑ | 101 | Kirt Manwaring | .05 | .02 |
| ❑ | 102 | Jaime Navarro | .05 | .02 |
| ❑ | 103 | Dickie Thon | .05 | .02 |
| ❑ | 104 | Brian Downing | .05 | .02 |
| ❑ | 105 | Jim Abbott | .10 | .05 |
| ❑ | 106 | Tom Brookens | .05 | .02 |
| ❑ | 107 | Darryl Hamilton UER (Bio info is for Jeff Hamilton) | .05 | .02 |
| ❑ | 108 | Bryan Harvey | .05 | .02 |
| ❑ | 109 | Greg A. Harris UER (Shown pitching lefty; bio says righty) | .05 | .02 |
| ❑ | 110 | Greg Swindell | .05 | .02 |
| ❑ | 111 | Juan Berenguer | .05 | .02 |
| ❑ | 112 | Mike Heath | .05 | .02 |
| ❑ | 113 | Scott Bradley | .05 | .02 |
| ❑ | 114 | Jack Morris | .10 | .05 |
| ❑ | 115 | Barry Jones | .05 | .02 |
| ❑ | 116 | Kevin Romine | .05 | .02 |
| ❑ | 117 | Garry Templeton | .05 | .02 |
| ❑ | 118 | Scott Sanderson | .05 | .02 |
| ❑ | 119 | Roberto Kelly | .05 | .02 |
| ❑ | 120 | George Brett | .40 | .18 |
| ❑ | 121 | Oddibe McDowell | .05 | .02 |

❑ 122 Jim Acker .05 .02
❑ 123 Bill Swift UER .05 .02
(Born 12/27/61;
should be 10/27)
❑ 124 Eric King .05 .02
❑ 125 Jay Buhner .10 .05
❑ 126 Matt Young .05 .02
❑ 127 Alvaro Espinoza .05 .02
❑ 128 Greg Hibbard .05 .02
❑ 129 Jeff M. Robinson .05 .02
❑ 130 Mike Greenwell .05 .02
❑ 131 Dion James .05 .02
❑ 132 Donn Pall UER .05 .02
(1988 ERA in stats 0.00)
❑ 133 Lloyd Moseby .05 .02
❑ 134 Randy Velarde .05 .02
❑ 135 Allan Anderson .05 .02
❑ 136 Mark Davis .05 .02
❑ 137 Eric Davis .10 .05
❑ 138 Phil Stephenson .05 .02
❑ 139 Felix Fermin .05 .02
❑ 140 Pedro Guerrero .05 .02
❑ 141 Charlie Hough .10 .05
❑ 142 Mike Henneman .05 .02
❑ 143 Jeff Montgomery .10 .05
❑ 144 Lenny Harris .05 .02
❑ 145 Bruce Hurst .05 .02
❑ 146 Eric Anthony .05 .02
❑ 147 Paul Assenmacher .05 .02
❑ 148 Jesse Barfield .05 .02
❑ 149 Carlos Quintana .05 .02
❑ 150 Dave Stewart .10 .05
❑ 151 Roy Smith .05 .02
❑ 152 Paul Gibson .05 .02
❑ 153 Mickey Hatcher .05 .02
❑ 154 Jim Eisenreich .05 .02
❑ 155 Kenny Rogers .05 .02
❑ 156 Dave Schmidt .05 .02
❑ 157 Lance Johnson .05 .02
❑ 158 Dave West .05 .02
❑ 159 Steve Balboni .05 .02
❑ 160 Jeff Brantley .05 .02
❑ 161 Craig Biggio .15 .07
❑ 162 Brook Jacoby .05 .02
❑ 163 Dan Gladden .05 .02
❑ 164 Jeff Reardon UER .10 .05
(Total IP shown as
943.2; should be 943.1)
❑ 165 Mark Carreon .05 .02
❑ 166 Mel Hall .05 .02
❑ 167 Gary Mielke .05 .02
❑ 168 Cecil Fielder .10 .05
❑ 169 Darrin Jackson .05 .02
❑ 170 Rick Aguilera .10 .05
❑ 171 Walt Weiss .05 .02
❑ 172 Steve Farr .05 .02
❑ 173 Jody Reed .05 .02
❑ 174 Mike Jeffcoat .05 .02
❑ 175 Mark Grace .20 .09
❑ 176 Larry Sheets .05 .02
❑ 177 Bill Gullickson .05 .02
❑ 178 Chris Gwynn .05 .02
❑ 179 Melido Perez .05 .02
❑ 180 Sid Fernandez UER .05 .02
(779 runs in 1990)
❑ 181 Tim Burke .05 .02
❑ 182 Gary Pettis .05 .02
❑ 183 Rob Murphy .05 .02
❑ 184 Craig Lefferts .05 .02
❑ 185 Howard Johnson .05 .02
❑ 186 Ken Caminiti .10 .05
❑ 187 Tim Belcher .05 .02
❑ 188 Greg Cadaret .05 .02
❑ 189 Matt Williams .15 .07
❑ 190 Dave Magadan .05 .02
❑ 191 Geno Petralli .05 .02
❑ 192 Jeff D. Robinson .05 .02
❑ 193 Jim Deshales .05 .02
❑ 194 Willie Randolph .10 .05
❑ 195 George Bell .05 .02
❑ 196 Hubie Brooks .05 .02
❑ 197 Tom Gordon .05 .02
❑ 198 Mike Fitzgerald .05 .02
❑ 199 Mike Pagliarulo .05 .02
❑ 200 Kirby Puckett .50 .23
❑ 201 Shawon Dunston .05 .02
❑ 202 Dennis Boyd .05 .02
❑ 203 Junior Felix UER .05 .02
(Text has him in NL)
❑ 204 Alejandro Pena .05 .02
❑ 205 Pete Smith .05 .02
❑ 206 Tom Glavine UER .20 .09
(Lefty spelled leftie)
❑ 207 Luis Salazar .05 .02
❑ 208 John Smoltz .10 .05
❑ 209 Doug Dascenzo .05 .02
❑ 210 Tim Wallach .05 .02
❑ 211 Greg Gagne .05 .02
❑ 212 Mark Gubicza .05 .02
❑ 213 Mark Parent .05 .02
❑ 214 Ken Oberkfell .05 .02
❑ 215 Gary Carter .15 .07
❑ 216 Rafael Palmeiro .20 .09
❑ 217 Tom Niedenfuer .05 .02
❑ 218 Dave LaPoint .05 .02
❑ 219 Jeff Treadway .05 .02
❑ 220 Mitch Williams UER .05 .02
('89 ERA shown as 2.76;
should be 2.64)
❑ 221 Jose DeLeon .05 .02
❑ 222 Mike LaValliere .05 .02
❑ 223 Darrel Akerfelds .05 .02
❑ 224A Kent Anderson ERR .10 .05
(First line, flachy
should read flashy)
❑ 224B Kent Anderson COR .10 .05
(Corrected in
factory sets)
❑ 225 Dwight Evans .10 .05
❑ 226 Gary Redus .05 .02
❑ 227 Paul O'Neill .10 .05
❑ 228 Marty Barrett .05 .02
❑ 229 Tom Browning .05 .02
❑ 230 Terry Pendleton .10 .05
❑ 231 Jack Armstrong .05 .02
❑ 232 Mike Boddicker .05 .02
❑ 233 Neal Heaton .05 .02
❑ 234 Marquis Grissom .05 .02
❑ 235 Bert Blyleven .10 .05
❑ 236 Curt Young .05 .02
❑ 237 Don Carman .05 .02
❑ 238 Charlie Hayes .05 .02
❑ 239 Mark Knudson .05 .02
❑ 240 Todd Zeile .10 .05
❑ 241 Larry Walker UER .20 .09
(Maple River, should
be Maple Ridge)
❑ 242 Jerald Clark .05 .02
❑ 243 Jeff Ballard .05 .02
❑ 244 Jeff King .05 .02
❑ 245 Tom Brunansky .05 .02
❑ 246 Darren Daulton .10 .05
❑ 247 Scott Terry .05 .02
❑ 248 Rob Deer .05 .02
❑ 249 Brady Anderson UER .20 .09
(1990 Hagerstown 1 hit,
should say 13 hits)
❑ 250 Len Dykstra .10 .05
❑ 251 Greg W. Harris .05 .02
❑ 252 Mike Hartley .05 .02
❑ 253 Joey Cora .05 .02
❑ 254 Ivan Calderon .05 .02
❑ 255 Ted Power .05 .02
❑ 256 Sammy Sosa .50 .23
❑ 257 Steve Buechele .05 .02
❑ 258 Mike Devereaux UER .05 .02
(No comma between
city and state)
❑ 259 Brad Komminsk UER .05 .02
(Last text line,
Ba should be BA)
❑ 260 Ted Higuera .05 .02
❑ 261 Shawn Abner .05 .02
❑ 262 Dave Valle .05 .02
❑ 263 Jeff Huson .05 .02
❑ 264 Edgar Martinez .15 .07
❑ 265 Carlton Fisk .20 .09
❑ 266 Steve Finley .10 .05
❑ 267 John Wetteland .20 .09
❑ 268 Kevin Appier .10 .05
❑ 269 Steve Lyons .05 .02
❑ 270 Mickey Tettleton .05 .02
❑ 271 Luis Rivera .05 .02
❑ 272 Steve Jeltz .05 .02
❑ 273 R.J. Reynolds .05 .02
❑ 274 Carlos Martinez .05 .02
❑ 275 Dan Plesac .05 .02
❑ 276 Mike Morgan UER .05 .02
(Total IP shown as
1149.1; should be 1149)
❑ 277 Jeff Russell .05 .02
❑ 278 Pete Incaviglia .05 .02
❑ 279 Kevin Seitzer UER .05 .02
(Bio has 200 hits twice
and .300 four times;
should be once and
three times)
❑ 280 Bobby Thigpen .05 .02
❑ 281 Stan Javier UER .05 .02
(Born 1/9;
should say 9/1)
❑ 282 Henry Cotto .05 .02
❑ 283 Gary Wayne .05 .02
❑ 284 Shane Mack .05 .02
❑ 285 Brian Holman .05 .02
❑ 286 Gerald Perry .05 .02
❑ 287 Steve Crawford .05 .02
❑ 288 Nelson Liriano .05 .02
❑ 289 Don Aase .05 .02
❑ 290 Randy Johnson .30 .14
❑ 291 Harold Baines .10 .05
❑ 292 Kent Hrbek .10 .05
❑ 293A Les Lancaster ERR .05 .02
(No comma between
Dallas and Texas)
❑ 293B Les Lancaster COR .05 .02
(Corrected in
factory sets)
❑ 294 Jeff Musselman .05 .02
❑ 295 Kurt Stillwell .05 .02
❑ 296 Stan Belinda .05 .02
❑ 297 Lou Whitaker .10 .05
❑ 298 Glenn Wilson .05 .02
❑ 299 Omar Vizquel UER .20 .09
(Born 5/15; should be
4/24; there is a decimal
before GP total for '90)
❑ 300 Ramon Martinez .05 .02
❑ 301 Dwight Smith .05 .02
❑ 302 Tim Crews .05 .02
❑ 303 Lance Blankenship .05 .02
❑ 304 Sid Bream .05 .02
❑ 305 Rafael Ramirez .05 .02
❑ 306 Steve Wilson .05 .02
❑ 307 Mackey Sasser .05 .02
❑ 308 Franklin Stubbs .05 .02
❑ 309 Jack Daugherty UER .05 .02
(Born 6/3/60;
should say July)
❑ 310 Eddie Murray .20 .09
❑ 311 Bob Welch .05 .02
❑ 312 Brian Harper .05 .02
❑ 313 Lance McCullers .05 .02
❑ 314 Dave Smith .05 .02
❑ 315 Bobby Bonilla .10 .05
❑ 316 Jerry Don Gleaton .05 .02
❑ 317 Greg Maddux .50 .23
❑ 318 Keith Miller .05 .02
❑ 319 Mark Portugal .05 .02
❑ 320 Robin Ventura .20 .09
❑ 321 Bob Ojeda .05 .02
❑ 322 Mike Harkey .05 .02
❑ 323 Jay Bell .10 .05
❑ 324 Mark McGwire .75 .35
❑ 325 Gary Gaetti .10 .05
❑ 326 Jeff Pico .05 .02
❑ 327 Kevin McReynolds .05 .02
❑ 328 Frank Tanana .05 .02
❑ 329 Eric Yelding UER .05 .02
(Listed as 6'3";
should be 5'11")
❑ 330 Barry Bonds .30 .14
❑ 331 Brian McRae RC UER .10 .05
(No comma between
city and state)
❑ 332 Pedro Munoz RC .05 .02
❑ 333 Daryl Irvine .05 .02
❑ 334 Chris Hoiles .05 .02

❑ 335 Thomas Howard .05 .02
❑ 336 Jeff Schulz .05 .02
❑ 337 Jeff Manto .05 .02
❑ 338 Beau Allred .05 .02
❑ 339 Mike Bordick RC .50 .23
❑ 340 Todd Hundley .05 .02
❑ 341 Jim Vatcher UER .05 .02 (Height 6'9"; should be 5'9")
❑ 342 Luis Sojo .05 .02
❑ 343 Jose Offerman UER .05 .02 (Born 1969; should say 1968)
❑ 344 Pete Coachman .05 .02
❑ 345 Mike Benjamin .05 .02
❑ 346 Ozzie Canseco .05 .02
❑ 347 Tim McIntosh .05 .02
❑ 348 Phil Plantier RC .05 .02
❑ 349 Terry Shumpert .05 .02
❑ 350 Darren Lewis .10 .05
❑ 351 David Walsh .05 .02
❑ 352A Scott Chiamparino .10 .05 ERR (Bats left; should be right)
❑ 352B Scott Chiamparino .10 .05 COR (corrected in factory sets)
❑ 353 Julio Valera .05 .02 UER (Progressed misspelled as progessed)
❑ 354 Anthony Telford .05 .02
❑ 355 Kevin Wickander .05 .02
❑ 356 Tim Naehring .05 .02
❑ 357 Jim Poole .05 .02
❑ 358 Mark Whiten UER .05 .02 (Shown hitting lefty; bio says righty)
❑ 359 Terry Wells .05 .02
❑ 360 Rafael Valdez .05 .02
❑ 361 Mel Stottlemyre Jr. .05 .02
❑ 362 David Segui .05 .02
❑ 363 Paul Abbott .05 .02
❑ 364 Steve Howard .05 .02
❑ 365 Karl Rhodes .05 .02
❑ 366 Rafael Novoa .05 .02
❑ 367 Joe Grahe RC .05 .02
❑ 368 Darren Reed .05 .02
❑ 369 Jeff McKnight .05 .02
❑ 370 Scott Leius .05 .02
❑ 371 Mark Dewey .05 .02
❑ 372 Mark Lee UER .05 .02 (Shown hitting lefty; bio says righty. Born in Dakota; should say North Dakota)
❑ 373 Rosario Rodriguez .05 .02 (Shown hitting lefty; bio says righty) UER
❑ 374 Chuck McElroy .05 .02
❑ 375 Mike Bell .05 .02
❑ 376 Mickey Morandini .05 .02
❑ 377 Bill Haselman .05 .02
❑ 378 Dave Pavlas .05 .02
❑ 379 Derrick May .05 .02
❑ 380 Jeromy Burnitz FDP RC .50 .23
❑ 381 Donald Peters FDP .05 .02
❑ 382 Alex Fernandez FDP .10 .05
❑ 383 Mike Mussina FDP RC 1.25 .55
❑ 384 Dan Smith FDP RC .05 .02
❑ 385 Lance Dickson FDP RC .05 .02
❑ 386 Carl Everett FDP RC 1.00 .45
❑ 387 Tom Nevers FDP RC .05 .02
❑ 388 Adam Hyzdu FDP RC .05 .02
❑ 389 Todd Van Poppel FDP RC .05 .02
❑ 390 Rondell White FDP RC .40 .18
❑ 391 Marc Newfield FDP RC .05 .02
❑ 392 Julio Franco AS .05 .02
❑ 393 Wade Boggs AS .10 .05
❑ 394 Ozzie Guillen AS .05 .02
❑ 395 Cecil Fielder AS .05 .02
❑ 396 Ken Griffey Jr. AS .50 .35
❑ 397 Rickey Henderson AS .10 .05
❑ 398 Jose Canseco AS .10 .05
❑ 399 Roger Clemens AS .20 .09
❑ 400 Sandy Alomar Jr. AS .05 .02
❑ 401 Bobby Thigpen AS .05 .02
❑ 402 Bobby Bonilla MB .05 .02
❑ 403 Eric Davis MB .05 .02
❑ 404 Fred McGriff MB .10 .05
❑ 405 Glenn Davis MB .05 .02
❑ 406 Kevin Mitchell MB .05 .02
❑ 407 Rob Dibble KM .05 .02
❑ 408 Ramon Martinez KM .05 .02
❑ 409 David Cone KM .05 .02
❑ 410 Bobby Witt KM .05 .02
❑ 411 Mark Langston KM .05 .02
❑ 412 Bo Jackson RIF .10 .05
❑ 413 Shawon Dunston RIF .05 .02 UER (In the baseball; should say in baseball)
❑ 414 Jesse Barfield RIF .05 .02
❑ 415 Ken Caminiti RIF .05 .02
❑ 416 Benito Santiago RIF .05 .02
❑ 417 Nolan Ryan HL .50 .18
❑ 418 Bobby Thigpen HL UER .05 .02 (Back refers to Hal McRae Jr.; should say Brian McRae)
❑ 419 Ramon Martinez HL .05 .02
❑ 420 Bo Jackson HL .10 .05
❑ 421 Carlton Fisk HL .10 .05
❑ 422 Jimmy Key .10 .05
❑ 423 Junior Noboa .05 .02
❑ 424 Al Newman .05 .02
❑ 425 Pat Borders .05 .02
❑ 426 Von Hayes .05 .02
❑ 427 Tim Teufel .05 .02
❑ 428 Eric Plunk UER .05 .02 (Text says Eric's had, no apostrophe needed)
❑ 429 John Moses .05 .02
❑ 430 Mike Witt .05 .02
❑ 431 Otis Nixon .05 .02
❑ 432 Tony Fernandez .05 .02
❑ 433 Rance Mulliniks .05 .02
❑ 434 Dan Petry .05 .02
❑ 435 Bob Geren .05 .02
❑ 436 Steve Frey .05 .02
❑ 437 Jamie Moyer .05 .02
❑ 438 Junior Ortiz .05 .02
❑ 439 Tom O'Malley .05 .02
❑ 440 Pat Combs .05 .02
❑ 441 Jose Canseco DT .25 .11
❑ 442 Alfredo Griffin .05 .02
❑ 443 Andres Galarraga .15 .07
❑ 444 Bryn Smith .05 .02
❑ 445 Andre Dawson .15 .07
❑ 446 Juan Samuel .05 .02
❑ 447 Mike Aldrete .05 .02
❑ 448 Ron Gant .10 .05
❑ 449 Fernando Valenzuela .10 .05
❑ 450 Vince Coleman UER .05 .02 (Should say topped majors in steals four times, not three times)
❑ 451 Kevin Mitchell .05 .02
❑ 452 Spike Owen .05 .02
❑ 453 Mike Bielecki .05 .02
❑ 454 Dennis Martinez .10 .05
❑ 455 Brett Butler .10 .05
❑ 456 Ron Darling .05 .02
❑ 457 Dennis Rasmussen .05 .02
❑ 458 Ken Howell .05 .02
❑ 459 Steve Bedrosian .05 .02
❑ 460 Frank Viola .05 .02
❑ 461 Jose Lind .05 .02
❑ 462 Chris Sabo .05 .02
❑ 463 Dante Bichette .20 .09
❑ 464 Rick Mahler .05 .02
❑ 465 John Smiley .05 .02
❑ 466 Devon White .05 .02
❑ 467 John Orton .05 .02
❑ 468 Mike Stanton .05 .02
❑ 469 Billy Hatcher .05 .02
❑ 470 Wally Joyner .10 .05
❑ 471 Gene Larkin .05 .02
❑ 472 Doug Drabek .05 .02
❑ 473 Gary Sheffield .20 .09
❑ 474 David Wells .10 .05
❑ 475 Andy Van Slyke .10 .05
❑ 476 Mike Gallego .05 .02
❑ 477 B.J. Surhoff .10 .05
❑ 478 Gene Nelson .05 .02
❑ 479 Mariano Duncan .05 .02
❑ 480 Fred McGriff .20 .09
❑ 481 Jerry Browne .05 .02
❑ 482 Alvin Davis .05 .02
❑ 483 Bill Wegman .05 .02
❑ 484 Dave Parker .10 .05
❑ 485 Dennis Eckersley .10 .05
❑ 486 Erik Hanson UER .05 .02 (Basketball misspelled as baseketball)
❑ 487 Bill Ripken .05 .02
❑ 488 Tom Candiotti .05 .02
❑ 489 Mike Schooler .05 .02
❑ 490 Gregg Olson .05 .02
❑ 491 Chris James .05 .02
❑ 492 Pete Harnisch .05 .02
❑ 493 Julio Franco .05 .02
❑ 494 Greg Briley .05 .02
❑ 495 Ruben Sierra .05 .02
❑ 496 Steve Olin .05 .02
❑ 497 Mike Fetters .05 .02
❑ 498 Mark Williamson .05 .02
❑ 499 Bob Tewksbury .05 .02
❑ 500 Tony Gwynn .40 .18
❑ 501 Randy Myers .10 .05
❑ 502 Keith Comstock .05 .02
❑ 503 Craig Worthington UER .05 .02 (DeCinces misspelled DiCinces on back)
❑ 504 Mark Eichhorn UER .05 .02 (Stats incomplete, doesn't have '89 Braves stint)
❑ 505 Barry Larkin .20 .09
❑ 506 Dave Johnson .05 .02
❑ 507 Bobby Witt .05 .02
❑ 508 Joe Orsulak .05 .02
❑ 509 Pete O'Brien .05 .02
❑ 510 Brad Arnsberg .05 .02
❑ 511 Storm Davis .05 .02
❑ 512 Bob Milacki .05 .02
❑ 513 Bill Pecota .05 .02
❑ 514 Glenallen Hill .05 .02
❑ 515 Danny Tartabull .05 .02
❑ 516 Mike Moore .05 .02
❑ 517 Ron Robinson UER .05 .02 (577 K's in 1990)
❑ 518 Mark Gardner .05 .02
❑ 519 Rick Wrona .05 .02
❑ 520 Mike Scioscia .05 .02
❑ 521 Frank Wills .05 .02
❑ 522 Greg Brock .05 .02
❑ 523 Jack Clark .10 .05
❑ 524 Bruce Ruffin .05 .02
❑ 525 Robin Yount .20 .09
❑ 526 Tom Foley .05 .02
❑ 527 Pat Perry .05 .02
❑ 528 Greg Vaughn .20 .09
❑ 529 Wally Whitehurst .05 .02
❑ 530 Norm Charlton .05 .02
❑ 531 Marvell Wynne .05 .02
❑ 532 Jim Gantner .05 .02
❑ 533 Greg Litton .05 .02
❑ 534 Manny Lee .05 .02
❑ 535 Scott Bailes .05 .02
❑ 536 Charlie Leibrandt .05 .02
❑ 537 Roger McDowell .05 .02
❑ 538 Andy Benes .05 .02
❑ 539 Rick Honeycutt .05 .02
❑ 540 Dwight Gooden .10 .05
❑ 541 Scott Garrelts .05 .02
❑ 542 Dave Clark .05 .02
❑ 543 Lonnie Smith .05 .02
❑ 544 Rick Reuschel .05 .02
❑ 545 Delino DeShields UER .10 .05 (Rockford misspelled as Rock Ford in '88)
❑ 546 Mike Sharperson .05 .02
❑ 547 Mike Kingery .05 .02
❑ 548 Terry Kennedy .05 .02
❑ 549 David Cone .10 .05
❑ 550 Orel Hershiser .10 .05
❑ 551 Matt Nokes .05 .02
❑ 552 Eddie Williams .05 .02
❑ 553 Frank DiPino .05 .02

| |  |  | | |
|---|---|---|---|---|
| ❑ | 554 | Fred Lynn | .05 | .02 |
| ❑ | 555 | Alex Cole | .05 | .02 |
| ❑ | 556 | Terry Leach | .05 | .02 |
| ❑ | 557 | Chet Lemon | .05 | .02 |
| ❑ | 558 | Paul Mirabella | .05 | .02 |
| ❑ | 559 | Bill Long | .05 | .02 |
| ❑ | 560 | Phil Bradley | .05 | .02 |
| ❑ | 561 | Duane Ward | .05 | .02 |
| ❑ | 562 | Dave Bergman | .05 | .02 |
| ❑ | 563 | Eric Show | .05 | .02 |
| ❑ | 564 | Xavier Hernandez | .05 | .02 |
| ❑ | 565 | Jeff Parrett | .05 | .02 |
| ❑ | 566 | Chuck Cary | .05 | .02 |
| ❑ | 567 | Ken Hill | .05 | .02 |
| ❑ | 568 | Bob Welch Hand (Complement should be compliment) UER | .05 | .02 |
| ❑ | 569 | John Mitchell | .05 | .02 |
| ❑ | 570 | Travis Fryman | .20 | .09 |
| ❑ | 571 | Derek Lilliquist | .05 | .02 |
| ❑ | 572 | Steve Lake | .05 | .02 |
| ❑ | 573 | John Barfield | .05 | .02 |
| ❑ | 574 | Randy Bush | .05 | .02 |
| ❑ | 575 | Joe Magrane | .05 | .02 |
| ❑ | 576 | Eddie Diaz | .05 | .02 |
| ❑ | 577 | Casey Candaele | .05 | .02 |
| ❑ | 578 | Jesse Orosco | .05 | .02 |
| ❑ | 579 | Tom Henke | .05 | .02 |
| ❑ | 580 | Rick Cerone UER (Actually his third go-round with Yankees) | .05 | .02 |
| ❑ | 581 | Drew Hall | .05 | .02 |
| ❑ | 582 | Tony Castillo | .05 | .02 |
| ❑ | 583 | Jimmy Jones | .05 | .02 |
| ❑ | 584 | Rick Reed | .05 | .02 |
| ❑ | 585 | Joe Girardi | .10 | .05 |
| ❑ | 586 | Jeff Gray | .05 | .02 |
| ❑ | 587 | Luis Polonia | .05 | .02 |
| ❑ | 588 | Joe Klink | .05 | .02 |
| ❑ | 589 | Rex Hudler | .05 | .02 |
| ❑ | 590 | Kirk McCaskill | .05 | .02 |
| ❑ | 591 | Juan Agosto | .05 | .02 |
| ❑ | 592 | Wes Gardner | .05 | .02 |
| ❑ | 593 | Rich Rodriguez | .05 | .02 |
| ❑ | 594 | Mitch Webster | .05 | .02 |
| ❑ | 595 | Kelly Gruber | .05 | .02 |
| ❑ | 596 | Dale Mohorcic | .05 | .02 |
| ❑ | 597 | Willie McGee | .10 | .05 |
| ❑ | 598 | Bill Krueger | .05 | .02 |
| ❑ | 599 | Bob Walk UER (Cards says he's 33, but actually he's 34) | .05 | .02 |
| ❑ | 600 | Kevin Maas | .05 | .02 |
| ❑ | 601 | Danny Jackson | .05 | .02 |
| ❑ | 602 | Craig McMurtry UER (Anonymously misspelled anonimously) | .05 | .02 |
| ❑ | 603 | Curtis Wilkerson | .05 | .02 |
| ❑ | 604 | Adam Peterson | .05 | .02 |
| ❑ | 605 | Sam Horn | .05 | .02 |
| ❑ | 606 | Tommy Gregg | .05 | .02 |
| ❑ | 607 | Ken Dayley | .05 | .02 |
| ❑ | 608 | Carmelo Castillo | .05 | .02 |
| ❑ | 609 | John Shelby | .05 | .02 |
| ❑ | 610 | Don Slaught | .05 | .02 |
| ❑ | 611 | Calvin Schiraldi | .05 | .02 |
| ❑ | 612 | Dennis Lamp | .05 | .02 |
| ❑ | 613 | Andres Thomas | .05 | .02 |
| ❑ | 614 | Jose Gonzalez | .05 | .02 |
| ❑ | 615 | Randy Ready | .05 | .02 |
| ❑ | 616 | Kevin Bass | .05 | .02 |
| ❑ | 617 | Mike Marshall | .05 | .02 |
| ❑ | 618 | Daryl Boston | .05 | .02 |
| ❑ | 619 | Andy McGaffigan | .05 | .02 |
| ❑ | 620 | Joe Oliver | .05 | .02 |
| ❑ | 621 | Jim Gott | .05 | .02 |
| ❑ | 622 | Jose Oquendo | .05 | .02 |
| ❑ | 623 | Jose DeJesus | .05 | .02 |
| ❑ | 624 | Mike Brumley | .05 | .02 |
| ❑ | 625 | John Olerud | .15 | .07 |
| ❑ | 626 | Ernest Riles | .05 | .02 |
| ❑ | 627 | Gene Harris | .05 | .02 |
| ❑ | 628 | Jose Uribe | .05 | .02 |
| ❑ | 629 | Darnell Coles | .05 | .02 |
| ❑ | 630 | Carney Lansford | .10 | .05 |
| ❑ | 631 | Tim Leary | .05 | .02 |
| ❑ | 632 | Tim Hulett | .05 | .02 |
| ❑ | 633 | Kevin Elster | .05 | .02 |
| ❑ | 634 | Tony Fossas | .05 | .02 |
| ❑ | 635 | Francisco Oliveras | .05 | .02 |
| ❑ | 636 | Bob Patterson | .05 | .02 |
| ❑ | 637 | Gary Ward | .05 | .02 |
| ❑ | 638 | Rene Gonzales | .05 | .02 |
| ❑ | 639 | Don Robinson | .05 | .02 |
| ❑ | 640 | Darryl Strawberry | .10 | .05 |
| ❑ | 641 | Dave Anderson | .05 | .02 |
| ❑ | 642 | Scott Scudder | .05 | .02 |
| ❑ | 643 | Reggie Harris UER (Hepatitis misspelled as hepititis) | .05 | .02 |
| ❑ | 644 | Dave Henderson | .05 | .02 |
| ❑ | 645 | Ben McDonald | .05 | .02 |
| ❑ | 646 | Bob Kipper | .05 | .02 |
| ❑ | 647 | Hal Morris UER (It's should be its) | .05 | .02 |
| ❑ | 648 | Tim Birtsas | .05 | .02 |
| ❑ | 649 | Steve Searcy | .05 | .02 |
| ❑ | 650 | Dale Murphy | .20 | .09 |
| ❑ | 651 | Ron Oester | .05 | .02 |
| ❑ | 652 | Mike LaCoss | .05 | .02 |
| ❑ | 653 | Ron Jones | .05 | .02 |
| ❑ | 654 | Kelly Downs | .05 | .02 |
| ❑ | 655 | Roger Clemens | .40 | .18 |
| ❑ | 656 | Herm Winningham | .05 | .02 |
| ❑ | 657 | Trevor Wilson | .05 | .02 |
| ❑ | 658 | Jose Rijo | .05 | .02 |
| ❑ | 659 | Dann Bilardello UER (Bio has 13 games, 1 hit, and 32 AB; stats show 19, 2, and 37) | .05 | .02 |
| ❑ | 660 | Gregg Jefferies | .05 | .02 |
| ❑ | 661 | Doug Drabek AS UER (Through is mis-spelled though) | .05 | .02 |
| ❑ | 662 | Randy Myers AS | .05 | .02 |
| ❑ | 663 | Benny Santiago AS | .05 | .02 |
| ❑ | 664 | Will Clark AS | .10 | .05 |
| ❑ | 665 | Ryne Sandberg AS | .20 | .09 |
| ❑ | 666 | Barry Larkin AS UER (Line 13, coolly misspelled cooly) | .10 | .05 |
| ❑ | 667 | Matt Williams AS | .10 | .05 |
| ❑ | 668 | Barry Bonds AS | .20 | .09 |
| ❑ | 669 | Eric Davis AS | .05 | .02 |
| ❑ | 670 | Bobby Bonilla AS | .05 | .02 |
| ❑ | 671 | Chipper Jones FDP RC | 4.00 | 1.80 |
| ❑ | 672 | Eric Christopherson RC FDP | .05 | .02 |
| ❑ | 673 | Robbie Beckett FDP RC | .05 | .02 |
| ❑ | 674 | Shane Andrews FDP RC | .25 | .11 |
| ❑ | 675 | Steve Karsay FDP RC | .25 | .11 |
| ❑ | 676 | Aaron Holbert FDP RC | .05 | .02 |
| ❑ | 677 | Donovan Osborne FDP RC | .05 | .02 |
| ❑ | 678 | Todd Ritchie FDP RC | .05 | .02 |
| ❑ | 679 | Ron Walden FDP RC | .05 | .02 |
| ❑ | 680 | Tim Costo FDP RC | .05 | .02 |
| ❑ | 681 | Dan Wilson FDP RC | .20 | .09 |
| ❑ | 682 | Kurt Miller FDP RC | .05 | .02 |
| ❑ | 683 | Mike Lieberthal FDP RC | .50 | .23 |
| ❑ | 684 | Roger Clemens KM | .20 | .09 |
| ❑ | 685 | Dwight Gooden KM | .05 | .02 |
| ❑ | 686 | Nolan Ryan KM | .50 | .18 |
| ❑ | 687 | Frank Viola KM | .05 | .02 |
| ❑ | 688 | Erik Hanson KM | .05 | .02 |
| ❑ | 689 | Matt Williams MB | .10 | .05 |
| ❑ | 690 | Jose Canseco MB UER (Mammoth misspelled as monmouth) | .10 | .05 |
| ❑ | 691 | Darryl Strawberry MB | .05 | .02 |
| ❑ | 692 | Bo Jackson MB | .10 | .05 |
| ❑ | 693 | Cecil Fielder MB | .05 | .02 |
| ❑ | 694 | Sandy Alomar Jr. RF | .05 | .02 |
| ❑ | 695 | Cory Snyder RF | .05 | .02 |
| ❑ | 696 | Eric Davis RF | .05 | .02 |
| ❑ | 697 | Ken Griffey Jr. RF | .50 | .35 |
| ❑ | 698 | Andy Van Slyke RF UER (Line 2, outfielders does not need) | .05 | .02 |
| ❑ | 699 | Mark Langston NH Mike Witt | .05 | .02 |
| ❑ | 700 | Randy Johnson NH | .20 | .09 |
| ❑ | 701 | Nolan Ryan NH | .50 | .18 |
| ❑ | 702 | Dave Stewart NH | .05 | .02 |
| ❑ | 703 | Fernando Valenzuela NH | .05 | .02 |
| ❑ | 704 | Andy Hawkins NH | .05 | .02 |
| ❑ | 705 | Melido Perez NH | .05 | .02 |
| ❑ | 706 | Terry Mulholland NH | .05 | .02 |
| ❑ | 707 | Dave Stieb NH | .05 | .02 |
| ❑ | 708 | Brian Barnes RC | .05 | .02 |
| ❑ | 709 | Bernard Gilkey | .10 | .05 |
| ❑ | 710 | Steve Decker | .05 | .02 |
| ❑ | 711 | Paul Faries | .05 | .02 |
| ❑ | 712 | Paul Marak | .05 | .02 |
| ❑ | 713 | Wes Chamberlain RC | .05 | .02 |
| ❑ | 714 | Kevin Belcher | .05 | .02 |
| ❑ | 715 | Dan Boone UER (IP adds up to 101, but card has 101.2) | .05 | .02 |
| ❑ | 716 | Steve Adkins | .05 | .02 |
| ❑ | 717 | Geronimo Pena | .05 | .02 |
| ❑ | 718 | Howard Farmer | .05 | .02 |
| ❑ | 719 | Mark Leonard | .05 | .02 |
| ❑ | 720 | Tom Lampkin | .05 | .02 |
| ❑ | 721 | Mike Gardiner | .05 | .02 |
| ❑ | 722 | Jeff Conine RC | .20 | .09 |
| ❑ | 723 | Efrain Valdez | .05 | .02 |
| ❑ | 724 | Chuck Malone | .05 | .02 |
| ❑ | 725 | Leo Gomez | .05 | .02 |
| ❑ | 726 | Paul McClellan | .05 | .02 |
| ❑ | 727 | Mark Leiter RC | .05 | .02 |
| ❑ | 728 | Rich DeLucia UER (Line 2, all told is written alltold) | .05 | .02 |
| ❑ | 729 | Mel Rojas | .10 | .05 |
| ❑ | 730 | Hector Wagner | .05 | .02 |
| ❑ | 731 | Ray Lankford | .20 | .09 |
| ❑ | 732 | Turner Ward RC | .05 | .02 |
| ❑ | 733 | Gerald Alexander | .05 | .02 |
| ❑ | 734 | Scott Anderson | .05 | .02 |
| ❑ | 735 | Tony Perezchica | .05 | .02 |
| ❑ | 736 | Jimmy Kremers | .05 | .02 |
| ❑ | 737 | American Flag (Pray for Peace) | .20 | .09 |
| ❑ | 738 | Mike York | .05 | .02 |
| ❑ | 739 | Mike Rochford | .05 | .02 |
| ❑ | 740 | Scott Aldred | .05 | .02 |
| ❑ | 741 | Rico Brogna | .15 | .07 |
| ❑ | 742 | Dave Burba RC | .05 | .02 |
| ❑ | 743 | Ray Stephens | .05 | .02 |
| ❑ | 744 | Eric Gunderson | .05 | .02 |
| ❑ | 745 | Troy Afenir | .05 | .02 |
| ❑ | 746 | Jeff Shaw | .05 | .02 |
| ❑ | 747 | Orlando Merced RC | .05 | .02 |
| ❑ | 748 | Omar Olivares UER RC (Line 9, league is misspelled legaue) | .05 | .02 |
| ❑ | 749 | Jerry Kutzler | .05 | .02 |
| ❑ | 750 | Mo Vaughn UER (44 SB's in 1990) | .10 | .05 |
| ❑ | 751 | Matt Stark | .05 | .02 |
| ❑ | 752 | Randy Hennis | .05 | .02 |
| ❑ | 753 | Andujar Cedeno | .05 | .02 |
| ❑ | 754 | Kelvin Torve | .05 | .02 |
| ❑ | 755 | Joe Kraemer | .05 | .02 |
| ❑ | 756 | Phil Clark RC | .05 | .02 |
| ❑ | 757 | Ed Vosberg | .05 | .02 |
| ❑ | 758 | Mike Perez RC | .05 | .02 |
| ❑ | 759 | Scott Lewis | .05 | .02 |
| ❑ | 760 | Steve Chitren | .05 | .02 |
| ❑ | 761 | Ray Young | .05 | .02 |
| ❑ | 762 | Andres Santana | .05 | .02 |
| ❑ | 763 | Rodney McCray | .05 | .02 |
| ❑ | 764 | Sean Berry UER RC (Name misspelled Barry on card front) | .10 | .05 |
| ❑ | 765 | Brent Mayne | .05 | .02 |
| ❑ | 766 | Mike Simms | .05 | .02 |
| ❑ | 767 | Glenn Sutko | .05 | .02 |
| ❑ | 768 | Gary DiSarcina | .05 | .02 |
| ❑ | 769 | George Brett HL | .20 | .09 |
| ❑ | 770 | Cecil Fielder HL | .05 | .02 |
| ❑ | 771 | Jim Presley | .05 | .02 |
| ❑ | 772 | John Dopson | .05 | .02 |
| ❑ | 773 | Bo Jackson Breaker | .10 | .05 |
| ❑ | 774 | Brent Knackert UER (Born in 1954. Shown throwing righty, but bio says lefty) | .05 | .02 |

| | No. | Player | MINT | NRMT |
|---|---|---|---|---|
| ❑ | 775 | Bill Doran UER (Reds in NL East) | .05 | .02 |
| ❑ | 776 | Dick Schofield | .05 | .02 |
| ❑ | 777 | Nelson Santovenia | .05 | .02 |
| ❑ | 778 | Mark Guthrie | .05 | .02 |
| ❑ | 779 | Mark Lemke | .05 | .02 |
| ❑ | 780 | Terry Steinbach | .10 | .05 |
| ❑ | 781 | Tom Bolton | .05 | .02 |
| ❑ | 782 | Randy Tomlin RC | .05 | .02 |
| ❑ | 783 | Jeff Kunkel | .05 | .02 |
| ❑ | 784 | Felix Jose | .05 | .02 |
| ❑ | 785 | Rick Sutcliffe | .10 | .05 |
| ❑ | 786 | John Cerutti | .05 | .02 |
| ❑ | 787 | Jose Vizcaino UER (Offerman, not Opperman) | .05 | .02 |
| ❑ | 788 | Curt Schilling | .10 | .05 |
| ❑ | 789 | Ed Whitson | .05 | .02 |
| ❑ | 790 | Tony Pena | .05 | .02 |
| ❑ | 791 | John Candelaria | .05 | .02 |
| ❑ | 792 | Carmelo Martinez | .05 | .02 |
| ❑ | 793 | Sandy Alomar Jr. UER (Indian's should say Indians') | .10 | .05 |
| ❑ | 794 | Jim Neidlinger | .05 | .02 |
| ❑ | 795 | Barry Larkin WS and Chris Sabo | .10 | .05 |
| ❑ | 796 | Paul Sorrento | .10 | .05 |
| ❑ | 797 | Tom Pagnozzi | .05 | .02 |
| ❑ | 798 | Tino Martinez | .10 | .05 |
| ❑ | 799 | Scott Ruskin UER (Text says first three seasons but lists averages for four) | .05 | .02 |
| ❑ | 800 | Kirk Gibson | .10 | .05 |
| ❑ | 801 | Walt Terrell | .05 | .02 |
| ❑ | 802 | John Russell | .05 | .02 |
| ❑ | 803 | Chili Davis | .10 | .05 |
| ❑ | 804 | Chris Nabholz | .05 | .02 |
| ❑ | 805 | Juan Gonzalez | .25 | .11 |
| ❑ | 806 | Ron Hassey | .05 | .02 |
| ❑ | 807 | Todd Worrell | .05 | .02 |
| ❑ | 808 | Tommy Greene | .05 | .02 |
| ❑ | 809 | Joel Skinner UER (Joel, not Bob, was drafted in 1979) | .05 | .02 |
| ❑ | 810 | Benito Santiago | .05 | .02 |
| ❑ | 811 | Pat Tabler UER (Line 3, always misspelled alway) | .05 | .02 |
| ❑ | 812 | Scott Erickson UER (Record spelled rcord) | .05 | .02 |
| ❑ | 813 | Moises Alou | .20 | .09 |
| ❑ | 814 | Dale Sveum | .05 | .02 |
| ❑ | 815 | Ryne Sandberg MANYR | .20 | .09 |
| ❑ | 816 | Rick Dempsey | .05 | .02 |
| ❑ | 817 | Scott Bankhead | .05 | .02 |
| ❑ | 818 | Jason Grimsley | .05 | .02 |
| ❑ | 819 | Doug Jennings | .05 | .02 |
| ❑ | 820 | Tom Herr | .05 | .02 |
| ❑ | 821 | Rob Ducey | .05 | .02 |
| ❑ | 822 | Luis Quinones | .05 | .02 |
| ❑ | 823 | Greg Minton | .05 | .02 |
| ❑ | 824 | Mark Grant | .05 | .02 |
| ❑ | 825 | Ozzie Smith UER (Shortstop misspelled shortsop) | .25 | .11 |
| ❑ | 826 | Dave Eiland | .05 | .02 |
| ❑ | 827 | Danny Heep | .05 | .02 |
| ❑ | 828 | Hensley Meulens | .05 | .02 |
| ❑ | 829 | Charlie O'Brien | .05 | .02 |
| ❑ | 830 | Glenn Davis | .05 | .02 |
| ❑ | 831 | John Marzano UER (International mis-spelled Internaional) | .05 | .02 |
| ❑ | 832 | Steve Ontiveros | .05 | .02 |
| ❑ | 833 | Ron Karkovice | .05 | .02 |
| ❑ | 834 | Jerry Goff | .05 | .02 |
| ❑ | 835 | Ken Griffey Sr. | .10 | .05 |
| ❑ | 836 | Kevin Reimer | .05 | .02 |
| ❑ | 837 | Randy Kutcher UER (Infectious mis-spelled infectous) | .05 | .02 |
| ❑ | 838 | Mike Blowers | .05 | .02 |
| ❑ | 839 | Mike Macfarlane | .05 | .02 |
| ❑ | 840 | Frank Thomas UER (1989 Sarasota stats, 15 games but 188 AB) | .50 | .23 |
| ❑ | 841 | The Griffeys Ken Griffey Jr. Ken Griffey Sr. | .75 | .35 |
| ❑ | 842 | Jack Howell | .05 | .02 |
| ❑ | 843 | Goose Gozzo | .05 | .02 |
| ❑ | 844 | Gerald Young | .05 | .02 |
| ❑ | 845 | Zane Smith | .05 | .02 |
| ❑ | 846 | Kevin Brown | .15 | .07 |
| ❑ | 847 | Sil Campusano | .05 | .02 |
| ❑ | 848 | Larry Andersen | .05 | .02 |
| ❑ | 849 | Cal Ripken FRAN | .40 | .18 |
| ❑ | 850 | Roger Clemens FRAN | .20 | .09 |
| ❑ | 851 | Sandy Alomar Jr. FRAN | .05 | .02 |
| ❑ | 852 | Alan Trammell FRAN | .05 | .02 |
| ❑ | 853 | George Brett FRAN | .20 | .09 |
| ❑ | 854 | Robin Yount FRAN | .10 | .05 |
| ❑ | 855 | Kirby Puckett FRAN | .25 | .11 |
| ❑ | 856 | Don Mattingly FRAN | .25 | .09 |
| ❑ | 857 | Rickey Henderson FRAN | .10 | .05 |
| ❑ | 858 | Ken Griffey Jr. FRAN | .50 | .35 |
| ❑ | 859 | Ruben Sierra FRAN | .05 | .02 |
| ❑ | 860 | John Olerud FRAN | .15 | .07 |
| ❑ | 861 | Dave Justice FRAN | .10 | .05 |
| ❑ | 862 | Ryne Sandberg FRAN | .20 | .09 |
| ❑ | 863 | Eric Davis FRAN | .05 | .02 |
| ❑ | 864 | Darryl Strawberry FRAN | .05 | .02 |
| ❑ | 865 | Tim Wallach FRAN | .05 | .02 |
| ❑ | 866 | Dwight Gooden FRAN | .05 | .02 |
| ❑ | 867 | Len Dykstra FRAN | .05 | .02 |
| ❑ | 868 | Barry Bonds FRAN | .20 | .09 |
| ❑ | 869 | Todd Zeile FRAN UER (Powerful misspelled as poweful) | .05 | .02 |
| ❑ | 870 | Benito Santiago FRAN | .05 | .02 |
| ❑ | 871 | Will Clark FRAN | .10 | .05 |
| ❑ | 872 | Craig Biggio FRAN | .10 | .05 |
| ❑ | 873 | Wally Joyner FRAN | .05 | .02 |
| ❑ | 874 | Frank Thomas FRAN | .20 | .09 |
| ❑ | 875 | Rickey Henderson MVP | .10 | .05 |
| ❑ | 876 | Barry Bonds MVP | .20 | .09 |
| ❑ | 877 | Bob Welch CY | .05 | .02 |
| ❑ | 878 | Doug Drabek CY | .05 | .02 |
| ❑ | 879 | Sandy Alomar Jr. ROY | .10 | .05 |
| ❑ | 880 | Dave Justice ROY | .10 | .05 |
| ❑ | 881 | Damon Berryhill | .05 | .02 |
| ❑ | 882 | Frank Viola DT | .05 | .02 |
| ❑ | 883 | Dave Stewart DT | .05 | .02 |
| ❑ | 884 | Doug Jones DT | .05 | .02 |
| ❑ | 885 | Randy Myers DT | .05 | .02 |
| ❑ | 886 | Will Clark DT | .10 | .05 |
| ❑ | 887 | Roberto Alomar DT | .10 | .05 |
| ❑ | 888 | Barry Larkin DT | .10 | .05 |
| ❑ | 889 | Wade Boggs DT | .25 | .11 |
| ❑ | 890 | Rickey Henderson DT | .25 | .11 |
| ❑ | 891 | Kirby Puckett DT | .50 | .23 |
| ❑ | 892 | Ken Griffey Jr DT | 1.00 | .45 |
| ❑ | 893 | Benny Santiago DT | .05 | .02 |

## 1991 Score Rookie/Traded

| | | | MINT | NRMT |
|---|---|---|---|---|
| | | COMP.FACT.SET (110) | 8.00 | 3.60 |
| ❑ | 1T | Bo Jackson | .10 | .05 |
| ❑ | 2T | Mike Flanagan | .05 | .02 |
| ❑ | 3T | Pete Incaviglia | .05 | .02 |
| ❑ | 4T | Jack Clark | .10 | .05 |
| ❑ | 5T | Hubie Brooks | .05 | .02 |
| ❑ | 6T | Ivan Calderon | .05 | .02 |
| ❑ | 7T | Glenn Davis | .05 | .02 |
| ❑ | 8T | Wally Backman | .05 | .02 |
| ❑ | 9T | Dave Smith | .05 | .02 |
| ❑ | 10T | Tim Raines | .10 | .05 |
| ❑ | 11T | Joe Carter | .10 | .05 |
| ❑ | 12T | Sid Bream | .05 | .02 |
| ❑ | 13T | George Bell | .05 | .02 |
| ❑ | 14T | Steve Bedrosian | .05 | .02 |
| ❑ | 15T | Willie Wilson | .05 | .02 |
| ❑ | 16T | Darryl Strawberry | .10 | .05 |
| ❑ | 17T | Danny Jackson | .05 | .02 |
| ❑ | 18T | Kirk Gibson | .10 | .05 |
| ❑ | 19T | Willie McGee | .10 | .05 |
| ❑ | 20T | Junior Felix | .05 | .02 |
| ❑ | 21T | Steve Farr | .05 | .02 |
| ❑ | 22T | Pat Tabler | .05 | .02 |
| ❑ | 23T | Brett Butler | .10 | .05 |
| ❑ | 24T | Danny Darwin | .05 | .02 |
| ❑ | 25T | Mickey Tettleton | .05 | .02 |
| ❑ | 26T | Gary Carter | .15 | .07 |
| ❑ | 27T | Mitch Williams | .05 | .02 |
| ❑ | 28T | Candy Maldonado | .05 | .02 |
| ❑ | 29T | Otis Nixon | .05 | .02 |
| ❑ | 30T | Brian Downing | .05 | .02 |
| ❑ | 31T | Tom Candiotti | .05 | .02 |
| ❑ | 32T | John Candelaria | .05 | .02 |
| ❑ | 33T | Rob Murphy | .05 | .02 |
| ❑ | 34T | Deion Sanders | .10 | .05 |
| ❑ | 35T | Willie Randolph | .10 | .05 |
| ❑ | 36T | Pete Harnisch | .05 | .02 |
| ❑ | 37T | Dante Bichette | .25 | .11 |
| ❑ | 38T | Garry Templeton | .05 | .02 |
| ❑ | 39T | Gary Gaetti | .10 | .05 |
| ❑ | 40T | John Cerutti | .05 | .02 |
| ❑ | 41T | Rick Cerone | .05 | .02 |
| ❑ | 42T | Mike Pagliarulo | .05 | .02 |
| ❑ | 43T | Ron Hassey | .05 | .02 |
| ❑ | 44T | Roberto Alomar | .25 | .11 |
| ❑ | 45T | Mike Boddicker | .05 | .02 |
| ❑ | 46T | Bud Black | .05 | .02 |
| ❑ | 47T | Rob Deer | .05 | .02 |
| ❑ | 48T | Devon White | .05 | .02 |
| ❑ | 49T | Luis Sojo | .05 | .02 |
| ❑ | 50T | Terry Pendleton | .10 | .05 |
| ❑ | 51T | Kevin Gross | .05 | .02 |
| ❑ | 52T | Mike Huff | .05 | .02 |
| ❑ | 53T | Dave Righetti | .05 | .02 |
| ❑ | 54T | Matt Young | .05 | .02 |
| ❑ | 55T | Earnest Riles | .05 | .02 |
| ❑ | 56T | Bill Gullickson | .05 | .02 |
| ❑ | 57T | Vince Coleman | .05 | .02 |
| ❑ | 58T | Fred McGriff | .25 | .11 |
| ❑ | 59T | Franklin Stubbs | .05 | .02 |
| ❑ | 60T | Eric King | .05 | .02 |
| ❑ | 61T | Cory Snyder | .05 | .02 |
| ❑ | 62T | Dwight Evans | .10 | .05 |
| ❑ | 63T | Gerald Perry | .05 | .02 |
| ❑ | 64T | Eric Show | .05 | .02 |
| ❑ | 65T | Shawn Hillegas | .05 | .02 |
| ❑ | 66T | Tony Fernandez | .05 | .02 |
| ❑ | 67T | Tim Teufel | .05 | .02 |
| ❑ | 68T | Mitch Webster | .05 | .02 |
| ❑ | 69T | Mike Heath | .05 | .02 |
| ❑ | 70T | Chili Davis | .10 | .05 |
| ❑ | 71T | Larry Andersen | .05 | .02 |
| ❑ | 72T | Gary Varsho | .05 | .02 |
| ❑ | 73T | Juan Berenguer | .05 | .02 |
| ❑ | 74T | Jack Morris | .10 | .05 |
| ❑ | 75T | Barry Jones | .05 | .02 |
| ❑ | 76T | Rafael Belliard | .05 | .02 |
| ❑ | 77T | Steve Buechele | .05 | .02 |
| ❑ | 78T | Scott Sanderson | .05 | .02 |
| ❑ | 79T | Bob Ojeda | .05 | .02 |
| ❑ | 80T | Curt Schilling | .10 | .05 |
| ❑ | 81T | Brian Drahman | .05 | .02 |
| ❑ | 82T | Ivan Rodriguez RC | 4.00 | 1.80 |
| ❑ | 83T | David Howard | .05 | .02 |
| ❑ | 84T | Heathcliff Slocumb RC | .05 | .02 |
| ❑ | 85T | Mike Timlin RC | .05 | .02 |
| ❑ | 86T | Darryl Kile | .10 | .05 |
| ❑ | 87T | Pete Schourek RC | .10 | .05 |
| ❑ | 88T | Bruce Walton | .05 | .02 |
| ❑ | 89T | Al Osuna RC | .05 | .02 |

| | | |
|---|---|---|
| ❑ 90T Gary Scott RC | .05 | .02 |
| ❑ 91T Doug Simons | .05 | .02 |
| ❑ 92T Chris Jones RC | .05 | .02 |
| ❑ 93T Chuck Knoblauch | .10 | .05 |
| ❑ 94T Dana Allison RC | .05 | .02 |
| ❑ 95T Erik Pappas | .05 | .02 |
| ❑ 96T Jeff Bagwell RC | 4.00 | 1.80 |
| ❑ 97T Kirk Dressendorfer RC | .05 | .02 |
| ❑ 98T Freddie Benavides | .05 | .02 |
| ❑ 99T Luis Gonzalez RC | .75 | .35 |
| ❑ 100T Wade Taylor | .05 | .02 |
| ❑ 101T Ed Sprague | .05 | .02 |
| ❑ 102T Bob Scanlan | .05 | .02 |
| ❑ 103T Rick Wilkins RC | .05 | .02 |
| ❑ 104T Chris Donnels | .05 | .02 |
| ❑ 105T Joe Slusarski | .05 | .02 |
| ❑ 106T Mark Lewis | .05 | .02 |
| ❑ 107T Pat Kelly RC | .05 | .02 |
| ❑ 108T John Briscoe | .05 | .02 |
| ❑ 109T Luis Lopez RC | .05 | .02 |
| ❑ 110T Jeff Johnson | .05 | .02 |

## 1992 Score

| | MINT | NRMT |
|---|---|---|
| COMPLETE SET (893) | 15.00 | 6.75 |
| COMP.FACT.SET (910) | 20.00 | 9.00 |
| COMPLETE SERIES 1 (442) | 8.00 | 3.60 |
| COMPLETE SERIES 2 (451) | 8.00 | 3.60 |
| COMMON CARD (1-893) | .05 | .02 |

| | | |
|---|---|---|
| ❑ 1 Ken Griffey Jr. | .75 | .35 |
| ❑ 2 Nolan Ryan | 1.00 | .45 |
| ❑ 3 Will Clark | .20 | .09 |
| ❑ 4 Dave Justice | .10 | .05 |
| ❑ 5 Dave Henderson | .05 | .02 |
| ❑ 6 Bret Saberhagen | .10 | .05 |
| ❑ 7 Fred McGriff | .10 | .05 |
| ❑ 8 Erik Hanson | .05 | .02 |
| ❑ 9 Darryl Strawberry | .10 | .05 |
| ❑ 10 Dwight Gooden | .10 | .05 |
| ❑ 11 Juan Gonzalez | .20 | .09 |
| ❑ 12 Mark Langston | .05 | .02 |
| ❑ 13 Lonnie Smith | .05 | .02 |
| ❑ 14 Jeff Montgomery | .10 | .05 |
| ❑ 15 Roberto Alomar | .20 | .09 |
| ❑ 16 Delino DeShields | .10 | .05 |
| ❑ 17 Steve Bedrosian | .05 | .02 |
| ❑ 18 Terry Pendleton | .10 | .05 |
| ❑ 19 Mark Carreon | .05 | .02 |
| ❑ 20 Mark McGwire | .75 | .35 |
| ❑ 21 Roger Clemens | .40 | .18 |
| ❑ 22 Chuck Crim | .05 | .02 |
| ❑ 23 Don Mattingly | .50 | .23 |
| ❑ 24 Dickie Thon | .05 | .02 |
| ❑ 25 Ron Gant | .10 | .05 |
| ❑ 26 Milt Cuyler | .05 | .02 |
| ❑ 27 Mike Macfarlane | .05 | .02 |
| ❑ 28 Dan Gladden | .05 | .02 |
| ❑ 29 Melido Perez | .05 | .02 |
| ❑ 30 Willie Randolph | .10 | .05 |
| ❑ 31 Albert Belle | .10 | .05 |
| ❑ 32 Dave Winfield | .20 | .09 |
| ❑ 33 Jimmy Jones | .05 | .02 |
| ❑ 34 Kevin Gross | .05 | .02 |
| ❑ 35 Andres Galarraga | .10 | .05 |
| ❑ 36 Mike Devereaux | .05 | .02 |
| ❑ 37 Chris Bosio | .05 | .02 |
| ❑ 38 Mike LaValliere | .05 | .02 |
| ❑ 39 Gary Gaetti | .10 | .05 |
| ❑ 40 Felix Jose | .05 | .02 |
| ❑ 41 Alvaro Espinoza | .05 | .02 |
| ❑ 42 Rick Aguilera | .10 | .05 |
| ❑ 43 Mike Gallego | .05 | .02 |
| ❑ 44 Eric Davis | .10 | .05 |
| ❑ 45 George Bell | .05 | .02 |
| ❑ 46 Tom Brunansky | .05 | .02 |
| ❑ 47 Steve Farr | .05 | .02 |
| ❑ 48 Duane Ward | .05 | .02 |
| ❑ 49 David Wells | .10 | .05 |
| ❑ 50 Cecil Fielder | .10 | .05 |
| ❑ 51 Walt Weiss | .05 | .02 |
| ❑ 52 Todd Zeile | .05 | .02 |
| ❑ 53 Doug Jones | .05 | .02 |
| ❑ 54 Bob Walk | .05 | .02 |
| ❑ 55 Rafael Palmeiro | .20 | .09 |
| ❑ 56 Rob Deer | .05 | .02 |
| ❑ 57 Paul O'Neill | .10 | .05 |
| ❑ 58 Jeff Reardon | .10 | .05 |
| ❑ 59 Randy Ready | .05 | .02 |
| ❑ 60 Scott Erickson | .05 | .02 |
| ❑ 61 Paul Molitor | .20 | .09 |
| ❑ 62 Jack McDowell | .05 | .02 |
| ❑ 63 Jim Acker | .05 | .02 |
| ❑ 64 Jay Buhner | .10 | .05 |
| ❑ 65 Travis Fryman | .10 | .05 |
| ❑ 66 Marquis Grissom | .05 | .02 |
| ❑ 67 Mike Harkey | .05 | .02 |
| ❑ 68 Luis Polonia | .05 | .02 |
| ❑ 69 Ken Caminiti | .10 | .05 |
| ❑ 70 Chris Sabo | .05 | .02 |
| ❑ 71 Gregg Olson | .05 | .02 |
| ❑ 72 Carlton Fisk | .20 | .09 |
| ❑ 73 Juan Samuel | .05 | .02 |
| ❑ 74 Todd Stottlemyre | .10 | .05 |
| ❑ 75 Andre Dawson | .10 | .05 |
| ❑ 76 Alvin Davis | .05 | .02 |
| ❑ 77 Bill Doran | .05 | .02 |
| ❑ 78 B.J. Surhoff | .10 | .05 |
| ❑ 79 Kirk McCaskill | .05 | .02 |
| ❑ 80 Dale Murphy | .20 | .09 |
| ❑ 81 Jose DeLeon | .05 | .02 |
| ❑ 82 Alex Fernandez | .10 | .05 |
| ❑ 83 Ivan Calderon | .05 | .02 |
| ❑ 84 Brent Mayne | .05 | .02 |
| ❑ 85 Jody Reed | .05 | .02 |
| ❑ 86 Randy Tomlin | .05 | .02 |
| ❑ 87 Randy Milligan | .05 | .02 |
| ❑ 88 Pascual Perez | .05 | .02 |
| ❑ 89 Hensley Meulens | .05 | .02 |
| ❑ 90 Joe Carter | .10 | .05 |
| ❑ 91 Mike Moore | .05 | .02 |
| ❑ 92 Ozzie Guillen | .05 | .02 |
| ❑ 93 Shawn Hillegas | .05 | .02 |
| ❑ 94 Chili Davis | .10 | .05 |
| ❑ 95 Vince Coleman | .05 | .02 |
| ❑ 96 Jimmy Key | .10 | .05 |
| ❑ 97 Billy Ripken | .05 | .02 |
| ❑ 98 Dave Smith | .05 | .02 |
| ❑ 99 Tom Bolton | .05 | .02 |
| ❑ 100 Barry Larkin | .10 | .05 |
| ❑ 101 Kenny Rogers | .05 | .02 |
| ❑ 102 Mike Boddicker | .05 | .02 |
| ❑ 103 Kevin Elster | .05 | .02 |
| ❑ 104 Ken Hill | .05 | .02 |
| ❑ 105 Charlie Leibrandt | .05 | .02 |
| ❑ 106 Pat Combs | .05 | .02 |
| ❑ 107 Hubie Brooks | .05 | .02 |
| ❑ 108 Julio Franco | .05 | .02 |
| ❑ 109 Vicente Palacios | .05 | .02 |
| ❑ 110 Kal Daniels | .05 | .02 |
| ❑ 111 Bruce Hurst | .05 | .02 |
| ❑ 112 Willie McGee | .10 | .05 |
| ❑ 113 Ted Power | .05 | .02 |
| ❑ 114 Milt Thompson | .05 | .02 |
| ❑ 115 Doug Drabek | .05 | .02 |
| ❑ 116 Rafael Belliard | .05 | .02 |
| ❑ 117 Scott Garrelts | .05 | .02 |
| ❑ 118 Terry Mulholland | .05 | .02 |
| ❑ 119 Jay Howell | .05 | .02 |
| ❑ 120 Danny Jackson | .05 | .02 |
| ❑ 121 Scott Ruskin | .05 | .02 |
| ❑ 122 Robin Ventura | .10 | .05 |
| ❑ 123 Bip Roberts | .05 | .02 |
| ❑ 124 Jeff Russell | .05 | .02 |
| ❑ 125 Hal Morris | .05 | .02 |
| ❑ 126 Teddy Higuera | .05 | .02 |
| ❑ 127 Luis Sojo | .05 | .02 |
| ❑ 128 Carlos Baerga | .05 | .02 |
| ❑ 129 Jeff Ballard | .05 | .02 |
| ❑ 130 Tom Gordon | .05 | .02 |
| ❑ 131 Sid Bream | .05 | .02 |
| ❑ 132 Rance Mulliniks | .05 | .02 |
| ❑ 133 Andy Benes | .05 | .02 |
| ❑ 134 Mickey Tettleton | .05 | .02 |
| ❑ 135 Rich DeLucia | .05 | .02 |
| ❑ 136 Tom Pagnozzi | .05 | .02 |
| ❑ 137 Harold Baines | .10 | .05 |
| ❑ 138 Danny Darwin | .05 | .02 |
| ❑ 139 Kevin Bass | .05 | .02 |
| ❑ 140 Chris Nabholz | .05 | .02 |
| ❑ 141 Pete O'Brien | .05 | .02 |
| ❑ 142 Jeff Treadway | .05 | .02 |
| ❑ 143 Mickey Morandini | .05 | .02 |
| ❑ 144 Eric King | .05 | .02 |
| ❑ 145 Danny Tartabull | .05 | .02 |
| ❑ 146 Lance Johnson | .05 | .02 |
| ❑ 147 Casey Candaele | .05 | .02 |
| ❑ 148 Felix Fermin | .05 | .02 |
| ❑ 149 Rich Rodriguez | .05 | .02 |
| ❑ 150 Dwight Evans | .10 | .05 |
| ❑ 151 Joe Klink | .05 | .02 |
| ❑ 152 Kevin Reimer | .05 | .02 |
| ❑ 153 Orlando Merced | .05 | .02 |
| ❑ 154 Mel Hall | .05 | .02 |
| ❑ 155 Randy Myers | .10 | .05 |
| ❑ 156 Greg A. Harris | .05 | .02 |
| ❑ 157 Jeff Brantley | .05 | .02 |
| ❑ 158 Jim Eisenreich | .05 | .02 |
| ❑ 159 Luis Rivera | .05 | .02 |
| ❑ 160 Cris Carpenter | .05 | .02 |
| ❑ 161 Bruce Ruffin | .05 | .02 |
| ❑ 162 Omar Vizquel | .10 | .05 |
| ❑ 163 Gerald Alexander | .05 | .02 |
| ❑ 164 Mark Guthrie | .05 | .02 |
| ❑ 165 Scott Lewis | .05 | .02 |
| ❑ 166 Bill Sampen | .05 | .02 |
| ❑ 167 Dave Anderson | .05 | .02 |
| ❑ 168 Kevin McReynolds | .05 | .02 |
| ❑ 169 Jose Vizcaino | .05 | .02 |
| ❑ 170 Bob Geren | .05 | .02 |
| ❑ 171 Mike Morgan | .05 | .02 |
| ❑ 172 Jim Gott | .05 | .02 |
| ❑ 173 Mike Pagliarulo | .05 | .02 |
| ❑ 174 Mike Jeffcoat | .05 | .02 |
| ❑ 175 Craig Lefferts | .05 | .02 |
| ❑ 176 Steve Finley | .10 | .05 |
| ❑ 177 Wally Backman | .05 | .02 |
| ❑ 178 Kent Mercker | .05 | .02 |
| ❑ 179 John Cerutti | .05 | .02 |
| ❑ 180 Jay Bell | .10 | .05 |
| ❑ 181 Dale Sveum | .05 | .02 |
| ❑ 182 Greg Gagne | .05 | .02 |
| ❑ 183 Donnie Hill | .05 | .02 |
| ❑ 184 Rex Hudler | .05 | .02 |
| ❑ 185 Pat Kelly | .05 | .02 |
| ❑ 186 Jeff D. Robinson | .05 | .02 |
| ❑ 187 Jeff Gray | .05 | .02 |
| ❑ 188 Jerry Willard | .05 | .02 |
| ❑ 189 Carlos Quintana | .05 | .02 |
| ❑ 190 Dennis Eckersley | .10 | .05 |
| ❑ 191 Kelly Downs | .05 | .02 |
| ❑ 192 Gregg Jefferies | .05 | .02 |
| ❑ 193 Darrin Fletcher | .05 | .02 |
| ❑ 194 Mike Jackson | .05 | .02 |
| ❑ 195 Eddie Murray | .20 | .09 |
| ❑ 196 Bill Landrum | .05 | .02 |
| ❑ 197 Eric Yelding | .05 | .02 |
| ❑ 198 Devon White | .05 | .02 |
| ❑ 199 Larry Walker | .10 | .05 |
| ❑ 200 Ryne Sandberg | .25 | .11 |
| ❑ 201 Dave Magadan | .05 | .02 |
| ❑ 202 Steve Chitren | .05 | .02 |
| ❑ 203 Scott Fletcher | .05 | .02 |
| ❑ 204 Dwayne Henry | .05 | .02 |
| ❑ 205 Scott Coolbaugh | .05 | .02 |
| ❑ 206 Tracy Jones | .05 | .02 |
| ❑ 207 Von Hayes | .05 | .02 |
| ❑ 208 Bob Melvin | .05 | .02 |
| ❑ 209 Scott Scudder | .05 | .02 |

❑ 210 Luis Gonzalez .10 .05
❑ 211 Scott Sanderson .05 .02
❑ 212 Chris Donnels .05 .02
❑ 213 Heathcliff Slocumb .05 .02
❑ 214 Mike Timlin .05 .02
❑ 215 Brian Harper .05 .02
❑ 216 Juan Berenguer UER .05 .02
(Decimal point missing in IP total)
❑ 217 Mike Henneman .05 .02
❑ 218 Bill Spiers .05 .02
❑ 219 Scott Terry .05 .02
❑ 220 Frank Viola .05 .02
❑ 221 Mark Eichhorn .05 .02
❑ 222 Ernest Riles .05 .02
❑ 223 Ray Lankford .20 .09
❑ 224 Pete Harnisch .05 .02
❑ 225 Bobby Bonilla .10 .05
❑ 226 Mike Scioscia .05 .02
❑ 227 Joel Skinner .05 .02
❑ 228 Brian Holman .05 .02
❑ 229 Gilberto Reyes .05 .02
❑ 230 Matt Williams .10 .05
❑ 231 Jaime Navarro .05 .02
❑ 232 Jose Rijo .05 .02
❑ 233 Atlee Hammaker .05 .02
❑ 234 Tim Teufel .05 .02
❑ 235 John Kruk .10 .05
❑ 236 Kurt Stillwell .05 .02
❑ 237 Dan Pasqua .05 .02
❑ 238 Tim Crews .05 .02
❑ 239 Dave Gallagher .05 .02
❑ 240 Leo Gomez .05 .02
❑ 241 Steve Avery .05 .02
❑ 242 Bill Gullickson .05 .02
❑ 243 Mark Portugal .05 .02
❑ 244 Lee Guetterman .05 .02
❑ 245 Benito Santiago .05 .02
❑ 246 Jim Gantner .05 .02
❑ 247 Robby Thompson .05 .02
❑ 248 Terry Shumpert .05 .02
❑ 249 Mike Bell .05 .02
❑ 250 Harold Reynolds .05 .02
❑ 251 Mike Felder .05 .02
❑ 252 Bill Pecota .05 .02
❑ 253 Bill Krueger .05 .02
❑ 254 Alfredo Griffin .05 .02
❑ 255 Lou Whitaker .10 .05
❑ 256 Roy Smith .05 .02
❑ 257 Jerald Clark .05 .02
❑ 258 Sammy Sosa .40 .18
❑ 259 Tim Naehring .05 .02
❑ 260 Dave Righetti .05 .02
❑ 261 Paul Gibson .05 .02
❑ 262 Chris James .05 .02
❑ 263 Larry Andersen .05 .02
❑ 264 Storm Davis .05 .02
❑ 265 Jose Lind .05 .02
❑ 266 Greg Hibbard .05 .02
❑ 267 Norm Charlton .05 .02
❑ 268 Paul Kilgus .05 .02
❑ 269 Greg Maddux .50 .23
❑ 270 Ellis Burks .10 .05
❑ 271 Frank Tanana .05 .02
❑ 272 Gene Larkin .05 .02
❑ 273 Ron Hassey .05 .02
❑ 274 Jeff M. Robinson .05 .02
❑ 275 Steve Howe .05 .02
❑ 276 Daryl Boston .05 .02
❑ 277 Mark Lee .05 .02
❑ 278 Jose Segura .05 .02
❑ 279 Lance Blankenship .05 .02
❑ 280 Don Slaught .05 .02
❑ 281 Russ Swan .05 .02
❑ 282 Bob Tewksbury .05 .02
❑ 283 Geno Petralli .05 .02
❑ 284 Shane Mack .05 .02
❑ 285 Bob Scanlan .05 .02
❑ 286 Tim Leary .05 .02
❑ 287 John Smoltz .10 .05
❑ 288 Pat Borders .05 .02
❑ 289 Mark Davidson .05 .02
❑ 290 Sam Horn .05 .02
❑ 291 Lenny Harris .05 .02
❑ 292 Franklin Stubbs .05 .02
❑ 293 Thomas Howard .05 .02
❑ 294 Steve Lyons .05 .02
❑ 295 Francisco Oliveras .05 .02
❑ 296 Terry Leach .05 .02
❑ 297 Barry Jones .05 .02
❑ 298 Lance Parrish .05 .02
❑ 299 Wally Whitehurst .05 .02
❑ 300 Bob Welch .05 .02
❑ 301 Charlie Hayes .05 .02
❑ 302 Charlie Hough .10 .05
❑ 303 Gary Redus .05 .02
❑ 304 Scott Bradley .05 .02
❑ 305 Jose Oquendo .05 .02
❑ 306 Pete Incaviglia .05 .02
❑ 307 Marvin Freeman .05 .02
❑ 308 Gary Pettis .05 .02
❑ 309 Joe Slusarski .05 .02
❑ 310 Kevin Seitzer .05 .02
❑ 311 Jeff Reed .05 .02
❑ 312 Pat Tabler .05 .02
❑ 313 Mike Maddux .05 .02
❑ 314 Bob Milacki .05 .02
❑ 315 Eric Anthony .05 .02
❑ 316 Dante Bichette .10 .05
❑ 317 Steve Decker .05 .02
❑ 318 Jack Clark .10 .05
❑ 319 Doug Dascenzo .05 .02
❑ 320 Scott Leius .05 .02
❑ 321 Jim Lindeman .05 .02
❑ 322 Bryan Harvey .05 .02
❑ 323 Spike Owen .05 .02
❑ 324 Roberto Kelly .05 .02
❑ 325 Stan Belinda .05 .02
❑ 326 Joey Cora .05 .02
❑ 327 Jeff Innis .05 .02
❑ 328 Willie Wilson .05 .02
❑ 329 Juan Agosto .05 .02
❑ 330 Charles Nagy .05 .02
❑ 331 Scott Bailes .05 .02
❑ 332 Pete Schourek .05 .02
❑ 333 Mike Flanagan .05 .02
❑ 334 Omar Olivares .05 .02
❑ 335 Dennis Lamp .05 .02
❑ 336 Tommy Greene .05 .02
❑ 337 Randy Velarde .05 .02
❑ 338 Tom Lampkin .05 .02
❑ 339 John Russell .05 .02
❑ 340 Bob Kipper .05 .02
❑ 341 Todd Burns .05 .02
❑ 342 Ron Jones .05 .02
❑ 343 Dave Valle .05 .02
❑ 344 Mike Heath .05 .02
❑ 345 John Olerud .10 .05
❑ 346 Gerald Young .05 .02
❑ 347 Ken Patterson .05 .02
❑ 348 Les Lancaster .05 .02
❑ 349 Steve Crawford .05 .02
❑ 350 John Candelaria .05 .02
❑ 351 Mike Aldrete .05 .02
❑ 352 Mariano Duncan .05 .02
❑ 353 Julio Machado .05 .02
❑ 354 Ken Williams .05 .02
❑ 355 Walt Terrell .05 .02
❑ 356 Mitch Williams .05 .02
❑ 357 Al Newman .05 .02
❑ 358 Bud Black .05 .02
❑ 359 Joe Hesketh .05 .02
❑ 360 Paul Assenmacher .05 .02
❑ 361 Bo Jackson .10 .05
❑ 362 Jeff Blauser .05 .02
❑ 363 Mike Brumley .05 .02
❑ 364 Jim Deshaies .05 .02
❑ 365 Brady Anderson .10 .05
❑ 366 Chuck McElroy .05 .02
❑ 367 Matt Merullo .05 .02
❑ 368 Tim Belcher .05 .02
❑ 369 Luis Aquino .05 .02
❑ 370 Joe Oliver .05 .02
❑ 371 Greg Swindell .05 .02
❑ 372 Lee Stevens .10 .05
❑ 373 Mark Knudson .05 .02
❑ 374 Bill Wegman .05 .02
❑ 375 Jerry Don Gleaton .05 .02
❑ 376 Pedro Guerrero .05 .02
❑ 377 Randy Bush .05 .02
❑ 378 Greg W. Harris .05 .02
❑ 379 Eric Plunk .05 .02
❑ 380 Jose DeJesus .05 .02
❑ 381 Bobby Witt .05 .02
❑ 382 Curtis Wilkerson .05 .02
❑ 383 Gene Nelson .05 .02
❑ 384 Wes Chamberlain .05 .02
❑ 385 Tom Henke .05 .02
❑ 386 Mark Lemke .05 .02
❑ 387 Greg Briley .05 .02
❑ 388 Rafael Ramirez .05 .02
❑ 389 Tony Fossas .05 .02
❑ 390 Henry Cotto .05 .02
❑ 391 Tim Hulett .05 .02
❑ 392 Dean Palmer .10 .05
❑ 393 Glenn Braggs .05 .02
❑ 394 Mark Salas .05 .02
❑ 395 Rusty Meacham .05 .02
❑ 396 Andy Ashby .10 .05
❑ 397 Jose Melendez .05 .02
❑ 398 Warren Newson .05 .02
❑ 399 Frank Castillo .05 .02
❑ 400 Chito Martinez .05 .02
❑ 401 Bernie Williams .20 .09
❑ 402 Derek Bell .10 .05
❑ 403 Javier Ortiz .05 .02
❑ 404 Tim Sherrill .05 .02
❑ 405 Rob MacDonald .05 .02
❑ 406 Phil Plantier .05 .02
❑ 407 Troy Afenir .05 .02
❑ 408 Gino Minutelli .05 .02
❑ 409 Reggie Jefferson .10 .05
❑ 410 Mike Remlinger .05 .02
❑ 411 Carlos Rodriguez .05 .02
❑ 412 Joe Redfield .05 .02
❑ 413 Alonzo Powell .05 .02
❑ 414 Scott Livingstone UER .05 .02
(Travis Fryman, not Woody, should be referenced on back)
❑ 415 Scott Kamieniecki .05 .02
❑ 416 Tim Spehr .05 .02
❑ 417 Brian Hunter .05 .02
❑ 418 Ced Landrum .05 .02
❑ 419 Bret Barberie .05 .02
❑ 420 Kevin Morton .05 .02
❑ 421 Doug Henry RC .05 .02
❑ 422 Doug Piatt .05 .02
❑ 423 Pat Rice .05 .02
❑ 424 Juan Guzman .05 .02
❑ 425 Nolan Ryan NH .50 .18
❑ 426 Tommy Greene NH .05 .02
❑ 427 Bob Milacki and .05 .02
Mike Flanagan NH (Mark Williamson and Gregg Olson)
❑ 428 Wilson Alvarez NH .05 .02
❑ 429 Otis Nixon HL .05 .02
❑ 430 Rickey Henderson HL .10 .05
❑ 431 Cecil Fielder AS .05 .02
❑ 432 Julio Franco AS .05 .02
❑ 433 Cal Ripken AS .40 .09
❑ 434 Wade Boggs AS .20 .09
❑ 435 Joe Carter AS .05 .02
❑ 436 Ken Griffey Jr. AS .60 .25
❑ 437 Ruben Sierra AS .05 .02
❑ 438 Scott Erickson AS .05 .02
❑ 439 Tom Henke AS .05 .02
❑ 440 Terry Steinbach AS .05 .02
❑ 441 Rickey Henderson DT .25 .11
❑ 442 Ryne Sandberg DT .25 .11
❑ 443 Otis Nixon .05 .02
❑ 444 Scott Radinsky .05 .02
❑ 445 Mark Grace .20 .09
❑ 446 Tony Pena .05 .02
❑ 447 Billy Hatcher .05 .02
❑ 448 Glenallen Hill .05 .02
❑ 449 Chris Gwynn .05 .02
❑ 450 Tom Glavine .10 .05
❑ 451 John Habyan .05 .02
❑ 452 Al Osuna .05 .02
❑ 453 Tony Phillips .05 .02
❑ 454 Greg Cadaret .05 .02
❑ 455 Rob Dibble .05 .02
❑ 456 Rick Honeycutt .05 .02
❑ 457 Jerome Walton .05 .02
❑ 458 Mookie Wilson .10 .05
❑ 459 Mark Gubicza .05 .02

❑ 460 Craig Biggio .10 .05
❑ 461 Dave Cochrane .05 .02
❑ 462 Keith Miller .05 .02
❑ 463 Alex Cole .05 .02
❑ 464 Pete Smith .05 .02
❑ 465 Brett Butler .10 .05
❑ 466 Jeff Huson .05 .02
❑ 467 Steve Lake .05 .02
❑ 468 Lloyd Moseby .05 .02
❑ 469 Tim McIntosh .05 .02
❑ 470 Dennis Martinez .10 .05
❑ 471 Greg Myers .05 .02
❑ 472 Mackey Sasser .05 .02
❑ 473 Junior Ortiz .05 .02
❑ 474 Greg Olson .05 .02
❑ 475 Steve Sax .05 .02
❑ 476 Ricky Jordan .05 .02
❑ 477 Max Venable .05 .02
❑ 478 Brian McRae .05 .02
❑ 479 Doug Simons .05 .02
❑ 480 Rickey Henderson .25 .11
❑ 481 Gary Varsho .05 .02
❑ 482 Carl Willis .05 .02
❑ 483 Rick Wilkins .05 .02
❑ 484 Donn Pall .05 .02
❑ 485 Edgar Martinez .10 .05
❑ 486 Tom Foley .05 .02
❑ 487 Mark Williamson .05 .02
❑ 488 Jack Armstrong .05 .02
❑ 489 Gary Carter .10 .05
❑ 490 Ruben Sierra .05 .02
❑ 491 Gerald Perry .05 .02
❑ 492 Rob Murphy .05 .02
❑ 493 Zane Smith .05 .02
❑ 494 Darryl Kile .10 .05
❑ 495 Kelly Gruber .05 .02
❑ 496 Jerry Browne .05 .02
❑ 497 Darryl Hamilton .05 .02
❑ 498 Mike Stanton .05 .02
❑ 499 Mark Leonard .05 .02
❑ 500 Jose Canseco .25 .11
❑ 501 Dave Martinez .05 .02
❑ 502 Jose Guzman .05 .02
❑ 503 Terry Kennedy .05 .02
❑ 504 Ed Sprague .05 .02
❑ 505 Frank Thomas UER .40 .18
(His Gulf Coast League stats are wrong)
❑ 506 Darren Daulton .10 .05
❑ 507 Kevin Tapani .05 .02
❑ 508 Luis Salazar .05 .02
❑ 509 Paul Faries .05 .02
❑ 510 Sandy Alomar Jr. .10 .05
❑ 511 Jeff King .05 .02
❑ 512 Gary Thurman .05 .02
❑ 513 Chris Hammond .05 .02
❑ 514 Pedro Munoz .05 .02
❑ 515 Alan Trammell .10 .05
❑ 516 Geronimo Pena .05 .02
❑ 517 Rodney McCray UER .05 .02
(Stole 6 bases in 1990, not 5; career totals are correct at 7)
❑ 518 Manny Lee .05 .02
❑ 519 Junior Felix .05 .02
❑ 520 Kirk Gibson .10 .05
❑ 521 Darrin Jackson .05 .02
❑ 522 John Burkett .05 .02
❑ 523 Jeff Johnson .05 .02
❑ 524 Jim Corsi .05 .02
❑ 525 Robin Yount .20 .09
❑ 526 Jamie Quirk .05 .02
❑ 527 Bob Ojeda .05 .02
❑ 528 Mark Lewis .05 .02
❑ 529 Bryn Smith .05 .02
❑ 530 Kent Hrbek .10 .05
❑ 531 Dennis Boyd .05 .02
❑ 532 Ron Karkovice .05 .02
❑ 533 Don August .05 .02
❑ 534 Todd Frohwirth .05 .02
❑ 535 Wally Joyner .10 .05
❑ 536 Dennis Rasmussen .05 .02
❑ 537 Andy Allanson .05 .02
❑ 538 Rich Gossage .10 .05
❑ 539 John Marzano .05 .02
❑ 540 Cal Ripken .75 .35
❑ 541 Bill Swift UER .05 .02
(Brewers logo on front)
❑ 542 Kevin Appier .10 .05
❑ 543 Dave Bergman .05 .02
❑ 544 Bernard Gilkey .10 .05
❑ 545 Mike Greenwell .05 .02
❑ 546 Jose Uribe .05 .02
❑ 547 Jesse Orosco .05 .02
❑ 548 Bob Patterson .05 .02
❑ 549 Mike Stanley .05 .02
❑ 550 Howard Johnson .05 .02
❑ 551 Joe Orsulak .05 .02
❑ 552 Dick Schofield .05 .02
❑ 553 Dave Hollins .05 .02
❑ 554 David Segui .05 .02
❑ 555 Barry Bonds .30 .14
❑ 556 Mo Vaughn .10 .05
❑ 557 Craig Wilson .05 .02
❑ 558 Bobby Rose .05 .02
❑ 559 Rod Nichols .05 .02
❑ 560 Len Dykstra .10 .05
❑ 561 Craig Grebeck .05 .02
❑ 562 Darren Lewis .05 .02
❑ 563 Todd Denzinger .05 .02
❑ 564 Ed Whitson .05 .02
❑ 565 Jesse Barfield .05 .02
❑ 566 Lloyd McClendon .05 .02
❑ 567 Dan Plesac .05 .02
❑ 568 Danny Cox .05 .02
❑ 569 Skeeter Barnes .05 .02
❑ 570 Bobby Thigpen .05 .02
❑ 571 Deion Sanders .20 .09
❑ 572 Chuck Knoblauch .10 .05
❑ 573 Matt Nokes .05 .02
❑ 574 Herm Winningham .05 .02
❑ 575 Tom Candiotti .05 .02
❑ 576 Jeff Bagwell .40 .18
❑ 577 Brook Jacoby .05 .02
❑ 578 Chico Walker .05 .02
❑ 579 Brian Downing .05 .02
❑ 580 Dave Stewart .10 .05
❑ 581 Francisco Cabrera .05 .02
❑ 582 Rene Gonzales .05 .02
❑ 583 Stan Javier .05 .02
❑ 584 Randy Johnson .25 .11
❑ 585 Chuck Finley .10 .05
❑ 586 Mark Gardner .05 .02
❑ 587 Mark Whiten .05 .02
❑ 588 Garry Templeton .05 .02
❑ 589 Gary Sheffield .20 .09
❑ 590 Ozzie Smith .25 .11
❑ 591 Candy Maldonado .05 .02
❑ 592 Mike Sharperson .05 .02
❑ 593 Carlos Martinez .05 .02
❑ 594 Scott Bankhead .05 .02
❑ 595 Tim Wallach .05 .02
❑ 596 Tino Martinez .10 .05
❑ 597 Roger McDowell .05 .02
❑ 598 Cory Snyder .05 .02
❑ 599 Andujar Cedeno .05 .02
❑ 600 Kirby Puckett .50 .23
❑ 601 Rick Parker .05 .02
❑ 602 Todd Hundley .05 .02
❑ 603 Greg Litton .05 .02
❑ 604 Dave Johnson .05 .02
❑ 605 John Franco .10 .05
❑ 606 Mike Fetters .05 .02
❑ 607 Luis Alicea .05 .02
❑ 608 Trevor Wilson .05 .02
❑ 609 Rob Ducey .05 .02
❑ 610 Ramon Martinez .05 .02
❑ 611 Dave Burba .05 .02
❑ 612 Dwight Smith .05 .02
❑ 613 Kevin Maas .05 .02
❑ 614 John Costello .05 .02
❑ 615 Glenn Davis .05 .02
❑ 616 Shawn Abner .05 .02
❑ 617 Scott Hemond .05 .02
❑ 618 Tom Prince .05 .02
❑ 619 Wally Ritchie .05 .02
❑ 620 Jim Abbott .10 .05
❑ 621 Charlie O'Brien .05 .02
❑ 622 Jack Daugherty .05 .02
❑ 623 Tommy Gregg .05 .02
❑ 624 Jeff Shaw .05 .02
❑ 625 Tony Gwynn .40 .18
❑ 626 Mark Leiter .05 .02
❑ 627 Jim Clancy .05 .02
❑ 628 Tim Layana .05 .02
❑ 629 Jeff Schaefer .05 .02
❑ 630 Lee Smith .10 .05
❑ 631 Wade Taylor .05 .02
❑ 632 Mike Simms .05 .02
❑ 633 Terry Steinbach .05 .02
❑ 634 Shawon Dunston .05 .02
❑ 635 Tim Raines .10 .05
❑ 636 Kirt Manwaring .05 .02
❑ 637 Warren Cromartie .05 .02
❑ 638 Luis Quinones .05 .02
❑ 639 Greg Vaughn .10 .05
❑ 640 Kevin Mitchell .10 .05
❑ 641 Chris Hoiles .05 .02
❑ 642 Tom Browning .05 .02
❑ 643 Mitch Webster .05 .02
❑ 644 Steve Olin .05 .02
❑ 645 Tony Fernandez .05 .02
❑ 646 Juan Bell .05 .02
❑ 647 Joe Boever .05 .02
❑ 648 Carney Lansford .10 .05
❑ 649 Mike Benjamin .05 .02
❑ 650 George Brett .40 .18
❑ 651 Tim Burke .05 .02
❑ 652 Jack Morris .10 .05
❑ 653 Orel Hershiser .10 .05
❑ 654 Mike Schooler .05 .02
❑ 655 Andy Van Slyke .10 .05
❑ 656 Dave Stieb .05 .02
❑ 657 Dave Clark .05 .02
❑ 658 Ben McDonald .05 .02
❑ 659 John Smiley .05 .02
❑ 660 Wade Boggs .25 .11
❑ 661 Eric Bullock .05 .02
❑ 662 Eric Show .05 .02
❑ 663 Lenny Webster .05 .02
❑ 664 Mike Huff .05 .02
❑ 665 Rick Sutcliffe .10 .05
❑ 666 Jeff Manto .05 .02
❑ 667 Mike Fitzgerald .05 .02
❑ 668 Matt Young .05 .02
❑ 669 Dave West .05 .02
❑ 670 Mike Hartley .05 .02
❑ 671 Curt Schilling .10 .05
❑ 672 Brian Bohanon .05 .02
❑ 673 Cecil Espy .05 .02
❑ 674 Joe Grahe .05 .02
❑ 675 Sid Fernandez .05 .02
❑ 676 Edwin Nunez .05 .02
❑ 677 Hector Villanueva .05 .02
❑ 678 Sean Berry .05 .02
❑ 679 Dave Eiland .05 .02
❑ 680 David Cone .10 .05
❑ 681 Mike Bordick .05 .02
❑ 682 Tony Castillo .05 .02
❑ 683 John Barfield .05 .02
❑ 684 Jeff Hamilton .05 .02
❑ 685 Ken Dayley .05 .02
❑ 686 Carmelo Martinez .05 .02
❑ 687 Mike Capel .05 .02
❑ 688 Scott Chiamparino .05 .02
❑ 689 Rich Gedman .05 .02
❑ 690 Rich Monteleone .05 .02
❑ 691 Alejandro Pena .05 .02
❑ 692 Oscar Azocar .05 .02
❑ 693 Jim Poole .05 .02
❑ 694 Mike Gardiner .05 .02
❑ 695 Steve Buechele .05 .02
❑ 696 Rudy Seanez .05 .02
❑ 697 Paul Abbott .05 .02
❑ 698 Steve Searcy .05 .02
❑ 699 Jose Offerman .05 .02
❑ 700 Ivan Rodriguez .40 .18
❑ 701 Joe Girardi .10 .05
❑ 702 Tony Perezchica .05 .02
❑ 703 Paul McClellan .05 .02
❑ 704 David Howard .05 .02
❑ 705 Dan Petry .05 .02
❑ 706 Jack Howell .05 .02
❑ 707 Jose Mesa .05 .02
❑ 708 Randy St. Claire .05 .02
❑ 709 Kevin Brown .10 .05
❑ 710 Ron Darling .05 .02
❑ 711 Jason Grimsley .05 .02

❑ 712 John Orton .05 .02
❑ 713 Shawn Boskie .05 .02
❑ 714 Pat Clements .05 .02
❑ 715 Brian Barnes .05 .02
❑ 716 Luis Lopez .05 .02
❑ 717 Bob McClure .05 .02
❑ 718 Mark Davis .05 .02
❑ 719 Dann Bilardello .05 .02
❑ 720 Tom Edens .05 .02
❑ 721 Willie Fraser .05 .02
❑ 722 Curt Young .05 .02
❑ 723 Neal Heaton .05 .02
❑ 724 Craig Worthington .05 .02
❑ 725 Mel Rojas .05 .02
❑ 726 Daryl Irvine .05 .02
❑ 727 Roger Mason .05 .02
❑ 728 Kirk Dressendorfer .05 .02
❑ 729 Scott Aldred .05 .02
❑ 730 Willie Blair .05 .02
❑ 731 Allan Anderson .05 .02
❑ 732 Dana Kiecker .05 .02
❑ 733 Jose Gonzalez .05 .02
❑ 734 Brian Drahman .05 .02
❑ 735 Brad Komminsk .05 .02
❑ 736 Arthur Rhodes .05 .02
❑ 737 Terry Mathews .05 .02
❑ 738 Jeff Fassero .05 .02
❑ 739 Mike Magnante RC .05 .02
❑ 740 Kip Gross .05 .02
❑ 741 Jim Hunter .05 .02
❑ 742 Jose Mota .05 .02
❑ 743 Joe Bitker .05 .02
❑ 744 Tim Mauser .05 .02
❑ 745 Ramon Garcia .05 .02
❑ 746 Rod Beck RC .20 .09
❑ 747 Jim Austin .05 .02
❑ 748 Keith Mitchell .05 .02
❑ 749 Wayne Rosenthal .05 .02
❑ 750 Bryan Hickerson RC .05 .02
❑ 751 Bruce Egloff .05 .02
❑ 752 John Wehner .05 .02
❑ 753 Darren Holmes .05 .02
❑ 754 Dave Hansen .05 .02
❑ 755 Mike Mussina .30 .14
❑ 756 Anthony Young .05 .02
❑ 757 Ron Tingley .05 .02
❑ 758 Ricky Bones .05 .02
❑ 759 Mark Wohlers .05 .02
❑ 760 Wilson Alvarez .05 .02
❑ 761 Harvey Pulliam .05 .02
❑ 762 Ryan Bowen .05 .02
❑ 763 Terry Bross .05 .02
❑ 764 Joel Johnston .05 .02
❑ 765 Terry McDaniel .05 .02
❑ 766 Esteban Beltre .05 .02
❑ 767 Rob Maurer .05 .02
❑ 768 Ted Wood .05 .02
❑ 769 Mo Sanford .05 .02
❑ 770 Jeff Carter .05 .02
❑ 771 Gil Heredia RC .05 .02
❑ 772 Monty Fariss .05 .02
❑ 773 Will Clark AS .10 .05
❑ 774 Ryne Sandberg AS .20 .09
❑ 775 Barry Larkin AS .10 .05
❑ 776 Howard Johnson AS .05 .02
❑ 777 Barry Bonds AS .20 .09
❑ 778 Brett Butler AS .05 .02
❑ 779 Tony Gwynn AS .20 .09
❑ 780 Ramon Martinez AS .05 .02
❑ 781 Lee Smith AS .05 .02
❑ 782 Mike Scioscia AS .05 .02
❑ 783 Dennis Martinez HL UER .05 .02
(Card has both 13th and 15th perfect game in Major League history)
❑ 784 Dennis Martinez NH .05 .02
❑ 785 Mark Gardner NH .05 .02
❑ 786 Bret Saberhagen NH .05 .02
❑ 787 Kent Mercker NH .05 .02
Mark Wohlers
Alejandro Pena
❑ 788 Cal Ripken MVP .40 .18
❑ 789 Terry Pendleton MVP .05 .02
❑ 790 Roger Clemens CY .20 .09
❑ 791 Tom Glavine CY .10 .05
❑ 792 Chuck Knoblauch ROY .05 .02
❑ 793 Jeff Bagwell ROY .10 .05
❑ 794 Cal Ripken MANYR .40 .18
❑ 795 David Cone HL .05 .02
❑ 796 Kirby Puckett HL .25 .09
❑ 797 Steve Avery HL .05 .02
❑ 798 Jack Morris HL .05 .02
❑ 799 Allen Watson DC RC .05 .02
❑ 800 Manny Ramirez DC RC 1.50 .70
❑ 801 Cliff Floyd DC RC .50 .23
❑ 802 Al Shirley DC RC .05 .02
❑ 803 Brian Barber DC RC .05 .02
❑ 804 Jon Farrell DC RC .05 .02
❑ 805 Brent Gates DC RC .05 .02
❑ 806 Scott Ruffcorn DC RC .05 .02
❑ 807 Tyrone Hill DC RC .05 .02
❑ 808 Benji Gil DC RC .05 .02
❑ 809 Aaron Sele DC RC .50 .23
❑ 810 Tyler Green DC RC .05 .02
❑ 811 Chris Jones .05 .02
❑ 812 Steve Wilson .05 .02
❑ 813 Freddie Benavides .05 .02
❑ 814 Don Wakamatsu .05 .02
❑ 815 Mike Humphreys .05 .02
❑ 816 Scott Servais .05 .02
❑ 817 Rico Rossy .05 .02
❑ 818 John Ramos .05 .02
❑ 819 Rob Mallicoat .05 .02
❑ 820 Milt Hill .05 .02
❑ 821 Carlos Garcia .05 .02
❑ 822 Stan Royer .05 .02
❑ 823 Jeff Plympton .05 .02
❑ 824 Braulio Castillo .05 .02
❑ 825 David Haas .05 .02
❑ 826 Luis Mercedes .05 .02
❑ 827 Eric Karros .20 .09
❑ 828 Shawn Hare RC .05 .02
❑ 829 Reggie Sanders .05 .02
❑ 830 Tom Goodwin .10 .05
❑ 831 Dan Gakeler .05 .02
❑ 832 Stacy Jones .05 .02
❑ 833 Kim Batiste .05 .02
❑ 834 Cal Eldred .05 .02
❑ 835 Chris George .05 .02
❑ 836 Wayne Housie .05 .02
❑ 837 Mike Ignasiak .05 .02
❑ 838 Josias Manzanillo RC .05 .02
❑ 839 Jim Olander .05 .02
❑ 840 Gary Cooper .05 .02
❑ 841 Royce Clayton .05 .02
❑ 842 Hector Fajardo RC .05 .02
❑ 843 Blaine Beatty .05 .02
❑ 844 Jorge Pedre .05 .02
❑ 845 Kenny Lofton .25 .11
❑ 846 Scott Brosius RC .25 .11
❑ 847 Chris Cron .05 .02
❑ 848 Denis Boucher .05 .02
❑ 849 Kyle Abbott .05 .02
❑ 850 Bob Zupcic RC .05 .02
❑ 851 Rheal Cormier .05 .02
❑ 852 Jim Lewis .05 .02
❑ 853 Anthony Telford .05 .02
❑ 854 Cliff Brantley .05 .02
❑ 855 Kevin Campbell .05 .02
❑ 856 Craig Shipley .05 .02
❑ 857 Chuck Carr .05 .02
❑ 858 Tony Eusebio .20 .09
❑ 859 Jim Thome .40 .18
❑ 860 Vinny Castilla RC 1.00 .45
❑ 861 Dann Howitt .05 .02
❑ 862 Kevin Ward .05 .02
❑ 863 Steve Wapnick .05 .02
❑ 864 Rod Brewer RC .05 .02
❑ 865 Todd Van Poppel .05 .02
❑ 866 Jose Hernandez RC .05 .02
❑ 867 Amalio Carreno .05 .02
❑ 868 Calvin Jones .05 .02
❑ 869 Jeff Gardner .05 .02
❑ 870 Jarvis Brown .05 .02
❑ 871 Eddie Taubensee RC .10 .05
❑ 872 Andy Mota .05 .02
❑ 873 Chris Haney .05 .02
❑ 874 Roberto Hernandez .05 .02
❑ 875 Laddie Renfroe .05 .02
❑ 876 Scott Cooper .05 .02
❑ 877 Armando Reynoso RC .05 .02
❑ 878 Ty Cobb MEMO .25 .11
❑ 879 Babe Ruth MEMO .40 .18
❑ 880 Honus Wagner MEMO .20 .09
❑ 881 Lou Gehrig MEMO .25 .11
❑ 882 Satchel Paige MEMO .20 .09
❑ 883 Will Clark DT .10 .05
❑ 884 Cal Ripken DT 2.00 .90
❑ 885 Wade Boggs DT .25 .11
❑ 886 Kirby Puckett DT .50 .23
❑ 887 Tony Gwynn DT .20 .09
❑ 888 Craig Biggio DT .10 .05
❑ 889 Scott Erickson DT .05 .02
❑ 890 Tom Glavine DT .10 .05
❑ 891 Rob Dibble DT .05 .02
❑ 892 Mitch Williams DT .05 .02
❑ 893 Frank Thomas DT .40 .18
❑ X672 Chuck Knoblauch AU 50.00 22.00
(1990 Score card, autographed with special hologram on back)

## 1992 Score Rookie/Traded

| | MINT | NRMT |
|---|---|---|
| COMP.FACT.SET (110) | 15.00 | 6.75 |

❑ 1T Gary Sheffield .75 .35
❑ 2T Kevin Seitzer .15 .07
❑ 3T Danny Tartabull .15 .07
❑ 4T Steve Sax .15 .07
❑ 5T Bobby Bonilla .30 .14
❑ 6T Frank Viola .15 .07
❑ 7T Dave Winfield .75 .35
❑ 8T Rick Sutcliffe .30 .14
❑ 9T Jose Canseco 1.00 .45
❑ 10T Greg Swindell .15 .07
❑ 11T Eddie Murray .75 .35
❑ 12T Randy Myers .30 .14
❑ 13T Wally Joyner .30 .14
❑ 14T Kenny Lofton 2.50 1.10
❑ 15T Jack Morris .30 .14
❑ 16T Charlie Hayes .15 .07
❑ 17T Pete Incaviglia .15 .07
❑ 18T Kevin Mitchell .30 .14
❑ 19T Kurt Stillwell .15 .07
❑ 20T Bret Saberhagen .30 .14
❑ 21T Steve Buechele .15 .07
❑ 22T John Smiley .15 .07
❑ 23T Sammy Sosa 1.50 .70
❑ 24T George Bell .15 .07
❑ 25T Curt Schilling .30 .14
❑ 26T Dick Schofield .15 .07
❑ 27T David Cone .30 .14
❑ 28T Dan Gladden .15 .07
❑ 29T Kirk McCaskill .15 .07
❑ 30T Mike Gallego .15 .07
❑ 31T Kevin McReynolds .15 .07
❑ 32T Bill Swift .15 .07
❑ 33T Dave Martinez .15 .07
❑ 34T Storm Davis .15 .07
❑ 35T Willie Randolph .30 .14
❑ 36T Melido Perez .15 .07
❑ 37T Mark Carreon .15 .07
❑ 38T Doug Jones .15 .07
❑ 39T Gregg Jefferies .15 .07
❑ 40T Mike Jackson .15 .07
❑ 41T Dickie Thon .15 .07
❑ 42T Eric King .15 .07

| | | | |
|---|---|---|---|
| ❑ 43T | Herm Winningham | .15 | .07 |
| ❑ 44T | Derek Lilliquist | .15 | .07 |
| ❑ 45T | Dave Anderson | .15 | .07 |
| ❑ 46T | Jeff Reardon | .30 | .14 |
| ❑ 47T | Scott Bankhead | .15 | .07 |
| ❑ 48T | Cory Snyder | .15 | .07 |
| ❑ 49T | Al Newman | .15 | .07 |
| ❑ 50T | Keith Miller | .15 | .07 |
| ❑ 51T | Dave Burba | .15 | .07 |
| ❑ 52T | Bill Pecota | .15 | .07 |
| ❑ 53T | Chuck Crim | .15 | .07 |
| ❑ 54T | Mariano Duncan | .15 | .07 |
| ❑ 55T | Dave Gallagher | .15 | .07 |
| ❑ 56T | Chris Gwynn | .15 | .07 |
| ❑ 57T | Scott Ruskin | .15 | .07 |
| ❑ 58T | Jack Armstrong | .15 | .07 |
| ❑ 59T | Gary Carter | .50 | .23 |
| ❑ 60T | Andres Galarraga | .50 | .23 |
| ❑ 61T | Ken Hill | .15 | .07 |
| ❑ 62T | Eric Davis | .30 | .14 |
| ❑ 63T | Ruben Sierra | .15 | .07 |
| ❑ 64T | Darrin Fletcher | .15 | .07 |
| ❑ 65T | Tim Belcher | .15 | .07 |
| ❑ 66T | Mike Morgan | .15 | .07 |
| ❑ 67T | Scott Scudder | .15 | .07 |
| ❑ 68T | Tom Candiotti | .15 | .07 |
| ❑ 69T | Hubie Brooks | .15 | .07 |
| ❑ 70T | Kal Daniels | .15 | .07 |
| ❑ 71T | Bruce Ruffin | .15 | .07 |
| ❑ 72T | Billy Hatcher | .15 | .07 |
| ❑ 73T | Bob Melvin | .15 | .07 |
| ❑ 74T | Lee Guetterman | .15 | .07 |
| ❑ 75T | Rene Gonzales | .15 | .07 |
| ❑ 76T | Kevin Bass | .15 | .07 |
| ❑ 77T | Tom Bolton | .15 | .07 |
| ❑ 78T | John Wetteland | .30 | .14 |
| ❑ 79T | Bip Roberts | .15 | .07 |
| ❑ 80T | Pat Listach RC | .15 | .07 |
| ❑ 81T | John Doherty RC | .15 | .07 |
| ❑ 82T | Sam Militello | .15 | .07 |
| ❑ 83T | Brian Jordan RC | 1.50 | .70 |
| ❑ 84T | Jeff Kent RC | 5.00 | 2.20 |
| ❑ 85T | Dave Fleming | .15 | .07 |
| ❑ 86T | Jeff Tackett | .15 | .07 |
| ❑ 87T | Chad Curtis RC | .50 | .23 |
| ❑ 88T | Eric Fox RC | .15 | .07 |
| ❑ 89T | Denny Neagle | .50 | .23 |
| ❑ 90T | Donovan Osborne | .15 | .07 |
| ❑ 91T | Carlos Hernandez | .15 | .07 |
| ❑ 92T | Tim Wakefield RC | .75 | .35 |
| ❑ 93T | Tim Salmon | 2.50 | 1.10 |
| ❑ 94T | Dave Nilsson | .30 | .14 |
| ❑ 95T | Mike Perez | .15 | .07 |
| ❑ 96T | Pat Hentgen | .15 | .07 |
| ❑ 97T | Frank Seminara RC | .15 | .07 |
| ❑ 98T | Ruben Amaro | .15 | .07 |
| ❑ 99T | Archi Cianfrocco RC | .15 | .07 |
| ❑ 100T | Andy Stankiewicz | .15 | .07 |
| ❑ 101T | Jim Bullinger | .15 | .07 |
| ❑ 102T | Pat Mahomes RC | .15 | .07 |
| ❑ 103T | Hipolito Pichardo RC | .15 | .07 |
| ❑ 104T | Bret Boone | .75 | .35 |
| ❑ 105T | John Vander Wal | .15 | .07 |
| ❑ 106T | Vince Horsman | .15 | .07 |
| ❑ 107T | James Austin | .15 | .07 |
| ❑ 108T | Brian Williams RC | .15 | .07 |
| ❑ 109T | Dan Walters | .15 | .07 |
| ❑ 110T | Wil Cordero | .15 | .07 |

## 1993 Score

| | | MINT | NRMT |
|---|---|---|---|
| COMPLETE SET (660) | | 40.00 | 18.00 |
| ❑ 1 | Ken Griffey Jr. | 1.50 | .70 |
| ❑ 2 | Gary Sheffield | .40 | .18 |
| ❑ 3 | Frank Thomas | .75 | .35 |
| ❑ 4 | Ryne Sandberg | .50 | .23 |
| ❑ 5 | Larry Walker | .20 | .09 |
| ❑ 6 | Cal Ripken Jr. | 1.50 | .70 |
| ❑ 7 | Roger Clemens | .75 | .35 |
| ❑ 8 | Bobby Bonilla | .20 | .09 |
| ❑ 9 | Carlos Baerga | .10 | .05 |
| ❑ 10 | Darren Daulton | .20 | .09 |
| ❑ 11 | Travis Fryman | .20 | .09 |
| ❑ 12 | Andy Van Slyke | .20 | .09 |

| | | | |
|---|---|---|---|
| ❑ 13 | Jose Canseco | .50 | .23 |
| ❑ 14 | Roberto Alomar | .40 | .18 |
| ❑ 15 | Tom Glavine | .30 | .14 |
| ❑ 16 | Barry Larkin | .40 | .18 |
| ❑ 17 | Gregg Jefferies | .10 | .05 |
| ❑ 18 | Craig Biggio | .30 | .14 |
| ❑ 19 | Shane Mack | .10 | .05 |
| ❑ 20 | Brett Butler | .20 | .09 |
| ❑ 21 | Dennis Eckersley | .20 | .09 |
| ❑ 22 | Will Clark | .40 | .18 |
| ❑ 23 | Don Mattingly | 1.00 | .45 |
| ❑ 24 | Tony Gwynn | .75 | .35 |
| ❑ 25 | Ivan Rodriguez | .50 | .23 |
| ❑ 26 | Shawon Dunston | .10 | .05 |
| ❑ 27 | Mike Mussina | .40 | .18 |
| ❑ 28 | Marquis Grissom | .10 | .05 |
| ❑ 29 | Charles Nagy | .10 | .05 |
| ❑ 30 | Len Dykstra | .20 | .09 |
| ❑ 31 | Cecil Fielder | .20 | .09 |
| ❑ 32 | Jay Bell | .20 | .09 |
| ❑ 33 | B.J. Surhoff | .20 | .09 |
| ❑ 34 | Bob Tewksbury | .10 | .05 |
| ❑ 35 | Danny Tartabull | .10 | .05 |
| ❑ 36 | Terry Pendleton | .20 | .09 |
| ❑ 37 | Jack Morris | .20 | .09 |
| ❑ 38 | Hal Morris | .10 | .05 |
| ❑ 39 | Luis Polonia | .10 | .05 |
| ❑ 40 | Ken Caminiti | .20 | .09 |
| ❑ 41 | Robin Ventura | .20 | .09 |
| ❑ 42 | Darryl Strawberry | .20 | .09 |
| ❑ 43 | Wally Joyner | .20 | .09 |
| ❑ 44 | Fred McGriff | .30 | .14 |
| ❑ 45 | Kevin Tapani | .10 | .05 |
| ❑ 46 | Matt Williams | .30 | .14 |
| ❑ 47 | Robin Yount | .30 | .14 |
| ❑ 48 | Ken Hill | .10 | .05 |
| ❑ 49 | Edgar Martinez | .30 | .14 |
| ❑ 50 | Mark Grace | .40 | .18 |
| ❑ 51 | Juan Gonzalez | .40 | .18 |
| ❑ 52 | Curt Schilling | .20 | .09 |
| ❑ 53 | Dwight Gooden | .20 | .09 |
| ❑ 54 | Chris Hoiles | .10 | .05 |
| ❑ 55 | Frank Viola | .10 | .05 |
| ❑ 56 | Ray Lankford | .30 | .14 |
| ❑ 57 | George Brett | .75 | .35 |
| ❑ 58 | Kenny Lofton | .20 | .09 |
| ❑ 59 | Nolan Ryan | 2.00 | .90 |
| ❑ 60 | Mickey Tettleton | .10 | .05 |
| ❑ 61 | John Smoltz | .20 | .09 |
| ❑ 62 | Howard Johnson | .10 | .05 |
| ❑ 63 | Eric Karros | .30 | .14 |
| ❑ 64 | Rick Aguilera | .10 | .05 |
| ❑ 65 | Steve Finley | .20 | .09 |
| ❑ 66 | Mark Langston | .10 | .05 |
| ❑ 67 | Bill Swift | .10 | .05 |
| ❑ 68 | John Olerud | .30 | .14 |
| ❑ 69 | Kevin McReynolds | .10 | .05 |
| ❑ 70 | Jack McDowell | .10 | .05 |
| ❑ 71 | Rickey Henderson | .50 | .23 |
| ❑ 72 | Brian Harper | .10 | .05 |
| ❑ 73 | Mike Morgan | .10 | .05 |
| ❑ 74 | Rafael Palmeiro | .40 | .18 |
| ❑ 75 | Dennis Martinez | .20 | .09 |
| ❑ 76 | Tino Martinez | .20 | .09 |
| ❑ 77 | Eddie Murray | .40 | .18 |
| ❑ 78 | Ellis Burks | .20 | .09 |
| ❑ 79 | John Kruk | .20 | .09 |
| ❑ 80 | Gregg Olson | .10 | .05 |
| ❑ 81 | Bernard Gilkey | .10 | .05 |
| ❑ 82 | Milt Cuyler | .10 | .05 |
| ❑ 83 | Mike LaValliere | .10 | .05 |
| ❑ 84 | Albert Belle | .30 | .14 |
| ❑ 85 | Bip Roberts | .10 | .05 |
| ❑ 86 | Melido Perez | .10 | .05 |
| ❑ 87 | Otis Nixon | .10 | .05 |
| ❑ 88 | Bill Spiers | .10 | .05 |
| ❑ 89 | Jeff Bagwell | .50 | .23 |
| ❑ 90 | Orel Hershiser | .20 | .09 |
| ❑ 91 | Andy Benes | .10 | .05 |
| ❑ 92 | Devon White | .10 | .05 |
| ❑ 93 | Willie McGee | .20 | .09 |
| ❑ 94 | Ozzie Guillen | .10 | .05 |
| ❑ 95 | Ivan Calderon | .10 | .05 |
| ❑ 96 | Keith Miller | .10 | .05 |
| ❑ 97 | Steve Buechele | .10 | .05 |
| ❑ 98 | Kent Hrbek | .20 | .09 |
| ❑ 99 | Dave Hollins | .10 | .05 |
| ❑ 100 | Mike Bordick | .10 | .05 |
| ❑ 101 | Randy Tomlin | .10 | .05 |
| ❑ 102 | Omar Vizquel | .20 | .09 |
| ❑ 103 | Lee Smith | .20 | .09 |
| ❑ 104 | Leo Gomez | .10 | .05 |
| ❑ 105 | Jose Rijo | .10 | .05 |
| ❑ 106 | Mark Whiten | .10 | .05 |
| ❑ 107 | Dave Justice | .30 | .14 |
| ❑ 108 | Eddie Taubensee | .10 | .05 |
| ❑ 109 | Lance Johnson | .10 | .05 |
| ❑ 110 | Felix Jose | .10 | .05 |
| ❑ 111 | Mike Harkey | .10 | .05 |
| ❑ 112 | Randy Milligan | .10 | .05 |
| ❑ 113 | Anthony Young | .10 | .05 |
| ❑ 114 | Rico Brogna | .20 | .09 |
| ❑ 115 | Bret Saberhagen | .20 | .09 |
| ❑ 116 | Sandy Alomar Jr. | .20 | .09 |
| ❑ 117 | Terry Mulholland | .10 | .05 |
| ❑ 118 | Darryl Hamilton | .10 | .05 |
| ❑ 119 | Todd Zeile | .10 | .05 |
| ❑ 120 | Bernie Williams | .40 | .18 |
| ❑ 121 | Zane Smith | .10 | .05 |
| ❑ 122 | Derek Bell | .10 | .05 |
| ❑ 123 | Deion Sanders | .30 | .14 |
| ❑ 124 | Luis Sojo | .10 | .05 |
| ❑ 125 | Joe Oliver | .10 | .05 |
| ❑ 126 | Craig Grebeck | .10 | .05 |
| ❑ 127 | Andujar Cedeno | .10 | .05 |
| ❑ 128 | Brian McRae | .10 | .05 |
| ❑ 129 | Jose Offerman | .10 | .05 |
| ❑ 130 | Pedro Munoz | .10 | .05 |
| ❑ 131 | Bud Black | .10 | .05 |
| ❑ 132 | Mo Vaughn | .20 | .09 |
| ❑ 133 | Bruce Hurst | .10 | .05 |
| ❑ 134 | Dave Henderson | .10 | .05 |
| ❑ 135 | Tom Pagnozzi | .10 | .05 |
| ❑ 136 | Erik Hanson | .10 | .05 |
| ❑ 137 | Orlando Merced | .10 | .05 |
| ❑ 138 | Dean Palmer | .20 | .09 |
| ❑ 139 | John Franco | .20 | .09 |
| ❑ 140 | Brady Anderson | .20 | .09 |
| ❑ 141 | Ricky Jordan | .10 | .05 |
| ❑ 142 | Jeff Blauser | .10 | .05 |
| ❑ 143 | Sammy Sosa | .75 | .35 |
| ❑ 144 | Bob Walk | .10 | .05 |
| ❑ 145 | Delino DeShields | .20 | .09 |
| ❑ 146 | Kevin Brown | .30 | .14 |
| ❑ 147 | Mark Lemke | .10 | .05 |
| ❑ 148 | Chuck Knoblauch | .20 | .09 |
| ❑ 149 | Chris Sabo | .10 | .05 |
| ❑ 150 | Bobby Witt | .10 | .05 |
| ❑ 151 | Luis Gonzalez | .20 | .09 |
| ❑ 152 | Ron Karkovice | .10 | .05 |
| ❑ 153 | Jeff Brantley | .10 | .05 |
| ❑ 154 | Kevin Appier | .20 | .09 |
| ❑ 155 | Darrin Jackson | .10 | .05 |
| ❑ 156 | Kelly Gruber | .10 | .05 |
| ❑ 157 | Royce Clayton | .10 | .05 |
| ❑ 158 | Chuck Finley | .20 | .09 |
| ❑ 159 | Jeff King | .10 | .05 |
| ❑ 160 | Greg Vaughn | .20 | .09 |
| ❑ 161 | Geronimo Pena | .10 | .05 |
| ❑ 162 | Steve Farr | .10 | .05 |
| ❑ 163 | Jose Oquendo | .10 | .05 |
| ❑ 164 | Mark Lewis | .10 | .05 |
| ❑ 165 | John Wetteland | .20 | .09 |
| ❑ 166 | Mike Henneman | .10 | .05 |

| # | Player | | |
|---|---|---|---|
| 167 | Todd Hundley | .10 | .05 |
| 168 | Wes Chamberlain | .10 | .05 |
| 169 | Steve Avery | .10 | .05 |
| 170 | Mike Devereaux | .10 | .05 |
| 171 | Reggie Sanders | .10 | .05 |
| 172 | Jay Buhner | .20 | .09 |
| 173 | Eric Anthony | .10 | .05 |
| 174 | John Burkett | .10 | .05 |
| 175 | Tom Candiotti | .10 | .05 |
| 176 | Phil Plantier | .10 | .05 |
| 177 | Doug Henry | .10 | .05 |
| 178 | Scott Leius | .10 | .05 |
| 179 | Kirt Manwaring | .10 | .05 |
| 180 | Jeff Parrett | .10 | .05 |
| 181 | Don Slaught | .10 | .05 |
| 182 | Scott Radinsky | .10 | .05 |
| 183 | Luis Alicea | .10 | .05 |
| 184 | Tom Gordon | .10 | .05 |
| 185 | Rick Wilkins | .10 | .05 |
| 186 | Todd Stottlemyre | .10 | .05 |
| 187 | Moises Alou | .20 | .09 |
| 188 | Joe Grahe | .10 | .05 |
| 189 | Jeff Kent | .40 | .18 |
| 190 | Bill Wegman | .10 | .05 |
| 191 | Kim Batiste | .10 | .05 |
| 192 | Matt Nokes | .10 | .05 |
| 193 | Mark Wohlers | .10 | .05 |
| 194 | Paul Sorrento | .10 | .05 |
| 195 | Chris Hammond | .10 | .05 |
| 196 | Scott Livingstone | .10 | .05 |
| 197 | Doug Jones | .10 | .05 |
| 198 | Scott Cooper | .10 | .05 |
| 199 | Ramon Martinez | .10 | .05 |
| 200 | Dave Valle | .10 | .05 |
| 201 | Mariano Duncan | .10 | .05 |
| 202 | Ben McDonald | .10 | .05 |
| 203 | Darren Lewis | .10 | .05 |
| 204 | Kenny Rogers | .10 | .05 |
| 205 | Manuel Lee | .10 | .05 |
| 206 | Scott Erickson | .10 | .05 |
| 207 | Dan Gladden | .10 | .05 |
| 208 | Bob Welch | .10 | .05 |
| 209 | Greg Olson | .10 | .05 |
| 210 | Dan Pasqua | .10 | .05 |
| 211 | Tim Wallach | .10 | .05 |
| 212 | Jeff Montgomery | .20 | .09 |
| 213 | Derrick May | .10 | .05 |
| 214 | Ed Sprague | .10 | .05 |
| 215 | David Haas | .10 | .05 |
| 216 | Darrin Fletcher | .10 | .05 |
| 217 | Brian Jordan | .20 | .09 |
| 218 | Jaime Navarro | .10 | .05 |
| 219 | Randy Velarde | .10 | .05 |
| 220 | Ron Gant | .20 | .09 |
| 221 | Paul Quantrill | .10 | .05 |
| 222 | Damion Easley | .10 | .05 |
| 223 | Charlie Hough | .20 | .09 |
| 224 | Brad Brink | .10 | .05 |
| 225 | Barry Manuel | .10 | .05 |
| 226 | Kevin Koslofski | .10 | .05 |
| 227 | Ryan Thompson | .10 | .05 |
| 228 | Mike Munoz | .10 | .05 |
| 229 | Dan Wilson | .20 | .09 |
| 230 | Peter Hoy | .10 | .05 |
| 231 | Pedro Astacio | .20 | .09 |
| 232 | Matt Stairs | .10 | .05 |
| 233 | Jeff Reboulet | .10 | .05 |
| 234 | Manny Alexander | .10 | .05 |
| 235 | Willie Banks | .10 | .05 |
| 236 | John Jaha | .10 | .05 |
| 237 | Scooter Tucker | .10 | .05 |
| 238 | Russ Springer | .10 | .05 |
| 239 | Paul Miller | .10 | .05 |
| 240 | Dan Peltier | .10 | .05 |
| 241 | Ozzie Canseco | .10 | .05 |
| 242 | Ben Rivera | .10 | .05 |
| 243 | John Valentin | .10 | .05 |
| 244 | Henry Rodriguez | .10 | .05 |
| 245 | Derek Parks | .10 | .05 |
| 246 | Carlos Garcia | .10 | .05 |
| 247 | Tim Pugh RC | .10 | .05 |
| 248 | Melvin Nieves | .10 | .05 |
| 249 | Rich Amaral | .10 | .05 |
| 250 | Willie Greene | .10 | .05 |
| 251 | Tim Scott | .10 | .05 |
| 252 | Dave Silvestri | .10 | .05 |
| 253 | Rob Mallicoat | .10 | .05 |
| 254 | Donald Harris | .10 | .05 |
| 255 | Craig Colbert | .10 | .05 |
| 256 | Jose Guzman | .10 | .05 |
| 257 | Domingo Martinez RC | .10 | .05 |
| 258 | William Suero | .10 | .05 |
| 259 | Juan Guerrero | .10 | .05 |
| 260 | J.T. Snow RC | .50 | .23 |
| 261 | Tony Pena | .10 | .05 |
| 262 | Tim Fortugno | .10 | .05 |
| 263 | Tom Marsh | .10 | .05 |
| 264 | Kurt Knudsen | .10 | .05 |
| 265 | Tim Costo | .10 | .05 |
| 266 | Steve Shifflett | .10 | .05 |
| 267 | Billy Ashley | .10 | .05 |
| 268 | Jerry Nielsen | .10 | .05 |
| 269 | Pete Young | .10 | .05 |
| 270 | Johnny Guzman | .10 | .05 |
| 271 | Greg Colbrunn | .10 | .05 |
| 272 | Jeff Nelson | .10 | .05 |
| 273 | Kevin Young | .20 | .09 |
| 274 | Jeff Frye | .10 | .05 |
| 275 | J.T. Bruett | .10 | .05 |
| 276 | Todd Pratt RC | .25 | .11 |
| 277 | Mike Butcher | .10 | .05 |
| 278 | John Flaherty | .10 | .05 |
| 279 | John Patterson | .10 | .05 |
| 280 | Eric Hillman | .10 | .05 |
| 281 | Bien Figueroa | .10 | .05 |
| 282 | Shane Reynolds | .10 | .05 |
| 283 | Rich Rowland | .10 | .05 |
| 284 | Steve Foster | .10 | .05 |
| 285 | Dave Milicki | .10 | .05 |
| 286 | Mike Piazza | 2.00 | .90 |
| 287 | Mike Trombley | .10 | .05 |
| 288 | Jim Pena | .10 | .05 |
| 289 | Bob Ayrault | .10 | .05 |
| 290 | Henry Mercedes | .10 | .05 |
| 291 | Bob Wickman | .10 | .05 |
| 292 | Jacob Brumfield | .10 | .05 |
| 293 | David Hulse RC | .10 | .05 |
| 294 | Ryan Klesko | .40 | .18 |
| 295 | Doug Linton | .10 | .05 |
| 296 | Steve Cooke | .10 | .05 |
| 297 | Eddie Zosky | .10 | .05 |
| 298 | Gerald Williams | .10 | .05 |
| 299 | Jonathan Hurst | .10 | .05 |
| 300 | Larry Carter | .10 | .05 |
| 301 | William Pennyfeather | .10 | .05 |
| 302 | Cesar Hernandez | .10 | .05 |
| 303 | Steve Hosey | .10 | .05 |
| 304 | Blas Minor | .10 | .05 |
| 305 | Jeff Grotewald | .10 | .05 |
| 306 | Bernardo Brito | .10 | .05 |
| 307 | Rafael Bournigal | .10 | .05 |
| 308 | Jeff Branson | .10 | .05 |
| 309 | Tom Quinlan RC | .10 | .05 |
| 310 | Pat Gomez RC | .10 | .05 |
| 311 | Sterling Hitchcock RC | .20 | .09 |
| 312 | Kent Bottenfield | .10 | .05 |
| 313 | Alan Trammell | .30 | .14 |
| 314 | Cris Colon | .10 | .05 |
| 315 | Paul Wagner | .10 | .05 |
| 316 | Matt Maysey | .10 | .05 |
| 317 | Mike Stanton | .10 | .05 |
| 318 | Rick Trlicek | .10 | .05 |
| 319 | Kevin Rogers | .10 | .05 |
| 320 | Mark Clark | .10 | .05 |
| 321 | Pedro Martinez | 1.00 | .45 |
| 322 | Al Martin | .10 | .05 |
| 323 | Mike Macfarlane | .10 | .05 |
| 324 | Rey Sanchez | .10 | .05 |
| 325 | Roger Pavlik | .10 | .05 |
| 326 | Troy Neel | .10 | .05 |
| 327 | Kerry Woodson | .10 | .05 |
| 328 | Wayne Kirby | .10 | .05 |
| 329 | Ken Ryan RC | .10 | .05 |
| 330 | Jesse Levis | .10 | .05 |
| 331 | James Austin | .10 | .05 |
| 332 | Dan Walters | .10 | .05 |
| 333 | Brian Williams | .10 | .05 |
| 334 | Wil Cordero | .10 | .05 |
| 335 | Bret Boone | .20 | .09 |
| 336 | Hipolito Pichardo | .10 | .05 |
| 337 | Pat Mahomes | .10 | .05 |
| 338 | Andy Stankiewicz | .10 | .05 |
| 339 | Jim Bullinger | .10 | .05 |
| 340 | Archi Cianfrocco | .10 | .05 |
| 341 | Ruben Amaro | .10 | .05 |
| 342 | Frank Seminara | .10 | .05 |
| 343 | Pat Hentgen | .10 | .05 |
| 344 | Dave Nilsson | .20 | .09 |
| 345 | Mike Perez | .10 | .05 |
| 346 | Tim Salmon | .20 | .09 |
| 347 | Tim Wakefield | .10 | .05 |
| 348 | Carlos Hernandez | .10 | .05 |
| 349 | Donovan Osborne | .10 | .05 |
| 350 | Denny Neagle | .20 | .09 |
| 351 | Sam Militello | .10 | .05 |
| 352 | Eric Fox | .10 | .05 |
| 353 | John Doherty | .10 | .05 |
| 354 | Chad Curtis | .10 | .05 |
| 355 | Jeff Tackett | .10 | .05 |
| 356 | Dave Fleming | .10 | .05 |
| 357 | Pat Listach | .10 | .05 |
| 358 | Kevin Wickander | .10 | .05 |
| 359 | John Vander Wal | .10 | .05 |
| 360 | Arthur Rhodes | .10 | .05 |
| 361 | Bob Scanlan | .10 | .05 |
| 362 | Bob Zupcic | .10 | .05 |
| 363 | Mel Rojas | .10 | .05 |
| 364 | Jim Thome | .30 | .14 |
| 365 | Bill Pecota | .10 | .05 |
| 366 | Mark Carreon | .10 | .05 |
| 367 | Mitch Williams | .10 | .05 |
| 368 | Cal Eldred | .10 | .05 |
| 369 | Stan Belinda | .10 | .05 |
| 370 | Pat Kelly | .10 | .05 |
| 371 | Rheal Cormier | .10 | .05 |
| 372 | Juan Guzman | .10 | .05 |
| 373 | Damon Berryhill | .10 | .05 |
| 374 | Gary DiSarcina | .10 | .05 |
| 375 | Norm Charlton | .10 | .05 |
| 376 | Roberto Hernandez | .10 | .05 |
| 377 | Scott Kamieniecki | .10 | .05 |
| 378 | Rusty Meacham | .10 | .05 |
| 379 | Kurt Stillwell | .10 | .05 |
| 380 | Lloyd McClendon | .10 | .05 |
| 381 | Mark Leonard | .10 | .05 |
| 382 | Jerry Browne | .10 | .05 |
| 383 | Glenn Davis | .10 | .05 |
| 384 | Randy Johnson | .50 | .23 |
| 385 | Mike Greenwell | .10 | .05 |
| 386 | Scott Chiamparino | .10 | .05 |
| 387 | George Bell | .10 | .05 |
| 388 | Steve Olin | .10 | .05 |
| 389 | Chuck McElroy | .10 | .05 |
| 390 | Mark Gardner | .10 | .05 |
| 391 | Rod Beck | .10 | .05 |
| 392 | Dennis Rasmussen | .10 | .05 |
| 393 | Charlie Leibrandt | .10 | .05 |
| 394 | Julio Franco | .10 | .05 |
| 395 | Pete Harnisch | .10 | .05 |
| 396 | Sid Bream | .10 | .05 |
| 397 | Milt Thompson | .10 | .05 |
| 398 | Glenallen Hill | .10 | .05 |
| 399 | Chico Walker | .10 | .05 |
| 400 | Alex Cole | .10 | .05 |
| 401 | Trevor Wilson | .10 | .05 |
| 402 | Jeff Conine | .10 | .05 |
| 403 | Kyle Abbott | .10 | .05 |
| 404 | Tom Browning | .10 | .05 |
| 405 | Jerald Clark | .10 | .05 |
| 406 | Vince Horsman | .10 | .05 |
| 407 | Kevin Mitchell | .20 | .09 |
| 408 | Pete Smith | .10 | .05 |
| 409 | Jeff Innis | .10 | .05 |
| 410 | Mike Timlin | .10 | .05 |
| 411 | Charlie Hayes | .10 | .05 |
| 412 | Alex Fernandez | .20 | .09 |
| 413 | Jeff Russell | .10 | .05 |
| 414 | Jody Reed | .10 | .05 |
| 415 | Mickey Morandini | .10 | .05 |
| 416 | Darnell Coles | .10 | .05 |
| 417 | Xavier Hernandez | .10 | .05 |
| 418 | Steve Sax | .10 | .05 |
| 419 | Joe Girardi | .20 | .09 |
| 420 | Mike Fetters | .10 | .05 |
| 421 | Danny Jackson | .10 | .05 |
| 422 | Jim Gott | .10 | .05 |
| 423 | Tim Belcher | .10 | .05 |
| 424 | Jose Mesa | .10 | .05 |

❑ 425 Junior Felix .10 .05
❑ 426 Thomas Howard .10 .05
❑ 427 Julio Valera .10 .05
❑ 428 Dante Bichette .20 .09
❑ 429 Mike Sharperson .10 .05
❑ 430 Darryl Kile .20 .09
❑ 431 Lonnie Smith .10 .05
❑ 432 Monty Fariss .10 .05
❑ 433 Reggie Jefferson .20 .09
❑ 434 Bob McClure .10 .05
❑ 435 Craig Lefferts .10 .05
❑ 436 Duane Ward .10 .05
❑ 437 Shawn Abner .10 .05
❑ 438 Roberto Kelly .10 .05
❑ 439 Paul O'Neill .20 .09
❑ 440 Alan Mills .10 .05
❑ 441 Roger Mason .10 .05
❑ 442 Gary Pettis .10 .05
❑ 443 Steve Lake .10 .05
❑ 444 Gene Larkin .10 .05
❑ 445 Larry Andersen .10 .05
❑ 446 Doug Dascenzo .10 .05
❑ 447 Daryl Boston .10 .05
❑ 448 John Candolaria .10 .05
❑ 449 Storm Davis .10 .05
❑ 450 Tom Edens .10 .05
❑ 451 Mike Maddux .10 .05
❑ 452 Tim Naehring .10 .05
❑ 453 John Orton .10 .05
❑ 454 Joey Cora .10 .05
❑ 455 Chuck Crim .10 .05
❑ 456 Dan Plesac .10 .05
❑ 457 Mike Bielecki .10 .05
❑ 458 Terry Jorgensen .10 .05
❑ 459 John Habyan .10 .05
❑ 460 Pete O'Brien .10 .05
❑ 461 Jeff Treadway .10 .05
❑ 462 Frank Castillo .10 .05
❑ 463 Jimmy Jones .10 .05
❑ 464 Tommy Greene .10 .05
❑ 465 Tracy Woodson .10 .05
❑ 466 Rich Rodriguez .10 .05
❑ 467 Joe Hesketh .10 .05
❑ 468 Greg Myers .10 .05
❑ 469 Kirk McCaskill .10 .05
❑ 470 Ricky Bones .10 .05
❑ 471 Lenny Webster .10 .05
❑ 472 Francisco Cabrera .10 .05
❑ 473 Turner Ward .10 .05
❑ 474 Dwayne Henry .10 .05
❑ 475 Al Osuna .10 .05
❑ 476 Craig Wilson .10 .05
❑ 477 Chris Nabholz .10 .05
❑ 478 Rafael Belliard .10 .05
❑ 479 Terry Leach .10 .05
❑ 480 Tim Teufel .10 .05
❑ 481 Dennis Eckersley AW .10 .05
❑ 482 Barry Bonds AW .30 .14
❑ 483 Dennis Eckersley AW .10 .05
❑ 484 Greg Maddux AW .50 .23
❑ 485 Pat Listach AW .10 .05
❑ 486 Eric Karros AW .10 .05
❑ 487 Jamie Arnold DP RC .10 .05
❑ 488 B.J. Wallace DP .10 .05
❑ 489 Derek Jeter DP RC 15.00 6.75
❑ 490 Jason Kendall DP RC 1.25 .55
❑ 491 Rick Helling DP .20 .09
❑ 492 Derek Wallace DP RC .10 .05
❑ 493 Sean Lowe DP RC .10 .05
❑ 494 Shannon Stewart DP RC 1.00 .45
❑ 495 Benji Grigsby DP RC .10 .05
❑ 496 Todd Steverson DP RC .10 .05
❑ 497 Dan Serafini DP RC .10 .05
❑ 498 Michael Tucker DP .40 .18
❑ 499 Chris Roberts DP .10 .05
❑ 500 Pete Janicki DP RC .10 .05
❑ 501 Jeff Schmidt DP RC .10 .05
❑ 502 Edgar Martinez AS .20 .09
❑ 503 Omar Vizquel AS .20 .09
❑ 504 Ken Griffey Jr. AS .75 .35
❑ 505 Kirby Puckett AS .50 .23
❑ 506 Joe Carter AS .10 .05
❑ 507 Ivan Rodriguez AS .30 .14
❑ 508 Jack Morris AS .10 .05
❑ 509 Dennis Eckersley AS .10 .05
❑ 510 Frank Thomas AS .40 .18
❑ 511 Roberto Alomar AS .20 .09
❑ 512 Mickey Morandini AS .10 .05
❑ 513 Dennis Eckersley HL .10 .05
❑ 514 Jeff Reardon HL .10 .05
❑ 515 Danny Tartabull HL .10 .05
❑ 516 Bip Roberts HL .10 .05
❑ 517 George Brett HL .40 .18
❑ 518 Robin Yount HL .30 .14
❑ 519 Kevin Gross HL .10 .05
❑ 520 Ed Sprague WS .10 .05
❑ 521 Dave Winfield WS .20 .09
❑ 522 Ozzie Smith AS .30 .14
❑ 523 Barry Bonds AS .40 .18
❑ 524 Andy Van Slyke AS .10 .05
❑ 525 Tony Gwynn AS .40 .18
❑ 526 Darren Daulton AS .10 .05
❑ 527 Greg Maddux AS .50 .23
❑ 528 Fred McGriff AS .30 .14
❑ 529 Lee Smith AS .10 .05
❑ 530 Ryne Sandberg AS .30 .14
❑ 531 Gary Sheffield AS .20 .09
❑ 532 Ozzie Smith DT .30 .14
❑ 533 Kirby Puckett DT .50 .23
❑ 534 Gary Sheffield DT .20 .09
❑ 535 Andy Van Slyke DT .10 .05
❑ 536 Ken Griffey Jr. DT .75 .35
❑ 537 Ivan Rodriguez DT .30 .14
❑ 538 Charles Nagy DT .10 .05
❑ 539 Tom Glavine DT .20 .09
❑ 540 Dennis Eckersley DT .10 .05
❑ 541 Frank Thomas DT .40 .18
❑ 542 Roberto Alomar DT .20 .09
❑ 543 Sean Berry .10 .05
❑ 544 Mike Schooler .10 .05
❑ 545 Chuck Carr .10 .05
❑ 546 Lenny Harris .10 .05
❑ 547 Gary Scott .10 .05
❑ 548 Derek Lilliquist .10 .05
❑ 549 Brian Hunter .10 .05
❑ 550 Kirby Puckett MOY .50 .23
❑ 551 Jim Eisenreich .10 .05
❑ 552 Andre Dawson .30 .14
❑ 553 David Nied .10 .05
❑ 554 Spike Owen .10 .05
❑ 555 Greg Gagne .10 .05
❑ 556 Sid Fernandez .10 .05
❑ 557 Mark McGwire 1.50 .70
❑ 558 Bryan Harvey .10 .05
❑ 559 Harold Reynolds .10 .05
❑ 560 Barry Bonds .60 .25
❑ 561 Eric Wedge RC .10 .05
❑ 562 Ozzie Smith .50 .23
❑ 563 Rick Sutcliffe .20 .09
❑ 564 Jeff Reardon .20 .09
❑ 565 Alex Arias .10 .05
❑ 566 Greg Swindell .10 .05
❑ 567 Brook Jacoby .10 .05
❑ 568 Pete Incaviglia .10 .05
❑ 569 Butch Henry .10 .05
❑ 570 Eric Davis .20 .09
❑ 571 Kevin Seitzer .10 .05
❑ 572 Tony Fernandez .10 .05
❑ 573 Steve Reed RC .10 .05
❑ 574 Cory Snyder .10 .05
❑ 575 Joe Carter .20 .09
❑ 576 Greg Maddux 1.00 .45
❑ 577 Bert Blyleven UER .20 .09
(Should say 3701
career strikeouts)
❑ 578 Kevin Bass .10 .05
❑ 579 Carlton Fisk .40 .18
❑ 580 Doug Drabek .10 .05
❑ 581 Mark Gubicza .10 .05
❑ 582 Bobby Thigpen .10 .05
❑ 583 Chili Davis .20 .09
❑ 584 Scott Bankhead .10 .05
❑ 585 Harold Baines .20 .09
❑ 586 Eric Young .10 .05
❑ 587 Lance Parrish .10 .05
❑ 588 Juan Bell .10 .05
❑ 589 Bob Ojeda .10 .05
❑ 590 Joe Orsulak .10 .05
❑ 591 Benito Santiago .10 .05
❑ 592 Wade Boggs .50 .23
❑ 593 Robby Thompson .10 .05
❑ 594 Eric Plunk .10 .05
❑ 595 Hensley Meulens .10 .05
❑ 596 Lou Whitaker .20 .09
❑ 597 Dale Murphy .30 .14
❑ 598 Paul Molitor .40 .18
❑ 599 Greg W. Harris .10 .05
❑ 600 Darren Holmes .10 .05
❑ 601 Dave Martinez .10 .05
❑ 602 Tom Henke .10 .05
❑ 603 Mike Benjamin .10 .05
❑ 604 Rene Gonzales .10 .05
❑ 605 Roger McDowell .10 .05
❑ 606 Kirby Puckett 1.00 .45
❑ 607 Randy Myers .20 .09
❑ 608 Ruben Sierra .10 .05
❑ 609 Wilson Alvarez .10 .05
❑ 610 David Segui .10 .05
❑ 611 Juan Samuel .10 .05
❑ 612 Tom Brunansky .10 .05
❑ 613 Willie Randolph .20 .09
❑ 614 Tony Phillips .10 .05
❑ 615 Candy Maldonado .10 .05
❑ 616 Chris Bosio .10 .05
❑ 617 Bret Barberie .10 .05
❑ 618 Scott Sanderson .10 .05
❑ 619 Ron Darling .10 .05
❑ 620 Dave Winfield .40 .18
❑ 621 Mike Felder .10 .05
❑ 622 Greg Hibbard .10 .05
❑ 623 Mike Scioscia .10 .05
❑ 624 John Smiley .10 .05
❑ 625 Alejandro Pena .10 .05
❑ 626 Terry Steinbach .10 .05
❑ 627 Freddie Benavides .10 .05
❑ 628 Kevin Reimer .10 .05
❑ 629 Braulio Castillo .10 .05
❑ 630 Dave Stieb .10 .05
❑ 631 Dave Magadan .10 .05
❑ 632 Scott Fletcher .10 .05
❑ 633 Cris Carpenter .10 .05
❑ 634 Kevin Maas .10 .05
❑ 635 Todd Worrell .10 .05
❑ 636 Rob Deer .10 .05
❑ 637 Dwight Smith .10 .05
❑ 638 Chito Martinez .10 .05
❑ 639 Jimmy Key .20 .09
❑ 640 Greg A. Harris .10 .05
❑ 641 Mike Moore .10 .05
❑ 642 Pat Borders .10 .05
❑ 643 Bill Gullickson .10 .05
❑ 644 Gary Gaetti .20 .09
❑ 645 David Howard .10 .05
❑ 646 Jim Abbott .20 .09
❑ 647 Willie Wilson .10 .05
❑ 648 David Wells .20 .09
❑ 649 Andres Galarraga .30 .14
❑ 650 Vince Coleman .10 .05
❑ 651 Rob Dibble .10 .05
❑ 652 Frank Tanana .10 .05
❑ 653 Steve Decker .10 .05
❑ 654 David Cone .20 .09
❑ 655 Jack Armstrong .10 .05
❑ 656 Dave Stewart .20 .09
❑ 657 Billy Hatcher .10 .05
❑ 658 Tim Raines .20 .09
❑ 659 Walt Weiss .10 .05
❑ 660 Jose Lind .10 .05

**1994 Score**

| | MINT | NRMT |
|---|---|---|
| COMPLETE SET (660) | 24.00 | 11.00 |
| COMPLETE SERIES 1 (330) | 12.00 | 5.50 |
| COMPLETE SERIES 2 (330) | 12.00 | 5.50 |
| COMMON CARD (1-660) | .10 | .05 |
| ❑ 1 Barry Bonds | .60 | .25 |
| ❑ 2 John Olerud | .20 | .09 |
| ❑ 3 Ken Griffey Jr. | 1.50 | .70 |
| ❑ 4 Jeff Bagwell | .50 | .23 |
| ❑ 5 John Burkett | .10 | .05 |
| ❑ 6 Jack McDowell | .10 | .05 |
| ❑ 7 Albert Belle | .25 | .11 |
| ❑ 8 Andres Galarraga | .25 | .11 |
| ❑ 9 Mike Mussina | .40 | .18 |
| ❑ 10 Will Clark | .40 | .18 |
| ❑ 11 Travis Fryman | .20 | .09 |
| ❑ 12 Tony Gwynn | .75 | .35 |
| ❑ 13 Robin Yount | .40 | .18 |
| ❑ 14 Dave Magadan | .10 | .05 |
| ❑ 15 Paul O'Neill | .20 | .09 |
| ❑ 16 Ray Lankford | .20 | .09 |
| ❑ 17 Damion Easley | .10 | .05 |
| ❑ 18 Andy Van Slyke | .20 | .09 |
| ❑ 19 Brian McRae | .10 | .05 |
| ❑ 20 Ryne Sandberg | .50 | .23 |
| ❑ 21 Kirby Puckett | 1.00 | .45 |
| ❑ 22 Dwight Gooden | .20 | .09 |
| ❑ 23 Don Mattingly | 1.00 | .45 |
| ❑ 24 Kevin Mitchell | .10 | .05 |
| ❑ 25 Roger Clemens | .75 | .35 |
| ❑ 26 Eric Karros | .20 | .09 |
| ❑ 27 Juan Gonzalez | .40 | .18 |
| ❑ 28 John Kruk | .20 | .09 |
| ❑ 29 Gregg Jefferies | .10 | .05 |
| ❑ 30 Tom Glavine | .40 | .18 |
| ❑ 31 Ivan Rodriguez | .50 | .23 |
| ❑ 32 Jay Bell | .20 | .09 |
| ❑ 33 Randy Johnson | .50 | .23 |
| ❑ 34 Darren Daulton | .20 | .09 |
| ❑ 35 Rickey Henderson | .50 | .23 |
| ❑ 36 Eddie Murray | .40 | .18 |
| ❑ 37 Brian Harper | .10 | .05 |
| ❑ 38 Delino DeShields | .10 | .05 |
| ❑ 39 Jose Lind | .10 | .05 |
| ❑ 40 Benito Santiago | .10 | .05 |
| ❑ 41 Frank Thomas | .75 | .35 |
| ❑ 42 Mark Grace | .40 | .18 |
| ❑ 43 Roberto Alomar | .40 | .18 |
| ❑ 44 Andy Benes | .10 | .05 |
| ❑ 45 Luis Polonia | .10 | .05 |
| ❑ 46 Brett Butler | .20 | .09 |
| ❑ 47 Terry Steinbach | .10 | .05 |
| ❑ 48 Craig Biggio | .25 | .11 |
| ❑ 49 Greg Vaughn | .20 | .09 |
| ❑ 50 Charlie Hayes | .10 | .05 |
| ❑ 51 Mickey Tettleton | .10 | .05 |
| ❑ 52 Jose Rijo | .10 | .05 |
| ❑ 53 Carlos Baerga | .10 | .05 |
| ❑ 54 Jeff Blauser | .10 | .05 |
| ❑ 55 Leo Gomez | .10 | .05 |
| ❑ 56 Bob Tewksbury | .10 | .05 |
| ❑ 57 Mo Vaughn | .20 | .09 |
| ❑ 58 Orlando Merced | .10 | .05 |
| ❑ 59 Tino Martinez | .20 | .09 |
| ❑ 60 Lenny Dykstra | .20 | .09 |
| ❑ 61 Jose Canseco | .50 | .23 |
| ❑ 62 Tony Fernandez | .10 | .05 |
| ❑ 63 Donovan Osborne | .10 | .05 |
| ❑ 64 Ken Hill | .10 | .05 |
| ❑ 65 Kent Hrbek | .20 | .09 |
| ❑ 66 Bryan Harvey | .10 | .05 |
| ❑ 67 Wally Joyner | .20 | .09 |
| ❑ 68 Derrick May | .10 | .05 |
| ❑ 69 Lance Johnson | .10 | .05 |
| ❑ 70 Willie McGee | .20 | .09 |
| ❑ 71 Mark Langston | .10 | .05 |
| ❑ 72 Terry Pendleton | .20 | .09 |
| ❑ 73 Joe Carter | .20 | .09 |
| ❑ 74 Barry Larkin | .40 | .18 |
| ❑ 75 Jimmy Key | .20 | .09 |
| ❑ 76 Joe Girardi | .10 | .05 |
| ❑ 77 B.J. Surhoff | .20 | .09 |
| ❑ 78 Pete Harnisch | .10 | .05 |
| ❑ 79 Lou Whitaker UER (Milt Cuyler pictured on front) | .20 | .09 |
| ❑ 80 Cory Snyder | .10 | .05 |
| ❑ 81 Kenny Lofton | .20 | .09 |
| ❑ 82 Fred McGriff | .25 | .11 |
| ❑ 83 Mike Greenwell | .10 | .05 |
| ❑ 84 Mike Perez | .10 | .05 |
| ❑ 85 Cal Ripken | 1.50 | .70 |
| ❑ 86 Don Slaught | .10 | .05 |
| ❑ 87 Omar Vizquel | .20 | .09 |
| ❑ 88 Curt Schilling | .20 | .09 |
| ❑ 89 Chuck Knoblauch | .20 | .09 |
| ❑ 90 Moises Alou | .20 | .09 |
| ❑ 91 Greg Gagne | .10 | .05 |
| ❑ 92 Bret Saberhagen | .20 | .09 |
| ❑ 93 Ozzie Guillen | .10 | .05 |
| ❑ 94 Matt Williams | .25 | .11 |
| ❑ 95 Chad Curtis | .10 | .05 |
| ❑ 96 Mike Harkey | .10 | .05 |
| ❑ 97 Devon White | .10 | .05 |
| ❑ 98 Walt Weiss | .10 | .05 |
| ❑ 99 Kevin Brown | .20 | .09 |
| ❑ 100 Gary Sheffield | .40 | .18 |
| ❑ 101 Wade Boggs | .50 | .23 |
| ❑ 102 Orel Hershiser | .20 | .09 |
| ❑ 103 Tony Phillips | .10 | .05 |
| ❑ 104 Andujar Cedeno | .10 | .05 |
| ❑ 105 Bill Spiers | .10 | .05 |
| ❑ 106 Otis Nixon | .10 | .05 |
| ❑ 107 Felix Fermin | .10 | .05 |
| ❑ 108 Bip Roberts | .10 | .05 |
| ❑ 109 Dennis Eckersley | .20 | .09 |
| ❑ 110 Dante Bichette | .20 | .09 |
| ❑ 111 Ben McDonald | .10 | .05 |
| ❑ 112 Jim Poole | .10 | .05 |
| ❑ 113 John Dopson | .10 | .05 |
| ❑ 114 Rob Dibble | .10 | .05 |
| ❑ 115 Jeff Treadway | .10 | .05 |
| ❑ 116 Ricky Jordan | .10 | .05 |
| ❑ 117 Mike Henneman | .10 | .05 |
| ❑ 118 Willie Blair | .10 | .05 |
| ❑ 119 Doug Henry | .10 | .05 |
| ❑ 120 Gerald Perry | .10 | .05 |
| ❑ 121 Greg Myers | .10 | .05 |
| ❑ 122 John Franco | .20 | .09 |
| ❑ 123 Roger Mason | .10 | .05 |
| ❑ 124 Chris Hammond | .10 | .05 |
| ❑ 125 Hubie Brooks | .10 | .05 |
| ❑ 126 Kent Mercker | .10 | .05 |
| ❑ 127 Jim Abbott | .20 | .09 |
| ❑ 128 Kevin Bass | .10 | .05 |
| ❑ 129 Rick Aguilera | .10 | .05 |
| ❑ 130 Mitch Webster | .10 | .05 |
| ❑ 131 Eric Plunk | .10 | .05 |
| ❑ 132 Mark Carreon | .10 | .05 |
| ❑ 133 Dave Stewart | .20 | .09 |
| ❑ 134 Willie Wilson | .10 | .05 |
| ❑ 135 Dave Fleming | .10 | .05 |
| ❑ 136 Jeff Tackett | .10 | .05 |
| ❑ 137 Geno Petralli | .10 | .05 |
| ❑ 138 Gene Harris | .10 | .05 |
| ❑ 139 Scott Bankhead | .10 | .05 |
| ❑ 140 Trevor Wilson | .10 | .05 |
| ❑ 141 Alvaro Espinoza | .10 | .05 |
| ❑ 142 Ryan Bowen | .10 | .05 |
| ❑ 143 Mike Moore | .10 | .05 |
| ❑ 144 Bill Pecota | .10 | .05 |
| ❑ 145 Jaime Navarro | .10 | .05 |
| ❑ 146 Jack Daugherty | .10 | .05 |
| ❑ 147 Bob Wickman | .10 | .05 |
| ❑ 148 Chris Jones | .10 | .05 |
| ❑ 149 Todd Stottlemyre | .10 | .05 |
| ❑ 150 Brian Williams | .10 | .05 |
| ❑ 151 Chuck Finley | .20 | .09 |
| ❑ 152 Lenny Harris | .10 | .05 |
| ❑ 153 Alex Fernandez | .10 | .05 |
| ❑ 154 Candy Maldonado | .10 | .05 |
| ❑ 155 Jeff Montgomery | .10 | .05 |
| ❑ 156 David West | .25 | .11 |
| ❑ 157 Mark Williamson | .10 | .05 |
| ❑ 158 Milt Thompson | .10 | .05 |
| ❑ 159 Ron Darling | .10 | .05 |
| ❑ 160 Stan Belinda | .10 | .05 |
| ❑ 161 Henry Cotto | .10 | .05 |
| ❑ 162 Mel Rojas | .10 | .05 |
| ❑ 163 Doug Strange | .10 | .05 |
| ❑ 164 Rene Arocha | .10 | .05 |
| ❑ 165 Tim Hulett | .10 | .05 |
| ❑ 166 Steve Avery | .10 | .05 |
| ❑ 167 Jim Thome | .25 | .11 |
| ❑ 168 Tom Browning | .10 | .05 |
| ❑ 169 Mario Diaz | .10 | .05 |
| ❑ 170 Steve Reed | .10 | .05 |
| ❑ 171 Scott Livingstone | .10 | .05 |
| ❑ 172 Chris Donnels | .10 | .05 |
| ❑ 173 John Jaha | .10 | .05 |
| ❑ 174 Carlos Hernandez | .10 | .05 |
| ❑ 175 Dion James | .10 | .05 |
| ❑ 176 Bud Black | .10 | .05 |
| ❑ 177 Tony Castillo | .10 | .05 |
| ❑ 178 Jose Guzman | .10 | .05 |
| ❑ 179 Torey Lovullo | .10 | .05 |
| ❑ 180 John Vander Wal | .10 | .05 |
| ❑ 181 Mike LaValliere | .10 | .05 |
| ❑ 182 Sid Fernandez | .10 | .05 |
| ❑ 183 Brent Mayne | .10 | .05 |
| ❑ 184 Terry Mulholland | .10 | .05 |
| ❑ 185 Willie Banks | .10 | .05 |
| ❑ 186 Steve Cooke | .10 | .05 |
| ❑ 187 Brent Gates | .10 | .05 |
| ❑ 188 Erik Pappas | .10 | .05 |
| ❑ 189 Bill Haselman | .10 | .05 |
| ❑ 190 Fernando Valenzuela | .20 | .09 |
| ❑ 191 Gary Redus | .10 | .05 |
| ❑ 192 Danny Darwin | .10 | .05 |
| ❑ 193 Mark Portugal | .10 | .05 |
| ❑ 194 Derek Lilliquist | .10 | .05 |
| ❑ 195 Charlie O'Brien | .10 | .05 |
| ❑ 196 Matt Nokes | .10 | .05 |
| ❑ 197 Danny Sheaffer | .10 | .05 |
| ❑ 198 Bill Gullickson | .10 | .05 |
| ❑ 199 Alex Arias | .10 | .05 |
| ❑ 200 Mike Fetters | .10 | .05 |
| ❑ 201 Brian Jordan | .20 | .09 |
| ❑ 202 Joe Grahe | .10 | .05 |
| ❑ 203 Tom Candiotti | .10 | .05 |
| ❑ 204 Jeremy Hernandez | .10 | .05 |
| ❑ 205 Mike Stanton | .10 | .05 |
| ❑ 206 David Howard | .10 | .05 |
| ❑ 207 Darren Holmes | .10 | .05 |
| ❑ 208 Rick Honeycutt | .10 | .05 |
| ❑ 209 Danny Jackson | .10 | .05 |
| ❑ 210 Rich Amaral | .10 | .05 |
| ❑ 211 Blas Minor | .10 | .05 |
| ❑ 212 Kenny Rogers | .10 | .05 |
| ❑ 213 Jim Leyritz | .10 | .05 |
| ❑ 214 Mike Morgan | .10 | .05 |
| ❑ 215 Dan Gladden | .10 | .05 |
| ❑ 216 Randy Velarde | .10 | .05 |
| ❑ 217 Mitch Williams | .10 | .05 |
| ❑ 218 Hipolito Pichardo | .10 | .05 |
| ❑ 219 Dave Burba | .10 | .05 |
| ❑ 220 Wilson Alvarez | .10 | .05 |
| ❑ 221 Bob Zupcic | .10 | .05 |
| ❑ 222 Francisco Cabrera | .10 | .05 |
| ❑ 223 Julio Valera | .10 | .05 |
| ❑ 224 Paul Assenmacher | .10 | .05 |
| ❑ 225 Jeff Branson | .10 | .05 |
| ❑ 226 Todd Frohwirth | .10 | .05 |
| ❑ 227 Armando Reynoso | .10 | .05 |
| ❑ 228 Rich Rowland | .10 | .05 |
| ❑ 229 Freddie Benavides | .10 | .05 |
| ❑ 230 Wayne Kirby | .10 | .05 |
| ❑ 231 Darryl Kile | .20 | .09 |
| ❑ 232 Skeeter Barnes | .10 | .05 |
| ❑ 233 Ramon Martinez | .10 | .05 |
| ❑ 234 Tom Gordon | .10 | .05 |
| ❑ 235 Dave Gallagher | .10 | .05 |
| ❑ 236 Ricky Bones | .10 | .05 |
| ❑ 237 Larry Andersen | .10 | .05 |
| ❑ 238 Pat Meares | .10 | .05 |
| ❑ 239 Zane Smith | .10 | .05 |
| ❑ 240 Tim Leary | .10 | .05 |
| ❑ 241 Phil Clark | .10 | .05 |
| ❑ 242 Danny Cox | .10 | .05 |
| ❑ 243 Mike Jackson | .10 | .05 |
| ❑ 244 Mike Gallego | .10 | .05 |
| ❑ 245 Lee Smith | .20 | .09 |
| ❑ 246 Todd Jones | .10 | .05 |
| ❑ 247 Steve Bedrosian | .10 | .05 |
| ❑ 248 Troy Neel | .10 | .05 |
| ❑ 249 Jose Bautista | .10 | .05 |
| ❑ 250 Steve Frey | .10 | .05 |

| No. | Card | | |
|---|---|---|---|
| 251 | Jeff Reardon | .20 | .09 |
| 252 | Stan Javier | .10 | .05 |
| 253 | Mo Sanford | .10 | .05 |
| 254 | Steve Sax | .10 | .05 |
| 255 | Luis Aquino | .10 | .05 |
| 256 | Domingo Jean | .10 | .05 |
| 257 | Scott Servais | .10 | .05 |
| 258 | Brad Pennington | .10 | .05 |
| 259 | Dave Hansen | .10 | .05 |
| 260 | Rich Gossage | .20 | .09 |
| 261 | Jeff Fassero | .10 | .05 |
| 262 | Junior Ortiz | .10 | .05 |
| 263 | Anthony Young | .10 | .05 |
| 264 | Chris Bosio | .10 | .05 |
| 265 | Ruben Amaro | .10 | .05 |
| 266 | Mark Eichhorn | .10 | .05 |
| 267 | Dave Clark | .10 | .05 |
| 268 | Gary Thurman | .10 | .05 |
| 269 | Les Lancaster | .10 | .05 |
| 270 | Jamie Moyer | .10 | .05 |
| 271 | Ricky Gutierrez | .10 | .05 |
| 272 | Greg A. Harris | .10 | .05 |
| 273 | Mike Benjamin | .10 | .05 |
| 274 | Gene Nelson | .10 | .05 |
| 275 | Damon Berryhill | .10 | .05 |
| 276 | Scott Radinsky | .10 | .05 |
| 277 | Mike Aldrete | .10 | .05 |
| 278 | Jerry DiPoto | .10 | .05 |
| 279 | Chris Haney | .10 | .05 |
| 280 | Richie Lewis | .10 | .05 |
| 281 | Jarvis Brown | .10 | .05 |
| 282 | Juan Bell | .10 | .05 |
| 283 | Joe Klink | .10 | .05 |
| 284 | Graeme Lloyd | .10 | .05 |
| 285 | Casey Candaele | .10 | .05 |
| 286 | Bob MacDonald | .10 | .05 |
| 287 | Mike Sharperson | .10 | .05 |
| 288 | Gene Larkin | .10 | .05 |
| 289 | Brian Barnes | .10 | .05 |
| 290 | David McCarty | .10 | .05 |
| 291 | Jeff Innis | .10 | .05 |
| 292 | Bob Patterson | .10 | .05 |
| 293 | Ben Rivera | .10 | .05 |
| 294 | John Habyan | .10 | .05 |
| 295 | Rich Rodriquez | .10 | .05 |
| 296 | Edwin Nunez | .10 | .05 |
| 297 | Rod Brewer | .10 | .05 |
| 298 | Mike Timlin | .10 | .05 |
| 299 | Jesse Orosco | .10 | .05 |
| 300 | Gary Gaetti | .20 | .09 |
| 301 | Todd Benzinger | .10 | .05 |
| 302 | Jeff Nelson | .10 | .05 |
| 303 | Rafael Belliard | .10 | .05 |
| 304 | Matt Whiteside | .10 | .05 |
| 305 | Vinny Castilla | .20 | .09 |
| 306 | Matt Turner | .10 | .05 |
| 307 | Eduardo Perez | .10 | .05 |
| 308 | Joel Johnston | .10 | .05 |
| 309 | Chris Gomez | .10 | .05 |
| 310 | Pat Rapp | .10 | .05 |
| 311 | Jim Tatum | .10 | .05 |
| 312 | Kirk Rueter | .10 | .05 |
| 313 | John Flaherty | .10 | .05 |
| 314 | Tom Kramer | .10 | .05 |
| 315 | Mark Whiten | .10 | .05 |
| 316 | Chris Bosio | .10 | .05 |
| 317 | Baltimore Orioles CL | .10 | .05 |
| 318 | Boston Red Sox CL UER (Viola listed as 316; should be 331) | .10 | .05 |
| 319 | California Angels CL | .10 | .05 |
| 320 | Chicago White Sox CL | .10 | .05 |
| 321 | Cleveland Indians CL | .10 | .05 |
| 322 | Detroit Tigers CL | .10 | .05 |
| 323 | Kansas City Royals CL | .10 | .05 |
| 324 | Milwaukee Brewers CL | .10 | .05 |
| 325 | Minnesota Twins CL | .10 | .05 |
| 326 | New York Yankees CL | .10 | .05 |
| 327 | Oakland Athletics CL | .10 | .05 |
| 328 | Seattle Mariners CL | .10 | .05 |
| 329 | Texas Rangers CL | .10 | .05 |
| 330 | Toronto Blue Jays CL | .10 | .05 |
| 331 | Frank Viola | .10 | .05 |
| 332 | Ron Gant | .20 | .09 |
| 333 | Charles Nagy | .10 | .05 |
| 334 | Roberto Kelly | .10 | .05 |
| 335 | Brady Anderson | .20 | .09 |
| 336 | Alex Cole | .10 | .05 |
| 337 | Alan Trammell | .25 | .11 |
| 338 | Derek Bell | .10 | .05 |
| 339 | Bernie Williams | .40 | .18 |
| 340 | Jose Offerman | .10 | .05 |
| 341 | Bill Wegman | .10 | .05 |
| 342 | Ken Caminiti | .20 | .09 |
| 343 | Pat Borders | .10 | .05 |
| 344 | Kirt Manwaring | .10 | .05 |
| 345 | Chili Davis | .20 | .09 |
| 346 | Steve Buechele | .10 | .05 |
| 347 | Robin Ventura | .20 | .09 |
| 348 | Teddy Higuera | .10 | .05 |
| 349 | Jerry Browne | .10 | .05 |
| 350 | Scott Kamieniecki | .10 | .05 |
| 351 | Kevin Tapani | .10 | .05 |
| 352 | Marquis Grissom | .10 | .05 |
| 353 | Jay Buhner | .20 | .09 |
| 354 | Dave Hollins | .10 | .05 |
| 355 | Dan Wilson | .10 | .05 |
| 356 | Bob Walk | .10 | .05 |
| 357 | Chris Hoiles | .10 | .05 |
| 358 | Todd Zeile | .10 | .05 |
| 359 | Kevin Appier | .20 | .09 |
| 360 | Chris Sabo | .10 | .05 |
| 361 | David Segui | .10 | .05 |
| 362 | Jerald Clark | .10 | .05 |
| 363 | Tony Pena | .10 | .05 |
| 364 | Steve Finley | .20 | .09 |
| 365 | Roger Pavlik | .10 | .05 |
| 366 | John Smoltz | .20 | .09 |
| 367 | Scott Fletcher | .10 | .05 |
| 368 | Jody Reed | .10 | .05 |
| 369 | David Wells | .20 | .09 |
| 370 | Jose Vizcaino | .10 | .05 |
| 371 | Pat Listach | .10 | .05 |
| 372 | Orestes Destrade | .10 | .05 |
| 373 | Danny Tartabull | .10 | .05 |
| 374 | Greg W. Harris | .10 | .05 |
| 375 | Juan Guzman | .10 | .05 |
| 376 | Larry Walker | .20 | .09 |
| 377 | Gary DiSarcina | .10 | .05 |
| 378 | Bobby Bonilla | .20 | .09 |
| 379 | Tim Raines | .20 | .09 |
| 380 | Tommy Greene | .10 | .05 |
| 381 | Chris Gwynn | .10 | .05 |
| 382 | Jeff King | .10 | .05 |
| 383 | Shane Mack | .10 | .05 |
| 384 | Ozzie Smith | .50 | .23 |
| 385 | Eddie Zambrano RC | .10 | .05 |
| 386 | Mike Devereaux | .10 | .05 |
| 387 | Erik Hanson | .10 | .05 |
| 388 | Scott Cooper | .10 | .05 |
| 389 | Dean Palmer | .20 | .09 |
| 390 | John Wetteland | .20 | .09 |
| 391 | Reggie Jefferson | .10 | .05 |
| 392 | Mark Lemke | .10 | .05 |
| 393 | Cecil Fielder | .20 | .09 |
| 394 | Reggie Sanders | .10 | .05 |
| 395 | Darryl Hamilton | .10 | .05 |
| 396 | Daryl Boston | .10 | .05 |
| 397 | Pat Kelly | .10 | .05 |
| 398 | Joe Orsulak | .10 | .05 |
| 399 | Ed Sprague | .10 | .05 |
| 400 | Eric Anthony | .10 | .05 |
| 401 | Scott Sanderson | .10 | .05 |
| 402 | Jim Gott | .10 | .05 |
| 403 | Ron Karkovice | .10 | .05 |
| 404 | Phil Plantier | .10 | .05 |
| 405 | David Cone | .20 | .09 |
| 406 | Robby Thompson | .10 | .05 |
| 407 | Dave Winfield | .40 | .18 |
| 408 | Dwight Smith | .10 | .05 |
| 409 | Ruben Sierra | .10 | .05 |
| 410 | Jack Armstrong | .10 | .05 |
| 411 | Mike Felder | .10 | .05 |
| 412 | Wil Cordero | .10 | .05 |
| 413 | Julio Franco | .10 | .05 |
| 414 | Howard Johnson | .10 | .05 |
| 415 | Mark McLemore | .10 | .05 |
| 416 | Pete Incaviglia | .10 | .05 |
| 417 | John Valentin | .10 | .05 |
| 418 | Tim Wakefield | .10 | .05 |
| 419 | Jose Mesa | .10 | .05 |
| 420 | Bernard Gilkey | .10 | .05 |
| 421 | Kirk Gibson | .20 | .09 |
| 422 | Dave Justice | .25 | .11 |
| 423 | Tom Brunansky | .10 | .05 |
| 424 | John Smiley | .10 | .05 |
| 425 | Kevin Maas | .10 | .05 |
| 426 | Doug Drabek | .10 | .05 |
| 427 | Paul Molitor | .40 | .18 |
| 428 | Darryl Strawberry | .20 | .09 |
| 429 | Tim Naehring | .10 | .05 |
| 430 | Bill Swift | .10 | .05 |
| 431 | Ellis Burks | .20 | .09 |
| 432 | Greg Hibbard | .10 | .05 |
| 433 | Felix Jose | .10 | .05 |
| 434 | Bret Barberie | .10 | .05 |
| 435 | Pedro Munoz | .10 | .05 |
| 436 | Darrin Fletcher | .10 | .05 |
| 437 | Bobby Witt | .10 | .05 |
| 438 | Wes Chamberlain | .10 | .05 |
| 439 | Mackey Sasser | .10 | .05 |
| 440 | Mark Whiten | .10 | .05 |
| 441 | Harold Reynolds | .10 | .05 |
| 442 | Greg Olson | .10 | .05 |
| 443 | Billy Hatcher | .10 | .05 |
| 444 | Joe Oliver | .10 | .05 |
| 445 | Sandy Alomar Jr. | .20 | .09 |
| 446 | Tim Wallach | .10 | .05 |
| 447 | Karl Rhodes | .10 | .05 |
| 448 | Royce Clayton | .10 | .05 |
| 449 | Cal Eldred | .10 | .05 |
| 450 | Rick Wilkins | .10 | .05 |
| 451 | Mike Stanley | .10 | .05 |
| 452 | Charlie Hough | .20 | .09 |
| 453 | Jack Morris | .20 | .09 |
| 454 | Jon Ratliff RC | .10 | .05 |
| 455 | Rene Gonzales | .10 | .05 |
| 456 | Eddie Taubensee | .10 | .05 |
| 457 | Roberto Hernandez | .10 | .05 |
| 458 | Todd Hundley | .10 | .05 |
| 459 | Mike Macfarlane | .10 | .05 |
| 460 | Mickey Morandini | .10 | .05 |
| 461 | Scott Erickson | .10 | .05 |
| 462 | Lonnie Smith | .10 | .05 |
| 463 | Dave Henderson | .10 | .05 |
| 464 | Ryan Klesko | .20 | .09 |
| 465 | Edgar Martinez | .25 | .11 |
| 466 | Tom Pagnozzi | .10 | .05 |
| 467 | Charlie Leibrandt | .10 | .05 |
| 468 | Brian Anderson RC | .20 | .09 |
| 469 | Harold Baines | .20 | .09 |
| 470 | Tim Belcher | .10 | .05 |
| 471 | Andre Dawson | .25 | .11 |
| 472 | Eric Young | .10 | .05 |
| 473 | Paul Sorrento | .10 | .05 |
| 474 | Luis Gonzalez | .20 | .09 |
| 475 | Rob Deer | .10 | .05 |
| 476 | Mike Piazza | 1.25 | .55 |
| 477 | Kevin Reimer | .10 | .05 |
| 478 | Jeff Gardner | .10 | .05 |
| 479 | Melido Perez | .10 | .05 |
| 480 | Darren Lewis | .10 | .05 |
| 481 | Duane Ward | .10 | .05 |
| 482 | Rey Sanchez | .10 | .05 |
| 483 | Mark Lewis | .10 | .05 |
| 484 | Jeff Conine | .10 | .05 |
| 485 | Joey Cora | .10 | .05 |
| 486 | Trot Nixon RC | .75 | .35 |
| 487 | Kevin McReynolds | .10 | .05 |
| 488 | Mike Lansing | .10 | .05 |
| 489 | Mike Pagliarulo | .10 | .05 |
| 490 | Mariano Duncan | .10 | .05 |
| 491 | Mike Bordick | .10 | .05 |
| 492 | Kevin Young | .10 | .05 |
| 493 | Dave Valle | .10 | .05 |
| 494 | Wayne Gomes RC | .10 | .05 |
| 495 | Rafael Palmeiro | .40 | .18 |
| 496 | Deion Sanders | .20 | .09 |
| 497 | Rick Sutcliffe | .20 | .09 |
| 498 | Randy Milligan | .10 | .05 |
| 499 | Carlos Quintana | .10 | .05 |
| 500 | Chris Turner | .10 | .05 |
| 501 | Thomas Howard | .10 | .05 |
| 502 | Greg Swindell | .10 | .05 |
| 503 | Chad Kreuter | .10 | .05 |
| 504 | Eric Davis | .20 | .09 |
| 505 | Dickie Thon | .10 | .05 |
| 506 | Matt Drews RC | .10 | .05 |

| | | MINT | NRMT |
|---|---|---|---|
| ❑ | 507 Spike Owen | .10 | .05 |
| ❑ | 508 Rod Beck | .10 | .05 |
| ❑ | 509 Pat Hentgen | .10 | .05 |
| ❑ | 510 Sammy Sosa | .75 | .35 |
| ❑ | 511 J.T. Snow | .20 | .09 |
| ❑ | 512 Chuck Carr | .10 | .05 |
| ❑ | 513 Bo Jackson | .20 | .09 |
| ❑ | 514 Dennis Martinez | .20 | .09 |
| ❑ | 515 Phil Hiatt | .10 | .05 |
| ❑ | 516 Jeff Kent | .25 | .11 |
| ❑ | 517 Brooks Kieschnick RC | .10 | .05 |
| ❑ | 518 Kirk Presley RC | .10 | .05 |
| ❑ | 519 Kevin Seitzer | .10 | .05 |
| ❑ | 520 Carlos Garcia | .10 | .05 |
| ❑ | 521 Mike Blowers | .10 | .05 |
| ❑ | 522 Luis Alicea | .10 | .05 |
| ❑ | 523 David Hulse | .10 | .05 |
| ❑ | 524 Greg Maddux UER (Career strikeout totals listed as 113; should be 1134) | 1.00 | .45 |
| ❑ | 525 Gregg Olson | .10 | .05 |
| ❑ | 526 Hal Morris | .10 | .05 |
| ❑ | 527 Daron Kirkreit | .10 | .05 |
| ❑ | 528 David Nied | .10 | .05 |
| ❑ | 529 Jeff Russell | .10 | .05 |
| ❑ | 530 Kevin Gross | .10 | .05 |
| ❑ | 531 John Doherty | .10 | .05 |
| ❑ | 532 Matt Brunson RC | .10 | .05 |
| ❑ | 533 Dave Nilsson | .10 | .05 |
| ❑ | 534 Randy Myers | .10 | .05 |
| ❑ | 535 Steve Farr | .10 | .05 |
| ❑ | 536 Billy Wagner RC | .40 | .18 |
| ❑ | 537 Darnell Coles | .10 | .05 |
| ❑ | 538 Frank Tanana | .10 | .05 |
| ❑ | 539 Tim Salmon | .20 | .09 |
| ❑ | 540 Kim Batiste | .10 | .05 |
| ❑ | 541 George Bell | .10 | .05 |
| ❑ | 542 Tom Henke | .10 | .05 |
| ❑ | 543 Sam Horn | .10 | .05 |
| ❑ | 544 Doug Jones | .10 | .05 |
| ❑ | 545 Scott Leius | .10 | .05 |
| ❑ | 546 Al Martin | .10 | .05 |
| ❑ | 547 Bob Welch | .10 | .05 |
| ❑ | 548 Scott Christman RC | .10 | .05 |
| ❑ | 549 Norm Charlton | .10 | .05 |
| ❑ | 550 Mark McGwire | 1.50 | .70 |
| ❑ | 551 Greg McMichael | .10 | .05 |
| ❑ | 552 Tim Costo | .10 | .05 |
| ❑ | 553 Rodney Bolton | .10 | .05 |
| ❑ | 554 Pedro Martinez | .60 | .25 |
| ❑ | 555 Marc Valdes | .10 | .05 |
| ❑ | 556 Darrell Whitmore | .10 | .05 |
| ❑ | 557 Tim Bogar | .10 | .05 |
| ❑ | 558 Steve Karsay | .10 | .05 |
| ❑ | 559 Danny Bautista | .10 | .05 |
| ❑ | 560 Jeffrey Hammonds | .20 | .09 |
| ❑ | 561 Aaron Sele | .20 | .09 |
| ❑ | 562 Russ Springer | .10 | .05 |
| ❑ | 563 Jason Bere | .10 | .05 |
| ❑ | 564 Billy Brewer | .10 | .05 |
| ❑ | 565 Sterling Hitchcock | .10 | .05 |
| ❑ | 566 Bobby Munoz | .10 | .05 |
| ❑ | 567 Craig Paquette | .10 | .05 |
| ❑ | 568 Bret Boone | .20 | .09 |
| ❑ | 569 Dan Peltier | .10 | .05 |
| ❑ | 570 Jeromy Burnitz | .20 | .09 |
| ❑ | 571 John Wasdin RC | .20 | .09 |
| ❑ | 572 Chipper Jones | 1.00 | .45 |
| ❑ | 573 Jamey Wright RC | .20 | .09 |
| ❑ | 574 Jeff Granger | .10 | .05 |
| ❑ | 575 Jay Powell RC | .25 | .11 |
| ❑ | 576 Ryan Thompson | .10 | .05 |
| ❑ | 577 Lou Frazier | .10 | .05 |
| ❑ | 578 Paul Wagner | .10 | .05 |
| ❑ | 579 Brad Ausmus | .10 | .05 |
| ❑ | 580 Jack Voigt | .10 | .05 |
| ❑ | 581 Kevin Rogers | .10 | .05 |
| ❑ | 582 Damon Buford | .10 | .05 |
| ❑ | 583 Paul Quantrill | .10 | .05 |
| ❑ | 584 Marc Newfield | .10 | .05 |
| ❑ | 585 Derrek Lee RC | .40 | .18 |
| ❑ | 586 Shane Reynolds | .10 | .05 |
| ❑ | 587 Cliff Floyd | .20 | .09 |
| ❑ | 588 Jeff Schwarz | .10 | .05 |
| ❑ | 589 Ross Powell RC | .10 | .05 |
| ❑ | 590 Gerald Williams | .10 | .05 |
| ❑ | 591 Mike Trombley | .10 | .05 |
| ❑ | 592 Ken Ryan | .10 | .05 |
| ❑ | 593 John O'Donoghue | .10 | .05 |
| ❑ | 594 Rod Correia | .10 | .05 |
| ❑ | 595 Darrell Sherman | .10 | .05 |
| ❑ | 596 Steve Scarsone | .10 | .05 |
| ❑ | 597 Sherman Obando | .10 | .05 |
| ❑ | 598 Kurt Abbott RC | .10 | .05 |
| ❑ | 599 Dave Telgheder | .10 | .05 |
| ❑ | 600 Rick Trlicek | .10 | .05 |
| ❑ | 601 Carl Everett | .20 | .09 |
| ❑ | 602 Luis Ortiz | .10 | .05 |
| ❑ | 603 Larry Luebbers | .10 | .05 |
| ❑ | 604 Kevin Roberson | .10 | .05 |
| ❑ | 605 Butch Huskey | .10 | .05 |
| ❑ | 606 Benji Gil | .10 | .05 |
| ❑ | 607 Todd Van Poppel | .10 | .05 |
| ❑ | 608 Mark Hutton | .10 | .05 |
| ❑ | 609 Chip Hale | .10 | .05 |
| ❑ | 610 Matt Maysey | .10 | .05 |
| ❑ | 611 Scott Ruffcorn | .10 | .05 |
| ❑ | 612 Hilly Hathaway | .10 | .05 |
| ❑ | 613 Allen Watson | .10 | .05 |
| ❑ | 614 Carlos Delgado | .60 | .25 |
| ❑ | 615 Roberto Mejia | .10 | .05 |
| ❑ | 616 Turk Wendell | .10 | .05 |
| ❑ | 617 Tony Tarasco | .10 | .05 |
| ❑ | 618 Raul Mondesi | .20 | .09 |
| ❑ | 619 Kevin Stocker | .10 | .05 |
| ❑ | 620 Javier Lopez | .20 | .09 |
| ❑ | 621 Keith Kessinger | .10 | .05 |
| ❑ | 622 Bob Hamelin | .10 | .05 |
| ❑ | 623 John Roper | .10 | .05 |
| ❑ | 624 Lenny Dykstra WS | .10 | .05 |
| ❑ | 625 Joe Carter WS | .10 | .05 |
| ❑ | 626 Jim Abbott HL | .10 | .05 |
| ❑ | 627 Lee Smith HL | .10 | .05 |
| ❑ | 628 Ken Griffey Jr. HL | .75 | .35 |
| ❑ | 629 Dave Winfield HL | .20 | .09 |
| ❑ | 630 Darryl Kile HL | .10 | .05 |
| ❑ | 631 Frank Thomas AL MVP | .40 | .18 |
| ❑ | 632 Barry Bonds NL MVP | .40 | .18 |
| ❑ | 633 Jack McDowell AL CY | .10 | .05 |
| ❑ | 634 Greg Maddux NL CY | .50 | .23 |
| ❑ | 635 Tim Salmon AL ROY | .10 | .05 |
| ❑ | 636 Mike Piazza NL ROY | .60 | .25 |
| ❑ | 637 Brian Turang RC | .10 | .05 |
| ❑ | 638 Rondell White | .20 | .09 |
| ❑ | 639 Nigel Wilson | .10 | .05 |
| ❑ | 640 Torii Hunter RC | .10 | .05 |
| ❑ | 641 Salomon Torres | .10 | .05 |
| ❑ | 642 Kevin Higgins | .10 | .05 |
| ❑ | 643 Eric Wedge | .10 | .05 |
| ❑ | 644 Roger Salkeld | .10 | .05 |
| ❑ | 645 Manny Ramirez | .60 | .25 |
| ❑ | 646 Jeff McNeely | .10 | .05 |
| ❑ | 647 Atlanta Braves CL | .10 | .05 |
| ❑ | 648 Chicago Cubs CL | .10 | .05 |
| ❑ | 649 Cincinnati Reds CL | .10 | .05 |
| ❑ | 650 Colorado Rockies CL | .10 | .05 |
| ❑ | 651 Florida Marlins CL | .10 | .05 |
| ❑ | 652 Houston Astros CL | .10 | .05 |
| ❑ | 653 Los Angeles Dodgers CL | .10 | .05 |
| ❑ | 654 Montreal Expos CL | .10 | .05 |
| ❑ | 655 New York Mets CL | .10 | .05 |
| ❑ | 656 Philadelphia Phillies CL | .10 | .05 |
| ❑ | 657 Pittsburgh Pirates CL | .10 | .05 |
| ❑ | 658 St. Louis Cardinals CL | .10 | .05 |
| ❑ | 659 San Diego Padres CL | .10 | .05 |
| ❑ | 660 San Francisco Giants CL | .10 | .05 |

## 1994 Score Rookie/Traded

| | | MINT | NRMT |
|---|---|---|---|
| | COMPLETE SET (165) | 15.00 | 6.75 |
| | COMMON CARD (RT1-RT165) | .15 | .07 |
| ❑ | RT1 Will Clark | .60 | .25 |
| ❑ | RT2 Lee Smith | .25 | .11 |
| ❑ | RT3 Bo Jackson | .25 | .11 |
| ❑ | RT4 Ellis Burks | .25 | .11 |
| ❑ | RT5 Eddie Murray | .60 | .25 |
| ❑ | RT6 Delino DeShields | .15 | .07 |
| ❑ | RT7 Erik Hanson | .15 | .07 |

| | | MINT | NRMT |
|---|---|---|---|
| ❑ | RT8 Rafael Palmeiro | .60 | .25 |
| ❑ | RT9 Luis Polonia | .15 | .07 |
| ❑ | RT10 Omar Vizquel | .25 | .11 |
| ❑ | RT11 Kurt Abbott | .15 | .07 |
| ❑ | RT12 Vince Coleman | .15 | .07 |
| ❑ | RT13 Rickey Henderson | .75 | .35 |
| ❑ | RT14 Terry Mulholland | .15 | .07 |
| ❑ | RT15 Greg Hibbard | .15 | .07 |
| ❑ | RT16 Walt Weiss | .15 | .07 |
| ❑ | RT17 Chris Sabo | .15 | .07 |
| ❑ | RT18 Dave Henderson | .15 | .07 |
| ❑ | RT19 Rick Sutcliffe | .25 | .11 |
| ❑ | RT20 Harold Reynolds | .15 | .07 |
| ❑ | RT21 Jack Morris | .25 | .11 |
| ❑ | RT22 Dan Wilson | .15 | .07 |
| ❑ | RT23 Dave Magadan | .15 | .07 |
| ❑ | RT24 Dennis Martinez | .25 | .11 |
| ❑ | RT25 Wes Chamberlain | .15 | .07 |
| ❑ | RT26 Otis Nixon | .15 | .07 |
| ❑ | RT27 Eric Anthony | .15 | .07 |
| ❑ | RT28 Randy Milligan | .15 | .07 |
| ❑ | RT29 Julio Franco | .15 | .07 |
| ❑ | RT30 Kevin McReynolds | .15 | .07 |
| ❑ | RT31 Anthony Young | .15 | .07 |
| ❑ | RT32 Brian Harper | .15 | .07 |
| ❑ | RT33 Gene Harris | .15 | .07 |
| ❑ | RT34 Eddie Taubensee | .15 | .07 |
| ❑ | RT35 David Segui | .15 | .07 |
| ❑ | RT36 Stan Javier | .15 | .07 |
| ❑ | RT37 Felix Fermin | .15 | .07 |
| ❑ | RT38 Darrin Jackson | .15 | .07 |
| ❑ | RT39 Tony Fernandez | .15 | .07 |
| ❑ | RT40 Jose Vizcaino | .15 | .07 |
| ❑ | RT41 Willie Banks | .15 | .07 |
| ❑ | RT42 Brian Hunter | .15 | .07 |
| ❑ | RT43 Reggie Jefferson | .15 | .07 |
| ❑ | RT44 Junior Felix | .15 | .07 |
| ❑ | RT45 Jack Armstrong | .15 | .07 |
| ❑ | RT46 Bip Roberts | .15 | .07 |
| ❑ | RT47 Jerry Browne | .15 | .07 |
| ❑ | RT48 Marvin Freeman | .15 | .07 |
| ❑ | RT49 Jody Reed | .15 | .07 |
| ❑ | RT50 Alex Cole | .15 | .07 |
| ❑ | RT51 Sid Fernandez | .15 | .07 |
| ❑ | RT52 Pete Smith | .15 | .07 |
| ❑ | RT53 Xavier Hernandez | .15 | .07 |
| ❑ | RT54 Scott Sanderson | .15 | .07 |
| ❑ | RT55 Turner Ward | .15 | .07 |
| ❑ | RT56 Rex Hudler | .15 | .07 |
| ❑ | RT57 Deion Sanders | .25 | .11 |
| ❑ | RT58 Sid Bream | .15 | .07 |
| ❑ | RT59 Tony Pena | .15 | .07 |
| ❑ | RT60 Bret Boone | .25 | .11 |
| ❑ | RT61 Bobby Ayala | .15 | .07 |
| ❑ | RT62 Pedro Martinez | 1.00 | .45 |
| ❑ | RT63 Howard Johnson | .15 | .07 |
| ❑ | RT64 Mark Portugal | .15 | .07 |
| ❑ | RT65 Roberto Kelly | .15 | .07 |
| ❑ | RT66 Spike Owen | .15 | .07 |
| ❑ | RT67 Jeff Treadway | .15 | .07 |
| ❑ | RT68 Mike Harkey | .15 | .07 |
| ❑ | RT69 Doug Jones | .15 | .07 |
| ❑ | RT70 Steve Farr | .15 | .07 |
| ❑ | RT71 Billy Taylor RC | .15 | .07 |
| ❑ | RT72 Manny Ramirez | 1.00 | .45 |
| ❑ | RT73 Bob Hamelin | .15 | .07 |
| ❑ | RT74 Steve Karsay | .15 | .07 |
| ❑ | RT75 Ryan Klesko | .25 | .11 |

❑ RT76 Cliff Floyd .25 .11
❑ RT77 Jeffrey Hammonds .25 .11
❑ RT78 Javier Lopez .25 .11
❑ RT79 Roger Salkeld .15 .07
❑ RT80 Hector Carrasco .15 .07
❑ RT81 Gerald Williams .15 .07
❑ RT82 Raul Mondesi .25 .11
❑ RT83 Sterling Hitchcock .15 .07
❑ RT84 Danny Bautista .15 .07
❑ RT85 Chris Turner .15 .07
❑ RT86 Shane Reynolds .15 .07
❑ RT87 Rondell White .25 .11
❑ RT88 Salomon Torres .15 .07
❑ RT89 Turk Wendell .15 .07
❑ RT90 Tony Tarasco .15 .07
❑ RT91 Shawn Green .75 .35
❑ RT92 Greg Colbrunn .15 .07
❑ RT93 Eddie Zambrano .15 .07
❑ RT94 Rich Becker .15 .07
❑ RT95 Chris Gomez .15 .07
❑ RT96 John Patterson .15 .07
❑ RT97 Derek Parks .15 .07
❑ RT98 Rich Rowland .15 .07
❑ RT99 James Mouton .15 .07
❑ RT100 Tim Hyers RC .15 .07
❑ RT101 Jose Valentin .15 .07
❑ RT102 Carlos Delgado 1.00 .45
❑ RT103 Robert Eenhoorn .15 .07
❑ RT104 John Hudek RC .15 .07
❑ RT105 Domingo Cedeno .15 .07
❑ RT106 Denny Hocking .15 .07
❑ RT107 Greg Pirkl .15 .07
❑ RT108 Mark Smith .15 .07
❑ RT109 Paul Shuey .15 .07
❑ RT110 Jorge Fabregas .15 .07
❑ RT111 Rikkert Faneyte RC .15 .07
❑ RT112 Rob Butler .15 .07
❑ RT113 Darren Oliver RC .25 .11
❑ RT114 Troy O'Leary .15 .07
❑ RT115 Scott Brow .15 .07
❑ RT116 Tony Eusebio .15 .07
❑ RT117 Carlos Reyes .15 .07
❑ RT118 J.R. Phillips .15 .07
❑ RT119 Alex Diaz .15 .07
❑ RT120 Charles Johnson .25 .11
❑ RT121 Nate Minchey .15 .07
❑ RT122 Scott Sanders .15 .07
❑ RT123 Daryl Boston .15 .07
❑ RT124 Joey Hamilton .15 .07
❑ RT125 Brian Anderson .25 .11
❑ RT126 Dan Miceli .15 .07
❑ RT127 Tom Brunansky .15 .07
❑ RT128 Dave Staton .15 .07
❑ RT129 Mike Oquist .15 .07
❑ RT130 John Mabry RC .15 .07
❑ RT131 Norberto Martin .15 .07
❑ RT132 Hector Fajardo .15 .07
❑ RT133 Mark Hutton .15 .07
❑ RT134 Fernando Vina .15 .07
❑ RT135 Lee Tinsley .15 .07
❑ RT136 Chan Ho Park RC .75 .35
❑ RT137 Paul Spoljaric .15 .07
❑ RT138 Matias Carrillo .15 .07
❑ RT139 Mark Kiefer .15 .07
❑ RT140 Stan Royer .15 .07
❑ RT141 Bryan Eversgerd .15 .07
❑ RT142 Brian L. Hunter .15 .07
❑ RT143 Joe Hall .15 .07
❑ RT144 Johnny Ruffin .15 .07
❑ RT145 Alex Gonzalez .15 .07
❑ RT146 Keith Lockhart RC .15 .07
❑ RT147 Tom Marsh .15 .07
❑ RT148 Tony Longmire .15 .07
❑ RT149 Keith Mitchell .15 .07
❑ RT150 Melvin Nieves .15 .07
❑ RT151 Kelly Stinnett RC .15 .07
❑ RT152 Miguel Jimenez .15 .07
❑ RT153 Jeff Juden .15 .07
❑ RT154 Matt Walbeck .15 .07
❑ RT155 Marc Newfield .15 .07
❑ RT156 Matt Mieske .15 .07
❑ RT157 Marcus Moore .15 .07
❑ RT158 Jose Lima RC SP 5.00 2.20
❑ RT159 Mike Kelly .15 .07
❑ RT160 Jim Edmonds .75 .35
❑ RT161 Steve Trachsel .15 .07
❑ RT162 Greg Blosser .15 .07
❑ RT163 Marc Acre RC .15 .07
❑ RT164 AL Checklist .15 .07
❑ RT165 NL Checklist .15 .07
❑ HC1 Alex Rodriguez 500.00 220.00
Call-Up Redemption
❑ NNO September Call-Up Trade EXP

## 1995 Score

| | MINT | NRMT |
|---|---|---|
| COMPLETE SET (605) | 24.00 | 11.00 |
| COMPLETE SERIES 1 (330) | 12.00 | 5.50 |
| COMPLETE SERIES 2 (275) | 12.00 | 5.50 |
| COMMON CARD (1-605) | .10 | .05 |

❑ 1 Frank Thomas .75 .35
❑ 2 Roberto Alomar .40 .18
❑ 3 Cal Ripken 1.50 .70
❑ 4 Jose Canseco .50 .23
❑ 5 Matt Williams .25 .11
❑ 6 Esteban Beltre .10 .05
❑ 7 Domingo Cedeno .10 .05
❑ 8 John Valentin .10 .05
❑ 9 Glenallen Hill .10 .05
❑ 10 Rafael Belliard .10 .05
❑ 11 Randy Myers .10 .05
❑ 12 Mo Vaughn .20 .09
❑ 13 Hector Carrasco .10 .05
❑ 14 Chili Davis .20 .09
❑ 15 Dante Bichette .20 .09
❑ 16 Darrin Jackson .10 .05
❑ 17 Mike Piazza 1.25 .55
❑ 18 Junior Felix .10 .05
❑ 19 Moises Alou .20 .09
❑ 20 Mark Gubicza .10 .05
❑ 21 Bret Saberhagen .20 .09
❑ 22 Lenny Dykstra .20 .09
❑ 23 Steve Howe .10 .05
❑ 24 Mark Dewey .10 .05
❑ 25 Brian Harper .10 .05
❑ 26 Ozzie Smith .50 .23
❑ 27 Scott Erickson .10 .05
❑ 28 Tony Gwynn .75 .35
❑ 29 Bob Welch .10 .05
❑ 30 Barry Bonds .60 .25
❑ 31 Leo Gomez .10 .05
❑ 32 Greg Maddux 1.00 .45
❑ 33 Mike Greenwell .10 .05
❑ 34 Sammy Sosa .75 .35
❑ 35 Darnell Coles .10 .05
❑ 36 Tommy Greene .10 .05
❑ 37 Will Clark .40 .18
❑ 38 Steve Ontiveros .10 .05
❑ 39 Stan Javier .10 .05
❑ 40 Bip Roberts .10 .05
❑ 41 Paul O'Neill .20 .09
❑ 42 Bill Haselman .10 .05
❑ 43 Shane Mack .10 .05
❑ 44 Orlando Merced .10 .05
❑ 45 Kevin Seitzer .10 .05
❑ 46 Trevor Hoffman .20 .09
❑ 47 Greg Gagne .10 .05
❑ 48 Jeff Kent .25 .11
❑ 49 Tony Phillips .10 .05
❑ 50 Ken Hill .10 .05
❑ 51 Carlos Baerga .10 .05
❑ 52 Henry Rodriguez .10 .05
❑ 53 Scott Sanderson .10 .05
❑ 54 Jeff Conine .10 .05
❑ 55 Chris Turner .10 .05
❑ 56 Ken Caminiti .20 .09
❑ 57 Harold Baines .20 .09
❑ 58 Charlie Hayes .10 .05
❑ 59 Roberto Kelly .10 .05
❑ 60 John Olerud .20 .09
❑ 61 Tim Davis .10 .05
❑ 62 Rich Rowland .10 .05
❑ 63 Rey Sanchez .10 .05
❑ 64 Junior Ortiz .10 .05
❑ 65 Ricky Gutierrez .10 .05
❑ 66 Rex Hudler .10 .05
❑ 67 Johnny Ruffin .10 .05
❑ 68 Jay Buhner .20 .09
❑ 69 Tom Pagnozzi .10 .05
❑ 70 Julio Franco .10 .05
❑ 71 Eric Young .10 .05
❑ 72 Mike Bordick .10 .05
❑ 73 Don Slaught .10 .05
❑ 74 Goose Gossage .20 .09
❑ 75 Lonnie Smith .10 .05
❑ 76 Jimmy Key .20 .09
❑ 77 Dave Hollins .10 .05
❑ 78 Mickey Tettleton .10 .05
❑ 79 Luis Gonzalez .10 .05
❑ 80 Dave Winfield .40 .18
❑ 81 Ryan Thompson .10 .05
❑ 82 Felix Jose .10 .05
❑ 83 Rusty Meacham .10 .05
❑ 84 Darryl Hamilton .10 .05
❑ 85 John Wetteland .20 .09
❑ 86 Tom Brunansky .10 .05
❑ 87 Mark Lemke .10 .05
❑ 88 Spike Owen .10 .05
❑ 89 Shawon Dunston .10 .05
❑ 90 Wilson Alvarez .10 .05
❑ 91 Lee Smith .20 .09
❑ 92 Scott Kamieniecki .10 .05
❑ 93 Jacob Brumfield .10 .05
❑ 94 Kirk Gibson .20 .09
❑ 95 Joe Girardi .10 .05
❑ 96 Mike Macfarlane .10 .05
❑ 97 Greg Colbrunn .10 .05
❑ 98 Ricky Bones .10 .05
❑ 99 Delino DeShields .10 .05
❑ 100 Pat Meares .10 .05
❑ 101 Jeff Fassero .10 .05
❑ 102 Jim Leyritz .10 .05
❑ 103 Gary Redus .10 .05
❑ 104 Terry Steinbach .10 .05
❑ 105 Kevin McReynolds .10 .05
❑ 106 Felix Fermin .10 .05
❑ 107 Danny Jackson .10 .05
❑ 108 Chris James .10 .05
❑ 109 Jeff King .10 .05
❑ 110 Pat Hentgen .10 .05
❑ 111 Gerald Perry .10 .05
❑ 112 Tim Raines .20 .09
❑ 113 Eddie Williams .10 .05
❑ 114 Jamie Moyer .10 .05
❑ 115 Bud Black .10 .05
❑ 116 Chris Gomez .10 .05
❑ 117 Luis Lopez .10 .05
❑ 118 Roger Clemens .75 .35
❑ 119 Javier Lopez .20 .09
❑ 120 Dave Nilsson .10 .05
❑ 121 Karl Rhodes .10 .05
❑ 122 Rick Aguilera .10 .05
❑ 123 Tony Fernandez .10 .05
❑ 124 Bernie Williams .40 .18
❑ 125 James Mouton .10 .05
❑ 126 Mark Langston .10 .05
❑ 127 Mike Lansing .10 .05
❑ 128 Tino Martinez .20 .09
❑ 129 Joe Orsulak .10 .05
❑ 130 David Hulse .10 .05
❑ 131 Pete Incaviglia .10 .05
❑ 132 Mark Clark .10 .05
❑ 133 Tony Eusebio .10 .05
❑ 134 Chuck Finley .20 .09
❑ 135 Lou Frazier .10 .05
❑ 136 Craig Grebeck .10 .05
❑ 137 Kelly Stinnett .10 .05
❑ 138 Paul Shuey .10 .05

❑ 139 David Nied .10 .05
❑ 140 Billy Brewer .10 .05
❑ 141 Dave Weathers .10 .05
❑ 142 Scott Leius .10 .05
❑ 143 Brian Jordan .20 .09
❑ 144 Melido Perez .10 .05
❑ 145 Tony Tarasco .10 .05
❑ 146 Dan Wilson .10 .05
❑ 147 Rondell White .20 .09
❑ 148 Mike Henneman .10 .05
❑ 149 Brian Johnson .10 .05
❑ 150 Tom Henke .10 .05
❑ 151 John Patterson .10 .05
❑ 152 Bobby Witt .10 .05
❑ 153 Eddie Taubensee .10 .05
❑ 154 Pat Borders .10 .05
❑ 155 Ramon Martinez .10 .05
❑ 156 Mike Kingery .10 .05
❑ 157 Zane Smith .10 .05
❑ 158 Benito Santiago .10 .05
❑ 159 Matias Carrillo .10 .05
❑ 160 Scott Brosius .20 .09
❑ 161 Dave Clark .10 .05
❑ 162 Mark McLemore .10 .05
❑ 163 Curt Schilling .20 .09
❑ 164 J.T. Snow .20 .09
❑ 165 Rod Beck .10 .05
❑ 166 Scott Fletcher .10 .05
❑ 167 Bob Tewksbury .10 .05
❑ 168 Mike LaValliere .10 .05
❑ 169 Dave Hansen .10 .05
❑ 170 Pedro Martinez .50 .23
❑ 171 Kirk Rueter .10 .05
❑ 172 Jose Lind .10 .05
❑ 173 Luis Alicea .10 .05
❑ 174 Mike Moore .10 .05
❑ 175 Andy Ashby .10 .05
❑ 176 Jody Reed .10 .05
❑ 177 Darryl Kile .20 .09
❑ 178 Carl Willis .10 .05
❑ 179 Jeromy Burnitz .20 .09
❑ 180 Mike Gallego .10 .05
❑ 181 Bill VanLandingham .10 .05
❑ 182 Sid Fernandez .10 .05
❑ 183 Kim Batiste .10 .05
❑ 184 Greg Myers .10 .05
❑ 185 Steve Avery .10 .05
❑ 186 Steve Farr .10 .05
❑ 187 Robb Nen .10 .05
❑ 188 Dan Pasqua .10 .05
❑ 189 Bruce Ruffin .10 .05
❑ 190 Jose Valentin .10 .05
❑ 191 Willie Banks .10 .05
❑ 192 Mike Aldrete .10 .05
❑ 193 Randy Milligan .10 .05
❑ 194 Steve Karsay .10 .05
❑ 195 Mike Stanley .10 .05
❑ 196 Jose Mesa .10 .05
❑ 197 Tom Browning .10 .05
❑ 198 John Vander Wal .10 .05
❑ 199 Kevin Brown .25 .11
❑ 200 Mike Oquist .10 .05
❑ 201 Greg Swindell .10 .05
❑ 202 Eddie Zambrano .10 .05
❑ 203 Joe Boever .10 .05
❑ 204 Gary Varsho .10 .05
❑ 205 Chris Gwynn .10 .05
❑ 206 David Howard .10 .05
❑ 207 Jerome Walton .10 .05
❑ 208 Danny Darwin .10 .05
❑ 209 Darryl Strawberry .20 .09
❑ 210 Todd Van Poppel .10 .05
❑ 211 Scott Livingstone .10 .05
❑ 212 Dave Fleming .10 .05
❑ 213 Todd Worrell .10 .05
❑ 214 Carlos Delgado .40 .18
❑ 215 Bill Pecota .10 .05
❑ 216 Jim Lindeman .10 .05
❑ 217 Rick White .10 .05
❑ 218 Jose Oquendo .10 .05
❑ 219 Tony Castillo .10 .05
❑ 220 Fernando Vina .10 .05
❑ 221 Jeff Bagwell .50 .23
❑ 222 Randy Johnson .50 .23
❑ 223 Albert Belle .25 .11
❑ 224 Chuck Carr .10 .05
❑ 225 Mark Leiter .10 .05
❑ 226 Hal Morris .10 .05
❑ 227 Robin Ventura .20 .09
❑ 228 Mike Munoz .10 .05
❑ 229 Jim Thome .25 .11
❑ 230 Mario Diaz .10 .05
❑ 231 John Doherty .10 .05
❑ 232 Bobby Jones .10 .05
❑ 233 Raul Mondesi .20 .09
❑ 234 Ricky Jordan .10 .05
❑ 235 John Jaha .10 .05
❑ 236 Carlos Garcia .10 .05
❑ 237 Kirby Puckett 1.00 .45
❑ 238 Orel Hershiser .20 .09
❑ 239 Don Mattingly 1.00 .45
❑ 240 Sid Bream .10 .05
❑ 241 Brent Gates .10 .05
❑ 242 Tony Longmire .10 .05
❑ 243 Robby Thompson .10 .05
❑ 244 Rick Sutcliffe .20 .09
❑ 245 Dean Palmer .20 .09
❑ 246 Marquis Grissom .10 .05
❑ 247 Paul Molitor .40 .18
❑ 248 Mark Carreon .10 .05
❑ 249 Jack Voigt .10 .05
❑ 250 Greg McMichael UER .10 .05
(Photo on front is Mike Stanton)
❑ 251 Damon Berryhill .10 .05
❑ 252 Brian Dorsett .10 .05
❑ 253 Jim Edmonds .40 .18
❑ 254 Barry Larkin .40 .18
❑ 255 Jack McDowell .10 .05
❑ 256 Wally Joyner .20 .09
❑ 257 Eddie Murray .40 .18
❑ 258 Lenny Webster .10 .05
❑ 259 Milt Cuyler .10 .05
❑ 260 Todd Benzinger .10 .05
❑ 261 Vince Coleman .10 .05
❑ 262 Todd Stottlemyre .10 .05
❑ 263 Turner Ward .10 .05
❑ 264 Ray Lankford .20 .09
❑ 265 Matt Walbeck .10 .05
❑ 266 Deion Sanders .20 .09
❑ 267 Gerald Williams .10 .05
❑ 268 Jim Gott .10 .05
❑ 269 Jeff Frye .10 .05
❑ 270 Jose Rijo .10 .05
❑ 271 Dave Justice .25 .11
❑ 272 Ismael Valdes .10 .05
❑ 273 Ben McDonald .10 .05
❑ 274 Darren Lewis .10 .05
❑ 275 Graeme Lloyd .10 .05
❑ 276 Luis Ortiz .10 .05
❑ 277 Julian Tavarez .10 .05
❑ 278 Mark Dalesandro .10 .05
❑ 279 Brett Merriman .10 .05
❑ 280 Ricky Bottalico .10 .05
❑ 281 Robert Eenhoorn .10 .05
❑ 282 Rikkert Faneyte .10 .05
❑ 283 Mike Kelly .10 .05
❑ 284 Mark Smith .10 .05
❑ 285 Turk Wendell .10 .05
❑ 286 Greg Blosser .10 .05
❑ 287 Garey Ingram .10 .05
❑ 288 Jorge Fabregas .10 .05
❑ 289 Blaise Ilsley .10 .05
❑ 290 Joe Hall .10 .05
❑ 291 Orlando Miller .10 .05
❑ 292 Jose Lima .10 .05
❑ 293 Greg O'Halloran RC .10 .05
❑ 294 Mark Kiefer .10 .05
❑ 295 Jose Oliva .10 .05
❑ 296 Rich Becker .10 .05
❑ 297 Brian L. Hunter .10 .05
❑ 298 Dave Silvestri .10 .05
❑ 299 Armando Benitez .20 .09
❑ 300 Darren Dreifort .20 .09
❑ 301 John Mabry .10 .05
❑ 302 Greg Pirkl .10 .05
❑ 303 J.R. Phillips .10 .05
❑ 304 Shawn Green .40 .18
❑ 305 Roberto Petagine .10 .05
❑ 306 Keith Lockhart .10 .05
❑ 307 Jonathan Hurst .10 .05
❑ 308 Paul Spoljaric .10 .05
❑ 309 Mike Lieberthal .20 .09
❑ 310 Garret Anderson .20 .09
❑ 311 John Johnstone .10 .05
❑ 312 Alex Rodriguez 1.50 .70
❑ 313 Kent Mercker HL .10 .05
❑ 314 John Valentin HL .10 .05
❑ 315 Kenny Rogers HL .10 .05
❑ 316 Fred McGriff HL .10 .05
❑ 317 Team Checklists .10 .05
❑ 318 Team Checklists .10 .05
❑ 319 Team Checklists .10 .05
❑ 320 Team Checklists .10 .05
❑ 321 Team Checklists .10 .05
❑ 322 Team Checklists .10 .05
❑ 323 Team Checklists .10 .05
❑ 324 Team Checklists .10 .05
❑ 325 Team Checklists .10 .05
❑ 326 Team Checklists .10 .05
❑ 327 Team Checklists .10 .05
❑ 328 Team Checklists .10 .05
❑ 329 Team Checklists .10 .05
❑ 330 Team Checklists .10 .05
❑ 331 Pedro Munoz .10 .05
❑ 332 Ryan Klesko .20 .09
❑ 333 Andre Dawson .25 .11
❑ 334 Derrick May .10 .05
❑ 335 Aaron Sele .20 .09
❑ 336 Kevin Mitchell .10 .05
❑ 337 Steve Trachsel .10 .05
❑ 338 Andres Galarraga .25 .11
❑ 339 Terry Pendleton .20 .09
❑ 340 Gary Sheffield .40 .18
❑ 341 Travis Fryman .20 .09
❑ 342 Bo Jackson .20 .09
❑ 343 Gary Gaetti .20 .09
❑ 344 Brett Butler .20 .09
❑ 345 B.J. Surhoff .20 .09
❑ 346 Larry Walker .20 .09
❑ 347 Kevin Tapani .10 .05
❑ 348 Rick Wilkins .10 .05
❑ 349 Wade Boggs .50 .23
❑ 350 Mariano Duncan .10 .05
❑ 351 Ruben Sierra .10 .05
❑ 352 Andy Van Slyke .20 .09
❑ 353 Reggie Jefferson .10 .05
❑ 354 Gregg Jefferies .10 .05
❑ 355 Tim Naehring .10 .05
❑ 356 John Roper .10 .05
❑ 357 Joe Carter .20 .09
❑ 358 Kurt Abbott .10 .05
❑ 359 Lenny Harris .10 .05
❑ 360 Lance Johnson .10 .05
❑ 361 Brian Anderson .10 .05
❑ 362 Jim Eisenreich .10 .05
❑ 363 Jerry Browne .10 .05
❑ 364 Mark Grace .40 .18
❑ 365 Devon White .20 .09
❑ 366 Reggie Sanders .10 .05
❑ 367 Ivan Rodriguez .50 .23
❑ 368 Kirt Manwaring .10 .05
❑ 369 Pat Kelly .10 .05
❑ 370 Ellis Burks .20 .09
❑ 371 Charles Nagy .10 .05
❑ 372 Kevin Bass .10 .05
❑ 373 Lou Whitaker .20 .09
❑ 374 Rene Arocha .10 .05
❑ 375 Derek Parks .10 .05
❑ 376 Mark Whiten .10 .05
❑ 377 Mark McGwire 1.50 .70
❑ 378 Doug Drabek .10 .05
❑ 379 Greg Vaughn .20 .09
❑ 380 Al Martin .10 .05
❑ 381 Ron Darling .10 .05
❑ 382 Tim Wallach .10 .05
❑ 383 Alan Trammell .25 .11
❑ 384 Randy Velarde .10 .05
❑ 385 Chris Sabo .10 .05
❑ 386 Wil Cordero .10 .05
❑ 387 Darrin Fletcher .10 .05
❑ 388 David Segui .10 .05
❑ 389 Steve Buechele .10 .05
❑ 390 Dave Gallagher .10 .05
❑ 391 Thomas Howard .10 .05
❑ 392 Chad Curtis .10 .05
❑ 393 Cal Eldred .10 .05
❑ 394 Jason Bere .10 .05
❑ 395 Bret Barberie .10 .05

❑ 396 Paul Sorrento .10 .05
❑ 397 Steve Finley .20 .09
❑ 398 Cecil Fielder .20 .09
❑ 399 Eric Karros .20 .09
❑ 400 Jeff Montgomery .10 .05
❑ 401 Cliff Floyd .20 .09
❑ 402 Matt Mieske .10 .05
❑ 403 Brian Hunter .10 .05
❑ 404 Alex Cole .10 .05
❑ 405 Kevin Stocker .10 .05
❑ 406 Eric Davis .20 .09
❑ 407 Marvin Freeman .10 .05
❑ 408 Dennis Eckersley .20 .09
❑ 409 Todd Zeile .10 .05
❑ 410 Keith Mitchell .10 .05
❑ 411 Andy Benes .10 .05
❑ 412 Juan Bell .10 .05
❑ 413 Royce Clayton .10 .05
❑ 414 Ed Sprague .10 .05
❑ 415 Mike Mussina .40 .18
❑ 416 Todd Hundley .10 .05
❑ 417 Pat Listach .10 .05
❑ 418 Joe Oliver .10 .05
❑ 419 Rafael Palmeiro .40 .18
❑ 420 Tim Salmon .20 .09
❑ 421 Brady Anderson .20 .09
❑ 422 Kenny Lofton .20 .09
❑ 423 Craig Biggio .25 .11
❑ 424 Bobby Bonilla .20 .09
❑ 425 Kenny Rogers .10 .05
❑ 426 Derek Bell .10 .05
❑ 427 Scott Cooper .10 .05
❑ 428 Ozzie Guillen .10 .05
❑ 429 Omar Vizquel .20 .09
❑ 430 Phil Plantier .10 .05
❑ 431 Chuck Knoblauch .20 .09
❑ 432 Darren Daulton .20 .09
❑ 433 Bob Hamelin .10 .05
❑ 434 Tom Glavine .40 .18
❑ 435 Walt Weiss .10 .05
❑ 436 Jose Vizcaino .10 .05
❑ 437 Ken Griffey Jr. 1.50 .70
❑ 438 Jay Bell .20 .09
❑ 439 Juan Gonzalez .40 .18
❑ 440 Jeff Blauser .10 .05
❑ 441 Rickey Henderson .50 .23
❑ 442 Bobby Ayala .10 .05
❑ 443 David Cone .20 .09
❑ 444 Pedro Martinez .50 .23
❑ 445 Manny Ramirez .50 .23
❑ 446 Mark Portugal .10 .05
❑ 447 Damion Easley .10 .05
❑ 448 Gary DiSarcina .10 .05
❑ 449 Roberto Hernandez .10 .05
❑ 450 Jeffrey Hammonds .20 .09
❑ 451 Jeff Treadway .10 .05
❑ 452 Jim Abbott .20 .09
❑ 453 Carlos Rodriguez .10 .05
❑ 454 Joey Cora .10 .05
❑ 455 Bret Boone .20 .09
❑ 456 Danny Tartabull .10 .05
❑ 457 John Franco .20 .09
❑ 458 Roger Salkeld .10 .05
❑ 459 Fred McGriff .25 .11
❑ 460 Pedro Astacio .10 .05
❑ 461 Jon Lieber .10 .05
❑ 462 Luis Polonia .10 .05
❑ 463 Geronimo Pena .10 .05
❑ 464 Tom Gordon .10 .05
❑ 465 Brad Ausmus .10 .05
❑ 466 Willie McGee .20 .09
❑ 467 Doug Jones .10 .05
❑ 468 John Smoltz .20 .09
❑ 469 Troy Neel .10 .05
❑ 470 Luis Sojo .10 .05
❑ 471 John Smiley .10 .05
❑ 472 Rafael Bournigal .10 .05
❑ 473 Bill Taylor .10 .05
❑ 474 Juan Guzman .10 .05
❑ 475 Dave Magadan .10 .05
❑ 476 Mike Devereaux .10 .05
❑ 477 Andujar Cedeno .10 .05
❑ 478 Edgar Martinez .25 .11
❑ 479 Milt Thompson .10 .05
❑ 480 Allen Watson .10 .05
❑ 481 Ron Karkovice .10 .05
❑ 482 Joey Hamilton .10 .05
❑ 483 Vinny Castilla .20 .09
❑ 484 Tim Belcher .10 .05
❑ 485 Bernard Gilkey .10 .05
❑ 486 Scott Servais .10 .05
❑ 487 Cory Snyder .10 .05
❑ 488 Mel Rojas .10 .05
❑ 489 Carlos Reyes .10 .05
❑ 490 Chip Hale .10 .05
❑ 491 Bill Swift .10 .05
❑ 492 Pat Rapp .10 .05
❑ 493 Brian McRae .10 .05
❑ 494 Mickey Morandini .10 .05
❑ 495 Tony Pena .10 .05
❑ 496 Danny Bautista .10 .05
❑ 497 Armando Reynoso .10 .05
❑ 498 Ken Ryan .10 .05
❑ 499 Billy Ripken .10 .05
❑ 500 Pat Mahomes .10 .05
❑ 501 Mark Acre .10 .05
❑ 502 Geronimo Berroa .10 .05
❑ 503 Norberto Martin .10 .05
❑ 504 Chad Kreuter .10 .05
❑ 505 Howard Johnson .10 .05
❑ 506 Eric Anthony .10 .05
❑ 507 Mark Wohlers .10 .05
❑ 508 Scott Sanders .10 .05
❑ 509 Pete Harnisch .10 .05
❑ 510 Wes Chamberlain .10 .05
❑ 511 Tom Candiotti .10 .05
❑ 512 Albie Lopez .10 .05
❑ 513 Denny Neagle .20 .09
❑ 514 Sean Berry .10 .05
❑ 515 Billy Hatcher .10 .05
❑ 516 Todd Jones .10 .05
❑ 517 Wayne Kirby .10 .05
❑ 518 Butch Henry .10 .05
❑ 519 Sandy Alomar Jr. .20 .09
❑ 520 Kevin Appier .20 .09
❑ 521 Roberto Mejia .10 .05
❑ 522 Steve Cooke .10 .05
❑ 523 Terry Shumpert .10 .05
❑ 524 Mike Jackson .10 .05
❑ 525 Kent Mercker .10 .05
❑ 526 David Wells .20 .09
❑ 527 Juan Samuel .10 .05
❑ 528 Salomon Torres .10 .05
❑ 529 Duane Ward .10 .05
❑ 530 Rob Dibble .10 .05
❑ 531 Mike Blowers .10 .05
❑ 532 Mark Eichhorn .10 .05
❑ 533 Alex Diaz .10 .05
❑ 534 Dan Miceli .10 .05
❑ 535 Jeff Branson .10 .05
❑ 536 Dave Stevens .10 .05
❑ 537 Charlie O'Brien .10 .05
❑ 538 Shane Reynolds .10 .05
❑ 539 Rich Amaral .10 .05
❑ 540 Rusty Greer .20 .09
❑ 541 Alex Arias .10 .05
❑ 542 Eric Plunk .10 .05
❑ 543 John Hudek .10 .05
❑ 544 Kirk McCaskill .10 .05
❑ 545 Jeff Reboulet .10 .05
❑ 546 Sterling Hitchcock .10 .05
❑ 547 Warren Newson .10 .05
❑ 548 Bryan Harvey .10 .05
❑ 549 Mike Huff .10 .05
❑ 550 Lance Parrish .10 .05
❑ 551 Ken Griffey Jr. HIT .75 .35
❑ 552 Matt Williams HIT .20 .09
❑ 553 Roberto Alomar HIT UER .20 .09
(Card says he's a NL All-Star; he plays in the AL)
❑ 554 Jeff Bagwell HIT .40 .18
❑ 555 Dave Justice HIT .10 .05
❑ 556 Cal Ripken Jr. HIT .75 .35
❑ 557 Albert Belle HIT .10 .05
❑ 558 Mike Piazza HIT .60 .25
❑ 559 Kirby Puckett HIT .50 .18
❑ 560 Wade Boggs HIT .20 .09
❑ 561 Tony Gwynn HIT UER .40 .18
(Card has him winning AL batting titles; he's played whole career in the NL)
❑ 562 Barry Bonds HIT .25 .11
❑ 563 Mo Vaughn HIT .20 .09
❑ 564 Don Mattingly HIT .50 .18
❑ 565 Carlos Baerga HIT .10 .05
❑ 566 Paul Molitor HIT .20 .09
❑ 567 Raul Mondesi HIT .10 .05
❑ 568 Manny Ramirez HIT .25 .11
❑ 569 Alex Rodriguez HIT .75 .35
❑ 570 Will Clark HIT .20 .09
❑ 571 Frank Thomas HIT .40 .18
❑ 572 Moises Alou HIT .10 .05
❑ 573 Jeff Conine HIT .10 .05
❑ 574 Joe Ausanio .10 .05
❑ 575 Charles Johnson .20 .09
❑ 576 Ernie Young .10 .05
❑ 577 Jeff Granger .10 .05
❑ 578 Robert Perez .10 .05
❑ 579 Melvin Nieves .10 .05
❑ 580 Gar Finnvold .10 .05
❑ 581 Duane Singleton .10 .05
❑ 582 Chan Ho Park .20 .09
❑ 583 Fausto Cruz .10 .05
❑ 584 Dave Staton .10 .05
❑ 585 Denny Hocking .10 .05
❑ 586 Nate Minchey .10 .05
❑ 587 Marc Newfield .10 .05
❑ 588 Jayhawk Owens UER .10 .05
(Front Photo is Jim Tatum)
❑ 589 Darren Bragg .10 .05
❑ 590 Kevin King .10 .05
❑ 591 Kurt Miller .10 .05
❑ 592 Aaron Small .10 .05
❑ 593 Troy O'Leary .10 .05
❑ 594 Phil Stidham .10 .05
❑ 595 Steve Dunn .10 .05
❑ 596 Cory Bailey .10 .05
❑ 597 Alex Gonzalez .10 .05
❑ 598 Jim Bowie RC .10 .05
❑ 599 Jeff Cirillo .20 .09
❑ 600 Mark Hutton .10 .05
❑ 601 Russ Davis .10 .05
❑ 602 Checklist .10 .05
❑ 603 Checklist .10 .05
❑ 604 Checklist .10 .05
❑ 605 Checklist .10 .05
❑ RG1 R.Klesko Rook.Great 1.00 .45
❑ SG1 Ryan Klesko AU6100 10.00 4.50
❑ NNO Trade Hall of Gold 1.00 .45

## 1996 Score

| | MINT | NRMT |
|---|---|---|
| COMPLETE SET (517) | 24.00 | 11.00 |
| COMPLETE SERIES 1 (275) | 12.00 | 5.50 |
| COMPLETE SERIES 2 (242) | 12.00 | 5.50 |

❑ 1 Will Clark .40 .18
❑ 2 Rich Becker .10 .05
❑ 3 Ryan Klesko .20 .09
❑ 4 Jim Edmonds .40 .18
❑ 5 Barry Larkin .40 .18
❑ 6 Jim Thome .25 .11
❑ 7 Raul Mondesi .20 .09
❑ 8 Don Mattingly 1.00 .45
❑ 9 Jeff Conine .10 .05
❑ 10 Rickey Henderson .50 .23
❑ 11 Chad Curtis .10 .05
❑ 12 Darren Daulton .20 .09
❑ 13 Larry Walker .20 .09
❑ 14 Carlos Garcia .10 .05

❑ 15 Carlos Baerga .10 .05
❑ 16 Tony Gwynn .75 .35
❑ 17 Jon Nunnally .10 .05
❑ 18 Deion Sanders .20 .09
❑ 19 Mark Grace .40 .18
❑ 20 Alex Rodriguez 1.25 .55
❑ 21 Frank Thomas .75 .35
❑ 22 Brian Jordan .20 .09
❑ 23 J.T. Snow .20 .09
❑ 24 Shawn Green .40 .18
❑ 25 Tim Wakefield .10 .05
❑ 26 Curtis Goodwin .10 .05
❑ 27 John Smoltz .20 .09
❑ 28 Devon White .20 .09
❑ 29 Johnny Damon .25 .11
❑ 30 Tim Salmon .25 .11
❑ 31 Rafael Palmeiro .40 .18
❑ 32 Bernard Gilkey .10 .05
❑ 33 John Valentin .10 .05
❑ 34 Randy Johnson .50 .23
❑ 35 Garret Anderson .20 .09
❑ 36 Rikkert Faneyte .10 .05
❑ 37 Ray Durham .20 .09
❑ 38 Bip Roberts .10 .05
❑ 39 Jaime Navarro .10 .05
❑ 40 Mark Johnson .10 .05
❑ 41 Darren Lewis .10 .05
❑ 42 Tyler Green .10 .05
❑ 43 Bill Pulsipher .10 .05
❑ 44 Jason Giambi .40 .18
❑ 45 Kevin Ritz .10 .05
❑ 46 Jack McDowell .10 .05
❑ 47 Felipe Lira .10 .05
❑ 48 Rico Brogna .10 .05
❑ 49 Terry Pendleton .20 .09
❑ 50 Rondell White .20 .09
❑ 51 Andre Dawson .25 .11
❑ 52 Kirby Puckett 1.00 .45
❑ 53 Wally Joyner .20 .09
❑ 54 B.J. Surhoff .20 .09
❑ 55 Randy Velarde .10 .05
❑ 56 Greg Vaughn .20 .09
❑ 57 Roberto Alomar .40 .18
❑ 58 David Justice .25 .11
❑ 59 Kevin Seitzer .10 .05
❑ 60 Cal Ripken 1.50 .70
❑ 61 Ozzie Smith .50 .23
❑ 62 Mo Vaughn .20 .09
❑ 63 Ricky Bones .10 .05
❑ 64 Gary DiSarcina .10 .05
❑ 65 Matt Williams .25 .11
❑ 66 Wilson Alvarez .10 .05
❑ 67 Lenny Dykstra .20 .09
❑ 68 Brian McRae .10 .05
❑ 69 Todd Stottlemyre .10 .05
❑ 70 Bret Boone .20 .09
❑ 71 Sterling Hitchcock .10 .05
❑ 72 Albert Belle .25 .11
❑ 73 Todd Hundley .10 .05
❑ 74 Vinny Castilla .20 .09
❑ 75 Moises Alou .20 .09
❑ 76 Cecil Fielder .20 .09
❑ 77 Brad Radke .20 .09
❑ 78 Quilvio Veras .10 .05
❑ 79 Eddie Murray .40 .18
❑ 80 James Mouton .10 .05
❑ 81 Pat Listach .10 .05
❑ 82 Mark Gubicza .10 .05
❑ 83 Dave Winfield .40 .18
❑ 84 Fred McGriff .25 .11
❑ 85 Darryl Hamilton .10 .05
❑ 86 Jeffrey Hammonds .20 .09
❑ 87 Pedro Munoz .10 .05
❑ 88 Craig Biggio .25 .11
❑ 89 Cliff Floyd .20 .09
❑ 90 Tim Naehring .10 .05
❑ 91 Brett Butler .20 .09
❑ 92 Kevin Foster .10 .05
❑ 93 Pat Kelly .10 .05
❑ 94 John Smiley .10 .05
❑ 95 Terry Steinbach .10 .05
❑ 96 Orel Hershiser .20 .09
❑ 97 Darrin Fletcher .10 .05
❑ 98 Walt Weiss .10 .05
❑ 99 John Wetteland .20 .09
❑ 100 Alan Trammell .25 .11
❑ 101 Steve Avery .10 .05
❑ 102 Tony Eusebio .10 .05
❑ 103 Sandy Alomar Jr. .20 .09
❑ 104 Joe Girardi .10 .05
❑ 105 Rick Aguilera .10 .05
❑ 106 Tony Tarasco .10 .05
❑ 107 Chris Hammond .10 .05
❑ 108 Mike Macfarlane .10 .05
❑ 109 Doug Drabek .10 .05
❑ 110 Derek Bell .10 .05
❑ 111 Ed Sprague .10 .05
❑ 112 Todd Hollandsworth .10 .05
❑ 113 Otis Nixon .10 .05
❑ 114 Keith Lockhart .10 .05
❑ 115 Donovan Osborne .10 .05
❑ 116 Dave Magadan .10 .05
❑ 117 Edgar Martinez .25 .11
❑ 118 Chuck Carr .10 .05
❑ 119 J.R. Phillips .10 .05
❑ 120 Sean Bergman .10 .05
❑ 121 Andujar Cedeno .10 .05
❑ 122 Eric Young .10 .05
❑ 123 Al Martin .10 .05
❑ 124 Mark Lemke .10 .05
❑ 125 Jim Eisenreich .10 .05
❑ 126 Benito Santiago .10 .05
❑ 127 Ariel Prieto .10 .05
❑ 128 Jim Bullinger .10 .05
❑ 129 Russ Davis .10 .05
❑ 130 Jim Abbott .20 .09
❑ 131 Jason Isringhausen .20 .09
❑ 132 Carlos Perez .10 .05
❑ 133 David Segui .10 .05
❑ 134 Troy O'Leary .10 .05
❑ 135 Pat Meares .10 .05
❑ 136 Chris Hoiles .10 .05
❑ 137 Ismael Valdes .10 .05
❑ 138 Jose Oliva .10 .05
❑ 139 Carlos Delgado .40 .18
❑ 140 Tom Goodwin .10 .05
❑ 141 Bob Tewksbury .10 .05
❑ 142 Chris Gomez .10 .05
❑ 143 Jose Oquendo .10 .05
❑ 144 Mark Lewis .10 .05
❑ 145 Salomon Torres .10 .05
❑ 146 Luis Gonzalez .20 .09
❑ 147 Mark Carreon .10 .05
❑ 148 Lance Johnson .10 .05
❑ 149 Melvin Nieves .10 .05
❑ 150 Lee Smith .20 .09
❑ 151 Jacob Brumfield .10 .05
❑ 152 Armando Benitez .10 .05
❑ 153 Curt Schilling .20 .09
❑ 154 Javier Lopez .20 .09
❑ 155 Frank Rodriguez .10 .05
❑ 156 Alex Gonzalez .10 .05
❑ 157 Todd Worrell .10 .05
❑ 158 Benji Gil .10 .05
❑ 159 Greg Gagne .10 .05
❑ 160 Tom Henke .10 .05
❑ 161 Randy Myers .10 .05
❑ 162 Joey Cora .10 .05
❑ 163 Scott Ruffcorn .10 .05
❑ 164 W. VanLandingham .10 .05
❑ 165 Tony Phillips .10 .05
❑ 166 Eddie Williams .10 .05
❑ 167 Bobby Bonilla .20 .09
❑ 168 Denny Neagle .20 .09
❑ 169 Troy Percival .10 .05
❑ 170 Billy Ashley .10 .05
❑ 171 Andy Van Slyke .20 .09
❑ 172 Jose Offerman .10 .05
❑ 173 Mark Parent .10 .05
❑ 174 Edgardo Alfonzo .20 .09
❑ 175 Trevor Hoffman .20 .09
❑ 176 David Cone .20 .09
❑ 177 Dan Wilson .10 .05
❑ 178 Steve Ontiveros .10 .05
❑ 179 Dean Palmer .20 .09
❑ 180 Mike Kelly .10 .05
❑ 181 Jim Leyritz .10 .05
❑ 182 Ron Karkovice .10 .05
❑ 183 Kevin Brown .25 .11
❑ 184 Jose Valentin .10 .05
❑ 185 Jorge Fabregas .10 .05
❑ 186 Jose Mesa .10 .05
❑ 187 Brent Mayne .10 .05
❑ 188 Carl Everett .20 .09
❑ 189 Paul Sorrento .10 .05
❑ 190 Pete Schourek .10 .05
❑ 191 Scott Kamieniecki .10 .05
❑ 192 Roberto Hernandez .10 .05
❑ 193 Randy Johnson RR .20 .09
❑ 194 Greg Maddux RR .50 .23
❑ 195 Hideo Nomo RR .20 .09
❑ 196 David Cone RR .10 .05
❑ 197 Mike Mussina RR .20 .09
❑ 198 Andy Benes RR .10 .05
❑ 199 Kevin Appier RR .10 .05
❑ 200 John Smoltz RR .10 .05
❑ 201 John Wetteland RR .10 .05
❑ 202 Mark Wohlers RR .10 .05
❑ 203 Stan Belinda .10 .05
❑ 204 Brian Anderson .10 .05
❑ 205 Mike Devereaux .10 .05
❑ 206 Mark Wohlers .10 .05
❑ 207 Omar Vizquel .20 .09
❑ 208 Jose Rijo .10 .05
❑ 209 Willie Blair .10 .05
❑ 210 Jamie Moyer .10 .05
❑ 211 Craig Shipley .10 .05
❑ 212 Shane Reynolds .10 .05
❑ 213 Chad Fonville .10 .05
❑ 214 Jose Vizcaino .10 .05
❑ 215 Sid Fernandez .10 .05
❑ 216 Andy Ashby .10 .05
❑ 217 Frank Castillo .10 .05
❑ 218 Kevin Tapani .10 .05
❑ 219 Kent Mercker .10 .05
❑ 220 Karim Garcia .10 .05
❑ 221 Antonio Osuna .10 .05
❑ 222 Tim Unroe .10 .05
❑ 223 Johnny Damon .25 .11
❑ 224 LaTroy Hawkins .10 .05
❑ 225 Mariano Rivera .20 .09
❑ 226 Jose Alberro .10 .05
❑ 227 Angel Martinez .10 .05
❑ 228 Jason Schmidt .10 .05
❑ 229 Tony Clark .10 .05
❑ 230 Kevin Jordan UER .10 .05
(Ricky Jordan pictured on both sides)
❑ 231 Mark Thompson .10 .05
❑ 232 Jim Dougherty .10 .05
❑ 233 Roger Cedeno .10 .05
❑ 234 Ugueth Urbina .20 .09
❑ 235 Ricky Otero .10 .05
❑ 236 Mark Smith .10 .05
❑ 237 Brian Barber .10 .05
❑ 238 Kevin Flora .10 .05
❑ 239 Joe Rosselli .10 .05
❑ 240 Derek Jeter 1.50 .70
❑ 241 Michael Tucker .10 .05
❑ 242 Ben Blomdahl .10 .05
❑ 243 Joe Vitiello .10 .05
❑ 244 Todd Steverson .10 .05
❑ 245 James Baldwin .10 .05
❑ 246 Alan Embree .10 .05
❑ 247 Shannon Penn .10 .05
❑ 248 Chris Stynes .10 .05
❑ 249 Oscar Munoz .10 .05
❑ 250 Jose Herrera .10 .05
❑ 251 Scott Sullivan .10 .05
❑ 252 Reggie Williams .10 .05
❑ 253 Mark Grudzielanek .10 .05
❑ 254 Steve Rodriguez .10 .05
❑ 255 Terry Bradshaw .10 .05
❑ 256 F.P. Santangelo .10 .05
❑ 257 Lyle Mouton .10 .05
❑ 258 George Williams .10 .05
❑ 259 Larry Thomas .10 .05
❑ 260 Rudy Pemberton .10 .05
❑ 261 Jim Pittsley .10 .05
❑ 262 Les Norman .10 .05
❑ 263 Ruben Rivera .10 .05
❑ 264 Cesar Devarez .10 .05
❑ 265 Greg Zaun .10 .05
❑ 266 Dustin Hermanson .10 .05
❑ 267 John Frascatore .10 .05
❑ 268 Joe Randa .10 .05
❑ 269 Jeff Bagwell CL .40 .18
❑ 270 Mike Piazza CL .60 .25
❑ 271 Dante Bichette CL .10 .05

❑ 272 Frank Thomas CL .40 .18
❑ 273 Ken Griffey Jr. CL .75 .35
❑ 274 Cal Ripken CL .75 .35
❑ 275 Greg Maddux CL .20 .09
Albert Belle
❑ 276 Greg Maddux 1.00 .45
❑ 277 Pedro Martinez .50 .23
❑ 278 Bobby Higginson .20 .09
❑ 279 Ray Lankford .20 .09
❑ 280 Shawon Dunston .10 .05
❑ 281 Gary Sheffield .40 .18
❑ 282 Ken Griffey Jr. 1.50 .70
❑ 283 Paul Molitor .40 .18
❑ 284 Kevin Appier .20 .09
❑ 285 Chuck Knoblauch .20 .09
❑ 286 Alex Fernandez .10 .05
❑ 287 Steve Finley .20 .09
❑ 288 Jeff Blauser .10 .05
❑ 289 Charles Johnson .20 .09
❑ 290 John Franco .20 .09
❑ 291 Mark Langston .10 .05
❑ 292 Bret Saberhagen .20 .09
❑ 293 John Mabry .10 .05
❑ 294 Ramon Martinez .10 .05
❑ 295 Mike Blowers .10 .05
❑ 296 Paul O'Neill .20 .09
❑ 297 Dave Nilsson .10 .05
❑ 298 Dante Bichette .20 .09
❑ 299 Marty Cordova .10 .05
❑ 300 Jay Bell .20 .09
❑ 301 Mike Mussina .40 .18
❑ 302 Ivan Rodriguez .50 .23
❑ 303 Jose Canseco .50 .23
❑ 304 Jeff Bagwell .50 .23
❑ 305 Manny Ramirez .50 .23
❑ 306 Dennis Martinez .20 .09
❑ 307 Charlie Hayes .10 .05
❑ 308 Joe Carter .20 .09
❑ 309 Travis Fryman .20 .09
❑ 310 Mark McGwire 1.50 .70
❑ 311 Reggie Sanders UER .10 .05
(Photo on front is John Roper)
❑ 312 Julian Tavarez .10 .05
❑ 313 Jeff Montgomery .10 .05
❑ 314 Andy Benes .10 .05
❑ 315 John Jaha .10 .05
❑ 316 Jeff Kent .25 .11
❑ 317 Mike Piazza 1.25 .55
❑ 318 Erik Hanson .10 .05
❑ 319 Kenny Rogers .10 .05
❑ 320 Hideo Nomo .40 .18
❑ 321 Gregg Jefferies .10 .05
❑ 322 Chipper Jones 1.00 .45
❑ 323 Jay Buhner .20 .09
❑ 324 Dennis Eckersley .20 .09
❑ 325 Kenny Lofton .20 .09
❑ 326 Robin Ventura .20 .09
❑ 327 Tom Glavine .40 .18
❑ 328 Tim Salmon .20 .09
❑ 329 Andres Galarraga .25 .11
❑ 330 Hal Morris .10 .05
❑ 331 Brady Anderson .20 .09
❑ 332 Chili Davis .20 .09
❑ 333 Roger Clemens .75 .35
❑ 334 Marquis Grissom .10 .05
❑ 335 Mike Greenwell UER .10 .05
(Name spelled Jeff on front)
❑ 336 Sammy Sosa .75 .35
❑ 337 Ron Gant .10 .05
❑ 338 Ken Caminiti .20 .09
❑ 339 Danny Tartabull .10 .05
❑ 340 Barry Bonds .60 .25
❑ 341 Ben McDonald .10 .05
❑ 342 Ruben Sierra .10 .05
❑ 343 Bernie Williams .40 .18
❑ 344 Wil Cordero .10 .05
❑ 345 Wade Boggs .50 .23
❑ 346 Gary Gaetti .20 .09
❑ 347 Greg Colbrunn .10 .05
❑ 348 Juan Gonzalez .40 .18
❑ 349 Marc Newfield .10 .05
❑ 350 Charles Nagy .10 .05
❑ 351 Robby Thompson .10 .05
❑ 352 Roberto Petagine .10 .05
❑ 353 Darryl Strawberry .20 .09
❑ 354 Tino Martinez .20 .09
❑ 355 Eric Karros .20 .09
❑ 356 Cal Ripken SS .75 .35
❑ 357 Cecil Fielder SS .10 .05
❑ 358 Kirby Puckett SS .50 .23
❑ 359 Jim Edmonds SS .20 .09
❑ 360 Matt Williams SS .20 .09
❑ 361 Alex Rodriguez SS .60 .25
❑ 362 Barry Larkin SS .10 .05
❑ 363 Rafael Palmeiro SS .10 .05
❑ 364 David Cone SS .10 .05
❑ 365 Roberto Alomar SS .20 .09
❑ 366 Eddie Murray SS .20 .09
❑ 367 Randy Johnson SS .20 .09
❑ 368 Ryan Klesko SS .10 .05
❑ 369 Raul Mondesi SS .10 .05
❑ 370 Mo Vaughn SS .20 .09
❑ 371 Will Clark SS .20 .09
❑ 372 Carlos Baerga SS .10 .05
❑ 373 Frank Thomas SS .40 .18
❑ 374 Larry Walker SS .20 .09
❑ 375 Garret Anderson SS .10 .05
❑ 376 Edgar Martinez SS .20 .09
❑ 377 Don Mattingly SS .50 .18
❑ 378 Tony Gwynn SS .40 .18
❑ 379 Albert Belle SS .10 .05
❑ 380 Jason Isringhausen SS .10 .05
❑ 381 Ruben Rivera SS .10 .05
❑ 382 Johnny Damon SS .10 .05
❑ 383 Karim Garcia SS .10 .05
❑ 384 Derek Jeter SS .75 .35
❑ 385 David Justice SS .10 .05
❑ 386 Royce Clayton .10 .05
❑ 387 Mark Whiten .10 .05
❑ 388 Mickey Tettleton .10 .05
❑ 389 Steve Trachsel .10 .05
❑ 390 Danny Bautista .10 .05
❑ 391 Midre Cummings .10 .05
❑ 392 Scott Leius .10 .05
❑ 393 Manny Alexander .10 .05
❑ 394 Brent Gates .10 .05
❑ 395 Rey Sanchez .10 .05
❑ 396 Andy Pettitte .20 .09
❑ 397 Jeff Cirillo .20 .09
❑ 398 Kurt Abbott .10 .05
❑ 399 Lee Tinsley .10 .05
❑ 400 Paul Assenmacher .10 .05
❑ 401 Scott Erickson .10 .05
❑ 402 Todd Zeile .10 .05
❑ 403 Tom Pagnozzi .10 .05
❑ 404 Ozzie Guillen .10 .05
❑ 405 Jeff Frye .10 .05
❑ 406 Kirt Manwaring .10 .05
❑ 407 Chad Ogea .10 .05
❑ 408 Harold Baines .20 .09
❑ 409 Jason Bere .10 .05
❑ 410 Chuck Finley .20 .09
❑ 411 Jeff Fassero .10 .05
❑ 412 Joey Hamilton .10 .05
❑ 413 John Olerud .20 .09
❑ 414 Kevin Stocker .10 .05
❑ 415 Eric Anthony .10 .05
❑ 416 Aaron Sele .20 .09
❑ 417 Chris Bosio .10 .05
❑ 418 Michael Mimbs .10 .05
❑ 419 Orlando Miller .10 .05
❑ 420 Stan Javier .10 .05
❑ 421 Matt Mieske .10 .05
❑ 422 Jason Bates .10 .05
❑ 423 Orlando Merced .10 .05
❑ 424 John Flaherty .10 .05
❑ 425 Reggie Jefferson .10 .05
❑ 426 Scott Stahoviak .10 .05
❑ 427 John Burkett .10 .05
❑ 428 Rod Beck .10 .05
❑ 429 Bill Swift .10 .05
❑ 430 Scott Cooper .10 .05
❑ 431 Mel Rojas .10 .05
❑ 432 Todd Van Poppel .10 .05
❑ 433 Bobby Jones .10 .05
❑ 434 Mike Harkey .10 .05
❑ 435 Sean Berry .10 .05
❑ 436 Glenallen Hill .10 .05
❑ 437 Ryan Thompson .10 .05
❑ 438 Luis Alicea .10 .05
❑ 439 Esteban Loaiza .10 .05
❑ 440 Jeff Reboulet .10 .05
❑ 441 Vince Coleman .10 .05
❑ 442 Ellis Burks .20 .09
❑ 443 Allen Battle .10 .05
❑ 444 Jimmy Key .20 .09
❑ 445 Ricky Bottalico .10 .05
❑ 446 Delino DeShields .10 .05
❑ 447 Albie Lopez .10 .05
❑ 448 Mark Petkovsek .10 .05
❑ 449 Tim Raines .20 .09
❑ 450 Bryan Harvey .10 .05
❑ 451 Pat Hentgen .10 .05
❑ 452 Tim Laker .10 .05
❑ 453 Tom Gordon .10 .05
❑ 454 Phil Plantier .10 .05
❑ 455 Ernie Young .10 .05
❑ 456 Pete Harnisch .10 .05
❑ 457 Roberto Kelly .10 .05
❑ 458 Mark Portugal .10 .05
❑ 459 Mark Leiter .10 .05
❑ 460 Tony Pena .10 .05
❑ 461 Roger Pavlik .10 .05
❑ 462 Jeff King .10 .05
❑ 463 Bryan Rekar .10 .05
❑ 464 Al Leiter .20 .09
❑ 465 Phil Nevin .20 .09
❑ 466 Jose Lima .10 .05
❑ 467 Mike Stanley .10 .05
❑ 468 David McCarty .10 .05
❑ 469 Herb Perry .10 .05
❑ 470 Geronimo Berroa .10 .05
❑ 471 David Wells .20 .09
❑ 472 Vaughn Eshelman .10 .05
❑ 473 Greg Swindell .10 .05
❑ 474 Steve Sparks .10 .05
❑ 475 Luis Sojo .10 .05
❑ 476 Derrick May .10 .05
❑ 477 Joe Oliver .10 .05
❑ 478 Alex Arias .10 .05
❑ 479 Brad Ausmus .10 .05
❑ 480 Gabe White .10 .05
❑ 481 Pat Rapp .10 .05
❑ 482 Damon Buford .10 .05
❑ 483 Turk Wendell .10 .05
❑ 484 Jeff Brantley .10 .05
❑ 485 Curtis Leskanic .10 .05
❑ 486 Robb Nen .10 .05
❑ 487 Lou Whitaker .20 .09
❑ 488 Melido Perez .10 .05
❑ 489 Luis Polonia .10 .05
❑ 490 Scott Brosius .20 .09
❑ 491 Robert Perez .10 .05
❑ 492 Mike Sweeney RC 1.50 .70
❑ 493 Mark Loretta .10 .05
❑ 494 Alex Ochoa .10 .05
❑ 495 Matt Lawton RC .50 .23
❑ 496 Shawn Estes .20 .09
❑ 497 John Wasdin .10 .05
❑ 498 Marc Kroon .10 .05
❑ 499 Chris Snopek .10 .05
❑ 500 Jeff Suppan .10 .05
❑ 501 Terrell Wade .10 .05
❑ 502 Marvin Benard RC .10 .05
❑ 503 Chris Widger .10 .05
❑ 504 Quinton McCracken .10 .05
❑ 505 Bob Wolcott .10 .05
❑ 506 C.J. Nitkowski .10 .05
❑ 507 Aaron Ledesma .10 .05
❑ 508 Scott Hatteberg .10 .05
❑ 509 Jimmy Haynes .10 .05
❑ 510 Howard Battle .10 .05
❑ 511 Marty Cordova CL .10 .05
❑ 512 Randy Johnson CL .20 .09
❑ 513 Mo Vaughn CL .20 .09
❑ 514 Chan Ho Park CL .10 .05
❑ 515 Greg Maddux CL .50 .23
❑ 516 Barry Larkin CL .20 .09
❑ 517 Tom Glavine CL .20 .09
❑ NNO Cal Ripken 2131 20.00 9.00

## 1997 Score

| | MINT | NRMT |
|---|---|---|
| COMPLETE SET (551) | 40.00 | 18.00 |
| COMP.FACT.SET (551) | 40.00 | 18.00 |
| COMPLETE SERIES 1 (330) | 15.00 | 6.75 |
| COMPLETE SERIES 2 (221) | 25.00 | 11.00 |

COMMON CARD (1-551) .10 .05

| |  |  | | |
|---|---|---|---|---|
| ❑ | 1 | Jeff Bagwell | .50 | .23 |
| ❑ | 2 | Mickey Tettleton | .10 | .05 |
| ❑ | 3 | Johnny Damon | .15 | .07 |
| ❑ | 4 | Jeff Conine | .10 | .05 |
| ❑ | 5 | Bernie Williams | .40 | .18 |
| ❑ | 6 | Will Clark | .40 | .18 |
| ❑ | 7 | Ryan Klesko | .15 | .07 |
| ❑ | 8 | Cecil Fielder | .15 | .07 |
| ❑ | 9 | Paul Wilson | .10 | .05 |
| ❑ | 10 | Gregg Jefferies | .10 | .05 |
| ❑ | 11 | Chili Davis | .15 | .07 |
| ❑ | 12 | Albert Belle | .25 | .11 |
| ❑ | 13 | Ken Hill | .10 | .05 |
| ❑ | 14 | Cliff Floyd | .15 | .07 |
| ❑ | 15 | Jaime Navarro | .10 | .05 |
| ❑ | 16 | Ismael Valdes | .10 | .05 |
| ❑ | 17 | Jeff King | .10 | .05 |
| ❑ | 18 | Chris Bosio | .10 | .05 |
| ❑ | 19 | Reggie Sanders | .10 | .05 |
| ❑ | 20 | Darren Daulton | .15 | .07 |
| ❑ | 21 | Ken Caminiti | .15 | .07 |
| ❑ | 22 | Mike Piazza | 1.25 | .55 |
| ❑ | 23 | Chad Mottola | .10 | .05 |
| ❑ | 24 | Darin Erstad | .50 | .23 |
| ❑ | 25 | Dante Bichette | .15 | .07 |
| ❑ | 26 | Frank Thomas | .75 | .35 |
| ❑ | 27 | Ben McDonald | .10 | .05 |
| ❑ | 28 | Raul Casanova | .10 | .05 |
| ❑ | 29 | Kevin Ritz | .10 | .05 |
| ❑ | 30 | Garret Anderson | .15 | .07 |
| ❑ | 31 | Jason Kendall | .15 | .07 |
| ❑ | 32 | Billy Wagner | .10 | .05 |
| ❑ | 33 | Dave Justice | .25 | .11 |
| ❑ | 34 | Marty Cordova | .10 | .05 |
| ❑ | 35 | Derek Jeter | 1.50 | .70 |
| ❑ | 36 | Trevor Hoffman | .15 | .07 |
| ❑ | 37 | Geronimo Berroa | .10 | .05 |
| ❑ | 38 | Walt Weiss | .10 | .05 |
| ❑ | 39 | Kirt Manwaring | .10 | .05 |
| ❑ | 40 | Alex Gonzalez | .10 | .05 |
| ❑ | 41 | Sean Berry | .10 | .05 |
| ❑ | 42 | Kevin Appier | .15 | .07 |
| ❑ | 43 | Rusty Greer | .15 | .07 |
| ❑ | 44 | Pete Incaviglia | .10 | .05 |
| ❑ | 45 | Rafael Palmeiro | .40 | .18 |
| ❑ | 46 | Eddie Murray | .40 | .18 |
| ❑ | 47 | Moises Alou | .15 | .07 |
| ❑ | 48 | Mark Lewis | .10 | .05 |
| ❑ | 49 | Hal Morris | .10 | .05 |
| ❑ | 50 | Edgar Renteria | .15 | .07 |
| ❑ | 51 | Rickey Henderson | .50 | .23 |
| ❑ | 52 | Pat Listach | .10 | .05 |
| ❑ | 53 | John Wasdin | .10 | .05 |
| ❑ | 54 | James Baldwin | .15 | .07 |
| ❑ | 55 | Brian Jordan | .15 | .07 |
| ❑ | 56 | Edgar Martinez | .25 | .11 |
| ❑ | 57 | Wil Cordero | .10 | .05 |
| ❑ | 58 | Danny Tartabull | .10 | .05 |
| ❑ | 59 | Keith Lockhart | .10 | .05 |
| ❑ | 60 | Rico Brogna | .10 | .05 |
| ❑ | 61 | Ricky Bottalico | .10 | .05 |
| ❑ | 62 | Terry Pendleton | .15 | .07 |
| ❑ | 63 | Bret Boone | .15 | .07 |
| ❑ | 64 | Charlie Hayes | .10 | .05 |
| ❑ | 65 | Marc Newfield | .10 | .05 |
| ❑ | 66 | Sterling Hitchcock | .10 | .05 |
| ❑ | 67 | Roberto Alomar | .40 | .18 |
| ❑ | 68 | John Jaha | .10 | .05 |
| ❑ | 69 | Greg Colbrunn | .10 | .05 |
| ❑ | 70 | Sal Fasano | .10 | .05 |
| ❑ | 71 | Brooks Kieschnick | .10 | .05 |
| ❑ | 72 | Pedro Martinez | .50 | .23 |
| ❑ | 73 | Kevin Elster | .10 | .05 |
| ❑ | 74 | Ellis Burks | .15 | .07 |
| ❑ | 75 | Chuck Finley | .15 | .07 |
| ❑ | 76 | John Olerud | .15 | .07 |
| ❑ | 77 | Jay Bell | .15 | .07 |
| ❑ | 78 | Allen Watson | .10 | .05 |
| ❑ | 79 | Darryl Strawberry | .15 | .07 |
| ❑ | 80 | Orlando Miller | .10 | .05 |
| ❑ | 81 | Jose Herrera | .10 | .05 |
| ❑ | 82 | Andy Pettitte | .15 | .07 |
| ❑ | 83 | Juan Guzman | .10 | .05 |
| ❑ | 84 | Alan Benes | .10 | .05 |
| ❑ | 85 | Jack McDowell | .10 | .05 |
| ❑ | 86 | Ugueth Urbina | .10 | .05 |
| ❑ | 87 | Rocky Coppinger | .10 | .05 |
| ❑ | 88 | Jeff Cirillo | .15 | .07 |
| ❑ | 89 | Tom Glavine | .40 | .18 |
| ❑ | 90 | Robby Thompson | .10 | .05 |
| ❑ | 91 | Barry Bonds | .60 | .25 |
| ❑ | 92 | Carlos Delgado | .40 | .18 |
| ❑ | 93 | Mo Vaughn | .15 | .07 |
| ❑ | 94 | Ryne Sandberg | .50 | .23 |
| ❑ | 95 | Alex Rodriguez | 1.25 | .55 |
| ❑ | 96 | Brady Anderson | .15 | .07 |
| ❑ | 97 | Scott Brosius | .15 | .07 |
| ❑ | 98 | Dennis Eckersley | .15 | .07 |
| ❑ | 99 | Brian McRae | .10 | .05 |
| ❑ | 100 | Rey Ordonez | .10 | .05 |
| ❑ | 101 | John Valentin | .10 | .05 |
| ❑ | 102 | Brett Butler | .15 | .07 |
| ❑ | 103 | Eric Karros | .15 | .07 |
| ❑ | 104 | Harold Baines | .15 | .07 |
| ❑ | 105 | Javier Lopez | .15 | .07 |
| ❑ | 106 | Alan Trammell | .25 | .11 |
| ❑ | 107 | Jim Thome | .25 | .11 |
| ❑ | 108 | Frank Rodriguez | .10 | .05 |
| ❑ | 109 | Bernard Gilkey | .10 | .05 |
| ❑ | 110 | Reggie Jefferson | .10 | .05 |
| ❑ | 111 | Scott Stahoviak | .10 | .05 |
| ❑ | 112 | Steve Gibralter | .10 | .05 |
| ❑ | 113 | Todd Hollandsworth | .10 | .05 |
| ❑ | 114 | Ruben Rivera | .10 | .05 |
| ❑ | 115 | Dennis Martinez | .15 | .07 |
| ❑ | 116 | Mariano Rivera | .15 | .07 |
| ❑ | 117 | John Smoltz | .15 | .07 |
| ❑ | 118 | John Mabry | .10 | .05 |
| ❑ | 119 | Tom Gordon | .10 | .05 |
| ❑ | 120 | Alex Ochoa | .10 | .05 |
| ❑ | 121 | Jamey Wright | .10 | .05 |
| ❑ | 122 | Dave Nilsson | .10 | .05 |
| ❑ | 123 | Bobby Bonilla | .15 | .07 |
| ❑ | 124 | Al Leiter | .15 | .07 |
| ❑ | 125 | Rick Aguilera | .10 | .05 |
| ❑ | 126 | Jeff Brantley | .10 | .05 |
| ❑ | 127 | Kevin Brown | .15 | .07 |
| ❑ | 128 | George Arias | .10 | .05 |
| ❑ | 129 | Darren Oliver | .10 | .05 |
| ❑ | 130 | Bill Pulsipher | .10 | .05 |
| ❑ | 131 | Roberto Hernandez | .10 | .05 |
| ❑ | 132 | Delino DeShields | .10 | .05 |
| ❑ | 133 | Mark Grudzielanek | .10 | .05 |
| ❑ | 134 | John Wetteland | .15 | .07 |
| ❑ | 135 | Carlos Baerga | .10 | .05 |
| ❑ | 136 | Paul Sorrento | .10 | .05 |
| ❑ | 137 | Leo Gomez | .10 | .05 |
| ❑ | 138 | Andy Ashby | .10 | .05 |
| ❑ | 139 | Julio Franco | .15 | .07 |
| ❑ | 140 | Brian Hunter | .10 | .05 |
| ❑ | 141 | Jermaine Dye | .15 | .07 |
| ❑ | 142 | Tony Clark | .10 | .05 |
| ❑ | 143 | Ruben Sierra | .10 | .05 |
| ❑ | 144 | Donovan Osborne | .10 | .05 |
| ❑ | 145 | Mark McLemore | .10 | .05 |
| ❑ | 146 | Terry Steinbach | .10 | .05 |
| ❑ | 147 | Bob Wells | .10 | .05 |
| ❑ | 148 | Chan Ho Park | .15 | .07 |
| ❑ | 149 | Tim Salmon | .15 | .07 |
| ❑ | 150 | Paul O'Neill | .15 | .07 |
| ❑ | 151 | Cal Ripken | 1.50 | .70 |
| ❑ | 152 | Wally Joyner | .15 | .07 |
| ❑ | 153 | Omar Vizquel | .15 | .07 |
| ❑ | 154 | Mike Mussina | .40 | .18 |
| ❑ | 155 | Andres Galarraga | .25 | .11 |
| ❑ | 156 | Ken Griffey Jr. | 1.50 | .70 |
| ❑ | 157 | Kenny Lofton | .15 | .07 |
| ❑ | 158 | Ray Durham | .15 | .07 |
| ❑ | 159 | Hideo Nomo | .40 | .18 |
| ❑ | 160 | Ozzie Guillen | .10 | .05 |
| ❑ | 161 | Roger Pavlik | .10 | .05 |
| ❑ | 162 | Manny Ramirez | .50 | .23 |
| ❑ | 163 | Mark Lemke | .10 | .05 |
| ❑ | 164 | Mike Stanley | .10 | .05 |
| ❑ | 165 | Chuck Knoblauch | .15 | .07 |
| ❑ | 166 | Kimera Bartee | .10 | .05 |
| ❑ | 167 | Wade Boggs | .50 | .23 |
| ❑ | 168 | Jay Buhner | .15 | .07 |
| ❑ | 169 | Eric Young | .10 | .05 |
| ❑ | 170 | Jose Canseco | .50 | .23 |
| ❑ | 171 | Dwight Gooden | .15 | .07 |
| ❑ | 172 | Fred McGriff | .25 | .11 |
| ❑ | 173 | Sandy Alomar Jr. | .15 | .07 |
| ❑ | 174 | Andy Benes | .10 | .05 |
| ❑ | 175 | Dean Palmer | .15 | .07 |
| ❑ | 176 | Larry Walker | .15 | .07 |
| ❑ | 177 | Charles Nagy | .10 | .05 |
| ❑ | 178 | David Cone | .15 | .07 |
| ❑ | 179 | Mark Grace | .40 | .18 |
| ❑ | 180 | Robin Ventura | .15 | .07 |
| ❑ | 181 | Roger Clemens | .75 | .35 |
| ❑ | 182 | Bobby Witt | .10 | .05 |
| ❑ | 183 | Vinny Castilla | .15 | .07 |
| ❑ | 184 | Gary Sheffield | .40 | .18 |
| ❑ | 185 | Dan Wilson | .10 | .05 |
| ❑ | 186 | Roger Cedeno | .10 | .05 |
| ❑ | 187 | Mark McGwire | 1.50 | .70 |
| ❑ | 188 | Darren Bragg | .10 | .05 |
| ❑ | 189 | Quinton McCracken | .10 | .05 |
| ❑ | 190 | Randy Myers | .10 | .05 |
| ❑ | 191 | Jeromy Burnitz | .15 | .07 |
| ❑ | 192 | Randy Johnson | .50 | .23 |
| ❑ | 193 | Chipper Jones | 1.00 | .45 |
| ❑ | 194 | Greg Vaughn | .15 | .07 |
| ❑ | 195 | Travis Fryman | .15 | .07 |
| ❑ | 196 | Tim Naehring | .10 | .05 |
| ❑ | 197 | B.J. Surhoff | .15 | .07 |
| ❑ | 198 | Juan Gonzalez | .40 | .18 |
| ❑ | 199 | Terrell Wade | .10 | .05 |
| ❑ | 200 | Jeff Frye | .10 | .05 |
| ❑ | 201 | Joey Cora | .10 | .05 |
| ❑ | 202 | Raul Mondesi | .15 | .07 |
| ❑ | 203 | Ivan Rodriguez | .50 | .23 |
| ❑ | 204 | Armando Reynoso | .10 | .05 |
| ❑ | 205 | Jeffrey Hammonds | .15 | .07 |
| ❑ | 206 | Darren Dreifort | .15 | .07 |
| ❑ | 207 | Kevin Seitzer | .10 | .05 |
| ❑ | 208 | Tino Martinez | .15 | .07 |
| ❑ | 209 | Jim Bruske | .10 | .05 |
| ❑ | 210 | Jeff Suppan | .10 | .05 |
| ❑ | 211 | Mark Carreon | .10 | .05 |
| ❑ | 212 | Wilson Alvarez | .10 | .05 |
| ❑ | 213 | John Burkett | .10 | .05 |
| ❑ | 214 | Tony Phillips | .10 | .05 |
| ❑ | 215 | Greg Maddux | 1.00 | .45 |
| ❑ | 216 | Mark Whiten | .10 | .05 |
| ❑ | 217 | Curtis Pride | .10 | .05 |
| ❑ | 218 | Lyle Mouton | .10 | .05 |
| ❑ | 219 | Todd Hundley | .10 | .05 |
| ❑ | 220 | Greg Gagne | .10 | .05 |
| ❑ | 221 | Rich Amaral | .10 | .05 |
| ❑ | 222 | Tom Goodwin | .10 | .05 |
| ❑ | 223 | Chris Hoiles | .10 | .05 |
| ❑ | 224 | Jayhawk Owens | .10 | .05 |
| ❑ | 225 | Kenny Rogers | .10 | .05 |
| ❑ | 226 | Mike Greenwell | .10 | .05 |
| ❑ | 227 | Mark Wohlers | .10 | .05 |
| ❑ | 228 | Henry Rodriguez | .10 | .05 |
| ❑ | 229 | Robert Perez | .10 | .05 |
| ❑ | 230 | Jeff Kent | .25 | .11 |
| ❑ | 231 | Darryl Hamilton | .10 | .05 |
| ❑ | 232 | Alex Fernandez | .10 | .05 |
| ❑ | 233 | Ron Karkovice | .10 | .05 |
| ❑ | 234 | Jimmy Haynes | .10 | .05 |
| ❑ | 235 | Craig Biggio | .25 | .11 |
| ❑ | 236 | Ray Lankford | .15 | .07 |
| ❑ | 237 | Lance Johnson | .10 | .05 |
| ❑ | 238 | Matt Williams | .25 | .11 |

❑ 239 Chad Curtis .10 .05
❑ 240 Mark Thompson .10 .05
❑ 241 Jason Giambi .40 .18
❑ 242 Barry Larkin .40 .18
❑ 243 Paul Molitor .40 .18
❑ 244 Sammy Sosa .75 .35
❑ 245 Kevin Tapani .10 .05
❑ 246 Marquis Grissom .10 .05
❑ 247 Joe Carter .15 .07
❑ 248 Ramon Martinez .10 .05
❑ 249 Tony Gwynn .75 .35
❑ 250 Andy Fox .10 .05
❑ 251 Troy O'Leary .10 .05
❑ 252 Warren Newson .10 .05
❑ 253 Troy Percival .10 .05
❑ 254 Jamie Moyer .10 .05
❑ 255 Danny Graves .10 .05
❑ 256 David Wells .15 .07
❑ 257 Todd Zeile .10 .05
❑ 258 Raul Ibanez .10 .05
❑ 259 Tyler Houston .10 .05
❑ 260 LaTroy Hawkins .10 .05
❑ 261 Joey Hamilton .10 .05
❑ 262 Mike Sweeney .15 .07
❑ 263 Brant Brown .10 .05
❑ 264 Pat Hentgen .10 .05
❑ 265 Mark Johnson .10 .05
❑ 266 Robb Nen .10 .05
❑ 267 Justin Thompson .10 .05
❑ 268 Ron Gant .10 .05
❑ 269 Jeff D'Amico .10 .05
❑ 270 Shawn Estes .15 .07
❑ 271 Derek Bell .10 .05
❑ 272 Fernando Valenzuela .15 .07
❑ 273 Tom Pagnozzi .10 .05
❑ 274 John Burke .10 .05
❑ 275 Ed Sprague .10 .05
❑ 276 F.P. Santangelo .10 .05
❑ 277 Todd Greene .10 .05
❑ 278 Butch Huskey .10 .05
❑ 279 Steve Finley .15 .07
❑ 280 Eric Davis .15 .07
❑ 281 Shawn Green .40 .18
❑ 282 Al Martin .10 .05
❑ 283 Michael Tucker .10 .05
❑ 284 Shane Reynolds .10 .05
❑ 285 Matt Mieske .10 .05
❑ 286 Jose Rosado .10 .05
❑ 287 Mark Langston .10 .05
❑ 288 Ralph Milliard .10 .05
❑ 289 Mike Lansing .10 .05
❑ 290 Scott Servais .10 .05
❑ 291 Royce Clayton .10 .05
❑ 292 Mike Grace .10 .05
❑ 293 James Mouton .10 .05
❑ 294 Charles Johnson .15 .07
❑ 295 Gary Gaetti .15 .07
❑ 296 Kevin Mitchell .10 .05
❑ 297 Carlos Garcia .10 .05
❑ 298 Desi Relaford .10 .05
❑ 299 Jason Thompson .10 .05
❑ 300 Osvaldo Fernandez .10 .05
❑ 301 Fernando Vina .10 .05
❑ 302 Jose Offerman .10 .05
❑ 303 Yamil Benitez .10 .05
❑ 304 J.T. Snow .15 .07
❑ 305 Rafael Bournigal .10 .05
❑ 306 Jason Isringhausen .10 .05
❑ 307 Bobby Higginson .15 .07
❑ 308 Nerio Rodriguez RC .10 .05
❑ 309 Brian Giles RC 1.50 .70
❑ 310 Andruw Jones .50 .23
❑ 311 Tony Graffanino .10 .05
❑ 312 Arquimedez Pozo .10 .05
❑ 313 Jermaine Allensworth .10 .05
❑ 314 Jeff Darwin .10 .05
❑ 315 George Williams .10 .05
❑ 316 Karim Garcia .10 .05
❑ 317 Trey Beamon .10 .05
❑ 318 Mac Suzuki .10 .05
❑ 319 Robin Jennings .10 .05
❑ 320 Danny Patterson .10 .05
❑ 321 Damon Mashore .10 .05
❑ 322 Wendell Magee .10 .05
❑ 323 Dax Jones .10 .05
❑ 324 Kevin Brown .15 .07
❑ 325 Marvin Benard .10 .05
❑ 326 Mike Cameron .15 .07
❑ 327 Marcus Jensen .10 .05
❑ 328 Eddie Murray CL .15 .07
❑ 329 Paul Molitor CL .15 .07
❑ 330 Todd Hundley CL .10 .05
❑ 331 Norm Charlton .10 .05
❑ 332 Bruce Ruffin .10 .05
❑ 333 John Wetteland .15 .07
❑ 334 Marquis Grissom .10 .05
❑ 335 Sterling Hitchcock .10 .05
❑ 336 John Olerud .15 .07
❑ 337 David Wells .15 .07
❑ 338 Chili Davis .15 .07
❑ 339 Mark Lewis .10 .05
❑ 340 Kenny Lofton .15 .07
❑ 341 Alex Fernandez .10 .05
❑ 342 Ruben Sierra .10 .05
❑ 343 Delino DeShields .10 .05
❑ 344 John Wasdin .10 .05
❑ 345 Dennis Martinez .15 .07
❑ 346 Kevin Elster .10 .05
❑ 347 Bobby Bonilla .15 .07
❑ 348 Jaime Navarro .10 .05
❑ 349 Chad Curtis .10 .05
❑ 350 Terry Steinbach .10 .05
❑ 351 Ariel Prieto .10 .05
❑ 352 Jeff Kent .25 .11
❑ 353 Carlos Garcia .10 .05
❑ 354 Mark Whiten .10 .05
❑ 355 Todd Zeile .10 .05
❑ 356 Eric Davis .15 .07
❑ 357 Greg Colbrunn .10 .05
❑ 358 Moises Alou .15 .07
❑ 359 Allen Watson .10 .05
❑ 360 Jose Canseco .50 .23
❑ 361 Matt Williams .25 .11
❑ 362 Jeff King .10 .05
❑ 363 Darryl Hamilton .10 .05
❑ 364 Mark Clark .10 .05
❑ 365 J.T. Snow .15 .07
❑ 366 Kevin Mitchell .10 .05
❑ 367 Orlando Miller .10 .05
❑ 368 Rico Brogna .10 .05
❑ 369 Mike James .10 .05
❑ 370 Brad Ausmus .10 .05
❑ 371 Darryl Kile .15 .07
❑ 372 Edgardo Alfonzo .15 .07
❑ 373 Julian Tavarez .10 .05
❑ 374 Darren Lewis .10 .05
❑ 375 Steve Karsay .10 .05
❑ 376 Lee Stevens .10 .05
❑ 377 Albie Lopez .10 .05
❑ 378 Orel Hershiser .15 .07
❑ 379 Lee Smith .15 .07
❑ 380 Rick Helling .15 .07
❑ 381 Carlos Perez .10 .05
❑ 382 Tony Tarasco .10 .05
❑ 383 Melvin Nieves .10 .05
❑ 384 Benji Gil .10 .05
❑ 385 Devon White .15 .07
❑ 386 Armando Benitez .10 .05
❑ 387 Bill Swift .10 .05
❑ 388 John Smiley .10 .05
❑ 389 Midre Cummings .10 .05
❑ 390 Tim Belcher .10 .05
❑ 391 Tim Raines .15 .07
❑ 392 Todd Worrell .10 .05
❑ 393 Quilvio Veras .10 .05
❑ 394 Matt Lawton .15 .07
❑ 395 Aaron Sele .15 .07
❑ 396 Bip Roberts .10 .05
❑ 397 Denny Neagle .15 .07
❑ 398 Tyler Green .10 .05
❑ 399 Hipolito Pichardo .10 .05
❑ 400 Scott Erickson .10 .05
❑ 401 Bobby Jones .10 .05
❑ 402 Jim Edmonds .40 .18
❑ 403 Chad Ogea .10 .05
❑ 404 Cal Eldred .10 .05
❑ 405 Pat Listach .10 .05
❑ 406 Todd Stottlemyre .10 .05
❑ 407 Phil Nevin .15 .07
❑ 408 Otis Nixon .10 .05
❑ 409 Billy Ashley .10 .05
❑ 410 Jimmy Key .15 .07
❑ 411 Mike Timlin .10 .05
❑ 412 Joe Vitiello .10 .05
❑ 413 Rondell White .15 .07
❑ 414 Jeff Fassero .10 .05
❑ 415 Rex Hudler .10 .05
❑ 416 Curt Schilling .15 .07
❑ 417 Rich Becker .10 .05
❑ 418 William Van Landingham .10 .05
❑ 419 Chris Snopek .10 .05
❑ 420 David Segui .10 .05
❑ 421 Eddie Murray .40 .18
❑ 422 Shane Andrews .10 .05
❑ 423 Gary DiSarcina .10 .05
❑ 424 Brian Hunter .10 .05
❑ 425 Willie Greene .10 .05
❑ 426 Felipe Crespo .10 .05
❑ 427 Jason Bates .10 .05
❑ 428 Albert Belle .25 .11
❑ 429 Rey Sanchez .10 .05
❑ 430 Roger Clemens .75 .35
❑ 431 Deion Sanders .15 .07
❑ 432 Ernie Young .10 .05
❑ 433 Jay Bell .15 .07
❑ 434 Jeff Blauser .10 .05
❑ 435 Lenny Dykstra .15 .07
❑ 436 Chuck Carr .10 .05
❑ 437 Russ Davis .10 .05
❑ 438 Carl Everett .15 .07
❑ 439 Damion Easley .10 .05
❑ 440 Pat Kelly .10 .05
❑ 441 Pat Rapp .10 .05
❑ 442 Dave Justice .25 .11
❑ 443 Graeme Lloyd .10 .05
❑ 444 Damon Buford .10 .05
❑ 445 Jose Valentin .10 .05
❑ 446 Jason Schmidt .10 .05
❑ 447 Dave Martinez .10 .05
❑ 448 Danny Tartabull .10 .05
❑ 449 Jose Vizcaino .10 .05
❑ 450 Steve Avery .10 .05
❑ 451 Mike Devereaux .10 .05
❑ 452 Jim Eisenreich .10 .05
❑ 453 Mark Leiter .10 .05
❑ 454 Roberto Kelly .10 .05
❑ 455 Benito Santiago .10 .05
❑ 456 Steve Trachsel .10 .05
❑ 457 Gerald Williams .10 .05
❑ 458 Pete Schourek .10 .05
❑ 459 Esteban Loaiza .10 .05
❑ 460 Mel Rojas .10 .05
❑ 461 Tim Wakefield .10 .05
❑ 462 Tony Fernandez .10 .05
❑ 463 Doug Drabek .10 .05
❑ 464 Joe Girardi .10 .05
❑ 465 Mike Bordick .10 .05
❑ 466 Jim Leyritz .10 .05
❑ 467 Erik Hanson .10 .05
❑ 468 Michael Tucker .10 .05
❑ 469 Tony Womack RC .50 .23
❑ 470 Doug Glanville .10 .05
❑ 471 Rudy Pemberton .10 .05
❑ 472 Keith Lockhart .10 .05
❑ 473 Nomar Garciaparra 1.25 .55
❑ 474 Scott Rolen .40 .18
❑ 475 Jason Dickson .10 .05
❑ 476 Glendon Rusch .10 .05
❑ 477 Todd Walker .10 .05
❑ 478 Dmitri Young .15 .07
❑ 479 Rod Myers .10 .05
❑ 480 Wilton Guerrero .10 .05
❑ 481 Jorge Posada .15 .07
❑ 482 Brant Brown .10 .05
❑ 483 Bubba Trammell RC .15 .07
❑ 484 Jose Guillen .10 .05
❑ 485 Scott Spiezio .10 .05
❑ 486 Bob Abreu .15 .07
❑ 487 Chris Holt .10 .05
❑ 488 Deivi Cruz RC .50 .23
❑ 489 Vladimir Guerrero .75 .35
❑ 490 Julio Santana .10 .05
❑ 491 Ray Montgomery RC .10 .05
❑ 492 Kevin Orie .10 .05
❑ 493 Todd Hundley GY .10 .05
❑ 494 Tim Salmon GY .10 .05
❑ 495 Albert Belle GY .15 .07
❑ 496 Manny Ramirez GY .25 .11

❑ 497 Rafael Palmeiro GY ...... .15 .07
❑ 498 Juan Gonzalez GY ....... .15 .07
❑ 499 Ken Griffey Jr. GY ........ .75 .35
❑ 500 Andruw Jones GY ......... .25 .11
❑ 501 Mike Piazza GY ............ .60 .25
❑ 502 Jeff Bagwell GY ............ .25 .11
❑ 503 Bernie Williams GY ....... .15 .07
❑ 504 Barry Bonds GY ........... .40 .18
❑ 505 Ken Caminiti GY ........... .10 .05
❑ 506 Darin Erstad GY ........... .25 .11
❑ 507 Alex Rodriguez GY ........ .60 .25
❑ 508 Frank Thomas GY .......... .40 .18
❑ 509 Chipper Jones GY .......... .50 .23
❑ 510 Mo Vaughn GY .............. .10 .05
❑ 511 Mark McGwire GY .......... .75 .35
❑ 512 Fred McGriff GY ........... .15 .07
❑ 513 Jay Buhner GY ............. .10 .05
❑ 514 Gary Sheffield GY ......... .15 .07
❑ 515 Jim Thome GY .............. .15 .07
❑ 516 Dean Palmer GY ............ .10 .05
❑ 517 Henry Rodriguez GY ...... .10 .05
❑ 518 Andy Pettitte RF ........... .10 .05
❑ 519 Mike Mussina RF ........... .15 .07
❑ 520 Greg Maddux RF ............ .50 .23
❑ 521 John Smoltz RF ............. .10 .05
❑ 522 Hideo Nomo RF .............. .15 .07
❑ 523 Troy Percival RF ........... .10 .05
❑ 524 John Wetteland RF ......... .10 .05
❑ 525 Roger Clemens RF .......... .40 .18
❑ 526 Charles Nagy RF ............ .10 .05
❑ 527 Mariano Rivera RF ......... .10 .05
❑ 528 Tom Glavine RF ............. .15 .07
❑ 529 Randy Johnson RF .......... .25 .11
❑ 530 Jason Isringhausen RF .. .10 .05
❑ 531 Alex Fernandez RF ......... .10 .05
❑ 532 Kevin Brown RF ............. .10 .05
❑ 533 Chuck Knoblauch TG .... .10 .05
❑ 534 Rusty Greer TG ............. .10 .05
❑ 535 Tony Gwynn TG ............. .40 .18
❑ 536 Ryan Klesko TG ............ .10 .05
❑ 537 Ryne Sandberg TG ......... .25 .11
❑ 538 Barry Larkin TG ............. .15 .07
❑ 539 Will Clark TG ................ .15 .07
❑ 540 Kenny Lofton TG ........... .10 .05
❑ 541 Paul Molitor TG ............. .15 .07
❑ 542 Roberto Alomar TG ........ .15 .07
❑ 543 Rey Ordonez TG ............ .10 .05
❑ 544 Jason Giambi TG ........... .15 .07
❑ 545 Derek Jeter TG .............. .75 .35
❑ 546 Cal Ripken TG ............... .75 .35
❑ 547 Ivan Rodriguez TG ......... .25 .11
❑ 548 Ken Griffey Jr. CL .......... .75 .35
❑ 549 Frank Thomas CL ........... .40 .18
❑ 550 Mike Piazza CL .............. .60 .25
❑ 551A Hideki Irabu SP ........... 5.00 2.20
❑ 551B Hideki Irabu ................ 5.00 2.20
Japanese SP

## 1998 Score

| | MINT | NRMT |
|---|---|---|
| COMPLETE SET (270) | 50.00 | 22.00 |
| COMMON CARD (1-270) | .10 | .05 |

❑ 1 Andruw Jones .................. .40 .18
❑ 2 Dan Wilson ...................... .10 .05
❑ 3 Hideo Nomo ..................... .40 .18
❑ 4 Chuck Carr ...................... .10 .05
❑ 5 Barry Bonds ..................... .60 .25
❑ 6 Jack McDowell ................. .10 .05
❑ 7 Albert Belle ...................... .25 .11
❑ 8 Francisco Cordova ........... .10 .05
❑ 9 Greg Maddux ................... 1.00 .45
❑ 10 Alex Rodriguez .............. 1.25 .55
❑ 11 Steve Avery .................... .10 .05
❑ 12 Chuck McElroy ............... .10 .05
❑ 13 Larry Walker ................... .15 .07
❑ 14 Hideki Irabu ................... .10 .05
❑ 15 Roberto Alomar ............... .40 .18
❑ 16 Neifi Perez ..................... .10 .05
❑ 17 Jim Thome ...................... .25 .11
❑ 18 Rickey Henderson ........... .50 .23
❑ 19 Andres Galarraga ............ .25 .11
❑ 20 Jeff Fassero .................... .10 .05
❑ 21 Kevin Young .................... .15 .07
❑ 22 Derek Jeter ..................... 1.50 .70
❑ 23 Andy Benes ..................... .10 .05
❑ 24 Mike Piazza ..................... 1.25 .55
❑ 25 Todd Stottlemyre ............. .10 .05
❑ 26 Michael Tucker ................ .10 .05
❑ 27 Denny Neagle .................. .10 .05
❑ 28 Javier Lopez .................... .15 .07
❑ 29 Aaron Sele ...................... .15 .07
❑ 30 Ryan Klesko .................... .15 .07
❑ 31 Dennis Eckersley ............. .15 .07
❑ 32 Quinton McCracken ......... .10 .05
❑ 33 Brian Anderson ................ .10 .05
❑ 34 Ken Griffey Jr. ................. 1.50 .70
❑ 35 Shawn Estes .................... .10 .05
❑ 36 Tim Wakefield .................. .10 .05
❑ 37 Jimmy Key ....................... .15 .07
❑ 38 Jeff Bagwell ..................... .50 .23
❑ 39 Edgardo Alfonzo .............. .15 .07
❑ 40 Mike Cameron .................. .15 .07
❑ 41 Mark McGwire .................. 1.50 .70
❑ 42 Tino Martinez ................... .15 .07
❑ 43 Cal Ripken ........................ 1.50 .70
❑ 44 Curtis Goodwin ................. .10 .05
❑ 45 Bobby Ayala ..................... .10 .05
❑ 46 Sandy Alomar Jr. .............. .15 .07
❑ 47 Bobby Jones ..................... .10 .05
❑ 48 Omar Vizquel .................... .15 .07
❑ 49 Roger Clemens .................. .75 .35
❑ 50 Tony Gwynn ...................... .75 .35
❑ 51 Chipper Jones ................... 1.00 .45
❑ 52 Ron Coomer ...................... .10 .05
❑ 53 Dmitri Young ..................... .15 .07
❑ 54 Brian Giles ........................ .15 .07
❑ 55 Steve Finley ...................... .15 .07
❑ 56 David Cone ........................ .15 .07
❑ 57 Andy Pettitte ..................... .15 .07
❑ 58 Wilton Guerrero ................. .10 .05
❑ 59 Deion Sanders ................... .15 .07
❑ 60 Carlos Delgado .................. .40 .18
❑ 61 Jason Giambi ..................... .40 .18
❑ 62 Ozzie Guillen ..................... .10 .05
❑ 63 Jay Bell .............................. .15 .07
❑ 64 Barry Larkin ....................... .40 .18
❑ 65 Sammy Sosa ...................... .75 .35
❑ 66 Bernie Williams .................. .40 .18
❑ 67 Terry Steinbach .................. .10 .05
❑ 68 Scott Rolen ........................ .40 .18
❑ 69 Melvin Nieves ..................... .10 .05
❑ 70 Craig Biggio ........................ .25 .11
❑ 71 Todd Greene ....................... .10 .05
❑ 72 Greg Gagne ........................ .10 .05
❑ 73 Shigetoshi Hasegawa ......... .15 .07
❑ 74 Mark McLemore .................. .10 .05
❑ 75 Darren Bragg ...................... .10 .05
❑ 76 Brett Butler ......................... .15 .07
❑ 77 Ron Gant ............................ .15 .07
❑ 78 Mike Difelice RC ................. .10 .05
❑ 79 Charles Nagy ...................... .10 .05
❑ 80 Scott Hatteberg ................... .10 .05
❑ 81 Brady Anderson .................. .15 .07
❑ 82 Jay Buhner .......................... .15 .07
❑ 83 Todd Hollandsworth ............ .10 .05
❑ 84 Geronimo Berroa ................. .10 .05
❑ 85 Jeff Suppan ......................... .10 .05
❑ 86 Pedro Martinez .................... .50 .23
❑ 87 Roger Cedeno ...................... .10 .05
❑ 88 Ivan Rodriguez .................... .50 .23
❑ 89 Jaime Navarro ...................... .10 .05
❑ 90 Chris Hoiles ......................... .10 .05
❑ 91 Nomar Garciaparra ............. 1.25 .55
❑ 92 Rafael Palmeiro .................. .40 .18
❑ 93 Darin Erstad ........................ .40 .18
❑ 94 Kenny Lofton ....................... .15 .07
❑ 95 Mike Timlin .......................... .10 .05
❑ 96 Chris Clemons ..................... .10 .05
❑ 97 Vinny Castilla ...................... .15 .07
❑ 98 Charlie Hayes ...................... .10 .05
❑ 99 Lyle Mouton ......................... .10 .05
❑ 100 Jason Dickson .................... .10 .05
❑ 101 Justin Thompson ................ .10 .05
❑ 102 Pat Kelly ............................. .10 .05
❑ 103 Chan Ho Park ..................... .15 .07
❑ 104 Ray Lankford ...................... .15 .07
❑ 105 Frank Thomas ..................... .75 .35
❑ 106 Jermaine Allensworth .... .10 .05
❑ 107 Doug Drabek ....................... .10 .05
❑ 108 Todd Hundley ...................... .10 .05
❑ 109 Carl Everett ......................... .15 .07
❑ 110 Edgar Martinez .................... .25 .11
❑ 111 Robin Ventura ...................... .15 .07
❑ 112 John Wetteland .................... .15 .07
❑ 113 Mariano Rivera ..................... .15 .07
❑ 114 Jose Rosado ........................ .10 .05
❑ 115 Ken Caminiti ......................... .15 .07
❑ 116 Paul O'Neill ........................... .15 .07
❑ 117 Tim Salmon ........................... .15 .07
❑ 118 Eduardo Perez ...................... .10 .05
❑ 119 Mike Jackson ........................ .10 .05
❑ 120 John Smoltz .......................... .15 .07
❑ 121 Brant Brown .......................... .10 .05
❑ 122 John Mabry ........................... .10 .05
❑ 123 Chuck Knoblauch .................. .15 .07
❑ 124 Reggie Sanders ..................... .10 .05
❑ 125 Ken Hill ................................. .10 .05
❑ 126 Mike Mussina ........................ .40 .18
❑ 127 Chad Curtis ........................... .10 .05
❑ 128 Todd Worrell .......................... .10 .05
❑ 129 Chris Widger .......................... .10 .05
❑ 130 Damon Mashore ..................... .10 .05
❑ 131 Kevin Brown ........................... .25 .11
❑ 132 Bip Roberts ............................ .10 .05
❑ 133 Tim Naehring .......................... .10 .05
❑ 134 Dave Martinez ........................ .10 .05
❑ 135 Jeff Blauser ............................ .10 .05
❑ 136 David Justice .......................... .25 .11
❑ 137 Dave Hollins ........................... .10 .05
❑ 138 Pat Hentgen ............................ .10 .05
❑ 139 Darren Daulton ....................... .15 .07
❑ 140 Ramon Martinez ...................... .10 .05
❑ 141 Raul Casanova ........................ .10 .05
❑ 142 Tom Glavine ............................ .40 .18
❑ 143 J.T. Snow ................................ .15 .07
❑ 144 Tony Graffanino ...................... .10 .05
❑ 145 Randy Johnson ....................... .50 .23
❑ 146 Orlando Merced ...................... .10 .05
❑ 147 Jeff Juden ............................... .10 .05
❑ 148 Darryl Kile ............................... .15 .07
❑ 149 Ray Durham ............................ .15 .07
❑ 150 Alex Fernandez ....................... .10 .05
❑ 151 Joey Cora ................................ .10 .05
❑ 152 Royce Clayton ......................... .10 .05
❑ 153 Randy Myers ........................... .15 .07
❑ 154 Charles Johnson ..................... .15 .07
❑ 155 Alan Benes .............................. .10 .05
❑ 156 Mike Bordick ........................... .10 .05
❑ 157 Heathcliff Slocumb ................. .10 .05
❑ 158 Roger Bailey ........................... .10 .05
❑ 159 Reggie Jefferson ..................... .10 .05
❑ 160 Ricky Bottalico ........................ .10 .05
❑ 161 Scott Erickson ......................... .10 .05
❑ 162 Matt Williams .......................... .25 .11
❑ 163 Robb Nen ................................ .10 .05
❑ 164 Matt Stairs ............................... .10 .05
❑ 165 Ismael Valdes .......................... .10 .05
❑ 166 Lee Stevens ............................. .10 .05
❑ 167 Gary DiSarcina ......................... .10 .05
❑ 168 Brad Radke ............................... .15 .07
❑ 169 Mike Lansing ............................ .10 .05
❑ 170 Armando Benitez ...................... .10 .05
❑ 171 Mike James .............................. .10 .05
❑ 172 Russ Davis ................................ .10 .05
❑ 173 Lance Johnson .......................... .10 .05
❑ 174 Joey Hamilton ........................... .10 .05
❑ 175 John Valentin ............................ .10 .05
❑ 176 David Segui ............................... .10 .05

| | | | |
|---|---|---|---|
| ❑ 177 | David Wells | .15 | .07 |
| ❑ 178 | Delino DeShields | .10 | .05 |
| ❑ 179 | Eric Karros | .15 | .07 |
| ❑ 180 | Jim Leyritz | .10 | .05 |
| ❑ 181 | Raul Mondesi | .15 | .07 |
| ❑ 182 | Travis Fryman | .15 | .07 |
| ❑ 183 | Todd Zeile | .15 | .07 |
| ❑ 184 | Brian Jordan | .15 | .07 |
| ❑ 185 | Rey Ordonez | .10 | .05 |
| ❑ 186 | Jim Edmonds | .40 | .18 |
| ❑ 187 | Terrell Wade | .10 | .05 |
| ❑ 188 | Marquis Grissom | .10 | .05 |
| ❑ 189 | Chris Snopek | .10 | .05 |
| ❑ 190 | Shane Reynolds | .10 | .05 |
| ❑ 191 | Jeff Frye | .10 | .05 |
| ❑ 192 | Paul Sorrento | .10 | .05 |
| ❑ 193 | James Baldwin | .10 | .05 |
| ❑ 194 | Brian McRae | .10 | .05 |
| ❑ 195 | Fred McGriff | .25 | .11 |
| ❑ 196 | Troy Percival | .10 | .05 |
| ❑ 197 | Rich Amaral | .10 | .05 |
| ❑ 198 | Juan Guzman | .10 | .05 |
| ❑ 199 | Cecil Fielder | .15 | .07 |
| ❑ 200 | Willie Blair | .10 | .05 |
| ❑ 201 | Chili Davis | .15 | .07 |
| ❑ 202 | Gary Gaetti | .15 | .07 |
| ❑ 203 | B.J. Surhoff | .15 | .07 |
| ❑ 204 | Steve Cooke | .10 | .05 |
| ❑ 205 | Chuck Finley | .15 | .07 |
| ❑ 206 | Jeff Kent | .25 | .11 |
| ❑ 207 | Ben McDonald | .10 | .05 |
| ❑ 208 | Jeffrey Hammonds | .15 | .07 |
| ❑ 209 | Tom Goodwin | .10 | .05 |
| ❑ 210 | Billy Ashley | .10 | .05 |
| ❑ 211 | Wil Cordero | .10 | .05 |
| ❑ 212 | Shawon Dunston | .10 | .05 |
| ❑ 213 | Tony Phillips | .10 | .05 |
| ❑ 214 | Jamie Moyer | .10 | .05 |
| ❑ 215 | John Jaha | .15 | .07 |
| ❑ 216 | Troy O'Leary | .10 | .05 |
| ❑ 217 | Brad Ausmus | .10 | .05 |
| ❑ 218 | Garret Anderson | .15 | .07 |
| ❑ 219 | Wilson Alvarez | .10 | .05 |
| ❑ 220 | Kent Mercker | .10 | .05 |
| ❑ 221 | Wade Boggs | .50 | .23 |
| ❑ 222 | Mark Wohlers | .10 | .05 |
| ❑ 223 | Kevin Appier | .15 | .07 |
| ❑ 224 | Tony Fernandez | .10 | .05 |
| ❑ 225 | Ugueth Urbina | .10 | .05 |
| ❑ 226 | Gregg Jefferies | .10 | .05 |
| ❑ 227 | Mo Vaughn | .15 | .07 |
| ❑ 228 | Arthur Rhodes | .10 | .05 |
| ❑ 229 | Jorge Fabregas | .10 | .05 |
| ❑ 230 | Mark Gardner | .10 | .05 |
| ❑ 231 | Shane Mack | .10 | .05 |
| ❑ 232 | Jorge Posada | .10 | .05 |
| ❑ 233 | Jose Cruz Jr. | .15 | .07 |
| ❑ 234 | Paul Konerko | .15 | .07 |
| ❑ 235 | Derrek Lee | .10 | .05 |
| ❑ 236 | Steve Woodard | .10 | .05 |
| ❑ 237 | Todd Dunwoody | .10 | .05 |
| ❑ 238 | Fernando Tatis | .15 | .07 |
| ❑ 239 | Jacob Cruz | .10 | .05 |
| ❑ 240 | Pokey Reese | .15 | .07 |
| ❑ 241 | Mark Kotsay | .15 | .07 |
| ❑ 242 | Matt Morris | .10 | .05 |
| ❑ 243 | Antone Williamson | .10 | .05 |
| ❑ 244 | Ben Grieve | .15 | .07 |
| ❑ 245 | Ryan McGuire | .10 | .05 |
| ❑ 246 | Lou Collier | .10 | .05 |
| ❑ 247 | Shannon Stewart | .15 | .07 |
| ❑ 248 | Brett Tomko | .10 | .05 |
| ❑ 249 | Bobby Estalella | .10 | .05 |
| ❑ 250 | Livan Hernandez | .10 | .05 |
| ❑ 251 | Todd Helton | .50 | .23 |
| ❑ 252 | Jaret Wright | .10 | .05 |
| ❑ 253 | Darryl Hamilton IM | .10 | .05 |
| ❑ 254 | Stan Javier IM | .10 | .05 |
| ❑ 255 | Glenallen Hill IM | .10 | .05 |
| ❑ 256 | Mark Gardner IM | .10 | .05 |
| ❑ 257 | Cal Ripken IM | .75 | .35 |
| ❑ 258 | Mike Mussina IM | .15 | .07 |
| ❑ 259 | Mike Piazza IM | .60 | .25 |
| ❑ 260 | Sammy Sosa IM | .40 | .18 |
| ❑ 261 | Todd Hundley IM | .10 | .05 |
| ❑ 262 | Eric Karros IM | .10 | .05 |
| ❑ 263 | Denny Neagle IM | .10 | .05 |
| ❑ 264 | Jeromy Burnitz IM | .10 | .05 |
| ❑ 265 | Greg Maddux IM | .50 | .23 |
| ❑ 266 | Tony Clark IM | .10 | .05 |
| ❑ 267 | Vladimir Guerrero IM | .25 | .11 |
| ❑ 268 | Cal Ripken CL UER | .75 | .35 |
| ❑ 269 | Ken Griffey Jr. CL | .75 | .35 |
| ❑ 270 | Mark McGwire CL | .75 | .35 |
| ❑ NNO | Checklist All-Star Edition | .25 | .11 |
| ❑ NNO | Checklist Regular Issue | .10 | .05 |

## 1998 Score Rookie/Traded

| | MINT | NRMT |
|---|---|---|
| COMPLETE SET (270) | 40.00 | 18.00 |
| COMMON SP (1-50) | .25 | .11 |
| COMMON CARD (51-270) | .10 | .05 |

| | | | |
|---|---|---|---|
| ❑ 1 | Tony Clark | .25 | .11 |
| ❑ 2 | Juan Gonzalez | .60 | .25 |
| ❑ 3 | Frank Thomas | 1.25 | .55 |
| ❑ 4 | Greg Maddux | 1.50 | .70 |
| ❑ 5 | Barry Larkin | .60 | .25 |
| ❑ 6 | Derek Jeter | 2.50 | 1.10 |
| ❑ 7 | Randy Johnson | .75 | .35 |
| ❑ 8 | Roger Clemens | 1.25 | .55 |
| ❑ 9 | Tony Gwynn | 1.25 | .55 |
| ❑ 10 | Barry Bonds | 1.00 | .45 |
| ❑ 11 | Jim Edmonds | .60 | .25 |
| ❑ 12 | Bernie Williams | .60 | .25 |
| ❑ 13 | Ken Griffey Jr. | 2.50 | 1.10 |
| ❑ 14 | Tim Salmon | .30 | .14 |
| ❑ 15 | Mo Vaughn | .30 | .14 |
| ❑ 16 | David Justice | .40 | .18 |
| ❑ 17 | Jose Cruz Jr. | .30 | .14 |
| ❑ 18 | Andruw Jones | .60 | .25 |
| ❑ 19 | Sammy Sosa | 1.25 | .55 |
| ❑ 20 | Jeff Bagwell | .75 | .35 |
| ❑ 21 | Scott Rolen | .60 | .25 |
| ❑ 22 | Darin Erstad | .60 | .25 |
| ❑ 23 | Andy Pettitte | .30 | .14 |
| ❑ 24 | Mike Mussina | .60 | .25 |
| ❑ 25 | Mark McGwire | 2.50 | 1.10 |
| ❑ 26 | Hideo Nomo | .60 | .25 |
| ❑ 27 | Chipper Jones | 1.50 | .70 |
| ❑ 28 | Cal Ripken | 2.50 | 1.10 |
| ❑ 29 | Chuck Knoblauch | .30 | .14 |
| ❑ 30 | Alex Rodriguez | 2.00 | .90 |
| ❑ 31 | Jim Thome | .40 | .18 |
| ❑ 32 | Mike Piazza | 2.00 | .90 |
| ❑ 33 | Ivan Rodriguez | .75 | .35 |
| ❑ 34 | Roberto Alomar | .60 | .25 |
| ❑ 35 | Nomar Garciaparra | 2.00 | .90 |
| ❑ 36 | Albert Belle | .40 | .18 |
| ❑ 37 | Vladimir Guerrero | 1.00 | .45 |
| ❑ 38 | Raul Mondesi | .30 | .14 |
| ❑ 39 | Larry Walker | .30 | .14 |
| ❑ 40 | Manny Ramirez | .75 | .35 |
| ❑ 41 | Tino Martinez | .30 | .14 |
| ❑ 42 | Craig Biggio | .40 | .18 |
| ❑ 43 | Jay Buhner | .30 | .14 |
| ❑ 44 | Kenny Lofton | .30 | .14 |
| ❑ 45 | Pedro Martinez | .75 | .35 |
| ❑ 46 | Edgar Martinez | .40 | .18 |
| ❑ 47 | Gary Sheffield | .60 | .25 |
| ❑ 48 | Jose Guillen | .25 | .11 |
| ❑ 49 | Ken Caminiti | .30 | .14 |
| ❑ 50 | Bobby Higginson | .30 | .14 |
| ❑ 51 | Alan Benes | .10 | .05 |
| ❑ 52 | Shawn Green | .40 | .18 |
| ❑ 53 | Ron Coomer | .10 | .05 |
| ❑ 54 | Charles Nagy | .10 | .05 |
| ❑ 55 | Steve Karsay | .10 | .05 |
| ❑ 56 | Matt Morris | .10 | .05 |
| ❑ 57 | Bobby Jones | .10 | .05 |
| ❑ 58 | Jason Kendall | .15 | .07 |
| ❑ 59 | Jeff Conine | .10 | .05 |
| ❑ 60 | Joe Girardi | .10 | .05 |
| ❑ 61 | Mark Kotsay | .15 | .07 |
| ❑ 62 | Eric Karros | .15 | .07 |
| ❑ 63 | Bartolo Colon | .15 | .07 |
| ❑ 64 | Mariano Rivera | .15 | .07 |
| ❑ 65 | Alex Gonzalez | .10 | .05 |
| ❑ 66 | Scott Spiezio | .10 | .05 |
| ❑ 67 | Luis Castillo | .15 | .07 |
| ❑ 68 | Joey Cora | .10 | .05 |
| ❑ 69 | Mark McLemore | .10 | .05 |
| ❑ 70 | Reggie Jefferson | .10 | .05 |
| ❑ 71 | Lance Johnson | .10 | .05 |
| ❑ 72 | Damian Jackson | .10 | .05 |
| ❑ 73 | Jeff D'Amico | .10 | .05 |
| ❑ 74 | David Ortiz | .10 | .05 |
| ❑ 75 | J.T. Snow | .15 | .07 |
| ❑ 76 | Todd Hundley | .10 | .05 |
| ❑ 77 | Billy Wagner | .10 | .05 |
| ❑ 78 | Vinny Castilla | .15 | .07 |
| ❑ 79 | Ismael Valdes | .10 | .05 |
| ❑ 80 | Neifi Perez | .10 | .05 |
| ❑ 81 | Derek Bell | .10 | .05 |
| ❑ 82 | Ryan Klesko | .15 | .07 |
| ❑ 83 | Rey Ordonez | .10 | .05 |
| ❑ 84 | Carlos Garcia | .10 | .05 |
| ❑ 85 | Curt Schilling | .15 | .07 |
| ❑ 86 | Robin Ventura | .15 | .07 |
| ❑ 87 | Pat Hentgen | .10 | .05 |
| ❑ 88 | Glendon Rusch | .10 | .05 |
| ❑ 89 | Hideki Irabu | .10 | .05 |
| ❑ 90 | Antone Williamson | .10 | .05 |
| ❑ 91 | Denny Neagle | .10 | .05 |
| ❑ 92 | Kevin Orie | .10 | .05 |
| ❑ 93 | Reggie Sanders | .10 | .05 |
| ❑ 94 | Brady Anderson | .15 | .07 |
| ❑ 95 | Andy Benes | .10 | .05 |
| ❑ 96 | John Valentin | .10 | .05 |
| ❑ 97 | Bobby Bonilla | .15 | .07 |
| ❑ 98 | Walt Weiss | .10 | .05 |
| ❑ 99 | Robin Jennings | .10 | .05 |
| ❑ 100 | Marty Cordova | .10 | .05 |
| ❑ 101 | Brad Ausmus | .10 | .05 |
| ❑ 102 | Brian Rose | .10 | .05 |
| ❑ 103 | Calvin Maduro | .10 | .05 |
| ❑ 104 | Raul Casanova | .10 | .05 |
| ❑ 105 | Jeff King | .10 | .05 |
| ❑ 106 | Sandy Alomar Jr. | .15 | .07 |
| ❑ 107 | Tim Naehring | .10 | .05 |
| ❑ 108 | Mike Cameron | .15 | .07 |
| ❑ 109 | Omar Vizquel | .15 | .07 |
| ❑ 110 | Brad Radke | .15 | .07 |
| ❑ 111 | Jeff Fassero | .10 | .05 |
| ❑ 112 | Deivi Cruz | .10 | .05 |
| ❑ 113 | Dave Hollins | .10 | .05 |
| ❑ 114 | Dean Palmer | .15 | .07 |
| ❑ 115 | Esteban Loaiza | .10 | .05 |
| ❑ 116 | Brian Giles | .15 | .07 |
| ❑ 117 | Steve Finley | .15 | .07 |
| ❑ 118 | Jose Canseco | .50 | .23 |
| ❑ 119 | Al Martin | .10 | .05 |
| ❑ 120 | Eric Young | .10 | .05 |
| ❑ 121 | Curtis Goodwin | .10 | .05 |
| ❑ 122 | Ellis Burks | .15 | .07 |
| ❑ 123 | Mike Hampton | .15 | .07 |
| ❑ 124 | Lou Collier | .10 | .05 |
| ❑ 125 | John Olerud | .15 | .07 |
| ❑ 126 | Ramon Martinez | .10 | .05 |
| ❑ 127 | Todd Dunwoody | .10 | .05 |
| ❑ 128 | Jermaine Allensworth | .10 | .05 |
| ❑ 129 | Eduardo Perez | .10 | .05 |
| ❑ 130 | Dante Bichette | .15 | .07 |
| ❑ 131 | Edgar Renteria | .10 | .05 |
| ❑ 132 | Bob Abreu | .15 | .07 |
| ❑ 133 | Rondell White | .15 | .07 |
| ❑ 134 | Michael Coleman | .10 | .05 |
| ❑ 135 | Jason Giambi | .40 | .18 |

| Card | Player | MINT | NRMT |
|---|---|---|---|
| ❑ 136 | Brant Brown | .10 | .05 |
| ❑ 137 | Michael Tucker | .10 | .05 |
| ❑ 138 | Dave Nilsson | .10 | .05 |
| ❑ 139 | Benito Santiago | .10 | .05 |
| ❑ 140 | Ray Durham | .15 | .07 |
| ❑ 141 | Jeff Kent | .25 | .11 |
| ❑ 142 | Matt Stairs | .10 | .05 |
| ❑ 143 | Kevin Young | .15 | .07 |
| ❑ 144 | Eric Davis | .15 | .07 |
| ❑ 145 | John Wetteland | .15 | .07 |
| ❑ 146 | Esteban Yan RC | .25 | .11 |
| ❑ 147 | Wilton Guerrero | .10 | .05 |
| ❑ 148 | Moises Alou | .15 | .07 |
| ❑ 149 | Edgardo Alfonzo | .15 | .07 |
| ❑ 150 | Andy Ashby | .10 | .05 |
| ❑ 151 | Todd Walker | .10 | .05 |
| ❑ 152 | Jermaine Dye | .15 | .07 |
| ❑ 153 | Brian Hunter | .10 | .05 |
| ❑ 154 | Shawn Estes | .10 | .05 |
| ❑ 155 | Bernard Gilkey | .10 | .05 |
| ❑ 156 | Tony Womack | .10 | .05 |
| ❑ 157 | John Smoltz | .15 | .07 |
| ❑ 158 | Delino DeShields | .10 | .05 |
| ❑ 159 | Jacob Cruz | .10 | .05 |
| ❑ 160 | Javier Valentin | .10 | .05 |
| ❑ 161 | Chris Hoiles | .10 | .05 |
| ❑ 162 | Garret Anderson | .15 | .07 |
| ❑ 163 | Dan Wilson | .10 | .05 |
| ❑ 164 | Paul O'Neill | .15 | .07 |
| ❑ 165 | Matt Williams | .25 | .11 |
| ❑ 166 | Travis Fryman | .15 | .07 |
| ❑ 167 | Javier Lopez | .15 | .07 |
| ❑ 168 | Ray Lankford | .15 | .07 |
| ❑ 169 | Bobby Estalella | .10 | .05 |
| ❑ 170 | Henry Rodriguez | .10 | .05 |
| ❑ 171 | Quinton McCracken | .10 | .05 |
| ❑ 172 | Jaret Wright | .10 | .05 |
| ❑ 173 | Darryl Kile | .15 | .07 |
| ❑ 174 | Wade Boggs | .50 | .23 |
| ❑ 175 | Orel Hershiser | .15 | .07 |
| ❑ 176 | B.J. Surhoff | .15 | .07 |
| ❑ 177 | Fernando Tatis | .15 | .07 |
| ❑ 178 | Carlos Delgado | .40 | .18 |
| ❑ 179 | Jorge Fabregas | .10 | .05 |
| ❑ 180 | Tony Saunders | .10 | .05 |
| ❑ 181 | Devon White | .10 | .05 |
| ❑ 182 | Dmitri Young | .15 | .07 |
| ❑ 183 | Ryan McGuire | .10 | .05 |
| ❑ 184 | Mark Bellhorn | .10 | .05 |
| ❑ 185 | Joe Carter | .15 | .07 |
| ❑ 186 | Kevin Stocker | .10 | .05 |
| ❑ 187 | Mike Lansing | .10 | .05 |
| ❑ 188 | Jason Dickson | .10 | .05 |
| ❑ 189 | Charles Johnson | .15 | .07 |
| ❑ 190 | Will Clark | .40 | .18 |
| ❑ 191 | Shannon Stewart | .15 | .07 |
| ❑ 192 | Johnny Damon | .15 | .07 |
| ❑ 193 | Todd Greene | .10 | .05 |
| ❑ 194 | Carlos Baerga | .10 | .05 |
| ❑ 195 | David Cone | .15 | .07 |
| ❑ 196 | Pokey Reese | .15 | .07 |
| ❑ 197 | Livan Hernandez | .10 | .05 |
| ❑ 198 | Tom Glavine | .40 | .18 |
| ❑ 199 | Geronimo Berroa | .10 | .05 |
| ❑ 200 | Darryl Hamilton | .10 | .05 |
| ❑ 201 | Terry Steinbach | .10 | .05 |
| ❑ 202 | Robb Nen | .10 | .05 |
| ❑ 203 | Ron Gant | .15 | .07 |
| ❑ 204 | Rafael Palmeiro | .40 | .18 |
| ❑ 205 | Rickey Henderson | .50 | .23 |
| ❑ 206 | Justin Thompson | .10 | .05 |
| ❑ 207 | Jeff Suppan | .10 | .05 |
| ❑ 208 | Kevin Brown | .25 | .11 |
| ❑ 209 | Jimmy Key | .15 | .07 |
| ❑ 210 | Brian Jordan | .15 | .07 |
| ❑ 211 | Aaron Sele | .15 | .07 |
| ❑ 212 | Fred McGriff | .25 | .11 |
| ❑ 213 | Jay Bell | .15 | .07 |
| ❑ 214 | Andres Galarraga | .25 | .11 |
| ❑ 215 | Mark Grace | .40 | .18 |
| ❑ 216 | Brett Tomko | .10 | .05 |
| ❑ 217 | Francisco Cordova | .10 | .05 |
| ❑ 218 | Rusty Greer | .15 | .07 |
| ❑ 219 | Bubba Trammell | .10 | .05 |
| ❑ 220 | Derrek Lee | .10 | .05 |
| ❑ 221 | Brian Anderson | .10 | .05 |
| ❑ 222 | Mark Grudzielanek | .10 | .05 |
| ❑ 223 | Marquis Grissom | .10 | .05 |
| ❑ 224 | Gary DiSarcina | .10 | .05 |
| ❑ 225 | Jim Leyritz | .10 | .05 |
| ❑ 226 | Jeffrey Hammonds | .15 | .07 |
| ❑ 227 | Karim Garcia | .10 | .05 |
| ❑ 228 | Chan Ho Park | .15 | .07 |
| ❑ 229 | Brooks Kieschnick | .10 | .05 |
| ❑ 230 | Trey Beamon | .10 | .05 |
| ❑ 231 | Kevin Appier | .15 | .07 |
| ❑ 232 | Wally Joyner | .15 | .07 |
| ❑ 233 | Richie Sexson | .25 | .11 |
| ❑ 234 | Frank Catalanotto RC | .25 | .11 |
| ❑ 235 | Rafael Medina | .10 | .05 |
| ❑ 236 | Travis Lee | .15 | .07 |
| ❑ 237 | Eli Marrero | .10 | .05 |
| ❑ 238 | Carl Pavano | .10 | .05 |
| ❑ 239 | Enrique Wilson | .10 | .05 |
| ❑ 240 | Richard Hidalgo | .15 | .07 |
| ❑ 241 | Todd Helton | .50 | .23 |
| ❑ 242 | Ben Grieve | .15 | .07 |
| ❑ 243 | Mario Valdez | .10 | .05 |
| ❑ 244 | Magglio Ordonez RC | 1.50 | .70 |
| ❑ 245 | Juan Encarnacion | .15 | .07 |
| ❑ 246 | Russell Branyan | .15 | .07 |
| ❑ 247 | Sean Casey | .15 | .07 |
| ❑ 248 | Abraham Nunez | .10 | .05 |
| ❑ 249 | Brad Fullmer | .15 | .07 |
| ❑ 250 | Paul Konerko | .15 | .07 |
| ❑ 251 | Miguel Tejada | .40 | .18 |
| ❑ 252 | Mike Lowell RC | .50 | .23 |
| ❑ 253 | Ken Griffey Jr. ST | .75 | .35 |
| ❑ 254 | Frank Thomas ST | .40 | .18 |
| ❑ 255 | Alex Rodriguez ST | .60 | .25 |
| ❑ 256 | Jose Cruz Jr. ST | .10 | .05 |
| ❑ 257 | Jeff Bagwell ST | .25 | .11 |
| ❑ 258 | Chipper Jones ST | .50 | .23 |
| ❑ 259 | Mo Vaughn ST | .15 | .07 |
| ❑ 260 | Nomar Garciaparra ST | .60 | .25 |
| ❑ 261 | Jim Thome ST | .10 | .05 |
| ❑ 262 | Derek Jeter ST | .75 | .35 |
| ❑ 263 | Mike Piazza ST | .60 | .25 |
| ❑ 264 | Tony Gwynn ST | .40 | .18 |
| ❑ 265 | Scott Rolen ST | .40 | .18 |
| ❑ 266 | Andruw Jones ST | .15 | .07 |
| ❑ 267 | Cal Ripken ST | .75 | .35 |
| ❑ 268 | Checklist 1 | .10 | .05 |
| ❑ 269 | Checklist 2 | .10 | .05 |
| ❑ 270 | Checklist 3 | .10 | .05 |
| ❑ S250 | Paul Konerko AU500 | 10.00 | 4.50 |

## 1993 Select

| | MINT | NRMT |
|---|---|---|
| COMPLETE SET (405) | 20.00 | 9.00 |

| Card | Player | MINT | NRMT |
|---|---|---|---|
| ❑ 1 | Barry Bonds | .60 | .25 |
| ❑ 2 | Ken Griffey Jr. | 1.50 | .70 |
| ❑ 3 | Will Clark | .40 | .18 |
| ❑ 4 | Kirby Puckett | 1.00 | .45 |
| ❑ 5 | Tony Gwynn | .75 | .35 |
| ❑ 6 | Frank Thomas | .75 | .35 |
| ❑ 7 | Tom Glavine | .25 | .11 |
| ❑ 8 | Roberto Alomar | .40 | .18 |
| ❑ 9 | Andre Dawson | .25 | .11 |
| ❑ 10 | Ron Darling | .10 | .05 |
| ❑ 11 | Bobby Bonilla | .15 | .07 |
| ❑ 12 | Danny Tartabull | .10 | .05 |
| ❑ 13 | Darren Daulton | .15 | .07 |
| ❑ 14 | Roger Clemens | .75 | .35 |
| ❑ 15 | Ozzie Smith | .50 | .23 |
| ❑ 16 | Mark McGwire | 1.50 | .70 |
| ❑ 17 | Terry Pendleton | .15 | .07 |
| ❑ 18 | Cal Ripken | 1.50 | .70 |
| ❑ 19 | Fred McGriff | .25 | .11 |
| ❑ 20 | Cecil Fielder | .15 | .07 |
| ❑ 21 | Darryl Strawberry | .15 | .07 |
| ❑ 22 | Robin Yount | .25 | .11 |
| ❑ 23 | Barry Larkin | .40 | .18 |
| ❑ 24 | Don Mattingly | 1.00 | .45 |
| ❑ 25 | Craig Biggio | .25 | .11 |
| ❑ 26 | Sandy Alomar Jr. | .15 | .07 |
| ❑ 27 | Larry Walker | .15 | .07 |
| ❑ 28 | Junior Felix | .10 | .05 |
| ❑ 29 | Eddie Murray | .40 | .18 |
| ❑ 30 | Robin Ventura | .15 | .07 |
| ❑ 31 | Greg Maddux | 1.00 | .45 |
| ❑ 32 | Dave Winfield | .40 | .18 |
| ❑ 33 | John Kruk | .15 | .07 |
| ❑ 34 | Wally Joyner | .15 | .07 |
| ❑ 35 | Andy Van Slyke | .15 | .07 |
| ❑ 36 | Chuck Knoblauch | .15 | .07 |
| ❑ 37 | Tom Pagnozzi | .10 | .05 |
| ❑ 38 | Dennis Eckersley | .15 | .07 |
| ❑ 39 | Dave Justice | .25 | .11 |
| ❑ 40 | Juan Gonzalez | .40 | .18 |
| ❑ 41 | Gary Sheffield | .40 | .18 |
| ❑ 42 | Paul Molitor | .40 | .18 |
| ❑ 43 | Delino DeShields | .15 | .07 |
| ❑ 44 | Travis Fryman | .15 | .07 |
| ❑ 45 | Hal Morris | .10 | .05 |
| ❑ 46 | Greg Olson | .10 | .05 |
| ❑ 47 | Ken Caminiti | .15 | .07 |
| ❑ 48 | Wade Boggs | .50 | .23 |
| ❑ 49 | Orel Hershiser | .15 | .07 |
| ❑ 50 | Albert Belle | .25 | .11 |
| ❑ 51 | Bill Swift | .10 | .05 |
| ❑ 52 | Mark Langston | .10 | .05 |
| ❑ 53 | Joe Girardi | .15 | .07 |
| ❑ 54 | Keith Miller | .10 | .05 |
| ❑ 55 | Gary Carter | .25 | .11 |
| ❑ 56 | Brady Anderson | .15 | .07 |
| ❑ 57 | Dwight Gooden | .15 | .07 |
| ❑ 58 | Julio Franco | .10 | .05 |
| ❑ 59 | Lenny Dykstra | .15 | .07 |
| ❑ 60 | Mickey Tettleton | .10 | .05 |
| ❑ 61 | Randy Tomlin | .10 | .05 |
| ❑ 62 | B.J. Surhoff | .15 | .07 |
| ❑ 63 | Todd Zeile | .10 | .05 |
| ❑ 64 | Roberto Kelly | .10 | .05 |
| ❑ 65 | Rob Dibble | .10 | .05 |
| ❑ 66 | Leo Gomez | .10 | .05 |
| ❑ 67 | Doug Jones | .10 | .05 |
| ❑ 68 | Ellis Burks | .15 | .07 |
| ❑ 69 | Mike Scioscia | .10 | .05 |
| ❑ 70 | Charles Nagy | .10 | .05 |
| ❑ 71 | Cory Snyder | .10 | .05 |
| ❑ 72 | Devon White | .10 | .05 |
| ❑ 73 | Mark Grace | .40 | .18 |
| ❑ 74 | Luis Polonia | .10 | .05 |
| ❑ 75 | John Smiley 2X | .10 | .05 |
| ❑ 76 | Carlton Fisk | .40 | .18 |
| ❑ 77 | Luis Sojo | .10 | .05 |
| ❑ 78 | George Brett | .75 | .35 |
| ❑ 79 | Mitch Williams | .10 | .05 |
| ❑ 80 | Kent Hrbek | .15 | .07 |
| ❑ 81 | Jay Bell | .15 | .07 |
| ❑ 82 | Edgar Martinez | .25 | .11 |
| ❑ 83 | Lee Smith | .15 | .07 |
| ❑ 84 | Deion Sanders | .25 | .11 |
| ❑ 85 | Bill Gullickson | .10 | .05 |
| ❑ 86 | Paul O'Neill | .15 | .07 |
| ❑ 87 | Kevin Seitzer | .10 | .05 |
| ❑ 88 | Steve Finley | .15 | .07 |
| ❑ 89 | Mel Hall | .10 | .05 |
| ❑ 90 | Nolan Ryan | 2.00 | .90 |
| ❑ 91 | Eric Davis | .15 | .07 |
| ❑ 92 | Mike Mussina | .40 | .18 |
| ❑ 93 | Tony Fernandez | .10 | .05 |
| ❑ 94 | Frank Viola | .10 | .05 |
| ❑ 95 | Matt Williams | .25 | .11 |
| ❑ 96 | Joe Carter | .15 | .07 |
| ❑ 97 | Ryne Sandberg | .50 | .23 |
| ❑ 98 | Jim Abbott | .15 | .07 |

❑ 99 Marquis Grissom .10 .05
❑ 100 George Bell .10 .05
❑ 101 Howard Johnson .10 .05
❑ 102 Kevin Appier .15 .07
❑ 103 Dale Murphy .25 .11
❑ 104 Shane Mack .10 .05
❑ 105 Jose Lind .10 .05
❑ 106 Rickey Henderson .50 .23
❑ 107 Bob Tewksbury .10 .05
❑ 108 Kevin Mitchell .15 .07
❑ 109 Steve Avery .10 .05
❑ 110 Candy Maldonado .10 .05
❑ 111 Bip Roberts .10 .05
❑ 112 Lou Whitaker .15 .07
❑ 113 Jeff Bagwell .50 .23
❑ 114 Dante Bichette .15 .07
❑ 115 Brett Butler .15 .07
❑ 116 Melido Perez .10 .05
❑ 117 Andy Benes .10 .05
❑ 118 Randy Johnson .50 .23
❑ 119 Willie McGee .15 .07
❑ 120 Jody Reed .10 .05
❑ 121 Shawon Dunston .10 .05
❑ 122 Carlos Baerga .10 .05
❑ 123 Bret Saberhagen .15 .07
❑ 124 John Olerud .25 .11
❑ 125 Ivan Calderon .10 .05
❑ 126 Bryan Harvey .10 .05
❑ 127 Terry Mulholland .10 .05
❑ 128 Ozzie Guillen .10 .05
❑ 129 Steve Buechele .10 .05
❑ 130 Kevin Tapani .10 .05
❑ 131 Felix Jose .10 .05
❑ 132 Terry Steinbach .10 .05
❑ 133 Ron Gant .15 .07
❑ 134 Harold Reynolds .10 .05
❑ 135 Chris Sabo .10 .05
❑ 136 Ivan Rodriguez .50 .23
❑ 137 Eric Anthony .10 .05
❑ 138 Mike Henneman .10 .05
❑ 139 Robby Thompson .10 .05
❑ 140 Scott Fletcher .10 .05
❑ 141 Bruce Hurst .10 .05
❑ 142 Kevin Maas .10 .05
❑ 143 Tom Candiotti .10 .05
❑ 144 Chris Hoiles .10 .05
❑ 145 Mike Morgan .10 .05
❑ 146 Mark Whiten .10 .05
❑ 147 Dennis Martinez .15 .07
❑ 148 Tony Pena .10 .05
❑ 149 Dave Magadan .10 .05
❑ 150 Mark Lewis .10 .05
❑ 151 Mariano Duncan .10 .05
❑ 152 Gregg Jefferies .10 .05
❑ 153 Doug Drabek .10 .05
❑ 154 Brian Harper .10 .05
❑ 155 Ray Lankford .25 .11
❑ 156 Carney Lansford .15 .07
❑ 157 Mike Sharperson .10 .05
❑ 158 Jack Morris .15 .07
❑ 159 Otis Nixon .10 .05
❑ 160 Steve Sax .10 .05
❑ 161 Mark Lemke .10 .05
❑ 162 Rafael Palmeiro .40 .18
❑ 163 Jose Rijo .10 .05
❑ 164 Omar Vizquel .15 .07
❑ 165 Sammy Sosa .75 .35
❑ 166 Milt Cuyler .10 .05
❑ 167 John Franco .15 .07
❑ 168 Darryl Hamilton .10 .05
❑ 169 Ken Hill .10 .05
❑ 170 Mike Devereaux .10 .05
❑ 171 Don Slaught .10 .05
❑ 172 Steve Farr .10 .05
❑ 173 Bernard Gilkey .10 .05
❑ 174 Mike Fetters .10 .05
❑ 175 Vince Coleman .10 .05
❑ 176 Kevin McReynolds .10 .05
❑ 177 John Smoltz .15 .07
❑ 178 Greg Gagne .10 .05
❑ 179 Greg Swindell .10 .05
❑ 180 Juan Guzman .10 .05
❑ 181 Kal Daniels .10 .05
❑ 182 Rick Sutcliffe .15 .07
❑ 183 Orlando Merced .10 .05
❑ 184 Bill Wegman .10 .05
❑ 185 Mark Gardner .10 .05
❑ 186 Rob Deer .10 .05
❑ 187 Dave Hollins .10 .05
❑ 188 Jack Clark .10 .05
❑ 189 Brian Hunter .10 .05
❑ 190 Tim Wallach .10 .05
❑ 191 Tim Belcher .10 .05
❑ 192 Walt Weiss .10 .05
❑ 193 Kurt Stillwell .10 .05
❑ 194 Charlie Hayes .10 .05
❑ 195 Willie Randolph .15 .07
❑ 196 Jack McDowell .10 .05
❑ 197 Jose Offerman .10 .05
❑ 198 Chuck Finley .15 .07
❑ 199 Darrin Jackson .10 .05
❑ 200 Kelly Gruber .10 .05
❑ 201 John Wetteland .15 .07
❑ 202 Jay Buhner .15 .07
❑ 203 Mike LaValliere .10 .05
❑ 204 Kevin Brown .25 .11
❑ 205 Luis Gonzalez .15 .07
❑ 206 Rick Aguilera .10 .05
❑ 207 Norm Charlton .10 .05
❑ 208 Mike Bordick .10 .05
❑ 209 Charlie Leibrandt .10 .05
❑ 210 Tom Brunansky .10 .05
❑ 211 Tom Henke .10 .05
❑ 212 Randy Milligan .10 .05
❑ 213 Ramon Martinez .10 .05
❑ 214 Mo Vaughn .15 .07
❑ 215 Randy Myers .15 .07
❑ 216 Greg Hibbard .10 .05
❑ 217 Wes Chamberlain .10 .05
❑ 218 Tony Phillips .10 .05
❑ 219 Pete Harnisch .10 .05
❑ 220 Mike Gallego .10 .05
❑ 221 Bud Black .10 .05
❑ 222 Greg Vaughn .15 .07
❑ 223 Milt Thompson .10 .05
❑ 224 Ben McDonald .10 .05
❑ 225 Billy Hatcher .10 .05
❑ 226 Paul Sorrento .10 .05
❑ 227 Mark Gubicza .10 .05
❑ 228 Mike Greenwell .10 .05
❑ 229 Curt Schilling .15 .07
❑ 230 Alan Trammell .25 .11
❑ 231 Zane Smith .10 .05
❑ 232 Bobby Thigpen .10 .05
❑ 233 Greg Olson .10 .05
❑ 234 Joe Orsulak .10 .05
❑ 235 Joe Oliver .10 .05
❑ 236 Tim Raines .15 .07
❑ 237 Juan Samuel .10 .05
❑ 238 Chili Davis .15 .07
❑ 239 Spike Owen .10 .05
❑ 240 Dave Stewart .15 .07
❑ 241 Jim Eisenreich .10 .05
❑ 242 Phil Plantier .10 .05
❑ 243 Sid Fernandez .10 .05
❑ 244 Dan Gladden .10 .05
❑ 245 Mickey Morandini .10 .05
❑ 246 Tino Martinez .15 .07
❑ 247 Kirt Manwaring .10 .05
❑ 248 Dean Palmer .15 .07
❑ 249 Tom Browning .10 .05
❑ 250 Brian McRae .10 .05
❑ 251 Scott Leius .10 .05
❑ 252 Bert Blyleven .15 .07
❑ 253 Scott Erickson .10 .05
❑ 254 Bob Welch .10 .05
❑ 255 Pat Kelly .10 .05
❑ 256 Felix Fermin .10 .05
❑ 257 Harold Baines .15 .07
❑ 258 Duane Ward .10 .05
❑ 259 Bill Spiers .10 .05
❑ 260 Jaime Navarro .10 .05
❑ 261 Scott Sanderson .10 .05
❑ 262 Gary Gaetti .15 .07
❑ 263 Bob Ojeda .10 .05
❑ 264 Jeff Montgomery .15 .07
❑ 265 Scott Bankhead .10 .05
❑ 266 Lance Johnson .10 .05
❑ 267 Rafael Belliard .10 .05
❑ 268 Kevin Reimer .10 .05
❑ 269 Benito Santiago .10 .05
❑ 270 Mike Moore .10 .05
❑ 271 Dave Fleming .10 .05
❑ 272 Moises Alou .15 .07
❑ 273 Pat Listach .10 .05
❑ 274 Reggie Sanders .10 .05
❑ 275 Kenny Lofton .15 .07
❑ 276 Donovan Osborne .10 .05
❑ 277 Rusty Meacham .10 .05
❑ 278 Eric Karros .25 .11
❑ 279 Andy Stankiewicz .10 .05
❑ 280 Brian Jordan .15 .07
❑ 281 Gary DiSarcina .10 .05
❑ 282 Mark Wohlers .10 .05
❑ 283 Dave Nilsson .15 .07
❑ 284 Anthony Young .10 .05
❑ 285 Jim Bullinger .10 .05
❑ 286 Derek Bell .10 .05
❑ 287 Brian Williams .10 .05
❑ 288 Julio Valera .10 .05
❑ 289 Dan Walters .10 .05
❑ 290 Chad Curtis .10 .05
❑ 291 Michael Tucker DP .40 .18
❑ 292 Bob Zupcic .10 .05
❑ 293 Todd Hundley .10 .05
❑ 294 Jeff Tackett .10 .05
❑ 295 Greg Colbrunn .10 .05
❑ 296 Cal Eldred .10 .05
❑ 297 Chris Roberts DP .10 .05
❑ 298 John Doherty .10 .05
❑ 299 Denny Neagle .15 .07
❑ 300 Arthur Rhodes .10 .05
❑ 301 Mark Clark .10 .05
❑ 302 Scott Cooper .10 .05
❑ 303 Jamie Arnold DP RC .10 .05
❑ 304 Jim Thome .25 .11
❑ 305 Frank Seminara .10 .05
❑ 306 Kurt Knudsen .10 .05
❑ 307 Tim Wakefield .10 .05
❑ 308 John Jaha .10 .05
❑ 309 Pat Hentgen .10 .05
❑ 310 B.J. Wallace DP .10 .05
❑ 311 Roberto Hernandez .10 .05
❑ 312 Hipolito Pichardo .10 .05
❑ 313 Eric Fox .10 .05
❑ 314 Willie Banks .10 .05
❑ 315 Sam Militello .10 .05
❑ 316 Vince Horsman .10 .05
❑ 317 Carlos Hernandez .10 .05
❑ 318 Jeff Kent .40 .18
❑ 319 Mike Perez .10 .05
❑ 320 Scott Livingstone .10 .05
❑ 321 Jeff Conine .10 .05
❑ 322 James Austin .10 .05
❑ 323 John Vander Wal .10 .05
❑ 324 Pat Mahomes .10 .05
❑ 325 Pedro Astacio .15 .07
❑ 326 Bret Boone UER .15 .07
(Misspelled Brett)
❑ 327 Matt Stairs .10 .05
❑ 328 Damion Easley .10 .05
❑ 329 Ben Rivera .10 .05
❑ 330 Reggie Jefferson .15 .07
❑ 331 Luis Mercedes .10 .05
❑ 332 Kyle Abbott .10 .05
❑ 333 Eddie Taubensee .10 .05
❑ 334 Tim McIntosh .10 .05
❑ 335 Phil Clark .10 .05
❑ 336 Wil Cordero .10 .05
❑ 337 Russ Springer .10 .05
❑ 338 Craig Colbert .10 .05
❑ 339 Tim Salmon .15 .07
❑ 340 Braulio Castillo .10 .05
❑ 341 Donald Harris .10 .05
❑ 342 Eric Young .10 .05
❑ 343 Bob Wickman .10 .05
❑ 344 John Valentin .10 .05
❑ 345 Dan Wilson .15 .07
❑ 346 Steve Hosey .10 .05
❑ 347 Mike Piazza 2.00 .90
❑ 348 Willie Greene .10 .05
❑ 349 Tom Goodwin .10 .05
❑ 350 Eric Hillman .10 .05
❑ 351 Steve Reed RC .10 .05
❑ 352 Dan Serafini DP RC .10 .05
❑ 353 Todd Steverson DP RC .10 .05
❑ 354 Benji Grigsby DP RC .10 .05
❑ 355 Shannon Stewart DP RC 1.00 .45

| Card | Player | Mint | NRMT |
|---|---|---|---|
| ❑ 356 | Sean Lowe DP RC | .10 | .05 |
| ❑ 357 | Derek Wallace DP RC | .10 | .05 |
| ❑ 358 | Rick Helling DP | .15 | .07 |
| ❑ 359 | Jason Kendall DP RC | 1.25 | .55 |
| ❑ 360 | Derek Jeter DP RC | 12.00 | 5.50 |
| ❑ 361 | David Cone | .15 | .07 |
| ❑ 362 | Jeff Reardon | .15 | .07 |
| ❑ 363 | Bobby Witt | .10 | .05 |
| ❑ 364 | Jose Canseco | .50 | .23 |
| ❑ 365 | Jeff Russell | .10 | .05 |
| ❑ 366 | Ruben Sierra | .10 | .05 |
| ❑ 367 | Alan Mills | .10 | .05 |
| ❑ 368 | Matt Nokes | .10 | .05 |
| ❑ 369 | Pat Borders | .10 | .05 |
| ❑ 370 | Pedro Munoz | .10 | .05 |
| ❑ 371 | Danny Jackson | .10 | .05 |
| ❑ 372 | Geronimo Pena | .10 | .05 |
| ❑ 373 | Craig Lefferts | .10 | .05 |
| ❑ 374 | Joe Grahe | .10 | .05 |
| ❑ 375 | Roger McDowell | .10 | .05 |
| ❑ 376 | Jimmy Key | .15 | .07 |
| ❑ 377 | Steve Olin | .10 | .05 |
| ❑ 378 | Glenn Davis | .10 | .05 |
| ❑ 379 | Rene Gonzales | .10 | .05 |
| ❑ 380 | Manuel Lee | .10 | .05 |
| ❑ 381 | Ron Karkovice | .10 | .05 |
| ❑ 382 | Sid Bream | .10 | .05 |
| ❑ 383 | Gerald Williams | .10 | .05 |
| ❑ 384 | Lenny Harris | .10 | .05 |
| ❑ 385 | J.T. Snow RC | .50 | .23 |
| ❑ 386 | Dave Stieb | .10 | .05 |
| ❑ 387 | Kirk McCaskill | .10 | .05 |
| ❑ 388 | Lance Parrish | .10 | .05 |
| ❑ 389 | Craig Grebeck | .10 | .05 |
| ❑ 390 | Rick Wilkins | .10 | .05 |
| ❑ 391 | Manny Alexander | .10 | .05 |
| ❑ 392 | Mike Schooler | .10 | .05 |
| ❑ 393 | Bernie Williams | .40 | .18 |
| ❑ 394 | Kevin Koslofski | .10 | .05 |
| ❑ 395 | Willie Wilson | .10 | .05 |
| ❑ 396 | Jeff Parrett | .10 | .05 |
| ❑ 397 | Mike Harkey | .10 | .05 |
| ❑ 398 | Frank Tanana | .10 | .05 |
| ❑ 399 | Doug Henry | .10 | .05 |
| ❑ 400 | Royce Clayton | .10 | .05 |
| ❑ 401 | Eric Wedge RC | .10 | .05 |
| ❑ 402 | Derrick May | .10 | .05 |
| ❑ 403 | Carlos Garcia | .10 | .05 |
| ❑ 404 | Henry Rodriguez | .10 | .05 |
| ❑ 405 | Ryan Klesko | .40 | .18 |

## 1993 Select Rookie/Traded

| | MINT | NRMT |
|---|---|---|
| COMPLETE SET (150) | 15.00 | 6.75 |

| Card | Player | Mint | NRMT |
|---|---|---|---|
| ❑ 1T | Rickey Henderson | 1.50 | .70 |
| ❑ 2T | Rob Deer | .30 | .14 |
| ❑ 3T | Tim Belcher | .30 | .14 |
| ❑ 4T | Gary Sheffield | 1.25 | .55 |
| ❑ 5T | Fred McGriff | .75 | .35 |
| ❑ 6T | Mark Whiten | .30 | .14 |
| ❑ 7T | Jeff Russell | .30 | .14 |
| ❑ 8T | Harold Baines | .50 | .23 |
| ❑ 9T | Dave Winfield | 1.25 | .55 |
| ❑ 10T | Ellis Burks | .50 | .23 |
| ❑ 11T | Andre Dawson | .75 | .35 |
| ❑ 12T | Gregg Jefferies | .30 | .14 |
| ❑ 13T | Jimmy Key | .50 | .23 |
| ❑ 14T | Harold Reynolds | .30 | .14 |
| ❑ 15T | Tom Henke | .30 | .14 |
| ❑ 16T | Paul Molitor | 1.25 | .55 |
| ❑ 17T | Wade Boggs | 1.50 | .70 |
| ❑ 18T | David Cone | .50 | .23 |
| ❑ 19T | Tony Fernandez | .30 | .14 |
| ❑ 20T | Roberto Kelly | .30 | .14 |
| ❑ 21T | Paul O'Neill | .50 | .23 |
| ❑ 22T | Jose Lind | .30 | .14 |
| ❑ 23T | Barry Bonds | 2.00 | .90 |
| ❑ 24T | Dave Stewart | .50 | .23 |
| ❑ 25T | Randy Myers | .50 | .23 |
| ❑ 26T | Benito Santiago | .30 | .14 |
| ❑ 27T | Tim Wallach | .30 | .14 |
| ❑ 28T | Greg Gagne | .30 | .14 |
| ❑ 29T | Kevin Mitchell | .50 | .23 |
| ❑ 30T | Jim Abbott | .50 | .23 |
| ❑ 31T | Lee Smith | .50 | .23 |
| ❑ 32T | Bobby Munoz | .30 | .14 |
| ❑ 33T | Mo Sanford | .30 | .14 |
| ❑ 34T | John Roper | .30 | .14 |
| ❑ 35T | David Hulse RC | .30 | .14 |
| ❑ 36T | Pedro Martinez | 3.00 | 1.35 |
| ❑ 37T | Chuck Carr | .30 | .14 |
| ❑ 38T | Armando Reynoso | .30 | .14 |
| ❑ 39T | Ryan Thompson | .30 | .14 |
| ❑ 40T | Carlos Garcia | .30 | .14 |
| ❑ 41T | Matt Whiteside RC | .30 | .14 |
| ❑ 42T | Benji Gil | .30 | .14 |
| ❑ 43T | Rodney Bolton | .30 | .14 |
| ❑ 44T | J.T. Snow | 1.25 | .55 |
| ❑ 45T | David McCarty | .30 | .14 |
| ❑ 46T | Paul Quantrill | .30 | .14 |
| ❑ 47T | Al Martin | .30 | .14 |
| ❑ 48T | Lance Painter RC | .30 | .14 |
| ❑ 49T | Lou Frazier RC | .30 | .14 |
| ❑ 50T | Eduardo Perez | .30 | .14 |
| ❑ 51T | Kevin Young | .50 | .23 |
| ❑ 52T | Mike Trombley | .30 | .14 |
| ❑ 53T | Sterling Hitchcock RC | 2.00 | .90 |
| ❑ 54T | Tim Bogar RC | .30 | .14 |
| ❑ 55T | Hilly Hathaway RC | .30 | .14 |
| ❑ 56T | Wayne Kirby | .30 | .14 |
| ❑ 57T | Craig Paquette | .30 | .14 |
| ❑ 58T | Bret Boone | .50 | .23 |
| ❑ 59T | Greg McMichael RC | .30 | .14 |
| ❑ 60T | Mike Lansing RC | .50 | .23 |
| ❑ 61T | Brent Gates | .30 | .14 |
| ❑ 62T | Rene Arocha RC | .30 | .14 |
| ❑ 63T | Ricky Gutierrez | .30 | .14 |
| ❑ 64T | Kevin Rogers | .30 | .14 |
| ❑ 65T | Ken Ryan RC | .30 | .14 |
| ❑ 66T | Phil Hiatt | .30 | .14 |
| ❑ 67T | Pat Meares RC | .30 | .14 |
| ❑ 68T | Troy Neel | .30 | .14 |
| ❑ 69T | Steve Cooke | .30 | .14 |
| ❑ 70T | Sherman Obando RC | .30 | .14 |
| ❑ 71T | Blas Minor | .30 | .14 |
| ❑ 72T | Angel Miranda | .30 | .14 |
| ❑ 73T | Tom Kramer RC | .30 | .14 |
| ❑ 74T | Chip Hale | .30 | .14 |
| ❑ 75T | Brad Pennington | .30 | .14 |
| ❑ 76T | Graeme Lloyd RC | .30 | .14 |
| ❑ 77T | Darrell Whitmore RC | .30 | .14 |
| ❑ 78T | David Nied | .30 | .14 |
| ❑ 79T | Todd Van Poppel | .30 | .14 |
| ❑ 80T | Chris Gomez RC | .50 | .23 |
| ❑ 81T | Jason Bere | .30 | .14 |
| ❑ 82T | Jeffrey Hammonds | .50 | .23 |
| ❑ 83T | Brad Ausmus | .30 | .14 |
| ❑ 84T | Kevin Stocker | .30 | .14 |
| ❑ 85T | Jeromy Burnitz | .50 | .23 |
| ❑ 86T | Aaron Sele | 1.25 | .55 |
| ❑ 87T | Roberto Mejia RC | .30 | .14 |
| ❑ 88T | Kirk Rueter RC | 1.00 | .45 |
| ❑ 89T | Kevin Roberson RC | .30 | .14 |
| ❑ 90T | Allen Watson | .30 | .14 |
| ❑ 91T | Charlie Leibrandt | .30 | .14 |
| ❑ 92T | Eric Davis | .50 | .23 |
| ❑ 93T | Jody Reed | .30 | .14 |
| ❑ 94T | Danny Jackson | .30 | .14 |
| ❑ 95T | Gary Gaetti | .50 | .23 |
| ❑ 96T | Norm Charlton | .30 | .14 |
| ❑ 97T | Doug Drabek | .30 | .14 |
| ❑ 98T | Scott Fletcher | .30 | .14 |
| ❑ 99T | Greg Swindell | .30 | .14 |
| ❑ 100T | John Smiley | .30 | .14 |
| ❑ 101T | Kevin Reimer | .30 | .14 |
| ❑ 102T | Andres Galarraga | .75 | .35 |
| ❑ 103T | Greg Hibbard | .30 | .14 |
| ❑ 104T | Chris Hammond | .30 | .14 |
| ❑ 105T | Darnell Coles | .30 | .14 |
| ❑ 106T | Mike Felder | .30 | .14 |
| ❑ 107T | Jose Guzman | .30 | .14 |
| ❑ 108T | Chris Bosio | .30 | .14 |
| ❑ 109T | Spike Owen | .30 | .14 |
| ❑ 110T | Felix Jose | .30 | .14 |
| ❑ 111T | Cory Snyder | .30 | .14 |
| ❑ 112T | Craig Lefferts | .30 | .14 |
| ❑ 113T | David Wells | .50 | .23 |
| ❑ 114T | Pete Incaviglia | .30 | .14 |
| ❑ 115T | Mike Pagliarulo | .30 | .14 |
| ❑ 116T | Dave Magadan | .30 | .14 |
| ❑ 117T | Charlie Hough | .50 | .23 |
| ❑ 118T | Ivan Calderon | .30 | .14 |
| ❑ 119T | Manuel Lee | .30 | .14 |
| ❑ 120T | Bob Patterson | .30 | .14 |
| ❑ 121T | Bob Ojeda | .30 | .14 |
| ❑ 122T | Scott Bankhead | .30 | .14 |
| ❑ 123T | Greg Maddux | 3.00 | 1.35 |
| ❑ 124T | Chili Davis | .50 | .23 |
| ❑ 125T | Milt Thompson | .30 | .14 |
| ❑ 126T | Dave Martinez | .30 | .14 |
| ❑ 127T | Frank Tanana | .30 | .14 |
| ❑ 128T | Phil Plantier | .30 | .14 |
| ❑ 129T | Juan Samuel | .30 | .14 |
| ❑ 130T | Eric Young | .30 | .14 |
| ❑ 131T | Joe Orsulak | .30 | .14 |
| ❑ 132T | Derek Bell | .30 | .14 |
| ❑ 133T | Darrin Jackson | .30 | .14 |
| ❑ 134T | Tom Brunansky | .30 | .14 |
| ❑ 135T | Jeff Reardon | .50 | .23 |
| ❑ 136T | Kevin Higgins | .30 | .14 |
| ❑ 137T | Joel Johnston | .30 | .14 |
| ❑ 138T | Rick Trlicek | .30 | .14 |
| ❑ 139T | Richie Lewis RC | .30 | .14 |
| ❑ 140T | Jeff Gardner | .30 | .14 |
| ❑ 141T | Jack Voigt RC | .30 | .14 |
| ❑ 142T | Rod Correia RC | .30 | .14 |
| ❑ 143T | Billy Brewer | .30 | .14 |
| ❑ 144T | Terry Jorgensen | .30 | .14 |
| ❑ 145T | Rich Amaral | .30 | .14 |
| ❑ 146T | Sean Berry | .30 | .14 |
| ❑ 147T | Dan Peltier | .30 | .14 |
| ❑ 148T | Paul Wagner | .30 | .14 |
| ❑ 149T | Damon Buford | .30 | .14 |
| ❑ 150T | Wil Cordero | .30 | .14 |
| ❑ NR1 | Nolan Ryan Tribute | 50.00 | 22.00 |
| ❑ ROY1 | Tim Salmon AL ROY | 6.00 | 2.70 |
| ❑ ROY2 | Mike Piazza NL ROY | 40.00 | 18.00 |

## 1994 Select

| | MINT | NRMT |
|---|---|---|
| COMPLETE SET (420) | 25.00 | 11.00 |
| COMPLETE SERIES 1 (210) | 15.00 | 6.75 |
| COMPLETE SERIES 2 (210) | 10.00 | 4.50 |

| Card | Player | Mint | NRMT |
|---|---|---|---|
| ❑ 1 | Ken Griffey Jr. | 2.50 | 1.10 |
| ❑ 2 | Greg Maddux | 1.50 | .70 |
| ❑ 3 | Paul Molitor | .60 | .25 |
| ❑ 4 | Mike Piazza | 2.00 | .90 |

| | No. | Player | Price | Price |
|---|---|---|---|---|
| ❑ | 5 | Jay Bell | .30 | .14 |
| ❑ | 6 | Frank Thomas | 1.25 | .55 |
| ❑ | 7 | Barry Larkin | .60 | .25 |
| ❑ | 8 | Paul O'Neill | .30 | .14 |
| ❑ | 9 | Darren Daulton | .30 | .14 |
| ❑ | 10 | Mike Greenwell | .15 | .07 |
| ❑ | 11 | Chuck Carr | .15 | .07 |
| ❑ | 12 | Joe Carter | .30 | .14 |
| ❑ | 13 | Lance Johnson | .15 | .07 |
| ❑ | 14 | Jeff Blauser | .15 | .07 |
| ❑ | 15 | Chris Hoiles | .15 | .07 |
| ❑ | 16 | Rick Wilkins | .15 | .07 |
| ❑ | 17 | Kirby Puckett | 1.50 | .70 |
| ❑ | 18 | Larry Walker | .30 | .14 |
| ❑ | 19 | Randy Johnson | .75 | .35 |
| ❑ | 20 | Bernard Gilkey | .15 | .07 |
| ❑ | 21 | Devon White | .15 | .07 |
| ❑ | 22 | Randy Myers | .15 | .07 |
| ❑ | 23 | Don Mattingly | 1.50 | .70 |
| ❑ | 24 | John Kruk | .30 | .14 |
| ❑ | 25 | Ozzie Guillen | .15 | .07 |
| ❑ | 26 | Jeff Conine | .15 | .07 |
| ❑ | 27 | Mike Macfarlane | .15 | .07 |
| ❑ | 28 | Dave Hollins | .15 | .07 |
| ❑ | 29 | Chuck Knoblauch | .30 | .14 |
| ❑ | 30 | Ozzie Smith | .75 | .35 |
| ❑ | 31 | Harold Baines | .30 | .14 |
| ❑ | 32 | Ryne Sandberg | .75 | .35 |
| ❑ | 33 | Ron Karkovice | .15 | .07 |
| ❑ | 34 | Terry Pendleton | .30 | .14 |
| ❑ | 35 | Wally Joyner | .30 | .14 |
| ❑ | 36 | Mike Mussina | .60 | .25 |
| ❑ | 37 | Felix Jose | .15 | .07 |
| ❑ | 38 | Derrick May | .15 | .07 |
| ❑ | 39 | Scott Cooper | .15 | .07 |
| ❑ | 40 | Jose Rijo | .15 | .07 |
| ❑ | 41 | Robin Ventura | .30 | .14 |
| ❑ | 42 | Charlie Hayes | .15 | .07 |
| ❑ | 43 | Jimmy Key | .30 | .14 |
| ❑ | 44 | Eric Karros | .30 | .14 |
| ❑ | 45 | Ruben Sierra | .15 | .07 |
| ❑ | 46 | Ryan Thompson | .15 | .07 |
| ❑ | 47 | Brian McRae | .15 | .07 |
| ❑ | 48 | Pat Hentgen | .15 | .07 |
| ❑ | 49 | John Valentin | .15 | .07 |
| ❑ | 50 | Al Martin | .15 | .07 |
| ❑ | 51 | Jose Lind | .15 | .07 |
| ❑ | 52 | Kevin Stocker | .15 | .07 |
| ❑ | 53 | Mike Gallego | .15 | .07 |
| ❑ | 54 | Dwight Gooden | .30 | .14 |
| ❑ | 55 | Brady Anderson | .30 | .14 |
| ❑ | 56 | Jeff King | .15 | .07 |
| ❑ | 57 | Mark McGwire | 2.50 | 1.10 |
| ❑ | 58 | Sammy Sosa | 1.25 | .55 |
| ❑ | 59 | Ryan Bowen | .15 | .07 |
| ❑ | 60 | Mark Lemke | .15 | .07 |
| ❑ | 61 | Roger Clemens | 1.25 | .55 |
| ❑ | 62 | Brian Jordan | .30 | .14 |
| ❑ | 63 | Andres Galarraga | .30 | .14 |
| ❑ | 64 | Kevin Appier | .30 | .14 |
| ❑ | 65 | Don Slaught | .15 | .07 |
| ❑ | 66 | Mike Blowers | .15 | .07 |
| ❑ | 67 | Wes Chamberlain | .15 | .07 |
| ❑ | 68 | Troy Neel | .15 | .07 |
| ❑ | 69 | John Wetteland | .30 | .14 |
| ❑ | 70 | Joe Girardi | .15 | .07 |
| ❑ | 71 | Reggie Sanders | .15 | .07 |
| ❑ | 72 | Edgar Martinez | .30 | .14 |
| ❑ | 73 | Todd Hundley | .15 | .07 |
| ❑ | 74 | Pat Borders | .15 | .07 |
| ❑ | 75 | Roberto Mejia | .15 | .07 |
| ❑ | 76 | David Cone | .30 | .14 |
| ❑ | 77 | Tony Gwynn | 1.25 | .55 |
| ❑ | 78 | Jim Abbott | .30 | .14 |
| ❑ | 79 | Jay Buhner | .30 | .14 |
| ❑ | 80 | Mark McLemore | .15 | .07 |
| ❑ | 81 | Wil Cordero | .15 | .07 |
| ❑ | 82 | Pedro Astacio | .15 | .07 |
| ❑ | 83 | Bob Tewksbury | .15 | .07 |
| ❑ | 84 | Dave Winfield | .60 | .25 |
| ❑ | 85 | Jeff Kent | .30 | .14 |
| ❑ | 86 | Todd Van Poppel | .15 | .07 |
| ❑ | 87 | Steve Avery | .15 | .07 |
| ❑ | 88 | Mike Lansing | .15 | .07 |
| ❑ | 89 | Lenny Dykstra | .30 | .14 |
| ❑ | 90 | Jose Guzman | .15 | .07 |
| ❑ | 91 | Brian R. Hunter | .15 | .07 |
| ❑ | 92 | Tim Raines | .30 | .14 |
| ❑ | 93 | Andre Dawson | .30 | .14 |
| ❑ | 94 | Joe Orsulak | .15 | .07 |
| ❑ | 95 | Ricky Jordan | .15 | .07 |
| ❑ | 96 | Billy Hatcher | .15 | .07 |
| ❑ | 97 | Jack McDowell | .15 | .07 |
| ❑ | 98 | Tom Pagnozzi | .15 | .07 |
| ❑ | 99 | Darryl Strawberry | .30 | .14 |
| ❑ | 100 | Mike Stanley | .15 | .07 |
| ❑ | 101 | Bret Saberhagen | .30 | .14 |
| ❑ | 102 | Willie Greene | .15 | .07 |
| ❑ | 103 | Bryan Harvey | .15 | .07 |
| ❑ | 104 | Tim Bogar | .15 | .07 |
| ❑ | 105 | Jack Voigt | .15 | .07 |
| ❑ | 106 | Brad Ausmus | .15 | .07 |
| ❑ | 107 | Ramon Martinez | .15 | .07 |
| ❑ | 108 | Mike Perez | .15 | .07 |
| ❑ | 109 | Jeff Montgomery | .15 | .07 |
| ❑ | 110 | Danny Darwin | .15 | .07 |
| ❑ | 111 | Wilson Alvarez | .15 | .07 |
| ❑ | 112 | Kevin Mitchell | .15 | .07 |
| ❑ | 113 | David Nied | .15 | .07 |
| ❑ | 114 | Rich Amaral | .15 | .07 |
| ❑ | 115 | Stan Javier | .15 | .07 |
| ❑ | 116 | Mo Vaughn | .30 | .14 |
| ❑ | 117 | Ben McDonald | .15 | .07 |
| ❑ | 118 | Tom Gordon | .15 | .07 |
| ❑ | 119 | Carlos Garcia | .15 | .07 |
| ❑ | 120 | Phil Plantier | .15 | .07 |
| ❑ | 121 | Mike Morgan | .15 | .07 |
| ❑ | 122 | Pat Meares | .15 | .07 |
| ❑ | 123 | Kevin Young | .15 | .07 |
| ❑ | 124 | Jeff Fassero | .15 | .07 |
| ❑ | 125 | Gene Harris | .15 | .07 |
| ❑ | 126 | Bob Welch | .15 | .07 |
| ❑ | 127 | Walt Weiss | .15 | .07 |
| ❑ | 128 | Bobby Witt | .15 | .07 |
| ❑ | 129 | Andy Van Slyke | .30 | .14 |
| ❑ | 130 | Steve Cooke | .15 | .07 |
| ❑ | 131 | Mike Devereaux | .15 | .07 |
| ❑ | 132 | Joey Cora | .15 | .07 |
| ❑ | 133 | Bret Barberie | .15 | .07 |
| ❑ | 134 | Orel Hershiser | .30 | .14 |
| ❑ | 135 | Ed Sprague | .15 | .07 |
| ❑ | 136 | Shawon Dunston | .15 | .07 |
| ❑ | 137 | Alex Arias | .15 | .07 |
| ❑ | 138 | Archi Cianfrocco | .15 | .07 |
| ❑ | 139 | Tim Wallach | .15 | .07 |
| ❑ | 140 | Bernie Williams | .60 | .25 |
| ❑ | 141 | Karl Rhodes | .15 | .07 |
| ❑ | 142 | Pat Kelly | .15 | .07 |
| ❑ | 143 | Dave Magadan | .15 | .07 |
| ❑ | 144 | Kevin Tapani | .15 | .07 |
| ❑ | 145 | Eric Young | .15 | .07 |
| ❑ | 146 | Derek Bell | .15 | .07 |
| ❑ | 147 | Dante Bichette | .30 | .14 |
| ❑ | 148 | Geronimo Pena | .15 | .07 |
| ❑ | 149 | Joe Oliver | .15 | .07 |
| ❑ | 150 | Orestes Destrade | .15 | .07 |
| ❑ | 151 | Tim Naehring | .15 | .07 |
| ❑ | 152 | Ray Lankford | .30 | .14 |
| ❑ | 153 | Phil Clark | .15 | .07 |
| ❑ | 154 | David McCarty | .15 | .07 |
| ❑ | 155 | Tommy Greene | .15 | .07 |
| ❑ | 156 | Wade Boggs | .75 | .35 |
| ❑ | 157 | Kevin Gross | .15 | .07 |
| ❑ | 158 | Hal Morris | .15 | .07 |
| ❑ | 159 | Moises Alou | .30 | .14 |
| ❑ | 160 | Rick Aguilera | .15 | .07 |
| ❑ | 161 | Curt Schilling | .30 | .14 |
| ❑ | 162 | Chip Hale | .15 | .07 |
| ❑ | 163 | Tino Martinez | .30 | .14 |
| ❑ | 164 | Mark Whiten | .15 | .07 |
| ❑ | 165 | Dave Stewart | .30 | .14 |
| ❑ | 166 | Steve Buechele | .15 | .07 |
| ❑ | 167 | Bobby Jones | .15 | .07 |
| ❑ | 168 | Darrin Fletcher | .15 | .07 |
| ❑ | 169 | John Smiley | .15 | .07 |
| ❑ | 170 | Cory Snyder | .15 | .07 |
| ❑ | 171 | Scott Erickson | .15 | .07 |
| ❑ | 172 | Kirk Rueter | .15 | .07 |
| ❑ | 173 | Dave Fleming | .15 | .07 |
| ❑ | 174 | John Smoltz | .30 | .14 |
| ❑ | 175 | Ricky Gutierrez | .15 | .07 |
| ❑ | 176 | Mike Bordick | .15 | .07 |
| ❑ | 177 | Chan Ho Park RC | .60 | .25 |
| ❑ | 178 | Alex Gonzalez | .15 | .07 |
| ❑ | 179 | Steve Karsay | .15 | .07 |
| ❑ | 180 | Jeffrey Hammonds | .30 | .14 |
| ❑ | 181 | Manny Ramirez | 1.00 | .45 |
| ❑ | 182 | Salomon Torres | .15 | .07 |
| ❑ | 183 | Raul Mondesi | .30 | .14 |
| ❑ | 184 | James Mouton | .15 | .07 |
| ❑ | 185 | Cliff Floyd | .30 | .14 |
| ❑ | 186 | Danny Bautista | .15 | .07 |
| ❑ | 187 | Kurt Abbott RC | .15 | .07 |
| ❑ | 188 | Javier Lopez | .30 | .14 |
| ❑ | 189 | John Patterson | .15 | .07 |
| ❑ | 190 | Greg Blosser | .15 | .07 |
| ❑ | 191 | Bob Hamelin | .15 | .07 |
| ❑ | 192 | Tony Eusebio | .15 | .07 |
| ❑ | 193 | Carlos Delgado | 1.00 | .45 |
| ❑ | 194 | Chris Gomez | .15 | .07 |
| ❑ | 195 | Kelly Stinnett RC | .15 | .07 |
| ❑ | 196 | Shane Reynolds | .15 | .07 |
| ❑ | 197 | Ryan Klesko | .30 | .14 |
| ❑ | 198 | Jim Edmonds UER (Mark Dalesandro pictured on front) | .75 | .35 |
| ❑ | 199 | James Hurst RC | .15 | .07 |
| ❑ | 200 | Dave Staton | .15 | .07 |
| ❑ | 201 | Rondell White | .30 | .14 |
| ❑ | 202 | Keith Mitchell | .15 | .07 |
| ❑ | 203 | Darren Oliver RC | .30 | .14 |
| ❑ | 204 | Mike Matheny RC | .15 | .07 |
| ❑ | 205 | Chris Turner | .15 | .07 |
| ❑ | 206 | Matt Mieske | .15 | .07 |
| ❑ | 207 | NL Team Checklist | .15 | .07 |
| ❑ | 208 | NL Team Checklist | .15 | .07 |
| ❑ | 209 | AL Team Checklist | .15 | .07 |
| ❑ | 210 | AL Team Checklist | .15 | .07 |
| ❑ | 211 | Barry Bonds | 1.00 | .45 |
| ❑ | 212 | Juan Gonzalez | .60 | .25 |
| ❑ | 213 | Jim Eisenreich | .15 | .07 |
| ❑ | 214 | Ivan Rodriguez | .75 | .35 |
| ❑ | 215 | Tony Phillips | .15 | .07 |
| ❑ | 216 | John Jaha | .15 | .07 |
| ❑ | 217 | Lee Smith | .30 | .14 |
| ❑ | 218 | Bip Roberts | .15 | .07 |
| ❑ | 219 | Dave Hansen | .15 | .07 |
| ❑ | 220 | Pat Listach | .15 | .07 |
| ❑ | 221 | Willie McGee | .30 | .14 |
| ❑ | 222 | Damion Easley | .15 | .07 |
| ❑ | 223 | Dean Palmer | .30 | .14 |
| ❑ | 224 | Mike Moore | .15 | .07 |
| ❑ | 225 | Brian Harper | .15 | .07 |
| ❑ | 226 | Gary DiSarcina | .15 | .07 |
| ❑ | 227 | Delino DeShields | .15 | .07 |
| ❑ | 228 | Otis Nixon | .15 | .07 |
| ❑ | 229 | Roberto Alomar | .60 | .25 |
| ❑ | 230 | Mark Grace | .60 | .25 |
| ❑ | 231 | Kenny Lofton | .30 | .14 |
| ❑ | 232 | Gregg Jefferies | .15 | .07 |
| ❑ | 233 | Cecil Fielder | .30 | .14 |
| ❑ | 234 | Jeff Bagwell | .75 | .35 |
| ❑ | 235 | Albert Belle | .30 | .14 |
| ❑ | 236 | Dave Justice | .30 | .14 |
| ❑ | 237 | Tom Henke | .15 | .07 |
| ❑ | 238 | Bobby Bonilla | .30 | .14 |
| ❑ | 239 | John Olerud | .30 | .14 |
| ❑ | 240 | Robby Thompson | .15 | .07 |
| ❑ | 241 | Dave Valle | .15 | .07 |
| ❑ | 242 | Marquis Grissom | .15 | .07 |
| ❑ | 243 | Greg Swindell | .15 | .07 |
| ❑ | 244 | Todd Zeile | .15 | .07 |
| ❑ | 245 | Dennis Eckersley | .30 | .14 |
| ❑ | 246 | Jose Offerman | .15 | .07 |
| ❑ | 247 | Greg McMichael | .15 | .07 |
| ❑ | 248 | Tim Belcher | .15 | .07 |
| ❑ | 249 | Cal Ripken Jr. | 2.50 | 1.10 |
| ❑ | 250 | Tom Glavine | .60 | .25 |
| ❑ | 251 | Luis Polonia | .15 | .07 |
| ❑ | 252 | Bill Swift | .15 | .07 |
| ❑ | 253 | Juan Guzman | .15 | .07 |
| ❑ | 254 | Rickey Henderson | .75 | .35 |
| ❑ | 255 | Terry Mulholland | .15 | .07 |
| ❑ | 256 | Gary Sheffield | .60 | .25 |
| ❑ | 257 | Terry Steinbach | .15 | .07 |
| ❑ | 258 | Brett Butler | .30 | .14 |
| ❑ | 259 | Jason Bere | .15 | .07 |
| ❑ | 260 | Doug Strange | .15 | .07 |
| ❑ | 261 | Kent Hrbek | .30 | .14 |

| | | |
|---|---|---|
| ❑ 262 Graeme Lloyd | .15 | .07 |
| ❑ 263 Lou Frazier | .15 | .07 |
| ❑ 264 Charles Nagy | .15 | .07 |
| ❑ 265 Bret Boone | .30 | .14 |
| ❑ 266 Kirk Gibson | .30 | .14 |
| ❑ 267 Kevin Brown | .30 | .14 |
| ❑ 268 Fred McGriff | .30 | .14 |
| ❑ 269 Matt Williams | .30 | .14 |
| ❑ 270 Greg Gagne | .15 | .07 |
| ❑ 271 Mariano Duncan | .15 | .07 |
| ❑ 272 Jeff Russell | .15 | .07 |
| ❑ 273 Eric Davis | .30 | .14 |
| ❑ 274 Shane Mack | .15 | .07 |
| ❑ 275 Jose Vizcaino | .15 | .07 |
| ❑ 276 Jose Canseco | .75 | .35 |
| ❑ 277 Roberto Hernandez | .15 | .07 |
| ❑ 278 Royce Clayton | .15 | .07 |
| ❑ 279 Carlos Baerga | .15 | .07 |
| ❑ 280 Pete Incaviglia | .15 | .07 |
| ❑ 281 Brent Gates | .15 | .07 |
| ❑ 282 Jeromy Burnitz | .30 | .14 |
| ❑ 283 Chili Davis | .30 | .14 |
| ❑ 284 Pete Harnisch | .15 | .07 |
| ❑ 285 Alan Trammell | .30 | .14 |
| ❑ 286 Eric Anthony | .15 | .07 |
| ❑ 287 Ellis Burks | .30 | .14 |
| ❑ 288 Julio Franco | .15 | .07 |
| ❑ 289 Jack Morris | .30 | .14 |
| ❑ 290 Erik Hanson | .15 | .07 |
| ❑ 291 Chuck Finley | .30 | .14 |
| ❑ 292 Reggie Jefferson | .15 | .07 |
| ❑ 293 Kevin McReynolds | .15 | .07 |
| ❑ 294 Greg Hibbard | .15 | .07 |
| ❑ 295 Travis Fryman | .30 | .14 |
| ❑ 296 Craig Biggio | .30 | .14 |
| ❑ 297 Kenny Rogers | .15 | .07 |
| ❑ 298 Dave Henderson | .15 | .07 |
| ❑ 299 Jim Thome | .30 | .14 |
| ❑ 300 Rene Arocha | .15 | .07 |
| ❑ 301 Pedro Munoz | .15 | .07 |
| ❑ 302 David Hulse | .15 | .07 |
| ❑ 303 Greg Vaughn | .30 | .14 |
| ❑ 304 Darren Lewis | .15 | .07 |
| ❑ 305 Deion Sanders | .30 | .14 |
| ❑ 306 Danny Tartabull | .15 | .07 |
| ❑ 307 Darryl Hamilton | .15 | .07 |
| ❑ 308 Andujar Cedeno | .15 | .07 |
| ❑ 309 Tim Salmon | .30 | .14 |
| ❑ 310 Tony Fernandez | .15 | .07 |
| ❑ 311 Alex Fernandez | .15 | .07 |
| ❑ 312 Roberto Kelly | .15 | .07 |
| ❑ 313 Harold Reynolds | .15 | .07 |
| ❑ 314 Chris Sabo | .15 | .07 |
| ❑ 315 Howard Johnson | .15 | .07 |
| ❑ 316 Mark Portugal | .15 | .07 |
| ❑ 317 Rafael Palmeiro | .60 | .25 |
| ❑ 318 Pete Smith | .15 | .07 |
| ❑ 319 Will Clark | .60 | .25 |
| ❑ 320 Henry Rodriguez | .15 | .07 |
| ❑ 321 Omar Vizquel | .30 | .14 |
| ❑ 322 David Segui | .15 | .07 |
| ❑ 323 Lou Whitaker | .30 | .14 |
| ❑ 324 Felix Fermin | .15 | .07 |
| ❑ 325 Spike Owen | .15 | .07 |
| ❑ 326 Darryl Kile | .30 | .14 |
| ❑ 327 Chad Kreuter | .15 | .07 |
| ❑ 328 Rod Beck | .15 | .07 |
| ❑ 329 Eddie Murray | .60 | .25 |
| ❑ 330 B.J. Surhoff | .30 | .14 |
| ❑ 331 Mickey Tettleton | .15 | .07 |
| ❑ 332 Pedro Martinez | 1.00 | .45 |
| ❑ 333 Roger Pavlik | .15 | .07 |
| ❑ 334 Eddie Taubensee | .15 | .07 |
| ❑ 335 John Doherty | .15 | .07 |
| ❑ 336 Jody Reed | .15 | .07 |
| ❑ 337 Aaron Sele | .30 | .14 |
| ❑ 338 Leo Gomez | .15 | .07 |
| ❑ 339 Dave Nilsson | .15 | .07 |
| ❑ 340 Rob Dibble | .15 | .07 |
| ❑ 341 John Burkett | .15 | .07 |
| ❑ 342 Wayne Kirby | .15 | .07 |
| ❑ 343 Dan Wilson | .15 | .07 |
| ❑ 344 Armando Reynoso | .15 | .07 |
| ❑ 345 Chad Curtis | .15 | .07 |
| ❑ 346 Dennis Martinez | .30 | .14 |
| ❑ 347 Cal Eldred | .15 | .07 |
| ❑ 348 Luis Gonzalez | .30 | .14 |
| ❑ 349 Doug Drabek | .15 | .07 |
| ❑ 350 Jim Leyritz | .15 | .07 |
| ❑ 351 Mark Langston | .15 | .07 |
| ❑ 352 Darrin Jackson | .15 | .07 |
| ❑ 353 Sid Fernandez | .15 | .07 |
| ❑ 354 Benito Santiago | .15 | .07 |
| ❑ 355 Kevin Seitzer | .15 | .07 |
| ❑ 356 Bo Jackson | .30 | .14 |
| ❑ 357 David Wells | .30 | .14 |
| ❑ 358 Paul Sorrento | .15 | .07 |
| ❑ 359 Ken Caminiti | .30 | .14 |
| ❑ 360 Eduardo Perez | .15 | .07 |
| ❑ 361 Orlando Merced | .15 | .07 |
| ❑ 362 Steve Finley | .30 | .14 |
| ❑ 363 Andy Benes | .15 | .07 |
| ❑ 364 Manuel Lee | .15 | .07 |
| ❑ 365 Todd Benzinger | .15 | .07 |
| ❑ 366 Sandy Alomar Jr. | .30 | .14 |
| ❑ 367 Rex Hudler | .15 | .07 |
| ❑ 368 Mike Henneman | .15 | .07 |
| ❑ 369 Vince Coleman | .15 | .07 |
| ❑ 370 Kirt Manwaring | .15 | .07 |
| ❑ 371 Ken Hill | .15 | .07 |
| ❑ 372 Glenallen Hill | .15 | .07 |
| ❑ 373 Sean Berry | .15 | .07 |
| ❑ 374 Geronimo Berroa | .15 | .07 |
| ❑ 375 Duane Ward | .15 | .07 |
| ❑ 376 Allen Watson | .15 | .07 |
| ❑ 377 Marc Newfield | .15 | .07 |
| ❑ 378 Dan Miceli | .15 | .07 |
| ❑ 379 Denny Hocking | .15 | .07 |
| ❑ 380 Mark Kiefer | .15 | .07 |
| ❑ 381 Tony Tarasco | .15 | .07 |
| ❑ 382 Tony Longmire | .15 | .07 |
| ❑ 383 Brian Anderson RC | .30 | .14 |
| ❑ 384 Fernando Vina | .15 | .07 |
| ❑ 385 Hector Carrasco | .15 | .07 |
| ❑ 386 Mike Kelly | .15 | .07 |
| ❑ 387 Greg Colbrunn | .15 | .07 |
| ❑ 388 Roger Salkeld | .15 | .07 |
| ❑ 389 Steve Trachsel | .15 | .07 |
| ❑ 390 Rich Becker | .15 | .07 |
| ❑ 391 Billy Taylor RC | .15 | .07 |
| ❑ 392 Rich Rowland | .15 | .07 |
| ❑ 393 Carl Everett | .30 | .14 |
| ❑ 394 Johnny Ruffin | .15 | .07 |
| ❑ 395 Keith Lockhart RC | .15 | .07 |
| ❑ 396 J.R. Phillips | .15 | .07 |
| ❑ 397 Sterling Hitchcock | .15 | .07 |
| ❑ 398 Jorge Fabregas | .15 | .07 |
| ❑ 399 Jeff Granger | .15 | .07 |
| ❑ 400 Eddie Zambrano RC | .15 | .07 |
| ❑ 401 Rikkert Faneyte RC | .15 | .07 |
| ❑ 402 Gerald Williams | .15 | .07 |
| ❑ 403 Joey Hamilton | .15 | .07 |
| ❑ 404 Joe Hall RC | .15 | .07 |
| ❑ 405 John Hudek RC | .15 | .07 |
| ❑ 406 Roberto Petagine | .15 | .07 |
| ❑ 407 Charles Johnson | .30 | .14 |
| ❑ 408 Mark Smith | .15 | .07 |
| ❑ 409 Jeff Juden | .15 | .07 |
| ❑ 410 Carlos Pulido RC | .15 | .07 |
| ❑ 411 Paul Shuey | .15 | .07 |
| ❑ 412 Rob Butler | .15 | .07 |
| ❑ 413 Mark Acre RC | .15 | .07 |
| ❑ 414 Greg Pirkl | .15 | .07 |
| ❑ 415 Melvin Nieves | .15 | .07 |
| ❑ 416 Tim Hyers RC | .15 | .07 |
| ❑ 417 NL Checklist | .15 | .07 |
| ❑ 418 NL Checklist | .15 | .07 |
| ❑ 419 AL Checklist | .15 | .07 |
| ❑ 420 AL Checklist | .15 | .07 |
| ❑ RY1 Carlos Delgado | 6.00 | 2.70 |
| ❑ SS1 Cal Ripken Jr. Salute | 20.00 | 9.00 |
| ❑ SS2 Dave Winfield Salute | 4.00 | 1.80 |
| ❑ MVP1 Paul Molitor | 5.00 | 2.20 |

# 1995 Select

| | MINT | NRMT |
|---|---|---|
| COMPLETE SET (250) | 15.00 | 6.75 |
| COMMON CARD (1-250) | .10 | .05 |

| | | |
|---|---|---|
| ❑ 1 Cal Ripken Jr. | 1.50 | .70 |
| ❑ 2 Robin Ventura | .15 | .07 |
| ❑ 3 Al Martin | .10 | .05 |
| ❑ 4 Jeff Frye | .10 | .05 |
| ❑ 5 Darryl Strawberry | .15 | .07 |
| ❑ 6 Chan Ho Park | .15 | .07 |
| ❑ 7 Steve Avery | .10 | .05 |
| ❑ 8 Bret Boone | .15 | .07 |
| ❑ 9 Danny Tartabull | .10 | .05 |
| ❑ 10 Dante Bichette | .15 | .07 |
| ❑ 11 Rondell White | .15 | .07 |
| ❑ 12 Dave McCarty | .10 | .05 |
| ❑ 13 Bernard Gilkey | .10 | .05 |
| ❑ 14 Mark McGwire | 1.50 | .70 |
| ❑ 15 Ruben Sierra | .10 | .05 |
| ❑ 16 Wade Boggs | .50 | .23 |
| ❑ 17 Mike Piazza | 1.25 | .55 |
| ❑ 18 Jeffrey Hammonds | .15 | .07 |
| ❑ 19 Mike Mussina | .40 | .18 |
| ❑ 20 Darryl Kile | .15 | .07 |
| ❑ 21 Greg Maddux | 1.00 | .45 |
| ❑ 22 Frank Thomas | .75 | .35 |
| ❑ 23 Kevin Appier | .15 | .07 |
| ❑ 24 Jay Bell | .15 | .07 |
| ❑ 25 Kirk Gibson | .15 | .07 |
| ❑ 26 Pat Hentgen | .10 | .05 |
| ❑ 27 Joey Hamilton | .10 | .05 |
| ❑ 28 Bernie Williams | .25 | .11 |
| ❑ 29 Aaron Sele | .15 | .07 |
| ❑ 30 Delino DeShields | .10 | .05 |
| ❑ 31 Danny Bautista | .10 | .05 |
| ❑ 32 Jim Thome | .25 | .11 |
| ❑ 33 Rikkert Faneyte | .10 | .05 |
| ❑ 34 Roberto Alomar | .40 | .18 |
| ❑ 35 Paul Molitor | .40 | .18 |
| ❑ 36 Allen Watson | .10 | .05 |
| ❑ 37 Jeff Bagwell | .50 | .23 |
| ❑ 38 Jay Buhner | .15 | .07 |
| ❑ 39 Marquis Grissom | .10 | .05 |
| ❑ 40 Jim Edmonds | .40 | .18 |
| ❑ 41 Ryan Klesko | .15 | .07 |
| ❑ 42 Fred McGriff | .25 | .11 |
| ❑ 43 Tony Tarasco | .10 | .05 |
| ❑ 44 Darren Daulton | .15 | .07 |
| ❑ 45 Marc Newfield | .10 | .05 |
| ❑ 46 Barry Bonds | .60 | .25 |
| ❑ 47 Bobby Bonilla | .15 | .07 |
| ❑ 48 Greg Pirkl | .10 | .05 |
| ❑ 49 Steve Karsay | .10 | .05 |
| ❑ 50 Bob Hamelin | .10 | .05 |
| ❑ 51 Javier Lopez | .15 | .07 |
| ❑ 52 Barry Larkin | .40 | .18 |
| ❑ 53 Kevin Young | .10 | .05 |
| ❑ 54 Sterling Hitchcock | .10 | .05 |
| ❑ 55 Tom Glavine | .40 | .18 |
| ❑ 56 Carlos Delgado | .40 | .18 |
| ❑ 57 Darren Oliver | .10 | .05 |
| ❑ 58 Cliff Floyd | .15 | .07 |
| ❑ 59 Tim Salmon | .15 | .07 |
| ❑ 60 Albert Belle | .15 | .07 |
| ❑ 61 Salomon Torres | .10 | .05 |
| ❑ 62 Gary Sheffield | .40 | .18 |
| ❑ 63 Ivan Rodriguez | .50 | .23 |
| ❑ 64 Charles Nagy | .10 | .05 |
| ❑ 65 Eduardo Perez | .10 | .05 |
| ❑ 66 Terry Steinbach | .10 | .05 |
| ❑ 67 Dave Justice | .25 | .11 |
| ❑ 68 Jason Bere | .10 | .05 |

| No. | Player | MINT | NRMT |
|---|---|---|---|
| 69 | Dave Nilsson | .10 | .05 |
| 70 | Brian Anderson | .10 | .05 |
| 71 | Billy Ashley | .10 | .05 |
| 72 | Roger Clemens | .75 | .35 |
| 73 | Jimmy Key | .15 | .07 |
| 74 | Wally Joyner | .15 | .07 |
| 75 | Andy Benes | .10 | .05 |
| 76 | Ray Lankford | .15 | .07 |
| 77 | Jeff Kent | .25 | .11 |
| 78 | Moises Alou | .15 | .07 |
| 79 | Kirby Puckett | 1.00 | .45 |
| 80 | Joe Carter | .15 | .07 |
| 81 | Manny Ramirez | .50 | .23 |
| 82 | J.R. Phillips | .10 | .05 |
| 83 | Matt Mieske | .10 | .05 |
| 84 | John Olerud | .15 | .07 |
| 85 | Andres Galarraga | .25 | .11 |
| 86 | Juan Gonzalez | .40 | .18 |
| 87 | Pedro Martinez | .50 | .23 |
| 88 | Dean Palmer | .15 | .07 |
| 89 | Ken Griffey Jr. | 1.50 | .70 |
| 90 | Brian Jordan | .15 | .07 |
| 91 | Hal Morris | .10 | .05 |
| 92 | Lenny Dykstra | .15 | .07 |
| 93 | Wil Cordero | .10 | .05 |
| 94 | Tony Gwynn | .75 | .35 |
| 95 | Alex Gonzalez | .10 | .05 |
| 96 | Cecil Fielder | .15 | .07 |
| 97 | Mo Vaughn | .15 | .07 |
| 98 | John Valentin | .10 | .05 |
| 99 | Will Clark | .40 | .18 |
| 100 | Geronimo Pena | .10 | .05 |
| 101 | Don Mattingly | 1.00 | .45 |
| 102 | Charles Johnson | .15 | .07 |
| 103 | Raul Mondesi | .15 | .07 |
| 104 | Reggie Sanders | .10 | .05 |
| 105 | Royce Clayton | .10 | .05 |
| 106 | Reggie Jefferson | .10 | .05 |
| 107 | Craig Biggio | .25 | .11 |
| 108 | Jack McDowell | .10 | .05 |
| 109 | James Mouton | .10 | .05 |
| 110 | Mike Greenwell | .10 | .05 |
| 111 | David Cone | .15 | .07 |
| 112 | Matt Williams | .25 | .11 |
| 113 | Garret Anderson | .15 | .07 |
| 114 | Carlos Garcia | .10 | .05 |
| 115 | Alex Fernandez | .10 | .05 |
| 116 | Deion Sanders | .15 | .07 |
| 117 | Chili Davis | .15 | .07 |
| 118 | Mike Kelly | .10 | .05 |
| 119 | Jeff Conine | .10 | .05 |
| 120 | Kenny Lofton | .15 | .07 |
| 121 | Rafael Palmeiro | .40 | .18 |
| 122 | Chuck Knoblauch | .15 | .07 |
| 123 | Ozzie Smith | .50 | .23 |
| 124 | Carlos Baerga | .10 | .05 |
| 125 | Brett Butler | .15 | .07 |
| 126 | Sammy Sosa | .75 | .35 |
| 127 | Ellis Burks | .15 | .07 |
| 128 | Bret Saberhagen | .15 | .07 |
| 129 | Doug Drabek | .10 | .05 |
| 130 | Dennis Martinez | .15 | .07 |
| 131 | Paul O'Neill | .15 | .07 |
| 132 | Travis Fryman | .15 | .07 |
| 133 | Brent Gates | .10 | .05 |
| 134 | Rickey Henderson | .50 | .23 |
| 135 | Randy Johnson | .50 | .23 |
| 136 | Mark Langston | .10 | .05 |
| 137 | Greg Colbrunn | .10 | .05 |
| 138 | Jose Rijo | .10 | .05 |
| 139 | Bryan Harvey | .10 | .05 |
| 140 | Dennis Eckersley | .15 | .07 |
| 141 | Ron Gant | .10 | .05 |
| 142 | Carl Everett | .15 | .07 |
| 143 | Jeff Granger | .10 | .05 |
| 144 | Ben McDonald | .10 | .05 |
| 145 | Kurt Abbott UER (Mariners logo on front) | .10 | .05 |
| 146 | Jim Abbott | .15 | .07 |
| 147 | Jason Jacome | .10 | .05 |
| 148 | Rico Brogna | .10 | .05 |
| 149 | Cal Eldred | .10 | .05 |
| 150 | Rich Becker | .10 | .05 |
| 151 | Pete Harnisch | .10 | .05 |
| 152 | Roberto Petagine | .10 | .05 |
| 153 | Jacob Brumfield | .10 | .05 |
| 154 | Todd Hundley | .10 | .05 |
| 155 | Roger Cedeno | .10 | .05 |
| 156 | Harold Baines | .15 | .07 |
| 157 | Steve Dunn | .10 | .05 |
| 158 | Tim Belk | .10 | .05 |
| 159 | Marty Cordova | .10 | .05 |
| 160 | Russ Davis | .10 | .05 |
| 161 | Jose Malave | .10 | .05 |
| 162 | Brian Hunter | .10 | .05 |
| 163 | Andy Pettitte | .25 | .11 |
| 164 | Brooks Kieschnick | .10 | .05 |
| 165 | Midre Cummings | .10 | .05 |
| 166 | Frank Rodriguez | .10 | .05 |
| 167 | Chad Mottola | .10 | .05 |
| 168 | Brian Barber | .10 | .05 |
| 169 | Tim Unroe RC | .10 | .05 |
| 170 | Shane Andrews | .10 | .05 |
| 171 | Kevin Flora | .10 | .05 |
| 172 | Ray Durham | .15 | .07 |
| 173 | Chipper Jones | 1.00 | .45 |
| 174 | Butch Huskey | .10 | .05 |
| 175 | Ray McDavid | .10 | .05 |
| 176 | Jeff Cirillo | .15 | .07 |
| 177 | Terry Pendleton | .15 | .07 |
| 178 | Scott Ruffcorn | .10 | .05 |
| 179 | Ray Holbert | .10 | .05 |
| 180 | Joe Randa | .10 | .05 |
| 181 | Jose Oliva | .10 | .05 |
| 182 | Andy Van Slyke | .15 | .07 |
| 183 | Albie Lopez | .10 | .05 |
| 184 | Chad Curtis | .10 | .05 |
| 185 | Ozzie Guillen | .10 | .05 |
| 186 | Chad Ogea | .10 | .05 |
| 187 | Dan Wilson | .10 | .05 |
| 188 | Tony Fernandez | .10 | .05 |
| 189 | John Smoltz | .15 | .07 |
| 190 | Willie Greene | .10 | .05 |
| 191 | Darren Lewis | .10 | .05 |
| 192 | Orlando Miller | .10 | .05 |
| 193 | Kurt Miller | .10 | .05 |
| 194 | Andrew Lorraine | .10 | .05 |
| 195 | Ernie Young | .10 | .05 |
| 196 | Jimmy Haynes | .10 | .05 |
| 197 | Raul Casanova RC | .10 | .05 |
| 198 | Joe Vitiello | .10 | .05 |
| 199 | Brad Woodall RC | .10 | .05 |
| 200 | Juan Acevedo RC | .10 | .05 |
| 201 | Michael Tucker | .10 | .05 |
| 202 | Shawn Green | .40 | .18 |
| 203 | Alex Rodriguez | 1.50 | .70 |
| 204 | Julian Tavarez | .10 | .05 |
| 205 | Jose Lima | .10 | .05 |
| 206 | Wilson Alvarez | .10 | .05 |
| 207 | Rich Aude | .10 | .05 |
| 208 | Armando Benitez | .15 | .07 |
| 209 | Dwayne Hosey | .10 | .05 |
| 210 | Gabe White | .10 | .05 |
| 211 | Joey Eischen | .10 | .05 |
| 212 | Bill Pulsipher | .10 | .05 |
| 213 | Robby Thompson | .10 | .05 |
| 214 | Toby Borland | .10 | .05 |
| 215 | Rusty Greer | .15 | .07 |
| 216 | Fausto Cruz | .10 | .05 |
| 217 | Luis Ortiz | .10 | .05 |
| 218 | Duane Singleton | .10 | .05 |
| 219 | Troy Percival | .10 | .05 |
| 220 | Gregg Jefferies | .10 | .05 |
| 221 | Mark Grace | .40 | .18 |
| 222 | Mickey Tettleton | .10 | .05 |
| 223 | Phil Plantier | .10 | .05 |
| 224 | Larry Walker | .15 | .07 |
| 225 | Ken Caminiti | .15 | .07 |
| 226 | Dave Winfield | .40 | .18 |
| 227 | Brady Anderson | .15 | .07 |
| 228 | Kevin Brown | .15 | .07 |
| 229 | Andujar Cedeno | .10 | .05 |
| 230 | Roberto Kelly | .10 | .05 |
| 231 | Jose Canseco | .50 | .23 |
| 232 | Scott Ruffcorn ST | .10 | .05 |
| 233 | Billy Ashley ST | .10 | .05 |
| 234 | J.R. Phillips ST | .10 | .05 |
| 235 | Chipper Jones ST | .50 | .23 |
| 236 | Charles Johnson ST | .10 | .05 |
| 237 | Midre Cummings ST | .10 | .05 |
| 238 | Brian L.Hunter ST | .10 | .05 |
| 239 | Garret Anderson ST | .15 | .07 |
| 240 | Shawn Green ST | .15 | .07 |
| 241 | Alex Rodriguez ST | .75 | .35 |
| 242 | Frank Thomas CL | .40 | .18 |
| 243 | Ken Griffey Jr. CL | .75 | .35 |
| 244 | Albert Belle CL | .10 | .05 |
| 245 | Cal Ripken Jr. CL | .75 | .35 |
| 246 | Barry Bonds CL | .40 | .18 |
| 247 | Raul Mondesi CL | .15 | .07 |
| 248 | Mike Piazza CL | .60 | .25 |
| 249 | Jeff Bagwell CL | .25 | .11 |
| 250 | Jeff Bagwell, Ken Griffey Jr., Frank Thomas, Mike Piazza CL | .75 | .35 |
| 251S | Hideo Nomo | 1.00 | .45 |

## 1996 Select

| | MINT | NRMT |
|---|---|---|
| COMPLETE SET (200) | 15.00 | 6.75 |
| COMMON CARD (1-200) | .10 | .05 |

| No. | Player | MINT | NRMT |
|---|---|---|---|
| 1 | Wade Boggs | .50 | .23 |
| 2 | Shawn Green | .40 | .18 |
| 3 | Andres Galarraga | .25 | .11 |
| 4 | Bill Pulsipher | .10 | .05 |
| 5 | Chuck Knoblauch | .20 | .09 |
| 6 | Ken Griffey Jr. | 1.50 | .70 |
| 7 | Greg Maddux | 1.00 | .45 |
| 8 | Manny Ramirez | .50 | .23 |
| 9 | Ivan Rodriguez | .50 | .23 |
| 10 | Tim Salmon | .20 | .09 |
| 11 | Frank Thomas | .75 | .35 |
| 12 | Jeff Bagwell | .50 | .23 |
| 13 | Travis Fryman | .20 | .09 |
| 14 | Kenny Lofton | .20 | .09 |
| 15 | Matt Williams | .25 | .11 |
| 16 | Jay Bell | .20 | .09 |
| 17 | Ken Caminiti | .20 | .09 |
| 18 | Ray Lankford | .20 | .09 |
| 19 | Cal Ripken | 1.50 | .70 |
| 20 | Roger Clemens | .75 | .35 |
| 21 | Carlos Baerga | .10 | .05 |
| 22 | Mike Piazza | 1.25 | .55 |
| 23 | Gregg Jefferies | .10 | .05 |
| 24 | Reggie Sanders | .10 | .05 |
| 25 | Rondell White | .20 | .09 |
| 26 | Sammy Sosa | .75 | .35 |
| 27 | Kevin Appier | .20 | .09 |
| 28 | Kevin Seitzer | .10 | .05 |
| 29 | Gary Sheffield | .40 | .18 |
| 30 | Mike Mussina | .40 | .18 |
| 31 | Mark McGwire | 1.50 | .70 |
| 32 | Barry Larkin | .40 | .18 |
| 33 | Marc Newfield | .10 | .05 |
| 34 | Ismael Valdes | .10 | .05 |
| 35 | Marty Cordova | .10 | .05 |
| 36 | Albert Belle | .25 | .11 |
| 37 | Johnny Damon | .25 | .11 |
| 38 | Garret Anderson | .20 | .09 |
| 39 | Cecil Fielder | .20 | .09 |
| 40 | John Mabry | .10 | .05 |
| 41 | Chipper Jones | 1.00 | .45 |
| 42 | Omar Vizquel | .20 | .09 |
| 43 | Jose Rijo | .10 | .05 |
| 44 | Charles Johnson | .20 | .09 |
| 45 | Alex Rodriguez | 1.25 | .55 |
| 46 | Rico Brogna | .10 | .05 |

| Card | MINT | NRMT |
|---|---|---|
| ❑ 47 Joe Carter | .20 | .09 |
| ❑ 48 Mo Vaughn | .20 | .09 |
| ❑ 49 Moises Alou | .20 | .09 |
| ❑ 50 Raul Mondesi | .20 | .09 |
| ❑ 51 Robin Ventura | .20 | .09 |
| ❑ 52 Jim Thome | .25 | .11 |
| ❑ 53 David Justice | .25 | .11 |
| ❑ 54 Jeff King | .10 | .05 |
| ❑ 55 Brian L.Hunter | .10 | .05 |
| ❑ 56 Juan Gonzalez | .40 | .18 |
| ❑ 57 John Olerud | .20 | .09 |
| ❑ 58 Rafael Palmeiro | .40 | .18 |
| ❑ 59 Tony Gwynn | .75 | .35 |
| ❑ 60 Eddie Murray | .40 | .18 |
| ❑ 61 Jason Isringhausen | .20 | .09 |
| ❑ 62 Dante Bichette | .20 | .09 |
| ❑ 63 Randy Johnson | .50 | .23 |
| ❑ 64 Kirby Puckett | 1.00 | .45 |
| ❑ 65 Jim Edmonds | .40 | .18 |
| ❑ 66 David Cone | .20 | .09 |
| ❑ 67 Ozzie Smith | .50 | .23 |
| ❑ 68 Fred McGriff | .25 | .11 |
| ❑ 69 Darren Daulton | .20 | .09 |
| ❑ 70 Edgar Martinez | .25 | .11 |
| ❑ 71 J.T. Snow | .20 | .09 |
| ❑ 72 Butch Huskey | .10 | .05 |
| ❑ 73 Hideo Nomo | .40 | .18 |
| ❑ 74 Pedro Martinez | .50 | .23 |
| ❑ 75 Bobby Bonilla | .20 | .09 |
| ❑ 76 Jeff Conine | .10 | .05 |
| ❑ 77 Ryan Klesko | .20 | .09 |
| ❑ 78 Bernie Williams | .40 | .18 |
| ❑ 79 Andre Dawson | .25 | .11 |
| ❑ 80 Trevor Hoffman | .20 | .09 |
| ❑ 81 Mark Grace | .40 | .18 |
| ❑ 82 Benji Gil | .10 | .05 |
| ❑ 83 Eric Karros | .20 | .09 |
| ❑ 84 Pete Schourek | .10 | .05 |
| ❑ 85 Edgardo Alfonzo | .20 | .09 |
| ❑ 86 Jay Buhner | .20 | .09 |
| ❑ 87 Vinny Castilla | .20 | .09 |
| ❑ 88 Bret Boone | .20 | .09 |
| ❑ 89 Ray Durham | .20 | .09 |
| ❑ 90 Brian Jordan | .20 | .09 |
| ❑ 91 Jose Canseco | .50 | .23 |
| ❑ 92 Paul O'Neill | .20 | .09 |
| ❑ 93 Chili Davis | .20 | .09 |
| ❑ 94 Tom Glavine | .40 | .18 |
| ❑ 95 Julian Tavarez | .10 | .05 |
| ❑ 96 Derek Bell | .10 | .05 |
| ❑ 97 Will Clark | .40 | .18 |
| ❑ 98 Larry Walker | .20 | .09 |
| ❑ 99 Denny Neagle | .20 | .09 |
| ❑ 100 Alex Fernandez | .10 | .05 |
| ❑ 101 Barry Bonds | .60 | .25 |
| ❑ 102 Ben McDonald | .10 | .05 |
| ❑ 103 Andy Pettitte | .20 | .09 |
| ❑ 104 Tino Martinez | .20 | .09 |
| ❑ 105 Sterling Hitchcock | .10 | .05 |
| ❑ 106 Royce Clayton | .10 | .05 |
| ❑ 107 Jim Abbott | .20 | .09 |
| ❑ 108 Rickey Henderson | .50 | .23 |
| ❑ 109 Ramon Martinez | .10 | .05 |
| ❑ 110 Paul Molitor | .40 | .18 |
| ❑ 111 Dennis Eckersley | .20 | .09 |
| ❑ 112 Alex Gonzalez | .10 | .05 |
| ❑ 113 Marquis Grissom | .10 | .05 |
| ❑ 114 Greg Vaughn | .20 | .09 |
| ❑ 115 Lance Johnson | .10 | .05 |
| ❑ 116 Todd Stottlemyre | .10 | .05 |
| ❑ 117 Jack McDowell | .10 | .05 |
| ❑ 118 Ruben Sierra | .10 | .05 |
| ❑ 119 Brady Anderson | .20 | .09 |
| ❑ 120 Julio Franco | .10 | .05 |
| ❑ 121 Brooks Kieschnick | .10 | .05 |
| ❑ 122 Roberto Alomar | .40 | .18 |
| ❑ 123 Greg Gagne | .10 | .05 |
| ❑ 124 Wally Joyner | .20 | .09 |
| ❑ 125 John Smoltz | .20 | .09 |
| ❑ 126 John Valentin | .10 | .05 |
| ❑ 127 Russ Davis | .10 | .05 |
| ❑ 128 Joe Vitiello | .10 | .05 |
| ❑ 129 Shawon Dunston | .10 | .05 |
| ❑ 130 Frank Rodriguez | .10 | .05 |
| ❑ 131 Charlie Hayes | .10 | .05 |
| ❑ 132 Andy Benes | .10 | .05 |
| ❑ 133 B.J. Surhoff | .20 | .09 |
| ❑ 134 Dave Nilsson | .10 | .05 |
| ❑ 135 Carlos Delgado | .40 | .18 |
| ❑ 136 Walt Weiss | .10 | .05 |
| ❑ 137 Mike Stanley | .10 | .05 |
| ❑ 138 Greg Colbrunn | .10 | .05 |
| ❑ 139 Mike Kelly | .10 | .05 |
| ❑ 140 Ryne Sandberg | .50 | .23 |
| ❑ 141 Lee Smith | .20 | .09 |
| ❑ 142 Dennis Martinez | .20 | .09 |
| ❑ 143 Bernard Gilkey | .10 | .05 |
| ❑ 144 Lenny Dykstra | .20 | .09 |
| ❑ 145 Danny Tartabull | .10 | .05 |
| ❑ 146 Dean Palmer | .20 | .09 |
| ❑ 147 Craig Biggio | .25 | .11 |
| ❑ 148 Juan Acevedo | .10 | .05 |
| ❑ 149 Michael Tucker | .10 | .05 |
| ❑ 150 Bobby Higginson | .20 | .09 |
| ❑ 151 Ken Griffey Jr. LUL | .75 | .35 |
| ❑ 152 Frank Thomas LUL | .40 | .18 |
| ❑ 153 Cal Ripken LUL | .75 | .35 |
| ❑ 154 Albert Belle LUL | .10 | .05 |
| ❑ 155 Mike Piazza LUL | .60 | .25 |
| ❑ 156 Barry Bonds LUL | .25 | .11 |
| ❑ 157 Sammy Sosa LUL | .40 | .18 |
| ❑ 158 Mo Vaughn LUL | .20 | .09 |
| ❑ 159 Greg Maddux LUL | .50 | .23 |
| ❑ 160 Jeff Bagwell LUL | .40 | .18 |
| ❑ 161 Derek Jeter | 1.50 | .70 |
| ❑ 162 Paul Wilson | .10 | .05 |
| ❑ 163 Chris Snopek | .10 | .05 |
| ❑ 164 Jason Schmidt | .10 | .05 |
| ❑ 165 Jimmy Haynes | .10 | .05 |
| ❑ 166 George Arias | .10 | .05 |
| ❑ 167 Steve Gibralter | .10 | .05 |
| ❑ 168 Bob Wolcott | .10 | .05 |
| ❑ 169 Jason Kendall | .20 | .09 |
| ❑ 170 Greg Zaun | .10 | .05 |
| ❑ 171 Quinton McCracken | .10 | .05 |
| ❑ 172 Alan Benes | .10 | .05 |
| ❑ 173 Rey Ordonez | .20 | .09 |
| ❑ 174 Livan Hernandez RC | .50 | .23 |
| ❑ 175 Osvaldo Fernandez | .10 | .05 |
| ❑ 176 Marc Barcelo | .10 | .05 |
| ❑ 177 Sal Fasano | .10 | .05 |
| ❑ 178 Mike Grace | .10 | .05 |
| ❑ 179 Chan Ho Park | .20 | .09 |
| ❑ 180 Robert Perez | .10 | .05 |
| ❑ 181 Todd Hollandsworth | .10 | .05 |
| ❑ 182 Wilton Guerrero RC | .25 | .11 |
| ❑ 183 John Wasdin | .10 | .05 |
| ❑ 184 Jim Pittsley | .10 | .05 |
| ❑ 185 LaTroy Hawkins | .10 | .05 |
| ❑ 186 Jay Powell | .10 | .05 |
| ❑ 187 Felipe Crespo | .10 | .05 |
| ❑ 188 Jermaine Dye | .20 | .09 |
| ❑ 189 Bob Abreu | .50 | .23 |
| ❑ 190 Matt Luke | .10 | .05 |
| ❑ 191 Richard Hidalgo | .20 | .09 |
| ❑ 192 Karim Garcia | .10 | .05 |
| ❑ 193 Marvin Benard RC | .10 | .05 |
| ❑ 194 Andy Fox | .10 | .05 |
| ❑ 195 Terrell Wade | .10 | .05 |
| ❑ 196 Frank Thomas CL | .40 | .18 |
| ❑ 197 Ken Griffey Jr. CL | .75 | .35 |
| ❑ 198 Greg Maddux CL | .50 | .23 |
| ❑ 199 Mike Piazza CL | .60 | .25 |
| ❑ 200 Cal Ripken CL | .75 | .35 |

## 1997 Select

| | MINT | NRMT |
|---|---|---|
| COMPLETE SET (200) | 70.00 | 32.00 |
| COMPLETE SERIES 1 (150) | 40.00 | 18.00 |
| COMPLETE HI SERIES (50) | 30.00 | 13.50 |
| COMMON RED (1-150) | .15 | .07 |
| COMMON BLUE (1-150) | .30 | .14 |
| COMMON CARD (151-200) | .30 | .14 |
| ❑ 1 Juan Gonzalez B | 1.25 | .55 |
| ❑ 2 Mo Vaughn B | .50 | .23 |
| ❑ 3 Tony Gwynn R | 1.25 | .55 |
| ❑ 4 Manny Ramirez B | 1.50 | .70 |
| ❑ 5 Jose Canseco R | .75 | .35 |
| ❑ 6 David Cone R | .15 | .07 |
| ❑ 7 Chan Ho Park R | .25 | .11 |

| Card | MINT | NRMT |
|---|---|---|
| ❑ 8 Frank Thomas B | 2.50 | 1.10 |
| ❑ 9 Todd Hollandsworth R | .15 | .07 |
| ❑ 10 Marty Cordova R | .15 | .07 |
| ❑ 11 Gary Sheffield B | 1.25 | .55 |
| ❑ 12 John Smoltz B | .50 | .23 |
| ❑ 13 Mark Grudzielanek R | .15 | .07 |
| ❑ 14 Sammy Sosa B | 2.50 | 1.10 |
| ❑ 15 Paul Molitor R | .60 | .25 |
| ❑ 16 Kevin Brown R | .25 | .11 |
| ❑ 17 Albert Belle B | .75 | .35 |
| ❑ 18 Eric Young R | .15 | .07 |
| ❑ 19 John Wetteland R | .25 | .11 |
| ❑ 20 Ryan Klesko B | .50 | .23 |
| ❑ 21 Joe Carter R | .25 | .11 |
| ❑ 22 Alex Ochoa R | .15 | .07 |
| ❑ 23 Greg Maddux B | 3.00 | 1.35 |
| ❑ 24 Roger Clemens B | 2.50 | 1.10 |
| ❑ 25 Ivan Rodriguez B | 1.50 | .70 |
| ❑ 26 Barry Bonds B | 2.00 | .90 |
| ❑ 27 Kenny Lofton B | .50 | .23 |
| ❑ 28 Javy Lopez R | .25 | .11 |
| ❑ 29 Hideo Nomo B | 1.25 | .55 |
| ❑ 30 Rusty Greer R | .25 | .11 |
| ❑ 31 Rafael Palmeiro R | .60 | .25 |
| ❑ 32 Mike Piazza B | 4.00 | 1.80 |
| ❑ 33 Ryne Sandberg R | .75 | .35 |
| ❑ 34 Wade Boggs R | .75 | .35 |
| ❑ 35 Jim Thome B | .75 | .35 |
| ❑ 36 Ken Caminiti B | .50 | .23 |
| ❑ 37 Mark Grace R | .60 | .25 |
| ❑ 38 Brian Jordan B | .50 | .23 |
| ❑ 39 Craig Biggio R | .40 | .18 |
| ❑ 40 Henry Rodriguez R | .15 | .07 |
| ❑ 41 Dean Palmer R | .25 | .11 |
| ❑ 42 Jason Kendall R | .25 | .11 |
| ❑ 43 Bill Pulsipher R | .15 | .07 |
| ❑ 44 Tim Salmon B | .50 | .23 |
| ❑ 45 Marc Newfield R | .15 | .07 |
| ❑ 46 Pat Hentgen R | .15 | .07 |
| ❑ 47 Ken Griffey Jr. B | 5.00 | 2.20 |
| ❑ 48 Paul Wilson R | .15 | .07 |
| ❑ 49 Jay Buhner B | .50 | .23 |
| ❑ 50 Rickey Henderson R | .75 | .35 |
| ❑ 51 Jeff Bagwell B | 1.50 | .70 |
| ❑ 52 Cecil Fielder R | .25 | .11 |
| ❑ 53 Alex Rodriguez B | 4.00 | 1.80 |
| ❑ 54 John Jaha R | .15 | .07 |
| ❑ 55 Brady Anderson B | .50 | .23 |
| ❑ 56 Andres Galarraga R | .40 | .18 |
| ❑ 57 Raul Mondesi R | .25 | .11 |
| ❑ 58 Andy Pettitte R | .25 | .11 |
| ❑ 59 Roberto Alomar B | 1.25 | .55 |
| ❑ 60 Derek Jeter B | 5.00 | 2.20 |
| ❑ 61 Charles Johnson R | .15 | .07 |
| ❑ 62 Travis Fryman R | .25 | .11 |
| ❑ 63 Chipper Jones B | 3.00 | 1.35 |
| ❑ 64 Edgar Martinez R | .40 | .18 |
| ❑ 65 Bobby Bonilla R | .25 | .11 |
| ❑ 66 Greg Vaughn R | .25 | .11 |
| ❑ 67 Bobby Higginson R | .25 | .11 |
| ❑ 68 Garret Anderson R | .25 | .11 |
| ❑ 69 Chuck Knoblauch B | .50 | .23 |
| ❑ 70 Jermaine Dye R | .25 | .11 |
| ❑ 71 Cal Ripken B | 5.00 | 2.20 |
| ❑ 72 Jason Giambi R | .60 | .25 |
| ❑ 73 Trey Beamon R | .15 | .07 |
| ❑ 74 Shawn Green R | .60 | .25 |
| ❑ 75 Mark McGwire B | 5.00 | 2.20 |

- ❑ 76 Carlos Delgado R .60 .25
- ❑ 77 Jason Isringhausen R .15 .07
- ❑ 78 Randy Johnson B 1.50 .70
- ❑ 79 Troy Percival B .30 .14
- ❑ 80 Ron Gant R .15 .07
- ❑ 81 Ellis Burks R .25 .11
- ❑ 82 Mike Mussina B 1.25 .55
- ❑ 83 Todd Hundley R .15 .07
- ❑ 84 Jim Edmonds R .60 .25
- ❑ 85 Charles Nagy R .15 .07
- ❑ 86 Dante Bichette B .50 .23
- ❑ 87 Mariano Rivera R .25 .11
- ❑ 88 Matt Williams B .75 .35
- ❑ 89 Rondell White R .25 .11
- ❑ 90 Steve Finley R .25 .11
- ❑ 91 Alex Fernandez R .15 .07
- ❑ 92 Barry Larkin R .60 .25
- ❑ 93 Tom Goodwin R .15 .07
- ❑ 94 Will Clark R .60 .25
- ❑ 95 Michael Tucker R .15 .07
- ❑ 96 Derek Bell R .15 .07
- ❑ 97 Larry Walker R .25 .11
- ❑ 98 Alan Benes R .15 .07
- ❑ 99 Tom Glavine R .60 .25
- ❑ 100 Darin Erstad B 1.50 .70
- ❑ 101 Andruw Jones B 1.50 .70
- ❑ 102 Scott Rolen R .60 .25
- ❑ 103 Todd Walker B .30 .14
- ❑ 104 Dmitri Young R .25 .11
- ❑ 105 Vladimir Guerrero B 2.50 1.10
- ❑ 106 Nomar Garciaparra R 2.00 .90
- ❑ 107 Danny Patterson R .15 .07
- ❑ 108 Karim Garcia R .15 .07
- ❑ 109 Todd Greene R .15 .07
- ❑ 110 Ruben Rivera R .15 .07
- ❑ 111 Raul Casanova R .15 .07
- ❑ 112 Mike Cameron R .25 .11
- ❑ 113 Bartolo Colon R .25 .11
- ❑ 114 Rod Myers R .15 .07
- ❑ 115 Todd Dunn R .15 .07
- ❑ 116 Torii Hunter R .15 .07
- ❑ 117 Jason Dickson R .15 .07
- ❑ 118 Eugene Kingsale R .15 .07
- ❑ 119 Rafael Medina R .15 .07
- ❑ 120 Raul Ibanez R .15 .07
- ❑ 121 Bobby Henley R RC .15 .07
- ❑ 122 Scott Spiezio R .15 .07
- ❑ 123 Bobby Smith R .15 .07
- ❑ 124 J.J. Johnson R .15 .07
- ❑ 125 Bubba Trammell R RC .25 .11
- ❑ 126 Jeff Abbott R .15 .07
- ❑ 127 Neifi Perez R .15 .07
- ❑ 128 Derrek Lee R .15 .07
- ❑ 129 Kevin Brown C R .15 .07
- ❑ 130 Mendy Lopez R .15 .07
- ❑ 131 Kevin Orie R .15 .07
- ❑ 132 Ryan Jones R .15 .07
- ❑ 133 Juan Encarnacion R .25 .11
- ❑ 134 Jose Guillen B .15 .07
- ❑ 135 Greg Norton R .15 .07
- ❑ 136 Richie Sexson R .25 .11
- ❑ 137 Jay Payton R .25 .11
- ❑ 138 Bob Abreu R .25 .11
- ❑ 139 Ron Belliard R RC 1.50 .70
- ❑ 140 Wilton Guerrero B .30 .14
- ❑ 141 Alex Rodriguez SS B 2.00 .90
- ❑ 142 Juan Gonzalez SS B .50 .23
- ❑ 143 Ken Caminiti SS B .30 .14
- ❑ 144 Frank Thomas SS B 1.25 .55
- ❑ 145 Ken Griffey Jr. SS B 2.50 1.10
- ❑ 146 John Smoltz SS B .30 .14
- ❑ 147 Mike Piazza SS B 2.00 .90
- ❑ 148 Derek Jeter SS B 2.50 1.10
- ❑ 149 Frank Thomas CL R .60 .25
- ❑ 150 Ken Griffey Jr. CL R 1.25 .55
- ❑ 151 Jose Cruz Jr. RC 5.00 2.20
- ❑ 152 Moises Alou .50 .23
- ❑ 153 Hideki Irabu RC 1.50 .70
- ❑ 154 Glendon Rusch .30 .14
- ❑ 155 Ron Coomer .30 .14
- ❑ 156 Jeremi Gonzalez RC .30 .14
- ❑ 157 Fernando Tatis RC 5.00 2.20
- ❑ 158 John Olerud .50 .23
- ❑ 159 Rickey Henderson 1.50 .70
- ❑ 160 Shannon Stewart .50 .23
- ❑ 161 Kevin Polcovich RC .30 .14
- ❑ 162 Jose Rosado .30 .14
- ❑ 163 Ray Lankford .50 .23
- ❑ 164 David Justice .75 .35
- ❑ 165 Mark Kotsay RC 2.00 .90
- ❑ 166 Deivi Cruz RC 2.50 1.10
- ❑ 167 Billy Wagner .30 .14
- ❑ 168 Jacob Cruz .30 .14
- ❑ 169 Matt Morris .30 .14
- ❑ 170 Brian Banks .30 .14
- ❑ 171 Brett Tomko .30 .14
- ❑ 172 Todd Helton 2.00 .90
- ❑ 173 Eric Young .30 .14
- ❑ 174 Bernie Williams 1.25 .55
- ❑ 175 Jeff Fassero .30 .14
- ❑ 176 Ryan McGuire .30 .14
- ❑ 177 Darryl Kile .50 .23
- ❑ 178 Kelvim Escobar RC 1.50 .70
- ❑ 179 Dave Nilsson .30 .14
- ❑ 180 Geronimo Berroa .30 .14
- ❑ 181 Livan Hernandez .50 .23
- ❑ 182 Tony Womack RC 2.50 1.10
- ❑ 183 Deion Sanders .50 .23
- ❑ 184 Jeff Kent .75 .35
- ❑ 185 Brian Hunter .30 .14
- ❑ 186 Jose Malave .30 .14
- ❑ 187 Steve Woodard RC 1.50 .70
- ❑ 188 Brad Radke .50 .23
- ❑ 189 Todd Dunwoody .30 .14
- ❑ 190 Joey Hamilton .30 .14
- ❑ 191 Denny Neagle .50 .23
- ❑ 192 Bobby Jones .30 .14
- ❑ 193 Tony Clark .30 .14
- ❑ 194 Jaret Wright RC 1.50 .70
- ❑ 195 Matt Stairs .30 .14
- ❑ 196 Francisco Cordova .30 .14
- ❑ 197 Justin Thompson .30 .14
- ❑ 198 Pokey Reese .50 .23
- ❑ 199 Garrett Stephenson .30 .14
- ❑ 200 Carl Everett .50 .23

## 1995 Select Certified

| | MINT | NRMT |
|---|---|---|
| COMPLETE SET (135) | 40.00 | 18.00 |
| COMMON CARD (1-135) | .25 | .11 |

- ❑ 1 Barry Bonds 1.50 .70
- ❑ 2 Reggie Sanders .25 .11
- ❑ 3 Terry Steinbach .25 .11
- ❑ 4 Eduardo Perez .25 .11
- ❑ 5 Frank Thomas 2.00 .90
- ❑ 6 Wil Cordero .25 .11
- ❑ 7 John Olerud .50 .23
- ❑ 8 Deion Sanders .50 .23
- ❑ 9 Mike Mussina 1.00 .45
- ❑ 10 Mo Vaughn .50 .23
- ❑ 11 Will Clark 1.00 .45
- ❑ 12 Chili Davis .50 .23
- ❑ 13 Jimmy Key .50 .23
- ❑ 14 Eddie Murray 1.00 .45
- ❑ 15 Bernard Gilkey .25 .11
- ❑ 16 David Cone .50 .23
- ❑ 17 Tim Salmon .50 .23
- ❑ 19 Steve Ontiveros .25 .11
- ❑ 20 Andres Galarraga .75 .35
- ❑ 21 Don Mattingly 2.50 1.10
- ❑ 22 Kevin Appier .50 .23
- ❑ 23 Paul Molitor 1.00 .45
- ❑ 24 Edgar Martinez .75 .35
- ❑ 25 Andy Benes .25 .11
- ❑ 26 Rafael Palmeiro 1.00 .45
- ❑ 27 Barry Larkin 1.00 .45
- ❑ 28 Gary Sheffield 1.00 .45
- ❑ 29 Wally Joyner .50 .23
- ❑ 30 Wade Boggs 1.25 .55
- ❑ 31 Rico Brogna .25 .11
- ❑ 32 Eddie Murray 3000th Hit .50 .23
- ❑ 33 Kirby Puckett 2.50 1.10
- ❑ 34 Bobby Bonilla .50 .23
- ❑ 35 Hal Morris .25 .11
- ❑ 36 Moises Alou .50 .23
- ❑ 37 Javier Lopez .50 .23
- ❑ 38 Chuck Knoblauch .50 .23
- ❑ 39 Mike Piazza 3.00 1.35
- ❑ 40 Travis Fryman .50 .23
- ❑ 41 Rickey Henderson 1.25 .55
- ❑ 42 Jim Thome .75 .35
- ❑ 43 Carlos Baerga .25 .11
- ❑ 44 Dean Palmer .50 .23
- ❑ 45 Kirk Gibson .50 .23
- ❑ 46 Bret Saberhagen .50 .23
- ❑ 47 Cecil Fielder .50 .23
- ❑ 48 Manny Ramirez 1.25 .55
- ❑ 49 Derek Bell .25 .11
- ❑ 50 Mark McGwire 4.00 1.80
- ❑ 51 Jim Edmonds 1.00 .45
- ❑ 52 Robin Ventura .50 .23
- ❑ 53 Ryan Klesko .50 .23
- ❑ 54 Jeff Bagwell 1.25 .55
- ❑ 55 Ozzie Smith 1.25 .55
- ❑ 56 Albert Belle .75 .35
- ❑ 57 Darren Daulton .50 .23
- ❑ 58 Jeff Conine .25 .11
- ❑ 59 Greg Maddux 2.50 1.10
- ❑ 60 Lenny Dykstra .50 .23
- ❑ 61 Randy Johnson 1.25 .55
- ❑ 62 Fred McGriff .75 .35
- ❑ 63 Ray Lankford .50 .23
- ❑ 64 David Justice .75 .35
- ❑ 65 Paul O'Neill .50 .23
- ❑ 66 Tony Gwynn 2.00 .90
- ❑ 67 Matt Williams .75 .35
- ❑ 68 Dante Bichette .50 .23
- ❑ 69 Craig Biggio .75 .35
- ❑ 70 Ken Griffey Jr. 4.00 1.80
- ❑ 71 J.T. Snow .50 .23
- ❑ 72 Cal Ripken 4.00 1.80
- ❑ 73 Jay Bell .50 .23
- ❑ 74 Joe Carter .50 .23
- ❑ 75 Roberto Alomar 1.00 .45
- ❑ 76 Benji Gil .25 .11
- ❑ 77 Ivan Rodriguez 1.25 .55
- ❑ 78 Raul Mondesi .50 .23
- ❑ 79 Cliff Floyd .50 .23
- ❑ 80 Eric Karros 1.00 .45
  Mike Piazza
  Raul Mondesi
- ❑ 81 Royce Clayton .25 .11
- ❑ 82 Billy Ashley .25 .11
- ❑ 83 Joey Hamilton .25 .11
- ❑ 84 Sammy Sosa 2.00 .90
- ❑ 85 Jason Bere .25 .11
- ❑ 86 Dennis Martinez .50 .23
- ❑ 87 Greg Vaughn .50 .23
- ❑ 88 Roger Clemens 2.00 .90
- ❑ 89 Larry Walker .50 .23
- ❑ 90 Mark Grace 1.00 .45
- ❑ 91 Kenny Lofton .50 .23
- ❑ 92 Carlos Perez RC .50 .23
- ❑ 93 Roger Cedeno .25 .11
- ❑ 94 Scott Ruffcorn .25 .11
- ❑ 95 Jim Pittsley .25 .11
- ❑ 96 Andy Pettitte .75 .35
- ❑ 97 James Baldwin .50 .23
- ❑ 98 Hideo Nomo RC 2.50 1.10
- ❑ 99 Ismael Valdes .25 .11
- ❑ 100 Armando Benitez .50 .23
- ❑ 101 Jose Malave .25 .11
- ❑ 102 Bob Higginson RC 1.50 .70
- ❑ 103 LaTroy Hawkins .25 .11
- ❑ 104 Russ Davis .25 .11
- ❑ 105 Shawn Green 1.00 .45
- ❑ 106 Joe Vitiello .25 .11
- ❑ 107 Chipper Jones 2.50 1.10

| Card | MINT | NRMT |
|---|---|---|
| 108 Shane Andrews | .25 | .11 |
| 109 Jose Oliva | .25 | .11 |
| 110 Ray Durham | .50 | .23 |
| 111 Jon Nunnally | .25 | .11 |
| 112 Alex Gonzalez | .25 | .11 |
| 113 Vaughn Eshelman | .25 | .11 |
| 114 Marty Cordova | .25 | .11 |
| 115 Mark Grudzielanek RC | .50 | .23 |
| 116 Brian L.Hunter | .25 | .11 |
| 117 Charles Johnson | .50 | .23 |
| 118 Alex Rodriguez | 4.00 | 1.80 |
| 119 David Bell | .25 | .11 |
| 120 Todd Hollandsworth | .25 | .11 |
| 121 Joe Randa | .25 | .11 |
| 122 Derek Jeter | 4.00 | 1.80 |
| 123 Frank Rodriguez | .25 | .11 |
| 124 Curtis Goodwin | .25 | .11 |
| 125 Bill Pulsipher | .25 | .11 |
| 126 John Mabry | .25 | .11 |
| 127 Julian Tavarez | .25 | .11 |
| 128 Edgardo Alfonzo | 1.00 | .45 |
| 129 Orlando Miller | .25 | .11 |
| 130 Juan Acevedo RC | .25 | .11 |
| 131 Jeff Cirillo | .50 | .23 |
| 132 Roberto Petagine | .25 | .11 |
| 133 Antonio Osuna | .25 | .11 |
| 134 Michael Tucker | .25 | .11 |
| 135 Garret Anderson | .50 | .23 |
| 2131 Cal Ripken TRIB | 4.00 | 1.80 |

## 1996 Select Certified

| | MINT | NRMT |
|---|---|---|
| COMPLETE SET (144) | 40.00 | 18.00 |
| COMMON CARD (1-144) | .20 | .09 |

| Card | MINT | NRMT |
|---|---|---|
| 1 Frank Thomas | 1.50 | .70 |
| 2 Tino Martinez | .30 | .14 |
| 3 Gary Sheffield | .75 | .35 |
| 4 Kenny Lofton | .30 | .14 |
| 5 Joe Carter | .30 | .14 |
| 6 Alex Rodriguez | 2.50 | 1.10 |
| 7 Chipper Jones | 2.00 | .90 |
| 8 Roger Clemens | 1.50 | .70 |
| 9 Jay Bell | .30 | .14 |
| 10 Eddie Murray | .75 | .35 |
| 11 Will Clark | .75 | .35 |
| 12 Mike Mussina | .75 | .35 |
| 13 Hideo Nomo | .75 | .35 |
| 14 Andres Galarraga | .50 | .23 |
| 15 Marc Newfield | .20 | .09 |
| 16 Jason Isringhausen | .30 | .14 |
| 17 Randy Johnson | 1.00 | .45 |
| 18 Chuck Knoblauch | .30 | .14 |
| 19 J.T. Snow | .30 | .14 |
| 20 Mark McGwire | 3.00 | 1.35 |
| 21 Tony Gwynn | 1.50 | .70 |
| 22 Albert Belle | .50 | .23 |
| 23 Gregg Jefferies | .20 | .09 |
| 24 Reggie Sanders | .20 | .09 |
| 25 Bernie Williams | .75 | .35 |
| 26 Ray Lankford | .30 | .14 |
| 27 Johnny Damon | .50 | .23 |
| 28 Ryne Sandberg | 1.00 | .45 |
| 29 Rondell White | .30 | .14 |
| 30 Mike Piazza | 2.50 | 1.10 |
| 31 Barry Bonds | 1.25 | .55 |
| 32 Greg Maddux | 2.00 | .90 |
| 33 Craig Biggio | .50 | .23 |
| 34 John Valentin | .20 | .09 |
| 35 Ivan Rodriguez | 1.00 | .45 |
| 36 Rico Brogna | .20 | .09 |
| 37 Tim Salmon | .30 | .14 |
| 38 Sterling Hitchcock | .20 | .09 |
| 39 Charles Johnson | .30 | .14 |
| 40 Travis Fryman | .30 | .14 |
| 41 Barry Larkin | .75 | .35 |
| 42 Tom Glavine | .75 | .35 |
| 43 Marty Cordova | .20 | .09 |
| 44 Shawn Green | .75 | .35 |
| 45 Ben McDonald | .20 | .09 |
| 46 Robin Ventura | .30 | .14 |
| 47 Ken Griffey Jr. | 3.00 | 1.35 |
| 48 Orlando Merced | .20 | .09 |
| 49 Paul O'Neill | .30 | .14 |
| 50 Ozzie Smith | 1.00 | .45 |
| 51 Manny Ramirez | 1.00 | .45 |
| 52 Ismael Valdes | .20 | .09 |
| 53 Cal Ripken | 3.00 | 1.35 |
| 54 Jeff Bagwell | 1.00 | .45 |
| 55 Greg Vaughn | .30 | .14 |
| 56 Juan Gonzalez | .75 | .35 |
| 57 Raul Mondesi | .30 | .14 |
| 58 Carlos Baerga | .20 | .09 |
| 59 Sammy Sosa | 1.50 | .70 |
| 60 Mike Kelly | .20 | .09 |
| 61 Edgar Martinez | .50 | .23 |
| 62 Kirby Puckett | 2.00 | .90 |
| 63 Cecil Fielder | .30 | .14 |
| 64 David Cone | .30 | .14 |
| 65 Moises Alou | .30 | .14 |
| 66 Fred McGriff | .50 | .23 |
| 67 Mo Vaughn | .30 | .14 |
| 68 Edgardo Alfonzo | .30 | .14 |
| 69 Jim Thome | .50 | .23 |
| 70 Rickey Henderson | 1.00 | .45 |
| 71 Dante Bichette | .30 | .14 |
| 72 Lenny Dykstra | .30 | .14 |
| 73 Benji Gil | .20 | .09 |
| 74 Wade Boggs | 1.00 | .45 |
| 75 Jim Edmonds | .75 | .35 |
| 76 Michael Tucker | .20 | .09 |
| 77 Carlos Delgado | .75 | .35 |
| 78 Butch Huskey | .20 | .09 |
| 79 Billy Ashley | .20 | .09 |
| 80 Dean Palmer | .30 | .14 |
| 81 Paul Molitor | .75 | .35 |
| 82 Ryan Klesko | .30 | .14 |
| 83 Brian L.Hunter | .20 | .09 |
| 84 Jay Buhner | .30 | .14 |
| 85 Larry Walker | .30 | .14 |
| 86 Mike Bordick | .20 | .09 |
| 87 Matt Williams | .50 | .23 |
| 88 Jack McDowell | .20 | .09 |
| 89 Hal Morris | .20 | .09 |
| 90 Brian Jordan | .30 | .14 |
| 91 Andy Pettitte | .30 | .14 |
| 92 Melvin Nieves | .20 | .09 |
| 93 Pedro Martinez | 1.00 | .45 |
| 94 Mark Grace | .75 | .35 |
| 95 Garret Anderson | .30 | .14 |
| 96 Andre Dawson | .50 | .23 |
| 97 Ray Durham | .30 | .14 |
| 98 Jose Canseco | 1.00 | .45 |
| 99 Roberto Alomar | .75 | .35 |
| 100 Derek Jeter | 3.00 | 1.35 |
| 101 Alan Benes | .20 | .09 |
| 102 Karim Garcia | .20 | .09 |
| 103 Robin Jennings | .20 | .09 |
| 104 Bob Abreu | 1.00 | .45 |
| 105 Sal Fasano UER (Name on front is Livan Hernandez) | .20 | .09 |
| 106 Steve Gibralter | .20 | .09 |
| 107 Jermaine Dye | .30 | .14 |
| 108 Jason Kendall | .30 | .14 |
| 109 Mike Grace RC | .20 | .09 |
| 110 Jason Schmidt | .20 | .09 |
| 111 Paul Wilson | .20 | .09 |
| 112 Rey Ordonez | .30 | .14 |
| 113 Wilton Guerrero RC | .50 | .23 |
| 114 Brooks Kieschnick | .20 | .09 |
| 115 George Arias | .20 | .09 |
| 116 Osvaldo Fernandez RC | .20 | .09 |
| 117 Todd Hollandsworth | .20 | .09 |
| 118 John Wasdin | .20 | .09 |
| 119 Eric Owens | .20 | .09 |
| 120 Chan Ho Park | .30 | .14 |
| 121 Mark Loretta | .20 | .09 |
| 122 Richard Hidalgo | .30 | .14 |
| 123 Jeff Suppan | .20 | .09 |
| 124 Jim Pittsley | .20 | .09 |
| 125 LaTroy Hawkins | .20 | .09 |
| 126 Chris Snopek | .20 | .09 |
| 127 Justin Thompson | .20 | .09 |
| 128 Jay Powell | .20 | .09 |
| 129 Alex Ochoa | .20 | .09 |
| 130 Felipe Crespo | .20 | .09 |
| 131 Matt Lawton RC | 1.00 | .45 |
| 132 Jimmy Haynes | .20 | .09 |
| 133 Terrell Wade | .20 | .09 |
| 134 Ruben Rivera | .20 | .09 |
| 135 Frank Thomas PP | .75 | .35 |
| 136 Ken Griffey Jr. PP | 1.50 | .70 |
| 137 Greg Maddux PP | 1.00 | .45 |
| 138 Mike Piazza PP | 1.25 | .55 |
| 139 Cal Ripken PP | 1.50 | .70 |
| 140 Albert Belle PP | .20 | .09 |
| 141 Mo Vaughn PP | .30 | .14 |
| 142 Chipper Jones PP | 1.00 | .45 |
| 143 Hideo Nomo PP | .30 | .14 |
| 144 Ryan Klesko PP | .20 | .09 |

## 2000 SkyBox

| | MINT | NRMT |
|---|---|---|
| COMP.MASTER SET (300) | 120.00 | 55.00 |
| COMP.SET w/o SP's (250) | 40.00 | 18.00 |
| COMMON CARD (1-250) | .15 | .07 |
| MINOR STARS | .25 | .11 |
| SEMISTARS | .40 | .18 |
| UNLISTED STARS | .60 | .25 |
| COMMON SP (201S-240S) | 2.00 | .90 |
| SP MINOR STARS | 2.00 | .90 |
| SP SEMISTARS | 2.50 | 1.10 |
| SP UNLISTED STARS | 4.00 | 1.80 |
| COMMON DUAL SP (241S-250S) | 1.00 | .45 |
| DUAL SP MINOR STARS | 1.00 | .45 |
| DUAL SP SEMISTARS | 1.00 | .45 |
| DUAL SP UNLISTED STARS | 1.00 | .45 |

| Card | MINT | NRMT |
|---|---|---|
| 1 Cal Ripken | 2.50 | 1.10 |
| 2 Ivan Rodriguez | .75 | .35 |
| 3 Chipper Jones | 1.50 | .70 |
| 4 Dean Palmer | .25 | .11 |
| 5 Devon White | .15 | .07 |
| 6 Ugueth Urbina | .15 | .07 |
| 7 Doug Glanville | .15 | .07 |
| 8 Damian Jackson | .15 | .07 |
| 9 Jose Canseco | .75 | .35 |
| 10 Billy Koch | .25 | .11 |
| 11 Brady Anderson | .25 | .11 |
| 12 Vladimir Guerrero | 1.00 | .45 |
| 13 Dan Wilson | .15 | .07 |
| 14 Kevin Brown | .40 | .18 |
| 15 Eddie Taubensee | .15 | .07 |
| 16 Jose Lima | .15 | .07 |
| 17 Greg Maddux | 1.50 | .70 |
| 18 Manny Ramirez | .75 | .35 |
| 19 Brad Fullmer | .25 | .11 |
| 20 Ron Gant | .25 | .11 |
| 21 Edgar Martinez | .40 | .18 |
| 22 Pokey Reese | .25 | .11 |

❑ 23 Jason Varitek .25 .11
❑ 24 Neifi Perez .15 .07
❑ 25 Shane Reynolds .15 .07
❑ 26 Robin Ventura .40 .18
❑ 27 Scott Rolen .60 .25
❑ 28 Trevor Hoffman .25 .11
❑ 29 John Valentin .15 .07
❑ 30 Shannon Stewart .25 .11
❑ 31 Troy Glaus .75 .35
❑ 32 Kerry Wood .25 .11
❑ 33 Jim Thome .40 .18
❑ 34 Rafael Roque .15 .07
❑ 35 Tino Martinez .25 .11
❑ 36 Jeffrey Hammonds .25 .11
❑ 37 Orlando Hernandez .25 .11
❑ 38 Kris Benson .25 .11
❑ 39 Fred McGriff .40 .18
❑ 40 Brian Jordan .25 .11
❑ 41 Trot Nixon .25 .11
❑ 42 Matt Clement .15 .07
❑ 43 Ray Durham .25 .11
❑ 44 Johnny Damon .25 .11
❑ 45 Todd Hollandsworth .15 .07
❑ 46 Edgardo Alfonzo .25 .11
❑ 47 Tim Hudson .60 .25
❑ 48 Tony Gwynn 1.25 .55
❑ 49 Barry Bonds 1.00 .45
❑ 50 Andruw Jones .60 .25
❑ 51 Pedro Martinez .75 .35
❑ 52 Mike Hampton .25 .11
❑ 53 Miguel Tejada .25 .11
❑ 54 Kevin Young .15 .07
❑ 55 J.T. Snow .25 .11
❑ 56 Carlos Delgado .60 .25
❑ 57 Bobby Howry .15 .07
❑ 58 Andres Galarraga .40 .18
❑ 59 Paul Konerko .25 .11
❑ 60 Mike Cameron .15 .07
❑ 61 Jeremy Giambi .15 .07
❑ 62 Todd Hundley .15 .07
❑ 63 Al Leiter .15 .07
❑ 64 Matt Stairs .15 .07
❑ 65 Edgar Renteria .15 .07
❑ 66 Jeff Kent .40 .18
❑ 67 John Wetteland .25 .11
❑ 68 Nomar Garciaparra 2.00 .90
❑ 69 Jeff Weaver .15 .07
❑ 70 Matt Williams .40 .18
❑ 71 Kyle Farnsworth .15 .07
❑ 72 Brad Radke .25 .11
❑ 73 Eric Chavez .25 .11
❑ 74 J.D. Drew .60 .25
❑ 75 Steve Finley .25 .11
❑ 76 Pete Harnisch .15 .07
❑ 77 Chad Kreuter .15 .07
❑ 78 Todd Pratt .15 .07
❑ 79 John Jaha .15 .07
❑ 80 Armando Rios .15 .07
❑ 81 Luis Gonzalez .25 .11
❑ 82 Ryan Minor .15 .07
❑ 83 Juan Gonzalez .60 .25
❑ 84 Rickey Henderson .75 .35
❑ 85 Jason Giambi .60 .25
❑ 86 Shawn Estes .15 .07
❑ 87 Chad Curtis .15 .07
❑ 88 Jeff Cirillo .25 .11
❑ 89 Juan Encarnacion .25 .11
❑ 90 Tony Womack .15 .07
❑ 91 Mike Mussina .60 .25
❑ 92 Jeff Bagwell .75 .35
❑ 93 Rey Ordonez .15 .07
❑ 94 Joe McEwing .15 .07
❑ 95 Robb Nen .15 .07
❑ 96 Will Clark .60 .25
❑ 97 Chris Singleton .25 .11
❑ 98 Jason Kendall .25 .11
❑ 99 Ken Griffey Jr. 2.50 1.10
❑ 100 Rusty Greer .25 .11
❑ 101 Charles Johnson .25 .11
❑ 102 Carlos Lee .25 .11
❑ 103 Brad Ausmus .15 .07
❑ 104 Preston Wilson .25 .11
❑ 105 Ronnie Belliard .15 .07
❑ 106 Mike Lieberthal .25 .11
❑ 107 Alex Rodriguez 2.00 .90
❑ 108 Jay Bell .25 .11
❑ 109 Frank Thomas 1.25 .55
❑ 110 Adrian Beltre .25 .11
❑ 111 Ron Coomer .15 .07
❑ 112 Ben Grieve .25 .11
❑ 113 Darryl Kile .25 .11
❑ 114 Erubiel Durazo .25 .11
❑ 115 Magglio Ordonez .25 .11
❑ 116 Gary Sheffield .60 .25
❑ 117 Joe Mays .15 .07
❑ 118 Fernando Tatis .25 .11
❑ 119 David Wells .25 .11
❑ 120 Tim Salmon .25 .11
❑ 121 Troy O'Leary .15 .07
❑ 122 Roberto Alomar .60 .25
❑ 123 Damion Easley .15 .07
❑ 124 Brant Brown .15 .07
❑ 125 Carlos Beltran .25 .11
❑ 126 Eric Karros .25 .11
❑ 127 Geoff Jenkins .25 .11
❑ 128 Roger Clemens 1.25 .55
❑ 129 Warren Morris .15 .07
❑ 130 Eric Owens .15 .07
❑ 131 Jose Cruz Jr. .25 .11
❑ 132 Mo Vaughn .25 .11
❑ 133 Eric Young .15 .07
❑ 134 Kenny Lofton .25 .11
❑ 135 Marquis Grissom .15 .07
❑ 136 A.J. Burnett .25 .11
❑ 137 Bernie Williams .60 .25
❑ 138 Javy Lopez .25 .11
❑ 139 Jose Offerman .15 .07
❑ 140 Sean Casey .25 .11
❑ 141 Alex Gonzalez .15 .07
❑ 142 Carlos Febles .15 .07
❑ 143 Mike Piazza 2.00 .90
❑ 144 Curt Schilling .25 .11
❑ 145 Ben Davis .15 .07
❑ 146 Rafael Palmeiro .60 .25
❑ 147 Scott Williamson .15 .07
❑ 148 Darin Erstad .60 .25
❑ 149 Joe Girardi .15 .07
❑ 150 Gerald Williams .15 .07
❑ 151 Richie Sexson .25 .11
❑ 152 Corey Koskie .15 .07
❑ 153 Paul O'Neill .25 .11
❑ 154 Chad Hermansen .15 .07
❑ 155 Randy Johnson .75 .35
❑ 156 Henry Rodriguez .15 .07
❑ 157 Bartolo Colon .25 .11
❑ 158 Tony Clark .15 .07
❑ 159 Mike Lowell .15 .07
❑ 160 Moises Alou .25 .11
❑ 161 Todd Walker .15 .07
❑ 162 Mariano Rivera .25 .11
❑ 163 Mark McGwire 2.50 1.10
❑ 164 Roberto Hernandez .15 .07
❑ 165 Larry Walker .25 .11
❑ 166 Albert Belle .40 .18
❑ 167 Barry Larkin .60 .25
❑ 168 Rolando Arrojo .15 .07
❑ 169 Mark Kotsay .15 .07
❑ 170 Ken Caminiti .25 .11
❑ 171 Dermal Brown .25 .11
❑ 172 Michael Barrett .15 .07
❑ 173 Jay Buhner .25 .11
❑ 174 Ruben Mateo .25 .11
❑ 175 Jim Edmonds .60 .25
❑ 176 Sammy Sosa 1.25 .55
❑ 177 Omar Vizquel .25 .11
❑ 178 Todd Helton .75 .35
❑ 179 Kevin Barker .15 .07
❑ 180 Derek Jeter 2.50 1.10
❑ 181 Brian Giles .25 .11
❑ 182 Greg Vaughn .25 .11
❑ 183 Roy Halladay .15 .07
❑ 184 Tom Glavine .60 .25
❑ 185 Craig Biggio .40 .18
❑ 186 Jose Vidro .15 .07
❑ 187 Andy Ashby .15 .07
❑ 188 Freddy Garcia .25 .11
❑ 189 Garret Anderson .25 .11
❑ 190 Mark Grace .60 .25
❑ 191 Travis Fryman .25 .11
❑ 192 Jeromy Burnitz .25 .11
❑ 193 Jacque Jones .25 .11
❑ 194 David Cone .25 .11
❑ 195 Ryan Rupe .15 .07
❑ 196 John Smoltz .25 .11
❑ 197 Daryle Ward .25 .11
❑ 198 Rondell White .25 .11
❑ 199 Bobby Abreu .25 .11
❑ 200 Justin Thompson .15 .07
❑ 201 Norm Hutchins .15 .07
❑ 201S Norm Hutchins SP 2.00 .90
❑ 202 Ramon Ortiz .25 .11
❑ 202S Ramon Ortiz SP 2.00 .90
❑ 203 Dan Wheeler .15 .07
❑ 203S Dan Wheeler SP 2.00 .90
❑ 204 Matt Riley .25 .11
❑ 204S Matt Riley SP 2.00 .90
❑ 205 Steve Lomasney .15 .07
❑ 205S Steve Lomasney SP 2.00 .90
❑ 206 Chad Meyers .15 .07
❑ 206S Chad Meyers SP 2.00 .90
❑ 207 Gary Glover RC .25 .11
❑ 207S Gary Glover SP 2.00 .90
❑ 208 Joe Crede .60 .25
❑ 208S Joe Crede SP 4.00 1.80
❑ 209 Kip Wells .25 .11
❑ 209S Kip Wells SP 2.00 .90
❑ 210 Travis Dawkins .25 .11
❑ 210S Travis Dawkins SP 2.00 .90
❑ 211 Denny Stark RC .25 .11
❑ 211S Denny Stark SP 2.00 .90
❑ 212 Ben Petrick .15 .07
❑ 212S Ben Petrick SP 2.00 .90
❑ 213 Eric Munson .60 .25
❑ 213S Eric Munson SP 4.00 1.80
❑ 214 Josh Beckett .60 .25
❑ 214S Josh Beckett SP 4.00 1.80
❑ 215 Pablo Ozuna .15 .07
❑ 215S Pablo Ozuna SP 2.00 .90
❑ 216 Brad Penny .25 .11
❑ 216S Brad Penny SP 2.00 .90
❑ 217 Julio Ramirez .15 .07
❑ 217S Julio Ramirez SP 2.00 .90
❑ 218 Danny Peoples .15 .07
❑ 218S Danny Peoples SP 2.00 .90
❑ 219 Wilfredo Rodriguez RC .60 .25
❑ 219S Wilfredo Rodriguez SP 3.00 1.35
❑ 220 Julio Lugo .15 .07
❑ 220S Julio Lugo SP 2.00 .90
❑ 221 Mark Quinn .25 .11
❑ 221S Mark Quinn SP 2.00 .90
❑ 222 Eric Gagne .15 .07
❑ 222S Eric Gagne SP 2.00 .90
❑ 223 Chad Green .15 .07
❑ 223S Chad Green SP 2.00 .90
❑ 224 Tony Armas Jr. .25 .11
❑ 224S Tony Armas Jr. SP 2.00 .90
❑ 225 Milton Bradley .25 .11
❑ 225S Milton Bradley SP 2.00 .90
❑ 226 Rob Bell .15 .07
❑ 226S Rob Bell SP 2.00 .90
❑ 227 Alfonso Soriano .25 .11
❑ 227S Alfonso Soriano SP .25 .11
❑ 228 Wily Pena .25 .11
❑ 228S Wily Pena SP 2.00 .90
❑ 229 Nick Johnson .25 .11
❑ 229S Nick Johnson SP 2.00 .90
❑ 230 Ed Yarnall .15 .07
❑ 230S Ed Yarnall SP 2.00 .90
❑ 231 Ryan Bradley .15 .07
❑ 231S Ryan Bradley SP 2.00 .90
❑ 232 Adam Piatt .60 .25
❑ 232S Adam Piatt SP 4.00 1.80
❑ 233 Chad Harville .15 .07
❑ 233S Chad Harville SP 2.00 .90
❑ 234 Alex Sanchez .15 .07
❑ 234S Alex Sanchez SP 2.00 .90
❑ 235 Michael Coleman .15 .07
❑ 235S Michael Coleman SP 2.00 .90
❑ 236 Pat Burrell 1.00 .45
❑ 236S Pat Burrell SP 6.00 2.70
❑ 237 Wascar Serrano RC .50 .23
❑ 237S Wascar Serrano SP 2.50 1.10
❑ 238 Rick Ankiel 1.25 .55
❑ 238S Rick Ankiel SP 8.00 3.60
❑ 239 Mike Lamb RC .60 .25
❑ 239S Mike Lamb SP 3.00 1.35
❑ 240 Vernon Wells .25 .11
❑ 240S Vernon Wells SP 2.00 .90

❑ 241 Jorge Toca .15 .07
Geofrey Tomlinson
❑ 241S Jorge Toca 1.00 .45
Geofrey Tomlinson SP
❑ 242 Josh Phelps RC .40 .18
Shea Hillenbrand
❑ 242S Josh Phelps 1.00 .45
Shea Hillenbrand SP
❑ 243 Aaron Myette .25 .11
Doug Davis
❑ 243S Aaron Myette 1.00 .45
Doug Davis SP
❑ 244 Brett Laxton .15 .07
Rob Ramsay
❑ 244S Brett Laxton 1.00 .45
Rob Ramsay SP
❑ 245 B.J. Ryan .15 .07
Corey Lee
❑ 245S B.J.Ryan 1.00 .45
Corey Lee SP
❑ 246 Chris Haas .50 .23
Wilton Veras
❑ 246S Chris Haas 1.00 .45
Wilton Veras SP
❑ 247 Jimmy Anderson .15 .07
Kyle Peterson
❑ 247S Jimmy Anderson 1.00 .45
Kyle Peterson SP
❑ 248 Jason Dewey .15 .07
Giuseppe Chiaramonte
❑ 248S Jason Dewey 1.00 .45
Giuseppe Chiaramonte SP
❑ 249 Guillermo Mota .15 .07
Orber Moreno
❑ 249S Guillermo Mota 1.00 .45
Orber Moreno SP
❑ 250 Julio Zuleta RC .40 .18
Steve Cox
❑ 250S Julio Zuleta 1.00 .45
Steve Cox SP

## 2000 SkyBox Dominion

| | MINT | NRMT |
|---|---|---|
| COMPLETE SET (300) | 40.00 | 18.00 |
| COMMON CARD (1-250) | .10 | .05 |
| COMMON PROS (251-300) | .25 | .11 |

❑ 1 Mark McGwire LL .75 .35
Ken.Griffey Jr.
❑ 2 Mark McGwire LL .75 .35
Manny Ramirez
❑ 3 Larry Walker LL .60 .25
Nomar Garciaparra
❑ 4 Tony Womack LL .10 .05
Brian Hunter
❑ 5 Mike Hampton LL .15 .07
Pedro Martinez
❑ 6 Randy Johnson LL .15 .07
Pedro Martinez
❑ 7 Randy Johnson LL .15 .07
Pedro Martinez
❑ 8 Ugueth Urbina LL .10 .05
Mariano Rivera
❑ 9 Vinny Castilla HL .10 .05
❑ 10 Orioles/Cuban Nat'l HL .10 .05
❑ 11 Jose Canseco HL .25 .11
❑ 12 Fernando Tatis HL .10 .05
❑ 13 Robin Ventura HL .15 .07
❑ 14 Roger Clemens HL .40 .18
❑ 15 Jose Jimenez HL .10 .05
❑ 16 David Cone HL .15 .07
❑ 17 Mark McGwire HL .75 .35
❑ 18 Cal Ripken HL .75 .35
❑ 19 Tony Gwynn HL .40 .18
❑ 20 Wade Boggs HL .25 .11
❑ 21 Ivan Rodriguez HL .25 .11
❑ 22 Chuck Finley HL UER .10 .05
❑ 23 Eric Milton HL .10 .05
❑ 24 Adrian Beltre .15 .07
❑ 25 Brad Radke .15 .07
❑ 26 Derek Bell .10 .05
❑ 27 Garret Anderson .15 .07
❑ 28 Ivan Rodriguez .50 .23
❑ 29 Jeff Kent .25 .11
❑ 30 Jeremy Giambi .10 .05
❑ 31 John Franco .15 .07
❑ 32 Jose Hernandez .10 .05
❑ 33 Jose Offerman .10 .05
❑ 34 Jose Rosado .10 .05
❑ 35 Kevin Appier .10 .05
❑ 36 Kris Benson .15 .07
❑ 37 Mark McGwire 1.50 .70
❑ 38 Matt Williams .25 .11
❑ 39 Paul O'Neill .15 .07
❑ 40 Rickey Henderson .50 .23
❑ 41 Todd Greene .10 .05
❑ 42 Russ Ortiz .15 .07
❑ 43 Sean Casey .15 .07
❑ 44 Tony Womack .10 .05
❑ 45 Troy O'Leary .10 .05
❑ 46 Ugueth Urbina .10 .05
❑ 47 Tom Glavine .40 .18
❑ 48 Mike Mussina .40 .18
❑ 49 Carlos Febles .10 .05
❑ 50 Jon Lieber .10 .05
❑ 51 Juan Gonzalez .40 .18
❑ 52 Matt Clement .10 .05
❑ 53 Moises Alou .15 .07
❑ 54 Ray Durham .15 .07
❑ 55 Robb Nen .10 .05
❑ 56 Tino Martinez .15 .07
❑ 57 Troy Glaus .50 .23
❑ 58 Curt Schilling .15 .07
❑ 59 Mike Sweeney .15 .07
❑ 60 Steve Finley .15 .07
❑ 61 Roger Cedeno .10 .05
❑ 62 Bobby Jones .10 .05
❑ 63 John Smoltz .15 .07
❑ 64 Darin Erstad .40 .18
❑ 65 Carlos Delgado .40 .18
❑ 66 Ray Lankford .15 .07
❑ 67 Todd Stottlemyre .10 .05
❑ 68 Andy Ashby .10 .05
❑ 69 Bob Abreu .15 .07
❑ 70 Chuck Finley .15 .07
❑ 71 Damion Easley .10 .05
❑ 72 Dustin Hermanson .10 .05
❑ 73 Frank Thomas .75 .35
❑ 74 Kevin Brown .25 .11
❑ 75 Kevin Millwood .15 .07
❑ 76 Mark Grace .40 .18
❑ 77 Matt Stairs .10 .05
❑ 78 Mike Hampton .15 .07
❑ 79 Omar Vizquel .15 .07
❑ 80 Preston Wilson .15 .07
❑ 81 Robin Ventura .25 .11
❑ 82 Todd Helton .50 .23
❑ 83 Tony Clark .10 .05
❑ 84 Al Leiter .10 .05
❑ 85 Alex Fernandez .10 .05
❑ 86 Bernie Williams .40 .18
❑ 87 Edgar Martinez .25 .11
❑ 88 Edgar Renteria .10 .05
❑ 89 Fred McGriff .25 .11
❑ 90 Jermaine Dye .15 .07
❑ 91 Joe McEwing .10 .05
❑ 92 John Halama .10 .05
❑ 93 Lee Stevens .10 .05
❑ 94 Matt Lawton .10 .05
❑ 95 Mike Piazza 1.25 .55
❑ 96 Pete Harnisch .10 .05
❑ 97 Scott Karl .10 .05
❑ 98 Tony Fernandez .10 .05
❑ 99 Sammy Sosa .75 .35
❑ 100 Bobby Higginson .10 .05
❑ 101 Tony Gwynn .75 .35
❑ 102 J.D. Drew .40 .18
❑ 103 Roberto Hernandez .10 .05
❑ 104 Rondell White .15 .07
❑ 105 David Nilsson .10 .05
❑ 106 Shane Reynolds .10 .05
❑ 107 Jaret Wright .10 .05
❑ 108 Jeff Bagwell .50 .23
❑ 109 Jay Bell .15 .07
❑ 110 Kevin Tapani .10 .05
❑ 111 Michael Barrett .10 .05
❑ 112 Neifi Perez .10 .05
❑ 113 Pat Hengen .10 .05
❑ 114 Roger Clemens .75 .35
❑ 115 Travis Fryman .15 .07
❑ 116 Aaron Sele .10 .05
❑ 117 Eric Davis .15 .07
❑ 118 Trevor Hoffman .15 .07
❑ 119 Chris Singleton .15 .07
❑ 120 Ryan Klesko .15 .07
❑ 121 Scott Rolen .40 .18
❑ 122 Jorge Posada .15 .07
❑ 123 Abraham Nunez .10 .05
❑ 124 Alex Gonzalez .10 .05
❑ 125 B.J. Surhoff .15 .07
❑ 126 Barry Bonds .60 .25
❑ 127 Billy Koch .15 .07
❑ 128 Billy Wagner .10 .05
❑ 129 Brad Ausmus .10 .05
❑ 130 Bret Boone .10 .05
❑ 131 Cal Ripken 1.50 .70
❑ 132 Chad Allen .10 .05
❑ 133 Chris Carpenter .10 .05
❑ 134 Craig Biggio .25 .11
❑ 135 Dante Bichette .15 .07
❑ 136 Dean Palmer .15 .07
❑ 137 Derek Jeter 1.50 .70
❑ 138 Ellis Burks .15 .07
❑ 139 Freddy Garcia .15 .07
❑ 140 Gabe Kapler .15 .07
❑ 141 Greg Maddux 1.00 .45
❑ 142 Greg Vaughn .15 .07
❑ 143 Jason Kendall .15 .07
❑ 144 Jim Parque .10 .05
❑ 145 John Valentin .10 .05
❑ 146 Jose Vidro .10 .05
❑ 147 Ken Griffey Jr. 1.50 .70
❑ 148 Kenny Lofton .15 .07
❑ 149 Kenny Rogers .10 .05
❑ 150 Kent Bottenfield .10 .05
❑ 151 Chuck Knoblauch .15 .07
❑ 152 Larry Walker .15 .07
❑ 153 Manny Ramirez .50 .23
❑ 154 Mickey Morandini .10 .05
❑ 155 Mike Cameron .10 .05
❑ 156 Mike Lieberthal .15 .07
❑ 157 Mo Vaughn .15 .07
❑ 158 Randy Johnson .50 .23
❑ 159 Rey Ordonez .10 .05
❑ 160 Roberto Alomar .40 .18
❑ 161 Scott Williamson .10 .05
❑ 162 Shawn Estes .10 .05
❑ 163 Tim Wakefield .10 .05
❑ 164 Tony Batista .15 .07
❑ 165 Will Clark .40 .18
❑ 166 Wade Boggs .50 .23
❑ 167 David Cone .15 .07
❑ 168 Doug Glanville .10 .05
❑ 169 Jeff Cirillo .15 .07
❑ 170 John Jaha .10 .05
❑ 171 Mariano Rivera .15 .07
❑ 172 Tom Gordon .10 .05
❑ 173 Wally Joyner .15 .07
❑ 174 Alex Gonzalez .10 .05
❑ 175 Andruw Jones .40 .18
❑ 176 Barry Larkin .40 .18
❑ 177 Bartolo Colon .15 .07
❑ 178 Brian Giles .15 .07
❑ 179 Carlos Lee .15 .07
❑ 180 Darren Dreifort .10 .05
❑ 181 Eric Chavez .15 .07
❑ 182 Henry Rodriguez .10 .05
❑ 183 Ismael Valdes .10 .05
❑ 184 Jason Giambi .40 .18

❑ 185 John Wetteland .15 .07
❑ 186 Juan Encarnacion .15 .07
❑ 187 Luis Gonzalez .15 .07
❑ 188 Reggie Sanders .10 .05
❑ 189 Richard Hidalgo .15 .07
❑ 190 Ryan Rupe .10 .05
❑ 191 Sean Berry .10 .05
❑ 192 Rick Helling .15 .07
❑ 193 Randy Wolf .10 .05
❑ 194 Cliff Floyd .15 .07
❑ 195 Jose Lima .10 .05
❑ 196 Chipper Jones 1.00 .45
❑ 197 Charles Johnson .15 .07
❑ 198 Nomar Garciaparra 1.25 .55
❑ 199 Maggio Ordonez .15 .07
❑ 200 Shawn Green .40 .18
❑ 201 Travis Lee .10 .05
❑ 202 Jose Canseco .50 .23
❑ 203 Fernando Tatis .15 .07
❑ 204 Bruce Aven .10 .05
❑ 205 Johnny Damon .15 .07
❑ 206 Gary Sheffield .40 .18
❑ 207 Ken Caminiti .15 .07
❑ 208 Ben Grieve .15 .07
❑ 209 Sidney Ponson .10 .05
❑ 210 Vinny Castilla .15 .07
❑ 211 Alex Rodriguez 1.25 .55
❑ 212 Chris Widger .10 .05
❑ 213 Carl Pavano .10 .05
❑ 214 J.T. Snow .15 .07
❑ 215 Jim Thome .25 .11
❑ 216 Kevin Young .10 .05
❑ 217 Mike Sirotka .10 .05
❑ 218 Rafael Palmeiro .40 .18
❑ 219 Rico Brogna .10 .05
❑ 220 Todd Walker .10 .05
❑ 221 Todd Zeile .15 .07
❑ 222 Brian Rose .10 .05
❑ 223 Chris Fussell .10 .05
❑ 224 Corey Koskie .10 .05
❑ 225 Rich Aurilia .10 .05
❑ 226 Geoff Jenkins .15 .07
❑ 227 Pedro Martinez .50 .23
❑ 228 Todd Hundley .10 .05
❑ 229 Brian Jordan .15 .07
❑ 230 Cristian Guzman .10 .05
❑ 231 Raul Mondesi .15 .07
❑ 232 Tim Hudson .40 .18
❑ 233 Albert Belle .25 .11
❑ 234 Andy Pettitte .15 .07
❑ 235 Brady Anderson .15 .07
❑ 236 Brian Bohanon .10 .05
❑ 237 Carlos Beltran .15 .07
❑ 238 Doug Mientkiewicz .10 .05
❑ 239 Jason Schmidt .10 .05
❑ 240 Jeff Zimmerman .10 .05
❑ 241 John Olerud .15 .07
❑ 242 Paul Byrd .10 .05
❑ 243 Vladimir Guerrero .50 .23
❑ 244 Warren Morris .10 .05
❑ 245 Eric Karros .15 .07
❑ 246 Jeff Weaver .10 .05
❑ 247 Jeromy Burnitz .15 .07
❑ 248 David Bell .10 .05
❑ 249 Rusty Greer .15 .07
❑ 250 Kevin Stocker .10 .05
❑ 251 Shea Hillenbrand PROS .25 .11
❑ 252 Alfonso Soriano PROS .40 .18
❑ 253 Micah Bowie PROS .25 .11
❑ 254 Gary Matthews Jr. PROS .25 .11
❑ 255 Lance Berkman PROS .40 .18
❑ 256 Pat Burrell PROS 1.25 .55
❑ 257 Ruben Mateo PROS .40 .18
❑ 258 Kip Wells PROS .40 .18
❑ 259 Wilton Veras PROS .40 .18
❑ 260 Ben Davis PROS .25 .11
❑ 261 Eric Munson PROS .75 .35
❑ 262 Ramon Hernandez PROS .25 .11
❑ 263 Tony Armas Jr. PROS .40 .18
❑ 264 Erubiel Durazo PROS .40 .18
❑ 265 Chad Meyers PROS .25 .11
❑ 266 Rick Ankiel PROS 1.50 .70
❑ 267 Ramon Ortiz PROS .40 .18
❑ 268 Adam Kennedy PROS .40 .18
❑ 269 Vernon Wells PROS .40 .18
❑ 270 Chad Hermansen PROS .25 .11
❑ 271 Norm Hutchins .25 .11
Trent Durrington
❑ 272 Gabe Molina .25 .11
B.J. Ryan
❑ 273 Juan Pena .60 .25
Tomakazu Ohka RC
❑ 274 Pat Daneker .25 .11
Aaron Myette
❑ 275 Jason Rakers .40 .18
Russ Branyan
❑ 276 Beiker Graterol .25 .11
Dave Borkowski
❑ 277 Mark Quinn .40 .18
Dan Reichert
❑ 278 Mark Redman .40 .18
Jacque Jones
❑ 279 Ed Yarnall .75 .35
Wily Pena
❑ 280 Chad Harville .25 .11
Brett Laxton
❑ 281 Aaron Scheffer .40 .18
Gil Meche
❑ 282 Jim Morris .25 .11
Dan Wheeler
❑ 283 Danny Kolb .25 .11
Kelly Dransfeldt
❑ 284 Peter Munro .25 .11
Casey Blake
❑ 285 Rob Ryan .40 .18
Byung-Hyun Kim
❑ 286 Derrin Ebert .25 .11
Pascual Matos
❑ 287 Richard Barker .25 .11
Kyle Farnsworth
❑ 288 Jason LaRue .25 .11
Travis Dawkins
❑ 289 Chris Sexton .25 .11
Edgard Clemente
❑ 290 Amaury Garcia .40 .18
A.J. Burnett
❑ 291 Carlos Hernandez .40 .18
Daryle Ward
❑ 292 Eric Gagne .50 .23
Jeff R.Williams RC
❑ 293 Kyle Peterson .25 .11
Kevin Barker
❑ 294 Fernando Seguignol .25 .11
Guillermo Mota
❑ 295 Melvin Mora .25 .11
Octavio Dotel
❑ 296 Anthony Shumaker .25 .11
Cliff Politte
❑ 297 Yamid Haad .25 .11
Jimmy Anderson
❑ 298 Rick Heiserman .25 .11
Chad Hutchinson
❑ 299 Mike Darr .40 .18
Wiki Gonzalez
❑ 300 Joe Nathan .25 .11
Calvin Murray
❑ P211 Alex Rodriguez Promo 2.00

## 1993 SP

| | MINT | NRMT |
|---|---|---|
| COMPLETE SET (290) | 160.00 | 70.00 |
| COMMON CARD (1-270) | .40 | .11 |
| FOIL PROSPECTS (271-290) | 1.00 | .23 |
| FOIL MINOR STARS | 2.00 | |
| FOIL SEMISTARS | 3.00 | |
| FOIL UNLISTED STARS | 5.00 | |

❑ 1 Roberto Alomar AS 1.50 .70
❑ 2 Wade Boggs AS 2.00 .90
❑ 3 Joe Carter AS .25 .11
❑ 4 Ken Griffey Jr. AS 6.00 2.70
❑ 5 Mark Langston AS .25 .11
❑ 6 John Olerud AS 1.00 .45
❑ 7 Kirby Puckett AS 4.00 1.80
❑ 8 Cal Ripken Jr. AS 6.00 2.70
❑ 9 Ivan Rodriguez AS 2.00 .90
❑ 10 Barry Bonds AS 2.50 1.10
❑ 11 Darren Daulton AS .50 .23
❑ 12 Marquis Grissom AS .25 .11
❑ 13 David Justice AS 1.00 .45
❑ 14 John Kruk AS .50 .23
❑ 15 Barry Larkin AS 1.50 .70
❑ 16 Terry Mulholland AS .25 .11
❑ 17 Ryne Sandberg AS 2.00 .90
❑ 18 Gary Sheffield AS 1.50 .70
❑ 19 Chad Curtis .25 .11
❑ 20 Chili Davis .50 .23
❑ 21 Gary DiSarcina .25 .11
❑ 22 Damion Easley .25 .11
❑ 23 Chuck Finley .50 .23
❑ 24 Luis Polonia .25 .11
❑ 25 Tim Salmon .50 .23
❑ 26 J.T. Snow RC 2.00 .90
❑ 27 Russ Springer .25 .11
❑ 28 Jeff Bagwell 2.00 .90
❑ 29 Craig Biggio 1.00 .45
❑ 30 Ken Caminiti .50 .23
❑ 31 Andujar Cedeno .25 .11
❑ 32 Doug Drabek .25 .11
❑ 33 Steve Finley .50 .23
❑ 34 Luis Gonzalez .50 .23
❑ 35 Pete Harnisch .25 .11
❑ 36 Darryl Kile .50 .23
❑ 37 Mike Bordick .25 .11
❑ 38 Dennis Eckersley .50 .23
❑ 39 Brent Gates .25 .11
❑ 40 Rickey Henderson 2.00 .90
❑ 41 Mark McGwire 6.00 2.70
❑ 42 Craig Paquette .25 .11
❑ 43 Ruben Sierra .25 .11
❑ 44 Terry Steinbach .25 .11
❑ 45 Todd Van Poppel .25 .11
❑ 46 Pat Borders .25 .11
❑ 47 Tony Fernandez .25 .11
❑ 48 Juan Guzman .25 .11
❑ 49 Pat Hentgen .25 .11
❑ 50 Paul Molitor 1.50 .70
❑ 51 Jack Morris .50 .23
❑ 52 Ed Sprague .25 .11
❑ 53 Duane Ward .25 .11
❑ 54 Devon White .25 .11
❑ 55 Steve Avery .25 .11
❑ 56 Jeff Blauser .25 .11
❑ 57 Ron Gant .50 .23
❑ 58 Tom Glavine 1.00 .45
❑ 59 Greg Maddux 4.00 1.80
❑ 60 Fred McGriff 1.00 .45
❑ 61 Terry Pendleton .50 .23
❑ 62 Deion Sanders 1.00 .45
❑ 63 John Smoltz .50 .23
❑ 64 Cal Eldred .25 .11
❑ 65 Darryl Hamilton .25 .11
❑ 66 John Jaha .25 .11
❑ 67 Pat Listach .25 .11
❑ 68 Jaime Navarro .25 .11
❑ 69 Kevin Reimer .25 .11
❑ 70 B.J. Surhoff .50 .23
❑ 71 Greg Vaughn .50 .23
❑ 72 Robin Yount 1.00 .45
❑ 73 Rene Arocha RC .25 .11
❑ 74 Bernard Gilkey .25 .11
❑ 75 Gregg Jefferies .25 .11
❑ 76 Ray Lankford 1.00 .45
❑ 77 Tom Pagnozzi .25 .11
❑ 78 Lee Smith .50 .23
❑ 79 Ozzie Smith 2.00 .90
❑ 80 Bob Tewksbury .25 .11
❑ 81 Mark Whiten .25 .11
❑ 82 Steve Buechele .25 .11

| No. | Player | Mint | NrMt |
|---|---|---|---|
| 83 | Mark Grace | 1.50 | .70 |
| 84 | Jose Guzman | .25 | .11 |
| 85 | Derrick May | .25 | .11 |
| 86 | Mike Morgan | .25 | .11 |
| 87 | Randy Myers | .50 | .23 |
| 88 | Kevin Roberson RC | .25 | .11 |
| 89 | Sammy Sosa | 3.00 | 1.35 |
| 90 | Rick Wilkins | .25 | .11 |
| 91 | Brett Butler | .50 | .23 |
| 92 | Eric Davis | .50 | .23 |
| 93 | Orel Hershiser | .50 | .23 |
| 94 | Eric Karros | 1.00 | .45 |
| 95 | Ramon Martinez | .25 | .11 |
| 96 | Raul Mondesi | .50 | .23 |
| 97 | Jose Offerman | .25 | .11 |
| 98 | Mike Piazza | 8.00 | 3.60 |
| 99 | Darryl Strawberry | .50 | .23 |
| 100 | Moises Alou | .50 | .23 |
| 101 | Wil Cordero | .25 | .11 |
| 102 | Delino DeShields | .50 | .23 |
| 103 | Darrin Fletcher | .25 | .11 |
| 104 | Ken Hill | .25 | .11 |
| 105 | Mike Lansing RC | .50 | .23 |
| 106 | Dennis Martinez | .50 | .23 |
| 107 | Larry Walker | .50 | .23 |
| 108 | John Wetteland | .50 | .23 |
| 109 | Rod Beck | .25 | .11 |
| 110 | John Burkett | .25 | .11 |
| 111 | Will Clark | 1.50 | .70 |
| 112 | Royce Clayton | .25 | .11 |
| 113 | Darren Lewis | .25 | .11 |
| 114 | Willie McGee | .50 | .23 |
| 115 | Bill Swift | .25 | .11 |
| 116 | Robby Thompson | .25 | .11 |
| 117 | Matt Williams | 1.00 | .45 |
| 118 | Sandy Alomar Jr. | .50 | .23 |
| 119 | Carlos Baerga | .25 | .11 |
| 120 | Albert Belle | 1.00 | .45 |
| 121 | Reggie Jefferson | .50 | .23 |
| 122 | Wayne Kirby | .25 | .11 |
| 123 | Kenny Lofton | 1.50 | .70 |
| 124 | Carlos Martinez | .25 | .11 |
| 125 | Charles Nagy | .25 | .11 |
| 126 | Paul Sorrento | .25 | .11 |
| 127 | Rich Amaral | .25 | .11 |
| 128 | Jay Buhner | .50 | .23 |
| 129 | Norm Charlton | .25 | .11 |
| 130 | Dave Fleming | .25 | .11 |
| 131 | Erik Hanson | .25 | .11 |
| 132 | Randy Johnson | 2.00 | .90 |
| 133 | Edgar Martinez | 1.00 | .45 |
| 134 | Tino Martinez | .50 | .23 |
| 135 | Omar Vizquel | .50 | .23 |
| 136 | Bret Barberie | .25 | .11 |
| 137 | Chuck Carr | .25 | .11 |
| 138 | Jeff Conine | .25 | .11 |
| 139 | Orestes Destrade | .25 | .11 |
| 140 | Chris Hammond | .25 | .11 |
| 141 | Bryan Harvey | .25 | .11 |
| 142 | Benito Santiago | .25 | .11 |
| 143 | Walt Weiss | .25 | .11 |
| 144 | Darrell Whitmore RC | .25 | .11 |
| 145 | Tim Bogar RC | .25 | .11 |
| 146 | Bobby Bonilla | .50 | .23 |
| 147 | Jeromy Burnitz | .50 | .23 |
| 148 | Vince Coleman | .25 | .11 |
| 149 | Dwight Gooden | .50 | .23 |
| 150 | Todd Hundley | .25 | .11 |
| 151 | Howard Johnson | .25 | .11 |
| 152 | Eddie Murray | 1.50 | .70 |
| 153 | Bret Saberhagen | .50 | .23 |
| 154 | Brady Anderson | .50 | .23 |
| 155 | Mike Devereaux | .25 | .11 |
| 156 | Jeffrey Hammonds | .50 | .23 |
| 157 | Chris Hoiles | .25 | .11 |
| 158 | Ben McDonald | .25 | .11 |
| 159 | Mark McLemore | .25 | .11 |
| 160 | Mike Mussina | 1.50 | .70 |
| 161 | Gregg Olson | .25 | .11 |
| 162 | David Segui | .25 | .11 |
| 163 | Derek Bell | .25 | .11 |
| 164 | Andy Benes | .25 | .11 |
| 165 | Archi Cianfrocco | .25 | .11 |
| 166 | Ricky Gutierrez | .25 | .11 |
| 167 | Tony Gwynn | 3.00 | 1.35 |
| 168 | Gene Harris | .25 | .11 |
| 169 | Trevor Hoffman | 1.50 | .70 |
| 170 | Ray McDavid RC | .25 | .11 |
| 171 | Phil Plantier | .25 | .11 |
| 172 | Mariano Duncan | .25 | .11 |
| 173 | Len Dykstra | .50 | .23 |
| 174 | Tommy Greene | .25 | .11 |
| 175 | Dave Hollins | .25 | .11 |
| 176 | Pete Incaviglia | .25 | .11 |
| 177 | Mickey Morandini | .25 | .11 |
| 178 | Curt Schilling | .50 | .23 |
| 179 | Kevin Stocker | .25 | .11 |
| 180 | Mitch Williams | .25 | .11 |
| 181 | Stan Belinda | .25 | .11 |
| 182 | Jay Bell | .50 | .23 |
| 183 | Steve Cooke | .25 | .11 |
| 184 | Carlos Garcia | .25 | .11 |
| 185 | Jeff King | .25 | .11 |
| 186 | Orlando Merced | .25 | .11 |
| 187 | Don Slaught | .25 | .11 |
| 188 | Andy Van Slyke | .50 | .23 |
| 189 | Kevin Young | .50 | .23 |
| 190 | Kevin Brown | 1.00 | .45 |
| 191 | Jose Canseco | 2.00 | .90 |
| 192 | Julio Franco | .25 | .11 |
| 193 | Benji Gil | .25 | .11 |
| 194 | Juan Gonzalez | 1.50 | .70 |
| 195 | Tom Henke | .25 | .11 |
| 196 | Rafael Palmeiro | 1.50 | .70 |
| 197 | Dean Palmer | .50 | .23 |
| 198 | Nolan Ryan | 8.00 | 3.60 |
| 199 | Roger Clemens | 3.00 | 1.35 |
| 200 | Scott Cooper | .25 | .11 |
| 201 | Andre Dawson | 1.00 | .45 |
| 202 | Mike Greenwell | .25 | .11 |
| 203 | Carlos Quintana | .25 | .11 |
| 204 | Jeff Russell | .25 | .11 |
| 205 | Aaron Sele | 1.50 | .70 |
| 206 | Mo Vaughn | .50 | .23 |
| 207 | Frank Viola | .25 | .11 |
| 208 | Rob Dibble | .25 | .11 |
| 209 | Roberto Kelly | .25 | .11 |
| 210 | Kevin Mitchell | .50 | .23 |
| 211 | Hal Morris | .25 | .11 |
| 212 | Joe Oliver | .25 | .11 |
| 213 | Jose Rijo | .25 | .11 |
| 214 | Bip Roberts | .25 | .11 |
| 215 | Chris Sabo | .25 | .11 |
| 216 | Reggie Sanders | .25 | .11 |
| 217 | Dante Bichette | .50 | .23 |
| 218 | Jerald Clark | .25 | .11 |
| 219 | Alex Cole | .25 | .11 |
| 220 | Andres Galarraga | 1.00 | .45 |
| 221 | Joe Girardi | .50 | .23 |
| 222 | Charlie Hayes | .25 | .11 |
| 223 | Roberto Mejia RC | .25 | .11 |
| 224 | Armando Reynoso | .25 | .11 |
| 225 | Eric Young | .25 | .11 |
| 226 | Kevin Appier | .50 | .23 |
| 227 | George Brett | 3.00 | 1.35 |
| 228 | David Cone | .50 | .23 |
| 229 | Phil Hiatt | .25 | .11 |
| 230 | Felix Jose | .25 | .11 |
| 231 | Wally Joyner | .50 | .23 |
| 232 | Mike Macfarlane | .25 | .11 |
| 233 | Brian McRae | .25 | .11 |
| 234 | Jeff Montgomery | .50 | .23 |
| 235 | Rob Deer | .25 | .11 |
| 236 | Cecil Fielder | .50 | .23 |
| 237 | Travis Fryman | .50 | .23 |
| 238 | Mike Henneman | .25 | .11 |
| 239 | Tony Phillips | .25 | .11 |
| 240 | Mickey Tettleton | .25 | .11 |
| 241 | Alan Trammell | 1.00 | .45 |
| 242 | David Wells | .50 | .23 |
| 243 | Lou Whitaker | .50 | .23 |
| 244 | Rick Aguilera | .25 | .11 |
| 245 | Scott Erickson | .25 | .11 |
| 246 | Brian Harper | .25 | .11 |
| 247 | Kent Hrbek | .50 | .23 |
| 248 | Chuck Knoblauch | .50 | .23 |
| 249 | Shane Mack | .25 | .11 |
| 250 | David McCarty | .25 | .11 |
| 251 | Pedro Munoz | .25 | .11 |
| 252 | Dave Winfield | 1.50 | .70 |
| 253 | Alex Fernandez | .50 | .23 |
| 254 | Ozzie Guillen | .25 | .11 |
| 255 | Bo Jackson | .50 | .23 |
| 256 | Lance Johnson | .25 | .11 |
| 257 | Ron Karkovice | .25 | .11 |
| 258 | Jack McDowell | .25 | .11 |
| 259 | Tim Raines | .50 | .23 |
| 260 | Frank Thomas | 3.00 | 1.35 |
| 261 | Robin Ventura | .50 | .23 |
| 262 | Jim Abbott | .50 | .23 |
| 263 | Steve Farr | .25 | .11 |
| 264 | Jimmy Key | .50 | .23 |
| 265 | Don Mattingly | 4.00 | 1.80 |
| 266 | Paul O'Neill | .50 | .23 |
| 267 | Mike Stanley | .25 | .11 |
| 268 | Danny Tartabull | .25 | .11 |
| 269 | Bob Wickman | .25 | .11 |
| 270 | Bernie Williams | 1.50 | .70 |
| 271 | Jason Bere FOIL | .50 | .23 |
| 272 | Roger Cedeno FOIL RC | 4.00 | 1.80 |
| 273 | Johnny Damon FOIL RC | 12.00 | 5.50 |
| 274 | Russ Davis FOIL RC | 2.00 | .90 |
| 275 | Carlos Delgado FOIL | 5.00 | 2.20 |
| 276 | Carl Everett FOIL | 3.00 | 1.35 |
| 277 | Cliff Floyd FOIL | .50 | .23 |
| 278 | Alex Gonzalez FOIL | .50 | .23 |
| 279 | Derek Jeter FOIL RC | 120.00 | 55.00 |
| 280 | Chipper Jones FOIL | 8.00 | 3.60 |
| 281 | Javier Lopez FOIL | .50 | .23 |
| 282 | Chad Mottola FOIL RC | .50 | .23 |
| 283 | Marc Newfield FOIL | .50 | .23 |
| 284 | Eduardo Perez FOIL | .50 | .23 |
| 285 | Manny Ramirez FOIL | 6.00 | 2.70 |
| 286 | Todd Steverson FOIL RC | .50 | .23 |
| 287 | Michael Tucker FOIL | 1.50 | .70 |
| 288 | Allen Watson FOIL | .50 | .23 |
| 289 | Rondell White FOIL | 1.00 | .45 |
| 290 | Dmitri Young FOIL | 2.00 | .90 |

## 1994 SP

| | MINT | NRMT |
|---|---|---|
| COMPLETE SET (200) | 140.00 | 65.00 |
| COMMON FOIL (1-20) | .50 | .23 |
| COMMON CARD (21-200) | .20 | .09 |

| No. | Player | Mint | NrMt |
|---|---|---|---|
| 1 | Mike Bell FOIL RC | .50 | .23 |
| 2 | D.J. Boston FOIL RC | .50 | .23 |
| 3 | Johnny Damon FOIL | .75 | .35 |
| 4 | Brad Fullmer FOIL RC | 5.00 | 2.20 |
| 5 | Joey Hamilton FOIL | .20 | .09 |
| 6 | Todd Hollandsworth FOIL | .20 | .09 |
| 7 | Brian L. Hunter FOIL | .20 | .09 |
| 8 | LaTroy Hawkins FOIL RC | .75 | .23 |
| 9 | Brooks Kieschnick FOIL RC | .50 | .23 |
| 10 | Derrek Lee FOIL RC | 2.00 | .90 |
| 11 | Trot Nixon FOIL RC | 5.00 | 2.20 |
| 12 | Alex Ochoa FOIL | .50 | .23 |
| 13 | Chan Ho Park FOIL RC | 3.00 | 1.35 |
| 14 | Kirk Presley FOIL RC | .50 | .23 |
| 15 | Alex Rodriguez FOIL RC ! | 100.00 | 45.00 |
| 16 | Jose Silva FOIL RC | .50 | .23 |
| 17 | Terrell Wade FOIL RC | .50 | .23 |
| 18 | Billy Wagner FOIL RC | 2.00 | .90 |
| 19 | Glenn Williams FOIL RC | .75 | .35 |
| 20 | Preston Wilson FOIL | 2.00 | .90 |
| 21 | Brian Anderson RC | .75 | .35 |
| 22 | Chad Curtis | .20 | .09 |
| 23 | Chili Davis | .40 | .18 |
| 24 | Bo Jackson | .40 | .18 |

❑ 25 Mark Langston .20 .09
❑ 26 Tim Salmon .40 .18
❑ 27 Jeff Bagwell 1.00 .45
❑ 28 Craig Biggio .50 .23
❑ 29 Ken Caminiti .40 .18
❑ 30 Doug Drabek .20 .09
❑ 31 John Hudek RC .20 .09
❑ 32 Greg Swindell .20 .09
❑ 33 Brent Gates .20 .09
❑ 34 Rickey Henderson 1.00 .45
❑ 35 Steve Karsay .20 .09
❑ 36 Mark McGwire 3.00 1.35
❑ 37 Ruben Sierra .20 .09
❑ 38 Terry Steinbach .20 .09
❑ 39 Roberto Alomar .75 .35
❑ 40 Joe Carter .40 .18
❑ 41 Carlos Delgado 1.25 .55
❑ 42 Alex Gonzalez .20 .09
❑ 43 Juan Guzman .20 .09
❑ 44 Paul Molitor .75 .35
❑ 45 John Olerud .40 .18
❑ 46 Devon White .20 .09
❑ 47 Steve Avery .20 .09
❑ 48 Jeff Blauser .20 .09
❑ 49 Tom Glavine .75 .35
❑ 50 David Justice .50 .23
❑ 51 Roberto Kelly .20 .09
❑ 52 Ryan Klesko .40 .18
❑ 53 Javier Lopez .40 .18
❑ 54 Greg Maddux 2.00 .90
❑ 55 Fred McGriff .50 .23
❑ 56 Ricky Bones .20 .09
❑ 57 Cal Eldred .20 .09
❑ 58 Brian Harper .20 .09
❑ 59 Pat Listach .20 .09
❑ 60 B.J. Surhoff .40 .18
❑ 61 Greg Vaughn .40 .18
❑ 62 Bernard Gilkey .20 .09
❑ 63 Gregg Jefferies .20 .09
❑ 64 Ray Lankford .40 .18
❑ 65 Ozzie Smith 1.00 .45
❑ 66 Bob Tewksbury .20 .09
❑ 67 Mark Whiten .20 .09
❑ 68 Todd Zeile .20 .09
❑ 69 Mark Grace .75 .35
❑ 70 Randy Myers .20 .09
❑ 71 Ryne Sandberg 1.00 .45
❑ 72 Sammy Sosa 1.50 .70
❑ 73 Steve Trachsel .20 .09
❑ 74 Rick Wilkins .20 .09
❑ 75 Brett Butler .40 .18
❑ 76 Delino DeShields .20 .09
❑ 77 Orel Hershiser .40 .18
❑ 78 Eric Karros .40 .18
❑ 79 Raul Mondesi .40 .18
❑ 80 Mike Piazza 2.50 1.10
❑ 81 Tim Wallach .20 .09
❑ 82 Moises Alou .40 .18
❑ 83 Cliff Floyd .40 .18
❑ 84 Marquis Grissom .20 .09
❑ 85 Pedro Martinez 1.25 .55
❑ 86 Larry Walker .40 .18
❑ 87 John Wetteland .40 .18
❑ 88 Rondell White .40 .18
❑ 89 Rod Beck .20 .09
❑ 90 Barry Bonds 1.25 .55
❑ 91 John Burkett .20 .09
❑ 92 Royce Clayton .20 .09
❑ 93 Billy Swift .20 .09
❑ 94 Robby Thompson .20 .09
❑ 95 Matt Williams .50 .23
❑ 96 Carlos Baerga .20 .09
❑ 97 Albert Belle .50 .23
❑ 98 Kenny Lofton .40 .18
❑ 99 Dennis Martinez .40 .18
❑ 100 Eddie Murray .75 .35
❑ 101 Manny Ramirez 1.25 .55
❑ 102 Eric Anthony .20 .09
❑ 103 Chris Bosio .20 .09
❑ 104 Jay Buhner .40 .18
❑ 105 Ken Griffey Jr. 3.00 1.35
❑ 106 Randy Johnson 1.00 .45
❑ 107 Edgar Martinez .50 .23
❑ 108 Chuck Carr .20 .09
❑ 109 Jeff Conine .20 .09
❑ 110 Carl Everett .40 .18
❑ 111 Chris Hammond .20 .09
❑ 112 Bryan Harvey .20 .09
❑ 113 Charles Johnson .40 .18
❑ 114 Gary Sheffield .75 .35
❑ 115 Bobby Bonilla .40 .18
❑ 116 Dwight Gooden .40 .18
❑ 117 Todd Hundley .20 .09
❑ 118 Bobby Jones .20 .09
❑ 119 Jeff Kent .50 .23
❑ 120 Bret Saberhagen .40 .18
❑ 121 Jeffrey Hammonds .40 .18
❑ 122 Chris Hoiles .20 .09
❑ 123 Ben McDonald .20 .09
❑ 124 Mike Mussina .75 .35
❑ 125 Rafael Palmeiro .75 .35
❑ 126 Cal Ripken Jr. 3.00 1.35
❑ 127 Lee Smith .40 .18
❑ 128 Derek Bell .20 .09
❑ 129 Andy Benes .20 .09
❑ 130 Tony Gwynn 1.50 .70
❑ 131 Trevor Hoffman .40 .18
❑ 132 Phil Plantier .20 .09
❑ 133 Bip Roberts .20 .09
❑ 134 Darren Daulton .40 .18
❑ 135 Lenny Dykstra .40 .18
❑ 136 Dave Hollins .20 .09
❑ 137 Danny Jackson .20 .09
❑ 138 John Kruk .40 .18
❑ 139 Kevin Stocker .20 .09
❑ 140 Jay Bell .40 .18
❑ 141 Carlos Garcia .20 .09
❑ 142 Jeff King .20 .09
❑ 143 Orlando Merced .20 .09
❑ 144 Andy Van Slyke .40 .18
❑ 145 Rick White .20 .09
❑ 146 Jose Canseco 1.00 .45
❑ 147 Will Clark .75 .35
❑ 148 Juan Gonzalez .75 .35
❑ 149 Rick Helling .40 .18
❑ 150 Dean Palmer .40 .18
❑ 151 Ivan Rodriguez 1.00 .45
❑ 152 Roger Clemens 1.50 .70
❑ 153 Scott Cooper .20 .09
❑ 154 Andre Dawson .50 .23
❑ 155 Mike Greenwell .20 .09
❑ 156 Aaron Sele .40 .18
❑ 157 Mo Vaughn .40 .18
❑ 158 Bret Boone .40 .18
❑ 159 Barry Larkin .75 .35
❑ 160 Kevin Mitchell .20 .09
❑ 161 Jose Rijo .20 .09
❑ 162 Deion Sanders .40 .18
❑ 163 Reggie Sanders .20 .09
❑ 164 Dante Bichette .40 .18
❑ 165 Ellis Burks .40 .18
❑ 166 Andres Galarraga .50 .23
❑ 167 Charlie Hayes .20 .09
❑ 168 David Nied .20 .09
❑ 169 Walt Weiss .20 .09
❑ 170 Kevin Appier .40 .18
❑ 171 David Cone .40 .18
❑ 172 Jeff Granger .20 .09
❑ 173 Felix Jose .20 .09
❑ 174 Wally Joyner .40 .18
❑ 175 Brian McRae .20 .09
❑ 176 Cecil Fielder .40 .18
❑ 177 Travis Fryman .40 .18
❑ 178 Mike Henneman .20 .09
❑ 179 Tony Phillips .20 .09
❑ 180 Mickey Tettleton .20 .09
❑ 181 Alan Trammell .50 .23
❑ 182 Rick Aguilera .20 .09
❑ 183 Rich Becker .20 .09
❑ 184 Scott Erickson .20 .09
❑ 185 Chuck Knoblauch .40 .18
❑ 186 Kirby Puckett 2.00 .90
❑ 187 Dave Winfield .75 .35
❑ 188 Wilson Alvarez .20 .09
❑ 189 Jason Bere .20 .09
❑ 190 Alex Fernandez .20 .09
❑ 191 Julio Franco .20 .09
❑ 192 Jack McDowell .20 .09
❑ 193 Frank Thomas 1.50 .70
❑ 194 Robin Ventura .40 .18
❑ 195 Jim Abbott .40 .18
❑ 196 Wade Boggs 1.00 .45
❑ 197 Jimmy Key .40 .18
❑ 198 Don Mattingly 2.00 .90
❑ 199 Paul O'Neill .40 .18
❑ 200 Danny Tartabull .20 .09
❑ P24 Ken Griffey Jr. Promo 3.00 1.35

## 1995 SP

| | MINT | NRMT |
|---|---|---|
| COMPLETE SET (207) | 40.00 | 18.00 |
| COMMON CARD (1-207) | .20 | .09 |
| FOIL PROSPECTS (5-24) | .25 | .11 |

❑ 1 Cal Ripken Salute 3.00 1.35
❑ 2 Nolan Ryan Salute 4.00 1.80
❑ 3 George Brett Salute 1.50 .70
❑ 4 Mike Schmidt Salute 1.25 .55
❑ 5 Dustin Hermanson FOIL .20 .11
❑ 6 Antonio Osuna FOIL .25 .11
❑ 7 Mark Grudzielanek FOIL RC .40 .18
❑ 8 Ray Durham FOIL .40 .18
❑ 9 Ugueth Urbina FOIL .25 .11
❑ 10 Ruben Rivera FOIL .20 .11
❑ 11 Curtis Goodwin FOIL .25 .11
❑ 12 Jimmy Hurst FOIL .25 .11
❑ 13 Jose Malave FOIL .25 .11
❑ 14 Hideo Nomo FOIL RC 2.00 .90
❑ 15 Juan Acevedo RC FOIL .25 .11
❑ 16 Tony Clark FOIL .40 .18
❑ 17 Jim Pittsley FOIL .25 .11
❑ 18 Freddy Garcia RC FOIL .25 .11
❑ 19 Carlos Perez RC FOIL .40 .11
❑ 20 Raul Casanova FOIL RC .25 .11
❑ 21 Quilvio Veras FOIL .25 .11
❑ 22 Edgardo Alfonzo FOIL .75 .35
❑ 23 Marty Cordova FOIL .25 .11
❑ 24 C.J. Nitkowski FOIL .25 .11
❑ 25 Wade Boggs CL .40 .18
❑ 26 Dave Winfield CL .40 .18
❑ 27 Eddie Murray CL .40 .18
❑ 28 David Justice .50 .23
❑ 29 Marquis Grissom .20 .09
❑ 30 Fred McGriff .50 .23
❑ 31 Greg Maddux 2.00 .90
❑ 32 Tom Glavine .75 .35
❑ 33 Steve Avery .20 .09
❑ 34 Chipper Jones 2.00 .90
❑ 35 Sammy Sosa 1.50 .70
❑ 36 Jaime Navarro .20 .09
❑ 37 Randy Myers .20 .09
❑ 38 Mark Grace .75 .35
❑ 39 Todd Zeile .20 .09
❑ 40 Brian McRae .20 .09
❑ 41 Reggie Sanders .20 .09
❑ 42 Ron Gant .20 .09
❑ 43 Deion Sanders .40 .18
❑ 44 Bret Boone .40 .18
❑ 45 Barry Larkin .75 .35
❑ 46 Jose Rijo .20 .09
❑ 47 Jason Bates .20 .09
❑ 48 Andres Galarraga .50 .23
❑ 49 Bill Swift .20 .09
❑ 50 Larry Walker .40 .18
❑ 51 Vinny Castilla .40 .18
❑ 52 Dante Bichette .40 .18
❑ 53 Jeff Conine .20 .09
❑ 54 John Burkett .20 .09
❑ 55 Gary Sheffield .75 .35

❑ 56 Andre Dawson .50 .23
❑ 57 Terry Pendleton .40 .18
❑ 58 Charles Johnson .40 .18
❑ 59 Brian L. Hunter .20 .09
❑ 60 Jeff Bagwell 1.00 .45
❑ 61 Craig Biggio .50 .23
❑ 62 Phil Nevin .40 .18
❑ 63 Doug Drabek .20 .09
❑ 64 Derek Bell .20 .09
❑ 65 Raul Mondesi .40 .18
❑ 66 Eric Karros .40 .18
❑ 67 Roger Cedeno .20 .09
❑ 68 Delino DeShields .20 .09
❑ 69 Ramon Martinez .20 .09
❑ 70 Mike Piazza 2.50 1.10
❑ 71 Billy Ashley .20 .09
❑ 72 Jeff Fassero .20 .09
❑ 73 Shane Andrews .20 .09
❑ 74 Wil Cordero .20 .09
❑ 75 Tony Tarasco .20 .09
❑ 76 Rondell White .40 .18
❑ 77 Pedro Martinez 1.00 .45
❑ 78 Moises Alou .40 .18
❑ 79 Rico Brogna .20 .09
❑ 80 Bobby Bonilla .40 .18
❑ 81 Jeff Kent .50 .23
❑ 82 Brett Butler .40 .18
❑ 83 Bobby Jones .20 .09
❑ 84 Bill Pulsipher .20 .09
❑ 85 Bret Saberhagen .40 .18
❑ 86 Gregg Jefferies .20 .09
❑ 87 Lenny Dykstra .40 .18
❑ 88 Dave Hollins .20 .09
❑ 89 Charlie Hayes .20 .09
❑ 90 Darren Daulton .40 .18
❑ 91 Curt Schilling .40 .18
❑ 92 Heathcliff Slocumb .20 .09
❑ 93 Carlos Garcia .20 .09
❑ 94 Denny Neagle .40 .18
❑ 95 Jay Bell .40 .18
❑ 96 Orlando Merced .20 .09
❑ 97 Dave Clark .20 .09
❑ 98 Bernard Gilkey .20 .09
❑ 99 Scott Cooper .20 .09
❑ 100 Ozzie Smith 1.00 .45
❑ 101 Tom Henke .20 .09
❑ 102 Ken Hill .20 .09
❑ 103 Brian Jordan .40 .18
❑ 104 Ray Lankford .40 .18
❑ 105 Tony Gwynn 1.50 .70
❑ 106 Andy Benes .20 .09
❑ 107 Ken Caminiti .40 .18
❑ 108 Steve Finley .40 .18
❑ 109 Joey Hamilton .20 .09
❑ 110 Bip Roberts .20 .09
❑ 111 Eddie Williams .20 .09
❑ 112 Rod Beck .20 .09
❑ 113 Matt Williams .50 .23
❑ 114 Glenallen Hill .20 .09
❑ 115 Barry Bonds 1.25 .55
❑ 116 Robby Thompson .20 .09
❑ 117 Mark Portugal .20 .09
❑ 118 Brady Anderson .40 .18
❑ 119 Mike Mussina .75 .35
❑ 120 Rafael Palmeiro .75 .35
❑ 121 Chris Hoiles .20 .09
❑ 122 Harold Baines .40 .18
❑ 123 Jeffrey Hammonds .40 .18
❑ 124 Tim Naehring .20 .09
❑ 125 Mo Vaughn .40 .18
❑ 126 Mike Macfarlane .20 .09
❑ 127 Roger Clemens 1.50 .70
❑ 128 John Valentin .20 .09
❑ 129 Aaron Sele .40 .18
❑ 130 Jose Canseco 1.00 .45
❑ 131 J.T. Snow .40 .18
❑ 132 Mark Langston .20 .09
❑ 133 Chili Davis .40 .18
❑ 134 Chuck Finley .40 .18
❑ 135 Tim Salmon .40 .18
❑ 136 Tony Phillips .20 .09
❑ 137 Jason Bere .20 .09
❑ 138 Robin Ventura .40 .18
❑ 139 Tim Raines .40 .18
❑ 140 Frank Thomas COR 1.50 .70
❑ 140A Frank Thomas ERR 8.00 3.60
❑ 141 Alex Fernandez .20 .09
❑ 142 Jim Abbott .40 .18
❑ 143 Wilson Alvarez .20 .09
❑ 144 Carlos Baerga .20 .09
❑ 145 Albert Belle .50 .23
❑ 146 Jim Thome .50 .23
❑ 147 Dennis Martinez .40 .18
❑ 148 Eddie Murray .75 .35
❑ 149 Dave Winfield .75 .35
❑ 150 Kenny Lofton .50 .23
❑ 151 Manny Ramirez 1.00 .45
❑ 152 Chad Curtis .20 .09
❑ 153 Lou Whitaker .40 .18
❑ 154 Alan Trammell .50 .23
❑ 155 Cecil Fielder .40 .18
❑ 156 Kirk Gibson .40 .18
❑ 157 Michael Tucker .20 .09
❑ 158 Jon Nunnally .20 .09
❑ 159 Wally Joyner .40 .18
❑ 160 Kevin Appier .40 .18
❑ 161 Jeff Montgomery .20 .09
❑ 162 Greg Gagne .20 .09
❑ 163 Ricky Bones .20 .09
❑ 164 Cal Eldred .20 .09
❑ 165 Greg Vaughn .40 .18
❑ 166 Kevin Seitzer .20 .09
❑ 167 Jose Valentin .20 .09
❑ 168 Joe Oliver .20 .09
❑ 169 Rick Aguilera .20 .09
❑ 170 Kirby Puckett 2.00 .90
❑ 171 Scott Stahoviak .20 .09
❑ 172 Kevin Tapani .20 .09
❑ 173 Chuck Knoblauch .40 .18
❑ 174 Rich Becker .20 .09
❑ 175 Don Mattingly 2.00 .90
❑ 176 Jack McDowell .20 .09
❑ 177 Jimmy Key .40 .18
❑ 178 Paul O'Neill .40 .18
❑ 179 John Wetteland .40 .18
❑ 180 Wade Boggs 1.00 .45
❑ 181 Derek Jeter 3.00 1.35
❑ 182 Rickey Henderson 1.00 .45
❑ 183 Terry Steinbach .20 .09
❑ 184 Ruben Sierra .20 .09
❑ 185 Mark McGwire 3.00 1.35
❑ 186 Todd Stottlemyre .20 .09
❑ 187 Dennis Eckersley .40 .18
❑ 188 Alex Rodriguez 3.00 1.35
❑ 189 Randy Johnson 1.00 .45
❑ 190 Ken Griffey Jr. 3.00 1.35
❑ 191 Tino Martinez UER .40 .18
(Mike Blowers pictured on back)
❑ 192 Jay Buhner .40 .18
❑ 193 Edgar Martinez .50 .23
❑ 194 Mickey Tettleton .20 .09
❑ 195 Juan Gonzalez .75 .35
❑ 196 Benji Gil .20 .09
❑ 197 Dean Palmer .40 .18
❑ 198 Ivan Rodriguez 1.00 .45
❑ 199 Kenny Rogers .20 .09
❑ 200 Will Clark .75 .35
❑ 201 Roberto Alomar .75 .35
❑ 202 David Cone .40 .18
❑ 203 Paul Molitor .75 .35
❑ 204 Shawn Green .75 .35
❑ 205 Joe Carter .40 .18
❑ 206 Alex Gonzalez .20 .09
❑ 207 Pat Hentgen .20 .09
❑ P100 Ken Griffey Jr. Promo 3.00 1.35
❑ AU190 Ken Griffey Jr. AU 200.00 90.00

## 1996 SP

| | MINT | NRMT |
|---|---|---|
| COMPLETE SET (188) | 40.00 | 18.00 |

❑ 1 Rey Ordonez FOIL .40 .18
❑ 2 George Arias FOIL .20 .09
❑ 3 Osvaldo Fernandez FOIL .20 .09
❑ 4 Darin Erstad FOIL RC 25.00 11.00
❑ 5 Paul Wilson FOIL .20 .09
❑ 6 Richard Hidalgo FOIL .40 .18
❑ 7 Justin Thompson FOIL .20 .09
❑ 8 Jimmy Haynes FOIL .20 .09
❑ 9 Edgar Renteria FOIL .20 .09
❑ 10 Ruben Rivera FOIL .20 .09

❑ 11 Chris Snopek FOIL .20 .09
❑ 12 Billy Wagner FOIL .20 .09
❑ 13 Mike Grace FOIL RC .20 .09
❑ 14 Todd Greene FOIL .20 .09
❑ 15 Karim Garcia FOIL .20 .09
❑ 16 John Wasdin FOIL .20 .09
❑ 17 Jason Kendall FOIL .40 .18
❑ 18 Bob Abreu FOIL 1.00 .45
❑ 19 Jermaine Dye FOIL .40 .18
❑ 20 Jason Schmidt FOIL .20 .09
❑ 21 Javy Lopez .40 .18
❑ 22 Ryan Klesko .40 .18
❑ 23 Tom Glavine .75 .35
❑ 24 John Smoltz .40 .18
❑ 25 Greg Maddux 2.00 .90
❑ 26 Chipper Jones 2.00 .90
❑ 27 Fred McGriff .50 .23
❑ 28 David Justice .50 .23
❑ 29 Roberto Alomar .75 .35
❑ 30 Cal Ripken 3.00 1.35
❑ 31 B.J. Surhoff .40 .18
❑ 32 Bobby Bonilla .40 .18
❑ 33 Mike Mussina .75 .35
❑ 34 Randy Myers .20 .09
❑ 35 Rafael Palmeiro .75 .35
❑ 36 Brady Anderson .40 .18
❑ 37 Tim Naehring .20 .09
❑ 38 Jose Canseco 1.00 .45
❑ 39 Roger Clemens 1.50 .70
❑ 40 Mo Vaughn .40 .18
❑ 41 Jose Valentin .20 .09
❑ 42 Kevin Mitchell .20 .09
❑ 43 Chili Davis .40 .18
❑ 44 Garret Anderson .40 .18
❑ 45 Tim Salmon .40 .18
❑ 46 Chuck Finley .40 .18
❑ 47 Troy Percival .40 .18
❑ 48 Jim Abbott .40 .18
❑ 49 J.T. Snow .40 .18
❑ 50 Jim Edmonds .75 .35
❑ 51 Sammy Sosa 1.50 .70
❑ 52 Brian McRae .20 .09
❑ 53 Ryne Sandberg 1.00 .45
❑ 54 Jaime Navarro .75 .35
❑ 55 Mark Grace .50 .23
❑ 56 Harold Baines .40 .18
❑ 57 Robin Ventura .40 .18
❑ 58 Tony Phillips .20 .09
❑ 59 Alex Fernandez .20 .09
❑ 60 Frank Thomas 1.50 .70
❑ 61 Ray Durham .40 .18
❑ 62 Bret Boone .40 .18
❑ 63 Reggie Sanders .40 .18
❑ 64 Pete Schourek .20 .09
❑ 65 Barry Larkin .75 .35
❑ 66 John Smiley .20 .09
❑ 67 Carlos Baerga .20 .09
❑ 68 Jim Thome .50 .23
❑ 69 Eddie Murray .75 .35
❑ 70 Albert Belle .50 .23
❑ 71 Dennis Martinez .40 .18
❑ 72 Jack McDowell .20 .09
❑ 73 Kenny Lofton .40 .18
❑ 74 Manny Ramirez 1.00 .45
❑ 75 Dante Bichette .40 .18
❑ 76 Vinny Castilla .40 .18
❑ 77 Andres Galarraga .50 .23
❑ 78 Walt Weiss .20 .09

❑ 79 Ellis Burks .40 .18
❑ 80 Larry Walker .40 .18
❑ 81 Cecil Fielder .40 .18
❑ 82 Melvin Nieves .20 .09
❑ 83 Travis Fryman .40 .18
❑ 84 Chad Curtis .20 .09
❑ 85 Alan Trammell .50 .23
❑ 86 Gary Sheffield .75 .35
❑ 87 Charles Johnson .40 .18
❑ 88 Andre Dawson .50 .23
❑ 89 Jeff Conine .20 .09
❑ 90 Greg Colbrunn .20 .09
❑ 91 Derek Bell .20 .09
❑ 92 Brian L.Hunter .20 .09
❑ 93 Doug Drabek .20 .09
❑ 94 Craig Biggio .50 .23
❑ 95 Jeff Bagwell 1.00 .45
❑ 96 Kevin Appier .40 .18
❑ 97 Jeff Montgomery .20 .09
❑ 98 Michael Tucker .20 .09
❑ 99 Bip Roberts .20 .09
❑ 100 Johnny Damon .50 .23
❑ 101 Eric Karros .40 .18
❑ 102 Raul Mondesi .40 .18
❑ 103 Ramon Martinez .20 .09
❑ 104 Ismael Valdes .20 .09
❑ 105 Mike Piazza 2.50 1.10
❑ 106 Hideo Nomo .75 .35
❑ 107 Chan Ho Park .40 .18
❑ 108 Ben McDonald .20 .09
❑ 109 Kevin Seitzer .20 .09
❑ 110 Greg Vaughn .40 .18
❑ 111 Jose Valentin .20 .09
❑ 112 Rick Aguilera .20 .09
❑ 113 Marty Cordova .20 .09
❑ 114 Brad Radke .40 .18
❑ 115 Kirby Puckett 2.00 .90
❑ 116 Chuck Knoblauch .40 .18
❑ 117 Paul Molitor .75 .35
❑ 118 Pedro Martinez 1.00 .45
❑ 119 Mike Lansing .20 .09
❑ 120 Rondell White .40 .18
❑ 121 Moises Alou .40 .18
❑ 122 Mark Grudzielanek .20 .09
❑ 123 Jeff Fassero .20 .09
❑ 124 Rico Brogna .20 .09
❑ 125 Jason Isringhausen .40 .18
❑ 126 Jeff Kent .50 .23
❑ 127 Bernard Gilkey .20 .09
❑ 128 Todd Hundley .20 .09
❑ 129 David Cone .40 .18
❑ 130 Andy Pettitte .40 .18
❑ 131 Wade Boggs 1.00 .45
❑ 132 Paul O'Neill .40 .18
❑ 133 Ruben Sierra .20 .09
❑ 134 John Wetteland .40 .18
❑ 135 Derek Jeter 3.00 1.35
❑ 136 Geronimo Berroa .20 .09
❑ 137 Terry Steinbach .20 .09
❑ 138 Ariel Prieto .20 .09
❑ 139 Scott Brosius .40 .18
❑ 140 Mark McGwire 3.00 1.35
❑ 141 Lenny Dykstra .40 .18
❑ 142 Todd Zeile .20 .09
❑ 143 Benito Santiago .20 .09
❑ 144 Mickey Morandini .20 .09
❑ 145 Gregg Jefferies .20 .09
❑ 146 Denny Neagle .40 .18
❑ 147 Orlando Merced .20 .09
❑ 148 Charlie Hayes .20 .09
❑ 149 Carlos Garcia .20 .09
❑ 150 Jay Bell .40 .18
❑ 151 Ray Lankford .40 .18
❑ 152 Alan Benes .20 .09
Andy Benes
❑ 153 Dennis Eckersley .40 .18
❑ 154 Gary Gaetti .40 .18
❑ 155 Ozzie Smith 1.00 .45
❑ 156 Ron Gant .20 .09
❑ 157 Brian Jordan .40 .18
❑ 158 Ken Caminiti .40 .18
❑ 159 Rickey Henderson 1.00 .45
❑ 160 Tony Gwynn 1.50 .70
❑ 161 Wally Joyner .40 .18
❑ 162 Andy Ashby .20 .09
❑ 163 Steve Finley .40 .18
❑ 164 Glenallen Hill .20 .09
❑ 165 Matt Williams .50 .23
❑ 166 Barry Bonds 1.25 .55
❑ 167 William VanLandingham .20 .09
❑ 168 Rod Beck .20 .09
❑ 169 Randy Johnson 1.00 .45
❑ 170 Ken Griffey Jr. 3.00 1.35
❑ 171 Alex Rodriguez 2.50 1.10
❑ 172 Edgar Martinez .50 .23
❑ 173 Jay Buhner .40 .18
❑ 174 Russ Davis .20 .09
❑ 175 Juan Gonzalez .75 .35
❑ 176 Mickey Tettleton .20 .09
❑ 177 Will Clark .75 .35
❑ 178 Ken Hill .20 .09
❑ 179 Dean Palmer .40 .18
❑ 180 Ivan Rodriguez 1.00 .45
❑ 181 Carlos Delgado .75 .35
❑ 182 Alex Gonzalez .20 .09
❑ 183 Shawn Green .75 .35
❑ 184 Juan Guzman .20 .09
❑ 185 Joe Carter .40 .18
❑ 186 Hideo Nomo CL UER .40 .18
(Checklist lists Livan Hernandez as #1)
❑ 187 Cal Ripken CL 1.50 .70
❑ 188 Ken Griffey Jr. CL 1.50 .70

## 1997 SP

| | MINT | NRMT |
|---|---|---|
| COMPLETE SET (184) | 50.00 | 22.00 |
| COMMON (1-159/181-184) | .20 | .09 |

❑ 1 Andruw Jones FOIL 1.00 .45
❑ 2 Kevin Orie FOIL .20 .09
❑ 3 Nomar Garciaparra FOIL 2.50 1.10
❑ 4 Jose Guillen FOIL .20 .09
❑ 5 Todd Walker FOIL .20 .09
❑ 6 Derrick Gibson FOIL .20 .09
❑ 7 Aaron Boone FOIL .20 .09
❑ 8 Bartolo Colon FOIL .30 .14
❑ 9 Derrek Lee FOIL .20 .09
❑ 10 Vladimir Guerrero FOIL 1.50 .70
❑ 11 Wilton Guerrero FOIL .20 .09
❑ 12 Luis Castillo FOIL .30 .14
❑ 13 Jason Dickson FOIL .20 .09
❑ 14 Bubba Trammell FOIL RC .30 .14
❑ 15 Jose Cruz Jr. FOIL RC 2.00 .90
❑ 16 Eddie Murray .75 .35
❑ 17 Darin Erstad 1.00 .45
❑ 18 Garret Anderson .30 .14
❑ 19 Jim Edmonds .75 .35
❑ 20 Tim Salmon .30 .14
❑ 21 Chuck Finley .30 .14
❑ 22 John Smoltz .30 .14
❑ 23 Greg Maddux 2.00 .90
❑ 24 Kenny Lofton .30 .14
❑ 25 Chipper Jones 2.00 .90
❑ 26 Ryan Klesko .30 .14
❑ 27 Javy Lopez .30 .14
❑ 28 Fred McGriff .50 .23
❑ 29 Roberto Alomar .75 .35
❑ 30 Rafael Palmeiro .75 .35
❑ 31 Mike Mussina .75 .35
❑ 32 Brady Anderson .30 .14
❑ 33 Rocky Coppinger .20 .09
❑ 34 Cal Ripken 3.00 1.35
❑ 35 Mo Vaughn .30 .14
❑ 36 Steve Avery .20 .09
❑ 37 Tom Gordon .20 .09
❑ 38 Tim Naehring .20 .09
❑ 39 Troy O'Leary .20 .09
❑ 40 Sammy Sosa 1.50 .70
❑ 41 Brian McRae .20 .09
❑ 42 Mel Rojas .20 .09
❑ 43 Ryne Sandberg 1.00 .45
❑ 44 Mark Grace .75 .35
❑ 45 Albert Belle .50 .23
❑ 46 Robin Ventura .30 .14
❑ 47 Roberto Hernandez .20 .09
❑ 48 Ray Durham .30 .14
❑ 49 Harold Baines .30 .14
❑ 50 Frank Thomas 1.50 .70
❑ 51 Bret Boone .30 .14
❑ 52 Reggie Sanders .20 .09
❑ 53 Deion Sanders .30 .14
❑ 54 Hal Morris .20 .09
❑ 55 Barry Larkin .75 .35
❑ 56 Jim Thome .50 .23
❑ 57 Marquis Grissom .20 .09
❑ 58 David Justice .50 .23
❑ 59 Charles Nagy .20 .09
❑ 60 Manny Ramirez 1.00 .45
❑ 61 Matt Williams .50 .23
❑ 62 Jack McDowell .20 .09
❑ 63 Vinny Castilla .30 .14
❑ 64 Dante Bichette .30 .14
❑ 65 Andres Galarraga .50 .23
❑ 66 Ellis Burks .30 .14
❑ 67 Larry Walker .30 .14
❑ 68 Eric Young .20 .09
❑ 69 Brian L. Hunter .20 .09
❑ 70 Travis Fryman .30 .14
❑ 71 Tony Clark .20 .09
❑ 72 Bobby Higginson .30 .14
❑ 73 Melvin Nieves .20 .09
❑ 74 Jeff Conine .20 .09
❑ 75 Gary Sheffield .75 .35
❑ 76 Moises Alou .30 .14
❑ 77 Edgar Renteria .20 .09
❑ 78 Alex Fernandez .20 .09
❑ 79 Charles Johnson .30 .14
❑ 80 Bobby Bonilla .30 .14
❑ 81 Darryl Kile .30 .14
❑ 82 Derek Bell .20 .09
❑ 83 Shane Reynolds .20 .09
❑ 84 Craig Biggio .50 .23
❑ 85 Jeff Bagwell 1.00 .45
❑ 86 Billy Wagner .20 .09
❑ 87 Chili Davis .30 .14
❑ 88 Kevin Appier .30 .14
❑ 89 Jay Bell .30 .14
❑ 90 Johnny Damon .30 .14
❑ 91 Jeff King .20 .09
❑ 92 Hideo Nomo .75 .35
❑ 93 Todd Hollandsworth .20 .09
❑ 94 Eric Karros .30 .14
❑ 95 Mike Piazza 2.50 1.10
❑ 96 Ramon Martinez .20 .09
❑ 97 Todd Worrell .20 .09
❑ 98 Raul Mondesi .30 .14
❑ 99 Dave Nilsson .20 .09
❑ 100 John Jaha .20 .09
❑ 101 Jose Valentin .20 .09
❑ 102 Jeff Cirillo .30 .14
❑ 103 Jeff D'Amico .20 .09
❑ 104 Ben McDonald .20 .09
❑ 105 Paul Molitor .75 .35
❑ 106 Rich Becker .20 .09
❑ 107 Frank Rodriguez .20 .09
❑ 108 Marty Cordova .20 .09
❑ 109 Terry Steinbach .20 .09
❑ 110 Chuck Knoblauch .30 .14
❑ 111 Mark Grudzielanek .20 .09
❑ 112 Mike Lansing .20 .09
❑ 113 Pedro Martinez 1.00 .45
❑ 114 Henry Rodriguez .20 .09
❑ 115 Rondell White .30 .14
❑ 116 Rey Ordonez .20 .09
❑ 117 Carlos Baerga .20 .09
❑ 118 Lance Johnson .20 .09
❑ 119 Bernard Gilkey .20 .09
❑ 120 Todd Hundley .20 .09
❑ 121 John Franco .30 .14

❑ 122 Bernie Williams .75 .35
❑ 123 David Cone .30 .14
❑ 124 Cecil Fielder .30 .14
❑ 125 Derek Jeter 3.00 1.35
❑ 126 Tino Martinez .30 .14
❑ 127 Mariano Rivera .30 .14
❑ 128 Andy Pettitte .30 .14
❑ 129 Wade Boggs 1.00 .45
❑ 130 Mark McGwire 3.00 1.35
❑ 131 Jose Canseco 1.00 .45
❑ 132 Geronimo Berroa .20 .09
❑ 133 Jason Giambi .75 .35
❑ 134 Ernie Young .20 .09
❑ 135 Scott Rolen .75 .35
❑ 136 Ricky Bottalico .20 .09
❑ 137 Curt Schilling .30 .14
❑ 138 Gregg Jefferies .20 .09
❑ 139 Mickey Morandini .20 .09
❑ 140 Jason Kendall .30 .14
❑ 141 Kevin Elster .20 .09
❑ 142 Al Martin .20 .09
❑ 143 Joe Randa .20 .09
❑ 144 Jason Schmidt .20 .09
❑ 145 Ray Lankford .30 .14
❑ 146 Brian Jordan .30 .14
❑ 147 Andy Benes .20 .09
❑ 148 Alan Benes .20 .09
❑ 149 Gary Gaetti .30 .14
❑ 150 Ron Gant .20 .09
❑ 151 Dennis Eckersley .30 .14
❑ 152 Rickey Henderson 1.00 .45
❑ 153 Joey Hamilton .20 .09
❑ 154 Ken Caminiti .30 .14
❑ 155 Tony Gwynn 1.50 .70
❑ 156 Steve Finley .30 .14
❑ 157 Trevor Hoffman .30 .14
❑ 158 Greg Vaughn .30 .14
❑ 159 J.T.Snow .30 .14
❑ 160 Barry Bonds 1.25 .55
❑ 161 Glenallen Hill .20 .09
❑ 162 Bill Van Landingham .20 .09
❑ 163 Jeff Kent .50 .23
❑ 164 Jay Buhner .30 .14
❑ 165 Ken Griffey Jr. 3.00 1.35
❑ 166 Alex Rodriguez 2.50 1.10
❑ 167 Randy Johnson 1.00 .45
❑ 168 Edgar Martinez .50 .23
❑ 169 Dan Wilson .20 .09
❑ 170 Ivan Rodriguez 1.00 .45
❑ 171 Roger Pavlik .20 .09
❑ 172 Will Clark .75 .35
❑ 173 Dean Palmer .30 .14
❑ 174 Rusty Greer .30 .14
❑ 175 Juan Gonzalez .75 .35
❑ 176 John Wetteland .30 .14
❑ 177 Joe Carter .30 .14
❑ 178 Ed Sprague .20 .09
❑ 179 Carlos Delgado .75 .35
❑ 180 Roger Clemens 1.50 .70
❑ 181 Juan Guzman .20 .09
❑ 182 Pat Hentgen .20 .09
❑ 183 Ken Griffey Jr. CL 1.50 .70
❑ 184 Hideki Irabu RC .60 .25

## 1998 SP Authentic

| | MINT | NRMT |
|---|---|---|
| COMPLETE SET (198) | 80.00 | 36.00 |

❑ 1 Travis Lee FOIL .30 .14
❑ 2 Mike Caruso FOIL .20 .09
❑ 3 Kerry Wood FOIL 1.50 .70
❑ 4 Mark Kotsay FOIL .30 .14
❑ 5 Magglio Ordonez FOIL RC 20.00 9.00
❑ 6 Scott Elarton FOIL .30 .14
❑ 7 Carl Pavano FOIL .20 .09
❑ 8 A.J. Hinch FOIL .20 .09
❑ 9 Rolando Arrojo FOIL RC 1.50 .70
❑ 10 Ben Grieve FOIL .30 .14
❑ 11 Gabe Alvarez FOIL .20 .09
❑ 12 Mike Kinkade FOIL RC 1.00 .45
❑ 13 Bruce Chen FOIL .20 .09
❑ 14 Juan Encarnacion FOIL .30 .14
❑ 15 Todd Helton FOIL 1.00 .45
❑ 16 Aaron Boone FOIL .20 .09
❑ 17 Sean Casey FOIL .30 .14
❑ 18 Ramon Hernandez FOIL .20 .09
❑ 19 Daryle Ward FOIL .30 .14
❑ 20 Paul Konerko FOIL .30 .14
❑ 21 David Ortiz FOIL .20 .09
❑ 22 Derrek Lee FOIL .20 .09
❑ 23 Brad Fullmer FOIL .30 .14
❑ 24 Javier Vazquez FOIL .20 .09
❑ 25 Miguel Tejada FOIL .75 .35
❑ 26 Dave Dellucci FOIL RC .20 .09
❑ 27 Alex Gonzalez FOIL .20 .09
❑ 28 Matt Clement FOIL .30 .14
❑ 29 Masato Yoshii FOIL RC 1.50 .70
❑ 30 Russell Branyan FOIL .30 .14
❑ 31 Chuck Finley .30 .14
❑ 32 Jim Edmonds .75 .35
❑ 33 Darin Erstad .75 .35
❑ 34 Jason Dickson .20 .09
❑ 35 Tim Salmon .30 .14
❑ 36 Cecil Fielder .30 .14
❑ 37 Todd Greene .20 .09
❑ 38 Andy Benes .20 .09
❑ 39 Jay Bell .30 .14
❑ 40 Matt Williams .50 .23
❑ 41 Brian Anderson .20 .09
❑ 42 Karim Garcia .20 .09
❑ 43 Javy Lopez .30 .14
❑ 44 Tom Glavine .75 .35
❑ 45 Greg Maddux 2.00 .90
❑ 46 Andruw Jones .75 .35
❑ 47 Chipper Jones 2.00 .90
❑ 48 Ryan Klesko .30 .14
❑ 49 John Smoltz .30 .14
❑ 50 Andres Galarraga .50 .23
❑ 51 Rafael Palmeiro .75 .35
❑ 52 Mike Mussina .75 .35
❑ 53 Roberto Alomar .75 .35
❑ 54 Joe Carter .30 .14
❑ 55 Cal Ripken 3.00 1.35
❑ 56 Brady Anderson .30 .14
❑ 57 Mo Vaughn .30 .14
❑ 58 John Valentin .20 .09
❑ 59 Dennis Eckersley .30 .14
❑ 60 Nomar Garciaparra 2.50 1.10
❑ 61 Pedro Martinez 1.00 .45
❑ 62 Jeff Blauser .20 .09
❑ 63 Kevin Orie .20 .09
❑ 64 Henry Rodriguez .20 .09
❑ 65 Mark Grace .75 .35
❑ 66 Albert Belle .50 .23
❑ 67 Mike Cameron .30 .14
❑ 68 Robin Ventura .30 .14
❑ 69 Frank Thomas 1.50 .70
❑ 70 Barry Larkin .75 .35
❑ 71 Brett Tomko .20 .09
❑ 72 Willie Greene .20 .09
❑ 73 Reggie Sanders .20 .09
❑ 74 Sandy Alomar Jr. .30 .14
❑ 75 Kenny Lofton .30 .14
❑ 76 Jaret Wright .20 .09
❑ 77 David Justice .50 .23
❑ 78 Omar Vizquel .30 .14
❑ 79 Manny Ramirez 1.00 .45
❑ 80 Jim Thome .50 .23
❑ 81 Travis Fryman .30 .14
❑ 82 Neifi Perez .20 .09
❑ 83 Mike Lansing .20 .09
❑ 84 Vinny Castilla .30 .14
❑ 85 Larry Walker .30 .14
❑ 86 Dante Bichette .30 .14
❑ 87 Darryl Kile .30 .14
❑ 88 Justin Thompson .20 .09
❑ 89 Damion Easley .20 .09
❑ 90 Tony Clark .20 .09
❑ 91 Bobby Higginson .30 .14
❑ 92 Brian Hunter .20 .09
❑ 93 Edgar Renteria .20 .09
❑ 94 Craig Counsell .20 .09
❑ 95 Mike Piazza 2.50 1.10
❑ 96 Livan Hernandez .20 .09
❑ 97 Todd Zeile .30 .14
❑ 98 Richard Hidalgo .30 .14
❑ 99 Moises Alou .30 .14
❑ 100 Jeff Bagwell 1.00 .45
❑ 101 Mike Hampton .30 .14
❑ 102 Craig Biggio .50 .23
❑ 103 Dean Palmer .30 .14
❑ 104 Tim Belcher .20 .09
❑ 105 Jeff King .20 .09
❑ 106 Jeff Conine .20 .09
❑ 107 Johnny Damon .30 .14
❑ 108 Hideo Nomo .75 .35
❑ 109 Raul Mondesi .30 .14
❑ 110 Gary Sheffield .75 .35
❑ 111 Ramon Martinez .20 .09
❑ 112 Chan Ho Park .30 .14
❑ 113 Eric Young .20 .09
❑ 114 Charles Johnson .30 .14
❑ 115 Eric Karros .30 .14
❑ 116 Bobby Bonilla .30 .14
❑ 117 Jeromy Burnitz .30 .14
❑ 118 Cal Eldred .20 .09
❑ 119 Jeff D'Amico .20 .09
❑ 120 Marquis Grissom .20 .09
❑ 121 Dave Nilsson .20 .09
❑ 122 Brad Radke .30 .14
❑ 123 Marty Cordova .20 .09
❑ 124 Ron Coomer .20 .09
❑ 125 Paul Molitor .75 .35
❑ 126 Todd Walker .20 .09
❑ 127 Rondell White .30 .14
❑ 128 Mark Grudzielanek .20 .09
❑ 129 Carlos Perez .20 .09
❑ 130 Vladimir Guerrero 1.25 .55
❑ 131 Dustin Hermanson .20 .09
❑ 132 Butch Huskey .20 .09
❑ 133 John Franco .30 .14
❑ 134 Rey Ordonez .20 .09
❑ 135 Todd Hundley .20 .09
❑ 136 Edgardo Alfonzo .30 .14
❑ 137 Bobby Jones .20 .09
❑ 138 John Olerud .30 .14
❑ 139 Chili Davis .30 .14
❑ 140 Tino Martinez .30 .14
❑ 141 Andy Pettitte .30 .14
❑ 142 Chuck Knoblauch .30 .14
❑ 143 Bernie Williams .75 .35
❑ 144 David Cone .30 .14
❑ 145 Derek Jeter 3.00 1.35
❑ 146 Paul O'Neill .30 .14
❑ 147 Rickey Henderson 1.00 .45
❑ 148 Jason Giambi .75 .35
❑ 149 Kenny Rogers .20 .09
❑ 150 Scott Rolen .75 .35
❑ 151 Curt Schilling .30 .14
❑ 152 Ricky Bottalico .20 .09
❑ 153 Mike Lieberthal .30 .14
❑ 154 Francisco Cordova .20 .09
❑ 155 Jose Guillen .20 .09
❑ 156 Jason Schmidt .20 .09
❑ 157 Jason Kendall .30 .14
❑ 158 Kevin Young .30 .14
❑ 159 Delino DeShields .20 .09
❑ 160 Mark McGwire 3.00 1.35
❑ 161 Ray Lankford .30 .14
❑ 162 Brian Jordan .30 .14
❑ 163 Ron Gant .30 .14
❑ 164 Todd Stottlemyre .20 .09
❑ 165 Ken Caminiti .30 .14
❑ 166 Kevin Brown .50 .23
❑ 167 Trevor Hoffman .30 .14
❑ 168 Steve Finley .30 .14
❑ 169 Wally Joyner .30 .14
❑ 170 Tony Gwynn 1.50 .70
❑ 171 Shawn Estes .20 .09
❑ 172 J.T. Snow .30 .14

| Card | MINT | NRMT |
|---|---|---|
| ❑ 173 Jeff Kent | .50 | .23 |
| ❑ 174 Robb Nen | .20 | .09 |
| ❑ 175 Barry Bonds | 1.25 | .55 |
| ❑ 176 Randy Johnson | 1.00 | .45 |
| ❑ 177 Edgar Martinez | .50 | .23 |
| ❑ 178 Jay Buhner | .30 | .14 |
| ❑ 179 Alex Rodriguez | 2.50 | 1.10 |
| ❑ 180 Ken Griffey Jr. | 3.00 | 1.35 |
| ❑ 181 Ken Cloude | .20 | .09 |
| ❑ 182 Wade Boggs | 1.00 | .45 |
| ❑ 183 Tony Saunders | .20 | .09 |
| ❑ 184 Wilson Alvarez | .20 | .09 |
| ❑ 185 Fred McGriff | .50 | .23 |
| ❑ 186 Roberto Hernandez | .20 | .09 |
| ❑ 187 Kevin Stocker | .20 | .09 |
| ❑ 188 Fernando Tatis | .30 | .14 |
| ❑ 189 Will Clark | .75 | .35 |
| ❑ 190 Juan Gonzalez | .75 | .35 |
| ❑ 191 Rusty Greer | .30 | .14 |
| ❑ 192 Ivan Rodriguez | 1.00 | .45 |
| ❑ 193 Jose Canseco | 1.00 | .45 |
| ❑ 194 Carlos Delgado | .75 | .35 |
| ❑ 195 Roger Clemens | 1.50 | .70 |
| ❑ 196 Pat Hentgen | .20 | .09 |
| ❑ 197 Randy Myers | .30 | .14 |
| ❑ 198 Ken Griffey Jr. CL | 1.50 | .70 |
| ❑ S123 Ken Griffey Jr. Sample | 3.00 | 1.35 |

## 1999 SP Authentic

| | MINT | NRMT |
|---|---|---|
| COMPLETE SET (135) | 400.00 | 180.00 |
| COMP.SET w/o SP's (90) | 25.00 | 11.00 |
| COMMON CARD (1-90) | .20 | .09 |
| COMMON FW (91-120) | 10.00 | 4.50 |
| COMMON STR (121-135) | 2.50 | 1.10 |

| Card | MINT | NRMT |
|---|---|---|
| ❑ 1 Mo Vaughn | .30 | .14 |
| ❑ 2 Jim Edmonds | .75 | .35 |
| ❑ 3 Darin Erstad | .75 | .35 |
| ❑ 4 Travis Lee | .20 | .09 |
| ❑ 5 Matt Williams | .50 | .23 |
| ❑ 6 Randy Johnson | 1.00 | .45 |
| ❑ 7 Chipper Jones | 2.00 | .90 |
| ❑ 8 Greg Maddux | 2.00 | .90 |
| ❑ 9 Andruw Jones | .75 | .35 |
| ❑ 10 Andres Galarraga | .50 | .23 |
| ❑ 11 Tom Glavine | .75 | .35 |
| ❑ 12 Cal Ripken | 3.00 | 1.35 |
| ❑ 13 Brady Anderson | .30 | .14 |
| ❑ 14 Albert Belle | .50 | .23 |
| ❑ 15 Nomar Garciaparra | 2.50 | 1.10 |
| ❑ 16 Donnie Sadler | .20 | .09 |
| ❑ 17 Pedro Martinez | 1.00 | .45 |
| ❑ 18 Sammy Sosa | 1.50 | .70 |
| ❑ 19 Kerry Wood | .30 | .14 |
| ❑ 20 Mark Grace | .75 | .35 |
| ❑ 21 Mike Caruso | .20 | .09 |
| ❑ 22 Frank Thomas | 1.50 | .70 |
| ❑ 23 Paul Konerko | .30 | .14 |
| ❑ 24 Sean Casey | .30 | .14 |
| ❑ 25 Barry Larkin | .75 | .35 |
| ❑ 26 Kenny Lofton | .30 | .14 |
| ❑ 27 Manny Ramirez | 1.00 | .45 |
| ❑ 28 Jim Thome | .50 | .23 |
| ❑ 29 Bartolo Colon | .30 | .14 |
| ❑ 30 Jaret Wright | .20 | .09 |
| ❑ 31 Larry Walker | .30 | .14 |
| ❑ 32 Todd Helton | 1.00 | .45 |
| ❑ 33 Tony Clark | .20 | .09 |
| ❑ 34 Dean Palmer | .30 | .14 |
| ❑ 35 Mark Kotsay | .20 | .09 |
| ❑ 36 Cliff Floyd | .30 | .14 |
| ❑ 37 Ken Caminiti | .30 | .14 |
| ❑ 38 Craig Biggio | .50 | .23 |
| ❑ 39 Jeff Bagwell | 1.00 | .45 |
| ❑ 40 Moises Alou | .30 | .14 |
| ❑ 41 Johnny Damon | .30 | .14 |
| ❑ 42 Larry Sutton | .20 | .09 |
| ❑ 43 Kevin Brown | .50 | .23 |
| ❑ 44 Gary Sheffield | .75 | .35 |
| ❑ 45 Raul Mondesi | .30 | .14 |
| ❑ 46 Jeromy Burnitz | .30 | .14 |
| ❑ 47 Jeff Cirillo | .30 | .14 |
| ❑ 48 Todd Walker | .20 | .09 |
| ❑ 49 David Ortiz | .20 | .09 |
| ❑ 50 Brad Radke | .30 | .14 |
| ❑ 51 Vladimir Guerrero | 1.25 | .55 |
| ❑ 52 Rondell White | .30 | .14 |
| ❑ 53 Brad Fullmer | .30 | .14 |
| ❑ 54 Mike Piazza | 2.50 | 1.10 |
| ❑ 55 Robin Ventura | .30 | .14 |
| ❑ 56 John Olerud | .30 | .14 |
| ❑ 57 Derek Jeter | 3.00 | 1.35 |
| ❑ 58 Tino Martinez | .30 | .14 |
| ❑ 59 Bernie Williams | .75 | .35 |
| ❑ 60 Roger Clemens | 1.50 | .70 |
| ❑ 61 Ben Grieve | .30 | .14 |
| ❑ 62 Miguel Tejada | .30 | .14 |
| ❑ 63 A.J. Hinch | .20 | .09 |
| ❑ 64 Scott Rolen | .75 | .35 |
| ❑ 65 Curt Schilling | .30 | .14 |
| ❑ 66 Doug Glanville | .20 | .09 |
| ❑ 67 Aramis Ramirez | .20 | .09 |
| ❑ 68 Tony Womack | .20 | .09 |
| ❑ 69 Jason Kendall | .30 | .14 |
| ❑ 70 Tony Gwynn | 1.50 | .70 |
| ❑ 71 Wally Joyner | .30 | .14 |
| ❑ 72 Greg Vaughn | .30 | .14 |
| ❑ 73 Barry Bonds | 1.25 | .55 |
| ❑ 74 Ellis Burks | .30 | .14 |
| ❑ 75 Jeff Kent | .50 | .23 |
| ❑ 76 Ken Griffey Jr. | 3.00 | 1.35 |
| ❑ 77 Alex Rodriguez | 2.50 | 1.10 |
| ❑ 78 Edgar Martinez | .50 | .23 |
| ❑ 79 Mark McGwire | 3.00 | 1.35 |
| ❑ 80 Eli Marrero | .20 | .09 |
| ❑ 81 Matt Morris | .20 | .09 |
| ❑ 82 Rolando Arrojo | .20 | .09 |
| ❑ 83 Quinton McCracken | .20 | .09 |
| ❑ 84 Jose Canseco | 1.00 | .45 |
| ❑ 85 Ivan Rodriguez | 1.00 | .45 |
| ❑ 86 Juan Gonzalez | .75 | .35 |
| ❑ 87 Royce Clayton | .20 | .09 |
| ❑ 88 Shawn Green | .75 | .35 |
| ❑ 89 Jose Cruz Jr. | .30 | .14 |
| ❑ 90 Carlos Delgado | .75 | .35 |
| ❑ 91 Troy Glaus FW | 30.00 | 13.50 |
| ❑ 92 George Lombard FW | 10.00 | 4.50 |
| ❑ 93 Ryan Minor FW | 10.00 | 4.50 |
| ❑ 94 Calvin Pickering FW | 10.00 | 4.50 |
| ❑ 95 Jin Ho Cho FW | 10.00 | 4.50 |
| ❑ 96 Russ Branyan FW | 10.00 | 4.50 |
| ❑ 97 Derrick Gibson FW | 10.00 | 4.50 |
| ❑ 98 Gabe Kapler FW | 10.00 | 4.50 |
| ❑ 99 Matt Anderson FW | 10.00 | 4.50 |
| ❑ 100 Preston Wilson FW | 10.00 | 4.50 |
| ❑ 101 Alex Gonzalez FW | 10.00 | 4.50 |
| ❑ 102 Carlos Beltran FW | 10.00 | 4.50 |
| ❑ 103 Dee Brown FW | 10.00 | 4.50 |
| ❑ 104 Jeremy Giambi FW | 10.00 | 4.50 |
| ❑ 105 Angel Pena FW | 10.00 | 4.50 |
| ❑ 106 Geoff Jenkins FW | 10.00 | 4.50 |
| ❑ 107 Corey Koskie FW | 10.00 | 4.50 |
| ❑ 108 A.J. Pierzynski FW | 10.00 | 4.50 |
| ❑ 109 Michael Barrett FW | 10.00 | 4.50 |
| ❑ 110 Fernando Seguignol FW | 10.00 | 4.50 |
| ❑ 111 Mike Kinkade FW | 10.00 | 4.50 |
| ❑ 112 Ricky Ledee FW | 10.00 | 4.50 |
| ❑ 113 Mike Lowell FW | 10.00 | 4.50 |
| ❑ 114 Eric Chavez FW | 10.00 | 4.50 |
| ❑ 115 Matt Clement FW | 10.00 | 4.50 |
| ❑ 116 Shane Monahan FW | 10.00 | 4.50 |
| ❑ 117 J.D. Drew FW | 20.00 | 9.00 |
| ❑ 118 Bubba Trammell FW | 10.00 | 4.50 |
| ❑ 119 Kevin Witt FW | 10.00 | 4.50 |
| ❑ 120 Roy Halladay FW | 10.00 | 4.50 |
| ❑ 121 Mark McGwire STR | 20.00 | 9.00 |
| ❑ 122 Mark McGwire STR<br>Sammy Sosa | 15.00 | 6.75 |
| ❑ 123 Sammy Sosa STR | 10.00 | 4.50 |
| ❑ 124 Ken Griffey Jr. STR | 20.00 | 9.00 |
| ❑ 125 Cal Ripken STR | 20.00 | 9.00 |
| ❑ 126 Juan Gonzalez STR | 5.00 | 2.20 |
| ❑ 127 Kerry Wood STR | 2.50 | 1.10 |
| ❑ 128 Trevor Hoffman STR | 2.50 | 1.10 |
| ❑ 129 Barry Bonds STR | 8.00 | 3.60 |
| ❑ 130 Alex Rodriguez STR | 15.00 | 6.75 |
| ❑ 131 Ben Grieve STR | 2.50 | 1.10 |
| ❑ 132 Tom Glavine STR | 5.00 | 2.20 |
| ❑ 133 David Wells STR | 2.50 | 1.10 |
| ❑ 134 Mike Piazza STR | 15.00 | 6.75 |
| ❑ 135 Scott Brosius STR | 2.50 | 1.10 |

## 2000 SP Authentic

| | MINT | NRMT |
|---|---|---|
| COMPLETE SET (196) | | |
| COMPLETE BASIC SET (135) | 500.00 | 220.00 |
| COMPLETE UPDATE SET (61) | | |
| COMP.BASIC w/o SP's (90) | 25.00 | 11.00 |
| COMMON CARD (1-90) | .20 | .09 |
| COMMON SUP (91-105) | 5.00 | 2.20 |
| COMMON FW (106-135) | 10.00 | 4.50 |
| COMMON FW (136-164) | | |
| COMMON CARD (166-195) | | |

| Card | MINT | NRMT |
|---|---|---|
| ❑ 1 Mo Vaughn | .30 | .14 |
| ❑ 2 Troy Glaus | 1.00 | .45 |
| ❑ 3 Jason Giambi | .75 | .35 |
| ❑ 4 Tim Hudson | .75 | .35 |
| ❑ 5 Eric Chavez | .30 | .14 |
| ❑ 6 Shannon Stewart | .30 | .14 |
| ❑ 7 Raul Mondesi | .30 | .14 |
| ❑ 8 Carlos Delgado | .75 | .35 |
| ❑ 9 Jose Canseco | 1.00 | .45 |
| ❑ 10 Vinny Castilla | .30 | .14 |
| ❑ 11 Greg Vaughn | .30 | .14 |
| ❑ 12 Manny Ramirez | 1.00 | .45 |
| ❑ 13 Roberto Alomar | .75 | .35 |
| ❑ 14 Jim Thome | .50 | .23 |
| ❑ 15 Richie Sexson | .30 | .14 |
| ❑ 16 Alex Rodriguez | 2.50 | 1.10 |
| ❑ 17 Freddy Garcia | .30 | .14 |
| ❑ 18 John Olerud | .30 | .14 |
| ❑ 19 Albert Belle | .50 | .23 |
| ❑ 20 Cal Ripken | 3.00 | 1.35 |
| ❑ 21 Mike Mussina | .75 | .35 |
| ❑ 22 Ivan Rodriguez | 1.00 | .45 |
| ❑ 23 Gabe Kapler | .30 | .14 |
| ❑ 24 Rafael Palmeiro | .75 | .35 |
| ❑ 25 Nomar Garciaparra | 2.50 | 1.10 |
| ❑ 26 Pedro Martinez | 1.00 | .45 |
| ❑ 27 Carl Everett | .30 | .14 |
| ❑ 28 Carlos Beltran | .30 | .14 |
| ❑ 29 Jermaine Dye | .30 | .14 |
| ❑ 30 Juan Gonzalez | .75 | .35 |
| ❑ 31 Dean Palmer | .30 | .14 |
| ❑ 32 Corey Koskie | .20 | .09 |
| ❑ 33 Jacque Jones | .30 | .14 |
| ❑ 34 Frank Thomas | 1.50 | .70 |
| ❑ 35 Paul Konerko | .30 | .14 |

| | | | |
|---|---|---|---|
| ❑ 36 | Magglio Ordonez | .30 | .14 |
| ❑ 37 | Bernie Williams | .75 | .35 |
| ❑ 38 | Derek Jeter | 3.00 | 1.35 |
| ❑ 39 | Roger Clemens | 1.50 | .70 |
| ❑ 40 | Mariano Rivera | .30 | .14 |
| ❑ 41 | Jeff Bagwell | 1.00 | .45 |
| ❑ 42 | Craig Biggio | .50 | .23 |
| ❑ 43 | Jose Lima | .20 | .09 |
| ❑ 44 | Moises Alou | .30 | .14 |
| ❑ 45 | Chipper Jones | 2.00 | .90 |
| ❑ 46 | Greg Maddux | 2.00 | .90 |
| ❑ 47 | Andruw Jones | .75 | .35 |
| ❑ 48 | Andres Galarraga | .50 | .23 |
| ❑ 49 | Jeromy Burnitz | .30 | .14 |
| ❑ 50 | Geoff Jenkins | .30 | .14 |
| ❑ 51 | Mark McGwire | 3.00 | 1.35 |
| ❑ 52 | Fernando Tatis | .30 | .14 |
| ❑ 53 | J.D. Drew | .75 | .35 |
| ❑ 54 | Sammy Sosa | 1.50 | .70 |
| ❑ 55 | Kerry Wood | .30 | .14 |
| ❑ 56 | Mark Grace | .75 | .35 |
| ❑ 57 | Matt Williams | .50 | .23 |
| ❑ 58 | Randy Johnson | 1.00 | .45 |
| ❑ 59 | Erubiel Durazo | .30 | .14 |
| ❑ 60 | Gary Sheffield | .75 | .35 |
| ❑ 61 | Kevin Brown | .50 | .23 |
| ❑ 62 | Shawn Green | .75 | .35 |
| ❑ 63 | Vladimir Guerrero | 1.25 | .55 |
| ❑ 64 | Michael Barrett | .20 | .09 |
| ❑ 65 | Barry Bonds | 1.25 | .55 |
| ❑ 66 | Jeff Kent | .50 | .23 |
| ❑ 67 | Russ Ortiz | .20 | .09 |
| ❑ 68 | Preston Wilson | .30 | .14 |
| ❑ 69 | Mike Lowell | .30 | .14 |
| ❑ 70 | Mike Piazza | 2.50 | 1.10 |
| ❑ 71 | Mike Hampton | .30 | .14 |
| ❑ 72 | Robin Ventura | .30 | .14 |
| ❑ 73 | Edgardo Alfonzo | .30 | .14 |
| ❑ 74 | Tony Gwynn | 1.50 | .70 |
| ❑ 75 | Ryan Klesko | .30 | .14 |
| ❑ 76 | Trevor Hoffman | .30 | .14 |
| ❑ 77 | Scott Rolen | .75 | .35 |
| ❑ 78 | Bob Abreu | .30 | .14 |
| ❑ 79 | Mike Lieberthal | .30 | .14 |
| ❑ 80 | Curt Schilling | .30 | .14 |
| ❑ 81 | Jason Kendall | .30 | .14 |
| ❑ 82 | Brian Giles | .30 | .14 |
| ❑ 83 | Kris Benson | .30 | .14 |
| ❑ 84 | Ken Griffey Jr. | 3.00 | 1.35 |
| ❑ 85 | Sean Casey | .30 | .14 |
| ❑ 86 | Pokey Reese | .30 | .14 |
| ❑ 87 | Barry Larkin | .75 | .35 |
| ❑ 88 | Larry Walker | .30 | .14 |
| ❑ 89 | Todd Helton | 1.00 | .45 |
| ❑ 90 | Jeff Cirillo | .30 | .14 |
| ❑ 91 | Ken Griffey Jr. SUP | 20.00 | 9.00 |
| ❑ 92 | Mark McGwire SUP | 20.00 | 9.00 |
| ❑ 93 | Chipper Jones SUP | 12.00 | 5.50 |
| ❑ 94 | Derek Jeter SUP | 20.00 | 9.00 |
| ❑ 95 | Shawn Green SUP | 5.00 | 2.20 |
| ❑ 96 | Pedro Martinez SUP | 6.00 | 2.70 |
| ❑ 97 | Mike Piazza SUP | 15.00 | 6.75 |
| ❑ 98 | Alex Rodriguez SUP | 15.00 | 6.75 |
| ❑ 99 | Jeff Bagwell SUP | 6.00 | 2.70 |
| ❑ 100 | Cal Ripken SUP | 20.00 | 9.00 |
| ❑ 101 | Sammy Sosa SUP | 10.00 | 4.50 |
| ❑ 102 | Barry Bonds SUP | 8.00 | 3.60 |
| ❑ 103 | Jose Canseco SUP | 6.00 | 2.70 |
| ❑ 104 | Nomar Garciaparra SUP | 15.00 | 6.75 |
| ❑ 105 | Ivan Rodriguez SUP | 6.00 | 2.70 |
| ❑ 106 | Rick Ankiel FW | 30.00 | 13.50 |
| ❑ 107 | Pat Burrell FW | 25.00 | 11.00 |
| ❑ 108 | Vernon Wells FW | 10.00 | 4.50 |
| ❑ 109 | Nick Johnson FW | 10.00 | 4.50 |
| ❑ 110 | Kip Wells FW | 10.00 | 4.50 |
| ❑ 111 | Matt Riley FW | 10.00 | 4.50 |
| ❑ 112 | Alfonso Soriano FW | 10.00 | 4.50 |
| ❑ 113 | Josh Beckett FW | 15.00 | 6.75 |
| ❑ 114 | Danys Baez FW RC | 15.00 | 6.75 |
| ❑ 115 | Travis Dawkins FW | 10.00 | 4.50 |
| ❑ 116 | Eric Gagne FW | 10.00 | 4.50 |
| ❑ 117 | Mike Lamb FW RC | 12.00 | 5.50 |
| ❑ 118 | Eric Munson FW | 15.00 | 6.75 |
| ❑ 119 | Wilfredo Rodriguez FW RC | 10.00 | 4.50 |
| ❑ 120 | Kazuhiro Sasaki FW RC | 50.00 | 22.00 |
| ❑ 121 | Chad Hutchinson FW | 10.00 | 4.50 |
| ❑ 122 | Peter Bergeron FW | 10.00 | 4.50 |
| ❑ 123 | Wascar Serrano FW RC | 10.00 | 4.50 |
| ❑ 124 | Tony Armas Jr. FW | 10.00 | 4.50 |
| ❑ 125 | Ramon Ortiz FW | 10.00 | 4.50 |
| ❑ 126 | Adam Kennedy FW | 10.00 | 4.50 |
| ❑ 127 | Joe Crede FW | 15.00 | 6.75 |
| ❑ 128 | Roosevelt Brown FW | 10.00 | 4.50 |
| ❑ 129 | Mark Mulder FW | 10.00 | 4.50 |
| ❑ 130 | Brad Penny FW | 10.00 | 4.50 |
| ❑ 131 | Terrence Long FW | 10.00 | 4.50 |
| ❑ 132 | Ruben Mateo FW | 10.00 | 4.50 |
| ❑ 133 | Wily Mo Pena FW | 10.00 | 4.50 |
| ❑ 134 | Rafael Furcal FW | 40.00 | 18.00 |
| ❑ 135 | Mario Encarnacion FW | 10.00 | 4.50 |
| ❑ 136 | Barry Zito FW RC | | |
| ❑ 137 | Aaron McNeal FW RC | | |
| ❑ 138 | Timo Perez FW RC | | |
| ❑ 139 | Sun Woo Kim FW RC | | |
| ❑ 140 | Xavier Nady FW RC | | |
| ❑ 141 | Matt Wheatland FW RC | | |
| ❑ 142 | Brent Abernathy FW RC | | |
| ❑ 143 | Cory Vance FW RC | | |
| ❑ 144 | Scott Heard FW RC | | |
| ❑ 145 | Mike Meyers FW RC | | |
| ❑ 146 | Ben Diggins FW RC | | |
| ❑ 147 | Luis Matos FW RC | | |
| ❑ 148 | Ben Sheets FW RC | | |
| ❑ 149 | Kurt Ainsworth FW RC | | |
| ❑ 150 | Dave Krynzel FW RC | | |
| ❑ 151 | Alex Cabrera FW RC | | |
| ❑ 152 | Mike Tonis FW RC | | |
| ❑ 153 | Dane Sardinha FW RC | | |
| ❑ 154 | Koith Ginter FW RC | | |
| ❑ 155 | David Espinosa FW RC | | |
| ❑ 156 | Joe Torres FW RC | | |
| ❑ 157 | Daylan Holt FW RC | | |
| ❑ 158 | Koyie Hill FW RC | | |
| ❑ 159 | Brad Wilkerson FW RC | | |
| ❑ 160 | Juan Pierre FW RC | | |
| ❑ 161 | Matt Ginter FW RC | | |
| ❑ 162 | Dane Artman FW RC | | |
| ❑ 163 | Jon Rauch FW RC | | |
| ❑ 164 | Sean Burnett FW RC | | |
| ❑ 165 | Does Not Exist | | |
| ❑ 166 | Darin Erstad | | |
| ❑ 167 | Ben Grieve | | |
| ❑ 168 | David Wells | | |
| ❑ 169 | Fred McGriff | | |
| ❑ 170 | Bob Wickman | | |
| ❑ 171 | Al Martin | | |
| ❑ 172 | Melvin Mora | | |
| ❑ 173 | Ricky Ledee | | |
| ❑ 174 | Dante Bichette | | |
| ❑ 175 | Mike Sweeney | | |
| ❑ 176 | Bobby Higginson | | |
| ❑ 177 | Matt Lawton | | |
| ❑ 178 | Charles Johnson | | |
| ❑ 179 | David Justice | | |
| ❑ 180 | Richard Hidalgo | | |
| ❑ 181 | B.J. Surhoff | | |
| ❑ 182 | Richie Sexson | | |
| ❑ 183 | Jim Edmonds | | |
| ❑ 184 | Rondell White | | |
| ❑ 185 | Curt Schilling | | |
| ❑ 186 | Tom Goodwin | | |
| ❑ 187 | Jose Vidro | | |
| ❑ 188 | Ellis Burks | | |
| ❑ 189 | Henry Rodriguez | | |
| ❑ 190 | Mike Bordick | | |
| ❑ 191 | Eric Owens | | |
| ❑ 192 | Travis Lee | | |
| ❑ 193 | Kevin Young | | |
| ❑ 194 | Aaron Boone | | |
| ❑ 195 | Todd Hollandsworth | | |
| ❑ SPA | Ken Griffey Jr. Sample | 3.00 | 1.35 |

## 1999 SP Signature

| | | MINT | NRMT |
|---|---|---|---|
| COMPLETE SET (180) | | 250.00 | 110.00 |
| ❑ 1 | Nomar Garciaparra | 6.00 | 2.70 |
| ❑ 2 | Ken Griffey Jr. | 8.00 | 3.60 |
| ❑ 3 | J.D. Drew | 2.00 | .90 |
| ❑ 4 | Alex Rodriguez | 6.00 | 2.70 |
| ❑ 5 | Juan Gonzalez | 2.00 | .90 |
| ❑ 6 | Mo Vaughn | .75 | .35 |
| ❑ 7 | Greg Maddux | 5.00 | 2.20 |
| ❑ 8 | Chipper Jones | 5.00 | 2.20 |
| ❑ 9 | Frank Thomas | 4.00 | 1.80 |
| ❑ 10 | Vladimir Guerrero | 3.00 | 1.35 |
| ❑ 11 | Mike Piazza | 6.00 | 2.70 |
| ❑ 12 | Eric Chavez | .75 | .35 |
| ❑ 13 | Tony Gwynn | 4.00 | 1.80 |
| ❑ 14 | Orlando Hernandez | .75 | .35 |
| ❑ 15 | Pat Burrell RC | 30.00 | 13.50 |
| ❑ 16 | Darin Erstad | 2.00 | .90 |
| ❑ 17 | Greg Vaughn | .75 | .35 |
| ❑ 18 | Russ Branyan | .75 | .35 |
| ❑ 19 | Gabe Kapler | .75 | .35 |
| ❑ 20 | Craig Biggio | 1.25 | .55 |
| ❑ 21 | Troy Glaus | 3.00 | 1.35 |
| ❑ 22 | Pedro Martinez | 2.50 | 1.10 |
| ❑ 23 | Carlos Beltran | .75 | .35 |
| ❑ 24 | Derrek Lee | .50 | .23 |
| ❑ 25 | Manny Ramirez | 2.50 | 1.10 |
| ❑ 26 | Shea Hillenbrand RC | 1.50 | .70 |
| ❑ 27 | Carlos Lee | .75 | .35 |
| ❑ 28 | Angel Pena | .50 | .23 |
| ❑ 29 | Rafael Roque RC | .50 | .23 |
| ❑ 30 | Octavio Dotel | .50 | .23 |
| ❑ 31 | Jeromy Burnitz | .75 | .35 |
| ❑ 32 | Jeremy Giambi | .50 | .23 |
| ❑ 33 | Andruw Jones | 2.00 | .90 |
| ❑ 34 | Todd Helton | 2.50 | 1.10 |
| ❑ 35 | Scott Rolen | 2.00 | .90 |
| ❑ 36 | Jason Kendall | .75 | .35 |
| ❑ 37 | Trevor Hoffman | .75 | .35 |
| ❑ 38 | Barry Bonds | 3.00 | 1.35 |
| ❑ 39 | Ivan Rodriguez | 2.50 | 1.10 |
| ❑ 40 | Roy Halladay | .50 | .23 |
| ❑ 41 | Rickey Henderson | 2.50 | 1.10 |
| ❑ 42 | Ryan Minor | .50 | .23 |
| ❑ 43 | Brian Jordan | .75 | .35 |
| ❑ 44 | Alex Gonzalez | .50 | .23 |
| ❑ 45 | Raul Mondesi | .75 | .35 |
| ❑ 46 | Corey Koskie | .50 | .23 |
| ❑ 47 | Paul O'Neill | .75 | .35 |
| ❑ 48 | Todd Walker | .50 | .23 |
| ❑ 49 | Carlos Febles | .50 | .23 |
| ❑ 50 | Travis Fryman | .75 | .35 |
| ❑ 51 | Albert Belle | 1.25 | .55 |
| ❑ 52 | Travis Lee | .50 | .23 |
| ❑ 53 | Bruce Chen | .50 | .23 |
| ❑ 54 | Reggie Taylor | .50 | .23 |
| ❑ 55 | Jerry Hairston Jr. | .75 | .35 |
| ❑ 56 | Carlos Guillen | .50 | .23 |
| ❑ 57 | Michael Barrett | .50 | .23 |
| ❑ 58 | Jason Conti | .50 | .23 |
| ❑ 59 | Joe Lawrence | .75 | .35 |
| ❑ 60 | Jeff Cirillo | .75 | .35 |
| ❑ 61 | Juan Melo | .50 | .23 |
| ❑ 62 | Chad Hermansen | .50 | .23 |
| ❑ 63 | Ruben Mateo | .75 | .35 |
| ❑ 64 | Ben Davis | .50 | .23 |
| ❑ 65 | Mike Caruso | .50 | .23 |
| ❑ 66 | Jason Giambi | 2.00 | .90 |
| ❑ 67 | Jose Canseco | 2.50 | 1.10 |
| ❑ 68 | Chad Hutchinson RC | 2.50 | 1.10 |
| ❑ 69 | Mitch Meluskey | .50 | .23 |
| ❑ 70 | Adrian Beltre | .75 | .35 |
| ❑ 71 | Mark Kotsay | .50 | .23 |
| ❑ 72 | Juan Encarnacion | .75 | .35 |
| ❑ 73 | Dermal Brown | .75 | .35 |

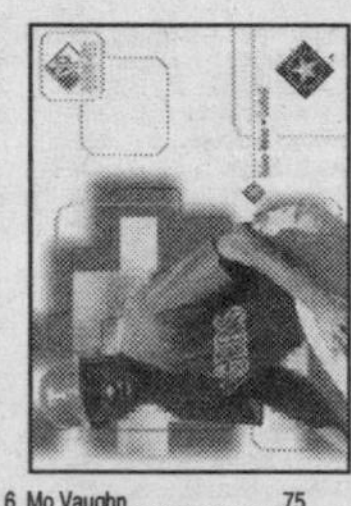

|  | | |
|---|---|---|
| ☐ 74 Kevin Witt | .50 | .23 |
| ☐ 75 Vinny Castilla | .75 | .35 |
| ☐ 76 Aramis Ramirez | .50 | .23 |
| ☐ 77 Marlon Anderson | .50 | .23 |
| ☐ 78 Mike Kinkade | .50 | .23 |
| ☐ 79 Kevin Barker | .50 | .23 |
| ☐ 80 Ron Belliard | .50 | .23 |
| ☐ 81 Chris Haas | .50 | .23 |
| ☐ 82 Bob Henley | .50 | .23 |
| ☐ 83 Fernando Seguignol | .50 | .23 |
| ☐ 84 Damon Minor | .50 | .23 |
| ☐ 85 A.J. Burnett RC | 3.00 | 1.35 |
| ☐ 86 Calvin Pickering | .50 | .23 |
| ☐ 87 Mike Darr | .50 | .23 |
| ☐ 88 Cesar King | .50 | .23 |
| ☐ 89 Rob Bell | .50 | .23 |
| ☐ 90 Derrick Gibson | .50 | .23 |
| ☐ 91 Orber Moreno RC | 1.50 | .70 |
| ☐ 92 Robert Fick | .50 | .23 |
| ☐ 93 Doug Mientkiewicz RC | 1.50 | .70 |
| ☐ 94 A.J. Pierzynski | .50 | .23 |
| ☐ 95 Orlando Palmeiro | .50 | .23 |
| ☐ 96 Sidney Ponson | .50 | .23 |
| ☐ 97 Ivanon Coffie RC | 1.50 | .70 |
| ☐ 98 Juan Pena RC | 1.50 | .70 |
| ☐ 99 Matt Karchner | .50 | .23 |
| ☐ 100 Carlos Castillo | .50 | .23 |
| ☐ 101 Bryan Ward RC | .50 | .23 |
| ☐ 102 Mario Valdez | .50 | .23 |
| ☐ 103 Billy Wagner | .50 | .23 |
| ☐ 104 Miguel Tejada | .75 | .35 |
| ☐ 105 Jose Cruz Jr. | .75 | .35 |
| ☐ 106 George Lombard | .50 | .23 |
| ☐ 107 Geoff Jenkins | .75 | .35 |
| ☐ 108 Ray Lankford | .75 | .35 |
| ☐ 109 Todd Stottlemyre | .50 | .23 |
| ☐ 110 Mike Lowell | .75 | .35 |
| ☐ 111 Matt Clement | .50 | .23 |
| ☐ 112 Scott Brosius | .75 | .35 |
| ☐ 113 Preston Wilson | .75 | .35 |
| ☐ 114 Bartolo Colon | .75 | .35 |
| ☐ 115 Rolando Arrojo | .50 | .23 |
| ☐ 116 Jose Guillen | .50 | .23 |
| ☐ 117 Ron Gant | .75 | .35 |
| ☐ 118 Ricky Ledee | .50 | .23 |
| ☐ 119 Carlos Delgado | 2.00 | .90 |
| ☐ 120 Abraham Nunez | .50 | .23 |
| ☐ 121 John Olerud | .75 | .35 |
| ☐ 122 Chan Ho Park | .75 | .35 |
| ☐ 123 Brad Radke | .75 | .35 |
| ☐ 124 Al Leiter | .75 | .35 |
| ☐ 125 Gary Matthews Jr. | .50 | .23 |
| ☐ 126 F.P. Santangelo | .50 | .23 |
| ☐ 127 Brad Fullmer | .75 | .35 |
| ☐ 128 Matt Anderson | .50 | .23 |
| ☐ 129 A.J. Hinch | .50 | .23 |
| ☐ 130 Sterling Hitchcock | .50 | .23 |
| ☐ 131 Edgar Martinez | 1.25 | .55 |
| ☐ 132 Fernando Tatis | .75 | .35 |
| ☐ 133 Bobby Smith | .50 | .23 |
| ☐ 134 Paul Konerko | .75 | .35 |
| ☐ 135 Sean Casey | .75 | .35 |
| ☐ 136 Donnie Sadler | .50 | .23 |
| ☐ 137 Denny Neagle | .50 | .23 |
| ☐ 138 Sandy Alomar Jr. | .75 | .35 |
| ☐ 139 Mariano Rivera | .75 | .35 |
| ☐ 140 Emil Brown | .50 | .23 |
| ☐ 141 J.T. Snow | .75 | .35 |
| ☐ 142 Eli Marrero | .50 | .23 |
| ☐ 143 Rusty Greer | .75 | .35 |
| ☐ 144 Johnny Damon | .75 | .35 |
| ☐ 145 Damion Easley | .50 | .23 |
| ☐ 146 Eric Milton | .50 | .23 |
| ☐ 147 Rico Brogna | .50 | .23 |
| ☐ 148 Ray Durham | .75 | .35 |
| ☐ 149 Wally Joyner | .75 | .35 |
| ☐ 150 Royce Clayton | .50 | .23 |
| ☐ 151 David Ortiz | .50 | .23 |
| ☐ 152 Wade Boggs | 2.50 | 1.10 |
| ☐ 153 Ugueth Urbina | .50 | .23 |
| ☐ 154 Richard Hidalgo | .75 | .35 |
| ☐ 155 Bob Abreu | .75 | .35 |
| ☐ 156 Robb Nen | .50 | .23 |
| ☐ 157 David Segui | .50 | .23 |
| ☐ 158 Sean Berry | .50 | .23 |
| ☐ 159 Kevin Tapani | .50 | .23 |
| ☐ 160 Jason Varitek | .75 | .35 |
| ☐ 161 Fernando Vina | .50 | .23 |
| ☐ 162 Jim Leyritz | .50 | .23 |
| ☐ 163 Enrique Wilson | .50 | .23 |
| ☐ 164 Jim Parque | .50 | .23 |
| ☐ 165 Doug Glanville | .50 | .23 |
| ☐ 166 Jesus Sanchez | .50 | .23 |
| ☐ 167 Nolan Ryan | 15.00 | 6.75 |
| ☐ 168 Robin Yount | 3.00 | 1.35 |
| ☐ 169 Stan Musial | 6.00 | 2.70 |
| ☐ 170 Tom Seaver | 5.00 | 2.20 |
| ☐ 171 Mike Schmidt | 5.00 | 2.20 |
| ☐ 172 Willie Stargell | 2.00 | .90 |
| ☐ 173 Rollie Fingers | 1.00 | .45 |
| ☐ 174 Willie McCovey | 3.00 | 1.35 |
| ☐ 175 Harmon Killebrew | 3.00 | 1.35 |
| ☐ 176 Eddie Mathews | 3.00 | 1.35 |
| ☐ 177 Reggie Jackson | 5.00 | 2.20 |
| ☐ 178 Frank Robinson | 3.00 | 1.35 |
| ☐ 179 Ken Griffey Sr. | 1.00 | .45 |
| ☐ 180 Eddie Murray | 4.00 | 1.80 |
| ☐ S1 Ken Griffey Jr. Sample | 3.00 | 1.35 |

## 1996 SPx

| | MINT | NRMT |
|---|---|---|
| COMPLETE SET (60) | 80.00 | 36.00 |
| COMMON CARD (1-60) | .60 | .35 |
| ☐ 1 Greg Maddux | 4.00 | 1.80 |
| ☐ 2 Chipper Jones | 4.00 | 1.80 |
| ☐ 3 Fred McGriff | 1.25 | .55 |
| ☐ 4 Tom Glavine | 1.50 | .70 |
| ☐ 5 Cal Ripken | 6.00 | 2.70 |
| ☐ 6 Roberto Alomar | 1.50 | .70 |
| ☐ 7 Rafael Palmeiro | 1.50 | .70 |
| ☐ 8 Jose Canseco | 2.00 | .90 |
| ☐ 9 Roger Clemens | 3.00 | 1.35 |
| ☐ 10 Mo Vaughn | 1.00 | .45 |
| ☐ 11 Jim Edmonds | 1.50 | .70 |
| ☐ 12 Tim Salmon | 1.00 | .45 |
| ☐ 13 Sammy Sosa | 3.00 | 1.35 |
| ☐ 14 Ryne Sandberg | 2.00 | .90 |
| ☐ 15 Mark Grace | 1.50 | .70 |
| ☐ 16 Frank Thomas | 3.00 | 1.35 |
| ☐ 17 Barry Larkin | 1.50 | .70 |
| ☐ 18 Kenny Lofton | 1.00 | .45 |
| ☐ 19 Albert Belle | 1.25 | .55 |
| ☐ 20 Eddie Murray | 1.50 | .70 |
| ☐ 21 Manny Ramirez | 2.00 | .90 |
| ☐ 22 Dante Bichette | 1.00 | .45 |
| ☐ 23 Larry Walker | 1.00 | .45 |
| ☐ 24 Vinny Castilla | 1.00 | .45 |
| ☐ 25 Andres Galarraga | 1.25 | .55 |
| ☐ 26 Cecil Fielder | 1.00 | .45 |
| ☐ 27 Gary Sheffield | 1.50 | .70 |
| ☐ 28 Craig Biggio | 1.25 | .55 |
| ☐ 29 Jeff Bagwell | 2.00 | .90 |
| ☐ 30 Derek Bell | .75 | .35 |
| ☐ 31 Johnny Damon | 1.25 | .55 |
| ☐ 32 Eric Karros | 1.00 | .45 |
| ☐ 33 Mike Piazza | 5.00 | 2.20 |
| ☐ 34 Raul Mondesi | 1.00 | .45 |
| ☐ 35 Hideo Nomo | 1.50 | .70 |
| ☐ 36 Kirby Puckett | 4.00 | 1.80 |
| ☐ 37 Paul Molitor | 1.50 | .70 |
| ☐ 38 Marty Cordova | .75 | .35 |
| ☐ 39 Rondell White | 1.00 | .45 |
| ☐ 40 Jason Isringhausen | 1.00 | .45 |
| ☐ 41 Paul Wilson | .75 | .35 |
| ☐ 42 Rey Ordonez | 1.00 | .45 |
| ☐ 43 Derek Jeter | 6.00 | 2.70 |
| ☐ 44 Wade Boggs | 2.00 | .90 |
| ☐ 45 Mark McGwire | 6.00 | 2.70 |
| ☐ 46 Jason Kendall | 1.00 | .45 |
| ☐ 47 Ron Gant | .75 | .35 |
| ☐ 48 Ozzie Smith | 2.00 | .90 |
| ☐ 49 Tony Gwynn | 3.00 | 1.35 |
| ☐ 50 Ken Caminiti | 1.00 | .45 |
| ☐ 51 Barry Bonds | 2.50 | 1.10 |
| ☐ 52 Matt Williams | 1.25 | .55 |
| ☐ 53 Osvaldo Fernandez | .75 | .35 |
| ☐ 54 Jay Buhner | 1.00 | .45 |
| ☐ 55 Ken Griffey Jr. | 6.00 | 2.70 |
| ☐ 56 Randy Johnson | 2.00 | .90 |
| ☐ 57 Alex Rodriguez | 5.00 | 2.20 |
| ☐ 58 Juan Gonzalez | 1.50 | .70 |
| ☐ 59 Joe Carter | 1.00 | .45 |
| ☐ 60 Carlos Delgado | 1.50 | .70 |
| ☐ KG1 Ken Griffey Jr. Comm. | 12.00 | 5.50 |
| ☐ MP1 Mike Piazza Trib. | 8.00 | 3.60 |
| ☐ KGA1 Ken Griffey Jr. Auto | 200.00 | 90.00 |
| ☐ MPA1 Mike Piazza Auto. | 150.00 | 70.00 |

## 1997 SPx

| | MINT | NRMT |
|---|---|---|
| COMPLETE SET (50) | 60.00 | 27.00 |
| COMMON CARD (1-50) | .50 | .23 |
| ☐ 1 Eddie Murray | 1.25 | .55 |
| ☐ 2 Darin Erstad | 1.50 | .70 |
| ☐ 3 Tim Salmon | .60 | .25 |
| ☐ 4 Andruw Jones | 1.50 | .70 |
| ☐ 5 Chipper Jones | 3.00 | 1.35 |
| ☐ 6 John Smoltz | .60 | .25 |
| ☐ 7 Greg Maddux | 3.00 | 1.35 |
| ☐ 8 Kenny Lofton | .60 | .25 |
| ☐ 9 Roberto Alomar | 1.25 | .55 |
| ☐ 10 Rafael Palmeiro | 1.25 | .55 |
| ☐ 11 Brady Anderson | .60 | .25 |
| ☐ 12 Cal Ripken | 5.00 | 2.20 |
| ☐ 13 Nomar Garciaparra | 4.00 | 1.80 |
| ☐ 14 Mo Vaughn | .60 | .25 |
| ☐ 15 Ryne Sandberg | 1.50 | .70 |
| ☐ 16 Sammy Sosa | 2.50 | 1.10 |
| ☐ 17 Frank Thomas | 2.50 | 1.10 |
| ☐ 18 Albert Belle | .75 | .35 |
| ☐ 19 Barry Larkin | 1.25 | .55 |
| ☐ 20 Deion Sanders | .60 | .25 |
| ☐ 21 Manny Ramirez | 1.50 | .70 |
| ☐ 22 Jim Thome | .75 | .35 |
| ☐ 23 Dante Bichette | .60 | .25 |
| ☐ 24 Andres Galarraga | .75 | .35 |
| ☐ 25 Larry Walker | .60 | .25 |
| ☐ 26 Gary Sheffield | 1.25 | .55 |
| ☐ 27 Jeff Bagwell | 1.50 | .70 |
| ☐ 28 Raul Mondesi | .60 | .25 |
| ☐ 29 Hideo Nomo | 1.25 | .55 |
| ☐ 30 Mike Piazza | 4.00 | 1.80 |
| ☐ 31 Paul Molitor | 1.25 | .55 |
| ☐ 32 Todd Walker | .50 | .23 |
| ☐ 33 Vladimir Guerrero | 2.50 | 1.10 |
| ☐ 34 Todd Hundley | .50 | .23 |
| ☐ 35 Andy Pettitte | .60 | .25 |
| ☐ 36 Derek Jeter | 5.00 | 2.20 |
| ☐ 37 Jose Canseco | 1.50 | .70 |

| | | |
|---|---|---|
| ❑ 38 Mark McGwire | 5.00 | 2.20 |
| ❑ 39 Scott Rolen | 1.25 | .55 |
| ❑ 40 Ron Gant | .50 | .23 |
| ❑ 41 Ken Caminiti | .60 | .25 |
| ❑ 42 Tony Gwynn | 2.50 | 1.10 |
| ❑ 43 Barry Bonds | 2.00 | .90 |
| ❑ 44 Jay Buhner | .60 | .25 |
| ❑ 45 Ken Griffey Jr. | 5.00 | 2.20 |
| ❑ 46 Alex Rodriguez | 4.00 | 1.80 |
| ❑ 47 Jose Cruz Jr. RC | 3.00 | 1.35 |
| ❑ 48 Juan Gonzalez | 1.25 | .55 |
| ❑ 49 Ivan Rodriguez | 1.50 | .70 |
| ❑ 50 Roger Clemens | 2.50 | 1.10 |
| ❑ S45 Ken Griffey Jr. SAMPLE | 3.00 | 1.35 |

## 1998 SPx Finite

| | MINT | NRMT |
|---|---|---|
| COMP.YM SER.1 (30) | 60.00 | 27.00 |
| COMMON YM (1-30) | .75 | .35 |
| COMP.PE SER.1 (20) | 150.00 | 70.00 |
| COMMON PE (31-50) | 2.00 | .90 |
| COMP.BASIC SER.1 (90) | 100.00 | 45.00 |
| COMMON CARD (51-140) | .50 | .23 |
| COMP.SF SER.1 (30) | 120.00 | 55.00 |
| COMMON SF (141-170) | 1.00 | .45 |
| COMP.HG SER.1 (10) | 200.00 | 90.00 |
| COMMON HG (171-180) | 10.00 | 4.50 |
| COMP.YM SER.2 (30) | 120.00 | 55.00 |
| COMMON YM (181-210) | 1.50 | .70 |
| COMP.PP SER.2 (30) | 100.00 | 45.00 |
| COMMON PP (211-240) | 1.00 | .45 |
| COMP.BASIC SER.2 (90) | 60.00 | 27.00 |
| COMMON CARD (241-330) | .50 | .23 |
| COMP.TW SER.2 (20) | 40.00 | 18.00 |
| COMMON TW (331-350) | 1.25 | .55 |
| COMP.CG SER.2 (10) | 200.00 | 90.00 |
| COMMON CG (351-360) | 8.00 | 3.60 |

| | | |
|---|---|---|
| ❑ 1 Nomar Garciaparra YM | 10.00 | 4.50 |
| ❑ 2 Miguel Tejada YM | 3.00 | 1.35 |
| ❑ 3 Mike Cameron YM | 1.25 | .55 |
| ❑ 4 Ken Cloude YM | .75 | .35 |
| ❑ 5 Jaret Wright YM | .75 | .35 |
| ❑ 6 Mark Kotsay YM | 1.25 | .55 |
| ❑ 7 Craig Counsell YM | .75 | .35 |
| ❑ 8 Jose Guillen YM | .75 | .35 |
| ❑ 9 Neifi Perez YM | .75 | .35 |
| ❑ 10 Jose Cruz Jr. YM | 1.25 | .55 |
| ❑ 11 Brett Tomko YM | .75 | .35 |
| ❑ 12 Matt Morris YM | .75 | .35 |
| ❑ 13 Justin Thompson YM | .75 | .35 |
| ❑ 14 Jeremi Gonzalez YM | .75 | .35 |
| ❑ 15 Scott Rolen YM | 3.00 | 1.35 |
| ❑ 16 Vladimir Guerrero YM | 5.00 | 2.20 |
| ❑ 17 Brad Fullmer YM | 1.25 | .55 |
| ❑ 18 Brian Giles YM | 1.25 | .55 |
| ❑ 19 Todd Dunwoody YM | .75 | .35 |
| ❑ 20 Ben Grieve YM | 1.25 | .55 |
| ❑ 21 Juan Encarnacion YM | 1.25 | .55 |
| ❑ 22 Aaron Boone YM | .75 | .35 |
| ❑ 23 Richie Sexson YM | 2.00 | .90 |
| ❑ 24 Richard Hidalgo YM | 1.25 | .55 |
| ❑ 25 Andruw Jones YM | 3.00 | 1.35 |
| ❑ 26 Todd Helton YM | 4.00 | 1.80 |
| ❑ 27 Paul Konerko YM | 1.25 | .55 |
| ❑ 28 Dante Powell YM | .75 | .35 |
| ❑ 29 Eli Marrero YM | .75 | .35 |
| ❑ 30 Derek Jeter YM | 12.00 | 5.50 |
| ❑ 31 Mike Piazza PE | 15.00 | 6.75 |
| ❑ 32 Tony Clark PE | 2.00 | .90 |
| ❑ 33 Larry Walker PE | | |
| ❑ 34 Jim Thome PE | 3.00 | 1.35 |
| ❑ 35 Juan Gonzalez PE | 5.00 | 2.20 |
| ❑ 36 Jeff Bagwell PE | 6.00 | 2.70 |
| ❑ 37 Jay Buhner PE | | |
| ❑ 38 Tim Salmon PE | | |
| ❑ 39 Albert Belle PE | 3.00 | 1.35 |
| ❑ 40 Mark McGwire PE | 20.00 | 9.00 |
| ❑ 41 Sammy Sosa PE | 10.00 | 4.50 |
| ❑ 42 Mo Vaughn PE | | |
| ❑ 43 Manny Ramirez PE | 6.00 | 2.70 |
| ❑ 44 Tino Martinez PE | | |
| ❑ 45 Frank Thomas PE | 10.00 | 4.50 |
| ❑ 46 Nomar Garciaparra PE | 15.00 | 6.75 |
| ❑ 47 Alex Rodriguez PE | 15.00 | 6.75 |
| ❑ 48 Chipper Jones PE | 12.00 | 5.50 |
| ❑ 49 Barry Bonds PE | 8.00 | 3.60 |
| ❑ 50 Ken Griffey Jr. PE | 20.00 | 9.00 |
| ❑ 51 Jason Dickson | .50 | .23 |
| ❑ 52 Jim Edmonds | 2.00 | .90 |
| ❑ 53 Darin Erstad | 2.00 | .90 |
| ❑ 54 Tim Salmon | .75 | .35 |
| ❑ 55 Chipper Jones | 5.00 | 2.20 |
| ❑ 56 Ryan Klesko | .75 | .35 |
| ❑ 57 Tom Glavine | 2.00 | .90 |
| ❑ 58 Denny Neagle | .50 | .23 |
| ❑ 59 John Smoltz | .75 | .35 |
| ❑ 60 Javy Lopez | .75 | .35 |
| ❑ 61 Roberto Alomar | 2.00 | .90 |
| ❑ 62 Rafael Palmeiro | 2.00 | .90 |
| ❑ 63 Mike Mussina | 2.00 | .90 |
| ❑ 64 Cal Ripken | 8.00 | 3.60 |
| ❑ 65 Mo Vaughn | .75 | .35 |
| ❑ 66 Tim Naehring | .50 | .23 |
| ❑ 67 John Valentin | .50 | .23 |
| ❑ 68 Mark Grace | 2.00 | .90 |
| ❑ 69 Kevin Orie | .50 | .23 |
| ❑ 70 Sammy Sosa | 4.00 | 1.80 |
| ❑ 71 Albert Belle | 1.25 | .55 |
| ❑ 72 Frank Thomas | 4.00 | 1.80 |
| ❑ 73 Robin Ventura | .75 | .35 |
| ❑ 74 David Justice | 1.25 | .55 |
| ❑ 75 Kenny Lofton | .75 | .35 |
| ❑ 76 Omar Vizquel | .75 | .35 |
| ❑ 77 Manny Ramirez | 2.50 | 1.10 |
| ❑ 78 Jim Thome | 1.25 | .55 |
| ❑ 79 Dante Bichette | .75 | .35 |
| ❑ 80 Larry Walker | .75 | .35 |
| ❑ 81 Vinny Castilla | .75 | .35 |
| ❑ 82 Ellis Burks | .75 | .35 |
| ❑ 83 Bobby Higginson | .75 | .35 |
| ❑ 84 Brian Hunter | .50 | .23 |
| ❑ 85 Tony Clark | .50 | .23 |
| ❑ 86 Mike Hampton | .75 | .35 |
| ❑ 87 Jeff Bagwell | 2.50 | 1.10 |
| ❑ 88 Craig Biggio | 1.25 | .55 |
| ❑ 89 Derek Bell | .75 | .35 |
| ❑ 90 Mike Piazza | 6.00 | 2.70 |
| ❑ 91 Ramon Martinez | .50 | .23 |
| ❑ 92 Raul Mondesi | .75 | .35 |
| ❑ 93 Hideo Nomo | 2.00 | .90 |
| ❑ 94 Eric Karros | .75 | .35 |
| ❑ 95 Paul Molitor | 2.00 | .90 |
| ❑ 96 Marty Cordova | .50 | .23 |
| ❑ 97 Brad Radke | .75 | .35 |
| ❑ 98 Mark Grudzielanek | .50 | .23 |
| ❑ 99 Carlos Perez | .50 | .23 |
| ❑ 100 Rondell White | .75 | .35 |
| ❑ 101 Todd Hundley | .50 | .23 |
| ❑ 102 Edgardo Alfonzo | .75 | .35 |
| ❑ 103 John Franco | .75 | .35 |
| ❑ 104 John Olerud | .75 | .35 |
| ❑ 105 Tino Martinez | .75 | .35 |
| ❑ 106 David Cone | .75 | .35 |
| ❑ 107 Paul O'Neill | .75 | .35 |
| ❑ 108 Andy Pettitte | .75 | .35 |
| ❑ 109 Bernie Williams | 2.00 | .90 |
| ❑ 110 Rickey Henderson | 2.50 | 1.10 |
| ❑ 111 Jason Giambi | 2.00 | .90 |
| ❑ 112 Matt Stairs | .50 | .23 |
| ❑ 113 Gregg Jefferies | .50 | .23 |
| ❑ 114 Rico Brogna | .50 | .23 |
| ❑ 115 Curt Schilling | .75 | .35 |
| ❑ 116 Jason Schmidt | .50 | .23 |
| ❑ 117 Jose Guillen | .50 | .23 |
| ❑ 118 Kevin Young | .75 | .35 |
| ❑ 119 Ray Lankford | .75 | .35 |
| ❑ 120 Mark McGwire | 8.00 | 3.60 |
| ❑ 121 Delino DeShields | .50 | .23 |
| ❑ 122 Ken Caminiti | .75 | .35 |
| ❑ 123 Tony Gwynn | 4.00 | 1.80 |
| ❑ 124 Trevor Hoffman | .75 | .35 |
| ❑ 125 Barry Bonds | 3.00 | 1.35 |
| ❑ 126 Jeff Kent | 1.25 | .55 |
| ❑ 127 Shawn Estes | .50 | .23 |
| ❑ 128 J.T. Snow | .75 | .35 |
| ❑ 129 Jay Buhner | .75 | .35 |
| ❑ 130 Ken Griffey Jr. | 8.00 | 3.60 |
| ❑ 131 Dan Wilson | .50 | .23 |
| ❑ 132 Edgar Martinez | 1.25 | .55 |
| ❑ 133 Alex Rodriguez | 6.00 | 2.70 |
| ❑ 134 Rusty Greer | .75 | .35 |
| ❑ 135 Juan Gonzalez | .75 | .35 |
| ❑ 136 Fernando Tatis | .75 | .35 |
| ❑ 137 Ivan Rodriguez | 2.50 | 1.10 |
| ❑ 138 Carlos Delgado | 2.00 | .90 |
| ❑ 139 Pat Hentgen | .50 | .23 |
| ❑ 140 Roger Clemens | 4.00 | 1.80 |
| ❑ 141 Chipper Jones SF | 6.00 | 2.70 |
| ❑ 142 Greg Maddux SF | 6.00 | 2.70 |
| ❑ 143 Rafael Palmeiro SF | 2.50 | 1.10 |
| ❑ 144 Mike Mussina SF | 2.50 | 1.10 |
| ❑ 145 Cal Ripken SF | 10.00 | 4.50 |
| ❑ 146 Nomar Garciaparra SF | 8.00 | 3.60 |
| ❑ 147 Mo Vaughn SF | 1.00 | .45 |
| ❑ 148 Sammy Sosa SF | 5.00 | 2.20 |
| ❑ 149 Albert Belle SF | 1.50 | .70 |
| ❑ 150 Frank Thomas SF | 5.00 | 2.20 |
| ❑ 151 Jim Thome SF | 1.50 | .70 |
| ❑ 152 Kenny Lofton SF | 1.00 | .45 |
| ❑ 153 Manny Ramirez SF | 3.00 | 1.35 |
| ❑ 154 Larry Walker SF | 1.00 | .45 |
| ❑ 155 Jeff Bagwell SF | 3.00 | 1.35 |
| ❑ 156 Craig Biggio SF | 1.50 | .70 |
| ❑ 157 Mike Piazza SF | 8.00 | 3.60 |
| ❑ 158 Paul Molitor SF | 2.50 | 1.10 |
| ❑ 159 Derek Jeter SF | 10.00 | 4.50 |
| ❑ 160 Tino Martinez SF | 1.00 | .45 |
| ❑ 161 Curt Schilling SF | 1.00 | .45 |
| ❑ 162 Mark McGwire SF | 10.00 | 4.50 |
| ❑ 163 Tony Gwynn SF | 5.00 | 2.20 |
| ❑ 164 Barry Bonds SF | 4.00 | 1.80 |
| ❑ 165 Ken Griffey Jr. SF | 10.00 | 4.50 |
| ❑ 166 Randy Johnson SF | 3.00 | 1.35 |
| ❑ 167 Alex Rodriguez SF | 8.00 | 3.60 |
| ❑ 168 Juan Gonzalez SF | 2.50 | 1.10 |
| ❑ 169 Ivan Rodriguez SF | 3.00 | 1.35 |
| ❑ 170 Roger Clemens SF | 5.00 | 2.20 |
| ❑ 171 Greg Maddux HG | 20.00 | 9.00 |
| ❑ 172 Cal Ripken HG | 30.00 | 13.50 |
| ❑ 173 Frank Thomas HG | 15.00 | 6.75 |
| ❑ 174 Jeff Bagwell HG | 10.00 | 4.50 |
| ❑ 175 Mike Piazza HG | 25.00 | 11.00 |
| ❑ 176 Mark McGwire HG | 30.00 | 13.50 |
| ❑ 177 Barry Bonds HG | 12.00 | 5.50 |
| ❑ 178 Ken Griffey Jr. HG | 30.00 | 13.50 |
| ❑ 179 Alex Rodriguez HG | 25.00 | 11.00 |
| ❑ 180 Roger Clemens HG | 15.00 | 6.75 |
| ❑ 181 Mike Caruso YM | 1.50 | .70 |
| ❑ 182 David Ortiz YM | 1.50 | .70 |
| ❑ 183 Gabe Alvarez YM | 1.50 | .70 |
| ❑ 184 Gary Matthews Jr. YM RC | 1.50 | .70 |
| ❑ 185 Kerry Wood YM | 4.00 | 1.80 |
| ❑ 186 Carl Pavano YM | 1.50 | .70 |
| ❑ 187 Alex Gonzalez YM | 1.50 | .70 |
| ❑ 188 Masato Yoshii YM RC | 8.00 | 3.60 |
| ❑ 189 Larry Sutton YM | 1.50 | .70 |
| ❑ 190 Russell Branyan YM | 2.00 | .90 |
| ❑ 191 Bruce Chen YM | 1.50 | .70 |
| ❑ 192 Rolando Arrojo YM RC | 8.00 | 3.60 |
| ❑ 193 Ryan Christenson YM RC | 1.50 | .70 |
| ❑ 194 Cliff Politte YM | 1.50 | .70 |
| ❑ 195 A.J. Hinch YM | 1.50 | .70 |
| ❑ 196 Kevin Witt YM | 1.50 | .70 |
| ❑ 197 Daryle Ward YM | 2.00 | .90 |
| ❑ 198 Corey Koskie YM RC | 10.00 | 4.50 |
| ❑ 199 Mike Lowell YM RC | 15.00 | 6.75 |
| ❑ 200 Travis Lee YM | 2.00 | .90 |
| ❑ 201 Kevin Millwood YM RC | 15.00 | 6.75 |

❑ 202 Robert Smith YM .......... 1.50 .70
❑ 203 Magglio Ordonez YM RC 40.00 18.00
❑ 204 Eric Milton YM .......... 2.00 .90
❑ 205 Geoff Jenkins YM .......... 2.00 .90
❑ 206 Rich Butler YM RC .......... 1.50 .70
❑ 207 Mike Kinkade YM RC .. 2.00 .90
❑ 208 Braden Looper YM .......... 1.50 .70
❑ 209 Matt Clement YM .......... 2.00 .90
❑ 210 Derrek Lee YM .......... 2.00 .90
❑ 211 Randy Johnson PP .......... 3.00 1.35
❑ 212 John Smoltz PP .......... 1.00 .40
❑ 213 Roger Clemens PP .......... 5.00 2.20
❑ 214 Curt Schilling PP .......... 1.00 .40
❑ 215 Pedro Martinez PP .......... 3.00 1.35
❑ 216 Vinny Castilla PP .......... 1.00 .40
❑ 217 Jose Cruz Jr. PP .......... 1.00 .40
❑ 218 Jim Thome PP .......... 1.50 .70
❑ 219 Alex Rodriguez PP .......... 8.00 3.60
❑ 220 Frank Thomas PP .......... 5.00 2.20
❑ 221 Tim Salmon PP .......... 1.00 .40
❑ 222 Larry Walker PP .......... 1.00 .40
❑ 223 Albert Belle PP .......... 1.50 .70
❑ 224 Manny Ramirez PP .......... 3.00 1.35
❑ 225 Mark McGwire PP .......... 10.00 4.50
❑ 226 Mo Vaughn PP .......... 1.00 .40
❑ 227 Andres Galarraga PP .. 1.50 .70
❑ 228 Scott Rolen PP .......... 2.50 1.10
❑ 229 Travis Lee PP .......... 1.00 .40
❑ 230 Mike Piazza PP .......... 8.00 3.60
❑ 231 Nomar Garciaparra PP 8.00 3.60
❑ 232 Andruw Jones PP .......... 2.50 1.10
❑ 233 Barry Bonds PP .......... 4.00 1.80
❑ 234 Jeff Bagwell PP .......... 3.00 1.35
❑ 235 Juan Gonzalez PP .......... 2.50 1.10
❑ 236 Tino Martinez PP .......... 1.00 .40
❑ 237 Vladimir Guerrero PP .. 4.00 1.80
❑ 238 Rafael Palmeiro PP .......... 2.50 1.10
❑ 239 Russell Branyan PP .......... 1.00 .40
❑ 240 Ken Griffey Jr. PP .......... 10.00 4.50
❑ 241 Cecil Fielder .......... .75 .35
❑ 242 Chuck Finley .......... .75 .35
❑ 243 Jay Bell .......... .75 .35
❑ 244 Andy Benes .......... .50 .23
❑ 245 Matt Williams .......... 1.25 .55
❑ 246 Brian Anderson .......... .50 .23
❑ 247 Dave Dellucci RC .......... .50 .23
❑ 248 Andres Galarraga .......... 1.25 .55
❑ 249 Andruw Jones .......... 2.00 .90
❑ 250 Greg Maddux .......... 5.00 2.20
❑ 251 Brady Anderson .......... .75 .35
❑ 252 Joe Carter .......... .75 .35
❑ 253 Eric Davis .......... .75 .35
❑ 254 Pedro Martinez .......... 2.50 1.10
❑ 255 Nomar Garciaparra .......... 6.00 2.70
❑ 256 Dennis Eckersley .......... .75 .35
❑ 257 Henry Rodriguez .......... .50 .23
❑ 258 Jeff Blauser .......... .50 .23
❑ 259 Jaime Navarro .......... .50 .23
❑ 260 Ray Durham .......... .75 .35
❑ 261 Chris Stynes .......... .50 .23
❑ 262 Willie Greene .......... .50 .23
❑ 263 Reggie Sanders .......... .50 .23
❑ 264 Bret Boone .......... .75 .35
❑ 265 Barry Larkin .......... 2.00 .90
❑ 266 Travis Fryman .......... .75 .35
❑ 267 Charles Nagy .......... .50 .23
❑ 268 Sandy Alomar Jr. .......... .75 .35
❑ 269 Darryl Kile .......... .75 .35
❑ 270 Mike Lansing .......... .50 .23
❑ 271 Pedro Astacio .......... .50 .23
❑ 272 Damion Easley .......... .50 .23
❑ 273 Joe Randa .......... .50 .23
❑ 274 Luis Gonzalez .......... .75 .35
❑ 275 Mike Piazza .......... 6.00 2.70
❑ 276 Todd Zeile .......... .75 .35
❑ 277 Edgar Renteria .......... .50 .23
❑ 278 Livan Hernandez .......... .50 .23
❑ 279 Cliff Floyd .......... .75 .35
❑ 280 Moises Alou .......... .75 .35
❑ 281 Billy Wagner .......... .50 .23
❑ 282 Jeff King .......... .50 .23
❑ 283 Hal Morris .......... .50 .23
❑ 284 Johnny Damon .......... .75 .35
❑ 285 Dean Palmer .......... .75 .35
❑ 286 Tim Belcher .......... .50 .23
❑ 287 Eric Young .......... .50 .23
❑ 288 Bobby Bonilla .......... .75 .35
❑ 289 Gary Sheffield .......... 2.00 .90
❑ 290 Chan Ho Park .......... .75 .35
❑ 291 Charles Johnson .......... .75 .35
❑ 292 Jeff Cirillo .......... .75 .35
❑ 293 Jeromy Burnitz .......... .75 .35
❑ 294 Jose Valentin .......... .50 .23
❑ 295 Marquis Grissom .......... .50 .23
❑ 296 Todd Walker .......... .50 .23
❑ 297 Terry Steinbach .......... .50 .23
❑ 298 Rick Aguilera .......... .50 .23
❑ 299 Vladimir Guerrero .......... 3.00 1.35
❑ 300 Rey Ordonez .......... .50 .23
❑ 301 Butch Huskey .......... .50 .23
❑ 302 Bernard Gilkey .......... .50 .23
❑ 303 Mariano Rivera .......... .75 .35
❑ 304 Chuck Knoblauch .......... .75 .35
❑ 305 Derek Jeter .......... 8.00 3.60
❑ 306 Ricky Bottalico .......... .50 .23
❑ 307 Bob Abreu .......... .75 .35
❑ 308 Scott Rolen .......... 2.00 .90
❑ 309 Al Martin .......... .50 .23
❑ 310 Jason Kendall .......... .75 .35
❑ 311 Brian Jordan .......... .75 .35
❑ 312 Ron Gant .......... .75 .35
❑ 313 Todd Stottlemyre .......... .50 .23
❑ 314 Greg Vaughn .......... .75 .35
❑ 315 Kevin Brown .......... 1.25 .55
❑ 316 Wally Joyner .......... .75 .35
❑ 317 Robb Nen .......... .50 .23
❑ 318 Orel Hershiser .......... .75 .35
❑ 319 Russ Davis .......... .50 .23
❑ 320 Randy Johnson .......... 2.50 1.10
❑ 321 Quinton McCracken .......... .50 .23
❑ 322 Tony Saunders .......... .50 .23
❑ 323 Wilson Alvarez .......... .50 .23
❑ 324 Wade Boggs .......... 2.50 1.10
❑ 325 Fred McGriff .......... 1.25 .55
❑ 326 Lee Stevens .......... .50 .23
❑ 327 John Wetteland .......... .75 .35
❑ 328 Jose Canseco .......... 2.50 1.10
❑ 329 Randy Myers .......... .75 .35
❑ 330 Jose Cruz Jr. .......... .75 .35
❑ 331 Matt Williams TW .......... 3.00 1.35
❑ 332 Andres Galarraga TW .. 3.00 1.35
❑ 333 Walt Weiss TW .......... 2.00 .90
❑ 334 Joe Carter TW .......... 2.00 .90
❑ 335 Pedro Martinez TW .......... 6.00 2.70
❑ 336 Henry Rodriguez TW .......... 1.25 .55
❑ 337 Travis Fryman TW .......... 2.00 .90
❑ 338 Darryl Kile TW .......... 2.00 .90
❑ 339 Mike Lansing TW .......... 1.25 .55
❑ 340 Mike Piazza TW .......... 15.00 6.75
❑ 341 Moises Alou TW .......... 2.00 .90
❑ 342 Charles Johnson TW .......... 2.00 .90
❑ 343 Chuck Knoblauch TW .. 2.00 .90
❑ 344 Rickey Henderson TW 6.00 2.70
❑ 345 Kevin Brown TW .......... 3.00 1.35
❑ 346 Orel Hershiser TW .......... 2.00 .90
❑ 347 Wade Boggs TW .......... 6.00 2.70
❑ 348 Fred McGriff TW .......... 3.00 1.35
❑ 349 Jose Canseco TW .......... 6.00 2.70
❑ 350 Gary Sheffield TW .......... 5.00 2.20
❑ 351 Travis Lee CG .......... 8.00 3.60
❑ 352 Nomar Garciaparra CG 25.00 11.00
❑ 353 Frank Thomas CG .......... 15.00 6.75
❑ 354 Cal Ripken CG .......... 30.00 13.50
❑ 355 Mark McGwire CG .......... 30.00 13.50
❑ 356 Mike Piazza CG .......... 25.00 11.00
❑ 357 Alex Rodriguez CG .......... 25.00 11.00
❑ 358 Barry Bonds CG .......... 12.00 5.50
❑ 359 Tony Gwynn CG .......... 15.00 6.75
❑ 360 Ken Griffey Jr. CG .......... 30.00 13.50

## 1999 SPx

| | MINT | NRMT |
|---|---|---|
| COMPLETE SET (120) | 550.00 | 250.00 |
| COMP.SET w/o SP's (80) | 50.00 | 22.00 |
| COMMON MCGWIRE (1-10) | 4.00 | 1.80 |
| COMMON CARD (11-80) | .25 | .11 |
| COMMON SP (81-120) | 12.00 | 5.50 |

❑ 1 Mark McGwire 61 .......... 4.00 1.80
❑ 2 Mark McGwire 62 .......... 4.00 1.80
❑ 3 Mark McGwire 63 .......... 4.00 1.80
❑ 4 Mark McGwire 64 .......... 4.00 1.80
❑ 5 Mark McGwire 65 .......... 4.00 1.80
❑ 6 Mark McGwire 66 .......... 4.00 1.80
❑ 7 Mark McGwire 67 .......... 4.00 1.80
❑ 8 Mark McGwire 68 .......... 4.00 1.80
❑ 9 Mark McGwire 69 .......... 4.00 1.80
❑ 10 Mark McGwire 70 .......... 5.00 2.20
❑ 11 Mo Vaughn .......... .40 .18
❑ 12 Darin Erstad .......... 1.00 .45
❑ 13 Travis Lee .......... .25 .11
❑ 14 Randy Johnson .......... 1.25 .55
❑ 15 Matt Williams .......... .60 .25
❑ 16 Chipper Jones .......... 2.50 1.10
❑ 17 Greg Maddux .......... 2.50 1.10
❑ 18 Andruw Jones .......... 1.00 .45
❑ 19 Andres Galarraga .......... .60 .25
❑ 20 Cal Ripken .......... 4.00 1.80
❑ 21 Albert Belle .......... .60 .25
❑ 22 Mike Mussina .......... 1.00 .45
❑ 23 Nomar Garciaparra .......... 3.00 1.35
❑ 24 Pedro Martinez .......... 1.25 .55
❑ 25 John Valentin .......... .25 .11
❑ 26 Kerry Wood .......... .40 .18
❑ 27 Sammy Sosa .......... 2.00 .90
❑ 28 Mark Grace .......... 1.00 .45
❑ 29 Frank Thomas .......... 2.00 .90
❑ 30 Mike Caruso .......... .25 .11
❑ 31 Barry Larkin .......... 1.00 .45
❑ 32 Sean Casey .......... .40 .18
❑ 33 Jim Thome .......... .60 .25
❑ 34 Kenny Lofton .......... .40 .18
❑ 35 Manny Ramirez .......... 1.25 .55
❑ 36 Larry Walker .......... .40 .18
❑ 37 Todd Helton .......... 1.25 .55
❑ 38 Vinny Castilla .......... .40 .18
❑ 39 Tony Clark .......... .25 .11
❑ 40 Derrek Lee .......... .25 .11
❑ 41 Mark Kotsay .......... .25 .11
❑ 42 Jeff Bagwell .......... 1.25 .55
❑ 43 Craig Biggio .......... .60 .25
❑ 44 Moises Alou .......... .40 .18
❑ 45 Larry Sutton .......... .25 .11
❑ 46 Johnny Damon .......... .40 .18
❑ 47 Gary Sheffield .......... 1.00 .45
❑ 48 Raul Mondesi .......... .40 .18
❑ 49 Jeromy Burnitz .......... .40 .18
❑ 50 Todd Walker .......... .25 .11
❑ 51 David Ortiz .......... .25 .11
❑ 52 Vladimir Guerrero .......... 1.50 .70
❑ 53 Rondell White .......... .40 .18
❑ 54 Mike Piazza .......... 3.00 1.35
❑ 55 Derek Jeter .......... 4.00 1.80
❑ 56 Tino Martinez .......... .40 .18

| | | |
|---|---|---|
| ❑ 57 Roger Clemens | 2.00 | .90 |
| ❑ 58 Ben Grieve | .40 | .18 |
| ❑ 59 A.J. Hinch | .25 | .11 |
| ❑ 60 Scott Rolen | 1.00 | .45 |
| ❑ 61 Doug Glanville | .25 | .11 |
| ❑ 62 Aramis Ramirez | .25 | .11 |
| ❑ 63 Jose Guillen | .25 | .11 |
| ❑ 64 Tony Gwynn | 2.00 | .90 |
| ❑ 65 Greg Vaughn | .40 | .18 |
| ❑ 66 Ruben Rivera | .25 | .11 |
| ❑ 67 Barry Bonds | 1.50 | .70 |
| ❑ 68 J.T. Snow | .40 | .18 |
| ❑ 69 Alex Rodriguez | 3.00 | 1.35 |
| ❑ 70 Ken Griffey Jr. | 4.00 | 1.80 |
| ❑ 71 Jay Buhner | .40 | .18 |
| ❑ 72 Mark McGwire | 4.00 | 1.80 |
| ❑ 73 Fernando Tatis | .40 | .18 |
| ❑ 74 Quinton McCracken | .25 | .11 |
| ❑ 75 Wade Boggs | 1.25 | .55 |
| ❑ 76 Ivan Rodriguez | 1.25 | .55 |
| ❑ 77 Juan Gonzalez | 1.00 | .45 |
| ❑ 78 Rafael Palmeiro | 1.00 | .45 |
| ❑ 79 Jose Cruz Jr. | .40 | .18 |
| ❑ 80 Carlos Delgado | 1.00 | .45 |
| ❑ 81 Troy Glaus SP | 40.00 | 18.00 |
| ❑ 82 Vladimir Nunez SP | 12.00 | 5.50 |
| ❑ 83 George Lombard SP | 12.00 | 5.50 |
| ❑ 84 Bruce Chen SP | 12.00 | 5.50 |
| ❑ 85 Ryan Minor SP | 12.00 | 5.50 |
| ❑ 86 Calvin Pickering SP | 12.00 | 5.50 |
| ❑ 87 Jin Ho Cho SP | 12.00 | 5.50 |
| ❑ 88 Russ Branyan SP | 12.00 | 5.50 |
| ❑ 89 Derrick Gibson SP | 12.00 | 5.50 |
| ❑ 90 Gabe Kapler SP AU | 30.00 | 13.50 |
| ❑ 91 Matt Anderson SP | 12.00 | 5.50 |
| ❑ 92 Robert Fick SP | 12.00 | 5.50 |
| ❑ 93 Juan Encarnacion SP | 12.00 | 5.50 |
| ❑ 94 Preston Wilson SP | 12.00 | 5.50 |
| ❑ 95 Alex Gonzalez SP | 12.00 | 5.50 |
| ❑ 96 Carlos Beltran SP | 12.00 | 5.50 |
| ❑ 97 Jeremy Giambi SP | 12.00 | 5.50 |
| ❑ 98 Dee Brown SP | 12.00 | 5.50 |
| ❑ 99 Adrian Beltre SP | 12.00 | 5.50 |
| ❑ 100 Alex Cora SP | 12.00 | 5.50 |
| ❑ 101 Angel Pena SP | 12.00 | 5.50 |
| ❑ 102 Geoff Jenkins SP | 12.00 | 5.50 |
| ❑ 103 Ronnie Belliard SP | 12.00 | 5.50 |
| ❑ 104 Corey Koskie SP | 12.00 | 5.50 |
| ❑ 105 A.J. Pierzynski SP | 12.00 | 5.50 |
| ❑ 106 Michael Barrett SP | 12.00 | 5.50 |
| ❑ 107 Fernando Seguignol SP | 12.00 | 5.50 |
| ❑ 108 Mike Kinkade SP | 12.00 | 5.50 |
| ❑ 109 Mike Lowell SP | 12.00 | 5.50 |
| ❑ 110 Ricky Ledee SP | 12.00 | 5.50 |
| ❑ 111 Eric Chavez SP | 12.00 | 5.50 |
| ❑ 112 Abraham Nunez SP | 12.00 | 5.50 |
| ❑ 113 Matt Clement SP | 12.00 | 5.50 |
| ❑ 114 Ben Davis SP | 12.00 | 5.50 |
| ❑ 115 Mike Darr SP | 12.00 | 5.50 |
| ❑ 116 Ramon E.Martinez SP RC | 12.00 | 5.50 |
| ❑ 117 Carlos Guillen SP | 12.00 | 5.50 |
| ❑ 118 Shane Monahan SP | 12.00 | 5.50 |
| ❑ 119 J.D. Drew SP AU | 60.00 | 27.00 |
| ❑ 120 Kevin Witt SP | 12.00 | 5.50 |
| ❑ 24EAST Ken Griffey Jr. Sample | 3.00 | 1.35 |

## 2000 SPx

| | MINT | NRMT |
|---|---|---|
| COMPLETE SET (196) | 1900.00 | 850.00 |
| COMP.BASIC SET (120) | 1000.00 | 450.00 |
| COMP.UPDATE SET (76) | 900.00 | 400.00 |
| COMP.BASIC w/o SP's (90) | 40.00 | 18.00 |
| COMP.UPDATE w/o SP's (30) | 15.00 | 6.75 |
| COMMON CARD (1-90) | .25 | .11 |
| COMMON CARD (91-120) | 20.00 | 9.00 |
| COMMON (121-135/182-196) | 10.00 | 4.50 |
| COMMON CARD (136-151) | 15.00 | 6.75 |
| COMMON CARD (152-181) | .40 | .18 |

| | | |
|---|---|---|
| ❑ 1 Troy Glaus | 1.25 | .55 |
| ❑ 2 Mo Vaughn | .40 | .18 |
| ❑ 3 Ramon Ortiz | .40 | .18 |
| ❑ 4 Jeff Bagwell | 1.25 | .55 |
| ❑ 5 Moises Alou | .40 | .18 |
| ❑ 6 Craig Biggio | .60 | .25 |
| ❑ 7 Jose Lima | .25 | .11 |
| ❑ 8 Jason Giambi | 1.00 | .45 |
| ❑ 9 John Jaha | .25 | .11 |
| ❑ 10 Matt Stairs | .25 | .11 |
| ❑ 11 Chipper Jones | 2.50 | 1.10 |
| ❑ 12 Greg Maddux | 2.50 | 1.10 |
| ❑ 13 Andres Galarraga | .60 | .25 |
| ❑ 14 Andruw Jones | 1.00 | .45 |
| ❑ 15 Jeromy Burnitz | .40 | .18 |
| ❑ 16 Ron Belliard | .25 | .11 |
| ❑ 17 Carlos Delgado | 1.00 | .45 |
| ❑ 18 David Wells | .40 | .18 |
| ❑ 19 Tony Batista | .40 | .18 |
| ❑ 20 Shannon Stewart | .40 | .18 |
| ❑ 21 Sammy Sosa | 2.00 | .90 |
| ❑ 22 Mark Grace | 1.00 | .45 |
| ❑ 23 Henry Rodriguez | .25 | .11 |
| ❑ 24 Mark McGwire | 4.00 | 1.80 |
| ❑ 25 J.D. Drew | 1.00 | .45 |
| ❑ 26 Luis Gonzalez | .40 | .18 |
| ❑ 27 Randy Johnson | 1.25 | .55 |
| ❑ 28 Matt Williams | .60 | .25 |
| ❑ 29 Steve Finley | .40 | .18 |
| ❑ 30 Shawn Green | 1.00 | .45 |
| ❑ 31 Kevin Brown | .60 | .25 |
| ❑ 32 Gary Sheffield | 1.00 | .45 |
| ❑ 33 Jose Canseco | 1.25 | .55 |
| ❑ 34 Greg Vaughn | .40 | .18 |
| ❑ 35 Vladimir Guerrero | 1.50 | .70 |
| ❑ 36 Michael Barrett | .25 | .11 |
| ❑ 37 Russ Ortiz | .40 | .18 |
| ❑ 38 Barry Bonds | 1.50 | .70 |
| ❑ 39 Jeff Kent | .60 | .25 |
| ❑ 40 Richie Sexson | .40 | .18 |
| ❑ 41 Manny Ramirez | 1.25 | .55 |
| ❑ 42 Jim Thome | .40 | .18 |
| ❑ 43 Roberto Alomar | 1.00 | .45 |
| ❑ 44 Edgar Martinez | .60 | .25 |
| ❑ 45 Alex Rodriguez | 3.00 | 1.35 |
| ❑ 46 John Olerud | .40 | .18 |
| ❑ 47 Alex Gonzalez | .25 | .11 |
| ❑ 48 Cliff Floyd | .40 | .18 |
| ❑ 49 Mike Piazza | 3.00 | 1.35 |
| ❑ 50 Al Leiter | .25 | .11 |
| ❑ 51 Robin Ventura | .60 | .25 |
| ❑ 52 Edgardo Alfonzo | .40 | .18 |
| ❑ 53 Albert Belle | .60 | .25 |
| ❑ 54 Cal Ripken | 4.00 | 1.80 |
| ❑ 55 B.J. Surhoff | .40 | .18 |
| ❑ 56 Tony Gwynn | 2.00 | .90 |
| ❑ 57 Trevor Hoffman | .40 | .18 |
| ❑ 58 Brian Giles | .40 | .18 |
| ❑ 59 Jason Kendall | .40 | .18 |
| ❑ 60 Kris Benson | .40 | .18 |
| ❑ 61 Bob Abreu | .40 | .18 |
| ❑ 62 Scott Rolen | 1.00 | .45 |
| ❑ 63 Curt Schilling | .40 | .18 |
| ❑ 64 Mike Lieberthal | .40 | .18 |
| ❑ 65 Sean Casey | .40 | .18 |
| ❑ 66 Dante Bichette | .40 | .18 |
| ❑ 67 Ken Griffey Jr. | 4.00 | 1.80 |
| ❑ 68 Pokey Reese | .40 | .18 |
| ❑ 69 Mike Sweeney | .40 | .18 |
| ❑ 70 Carlos Febles | .25 | .11 |
| ❑ 71 Ivan Rodriguez | 1.25 | .55 |
| ❑ 72 Ruben Mateo | .40 | .18 |
| ❑ 73 Rafael Palmeiro | 1.00 | .45 |
| ❑ 74 Larry Walker | .40 | .18 |
| ❑ 75 Todd Helton | 1.25 | .55 |
| ❑ 76 Nomar Garciaparra | 3.00 | 1.35 |
| ❑ 77 Pedro Martinez | 1.25 | .55 |
| ❑ 78 Troy O'Leary | .25 | .11 |
| ❑ 79 Jacque Jones | .40 | .18 |
| ❑ 80 Corey Koskie | .25 | .11 |
| ❑ 81 Juan Gonzalez | 1.00 | .45 |
| ❑ 82 Dean Palmer | .40 | .18 |
| ❑ 83 Juan Encarnacion | .40 | .18 |
| ❑ 84 Frank Thomas | 2.00 | .90 |
| ❑ 85 Magglio Ordonez | .40 | .18 |
| ❑ 86 Paul Konerko | .40 | .18 |
| ❑ 87 Bernie Williams | 1.00 | .45 |
| ❑ 88 Derek Jeter | 4.00 | 1.80 |
| ❑ 89 Roger Clemens | 2.00 | .90 |
| ❑ 90 Orlando Hernandez | .40 | .18 |
| ❑ 91 Vernon Wells/1500 AU | 20.00 | 9.00 |
| ❑ 92 Rick Ankiel/1500 AU | 80.00 | 36.00 |
| ❑ 93 Eric Chavez/1500 AU | 25.00 | 11.00 |
| ❑ 94 Alfonso Soriano/1500 AU | 25.00 | 11.00 |
| ❑ 95 Eric Gagne/1500 AU | 20.00 | 9.00 |
| ❑ 96 Rob Bell/1500 AU | 20.00 | 9.00 |
| ❑ 97 Matt Riley/1500 AU | 20.00 | 9.00 |
| ❑ 98 Josh Beckett/1500 AU | 40.00 | 18.00 |
| ❑ 99 Ben Petrick/1500 AU | 20.00 | 9.00 |
| ❑ 100 Rob Ramsay/1500 AU | 20.00 | 9.00 |
| ❑ 101 Scott Williamson/1500 AU | 20.00 | 9.00 |
| ❑ 102 Doug Davis/1500 AU | 20.00 | 9.00 |
| ❑ 103 Eric Munson/1500 AU* | 40.00 | 18.00 |
| ❑ 104 Pat Burrell/500 AU | 120.00 | 55.00 |
| ❑ 105 Jim Morris/1500 AU | 20.00 | 9.00 |
| ❑ 106 Gabe Kapler/500 AU | 50.00 | 22.00 |
| ❑ 107 Lance Berkman/1000 | 20.00 | 9.00 |
| ❑ 108 Erubiel Durazo/1500 AU | 20.00 | 9.00 |
| ❑ 109 Tim Hudson/1500 AU | 50.00 | 22.00 |
| ❑ 110 Ben Davis/1500 AU* | 20.00 | 9.00 |
| ❑ 111 Nick Johnson/1500 AU | 25.00 | 11.00 |
| ❑ 112 Octavio Dotel/1500 AU | 20.00 | 9.00 |
| ❑ 113 Jerry Hairston/1000 | 20.00 | 9.00 |
| ❑ 114 Ruben Mateo/1000 | 20.00 | 9.00 |
| ❑ 115 Chris Singleton/1000 | 20.00 | 9.00 |
| ❑ 116 Bruce Chen/1500 AU | 20.00 | 9.00 |
| ❑ 117 Derrick Gibson/1000 | 20.00 | 9.00 |
| ❑ 118 Carlos Beltran/500 AU | 40.00 | 18.00 |
| ❑ 119 Freddy Garcia/1500 AU | 20.00 | 9.00 |
| ❑ 120 Preston Wilson/1500 AU | 20.00 | 9.00 |
| ❑ 121 Brad Wilkerson/1600 RC | 15.00 | 6.75 |
| ❑ 122 Roy Oswalt/1600 RC | 15.00 | 6.75 |
| ❑ 123 Wascar Serrano/1600 RC | 10.00 | 4.50 |
| ❑ 124 Sean Burnett/1600 RC | 15.00 | 6.75 |
| ❑ 125 Alex Cabrera/1600 RC | 10.00 | 4.50 |
| ❑ 126 Timo Perez/1600 RC | 15.00 | 6.75 |
| ❑ 127 Juan Pierre/1600 RC | 12.00 | 5.50 |
| ❑ 128 Daylan Holt/1600 RC | 15.00 | 6.75 |
| ❑ 129 Tomokazu Ohka/1600 RC | 15.00 | 6.75 |
| ❑ 130 Kazuhiro Sasaki/1600 RC | 25.00 | 11.00 |
| ❑ 131 Kurt Ainsworth/1600 RC | 20.00 | 9.00 |
| ❑ 132 Brent Abernathy/1600 RC | 10.00 | 4.50 |
| ❑ 133 Danys Baez/1600 RC | 15.00 | 6.75 |
| ❑ 134 Brad Cresse/1600 RC | 40.00 | 18.00 |
| ❑ 135 Ryan Franklin/1600 RC | 10.00 | 4.50 |
| ❑ 136 Mike Lamb/1500 AU RC | 20.00 | 9.00 |
| ❑ 137 David Espinosa/1500 AU RC | 40.00 | 18.00 |
| ❑ 138 Matt Wheatland/1500 AU RC | 30.00 | 13.50 |
| ❑ 139 Xavier Nady/1500 AU RC | 80.00 | 36.00 |
| ❑ 140 Scott Heard/1500 AU RC | 25.00 | 11.00 |
| ❑ 141 Pasqual Coco/1500 AU RC | 15.00 | 6.75 |
| ❑ 142 Justin Miller/1500 AU RC | 15.00 | 6.75 |
| ❑ 143 Dave Krynzel/150 AU RC | 30.00 | 13.50 |
| ❑ 144 Dane Sardinha/1500 AU RC | 25.00 | 11.00 |
| ❑ 145 Ben Sheets/1500 AU RC | 100.00 | 45.00 |
| ❑ 146 Leo Estrella/1500 AU RC | 15.00 | 6.75 |
| ❑ 147 Ben Diggins/1500 AU RC | 25.00 | 11.00 |
| ❑ 148 Barry Zito/1500 AU RC | 80.00 | 36.00 |

| No. | Player | MINT | NRMT |
|---|---|---|---|
| 149 | Joe Torres/1500 AU RC | 25.00 | 11.00 |
| 150 | Mike Meyers/1500 AU RC | 15.00 | 6.75 |
| 151 | Kris Wilson/1500 AU RC | 15.00 | 6.75 |
| 152 | Darin Erstad | 1.50 | .70 |
| 153 | Richard Hidalgo | .60 | .25 |
| 154 | Eric Chavez | .60 | .25 |
| 155 | B.J. Surhoff | .60 | .25 |
| 156 | Richie Sexson | .60 | .25 |
| 157 | Raul Mondesi | .60 | .25 |
| 158 | Rondell White | .60 | .25 |
| 159 | Jim Edmonds | 1.25 | .55 |
| 160 | Curt Schilling | .60 | .25 |
| 161 | Tom Goodwin | .40 | .18 |
| 162 | Fred McGriff | 1.00 | .45 |
| 163 | Jose Vidro | .60 | .25 |
| 164 | Ellis Burks | .60 | .25 |
| 165 | David Segui | .40 | .18 |
| 166 | Aaron Sele | .60 | .25 |
| 167 | Henry Rodriguez | .40 | .18 |
| 168 | Mike Bordick | .40 | .18 |
| 169 | Mike Mussina | 1.50 | .70 |
| 170 | Ryan Klesko | .60 | .25 |
| 171 | Kevin Young | .40 | .18 |
| 172 | Travis Lee | .40 | .18 |
| 173 | Aaron Boone | .40 | .18 |
| 174 | Jermaine Dye | .60 | .25 |
| 175 | Ricky Ledee | .40 | .18 |
| 176 | Jeffrey Hammonds | .60 | .25 |
| 177 | Carl Everett | .60 | .25 |
| 178 | Matt Lawton | .60 | .25 |
| 179 | Bobby Higginson | .60 | .25 |
| 180 | Charles Johnson | .60 | .25 |
| 181 | David Justice | 1.00 | .45 |
| 182 | Joey Nation/1600 RC | 10.00 | 4.50 |
| 183 | Rico Washington/1600 RC | 10.00 | 4.50 |
| 184 | Luis Matos/1600 RC | 12.00 | 5.50 |
| 185 | Chris Wakeland/1600 RC | 10.00 | 4.50 |
| 186 | Sun Woo Kim/1600 RC | 12.00 | 5.50 |
| 187 | Keith Ginter/1600 RC | 15.00 | 6.75 |
| 188 | Geraldo Guzman/1600 RC | 10.00 | 4.50 |
| 189 | Jay Spurgeon/1600 RC | 10.00 | 4.50 |
| 190 | Jace Brewer/1600 RC | 10.00 | 4.50 |
| 191 | Juan Guzman/1600 RC | 10.00 | 4.50 |
| 192 | Ross Gload/1600 RC | 10.00 | 4.50 |
| 193 | Paxton Crawford/1600 RC | 10.00 | 4.50 |
| 194 | Ryan Kohlmeier/1600 RC | 10.00 | 4.50 |
| 195 | Julio Zuleta/1600 RC | 10.00 | 4.50 |
| 196 | Matt Ginter/1600 RC | 10.00 | 4.50 |

## 1991 Stadium Club

| | MINT | NRMT |
|---|---|---|
| COMPLETE SET (600) | 80.00 | 36.00 |
| COMPLETE SERIES 1 (300) | 50.00 | 22.00 |
| COMPLETE SERIES 2 (300) | 30.00 | 13.50 |

| No. | Player | MINT | NRMT |
|---|---|---|---|
| 1 | Dave Stewart TUX | 1.00 | .45 |
| 2 | Wally Joyner | .50 | .23 |
| 3 | Shawon Dunston | .25 | .11 |
| 4 | Darren Daulton | .50 | .23 |
| 5 | Will Clark | 1.00 | .45 |
| 6 | Sammy Sosa | 2.50 | 1.10 |
| 7 | Dan Plesac | .25 | .11 |
| 8 | Marquis Grissom | .25 | .11 |
| 9 | Erik Hanson | .25 | .11 |
| 10 | Geno Petralli | .25 | .11 |
| 11 | Jose Rijo | .25 | .11 |
| 12 | Carlos Quintana | .25 | .11 |
| 13 | Junior Ortiz | .25 | .11 |
| 14 | Bob Walk | .25 | .11 |
| 15 | Mike Macfarlane | .25 | .11 |
| 16 | Eric Yelding | .25 | .11 |
| 17 | Bryn Smith | .25 | .11 |
| 18 | Bip Roberts | .25 | .11 |
| 19 | Mike Scioscia | .25 | .11 |
| 20 | Mark Williamson | .25 | .11 |
| 21 | Don Mattingly | 2.50 | 1.10 |
| 22 | John Franco | .50 | .23 |
| 23 | Chet Lemon | .25 | .11 |
| 24 | Tom Henke | .25 | .11 |
| 25 | Jerry Browne | .25 | .11 |
| 26 | Dave Justice | 1.00 | .45 |
| 27 | Mark Langston | .25 | .11 |
| 28 | Damon Berryhill | .25 | .11 |
| 29 | Kevin Bass | .25 | .11 |
| 30 | Scott Fletcher | .25 | .11 |
| 31 | Moises Alou | 1.50 | .70 |
| 32 | Dave Valle | .25 | .11 |
| 33 | Jody Reed | .25 | .11 |
| 34 | Dave West | .25 | .11 |
| 35 | Kevin McReynolds | .25 | .11 |
| 36 | Pat Combs | .25 | .11 |
| 37 | Eric Davis | .50 | .23 |
| 38 | Bret Saberhagen | .50 | .23 |
| 39 | Stan Javier | .25 | .11 |
| 40 | Chuck Cary | .25 | .11 |
| 41 | Tony Phillips | .25 | .11 |
| 42 | Lee Smith | .50 | .23 |
| 43 | Tim Teufel | .25 | .11 |
| 44 | Lance Dickson RC | .25 | .11 |
| 45 | Greg Litton | .25 | .11 |
| 46 | Ted Higuera | .25 | .11 |
| 47 | Edgar Martinez | .50 | .23 |
| 48 | Steve Avery | .25 | .11 |
| 49 | Walt Weiss | .25 | .11 |
| 50 | David Segui | .25 | .11 |
| 51 | Andy Benes | .25 | .11 |
| 52 | Karl Rhodes | .25 | .11 |
| 53 | Neal Heaton | .25 | .11 |
| 54 | Danny Gladden | .25 | .11 |
| 55 | Luis Rivera | .25 | .11 |
| 56 | Kevin Brown | .50 | .23 |
| 57 | Frank Thomas | 2.50 | 1.10 |
| 58 | Terry Mulholland | .25 | .11 |
| 59 | Dick Schofield | .25 | .11 |
| 60 | Ron Darling | .25 | .11 |
| 61 | Sandy Alomar Jr. | .50 | .23 |
| 62 | Dave Stieb | .25 | .11 |
| 63 | Alan Trammell | .50 | .23 |
| 64 | Matt Nokes | .25 | .11 |
| 65 | Lenny Harris | .25 | .11 |
| 66 | Milt Thompson | .25 | .11 |
| 67 | Storm Davis | .25 | .11 |
| 68 | Joe Oliver | .25 | .11 |
| 69 | Andres Galarraga | .50 | .23 |
| 70 | Ozzie Guillen | .25 | .11 |
| 71 | Ken Howell | .25 | .11 |
| 72 | Garry Templeton | .25 | .11 |
| 73 | Derrick May | .25 | .11 |
| 74 | Xavier Hernandez | .25 | .11 |
| 75 | Dave Parker | .50 | .23 |
| 76 | Rick Aguilera | .50 | .23 |
| 77 | Robby Thompson | .25 | .11 |
| 78 | Pete Incaviglia | .25 | .11 |
| 79 | Bob Welch | .25 | .11 |
| 80 | Randy Milligan | .25 | .11 |
| 81 | Chuck Finley | .50 | .23 |
| 82 | Alvin Davis | .25 | .11 |
| 83 | Tim Naehring | .25 | .11 |
| 84 | Jay Bell | .50 | .23 |
| 85 | Joe Magrane | .25 | .11 |
| 86 | Howard Johnson | .25 | .11 |
| 87 | Jack McDowell | .25 | .11 |
| 88 | Kevin Seitzer | .25 | .11 |
| 89 | Bruce Ruffin | .25 | .11 |
| 90 | Fernando Valenzuela | .50 | .23 |
| 91 | Terry Kennedy | .25 | .11 |
| 92 | Barry Larkin | 1.00 | .45 |
| 93 | Larry Walker | 1.00 | .45 |
| 94 | Luis Salazar | .25 | .11 |
| 95 | Gary Sheffield | 1.00 | .45 |
| 96 | Bobby Witt | .25 | .11 |
| 97 | Lonnie Smith | .25 | .11 |
| 98 | Bryan Harvey | .25 | .11 |
| 99 | Mookie Wilson | .50 | .23 |
| 100 | Dwight Gooden | .50 | .23 |
| 101 | Lou Whitaker | .50 | .23 |
| 102 | Ron Karkovice | .25 | .11 |
| 103 | Jesse Barfield | .25 | .11 |
| 104 | Jose DeJesus | .25 | .11 |
| 105 | Benito Santiago | .25 | .11 |
| 106 | Brian Holman | .25 | .11 |
| 107 | Rafael Ramirez | .25 | .11 |
| 108 | Ellis Burks | .50 | .23 |
| 109 | Mike Bielecki | .25 | .11 |
| 110 | Kirby Puckett | 2.50 | 1.10 |
| 111 | Terry Shumpert | .25 | .11 |
| 112 | Chuck Crim | .25 | .11 |
| 113 | Todd Benzinger | .25 | .11 |
| 114 | Brian Barnes RC | .25 | .11 |
| 115 | Carlos Baerga | .25 | .11 |
| 116 | Kal Daniels | .25 | .11 |
| 117 | Dave Johnson | .25 | .11 |
| 118 | Andy Van Slyke | .50 | .23 |
| 119 | John Burkett | .25 | .11 |
| 120 | Rickey Henderson | 1.25 | .55 |
| 121 | Tim Jones | .25 | .11 |
| 122 | Daryl Irvine | .25 | .11 |
| 123 | Ruben Sierra | .25 | .11 |
| 124 | Jim Abbott | .50 | .23 |
| 125 | Daryl Boston | .25 | .11 |
| 126 | Greg Maddux | 2.50 | 1.10 |
| 127 | Von Hayes | .25 | .11 |
| 128 | Mike Fitzgerald | .25 | .11 |
| 129 | Wayne Edwards | .25 | .11 |
| 130 | Greg Briley | .25 | .11 |
| 131 | Rob Dibble | .25 | .11 |
| 132 | Gene Larkin | .25 | .11 |
| 133 | David Wells | .50 | .23 |
| 134 | Steve Balboni | .25 | .11 |
| 135 | Greg Vaughn | 1.00 | .45 |
| 136 | Mark Davis | .25 | .11 |
| 137 | Dave Rhode | .25 | .11 |
| 138 | Eric Show | .25 | .11 |
| 139 | Bobby Bonilla | .50 | .23 |
| 140 | Dana Kiecker | .25 | .11 |
| 141 | Gary Pettis | .25 | .11 |
| 142 | Dennis Boyd | .25 | .11 |
| 143 | Mike Benjamin | .25 | .11 |
| 144 | Luis Polonia | .25 | .11 |
| 145 | Doug Jones | .25 | .11 |
| 146 | Al Newman | .25 | .11 |
| 147 | Alex Fernandez | .50 | .23 |
| 148 | Bill Doran | .25 | .11 |
| 149 | Kevin Elster | .25 | .11 |
| 150 | Len Dykstra | .50 | .23 |
| 151 | Mike Gallego | .25 | .11 |
| 152 | Tim Belcher | .25 | .11 |
| 153 | Jay Buhner | .50 | .23 |
| 154 | Ozzie Smith UER (Rookie card is 1979, but card back says '78) | 1.25 | .55 |
| 155 | Jose Canseco | 1.25 | .55 |
| 156 | Gregg Olson | .25 | .11 |
| 157 | Charlie O'Brien | .25 | .11 |
| 158 | Frank Tanana | .25 | .11 |
| 159 | George Brett | 2.00 | .90 |
| 160 | Jeff Huson | .25 | .11 |
| 161 | Kevin Tapani | .25 | .11 |
| 162 | Jerome Walton | .25 | .11 |
| 163 | Charlie Hayes | .25 | .11 |
| 164 | Chris Bosio | .25 | .11 |
| 165 | Chris Sabo | .25 | .11 |
| 166 | Lance Parrish | .25 | .11 |
| 167 | Don Robinson | .25 | .11 |
| 168 | Manny Lee | .25 | .11 |
| 169 | Dennis Rasmussen | .25 | .11 |
| 170 | Wade Boggs | 1.25 | .55 |
| 171 | Bob Geren | .25 | .11 |
| 172 | Mackey Sasser | .25 | .11 |
| 173 | Julio Franco | .25 | .11 |
| 174 | Otis Nixon | .25 | .11 |
| 175 | Bert Blyleven | .50 | .23 |
| 176 | Craig Biggio | .50 | .23 |
| 177 | Eddie Murray | 1.00 | .45 |
| 178 | Randy Tomlin RC | .25 | .11 |
| 179 | Tino Martinez | .50 | .23 |
| 180 | Carlton Fisk | 1.00 | .45 |
| 181 | Dwight Smith | .25 | .11 |
| 182 | Scott Garrelts | .25 | .11 |

| |  |  | | |
|---|---|---|---|---|
| ❑ | 183 | Jim Gantner | .25 | .11 |
| ❑ | 184 | Dickie Thon | .25 | .11 |
| ❑ | 185 | John Farrell | .25 | .11 |
| ❑ | 186 | Cecil Fielder | .50 | .23 |
| ❑ | 187 | Glenn Braggs | .25 | .11 |
| ❑ | 188 | Allan Anderson | .25 | .11 |
| ❑ | 189 | Kurt Stillwell | .25 | .11 |
| ❑ | 190 | Jose Oquendo | .25 | .11 |
| ❑ | 191 | Joe Orsulak | .25 | .11 |
| ❑ | 192 | Ricky Jordan | .25 | .11 |
| ❑ | 193 | Kelly Downs | .25 | .11 |
| ❑ | 194 | Delino DeShields | .50 | .23 |
| ❑ | 195 | Omar Vizquel | 1.00 | .45 |
| ❑ | 196 | Mark Carreon | .25 | .11 |
| ❑ | 197 | Mike Harkey | .25 | .11 |
| ❑ | 198 | Jack Howell | .25 | .11 |
| ❑ | 199 | Lance Johnson | .25 | .11 |
| ❑ | 200 | Nolan Ryan TUX | 5.00 | 2.20 |
| ❑ | 201 | John Marzano | .25 | .11 |
| ❑ | 202 | Doug Drabek | .25 | .11 |
| ❑ | 203 | Mark Lemke | .25 | .11 |
| ❑ | 204 | Steve Sax | .25 | .11 |
| ❑ | 205 | Greg Harris | .25 | .11 |
| ❑ | 206 | B.J. Surhoff | .50 | .23 |
| ❑ | 207 | Todd Burns | .25 | .11 |
| ❑ | 208 | Jose Gonzalez | .25 | .11 |
| ❑ | 209 | Mike Scott | .25 | .11 |
| ❑ | 210 | Dave Magadan | .25 | .11 |
| ❑ | 211 | Dante Bichette | 1.00 | .45 |
| ❑ | 212 | Trevor Wilson | .25 | .11 |
| ❑ | 213 | Hector Villanueva | .25 | .11 |
| ❑ | 214 | Dan Pasqua | .25 | .11 |
| ❑ | 215 | Greg Colbrunn RC | .25 | .11 |
| ❑ | 216 | Mike Jeffcoat | .25 | .11 |
| ❑ | 217 | Harold Reynolds | .25 | .11 |
| ❑ | 218 | Paul O'Neill | .50 | .23 |
| ❑ | 219 | Mark Guthrie | .25 | .11 |
| ❑ | 220 | Barry Bonds | 1.50 | .70 |
| ❑ | 221 | Jimmy Key | .50 | .23 |
| ❑ | 222 | Billy Ripken | .25 | .11 |
| ❑ | 223 | Tom Pagnozzi | .25 | .11 |
| ❑ | 224 | Bo Jackson | .50 | .23 |
| ❑ | 225 | Sid Fernandez | .25 | .11 |
| ❑ | 226 | Mike Marshall | .25 | .11 |
| ❑ | 227 | John Kruk | .50 | .23 |
| ❑ | 228 | Mike Fetters | .25 | .11 |
| ❑ | 229 | Eric Anthony | .25 | .11 |
| ❑ | 230 | Ryne Sandberg | 1.25 | .55 |
| ❑ | 231 | Carney Lansford | .50 | .23 |
| ❑ | 232 | Melido Perez | .25 | .11 |
| ❑ | 233 | Jose Lind | .25 | .11 |
| ❑ | 234 | Darryl Hamilton | .25 | .11 |
| ❑ | 235 | Tom Browning | .25 | .11 |
| ❑ | 236 | Spike Owen | .25 | .11 |
| ❑ | 237 | Juan Gonzalez | 2.50 | 1.10 |
| ❑ | 238 | Felix Fermin | .25 | .11 |
| ❑ | 239 | Keith Miller | .25 | .11 |
| ❑ | 240 | Mark Gubicza | .25 | .11 |
| ❑ | 241 | Kent Anderson | .25 | .11 |
| ❑ | 242 | Alvaro Espinoza | .25 | .11 |
| ❑ | 243 | Dale Murphy | 1.00 | .45 |
| ❑ | 244 | Orel Hershiser | .50 | .23 |
| ❑ | 245 | Paul Molitor | 1.00 | .45 |
| ❑ | 246 | Eddie Whitson | .25 | .11 |
| ❑ | 247 | Joe Girardi | .50 | .23 |
| ❑ | 248 | Kent Hrbek | .50 | .23 |
| ❑ | 249 | Bill Sampen | .25 | .11 |
| ❑ | 250 | Kevin Mitchell | .25 | .11 |
| ❑ | 251 | Mariano Duncan | .25 | .11 |
| ❑ | 252 | Scott Bradley | .25 | .11 |
| ❑ | 253 | Mike Greenwell | .25 | .11 |
| ❑ | 254 | Tom Gordon | .25 | .11 |
| ❑ | 255 | Todd Zeile | .50 | .23 |
| ❑ | 256 | Bobby Thigpen | .25 | .11 |
| ❑ | 257 | Gregg Jefferies | .25 | .11 |
| ❑ | 258 | Kenny Rogers | .25 | .11 |
| ❑ | 259 | Shane Mack | .25 | .11 |
| ❑ | 260 | Zane Smith | .25 | .11 |
| ❑ | 261 | Mitch Williams | .25 | .11 |
| ❑ | 262 | Jim Deshaies | .25 | .11 |
| ❑ | 263 | Dave Winfield | 1.00 | .45 |
| ❑ | 264 | Ben McDonald | .25 | .11 |
| ❑ | 265 | Randy Ready | .25 | .11 |
| ❑ | 266 | Pat Borders | .25 | .11 |
| ❑ | 267 | Jose Uribe | .25 | .11 |
| ❑ | 268 | Derek Lilliquist | .25 | .11 |
| ❑ | 269 | Greg Brock | .25 | .11 |
| ❑ | 270 | Ken Griffey Jr. | 5.00 | 2.20 |
| ❑ | 271 | Jeff Gray | .25 | .11 |
| ❑ | 272 | Danny Tartabull | .25 | .11 |
| ❑ | 273 | Dennis Martinez | .50 | .23 |
| ❑ | 274 | Robin Ventura | 1.00 | .45 |
| ❑ | 275 | Randy Myers | .50 | .23 |
| ❑ | 276 | Jack Daugherty | .25 | .11 |
| ❑ | 277 | Greg Gagne | .25 | .11 |
| ❑ | 278 | Jay Howell | .25 | .11 |
| ❑ | 279 | Mike LaValliere | .25 | .11 |
| ❑ | 280 | Rex Hudler | .25 | .11 |
| ❑ | 281 | Mike Simms | .25 | .11 |
| ❑ | 282 | Kevin Maas | .25 | .11 |
| ❑ | 283 | Jeff Ballard | .25 | .11 |
| ❑ | 284 | Dave Henderson | .25 | .11 |
| ❑ | 285 | Pete O'Brien | .25 | .11 |
| ❑ | 286 | Brook Jacoby | .25 | .11 |
| ❑ | 287 | Mike Henneman | .25 | .11 |
| ❑ | 288 | Greg Olson | .25 | .11 |
| ❑ | 289 | Greg Myers | .25 | .11 |
| ❑ | 290 | Mark Grace | 1.00 | .45 |
| ❑ | 291 | Shawn Abner | .25 | .11 |
| ❑ | 292 | Frank Viola | .25 | .11 |
| ❑ | 293 | Lee Stevens | .50 | .23 |
| ❑ | 294 | Jason Grimsley | .25 | .11 |
| ❑ | 295 | Matt Williams | .50 | .23 |
| ❑ | 296 | Ron Robinson | .25 | .11 |
| ❑ | 297 | Tom Brunansky | .25 | .11 |
| ❑ | 298 | Checklist 1-100 | .25 | .11 |
| ❑ | 299 | Checklist 101-200 | .25 | .11 |
| ❑ | 300 | Checklist 201-300 | .25 | .11 |
| ❑ | 301 | Darryl Strawberry | .50 | .23 |
| ❑ | 302 | Bud Black | .25 | .11 |
| ❑ | 303 | Harold Baines | .50 | .23 |
| ❑ | 304 | Roberto Alomar | 1.00 | .45 |
| ❑ | 305 | Norm Charlton | .25 | .11 |
| ❑ | 306 | Gary Thurman | .25 | .11 |
| ❑ | 307 | Mike Felder | .25 | .11 |
| ❑ | 308 | Tony Gwynn | 2.00 | .90 |
| ❑ | 309 | Roger Clemens | 2.00 | .90 |
| ❑ | 310 | Andre Dawson | .50 | .23 |
| ❑ | 311 | Scott Radinsky | .25 | .11 |
| ❑ | 312 | Bob Melvin | .25 | .11 |
| ❑ | 313 | Kirk McCaskill | .25 | .11 |
| ❑ | 314 | Pedro Guerrero | .25 | .11 |
| ❑ | 315 | Walt Terrell | .25 | .11 |
| ❑ | 316 | Sam Horn | .25 | .11 |
| ❑ | 317 | Wes Chamberlain RC UER (Card listed as 1989; Debut card, should be 1990) | .25 | .11 |
| ❑ | 318 | Pedro Munoz RC | .25 | .11 |
| ❑ | 319 | Roberto Kelly | .25 | .11 |
| ❑ | 320 | Mark Portugal | .25 | .11 |
| ❑ | 321 | Tim McIntosh | .25 | .11 |
| ❑ | 322 | Jesse Orosco | .25 | .11 |
| ❑ | 323 | Gary Green | .25 | .11 |
| ❑ | 324 | Greg Harris | .25 | .11 |
| ❑ | 325 | Hubie Brooks | .25 | .11 |
| ❑ | 326 | Chris Nabholz | .25 | .11 |
| ❑ | 327 | Terry Pendleton | .50 | .23 |
| ❑ | 328 | Eric King | .25 | .11 |
| ❑ | 329 | Chili Davis | .50 | .23 |
| ❑ | 330 | Anthony Telford | .25 | .11 |
| ❑ | 331 | Kelly Gruber | .25 | .11 |
| ❑ | 332 | Dennis Eckersley | .50 | .23 |
| ❑ | 333 | Mel Hall | .25 | .11 |
| ❑ | 334 | Bob Kipper | .25 | .11 |
| ❑ | 335 | Willie McGee | .50 | .23 |
| ❑ | 336 | Steve Olin | .25 | .11 |
| ❑ | 337 | Steve Buechele | .25 | .11 |
| ❑ | 338 | Scott Leius | .25 | .11 |
| ❑ | 339 | Hal Morris | .25 | .11 |
| ❑ | 340 | Jose Offerman | .25 | .11 |
| ❑ | 341 | Kent Mercker | .25 | .11 |
| ❑ | 342 | Ken Griffey Sr. | .50 | .23 |
| ❑ | 343 | Pete Harnisch | .25 | .11 |
| ❑ | 344 | Kirk Gibson | .50 | .23 |
| ❑ | 345 | Dave Smith | .25 | .11 |
| ❑ | 346 | Dave Martinez | .25 | .11 |
| ❑ | 347 | Atlee Hammaker | .25 | .11 |
| ❑ | 348 | Brian Downing | .25 | .11 |
| ❑ | 349 | Todd Hundley | 1.50 | .70 |
| ❑ | 350 | Candy Maldonado | .25 | .11 |
| ❑ | 351 | Dwight Evans | .50 | .23 |
| ❑ | 352 | Steve Searcy | .25 | .11 |
| ❑ | 353 | Gary Gaetti | .50 | .23 |
| ❑ | 354 | Jeff Reardon | .50 | .23 |
| ❑ | 355 | Travis Fryman | 1.00 | .45 |
| ❑ | 356 | Dave Righetti | .25 | .11 |
| ❑ | 357 | Fred McGriff | 1.00 | .45 |
| ❑ | 358 | Don Slaught | .25 | .11 |
| ❑ | 359 | Gene Nelson | .25 | .11 |
| ❑ | 360 | Billy Spiers | .25 | .11 |
| ❑ | 361 | Lee Guetterman | .25 | .11 |
| ❑ | 362 | Darren Lewis | .50 | .23 |
| ❑ | 363 | Duane Ward | .25 | .11 |
| ❑ | 364 | Lloyd Moseby | .25 | .11 |
| ❑ | 365 | John Smoltz | .50 | .23 |
| ❑ | 366 | Felix Jose | .25 | .11 |
| ❑ | 367 | David Cone | .50 | .23 |
| ❑ | 368 | Wally Backman | .25 | .11 |
| ❑ | 369 | Jeff Montgomery | .50 | .23 |
| ❑ | 370 | Rich Garces RC | .25 | .11 |
| ❑ | 371 | Billy Hatcher | .25 | .11 |
| ❑ | 372 | Bill Swift | .25 | .11 |
| ❑ | 373 | Jim Eisenreich | .25 | .11 |
| ❑ | 374 | Rob Ducey | .25 | .11 |
| ❑ | 375 | Tim Crews | .25 | .11 |
| ❑ | 376 | Steve Finley | .50 | .23 |
| ❑ | 377 | Jeff Blauser | .25 | .11 |
| ❑ | 378 | Willie Wilson | .25 | .11 |
| ❑ | 379 | Gerald Perry | .25 | .11 |
| ❑ | 380 | Jose Mesa | .25 | .11 |
| ❑ | 381 | Pat Kelly RC | .25 | .11 |
| ❑ | 382 | Matt Merullo | .25 | .11 |
| ❑ | 383 | Ivan Calderon | .25 | .11 |
| ❑ | 384 | Scott Chiamparino | .25 | .11 |
| ❑ | 385 | Lloyd McClendon | .25 | .11 |
| ❑ | 386 | Dave Bergman | .25 | .11 |
| ❑ | 387 | Ed Sprague | .25 | .11 |
| ❑ | 388 | Jeff Bagwell RC | 8.00 | 3.60 |
| ❑ | 389 | Brett Butler | .50 | .23 |
| ❑ | 390 | Larry Andersen | .25 | .11 |
| ❑ | 391 | Glenn Davis | .25 | .11 |
| ❑ | 392 | Alex Cole UER (Front photo actually Otis Nixon) | .25 | .11 |
| ❑ | 393 | Mike Heath | .25 | .11 |
| ❑ | 394 | Danny Darwin | .25 | .11 |
| ❑ | 395 | Steve Lake | .25 | .11 |
| ❑ | 396 | Tim Layana | .25 | .11 |
| ❑ | 397 | Terry Leach | .25 | .11 |
| ❑ | 398 | Bill Wegman | .25 | .11 |
| ❑ | 399 | Mark McGwire | 4.00 | 1.80 |
| ❑ | 400 | Mike Boddicker | .25 | .11 |
| ❑ | 401 | Steve Howe | .25 | .11 |
| ❑ | 402 | Bernard Gilkey | .50 | .23 |
| ❑ | 403 | Thomas Howard | .25 | .11 |
| ❑ | 404 | Rafael Belliard | .25 | .11 |
| ❑ | 405 | Tom Candiotti | .25 | .11 |
| ❑ | 406 | Rene Gonzales | .25 | .11 |
| ❑ | 407 | Chuck McElroy | .25 | .11 |
| ❑ | 408 | Paul Sorrento | .50 | .23 |
| ❑ | 409 | Randy Johnson | 1.50 | .70 |
| ❑ | 410 | Brady Anderson | 1.00 | .45 |
| ❑ | 411 | Dennis Cook | .25 | .11 |
| ❑ | 412 | Mickey Tettleton | .25 | .11 |
| ❑ | 413 | Mike Stanton | .25 | .11 |
| ❑ | 414 | Ken Oberkfell | .25 | .11 |
| ❑ | 415 | Rick Honeycutt | .25 | .11 |
| ❑ | 416 | Nelson Santovenia | .25 | .11 |
| ❑ | 417 | Bob Tewksbury | .25 | .11 |
| ❑ | 418 | Brent Mayne | .25 | .11 |
| ❑ | 419 | Steve Farr | .25 | .11 |
| ❑ | 420 | Phil Stephenson | .25 | .11 |
| ❑ | 421 | Jeff Russell | .25 | .11 |
| ❑ | 422 | Chris James | .25 | .11 |
| ❑ | 423 | Tim Leary | .25 | .11 |
| ❑ | 424 | Gary Carter | .50 | .23 |
| ❑ | 425 | Glenallen Hill | .25 | .11 |
| ❑ | 426 | Matt Young UER (Card mentions 83T/Tr as RC, but 84T shown) | .25 | .11 |
| ❑ | 427 | Sid Bream | .25 | .11 |
| ❑ | 428 | Greg Swindell | .25 | .11 |
| ❑ | 429 | Scott Aldred | .25 | .11 |
| ❑ | 430 | Cal Ripken | 4.00 | 1.80 |
| ❑ | 431 | Bill Landrum | .25 | .11 |
| ❑ | 432 | Earnest Riles | .25 | .11 |
| ❑ | 433 | Danny Jackson | .25 | .11 |
| ❑ | 434 | Casey Candaele | .25 | .11 |

| | | | |
|---|---|---|---|
| ❑ 435 | Ken Hill | .25 | .11 |
| ❑ 436 | Jaime Navarro | .25 | .11 |
| ❑ 437 | Lance Blankenship | .25 | .11 |
| ❑ 438 | Randy Velarde | .25 | .11 |
| ❑ 439 | Frank DiPino | .25 | .11 |
| ❑ 440 | Carl Nichols | .25 | .11 |
| ❑ 441 | Jeff M. Robinson | .25 | .11 |
| ❑ 442 | Deion Sanders | .50 | .23 |
| ❑ 443 | Vicente Palacios | .25 | .11 |
| ❑ 444 | Devon White | .25 | .11 |
| ❑ 445 | John Cerutti | .25 | .11 |
| ❑ 446 | Tracy Jones | .25 | .11 |
| ❑ 447 | Jack Morris | .50 | .23 |
| ❑ 448 | Mitch Webster | .25 | .11 |
| ❑ 449 | Bob Ojeda | .25 | .11 |
| ❑ 450 | Oscar Azocar | .25 | .11 |
| ❑ 451 | Luis Aquino | .25 | .11 |
| ❑ 452 | Mark Whiten | .25 | .11 |
| ❑ 453 | Stan Belinda | .25 | .11 |
| ❑ 454 | Ron Gant | .50 | .23 |
| ❑ 455 | Jose DeLeon | .25 | .11 |
| ❑ 456 | Mark Salas UER (Back has 85T photo, but calls it 86T) | .25 | .11 |
| ❑ 457 | Junior Felix | .25 | .11 |
| ❑ 458 | Wally Whitehurst | .25 | .11 |
| ❑ 459 | Phil Plantier RC | .25 | .11 |
| ❑ 460 | Juan Berenguer | .25 | .11 |
| ❑ 461 | Franklin Stubbs | .25 | .11 |
| ❑ 462 | Joe Boever | .25 | .11 |
| ❑ 463 | Tim Wallach | .25 | .11 |
| ❑ 464 | Mike Moore | .25 | .11 |
| ❑ 465 | Albert Belle | .50 | .23 |
| ❑ 466 | Mike Witt | .25 | .11 |
| ❑ 467 | Craig Worthington | .25 | .11 |
| ❑ 468 | Jerald Clark | .25 | .11 |
| ❑ 469 | Scott Terry | .25 | .11 |
| ❑ 470 | Milt Cuyler | .25 | .11 |
| ❑ 471 | John Smiley | .25 | .11 |
| ❑ 472 | Charles Nagy | .25 | .11 |
| ❑ 473 | Alan Mills | .25 | .11 |
| ❑ 474 | John Russell | .25 | .11 |
| ❑ 475 | Bruce Hurst | .25 | .11 |
| ❑ 476 | Andujar Cedeno | .25 | .11 |
| ❑ 477 | Dave Eiland | .25 | .11 |
| ❑ 478 | Brian McRae RC | .50 | .23 |
| ❑ 479 | Mike LaCoss | .25 | .11 |
| ❑ 480 | Chris Gwynn | .25 | .11 |
| ❑ 481 | Jamie Moyer | .25 | .11 |
| ❑ 482 | John Olerud | .50 | .23 |
| ❑ 483 | Efrain Valdez | .25 | .11 |
| ❑ 484 | Sil Campusano | .25 | .11 |
| ❑ 485 | Pascual Perez | .25 | .11 |
| ❑ 486 | Gary Redus | .25 | .11 |
| ❑ 487 | Andy Hawkins | .25 | .11 |
| ❑ 488 | Cory Snyder | .25 | .11 |
| ❑ 489 | Chris Hoiles | .25 | .11 |
| ❑ 490 | Ron Hassey | .25 | .11 |
| ❑ 491 | Gary Wayne | .25 | .11 |
| ❑ 492 | Mark Lewis | .25 | .11 |
| ❑ 493 | Scott Coolbaugh | .25 | .11 |
| ❑ 494 | Gerald Young | .25 | .11 |
| ❑ 495 | Juan Samuel | .25 | .11 |
| ❑ 496 | Willie Fraser | .25 | .11 |
| ❑ 497 | Jeff Treadway | .25 | .11 |
| ❑ 498 | Vince Coleman | .25 | .11 |
| ❑ 499 | Cris Carpenter | .25 | .11 |
| ❑ 500 | Jack Clark | .50 | .23 |
| ❑ 501 | Kevin Appier | .50 | .23 |
| ❑ 502 | Rafael Palmeiro | 1.00 | .45 |
| ❑ 503 | Hensley Meulens | .25 | .11 |
| ❑ 504 | George Bell | .25 | .11 |
| ❑ 505 | Tony Pena | .25 | .11 |
| ❑ 506 | Roger McDowell | .25 | .11 |
| ❑ 507 | Luis Sojo | .25 | .11 |
| ❑ 508 | Mike Schooler | .25 | .11 |
| ❑ 509 | Robin Yount | 1.00 | .45 |
| ❑ 510 | Jack Armstrong | .25 | .11 |
| ❑ 511 | Rick Cerone | .25 | .11 |
| ❑ 512 | Curt Wilkerson | .25 | .11 |
| ❑ 513 | Joe Carter | .50 | .23 |
| ❑ 514 | Tim Burke | .25 | .11 |
| ❑ 515 | Tony Fernandez | .25 | .11 |
| ❑ 516 | Ramon Martinez | .25 | .11 |
| ❑ 517 | Tim Hulett | .25 | .11 |
| ❑ 518 | Terry Steinbach | .50 | .23 |
| ❑ 519 | Pete Smith | .25 | .11 |
| ❑ 520 | Ken Caminiti | .50 | .23 |
| ❑ 521 | Shawn Boskie | .25 | .11 |
| ❑ 522 | Mike Pagliarulo | .25 | .11 |
| ❑ 523 | Tim Raines | .50 | .23 |
| ❑ 524 | Alfredo Griffin | .25 | .11 |
| ❑ 525 | Henry Cotto | .25 | .11 |
| ❑ 526 | Mike Stanley | .25 | .11 |
| ❑ 527 | Charlie Leibrandt | .25 | .11 |
| ❑ 528 | Jeff King | .25 | .11 |
| ❑ 529 | Eric Plunk | .25 | .11 |
| ❑ 530 | Tom Lampkin | .25 | .11 |
| ❑ 531 | Steve Bedrosian | .25 | .11 |
| ❑ 532 | Tom Herr | .25 | .11 |
| ❑ 533 | Craig Lefferts | .25 | .11 |
| ❑ 534 | Jeff Reed | .25 | .11 |
| ❑ 535 | Mickey Morandini | .25 | .11 |
| ❑ 536 | Greg Cadaret | .25 | .11 |
| ❑ 537 | Ray Lankford | 2.00 | .90 |
| ❑ 538 | John Candelaria | .25 | .11 |
| ❑ 539 | Rob Deer | .25 | .11 |
| ❑ 540 | Brad Arnsberg | .25 | .11 |
| ❑ 541 | Mike Sharperson | .25 | .11 |
| ❑ 542 | Jeff D. Robinson | .25 | .11 |
| ❑ 543 | Mo Vaughn | 2.00 | .90 |
| ❑ 544 | Jeff Parrett | .25 | .11 |
| ❑ 545 | Willie Randolph | .50 | .23 |
| ❑ 546 | Herm Winningham | .25 | .11 |
| ❑ 547 | Jeff Innis | .25 | .11 |
| ❑ 548 | Chuck Knoblauch | 1.25 | .55 |
| ❑ 549 | Tommy Greene UER (Born in North Carolina, not South Carolina) | .25 | .11 |
| ❑ 550 | Jeff Hamilton | .25 | .11 |
| ❑ 551 | Barry Jones | .25 | .11 |
| ❑ 552 | Ken Dayley | .25 | .11 |
| ❑ 553 | Rick Dempsey | .25 | .11 |
| ❑ 554 | Greg Smith | .25 | .11 |
| ❑ 555 | Mike Devereaux | .25 | .11 |
| ❑ 556 | Keith Comstock | .25 | .11 |
| ❑ 557 | Paul Faries | .25 | .11 |
| ❑ 558 | Tom Glavine | 1.00 | .45 |
| ❑ 559 | Craig Grebeck | .25 | .11 |
| ❑ 560 | Scott Erickson | .25 | .11 |
| ❑ 561 | Joel Skinner | .25 | .11 |
| ❑ 562 | Mike Morgan | .25 | .11 |
| ❑ 563 | Dave Gallagher | .25 | .11 |
| ❑ 564 | Todd Stottlemyre | .50 | .23 |
| ❑ 565 | Rich Rodriguez | .25 | .11 |
| ❑ 566 | Craig Wilson | .25 | .11 |
| ❑ 567 | Jeff Brantley | .25 | .11 |
| ❑ 568 | Scott Kamieniecki RC | .25 | .11 |
| ❑ 569 | Steve Decker RC | .25 | .11 |
| ❑ 570 | Juan Agosto | .25 | .11 |
| ❑ 571 | Tommy Gregg | .25 | .11 |
| ❑ 572 | Kevin Wickander | .25 | .11 |
| ❑ 573 | Jamie Quirk UER (Rookie card is 1976, but card back is 1990) | .25 | .11 |
| ❑ 574 | Jerry Don Gleaton | .25 | .11 |
| ❑ 575 | Chris Hammond | .25 | .11 |
| ❑ 576 | Luis Gonzalez RC | 1.50 | .70 |
| ❑ 577 | Russ Swan | .25 | .11 |
| ❑ 578 | Jeff Conine RC | 1.00 | .45 |
| ❑ 579 | Charlie Hough | .50 | .23 |
| ❑ 580 | Jeff Kunkel | .25 | .11 |
| ❑ 581 | Darrel Akerfelds | .25 | .11 |
| ❑ 582 | Jeff Manto | .25 | .11 |
| ❑ 583 | Alejandro Pena | .25 | .11 |
| ❑ 584 | Mark Davidson | .25 | .11 |
| ❑ 585 | Bob MacDonald RC | .25 | .11 |
| ❑ 586 | Paul Assenmacher | .25 | .11 |
| ❑ 587 | Dan Wilson RC | 1.00 | .45 |
| ❑ 588 | Tom Bolton | .25 | .11 |
| ❑ 589 | Brian Harper | .25 | .11 |
| ❑ 590 | John Habyan | .25 | .11 |
| ❑ 591 | John Orton | .25 | .11 |
| ❑ 592 | Mark Gardner | .25 | .11 |
| ❑ 593 | Turner Ward RC | .25 | .11 |
| ❑ 594 | Bob Patterson | .25 | .11 |
| ❑ 595 | Ed Nunez | .25 | .11 |
| ❑ 596 | Gary Scott RC UER (Major League Batting Record should be Minor League) | .25 | .11 |
| ❑ 597 | Scott Bankhead | .25 | .11 |
| ❑ 598 | Checklist 301-400 | .25 | .11 |
| ❑ 599 | Checklist 401-500 | .25 | .11 |
| ❑ 600 | Checklist 501-600 | .25 | .11 |

## 1992 Stadium Club Dome

| | | MINT | NRMT |
|---|---|---|---|
| COMP.FACT.SET (200) | | 25.00 | 11.00 |
| ❑ 1 | Terry Adams RC | .25 | .11 |
| ❑ 2 | Tommy Adams RC | .10 | .05 |
| ❑ 3 | Rick Aguilera | .20 | .09 |
| ❑ 4 | Ron Allen RC | .10 | .05 |
| ❑ 5 | Roberto Alomar | .40 | .18 |
| ❑ 6 | Sandy Alomar Jr. | .20 | .09 |
| ❑ 7 | Greg Anthony RC | .10 | .05 |
| ❑ 8 | James Austin RC | .10 | .05 |
| ❑ 9 | Steve Avery | .10 | .05 |
| ❑ 10 | Harold Baines | .20 | .09 |
| ❑ 11 | Brian Barber RC | .10 | .05 |
| ❑ 12 | Jon Barnes RC | .10 | .05 |
| ❑ 13 | George Bell | .10 | .05 |
| ❑ 14 | Doug Bennett RC | .10 | .05 |
| ❑ 15 | Sean Bergman RC | .10 | .05 |
| ❑ 16 | Craig Biggio | .25 | .11 |
| ❑ 17 | Bill Bliss RC | .10 | .05 |
| ❑ 18 | Wade Boggs | .50 | .23 |
| ❑ 19 | Bobby Bonilla | .20 | .09 |
| ❑ 20 | Russell Brock RC | .10 | .05 |
| ❑ 21 | Tarrik Brock RC | .10 | .05 |
| ❑ 22 | Tom Browning | .10 | .05 |
| ❑ 23 | Brett Butler | .20 | .09 |
| ❑ 24 | Ivan Calderon | .10 | .05 |
| ❑ 25 | Joe Carter | .20 | .09 |
| ❑ 26 | Joe Caruso RC | .10 | .05 |
| ❑ 27 | Dan Cholowsky RC | .10 | .05 |
| ❑ 28 | Will Clark | .40 | .18 |
| ❑ 29 | Roger Clemens | .75 | .35 |
| ❑ 30 | Shawn Curran RC | .10 | .05 |
| ❑ 31 | Chris Curtis RC | .10 | .05 |
| ❑ 32 | Chili Davis | .20 | .09 |
| ❑ 33 | Andre Dawson | .25 | .11 |
| ❑ 34 | Joe DeBerry RC | .10 | .05 |
| ❑ 35 | John Dettmer | .10 | .05 |
| ❑ 36 | Rob Dibble | .10 | .05 |
| ❑ 37 | John Donati RC | .10 | .05 |
| ❑ 38 | Dave Doorneweerd RC | .10 | .05 |
| ❑ 39 | Darren Dreifort | .20 | .09 |
| ❑ 40 | Mike Durant RC | .10 | .05 |
| ❑ 41 | Chris Durkin RC | .10 | .05 |
| ❑ 42 | Dennis Eckersley | .20 | .09 |
| ❑ 43 | Brian Edmondson RC | .10 | .05 |
| ❑ 44 | Vaughn Eshelman RC | .10 | .05 |
| ❑ 45 | Shawn Estes RC | .75 | .35 |
| ❑ 46 | Jorge Fabregas RC | .10 | .05 |
| ❑ 47 | Jon Farrell RC | .10 | .05 |
| ❑ 48 | Cecil Fielder | .20 | .09 |
| ❑ 49 | Carlton Fisk | .40 | .18 |
| ❑ 50 | Tim Flannelly RC | .10 | .05 |
| ❑ 51 | Cliff Floyd RC | 1.50 | .70 |
| ❑ 52 | Julio Franco | .10 | .05 |
| ❑ 53 | Greg Gagne | .10 | .05 |
| ❑ 54 | Chris Gambs RC | .10 | .05 |
| ❑ 55 | Ron Gant | .20 | .09 |
| ❑ 56 | Brent Gates RC | .10 | .05 |
| ❑ 57 | Dwayne Gerald RC | .10 | .05 |
| ❑ 58 | Jason Giambi | 3.00 | 1.35 |

❑ 59 Benji Gil RC .10 .05
❑ 60 Mark Gipner RC .10 .05
❑ 61 Danny Gladden .10 .05
❑ 62 Tom Glavine .25 .11
❑ 63 Jimmy Gonzalez RC .10 .05
❑ 64 Jeff Granger .10 .05
❑ 65 Dan Grapenthien RC .10 .05
❑ 66 Dennis Gray RC .10 .05
❑ 67 Shawn Green RC 8.00 3.60
❑ 68 Tyler Green RC .10 .05
❑ 69 Todd Greene .10 .05
❑ 70 Ken Griffey Jr. 1.50 .70
❑ 71 Kelly Gruber .10 .05
❑ 72 Ozzie Guillen .10 .05
❑ 73 Tony Gwynn .75 .35
❑ 74 Shane Halter RC .10 .05
❑ 75 Jeffrey Hammonds 1.00 .45
❑ 76 Larry Hanlon RC .10 .05
❑ 77 Pete Harnisch .10 .05
❑ 78 Mike Harrison RC .10 .05
❑ 79 Bryan Harvey .10 .05
❑ 80 Scott Hatteberg RC .10 .05
❑ 81 Rick Helling .20 .09
❑ 82 Dave Henderson .10 .05
❑ 83 Rickey Henderson .50 .23
❑ 84 Tyrone Hill RC .10 .05
❑ 85 Todd Hollandsworth RC .50 .23
❑ 86 Brian Holliday RC .10 .05
❑ 87 Terry Horn RC .10 .05
❑ 88 Jeff Hostetler RC .10 .05
❑ 89 Kent Hrbek .20 .09
❑ 90 Mark Hubbard RC .10 .05
❑ 91 Charles Johnson .75 .35
❑ 92 Howard Johnson .10 .05
❑ 93 Todd Johnson .10 .05
❑ 94 Bobby Jones RC .40 .18
❑ 95 Dan Jones RC .10 .05
❑ 96 Felix Jose .10 .05
❑ 97 David Justice .25 .11
❑ 98 Jimmy Key .20 .09
❑ 99 Marc Kroon RC .10 .05
❑ 100 John Kruk .20 .09
❑ 101 Mark Langston .10 .05
❑ 102 Barry Larkin .25 .11
❑ 103 Mike LaValliere .10 .05
❑ 104 Scott Leius .10 .05
❑ 105 Mark Lemke .10 .05
❑ 106 Donnie Leshnock .10 .05
❑ 107 Jimmy Lewis RC .10 .05
❑ 108 Shane Livesy RC .10 .05
❑ 109 Ryan Long RC .10 .05
❑ 110 Trevor Mallory RC .10 .05
❑ 111 Dennis Martinez .20 .09
❑ 112 Justin Mashore RC .10 .05
❑ 113 Jason McDonald .10 .05
❑ 114 Jack McDowell .10 .05
❑ 115 Tom McKinnon RC .10 .05
❑ 116 Billy McMillon .10 .05
❑ 117 Buck McNabb RC .20 .09
❑ 118 Jim Mecir RC .10 .05
❑ 119 Dan Melendez .10 .05
❑ 120 Shawn Miller RC .10 .05
❑ 121 Trever Miller RC .10 .05
❑ 122 Paul Molitor .40 .18
❑ 123 Vincent Moore RC .10 .05
❑ 124 Mike Morgan .10 .05
❑ 125 Jack Morris WS .10 .05
❑ 126 Jack Morris AS .10 .05
❑ 127 Sean Mulligan RC .10 .05
❑ 128 Eddie Murray AS .40 .18
❑ 129 Mike Neill RC .10 .05
❑ 130 Phil Nevin 1.00 .45
❑ 131 Mark O'Brien RC .10 .05
❑ 132 Alex Ochoa RC .50 .23
❑ 133 Chad Ogea RC .25 .11
❑ 134 Greg Olson .10 .05
❑ 135 Paul O'Neill .20 .09
❑ 136 Jared Osentowski RC .10 .05
❑ 137 Mike Pagliarulo .10 .05
❑ 138 Rafael Palmeiro .40 .18
❑ 139 Rodney Pedraza RC .10 .05
❑ 140 Tony Phillips (P) .10 .05
❑ 141 Scott Pisciotta RC .10 .05
❑ 142 Christopher Pritchett RC .10 .05
❑ 143 Jason Pruitt RC .10 .05
❑ 144 Kirby Puckett WS UER 1.00 .45
(Championship series
AB and BA is wrong)
❑ 145 Kirby Puckett AS 1.00 .45
❑ 146 Manny Ramirez RC 8.00 3.60
❑ 147 Eddie Ramos RC .10 .05
❑ 148 Mark Ratekin RC .10 .05
❑ 149 Jeff Reardon .20 .09
❑ 150 Sean Rees RC .10 .05
❑ 151 Pokey Reese RC 1.00 .45
❑ 152 Desmond Relaford RC .50 .23
❑ 153 Eric Richardson RC .10 .05
❑ 154 Cal Ripken 1.50 .70
❑ 155 Chris Roberts .10 .05
❑ 156 Mike Robertson RC .10 .05
❑ 157 Steve Rodriguez .10 .05
❑ 158 Mike Rossiter RC .10 .05
❑ 159 Scott Ruffcorn RC .10 .05
❑ 160 Chris Sabo .10 .05
❑ 161 Juan Samuel .10 .05
❑ 162 Ryne Sandberg UER .50 .23
(On 5th line, prior
misspelled as prilor)
❑ 163 Scott Sanderson .10 .05
❑ 164 Benny Santiago .10 .05
❑ 165 Gene Schall RC .10 .05
❑ 166 Chad Schoenvogel RC .10 .05
❑ 167 Chris Seelbach RC .10 .05
❑ 168 Aaron Sele RC 1.00 .45
❑ 169 Basil Shabazz RC .10 .05
❑ 170 Al Shirley RC .10 .05
❑ 171 Paul Shuey .10 .05
❑ 172 Ruben Sierra .10 .05
❑ 173 John Smiley .10 .05
❑ 174 Lee Smith .20 .09
❑ 175 Ozzie Smith .50 .23
❑ 176 Tim Smith RC .10 .05
❑ 177 Zane Smith .10 .05
❑ 178 John Smoltz .20 .09
❑ 179 Scott Stahoviak RC .10 .05
❑ 180 Kennie Steenstra .10 .05
❑ 181 Kevin Stocker RC .10 .05
❑ 182 Chris Stynes RC .40 .18
❑ 183 Danny Tartabull .10 .05
❑ 184 Brien Taylor RC .10 .05
❑ 185 Todd Taylor .10 .05
❑ 186 Larry Thomas RC .10 .05
❑ 187 Ozzie Timmons RC .20 .09
(See also 188)
❑ 188 David Tuttle UER .10 .05
(Mistakenly numbered
as 187 on card)
❑ 189 Andy Van Slyke .20 .09
❑ 190 Frank Viola .10 .05
❑ 191 Michael Walkden RC .10 .05
❑ 192 Jeff Ware .10 .05
❑ 193 Allen Watson RC .10 .05
❑ 194 Steve Whitaker RC .10 .05
❑ 195 Jerry Willard .10 .05
❑ 196 Craig Wilson .10 .05
❑ 197 Chris Wimmer .10 .05
❑ 198 Steve Wojciechowski RC .10 .05
❑ 199 Joel Wolfe RC .10 .05
❑ 200 Ivan Zweig .10 .05

## 1992 Stadium Club

| | MINT | NRMT |
|---|---|---|
| COMPLETE SET (900) | 45.00 | 20.00 |
| COMPLETE SERIES 1 (300) | 15.00 | 6.75 |
| COMPLETE SERIES 2 (300) | 15.00 | 6.75 |
| COMPLETE SERIES 3 (300) | 15.00 | 6.75 |

❑ 1 Cal Ripken UER 1.50 .70
(Misspelled Ripkin
on card back)
❑ 2 Eric Yelding .10 .05
❑ 3 Geno Petralli .10 .05
❑ 4 Wally Backman .10 .05
❑ 5 Milt Cuyler .10 .05
❑ 6 Kevin Bass .10 .05
❑ 7 Dante Bichette .25 .11
❑ 8 Ray Lankford .40 .18
❑ 9 Mel Hall .10 .05
❑ 10 Joe Carter .20 .09
❑ 11 Juan Samuel .10 .05
❑ 12 Jeff Montgomery .20 .09
❑ 13 Glenn Braggs .10 .05
❑ 14 Henry Cotto .10 .05
❑ 15 Deion Sanders .40 .18
❑ 16 Dick Schofield .10 .05
❑ 17 David Cone .20 .09
❑ 18 Chili Davis .20 .09
❑ 19 Tom Foley .10 .05
❑ 20 Ozzie Guillen .10 .05
❑ 21 Luis Salazar .10 .05
❑ 22 Terry Steinbach .10 .05
❑ 23 Chris James .10 .05
❑ 24 Jeff King .10 .05
❑ 25 Carlos Quintana .10 .05
❑ 26 Mike Maddux .10 .05
❑ 27 Tommy Greene .10 .05
❑ 28 Jeff Russell .10 .05
❑ 29 Steve Finley .20 .09
❑ 30 Mike Flanagan .10 .05
❑ 31 Darren Lewis .10 .05
❑ 32 Mark Lee .10 .05
❑ 33 Willie Fraser .10 .05
❑ 34 Mike Henneman .10 .05
❑ 35 Kevin Maas .10 .05
❑ 36 Dave Hansen .10 .05
❑ 37 Erik Hanson .10 .05
❑ 38 Bill Doran .10 .05
❑ 39 Mike Boddicker .10 .05
❑ 40 Vince Coleman .10 .05
❑ 41 Devon White .10 .05
❑ 42 Mark Gardner .10 .05
❑ 43 Scott Lewis .10 .05
❑ 44 Juan Berenguer .10 .05
❑ 45 Carney Lansford .20 .09
❑ 46 Curt Wilkerson .10 .05
❑ 47 Shane Mack .10 .05
❑ 48 Bip Roberts .10 .05
❑ 49 Greg A. Harris .10 .05
❑ 50 Ryne Sandberg .50 .23
❑ 51 Mark Whiten .10 .05
❑ 52 Jack McDowell .10 .05
❑ 53 Jimmy Jones .10 .05
❑ 54 Steve Lake .10 .05
❑ 55 Bud Black .10 .05
❑ 56 Dave Valle .10 .05
❑ 57 Kevin Reimer .10 .05
❑ 58 Rich Gedman UER .10 .05
(Wrong BARS chart used)
❑ 59 Travis Fryman .20 .09
❑ 60 Steve Avery .10 .05
❑ 61 Francisco de la Rosa .10 .05
❑ 62 Scott Hemond .10 .05
❑ 63 Hal Morris .10 .05
❑ 64 Hensley Meulens .10 .05
❑ 65 Frank Castillo .10 .05
❑ 66 Gene Larkin .10 .05
❑ 67 Jose DeLeon .10 .05
❑ 68 Al Osuna .10 .05
❑ 69 Dave Cochrane .10 .05
❑ 70 Robin Ventura .20 .09
❑ 71 John Cerutti .10 .05
❑ 72 Kevin Gross .10 .05
❑ 73 Ivan Calderon .10 .05
❑ 74 Mike Macfarlane .10 .05
❑ 75 Stan Belinda .10 .05
❑ 76 Shawn Hillegas .10 .05
❑ 77 Pat Borders .10 .05
❑ 78 Jim Vatcher .10 .05
❑ 79 Bobby Rose .10 .05

❑ 80 Roger Clemens .75 .35
❑ 81 Craig Worthington .10 .05
❑ 82 Jeff Treadway .10 .05
❑ 83 Jamie Quirk .10 .05
❑ 84 Randy Bush .10 .05
❑ 85 Anthony Young .10 .05
❑ 86 Trevor Wilson .10 .05
❑ 87 Jaime Navarro .10 .05
❑ 88 Les Lancaster .10 .05
❑ 89 Pat Kelly .10 .05
❑ 90 Alvin Davis .10 .05
❑ 91 Larry Andersen .10 .05
❑ 92 Rob Deer .10 .05
❑ 93 Mike Sharperson .10 .05
❑ 94 Lance Parrish .10 .05
❑ 95 Cecil Espy .10 .05
❑ 96 Tim Spehr .10 .05
❑ 97 Dave Stieb .10 .05
❑ 98 Terry Mulholland .10 .05
❑ 99 Dennis Boyd .10 .05
❑ 100 Barry Larkin .25 .11
❑ 101 Ryan Bowen .10 .05
❑ 102 Felix Fermin .10 .05
❑ 103 Luis Alicea .10 .05
❑ 104 Tim Hulett .10 .05
❑ 105 Rafael Belliard .10 .05
❑ 106 Mike Gallego .10 .05
❑ 107 Dave Righetti .10 .05
❑ 108 Jeff Schaefer .10 .05
❑ 109 Ricky Bones .10 .05
❑ 110 Scott Erickson .10 .05
❑ 111 Matt Nokes .10 .05
❑ 112 Bob Scanlan .10 .05
❑ 113 Tom Candiotti .10 .05
❑ 114 Sean Berry .10 .05
❑ 115 Kevin Morton .10 .05
❑ 116 Scott Fletcher .10 .05
❑ 117 B.J. Surhoff .20 .09
❑ 118 Dave Magadan UER .10 .05
(Born Tampa, not Tamps)
❑ 119 Bill Gullickson .10 .05
❑ 120 Marquis Grissom .10 .05
❑ 121 Lenny Harris .10 .05
❑ 122 Wally Joyner .20 .09
❑ 123 Kevin Brown .25 .11
❑ 124 Braulio Castillo .10 .05
❑ 125 Eric King .10 .05
❑ 126 Mark Portugal .10 .05
❑ 127 Calvin Jones .10 .05
❑ 128 Mike Heath .10 .05
❑ 129 Todd Van Poppel .10 .05
❑ 130 Benny Santiago .10 .05
❑ 131 Gary Thurman .10 .05
❑ 132 Joe Girardi .20 .09
❑ 133 Dave Eiland .10 .05
❑ 134 Orlando Merced .10 .05
❑ 135 Joe Orsulak .10 .05
❑ 136 John Burkett .10 .05
❑ 137 Ken Dayley .10 .05
❑ 138 Ken Hill .10 .05
❑ 139 Walt Terrell .10 .05
❑ 140 Mike Scioscia .10 .05
❑ 141 Junior Felix .10 .05
❑ 142 Ken Caminiti .20 .09
❑ 143 Carlos Baerga .10 .05
❑ 144 Tony Fossas .10 .05
❑ 145 Craig Grebeck .10 .05
❑ 146 Scott Bradley .10 .05
❑ 147 Kent Mercker .10 .05
❑ 148 Derrick May .10 .05
❑ 149 Jerald Clark .10 .05
❑ 150 George Brett .75 .35
❑ 151 Luis Quinones .10 .05
❑ 152 Mike Pagliarulo .10 .05
❑ 153 Jose Guzman .10 .05
❑ 154 Charlie O'Brien .10 .05
❑ 155 Darren Holmes .10 .05
❑ 156 Joe Boever .10 .05
❑ 157 Rich Monteleone .10 .05
❑ 158 Reggie Harris .10 .05
❑ 159 Roberto Alomar .40 .18
❑ 160 Robby Thompson .10 .05
❑ 161 Chris Hoiles .10 .05
❑ 162 Tom Pagnozzi .10 .05
❑ 163 Omar Vizquel .20 .09
❑ 164 John Candelaria .10 .05
❑ 165 Terry Shumpert .10 .05
❑ 166 Andy Mota .10 .05
❑ 167 Scott Bailes .10 .05
❑ 168 Jeff Blauser .10 .05
❑ 169 Steve Olin .10 .05
❑ 170 Doug Drabek .10 .05
❑ 171 Dave Bergman .10 .05
❑ 172 Eddie Whitson .10 .05
❑ 173 Gilberto Reyes .10 .05
❑ 174 Mark Grace .40 .18
❑ 175 Paul O'Neill .20 .09
❑ 176 Greg Cadaret .10 .05
❑ 177 Mark Williamson .10 .05
❑ 178 Casey Candaele .10 .05
❑ 179 Candy Maldonado .10 .05
❑ 180 Lee Smith .20 .09
❑ 181 Harold Reynolds .10 .05
❑ 182 David Justice .25 .11
❑ 183 Lenny Webster .10 .05
❑ 184 Donn Pall .10 .05
❑ 185 Gerald Alexander .10 .05
❑ 186 Jack Clark .20 .09
❑ 187 Stan Javier .10 .05
❑ 188 Ricky Jordan .10 .05
❑ 189 Franklin Stubbs .10 .05
❑ 190 Dennis Eckersley .20 .09
❑ 191 Danny Tartabull .10 .05
❑ 192 Pete O'Brien .10 .05
❑ 193 Mark Lewis .10 .05
❑ 194 Mike Felder .10 .05
❑ 195 Mickey Tettleton .10 .05
❑ 196 Dwight Smith .10 .05
❑ 197 Shawn Abner .10 .05
❑ 198 Jim Leyritz UER .10 .05
(Career totals less than 1991 totals)
❑ 199 Mike Devereaux .10 .05
❑ 200 Craig Biggio .25 .11
❑ 201 Kevin Elster .10 .05
❑ 202 Rance Mulliniks .10 .05
❑ 203 Tony Fernandez .10 .05
❑ 204 Allan Anderson .10 .05
❑ 205 Herm Winningham .10 .05
❑ 206 Tim Jones .10 .05
❑ 207 Ramon Martinez .10 .05
❑ 208 Teddy Higuera .10 .05
❑ 209 John Kruk .20 .09
❑ 210 Jim Abbott .20 .09
❑ 211 Dean Palmer .20 .09
❑ 212 Mark Davis .10 .05
❑ 213 Jay Buhner .20 .09
❑ 214 Jesse Barfield .10 .05
❑ 215 Kevin Mitchell .20 .09
❑ 216 Mike LaValliere .10 .05
❑ 217 Mark Wohlers .10 .05
❑ 218 Dave Henderson .10 .05
❑ 219 Dave Smith .10 .05
❑ 220 Albert Belle .25 .11
❑ 221 Spike Owen .10 .05
❑ 222 Jeff Gray .10 .05
❑ 223 Paul Gibson .10 .05
❑ 224 Bobby Thigpen .10 .05
❑ 225 Mike Mussina .60 .25
❑ 226 Darrin Jackson .10 .05
❑ 227 Luis Gonzalez .25 .11
❑ 228 Greg Briley .10 .05
❑ 229 Brent Mayne .10 .05
❑ 230 Paul Molitor .40 .18
❑ 231 Al Leiter .20 .09
❑ 232 Andy Van Slyke .20 .09
❑ 233 Ron Tingley .10 .05
❑ 234 Bernard Gilkey .20 .09
❑ 235 Kent Hrbek .20 .09
❑ 236 Eric Karros .40 .18
❑ 237 Randy Velarde .10 .05
❑ 238 Andy Allanson .10 .05
❑ 239 Willie McGee .20 .09
❑ 240 Juan Gonzalez .40 .18
❑ 241 Karl Rhodes .10 .05
❑ 242 Luis Mercedes .10 .05
❑ 243 Bill Swift .10 .05
❑ 244 Tommy Gregg .10 .05
❑ 245 David Howard .10 .05
❑ 246 Dave Hollins .10 .05
❑ 247 Kip Gross .10 .05
❑ 248 Walt Weiss .10 .05
❑ 249 Mackey Sasser .10 .05
❑ 250 Cecil Fielder .20 .09
❑ 251 Jerry Browne .10 .05
❑ 252 Doug Dascenzo .10 .05
❑ 253 Darryl Hamilton .10 .05
❑ 254 Dann Bilardello .10 .05
❑ 255 Luis Rivera .10 .05
❑ 256 Larry Walker .25 .11
❑ 257 Ron Karkovice .10 .05
❑ 258 Bob Tewksbury .10 .05
❑ 259 Jimmy Key .20 .09
❑ 260 Bernie Williams .40 .18
❑ 261 Gary Wayne .10 .05
❑ 262 Mike Simms UER .10 .05
(Reversed negative)
❑ 263 John Orton .10 .05
❑ 264 Marvin Freeman .10 .05
❑ 265 Mike Jeffcoat .10 .05
❑ 266 Roger Mason .10 .05
❑ 267 Edgar Martinez .25 .11
❑ 268 Henry Rodriguez .10 .05
❑ 269 Sam Horn .10 .05
❑ 270 Brian McRae .10 .05
❑ 271 Kirt Manwaring .10 .05
❑ 272 Mike Bordick .10 .05
❑ 273 Chris Sabo .10 .05
❑ 274 Jim Olander .10 .05
❑ 275 Greg W. Harris .10 .05
❑ 276 Dan Gakeler .10 .05
❑ 277 Bill Sampen .10 .05
❑ 278 Joel Skinner .10 .05
❑ 279 Curt Schilling .20 .09
❑ 280 Dale Murphy .40 .18
❑ 281 Lee Stevens .20 .09
❑ 282 Lonnie Smith .10 .05
❑ 283 Manuel Lee .10 .05
❑ 284 Shawn Boskie .10 .05
❑ 285 Kevin Seitzer .10 .05
❑ 286 Stan Royer .10 .05
❑ 287 John Dopson .10 .05
❑ 288 Scott Bullett RC .10 .05
❑ 289 Ken Patterson .10 .05
❑ 290 Todd Hundley .10 .05
❑ 291 Tim Leary .10 .05
❑ 292 Brett Butler .20 .09
❑ 293 Gregg Olson .10 .05
❑ 294 Jeff Brantley .10 .05
❑ 295 Brian Holman .10 .05
❑ 296 Brian Harper .10 .05
❑ 297 Brian Bohanon .10 .05
❑ 298 Checklist 1-100 .10 .05
❑ 299 Checklist 101-200 .10 .05
❑ 300 Checklist 201-300 .10 .05
❑ 301 Frank Thomas .75 .35
❑ 302 Lloyd McClendon .10 .05
❑ 303 Brady Anderson .25 .11
❑ 304 Julio Valera .10 .05
❑ 305 Mike Aldrete .10 .05
❑ 306 Joe Oliver .10 .05
❑ 307 Todd Stottlemyre .20 .09
❑ 308 Rey Sanchez RC .10 .05
❑ 309 Gary Sheffield UER .40 .18
(Listed as 5'1", should be 5'11")
❑ 310 Andujar Cedeno .10 .05
❑ 311 Kenny Rogers .10 .05
❑ 312 Bruce Hurst .10 .05
❑ 313 Mike Schooler .10 .05
❑ 314 Mike Benjamin .10 .05
❑ 315 Chuck Finley .20 .09
❑ 316 Mark Lemke .10 .05
❑ 317 Scott Livingstone .10 .05
❑ 318 Chris Nabholz .10 .05
❑ 319 Mike Humphreys .10 .05
❑ 320 Pedro Guerrero .10 .05
❑ 321 Willie Banks .10 .05
❑ 322 Tom Goodwin .20 .09
❑ 323 Hector Wagner .10 .05
❑ 324 Wally Ritchie .10 .05
❑ 325 Mo Vaughn .20 .09
❑ 326 Joe Klink .10 .05
❑ 327 Cal Eldred .10 .05
❑ 328 Daryl Boston .10 .05
❑ 329 Mike Huff .10 .05
❑ 330 Jeff Bagwell .75 .35
❑ 331 Bob Milacki .10 .05

| | | | | |
|---|---|---|---|---|
| ❑ | 332 | Tom Prince | .10 | .05 |
| ❑ | 333 | Pat Tabler | .10 | .05 |
| ❑ | 334 | Ced Landrum | .10 | .05 |
| ❑ | 335 | Reggie Jefferson | .20 | .09 |
| ❑ | 336 | Mo Sanford | .10 | .05 |
| ❑ | 337 | Kevin Ritz | .10 | .05 |
| ❑ | 338 | Gerald Perry | .10 | .05 |
| ❑ | 339 | Jeff Hamilton | .10 | .05 |
| ❑ | 340 | Tim Wallach | .10 | .05 |
| ❑ | 341 | Jeff Huson | .10 | .05 |
| ❑ | 342 | Jose Melendez | .10 | .05 |
| ❑ | 343 | Willie Wilson | .10 | .05 |
| ❑ | 344 | Mike Stanton | .10 | .05 |
| ❑ | 345 | Joel Johnston | .10 | .05 |
| ❑ | 346 | Lee Guetterman | .10 | .05 |
| ❑ | 347 | Francisco Oliveras | .10 | .05 |
| ❑ | 348 | Dave Burba | .10 | .05 |
| ❑ | 349 | Tim Crews | .10 | .05 |
| ❑ | 350 | Scott Leius | .10 | .05 |
| ❑ | 351 | Danny Cox | .10 | .05 |
| ❑ | 352 | Wayne Housie | .10 | .05 |
| ❑ | 353 | Chris Donnels | .10 | .05 |
| ❑ | 354 | Chris George | .10 | .05 |
| ❑ | 355 | Gerald Young | .10 | .05 |
| ❑ | 356 | Roberto Hernandez | .10 | .05 |
| ❑ | 357 | Neal Heaton | .10 | .05 |
| ❑ | 358 | Todd Frohwirth | .10 | .05 |
| ❑ | 359 | Jose Vizcaino | .10 | .05 |
| ❑ | 360 | Jim Thome | .75 | .35 |
| ❑ | 361 | Craig Wilson | .10 | .05 |
| ❑ | 362 | Dave Haas | .10 | .05 |
| ❑ | 363 | Billy Hatcher | .10 | .05 |
| ❑ | 364 | John Barfield | .10 | .05 |
| ❑ | 365 | Luis Aquino | .10 | .05 |
| ❑ | 366 | Charlie Leibrandt | .10 | .05 |
| ❑ | 367 | Howard Farmer | .10 | .05 |
| ❑ | 368 | Bryn Smith | .10 | .05 |
| ❑ | 369 | Mickey Morandini | .10 | .05 |
| ❑ | 370 | Jose Canseco (See also 597) | .50 | .23 |
| ❑ | 371 | Jose Uribe | .10 | .05 |
| ❑ | 372 | Bob MacDonald | .10 | .05 |
| ❑ | 373 | Luis Sojo | .10 | .05 |
| ❑ | 374 | Craig Shipley | .10 | .05 |
| ❑ | 375 | Scott Bankhead | .10 | .05 |
| ❑ | 376 | Greg Gagne | .10 | .05 |
| ❑ | 377 | Scott Cooper | .10 | .05 |
| ❑ | 378 | Jose Offerman | .10 | .05 |
| ❑ | 379 | Bill Spiers | .10 | .05 |
| ❑ | 380 | John Smiley | .10 | .05 |
| ❑ | 381 | Jeff Carter | .10 | .05 |
| ❑ | 382 | Heathcliff Slocumb | .10 | .05 |
| ❑ | 383 | Jeff Tackett | .10 | .05 |
| ❑ | 384 | John Kiely | .10 | .05 |
| ❑ | 385 | John Vander Wal | .10 | .05 |
| ❑ | 386 | Omar Olivares | .10 | .05 |
| ❑ | 387 | Ruben Sierra | .10 | .05 |
| ❑ | 388 | Tom Gordon | .10 | .05 |
| ❑ | 389 | Charles Nagy | .10 | .05 |
| ❑ | 390 | Dave Stewart | .20 | .09 |
| ❑ | 391 | Pete Harnisch | .10 | .05 |
| ❑ | 392 | Tim Burke | .10 | .05 |
| ❑ | 393 | Roberto Kelly | .10 | .05 |
| ❑ | 394 | Freddie Benavides | .10 | .05 |
| ❑ | 395 | Tom Glavine | .25 | .11 |
| ❑ | 396 | Wes Chamberlain | .10 | .05 |
| ❑ | 397 | Eric Gunderson | .10 | .05 |
| ❑ | 398 | Dave West | .10 | .05 |
| ❑ | 399 | Ellis Burks | .20 | .09 |
| ❑ | 400 | Ken Griffey Jr. | 1.50 | .70 |
| ❑ | 401 | Thomas Howard | .10 | .05 |
| ❑ | 402 | Juan Guzman | .10 | .05 |
| ❑ | 403 | Mitch Webster | .10 | .05 |
| ❑ | 404 | Matt Merullo | .10 | .05 |
| ❑ | 405 | Steve Buechele | .10 | .05 |
| ❑ | 406 | Danny Jackson | .10 | .05 |
| ❑ | 407 | Felix Jose | .10 | .05 |
| ❑ | 408 | Doug Piatt | .10 | .05 |
| ❑ | 409 | Jim Eisenreich | .10 | .05 |
| ❑ | 410 | Bryan Harvey | .10 | .05 |
| ❑ | 411 | Jim Austin | .10 | .05 |
| ❑ | 412 | Jim Poole | .10 | .05 |
| ❑ | 413 | Glenallen Hill | .10 | .05 |
| ❑ | 414 | Gene Nelson | .10 | .05 |
| ❑ | 415 | Ivan Rodriguez | .75 | .35 |
| ❑ | 416 | Frank Tanana | .10 | .05 |
| ❑ | 417 | Steve Decker | .10 | .05 |
| ❑ | 418 | Jason Grimsley | .10 | .05 |
| ❑ | 419 | Tim Layana | .10 | .05 |
| ❑ | 420 | Don Mattingly | 1.00 | .45 |
| ❑ | 421 | Jerome Walton | .10 | .05 |
| ❑ | 422 | Rob Ducey | .10 | .05 |
| ❑ | 423 | Andy Benes | .10 | .05 |
| ❑ | 424 | John Marzano | .10 | .05 |
| ❑ | 425 | Gene Harris | .10 | .05 |
| ❑ | 426 | Tim Raines | .20 | .09 |
| ❑ | 427 | Bret Barberie | .10 | .05 |
| ❑ | 428 | Harvey Pulliam | .10 | .05 |
| ❑ | 429 | Cris Carpenter | .10 | .05 |
| ❑ | 430 | Howard Johnson | .10 | .05 |
| ❑ | 431 | Orel Hershiser | .20 | .09 |
| ❑ | 432 | Brian Hunter | .10 | .05 |
| ❑ | 433 | Kevin Tapani | .10 | .05 |
| ❑ | 434 | Rick Reed | .10 | .05 |
| ❑ | 435 | Ron Witmeyer RC | .10 | .05 |
| ❑ | 436 | Gary Gaetti | .20 | .09 |
| ❑ | 437 | Alex Cole | .10 | .05 |
| ❑ | 438 | Chito Martinez | .10 | .05 |
| ❑ | 439 | Greg Litton | .10 | .05 |
| ❑ | 440 | Julio Franco | .10 | .05 |
| ❑ | 441 | Mike Munoz | .10 | .05 |
| ❑ | 442 | Erik Pappas | .10 | .05 |
| ❑ | 443 | Pat Combs | .10 | .05 |
| ❑ | 444 | Lance Johnson | .10 | .05 |
| ❑ | 445 | Ed Sprague | .10 | .05 |
| ❑ | 446 | Mike Greenwell | .10 | .05 |
| ❑ | 447 | Milt Thompson | .10 | .05 |
| ❑ | 448 | Mike Magnante RC | .10 | .05 |
| ❑ | 449 | Chris Haney | .10 | .05 |
| ❑ | 450 | Robin Yount | .40 | .18 |
| ❑ | 451 | Rafael Ramirez | .10 | .05 |
| ❑ | 452 | Gino Minutelli | .10 | .05 |
| ❑ | 453 | Tom Lampkin | .10 | .05 |
| ❑ | 454 | Tony Perezchica | .10 | .05 |
| ❑ | 455 | Dwight Gooden | .20 | .09 |
| ❑ | 456 | Mark Guthrie | .10 | .05 |
| ❑ | 457 | Jay Howell | .10 | .05 |
| ❑ | 458 | Gary DiSarcina | .10 | .05 |
| ❑ | 459 | John Smoltz | .20 | .09 |
| ❑ | 460 | Will Clark | .40 | .18 |
| ❑ | 461 | Dave Otto | .10 | .05 |
| ❑ | 462 | Rob Maurer | .10 | .05 |
| ❑ | 463 | Dwight Evans | .20 | .09 |
| ❑ | 464 | Tom Brunansky | .10 | .05 |
| ❑ | 465 | Shawn Hare RC | .10 | .05 |
| ❑ | 466 | Geronimo Pena | .10 | .05 |
| ❑ | 467 | Alex Fernandez | .20 | .09 |
| ❑ | 468 | Greg Myers | .10 | .05 |
| ❑ | 469 | Jeff Fassero | .10 | .05 |
| ❑ | 470 | Len Dykstra | .20 | .09 |
| ❑ | 471 | Jeff Johnson | .10 | .05 |
| ❑ | 472 | Russ Swan | .10 | .05 |
| ❑ | 473 | Archie Corbin | .10 | .05 |
| ❑ | 474 | Chuck McElroy | .10 | .05 |
| ❑ | 475 | Mark McGwire | 1.50 | .70 |
| ❑ | 476 | Wally Whitehurst | .10 | .05 |
| ❑ | 477 | Tim McIntosh | .10 | .05 |
| ❑ | 478 | Sid Bream | .10 | .05 |
| ❑ | 479 | Jeff Juden | .10 | .05 |
| ❑ | 480 | Carlton Fisk | .40 | .18 |
| ❑ | 481 | Jeff Plympton | .10 | .05 |
| ❑ | 482 | Carlos Martinez | .10 | .05 |
| ❑ | 483 | Jim Gott | .10 | .05 |
| ❑ | 484 | Bob McClure | .10 | .05 |
| ❑ | 485 | Tim Teufel | .10 | .05 |
| ❑ | 486 | Vicente Palacios | .10 | .05 |
| ❑ | 487 | Jeff Reed | .10 | .05 |
| ❑ | 488 | Tony Phillips | .10 | .05 |
| ❑ | 489 | Mel Rojas | .10 | .05 |
| ❑ | 490 | Ben McDonald | .10 | .05 |
| ❑ | 491 | Andres Santana | .10 | .05 |
| ❑ | 492 | Chris Beasley | .10 | .05 |
| ❑ | 493 | Mike Timlin | .10 | .05 |
| ❑ | 494 | Brian Downing | .10 | .05 |
| ❑ | 495 | Kirk Gibson | .20 | .09 |
| ❑ | 496 | Scott Sanderson | .10 | .05 |
| ❑ | 497 | Nick Esasky | .10 | .05 |
| ❑ | 498 | Johnny Guzman RC | .10 | .05 |
| ❑ | 499 | Mitch Williams | .10 | .05 |
| ❑ | 500 | Kirby Puckett | 1.00 | .45 |
| ❑ | 501 | Mike Harkey | .10 | .05 |
| ❑ | 502 | Jim Gantner | .10 | .05 |
| ❑ | 503 | Bruce Egloff | .10 | .05 |
| ❑ | 504 | Josias Manzanillo RC | .10 | .05 |
| ❑ | 505 | Delino DeShields | .20 | .09 |
| ❑ | 506 | Rheal Cormier | .10 | .05 |
| ❑ | 507 | Jay Bell | .20 | .09 |
| ❑ | 508 | Rich Rowland RC | .10 | .05 |
| ❑ | 509 | Scott Servais | .10 | .05 |
| ❑ | 510 | Terry Pendleton | .20 | .09 |
| ❑ | 511 | Rich DeLucia | .10 | .05 |
| ❑ | 512 | Warren Newson | .10 | .05 |
| ❑ | 513 | Paul Faries | .10 | .05 |
| ❑ | 514 | Kal Daniels | .10 | .05 |
| ❑ | 515 | Jarvis Brown | .10 | .05 |
| ❑ | 516 | Rafael Palmeiro | .40 | .18 |
| ❑ | 517 | Kelly Downs | .10 | .05 |
| ❑ | 518 | Steve Chitren | .10 | .05 |
| ❑ | 519 | Moises Alou | .40 | .18 |
| ❑ | 520 | Wade Boggs | .50 | .23 |
| ❑ | 521 | Pete Schourek | .10 | .05 |
| ❑ | 522 | Scott Terry | .10 | .05 |
| ❑ | 523 | Kevin Appier | .20 | .09 |
| ❑ | 524 | Gary Redus | .10 | .05 |
| ❑ | 525 | George Bell | .10 | .05 |
| ❑ | 526 | Jeff Kaiser | .10 | .05 |
| ❑ | 527 | Alvaro Espinoza | .10 | .05 |
| ❑ | 528 | Luis Polonia | .10 | .05 |
| ❑ | 529 | Darren Daulton | .20 | .09 |
| ❑ | 530 | Norm Charlton | .10 | .05 |
| ❑ | 531 | John Olerud | .20 | .09 |
| ❑ | 532 | Dan Plesac | .10 | .05 |
| ❑ | 533 | Billy Ripken | .10 | .05 |
| ❑ | 534 | Rod Nichols | .10 | .05 |
| ❑ | 535 | Joey Cora | .10 | .05 |
| ❑ | 536 | Harold Baines | .20 | .09 |
| ❑ | 537 | Bob Ojeda | .10 | .05 |
| ❑ | 538 | Mark Leonard | .10 | .05 |
| ❑ | 539 | Danny Darwin | .10 | .05 |
| ❑ | 540 | Shawon Dunston | .10 | .05 |
| ❑ | 541 | Pedro Munoz | .10 | .05 |
| ❑ | 542 | Mark Gubicza | .10 | .05 |
| ❑ | 543 | Kevin Baez | .10 | .05 |
| ❑ | 544 | Todd Zeile | .10 | .05 |
| ❑ | 545 | Don Slaught | .10 | .05 |
| ❑ | 546 | Tony Eusebio | .40 | .18 |
| ❑ | 547 | Alonzo Powell | .10 | .05 |
| ❑ | 548 | Gary Pettis | .10 | .05 |
| ❑ | 549 | Brian Barnes | .10 | .05 |
| ❑ | 550 | Lou Whitaker | .20 | .09 |
| ❑ | 551 | Keith Mitchell | .10 | .05 |
| ❑ | 552 | Oscar Azocar | .10 | .05 |
| ❑ | 553 | Stu Cole RC | .10 | .05 |
| ❑ | 554 | Steve Wapnick | .10 | .05 |
| ❑ | 555 | Derek Bell | .10 | .05 |
| ❑ | 556 | Luis Lopez | .10 | .05 |
| ❑ | 557 | Anthony Telford | .10 | .05 |
| ❑ | 558 | Tim Mauser | .10 | .05 |
| ❑ | 559 | Glen Sutko | .10 | .05 |
| ❑ | 560 | Darryl Strawberry | .20 | .09 |
| ❑ | 561 | Tom Bolton | .10 | .05 |
| ❑ | 562 | Cliff Young | .10 | .05 |
| ❑ | 563 | Bruce Walton | .10 | .05 |
| ❑ | 564 | Chico Walker | .10 | .05 |
| ❑ | 565 | John Franco | .20 | .09 |
| ❑ | 566 | Paul McClellan | .10 | .05 |
| ❑ | 567 | Paul Abbott | .10 | .05 |
| ❑ | 568 | Gary Varsho | .10 | .05 |
| ❑ | 569 | Carlos Maldonado RC | .10 | .05 |
| ❑ | 570 | Kelly Gruber | .10 | .05 |
| ❑ | 571 | Jose Oquendo | .10 | .05 |
| ❑ | 572 | Steve Frey | .10 | .05 |
| ❑ | 573 | Tino Martinez | .20 | .09 |
| ❑ | 574 | Bill Haselman | .10 | .05 |
| ❑ | 575 | Eric Anthony | .10 | .05 |
| ❑ | 576 | John Habyan | .10 | .05 |
| ❑ | 577 | Jeff McNeely | .10 | .05 |
| ❑ | 578 | Chris Bosio | .10 | .05 |
| ❑ | 579 | Joe Grahe | .10 | .05 |
| ❑ | 580 | Fred McGriff | .25 | .11 |
| ❑ | 581 | Rick Honeycutt | .10 | .05 |
| ❑ | 582 | Matt Williams | .25 | .11 |
| ❑ | 583 | Cliff Brantley | .10 | .05 |
| ❑ | 584 | Rob Dibble | .10 | .05 |
| ❑ | 585 | Skeeter Barnes | .10 | .05 |
| ❑ | 586 | Greg Hibbard | .10 | .05 |
| ❑ | 587 | Randy Milligan | .10 | .05 |
| ❑ | 588 | Checklist 301-400 | .10 | .05 |

❑ 589 Checklist 401-500 .10 .05
❑ 590 Checklist 501-600 .10 .05
❑ 591 Frank Thomas MC .40 .18
❑ 592 David Justice MC .10 .05
❑ 593 Roger Clemens MC .40 .18
❑ 594 Steve Avery MC .10 .05
❑ 595 Cal Ripken MC .75 .35
❑ 596 Barry Larkin MC UER .20 .09
(Ranked in AL; should be NL)
❑ 597 Jose Canseco MC UER .20 .09
(Mistakenly numbered 370 on card back)
❑ 598 Will Clark MC .20 .09
❑ 599 Cecil Fielder MC .10 .05
❑ 600 Ryne Sandberg MC .40 .18
❑ 601 Chuck Knoblauch MC .10 .05
❑ 602 Dwight Gooden MC .10 .05
❑ 603 Ken Griffey Jr. MC 1.25 .55
❑ 604 Barry Bonds MC .40 .18
❑ 605 Nolan Ryan MC .75 .35
❑ 606 Jeff Bagwell MC .25 .11
❑ 607 Robin Yount MC .20 .09
❑ 608 Bobby Bonilla MC .10 .05
❑ 609 George Brett MC .40 .18
❑ 610 Howard Johnson MC .10 .05
❑ 611 Esteban Beltre .10 .05
❑ 612 Mike Christopher .10 .05
❑ 613 Troy Afenir .10 .05
❑ 614 Mariano Duncan .10 .05
❑ 615 Doug Henry RC .10 .05
❑ 616 Doug Jones .10 .05
❑ 617 Alvin Davis .10 .05
❑ 618 Craig Lefferts .10 .05
❑ 619 Kevin McReynolds .10 .05
❑ 620 Barry Bonds .60 .25
❑ 621 Turner Ward .10 .05
❑ 622 Joe Magrane .10 .05
❑ 623 Mark Parent .10 .05
❑ 624 Tom Browning .10 .05
❑ 625 John Smiley .10 .05
❑ 626 Steve Wilson .10 .05
❑ 627 Mike Gallego .10 .05
❑ 628 Sammy Sosa .75 .35
❑ 629 Rico Rossy .10 .05
❑ 630 Royce Clayton .10 .05
❑ 631 Clay Parker .10 .05
❑ 632 Pete Smith .10 .05
❑ 633 Jeff McKnight .10 .05
❑ 634 Jack Daugherty .10 .05
❑ 635 Steve Sax .10 .05
❑ 636 Joe Hesketh .10 .05
❑ 637 Vince Horsman .10 .05
❑ 638 Eric King .10 .05
❑ 639 Joe Boever .10 .05
❑ 640 Jack Morris .20 .09
❑ 641 Arthur Rhodes .10 .05
❑ 642 Bob Melvin .10 .05
❑ 643 Rick Wilkins .10 .05
❑ 644 Scott Scudder .10 .05
❑ 645 Bip Roberts .10 .05
❑ 646 Julio Valera .10 .05
❑ 647 Kevin Campbell .10 .05
❑ 648 Steve Searcy .10 .05
❑ 649 Scott Kamieniecki .10 .05
❑ 650 Kurt Stillwell .10 .05
❑ 651 Bob Welch .10 .05
❑ 652 Andres Galarraga .25 .11
❑ 653 Mike Jackson .10 .05
❑ 654 Bo Jackson .20 .09
❑ 655 Sid Fernandez .10 .05
❑ 656 Mike Bielecki .10 .05
❑ 657 Jeff Reardon .20 .09
❑ 658 Wayne Rosenthal .10 .05
❑ 659 Eric Bullock .10 .05
❑ 660 Eric Davis .20 .09
❑ 661 Randy Tomlin .10 .05
❑ 662 Tom Edens .10 .05
❑ 663 Rob Murphy .10 .05
❑ 664 Leo Gomez .10 .05
❑ 665 Greg Maddux 1.00 .45
❑ 666 Greg Vaughn .25 .11
❑ 667 Wade Taylor .10 .05
❑ 668 Brad Arnsberg .10 .05
❑ 669 Mike Moore .10 .05
❑ 670 Mark Langston .10 .05
❑ 671 Barry Jones .10 .05
❑ 672 Bill Landrum .10 .05
❑ 673 Greg Swindell .10 .05
❑ 674 Wayne Edwards .10 .05
❑ 675 Greg Olson .10 .05
❑ 676 Bill Pulsipher RC .10 .05
❑ 677 Bobby Witt .10 .05
❑ 678 Mark Carreon .10 .05
❑ 679 Patrick Lennon .10 .05
❑ 680 Ozzie Smith .50 .23
❑ 681 John Briscoe .10 .05
❑ 682 Matt Young .10 .05
❑ 683 Jeff Conine .10 .05
❑ 684 Phil Stephenson .10 .05
❑ 685 Ron Darling .10 .05
❑ 686 Bryan Hickerson RC .10 .05
❑ 687 Dale Sveum .10 .05
❑ 688 Kirk McCaskill .10 .05
❑ 689 Rich Amaral .10 .05
❑ 690 Danny Tartabull .10 .05
❑ 691 Donald Harris .10 .05
❑ 692 Doug Davis .10 .05
❑ 693 John Farrell .10 .05
❑ 694 Paul Gibson .10 .05
❑ 695 Kenny Lofton .50 .23
❑ 696 Mike Fetters .10 .05
❑ 697 Rosario Rodriguez .10 .05
❑ 698 Chris Jones .10 .05
❑ 699 Jeff Manto .10 .05
❑ 700 Rick Sutcliffe .20 .09
❑ 701 Scott Bankhead .10 .05
❑ 702 Donnie Hill .10 .05
❑ 703 Todd Worrell .10 .05
❑ 704 Rene Gonzales .10 .05
❑ 705 Rick Cerone .10 .05
❑ 706 Tony Pena .10 .05
❑ 707 Paul Sorrento .10 .05
❑ 708 Gary Scott .10 .05
❑ 709 Junior Noboa .10 .05
❑ 710 Wally Joyner .20 .09
❑ 711 Charlie Hayes .10 .05
❑ 712 Rich Rodriguez .10 .05
❑ 713 Rudy Seanez .10 .05
❑ 714 Jim Bullinger .10 .05
❑ 715 Jeff M. Robinson .10 .05
❑ 716 Jeff Branson .10 .05
❑ 717 Andy Ashby .20 .09
❑ 718 Dave Burba .10 .05
❑ 719 Rich Gossage .20 .09
❑ 720 Randy Johnson .50 .23
❑ 721 David Wells .20 .09
❑ 722 Paul Kilgus .10 .05
❑ 723 Dave Martinez .10 .05
❑ 724 Denny Neagle .25 .11
❑ 725 Andy Stankiewicz .10 .05
❑ 726 Rick Aguilera .20 .09
❑ 727 Junior Ortiz .10 .05
❑ 728 Storm Davis .10 .05
❑ 729 Don Robinson .10 .05
❑ 730 Ron Gant .20 .09
❑ 731 Paul Assenmacher .10 .05
❑ 732 Mike Gardiner .10 .05
❑ 733 Milt Hill .10 .05
❑ 734 Jeremy Hernandez RC .10 .05
❑ 735 Ken Hill .10 .05
❑ 736 Xavier Hernandez .10 .05
❑ 737 Gregg Jefferies .10 .05
❑ 738 Dick Schofield .10 .05
❑ 739 Ron Robinson .10 .05
❑ 740 Sandy Alomar Jr. .20 .09
❑ 741 Mike Stanley .10 .05
❑ 742 Butch Henry RC .10 .05
❑ 743 Floyd Bannister .10 .05
❑ 744 Brian Drahman .10 .05
❑ 745 Dave Winfield .40 .18
❑ 746 Bob Walk .10 .05
❑ 747 Chris James .10 .05
❑ 748 Don Prybylinski RC .10 .05
❑ 749 Dennis Rasmussen .10 .05
❑ 750 Rickey Henderson .50 .23
❑ 751 Chris Hammond .10 .05
❑ 752 Bob Kipper .10 .05
❑ 753 Dave Rohde .10 .05
❑ 754 Hubie Brooks .10 .05
❑ 755 Bret Saberhagen .20 .09
❑ 756 Jeff D. Robinson .10 .05
❑ 757 Pat Listach RC .10 .05
❑ 758 Bill Wegman .10 .05
❑ 759 John Wetteland .20 .09
❑ 760 Phil Plantier .10 .05
❑ 761 Wilson Alvarez .10 .05
❑ 762 Scott Aldred .10 .05
❑ 763 Armando Reynoso RC .10 .05
❑ 764 Todd Benzinger .10 .05
❑ 765 Kevin Mitchell .20 .09
❑ 766 Gary Sheffield .40 .18
❑ 767 Allan Anderson .10 .05
❑ 768 Rusty Meacham .10 .05
❑ 769 Rick Parker .10 .05
❑ 770 Nolan Ryan 2.00 .90
❑ 771 Jeff Ballard .10 .05
❑ 772 Cory Snyder .10 .05
❑ 773 Denis Boucher .10 .05
❑ 774 Jose Gonzalez .10 .05
❑ 775 Juan Guerrero .10 .05
❑ 776 Ed Nunez .10 .05
❑ 777 Scott Ruskin .10 .05
❑ 778 Terry Leach .10 .05
❑ 779 Carl Willis .10 .05
❑ 780 Bobby Bonilla .20 .09
❑ 781 Duane Ward .10 .05
❑ 782 Joe Slusarski .10 .05
❑ 783 David Segui .10 .05
❑ 784 Kirk Gibson .20 .09
❑ 785 Frank Viola .10 .05
❑ 786 Keith Miller .10 .05
❑ 787 Mike Morgan .10 .05
❑ 788 Kim Batiste .10 .05
❑ 789 Sergio Valdez .10 .05
❑ 790 Eddie Taubensee RC .20 .09
❑ 791 Jack Armstrong .10 .05
❑ 792 Scott Fletcher .10 .05
❑ 793 Steve Farr .10 .05
❑ 794 Dan Pasqua .10 .05
❑ 795 Eddie Murray .40 .18
❑ 796 John Morris .10 .05
❑ 797 Francisco Cabrera .10 .05
❑ 798 Mike Perez .10 .05
❑ 799 Ted Wood .10 .05
❑ 800 Jose Rijo .10 .05
❑ 801 Danny Gladden .10 .05
❑ 802 Archi Cianfrocco RC .10 .05
❑ 803 Monty Fariss .10 .05
❑ 804 Roger McDowell .10 .05
❑ 805 Randy Myers .20 .09
❑ 806 Kirk Dressendorfer .10 .05
❑ 807 Zane Smith .10 .05
❑ 808 Glenn Davis .10 .05
❑ 809 Torey Lovullo .10 .05
❑ 810 Andre Dawson .25 .11
❑ 811 Bill Pecota .10 .05
❑ 812 Ted Power .10 .05
❑ 813 Willie Blair .10 .05
❑ 814 Dave Fleming .10 .05
❑ 815 Chris Gwynn .10 .05
❑ 816 Jody Reed .10 .05
❑ 817 Mark Dewey .10 .05
❑ 818 Kyle Abbott .10 .05
❑ 819 Tom Henke .10 .05
❑ 820 Kevin Seitzer .10 .05
❑ 821 Al Newman .10 .05
❑ 822 Tim Sherrill .10 .05
❑ 823 Chuck Crim .10 .05
❑ 824 Darren Reed .10 .05
❑ 825 Tony Gwynn .75 .35
❑ 826 Steve Foster .10 .05
❑ 827 Steve Howe .10 .05
❑ 828 Brook Jacoby .10 .05
❑ 829 Rodney McCray .10 .05
❑ 830 Chuck Knoblauch .20 .09
❑ 831 John Wehner .10 .05
❑ 832 Scott Garrelts .10 .05
❑ 833 Alejandro Pena .10 .05
❑ 834 Jeff Parrett UER .10 .05
(Kentucky)
❑ 835 Juan Bell .10 .05
❑ 836 Lance Dickson .10 .05
❑ 837 Darryl Kile .20 .09
❑ 838 Efrain Valdez .10 .05
❑ 839 Bob Zupcic RC .10 .05
❑ 840 George Bell .10 .05
❑ 841 Dave Gallagher .10 .05

| No. | Player | MINT | NRMT |
|---|---|---|---|
| ❑ 842 | Tim Belcher | .10 | .05 |
| ❑ 843 | Jeff Shaw | .10 | .05 |
| ❑ 844 | Mike Fitzgerald | .10 | .05 |
| ❑ 845 | Gary Carter | .25 | .11 |
| ❑ 846 | John Russell | .10 | .05 |
| ❑ 847 | Eric Hillman RC | .10 | .05 |
| ❑ 848 | Mike Witt | .10 | .05 |
| ❑ 849 | Curt Wilkerson | .10 | .05 |
| ❑ 850 | Alan Trammell | .25 | .11 |
| ❑ 851 | Rex Hudler | .10 | .05 |
| ❑ 852 | Mike Walkden RC | .10 | .05 |
| ❑ 853 | Kevin Ward | .10 | .05 |
| ❑ 854 | Tim Naehring | .10 | .05 |
| ❑ 855 | Bill Swift | .10 | .05 |
| ❑ 856 | Damon Berryhill | .10 | .05 |
| ❑ 857 | Mark Eichhorn | .10 | .05 |
| ❑ 858 | Hector Villanueva | .10 | .05 |
| ❑ 859 | Jose Lind | .10 | .05 |
| ❑ 860 | Dennis Martinez | .20 | .09 |
| ❑ 861 | Bill Krueger | .10 | .05 |
| ❑ 862 | Mike Kingery | .10 | .05 |
| ❑ 863 | Jeff Innis | .10 | .05 |
| ❑ 864 | Derek Lilliquist | .10 | .05 |
| ❑ 865 | Reggie Sanders | .10 | .05 |
| ❑ 866 | Ramon Garcia | .10 | .05 |
| ❑ 867 | Bruce Ruffin | .10 | .05 |
| ❑ 868 | Dickie Thon | .10 | .05 |
| ❑ 869 | Melido Perez | .10 | .05 |
| ❑ 870 | Ruben Amaro | .10 | .05 |
| ❑ 871 | Alan Mills | .10 | .05 |
| ❑ 872 | Matt Sinatro | .10 | .05 |
| ❑ 873 | Eddie Zosky | .10 | .05 |
| ❑ 874 | Pete Incaviglia | .10 | .05 |
| ❑ 875 | Tom Candiotti | .10 | .05 |
| ❑ 876 | Bob Patterson | .10 | .05 |
| ❑ 877 | Neal Heaton | .10 | .05 |
| ❑ 878 | Terrel Hansen RC | .10 | .05 |
| ❑ 879 | Dave Eiland | .10 | .05 |
| ❑ 880 | Von Hayes | .10 | .05 |
| ❑ 881 | Tim Scott | .10 | .05 |
| ❑ 882 | Otis Nixon | .10 | .05 |
| ❑ 883 | Herm Winningham | .10 | .05 |
| ❑ 884 | Dion James | .10 | .05 |
| ❑ 885 | Dave Wainhouse | .10 | .05 |
| ❑ 886 | Frank DiPino | .10 | .05 |
| ❑ 887 | Dennis Cook | .10 | .05 |
| ❑ 888 | Jose Mesa | .10 | .05 |
| ❑ 889 | Mark Leiter | .10 | .05 |
| ❑ 890 | Willie Randolph | .20 | .09 |
| ❑ 891 | Craig Colbert | .10 | .05 |
| ❑ 892 | Dwayne Henry | .10 | .05 |
| ❑ 893 | Jim Lindeman | .10 | .05 |
| ❑ 894 | Charlie Hough | .20 | .09 |
| ❑ 895 | Gil Heredia RC | .10 | .05 |
| ❑ 896 | Scott Chiamparino | .10 | .05 |
| ❑ 897 | Lance Blankenship | .10 | .05 |
| ❑ 898 | Checklist 601-700 | .10 | .05 |
| ❑ 899 | Checklist 701-800 | .10 | .05 |
| ❑ 900 | Checklist 801-900 | .10 | .05 |

## 1993 Stadium Club Murphy

| | MINT | NRMT |
|---|---|---|
| COMP.FACT.SET (212) | 100.00 | 45.00 |
| COMPLETE SET (200) | 25.00 | 11.00 |

| No. | Player | MINT | NRMT |
|---|---|---|---|
| ❑ 1 | Dave Winfield | .60 | .25 |
| ❑ 2 | Juan Guzman | .15 | .07 |
| ❑ 3 | Tony Gwynn | 1.25 | .55 |
| ❑ 4 | Chris Roberts | .15 | .07 |
| ❑ 5 | Benny Santiago | .15 | .07 |
| ❑ 6 | Sherard Clinkscales RC | .15 | .07 |
| ❑ 7 | Jon Nunnally RC | .30 | .14 |
| ❑ 8 | Chuck Knoblauch | .30 | .14 |
| ❑ 9 | Bob Wolcott RC | .30 | .14 |
| ❑ 10 | Steve Rodriguez | .15 | .07 |
| ❑ 11 | Mark Williams RC | .15 | .07 |
| ❑ 12 | Danny Clyburn RC | .15 | .07 |
| ❑ 13 | Darren Dreifort | .15 | .07 |
| ❑ 14 | Andy Van Slyke | .30 | .14 |
| ❑ 15 | Wade Boggs | .75 | .35 |
| ❑ 16 | Scott Patton RC | .15 | .07 |
| ❑ 17 | Gary Sheffield | .60 | .25 |
| ❑ 18 | Ron Villone | .15 | .07 |
| ❑ 19 | Roberto Alomar | .60 | .25 |
| ❑ 20 | Marc Valdes | .15 | .07 |
| ❑ 21 | Daron Kirkreit | .15 | .07 |
| ❑ 22 | Jeff Granger | .15 | .07 |
| ❑ 23 | Levon Largusa RC | .15 | .07 |
| ❑ 24 | Jimmy Key | .30 | .14 |
| ❑ 25 | Kevin Pearson RC | .15 | .07 |
| ❑ 26 | Michael Moore RC | .15 | .07 |
| ❑ 27 | Preston Wilson RC | 8.00 | 3.60 |
| ❑ 28 | Kirby Puckett | 1.50 | .70 |
| ❑ 29 | Tim Crabtree RC | .15 | .07 |
| ❑ 30 | Bip Roberts | .15 | .07 |
| ❑ 31 | Kelly Gruber | .15 | .07 |
| ❑ 32 | Tony Fernandez | .15 | .07 |
| ❑ 33 | Jason Angel RC | .15 | .07 |
| ❑ 34 | Calvin Murray | .15 | .07 |
| ❑ 35 | Chad McConnell | .15 | .07 |
| ❑ 36 | Jason Moler | .15 | .07 |
| ❑ 37 | Mark Lemke | .15 | .07 |
| ❑ 38 | Tom Knauss RC | .15 | .07 |
| ❑ 39 | Larry Mitchell RC | .15 | .07 |
| ❑ 40 | Doug Mirabelli RC | .15 | .07 |
| ❑ 41 | Everett Stull II RC | .15 | .07 |
| ❑ 42 | Chris Wimmer | .15 | .07 |
| ❑ 43 | Dan Serafini RC | .15 | .07 |
| ❑ 44 | Ryne Sandberg | .75 | .35 |
| ❑ 45 | Steve Lyons RC | .15 | .07 |
| ❑ 46 | Ryan Freeburg RC | .15 | .07 |
| ❑ 47 | Ruben Sierra | .15 | .07 |
| ❑ 48 | David Mysel RC | .15 | .07 |
| ❑ 49 | Joe Hamilton RC | .15 | .07 |
| ❑ 50 | Steve Rodriguez | .15 | .07 |
| ❑ 51 | Tim Wakefield | .15 | .07 |
| ❑ 52 | Scott Gentile RC | .15 | .07 |
| ❑ 53 | Doug Jones | .15 | .07 |
| ❑ 54 | Willie Brown RC | .15 | .07 |
| ❑ 55 | Chad Mottola RC | .15 | .07 |
| ❑ 56 | Ken Griffey Jr. | 2.50 | 1.10 |
| ❑ 57 | Jon Lieber RC | 1.00 | .45 |
| ❑ 58 | Dennis Martinez | .30 | .14 |
| ❑ 59 | Joe Petcka RC | .15 | .07 |
| ❑ 60 | Benji Simonton RC | .15 | .07 |
| ❑ 61 | Brett Backlund RC | .15 | .07 |
| ❑ 62 | Damon Berryhill | .15 | .07 |
| ❑ 63 | Juan Guzman | .15 | .07 |
| ❑ 64 | Doug Hecker RC | .15 | .07 |
| ❑ 65 | Jamie Arnold RC | .15 | .07 |
| ❑ 66 | Bob Tewksbury | .15 | .07 |
| ❑ 67 | Tim Leger RC | .15 | .07 |
| ❑ 68 | Todd Etler RC | .15 | .07 |
| ❑ 69 | Lloyd McClendon | .15 | .07 |
| ❑ 70 | Kurt Ehmann RC | .15 | .07 |
| ❑ 71 | Rick Magdaleno RC | .15 | .07 |
| ❑ 72 | Tom Pagnozzi | .15 | .07 |
| ❑ 73 | Jeffrey Hammonds | .30 | .14 |
| ❑ 74 | Joe Carter | .30 | .14 |
| ❑ 75 | Chris Holt RC | .15 | .07 |
| ❑ 76 | Charles Johnson | 1.00 | .45 |
| ❑ 77 | Bob Walk | .15 | .07 |
| ❑ 78 | Fred McGriff | .40 | .18 |
| ❑ 79 | Tom Evans RC | .30 | .14 |
| ❑ 80 | Scott Klingenbeck RC | .15 | .07 |
| ❑ 81 | Chad McConnell | .15 | .07 |
| ❑ 82 | Chris Eddy RC | .15 | .07 |
| ❑ 83 | Phil Nevin | .30 | .14 |
| ❑ 84 | John Kruk | .30 | .14 |
| ❑ 85 | Tony Sheffield RC | .15 | .07 |
| ❑ 86 | John Smoltz | .30 | .14 |
| ❑ 87 | Trevor Humphry RC | .15 | .07 |
| ❑ 88 | Charles Nagy | .15 | .07 |
| ❑ 89 | Sean Runyan RC | .15 | .07 |
| ❑ 90 | Mike Gulan RC | .15 | .07 |
| ❑ 91 | Darren Daulton | .30 | .14 |
| ❑ 92 | Otis Nixon | .15 | .07 |
| ❑ 93 | Nomar Garciaparra | 25.00 | 11.00 |
| ❑ 94 | Larry Walker | .30 | .14 |
| ❑ 95 | Hut Smith RC | .15 | .07 |
| ❑ 96 | Rick Helling | .30 | .14 |
| ❑ 97 | Roger Clemens | 1.25 | .55 |
| ❑ 98 | Ron Gant | .30 | .14 |
| ❑ 99 | Kenny Felder RC | .15 | .07 |
| ❑ 100 | Steve Murphy RC | .15 | .07 |
| ❑ 101 | Mike Smith RC | .15 | .07 |
| ❑ 102 | Terry Pendleton | .30 | .14 |
| ❑ 103 | Tim Davis | .15 | .07 |
| ❑ 104 | Jeff Patzke RC | .30 | .14 |
| ❑ 105 | Craig Wilson | .15 | .07 |
| ❑ 106 | Tom Glavine | .40 | .18 |
| ❑ 107 | Mark Langston | .15 | .07 |
| ❑ 108 | Mark Thompson RC | .15 | .07 |
| ❑ 109 | Eric Owens RC | 4.00 | 1.80 |
| ❑ 110 | Keith Johnson RC | .15 | .07 |
| ❑ 111 | Robin Ventura | .30 | .14 |
| ❑ 112 | Ed Sprague | .15 | .07 |
| ❑ 113 | Jeff Schmidt RC | .15 | .07 |
| ❑ 114 | Don Wengert RC | .15 | .07 |
| ❑ 115 | Craig Biggio | .40 | .18 |
| ❑ 116 | Kenny Carlyle RC | .15 | .07 |
| ❑ 117 | Derek Jeter RC | 50.00 | 22.00 |
| ❑ 118 | Manuel Lee | .15 | .07 |
| ❑ 119 | Jeff Haas RC | .15 | .07 |
| ❑ 120 | Roger Bailey RC | .15 | .07 |
| ❑ 121 | Sean Lowe RC | .15 | .07 |
| ❑ 122 | Rick Aguilera | .15 | .07 |
| ❑ 123 | Sandy Alomar Jr. | .30 | .14 |
| ❑ 124 | Derek Wallace RC | .15 | .07 |
| ❑ 125 | B.J. Wallace | .15 | .07 |
| ❑ 126 | Greg Maddux | 1.50 | .70 |
| ❑ 127 | Tim Moore RC | .15 | .07 |
| ❑ 128 | Lee Smith | .30 | .14 |
| ❑ 129 | Todd Steverson RC | .15 | .07 |
| ❑ 130 | Chris Widger RC | 1.00 | .45 |
| ❑ 131 | Paul Molitor | .60 | .25 |
| ❑ 132 | Chris Smith RC | .15 | .07 |
| ❑ 133 | Chris Gomez RC | .30 | .14 |
| ❑ 134 | Jimmy Baron RC | .15 | .07 |
| ❑ 135 | John Smoltz | .30 | .14 |
| ❑ 136 | Pat Borders | .15 | .07 |
| ❑ 137 | Donnie Leshnock | .15 | .07 |
| ❑ 138 | Gus Gandarillos RC | .15 | .07 |
| ❑ 139 | Will Clark | .60 | .25 |
| ❑ 140 | Ryan Luzinski RC | .15 | .07 |
| ❑ 141 | Cal Ripken | 2.50 | 1.10 |
| ❑ 142 | B.J. Wallace | .15 | .07 |
| ❑ 143 | Trey Beamon RC | .30 | .14 |
| ❑ 144 | Norm Charlton | .15 | .07 |
| ❑ 145 | Mike Mussina | .60 | .25 |
| ❑ 146 | Billy Owens RC | .15 | .07 |
| ❑ 147 | Ozzie Smith | .75 | .35 |
| ❑ 148 | Jason Kendall RC | 10.00 | 4.50 |
| ❑ 149 | Mike Matthews RC | .15 | .07 |
| ❑ 150 | David Spykstra RC | .15 | .07 |
| ❑ 151 | Benji Grigsby RC | .15 | .07 |
| ❑ 152 | Sean Smith RC | .15 | .07 |
| ❑ 153 | Mark McGwire | 2.50 | 1.10 |
| ❑ 154 | David Cone | .30 | .14 |
| ❑ 155 | Shon Walker RC | .15 | .07 |
| ❑ 156 | Jason Giambi | 1.00 | .45 |
| ❑ 157 | Jack McDowell | .15 | .07 |
| ❑ 158 | Paxton Briley RC | .15 | .07 |
| ❑ 159 | Edgar Martinez | .40 | .18 |
| ❑ 160 | Brian Sackinsky RC | .15 | .07 |
| ❑ 161 | Barry Bonds | 1.00 | .45 |
| ❑ 162 | Roberto Kelly | .15 | .07 |
| ❑ 163 | Jeff Alkire | .15 | .07 |
| ❑ 164 | Mike Sharperson | .15 | .07 |
| ❑ 165 | Jamie Taylor RC | .15 | .07 |
| ❑ 166 | John Saffer RC | .15 | .07 |
| ❑ 167 | Jerry Browne | .15 | .07 |
| ❑ 168 | Travis Fryman | .30 | .14 |
| ❑ 169 | Brady Anderson | .30 | .14 |
| ❑ 170 | Chris Roberts | .15 | .07 |
| ❑ 171 | Lloyd Peever RC | .15 | .07 |
| ❑ 172 | Francisco Cabrera | .15 | .07 |
| ❑ 173 | Ramiro Martinez RC | .15 | .07 |

| | No. | Player | Mint | Nrmt |
|---|---|---|---|---|
| ❑ | 174 | Jeff Alkire | .15 | .07 |
| ❑ | 175 | Ivan Rodriguez | .75 | .35 |
| ❑ | 176 | Kevin Brown | .40 | .18 |
| ❑ | 177 | Chad Roper RC | .15 | .07 |
| ❑ | 178 | Rod Henderson RC | .15 | .07 |
| ❑ | 179 | Dennis Eckersley | .30 | .14 |
| ❑ | 180 | Shannon Stewart RC | 8.00 | 3.60 |
| ❑ | 181 | DeShawn Warren RC | .15 | .07 |
| ❑ | 182 | Lonnie Smith | .15 | .07 |
| ❑ | 183 | Willie Adams | .15 | .07 |
| ❑ | 184 | Jeff Montgomery | .30 | .14 |
| ❑ | 185 | Damon Hollins RC | .15 | .07 |
| ❑ | 186 | Byron Mathews RC | .15 | .07 |
| ❑ | 187 | Harold Baines | .30 | .14 |
| ❑ | 188 | Rick Greene | .15 | .07 |
| ❑ | 189 | Carlos Baerga | .15 | .07 |
| ❑ | 190 | Brandon Cromer RC | .15 | .07 |
| ❑ | 191 | Roberto Alomar | .60 | .25 |
| ❑ | 192 | Rich Ireland RC | .15 | .07 |
| ❑ | 193 | Steve Montgomery RC | .15 | .07 |
| ❑ | 194 | Brant Brown RC | .30 | .14 |
| ❑ | 195 | Ritchie Moody RC | .15 | .07 |
| ❑ | 196 | Michael Tucker | .60 | .25 |
| ❑ | 197 | Jason Varitek | 1.50 | .70 |
| ❑ | 198 | David Manning RC | .15 | .07 |
| ❑ | 199 | Marquis Riley RC | .15 | .07 |
| ❑ | 200 | Jason Giambi | 1.00 | .45 |

## 1993 Stadium Club

| | MINT | NRMT |
|---|---|---|
| COMPLETE SET (750) | 50.00 | 22.00 |
| COMPLETE SERIES 1 (300) | 15.00 | 6.75 |
| COMPLETE SERIES 2 (300) | 20.00 | 9.00 |
| COMPLETE SERIES 3 (150) | 15.00 | 6.75 |
| COMMON CARD (1-750) | .15 | .07 |

| | No. | Player | Mint | Nrmt |
|---|---|---|---|---|
| ❑ | 1 | Pat Borders | .15 | .07 |
| ❑ | 2 | Greg Maddux | 1.50 | .70 |
| ❑ | 3 | Daryl Boston | .15 | .07 |
| ❑ | 4 | Bob Ayrault | .15 | .07 |
| ❑ | 5 | Tony Phillips IF | .15 | .07 |
| ❑ | 6 | Damion Easley | .15 | .07 |
| ❑ | 7 | Kip Gross | .15 | .07 |
| ❑ | 8 | Jim Thome | .40 | .18 |
| ❑ | 9 | Tim Belcher | .15 | .07 |
| ❑ | 10 | Gary Wayne | .15 | .07 |
| ❑ | 11 | Sam Militello | .15 | .07 |
| ❑ | 12 | Mike Magnante | .15 | .07 |
| ❑ | 13 | Tim Wakefield | .15 | .07 |
| ❑ | 14 | Tim Hulett | .15 | .07 |
| ❑ | 15 | Rheal Cormier | .15 | .07 |
| ❑ | 16 | Juan Guerrero | .15 | .07 |
| ❑ | 17 | Rich Gossage | .30 | .14 |
| ❑ | 18 | Tim Laker RC | .15 | .07 |
| ❑ | 19 | Darrin Jackson | .15 | .07 |
| ❑ | 20 | Jack Clark | .15 | .07 |
| ❑ | 21 | Roberto Hernandez | .15 | .07 |
| ❑ | 22 | Dean Palmer | .30 | .14 |
| ❑ | 23 | Harold Reynolds | .15 | .07 |
| ❑ | 24 | Dan Plesac | .15 | .07 |
| ❑ | 25 | Brent Mayne | .15 | .07 |
| ❑ | 26 | Pat Hentgen | .15 | .07 |
| ❑ | 27 | Luis Sojo | .15 | .07 |
| ❑ | 28 | Ron Gant | .30 | .14 |
| ❑ | 29 | Paul Gibson | .15 | .07 |
| ❑ | 30 | Bip Roberts | .15 | .07 |
| ❑ | 31 | Mickey Tettleton | .15 | .07 |
| ❑ | 32 | Randy Velarde | .15 | .07 |
| ❑ | 33 | Brian McRae | .15 | .07 |
| ❑ | 34 | Wes Chamberlain | .15 | .07 |
| ❑ | 35 | Wayne Kirby | .15 | .07 |
| ❑ | 36 | Rey Sanchez | .15 | .07 |
| ❑ | 37 | Jesse Orosco | .15 | .07 |
| ❑ | 38 | Mike Stanton | .15 | .07 |
| ❑ | 39 | Royce Clayton | .15 | .07 |
| ❑ | 40 | Cal Ripken UER (Place of birth Havre de Grave; should be Havre de Grace) | 2.50 | 1.10 |
| ❑ | 41 | John Dopson | .15 | .07 |
| ❑ | 42 | Gene Larkin | .15 | .07 |
| ❑ | 43 | Tim Raines | .30 | .14 |
| ❑ | 44 | Randy Myers | .30 | .14 |
| ❑ | 45 | Clay Parker | .15 | .07 |
| ❑ | 46 | Mike Scioscia | .15 | .07 |
| ❑ | 47 | Pete Incaviglia | .15 | .07 |
| ❑ | 48 | Todd Van Poppel | .15 | .07 |
| ❑ | 49 | Ray Lankford | .40 | .18 |
| ❑ | 50 | Eddie Murray | .60 | .25 |
| ❑ | 51 | Barry Bonds COR | 1.00 | .45 |
| ❑ | 51A | Barry Bonds ERR (Missing four stars over name to indicate NL MVP) | .60 | .25 |
| ❑ | 52 | Gary Thurman | .15 | .07 |
| ❑ | 53 | Bob Wickman | .15 | .07 |
| ❑ | 54 | Joey Cora | .15 | .07 |
| ❑ | 55 | Kenny Rogers | .15 | .07 |
| ❑ | 56 | Mike Devereaux | .15 | .07 |
| ❑ | 57 | Kevin Seitzer | .15 | .07 |
| ❑ | 58 | Rafael Belliard | .15 | .07 |
| ❑ | 59 | David Wells | .30 | .14 |
| ❑ | 60 | Mark Clark | .15 | .07 |
| ❑ | 61 | Carlos Baerga | .15 | .07 |
| ❑ | 62 | Scott Brosius | .30 | .14 |
| ❑ | 63 | Jeff Grotewold | .15 | .07 |
| ❑ | 64 | Rick Wrona | .15 | .07 |
| ❑ | 65 | Kurt Knudsen | .15 | .07 |
| ❑ | 66 | Lloyd McClendon | .15 | .07 |
| ❑ | 67 | Omar Vizquel | .30 | .14 |
| ❑ | 68 | Jose Vizcaino | .15 | .07 |
| ❑ | 69 | Rob Ducey | .15 | .07 |
| ❑ | 70 | Casey Candaele | .15 | .07 |
| ❑ | 71 | Ramon Martinez | .15 | .07 |
| ❑ | 72 | Todd Hundley | .15 | .07 |
| ❑ | 73 | John Marzano | .15 | .07 |
| ❑ | 74 | Derek Parks | .15 | .07 |
| ❑ | 75 | Jack McDowell | .15 | .07 |
| ❑ | 76 | Tim Scott | .15 | .07 |
| ❑ | 77 | Mike Mussina | .60 | .25 |
| ❑ | 78 | Delino DeShields | .30 | .14 |
| ❑ | 79 | Chris Bosio | .15 | .07 |
| ❑ | 80 | Mike Bordick | .15 | .07 |
| ❑ | 81 | Rod Beck | .15 | .07 |
| ❑ | 82 | Ted Power | .15 | .07 |
| ❑ | 83 | John Kruk | .30 | .14 |
| ❑ | 84 | Steve Shifflett | .15 | .07 |
| ❑ | 85 | Danny Tartabull | .15 | .07 |
| ❑ | 86 | Mike Greenwell | .15 | .07 |
| ❑ | 87 | Jose Melendez | .15 | .07 |
| ❑ | 88 | Craig Wilson | .15 | .07 |
| ❑ | 89 | Melvin Nieves | .15 | .07 |
| ❑ | 90 | Ed Sprague | .15 | .07 |
| ❑ | 91 | Willie McGee | .30 | .14 |
| ❑ | 92 | Joe Orsulak | .15 | .07 |
| ❑ | 93 | Jeff King | .15 | .07 |
| ❑ | 94 | Dan Pasqua | .15 | .07 |
| ❑ | 95 | Brian Harper | .15 | .07 |
| ❑ | 96 | Joe Oliver | .15 | .07 |
| ❑ | 97 | Shane Turner | .15 | .07 |
| ❑ | 98 | Lenny Harris | .15 | .07 |
| ❑ | 99 | Jeff Parrett | .15 | .07 |
| ❑ | 100 | Luis Polonia | .15 | .07 |
| ❑ | 101 | Kent Bottenfield | .15 | .07 |
| ❑ | 102 | Albert Belle | .40 | .18 |
| ❑ | 103 | Mike Maddux | .15 | .07 |
| ❑ | 104 | Randy Tomlin | .15 | .07 |
| ❑ | 105 | Andy Stankiewicz | .15 | .07 |
| ❑ | 106 | Rico Rossy | .15 | .07 |
| ❑ | 107 | Joe Hesketh | .15 | .07 |
| ❑ | 108 | Dennis Powell | .15 | .07 |
| ❑ | 109 | Derrick May | .15 | .07 |
| ❑ | 110 | Pete Harnisch | .15 | .07 |
| ❑ | 111 | Kent Mercker | .15 | .07 |
| ❑ | 112 | Scott Fletcher | .15 | .07 |
| ❑ | 113 | Rex Hudler | .15 | .07 |
| ❑ | 114 | Chico Walker | .15 | .07 |
| ❑ | 115 | Rafael Palmeiro | .60 | .25 |
| ❑ | 116 | Mark Leiter | .15 | .07 |
| ❑ | 117 | Pedro Munoz | .15 | .07 |
| ❑ | 118 | Jim Bullinger | .15 | .07 |
| ❑ | 119 | Ivan Calderon | .15 | .07 |
| ❑ | 120 | Mike Timlin | .15 | .07 |
| ❑ | 121 | Rene Gonzales | .15 | .07 |
| ❑ | 122 | Greg Vaughn | .30 | .14 |
| ❑ | 123 | Mike Flanagan | .15 | .07 |
| ❑ | 124 | Mike Hartley | .15 | .07 |
| ❑ | 125 | Jeff Montgomery | .30 | .14 |
| ❑ | 126 | Mike Gallego | .15 | .07 |
| ❑ | 127 | Don Slaught | .15 | .07 |
| ❑ | 128 | Charlie O'Brien | .15 | .07 |
| ❑ | 129 | Jose Offerman (Can be found with hometown missing on back) | .15 | .07 |
| ❑ | 130 | Mark Wohlers | .15 | .07 |
| ❑ | 131 | Eric Fox | .15 | .07 |
| ❑ | 132 | Doug Strange | .15 | .07 |
| ❑ | 133 | Jeff Frye | .15 | .07 |
| ❑ | 134 | Wade Boggs UER (Redundantly lists lefty breakdown) | .75 | .35 |
| ❑ | 135 | Lou Whitaker | .30 | .14 |
| ❑ | 136 | Craig Grebeck | .15 | .07 |
| ❑ | 137 | Rich Rodriguez | .15 | .07 |
| ❑ | 138 | Jay Bell | .30 | .14 |
| ❑ | 139 | Felix Fermin | .15 | .07 |
| ❑ | 140 | Dennis Martinez | .30 | .14 |
| ❑ | 141 | Eric Anthony | .15 | .07 |
| ❑ | 142 | Roberto Alomar | .60 | .25 |
| ❑ | 143 | Darren Lewis | .15 | .07 |
| ❑ | 144 | Mike Blowers | .15 | .07 |
| ❑ | 145 | Scott Bankhead | .15 | .07 |
| ❑ | 146 | Jeff Reboulet | .15 | .07 |
| ❑ | 147 | Frank Viola | .15 | .07 |
| ❑ | 148 | Bill Pecota | .15 | .07 |
| ❑ | 149 | Carlos Hernandez | .15 | .07 |
| ❑ | 150 | Bobby Witt | .15 | .07 |
| ❑ | 151 | Sid Bream | .15 | .07 |
| ❑ | 152 | Todd Zeile | .15 | .07 |
| ❑ | 153 | Dennis Cook | .15 | .07 |
| ❑ | 154 | Brian Bohanon | .15 | .07 |
| ❑ | 155 | Pat Kelly | .15 | .07 |
| ❑ | 156 | Milt Cuyler | .15 | .07 |
| ❑ | 157 | Juan Bell | .15 | .07 |
| ❑ | 158 | Randy Milligan | .15 | .07 |
| ❑ | 159 | Mark Gardner | .15 | .07 |
| ❑ | 160 | Pat Tabler | .15 | .07 |
| ❑ | 161 | Jeff Reardon | .30 | .14 |
| ❑ | 162 | Ken Patterson | .15 | .07 |
| ❑ | 163 | Bobby Bonilla | .30 | .14 |
| ❑ | 164 | Tony Pena | .15 | .07 |
| ❑ | 165 | Greg Swindell | .15 | .07 |
| ❑ | 166 | Kirk McCaskill | .15 | .07 |
| ❑ | 167 | Doug Drabek | .15 | .07 |
| ❑ | 168 | Franklin Stubbs | .15 | .07 |
| ❑ | 169 | Ron Tingley | .15 | .07 |
| ❑ | 170 | Willie Banks | .15 | .07 |
| ❑ | 171 | Sergio Valdez | .15 | .07 |
| ❑ | 172 | Mark Lemke | .15 | .07 |
| ❑ | 173 | Robin Yount | .40 | .18 |
| ❑ | 174 | Storm Davis | .15 | .07 |
| ❑ | 175 | Dan Walters | .15 | .07 |
| ❑ | 176 | Steve Farr | .15 | .07 |
| ❑ | 177 | Curt Wilkerson | .15 | .07 |
| ❑ | 178 | Luis Alicea | .15 | .07 |
| ❑ | 179 | Russ Swan | .15 | .07 |
| ❑ | 180 | Mitch Williams | .15 | .07 |
| ❑ | 181 | Wilson Alvarez | .15 | .07 |
| ❑ | 182 | Carl Willis | .15 | .07 |
| ❑ | 183 | Craig Biggio | .40 | .18 |
| ❑ | 184 | Sean Berry | .15 | .07 |
| ❑ | 185 | Trevor Wilson | .15 | .07 |
| ❑ | 186 | Jeff Tackett | .15 | .07 |
| ❑ | 187 | Ellis Burks | .30 | .14 |
| ❑ | 188 | Jeff Branson | .15 | .07 |
| ❑ | 189 | Matt Nokes | .15 | .07 |
| ❑ | 190 | John Smiley | .15 | .07 |
| ❑ | 191 | Danny Gladden | .15 | .07 |
| ❑ | 192 | Mike Boddicker | .15 | .07 |
| ❑ | 193 | Roger Pavlik | .15 | .07 |

| | | | |
|---|---|---|---|
| ❑ 194 | Paul Sorrento | .15 | .07 |
| ❑ 195 | Vince Coleman | .15 | .07 |
| ❑ 196 | Gary DiSarcina | .15 | .07 |
| ❑ 197 | Rafael Bournigal | .15 | .07 |
| ❑ 198 | Mike Schooler | .15 | .07 |
| ❑ 199 | Scott Ruskin | .15 | .07 |
| ❑ 200 | Frank Thomas | 1.25 | .55 |
| ❑ 201 | Kyle Abbott | .15 | .07 |
| ❑ 202 | Mike Perez | .15 | .07 |
| ❑ 203 | Andre Dawson | .40 | .18 |
| ❑ 204 | Bill Swift | .15 | .07 |
| ❑ 205 | Alejandro Pena | .15 | .07 |
| ❑ 206 | Dave Winfield | .60 | .25 |
| ❑ 207 | Andujar Cedeno | .15 | .07 |
| ❑ 208 | Terry Steinbach | .15 | .07 |
| ❑ 209 | Chris Hammond | .15 | .07 |
| ❑ 210 | Todd Burns | .15 | .07 |
| ❑ 211 | Hipolito Pichardo | .15 | .07 |
| ❑ 212 | John Kiely | .15 | .07 |
| ❑ 213 | Tim Teufel | .15 | .07 |
| ❑ 214 | Lee Guetterman | .15 | .07 |
| ❑ 215 | Geronimo Pena | .15 | .07 |
| ❑ 216 | Brett Butler | .30 | .14 |
| ❑ 217 | Bryan Hickerson | .15 | .07 |
| ❑ 218 | Rick Trlicek | .15 | .07 |
| ❑ 219 | Lee Stevens | .30 | .14 |
| ❑ 220 | Roger Clemens | 1.25 | .55 |
| ❑ 221 | Carlton Fisk | .60 | .25 |
| ❑ 222 | Chili Davis | .30 | .14 |
| ❑ 223 | Walt Terrell | .15 | .07 |
| ❑ 224 | Jim Eisenreich | .15 | .07 |
| ❑ 225 | Ricky Bones | .15 | .07 |
| ❑ 226 | Henry Rodriguez | .15 | .07 |
| ❑ 227 | Ken Hill | .15 | .07 |
| ❑ 228 | Rick Wilkins | .15 | .07 |
| ❑ 229 | Ricky Jordan | .15 | .07 |
| ❑ 230 | Bernard Gilkey | .15 | .07 |
| ❑ 231 | Tim Fortugno | .15 | .07 |
| ❑ 232 | Geno Petralli | .15 | .07 |
| ❑ 233 | Jose Rijo | .15 | .07 |
| ❑ 234 | Jim Leyritz | .15 | .07 |
| ❑ 235 | Kevin Campbell | .15 | .07 |
| ❑ 236 | Al Osuna | .15 | .07 |
| ❑ 237 | Pete Smith | .15 | .07 |
| ❑ 238 | Pete Schourek | .15 | .07 |
| ❑ 239 | Moises Alou | .30 | .14 |
| ❑ 240 | Donn Pall | .15 | .07 |
| ❑ 241 | Denny Neagle | .30 | .14 |
| ❑ 242 | Dan Peltier | .15 | .07 |
| ❑ 243 | Scott Scudder | .15 | .07 |
| ❑ 244 | Juan Guzman | .15 | .07 |
| ❑ 245 | Dave Burba | .15 | .07 |
| ❑ 246 | Rick Sutcliffe | .30 | .14 |
| ❑ 247 | Tony Fossas | .15 | .07 |
| ❑ 248 | Mike Munoz | .15 | .07 |
| ❑ 249 | Tim Salmon | .30 | .14 |
| ❑ 250 | Rob Murphy | .15 | .07 |
| ❑ 251 | Roger McDowell | .15 | .07 |
| ❑ 252 | Lance Parrish | .15 | .07 |
| ❑ 253 | Cliff Brantley | .15 | .07 |
| ❑ 254 | Scott Leius | .15 | .07 |
| ❑ 255 | Carlos Martinez | .15 | .07 |
| ❑ 256 | Vince Horsman | .15 | .07 |
| ❑ 257 | Oscar Azocar | .15 | .07 |
| ❑ 258 | Craig Shipley | .15 | .07 |
| ❑ 259 | Ben McDonald | .15 | .07 |
| ❑ 260 | Jeff Brantley | .15 | .07 |
| ❑ 261 | Damon Berryhill | .15 | .07 |
| ❑ 262 | Joe Grahe | .15 | .07 |
| ❑ 263 | Dave Hansen | .15 | .07 |
| ❑ 264 | Rich Amaral | .15 | .07 |
| ❑ 265 | Tim Pugh RC | .15 | .07 |
| ❑ 266 | Dion James | .15 | .07 |
| ❑ 267 | Frank Tanana | .15 | .07 |
| ❑ 268 | Stan Belinda | .15 | .07 |
| ❑ 269 | Jeff Kent | .60 | .25 |
| ❑ 270 | Bruce Ruffin | .15 | .07 |
| ❑ 271 | Xavier Hernandez | .15 | .07 |
| ❑ 272 | Darrin Fletcher | .15 | .07 |
| ❑ 273 | Tino Martinez | .30 | .14 |
| ❑ 274 | Benny Santiago | .15 | .07 |
| ❑ 275 | Scott Radinsky | .15 | .07 |
| ❑ 276 | Mariano Duncan | .15 | .07 |
| ❑ 277 | Kenny Lofton | .30 | .14 |
| ❑ 278 | Dwight Smith | .15 | .07 |
| ❑ 279 | Joe Carter | .30 | .14 |
| ❑ 280 | Tim Jones | .15 | .07 |
| ❑ 281 | Jeff Huson | .15 | .07 |
| ❑ 282 | Phil Plantier | .15 | .07 |
| ❑ 283 | Kirby Puckett | 1.50 | .70 |
| ❑ 284 | Johnny Guzman | .15 | .07 |
| ❑ 285 | Mike Morgan | .15 | .07 |
| ❑ 286 | Chris Sabo | .15 | .07 |
| ❑ 287 | Matt Williams | .40 | .18 |
| ❑ 288 | Checklist 1-100 | .15 | .07 |
| ❑ 289 | Checklist 101-200 | .15 | .07 |
| ❑ 290 | Checklist 201-300 | .15 | .07 |
| ❑ 291 | Dennis Eckersley MC | .15 | .07 |
| ❑ 292 | Eric Karros MC | .15 | .07 |
| ❑ 293 | Pat Listach MC | .15 | .07 |
| ❑ 294 | Andy Van Slyke MC | .15 | .07 |
| ❑ 295 | Robin Ventura MC | .30 | .14 |
| ❑ 296 | Tom Glavine MC | .30 | .14 |
| ❑ 297 | Juan Gonzalez MC UER (Misspelled Gonzales) | .30 | .14 |
| ❑ 298 | Travis Fryman MC | .15 | .07 |
| ❑ 299 | Larry Walker MC | .30 | .14 |
| ❑ 300 | Gary Sheffield MC | .30 | .14 |
| ❑ 301 | Chuck Finley | .30 | .14 |
| ❑ 302 | Luis Gonzalez | .30 | .14 |
| ❑ 303 | Darryl Hamilton | .15 | .07 |
| ❑ 304 | Bien Figueroa | .15 | .07 |
| ❑ 305 | Ron Darling | .15 | .07 |
| ❑ 306 | Jonathan Hurst | .15 | .07 |
| ❑ 307 | Mike Sharperson | .15 | .07 |
| ❑ 308 | Mike Christopher | .15 | .07 |
| ❑ 309 | Marvin Freeman | .15 | .07 |
| ❑ 310 | Jay Buhner | .30 | .14 |
| ❑ 311 | Butch Henry | .15 | .07 |
| ❑ 312 | Greg W. Harris | .15 | .07 |
| ❑ 313 | Darren Daulton | .30 | .14 |
| ❑ 314 | Chuck Knoblauch | .30 | .14 |
| ❑ 315 | Greg A. Harris | .15 | .07 |
| ❑ 316 | John Franco | .30 | .14 |
| ❑ 317 | John Wehner | .15 | .07 |
| ❑ 318 | Donald Harris | .15 | .07 |
| ❑ 319 | Benny Santiago | .15 | .07 |
| ❑ 320 | Larry Walker | .30 | .14 |
| ❑ 321 | Randy Knorr | .15 | .07 |
| ❑ 322 | Ramon Martinez RC | .30 | .14 |
| ❑ 323 | Mike Stanley | .15 | .07 |
| ❑ 324 | Bill Wegman | .15 | .07 |
| ❑ 325 | Tom Candiotti | .15 | .07 |
| ❑ 326 | Glenn Davis | .15 | .07 |
| ❑ 327 | Chuck Crim | .15 | .07 |
| ❑ 328 | Scott Livingstone | .15 | .07 |
| ❑ 329 | Eddie Taubensee | .15 | .07 |
| ❑ 330 | George Bell | .15 | .07 |
| ❑ 331 | Edgar Martinez | .40 | .18 |
| ❑ 332 | Paul Assenmacher | .15 | .07 |
| ❑ 333 | Steve Hosey | .15 | .07 |
| ❑ 334 | Mo Vaughn | .30 | .14 |
| ❑ 335 | Bret Saberhagen | .30 | .14 |
| ❑ 336 | Mike Trombley | .15 | .07 |
| ❑ 337 | Mark Lewis | .15 | .07 |
| ❑ 338 | Terry Pendleton | .30 | .14 |
| ❑ 339 | Dave Hollins | .15 | .07 |
| ❑ 340 | Jeff Conine | .15 | .07 |
| ❑ 341 | Bob Tewksbury | .15 | .07 |
| ❑ 342 | Billy Ashley | .15 | .07 |
| ❑ 343 | Zane Smith | .15 | .07 |
| ❑ 344 | John Wetteland | .30 | .14 |
| ❑ 345 | Chris Hoiles | .15 | .07 |
| ❑ 346 | Frank Castillo | .15 | .07 |
| ❑ 347 | Bruce Hurst | .15 | .07 |
| ❑ 348 | Kevin McReynolds | .15 | .07 |
| ❑ 349 | Dave Henderson | .15 | .07 |
| ❑ 350 | Ryan Bowen | .15 | .07 |
| ❑ 351 | Sid Fernandez | .15 | .07 |
| ❑ 352 | Mark Whiten | .15 | .07 |
| ❑ 353 | Nolan Ryan | 3.00 | 1.35 |
| ❑ 354 | Rick Aguilera | .15 | .07 |
| ❑ 355 | Mark Langston | .15 | .07 |
| ❑ 356 | Jack Morris | .30 | .14 |
| ❑ 357 | Rob Deer | .15 | .07 |
| ❑ 358 | Dave Fleming | .15 | .07 |
| ❑ 359 | Lance Johnson | .15 | .07 |
| ❑ 360 | Joe Millette | .15 | .07 |
| ❑ 361 | Wil Cordero | .15 | .07 |
| ❑ 362 | Chito Martinez | .15 | .07 |
| ❑ 363 | Scott Servais | .15 | .07 |
| ❑ 364 | Bernie Williams | .60 | .25 |
| ❑ 365 | Pedro Martinez | 1.50 | .70 |
| ❑ 366 | Ryne Sandberg | .75 | .35 |
| ❑ 367 | Brad Ausmus | .15 | .07 |
| ❑ 368 | Scott Cooper | .15 | .07 |
| ❑ 369 | Rob Dibble | .15 | .07 |
| ❑ 370 | Walt Weiss | .15 | .07 |
| ❑ 371 | Mark Davis | .15 | .07 |
| ❑ 372 | Orlando Merced | .15 | .07 |
| ❑ 373 | Mike Jackson | .15 | .07 |
| ❑ 374 | Kevin Appier | .30 | .14 |
| ❑ 375 | Esteban Beltre | .15 | .07 |
| ❑ 376 | Joe Slusarski | .15 | .07 |
| ❑ 377 | William Suero | .15 | .07 |
| ❑ 378 | Pete O'Brien | .15 | .07 |
| ❑ 379 | Alan Embree | .15 | .07 |
| ❑ 380 | Lenny Webster | .15 | .07 |
| ❑ 381 | Eric Davis | .30 | .14 |
| ❑ 382 | Duane Ward | .15 | .07 |
| ❑ 383 | John Habyan | .15 | .07 |
| ❑ 384 | Jeff Bagwell | .75 | .35 |
| ❑ 385 | Ruben Amaro | .15 | .07 |
| ❑ 386 | Julio Valera | .15 | .07 |
| ❑ 387 | Robin Ventura | .30 | .14 |
| ❑ 388 | Archi Cianfrocco | .15 | .07 |
| ❑ 389 | Skeeter Barnes | .15 | .07 |
| ❑ 390 | Tim Costo | .15 | .07 |
| ❑ 391 | Luis Mercedes | .15 | .07 |
| ❑ 392 | Jeremy Hernandez | .15 | .07 |
| ❑ 393 | Shawon Dunston | .15 | .07 |
| ❑ 394 | Andy Van Slyke | .30 | .14 |
| ❑ 395 | Kevin Maas | .15 | .07 |
| ❑ 396 | Kevin Brown | .40 | .18 |
| ❑ 397 | J.T. Bruett | .15 | .07 |
| ❑ 398 | Darryl Strawberry | .30 | .14 |
| ❑ 399 | Tom Pagnozzi | .15 | .07 |
| ❑ 400 | Sandy Alomar Jr. | .30 | .14 |
| ❑ 401 | Keith Miller | .15 | .07 |
| ❑ 402 | Rich DeLucia | .15 | .07 |
| ❑ 403 | Shawn Abner | .15 | .07 |
| ❑ 404 | Howard Johnson | .15 | .07 |
| ❑ 405 | Mike Benjamin | .15 | .07 |
| ❑ 406 | Roberto Mejia RC | .15 | .07 |
| ❑ 407 | Mike Butcher | .15 | .07 |
| ❑ 408 | Deion Sanders UER (Braves on front and Yankees on back) | .40 | .18 |
| ❑ 409 | Todd Stottlemyre | .15 | .07 |
| ❑ 410 | Scott Kamieniecki | .15 | .07 |
| ❑ 411 | Doug Jones | .15 | .07 |
| ❑ 412 | John Burkett | .15 | .07 |
| ❑ 413 | Lance Blankenship | .15 | .07 |
| ❑ 414 | Jeff Parrett | .15 | .07 |
| ❑ 415 | Barry Larkin | .60 | .25 |
| ❑ 416 | Alan Trammell | .40 | .18 |
| ❑ 417 | Mark Kiefer | .15 | .07 |
| ❑ 418 | Gregg Olson | .15 | .07 |
| ❑ 419 | Mark Grace | .60 | .25 |
| ❑ 420 | Shane Mack | .15 | .07 |
| ❑ 421 | Bob Walk | .15 | .07 |
| ❑ 422 | Curt Schilling | .30 | .14 |
| ❑ 423 | Erik Hanson | .15 | .07 |
| ❑ 424 | George Brett | 1.25 | .55 |
| ❑ 425 | Reggie Jefferson | .30 | .14 |
| ❑ 426 | Mark Portugal | .15 | .07 |
| ❑ 427 | Ron Karkovice | .15 | .07 |
| ❑ 428 | Matt Young | .15 | .07 |
| ❑ 429 | Troy Neel | .15 | .07 |
| ❑ 430 | Hector Fajardo | .15 | .07 |
| ❑ 431 | Dave Righetti | .15 | .07 |
| ❑ 432 | Pat Listach | .15 | .07 |
| ❑ 433 | Jeff Innis | .15 | .07 |
| ❑ 434 | Bob MacDonald | .15 | .07 |
| ❑ 435 | Brian Jordan | .30 | .14 |
| ❑ 436 | Jeff Blauser | .15 | .07 |
| ❑ 437 | Mike Myers RC | .15 | .07 |
| ❑ 438 | Frank Seminara | .15 | .07 |
| ❑ 439 | Rusty Meacham | .15 | .07 |
| ❑ 440 | Greg Briley | .15 | .07 |
| ❑ 441 | Derek Lilliquist | .15 | .07 |
| ❑ 442 | John Vander Wal | .15 | .07 |
| ❑ 443 | Scott Erickson | .15 | .07 |
| ❑ 444 | Bob Scanlan | .15 | .07 |
| ❑ 445 | Todd Frohwirth | .15 | .07 |
| ❑ 446 | Tom Goodwin | .15 | .07 |
| ❑ 447 | William Pennyfeather | .15 | .07 |
| ❑ 448 | Travis Fryman | .30 | .14 |

| | | | |
|---|---|---|---|
| ❑ 449 | Mickey Morandini | .15 | .07 |
| ❑ 450 | Greg Olson | .15 | .07 |
| ❑ 451 | Trevor Hoffman | .60 | .25 |
| ❑ 452 | Dave Magadan | .15 | .07 |
| ❑ 453 | Shawn Jeter | .15 | .07 |
| ❑ 454 | Andres Galarraga | .40 | .18 |
| ❑ 455 | Ted Wood | .15 | .07 |
| ❑ 456 | Freddie Benavides | .15 | .07 |
| ❑ 457 | Junior Felix | .15 | .07 |
| ❑ 458 | Alex Cole | .15 | .07 |
| ❑ 459 | John Orton | .15 | .07 |
| ❑ 460 | Eddie Zosky | .15 | .07 |
| ❑ 461 | Dennis Eckersley | .30 | .14 |
| ❑ 462 | Lee Smith | .30 | .14 |
| ❑ 463 | John Smoltz | .30 | .14 |
| ❑ 464 | Ken Caminiti | .30 | .14 |
| ❑ 465 | Melido Perez | .15 | .07 |
| ❑ 466 | Tom Marsh | .15 | .07 |
| ❑ 467 | Jeff Nelson | .15 | .07 |
| ❑ 468 | Jesse Levis | .15 | .07 |
| ❑ 469 | Chris Nabholz | .15 | .07 |
| ❑ 470 | Mike Macfarlane | .15 | .07 |
| ❑ 471 | Reggie Sanders | .15 | .07 |
| ❑ 472 | Chuck McElroy | .15 | .07 |
| ❑ 473 | Kevin Gross | .15 | .07 |
| ❑ 474 | Matt Whiteside RC | .15 | .07 |
| ❑ 475 | Cal Eldred | .15 | .07 |
| ❑ 476 | Dave Gallagher | .15 | .07 |
| ❑ 477 | Len Dykstra | .30 | .14 |
| ❑ 478 | Mark McGwire | 2.50 | 1.10 |
| ❑ 479 | David Segui | .15 | .07 |
| ❑ 480 | Mike Henneman | .15 | .07 |
| ❑ 481 | Bret Barberie | .15 | .07 |
| ❑ 482 | Steve Sax | .15 | .07 |
| ❑ 483 | Dave Valle | .15 | .07 |
| ❑ 484 | Danny Darwin | .15 | .07 |
| ❑ 485 | Devon White | .15 | .07 |
| ❑ 486 | Eric Plunk | .15 | .07 |
| ❑ 487 | Jim Gott | .15 | .07 |
| ❑ 488 | Scooter Tucker | .15 | .07 |
| ❑ 489 | Omar Olivares | .15 | .07 |
| ❑ 490 | Greg Myers | .15 | .07 |
| ❑ 491 | Brian Hunter | .15 | .07 |
| ❑ 492 | Kevin Tapani | .15 | .07 |
| ❑ 493 | Rich Monteleone | .15 | .07 |
| ❑ 494 | Steve Buechele | .15 | .07 |
| ❑ 495 | Bo Jackson | .30 | .14 |
| ❑ 496 | Mike LaValliere | .15 | .07 |
| ❑ 497 | Mark Leonard | .15 | .07 |
| ❑ 498 | Daryl Boston | .15 | .07 |
| ❑ 499 | Jose Canseco | .75 | .35 |
| ❑ 500 | Brian Barnes | .15 | .07 |
| ❑ 501 | Randy Johnson | .75 | .35 |
| ❑ 502 | Tim McIntosh | .15 | .07 |
| ❑ 503 | Cecil Fielder | .30 | .14 |
| ❑ 504 | Derek Bell | .15 | .07 |
| ❑ 505 | Kevin Koslofski | .15 | .07 |
| ❑ 506 | Darren Holmes | .15 | .07 |
| ❑ 507 | Brady Anderson | .30 | .14 |
| ❑ 508 | John Valentin | .15 | .07 |
| ❑ 509 | Jerry Browne | .15 | .07 |
| ❑ 510 | Fred McGriff | .40 | .18 |
| ❑ 511 | Pedro Astacio | .30 | .14 |
| ❑ 512 | Gary Gaetti | .30 | .14 |
| ❑ 513 | John Burke RC | .15 | .07 |
| ❑ 514 | Dwight Gooden | .30 | .14 |
| ❑ 515 | Thomas Howard | .15 | .07 |
| ❑ 516 | Darrell Whitmore RC UER (11 games played in 1992; should be 121) | .15 | .07 |
| ❑ 517 | Ozzie Guillen | .15 | .07 |
| ❑ 518 | Darryl Kile | .30 | .14 |
| ❑ 519 | Rich Rowland | .15 | .07 |
| ❑ 520 | Carlos Delgado | 1.25 | .55 |
| ❑ 521 | Doug Henry | .15 | .07 |
| ❑ 522 | Greg Colbrunn | .15 | .07 |
| ❑ 523 | Tom Gordon | .15 | .07 |
| ❑ 524 | Ivan Rodriguez | .75 | .35 |
| ❑ 525 | Kent Hrbek | .30 | .14 |
| ❑ 526 | Eric Young | .15 | .07 |
| ❑ 527 | Rod Brewer | .15 | .07 |
| ❑ 528 | Eric Karros | .40 | .18 |
| ❑ 529 | Marquis Grissom | .15 | .07 |
| ❑ 530 | Rico Brogna | .30 | .14 |
| ❑ 531 | Sammy Sosa | 1.25 | .55 |
| ❑ 532 | Bret Boone | .30 | .14 |
| ❑ 533 | Luis Rivera | .15 | .07 |
| ❑ 534 | Hal Morris | .15 | .07 |
| ❑ 535 | Monty Fariss | .15 | .07 |
| ❑ 536 | Leo Gomez | .15 | .07 |
| ❑ 537 | Wally Joyner | .30 | .14 |
| ❑ 538 | Tony Gwynn | 1.25 | .55 |
| ❑ 539 | Mike Williams | .15 | .07 |
| ❑ 540 | Juan Gonzalez | .60 | .25 |
| ❑ 541 | Ryan Klesko | .60 | .25 |
| ❑ 542 | Ryan Thompson | .15 | .07 |
| ❑ 543 | Chad Curtis | .15 | .07 |
| ❑ 544 | Orel Hershiser | .30 | .14 |
| ❑ 545 | Carlos Garcia | .15 | .07 |
| ❑ 546 | Bob Welch | .15 | .07 |
| ❑ 547 | Vinny Castilla | .75 | .35 |
| ❑ 548 | Ozzie Smith | .75 | .35 |
| ❑ 549 | Luis Salazar | .15 | .07 |
| ❑ 550 | Mark Guthrie | .15 | .07 |
| ❑ 551 | Charles Nagy | .15 | .07 |
| ❑ 552 | Alex Fernandez | .30 | .14 |
| ❑ 553 | Mel Rojas | .15 | .07 |
| ❑ 554 | Orestes Destrade | .15 | .07 |
| ❑ 555 | Mark Gubicza | .15 | .07 |
| ❑ 556 | Steve Finley | .30 | .14 |
| ❑ 557 | Don Mattingly | 1.50 | .70 |
| ❑ 558 | Rickey Henderson | .75 | .35 |
| ❑ 559 | Tommy Greene | .15 | .07 |
| ❑ 560 | Arthur Rhodes | .15 | .07 |
| ❑ 561 | Alfredo Griffin | .15 | .07 |
| ❑ 562 | Will Clark | .60 | .25 |
| ❑ 563 | Bob Zupcic | .15 | .07 |
| ❑ 564 | Chuck Carr | .15 | .07 |
| ❑ 565 | Henry Cotto | .15 | .07 |
| ❑ 566 | Billy Spiers | .15 | .07 |
| ❑ 567 | Jack Armstrong | .15 | .07 |
| ❑ 568 | Kurt Stillwell | .15 | .07 |
| ❑ 569 | David McCarty | .15 | .07 |
| ❑ 570 | Joe Vitiello | .15 | .07 |
| ❑ 571 | Gerald Williams | .15 | .07 |
| ❑ 572 | Dale Murphy | .40 | .18 |
| ❑ 573 | Scott Aldred | .15 | .07 |
| ❑ 574 | Bill Gullickson | .15 | .07 |
| ❑ 575 | Bobby Thigpen | .15 | .07 |
| ❑ 576 | Glenallen Hill | .15 | .07 |
| ❑ 577 | Dwayne Henry | .15 | .07 |
| ❑ 578 | Calvin Jones | .15 | .07 |
| ❑ 579 | Al Martin | .15 | .07 |
| ❑ 580 | Ruben Sierra | .15 | .07 |
| ❑ 581 | Andy Benes | .15 | .07 |
| ❑ 582 | Anthony Young | .15 | .07 |
| ❑ 583 | Shawn Boskie | .15 | .07 |
| ❑ 584 | Scott Pose RC | .15 | .07 |
| ❑ 585 | Mike Piazza | 3.00 | 1.35 |
| ❑ 586 | Donovan Osborne | .15 | .07 |
| ❑ 587 | James Austin | .15 | .07 |
| ❑ 588 | Checklist 301-400 | .15 | .07 |
| ❑ 589 | Checklist 401-500 | .15 | .07 |
| ❑ 590 | Checklist 501-600 | .15 | .07 |
| ❑ 591 | Ken Griffey Jr. MC | 1.25 | .55 |
| ❑ 592 | Ivan Rodriguez MC | .40 | .18 |
| ❑ 593 | Carlos Baerga MC | .15 | .07 |
| ❑ 594 | Fred McGriff MC | .30 | .14 |
| ❑ 595 | Mark McGwire MC | 1.25 | .55 |
| ❑ 596 | Roberto Alomar MC | .30 | .14 |
| ❑ 597 | Kirby Puckett MC | .75 | .35 |
| ❑ 598 | Marquis Grissom MC | .15 | .07 |
| ❑ 599 | John Smoltz MC | .30 | .14 |
| ❑ 600 | Ryne Sandberg MC | .40 | .18 |
| ❑ 601 | Wade Boggs | .75 | .35 |
| ❑ 602 | Jeff Reardon | .30 | .14 |
| ❑ 603 | Billy Ripken | .15 | .07 |
| ❑ 604 | Bryan Harvey | .15 | .07 |
| ❑ 605 | Carlos Quintana | .15 | .07 |
| ❑ 606 | Greg Hibbard | .15 | .07 |
| ❑ 607 | Ellis Burks | .30 | .14 |
| ❑ 608 | Greg Swindell | .15 | .07 |
| ❑ 609 | Dave Winfield | .60 | .25 |
| ❑ 610 | Charlie Hough | .30 | .14 |
| ❑ 611 | Chili Davis | .30 | .14 |
| ❑ 612 | Jody Reed | .15 | .07 |
| ❑ 613 | Mark Williamson | .15 | .07 |
| ❑ 614 | Phil Plantier | .15 | .07 |
| ❑ 615 | Jim Abbott | .30 | .14 |
| ❑ 616 | Dante Bichette | .30 | .14 |
| ❑ 617 | Mark Eichhorn | .15 | .07 |
| ❑ 618 | Gary Sheffield | .60 | .25 |
| ❑ 619 | Richie Lewis RC | .15 | .07 |
| ❑ 620 | Joe Girardi | .30 | .14 |
| ❑ 621 | Jaime Navarro | .15 | .07 |
| ❑ 622 | Willie Wilson | .15 | .07 |
| ❑ 623 | Scott Fletcher | .15 | .07 |
| ❑ 624 | Bud Black | .15 | .07 |
| ❑ 625 | Tom Brunansky | .15 | .07 |
| ❑ 626 | Steve Avery | .15 | .07 |
| ❑ 627 | Paul Molitor | .60 | .25 |
| ❑ 628 | Gregg Jefferies | .15 | .07 |
| ❑ 629 | Dave Stewart | .30 | .14 |
| ❑ 630 | Javier Lopez | .30 | .14 |
| ❑ 631 | Greg Gagne | .15 | .07 |
| ❑ 632 | Roberto Kelly | .15 | .07 |
| ❑ 633 | Mike Fetters | .15 | .07 |
| ❑ 634 | Ozzie Canseco | .15 | .07 |
| ❑ 635 | Jeff Russell | .15 | .07 |
| ❑ 636 | Pete Incaviglia | .15 | .07 |
| ❑ 637 | Tom Henke | .15 | .07 |
| ❑ 638 | Chipper Jones | 2.00 | .90 |
| ❑ 639 | Jimmy Key | .30 | .14 |
| ❑ 640 | Dave Martinez | .15 | .07 |
| ❑ 641 | Dave Stieb | .15 | .07 |
| ❑ 642 | Milt Thompson | .15 | .07 |
| ❑ 643 | Alan Mills | .15 | .07 |
| ❑ 644 | Tony Fernandez | .15 | .07 |
| ❑ 645 | Randy Bush | .15 | .07 |
| ❑ 646 | Joe Magrane | .15 | .07 |
| ❑ 647 | Ivan Calderon | .15 | .07 |
| ❑ 648 | Jose Guzman | .15 | .07 |
| ❑ 649 | John Olerud | .40 | .18 |
| ❑ 650 | Tom Glavine | .40 | .18 |
| ❑ 651 | Julio Franco | .15 | .07 |
| ❑ 652 | Armando Reynoso | .15 | .07 |
| ❑ 653 | Felix Jose | .15 | .07 |
| ❑ 654 | Ben Rivera | .15 | .07 |
| ❑ 655 | Andre Dawson | .40 | .18 |
| ❑ 656 | Mike Harkey | .15 | .07 |
| ❑ 657 | Kevin Seitzer | .15 | .07 |
| ❑ 658 | Lonnie Smith | .15 | .07 |
| ❑ 659 | Norm Charlton | .15 | .07 |
| ❑ 660 | David Justice | .40 | .18 |
| ❑ 661 | Fernando Valenzuela | .30 | .14 |
| ❑ 662 | Dan Wilson | .30 | .14 |
| ❑ 663 | Mark Gardner | .15 | .07 |
| ❑ 664 | Doug Dascenzo | .15 | .07 |
| ❑ 665 | Greg Maddux | 1.50 | .70 |
| ❑ 666 | Harold Baines | .30 | .14 |
| ❑ 667 | Randy Myers | .30 | .14 |
| ❑ 668 | Harold Reynolds | .15 | .07 |
| ❑ 669 | Candy Maldonado | .15 | .07 |
| ❑ 670 | Al Leiter | .30 | .14 |
| ❑ 671 | Jerald Clark | .15 | .07 |
| ❑ 672 | Doug Drabek | .15 | .07 |
| ❑ 673 | Kirk Gibson | .30 | .14 |
| ❑ 674 | Steve Reed RC | .15 | .07 |
| ❑ 675 | Mike Felder | .15 | .07 |
| ❑ 676 | Ricky Gutierrez | .15 | .07 |
| ❑ 677 | Spike Owen | .15 | .07 |
| ❑ 678 | Otis Nixon | .15 | .07 |
| ❑ 679 | Scott Sanderson | .15 | .07 |
| ❑ 680 | Mark Carreon | .15 | .07 |
| ❑ 681 | Troy Percival | .15 | .07 |
| ❑ 682 | Kevin Stocker | .15 | .07 |
| ❑ 683 | Jim Converse RC | .15 | .07 |
| ❑ 684 | Barry Bonds | 1.00 | .45 |
| ❑ 685 | Greg Gohr | .15 | .07 |
| ❑ 686 | Tim Wallach | .15 | .07 |
| ❑ 687 | Matt Mieske | .15 | .07 |
| ❑ 688 | Robby Thompson | .15 | .07 |
| ❑ 689 | Brien Taylor | .15 | .07 |
| ❑ 690 | Kirt Manwaring | .15 | .07 |
| ❑ 691 | Mike Lansing RC | .30 | .14 |
| ❑ 692 | Steve Decker | .15 | .07 |
| ❑ 693 | Mike Moore | .15 | .07 |
| ❑ 694 | Kevin Mitchell | .30 | .14 |
| ❑ 695 | Phil Hiatt | .15 | .07 |
| ❑ 696 | Tony Tarasco RC | .15 | .07 |
| ❑ 697 | Benji Gil | .15 | .07 |
| ❑ 698 | Jeff Juden | .15 | .07 |
| ❑ 699 | Kevin Reimer | .15 | .07 |
| ❑ 700 | Andy Ashby | .30 | .14 |
| ❑ 701 | John Jaha | .15 | .07 |
| ❑ 702 | Tim Bogar RC | .15 | .07 |
| ❑ 703 | David Cone | .30 | .14 |
| ❑ 704 | Willie Greene | .15 | .07 |

| | No. | Player | MINT | NRMT |
|---|---|---|---|---|
| ❑ | 705 | David Hulse RC | .15 | .07 |
| ❑ | 706 | Cris Carpenter | .15 | .07 |
| ❑ | 707 | Ken Griffey Jr. | 2.50 | 1.10 |
| ❑ | 708 | Steve Bedrosian | .15 | .07 |
| ❑ | 709 | Dave Nilsson | .30 | .14 |
| ❑ | 710 | Paul Wagner | .15 | .07 |
| ❑ | 711 | B.J. Surhoff | .30 | .14 |
| ❑ | 712 | Rene Arocha RC | .15 | .07 |
| ❑ | 713 | Manuel Lee | .15 | .07 |
| ❑ | 714 | Brian Williams | .15 | .07 |
| ❑ | 715 | Sherman Obando RC | .15 | .07 |
| ❑ | 716 | Terry Mulholland | .15 | .07 |
| ❑ | 717 | Paul O'Neill | .30 | .14 |
| ❑ | 718 | David Nied | .15 | .07 |
| ❑ | 719 | J.T. Snow RC | .75 | .35 |
| ❑ | 720 | Nigel Wilson | .15 | .07 |
| ❑ | 721 | Mike Bielecki | .15 | .07 |
| ❑ | 722 | Kevin Young | .30 | .14 |
| ❑ | 723 | Charlie Leibrandt | .15 | .07 |
| ❑ | 724 | Frank Bolick | .15 | .07 |
| ❑ | 725 | Jon Shave RC | .15 | .07 |
| ❑ | 726 | Steve Cooke | .15 | .07 |
| ❑ | 727 | Domingo Martinez RC | .15 | .07 |
| ❑ | 728 | Todd Worrell | .15 | .07 |
| ❑ | 729 | Jose Lind | .15 | .07 |
| ❑ | 730 | Jim Tatum RC | .15 | .07 |
| ❑ | 731 | Mike Hampton | .60 | .25 |
| ❑ | 732 | Mike Draper | .15 | .07 |
| ❑ | 733 | Henry Mercedes | .15 | .07 |
| ❑ | 734 | John Johnstone RC | .15 | .07 |
| ❑ | 735 | Mitch Webster | .15 | .07 |
| ❑ | 736 | Russ Springer | .15 | .07 |
| ❑ | 737 | Rob Natal | .15 | .07 |
| ❑ | 738 | Steve Howe | .15 | .07 |
| ❑ | 739 | Darrell Sherman RC | .15 | .07 |
| ❑ | 740 | Pat Mahomes | .15 | .07 |
| ❑ | 741 | Alex Arias | .15 | .07 |
| ❑ | 742 | Damon Buford | .15 | .07 |
| ❑ | 743 | Charlie Hayes | .15 | .07 |
| ❑ | 744 | Guillermo Velasquez | .15 | .07 |
| ❑ | 745 | Checklist 601-750 UER | .15 | .07 |
| | | (650 Tom Glavine) | | |
| ❑ | 746 | Frank Thomas MC | .60 | .25 |
| ❑ | 747 | Barry Bonds MC | .40 | .18 |
| ❑ | 748 | Roger Clemens MC | .60 | .25 |
| ❑ | 749 | Joe Carter MC | .15 | .07 |
| ❑ | 750 | Greg Maddux MC | .75 | .35 |

## 1994 Stadium Club

| | MINT | NRMT |
|---|---|---|
| COMPLETE SET (720) | 55.00 | 25.00 |
| COMPLETE SERIES 1 (270) | 20.00 | 9.00 |
| COMPLETE SERIES 2 (270) | 20.00 | 9.00 |
| COMPLETE SERIES 3 (180) | 15.00 | 6.75 |
| COMMON CARD (1-720) | .15 | .07 |

| | No. | Player | MINT | NRMT |
|---|---|---|---|---|
| ❑ | 1 | Robin Yount | .60 | .25 |
| ❑ | 2 | Rick Wilkins | .15 | .07 |
| ❑ | 3 | Steve Scarsone | .15 | .07 |
| ❑ | 4 | Gary Sheffield | .60 | .25 |
| ❑ | 5 | George Brett UER | 1.25 | .55 |
| | | (Birthdate listed as 1963; should be 1953) | | |
| ❑ | 6 | Al Martin | .15 | .07 |
| ❑ | 7 | Joe Oliver | .15 | .07 |
| ❑ | 8 | Stan Belinda | .15 | .07 |
| ❑ | 9 | Denny Hocking | .15 | .07 |
| ❑ | 10 | Roberto Alomar | .60 | .25 |
| ❑ | 11 | Luis Polonia | .15 | .07 |
| ❑ | 12 | Scott Hemond | .15 | .07 |
| ❑ | 13 | Jody Reed | .15 | .07 |
| ❑ | 14 | Mel Rojas | .15 | .07 |
| ❑ | 15 | Junior Ortiz | .15 | .07 |
| ❑ | 16 | Harold Baines | .30 | .14 |
| ❑ | 17 | Brad Pennington | .15 | .07 |
| ❑ | 18 | Jay Bell | .30 | .14 |
| ❑ | 19 | Tom Henke | .15 | .07 |
| ❑ | 20 | Jeff Branson | .15 | .07 |
| ❑ | 21 | Roberto Mejia | .15 | .07 |
| ❑ | 22 | Pedro Munoz | .15 | .07 |
| ❑ | 23 | Matt Nokes | .15 | .07 |
| ❑ | 24 | Jack McDowell | .15 | .07 |
| ❑ | 25 | Cecil Fielder | .30 | .14 |
| ❑ | 26 | Tony Fossas | .15 | .07 |
| ❑ | 27 | Jim Eisenreich | .15 | .07 |
| ❑ | 28 | Anthony Young | .15 | .07 |
| ❑ | 29 | Chuck Carr | .15 | .07 |
| ❑ | 30 | Jeff Treadway | .15 | .07 |
| ❑ | 31 | Chris Nabholz | .15 | .07 |
| ❑ | 32 | Tom Candiotti | .15 | .07 |
| ❑ | 33 | Mike Maddux | .15 | .07 |
| ❑ | 34 | Nolan Ryan | 3.00 | 1.35 |
| ❑ | 35 | Luis Gonzalez | .30 | .14 |
| ❑ | 36 | Tim Salmon | .30 | .14 |
| ❑ | 37 | Mark Whiten | .15 | .07 |
| ❑ | 38 | Roger McDowell | .15 | .07 |
| ❑ | 39 | Royce Clayton | .15 | .07 |
| ❑ | 40 | Troy Neel | .15 | .07 |
| ❑ | 41 | Mike Harkey | .15 | .07 |
| ❑ | 42 | Darrin Fletcher | .15 | .07 |
| ❑ | 43 | Wayne Kirby | .15 | .07 |
| ❑ | 44 | Rich Amaral | .15 | .07 |
| ❑ | 45 | Robb Nen UER | .15 | .07 |
| | | (Nenn on back) | | |
| ❑ | 46 | Tim Teufel | .15 | .07 |
| ❑ | 47 | Steve Cooke | .15 | .07 |
| ❑ | 48 | Jeff McNeely | .15 | .07 |
| ❑ | 49 | Jeff Montgomery | .15 | .07 |
| ❑ | 50 | Skeeter Barnes | .15 | .07 |
| ❑ | 51 | Scott Stahoviak | .15 | .07 |
| ❑ | 52 | Pat Kelly | .15 | .07 |
| ❑ | 53 | Brady Anderson | .30 | .14 |
| ❑ | 54 | Mariano Duncan | .15 | .07 |
| ❑ | 55 | Brian Bohanon | .15 | .07 |
| ❑ | 56 | Jerry Spradlin | .15 | .07 |
| ❑ | 57 | Ron Karkovice | .15 | .07 |
| ❑ | 58 | Jeff Gardner | .15 | .07 |
| ❑ | 59 | Bobby Bonilla | .30 | .14 |
| ❑ | 60 | Tino Martinez | .30 | .14 |
| ❑ | 61 | Todd Benzinger | .15 | .07 |
| ❑ | 62 | Steve Trachsel | .15 | .07 |
| ❑ | 63 | Brian Jordan | .30 | .14 |
| ❑ | 64 | Steve Bedrosian | .15 | .07 |
| ❑ | 65 | Brent Gates | .15 | .07 |
| ❑ | 66 | Shawn Green | .75 | .35 |
| ❑ | 67 | Sean Berry | .15 | .07 |
| ❑ | 68 | Joe Klink | .15 | .07 |
| ❑ | 69 | Fernando Valenzuela | .30 | .14 |
| ❑ | 70 | Andy Tomberlin | .15 | .07 |
| ❑ | 71 | Tony Pena | .15 | .07 |
| ❑ | 72 | Eric Young | .15 | .07 |
| ❑ | 73 | Chris Gomez | .15 | .07 |
| ❑ | 74 | Paul O'Neill | .30 | .14 |
| ❑ | 75 | Ricky Gutierrez | .15 | .07 |
| ❑ | 76 | Brad Holman | .15 | .07 |
| ❑ | 77 | Lance Painter | .15 | .07 |
| ❑ | 78 | Mike Butcher | .15 | .07 |
| ❑ | 79 | Sid Bream | .15 | .07 |
| ❑ | 80 | Sammy Sosa | 1.25 | .55 |
| ❑ | 81 | Felix Fermin | .15 | .07 |
| ❑ | 82 | Todd Hundley | .15 | .07 |
| ❑ | 83 | Kevin Higgins | .15 | .07 |
| ❑ | 84 | Todd Pratt | .15 | .07 |
| ❑ | 85 | Ken Griffey Jr. | 2.50 | 1.10 |
| ❑ | 86 | John O'Donoghue | .15 | .07 |
| ❑ | 87 | Rick Renteria | .15 | .07 |
| ❑ | 88 | John Burkett | .15 | .07 |
| ❑ | 89 | Jose Vizcaino | .15 | .07 |
| ❑ | 90 | Kevin Seitzer | .15 | .07 |
| ❑ | 91 | Bobby Witt | .15 | .07 |
| ❑ | 92 | Chris Turner | .15 | .07 |
| ❑ | 93 | Omar Vizquel | .30 | .14 |
| ❑ | 94 | David Justice | .40 | .18 |
| ❑ | 95 | David Segui | .15 | .07 |
| ❑ | 96 | Dave Hollins | .15 | .07 |
| ❑ | 97 | Doug Strange | .15 | .07 |
| ❑ | 98 | Jerald Clark | .15 | .07 |
| ❑ | 99 | Mike Moore | .15 | .07 |
| ❑ | 100 | Joey Cora | .15 | .07 |
| ❑ | 101 | Scott Kamieniecki | .15 | .07 |
| ❑ | 102 | Andy Benes | .15 | .07 |
| ❑ | 103 | Chris Bosio | .15 | .07 |
| ❑ | 104 | Rey Sanchez | .15 | .07 |
| ❑ | 105 | John Jaha | .15 | .07 |
| ❑ | 106 | Otis Nixon | .15 | .07 |
| ❑ | 107 | Rickey Henderson | .75 | .35 |
| ❑ | 108 | Jeff Bagwell | .75 | .35 |
| ❑ | 109 | Gregg Jefferies | .15 | .07 |
| ❑ | 110 | Roberto Alomar | .40 | .18 |
| | | Paul Molitor | | |
| | | John Olerud | | |
| ❑ | 111 | Ron Gant | .30 | .14 |
| | | David Justice | | |
| | | Fred McGriff | | |
| ❑ | 112 | Juan Gonzalez | .30 | .14 |
| | | Rafael Palmeiro | | |
| | | Dean Palmer | | |
| ❑ | 113 | Greg Swindell | .15 | .07 |
| ❑ | 114 | Bill Haselman | .15 | .07 |
| ❑ | 115 | Phil Plantier | .15 | .07 |
| ❑ | 116 | Ivan Rodriguez | .75 | .35 |
| ❑ | 117 | Kevin Tapani | .15 | .07 |
| ❑ | 118 | Mike LaValliere | .15 | .07 |
| ❑ | 119 | Tim Costo | .15 | .07 |
| ❑ | 120 | Mickey Morandini | .15 | .07 |
| ❑ | 121 | Brett Butler | .30 | .14 |
| ❑ | 122 | Tom Pagnozzi | .15 | .07 |
| ❑ | 123 | Ron Gant | .30 | .14 |
| ❑ | 124 | Damion Easley | .15 | .07 |
| ❑ | 125 | Dennis Eckersley | .30 | .14 |
| ❑ | 126 | Matt Mieske | .15 | .07 |
| ❑ | 127 | Cliff Floyd | .30 | .14 |
| ❑ | 128 | Julian Tavarez RC | .15 | .07 |
| ❑ | 129 | Arthur Rhodes | .15 | .07 |
| ❑ | 130 | Dave West | .15 | .07 |
| ❑ | 131 | Tim Naehring | .15 | .07 |
| ❑ | 132 | Freddie Benavides | .15 | .07 |
| ❑ | 133 | Paul Assenmacher | .15 | .07 |
| ❑ | 134 | David McCarty | .15 | .07 |
| ❑ | 135 | Jose Lind | .15 | .07 |
| ❑ | 136 | Reggie Sanders | .15 | .07 |
| ❑ | 137 | Don Slaught | .15 | .07 |
| ❑ | 138 | Andujar Cedeno | .15 | .07 |
| ❑ | 139 | Rob Deer | .15 | .07 |
| ❑ | 140 | Mike Piazza UER | 2.00 | .90 |
| | | (Listed as outfielder) | | |
| ❑ | 141 | Moises Alou | .30 | .14 |
| ❑ | 142 | Tom Foley | .15 | .07 |
| ❑ | 143 | Benito Santiago | .15 | .07 |
| ❑ | 144 | Sandy Alomar Jr. | .30 | .14 |
| ❑ | 145 | Carlos Hernandez | .15 | .07 |
| ❑ | 146 | Luis Alicea | .15 | .07 |
| ❑ | 147 | Tom Lampkin | .15 | .07 |
| ❑ | 148 | Ryan Klesko | .30 | .14 |
| ❑ | 149 | Juan Guzman | .15 | .07 |
| ❑ | 150 | Scott Servais | .15 | .07 |
| ❑ | 151 | Tony Gwynn | 1.25 | .55 |
| ❑ | 152 | Tim Wakefield | .15 | .07 |
| ❑ | 153 | David Nied | .15 | .07 |
| ❑ | 154 | Chris Haney | .15 | .07 |
| ❑ | 155 | Danny Bautista | .15 | .07 |
| ❑ | 156 | Randy Velarde | .15 | .07 |
| ❑ | 157 | Darrin Jackson | .15 | .07 |
| ❑ | 158 | J.R. Phillips | .15 | .07 |
| ❑ | 159 | Greg Gagne | .15 | .07 |
| ❑ | 160 | Luis Aquino | .15 | .07 |
| ❑ | 161 | John Vander Wal | .15 | .07 |
| ❑ | 162 | Randy Myers | .15 | .07 |
| ❑ | 163 | Ted Power | .15 | .07 |
| ❑ | 164 | Scott Brosius | .30 | .14 |
| ❑ | 165 | Len Dykstra | .30 | .14 |
| ❑ | 166 | Jacob Brumfield | .15 | .07 |
| ❑ | 167 | Bo Jackson | .30 | .14 |
| ❑ | 168 | Eddie Taubensee | .15 | .07 |
| ❑ | 169 | Carlos Baerga | .15 | .07 |
| ❑ | 170 | Tim Bogar | .15 | .07 |
| ❑ | 171 | Jose Canseco | .75 | .35 |
| ❑ | 172 | Greg Blosser UER | .15 | .07 |
| | | (Gregg on front) | | |

| |  |  | | |
|---|---|---|---|---|
| ❑ | 173 | Chili Davis | .30 | .14 |
| ❑ | 174 | Randy Knorr | .15 | .07 |
| ❑ | 175 | Mike Perez | .15 | .07 |
| ❑ | 176 | Henry Rodriguez | .15 | .07 |
| ❑ | 177 | Brian Turang RC | .15 | .07 |
| ❑ | 178 | Roger Pavlik | .15 | .07 |
| ❑ | 179 | Aaron Sele | .30 | .14 |
| ❑ | 180 | Fred McGriff<br>Gary Sheffield | .60 | .25 |
| ❑ | 181 | J.T. Snow<br>Tim Salmon | .30 | .14 |
| ❑ | 182 | Roberto Hernandez | .15 | .07 |
| ❑ | 183 | Jeff Reboulet | .15 | .07 |
| ❑ | 184 | John Doherty | .15 | .07 |
| ❑ | 185 | Danny Sheaffer | .15 | .07 |
| ❑ | 186 | Bip Roberts | .15 | .07 |
| ❑ | 187 | Dennis Martinez | .30 | .14 |
| ❑ | 188 | Darryl Hamilton | .15 | .07 |
| ❑ | 189 | Eduardo Perez | .15 | .07 |
| ❑ | 190 | Pete Harnisch | .15 | .07 |
| ❑ | 191 | Rich Gossage | .30 | .14 |
| ❑ | 192 | Mickey Tettleton | .15 | .07 |
| ❑ | 193 | Lenny Webster | .15 | .07 |
| ❑ | 194 | Lance Johnson | .15 | .07 |
| ❑ | 195 | Don Mattingly | 1.50 | .70 |
| ❑ | 196 | Gregg Olson | .15 | .07 |
| ❑ | 197 | Mark Gubicza | .15 | .07 |
| ❑ | 198 | Scott Fletcher | .15 | .07 |
| ❑ | 199 | Jon Shave | .15 | .07 |
| ❑ | 200 | Tim Mauser | .15 | .07 |
| ❑ | 201 | Jeromy Burnitz | .30 | .14 |
| ❑ | 202 | Rob Dibble | .15 | .07 |
| ❑ | 203 | Will Clark | .60 | .25 |
| ❑ | 204 | Steve Buechele | .15 | .07 |
| ❑ | 205 | Brian Williams | .15 | .07 |
| ❑ | 206 | Carlos Garcia | .15 | .07 |
| ❑ | 207 | Mark Clark | .15 | .07 |
| ❑ | 208 | Rafael Palmeiro | .60 | .25 |
| ❑ | 209 | Eric Davis | .30 | .14 |
| ❑ | 210 | Pat Meares | .15 | .07 |
| ❑ | 211 | Chuck Finley | .30 | .14 |
| ❑ | 212 | Jason Bere | .15 | .07 |
| ❑ | 213 | Gary DiSarcina | .15 | .07 |
| ❑ | 214 | Tony Fernandez | .15 | .07 |
| ❑ | 215 | B.J. Surhoff | .30 | .14 |
| ❑ | 216 | Lee Guetterman | .15 | .07 |
| ❑ | 217 | Tim Wallach | .15 | .07 |
| ❑ | 218 | Kirt Manwaring | .15 | .07 |
| ❑ | 219 | Albert Belle | .40 | .18 |
| ❑ | 220 | Dwight Gooden | .30 | .14 |
| ❑ | 221 | Archi Cianfrocco | .15 | .07 |
| ❑ | 222 | Terry Mulholland | .15 | .07 |
| ❑ | 223 | Hipolito Pichardo | .15 | .07 |
| ❑ | 224 | Kent Hrbek | .30 | .14 |
| ❑ | 225 | Craig Grebeck | .15 | .07 |
| ❑ | 226 | Todd Jones | .15 | .07 |
| ❑ | 227 | Mike Bordick | .15 | .07 |
| ❑ | 228 | John Olerud | .30 | .14 |
| ❑ | 229 | Jeff Blauser | .15 | .07 |
| ❑ | 230 | Alex Arias | .15 | .07 |
| ❑ | 231 | Bernard Gilkey | .15 | .07 |
| ❑ | 232 | Denny Neagle | .15 | .07 |
| ❑ | 233 | Pedro Borbon | .15 | .07 |
| ❑ | 234 | Dick Schofield | .15 | .07 |
| ❑ | 235 | Matias Carrillo | .15 | .07 |
| ❑ | 236 | Juan Bell | .15 | .07 |
| ❑ | 237 | Mike Hampton | .15 | .07 |
| ❑ | 238 | Barry Bonds | 1.00 | .45 |
| ❑ | 239 | Cris Carpenter | .15 | .07 |
| ❑ | 240 | Eric Karros | .30 | .14 |
| ❑ | 241 | Greg McMichael | .15 | .07 |
| ❑ | 242 | Pat Hentgen | .15 | .07 |
| ❑ | 243 | Tim Pugh | .15 | .07 |
| ❑ | 244 | Vinny Castilla | .30 | .14 |
| ❑ | 245 | Charlie Hough | .30 | .14 |
| ❑ | 246 | Bobby Munoz | .15 | .07 |
| ❑ | 247 | Kevin Baez | .15 | .07 |
| ❑ | 248 | Todd Frohwirth | .15 | .07 |
| ❑ | 249 | Charlie Hayes | .15 | .07 |
| ❑ | 250 | Mike Macfarlane | .15 | .07 |
| ❑ | 251 | Danny Darwin | .15 | .07 |
| ❑ | 252 | Ben Rivera | .15 | .07 |
| ❑ | 253 | Dave Henderson | .15 | .07 |
| ❑ | 254 | Steve Avery | .15 | .07 |
| ❑ | 255 | Tim Belcher | .15 | .07 |
| ❑ | 256 | Dan Plesac | .15 | .07 |
| ❑ | 257 | Jim Thome | .40 | .18 |
| ❑ | 258 | Albert Belle HR | .15 | .07 |
| ❑ | 259 | Barry Bonds HR | .60 | .25 |
| ❑ | 260 | Ron Gant HR | .15 | .07 |
| ❑ | 261 | Juan Gonzalez HR | .60 | .25 |
| ❑ | 262 | Ken Griffey Jr. HR | 1.25 | .55 |
| ❑ | 263 | David Justice HR | .15 | .07 |
| ❑ | 264 | Fred McGriff HR | .15 | .07 |
| ❑ | 265 | Rafael Palmeiro HR | .30 | .14 |
| ❑ | 266 | Mike Piazza HR | 1.00 | .45 |
| ❑ | 267 | Frank Thomas HR | .60 | .25 |
| ❑ | 268 | Matt Williams HR | .15 | .07 |
| ❑ | 269 | Checklist 1-135 | .15 | .07 |
| ❑ | 270 | Checklist 136-270 | .15 | .07 |
| ❑ | 271 | Mike Stanley | .15 | .07 |
| ❑ | 272 | Tony Tarasco | .15 | .07 |
| ❑ | 273 | Teddy Higuera | .15 | .07 |
| ❑ | 274 | Ryan Thompson | .15 | .07 |
| ❑ | 275 | Rick Aguilera | .15 | .07 |
| ❑ | 276 | Ramon Martinez | .15 | .07 |
| ❑ | 277 | Orlando Merced | .15 | .07 |
| ❑ | 278 | Guillermo Velasquez | .15 | .07 |
| ❑ | 279 | Mark Hutton | .15 | .07 |
| ❑ | 280 | Larry Walker | .30 | .14 |
| ❑ | 281 | Kevin Gross | .15 | .07 |
| ❑ | 282 | Jose Offerman | .15 | .07 |
| ❑ | 283 | Jim Leyritz | .15 | .07 |
| ❑ | 284 | Jamie Moyer | .15 | .07 |
| ❑ | 285 | Frank Thomas | 1.25 | .55 |
| ❑ | 286 | Derek Bell | .15 | .07 |
| ❑ | 287 | Derrick May | .15 | .07 |
| ❑ | 288 | Dave Winfield | .60 | .25 |
| ❑ | 289 | Curt Schilling | .30 | .14 |
| ❑ | 290 | Carlos Quintana | .15 | .07 |
| ❑ | 291 | Bob Natal | .15 | .07 |
| ❑ | 292 | David Cone | .30 | .14 |
| ❑ | 293 | Al Osuna | .15 | .07 |
| ❑ | 294 | Bob Hamelin | .15 | .07 |
| ❑ | 295 | Chad Curtis | .15 | .07 |
| ❑ | 296 | Danny Jackson | .15 | .07 |
| ❑ | 297 | Bob Welch | .15 | .07 |
| ❑ | 298 | Felix Jose | .15 | .07 |
| ❑ | 299 | Jay Buhner | .30 | .14 |
| ❑ | 300 | Joe Carter | .30 | .14 |
| ❑ | 301 | Kenny Lofton | .30 | .14 |
| ❑ | 302 | Kirk Rueter | .15 | .07 |
| ❑ | 303 | Kim Batiste | .15 | .07 |
| ❑ | 304 | Mike Morgan | .15 | .07 |
| ❑ | 305 | Pat Borders | .15 | .07 |
| ❑ | 306 | Rene Arocha | .15 | .07 |
| ❑ | 307 | Ruben Sierra | .15 | .07 |
| ❑ | 308 | Steve Finley | .30 | .14 |
| ❑ | 309 | Travis Fryman | .30 | .14 |
| ❑ | 310 | Zane Smith | .15 | .07 |
| ❑ | 311 | Willie Wilson | .15 | .07 |
| ❑ | 312 | Trevor Hoffman | .30 | .14 |
| ❑ | 313 | Terry Pendleton | .30 | .14 |
| ❑ | 314 | Salomon Torres | .15 | .07 |
| ❑ | 315 | Robin Ventura | .30 | .14 |
| ❑ | 316 | Randy Tomlin | .15 | .07 |
| ❑ | 317 | Dave Stewart | .30 | .14 |
| ❑ | 318 | Mike Benjamin | .15 | .07 |
| ❑ | 319 | Matt Turner | .15 | .07 |
| ❑ | 320 | Manny Ramirez | 1.00 | .45 |
| ❑ | 321 | Kevin Young | .15 | .07 |
| ❑ | 322 | Ken Caminiti | .30 | .14 |
| ❑ | 323 | Joe Girardi | .15 | .07 |
| ❑ | 324 | Jeff McKnight | .15 | .07 |
| ❑ | 325 | Gene Harris | .15 | .07 |
| ❑ | 326 | Devon White | .15 | .07 |
| ❑ | 327 | Darryl Kile | .30 | .14 |
| ❑ | 328 | Craig Paquette | .15 | .07 |
| ❑ | 329 | Cal Eldred | .15 | .07 |
| ❑ | 330 | Bill Swift | .15 | .07 |
| ❑ | 331 | Alan Trammell | .40 | .18 |
| ❑ | 332 | Armando Reynoso | .15 | .07 |
| ❑ | 333 | Brent Mayne | .15 | .07 |
| ❑ | 334 | Chris Donnels | .15 | .07 |
| ❑ | 335 | Darryl Strawberry | .30 | .14 |
| ❑ | 336 | Dean Palmer | .30 | .14 |
| ❑ | 337 | Frank Castillo | .15 | .07 |
| ❑ | 338 | Jeff King | .15 | .07 |
| ❑ | 339 | John Franco | .30 | .14 |
| ❑ | 340 | Kevin Appier | .30 | .14 |
| ❑ | 341 | Lance Blankenship | .15 | .07 |
| ❑ | 342 | Mark McLemore | .15 | .07 |
| ❑ | 343 | Pedro Astacio | .15 | .07 |
| ❑ | 344 | Rich Batchelor | .15 | .07 |
| ❑ | 345 | Ryan Bowen | .15 | .07 |
| ❑ | 346 | Terry Steinbach | .15 | .07 |
| ❑ | 347 | Troy O'Leary | .15 | .07 |
| ❑ | 348 | Willie Blair | .15 | .07 |
| ❑ | 349 | Wade Boggs | .75 | .35 |
| ❑ | 350 | Tim Raines | .30 | .14 |
| ❑ | 351 | Scott Livingstone | .15 | .07 |
| ❑ | 352 | Rod Correia | .15 | .07 |
| ❑ | 353 | Ray Lankford | .30 | .14 |
| ❑ | 354 | Pat Listach | .15 | .07 |
| ❑ | 355 | Milt Thompson | .15 | .07 |
| ❑ | 356 | Miguel Jimenez | .15 | .07 |
| ❑ | 357 | Marc Newfield | .15 | .07 |
| ❑ | 358 | Mark McGwire | 2.50 | 1.10 |
| ❑ | 359 | Kirby Puckett | 1.50 | .70 |
| ❑ | 360 | Kent Mercker | .15 | .07 |
| ❑ | 361 | John Kruk | .30 | .14 |
| ❑ | 362 | Jeff Kent | .40 | .18 |
| ❑ | 363 | Hal Morris | .15 | .07 |
| ❑ | 364 | Edgar Martinez | .40 | .18 |
| ❑ | 365 | Dave Magadan | .15 | .07 |
| ❑ | 366 | Dante Bichette | .30 | .14 |
| ❑ | 367 | Chris Hammond | .15 | .07 |
| ❑ | 368 | Bret Saberhagen | .30 | .14 |
| ❑ | 369 | Billy Ripken | .15 | .07 |
| ❑ | 370 | Bill Gullickson | .15 | .07 |
| ❑ | 371 | Andre Dawson | .40 | .18 |
| ❑ | 372 | Roberto Kelly | .15 | .07 |
| ❑ | 373 | Cal Ripken | 2.50 | 1.10 |
| ❑ | 374 | Craig Biggio | .40 | .18 |
| ❑ | 375 | Dan Pasqua | .15 | .07 |
| ❑ | 376 | Dave Nilsson | .15 | .07 |
| ❑ | 377 | Duane Ward | .15 | .07 |
| ❑ | 378 | Greg Vaughn | .30 | .14 |
| ❑ | 379 | Jeff Fassero | .15 | .07 |
| ❑ | 380 | Jerry DiPoto | .15 | .07 |
| ❑ | 381 | John Patterson | .15 | .07 |
| ❑ | 382 | Kevin Brown | .30 | .14 |
| ❑ | 383 | Kevin Roberson | .15 | .07 |
| ❑ | 384 | Joe Orsulak | .15 | .07 |
| ❑ | 385 | Hilly Hathaway | .15 | .07 |
| ❑ | 386 | Mike Greenwell | .15 | .07 |
| ❑ | 387 | Orestes Destrade | .15 | .07 |
| ❑ | 388 | Mike Gallego | .15 | .07 |
| ❑ | 389 | Ozzie Guillen | .15 | .07 |
| ❑ | 390 | Raul Mondesi | .30 | .14 |
| ❑ | 391 | Scott Lydy | .15 | .07 |
| ❑ | 392 | Tom Urbani | .15 | .07 |
| ❑ | 393 | Wil Cordero | .15 | .07 |
| ❑ | 394 | Tony Longmire | .15 | .07 |
| ❑ | 395 | Todd Zeile | .15 | .07 |
| ❑ | 396 | Scott Cooper | .15 | .07 |
| ❑ | 397 | Ryne Sandberg | .75 | .35 |
| ❑ | 398 | Ricky Bones | .15 | .07 |
| ❑ | 399 | Phil Clark | .15 | .07 |
| ❑ | 400 | Orel Hershiser | .30 | .14 |
| ❑ | 401 | Mike Henneman | .15 | .07 |
| ❑ | 402 | Mark Lemke | .15 | .07 |
| ❑ | 403 | Mark Grace | .60 | .25 |
| ❑ | 404 | Ken Ryan | .15 | .07 |
| ❑ | 405 | John Smoltz | .30 | .14 |
| ❑ | 406 | Jeff Conine | .15 | .07 |
| ❑ | 407 | Greg Harris | .15 | .07 |
| ❑ | 408 | Doug Drabek | .15 | .07 |
| ❑ | 409 | Dave Fleming | .15 | .07 |
| ❑ | 410 | Danny Tartabull | .15 | .07 |
| ❑ | 411 | Chad Kreuter | .15 | .07 |
| ❑ | 412 | Brad Ausmus | .15 | .07 |
| ❑ | 413 | Ben McDonald | .15 | .07 |
| ❑ | 414 | Barry Larkin | .60 | .25 |
| ❑ | 415 | Bret Barberie | .15 | .07 |
| ❑ | 416 | Chuck Knoblauch | .30 | .14 |
| ❑ | 417 | Ozzie Smith | .75 | .35 |
| ❑ | 418 | Ed Sprague | .15 | .07 |
| ❑ | 419 | Matt Williams | .40 | .18 |
| ❑ | 420 | Jeremy Hernandez | .15 | .07 |
| ❑ | 421 | Jose Bautista | .15 | .07 |
| ❑ | 422 | Kevin Mitchell | .15 | .07 |
| ❑ | 423 | Manuel Lee | .15 | .07 |
| ❑ | 424 | Mike Devereaux | .15 | .07 |
| ❑ | 425 | Omar Olivares | .15 | .07 |
| ❑ | 426 | Rafael Belliard | .15 | .07 |
| ❑ | 427 | Richie Lewis | .15 | .07 |
| ❑ | 428 | Ron Darling | .15 | .07 |

❑ 429 Shane Mack .15 .07
❑ 430 Tim Hulett .15 .07
❑ 431 Wally Joyner .30 .14
❑ 432 Wes Chamberlain .15 .07
❑ 433 Tom Browning .15 .07
❑ 434 Scott Radinsky .15 .07
❑ 435 Rondell White .30 .14
❑ 436 Rod Beck .15 .07
❑ 437 Rheal Cormier .15 .07
❑ 438 Randy Johnson .75 .35
❑ 439 Pete Schourek .15 .07
❑ 440 Mo Vaughn .30 .14
❑ 441 Mike Timlin .15 .07
❑ 442 Mark Langston .15 .07
❑ 443 Lou Whitaker .30 .14
❑ 444 Kevin Stocker .15 .07
❑ 445 Ken Hill .15 .07
❑ 446 John Wetteland .30 .14
❑ 447 J.T. Snow .30 .14
❑ 448 Erik Pappas .15 .07
❑ 449 David Hulse .15 .07
❑ 450 Darren Daulton .30 .14
❑ 451 Chris Hoiles .15 .07
❑ 452 Bryan Harvey .15 .07
❑ 453 Darren Lewis .15 .07
❑ 454 Andres Galarraga .40 .18
❑ 455 Joe Hesketh .15 .07
❑ 456 Jose Valentin .15 .07
❑ 457 Dan Peltier .15 .07
❑ 458 Joe Boever .15 .07
❑ 459 Kevin Rogers .15 .07
❑ 460 Craig Shipley .15 .07
❑ 461 Alvaro Espinoza .15 .07
❑ 462 Wilson Alvarez .15 .07
❑ 463 Cory Snyder .15 .07
❑ 464 Candy Maldonado .15 .07
❑ 465 Blas Minor .15 .07
❑ 466 Rod Bolton .15 .07
❑ 467 Kenny Rogers .15 .07
❑ 468 Greg Myers .15 .07
❑ 469 Jimmy Key .30 .14
❑ 470 Tony Castillo .15 .07
❑ 471 Mike Stanton .15 .07
❑ 472 Deion Sanders .30 .14
❑ 473 Tito Navarro .15 .07
❑ 474 Mike Gardiner .15 .07
❑ 475 Steve Reed .15 .07
❑ 476 John Roper .15 .07
❑ 477 Mike Trombley .15 .07
❑ 478 Charles Nagy .15 .07
❑ 479 Larry Casian .15 .07
❑ 480 Eric Hillman .15 .07
❑ 481 Bill Wertz .15 .07
❑ 482 Jeff Schwarz .15 .07
❑ 483 John Valentin .15 .07
❑ 484 Carl Willis .15 .07
❑ 485 Gary Gaetti .30 .14
❑ 486 Bill Pecota .15 .07
❑ 487 John Smiley .15 .07
❑ 488 Mike Mussina .60 .25
❑ 489 Mike Ignasiak .15 .07
❑ 490 Billy Brewer .15 .07
❑ 491 Jack Voigt .15 .07
❑ 492 Mike Munoz .15 .07
❑ 493 Lee Tinsley .15 .07
❑ 494 Bob Wickman .15 .07
❑ 495 Roger Salkeld .15 .07
❑ 496 Thomas Howard .15 .07
❑ 497 Mark Davis .15 .07
❑ 498 Dave Clark .15 .07
❑ 499 Turk Wendell .15 .07
❑ 500 Rafael Bournigal .15 .07
❑ 501 Chip Hale .15 .07
❑ 502 Matt Whiteside .15 .07
❑ 503 Brian Koelling .15 .07
❑ 504 Jeff Reed .15 .07
❑ 505 Paul Wagner .15 .07
❑ 506 Torey Lovullo .15 .07
❑ 507 Curt Leskanic .15 .07
❑ 508 Derek Lilliquist .15 .07
❑ 509 Joe Magrane .15 .07
❑ 510 Mackey Sasser .15 .07
❑ 511 Lloyd McClendon .15 .07
❑ 512 Jayhawk Owens .15 .07
❑ 513 Woody Williams .15 .07
❑ 514 Gary Redus .15 .07
❑ 515 Tim Spehr .15 .07
❑ 516 Jim Abbott .30 .14
❑ 517 Lou Frazier .15 .07
❑ 518 Erik Plantenberg RC .15 .07
❑ 519 Tim Worrell .15 .07
❑ 520 Brian McRae .15 .07
❑ 521 Chan Ho Park RC .75 .35
❑ 522 Mark Wohlers .15 .07
❑ 523 Geronimo Pena .15 .07
❑ 524 Andy Ashby .15 .07
❑ 525 Tim Raines .15 .07
Andre Dawson TALE
❑ 526 Paul Molitor TALE .30 .14
❑ 527 Joe Carter DL .15 .07
❑ 528 Frank Thomas DL UER .60 .25
(Listed as third in RBI in 1993; was actually second)
❑ 529 Ken Griffey Jr. DL 1.25 .55
❑ 530 David Justice DL .15 .07
❑ 531 Gregg Jefferies DL .15 .07
❑ 532 Barry Bonds DL .60 .25
❑ 533 John Kruk QS .15 .07
❑ 534 Roger Clemens QS .60 .25
❑ 535 Cecil Fielder QS .15 .07
❑ 536 Ruben Sierra QS .15 .07
❑ 537 Tony Gwynn QS .60 .25
❑ 538 Tom Glavine QS .30 .14
❑ 539 Checklist 271-405 UER .15 .07
(Number on back is 269)
❑ 540 Checklist 406-540 UER .15 .07
(Numbered 270 on back)
❑ 541 Ozzie Smith ATL .60 .25
❑ 542 Eddie Murray ATL .30 .14
❑ 543 Lee Smith ATL .15 .07
❑ 544 Greg Maddux 1.50 .70
❑ 545 Denis Boucher .15 .07
❑ 546 Mark Gardner .15 .07
❑ 547 Bo Jackson .30 .14
❑ 548 Eric Anthony .15 .07
❑ 549 Delino DeShields .15 .07
❑ 550 Turner Ward .15 .07
❑ 551 Scott Sanderson .15 .07
❑ 552 Hector Carrasco .15 .07
❑ 553 Tony Phillips .15 .07
❑ 554 Melido Perez .15 .07
❑ 555 Mike Felder .15 .07
❑ 556 Jack Morris .30 .14
❑ 557 Rafael Palmeiro .60 .25
❑ 558 Shane Reynolds .15 .07
❑ 559 Pete Incaviglia .15 .07
❑ 560 Greg Harris .15 .07
❑ 561 Matt Walbeck .15 .07
❑ 562 Todd Van Poppel .15 .07
❑ 563 Todd Stottlemyre .15 .07
❑ 564 Ricky Bones .15 .07
❑ 565 Mike Jackson .15 .07
❑ 566 Kevin McReynolds .15 .07
❑ 567 Melvin Nieves .15 .07
❑ 568 Juan Gonzalez .60 .25
❑ 569 Frank Viola .15 .07
❑ 570 Vince Coleman .15 .07
❑ 571 Brian Anderson RC .30 .14
❑ 572 Omar Vizquel .30 .14
❑ 573 Bernie Williams .60 .25
❑ 574 Tom Glavine .60 .25
❑ 575 Mitch Williams .15 .07
❑ 576 Shawon Dunston .15 .07
❑ 577 Mike Lansing .15 .07
❑ 578 Greg Pirkl .15 .07
❑ 579 Sid Fernandez .15 .07
❑ 580 Doug Jones .15 .07
❑ 581 Walt Weiss .15 .07
❑ 582 Tim Belcher .15 .07
❑ 583 Alex Fernandez .15 .07
❑ 584 Alex Cole .15 .07
❑ 585 Greg Cadaret .15 .07
❑ 586 Bob Tewksbury .15 .07
❑ 587 Dave Hansen .15 .07
❑ 588 Kurt Abbott RC .15 .07
❑ 589 Rick White RC .15 .07
❑ 590 Kevin Bass .15 .07
❑ 591 Geronimo Berroa .15 .07
❑ 592 Jaime Navarro .15 .07
❑ 593 Steve Farr .15 .07
❑ 594 Jack Armstrong .15 .07
❑ 595 Steve Howe .15 .07
❑ 596 Jose Rijo .15 .07
❑ 597 Otis Nixon .15 .07
❑ 598 Robby Thompson .15 .07
❑ 599 Kelly Stinnett RC .15 .07
❑ 600 Carlos Delgado 1.00 .45
❑ 601 Brian Johnson RC .15 .07
❑ 602 Gregg Olson .15 .07
❑ 603 Jim Edmonds .75 .35
❑ 604 Mike Blowers .15 .07
❑ 605 Lee Smith .30 .14
❑ 606 Pat Rapp .15 .07
❑ 607 Mike Magnante .15 .07
❑ 608 Karl Rhodes .15 .07
❑ 609 Jeff Juden .15 .07
❑ 610 Rusty Meacham .15 .07
❑ 611 Pedro Martinez .75 .07
❑ 612 Todd Worrell .15 .07
❑ 613 Stan Javier .15 .07
❑ 614 Mike Hampton .15 .07
❑ 615 Jose Guzman .15 .07
❑ 616 Xavier Hernandez .15 .07
❑ 617 David Wells .30 .14
❑ 618 John Habyan .15 .07
❑ 619 Chris Nabholz .15 .07
❑ 620 Bobby Jones .15 .07
❑ 621 Chris James .15 .07
❑ 622 Ellis Burks .30 .14
❑ 623 Erik Hanson .15 .07
❑ 624 Pat Meares .15 .07
❑ 625 Harold Reynolds .15 .07
❑ 626 Bob Hamelin RR .15 .07
❑ 627 Manny Ramirez RR .40 .18
❑ 628 Ryan Klesko RR .15 .07
❑ 629 Carlos Delgado RR .60 .25
❑ 630 Javier Lopez RR .30 .14
❑ 631 Steve Karsay RR .15 .07
❑ 632 Rick Helling RR .30 .14
❑ 633 Steve Trachsel RR .15 .07
❑ 634 Hector Carrasco RR .15 .07
❑ 635 Andy Stankiewicz .15 .07
❑ 636 Paul Sorrento .15 .07
❑ 637 Scott Erickson .15 .07
❑ 638 Chipper Jones 1.50 .70
❑ 639 Luis Polonia .15 .07
❑ 640 Howard Johnson .15 .07
❑ 641 John Dopson .15 .07
❑ 642 Jody Reed .15 .07
❑ 643 Lonnie Smith UER .15 .07
(Card numbered 543)
❑ 644 Mark Portugal .15 .07
❑ 645 Paul Molitor .60 .25
❑ 646 Paul Assenmacher .15 .07
❑ 647 Hubie Brooks .15 .07
❑ 648 Gary Wayne .15 .07
❑ 649 Sean Berry .15 .07
❑ 650 Roger Clemens 1.25 .55
❑ 651 Brian L. Hunter .15 .07
❑ 652 Wally Whitehurst .15 .07
❑ 653 Allen Watson .15 .07
❑ 654 Rickey Henderson .75 .35
❑ 655 Sid Bream .15 .07
❑ 656 Dan Wilson .15 .07
❑ 657 Ricky Jordan .15 .07
❑ 658 Sterling Hitchcock .15 .07
❑ 659 Darrin Jackson .15 .07
❑ 660 Junior Felix .15 .07
❑ 661 Tom Brunansky .15 .07
❑ 662 Jose Vizcaino .15 .07
❑ 663 Mark Leiter .15 .07
❑ 664 Gil Heredia .15 .07
❑ 665 Fred McGriff .40 .18
❑ 666 Will Clark .60 .25
❑ 667 Al Leiter .30 .14
❑ 668 James Mouton .15 .07
❑ 669 Billy Bean .15 .07
❑ 670 Scott Leius .15 .07
❑ 671 Bret Boone .30 .14
❑ 672 Darren Holmes .15 .07
❑ 673 Dave Weathers .15 .07
❑ 674 Eddie Murray .60 .25
❑ 675 Felix Fermin .15 .07
❑ 676 Chris Sabo .15 .07
❑ 677 Billy Spiers .15 .07
❑ 678 Aaron Sele .30 .14
❑ 679 Juan Samuel .15 .07
❑ 680 Julio Franco .15 .07

| No. | Player | MINT | NRMT |
|---|---|---|---|
| 681 | Heathcliff Slocumb | .15 | .07 |
| 682 | Dennis Martinez | .30 | .14 |
| 683 | Jerry Browne | .15 | .07 |
| 684 | Pedro Martinez RC | .15 | .07 |
| 685 | Rex Hudler | .15 | .07 |
| 686 | Willie McGee | .30 | .14 |
| 687 | Andy Van Slyke | .30 | .14 |
| 688 | Pat Mahomes | .15 | .07 |
| 689 | Dave Henderson | .15 | .07 |
| 690 | Tony Eusebio | .15 | .07 |
| 691 | Rick Sutcliffe | .30 | .14 |
| 692 | Willie Banks | .15 | .07 |
| 693 | Alan Mills | .15 | .07 |
| 694 | Jeff Treadway | .15 | .07 |
| 695 | Alex Gonzalez | .15 | .07 |
| 696 | David Segui | .15 | .07 |
| 697 | Rick Helling | .30 | .14 |
| 698 | Bip Roberts | .15 | .07 |
| 699 | Jeff Cirillo RC | 2.00 | .90 |
| 700 | Terry Mulholland | .15 | .07 |
| 701 | Marvin Freeman | .15 | .07 |
| 702 | Jason Bere | .15 | .07 |
| 703 | Javier Lopez | .30 | .14 |
| 704 | Greg Hibbard | .15 | .07 |
| 705 | Tommy Greene | .15 | .07 |
| 706 | Marquis Grissom | .15 | .07 |
| 707 | Brian Harper | .15 | .07 |
| 708 | Steve Karsay | .15 | .07 |
| 709 | Jeff Brantley | .15 | .07 |
| 710 | Jeff Russell | .15 | .07 |
| 711 | Bryan Hickerson | .15 | .07 |
| 712 | Jim Pittsley RC | .15 | .07 |
| 713 | Bobby Ayala | .15 | .07 |
| 714 | John Smoltz | .30 | .14 |
| 715 | Jose Rijo | .15 | .07 |
| 716 | Greg Maddux | .75 | .35 |
| 717 | Matt Williams | .40 | .18 |
| 718 | Frank Thomas | .60 | .25 |
| 719 | Ryne Sandberg | .60 | .25 |
| 720 | Checklist | .15 | .07 |

## 1995 Stadium Club

| | MINT | NRMT |
|---|---|---|
| COMPLETE SET (630) | 60.00 | 27.00 |
| COMPLETE SERIES 1 (270) | 25.00 | 11.00 |
| COMPLETE SERIES 2 (225) | 20.00 | 9.00 |
| COMPLETE SERIES 3 (135) | 15.00 | 6.75 |
| COMMON CARD (1-630) | .15 | .07 |

| No. | Player | MINT | NRMT |
|---|---|---|---|
| 1 | Cal Ripken | 2.50 | 1.10 |
| 2 | Bo Jackson | .30 | .14 |
| 3 | Bryan Harvey | .15 | .07 |
| 4 | Curt Schilling | .30 | .14 |
| 5 | Bruce Ruffin | .15 | .07 |
| 6 | Travis Fryman | .30 | .14 |
| 7 | Jim Abbott | .30 | .14 |
| 8 | David McCarty | .15 | .07 |
| 9 | Gary Gaetti | .30 | .14 |
| 10 | Roger Clemens | 1.25 | .55 |
| 11 | Carlos Garcia | .15 | .07 |
| 12 | Lee Smith | .30 | .14 |
| 13 | Bobby Ayala | .15 | .07 |
| 14 | Charles Nagy | .15 | .07 |
| 15 | Lou Frazier | .15 | .07 |
| 16 | Rene Arocha | .15 | .07 |
| 17 | Carlos Delgado | .60 | .25 |
| 18 | Steve Finley | .30 | .14 |
| 19 | Ryan Klesko | .30 | .14 |
| 20 | Cal Eldred | .15 | .07 |
| 21 | Rey Sanchez | .15 | .07 |
| 22 | Ken Hill | .15 | .07 |
| 23 | Benito Santiago | .15 | .07 |
| 24 | Julian Tavarez | .15 | .07 |
| 25 | Jose Vizcaino | .15 | .07 |
| 26 | Andy Benes | .15 | .07 |
| 27 | Mariano Duncan | .15 | .07 |
| 28 | Checklist A | .15 | .07 |
| 29 | Shawon Dunston | .15 | .07 |
| 30 | Rafael Palmeiro | .60 | .25 |
| 31 | Dean Palmer | .30 | .14 |
| 32 | Andres Galarraga | .40 | .18 |
| 33 | Joey Cora | .15 | .07 |
| 34 | Mickey Tettleton | .15 | .07 |
| 35 | Barry Larkin | .60 | .25 |
| 36 | Carlos Baerga | .15 | .07 |
| 37 | Orel Hershiser | .30 | .14 |
| 38 | Jody Reed | .15 | .07 |
| 39 | Paul Molitor | .60 | .25 |
| 40 | Jim Edmonds | .60 | .25 |
| 41 | Bob Tewksbury | .15 | .07 |
| 42 | John Patterson | .15 | .07 |
| 43 | Ray McDavid | .15 | .07 |
| 44 | Zane Smith | .15 | .07 |
| 45 | Bret Saberhagen SE | .30 | .14 |
| 46 | Greg Maddux SE | .75 | .35 |
| 47 | Frank Thomas SE | .60 | .25 |
| 48 | Carlos Baerga SE | .15 | .07 |
| 49 | Billy Spiers | .15 | .07 |
| 50 | Stan Javier | .15 | .07 |
| 51 | Rex Hudler | .15 | .07 |
| 52 | Denny Hocking | .15 | .07 |
| 53 | Todd Worrell | .15 | .07 |
| 54 | Mark Clark | .15 | .07 |
| 55 | Hipolito Pichardo | .15 | .07 |
| 56 | Bob Wickman | .15 | .07 |
| 57 | Raul Mondesi | .30 | .14 |
| 58 | Steve Cooke | .15 | .07 |
| 59 | Rod Beck | .15 | .07 |
| 60 | Tim Davis | .15 | .07 |
| 61 | Jeff Kent | .40 | .18 |
| 62 | John Valentin | .15 | .07 |
| 63 | Alex Arias | .15 | .07 |
| 64 | Steve Reed | .15 | .07 |
| 65 | Ozzie Smith | .75 | .35 |
| 66 | Terry Pendleton | .30 | .14 |
| 67 | Kenny Rogers | .15 | .07 |
| 68 | Vince Coleman | .15 | .07 |
| 69 | Tom Pagnozzi | .15 | .07 |
| 70 | Roberto Alomar | .60 | .25 |
| 71 | Darrin Jackson | .15 | .07 |
| 72 | Dennis Eckersley | .30 | .14 |
| 73 | Jay Buhner | .30 | .14 |
| 74 | Darren Lewis | .15 | .07 |
| 75 | Dave Weathers | .15 | .07 |
| 76 | Matt Walbeck | .15 | .07 |
| 77 | Brad Ausmus | .15 | .07 |
| 78 | Danny Bautista | .15 | .07 |
| 79 | Bob Hamelin | .15 | .07 |
| 80 | Steve Trachsel | .15 | .07 |
| 81 | Ken Ryan | .15 | .07 |
| 82 | Chris Turner | .15 | .07 |
| 83 | David Segui | .15 | .07 |
| 84 | Ben McDonald | .15 | .07 |
| 85 | Wade Boggs | .75 | .35 |
| 86 | John Vander Wal | .15 | .07 |
| 87 | Sandy Alomar Jr. | .30 | .14 |
| 88 | Ron Karkovice | .15 | .07 |
| 89 | Doug Jones | .15 | .07 |
| 90 | Gary Sheffield | .60 | .25 |
| 91 | Ken Caminiti | .30 | .14 |
| 92 | Chris Bosio | .15 | .07 |
| 93 | Kevin Tapani | .15 | .07 |
| 94 | Walt Weiss | .15 | .07 |
| 95 | Erik Hanson | .15 | .07 |
| 96 | Ruben Sierra | .15 | .07 |
| 97 | Nomar Garciaparra | 4.00 | 1.80 |
| 98 | Terrence Long | .60 | .25 |
| 99 | Jacob Shumate | .15 | .07 |
| 100 | Paul Wilson | .15 | .07 |
| 101 | Kevin Witt | .30 | .14 |
| 102 | Paul Konerko | .60 | .25 |
| 103 | Ben Grieve | 1.00 | .45 |
| 104 | Mark Johnson RC | .15 | .07 |
| 105 | Cade Gaspar RC | .15 | .07 |
| 106 | Mark Farris RC | .15 | .07 |
| 107 | Dustin Hermanson | .15 | .07 |
| 108 | Scott Elarton RC | 1.50 | .70 |
| 109 | Doug Million | .15 | .07 |
| 110 | Matt Smith RC | .15 | .07 |
| 111 | Brian Buchanan RC | .15 | .07 |
| 112 | Jayson Peterson RC | .15 | .07 |
| 113 | Bret Wagner RC | .15 | .07 |
| 114 | C.J. Nitkowski RC | .15 | .07 |
| 115 | Ramon Castro RC | .30 | .14 |
| 116 | Rafael Bournigal | .15 | .07 |
| 117 | Jeff Fassero | .15 | .07 |
| 118 | Bobby Bonilla | .30 | .14 |
| 119 | Ricky Gutierrez | .15 | .07 |
| 120 | Roger Pavlik | .15 | .07 |
| 121 | Mike Greenwell | .15 | .07 |
| 122 | Deion Sanders | .30 | .14 |
| 123 | Charlie Hayes | .15 | .07 |
| 124 | Paul O'Neill | .30 | .14 |
| 125 | Jay Bell | .30 | .14 |
| 126 | Royce Clayton | .15 | .07 |
| 127 | Willie Banks | .15 | .07 |
| 128 | Mark Wohlers | .15 | .07 |
| 129 | Todd Jones | .15 | .07 |
| 130 | Todd Stottlemyre | .15 | .07 |
| 131 | Will Clark | .60 | .25 |
| 132 | Wilson Alvarez | .15 | .07 |
| 133 | Chili Davis | .30 | .14 |
| 134 | Dave Burba | .15 | .07 |
| 135 | Chris Hoiles | .15 | .07 |
| 136 | Jeff Blauser | .15 | .07 |
| 137 | Jeff Reboulet | .15 | .07 |
| 138 | Bret Saberhagen | .30 | .14 |
| 139 | Kirk Rueter | .15 | .07 |
| 140 | Dave Nilsson | .15 | .07 |
| 141 | Pat Borders | .15 | .07 |
| 142 | Ron Darling | .15 | .07 |
| 143 | Derek Bell | .15 | .07 |
| 144 | Dave Hollins | .15 | .07 |
| 145 | Juan Gonzalez | .60 | .25 |
| 146 | Andre Dawson | .40 | .18 |
| 147 | Jim Thome | .40 | .18 |
| 148 | Larry Walker | .30 | .14 |
| 149 | Mike Piazza | 2.00 | .90 |
| 150 | Mike Perez | .15 | .07 |
| 151 | Steve Avery | .15 | .07 |
| 152 | Dan Wilson | .15 | .07 |
| 153 | Andy Van Slyke | .30 | .14 |
| 154 | Junior Felix | .15 | .07 |
| 155 | Jack McDowell | .15 | .07 |
| 156 | Danny Tartabull | .15 | .07 |
| 157 | Willie Blair | .15 | .07 |
| 158 | Wm.VanLandingham | .15 | .07 |
| 159 | Robb Nen | .15 | .07 |
| 160 | Lee Tinsley | .15 | .07 |
| 161 | Ismael Valdes | .15 | .07 |
| 162 | Juan Guzman | .15 | .07 |
| 163 | Scott Servais | .15 | .07 |
| 164 | Cliff Floyd | .30 | .14 |
| 165 | Allen Watson | .15 | .07 |
| 166 | Eddie Taubensee | .15 | .07 |
| 167 | Scott Hemond | .15 | .07 |
| 168 | Jeff Tackett | .15 | .07 |
| 169 | Chad Curtis | .15 | .07 |
| 170 | Rico Brogna | .15 | .07 |
| 171 | Luis Polonia | .15 | .07 |
| 172 | Checklist B | .15 | .07 |
| 173 | Lance Johnson | .15 | .07 |
| 174 | Sammy Sosa | 1.25 | .55 |
| 175 | Mike Macfarlane | .15 | .07 |
| 176 | Darryl Hamilton | .15 | .07 |
| 177 | Rick Aguilera | .15 | .07 |
| 178 | Dave West | .15 | .07 |
| 179 | Mike Gallego | .15 | .07 |
| 180 | Marc Newfield | .15 | .07 |
| 181 | Steve Buechele | .15 | .07 |
| 182 | David Wells | .30 | .14 |
| 183 | Tom Glavine | .60 | .25 |
| 184 | Joe Girardi | .15 | .07 |
| 185 | Craig Biggio | .40 | .18 |
| 186 | Eddie Murray | .60 | .25 |
| 187 | Kevin Gross | .15 | .07 |
| 188 | Sid Fernandez | .15 | .07 |
| 189 | John Franco | .30 | .14 |
| 190 | Bernard Gilkey | .15 | .07 |

❑ 191 Matt Williams .40 .18
❑ 192 Darrin Fletcher .15 .07
❑ 193 Jeff Conine .15 .07
❑ 194 Ed Sprague .15 .07
❑ 195 Eduardo Perez .15 .07
❑ 196 Scott Livingstone .15 .07
❑ 197 Ivan Rodriguez .75 .35
❑ 198 Orlando Merced .15 .07
❑ 199 Ricky Bones .15 .07
❑ 200 Javier Lopez .30 .14
❑ 201 Miguel Jimenez .15 .07
❑ 202 Terry McGriff .15 .07
❑ 203 Mike Lieberthal .30 .14
❑ 204 David Cone .30 .14
❑ 205 Todd Hundley .15 .07
❑ 206 Ozzie Guillen .15 .07
❑ 207 Alex Cole .15 .07
❑ 208 Tony Phillips .15 .07
❑ 209 Jim Eisenreich .15 .07
❑ 210 Greg Vaughn BES .15 .07
❑ 211 Barry Larkin BES .30 .14
❑ 212 Don Mattingly BES .75 .25
❑ 213 Mark Grace BES .30 .14
❑ 214 Jose Canseco BES .40 .18
❑ 215 Joe Carter BES .15 .07
❑ 216 David Cone BES .15 .07
❑ 217 Sandy Alomar Jr. BES .15 .07
❑ 218 Al Martin BES .15 .07
❑ 219 Roberto Kelly BES .15 .07
❑ 220 Paul Sorrento .15 .07
❑ 221 Tony Fernandez .15 .07
❑ 222 Stan Belinda .15 .07
❑ 223 Mike Stanley .15 .07
❑ 224 Doug Drabek .15 .07
❑ 225 Todd Van Poppel .15 .07
❑ 226 Matt Mieske .15 .07
❑ 227 Tino Martinez .30 .14
❑ 228 Andy Ashby .15 .07
❑ 229 Midre Cummings .15 .07
❑ 230 Jeff Frye .15 .07
❑ 231 Hal Morris .15 .07
❑ 232 Jose Lind .15 .07
❑ 233 Shawn Green .60 .25
❑ 234 Rafael Belliard .15 .07
❑ 235 Randy Myers .15 .07
❑ 236 Frank Thomas CE .60 .25
❑ 237 Darren Daulton CE .15 .07
❑ 238 Sammy Sosa CE .60 .25
❑ 239 Cal Ripken CE 1.25 .55
❑ 240 Jeff Bagwell CE .60 .25
❑ 241 Ken Griffey Jr. 2.50 1.10
❑ 242 Brett Butler .30 .14
❑ 243 Derrick May .15 .07
❑ 244 Pat Listach .15 .07
❑ 245 Mike Bordick .15 .07
❑ 246 Mark Langston .15 .07
❑ 247 Randy Velarde .15 .07
❑ 248 Julio Franco .15 .07
❑ 249 Chuck Knoblauch .30 .14
❑ 250 Bill Gullickson .15 .07
❑ 251 Dave Henderson .15 .07
❑ 252 Bret Boone .30 .14
❑ 253 Al Martin .15 .07
❑ 254 Armando Benitez .30 .14
❑ 255 Wil Cordero .15 .07
❑ 256 Al Leiter .30 .14
❑ 257 Luis Gonzalez .15 .07
❑ 258 Charlie O'Brien .15 .07
❑ 259 Tim Wallach .15 .07
❑ 260 Scott Sanders .15 .07
❑ 261 Tom Henke .15 .07
❑ 262 Otis Nixon .15 .07
❑ 263 Darren Daulton .30 .14
❑ 264 Manny Ramirez .75 .35
❑ 265 Bret Barberie .15 .07
❑ 266 Mel Rojas .15 .07
❑ 267 John Burkett .15 .07
❑ 268 Brady Anderson .30 .14
❑ 269 John Roper .15 .07
❑ 270 Shane Reynolds .15 .07
❑ 271 Barry Bonds 1.00 .45
❑ 272 Alex Fernandez .15 .07
❑ 273 Brian McRae .15 .07
❑ 274 Todd Zeile .15 .07
❑ 275 Greg Swindell .15 .07
❑ 276 Johnny Ruffin .15 .07
❑ 277 Troy Neel .15 .07
❑ 278 Eric Karros .30 .14
❑ 279 John Hudek .15 .07
❑ 280 Thomas Howard .15 .07
❑ 281 Joe Carter .30 .14
❑ 282 Mike Devereaux .15 .07
❑ 283 Butch Henry .15 .07
❑ 284 Reggie Jefferson .15 .07
❑ 285 Mark Lemke .15 .07
❑ 286 Jeff Montgomery .15 .07
❑ 287 Ryan Thompson .15 .07
❑ 288 Paul Shuey .15 .07
❑ 289 Mark McGwire 2.50 1.10
❑ 290 Bernie Williams .60 .25
❑ 291 Mickey Morandini .15 .07
❑ 292 Scott Leius .15 .07
❑ 293 David Hulse .15 .07
❑ 294 Greg Gagne .15 .07
❑ 295 Moises Alou .30 .14
❑ 296 Geronimo Berroa .15 .07
❑ 297 Eddie Zambrano .15 .07
❑ 298 Alan Trammell .40 .18
❑ 299 Don Slaught .15 .07
❑ 300 Jose Rijo .15 .07
❑ 301 Joe Ausanio .15 .07
❑ 302 Tim Raines .30 .14
❑ 303 Melido Perez .15 .07
❑ 304 Kent Mercker .15 .07
❑ 305 James Mouton .15 .07
❑ 306 Luis Lopez .15 .07
❑ 307 Mike Kingery .15 .07
❑ 308 Willie Greene .15 .07
❑ 309 Cecil Fielder .30 .14
❑ 310 Scott Kamieniecki .15 .07
❑ 311 Mike Greenwell BES .15 .07
❑ 312 Bobby Bonilla BES .30 .14
❑ 313 Andres Galarraga BES .40 .18
❑ 314 Cal Ripken BES 1.25 .55
❑ 315 Matt Williams BES .30 .14
❑ 316 Tom Pagnozzi BES .15 .07
❑ 317 Len Dykstra BES .15 .07
❑ 318 Frank Thomas BES .60 .25
❑ 319 Kirby Puckett BES .75 .25
❑ 320 Mike Piazza BES 1.00 .45
❑ 321 Jason Jacome .15 .07
❑ 322 Brian Hunter .15 .07
❑ 323 Brent Gates .15 .07
❑ 324 Jim Converse .15 .07
❑ 325 Damion Easley .15 .07
❑ 326 Dante Bichette .30 .14
❑ 327 Kurt Abbott .15 .07
❑ 328 Scott Cooper .15 .07
❑ 329 Mike Henneman .15 .07
❑ 330 Orlando Miller .15 .07
❑ 331 John Kruk .30 .14
❑ 332 Jose Oliva .15 .07
❑ 333 Reggie Sanders .15 .07
❑ 334 Omar Vizquel .30 .14
❑ 335 Devon White .30 .14
❑ 336 Mike Morgan .15 .07
❑ 337 J.R. Phillips .15 .07
❑ 338 Gary DiSarcina .15 .07
❑ 339 Joey Hamilton .15 .07
❑ 340 Randy Johnson .75 .35
❑ 341 Jim Leyritz .15 .07
❑ 342 Bobby Jones .15 .07
❑ 343 Jaime Navarro .15 .07
❑ 344 Bip Roberts .15 .07
❑ 345 Steve Karsay .15 .07
❑ 346 Kevin Stocker .15 .07
❑ 347 Jose Canseco .75 .35
❑ 348 Bill Wegman .15 .07
❑ 349 Rondell White .30 .14
❑ 350 Mo Vaughn .30 .14
❑ 351 Joe Orsulak .15 .07
❑ 352 Pat Meares .15 .07
❑ 353 Albie Lopez .15 .07
❑ 354 Edgar Martinez .40 .18
❑ 355 Brian Jordan .30 .14
❑ 356 Tommy Greene .15 .07
❑ 357 Chuck Carr .15 .07
❑ 358 Pedro Astacio .15 .07
❑ 359 Russ Davis .15 .07
❑ 360 Chris Hammond .15 .07
❑ 361 Gregg Jefferies .15 .07
❑ 362 Shane Mack .15 .07
❑ 363 Fred McGriff .40 .18
❑ 364 Pat Rapp .15 .07
❑ 365 Bill Swift .15 .07
❑ 366 Checklist .15 .07
❑ 367 Robin Ventura .30 .14
❑ 368 Bobby Witt .15 .07
❑ 369 Karl Rhodes .15 .07
❑ 370 Eddie Williams .15 .07
❑ 371 John Jaha .15 .07
❑ 372 Steve Howe .15 .07
❑ 373 Leo Gomez .15 .07
❑ 374 Hector Fajardo .15 .07
❑ 375 Jeff Bagwell .75 .35
❑ 376 Mark Acre .15 .07
❑ 377 Wayne Kirby .15 .07
❑ 378 Mark Portugal .15 .07
❑ 379 Jesus Tavarez .15 .07
❑ 380 Jim Lindeman .15 .07
❑ 381 Don Mattingly 1.50 .70
❑ 382 Trevor Hoffman .30 .14
❑ 383 Chris Gomez .15 .07
❑ 384 Garret Anderson .30 .14
❑ 385 Bobby Munoz .15 .07
❑ 386 Jon Lieber .15 .07
❑ 387 Rick Helling .30 .14
❑ 388 Marvin Freeman .15 .07
❑ 389 Juan Castillo .15 .07
❑ 390 Jeff Cirillo .30 .14
❑ 391 Sean Berry .15 .07
❑ 392 Hector Carrasco .15 .07
❑ 393 Mark Grace .60 .25
❑ 394 Pat Kelly .15 .07
❑ 395 Tim Naehring .15 .07
❑ 396 Greg Pirkl .15 .07
❑ 397 John Smoltz .30 .14
❑ 398 Robby Thompson .15 .07
❑ 399 Rick White .15 .07
❑ 400 Frank Thomas 1.25 .55
❑ 401 Jeff Conine CS .15 .07
❑ 402 Jose Valentin CS .15 .07
❑ 403 Carlos Baerga CS .15 .07
❑ 404 Rick Aguilera CS .15 .07
❑ 405 Wilson Alvarez CS .15 .07
❑ 406 Juan Gonzalez CS .30 .14
❑ 407 Barry Larkin CS .30 .14
❑ 408 Ken Hill CS .15 .07
❑ 409 Chuck Carr CS .15 .07
❑ 410 Tim Raines CS .15 .07
❑ 411 Bryan Eversgerd .15 .07
❑ 412 Phil Plantier .15 .07
❑ 413 Josias Manzanillo .15 .07
❑ 414 Roberto Kelly .15 .07
❑ 415 Rickey Henderson .75 .35
❑ 416 John Smiley .15 .07
❑ 417 Kevin Brown .40 .18
❑ 418 Jimmy Key .30 .14
❑ 419 Wally Joyner .30 .14
❑ 420 Roberto Hernandez .15 .07
❑ 421 Felix Fermin .15 .07
❑ 422 Checklist .15 .07
❑ 423 Greg Vaughn .30 .14
❑ 424 Ray Lankford .30 .14
❑ 425 Greg Maddux 1.50 .70
❑ 426 Mike Mussina .60 .25
❑ 427 Geronimo Pena .15 .07
❑ 428 David Nied .15 .07
❑ 429 Scott Erickson .15 .07
❑ 430 Kevin Mitchell .15 .07
❑ 431 Mike Lansing .15 .07
❑ 432 Brian Anderson .15 .07
❑ 433 Jeff King .15 .07
❑ 434 Ramon Martinez .15 .07
❑ 435 Kevin Seitzer .15 .07
❑ 436 Salomon Torres .15 .07
❑ 437 Brian L.Hunter .15 .07
❑ 438 Melvin Nieves .15 .07
❑ 439 Mike Kelly .15 .07
❑ 440 Marquis Grissom .15 .07
❑ 441 Chuck Finley .30 .14
❑ 442 Len Dykstra .30 .14
❑ 443 Ellis Burks .30 .14
❑ 444 Harold Baines .30 .14
❑ 445 Kevin Appier .30 .14
❑ 446 David Justice .40 .18
❑ 447 Darryl Kile .30 .14
❑ 448 John Olerud .30 .14

| No. | Player | Mint | NrMt |
|---|---|---|---|
| ❑ 449 | Greg McMichael | .15 | .07 |
| ❑ 450 | Kirby Puckett | 1.50 | .70 |
| ❑ 451 | Jose Valentin | .15 | .07 |
| ❑ 452 | Rick Wilkins | .15 | .07 |
| ❑ 453 | Arthur Rhodes | .15 | .07 |
| ❑ 454 | Pat Hentgen | .15 | .07 |
| ❑ 455 | Tom Gordon | .15 | .07 |
| ❑ 456 | Tom Candiotti | .15 | .07 |
| ❑ 457 | Jason Bere | .15 | .07 |
| ❑ 458 | Wes Chamberlain | .15 | .07 |
| ❑ 459 | Greg Colbrunn | .15 | .07 |
| ❑ 460 | John Doherty | .15 | .07 |
| ❑ 461 | Kevin Foster | .15 | .07 |
| ❑ 462 | Mark Whiten | .15 | .07 |
| ❑ 463 | Terry Steinbach | .15 | .07 |
| ❑ 464 | Aaron Sele | .30 | .14 |
| ❑ 465 | Kirt Manwaring | .15 | .07 |
| ❑ 466 | Darren Hall | .15 | .07 |
| ❑ 467 | Delino DeShields | .15 | .07 |
| ❑ 468 | Andujar Cedeno | .15 | .07 |
| ❑ 469 | Billy Ashley | .15 | .07 |
| ❑ 470 | Kenny Lofton | .30 | .14 |
| ❑ 471 | Pedro Munoz | .15 | .07 |
| ❑ 472 | John Wetteland | .30 | .14 |
| ❑ 473 | Tim Salmon | .30 | .14 |
| ❑ 474 | Denny Neagle | .30 | .14 |
| ❑ 475 | Tony Gwynn | 1.25 | .55 |
| ❑ 476 | Vinny Castilla | .30 | .14 |
| ❑ 477 | Steve Dreyer | .15 | .07 |
| ❑ 478 | Jeff Shaw | .15 | .07 |
| ❑ 479 | Chad Ogea | .15 | .07 |
| ❑ 480 | Scott Ruffcorn | .15 | .07 |
| ❑ 481 | Lou Whitaker | .30 | .14 |
| ❑ 482 | J.T. Snow | .30 | .14 |
| ❑ 483 | Rich Rowland | .15 | .07 |
| ❑ 484 | Donny Martinez | .30 | .14 |
| ❑ 485 | Pedro Martinez | .75 | .35 |
| ❑ 486 | Rusty Greer | .30 | .14 |
| ❑ 487 | Dave Fleming | .15 | .07 |
| ❑ 488 | John Dettmer | .15 | .07 |
| ❑ 489 | Albert Belle | .40 | .18 |
| ❑ 490 | Ravelo Manzanillo | .15 | .07 |
| ❑ 491 | Henry Rodriguez | .15 | .07 |
| ❑ 492 | Andrew Lorraine | .15 | .07 |
| ❑ 493 | Dwayne Hosey | .15 | .07 |
| ❑ 494 | Mike Blowers | .15 | .07 |
| ❑ 495 | Turner Ward | .15 | .07 |
| ❑ 496 | Fred McGriff EC | .15 | .07 |
| ❑ 497 | Sammy Sosa EC | .60 | .25 |
| ❑ 498 | Barry Larkin EC | .30 | .14 |
| ❑ 499 | Andres Galarraga EC | .40 | .18 |
| ❑ 500 | Gary Sheffield EC | .30 | .14 |
| ❑ 501 | Jeff Bagwell EC | .60 | .25 |
| ❑ 502 | Mike Piazza EC | 1.00 | .45 |
| ❑ 503 | Moises Alou EC | .15 | .07 |
| ❑ 504 | Bobby Bonilla EC | .30 | .14 |
| ❑ 505 | Darren Daulton EC | .15 | .07 |
| ❑ 506 | Jeff King EC | .15 | .07 |
| ❑ 507 | Ray Lankford EC | .15 | .07 |
| ❑ 508 | Tony Gwynn EC | .60 | .25 |
| ❑ 509 | Barry Bonds EC | .40 | .18 |
| ❑ 510 | Cal Ripken EC | 1.25 | .55 |
| ❑ 511 | Mo Vaughn EC | .30 | .14 |
| ❑ 512 | Tim Salmon EC | .15 | .07 |
| ❑ 513 | Frank Thomas EC | .60 | .25 |
| ❑ 514 | Albert Belle EC | .15 | .07 |
| ❑ 515 | Cecil Fielder EC | .15 | .07 |
| ❑ 516 | Kevin Appier EC | .15 | .07 |
| ❑ 517 | Greg Vaughn EC | .15 | .07 |
| ❑ 518 | Kirby Puckett EC | .75 | .35 |
| ❑ 519 | Paul O'Neill EC | .15 | .07 |
| ❑ 520 | Ruben Sierra EC | .15 | .07 |
| ❑ 521 | Ken Griffey Jr. EC | 1.25 | .55 |
| ❑ 522 | Will Clark EC | .30 | .14 |
| ❑ 523 | Joe Carter EC | .15 | .07 |
| ❑ 524 | Antonio Osuna | .15 | .07 |
| ❑ 525 | Glenallen Hill | .15 | .07 |
| ❑ 526 | Alex Gonzalez | .15 | .07 |
| ❑ 527 | Dave Stewart | .30 | .14 |
| ❑ 528 | Ron Gant | .15 | .07 |
| ❑ 529 | Jason Bates | .15 | .07 |
| ❑ 530 | Mike Macfarlane | .15 | .07 |
| ❑ 531 | Esteban Loaiza | .15 | .07 |
| ❑ 532 | Joe Randa | .15 | .07 |
| ❑ 533 | Dave Winfield | .60 | .25 |
| ❑ 534 | Danny Darwin | .15 | .07 |
| ❑ 535 | Pete Harnisch | .15 | .07 |
| ❑ 536 | Joey Cora | .15 | .07 |
| ❑ 537 | Jaime Navarro | .15 | .07 |
| ❑ 538 | Marty Cordova | .15 | .07 |
| ❑ 539 | Andujar Cedeno | .15 | .07 |
| ❑ 540 | Mickey Tettleton | .15 | .07 |
| ❑ 541 | Andy Van Slyke | .30 | .14 |
| ❑ 542 | Carlos Perez RC | .30 | .14 |
| ❑ 543 | Chipper Jones | 1.50 | .70 |
| ❑ 544 | Tony Fernandez | .15 | .07 |
| ❑ 545 | Tom Henke | .15 | .07 |
| ❑ 546 | Pat Borders | .15 | .07 |
| ❑ 547 | Chad Curtis | .15 | .07 |
| ❑ 548 | Ray Durham | .30 | .14 |
| ❑ 549 | Joe Oliver | .15 | .07 |
| ❑ 550 | Jose Mesa | .15 | .07 |
| ❑ 551 | Steve Finley | .30 | .14 |
| ❑ 552 | Otis Nixon | .15 | .07 |
| ❑ 553 | Jacob Brumfield | .15 | .07 |
| ❑ 554 | Bill Swift | .15 | .07 |
| ❑ 555 | Quilvio Veras | .15 | .07 |
| ❑ 556 | Hideo Nomo RC UER (Wins and IP totals reversed) | 1.50 | .70 |
| ❑ 557 | Joe Vitiello | .15 | .07 |
| ❑ 558 | Mike Perez | .15 | .07 |
| ❑ 559 | Charlie Hayes | .15 | .07 |
| ❑ 560 | Brad Radke RC | 1.00 | .45 |
| ❑ 561 | Darren Bragg | .15 | .07 |
| ❑ 562 | Orel Hershiser | .30 | .14 |
| ❑ 563 | Edgardo Alfonzo | .60 | .25 |
| ❑ 564 | Doug Jones | .15 | .07 |
| ❑ 565 | Andy Pettitte | .40 | .18 |
| ❑ 566 | Benito Santiago | .15 | .07 |
| ❑ 567 | John Burkett | .15 | .07 |
| ❑ 568 | Brad Clontz | .15 | .07 |
| ❑ 569 | Jim Abbott | .30 | .14 |
| ❑ 570 | Joe Rosselli | .15 | .07 |
| ❑ 571 | Mark Grudzielanek RC | .30 | .14 |
| ❑ 572 | Dustin Hermanson | .15 | .07 |
| ❑ 573 | Benji Gil | .15 | .07 |
| ❑ 574 | Mark Whiten | .15 | .07 |
| ❑ 575 | Mike Ignasiak | .15 | .07 |
| ❑ 576 | Kevin Ritz | .15 | .07 |
| ❑ 577 | Paul Quantrill | .15 | .07 |
| ❑ 578 | Andre Dawson | .40 | .18 |
| ❑ 579 | Jerald Clark | .15 | .07 |
| ❑ 580 | Frank Rodriguez | .15 | .07 |
| ❑ 581 | Mark Kiefer | .15 | .07 |
| ❑ 582 | Trevor Wilson | .15 | .07 |
| ❑ 583 | Gary Wilson RC | .15 | .07 |
| ❑ 584 | Andy Stankiewicz | .15 | .07 |
| ❑ 585 | Felipe Lira | .15 | .07 |
| ❑ 586 | Mike Mimbs RC | .15 | .07 |
| ❑ 587 | Jon Nunnally | .15 | .07 |
| ❑ 588 | Tomas Perez RC | .15 | .07 |
| ❑ 589 | Checklist | .15 | .07 |
| ❑ 590 | Todd Hollandsworth | .15 | .07 |
| ❑ 591 | Roberto Petagine | .15 | .07 |
| ❑ 592 | Mariano Rivera | .30 | .14 |
| ❑ 593 | Mark McLemore | .15 | .07 |
| ❑ 594 | Bobby Witt | .15 | .07 |
| ❑ 595 | Jose Offerman | .15 | .07 |
| ❑ 596 | Jason Christiansen RC | .15 | .07 |
| ❑ 597 | Jeff Manto | .15 | .07 |
| ❑ 598 | Jim Dougherty RC | .15 | .07 |
| ❑ 599 | Juan Acevedo RC | .15 | .07 |
| ❑ 600 | Troy O'Leary | .15 | .07 |
| ❑ 601 | Ron Villone | .15 | .07 |
| ❑ 602 | Tripp Cromer | .15 | .07 |
| ❑ 603 | Steve Scarsone | .15 | .07 |
| ❑ 604 | Lance Parrish | .15 | .07 |
| ❑ 605 | Ozzie Timmons | .15 | .07 |
| ❑ 606 | Ray Holbert | .15 | .07 |
| ❑ 607 | Tony Phillips | .15 | .07 |
| ❑ 608 | Phil Plantier | .15 | .07 |
| ❑ 609 | Shane Andrews | .15 | .07 |
| ❑ 610 | Heathcliff Slocumb | .15 | .07 |
| ❑ 611 | Bobby Higginson RC | 1.00 | .45 |
| ❑ 612 | Bob Tewksbury | .15 | .07 |
| ❑ 613 | Terry Pendleton | .30 | .14 |
| ❑ 614 | Scott Cooper TA | .15 | .07 |
| ❑ 615 | John Wetteland TA | .15 | .07 |
| ❑ 616 | Ken Hill TA | .15 | .07 |
| ❑ 617 | Marquis Grissom TA | .15 | .07 |
| ❑ 618 | Larry Walker TA | .30 | .14 |
| ❑ 619 | Derek Bell TA | .15 | .07 |
| ❑ 620 | David Cone TA | .15 | .07 |
| ❑ 621 | Ken Caminiti TA | .15 | .07 |
| ❑ 622 | Jack McDowell TA | .15 | .07 |
| ❑ 623 | Vaughn Eshelman TA | .15 | .07 |
| ❑ 624 | Brian McRae TA | .15 | .07 |
| ❑ 625 | Gregg Jefferies TA | .15 | .07 |
| ❑ 626 | Kevin Brown TA | .15 | .07 |
| ❑ 627 | Lee Smith TA | .15 | .07 |
| ❑ 628 | Tony Tarasco TA | .15 | .07 |
| ❑ 629 | Brett Butler TA | .15 | .07 |
| ❑ 630 | Jose Canseco TA | .40 | .18 |

## 1996 Stadium Club

| | MINT | NRMT |
|---|---|---|
| COMPLETE SET (450) | 90.00 | 40.00 |
| COMP.CEREAL SET (454) | 90.00 | 40.00 |
| COMPLETE SERIES 1 (225) | 50.00 | 22.00 |
| COMPLETE SERIES 2 (225) | 40.00 | 18.00 |
| COMMON (1-180/271-450) | .15 | .07 |
| COMMON TSC SP (181-270) | .25 | .11 |

| No. | Player | Mint | NrMt |
|---|---|---|---|
| ❑ 1 | Hideo Nomo | .60 | .25 |
| ❑ 2 | Paul Molitor | .60 | .25 |
| ❑ 3 | Garret Anderson | .25 | .11 |
| ❑ 4 | Jose Mesa | .15 | .07 |
| ❑ 5 | Vinny Castilla | .25 | .11 |
| ❑ 6 | Mike Mussina | .60 | .25 |
| ❑ 7 | Ray Durham | .25 | .11 |
| ❑ 8 | Jack McDowell | .15 | .07 |
| ❑ 9 | Juan Gonzalez | .60 | .25 |
| ❑ 10 | Chipper Jones | 1.50 | .70 |
| ❑ 11 | Deion Sanders | .25 | .11 |
| ❑ 12 | Rondell White | .25 | .11 |
| ❑ 13 | Tom Henke | .15 | .07 |
| ❑ 14 | Derek Bell | .15 | .07 |
| ❑ 15 | Randy Myers | .15 | .07 |
| ❑ 16 | Randy Johnson | .75 | .35 |
| ❑ 17 | Len Dykstra | .25 | .11 |
| ❑ 18 | Bill Pulsipher | .15 | .07 |
| ❑ 19 | Greg Colbrunn | .15 | .07 |
| ❑ 20 | David Wells | .25 | .11 |
| ❑ 21 | Chad Curtis | .15 | .07 |
| ❑ 22 | Roberto Hernandez SP | 5.00 | 2.20 |
| ❑ 23 | Kirby Puckett | 1.50 | .70 |
| ❑ 24 | Joe Vitiello | .15 | .07 |
| ❑ 25 | Roger Clemens | 1.25 | .55 |
| ❑ 26 | Al Martin | .15 | .07 |
| ❑ 27 | Chad Ogea | .15 | .07 |
| ❑ 28 | David Segui | .15 | .07 |
| ❑ 29 | Joey Hamilton | .15 | .07 |
| ❑ 30 | Dan Wilson | .15 | .07 |
| ❑ 31 | Chad Fonville | .15 | .07 |
| ❑ 32 | Bernard Gilkey | .15 | .07 |
| ❑ 33 | Kevin Seitzer | .15 | .07 |
| ❑ 34 | Shawn Green | .60 | .25 |
| ❑ 35 | Rick Aguilera | .15 | .07 |
| ❑ 36 | Gary DiSarcina | .15 | .07 |
| ❑ 37 | Jaime Navarro | .15 | .07 |
| ❑ 38 | Doug Jones | .15 | .07 |
| ❑ 39 | Brent Gates | .15 | .07 |
| ❑ 40 | Dean Palmer | .25 | .11 |
| ❑ 41 | Pat Rapp | .15 | .07 |
| ❑ 42 | Tony Clark | .15 | .07 |
| ❑ 43 | Bill Swift | .15 | .07 |
| ❑ 44 | Randy Velarde | .15 | .07 |
| ❑ 45 | Matt Williams | .40 | .18 |
| ❑ 46 | John Mabry | .15 | .07 |

❑ 47 Mike Fetters .15 .07
❑ 48 Orlando Miller .15 .07
❑ 49 Tom Glavine .60 .25
❑ 50 Delino DeShields .15 .07
❑ 51 Scott Erickson .15 .07
❑ 52 Andy Van Slyke .25 .11
❑ 53 Jim Bullinger .15 .07
❑ 54 Lyle Mouton .15 .07
❑ 55 Bret Saberhagen .25 .11
❑ 56 Benito Santiago .15 .07
❑ 57 Dan Miceli .15 .07
❑ 58 Carl Everett .25 .11
❑ 59 Rod Beck .15 .07
❑ 60 Phil Nevin .25 .11
❑ 61 Jason Giambi .60 .25
❑ 62 Paul Menhart .15 .07
❑ 63 Eric Karros .25 .11
❑ 64 Allen Watson .15 .07
❑ 65 Jeff Cirillo .25 .11
❑ 66 Lee Smith .25 .11
❑ 67 Sean Berry .15 .07
❑ 68 Luis Sojo .15 .07
❑ 69 Jeff Montgomery .15 .07
❑ 70 Todd Hundley .15 .07
❑ 71 John Burkett .15 .07
❑ 72 Mark Gubicza .15 .07
❑ 73 Don Mattingly 1.00 .45
❑ 74 Jeff Brantley .15 .07
❑ 75 Matt Walbeck .15 .07
❑ 76 Steve Parris .15 .07
❑ 77 Ken Caminiti .25 .11
❑ 78 Kirt Manwaring .15 .07
❑ 79 Greg Vaughn .25 .11
❑ 80 Pedro Martinez .75 .35
❑ 81 Benji Gil .15 .07
❑ 82 Heathcliff Slocumb .15 .07
❑ 83 Joe Girardi .15 .07
❑ 84 Sean Bergman .15 .07
❑ 85 Matt Karchner .15 .07
❑ 86 Butch Huskey .15 .07
❑ 87 Mike Morgan .15 .07
❑ 88 Todd Worrell .15 .07
❑ 89 Mike Bordick .15 .07
❑ 90 Bip Roberts .15 .07
❑ 91 Mike Hampton .25 .11
❑ 92 Troy O'Leary .15 .07
❑ 93 Wally Joyner .25 .11
❑ 94 Dave Stevens .15 .07
❑ 95 Cecil Fielder .25 .11
❑ 96 Wade Boggs .75 .35
❑ 97 Hal Morris .15 .07
❑ 98 Mickey Tettleton .15 .07
❑ 99 Jeff Kent .40 .18
❑ 100 Denny Martinez .25 .11
❑ 101 Luis Gonzalez .25 .11
❑ 102 John Jaha .15 .07
❑ 103 Javier Lopez .25 .11
❑ 104 Mark McGwire 2.50 1.10
❑ 105 Ken Griffey Jr. 2.50 1.10
❑ 106 Darren Daulton .25 .11
❑ 107 Bryan Rekar .15 .07
❑ 108 Mike Macfarlane .15 .07
❑ 109 Gary Gaetti .25 .11
❑ 110 Shane Reynolds .15 .07
❑ 111 Pat Meares .15 .07
❑ 112 Jason Schmidt .15 .07
❑ 113 Otis Nixon .15 .07
❑ 114 John Franco .25 .11
❑ 115 Marc Newfield .15 .07
❑ 116 Andy Benes .15 .07
❑ 117 Ozzie Guillen .15 .07
❑ 118 Brian Jordan .25 .11
❑ 119 Terry Pendleton .25 .11
❑ 120 Chuck Finley .25 .11
❑ 121 Scott Stahoviak .15 .07
❑ 122 Sid Fernandez .15 .07
❑ 123 Derek Jeter 2.50 1.10
❑ 124 John Smiley .15 .07
❑ 125 David Bell .15 .07
❑ 126 Brett Butler .25 .11
❑ 127 Doug Drabek .15 .07
❑ 128 J.T. Snow .25 .11
❑ 129 Joe Carter .25 .11
❑ 130 Dennis Eckersley .25 .11
❑ 131 Marty Cordova .15 .07
❑ 132 Greg Maddux 1.50 .70
❑ 133 Tom Goodwin .15 .07
❑ 134 Andy Ashby .15 .07
❑ 135 Paul Sorrento .15 .07
❑ 136 Ricky Bones .15 .07
❑ 137 Shawon Dunston .15 .07
❑ 138 Moises Alou .25 .11
❑ 139 Mickey Morandini .15 .07
❑ 140 Ramon Martinez .15 .07
❑ 141 Royce Clayton .15 .07
❑ 142 Brad Ausmus .15 .07
❑ 143 Kenny Rogers .15 .07
❑ 144 Tim Naehring .15 .07
❑ 145 Chris Gomez .15 .07
❑ 146 Bobby Bonilla .25 .11
❑ 147 Wilson Alvarez .15 .07
❑ 148 Johnny Damon .25 .11
❑ 149 Pat Hentgen .15 .07
❑ 150 Andres Galarraga .40 .18
❑ 151 David Cone .25 .11
❑ 152 Lance Johnson .15 .07
❑ 153 Carlos Garcia .15 .07
❑ 154 Doug Johns .15 .07
❑ 155 Midre Cummings .15 .07
❑ 156 Steve Sparks .15 .07
❑ 157 Sandy Martinez .15 .07
❑ 158 Wm. Van Landingham .15 .07
❑ 159 David Justice .40 .18
❑ 160 Mark Grace .60 .25
❑ 161 Robb Nen .15 .07
❑ 162 Mike Greenwell .15 .07
❑ 163 Brad Radke .25 .11
❑ 164 Edgardo Alfonzo .25 .11
❑ 165 Mark Leiter .15 .07
❑ 166 Walt Weiss .15 .07
❑ 167 Mel Rojas .15 .07
❑ 168 Bret Boone .25 .11
❑ 169 Ricky Bottalico .15 .07
❑ 170 Bobby Higginson .25 .11
❑ 171 Trevor Hoffman .25 .11
❑ 172 Jay Bell .25 .11
❑ 173 Gabe White .15 .07
❑ 174 Curtis Goodwin .15 .07
❑ 175 Tyler Green .15 .07
❑ 176 Roberto Alomar .60 .25
❑ 177 Sterling Hitchcock .15 .07
❑ 178 Ryan Klesko .25 .11
❑ 179 Donne Wall .15 .07
❑ 180 Brian McRae .15 .07
❑ 181 Will Clark TSC SP .75 .35
❑ 182 Frank Thomas TSC SP 1.50 .70
❑ 183 Jeff Bagwell TSC SP 1.00 .45
❑ 184 Mo Vaughn TSC SP .40 .18
❑ 185 Tino Martinez TSC SP .40 .18
❑ 186 Craig Biggio TSC SP .50 .23
❑ 187 C. Knoblauch TSC SP .40 .18
❑ 188 Carlos Baerga TSC SP .25 .11
❑ 189 Quilvio Veras TSC SP .25 .11
❑ 190 Luis Alicea TSC SP .25 .11
❑ 191 Jim Thome TSC SP .50 .23
❑ 192 Mike Blowers TSC SP .25 .11
❑ 193 Robin Ventura TSC SP .40 .18
❑ 194 Jeff King TSC SP .25 .11
❑ 195 Tony Phillips TSC SP .25 .11
❑ 196 John Valentin TSC SP .25 .11
❑ 197 Barry Larkin TSC SP .75 .35
❑ 198 Cal Ripken TSC SP 3.00 1.35
❑ 199 Omar Vizquel TSC SP .40 .18
❑ 200 Kurt Abbott TSC SP .25 .11
❑ 201 Albert Belle TSC SP .25 .11
❑ 202 Barry Bonds TSC SP 1.25 .55
❑ 203 Ron Gant TSC SP .25 .11
❑ 204 Dante Bichette TSC SP .40 .18
❑ 205 Jeff Conine TSC SP .25 .11
❑ 206 Jim Edmonds TSC SP UER .75 .35
(Greg Myers pictured on front)
❑ 207 Stan Javier TSC SP .25 .11
❑ 208 Kenny Lofton TSC SP .40 .18
❑ 209 Ray Lankford TSC SP .40 .18
❑ 210 Bernie Williams TSC SP .75 .35
❑ 211 Jay Buhner TSC SP .40 .18
❑ 212 Paul O'Neill TSC SP .40 .18
❑ 213 Tim Salmon TSC SP .40 .18
❑ 214 Reggie Sanders TSC SP .25 .11
❑ 215 Manny Ramirez TSC SP 1.00 .45
❑ 216 Mike Piazza TSC SP 2.50 1.10
❑ 217 Mike Stanley TSC SP .25 .11
❑ 218 Tony Eusebio TSC SP .25 .11
❑ 219 Chris Hoiles TSC SP .25 .11
❑ 220 Ron Karkovice TSC SP .25 .11
❑ 221 Edgar Martinez TSC SP .50 .23
❑ 222 Chili Davis TSC SP .40 .18
❑ 223 Jose Canseco TSC SP 1.00 .45
❑ 224 Eddie Murray TSC SP .75 .35
❑ 225 Geronimo Berroa TSC SP .25 .11
❑ 226 Chipper Jones TSC SP 2.00 .90
❑ 227 Garret Anderson TSC SP .40 .18
❑ 228 Marty Cordova TSC SP .25 .11
❑ 229 Jon Nunnally TSC SP .25 .11
❑ 230 Brian L.Hunter TSC SP .25 .11
❑ 231 Shawn Green TSC SP .75 .35
❑ 232 Ray Durham TSC SP .40 .18
❑ 233 Alex Gonzalez TSC SP .25 .11
❑ 234 Bobby Higginson TSC SP .40 .18
❑ 235 Randy Johnson TSC SP 1.00 .45
❑ 236 Al Leiter TSC SP .40 .18
❑ 237 Tom Glavine TSC SP .75 .35
❑ 238 Kenny Rogers TSC SP .25 .11
❑ 239 Mike Hampton TSC SP .40 .18
❑ 240 David Wells TSC SP .40 .18
❑ 241 Jim Abbott TSC SP .40 .18
❑ 242 Denny Neagle TSC SP .40 .18
❑ 243 Wilson Alvarez TSC SP .25 .11
❑ 244 John Smiley TSC SP .25 .11
❑ 245 Greg Maddux TSC SP 2.00 .90
❑ 246 Andy Ashby TSC SP .25 .11
❑ 247 Hideo Nomo TSC SP .75 .35
❑ 248 Pat Rapp TSC SP .25 .11
❑ 249 Tim Wakefield TSC SP .25 .11
❑ 250 John Smoltz TSC SP .40 .18
❑ 251 Joey Hamilton TSC SP .25 .11
❑ 252 Frank Castillo TSC SP .25 .11
❑ 253 Denny Martinez TSC SP .40 .18
❑ 254 Jaime Navarro TSC SP .25 .11
❑ 255 Karim Garcia TSC SP .25 .11
❑ 256 Bob Abreu TSC SP 1.00 .45
❑ 257 Butch Huskey TSC SP .25 .11
❑ 258 Ruben Rivera TSC SP .25 .11
❑ 259 Johnny Damon TSC SP .40 .18
❑ 260 Derek Jeter TSC SP 3.00 1.35
❑ 261 D. Eckersley TSC SP .40 .18
❑ 262 Jose Mesa TSC SP .25 .11
❑ 263 Tom Henke TSC SP .25 .11
❑ 264 Rick Aguilera TSC SP .25 .11
❑ 265 Randy Myers TSC SP .25 .11
❑ 266 John Franco TSC SP .40 .18
❑ 267 Jeff Brantley TSC SP .25 .11
❑ 268 John Wetteland TSC SP .40 .18
❑ 269 Mark Wohlers TSC SP .25 .11
❑ 270 Rod Beck TSC SP .25 .11
❑ 271 Barry Larkin .60 .25
❑ 272 Paul O'Neill .25 .11
❑ 273 Bobby Jones .15 .07
❑ 274 Will Clark .60 .25
❑ 275 Steve Avery .15 .07
❑ 276 Jim Edmonds .60 .25
❑ 277 John Olerud .25 .11
❑ 278 Carlos Perez .15 .07
❑ 279 Chris Hoiles .15 .07
❑ 280 Jeff Conine .15 .07
❑ 281 Jim Eisenreich .15 .07
❑ 282 Jason Jacome .15 .07
❑ 283 Ray Lankford .25 .11
❑ 284 John Wasdin .15 .07
❑ 285 Frank Thomas 1.25 .55
❑ 286 Jason Isringhausen .25 .11
❑ 287 Glenallen Hill .15 .07
❑ 288 Esteban Loaiza .15 .07
❑ 289 Bernie Williams .60 .25
❑ 290 Curtis Leskanic .15 .07
❑ 291 Scott Cooper .15 .07
❑ 292 Curt Schilling .25 .11
❑ 293 Eddie Murray .60 .25
❑ 294 Rick Krivda .15 .07
❑ 295 Domingo Cedeno .15 .07
❑ 296 Jeff Fassero .15 .07
❑ 297 Albert Belle .40 .18
❑ 298 Craig Biggio .40 .18
❑ 299 Fernando Vina .15 .07
❑ 300 Edgar Martinez .40 .18
❑ 301 Tony Gwynn 1.25 .55
❑ 302 Felipe Lira .15 .07

| No. | Player | Mint | NrMt |
|---|---|---|---|
| 303 | Mo Vaughn | .25 | .11 |
| 304 | Alex Fernandez | .15 | .07 |
| 305 | Keith Lockhart | .15 | .07 |
| 306 | Roger Pavlik | .15 | .07 |
| 307 | Lee Tinsley | .15 | .07 |
| 308 | Omar Vizquel | .25 | .11 |
| 309 | Scott Servais | .15 | .07 |
| 310 | Danny Tartabull | .15 | .07 |
| 311 | Chili Davis | .25 | .11 |
| 312 | Cal Eldred | .15 | .07 |
| 313 | Roger Cedeno | .15 | .07 |
| 314 | Chris Hammond | .15 | .07 |
| 315 | Rusty Greer | .25 | .11 |
| 316 | Brady Anderson | .25 | .11 |
| 317 | Ron Villone | .15 | .07 |
| 318 | Mark Carreon | .15 | .07 |
| 319 | Larry Walker | .25 | .11 |
| 320 | Pete Harnisch | .15 | .07 |
| 321 | Robin Ventura | .25 | .11 |
| 322 | Tim Belcher | .15 | .07 |
| 323 | Tony Tarasco | .15 | .07 |
| 324 | Juan Guzman | .15 | .07 |
| 325 | Kenny Lofton | .25 | .11 |
| 326 | Kevin Foster | .15 | .07 |
| 327 | Wil Cordero | .15 | .07 |
| 328 | Troy Percival | .15 | .07 |
| 329 | Turk Wendell | .15 | .07 |
| 330 | Thomas Howard | .15 | .07 |
| 331 | Carlos Baerga | .15 | .07 |
| 332 | B.J. Surhoff | .25 | .11 |
| 333 | Jay Buhner | .25 | .11 |
| 334 | Andujar Cedeno | .15 | .07 |
| 335 | Jeff King | .15 | .07 |
| 336 | Dante Bichette | .25 | .11 |
| 337 | Alan Trammell | .40 | .10 |
| 338 | Scott Leius | .15 | .07 |
| 339 | Chris Snopek | .15 | .07 |
| 340 | Roger Bailey | .15 | .07 |
| 341 | Jacob Brumfield | .15 | .07 |
| 342 | Jose Canseco | .75 | .35 |
| 343 | Rafael Palmeiro | .60 | .25 |
| 344 | Quilvio Veras | .15 | .07 |
| 345 | Darrin Fletcher | .15 | .07 |
| 346 | Carlos Delgado | .60 | .25 |
| 347 | Tony Eusebio | .15 | .07 |
| 348 | Ismael Valdes | .15 | .07 |
| 349 | Terry Steinbach | .15 | .07 |
| 350 | Orel Hershiser | .25 | .11 |
| 351 | Kurt Abbott | .15 | .07 |
| 352 | Jody Reed | .15 | .07 |
| 353 | David Howard | .15 | .07 |
| 354 | Ruben Sierra | .15 | .07 |
| 355 | John Ericks | .15 | .07 |
| 356 | Buck Showalter MG | .15 | .07 |
| 357 | Jim Thome | .40 | .18 |
| 358 | Geronimo Berroa | .15 | .07 |
| 359 | Robby Thompson | .15 | .07 |
| 360 | Jose Vizcaino | .15 | .07 |
| 361 | Jeff Frye | .15 | .07 |
| 362 | Kevin Appier | .25 | .11 |
| 363 | Pat Kelly | .15 | .07 |
| 364 | Ron Gant | .15 | .07 |
| 365 | Luis Alicea | .15 | .07 |
| 366 | Armando Benitez | .15 | .07 |
| 367 | Rico Brogna | .15 | .07 |
| 368 | Manny Ramirez | .75 | .35 |
| 369 | Mike Lansing | .15 | .07 |
| 370 | Sammy Sosa | 1.25 | .55 |
| 371 | Don Wengert | .15 | .07 |
| 372 | Dave Nilsson | .15 | .07 |
| 373 | Sandy Alomar Jr. | .25 | .11 |
| 374 | Joey Cora | .15 | .07 |
| 375 | Larry Thomas | .15 | .07 |
| 376 | John Valentin | .15 | .07 |
| 377 | Kevin Ritz | .15 | .07 |
| 378 | Steve Finley | .25 | .11 |
| 379 | Frank Rodriguez | .15 | .07 |
| 380 | Ivan Rodriguez | .75 | .35 |
| 381 | Alex Ochoa | .15 | .07 |
| 382 | Mark Lemke | .15 | .07 |
| 383 | Scott Brosius | .25 | .11 |
| 384 | James Mouton | .15 | .07 |
| 385 | Mark Langston | .15 | .07 |
| 386 | Ed Sprague | .15 | .07 |
| 387 | Joe Oliver | .15 | .07 |
| 388 | Steve Ontiveros | .15 | .07 |
| 389 | Rey Sanchez | .15 | .07 |
| 390 | Mike Henneman | .15 | .07 |
| 391 | Jose Valentin | .15 | .07 |
| 392 | Tom Candiotti | .15 | .07 |
| 393 | Damon Buford | .15 | .07 |
| 394 | Erik Hanson | .15 | .07 |
| 395 | Mark Smith | .15 | .07 |
| 396 | Pete Schourek | .15 | .07 |
| 397 | John Flaherty | .15 | .07 |
| 398 | Dave Martinez | .15 | .07 |
| 399 | Tommy Greene | .15 | .07 |
| 400 | Gary Sheffield | .60 | .25 |
| 401 | Glenn Dishman | .15 | .07 |
| 402 | Barry Bonds | 1.00 | .45 |
| 403 | Tom Pagnozzi | .15 | .07 |
| 404 | Todd Stottlemyre | .15 | .07 |
| 405 | Tim Salmon | .25 | .11 |
| 406 | John Hudek | .15 | .07 |
| 407 | Fred McGriff | .40 | .18 |
| 408 | Orlando Merced | .15 | .07 |
| 409 | Brian Barber | .15 | .07 |
| 410 | Ryan Thompson | .15 | .07 |
| 411 | Mariano Rivera | .25 | .11 |
| 412 | Eric Young | .15 | .07 |
| 413 | Chris Bosio | .15 | .07 |
| 414 | Chuck Knoblauch | .25 | .11 |
| 415 | Jamie Moyer | .15 | .07 |
| 416 | Chan Ho Park | .25 | .11 |
| 417 | Mark Portugal | .15 | .07 |
| 418 | Tim Raines | .25 | .11 |
| 419 | Antonio Osuna | .15 | .07 |
| 420 | Todd Zeile | .15 | .07 |
| 421 | Steve Wojciechowski | .15 | .07 |
| 422 | Marquis Grissom | .15 | .07 |
| 423 | Norm Charlton | .15 | .07 |
| 424 | Cal Ripken | 2.50 | 1.10 |
| 425 | Gregg Jefferies | .15 | .07 |
| 426 | Mike Stanton | .15 | .07 |
| 427 | Tony Fernandez | .15 | .07 |
| 428 | Jose Rijo | .15 | .07 |
| 429 | Jeff Bagwell | .75 | .35 |
| 430 | Raul Mondesi | .25 | .11 |
| 431 | Travis Fryman | .25 | .11 |
| 432 | Ron Karkovice | .15 | .07 |
| 433 | Alan Benes | .15 | .07 |
| 434 | Tony Phillips | .15 | .07 |
| 435 | Reggie Sanders | .15 | .07 |
| 436 | Andy Pettitte | .25 | .11 |
| 437 | Matt Lawton RC | .75 | .35 |
| 438 | Jeff Blauser | .15 | .07 |
| 439 | Michael Tucker | .15 | .07 |
| 440 | Mark Loretta | .15 | .07 |
| 441 | Charlie Hayes | .15 | .07 |
| 442 | Mike Piazza | 2.00 | .90 |
| 443 | Shane Andrews | .15 | .07 |
| 444 | Jeff Suppan | .15 | .07 |
| 445 | Steve Rodriguez | .15 | .07 |
| 446 | Mike Matheny | .15 | .07 |
| 447 | Trenidad Hubbard | .15 | .07 |
| 448 | Denny Hocking | .15 | .07 |
| 449 | Mark Grudzielanek | .15 | .07 |
| 450 | Joe Randa | .15 | .07 |

## 1997 Stadium Club

| | MINT | NRMT |
|---|---|---|
| COMPLETE SET (390) | 90.00 | 40.00 |
| COMPLETE SERIES 1 (195) | 50.00 | 22.00 |
| COMPLETE SERIES 2 (195) | 40.00 | 18.00 |
| COMMON (1-180/196-375) | .15 | .07 |
| COM.SP (181-195/376-390) | .50 | .23 |

| No. | Player | Mint | NrMt |
|---|---|---|---|
| 1 | Chipper Jones | 1.50 | .70 |
| 2 | Gary Sheffield | .60 | .25 |
| 3 | Kenny Lofton | .25 | .11 |
| 4 | Brian Jordan | .25 | .11 |
| 5 | Mark McGwire | 2.50 | 1.10 |
| 6 | Charles Nagy | .15 | .07 |
| 7 | Tim Salmon | .25 | .11 |
| 8 | Cal Ripken | 2.50 | 1.10 |
| 9 | Jeff Conine | .15 | .07 |
| 10 | Paul Molitor | .60 | .25 |
| 11 | Mariano Rivera | .25 | .11 |
| 12 | Pedro Martinez | .75 | .35 |
| 13 | Jeff Bagwell | .75 | .35 |
| 14 | Bobby Bonilla | .25 | .11 |
| 15 | Barry Bonds | 1.00 | .45 |
| 16 | Ryan Klesko | .25 | .11 |
| 17 | Barry Larkin | .60 | .25 |
| 18 | Jim Thome | .40 | .18 |
| 19 | Jay Buhner | .25 | .11 |
| 20 | Juan Gonzalez | .60 | .25 |
| 21 | Mike Mussina | .60 | .25 |
| 22 | Kevin Appier | .25 | .11 |
| 23 | Eric Karros | .25 | .11 |
| 24 | Steve Finley | .25 | .11 |
| 25 | Ed Sprague | .15 | .07 |
| 26 | Bernard Gilkey | .15 | .07 |
| 27 | Tony Phillips | .15 | .07 |
| 28 | Henry Rodriguez | .15 | .07 |
| 29 | John Smoltz | .25 | .11 |
| 30 | Dante Bichette | .25 | .11 |
| 31 | Mike Piazza | 2.00 | .90 |
| 32 | Paul O'Neill | .25 | .11 |
| 33 | Billy Wagner | .15 | .07 |
| 34 | Reggie Sanders | .15 | .07 |
| 35 | John Jaha | .15 | .07 |
| 36 | Eddie Murray | .60 | .25 |
| 37 | Eric Young | .15 | .07 |
| 38 | Roberto Hernandez | .15 | .07 |
| 39 | Pat Hentgen | .15 | .07 |
| 40 | Sammy Sosa | 1.25 | .55 |
| 41 | Todd Hundley | .15 | .07 |
| 42 | Mo Vaughn | .25 | .11 |
| 43 | Robin Ventura | .25 | .11 |
| 44 | Mark Grudzielanek | .15 | .07 |
| 45 | Shane Reynolds | .15 | .07 |
| 46 | Andy Pettitte | .25 | .11 |
| 47 | Fred McGriff | .40 | .18 |
| 48 | Rey Ordonez | .15 | .07 |
| 49 | Will Clark | .60 | .25 |
| 50 | Ken Griffey Jr. | 2.50 | 1.10 |
| 51 | Todd Worrell | .15 | .07 |
| 52 | Rusty Greer | .25 | .11 |
| 53 | Mark Grace | .60 | .25 |
| 54 | Tom Glavine | .60 | .25 |
| 55 | Derek Jeter | 2.50 | 1.10 |
| 56 | Rafael Palmeiro | .60 | .25 |
| 57 | Bernie Williams | .60 | .25 |
| 58 | Marty Cordova | .15 | .07 |
| 59 | Andres Galarraga | .40 | .18 |
| 60 | Ken Caminiti | .25 | .11 |
| 61 | Garret Anderson | .25 | .11 |
| 62 | Denny Martinez | .25 | .11 |
| 63 | Mike Greenwell | .15 | .07 |
| 64 | David Segui | .15 | .07 |
| 65 | Julio Franco | .25 | .11 |
| 66 | Rickey Henderson | .75 | .35 |
| 67 | Ozzie Guillen | .15 | .07 |
| 68 | Pete Harnisch | .15 | .07 |
| 69 | Chan Ho Park | .25 | .11 |
| 70 | Harold Baines | .25 | .11 |
| 71 | Mark Clark | .15 | .07 |
| 72 | Steve Avery | .15 | .07 |
| 73 | Brian Hunter | .15 | .07 |
| 74 | Pedro Astacio | .15 | .07 |
| 75 | Jack McDowell | .15 | .07 |
| 76 | Gregg Jefferies | .15 | .07 |
| 77 | Jason Kendall | .25 | .11 |
| 78 | Todd Walker | .15 | .07 |
| 79 | B.J. Surhoff | .25 | .11 |
| 80 | Moises Alou | .25 | .11 |
| 81 | Fernando Vina | .15 | .07 |
| 82 | Darryl Strawberry | .25 | .11 |

❑ 83 Jose Rosado .15 .07
❑ 84 Chris Gomez .15 .07
❑ 85 Chili Davis .25 .11
❑ 86 Alan Benes .15 .07
❑ 87 Todd Hollandsworth .15 .07
❑ 88 Jose Vizcaino .15 .07
❑ 89 Edgardo Alfonzo .25 .11
❑ 90 Ruben Rivera .15 .07
❑ 91 Donovan Osborne .15 .07
❑ 92 Doug Glanville .15 .07
❑ 93 Gary DiSarcina .15 .07
❑ 94 Brooks Kieschnick .15 .07
❑ 95 Bobby Jones .15 .07
❑ 96 Raul Casanova .15 .07
❑ 97 Jermaine Allensworth .15 .07
❑ 98 Kenny Rogers .15 .07
❑ 99 Mark McLemore .15 .07
❑ 100 Jeff Fassero .15 .07
❑ 101 Sandy Alomar Jr. .25 .11
❑ 102 Chuck Finley .25 .11
❑ 103 Eric Owens .15 .07
❑ 104 Billy McMillon .15 .07
❑ 105 Dwight Gooden .25 .11
❑ 106 Sterling Hitchcock .15 .07
❑ 107 Doug Drabek .15 .07
❑ 108 Paul Wilson .15 .07
❑ 109 Chris Snopek .15 .07
❑ 110 Al Leiter .25 .11
❑ 111 Bob Tewksbury .15 .07
❑ 112 Todd Greene .15 .07
❑ 113 Jose Valentin .15 .07
❑ 114 Delino DeShields .15 .07
❑ 115 Mike Bordick .15 .07
❑ 116 Pat Meares .15 .07
❑ 117 Mariano Duncan .15 .07
❑ 118 Steve Trachsel .15 .07
❑ 119 Luis Castillo .25 .11
❑ 120 Andy Benes .15 .07
❑ 121 Donne Wall .15 .07
❑ 122 Alex Gonzalez .15 .07
❑ 123 Dan Wilson .15 .07
❑ 124 Omar Vizquel .25 .11
❑ 125 Devon White .25 .11
❑ 126 Darryl Hamilton .15 .07
❑ 127 Orlando Merced .15 .07
❑ 128 Royce Clayton .15 .07
❑ 129 William VanLandingham .15 .07
❑ 130 Terry Steinbach .15 .07
❑ 131 Jeff Blauser .15 .07
❑ 132 Jeff Cirillo .25 .11
❑ 133 Roger Pavlik .15 .07
❑ 134 Danny Tartabull .15 .07
❑ 135 Jeff Montgomery .15 .07
❑ 136 Bobby Higginson .25 .11
❑ 137 Mike Grace .15 .07
❑ 138 Kevin Elster .15 .07
❑ 139 Brian Giles RC 2.50 1.10
❑ 140 Rod Beck .15 .07
❑ 141 Ismael Valdes .15 .07
❑ 142 Scott Brosius .25 .11
❑ 143 Mike Fetters .15 .07
❑ 144 Gary Gaetti .25 .11
❑ 145 Mike Lansing .15 .07
❑ 146 Glenallen Hill .15 .07
❑ 147 Shawn Green .60 .25
❑ 148 Mel Rojas .15 .07
❑ 149 Joey Cora .15 .07
❑ 150 John Smiley .15 .07
❑ 151 Marvin Benard .15 .07
❑ 152 Curt Schilling .25 .11
❑ 153 Dave Nilsson .15 .07
❑ 154 Edgar Renteria .25 .11
❑ 155 Joey Hamilton .15 .07
❑ 156 Carlos Garcia .15 .07
❑ 157 Nomar Garciaparra 2.00 .90
❑ 158 Kevin Ritz .15 .07
❑ 159 Keith Lockhart .15 .07
❑ 160 Justin Thompson .15 .07
❑ 161 Terry Adams .15 .07
❑ 162 Jamey Wright .15 .07
❑ 163 Otis Nixon .15 .07
❑ 164 Michael Tucker .15 .07
❑ 165 Mike Stanley .15 .07
❑ 166 Ben McDonald .15 .07
❑ 167 John Mabry .15 .07
❑ 168 Troy O'Leary .15 .07
❑ 169 Mel Nieves .15 .07
❑ 170 Bret Boone .25 .11
❑ 171 Mike Timlin .15 .07
❑ 172 Scott Rolen .60 .25
❑ 173 Reggie Jefferson .15 .07
❑ 174 Neifi Perez .15 .07
❑ 175 Brian McRae .15 .07
❑ 176 Tom Goodwin .15 .07
❑ 177 Aaron Sele .25 .11
❑ 178 Benito Santiago .15 .07
❑ 179 Frank Rodriguez .15 .07
❑ 180 Eric Davis .25 .11
❑ 181 Andruw Jones 2000 SP 1.50 .70
❑ 182 Todd Walker 2000 SP .50 .23
❑ 183 Wes Helms 2000 SP .50 .23
❑ 184 Nelson Figueroa 2000 SP RC .50 .23
❑ 185 V. Guerrero 2000 SP 2.50 1.10
❑ 186 Billy McMillon 2000 SP .50 .23
❑ 187 Todd Helton 2000 SP 2.00 .90
❑ 188 N. Garciaparra 2000 SP 4.00 1.80
❑ 189 K. Maeda 2000 SP .50 .23
❑ 190 Russell Branyan 2000 SP .60 .25
❑ 191 Glendon Rusch 2000 SP .50 .23
❑ 192 Bartolo Colon 2000 SP .60 .25
❑ 193 Scott Rolen 2000 SP 1.25 .55
❑ 194 A. Echevarria 2000 SP .50 .23
❑ 195 Bob Abreu 2000 SP .60 .25
❑ 196 Greg Maddux 1.50 .70
❑ 197 Joe Carter .25 .11
❑ 198 Alex Ochoa .15 .07
❑ 199 Ellis Burks .25 .11
❑ 200 Ivan Rodriguez .75 .35
❑ 201 Marquis Grissom .15 .07
❑ 202 Trevor Hoffman .25 .11
❑ 203 Matt Williams .40 .18
❑ 204 Carlos Delgado .60 .25
❑ 205 Ramon Martinez .15 .07
❑ 206 Chuck Knoblauch .25 .11
❑ 207 Juan Guzman .15 .07
❑ 208 Derek Bell .15 .07
❑ 209 Roger Clemens 1.25 .55
❑ 210 Vladimir Guerrero 1.25 .55
❑ 211 Cecil Fielder .25 .11
❑ 212 Hideo Nomo .60 .25
❑ 213 Frank Thomas 1.25 .55
❑ 214 Greg Vaughn .25 .11
❑ 215 Javy Lopez .25 .11
❑ 216 Raul Mondesi .25 .11
❑ 217 Wade Boggs .75 .35
❑ 218 Carlos Baerga .15 .07
❑ 219 Tony Gwynn 1.25 .55
❑ 220 Tino Martinez .25 .11
❑ 221 Vinny Castilla .25 .11
❑ 222 Lance Johnson .15 .07
❑ 223 David Justice .40 .18
❑ 224 Rondell White .25 .11
❑ 225 Dean Palmer .25 .11
❑ 226 Jim Edmonds .60 .25
❑ 227 Albert Belle .40 .18
❑ 228 Alex Fernandez .15 .07
❑ 229 Ryne Sandberg .75 .35
❑ 230 Jose Mesa .15 .07
❑ 231 David Cone .25 .11
❑ 232 Troy Percival .15 .07
❑ 233 Edgar Martinez .40 .18
❑ 234 Jose Canseco .75 .35
❑ 235 Kevin Brown .25 .11
❑ 236 Ray Lankford .25 .11
❑ 237 Karim Garcia .15 .07
❑ 238 J.T. Snow .25 .11
❑ 239 Dennis Eckersley .25 .11
❑ 240 Roberto Alomar .60 .25
❑ 241 John Valentin .15 .07
❑ 242 Ron Gant .15 .07
❑ 243 Geronimo Berroa .15 .07
❑ 244 Manny Ramirez .75 .35
❑ 245 Travis Fryman .25 .11
❑ 246 Denny Neagle .25 .11
❑ 247 Randy Johnson .75 .35
❑ 248 Darin Erstad .75 .35
❑ 249 Mark Wohlers .15 .07
❑ 250 Ken Hill .15 .07
❑ 251 Larry Walker .25 .11
❑ 252 Craig Biggio .40 .18
❑ 253 Brady Anderson .25 .11
❑ 254 John Wetteland .25 .11
❑ 255 Andruw Jones .75 .35
❑ 256 Turk Wendell .15 .07
❑ 257 Jason Isringhausen .15 .07
❑ 258 Jaime Navarro .15 .07
❑ 259 Sean Berry .15 .07
❑ 260 Albie Lopez .15 .07
❑ 261 Jay Bell .25 .11
❑ 262 Bobby Witt .15 .07
❑ 263 Tony Clark .15 .07
❑ 264 Tim Wakefield .15 .07
❑ 265 Brad Radke .25 .11
❑ 266 Tim Belcher .15 .07
❑ 267 Nerio Rodriguez RC .15 .07
❑ 268 Roger Cedeno .15 .07
❑ 269 Tim Naehring .15 .07
❑ 270 Kevin Tapani .15 .07
❑ 271 Joe Randa .15 .07
❑ 272 Randy Myers .15 .07
❑ 273 Dave Burba .15 .07
❑ 274 Mike Sweeney .25 .11
❑ 275 Danny Graves .15 .07
❑ 276 Chad Mottola .15 .07
❑ 277 Ruben Sierra .15 .07
❑ 278 Norm Charlton .15 .07
❑ 279 Scott Servais .15 .07
❑ 280 Jacob Cruz .15 .07
❑ 281 Mike Macfarlane .15 .07
❑ 282 Rich Becker .15 .07
❑ 283 Shannon Stewart .25 .11
❑ 284 Gerald Williams .15 .07
❑ 285 Jody Reed .15 .07
❑ 286 Jeff D'Amico .15 .07
❑ 287 Walt Weiss .15 .07
❑ 288 Jim Leyritz .15 .07
❑ 289 Francisco Cordova .15 .07
❑ 290 F.P. Santangelo .15 .07
❑ 291 Scott Erickson .15 .07
❑ 292 Hal Morris .15 .07
❑ 293 Ray Durham .25 .11
❑ 294 Andy Ashby .15 .07
❑ 295 Darryl Kile .25 .11
❑ 296 Jose Paniagua .15 .07
❑ 297 Mickey Tettleton .15 .07
❑ 298 Joe Girardi .15 .07
❑ 299 Rocky Coppinger .15 .07
❑ 300 Bob Abreu .25 .11
❑ 301 John Olerud .25 .11
❑ 302 Paul Shuey .15 .07
❑ 303 Jeff Brantley .15 .07
❑ 304 Bob Wells .15 .07
❑ 305 Kevin Seitzer .15 .07
❑ 306 Shawon Dunston .15 .07
❑ 307 Jose Herrera .15 .07
❑ 308 Butch Huskey .15 .07
❑ 309 Jose Offerman .15 .07
❑ 310 Rick Aguilera .15 .07
❑ 311 Greg Gagne .15 .07
❑ 312 John Burkett .15 .07
❑ 313 Mark Thompson .15 .07
❑ 314 Alvaro Espinoza .15 .07
❑ 315 Todd Stottlemyre .15 .07
❑ 316 Al Martin .15 .07
❑ 317 James Baldwin .25 .11
❑ 318 Cal Eldred .15 .07
❑ 319 Sid Fernandez .15 .07
❑ 320 Mickey Morandini .15 .07
❑ 321 Robb Nen .15 .07
❑ 322 Mark Lemke .15 .07
❑ 323 Pete Schourek .15 .07
❑ 324 Marcus Jensen .15 .07
❑ 325 Rich Aurilia .25 .11
❑ 326 Jeff King .15 .07
❑ 327 Scott Stahoviak .15 .07
❑ 328 Ricky Otero .15 .07
❑ 329 Antonio Osuna .15 .07
❑ 330 Chris Hoiles .15 .07
❑ 331 Luis Gonzalez .25 .11
❑ 332 Wil Cordero .15 .07
❑ 333 Johnny Damon .25 .11
❑ 334 Mark Langston .15 .07
❑ 335 Orlando Miller .15 .07
❑ 336 Jason Giambi .60 .25
❑ 337 Damian Jackson .15 .07
❑ 338 David Wells .25 .11
❑ 339 Bip Roberts .15 .07
❑ 340 Matt Ruebel .15 .07

❑ 341 Tom Candiotti .15 .07
❑ 342 Wally Joyner .25 .11
❑ 343 Jimmy Key .25 .11
❑ 344 Tony Batista .60 .25
❑ 345 Paul Sorrento .15 .07
❑ 346 Ron Karkovice .15 .07
❑ 347 Wilson Alvarez .15 .07
❑ 348 John Flaherty .15 .07
❑ 349 Rey Sanchez .15 .07
❑ 350 John Vander Wal .15 .07
❑ 351 Jermaine Dye .25 .11
❑ 352 Mike Hampton .25 .11
❑ 353 Greg Colbrunn .15 .07
❑ 354 Heathcliff Slocumb .15 .07
❑ 355 Ricky Bottalico .15 .07
❑ 356 Marty Janzen .15 .07
❑ 357 Orel Hershiser .25 .11
❑ 358 Rex Hudler .15 .07
❑ 359 Amaury Telemaco .15 .07
❑ 360 Darrin Fletcher .15 .07
❑ 361 Brant Brown UER .15 .07
(Card numbered 351)
❑ 362 Russ Davis .15 .07
❑ 363 Allen Watson .15 .07
❑ 364 Mike Lieberthal .25 .11
❑ 365 Dave Stevens .15 .07
❑ 366 Jay Powell .15 .07
❑ 367 Tony Fossas .15 .07
❑ 368 Bob Wolcott .15 .07
❑ 369 Mark Loretta .15 .07
❑ 370 Shawn Estes .25 .11
❑ 371 Sandy Martinez .15 .07
❑ 372 Wendell Magee Jr. .15 .07
❑ 373 John Franco .25 .11
❑ 374 Tom Pagnozzi UER .15 .07
(Misnumbered as 274)
❑ 375 Willie Adams .15 .07
❑ 376 Chipper Jones SS SP .. 3.00 1.35
❑ 377 Mo Vaughn SS SP .60 .25
❑ 378 Frank Thomas SS SP .. 2.50 1.10
❑ 379 Albert Belle SS SP .75 .35
❑ 380 Andres Galarraga SS SP .75 .35
❑ 381 Gary Sheffield SS SP .. 1.25 .55
❑ 382 Jeff Bagwell SS SP 1.50 .70
❑ 383 Mike Piazza SS SP 4.00 1.80
❑ 384 Mark McGwire SS SP .. 5.00 2.20
❑ 385 Ken Griffey Jr. SS SP 5.00 2.20
❑ 386 Barry Bonds SS SP 2.00 .90
❑ 387 Juan Gonzalez SS SP .. 1.25 .55
❑ 388 Brady Anderson SS SP .. .60 .25
❑ 389 Ken Caminiti SS SP .60 .25
❑ 390 Jay Buhner SS SP .60 .25

## 1998 Stadium Club

| | MINT | NRMT |
|---|---|---|
| COMPLETE SET (400) | 80.00 | 36.00 |
| COMPLETE SERIES 1 (200) | 40.00 | 18.00 |
| COMPLETE SERIES 2 (200) | 40.00 | 18.00 |
| COMMON CARD (1-400) | .15 | .07 |

❑ 1 Chipper Jones 1.50 .70
❑ 2 Frank Thomas 1.25 .55
❑ 3 Vladimir Guerrero 1.00 .45
❑ 4 Ellis Burks .25 .11
❑ 5 John Franco .25 .11
❑ 6 Paul Molitor .60 .25
❑ 7 Rusty Greer .25 .11
❑ 8 Todd Hundley .15 .07
❑ 9 Brett Tomko .15 .07
❑ 10 Eric Karros .25 .11
❑ 11 Mike Cameron .25 .11
❑ 12 Jim Edmonds .25 .11
❑ 13 Bernie Williams .60 .25
❑ 14 Denny Neagle .15 .07
❑ 15 Jason Dickson .15 .07
❑ 16 Sammy Sosa 1.25 .55
❑ 17 Brian Jordan .25 .11
❑ 18 Jose Vidro .15 .07
❑ 19 Scott Spiezio .15 .07
❑ 20 Jay Buhner .25 .11
❑ 21 Jim Thome .40 .18
❑ 22 Sandy Alomar Jr. .25 .11
❑ 23 Livan Hernandez .15 .07
❑ 24 Roberto Alomar .60 .25
❑ 25 Chris Gomez .15 .07
❑ 26 John Wetteland .25 .11
❑ 27 Willie Greene .15 .07
❑ 28 Gregg Jefferies .15 .07
❑ 29 Johnny Damon .25 .11
❑ 30 Barry Larkin .60 .25
❑ 31 Chuck Knoblauch .25 .11
❑ 32 Mo Vaughn .25 .11
❑ 33 Tony Clark .15 .07
❑ 34 Marty Cordova .15 .07
❑ 35 Vinny Castilla .25 .11
❑ 36 Jeff King .15 .07
❑ 37 Reggie Jefferson .15 .07
❑ 38 Mariano Rivera .25 .11
❑ 39 Jermaine Allensworth .15 .07
❑ 40 Livan Hernandez .15 .07
❑ 41 Heathcliff Slocumb .15 .07
❑ 42 Jacob Cruz .15 .07
❑ 43 Barry Bonds 1.00 .45
❑ 44 Dave Magadan .15 .07
❑ 45 Chan Ho Park .25 .11
❑ 46 Jeremi Gonzalez .15 .07
❑ 47 Jeff Cirillo .25 .11
❑ 48 Delino DeShields .15 .07
❑ 49 Craig Biggio .40 .18
❑ 50 Benito Santiago .15 .07
❑ 51 Mark Clark .15 .07
❑ 52 Fernando Vina .15 .07
❑ 53 F.P. Santangelo .15 .07
❑ 54 Pep Harris .15 .07
❑ 55 Edgar Renteria .15 .07
❑ 56 Jeff Bagwell .75 .35
❑ 57 Jimmy Key .25 .11
❑ 58 Bartolo Colon .25 .11
❑ 59 Curt Schilling .25 .11
❑ 60 Steve Finley .25 .11
❑ 61 Andy Ashby .15 .07
❑ 62 John Burkett .15 .07
❑ 63 Orel Hershiser .25 .11
❑ 64 Pokey Reese .25 .11
❑ 65 Scott Servais .15 .07
❑ 66 Todd Jones .15 .07
❑ 67 Javy Lopez .25 .11
❑ 68 Robin Ventura .25 .11
❑ 69 Miguel Tejada .60 .25
❑ 70 Raul Casanova .15 .07
❑ 71 Reggie Sanders .15 .07
❑ 72 Edgardo Alfonzo .25 .11
❑ 73 Dean Palmer .25 .11
❑ 74 Todd Stottlemyre .15 .07
❑ 75 David Wells .25 .11
❑ 76 Troy Percival .15 .07
❑ 77 Albert Belle .40 .18
❑ 78 Pat Hentgen .15 .07
❑ 79 Brian Hunter .15 .07
❑ 80 Richard Hidalgo .25 .11
❑ 81 Darren Oliver .15 .07
❑ 82 Mark Wohlers .15 .07
❑ 83 Cal Ripken 2.50 1.10
❑ 84 Hideo Nomo .60 .25
❑ 85 Derrek Lee .15 .07
❑ 86 Stan Javier .15 .07
❑ 87 Rey Ordonez .15 .07
❑ 88 Randy Johnson .75 .35
❑ 89 Jeff Kent .40 .18
❑ 90 Brian McRae .15 .07
❑ 91 Manny Ramirez .75 .35
❑ 92 Trevor Hoffman .25 .11
❑ 93 Doug Glanville .15 .07
❑ 94 Todd Walker .15 .07
❑ 95 Andy Benes .15 .07
❑ 96 Jason Schmidt .15 .07
❑ 97 Mike Matheny .15 .07
❑ 98 Tim Naehring .15 .07
❑ 99 Keith Lockhart .15 .07
❑ 100 Jose Rosado .15 .07
❑ 101 Roger Clemens 1.25 .55
❑ 102 Pedro Astacio .15 .07
❑ 103 Mark Bellhorn .15 .07
❑ 104 Paul O'Neill .25 .11
❑ 105 Darin Erstad .60 .25
❑ 106 Mike Lieberthal .25 .11
❑ 107 Wilson Alvarez .15 .07
❑ 108 Mike Mussina .60 .25
❑ 109 George Williams .15 .07
❑ 110 Cliff Floyd .25 .11
❑ 111 Shawn Estes .15 .07
❑ 112 Mark Grudzielanek .15 .07
❑ 113 Tony Gwynn 1.25 .55
❑ 114 Alan Benes .15 .07
❑ 115 Terry Steinbach .15 .07
❑ 116 Greg Maddux 1.50 .70
❑ 117 Andy Pettitte .25 .11
❑ 118 Dave Nilsson .15 .07
❑ 119 Deivi Cruz .15 .07
❑ 120 Carlos Delgado .60 .25
❑ 121 Scott Hatteberg .15 .07
❑ 122 John Olerud .25 .11
❑ 123 Todd Dunwoody .15 .07
❑ 124 Garret Anderson .25 .11
❑ 125 Royce Clayton .15 .07
❑ 126 Dante Powell .15 .07
❑ 127 Tom Glavine .60 .25
❑ 128 Gary DiSarcina .15 .07
❑ 129 Terry Adams .15 .07
❑ 130 Raul Mondesi .25 .11
❑ 131 Dan Wilson .15 .07
❑ 132 Al Martin .15 .07
❑ 133 Mickey Morandini .15 .07
❑ 134 Rafael Palmeiro .60 .25
❑ 135 Juan Encarnacion .25 .11
❑ 136 Jim Pittsley .15 .07
❑ 137 Magglio Ordonez RC 2.50 1.10
❑ 138 Will Clark .60 .25
❑ 139 Todd Helton .75 .35
❑ 140 Kelvim Escobar .15 .07
❑ 141 Esteban Loaiza .15 .07
❑ 142 John Jaha .25 .11
❑ 143 Jeff Fassero .15 .07
❑ 144 Harold Baines .25 .11
❑ 145 Butch Huskey .15 .07
❑ 146 Pat Meares .15 .07
❑ 147 Brian Giles .25 .11
❑ 148 Ramiro Mendoza .15 .07
❑ 149 John Smoltz .25 .11
❑ 150 Felix Martinez .15 .07
❑ 151 Jose Valentin .15 .07
❑ 152 Brad Rigby .15 .07
❑ 153 Ed Sprague .15 .07
❑ 154 Mike Hampton .25 .11
❑ 155 Carlos Perez .15 .07
❑ 156 Ray Lankford .25 .11
❑ 157 Bobby Bonilla .25 .11
❑ 158 Bill Mueller .15 .07
❑ 159 Jeffrey Hammonds .25 .11
❑ 160 Charles Nagy .15 .07
❑ 161 Rich Loiselle RC .15 .07
❑ 162 Al Leiter .25 .11
❑ 163 Larry Walker .25 .11
❑ 164 Chris Hoiles .15 .07
❑ 165 Jeff Montgomery .15 .07
❑ 166 Francisco Cordova .15 .07
❑ 167 James Baldwin .15 .07
❑ 168 Mark McLemore .15 .07
❑ 169 Kevin Appier .25 .11
❑ 170 Jamey Wright .15 .07
❑ 171 Nomar Garciaparra 2.00 .90
❑ 172 Matt Franco .15 .07
❑ 173 Armando Benitez .15 .07
❑ 174 Jeromy Burnitz .25 .11
❑ 175 Ismael Valdes .15 .07
❑ 176 Lance Johnson .15 .07
❑ 177 Paul Sorrento .15 .07
❑ 178 Rondell White .25 .11
❑ 179 Kevin Elster .15 .07

| | | | |
|---|---|---|---|
| ❑ 180 | Jason Giambi | .60 | .25 |
| ❑ 181 | Carlos Baerga | .15 | .07 |
| ❑ 182 | Russ Davis | .15 | .07 |
| ❑ 183 | Ryan McGuire | .15 | .07 |
| ❑ 184 | Eric Young | .15 | .07 |
| ❑ 185 | Ron Gant | .25 | .11 |
| ❑ 186 | Manny Alexander | .15 | .07 |
| ❑ 187 | Scott Karl | .15 | .07 |
| ❑ 188 | Brady Anderson | .25 | .11 |
| ❑ 189 | Randall Simon | .15 | .07 |
| ❑ 190 | Tim Belcher | .15 | .07 |
| ❑ 191 | Jaret Wright | .15 | .07 |
| ❑ 192 | Dante Bichette | .25 | .11 |
| ❑ 193 | John Valentin | .15 | .07 |
| ❑ 194 | Darren Bragg | .15 | .07 |
| ❑ 195 | Mike Sweeney | .25 | .11 |
| ❑ 196 | Craig Counsell | .15 | .07 |
| ❑ 197 | Jaime Navarro | .15 | .07 |
| ❑ 198 | Todd Dunn | .15 | .07 |
| ❑ 199 | Ken Griffey Jr. | 2.50 | 1.10 |
| ❑ 200 | Juan Gonzalez | .60 | .25 |
| ❑ 201 | Billy Wagner | .15 | .07 |
| ❑ 202 | Tino Martinez | .25 | .11 |
| ❑ 203 | Mark McGwire | 2.50 | 1.10 |
| ❑ 204 | Jeff D'Amico | .15 | .07 |
| ❑ 205 | Rico Brogna | .15 | .07 |
| ❑ 206 | Todd Hollandsworth | .15 | .07 |
| ❑ 207 | Chad Curtis | .15 | .07 |
| ❑ 208 | Tom Goodwin | .15 | .07 |
| ❑ 209 | Neifi Perez | .15 | .07 |
| ❑ 210 | Derek Bell | .15 | .07 |
| ❑ 211 | Quilvio Veras | .15 | .07 |
| ❑ 212 | Greg Vaughn | .25 | .11 |
| ❑ 213 | Kirk Rueter | .15 | .07 |
| ❑ 214 | Arthur Rhodes | .15 | .07 |
| ❑ 215 | Cal Eldred | .15 | .07 |
| ❑ 216 | Bill Taylor | .15 | .07 |
| ❑ 217 | Todd Greene | .15 | .07 |
| ❑ 218 | Mario Valdez | .15 | .07 |
| ❑ 219 | Ricky Bottalico | .15 | .07 |
| ❑ 220 | Frank Rodriguez | .15 | .07 |
| ❑ 221 | Rich Becker | .15 | .07 |
| ❑ 222 | Roberto Duran RC | .25 | .11 |
| ❑ 223 | Ivan Rodriguez | .75 | .35 |
| ❑ 224 | Mike Jackson | .15 | .07 |
| ❑ 225 | Deion Sanders | .25 | .11 |
| ❑ 226 | Tony Womack | .15 | .07 |
| ❑ 227 | Mark Kotsay | .25 | .11 |
| ❑ 228 | Steve Trachsel | .15 | .07 |
| ❑ 229 | Ryan Klesko | .25 | .11 |
| ❑ 230 | Ken Cloude | .15 | .07 |
| ❑ 231 | Luis Gonzalez | .25 | .11 |
| ❑ 232 | Gary Gaetti | .25 | .11 |
| ❑ 233 | Michael Tucker | .15 | .07 |
| ❑ 234 | Shawn Green | .60 | .25 |
| ❑ 235 | Ariel Prieto | .15 | .07 |
| ❑ 236 | Kirt Manwaring | .15 | .07 |
| ❑ 237 | Omar Vizquel | .25 | .11 |
| ❑ 238 | Matt Beech | .15 | .07 |
| ❑ 239 | Justin Thompson | .15 | .07 |
| ❑ 240 | Bret Boone | .25 | .11 |
| ❑ 241 | Derek Jeter | 2.50 | 1.10 |
| ❑ 242 | Ken Caminiti | .25 | .11 |
| ❑ 243 | Jose Offerman | .15 | .07 |
| ❑ 244 | Kevin Tapani | .15 | .07 |
| ❑ 245 | Jason Kendall | .25 | .11 |
| ❑ 246 | Jose Guillen | .15 | .07 |
| ❑ 247 | Mike Bordick | .15 | .07 |
| ❑ 248 | Dustin Hermanson | .15 | .07 |
| ❑ 249 | Darrin Fletcher | .15 | .07 |
| ❑ 250 | Dave Hollins | .15 | .07 |
| ❑ 251 | Ramon Martinez | .15 | .07 |
| ❑ 252 | Hideki Irabu | .15 | .07 |
| ❑ 253 | Mark Grace | .60 | .25 |
| ❑ 254 | Jason Isringhausen | .15 | .07 |
| ❑ 255 | Jose Cruz Jr. | .25 | .11 |
| ❑ 256 | Brian Johnson | .15 | .07 |
| ❑ 257 | Brad Ausmus | .15 | .07 |
| ❑ 258 | Andruw Jones | .60 | .25 |
| ❑ 259 | Doug Jones | .15 | .07 |
| ❑ 260 | Jeff Shaw | .15 | .07 |
| ❑ 261 | Chuck Finley | .25 | .11 |
| ❑ 262 | Gary Sheffield | .60 | .25 |
| ❑ 263 | David Segui | .15 | .07 |
| ❑ 264 | John Smiley | .15 | .07 |
| ❑ 265 | Tim Salmon | .25 | .11 |
| ❑ 266 | J.T. Snow | .25 | .11 |
| ❑ 267 | Alex Fernandez | .15 | .07 |
| ❑ 268 | Matt Stairs | .15 | .07 |
| ❑ 269 | B.J. Surhoff | .25 | .11 |
| ❑ 270 | Keith Foulke | .15 | .07 |
| ❑ 271 | Edgar Martinez | .40 | .18 |
| ❑ 272 | Shannon Stewart | .25 | .11 |
| ❑ 273 | Eduardo Perez | .15 | .07 |
| ❑ 274 | Wally Joyner | .25 | .11 |
| ❑ 275 | Kevin Young | .25 | .11 |
| ❑ 276 | Eli Marrero | .15 | .07 |
| ❑ 277 | Brad Radke | .25 | .11 |
| ❑ 278 | Jamie Moyer | .15 | .07 |
| ❑ 279 | Joe Girardi | .15 | .07 |
| ❑ 280 | Troy O'Leary | .15 | .07 |
| ❑ 281 | Jeff Frye | .15 | .07 |
| ❑ 282 | Jose Offerman | .15 | .07 |
| ❑ 283 | Scott Erickson | .15 | .07 |
| ❑ 284 | Sean Berry | .15 | .07 |
| ❑ 285 | Shigetoshi Hasegawa | .25 | .11 |
| ❑ 286 | Felix Heredia | .15 | .07 |
| ❑ 287 | Willie McGee | .25 | .11 |
| ❑ 288 | Alex Rodriguez | 2.00 | .90 |
| ❑ 289 | Ugueth Urbina | .15 | .07 |
| ❑ 290 | Jon Lieber | .15 | .07 |
| ❑ 291 | Fernando Tatis | .25 | .11 |
| ❑ 292 | Chris Stynes | .15 | .07 |
| ❑ 293 | Bernard Gilkey | .15 | .07 |
| ❑ 294 | Joey Hamilton | .15 | .07 |
| ❑ 295 | Matt Karchner | .15 | .07 |
| ❑ 296 | Paul Wilson | .15 | .07 |
| ❑ 297 | Damion Easley | .15 | .07 |
| ❑ 298 | Kevin Millwood RC | 1.00 | .45 |
| ❑ 299 | Ellis Burks | .25 | .11 |
| ❑ 300 | Jerry DiPoto | .15 | .07 |
| ❑ 301 | Jermaine Dye | .25 | .11 |
| ❑ 302 | Travis Lee | .25 | .11 |
| ❑ 303 | Ron Coomer | .15 | .07 |
| ❑ 304 | Matt Williams | .40 | .18 |
| ❑ 305 | Bobby Higginson | .25 | .11 |
| ❑ 306 | Jorge Fabregas | .15 | .07 |
| ❑ 307 | Jon Nunnally | .15 | .07 |
| ❑ 308 | Jay Bell | .25 | .11 |
| ❑ 309 | Jason Schmidt | .15 | .07 |
| ❑ 310 | Andy Benes | .15 | .07 |
| ❑ 311 | Sterling Hitchcock | .15 | .07 |
| ❑ 312 | Jeff Suppan | .15 | .07 |
| ❑ 313 | Shane Reynolds | .15 | .07 |
| ❑ 314 | Willie Blair | .15 | .07 |
| ❑ 315 | Scott Rolen | .60 | .25 |
| ❑ 316 | Wilson Alvarez | .15 | .07 |
| ❑ 317 | David Justice | .40 | .18 |
| ❑ 318 | Fred McGriff | .40 | .18 |
| ❑ 319 | Bobby Jones | .15 | .07 |
| ❑ 320 | Wade Boggs | .75 | .35 |
| ❑ 321 | Tim Wakefield | .15 | .07 |
| ❑ 322 | Tony Saunders | .15 | .07 |
| ❑ 323 | David Cone | .25 | .11 |
| ❑ 324 | Roberto Hernandez | .15 | .07 |
| ❑ 325 | Jose Canseco | .75 | .35 |
| ❑ 326 | Kevin Stocker | .15 | .07 |
| ❑ 327 | Gerald Williams | .15 | .07 |
| ❑ 328 | Quinton McCracken | .15 | .07 |
| ❑ 329 | Mark Gardner | .15 | .07 |
| ❑ 330 | Ben Grieve | .25 | .11 |
| ❑ 331 | Kevin Brown | .40 | .18 |
| ❑ 332 | Mike Lowell | .60 | .25 |
| ❑ 333 | Jed Hansen | .15 | .07 |
| ❑ 334 | Abraham Nunez | .15 | .07 |
| ❑ 335 | John Thomson | .15 | .07 |
| ❑ 336 | Masato Yoshii RC | .50 | .23 |
| ❑ 337 | Mike Piazza | 2.00 | .90 |
| ❑ 338 | Brad Fullmer | .25 | .11 |
| ❑ 339 | Ray Durham | .25 | .11 |
| ❑ 340 | Kerry Wood | .60 | .25 |
| ❑ 341 | Kevin Polcovich | .15 | .07 |
| ❑ 342 | Russ Johnson | .15 | .07 |
| ❑ 343 | Darryl Hamilton | .15 | .07 |
| ❑ 344 | David Ortiz | .15 | .07 |
| ❑ 345 | Kevin Orie | .15 | .07 |
| ❑ 346 | Mike Caruso | .15 | .07 |
| ❑ 347 | Juan Guzman | .15 | .07 |
| ❑ 348 | Ruben Rivera | .15 | .07 |
| ❑ 349 | Rick Aguilera | .15 | .07 |
| ❑ 350 | Bobby Estalella | .15 | .07 |
| ❑ 351 | Bobby Witt | .15 | .07 |
| ❑ 352 | Paul Konerko | .25 | .11 |
| ❑ 353 | Matt Morris | .15 | .07 |
| ❑ 354 | Carl Pavano | .15 | .07 |
| ❑ 355 | Todd Zeile | .25 | .11 |
| ❑ 356 | Kevin Brown TR | .40 | .18 |
| ❑ 357 | Alex Gonzalez | .15 | .07 |
| ❑ 358 | Chuck Knoblauch TR | .25 | .11 |
| ❑ 359 | Joey Cora | .15 | .07 |
| ❑ 360 | Mike Lansing TR | .15 | .07 |
| ❑ 361 | Adrian Beltre | .25 | .11 |
| ❑ 362 | Dennis Eckersley TR | .25 | .11 |
| ❑ 363 | A.J. Hinch | .15 | .07 |
| ❑ 364 | Kenny Lofton TR | .25 | .11 |
| ❑ 365 | Alex Gonzalez | .15 | .07 |
| ❑ 366 | Henry Rodriguez TR | .15 | .07 |
| ❑ 367 | Mike Stoner RC | .15 | .07 |
| ❑ 368 | Darryl Kile TR | .25 | .11 |
| ❑ 369 | Kevin McGlinchy | .15 | .07 |
| ❑ 370 | Walt Weiss TR | .15 | .07 |
| ❑ 371 | Kris Benson | .25 | .11 |
| ❑ 372 | Cecil Fielder TR | .25 | .11 |
| ❑ 373 | Dermal Brown | .25 | .11 |
| ❑ 374 | Rod Beck TR | .15 | .07 |
| ❑ 375 | Eric Milton | .15 | .07 |
| ❑ 376 | Travis Fryman TR | .25 | .11 |
| ❑ 377 | Preston Wilson | .25 | .11 |
| ❑ 378 | Chili Davis TR | .25 | .11 |
| ❑ 379 | Travis Lee | .25 | .11 |
| ❑ 380 | Jim Leyritz TR | .15 | .07 |
| ❑ 381 | Vernon Wells | .40 | .18 |
| ❑ 382 | Joe Carter TR | .25 | .11 |
| ❑ 383 | J.J. Davis | .25 | .11 |
| ❑ 384 | Marquis Grissom TR | .15 | .07 |
| ❑ 385 | Mike Cuddyer RC | .75 | .35 |
| ❑ 386 | Rickey Henderson TR | .75 | .35 |
| ❑ 387 | Chris Enochs RC | .40 | .18 |
| ❑ 388 | Andres Galarraga TR | .40 | .18 |
| ❑ 389 | Jason Dellaero | .15 | .07 |
| ❑ 390 | Robb Nen TR | .15 | .07 |
| ❑ 391 | Mark Mangum | .15 | .07 |
| ❑ 392 | Jeff Blauser TR | .15 | .07 |
| ❑ 393 | Adam Kennedy | .25 | .11 |
| ❑ 394 | Bob Abreu TR | .25 | .11 |
| ❑ 395 | Jack Cust RC | 1.25 | .55 |
| ❑ 396 | Jose Vizcaino TR | .15 | .07 |
| ❑ 397 | Jon Garland | .15 | .07 |
| ❑ 398 | Pedro Martinez TR | .75 | .35 |
| ❑ 399 | Aaron Akin | .15 | .07 |
| ❑ 400 | Jeff Conine TR | .15 | .07 |
| ❑ NNO | C. Ripken Sound Chip 1 | 15.00 | 6.75 |
| ❑ NNO | C. Ripken Sound Chip 2 | 15.00 | 6.75 |

## 1999 Stadium Club

| | MINT | NRMT |
|---|---|---|
| COMPLETE SET (355) | 125.00 | 55.00 |
| COMPLETE SERIES 1 (170) | 65.00 | 29.00 |
| COMP.SER.1 w/o SP's (150) | 25.00 | 11.00 |
| COMPLETE SERIES 2 (185) | 60.00 | 27.00 |
| COMP.SER.2 w/o SP's (165) | 25.00 | 11.00 |
| COMMON CARD (1-140/161-170) | .15 | .07 |
| COMMON CARD (171-335) | .15 | .07 |
| COMM.SP (141-160/336-355) | 1.00 | .45 |

| | | | |
|---|---|---|---|
| ❑ 1 | Alex Rodriguez | 2.00 | .90 |
| ❑ 2 | Chipper Jones | 1.50 | .70 |
| ❑ 3 | Rusty Greer | .25 | .11 |
| ❑ 4 | Jim Edmonds | .60 | .25 |

❑ 5 Ron Gant .25 .11
❑ 6 Kevin Polcovich .15 .07
❑ 7 Darryl Strawberry .25 .11
❑ 8 Bill Mueller .15 .07
❑ 9 Vinny Castilla .25 .11
❑ 10 Wade Boggs .75 .35
❑ 11 Jose Lima .15 .07
❑ 12 Darren Dreifort .15 .07
❑ 13 Jay Bell .25 .11
❑ 14 Ben Grieve .25 .11
❑ 15 Shawn Green .60 .25
❑ 16 Andres Galarraga .40 .18
❑ 17 Bartolo Colon .25 .11
❑ 18 Francisco Cordova .15 .07
❑ 19 Paul O'Neill .25 .11
❑ 20 Trevor Hoffman .25 .11
❑ 21 Darren Oliver .15 .07
❑ 22 John Franco .25 .11
❑ 23 Eli Marrero .15 .07
❑ 24 Roberto Hernandez .15 .07
❑ 25 Craig Biggio .40 .18
❑ 26 Brad Fullmer .25 .11
❑ 27 Scott Erickson .15 .07
❑ 28 Tom Gordon .15 .07
❑ 29 Brian Hunter .15 .07
❑ 30 Raul Mondesi .25 .11
❑ 31 Rick Reed .15 .07
❑ 32 Jose Canseco .75 .35
❑ 33 Robb Nen .15 .07
❑ 34 Turner Ward .15 .07
❑ 35 Orlando Hernandez .25 .11
❑ 36 Jeff Shaw .15 .07
❑ 37 Matt Lawton .25 .11
❑ 38 David Wells .25 .11
❑ 39 Bob Abreu .25 .11
❑ 40 Jeromy Burnitz .25 .11
❑ 41 Deivi Cruz .15 .07
❑ 42 Derek Bell .15 .07
❑ 43 Rico Brogna .15 .07
❑ 44 Dmitri Young .25 .11
❑ 45 Chuck Knoblauch .25 .11
❑ 46 Johnny Damon .25 .11
❑ 47 Brian Meadows .15 .07
❑ 48 Jeremi Gonzalez .15 .07
❑ 49 Gary DiSarcina .15 .07
❑ 50 Frank Thomas 1.25 .55
❑ 51 F.P. Santangelo .15 .07
❑ 52 Tom Candiotti .15 .07
❑ 53 Shane Reynolds .15 .07
❑ 54 Rod Beck .15 .07
❑ 55 Rey Ordonez .15 .07
❑ 56 Todd Helton .75 .35
❑ 57 Mickey Morandini .15 .07
❑ 58 Jorge Posada .25 .11
❑ 59 Mike Mussina .60 .25
❑ 60 Al Leiter .25 .11
❑ 61 David Segui .15 .07
❑ 62 Brian McRae .15 .07
❑ 63 Fred McGriff .40 .18
❑ 64 Brett Tomko .15 .07
❑ 65 Derek Jeter 2.50 1.10
❑ 66 Sammy Sosa 1.25 .55
❑ 67 Kenny Rogers .15 .07
❑ 68 Dave Nilsson .15 .07
❑ 69 Eric Young .15 .07
❑ 70 Mark McGwire 2.50 1.10
❑ 71 Kenny Lofton .25 .11
❑ 72 Tom Glavine .60 .25
❑ 73 Joey Hamilton .15 .07
❑ 74 John Valentin .15 .07
❑ 75 Mariano Rivera .25 .11
❑ 76 Ray Durham .25 .11
❑ 77 Tony Clark .15 .07
❑ 78 Livan Hernandez .15 .07
❑ 79 Rickey Henderson .75 .35
❑ 80 Vladimir Guerrero 1.00 .45
❑ 81 J.T. Snow .25 .11
❑ 82 Juan Guzman .15 .07
❑ 83 Darryl Hamilton .15 .07
❑ 84 Matt Anderson .15 .07
❑ 85 Travis Lee .15 .07
❑ 86 Joe Randa .15 .07
❑ 87 Dave Dellucci .15 .07
❑ 88 Moises Alou .25 .11
❑ 89 Alex Gonzalez .15 .07
❑ 90 Tony Womack .15 .07
❑ 91 Neifi Perez .15 .07
❑ 92 Travis Fryman .25 .11
❑ 93 Masato Yoshii .25 .11
❑ 94 Woody Williams .15 .07
❑ 95 Ray Lankford .25 .11
❑ 96 Roger Clemens 1.25 .55
❑ 97 Dustin Hermanson .15 .07
❑ 98 Joe Carter .25 .11
❑ 99 Jason Schmidt .15 .07
❑ 100 Greg Maddux 1.50 .70
❑ 101 Kevin Tapani .15 .07
❑ 102 Charles Johnson .25 .11
❑ 103 Derrek Lee .15 .07
❑ 104 Pete Harnisch .15 .07
❑ 105 Dante Bichette .25 .11
❑ 106 Scott Brosius .25 .11
❑ 107 Mike Caruso .15 .07
❑ 108 Eddie Taubensee .15 .07
❑ 109 Jeff Fassero .15 .07
❑ 110 Marquis Grissom .15 .07
❑ 111 Jose Hernandez .15 .07
❑ 112 Chan Ho Park .25 .11
❑ 113 Wally Joyner .25 .11
❑ 114 Bobby Estalella .15 .07
❑ 115 Pedro Martinez .75 .35
❑ 116 Shawn Estes .15 .07
❑ 117 Walt Weiss .15 .07
❑ 118 John Mabry .15 .07
❑ 119 Brian Johnson .15 .07
❑ 120 Jim Thome .40 .18
❑ 121 Bill Spiers .15 .07
❑ 122 John Olerud .25 .11
❑ 123 Jeff King .15 .07
❑ 124 Tim Belcher .15 .07
❑ 125 John Wetteland .25 .11
❑ 126 Tony Gwynn 1.25 .55
❑ 127 Brady Anderson .25 .11
❑ 128 Randy Winn .15 .07
❑ 129 Andy Fox .15 .07
❑ 130 Eric Karros .25 .11
❑ 131 Kevin Millwood .25 .11
❑ 132 Andy Benes .15 .07
❑ 133 Andy Ashby .15 .07
❑ 134 Ron Coomer .15 .07
❑ 135 Juan Gonzalez .60 .25
❑ 136 Randy Johnson .75 .35
❑ 137 Aaron Sele .25 .11
❑ 138 Edgardo Alfonzo .25 .11
❑ 139 B.J. Surhoff .25 .11
❑ 140 Jose Vizcaino .15 .07
❑ 141 Chad Moeller SP RC 1.00 .45
❑ 142 Mike Zywica SP RC 1.00 .45
❑ 143 Angel Pena SP 1.00 .45
❑ 144 Nick Johnson SP RC 4.00 1.80
❑ 145 G. Chiaramonte SP RC 1.25 .55
❑ 146 Kit Pellow SP RC 1.00 .45
❑ 147 Clayton Andrews SP RC 1.00 .45
❑ 148 Jerry Hairston Jr. SP 1.25 .55
❑ 149 Jason Tyner SP RC 1.50 .70
❑ 150 Chip Ambres SP RC 1.25 .55
❑ 151 Pat Burrell SP RC 10.00 4.50
❑ 152 Josh McKinley SP RC 1.00 .45
❑ 153 Choo Freeman SP RC 1.25 .55
❑ 154 Rick Elder SP RC 1.00 .45
❑ 155 Eric Valent SP RC 2.00 .90
❑ 156 Jeff Winchester SP RC 1.50 .70
❑ 157 Mike Nannini SP RC 1.25 .55
❑ 158 Mamon Tucker SP RC 1.00 .45
❑ 159 Nate Bump SP RC 1.00 .45
❑ 160 Andy Brown SP RC 1.50 .70
❑ 161 Troy Glaus 1.00 .45
❑ 162 Adrian Beltre .25 .11
❑ 163 Mitch Meluskey .15 .07
❑ 164 Alex Gonzalez .15 .07
❑ 165 George Lombard .15 .07
❑ 166 Eric Chavez .25 .11
❑ 167 Ruben Mateo .25 .11
❑ 168 Calvin Pickering .15 .07
❑ 169 Gabe Kapler .25 .11
❑ 170 Bruce Chen .15 .07
❑ 171 Darin Erstad .60 .25
❑ 172 Sandy Alomar Jr. .25 .11
❑ 173 Miguel Cairo .15 .07
❑ 174 Jason Kendall .25 .11
❑ 175 Cal Ripken 2.50 1.10
❑ 176 Darryl Kile .25 .11
❑ 177 David Cone .25 .11
❑ 178 Mike Sweeney .25 .11
❑ 179 Royce Clayton .15 .07
❑ 180 Curt Schilling .25 .11
❑ 181 Barry Larkin .60 .25
❑ 182 Eric Milton .15 .07
❑ 183 Ellis Burks .25 .11
❑ 184 A.J. Hinch .15 .07
❑ 185 Garret Anderson .25 .11
❑ 186 Sean Bergman .15 .07
❑ 187 Shannon Stewart .25 .11
❑ 188 Bernard Gilkey .15 .07
❑ 189 Jeff Blauser .15 .07
❑ 190 Andruw Jones .60 .25
❑ 191 Omar Daal .15 .07
❑ 192 Jeff Kent .40 .18
❑ 193 Mark Kotsay .15 .07
❑ 194 Dave Burba .15 .07
❑ 195 Bobby Higginson .25 .11
❑ 196 Hideki Irabu .15 .07
❑ 197 Jamie Moyer .15 .07
❑ 198 Doug Glanville .15 .07
❑ 199 Quinton McCracken .15 .07
❑ 200 Ken Griffey Jr. 2.50 1.10
❑ 201 Mike Lieberthal .25 .11
❑ 202 Carl Everett .25 .11
❑ 203 Omar Vizquel .25 .11
❑ 204 Mike Lansing .15 .07
❑ 205 Manny Ramirez .75 .35
❑ 206 Ryan Klesko .25 .11
❑ 207 Jeff Montgomery .15 .07
❑ 208 Chad Curtis .15 .07
❑ 209 Rick Helling .25 .11
❑ 210 Justin Thompson .15 .07
❑ 211 Tom Goodwin .15 .07
❑ 212 Todd Dunwoody .15 .07
❑ 213 Kevin Young .25 .11
❑ 214 Tony Saunders .15 .07
❑ 215 Gary Sheffield .60 .25
❑ 216 Jaret Wright .15 .07
❑ 217 Quilvio Veras .15 .07
❑ 218 Marty Cordova .15 .07
❑ 219 Tino Martinez .25 .11
❑ 220 Scott Rolen .60 .25
❑ 221 Fernando Tatis .25 .11
❑ 222 Damion Easley .15 .07
❑ 223 Aramis Ramirez .15 .07
❑ 224 Brad Radke .25 .11
❑ 225 Nomar Garciaparra 3.00 1.35
❑ 226 Magglio Ordonez .40 .18
❑ 227 Andy Pettitte .25 .11
❑ 228 David Ortiz .15 .07
❑ 229 Todd Jones .15 .07
❑ 230 Larry Walker .25 .11
❑ 231 Tim Wakefield .15 .07
❑ 232 Jose Guillen .15 .07
❑ 233 Gregg Olson .15 .07
❑ 234 Ricky Gutierrez .15 .07
❑ 235 Todd Walker .15 .07
❑ 236 Abraham Nunez .15 .07
❑ 237 Sean Casey .25 .11
❑ 238 Greg Norton .15 .07
❑ 239 Bret Saberhagen .25 .11
❑ 240 Bernie Williams .60 .25
❑ 241 Tim Salmon .25 .11
❑ 242 Jason Giambi .60 .25
❑ 243 Fernando Vina .15 .07
❑ 244 Darrin Fletcher .15 .07
❑ 245 Greg Vaughn .25 .11
❑ 246 Dennis Reyes .15 .07
❑ 247 Hideo Nomo .60 .25
❑ 248 Kevin Stocker .15 .07
❑ 249 Mike Hampton .25 .11
❑ 250 Kerry Wood .25 .11
❑ 251 Ismael Valdes .15 .07
❑ 252 Pat Hentgen .15 .07
❑ 253 Scott Spiezio .15 .07
❑ 254 Chuck Finley .25 .11
❑ 255 Troy Glaus 1.00 .45
❑ 256 Bobby Jones .15 .07
❑ 257 Wayne Gomes .15 .07
❑ 258 Rondell White .25 .11
❑ 259 Todd Zeile .25 .11
❑ 260 Matt Williams .40 .18
❑ 261 Henry Rodriguez .15 .07
❑ 262 Matt Stairs .15 .07

| | MINT | NRMT |
|---|---|---|
| ❑ 263 Jose Valentin | .15 | .07 |
| ❑ 264 David Justice | .40 | .18 |
| ❑ 265 Javy Lopez | .25 | .11 |
| ❑ 266 Matt Morris | .15 | .07 |
| ❑ 267 Steve Trachsel | .15 | .07 |
| ❑ 268 Edgar Martinez | .40 | .18 |
| ❑ 269 Al Martin | .15 | .07 |
| ❑ 270 Ivan Rodriguez | .75 | .35 |
| ❑ 271 Carlos Delgado | .60 | .25 |
| ❑ 272 Mark Grace | .60 | .25 |
| ❑ 273 Ugueth Urbina | .15 | .07 |
| ❑ 274 Jay Buhner | .25 | .11 |
| ❑ 275 Mike Piazza | 2.00 | .90 |
| ❑ 276 Rick Aguilera | .15 | .07 |
| ❑ 277 Javier Valentin | .15 | .07 |
| ❑ 278 Brian Anderson | .15 | .07 |
| ❑ 279 Cliff Floyd | .25 | .11 |
| ❑ 280 Barry Bonds | 1.00 | .45 |
| ❑ 281 Troy O'Leary | .15 | .07 |
| ❑ 282 Seth Greisinger | .15 | .07 |
| ❑ 283 Mark Grudzielanek | .15 | .07 |
| ❑ 284 Jose Cruz Jr. | .25 | .11 |
| ❑ 285 Jeff Bagwell | .75 | .35 |
| ❑ 286 John Smoltz | .25 | .11 |
| ❑ 287 Jeff Cirillo | .25 | .11 |
| ❑ 288 Richie Sexson | .25 | .11 |
| ❑ 289 Charles Nagy | .15 | .07 |
| ❑ 290 Pedro Martinez | .75 | .35 |
| ❑ 291 Juan Encarnacion | .25 | .11 |
| ❑ 292 Phil Nevin | .25 | .11 |
| ❑ 293 Terry Steinbach | .15 | .07 |
| ❑ 294 Miguel Tejada | .25 | .11 |
| ❑ 295 Dan Wilson | .15 | .07 |
| ❑ 296 Chris Peters | .15 | .07 |
| ❑ 297 Brian Moehler | .15 | .07 |
| ❑ 298 Jason Christiansen | .15 | .07 |
| ❑ 299 Kelly Stinnett | .15 | .07 |
| ❑ 300 Dwight Gooden | .25 | .11 |
| ❑ 301 Randy Velarde | .15 | .07 |
| ❑ 302 Kirt Manwaring | .15 | .07 |
| ❑ 303 Jeff Abbott | .15 | .07 |
| ❑ 304 Dave Hollins | .15 | .07 |
| ❑ 305 Kerry Ligtenberg | .15 | .07 |
| ❑ 306 Aaron Boone | .15 | .07 |
| ❑ 307 Carlos Hernandez | .15 | .07 |
| ❑ 308 Mike Difelice | .15 | .07 |
| ❑ 309 Brian Meadows | .15 | .07 |
| ❑ 310 Tim Bogar | .15 | .07 |
| ❑ 311 Greg Vaughn TR | .25 | .11 |
| ❑ 312 Brant Brown TR | .15 | .07 |
| ❑ 313 Steve Finley TR | .25 | .11 |
| ❑ 314 Bret Boone TR | .25 | .11 |
| ❑ 315 Albert Belle TR | .40 | .18 |
| ❑ 316 Robin Ventura TR | .25 | .11 |
| ❑ 317 Eric Davis TR | .25 | .11 |
| ❑ 318 Todd Hundley TR | .15 | .07 |
| ❑ 319 Roger Clemens TR | .60 | .25 |
| ❑ 320 Kevin Brown TR | .40 | .18 |
| ❑ 321 Jose Offerman TR | .15 | .07 |
| ❑ 322 Brian Jordan TR | .25 | .11 |
| ❑ 323 Mike Cameron TR | .15 | .07 |
| ❑ 324 Bobby Bonilla TR | .25 | .11 |
| ❑ 325 Roberto Alomar TR | .60 | .25 |
| ❑ 326 Ken Caminiti TR | .25 | .11 |
| ❑ 327 Todd Stottlemyre TR | .15 | .07 |
| ❑ 328 Randy Johnson TR | .60 | .25 |
| ❑ 329 Luis Gonzalez TR | .25 | .11 |
| ❑ 330 Rafael Palmeiro TR | .60 | .25 |
| ❑ 331 Devon White TR | .15 | .07 |
| ❑ 332 Will Clark TR | .60 | .25 |
| ❑ 333 Dean Palmer TR | .25 | .11 |
| ❑ 334 Gregg Jefferies TR | .15 | .07 |
| ❑ 335 Mo Vaughn TR | .25 | .11 |
| ❑ 336 Brad Lidge SP RC | 1.00 | .45 |
| ❑ 337 Chris George SP RC | 1.50 | .70 |
| ❑ 338 Austin Kearns SP RC | 4.00 | 1.80 |
| ❑ 339 Matt Belisle SP RC | 1.50 | .70 |
| ❑ 340 Nate Cornejo SP RC | 1.00 | .45 |
| ❑ 341 Matt Holliday SP RC | 1.50 | .70 |
| ❑ 342 J.M. Gold SP RC | 1.00 | .45 |
| ❑ 343 Matt Roney SP RC | 1.00 | .45 |
| ❑ 344 Seth Etherton SP RC | 1.00 | .45 |
| ❑ 345 Adam Everett SP RC | 1.25 | .55 |
| ❑ 346 Marlon Anderson SP | 1.00 | .45 |
| ❑ 347 Ron Belliard SP | 1.00 | .45 |
| ❑ 348 Fernando Seguignol SP | 1.00 | .45 |
| ❑ 349 Michael Barrett SP | 1.00 | .45 |
| ❑ 350 Dernell Stenson SP | 1.25 | .55 |
| ❑ 351 Ryan Anderson SP | 1.25 | .55 |
| ❑ 352 Ramon Hernandez SP | 1.00 | .45 |
| ❑ 353 Jeremy Giambi SP | 1.00 | .45 |
| ❑ 354 Ricky Ledee SP | 1.00 | .45 |
| ❑ 355 Carlos Lee SP | 1.25 | .55 |

## 2000 Stadium Club

| | MINT | NRMT |
|---|---|---|
| COMPLETE SET (250) | 250.00 | 110.00 |
| COMP.SET w/o SP'S (200) | 30.00 | 13.50 |
| COMMON CARD (1-200) | .15 | .07 |
| COMMON SP (201-250) | 3.00 | 1.35 |
| ❑ 1 Nomar Garciaparra | 2.00 | .90 |
| ❑ 2 Brian Jordan | .25 | .11 |
| ❑ 3 Mark Grace | .60 | .25 |
| ❑ 4 Jeromy Burnitz | .25 | .11 |
| ❑ 5 Shane Reynolds | .15 | .07 |
| ❑ 6 Alex Gonzalez | .15 | .07 |
| ❑ 7 Jose Offerman | .15 | .07 |
| ❑ 8 Orlando Hernandez | .25 | .11 |
| ❑ 9 Mike Caruso | .15 | .07 |
| ❑ 10 Tony Clark | .15 | .07 |
| ❑ 11 Sean Casey | .25 | .11 |
| ❑ 12 Johnny Damon | .25 | .11 |
| ❑ 13 Dante Bichette | .25 | .11 |
| ❑ 14 Kevin Young | .15 | .07 |
| ❑ 15 Juan Gonzalez | .60 | .25 |
| ❑ 16 Chipper Jones | 1.50 | .70 |
| ❑ 17 Quilvio Veras | .15 | .07 |
| ❑ 18 Trevor Hoffman | .25 | .11 |
| ❑ 19 Roger Cedeno | .15 | .07 |
| ❑ 20 Ellis Burks | .25 | .11 |
| ❑ 21 Richie Sexson | .25 | .11 |
| ❑ 22 Gary Sheffield | .60 | .25 |
| ❑ 23 Delino DeShields | .15 | .07 |
| ❑ 24 Wade Boggs | .75 | .35 |
| ❑ 25 Ray Lankford | .25 | .11 |
| ❑ 26 Kevin Appier | .15 | .07 |
| ❑ 27 Roy Halladay | .15 | .07 |
| ❑ 28 Harold Baines | .25 | .11 |
| ❑ 29 Todd Zeile | .25 | .11 |
| ❑ 30 Barry Larkin | .60 | .25 |
| ❑ 31 Ron Coomer | .15 | .07 |
| ❑ 32 Jorge Posada | .25 | .11 |
| ❑ 33 Magglio Ordonez | .25 | .11 |
| ❑ 34 Brian Giles | .25 | .11 |
| ❑ 35 Jeff Kent | .40 | .18 |
| ❑ 36 Henry Rodriguez | .15 | .07 |
| ❑ 37 Fred McGriff | .40 | .18 |
| ❑ 38 Shawn Green | .60 | .25 |
| ❑ 39 Derek Bell | .15 | .07 |
| ❑ 40 Ben Grieve | .25 | .11 |
| ❑ 41 Dave Nilsson | .15 | .07 |
| ❑ 42 Mo Vaughn | .25 | .11 |
| ❑ 43 Rondell White | .25 | .11 |
| ❑ 44 Doug Glanville | .15 | .07 |
| ❑ 45 Paul O'Neill | .25 | .11 |
| ❑ 46 Carlos Lee | .25 | .11 |
| ❑ 47 Vinny Castilla | .25 | .11 |
| ❑ 48 Mike Sweeney | .25 | .11 |
| ❑ 49 Rico Brogna | .15 | .07 |
| ❑ 50 Alex Rodriguez | 2.00 | .90 |
| ❑ 51 Luis Castillo | .25 | .11 |
| ❑ 52 Kevin Brown | .40 | .18 |
| ❑ 53 Jose Vidro | .15 | .07 |
| ❑ 54 John Smoltz | .25 | .11 |
| ❑ 55 Garret Anderson | .25 | .11 |
| ❑ 56 Matt Stairs | .15 | .07 |
| ❑ 57 Omar Vizquel | .25 | .11 |
| ❑ 58 Tom Goodwin | .15 | .07 |
| ❑ 59 Scott Brosius | .25 | .11 |
| ❑ 60 Robin Ventura | .40 | .18 |
| ❑ 61 B.J. Surhoff | .25 | .11 |
| ❑ 62 Andy Ashby | .15 | .07 |
| ❑ 63 Chris Widger | .15 | .07 |
| ❑ 64 Tim Hudson | .60 | .25 |
| ❑ 65 Javy Lopez | .25 | .11 |
| ❑ 66 Tim Salmon | .25 | .11 |
| ❑ 67 Warren Morris | .15 | .07 |
| ❑ 68 John Wetteland | .25 | .11 |
| ❑ 69 Gabe Kapler | .25 | .11 |
| ❑ 70 Bernie Williams | .60 | .25 |
| ❑ 71 Rickey Henderson | .75 | .35 |
| ❑ 72 Andruw Jones | .60 | .25 |
| ❑ 73 Eric Young | .15 | .07 |
| ❑ 74 Bob Abreu | .25 | .11 |
| ❑ 75 David Cone | .25 | .11 |
| ❑ 76 Rusty Greer | .25 | .11 |
| ❑ 77 Ron Belliard | .15 | .07 |
| ❑ 78 Troy Glaus | .75 | .35 |
| ❑ 79 Mike Hampton | .25 | .11 |
| ❑ 80 Miguel Tejada | .25 | .11 |
| ❑ 81 Jeff Cirillo | .25 | .11 |
| ❑ 82 Todd Hundley | .15 | .07 |
| ❑ 83 Roberto Alomar | .75 | .35 |
| ❑ 84 Charles Johnson | .25 | .11 |
| ❑ 85 Rafael Palmeiro | .60 | .25 |
| ❑ 86 Doug Mientkiewicz | .15 | .07 |
| ❑ 87 Mariano Rivera | .25 | .11 |
| ❑ 88 Neifi Perez | .15 | .07 |
| ❑ 89 Jermaine Dye | .25 | .11 |
| ❑ 90 Ivan Rodriguez | .75 | .35 |
| ❑ 91 Jay Buhner | .25 | .11 |
| ❑ 92 Pokey Reese | .25 | .11 |
| ❑ 93 John Olerud | .25 | .11 |
| ❑ 94 Brady Anderson | .25 | .11 |
| ❑ 95 Manny Ramirez | .75 | .35 |
| ❑ 96 Keith Osik | .15 | .07 |
| ❑ 97 Mickey Morandini | .15 | .07 |
| ❑ 98 Matt Williams | .40 | .18 |
| ❑ 99 Eric Karros | .25 | .11 |
| ❑ 100 Ken Griffey Jr. | 2.50 | 1.10 |
| ❑ 101 Bret Boone | .15 | .07 |
| ❑ 102 Ryan Klesko | .25 | .11 |
| ❑ 103 Craig Biggio | .40 | .18 |
| ❑ 104 John Jaha | .15 | .07 |
| ❑ 105 Vladimir Guerrero | 1.00 | .45 |
| ❑ 106 Devon White | .15 | .07 |
| ❑ 107 Tony Womack | .15 | .07 |
| ❑ 108 Marvin Benard | .15 | .07 |
| ❑ 109 Kenny Lofton | .25 | .11 |
| ❑ 110 Preston Wilson | .25 | .11 |
| ❑ 111 Al Leiter | .15 | .07 |
| ❑ 112 Reggie Sanders | .15 | .07 |
| ❑ 113 Scott Williamson | .15 | .07 |
| ❑ 114 Deivi Cruz | .15 | .07 |
| ❑ 115 Carlos Beltran | .25 | .11 |
| ❑ 116 Ray Durham | .25 | .11 |
| ❑ 117 Ricky Ledee | .15 | .07 |
| ❑ 118 Torii Hunter | .15 | .07 |
| ❑ 119 John Valentin | .15 | .07 |
| ❑ 120 Scott Rolen | .60 | .25 |
| ❑ 121 Jason Kendall | .25 | .11 |
| ❑ 122 Dave Martinez | .15 | .07 |
| ❑ 123 Jim Thome | .40 | .18 |
| ❑ 124 David Bell | .15 | .07 |
| ❑ 125 Jose Canseco | .75 | .35 |
| ❑ 126 Jose Lima | .15 | .07 |
| ❑ 127 Carl Everett | .25 | .11 |
| ❑ 128 Kevin Millwood | .25 | .11 |
| ❑ 129 Bill Spiers | .15 | .07 |
| ❑ 130 Omar Daal | .15 | .07 |
| ❑ 131 Miguel Cairo | .15 | .07 |
| ❑ 132 Mark Grudzielanek | .15 | .07 |
| ❑ 133 David Justice | .40 | .18 |
| ❑ 134 Russ Ortiz | .25 | .11 |
| ❑ 135 Mike Piazza | 2.00 | .90 |
| ❑ 136 Brian Meadows | .15 | .07 |
| ❑ 137 Tony Gwynn | 1.25 | .55 |
| ❑ 138 Cal Ripken | 2.50 | 1.10 |

❑ 139 Kris Benson .25 .11
❑ 140 Larry Walker .25 .11
❑ 141 Cristian Guzman .15 .07
❑ 142 Tino Martinez .25 .11
❑ 143 Chris Singleton .25 .11
❑ 144 Lee Stevens .15 .07
❑ 145 Rey Ordonez .15 .07
❑ 146 Russ Davis .15 .07
❑ 147 J.T. Snow .25 .11
❑ 148 Luis Gonzalez .25 .11
❑ 149 Marquis Grissom .15 .07
❑ 150 Greg Maddux 1.50 .70
❑ 151 Fernando Tatis .25 .11
❑ 152 Jason Giambi .60 .25
❑ 153 Carlos Delgado .60 .25
❑ 154 Joe McEwing .15 .07
❑ 155 Raul Mondesi .25 .11
❑ 156 Rich Aurilia .15 .07
❑ 157 Alex Fernandez .15 .07
❑ 158 Albert Belle .40 .18
❑ 159 Pat Meares .15 .07
❑ 160 Mike Lieberthal .25 .11
❑ 161 Mike Cameron .15 .07
❑ 162 Juan Encarnacion .25 .11
❑ 163 Chuck Knoblauch .25 .11
❑ 164 Pedro Martinez .75 .35
❑ 165 Randy Johnson .75 .35
❑ 166 Shannon Stewart .25 .11
❑ 167 Jeff Bagwell .75 .35
❑ 168 Edgar Renteria .15 .07
❑ 169 Barry Bonds 1.00 .45
❑ 170 Steve Finley .25 .11
❑ 171 Brian Hunter .15 .07
❑ 172 Tom Glavine .60 .25
❑ 173 Mark Kotsay .15 .07
❑ 174 Tony Fernandez .15 .07
❑ 175 Sammy Sosa 1.25 .55
❑ 176 Geoff Jenkins .25 .11
❑ 177 Adrian Beltre .25 .11
❑ 178 Jay Bell .25 .11
❑ 179 Mike Bordick .15 .07
❑ 180 Ed Sprague .15 .07
❑ 181 Dave Roberts .15 .07
❑ 182 Greg Vaughn .25 .11
❑ 183 Brian Daubach .15 .07
❑ 184 Damion Easley .15 .07
❑ 185 Carlos Febles .15 .07
❑ 186 Kevin Tapani .15 .07
❑ 187 Frank Thomas 1.25 .55
❑ 188 Roger Clemens 1.25 .55
❑ 189 Mike Benjamin .15 .07
❑ 190 Curt Schilling .25 .11
❑ 191 Edgardo Alfonzo .25 .11
❑ 192 Mike Mussina .60 .25
❑ 193 Todd Helton .75 .35
❑ 194 Todd Jones .15 .07
❑ 195 Dean Palmer .25 .11
❑ 196 John Flaherty .15 .07
❑ 197 Derek Jeter 2.50 1.10
❑ 198 Todd Walker .15 .07
❑ 199 Brad Ausmus .15 .07
❑ 200 Mark McGwire 2.50 1.10
❑ 201 Erubiel Durazo SP 4.00 1.80
❑ 202 Nick Johnson SP 4.00 1.80
❑ 203 Ruben Mateo SP 4.00 1.80
❑ 204 Lance Berkman SP 4.00 1.80
❑ 205 Pat Burrell SP 8.00 3.60
❑ 206 Pablo Ozuna SP 3.00 1.35
❑ 207 Roosevelt Brown SP 3.00 1.35
❑ 208 Alfonso Soriano SP 4.00 1.80
❑ 209 A.J. Burnett SP 4.00 1.80
❑ 210 Rafael Furcal SP 12.00 5.50
❑ 211 Scott Morgan SP 3.00 1.35
❑ 212 Adam Piatt SP 5.00 2.20
❑ 213 Dee Brown SP 4.00 1.80
❑ 214 Corey Patterson SP 8.00 3.60
❑ 215 Mickey Lopez SP 3.00 1.35
❑ 216 Rob Ryan SP 3.00 1.35
❑ 217 Sean Burroughs SP 5.00 2.20
❑ 218 Jack Cust SP 4.00 1.80
❑ 219 John Patterson SP 3.00 1.35
❑ 220 Kit Pellow SP 3.00 1.35
❑ 221 Chad Hermansen SP 3.00 1.35
❑ 222 Daryle Ward SP 4.00 1.80
❑ 223 Jayson Werth SP 3.00 1.35
❑ 224 Jason Standridge SP 3.00 1.35
❑ 225 Mark Mulder SP 4.00 1.80
❑ 226 Peter Bergeron SP 3.00 1.35
❑ 227 Willi Mo Pena SP 4.00 1.80
❑ 228 Aramis Ramirez SP 3.00 1.35
❑ 229 John Sneed SP RC 3.00 1.35
❑ 230 Wilton Veras SP 4.00 1.80
❑ 231 Josh Hamilton SP 8.00 3.60
❑ 232 Eric Munson SP 5.00 2.20
❑ 233 Bobby Bradley SP RC 10.00 4.50
❑ 234 Larry Bigbie SP RC 4.00 1.80
❑ 235 B.J. Garbe SP RC 6.00 2.70
❑ 236 Brett Myers SP RC 4.00 1.80
❑ 237 Jason Stumm SP RC 4.00 1.80
❑ 238 Corey Myers SP RC 3.00 1.35
❑ 239 Ryan Christianson SP RC 5.00 2.20
❑ 240 David Walling SP 3.00 1.35
❑ 241 Josh Girdley SP 3.00 1.35
❑ 242 Omar Ortiz SP 3.00 1.35
❑ 243 Jason Jennings SP 3.00 1.35
❑ 244 Kyle Snyder SP 3.00 1.35
❑ 245 Jay Gehrke SP 3.00 1.35
❑ 246 Mike Paradis SP 3.00 1.35
❑ 247 Chance Caple SP RC 3.00 1.35
❑ 248 Ben Christensen SP RC 5.00 2.20
❑ 249 Brad Baker SP RC 5.00 2.20
❑ 250 Rick Asadoorian SP RC 12.00 5.50

## 2000 Stadium Club Chrome

| | MINT | NRMT |
|---|---|---|
| COMPLETE SET (250) | 200.00 | 90.00 |

❑ 1 Nomar Garciaparra 6.00 2.70
❑ 2 Brian Jordan .75 .35
❑ 3 Mark Grace 2.00 .90
❑ 4 Jeromy Burnitz .75 .35
❑ 5 Shane Reynolds .50 .23
❑ 6 Alex Gonzalez .50 .23
❑ 7 Jose Offerman .50 .23
❑ 8 Orlando Hernandez .75 .35
❑ 9 Mike Caruso .50 .23
❑ 10 Tony Clark .50 .23
❑ 11 Sean Casey .75 .35
❑ 12 Johnny Damon .75 .35
❑ 13 Dante Bichette .75 .35
❑ 14 Kevin Young .50 .23
❑ 15 Juan Gonzalez 2.00 .90
❑ 16 Chipper Jones 5.00 2.20
❑ 17 Quilvio Veras .50 .23
❑ 18 Trevor Hoffman .75 .35
❑ 19 Roger Cedeno .50 .23
❑ 20 Ellis Burks .75 .35
❑ 21 Richie Sexson .75 .35
❑ 22 Gary Sheffield 2.00 .90
❑ 23 Delino DeShields .50 .23
❑ 24 Wade Boggs 2.50 1.10
❑ 25 Ray Lankford .75 .35
❑ 26 Kevin Appier .50 .23
❑ 27 Roy Halladay .50 .23
❑ 28 Harold Baines .75 .35
❑ 29 Todd Zeile .75 .35
❑ 30 Barry Larkin 2.00 .90
❑ 31 Ron Coomer .50 .23
❑ 32 Jorge Posada .75 .35
❑ 33 Magglio Ordonez .75 .35
❑ 34 Brian Giles .75 .35
❑ 35 Jeff Kent 1.25 .55
❑ 36 Henry Rodriguez .50 .23
❑ 37 Fred McGriff 1.25 .55
❑ 38 Shawn Green 2.00 .90
❑ 39 Derek Bell .50 .23
❑ 40 Ben Grieve .75 .35
❑ 41 Dave Nilsson .50 .23
❑ 42 Mo Vaughn .75 .35
❑ 43 Rondell White .75 .35
❑ 44 Doug Glanville .50 .23
❑ 45 Paul O'Neill .75 .35
❑ 46 Carlos Lee .75 .35
❑ 47 Vinny Castilla .75 .35
❑ 48 Mike Sweeney .75 .35
❑ 49 Rico Brogna .50 .23
❑ 50 Alex Rodriguez 6.00 2.70
❑ 51 Luis Castillo .75 .35
❑ 52 Kevin Brown 1.25 .55
❑ 53 Jose Vidro .50 .23
❑ 54 John Smoltz .75 .35
❑ 55 Garret Anderson .75 .35
❑ 56 Matt Stairs .50 .23
❑ 57 Omar Vizquel .75 .35
❑ 58 Tom Goodwin .50 .23
❑ 59 Scott Brosius .75 .35
❑ 60 Robin Ventura 1.25 .55
❑ 61 B.J. Surhoff .75 .35
❑ 62 Andy Ashby .50 .23
❑ 63 Chris Widger .50 .23
❑ 64 Tim Hudson 2.00 .90
❑ 65 Javy Lopez .75 .35
❑ 66 Tim Salmon .75 .35
❑ 67 Warren Morris .50 .23
❑ 68 John Wetteland .75 .35
❑ 69 Gabe Kapler .75 .35
❑ 70 Bernie Williams 2.00 .90
❑ 71 Rickey Henderson 2.50 1.10
❑ 72 Andruw Jones 2.00 .90
❑ 73 Eric Young .50 .23
❑ 74 Bob Abreu .75 .35
❑ 75 David Cone .75 .35
❑ 76 Rusty Greer .75 .35
❑ 77 Ron Belliard .50 .23
❑ 78 Troy Glaus 2.50 1.10
❑ 79 Mike Hampton .75 .35
❑ 80 Miguel Tejada .75 .35
❑ 81 Jeff Cirillo .75 .35
❑ 82 Todd Hundley .50 .23
❑ 83 Roberto Alomar 2.00 .90
❑ 84 Charles Johnson .75 .35
❑ 85 Rafael Palmeiro 2.00 .90
❑ 86 Doug Mientkiewicz .50 .23
❑ 87 Mariano Rivera .75 .35
❑ 88 Neifi Perez .50 .23
❑ 89 Jermiane Dye .75 .35
❑ 90 Ivan Rodriguez 2.50 1.10
❑ 91 Jay Buhner .75 .35
❑ 92 Pokey Reese .75 .35
❑ 93 John Olerud .75 .35
❑ 94 Brady Anderson .75 .35
❑ 95 Manny Ramirez 2.50 1.10
❑ 96 Keith Osik .50 .23
❑ 97 Mickey Morandini .50 .23
❑ 98 Matt Williams 1.25 .55
❑ 99 Eric Karros .75 .35
❑ 100 Ken Griffey Jr. 8.00 3.60
❑ 101 Bret Boone .50 .23
❑ 102 Ryan Klesko .75 .35
❑ 103 Craig Biggio 1.25 .55
❑ 104 John Jaha .50 .23
❑ 105 Vladimir Guerrero 2.50 1.10
❑ 106 Devon White .50 .23
❑ 107 Tony Womack .50 .23
❑ 108 Marvin Benard .50 .23
❑ 109 Kenny Lofton .75 .35
❑ 110 Preston Wilson .75 .35
❑ 111 Al Leiter .50 .23
❑ 112 Reggie Sanders .50 .23
❑ 113 Scott Williamson .50 .23
❑ 114 Deivi Cruz .50 .23
❑ 115 Carlos Beltran .75 .35
❑ 116 Ray Durham .75 .35
❑ 117 Ricky Ledee .50 .23
❑ 118 Torii Hunter .50 .23
❑ 119 John Valentin .50 .23
❑ 120 Scott Rolen 2.00 .90
❑ 121 Jason Kendall .75 .35

| # | Player | Mint | Nrmt |
|---|---|---|---|
| ❑ 122 | Dave Martinez | .50 | .23 |
| ❑ 123 | Jim Thome | 1.25 | .55 |
| ❑ 124 | David Bell | .50 | .23 |
| ❑ 125 | Jose Canseco | 2.50 | 1.10 |
| ❑ 126 | Jose Lima | .50 | .23 |
| ❑ 127 | Carl Everett | .75 | .35 |
| ❑ 128 | Kevin Millwood | .75 | .35 |
| ❑ 129 | Bill Spiers | .50 | .23 |
| ❑ 130 | Omar Daal | .50 | .23 |
| ❑ 131 | Miguel Cairo | .50 | .23 |
| ❑ 132 | Mark Grudzielanek | .50 | .23 |
| ❑ 133 | David Justice | 1.25 | .55 |
| ❑ 134 | Russ Ortiz | .75 | .35 |
| ❑ 135 | Mike Piazza | 6.00 | 2.70 |
| ❑ 136 | Brian Meadows | .50 | .23 |
| ❑ 137 | Tony Gwynn | 4.00 | 1.80 |
| ❑ 138 | Cal Ripken | 8.00 | 3.60 |
| ❑ 139 | Kris Benson | .75 | .35 |
| ❑ 140 | Larry Walker | .75 | .35 |
| ❑ 141 | Cristian Guzman | .50 | .23 |
| ❑ 142 | Tino Martinez | .75 | .35 |
| ❑ 143 | Chris Singleton | .75 | .35 |
| ❑ 144 | Lee Stevens | .50 | .23 |
| ❑ 145 | Rey Ordonez | .50 | .23 |
| ❑ 146 | Russ Davis | .50 | .23 |
| ❑ 147 | J.T. Snow | .75 | .35 |
| ❑ 148 | Luis Gonzalez | .75 | .35 |
| ❑ 149 | Marquis Grissom | .50 | .23 |
| ❑ 150 | Greg Maddux | 5.00 | 2.20 |
| ❑ 151 | Fernando Tatis | .75 | .35 |
| ❑ 152 | Jason Giambi | 2.00 | .90 |
| ❑ 153 | Carlos Delgado | 2.00 | .90 |
| ❑ 154 | Joe McEwing | .50 | .23 |
| ❑ 155 | Raul Mondesi | .75 | .35 |
| ❑ 156 | Rich Aurilia | .50 | .23 |
| ❑ 157 | Alex Fernandez | .50 | .23 |
| ❑ 158 | Albert Belle | 1.25 | .55 |
| ❑ 159 | Pat Meares | .50 | .23 |
| ❑ 160 | Mike Lieberthal | .75 | .35 |
| ❑ 161 | Mike Cameron | .50 | .23 |
| ❑ 162 | Juan Encarnacion | .75 | .35 |
| ❑ 163 | Chuck Knoblauch | .75 | .35 |
| ❑ 164 | Pedro Martinez | 2.50 | 1.10 |
| ❑ 165 | Randy Johnson | 2.50 | 1.10 |
| ❑ 166 | Shannon Stewart | .75 | .35 |
| ❑ 167 | Jeff Bagwell | 2.50 | 1.10 |
| ❑ 168 | Edgar Renteria | .50 | .23 |
| ❑ 169 | Barry Bonds | 3.00 | 1.35 |
| ❑ 170 | Steve Finley | .75 | .35 |
| ❑ 171 | Brian Hunter | .50 | .23 |
| ❑ 172 | Tom Glavine | 2.00 | .90 |
| ❑ 173 | Mark Kotsay | .50 | .23 |
| ❑ 174 | Tony Fernandez | .50 | .23 |
| ❑ 175 | Sammy Sosa | 4.00 | 1.80 |
| ❑ 176 | Geoff Jenkins | .75 | .35 |
| ❑ 177 | Adrian Beltre | .75 | .35 |
| ❑ 178 | Jay Bell | .75 | .35 |
| ❑ 179 | Mike Bordick | .50 | .23 |
| ❑ 180 | Ed Sprague | .50 | .23 |
| ❑ 181 | Dave Roberts | .50 | .23 |
| ❑ 182 | Greg Vaughn | .75 | .35 |
| ❑ 183 | Brian Daubach | .50 | .23 |
| ❑ 184 | Damion Easley | .50 | .23 |
| ❑ 185 | Carlos Febles | .50 | .23 |
| ❑ 186 | Kevin Tapani | .50 | .23 |
| ❑ 187 | Frank Thomas | 4.00 | 1.80 |
| ❑ 188 | Roger Clemens | 4.00 | 1.80 |
| ❑ 189 | Mike Benjamin | .50 | .23 |
| ❑ 190 | Curt Schilling | .75 | .35 |
| ❑ 191 | Edgardo Alfonzo | .75 | .35 |
| ❑ 192 | Mike Mussina | 2.00 | .90 |
| ❑ 193 | Todd Helton | 2.50 | 1.10 |
| ❑ 194 | Todd Jones | .50 | .23 |
| ❑ 195 | Dean Palmer | .75 | .35 |
| ❑ 196 | John Flaherty | .50 | .23 |
| ❑ 197 | Derek Jeter | 8.00 | 3.60 |
| ❑ 198 | Todd Walker | .50 | .23 |
| ❑ 199 | Brad Ausmus | .50 | .23 |
| ❑ 200 | Mark McGwire | 8.00 | 3.60 |
| ❑ 201 | Erubiel Durazo | .75 | .35 |
| ❑ 202 | Nick Johnson | .75 | .35 |
| ❑ 203 | Ruben Mateo | .75 | .35 |
| ❑ 204 | Lance Berkman | .75 | .35 |
| ❑ 205 | Pat Burrell | 3.00 | 1.35 |
| ❑ 206 | Pablo Ozuna | .50 | .23 |
| ❑ 207 | Roosevelt Brown | .50 | .23 |
| ❑ 208 | Alfonso Soriano | .75 | .35 |
| ❑ 209 | A.J. Burnett | .75 | .35 |
| ❑ 210 | Rafael Furcal | 5.00 | 2.20 |
| ❑ 211 | Scott Morgan | .50 | .23 |
| ❑ 212 | Adam Piatt | 2.00 | .90 |
| ❑ 213 | Dee Brown | .75 | .35 |
| ❑ 214 | Corey Patterson | 3.00 | 1.35 |
| ❑ 215 | Mickey Lopez | .50 | .23 |
| ❑ 216 | Rob Ryan | .50 | .23 |
| ❑ 217 | Sean Burroughs | 2.00 | .90 |
| ❑ 218 | Jack Cust | .75 | .35 |
| ❑ 219 | John Patterson | .50 | .23 |
| ❑ 220 | Kit Pellow | .50 | .23 |
| ❑ 221 | Chad Hermansen | .50 | .23 |
| ❑ 222 | Daryle Ward | .75 | .35 |
| ❑ 223 | Jayson Werth | .50 | .23 |
| ❑ 224 | Jason Standridge | .50 | .23 |
| ❑ 225 | Mark Mulder | .75 | .35 |
| ❑ 226 | Peter Bergeron | .50 | .23 |
| ❑ 227 | Willi Mo Pena | .75 | .35 |
| ❑ 228 | Aramis Ramirez | .50 | .23 |
| ❑ 229 | John Sneed RC | 2.00 | .90 |
| ❑ 230 | Wilton Veras | .75 | .35 |
| ❑ 231 | Josh Hamilton | 3.00 | 1.35 |
| ❑ 232 | Eric Munson | 2.00 | .90 |
| ❑ 233 | Bobby Bradley RC | 5.00 | 2.20 |
| ❑ 234 | Larry Bigbie RC | 2.00 | .90 |
| ❑ 235 | B.J. Garbe RC | 3.00 | 1.35 |
| ❑ 236 | Brett Myers RC | 2.00 | .90 |
| ❑ 237 | Jason Stumm RC | 2.00 | .90 |
| ❑ 238 | Corey Myers RC | 1.50 | .70 |
| ❑ 239 | Ryan Christianson RC | 2.50 | 1.10 |
| ❑ 240 | David Walling | .50 | .23 |
| ❑ 241 | Josh Girdley | .50 | .23 |
| ❑ 242 | Omar Ortiz | .50 | .23 |
| ❑ 243 | Jason Jennings | .50 | .23 |
| ❑ 244 | Kyle Snyder | .50 | .23 |
| ❑ 245 | Jay Gehrke | .50 | .23 |
| ❑ 246 | Mike Paradis | .50 | .23 |
| ❑ 247 | Chance Caple RC | 1.50 | .70 |
| ❑ 248 | Ben Christensen RC | 2.50 | 1.10 |
| ❑ 249 | Brad Baker RC | 2.50 | 1.10 |
| ❑ 250 | Rick Asadoorian RC | 6.00 | 2.70 |

## 2001 Stadium Club

| | MINT | NRMT |
|---|---|---|
| COMPLETE SET (200) | 120.00 | 55.00 |
| COMP.SET w/o SP's (175) | 25.00 | 11.00 |
| COMMON CARD (1-150) | .15 | .07 |
| COMMON SP (151-200) | 3.00 | 1.35 |

| # | Player | Mint | Nrmt |
|---|---|---|---|
| ❑ 1 | Nomar Garciaparra | 2.00 | .90 |
| ❑ 2 | Chipper Jones | 1.50 | .70 |
| ❑ 3 | Jeff Bagwell | .75 | .35 |
| ❑ 4 | Chad Kreuter | .15 | .07 |
| ❑ 5 | Randy Johnson | .75 | .35 |
| ❑ 6 | Mike Hampton | .25 | .11 |
| ❑ 7 | Barry Larkin | .50 | .23 |
| ❑ 8 | Bernie Williams | .50 | .23 |
| ❑ 9 | Chris Singleton | .25 | .11 |
| ❑ 10 | Larry Walker | .25 | .11 |
| ❑ 11 | Brad Ausmus | .15 | .07 |
| ❑ 12 | Ron Coomer | .15 | .07 |
| ❑ 13 | Edgardo Alfonzo | .25 | .11 |
| ❑ 14 | Delino DeShields | .15 | .07 |
| ❑ 15 | Tony Gwynn | 1.25 | .55 |
| ❑ 16 | Andruw Jones | .60 | .25 |
| ❑ 17 | Raul Mondesi | .25 | .11 |
| ❑ 18 | Troy Glaus | .75 | .35 |
| ❑ 19 | Ben Grieve | .25 | .11 |
| ❑ 20 | Sammy Sosa | 1.25 | .55 |
| ❑ 21 | Fernando Vina | .25 | .11 |
| ❑ 22 | Jeromy Burnitz | .25 | .11 |
| ❑ 23 | Jay Bell | .25 | .11 |
| ❑ 24 | Pete Harnisch | .15 | .07 |
| ❑ 25 | Barry Bonds | 1.00 | .45 |
| ❑ 26 | Eric Karros | .25 | .11 |
| ❑ 27 | Alex Gonzalez | .15 | .07 |
| ❑ 28 | Mike Lieberthal | .25 | .11 |
| ❑ 29 | Juan Encarnacion | .25 | .11 |
| ❑ 30 | Derek Jeter | 2.50 | 1.10 |
| ❑ 31 | Luis Sojo | .15 | .07 |
| ❑ 32 | Eric Milton | .25 | .11 |
| ❑ 33 | Aaron Boone | .15 | .07 |
| ❑ 34 | Roberto Alomar | .60 | .25 |
| ❑ 35 | John Olerud | .25 | .11 |
| ❑ 36 | Orlando Cabrera | .15 | .07 |
| ❑ 37 | Shawn Green | .50 | .23 |
| ❑ 38 | Roger Cedeno | .15 | .07 |
| ❑ 39 | Garret Anderson | .25 | .11 |
| ❑ 40 | Jim Thome | .40 | .18 |
| ❑ 41 | Gabe Kapler | .25 | .11 |
| ❑ 42 | Mo Vaughn | .25 | .11 |
| ❑ 43 | Sean Casey | .25 | .11 |
| ❑ 44 | Preston Wilson | .25 | .11 |
| ❑ 45 | Javy Lopez | .25 | .11 |
| ❑ 46 | Ryan Klesko | .25 | .11 |
| ❑ 47 | Ray Durham | .25 | .11 |
| ❑ 48 | Dean Palmer | .25 | .11 |
| ❑ 49 | Jorge Posada | .25 | .11 |
| ❑ 50 | Alex Rodriguez | 2.00 | .90 |
| ❑ 51 | Tom Glavine | .50 | .23 |
| ❑ 52 | Ray Lankford | .25 | .11 |
| ❑ 53 | Jose Canseco | .75 | .35 |
| ❑ 54 | Tim Salmon | .25 | .11 |
| ❑ 55 | Cal Ripken | 2.50 | 1.10 |
| ❑ 56 | Bob Abreu | .25 | .11 |
| ❑ 57 | Robin Ventura | .25 | .11 |
| ❑ 58 | Damion Easley | .15 | .07 |
| ❑ 59 | Paul O'Neill | .25 | .11 |
| ❑ 60 | Ivan Rodriguez | .75 | .35 |
| ❑ 61 | Carl Everett | .25 | .11 |
| ❑ 62 | Doug Glanville | .15 | .07 |
| ❑ 63 | Jeff Kent | .40 | .18 |
| ❑ 64 | Jay Buhner | .25 | .11 |
| ❑ 65 | Cliff Floyd | .25 | .11 |
| ❑ 66 | Rick Ankiel | .75 | .35 |
| ❑ 67 | Mark Grace | .60 | .25 |
| ❑ 68 | Brian Jordan | .25 | .11 |
| ❑ 69 | Craig Biggio | .40 | .18 |
| ❑ 70 | Carlos Delgado | .60 | .25 |
| ❑ 71 | Brad Radke | .25 | .11 |
| ❑ 72 | Greg Maddux | 1.50 | .70 |
| ❑ 73 | Al Leiter | .25 | .11 |
| ❑ 74 | Pokey Reese | .25 | .11 |
| ❑ 75 | Todd Helton | .75 | .35 |
| ❑ 76 | Mariano Rivera | .25 | .11 |
| ❑ 77 | Shane Spencer | .15 | .07 |
| ❑ 78 | Jason Kendall | .25 | .11 |
| ❑ 79 | Chuck Knoblauch | .25 | .11 |
| ❑ 80 | Scott Rolen | .50 | .23 |
| ❑ 81 | Jose Offerman | .15 | .07 |
| ❑ 82 | J.T. Snow | .25 | .11 |
| ❑ 83 | Pat Meares | .15 | .07 |
| ❑ 84 | Quilvio Veras | .15 | .07 |
| ❑ 85 | Edgar Renteria | .15 | .07 |
| ❑ 86 | Luis Matos | .15 | .07 |
| ❑ 87 | Adrian Beltre | .25 | .11 |
| ❑ 88 | Luis Gonzalez | .25 | .11 |
| ❑ 89 | Rickey Henderson | .75 | .35 |
| ❑ 90 | Brian Giles | .25 | .11 |
| ❑ 91 | Carlos Febles | .15 | .07 |
| ❑ 92 | Tino Martinez | .25 | .11 |
| ❑ 93 | Magglio Ordonez | .25 | .11 |
| ❑ 94 | Rafael Furcal | 1.00 | .45 |
| ❑ 95 | Mike Mussina | .60 | .25 |
| ❑ 96 | Gary Sheffield | .50 | .23 |
| ❑ 97 | Kenny Lofton | .25 | .11 |
| ❑ 98 | Fred McGriff | .40 | .18 |
| ❑ 99 | Ken Caminiti | .25 | .11 |
| ❑ 100 | Mark McGwire | 2.50 | 1.10 |
| ❑ 101 | Tom Goodwin | .15 | .07 |
| ❑ 102 | Mark Grudzielanek | .15 | .07 |

❑ 103 Derek Bell .15 .07
❑ 104 Mike Lowell .25 .11
❑ 105 Jeff Cirillo .25 .11
❑ 106 Orlando Hernandez .25 .11
❑ 107 Jose Valentin .15 .07
❑ 108 Warren Morris .15 .07
❑ 109 Mike Williams .15 .07
❑ 110 Greg Vaughn .25 .11
❑ 111 Jose Vidro .25 .11
❑ 112 Omar Vizquel .25 .11
❑ 113 Vinny Castilla .25 .11
❑ 114 Gregg Jefferies .15 .07
❑ 115 Kevin Brown .25 .11
❑ 116 Shannon Stewart .25 .11
❑ 117 Marquis Grissom .15 .07
❑ 118 Manny Ramirez .75 .35
❑ 119 Albert Belle .40 .18
❑ 120 Bret Boone .25 .11
❑ 121 Johnny Damon .25 .11
❑ 122 Juan Gonzalez .50 .23
❑ 123 David Justice .40 .18
❑ 124 Jeffrey Hammonds .25 .11
❑ 125 Ken Griffey Jr. 2.50 1.10
❑ 126 Mike Sweeney .25 .11
❑ 127 Tony Clark .15 .07
❑ 128 Todd Zeile .25 .11
❑ 129 Mark Johnson .15 .07
❑ 130 Matt Williams .40 .18
❑ 131 Geoff Jenkins .25 .11
❑ 132 Jason Giambi .60 .25
❑ 133 Steve Finley .25 .11
❑ 134 Derek Lee .25 .11
❑ 135 Royce Clayton .15 .07
❑ 136 Joe Randa .25 .11
❑ 137 Rafael Palmeiro .50 .23
❑ 138 Kevin Young .15 .07
❑ 139 Mike Redmond .15 .07
❑ 140 Vladimir Guerrero 1.00 .45
❑ 141 Greg Vaughn .25 .11
❑ 142 Jermaine Dye .25 .11
❑ 143 Roger Clemens 1.25 .55
❑ 144 Denny Hocking .15 .07
❑ 145 Frank Thomas 1.25 .55
❑ 146 Carlos Beltran .25 .11
❑ 147 Eric Young .15 .07
❑ 148 Pat Burrell .60 .25
❑ 149 Pedro Martinez .75 .35
❑ 150 Mike Piazza 2.00 .90
❑ 151 Adrian Gonzalez 1.25 .55
❑ 152 Adam Johnson .50 .23
❑ 153 Luis Montanez SP RC 15.00 6.75
❑ 154 Mike Stodolka .50 .23
❑ 155 Phil Dumatrait .50 .23
❑ 156 Sean Burnett SP 3.00 1.35
❑ 157 Dominic Rich SP RC 3.00 1.35
❑ 158 Adam Wainwright 1.00 .45
❑ 159 Scott Thorman .50 .23
❑ 160 Scott Heard .50 .23
❑ 161 Chad Petty SP RC 3.00 1.35
❑ 162 Matt Wheatland SP 4.00 1.80
❑ 163 Bryan Digby .50 .23
❑ 164 Rocco Baldelli 1.00 .45
❑ 165 Grady Sizemore .50 .23
❑ 166 Brian Sellier SP RC 3.00 1.35
❑ 167 Rick Brosseau SP RC 3.00 1.35
❑ 168 Shawn Fagan SP RC 3.00 1.35
❑ 169 Sean Smith SP 3.00 1.35
❑ 170 Chris Bass SP RC 3.00 1.35
❑ 171 Corey Patterson 1.00 .45
❑ 172 Sean Burroughs .75 .35
❑ 173 Ben Petrick .50 .23
❑ 174 Mike Glendenning .50 .23
❑ 175 Barry Zito 2.00 .90
❑ 176 Milton Bradley .50 .23
❑ 177 Bobby Bradley 1.00 .45
❑ 178 Jason Hart 1.00 .45
❑ 179 Ryan Anderson .50 .23
❑ 180 Ben Sheets 1.50 .70
❑ 181 Adam Everett .50 .23
❑ 182 Alfonso Soriano .50 .23
❑ 183 Josh Hamilton 1.00 .45
❑ 184 Eric Munson .50 .23
❑ 185 Chin Feng Chen 2.00 .90
❑ 186 Tim Christman SP RC 3.00 1.35
❑ 187 J.R. House SP 8.00 3.60
❑ 188 Brandon Parker SP RC 3.00 1.35
❑ 189 Sean Fesh SP RC 3.00 1.35
❑ 190 Joel Pineiro SP 3.00 1.35
❑ 191 Oscar Ramirez SP RC 3.00 1.35
❑ 192 Alex Santos SP RC 3.00 1.35
❑ 193 Eddy Reyes SP RC 3.00 1.35
❑ 194 Mike Jacobs SP RC 3.00 1.35
❑ 195 Erick Almonte SP RC 3.00 1.35
❑ 196 Brandon Claussen SP RC 3.00 1.35
❑ 197 Kris Keller SP RC 3.00 1.35
❑ 198 Wilson Betemit SP RC 10.00 4.50
❑ 199 Andy Phillips SP RC 3.00 1.35
❑ 200 Adam Pettyjohn SP RC 5.00 2.20

## 1991 Studio

| | MINT | NRMT |
|---|---|---|
| COMPLETE SET (264) | 15.00 | 6.75 |

❑ 1 Glenn Davis .10 .05
❑ 2 Dwight Evans .20 .09
❑ 3 Leo Gomez .10 .05
❑ 4 Chris Hoiles .10 .05
❑ 5 Sam Horn .10 .05
❑ 6 Ben McDonald .10 .05
❑ 7 Randy Milligan .10 .05
❑ 8 Gregg Olson .10 .05
❑ 9 Cal Ripken 1.50 .70
❑ 10 David Segui .10 .05
❑ 11 Wade Boggs .50 .23
❑ 12 Ellis Burks .20 .09
❑ 13 Jack Clark .20 .09
❑ 14 Roger Clemens .75 .35
❑ 15 Mike Greenwell .10 .05
❑ 16 Tim Naehring .10 .05
❑ 17 Tony Pena .10 .05
❑ 18 Phil Plantier RC .10 .05
❑ 19 Jeff Reardon .20 .09
❑ 20 Mo Vaughn .50 .23
❑ 21 Jimmie Reese CO .20 .09
❑ 22 Jim Abbott UER .20 .09
(Born in 1967, not 1969)
❑ 23 Bert Blyleven .20 .09
❑ 24 Chuck Finley .20 .09
❑ 25 Gary Gaetti .20 .09
❑ 26 Wally Joyner .20 .09
❑ 27 Mark Langston .10 .05
❑ 28 Kirk McCaskill .10 .05
❑ 29 Lance Parrish .10 .05
❑ 30 Dave Winfield .40 .18
❑ 31 Alex Fernandez .20 .09
❑ 32 Carlton Fisk .40 .18
❑ 33 Scott Fletcher .10 .05
❑ 34 Greg Hibbard .10 .05
❑ 35 Charlie Hough .20 .09
❑ 36 Jack McDowell .10 .05
❑ 37 Tim Raines .20 .09
❑ 38 Sammy Sosa 1.00 .45
❑ 39 Bobby Thigpen .10 .05
❑ 40 Frank Thomas 1.00 .45
❑ 41 Sandy Alomar Jr. .20 .09
❑ 42 John Farrell .10 .05
❑ 43 Glenallen Hill .10 .05
❑ 44 Brook Jacoby .10 .05
❑ 45 Chris James .10 .05
❑ 46 Doug Jones .10 .05
❑ 47 Eric King .10 .05
❑ 48 Mark Lewis .10 .05
❑ 49 Greg Swindell UER .10 .05
(Photo actually Turner Ward)
❑ 50 Mark Whiten .10 .05
❑ 51 Milt Cuyler .10 .05
❑ 52 Rob Deer .10 .05
❑ 53 Cecil Fielder .20 .09
❑ 54 Travis Fryman .40 .18
❑ 55 Bill Gullickson .10 .05
❑ 56 Lloyd Moseby .10 .05
❑ 57 Frank Tanana .10 .05
❑ 58 Mickey Tettleton .10 .05
❑ 59 Alan Trammell .25 .11
❑ 60 Lou Whitaker .20 .09
❑ 61 Mike Boddicker .10 .05
❑ 62 George Brett .75 .35
❑ 63 Jeff Conine RC .40 .18
❑ 64 Warren Cromartie .10 .05
❑ 65 Storm Davis .10 .05
❑ 66 Kirk Gibson .20 .09
❑ 67 Mark Gubicza .10 .05
❑ 68 Brian McRae RC .20 .09
❑ 69 Bret Saberhagen .20 .09
❑ 70 Kurt Stillwell .10 .05
❑ 71 Tim McIntosh .10 .05
❑ 72 Candy Maldonado .10 .05
❑ 73 Paul Molitor .40 .18
❑ 74 Willie Randolph .20 .09
❑ 75 Ron Robinson .10 .05
❑ 76 Gary Sheffield .40 .18
❑ 77 Franklin Stubbs .10 .05
❑ 78 B.J. Surhoff .20 .09
❑ 79 Greg Vaughn .40 .18
❑ 80 Robin Yount .40 .18
❑ 81 Rick Aguilera .20 .09
❑ 82 Steve Bedrosian .10 .05
❑ 83 Scott Erickson .10 .05
❑ 84 Greg Gagne .10 .05
❑ 85 Dan Gladden .10 .05
❑ 86 Brian Harper .10 .05
❑ 87 Kent Hrbek .20 .09
❑ 88 Shane Mack .10 .05
❑ 89 Jack Morris .20 .09
❑ 90 Kirby Puckett 1.00 .45
❑ 91 Jesse Barfield .10 .05
❑ 92 Steve Farr .10 .05
❑ 93 Steve Howe .10 .05
❑ 94 Roberto Kelly .10 .05
❑ 95 Tim Leary .10 .05
❑ 96 Kevin Maas .10 .05
❑ 97 Don Mattingly 1.00 .45
❑ 98 Hensley Meulens .10 .05
❑ 99 Scott Sanderson .10 .05
❑ 100 Steve Sax .10 .05
❑ 101 Jose Canseco .50 .23
❑ 102 Dennis Eckersley .20 .09
❑ 103 Dave Henderson .10 .05
❑ 104 Rickey Henderson .50 .23
❑ 105 Rick Honeycutt .10 .05
❑ 106 Mark McGwire 1.50 .70
❑ 107 Dave Stewart UER .10 .05
(No-hitter against Toronto, not Texas)
❑ 108 Eric Show .10 .05
❑ 109 Todd Van Poppel RC .10 .05
❑ 110 Bob Welch .10 .05
❑ 111 Alvin Davis .10 .05
❑ 112 Ken Griffey Jr. 2.00 .90
❑ 113 Ken Griffey Sr. .20 .09
❑ 114 Erik Hanson UER .10 .05
(Misspelled Eric)
❑ 115 Brian Holman .10 .05
❑ 116 Randy Johnson .60 .25
❑ 117 Edgar Martinez .25 .11
❑ 118 Tino Martinez .20 .09
❑ 119 Harold Reynolds .10 .05
❑ 120 David Valle .10 .05
❑ 121 Kevin Belcher .10 .05
❑ 122 Scott Chiamparino .10 .05
❑ 123 Julio Franco .10 .05
❑ 124 Juan Gonzalez .50 .23
❑ 125 Rich Gossage .20 .09
❑ 126 Jeff Kunkel .10 .05
❑ 127 Rafael Palmeiro .40 .18
❑ 128 Nolan Ryan 2.00 .90
❑ 129 Ruben Sierra .10 .05
❑ 130 Bobby Witt .10 .05

| |  |  | | |
|---|---|---|---|---|
| ❑ | 131 | Roberto Alomar | .40 | .18 |
| ❑ | 132 | Tom Candiotti | .10 | .05 |
| ❑ | 133 | Joe Carter | .20 | .09 |
| ❑ | 134 | Ken Dayley | .10 | .05 |
| ❑ | 135 | Kelly Gruber | .10 | .05 |
| ❑ | 136 | John Olerud | .25 | .11 |
| ❑ | 137 | Dave Stieb | .10 | .05 |
| ❑ | 138 | Turner Ward RC | .10 | .05 |
| ❑ | 139 | Devon White | .10 | .05 |
| ❑ | 140 | Mookie Wilson | .20 | .09 |
| ❑ | 141 | Steve Avery | .10 | .05 |
| ❑ | 142 | Sid Bream | .10 | .05 |
| ❑ | 143 | Nick Esasky UER (Homers abbreviated RH) | .10 | .05 |
| ❑ | 144 | Ron Gant | .20 | .09 |
| ❑ | 145 | Tom Glavine | .40 | .18 |
| ❑ | 146 | David Justice | .40 | .18 |
| ❑ | 147 | Kelly Mann | .10 | .05 |
| ❑ | 148 | Terry Pendleton | .20 | .09 |
| ❑ | 149 | John Smoltz | .20 | .09 |
| ❑ | 150 | Jeff Treadway | .10 | .05 |
| ❑ | 151 | George Bell | .10 | .05 |
| ❑ | 152 | Shawn Boskie | .10 | .05 |
| ❑ | 153 | Andre Dawson | .25 | .11 |
| ❑ | 154 | Lance Dickson RC | .10 | .05 |
| ❑ | 155 | Shawon Dunston | .10 | .05 |
| ❑ | 156 | Joe Girardi | .20 | .09 |
| ❑ | 157 | Mark Grace | .40 | .18 |
| ❑ | 158 | Ryne Sandberg | .50 | .23 |
| ❑ | 159 | Gary Scott RC | .10 | .05 |
| ❑ | 160 | Dave Smith | .10 | .05 |
| ❑ | 161 | Tom Browning | .10 | .05 |
| ❑ | 162 | Eric Davis | .20 | .09 |
| ❑ | 163 | Rob Dibble | .10 | .05 |
| ❑ | 164 | Mariano Duncan | .10 | .05 |
| ❑ | 165 | Chris Hammond | .10 | .05 |
| ❑ | 166 | Billy Hatcher | .10 | .05 |
| ❑ | 167 | Barry Larkin | .40 | .18 |
| ❑ | 168 | Hal Morris | .10 | .05 |
| ❑ | 169 | Paul O'Neill | .20 | .09 |
| ❑ | 170 | Chris Sabo | .10 | .05 |
| ❑ | 171 | Eric Anthony | .10 | .05 |
| ❑ | 172 | Jeff Bagwell RC | 3.00 | 1.35 |
| ❑ | 173 | Craig Biggio | .25 | .11 |
| ❑ | 174 | Ken Caminiti | .20 | .09 |
| ❑ | 175 | Jim Deshaies | .10 | .05 |
| ❑ | 176 | Steve Finley | .20 | .09 |
| ❑ | 177 | Pete Harnisch | .10 | .05 |
| ❑ | 178 | Darryl Kile | .20 | .09 |
| ❑ | 179 | Curt Schilling | .20 | .09 |
| ❑ | 180 | Mike Scott | .10 | .05 |
| ❑ | 181 | Brett Butler | .20 | .09 |
| ❑ | 182 | Gary Carter | .25 | .11 |
| ❑ | 183 | Orel Hershiser | .20 | .09 |
| ❑ | 184 | Ramon Martinez | .10 | .05 |
| ❑ | 185 | Eddie Murray | .40 | .18 |
| ❑ | 186 | Jose Offerman | .10 | .05 |
| ❑ | 187 | Bob Ojeda | .10 | .05 |
| ❑ | 188 | Juan Samuel | .10 | .05 |
| ❑ | 189 | Mike Scioscia | .10 | .05 |
| ❑ | 190 | Darryl Strawberry | .20 | .09 |
| ❑ | 191 | Moises Alou | .40 | .18 |
| ❑ | 192 | Brian Barnes | .10 | .05 |
| ❑ | 193 | Oil Can Boyd | .10 | .05 |
| ❑ | 194 | Ivan Calderon | .10 | .05 |
| ❑ | 195 | Delino DeShields | .20 | .09 |
| ❑ | 196 | Mike Fitzgerald | .10 | .05 |
| ❑ | 197 | Andres Galarraga | .25 | .11 |
| ❑ | 198 | Marquis Grissom | .10 | .05 |
| ❑ | 199 | Bill Sampen | .10 | .05 |
| ❑ | 200 | Tim Wallach | .10 | .05 |
| ❑ | 201 | Daryl Boston | .10 | .05 |
| ❑ | 202 | Vince Coleman | .10 | .05 |
| ❑ | 203 | John Franco | .20 | .09 |
| ❑ | 204 | Dwight Gooden | .20 | .09 |
| ❑ | 205 | Tom Herr | .10 | .05 |
| ❑ | 206 | Gregg Jefferies | .10 | .05 |
| ❑ | 207 | Howard Johnson | .10 | .05 |
| ❑ | 208 | Dave Magadan UER (Born 1862, should be 1962) | .10 | .05 |
| ❑ | 209 | Kevin McReynolds | .10 | .05 |
| ❑ | 210 | Frank Viola | .10 | .05 |
| ❑ | 211 | Wes Chamberlain RC | .10 | .05 |
| ❑ | 212 | Darren Daulton | .20 | .09 |
| ❑ | 213 | Len Dykstra | .20 | .09 |
| ❑ | 214 | Charlie Hayes | .10 | .05 |
| ❑ | 215 | Ricky Jordan | .10 | .05 |
| ❑ | 216 | Steve Lake (Pictured with parrot on his shoulder) | .20 | .09 |
| ❑ | 217 | Roger McDowell | .10 | .05 |
| ❑ | 218 | Mickey Morandini | .10 | .05 |
| ❑ | 219 | Terry Mulholland | .10 | .05 |
| ❑ | 220 | Dale Murphy | .40 | .18 |
| ❑ | 221 | Jay Bell | .20 | .09 |
| ❑ | 222 | Barry Bonds | .60 | .25 |
| ❑ | 223 | Bobby Bonilla | .20 | .09 |
| ❑ | 224 | Doug Drabek | .10 | .05 |
| ❑ | 225 | Bill Landrum | .10 | .05 |
| ❑ | 226 | Mike LaValliere | .10 | .05 |
| ❑ | 227 | Jose Lind | .10 | .05 |
| ❑ | 228 | Don Slaught | .10 | .05 |
| ❑ | 229 | John Smiley | .10 | .05 |
| ❑ | 230 | Andy Van Slyke | .20 | .09 |
| ❑ | 231 | Bernard Gilkey | .20 | .09 |
| ❑ | 232 | Pedro Guerrero | .10 | .05 |
| ❑ | 233 | Rex Hudler | .10 | .05 |
| ❑ | 234 | Ray Lankford | .40 | .18 |
| ❑ | 235 | Joe Magrane | .10 | .05 |
| ❑ | 236 | Jose Oquendo | .10 | .05 |
| ❑ | 237 | Lee Smith | .20 | .09 |
| ❑ | 238 | Ozzie Smith | .50 | .23 |
| ❑ | 239 | Milt Thompson | .10 | .05 |
| ❑ | 240 | Todd Zeile | .20 | .09 |
| ❑ | 241 | Larry Andersen | .10 | .05 |
| ❑ | 242 | Andy Benes | .10 | .05 |
| ❑ | 243 | Paul Faries | .10 | .05 |
| ❑ | 244 | Tony Fernandez | .10 | .05 |
| ❑ | 245 | Tony Gwynn | .75 | .35 |
| ❑ | 246 | Atlee Hammaker | .10 | .05 |
| ❑ | 247 | Fred McGriff | .40 | .18 |
| ❑ | 248 | Bip Roberts | .10 | .05 |
| ❑ | 249 | Bentio Santiago | .10 | .05 |
| ❑ | 250 | Ed Whitson | .10 | .05 |
| ❑ | 251 | Dave Anderson | .10 | .05 |
| ❑ | 252 | Mike Benjamin | .10 | .05 |
| ❑ | 253 | John Burkett UER (Front photo actually Trevor Wilson) | .10 | .05 |
| ❑ | 254 | Will Clark | .40 | .18 |
| ❑ | 255 | Scott Garrelts | .10 | .05 |
| ❑ | 256 | Willie McGee | .20 | .09 |
| ❑ | 257 | Kevin Mitchell | .10 | .05 |
| ❑ | 258 | Dave Righetti | .10 | .05 |
| ❑ | 259 | Matt Williams | .25 | .11 |
| ❑ | 260 | Bud Black Steve Decker | .10 | .05 |
| ❑ | 261 | Sparky Anderson MG CL | .20 | .09 |
| ❑ | 262 | Tom Lasorda MG CL | .25 | .11 |
| ❑ | 263 | Tony LaRussa MG CL | .20 | .09 |
| ❑ | NNO | Title Card | .10 | .05 |

# 1992 Studio

| | MINT | NRMT |
|---|---|---|
| COMPLETE SET (264) | 15.00 | 6.75 |

| |  |  | | |
|---|---|---|---|---|
| ❑ | 1 | Steve Avery | .05 | .02 |
| ❑ | 2 | Sid Bream | .05 | .02 |
| ❑ | 3 | Ron Gant | .10 | .05 |
| ❑ | 4 | Tom Glavine | .15 | .07 |
| ❑ | 5 | David Justice | .15 | .07 |
| ❑ | 6 | Mark Lemke | .05 | .02 |
| ❑ | 7 | Greg Olson | .05 | .02 |
| ❑ | 8 | Terry Pendleton | .10 | .05 |
| ❑ | 9 | Deion Sanders | .30 | .14 |
| ❑ | 10 | John Smoltz | .10 | .05 |
| ❑ | 11 | Doug Dascenzo | .05 | .02 |
| ❑ | 12 | Andre Dawson | .15 | .07 |
| ❑ | 13 | Joe Girardi | .10 | .05 |
| ❑ | 14 | Mark Grace | .30 | .14 |
| ❑ | 15 | Greg Maddux | .75 | .35 |
| ❑ | 16 | Chuck McElroy | .05 | .02 |
| ❑ | 17 | Mike Morgan | .05 | .02 |
| ❑ | 18 | Ryne Sandberg | .40 | .18 |
| ❑ | 19 | Gary Scott | .05 | .02 |
| ❑ | 20 | Sammy Sosa | .60 | .25 |
| ❑ | 21 | Norm Charlton | .05 | .02 |
| ❑ | 22 | Rob Dibble | .05 | .02 |
| ❑ | 23 | Barry Larkin | .15 | .07 |
| ❑ | 24 | Hal Morris | .05 | .02 |
| ❑ | 25 | Paul O'Neill | .10 | .05 |
| ❑ | 26 | Jose Rijo | .05 | .02 |
| ❑ | 27 | Bip Roberts | .05 | .02 |
| ❑ | 28 | Chris Sabo | .05 | .02 |
| ❑ | 29 | Reggie Sanders | .05 | .02 |
| ❑ | 30 | Greg Swindell | .05 | .02 |
| ❑ | 31 | Jeff Bagwell | .60 | .25 |
| ❑ | 32 | Craig Biggio | .15 | .07 |
| ❑ | 33 | Ken Caminiti | .10 | .05 |
| ❑ | 34 | Andujar Cedeno | .05 | .02 |
| ❑ | 35 | Steve Finley | .10 | .05 |
| ❑ | 36 | Pete Harnisch | .05 | .02 |
| ❑ | 37 | Butch Henry RC | .05 | .02 |
| ❑ | 38 | Doug Jones | .05 | .02 |
| ❑ | 39 | Darryl Kile | .10 | .05 |
| ❑ | 40 | Eddie Taubensee RC | .10 | .05 |
| ❑ | 41 | Brett Butler | .10 | .05 |
| ❑ | 42 | Tom Candiotti | .05 | .02 |
| ❑ | 43 | Eric Davis | .10 | .05 |
| ❑ | 44 | Orel Hershiser | .10 | .05 |
| ❑ | 45 | Eric Karros | .30 | .14 |
| ❑ | 46 | Ramon Martinez | .05 | .02 |
| ❑ | 47 | Jose Offerman | .05 | .02 |
| ❑ | 48 | Mike Scioscia | .05 | .02 |
| ❑ | 49 | Mike Sharperson | .05 | .02 |
| ❑ | 50 | Darryl Strawberry | .10 | .05 |
| ❑ | 51 | Bret Barberie | .05 | .02 |
| ❑ | 52 | Ivan Calderon | .05 | .02 |
| ❑ | 53 | Gary Carter | .15 | .07 |
| ❑ | 54 | Delino DeShields | .10 | .05 |
| ❑ | 55 | Marquis Grissom | .05 | .02 |
| ❑ | 56 | Ken Hill | .05 | .02 |
| ❑ | 57 | Dennis Martinez | .10 | .05 |
| ❑ | 58 | Spike Owen | .05 | .02 |
| ❑ | 59 | Larry Walker | .15 | .07 |
| ❑ | 60 | Tim Wallach | .05 | .02 |
| ❑ | 61 | Bobby Bonilla | .10 | .05 |
| ❑ | 62 | Tim Burke | .05 | .02 |
| ❑ | 63 | Vince Coleman | .05 | .02 |
| ❑ | 64 | John Franco | .10 | .05 |
| ❑ | 65 | Dwight Gooden | .10 | .05 |
| ❑ | 66 | Todd Hundley | .05 | .02 |
| ❑ | 67 | Howard Johnson | .05 | .02 |
| ❑ | 68 | Eddie Murray UER (He's not all-time switch homer leader, but he has most games with homers from both sides) | .30 | .14 |
| ❑ | 69 | Bret Saberhagen | .10 | .05 |
| ❑ | 70 | Anthony Young | .05 | .02 |
| ❑ | 71 | Kim Batiste | .05 | .02 |
| ❑ | 72 | Wes Chamberlain | .05 | .02 |
| ❑ | 73 | Darren Daulton | .10 | .05 |
| ❑ | 74 | Mariano Duncan | .05 | .02 |
| ❑ | 75 | Len Dykstra | .10 | .05 |
| ❑ | 76 | John Kruk | .10 | .05 |
| ❑ | 77 | Mickey Morandini | .05 | .02 |
| ❑ | 78 | Terry Mulholland | .05 | .02 |
| ❑ | 79 | Dale Murphy | .30 | .14 |
| ❑ | 80 | Mitch Williams | .05 | .02 |
| ❑ | 81 | Jay Bell | .10 | .05 |
| ❑ | 82 | Barry Bonds | .50 | .23 |
| ❑ | 83 | Steve Buechele | .05 | .02 |
| ❑ | 84 | Doug Drabek | .05 | .02 |
| ❑ | 85 | Mike LaValliere | .05 | .02 |
| ❑ | 86 | Jose Lind | .05 | .02 |
| ❑ | 87 | Denny Neagle | .15 | .07 |
| ❑ | 88 | Randy Tomlin | .05 | .02 |

❑ 89 Andy Van Slyke .10 .05
❑ 90 Gary Varsho .05 .02
❑ 91 Pedro Guerrero .05 .02
❑ 92 Rex Hudler .05 .02
❑ 93 Brian Jordan RC .75 .35
❑ 94 Felix Jose .05 .02
❑ 95 Donovan Osborne .05 .02
❑ 96 Tom Pagnozzi .05 .02
❑ 97 Lee Smith .10 .05
❑ 98 Ozzie Smith .40 .18
❑ 99 Todd Worrell .05 .02
❑ 100 Todd Zeile .05 .02
❑ 101 Andy Benes .05 .02
❑ 102 Jerald Clark .05 .02
❑ 103 Tony Fernandez .05 .02
❑ 104 Tony Gwynn .60 .25
❑ 105 Greg W. Harris .05 .02
❑ 106 Fred McGriff .15 .07
❑ 107 Benito Santiago .05 .02
❑ 108 Gary Sheffield .30 .14
❑ 109 Kurt Stillwell .05 .02
❑ 110 Tim Teufel .05 .02
❑ 111 Kevin Bass .05 .02
❑ 112 Jeff Brantley .05 .02
❑ 113 John Burkett .05 .02
❑ 114 Will Clark .30 .14
❑ 115 Royce Clayton .05 .02
❑ 116 Mike Jackson .05 .02
❑ 117 Darren Lewis .05 .02
❑ 118 Bill Swift .05 .02
❑ 119 Robby Thompson .05 .02
❑ 120 Matt Williams .15 .07
❑ 121 Brady Anderson .15 .07
❑ 122 Glenn Davis .05 .02
❑ 123 Mike Devereaux .05 .02
❑ 124 Chris Hoiles .05 .02
❑ 125 Sam Horn .05 .02
❑ 126 Ben McDonald .05 .02
❑ 127 Mike Mussina .50 .23
❑ 128 Gregg Olson .05 .02
❑ 129 Cal Ripken Jr. 1.25 .55
❑ 130 Rick Sutcliffe .10 .05
❑ 131 Wade Boggs .40 .18
❑ 132 Roger Clemens .60 .25
❑ 133 Greg A. Harris .05 .02
❑ 134 Tim Naehring .05 .02
❑ 135 Tony Pena .05 .02
❑ 136 Phil Plantier .05 .02
❑ 137 Jeff Reardon .10 .05
❑ 138 Jody Reed .05 .02
❑ 139 Mo Vaughn .40 .18
❑ 140 Frank Viola .05 .02
❑ 141 Jim Abbott .10 .05
❑ 142 Hubie Brooks .05 .02
❑ 143 Chad Curtis RC .40 .18
❑ 144 Gary DiSarcina .05 .02
❑ 145 Chuck Finley .10 .05
❑ 146 Bryan Harvey .05 .02
❑ 147 Von Hayes .05 .02
❑ 148 Mark Langston .05 .02
❑ 149 Lance Parrish .05 .02
❑ 150 Lee Stevens .10 .05
❑ 151 George Bell .05 .02
❑ 152 Alex Fernandez .10 .05
❑ 153 Greg Hibbard .05 .02
❑ 154 Lance Johnson .05 .02
❑ 155 Kirk McCaskill .05 .02
❑ 156 Tim Raines .10 .05
❑ 157 Steve Sax .05 .02
❑ 158 Bobby Thigpen .05 .02
❑ 159 Frank Thomas .60 .25
❑ 160 Robin Ventura .10 .05
❑ 161 Sandy Alomar Jr. .10 .05
❑ 162 Jack Armstrong .05 .02
❑ 163 Carlos Baerga .05 .02
❑ 164 Albert Belle .15 .07
❑ 165 Alex Cole .05 .02
❑ 166 Glenallen Hill .05 .02
❑ 167 Mark Lewis .05 .02
❑ 168 Kenny Lofton .40 .18
❑ 169 Paul Sorrento .05 .02
❑ 170 Mark Whiten .05 .02
❑ 171 Milt Cuyler .05 .02
❑ 172 Rob Deer .05 .02
❑ 173 Cecil Fielder .10 .05
❑ 174 Travis Fryman .10 .05
❑ 175 Mike Henneman .05 .02
❑ 176 Tony Phillips .05 .02
❑ 177 Frank Tanana .05 .02
❑ 178 Mickey Tettleton .05 .02
❑ 179 Alan Trammell .15 .07
❑ 180 Lou Whitaker .10 .05
❑ 181 George Brett .60 .25
❑ 182 Tom Gordon .05 .02
❑ 183 Mark Gubicza .05 .02
❑ 184 Gregg Jefferies .05 .02
❑ 185 Wally Joyner .10 .05
❑ 186 Brent Mayne .05 .02
❑ 187 Brian McRae .05 .02
❑ 188 Kevin McReynolds .05 .02
❑ 189 Keith Miller .05 .02
❑ 190 Jeff Montgomery .10 .05
❑ 191 Dante Bichette .15 .07
❑ 192 Ricky Bones .05 .02
❑ 193 Scott Fletcher .05 .02
❑ 194 Paul Molitor .30 .14
❑ 195 Jaime Navarro .05 .02
❑ 196 Franklin Stubbs .05 .02
❑ 197 B.J. Surhoff .10 .05
❑ 198 Greg Vaughn .15 .07
❑ 199 Bill Wegman .05 .02
❑ 200 Robin Yount .30 .14
❑ 201 Rick Aguilera .10 .05
❑ 202 Scott Erickson .05 .02
❑ 203 Greg Gagne .05 .02
❑ 204 Brian Harper .05 .02
❑ 205 Kent Hrbek .10 .05
❑ 206 Scott Leius .05 .02
❑ 207 Shane Mack .05 .02
❑ 208 Pat Mahomes RC .05 .02
❑ 209 Kirby Puckett .75 .35
❑ 210 John Smiley .05 .02
❑ 211 Mike Gallego .05 .02
❑ 212 Charlie Hayes .05 .02
❑ 213 Pat Kelly .05 .02
❑ 214 Roberto Kelly .05 .02
❑ 215 Kevin Maas .05 .02
❑ 216 Don Mattingly .75 .35
❑ 217 Matt Nokes .05 .02
❑ 218 Melido Perez .05 .02
❑ 219 Scott Sanderson .05 .02
❑ 220 Danny Tartabull .05 .02
❑ 221 Harold Baines .10 .05
❑ 222 Jose Canseco .40 .18
❑ 223 Dennis Eckersley .10 .05
❑ 224 Dave Henderson .05 .02
❑ 225 Carney Lansford .10 .05
❑ 226 Mark McGwire 1.25 .55
❑ 227 Mike Moore .05 .02
❑ 228 Randy Ready .05 .02
❑ 229 Terry Steinbach .05 .02
❑ 230 Dave Stewart .10 .05
❑ 231 Jay Buhner .10 .05
❑ 232 Ken Griffey Jr. 1.25 .55
❑ 233 Erik Hanson .05 .02
❑ 234 Randy Johnson .40 .18
❑ 235 Edgar Martinez .15 .07
❑ 236 Tino Martinez .10 .05
❑ 237 Kevin Mitchell .10 .05
❑ 238 Pete O'Brien .05 .02
❑ 239 Harold Reynolds .05 .02
❑ 240 David Valle .05 .02
❑ 241 Julio Franco .05 .02
❑ 242 Juan Gonzalez .30 .14
❑ 243 Jose Guzman .05 .02
❑ 244 Rafael Palmeiro .30 .14
❑ 245 Dean Palmer .10 .05
❑ 246 Ivan Rodriguez .60 .25
❑ 247 Jeff Russell .05 .02
❑ 248 Nolan Ryan 1.50 .70
❑ 249 Ruben Sierra .05 .02
❑ 250 Dickie Thon .05 .02
❑ 251 Roberto Alomar .30 .14
❑ 252 Derek Bell .10 .05
❑ 253 Pat Borders .05 .02
❑ 254 Joe Carter .10 .05
❑ 255 Kelly Gruber .05 .02
❑ 256 Juan Guzman .05 .02
❑ 257 Jack Morris .10 .05
❑ 258 John Olerud .10 .05
❑ 259 Devon White .05 .02
❑ 260 Dave Winfield .30 .14
❑ 261 Checklist .05 .02
❑ 262 Checklist .05 .02
❑ 263 Checklist .05 .02
❑ 264 History Card .05 .02

## 1993 Studio

| | MINT | NRMT |
|---|---|---|
| COMPLETE SET (220) | 20.00 | 9.00 |
| COMMON CARD (1-220) | .12 | .05 |

❑ 1 Dennis Eckersley .25 .11
❑ 2 Chad Curtis .10 .05
❑ 3 Eric Anthony .10 .05
❑ 4 Roberto Alomar .50 .23
❑ 5 Steve Avery .10 .05
❑ 6 Cal Eldred .10 .05
❑ 7 Bernard Gilkey .10 .05
❑ 8 Steve Buechele .10 .05
❑ 9 Brett Butler .25 .11
❑ 10 Terry Mulholland .10 .05
❑ 11 Moises Alou .25 .11
❑ 12 Barry Bonds .75 .35
❑ 13 Sandy Alomar Jr. .25 .11
❑ 14 Chris Bosio .10 .05
❑ 15 Scott Sanderson .10 .05
❑ 16 Bobby Bonilla .25 .11
❑ 17 Brady Anderson .25 .11
❑ 18 Derek Bell .10 .05
❑ 19 Wes Chamberlain .10 .05
❑ 20 Jay Bell .25 .11
❑ 21 Kevin Brown .30 .14
❑ 22 Roger Clemens 1.00 .45
❑ 23 Roberto Kelly .10 .05
❑ 24 Dante Bichette .25 .11
❑ 25 George Brett 1.00 .45
❑ 26 Rob Deer .10 .05
❑ 27 Brian Harper .10 .05
❑ 28 George Bell .10 .05
❑ 29 Jim Abbott .25 .11
❑ 30 Dave Henderson .10 .05
❑ 31 Wade Boggs .60 .25
❑ 32 Chili Davis .25 .11
❑ 33 Ellis Burks .25 .11
❑ 34 Jeff Bagwell .60 .25
❑ 35 Kent Hrbek .25 .11
❑ 36 Pat Borders .10 .05
❑ 37 Cecil Fielder .25 .11
❑ 38 Sid Bream .10 .05
❑ 39 Greg Gagne .10 .05
❑ 40 Darryl Hamilton .10 .05
❑ 41 Jerald Clark .10 .05
❑ 42 Mark Grace .50 .23
❑ 43 Barry Larkin .50 .23
❑ 44 John Burkett .10 .05
❑ 45 Scott Cooper .10 .05
❑ 46 Mike Lansing RC .25 .11
❑ 47 Jose Canseco .60 .25
❑ 48 Will Clark .50 .23
❑ 49 Carlos Garcia .10 .05
❑ 50 Carlos Baerga .10 .05
❑ 51 Darren Daulton .25 .11
❑ 52 Jay Buhner .25 .11
❑ 53 Andy Benes .10 .05
❑ 54 Jeff Conine .10 .05
❑ 55 Mike Devereaux .10 .05
❑ 56 Vince Coleman .10 .05
❑ 57 Terry Steinbach .10 .05

❑ 58 J.T. Snow RC .60 .25
❑ 59 Greg Swindell .10 .05
❑ 60 Devon White .10 .05
❑ 61 John Smoltz .25 .11
❑ 62 Todd Zeile .10 .05
❑ 63 Rick Wilkins .10 .05
❑ 64 Tim Wallach .10 .05
❑ 65 John Wetteland .25 .11
❑ 66 Matt Williams .30 .14
❑ 67 Paul Sorrento .10 .05
❑ 68 David Valle .10 .05
❑ 69 Walt Weiss .10 .05
❑ 70 John Franco .25 .11
❑ 71 Nolan Ryan 2.50 1.10
❑ 72 Frank Viola .10 .05
❑ 73 Chris Sabo .10 .05
❑ 74 David Nied .10 .05
❑ 75 Kevin McReynolds .10 .05
❑ 76 Lou Whitaker .25 .11
❑ 77 Dave Winfield .50 .23
❑ 78 Robin Ventura .25 .11
❑ 79 Spike Owen .10 .05
❑ 80 Cal Ripken Jr. 2.00 .90
❑ 81 Dan Walters .10 .05
❑ 82 Mitch Williams .10 .05
❑ 83 Tim Wakefield .10 .05
❑ 84 Rickey Henderson .60 .25
❑ 85 Gary DiSarcina .10 .05
❑ 86 Craig Biggio .30 .14
❑ 87 Joe Carter .25 .11
❑ 88 Ron Gant .25 .11
❑ 89 John Jaha .10 .05
❑ 90 Gregg Jefferies .10 .05
❑ 91 Jose Guzman .10 .05
❑ 92 Eric Karros .30 .14
❑ 93 Wil Cordero .10 .05
❑ 94 Royce Clayton .10 .05
❑ 95 Albert Belle .30 .14
❑ 96 Ken Griffey Jr. 2.00 .90
❑ 97 Orestes Destrade .10 .05
❑ 98 Tony Fernandez .10 .05
❑ 99 Leo Gomez .10 .05
❑ 100 Tony Gwynn 1.00 .45
❑ 101 Len Dykstra .25 .11
❑ 102 Jeff King .10 .05
❑ 103 Julio Franco .10 .05
❑ 104 Andre Dawson .30 .14
❑ 105 Randy Milligan .10 .05
❑ 106 Alex Cole .10 .05
❑ 107 Phil Hiatt .10 .05
❑ 108 Travis Fryman .25 .11
❑ 109 Chuck Knoblauch .25 .11
❑ 110 Bo Jackson .25 .11
❑ 111 Pat Kelly .10 .05
❑ 112 Bret Saberhagen .25 .11
❑ 113 Ruben Sierra .10 .05
❑ 114 Tim Salmon .25 .11
❑ 115 Doug Jones .10 .05
❑ 116 Ed Sprague .10 .05
❑ 117 Terry Pendleton .25 .11
❑ 118 Robin Yount .30 .14
❑ 119 Mark Whiten .10 .05
❑ 120 Checklist 1-110 .10 .05
❑ 121 Sammy Sosa 1.00 .45
❑ 122 Darryl Strawberry .25 .11
❑ 123 Larry Walker .25 .11
❑ 124 Robby Thompson .10 .05
❑ 125 Carlos Martinez .10 .05
❑ 126 Edgar Martinez .30 .14
❑ 127 Benito Santiago .10 .05
❑ 128 Howard Johnson .10 .05
❑ 129 Harold Reynolds .10 .05
❑ 130 Craig Shipley .10 .05
❑ 131 Curt Schilling .25 .11
❑ 132 Andy Van Slyke .25 .11
❑ 133 Ivan Rodriguez .60 .25
❑ 134 Mo Vaughn .25 .11
❑ 135 Bip Roberts .10 .05
❑ 136 Charlie Hayes .10 .05
❑ 137 Brian McRae .10 .05
❑ 138 Mickey Tettleton .10 .05
❑ 139 Frank Thomas 1.00 .45
❑ 140 Paul O'Neill .25 .11
❑ 141 Mark McGwire 2.00 .90
❑ 142 Damion Easley .10 .05
❑ 143 Ken Caminiti .25 .11
❑ 144 Juan Guzman .10 .05
❑ 145 Tom Glavine .30 .14
❑ 146 Pat Listach .10 .05
❑ 147 Lee Smith .25 .11
❑ 148 Derrick May .10 .05
❑ 149 Ramon Martinez .10 .05
❑ 150 Delino DeShields .25 .11
❑ 151 Kirt Manwaring .10 .05
❑ 152 Reggie Jefferson .25 .11
❑ 153 Randy Johnson .60 .25
❑ 154 Dave Magadan .10 .05
❑ 155 Dwight Gooden .25 .11
❑ 156 Chris Hoiles .10 .05
❑ 157 Fred McGriff .30 .14
❑ 158 Dave Hollins .10 .05
❑ 159 Al Martin .10 .05
❑ 160 Juan Gonzalez .50 .23
❑ 161 Mike Greenwell .10 .05
❑ 162 Kevin Mitchell .25 .11
❑ 163 Andres Galarraga .30 .14
❑ 164 Wally Joyner .25 .11
❑ 165 Kirk Gibson .25 .11
❑ 166 Pedro Munoz .10 .05
❑ 167 Ozzie Guillen .10 .05
❑ 168 Jimmy Key .25 .11
❑ 169 Kevin Seitzer .10 .05
❑ 170 Luis Polonia .10 .05
❑ 171 Luis Gonzalez .25 .11
❑ 172 Paul Molitor .50 .23
❑ 173 David Justice .30 .14
❑ 174 B.J. Surhoff .25 .11
❑ 175 Ray Lankford .30 .14
❑ 176 Ryne Sandberg .60 .25
❑ 177 Jody Reed .10 .05
❑ 178 Marquis Grissom .10 .05
❑ 179 Willie McGee .25 .11
❑ 180 Kenny Lofton .25 .11
❑ 181 Junior Felix .10 .05
❑ 182 Jose Offerman .10 .05
❑ 183 John Kruk .25 .11
❑ 184 Orlando Merced .10 .05
❑ 185 Rafael Palmeiro .50 .23
❑ 186 Billy Hatcher .10 .05
❑ 187 Joe Oliver .10 .05
❑ 188 Joe Girardi .25 .11
❑ 189 Jose Lind .10 .05
❑ 190 Harold Baines .25 .11
❑ 191 Mike Pagliarulo .10 .05
❑ 192 Lance Johnson .10 .05
❑ 193 Don Mattingly 1.25 .55
❑ 194 Doug Drabek .10 .05
❑ 195 John Olerud .30 .14
❑ 196 Greg Maddux 1.25 .55
❑ 197 Greg Vaughn .25 .11
❑ 198 Tom Pagnozzi .10 .05
❑ 199 Willie Wilson .10 .05
❑ 200 Jack McDowell .10 .05
❑ 201 Mike Piazza 2.50 1.10
❑ 202 Mike Mussina .50 .23
❑ 203 Charles Nagy .10 .05
❑ 204 Tino Martinez .25 .11
❑ 205 Charlie Hough .25 .11
❑ 206 Todd Hundley .10 .05
❑ 207 Gary Sheffield .50 .23
❑ 208 Mickey Morandini .10 .05
❑ 209 Don Slaught .10 .05
❑ 210 Dean Palmer .25 .11
❑ 211 Jose Rijo .10 .05
❑ 212 Vinny Castilla .60 .25
❑ 213 Tony Phillips .10 .05
❑ 214 Kirby Puckett 1.25 .55
❑ 215 Tim Raines .25 .11
❑ 216 Otis Nixon .10 .05
❑ 217 Ozzie Smith .60 .25
❑ 218 Jose Vizcaino .10 .05
❑ 219 Randy Tomlin .10 .05
❑ 220 Checklist 111-220 .10 .05

## 1994 Studio

| | MINT | NRMT |
|---|---|---|
| COMPLETE SET (220) | 15.00 | 6.75 |

❑ 1 Dennis Eckersley .30 .14
❑ 2 Brent Gates .15 .07
❑ 3 Rickey Henderson .75 .35
❑ 4 Mark McGwire 2.50 1.10
❑ 5 Troy Neel .15 .07
❑ 6 Ruben Sierra .15 .07
❑ 7 Terry Steinbach .15 .07
❑ 8 Chad Curtis .15 .07
❑ 9 Chili Davis .30 .14
❑ 10 Gary DiSarcina .15 .07
❑ 11 Damion Easley .15 .07
❑ 12 Bo Jackson .30 .14
❑ 13 Mark Langston .15 .07
❑ 14 Eduardo Perez .15 .07
❑ 15 Tim Salmon .30 .14
❑ 16 Jeff Bagwell .75 .35
❑ 17 Craig Biggio .40 .18
❑ 18 Ken Caminiti .30 .14
❑ 19 Andujar Cedeno .15 .07
❑ 20 Doug Drabek .15 .07
❑ 21 Steve Finley .30 .14
❑ 22 Luis Gonzalez .30 .14
❑ 23 Darryl Kile .30 .14
❑ 24 Roberto Alomar .60 .25
❑ 25 Pat Borders .15 .07
❑ 26 Joe Carter .30 .14
❑ 27 Carlos Delgado 1.00 .45
❑ 28 Pat Hentgen .15 .07
❑ 29 Paul Molitor .60 .25
❑ 30 John Olerud .30 .14
❑ 31 Ed Sprague .15 .07
❑ 32 Devon White .15 .07
❑ 33 Steve Avery .15 .07
❑ 34 Tom Glavine .60 .25
❑ 35 David Justice .40 .18
❑ 36 Roberto Kelly .15 .07
❑ 37 Ryan Klesko .30 .14
❑ 38 Javier Lopez .30 .14
❑ 39 Greg Maddux 1.50 .70
❑ 40 Fred McGriff .40 .18
❑ 41 Terry Pendleton .30 .14
❑ 42 Ricky Bones .15 .07
❑ 43 Darryl Hamilton .15 .07
❑ 44 Brian Harper .15 .07
❑ 45 John Jaha .15 .07
❑ 46 Dave Nilsson .15 .07
❑ 47 Kevin Seitzer .15 .07
❑ 48 Greg Vaughn .30 .14
❑ 49 Turner Ward .15 .07
❑ 50 Bernard Gilkey .15 .07
❑ 51 Gregg Jefferies .15 .07
❑ 52 Ray Lankford .30 .14
❑ 53 Tom Pagnozzi .15 .07

❑ 54 Ozzie Smith .75 .35
❑ 55 Bob Tewksbury .15 .07
❑ 56 Mark Whiten .15 .07
❑ 57 Todd Zeile .15 .07
❑ 58 Steve Buechele .15 .07
❑ 59 Shawon Dunston .15 .07
❑ 60 Mark Grace .60 .25
❑ 61 Derrick May .15 .07
❑ 62 Karl Rhodes .15 .07
❑ 63 Ryne Sandberg .75 .35
❑ 64 Sammy Sosa 1.25 .55
❑ 65 Rick Wilkins .15 .07
❑ 66 Brett Butler .30 .14
❑ 67 Delino DeShields .15 .07
❑ 68 Orel Hershiser .30 .14
❑ 69 Eric Karros .30 .14
❑ 70 Raul Mondesi .30 .14
❑ 71 Jose Offerman .15 .07
❑ 72 Mike Piazza 2.00 .90
❑ 73 Tim Wallach .15 .07
❑ 74 Moises Alou .30 .14
❑ 75 Sean Berry .15 .07
❑ 76 Wil Cordero .15 .07
❑ 77 Cliff Floyd .30 .14
❑ 78 Marquis Grissom .15 .07
❑ 79 Ken Hill .15 .07
❑ 80 Larry Walker .30 .14
❑ 81 John Wetteland .30 .14
❑ 82 Rod Beck .15 .07
❑ 83 Barry Bonds 1.00 .45
❑ 84 Royce Clayton .15 .07
❑ 85 Darren Lewis .15 .07
❑ 86 Willie McGee .30 .14
❑ 87 Bill Swift .15 .07
❑ 88 Robby Thompson .15 .07
❑ 89 Matt Williams .40 .18
❑ 90 Sandy Alomar Jr. .30 .14
❑ 91 Carlos Baerga .15 .07
❑ 92 Albert Belle .40 .18
❑ 93 Kenny Lofton .30 .14
❑ 94 Eddie Murray .60 .25
❑ 95 Manny Ramirez 1.00 .45
❑ 96 Paul Sorrento .15 .07
❑ 97 Jim Thome .40 .18
❑ 98 Rich Amaral .15 .07
❑ 99 Eric Anthony .15 .07
❑ 100 Jay Buhner .30 .14
❑ 101 Ken Griffey Jr. 2.50 1.10
❑ 102 Randy Johnson .75 .35
❑ 103 Edgar Martinez .40 .18
❑ 104 Tino Martinez .30 .14
❑ 105 Kurt Abbott RC .15 .07
❑ 106 Bret Barberie .15 .07
❑ 107 Chuck Carr .15 .07
❑ 108 Jeff Conine .15 .07
❑ 109 Chris Hammond .15 .07
❑ 110 Bryan Harvey .15 .07
❑ 111 Benito Santiago .15 .07
❑ 112 Gary Sheffield .60 .25
❑ 113 Bobby Bonilla .30 .14
❑ 114 Dwight Gooden .30 .14
❑ 115 Todd Hundley .15 .07
❑ 116 Bobby Jones .15 .07
❑ 117 Jeff Kent .40 .18
❑ 118 Kevin McReynolds .15 .07
❑ 119 Bret Saberhagen .30 .14
❑ 120 Ryan Thompson .15 .07
❑ 121 Harold Baines .30 .14
❑ 122 Mike Devereaux .15 .07
❑ 123 Jeffrey Hammonds .30 .14
❑ 124 Ben McDonald .15 .07
❑ 125 Mike Mussina .60 .25
❑ 126 Rafael Palmeiro .60 .25
❑ 127 Cal Ripken Jr. 2.50 1.10
❑ 128 Lee Smith .30 .14
❑ 129 Brad Ausmus .15 .07
❑ 130 Derek Bell .15 .07
❑ 131 Andy Benes .15 .07
❑ 132 Tony Gwynn 1.25 .55
❑ 133 Trevor Hoffman .30 .14
❑ 134 Scott Livingstone .15 .07
❑ 135 Phil Plantier .15 .07
❑ 136 Darren Daulton .30 .14
❑ 137 Mariano Duncan .15 .07
❑ 138 Lenny Dykstra .30 .14
❑ 139 Dave Hollins .15 .07
❑ 140 Pete Incaviglia .15 .07
❑ 141 Danny Jackson .15 .07
❑ 142 John Kruk .30 .14
❑ 143 Kevin Stocker .15 .07
❑ 144 Jay Bell .30 .14
❑ 145 Carlos Garcia .15 .07
❑ 146 Jeff King .15 .07
❑ 147 Al Martin .15 .07
❑ 148 Orlando Merced .15 .07
❑ 149 Don Slaught .15 .07
❑ 150 Andy Van Slyke .30 .14
❑ 151 Kevin Brown .30 .14
❑ 152 Jose Canseco .75 .35
❑ 153 Will Clark .60 .25
❑ 154 Juan Gonzalez .60 .25
❑ 155 David Hulse .15 .07
❑ 156 Dean Palmer .30 .14
❑ 157 Ivan Rodriguez .75 .35
❑ 158 Kenny Rogers .15 .07
❑ 159 Roger Clemens 1.25 .55
❑ 160 Scott Cooper .15 .07
❑ 161 Andre Dawson .40 .18
❑ 162 Mike Greenwell .15 .07
❑ 163 Otis Nixon .15 .07
❑ 164 Aaron Sele .30 .14
❑ 165 John Valentin .15 .07
❑ 166 Mo Vaughn .30 .14
❑ 167 Bret Boone .30 .14
❑ 168 Barry Larkin .60 .25
❑ 169 Kevin Mitchell .15 .07
❑ 170 Hal Morris .15 .07
❑ 171 Jose Rijo .15 .07
❑ 172 Deion Sanders .30 .14
❑ 173 Reggie Sanders .15 .07
❑ 174 John Smiley .15 .07
❑ 175 Dante Bichette .30 .14
❑ 176 Ellis Burks .30 .14
❑ 177 Andres Galarraga .40 .18
❑ 178 Joe Girardi .15 .07
❑ 179 Charlie Hayes .15 .07
❑ 180 Roberto Mejia .15 .07
❑ 181 Walt Weiss .15 .07
❑ 182 David Cone .30 .14
❑ 183 Gary Gaetti .30 .14
❑ 184 Greg Gagne .15 .07
❑ 185 Felix Jose .15 .07
❑ 186 Wally Joyner .30 .14
❑ 187 Mike Macfarlane .15 .07
❑ 188 Brian McRae .15 .07
❑ 189 Eric Davis .30 .14
❑ 190 Cecil Fielder .30 .14
❑ 191 Travis Fryman .30 .14
❑ 192 Tony Phillips .15 .07
❑ 193 Mickey Tettleton .15 .07
❑ 194 Alan Trammell .40 .18
❑ 195 Lou Whitaker .30 .14
❑ 196 Kent Hrbek .30 .14
❑ 197 Chuck Knoblauch .30 .14
❑ 198 Shane Mack .15 .07
❑ 199 Pat Meares .15 .07
❑ 200 Kirby Puckett 1.50 .70
❑ 201 Matt Walbeck .15 .07
❑ 202 Dave Winfield .60 .25
❑ 203 Wilson Alvarez .15 .07
❑ 204 Alex Fernandez .15 .07
❑ 205 Julio Franco .15 .07
❑ 206 Ozzie Guillen .15 .07
❑ 207 Jack McDowell .15 .07
❑ 208 Tim Raines .30 .14
❑ 209 Frank Thomas 1.25 .55
❑ 210 Robin Ventura .30 .14
❑ 211 Jim Abbott .30 .14
❑ 212 Wade Boggs .75 .35
❑ 213 Pat Kelly .15 .07
❑ 214 Jimmy Key .30 .14
❑ 215 Don Mattingly 1.50 .70
❑ 216 Paul O'Neill .30 .14
❑ 217 Mike Stanley .15 .07
❑ 218 Danny Tartabull .15 .07
❑ 219 Checklist .15 .07
❑ 220 Checklist .15 .07

## 1995 Studio

| | MINT | NRMT |
|---|---|---|
| COMPLETE SET (200) | 60.00 | 27.00 |

❑ 1 Frank Thomas 1.50 .70
❑ 2 Jeff Bagwell 1.00 .45
❑ 3 Don Mattingly 2.00 .90
❑ 4 Mike Piazza 2.50 1.10
❑ 5 Ken Griffey Jr. 3.00 1.35
❑ 6 Greg Maddux 2.00 .90
❑ 7 Barry Bonds 1.25 .55
❑ 8 Cal Ripken Jr. 3.00 1.35
❑ 9 Jose Canseco 1.00 .45
❑ 10 Paul Molitor .75 .35
❑ 11 Kenny Lofton .40 .18
❑ 12 Will Clark .75 .35
❑ 13 Tim Salmon .40 .18
❑ 14 Joe Carter .40 .18
❑ 15 Albert Belle .40 .18
❑ 16 Roger Clemens 1.50 .70
❑ 17 Roberto Alomar .75 .35
❑ 18 Alex Rodriguez 3.00 1.35
❑ 19 Raul Mondesi .40 .18
❑ 20 Deion Sanders .40 .18
❑ 21 Juan Gonzalez .75 .35
❑ 22 Kirby Puckett 2.00 .90
❑ 23 Fred McGriff .40 .18
❑ 24 Matt Williams .40 .18
❑ 25 Tony Gwynn 1.50 .70
❑ 26 Cliff Floyd .40 .18
❑ 27 Travis Fryman .40 .18
❑ 28 Shawn Green .75 .35
❑ 29 Mike Mussina .75 .35
❑ 30 Bob Hamelin .20 .09
❑ 31 David Justice .40 .18
❑ 32 Manny Ramirez 1.00 .45
❑ 33 David Cone .40 .18
❑ 34 Marquis Grissom .20 .09
❑ 35 Moises Alou .40 .18
❑ 36 Carlos Baerga .20 .09
❑ 37 Barry Larkin .75 .35
❑ 38 Robin Ventura .40 .18
❑ 39 Mo Vaughn .40 .18
❑ 40 Jeffrey Hammonds .40 .18
❑ 41 Ozzie Smith 1.00 .45
❑ 42 Andres Galarraga .40 .18
❑ 43 Carlos Delgado .75 .35
❑ 44 Lenny Dykstra .40 .18
❑ 45 Cecil Fielder .40 .18
❑ 46 Wade Boggs 1.00 .45
❑ 47 Gregg Jefferies .20 .09
❑ 48 Randy Johnson 1.00 .45
❑ 49 Rafael Palmeiro .75 .35
❑ 50 Craig Biggio .40 .18
❑ 51 Steve Avery .20 .09
❑ 52 Ricky Bottalico .20 .09
❑ 53 Chris Gomez .20 .09
❑ 54 Carlos Garcia .20 .09
❑ 55 Brian Anderson .20 .09
❑ 56 Wilson Alvarez .20 .09
❑ 57 Roberto Kelly .20 .09
❑ 58 Larry Walker .40 .18
❑ 59 Dean Palmer .40 .18
❑ 60 Rick Aguilera .20 .09
❑ 61 Javier Lopez .40 .18
❑ 62 Shawon Dunston .20 .09
❑ 63 Wm. VanLandingham .20 .09

| Card | Player | | |
|---|---|---|---|
| ❑ 64 | Jeff Kent | .40 | .18 |
| ❑ 65 | David McCarty | .20 | .09 |
| ❑ 66 | Armando Benitez | .40 | .18 |
| ❑ 67 | Brett Butler | .40 | .18 |
| ❑ 68 | Bernard Gilkey | .20 | .09 |
| ❑ 69 | Joey Hamilton | .20 | .09 |
| ❑ 70 | Chad Curtis | .20 | .09 |
| ❑ 71 | Dante Bichette | .40 | .18 |
| ❑ 72 | Chuck Carr | .20 | .09 |
| ❑ 73 | Pedro Martinez | 1.00 | .45 |
| ❑ 74 | Ramon Martinez | .20 | .09 |
| ❑ 75 | Rondell White | .40 | .18 |
| ❑ 76 | Alex Fernandez | .20 | .09 |
| ❑ 77 | Dennis Martinez | .40 | .18 |
| ❑ 78 | Sammy Sosa | 1.50 | .70 |
| ❑ 79 | Bernie Williams | .75 | .35 |
| ❑ 80 | Lou Whitaker | .40 | .18 |
| ❑ 81 | Kurt Abbott | .20 | .09 |
| ❑ 82 | Tino Martinez | .40 | .18 |
| ❑ 83 | Willie Greene | .20 | .09 |
| ❑ 84 | Garret Anderson | .40 | .18 |
| ❑ 85 | Jose Rijo | .20 | .09 |
| ❑ 86 | Jeff Montgomery | .20 | .09 |
| ❑ 87 | Mark Langston | .20 | .09 |
| ❑ 88 | Reggie Sanders | .20 | .09 |
| ❑ 89 | Rusty Greer | .40 | .18 |
| ❑ 90 | Delino DeShields | .20 | .09 |
| ❑ 91 | Jason Bere | .20 | .09 |
| ❑ 92 | Lee Smith | .40 | .18 |
| ❑ 93 | Devon White | .40 | .18 |
| ❑ 94 | John Wetteland | .40 | .18 |
| ❑ 95 | Luis Gonzalez | .20 | .09 |
| ❑ 96 | Greg Vaughn | .40 | .18 |
| ❑ 97 | Lance Johnson | .20 | .09 |
| ❑ 98 | Alan Trammell | .40 | .18 |
| ❑ 99 | Bret Saberhagen | .40 | .18 |
| ❑ 100 | Jack McDowell | .20 | .09 |
| ❑ 101 | Trevor Hoffman | .40 | .18 |
| ❑ 102 | Dave Nilsson | .20 | .09 |
| ❑ 103 | Bryan Harvey | .20 | .09 |
| ❑ 104 | Chuck Knoblauch | .40 | .18 |
| ❑ 105 | Bobby Bonilla | .40 | .18 |
| ❑ 106 | Hal Morris | .20 | .09 |
| ❑ 107 | Mark Whiten | .20 | .09 |
| ❑ 108 | Phil Plantier | .20 | .09 |
| ❑ 109 | Ryan Klesko | .40 | .18 |
| ❑ 110 | Greg Gagne | .20 | .09 |
| ❑ 111 | Ruben Sierra | .20 | .09 |
| ❑ 112 | J.R. Phillips | .20 | .09 |
| ❑ 113 | Terry Steinbach | .20 | .09 |
| ❑ 114 | Jay Buhner | .40 | .18 |
| ❑ 115 | Ken Caminiti | .40 | .18 |
| ❑ 116 | Gary DiSarcina | .20 | .09 |
| ❑ 117 | Ivan Rodriguez | 1.00 | .45 |
| ❑ 118 | Bip Roberts | .20 | .09 |
| ❑ 119 | Jay Bell | .40 | .18 |
| ❑ 120 | Ken Hill | .20 | .09 |
| ❑ 121 | Mike Greenwell | .20 | .09 |
| ❑ 122 | Rick Wilkins | .20 | .09 |
| ❑ 123 | Rickey Henderson | 1.00 | .45 |
| ❑ 124 | Dave Hollins | .20 | .09 |
| ❑ 125 | Terry Pendleton | .40 | .18 |
| ❑ 126 | Rich Becker | .20 | .09 |
| ❑ 127 | Billy Ashley | .20 | .09 |
| ❑ 128 | Derek Bell | .20 | .09 |
| ❑ 129 | Dennis Eckersley | .40 | .18 |
| ❑ 130 | Andujar Cedeno | .20 | .09 |
| ❑ 131 | John Jaha | .20 | .09 |
| ❑ 132 | Chuck Finley | .40 | .18 |
| ❑ 133 | Steve Finley | .40 | .18 |
| ❑ 134 | Danny Tartabull | .20 | .09 |
| ❑ 135 | Jeff Conine | .20 | .09 |
| ❑ 136 | Jon Lieber | .20 | .09 |
| ❑ 137 | Jim Abbott | .40 | .18 |
| ❑ 138 | Steve Trachsel | .20 | .09 |
| ❑ 139 | Bret Boone | .40 | .18 |
| ❑ 140 | Charles Johnson | .40 | .18 |
| ❑ 141 | Mark McGwire | 3.00 | 1.35 |
| ❑ 142 | Eddie Murray | .75 | .35 |
| ❑ 143 | Doug Drabek | .20 | .09 |
| ❑ 144 | Steve Cooke | .20 | .09 |
| ❑ 145 | Kevin Seitzer | .20 | .09 |
| ❑ 146 | Rod Beck | .20 | .09 |
| ❑ 147 | Eric Karros | .40 | .18 |
| ❑ 148 | Tim Raines | .40 | .18 |
| ❑ 149 | Joe Girardi | .20 | .09 |
| ❑ 150 | Aaron Sele | .40 | .18 |
| ❑ 151 | Robby Thompson | .20 | .09 |
| ❑ 152 | Chan Ho Park | .40 | .18 |
| ❑ 153 | Ellis Burks | .40 | .18 |
| ❑ 154 | Brian McRae | .20 | .09 |
| ❑ 155 | Jimmy Key | .40 | .18 |
| ❑ 156 | Rico Brogna | .20 | .09 |
| ❑ 157 | Ozzie Guillen | .20 | .09 |
| ❑ 158 | Chili Davis | .40 | .18 |
| ❑ 159 | Darren Daulton | .40 | .18 |
| ❑ 160 | Chipper Jones | 2.00 | .90 |
| ❑ 161 | Walt Weiss | .20 | .09 |
| ❑ 162 | Paul O'Neill | .40 | .18 |
| ❑ 163 | Al Martin | .20 | .09 |
| ❑ 164 | John Valentin | .20 | .09 |
| ❑ 165 | Tim Wallach | .20 | .09 |
| ❑ 166 | Scott Erickson | .20 | .09 |
| ❑ 167 | Ryan Thompson | .20 | .09 |
| ❑ 168 | Todd Zeile | .20 | .09 |
| ❑ 169 | Scott Cooper | .20 | .09 |
| ❑ 170 | Matt Mieske | .20 | .09 |
| ❑ 171 | Allen Watson | .20 | .09 |
| ❑ 172 | Brian L.Hunter | .20 | .09 |
| ❑ 173 | Kevin Stocker | .20 | .09 |
| ❑ 174 | Cal Eldred | .20 | .09 |
| ❑ 175 | Tony Phillips | .20 | .09 |
| ❑ 176 | Ben McDonald | .20 | .09 |
| ❑ 177 | Mark Grace | .75 | .35 |
| ❑ 178 | Midre Cummings | .20 | .09 |
| ❑ 179 | Orlando Merced | .20 | .09 |
| ❑ 180 | Jeff King | .20 | .09 |
| ❑ 181 | Gary Sheffield | .75 | .35 |
| ❑ 182 | Tom Glavine | .75 | .35 |
| ❑ 183 | Edgar Martinez | .40 | .18 |
| ❑ 184 | Steve Karsay | .20 | .09 |
| ❑ 185 | Pat Listach | .20 | .09 |
| ❑ 186 | Wil Cordero | .20 | .09 |
| ❑ 187 | Brady Anderson | .40 | .18 |
| ❑ 188 | Bobby Jones | .20 | .09 |
| ❑ 189 | Andy Benes | .20 | .09 |
| ❑ 190 | Ray Lankford | .40 | .18 |
| ❑ 191 | John Doherty | .20 | .09 |
| ❑ 192 | Wally Joyner | .40 | .18 |
| ❑ 193 | Jim Thome | .40 | .18 |
| ❑ 194 | Royce Clayton | .20 | .09 |
| ❑ 195 | John Olerud | .40 | .18 |
| ❑ 196 | Steve Buechele | .20 | .09 |
| ❑ 197 | Harold Baines | .40 | .18 |
| ❑ 198 | Geronimo Berroa | .20 | .09 |
| ❑ 199 | Checklist | .20 | .09 |
| ❑ 200 | Checklist | .20 | .09 |

## 1996 Studio

| | | MINT | NRMT |
|---|---|---|---|
| COMPLETE SET (150) | | 15.00 | 6.75 |
| ❑ 1 | Cal Ripken | 2.00 | .90 |
| ❑ 2 | Alex Gonzalez | .15 | .07 |
| ❑ 3 | Roger Cedeno | .15 | .07 |
| ❑ 4 | Todd Hollandsworth | .15 | .07 |
| ❑ 5 | Gregg Jefferies | .15 | .07 |
| ❑ 6 | Ryne Sandberg | .60 | .25 |
| ❑ 7 | Eric Karros | .25 | .11 |
| ❑ 8 | Jeff Conine | .15 | .07 |
| ❑ 9 | Rafael Palmeiro | .50 | .23 |
| ❑ 10 | Bip Roberts | .15 | .07 |
| ❑ 11 | Roger Clemens | 1.00 | .45 |
| ❑ 12 | Tom Glavine | .50 | .23 |
| ❑ 13 | Jason Giambi | .50 | .23 |
| ❑ 14 | Rey Ordonez | .25 | .11 |
| ❑ 15 | Chan Ho Park | .25 | .11 |
| ❑ 16 | Vinny Castilla | .25 | .11 |
| ❑ 17 | Butch Huskey | .15 | .07 |
| ❑ 18 | Greg Maddux | 1.25 | .55 |
| ❑ 19 | Bernard Gilkey | .15 | .07 |
| ❑ 20 | Marquis Grissom | .15 | .07 |
| ❑ 21 | Chuck Knoblauch | .25 | .11 |
| ❑ 22 | Ozzie Smith | .60 | .25 |
| ❑ 23 | Garret Anderson | .25 | .11 |
| ❑ 24 | J.T. Snow | .25 | .11 |
| ❑ 25 | John Valentin | .15 | .07 |
| ❑ 26 | Barry Larkin | .50 | .23 |
| ❑ 27 | Bobby Bonilla | .25 | .11 |
| ❑ 28 | Todd Zeile | .15 | .07 |
| ❑ 29 | Roberto Alomar | .50 | .23 |
| ❑ 30 | Ramon Martinez | .15 | .07 |
| ❑ 31 | Jeff King | .15 | .07 |
| ❑ 32 | Dennis Eckersley | .25 | .11 |
| ❑ 33 | Derek Jeter | 2.00 | .90 |
| ❑ 34 | Edgar Martinez | .30 | .14 |
| ❑ 35 | Geronimo Berroa | .15 | .07 |
| ❑ 36 | Hal Morris | .15 | .07 |
| ❑ 37 | Troy Percival | .15 | .07 |
| ❑ 38 | Jason Isringhausen | .25 | .11 |
| ❑ 39 | Greg Vaughn | .25 | .11 |
| ❑ 40 | Robin Ventura | .25 | .11 |
| ❑ 41 | Craig Biggio | .30 | .14 |
| ❑ 42 | Will Clark | .50 | .23 |
| ❑ 43 | Sammy Sosa | 1.00 | .45 |
| ❑ 44 | Bernie Williams | .50 | .23 |
| ❑ 45 | Kenny Lofton | .25 | .11 |
| ❑ 46 | Wade Boggs | .60 | .25 |
| ❑ 47 | Javy Lopez | .25 | .11 |
| ❑ 48 | Reggie Sanders | .15 | .07 |
| ❑ 49 | Jeff Bagwell | .60 | .25 |
| ❑ 50 | Fred McGriff | .30 | .14 |
| ❑ 51 | Charles Johnson | .25 | .11 |
| ❑ 52 | Darren Daulton | .25 | .11 |
| ❑ 53 | Jose Canseco | .60 | .25 |
| ❑ 54 | Cecil Fielder | .25 | .11 |
| ❑ 55 | Hideo Nomo | .50 | .23 |
| ❑ 56 | Tim Salmon | .25 | .11 |
| ❑ 57 | Carlos Delgado | .50 | .23 |
| ❑ 58 | David Cone | .25 | .11 |
| ❑ 59 | Tim Raines | .25 | .11 |
| ❑ 60 | Lyle Mouton | .15 | .07 |
| ❑ 61 | Wally Joyner | .25 | .11 |
| ❑ 62 | Bret Boone | .25 | .11 |
| ❑ 63 | Raul Mondesi | .25 | .11 |
| ❑ 64 | Gary Sheffield | .50 | .23 |
| ❑ 65 | Alex Rodriguez | 1.50 | .70 |
| ❑ 66 | Russ Davis | .15 | .07 |
| ❑ 67 | Checklist | .15 | .07 |
| ❑ 68 | Marty Cordova | .15 | .07 |
| ❑ 69 | Ruben Sierra | .15 | .07 |
| ❑ 70 | Jose Mesa | .15 | .07 |
| ❑ 71 | Matt Williams | .30 | .14 |
| ❑ 72 | Chipper Jones | 1.25 | .55 |
| ❑ 73 | Randy Johnson | .60 | .25 |
| ❑ 74 | Kirby Puckett | 1.25 | .55 |
| ❑ 75 | Jim Edmonds | .50 | .23 |
| ❑ 76 | Barry Bonds | .75 | .35 |
| ❑ 77 | David Segui | .15 | .07 |
| ❑ 78 | Larry Walker | .25 | .11 |
| ❑ 79 | Jason Kendall | .25 | .11 |
| ❑ 80 | Mike Piazza | 1.50 | .70 |
| ❑ 81 | Brian L.Hunter | .15 | .07 |
| ❑ 82 | Julio Franco | .15 | .07 |
| ❑ 83 | Jay Bell | .25 | .11 |
| ❑ 84 | Kevin Seitzer | .15 | .07 |
| ❑ 85 | John Smoltz | .25 | .11 |
| ❑ 86 | Joe Carter | .25 | .11 |
| ❑ 87 | Ray Durham | .25 | .11 |
| ❑ 88 | Carlos Baerga | .15 | .07 |
| ❑ 89 | Ron Gant | .15 | .07 |
| ❑ 90 | Orlando Merced | .15 | .07 |
| ❑ 91 | Lee Smith | .25 | .11 |
| ❑ 92 | Pedro Martinez | .60 | .25 |
| ❑ 93 | Frank Thomas | 1.00 | .45 |
| ❑ 94 | Al Martin | .15 | .07 |
| ❑ 95 | Chad Curtis | .15 | .07 |
| ❑ 96 | Eddie Murray | .50 | .23 |
| ❑ 97 | Rusty Greer | .25 | .11 |

❑ 98 Jay Buhner .25 .11
❑ 99 Rico Brogna .15 .07
❑ 100 Todd Hundley .15 .07
❑ 101 Moises Alou .25 .11
❑ 102 Chili Davis .25 .11
❑ 103 Ismael Valdes .15 .07
❑ 104 Mo Vaughn .25 .11
❑ 105 Juan Gonzalez .50 .23
❑ 106 Mark Grudzielanek .15 .07
❑ 107 Derek Bell .15 .07
❑ 108 Shawn Green .50 .23
❑ 109 David Justice .30 .14
❑ 110 Paul O'Neill .25 .11
❑ 111 Kevin Appier .25 .11
❑ 112 Ray Lankford .25 .11
❑ 113 Travis Fryman .25 .11
❑ 114 Manny Ramirez .60 .25
❑ 115 Brooks Kieschnick .15 .07
❑ 116 Ken Griffey Jr. 2.00 .90
❑ 117 Jeffrey Hammonds .25 .11
❑ 118 Mark McGwire 2.00 .90
❑ 119 Denny Neagle .25 .11
❑ 120 Quilvio Veras .15 .07
❑ 121 Alan Benes .15 .07
❑ 122 Rondell White .25 .11
❑ 123 Osvaldo Fernandez RC .15 .07
❑ 124 Andres Galarraga .30 .14
❑ 125 Johnny Damon .30 .14
❑ 126 Lenny Dykstra .25 .11
❑ 127 Jason Schmidt .15 .07
❑ 128 Mike Mussina .50 .23
❑ 129 Ken Caminiti .25 .11
❑ 130 Michael Tucker .15 .07
❑ 131 LaTroy Hawkins .15 .07
❑ 132 Checklist .15 .07
❑ 133 Delino DeShields .15 .07
❑ 134 Dave Nilsson .15 .07
❑ 135 Jack McDowell .15 .07
❑ 136 Joey Hamilton .15 .07
❑ 137 Dante Bichette .25 .11
❑ 138 Paul Molitor .50 .23
❑ 139 Ivan Rodriguez .60 .25
❑ 140 Mark Grace .50 .23
❑ 141 Paul Wilson .15 .07
❑ 142 Orel Hershiser .25 .11
❑ 143 Albert Belle .30 .14
❑ 144 Tino Martinez .25 .11
❑ 145 Tony Gwynn 1.00 .45
❑ 146 George Arias .15 .07
❑ 147 Brian Jordan .25 .11
❑ 148 Brian McRae .15 .07
❑ 149 Rickey Henderson .60 .25
❑ 150 Ryan Klesko .25 .11

## 1997 Studio

| | MINT | NRMT |
|---|---|---|
| COMPLETE SET (165) | 60.00 | 27.00 |
| COMMON CARD (1-165) | .15 | .07 |

❑ 1 Frank Thomas 1.25 .55
❑ 2 Gary Sheffield .60 .25
❑ 3 Jason Isringhausen .15 .07
❑ 4 Ron Gant .15 .07
❑ 5 Andy Pettitte .25 .11
❑ 6 Todd Hollandsworth .15 .07
❑ 7 Troy Percival .15 .07
❑ 8 Mark McGwire 2.50 1.10
❑ 9 Barry Larkin .60 .25
❑ 10 Ken Caminiti .25 .11
❑ 11 Paul Molitor .60 .25
❑ 12 Travis Fryman .25 .11
❑ 13 Kevin Brown .25 .11
❑ 14 Robin Ventura .25 .11
❑ 15 Andres Galarraga .40 .18
❑ 16 Ken Griffey Jr. 2.50 1.10
❑ 17 Roger Clemens 1.25 .55
❑ 18 Alan Benes .15 .07
❑ 19 Dave Justice .40 .18
❑ 20 Damon Buford .15 .07
❑ 21 Mike Piazza 2.00 .90
❑ 22 Ray Durham .25 .11
❑ 23 Billy Wagner .15 .07
❑ 24 Dean Palmer .25 .11
❑ 25 David Cone .25 .11
❑ 26 Ruben Sierra .15 .07
❑ 27 Henry Rodriguez .15 .07
❑ 28 Ray Lankford .25 .11
❑ 29 Jamey Wright .15 .07
❑ 30 Brady Anderson .25 .11
❑ 31 Tino Martinez .25 .11
❑ 32 Manny Ramirez .75 .35
❑ 33 Jeff Conine .15 .07
❑ 34 Dante Bichette .25 .11
❑ 35 Jose Canseco .75 .35
❑ 36 Mo Vaughn .25 .11
❑ 37 Sammy Sosa 1.25 .55
❑ 38 Mark Grudzielanek .15 .07
❑ 39 Mike Mussina .60 .25
❑ 40 Bill Pulsipher .15 .07
❑ 41 Ryne Sandberg .75 .35
❑ 42 Rickey Henderson .75 .35
❑ 43 Alex Rodriguez 2.00 .90
❑ 44 Eddie Murray .60 .25
❑ 45 Ernie Young .15 .07
❑ 46 Joey Hamilton .15 .07
❑ 47 Wade Boggs .75 .35
❑ 48 Rusty Greer .25 .11
❑ 49 Carlos Delgado .60 .25
❑ 50 Ellis Burks .25 .11
❑ 51 Cal Ripken 2.50 1.10
❑ 52 Alex Fernandez .15 .07
❑ 53 Wally Joyner .25 .11
❑ 54 James Baldwin .25 .11
❑ 55 Juan Gonzalez .60 .25
❑ 56 John Smoltz .25 .11
❑ 57 Omar Vizquel .25 .11
❑ 58 Shane Reynolds .15 .07
❑ 59 Barry Bonds 1.00 .45
❑ 60 Jason Kendall .25 .11
❑ 61 Marty Cordova .15 .07
❑ 62 Charles Johnson .25 .11
❑ 63 John Jaha .15 .07
❑ 64 Chan Ho Park .25 .11
❑ 65 Jermaine Allensworth .15 .07
❑ 66 Mark Grace .60 .25
❑ 67 Tim Salmon .25 .11
❑ 68 Edgar Martinez .40 .18
❑ 69 Marquis Grissom .15 .07
❑ 70 Craig Biggio .40 .18
❑ 71 Bobby Higginson .25 .11
❑ 72 Kevin Seitzer .15 .07
❑ 73 Hideo Nomo .60 .25
❑ 74 Dennis Eckersley .25 .11
❑ 75 Bobby Bonilla .25 .11
❑ 76 Dwight Gooden .25 .11
❑ 77 Jeff Cirillo .25 .11
❑ 78 Brian McRae .15 .07
❑ 79 Chipper Jones 1.50 .70
❑ 80 Jeff Fassero .15 .07
❑ 81 Fred McGriff .40 .18
❑ 82 Garret Anderson .25 .11
❑ 83 Eric Karros .25 .11
❑ 84 Derek Bell .15 .07
❑ 85 Kenny Lofton .25 .11
❑ 86 John Mabry .15 .07
❑ 87 Pat Hentgen .15 .07
❑ 88 Greg Maddux 1.50 .70
❑ 89 Jason Giambi .60 .25
❑ 90 Al Martin .15 .07
❑ 91 Derek Jeter 2.50 1.10
❑ 92 Rey Ordonez .15 .07
❑ 93 Will Clark .60 .25
❑ 94 Kevin Appier .25 .11
❑ 95 Roberto Alomar .60 .25
❑ 96 Joe Carter .25 .11
❑ 97 Bernie Williams .60 .25
❑ 98 Albert Belle .40 .18
❑ 99 Greg Vaughn .25 .11
❑ 100 Tony Clark .15 .07
❑ 101 Matt Williams .40 .18
❑ 102 Jeff Bagwell .75 .35
❑ 103 Reggie Sanders .15 .07
❑ 104 Mariano Rivera .25 .11
❑ 105 Larry Walker .25 .11
❑ 106 Shawn Green .60 .25
❑ 107 Alex Ochoa .15 .07
❑ 108 Ivan Rodriguez .75 .35
❑ 109 Eric Young .15 .07
❑ 110 Javier Lopez .25 .11
❑ 111 Brian Hunter .15 .07
❑ 112 Raul Mondesi SP 5.00 2.20
❑ 113 Randy Johnson .75 .35
❑ 114 Tony Phillips .15 .07
❑ 115 Carlos Garcia .15 .07
❑ 116 Moises Alou .25 .11
❑ 117 Paul O'Neill .25 .11
❑ 118 Jim Thome .40 .18
❑ 119 Jermaine Dye .25 .11
❑ 120 Wilson Alvarez .15 .07
❑ 121 Rondell White .25 .11
❑ 122 Michael Tucker .15 .07
❑ 123 Mike Lansing .15 .07
❑ 124 Tony Gwynn 1.25 .55
❑ 125 Ryan Klesko .25 .11
❑ 126 Jim Edmonds .60 .25
❑ 127 Chuck Knoblauch .25 .11
❑ 128 Rafael Palmeiro .60 .25
❑ 129 Jay Buhner .25 .11
❑ 130 Tom Glavine .60 .25
❑ 131 Julio Franco .25 .11
❑ 132 Cecil Fielder .25 .11
❑ 133 Paul Wilson SP 4.00 1.80
❑ 134 Deion Sanders .25 .11
❑ 135 Alex Gonzalez .15 .07
❑ 136 Charles Nagy .15 .07
❑ 137 Andy Ashby SP 4.00 1.80
❑ 138 Edgar Renteria .25 .11
❑ 139 Pedro Martinez .75 .35
❑ 140 Brian Jordan .25 .11
❑ 141 Todd Hundley .15 .07
❑ 142 Marc Newfield .15 .07
❑ 143 Darryl Strawberry .25 .11
❑ 144 Dan Wilson .15 .07
❑ 145 Brian Giles RC 2.50 1.10
❑ 146 F.P. Santangelo .15 .07
❑ 147 Shannon Stewart SP 5.00 2.20
❑ 148 Scott Spiezio .15 .07
❑ 149 Andruw Jones .75 .35
❑ 150 Karim Garcia .15 .07
❑ 151 Vladimir Guerrero 1.25 .55
❑ 152 George Arias .15 .07

| | No. | Player | Mint | Nrmt |
|---|---|---|---|---|
| ❑ | 153 | Brooks Kieschnick | .15 | .07 |
| ❑ | 154 | Todd Walker | .15 | .07 |
| ❑ | 155 | Scott Rolen | .60 | .25 |
| ❑ | 156 | Todd Greene | .15 | .07 |
| ❑ | 157 | Dmitri Young | .25 | .11 |
| ❑ | 158 | Ruben Rivera | .15 | .07 |
| ❑ | 159 | Bartolo Colon | .25 | .11 |
| ❑ | 160 | Nomar Garciaparra | 2.00 | .90 |
| ❑ | 161 | Bob Abreu SP | 8.00 | 3.60 |
| ❑ | 162 | Darin Erstad | .75 | .35 |
| ❑ | 163 | Ken Griffey Jr. CL | 1.25 | .55 |
| ❑ | 164 | Frank Thomas CL | .60 | .25 |
| ❑ | 165 | Alex Rodriguez CL | 1.00 | .45 |

## 1998 Studio

| | MINT | NRMT |
|---|---|---|
| COMPLETE SET (220) | 50.00 | 22.00 |

| | No. | Player | Mint | Nrmt |
|---|---|---|---|---|
| ❑ | 1 | Tony Clark | .15 | .07 |
| ❑ | 2 | Jose Cruz Jr. | .25 | .11 |
| ❑ | 3 | Ivan Rodriguez | .75 | .35 |
| ❑ | 4 | Mo Vaughn | .25 | .11 |
| ❑ | 5 | Kenny Lofton | .25 | .11 |
| ❑ | 6 | Will Clark | .60 | .25 |
| ❑ | 7 | Barry Larkin | .60 | .25 |
| ❑ | 8 | Jay Bell | .25 | .11 |
| ❑ | 9 | Kevin Young | .25 | .11 |
| ❑ | 10 | Francisco Cordova | .15 | .07 |
| ❑ | 11 | Justin Thompson | .15 | .07 |
| ❑ | 12 | Paul Molitor | .60 | .25 |
| ❑ | 13 | Jeff Bagwell | .75 | .35 |
| ❑ | 14 | Jose Canseco | .75 | .35 |
| ❑ | 15 | Scott Rolen | .60 | .25 |
| ❑ | 16 | Wilton Guerrero | .15 | .07 |
| ❑ | 17 | Shannon Stewart | .25 | .11 |
| ❑ | 18 | Hideki Irabu | .15 | .07 |
| ❑ | 19 | Michael Tucker | .15 | .07 |
| ❑ | 20 | Joe Carter | .25 | .11 |
| ❑ | 21 | Gabe Alvarez | .15 | .07 |
| ❑ | 22 | Ricky Ledee | .15 | .07 |
| ❑ | 23 | Karim Garcia | .15 | .07 |
| ❑ | 24 | Eli Marrero | .15 | .07 |
| ❑ | 25 | Scott Elarton | .25 | .11 |
| ❑ | 26 | Mario Valdez | .15 | .07 |
| ❑ | 27 | Ben Grieve | .25 | .11 |
| ❑ | 28 | Paul Konerko | .25 | .11 |
| ❑ | 29 | Esteban Yan RC | .40 | .18 |
| ❑ | 30 | Esteban Loaiza | .15 | .07 |
| ❑ | 31 | Delino DeShields | .15 | .07 |
| ❑ | 32 | Bernie Williams | .60 | .25 |
| ❑ | 33 | Joe Randa | .15 | .07 |
| ❑ | 34 | Randy Johnson | .75 | .35 |
| ❑ | 35 | Brett Tomko | .15 | .07 |
| ❑ | 36 | Todd Erdos RC | .25 | .11 |
| ❑ | 37 | Bobby Higginson | .25 | .11 |
| ❑ | 38 | Jason Kendall | .25 | .11 |
| ❑ | 39 | Ray Lankford | .25 | .11 |
| ❑ | 40 | Mark Grace | .60 | .25 |
| ❑ | 41 | Andy Pettitte | .25 | .11 |
| ❑ | 42 | Alex Rodriguez | 2.00 | .90 |
| ❑ | 43 | Hideo Nomo | .60 | .25 |
| ❑ | 44 | Sammy Sosa | 1.25 | .55 |
| ❑ | 45 | J.T. Snow | .25 | .11 |
| ❑ | 46 | Jason Varitek | .25 | .11 |
| ❑ | 47 | Vinny Castilla | .25 | .11 |
| ❑ | 48 | Neifi Perez | .15 | .07 |
| ❑ | 49 | Todd Walker | .15 | .07 |
| ❑ | 50 | Mike Cameron | .25 | .11 |
| ❑ | 51 | Jeffrey Hammonds | .25 | .11 |
| ❑ | 52 | Deivi Cruz | .15 | .07 |
| ❑ | 53 | Brian Hunter | .15 | .07 |
| ❑ | 54 | Al Martin | .15 | .07 |
| ❑ | 55 | Ron Coomer | .15 | .07 |
| ❑ | 56 | Chan Ho Park | .25 | .11 |
| ❑ | 57 | Pedro Martinez | .75 | .35 |
| ❑ | 58 | Darin Erstad | .60 | .25 |
| ❑ | 59 | Albert Belle | .40 | .18 |
| ❑ | 60 | Nomar Garciaparra | 2.00 | .90 |
| ❑ | 61 | Tony Gwynn | 1.25 | .55 |
| ❑ | 62 | Mike Piazza | 2.00 | .90 |
| ❑ | 63 | Todd Helton | .75 | .35 |
| ❑ | 64 | David Ortiz | .15 | .07 |
| ❑ | 65 | Todd Dunwoody | .15 | .07 |
| ❑ | 66 | Orlando Cabrera | .15 | .07 |
| ❑ | 67 | Ken Cloude | .15 | .07 |
| ❑ | 68 | Andy Benes | .15 | .07 |
| ❑ | 69 | Mariano Rivera | .25 | .11 |
| ❑ | 70 | Cecil Fielder | .25 | .11 |
| ❑ | 71 | Brian Jordan | .25 | .11 |
| ❑ | 72 | Darryl Kile | .25 | .11 |
| ❑ | 73 | Reggie Jefferson | .15 | .07 |
| ❑ | 74 | Shawn Estes | .15 | .07 |
| ❑ | 75 | Bobby Bonilla | .25 | .11 |
| ❑ | 76 | Denny Neagle | .15 | .07 |
| ❑ | 77 | Robin Ventura | .25 | .11 |
| ❑ | 78 | Omar Vizquel | .25 | .11 |
| ❑ | 79 | Craig Biggio | .40 | .18 |
| ❑ | 80 | Moises Alou | .25 | .11 |
| ❑ | 81 | Garret Anderson | .25 | .11 |
| ❑ | 82 | Eric Karros | .25 | .11 |
| ❑ | 83 | Dante Bichette | .25 | .11 |
| ❑ | 84 | Charles Johnson | .25 | .11 |
| ❑ | 85 | Rusty Greer | .25 | .11 |
| ❑ | 86 | Travis Fryman | .25 | .11 |
| ❑ | 87 | Fernando Tatis | .25 | .11 |
| ❑ | 88 | Wilson Alvarez | .15 | .07 |
| ❑ | 89 | Carl Pavano | .15 | .07 |
| ❑ | 90 | Brian Rose | .15 | .07 |
| ❑ | 91 | Geoff Jenkins | .25 | .11 |
| ❑ | 92 | Magglio Ordonez RC | 2.50 | 1.10 |
| ❑ | 93 | David Segui | .15 | .07 |
| ❑ | 94 | David Cone | .25 | .11 |
| ❑ | 95 | John Smoltz | .25 | .11 |
| ❑ | 96 | Jim Thome | .40 | .18 |
| ❑ | 97 | Gary Sheffield | .60 | .25 |
| ❑ | 98 | Barry Bonds | 1.00 | .45 |
| ❑ | 99 | Andres Galarraga | .40 | .18 |
| ❑ | 100 | Brad Fullmer | .25 | .11 |
| ❑ | 101 | Bobby Estalella | .15 | .07 |
| ❑ | 102 | Enrique Wilson | .15 | .07 |
| ❑ | 103 | Frank Catalanotto RC | .40 | .18 |
| ❑ | 104 | Mike Lowell RC | .75 | .35 |
| ❑ | 105 | Kevin Orie | .15 | .07 |
| ❑ | 106 | Matt Morris | .15 | .07 |
| ❑ | 107 | Pokey Reese | .25 | .11 |
| ❑ | 108 | Shawn Green | .60 | .25 |
| ❑ | 109 | Tony Womack | .15 | .07 |
| ❑ | 110 | Ken Caminiti | .25 | .11 |
| ❑ | 111 | Roberto Alomar | .60 | .25 |
| ❑ | 112 | Ken Griffey Jr. | 2.50 | 1.10 |
| ❑ | 113 | Cal Ripken | 2.50 | 1.10 |
| ❑ | 114 | Lou Collier | .15 | .07 |
| ❑ | 115 | Larry Walker | .25 | .11 |
| ❑ | 116 | Fred McGriff | .40 | .18 |
| ❑ | 117 | Jim Edmonds | .60 | .25 |
| ❑ | 118 | Edgar Martinez | .40 | .18 |
| ❑ | 119 | Matt Williams | .40 | .18 |
| ❑ | 120 | Ismael Valdes | .15 | .07 |
| ❑ | 121 | Bartolo Colon | .25 | .11 |
| ❑ | 122 | Jeff Cirillo | .25 | .11 |
| ❑ | 123 | Steve Woodard | .15 | .07 |
| ❑ | 124 | Kevin Millwood RC | 1.00 | .45 |
| ❑ | 125 | Derrick Gibson | .15 | .07 |
| ❑ | 126 | Jacob Cruz | .15 | .07 |
| ❑ | 127 | Russell Branyan | .25 | .11 |
| ❑ | 128 | Sean Casey | .25 | .11 |
| ❑ | 129 | Derrek Lee | .15 | .07 |
| ❑ | 130 | Paul O'Neill | .25 | .11 |
| ❑ | 131 | Brad Radke | .25 | .11 |
| ❑ | 132 | Kevin Appier | .25 | .11 |
| ❑ | 133 | John Olerud | .25 | .11 |
| ❑ | 134 | Alan Benes | .15 | .07 |
| ❑ | 135 | Todd Greene | .15 | .07 |
| ❑ | 136 | Carlos Mendoza RC | .25 | .11 |
| ❑ | 137 | Wade Boggs | .75 | .35 |
| ❑ | 138 | Jose Guillen | .15 | .07 |
| ❑ | 139 | Tino Martinez | .25 | .11 |
| ❑ | 140 | Aaron Boone | .15 | .07 |
| ❑ | 141 | Abraham Nunez | .15 | .07 |
| ❑ | 142 | Preston Wilson | .25 | .11 |
| ❑ | 143 | Randall Simon | .15 | .07 |
| ❑ | 144 | Dennis Reyes | .15 | .07 |
| ❑ | 145 | Mark Kotsay | .25 | .11 |
| ❑ | 146 | Richard Hidalgo | .25 | .11 |
| ❑ | 147 | Travis Lee | .25 | .11 |
| ❑ | 148 | Hanley Frias RC | .15 | .07 |
| ❑ | 149 | Ruben Rivera | .15 | .07 |
| ❑ | 150 | Rafael Medina | .15 | .07 |
| ❑ | 151 | Dave Nilsson | .15 | .07 |
| ❑ | 152 | Curt Schilling | .25 | .11 |
| ❑ | 153 | Brady Anderson | .25 | .11 |
| ❑ | 154 | Carlos Delgado | .60 | .25 |
| ❑ | 155 | Jason Giambi | .60 | .25 |
| ❑ | 156 | Pat Hentgen | .15 | .07 |
| ❑ | 157 | Tom Glavine | .60 | .25 |
| ❑ | 158 | Ryan Klesko | .25 | .11 |
| ❑ | 159 | Chipper Jones | 1.50 | .70 |
| ❑ | 160 | Juan Gonzalez | .60 | .25 |
| ❑ | 161 | Mark McGwire | 2.50 | 1.10 |
| ❑ | 162 | Vladimir Guerrero | 1.00 | .45 |
| ❑ | 163 | Derek Jeter | 2.50 | 1.10 |
| ❑ | 164 | Manny Ramirez | .75 | .35 |
| ❑ | 165 | Mike Mussina | .60 | .25 |
| ❑ | 166 | Rafael Palmeiro | .60 | .25 |
| ❑ | 167 | Henry Rodriguez | .15 | .07 |
| ❑ | 168 | Jeff Suppan | .15 | .07 |
| ❑ | 169 | Eric Milton | .15 | .07 |
| ❑ | 170 | Scott Spiezio | .15 | .07 |
| ❑ | 171 | Wilson Delgado | .15 | .07 |
| ❑ | 172 | Bubba Trammell | .15 | .07 |
| ❑ | 173 | Ellis Burks | .25 | .11 |
| ❑ | 174 | Jason Dickson | .15 | .07 |
| ❑ | 175 | Butch Huskey | .15 | .07 |
| ❑ | 176 | Edgardo Alfonzo | .25 | .11 |
| ❑ | 177 | Eric Young | .15 | .07 |
| ❑ | 178 | Marquis Grissom | .15 | .07 |
| ❑ | 179 | Lance Johnson | .15 | .07 |
| ❑ | 180 | Kevin Brown | .40 | .18 |
| ❑ | 181 | Sandy Alomar Jr. | .25 | .11 |
| ❑ | 182 | Todd Hundley | .15 | .07 |
| ❑ | 183 | Rondell White | .25 | .11 |
| ❑ | 184 | Javier Lopez | .25 | .11 |
| ❑ | 185 | Damian Jackson | .15 | .07 |
| ❑ | 186 | Raul Mondesi | .25 | .11 |
| ❑ | 187 | Rickey Henderson | .75 | .35 |
| ❑ | 188 | David Justice | .40 | .18 |
| ❑ | 189 | Jay Buhner | .25 | .11 |
| ❑ | 190 | Jaret Wright | .15 | .07 |
| ❑ | 191 | Miguel Tejada | .60 | .25 |
| ❑ | 192 | Ron Wright | .15 | .07 |
| ❑ | 193 | Livan Hernandez | .15 | .07 |
| ❑ | 194 | A.J. Hinch | .15 | .07 |
| ❑ | 195 | Richie Sexson | .40 | .18 |
| ❑ | 196 | Bob Abreu | .25 | .11 |
| ❑ | 197 | Louis Castillo | .25 | .11 |
| ❑ | 198 | Michael Coleman | .15 | .07 |
| ❑ | 199 | Greg Maddux | 1.50 | .70 |
| ❑ | 200 | Frank Thomas | 1.25 | .55 |
| ❑ | 201 | Andruw Jones | .60 | .25 |
| ❑ | 202 | Roger Clemens | 1.25 | .55 |
| ❑ | 203 | Tim Salmon | .25 | .11 |
| ❑ | 204 | Chuck Knoblauch | .25 | .11 |
| ❑ | 205 | Wes Helms | .15 | .07 |
| ❑ | 206 | Juan Encarnacion | .25 | .11 |
| ❑ | 207 | Russ Davis | .15 | .07 |
| ❑ | 208 | John Valentin | .15 | .07 |
| ❑ | 209 | Tony Saunders | .15 | .07 |
| ❑ | 210 | Mike Sweeney | .25 | .11 |
| ❑ | 211 | Steve Finley | .25 | .11 |
| ❑ | 212 | Dave Dellucci RC | .15 | .07 |
| ❑ | 213 | Edgar Renteria | .15 | .07 |
| ❑ | 214 | Jeremi Gonzalez | .15 | .07 |
| ❑ | CL1 | Jeff Bagwell CL | .60 | .25 |
| ❑ | CL2 | Mike Piazza CL | 1.00 | .45 |
| ❑ | CL3 | Greg Maddux CL | .75 | .35 |
| ❑ | CL4 | Cal Ripken CL | 1.25 | .55 |
| ❑ | CL5 | Frank Thomas CL | .60 | .25 |
| ❑ | CL6 | Ken Griffey Jr. CL | 1.25 | .55 |

❑ 93 Butch Huskey .15 .07
❑ 94 Garret Anderson .25 .11
❑ 95 Mike Bordick .15 .07
❑ 96 Dave Justice .40 .18
❑ 97 Chad Curtis .15 .07
❑ 98 Carlos Baerga .15 .07
❑ 99 Jason Isringhausen .25 .11
❑ 100 Gary Sheffield .60 .25
❑ 101 Roger Clemens 1.25 .55
❑ 102 Ozzie Smith .75 .35
❑ 103 Ramon Martinez .15 .07
❑ 104 Paul O'Neill .25 .11
❑ 105 Will Clark .60 .25
❑ 106 Tom Glavine .60 .25
❑ 107 Barry Bonds 1.00 .45
❑ 108 Barry Larkin .60 .25
❑ 109 Derek Bell .15 .07
❑ 110 Randy Johnson .75 .35
❑ 111 Jeff Conine .15 .07
❑ 112 John Mabry .15 .07
❑ 113 Julian Tavarez .15 .07
❑ 114 Gary DiSarcina .15 .07
❑ 115 Andres Galarraga .40 .18
❑ 116 Marc Newfield .15 .07
❑ 117 Frank Rodriguez .15 .07
❑ 118 Brady Anderson .25 .11
❑ 119 Mike Mussina .60 .25
❑ 120 Orlando Merced .15 .07
❑ 121 Melvin Nieves .15 .07
❑ 122 Brian Jordan .25 .11
❑ 123 Rafael Palmeiro .60 .25
❑ 124 Johnny Damon .25 .11
❑ 125 Wil Cordero .15 .07
❑ 126 Chipper Jones 1.50 .70
❑ 127 Eric Karros .25 .11
❑ 128 Darren Daulton .25 .11
❑ 129 Vinny Castilla .25 .11
❑ 130 Joe Carter .25 .11
❑ 131 Bernie Williams .60 .25
❑ 132 Bernard Gilkey .15 .07
❑ 133 Bret Boone .25 .11
❑ 134 Tony Gwynn 1.25 .55
❑ 135 Dave Nilsson .15 .07
❑ 136 Ryan Klesko .25 .11
❑ 137 Paul Molitor .60 .25
❑ 138 John Olerud .25 .11
❑ 139 Craig Biggio .40 .18
❑ 140 John Valentin .15 .07
❑ 141 Chuck Knoblauch .25 .11
❑ 142 Edgar Martinez .40 .18
❑ 143 Rico Brogna .15 .07
❑ 144 Dean Palmer .25 .11
❑ 145 Mark Grace .60 .25
❑ 146 Roberto Alomar .60 .25
❑ 147 Alex Fernandez .15 .07
❑ 148 Andre Dawson .40 .18
❑ 149 Wade Boggs .75 .35
❑ 150 Mark Lewis .15 .07
❑ 151 Gary Gaetti .25 .11
❑ 152 Paul Wilson .40 .18
Roger Clemens
❑ 153 Rey Ordonez .25 .11
Ozzie Smith
❑ 154 Derek Jeter 1.00 .45
Cal Ripken
❑ 155 Andy Benes .15 .07
Alan Benes
❑ 156 Jason Kendall .60 .25
Mike Piazza
❑ 157 Ryan Klesko .60 .25
Frank Thomas
❑ 158 Johnny Damon .75 .35
Ken Griffey Jr.
❑ 159 Karim Garcia .60 .25
Sammy Sosa
❑ 160 Raul Mondesi .25 .11
Tim Salmon
❑ 161 Chipper Jones .60 .25
Matt Williams
❑ 162 Rey Ordonez .15 .07
❑ 163 Bob Wolcott .15 .07
❑ 164 Brooks Kieschnick .15 .07
❑ 165 Steve Gibralter .15 .07
❑ 166 Bob Abreu .75 .35
❑ 167 Greg Zaun .15 .07
❑ 168 Tavo Alvarez .15 .07
❑ 169 Sal Fasano .15 .07
❑ 170 George Arias .15 .07
❑ 171 Derek Jeter 2.50 1.10
❑ 172 Livan Hernandez RC .75 .35
❑ 173 Alan Benes .15 .07
❑ 174 George Williams .15 .07
❑ 175 John Wasdin .15 .07
❑ 176 Chan Ho Park .25 .11
❑ 177 Paul Wilson .15 .07
❑ 178 Jeff Suppan .15 .07
❑ 179 Quinton McCracken .15 .07
❑ 180 Wilton Guerrero RC .40 .18
❑ 181 Eric Owens .15 .07
❑ 182 Felipe Crespo .15 .07
❑ 183 LaTroy Hawkins .15 .07
❑ 184 Jason Schmidt .15 .07
❑ 185 Terrell Wade .15 .07
❑ 186 Mike Grace RC .15 .07
❑ 187 Chris Snopek .15 .07
❑ 188 Jason Kendall .25 .11
❑ 189 Todd Hollandsworth .15 .07
❑ 190 Jim Pittsley .15 .07
❑ 191 Jermaine Dye .25 .11
❑ 192 Mike Busby RC .15 .07
❑ 193 Richard Hidalgo .25 .11
❑ 194 Tyler Houston .15 .07
❑ 195 Jimmy Haynes .15 .07
❑ 196 Karim Garcia .15 .07
❑ 197 Ken Griffey Jr. CL 1.25 .55
❑ 198 Frank Thomas CL .60 .25
❑ 199 Greg Maddux CL .75 .35
❑ 200 Cal Ripken CL 1.25 .55

## 1952 Topps

| | NRMT | VG-E |
|---|---|---|
| COMPLETE SET (407) | 65000.00 | 29200.00 |
| COMMON CARD (1-80) | 60.00 | 27.00 |
| *RED/BLACK BACKS 1-80 SAME VALUE | | |
| COMMON CARD (81-250) | 40.00 | 18.00 |
| COMMON CARD (251-310) | 50.00 | 22.00 |
| COMMON CARD (311-407) | 250.00 | 110.00 |
| WRAPPER (1-CENT) | 250.00 | 110.00 |
| WRAPPER (5-CENT) | 100.00 | 45.00 |

❑ 1 Andy Pafko 3000.00 300.00
❑ 2 Pete Runnels RC I 250.00 110.00
❑ 3 Hank Thompson 70.00 32.00
❑ 4 Don Lenhardt 60.00 27.00
❑ 5 Larry Jansen 70.00 32.00
❑ 6 Grady Hatton 60.00 27.00
❑ 7 Wayne Terwilliger 60.00 27.00
❑ 8 Fred Marsh 60.00 27.00
❑ 9 Robert Hogue 60.00 27.00
❑ 10 Al Rosen 70.00 32.00
❑ 11 Phil Rizzuto 350.00 160.00
❑ 12 Monty Basgall 60.00 27.00
❑ 13 Johnny Wyrostek 60.00 27.00
❑ 14 Bob Elliott 70.00 32.00
❑ 15 Johnny Pesky 70.00 32.00
❑ 16 Gene Hermanski 60.00 27.00
❑ 17 Jim Hegan 70.00 32.00
❑ 18 Merrill Combs 60.00 27.00
❑ 19 Johnny Bucha 60.00 27.00
❑ 20 Billy Loes RC ! 125.00 55.00
❑ 21 Ferris Fain 70.00 32.00
❑ 22 Dom DiMaggio 100.00 45.00
❑ 23 Billy Goodman 70.00 32.00
❑ 24 Luke Easter 80.00 36.00
❑ 25 Johnny Groth 60.00 27.00
❑ 26 Monte Irvin 125.00 55.00
❑ 27 Sam Jethroe 70.00 32.00
❑ 28 Jerry Priddy 60.00 27.00
❑ 29 Ted Kluszewski 125.00 55.00
❑ 30 Mel Parnell 70.00 32.00
❑ 31 Gus Zernial 80.00 36.00
(Posed with seven baseballs)
❑ 32 Eddie Robinson 60.00 27.00
❑ 33 Warren Spahn 250.00 110.00
❑ 34 Elmer Valo 60.00 27.00
❑ 35 Hank Sauer 70.00 32.00
❑ 36 Gil Hodges 250.00 110.00
❑ 37 Duke Snider 400.00 180.00
❑ 38 Wally Westlake 60.00 27.00
❑ 39 Dizzy Trout 70.00 32.00
❑ 40 Irv Noren 70.00 32.00
❑ 41 Bob Wellman 60.00 27.00
❑ 42 Lou Kretlow 60.00 27.00
❑ 43 Ray Scarborough 60.00 27.00
❑ 44 Con Dempsey 60.00 27.00
❑ 45 Eddie Joost 60.00 27.00
❑ 46 Gordon Goldsberry 60.00 27.00
❑ 47 Willie Jones 70.00 32.00
❑ 48A Joe Page COR 125.00 55.00
❑ 48B Joe Page ERR 300.00 135.00
(Bio for Sain)
❑ 49A Johnny Sain COR 125.00 55.00
❑ 49B Johnny Sain ERR 300.00 135.00
(Bio for Page)
❑ 50 Marv Rickert 60.00 27.00
❑ 51 Jim Russell 60.00 27.00
❑ 52 Don Mueller 70.00 32.00
❑ 53 Chris Van Cuyk 60.00 27.00
❑ 54 Leo Kiely 60.00 27.00
❑ 55 Ray Boone 80.00 36.00
❑ 56 Tommy Glaviano 60.00 27.00
❑ 57 Ed Lopat 100.00 45.00
❑ 58 Bob Mahoney 60.00 27.00
❑ 59 Robin Roberts 175.00 80.00
❑ 60 Sid Hudson 60.00 27.00
❑ 61 Tookie Gilbert 60.00 27.00
❑ 62 Chuck Stobbs 60.00 27.00
❑ 63 Howie Pollet 60.00 27.00
❑ 64 Roy Sievers 70.00 32.00
❑ 65 Enos Slaughter 175.00 80.00
❑ 66 Preacher Roe 100.00 45.00
❑ 67 Allie Reynolds 100.00 45.00
❑ 68 Cliff Chambers 60.00 27.00
❑ 69 Virgil Stallcup 60.00 27.00
❑ 70 Al Zarilla 60.00 27.00
❑ 71 Tom Upton 60.00 27.00
❑ 72 Karl Olson 60.00 27.00
❑ 73 Bill Werle 60.00 27.00
❑ 74 Andy Hansen 60.00 27.00
❑ 75 Wes Westrum 70.00 32.00
❑ 76 Eddie Stanky 70.00 32.00
❑ 77 Bob Kennedy 70.00 32.00
❑ 78 Ellis Kinder 60.00 27.00
❑ 79 Gerry Staley 60.00 27.00
❑ 80 Herman Wehmeier 80.00 36.00
❑ 81 Vernon Law 80.00 36.00
❑ 82 Duane Pillette 40.00 18.00
❑ 83 Billy Johnson 40.00 18.00
❑ 84 Vern Stephens 50.00 22.00
❑ 85 Bob Kuzava 50.00 22.00
❑ 86 Ted Gray 40.00 18.00
❑ 87 Dale Coogan 40.00 18.00
❑ 88 Bob Feller 250.00 110.00
❑ 89 Johnny Lipon 40.00 18.00
❑ 90 Mickey Grasso 40.00 18.00
❑ 91 Red Schoendienst 100.00 45.00
❑ 92 Dale Mitchell 50.00 22.00
❑ 93 Al Sima 40.00 18.00
❑ 94 Sam Mele 40.00 18.00
❑ 95 Ken Holcombe 40.00 18.00
❑ 96 Willard Marshall 40.00 18.00
❑ 97 Earl Torgeson 40.00 18.00
❑ 98 Billy Pierce 50.00 22.00
❑ 99 Gene Woodling 60.00 27.00
❑ 100 Del Rice 40.00 18.00
❑ 101 Max Lanier 40.00 18.00
❑ 102 Bill Kennedy 40.00 18.00
❑ 103 Cliff Mapes 40.00 18.00
❑ 104 Don Kolloway 40.00 18.00

❑ 105 Johnny Pramesa 40.00 18.00
❑ 106 Mickey Vernon 60.00 27.00
❑ 107 Connie Ryan 40.00 18.00
❑ 108 Jim Konstanty 60.00 27.00
❑ 109 Ted Wilks 40.00 18.00
❑ 110 Dutch Leonard 40.00 18.00
❑ 111 Peanuts Lowrey 40.00 18.00
❑ 112 Hank Majeski 40.00 18.00
❑ 113 Dick Sisler 50.00 22.00
❑ 114 Willard Ramsdell 40.00 18.00
❑ 115 Red Munger 40.00 18.00
❑ 116 Carl Scheib 40.00 18.00
❑ 117 Sherm Lollar 50.00 22.00
❑ 118 Ken Raffensberger 40.00 18.00
❑ 119 Mickey McDermott 40.00 18.00
❑ 120 Bob Chakales 40.00 18.00
❑ 121 Gus Niarhos 40.00 18.00
❑ 122 Jackie Jensen 80.00 36.00
❑ 123 Eddie Yost 50.00 22.00
❑ 124 Monte Kennedy 40.00 18.00
❑ 125 Bill Rigney 40.00 18.00
❑ 126 Fred Hutchinson 50.00 22.00
❑ 127 Paul Minner 40.00 18.00
❑ 128 Don Bollweg 40.00 18.00
❑ 129 Johnny Mize 150.00 70.00
❑ 130 Sheldon Jones 40.00 18.00
❑ 131 Morrie Martin 40.00 18.00
❑ 132 Clyde Kluttz 40.00 18.00
❑ 133 Al Widmar 40.00 18.00
❑ 134 Joe Tipton 40.00 18.00
❑ 135 Dixie Howell 40.00 18.00
❑ 136 Johnny Schmitz 40.00 18.00
❑ 137 Roy McMillan RC 50.00 22.00
❑ 138 Bill MacDonald 40.00 18.00
❑ 139 Ken Wood 40.00 18.00
❑ 140 Johnny Antonelli 60.00 27.00
❑ 141 Clint Hartung 40.00 18.00
❑ 142 Harry Perkowski 40.00 18.00
❑ 143 Les Moss 40.00 18.00
❑ 144 Ed Blake 40.00 18.00
❑ 145 Joe Haynes 40.00 18.00
❑ 146 Frank House 40.00 18.00
❑ 147 Bob Young 40.00 18.00
❑ 148 Johnny Klippstein 40.00 18.00
❑ 149 Dick Kryhoski 40.00 18.00
❑ 150 Ted Beard 40.00 18.00
❑ 151 Wally Post RC 50.00 22.00
❑ 152 Al Evans 40.00 18.00
❑ 153 Bob Rush 40.00 18.00
❑ 154 Joe Muir 40.00 18.00
❑ 155 Frank Overmire 40.00 18.00
❑ 156 Frank Hiller 40.00 18.00
❑ 157 Bob Usher 40.00 18.00
❑ 158 Eddie Waitkus 40.00 18.00
❑ 159 Saul Rogovin 40.00 18.00
❑ 160 Owen Friend 40.00 18.00
❑ 161 Bud Byerly 40.00 18.00
❑ 162 Del Crandall 50.00 22.00
❑ 163 Stan Rojek 40.00 18.00
❑ 164 Walt Dubiel 40.00 18.00
❑ 165 Eddie Kazak 40.00 18.00
❑ 166 Paul LaPalme 40.00 18.00
❑ 167 Bill Howerton 40.00 18.00
❑ 168 Charlie Silvera RC 60.00 27.00
❑ 169 Howie Judson 40.00 18.00
❑ 170 Gus Bell 50.00 22.00
❑ 171 Ed Erautt 40.00 18.00
❑ 172 Eddie Miksis 40.00 18.00
❑ 173 Roy Smalley 40.00 18.00
❑ 174 Clarence Marshall 50.00 22.00
❑ 175 Billy Martin RC 400.00 180.00
❑ 176 Hank Edwards 40.00 18.00
❑ 177 Bill Wight 40.00 18.00
❑ 178 Cass Michaels 40.00 18.00
❑ 179 Frank Smith 40.00 18.00
❑ 180 Charlie Maxwell RC 50.00 22.00
❑ 181 Bob Swift 40.00 18.00
❑ 182 Billy Hitchcock 40.00 18.00
❑ 183 Erv Dusak 40.00 18.00
❑ 184 Bob Ramazzotti 40.00 18.00
❑ 185 Bill Nicholson 50.00 22.00
❑ 186 Walt Masterson 40.00 18.00
❑ 187 Bob Miller 40.00 18.00
❑ 188 Clarence Podbielan 40.00 18.00
❑ 189 Pete Reiser 60.00 27.00
❑ 190 Don Johnson 40.00 18.00
❑ 191 Yogi Berra 600.00 275.00
❑ 192 Myron Ginsberg 40.00 18.00
❑ 193 Harry Simpson 50.00 22.00
❑ 194 Joe Hatton 40.00 18.00
❑ 195 Minnie Minoso RC 150.00 70.00
❑ 196 Solly Hemus RC 60.00 27.00
❑ 197 George Strickland 40.00 18.00
❑ 198 Phil Haugstad 40.00 18.00
❑ 199 George Zuverink 40.00 18.00
❑ 200 Ralph Houk RC 80.00 36.00
❑ 201 Alex Kellner 40.00 18.00
❑ 202 Joe Collins RC 60.00 27.00
❑ 203 Curt Simmons 60.00 27.00
❑ 204 Ron Northey 40.00 18.00
❑ 205 Clyde King 60.00 27.00
❑ 206 Joe Ostrowski 40.00 18.00
❑ 207 Mickey Harris 40.00 18.00
❑ 208 Marlin Stuart 40.00 18.00
❑ 209 Howie Fox 40.00 18.00
❑ 210 Dick Fowler 40.00 18.00
❑ 211 Ray Coleman 40.00 18.00
❑ 212 Ned Garver 40.00 18.00
❑ 213 Nippy Jones 40.00 18.00
❑ 214 Johnny Hopp 50.00 22.00
❑ 215 Hank Bauer 80.00 36.00
❑ 216 Richie Ashburn 200.00 90.00
❑ 217 Snuffy Stirnweiss 50.00 22.00
❑ 218 Clyde McCullough 40.00 18.00
❑ 219 Bobby Shantz 60.00 27.00
❑ 220 Joe Presko 40.00 18.00
❑ 221 Granny Hamner 40.00 18.00
❑ 222 Hoot Evers 40.00 18.00
❑ 223 Del Ennis 50.00 22.00
❑ 224 Bruce Edwards 40.00 18.00
❑ 225 Frank Baumholtz 40.00 18.00
❑ 226 Dave Philley 40.00 18.00
❑ 227 Joe Garagiola 80.00 36.00
❑ 228 Al Brazle 40.00 18.00
❑ 229 Gene Bearden UER 40.00 18.00
(Misspelled Beardon)
❑ 230 Matt Batts 40.00 18.00
❑ 231 Sam Zoldak 40.00 18.00
❑ 232 Billy Cox 50.00 22.00
❑ 233 Bob Friend RC 60.00 27.00
❑ 234 Steve Souchock 40.00 18.00
❑ 235 Walt Dropo 40.00 18.00
❑ 236 Ed Fitzgerald 40.00 18.00
❑ 237 Jerry Coleman 60.00 27.00
❑ 238 Art Houtteman 40.00 18.00
❑ 239 Rocky Bridges 50.00 22.00
❑ 240 Jack Phillips 40.00 18.00
❑ 241 Tommy Byrne 40.00 18.00
❑ 242 Tom Poholsky 40.00 18.00
❑ 243 Larry Doby 80.00 36.00
❑ 244 Vic Wertz 40.00 18.00
❑ 245 Sherry Robertson 40.00 18.00
❑ 246 George Kell 80.00 36.00
❑ 247 Randy Gumpert 40.00 18.00
❑ 248 Frank Shea 40.00 18.00
❑ 249 Bobby Adams 40.00 18.00
❑ 250 Carl Erskine 100.00 45.00
❑ 251 Chico Carrasquel 50.00 22.00
❑ 252 Vern Bickford 50.00 22.00
❑ 253 Johnny Berardino 100.00 45.00
❑ 254 Joe Dobson 50.00 22.00
❑ 255 Clyde Vollmer 50.00 22.00
❑ 256 Pete Suder 50.00 22.00
❑ 257 Bobby Avila 60.00 27.00
❑ 258 Steve Gromek 60.00 27.00
❑ 259 Bob Addis 50.00 22.00
❑ 260 Pete Castiglione 50.00 22.00
❑ 261 Willie Mays 2500.00 1100.00
❑ 262 Virgil Trucks 60.00 27.00
❑ 263 Harry Brecheen 60.00 27.00
❑ 264 Roy Hartsfield 50.00 22.00
❑ 265 Chuck Diering 50.00 22.00
❑ 266 Murry Dickson 50.00 22.00
❑ 267 Sid Gordon 60.00 27.00
❑ 268 Bob Lemon 150.00 70.00
❑ 269 Willard Nixon 50.00 22.00
❑ 270 Lou Brissie 50.00 22.00
❑ 271 Jim Delsing 60.00 27.00
❑ 272 Mike Garcia 75.00 34.00
❑ 273 Erv Palica 50.00 22.00
❑ 274 Ralph Branca 125.00 55.00
❑ 275 Pat Mullin 50.00 22.00
❑ 276 Jim Wilson 50.00 22.00
❑ 277 Early Wynn 150.00 70.00
❑ 278 Allie Clark 50.00 22.00
❑ 279 Eddie Stewart 50.00 22.00
❑ 280 Cloyd Boyer 75.00 34.00
❑ 281 Tommy Brown SP 75.00 34.00
❑ 282 Birdie Tebbetts SP 75.00 34.00
❑ 283 Phil Masi SP 60.00 27.00
❑ 284 Hank Arft SP 60.00 27.00
❑ 285 Cliff Fannin SP 60.00 27.00
❑ 286 Joe DeMaestri SP 60.00 27.00
❑ 287 Steve Bilko SP 60.00 27.00
❑ 288 Chet Nichols SP 75.00 34.00
❑ 289 Tommy Holmes SP 90.00 40.00
❑ 290 Joe Astroth SP 60.00 27.00
❑ 291 Gil Coan SP 60.00 27.00
❑ 292 Floyd Baker SP 60.00 27.00
❑ 293 Sibby Sisti SP 60.00 27.00
❑ 294 Walker Cooper SP 60.00 27.00
❑ 295 Phil Cavarretta SP 75.00 34.00
❑ 296 Red Rolfe MG SP 60.00 27.00
❑ 297 Andy Seminick SP 60.00 27.00
❑ 298 Bob Ross SP 60.00 27.00
❑ 299 Ray Murray SP 75.00 34.00
❑ 300 Barney McCosky SP 75.00 34.00
❑ 301 Bob Porterfield 50.00 22.00
❑ 302 Max Surkont 50.00 22.00
❑ 303 Harry Dorish 50.00 22.00
❑ 304 Sam Dente 50.00 22.00
❑ 305 Paul Richards MG 60.00 27.00
❑ 306 Lou Sleater 50.00 22.00
❑ 307 Frank Campos 50.00 22.00
❑ 308 Luis Aloma 50.00 22.00
❑ 309 Jim Busby 60.00 27.00
❑ 310 George Metkovich 90.00 40.00
❑ 311 Mickey Mantle 18000.00 8100.00
❑ 312 Jackie Robinson DP 2000.00 900.00
❑ 313 Bobby Thomson DP 300.00 135.00
❑ 314 Roy Campanella 2200.00 1000.00
❑ 315 Leo Durocher MG 400.00 180.00
❑ 316 Dave Williams RC 300.00 135.00
❑ 317 Conrado Marrero 300.00 135.00
❑ 318 Harold Gregg 300.00 135.00
❑ 319 Al Walker 250.00 110.00
❑ 320 John Rutherford RC 300.00 135.00
❑ 321 Joe Black RC 350.00 160.00
❑ 322 Randy Jackson 300.00 135.00
❑ 323 Bubba Church 250.00 110.00
❑ 324 Warren Hacker 250.00 110.00
❑ 325 Bill Serena 300.00 135.00
❑ 326 George Shuba RC 400.00 180.00
❑ 327 Al Wilson 250.00 110.00
❑ 328 Bob Borkowski 300.00 135.00
❑ 329 Ike Delock 300.00 135.00
❑ 330 Turk Lown 300.00 135.00
❑ 331 Tom Morgan 300.00 135.00
❑ 332 Anthony Bartirome 300.00 135.00
❑ 333 Pee Wee Reese 1600.00 700.00
❑ 334 Wilmer Mizell RC 300.00 135.00
❑ 335 Ted Lepcio 250.00 110.00
❑ 336 Dave Koslo 250.00 110.00
❑ 337 Jim Hearn 300.00 135.00
❑ 338 Sal Yvars 300.00 135.00
❑ 339 Russ Meyer 300.00 135.00
❑ 340 Bob Hooper 300.00 135.00
❑ 341 Hal Jeffcoat 300.00 135.00
❑ 342 Clem Labine RC 400.00 180.00
❑ 343 Dick Gernert 250.00 110.00
❑ 344 Ewell Blackwell 300.00 135.00
❑ 345 Sammy White 250.00 110.00
❑ 346 George Spencer 250.00 110.00
❑ 347 Joe Adcock 300.00 135.00
❑ 348 Robert Kelly 250.00 110.00
❑ 349 Bob Cain 300.00 135.00
❑ 350 Cal Abrams 300.00 135.00
❑ 351 Alvin Dark 300.00 135.00
❑ 352 Karl Drews 300.00 135.00
❑ 353 Bobby Del Greco 300.00 135.00
❑ 354 Fred Hatfield 300.00 135.00
❑ 355 Bobby Morgan 300.00 135.00
❑ 356 Toby Atwell 300.00 135.00
❑ 357 Smoky Burgess 300.00 135.00
❑ 358 John Kucab 300.00 135.00
❑ 359 Dee Fondy 250.00 110.00
❑ 360 George Crowe RC 300.00 135.00
❑ 361 William Posedel CO 250.00 110.00

| No. | Player | NRMT | VG-E |
|---|---|---|---|
| 362 | Ken Heintzelman | 300.00 | 135.00 |
| 363 | Dick Rozek | 300.00 | 135.00 |
| 364 | Clyde Sukeforth CO | 300.00 | 135.00 |
| 365 | Cookie Lavagetto CO | 350.00 | 160.00 |
| 366 | Dave Madison | 250.00 | 110.00 |
| 367 | Ben Thorpe | 300.00 | 135.00 |
| 368 | Ed Wright | 300.00 | 135.00 |
| 369 | Dick Groat RC | 350.00 | 160.00 |
| 370 | Billy Hoeft RC | 300.00 | 135.00 |
| 371 | Bobby Hofman | 250.00 | 110.00 |
| 372 | Gil McDougald RC | 400.00 | 180.00 |
| 373 | Jim Turner RC CO | 400.00 | 180.00 |
| 374 | John Benton | 250.00 | 110.00 |
| 375 | John Merson | 250.00 | 110.00 |
| 376 | Faye Throneberry | 250.00 | 110.00 |
| 377 | Chuck Dressen MG | 350.00 | 160.00 |
| 378 | Leroy Fusselman | 300.00 | 135.00 |
| 379 | Joe Rossi | 250.00 | 110.00 |
| 380 | Clem Koshorek | 250.00 | 110.00 |
| 381 | Milton Stock CO | 300.00 | 135.00 |
| 382 | Sam Jones RC | 350.00 | 160.00 |
| 383 | Del Wilber | 250.00 | 110.00 |
| 384 | Frank Crosetti CO | 400.00 | 180.00 |
| 385 | Herman Franks CO RC | 250.00 | 110.00 |
| 386 | John Yuhas | 300.00 | 135.00 |
| 387 | Billy Meyer MG | 250.00 | 110.00 |
| 388 | Bob Chipman | 250.00 | 110.00 |
| 389 | Ben Wade | 300.00 | 135.00 |
| 390 | Glenn Nelson | 300.00 | 135.00 |
| 391 | Ben Chapman UER CO (Photo actually Sam Chapman) | 250.00 | 110.00 |
| 392 | Hoyt Wilhelm RC ! | 750.00 | 350.00 |
| 393 | Ebba St.Claire | 300.00 | 135.00 |
| 394 | Billy Herman CO | 400.00 | 180.00 |
| 395 | Jake Pitler CO | 300.00 | 135.00 |
| 396 | Dick Williams RC | 400.00 | 180.00 |
| 397 | Forrest Main | 250.00 | 110.00 |
| 398 | Hal Rice | 250.00 | 110.00 |
| 399 | Jim Fridley | 250.00 | 110.00 |
| 400 | Bill Dickey CO | 800.00 | 350.00 |
| 401 | Bob Schultz | 300.00 | 135.00 |
| 402 | Earl Harrist | 300.00 | 135.00 |
| 403 | Bill Miller | 300.00 | 135.00 |
| 404 | Dick Brodowski | 300.00 | 135.00 |
| 405 | Eddie Pellagrini | 300.00 | 135.00 |
| 406 | Joe Nuxhall RC | 400.00 | 180.00 |
| 407 | Eddie Mathews RC ! | 5000.00 | 1250.00 |

## 1953 Topps

| | NRMT | VG-E |
|---|---|---|
| COMPLETE SET (274) | 13500.00 | 6100.00 |
| COMMON CARD (1-165) | 30.00 | 13.50 |
| COMMON CARD (166-220) | 25.00 | 11.00 |
| COMMON DP (1-220) | 15.00 | 6.75 |
| COMMON CARD (221-280) | 100.00 | 45.00 |
| NOT ISSUED (253/261/267) | | |
| NOT ISSUED (268/271/275) | | |
| WRAP.(1-CENT, DATED) | 200.00 | 90.00 |
| WRAP.(1-CENT,NO DATE) | 300.00 | 135.00 |
| WRAP.(5-CENT, DATED) | 400.00 | 180.00 |
| WRAP.(5-CENT,NO DATE) | 350.00 | 160.00 |

| No. | Player | NRMT | VG-E |
|---|---|---|---|
| 1 | Jackie Robinson DP | 700.00 | 190.00 |
| 2 | Luke Easter DP | 20.00 | 9.00 |
| 3 | George Crowe | 40.00 | 18.00 |
| 4 | Ben Wade | 30.00 | 13.50 |
| 5 | Joe Dobson | 30.00 | 13.50 |
| 6 | Sam Jones | 40.00 | 18.00 |
| 7 | Bob Borkowski DP | 15.00 | 6.75 |
| 8 | Clem Koshorek DP | 15.00 | 6.75 |
| 9 | Joe Collins | 60.00 | 27.00 |
| 10 | Smoky Burgess SP | 70.00 | 32.00 |
| 11 | Sal Yvars | 30.00 | 13.50 |
| 12 | Howie Judson DP | 15.00 | 6.75 |
| 13 | Conrado Marrero DP | 15.00 | 6.75 |
| 14 | Clem Labine DP | 20.00 | 9.00 |
| 15 | Bobo Newsom DP | 20.00 | 9.00 |
| 16 | Peanuts Lowrey DP | 15.00 | 6.75 |
| 17 | Billy Hitchcock | 30.00 | 13.50 |
| 18 | Ted Lepcio DP | 15.00 | 6.75 |
| 19 | Mel Parnell DP | 30.00 | 13.50 |
| 20 | Hank Thompson | 40.00 | 18.00 |
| 21 | Billy Johnson | 30.00 | 13.50 |
| 22 | Howie Fox | 30.00 | 13.50 |
| 23 | Toby Atwell DP | 15.00 | 6.75 |
| 24 | Ferris Fain | 40.00 | 18.00 |
| 25 | Ray Boone | 40.00 | 18.00 |
| 26 | Dale Mitchell DP | 40.00 | 18.00 |
| 27 | Roy Campanella DP | 200.00 | 90.00 |
| 28 | Eddie Pellagrini | 30.00 | 13.50 |
| 29 | Hal Jeffcoat | 30.00 | 13.50 |
| 30 | Willard Nixon | 30.00 | 13.50 |
| 31 | Ewell Blackwell | 60.00 | 27.00 |
| 32 | Clyde Vollmer | 30.00 | 13.50 |
| 33 | Bob Kennedy DP | 15.00 | 6.75 |
| 34 | George Shuba | 40.00 | 18.00 |
| 35 | Irv Noren DP | 15.00 | 6.75 |
| 36 | Johnny Groth DP | 15.00 | 6.75 |
| 37 | Eddie Mathews DP | 150.00 | 70.00 |
| 38 | Jim Hearn DP | 15.00 | 6.75 |
| 39 | Eddie Miksis | 30.00 | 13.50 |
| 40 | John Lipon | 30.00 | 13.50 |
| 41 | Enos Slaughter | 80.00 | 36.00 |
| 42 | Gus Zernial DP | 30.00 | 13.50 |
| 43 | Gil McDougald | 60.00 | 27.00 |
| 44 | Ellis Kinder SP | 35.00 | 16.00 |
| 45 | Grady Hatton DP | 15.00 | 6.75 |
| 46 | Johnny Klippstein DP | 15.00 | 6.75 |
| 47 | Bubba Church DP | 15.00 | 6.75 |
| 48 | Bob Del Greco DP | 15.00 | 6.75 |
| 49 | Faye Throneberry DP | 15.00 | 6.75 |
| 50 | Chuck Dressen MG DP | 20.00 | 9.00 |
| 51 | Frank Campos DP | 15.00 | 6.75 |
| 52 | Ted Gray DP | 15.00 | 6.75 |
| 53 | Sherm Lollar DP | 30.00 | 13.50 |
| 54 | Bob Feller DP | 125.00 | 55.00 |
| 55 | Maurice McDermott DP | 15.00 | 6.75 |
| 56 | Gerry Staley DP | 15.00 | 6.75 |
| 57 | Carl Scheib | 30.00 | 13.50 |
| 58 | George Metkovich | 30.00 | 13.50 |
| 59 | Karl Drews DP | 15.00 | 6.75 |
| 60 | Cloyd Boyer DP | 15.00 | 6.75 |
| 61 | Early Wynn SP | 110.00 | 50.00 |
| 62 | Monte Irvin DP | 35.00 | 16.00 |
| 63 | Gus Niarhos DP | 15.00 | 6.75 |
| 64 | Dave Philley | 30.00 | 13.50 |
| 65 | Earl Harrist | 30.00 | 13.50 |
| 66 | Minnie Minoso | 60.00 | 27.00 |
| 67 | Roy Sievers DP | 30.00 | 13.50 |
| 68 | Del Rice | 30.00 | 13.50 |
| 69 | Dick Brodowski | 30.00 | 13.50 |
| 70 | Ed Yuhas | 30.00 | 13.50 |
| 71 | Tony Bartirome | 30.00 | 13.50 |
| 72 | Fred Hutchinson MG SP | 50.00 | 22.00 |
| 73 | Eddie Robinson | 30.00 | 13.50 |
| 74 | Joe Rossi | 30.00 | 13.50 |
| 75 | Mike Garcia | 40.00 | 18.00 |
| 76 | Pee Wee Reese | 175.00 | 80.00 |
| 77 | Johnny Mize DP | 80.00 | 36.00 |
| 78 | Red Schoendienst | 80.00 | 36.00 |
| 79 | Johnny Wyrostek | 30.00 | 13.50 |
| 80 | Jim Hegan | 40.00 | 18.00 |
| 81 | Joe Black SP | 70.00 | 32.00 |
| 82 | Mickey Mantle | 3000.00 | 1350.00 |
| 83 | Howie Pollet | 30.00 | 13.50 |
| 84 | Bob Hooper DP | 15.00 | 6.75 |
| 85 | Bobby Morgan DP | 15.00 | 6.75 |
| 86 | Billy Martin | 125.00 | 55.00 |
| 87 | Ed Lopat | 60.00 | 27.00 |
| 88 | Willie Jones DP | 15.00 | 6.75 |
| 89 | Chuck Stobbs DP | 15.00 | 6.75 |
| 90 | Hank Edwards DP | 15.00 | 6.75 |
| 91 | Ebba St.Claire DP | 15.00 | 6.75 |
| 92 | Paul Minner DP | 15.00 | 6.75 |
| 93 | Hal Rice DP | 15.00 | 6.75 |
| 94 | Bill Kennedy DP | 15.00 | 6.75 |
| 95 | Willard Marshall DP | 15.00 | 6.75 |
| 96 | Virgil Trucks | 40.00 | 18.00 |
| 97 | Don Kolloway DP | 15.00 | 6.75 |
| 98 | Cal Abrams DP | 15.00 | 6.75 |
| 99 | Dave Madison | 30.00 | 13.50 |
| 100 | Bill Miller | 30.00 | 13.50 |
| 101 | Ted Wilks | 30.00 | 13.50 |
| 102 | Connie Ryan DP | 15.00 | 6.75 |
| 103 | Joe Astroth DP | 15.00 | 6.75 |
| 104 | Yogi Berra | 300.00 | 135.00 |
| 105 | Joe Nuxhall DP | 30.00 | 13.50 |
| 106 | Johnny Antonelli | 40.00 | 18.00 |
| 107 | Danny O'Connell DP | 15.00 | 6.75 |
| 108 | Bob Porterfield DP | 15.00 | 6.75 |
| 109 | Alvin Dark | 60.00 | 27.00 |
| 110 | Herman Wehmeier DP | 15.00 | 6.75 |
| 111 | Hank Sauer DP | 20.00 | 9.00 |
| 112 | Ned Garver DP | 15.00 | 6.75 |
| 113 | Jerry Priddy | 30.00 | 13.50 |
| 114 | Phil Rizzuto | 175.00 | 80.00 |
| 115 | George Spencer | 30.00 | 13.50 |
| 116 | Frank Smith DP | 15.00 | 6.75 |
| 117 | Sid Gordon DP | 15.00 | 6.75 |
| 118 | Gus Bell DP | 20.00 | 9.00 |
| 119 | Johnny Sain SP | 50.00 | 22.00 |
| 120 | Davey Williams | 40.00 | 18.00 |
| 121 | Walt Dropo | 40.00 | 18.00 |
| 122 | Elmer Valo | 30.00 | 13.50 |
| 123 | Tommy Byrne DP | 15.00 | 6.75 |
| 124 | Sibby Sisti DP | 15.00 | 6.75 |
| 125 | Dick Williams DP | 25.00 | 11.00 |
| 126 | Bill Connelly DP | 15.00 | 6.75 |
| 127 | Clint Courtney DP | 15.00 | 6.75 |
| 128 | Wilmer Mizell DP (Inconsistent design, logo on front with black birds) | 20.00 | 9.00 |
| 129 | Keith Thomas | 30.00 | 13.50 |
| 130 | Turk Lown DP | 15.00 | 6.75 |
| 131 | Harry Byrd DP | 15.00 | 6.75 |
| 132 | Tom Morgan | 30.00 | 13.50 |
| 133 | Gil Coan | 30.00 | 13.50 |
| 134 | Rube Walker | 40.00 | 18.00 |
| 135 | Al Rosen DP | 25.00 | 11.00 |
| 136 | Ken Heintzelman DP | 15.00 | 6.75 |
| 137 | John Rutherford DP | 15.00 | 6.75 |
| 138 | George Kell | 80.00 | 36.00 |
| 139 | Sammy White | 30.00 | 13.50 |
| 140 | Tommy Glaviano | 30.00 | 13.50 |
| 141 | Allie Reynolds DP | 25.00 | 11.00 |
| 142 | Vic Wertz | 40.00 | 18.00 |
| 143 | Billy Pierce ! | 60.00 | 27.00 |
| 144 | Bob Schultz DP | 15.00 | 6.75 |
| 145 | Harry Dorish DP | 15.00 | 6.75 |
| 146 | Granny Hamner | 30.00 | 13.50 |
| 147 | Warren Spahn | 150.00 | 70.00 |
| 148 | Mickey Grasso | 30.00 | 13.50 |
| 149 | Dom DiMaggio DP | 35.00 | 16.00 |
| 150 | Harry Simpson DP | 15.00 | 6.75 |
| 151 | Hoyt Wilhelm | 80.00 | 36.00 |
| 152 | Bob Adams DP | 15.00 | 6.75 |
| 153 | Andy Seminick DP | 15.00 | 6.75 |
| 154 | Dick Groat | 40.00 | 18.00 |
| 155 | Dutch Leonard | 30.00 | 13.50 |
| 156 | Jim Rivera DP | 30.00 | 13.50 |
| 157 | Bob Addis DP | 15.00 | 6.75 |
| 158 | Johnny Logan RC | 40.00 | 18.00 |
| 159 | Wayne Terwilliger DP | 15.00 | 6.75 |
| 160 | Bob Young | 30.00 | 13.50 |
| 161 | Vern Bickford DP | 15.00 | 6.75 |
| 162 | Ted Kluszewski | 60.00 | 27.00 |
| 163 | Fred Hatfield DP | 15.00 | 6.75 |
| 164 | Frank Shea DP | 15.00 | 6.75 |
| 165 | Billy Hoeft | 30.00 | 13.50 |
| 166 | Billy Hunter | 25.00 | 11.00 |
| 167 | Art Schult | 25.00 | 11.00 |
| 168 | Willard Schmidt | 25.00 | 11.00 |
| 169 | Dizzy Trout | 40.00 | 18.00 |
| 170 | Bill Werle | 25.00 | 11.00 |
| 171 | Bill Glynn | 25.00 | 11.00 |
| 172 | Rip Repulski | 25.00 | 11.00 |
| 173 | Preston Ward | 25.00 | 11.00 |

| ❑ | Card | NRMT | VG-E |
|---|---|---|---|
| ❑ | 174 Billy Loes | 40.00 | 18.00 |
| ❑ | 175 Ron Kline | 25.00 | 11.00 |
| ❑ | 176 Don Hoak RC | 40.00 | 18.00 |
| ❑ | 177 Jim Dyck | 25.00 | 11.00 |
| ❑ | 178 Jim Waugh | 25.00 | 11.00 |
| ❑ | 179 Gene Hermanski | 25.00 | 11.00 |
| ❑ | 180 Virgil Stallcup | 25.00 | 11.00 |
| ❑ | 181 Al Zarilla | 25.00 | 11.00 |
| ❑ | 182 Bobby Hofman | 25.00 | 11.00 |
| ❑ | 183 Stu Miller RC | 40.00 | 18.00 |
| ❑ | 184 Hal Brown | 25.00 | 11.00 |
| ❑ | 185 Jim Pendleton | 25.00 | 11.00 |
| ❑ | 186 Charlie Bishop | 25.00 | 11.00 |
| ❑ | 187 Jim Fridley | 25.00 | 11.00 |
| ❑ | 188 Andy Carey RC | 40.00 | 18.00 |
| ❑ | 189 Ray Jablonski | 25.00 | 11.00 |
| ❑ | 190 Dixie Walker CO | 40.00 | 18.00 |
| ❑ | 191 Ralph Kiner | 80.00 | 36.00 |
| ❑ | 192 Wally Westlake | 25.00 | 11.00 |
| ❑ | 193 Mike Clark | 25.00 | 11.00 |
| ❑ | 194 Eddie Kazak | 25.00 | 11.00 |
| ❑ | 195 Ed McGhee | 25.00 | 11.00 |
| ❑ | 196 Bob Keegan | 25.00 | 11.00 |
| ❑ | 197 Del Crandall | 40.00 | 18.00 |
| ❑ | 198 Forrest Main | 25.00 | 11.00 |
| ❑ | 199 Marion Fricano | 25.00 | 11.00 |
| ❑ | 200 Gordon Goldsberry | 25.00 | 11.00 |
| ❑ | 201 Paul LaPalme | 25.00 | 11.00 |
| ❑ | 202 Carl Sawatski | 25.00 | 11.00 |
| ❑ | 203 Cliff Fannin | 25.00 | 11.00 |
| ❑ | 204 Dick Bokelman | 25.00 | 11.00 |
| ❑ | 205 Vern Benson | 25.00 | 11.00 |
| ❑ | 206 Ed Bailey RC | 25.00 | 11.00 |
| ❑ | 207 Whitey Ford | 175.00 | 80.00 |
| ❑ | 208 Jim Wilson | 25.00 | 11.00 |
| ❑ | 209 Jim Greengrass | 25.00 | 11.00 |
| ❑ | 210 Bob Cerv RC | 40.00 | 18.00 |
| ❑ | 211 J.W. Porter | 25.00 | 11.00 |
| ❑ | 212 Jack Dittmer | 25.00 | 11.00 |
| ❑ | 213 Ray Scarborough | 25.00 | 11.00 |
| ❑ | 214 Bill Bruton RC | 40.00 | 18.00 |
| ❑ | 215 Gene Conley RC | 40.00 | 18.00 |
| ❑ | 216 Jim Hughes | 25.00 | 11.00 |
| ❑ | 217 Murray Wall | 25.00 | 11.00 |
| ❑ | 218 Les Fusselman | 25.00 | 11.00 |
| ❑ | 219 Pete Runnels UER (Photo actually Don Johnson) | 40.00 | 18.00 |
| ❑ | 220 Satchel Paige UER (Misspelled Satchell on card front) | 600.00 | 275.00 |
| ❑ | 221 Bob Milliken | 100.00 | 45.00 |
| ❑ | 222 Vic Janowicz DP RC | 60.00 | 27.00 |
| ❑ | 223 Johnny O'Brien DP | 50.00 | 22.00 |
| ❑ | 224 Lou Sleater DP | 100.00 | 45.00 |
| ❑ | 225 Bobby Shantz | 120.00 | 55.00 |
| ❑ | 226 Ed Erautt | 100.00 | 45.00 |
| ❑ | 227 Morrie Martin | 100.00 | 45.00 |
| ❑ | 228 Hal Newhouser | 150.00 | 70.00 |
| ❑ | 229 Rocky Krsnich | 100.00 | 45.00 |
| ❑ | 230 Johnny Lindell DP | 50.00 | 22.00 |
| ❑ | 231 Solly Hemus DP | 50.00 | 22.00 |
| ❑ | 232 Dick Kokos | 100.00 | 45.00 |
| ❑ | 233 Al Aber | 100.00 | 45.00 |
| ❑ | 234 Ray Murray DP | 50.00 | 22.00 |
| ❑ | 235 John Hetki DP | 50.00 | 22.00 |
| ❑ | 236 Harry Perkowski DP | 120.00 | 55.00 |
| ❑ | 237 Bud Podbielan DP | 50.00 | 22.00 |
| ❑ | 238 Cal Hogue DP | 50.00 | 22.00 |
| ❑ | 239 Jim Delsing | 100.00 | 45.00 |
| ❑ | 240 Fred Marsh | 100.00 | 45.00 |
| ❑ | 241 Al Sima DP | 50.00 | 22.00 |
| ❑ | 242 Charlie Silvera | 120.00 | 55.00 |
| ❑ | 243 Carlos Bernier DP | 50.00 | 22.00 |
| ❑ | 244 Willie Mays | 2700.00 | 1200.00 |
| ❑ | 245 Bill Norman CO | 100.00 | 45.00 |
| ❑ | 246 Roy Face DP RC | 80.00 | 36.00 |
| ❑ | 247 Mike Sandlock DP | 50.00 | 22.00 |
| ❑ | 248 Gene Stephens DP | 50.00 | 22.00 |
| ❑ | 249 Eddie O'Brien | 100.00 | 45.00 |
| ❑ | 250 Bob Wilson | 100.00 | 45.00 |
| ❑ | 251 Sid Hudson | 100.00 | 45.00 |
| ❑ | 252 Hank Foiles | 100.00 | 45.00 |
| ❑ | 253 Does not exist | | |
| ❑ | 254 Preacher Roe DP | 80.00 | 36.00 |
| ❑ | 255 Dixie Howell | 100.00 | 45.00 |
| ❑ | 256 Les Peden | 100.00 | 45.00 |
| ❑ | 257 Bob Boyd | 100.00 | 45.00 |
| ❑ | 258 Jim Gilliam RC | 300.00 | 135.00 |
| ❑ | 259 Roy McMillan DP | 100.00 | 45.00 |
| ❑ | 260 Sam Calderone | 100.00 | 45.00 |
| ❑ | 261 Does not exist | | |
| ❑ | 262 Bob Oldis | 100.00 | 45.00 |
| ❑ | 263 Johnny Podres RC | 300.00 | 135.00 |
| ❑ | 264 Gene Woodling DP | 100.00 | 45.00 |
| ❑ | 265 Jackie Jensen | 120.00 | 55.00 |
| ❑ | 266 Bob Cain | 100.00 | 45.00 |
| ❑ | 267 Does not exist | | |
| ❑ | 268 Does not exist | | |
| ❑ | 269 Duane Pillette | 100.00 | 45.00 |
| ❑ | 270 Vern Stephens | 120.00 | 55.00 |
| ❑ | 271 Does not exist | | |
| ❑ | 272 Bill Antonello | 100.00 | 45.00 |
| ❑ | 273 Harvey Haddix RC | 150.00 | 70.00 |
| ❑ | 274 John Riddle CO | 100.00 | 45.00 |
| ❑ | 275 Does not exist | | |
| ❑ | 276 Ken Raffensberger | 100.00 | 45.00 |
| ❑ | 277 Don Lund | 100.00 | 45.00 |
| ❑ | 278 Willie Miranda | 100.00 | 45.00 |
| ❑ | 279 Joe Coleman DP | 50.00 | 22.00 |
| ❑ | 280 Milt Bolling RC ! | 350.00 | 57.50 |

## 1954 Topps

| | NRMT | VG-E |
|---|---|---|
| COMPLETE SET (250) | 7500.00 | 3400.00 |
| COMMON (1-50/76-250) | 15.00 | 6.75 |
| COMMON CARD (51-75) | 25.00 | 11.00 |
| WRAP.(1-CENT, DATED) | 200.00 | 90.00 |
| WRAP.(1-CENT, UNDAT) | 150.00 | 70.00 |
| WRAP.(5-CENT, DATED) | 300.00 | 135.00 |
| WRAP.(5-CENT, UNDAT) | 250.00 | 110.00 |

| ❑ | Card | NRMT | VG-E |
|---|---|---|---|
| ❑ | 1 Ted Williams | 800.00 | 275.00 |
| ❑ | 2 Gus Zernial | 25.00 | 11.00 |
| ❑ | 3 Monte Irvin | 50.00 | 22.00 |
| ❑ | 4 Hank Sauer | 25.00 | 11.00 |
| ❑ | 5 Ed Lopat | 25.00 | 11.00 |
| ❑ | 6 Pete Runnels | 25.00 | 11.00 |
| ❑ | 7 Ted Kluszewski | 50.00 | 22.00 |
| ❑ | 8 Bob Young | 15.00 | 6.75 |
| ❑ | 9 Harvey Haddix | 25.00 | 11.00 |
| ❑ | 10 Jackie Robinson | 300.00 | 135.00 |
| ❑ | 11 Paul Leslie Smith | 15.00 | 6.75 |
| ❑ | 12 Del Crandall | 25.00 | 11.00 |
| ❑ | 13 Billy Martin | 80.00 | 36.00 |
| ❑ | 14 Preacher Roe | 25.00 | 11.00 |
| ❑ | 15 Al Rosen | 25.00 | 11.00 |
| ❑ | 16 Vic Janowicz | 25.00 | 11.00 |
| ❑ | 17 Phil Rizzuto | 100.00 | 45.00 |
| ❑ | 18 Walt Dropo | 25.00 | 11.00 |
| ❑ | 19 Johnny Lipon (Orioles team name on front; White Sox team on back; wearing a Red Sox cap) | 15.00 | 6.75 |
| ❑ | 20 Warren Spahn | 80.00 | 36.00 |
| ❑ | 21 Bobby Shantz | 25.00 | 11.00 |
| ❑ | 22 Jim Greengrass | 15.00 | 6.75 |
| ❑ | 23 Luke Easter | 25.00 | 11.00 |
| ❑ | 24 Granny Hamner | 15.00 | 6.75 |
| ❑ | 25 Harvey Kuenn RC ! | 40.00 | 18.00 |
| ❑ | 26 Ray Jablonski | 15.00 | 6.75 |
| ❑ | 27 Ferris Fain | 25.00 | 11.00 |
| ❑ | 28 Paul Minner | 15.00 | 6.75 |
| ❑ | 29 Jim Hegan | 25.00 | 11.00 |
| ❑ | 30 Eddie Mathews | 80.00 | 36.00 |
| ❑ | 31 Johnny Klippstein | 15.00 | 6.75 |
| ❑ | 32 Duke Snider | 175.00 | 80.00 |
| ❑ | 33 Johnny Schmitz | 15.00 | 6.75 |
| ❑ | 34 Jim Rivera | 15.00 | 6.75 |
| ❑ | 35 Jim Gilliam | 50.00 | 22.00 |
| ❑ | 36 Hoyt Wilhelm | 50.00 | 22.00 |
| ❑ | 37 Whitey Ford | 125.00 | 55.00 |
| ❑ | 38 Eddie Stanky MG | 25.00 | 11.00 |
| ❑ | 39 Sherm Lollar | 25.00 | 11.00 |
| ❑ | 40 Mel Parnell | 25.00 | 11.00 |
| ❑ | 41 Willie Jones | 15.00 | 6.75 |
| ❑ | 42 Don Mueller | 25.00 | 11.00 |
| ❑ | 43 Dick Groat | 25.00 | 11.00 |
| ❑ | 44 Ned Garver | 15.00 | 6.75 |
| ❑ | 45 Richie Ashburn | 80.00 | 36.00 |
| ❑ | 46 Ken Raffensberger | 15.00 | 6.75 |
| ❑ | 47 Ellis Kinder | 15.00 | 6.75 |
| ❑ | 48 Billy Hunter | 25.00 | 11.00 |
| ❑ | 49 Ray Murray | 15.00 | 6.75 |
| ❑ | 50 Yogi Berra | 200.00 | 90.00 |
| ❑ | 51 Johnny Lindell | 25.00 | 11.00 |
| ❑ | 52 Vic Power RC | 30.00 | 13.50 |
| ❑ | 53 Jack Dittmer | 25.00 | 11.00 |
| ❑ | 54 Vern Stephens | 30.00 | 13.50 |
| ❑ | 55 Phil Cavarretta MG | 30.00 | 13.50 |
| ❑ | 56 Willie Miranda | 25.00 | 11.00 |
| ❑ | 57 Luis Aloma | 25.00 | 11.00 |
| ❑ | 58 Bob Wilson | 25.00 | 11.00 |
| ❑ | 59 Gene Conley | 30.00 | 13.50 |
| ❑ | 60 Frank Baumholtz | 25.00 | 11.00 |
| ❑ | 61 Bob Cain | 25.00 | 11.00 |
| ❑ | 62 Eddie Robinson | 25.00 | 11.00 |
| ❑ | 63 Johnny Pesky | 30.00 | 13.50 |
| ❑ | 64 Hank Thompson | 25.00 | 11.00 |
| ❑ | 65 Bob Swift CO | 25.00 | 11.00 |
| ❑ | 66 Ted Lepcio | 25.00 | 11.00 |
| ❑ | 67 Jim Willis | 25.00 | 11.00 |
| ❑ | 68 Sam Calderone | 25.00 | 11.00 |
| ❑ | 69 Bud Podbielan | 25.00 | 11.00 |
| ❑ | 70 Larry Doby | 60.00 | 27.00 |
| ❑ | 71 Frank Smith | 25.00 | 11.00 |
| ❑ | 72 Preston Ward | 25.00 | 11.00 |
| ❑ | 73 Wayne Terwilliger | 25.00 | 11.00 |
| ❑ | 74 Bill Taylor | 25.00 | 11.00 |
| ❑ | 75 Fred Haney MG | 25.00 | 11.00 |
| ❑ | 76 Bob Scheffing CO | 15.00 | 6.75 |
| ❑ | 77 Ray Boone | 25.00 | 11.00 |
| ❑ | 78 Ted Kazanski | 15.00 | 6.75 |
| ❑ | 79 Andy Pafko | 25.00 | 11.00 |
| ❑ | 80 Jackie Jensen | 25.00 | 11.00 |
| ❑ | 81 Dave Hoskins | 15.00 | 6.75 |
| ❑ | 82 Milt Bolling | 15.00 | 6.75 |
| ❑ | 83 Joe Collins | 25.00 | 11.00 |
| ❑ | 84 Dick Cole | 15.00 | 6.75 |
| ❑ | 85 Bob Turley RC | 40.00 | 18.00 |
| ❑ | 86 Billy Herman CO | 25.00 | 11.00 |
| ❑ | 87 Roy Face | 25.00 | 11.00 |
| ❑ | 88 Matt Batts | 15.00 | 6.75 |
| ❑ | 89 Howie Pollet | 15.00 | 6.75 |
| ❑ | 90 Willie Mays | 500.00 | 220.00 |
| ❑ | 91 Bob Oldis | 15.00 | 6.75 |
| ❑ | 92 Wally Westlake | 15.00 | 6.75 |
| ❑ | 93 Sid Hudson | 15.00 | 6.75 |
| ❑ | 94 Ernie Banks RC ! | 750.00 | 350.00 |
| ❑ | 95 Hal Rice | 15.00 | 6.75 |
| ❑ | 96 Charlie Silvera | 25.00 | 11.00 |
| ❑ | 97 Jerald Hal Lane | 15.00 | 6.75 |
| ❑ | 98 Joe Black | 40.00 | 18.00 |
| ❑ | 99 Bobby Hofman | 15.00 | 6.75 |
| ❑ | 100 Bob Keegan | 15.00 | 6.75 |
| ❑ | 101 Gene Woodling | 25.00 | 11.00 |
| ❑ | 102 Gil Hodges | 80.00 | 36.00 |
| ❑ | 103 Jim Lemon RC | 15.00 | 6.75 |
| ❑ | 104 Mike Sandlock | 15.00 | 6.75 |
| ❑ | 105 Andy Carey | 25.00 | 11.00 |
| ❑ | 106 Dick Kokos | 15.00 | 6.75 |
| ❑ | 107 Duane Pillette | 15.00 | 6.75 |
| ❑ | 108 Thornton Kipper | 15.00 | 6.75 |
| ❑ | 109 Bill Bruton | 25.00 | 11.00 |
| ❑ | 110 Harry Dorish | 15.00 | 6.75 |
| ❑ | 111 Jim Delsing | 15.00 | 6.75 |
| ❑ | 112 Bill Renna | 15.00 | 6.75 |
| ❑ | 113 Bob Boyd | 15.00 | 6.75 |
| ❑ | 114 Dean Stone | 15.00 | 6.75 |

❑ 115 Rip Repulski ............ 15.00 6.75
❑ 116 Steve Bilko ............ 15.00 6.75
❑ 117 Solly Hemus ............ 15.00 6.75
❑ 118 Carl Scheib ............ 15.00 6.75
❑ 119 Johnny Antonelli ........ 25.00 11.00
❑ 120 Roy McMillan ............ 25.00 11.00
❑ 121 Clem Labine ............ 25.00 11.00
❑ 122 Johnny Logan ............ 25.00 11.00
❑ 123 Bobby Adams ............ 15.00 6.75
❑ 124 Marion Fricano ............ 15.00 6.75
❑ 125 Harry Perkowski ........ 15.00 6.75
❑ 126 Ben Wade ............ 15.00 6.75
❑ 127 Steve O'Neill MG........ 15.00 6.75
❑ 128 Hank Aaron RC ! .... 1500.00 700.00
❑ 129 Forrest Jacobs ............ 15.00 6.75
❑ 130 Hank Bauer ............ 25.00 11.00
❑ 131 Reno Bertoia ............ 25.00 11.00
❑ 132 Tommy Lasorda RC 200.00 90.00
❑ 133 Del Baker CO ............ 15.00 6.75
❑ 134 Cal Hogue ............ 15.00 6.75
❑ 135 Joe Presko ............ 15.00 6.75
❑ 136 Connie Ryan ............ 15.00 6.75
❑ 137 Wally Moon RC ............ 40.00 18.00
❑ 138 Bob Borkowski ............ 15.00 6.75
❑ 139 The O'Briens ............ 50.00 22.00
Johnny O'Brien
Eddie O'Brien
❑ 140 Tom Wright ............ 15.00 6.75
❑ 141 Joey Jay RC ............ 25.00 11.00
❑ 142 Tom Poholsky ............ 15.00 6.75
❑ 143 Rollie Hemsley CO .... 15.00 6.75
❑ 144 Bill Werle ............ 15.00 6.75
❑ 145 Elmer Valo ............ 15.00 6.75
❑ 146 Don Johnson ............ 15.00 6.75
❑ 147 Johnny Riddle CO ...... 15.00 6.75
❑ 148 Bob Trice ............ 15.00 6.75
❑ 149 Al Robertson ............ 15.00 6.75
❑ 150 Dick Kryhoski ............ 15.00 6.75
❑ 151 Alex Grammas ............ 15.00 6.75
❑ 152 Michael Blyzka ............ 15.00 6.75
❑ 153 Al Walker ............ 25.00 11.00
❑ 154 Mike Fornieles ............ 15.00 6.75
❑ 155 Bob Kennedy ............ 25.00 11.00
❑ 156 Joe Coleman ............ 25.00 11.00
❑ 157 Don Lenhardt ............ 25.00 11.00
❑ 158 Peanuts Lowrey ........ 15.00 6.75
❑ 159 Dave Philley ............ 15.00 6.75
❑ 160 Ralph Kress CO ........ 15.00 6.75
❑ 161 John Hetki ............ 15.00 6.75
❑ 162 Herman Wehmeier .... 15.00 6.75
❑ 163 Frank House ............ 15.00 6.75
❑ 164 Stu Miller ............ 25.00 11.00
❑ 165 Jim Pendleton ............ 15.00 6.75
❑ 166 Johnny Podres ............ 40.00 18.00
❑ 167 Don Lund ............ 15.00 6.75
❑ 168 Morrie Martin ............ 25.00 11.00
❑ 169 Jim Hughes ............ 40.00 18.00
❑ 170 James(Dusty) Rhodes RC 25.00 11.00
❑ 171 Leo Kiely ............ 15.00 6.75
❑ 172 Harold Brown ............ 15.00 6.75
❑ 173 Jack Harshman ............ 15.00 6.75
❑ 174 Tom Qualters ............ 15.00 6.75
❑ 175 Frank Leja RC ............ 25.00 11.00
❑ 176 Robert Keely CO ........ 15.00 6.75
❑ 177 Bob Milliken ............ 15.00 6.75
❑ 178 Bill Glynn UER ............ 15.00 6.75
(Spelled Gylnn on the front)
❑ 179 Gair Allie ............ 15.00 6.75
❑ 180 Wes Westrum ............ 25.00 11.00
❑ 181 Mel Roach ............ 15.00 6.75
❑ 182 Chuck Harmon ............ 15.00 6.75
❑ 183 Earle Combs CO ........ 25.00 11.00
❑ 184 Ed Bailey ............ 15.00 6.75
❑ 185 Chuck Stobbs ............ 15.00 6.75
❑ 186 Karl Olson ............ 15.00 6.75
❑ 187 Heinie Manush CO .... 25.00 11.00
❑ 188 Dave Jolly ............ 15.00 6.75
❑ 189 Bob Ross ............ 15.00 6.75
❑ 190 Ray Herbert ............ 15.00 6.75
❑ 191 John(Dick) Schofield RC 25.00 11.00
❑ 192 Ellis Deal CO ............ 15.00 6.75
❑ 193 Johnny Hopp CO ........ 25.00 11.00
❑ 194 Bill Sarni ............ 15.00 6.75
❑ 195 Billy Consolo RC ........ 15.00 6.75
❑ 196 Stan Jok ............ 15.00 6.75
❑ 197 Lynwood Rowe CO .... 25.00 11.00
("Schoolboy")
❑ 198 Carl Sawatski ............ 15.00 6.75
❑ 199 Glenn(Rocky) Nelson 15.00 6.75
❑ 200 Larry Jansen ............ 25.00 11.00
❑ 201 Al Kaline RC ............ 750.00 350.00
❑ 202 Bob Purkey RC ............ 25.00 11.00
❑ 203 Harry Brecheen CO.... 25.00 11.00
❑ 204 Angel Scull ............ 15.00 6.75
❑ 205 Johnny Sain ............ 40.00 18.00
❑ 206 Ray Crone ............ 15.00 6.75
❑ 207 Tom Oliver CO ............ 15.00 6.75
❑ 208 Grady Hatton ............ 15.00 6.75
❑ 209 Chuck Thompson ..... 15.00 6.75
❑ 210 Bob Buhl RC ............ 25.00 11.00
❑ 211 Don Hoak ............ 25.00 11.00
❑ 212 Bob Micelotta ............ 15.00 6.75
❑ 213 Johnny Fitzpatrick CO 15.00 6.75
❑ 214 Arnie Portocarrero...... 15.00 6.75
❑ 215 Ed McGhee ............ 25.00 11.00
❑ 216 Al Sima ............ 15.00 6.75
❑ 217 Paul Schreiber CO .... 15.00 6.75
❑ 218 Fred Marsh ............ 15.00 6.75
❑ 219 Chuck Kress ............ 15.00 6.75
❑ 220 Ruben Gomez ............ 25.00 11.00
❑ 221 Dick Brodowski ............ 15.00 6.75
❑ 222 Bill Wilson ............ 15.00 6.75
❑ 223 Joe Haynes CO............ 15.00 6.75
❑ 224 Dick Weik ............ 15.00 6.75
❑ 225 Don Liddle ............ 15.00 6.75
❑ 226 Jehosie Heard ............ 25.00 11.00
❑ 227 Colonel Mills CO ............ 15.00 6.75
❑ 228 Gene Hermanski ........ 15.00 6.75
❑ 229 Bob Talbot ............ 15.00 6.75
❑ 230 Bob Kuzava ............ 25.00 11.00
❑ 231 Roy Smalley ............ 15.00 6.75
❑ 232 Lou Limmer ............ 15.00 6.75
❑ 233 Augie Galan CO ........ 15.00 6.75
❑ 234 Jerry Lynch RC ............ 15.00 6.75
❑ 235 Vern Law ............ 25.00 11.00
❑ 236 Paul Penson ............ 15.00 6.75
❑ 237 Mike Ryba CO ............ 15.00 6.75
❑ 238 Al Aber ............ 15.00 6.75
❑ 239 Bill Skowron RC ...... 100.00 45.00
❑ 240 Sam Mele ............ 25.00 11.00
❑ 241 Robert Miller ............ 15.00 6.75
❑ 242 Curt Roberts ............ 15.00 6.75
❑ 243 Ray Blades CO ............ 15.00 6.75
❑ 244 Leroy Wheat ............ 15.00 6.75
❑ 245 Roy Sievers ............ 25.00 11.00
❑ 246 Howie Fox ............ 15.00 6.75
❑ 247 Ed Mayo CO ............ 15.00 6.75
❑ 248 Al Smith RC ............ 25.00 11.00
❑ 249 Wilmer Mizell ............ 25.00 11.00
❑ 250 Ted Williams ............ 800.00 325.00

## 1955 Topps

| | NRMT | VG-E |
|---|---|---|
| COMPLETE SET (206) | 7200.00 | 3200.00 |
| COMMON CARD (1-150) | 12.00 | 5.50 |
| COMMON CARD (151-160) | 20.00 | 9.00 |
| COMMON CARD (161-210) | 30.00 | 13.50 |
| WRAP.(1-CENT, DATED) | 150.00 | 70.00 |
| WRAP.(1-CENT, UNDAT) | 50.00 | 22.00 |
| WRAP.(5-CENT, DATED) | 150.00 | 70.00 |
| WRAP.(5-CENT, UNDAT) | 100.00 | 45.00 |

❑ 1 Dusty Rhodes ............ 75.00 15.00
❑ 2 Ted Williams ............ 600.00 275.00
❑ 3 Art Fowler ............ 15.00 6.75
❑ 4 Al Kaline ............ 150.00 70.00
❑ 5 Jim Gilliam ............ 40.00 18.00
❑ 6 Stan Hack MG ............ 25.00 11.00
❑ 7 Jim Hegan ............ 15.00 6.75
❑ 8 Harold Smith ............ 12.00 5.50
❑ 9 Robert Miller ............ 12.00 5.50
❑ 10 Bob Keegan ............ 12.00 5.50
❑ 11 Ferris Fain ............ 15.00 6.75
❑ 12 Vernon(Jake) Thies...... 12.00 5.50
❑ 13 Fred Marsh ............ 12.00 5.50
❑ 14 Jim Finigan ............ 12.00 5.50
❑ 15 Jim Pendleton ............ 12.00 5.50
❑ 16 Roy Sievers ............ 15.00 6.75
❑ 17 Bobby Hofman ............ 12.00 5.50
❑ 18 Russ Kemmerer ............ 12.00 5.50
❑ 19 Billy Herman CO ............ 15.00 6.75
❑ 20 Andy Carey ............ 15.00 6.75
❑ 21 Alex Grammas ............ 12.00 5.50
❑ 22 Bill Skowron ............ 40.00 18.00
❑ 23 Jack Parks ............ 12.00 5.50
❑ 24 Hal Newhouser ............ 40.00 18.00
❑ 25 Johnny Podres ............ 25.00 11.00
❑ 26 Dick Groat ............ 15.00 6.75
❑ 27 Billy Gardner ............ 15.00 6.75
❑ 28 Ernie Banks ............ 175.00 80.00
❑ 29 Herman Wehmeier ...... 12.00 5.50
❑ 30 Vic Power ............ 15.00 6.75
❑ 31 Warren Spahn ............ 100.00 45.00
❑ 32 Warren McGhee ............ 12.00 5.50
❑ 33 Tom Qualters ............ 12.00 5.50
❑ 34 Wayne Terwilliger ........ 12.00 5.50
❑ 35 Dave Jolly ............ 12.00 5.50
❑ 36 Leo Kiely ............ 12.00 5.50
❑ 37 Joe Cunningham RC.... 15.00 6.75
❑ 38 Bob Turley ............ 15.00 6.75
❑ 39 Bill Glynn ............ 12.00 5.50
❑ 40 Don Hoak ............ 15.00 6.75
❑ 41 Chuck Stobbs ............ 12.00 5.50
❑ 42 John(Windy) McCall .... 12.00 5.50
❑ 43 Harvey Haddix ............ 15.00 6.75
❑ 44 Harold Valentine ............ 12.00 5.50
❑ 45 Hank Sauer ............ 15.00 6.75
❑ 46 Ted Kazanski ............ 12.00 5.50
❑ 47 Hank Aaron UER........ 350.00 160.00
(Birth incorrectly
listed as 2/10)
❑ 48 Bob Kennedy ............ 15.00 6.75
❑ 49 J.W. Porter ............ 12.00 5.50
❑ 50 Jackie Robinson ........ 350.00 160.00
❑ 51 Jim Hughes ............ 15.00 6.75
❑ 52 Bill Tremel ............ 12.00 5.50
❑ 53 Bill Taylor ............ 12.00 5.50
❑ 54 Lou Limmer ............ 12.00 5.50
❑ 55 Rip Repulski ............ 12.00 5.50
❑ 56 Ray Jablonski ............ 12.00 5.50
❑ 57 Billy O'Dell ............ 12.00 5.50
❑ 58 Jim Rivera ............ 12.00 5.50
❑ 59 Gair Allie ............ 12.00 5.50
❑ 60 Dean Stone ............ 12.00 5.50
❑ 61 Forrest Jacobs ............ 12.00 5.50
❑ 62 Thornton Kipper ............ 12.00 5.50
❑ 63 Joe Collins ............ 15.00 6.75
❑ 64 Gus Triandos RC ............ 15.00 6.75
❑ 65 Ray Boone ............ 15.00 6.75
❑ 66 Ron Jackson ............ 12.00 5.50
❑ 67 Wally Moon ............ 15.00 6.75
❑ 68 Jim Davis ............ 12.00 5.50
❑ 69 Ed Bailey ............ 15.00 6.75
❑ 70 Al Rosen ............ 15.00 6.75
❑ 71 Ruben Gomez ............ 12.00 5.50
❑ 72 Karl Olson ............ 12.00 5.50
❑ 73 Jack Shepard ............ 12.00 5.50
❑ 74 Bob Borkowski ............ 12.00 5.50
❑ 75 Sandy Amoros RC ! ...... 40.00 10.00
❑ 76 Howie Pollet ............ 12.00 5.50
❑ 77 Arnie Portocarrero........ 12.00 5.50
❑ 78 Gordon Jones ............ 12.00 5.50
❑ 79 Clyde(Danny) Schell .... 12.00 5.50
❑ 80 Bob Grim RC ............ 15.00 6.75
❑ 81 Gene Conley ............ 15.00 6.75
❑ 82 Chuck Harmon ............ 12.00 5.50
❑ 83 Tom Brewer ............ 12.00 5.50
❑ 84 Camilo Pascual RC ...... 15.00 6.75

❑ 85 Don Mossi RC 25.00 11.00
❑ 86 Bill Wilson 12.00 5.50
❑ 87 Frank House 12.00 5.50
❑ 88 Bob Skinner RC 15.00 6.75
❑ 89 Joe Frazier 15.00 6.75
❑ 90 Karl Spooner RC 15.00 6.75
❑ 91 Milt Bolling 12.00 5.50
❑ 92 Don Zimmer RC 25.00 11.00
❑ 93 Steve Bilko 12.00 5.50
❑ 94 Reno Bertoia 12.00 5.50
❑ 95 Preston Ward 12.00 5.50
❑ 96 Chuck Bishop 12.00 5.50
❑ 97 Carlos Paula 12.00 5.50
❑ 98 John Riddle CO 12.00 5.50
❑ 99 Frank Leja 12.00 5.50
❑ 100 Monte Irvin 40.00 18.00
❑ 101 Johnny Gray 12.00 5.50
❑ 102 Wally Westlake 12.00 5.50
❑ 103 Chuck White 12.00 5.50
❑ 104 Jack Harshman 12.00 5.50
❑ 105 Chuck Diering 12.00 5.50
❑ 106 Frank Sullivan 12.00 5.50
❑ 107 Curt Roberts 12.00 5.50
❑ 108 Al Walker 15.00 6.75
❑ 109 Ed Lopat 15.00 6.75
❑ 110 Gus Zernial 15.00 6.75
❑ 111 Bob Milliken 15.00 6.75
❑ 112 Nelson King 12.00 5.50
❑ 113 Harry Brecheen CO 15.00 6.75
❑ 114 Louis Ortiz 12.00 5.50
❑ 115 Ellis Kinder 12.00 5.50
❑ 116 Tom Hurd 12.00 5.50
❑ 117 Mel Roach 12.00 5.50
❑ 118 Bob Purkey 12.00 5.50
❑ 119 Bob Lennon 12.00 5.50
❑ 120 Ted Kluszewski 75.00 34.00
❑ 121 Bill Renna 12.00 5.50
❑ 122 Carl Sawatski 12.00 5.50
❑ 123 Sandy Koufax RC ! 800.00 350.00
❑ 124 Harmon Killebrew RC ! 250.00 110.00
❑ 125 Ken Boyer RC 60.00 27.00
❑ 126 Dick Hall 12.00 5.50
❑ 127 Dale Long RC 15.00 6.75
❑ 128 Ted Lepcio 12.00 5.50
❑ 129 Elvin Tappe 15.00 6.75
❑ 130 Mayo Smith MG 12.00 5.50
❑ 131 Grady Hatton 12.00 5.50
❑ 132 Bob Trice 12.00 5.50
❑ 133 Dave Hoskins 12.00 5.50
❑ 134 Joey Jay 15.00 6.75
❑ 135 Johnny O'Brien 15.00 6.75
❑ 136 Veston(Bunky) Stewart 12.00 5.50
❑ 137 Harry Elliott 12.00 5.50
❑ 138 Ray Herbert 12.00 5.50
❑ 139 Steve Kraly 12.00 5.50
❑ 140 Mel Parnell 15.00 6.75
❑ 141 Tom Wright 12.00 5.50
❑ 142 Jerry Lynch 15.00 6.75
❑ 143 John(Dick) Schofield 15.00 6.75
❑ 144 John(Joe) Amalfitano RC 12.00 5.50
❑ 145 Elmer Valo 12.00 5.50
❑ 146 Dick Donovan RC 12.00 5.50
❑ 147 Hugh Pepper 12.00 5.50
❑ 148 Hector Brown 12.00 5.50
❑ 149 Ray Crone 12.00 5.50
❑ 150 Mike Higgins MG 12.00 5.50
❑ 151 Ralph Kress CO 20.00 9.00
❑ 152 Harry Agganis RC 80.00 36.00
❑ 153 Bud Podbielan 25.00 11.00
❑ 154 Willie Miranda 20.00 9.00
❑ 155 Eddie Mathews 125.00 55.00
❑ 156 Joe Black 50.00 22.00
❑ 157 Robert Miller 20.00 9.00
❑ 158 Tommy Carroll 25.00 11.00
❑ 159 Johnny Schmitz 20.00 9.00
❑ 160 Ray Narleski RC 20.00 9.00
❑ 161 Chuck Tanner RC 40.00 18.00
❑ 162 Joe Coleman 30.00 13.50
❑ 163 Faye Throneberry 30.00 13.50
❑ 164 Roberto Clemente RC ! 2000.00 900.00
❑ 165 Don Johnson 30.00 13.50
❑ 166 Hank Bauer 75.00 34.00
❑ 167 Thomas Casagrande 30.00 13.50
❑ 168 Duane Pillette 30.00 13.50
❑ 169 Bob Oldis 40.00 18.00
❑ 170 Jim Pearce DP 15.00 6.75
❑ 171 Dick Brodowski 30.00 13.50
❑ 172 Frank Baumholtz DP 15.00 6.75
❑ 173 Bob Kline 30.00 13.50
❑ 174 Rudy Minarcin 30.00 13.50
❑ 175 Does not exist
❑ 176 Norm Zauchin 30.00 13.50
❑ 177 Al Robertson 30.00 13.50
❑ 178 Bobby Adams 30.00 13.50
❑ 179 Jim Bolger 30.00 13.50
❑ 180 Clem Labine 60.00 27.00
❑ 181 Roy McMillan 40.00 18.00
❑ 182 Humberto Robinson 30.00 13.50
❑ 183 Anthony Jacobs 30.00 13.50
❑ 184 Harry Perkowski DP 15.00 6.75
❑ 185 Don Ferrarese 30.00 13.50
❑ 186 Does not exist
❑ 187 Gil Hodges 150.00 70.00
❑ 188 Charlie Silvera DP 15.00 6.75
❑ 189 Phil Rizzuto 150.00 70.00
❑ 190 Gene Woodling 40.00 18.00
❑ 191 Eddie Stanky MG 40.00 18.00
❑ 192 Jim Delsing 40.00 18.00
❑ 193 Johnny Sain 60.00 27.00
❑ 194 Willie Mays 500.00 220.00
❑ 195 Ed Roebuck RC 60.00 27.00
❑ 196 Gale Wade 30.00 13.50
❑ 197 Al Smith 60.00 27.00
❑ 198 Yogi Berra 250.00 110.00
❑ 199 Odbert Hamric 60.00 27.00
❑ 200 Jackie Jensen 60.00 27.00
❑ 201 Sherman Lollar ! 30.00 13.50
❑ 202 Jim Owens 30.00 13.50
❑ 203 Does not exist
❑ 204 Frank Smith 30.00 13.50
❑ 205 Gene Freese RC 40.00 18.00
❑ 206 Pete Daley 30.00 13.50
❑ 207 Billy Consolo 30.00 13.50
❑ 208 Ray Moore 40.00 18.00
❑ 209 Does not exist
❑ 210 Duke Snider 500.00 150.00

## 1956 Topps

| | NRMT | VG-E |
|---|---|---|
| COMPLETE SET (340) | 7000.00 | 3200.00 |
| COMMON CARD (1-100) | 10.00 | 4.50 |
| COMMON CARD (101-180) | 12.00 | 5.50 |
| COMMON CARD (261-340) | 12.00 | 5.50 |
| COMMON CARD (181-260) | 15.00 | 6.75 |
| WRAP.(1-CENT) | 250.00 | 110.00 |
| WRAP.(1-CENT, REPEAT) | 100.00 | 45.00 |
| WRAPPER (5-CENT) | 200.00 | 90.00 |

❑ 1 William Harridge PRES RC ! 100.00 28.00
❑ 2 Warren Giles PRES RC 40.00 18.00
❑ 3 Elmer Valo 15.00 6.75
❑ 4 Carlos Paula 15.00 6.75
❑ 5 Ted Williams 400.00 180.00
❑ 6 Ray Boone 25.00 11.00
❑ 7 Ron Negray 10.00 4.50
❑ 8 Walter Alston MG RC 40.00 18.00
❑ 9 Ruben Gomez DP 9.00 4.00
❑ 10 Warren Spahn 80.00 36.00
❑ 11A Chicago Cubs 30.00 13.50
(Centered)
❑ 11B Cubs Team 80.00 36.00
(Dated 1955)
❑ 11C Cubs Team 30.00 13.50
(Name at far left)
❑ 12 Andy Carey 15.00 6.75
❑ 13 Roy Face 15.00 6.75
❑ 14 Ken Boyer DP 15.00 6.75
❑ 15 Ernie Banks DP 90.00 40.00
❑ 16 Hector Lopez RC 15.00 6.75
❑ 17 Gene Conley 15.00 6.75
❑ 18 Dick Donovan 10.00 4.50
❑ 19 Chuck Diering 10.00 4.50
❑ 20 Al Kaline 100.00 45.00
❑ 21 Joe Collins DP 15.00 6.75
❑ 22 Jim Finigan 10.00 4.50
❑ 23 Fred Marsh 10.00 4.50
❑ 24 Dick Groat 15.00 6.75
❑ 25 Ted Kluszewski 75.00 34.00
❑ 26 Grady Hatton 10.00 4.50
❑ 27 Nelson Burbrink 10.00 4.50
❑ 28 Bobby Hofman 10.00 4.50
❑ 29 Jack Harshman 10.00 4.50
❑ 30 Jackie Robinson DP 200.00 90.00
❑ 31 Hank Aaron UER 300.00 135.00
(Small photo
actually Willie Mays)
❑ 32 Frank House 10.00 4.50
❑ 33 Roberto Clemente 375.00 170.00
❑ 34 Tom Brewer 10.00 4.50
❑ 35 Al Rosen 15.00 6.75
❑ 36 Rudy Minarcin 15.00 6.75
❑ 37 Alex Grammas 10.00 4.50
❑ 38 Bob Kennedy 15.00 6.75
❑ 39 Don Mossi 15.00 6.75
❑ 40 Bob Turley 15.00 6.75
❑ 41 Hank Sauer 15.00 6.75
❑ 42 Sandy Amoros 25.00 11.00
❑ 43 Ray Moore 10.00 4.50
❑ 44 Windy McCall 10.00 4.50
❑ 45 Gus Zernial 15.00 6.75
❑ 46 Gene Freese DP 9.00 4.00
❑ 47 Art Fowler 10.00 4.50
❑ 48 Jim Hegan 15.00 6.75
❑ 49 Pedro Ramos 10.00 4.50
❑ 50 Dusty Rhodes 15.00 6.75
❑ 51 Ernie Oravetz 10.00 4.50
❑ 52 Bob Grim 15.00 6.75
❑ 53 Arnie Portocarrero 10.00 4.50
❑ 54 Bob Keegan 10.00 4.50
❑ 55 Wally Moon 15.00 6.75
❑ 56 Dale Long 15.00 6.75
❑ 57 Duke Maas 10.00 4.50
❑ 58 Ed Roebuck 25.00 11.00
❑ 59 Jose Santiago 10.00 4.50
❑ 60 Mayo Smith MG DP 9.00 4.00
❑ 61 Bill Skowron 25.00 11.00
❑ 62 Hal Smith 15.00 6.75
❑ 63 Roger Craig RC 40.00 18.00
❑ 64 Luis Arroyo RC 10.00 4.50
❑ 65 Johnny O'Brien 15.00 6.75
❑ 66 Bob Speake 10.00 4.50
❑ 67 Vic Power 15.00 6.75
❑ 68 Chuck Stobbs 10.00 4.50
❑ 69 Chuck Tanner 15.00 6.75
❑ 70 Jim Rivera 10.00 4.50
❑ 71 Frank Sullivan 10.00 4.50
❑ 72A Phillies Team 30.00 13.50
(Centered)
❑ 72B Phillies Team 80.00 36.00
(Dated 1955)
❑ 72C Phillies Team 30.00 13.50
(Name at far left)
❑ 73 Wayne Terwilliger 10.00 4.50
❑ 74 Jim King 10.00 4.50
❑ 75 Roy Sievers DP 15.00 6.75
❑ 76 Ray Crone 10.00 4.50
❑ 77 Harvey Haddix 15.00 6.75
❑ 78 Herman Wehmeier 10.00 4.50
❑ 79 Sandy Koufax 350.00 160.00
❑ 80 Gus Triandos DP 10.00 4.50
❑ 81 Wally Westlake 10.00 4.50
❑ 82 Bill Renna 10.00 4.50
❑ 83 Karl Spooner 15.00 6.75
❑ 84 Babe Birrer 10.00 4.50
❑ 85A Cleveland Indians 30.00 13.50
(Centered)
❑ 85B Indians Team 80.00 36.00
(Dated 1955)
❑ 85C Indians Team 30.00 13.50

(Name at far left)
❑ 86 Ray Jablonski DP .......... 9.00 4.00
❑ 87 Dean Stone .................. 10.00 4.50
❑ 88 Johnny Kucks RC ........ 15.00 6.75
❑ 89 Norm Zauchin .............. 10.00 4.50
❑ 90A Cincinnati Redlegs .... 30.00 13.50
Team (Centered)
❑ 90B Reds Team ............... 80.00 36.00
(Dated 1955)
❑ 90C Reds Team ............... 30.00 13.50
(Name at far left)
❑ 91 Gail Harris .................... 10.00 4.50
❑ 92 Bob(Red) Wilson .......... 10.00 4.50
❑ 93 George Susce .............. 10.00 4.50
❑ 94 Ron Kline ....................... 10.00 4.50
❑ 95A Milwaukee Braves ...... 40.00 18.00
Team (Centered)
❑ 95B Braves Team ........... 80.00 36.00
(Dated 1955)
❑ 95C Braves Team ........... 40.00 18.00
(Name at far left)
❑ 96 Bill Tremel ................... 10.00 4.50
❑ 97 Jerry Lynch .................. 15.00 6.75
❑ 98 Camilo Pascual ............ 15.00 6.75
❑ 99 Don Zimmer ................ 25.00 11.00
❑ 100A Baltimore Orioles .... 35.00 16.00
Team (centered)
❑ 100B Orioles Team .......... 80.00 36.00
(Dated 1955)
❑ 100C Orioles Team .......... 35.00 16.00
(Name at far left)
❑ 101 Roy Campanella ...... 150.00 70.00
❑ 102 Jim Davis .................... 12.00 5.50
❑ 103 Willie Miranda ............ 12.00 5.50
❑ 104 Bob Lennon ................ 12.00 5.50
❑ 105 Al Smith ...................... 12.00 5.50
❑ 106 Joe Astroth ................ 12.00 5.50
❑ 107 Eddie Mathews .......... 80.00 36.00
❑ 108 Laurin Pepper ............ 12.00 5.50
❑ 109 Enos Slaughter .......... 40.00 18.00
❑ 110 Yogi Berra .................. 150.00 70.00
❑ 111 Boston Red Sox ........ 35.00 16.00
Team Card
❑ 112 Dee Fondy .................. 12.00 5.50
❑ 113 Phil Rizzuto .............. 125.00 55.00
❑ 114 Jim Owens ................ 15.00 6.75
❑ 115 Jackie Jensen ............ 15.00 6.75
❑ 116 Eddie O'Brien ............ 12.00 5.50
❑ 117 Virgil Trucks .............. 15.00 6.75
❑ 118 Nellie Fox .................. 60.00 27.00
❑ 119 Larry Jackson RC ...... 15.00 6.75
❑ 120 Richie Ashburn .......... 60.00 27.00
❑ 121 Pittsburgh Pirates ...... 35.00 16.00
Team Card
❑ 122 Willard Nixon .............. 12.00 5.50
❑ 123 Roy McMillan .............. 15.00 6.75
❑ 124 Don Kaiser ................ 12.00 5.50
❑ 125 Minnie Minoso ............ 40.00 18.00
❑ 126 Jim Brady .................. 12.00 5.50
❑ 127 Willie Jones ................ 15.00 6.75
❑ 128 Eddie Yost .................. 15.00 6.75
❑ 129 Jake Martin ................ 12.00 5.50
❑ 130 Willie Mays .............. 300.00 135.00
❑ 131 Bob Roselli ................ 12.00 5.50
❑ 132 Bobby Avila ................ 12.00 5.50
❑ 133 Ray Narleski .............. 12.00 5.50
❑ 134 St. Louis Cardinals .... 35.00 16.00
Team Card
❑ 135 Mickey Mantle ........ 1400.00 650.00
❑ 136 Johnny Logan ............ 15.00 6.75
❑ 137 Al Silvera .................... 12.00 5.50
❑ 138 Johnny Antonelli ........ 15.00 6.75
❑ 139 Tommy Carroll ............ 15.00 6.75
❑ 140 Herb Score RC .......... 60.00 27.00
❑ 141 Joe Frazier ................ 12.00 5.50
❑ 142 Gene Baker ................ 12.00 5.50
❑ 143 Jim Piersall ................ 15.00 6.75
❑ 144 Leroy Powell .............. 12.00 5.50
❑ 145 Gil Hodges ................ 60.00 27.00
❑ 146 Washington Nationals 35.00 16.00
Team Card
❑ 147 Earl Torgeson ............ 12.00 5.50
❑ 148 Alvin Dark .................. 15.00 6.75
❑ 149 Dixie Howell .............. 12.00 5.50
❑ 150 Duke Snider ............ 125.00 55.00
❑ 151 Spook Jacobs ............ 15.00 6.75
❑ 152 Billy Hoeft .................. 15.00 6.75
❑ 153 Frank Thomas ............ 15.00 6.75
❑ 154 Dave Pope ................ 12.00 5.50
❑ 155 Harvey Kuenn ............ 15.00 6.75
❑ 156 Wes Westrum ............ 15.00 6.75
❑ 157 Dick Brodowski .......... 12.00 5.50
❑ 158 Wally Post .................. 15.00 6.75
❑ 159 Clint Courtney ............ 12.00 5.50
❑ 160 Billy Pierce ................ 15.00 6.75
❑ 161 Joe DeMaestri ............ 12.00 5.50
❑ 162 Dave(Gus) Bell .......... 15.00 6.75
❑ 163 Gene Woodling .......... 15.00 6.75
❑ 164 Harmon Killebrew .... 100.00 45.00
❑ 165 Red Schoendienst ...... 40.00 18.00
❑ 166 Brooklyn Dodgers .... 200.00 90.00
Team Card
❑ 167 Harry Dorish .............. 12.00 5.50
❑ 168 Sammy White ............ 12.00 5.50
❑ 169 Bob Nelson ................ 12.00 5.50
❑ 170 Bill Virdon .................. 15.00 6.75
❑ 171 Jim Wilson .................. 12.00 5.50
❑ 172 Frank Torre RC .......... 15.00 6.75
❑ 173 Johnny Podres .......... 25.00 11.00
❑ 174 Glen Gorbous ............ 12.00 5.50
❑ 175 Del Crandall .............. 15.00 6.75
❑ 176 Alex Kellner ................ 12.00 5.50
❑ 177 Hank Bauer ................ 25.00 11.00
❑ 178 Joe Black .................. 15.00 6.75
❑ 179 Harry Chiti .................. 12.00 5.50
❑ 180 Robin Roberts ............ 50.00 22.00
❑ 181 Billy Martin .................. 60.00 27.00
❑ 182 Paul Minner ................ 15.00 6.75
❑ 183 Stan Lopata ................ 20.00 9.00
❑ 184 Don Bessent .............. 20.00 9.00
❑ 185 Bill Bruton .................. 20.00 9.00
❑ 186 Ron Jackson .............. 15.00 6.75
❑ 187 Early Wynn ................ 50.00 22.00
❑ 188 Chicago White Sox .... 50.00 22.00
Team Card
❑ 189 Ned Garver ................ 15.00 6.75
❑ 190 Carl Furillo .................. 30.00 13.50
❑ 191 Frank Lary .................. 20.00 9.00
❑ 192 Smoky Burgess .......... 20.00 9.00
❑ 193 Wilmer Mizell .............. 20.00 9.00
❑ 194 Monte Irvin ................ 30.00 13.50
❑ 195 George Kell ................ 30.00 13.50
❑ 196 Tom Poholsky ............ 15.00 6.75
❑ 197 Granny Hamner .......... 15.00 6.75
❑ 198 Ed Fitzgerald .............. 15.00 6.75
❑ 199 Hank Thompson ........ 20.00 9.00
❑ 200 Bob Feller ................ 100.00 45.00
❑ 201 Rip Repulski .............. 15.00 6.75
❑ 202 Jim Hearn .................. 15.00 6.75
❑ 203 Bill Tuttle .................. 15.00 6.75
❑ 204 Art Swanson .............. 15.00 6.75
❑ 205 Whitey Lockman ........ 20.00 9.00
❑ 206 Erv Palica .................. 15.00 6.75
❑ 207 Jim Small .................. 15.00 6.75
❑ 208 Elston Howard ............ 60.00 27.00
❑ 209 Max Surkont .............. 15.00 6.75
❑ 210 Mike Garcia ................ 20.00 9.00
❑ 211 Murry Dickson ............ 15.00 6.75
❑ 212 Johnny Temple .......... 15.00 6.75
❑ 213 Detroit Tigers .............. 60.00 27.00
Team Card
❑ 214 Bob Rush .................. 15.00 6.75
❑ 215 Tommy Byrne ............ 20.00 9.00
❑ 216 Jerry Schoonmaker .... 15.00 6.75
❑ 217 Billy Klaus .................. 15.00 6.75
❑ 218 Joe Nuxhall UER ........ 20.00 9.00
(Misspelled Nuxall)
❑ 219 Lew Burdette .............. 20.00 9.00
❑ 220 Del Ennis .................... 20.00 9.00
❑ 221 Bob Friend .................. 20.00 9.00
❑ 222 Dave Philley .............. 15.00 6.75
❑ 223 Randy Jackson .......... 15.00 6.75
❑ 224 Bud Podbielan ............ 15.00 6.75
❑ 225 Gil McDougald ............ 50.00 22.00
❑ 226 New York Giants ........ 75.00 34.00
Team Card
❑ 227 Russ Meyer ................ 15.00 6.75
❑ 228 Mickey Vernon ............ 20.00 9.00
❑ 229 Harry Brecheen CO .... 20.00 9.00
❑ 230 Chico Carrasquel ...... 15.00 6.75
❑ 231 Bob Hale .................... 15.00 6.75
❑ 232 Toby Atwell ................ 15.00 6.75
❑ 233 Carl Erskine ................ 30.00 13.50
❑ 234 Pete Runnels .............. 15.00 6.75
❑ 235 Don Newcombe .......... 50.00 22.00
❑ 236 Kansas City Athletics 35.00 16.00
Team Card
❑ 237 Jose Valdivielso ........ 15.00 6.75
❑ 238 Walt Dropo ................ 20.00 9.00
❑ 239 Harry Simpson .......... 15.00 6.75
❑ 240 Whitey Ford ............ 125.00 55.00
❑ 241 Don Mueller UER ...... 20.00 9.00
(6~ tall)
❑ 242 Hershell Freeman ...... 15.00 6.75
❑ 243 Sherm Lollar .............. 20.00 9.00
❑ 244 Bob Buhl .................... 30.00 13.50
❑ 245 Billy Goodman ............ 20.00 9.00
❑ 246 Tom Gorman .............. 15.00 6.75
❑ 247 Bill Sarni .................... 15.00 6.75
❑ 248 Bob Porterfield .......... 15.00 6.75
❑ 249 Johnny Klippstein ...... 15.00 6.75
❑ 250 Larry Doby .................. 30.00 13.50
❑ 251 New York Yankees .. 250.00 110.00
Team Card UER
(Don Larsen misspelled
as Larson on front)
❑ 252 Vern Law .................... 20.00 9.00
❑ 253 Irv Noren .................... 30.00 13.50
❑ 254 George Crowe ............ 15.00 6.75
❑ 255 Bob Lemon ................ 50.00 22.00
❑ 256 Tom Hurd .................. 15.00 6.75
❑ 257 Bobby Thomson ........ 30.00 13.50
❑ 258 Art Ditmar .................. 15.00 6.75
❑ 259 Sam Jones ................ 20.00 9.00
❑ 260 Pee Wee Reese ...... 125.00 55.00
❑ 261 Bobby Shantz ............ 15.00 6.75
❑ 262 Howie Pollet .............. 12.00 5.50
❑ 263 Bob Miller .................. 12.00 5.50
❑ 264 Ray Monzant .............. 12.00 5.50
❑ 265 Sandy Consuegra ...... 12.00 5.50
❑ 266 Don Ferrarese ............ 12.00 5.50
❑ 267 Bob Nieman .............. 12.00 5.50
❑ 268 Dale Mitchell .............. 15.00 6.75
❑ 269 Jack Meyer ................ 12.00 5.50
❑ 270 Billy Loes .................. 15.00 6.75
❑ 271 Foster Castleman ...... 12.00 5.50
❑ 272 Danny O'Connell ........ 12.00 5.50
❑ 273 Walker Cooper .......... 12.00 5.50
❑ 274 Frank Baumholtz ........ 12.00 5.50
❑ 275 Jim Greengrass .......... 12.00 5.50
❑ 276 George Zuverink ........ 12.00 5.50
❑ 277 Daryl Spencer ............ 12.00 5.50
❑ 278 Chet Nichols .............. 12.00 5.50
❑ 279 Johnny Groth .............. 12.00 5.50
❑ 280 Jim Gilliam .................. 40.00 18.00
❑ 281 Art Houtteman ............ 12.00 5.50
❑ 282 Warren Hacker .......... 12.00 5.50
❑ 283 Hal Smith RC ............ 15.00 6.75
❑ 284 Ike Delock .................. 12.00 5.50
❑ 285 Eddie Miksis .............. 12.00 5.50
❑ 286 Bill Wight .................... 12.00 5.50
❑ 287 Bobby Adams ............ 12.00 5.50
❑ 288 Bob Cerv .................... 40.00 18.00
❑ 289 Hal Jeffcoat ................ 12.00 5.50
❑ 290 Curt Simmons ............ 15.00 6.75
❑ 291 Frank Kellert .............. 12.00 5.50
❑ 292 Luis Aparicio RC ! .... 150.00 70.00
❑ 293 Stu Miller .................... 25.00 11.00
❑ 294 Ernie Johnson ............ 15.00 6.75
❑ 295 Clem Labine .............. 15.00 6.75
❑ 296 Andy Seminick .......... 12.00 5.50
❑ 297 Bob Skinner ................ 15.00 6.75
❑ 298 Johnny Schmitz .......... 12.00 5.50
❑ 299 Charlie Neal .............. 40.00 18.00
❑ 300 Vic Wertz .................... 15.00 6.75
❑ 301 Marv Grissom ............ 12.00 5.50
❑ 302 Eddie Robinson .......... 12.00 5.50
❑ 303 Jim Dyck .................... 12.00 5.50
❑ 304 Frank Malzone .......... 15.00 6.75
❑ 305 Brooks Lawrence ...... 12.00 5.50
❑ 306 Curt Roberts .............. 12.00 5.50
❑ 307 Hoyt Wilhelm .............. 40.00 18.00
❑ 308 Chuck Harmon .......... 12.00 5.50
❑ 309 Don Blasingame RC .. 15.00 6.75
❑ 310 Steve Gromek ............ 12.00 5.50
❑ 311 Hal Naragon .............. 12.00 5.50
❑ 312 Andy Pafko ................ 15.00 6.75
❑ 313 Gene Stephens .......... 12.00 5.50

❑ 314 Hobie Landrith 12.00 5.50
❑ 315 Milt Bolling 12.00 5.50
❑ 316 Jerry Coleman 15.00 6.75
❑ 317 Al Aber 12.00 5.50
❑ 318 Fred Hatfield 12.00 5.50
❑ 319 Jack Crimian 12.00 5.50
❑ 320 Joe Adcock 15.00 6.75
❑ 321 Jim Konstanty 15.00 6.75
❑ 322 Karl Olson 12.00 5.50
❑ 323 Willard Schmidt 12.00 5.50
❑ 324 Rocky Bridges 15.00 6.75
❑ 325 Don Liddle 12.00 5.50
❑ 326 Connie Johnson 12.00 5.50
❑ 327 Bob Wiesler 12.00 5.50
❑ 328 Preston Ward 12.00 5.50
❑ 329 Lou Berberet 12.00 5.50
❑ 330 Jim Busby 15.00 6.75
❑ 331 Dick Hall 12.00 5.50
❑ 332 Don Larsen 60.00 27.00
❑ 333 Rube Walker 12.00 5.50
❑ 334 Bob Miller 15.00 6.75
❑ 335 Don Hoak 15.00 6.75
❑ 336 Ellis Kinder 12.00 5.50
❑ 337 Bobby Morgan 12.00 5.50
❑ 338 Jim Delsing 12.00 5.50
❑ 339 Rance Pless 12.00 5.50
❑ 340 Mickey McDermott 60.00 12.00
❑ NNO Checklist 1/3 275.00 90.00
❑ NNO Checklist 2/4 275.00 90.00

## 1957 Topps

| | NRMT | VG-E |
|---|---|---|
| COMPLETE SET (407) | 7000.00 | 3200.00 |
| COMMON CARD (1-88) | 10.00 | 4.50 |
| COMMON CARD (89-176) | 8.00 | 3.60 |
| COMMON CARD (177-264) | 8.00 | 3.60 |
| COMMON CARD (265-352) | 20.00 | 9.00 |
| COMMON CARD (353-407) | 8.00 | 3.60 |
| COMMON DP (265-352) | 13.00 | 5.75 |
| WRAPPER (1-CENT) | 300.00 | 135.00 |
| WRAPPER (5-CENT) | 200.00 | 90.00 |

❑ 1 Ted Williams 500.00 150.00
❑ 2 Yogi Berra 135.00 60.00
❑ 3 Dale Long 20.00 9.00
❑ 4 Johnny Logan 20.00 9.00
❑ 5 Sal Maglie 20.00 9.00
❑ 6 Hector Lopez 15.00 6.75
❑ 7 Luis Aparicio 30.00 13.50
❑ 8 Don Mossi 15.00 6.75
❑ 9 Johnny Temple 15.00 6.75
❑ 10 Willie Mays 225.00 100.00
❑ 11 George Zuverink 10.00 4.50
❑ 12 Dick Groat 20.00 9.00
❑ 13 Wally Burnette 10.00 4.50
❑ 14 Bob Nieman 10.00 4.50
❑ 15 Robin Roberts 30.00 13.50
❑ 16 Walt Moryn 10.00 4.50
❑ 17 Billy Gardner 10.00 4.50
❑ 18 Don Drysdale RC ! 225.00 100.00
❑ 19 Bob Wilson 10.00 4.50
❑ 20 Hank Aaron UER 250.00 110.00
(Reverse negative photo on front)
❑ 21 Frank Sullivan 10.00 4.50
❑ 22 Jerry Snyder UER 10.00 4.50
(Photo actually Ed Fitzgerald)
❑ 23 Sherm Lollar 15.00 6.75
❑ 24 Bill Mazeroski RC 75.00 34.00
❑ 25 Whitey Ford 100.00 45.00
❑ 26 Bob Boyd 10.00 4.50
❑ 27 Ted Kazanski 10.00 4.50
❑ 28 Gene Conley 15.00 6.75
❑ 29 Whitey Herzog RC 30.00 13.50
❑ 30 Pee Wee Reese 75.00 34.00
❑ 31 Ron Northey 10.00 4.50
❑ 32 Hershell Freeman 10.00 4.50
❑ 33 Jim Small 10.00 4.50
❑ 34 Tom Sturdivant 15.00 6.75
❑ 35 Frank Robinson RC ! 200.00 90.00
❑ 36 Bob Grim 10.00 4.50
❑ 37 Frank Torre 15.00 6.75
❑ 38 Nellie Fox 50.00 22.00
❑ 39 Al Worthington 10.00 4.50
❑ 40 Early Wynn 30.00 13.50
❑ 41 Hal W. Smith 10.00 4.50
❑ 42 Dee Fondy 10.00 4.50
❑ 43 Connie Johnson 10.00 4.50
❑ 44 Joe DeMaestri 10.00 4.50
❑ 45 Carl Furillo 30.00 13.50
❑ 46 Robert J. Miller 10.00 4.50
❑ 47 Don Blasingame 10.00 4.50
❑ 48 Bill Bruton 15.00 6.75
❑ 49 Daryl Spencer 10.00 4.50
❑ 50 Herb Score 30.00 13.50
❑ 51 Clint Courtney 10.00 4.50
❑ 52 Lee Walls 10.00 4.50
❑ 53 Clem Labine 20.00 9.00
❑ 54 Elmer Valo 10.00 4.50
❑ 55 Ernie Banks 125.00 55.00
❑ 56 Dave Sisler 10.00 4.50
❑ 57 Jim Lemon 15.00 6.75
❑ 58 Ruben Gomez 10.00 4.50
❑ 59 Dick Williams 15.00 6.75
❑ 60 Billy Hoeft 15.00 6.75
❑ 61 Dusty Rhodes 15.00 6.75
❑ 62 Billy Martin 50.00 22.00
❑ 63 Ike Delock 10.00 4.50
❑ 64 Pete Runnels 15.00 6.75
❑ 65 Wally Moon 15.00 6.75
❑ 66 Brooks Lawrence 10.00 4.50
❑ 67 Chico Carrasquel 10.00 4.50
❑ 68 Ray Crone 10.00 4.50
❑ 69 Roy McMillan 15.00 6.75
❑ 70 Richie Ashburn 50.00 22.00
❑ 71 Murry Dickson 10.00 4.50
❑ 72 Bill Tuttle 10.00 4.50
❑ 73 George Crowe 10.00 4.50
❑ 74 Vito Valentinetti 10.00 4.50
❑ 75 Jimmy Piersall 15.00 6.75
❑ 76 Roberto Clemente 300.00 135.00
❑ 77 Paul Foytack 10.00 4.50
❑ 78 Vic Wertz 15.00 6.75
❑ 79 Lindy McDaniel RC 15.00 6.75
❑ 80 Gil Hodges 50.00 22.00
❑ 81 Herman Wehmeier 10.00 4.50
❑ 82 Elston Howard 30.00 13.50
❑ 83 Lou Skizas 10.00 4.50
❑ 84 Moe Drabowsky 15.00 6.75
❑ 85 Larry Doby 30.00 13.50
❑ 86 Bill Sarni 10.00 4.50
❑ 87 Tom Gorman 10.00 4.50
❑ 88 Harvey Kuenn 15.00 6.75
❑ 89 Roy Sievers 15.00 6.75
❑ 90 Warren Spahn 90.00 40.00
❑ 91 Mack Burk 8.00 3.60
❑ 92 Mickey Vernon 15.00 6.75
❑ 93 Hal Jeffcoat 8.00 3.60
❑ 94 Bobby Del Greco 8.00 3.60
❑ 95 Mickey Mantle 1000.00 450.00
❑ 96 Hank Aguirre 8.00 3.60
❑ 97 New York Yankees 90.00 40.00
Team Card
❑ 98 Alvin Dark 15.00 6.75
❑ 99 Bob Keegan 8.00 3.60
❑ 100 League Presidents 15.00 6.75
Warren Giles
Will Harridge
❑ 101 Chuck Stobbs 8.00 3.60
❑ 102 Ray Boone 15.00 6.75
❑ 103 Joe Nuxhall 15.00 6.75
❑ 104 Hank Foiles 8.00 3.60
❑ 105 Johnny Antonelli 15.00 6.75
❑ 106 Ray Moore 8.00 3.60
❑ 107 Jim Rivera 8.00 3.60
❑ 108 Tommy Byrne 15.00 6.75
❑ 109 Hank Thompson 8.00 3.60
❑ 110 Bill Virdon 15.00 6.75
❑ 111 Hal R. Smith 8.00 3.60
❑ 112 Tom Brewer 8.00 3.60
❑ 113 Wilmer Mizell 15.00 6.75
❑ 114 Milwaukee Braves 20.00 9.00
Team Card
❑ 115 Jim Gilliam 15.00 6.75
❑ 116 Mike Fornieles 8.00 3.60
❑ 117 Joe Adcock 20.00 9.00
❑ 118 Bob Porterfield 8.00 3.60
❑ 119 Stan Lopata 8.00 3.60
❑ 120 Bob Lemon 30.00 13.50
❑ 121 Clete Boyer RC 30.00 13.50
❑ 122 Ken Boyer 20.00 9.00
❑ 123 Steve Ridzik 8.00 3.60
❑ 124 Dave Philley 8.00 3.60
❑ 125 Al Kaline 100.00 45.00
❑ 126 Bob Wiesler 8.00 3.60
❑ 127 Bob Buhl 15.00 6.75
❑ 128 Ed Bailey 15.00 6.75
❑ 129 Saul Rogovin 8.00 3.60
❑ 130 Don Newcombe 20.00 9.00
❑ 131 Milt Bolling 8.00 3.60
❑ 132 Art Ditmar 15.00 6.75
❑ 133 Del Crandall 15.00 6.75
❑ 134 Don Kaiser 8.00 3.60
❑ 135 Bill Skowron 20.00 9.00
❑ 136 Jim Hegan 15.00 6.75
❑ 137 Bob Rush 8.00 3.60
❑ 138 Minnie Minoso 20.00 9.00
❑ 139 Lou Kretlow 8.00 3.60
❑ 140 Frank Thomas 15.00 6.75
❑ 141 Al Aber 8.00 3.60
❑ 142 Charley Thompson 8.00 3.60
❑ 143 Andy Pafko 15.00 6.75
❑ 144 Ray Narleski 8.00 3.60
❑ 145 Al Smith 8.00 3.60
❑ 146 Don Ferrarese 8.00 3.60
❑ 147 Al Walker 8.00 3.60
❑ 148 Don Mueller 15.00 6.75
❑ 149 Bob Kennedy 15.00 6.75
❑ 150 Bob Friend 15.00 6.75
❑ 151 Willie Miranda 8.00 3.60
❑ 152 Jack Harshman 8.00 3.60
❑ 153 Karl Olson 8.00 3.60
❑ 154 Red Schoendienst 30.00 13.50
❑ 155 Jim Brosnan 15.00 6.75
❑ 156 Gus Triandos 15.00 6.75
❑ 157 Wally Post 15.00 6.75
❑ 158 Curt Simmons 15.00 6.75
❑ 159 Solly Drake 8.00 3.60
❑ 160 Billy Pierce 15.00 6.75
❑ 161 Pittsburgh Pirates 15.00 6.75
Team Card
❑ 162 Jack Meyer 8.00 3.60
❑ 163 Sammy White 8.00 3.60
❑ 164 Tommy Carroll 8.00 3.60
❑ 165 Ted Kluszewski 90.00 40.00
❑ 166 Roy Face 15.00 6.75
❑ 167 Vic Power 15.00 6.75
❑ 168 Frank Lary 15.00 6.75
❑ 169 Herb Plews 8.00 3.60
❑ 170 Duke Snider 125.00 55.00
❑ 171 Boston Red Sox 15.00 6.75
Team Card
❑ 172 Gene Woodling 15.00 6.75
❑ 173 Roger Craig 15.00 6.75
❑ 174 Willie Jones 8.00 3.60
❑ 175 Don Larsen 30.00 13.50
❑ 176A Gene Baker ERR 350.00 160.00
(Misspelled Bakep on card back)
❑ 176B Gene Baker COR 15.00 6.75
❑ 177 Eddie Yost 15.00 6.75
❑ 178 Don Bessent 8.00 3.60
❑ 179 Ernie Oravetz 8.00 3.60
❑ 180 Gus Bell 15.00 6.75
❑ 181 Dick Donovan 8.00 3.60
❑ 182 Hobie Landrith 8.00 3.60
❑ 183 Chicago Cubs 15.00 6.75
Team Card

❑ 184 Tito Francona RC 8.00 3.60
❑ 185 Johnny Kucks 15.00 6.75
❑ 186 Jim King 15.00 6.75
❑ 187 Virgil Trucks 15.00 6.75
❑ 188 Felix Mantilla RC 15.00 6.75
❑ 189 Willard Nixon 8.00 3.60
❑ 190 Randy Jackson 8.00 3.60
❑ 191 Joe Margoneri 8.00 3.60
❑ 192 Jerry Coleman 15.00 6.75
❑ 193 Del Rice 8.00 3.60
❑ 194 Hal Brown 8.00 3.60
❑ 195 Bobby Avila 8.00 3.60
❑ 196 Larry Jackson 15.00 6.75
❑ 197 Hank Sauer 15.00 6.75
❑ 198 Detroit Tigers Team Card 15.00 6.75
❑ 199 Vern Law 15.00 6.75
❑ 200 Gil McDougald 15.00 6.75
❑ 201 Sandy Amoros 15.00 6.75
❑ 202 Dick Gernert 8.00 3.60
❑ 203 Hoyt Wilhelm 30.00 13.50
❑ 204 Kansas City Athletics Team Card 15.00 6.75
❑ 205 Charlie Maxwell 15.00 6.75
❑ 206 Willard Schmidt 8.00 3.60
❑ 207 Gordon(Billy) Hunter 8.00 3.60
❑ 208 Lou Burdette 15.00 6.75
❑ 209 Bob Skinner 15.00 6.75
❑ 210 Roy Campanella 150.00 70.00
❑ 211 Camilo Pascual 15.00 6.75
❑ 212 Rocky Colavito RC ! 150.00 70.00
❑ 213 Les Moss 8.00 3.60
❑ 214 Philadelphia Phillies Team Card 15.00 6.75
❑ 215 Enos Slaughter 30.00 13.50
❑ 216 Marv Grissom 8.00 3.60
❑ 217 Gene Stephens 8.00 3.60
❑ 218 Ray Jablonski 8.00 3.60
❑ 219 Tom Acker 8.00 3.60
❑ 220 Jackie Jensen 20.00 9.00
❑ 221 Dixie Howell 8.00 3.60
❑ 222 Alex Grammas 8.00 3.60
❑ 223 Frank House 8.00 3.60
❑ 224 Marv Blaylock 8.00 3.60
❑ 225 Harry Simpson 8.00 3.60
❑ 226 Preston Ward 8.00 3.60
❑ 227 Gerry Staley 8.00 3.60
❑ 228 Smoky Burgess UER 15.00 6.75
(Misspelled Smokey on card back)
❑ 229 George Susce 8.00 3.60
❑ 230 George Kell 30.00 13.50
❑ 231 Solly Hemus 8.00 3.60
❑ 232 Whitey Lockman 15.00 6.75
❑ 233 Art Fowler 8.00 3.60
❑ 234 Dick Cole 8.00 3.60
❑ 235 Tom Poholsky 8.00 3.60
❑ 236 Joe Ginsberg 8.00 3.60
❑ 237 Foster Castleman 8.00 3.60
❑ 238 Eddie Robinson 8.00 3.60
❑ 239 Tom Morgan 8.00 3.60
❑ 240 Hank Bauer 15.00 6.75
❑ 241 Joe Lonnett 8.00 3.60
❑ 242 Charlie Neal 15.00 6.75
❑ 243 St. Louis Cardinals Team Card 15.00 6.75
❑ 244 Billy Loes 15.00 6.75
❑ 245 Rip Repulski 8.00 3.60
❑ 246 Jose Valdivielso 8.00 3.60
❑ 247 Turk Lown 8.00 3.60
❑ 248 Jim Finigan 8.00 3.60
❑ 249 Dave Pope 8.00 3.60
❑ 250 Eddie Mathews 50.00 22.00
❑ 251 Baltimore Orioles Team Card 15.00 6.75
❑ 252 Carl Erskine 15.00 6.75
❑ 253 Gus Zernial 15.00 6.75
❑ 254 Ron Negray 8.00 3.60
❑ 255 Charlie Silvera 15.00 6.75
❑ 256 Ron Kline 8.00 3.60
❑ 257 Walt Dropo 8.00 3.60
❑ 258 Steve Gromek 8.00 3.60
❑ 259 Eddie O'Brien 8.00 3.60
❑ 260 Del Ennis 15.00 6.75
❑ 261 Bob Chakales 8.00 3.60
❑ 262 Bobby Thomson 15.00 6.75
❑ 263 George Strickland 8.00 3.60
❑ 264 Bob Turley 15.00 6.75
❑ 265 Harvey Haddix DP 13.00 5.75
❑ 266 Ken Kuhn DP 13.00 5.75
❑ 267 Danny Kravitz 20.00 9.00
❑ 268 Jack Collum 20.00 9.00
❑ 269 Bob Cerv 30.00 13.50
❑ 270 Washington Senators Team Card 60.00 27.00
❑ 271 Danny O'Connell DP 13.00 5.75
❑ 272 Bobby Shantz 30.00 13.50
❑ 273 Jim Davis 20.00 9.00
❑ 274 Don Hoak 15.00 6.75
❑ 275 Cleveland Indians Team Card UER 60.00 27.00
(Text on back credits Tribe with winning AL title in '28; the Yankees won that year.)
❑ 276 Jim Pyburn 20.00 9.00
❑ 277 Johnny Podres DP 45.00 20.00
❑ 278 Fred Hatfield DP 13.00 5.75
❑ 279 Bob Thurman 20.00 9.00
❑ 280 Alex Kellner 20.00 9.00
❑ 281 Gail Harris 20.00 9.00
❑ 282 Jack Dittmer DP 13.00 5.75
❑ 283 Wes Covington DP 13.00 5.75
❑ 284 Don Zimmer 45.00 20.00
❑ 285 Ned Garver 20.00 9.00
❑ 286 Bobby Richardson RC 125.00 55.00
❑ 287 Sam Jones 20.00 9.00
❑ 288 Ted Lepcio 20.00 9.00
❑ 289 Jim Bolger DP 13.00 5.75
❑ 290 Andy Carey DP 40.00 18.00
❑ 291 Windy McCall 20.00 9.00
❑ 292 Billy Klaus 20.00 9.00
❑ 293 Ted Abernathy 20.00 9.00
❑ 294 Rocky Bridges DP 13.00 5.75
❑ 295 Joe Collins DP 40.00 18.00
❑ 296 Johnny Klippstein 20.00 9.00
❑ 297 Jack Crimian 20.00 9.00
❑ 298 Irv Noren DP 13.00 5.75
❑ 299 Chuck Harmon 20.00 9.00
❑ 300 Mike Garcia 30.00 13.50
❑ 301 Sammy Esposito DP 20.00 9.00
❑ 302 Sandy Koufax DP 300.00 135.00
❑ 303 Billy Goodman 30.00 13.50
❑ 304 Joe Cunningham 30.00 13.50
❑ 305 Chico Fernandez 20.00 9.00
❑ 306 Darrell Johnson DP 13.00 5.75
❑ 307 Jack D. Phillips DP 13.00 5.75
❑ 308 Dick Hall 20.00 9.00
❑ 309 Jim Busby DP 13.00 5.75
❑ 310 Max Surkont DP 13.00 5.75
❑ 311 Al Pilarcik DP 13.00 5.75
❑ 312 Tony Kubek DP RC ! 90.00 40.00
❑ 313 Mel Parnell 15.00 6.75
❑ 314 Ed Bouchee DP 13.00 5.75
❑ 315 Lou Berberet DP 13.00 5.75
❑ 316 Billy O'Dell 20.00 9.00
❑ 317 New York Giants Team Card 75.00 34.00
❑ 318 Mickey McDermott 20.00 9.00
❑ 319 Gino Cimoli RC 20.00 9.00
❑ 320 Neil Chrisley 20.00 9.00
❑ 321 John(Red) Murff 20.00 9.00
❑ 322 Cincinnati Reds Team Card 75.00 34.00
❑ 323 Wes Westrum 30.00 13.50
❑ 324 Brooklyn Dodgers Team Card 125.00 55.00
❑ 325 Frank Bolling 20.00 9.00
❑ 326 Pedro Ramos 20.00 9.00
❑ 327 Jim Pendleton 20.00 9.00
❑ 328 Brooks Robinson RC ! 400.00 180.00
❑ 329 Chicago White Sox Team Card 60.00 27.00
❑ 330 Jim Wilson 20.00 9.00
❑ 331 Ray Katt 20.00 9.00
❑ 332 Bob Bowman 20.00 9.00
❑ 333 Ernie Johnson 20.00 9.00
❑ 334 Jerry Schoonmaker 20.00 9.00
❑ 335 Granny Hamner 20.00 9.00
❑ 336 Haywood Sullivan RC 40.00 18.00
❑ 337 Rene Valdes 20.00 9.00
❑ 338 Jim Bunning RC 125.00 55.00
❑ 339 Bob Speake 20.00 9.00
❑ 340 Bill Wight 20.00 9.00
❑ 341 Don Gross 20.00 9.00
❑ 342 Gene Mauch 30.00 13.50
❑ 343 Taylor Phillips 15.00 6.75
❑ 344 Paul LaPalme 20.00 9.00
❑ 345 Paul Smith 20.00 9.00
❑ 346 Dick Littlefield 20.00 9.00
❑ 347 Hal Naragon 20.00 9.00
❑ 348 Jim Hearn 20.00 9.00
❑ 349 Nellie King 20.00 9.00
❑ 350 Eddie Miksis 20.00 9.00
❑ 351 Dave Hillman 20.00 9.00
❑ 352 Ellis Kinder 20.00 9.00
❑ 353 Cal Neeman 8.00 3.60
❑ 354 W. (Rip) Coleman 8.00 3.60
❑ 355 Frank Malzone 15.00 6.75
❑ 356 Faye Throneberry 8.00 3.60
❑ 357 Earl Torgeson 8.00 3.60
❑ 358 Jerry Lynch 15.00 6.75
❑ 359 Tom Cheney 8.00 3.60
❑ 360 Johnny Groth 8.00 3.60
❑ 361 Curt Barclay 8.00 3.60
❑ 362 Roman Mejias 15.00 6.75
❑ 363 Eddie Kasko 8.00 3.60
❑ 364 Cal McLish 15.00 6.75
❑ 365 Ozzie Virgil 8.00 3.60
❑ 366 Ken Lehman 8.00 3.60
❑ 367 Ed Fitzgerald 8.00 3.60
❑ 368 Bob Purkey 8.00 3.60
❑ 369 Milt Graff 8.00 3.60
❑ 370 Warren Hacker 8.00 3.60
❑ 371 Bob Lennon 8.00 3.60
❑ 372 Norm Zauchin 8.00 3.60
❑ 373 Pete Whisenant 8.00 3.60
❑ 374 Don Cardwell 8.00 3.60
❑ 375 Jim Landis 15.00 6.75
❑ 376 Don Elston 8.00 3.60
❑ 377 Andre Rodgers 8.00 3.60
❑ 378 Elmer Singleton 8.00 3.60
❑ 379 Don Lee 8.00 3.60
❑ 380 Walker Cooper 8.00 3.60
❑ 381 Dean Stone 8.00 3.60
❑ 382 Jim Brideweser 8.00 3.60
❑ 383 Juan Pizarro 8.00 3.60
❑ 384 Bobby G. Smith 8.00 3.60
❑ 385 Art Houtteman 8.00 3.60
❑ 386 Lyle Luttrell 8.00 3.60
❑ 387 Jack Sanford RC 15.00 6.75
❑ 388 Pete Daley 8.00 3.60
❑ 389 Dave Jolly 8.00 3.60
❑ 390 Reno Bertoia 8.00 3.60
❑ 391 Ralph Terry RC 15.00 6.75
❑ 392 Chuck Tanner 15.00 6.75
❑ 393 Raul Sanchez 8.00 3.60
❑ 394 Luis Arroyo 15.00 6.75
❑ 395 Bubba Phillips 8.00 3.60
❑ 396 Casey Wise 8.00 3.60
❑ 397 Roy Smalley 8.00 3.60
❑ 398 Al Cicotte 15.00 6.75
❑ 399 Billy Consolo 8.00 3.60
❑ 400 Dodgers' Sluggers 250.00 110.00
Carl Furillo
Gil Hodges
Roy Campanella
Duke Snider
❑ 401 Earl Battey RC 15.00 6.75
❑ 402 Jim Pisoni 8.00 3.60
❑ 403 Dick Hyde 8.00 3.60
❑ 404 Harry Anderson 8.00 3.60
❑ 405 Duke Maas 8.00 3.60
❑ 406 Bob Hale 8.00 3.60
❑ 407 Yankee Power Hitters 500.00 150.00
Mickey Mantle
Yogi Berra
❑ CC1 Contest Card 90.00 22.00
Saturday, May 4th
Boston Red Sox vs. Cleveland Indians
Cincinnati Redlegs vs. New York Giants
❑ CC2 Contest Card 90.00 22.00
Saturday, May 25th
Detroit Tigers vs. Kansas City Athletics
Pittsburgh Pirates vs. Philadelphia Phillies

❑ CC3 Contest Card ......... 120.00 30.00
Saturday, June 22nd
Brooklyn Dodgers
vs. St. Louis Cardinals
Chicago White Sox
vs. New York Yankees
❑ CC4 Contest Card ......... 120.00 30.00
Saturday, July 19th
Milwaukee Braves
vs. New York Giants
Baltimore Orioles
vs. Kansas City Athletics
❑ NNO Checklist 1/2 ......... 250.00 75.00
❑ NNO Checklist 2/3 ......... 400.00 100.00
❑ NNO Checklist 3/4 ......... 750.00 170.00
❑ NNO Checklist 4/5 ......... 900.00 200.00
❑ NNO Lucky Penny Charm 100.00 45.00
and Key Chain
offer card

## 1958 Topps

| | NRMT | VG-E |
|---|---|---|
| COMP. MASTER SET (534) | 12000.00 | |
| COMPLETE SET (494) | 4800.00 | 2200.00 |
| COMMON CARD (1-110) | 12.00 | 5.50 |
| COMMON CARD (111-495) | 8.00 | 3.60 |
| WRAPPER (1-CENT) | 100.00 | 45.00 |
| WRAPPER (5-CENT) | 125.00 | 55.00 |

❑ 1 Ted Williams ............... 500.00 180.00
❑ 2A Bob Lemon ............... 30.00 13.50
❑ 2B Bob Lemon YT ........... 60.00 27.00
❑ 3 Alex Kellner ............... 12.00 5.50
❑ 4 Hank Foiles ............... 12.00 5.50
❑ 5 Willie Mays ............... 225.00 100.00
❑ 6 George Zuverink ........... 12.00 5.50
❑ 7 Dale Long ............... 15.00 6.75
❑ 8A Eddie Kasko ............... 12.00 5.50
❑ 8B Eddie Kasko YL ......... 45.00 20.00
❑ 9 Hank Bauer ............... 20.00 9.00
❑ 10 Lou Burdette ............... 20.00 9.00
❑ 11A Jim Rivera ............... 12.00 5.50
❑ 11B Jim Rivera YT ........... 45.00 20.00
❑ 12 George Crowe ............... 12.00 5.50
❑ 13A Billy Hoeft ............... 12.00 5.50
❑ 13B Billy Hoeft YL ........... 45.00 20.00
❑ 14 Rip Repulski ............... 12.00 5.50
❑ 15 Jim Lemon ............... 15.00 6.75
❑ 16 Charlie Neal ............... 15.00 6.75
❑ 17 Felix Mantilla ............... 12.00 5.50
❑ 18 Frank Sullivan ............... 12.00 5.50
❑ 19 New York Giants ......... 40.00 8.00
Team Card
(Checklist on back)
❑ 20A Gil McDougald ......... 20.00 9.00
❑ 20B Gil McDougald YL...... 60.00 27.00
❑ 21 Curt Barclay ............... 12.00 5.50
❑ 22 Hal Naragon ............... 12.00 5.50
❑ 23A Bill Tuttle ............... 12.00 5.50
❑ 23B Bill Tuttle YL ............ 45.00 20.00
❑ 24A Hobie Landrith ......... 12.00 5.50
❑ 24B Hobie Landrith YL...... 45.00 20.00
❑ 25 Don Drysdale ............. 75.00 34.00
❑ 26 Ron Jackson ............... 12.00 5.50
❑ 27 Bud Freeman ............... 12.00 5.50
❑ 28 Jim Busby ............... 12.00 5.50
❑ 29 Ted Lepcio ............... 12.00 5.50
❑ 30A Hank Aaron ............. 200.00 90.00
❑ 30B Hank Aaron YL ......... 500.00 220.00
❑ 31 Tex Clevenger ............. 12.00 5.50
❑ 32A J.W. Porter ............... 12.00 5.50
❑ 32B J.W. Porter YL ......... 45.00 20.00
❑ 33A Cal Neeman ............... 12.00 5.50
❑ 33B Cal Neeman YT ......... 45.00 20.00
❑ 34 Bob Thurman ............... 12.00 5.50
❑ 35A Don Mossi ............... 15.00 6.75
❑ 35B Don Mossi YT ........... 45.00 20.00
❑ 36 Ted Kazanski ............... 12.00 5.50
❑ 37 Mike McCormick UER RC 15.00 6.75
(Photo actually
Ray Monzant)
❑ 38 Dick Gernert ............... 12.00 5.50
❑ 39 Bob Martyn ............... 12.00 5.50
❑ 40 George Kell ............... 30.00 13.50
❑ 41 Dave Hillman ............... 12.00 5.50
❑ 42 John Roseboro RC ! .... 30.00 13.50
❑ 43 Sal Maglie ............... 15.00 6.75
❑ 44 Washington Senators .. 20.00 4.00
Team Card
(Checklist on back)
❑ 45 Dick Groat ............... 15.00 6.75
❑ 46A Lou Sleater ............... 12.00 5.50
❑ 46B Lou Sleater YL ......... 45.00 20.00
❑ 47 Roger Maris RC ! ...... 400.00 180.00
❑ 48 Chuck Harmon ............ 12.00 5.50
❑ 49 Smoky Burgess ........... 15.00 6.75
❑ 50A Billy Pierce ............... 15.00 6.75
❑ 50B Billy Pierce YT ......... 45.00 20.00
❑ 51 Del Rice ............... 12.00 5.50
❑ 52A Roberto Clemente.... 300.00 135.00
❑ 52B Roberto Clemente YT 500.00 220.00
❑ 53A Morrie Martin ............ 12.00 5.50
❑ 53B Morrie Martin YL ........ 45.00 20.00
❑ 54 Norm Siebern RC ........ 20.00 9.00
❑ 55 Chico Carrasquel ........ 12.00 5.50
❑ 56 Bill Fischer ............... 12.00 5.50
❑ 57A Tim Thompson ........... 12.00 5.50
❑ 57B Tim Thompson YL .... 45.00 20.00
❑ 58A Art Schult ............... 12.00 5.50
❑ 58B Art Schult YT ............ 45.00 20.00
❑ 59 Dave Sisler ............... 12.00 5.50
❑ 60A Del Ennis ............... 15.00 6.75
❑ 60B Del Ennis YL ............ 45.00 20.00
❑ 61A Darrell Johnson ......... 12.00 5.50
❑ 61B Darrell Johnson YL .... 45.00 20.00
❑ 62 Joe DeMaestri ............ 12.00 5.50
❑ 63 Joe Nuxhall ............... 15.00 6.75
❑ 64 Joe Lonnett ............... 12.00 5.50
❑ 65A Von McDaniel RC ...... 12.00 5.50
❑ 65B Von McDaniel YL RC 45.00 20.00
❑ 66 Lee Walls ............... 12.00 5.50
❑ 67 Joe Ginsberg ............. 12.00 5.50
❑ 68 Daryl Spencer ............ 12.00 5.50
❑ 69 Wally Burnette ............ 12.00 5.50
❑ 70A Al Kaline ............... 100.00 45.00
❑ 70B Al Kaline YL ........... 250.00 110.00
❑ 71 Dodgers Team ........... 60.00 12.00
(Checklist on back)
❑ 72 Bud Byerly ............... 12.00 5.50
❑ 73 Pete Daley ............... 12.00 5.50
❑ 74 Roy Face ............... 15.00 6.75
❑ 75 Gus Bell ............... 15.00 6.75
❑ 76A Dick Farrell ............... 12.00 5.50
❑ 76B Dick Farrell YT ......... 45.00 20.00
❑ 77A Don Zimmer ............. 15.00 6.75
❑ 77B Don Zimmer YT ........ 45.00 20.00
❑ 78A Ernie Johnson ........... 15.00 6.75
❑ 78B Ernie Johnson YL ...... 45.00 20.00
❑ 79A Dick Williams ........... 15.00 6.75
❑ 79B Dick Williams YT........ 45.00 20.00
❑ 80 Dick Drott ............... 12.00 5.50
❑ 81A Steve Boros RC ......... 12.00 5.50
❑ 81B Steve Boros YT RC .. 45.00 20.00
❑ 82 Ron Kline ............... 12.00 5.50
❑ 83 Bob Hazle RC ............ 12.00 5.50
❑ 84 Billy O'Dell ............... 12.00 5.50
❑ 85A Luis Aparicio ............ 30.00 13.50
❑ 85B Luis Aparicio YT ........ 75.00 34.00
❑ 86 Valmy Thomas ............ 12.00 5.50
❑ 87 Johnny Kucks ............ 12.00 5.50
❑ 88 Duke Snider ............... 75.00 34.00
❑ 89 Billy Klaus ............... 12.00 5.50
❑ 90 Robin Roberts ............ 30.00 13.50
❑ 91 Chuck Tanner ............. 15.00 6.75
❑ 92A Clint Courtney ........... 12.00 5.50
❑ 92B Clint Courtney YL ...... 45.00 20.00
❑ 93 Sandy Amoros ............ 15.00 6.75
❑ 94 Bob Skinner ............... 15.00 6.75
❑ 95 Frank Bolling ............... 12.00 5.50
❑ 96 Joe Durham ............... 12.00 5.50
❑ 97A Larry Jackson ........... 12.00 5.50
❑ 97B Larry Jackson YL ...... 45.00 20.00
❑ 98A Billy Hunter ............... 12.00 5.50
❑ 98B Billy Hunter YL ......... 45.00 20.00
❑ 99 Bobby Adams ............. 12.00 5.50
❑ 100A Early Wynn ............. 30.00 13.50
❑ 100B Early Wynn YT ........ 75.00 34.00
❑ 101A Bobby Richardson .. 30.00 13.50
❑ 101B Bobby Richardson YL 60.00 27.00
❑ 102 George Strickland ...... 12.00 5.50
❑ 103 Jerry Lynch ............... 15.00 6.75
❑ 104 Jim Pendleton ........... 12.00 5.50
❑ 105 Billy Gardner ............ 12.00 5.50
❑ 106 Dick Schofield ........... 15.00 6.75
❑ 107 Ossie Virgil ............... 12.00 5.50
❑ 108A Jim Landis ............... 12.00 5.50
❑ 108B Jim Landis YT ......... 45.00 20.00
❑ 109 Herb Plews ............... 12.00 5.50
❑ 110 Johnny Logan ............ 15.00 6.75
❑ 111 Stu Miller ............... 10.00 4.50
❑ 112 Gus Zernial ............... 10.00 4.50
❑ 113 Jerry Walker RC ......... 8.00 3.60
❑ 114 Irv Noren ............... 10.00 4.50
❑ 115 Jim Bunning ............. 30.00 13.50
❑ 116 Dave Philley ............. 8.00 3.60
❑ 117 Frank Torre ............... 10.00 4.50
❑ 118 Harvey Haddix ........... 10.00 4.50
❑ 119 Harry Chiti ............... 8.00 3.60
❑ 120 Johnny Podres .......... 10.00 4.50
❑ 121 Eddie Miksis ............. 8.00 3.60
❑ 122 Walt Moryn ............... 8.00 3.60
❑ 123 Dick Tomanek ............ 8.00 3.60
❑ 124 Bobby Usher ............. 8.00 3.60
❑ 125 Alvin Dark ............... 10.00 4.50
❑ 126 Stan Palys ............... 8.00 3.60
❑ 127 Tom Sturdivant .......... 10.00 4.50
❑ 128 Willie Kirkland ........... 8.00 3.60
❑ 129 Jim Derrington ........... 8.00 3.60
❑ 130 Jackie Jensen ........... 10.00 4.50
❑ 131 Bob Henrich ............... 8.00 3.60
❑ 132 Vern Law ............... 10.00 4.50
❑ 133 Russ Nixon RC ........... 8.00 3.60
❑ 134 Philadelphia Phillies .. 15.00 3.00
Team Card
(Checklist on back)
❑ 135 Mike(Moe) Drabowsky 10.00 4.50
❑ 136 Jim Finigan ............... 8.00 3.60
❑ 137 Russ Kemmerer .......... 8.00 3.60
❑ 138 Earl Torgeson ............ 8.00 3.60
❑ 139 George Brunet ........... 8.00 3.60
❑ 140 Wes Covington .......... 10.00 4.50
❑ 141 Ken Lehman ............... 8.00 3.60
❑ 142 Enos Slaughter ......... 25.00 11.00
❑ 143 Billy Muffett RC .......... 8.00 3.60
❑ 144 Bobby Morgan ............ 8.00 3.60
❑ 145 Never issued ...............
❑ 146 Dick Gray ............... 8.00 3.60
❑ 147 Don McMahon RC ....... 8.00 3.60
❑ 148 Billy Consolo ............ 8.00 3.60
❑ 149 Tom Acker ............... 8.00 3.60
❑ 150 Mickey Mantle .......... 800.00 350.00
❑ 151 Buddy Pritchard ......... 8.00 3.60
❑ 152 Johnny Antonelli ........ 10.00 4.50
❑ 153 Les Moss ............... 8.00 3.60
❑ 154 Harry Byrd ............... 8.00 3.60
❑ 155 Hector Lopez ............ 10.00 4.50
❑ 156 Dick Hyde ............... 8.00 3.60
❑ 157 Dee Fondy ............... 8.00 3.60
❑ 158 Cleveland Indians ...... 15.00 3.00
Team Card
(Checklist on back)
❑ 159 Taylor Phillips ........... 8.00 3.60
❑ 160 Don Hoak ............... 10.00 4.50
❑ 161 Don Larsen ............... 15.00 6.75
❑ 162 Gil Hodges ............... 40.00 18.00
❑ 163 Jim Wilson ............... 8.00 3.60
❑ 164 Bob Taylor ............... 8.00 3.60
❑ 165 Bob Nieman ............... 8.00 3.60
❑ 166 Danny O'Connell ......... 8.00 3.60

| | No. | Card | NrMT | VG-E |
|---|---|---|---|---|
| ❑ | 167 | Frank Baumann | 8.00 | 3.60 |
| ❑ | 168 | Joe Cunningham | 8.00 | 3.60 |
| ❑ | 169 | Ralph Terry | 10.00 | 4.50 |
| ❑ | 170 | Vic Wertz | 10.00 | 4.50 |
| ❑ | 171 | Harry Anderson | 8.00 | 3.60 |
| ❑ | 172 | Don Gross | 8.00 | 3.60 |
| ❑ | 173 | Eddie Yost | 8.00 | 3.60 |
| ❑ | 174 | Athletics Team | 15.00 | 3.00 |
| | | (Checklist on back) | | |
| ❑ | 175 | Marv Throneberry RC | 15.00 | 6.75 |
| ❑ | 176 | Bob Buhl | 10.00 | 4.50 |
| ❑ | 177 | Al Smith | 8.00 | 3.60 |
| ❑ | 178 | Ted Kluszewski | 25.00 | 11.00 |
| ❑ | 179 | Willie Miranda | 8.00 | 3.60 |
| ❑ | 180 | Lindy McDaniel | 10.00 | 4.50 |
| ❑ | 181 | Willie Jones | 8.00 | 3.60 |
| ❑ | 182 | Joe Caffie | 8.00 | 3.60 |
| ❑ | 183 | Dave Jolly | 8.00 | 3.60 |
| ❑ | 184 | Elvin Tappe | 8.00 | 3.60 |
| ❑ | 185 | Ray Boone | 10.00 | 4.50 |
| ❑ | 186 | Jack Meyer | 8.00 | 3.60 |
| ❑ | 187 | Sandy Koufax | 225.00 | 100.00 |
| ❑ | 188 | Milt Bolling UER | 8.00 | 3.60 |
| | | (Photo actually Lou Berberet) | | |
| ❑ | 189 | George Susce | 8.00 | 3.60 |
| ❑ | 190 | Red Schoendienst | 25.00 | 11.00 |
| ❑ | 191 | Art Ceccarelli | 8.00 | 3.60 |
| ❑ | 192 | Milt Graff | 8.00 | 3.60 |
| ❑ | 193 | Jerry Lumpe RC | 8.00 | 3.60 |
| ❑ | 194 | Roger Craig | 10.00 | 4.50 |
| ❑ | 195 | Whitey Lockman | 10.00 | 4.50 |
| ❑ | 196 | Mike Garcia | 10.00 | 4.50 |
| ❑ | 197 | Haywood Sullivan | 10.00 | 4.50 |
| ❑ | 198 | Bill Virdon | 10.00 | 4.50 |
| ❑ | 199 | Don Blasingame | 8.00 | 3.60 |
| ❑ | 200 | Bob Keegan | 8.00 | 3.60 |
| ❑ | 201 | Jim Bolger | 8.00 | 3.60 |
| ❑ | 202 | Woody Held RC | 8.00 | 3.60 |
| ❑ | 203 | Al Walker | 8.00 | 3.60 |
| ❑ | 204 | Leo Kiely | 8.00 | 3.60 |
| ❑ | 205 | Johnny Temple | 10.00 | 4.50 |
| ❑ | 206 | Bob Shaw RC | 8.00 | 3.60 |
| ❑ | 207 | Solly Hemus | 8.00 | 3.60 |
| ❑ | 208 | Cal McLish | 8.00 | 3.60 |
| ❑ | 209 | Bob Anderson | 8.00 | 3.60 |
| ❑ | 210 | Wally Moon | 10.00 | 4.50 |
| ❑ | 211 | Pete Burnside | 8.00 | 3.60 |
| ❑ | 212 | Bubba Phillips | 8.00 | 3.60 |
| ❑ | 213 | Red Wilson | 8.00 | 3.60 |
| ❑ | 214 | Willard Schmidt | 8.00 | 3.60 |
| ❑ | 215 | Jim Gilliam | 15.00 | 6.75 |
| ❑ | 216 | St. Louis Cardinals | 15.00 | 3.00 |
| | | Team Card | | |
| | | (Checklist on back) | | |
| ❑ | 217 | Jack Harshman | 8.00 | 3.60 |
| ❑ | 218 | Dick Rand | 8.00 | 3.60 |
| ❑ | 219 | Camilo Pascual | 10.00 | 4.50 |
| ❑ | 220 | Tom Brewer | 8.00 | 3.60 |
| ❑ | 221 | Jerry Kindall RC | 8.00 | 3.60 |
| ❑ | 222 | Bud Daley | 8.00 | 3.60 |
| ❑ | 223 | Andy Pafko | 10.00 | 4.50 |
| ❑ | 224 | Bob Grim | 10.00 | 4.50 |
| ❑ | 225 | Billy Goodman | 10.00 | 4.50 |
| ❑ | 226 | Bob Smith | 8.00 | 3.60 |
| ❑ | 227 | Gene Stephens | 8.00 | 3.60 |
| ❑ | 228 | Duke Maas | 8.00 | 3.60 |
| ❑ | 229 | Frank Zupo | 8.00 | 3.60 |
| ❑ | 230 | Richie Ashburn | 40.00 | 18.00 |
| ❑ | 231 | Lloyd Merritt | 8.00 | 3.60 |
| ❑ | 232 | Reno Bertoia | 8.00 | 3.60 |
| ❑ | 233 | Mickey Vernon | 10.00 | 4.50 |
| ❑ | 234 | Carl Sawatski | 8.00 | 3.60 |
| ❑ | 235 | Tom Gorman | 8.00 | 3.60 |
| ❑ | 236 | Ed Fitzgerald | 8.00 | 3.60 |
| ❑ | 237 | Bill Wight | 8.00 | 3.60 |
| ❑ | 238 | Bill Mazeroski | 30.00 | 13.50 |
| ❑ | 239 | Chuck Stobbs | 8.00 | 3.60 |
| ❑ | 240 | Bill Skowron | 25.00 | 11.00 |
| ❑ | 241 | Dick Littlefield | 8.00 | 3.60 |
| ❑ | 242 | Johnny Klippstein | 8.00 | 3.60 |
| ❑ | 243 | Larry Raines | 8.00 | 3.60 |
| ❑ | 244 | Don Demeter | 8.00 | 3.60 |
| ❑ | 245 | Frank Lary | 10.00 | 4.50 |
| ❑ | 246 | New York Yankees | 100.00 | 20.00 |
| | | Team Card | | |
| | | (Checklist on back) | | |
| ❑ | 247 | Casey Wise | 8.00 | 3.60 |
| ❑ | 248 | Herman Wehmeier | 8.00 | 3.60 |
| ❑ | 249 | Ray Moore | 8.00 | 3.60 |
| ❑ | 250 | Roy Sievers | 10.00 | 4.50 |
| ❑ | 251 | Warren Hacker | 8.00 | 3.60 |
| ❑ | 252 | Bob Trowbridge | 8.00 | 3.60 |
| ❑ | 253 | Don Mueller | 10.00 | 4.50 |
| ❑ | 254 | Alex Grammas | 8.00 | 3.60 |
| ❑ | 255 | Bob Turley | 10.00 | 4.50 |
| ❑ | 256 | Chicago White Sox | 15.00 | 3.00 |
| | | Team Card | | |
| | | (Checklist on back) | | |
| ❑ | 257 | Hal Smith | 8.00 | 3.60 |
| ❑ | 258 | Carl Erskine | 15.00 | 6.75 |
| ❑ | 259 | Al Pilarcik | 8.00 | 3.60 |
| ❑ | 260 | Frank Malzone | 10.00 | 4.50 |
| ❑ | 261 | Turk Lown | 8.00 | 3.60 |
| ❑ | 262 | Johnny Groth | 8.00 | 3.60 |
| ❑ | 263 | Eddie Bressoud | 10.00 | 4.50 |
| ❑ | 264 | Jack Sanford | 10.00 | 4.50 |
| ❑ | 265 | Pete Runnels | 10.00 | 4.50 |
| ❑ | 266 | Connie Johnson | 8.00 | 3.60 |
| ❑ | 267 | Sherm Lollar | 10.00 | 4.50 |
| ❑ | 268 | Granny Hamner | 8.00 | 3.60 |
| ❑ | 269 | Paul Smith | 8.00 | 3.60 |
| ❑ | 270 | Warren Spahn | 60.00 | 27.00 |
| ❑ | 271 | Billy Martin | 40.00 | 18.00 |
| ❑ | 272 | Ray Crone | 8.00 | 3.60 |
| ❑ | 273 | Hal Smith | 8.00 | 3.60 |
| ❑ | 274 | Rocky Bridges | 8.00 | 3.60 |
| ❑ | 275 | Elston Howard | 15.00 | 6.75 |
| ❑ | 276 | Bobby Avila | 8.00 | 3.60 |
| ❑ | 277 | Virgil Trucks | 10.00 | 4.50 |
| ❑ | 278 | Mack Burk | 8.00 | 3.60 |
| ❑ | 279 | Bob Boyd | 8.00 | 3.60 |
| ❑ | 280 | Jim Piersall | 10.00 | 4.50 |
| ❑ | 281 | Sammy Taylor | 8.00 | 3.60 |
| ❑ | 282 | Paul Foytack | 8.00 | 3.60 |
| ❑ | 283 | Ray Shearer | 8.00 | 3.60 |
| ❑ | 284 | Ray Katt | 8.00 | 3.60 |
| ❑ | 285 | Frank Robinson | 100.00 | 45.00 |
| ❑ | 286 | Gino Cimoli | 8.00 | 3.60 |
| ❑ | 287 | Sam Jones | 10.00 | 4.50 |
| ❑ | 288 | Harmon Killebrew | 90.00 | 40.00 |
| ❑ | 289 | Lou Burdette | 10.00 | 4.50 |
| | | Bobby Shantz | | |
| ❑ | 290 | Dick Donovan | 8.00 | 3.60 |
| ❑ | 291 | Don Landrum | 8.00 | 3.60 |
| ❑ | 292 | Ned Garver | 8.00 | 3.60 |
| ❑ | 293 | Gene Freese | 8.00 | 3.60 |
| ❑ | 294 | Hal Jeffcoat | 8.00 | 3.60 |
| ❑ | 295 | Minnie Minoso | 25.00 | 11.00 |
| ❑ | 296 | Ryne Duren RC | 15.00 | 6.75 |
| ❑ | 297 | Don Buddin | 8.00 | 3.60 |
| ❑ | 298 | Jim Hearn | 8.00 | 3.60 |
| ❑ | 299 | Harry Simpson | 8.00 | 3.60 |
| ❑ | 300 | Will Harridge PRES | 15.00 | 6.75 |
| | | Warren Giles | | |
| ❑ | 301 | Randy Jackson | 8.00 | 3.60 |
| ❑ | 302 | Mike Baxes | 8.00 | 3.60 |
| ❑ | 303 | Neil Chrisley | 8.00 | 3.60 |
| ❑ | 304 | Harvey Kuenn | 25.00 | 11.00 |
| | | Al Kaline | | |
| ❑ | 305 | Clem Labine | 10.00 | 4.50 |
| ❑ | 306 | Whammy Douglas | 8.00 | 3.60 |
| ❑ | 307 | Brooks Robinson | 100.00 | 45.00 |
| ❑ | 308 | Paul Giel | 10.00 | 4.50 |
| ❑ | 309 | Gail Harris | 8.00 | 3.60 |
| ❑ | 310 | Ernie Banks | 100.00 | 45.00 |
| ❑ | 311 | Bob Purkey | 8.00 | 3.60 |
| ❑ | 312 | Boston Red Sox | 15.00 | 3.00 |
| | | Team Card | | |
| | | (Checklist on back) | | |
| ❑ | 313 | Bob Rush | 8.00 | 3.60 |
| ❑ | 314 | Duke Snider | 50.00 | 22.00 |
| | | Walt Alston MG | | |
| ❑ | 315 | Bob Friend | 10.00 | 4.50 |
| ❑ | 316 | Tito Francona | 10.00 | 4.50 |
| ❑ | 317 | Albie Pearson | 10.00 | 4.50 |
| ❑ | 318 | Frank House | 8.00 | 3.60 |
| ❑ | 319 | Lou Skizas | 8.00 | 3.60 |
| ❑ | 320 | Whitey Ford | 60.00 | 27.00 |
| ❑ | 321 | Sluggers Supreme | 75.00 | 34.00 |
| | | Ted Kluszewski | | |
| | | Ted Williams | | |
| ❑ | 322 | Harding Peterson | 10.00 | 4.50 |
| ❑ | 323 | Elmer Valo | 8.00 | 3.60 |
| ❑ | 324 | Hoyt Wilhelm | 25.00 | 11.00 |
| ❑ | 325 | Joe Adcock | 10.00 | 4.50 |
| ❑ | 326 | Bob Miller | 8.00 | 3.60 |
| ❑ | 327 | Chicago Cubs | 15.00 | 3.00 |
| | | Team Card | | |
| | | (Checklist on back) | | |
| ❑ | 328 | Ike Delock | 8.00 | 3.60 |
| ❑ | 329 | Bob Cerv | 10.00 | 4.50 |
| ❑ | 330 | Ed Bailey | 10.00 | 4.50 |
| ❑ | 331 | Pedro Ramos | 8.00 | 3.60 |
| ❑ | 332 | Jim King | 8.00 | 3.60 |
| ❑ | 333 | Andy Carey | 10.00 | 4.50 |
| ❑ | 334 | Bob Friend | 10.00 | 4.50 |
| | | Billy Pierce | | |
| ❑ | 335 | Ruben Gomez | 8.00 | 3.60 |
| ❑ | 336 | Bert Hamric | 8.00 | 3.60 |
| ❑ | 337 | Hank Aguirre | 8.00 | 3.60 |
| ❑ | 338 | Walt Dropo | 10.00 | 4.50 |
| ❑ | 339 | Fred Hatfield | 8.00 | 3.60 |
| ❑ | 340 | Don Newcombe | 15.00 | 6.75 |
| ❑ | 341 | Pittsburgh Pirates | 15.00 | 3.00 |
| | | Team Card | | |
| | | (Checklist on back) | | |
| ❑ | 342 | Jim Brosnan | 10.00 | 4.50 |
| ❑ | 343 | Orlando Cepeda RC | 100.00 | 45.00 |
| ❑ | 344 | Bob Porterfield | 8.00 | 3.60 |
| ❑ | 345 | Jim Hegan | 10.00 | 4.50 |
| ❑ | 346 | Steve Bilko | 8.00 | 3.60 |
| ❑ | 347 | Don Rudolph | 8.00 | 3.60 |
| ❑ | 348 | Chico Fernandez | 8.00 | 3.60 |
| ❑ | 349 | Murry Dickson | 8.00 | 3.60 |
| ❑ | 350 | Ken Boyer | 25.00 | 11.00 |
| ❑ | 351 | Braves Fence Busters | 40.00 | 18.00 |
| | | Del Crandall | | |
| | | Eddie Mathews | | |
| | | Hank Aaron | | |
| | | Joe Adcock | | |
| ❑ | 352 | Herb Score | 15.00 | 6.75 |
| ❑ | 353 | Stan Lopata | 8.00 | 3.60 |
| ❑ | 354 | Art Ditmar | 10.00 | 4.50 |
| ❑ | 355 | Bill Bruton | 10.00 | 4.50 |
| ❑ | 356 | Bob Malkmus | 8.00 | 3.60 |
| ❑ | 357 | Danny McDevitt | 8.00 | 3.60 |
| ❑ | 358 | Gene Baker | 8.00 | 3.60 |
| ❑ | 359 | Billy Loes | 10.00 | 4.50 |
| ❑ | 360 | Roy McMillan | 10.00 | 4.50 |
| ❑ | 361 | Mike Fornieles | 8.00 | 3.60 |
| ❑ | 362 | Ray Jablonski | 8.00 | 3.60 |
| ❑ | 363 | Don Elston | 8.00 | 3.60 |
| ❑ | 364 | Earl Battey | 8.00 | 3.60 |
| ❑ | 365 | Tom Morgan | 8.00 | 3.60 |
| ❑ | 366 | Gene Green | 8.00 | 3.60 |
| ❑ | 367 | Jack Urban | 8.00 | 3.60 |
| ❑ | 368 | Rocky Colavito | 50.00 | 22.00 |
| ❑ | 369 | Ralph Lumenti | 8.00 | 3.60 |
| ❑ | 370 | Yogi Berra | 100.00 | 45.00 |
| ❑ | 371 | Marty Keough | 8.00 | 3.60 |
| ❑ | 372 | Don Cardwell | 8.00 | 3.60 |
| ❑ | 373 | Joe Pignatano | 8.00 | 3.60 |
| ❑ | 374 | Brooks Lawrence | 8.00 | 3.60 |
| ❑ | 375 | Pee Wee Reese | 75.00 | 34.00 |
| ❑ | 376 | Charley Rabe | 8.00 | 3.60 |
| ❑ | 377A | Milwaukee Braves | 15.00 | 6.75 |
| | | Team Card | | |
| | | (Alphabetical) | | |
| ❑ | 377B | Milwaukee Team | 100.00 | 20.00 |
| | | numerical checklist | | |
| ❑ | 378 | Hank Sauer | 10.00 | 4.50 |
| ❑ | 379 | Ray Herbert | 8.00 | 3.60 |
| ❑ | 380 | Charlie Maxwell | 10.00 | 4.50 |
| ❑ | 381 | Hal Brown | 8.00 | 3.60 |
| ❑ | 382 | Al Cicotte | 8.00 | 3.60 |
| ❑ | 383 | Lou Berberet | 8.00 | 3.60 |
| ❑ | 384 | John Goryl | 8.00 | 3.60 |
| ❑ | 385 | Wilmer Mizell | 10.00 | 4.50 |
| ❑ | 386 | Birdie's Sluggers | 15.00 | 6.75 |
| | | Ed Bailey | | |
| | | Birdie Tebbetts MG | | |
| | | Frank Robinson | | |
| ❑ | 387 | Wally Post | 10.00 | 4.50 |
| ❑ | 388 | Billy Moran | 8.00 | 3.60 |
| ❑ | 389 | Bill Taylor | 8.00 | 3.60 |
| ❑ | 390 | Del Crandall | 10.00 | 4.50 |
| ❑ | 391 | Dave Melton | 8.00 | 3.60 |

❑ 392 Bennie Daniels ........... 8.00 3.60
❑ 393 Tony Kubek ............... 30.00 13.50
❑ 394 Jim Grant RC ............ 8.00 3.60
❑ 395 Willard Nixon ............. 8.00 3.60
❑ 396 Dutch Dotterer ............ 8.00 3.60
❑ 397A Detroit Tigers ......... 15.00 6.75
Team Card
(Alphabetical)
❑ 397B Detroit Team .......... 100.00 20.00
numerical checklist
❑ 398 Gene Woodling .......... 10.00 4.50
❑ 399 Marv Grissom ............ 8.00 3.60
❑ 400 Nellie Fox ................ 30.00 13.50
❑ 401 Don Bessent .............. 8.00 3.60
❑ 402 Bobby Gene Smith ...... 8.00 3.60
❑ 403 Steve Korcheck ........... 8.00 3.60
❑ 404 Curt Simmons ........... 10.00 4.50
❑ 405 Ken Aspromonte .......... 8.00 3.60
❑ 406 Vic Power ................ 10.00 4.50
❑ 407 Carlton Willey ........... 10.00 4.50
❑ 408A Baltimore Orioles .... 15.00 6.75
Team Card
(Alphabetical)
❑ 408B Baltimore Team .... 100.00 20.00
numerical checklist
❑ 409 Frank Thomas ........... 10.00 4.50
❑ 410 Murray Wall ............... 8.00 3.60
❑ 411 Tony Taylor RC .......... 10.00 4.50
❑ 412 Gerry Staley ............. 8.00 3.60
❑ 413 Jim Davenport RC ....... 8.00 3.60
❑ 414 Sammy White ............ 8.00 3.60
❑ 415 Bob Bowman .............. 8.00 3.60
❑ 416 Foster Castleman ........ 8.00 3.60
❑ 417 Carl Furillo ............... 15.00 6.75
❑ 418 Mickey Mantle .......... 300.00 135.00
Hank Aaron
❑ 419 Bobby Shantz ........... 10.00 4.50
❑ 420 Vada Pinson RC ........ 40.00 18.00
❑ 421 Dixie Howell ............. 8.00 3.60
❑ 422 Norm Zauchin ............ 8.00 3.60
❑ 423 Phil Clark .................. 8.00 3.60
❑ 424 Larry Doby ................ 25.00 11.00
❑ 425 Sammy Esposito .......... 8.00 3.60
❑ 426 Johnny O'Brien .......... 10.00 4.50
❑ 427 Al Worthington ............ 8.00 3.60
❑ 428A Cincinnati Reds ........ 15.00 6.75
Team Card
(Alphabetical)
❑ 428B Cincinnati Team .... 100.00 20.00
numerical checklist
❑ 429 Gus Triandos ............. 10.00 4.50
❑ 430 Bobby Thomson ....... 10.00 4.50
❑ 431 Gene Conley ............ 10.00 4.50
❑ 432 John Powers .............. 8.00 3.60
❑ 433A Pancho Herrer ERR 650.00 300.00
❑ 433B Pancho Herrera COR 10.00 4.50
❑ 434 Harvey Kuenn ........... 10.00 4.50
❑ 435 Ed Roebuck .............. 10.00 4.50
❑ 436 Willie Mays .............. 75.00 34.00
Duke Snider
❑ 437 Bob Speake ................ 8.00 3.60
❑ 438 Whitey Herzog ........... 10.00 4.50
❑ 439 Ray Narleski .............. 8.00 3.60
❑ 440 Eddie Mathews .......... 50.00 22.00
❑ 441 Jim Marshall ............ 10.00 4.50
❑ 442 Phil Paine .................. 8.00 3.60
❑ 443 Billy Harrell SP .......... 20.00 9.00
❑ 444 Danny Kravitz ............ 8.00 3.60
❑ 445 Bob Smith ................. 8.00 3.60
❑ 446 Carroll Hardy SP ....... 20.00 9.00
❑ 447 Ray Monzant .............. 8.00 3.60
❑ 448 Charlie Lau RC .......... 10.00 4.50
❑ 449 Gene Fodge ............... 8.00 3.60
❑ 450 Preston Ward SP ...... 20.00 9.00
❑ 451 Joe Taylor ................. 8.00 3.60
❑ 452 Roman Mejias ............ 8.00 3.60
❑ 453 Tom Qualters ............. 8.00 3.60
❑ 454 Harry Hanebrink .......... 8.00 3.60
❑ 455 Hal Griggs ................. 8.00 3.60
❑ 456 Dick Brown ................ 8.00 3.60
❑ 457 Milt Pappas RC ......... 10.00 4.50
❑ 458 Julio Becquer ............. 8.00 3.60
❑ 459 Ron Blackburn ............. 8.00 3.60
❑ 460 Chuck Essegian .......... 8.00 3.60
❑ 461 Ed Mayer ................... 8.00 3.60
❑ 462 Gary Geiger SP .......... 20.00 9.00
❑ 463 Vito Valentinetti ........... 8.00 3.60
❑ 464 Curt Flood RC ........... 30.00 13.50
❑ 465 Arnie Portocarrero ....... 8.00 3.60
❑ 466 Pete Whisenant ........... 8.00 3.60
❑ 467 Glen Hobbie ............... 8.00 3.60
❑ 468 Bob Schmidt ............... 8.00 3.60
❑ 469 Don Ferrarese ............. 8.00 3.60
❑ 470 R.C. Stevens ............... 8.00 3.60
❑ 471 Lenny Green ............... 8.00 3.60
❑ 472 Joey Jay .................. 10.00 4.50
❑ 473 Bill Renna .................. 8.00 3.60
❑ 474 Roman Semproch ........ 8.00 3.60
❑ 475 Fred Haney AS MG and 25.00 7.50
Casey Stengel AS MG
(Checklist back)
❑ 476 Stan Musial AS TP .... 50.00 22.00
❑ 477 Bill Skowron AS.......... 10.00 4.50
❑ 478 Johnny Temple AS ...... 8.00 3.60
❑ 479 Nellie Fox AS ........... 15.00 6.75
❑ 480 Eddie Mathews AS .... 25.00 11.00
❑ 481 Frank Malzone AS........ 8.00 3.60
❑ 482 Ernie Banks AS ......... 40.00 18.00
❑ 483 Luis Aparicio AS ........ 15.00 6.75
❑ 484 Frank Robinson AS .... 30.00 13.50
❑ 485 Ted Williams AS ...... 125.00 55.00
❑ 486 Willie Mays AS ......... 50.00 22.00
❑ 487 Mickey Mantle AS TP 175.00 80.00
❑ 488 Hank Aaron AS .......... 60.00 27.00
❑ 489 Jackie Jensen AS ...... 10.00 4.50
❑ 490 Ed Bailey AS ............... 8.00 3.60
❑ 491 Sherm Lollar AS .......... 8.00 3.60
❑ 492 Bob Friend AS ............ 8.00 3.60
❑ 493 Bob Turley AS ........... 10.00 4.50
❑ 494 Warren Spahn AS ...... 25.00 11.00
❑ 495 Herb Score AS .......... 15.00 3.00
❑ xx Contest Cards ........... 40.00 18.00

## 1959 Topps

| | NRMT | VG-E |
|---|---|---|
| COMPLETE SET (572) | 4500.00 | 2000.00 |
| COMMON CARD (1-110) | 6.00 | 2.70 |
| COMMON CARD (111-506) | 4.00 | 1.80 |
| COMMON CARD (507-572) | 16.00 | 7.25 |
| WRAPPER (1-CENT) | 125.00 | 55.00 |
| WRAPPER (5-CENT) | 100.00 | 45.00 |

❑ 1 Ford Frick COMM RC ! .. 60.00 16.50
❑ 2 Eddie Yost ..................... 8.00 3.60
❑ 3 Don McMahon ................ 8.00 3.60
❑ 4 Albie Pearson ............... 8.00 3.60
❑ 5 Dick Donovan ............... 8.00 3.60
❑ 6 Alex Grammas .............. 6.00 2.70
❑ 7 Al Pilarcik ..................... 6.00 2.70
❑ 8 Phillies Team ................ 75.00 15.00
(Checklist on back)
❑ 9 Paul Giel ....................... 8.00 3.60
❑ 10 Mickey Mantle ........... 700.00 325.00
❑ 11 Billy Hunter ................. 8.00 3.60
❑ 12 Vern Law .................... 8.00 3.60
❑ 13 Dick Gernert ................ 6.00 2.70
❑ 14 Pete Whisenant ............ 6.00 2.70
❑ 15 Dick Drott ................... 6.00 2.70
❑ 16 Joe Pignatano .............. 6.00 2.70
❑ 17 Frank Thomas ............. 8.00 3.60
Danny Murtaugh MG
Ted Kluszewski
❑ 18 Jack Urban .................. 6.00 2.70
❑ 19 Eddie Bressoud ............. 6.00 2.70
❑ 20 Duke Snider .............. 60.00 27.00
❑ 21 Connie Johnson ........... 6.00 2.70
❑ 22 Al Smith ...................... 8.00 3.60
❑ 23 Murry Dickson .............. 8.00 3.60
❑ 24 Red Wilson .................. 6.00 2.70
❑ 25 Don Hoak .................... 8.00 3.60
❑ 26 Chuck Stobbs .............. 6.00 2.70
❑ 27 Andy Pafko .................. 8.00 3.60
❑ 28 Al Worthington .............. 6.00 2.70
❑ 29 Jim Bolger ................... 6.00 2.70
❑ 30 Nellie Fox .................. 30.00 13.50
❑ 31 Ken Lehman ................. 6.00 2.70
❑ 32 Don Buddin .................. 6.00 2.70
❑ 33 Ed Fitzgerald ................ 6.00 2.70
❑ 34 Al Kaline .................. 20.00 9.00
Charley Maxwell
❑ 35 Ted Kluszewski ........... 12.00 5.50
❑ 36 Hank Aguirre ................ 6.00 2.70
❑ 37 Gene Green ................. 6.00 2.70
❑ 38 Morrie Martin ................ 6.00 2.70
❑ 39 Ed Bouchee .................. 6.00 2.70
❑ 40A Warren Spahn ERR .. 75.00 34.00
(Born 1931)
❑ 40B Warren Spahn ERR 100.00 45.00
(Born 1931, but three
is partially obscured)
❑ 40C Warren Spahn COR .. 60.00 27.00
(Born 1921)
❑ 41 Bob Martyn .................. 6.00 2.70
❑ 42 Murray Wall .................. 6.00 2.70
❑ 43 Steve Bilko ................... 6.00 2.70
❑ 44 Vito Valentinetti ............ 6.00 2.70
❑ 45 Andy Carey .................. 8.00 3.60
❑ 46 Bill R. Henry ................. 6.00 2.70
❑ 47 Jim Finigan .................. 6.00 2.70
❑ 48 Orioles Team .............. 24.00 4.80
(Checklist on back)
❑ 49 Bill Hall ........................ 6.00 2.70
❑ 50 Willie Mays ............... 125.00 55.00
❑ 51 Rip Coleman ................. 6.00 2.70
❑ 52 Coot Veal ..................... 6.00 2.70
❑ 53 Stan Williams RC .......... 8.00 3.60
❑ 54 Mel Roach .................... 6.00 2.70
❑ 55 Tom Brewer .................. 6.00 2.70
❑ 56 Carl Sawatski ............... 6.00 2.70
❑ 57 Al Cicotte ..................... 6.00 2.70
❑ 58 Eddie Miksis ................. 6.00 2.70
❑ 59 Irv Noren ...................... 8.00 3.60
❑ 60 Bob Turley .................... 8.00 3.60
❑ 61 Dick Brown ................... 6.00 2.70
❑ 62 Tony Taylor .................. 8.00 3.60
❑ 63 Jim Hearn ..................... 6.00 2.70
❑ 64 Joe DeMaestri ............... 6.00 2.70
❑ 65 Frank Torre ................... 8.00 3.60
❑ 66 Joe Ginsberg ................. 6.00 2.70
❑ 67 Brooks Lawrence .......... 6.00 2.70
❑ 68 Dick Schofield ............... 8.00 3.60
❑ 69 Giants Team ............... 24.00 4.80
(Checklist on back)
❑ 70 Harvey Kuenn ............... 8.00 3.60
❑ 71 Don Bessent ................. 6.00 2.70
❑ 72 Bill Renna ..................... 6.00 2.70
❑ 73 Ron Jackson .................. 8.00 3.60
❑ 74 Jim Lemon .................... 8.00 3.60
Cookie Lavagetto MG
Roy Sievers
❑ 75 Sam Jones .................... 8.00 3.60
❑ 76 Bobby Richardson ........ 20.00 9.00
❑ 77 John Goryl .................... 6.00 2.70
❑ 78 Pedro Ramos ................. 6.00 2.70
❑ 79 Harry Chiti ..................... 6.00 2.70
❑ 80 Minnie Minoso ............. 12.00 5.50
❑ 81 Hal Jeffcoat ................... 6.00 2.70
❑ 82 Bob Boyd ...................... 6.00 2.70
❑ 83 Bob Smith ..................... 6.00 2.70
❑ 84 Reno Bertoia ................. 6.00 2.70
❑ 85 Harry Anderson .............. 6.00 2.70
❑ 86 Bob Keegan ................... 8.00 3.60
❑ 87 Danny O'Connell ............ 6.00 2.70
❑ 88 Herb Score ................. 12.00 5.50
❑ 89 Billy Gardner ................. 6.00 2.70
❑ 90 Bill Skowron ................ 12.00 5.50
❑ 91 Herb Moford .................. 6.00 2.70
❑ 92 Dave Philley .................. 6.00 2.70
❑ 93 Julio Becquer ................ 6.00 2.70

❑ 94 White Sox Team .......... 40.00 8.00
(Checklist on back)
❑ 95 Carl Willey .......... 6.00 2.70
❑ 96 Lou Berberet .......... 6.00 2.70
❑ 97 Jerry Lynch .......... 8.00 3.60
❑ 98 Arnie Portocarrero .......... 6.00 2.70
❑ 99 Ted Kazanski .......... 6.00 2.70
❑ 100 Bob Cerv .......... 8.00 3.60
❑ 101 Alex Kellner .......... 6.00 2.70
❑ 102 Felipe Alou RC .......... 30.00 13.50
❑ 103 Billy Goodman .......... 8.00 3.60
❑ 104 Del Rice .......... 8.00 3.60
❑ 105 Lee Walls .......... 6.00 2.70
❑ 106 Hal Woodeshick .......... 6.00 2.70
❑ 107 Norm Larker .......... 8.00 3.60
❑ 108 Zack Monroe .......... 8.00 3.60
❑ 109 Bob Schmidt .......... 6.00 2.70
❑ 110 George Witt .......... 8.00 3.60
❑ 111 Redlegs Team .......... 15.00 3.00
(Checklist on back)
❑ 112 Billy Consolo .......... 4.00 1.80
❑ 113 Taylor Phillips .......... 4.00 1.80
❑ 114 Earl Battey .......... 8.00 3.60
❑ 115 Mickey Vernon .......... 8.00 3.60
❑ 116 Bob Allison RP RC .... 12.00 5.50
❑ 117 John Blanchard RP RC 12.00 5.50
❑ 118 John Buzhardt RP .......... 5.00 2.20
❑ 119 John Callison RP RC 12.00 5.50
❑ 120 Chuck Coles RP .......... 5.00 2.20
❑ 121 Bob Conley RP .......... 5.00 2.20
❑ 122 Bennie Daniels RP .......... 5.00 2.20
❑ 123 Don Dillard RP .......... 5.00 2.20
❑ 124 Dan Dobbek RP .......... 5.00 2.20
❑ 125 Ron Fairly RP RC .......... 12.00 5.50
❑ 126 Ed Haas RP .......... 5.00 2.20
❑ 127 Kent Hadley RP .......... 5.00 2.20
❑ 128 Bob Hartman RP .......... 5.00 2.20
❑ 129 Frank Herrera RP .......... 5.00 2.20
❑ 130 Lou Jackson RP .......... 5.00 2.20
❑ 131 Deron Johnson RP RC 12.00 5.50
❑ 132 Don Lee RP .......... 5.00 2.20
❑ 133 Bob Lillis RP RC .......... 5.00 2.20
❑ 134 Jim McDaniel RP .......... 5.00 2.20
❑ 135 Gene Oliver RP .......... 5.00 2.20
❑ 136 Jim O'Toole RP RC .......... 5.00 2.20
❑ 137 Dick Ricketts RP .......... 5.00 2.20
❑ 138 John Romano RP RC .. 5.00 2.20
❑ 139 Ed Sadowski RP .......... 5.00 2.20
❑ 140 Charlie Secrest RP .......... 5.00 2.20
❑ 141 Joe Shipley RP .......... 5.00 2.20
❑ 142 Dick Stigman RP .......... 5.00 2.20
❑ 143 Willie Tasby RP RC .......... 5.00 2.20
❑ 144 Jerry Walker RP .......... 5.00 2.20
❑ 145 Dom Zanni RP .......... 5.00 2.20
❑ 146 Jerry Zimmerman RP .. 5.00 2.20
❑ 147 Cubs Clubbers .......... 30.00 13.50
Dale Long
Ernie Banks
Walt Moryn
❑ 148 Mike McCormick .......... 8.00 3.60
❑ 149 Jim Bunning .......... 20.00 9.00
❑ 150 Stan Musial .......... 125.00 55.00
❑ 151 Bob Malkmus .......... 4.00 1.80
❑ 152 Johnny Klippstein .......... 4.00 1.80
❑ 153 Jim Marshall .......... 4.00 1.80
❑ 154 Ray Herbert .......... 4.00 1.80
❑ 155 Enos Slaughter .......... 20.00 9.00
❑ 156 Ace Hurlers .......... 12.00 5.50
Billy Pierce
Robin Roberts
❑ 157 Felix Mantilla .......... 4.00 1.80
❑ 158 Walt Dropo .......... 4.00 1.80
❑ 159 Bob Shaw .......... 8.00 3.60
❑ 160 Dick Groat .......... 8.00 3.60
❑ 161 Frank Baumann .......... 4.00 1.80
❑ 162 Bobby G. Smith .......... 4.00 1.80
❑ 163 Sandy Koufax .......... 150.00 70.00
❑ 164 Johnny Groth .......... 4.00 1.80
❑ 165 Bill Bruton .......... 4.00 1.80
❑ 166 Destruction Crew .......... 30.00 13.50
Minnie Minoso
Rocky Colavito
(Misspelled Colovito on card back)
Larry Doby
❑ 167 Duke Maas .......... 4.00 1.80
❑ 168 Carroll Hardy .......... 4.00 1.80
❑ 169 Ted Abernathy .......... 4.00 1.80
❑ 170 Gene Woodling .......... 8.00 3.60
❑ 171 Willard Schmidt .......... 4.00 1.80
❑ 172 Athletics Team .......... 15.00 3.00
(Checklist on back)
❑ 173 Bill Monbouquette .......... 8.00 3.60
❑ 174 Jim Pendleton .......... 4.00 1.80
❑ 175 Dick Farrell .......... 8.00 3.60
❑ 176 Preston Ward .......... 4.00 1.80
❑ 177 John Briggs .......... 4.00 1.80
❑ 178 Ruben Amaro RC .......... 12.00 5.50
❑ 179 Don Rudolph .......... 4.00 1.80
❑ 180 Yogi Berra .......... 75.00 34.00
❑ 181 Bob Porterfield .......... 4.00 1.80
❑ 182 Milt Graff .......... 4.00 1.80
❑ 183 Stu Miller .......... 8.00 3.60
❑ 184 Harvey Haddix .......... 8.00 3.60
❑ 185 Jim Busby .......... 4.00 1.80
❑ 186 Mudcat Grant .......... 8.00 3.60
❑ 187 Bubba Phillips .......... 8.00 3.60
❑ 188 Juan Pizarro .......... 4.00 1.80
❑ 189 Neil Chrisley .......... 4.00 1.80
❑ 190 Bill Virdon .......... 8.00 3.60
❑ 191 Russ Kemmerer .......... 4.00 1.80
❑ 192 Charlie Beamon .......... 4.00 1.80
❑ 193 Sammy Taylor .......... 4.00 1.80
❑ 194 Jim Brosnan .......... 8.00 3.60
❑ 195 Rip Repulski .......... 4.00 1.80
❑ 196 Billy Moran .......... 4.00 1.80
❑ 197 Ray Semproch .......... 4.00 1.80
❑ 198 Jim Davenport .......... 8.00 3.60
❑ 199 Leo Kiely .......... 4.00 1.80
❑ 200 Warren Giles NL PRES 8.00 3.60
❑ 201 Tom Acker .......... 4.00 1.80
❑ 202 Roger Maris .......... 125.00 55.00
❑ 203 Ossie Virgil .......... 4.00 1.80
❑ 204 Casey Wise .......... 4.00 1.80
❑ 205 Don Larsen .......... 8.00 3.60
❑ 206 Carl Furillo .......... 12.00 5.50
❑ 207 George Strickland .......... 4.00 1.80
❑ 208 Willie Jones .......... 4.00 1.80
❑ 209 Lenny Green .......... 4.00 1.80
❑ 210 Ed Bailey .......... 4.00 1.80
❑ 211 Bob Blaylock .......... 4.00 1.80
❑ 212 Hank Aaron .......... 75.00 34.00
Eddie Mathews
❑ 213 Jim Rivera .......... 8.00 3.60
❑ 214 Marcelino Solis .......... 4.00 1.80
❑ 215 Jim Lemon .......... 8.00 3.60
❑ 216 Andre Rodgers .......... 4.00 1.80
❑ 217 Carl Erskine .......... 12.00 5.50
❑ 218 Roman Mejias .......... 4.00 1.80
❑ 219 George Zuverink .......... 4.00 1.80
❑ 220 Frank Malzone .......... 8.00 3.60
❑ 221 Bob Bowman .......... 4.00 1.80
❑ 222 Bobby Shantz .......... 8.00 3.60
❑ 223 Cardinals Team .......... 15.00 3.00
(Checklist on back)
❑ 224 Claude Osteen RC .......... 8.00 3.60
❑ 225 Johnny Logan .......... 8.00 3.60
❑ 226 Art Ceccarelli .......... 4.00 1.80
❑ 227 Hal W. Smith .......... 4.00 1.80
❑ 228 Don Gross .......... 4.00 1.80
❑ 229 Vic Power .......... 8.00 3.60
❑ 230 Bill Fischer .......... 4.00 1.80
❑ 231 Ellis Burton .......... 4.00 1.80
❑ 232 Eddie Kasko .......... 4.00 1.80
❑ 233 Paul Foytack .......... 4.00 1.80
❑ 234 Chuck Tanner .......... 8.00 3.60
❑ 235 Valmy Thomas .......... 4.00 1.80
❑ 236 Ted Bowsfield .......... 4.00 1.80
❑ 237 Run Preventers .......... 12.00 5.50
Gil McDougald
Bob Turley
Bobby Richardson
❑ 238 Gene Baker .......... 4.00 1.80
❑ 239 Bob Trowbridge .......... 4.00 1.80
❑ 240 Hank Bauer .......... 12.00 5.50
❑ 241 Billy Muffett .......... 4.00 1.80
❑ 242 Ron Samford .......... 4.00 1.80
❑ 243 Marv Grissom .......... 4.00 1.80
❑ 244 Ted Gray .......... 4.00 1.80
❑ 245 Ned Garver .......... 4.00 1.80
❑ 246 J.W. Porter .......... 4.00 1.80
❑ 247 Don Ferrarese .......... 4.00 1.80
❑ 248 Red Sox Team .......... 15.00 3.00
(Checklist on back)
❑ 249 Bobby Adams .......... 4.00 1.80
❑ 250 Billy O'Dell .......... 4.00 1.80
❑ 251 Clete Boyer .......... 12.00 5.50
❑ 252 Ray Boone .......... 8.00 3.60
❑ 253 Seth Morehead .......... 4.00 1.80
❑ 254 Zeke Bella .......... 4.00 1.80
❑ 255 Del Ennis .......... 8.00 3.60
❑ 256 Jerry Davie .......... 4.00 1.80
❑ 257 Leon Wagner RC .......... 8.00 3.60
❑ 258 Fred Kipp .......... 4.00 1.80
❑ 259 Jim Pisoni .......... 4.00 1.80
❑ 260 Early Wynn UER .......... 20.00 9.00
(1957 Cleevland)
❑ 261 Gene Stephens .......... 4.00 1.80
❑ 262 Johnny Podres .......... 12.00 5.50
Clem Labine
Don Drysdale
❑ 263 Bud Daley .......... 4.00 1.80
❑ 264 Chico Carrasquel .......... 4.00 1.80
❑ 265 Ron Kline .......... 4.00 1.80
❑ 266 Woody Held .......... 4.00 1.80
❑ 267 John Romonosky .......... 4.00 1.80
❑ 268 Tito Francona .......... 8.00 3.60
❑ 269 Jack Meyer .......... 4.00 1.80
❑ 270 Gil Hodges .......... 30.00 13.50
❑ 271 Orlando Pena .......... 4.00 1.80
❑ 272 Jerry Lumpe .......... 4.00 1.80
❑ 273 Joey Jay .......... 8.00 3.60
❑ 274 Jerry Kindall .......... 8.00 3.60
❑ 275 Jack Sanford .......... 8.00 3.60
❑ 276 Pete Daley .......... 4.00 1.80
❑ 277 Turk Lown .......... 8.00 3.60
❑ 278 Chuck Essegian .......... 4.00 1.80
❑ 279 Ernie Johnson .......... 4.00 1.80
❑ 280 Frank Bolling .......... 4.00 1.80
❑ 281 Walt Craddock .......... 4.00 1.80
❑ 282 R.C. Stevens .......... 4.00 1.80
❑ 283 Russ Heman .......... 4.00 1.80
❑ 284 Steve Korcheck .......... 4.00 1.80
❑ 285 Joe Cunningham .......... 4.00 1.80
❑ 286 Dean Stone .......... 4.00 1.80
❑ 287 Don Zimmer .......... 12.00 5.50
❑ 288 Dutch Dotterer .......... 4.00 1.80
❑ 289 Johnny Kucks .......... 8.00 3.60
❑ 290 Wes Covington .......... 4.00 1.80
❑ 291 Pedro Ramos .......... 4.00 1.80
Camilo Pascual
❑ 292 Dick Williams .......... 8.00 3.60
❑ 293 Ray Moore .......... 4.00 1.80
❑ 294 Hank Foiles .......... 4.00 1.80
❑ 295 Billy Martin .......... 30.00 13.50
❑ 296 Ernie Broglio RC .......... 4.00 1.80
❑ 297 Jackie Brandt .......... 4.00 1.80
❑ 298 Tex Clevenger .......... 4.00 1.80
❑ 299 Billy Klaus .......... 4.00 1.80
❑ 300 Richie Ashburn .......... 30.00 13.50
❑ 301 Earl Averill .......... 4.00 1.80
❑ 302 Don Mossi .......... 8.00 3.60
❑ 303 Marty Keough .......... 4.00 1.80
❑ 304 Cubs Team .......... 15.00 3.00
(Checklist on back)
❑ 305 Curt Raydon .......... 4.00 1.80
❑ 306 Jim Gilliam .......... 8.00 3.60
❑ 307 Curt Barclay .......... 4.00 1.80
❑ 308 Norm Siebern .......... 4.00 1.80
❑ 309 Sal Maglie .......... 8.00 3.60
❑ 310 Luis Aparicio .......... 20.00 9.00
❑ 311 Norm Zauchin .......... 4.00 1.80
❑ 312 Don Newcombe .......... 8.00 3.60
❑ 313 Frank House .......... 4.00 1.80
❑ 314 Don Cardwell .......... 4.00 1.80
❑ 315 Joe Adcock .......... 8.00 3.60
❑ 316A Ralph Lumenti UER .. 4.00 1.80
(Option)
(Photo actually Camilo Pascual)
❑ 316B Ralph Lumenti UER 80.00 36.00
(No option)
(Photo actually Camilo Pascual)
❑ 317 Willie Mays .......... 75.00 34.00
Richie Ashburn
❑ 318 Rocky Bridges .......... 4.00 1.80
❑ 319 Dave Hillman .......... 4.00 1.80

❑ 320 Bob Skinner 8.00 3.60
❑ 321A Bob Giallombardo 8.00 3.60
(Option)
❑ 321B Bob Giallombardo 80.00 36.00
(No option)
❑ 322A Harry Hanebrink 8.00 3.60
(Traded)
❑ 322B Harry Hanebrink 80.00 36.00
(No trade)
❑ 323 Frank Sullivan 4.00 1.80
❑ 324 Don Demeter 4.00 1.80
❑ 325 Ken Boyer 12.00 5.50
❑ 326 Marv Throneberry 8.00 3.60
❑ 327 Gary Bell 4.00 1.80
❑ 328 Lou Skizas 4.00 1.80
❑ 329 Tigers Team 15.00 3.00
(Checklist on back)
❑ 330 Gus Triandos 8.00 3.60
❑ 331 Steve Boros 4.00 1.80
❑ 332 Ray Monzant 4.00 1.80
❑ 333 Harry Simpson 4.00 1.80
❑ 334 Glen Hobbie 4.00 1.80
❑ 335 Johnny Temple 8.00 3.60
❑ 336A Billy Loes 8.00 3.60
(With traded line)
❑ 336B Billy Loes 80.00 36.00
(No trade)
❑ 337 George Crowe 4.00 1.80
❑ 338 Sparky Anderson RC ! 60.00 27.00
❑ 339 Roy Face 8.00 3.60
❑ 340 Roy Sievers 8.00 3.60
❑ 341 Tom Qualters 4.00 1.80
❑ 342 Ray Jablonski 4.00 1.80
❑ 343 Billy Hoeft 4.00 1.80
❑ 344 Russ Nixon 4.00 1.80
❑ 345 Gil McDougald 12.00 5.50
❑ 346 Dave Sisler 4.00 1.80
Tom Brewer
❑ 347 Bob Buhl 4.00 1.80
❑ 348 Ted Lepcio 4.00 1.80
❑ 349 Hoyt Wilhelm 20.00 9.00
❑ 350 Ernie Banks 75.00 34.00
❑ 351 Earl Torgeson 4.00 1.80
❑ 352 Robin Roberts 20.00 9.00
❑ 353 Curt Flood 8.00 3.60
❑ 354 Pete Burnside 4.00 1.80
❑ 355 Jimmy Piersall 8.00 3.60
❑ 356 Bob Mabe 4.00 1.80
❑ 357 Dick Stuart RC 8.00 3.60
❑ 358 Ralph Terry 8.00 3.60
❑ 359 Bill White RC 20.00 9.00
❑ 360 Al Kaline 60.00 27.00
❑ 361 Willard Nixon 4.00 1.80
❑ 362A Dolan Nichols 4.00 1.80
(With option line)
❑ 362B Dolan Nichols 80.00 36.00
(No option)
❑ 363 Bobby Avila 4.00 1.80
❑ 364 Danny McDevitt 4.00 1.80
❑ 365 Gus Bell 8.00 3.60
❑ 366 Humberto Robinson 4.00 1.80
❑ 367 Cal Neeman 4.00 1.80
❑ 368 Don Mueller 8.00 3.60
❑ 369 Dick Tomanek 4.00 1.80
❑ 370 Pete Runnels 8.00 3.60
❑ 371 Dick Brodowski 4.00 1.80
❑ 372 Jim Hegan 8.00 3.60
❑ 373 Herb Plews 4.00 1.80
❑ 374 Art Ditmar 8.00 3.60
❑ 375 Bob Nieman 4.00 1.80
❑ 376 Hal Naragon 4.00 1.80
❑ 377 John Antonelli 8.00 3.60
❑ 378 Gail Harris 4.00 1.80
❑ 379 Bob Miller 4.00 1.80
❑ 380 Hank Aaron 125.00 55.00
❑ 381 Mike Baxes 4.00 1.80
❑ 382 Curt Simmons 8.00 3.60
❑ 383 Words of Wisdom 12.00 5.50
Don Larsen
Casey Stengel MG
❑ 384 Dave Sisler 4.00 1.80
❑ 385 Sherm Lollar 8.00 3.60
❑ 386 Jim Delsing 4.00 1.80
❑ 387 Don Drysdale 50.00 22.00
❑ 388 Bob Will 4.00 1.80
❑ 389 Joe Nuxhall 8.00 3.60
❑ 390 Orlando Cepeda 20.00 9.00
❑ 391 Milt Pappas 8.00 3.60
❑ 392 Whitey Herzog 8.00 3.60
❑ 393 Frank Lary 8.00 3.60
❑ 394 Randy Jackson 4.00 1.80
❑ 395 Elston Howard 12.00 5.50
❑ 396 Bob Rush 4.00 1.80
❑ 397 Senators Team 15.00 3.00
(Checklist on back)
❑ 398 Wally Post 8.00 3.60
❑ 399 Larry Jackson 4.00 1.80
❑ 400 Jackie Jensen 8.00 3.60
❑ 401 Ron Blackburn 4.00 1.80
❑ 402 Hector Lopez 8.00 3.60
❑ 403 Clem Labine 8.00 3.60
❑ 404 Hank Sauer 8.00 3.60
❑ 405 Roy McMillan 8.00 3.60
❑ 406 Solly Drake 4.00 1.80
❑ 407 Moe Drabowsky 8.00 3.60
❑ 408 Nellie Fox 35.00 16.00
Luis Aparicio
❑ 409 Gus Zernial 8.00 3.60
❑ 410 Billy Pierce 8.00 3.60
❑ 411 Whitey Lockman 8.00 3.60
❑ 412 Stan Lopata 4.00 1.80
❑ 413 Camilo Pascual UER 8.00 3.60
(Listed as Camillo
on front and Pasqual
on back)
❑ 414 Dale Long 8.00 3.60
❑ 415 Bill Mazeroski 12.00 5.50
❑ 416 Haywood Sullivan 8.00 3.60
❑ 417 Virgil Trucks 8.00 3.60
❑ 418 Gino Cimoli 4.00 1.80
❑ 419 Braves Team 15.00 3.00
(Checklist on back)
❑ 420 Rocky Colavito 30.00 13.50
❑ 421 Herman Wehmeier 4.00 1.80
❑ 422 Hobie Landrith 4.00 1.80
❑ 423 Bob Grim 8.00 3.60
❑ 424 Ken Aspromonte 4.00 1.80
❑ 425 Del Crandall 8.00 3.60
❑ 426 Gerry Staley 8.00 3.60
❑ 427 Charlie Neal 8.00 3.60
❑ 428 Ron Kline 4.00 1.80
Bob Friend
Vernon Law
Roy Face
❑ 429 Bobby Thomson 8.00 3.60
❑ 430 Whitey Ford 60.00 27.00
❑ 431 Whammy Douglas 4.00 1.80
❑ 432 Smoky Burgess 8.00 3.60
❑ 433 Billy Harrell 4.00 1.80
❑ 434 Hal Griggs 4.00 1.80
❑ 435 Frank Robinson 50.00 22.00
❑ 436 Granny Hamner 4.00 1.80
❑ 437 Ike Delock 4.00 1.80
❑ 438 Sammy Esposito 4.00 1.80
❑ 439 Brooks Robinson 50.00 22.00
❑ 440 Lou Burdette 8.00 3.60
(Posing as if
lefthanded)
❑ 441 John Roseboro 8.00 3.60
❑ 442 Ray Narleski 4.00 1.80
❑ 443 Daryl Spencer 4.00 1.80
❑ 444 Ron Hansen RC 8.00 3.60
❑ 445 Cal McLish 4.00 1.80
❑ 446 Rocky Nelson 4.00 1.80
❑ 447 Bob Anderson 4.00 1.80
❑ 448 Vada Pinson UER 12.00 5.50
(Born: 8/8/38
should be 8/11/38)
❑ 449 Tom Gorman 4.00 1.80
❑ 450 Eddie Mathews 35.00 16.00
❑ 451 Jimmy Constable 4.00 1.80
❑ 452 Chico Fernandez 4.00 1.80
❑ 453 Les Moss 4.00 1.80
❑ 454 Phil Clark 4.00 1.80
❑ 455 Larry Doby 12.00 5.50
❑ 456 Jerry Casale 4.00 1.80
❑ 457 Dodgers Team 30.00 6.00
(Checklist on back)
❑ 458 Gordon Jones 4.00 1.80
❑ 459 Bill Tuttle 4.00 1.80
❑ 460 Bob Friend 8.00 3.60
❑ 461 Mickey Mantle HL 125.00 55.00
❑ 462 Rocky Colavito HL 12.00 5.50
❑ 463 Al Kaline HL 30.00 13.50
❑ 464 Willie Mays HL 40.00 18.00
54 World Series Catch
❑ 465 Roy Sievers HL 8.00 3.60
❑ 466 Billy Pierce HL 8.00 3.60
❑ 467 Hank Aaron HL 40.00 18.00
❑ 468 Duke Snider HL 20.00 9.00
❑ 469 Ernie Banks HL 20.00 9.00
❑ 470 Stan Musial HL 30.00 13.50
3,000 Hits
❑ 471 Tom Sturdivant 4.00 1.80
❑ 472 Gene Freese 4.00 1.80
❑ 473 Mike Fornieles 4.00 1.80
❑ 474 Moe Thacker 4.00 1.80
❑ 475 Jack Harshman 4.00 1.80
❑ 476 Indians Team 15.00 3.00
(Checklist on back)
❑ 477 Barry Latman 4.00 1.80
❑ 478 Roberto Clemente 225.00 100.00
❑ 479 Lindy McDaniel 8.00 3.60
❑ 480 Red Schoendienst 12.00 5.50
❑ 481 Charlie Maxwell 8.00 3.60
❑ 482 Russ Meyer 4.00 1.80
❑ 483 Clint Courtney 4.00 1.80
❑ 484 Willie Kirkland 4.00 1.80
❑ 485 Ryne Duren 8.00 3.60
❑ 486 Sammy White 4.00 1.80
❑ 487 Hal Brown 4.00 1.80
❑ 488 Walt Moryn 4.00 1.80
❑ 489 John Powers 4.00 1.80
❑ 490 Frank Thomas 8.00 3.60
❑ 491 Don Blasingame 4.00 1.80
❑ 492 Gene Conley 8.00 3.60
❑ 493 Jim Landis 8.00 3.60
❑ 494 Don Pavletich 4.00 1.80
❑ 495 Johnny Podres 12.00 5.50
❑ 496 Wayne Terwilliger UER 4.00 1.80
(Athlftics on front)
❑ 497 Hal R. Smith 4.00 1.80
❑ 498 Dick Hyde 4.00 1.80
❑ 499 Johnny O'Brien 8.00 3.60
❑ 500 Vic Wertz 8.00 3.60
❑ 501 Bob Tiefenauer 4.00 1.80
❑ 502 Alvin Dark 8.00 3.60
❑ 503 Jim Owens 4.00 1.80
❑ 504 Ossie Alvarez 4.00 1.80
❑ 505 Tony Kubek 12.00 5.50
❑ 506 Bob Purkey 4.00 1.80
❑ 507 Bob Hale 16.00 7.25
❑ 508 Art Fowler 16.00 7.25
❑ 509 Norm Cash RC 80.00 36.00
❑ 510 Yankees Team 125.00 25.00
(Checklist on back)
❑ 511 George Susce 16.00 7.25
❑ 512 George Altman 16.00 7.25
❑ 513 Tommy Carroll 16.00 7.25
❑ 514 Bob Gibson RC ! 250.00 110.00
❑ 515 Harmon Killebrew 125.00 55.00
❑ 516 Mike Garcia 20.00 9.00
❑ 517 Joe Koppe 16.00 7.25
❑ 518 Mike Cueller UER RC ! 30.00 13.50
(Sic, Cuellar)
❑ 519 Pete Runnels 20.00 9.00
Dick Gernert
Frank Malzone
❑ 520 Don Elston 16.00 7.25
❑ 521 Gary Geiger 16.00 7.25
❑ 522 Gene Snyder 16.00 7.25
❑ 523 Harry Bright 16.00 7.25
❑ 524 Larry Osborne 16.00 7.25
❑ 525 Jim Coates 20.00 9.00
❑ 526 Bob Speake 16.00 7.25
❑ 527 Solly Hemus 16.00 7.25
❑ 528 Pirates Team 75.00 15.00
(Checklist on back)
❑ 529 George Bamberger RC 20.00 9.00
❑ 530 Wally Moon 20.00 9.00
❑ 531 Ray Webster 16.00 7.25
❑ 532 Mark Freeman 16.00 7.25
❑ 533 Darrell Johnson 20.00 9.00
❑ 534 Faye Throneberry 16.00 7.25
❑ 535 Ruben Gomez 16.00 7.25
❑ 536 Danny Kravitz 16.00 7.25
❑ 537 Rudolph Arias 16.00 7.25
❑ 538 Chick King 16.00 7.25

| Card | NRMT | VG-E |
|---|---|---|
| ❑ 539 Gary Blaylock | 16.00 | 7.25 |
| ❑ 540 Willie Miranda | 16.00 | 7.25 |
| ❑ 541 Bob Thurman | 16.00 | 7.25 |
| ❑ 542 Jim Perry RC | 30.00 | 13.50 |
| ❑ 543 Bob Skinner | 150.00 | 70.00 |
| Bill Virdon | | |
| Roberto Clemente | | |
| ❑ 544 Lee Tate | 16.00 | 7.25 |
| ❑ 545 Tom Morgan | 16.00 | 7.25 |
| ❑ 546 Al Schroll | 16.00 | 7.25 |
| ❑ 547 Jim Baxes | 16.00 | 7.25 |
| ❑ 548 Elmer Singleton | 16.00 | 7.25 |
| ❑ 549 Howie Nunn | 16.00 | 7.25 |
| ❑ 550 Roy Campanella | 150.00 | 70.00 |
| (Symbol of Courage) | | |
| ❑ 551 Fred Haney AS MG | 16.00 | 7.25 |
| ❑ 552 Casey Stengel AS MG | 30.00 | 13.50 |
| ❑ 553 Orlando Cepeda AS | 30.00 | 13.50 |
| ❑ 554 Bill Skowron AS | 20.00 | 9.00 |
| ❑ 555 Bill Mazeroski AS | 30.00 | 13.50 |
| ❑ 556 Nellie Fox AS | 40.00 | 18.00 |
| ❑ 557 Ken Boyer AS | 30.00 | 13.50 |
| ❑ 558 Frank Malzone AS | 16.00 | 7.25 |
| ❑ 559 Ernie Banks AS | 60.00 | 27.00 |
| ❑ 560 Luis Aparicio AS | 40.00 | 18.00 |
| ❑ 561 Hank Aaron AS | 125.00 | 55.00 |
| ❑ 562 Al Kaline AS | 60.00 | 27.00 |
| ❑ 563 Willie Mays AS | 125.00 | 55.00 |
| ❑ 564 Mickey Mantle AS | 250.00 | 110.00 |
| ❑ 565 Wes Covington AS | 20.00 | 9.00 |
| ❑ 566 Roy Sievers AS | 16.00 | 7.25 |
| ❑ 567 Del Crandall AS | 16.00 | 7.25 |
| ❑ 568 Gus Triandos AS | 16.00 | 7.25 |
| ❑ 569 Bob Friend AS | 16.00 | 7.25 |
| ❑ 570 Bob Turley AS | 16.00 | 7.25 |
| ❑ 571 Warren Spahn AS | 40.00 | 18.00 |
| ❑ 572 Billy Pierce AS | 40.00 | 13.00 |

## 1960 Topps

| | NRMT | VG-E |
|---|---|---|
| COMPLETE SET (572) | 3500.00 | 1600.00 |
| COMMON CARD (1-440) | 4.00 | 1.80 |
| COMMON CARD (441-506) | 7.00 | 3.10 |
| COMMON CARD (507-572) | 16.00 | 7.25 |
| WRAPPER (1-CENT) | 900.00 | 400.00 |
| WRAP. (1-CENT REPEAT) | 500.00 | 220.00 |
| WRAPPER (5-CENT) | 40.00 | 18.00 |

| Card | NRMT | VG-E |
|---|---|---|
| ❑ 1 Early Wynn | 35.00 | 8.75 |
| ❑ 2 Roman Mejias | 4.00 | 1.80 |
| ❑ 3 Joe Adcock | 6.00 | 2.70 |
| ❑ 4 Bob Purkey | 4.00 | 1.80 |
| ❑ 5 Wally Moon | 6.00 | 2.70 |
| ❑ 6 Lou Berberet | 4.00 | 1.80 |
| ❑ 7 Master and Mentor | 25.00 | 11.00 |
| Willie Mays | | |
| Bill Rigney MG | | |
| ❑ 8 Bud Daley | 4.00 | 1.80 |
| ❑ 9 Faye Throneberry | 4.00 | 1.80 |
| ❑ 10 Ernie Banks | 50.00 | 22.00 |
| ❑ 11 Norm Siebern | 4.00 | 1.80 |
| ❑ 12 Milt Pappas | 6.00 | 2.70 |
| ❑ 13 Wally Post | 6.00 | 2.70 |
| ❑ 14 Jim Grant | 6.00 | 2.70 |
| ❑ 15 Pete Runnels | 6.00 | 2.70 |
| ❑ 16 Ernie Broglio | 6.00 | 2.70 |
| ❑ 17 Johnny Callison | 6.00 | 2.70 |
| ❑ 18 Dodgers Team | 50.00 | 10.00 |
| (Checklist on back) | | |
| ❑ 19 Felix Mantilla | 4.00 | 1.80 |
| ❑ 20 Roy Face | 6.00 | 2.70 |
| ❑ 21 Dutch Dotterer | 4.00 | 1.80 |
| ❑ 22 Rocky Bridges | 4.00 | 1.80 |
| ❑ 23 Eddie Fisher | 4.00 | 1.80 |
| ❑ 24 Dick Gray | 4.00 | 1.80 |
| ❑ 25 Roy Sievers | 6.00 | 2.70 |
| ❑ 26 Wayne Terwilliger | 4.00 | 1.80 |
| ❑ 27 Dick Drott | 4.00 | 1.80 |
| ❑ 28 Brooks Robinson | 50.00 | 22.00 |
| ❑ 29 Clem Labine | 6.00 | 2.70 |
| ❑ 30 Tito Francona | 4.00 | 1.80 |
| ❑ 31 Sammy Esposito | 4.00 | 1.80 |
| ❑ 32 Sophomore Stalwarts | 4.00 | 1.80 |
| Jim O'Toole | | |
| Vada Pinson | | |
| ❑ 33 Tom Morgan | 4.00 | 1.80 |
| ❑ 34 Sparky Anderson | 15.00 | 6.75 |
| ❑ 35 Whitey Ford | 50.00 | 22.00 |
| ❑ 36 Russ Nixon | 4.00 | 1.80 |
| ❑ 37 Bill Bruton | 4.00 | 1.80 |
| ❑ 38 Jerry Casale | 4.00 | 1.80 |
| ❑ 39 Earl Averill | 4.00 | 1.80 |
| ❑ 40 Joe Cunningham | 4.00 | 1.80 |
| ❑ 41 Barry Latman | 4.00 | 1.80 |
| ❑ 42 Hobie Landrith | 4.00 | 1.80 |
| ❑ 43 Senators Team | 10.00 | 2.00 |
| (Checklist on back) | | |
| ❑ 44 Bobby Locke | 4.00 | 1.80 |
| ❑ 45 Roy McMillan | 6.00 | 2.70 |
| ❑ 46 Jerry Fisher | 4.00 | 1.80 |
| ❑ 47 Don Zimmer | 6.00 | 2.70 |
| ❑ 48 Hal W. Smith | 4.00 | 1.80 |
| ❑ 49 Curt Raydon | 4.00 | 1.80 |
| ❑ 50 Al Kaline | 50.00 | 22.00 |
| ❑ 51 Jim Coates | 6.00 | 2.70 |
| ❑ 52 Dave Philley | 4.00 | 1.80 |
| ❑ 53 Jackie Brandt | 4.00 | 1.80 |
| ❑ 54 Mike Fornieles | 4.00 | 1.80 |
| ❑ 55 Bill Mazeroski | 10.00 | 4.50 |
| ❑ 56 Steve Korcheck | 4.00 | 1.80 |
| ❑ 57 Win Savers | 4.00 | 1.80 |
| Turk Lown | | |
| Gerry Staley | | |
| ❑ 58 Gino Cimoli | 4.00 | 1.80 |
| ❑ 59 Juan Pizarro | 4.00 | 1.80 |
| ❑ 60 Gus Triandos | 6.00 | 2.70 |
| ❑ 61 Eddie Kasko | 4.00 | 1.80 |
| ❑ 62 Roger Craig | 6.00 | 2.70 |
| ❑ 63 George Strickland | 4.00 | 1.80 |
| ❑ 64 Jack Meyer | 4.00 | 1.80 |
| ❑ 65 Elston Howard | 6.00 | 2.70 |
| ❑ 66 Bob Trowbridge | 4.00 | 1.80 |
| ❑ 67 Jose Pagan | 4.00 | 1.80 |
| ❑ 68 Dave Hillman | 4.00 | 1.80 |
| ❑ 69 Billy Goodman | 6.00 | 2.70 |
| ❑ 70 Lew Burdette | 6.00 | 2.70 |
| ❑ 71 Marty Keough | 4.00 | 1.80 |
| ❑ 72 Tigers Team | 25.00 | 5.00 |
| (Checklist on back) | | |
| ❑ 73 Bob Gibson | 50.00 | 22.00 |
| ❑ 74 Walt Moryn | 4.00 | 1.80 |
| ❑ 75 Vic Power | 6.00 | 2.70 |
| ❑ 76 Bill Fischer | 4.00 | 1.80 |
| ❑ 77 Hank Foiles | 4.00 | 1.80 |
| ❑ 78 Bob Grim | 4.00 | 1.80 |
| ❑ 79 Walt Dropo | 4.00 | 1.80 |
| ❑ 80 Johnny Antonelli | 6.00 | 2.70 |
| ❑ 81 Russ Snyder | 4.00 | 1.80 |
| ❑ 82 Ruben Gomez | 4.00 | 1.80 |
| ❑ 83 Tony Kubek | 15.00 | 6.75 |
| ❑ 84 Hal R. Smith | 4.00 | 1.80 |
| ❑ 85 Frank Lary | 6.00 | 2.70 |
| ❑ 86 Dick Gernert | 4.00 | 1.80 |
| ❑ 87 John Romonosky | 4.00 | 1.80 |
| ❑ 88 John Roseboro | 6.00 | 2.70 |
| ❑ 89 Hal Brown | 4.00 | 1.80 |
| ❑ 90 Bobby Avila | 4.00 | 1.80 |
| ❑ 91 Bennie Daniels | 4.00 | 1.80 |
| ❑ 92 Whitey Herzog | 6.00 | 2.70 |
| ❑ 93 Art Schult | 4.00 | 1.80 |
| ❑ 94 Leo Kiely | 4.00 | 1.80 |
| ❑ 95 Frank Thomas | 6.00 | 2.70 |
| ❑ 96 Ralph Terry | 6.00 | 2.70 |
| ❑ 97 Ted Lepcio | 4.00 | 1.80 |
| ❑ 98 Gordon Jones | 4.00 | 1.80 |
| ❑ 99 Lenny Green | 4.00 | 1.80 |
| ❑ 100 Nellie Fox | 20.00 | 9.00 |
| ❑ 101 Bob Miller | 4.00 | 1.80 |
| ❑ 102 Kent Hadley | 4.00 | 1.80 |
| ❑ 103 Dick Farrell | 6.00 | 2.70 |
| ❑ 104 Dick Schofield | 6.00 | 2.70 |
| ❑ 105 Larry Sherry RC | 6.00 | 2.70 |
| ❑ 106 Billy Gardner | 4.00 | 1.80 |
| ❑ 107 Carlton Willey | 4.00 | 1.80 |
| ❑ 108 Pete Daley | 4.00 | 1.80 |
| ❑ 109 Clete Boyer | 15.00 | 6.75 |
| ❑ 110 Cal McLish | 4.00 | 1.80 |
| ❑ 111 Vic Wertz | 6.00 | 2.70 |
| ❑ 112 Jack Harshman | 4.00 | 1.80 |
| ❑ 113 Bob Skinner | 4.00 | 1.80 |
| ❑ 114 Ken Aspromonte | 4.00 | 1.80 |
| ❑ 115 Fork and Knuckler | 6.00 | 2.70 |
| Roy Face | | |
| Hoyt Wilhelm | | |
| ❑ 116 Jim Rivera | 4.00 | 1.80 |
| ❑ 117 Tom Borland RP | 4.00 | 1.80 |
| ❑ 118 Bob Bruce RP | 4.00 | 1.80 |
| ❑ 119 Chico Cardenas RP | 6.00 | 2.70 |
| ❑ 120 Duke Carmel RP | 4.00 | 1.80 |
| ❑ 121 Camilo Carreon RP | 4.00 | 1.80 |
| ❑ 122 Don Dillard RP | 4.00 | 1.80 |
| ❑ 123 Dan Dobbek RP | 4.00 | 1.80 |
| ❑ 124 Jim Donohue RP | 4.00 | 1.80 |
| ❑ 125 Dick Ellsworth RP RC | 6.00 | 2.70 |
| ❑ 126 Chuck Estrada RP RC | 4.00 | 1.80 |
| ❑ 127 Ron Hansen RP | 6.00 | 2.70 |
| ❑ 128 Bill Harris RP | 4.00 | 1.80 |
| ❑ 129 Bob Hartman RP | 4.00 | 1.80 |
| ❑ 130 Frank Herrera RP | 4.00 | 1.80 |
| ❑ 131 Ed Hobaugh RP | 4.00 | 1.80 |
| ❑ 132 Frank Howard RP RC ! | 25.00 | 11.00 |
| ❑ 133 Manuel Javier RC RP | 6.00 | 2.70 |
| (Sic, Julian) | | |
| ❑ 134 Deron Johnson RP | 6.00 | 2.70 |
| ❑ 135 Ken Johnson RP | 4.00 | 1.80 |
| ❑ 136 Jim Kaat RP RC ! | 40.00 | 18.00 |
| ❑ 137 Lou Klimchock RP | 4.00 | 1.80 |
| ❑ 138 Art Mahaffey RP | 15.00 | 6.75 |
| ❑ 139 Carl Mathias RP | 4.00 | 1.80 |
| ❑ 140 Julio Navarro RP RC | 4.00 | 1.80 |
| ❑ 141 Jim Proctor RP | 4.00 | 1.80 |
| ❑ 142 Bill Short RP | 4.00 | 1.80 |
| ❑ 143 Al Spangler RP | 4.00 | 1.80 |
| ❑ 144 Al Stieglitz RP | 4.00 | 1.80 |
| ❑ 145 Jim Umbricht RP | 4.00 | 1.80 |
| ❑ 146 Ted Wieand RP | 4.00 | 1.80 |
| ❑ 147 Bob Will RP | 4.00 | 1.80 |
| ❑ 148 Carl Yastrzemski RP RC ! | 150.00 | 70.00 |
| ❑ 149 Bob Nieman | 4.00 | 1.80 |
| ❑ 150 Billy Pierce | 6.00 | 2.70 |
| ❑ 151 Giants Team | 10.00 | 2.00 |
| (Checklist on back) | | |
| ❑ 152 Gail Harris | 4.00 | 1.80 |
| ❑ 153 Bobby Thomson | 6.00 | 2.70 |
| ❑ 154 Jim Davenport | 6.00 | 2.70 |
| ❑ 155 Charlie Neal | 6.00 | 2.70 |
| ❑ 156 Art Ceccarelli | 4.00 | 1.80 |
| ❑ 157 Rocky Nelson | 6.00 | 2.70 |
| ❑ 158 Wes Covington | 6.00 | 2.70 |
| ❑ 159 Jim Piersall | 6.00 | 2.70 |
| ❑ 160 Rival All-Stars | 150.00 | 70.00 |
| Mickey Mantle | | |
| Ken Boyer | | |
| ❑ 161 Ray Narleski | 4.00 | 1.80 |
| ❑ 162 Sammy Taylor | 4.00 | 1.80 |
| ❑ 163 Hector Lopez | 6.00 | 2.70 |
| ❑ 164 Reds Team | 10.00 | 2.00 |
| (Checklist on back) | | |
| ❑ 165 Jack Sanford | 6.00 | 2.70 |
| ❑ 166 Chuck Essegian | 4.00 | 1.80 |
| ❑ 167 Valmy Thomas | 4.00 | 1.80 |
| ❑ 168 Alex Grammas | 4.00 | 1.80 |
| ❑ 169 Jake Striker | 4.00 | 1.80 |
| ❑ 170 Del Crandall | 6.00 | 2.70 |
| ❑ 171 Johnny Groth | 4.00 | 1.80 |
| ❑ 172 Willie Kirkland | 4.00 | 1.80 |
| ❑ 173 Billy Martin | 20.00 | 9.00 |
| ❑ 174 Indians Team | 10.00 | 2.00 |
| (Checklist on back) | | |

❑ 175 Pedro Ramos .......... 4.00 1.80
❑ 176 Vada Pinson .......... 6.00 2.70
❑ 177 Johnny Kucks .......... 4.00 1.80
❑ 178 Woody Held .......... 4.00 1.80
❑ 179 Rip Coleman .......... 4.00 1.80
❑ 180 Harry Simpson .......... 4.00 1.80
❑ 181 Billy Loes .......... 6.00 2.70
❑ 182 Glen Hobbie .......... 4.00 1.80
❑ 183 Eli Grba .......... 4.00 1.80
❑ 184 Gary Geiger .......... 4.00 1.80
❑ 185 Jim Owens .......... 4.00 1.80
❑ 186 Dave Sisler .......... 4.00 1.80
❑ 187 Jay Hook .......... 4.00 1.80
❑ 188 Dick Williams .......... 6.00 2.70
❑ 189 Don McMahon .......... 4.00 1.80
❑ 190 Gene Woodling .......... 6.00 2.70
❑ 191 Johnny Klippstein .......... 4.00 1.80
❑ 192 Danny O'Connell .......... 4.00 1.80
❑ 193 Dick Hyde .......... 4.00 1.80
❑ 194 Bobby Gene Smith .......... 4.00 1.80
❑ 195 Lindy McDaniel .......... 6.00 2.70
❑ 196 Andy Carey .......... 6.00 2.70
❑ 197 Ron Kline .......... 4.00 1.80
❑ 198 Jerry Lynch .......... 6.00 2.70
❑ 199 Dick Donovan .......... 6.00 2.70
❑ 200 Willie Mays .......... 100.00 45.00
❑ 201 Larry Osborne .......... 4.00 1.80
❑ 202 Fred Kipp .......... 4.00 1.80
❑ 203 Sammy White .......... 4.00 1.80
❑ 204 Ryne Duren .......... 6.00 2.70
❑ 205 Johnny Logan .......... 6.00 2.70
❑ 206 Claude Osteen .......... 6.00 2.70
❑ 207 Bob Boyd .......... 4.00 1.80
❑ 208 White Sox Team .......... 10.00 2.00
(Checklist on back)
❑ 209 Ron Blackburn .......... 4.00 1.80
❑ 210 Harmon Killebrew .......... 25.00 11.00
❑ 211 Taylor Phillips .......... 4.00 1.80
❑ 212 Walter Alston MG .......... 10.00 4.50
❑ 213 Chuck Dressen MG .......... 6.00 2.70
❑ 214 Jimmy Dykes MG .......... 6.00 2.70
❑ 215 Bob Elliott MG .......... 6.00 2.70
❑ 216 Joe Gordon MG .......... 6.00 2.70
❑ 217 Charlie Grimm MG .......... 6.00 2.70
❑ 218 Solly Hemus MG .......... 4.00 1.80
❑ 219 Fred Hutchinson MG .......... 6.00 2.70
❑ 220 Billy Jurges MG .......... 4.00 1.80
❑ 221 Cookie Lavagetto MG .. 4.00 1.80
❑ 222 Al Lopez MG .......... 10.00 4.50
❑ 223 Danny Murtaugh MG .......... 6.00 2.70
❑ 224 Paul Richards MG .......... 6.00 2.70
❑ 225 Bill Rigney MG .......... 4.00 1.80
❑ 226 Eddie Sawyer MG .......... 4.00 1.80
❑ 227 Casey Stengel MG .......... 15.00 6.75
❑ 228 Ernie Johnson .......... 6.00 2.70
❑ 229 Joe M. Morgan .......... 4.00 1.80
❑ 230 Mound Magicians .......... 10.00 4.50
Lou Burdette
Warren Spahn
Bob Buhl
❑ 231 Hal Naragon .......... 4.00 1.80
❑ 232 Jim Busby .......... 4.00 1.80
❑ 233 Don Elston .......... 4.00 1.80
❑ 234 Don Demeter .......... 4.00 1.80
❑ 235 Gus Bell .......... 6.00 2.70
❑ 236 Dick Ricketts .......... 4.00 1.80
❑ 237 Elmer Valo .......... 4.00 1.80
❑ 238 Danny Kravitz .......... 4.00 1.80
❑ 239 Joe Shipley .......... 4.00 1.80
❑ 240 Luis Aparicio .......... 15.00 6.75
❑ 241 Albie Pearson .......... 6.00 2.70
❑ 242 Cardinals Team .......... 10.00 2.00
(Checklist on back)
❑ 243 Bubba Phillips .......... 4.00 1.80
❑ 244 Hal Griggs .......... 4.00 1.80
❑ 245 Eddie Yost .......... 6.00 2.70
❑ 246 Lee Maye .......... 6.00 2.70
❑ 247 Gil McDougald .......... 10.00 4.50
❑ 248 Del Rice .......... 4.00 1.80
❑ 249 Earl Wilson RC .......... 6.00 2.70
❑ 250 Stan Musial .......... 100.00 45.00
❑ 251 Bob Malkmus .......... 4.00 1.80
❑ 252 Ray Herbert .......... 4.00 1.80
❑ 253 Eddie Bressoud .......... 4.00 1.80
❑ 254 Arnie Portocarrero .......... 4.00 1.80
❑ 255 Jim Gilliam .......... 6.00 2.70
❑ 256 Dick Brown .......... 4.00 1.80
❑ 257 Gordy Coleman RC .......... 4.00 1.80
❑ 258 Dick Groat .......... 6.00 2.70
❑ 259 George Altman .......... 4.00 1.80
❑ 260 Power Plus .......... 15.00 6.75
Rocky Colavito
Tito Francona
❑ 261 Pete Burnside .......... 4.00 1.80
❑ 262 Hank Bauer .......... 6.00 2.70
❑ 263 Darrell Johnson .......... 4.00 1.80
❑ 264 Robin Roberts .......... 15.00 6.75
❑ 265 Rip Repulski .......... 4.00 1.80
❑ 266 Joey Jay .......... 6.00 2.70
❑ 267 Jim Marshall .......... 4.00 1.80
❑ 268 Al Worthington .......... 4.00 1.80
❑ 269 Gene Green .......... 4.00 1.80
❑ 270 Bob Turley .......... 6.00 2.70
❑ 271 Julio Becquer .......... 4.00 1.80
❑ 272 Fred Green .......... 6.00 2.70
❑ 273 Neil Chrisley .......... 4.00 1.80
❑ 274 Tom Acker .......... 4.00 1.80
❑ 275 Curt Flood .......... 6.00 2.70
❑ 276 Ken McBride .......... 4.00 1.80
❑ 277 Harry Bright .......... 4.00 1.80
❑ 278 Stan Williams .......... 6.00 2.70
❑ 279 Chuck Tanner .......... 6.00 2.70
❑ 280 Frank Sullivan .......... 4.00 1.80
❑ 281 Ray Boone .......... 6.00 2.70
❑ 282 Joe Nuxhall .......... 6.00 2.70
❑ 283 John Blanchard .......... 6.00 2.70
❑ 284 Don Gross .......... 4.00 1.80
❑ 285 Harry Anderson .......... 4.00 1.80
❑ 286 Ray Semproch .......... 4.00 1.80
❑ 287 Felipe Alou .......... 6.00 2.70
❑ 288 Bob Mabe .......... 4.00 1.80
❑ 289 Willie Jones .......... 4.00 1.80
❑ 290 Jerry Lumpe .......... 4.00 1.80
❑ 291 Bob Keegan .......... 4.00 1.80
❑ 292 Dodger Backstops .......... 6.00 2.70
Joe Pignatano
John Roseboro
❑ 293 Gene Conley .......... 6.00 2.70
❑ 294 Tony Taylor .......... 6.00 2.70
❑ 295 Gil Hodges .......... 25.00 11.00
❑ 296 Nelson Chittum .......... 4.00 1.80
❑ 297 Reno Bertoia .......... 4.00 1.80
❑ 298 George Witt .......... 4.00 1.80
❑ 299 Earl Torgeson .......... 4.00 1.80
❑ 300 Hank Aaron .......... 100.00 45.00
❑ 301 Jerry Davie .......... 4.00 1.80
❑ 302 Phillies Team .......... 10.00 2.00
(Checklist on back)
❑ 303 Billy O'Dell .......... 4.00 1.80
❑ 304 Joe Ginsberg .......... 4.00 1.80
❑ 305 Richie Ashburn .......... 20.00 9.00
❑ 306 Frank Baumann .......... 4.00 1.80
❑ 307 Gene Oliver .......... 4.00 1.80
❑ 308 Dick Hall .......... 4.00 1.80
❑ 309 Bob Hale .......... 4.00 1.80
❑ 310 Frank Malzone .......... 6.00 2.70
❑ 311 Raul Sanchez .......... 4.00 1.80
❑ 312 Charley Lau .......... 6.00 2.70
❑ 313 Turk Lown .......... 4.00 1.80
❑ 314 Chico Fernandez .......... 4.00 1.80
❑ 315 Bobby Shantz .......... 10.00 4.50
❑ 316 Willie McCovey RC ! 125.00 55.00
❑ 317 Pumpsie Green .......... 6.00 2.70
❑ 318 Jim Baxes .......... 6.00 2.70
❑ 319 Joe Koppe .......... 6.00 2.70
❑ 320 Bob Allison .......... 6.00 2.70
❑ 321 Ron Fairly .......... 6.00 2.70
❑ 322 Willie Tasby .......... 6.00 2.70
❑ 323 John Romano .......... 6.00 2.70
❑ 324 Jim Perry .......... 6.00 2.70
❑ 325 Jim O'Toole .......... 6.00 2.70
❑ 326 Roberto Clemente .... 175.00 80.00
❑ 327 Ray Sadecki RC .......... 4.00 1.80
❑ 328 Earl Battey .......... 4.00 1.80
❑ 329 Zack Monroe .......... 4.00 1.80
❑ 330 Harvey Kuenn .......... 6.00 2.70
❑ 331 Henry Mason .......... 4.00 1.80
❑ 332 Yankees Team .......... 75.00 15.00
(Checklist on back)
❑ 333 Danny McDevitt .......... 4.00 1.80
❑ 334 Ted Abernathy .......... 4.00 1.80
❑ 335 Red Schoendienst .......... 15.00 6.75
❑ 336 Ike Delock .......... 4.00 1.80
❑ 337 Cal Neeman .......... 4.00 1.80
❑ 338 Ray Monzant .......... 4.00 1.80
❑ 339 Harry Chiti .......... 4.00 1.80
❑ 340 Harvey Haddix .......... 6.00 2.70
❑ 341 Carroll Hardy .......... 4.00 1.80
❑ 342 Casey Wise .......... 4.00 1.80
❑ 343 Sandy Koufax .......... 125.00 55.00
❑ 344 Clint Courtney .......... 4.00 1.80
❑ 345 Don Newcombe .......... 6.00 2.70
❑ 346 J.C. Martin UER .......... 6.00 2.70
(Face actually
Gary Peters)
❑ 347 Ed Bouchee .......... 4.00 1.80
❑ 348 Barry Shetrone .......... 4.00 1.80
❑ 349 Moe Drabowsky .......... 6.00 2.70
❑ 350 Mickey Mantle .......... 450.00 200.00
❑ 351 Don Nottebart .......... 4.00 1.80
❑ 352 Cincy Clouters .......... 10.00 4.50
Gus Bell
Frank Robinson
Jerry Lynch
❑ 353 Don Larsen .......... 6.00 2.70
❑ 354 Bob Lillis .......... 4.00 1.80
❑ 355 Bill White .......... 6.00 2.70
❑ 356 Joe Amalfitano .......... 4.00 1.80
❑ 357 Al Schroll .......... 4.00 1.80
❑ 358 Joe DeMaestri .......... 4.00 1.80
❑ 359 Buddy Gilbert .......... 4.00 1.80
❑ 360 Herb Score .......... 6.00 2.70
❑ 361 Bob Oldis .......... 6.00 2.70
❑ 362 Russ Kemmerer .......... 4.00 1.80
❑ 363 Gene Stephens .......... 4.00 1.80
❑ 364 Paul Foytack .......... 4.00 1.80
❑ 365 Minnie Minoso .......... 10.00 4.50
❑ 366 Dallas Green RC .......... 10.00 4.50
❑ 367 Bill Tuttle .......... 4.00 1.80
❑ 368 Daryl Spencer .......... 4.00 1.80
❑ 369 Billy Hoeft .......... 4.00 1.80
❑ 370 Bill Skowron .......... 10.00 4.50
❑ 371 Bud Byerly .......... 4.00 1.80
❑ 372 Frank House .......... 4.00 1.80
❑ 373 Don Hoak .......... 6.00 2.70
❑ 374 Bob Buhl .......... 6.00 2.70
❑ 375 Dale Long .......... 10.00 4.50
❑ 376 John Briggs .......... 4.00 1.80
❑ 377 Roger Maris .......... 100.00 45.00
❑ 378 Stu Miller .......... 6.00 2.70
❑ 379 Red Wilson .......... 4.00 1.80
❑ 380 Bob Shaw .......... 4.00 1.80
❑ 381 Braves Team .......... 10.00 2.00
(Checklist on back)
❑ 382 Ted Bowsfield .......... 4.00 1.80
❑ 383 Leon Wagner .......... 4.00 1.80
❑ 384 Don Cardwell .......... 4.00 1.80
❑ 385 Charlie Neal WS .......... 6.00 2.70
❑ 386 Charlie Neal WS .......... 6.00 2.70
❑ 387 Carl Furillo WS .......... 6.00 2.70
❑ 388 Gil Hodges WS .......... 10.00 4.50
❑ 389 Luis Aparicio WS .......... 12.00 5.50
Maury Wills
❑ 390 World Series Game 6 .. 6.00 2.70
❑ 391 World Series Summary 6.00 2.70
The Champs Celebrate
❑ 392 Tex Clevenger .......... 4.00 1.80
❑ 393 Smoky Burgess .......... 6.00 2.70
❑ 394 Norm Larker .......... 6.00 2.70
❑ 395 Hoyt Wilhelm .......... 15.00 6.75
❑ 396 Steve Bilko .......... 4.00 1.80
❑ 397 Don Blasingame .......... 4.00 1.80
❑ 398 Mike Cuellar .......... 6.00 2.70
❑ 399 Young Hill Stars .......... 6.00 2.70
Milt Pappas
Jack Fisher
Jerry Walker
❑ 400 Rocky Colavito .......... 20.00 9.00
❑ 401 Bob Duliba .......... 4.00 1.80
❑ 402 Dick Stuart .......... 15.00 6.75
❑ 403 Ed Sadowski .......... 4.00 1.80
❑ 404 Bob Rush .......... 4.00 1.80
❑ 405 Bobby Richardson .......... 15.00 6.75
❑ 406 Billy Klaus .......... 4.00 1.80
❑ 407 Gary Peters RC UER .. 6.00 2.70
(Face actually
J.C. Martin)
❑ 408 Carl Furillo .......... 10.00 4.50

❑ 409 Ron Samford ........ 4.00 1.80
❑ 410 Sam Jones ........ 6.00 2.70
❑ 411 Ed Bailey ........ 4.00 1.80
❑ 412 Bob Anderson ........ 4.00 1.80
❑ 413 Athletics Team ........ 10.00 2.00
(Checklist on back)
❑ 414 Don Williams ........ 4.00 1.80
❑ 415 Bob Cerv ........ 4.00 1.80
❑ 416 Humberto Robinson ........ 4.00 1.80
❑ 417 Chuck Cottier RC ........ 4.00 1.80
❑ 418 Don Mossi ........ 6.00 2.70
❑ 419 George Crowe ........ 4.00 1.80
❑ 420 Eddie Mathews ........ 40.00 18.00
❑ 421 Duke Maas ........ 4.00 1.80
❑ 422 John Powers ........ 4.00 1.80
❑ 423 Ed Fitzgerald ........ 4.00 1.80
❑ 424 Pete Whisenant ........ 4.00 1.80
❑ 425 Johnny Podres ........ 6.00 2.70
❑ 426 Ron Jackson ........ 4.00 1.80
❑ 427 Al Grunwald ........ 4.00 1.80
❑ 428 Al Smith ........ 4.00 1.80
❑ 429 AL Kings ........ 10.00 4.50
Nellie Fox
Harvey Kuenn
❑ 430 Art Ditmar ........ 4.00 1.80
❑ 431 Andre Rodgers ........ 4.00 1.80
❑ 432 Chuck Stobbs ........ 4.00 1.80
❑ 433 Irv Noren ........ 4.00 1.80
❑ 434 Brooks Lawrence ........ 6.00 2.70
❑ 435 Gene Freese ........ 4.00 1.80
❑ 436 Marv Throneberry ........ 6.00 2.70
❑ 437 Bob Friend ........ 6.00 2.70
❑ 438 Jim Coker ........ 4.00 1.80
❑ 439 Tom Brewer ........ 4.00 1.80
❑ 440 Jim Lemon ........ 6.00 2.70
❑ 441 Gary Bell ........ 10.00 4.50
❑ 442 Joe Pignatano ........ 7.00 3.10
❑ 443 Charlie Maxwell ........ 7.00 3.10
❑ 444 Jerry Kindall ........ 7.00 3.10
❑ 445 Warren Spahn ........ 50.00 22.00
❑ 446 Ellis Burton ........ 7.00 3.10
❑ 447 Ray Moore ........ 7.00 3.10
❑ 448 Jim Gentile RC ! ........ 15.00 6.75
❑ 449 Jim Brosnan ........ 7.00 3.10
❑ 450 Orlando Cepeda ........ 25.00 11.00
❑ 451 Curt Simmons ........ 7.00 3.10
❑ 452 Ray Webster ........ 7.00 3.10
❑ 453 Vern Law ........ 25.00 11.00
❑ 454 Hal Woodeshick ........ 7.00 3.10
❑ 455 Baltimore Coaches ........ 7.00 3.10
Eddie Robinson
Harry Brecheen
Luman Harris
❑ 456 Red Sox Coaches ........ 10.00 4.50
Rudy York
Billy Herman
Sal Maglie
Del Baker
❑ 457 Cubs Coaches ........ 7.00 3.10
Charlie Root
Lou Klein
Elvin Tappe
❑ 458 White Sox Coaches ........ 7.00 3.10
Johnny Cooney
Don Gutteridge
Tony Cuccinello
Ray Berres
❑ 459 Reds Coaches ........ 7.00 3.10
Reggie Otero
Cot Deal
Wally Moses
❑ 460 Indians Coaches ........ 15.00 6.75
Mel Harder
Jo-Jo White
Bob Lemon
Ralph(Red) Kress
❑ 461 Tigers Coaches ........ 10.00 4.50
Tom Ferrick
Luke Appling
Billy Hitchcock
❑ 462 Athletics Coaches ........ 7.00 3.10
Fred Fitzsimmons
Don Heffner
Walker Cooper
❑ 463 Dodgers Coaches ........ 7.00 3.10
Bobby Bragan
Pete Reiser
Joe Becker
Greg Mulleavy
❑ 464 Braves Coaches ........ 7.00 3.10
Bob Scheffing
Whitlow Wyatt
Andy Pafko
George Myatt
❑ 465 Yankees Coaches ........ 25.00 11.00
Bill Dickey
Ralph Houk
Frank Crosetti
Ed Lopat
❑ 466 Phillies Coaches ........ 7.00 3.10
Ken Silvestri
Dick Carter
Andy Cohen
❑ 467 Pirates Coaches ........ 7.00 3.10
Mickey Vernon
Frank Oceak
Sam Narron
Bill Burwell
❑ 468 Cardinals Coaches ........ 7.00 3.10
Johnny Keane
Howie Pollet
Ray Katt
Harry Walker
❑ 469 Giants Coaches ........ 7.00 3.10
Wes Westrum
Salty Parker
Bill Posedel
❑ 470 Senators Coaches ........ 7.00 3.10
Bob Swift
Ellis Clary
Sam Mele
❑ 471 Ned Garver ........ 7.00 3.10
❑ 472 Alvin Dark ........ 7.00 3.10
❑ 473 Al Cicotte ........ 7.00 3.10
❑ 474 Haywood Sullivan ........ 7.00 3.10
❑ 475 Don Drysdale ........ 40.00 18.00
❑ 476 Lou Johnson ........ 7.00 3.10
❑ 477 Don Ferrarese ........ 7.00 3.10
❑ 478 Frank Torre ........ 7.00 3.10
❑ 479 Georges Maranda ........ 7.00 3.10
❑ 480 Yogi Berra ........ 75.00 34.00
❑ 481 Wes Stock ........ 7.00 3.10
❑ 482 Frank Bolling ........ 7.00 3.10
❑ 483 Camilo Pascual ........ 7.00 3.10
❑ 484 Pirates Team ........ 40.00 8.00
(Checklist on back)
❑ 485 Ken Boyer ........ 15.00 6.75
❑ 486 Bobby Del Greco ........ 7.00 3.10
❑ 487 Tom Sturdivant ........ 7.00 3.10
❑ 488 Norm Cash ........ 25.00 11.00
❑ 489 Steve Ridzik ........ 7.00 3.10
❑ 490 Frank Robinson ........ 50.00 22.00
❑ 491 Mel Roach ........ 7.00 3.10
❑ 492 Larry Jackson ........ 7.00 3.10
❑ 493 Duke Snider ........ 50.00 22.00
❑ 494 Orioles Team ........ 25.00 5.00
(Checklist on back)
❑ 495 Sherm Lollar ........ 7.00 3.10
❑ 496 Bill Virdon ........ 10.00 4.50
❑ 497 John Tsitouris ........ 7.00 3.10
❑ 498 Al Pilarcik ........ 7.00 3.10
❑ 499 Johnny James ........ 10.00 4.50
❑ 500 Johnny Temple ........ 7.00 3.10
❑ 501 Bob Schmidt ........ 7.00 3.10
❑ 502 Jim Bunning ........ 25.00 11.00
❑ 503 Don Lee ........ 7.00 3.10
❑ 504 Seth Morehead ........ 7.00 3.10
❑ 505 Ted Kluszewski ........ 25.00 11.00
❑ 506 Lee Walls ........ 7.00 3.10
❑ 507 Dick Stigman ........ 16.00 7.25
❑ 508 Billy Consolo ........ 16.00 7.25
❑ 509 Tommy Davis RC ! ........ 25.00 11.00
❑ 510 Gerry Staley ........ 16.00 7.25
❑ 511 Ken Walters ........ 16.00 7.25
❑ 512 Joe Gibbon ........ 16.00 7.25
❑ 513 Chicago Cubs ........ 30.00 6.00
Team Card
(Checklist on back)
❑ 514 Steve Barber RC ........ 16.00 7.25
❑ 515 Stan Lopata ........ 16.00 7.25
❑ 516 Marty Kutyna ........ 16.00 7.25
❑ 517 Charlie James ........ 25.00 11.00
❑ 518 Tony Gonzalez ........ 16.00 7.25
❑ 519 Ed Roebuck ........ 16.00 7.25
❑ 520 Don Buddin ........ 16.00 7.25
❑ 521 Mike Lee ........ 16.00 7.25
❑ 522 Ken Hunt ........ 30.00 13.50
❑ 523 Clay Dalrymple ........ 16.00 7.25
❑ 524 Bill Henry ........ 16.00 7.25
❑ 525 Marv Breeding ........ 16.00 7.25
❑ 526 Paul Giel ........ 25.00 11.00
❑ 527 Jose Valdivielso ........ 25.00 11.00
❑ 528 Ben Johnson ........ 16.00 7.25
❑ 529 Norm Sherry RC ........ 20.00 9.00
❑ 530 Mike McCormick ........ 16.00 7.25
❑ 531 Sandy Amoros ........ 20.00 9.00
❑ 532 Mike Garcia ........ 20.00 9.00
❑ 533 Lu Clinton ........ 16.00 7.25
❑ 534 Ken MacKenzie ........ 16.00 7.25
❑ 535 Whitey Lockman ........ 16.00 7.25
❑ 536 Wynn Hawkins ........ 16.00 7.25
❑ 537 Boston Red Sox ........ 30.00 6.00
Team Card
(Checklist on back)
❑ 538 Frank Barnes ........ 16.00 7.25
❑ 539 Gene Baker ........ 16.00 7.25
❑ 540 Jerry Walker ........ 16.00 7.25
❑ 541 Tony Curry ........ 16.00 7.25
❑ 542 Ken Hamlin ........ 16.00 7.25
❑ 543 Elio Chacon ........ 16.00 7.25
❑ 544 Bill Monbouquette ........ 20.00 9.00
❑ 545 Carl Sawatski ........ 16.00 7.25
❑ 546 Hank Aguirre ........ 16.00 7.25
❑ 547 Bob Aspromonte ........ 20.00 9.00
❑ 548 Don Mincher ........ 16.00 7.25
❑ 549 John Buzhardt ........ 16.00 7.25
❑ 550 Jim Landis ........ 16.00 7.25
❑ 551 Ed Rakow ........ 16.00 7.25
❑ 552 Walt Bond ........ 16.00 7.25
❑ 553 Bill Skowron AS ........ 20.00 9.00
❑ 554 Willie McCovey AS ........ 35.00 16.00
❑ 555 Nellie Fox AS ........ 30.00 13.50
❑ 556 Charlie Neal AS ........ 16.00 7.25
❑ 557 Frank Malzone AS ........ 16.00 7.25
❑ 558 Eddie Mathews AS ........ 35.00 16.00
❑ 559 Luis Aparicio AS ........ 30.00 13.50
❑ 560 Ernie Banks AS ........ 60.00 27.00
❑ 561 Al Kaline AS ........ 60.00 27.00
❑ 562 Joe Cunningham AS ........ 16.00 7.25
❑ 563 Mickey Mantle AS ........ 250.00 110.00
❑ 564 Willie Mays AS ........ 100.00 45.00
❑ 565 Roger Maris AS ........ 100.00 45.00
❑ 566 Hank Aaron AS ........ 100.00 45.00
❑ 567 Sherm Lollar AS ........ 16.00 7.25
❑ 568 Del Crandall AS ........ 16.00 7.25
❑ 569 Camilo Pascual AS ........ 16.00 7.25
❑ 570 Don Drysdale AS ........ 35.00 16.00
❑ 571 Billy Pierce AS ........ 16.00 7.25
❑ 572 Johnny Antonelli AS ........ 30.00 9.00
❑ NNO Iron-on team transfer ........ 4.00 1.80

## 1961 Topps

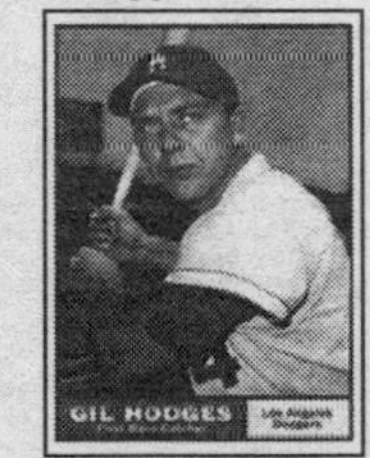


| | NRMT | VG-E |
|---|---|---|
| COMPLETE SET (587) | 4800.00 | 2200.00 |
| COMMON CARD (1-370) | 3.00 | 1.35 |
| COMMON CARD (371-446) | 4.00 | 1.80 |
| COMMON CARD (447-522) | 7.00 | 3.10 |
| COMMON CARD (523-589) | 30.00 | 13.50 |
| NOT ISSUED (587/588) | | |

WRAPPER (1-CENT) .......... 200.00 90.00
WRAP.(1-CENT, REPEAT) .. 100.00 45.00
WRAPPER (5-CENT) .......... 40.00 18.00

❑ 1 Dick Groat .......... 30.00 6.00
❑ 2 Roger Maris .......... 175.00 80.00
❑ 3 John Buzhardt .......... 3.00 1.35
❑ 4 Lenny Green .......... 3.00 1.35
❑ 5 John Romano .......... 3.00 1.35
❑ 6 Ed Roebuck .......... 3.00 1.35
❑ 7 White Sox Team .......... 8.00 3.60
❑ 8 Dick Williams .......... 6.00 2.70
❑ 9 Bob Purkey .......... 3.00 1.35
❑ 10 Brooks Robinson .......... 50.00 22.00
❑ 11 Curt Simmons .......... 6.00 2.70
❑ 12 Moe Thacker .......... 3.00 1.35
❑ 13 Chuck Cottier .......... 3.00 1.35
❑ 14 Don Mossi .......... 6.00 2.70
❑ 15 Willie Kirkland .......... 3.00 1.35
❑ 16 Billy Muffett .......... 3.00 1.35
❑ 17 Checklist 1 .......... 12.00 2.40
❑ 18 Jim Grant .......... 6.00 2.70
❑ 19 Clete Boyer .......... 8.00 3.60
❑ 20 Robin Roberts .......... 15.00 6.75
❑ 21 Zorro Versalles UER RC 8.00 3.60
(First name should
be Zoilo)
❑ 22 Clem Labine .......... 6.00 2.70
❑ 23 Don Demeter .......... 3.00 1.35
❑ 24 Ken Johnson .......... 6.00 2.70
❑ 25 Reds' Heavy Artillery .......... 8.00 3.60
Vada Pinson
Gus Bell
Frank Robinson
❑ 26 Wes Stock .......... 3.00 1.35
❑ 27 Jerry Kindall .......... 3.00 1.35
❑ 28 Hector Lopez .......... 6.00 2.70
❑ 29 Don Nottebart .......... 3.00 1.35
❑ 30 Nellie Fox .......... 15.00 6.75
❑ 31 Bob Schmidt .......... 3.00 1.35
❑ 32 Ray Sadecki .......... 3.00 1.35
❑ 33 Gary Geiger .......... 3.00 1.35
❑ 34 Wynn Hawkins .......... 3.00 1.35
❑ 35 Ron Santo RC .......... 40.00 18.00
❑ 36 Jack Kralick .......... 3.00 1.35
❑ 37 Charley Maxwell .......... 6.00 2.70
❑ 38 Bob Lillis .......... 3.00 1.35
❑ 39 Leo Posada .......... 3.00 1.35
❑ 40 Bob Turley .......... 6.00 2.70
❑ 41 NL Batting Leaders .......... 35.00 16.00
Dick Groat
Norm Larker
Willie Mays
Roberto Clemente
❑ 42 AL Batting Leaders .......... 8.00 3.60
Pete Runnels
Al Smith
Minnie Minoso
Bill Skowron
❑ 43 NL Home Run Leaders 30.00 13.50
Ernie Banks
Hank Aaron
Ed Mathews
Ken Boyer
❑ 44 AL Home Run Leaders 80.00 36.00
Mickey Mantle
Roger Maris
Jim Lemon
Rocky Colavito
❑ 45 NL ERA Leaders .......... 8.00 3.60
Mike McCormick
Ernie Broglio
Don Drysdale
Bob Friend
Stan Williams
❑ 46 AL ERA Leaders .......... 8.00 3.60
Frank Baumann
Jim Bunning
Art Ditmar
Hal Brown
❑ 47 NL Pitching Leaders .......... 8.00 3.60
Ernie Broglio
Warren Spahn
Vern Law
Lou Burdette
❑ 48 AL Pitching Leaders .......... 8.00 3.60
Chuck Estrada
Jim Perry UER
(Listed as an Oriole)
Bud Daley
Art Ditmar
Frank Lary
Milt Pappas
❑ 49 NL Strikeout Leaders .. 20.00 9.00
Don Drysdale
Sandy Koufax
Sam Jones
Ernie Broglio
❑ 50 AL Strikeout Leaders .......... 8.00 3.60
Jim Bunning
Pedro Ramos
Early Wynn
Frank Lary
❑ 51 Detroit Tigers .......... 8.00 3.60
Team Card
❑ 52 George Crowe .......... 3.00 1.35
❑ 53 Russ Nixon .......... 3.00 1.35
❑ 54 Earl Francis .......... 3.00 1.35
❑ 55 Jim Davenport .......... 6.00 2.70
❑ 56 Russ Kemmerer .......... 3.00 1.35
❑ 57 Marv Throneberry .......... 6.00 2.70
❑ 58 Joe Schaffernoth .......... 3.00 1.35
❑ 59 Jim Woods .......... 3.00 1.35
❑ 60 Woody Held .......... 3.00 1.35
❑ 61 Ron Piche .......... 3.00 1.35
❑ 62 Al Pilarcik .......... 3.00 1.35
❑ 63 Jim Kaat .......... 8.00 3.60
❑ 64 Alex Grammas .......... 3.00 1.35
❑ 65 Ted Kluszewski .......... 8.00 3.60
❑ 66 Bill Henry .......... 3.00 1.35
❑ 67 Ossie Virgil .......... 3.00 1.35
❑ 68 Deron Johnson .......... 6.00 2.70
❑ 69 Earl Wilson .......... 6.00 2.70
❑ 70 Bill Virdon .......... 6.00 2.70
❑ 71 Jerry Adair .......... 3.00 1.35
❑ 72 Stu Miller .......... 6.00 2.70
❑ 73 Al Spangler .......... 3.00 1.35
❑ 74 Joe Pignatano .......... 3.00 1.35
❑ 75 Lindy Shows Larry .......... 6.00 2.70
Lindy McDaniel
Larry Jackson
❑ 76 Harry Anderson .......... 3.00 1.35
❑ 77 Dick Stigman .......... 3.00 1.35
❑ 78 Lee Walls .......... 6.00 2.70
❑ 79 Joe Ginsberg .......... 3.00 1.35
❑ 80 Harmon Killebrew .......... 20.00 9.00
❑ 81 Tracy Stallard .......... 3.00 1.35
❑ 82 Joe Christopher .......... 3.00 1.35
❑ 83 Bob Bruce .......... 3.00 1.35
❑ 84 Lee Maye .......... 3.00 1.35
❑ 85 Jerry Walker .......... 3.00 1.35
❑ 86 Los Angeles Dodgers .... 8.00 3.60
Team Card
❑ 87 Joe Amalfitano .......... 3.00 1.35
❑ 88 Richie Ashburn .......... 15.00 6.75
❑ 89 Billy Martin .......... 15.00 6.75
❑ 90 Gerry Staley .......... 3.00 1.35
❑ 91 Walt Moryn .......... 3.00 1.35
❑ 92 Hal Naragon .......... 3.00 1.35
❑ 93 Tony Gonzalez .......... 3.00 1.35
❑ 94 Johnny Kucks .......... 3.00 1.35
❑ 95 Norm Cash .......... 8.00 3.60
❑ 96 Billy O'Dell .......... 3.00 1.35
❑ 97 Jerry Lynch .......... 6.00 2.70
❑ 98A Checklist 2 .......... 10.00 2.00
(Red "Checklist"
98 black on white)
❑ 98B Checklist 2 .......... 10.00 2.00
(Yellow "Checklist"
98 black on white)
❑ 98C Checklist 2 .......... 10.00 2.00
(Yellow "Checklist"
98 white on black;
no copyright)
❑ 99 Don Buddin UER .......... 3.00 1.35
(66 HR's)
❑ 100 Harvey Haddix .......... 6.00 2.70
❑ 101 Bubba Phillips .......... 3.00 1.35
❑ 102 Gene Stephens .......... 3.00 1.35
❑ 103 Ruben Amaro .......... 3.00 1.35
❑ 104 John Blanchard .......... 8.00 3.60
❑ 105 Carl Willey .......... 3.00 1.35
❑ 106 Whitey Herzog .......... 3.00 1.35
❑ 107 Seth Morehead .......... 3.00 1.35
❑ 108 Dan Dobbek .......... 3.00 1.35
❑ 109 Johnny Podres .......... 8.00 3.60
❑ 110 Vada Pinson .......... 8.00 3.60
❑ 111 Jack Meyer .......... 3.00 1.35
❑ 112 Chico Fernandez .......... 3.00 1.35
❑ 113 Mike Fornieles .......... 3.00 1.35
❑ 114 Hobie Landrith .......... 3.00 1.35
❑ 115 Johnny Antonelli .......... 6.00 2.70
❑ 116 Joe DeMaestri .......... 3.00 1.35
❑ 117 Dale Long .......... 6.00 2.70
❑ 118 Chris Cannizzaro .......... 3.00 1.35
❑ 119 A's Big Armor .......... 6.00 2.70
Norm Siebern
Hank Bauer
Jerry Lumpe
❑ 120 Eddie Mathews .......... 30.00 13.50
❑ 121 Eli Grba .......... 6.00 2.70
❑ 122 Chicago Cubs .......... 8.00 3.60
Team Card
❑ 123 Billy Gardner .......... 3.00 1.35
❑ 124 J.C. Martin .......... 3.00 1.35
❑ 125 Steve Barber .......... 3.00 1.35
❑ 126 Dick Stuart .......... 6.00 2.70
❑ 127 Ron Kline .......... 3.00 1.35
❑ 128 Rip Repulski .......... 3.00 1.35
❑ 129 Ed Hobaugh .......... 3.00 1.35
❑ 130 Norm Larker .......... 3.00 1.35
❑ 131 Paul Richards MG .......... 6.00 2.70
❑ 132 Al Lopez MG .......... 8.00 3.60
❑ 133 Ralph Houk MG .......... 6.00 2.70
❑ 134 Mickey Vernon MG .......... 6.00 2.70
❑ 135 Fred Hutchinson MG .... 6.00 2.70
❑ 136 Walter Alston MG .......... 8.00 3.60
❑ 137 Chuck Dressen MG .......... 6.00 2.70
❑ 138 Danny Murtaugh MG .... 6.00 2.70
❑ 139 Solly Hemus MG .......... 6.00 2.70
❑ 140 Gus Triandos .......... 6.00 2.70
❑ 141 Billy Williams RC .......... 60.00 27.00
❑ 142 Luis Arroyo .......... 6.00 2.70
❑ 143 Russ Snyder .......... 3.00 1.35
❑ 144 Jim Coker .......... 3.00 1.35
❑ 145 Bob Buhl .......... 6.00 2.70
❑ 146 Marty Keough .......... 3.00 1.35
❑ 147 Ed Rakow .......... 3.00 1.35
❑ 148 Julian Javier .......... 6.00 2.70
❑ 149 Bob Oldis .......... 3.00 1.35
❑ 150 Willie Mays .......... 100.00 45.00
❑ 151 Jim Donohue .......... 3.00 1.35
❑ 152 Earl Torgeson .......... 3.00 1.35
❑ 153 Don Lee .......... 3.00 1.35
❑ 154 Bobby Del Greco .......... 3.00 1.35
❑ 155 Johnny Temple .......... 6.00 2.70
❑ 156 Ken Hunt .......... 6.00 2.70
❑ 157 Cal McLish .......... 3.00 1.35
❑ 158 Pete Daley .......... 3.00 1.35
❑ 159 Orioles Team .......... 8.00 3.60
❑ 160 Whitey Ford UER .......... 50.00 22.00
(Incorrectly listed
as 5'0~ tall)
❑ 161 Sherman Jones UER .. 3.00 1.35
(Photo actually
Eddie Fisher)
❑ 162 Jay Hook .......... 3.00 1.35
❑ 163 Ed Sadowski .......... 3.00 1.35
❑ 164 Felix Mantilla .......... 3.00 1.35
❑ 165 Gino Cimoli .......... 3.00 1.35
❑ 166 Danny Kravitz .......... 3.00 1.35
❑ 167 San Francisco Giants .. 8.00 3.60
Team Card
❑ 168 Tommy Davis .......... 8.00 3.60
❑ 169 Don Elston .......... 3.00 1.35
❑ 170 Al Smith .......... 3.00 1.35
❑ 171 Paul Foytack .......... 3.00 1.35
❑ 172 Don Dillard .......... 3.00 1.35
❑ 173 Beantown Bombers .......... 6.00 2.70
Frank Malzone
Vic Wertz
Jackie Jensen
❑ 174 Ray Semproch .......... 3.00 1.35
❑ 175 Gene Freese .......... 3.00 1.35
❑ 176 Ken Aspromonte .......... 3.00 1.35
❑ 177 Don Larsen .......... 6.00 2.70
❑ 178 Bob Nieman .......... 3.00 1.35
❑ 179 Joe Koppe .......... 3.00 1.35

❑ 180 Bobby Richardson ...... 12.00 5.50
❑ 181 Fred Green ...... 3.00 1.35
❑ 182 Dave Nicholson ...... 3.00 1.35
❑ 183 Andre Rodgers ...... 3.00 1.35
❑ 184 Steve Bilko ...... 6.00 2.70
❑ 185 Herb Score ...... 6.00 2.70
❑ 186 Elmer Valo ...... 6.00 2.70
❑ 187 Billy Klaus ...... 3.00 1.35
❑ 188 Jim Marshall ...... 3.00 1.35
❑ 189A Checklist 3 ...... 10.00 2.00
(Copyright symbol
almost adjacent to
263 Ken Hamlin)
❑ 189B Checklist 3 ...... 10.00 2.00
(Copyright symbol
adjacent to
264 Glen Hobbie)
❑ 190 Stan Williams ...... 6.00 2.70
❑ 191 Mike de la Hoz ...... 3.00 1.35
❑ 192 Dick Brown ...... 3.00 1.35
❑ 193 Gene Conley ...... 6.00 2.70
❑ 194 Gordy Coleman ...... 6.00 2.70
❑ 195 Jerry Casale ...... 3.00 1.35
❑ 196 Ed Bouchee ...... 3.00 1.35
❑ 197 Dick Hall ...... 3.00 1.35
❑ 198 Carl Sawatski ...... 3.00 1.35
❑ 199 Bob Boyd ...... 3.00 1.35
❑ 200 Warren Spahn ...... 40.00 18.00
❑ 201 Pete Whisenant ...... 3.00 1.35
❑ 202 Al Neiger ...... 3.00 1.35
❑ 203 Eddie Bressoud ...... 3.00 1.35
❑ 204 Bob Skinner ...... 6.00 2.70
❑ 205 Billy Pierce ...... 6.00 2.70
❑ 206 Gene Green ...... 3.00 1.35
❑ 207 Dodger Southpaws ...... 30.00 13.50
Sandy Koufax
Johnny Podres
❑ 208 Larry Osborne ...... 3.00 1.35
❑ 209 Ken McBride ...... 3.00 1.35
❑ 210 Pete Runnels ...... 6.00 2.70
❑ 211 Bob Gibson ...... 40.00 18.00
❑ 212 Haywood Sullivan ...... 6.00 2.70
❑ 213 Bill Stafford ...... 3.00 1.35
❑ 214 Danny Murphy ...... 6.00 2.70
❑ 215 Gus Bell ...... 6.00 2.70
❑ 216 Ted Bowsfield ...... 3.00 1.35
❑ 217 Mel Roach ...... 3.00 1.35
❑ 218 Hal Brown ...... 3.00 1.35
❑ 219 Gene Mauch MG ...... 6.00 2.70
❑ 220 Alvin Dark MG ...... 6.00 2.70
❑ 221 Mike Higgins MG ...... 3.00 1.35
❑ 222 Jimmy Dykes MG ...... 6.00 2.70
❑ 223 Bob Scheffing MG ...... 3.00 1.35
❑ 224 Joe Gordon MG ...... 6.00 2.70
❑ 225 Bill Rigney MG ...... 6.00 2.70
❑ 226 Cookie Lavagetto MG ...... 6.00 2.70
❑ 227 Juan Pizarro ...... 3.00 1.35
❑ 228 New York Yankees ...... 60.00 27.00
Team Card
❑ 229 Rudy Hernandez ...... 3.00 1.35
❑ 230 Don Hoak ...... 6.00 2.70
❑ 231 Dick Drott ...... 3.00 1.35
❑ 232 Bill White ...... 6.00 2.70
❑ 233 Joey Jay ...... 6.00 2.70
❑ 234 Ted Lepcio ...... 3.00 1.35
❑ 235 Camilo Pascual ...... 6.00 2.70
❑ 236 Don Gile ...... 3.00 1.35
❑ 237 Billy Loes ...... 6.00 2.70
❑ 238 Jim Gilliam ...... 6.00 2.70
❑ 239 Dave Sisler ...... 3.00 1.35
❑ 240 Ron Hansen ...... 3.00 1.35
❑ 241 Al Cicotte ...... 3.00 1.35
❑ 242 Hal Smith ...... 3.00 1.35
❑ 243 Frank Lary ...... 6.00 2.70
❑ 244 Chico Cardenas ...... 6.00 2.70
❑ 245 Joe Adcock ...... 6.00 2.70
❑ 246 Bob Davis ...... 3.00 1.35
❑ 247 Billy Goodman ...... 6.00 2.70
❑ 248 Ed Keegan ...... 3.00 1.35
❑ 249 Cincinnati Reds ...... 8.00 3.60
Team Card
❑ 250 Buc Hill Aces ...... 6.00 2.70
Vern Law
Roy Face
❑ 251 Bill Bruton ...... 3.00 1.35
❑ 252 Bill Short ...... 3.00 1.35
❑ 253 Sammy Taylor ...... 3.00 1.35
❑ 254 Ted Sadowski ...... 6.00 2.70
❑ 255 Vic Power ...... 6.00 2.70
❑ 256 Billy Hoeft ...... 3.00 1.35
❑ 257 Carroll Hardy ...... 3.00 1.35
❑ 258 Jack Sanford ...... 6.00 2.70
❑ 259 John Schaive ...... 3.00 1.35
❑ 260 Don Drysdale ...... 30.00 13.50
❑ 261 Charlie Lau ...... 6.00 2.70
❑ 262 Tony Curry ...... 3.00 1.35
❑ 263 Ken Hamlin ...... 3.00 1.35
❑ 264 Glen Hobbie ...... 3.00 1.35
❑ 265 Tony Kubek ...... 12.00 5.50
❑ 266 Lindy McDaniel ...... 6.00 2.70
❑ 267 Norm Siebern ...... 3.00 1.35
❑ 268 Ike Delock ...... 3.00 1.35
❑ 269 Harry Chiti ...... 3.00 1.35
❑ 270 Bob Friend ...... 6.00 2.70
❑ 271 Jim Landis ...... 3.00 1.35
❑ 272 Tom Morgan ...... 3.00 1.35
❑ 273A Checklist 4 ...... 10.00 2.00
(Copyright symbol
adjacent to
336 Don Mincher)
❑ 273B Checklist 4 ...... 10.00 2.00
(Copyright symbol
adjacent to
339 Gene Baker)
❑ 274 Gary Bell ...... 3.00 1.35
❑ 275 Gene Woodling ...... 6.00 2.70
❑ 276 Ray Rippelmeyer ...... 3.00 1.35
❑ 277 Hank Foiles ...... 3.00 1.35
❑ 278 Don McMahon ...... 3.00 1.35
❑ 279 Jose Pagan ...... 3.00 1.35
❑ 280 Frank Howard ...... 8.00 3.60
❑ 281 Frank Sullivan ...... 3.00 1.35
❑ 282 Faye Throneberry ...... 3.00 1.35
❑ 283 Bob Anderson ...... 3.00 1.35
❑ 284 Dick Gernert ...... 3.00 1.35
❑ 285 Sherm Lollar ...... 6.00 2.70
❑ 286 George Witt ...... 3.00 1.35
❑ 287 Carl Yastrzemski ...... 50.00 22.00
❑ 288 Albie Pearson ...... 6.00 2.70
❑ 289 Ray Moore ...... 3.00 1.35
❑ 290 Stan Musial ...... 100.00 45.00
❑ 291 Tex Clevenger ...... 3.00 1.35
❑ 292 Jim Baumer ...... 3.00 1.35
❑ 293 Tom Sturdivant ...... 3.00 1.35
❑ 294 Don Blasingame ...... 3.00 1.35
❑ 295 Milt Pappas ...... 6.00 2.70
❑ 296 Wes Covington ...... 6.00 2.70
❑ 297 Athletics Team ...... 8.00 3.60
❑ 298 Jim Golden ...... 3.00 1.35
❑ 299 Clay Dalrymple ...... 3.00 1.35
❑ 300 Mickey Mantle ...... 400.00 180.00
❑ 301 Chet Nichols ...... 3.00 1.35
❑ 302 Al Heist ...... 3.00 1.35
❑ 303 Gary Peters ...... 6.00 2.70
❑ 304 Rocky Nelson ...... 3.00 1.35
❑ 305 Mike McCormick ...... 6.00 2.70
❑ 306 Bill Virdon WS ...... 8.00 3.60
❑ 307 Mickey Mantle WS ...... 80.00 36.00
❑ 308 Bobby Richardson WS 12.00 5.50
❑ 309 Gino Cimoli WS ...... 9.00 4.00
❑ 310 Roy Face WS ...... 9.00 4.00
❑ 311 Whitey Ford WS ...... 16.00 7.25
❑ 312 Bill Mazeroski WS ...... 20.00 9.00
Mazeroski Homer Wins it
❑ 313 World Series Summary 16.00 7.25
Pirates Celebrate
❑ 314 Bob Miller ...... 3.00 1.35
❑ 315 Earl Battey ...... 6.00 2.70
❑ 316 Bobby Gene Smith ...... 3.00 1.35
❑ 317 Jim Brewer ...... 3.00 1.35
❑ 318 Danny O'Connell ...... 3.00 1.35
❑ 319 Valmy Thomas ...... 3.00 1.35
❑ 320 Lou Burdette ...... 6.00 2.70
❑ 321 Marv Breeding ...... 3.00 1.35
❑ 322 Bill Kunkel ...... 6.00 2.70
❑ 323 Sammy Esposito ...... 3.00 1.35
❑ 324 Hank Aguirre ...... 3.00 1.35
❑ 325 Wally Moon ...... 6.00 2.70
❑ 326 Dave Hillman ...... 3.00 1.35
❑ 327 Matty Alou RC ...... 12.00 5.50
❑ 328 Jim O'Toole ...... 6.00 2.70
❑ 329 Julio Becquer ...... 3.00 1.35
❑ 330 Rocky Colavito ...... 20.00 9.00
❑ 331 Ned Garver ...... 3.00 1.35
❑ 332 Dutch Dotterer UER ...... 3.00 1.35
(Photo actually
Tommy Dotterer
Dutch's brother)
❑ 333 Fritz Brickell ...... 3.00 1.35
❑ 334 Walt Bond ...... 3.00 1.35
❑ 335 Frank Bolling ...... 3.00 1.35
❑ 336 Don Mincher ...... 6.00 2.70
❑ 337 Al's Aces ...... 8.00 3.60
Early Wynn
Al Lopez
Herb Score
❑ 338 Don Landrum ...... 3.00 1.35
❑ 339 Gene Baker ...... 3.00 1.35
❑ 340 Vic Wertz ...... 6.00 2.70
❑ 341 Jim Owens ...... 3.00 1.35
❑ 342 Clint Courtney ...... 3.00 1.35
❑ 343 Earl Robinson ...... 3.00 1.35
❑ 344 Sandy Koufax ...... 100.00 45.00
❑ 345 Jimmy Piersall ...... 8.00 3.60
❑ 346 Howie Nunn ...... 3.00 1.35
❑ 347 St. Louis Cardinals ...... 8.00 3.60
Team Card
❑ 348 Steve Boros ...... 3.00 1.35
❑ 349 Danny McDevitt ...... 3.00 1.35
❑ 350 Ernie Banks ...... 40.00 18.00
❑ 351 Jim King ...... 3.00 1.35
❑ 352 Bob Shaw ...... 3.00 1.35
❑ 353 Howie Bedell ...... 3.00 1.35
❑ 354 Billy Harrell ...... 6.00 2.70
❑ 355 Bob Allison ...... 8.00 3.60
❑ 356 Ryne Duren ...... 3.00 1.35
❑ 357 Daryl Spencer ...... 3.00 1.35
❑ 358 Earl Averill ...... 6.00 2.70
❑ 359 Dallas Green ...... 3.00 1.35
❑ 360 Frank Robinson ...... 40.00 18.00
❑ 361A Checklist 5 ...... 16.00 3.20
(No ad on back)
❑ 361B Checklist 5 ...... 16.00 3.20
(Special Feature
ad on back)
❑ 362 Frank Funk ...... 3.00 1.35
❑ 363 John Roseboro ...... 6.00 2.70
❑ 364 Moe Drabowsky ...... 6.00 2.70
❑ 365 Jerry Lumpe ...... 3.00 1.35
❑ 366 Eddie Fisher ...... 3.00 1.35
❑ 367 Jim Rivera ...... 3.00 1.35
❑ 368 Bennie Daniels ...... 3.00 1.35
❑ 369 Dave Philley ...... 3.00 1.35
❑ 370 Roy Face ...... 6.00 2.70
❑ 371 Bill Skowron SP ...... 50.00 22.00
❑ 372 Bob Hendley ...... 4.00 1.80
❑ 373 Boston Red Sox ...... 8.00 3.60
Team Card
❑ 374 Paul Giel ...... 4.00 1.80
❑ 375 Ken Boyer ...... 12.00 5.50
❑ 376 Mike Roarke RC ...... 6.00 2.70
❑ 377 Ruben Gomez ...... 4.00 1.80
❑ 378 Wally Post ...... 6.00 2.70
❑ 379 Bobby Shantz ...... 4.00 1.80
❑ 380 Minnie Minoso ...... 8.00 3.60
❑ 381 Dave Wickersham ...... 4.00 1.80
❑ 382 Frank Thomas ...... 6.00 2.70
❑ 383 Frisco First Liners ...... 6.00 2.70
Mike McCormick
Jack Sanford
Billy O'Dell
❑ 384 Chuck Essegian ...... 4.00 1.80
❑ 385 Jim Perry ...... 6.00 2.70
❑ 386 Joe Hicks ...... 4.00 1.80
❑ 387 Duke Maas ...... 4.00 1.80
❑ 388 Roberto Clemente ...... 135.00 60.00
❑ 389 Ralph Terry ...... 6.00 2.70
❑ 390 Del Crandall ...... 8.00 3.60
❑ 391 Winston Brown ...... 4.00 1.80
❑ 392 Reno Bertoia ...... 4.00 1.80
❑ 393 Batter Bafflers ...... 4.00 1.80
Don Cardwell
Glen Hobbie
❑ 394 Ken Walters ...... 4.00 1.80
❑ 395 Chuck Estrada ...... 6.00 2.70
❑ 396 Bob Aspromonte ...... 4.00 1.80
❑ 397 Hal Woodeshick ...... 4.00 1.80
❑ 398 Hank Bauer ...... 6.00 2.70

❑ 399 Cliff Cook 4.00 1.80
❑ 400 Vern Law 6.00 2.70
❑ 401 Babe Ruth HL 60.00 27.00
60th HR
❑ 402 Don Larsen HL SP 25.00 11.00
WS Perfect Game
❑ 403 Joe Oeschger HL 7.00 3.10
Leon Cadore
26 Inning Tie
❑ 404 Rogers Hornsby HL 12.00 5.50
.424 Season BA
❑ 405 Lou Gehrig HL 75.00 34.00
Consecutive Game Streak
❑ 406 Mickey Mantle HL 100.00 45.00
565 foot HR
❑ 407 Jack Chesbro HL 7.00 3.10
41 victories
❑ 408 C. Mathewson HL SP 20.00 9.00
267 Strikeouts
❑ 409 Walter Johnson SL 12.00 5.50
3 Shutouts in 4 days
❑ 410 Harvey Haddix HL 7.00 3.10
12 Perfect Innings
❑ 411 Tony Taylor 6.00 2.70
❑ 412 Larry Sherry 6.00 2.70
❑ 413 Eddie Yost 6.00 2.70
❑ 414 Dick Donovan 6.00 2.70
❑ 415 Hank Aaron 100.00 45.00
❑ 416 Dick Howser RC 8.00 3.60
❑ 417 Juan Marichal SP RC ! 100.00 45.00
❑ 418 Ed Bailey 6.00 2.70
❑ 419 Tom Borland 4.00 1.80
❑ 420 Ernie Broglio 6.00 2.70
❑ 421 Ty Cline SP 18.00 8.00
❑ 422 Bud Daley 4.00 1.80
❑ 423 Charlie Neal SP 18.00 8.00
❑ 424 Turk Lown 4.00 1.80
❑ 425 Yogi Berra 80.00 36.00
❑ 426 Milwaukee Braves 12.00 5.50
Team Card
(Back numbered 463)
❑ 427 Dick Ellsworth 6.00 2.70
❑ 428 Ray Barker SP 18.00 8.00
❑ 429 Al Kaline 50.00 22.00
❑ 430 Bill Mazeroski SP 50.00 22.00
❑ 431 Chuck Stobbs 4.00 1.80
❑ 432 Coot Veal 6.00 2.70
❑ 433 Art Mahaffey 4.00 1.80
❑ 434 Tom Brewer 4.00 1.80
❑ 435 Orlando Cepeda UER 12.00 5.50
(San Francis on
card front)
❑ 436 Jim Maloney SP RC ! 20.00 9.00
❑ 437A Checklist 6 16.00 3.20
440 Louis Aparicio
❑ 437B Checklist 6 16.00 3.20
440 Luis Aparicio
❑ 438 Curt Flood 8.00 3.60
❑ 439 Phil Regan RC 6.00 2.70
❑ 440 Luis Aparicio 12.00 5.50
❑ 441 Dick Bertell 4.00 1.80
❑ 442 Gordon Jones 4.00 1.80
❑ 443 Duke Snider 40.00 18.00
❑ 444 Joe Nuxhall 6.00 2.70
❑ 445 Frank Malzone 6.00 2.70
❑ 446 Bob Taylor 4.00 1.80
❑ 447 Harry Bright 7.00 3.10
❑ 448 Del Rice 15.00 6.75
❑ 449 Bob Bolin 7.00 3.10
❑ 450 Jim Lemon 7.00 3.10
❑ 451 Power for Ernie 7.00 3.10
Daryl Spencer
Bill White
Ernie Broglio
❑ 452 Bob Allen 7.00 3.10
❑ 453 Dick Schofield 7.00 3.10
❑ 454 Pumpsie Green 7.00 3.10
❑ 455 Early Wynn 15.00 6.75
❑ 456 Hal Bevan 7.00 3.10
❑ 457 Johnny James 7.00 3.10
(Listed as Angel,
but wearing Yankee
uniform and cap)
❑ 458 Willie Tasby 7.00 3.10
❑ 459 Terry Fox 10.00 4.50
❑ 460 Gil Hodges 25.00 11.00
❑ 461 Smoky Burgess 15.00 6.75
❑ 462 Lou Klimchock 7.00 3.10
❑ 463 Jack Fisher 7.00 3.10
(See also 426)
❑ 464 Lee Thomas RC 10.00 4.50
(Pictured with Yankee
cap but listed as
Los Angeles Angel)
❑ 465 Roy McMillan 15.00 6.75
❑ 466 Ron Moeller 7.00 3.10
❑ 467 Cleveland Indians 12.00 5.50
Team Card
❑ 468 John Callison 10.00 4.50
❑ 469 Ralph Lumenti 7.00 3.10
❑ 470 Roy Sievers 10.00 4.50
❑ 471 Phil Rizzuto MVP 25.00 11.00
❑ 472 Yogi Berra MVP 50.00 22.00
❑ 473 Bob Shantz MVP 7.00 3.10
❑ 474 Al Rosen MVP 10.00 4.50
❑ 475 Mickey Mantle MVP 175.00 80.00
❑ 476 Jackie Jensen MVP 10.00 4.50
❑ 477 Nellie Fox MVP 15.00 6.75
❑ 478 Roger Maris MVP 60.00 27.00
❑ 479 Jim Konstanty MVP 7.00 3.10
❑ 480 Roy Campanella MVP 40.00 18.00
❑ 481 Hank Sauer MVP 7.00 3.10
❑ 482 Willie Mays MVP 50.00 22.00
❑ 483 Don Newcombe MVP 10.00 4.50
❑ 484 Hank Aaron MVP 50.00 22.00
❑ 485 Ernie Banks MVP 40.00 18.00
❑ 486 Dick Groat MVP 10.00 4.50
❑ 487 Gene Oliver 7.00 3.10
❑ 488 Joe McClain 10.00 4.50
❑ 489 Walt Dropo 7.00 3.10
❑ 490 Jim Bunning 25.00 11.00
❑ 491 Philadelphia Phillies 12.00 5.50
Team Card
❑ 492 Ron Fairly 10.00 4.50
❑ 493 Don Zimmer UER 10.00 4.50
(Brooklyn A.L.)
❑ 494 Tom Cheney 15.00 6.75
❑ 495 Elston Howard 10.00 4.50
❑ 496 Ken MacKenzie 7.00 3.10
❑ 497 Willie Jones 7.00 3.10
❑ 498 Ray Herbert 7.00 3.10
❑ 499 Chuck Schilling 7.00 3.10
❑ 500 Harvey Kuenn 10.00 4.50
❑ 501 John DeMerit 7.00 3.10
❑ 502 Clarence Coleman RC 10.00 4.50
❑ 503 Tito Francona 7.00 3.10
❑ 504 Billy Consolo 7.00 3.10
❑ 505 Red Schoendienst 15.00 6.75
❑ 506 Willie Davis RC 15.00 6.75
❑ 507 Pete Burnside 7.00 3.10
❑ 508 Rocky Bridges 7.00 3.10
❑ 509 Camilo Carreon 7.00 3.10
❑ 510 Art Ditmar 7.00 3.10
❑ 511 Joe M. Morgan 7.00 3.10
❑ 512 Bob Will 7.00 3.10
❑ 513 Jim Brosnan 7.00 3.10
❑ 514 Jake Wood 7.00 3.10
❑ 515 Jackie Brandt 7.00 3.10
❑ 516 Checklist 7 16.00 3.20
❑ 517 Willie McCovey 40.00 18.00
❑ 518 Andy Carey 7.00 3.10
❑ 519 Jim Pagliaroni 7.00 3.10
❑ 520 Joe Cunningham 7.00 3.10
❑ 521 Brother Battery 7.00 3.10
Norm Sherry
Larry Sherry
❑ 522 Dick Farrell UER 15.00 6.75
(Phillies cap but
listed on Dodgers)
❑ 523 Joe Gibbon 30.00 13.50
❑ 524 Johnny Logan 30.00 13.50
❑ 525 Ron Perranoski RC 60.00 27.00
❑ 526 R.C. Stevens 30.00 13.50
❑ 527 Gene Leek 30.00 13.50
❑ 528 Pedro Ramos 30.00 13.50
❑ 529 Bob Roselli 30.00 13.50
❑ 530 Bob Malkmus 30.00 13.50
❑ 531 Jim Coates 50.00 22.00
❑ 532 Bob Hale 30.00 13.50
❑ 533 Jack Curtis 30.00 13.50
❑ 534 Eddie Kasko 40.00 18.00
❑ 535 Larry Jackson 30.00 13.50
❑ 536 Bill Tuttle 30.00 13.50
❑ 537 Bobby Locke 30.00 13.50
❑ 538 Chuck Hiller 30.00 13.50
❑ 539 Johnny Klippstein 30.00 13.50
❑ 540 Jackie Jensen 40.00 18.00
❑ 541 Roland Sheldon RC 40.00 18.00
❑ 542 Minnesota Twins 60.00 27.00
Team Card
❑ 543 Roger Craig 40.00 18.00
❑ 544 George Thomas 50.00 22.00
❑ 545 Hoyt Wilhelm 50.00 22.00
❑ 546 Marty Kutyna 30.00 13.50
❑ 547 Leon Wagner 30.00 13.50
❑ 548 Ted Wills 30.00 13.50
❑ 549 Hal R. Smith 30.00 13.50
❑ 550 Frank Baumann 30.00 13.50
❑ 551 George Altman 30.00 13.50
❑ 552 Jim Archer 30.00 13.50
❑ 553 Bill Fischer 30.00 13.50
❑ 554 Pittsburgh Pirates 70.00 32.00
Team Card
❑ 555 Sam Jones 30.00 13.50
❑ 556 Ken R. Hunt 30.00 13.50
❑ 557 Jose Valdivielso 30.00 13.50
❑ 558 Don Ferrarese 30.00 13.50
❑ 559 Jim Gentile 60.00 27.00
❑ 560 Barry Latman 40.00 18.00
❑ 561 Charley James 30.00 13.50
❑ 562 Bill Monbouquette 30.00 13.50
❑ 563 Bob Cerv 60.00 27.00
❑ 564 Don Cardwell 30.00 13.50
❑ 565 Felipe Alou 50.00 22.00
❑ 566 Paul Richards AS MG 30.00 13.50
❑ 567 Danny Murtaugh AS MG 30.00 13.50
❑ 568 Bill Skowron AS 50.00 22.00
❑ 569 Frank Herrera AS 40.00 18.00
❑ 570 Nellie Fox AS 60.00 27.00
❑ 571 Bill Mazeroski AS 50.00 22.00
❑ 572 Brooks Robinson AS 80.00 36.00
❑ 573 Ken Boyer AS 50.00 22.00
❑ 574 Luis Aparicio AS 60.00 27.00
❑ 575 Ernie Banks AS 80.00 36.00
❑ 576 Roger Maris AS 175.00 80.00
❑ 577 Hank Aaron AS 150.00 70.00
❑ 578 Mickey Mantle AS 400.00 180.00
❑ 579 Willie Mays AS 150.00 70.00
❑ 580 Al Kaline AS 80.00 36.00
❑ 581 Frank Robinson AS 80.00 36.00
❑ 582 Earl Battey AS 30.00 13.50
❑ 583 Del Crandall AS 30.00 13.50
❑ 584 Jim Perry AS 30.00 13.50
❑ 585 Bob Friend AS 30.00 13.50
❑ 586 Whitey Ford AS 100.00 45.00
❑ 589 Warren Spahn AS 100.00 30.00

## 1962 Topps

| | NRMT | VG-E |
|---|---|---|
| COMP. MASTER SET (611) | 10000.00 | 4500.00 |
| COMPLETE SET (598) | 4600.00 | 2100.00 |
| COMMON CARD (1-370) | 5.00 | 2.20 |
| COMMON CARD (371-446) | 6.00 | 2.70 |
| COMMON CARD (447-522) | 12.00 | 5.50 |
| COMMON CARD (523-598) | 20.00 | 9.00 |
| WRAPPER (1-CENT) | 100.00 | 45.00 |
| WRAPPER (5-CENT) | 30.00 | 13.50 |

❑ 1 Roger Maris 300.00 75.00

2 Jim Brosnan 5.00 2.20
3 Pete Runnels 5.00 2.20
4 John DeMerit 8.00 3.60
5 Sandy Koufax UER 135.00 60.00
(Struck ou 18)
6 Marv Breeding 5.00 2.20
7 Frank Thomas 10.00 4.50
8 Ray Herbert 5.00 2.20
9 Jim Davenport 8.00 3.60
10 Roberto Clemente 175.00 80.00
11 Tom Morgan 5.00 2.20
12 Harry Craft MG 8.00 3.60
13 Dick Howser 8.00 3.60
14 Bill White 8.00 3.60
15 Dick Donovan 5.00 2.20
16 Darrell Johnson 5.00 2.20
17 Johnny Callison 8.00 3.60
18 Managers' Dream 175.00 80.00
Mickey Mantle
Willie Mays
19 Ray Washburn 5.00 2.20
20 Rocky Colavito 15.00 6.75
21 Jim Kaat 8.00 3.60
22A Checklist 1 ERR 12.00 2.40
(121-176 on back)
22B Checklist 1 COR 12.00 2.40
23 Norm Larker 5.00 2.20
24 Tigers Team 10.00 4.50
25 Ernie Banks 50.00 22.00
26 Chris Cannizzaro 8.00 3.60
27 Chuck Cottier 5.00 2.20
28 Minnie Minoso 10.00 4.50
29 Casey Stengel MG 20.00 9.00
30 Eddie Mathews 40.00 18.00
31 Tom Tresh RC 15.00 6.75
32 John Roseboro 8.00 3.60
33 Don Larsen 8.00 3.60
34 Johnny Temple 8.00 3.60
35 Don Schwall 10.00 4.50
36 Don Leppert 5.00 2.20
37 Tribe Hill Trio 5.00 2.20
Barry Latman
Dick Stigman
Jim Perry
38 Gene Stephens 5.00 2.20
39 Joe Koppe 5.00 2.20
40 Orlando Cepeda 15.00 6.75
41 Cliff Cook 5.00 2.20
42 Jim King 5.00 2.20
43 Los Angeles Dodgers 10.00 4.50
Team Card
44 Don Taussig 5.00 2.20
45 Brooks Robinson 50.00 22.00
46 Jack Baldschun 5.00 2.20
47 Bob Will 5.00 2.20
48 Ralph Terry 8.00 3.60
49 Hal Jones 5.00 2.20
50 Stan Musial 100.00 45.00
51 AL Batting Leaders 8.00 3.60
Norm Cash
Jim Piersall
Al Kaline
Elston Howard
52 NL Batting Leaders 20.00 9.00
Roberto Clemente
Vada Pinson
Ken Boyer
Wally Moon
53 AL Home Run Leaders 100.00 45.00
Roger Maris
Mickey Mantle
Jim Gentile
Harmon Killebrew
54 NL Home Run Leaders 20.00 9.00
Orlando Cepeda
Willie Mays
Frank Robinson
55 AL ERA Leaders 8.00 3.60
Dick Donovan
Bill Stafford
Don Mossi
Milt Pappas
56 NL ERA Leaders 8.00 3.60
Warren Spahn
Jim O'Toole
Curt Simmons
Mike McCormick
57 AL Wins Leaders 8.00 3.60
Whitey Ford
Frank Lary
Steve Barber
Jim Bunning
58 NL Wins Leaders 8.00 3.60
Warren Spahn
Joe Jay
Jim O'Toole
59 AL Strikeout Leaders 8.00 3.60
Camilo Pascual
Whitey Ford
Jim Bunning
Juan Pizzaro
60 NL Strikeout Leaders 20.00 9.00
Sandy Koufax
Stan Williams
Don Drysdale
Jim O'Toole
61 Cardinals Team 10.00 4.50
62 Steve Boros 5.00 2.20
63 Tony Cloninger RC 8.00 3.60
64 Russ Snyder 5.00 2.20
65 Bobby Richardson 10.00 4.50
66 Cuno Barragan 5.00 2.20
67 Harvey Haddix 8.00 3.60
68 Ken Hunt 5.00 2.20
69 Phil Ortega 5.00 2.20
70 Harmon Killebrew 25.00 11.00
71 Dick LeMay 5.00 2.20
72 Bob's Pupils 5.00 2.20
Steve Boros
Bob Scheffing MG
Jake Wood
73 Nellie Fox 20.00 9.00
74 Bob Lillis 8.00 3.60
75 Milt Pappas 8.00 3.60
76 Howie Bedell 5.00 2.20
77 Tony Taylor 8.00 3.60
78 Gene Green 5.00 2.20
79 Ed Hobaugh 5.00 2.20
80 Vada Pinson 8.00 3.60
81 Jim Pagliaroni 5.00 2.20
82 Deron Johnson 8.00 3.60
83 Larry Jackson 5.00 2.20
84 Lenny Green 5.00 2.20
85 Gil Hodges 20.00 9.00
86 Donn Clendenon RC 8.00 3.60
87 Mike Roarke 5.00 2.20
88 Ralph Houk MG 8.00 3.60
(Berra in background)
89 Barney Schultz 5.00 2.20
90 Jimmy Piersall 8.00 3.60
91 J.C. Martin 5.00 2.20
92 Sam Jones 5.00 2.20
93 John Blanchard 8.00 3.60
94 Jay Hook 8.00 3.60
95 Don Hoak 8.00 3.60
96 Eli Grba 5.00 2.20
97 Tito Francona 5.00 2.20
98 Checklist 2 12.00 2.40
99 John (Boog) Powell RC 30.00 13.50
100 Warren Spahn 40.00 18.00
101 Carroll Hardy 5.00 2.20
102 Al Schroll 5.00 2.20
103 Don Blasingame 5.00 2.20
104 Ted Savage 5.00 2.20
105 Don Mossi 8.00 3.60
106 Carl Sawatski 5.00 2.20
107 Mike McCormick 8.00 3.60
108 Willie Davis 8.00 3.60
109 Bob Shaw 5.00 2.20
110 Bill Skowron 8.00 3.60
111 Dallas Green 8.00 3.60
112 Hank Foiles 5.00 2.20
113 Chicago White Sox 10.00 4.50
Team Card
114 Howie Koplitz 5.00 2.20
115 Bob Skinner 8.00 3.60
116 Herb Score 8.00 3.60
117 Gary Geiger 8.00 3.60
118 Julian Javier 8.00 3.60
119 Danny Murphy 5.00 2.20
120 Bob Purkey 5.00 2.20
121 Billy Hitchcock MG 5.00 2.20
122 Norm Bass 5.00 2.20
123 Mike de la Hoz 5.00 2.20
124 Bill Pleis 5.00 2.20
125 Gene Woodling 8.00 3.60
126 Al Cicotte 5.00 2.20
127 Pride of A's 5.00 2.20
Norm Siebern
Hank Bauer MG
Jerry Lumpe
128 Art Fowler 5.00 2.20
129A Lee Walls 5.00 2.20
(Facing right)
129B Lee Walls 30.00 13.50
(Facing left)
130 Frank Bolling 5.00 2.20
131 Pete Richert 5.00 2.20
132A Angels Team 10.00 4.50
(Without photo)
132B Angels Team 30.00 13.50
(With photo)
133 Felipe Alou 8.00 3.60
134A Billy Hoeft 5.00 2.20
(Facing right)
134B Billy Hoeft 30.00 13.50
(Facing straight)
135 Babe Ruth Special 1 20.00 9.00
Babe as a Boy
136 Babe Ruth Special 2 20.00 9.00
Babe Joins Yanks
137 Babe Ruth Special 3 20.00 9.00
With Miller Huggins
138 Babe Ruth Special 4 20.00 9.00
Famous Slugger
139A Babe Ruth Special 5 30.00 13.50
Babe Hits 60
139B Hal Reniff PORT RC 15.00 6.75
139C Hal Reniff RC ! 65.00 29.00
(Pitching)
140 Babe Ruth Special 6 60.00 27.00
With Lou Gehrig
141 Babe Ruth Special 7 20.00 9.00
Twilight Years
142 Babe Ruth Special 8 20.00 9.00
Coaching Dodgers
143 Babe Ruth Special 9 20.00 9.00
Greatest Sports Hero
144 Babe Ruth Special 10 20.00 9.00
Farewell Speech
145 Barry Latman 5.00 2.20
146 Don Demeter 5.00 2.20
147A Bill Kunkel PORT 5.00 2.20
147B Bill Kunkel 30.00 13.50
(Pitching pose)
148 Wally Post 5.00 2.20
149 Bob Duliba 5.00 2.20
150 Al Kaline 50.00 22.00
151 Johnny Klippstein 5.00 2.20
152 Mickey Vernon MG 8.00 3.60
153 Pumpsie Green 6.00 2.70
154 Lee Thomas 6.00 2.70
155 Stu Miller 6.00 2.70
156 Merritt Ranew 5.00 2.20
157 Wes Covington 8.00 3.60
158 Braves Team 15.00 6.75
159 Hal Reniff RC 8.00 3.60
160 Dick Stuart 8.00 3.60
161 Frank Baumann 5.00 2.20
162 Sammy Drake 5.00 2.20
163 Hot Corner Guard 8.00 3.60
Billy Gardner
Cletis Boyer
164 Hal Naragon 5.00 2.20
165 Jackie Brandt 5.00 2.20
166 Don Lee 5.00 2.20
167 Tim McCarver RC 30.00 13.50
168 Leo Posada 5.00 2.20
169 Bob Cerv 10.00 4.50
170 Ron Santo 15.00 6.75
171 Dave Sisler 5.00 2.20
172 Fred Hutchinson MG 8.00 3.60
173 Chico Fernandez 5.00 2.20
174A Carl Willey 5.00 2.20
(Capless)
174B Carl Willey 30.00 13.50
(With cap)
175 Frank Howard 10.00 4.50

| Card | Name | Price | Price |
|---|---|---|---|
| ❑ 176A | Eddie Yost PORT | 5.00 | 2.20 |
| ❑ 176B | Eddie Yost BATTING | 30.00 | 13.50 |
| ❑ 177 | Bobby Shantz | 8.00 | 3.60 |
| ❑ 178 | Camilo Carreon | 5.00 | 2.20 |
| ❑ 179 | Tom Sturdivant | 5.00 | 2.20 |
| ❑ 180 | Bob Allison | 10.00 | 4.50 |
| ❑ 181 | Paul Brown | 5.00 | 2.20 |
| ❑ 182 | Bob Nieman | 5.00 | 2.20 |
| ❑ 183 | Roger Craig | 8.00 | 3.60 |
| ❑ 184 | Haywood Sullivan | 8.00 | 3.60 |
| ❑ 185 | Roland Sheldon | 10.00 | 4.50 |
| ❑ 186 | Mack Jones | 5.00 | 2.20 |
| ❑ 187 | Gene Conley | 5.00 | 2.20 |
| ❑ 188 | Chuck Hiller | 5.00 | 2.20 |
| ❑ 189 | Dick Hall | 5.00 | 2.20 |
| ❑ 190A | Wally Moon PORT | 5.00 | 2.20 |
| ❑ 190B | Wally Moon BATTING | 30.00 | 13.50 |
| ❑ 191 | Jim Brewer | 5.00 | 2.20 |
| ❑ 192A | Checklist 3 | 12.00 | 2.40 |
| | (Without comma) | | |
| ❑ 192B | Checklist 3 | 16.00 | 3.20 |
| | (Comma after Checklist) | | |
| ❑ 193 | Eddie Kasko | 5.00 | 2.20 |
| ❑ 194 | Dean Chance RC | 8.00 | 3.60 |
| ❑ 195 | Joe Cunningham | 5.00 | 2.20 |
| ❑ 196 | Terry Fox | 5.00 | 2.20 |
| ❑ 197 | Daryl Spencer | 5.00 | 2.20 |
| ❑ 198 | Johnny Keane MG | 5.00 | 2.20 |
| ❑ 199 | Gaylord Perry RC ! | 80.00 | 36.00 |
| ❑ 200 | Mickey Mantle | 500.00 | 220.00 |
| ❑ 201 | Ike Delock | 5.00 | 2.20 |
| ❑ 202 | Carl Warwick | 5.00 | 2.20 |
| ❑ 203 | Jack Fisher | 5.00 | 2.20 |
| ❑ 204 | Johnny Weekly | 5.00 | 2.20 |
| ❑ 205 | Gene Freese | 5.00 | 2.20 |
| ❑ 206 | Senators Team | 10.00 | 4.50 |
| ❑ 207 | Pete Burnside | 5.00 | 2.20 |
| ❑ 208 | Billy Martin | 20.00 | 9.00 |
| ❑ 209 | Jim Fregosi RC | 15.00 | 6.75 |
| ❑ 210 | Roy Face | 8.00 | 3.60 |
| ❑ 211 | Midway Masters | 5.00 | 2.20 |
| | Frank Bolling | | |
| | Roy McMillan | | |
| ❑ 212 | Jim Owens | 5.00 | 2.20 |
| ❑ 213 | Richie Ashburn | 20.00 | 9.00 |
| ❑ 214 | Dom Zanni | 5.00 | 2.20 |
| ❑ 215 | Woody Held | 5.00 | 2.20 |
| ❑ 216 | Ron Kline | 5.00 | 2.20 |
| ❑ 217 | Walter Alston MG | 10.00 | 4.50 |
| ❑ 218 | Joe Torre RC | 40.00 | 18.00 |
| ❑ 219 | Al Downing RC | 8.00 | 3.60 |
| ❑ 220 | Roy Sievers | 8.00 | 3.60 |
| ❑ 221 | Bill Short | 5.00 | 2.20 |
| ❑ 222 | Jerry Zimmerman | 5.00 | 2.20 |
| ❑ 223 | Alex Grammas | 5.00 | 2.20 |
| ❑ 224 | Don Rudolph | 5.00 | 2.20 |
| ❑ 225 | Frank Malzone | 8.00 | 3.60 |
| ❑ 226 | San Francisco Giants | 10.00 | 4.50 |
| | Team Card | | |
| ❑ 227 | Bob Tiefenauer | 5.00 | 2.20 |
| ❑ 228 | Dale Long | 10.00 | 4.50 |
| ❑ 229 | Jesus McFarlane | 5.00 | 2.20 |
| ❑ 230 | Camilo Pascual | 8.00 | 3.60 |
| ❑ 231 | Ernie Bowman | 5.00 | 2.20 |
| ❑ 232 | World Series Game 1 | 10.00 | 4.50 |
| | Yanks win opener | | |
| ❑ 233 | Joey Jay WS | 10.00 | 4.50 |
| ❑ 234 | Roger Maris WS | 25.00 | 11.00 |
| ❑ 235 | Whitey Ford WS | 15.00 | 6.75 |
| | Sets new mark | | |
| ❑ 236 | World Series Game 5 | 8.00 | 3.60 |
| | Yanks crush Reds | | |
| ❑ 237 | World Series Summary | 8.00 | 3.60 |
| | Yanks celebrate | | |
| ❑ 238 | Norm Sherry | 5.00 | 2.20 |
| ❑ 239 | Cecil Butler | 5.00 | 2.20 |
| ❑ 240 | George Altman | 5.00 | 2.20 |
| ❑ 241 | Johnny Kucks | 5.00 | 2.20 |
| ❑ 242 | Mel McGaha MG | 5.00 | 2.20 |
| ❑ 243 | Robin Roberts | 15.00 | 6.75 |
| ❑ 244 | Don Gile | 5.00 | 2.20 |
| ❑ 245 | Ron Hansen | 5.00 | 2.20 |
| ❑ 246 | Art Ditmar | 5.00 | 2.20 |
| ❑ 247 | Joe Pignatano | 5.00 | 2.20 |
| ❑ 248 | Bob Aspromonte | 8.00 | 3.60 |
| ❑ 249 | Ed Keegan | 5.00 | 2.20 |
| ❑ 250 | Norm Cash | 10.00 | 4.50 |
| ❑ 251 | New York Yankees | 50.00 | 22.00 |
| | Team Card | | |
| ❑ 252 | Earl Francis | 5.00 | 2.20 |
| ❑ 253 | Harry Chiti MG | 5.00 | 2.20 |
| ❑ 254 | Gordon Windhorn | 5.00 | 2.20 |
| ❑ 255 | Juan Pizarro | 5.00 | 2.20 |
| ❑ 256 | Elio Chacon | 8.00 | 3.60 |
| ❑ 257 | Jack Spring | 5.00 | 2.20 |
| ❑ 258 | Marty Keough | 5.00 | 2.20 |
| ❑ 259 | Lou Klimchock | 5.00 | 2.20 |
| ❑ 260 | Billy Pierce | 8.00 | 3.60 |
| ❑ 261 | George Alusik | 5.00 | 2.20 |
| ❑ 262 | Bob Schmidt | 5.00 | 2.20 |
| ❑ 263 | The Right Pitch | 5.00 | 2.20 |
| | Bob Purkey | | |
| | Jim Turner CO | | |
| | Joe Jay | | |
| ❑ 264 | Dick Ellsworth | 8.00 | 3.60 |
| ❑ 265 | Joe Adcock | 8.00 | 3.60 |
| ❑ 266 | John Anderson | 5.00 | 2.20 |
| ❑ 267 | Dan Dobbek | 5.00 | 2.20 |
| ❑ 268 | Ken McBride | 5.00 | 2.20 |
| ❑ 269 | Bob Oldis | 5.00 | 2.20 |
| ❑ 270 | Dick Groat | 8.00 | 3.60 |
| ❑ 271 | Ray Rippelmeyer | 5.00 | 2.20 |
| ❑ 272 | Earl Robinson | 5.00 | 2.20 |
| ❑ 273 | Gary Bell | 5.00 | 2.20 |
| ❑ 274 | Sammy Taylor | 5.00 | 2.20 |
| ❑ 275 | Norm Siebern | 5.00 | 2.20 |
| ❑ 276 | Hal Kolstad | 5.00 | 2.20 |
| ❑ 277 | Checklist 4 | 16.00 | 3.20 |
| ❑ 278 | Ken Johnson | 8.00 | 3.60 |
| ❑ 279 | Hobie Landrith UER | 8.00 | 3.60 |
| | (Wrong birthdate) | | |
| ❑ 280 | Johnny Podres | 8.00 | 3.60 |
| ❑ 281 | Jake Gibbs | 10.00 | 4.50 |
| ❑ 282 | Dave Hillman | 5.00 | 2.20 |
| ❑ 283 | Charlie Smith | 5.00 | 2.20 |
| ❑ 284 | Ruben Amaro | 5.00 | 2.20 |
| ❑ 285 | Curt Simmons | 8.00 | 3.60 |
| ❑ 286 | Al Lopez MG | 10.00 | 4.50 |
| ❑ 287 | George Witt | 5.00 | 2.20 |
| ❑ 288 | Billy Williams | 30.00 | 13.50 |
| ❑ 289 | Mike Krsnich | 5.00 | 2.20 |
| ❑ 290 | Jim Gentile | 8.00 | 3.60 |
| ❑ 291 | Hal Stowe | 5.00 | 2.20 |
| ❑ 292 | Jerry Kindall | 5.00 | 2.20 |
| ❑ 293 | Bob Miller | 8.00 | 3.60 |
| ❑ 294 | Phillies Team | 10.00 | 4.50 |
| ❑ 295 | Vern Law | 8.00 | 3.60 |
| ❑ 296 | Ken Hamlin | 5.00 | 2.20 |
| ❑ 297 | Ron Perranoski | 8.00 | 3.60 |
| ❑ 298 | Bill Tuttle | 5.00 | 2.20 |
| ❑ 299 | Don Wert | 5.00 | 2.20 |
| ❑ 300 | Willie Mays | 150.00 | 70.00 |
| ❑ 301 | Galen Cisco RC | 5.00 | 2.20 |
| ❑ 302 | Johnny Edwards | 5.00 | 2.20 |
| ❑ 303 | Frank Torre | 8.00 | 3.60 |
| ❑ 304 | Dick Farrell | 8.00 | 3.60 |
| ❑ 305 | Jerry Lumpe | 5.00 | 2.20 |
| ❑ 306 | Redbird Rippers | 5.00 | 2.20 |
| | Lindy McDaniel | | |
| | Larry Jackson | | |
| ❑ 307 | Jim Grant | 8.00 | 3.60 |
| ❑ 308 | Neil Chrisley | 8.00 | 3.60 |
| ❑ 309 | Moe Morhardt | 5.00 | 2.20 |
| ❑ 310 | Whitey Ford | 50.00 | 22.00 |
| ❑ 311 | Tony Kubek IA | 8.00 | 3.60 |
| ❑ 312 | Warren Spahn IA | 15.00 | 6.75 |
| ❑ 313 | Roger Maris IA | 50.00 | 22.00 |
| | Blasts 61st | | |
| ❑ 314 | Rocky Colavito IA | 8.00 | 3.60 |
| ❑ 315 | Whitey Ford IA | 15.00 | 6.75 |
| ❑ 316 | Harmon Killebrew IA | 15.00 | 6.75 |
| ❑ 317 | Stan Musial IA | 20.00 | 9.00 |
| ❑ 318 | Mickey Mantle IA | 125.00 | 55.00 |
| ❑ 319 | Mike McCormick IA | 5.00 | 2.20 |
| ❑ 320 | Hank Aaron | 150.00 | 70.00 |
| ❑ 321 | Lee Stange | 5.00 | 2.20 |
| ❑ 322 | Alvin Dark MG | 8.00 | 3.60 |
| ❑ 323 | Don Landrum | 5.00 | 2.20 |
| ❑ 324 | Joe McClain | 5.00 | 2.20 |
| ❑ 325 | Luis Aparicio | 15.00 | 6.75 |
| ❑ 326 | Tom Parsons | 5.00 | 2.20 |
| ❑ 327 | Ozzie Virgil | 5.00 | 2.20 |
| ❑ 328 | Ken Walters | 5.00 | 2.20 |
| ❑ 329 | Bob Bolin | 5.00 | 2.20 |
| ❑ 330 | John Romano | 5.00 | 2.20 |
| ❑ 331 | Moe Drabowsky | 8.00 | 3.60 |
| ❑ 332 | Don Buddin | 5.00 | 2.20 |
| ❑ 333 | Frank Cipriani | 5.00 | 2.20 |
| ❑ 334 | Boston Red Sox | 10.00 | 4.50 |
| | Team Card | | |
| ❑ 335 | Bill Bruton | 5.00 | 2.20 |
| ❑ 336 | Billy Muffett | 5.00 | 2.20 |
| ❑ 337 | Jim Marshall | 8.00 | 3.60 |
| ❑ 338 | Billy Gardner | 5.00 | 2.20 |
| ❑ 339 | Jose Valdivielso | 5.00 | 2.20 |
| ❑ 340 | Don Drysdale | 50.00 | 22.00 |
| ❑ 341 | Mike Hershberger | 5.00 | 2.20 |
| ❑ 342 | Ed Rakow | 5.00 | 2.20 |
| ❑ 343 | Albie Pearson | 8.00 | 3.60 |
| ❑ 344 | Ed Bauta | 5.00 | 2.20 |
| ❑ 345 | Chuck Schilling | 5.00 | 2.20 |
| ❑ 346 | Jack Kralick | 5.00 | 2.20 |
| ❑ 347 | Chuck Hinton | 5.00 | 2.20 |
| ❑ 348 | Larry Burright | 8.00 | 3.60 |
| ❑ 349 | Paul Foytack | 5.00 | 2.20 |
| ❑ 350 | Frank Robinson | 50.00 | 22.00 |
| ❑ 351 | Braves' Backstops | 8.00 | 3.60 |
| | Joe Torre | | |
| | Del Crandall | | |
| ❑ 352 | Frank Sullivan | 5.00 | 2.20 |
| ❑ 353 | Bill Mazeroski | 10.00 | 4.50 |
| ❑ 354 | Roman Mejias | 8.00 | 3.60 |
| ❑ 355 | Steve Barber | 5.00 | 2.20 |
| ❑ 356 | Tom Haller RC | 5.00 | 2.20 |
| ❑ 357 | Jerry Walker | 5.00 | 2.20 |
| ❑ 358 | Tommy Davis | 8.00 | 3.60 |
| ❑ 359 | Bobby Locke | 5.00 | 2.20 |
| ❑ 360 | Yogi Berra | 80.00 | 36.00 |
| ❑ 361 | Bob Hendley | 5.00 | 2.20 |
| ❑ 362 | Ty Cline | 5.00 | 2.20 |
| ❑ 363 | Bob Roselli | 5.00 | 2.20 |
| ❑ 364 | Ken Hunt | 5.00 | 2.20 |
| ❑ 365 | Charlie Neal | 8.00 | 3.60 |
| ❑ 366 | Phil Regan | 8.00 | 3.60 |
| ❑ 367 | Checklist 5 | 16.00 | 3.20 |
| ❑ 368 | Bob Tillman | 5.00 | 2.20 |
| ❑ 369 | Ted Bowsfield | 5.00 | 2.20 |
| ❑ 370 | Ken Boyer | 10.00 | 4.50 |
| ❑ 371 | Earl Battey | 6.00 | 2.70 |
| ❑ 372 | Jack Curtis | 6.00 | 2.70 |
| ❑ 373 | Al Heist | 6.00 | 2.70 |
| ❑ 374 | Gene Mauch MG | 10.00 | 4.50 |
| ❑ 375 | Ron Fairly | 10.00 | 4.50 |
| ❑ 376 | Bud Daley | 8.00 | 3.60 |
| ❑ 377 | John Orsino | 6.00 | 2.70 |
| ❑ 378 | Bennie Daniels | 6.00 | 2.70 |
| ❑ 379 | Chuck Essegian | 6.00 | 2.70 |
| ❑ 380 | Lou Burdette | 10.00 | 4.50 |
| ❑ 381 | Chico Cardenas | 10.00 | 4.50 |
| ❑ 382 | Dick Williams | 8.00 | 3.60 |
| ❑ 383 | Ray Sadecki | 6.00 | 2.70 |
| ❑ 384 | K.C. Athletics | 10.00 | 4.50 |
| | Team Card | | |
| ❑ 385 | Early Wynn | 15.00 | 6.75 |
| ❑ 386 | Don Mincher | 8.00 | 3.60 |
| ❑ 387 | Lou Brock RC | 125.00 | 55.00 |
| ❑ 388 | Ryne Duren | 8.00 | 3.60 |
| ❑ 389 | Smoky Burgess | 10.00 | 4.50 |
| ❑ 390 | Orlando Cepeda AS | 10.00 | 4.50 |
| ❑ 391 | Bill Mazeroski AS | 10.00 | 4.50 |
| ❑ 392 | Ken Boyer AS UER | 8.00 | 3.60 |
| | (Batting Average mistakenly listed as .392) | | |
| ❑ 393 | Roy McMillan AS | 6.00 | 2.70 |
| ❑ 394 | Hank Aaron AS | 50.00 | 22.00 |
| ❑ 395 | Willie Mays AS | 50.00 | 22.00 |
| ❑ 396 | Frank Robinson AS | 15.00 | 6.75 |
| ❑ 397 | John Roseboro AS | 6.00 | 2.70 |
| ❑ 398 | Don Drysdale AS | 15.00 | 6.75 |
| ❑ 399 | Warren Spahn AS | 15.00 | 6.75 |
| ❑ 400 | Elston Howard | 10.00 | 4.50 |
| ❑ 401 | AL/NL Homer Kings | 60.00 | 27.00 |
| | Roger Maris | | |
| | Orlando Cepeda | | |
| ❑ 402 | Gino Cimoli | 6.00 | 2.70 |
| ❑ 403 | Chet Nichols | 6.00 | 2.70 |
| ❑ 404 | Tim Harkness | 8.00 | 3.60 |

❑ 405 Jim Perry 8.00 3.60
❑ 406 Bob Taylor 6.00 2.70
❑ 407 Hank Aguirre 6.00 2.70
❑ 408 Gus Bell 8.00 3.60
❑ 409 Pittsburgh Pirates 10.00 4.50
Team Card
❑ 410 Al Smith 6.00 2.70
❑ 411 Danny O'Connell 6.00 2.70
❑ 412 Charlie James 6.00 2.70
❑ 413 Matty Alou 10.00 4.50
❑ 414 Joe Gaines 6.00 2.70
❑ 415 Bill Virdon 10.00 4.50
❑ 416 Bob Scheffing MG 6.00 2.70
❑ 417 Joe Azcue 6.00 2.70
❑ 418 Andy Carey 6.00 2.70
❑ 419 Bob Bruce 8.00 3.60
❑ 420 Gus Triandos 8.00 3.60
❑ 421 Ken MacKenzie 8.00 3.60
❑ 422 Steve Bilko 6.00 2.70
❑ 423 Rival League 10.00 4.50
Relief Aces:
Roy Face
Hoyt Wilhelm
❑ 424 Al McBean RC 6.00 2.70
❑ 425 Carl Yastrzemski 125.00 55.00
❑ 426 Bob Farley 6.00 2.70
❑ 427 Jake Wood 6.00 2.70
❑ 428 Joe Hicks 6.00 2.70
❑ 429 Billy O'Dell 6.00 2.70
❑ 430 Tony Kubek 15.00 6.75
❑ 431 Bob Rodgers RC 8.00 3.60
❑ 432 Jim Pendleton 6.00 2.70
❑ 433 Jim Archer 6.00 2.70
❑ 434 Clay Dalrymple 6.00 2.70
❑ 435 Larry Sherry 8.00 3.60
❑ 436 Felix Mantilla 8.00 3.60
❑ 437 Ray Moore 6.00 2.70
❑ 438 Dick Brown 6.00 2.70
❑ 439 Jerry Buchek 6.00 2.70
❑ 440 Joey Jay 6.00 2.70
❑ 441 Checklist 6 16.00 7.25
❑ 442 Wes Stock 6.00 2.70
❑ 443 Del Crandall 8.00 3.60
❑ 444 Ted Wills 6.00 2.70
❑ 445 Vic Power 8.00 3.60
❑ 446 Don Elston 6.00 2.70
❑ 447 Willie Kirkland 12.00 5.50
❑ 448 Joe Gibbon 12.00 5.50
❑ 449 Jerry Adair 12.00 5.50
❑ 450 Jim O'Toole 15.00 6.75
❑ 451 Jose Tartabull RC 15.00 6.75
❑ 452 Earl Averill Jr. 12.00 5.50
❑ 453 Cal McLish 12.00 5.50
❑ 454 Floyd Robinson 12.00 5.50
❑ 455 Luis Arroyo 15.00 6.75
❑ 456 Joe Amalfitano 15.00 6.75
❑ 457 Lou Clinton 12.00 5.50
❑ 458A Bob Buhl 15.00 6.75
(Braves emblem
on cap)
❑ 458B Bob Buhl 50.00 22.00
(No emblem on cap)
❑ 459 Ed Bailey 12.00 5.50
❑ 460 Jim Bunning 20.00 9.00
❑ 461 Ken Hubbs RC 35.00 16.00
❑ 462A Willie Tasby 12.00 5.50
(Senators emblem
on cap)
❑ 462B Willie Tasby 50.00 22.00
(No emblem on cap)
❑ 463 Hank Bauer MG 15.00 6.75
❑ 464 Al Jackson RC 12.00 5.50
❑ 465 Reds Team 20.00 9.00
❑ 466 Norm Cash AS 15.00 6.75
❑ 467 Chuck Schilling AS 12.00 5.50
❑ 468 Brooks Robinson AS 25.00 11.00
❑ 469 Luis Aparicio AS 15.00 6.75
❑ 470 Al Kaline AS 25.00 11.00
❑ 471 Mickey Mantle AS 200.00 90.00
❑ 472 Rocky Colavito AS 15.00 6.75
❑ 473 Elston Howard AS 15.00 6.75
❑ 474 Frank Lary AS 12.00 5.50
❑ 475 Whitey Ford AS 15.00 6.75
❑ 476 Orioles Team 20.00 9.00
❑ 477 Andre Rodgers 12.00 5.50
❑ 478 Don Zimmer 20.00 9.00
(Shown with Mets cap,
but listed as with
Cincinnati)
❑ 479 Joel Horlen RC 12.00 5.50
❑ 480 Harvey Kuenn 15.00 6.75
❑ 481 Vic Wertz 15.00 6.75
❑ 482 Sam Mele MG 12.00 5.50
❑ 483 Don McMahon 12.00 5.50
❑ 484 Dick Schofield 12.00 5.50
❑ 485 Pedro Ramos 12.00 5.50
❑ 486 Jim Gilliam 15.00 6.75
❑ 487 Jerry Lynch 12.00 5.50
❑ 488 Hal Brown 12.00 5.50
❑ 489 Julio Gotay 12.00 5.50
❑ 490 Clete Boyer UER 15.00 6.75
(Reversed negative)
❑ 491 Leon Wagner 12.00 5.50
❑ 492 Hal W. Smith 15.00 6.75
❑ 493 Danny McDevitt 12.00 5.50
❑ 494 Sammy White 12.00 5.50
❑ 495 Don Cardwell 12.00 5.50
❑ 496 Wayne Causey 12.00 5.50
❑ 497 Ed Bouchee 15.00 6.75
❑ 498 Jim Donohue 12.00 5.50
❑ 499 Zoilo Versalles 15.00 6.75
❑ 500 Duke Snider 60.00 27.00
❑ 501 Claude Osteen 15.00 6.75
❑ 502 Hector Lopez 15.00 6.75
❑ 503 Danny Murtaugh MG 15.00 6.75
❑ 504 Eddie Bressoud 12.00 5.50
❑ 505 Juan Marichal 40.00 18.00
❑ 506 Charlie Maxwell 15.00 6.75
❑ 507 Ernie Broglio 15.00 6.75
❑ 508 Gordy Coleman 15.00 6.75
❑ 509 Dave Giusti RC 15.00 6.75
❑ 510 Jim Lemon 12.00 5.50
❑ 511 Bubba Phillips 12.00 5.50
❑ 512 Mike Fornieles 12.00 5.50
❑ 513 Whitey Herzog 15.00 6.75
❑ 514 Sherm Lollar 15.00 6.75
❑ 515 Stan Williams 15.00 6.75
❑ 516 Checklist 7 16.00 3.20
❑ 517 Dave Wickersham 12.00 5.50
❑ 518 Lee Maye 10.00 5.50
❑ 519 Bob Johnson 12.00 5.50
❑ 520 Bob Friend 15.00 6.75
❑ 521 Jacke Davis UER 12.00 5.50
(Listed as OF on
front and P on back)
❑ 522 Lindy McDaniel 15.00 6.75
❑ 523 Russ Nixon SP 30.00 13.50
❑ 524 Howie Nunn SP 30.00 13.50
❑ 525 George Thomas 20.00 9.00
❑ 526 Hal Woodeshick SP 30.00 13.50
❑ 527 Dick McAuliffe RC 30.00 13.50
❑ 528 Turk Lown 20.00 9.00
❑ 529 John Schaive SP 30.00 13.50
❑ 530 Bob Gibson SP 125.00 55.00
❑ 531 Bobby G. Smith 20.00 9.00
❑ 532 Dick Stigman 20.00 9.00
❑ 533 Charley Lau SP 30.00 13.50
❑ 534 Tony Gonzalez SP 30.00 13.50
❑ 535 Ed Roebuck 20.00 9.00
❑ 536 Dick Gernert 20.00 9.00
❑ 537 Cleveland Indians 50.00 22.00
Team Card
❑ 538 Jack Sanford 20.00 9.00
❑ 539 Billy Moran 20.00 9.00
❑ 540 Jim Landis SP 30.00 13.50
❑ 541 Don Nottebart SP 30.00 13.50
❑ 542 Dave Philley 20.00 9.00
❑ 543 Bob Allen SP 30.00 13.50
❑ 544 Willie McCovey SP 125.00 55.00
❑ 545 Hoyt Wilhelm SP 50.00 22.00
❑ 546 Moe Thacker SP 30.00 13.50
❑ 547 Don Ferrarese 20.00 9.00
❑ 548 Bobby Del Greco 20.00 9.00
❑ 549 Bill Rigney MG SP 30.00 13.50
❑ 550 Art Mahaffey SP 30.00 13.50
❑ 551 Harry Bright 20.00 9.00
❑ 552 Chicago Cubs SP 50.00 22.00
Team Card
❑ 553 Jim Coates 30.00 13.50
❑ 554 Bubba Morton SP 30.00 13.50
❑ 555 John Buzhardt SP 30.00 13.50
❑ 556 Al Spangler 20.00 9.00
❑ 557 Bob Anderson SP 30.00 13.50
❑ 558 John Goryl 20.00 9.00
❑ 559 Mike Higgins MG 20.00 9.00
❑ 560 Chuck Estrada SP 30.00 13.50
❑ 561 Gene Oliver SP 30.00 13.50
❑ 562 Bill Henry 20.00 9.00
❑ 563 Ken Aspromonte 20.00 9.00
❑ 564 Bob Grim 20.00 9.00
❑ 565 Jose Pagan 20.00 9.00
❑ 566 Marty Kutyna SP 30.00 13.50
❑ 567 Tracy Stallard SP 30.00 13.50
❑ 568 Jim Golden 20.00 9.00
❑ 569 Ed Sadowski SP 30.00 13.50
❑ 570 Bill Stafford SP 30.00 13.50
❑ 571 Billy Klaus SP 30.00 13.50
❑ 572 Bob G. Miller SP 30.00 13.50
❑ 573 Johnny Logan 20.00 9.00
❑ 574 Dean Stone 20.00 9.00
❑ 575 Red Schoendienst SP 50.00 22.00
❑ 576 Russ Kemmerer SP 30.00 13.50
❑ 577 Dave Nicholson SP 30.00 13.50
❑ 578 Jim Duffalo 20.00 9.00
❑ 579 Jim Schaffer SP 30.00 13.50
❑ 580 Bill Monbouquette 20.00 9.00
❑ 581 Mel Roach 20.00 9.00
❑ 582 Ron Piche 20.00 9.00
❑ 583 Larry Osborne 20.00 9.00
❑ 584 Minnesota Twins SP 60.00 27.00
Team Card
❑ 585 Glen Hobbie SP 30.00 13.50
❑ 586 Sammy Esposito SP 30.00 13.50
❑ 587 Frank Funk SP 30.00 13.50
❑ 588 Birdie Tebbetts MG 20.00 9.00
❑ 589 Bob Turley 30.00 13.50
❑ 590 Curt Flood 30.00 13.50
❑ 591 Rookie Pitchers SP 70.00 32.00
Sam McDowell RC
Ron Taylor
Ron Nischwitz
Art Quirk
Dick Radatz
❑ 592 Rookie Pitchers SP 70.00 32.00
Dan Pfister
Bo Belinsky
Dave Stenhouse
Jim Bouton RC
Joe Bonikowski
❑ 593 Rookie Pitchers SP 50.00 22.00
Jack Lamabe
Craig Anderson
Jack Hamilton
Bob Moorhead
Bob Veale
❑ 594 Rookie Catchers SP 75.00 34.00
Doc Edwards
Ken Retzer
Bob Uecker RC
Doug Camilli
Don Pavletich
❑ 595 Rookie Infielders SP 50.00 22.00
Bob Sadowski
Felix Torres
Marlan Coughtry
Ed Charles
❑ 596 Rookie Infielders SP 70.00 32.00
Bernie Allen
Joe Pepitone RC
Phil Linz
Rich Rollins
❑ 597 Rookie Infielders SP 50.00 22.00
Jim McKnight
Rod Kanehl
Amado Samuel
Denis Menke RC
❑ 598 Rookie Outfielders SP 80.00 23.00
Al Luplow
Manny Jimenez
Howie Goss
Jim Hickman
Ed Olivares RC

## 1963 Topps

| | NRMT | VG-E |
|---|---|---|
| COMPLETE SET (576) | 5000.00 | 2200.00 |
| COMMON CARD (1-196) | 4.00 | 1.80 |

COMMON CARD (197-283) ...... 5.00 2.20
COMMON CARD (284-370) ...... 5.00 2.20
COMMON CARD (371-446) ...... 5.00 2.20
COMMON CARD (447-522) .... 25.00 11.00
COMMON CARD (523-576) .... 15.00 6.75
WRAPPER (1-CENT) ............ 40.00 18.00
WRAPPER (5-CENT) ............ 30.00 13.50

❑ 1 NL Batting Leaders ........ 40.00 8.00
Tommy Davis
Frank Robinson
Stan Musial
Hank Aaron
Bill White
❑ 2 AL Batting Leaders ........ 50.00 22.00
Pete Runnels
Mickey Mantle
Floyd Robinson
Norm Siebern
Chuck Hinton
❑ 3 NL Home Run Leaders .. 40.00 18.00
Willie Mays
Hank Aaron
Frank Robinson
Orlando Cepeda
Ernie Banks
❑ 4 AL Home Run Leaders .. 20.00 9.00
Harmon Killebrew
Norm Cash
Rocky Colavito
Roger Maris
Jim Gentile
Leon Wagner
❑ 5 NL ERA Leaders ........... 25.00 11.00
Sandy Koufax
Bob Shaw
Bob Purkey
Bob Gibson
Don Drysdale
❑ 6 AL ERA Leaders ........... 10.00 4.50
Hank Aguirre
Robin Roberts
Whitey Ford
Eddie Fisher
Dean Chance
❑ 7 NL Pitching Leaders ...... 10.00 4.50
Don Drysdale
Jack Sanford
Bob Purkey
Billy O'Dell
Art Mahaffey
Joe Jay
❑ 8 AL Pitching Leaders ........ 8.00 3.60
Ralph Terry
Dick Donovan
Ray Herbert
Jim Bunning
Camilo Pascual
❑ 9 NL Strikeout Leaders .... 30.00 13.50
Don Drysdale
Sandy Koufax
Bob Gibson
Billy O'Dell
Dick Farrell
❑ 10 AL Strikeout Leaders...... 8.00 3.60
Camilo Pascual
Jim Bunning
Ralph Terry
Juan Pizarro
Jim Kaat
❑ 11 Lee Walls ..................... 4.00 1.80
❑ 12 Steve Barber .................. 4.00 1.80
❑ 13 Philadelphia Phillies ...... 8.00 3.60
Team Card
❑ 14 Pedro Ramos ............... 4.00 1.80
❑ 15 Ken Hubbs UER .......... 10.00 4.50
(No position listed
on front of card)
❑ 16 Al Smith......................... 4.00 1.80
❑ 17 Ryne Duren .................... 8.00 3.60
❑ 18 Buc Blasters ............... 80.00 36.00
Smoky Burgess
Dick Stuart
Bob Clemente
Bob Skinner
❑ 19 Pete Burnside ............... 4.00 1.80
❑ 20 Tony Kubek.................. 10.00 4.50
❑ 21 Marty Keough ............... 4.00 1.80
❑ 22 Curt Simmons ............... 8.00 3.60
❑ 23 Ed Lopat MG.................. 8.00 3.60
❑ 24 Bob Bruce ...................... 4.00 1.80
❑ 25 Al Kaline ..................... 45.00 20.00
❑ 26 Ray Moore...................... 4.00 1.80
❑ 27 Choo Choo Coleman...... 8.00 3.60
❑ 28 Mike Fornieles............... 4.00 1.80
❑ 29A 1962 Rookie Stars .... 10.00 4.50
Sammy Ellis
Ray Culp
John Boozer
Jesse Gonder
❑ 29B 1963 Rookie Stars ...... 4.00 1.80
Sammy Ellis
Ray Culp
John Boozer
Jesse Gonder
❑ 30 Harvey Kuenn ............... 8.00 3.60
❑ 31 Cal Koonce .................... 4.00 1.80
❑ 32 Tony Gonzalez .............. 4.00 1.80
❑ 33 Bo Belinsky .................. 8.00 3.60
❑ 34 Dick Schofield ............... 4.00 1.80
❑ 35 John Buzhardt............... 4.00 1.80
❑ 36 Jerry Kindall ................. 4.00 1.80
❑ 37 Jerry Lynch ................... 4.00 1.80
❑ 38 Bud Daley ..................... 8.00 3.60
❑ 39 Angels Team ................. 8.00 3.60
❑ 40 Vic Power ..................... 8.00 3.60
❑ 41 Charley Lau................... 8.00 3.60
❑ 42 Stan Williams ............... 8.00 3.60
(Listed as Yankee on
card but LA cap)
❑ 43 Veteran Masters ........... 8.00 3.60
Casey Stengel MG
Gene Woodling
❑ 44 Terry Fox....................... 4.00 1.80
❑ 45 Bob Aspromonte ........... 4.00 1.80
❑ 46 Tommie Aaron RC ........ 8.00 3.60
❑ 47 Don Lock ...................... 4.00 1.80
❑ 48 Birdie Tebbetts MG ........ 8.00 3.60
❑ 49 Dal Maxvill RC............... 8.00 3.60
❑ 50 Billy Pierce .................... 8.00 3.60
❑ 51 George Alusik ............... 4.00 1.80
❑ 52 Chuck Schilling ............. 4.00 1.80
❑ 53 Joe Moeller ................... 8.00 3.60
❑ 54A 1962 Rookie Stars .... 15.00 6.75
Nelson Mathews
Harry Fanok
Jack Cullen
Dave DeBusschere RC
❑ 54B 1963 Rookie Stars ...... 8.00 3.60
Nelson Mathews
Harry Fanok
Jack Cullen
Dave DeBusschere RC
❑ 55 Bill Virdon ..................... 8.00 3.60
❑ 56 Dennis Bennett .............. 4.00 1.80
❑ 57 Billy Moran ................... 4.00 1.80
❑ 58 Bob Will......................... 4.00 1.80
❑ 59 Craig Anderson ............. 4.00 1.80
❑ 60 Elston Howard............... 8.00 3.60
❑ 61 Ernie Bowman................ 4.00 1.80
❑ 62 Bob Hendley .................. 4.00 1.80
❑ 63 Reds Team .................... 8.00 3.60
❑ 64 Dick McAuliffe .............. 8.00 3.60
❑ 65 Jackie Brandt ............... 4.00 1.80
❑ 66 Mike Joyce .................... 4.00 1.80
❑ 67 Ed Charles .................... 4.00 1.80
❑ 68 Friendly Foes ............. 25.00 11.00
Duke Snider
Gil Hodges
❑ 69 Bud Zipfel ..................... 4.00 1.80
❑ 70 Jim O'Toole ................... 8.00 3.60
❑ 71 Bobby Wine.................... 8.00 3.60
❑ 72 Johnny Romano ............ 4.00 1.80
❑ 73 Bobby Bragan MG RC .. 8.00 3.60
❑ 74 Denny Lemaster ............ 4.00 1.80
❑ 75 Bob Allison .................... 8.00 3.60
❑ 76 Earl Wilson .................... 8.00 3.60
❑ 77 Al Spangler ................... 4.00 1.80
❑ 78 Marv Throneberry ......... 8.00 3.60
❑ 79 Checklist 1.................. 12.00 2.40
❑ 80 Jim Gilliam.................... 8.00 3.60
❑ 81 Jim Schaffer .................. 4.00 1.80
❑ 82 Ed Rakow ...................... 4.00 1.80
❑ 83 Charley James .............. 4.00 1.80
❑ 84 Ron Kline....................... 4.00 1.80
❑ 85 Tom Haller...................... 8.00 3.60
❑ 86 Charley Maxwell ............ 8.00 3.60
❑ 87 Bob Veale ..................... 8.00 3.60
❑ 88 Ron Hansen .................. 4.00 1.80
❑ 89 Dick Stigman.................. 4.00 1.80
❑ 90 Gordy Coleman.............. 8.00 3.60
❑ 91 Dallas Green.................. 8.00 3.60
❑ 92 Hector Lopez.................. 8.00 3.60
❑ 93 Galen Cisco................... 4.00 1.80
❑ 94 Bob Schmidt .................. 4.00 1.80
❑ 95 Larry Jackson ............... 4.00 1.80
❑ 96 Lou Clinton ................... 4.00 1.80
❑ 97 Bob Duliba..................... 4.00 1.80
❑ 98 George Thomas ............. 4.00 1.80
❑ 99 Jim Umbricht ................. 4.00 1.80
❑ 100 Joe Cunningham ......... 4.00 1.80
❑ 101 Joe Gibbon .................. 4.00 1.80
❑ 102A Checklist 2 ............. 12.00 2.40
(Red on yellow)
❑ 102B Checklist 2 ............. 12.00 2.40
(White on red)
❑ 103 Chuck Essegian .......... 4.00 1.80
❑ 104 Lew Krausse ................ 4.00 1.80
❑ 105 Ron Fairly .................... 8.00 3.60
❑ 106 Bobby Bolin.................. 4.00 1.80
❑ 107 Jim Hickman ................ 8.00 3.60
❑ 108 Hoyt Wilhelm.............. 10.00 4.50
❑ 109 Lee Maye .................... 4.00 1.80
❑ 110 Rich Rollins ................. 8.00 3.60
❑ 111 Al Jackson.................... 4.00 1.80
❑ 112 Dick Brown .................. 4.00 1.80
❑ 113 Don Landrum UER ...... 4.00 1.80
(Photo actually
Ron Santo)
❑ 114 Dan Osinski.................. 4.00 1.80
❑ 115 Carl Yastrzemski ........ 40.00 18.00
❑ 116 Jim Brosnan ................. 8.00 3.60
❑ 117 Jacke Davis.................. 4.00 1.80
❑ 118 Sherm Lollar ................ 4.00 1.80
❑ 119 Bob Lillis ..................... 4.00 1.80
❑ 120 Roger Maris............... 80.00 36.00
❑ 121 Jim Hannan.................. 4.00 1.80
❑ 122 Julio Gotay .................. 4.00 1.80
❑ 123 Frank Howard .............. 8.00 3.60
❑ 124 Dick Howser ................ 8.00 3.60
❑ 125 Robin Roberts ........... 15.00 6.75
❑ 126 Bob Uecker ............... 15.00 6.75
❑ 127 Bill Tuttle ..................... 4.00 1.80
❑ 128 Matty Alou ................... 8.00 3.60
❑ 129 Gary Bell ...................... 4.00 1.80
❑ 130 Dick Groat.................... 8.00 3.60
❑ 131 Washington Senators .. 8.00 3.60
Team Card
❑ 132 Jack Hamilton .............. 4.00 1.80
❑ 133 Gene Freese ................ 4.00 1.80
❑ 134 Bob Scheffing MG ........ 4.00 1.80
❑ 135 Richie Ashburn .......... 20.00 9.00
❑ 136 Ike Delock .................... 4.00 1.80
❑ 137 Mack Jones .................. 4.00 1.80
❑ 138 Pride of NL ................ 70.00 32.00
Willie Mays
Stan Musial
❑ 139 Earl Averill................... 4.00 1.80
❑ 140 Frank Lary.................... 8.00 3.60
❑ 141 Manny Mota RC .......... 8.00 3.60

❑ 142 Whitey Ford WS ........ 10.00 4.50
❑ 143 Jack Sanford WS ........ 8.00 3.60
❑ 144 Roger Maris WS ........ 15.00 6.75
❑ 145 Chuck Hiller WS ........ 8.00 3.60
❑ 146 Tom Tresh WS ........ 8.00 3.60
❑ 147 Billy Pierce WS ........ 8.00 3.60
❑ 148 Ralph Terry WS ........ 8.00 3.60
❑ 149 Marv Breeding ........ 4.00 1.80
❑ 150 Johnny Podres ........ 8.00 3.60
❑ 151 Pirates Team ........ 8.00 3.60
❑ 152 Ron Nischwitz ........ 4.00 1.80
❑ 153 Hal Smith ........ 4.00 1.80
❑ 154 Walter Alston MG ........ 8.00 3.60
❑ 155 Bill Stafford ........ 4.00 1.80
❑ 156 Roy McMillan ........ 8.00 3.60
❑ 157 Diego Segui RC ........ 8.00 3.60
❑ 158 Rookie Stars ........ 8.00 3.60
Rogelio Alvares
Dave Roberts
Tommy Harper RC
Bob Saverine
❑ 159 Jim Pagliaroni ........ 4.00 1.80
❑ 160 Juan Pizarro ........ 4.00 1.80
❑ 161 Frank Torre ........ 8.00 3.60
❑ 162 Twins Team ........ 8.00 3.60
❑ 163 Don Larsen ........ 8.00 3.60
❑ 164 Bubba Morton ........ 4.00 1.80
❑ 165 Jim Kaat ........ 8.00 3.60
❑ 166 Johnny Keane MG ........ 4.00 1.80
❑ 167 Jim Fregosi ........ 8.00 3.60
❑ 168 Russ Nixon ........ 4.00 1.80
❑ 169 Rookie Stars ........ 25.00 11.00
Dick Egan
Julio Navarro
Tommie Sisk
Gaylord Perry
❑ 170 Joe Adcock ........ 8.00 3.60
❑ 171 Steve Hamilton ........ 4.00 1.80
❑ 172 Gene Oliver ........ 4.00 1.80
❑ 173 Bombers' Best ........ 150.00 70.00
Tom Tresh
Mickey Mantle
Bobby Richardson
❑ 174 Larry Burright ........ 4.00 1.80
❑ 175 Bob Buhl ........ 8.00 3.60
❑ 176 Jim King ........ 4.00 1.80
❑ 177 Bubba Phillips ........ 4.00 1.80
❑ 178 Johnny Edwards ........ 4.00 1.80
❑ 179 Ron Piche ........ 4.00 1.80
❑ 180 Bill Skowron ........ 8.00 3.60
❑ 181 Sammy Esposito ........ 4.00 1.80
❑ 182 Albie Pearson ........ 8.00 3.60
❑ 183 Joe Pepitone ........ 8.00 3.60
❑ 184 Vern Law ........ 8.00 3.60
❑ 185 Chuck Hiller ........ 4.00 1.80
❑ 186 Jerry Zimmerman ........ 4.00 1.80
❑ 187 Willie Kirkland ........ 4.00 1.80
❑ 188 Eddie Bressoud ........ 4.00 1.80
❑ 189 Dave Giusti ........ 8.00 3.60
❑ 190 Minnie Minoso ........ 8.00 3.60
❑ 191 Checklist 3 ........ 12.00 2.40
❑ 192 Clay Dalrymple ........ 4.00 1.80
❑ 193 Andre Rodgers ........ 4.00 1.80
❑ 194 Joe Nuxhall ........ 8.00 3.60
❑ 195 Manny Jimenez ........ 4.00 1.80
❑ 196 Doug Camilli ........ 4.00 1.80
❑ 197 Roger Craig ........ 8.00 3.60
❑ 198 Lenny Green ........ 5.00 2.20
❑ 199 Joe Amalfitano ........ 5.00 2.20
❑ 200 Mickey Mantle ........ 500.00 220.00
❑ 201 Cecil Butler ........ 5.00 2.20
❑ 202 Boston Red Sox ........ 8.00 3.60
Team Card
❑ 203 Chico Cardenas ........ 8.00 3.60
❑ 204 Don Nottebart ........ 5.00 2.20
❑ 205 Luis Aparicio ........ 15.00 6.75
❑ 206 Ray Washburn ........ 5.00 2.20
❑ 207 Ken Hunt ........ 5.00 2.20
❑ 208 Rookie Stars ........ 5.00 2.20
Ron Herbel
John Miller
Wally Wolf
Ron Taylor
❑ 209 Hobie Landrith ........ 5.00 2.20
❑ 210 Sandy Koufax ! ........ 150.00 70.00
❑ 211 Fred Whitfield ........ 5.00 2.20
❑ 212 Glen Hobbie ........ 5.00 2.20
❑ 213 Billy Hitchcock MG ........ 5.00 2.20
❑ 214 Orlando Pena ........ 5.00 2.20
❑ 215 Bob Skinner ........ 8.00 3.60
❑ 216 Gene Conley ........ 8.00 3.60
❑ 217 Joe Christopher ........ 5.00 2.20
❑ 218 Tiger Twirlers ........ 8.00 3.60
Frank Lary
Don Mossi
Jim Bunning
❑ 219 Chuck Cottier ........ 5.00 2.20
❑ 220 Camilo Pascual ........ 8.00 3.60
❑ 221 Cookie Rojas RC ........ 8.00 3.60
❑ 222 Cubs Team ........ 8.00 3.60
❑ 223 Eddie Fisher ........ 5.00 2.20
❑ 224 Mike Roarke ........ 5.00 2.20
❑ 225 Joey Jay ........ 5.00 2.20
❑ 226 Julian Javier ........ 8.00 3.60
❑ 227 Jim Grant ........ 8.00 3.60
❑ 228 Rookie Stars ........ 50.00 22.00
Max Alvis
Bob Bailey
Tony Oliva
(Listed as Pedro)
Ed Kranepool RC
❑ 229 Willie Davis ........ 8.00 3.60
❑ 230 Pete Runnels ........ 8.00 3.60
❑ 231 Eli Grba UER ........ 5.00 2.20
(Large photo is
Ryne Duren)
❑ 232 Frank Malzone ........ 8.00 3.60
❑ 233 Casey Stengel MG ........ 20.00 9.00
❑ 234 Dave Nicholson ........ 5.00 2.20
❑ 235 Billy O'Dell ........ 5.00 2.20
❑ 236 Bill Bryan ........ 5.00 2.20
❑ 237 Jim Coates ........ 8.00 3.60
❑ 238 Lou Johnson ........ 5.00 2.20
❑ 239 Harvey Haddix ........ 8.00 3.60
❑ 240 Rocky Colavito ........ 15.00 6.75
❑ 241 Bob Smith ........ 5.00 2.20
❑ 242 Power Plus ........ 60.00 27.00
Ernie Banks
Hank Aaron
❑ 243 Don Leppert ........ 5.00 2.20
❑ 244 John Tsitouris ........ 5.00 2.20
❑ 245 Gil Hodges ........ 20.00 9.00
❑ 246 Lee Stange ........ 5.00 2.20
❑ 247 Yankees Team ........ 50.00 22.00
❑ 248 Tito Francona ........ 5.00 2.20
❑ 249 Leo Burke ........ 5.00 2.20
❑ 250 Stan Musial ........ 100.00 45.00
❑ 251 Jack Lamabe ........ 5.00 2.20
❑ 252 Ron Santo ........ 10.00 4.50
❑ 253 Rookie Stars ........ 5.00 2.20
Len Gabrielson
Pete Jernigan
John Wojcik
Deacon Jones
❑ 254 Mike Hershberger ........ 5.00 2.20
❑ 255 Bob Shaw ........ 5.00 2.20
❑ 256 Jerry Lumpe ........ 5.00 2.20
❑ 257 Hank Aguirre ........ 5.00 2.20
❑ 258 Alvin Dark MG ........ 8.00 3.60
❑ 259 Johnny Logan ........ 8.00 3.60
❑ 260 Jim Gentile ........ 8.00 3.60
❑ 261 Bob Miller ........ 5.00 2.20
❑ 262 Ellis Burton ........ 5.00 2.20
❑ 263 Dave Stenhouse ........ 5.00 2.20
❑ 264 Phil Linz ........ 5.00 2.20
❑ 265 Vada Pinson ........ 8.00 3.60
❑ 266 Bob Allen ........ 5.00 2.20
❑ 267 Carl Sawatski ........ 5.00 2.20
❑ 268 Don Demeter ........ 5.00 2.20
❑ 269 Don Mincher ........ 5.00 2.20
❑ 270 Felipe Alou ........ 8.00 3.60
❑ 271 Dean Stone ........ 5.00 2.20
❑ 272 Danny Murphy ........ 5.00 2.20
❑ 273 Sammy Taylor ........ 5.00 2.20
❑ 274 Checklist 4 ........ 12.00 2.40
❑ 275 Eddie Mathews ........ 30.00 13.50
❑ 276 Barry Shetrone ........ 5.00 2.20
❑ 277 Dick Farrell ........ 5.00 2.20
❑ 278 Chico Fernandez ........ 5.00 2.20
❑ 279 Wally Moon ........ 8.00 3.60
❑ 280 Bob Rodgers ........ 5.00 2.20
❑ 281 Tom Sturdivant ........ 5.00 2.20
❑ 282 Bobby Del Greco ........ 5.00 2.20
❑ 283 Roy Sievers ........ 8.00 3.60
❑ 284 Dave Sisler ........ 5.00 2.20
❑ 285 Dick Stuart ........ 8.00 3.60
❑ 286 Stu Miller ........ 8.00 3.60
❑ 287 Dick Bertell ........ 5.00 2.20
❑ 288 Chicago White Sox ........ 10.00 4.50
Team Card
❑ 289 Hal Brown ........ 5.00 2.20
❑ 290 Bill White ........ 8.00 3.60
❑ 291 Don Rudolph ........ 5.00 2.20
❑ 292 Pumpsie Green ........ 8.00 3.60
❑ 293 Bill Pleis ........ 5.00 2.20
❑ 294 Bill Rigney MG ........ 5.00 2.20
❑ 295 Ed Roebuck ........ 5.00 2.20
❑ 296 Doc Edwards ........ 5.00 2.20
❑ 297 Jim Golden ........ 5.00 2.20
❑ 298 Don Dillard ........ 5.00 2.20
❑ 299 Rookie Stars ........ 8.00 3.60
Dave Morehead
Bob Dustal
Tom Butters
Dan Schneider RC
❑ 300 Willie Mays ........ 150.00 70.00
❑ 301 Bill Fischer ........ 5.00 2.20
❑ 302 Whitey Herzog ........ 8.00 3.60
❑ 303 Earl Francis ........ 5.00 2.20
❑ 304 Harry Bright ........ 5.00 2.20
❑ 305 Don Hoak ........ 5.00 2.20
❑ 306 Star Receivers ........ 10.00 4.50
Earl Battey
Elston Howard
❑ 307 Chet Nichols ........ 5.00 2.20
❑ 308 Camilo Carreon ........ 5.00 2.20
❑ 309 Jim Brewer ........ 5.00 2.20
❑ 310 Tommy Davis ........ 8.00 3.60
❑ 311 Joe McClain ........ 5.00 2.20
❑ 312 Houston Colts ........ 25.00 11.00
Team Card
❑ 313 Ernie Broglio ........ 5.00 2.20
❑ 314 John Goryl ........ 5.00 2.20
❑ 315 Ralph Terry ........ 8.00 3.60
❑ 316 Norm Sherry ........ 8.00 3.60
❑ 317 Sam McDowell ........ 8.00 3.60
❑ 318 Gene Mauch MG ........ 8.00 3.60
❑ 319 Joe Gaines ........ 5.00 2.20
❑ 320 Warren Spahn ........ 60.00 27.00
❑ 321 Gino Cimoli ........ 5.00 2.20
❑ 322 Bob Turley ........ 8.00 3.60
❑ 323 Bill Mazeroski ........ 10.00 4.50
❑ 324 Rookie Stars ........ 8.00 3.60
George Williams
Pete Ward
Phil Roof
Vic Davalillo RC !
❑ 325 Jack Sanford ........ 5.00 2.20
❑ 326 Hank Foiles ........ 5.00 2.20
❑ 327 Paul Foytack ........ 5.00 2.20
❑ 328 Dick Williams ........ 8.00 3.60
❑ 329 Lindy McDaniel ........ 8.00 3.60
❑ 330 Chuck Hinton ........ 5.00 2.20
❑ 331 Series Foes ........ 8.00 3.60
Bill Stafford
Bill Pierce
❑ 332 Joel Horlen ........ 8.00 3.60
❑ 333 Carl Warwick ........ 5.00 2.20
❑ 334 Wynn Hawkins ........ 5.00 2.20
❑ 335 Leon Wagner ........ 5.00 2.20
❑ 336 Ed Bauta ........ 5.00 2.20
❑ 337 Dodgers Team ........ 25.00 11.00
❑ 338 Russ Kemmerer ........ 5.00 2.20
❑ 339 Ted Bowsfield ........ 5.00 2.20
❑ 340 Yogi Berra P/CO ........ 80.00 36.00
❑ 341 Jack Baldschun ........ 5.00 2.20
❑ 342 Gene Woodling ........ 8.00 3.60
❑ 343 Johnny Pesky MG ........ 8.00 3.60
❑ 344 Don Schwall ........ 5.00 2.20
❑ 345 Brooks Robinson ........ 60.00 27.00
❑ 346 Billy Hoeft ........ 5.00 2.20
❑ 347 Joe Torre ........ 15.00 6.75
❑ 348 Vic Wertz ........ 8.00 3.60
❑ 349 Zoilo Versalles ........ 8.00 3.60
❑ 350 Bob Purkey ........ 5.00 2.20
❑ 351 Al Luplow ........ 5.00 2.20
❑ 352 Ken Johnson ........ 5.00 2.20
❑ 353 Billy Williams ........ 30.00 13.50

❑ 354 Dom Zanni 5.00 2.20
❑ 355 Dean Chance 8.00 3.60
❑ 356 John Schaive 5.00 2.20
❑ 357 George Altman 5.00 2.20
❑ 358 Milt Pappas 8.00 3.60
❑ 359 Haywood Sullivan 8.00 3.60
❑ 360 Don Drysdale 60.00 27.00
❑ 361 Clete Boyer 10.00 4.50
❑ 362 Checklist 5 12.00 2.40
❑ 363 Dick Radatz 8.00 3.60
❑ 364 Howie Goss 5.00 2.20
❑ 365 Jim Bunning 20.00 9.00
❑ 366 Tony Taylor 8.00 3.60
❑ 367 Tony Cloninger 5.00 2.20
❑ 368 Ed Bailey 5.00 2.20
❑ 369 Jim Lemon 5.00 2.20
❑ 370 Dick Donovan 5.00 2.20
❑ 371 Rod Kanehl 8.00 3.60
❑ 372 Don Lee 5.00 2.20
❑ 373 Jim Campbell 5.00 2.20
❑ 374 Claude Osteen 8.00 3.60
❑ 375 Ken Boyer 15.00 6.75
❑ 376 John Wyatt 5.00 2.20
❑ 377 Baltimore Orioles 10.00 4.50
Team Card
❑ 378 Bill Henry 5.00 2.20
❑ 379 Bob Anderson 5.00 2.20
❑ 380 Ernie Banks UER 80.00 36.00
(Back has career Major
and Minor, but he
never played in Minors)
❑ 381 Frank Baumann 5.00 2.20
❑ 382 Ralph Houk MG 10.00 4.50
❑ 383 Pete Richert 5.00 2.20
❑ 384 Bob Tillman 5.00 2.20
❑ 385 Art Mahaffey 5.00 2.20
❑ 386 Rookie Stars 5.00 2.20
Ed Kirkpatrick
John Bateman RC
Larry Bearnarth
Garry Roggenburk
❑ 387 Al McBean 5.00 2.20
❑ 388 Jim Davenport 8.00 3.60
❑ 389 Frank Sullivan 5.00 2.20
❑ 390 Hank Aaron 125.00 55.00
❑ 391 Bill Dailey 5.00 2.20
❑ 392 Tribe Thumpers 5.00 2.20
Johnny Romano
Tito Francona
❑ 393 Ken MacKenzie 8.00 3.60
❑ 394 Tim McCarver 15.00 6.75
❑ 395 Don McMahon 5.00 2.20
❑ 396 Joe Koppe 5.00 2.20
❑ 397 Kansas City Athletics 10.00 4.50
Team Card
❑ 398 Boog Powell 25.00 11.00
❑ 399 Dick Ellsworth 5.00 2.20
❑ 400 Frank Robinson 60.00 27.00
❑ 401 Jim Bouton 15.00 6.75
❑ 402 Mickey Vernon MG 8.00 3.60
❑ 403 Ron Perranoski 8.00 3.60
❑ 404 Bob Oldis 5.00 2.20
❑ 405 Floyd Robinson 5.00 2.20
❑ 406 Howie Koplitz 5.00 2.20
❑ 407 Rookie Stars 8.00 3.60
Frank Kostro
Chico Ruiz
Larry Elliot
Dick Simpson
❑ 408 Billy Gardner 5.00 2.20
❑ 409 Roy Face 8.00 3.60
❑ 410 Earl Battey 5.00 2.20
❑ 411 Jim Constable 5.00 2.20
❑ 412 Dodger Big Three 50.00 22.00
Johnny Podres
Don Drysdale
Sandy Koufax
❑ 413 Jerry Walker 5.00 2.20
❑ 414 Ty Cline 5.00 2.20
❑ 415 Bob Gibson 60.00 27.00
❑ 416 Alex Grammas 5.00 2.20
❑ 417 Giants Team 10.00 4.50
❑ 418 John Orsino 5.00 2.20
❑ 419 Tracy Stallard 5.00 2.20
❑ 420 Bobby Richardson 15.00 6.75
❑ 421 Tom Morgan 5.00 2.20
❑ 422 Fred Hutchinson MG 8.00 3.60
❑ 423 Ed Hobaugh 5.00 2.20
❑ 424 Charlie Smith 5.00 2.20
❑ 425 Smoky Burgess 8.00 3.60
❑ 426 Barry Latman 5.00 2.20
❑ 427 Bernie Allen 5.00 2.20
❑ 428 Carl Boles 5.00 2.20
❑ 429 Lou Burdette 8.00 3.60
❑ 430 Norm Siebern 5.00 2.20
❑ 431A Checklist 6 12.00 2.40
(White on red)
❑ 431B Checklist 6 30.00 6.00
(Black on orange)
❑ 432 Roman Mejias 5.00 2.20
❑ 433 Denis Menke 5.00 2.20
❑ 434 John Callison 8.00 3.60
❑ 435 Woody Held 5.00 2.20
❑ 436 Tim Harkness 8.00 3.60
❑ 437 Bill Bruton 5.00 2.20
❑ 438 Wes Stock 5.00 2.20
❑ 439 Don Zimmer 8.00 3.60
❑ 440 Juan Marichal 30.00 13.50
❑ 441 Lee Thomas 8.00 3.60
❑ 442 J.C. Hartman 5.00 2.20
❑ 443 Jimmy Piersall 8.00 3.60
❑ 444 Jim Maloney 8.00 3.60
❑ 445 Norm Cash 10.00 4.50
❑ 446 Whitey Ford 60.00 27.00
❑ 447 Felix Mantilla 25.00 11.00
❑ 448 Jack Kralick 25.00 11.00
❑ 449 Jose Tartabull 25.00 11.00
❑ 450 Bob Friend 30.00 13.50
❑ 451 Indians Team 40.00 18.00
❑ 452 Barney Schultz 25.00 11.00
❑ 453 Jake Wood 25.00 11.00
❑ 454A Art Fowler 25.00 11.00
(Card number on
white background)
❑ 454B Art Fowler 30.00 13.50
(Card number on
orange background)
❑ 455 Ruben Amaro 25.00 11.00
❑ 456 Jim Coker 25.00 11.00
❑ 457 Tex Clevenger 25.00 11.00
❑ 458 Al Lopez MG 30.00 13.50
❑ 459 Dick LeMay 25.00 11.00
❑ 460 Del Crandall 30.00 13.50
❑ 461 Norm Bass 25.00 11.00
❑ 462 Wally Post 25.00 11.00
❑ 463 Joe Schaffernoth 25.00 11.00
❑ 464 Ken Aspromonte 25.00 11.00
❑ 465 Chuck Estrada 25.00 11.00
❑ 466 Rookie Stars SP 60.00 27.00
Nate Oliver
Tony Martinez
Bill Freehan RC !
Jerry Robinson
❑ 467 Phil Ortega 25.00 11.00
❑ 468 Carroll Hardy 30.00 13.50
❑ 469 Jay Hook 30.00 13.50
❑ 470 Tom Tresh SP 60.00 27.00
❑ 471 Ken Retzer 25.00 11.00
❑ 472 Lou Brock 80.00 36.00
❑ 473 New York Mets 100.00 45.00
Team Card
❑ 474 Jack Fisher 25.00 11.00
❑ 475 Gus Triandos 30.00 13.50
❑ 476 Frank Funk 25.00 11.00
❑ 477 Donn Clendenon 30.00 13.50
❑ 478 Paul Brown 25.00 11.00
❑ 479 Ed Brinkman 25.00 11.00
❑ 480 Bill Monbouquette 25.00 11.00
❑ 481 Bob Taylor 25.00 11.00
❑ 482 Felix Torres 25.00 11.00
❑ 483 Jim Owens UER 25.00 11.00
(Stat column for Wins
has an R instead)
❑ 484 Dale Long SP 30.00 13.50
❑ 485 Jim Landis 25.00 11.00
❑ 486 Ray Sadecki 25.00 11.00
❑ 487 John Roseboro 30.00 13.50
❑ 488 Jerry Adair 25.00 11.00
❑ 489 Paul Toth 25.00 11.00
❑ 490 Willie McCovey 100.00 45.00
❑ 491 Harry Craft MG 25.00 11.00
❑ 492 Dave Wickersham 25.00 11.00
❑ 493 Walt Bond 25.00 11.00
❑ 494 Phil Regan 25.00 11.00
❑ 495 Frank Thomas SP 30.00 13.50
❑ 496 Rookie Stars 30.00 13.50
Steve Dalkowski RC
Fred Newman
Jack Smith
Carl Bouldin
❑ 497 Bennie Daniels 25.00 11.00
❑ 498 Eddie Kasko 25.00 11.00
❑ 499 J.C. Martin 25.00 11.00
❑ 500 Harmon Killebrew SP 150.00 70.00
❑ 501 Joe Azcue 25.00 11.00
❑ 502 Daryl Spencer 25.00 11.00
❑ 503 Braves Team 40.00 18.00
❑ 504 Bob Johnson 25.00 11.00
❑ 505 Curt Flood 40.00 18.00
❑ 506 Gene Green 25.00 11.00
❑ 507 Roland Sheldon 30.00 13.50
❑ 508 Ted Savage 25.00 11.00
❑ 509A Checklist 7 30.00 6.00
(Copyright centered)
❑ 509B Checklist 7 30.00 6.00
(Copyright to right)
❑ 510 Ken McBride 25.00 11.00
❑ 511 Charlie Neal 30.00 13.50
❑ 512 Cal McLish 25.00 11.00
❑ 513 Gary Geiger 25.00 11.00
❑ 514 Larry Osborne 25.00 11.00
❑ 515 Don Elston 25.00 11.00
❑ 516 Purnell Goldy 25.00 11.00
❑ 517 Hal Woodeshick 25.00 11.00
❑ 518 Don Blasingame 25.00 11.00
❑ 519 Claude Raymond RC 25.00 11.00
❑ 520 Orlando Cepeda 30.00 13.50
❑ 521 Dan Pfister 25.00 11.00
❑ 522 Rookie Stars 30.00 13.50
Mel Nelson
Gary Peters
Jim Roland
Art Quirk
❑ 523 Bill Kunkel 15.00 6.75
❑ 524 Cardinals Team 30.00 13.50
❑ 525 Nellie Fox 50.00 22.00
❑ 526 Dick Hall 15.00 6.75
❑ 527 Ed Sadowski 15.00 6.75
❑ 528 Carl Willey 15.00 6.75
❑ 529 Wes Covington 15.00 6.75
❑ 530 Don Mossi 20.00 9.00
❑ 531 Sam Mele MG 15.00 6.75
❑ 532 Steve Boros 15.00 6.75
❑ 533 Bobby Shantz 20.00 9.00
❑ 534 Ken Walters 15.00 6.75
❑ 535 Jim Perry 20.00 9.00
❑ 536 Norm Larker 15.00 6.75
❑ 537 Rookie Stars 850.00 375.00
Pedro Gonzalez
Ken McMullen
Al Weis
Pete Rose RC !
❑ 538 George Brunet 15.00 6.75
❑ 539 Wayne Causey 15.00 6.75
❑ 540 Roberto Clemente 300.00 135.00
❑ 541 Ron Moeller 15.00 6.75
❑ 542 Lou Klimchock 15.00 6.75
❑ 543 Russ Snyder 15.00 6.75
❑ 544 Rookie Stars 50.00 22.00
Duke Carmel
Bill Haas
Rusty Staub RC
Dick Phillips
❑ 545 Jose Pagan 15.00 6.75
❑ 546 Hal Reniff 20.00 9.00
❑ 547 Gus Bell 15.00 6.75
❑ 548 Tom Satriano 15.00 6.75
❑ 549 Rookie Stars 15.00 6.75
Marcelino Lopez
Pete Lovrich
Paul Ratliff
Elmo Plaskett
❑ 550 Duke Snider 80.00 36.00
❑ 551 Billy Klaus 15.00 6.75
❑ 552 Detroit Tigers 50.00 22.00
Team Card
❑ 553 Rookie Stars 125.00 55.00
Brock Davis

| Card | NRMT | VG-E |
|---|---|---|
| Jim Gosger | | |
| Willie Stargell RC | | |
| John Herrnstein | | |
| ❑ 554 Hank Fischer | 15.00 | 6.75 |
| ❑ 555 John Blanchard | 20.00 | 9.00 |
| ❑ 556 Al Worthington | 15.00 | 6.75 |
| ❑ 557 Cuno Barragan | 15.00 | 6.75 |
| ❑ 558 Rookie Stars | 20.00 | 9.00 |
| Bill Faul | | |
| Ron Hunt RC | | |
| Al Moran | | |
| Bob Lipski | | |
| ❑ 559 Danny Murtaugh MG | 15.00 | 6.75 |
| ❑ 560 Ray Herbert | 15.00 | 6.75 |
| ❑ 561 Mike De La Hoz | 15.00 | 6.75 |
| ❑ 562 Rookie Stars | 30.00 | 13.50 |
| Randy Cardinal | | |
| Dave McNally | | |
| Ken Rowe | | |
| Don Rowe RC ! RC ! RC ! RC ! | | |
| ❑ 563 Mike McCormick | 15.00 | 6.75 |
| ❑ 564 George Banks | 15.00 | 6.75 |
| ❑ 565 Larry Sherry | 15.00 | 6.75 |
| ❑ 566 Cliff Cook | 15.00 | 6.75 |
| ❑ 567 Jim Duffalo | 15.00 | 6.75 |
| ❑ 568 Bob Sadowski | 15.00 | 6.75 |
| ❑ 569 Luis Arroyo | 20.00 | 9.00 |
| ❑ 570 Frank Bolling | 15.00 | 6.75 |
| ❑ 571 Johnny Klippstein | 15.00 | 6.75 |
| ❑ 572 Jack Spring | 15.00 | 6.75 |
| ❑ 573 Coot Veal | 15.00 | 6.75 |
| ❑ 574 Hal Kolstad | 15.00 | 6.75 |
| ❑ 575 Don Cardwell | 15.00 | 6.75 |
| ❑ 576 Johnny Temple | 30.00 | 11.00 |

## 1964 Topps

| | NRMT | VG-E |
|---|---|---|
| COMPLETE SET (587) | 3000.00 | 1350.00 |
| COMMON CARD (1-196) | 3.00 | 1.35 |
| COMMON CARD (197-370) | 4.00 | 1.80 |
| COMMON CARD (371-522) | 7.00 | 3.10 |
| COMMON CARD (523-587) | 16.00 | 7.25 |
| WRAPPER (1-CENT) | 100.00 | 45.00 |
| WRAP.(1-CENT, REPEAT) | 125.00 | 55.00 |
| WRAPPER (5-CENT) | 30.00 | 13.50 |
| WRAPPER (5-CENT, COIN) | 40.00 | 18.00 |

| Card | NRMT | VG-E |
|---|---|---|
| ❑ 1 NL ERA Leaders | 30.00 | 9.00 |
| Sandy Koufax | | |
| Dick Ellsworth | | |
| Bob Friend | | |
| ❑ 2 AL ERA Leaders | 8.00 | 3.60 |
| Gary Peters | | |
| Juan Pizarro | | |
| Camilo Pascual | | |
| ❑ 3 NL Pitching Leaders | 20.00 | 9.00 |
| Sandy Koufax | | |
| Juan Marichal | | |
| Warren Spahn | | |
| Jim Maloney | | |
| ❑ 4 AL Pitching Leaders | 8.00 | 3.60 |
| Whitey Ford | | |
| Camilo Pascual | | |
| Jim Bouton | | |
| ❑ 5 NL Strikeout Leaders | 15.00 | 6.75 |
| Sandy Koufax | | |
| Jim Maloney | | |
| Don Drysdale | | |
| ❑ 6 AL Strikeout Leaders | 8.00 | 3.60 |
| Camilo Pascual | | |
| Jim Bunning | | |
| Dick Stigman | | |
| ❑ 7 NL Batting Leaders | 20.00 | 9.00 |
| Tommy Davis | | |
| Roberto Clemente | | |
| Dick Groat | | |
| Hank Aaron | | |
| ❑ 8 AL Batting Leaders | 15.00 | 6.75 |
| Carl Yastrzemski | | |
| Al Kaline | | |
| Rich Rollins | | |
| ❑ 9 NL Home Run Leaders | 30.00 | 13.50 |
| Hank Aaron | | |
| Willie McCovey | | |
| Willie Mays | | |
| Orlando Cepeda | | |
| ❑ 10 AL Home Run Leaders | 8.00 | 3.60 |
| Harmon Killebrew | | |
| Dick Stuart | | |
| Bob Allison | | |
| ❑ 11 NL RBI Leaders | 15.00 | 6.75 |
| Hank Aaron | | |
| Ken Boyer | | |
| Bill White | | |
| ❑ 12 AL RBI Leaders | 8.00 | 3.60 |
| Dick Stuart | | |
| Al Kaline | | |
| Harmon Killebrew | | |
| ❑ 13 Hoyt Wilhelm | 12.00 | 5.50 |
| ❑ 14 Dodgers Rookies | 3.00 | 1.35 |
| Dick Nen RC | | |
| Nick Willhite | | |
| ❑ 15 Zoilo Versalles | 6.00 | 2.70 |
| ❑ 16 John Boozer | 3.00 | 1.35 |
| ❑ 17 Willie Kirkland | 3.00 | 1.35 |
| ❑ 18 Billy O'Dell | 3.00 | 1.35 |
| ❑ 19 Don Wert | 3.00 | 1.35 |
| ❑ 20 Bob Friend | 6.00 | 2.70 |
| ❑ 21 Yogi Berra MG | 35.00 | 16.00 |
| ❑ 22 Jerry Adair | 3.00 | 1.35 |
| ❑ 23 Chris Zachary | 3.00 | 1.35 |
| ❑ 24 Carl Sawatski | 3.00 | 1.35 |
| ❑ 25 Bill Monbouquette | 3.00 | 1.35 |
| ❑ 26 Gino Cimoli | 3.00 | 1.35 |
| ❑ 27 New York Mets | 8.00 | 3.60 |
| Team Card | | |
| ❑ 28 Claude Osteen | 6.00 | 2.70 |
| ❑ 29 Lou Brock | 35.00 | 16.00 |
| ❑ 30 Ron Perranoski | 6.00 | 2.70 |
| ❑ 31 Dave Nicholson | 3.00 | 1.35 |
| ❑ 32 Dean Chance | 6.00 | 2.70 |
| ❑ 33 Reds Rookies | 6.00 | 2.70 |
| Sammy Ellis | | |
| Mel Queen | | |
| ❑ 34 Jim Perry | 6.00 | 2.70 |
| ❑ 35 Eddie Mathews | 20.00 | 9.00 |
| ❑ 36 Hal Reniff | 3.00 | 1.35 |
| ❑ 37 Smoky Burgess | 6.00 | 2.70 |
| ❑ 38 Jim Wynn RC | 8.00 | 3.60 |
| ❑ 39 Hank Aguirre | 3.00 | 1.35 |
| ❑ 40 Dick Groat | 6.00 | 2.70 |
| ❑ 41 Friendly Foes | 8.00 | 3.60 |
| Willie McCovey | | |
| Leon Wagner | | |
| ❑ 42 Moe Drabowsky | 6.00 | 2.70 |
| ❑ 43 Roy Sievers | 6.00 | 2.70 |
| ❑ 44 Duke Carmel | 3.00 | 1.35 |
| ❑ 45 Milt Pappas | 6.00 | 2.70 |
| ❑ 46 Ed Brinkman | 3.00 | 1.35 |
| ❑ 47 Giants Rookies | 6.00 | 2.70 |
| Jesus Alou RC | | |
| Ron Herbel | | |
| ❑ 48 Bob Perry | 3.00 | 1.35 |
| ❑ 49 Bill Henry | 3.00 | 1.35 |
| ❑ 50 Mickey Mantle | 300.00 | 135.00 |
| ❑ 51 Pete Richert | 3.00 | 1.35 |
| ❑ 52 Chuck Hinton | 3.00 | 1.35 |
| ❑ 53 Denis Menke | 3.00 | 1.35 |
| ❑ 54 Sam Mele MG | 3.00 | 1.35 |
| ❑ 55 Ernie Banks | 35.00 | 16.00 |
| ❑ 56 Hal Brown | 3.00 | 1.35 |
| ❑ 57 Tim Harkness | 6.00 | 2.70 |
| ❑ 58 Don Demeter | 6.00 | 2.70 |
| ❑ 59 Ernie Broglio | 3.00 | 1.35 |
| ❑ 60 Frank Malzone | 6.00 | 2.70 |
| ❑ 61 Angel Backstops | 6.00 | 2.70 |
| Bob Rodgers | | |
| Ed Sadowski | | |
| ❑ 62 Ted Savage | 3.00 | 1.35 |
| ❑ 63 John Orsino | 3.00 | 1.35 |
| ❑ 64 Ted Abernathy | 3.00 | 1.35 |
| ❑ 65 Felipe Alou | 6.00 | 2.70 |
| ❑ 66 Eddie Fisher | 3.00 | 1.35 |
| ❑ 67 Tigers Team | 8.00 | 3.60 |
| ❑ 68 Willie Davis | 6.00 | 2.70 |
| ❑ 69 Clete Boyer | 6.00 | 2.70 |
| ❑ 70 Joe Torre | 8.00 | 3.60 |
| ❑ 71 Jack Spring | 3.00 | 1.35 |
| ❑ 72 Chico Cardenas | 6.00 | 2.70 |
| ❑ 73 Jimmie Hall | 8.00 | 3.60 |
| ❑ 74 Pirates Rookies | 3.00 | 1.35 |
| Bob Priddy | | |
| Tom Butters | | |
| ❑ 75 Wayne Causey | 3.00 | 1.35 |
| ❑ 76 Checklist 1 | 10.00 | 2.00 |
| ❑ 77 Jerry Walker | 3.00 | 1.35 |
| ❑ 78 Merritt Ranew | 3.00 | 1.35 |
| ❑ 79 Bob Heffner | 3.00 | 1.35 |
| ❑ 80 Vada Pinson | 8.00 | 3.60 |
| ❑ 81 All-Star Vets | 12.00 | 5.50 |
| Nellie Fox | | |
| Harmon Killebrew | | |
| ❑ 82 Jim Davenport | 6.00 | 2.70 |
| ❑ 83 Gus Triandos | 6.00 | 2.70 |
| ❑ 84 Carl Willey | 3.00 | 1.35 |
| ❑ 85 Pete Ward | 3.00 | 1.35 |
| ❑ 86 Al Downing | 6.00 | 2.70 |
| ❑ 87 St. Louis Cardinals | 6.00 | 2.70 |
| Team Card | | |
| ❑ 88 John Roseboro | 6.00 | 2.70 |
| ❑ 89 Boog Powell | 6.00 | 2.70 |
| ❑ 90 Earl Battey | 3.00 | 1.35 |
| ❑ 91 Bob Bailey | 6.00 | 2.70 |
| ❑ 92 Steve Ridzik | 3.00 | 1.35 |
| ❑ 93 Gary Geiger | 3.00 | 1.35 |
| ❑ 94 Braves Rookies | 3.00 | 1.35 |
| Jim Britton | | |
| Larry Maxie | | |
| ❑ 95 George Altman | 3.00 | 1.35 |
| ❑ 96 Bob Buhl | 6.00 | 2.70 |
| ❑ 97 Jim Fregosi | 6.00 | 2.70 |
| ❑ 98 Bill Bruton | 3.00 | 1.35 |
| ❑ 99 Al Stanek | 3.00 | 1.35 |
| ❑ 100 Elston Howard | 6.00 | 2.70 |
| ❑ 101 Walt Alston MG | 8.00 | 3.60 |
| ❑ 102 Checklist 2 | 10.00 | 2.00 |
| ❑ 103 Curt Flood | 6.00 | 2.70 |
| ❑ 104 Art Mahaffey | 6.00 | 2.70 |
| ❑ 105 Woody Held | 3.00 | 1.35 |
| ❑ 106 Joe Nuxhall | 6.00 | 2.70 |
| ❑ 107 White Sox Rookies | 3.00 | 1.35 |
| Bruce Howard | | |
| Frank Kreutzer | | |
| ❑ 108 John Wyatt | 3.00 | 1.35 |
| ❑ 109 Rusty Staub | 6.00 | 2.70 |
| ❑ 110 Albie Pearson | 6.00 | 2.70 |
| ❑ 111 Don Elston | 3.00 | 1.35 |
| ❑ 112 Bob Tillman | 3.00 | 1.35 |
| ❑ 113 Grover Powell | 6.00 | 2.70 |
| ❑ 114 Don Lock | 3.00 | 1.35 |
| ❑ 115 Frank Bolling | 3.00 | 1.35 |
| ❑ 116 Twins Rookies | 12.00 | 5.50 |
| Jay Ward | | |
| Tony Oliva | | |
| ❑ 117 Earl Francis | 3.00 | 1.35 |
| ❑ 118 John Blanchard | 6.00 | 2.70 |
| ❑ 119 Gary Kolb | 3.00 | 1.35 |
| ❑ 120 Don Drysdale | 20.00 | 9.00 |
| ❑ 121 Pete Runnels | 6.00 | 2.70 |
| ❑ 122 Don McMahon | 3.00 | 1.35 |
| ❑ 123 Jose Pagan | 3.00 | 1.35 |
| ❑ 124 Orlando Pena | 3.00 | 1.35 |
| ❑ 125 Pete Rose | 125.00 | 55.00 |
| ❑ 126 Russ Snyder | 3.00 | 1.35 |
| ❑ 127 Angels Rookies | 3.00 | 1.35 |
| Aubrey Gatewood | | |
| Dick Simpson | | |
| ❑ 128 Mickey Lolich RC | 20.00 | 9.00 |
| ❑ 129 Amado Samuel | 3.00 | 1.35 |

| # | Card | | |
|---|---|---|---|
| ❑ 130 | Gary Peters | 6.00 | 2.70 |
| ❑ 131 | Steve Boros | 3.00 | 1.35 |
| ❑ 132 | Braves Team | 6.00 | 2.70 |
| ❑ 133 | Jim Grant | 6.00 | 2.70 |
| ❑ 134 | Don Zimmer | 6.00 | 2.70 |
| ❑ 135 | Johnny Callison | 6.00 | 2.70 |
| ❑ 136 | Sandy Koufax WS | 20.00 | 9.00 |
| | Strikes out 15 | | |
| ❑ 137 | Willie Davis WS | 8.00 | 3.60 |
| ❑ 138 | Ron Fairly WS | 8.00 | 3.60 |
| ❑ 139 | Frank Howard WS | 8.00 | 3.60 |
| ❑ 140 | World Series Summary | 8.00 | 3.60 |
| | Dodgers celebrate | | |
| ❑ 141 | Danny Murtaugh MG | 6.00 | 2.70 |
| ❑ 142 | John Bateman | 3.00 | 1.35 |
| ❑ 143 | Bubba Phillips | 3.00 | 1.35 |
| ❑ 144 | Al Worthington | 3.00 | 1.35 |
| ❑ 145 | Norm Siebern | 3.00 | 1.35 |
| ❑ 146 | Indians Rookies | 30.00 | 13.50 |
| | Tommy John RC | | |
| | Bob Chance | | |
| ❑ 147 | Ray Sadecki | 3.00 | 1.35 |
| ❑ 148 | J.C. Martin | 3.00 | 1.35 |
| ❑ 149 | Paul Foytack | 3.00 | 1.35 |
| ❑ 150 | Willie Mays | 100.00 | 45.00 |
| ❑ 151 | Athletics Team | 6.00 | 2.70 |
| ❑ 152 | Denny Lemaster | 3.00 | 1.35 |
| ❑ 153 | Dick Williams | 6.00 | 2.70 |
| ❑ 154 | Dick Tracewski RC | 6.00 | 2.70 |
| ❑ 155 | Duke Snider | 30.00 | 13.50 |
| ❑ 156 | Bill Dailey | 3.00 | 1.35 |
| ❑ 157 | Gene Mauch MG | 6.00 | 2.70 |
| ❑ 158 | Ken Johnson | 3.00 | 1.35 |
| ❑ 159 | Charlie Dees | 3.00 | 1.35 |
| ❑ 160 | Ken Boyer | 6.00 | 2.70 |
| ❑ 161 | Dave McNally | 6.00 | 2.70 |
| ❑ 162 | Hitting Area | 6.00 | 2.70 |
| | Dick Sisler CO | | |
| | Vada Pinson | | |
| ❑ 163 | Donn Clendenon | 6.00 | 2.70 |
| ❑ 164 | Bud Daley | 3.00 | 1.35 |
| ❑ 165 | Jerry Lumpe | 3.00 | 1.35 |
| ❑ 166 | Marty Keough | 3.00 | 1.35 |
| ❑ 167 | Senators Rookies | 30.00 | 13.50 |
| | Mike Brumley | | |
| | Lou Piniella RC | | |
| ❑ 168 | Al Weis | 3.00 | 1.35 |
| ❑ 169 | Del Crandall | 6.00 | 2.70 |
| ❑ 170 | Dick Radatz | 6.00 | 2.70 |
| ❑ 171 | Ty Cline | 3.00 | 1.35 |
| ❑ 172 | Indians Team | 6.00 | 2.70 |
| ❑ 173 | Ryne Duren | 6.00 | 2.70 |
| ❑ 174 | Doc Edwards | 3.00 | 1.35 |
| ❑ 175 | Billy Williams | 12.00 | 5.50 |
| ❑ 176 | Tracy Stallard | 3.00 | 1.35 |
| ❑ 177 | Harmon Killebrew | 20.00 | 9.00 |
| ❑ 178 | Hank Bauer MG | 6.00 | 2.70 |
| ❑ 179 | Carl Warwick | 3.00 | 1.35 |
| ❑ 180 | Tommy Davis | 6.00 | 2.70 |
| ❑ 181 | Dave Wickersham | 3.00 | 1.35 |
| ❑ 182 | Sox Sockers | 15.00 | 6.75 |
| | Carl Yastrzemski | | |
| | Chuck Schilling | | |
| ❑ 183 | Ron Taylor | 3.00 | 1.35 |
| ❑ 184 | Al Luplow | 3.00 | 1.35 |
| ❑ 185 | Jim O'Toole | 6.00 | 2.70 |
| ❑ 186 | Roman Mejias | 3.00 | 1.35 |
| ❑ 187 | Ed Roebuck | 3.00 | 1.35 |
| ❑ 188 | Checklist 3 | 10.00 | 2.00 |
| ❑ 189 | Bob Hendley | 3.00 | 1.35 |
| ❑ 190 | Bobby Richardson | 8.00 | 3.60 |
| ❑ 191 | Clay Dalrymple | 6.00 | 2.70 |
| ❑ 192 | Cubs Rookies | 3.00 | 1.35 |
| | John Boccabella | | |
| | Billy Cowan | | |
| ❑ 193 | Jerry Lynch | 3.00 | 1.35 |
| ❑ 194 | John Goryl | 3.00 | 1.35 |
| ❑ 195 | Floyd Robinson | 3.00 | 1.35 |
| ❑ 196 | Jim Gentile | 3.00 | 1.35 |
| ❑ 197 | Frank Lary | 6.00 | 2.70 |
| ❑ 198 | Len Gabrielson | 4.00 | 1.80 |
| ❑ 199 | Joe Azcue | 4.00 | 1.80 |
| ❑ 200 | Sandy Koufax | 100.00 | 45.00 |
| ❑ 201 | Orioles Rookies | 6.00 | 2.70 |
| | Sam Bowens | | |
| | Wally Bunker | | |
| ❑ 202 | Galen Cisco | 6.00 | 2.70 |
| ❑ 203 | John Kennedy | 6.00 | 2.70 |
| ❑ 204 | Matty Alou | 6.00 | 2.70 |
| ❑ 205 | Nellie Fox | 12.00 | 5.50 |
| ❑ 206 | Steve Hamilton | 6.00 | 2.70 |
| ❑ 207 | Fred Hutchinson MG | 6.00 | 2.70 |
| ❑ 208 | Wes Covington | 6.00 | 2.70 |
| ❑ 209 | Bob Allen | 4.00 | 1.80 |
| ❑ 210 | Carl Yastrzemski | 40.00 | 18.00 |
| ❑ 211 | Jim Coker | 4.00 | 1.80 |
| ❑ 212 | Pete Lovrich | 4.00 | 1.80 |
| ❑ 213 | Angels Team | 6.00 | 2.70 |
| ❑ 214 | Ken McMullen | 6.00 | 2.70 |
| ❑ 215 | Ray Herbert | 4.00 | 1.80 |
| ❑ 216 | Mike de la Hoz | 4.00 | 1.80 |
| ❑ 217 | Jim King | 4.00 | 1.80 |
| ❑ 218 | Hank Fischer | 4.00 | 1.80 |
| ❑ 219 | Young Aces | 6.00 | 2.70 |
| | Al Downing | | |
| | Jim Bouton | | |
| ❑ 220 | Dick Ellsworth | 6.00 | 2.70 |
| ❑ 221 | Bob Saverine | 4.00 | 1.80 |
| ❑ 222 | Billy Pierce | 6.00 | 2.70 |
| ❑ 223 | George Banks | 4.00 | 1.80 |
| ❑ 224 | Tommie Sisk | 4.00 | 1.80 |
| ❑ 225 | Roger Maris | 60.00 | 27.00 |
| ❑ 226 | Colts Rookies | 6.00 | 2.70 |
| | Jerry Grote RC | | |
| | Larry Yellen | | |
| ❑ 227 | Barry Latman | 4.00 | 1.80 |
| ❑ 228 | Felix Mantilla | 4.00 | 1.80 |
| ❑ 229 | Charley Lau | 6.00 | 2.70 |
| ❑ 230 | Brooks Robinson | 40.00 | 18.00 |
| ❑ 231 | Dick Calmus | 4.00 | 1.80 |
| ❑ 232 | Al Lopez MG | 6.00 | 2.70 |
| ❑ 233 | Hal Smith | 4.00 | 1.80 |
| ❑ 234 | Gary Bell | 4.00 | 1.80 |
| ❑ 235 | Ron Hunt | 4.00 | 1.80 |
| ❑ 236 | Bill Faul | 4.00 | 1.80 |
| ❑ 237 | Cubs Team | 6.00 | 2.70 |
| ❑ 238 | Roy McMillan | 6.00 | 2.70 |
| ❑ 239 | Herm Starrette | 4.00 | 1.80 |
| ❑ 240 | Bill White | 6.00 | 2.70 |
| ❑ 241 | Jim Owens | 4.00 | 1.80 |
| ❑ 242 | Harvey Kuenn | 6.00 | 2.70 |
| ❑ 243 | Phillies Rookies | 30.00 | 13.50 |
| | Richie Allen RC | | |
| | John Hermstein | | |
| ❑ 244 | Tony LaRussa RC | 30.00 | 13.50 |
| ❑ 245 | Dick Stigman | 4.00 | 1.80 |
| ❑ 246 | Manny Mota | 6.00 | 2.70 |
| ❑ 247 | Dave DeBusschere | 6.00 | 2.70 |
| ❑ 248 | Johnny Pesky MG | 6.00 | 2.70 |
| ❑ 249 | Doug Camilli | 4.00 | 1.80 |
| ❑ 250 | Al Kaline | 40.00 | 18.00 |
| ❑ 251 | Choo Choo Coleman | 6.00 | 2.70 |
| ❑ 252 | Ken Aspromonte | 4.00 | 1.80 |
| ❑ 253 | Wally Post | 6.00 | 2.70 |
| ❑ 254 | Don Hoak | 6.00 | 2.70 |
| ❑ 255 | Lee Thomas | 6.00 | 2.70 |
| ❑ 256 | Johnny Weekly | 4.00 | 1.80 |
| ❑ 257 | San Francisco Giants | 6.00 | 2.70 |
| | Team Card | | |
| ❑ 258 | Garry Roggenburk | 4.00 | 1.80 |
| ❑ 259 | Harry Bright | 4.00 | 1.80 |
| ❑ 260 | Frank Robinson | 40.00 | 18.00 |
| ❑ 261 | Jim Hannan | 4.00 | 1.80 |
| ❑ 262 | Cards Rookies | 8.00 | 3.60 |
| | Mike Shannon RC | | |
| | Harry Fanok | | |
| ❑ 263 | Chuck Estrada | 4.00 | 1.80 |
| ❑ 264 | Jim Landis | 4.00 | 1.80 |
| ❑ 265 | Jim Bunning | 12.00 | 5.50 |
| ❑ 266 | Gene Freese | 4.00 | 1.80 |
| ❑ 267 | Wilbur Wood RC | 6.00 | 2.70 |
| ❑ 268 | Bill's Got It | 6.00 | 2.70 |
| | Danny Murtaugh MG | | |
| | Bill Virdon | | |
| ❑ 269 | Ellis Burton | 4.00 | 1.80 |
| ❑ 270 | Rich Rollins | 6.00 | 2.70 |
| ❑ 271 | Bob Sadowski | 4.00 | 1.80 |
| ❑ 272 | Jake Wood | 4.00 | 1.80 |
| ❑ 273 | Mel Nelson | 4.00 | 1.80 |
| ❑ 274 | Checklist 4 | 10.00 | 2.00 |
| ❑ 275 | John Tsitouris | 4.00 | 1.80 |
| ❑ 276 | Jose Tartabull | 6.00 | 2.70 |
| ❑ 277 | Ken Retzer | 4.00 | 1.80 |
| ❑ 278 | Bobby Shantz | 6.00 | 2.70 |
| ❑ 279 | Joe Koppe UER | 4.00 | 1.80 |
| | (Glove on wrong hand) | | |
| ❑ 280 | Juan Marichal | 12.00 | 5.50 |
| ❑ 281 | Yankees Rookies | 6.00 | 2.70 |
| | Jake Gibbs | | |
| | Tom Metcalf | | |
| ❑ 282 | Bob Bruce | 4.00 | 1.80 |
| ❑ 283 | Tom McCraw RC | 4.00 | 1.80 |
| ❑ 284 | Dick Schofield | 4.00 | 1.80 |
| ❑ 285 | Robin Roberts | 12.00 | 5.50 |
| ❑ 286 | Don Landrum | 4.00 | 1.80 |
| ❑ 287 | Red Sox Rookies | 50.00 | 22.00 |
| | Tony Conigliaro RC | | |
| | Bill Spanswick | | |
| ❑ 288 | Al Moran | 4.00 | 1.80 |
| ❑ 289 | Frank Funk | 4.00 | 1.80 |
| ❑ 290 | Bob Allison | 6.00 | 2.70 |
| ❑ 291 | Phil Ortega | 4.00 | 1.80 |
| ❑ 292 | Mike Roarke | 4.00 | 1.80 |
| ❑ 293 | Phillies Team | 6.00 | 2.70 |
| ❑ 294 | Ken L. Hunt | 4.00 | 1.80 |
| ❑ 295 | Roger Craig | 6.00 | 2.70 |
| ❑ 296 | Ed Kirkpatrick | 4.00 | 1.80 |
| ❑ 297 | Ken MacKenzie | 4.00 | 1.80 |
| ❑ 298 | Harry Craft MG | 4.00 | 1.80 |
| ❑ 299 | Bill Stafford | 4.00 | 1.80 |
| ❑ 300 | Hank Aaron | 100.00 | 45.00 |
| ❑ 301 | Larry Brown | 4.00 | 1.80 |
| ❑ 302 | Dan Pfister | 4.00 | 1.80 |
| ❑ 303 | Jim Campbell | 4.00 | 1.80 |
| ❑ 304 | Bob Johnson | 4.00 | 1.80 |
| ❑ 305 | Jack Lamabe | 4.00 | 1.80 |
| ❑ 306 | Giant Gunners | 40.00 | 18.00 |
| | Willie Mays | | |
| | Orlando Cepeda | | |
| ❑ 307 | Joe Gibbon | 4.00 | 1.80 |
| ❑ 308 | Gene Stephens | 4.00 | 1.80 |
| ❑ 309 | Paul Toth | 4.00 | 1.80 |
| ❑ 310 | Jim Gilliam | 6.00 | 2.70 |
| ❑ 311 | Tom Brown RC | 6.00 | 2.70 |
| ❑ 312 | Tigers Rookies | 4.00 | 1.80 |
| | Fritz Fisher | | |
| | Fred Gladding | | |
| ❑ 313 | Chuck Hiller | 4.00 | 1.80 |
| ❑ 314 | Jerry Buchek | 4.00 | 1.80 |
| ❑ 315 | Bo Belinsky | 6.00 | 2.70 |
| ❑ 316 | Gene Oliver | 4.00 | 1.80 |
| ❑ 317 | Al Smith | 4.00 | 1.80 |
| ❑ 318 | Minnesota Twins | 6.00 | 2.70 |
| | Team Card | | |
| ❑ 319 | Paul Brown | 4.00 | 1.80 |
| ❑ 320 | Rocky Colavito | 12.00 | 5.50 |
| ❑ 321 | Bob Lillis | 4.00 | 1.80 |
| ❑ 322 | George Brunet | 4.00 | 1.80 |
| ❑ 323 | John Buzhardt | 4.00 | 1.80 |
| ❑ 324 | Casey Stengel MG | 15.00 | 6.75 |
| ❑ 325 | Hector Lopez | 6.00 | 2.70 |
| ❑ 326 | Ron Brand | 4.00 | 1.80 |
| ❑ 327 | Don Blasingame | 4.00 | 1.80 |
| ❑ 328 | Bob Shaw | 4.00 | 1.80 |
| ❑ 329 | Russ Nixon | 4.00 | 1.80 |
| ❑ 330 | Tommy Harper | 6.00 | 2.70 |
| ❑ 331 | AL Bombers | 150.00 | 70.00 |
| | Roger Maris | | |
| | Norm Cash | | |
| | Mickey Mantle | | |
| | Al Kaline | | |
| ❑ 332 | Ray Washburn | 4.00 | 1.80 |
| ❑ 333 | Billy Moran | 4.00 | 1.80 |
| ❑ 334 | Lew Krausse | 4.00 | 1.80 |
| ❑ 335 | Don Mossi | 6.00 | 2.70 |
| ❑ 336 | Andre Rodgers | 4.00 | 1.80 |
| ❑ 337 | Dodgers Rookies | 6.00 | 2.70 |
| | Al Ferrara | | |
| | Jeff Torborg RC | | |
| ❑ 338 | Jack Kralick | 4.00 | 1.80 |
| ❑ 339 | Walt Bond | 4.00 | 1.80 |
| ❑ 340 | Joe Cunningham | 4.00 | 1.80 |
| ❑ 341 | Jim Roland | 4.00 | 1.80 |
| ❑ 342 | Willie Stargell | 30.00 | 13.50 |
| ❑ 343 | Senators Team | 6.00 | 2.70 |
| ❑ 344 | Phil Linz | 6.00 | 2.70 |
| ❑ 345 | Frank Thomas | 8.00 | 3.60 |
| ❑ 346 | Joey Jay | 4.00 | 1.80 |

❑ 347 Bobby Wine 6.00 2.70
❑ 348 Ed Lopat MG 6.00 2.70
❑ 349 Art Fowler 4.00 1.80
❑ 350 Willie McCovey 25.00 11.00
❑ 351 Dan Schneider 4.00 1.80
❑ 352 Eddie Bressoud 4.00 1.80
❑ 353 Wally Moon 6.00 2.70
❑ 354 Dave Giusti 4.00 1.80
❑ 355 Vic Power 6.00 2.70
❑ 356 Reds Rookies 6.00 2.70
Bill McCool
Chico Ruiz
❑ 357 Charley James 4.00 1.80
❑ 358 Ron Kline 4.00 1.80
❑ 359 Jim Schaffer 4.00 1.80
❑ 360 Joe Pepitone 12.00 5.50
❑ 361 Jay Hook 4.00 1.80
❑ 362 Checklist 5 10.00 2.00
❑ 363 Dick McAuliffe 6.00 2.70
❑ 364 Joe Gaines 4.00 1.80
❑ 365 Cal McLish 6.00 2.70
❑ 366 Nelson Mathews 4.00 1.80
❑ 367 Fred Whitfield 4.00 1.80
❑ 368 White Sox Rookies 6.00 2.70
Fritz Ackley
Don Buford RC
❑ 369 Jerry Zimmerman 4.00 1.80
❑ 370 Hal Woodeshick 4.00 1.80
❑ 371 Frank Howard 8.00 3.60
❑ 372 Howie Koplitz 7.00 3.10
❑ 373 Pirates Team 12.00 5.50
❑ 374 Bobby Bolin 7.00 3.10
❑ 375 Ron Santo 10.00 4.50
❑ 376 Dave Morehead 7.00 3.10
❑ 377 Bob Skinner 7.00 3.10
❑ 378 Braves Rookies 10.00 4.50
Woody Woodward RC
Jack Smith
❑ 379 Tony Gonzalez 7.00 3.10
❑ 380 Whitey Ford 40.00 18.00
❑ 381 Bob Taylor 7.00 3.10
❑ 382 Wes Stock 7.00 3.10
❑ 383 Bill Rigney MG 7.00 3.10
❑ 384 Ron Hansen 7.00 3.10
❑ 385 Curt Simmons 10.00 4.50
❑ 386 Lenny Green 7.00 3.10
❑ 387 Terry Fox 7.00 3.10
❑ 388 A's Rookies 10.00 4.50
John O'Donoghue RC
George Williams
❑ 389 Jim Umbricht 10.00 4.50
(Card back mentions
his death)
❑ 390 Orlando Cepeda 25.00 11.00
❑ 391 Sam McDowell 10.00 4.50
❑ 392 Jim Pagliaroni 7.00 3.10
❑ 393 Casey Teaches 15.00 6.75
Casey Stengel MG
Ed Kranepool
❑ 394 Bob Miller 7.00 3.10
❑ 395 Tom Tresh 10.00 4.50
❑ 396 Dennis Bennett 7.00 3.10
❑ 397 Chuck Cottier 7.00 3.10
❑ 398 Mets Rookies 10.00 4.50
Bill Haas
Dick Smith
❑ 399 Jackie Brandt 7.00 3.10
❑ 400 Warren Spahn 40.00 18.00
❑ 401 Charlie Maxwell 7.00 3.10
❑ 402 Tom Sturdivant 7.00 3.10
❑ 403 Reds Team 12.00 5.50
❑ 404 Tony Martinez 7.00 3.10
❑ 405 Ken McBride 7.00 3.10
❑ 406 Al Spangler 7.00 3.10
❑ 407 Bill Freehan 10.00 4.50
❑ 408 Cubs Rookies 7.00 3.10
Jim Stewart
Fred Burdette
❑ 409 Bill Fischer 7.00 3.10
❑ 410 Dick Stuart 10.00 4.50
❑ 411 Lee Walls 7.00 3.10
❑ 412 Ray Culp 10.00 4.50
❑ 413 Johnny Keane MG 7.00 3.10
❑ 414 Jack Sanford 7.00 3.10
❑ 415 Tony Kubek 15.00 6.75
❑ 416 Lee Maye 7.00 3.10
❑ 417 Don Cardwell 7.00 3.10
❑ 418 Orioles Rookies 10.00 4.50
Darold Knowles
Les Narum
❑ 419 Ken Harrelson RC 15.00 6.75
❑ 420 Jim Maloney 10.00 4.50
❑ 421 Camilo Carreon 7.00 3.10
❑ 422 Jack Fisher 7.00 3.10
❑ 423 Tops in NL 125.00 55.00
Hank Aaron
Willie Mays
❑ 424 Dick Bertell 7.00 3.10
❑ 425 Norm Cash 10.00 4.50
❑ 426 Bob Rodgers 7.00 3.10
❑ 427 Don Rudolph 7.00 3.10
❑ 428 Red Sox Rookies 7.00 3.10
Archie Skeen
Pete Smith
(Back states Archie
has retired)
❑ 429 Tim McCarver 10.00 4.50
❑ 430 Juan Pizarro 7.00 3.10
❑ 431 George Alusik 7.00 3.10
❑ 432 Ruben Amaro 10.00 4.50
❑ 433 Yankees Team 50.00 22.00
❑ 434 Don Nottebart 7.00 3.10
❑ 435 Vic Davalillo 7.00 3.10
❑ 436 Charlie Neal 10.00 4.50
❑ 437 Ed Bailey 7.00 3.10
❑ 438 Checklist 6 16.00 3.20
❑ 439 Harvey Haddix 10.00 4.50
❑ 440 Roberto Clemente UER 250.00 110.00
1960 Pittsburfh
❑ 441 Bob Duliba 7.00 3.10
❑ 442 Pumpsie Green 10.00 4.50
❑ 443 Chuck Dressen MG 10.00 4.50
❑ 444 Larry Jackson 7.00 3.10
❑ 445 Bill Skowron 10.00 4.50
❑ 446 Julian Javier 15.00 6.75
❑ 447 Ted Bowsfield 7.00 3.10
❑ 448 Cookie Rojas 10.00 4.50
❑ 449 Deron Johnson 10.00 4.50
❑ 450 Steve Barber 7.00 3.10
❑ 451 Joe Amalfitano 7.00 3.10
❑ 452 Giants Rookies 10.00 4.50
Gil Garrido
Jim Ray Hart RC
❑ 453 Frank Baumann 7.00 3.10
❑ 454 Tommie Aaron 10.00 4.50
❑ 455 Bernie Allen 7.00 3.10
❑ 456 Dodgers Rookies 10.00 4.50
Wes Parker RC
John Werhas
❑ 457 Jesse Gonder 7.00 3.10
❑ 458 Ralph Terry 10.00 4.50
❑ 459 Red Sox Rookies 7.00 3.10
Pete Charton
Dalton Jones
❑ 460 Bob Gibson 40.00 18.00
❑ 461 George Thomas 7.00 3.10
❑ 462 Birdie Tebbetts MG 7.00 3.10
❑ 463 Don Leppert 7.00 3.10
❑ 464 Dallas Green 15.00 6.75
❑ 465 Mike Hershberger 7.00 3.10
❑ 466 A's Rookies 10.00 4.50
Dick Green
Aurelio Monteagudo
❑ 467 Bob Aspromonte 7.00 3.10
❑ 468 Gaylord Perry 40.00 18.00
❑ 469 Cubs Rookies 10.00 4.50
Fred Norman
Sterling Slaughter
❑ 470 Jim Bouton 10.00 4.50
❑ 471 Gates Brown RC 10.00 4.50
❑ 472 Vern Law 10.00 4.50
❑ 473 Baltimore Orioles 12.00 5.50
Team Card
❑ 474 Larry Sherry 10.00 4.50
❑ 475 Ed Charles 7.00 3.10
❑ 476 Braves Rookies 15.00 6.75
Rico Carty RC
Dick Kelley
❑ 477 Mike Joyce 7.00 3.10
❑ 478 Dick Howser 10.00 4.50
❑ 479 Cardinals Rookies 7.00 3.10
Dave Bakenhaster
Johnny Lewis
❑ 480 Bob Purkey 7.00 3.10
❑ 481 Chuck Schilling 7.00 3.10
❑ 482 Phillies Rookies 10.00 4.50
John Briggs
Danny Cater
❑ 483 Fred Valentine 7.00 3.10
❑ 484 Bill Pleis 7.00 3.10
❑ 485 Tom Haller 7.00 3.10
❑ 486 Bob Kennedy MG 7.00 3.10
❑ 487 Mike McCormick 10.00 4.50
❑ 488 Yankees Rookies 15.00 6.75
Pete Mikkelsen
Bob Meyer
❑ 489 Julio Navarro 7.00 3.10
❑ 490 Ron Fairly 10.00 4.50
❑ 491 Ed Rakow 7.00 3.10
❑ 492 Colts Rookies 7.00 3.10
Jim Beauchamp RC
Mike White
❑ 493 Don Lee 7.00 3.10
❑ 494 Al Jackson 7.00 3.10
❑ 495 Bill Virdon 10.00 4.50
❑ 496 White Sox Team 12.00 5.50
❑ 497 Jeoff Long 7.00 3.10
❑ 498 Dave Stenhouse 7.00 3.10
❑ 499 Indians Rookies 7.00 3.10
Chico Salmon
Gordon Seyfried
❑ 500 Camilo Pascual 10.00 4.50
❑ 501 Bob Veale 10.00 4.50
❑ 502 Angels Rookies 7.00 3.10
Bobby Knoop RC
Bob Lee
❑ 503 Earl Wilson 7.00 3.10
❑ 504 Claude Raymond 7.00 3.10
❑ 505 Stan Williams 7.00 3.10
❑ 506 Bobby Bragan MG 7.00 3.10
❑ 507 Johnny Edwards 7.00 3.10
❑ 508 Diego Segui 7.00 3.10
❑ 509 Pirates Rookies 10.00 4.50
Gene Alley RC
Orlando McFarlane
❑ 510 Lindy McDaniel 10.00 4.50
❑ 511 Lou Jackson 10.00 4.50
❑ 512 Tigers Rookies 15.00 6.75
Willie Horton RC
Joe Sparma
❑ 513 Don Larsen 10.00 4.50
❑ 514 Jim Hickman 10.00 4.50
❑ 515 Johnny Romano 7.00 3.10
❑ 516 Twins Rookies 7.00 3.10
Jerry Arrigo
Dwight Siebler
❑ 517A Checklist 7 ERR 25.00 5.00
(incorrect numbering
sequence on back)
❑ 517B Checklist 7 COR 16.00 3.20
(Correct numbering
on back)
❑ 518 Carl Bouldin 7.00 3.10
❑ 519 Charlie Smith 7.00 3.10
❑ 520 Jack Baldschun 10.00 4.50
❑ 521 Tom Satriano 7.00 3.10
❑ 522 Bob Tiefenauer 7.00 3.10
❑ 523 Lou Burdette UER 20.00 9.00
(Pitching lefty)
❑ 524 Reds Rookies 16.00 7.25
Jim Dickson
Bobby Klaus
❑ 525 Al McBean 16.00 7.25
❑ 526 Lou Clinton 16.00 7.25
❑ 527 Larry Bearnarth 16.00 7.25
❑ 528 A's Rookies 20.00 9.00
Dave Duncan RC
Tommie Reynolds
❑ 529 Alvin Dark MG 20.00 9.00
❑ 530 Leon Wagner 16.00 7.25
❑ 531 Los Angeles Dodgers 25.00 11.00
Team Card
❑ 532 Twins Rookies 16.00 7.25
Bud Bloomfield
(Bloomfield photo
actually Jay Ward)
Joe Nossek RC
❑ 533 Johnny Klippstein 16.00 7.25

| | | NRMT | VG-E |
|---|---|---|---|
| ❑ 534 | Gus Bell | 16.00 | 7.25 |
| ❑ 535 | Phil Regan | 16.00 | 7.25 |
| ❑ 536 | Mets Rookies | 16.00 | 7.25 |
| | Larry Elliot | | |
| | John Stephenson | | |
| ❑ 537 | Dan Osinski | 16.00 | 7.25 |
| ❑ 538 | Minnie Minoso | 20.00 | 9.00 |
| ❑ 539 | Roy Face | 20.00 | 9.00 |
| ❑ 540 | Luis Aparicio | 40.00 | 18.00 |
| ❑ 541 | Braves Rookies | 80.00 | 36.00 |
| | Phil Roof | | |
| | Phil Niekro RC | | |
| ❑ 542 | Don Mincher | 16.00 | 7.25 |
| ❑ 543 | Bob Uecker | 40.00 | 18.00 |
| ❑ 544 | Colts Rookies | 16.00 | 7.25 |
| | Steve Hertz | | |
| | Joe Hoerner | | |
| ❑ 545 | Max Alvis | 16.00 | 7.25 |
| ❑ 546 | Joe Christopher | 16.00 | 7.25 |
| ❑ 547 | Gil Hodges MG | 30.00 | 13.50 |
| ❑ 548 | NL Rookies | 20.00 | 9.00 |
| | Wayne Schurr | | |
| | Paul Speckenbach | | |
| ❑ 549 | Joe Moeller | 16.00 | 7.25 |
| ❑ 550 | Ken Hubbs MEM | 40.00 | 18.00 |
| ❑ 551 | Billy Hoeft | 16.00 | 7.25 |
| ❑ 552 | Indians Rookies | 16.00 | 7.25 |
| | Tom Kelley | | |
| | Sonny Siebert | | |
| ❑ 553 | Jim Brewer | 16.00 | 7.25 |
| ❑ 554 | Hank Foiles | 16.00 | 7.25 |
| ❑ 555 | Lee Stange | 16.00 | 7.25 |
| ❑ 556 | Mets Rookies | 16.00 | 7.25 |
| | Steve Dillon | | |
| | Ron Locke | | |
| ❑ 557 | Leo Burke | 16.00 | 7.25 |
| ❑ 558 | Don Schwall | 16.00 | 7.25 |
| ❑ 559 | Dick Phillips | 16.00 | 7.25 |
| ❑ 560 | Dick Farrell | 16.00 | 7.25 |
| ❑ 561 | Phillies Rookies UER | 20.00 | 9.00 |
| | Dave Bennett | | |
| | (19 ... is 18) | | |
| | Rick Wise RC | | |
| ❑ 562 | Pedro Ramos | 16.00 | 7.25 |
| ❑ 563 | Dal Maxvill | 20.00 | 9.00 |
| ❑ 564 | AL Rookies | 20.00 | 9.00 |
| | Joe McCabe | | |
| | Jerry McNertney | | |
| ❑ 565 | Stu Miller | 16.00 | 7.25 |
| ❑ 566 | Ed Kranepool | 20.00 | 9.00 |
| ❑ 567 | Jim Kaat | 20.00 | 9.00 |
| ❑ 568 | NL Rookies | 16.00 | 7.25 |
| | Phil Gagliano | | |
| | Cap Peterson | | |
| ❑ 569 | Fred Newman | 16.00 | 7.25 |
| ❑ 570 | Bill Mazeroski | 20.00 | 9.00 |
| ❑ 571 | Gene Conley | 16.00 | 7.25 |
| ❑ 572 | AL Rookies | 16.00 | 7.25 |
| | Dave Gray | | |
| | Dick Egan | | |
| ❑ 573 | Jim Duffalo | 16.00 | 7.25 |
| ❑ 574 | Manny Jimenez | 16.00 | 7.25 |
| ❑ 575 | Tony Cloninger | 16.00 | 7.25 |
| ❑ 576 | Mets Rookies | 16.00 | 7.25 |
| | Jerry Hinsley | | |
| | Bill Wakefield | | |
| ❑ 577 | Gordy Coleman | 16.00 | 7.25 |
| ❑ 578 | Glen Hobbie | 16.00 | 7.25 |
| ❑ 579 | Red Sox Team | 25.00 | 11.00 |
| ❑ 580 | Johnny Podres | 20.00 | 9.00 |
| ❑ 581 | Yankees Rookies | 20.00 | 9.00 |
| | Pedro Gonzalez | | |
| | Archie Moore | | |
| ❑ 582 | Rod Kanehl | 20.00 | 9.00 |
| ❑ 583 | Tito Francona | 16.00 | 7.25 |
| ❑ 584 | Joel Horlen | 16.00 | 7.25 |
| ❑ 585 | Tony Taylor | 20.00 | 9.00 |
| ❑ 586 | Jimmy Piersall | 20.00 | 9.00 |
| ❑ 587 | Bennie Daniels ! | 20.00 | 8.00 |

## 1965 Topps

| | | NRMT | VG-E |
|---|---|---|---|
| COMPLETE SET (598) | | 3500.00 | 1600.00 |
| COMMON CARD (1-196) | | 2.00 | .90 |
| COMMON CARD (197-283) | | 2.50 | 1.10 |
| COMMON CARD (284-370) | | 4.00 | 1.80 |
| COMMON CARD (371-598) | | 7.00 | 3.10 |
| WRAPPER (1-CENT) | | 125.00 | 55.00 |
| WRAPPER (5-CENT) | | 100.00 | 45.00 |
| ❑ 1 | AL Batting Leaders | 20.00 | 6.00 |
| | Tony Oliva | | |
| | Elston Howard | | |
| | Brooks Robinson | | |
| ❑ 2 | NL Batting Leaders | 25.00 | 11.00 |
| | Roberto Clemente | | |
| | Hank Aaron | | |
| | Rico Carty | | |
| ❑ 3 | AL Home Run Leaders | 50.00 | 22.00 |
| | Harmon Killebrew | | |
| | Mickey Mantle | | |
| | Boog Powell | | |
| ❑ 4 | NL Home Run Leaders | 15.00 | 6.75 |
| | Willie Mays | | |
| | Billy Williams | | |
| | Jim Ray Hart | | |
| | Orlando Cepeda | | |
| | Johnny Callison | | |
| ❑ 5 | AL RBI Leaders | 40.00 | 18.00 |
| | Brooks Robinson | | |
| | Harmon Killebrew | | |
| | Mickey Mantle | | |
| | Dick Stuart | | |
| ❑ 6 | NL RBI Leaders | 12.00 | 5.50 |
| | Ken Boyer | | |
| | Willie Mays | | |
| | Ron Santo | | |
| ❑ 7 | AL ERA Leaders | 5.00 | 2.20 |
| | Dean Chance | | |
| | Joel Horlen | | |
| ❑ 8 | NL ERA Leaders | 20.00 | 9.00 |
| | Sandy Koufax | | |
| | Don Drysdale | | |
| ❑ 9 | AL Pitching Leaders | 5.00 | 2.20 |
| | Dean Chance | | |
| | Gary Peters | | |
| | Dave Wickersham | | |
| | Juan Pizarro | | |
| | Wally Bunker | | |
| ❑ 10 | NL Pitching Leaders | 5.00 | 2.20 |
| | Larry Jackson | | |
| | Ray Sadecki | | |
| | Juan Marichal | | |
| ❑ 11 | AL Strikeout Leaders | 5.00 | 2.20 |
| | Al Downing | | |
| | Dean Chance | | |
| | Camilo Pascual | | |
| ❑ 12 | NL Strikeout Leaders | 10.00 | 4.50 |
| | Bob Veale | | |
| | Don Drysdale | | |
| | Bob Gibson | | |
| ❑ 13 | Pedro Ramos | 4.00 | 1.80 |
| ❑ 14 | Len Gabrielson | 2.00 | .90 |
| ❑ 15 | Robin Roberts | 10.00 | 4.50 |
| ❑ 16 | Houston Rookie DP | 60.00 | 27.00 |
| | Joe Morgan RC ! | | |
| | Sonny Jackson | | |
| ❑ 17 | Johnny Romano | 2.00 | .90 |
| ❑ 18 | Bill McCool | 2.00 | .90 |
| ❑ 19 | Gates Brown | 4.00 | 1.80 |
| ❑ 20 | Jim Bunning | 10.00 | 4.50 |
| ❑ 21 | Don Blasingame | 2.00 | .90 |
| ❑ 22 | Charlie Smith | 2.00 | .90 |
| ❑ 23 | Bob Tiefenauer | 2.00 | .90 |
| ❑ 24 | Minnesota Twins | 6.00 | 2.70 |
| | Team Card | | |
| ❑ 25 | Al McBean | 2.00 | .90 |
| ❑ 26 | Bobby Knoop | 2.00 | .90 |
| ❑ 27 | Dick Bertell | 2.00 | .90 |
| ❑ 28 | Barney Schultz | 2.00 | .90 |
| ❑ 29 | Felix Mantilla | 2.00 | .90 |
| ❑ 30 | Jim Bouton | 6.00 | 2.70 |
| ❑ 31 | Mike White | 2.00 | .90 |
| ❑ 32 | Herman Franks MG | 2.00 | .90 |
| ❑ 33 | Jackie Brandt | 2.00 | .90 |
| ❑ 34 | Cal Koonce | 2.00 | .90 |
| ❑ 35 | Ed Charles | 2.00 | .90 |
| ❑ 36 | Bobby Wine | 2.00 | .90 |
| ❑ 37 | Fred Gladding | 2.00 | .90 |
| ❑ 38 | Jim King | 2.00 | .90 |
| ❑ 39 | Gerry Arrigo | 2.00 | .90 |
| ❑ 40 | Frank Howard | 6.00 | 2.70 |
| ❑ 41 | White Sox Rookies | 2.00 | .90 |
| | Bruce Howard | | |
| | Marv Staehle | | |
| ❑ 42 | Earl Wilson | 4.00 | 1.80 |
| ❑ 43 | Mike Shannon | 4.00 | 1.80 |
| | (Name in red, other | | |
| | Cardinals in yellow) | | |
| ❑ 44 | Wade Blasingame | 2.00 | .90 |
| ❑ 45 | Roy McMillan | 4.00 | 1.80 |
| ❑ 46 | Bob Lee | 2.00 | .90 |
| ❑ 47 | Tommy Harper | 4.00 | 1.80 |
| ❑ 48 | Claude Raymond | 4.00 | 1.80 |
| ❑ 49 | Orioles Rookies | 4.00 | 1.80 |
| | Curt Blefary RC | | |
| | John Miller | | |
| ❑ 50 | Juan Marichal | 10.00 | 4.50 |
| ❑ 51 | Bill Bryan | 2.00 | .90 |
| ❑ 52 | Ed Roebuck | 2.00 | .90 |
| ❑ 53 | Dick McAuliffe | 4.00 | 1.80 |
| ❑ 54 | Joe Gibbon | 2.00 | .90 |
| ❑ 55 | Tony Conigliaro | 15.00 | 6.75 |
| ❑ 56 | Ron Kline | 2.00 | .90 |
| ❑ 57 | Cardinals Team | 6.00 | 2.70 |
| ❑ 58 | Fred Talbot | 2.00 | .90 |
| ❑ 59 | Nate Oliver | 2.00 | .90 |
| ❑ 60 | Jim O'Toole | 4.00 | 1.80 |
| ❑ 61 | Chris Cannizzaro | 2.00 | .90 |
| ❑ 62 | Jim Kaat UER DP | 6.00 | 2.70 |
| | (Misspelled Katt) | | |
| ❑ 63 | Ty Cline | 2.00 | .90 |
| ❑ 64 | Lou Burdette | 4.00 | 1.80 |
| ❑ 65 | Tony Kubek | 6.00 | 2.70 |
| ❑ 66 | Bill Rigney MG | 2.00 | .90 |
| ❑ 67 | Harvey Haddix | 4.00 | 1.80 |
| ❑ 68 | Del Crandall | 4.00 | 1.80 |
| ❑ 69 | Bill Virdon | 4.00 | 1.80 |
| ❑ 70 | Bill Skowron | 6.00 | 2.70 |
| ❑ 71 | John O'Donoghue | 2.00 | .90 |
| ❑ 72 | Tony Gonzalez | 2.00 | .90 |
| ❑ 73 | Dennis Ribant | 2.00 | .90 |
| ❑ 74 | Red Sox Rookies | 10.00 | 4.50 |
| | Rico Petrocelli# RC | | |
| | Jerry Stephenson | | |
| ❑ 75 | Deron Johnson | 4.00 | 1.80 |
| ❑ 76 | Sam McDowell | 4.00 | 1.80 |
| ❑ 77 | Doug Camilli | 2.00 | .90 |
| ❑ 78 | Dal Maxvill | 2.00 | .90 |
| ❑ 79A | Checklist 1 | 10.00 | 2.00 |
| | (61 Cannizzaro) | | |
| ❑ 79B | Checklist 1 | 10.00 | 2.00 |
| | (61 C.Cannizzaro) | | |
| ❑ 80 | Turk Farrell | 2.00 | .90 |
| ❑ 81 | Don Buford | 4.00 | 1.80 |
| ❑ 82 | Braves Rookies | 6.00 | 2.70 |
| | Santos Alomar RC | | |
| | John Braun | | |
| ❑ 83 | George Thomas | 2.00 | .90 |
| ❑ 84 | Ron Herbel | 2.00 | .90 |
| ❑ 85 | Willie Smith | 2.00 | .90 |
| ❑ 86 | Les Narum | 2.00 | .90 |
| ❑ 87 | Nelson Mathews | 2.00 | .90 |
| ❑ 88 | Jack Lamabe | 2.00 | .90 |
| ❑ 89 | Mike Hershberger | 2.00 | .90 |
| ❑ 90 | Rich Rollins | 4.00 | 1.80 |
| ❑ 91 | Cubs Team | 6.00 | 2.70 |
| ❑ 92 | Dick Howser | 4.00 | 1.80 |
| ❑ 93 | Jack Fisher | 2.00 | .90 |
| ❑ 94 | Charlie Lau | 4.00 | 1.80 |

❑ 95 Bill Mazeroski DP 6.00 2.70
❑ 96 Sonny Siebert 4.00 1.80
❑ 97 Pedro Gonzalez 2.00 .90
❑ 98 Bob Miller 2.00 .90
❑ 99 Gil Hodges MG 6.00 2.70
❑ 100 Ken Boyer 10.00 4.50
❑ 101 Fred Newman 2.00 .90
❑ 102 Steve Boros 2.00 .90
❑ 103 Harvey Kuenn 4.00 1.80
❑ 104 Checklist 2 10.00 2.00
❑ 105 Chico Salmon 2.00 .90
❑ 106 Gene Oliver 2.00 .90
❑ 107 Phillies Rookies 4.00 1.80
Pat Corrales RC
Costen Shockley
❑ 108 Don Mincher 2.00 .90
❑ 109 Walt Bond 2.00 .90
❑ 110 Ron Santo 6.00 2.70
❑ 111 Lee Thomas 4.00 1.80
❑ 112 Derrell Griffith 2.00 .90
❑ 113 Steve Barber 2.00 .90
❑ 114 Jim Hickman 4.00 1.80
❑ 115 Bobby Richardson 10.00 4.50
❑ 116 Cardinals Rookies 4.00 1.80
Dave Dowling
Bob Tolan RC
❑ 117 Wes Stock 2.00 .90
❑ 118 Hal Lanier 4.00 1.80
❑ 119 John Kennedy 2.00 .90
❑ 120 Frank Robinson 35.00 16.00
❑ 121 Gene Alley 4.00 1.80
❑ 122 Bill Pleis 2.00 .90
❑ 123 Frank Thomas 4.00 1.80
❑ 124 Tom Satriano 2.00 .90
❑ 125 Juan Pizarro 2.00 .90
❑ 126 Dodgers Team 6.00 2.70
❑ 127 Frank Lary 2.00 .90
❑ 128 Vic Davalillo 2.00 .90
❑ 129 Bennie Daniels 2.00 .90
❑ 130 Al Kaline 35.00 16.00
❑ 131 Johnny Keane MG 2.00 .90
❑ 132 Mike Shannon WS 10.00 4.50
❑ 133 Mel Stottlemyre WS 6.00 2.70
❑ 134 Mickey Mantle WS 80.00 36.00
Mantle's Clutch HR
❑ 135 Ken Boyer WS 10.00 4.50
❑ 136 Tim McCarver WS 6.00 2.70
❑ 137 Jim Bouton WS 6.00 2.70
❑ 138 Bob Gibson WS 12.00 5.50
❑ 139 World Series Summary 6.00 2.70
Cards celebrate
❑ 140 Dean Chance 4.00 1.80
❑ 141 Charlie James 2.00 .90
❑ 142 Bill Monbouquette 2.00 .90
❑ 143 Pirates Rookies 2.00 .90
John Gelnar
Jerry May
❑ 144 Ed Kranepool 4.00 1.80
❑ 145 Luis Tiant RC 10.00 4.50
❑ 146 Ron Hansen 2.00 .90
❑ 147 Dennis Bennett 2.00 .90
❑ 148 Willie Kirkland 2.00 .90
❑ 149 Wayne Schurr 2.00 .90
❑ 150 Brooks Robinson 40.00 18.00
❑ 151 Athletics Team 6.00 2.70
❑ 152 Phil Ortega 2.00 .90
❑ 153 Norm Cash 6.00 2.70
❑ 154 Bob Humphreys 2.00 .90
❑ 155 Roger Maris 60.00 27.00
❑ 156 Bob Sadowski 2.00 .90
❑ 157 Zoilo Versalles 4.00 1.80
❑ 158 Dick Sisler 2.00 .90
❑ 159 Jim Duffalo 2.00 .90
❑ 160 Roberto Clemente UER 175.00 80.00
(1960 Pittsburfh)
❑ 161 Frank Baumann 2.00 .90
❑ 162 Russ Nixon 2.00 .90
❑ 163 Johnny Briggs 2.00 .90
❑ 164 Al Spangler 2.00 .90
❑ 165 Dick Ellsworth 2.00 .90
❑ 166 Indians Rookies 4.00 1.80
George Culver
Tommie Agee RC
❑ 167 Bill Wakefield 2.00 .90
❑ 168 Dick Green 2.00 .90
❑ 169 Dave Vineyard 2.00 .90

❑ 170 Hank Aaron 100.00 45.00
❑ 171 Jim Roland 2.00 .90
❑ 172 Jimmy Piersall 6.00 2.70
❑ 173 Detroit Tigers 6.00 2.70
Team Card
❑ 174 Joey Jay 2.00 .90
❑ 175 Bob Aspromonte 2.00 .90
❑ 176 Willie McCovey 20.00 9.00
❑ 177 Pete Mikkelsen 2.00 .90
❑ 178 Dalton Jones 2.00 .90
❑ 179 Hal Woodeshick 2.00 .90
❑ 180 Bob Allison 4.00 1.80
❑ 181 Senators Rookies 2.00 .90
Don Loun
Joe McCabe
❑ 182 Mike de la Hoz 2.00 .90
❑ 183 Dave Nicholson 2.00 .90
❑ 184 John Boozer 2.00 .90
❑ 185 Max Alvis 2.00 .90
❑ 186 Billy Cowan 2.00 .90
❑ 187 Casey Stengel MG 15.00 6.75
❑ 188 Sam Bowens 2.00 .90
❑ 189 Checklist 3 10.00 2.00
❑ 190 Bill White 6.00 2.70
❑ 191 Phil Regan 4.00 1.80
❑ 192 Jim Coker 2.00 .90
❑ 193 Gaylord Perry 15.00 6.75
❑ 194 Rookie Stars 2.00 .90
Bill Kelso
Rick Reichardt
❑ 195 Bob Veale 4.00 1.80
❑ 196 Ron Fairly 4.00 1.80
❑ 197 Diego Segui 2.50 1.10
❑ 198 Smoky Burgess 4.00 1.80
❑ 199 Bob Heffner 2.50 1.10
❑ 200 Joe Torre 6.00 2.70
❑ 201 Twins Rookies 4.00 1.80
Sandy Valdespino
Cesar Tovar RC
❑ 202 Leo Burke 2.50 1.10
❑ 203 Dallas Green 4.00 1.80
❑ 204 Russ Snyder 2.50 1.10
❑ 205 Warren Spahn 30.00 13.50
❑ 206 Willie Horton 4.00 1.80
❑ 207 Pete Rose 125.00 55.00
❑ 208 Tommy John 6.00 2.70
❑ 209 Pirates Team 6.00 2.70
❑ 210 Jim Fregosi 4.00 1.80
❑ 211 Steve Ridzik 2.50 1.10
❑ 212 Ron Brand 2.50 1.10
❑ 213 Jim Davenport 2.50 1.10
❑ 214 Bob Purkey 2.50 1.10
❑ 215 Pete Ward 2.50 1.10
❑ 216 Al Worthington 2.50 1.10
❑ 217 Walter Alston MG 6.00 2.70
❑ 218 Dick Schofield 2.50 1.10
❑ 219 Bob Meyer 2.50 1.10
❑ 220 Billy Williams 10.00 4.50
❑ 221 John Tsitouris 2.50 1.10
❑ 222 Bob Tillman 2.50 1.10
❑ 223 Dan Osinski 2.50 1.10
❑ 224 Bob Chance 2.50 1.10
❑ 225 Bo Belinsky 4.00 1.80
❑ 226 Yankees Rookies 6.00 2.70
Elvio Jimenez
Jake Gibbs
❑ 227 Bobby Klaus 2.50 1.10
❑ 228 Jack Sanford 2.50 1.10
❑ 229 Lou Clinton 2.50 1.10
❑ 230 Ray Sadecki 2.50 1.10
❑ 231 Jerry Adair 2.50 1.10
❑ 232 Steve Blass RC 4.00 1.80
❑ 233 Don Zimmer 4.00 1.80
❑ 234 White Sox Team 6.00 2.70
❑ 235 Chuck Hinton 2.50 1.10
❑ 236 Denny McLain RC 25.00 11.00
❑ 237 Bernie Allen 2.50 1.10
❑ 238 Joe Moeller 2.50 1.10
❑ 239 Doc Edwards 2.50 1.10
❑ 240 Bob Bruce 2.50 1.10
❑ 241 Mack Jones 2.50 1.10
❑ 242 George Brunet 2.50 1.10
❑ 243 Reds Rookies 4.00 1.80
Ted Davidson
Tommy Helms RC
❑ 244 Lindy McDaniel 4.00 1.80

❑ 245 Joe Pepitone 6.00 2.70
❑ 246 Tom Butters 4.00 1.80
❑ 247 Wally Moon 4.00 1.80
❑ 248 Gus Triandos 4.00 1.80
❑ 249 Dave McNally 4.00 1.80
❑ 250 Willie Mays 100.00 45.00
❑ 251 Billy Herman MG 4.00 1.80
❑ 252 Pete Richert 2.50 1.10
❑ 253 Danny Cater 2.50 1.10
❑ 254 Roland Sheldon 2.50 1.10
❑ 255 Camilo Pascual 4.00 1.80
❑ 256 Tito Francona 2.50 1.10
❑ 257 Jim Wynn 4.00 1.80
❑ 258 Larry Bearnarth 2.50 1.10
❑ 259 Tigers Rookies 6.00 2.70
Jim Northrup RC
Ray Oyler
❑ 260 Don Drysdale 20.00 9.00
❑ 261 Duke Carmel 2.50 1.10
❑ 262 Bud Daley 2.50 1.10
❑ 263 Marty Keough 2.50 1.10
❑ 264 Bob Buhl 4.00 1.80
❑ 265 Jim Pagliaroni 2.50 1.10
❑ 266 Bert Campaneris RC 10.00 4.50
❑ 267 Senators Team 6.00 2.70
❑ 268 Ken McBride 2.50 1.10
❑ 269 Frank Bolling 2.50 1.10
❑ 270 Milt Pappas 4.00 1.80
❑ 271 Don Wert 4.00 1.80
❑ 272 Chuck Schilling 2.50 1.10
❑ 273 Checklist 4 10.00 2.00
❑ 274 Lum Harris MG 2.50 1.10
❑ 275 Dick Groat 6.00 2.70
❑ 276 Hoyt Wilhelm 10.00 4.50
❑ 277 Johnny Lewis 2.50 1.10
❑ 278 Ken Retzer 2.50 1.10
❑ 279 Dick Tracewski 2.50 1.10
❑ 280 Dick Stuart 4.00 1.80
❑ 281 Bill Stafford 2.50 1.10
❑ 282 Giants Rookies 40.00 18.00
Dick Estelle
Masanori Murakami RC
❑ 283 Fred Whitfield 2.50 1.10
❑ 284 Nick Willhite 4.00 1.80
❑ 285 Ron Hunt 4.00 1.80
❑ 286 Athletics Rookies 4.00 1.80
Jim Dickson
Aurelio Monteagudo
❑ 287 Gary Kolb 4.00 1.80
❑ 288 Jack Hamilton 4.00 1.80
❑ 289 Gordy Coleman 6.00 2.70
❑ 290 Wally Bunker 6.00 2.70
❑ 291 Jerry Lynch 4.00 1.80
❑ 292 Larry Yellen 4.00 1.80
❑ 293 Angels Team 6.00 2.70
❑ 294 Tim McCarver 10.00 4.50
❑ 295 Dick Radatz 6.00 2.70
❑ 296 Tony Taylor 6.00 2.70
❑ 297 Dave DeBusschere 10.00 4.50
❑ 298 Jim Stewart 4.00 1.80
❑ 299 Jerry Zimmerman 4.00 1.80
❑ 300 Sandy Koufax 100.00 45.00
❑ 301 Birdie Tebbetts MG 6.00 2.70
❑ 302 Al Stanek 4.00 1.80
❑ 303 John Orsino 4.00 1.80
❑ 304 Dave Stenhouse 4.00 1.80
❑ 305 Rico Carty 6.00 2.70
❑ 306 Bubba Phillips 4.00 1.80
❑ 307 Barry Latman 4.00 1.80
❑ 308 Mets Rookies 6.00 2.70
Cleon Jones RC
Tom Parsons
❑ 309 Steve Hamilton 6.00 2.70
❑ 310 Johnny Callison 6.00 2.70
❑ 311 Orlando Pena 4.00 1.80
❑ 312 Joe Nuxhall 4.00 1.80
❑ 313 Jim Schaffer 4.00 1.80
❑ 314 Sterling Slaughter 4.00 1.80
❑ 315 Frank Malzone 6.00 2.70
❑ 316 Reds Team 6.00 2.70
❑ 317 Don McMahon 4.00 1.80
❑ 318 Matty Alou 6.00 2.70
❑ 319 Ken McMullen 4.00 1.80
❑ 320 Bob Gibson 50.00 22.00
❑ 321 Rusty Staub 10.00 4.50
❑ 322 Rick Wise 6.00 2.70

| No. | Card | NrMt | VgE |
|---|---|---|---|
| 323 | Hank Bauer MG | 6.00 | 2.70 |
| 324 | Bobby Locke | 4.00 | 1.80 |
| 325 | Donn Clendenon | 6.00 | 2.70 |
| 326 | Dwight Siebler | 4.00 | 1.80 |
| 327 | Denis Menke | 4.00 | 1.80 |
| 328 | Eddie Fisher | 4.00 | 1.80 |
| 329 | Hawk Taylor | 4.00 | 1.80 |
| 330 | Whitey Ford | 40.00 | 18.00 |
| 331 | Dodgers Rookies | 6.00 | 2.70 |
| | Al Ferrara | | |
| | John Purdin | | |
| 332 | Ted Abernathy | 4.00 | 1.80 |
| 333 | Tom Reynolds | 4.00 | 1.80 |
| 334 | Vic Roznovsky | 4.00 | 1.80 |
| 335 | Mickey Lolich | 6.00 | 2.70 |
| 336 | Woody Held | 4.00 | 1.80 |
| 337 | Mike Cuellar | 6.00 | 2.70 |
| 338 | Philadelphia Phillies | 6.00 | 2.70 |
| | Team Card | | |
| 339 | Ryne Duren | 6.00 | 2.70 |
| 340 | Tony Oliva | 20.00 | 9.00 |
| 341 | Bob Bolin | 4.00 | 1.80 |
| 342 | Bob Rodgers | 6.00 | 2.70 |
| 343 | Mike McCormick | 6.00 | 2.70 |
| 344 | Wes Parker | 6.00 | 2.70 |
| 345 | Floyd Robinson | 4.00 | 1.80 |
| 346 | Bobby Bragan MG | 4.00 | 1.80 |
| 347 | Roy Face | 6.00 | 2.70 |
| 348 | George Banks | 4.00 | 1.80 |
| 349 | Larry Miller | 4.00 | 1.80 |
| 350 | Mickey Mantle | 450.00 | 200.00 |
| 351 | Jim Perry | 6.00 | 2.70 |
| 352 | Alex Johnson RC | 6.00 | 2.70 |
| 353 | Jerry Lumpe | 4.00 | 1.80 |
| 354 | Cubs Rookies | 4.00 | 1.80 |
| | Billy Ott | | |
| | Jack Warner | | |
| 355 | Vada Pinson | 10.00 | 4.50 |
| 356 | Bill Spanswick | 4.00 | 1.80 |
| 357 | Carl Warwick | 4.00 | 1.80 |
| 358 | Albie Pearson | 6.00 | 2.70 |
| 359 | Ken Johnson | 4.00 | 1.80 |
| 360 | Orlando Cepeda | 15.00 | 6.75 |
| 361 | Checklist 5 | 12.00 | 2.40 |
| 362 | Don Schwall | 4.00 | 1.80 |
| 363 | Bob Johnson | 4.00 | 1.80 |
| 364 | Galen Cisco | 4.00 | 1.80 |
| 365 | Jim Gentile | 6.00 | 2.70 |
| 366 | Dan Schneider | 4.00 | 1.80 |
| 367 | Leon Wagner | 4.00 | 1.80 |
| 368 | White Sox Rookies | 6.00 | 2.70 |
| | Ken Berry | | |
| | Joel Gibson | | |
| 369 | Phil Linz | 6.00 | 2.70 |
| 370 | Tommy Davis | 6.00 | 2.70 |
| 371 | Frank Kreutzer | 7.00 | 3.10 |
| 372 | Clay Dalrymple | 7.00 | 3.10 |
| 373 | Curt Simmons | 7.00 | 3.10 |
| 374 | Angels Rookies | 7.00 | 3.10 |
| | Jose Cardenal RC | | |
| | Dick Simpson | | |
| 375 | Dave Wickersham | 7.00 | 3.10 |
| 376 | Jim Landis | 7.00 | 3.10 |
| 377 | Willie Stargell | 25.00 | 11.00 |
| 378 | Chuck Estrada | 7.00 | 3.10 |
| 379 | Giants Team | 7.00 | 3.10 |
| 380 | Rocky Colavito | 25.00 | 11.00 |
| 381 | Al Jackson | 7.00 | 3.10 |
| 382 | J.C. Martin | 7.00 | 3.10 |
| 383 | Felipe Alou | 15.00 | 6.75 |
| 384 | Johnny Klippstein | 7.00 | 3.10 |
| 385 | Carl Yastrzemski | 60.00 | 27.00 |
| 386 | Cubs Rookies | 7.00 | 3.10 |
| | Paul Jaeckel | | |
| | Fred Norman | | |
| 387 | Johnny Podres | 15.00 | 6.75 |
| 388 | John Blanchard | 15.00 | 6.75 |
| 389 | Don Larsen | 15.00 | 6.75 |
| 390 | Bill Freehan | 15.00 | 6.75 |
| 391 | Mel McGaha MG | 7.00 | 3.10 |
| 392 | Bob Friend | 15.00 | 6.75 |
| 393 | Ed Kirkpatrick | 7.00 | 3.10 |
| 394 | Jim Hannan | 7.00 | 3.10 |
| 395 | Jim Ray Hart | 7.00 | 3.10 |
| 396 | Frank Bertaina | 7.00 | 3.10 |
| 397 | Jerry Buchek | 7.00 | 3.10 |
| 398 | Reds Rookies | 15.00 | 6.75 |
| | Dan Neville | | |
| | Art Shamsky | | |
| 399 | Ray Herbert | 7.00 | 3.10 |
| 400 | Harmon Killebrew | 50.00 | 22.00 |
| 401 | Carl Willey | 7.00 | 3.10 |
| 402 | Joe Amalfitano | 7.00 | 3.10 |
| 403 | Boston Red Sox | 7.00 | 3.10 |
| | Team Card | | |
| 404 | Stan Williams | 7.00 | 3.10 |
| | (Listed as Indian | | |
| | but Yankee cap) | | |
| 405 | John Roseboro | 20.00 | 9.00 |
| 406 | Ralph Terry | 20.00 | 9.00 |
| 407 | Lee Maye | 7.00 | 3.10 |
| 408 | Larry Sherry | 7.00 | 3.10 |
| 409 | Astros Rookies | 15.00 | 6.75 |
| | Jim Beauchamp | | |
| | Larry Dierker RC | | |
| 410 | Luis Aparicio | 20.00 | 9.00 |
| 411 | Roger Craig | 15.00 | 6.75 |
| 412 | Bob Bailey | 7.00 | 3.10 |
| 413 | Hal Reniff | 7.00 | 3.10 |
| 414 | Al Lopez MG | 15.00 | 6.75 |
| 415 | Curt Flood | 15.00 | 6.75 |
| 416 | Jim Brewer | 7.00 | 3.10 |
| 417 | Ed Brinkman | 7.00 | 3.10 |
| 418 | Johnny Edwards | 7.00 | 3.10 |
| 419 | Ruben Amaro | 7.00 | 3.10 |
| 420 | Larry Jackson | 7.00 | 3.10 |
| 421 | Twins Rookies | 7.00 | 3.10 |
| | Gary Dotter | | |
| | Jay Ward | | |
| 422 | Aubrey Gatewood | 7.00 | 3.10 |
| 423 | Jesse Gonder | 7.00 | 3.10 |
| 424 | Gary Bell | 7.00 | 3.10 |
| 425 | Wayne Causey | 7.00 | 3.10 |
| 426 | Braves Team | 7.00 | 3.10 |
| 427 | Bob Saverine | 7.00 | 3.10 |
| 428 | Bob Shaw | 7.00 | 3.10 |
| 429 | Don Demeter | 7.00 | 3.10 |
| 430 | Gary Peters | 7.00 | 3.10 |
| 431 | Cards Rookies | 15.00 | 6.75 |
| | Nelson Briles RC | | |
| | Wayne Spiezio | | |
| 432 | Jim Grant | 15.00 | 6.75 |
| 433 | John Bateman | 7.00 | 3.10 |
| 434 | Dave Morehead | 7.00 | 3.10 |
| 435 | Willie Davis | 15.00 | 6.75 |
| 436 | Don Elston | 7.00 | 3.10 |
| 437 | Chico Cardenas | 15.00 | 6.75 |
| 438 | Harry Walker MG | 7.00 | 3.10 |
| 439 | Moe Drabowsky | 15.00 | 6.75 |
| 440 | Tom Tresh | 15.00 | 6.75 |
| 441 | Denny Lemaster | 7.00 | 3.10 |
| 442 | Vic Power | 7.00 | 3.10 |
| 443 | Checklist 6 | 12.00 | 2.40 |
| 444 | Bob Hendley | 7.00 | 3.10 |
| 445 | Don Lock | 7.00 | 3.10 |
| 446 | Art Mahaffey | 7.00 | 3.10 |
| 447 | Julian Javier | 15.00 | 6.75 |
| 448 | Lee Stange | 7.00 | 3.10 |
| 449 | Mets Rookies | 15.00 | 6.75 |
| | Jerry Hinsley | | |
| | Gary Kroll | | |
| 450 | Elston Howard | 15.00 | 6.75 |
| 451 | Jim Owens | 7.00 | 3.10 |
| 452 | Gary Geiger | 7.00 | 3.10 |
| 453 | Dodgers Rookies | 15.00 | 6.75 |
| | Willie Crawford | | |
| | John Werhas | | |
| 454 | Ed Rakow | 7.00 | 3.10 |
| 455 | Norm Siebern | 7.00 | 3.10 |
| 456 | Bill Henry | 7.00 | 3.10 |
| 457 | Bob Kennedy MG | 15.00 | 6.75 |
| 458 | John Buzhardt | 7.00 | 3.10 |
| 459 | Frank Kostro | 7.00 | 3.10 |
| 460 | Richie Allen | 40.00 | 18.00 |
| 461 | Braves Rookies | 50.00 | 22.00 |
| | Clay Carroll RC | | |
| | Phil Niekro | | |
| 462 | Lew Krausse UER | 7.00 | 3.10 |
| | (Photo actually | | |
| | Pete Lovrich) | | |
| 463 | Manny Mota | 15.00 | 6.75 |
| 464 | Ron Piche | 7.00 | 3.10 |
| 465 | Tom Haller | 15.00 | 6.75 |
| 466 | Senators Rookies | 7.00 | 3.10 |
| | Pete Craig | | |
| | Dick Nen | | |
| 467 | Ray Washburn | 7.00 | 3.10 |
| 468 | Larry Brown | 7.00 | 3.10 |
| 469 | Don Nottebart | 7.00 | 3.10 |
| 470 | Yogi Berra P/CO | 50.00 | 22.00 |
| 471 | Billy Hoeft | 7.00 | 3.10 |
| 472 | Don Pavletich UER | 7.00 | 3.10 |
| | Listed as a pitcher | | |
| 473 | Orioles Rookies | 15.00 | 6.75 |
| | Paul Blair | | |
| | Dave Johnson RC | | |
| 474 | Cookie Rojas | 15.00 | 6.75 |
| 475 | Clete Boyer | 15.00 | 6.75 |
| 476 | Billy O'Dell | 7.00 | 3.10 |
| 477 | Cards Rookies | 175.00 | 80.00 |
| | Fritz Ackley | | |
| | Steve Carlton RC | | |
| 478 | Wilbur Wood | 15.00 | 6.75 |
| 479 | Ken Harrelson | 15.00 | 6.75 |
| 480 | Joel Horlen | 7.00 | 3.10 |
| 481 | Cleveland Indians | 10.00 | 4.50 |
| | Team Card | | |
| 482 | Bob Priddy | 7.00 | 3.10 |
| 483 | George Smith | 7.00 | 3.10 |
| 484 | Ron Perranoski | 20.00 | 9.00 |
| 485 | Nellie Fox P/CO | 20.00 | 9.00 |
| 486 | Angels Rookies | 7.00 | 3.10 |
| | Tom Egan | | |
| | Pat Rogan | | |
| 487 | Woody Woodward | 15.00 | 6.75 |
| 488 | Ted Wills | 7.00 | 3.10 |
| 489 | Gene Mauch MG | 15.00 | 6.75 |
| 490 | Earl Battey | 7.00 | 3.10 |
| 491 | Tracy Stallard | 7.00 | 3.10 |
| 492 | Gene Freese | 7.00 | 3.10 |
| 493 | Tigers Rookies | 7.00 | 3.10 |
| | Bill Roman | | |
| | Bruce Brubaker | | |
| 494 | Jay Ritchie | 7.00 | 3.10 |
| 495 | Joe Christopher | 7.00 | 3.10 |
| 496 | Joe Cunningham | 7.00 | 3.10 |
| 497 | Giants Rookies | 15.00 | 6.75 |
| | Ken Henderson | | |
| | Jack Hiatt | | |
| 498 | Gene Stephens | 7.00 | 3.10 |
| 499 | Stu Miller | 15.00 | 6.75 |
| 500 | Eddie Mathews | 40.00 | 18.00 |
| 501 | Indians Rookies | 7.00 | 3.10 |
| | Ralph Gagliano | | |
| | Jim Rittwage | | |
| 502 | Don Cardwell | 7.00 | 3.10 |
| 503 | Phil Gagliano | 7.00 | 3.10 |
| 504 | Jerry Grote | 15.00 | 6.75 |
| 505 | Ray Culp | 7.00 | 3.10 |
| 506 | Sam Mele MG | 7.00 | 3.10 |
| 507 | Sammy Ellis | 7.00 | 3.10 |
| 508 | Checklist 7 | 12.00 | 2.40 |
| 509 | Red Sox Rookies | 7.00 | 3.10 |
| | Bob Guindon | | |
| | Gerry Vezendy | | |
| 510 | Ernie Banks | 80.00 | 36.00 |
| 511 | Ron Locke | 7.00 | 3.10 |
| 512 | Cap Peterson | 7.00 | 3.10 |
| 513 | New York Yankees | 40.00 | 18.00 |
| | Team Card | | |
| 514 | Joe Azcue | 7.00 | 3.10 |
| 515 | Vern Law | 15.00 | 6.75 |
| 516 | Al Weis | 7.00 | 3.10 |
| 517 | Angels Rookies | 15.00 | 6.75 |
| | Paul Schaal | | |
| | Jack Warner | | |
| 518 | Ken Rowe | 7.00 | 3.10 |
| 519 | Bob Uecker UER | 30.00 | 13.50 |
| | (Posing as a left-handed batter) | | |
| 520 | Tony Cloninger | 7.00 | 3.10 |
| 521 | Phillies Rookies | 7.00 | 3.10 |
| | Dave Bennett | | |
| | Morrie Stevens | | |
| 522 | Hank Aguirre | 7.00 | 3.10 |
| 523 | Mike Brumley SP | 12.00 | 5.50 |
| 524 | Dave Giusti SP | 12.00 | 5.50 |
| 525 | Eddie Bressoud | 7.00 | 3.10 |

❑ 526 Athletics Rookies SP .. 80.00 36.00
Rene Lachemann
Johnny Odom
Jim Hunter RC UER
(Tim on back)
Skip Lockwood
❑ 527 Jeff Torborg SP .......... 12.00 5.50
❑ 528 George Altman ........... 7.00 3.10
❑ 529 Jerry Fosnow SP ........ 12.00 5.50
❑ 530 Jim Maloney ............. 15.00 6.75
❑ 531 Chuck Hiller ............... 7.00 3.10
❑ 532 Hector Lopez ............. 15.00 6.75
❑ 533 Mets Rookies SP ........ 25.00 11.00
Dan Napoleon
Ron Swoboda RC
Tug McGraw
Jim Bethke
❑ 534 John Herrnstein ........... 7.00 3.10
❑ 535 Jack Kralick SP .......... 12.00 5.50
❑ 536 Andre Rodgers SP .... 12.00 5.50
❑ 537 Angels Rookies ........... 7.00 3.10
Marcelino Lopez
Phil Roof
Rudy May RC
❑ 538 Chuck Dressen SP MG 12.00 5.50
❑ 539 Herm Starrette ............. 7.00 3.10
❑ 540 Lou Brock SP ........... 50.00 22.00
❑ 541 White Sox Rookies ...... 7.00 3.10
Greg Bollo
Bob Locker
❑ 542 Lou Klimchock ............. 7.00 3.10
❑ 543 Ed Connolly SP ......... 12.00 5.50
❑ 544 Howie Reed ................. 7.00 3.10
❑ 545 Jesus Alou SP .......... 14.00 6.25
❑ 546 Indians Rookies ........... 7.00 3.10
Bill Davis
Mike Hedlund
Ray Barker
Floyd Weaver
❑ 547 Jake Wood SP .......... 12.00 5.50
❑ 548 Dick Stigman ............... 7.00 3.10
❑ 549 Cubs Rookies SP ...... 20.00 9.00
Roberto Pena
Glenn Beckert RC
❑ 550 Mel Stottlemyre RC SP 30.00 13.50
❑ 551 New York Mets SP .... 30.00 13.50
Team Card
❑ 552 Julio Gotay ................. 7.00 3.10
❑ 553 Astros Rookies ............ 7.00 3.10
Dan Coombs
Gene Ratliff
Jack McClure
❑ 554 Chico Ruiz SP ........... 12.00 5.50
❑ 555 Jack Baldschun SP .... 12.00 5.50
❑ 556 Red Schoendienst ...... 24.00 11.00
SP MG
❑ 557 Jose Santiago ............. 7.00 3.10
❑ 558 Tommie Sisk ............... 7.00 3.10
❑ 559 Ed Bailey SP ............. 12.00 5.50
❑ 560 Boog Powell SP ........ 24.00 11.00
❑ 561 Dodgers Rookies ........ 15.00 6.75
Dennis Daboll
Mike Kekich
Hector Valle
Jim Lefebvre RC
❑ 562 Billy Moran ................. 7.00 3.10
❑ 563 Julio Navarro .............. 7.00 3.10
❑ 564 Mel Nelson .................. 7.00 3.10
❑ 565 Ernie Broglio SP ........ 12.00 5.50
❑ 566 Yankees Rookies SP 12.00 5.50
Gil Blanco
Ross Moschitto
Art Lopez
❑ 567 Tommie Aaron ............. 7.00 3.10
❑ 568 Ron Taylor SP ........... 12.00 5.50
❑ 569 Gino Cimoli SP .......... 12.00 5.50
❑ 570 Claude Osteen SP .... 15.00 6.75
❑ 571 Ossie Virgil SP .......... 12.00 5.50
❑ 572 Baltimore Orioles SP .. 25.00 11.00
Team Card
❑ 573 Red Sox Rookies SP .. 24.00 11.00
Jim Lonborg RC
Gerry Moses
Bill Schlesinger
Mike Ryan
❑ 574 Roy Sievers ............... 15.00 6.75
❑ 575 Jose Pagan ................. 7.00 3.10
❑ 576 Terry Fox SP ............ 12.00 5.50
❑ 577 AL Rookie Stars SP .. 12.00 5.50
Darold Knowles
Don Buschhorn
Richie Scheinblum
❑ 578 Camilo Carreon SP .... 12.00 5.50
❑ 579 Dick Smith SP ........... 12.00 5.50
❑ 580 Jimmie Hall SP .......... 12.00 5.50
❑ 581 NL Rookie Stars SP .. 80.00 36.00
Tony Perez RC !
Dave Ricketts
Kevin Collins
❑ 582 Bob Schmidt SP ........ 12.00 5.50
❑ 583 Wes Covington SP .... 12.00 5.50
❑ 584 Harry Bright ............... 15.00 6.75
❑ 585 Hank Fischer ............... 7.00 3.10
❑ 586 Tom McCraw SP ....... 12.00 5.50
❑ 587 Joe Sparma ................ 7.00 3.10
❑ 588 Lenny Green ............... 7.00 3.10
❑ 589 Giants Rookies SP .... 12.00 5.50
Frank Linzy
Bob Schroder
❑ 590 John Wyatt ................. 7.00 3.10
❑ 591 Bob Skinner SP ......... 12.00 5.50
❑ 592 Frank Bork SP ........... 12.00 5.50
❑ 593 Tigers Rookies SP .... 12.00 5.50
Jackie Moore RC
John Sullivan
❑ 594 Joe Gaines ................. 7.00 3.10
❑ 595 Don Lee ..................... 7.00 3.10
❑ 596 Don Landrum SP ........ 12.00 5.50
❑ 597 Twins Rookies ............. 7.00 3.10
Joe Nossek
John Sevcik
Dick Reese
❑ 598 Al Downing SP ......... 24.00 7.25

## 1966 Topps

| | NRMT | VG-E |
|---|---|---|
| COMPLETE SET (598) | 4000.00 | 1800.00 |
| COMMON CARD (1-109) | 1.50 | .70 |
| COMMON CARD (110-283) | 2.00 | .90 |
| COMMON CARD (284-370) | 3.00 | 1.35 |
| COMMON CARD (371-446) | 5.00 | 2.20 |
| COMMON CARD (447-522) | 9.00 | 4.00 |
| COMMON CARD (523-598) | 15.00 | 6.75 |
| COMMON SP (523-598) | 30.00 | 13.50 |
| WRAPPER (5-CENT) | 25.00 | 11.00 |

❑ 1 Willie Mays ................. 150.00 47.50
❑ 2 Ted Abernathy ............... 1.50 .70
❑ 3 Sam Mele MG ................ 1.50 .70
❑ 4 Ray Culp ....................... 1.50 .70
❑ 5 Jim Fregosi ................... 4.00 1.80
❑ 6 Chuck Schilling .............. 1.50 .70
❑ 7 Tracy Stallard ................ 1.50 .70
❑ 8 Floyd Robinson .............. 1.50 .70
❑ 9 Clete Boyer ................... 4.00 1.80
❑ 10 Tony Cloninger ............ 1.50 .70
❑ 11 Senators Rookies ......... 1.50 .70
Brant Alyea
Pete Craig
❑ 12 John Tsitouris .............. 1.50 .70
❑ 13 Lou Johnson ................ 4.00 1.80
❑ 14 Norm Siebern ............... 1.50 .70
❑ 15 Vern Law ..................... 4.00 1.80
❑ 16 Larry Brown .................. 1.50 .70
❑ 17 John Stephenson .......... 1.50 .70
❑ 18 Roland Sheldon ............. 1.50 .70
❑ 19 San Francisco Giants .... 5.00 2.20
Team Card
❑ 20 Willie Horton ................. 4.00 1.80
❑ 21 Don Nottebart ............... 1.50 .70
❑ 22 Joe Nossek ................... 1.50 .70
❑ 23 Jack Sanford ................. 1.50 .70
❑ 24 Don Kessinger RC ........ 6.00 2.70
❑ 25 Pete Ward ..................... 1.50 .70
❑ 26 Ray Sadecki .................. 1.50 .70
❑ 27 Orioles Rookies ............. 1.50 .70
Darold Knowles
Andy Etchebarren
❑ 28 Phil Niekro .................. 20.00 9.00
❑ 29 Mike Brumley ................ 1.50 .70
❑ 30 Pete Rose DP ............. 40.00 18.00
❑ 31 Jack Cullen ................... 4.00 1.80
❑ 32 Adolfo Phillips ............... 1.50 .70
❑ 33 Jim Pagliaroni ............... 1.50 .70
❑ 34 Checklist 1 .................... 8.00 1.60
❑ 35 Ron Swoboda ................ 4.00 1.80
❑ 36 Jim Hunter UER .......... 20.00 9.00
(Stats say 1963 and
1964, should be
1964 and 1965)
❑ 37 Billy Herman MG ........... 4.00 1.80
❑ 38 Ron Nischwitz ............... 1.50 .70
❑ 39 Ken Henderson ............. 1.50 .70
❑ 40 Jim Grant ...................... 1.50 .70
❑ 41 Don LeJohn .................. 1.50 .70
❑ 42 Aubrey Gatewood .......... 1.50 .70
❑ 43A Don Landrum .............. 4.00 1.80
(Dark button on pants
showing)
❑ 43B Don Landrum ............ 20.00 9.00
(Button on pants
partially airbrushed)
❑ 43C Don Landrum .............. 4.00 1.80
(Button on pants
not showing)
❑ 44 Indians Rookies ............. 1.50 .70
Bill Davis
Tom Kelley
❑ 45 Jim Gentile .................... 4.00 1.80
❑ 46 Howie Koplitz ................ 1.50 .70
❑ 47 J.C. Martin .................... 1.50 .70
❑ 48 Paul Blair ...................... 4.00 1.80
❑ 49 Woody Woodward .......... 4.00 1.80
❑ 50 Mickey Mantle DP ...... 250.00 110.00
❑ 51 Gordon Richardson ....... 1.50 .70
❑ 52 Power Plus ................... 4.00 1.80
Wes Covington
Johnny Callison
❑ 53 Bob Duliba .................... 1.50 .70
❑ 54 Jose Pagan ................... 1.50 .70
❑ 55 Ken Harrelson ............... 4.00 1.80
❑ 56 Sandy Valdespino .......... 1.50 .70
❑ 57 Jim Lefebvre ................. 4.00 1.80
❑ 58 Dave Wickersham .......... 1.50 .70
❑ 59 Reds Team .................... 5.00 2.20
❑ 60 Curt Flood ..................... 6.00 2.70
❑ 61 Bob Bolin ...................... 1.50 .70
❑ 62A Merritt Ranew .............. 4.00 1.80
(With sold line)
❑ 62B Merritt Ranew ............ 30.00 13.50
(Without sold line)
❑ 63 Jim Stewart ................... 1.50 .70
❑ 64 Bob Bruce ..................... 1.50 .70
❑ 65 Leon Wagner ................. 1.50 .70
❑ 66 Al Weis ......................... 1.50 .70
❑ 67 Mets Rookies ................ 4.00 1.80
Cleon Jones
Dick Selma
❑ 68 Hal Reniff ...................... 1.50 .70
❑ 69 Ken Hamlin .................... 1.50 .70
❑ 70 Carl Yastrzemski .......... 30.00 13.50
❑ 71 Frank Carpin ................. 1.50 .70
❑ 72 Tony Perez .................. 25.00 11.00
❑ 73 Jerry Zimmerman ........... 1.50 .70
❑ 74 Don Mossi ..................... 4.00 1.80
❑ 75 Tommy Davis ................. 4.00 1.80
❑ 76 Red Schoendienst MG .. 4.00 1.80
❑ 77 John Orsino ................... 1.50 .70
❑ 78 Frank Linzy ................... 1.50 .70

❑ 79 Joe Pepitone ........ 4.00 1.80
❑ 80 Richie Allen ........ 6.00 2.70
❑ 81 Ray Oyler ........ 1.50 .70
❑ 82 Bob Hendley ........ 1.50 .70
❑ 83 Albie Pearson ........ 4.00 1.80
❑ 84 Braves Rookies ........ 1.50 .70
Jim Beauchamp
Dick Kelley
❑ 85 Eddie Fisher ........ 1.50 .70
❑ 86 John Bateman ........ 1.50 .70
❑ 87 Dan Napoleon ........ 1.50 .70
❑ 88 Fred Whitfield ........ 1.50 .70
❑ 89 Ted Davidson ........ 1.50 .70
❑ 90 Luis Aparicio ........ 8.00 3.60
❑ 91A Bob Uecker TR ........ 10.00 4.50
❑ 91B Bob Uecker NTR ........ 40.00 18.00
❑ 92 Yankees Team ........ 14.00 6.25
❑ 93 Jim Lonborg ........ 4.00 1.80
❑ 94 Matty Alou ........ 4.00 1.80
❑ 95 Pete Richert ........ 1.50 .70
❑ 96 Felipe Alou ........ 4.00 1.80
❑ 97 Jim Merritt ........ 1.50 .70
❑ 98 Don Demeter ........ 1.50 .70
❑ 99 Buc Belters ........ 6.00 2.70
Willie Stargell
Donn Clendenon
❑ 100 Sandy Koufax ........ 75.00 34.00
❑ 101A Checklist 2 ........ 16.00 3.20
(115 W. Spahn) ERR
❑ 101B Checklist 2 ........ 10.00 2.00
(115 Bill Henry) COR
❑ 102 Ed Kirkpatrick ........ 1.50 .70
❑ 103A Dick Groat TR ........ 4.00 1.80
❑ 103B Dick Groat NTR ........ 40.00 18.00
❑ 104A Alex Johnson TR ........ 4.00 1.80
❑ 104B Alex Johnson NTR .. 30.00 13.50
❑ 105 Milt Pappas ........ 4.00 1.80
❑ 106 Rusty Staub ........ 4.00 1.80
❑ 107 A's Rookies ........ 1.50 .70
Larry Stahl
Ron Tompkins
❑ 108 Bobby Klaus ........ 1.50 .70
❑ 109 Ralph Terry ........ 4.00 1.80
❑ 110 Ernie Banks ........ 30.00 13.50
❑ 111 Gary Peters ........ 2.00 .90
❑ 112 Manny Mota ........ 4.00 1.80
❑ 113 Hank Aguirre ........ 2.00 .90
❑ 114 Jim Gosger ........ 2.00 .90
❑ 115 Bill Henry ........ 2.00 .90
❑ 116 Walter Alston MG ........ 6.00 2.70
❑ 117 Jake Gibbs ........ 4.00 1.80
❑ 118 Mike McCormick ........ 4.00 1.80
❑ 119 Art Shamsky ........ 2.00 .90
❑ 120 Harmon Killebrew ........ 15.00 6.75
❑ 121 Ray Herbert ........ 2.00 .90
❑ 122 Joe Gaines ........ 2.00 .90
❑ 123 Pirates Rookies ........ 2.00 .90
Frank Bork
Jerry May
❑ 124 Tug McGraw ........ 4.00 1.80
❑ 125 Lou Brock ........ 20.00 9.00
❑ 126 Jim Palmer RC ! UER 100.00 45.00
(Described as a
left hander on
card back)
❑ 127 Ken Berry ........ 2.00 .90
❑ 128 Jim Landis ........ 2.00 .90
❑ 129 Jack Kralick ........ 2.00 .90
❑ 130 Joe Torre ........ 6.00 2.70
❑ 131 Angels Team ........ 5.00 2.20
❑ 132 Orlando Cepeda ........ 8.00 3.60
❑ 133 Don McMahon ........ 2.00 .90
❑ 134 Wes Parker ........ 4.00 1.80
❑ 135 Dave Morehead ........ 2.00 .90
❑ 136 Woody Held ........ 2.00 .90
❑ 137 Pat Corrales ........ 4.00 1.80
❑ 138 Roger Repoz ........ 2.00 .90
❑ 139 Cubs Rookies ........ 2.00 .90
Byron Browne
Don Young
❑ 140 Jim Maloney ........ 4.00 1.80
❑ 141 Tom McCraw ........ 2.00 .90
❑ 142 Don Dennis ........ 2.00 .90
❑ 143 Jose Tartabull ........ 4.00 1.80
❑ 144 Don Schwall ........ 2.00 .90
❑ 145 Bill Freehan ........ 4.00 1.80
❑ 146 George Altman ........ 2.00 .90
❑ 147 Lum Harris MG ........ 2.00 .90
❑ 148 Bob Johnson ........ 2.00 .90
❑ 149 Dick Nen ........ 2.00 .90
❑ 150 Rocky Colavito ........ 8.00 3.60
❑ 151 Gary Wagner ........ 2.00 .90
❑ 152 Frank Malzone ........ 4.00 1.80
❑ 153 Rico Carty ........ 4.00 1.80
❑ 154 Chuck Hiller ........ 2.00 .90
❑ 155 Marcelino Lopez ........ 2.00 .90
❑ 156 Double Play Combo ........ 2.00 .90
Dick Schofield
Hal Lanier
❑ 157 Rene Lachemann ........ 2.00 .90
❑ 158 Jim Brewer ........ 2.00 .90
❑ 159 Chico Ruiz ........ 2.00 .90
❑ 160 Whitey Ford ........ 25.00 11.00
❑ 161 Jerry Lumpe ........ 2.00 .90
❑ 162 Lee Maye ........ 2.00 .90
❑ 163 Tito Francona ........ 2.00 .90
❑ 164 White Sox Rookies ........ 4.00 1.80
Tommie Agee
Marv Staehle
❑ 165 Don Lock ........ 2.00 .90
❑ 166 Chris Krug ........ 2.00 .90
❑ 167 Boog Powell ........ 6.00 2.70
❑ 168 Dan Osinski ........ 2.00 .90
❑ 169 Duke Sims ........ 2.00 .90
❑ 170 Cookie Rojas ........ 4.00 1.80
❑ 171 Nick Willhite ........ 2.00 .90
❑ 172 Mets Team ........ 5.00 2.20
❑ 173 Al Spangler ........ 2.00 .90
❑ 174 Ron Taylor ........ 2.00 .90
❑ 175 Bert Campaneris ........ 4.00 1.80
❑ 176 Jim Davenport ........ 2.00 .90
❑ 177 Hector Lopez ........ 2.00 .90
❑ 178 Bob Tillman ........ 2.00 .90
❑ 179 Cards Rookies ........ 4.00 1.80
Dennis Aust
Bob Tolan
❑ 180 Vada Pinson ........ 4.00 1.80
❑ 181 Al Worthington ........ 2.00 .90
❑ 182 Jerry Lynch ........ 2.00 .90
❑ 183A Checklist 3 ........ 8.00 1.60
(Large print
on front)
❑ 183B Checklist 3 ........ 8.00 1.60
(Small print
on front)
❑ 184 Denis Menke ........ 2.00 .90
❑ 185 Bob Buhl ........ 4.00 1.80
❑ 186 Ruben Amaro ........ 2.00 .90
❑ 187 Chuck Dressen MG ........ 4.00 1.80
❑ 188 Al Luplow ........ 2.00 .90
❑ 189 John Roseboro ........ 4.00 1.80
❑ 190 Jimmie Hall ........ 2.00 .90
❑ 191 Darrell Sutherland ........ 2.00 .90
❑ 192 Vic Power ........ 4.00 1.80
❑ 193 Dave McNally ........ 4.00 1.80
❑ 194 Senators Team ........ 5.00 2.20
❑ 195 Joe Morgan ........ 15.00 6.75
❑ 196 Don Pavletich ........ 2.00 .90
❑ 197 Sonny Siebert ........ 2.00 .90
❑ 198 Mickey Stanley RC ........ 6.00 2.70
❑ 199 Chisox Clubbers ........ 4.00 1.80
Bill Skowron
Johnny Romano
Floyd Robinson
❑ 200 Eddie Mathews ........ 15.00 6.75
❑ 201 Jim Dickson ........ 2.00 .90
❑ 202 Clay Dalrymple ........ 2.00 .90
❑ 203 Jose Santiago ........ 2.00 .90
❑ 204 Cubs Team ........ 5.00 2.20
❑ 205 Tom Tresh ........ 4.00 1.80
❑ 206 Al Jackson ........ 2.00 .90
❑ 207 Frank Quilici ........ 2.00 .90
❑ 208 Bob Miller ........ 2.00 .90
❑ 209 Tigers Rookies ........ 4.00 1.80
Fritz Fisher
John Hiller RC
❑ 210 Bill Mazeroski ........ 6.00 2.70
❑ 211 Frank Kreutzer ........ 2.00 .90
❑ 212 Ed Kranepool ........ 4.00 1.80
❑ 213 Fred Newman ........ 2.00 .90
❑ 214 Tommy Harper ........ 4.00 1.80
❑ 215 NL Batting Leaders ........ 50.00 22.00
Bob Clemente
Hank Aaron
Willie Mays
❑ 216 AL Batting Leaders ........ 5.00 2.20
Tony Oliva
Carl Yastrzemski
Vic Davalillo
❑ 217 NL Home Run Leaders 20.00 9.00
Willie Mays
Willie McCovey
Billy Williams
❑ 218 AL Home Run Leaders 5.00 2.20
Tony Conigliaro
Norm Cash
Willie Horton
❑ 219 NL RBI Leaders ........ 12.00 5.50
Deron Johnson
Frank Robinson
Willie Mays
❑ 220 AL RBI Leaders ........ 5.00 2.20
Rocky Colavito
Willie Horton
Tony Oliva
❑ 221 NL ERA Leaders ........ 12.00 5.50
Sandy Koufax
Juan Marichal
Vern Law
❑ 222 AL ERA Leaders ........ 5.00 2.20
Sam McDowell
Eddie Fisher
Sonny Siebert
❑ 223 NL Pitching Leaders .. 12.00 5.50
Sandy Koufax
Tony Cloninger
Don Drysdale
❑ 224 AL Pitching Leaders ........ 5.00 2.20
Jim Grant
Mel Stottlemyre
Jim Kaat
❑ 225 NL Strikeout Leaders 12.00 5.50
Sandy Koufax
Bob Veale
Bob Gibson
❑ 226 AL Strikeout Leaders ........ 5.00 2.20
Sam McDowell
Mickey Lolich
Dennis McLain
Sonny Siebert
❑ 227 Russ Nixon ........ 2.00 .90
❑ 228 Larry Dierker ........ 4.00 1.80
❑ 229 Hank Bauer MG ........ 4.00 1.80
❑ 230 Johnny Callison ........ 4.00 1.80
❑ 231 Floyd Weaver ........ 2.00 .90
❑ 232 Glenn Beckert ........ 4.00 1.80
❑ 233 Dom Zanni ........ 2.00 .90
❑ 234 Yankees Rookies ........ 8.00 3.60
Rich Beck
Roy White RC
❑ 235 Don Cardwell ........ 2.00 .90
❑ 236 Mike Hershberger ........ 2.00 .90
❑ 237 Billy O'Dell ........ 2.00 .90
❑ 238 Dodgers Team ........ 5.00 2.20
❑ 239 Orlando Pena ........ 2.00 .90
❑ 240 Earl Battey ........ 2.00 .90
❑ 241 Dennis Ribant ........ 2.00 .90
❑ 242 Jesus Alou ........ 2.00 .90
❑ 243 Nelson Briles ........ 4.00 1.80
❑ 244 Astros Rookies ........ 2.00 .90
Chuck Harrison
Sonny Jackson
❑ 245 John Buzhardt ........ 2.00 .90
❑ 246 Ed Bailey ........ 2.00 .90
❑ 247 Carl Warwick ........ 2.00 .90
❑ 248 Pete Mikkelsen ........ 2.00 .90
❑ 249 Bill Rigney MG ........ 2.00 .90
❑ 250 Sammy Ellis ........ 2.00 .90
❑ 251 Ed Brinkman ........ 2.00 .90
❑ 252 Denny Lemaster ........ 2.00 .90
❑ 253 Don Wert ........ 2.00 .90
❑ 254 Phillies Rookies ........ 70.00 32.00
Ferguson Jenkins RC
Bill Sorrell
❑ 255 Willie Stargell ........ 20.00 9.00
❑ 256 Lew Krausse ........ 2.00 .90
❑ 257 Jeff Torborg ........ 4.00 1.80
❑ 258 Dave Giusti ........ 2.00 .90

| No. | Card | | |
|---|---|---|---|
| ❑ 259 | Boston Red Sox Team Card | 5.00 | 2.20 |
| ❑ 260 | Bob Shaw | 2.00 | .90 |
| ❑ 261 | Ron Hansen | 2.00 | .90 |
| ❑ 262 | Jack Hamilton | 2.00 | .90 |
| ❑ 263 | Tom Egan | 2.00 | .90 |
| ❑ 264 | Twins Rookies<br>Andy Kosco<br>Ted Uhlaender | 2.00 | .90 |
| ❑ 265 | Stu Miller | 4.00 | 1.80 |
| ❑ 266 | Pedro Gonzalez UER<br>(Misspelled Gonzales on card back) | 2.00 | .90 |
| ❑ 267 | Joe Sparma | 2.00 | .90 |
| ❑ 268 | John Blanchard | 2.00 | .90 |
| ❑ 269 | Don Heffner MG | 2.00 | .90 |
| ❑ 270 | Claude Osteen | 4.00 | 1.80 |
| ❑ 271 | Hal Lanier | 2.00 | .90 |
| ❑ 272 | Jack Baldschun | 2.00 | .90 |
| ❑ 273 | Astro Aces<br>Bob Aspromonte<br>Rusty Staub | 4.00 | 1.80 |
| ❑ 274 | Buster Narum | 2.00 | .90 |
| ❑ 275 | Tim McCarver | 4.00 | 1.80 |
| ❑ 276 | Jim Bouton | 4.00 | 1.80 |
| ❑ 277 | George Thomas | 2.00 | .90 |
| ❑ 278 | Cal Koonce | 2.00 | .90 |
| ❑ 279A | Checklist 4<br>(Player's cap black) | 8.00 | 1.60 |
| ❑ 279B | Checklist 4<br>(Player's cap red) | 8.00 | 1.60 |
| ❑ 280 | Bobby Knoop | 2.00 | .90 |
| ❑ 281 | Bruce Howard | 2.00 | .90 |
| ❑ 282 | Johnny Lewis | 2.00 | .90 |
| ❑ 283 | Jim Perry | 4.00 | 1.80 |
| ❑ 284 | Bobby Wine | 3.00 | 1.35 |
| ❑ 285 | Luis Tiant | 5.00 | 2.20 |
| ❑ 286 | Gary Geiger | 3.00 | 1.35 |
| ❑ 287 | Jack Aker | 3.00 | 1.35 |
| ❑ 288 | Dodgers Rookies<br>Bill Singer<br>Don Sutton RC | 50.00 | 22.00 |
| ❑ 289 | Larry Sherry | 3.00 | 1.35 |
| ❑ 290 | Ron Santo | 5.00 | 2.20 |
| ❑ 291 | Moe Drabowsky | 5.00 | 2.20 |
| ❑ 292 | Jim Coker | 3.00 | 1.35 |
| ❑ 293 | Mike Shannon | 5.00 | 2.20 |
| ❑ 294 | Steve Ridzik | 3.00 | 1.35 |
| ❑ 295 | Jim Ray Hart | 5.00 | 2.20 |
| ❑ 296 | Johnny Keane MG | 5.00 | 2.20 |
| ❑ 297 | Jim Owens | 3.00 | 1.35 |
| ❑ 298 | Rico Petrocelli | 5.00 | 2.20 |
| ❑ 299 | Lou Burdette | 5.00 | 2.20 |
| ❑ 300 | Bob Clemente | 150.00 | 70.00 |
| ❑ 301 | Greg Bollo | 3.00 | 1.35 |
| ❑ 302 | Ernie Bowman | 3.00 | 1.35 |
| ❑ 303 | Cleveland Indians Team Card | 5.00 | 2.20 |
| ❑ 304 | John Herrnstein | 3.00 | 1.35 |
| ❑ 305 | Camilo Pascual | 5.00 | 2.20 |
| ❑ 306 | Ty Cline | 3.00 | 1.35 |
| ❑ 307 | Clay Carroll | 5.00 | 2.20 |
| ❑ 308 | Tom Haller | 5.00 | 2.20 |
| ❑ 309 | Diego Segui | 3.00 | 1.35 |
| ❑ 310 | Frank Robinson | 40.00 | 18.00 |
| ❑ 311 | Reds Rookies<br>Tommy Helms<br>Dick Simpson | 5.00 | 2.20 |
| ❑ 312 | Bob Saverine | 3.00 | 1.35 |
| ❑ 313 | Chris Zachary | 3.00 | 1.35 |
| ❑ 314 | Hector Valle | 3.00 | 1.35 |
| ❑ 315 | Norm Cash | 5.00 | 2.20 |
| ❑ 316 | Jack Fisher | 3.00 | 1.35 |
| ❑ 317 | Dalton Jones | 3.00 | 1.35 |
| ❑ 318 | Harry Walker MG | 3.00 | 1.35 |
| ❑ 319 | Gene Freese | 3.00 | 1.35 |
| ❑ 320 | Bob Gibson | 25.00 | 11.00 |
| ❑ 321 | Rick Reichardt | 3.00 | 1.35 |
| ❑ 322 | Bill Faul | 3.00 | 1.35 |
| ❑ 323 | Ray Barker | 3.00 | 1.35 |
| ❑ 324 | John Boozer | 3.00 | 1.35 |
| ❑ 325 | Vic Davalillo | 3.00 | 1.35 |
| ❑ 326 | Braves Team | 5.00 | 2.20 |
| ❑ 327 | Bernie Allen | 3.00 | 1.35 |
| ❑ 328 | Jerry Grote | 5.00 | 2.20 |
| ❑ 329 | Pete Charton | 3.00 | 1.35 |
| ❑ 330 | Ron Fairly | 5.00 | 2.20 |
| ❑ 331 | Ron Herbel | 3.00 | 1.35 |
| ❑ 332 | Bill Bryan | 3.00 | 1.35 |
| ❑ 333 | Senators Rookies<br>Joe Coleman RC<br>Jim French | 3.00 | 1.35 |
| ❑ 334 | Marty Keough | 3.00 | 1.35 |
| ❑ 335 | Juan Pizarro | 3.00 | 1.35 |
| ❑ 336 | Gene Alley | 5.00 | 2.20 |
| ❑ 337 | Fred Gladding | 3.00 | 1.35 |
| ❑ 338 | Dal Maxvill | 3.00 | 1.35 |
| ❑ 339 | Del Crandall | 5.00 | 2.20 |
| ❑ 340 | Dean Chance | 5.00 | 2.20 |
| ❑ 341 | Wes Westrum MG | 5.00 | 2.20 |
| ❑ 342 | Bob Humphreys | 3.00 | 1.35 |
| ❑ 343 | Joe Christopher | 3.00 | 1.35 |
| ❑ 344 | Steve Blass | 5.00 | 2.20 |
| ❑ 345 | Bob Allison | 5.00 | 2.20 |
| ❑ 346 | Mike de la Hoz | 3.00 | 1.35 |
| ❑ 347 | Phil Regan | 5.00 | 2.20 |
| ❑ 348 | Orioles Team | 8.00 | 3.60 |
| ❑ 349 | Cap Peterson | 3.00 | 1.35 |
| ❑ 350 | Mel Stottlemyre | 8.00 | 3.60 |
| ❑ 351 | Fred Valentine | 3.00 | 1.35 |
| ❑ 352 | Bob Aspromonte | 3.00 | 1.35 |
| ❑ 353 | Al McBean | 3.00 | 1.35 |
| ❑ 354 | Smoky Burgess | 5.00 | 2.20 |
| ❑ 355 | Wade Blasingame | 3.00 | 1.35 |
| ❑ 356 | Red Sox Rookies<br>Owen Johnson<br>Ken Sanders | 3.00 | 1.35 |
| ❑ 357 | Gerry Arrigo | 3.00 | 1.35 |
| ❑ 358 | Charlie Smith | 3.00 | 1.35 |
| ❑ 359 | Johnny Briggs | 3.00 | 1.35 |
| ❑ 360 | Ron Hunt | 3.00 | 1.35 |
| ❑ 361 | Tom Satriano | 3.00 | 1.35 |
| ❑ 362 | Gates Brown | 5.00 | 2.20 |
| ❑ 363 | Checklist 5 | 10.00 | 2.00 |
| ❑ 364 | Nate Oliver | 3.00 | 1.35 |
| ❑ 365 | Roger Maris | 50.00 | 22.00 |
| ❑ 366 | Wayne Causey | 3.00 | 1.35 |
| ❑ 367 | Mel Nelson | 3.00 | 1.35 |
| ❑ 368 | Charlie Lau | 5.00 | 2.20 |
| ❑ 369 | Jim King | 3.00 | 1.35 |
| ❑ 370 | Chico Cardenas | 3.00 | 1.35 |
| ❑ 371 | Lee Stange | 5.00 | 2.20 |
| ❑ 372 | Harvey Kuenn | 8.00 | 3.60 |
| ❑ 373 | Giants Rookies<br>Jack Hiatt<br>Dick Estelle | 8.00 | 3.60 |
| ❑ 374 | Bob Locker | 5.00 | 2.20 |
| ❑ 375 | Donn Clendenon | 8.00 | 3.60 |
| ❑ 376 | Paul Schaal | 5.00 | 2.20 |
| ❑ 377 | Turk Farrell | 5.00 | 2.20 |
| ❑ 378 | Dick Tracewski | 5.00 | 2.20 |
| ❑ 379 | Cardinal Team | 10.00 | 4.50 |
| ❑ 380 | Tony Conigliaro | 10.00 | 4.50 |
| ❑ 381 | Hank Fischer | 5.00 | 2.20 |
| ❑ 382 | Phil Roof | 5.00 | 2.20 |
| ❑ 383 | Jackie Brandt | 5.00 | 2.20 |
| ❑ 384 | Al Downing | 8.00 | 3.60 |
| ❑ 385 | Ken Boyer | 10.00 | 4.50 |
| ❑ 386 | Gil Hodges MG | 8.00 | 3.60 |
| ❑ 387 | Howie Reed | 5.00 | 2.20 |
| ❑ 388 | Don Mincher | 5.00 | 2.20 |
| ❑ 389 | Jim O'Toole | 8.00 | 3.60 |
| ❑ 390 | Brooks Robinson | 50.00 | 22.00 |
| ❑ 391 | Chuck Hinton | 5.00 | 2.20 |
| ❑ 392 | Cubs Rookies<br>Bill Hands<br>Randy Hundley RC | 8.00 | 3.60 |
| ❑ 393 | George Brunet | 5.00 | 2.20 |
| ❑ 394 | Ron Brand | 5.00 | 2.20 |
| ❑ 395 | Len Gabrielson | 5.00 | 2.20 |
| ❑ 396 | Jerry Stephenson | 5.00 | 2.20 |
| ❑ 397 | Bill White | 8.00 | 3.60 |
| ❑ 398 | Danny Cater | 5.00 | 2.20 |
| ❑ 399 | Ray Washburn | 5.00 | 2.20 |
| ❑ 400 | Zoilo Versalles | 8.00 | 3.60 |
| ❑ 401 | Ken McMullen | 5.00 | 2.20 |
| ❑ 402 | Jim Hickman | 5.00 | 2.20 |
| ❑ 403 | Fred Talbot | 5.00 | 2.20 |
| ❑ 404 | Pittsburgh Pirates Team Card | 10.00 | 4.50 |
| ❑ 405 | Elston Howard | 8.00 | 3.60 |
| ❑ 406 | Joey Jay | 5.00 | 2.20 |
| ❑ 407 | John Kennedy | 5.00 | 2.20 |
| ❑ 408 | Lee Thomas | 8.00 | 3.60 |
| ❑ 409 | Billy Hoeft | 5.00 | 2.20 |
| ❑ 410 | Al Kaline | 40.00 | 18.00 |
| ❑ 411 | Gene Mauch MG | 5.00 | 2.20 |
| ❑ 412 | Sam Bowens | 5.00 | 2.20 |
| ❑ 413 | Johnny Romano | 5.00 | 2.20 |
| ❑ 414 | Dan Coombs | 5.00 | 2.20 |
| ❑ 415 | Max Alvis | 5.00 | 2.20 |
| ❑ 416 | Phil Ortega | 5.00 | 2.20 |
| ❑ 417 | Angels Rookies<br>Jim McGlothlin<br>Ed Sukla | 5.00 | 2.20 |
| ❑ 418 | Phil Gagliano | 5.00 | 2.20 |
| ❑ 419 | Mike Ryan | 5.00 | 2.20 |
| ❑ 420 | Juan Marichal | 15.00 | 6.75 |
| ❑ 421 | Roy McMillan | 8.00 | 3.60 |
| ❑ 422 | Ed Charles | 5.00 | 2.20 |
| ❑ 423 | Ernie Broglio | 5.00 | 2.20 |
| ❑ 424 | Reds Rookies<br>Lee May RC<br>Darrell Osteen | 10.00 | 4.50 |
| ❑ 425 | Bob Veale | 8.00 | 3.60 |
| ❑ 426 | White Sox Team | 10.00 | 4.50 |
| ❑ 427 | John Miller | 5.00 | 2.20 |
| ❑ 428 | Sandy Alomar | 5.00 | 2.20 |
| ❑ 429 | Bill Monbouquette | 5.00 | 2.20 |
| ❑ 430 | Don Drysdale | 20.00 | 9.00 |
| ❑ 431 | Walt Bond | 5.00 | 2.20 |
| ❑ 432 | Bob Heffner | 5.00 | 2.20 |
| ❑ 433 | Alvin Dark MG | 8.00 | 3.60 |
| ❑ 434 | Willie Kirkland | 5.00 | 2.20 |
| ❑ 435 | Jim Bunning | 15.00 | 6.75 |
| ❑ 436 | Julian Javier | 8.00 | 3.60 |
| ❑ 437 | Al Stanek | 5.00 | 2.20 |
| ❑ 438 | Willie Smith | 5.00 | 2.20 |
| ❑ 439 | Pedro Ramos | 5.00 | 2.20 |
| ❑ 440 | Deron Johnson | 8.00 | 3.60 |
| ❑ 441 | Tommie Sisk | 5.00 | 2.20 |
| ❑ 442 | Orioles Rookies<br>Ed Barnowski<br>Eddie Watt | 5.00 | 2.20 |
| ❑ 443 | Bill Wakefield | 5.00 | 2.20 |
| ❑ 444 | Checklist 6 | 10.00 | 2.00 |
| ❑ 445 | Jim Kaat | 10.00 | 4.50 |
| ❑ 446 | Mack Jones | 5.00 | 2.20 |
| ❑ 447 | Dick Ellsworth UER<br>(Photo actually Ken Hubbs) | 15.00 | 6.75 |
| ❑ 448 | Eddie Stanky MG | 9.00 | 4.00 |
| ❑ 449 | Joe Moeller | 9.00 | 4.00 |
| ❑ 450 | Tony Oliva | 15.00 | 6.75 |
| ❑ 451 | Barry Latman | 9.00 | 4.00 |
| ❑ 452 | Joe Azcue | 9.00 | 4.00 |
| ❑ 453 | Ron Kline | 9.00 | 4.00 |
| ❑ 454 | Jerry Buchek | 9.00 | 4.00 |
| ❑ 455 | Mickey Lolich | 15.00 | 6.75 |
| ❑ 456 | Red Sox Rookies<br>Darrell Brandon<br>Joe Foy | 9.00 | 4.00 |
| ❑ 457 | Joe Gibbon | 9.00 | 4.00 |
| ❑ 458 | Manny Jiminez | 9.00 | 4.00 |
| ❑ 459 | Bill McCool | 9.00 | 4.00 |
| ❑ 460 | Curt Blefary | 9.00 | 4.00 |
| ❑ 461 | Roy Face | 15.00 | 6.75 |
| ❑ 462 | Bob Rodgers | 9.00 | 4.00 |
| ❑ 463 | Philadelphia Phillies Team Card | 15.00 | 6.75 |
| ❑ 464 | Larry Bearnarth | 9.00 | 4.00 |
| ❑ 465 | Don Buford | 9.00 | 4.00 |
| ❑ 466 | Ken Johnson | 9.00 | 4.00 |
| ❑ 467 | Vic Roznovsky | 9.00 | 4.00 |
| ❑ 468 | Johnny Podres | 15.00 | 6.75 |
| ❑ 469 | Yankees Rookies<br>Bobby Murcer RC<br>Dooley Womack | 30.00 | 13.50 |
| ❑ 470 | Sam McDowell | 15.00 | 6.75 |
| ❑ 471 | Bob Skinner | 9.00 | 4.00 |
| ❑ 472 | Terry Fox | 9.00 | 4.00 |
| ❑ 473 | Rich Rollins | 9.00 | 4.00 |
| ❑ 474 | Dick Schofield | 9.00 | 4.00 |
| ❑ 475 | Dick Radatz | 9.00 | 4.00 |
| ❑ 476 | Bobby Bragan MG | 9.00 | 4.00 |
| ❑ 477 | Steve Barber | 9.00 | 4.00 |
| ❑ 478 | Tony Gonzalez | 9.00 | 4.00 |
| ❑ 479 | Jim Hannan | 9.00 | 4.00 |

❑ 480 Dick Stuart.................... 9.00 4.00
❑ 481 Bob Lee......................... 9.00 4.00
❑ 482 Cubs Rookies .............. 9.00 4.00
John Boccabella
Dave Dowling
❑ 483 Joe Nuxhall .................. 9.00 4.00
❑ 484 Wes Covington ............ 9.00 4.00
❑ 485 Bob Bailey..................... 9.00 4.00
❑ 486 Tommy John .............. 15.00 6.75
❑ 487 Al Ferrara .................... 9.00 4.00
❑ 488 George Banks ............. 9.00 4.00
❑ 489 Curt Simmons ............. 9.00 4.00
❑ 490 Bobby Richardson...... 25.00 11.00
❑ 491 Dennis Bennett ............ 9.00 4.00
❑ 492 Athletics Team .......... 15.00 6.75
❑ 493 Johnny Klippstein ........ 9.00 4.00
❑ 494 Gordy Coleman............ 9.00 4.00
❑ 495 Dick McAuliffe ........... 15.00 6.75
❑ 496 Lindy McDaniel ............ 9.00 4.00
❑ 497 Chris Cannizzaro.......... 9.00 4.00
❑ 498 Pirates Rookies............ 9.00 4.00
Luke Walker
Woody Fryman
❑ 499 Wally Bunker................ 9.00 4.00
❑ 500 Hank Aaron ............. 125.00 55.00
❑ 501 John O'Donoghue ........ 9.00 4.00
❑ 502 Lenny Green UER........ 9.00 4.00
(Born: aJn. 6, 1933)
❑ 503 Steve Hamilton .......... 15.00 6.75
❑ 504 Grady Hatton MG ........ 9.00 4.00
❑ 505 Jose Cardenal .............. 9.00 4.00
❑ 506 Bo Belinsky ................ 15.00 6.75
❑ 507 Johnny Edwards .......... 9.00 4.00
❑ 508 Steve Hargan RC ........ 9.00 4.00
❑ 509 Jake Wood .................. 9.00 4.00
❑ 510 Hoyt Wilhelm.............. 15.00 6.75
❑ 511 Giants Rookies ............ 9.00 4.00
Bob Barton
Tito Fuentes RC
❑ 512 Dick Stigman................ 9.00 4.00
❑ 513 Camilo Carreon............ 9.00 4.00
❑ 514 Hal Woodeshick .......... 9.00 4.00
❑ 515 Frank Howard ............ 15.00 6.75
❑ 516 Eddie Bressoud............ 9.00 4.00
❑ 517A Checklist 7 .............. 16.00 3.20
529 White Sox Rookies
544 Cardinals Rookies
❑ 517B Checklist 7 .............. 16.00 3.20
529 W. Sox Rookies
544 Cards Rookies
❑ 518 Braves Rookies............ 9.00 4.00
Herb Hippauf
Arnie Umbach
❑ 519 Bob Friend.................. 15.00 6.75
❑ 520 Jim Wynn .................. 15.00 6.75
❑ 521 John Wyatt .................. 9.00 4.00
❑ 522 Phil Linz........................ 9.00 4.00
❑ 523 Bob Sadowski ............ 15.00 6.75
❑ 524 Giants Rookies SP .... 30.00 13.50
Ollie Brown
Don Mason
❑ 525 Gary Bell SP ............. 30.00 13.50
❑ 526 Twins Team SP........ 100.00 45.00
❑ 527 Julio Navarro.............. 15.00 6.75
❑ 528 Jesse Gonder SP ...... 30.00 13.50
❑ 529 White Sox Rookies .... 15.00 6.75
Lee Elia
Dennis Higgins
Bill Voss
❑ 530 Robin Roberts............ 50.00 22.00
❑ 531 Joe Cunningham........ 15.00 6.75
❑ 532 Aurelio Monteagudo SP 30.00 13.50
❑ 533 Jerry Adair SP........... 30.00 13.50
❑ 534 Mets Rookies ............ 15.00 6.75
Dave Eilers
Rob Gardner
❑ 535 Willie Davis SP .......... 40.00 18.00
❑ 536 Dick Egan ................. 15.00 6.75
❑ 537 Herman Franks MG.... 15.00 6.75
❑ 538 Bob Allen SP.............. 30.00 13.50
❑ 539 Astros Rookies .......... 25.00 11.00
Bill Heath
Carroll Sembera
❑ 540 Denny McLain SP ...... 60.00 27.00
❑ 541 Gene Oliver SP.......... 30.00 13.50
❑ 542 George Smith ............ 15.00 6.75
❑ 543 Roger Craig SP......... 30.00 13.50
❑ 544 Cardinals Rookies SP 30.00 13.50
Joe Hoerner
George Kernek
Jimy Williams UER
(Misspelled Jimmy
on card)
❑ 545 Dick Green SP .......... 30.00 13.50
❑ 546 Dwight Siebler .......... 25.00 11.00
❑ 547 Horace Clarke RC SP 40.00 18.00
❑ 548 Gary Kroll SP ............ 30.00 13.50
❑ 549 Senators Rookies ...... 15.00 6.75
Al Closter
Casey Cox
❑ 550 Willie McCovey SP .. 100.00 45.00
❑ 551 Bob Purkey SP .......... 30.00 13.50
❑ 552 Birdie Tebbetts .......... 30.00 13.50
MG SP
❑ 553 Rookie Stars ............. 15.00 6.75
Pat Garrett
Jackie Warner
❑ 554 Jim Northrup SP ........ 30.00 13.50
❑ 555 Ron Perranoski SP .... 30.00 13.50
❑ 556 Mel Queen SP............ 30.00 13.50
❑ 557 Felix Mantilla SP ........ 30.00 13.50
❑ 558 Red Sox Rookies ...... 20.00 9.00
Guido Grilli
Pete Magrini
George Scott RC
❑ 559 Roberto Pena SP ...... 30.00 13.50
❑ 560 Joel Horlen .................. 8.00 3.60
❑ 561 ChooChoo Coleman SP 30.00 13.50
❑ 562 Russ Snyder ............. 25.00 11.00
❑ 563 Twins Rookies........... 15.00 6.75
Pete Cimino
Cesar Tovar
❑ 564 Bob Chance SP.......... 30.00 13.50
❑ 565 Jimmy Piersall SP ...... 40.00 18.00
❑ 566 Mike Cuellar SP ........ 30.00 13.50
❑ 567 Dick Howser SP ........ 40.00 18.00
❑ 568 Athletics Rookies....... 15.00 6.75
Paul Lindblad
Ron Stone
❑ 569 Orlando McFarlane SP 30.00 13.50
❑ 570 Art Mahaffey SP ........ 30.00 13.50
❑ 571 Dave Roberts SP ...... 30.00 13.50
❑ 572 Bob Priddy.................. 15.00 6.75
❑ 573 Derrell Griffith ............ 15.00 6.75
❑ 574 Mets Rookies ............ 15.00 6.75
Bill Hepler
Bill Murphy
❑ 575 Earl Wilson ................ 15.00 6.75
❑ 576 Dave Nicholson SP .... 30.00 13.50
❑ 577 Jack Lamabe SP........ 30.00 13.50
❑ 578 Chi Chi Olivo SP ........ 30.00 13.50
❑ 579 Orioles Rookies.......... 20.00 9.00
Frank Bertaina
Gene Brabender
Dave Johnson
❑ 580 Billy Williams SP ........ 60.00 27.00
❑ 581 Tony Martinez ............ 15.00 6.75
❑ 582 Garry Roggenburk...... 15.00 6.75
❑ 583 Tigers Team SP UER 125.00 55.00
(Text on back states Tigers
finished third in 1966 instead
of fourth.)
❑ 584 Yankees Rookies ...... 15.00 6.75
Frank Fernandez
Fritz Peterson
❑ 585 Tony Taylor ............... 25.00 11.00
❑ 586 Claude Raymond SP.. 30.00 13.50
❑ 587 Dick Bertell ................ 15.00 6.75
❑ 588 Athletics Rookies....... 15.00 6.75
Chuck Dobson
Ken Suarez
❑ 589 Lou Klimchock SP...... 30.00 13.50
❑ 590 Bill Skowron SP.......... 40.00 18.00
❑ 591 NL Rookies SP .......... 40.00 18.00
Bart Shirley
Grant Jackson RC
❑ 592 Andre Rodgers .......... 15.00 6.75
❑ 593 Doug Camilli SP ........ 30.00 13.50
❑ 594 Chico Salmon ............ 15.00 6.75
❑ 595 Larry Jackson ............ 15.00 6.75
❑ 596 Astros Rookies SP .... 30.00 13.50
Nate Colbert RC
Greg Sims
❑ 597 John Sullivan.............. 15.00 6.75
❑ 598 Gaylord Perry SP .... 175.00 50.00

## 1967 Topps

| | NRMT | VG-E |
|---|---|---|
| COMPLETE SET (609) ...... | 4600.00 | 2100.00 |
| COMMON CARD (1-109).......... | 1.50 | .70 |
| COMMON CARD (110-283)...... | 2.00 | .90 |
| COMMON CARD (284-370)...... | 2.50 | 1.10 |
| COMMON CARD (371-457)...... | 4.00 | 1.80 |
| COMMON CARD (458-533)...... | 6.00 | 2.70 |
| COMMON CARD (534-609).... | 16.00 | 7.25 |
| COMMON DP (534-609) ......... | 9.00 | 4.00 |
| WRAPPER (5-CENT)............ | 25.00 | 11.00 |

❑ 1 The Champs DP ........... 25.00 7.50
Frank Robinson
Hank Bauer MG
Brooks Robinson
❑ 2 Jack Hamilton ............... 1.50 .70
❑ 3 Duke Sims........................ 1.50 .70
❑ 4 Hal Lanier ........................ 1.50 .70
❑ 5 Whitey Ford UER ......... 20.00 9.00
(1953 listed as
1933 in stats on back)
❑ 6 Dick Simpson ................. 1.50 .70
❑ 7 Don McMahon................ 1.50 .70
❑ 8 Chuck Harrison .............. 1.50 .70
❑ 9 Ron Hansen ................... 1.50 .70
❑ 10 Matty Alou ................... 4.00 1.80
❑ 11 Barry Moore ................. 1.50 .70
❑ 12 Dodgers Rookies.......... 4.00 1.80
Jim Campanis
Bill Singer
❑ 13 Joe Sparma................... 1.50 .70
❑ 14 Phil Linz......................... 4.00 1.80
❑ 15 Earl Battey.................... 1.50 .70
❑ 16 Bill Hands ..................... 1.50 .70
❑ 17 Jim Gosger ................... 1.50 .70
❑ 18 Gene Oliver................... 1.50 .70
❑ 19 Jim McGlothlin.............. 1.50 .70
❑ 20 Orlando Cepeda ........... 8.00 3.60
❑ 21 Dave Bristol MG ........... 1.50 .70
❑ 22 Gene Brabender ........... 1.50 .70
❑ 23 Larry Elliot .................... 1.50 .70
❑ 24 Bob Allen...................... 1.50 .70
❑ 25 Elston Howard.............. 4.00 1.80
❑ 26A Bob Priddy NTR ........ 30.00 13.50
❑ 26B Bob Priddy TR ........... 4.00 1.80
❑ 27 Bob Saverine................. 1.50 .70
❑ 28 Barry Latman................. 1.50 .70
❑ 29 Tom McCraw ................ 1.50 .70
❑ 30 Al Kaline DP .............. 20.00 9.00
❑ 31 Jim Brewer .................... 1.50 .70
❑ 32 Bob Bailey..................... 4.00 1.80
❑ 33 Athletic Rookies ........... 6.00 2.70
Sal Bando RC
Randy Schwartz
❑ 34 Pete Cimino................... 1.50 .70
❑ 35 Rico Carty ..................... 4.00 1.80
❑ 36 Bob Tillman................... 1.50 .70
❑ 37 Rick Wise ..................... 4.00 1.80
❑ 38 Bob Johnson ................. 1.50 .70
❑ 39 Curt Simmons ............... 4.00 1.80
❑ 40 Rick Reichardt.............. 1.50 .70
❑ 41 Joe Hoerner .................. 1.50 .70

|  | | |
|---|---|---|
| ❑ 42 Mets Team | 10.00 | 4.50 |
| ❑ 43 Chico Salmon | 1.50 | .70 |
| ❑ 44 Joe Nuxhall | 4.00 | 1.80 |
| ❑ 45 Roger Maris | 50.00 | 22.00 |
| ❑ 45A Roger Maris | 100.00 | 45.00 |
| (Yankees listed as team; | | |
| blank back) | | |
| ❑ 46 Lindy McDaniel | 4.00 | 1.80 |
| ❑ 47 Ken McMullen | 1.50 | .70 |
| ❑ 48 Bill Freehan | 4.00 | 1.80 |
| ❑ 49 Roy Face | 4.00 | 1.80 |
| ❑ 50 Tony Oliva | 6.00 | 2.70 |
| ❑ 51 Astros Rookies | 1.50 | .70 |
| Dave Adlesh | | |
| Wes Bales | | |
| ❑ 52 Dennis Higgins | 1.50 | .70 |
| ❑ 53 Clay Dalrymple | 1.50 | .70 |
| ❑ 54 Dick Green | 1.50 | .70 |
| ❑ 55 Don Drysdale | 16.00 | 7.25 |
| ❑ 56 Jose Tartabull | 4.00 | 1.80 |
| ❑ 57 Pat Jarvis | 1.50 | .70 |
| ❑ 58A Paul Schaal | 1.50 | .70 |
| Green Bat | | |
| ❑ 58B Paul Schall | 1.50 | .70 |
| Normal Colored Bat | | |
| ❑ 59 Ralph Terry | 4.00 | 1.80 |
| ❑ 60 Luis Aparicio | 8.00 | 3.60 |
| ❑ 61 Gordy Coleman | 4.00 | 1.80 |
| ❑ 62 Frank Robinson CL | 8.00 | 1.60 |
| ❑ 63 Cards' Clubbers | 8.00 | 3.60 |
| Lou Brock | | |
| Curt Flood | | |
| ❑ 64 Fred Valentine | 1.50 | .70 |
| ❑ 65 Tom Haller | 4.00 | 1.80 |
| ❑ 66 Manny Mota | 4.00 | 1.80 |
| ❑ 67 Ken Berry | 1.50 | .70 |
| ❑ 68 Bob Buhl | 4.00 | 1.80 |
| ❑ 69 Vic Davalillo | 1.50 | .70 |
| ❑ 70 Ron Santo | 6.00 | 2.70 |
| ❑ 71 Camilo Pascual | 4.00 | 1.80 |
| ❑ 72 Tigers Rookies | 1.50 | .70 |
| George Korince | | |
| (Photo actually | | |
| James Murray Brown) | | |
| John (Tom) Matchick | | |
| ❑ 73 Rusty Staub | 6.00 | 2.70 |
| ❑ 74 Wes Stock | 1.50 | .70 |
| ❑ 75 George Scott | 4.00 | 1.80 |
| ❑ 76 Jim Barbieri | 1.50 | .70 |
| ❑ 77 Dooley Womack | 4.00 | 1.80 |
| ❑ 78 Pat Corrales | 4.00 | 1.80 |
| ❑ 79 Bubba Morton | 1.50 | .70 |
| ❑ 80 Jim Maloney | 4.00 | 1.80 |
| ❑ 81 Eddie Stanky MG | 4.00 | 1.80 |
| ❑ 82 Steve Barber | 1.50 | .70 |
| ❑ 83 Ollie Brown | 1.50 | .70 |
| ❑ 84 Tommie Sisk | 1.50 | .70 |
| ❑ 85 Johnny Callison | 4.00 | 1.80 |
| ❑ 86A Mike McCormick NTR | 30.00 | 13.50 |
| (Senators on front | | |
| and Senators on back) | | |
| ❑ 86B Mike McCormick TR | 4.00 | 1.80 |
| (Traded line | | |
| at end of bio; | | |
| Senators on front, | | |
| but Giants on back) | | |
| ❑ 87 George Altman | 1.50 | .70 |
| ❑ 88 Mickey Lolich | 4.00 | 1.80 |
| ❑ 89 Felix Millan | 4.00 | 1.80 |
| ❑ 90 Jim Nash | 1.50 | .70 |
| ❑ 91 Johnny Lewis | 1.50 | .70 |
| ❑ 92 Ray Washburn | 1.50 | .70 |
| ❑ 93 Yankees Rookies | 4.00 | 1.80 |
| Stan Bahnsen RC | | |
| Bobby Murcer | | |
| ❑ 94 Ron Fairly | 4.00 | 1.80 |
| ❑ 95 Sonny Siebert | 1.50 | .70 |
| ❑ 96 Art Shamsky | 1.50 | .70 |
| ❑ 97 Mike Cuellar | 4.00 | 1.80 |
| ❑ 98 Rich Rollins | 1.50 | .70 |
| ❑ 99 Lee Stange | 1.50 | .70 |
| ❑ 100 Frank Robinson DP | 14.00 | 6.25 |
| ❑ 101 Ken Johnson | 1.50 | .70 |
| ❑ 102 Philadelphia Phillies | 4.00 | 1.80 |
| Team Card | | |
| ❑ 103 Mickey Mantle CL | 20.00 | 4.00 |
| ❑ 104 Minnie Rojas | 1.50 | .70 |
| ❑ 105 Ken Boyer | 6.00 | 2.70 |
| ❑ 106 Randy Hundley | 4.00 | 1.80 |
| ❑ 107 Joel Horlen | 1.50 | .70 |
| ❑ 108 Alex Johnson | 4.00 | 1.80 |
| ❑ 109 Tribe Thumpers | 6.00 | 2.70 |
| Rocky Colavito | | |
| Leon Wagner | | |
| ❑ 110 Jack Aker | 4.00 | 1.80 |
| ❑ 111 John Kennedy | 2.00 | .90 |
| ❑ 112 Dave Wickersham | 2.00 | .90 |
| ❑ 113 Dave Nicholson | 2.00 | .90 |
| ❑ 114 Jack Baldschun | 2.00 | .90 |
| ❑ 115 Paul Casanova | 2.00 | .90 |
| ❑ 116 Herman Franks MG | 2.00 | .90 |
| ❑ 117 Darrell Brandon | 2.00 | .90 |
| ❑ 118 Bernie Allen | 2.00 | .90 |
| ❑ 119 Wade Blasingame | 2.00 | .90 |
| ❑ 120 Floyd Robinson | 2.00 | .90 |
| ❑ 121 Eddie Bressoud | 2.00 | .90 |
| ❑ 122 George Brunet | 2.00 | .90 |
| ❑ 123 Pirates Rookies | 4.00 | 1.80 |
| Jim Price | | |
| Luke Walker | | |
| ❑ 124 Jim Stewart | 2.00 | .90 |
| ❑ 125 Moe Drabowsky | 4.00 | 1.80 |
| ❑ 126 Tony Taylor | 2.00 | .90 |
| ❑ 127 John O'Donoghue | 2.00 | .90 |
| ❑ 128 Ed Spiezio | 2.00 | .90 |
| ❑ 129 Phil Roof | 2.00 | .90 |
| ❑ 130 Phil Regan | 4.00 | 1.80 |
| ❑ 131 Yankees Team | 10.00 | 4.50 |
| ❑ 132 Ozzie Virgil | 2.00 | .90 |
| ❑ 133 Ron Kline | 2.00 | .90 |
| ❑ 134 Gates Brown | 6.00 | 2.70 |
| ❑ 135 Deron Johnson | 4.00 | 1.80 |
| ❑ 136 Carroll Sembera | 2.00 | .90 |
| ❑ 137 Twins Rookies | 2.00 | .90 |
| Ron Clark | | |
| Jim Ollum | | |
| ❑ 138 Dick Kelley | 2.00 | .90 |
| ❑ 139 Dalton Jones | 4.00 | 1.80 |
| ❑ 140 Willie Stargell | 20.00 | 9.00 |
| ❑ 141 John Miller | 2.00 | .90 |
| ❑ 142 Jackie Brandt | 2.00 | .90 |
| ❑ 143 Sox Sockers | 2.00 | .90 |
| Pete Ward | | |
| Don Buford | | |
| ❑ 144 Bill Hepler | 2.00 | .90 |
| ❑ 145 Larry Brown | 2.00 | .90 |
| ❑ 146 Steve Carlton | 50.00 | 22.00 |
| ❑ 147 Tom Egan | 2.00 | .90 |
| ❑ 148 Adolfo Phillips | 2.00 | .90 |
| ❑ 149 Joe Moeller | 2.00 | .90 |
| ❑ 150 Mickey Mantle | 250.00 | 110.00 |
| ❑ 151 Moe Drabowsky WS | 4.00 | 1.80 |
| ❑ 152 Jim Palmer WS | 8.00 | 3.60 |
| ❑ 153 Paul Blair WS | 4.00 | 1.80 |
| ❑ 154 Brooks Robinson WS | 4.00 | 1.80 |
| Dave McNally | | |
| ❑ 155 World Series Summary | 4.00 | 1.80 |
| Winners celebrate | | |
| ❑ 156 Ron Herbel | 2.00 | .90 |
| ❑ 157 Danny Cater | 2.00 | .90 |
| ❑ 158 Jimmie Coker | 2.00 | .90 |
| ❑ 159 Bruce Howard | 2.00 | .90 |
| ❑ 160 Willie Davis | 4.00 | 1.80 |
| ❑ 161 Dick Williams MG | 4.00 | 1.80 |
| ❑ 162 Billy O'Dell | 2.00 | .90 |
| ❑ 163 Vic Roznovsky | 2.00 | .90 |
| ❑ 164 Dwight Siebler UER | 2.00 | .90 |
| (Last line of stats | | |
| shows 1960 Minnesota) | | |
| ❑ 165 Cleon Jones | 4.00 | 1.80 |
| ❑ 166 Eddie Mathews | 15.00 | 6.75 |
| ❑ 167 Senators Rookies | 2.00 | .90 |
| Joe Coleman | | |
| Tim Cullen | | |
| ❑ 168 Ray Culp | 2.00 | .90 |
| ❑ 169 Horace Clarke | 4.00 | 1.80 |
| ❑ 170 Dick McAuliffe | 4.00 | 1.80 |
| ❑ 171 Cal Koonce | 2.00 | .90 |
| ❑ 172 Bill Heath | 2.00 | .90 |
| ❑ 173 St. Louis Cardinals | 4.00 | 1.80 |
| Team Card | | |
| ❑ 174 Dick Radatz | 4.00 | 1.80 |
| ❑ 175 Bobby Knoop | 2.00 | .90 |
| ❑ 176 Sammy Ellis | 2.00 | .90 |
| ❑ 177 Tito Fuentes | 4.00 | 1.80 |
| ❑ 178 John Buzhardt | 2.00 | .90 |
| ❑ 179 Braves Rookies | 4.00 | 1.80 |
| Charles Vaughan | | |
| Cecil Upshaw | | |
| ❑ 180 Curt Blefary | 2.00 | .90 |
| ❑ 181 Terry Fox | 2.00 | .90 |
| ❑ 182 Ed Charles | 2.00 | .90 |
| ❑ 183 Jim Pagliaroni | 2.00 | .90 |
| ❑ 184 George Thomas | 2.00 | .90 |
| ❑ 185 Ken Holtzman RC | 4.00 | 1.80 |
| ❑ 186 Mets Maulers | 4.00 | 1.80 |
| Ed Kranepool | | |
| Ron Swoboda | | |
| ❑ 187 Pedro Ramos | 2.00 | .90 |
| ❑ 188 Ken Harrelson | 4.00 | 1.80 |
| ❑ 189 Chuck Hinton | 2.00 | .90 |
| ❑ 190 Turk Farrell | 2.00 | .90 |
| ❑ 191A Willie Mays CL | 10.00 | 2.00 |
| 214 Tom Kelley | | |
| ❑ 191B Willie Mays CL | 12.00 | 2.40 |
| 214 Dick Kelley | | |
| ❑ 192 Fred Gladding | 2.00 | .90 |
| ❑ 193 Jose Cardenal | 4.00 | 1.80 |
| ❑ 194 Bob Allison | 4.00 | 1.80 |
| ❑ 195 Al Jackson | 2.00 | .90 |
| ❑ 196 Johnny Romano | 2.00 | .90 |
| ❑ 197 Ron Perranoski | 4.00 | 1.80 |
| ❑ 198 Chuck Hiller | 2.00 | .90 |
| ❑ 199 Billy Hitchcock MG | 2.00 | .90 |
| ❑ 200 Willie Mays UER | 80.00 | 36.00 |
| ('63 Sna Francisco | | |
| on card back stats) | | |
| ❑ 201 Hal Reniff | 4.00 | 1.80 |
| ❑ 202 Johnny Edwards | 2.00 | .90 |
| ❑ 203 Al McBean | 2.00 | .90 |
| ❑ 204 Orioles Rookies | 6.00 | 2.70 |
| Mike Epstein | | |
| Tom Phoebus | | |
| ❑ 205 Dick Groat | 4.00 | 1.80 |
| ❑ 206 Dennis Bennett | 2.00 | .00 |
| ❑ 207 John Orsino | 2.00 | .90 |
| ❑ 208 Jack Lamabe | 2.00 | .90 |
| ❑ 209 Joe Nossek | 2.00 | .90 |
| ❑ 210 Bob Gibson | 20.00 | 9.00 |
| ❑ 211 Twins Team | 4.00 | 1.80 |
| ❑ 212 Chris Zachary | 2.00 | .90 |
| ❑ 213 Jay Johnstone RC | 4.00 | 1.80 |
| ❑ 214 Dick Kelley | 2.00 | .90 |
| ❑ 215 Ernie Banks | 20.00 | 9.00 |
| ❑ 216 Bengal Belters | 8.00 | 3.60 |
| Norm Cash | | |
| Al Kaline | | |
| ❑ 217 Rob Gardner | 2.00 | .90 |
| ❑ 218 Wes Parker | 4.00 | 1.80 |
| ❑ 219 Clay Carroll | 4.00 | 1.80 |
| ❑ 220 Jim Ray Hart | 4.00 | 1.80 |
| ❑ 221 Woody Fryman | 4.00 | 1.80 |
| ❑ 222 Reds Rookies | 4.00 | 1.80 |
| Darrell Osteen | | |
| Lee May | | |
| ❑ 223 Mike Ryan | 4.00 | 1.80 |
| ❑ 224 Walt Bond | 2.00 | .90 |
| ❑ 225 Mel Stottlemyre | 6.00 | 2.70 |
| ❑ 226 Julian Javier | 4.00 | 1.80 |
| ❑ 227 Paul Lindblad | 2.00 | .90 |
| ❑ 228 Gil Hodges MG | 6.00 | 2.70 |
| ❑ 229 Larry Jackson | 2.00 | .90 |
| ❑ 230 Boog Powell | 6.00 | 2.70 |
| ❑ 231 John Bateman | 2.00 | .90 |
| ❑ 232 Don Buford | 2.00 | .90 |
| ❑ 233 AL ERA Leaders | 4.00 | 1.80 |
| Gary Peters | | |
| Joel Horlen | | |
| Steve Hargan | | |
| ❑ 234 NL ERA Leaders | 15.00 | 6.75 |
| Sandy Koufax | | |
| Mike Cuellar | | |
| Juan Marichal | | |
| ❑ 235 AL Pitching Leaders | 6.00 | 2.70 |
| Jim Kaat | | |
| Denny McLain | | |
| Earl Wilson | | |
| ❑ 236 NL Pitching Leaders | 25.00 | 11.00 |

Sandy Koufax
Juan Marichal
Bob Gibson
Gaylord Perry
❑ 237 AL Strikeout Leaders.... 6.00 2.70
Sam McDowell
Jim Kaat
Earl Wilson
❑ 238 NL Strikeout Leaders 12.00 5.50
Sandy Koufax
Jim Bunning
Bob Veale
❑ 239 AL Batting Leaders ...... 9.00 4.00
Frank Robinson
Tony Oliva
Al Kaline
❑ 240 NL Batting Leaders ...... 6.00 2.70
Matty Alou
Felipe Alou
Rico Carty
❑ 241 AL RBI Leaders........... 9.00 4.00
Frank Robinson
Harmon Killebrew
Boog Powell
❑ 242 NL RBI Leaders.......... 25.00 11.00
Hank Aaron
Bob Clemente
Richie Allen
❑ 243 AL Home Run Leaders 9.00 4.00
Frank Robinson
Harmon Killebrew
Boog Powell
❑ 244 NL Home Run Leaders 20.00 9.00
Hank Aaron
Richie Allen
Willie Mays
❑ 245 Curt Flood .................... 6.00 2.70
❑ 246 Jim Perry ..................... 4.00 1.80
❑ 247 Jerry Lumpe ................ 2.00 .90
❑ 248 Gene Mauch MG.......... 4.00 1.80
❑ 249 Nick Willhite............... 2.00 .90
❑ 250 Hank Aaron UER........ 80.00 36.00
(Second 1961 in stats
should be 1962)
❑ 251 Woody Held................ 2.00 .90
❑ 252 Bob Bolin.................... 2.00 .90
❑ 253 Indians Rookies........... 2.00 .90
Bill Davis
Gus Gil
❑ 254 Milt Pappas ................. 4.00 1.80
(No facsimile auto-
graph on card front)
❑ 255 Frank Howard ............. 4.00 1.80
❑ 256 Bob Hendley ............... 2.00 .90
❑ 257 Charlie Smith.............. 2.00 .90
❑ 258 Lee Maye .................... 2.00 .90
❑ 259 Don Dennis ................. 2.00 .90
❑ 260 Jim Lefebvre ............... 4.00 1.80
❑ 261 John Wyatt ................. 2.00 .90
❑ 262 Athletics Team ........... 4.00 1.80
❑ 263 Hank Aguirre .............. 2.00 .90
❑ 264 Ron Swoboda ............. 4.00 1.80
❑ 265 Lou Burdette .............. 4.00 1.80
❑ 266 Pitt Power .................. 4.00 1.80
Willie Stargell
Donn Clendenon
❑ 267 Don Schwall ............... 2.00 .90
❑ 268 Johnny Briggs ............ 2.00 .90
❑ 269 Don Nottebart ............ 2.00 .90
❑ 270 Zoilo Versalles............ 2.00 .90
❑ 271 Eddie Watt.................. 2.00 .90
❑ 272 Cubs Rookies ............. 4.00 1.80
Bill Connors RC
Dave Dowling
❑ 273 Dick Lines .................. 2.00 .90
❑ 274 Bob Aspromonte ......... 2.00 .90
❑ 275 Fred Whitfield ............ 2.00 .90
❑ 276 Bruce Brubaker ........... 2.00 .90
❑ 277 Steve Whitaker ........... 6.00 2.70
❑ 278 Jim Kaat CL................ 8.00 1.60
❑ 279 Frank Linzy ................ 2.00 .90
❑ 280 Tony Conigliaro .......... 8.00 3.60
❑ 281 Bob Rodgers .............. 2.00 .90
❑ 282 John Odom ................ 2.00 .90
❑ 283 Gene Alley.................. 4.00 1.80
❑ 284 Johnny Podres ........... 4.00 1.80
❑ 285 Lou Brock .................. 20.00 9.00
❑ 286 Wayne Causey ........... 2.50 1.10
❑ 287 Mets Rookies ............. 2.50 1.10
Greg Goossen
Bart Shirley
❑ 288 Denny Lemaster ......... 2.50 1.10
❑ 289 Tom Tresh................... 5.00 2.20
❑ 290 Bill White .................... 5.00 2.20
❑ 291 Jim Hannan................. 2.50 1.10
❑ 292 Don Pavletich ............. 2.50 1.10
❑ 293 Ed Kirkpatrick ............. 2.50 1.10
❑ 294 Walter Alston MG ....... 8.00 3.60
❑ 295 Sam McDowell ........... 5.00 2.20
❑ 296 Glenn Beckert ............ 5.00 2.20
❑ 297 Dave Morehead........... 5.00 2.20
❑ 298 Ron Davis ................... 2.50 1.10
❑ 299 Norm Siebern ............. 2.50 1.10
❑ 300 Jim Kaat ..................... 5.00 2.20
❑ 301 Jesse Gonder ............. 2.50 1.10
❑ 302 Orioles Team............... 8.00 3.60
❑ 303 Gil Blanco ................... 2.50 1.10
❑ 304 Phil Gagliano............... 2.50 1.10
❑ 305 Earl Wilson ................. 5.00 2.20
❑ 306 Bud Harrelson RC........ 5.00 2.20
❑ 307 Jim Beauchamp .......... 2.50 1.10
❑ 308 Al Downing ................. 5.00 2.20
❑ 309 Hurlers Beware ........... 5.00 2.20
Johnny Callison
Richie Allen
❑ 310 Gary Peters ................ 2.50 1.10
❑ 311 Ed Brinkman ............... 2.50 1.10
❑ 312 Don Mincher ............... 2.50 1.10
❑ 313 Bob Lee....................... 2.50 1.10
❑ 314 Red Sox Rookies ........ 8.00 3.60
Mike Andrews
Reggie Smith RC
❑ 315 Billy Williams ............. 15.00 6.75
❑ 316 Jack Kralick ................ 2.50 1.10
❑ 317 Cesar Tovar ............... 2.50 1.10
❑ 318 Dave Giusti ................. 2.50 1.10
❑ 319 Paul Blair..................... 5.00 2.20
❑ 320 Gaylord Perry ............ 15.00 6.75
❑ 321 Mayo Smith MG .......... 2.50 1.10
❑ 322 Jose Pagan ................. 2.50 1.10
❑ 323 Mike Hershberger ........ 2.50 1.10
❑ 324 Hal Woodeshick .......... 2.50 1.10
❑ 325 Chico Cardenas .......... 5.00 2.20
❑ 326 Bob Uecker ............... 10.00 4.50
❑ 327 California Angels.......... 8.00 3.60
Team Card
❑ 328 Clete Boyer UER.......... 5.00 2.20
(Stats only go up
through 1965)
❑ 329 Charlie Lau ................. 5.00 2.20
❑ 330 Claude Osteen ............ 5.00 2.20
❑ 331 Joe Foy ...................... 5.00 2.20
❑ 332 Jesus Alou................... 2.50 1.10
❑ 333 Ferguson Jenkins ...... 20.00 9.00
❑ 334 Twin Terrors .............. 10.00 4.50
Bob Allison
Harmon Killebrew
❑ 335 Bob Veale ................... 5.00 2.20
❑ 336 Joe Azcue ................... 2.50 1.10
❑ 337 Joe Morgan ............... 15.00 6.75
❑ 338 Bob Locker .................. 2.50 1.10
❑ 339 Chico Ruiz................... 2.50 1.10
❑ 340 Joe Pepitone ............... 8.00 3.60
❑ 341 Giants Rookies ............ 2.50 1.10
Dick Dietz
Bill Sorrell
❑ 342 Hank Fischer................ 2.50 1.10
❑ 343 Tom Satriano................ 2.50 1.10
❑ 344 Ossie Chavarria ........... 2.50 1.10
❑ 345 Stu Miller ..................... 5.00 2.20
❑ 346 Jim Hickman ................ 2.50 1.10
❑ 347 Grady Hatton MG ......... 2.50 1.10
❑ 348 Tug McGraw ................ 5.00 2.20
❑ 349 Bob Chance ................ 2.50 1.10
❑ 350 Joe Torre..................... 8.00 3.60
❑ 351 Vern Law..................... 5.00 2.20
❑ 352 Ray Oyler ................... 2.50 1.10
❑ 353 Bill McCool .................. 2.50 1.10
❑ 354 Cubs Team .................. 8.00 3.60
❑ 355 Carl Yastrzemski........ 50.00 22.00
❑ 356 Larry Jaster ................ 2.50 1.10
❑ 357 Bill Skowron ............... 5.00 2.20
❑ 358 Ruben Amaro ............. 2.50 1.10
❑ 359 Dick Ellsworth ............ 2.50 1.10
❑ 360 Leon Wagner............... 2.50 1.10
❑ 361 Roberto Clemente CL 15.00 3.00
❑ 362 Darold Knowles............ 2.50 1.10
❑ 363 Dave Johnson ............. 5.00 2.20
❑ 364 Claude Raymond ........ 2.50 1.10
❑ 365 John Roseboro ........... 5.00 2.20
❑ 366 Andy Kosco ................. 2.50 1.10
❑ 367 Angels Rookies ........... 2.50 1.10
Bill Kelso
Don Wallace
❑ 368 Jack Hiatt .................... 2.50 1.10
❑ 369 Jim Hunter.................. 15.00 6.75
❑ 370 Tommy Davis ............. 5.00 2.20
❑ 371 Jim Lonborg ............... 8.00 3.60
❑ 372 Mike de la Hoz ........... 4.00 1.80
❑ 373 White Sox Rookies DP 4.00 1.80
Duane Josephson
Fred Klages
❑ 374A Mel Queen ERR DP 20.00 9.00
(Incomplete stat
line on back)
❑ 374B Mel Queen COR DP .. 4.00 1.80
(Complete stat
line on back)
❑ 375 Jake Gibbs .................. 8.00 3.60
❑ 376 Don Lock DP ............... 4.00 1.80
❑ 377 Luis Tiant..................... 8.00 3.60
❑ 378 Detroit Tigers................ 8.00 3.60
Team Card UER
(Willie Horton with
262 RBI's in 1966)
❑ 379 Jerry May DP .............. 4.00 1.80
❑ 380 Dean Chance DP ........ 4.00 1.80
❑ 381 Dick Schofield DP ....... 4.00 1.80
❑ 382 Dave McNally ............. 8.00 3.60
❑ 383 Ken Henderson DP ...... 4.00 1.80
❑ 384 Cardinals Rookies........ 4.00 1.80
Jim Cosman
Dick Hughes
❑ 385 Jim Fregosi ................. 8.00 3.60
(Batting wrong)
❑ 386 Dick Selma DP ............ 4.00 1.80
❑ 387 Cap Peterson DP ........ 4.00 1.80
❑ 388 Arnold Earley DP......... 4.00 1.80
❑ 389 Alvin Dark MG DP ....... 8.00 3.60
❑ 390 Jim Wynn DP .............. 8.00 3.60
❑ 391 Wilbur Wood DP .......... 8.00 3.60
❑ 392 Tommy Harper DP ...... 8.00 3.60
❑ 393 Jim Bouton DP ............ 8.00 3.60
❑ 394 Jake Wood DP ............ 4.00 1.80
❑ 395 Chris Short ................. 8.00 3.60
❑ 396 Atlanta Aces ............... 4.00 1.80
Denis Menke
Tony Cloninger
❑ 397 Willie Smith DP ........... 4.00 1.80
❑ 398 Jeff Torborg................. 8.00 3.60
❑ 399 Al Worthington DP....... 4.00 1.80
❑ 400 Bob Clemente DP .... 100.00 45.00
❑ 401 Jim Coates .................. 4.00 1.80
❑ 402A Phillies Rookies DP 20.00 9.00
Grant Jackson
Billy Wilson
Incomplete stat line
❑ 402B Phillies Rookies DP .. 8.00 3.60
Grant Jackson
Billy Wilson
❑ 403 Dick Nen ..................... 4.00 1.80
❑ 404 Nelson Briles .............. 8.00 3.60
❑ 405 Russ Snyder ............... 4.00 1.80
❑ 406 Lee Elia DP ................. 4.00 1.80
❑ 407 Reds Team .................. 8.00 3.60
❑ 408 Jim Northrup DP ......... 8.00 3.60
❑ 409 Ray Sadecki ............... 4.00 1.80
❑ 410 Lou Johnson DP ......... 4.00 1.80
❑ 411 Dick Howser DP ......... 4.00 1.80
❑ 412 Astros Rookies ........... 8.00 3.60
Norm Miller
Doug Rader RC
❑ 413 Jerry Grote ................. 4.00 1.80
❑ 414 Casey Cox................... 4.00 1.80
❑ 415 Sonny Jackson ........... 4.00 1.80
❑ 416 Roger Repoz............... 4.00 1.80
❑ 417A Bob Bruce ERR DP 30.00 13.50
(RBAVES on back)

❑ 417B Bob Bruce COR DP .. 4.00 1.80
❑ 418 Sam Mele MG .............. 4.00 1.80
❑ 419 Don Kessinger DP........ 8.00 3.60
❑ 420 Denny McLain ........... 12.00 5.50
❑ 421 Dal Maxvill DP .............. 4.00 1.80
❑ 422 Hoyt Wilhelm ............. 15.00 6.75
❑ 423 Fence Busters DP ...... 25.00 11.00
Willie Mays
Willie McCovey
❑ 424 Pedro Gonzalez .......... 4.00 1.80
❑ 425 Pete Mikkelsen ............ 4.00 1.80
❑ 426 Lou Clinton .................. 4.00 1.80
❑ 427A Ruben Gomez ERR DP 20.00 9.00
(Incomplete stat
line on back)
❑ 427B Ruben Gomez COR DP 4.00 1.80
(Complete stat
line on back)
❑ 428 Dodgers Rookies DP.... 8.00 3.60
Tom Hutton RC
Gene Michael
❑ 429 Garry Roggenburk DP.. 4.00 1.80
❑ 430 Pete Rose .................. 80.00 36.00
❑ 431 Ted Uhlaender ............ 4.00 1.80
❑ 432 Jimmie Hall DP ............ 4.00 1.80
❑ 433 Al Luplow DP................ 4.00 1.80
❑ 434 Eddie Fisher DP .......... 4.00 1.80
❑ 435 Mack Jones DP............ 4.00 1.80
❑ 436 Pete Ward .................. 4.00 1.80
❑ 437 Senators Team ............ 8.00 3.60
❑ 438 Chuck Dobson.............. 4.00 1.80
❑ 439 Byron Browne ............. 4.00 1.80
❑ 440 Steve Hargan .............. 4.00 1.80
❑ 441 Jim Davenport.............. 4.00 1.80
❑ 442 Yankees Rookies DP .. 8.00 3.60
Bill Robinson RC
Joe Verbanic
❑ 443 Tito Francona DP ........ 4.00 1.80
❑ 444 George Smith ............. 4.00 1.80
❑ 445 Don Sutton ................ 25.00 11.00
❑ 446 Russ Nixon DP ............ 4.00 1.80
❑ 447A Bo Belinsky ERR DP 5.00 2.20
(Incomplete stat
line on back)
❑ 447B Bo Belinsky COR DP 8.00 3.60
(Complete stat
line on back)
❑ 448 Harry Walker DP MG .. 4.00 1.80
❑ 449 Orlando Pena ............. 4.00 1.80
❑ 450 Richie Allen ................ 8.00 3.60
❑ 451 Fred Newman DP ........ 4.00 1.80
❑ 452 Ed Kranepool ............. 8.00 3.60
❑ 453 Aurelio Monteagudo DP 4.00 1.80
❑ 454A Juan Marichal CL .... 12.00 2.40
Missing left ear
❑ 454B Juan Marichal CL .... 12.00 2.40
Left ear showing
❑ 455 Tommie Agee ............ 8.00 3.60
❑ 456 Phil Niekro................ 15.00 6.75
❑ 457 Andy Etchebarren DP .. 8.00 3.60
❑ 458 Lee Thomas ................ 6.00 2.70
❑ 459 Senators Rookies ........ 6.00 2.70
Dick Bosman RC
Pete Craig
❑ 460 Harmon Killebrew ...... 60.00 27.00
❑ 461 Bob Miller .................. 12.00 5.50
❑ 462 Bob Barton .................. 6.00 2.70
❑ 463 Hill Aces .................... 12.00 5.50
Sam McDowell
Sonny Siebert
❑ 464 Dan Coombs ................ 6.00 2.70
❑ 465 Willie Horton .............. 12.00 5.50
❑ 466 Bobby Wine................. 6.00 2.70
❑ 467 Jim O'Toole ................. 6.00 2.70
❑ 468 Ralph Houk MG............ 6.00 2.70
❑ 469 Len Gabrielson ............ 6.00 2.70
❑ 470 Bob Shaw ................... 6.00 2.70
❑ 471 Rene Lachemann ........ 6.00 2.70
❑ 472 Rookies Pirates ........... 6.00 2.70
John Gelnar
George Spriggs
❑ 473 Jose Santiago .............. 6.00 2.70
❑ 474 Bob Tolan .................... 6.00 2.70
❑ 475 Jim Palmer ................. 80.00 36.00
❑ 476 Tony Perez SP ........... 60.00 27.00
❑ 477 Braves Team.............. 15.00 6.75
❑ 478 Bob Humphreys .......... 6.00 2.70
❑ 479 Gary Bell ..................... 6.00 2.70
❑ 480 Willie McCovey .......... 40.00 18.00
❑ 481 Leo Durocher MG ...... 20.00 9.00
❑ 482 Bill Monbouquette ........ 6.00 2.70
❑ 483 Jim Landis.................... 6.00 2.70
❑ 484 Jerry Adair.................... 6.00 2.70
❑ 485 Tim McCarver ........... 25.00 11.00
❑ 486 Twins Rookies.............. 6.00 2.70
Rich Reese
Bill Whitby
❑ 487 Tommie Reynolds ........ 6.00 2.70
❑ 488 Gerry Arrigo................. 6.00 2.70
❑ 489 Doug Clemens ............ 6.00 2.70
❑ 490 Tony Cloninger ............ 6.00 2.70
❑ 491 Sam Bowens ............... 6.00 2.70
❑ 492 Pittsburgh Pirates ...... 15.00 6.75
Team Card
❑ 493 Phil Ortega .................. 6.00 2.70
❑ 494 Bill Rigney MG ............ 6.00 2.70
❑ 495 Fritz Peterson .............. 6.00 2.70
❑ 496 Orlando McFarlane ...... 6.00 2.70
❑ 497 Ron Campbell .............. 6.00 2.70
❑ 498 Larry Dierker ............. 12.00 5.50
❑ 499 Indians Rookies........... 6.00 2.70
George Culver
Jose Vidal
❑ 500 Juan Marichal ........... 25.00 11.00
❑ 501 Jerry Zimmerman ........ 6.00 2.70
❑ 502 Derrell Griffith ............. 6.00 2.70
❑ 503 Los Angeles Dodgers 20.00 9.00
Team Card
❑ 504 Orlando Martinez.......... 6.00 2.70
❑ 505 Tommy Helms........... 12.00 5.50
❑ 506 Smoky Burgess ............ 6.00 2.70
❑ 507 Orioles Rookies........... 6.00 2.70
Ed Barnowski
Larry Haney RC
❑ 508 Dick Hall ..................... 6.00 2.70
❑ 509 Jim King ...................... 6.00 2.70
❑ 510 Bill Mazeroski ........... 20.00 9.00
❑ 511 Don Wert...................... 6.00 2.70
❑ 512 Red Schoendienst MG 25.00 11.00
❑ 513 Marcelino Lopez .......... 6.00 2.70
❑ 514 John Werhas............... 6.00 2.70
❑ 515 Bert Campaneris ....... 12.00 5.50
❑ 516 Giants Team ............. 15.00 6.75
❑ 517 Fred Talbot ............... 12.00 5.50
❑ 518 Denis Menke ............... 6.00 2.70
❑ 519 Ted Davidson .............. 6.00 2.70
❑ 520 Max Alvis..................... 6.00 2.70
❑ 521 Bird Bombers ........... 12.00 5.50
Boog Powell
Curt Blefary
❑ 522 John Stephenson ........ 6.00 2.70
❑ 523 Jim Merritt ................... 6.00 2.70
❑ 524 Felix Mantilla .............. 6.00 2.70
❑ 525 Ron Hunt..................... 6.00 2.70
❑ 526 Tigers Rookies ............ 6.00 2.70
Pat Dobson RC
George Korince
(See 67T-72)
❑ 527 Dennis Ribant .............. 6.00 2.70
❑ 528 Rico Petrocelli ........... 20.00 9.00
❑ 529 Gary Wagner................ 6.00 2.70
❑ 530 Felipe Alou ............... 12.00 5.50
❑ 531 Brooks Robinson CL .. 14.00 2.80
❑ 532 Jim Hicks..................... 6.00 2.70
❑ 533 Jack Fisher .................. 6.00 2.70
❑ 534 Hank Bauer MG DP .... 9.00 4.00
❑ 535 Donn Clendenon ....... 25.00 11.00
❑ 536 Cubs Rookies ............ 50.00 22.00
Joe Niekro RC
Paul Popovich
❑ 537 Chuck Estrada DP........ 9.00 4.00
❑ 538 J.C. Martin................ 16.00 7.25
❑ 539 Dick Egan DP ............. 9.00 4.00
❑ 540 Norm Cash ............... 50.00 22.00
❑ 541 Joe Gibbon ............... 16.00 7.25
❑ 542 Athletics Rookies DP.. 15.00 6.75
Rick Monday RC
Tony Pierce
❑ 543 Dan Schneider .......... 16.00 7.25
❑ 544 Cleveland Indians ...... 30.00 13.50
Team Card
❑ 545 Jim Grant.................. 25.00 11.00
❑ 546 Woody Woodward...... 25.00 11.00
❑ 547 Red Sox Rookies DP .. 9.00 4.00
Russ Gibson
Bill Rohr
❑ 548 Tony Gonzalez DP ...... 9.00 4.00
❑ 549 Jack Sanford ............ 16.00 7.25
❑ 550 Vada Pinson DP ....... 10.00 4.50
❑ 551 Doug Camilli DP .......... 9.00 4.00
❑ 552 Ted Savage............... 25.00 11.00
❑ 553 Yankees Rookies ...... 40.00 18.00
Mike Hegan RC
Thad Tillotson
❑ 554 Andre Rodgers DP ...... 9.00 4.00
❑ 555 Don Cardwell............. 25.00 11.00
❑ 556 Al Weis DP .................. 9.00 4.00
❑ 557 Al Ferrara ................. 25.00 11.00
❑ 558 Orioles Rookies......... 50.00 22.00
Mark Belanger RC
Bill Dillman
❑ 559 Dick Tracewski DP ...... 9.00 4.00
❑ 560 Jim Bunning ............. 60.00 27.00
❑ 561 Sandy Alomar ........... 40.00 18.00
❑ 562 Steve Blass DP ............ 9.00 4.00
❑ 563 Joe Adcock ............... 40.00 18.00
❑ 564 Astros Rookies DP ...... 9.00 4.00
Alonzo Harris
Aaron Pointer
❑ 565 Lew Krausse ............. 25.00 11.00
❑ 566 Gary Geiger DP........... 9.00 4.00
❑ 567 Steve Hamilton ......... 40.00 18.00
❑ 568 John Sullivan............. 40.00 18.00
❑ 569 AL Rookies DP ........ 200.00 90.00
Rod Carew RC !
Hank Allen
❑ 570 Maury Wills .............. 90.00 40.00
❑ 571 Larry Sherry ............. 25.00 11.00
❑ 572 Don Demeter............. 25.00 11.00
❑ 573 Chicago White Sox .... 30.00 13.50
Team Card UER
(Indians team
stats on back)
❑ 574 Jerry Duchek ............. 25.00 11.00
❑ 575 Dave Boswell ............ 16.00 7.25
❑ 576 NL Rookies ............... 40.00 18.00
Ramon Hernandez
Norm Gigon RC
❑ 577 Bill Short ................... 16.00 7.25
❑ 578 John Boccabella ........ 16.00 7.25
❑ 579 Bill Henry.................. 16.00 7.25
❑ 580 Rocky Colavito ....... 125.00 55.00
❑ 581 Mets Rookies .......... 500.00 220.00
Bill Denehy
Tom Seaver RC
❑ 582 Jim Owens DP ............ 9.00 4.00
❑ 583 Ray Barker ............... 40.00 18.00
❑ 584 Jimmy Piersall ........... 40.00 18.00
❑ 585 Wally Bunker............. 25.00 11.00
❑ 586 Manny Jimenez......... 16.00 7.25
❑ 587 NL Rookies ............... 40.00 18.00
Don Shaw
Gary Sutherland RC
❑ 588 Johnny Klippstein DP .. 9.00 4.00
❑ 589 Dave Ricketts DP ....... 9.00 4.00
❑ 590 Pete Richert ............. 16.00 7.25
❑ 591 Ty Cline.................... 25.00 11.00
❑ 592 NL Rookies ............... 25.00 11.00
Jim Shellenback
Ron Willis RC
❑ 593 Wes Westrum MG...... 50.00 22.00
❑ 594 Dan Osinski............... 40.00 18.00
❑ 595 Cookie Rojas............. 25.00 11.00
❑ 596 Galen Cisco DP........... 9.00 4.00
❑ 597 Ted Abernathy........... 16.00 7.25
❑ 598 White Sox Rookies .... 25.00 11.00
Walt Williams
Ed Stroud
❑ 599 Bob Duliba DP............. 9.00 4.00
❑ 600 Brooks Robinson .... 250.00 110.00
❑ 601 Bill Bryan DP .............. 9.00 4.00
❑ 602 Juan Pizarro ............. 40.00 18.00
❑ 603 Athletics Rookies....... 25.00 11.00
Tim Talton
Ramon Webster
❑ 604 Red Sox Team ........ 125.00 55.00
❑ 605 Mike Shannon ........... 50.00 22.00
❑ 606 Ron Taylor................ 25.00 11.00

| | | |
|---|---|---|
| ❑ 607 Mickey Stanley | 50.00 | 22.00 |
| ❑ 608 Cubs Rookies DP | 9.00 | 4.00 |
| Rich Nye | | |
| John Upham | | |
| ❑ 609 Tommy John | 80.00 | 27.00 |

## 1968 Topps

| | NRMT | VG-E |
|---|---|---|
| COMPLETE SET (598) | 3000.00 | 1350.00 |
| COMMON CARD (1-457) | 1.75 | .80 |
| COMMON CARD (458-598) | 3.50 | 1.55 |
| WRAPPER (5-CENT) | 25.00 | 11.00 |
| ❑ 1 NL Batting Leaders | 30.00 | 12.00 |
| Roberto Clemente | | |
| Tony Gonzalez | | |
| Matty Alou | | |
| ❑ 2 AL Batting Leaders | 14.00 | 6.25 |
| Carl Yastrzemski | | |
| Frank Robinson | | |
| Al Kaline | | |
| ❑ 3 NL RBI Leaders | 20.00 | 9.00 |
| Orlando Cepeda | | |
| Roberto Clemente | | |
| Hank Aaron | | |
| ❑ 4 AL RBI Leaders | 14.00 | 6.25 |
| Carl Yastrzemski | | |
| Harmon Killebrew | | |
| Frank Robinson | | |
| ❑ 5 NL Home Run Leaders | 8.00 | 3.60 |
| Hank Aaron | | |
| Jim Wynn | | |
| Ron Santo | | |
| Willie McCovey | | |
| ❑ 6 AL Home Run Leaders | 8.00 | 3.60 |
| Carl Yastrzemski | | |
| Harmon Killebrew | | |
| Frank Howard | | |
| ❑ 7 NL ERA Leaders | 4.00 | 1.80 |
| Phil Niekro | | |
| Jim Bunning | | |
| Chris Short | | |
| ❑ 8 AL ERA Leaders | 4.00 | 1.80 |
| Joel Horlen | | |
| Gary Peters | | |
| Sonny Siebert | | |
| ❑ 9 NL Pitching Leaders | 5.00 | 2.20 |
| Mike McCormick | | |
| Ferguson Jenkins | | |
| Jim Bunning | | |
| Claude Osteen | | |
| ❑ 10A AL Pitching Leaders | 5.00 | 2.20 |
| Jim Lonborg ERR | | |
| (Misspelled Lonberg | | |
| on card back) | | |
| Earl Wilson | | |
| Dean Chance | | |
| ❑ 10B AL Pitching Leaders | 5.00 | 2.20 |
| Jim Lonborg COR | | |
| Earl Wilson | | |
| Dean Chance | | |
| ❑ 11 NL Strikeout Leaders | 6.00 | 2.70 |
| Jim Bunning | | |
| Ferguson Jenkins | | |
| Gaylord Perry | | |
| ❑ 12 AL Strikeout Leaders | 4.00 | 1.80 |
| Jim Lonborg UER | | |
| (Misspelled Longberg | | |
| on card back) | | |
| Sam McDowell | | |
| Dean Chance | | |
| ❑ 13 Chuck Hartenstein | 1.75 | .80 |
| ❑ 14 Jerry McNertney | 1.75 | .80 |
| ❑ 15 Ron Hunt | 1.75 | .80 |
| ❑ 16 Indians Rookies | 6.00 | 2.70 |
| Lou Piniella | | |
| Richie Scheinblum | | |
| ❑ 17 Dick Hall | 1.75 | .80 |
| ❑ 18 Mike Hershberger | 1.75 | .80 |
| ❑ 19 Juan Pizarro | 1.75 | .80 |
| ❑ 20 Brooks Robinson | 25.00 | 11.00 |
| ❑ 21 Ron Davis | 1.75 | .80 |
| ❑ 22 Pat Dobson | 4.00 | 1.80 |
| ❑ 23 Chico Cardenas | 4.00 | 1.80 |
| ❑ 24 Bobby Locke | 1.75 | .80 |
| ❑ 25 Julian Javier | 4.00 | 1.80 |
| ❑ 26 Darrell Brandon | 1.75 | .80 |
| ❑ 27 Gil Hodges MG | 8.00 | 3.60 |
| ❑ 28 Ted Uhlaender | 1.75 | .80 |
| ❑ 29 Joe Verbanic | 1.75 | .80 |
| ❑ 30 Joe Torre | 6.00 | 2.70 |
| ❑ 31 Ed Stroud | 1.75 | .80 |
| ❑ 32 Joe Gibbon | 1.75 | .80 |
| ❑ 33 Pete Ward | 1.75 | .80 |
| ❑ 34 Al Ferrara | 1.75 | .80 |
| ❑ 35 Steve Hargan | 1.75 | .80 |
| ❑ 36 Pirates Rookies | 4.00 | 1.80 |
| Bob Moose | | |
| Bob Robertson | | |
| ❑ 37 Billy Williams | 8.00 | 3.60 |
| ❑ 38 Tony Pierce | 1.75 | .80 |
| ❑ 39 Cookie Rojas | 4.00 | 1.80 |
| ❑ 40 Denny McLain | 8.00 | 3.60 |
| ❑ 41 Julio Gotay | 1.75 | .80 |
| ❑ 42 Larry Haney | 1.75 | .80 |
| ❑ 43 Gary Bell | 1.75 | .80 |
| ❑ 44 Frank Kostro | 1.75 | .80 |
| ❑ 45 Tom Seaver | 50.00 | 22.00 |
| ❑ 46 Dave Ricketts | 1.75 | .80 |
| ❑ 47 Ralph Houk MG | 4.00 | 1.80 |
| ❑ 48 Ted Davidson | 1.75 | .80 |
| ❑ 49A Eddie Brinkman | 1.75 | .80 |
| (White team name) | | |
| ❑ 49B Eddie Brinkman | 50.00 | 22.00 |
| (Yellow team name) | | |
| ❑ 50 Willie Mays | 60.00 | 27.00 |
| ❑ 51 Bob Locker | 1.75 | .80 |
| ❑ 52 Hawk Taylor | 1.75 | .80 |
| ❑ 53 Gene Alley | 4.00 | 1.80 |
| ❑ 54 Stan Williams | 4.00 | 1.80 |
| ❑ 55 Felipe Alou | 4.00 | 1.80 |
| ❑ 56 Orioles Rookies | 1.75 | .80 |
| Dave Leonhard | | |
| Dave May RC | | |
| ❑ 57 Dan Schneider | 1.75 | .80 |
| ❑ 58 Eddie Mathews | 15.00 | 6.75 |
| ❑ 59 Don Lock | 1.75 | .80 |
| ❑ 60 Ken Holtzman | 4.00 | 1.80 |
| ❑ 61 Reggie Smith | 4.00 | 1.80 |
| ❑ 62 Chuck Dobson | 1.75 | .80 |
| ❑ 63 Dick Kenworthy | 1.75 | .80 |
| ❑ 64 Jim Merritt | 1.75 | .80 |
| ❑ 65 John Roseboro | 4.00 | 1.80 |
| ❑ 66A Casey Cox | 1.75 | .80 |
| (White team name) | | |
| ❑ 66B Casey Cox | 100.00 | 45.00 |
| (Yellow team name) | | |
| ❑ 67 Jim Kaat CL | 6.00 | 1.20 |
| ❑ 68 Ron Willis | 1.75 | .80 |
| ❑ 69 Tom Tresh | 4.00 | 1.80 |
| ❑ 70 Bob Veale | 4.00 | 1.80 |
| ❑ 71 Vern Fuller | 1.75 | .80 |
| ❑ 72 Tommy John | 6.00 | 2.70 |
| ❑ 73 Jim Ray Hart | 4.00 | 1.80 |
| ❑ 74 Milt Pappas | 4.00 | 1.80 |
| ❑ 75 Don Mincher | 1.75 | .80 |
| ❑ 76 Braves Rookies | 4.00 | 1.80 |
| Jim Britton | | |
| Ron Reed | | |
| ❑ 77 Don Wilson | 4.00 | 1.80 |
| ❑ 78 Jim Northrup | 6.00 | 2.70 |
| ❑ 79 Ted Kubiak | 1.75 | .80 |
| ❑ 80 Rod Carew | 50.00 | 22.00 |
| ❑ 81 Larry Jackson | 1.75 | .80 |
| ❑ 82 Sam Bowens | 1.75 | .80 |
| ❑ 83 John Stephenson | 1.75 | .80 |
| ❑ 84 Bob Tolan | 4.00 | 1.80 |
| ❑ 85 Gaylord Perry | 8.00 | 3.60 |
| ❑ 86 Willie Stargell | 8.00 | 3.60 |
| ❑ 87 Dick Williams MG | 4.00 | 1.80 |
| ❑ 88 Phil Regan | 4.00 | 1.80 |
| ❑ 89 Jake Gibbs | 4.00 | 1.80 |
| ❑ 90 Vada Pinson | 4.00 | 1.80 |
| ❑ 91 Jim Ollom | 1.75 | .80 |
| ❑ 92 Ed Kranepool | 4.00 | 1.80 |
| ❑ 93 Tony Cloninger | 1.75 | .80 |
| ❑ 94 Lee Maye | 1.75 | .80 |
| ❑ 95 Bob Aspromonte | 1.75 | .80 |
| ❑ 96 Senator Rookies | 1.75 | .80 |
| Frank Coggins | | |
| Dick Nold | | |
| ❑ 97 Tom Phoebus | 1.75 | .80 |
| ❑ 98 Gary Sutherland | 1.75 | .80 |
| ❑ 99 Rocky Colavito | 8.00 | 3.60 |
| ❑ 100 Bob Gibson | 25.00 | 11.00 |
| ❑ 101 Glenn Beckert | 4.00 | 1.80 |
| ❑ 102 Jose Cardenal | 4.00 | 1.80 |
| ❑ 103 Don Sutton | 8.00 | 3.60 |
| ❑ 104 Dick Dietz | 1.75 | .80 |
| ❑ 105 Al Downing | 4.00 | 1.80 |
| ❑ 106 Dalton Jones | 1.75 | .80 |
| ❑ 107A Juan Marichal CL | 6.00 | 1.20 |
| Tan wide mesh | | |
| ❑ 107B Juan Marichal CL | 6.00 | 1.20 |
| Brown fine mesh | | |
| ❑ 108 Don Pavletich | 1.75 | .80 |
| ❑ 109 Bert Campaneris | 4.00 | 1.80 |
| ❑ 110 Hank Aaron | 60.00 | 27.00 |
| ❑ 111 Rich Reese | 1.75 | .80 |
| ❑ 112 Woody Fryman | 1.75 | .80 |
| ❑ 113 Tigers Rookies | 4.00 | 1.80 |
| Tom Matchick | | |
| Daryl Patterson | | |
| ❑ 114 Ron Swoboda | 4.00 | 1.80 |
| ❑ 115 Sam McDowell | 4.00 | 1.80 |
| ❑ 116 Ken McMullen | 1.75 | .80 |
| ❑ 117 Larry Jaster | 1.75 | .80 |
| ❑ 118 Mark Belanger | 4.00 | 1.80 |
| ❑ 119 Ted Savage | 1.75 | .80 |
| ❑ 120 Mel Stottlemyre | 4.00 | 1.80 |
| ❑ 121 Jimmie Hall | 1.75 | .80 |
| ❑ 122 Gene Mauch MG | 4.00 | 1.80 |
| ❑ 123 Jose Santiago | 1.75 | .80 |
| ❑ 124 Nate Oliver | 1.75 | .80 |
| ❑ 125 Joel Horlen | 1.75 | .80 |
| ❑ 126 Bobby Etheridge | 1.75 | .80 |
| ❑ 127 Paul Lindblad | 1.75 | .80 |
| ❑ 128 Astros Rookies | 1.75 | .80 |
| Tom Dukes | | |
| Alonzo Harris | | |
| ❑ 129 Mickey Stanley | 6.00 | 2.70 |
| ❑ 130 Tony Perez | 8.00 | 3.60 |
| ❑ 131 Frank Bertaina | 1.75 | .80 |
| ❑ 132 Bud Harrelson | 4.00 | 1.80 |
| ❑ 133 Fred Whitfield | 1.75 | .80 |
| ❑ 134 Pat Jarvis | 1.75 | .80 |
| ❑ 135 Paul Blair | 4.00 | 1.80 |
| ❑ 136 Randy Hundley | 4.00 | 1.80 |
| ❑ 137 Twins Team | 4.00 | 1.80 |
| ❑ 138 Ruben Amaro | 1.75 | .80 |
| ❑ 139 Chris Short | 4.00 | 1.80 |
| ❑ 140 Tony Conigliaro | 8.00 | 3.60 |
| ❑ 141 Dal Maxvill | 1.75 | .80 |
| ❑ 142 White Sox Rookies | 1.75 | .80 |
| Buddy Bradford | | |
| Bill Voss | | |
| ❑ 143 Pete Cimino | 1.75 | .80 |
| ❑ 144 Joe Morgan | 12.00 | 5.50 |
| ❑ 145 Don Drysdale | 12.00 | 5.50 |
| ❑ 146 Sal Bando | 4.00 | 1.80 |
| ❑ 147 Frank Linzy | 1.75 | .80 |
| ❑ 148 Dave Bristol MG | 1.75 | .80 |
| ❑ 149 Bob Saverine | 1.75 | .80 |
| ❑ 150 Roberto Clemente | 75.00 | 34.00 |
| ❑ 151 Lou Brock WS | 10.00 | 4.50 |
| ❑ 152 Carl Yastrzemski WS | 10.00 | 4.50 |
| ❑ 153 Nellie Briles WS | 5.00 | 2.20 |
| ❑ 154 Bob Gibson WS | 10.00 | 4.50 |
| ❑ 155 Jim Lonborg WS | 5.00 | 2.20 |

❑ 156 Rico Petrocelli WS ...... 5.00 2.20
❑ 157 World Series Game 7 .. 5.00 2.20
St. Louis wins it
❑ 158 World Series Summary 5.00 2.20
Cardinals celebrate
❑ 159 Don Kessinger............. 4.00 1.80
❑ 160 Earl Wilson ................. 4.00 1.80
❑ 161 Norm Miller ................. 1.75 .80
❑ 162 Cards Rookies............. 4.00 1.80
Hal Gilson
Mike Torrez
❑ 163 Gene Brabender .......... 1.75 .80
❑ 164 Ramon Webster .......... 1.75 .80
❑ 165 Tony Oliva.................. 6.00 2.70
❑ 166 Claude Raymond ........ 1.75 .80
❑ 167 Elston Howard............ 6.00 2.70
❑ 168 Dodgers Team ........... 4.00 1.80
❑ 169 Bob Bolin.................... 1.75 .80
❑ 170 Jim Fregosi ................. 4.00 1.80
❑ 171 Don Nottebart ............. 1.75 .80
❑ 172 Walt Williams.............. 1.75 .80
❑ 173 John Boozer ............... 1.75 .80
❑ 174 Bob Tillman ................ 1.75 .80
❑ 175 Maury Wills ................ 6.00 2.70
❑ 176 Bob Allen.................... 1.75 .80
❑ 177 Mets Rookies .......... 800.00 350.00
Jerry Koosman
Nolan Ryan RC !
❑ 178 Don Wert..................... 4.00 1.80
❑ 179 Bill Stoneman ............. 1.75 .80
❑ 180 Curt Flood .................. 6.00 2.70
❑ 181 Jerry Zimmerman ....... 1.75 .80
❑ 182 Dave Giusti ................ 1.75 .80
❑ 183 Bob Kennedy MG ....... 4.00 1.80
❑ 184 Lou Johnson .............. 4.00 1.80
❑ 185 Tom Haller................... 1.75 .80
❑ 186 Eddie Watt................... 1.75 .80
❑ 187 Sonny Jackson ........... 1.75 .80
❑ 188 Cap Peterson ............. 1.75 .80
❑ 189 Bill Landis .................. 1.75 .80
❑ 190 Bill White .................... 4.00 1.80
❑ 191 Dan Frisella ................ 1.75 .80
❑ 192A Carl Yastrzemski CL.. 8.00 1.60
Special Baseball Playing Card
❑ 192B Carl Yastrzemski CL.. 8.00 1.60
Special Baseball
Playing Card Game
❑ 193 Jack Hamilton ............. 1.75 .80
❑ 194 Don Buford ................. 1.75 .80
❑ 195 Joe Pepitone .............. 4.00 1.80
❑ 196 Gary Nolan ................. 4.00 1.80
❑ 197 Larry Brown................. 1.75 .80
❑ 198 Roy Face .................... 4.00 1.80
❑ 199 A's Rookies ................ 1.75 .80
Roberto Rodriquez
Darrell Osteen
❑ 200 Orlando Cepeda .......... 8.00 3.60
❑ 201 Mike Marshall RC ....... 4.00 1.80
❑ 202 Adolfo Phillips ............ 1.75 .80
❑ 203 Dick Kelley ................. 1.75 .80
❑ 204 Andy Etchebarren ....... 1.75 .80
❑ 205 Juan Marichal ............ 8.00 3.60
❑ 206 Cal Ermer MG............. 1.75 .80
❑ 207 Carroll Sembera ......... 1.75 .80
❑ 208 Willie Davis ................ 4.00 1.80
❑ 209 Tim Cullen................... 1.75 .80
❑ 210 Gary Peters................. 1.75 .80
❑ 211 J.C. Martin.................. 1.75 .80
❑ 212 Dave Morehead........... 1.75 .80
❑ 213 Chico Ruiz................... 1.75 .80
❑ 214 Yankees Rookies ....... 4.00 1.80
Stan Bahnsen
Frank Fernandez
❑ 215 Jim Bunning ............... 8.00 3.60
❑ 216 Bubba Morton ............. 1.75 .80
❑ 217 Dick Farrell ................. 1.75 .80
❑ 218 Ken Suarez ................ 1.75 .80
❑ 219 Rob Gardner ............... 1.75 .80
❑ 220 Harmon Killebrew ...... 15.00 6.75
❑ 221 Braves Team............... 4.00 1.80
❑ 222 Jim Hardin................... 1.75 .80
❑ 223 Ollie Brown ................. 1.75 .80
❑ 224 Jack Aker .................... 1.75 .80
❑ 225 Richie Allen ................ 6.00 2.70
❑ 226 Jimmie Price .............. 1.75 .80
❑ 227 Joe Hoerner ............... 1.75 .80
❑ 228 Dodgers Rookies......... 4.00 1.80
Jack Billingham
Jim Fairey
❑ 229 Fred Klages................. 1.75 .80
❑ 230 Pete Rose ................ 50.00 22.00
❑ 231 Dave Baldwin ............. 1.75 .80
❑ 232 Denis Menke .............. 1.75 .80
❑ 233 George Scott............... 4.00 1.80
❑ 234 Bill Monbouquette ....... 1.75 .80
❑ 235 Ron Santo .................. 8.00 3.60
❑ 236 Tug McGraw ............... 6.00 2.70
❑ 237 Alvin Dark MG............. 4.00 1.80
❑ 238 Tom Satriano............... 1.75 .80
❑ 239 Bill Henry.................... 1.75 .80
❑ 240 Al Kaline ................... 25.00 11.00
❑ 241 Felix Millan ................ 1.75 .80
❑ 242 Moe Drabowsky ......... 4.00 1.80
❑ 243 Rich Rollins ................ 1.75 .80
❑ 244 John Donaldson ......... 1.75 .80
❑ 245 Tony Gonzalez ........... 1.75 .80
❑ 246 Fritz Peterson ............. 4.00 1.80
❑ 247 Reds Rookies .......... 125.00 55.00
Johnny Bench RC
Ron Tompkins
❑ 248 Fred Valentine............. 1.75 .80
❑ 249 Bill Singer .................. 1.75 .80
❑ 250 Carl Yastrzemski ....... 30.00 13.50
❑ 251 Manny Sanguillen RC .. 6.00 2.70
❑ 252 Angels Team............... 4.00 1.80
❑ 253 Dick Hughes ............... 1.75 .80
❑ 254 Cleon Jones ............... 4.00 1.80
❑ 255 Dean Chance ............. 4.00 1.80
❑ 256 Norm Cash ................ 6.00 2.70
❑ 257 Phil Niekro.................. 8.00 3.60
❑ 258 Cubs Rookies ............ 1.75 .80
Jose Arcia
Bill Schlesinger
❑ 259 Ken Boyer .................. 6.00 2.70
❑ 260 Jim Wynn ................... 4.00 1.80
❑ 261 Dave Duncan .............. 4.00 1.80
❑ 262 Rick Wise ................... 4.00 1.80
❑ 263 Horace Clarke............. 4.00 1.80
❑ 264 Ted Abernathy............. 1.75 .80
❑ 265 Tommy Davis ............. 4.00 1.80
❑ 266 Paul Popovich............. 1.75 .80
❑ 267 Herman Franks MG...... 1.75 .80
❑ 268 Bob Humphreys .......... 1.75 .80
❑ 269 Bob Tiefenauer ........... 1.75 .80
❑ 270 Matty Alou .................. 4.00 1.80
❑ 271 Bobby Knoop............... 1.75 .80
❑ 272 Ray Culp .................... 1.75 .80
❑ 273 Dave Johnson............. 4.00 1.80
❑ 274 Mike Cuellar ............... 4.00 1.80
❑ 275 Tim McCarver ............. 6.00 2.70
❑ 276 Jim Roland ................. 1.75 .80
❑ 277 Jerry Buchek............... 1.75 .80
❑ 278 Orlando Cepeda CL .... 6.00 1.20
❑ 279 Bill Hands ................... 1.75 .80
❑ 280 Mickey Mantle ......... 250.00 110.00
❑ 281 Jim Campanis ............. 1.75 .80
❑ 282 Rick Monday ............... 4.00 1.80
❑ 283 Mel Queen.................. 1.75 .80
❑ 284 Johnny Briggs ............ 1.75 .80
❑ 285 Dick McAuliffe ............ 6.00 2.70
❑ 286 Cecil Upshaw ............. 1.75 .80
❑ 287 White Sox Rookies ...... 1.75 .80
Mickey Abarbanel
Cisco Carlos
❑ 288 Dave Wickersham....... 1.75 .80
❑ 289 Woody Held................ 1.75 .80
❑ 290 Willie McCovey ......... 12.00 5.50
❑ 291 Dick Lines .................. 1.75 .80
❑ 292 Art Shamsky ............... 1.75 .80
❑ 293 Bruce Howard ............. 1.75 .80
❑ 294 Red Schoendienst MG 6.00 2.70
❑ 295 Sonny Siebert ............. 1.75 .80
❑ 296 Byron Browne ............. 1.75 .80
❑ 297 Russ Gibson ............... 1.75 .80
❑ 298 Jim Brewer ................. 1.75 .80
❑ 299 Gene Michael ............. 4.00 1.80
❑ 300 Rusty Staub................ 4.00 1.80
❑ 301 Twins Rookies............. 1.75 .80
George Mitterwald
Rick Renick
❑ 302 Gerry Arrigo................ 1.75 .80
❑ 303 Dick Green ................. 4.00 1.80
❑ 304 Sandy Valdespino ........ 1.75 .80
❑ 305 Minnie Rojas ............... 1.75 .80
❑ 306 Mike Ryan ................... 1.75 .80
❑ 307 John Hiller .................. 4.00 1.80
❑ 308 Pirates Team............... 4.00 1.80
❑ 309 Ken Henderson ........... 1.75 .80
❑ 310 Luis Aparicio ............... 8.00 3.60
❑ 311 Jack Lamabe............... 1.75 .80
❑ 312 Curt Blefary ................ 1.75 .80
❑ 313 Al Weis ....................... 1.75 .80
❑ 314 Red Sox Rookies ....... 1.75 .80
Bill Rohr
George Spriggs
❑ 315 Zoilo Versalles............. 1.75 .80
❑ 316 Steve Barber............... 1.75 .80
❑ 317 Ron Brand................... 1.75 .80
❑ 318 Chico Salmon ............. 1.75 .80
❑ 319 George Culver............. 1.75 .80
❑ 320 Frank Howard ............. 4.00 1.80
❑ 321 Leo Durocher MG ........ 6.00 2.70
❑ 322 Dave Boswell .............. 1.75 .80
❑ 323 Deron Johnson ........... 4.00 1.80
❑ 324 Jim Nash ..................... 1.75 .80
❑ 325 Manny Mota ................ 4.00 1.80
❑ 326 Dennis Ribant .............. 1.75 .80
❑ 327 Tony Taylor................. 4.00 1.80
❑ 328 Angels Rookies ........... 1.75 .80
Chuck Vinson
Jim Weaver
❑ 329 Duane Josephson ........ 1.75 .80
❑ 330 Roger Maris.............. 50.00 22.00
❑ 331 Dan Osinski................. 1.75 .80
❑ 332 Doug Rader................. 4.00 1.80
❑ 333 Ron Herbel ................. 1.75 .80
❑ 334 Orioles Team............... 4.00 1.80
❑ 335 Bob Allison ................. 4.00 1.80
❑ 336 John Purdin................. 1.75 .80
❑ 337 Bill Robinson ............... 4.00 1.80
❑ 338 Bob Johnson ............... 1.75 .80
❑ 339 Rich Nye ..................... 1.75 .80
❑ 340 Max Alvis..................... 1.75 .80
❑ 341 Jim Lemon MG ............ 1.75 .80
❑ 342 Ken Johnson ............... 1.75 .80
❑ 343 Jim Gosger .................. 1.75 .80
❑ 344 Donn Clendenon ......... 4.00 1.80
❑ 345 Bob Hendley ................ 1.75 .80
❑ 346 Jerry Adair ................... 1.75 .80
❑ 347 George Brunet............. 1.75 .80
❑ 348 Phillies Rookies........... 1.75 .80
Larry Colton
Dick Thoenen
❑ 349 Ed Spiezio .................. 4.00 1.80
❑ 350 Hoyt Wilhelm .............. 8.00 3.60
❑ 351 Bob Barton ................. 1.75 .80
❑ 352 Jackie Hernandez ........ 1.75 .80
❑ 353 Mack Jones................. 1.75 .80
❑ 354 Pete Richert ................ 1.75 .80
❑ 355 Ernie Banks ............... 25.00 11.00
❑ 356A Ken Holtzman CL ...... 6.00 1.20
Head centered within circle
❑ 356B Ken Holtzman ........... 6.00 1.20
Head shifted right
within circle
❑ 357 Len Gabrielson ............ 1.75 .80
❑ 358 Mike Epstein ............... 1.75 .80
❑ 359 Joe Moeller ................. 1.75 .80
❑ 360 Willie Horton ............... 6.00 2.70
❑ 361 Harmon Killebrew AS .. 8.00 3.60
❑ 362 Orlando Cepeda AS .... 5.00 2.20
❑ 363 Rod Carew AS ............ 8.00 3.60
❑ 364 Joe Morgan AS ............ 8.00 3.60
❑ 365 Brooks Robinson AS.... 8.00 3.60
❑ 366 Ron Santo AS ............. 5.00 2.20
❑ 367 Jim Fregosi AS ............ 5.00 2.20
❑ 368 Gene Alley AS............. 5.00 2.20
❑ 369 Carl Yastrzemski AS .. 10.00 4.50
❑ 370 Hank Aaron AS ......... 20.00 9.00
❑ 371 Tony Oliva AS ............. 6.00 2.70
❑ 372 Lou Brock AS .............. 8.00 3.60
❑ 373 Frank Robinson AS ..... 8.00 3.60
❑ 374 Bob Clemente AS ...... 30.00 13.50
❑ 375 Bill Freehan AS ........... 5.00 2.20
❑ 376 Tim McCarver AS ........ 3.00 1.35
❑ 377 Joel Horlen AS ............ 5.00 2.20
❑ 378 Bob Gibson AS ............ 8.00 3.60
❑ 379 Gary Peters AS............ 5.00 2.20

❑ 380 Ken Holtzman AS 5.00 2.20
❑ 381 Boog Powell 4.00 1.80
❑ 382 Ramon Hernandez 1.75 .80
❑ 383 Steve Whitaker 1.75 .80
❑ 384 Reds Rookies 6.00 2.70
Bill Henry
Hal McRae RC
❑ 385 Jim Hunter 10.00 4.50
❑ 386 Greg Goossen 1.75 .80
❑ 387 Joe Foy 1.75 .80
❑ 388 Ray Washburn 1.75 .80
❑ 389 Jay Johnstone 4.00 1.80
❑ 390 Bill Mazeroski 6.00 2.70
❑ 391 Bob Priddy 1.75 .80
❑ 392 Grady Hatton MG 1.75 .80
❑ 393 Jim Perry 4.00 1.80
❑ 394 Tommie Aaron 6.00 2.70
❑ 395 Camilo Pascual 4.00 1.80
❑ 396 Bobby Wine 1.75 .80
❑ 397 Vic Davalillo 1.75 .80
❑ 398 Jim Grant 1.75 .80
❑ 399 Ray Oyler 4.00 1.80
❑ 400A Mike McCormick 4.00 1.80
(Yellow letters)
❑ 400B Mike McCormick 150.00 70.00
(Team name in
white letters)
❑ 401 Mets Team 4.00 1.80
❑ 402 Mike Hegan 4.00 1.80
❑ 403 John Buzhardt 1.75 .80
❑ 404 Floyd Robinson 1.75 .80
❑ 405 Tommy Helms 4.00 1.80
❑ 406 Dick Ellsworth 1.75 .80
❑ 407 Gary Kolb 1.75 .80
❑ 408 Steve Carlton 30.00 13.50
❑ 409 Orioles Rookies 1.75 .80
Frank Peters
Ron Stone
❑ 410 Ferguson Jenkins 10.00 4.50
❑ 411 Ron Hansen 1.75 .80
❑ 412 Clay Carroll 4.00 1.80
❑ 413 Tom McCraw 1.75 .80
❑ 414 Mickey Lolich 8.00 3.60
❑ 415 Johnny Callison 4.00 1.80
❑ 416 Bill Rigney MG 1.75 .80
❑ 417 Willie Crawford 1.75 .80
❑ 418 Eddie Fisher 1.75 .80
❑ 419 Jack Hiatt 1.75 .80
❑ 420 Cesar Tovar 1.75 .80
❑ 421 Ron Taylor 1.75 .80
❑ 422 Rene Lachemann 1.75 .80
❑ 423 Fred Gladding 1.75 .80
❑ 424 Chicago White Sox 4.00 1.80
Team Card
❑ 425 Jim Maloney 4.00 1.80
❑ 426 Hank Allen 1.75 .80
❑ 427 Dick Calmus 1.75 .80
❑ 428 Vic Roznovsky 1.75 .80
❑ 429 Tommie Sisk 1.75 .80
❑ 430 Rico Petrocelli 4.00 1.80
❑ 431 Dooley Womack 1.75 .80
❑ 432 Indians Rookies 1.75 .80
Bill Davis
Jose Vidal
❑ 433 Bob Rodgers 1.75 .80
❑ 434 Ricardo Joseph 1.75 .80
❑ 435 Ron Perranoski 4.00 1.80
❑ 436 Hal Lanier 1.75 .80
❑ 437 Don Cardwell 1.75 .80
❑ 438 Lee Thomas 4.00 1.80
❑ 439 Lum Harris MG 1.75 .80
❑ 440 Claude Osteen 4.00 1.80
❑ 441 Alex Johnson 4.00 1.80
❑ 442 Dick Bosman 1.75 .80
❑ 443 Joe Azcue 1.75 .80
❑ 444 Jack Fisher 1.75 .80
❑ 445 Mike Shannon 4.00 1.80
❑ 446 Ron Kline 1.75 .80
❑ 447 Tigers Rookies 4.00 1.80
George Korince
Fred Lasher
❑ 448 Gary Wagner 1.75 .80
❑ 449 Gene Oliver 1.75 .80
❑ 450 Jim Kaat 6.00 2.70
❑ 451 Al Spangler 1.75 .80
❑ 452 Jesus Alou 1.75 .80
❑ 453 Sammy Ellis 1.75 .80
❑ 454A Frank Robinson CL 8.00 1.60
Cap complete within circle
❑ 454B Frank Robinson CL 8.00 1.60
Cap partially within circle
❑ 455 Rico Carty 4.00 1.80
❑ 456 John O'Donoghue 1.75 .80
❑ 457 Jim Lefebvre 4.00 1.80
❑ 458 Lew Krausse 6.00 2.70
❑ 459 Dick Simpson 3.50 1.55
❑ 460 Jim Lonborg 6.00 2.70
❑ 461 Chuck Hiller 3.50 1.55
❑ 462 Barry Moore 3.50 1.55
❑ 463 Jim Schaffer 3.50 1.55
❑ 464 Don McMahon 3.50 1.55
❑ 465 Tommie Agee 10.00 4.50
❑ 466 Bill Dillman 3.50 1.55
❑ 467 Dick Howser 10.00 4.50
❑ 468 Larry Sherry 3.50 1.55
❑ 469 Ty Cline 3.50 1.55
❑ 470 Bill Freehan 10.00 4.50
❑ 471 Orlando Pena 3.50 1.55
❑ 472 Walter Alston MG 6.00 2.70
❑ 473 Al Worthington 3.50 1.55
❑ 474 Paul Schaal 3.50 1.55
❑ 475 Joe Niekro 6.00 2.70
❑ 476 Woody Woodward 3.50 1.55
❑ 477 Philadelphia Phillies 6.00 2.70
Team Card
❑ 478 Dave McNally 6.00 2.70
❑ 479 Phil Gagliano 6.00 2.70
❑ 480 Manager's Dream 80.00 36.00
Tony Oliva
Chico Cardenas
Bob Clemente
❑ 481 John Wyatt 3.50 1.55
❑ 482 Jose Pagan 3.50 1.55
❑ 483 Darold Knowles 3.50 1.55
❑ 484 Phil Roof 3.50 1.55
❑ 485 Ken Berry 6.00 2.70
❑ 486 Cal Koonce 3.50 1.55
❑ 487 Lee May 10.00 4.50
❑ 488 Dick Tracewski 6.00 2.70
❑ 489 Wally Bunker 3.50 1.55
❑ 490 Super Stars 175.00 80.00
Harmon Killebrew
Willie Mays
Mickey Mantle
❑ 491 Denny Lemaster 3.50 1.55
❑ 492 Jeff Torborg 6.00 2.70
❑ 493 Jim McGlothlin 3.50 1.55
❑ 494 Ray Sadecki 3.50 1.55
❑ 495 Leon Wagner 3.50 1.55
❑ 496 Steve Hamilton 6.00 2.70
❑ 497 Cardinals Team 7.00 3.10
❑ 498 Bill Bryan 6.00 2.70
❑ 499 Steve Blass 6.00 2.70
❑ 500 Frank Robinson 30.00 13.50
❑ 501 John Odom 6.00 2.70
❑ 502 Mike Andrews 3.50 1.55
❑ 503 Al Jackson 6.00 2.70
❑ 504 Russ Snyder 3.50 1.55
❑ 505 Joe Sparma 10.00 4.50
❑ 506 Clarence Jones RC 3.50 1.55
❑ 507 Wade Blasingame 3.50 1.55
❑ 508 Duke Sims 3.50 1.55
❑ 509 Dennis Higgins 3.50 1.55
❑ 510 Ron Fairly 10.00 4.50
❑ 511 Bill Kelso 3.50 1.55
❑ 512 Grant Jackson 3.50 1.55
❑ 513 Hank Bauer MG 6.00 2.70
❑ 514 Al McBean 3.50 1.55
❑ 515 Russ Nixon 3.50 1.55
❑ 516 Pete Mikkelsen 3.50 1.55
❑ 517 Diego Segui 6.00 2.70
❑ 518A Clete Boyer CL ERR 12.00 2.40
539 AL Rookies
❑ 518B Clete Boyer CL COR 12.00 2.40
539 ML Rookies
❑ 519 Jerry Stephenson 3.50 1.55
❑ 520 Lou Brock 25.00 11.00
❑ 521 Don Shaw 3.50 1.55
❑ 522 Wayne Causey 3.50 1.55
❑ 523 John Tsitouris 3.50 1.55
❑ 524 Andy Kosco 6.00 2.70
❑ 525 Jim Davenport 3.50 1.55
❑ 526 Bill Denehy 3.50 1.55
❑ 527 Tito Francona 3.50 1.55
❑ 528 Tigers Team 60.00 27.00
❑ 529 Bruce Von Hoff 3.50 1.55
❑ 530 Bird Belters 40.00 18.00
Brooks Robinson
Frank Robinson
❑ 531 Chuck Hinton 3.50 1.55
❑ 532 Luis Tiant 6.00 2.70
❑ 533 Wes Parker 6.00 2.70
❑ 534 Bob Miller 6.00 2.70
❑ 535 Danny Cater 6.00 2.70
❑ 536 Bill Short 3.50 1.55
❑ 537 Norm Siebern 6.00 2.70
❑ 538 Manny Jimenez 6.00 2.70
❑ 539 Major League Rookies 3.50 1.55
Jim Ray
Mike Ferraro
❑ 540 Nelson Briles 6.00 2.70
❑ 541 Sandy Alomar 6.00 2.70
❑ 542 John Boccabella 3.50 1.55
❑ 543 Bob Lee 3.50 1.55
❑ 544 Mayo Smith MG 12.00 5.50
❑ 545 Lindy McDaniel 6.00 2.70
❑ 546 Roy White 6.00 2.70
❑ 547 Dan Coombs 3.50 1.55
❑ 548 Bernie Allen 3.50 1.55
❑ 549 Orioles Rookies 3.50 1.55
Curt Motton
Roger Nelson
❑ 550 Clete Boyer 6.00 2.70
❑ 551 Darrell Sutherland 3.50 1.55
❑ 552 Ed Kirkpatrick 3.50 1.55
❑ 553 Hank Aguirre 3.50 1.55
❑ 554 A's Team 10.00 4.50
❑ 555 Jose Tartabull 6.00 2.70
❑ 556 Dick Selma 3.50 1.55
❑ 557 Frank Quilici 6.00 2.70
❑ 558 Johnny Edwards 3.50 1.55
❑ 559 Pirates Rookies 3.50 1.55
Carl Taylor
Luke Walker
❑ 560 Paul Casanova 3.50 1.55
❑ 561 Lee Elia 3.50 1.55
❑ 562 Jim Bouton 6.00 2.70
❑ 563 Ed Charles 3.50 1.55
❑ 564 Eddie Stanky MG 6.00 2.70
❑ 565 Larry Dierker 6.00 2.70
❑ 566 Ken Harrelson 6.00 2.70
❑ 567 Clay Dalrymple 3.50 1.55
❑ 568 Willie Smith 3.50 1.55
❑ 569 NL Rookies 3.50 1.55
Ivan Murrell
Les Rohr
❑ 570 Rick Reichardt 3.50 1.55
❑ 571 Tony LaRussa 12.00 5.50
❑ 572 Don Bosch 3.50 1.55
❑ 573 Joe Coleman 3.50 1.55
❑ 574 Cincinnati Reds 10.00 4.50
Team Card
❑ 575 Jim Palmer 40.00 18.00
❑ 576 Dave Adlesh 3.50 1.55
❑ 577 Fred Talbot 3.50 1.55
❑ 578 Orlando Martinez 3.50 1.55
❑ 579 NL Rookies 10.00 4.50
Larry Hisle RC
Mike Lum
❑ 580 Bob Bailey 3.50 1.55
❑ 581 Garry Roggenburk 3.50 1.55
❑ 582 Jerry Grote 10.00 4.50
❑ 583 Gates Brown 10.00 4.50
❑ 584 Larry Shepard MG 3.50 1.55
❑ 585 Wilbur Wood 6.00 2.70
❑ 586 Jim Pagliaroni 6.00 2.70
❑ 587 Roger Repoz 3.50 1.55
❑ 588 Dick Schofield 3.50 1.55
❑ 589 Twins Rookies 3.50 1.55
Ron Clark
Moe Ogier
❑ 590 Tommy Harper 6.00 2.70
❑ 591 Dick Nen 3.50 1.55
❑ 592 John Bateman 3.50 1.55
❑ 593 Lee Stange 3.50 1.55
❑ 594 Phil Linz 6.00 2.70
❑ 595 Phil Ortega 3.50 1.55
❑ 596 Charlie Smith 3.50 1.55

❑ 597 Bill McCool .................. 3.50 1.55
❑ 598 Jerry May .................. 6.00 1.85

## 1969 Topps

| | NRMT | VG-E |
|---|---|---|
| COMP. MASTER SET (695) | 5000.00 | 2200.00 |
| COMPLETE SET (664) ...... | 2200.00 | 1000.00 |
| COMMON (1-218/328-512) ...... | 1.50 | .70 |
| COMMON CARD (219-327) ...... | 2.50 | 1.10 |
| COMMON CARD (513-588) ...... | 2.00 | .90 |
| COMMON CARD (589-664) ...... | 3.00 | 1.35 |
| WRAPPER (5-CENT) ............ | 20.00 | 9.00 |

❑ 1 AL Batting Leaders ........ 15.00 5.25
Carl Yastrzemski
Danny Cator
Tony Oliva
❑ 2 NL Batting Leaders .......... 7.00 3.10
Pete Rose
Matty Alou
Felipe Alou
❑ 3 AL RBI Leaders................ 3.50 1.55
Ken Harrelson
Frank Howard
Jim Northrup
❑ 4 NL RBI Leaders................ 6.00 2.70
Willie McCovey
Ron Santo
Billy Williams
❑ 5 AL Home Run Leaders .... 3.50 1.55
Frank Howard
Willie Horton
Ken Harrelson
❑ 6 NL Home Run Leaders .... 6.00 2.70
Willie McCovey
Richie Allen
Ernie Banks
❑ 7 AL ERA Leaders ............. 3.50 1.55
Luis Tiant
Sam McDowell
Dave McNally
❑ 8 NL ERA Leaders ............. 6.00 2.70
Bob Gibson
Bobby Bolin
Bob Veale
❑ 9 AL Pitching Leaders ........ 3.50 1.55
Denny McLain
Dave McNally
Luis Tiant
Mel Stottlemyre
❑ 10 NL Pitching Leaders ...... 7.00 3.10
Juan Marichal
Bob Gibson
Fergie Jenkins
❑ 11 AL Strikeout Leaders...... 3.50 1.55
Sam McDowell
Denny McLain
Luis Tiant
❑ 12 NL Strikeout Leaders .... 4.00 1.80
Bob Gibson
Fergie Jenkins
Bill Singer
❑ 13 Mickey Stanley ................ 2.50 1.10
❑ 14 Al McBean...................... 1.50 .70
❑ 15 Boog Powell .................. 4.00 1.80
❑ 16 Giants Rookies ................ 1.50 .70
Cesar Gutierrez
Rich Robertson
❑ 17 Mike Marshall ................ 2.50 1.10
❑ 18 Dick Schofield ................ 1.50 .70
❑ 19 Ken Suarez .................... 1.50 .70
❑ 20 Ernie Banks.................. 20.00 9.00
❑ 21 Jose Santiago ................ 1.50 .70
❑ 22 Jesus Alou...................... 2.50 1.10
❑ 23 Lew Krausse .................. 1.50 .70
❑ 24 Walt Alston MG .............. 4.00 1.80
❑ 25 Roy White ...................... 2.50 1.10
❑ 26 Clay Carroll .................... 2.50 1.10
❑ 27 Bernie Allen.................... 1.50 .70
❑ 28 Mike Ryan........................ 1.50 .70
❑ 29 Dave Morehead................ 1.50 .70
❑ 30 Bob Allison...................... 2.50 1.10
❑ 31 Mets Rookies .................. 2.50 1.10
Gary Gentry RC
Amos Otis
❑ 32 Sammy Ellis .................... 1.50 .70
❑ 33 Wayne Causey ................ 1.50 .70
❑ 34 Gary Peters...................... 1.50 .70
❑ 35 Joe Morgan.................... 10.00 4.50
❑ 36 Luke Walker .................... 1.50 .70
❑ 37 Curt Motton .................... 1.50 .70
❑ 38 Zoilo Versalles................ 2.50 1.10
❑ 39 Dick Hughes .................. 1.50 .70
❑ 40 Mayo Smith MG .............. 1.50 .70
❑ 41 Bob Barton .................... 1.50 .70
❑ 42 Tommy Harper ................ 2.50 1.10
❑ 43 Joe Niekro...................... 2.50 1.10
❑ 44 Danny Cater .................... 1.50 .70
❑ 45 Maury Wills .................... 2.50 1.10
❑ 46 Fritz Peterson ................ 2.50 1.10
❑ 47A Paul Popovich .............. 1.50 .70
(No helmet emblem)
❑ 47B Paul Popovich.............. 25.00 11.00
(C emblem on helmet)
❑ 48 Brant Alyea .................... 1.50 .70
❑ 49A Royals Rookies ERR .. 1.50 .70
Steve Jones
E. Rodriquez
❑ 49B Royals Rookies COR .. 1.50 .70
Steve Jones
E. Rodriguez
❑ 50 Roberto Clemente UER 60.00 27.00
Bats Right listed twice
❑ 51 Woody Fryman ................ 1.50 .70
❑ 52 Mike Andrews .................. 1.50 .70
❑ 53 Sonny Jackson ................ 1.50 .70
❑ 54 Cisco Carlos .................... 1.50 .70
❑ 55 Jerry Grote ...................... 2.50 1.10
❑ 56 Rich Reese ...................... 1.50 .70
❑ 57 Denny McLain CL ............ 6.00 1.20
❑ 58 Fred Gladding .................. 1.50 .70
❑ 59 Jay Johnstone.................. 2.50 1.10
❑ 60 Nelson Briles.................... 2.50 1.10
❑ 61 Jimmie Hall ...................... 1.50 .70
❑ 62 Chico Salmon .................. 1.50 .70
❑ 63 Jim Hickman .................... 2.50 1.10
❑ 64 Bill Monbouquette ............ 1.50 .70
❑ 65 Willie Davis .................... 2.50 1.10
❑ 66 Orioles Rookies................ 1.50 .70
Mike Adamson
Merv Rettenmund
❑ 67 Bill Stoneman .................. 2.50 1.10
❑ 68 Dave Duncan .................. 2.50 1.10
❑ 69 Steve Hamilton ................ 2.50 1.10
❑ 70 Tommy Helms.................. 2.50 1.10
❑ 71 Steve Whitaker ................ 2.50 1.10
❑ 72 Ron Taylor........................ 1.50 .70
❑ 73 Johnny Briggs .................. 1.50 .70
❑ 74 Preston Gomez MG ........ 2.50 1.10
❑ 75 Luis Aparicio .................. 6.00 2.70
❑ 76 Norm Miller .................... 1.50 .70
❑ 77A Ron Perranoski.............. 2.50 1.10
(No emblem on cap)
❑ 77B Ron Perranoski............ 25.00 11.00
(LA on cap)
❑ 78 Tom Satriano.................... 1.50 .70
❑ 79 Milt Pappas .................... 2.50 1.10
❑ 80 Norm Cash ...................... 2.50 1.10
❑ 81 Mel Queen........................ 1.50 .70
❑ 82 Pirates Rookies ................ 8.00 3.60
Rich Hebner
Al Oliver RC
❑ 83 Mike Ferraro .................... 2.50 1.10
❑ 84 Bob Humphreys .............. 1.50 .70
❑ 85 Lou Brock ...................... 20.00 9.00
❑ 86 Pete Richert .................... 1.50 .70
❑ 87 Horace Clarke.................. 2.50 1.10
❑ 88 Rich Nye .......................... 1.50 .70
❑ 89 Russ Gibson .................... 1.50 .70
❑ 90 Jerry Koosman ................ 2.50 1.10
❑ 91 Alvin Dark MG .................. 2.50 1.10
❑ 92 Jack Billingham ................ 2.50 1.10
❑ 93 Joe Foy ............................ 2.50 1.10
❑ 94 Hank Aguirre .................... 1.50 .70
❑ 95 Johnny Bench ................ 50.00 22.00
❑ 96 Denny Lemaster .............. 1.50 .70
❑ 97 Buddy Bradford ................ 1.50 .70
❑ 98 Dave Giusti ...................... 1.50 .70
❑ 99A Twins Rookies ............ 15.00 6.75
Danny Morris
Graig Nettles RC
(No loop)
❑ 99B Twins Rookies ............ 15.00 6.75
Danny Morris
Graig Nettles RC
(Errant loop in
upper left corner
of obverse)
❑ 100 Hank Aaron .................. 40.00 18.00
❑ 101 Daryl Patterson .............. 1.50 .70
❑ 102 Jim Davenport ................ 1.50 .70
❑ 103 Roger Repoz .................. 1.50 .70
❑ 104 Steve Blass .................... 2.50 1.10
❑ 105 Rick Monday .................. 2.50 1.10
❑ 106 Jim Hannan .................... 1.50 .70
❑ 107A Bob Gibson CL ERR .. 6.00 1.20
161 Jim Purdin
❑ 107B Bob Gibson CL COR 7.50 1.50
161 John Purdin
❑ 108 Tony Taylor .................... 2.50 1.10
❑ 109 Jim Lonborg .................. 2.50 1.10
❑ 110 Mike Shannon ................ 2.50 1.10
❑ 111 Johnny Morris ................ 1.50 .70
❑ 112 J.C. Martin...................... 2.50 1.10
❑ 113 Dave May ...................... 1.50 .70
❑ 114 Yankees Rookies .......... 2.50 1.10
Alan Closter
John Cumberland
❑ 115 Bill Hands ...................... 1.50 .70
❑ 116 Chuck Harrison .............. 1.50 .70
❑ 117 Jim Fairey ...................... 1.50 .70
❑ 118 Stan Williams ................ 1.50 .70
❑ 119 Doug Rader.................... 2.50 1.10
❑ 120 Pete Rose .................... 25.00 11.00
❑ 121 Joe Grzenda .................. 1.50 .70
❑ 122 Ron Fairly ...................... 2.50 1.10
❑ 123 Wilbur Wood .................. 2.50 1.10
❑ 124 Hank Bauer MG ............ 2.50 1.10
❑ 125 Ray Sadecki .................. 1.50 .70
❑ 126 Dick Tracewski .............. 1.50 .70
❑ 127 Kevin Collins .................. 2.50 1.10
❑ 128 Tommie Aaron................ 2.50 1.10
❑ 129 Bill McCool .................... 1.50 .70
❑ 130 Carl Yastrzemski ........ 20.00 9.00
❑ 131 Chris Cannizzaro............ 1.50 .70
❑ 132 Dave Baldwin ................ 1.50 .70
❑ 133 Johnny Callison.............. 2.50 1.10
❑ 134 Jim Weaver .................... 1.50 .70
❑ 135 Tommy Davis ................ 2.50 1.10
❑ 136 Cards Rookies................ 1.50 .70
Steve Huntz
Mike Torrez
❑ 137 Wally Bunker.................. 1.50 .70
❑ 138 John Bateman................ 1.50 .70
❑ 139 Andy Kosco .................... 1.50 .70
❑ 140 Jim Lefebvre .................. 2.50 1.10
❑ 141 Bill Dillman .................... 1.50 .70
❑ 142 Woody Woodward.......... 2.50 1.10
❑ 143 Joe Nossek .................... 1.50 .70
❑ 144 Bob Hendley .................. 2.50 1.10
❑ 145 Max Alvis........................ 1.50 .70
❑ 146 Jim Perry ........................ 2.50 1.10
❑ 147 Leo Durocher MG .......... 4.00 1.80
❑ 148 Lee Stange .................... 1.50 .70
❑ 149 Ollie Brown .................... 2.50 1.10
❑ 150 Denny McLain ................ 4.00 1.80
❑ 151A Clay Dalrymple ............ 1.50 .70
Portrait, Orioles
❑ 151B Clay Dalrymple .......... 15.00 6.75

| | | | |
|---|---|---|---|
| | Catching, Phillies | | |
| ❑ 152 | Tommie Sisk | 1.50 | .70 |
| ❑ 153 | Ed Brinkman | 1.50 | .70 |
| ❑ 154 | Jim Britton | 1.50 | .70 |
| ❑ 155 | Pete Ward | 1.50 | .70 |
| ❑ 156 | Houston Rookies | 1.50 | .70 |
| | Hal Gilson | | |
| | Leon McFadden | | |
| ❑ 157 | Bob Rodgers | 2.50 | 1.10 |
| ❑ 158 | Joe Gibbon | 1.50 | .70 |
| ❑ 159 | Jerry Adair | 1.50 | .70 |
| ❑ 160 | Vada Pinson | 2.50 | 1.10 |
| ❑ 161 | John Purdin | 1.50 | .70 |
| ❑ 162 | Bob Gibson WS | 8.00 | 3.60 |
| | Fans 17 | | |
| ❑ 163 | Willie Horton WS | 6.00 | 2.70 |
| ❑ 164 | Tim McCarver WS | 12.00 | 5.50 |
| | Roger Maris | | |
| ❑ 165 | Lou Brock WS | 8.00 | 3.60 |
| ❑ 166 | Al Kaline WS | 8.00 | 3.60 |
| ❑ 167 | Jim Northrup WS | 6.00 | 2.70 |
| ❑ 168 | Mickey Lolich WS | 8.00 | 3.60 |
| | Bob Gibson | | |
| ❑ 169 | Dick McAuliffe WS | 6.00 | 2.70 |
| | Denny McLain | | |
| | Willie Horton | | |
| ❑ 170 | Frank Howard | 2.50 | 1.10 |
| ❑ 171 | Glenn Beckert | 2.50 | 1.10 |
| ❑ 172 | Jerry Stephenson | 1.50 | .70 |
| ❑ 173 | White Sox Rookies | 1.50 | .70 |
| | Bob Christian | | |
| | Gerry Nyman | | |
| ❑ 174 | Grant Jackson | 1.50 | .70 |
| ❑ 175 | Jim Bunning | 6.00 | 2.70 |
| ❑ 176 | Joe Azcue | 1.50 | .70 |
| ❑ 177 | Ron Reed | 1.50 | .70 |
| ❑ 178 | Ray Oyler | 2.50 | 1.10 |
| ❑ 179 | Don Pavletich | 1.50 | .70 |
| ❑ 180 | Willie Horton | 2.50 | 1.10 |
| ❑ 181 | Mel Nelson | 1.50 | .70 |
| ❑ 182 | Bill Rigney MG | 1.50 | .70 |
| ❑ 183 | Don Shaw | 1.50 | .70 |
| ❑ 184 | Roberto Pena | 1.50 | .70 |
| ❑ 185 | Tom Phoebus | 1.50 | .70 |
| ❑ 186 | Johnny Edwards | 1.50 | .70 |
| ❑ 187 | Leon Wagner | 1.50 | .70 |
| ❑ 188 | Rick Wise | 2.50 | 1.10 |
| ❑ 189 | Red Sox Rookies | 1.50 | .70 |
| | Joe Lahoud | | |
| | John Thibodeau | | |
| ❑ 190 | Willie Mays | 60.00 | 27.00 |
| ❑ 191 | Lindy McDaniel | 2.50 | 1.10 |
| ❑ 192 | Jose Pagan | 1.50 | .70 |
| ❑ 193 | Don Cardwell | 2.50 | 1.10 |
| ❑ 194 | Ted Uhlaender | 1.50 | .70 |
| ❑ 195 | John Odom | 1.50 | .70 |
| ❑ 196 | Lum Harris MG | 1.50 | .70 |
| ❑ 197 | Dick Selma | 1.50 | .70 |
| ❑ 198 | Willie Smith | 1.50 | .70 |
| ❑ 199 | Jim French | 1.50 | .70 |
| ❑ 200 | Bob Gibson | 12.00 | 5.50 |
| ❑ 201 | Russ Snyder | 1.50 | .70 |
| ❑ 202 | Don Wilson | 2.50 | 1.10 |
| ❑ 203 | Dave Johnson | 2.50 | 1.10 |
| ❑ 204 | Jack Hiatt | 1.50 | .70 |
| ❑ 205 | Rick Reichardt | 1.50 | .70 |
| ❑ 206 | Phillies Rookies | 2.50 | 1.10 |
| | Larry Hisle | | |
| | Barry Lersch | | |
| ❑ 207 | Roy Face | 2.50 | 1.10 |
| ❑ 208A | Donn Clendenon | 2.50 | 1.10 |
| | Houston | | |
| ❑ 208B | Donn Clendenon | 15.00 | 6.75 |
| | Expos | | |
| ❑ 209 | Larry Haney UER | 1.50 | .70 |
| | (Reverse negative) | | |
| ❑ 210 | Felix Millan | 1.50 | .70 |
| ❑ 211 | Galen Cisco | 1.50 | .70 |
| ❑ 212 | Tom Tresh | 2.50 | 1.10 |
| ❑ 213 | Gerry Arrigo | 1.50 | .70 |
| ❑ 214 | Checklist 3 | 6.00 | 1.20 |
| | With 69T deckle CL | | |
| | on back (no player) | | |
| ❑ 215 | Rico Petrocelli | 2.50 | 1.10 |
| ❑ 216 | Don Sutton | 6.00 | 2.70 |
| ❑ 217 | John Donaldson | 1.50 | .70 |
| ❑ 218 | John Roseboro | 2.50 | 1.10 |
| ❑ 219 | Freddie Patek RC | 4.00 | 1.80 |
| ❑ 220 | Sam McDowell | 4.00 | 1.80 |
| ❑ 221 | Art Shamsky | 4.00 | 1.80 |
| ❑ 222 | Duane Josephson | 2.50 | 1.10 |
| ❑ 223 | Tom Dukes | 4.00 | 1.80 |
| ❑ 224 | Angels Rookies | 2.50 | 1.10 |
| | Bill Harrelson | | |
| | Steve Kealey | | |
| ❑ 225 | Don Kessinger | 4.00 | 1.80 |
| ❑ 226 | Bruce Howard | 2.50 | 1.10 |
| ❑ 227 | Frank Johnson | 2.50 | 1.10 |
| ❑ 228 | Dave Leonhard | 2.50 | 1.10 |
| ❑ 229 | Don Lock | 2.50 | 1.10 |
| ❑ 230 | Rusty Staub UER | 4.00 | 1.80 |
| | (For 1966 stats, Houston spelled | | |
| | Huoston) | | |
| ❑ 231 | Pat Dobson | 4.00 | 1.80 |
| ❑ 232 | Dave Ricketts | 2.50 | 1.10 |
| ❑ 233 | Steve Barber | 4.00 | 1.80 |
| ❑ 234 | Dave Bristol MG | 2.50 | 1.10 |
| ❑ 235 | Jim Hunter | 10.00 | 4.50 |
| ❑ 236 | Manny Mota | 4.00 | 1.80 |
| ❑ 237 | Bobby Cox RC | 10.00 | 4.50 |
| ❑ 238 | Ken Johnson | 2.50 | 1.10 |
| ❑ 239 | Bob Taylor | 4.00 | 1.80 |
| ❑ 240 | Ken Harrelson | 4.00 | 1.80 |
| ❑ 241 | Jim Brewer | 2.50 | 1.10 |
| ❑ 242 | Frank Kostro | 2.50 | 1.10 |
| ❑ 243 | Ron Kline | 2.50 | 1.10 |
| ❑ 244 | Indians Rookies | 4.00 | 1.80 |
| | Ray Fosse RC | | |
| | George Woodson | | |
| ❑ 245 | Ed Charles | 4.00 | 1.80 |
| ❑ 246 | Joe Coleman | 2.50 | 1.10 |
| ❑ 247 | Gene Oliver | 2.50 | 1.10 |
| ❑ 248 | Bob Priddy | 2.50 | 1.10 |
| ❑ 249 | Ed Spiezio | 4.00 | 1.80 |
| ❑ 250 | Frank Robinson | 20.00 | 9.00 |
| ❑ 251 | Ron Herbel | 2.50 | 1.10 |
| ❑ 252 | Chuck Cottier | 2.50 | 1.10 |
| ❑ 253 | Jerry Johnson | 2.50 | 1.10 |
| ❑ 254 | Joe Schultz MG | 4.00 | 1.80 |
| ❑ 255 | Steve Carlton | 30.00 | 13.50 |
| ❑ 256 | Gates Brown | 4.00 | 1.80 |
| ❑ 257 | Jim Ray | 2.50 | 1.10 |
| ❑ 258 | Jackie Hernandez | 4.00 | 1.80 |
| ❑ 259 | Bill Short | 2.50 | 1.10 |
| ❑ 260 | Reggie Jackson RC ! | 250.00 | 110.00 |
| ❑ 261 | Bob Johnson | 2.50 | 1.10 |
| ❑ 262 | Mike Kekich | 4.00 | 1.80 |
| ❑ 263 | Jerry May | 2.50 | 1.10 |
| ❑ 264 | Bill Landis | 2.50 | 1.10 |
| ❑ 265 | Chico Cardenas | 4.00 | 1.80 |
| ❑ 266 | Dodger Rookies | 4.00 | 1.80 |
| | Tom Hutton | | |
| | Alan Foster | | |
| ❑ 267 | Vicente Romo | 2.50 | 1.10 |
| ❑ 268 | Al Spangler | 2.50 | 1.10 |
| ❑ 269 | Al Weis | 4.00 | 1.80 |
| ❑ 270 | Mickey Lolich | 4.00 | 1.80 |
| ❑ 271 | Larry Stahl | 4.00 | 1.80 |
| ❑ 272 | Ed Stroud | 2.50 | 1.10 |
| ❑ 273 | Ron Willis | 2.50 | 1.10 |
| ❑ 274 | Clyde King MG | 2.50 | 1.10 |
| ❑ 275 | Vic Davalillo | 2.50 | 1.10 |
| ❑ 276 | Gary Wagner | 2.50 | 1.10 |
| ❑ 277 | Elrod Hendricks RC | 2.50 | 1.10 |
| ❑ 278 | Gary Geiger UER | 2.50 | 1.10 |
| | (Batting wrong) | | |
| ❑ 279 | Roger Nelson | 4.00 | 1.80 |
| ❑ 280 | Alex Johnson | 4.00 | 1.80 |
| ❑ 281 | Ted Kubiak | 2.50 | 1.10 |
| ❑ 282 | Pat Jarvis | 2.50 | 1.10 |
| ❑ 283 | Sandy Alomar | 4.00 | 1.80 |
| ❑ 284 | Expos Rookies | 4.00 | 1.80 |
| | Jerry Robertson | | |
| | Mike Wegener | | |
| ❑ 285 | Don Mincher | 4.00 | 1.80 |
| ❑ 286 | Dock Ellis RC | 4.00 | 1.80 |
| ❑ 287 | Jose Tartabull | 4.00 | 1.80 |
| ❑ 288 | Ken Holtzman | 4.00 | 1.80 |
| ❑ 289 | Bart Shirley | 2.50 | 1.10 |
| ❑ 290 | Jim Kaat | 4.00 | 1.80 |
| ❑ 291 | Vern Fuller | 2.50 | 1.10 |
| ❑ 292 | Al Downing | 4.00 | 1.80 |
| ❑ 293 | Dick Dietz | 2.50 | 1.10 |
| ❑ 294 | Jim Lemon MG | 2.50 | 1.10 |
| ❑ 295 | Tony Perez | 12.00 | 5.50 |
| ❑ 296 | Andy Messersmith RC | 4.00 | 1.80 |
| ❑ 297 | Deron Johnson | 2.50 | 1.10 |
| ❑ 298 | Dave Nicholson | 4.00 | 1.80 |
| ❑ 299 | Mark Belanger | 4.00 | 1.80 |
| ❑ 300 | Felipe Alou | 4.00 | 1.80 |
| ❑ 301 | Darrell Brandon | 4.00 | 1.80 |
| ❑ 302 | Jim Pagliaroni | 2.50 | 1.10 |
| ❑ 303 | Cal Koonce | 4.00 | 1.80 |
| ❑ 304 | Padres Rookies | 6.00 | 2.70 |
| | Bill Davis | | |
| | Clarence Gaston RC | | |
| ❑ 305 | Dick McAuliffe | 4.00 | 1.80 |
| ❑ 306 | Jim Grant | 4.00 | 1.80 |
| ❑ 307 | Gary Kolb | 2.50 | 1.10 |
| ❑ 308 | Wade Blasingame | 2.50 | 1.10 |
| ❑ 309 | Walt Williams | 2.50 | 1.10 |
| ❑ 310 | Tom Haller | 2.50 | 1.10 |
| ❑ 311 | Sparky Lyle RC | 10.00 | 4.50 |
| ❑ 312 | Lee Elia | 2.50 | 1.10 |
| ❑ 313 | Bill Robinson | 4.00 | 1.80 |
| ❑ 314 | Don Drysdale CL | 6.00 | 1.20 |
| ❑ 315 | Eddie Fisher | 2.50 | 1.10 |
| ❑ 316 | Hal Lanier | 2.50 | 1.10 |
| ❑ 317 | Bruce Look | 2.50 | 1.10 |
| ❑ 318 | Jack Fisher | 2.50 | 1.10 |
| ❑ 319 | Ken McMullen UER | 2.50 | 1.10 |
| | (Headings on back | | |
| | are for a pitcher) | | |
| ❑ 320 | Dal Maxvill | 2.50 | 1.10 |
| ❑ 321 | Jim McAndrew | 4.00 | 1.80 |
| ❑ 322 | Jose Vidal | 4.00 | 1.80 |
| ❑ 323 | Larry Miller | 2.50 | 1.10 |
| ❑ 324 | Tiger Rookies | 4.00 | 1.80 |
| | Les Cain | | |
| | Dave Campbell RC | | |
| ❑ 325 | Jose Cardenal | 4.00 | 1.80 |
| ❑ 326 | Gary Sutherland | 4.00 | 1.80 |
| ❑ 327 | Willie Crawford | 2.50 | 1.10 |
| ❑ 328 | Joel Horlen | 1.50 | .70 |
| ❑ 329 | Rick Joseph | 1.50 | .70 |
| ❑ 330 | Tony Conigliaro | 4.00 | 1.80 |
| ❑ 331 | Braves Rookies | 2.50 | 1.10 |
| | Gil Garrido | | |
| | Tom House RC | | |
| ❑ 332 | Fred Talbot | 1.50 | .70 |
| ❑ 333 | Ivan Murrell | 1.50 | .70 |
| ❑ 334 | Phil Roof | 1.50 | .70 |
| ❑ 335 | Bill Mazeroski | 4.00 | 1.80 |
| ❑ 336 | Jim Roland | 1.50 | .70 |
| ❑ 337 | Marty Martinez | 1.50 | .70 |
| ❑ 338 | Del Unser | 1.50 | .70 |
| ❑ 339 | Reds Rookies | 1.50 | .70 |
| | Steve Mingori | | |
| | Jose Pena | | |
| ❑ 340 | Dave McNally | 2.50 | 1.10 |
| ❑ 341 | Dave Adlesh | 1.50 | .70 |
| ❑ 342 | Bubba Morton | 1.50 | .70 |
| ❑ 343 | Dan Frisella | 1.50 | .70 |
| ❑ 344 | Tom Matchick | 1.50 | .70 |
| ❑ 345 | Frank Linzy | 1.50 | .70 |
| ❑ 346 | Wayne Comer | 1.50 | .70 |
| ❑ 347 | Randy Hundley | 2.50 | 1.10 |
| ❑ 348 | Steve Hargan | 1.50 | .70 |
| ❑ 349 | Dick Williams MG | 2.50 | 1.10 |
| ❑ 350 | Richie Allen | 4.00 | 1.80 |
| ❑ 351 | Carroll Sembera | 1.50 | .70 |
| ❑ 352 | Paul Schaal | 2.50 | 1.10 |
| ❑ 353 | Jeff Torborg | 2.50 | 1.10 |
| ❑ 354 | Nate Oliver | 1.50 | .70 |
| ❑ 355 | Phil Niekro | 6.00 | 2.70 |
| ❑ 356 | Frank Quilici | 1.50 | .70 |
| ❑ 357 | Carl Taylor | 1.50 | .70 |
| ❑ 358 | Athletics Rookies | 1.50 | .70 |
| | George Lauzerique | | |
| | Roberto Rodriquez | | |
| ❑ 359 | Dick Kelley | 1.50 | .70 |
| ❑ 360 | Jim Wynn | 2.50 | 1.10 |
| ❑ 361 | Gary Holman | 1.50 | .70 |
| ❑ 362 | Jim Maloney | 2.50 | 1.10 |
| ❑ 363 | Russ Nixon | 1.50 | .70 |
| ❑ 364 | Tommie Agee | 4.00 | 1.80 |
| ❑ 365 | Jim Fregosi | 2.50 | 1.10 |
| ❑ 366 | Bo Belinsky | 2.50 | 1.10 |

❑ 367 Lou Johnson ............... 2.50 1.10
❑ 368 Vic Roznovsky............. 1.50 .70
❑ 369 Bob Skinner MG .......... 2.50 1.10
❑ 370 Juan Marichal ............ 8.00 3.60
❑ 371 Sal Bando .................. 2.50 1.10
❑ 372 Adolfo Phillips ............ 1.50 .70
❑ 373 Fred Lasher................. 1.50 .70
❑ 374 Bob Tillman.................. 1.50 .70
❑ 375 Harmon Killebrew ...... 15.00 6.75
❑ 376 Royals Rookies ........... 1.50 .70
Mike Fiore
Jim Rooker RC
❑ 377 Gary Bell ..................... 2.50 1.10
❑ 378 Jose Herrera ............... 1.50 .70
❑ 379 Ken Boyer .................... 2.50 1.10
❑ 380 Stan Bahnsen .............. 2.50 1.10
❑ 381 Ed Kranepool .............. 2.50 1.10
❑ 382 Pat Corrales ............... 2.50 1.10
❑ 383 Casey Cox.................... 1.50 .70
❑ 384 Larry Shepard MG........ 1.50 .70
❑ 385 Orlando Cepeda .......... 6.00 2.70
❑ 386 Jim McGlothlin............. 1.50 .70
❑ 387 Bobby Klaus ................ 1.50 .70
❑ 388 Tom McCraw................. 1.50 .70
❑ 389 Dan Coombs................. 1.50 .70
❑ 390 Bill Freehan.................. 2.50 1.10
❑ 391 Ray Culp ...................... 1.50 .70
❑ 392 Bob Burda..................... 1.50 .70
❑ 393 Gene Brabender .......... 2.50 1.10
❑ 394 Pilots Rookies ............. 6.00 2.70
Lou Piniella
Marv Staehle
❑ 395 Chris Short .................. 1.50 .70
❑ 396 Jim Campanis .............. 1.50 .70
❑ 397 Chuck Dobson.............. 1.50 .70
❑ 398 Tito Francona .............. 1.50 .70
❑ 399 Bob Bailey.................... 2.50 1.10
❑ 400 Don Drysdale ............. 16.00 7.25
❑ 401 Jake Gibbs ................... 2.50 1.10
❑ 402 Ken Boswell ................. 2.50 1.10
❑ 403 Bob Miller ..................... 1.50 .70
❑ 404 Cubs Rookies .............. 2.50 1.10
Vic LaRose
Gary Ross
❑ 405 Lee May ....................... 2.50 1.10
❑ 406 Phil Ortega .................. 1.50 .70
❑ 407 Tom Egan ..................... 1.50 .70
❑ 408 Nate Colbert ................ 1.50 .70
❑ 409 Bob Moose ................... 1.50 .70
❑ 410 Al Kaline .................... 25.00 11.00
❑ 411 Larry Dierker ............... 2.50 1.10
❑ 412 Mickey Mantle CL DP 15.00 3.00
❑ 413 Roland Sheldon............ 2.50 1.10
❑ 414 Duke Sims.................... 1.50 .70
❑ 415 Ray Washburn ............ 1.50 .70
❑ 416 Willie McCovey AS ...... 7.00 3.10
❑ 417 Ken Harrelson AS ........ 6.00 2.70
❑ 418 Tommy Helms AS......... 6.00 2.70
❑ 419 Rod Carew AS .......... 10.00 4.50
❑ 420 Ron Santo AS .............. 4.00 1.80
❑ 421 Brooks Robinson AS.... 7.00 3.10
❑ 422 Don Kessinger AS........ 6.00 2.70
❑ 423 Bert Campaneris AS .... 4.00 1.80
❑ 424 Pete Rose AS ............ 14.00 6.25
❑ 425 Carl Yastrzemski AS .. 10.00 4.50
❑ 426 Curt Flood AS .............. 4.00 1.80
❑ 427 Tony Oliva AS .............. 4.00 1.80
❑ 428 Lou Brock AS ............... 6.00 2.70
❑ 429 Willie Horton AS .......... 6.00 2.70
❑ 430 Johnny Bench AS ...... 10.00 4.50
❑ 431 Bill Freehan AS ............ 4.00 1.80
❑ 432 Bob Gibson AS ............. 6.00 2.70
❑ 433 Denny McLain AS ........ 6.00 2.70
❑ 434 Jerry Koosman AS ....... 3.00 1.35
❑ 435 Sam McDowell AS ....... 2.50 1.10
❑ 436 Gene Alley.................... 2.50 1.10
❑ 437 Luis Alcaraz.................. 1.50 .70
❑ 438 Gary Waslewski .......... 1.50 .70
❑ 439 White Sox Rookies ...... 1.50 .70
Ed Herrmann
Dan Lazar
❑ 440A Willie McCovey ........ 15.00 6.75
❑ 440B Willie McCovey WL 100.00 45.00
(McCovey white)
❑ 441A Dennis Higgins ......... 1.50 .70
❑ 441B Dennis Higgins WL .. 20.00 9.00
(Higgins white)
❑ 442 Ty Cline ........................ 1.50 .70
❑ 443 Don Wert ....................... 1.50 .70
❑ 444A Joe Moeller................ 1.50 .70
❑ 444B Joe Moeller WL......... 20.00 9.00
(Moeller white)
❑ 445 Bobby Knoop................ 1.50 .70
❑ 446 Claude Raymond ........ 1.50 .70
❑ 447A Ralph Houk MG ........ 2.50 1.10
❑ 447B Ralph Houk WL......... 20.00 9.00
MG (Houk white)
❑ 448 Bob Tolan .................... 2.50 1.10
❑ 449 Paul Lindblad ............. 1.50 .70
❑ 450 Billy Williams .............. 7.00 3.10
❑ 451A Rich Rollins............... 2.50 1.10
❑ 451B Rich Rollins WL ...... 20.00 9.00
(Rich and 3B white)
❑ 452A Al Ferrara ................. 1.50 .70
❑ 452B Al Ferrara WL .......... 20.00 9.00
(Al and OF white)
❑ 453 Mike Cuellar ............... 2.50 1.10
❑ 454A Phillies Rookies ....... 2.50 1.10
Larry Colton
Don Money
❑ 454B Phillies Rookies WL 20.00 9.00
Larry Colton
Don Money
(Names in white)
❑ 455 Sonny Siebert ............. 1.50 .70
❑ 456 Bud Harrelson ............. 2.50 1.10
❑ 457 Dalton Jones ............... 1.50 .70
❑ 458 Curt Blefary ................. 1.50 .70
❑ 459 Dave Boswell .............. 1.50 .70
❑ 460 Joe Torre...................... 4.00 1.80
❑ 461A Mike Epstein ............. 1.50 .70
❑ 461B Mike Epstein WL...... 20.00 9.00
(Epstein white)
❑ 462 Red Schoendienst....... 2.50 1.10
MG
❑ 463 Dennis Ribant ............. 1.50 .70
❑ 464A Dave Marshall........... 1.50 .70
❑ 464B Dave Marshall WL .. 20.00 9.00
(Marshall white)
❑ 465 Tommy John ............... 4.00 1.80
❑ 466 John Boccabella .......... 2.50 1.10
❑ 467 Tommie Reynolds ....... 1.50 .70
❑ 468A Pirates Rookies......... 1.50 .70
Bruce Dal Canton
Bob Robertson
❑ 468B Pirates Rookies WL 20.00 9.00
Bruce Dal Canton
Bob Robertson
(Names in white)
❑ 469 Chico Ruiz................... 1.50 .70
❑ 470A Mel Stottlemyre......... 2.50 1.10
❑ 470B Mel Stottlemyre WL 30.00 13.50
(Stottlemyre white)
❑ 471A Ted Savage .............. 1.50 .70
❑ 471B Ted Savage WL ...... 20.00 9.00
(Savage white)
❑ 472 Jim Price ..................... 1.50 .70
❑ 473A Jose Arcia ................ 1.50 .70
❑ 473B Jose Arcia WL.......... 20.00 9.00
(Jose and 2B white)
❑ 474 Tom Murphy ................ 1.50 .70
❑ 475 Tim McCarver ............. 4.00 1.80
❑ 476A Boston Rookies......... 3.00 1.35
Ken Brett RC
Gerry Moses
❑ 476B Boston Rookies WL 30.00 13.50
Ken Brett RC
Gerry Moses
(Names in white)
❑ 477 Jeff James.................... 1.50 .70
❑ 478 Don Buford .................. 1.50 .70
❑ 479 Richie Scheinblum ...... 1.50 .70
❑ 480 Tom Seaver............... 70.00 32.00
❑ 481 Bill Melton ................... 2.50 1.10
❑ 482A Jim Gosger ............... 1.50 .70
❑ 482B Jim Gosger WL ........ 20.00 9.00
(Jim and OF white)
❑ 483 Ted Abernathy.............. 1.50 .70
❑ 484 Joe Gordon MG............ 2.50 1.10
❑ 485A Gaylord Perry ........ 10.00 4.50
❑ 485B Gaylord Perry WL .... 85.00 38.00
(Perry white)
❑ 486A Paul Casanova .......... 1.50 .70
❑ 486B Paul Casanova WL .. 20.00 9.00
(Casanova white)
❑ 487 Denis Menke ............... 1.50 .70
❑ 488 Joe Sparma.................. 1.50 .70
❑ 489 Clete Boyer ................. 2.50 1.10
❑ 490 Matty Alou ................... 2.50 1.10
❑ 491A Twins Rookies .......... 1.50 .70
Jerry Crider
George Mitterwald
❑ 491B Twins Rookies WL .. 20.00 9.00
Jerry Crider
George Mitterwald
(Names in white)
❑ 492 Tony Cloninger ............ 1.50 .70
❑ 493A Wes Parker................ 2.50 1.10
❑ 493B Wes Parker WL........ 20.00 9.00
(Parker white)
❑ 494 Ken Berry ..................... 1.50 .70
❑ 495 Bert Campaneris .......... 2.50 1.10
❑ 496 Larry Jaster .................. 1.50 .70
❑ 497 Julian Javier ................ 2.50 1.10
❑ 498 Juan Pizarro ................ 2.50 1.10
❑ 499 Astro Rookies ............. 1.50 .70
Don Bryant
Steve Shea
❑ 500A Mickey Mantle UER 300.00 135.00
(No Topps copy-
right on card back)
❑ 500B Mickey Mantle WL 1200.00 550.00
(Mantle in white;
no Topps copyright
on card back) UER
❑ 501A Tony Gonzalez ......... 2.50 1.10
❑ 501B Tony Gonzalez WL .. 20.00 9.00
(Tony and OF white)
❑ 502 Minnie Rojas ............... 1.50 .70
❑ 503 Larry Brown................. 1.50 .70
❑ 504 Brooks Robinson CL .... 7.00 1.40
❑ 505A Bobby Bolin............... 1.50 .70
❑ 505B Bobby Bolin WL ...... 20.00 9.00
(Bolin white)
❑ 506 Paul Blair..................... 2.50 1.10
❑ 507 Cookie Rojas............... 2.50 1.10
❑ 508 Moe Drabowsky ......... 2.50 1.10
❑ 509 Manny Sanguillen ....... 2.50 1.10
❑ 510 Rod Carew ................ 40.00 18.00
❑ 511A Diego Segui ............. 2.50 1.10
❑ 511B Diego Segui WL ...... 20.00 9.00
(Diego and P white)
❑ 512 Cleon Jones ............... 2.50 1.10
❑ 513 Camilo Pascual ........... 3.00 1.35
❑ 514 Mike Lum..................... 2.00 .90
❑ 515 Dick Green .................. 2.00 .90
❑ 516 Earl Weaver RC MG .. 20.00 9.00
❑ 517 Mike McCormick ......... 3.00 1.35
❑ 518 Fred Whitfield ............. 2.00 .90
❑ 519 Yankees Rookies ........ 2.00 .90
Jerry Kenney
Len Boehmer
❑ 520 Bob Veale .................... 3.00 1.35
❑ 521 George Thomas .......... 2.00 .90
❑ 522 Joe Hoerner ................ 2.00 .90
❑ 523 Bob Chance ................ 2.00 .90
❑ 524 Expos Rookies ............ 3.00 1.35
Jose Laboy
Floyd Wicker
❑ 525 Earl Wilson .................. 3.00 1.35
❑ 526 Hector Torres .............. 2.00 .90
❑ 527 Al Lopez MG................ 5.00 2.20
❑ 528 Claude Osteen ............ 3.00 1.35
❑ 529 Ed Kirkpatrick ............. 3.00 1.35
❑ 530 Cesar Tovar ................ 2.00 .90
❑ 531 Dick Farrell ................. 2.00 .90
❑ 532 Bird Hill Aces.............. 3.00 1.35
Tom Phoebus
Jim Hardin
Dave McNally
Mike Cuellar
❑ 533 Nolan Ryan ............. 300.00 135.00
❑ 534 Jerry McNertney ......... 3.00 1.35
❑ 535 Phil Regan................... 3.00 1.35
❑ 536 Padres Rookies........... 2.00 .90
Danny Breeden
Dave Roberts
❑ 537 Mike Paul .................... 2.00 .90

| | Card | NRMT | VG-E |
|---|---|---|---|
| ❑ 538 | Charlie Smith | 2.00 | .90 |
| ❑ 539 | Ted Shows How | 12.00 | 5.50 |
| | Mike Epstein | | |
| | Ted Williams MG | | |
| ❑ 540 | Curt Flood | 3.00 | 1.35 |
| ❑ 541 | Joe Verbanic | 2.00 | .90 |
| ❑ 542 | Bob Aspromonte | 2.00 | .90 |
| ❑ 543 | Fred Newman | 2.00 | .90 |
| ❑ 544 | Tigers Rookies | 2.00 | .90 |
| | Mike Kilkenny | | |
| | Ron Woods | | |
| ❑ 545 | Willie Stargell | 12.00 | 5.50 |
| ❑ 546 | Jim Nash | 2.00 | .90 |
| ❑ 547 | Billy Martin MG | 5.00 | 2.20 |
| ❑ 548 | Bob Locker | 2.00 | .90 |
| ❑ 549 | Ron Brand | 2.00 | .90 |
| ❑ 550 | Brooks Robinson | 30.00 | 13.50 |
| ❑ 551 | Wayne Granger | 2.00 | .90 |
| ❑ 552 | Dodgers Rookies | 3.00 | 1.35 |
| | Ted Sizemore RC | | |
| | Bill Sudakis | | |
| ❑ 553 | Ron Davis | 2.00 | .90 |
| ❑ 554 | Frank Bertaina | 2.00 | .90 |
| ❑ 555 | Jim Ray Hart | 3.00 | 1.35 |
| ❑ 556 | A's Stars | 3.00 | 1.35 |
| | Sal Bando | | |
| | Bert Campaneris | | |
| | Danny Cater | | |
| ❑ 557 | Frank Fernandez | 2.00 | .90 |
| ❑ 558 | Tom Burgmeier | 3.00 | 1.35 |
| ❑ 559 | Cardinals Rookies | 2.00 | .90 |
| | Joe Hague | | |
| | Jim Hicks | | |
| ❑ 560 | Luis Tiant | 3.00 | 1.35 |
| ❑ 561 | Ron Clark | 2.00 | .90 |
| ❑ 562 | Bob Watson RC | 8.00 | 3.60 |
| ❑ 563 | Marty Pattin | 3.00 | 1.35 |
| ❑ 564 | Gil Hodges MG | 10.00 | 4.50 |
| ❑ 565 | Hoyt Wilhelm | 8.00 | 3.60 |
| ❑ 566 | Ron Hansen | 2.00 | .90 |
| ❑ 567 | Pirates Rookies | 2.00 | .90 |
| | Elvio Jimenez | | |
| | Jim Shellenback | | |
| ❑ 568 | Cecil Upshaw | 2.00 | .90 |
| ❑ 569 | Billy Harris | 1.50 | .70 |
| ❑ 570 | Ron Santo | 8.00 | 3.60 |
| ❑ 571 | Cap Peterson | 2.00 | .90 |
| ❑ 572 | Giants Heroes | 16.00 | 7.25 |
| | Willie McCovey | | |
| | Juan Marichal | | |
| ❑ 573 | Jim Palmer | 30.00 | 13.50 |
| ❑ 574 | George Scott | 3.00 | 1.35 |
| ❑ 575 | Bill Singer | 3.00 | 1.35 |
| ❑ 576 | Phillies Rookies | 2.00 | .90 |
| | Ron Stone | | |
| | Bill Wilson | | |
| ❑ 577 | Mike Hegan | 3.00 | 1.35 |
| ❑ 578 | Don Bosch | 2.00 | .90 |
| ❑ 579 | Dave Nelson | 2.00 | .90 |
| ❑ 580 | Jim Northrup | 3.00 | 1.35 |
| ❑ 581 | Gary Nolan | 3.00 | 1.35 |
| ❑ 582A | Tony Oliva CL | 6.00 | 1.20 |
| | White circle on back | | |
| ❑ 582B | Tony Oliva CL | 7.50 | 1.50 |
| | Red circle on back | | |
| ❑ 583 | Clyde Wright | 2.00 | .90 |
| ❑ 584 | Don Mason | 2.00 | .90 |
| ❑ 585 | Ron Swoboda | 3.00 | 1.35 |
| ❑ 586 | Tim Cullen | 2.00 | .90 |
| ❑ 587 | Joe Rudi RC | 8.00 | 3.60 |
| ❑ 588 | Bill White | 3.00 | 1.35 |
| ❑ 589 | Joe Pepitone | 5.00 | 2.20 |
| ❑ 590 | Rico Carty | 5.00 | 2.20 |
| ❑ 591 | Mike Hedlund | 3.00 | 1.35 |
| ❑ 592 | Padres Rookies | 5.00 | 2.20 |
| | Rafael Robles | | |
| | Al Santorini | | |
| ❑ 593 | Don Nottebart | 3.00 | 1.35 |
| ❑ 594 | Dooley Womack | 3.00 | 1.35 |
| ❑ 595 | Lee Maye | 3.00 | 1.35 |
| ❑ 596 | Chuck Hartenstein | 3.00 | 1.35 |
| ❑ 597 | A.L. Rookies | 40.00 | 18.00 |
| | Bob Floyd | | |
| | Larry Burchart | | |
| | Rollie Fingers RC | | |
| ❑ 598 | Ruben Amaro | 3.00 | 1.35 |
| ❑ 599 | John Boozer | 3.00 | 1.35 |
| ❑ 600 | Tony Oliva | 8.00 | 3.60 |
| ❑ 601 | Tug McGraw | 8.00 | 3.60 |
| ❑ 602 | Cubs Rookies | 5.00 | 2.20 |
| | Alec Distaso | | |
| | Don Young | | |
| | Jim Qualls | | |
| ❑ 603 | Joe Keough | 3.00 | 1.35 |
| ❑ 604 | Bobby Etheridge | 3.00 | 1.35 |
| ❑ 605 | Dick Ellsworth | 3.00 | 1.35 |
| ❑ 606 | Gene Mauch MG | 5.00 | 2.20 |
| ❑ 607 | Dick Bosman | 3.00 | 1.35 |
| ❑ 608 | Dick Simpson | 3.00 | 1.35 |
| ❑ 609 | Phil Gagliano | 3.00 | 1.35 |
| ❑ 610 | Jim Hardin | 3.00 | 1.35 |
| ❑ 611 | Braves Rookies | 5.00 | 2.20 |
| | Bob Didier | | |
| | Walt Hriniak RC | | |
| | Gary Neibauer | | |
| ❑ 612 | Jack Aker | 5.00 | 2.20 |
| ❑ 613 | Jim Beauchamp | 3.00 | 1.35 |
| ❑ 614 | Houston Rookies | 3.00 | 1.35 |
| | Tom Griffin | | |
| | Skip Guinn | | |
| ❑ 615 | Len Gabrielson | 3.00 | 1.35 |
| ❑ 616 | Don McMahon | 3.00 | 1.35 |
| ❑ 617 | Jesse Gonder | 3.00 | 1.35 |
| ❑ 618 | Ramon Webster | 3.00 | 1.35 |
| ❑ 619 | Royals Rookies | 5.00 | 2.20 |
| | Bill Butler | | |
| | Pat Kelly | | |
| | Juan Rios | | |
| ❑ 620 | Dean Chance | 5.00 | 2.20 |
| ❑ 621 | Bill Voss | 3.00 | 1.35 |
| ❑ 622 | Dan Osinski | 3.00 | 1.35 |
| ❑ 623 | Hank Allen | 3.00 | 1.35 |
| ❑ 624 | NL Rookies | 5.00 | 2.20 |
| | Darrel Chaney | | |
| | Duffy Dyer RC | | |
| | Terry Harmon | | |
| ❑ 625 | Mack Jones UER | 5.00 | 2.20 |
| | (Batting wrong) | | |
| ❑ 626 | Gene Michael | 5.00 | 2.20 |
| ❑ 627 | George Stone | 3.00 | 1.35 |
| ❑ 628 | Red Sox Rookies | 5.00 | 2.20 |
| | Bill Conigliaro RC | | |
| | Syd O'Brien | | |
| | Fred Wenz | | |
| ❑ 629 | Jack Hamilton | 3.00 | 1.35 |
| ❑ 630 | Bobby Bonds RC ! | 30.00 | 13.50 |
| ❑ 631 | John Kennedy | 5.00 | 2.20 |
| ❑ 632 | Jon Warden | 3.00 | 1.35 |
| ❑ 633 | Harry Walker MG | 3.00 | 1.35 |
| ❑ 634 | Andy Etchebarren | 3.00 | 1.35 |
| ❑ 635 | George Culver | 3.00 | 1.35 |
| ❑ 636 | Woody Held | 3.00 | 1.35 |
| ❑ 637 | Padres Rookies | 5.00 | 2.20 |
| | Jerry DaVanon | | |
| | Frank Reberger | | |
| | Clay Kirby | | |
| ❑ 638 | Ed Sprague RC | 3.00 | 1.35 |
| ❑ 639 | Barry Moore | 3.00 | 1.35 |
| ❑ 640 | Ferguson Jenkins | 20.00 | 9.00 |
| ❑ 641 | NL Rookies | 5.00 | 2.20 |
| | Bobby Darwin | | |
| | John Miller | | |
| | Tommy Dean | | |
| ❑ 642 | John Hiller | 3.00 | 1.35 |
| ❑ 643 | Billy Cowan | 3.00 | 1.35 |
| ❑ 644 | Chuck Hinton | 3.00 | 1.35 |
| ❑ 645 | George Brunet | 3.00 | 1.35 |
| ❑ 646 | Expos Rookies | 5.00 | 2.20 |
| | Dan McGinn | | |
| | Carl Morton | | |
| ❑ 647 | Dave Wickersham | 3.00 | 1.35 |
| ❑ 648 | Bobby Wine | 5.00 | 2.20 |
| ❑ 649 | Al Jackson | 3.00 | 1.35 |
| ❑ 650 | Ted Williams MG | 20.00 | 9.00 |
| ❑ 651 | Gus Gil | 5.00 | 2.20 |
| ❑ 652 | Eddie Watt | 3.00 | 1.35 |
| ❑ 653 | Aurelio Rodriguez RC UER | 5.00 | 2.20 |
| | (Photo actually | | |
| | Angels' batboy) | | |
| ❑ 654 | White Sox Rookies | 5.00 | 2.20 |
| | Carlos May RC | | |
| | Don Secrist | | |
| | Rich Morales | | |
| ❑ 655 | Mike Hershberger | 3.00 | 1.35 |
| ❑ 656 | Dan Schneider | 3.00 | 1.35 |
| ❑ 657 | Bobby Murcer | 8.00 | 3.60 |
| ❑ 658 | AL Rookies | 3.00 | 1.35 |
| | Tom Hall | | |
| | Bill Burbach | | |
| | Jim Miles | | |
| ❑ 659 | Johnny Podres | 5.00 | 2.20 |
| ❑ 660 | Reggie Smith | 5.00 | 2.20 |
| ❑ 661 | Jim Merritt | 3.00 | 1.35 |
| ❑ 662 | Royals Rookies | 5.00 | 2.20 |
| | Dick Drago | | |
| | George Spriggs | | |
| | Bob Oliver | | |
| ❑ 663 | Dick Radatz | 5.00 | 2.20 |
| ❑ 664 | Ron Hunt | 5.00 | 1.35 |

## 1970 Topps

| | NRMT | VG-E |
|---|---|---|
| COMPLETE SET (720) | 1800.00 | 800.00 |
| COMMON CARD (1-372) | 1.00 | .45 |
| COMMON CARD (373-459) | 1.50 | .70 |
| COMMON CARD (460-546) | 2.00 | .90 |
| COMMON CARD (547-633) | 4.00 | 1.80 |
| COMMON CARD (634-720) | 10.00 | 4.50 |
| WRAPPER (10-CENT) | 20.00 | 9.00 |

| | Card | NRMT | VG-E |
|---|---|---|---|
| ❑ 1 | New York Mets | 25.00 | 7.75 |
| | Team Card | | |
| ❑ 2 | Diego Segui | 2.00 | .90 |
| ❑ 3 | Darrel Chaney | 1.00 | .45 |
| ❑ 4 | Tom Egan | 1.00 | .45 |
| ❑ 5 | Wes Parker | 2.00 | .90 |
| ❑ 6 | Grant Jackson | 1.00 | .45 |
| ❑ 7 | Indians Rookies | 1.00 | .45 |
| | Gary Boyd | | |
| | Russ Nagelson | | |
| ❑ 8 | Jose Martinez | 1.00 | .45 |
| ❑ 9 | Checklist 1 | 12.00 | 2.40 |
| ❑ 10 | Carl Yastrzemski | 15.00 | 6.75 |
| ❑ 11 | Nate Colbert | 1.00 | .45 |
| ❑ 12 | John Hiller | 1.00 | .45 |
| ❑ 13 | Jack Hiatt | 1.00 | .45 |
| ❑ 14 | Hank Allen | 1.00 | .45 |
| ❑ 15 | Larry Dierker | 2.00 | .90 |
| ❑ 16 | Charlie Metro MG | 1.00 | .45 |
| ❑ 17 | Hoyt Wilhelm | 6.00 | 2.70 |
| ❑ 18 | Carlos May | 1.00 | .45 |
| ❑ 19 | John Boccabella | 1.00 | .45 |
| ❑ 20 | Dave McNally | 2.00 | .90 |
| ❑ 21 | A's Rookies | 6.00 | 2.70 |
| | Vida Blue | | |
| | Gene Tenace RC | | |
| ❑ 22 | Ray Washburn | 1.00 | .45 |
| ❑ 23 | Bill Robinson | 2.00 | .90 |
| ❑ 24 | Dick Selma | 1.00 | .45 |
| ❑ 25 | Cesar Tovar | 1.00 | .45 |
| ❑ 26 | Tug McGraw | 4.00 | 1.80 |
| ❑ 27 | Chuck Hinton | 1.00 | .45 |
| ❑ 28 | Billy Wilson | 1.00 | .45 |
| ❑ 29 | Sandy Alomar | 2.00 | .90 |
| ❑ 30 | Matty Alou | 2.00 | .90 |
| ❑ 31 | Marty Pattin | 2.00 | .90 |
| ❑ 32 | Harry Walker MG | 1.00 | .45 |
| ❑ 33 | Don Wert | 1.00 | .45 |
| ❑ 34 | Willie Crawford | 1.00 | .45 |

❑ 35 Joel Horlen 1.00 .45
❑ 36 Red Rookies 2.00 .90
Danny Breeden
Bernie Carbo
❑ 37 Dick Drago 1.00 .45
❑ 38 Mack Jones 1.00 .45
❑ 39 Mike Nagy 1.00 .45
❑ 40 Rich Allen 2.00 .90
❑ 41 George Lauzerique 1.00 .45
❑ 42 Tito Fuentes 1.00 .45
❑ 43 Jack Aker 1.00 .45
❑ 44 Roberto Pena 1.00 .45
❑ 45 Dave Johnson 2.00 .90
❑ 46 Ken Rudolph 1.00 .45
❑ 47 Bob Miller 1.00 .45
❑ 48 Gil Garrido 1.00 .45
❑ 49 Tim Cullen 1.00 .45
❑ 50 Tommie Agee 2.00 .90
❑ 51 Bob Christian 1.00 .45
❑ 52 Bruce Dal Canton 1.00 .45
❑ 53 John Kennedy 1.00 .45
❑ 54 Jeff Torborg 2.00 .90
❑ 55 John Odom 1.00 .45
❑ 56 Phillies Rookies 1.00 .45
Joe Lis
Scott Reid
❑ 57 Pat Kelly 1.00 .45
❑ 58 Dave Marshall 1.00 .45
❑ 59 Dick Ellsworth 1.00 .45
❑ 60 Jim Wynn 2.00 .90
❑ 61 NL Batting Leaders 12.00 5.50
Pete Rose
Bob Clemente
Cleon Jones
❑ 62 AL Batting Leaders 4.00 1.80
Rod Carew
Reggie Smith
Tony Oliva
❑ 63 NL RBI Leaders 4.00 1.80
Willie McCovey
Ron Santo
Tony Perez
❑ 64 AL RBI Leaders 6.00 2.70
Harmon Killebrew
Boog Powell
Reggie Jackson
❑ 65 NL Home Run Leaders 6.00 2.70
Willie McCovey
Hank Aaron
Lee May
❑ 66 AL Home Run Leaders 6.00 2.70
Harmon Killebrew
Frank Howard
Reggie Jackson
❑ 67 NL ERA Leaders 6.00 2.70
Juan Marichal
Steve Carlton
Bob Gibson
❑ 68 AL ERA Leaders 2.00 .90
Dick Bosman
Jim Palmer
Mike Cuellar
❑ 69 NL Pitching Leaders 6.00 2.70
Tom Seaver
Phil Niekro
Fergie Jenkins
Juan Marichal
❑ 70 AL Pitching Leaders 2.00 .90
Dennis McLain
Mike Cuellar
Dave Boswell
Dave McNally
Jim Perry
Mel Stottlemyre
❑ 71 NL Strikeout Leaders 4.00 1.80
Fergie Jenkins
Bob Gibson
Bill Singer
❑ 72 AL Strikeout Leaders 2.00 .90
Sam McDowell
Mickey Lolich
Andy Messersmith
❑ 73 Wayne Granger 1.00 .45
❑ 74 Angels Rookies 1.00 .45
Greg Washburn
Wally Wolf
❑ 75 Jim Kaat 2.00 .90
❑ 76 Carl Taylor 1.00 .45
❑ 77 Frank Linzy 1.00 .45
❑ 78 Joe Lahoud 1.00 .45
❑ 79 Clay Kirby 1.00 .45
❑ 80 Don Kessinger 2.00 .90
❑ 81 Dave May 1.00 .45
❑ 82 Frank Fernandez 1.00 .45
❑ 83 Don Cardwell 1.00 .45
❑ 84 Paul Casanova 1.00 .45
❑ 85 Max Alvis 1.00 .45
❑ 86 Lum Harris MG 1.00 .45
❑ 87 Steve Renko 1.00 .45
❑ 88 Pilots Rookies 2.00 .90
Miguel Fuentes
Dick Baney
❑ 89 Juan Rios 1.00 .45
❑ 90 Tim McCarver 2.00 .90
❑ 91 Rich Morales 1.00 .45
❑ 92 George Culver 1.00 .45
❑ 93 Rick Renick 1.00 .45
❑ 94 Freddie Patek 2.00 .90
❑ 95 Earl Wilson 2.00 .90
❑ 96 Cardinals Rookies 2.00 .90
Leron Lee
Jerry Reuss RC
❑ 97 Joe Moeller 1.00 .45
❑ 98 Gates Brown 2.00 .90
❑ 99 Bobby Pfeil 1.00 .45
❑ 100 Mel Stottlemyre 2.00 .90
❑ 101 Bobby Floyd 1.00 .45
❑ 102 Joe Rudi 2.00 .90
❑ 103 Frank Reberger 1.00 .45
❑ 104 Gerry Moses 1.00 .45
❑ 105 Tony Gonzalez 1.00 .45
❑ 106 Darold Knowles 1.00 .45
❑ 107 Bobby Etheridge 1.00 .45
❑ 108 Tom Burgmeier 1.00 .45
❑ 109 Expos Rookies 1.00 .45
Garry Jestadt
Carl Morton
❑ 110 Bob Moose 1.00 .45
❑ 111 Mike Hegan 2.00 .90
❑ 112 Dave Nelson 1.00 .45
❑ 113 Jim Ray 1.00 .45
❑ 114 Gene Michael 1.00 .45
❑ 115 Alex Johnson 2.00 .90
❑ 116 Sparky Lyle 2.00 .90
❑ 117 Don Young 1.00 .45
❑ 118 George Mitterwald 1.00 .45
❑ 119 Chuck Taylor 1.00 .45
❑ 120 Sal Bando 2.00 .90
❑ 121 Orioles Rookies 1.00 .45
Fred Beene
Terry Crowley
❑ 122 George Stone 1.00 .45
❑ 123 Don Gutteridge MG 1.00 .45
❑ 124 Larry Jaster 1.00 .45
❑ 125 Deron Johnson 1.00 .45
❑ 126 Marty Martinez 1.00 .45
❑ 127 Joe Coleman 1.00 .45
❑ 128A Checklist 2 ERR 6.00 1.20
(226 R Perranoski)
❑ 128B Checklist 2 COR 6.00 1.20
(226 R. Perranoski)
❑ 129 Jimmie Price 1.00 .45
❑ 130 Ollie Brown 1.00 .45
❑ 131 Dodgers Rookies 1.00 .45
Ray Lamb
Bob Stinson
❑ 132 Jim McGlothlin 1.00 .45
❑ 133 Clay Carroll 1.00 .45
❑ 134 Danny Walton 1.00 .45
❑ 135 Dick Dietz 1.00 .45
❑ 136 Steve Hargan 1.00 .45
❑ 137 Art Shamsky 1.00 .45
❑ 138 Joe Foy 1.00 .45
❑ 139 Rich Nye 1.00 .45
❑ 140 Reggie Jackson 50.00 22.00
❑ 141 Pirates Rookies 2.00 .90
Dave Cash
Johnny Jeter
❑ 142 Fritz Peterson 1.00 .45
❑ 143 Phil Gagliano 1.00 .45
❑ 144 Ray Culp 1.00 .45
❑ 145 Rico Carty 2.00 .90
❑ 146 Danny Murphy 1.00 .45
❑ 147 Angel Hermoso 1.00 .45
❑ 148 Earl Weaver MG 4.00 1.80
❑ 149 Billy Champion 1.00 .45
❑ 150 Harmon Killebrew 8.00 3.60
❑ 151 Dave Roberts 1.00 .45
❑ 152 Ike Brown 1.00 .45
❑ 153 Gary Gentry 1.00 .45
❑ 154 Senators Rookies 1.00 .45
Jim Miles
Jan Dukes
❑ 155 Denis Menke 1.00 .45
❑ 156 Eddie Fisher 1.00 .45
❑ 157 Manny Mota 2.00 .90
❑ 158 Jerry McNertney 2.00 .90
❑ 159 Tommy Helms 2.00 .90
❑ 160 Phil Niekro 6.00 2.70
❑ 161 Richie Scheinblum 1.00 .45
❑ 162 Jerry Johnson 1.00 .45
❑ 163 Syd O'Brien 1.00 .45
❑ 164 Ty Cline 1.00 .45
❑ 165 Ed Kirkpatrick 1.00 .45
❑ 166 Al Oliver 2.00 .90
❑ 167 Bill Burbach 1.00 .45
❑ 168 Dave Watkins 1.00 .45
❑ 169 Tom Hall 1.00 .45
❑ 170 Billy Williams 6.00 2.70
❑ 171 Jim Nash 1.00 .45
❑ 172 Braves Rookies 2.00 .90
Garry Hill
Ralph Garr RC
❑ 173 Jim Hicks 1.00 .45
❑ 174 Ted Sizemore 2.00 .90
❑ 175 Dick Bosman 1.00 .45
❑ 176 Jim Ray Hart 2.00 .90
❑ 177 Jim Northrup 2.00 .90
❑ 178 Denny Lemaster 1.00 .45
❑ 179 Ivan Murrell 1.00 .45
❑ 180 Tommy John 2.00 .90
❑ 181 Sparky Anderson MG 6.00 2.70
❑ 182 Dick Hall 1.00 .45
❑ 183 Jerry Grote 1.00 .45
❑ 184 Ray Fosse 1.00 .45
❑ 185 Don Mincher 2.00 .90
❑ 186 Rick Joseph 1.00 .45
❑ 187 Mike Hedlund 1.00 .45
❑ 188 Manny Sanguillen 2.00 .90
❑ 189 Yankees Rookies 60.00 27.00
Thurman Munson RC
Dave McDonald
❑ 190 Joe Torre 4.00 1.80
❑ 191 Vicente Romo 1.00 .45
❑ 192 Jim Qualls 1.00 .45
❑ 193 Mike Wegener 1.00 .45
❑ 194 Chuck Manuel 1.00 .45
❑ 195 Tom Seaver NLCS 15.00 6.75
❑ 196 Ken Boswell NLCS 2.00 .90
❑ 197 Nolan Ryan NLCS 30.00 13.50
❑ 198 NL Playoff Summary 15.00 6.75
Mets celebrate
(Nolan Ryan)
❑ 199 Mike Cuellar ALCS 2.00 .90
❑ 200 Boog Powell ALCS 4.00 1.80
❑ 201 Boog Powell ALCS 2.00 .90
Andy Etchebarren)
❑ 202 AL Playoff Summary 2.00 .90
Orioles celebrate
❑ 203 Rudy May 1.00 .45
❑ 204 Len Gabrielson 1.00 .45
❑ 205 Bert Campaneris 2.00 .90
❑ 206 Clete Boyer 2.00 .90
❑ 207 Tigers Rookies 1.00 .45
Norman McRae
Bob Reed
❑ 208 Fred Gladding 1.00 .45
❑ 209 Ken Suarez 1.00 .45
❑ 210 Juan Marichal 6.00 2.70
❑ 211 Ted Williams MG 12.00 5.50
❑ 212 Al Santorini 1.00 .45
❑ 213 Andy Etchebarren 1.00 .45
❑ 214 Ken Boswell 1.00 .45
❑ 215 Reggie Smith 2.00 .90
❑ 216 Chuck Hartenstein 1.00 .45
❑ 217 Ron Hansen 1.00 .45
❑ 218 Ron Stone 1.00 .45
❑ 219 Jerry Kenney 1.00 .45

❑ 220 Steve Carlton 15.00 6.75
❑ 221 Ron Brand 1.00 .45
❑ 222 Jim Rooker 2.00 .90
❑ 223 Nate Oliver 1.00 .45
❑ 224 Steve Barber 2.00 .90
❑ 225 Lee May 2.00 .90
❑ 226 Ron Perranoski 2.00 .90
❑ 227 Astros Rookies 2.00 .90
John Mayberry RC
Bob Watkins
❑ 228 Aurelio Rodriguez 1.00 .45
❑ 229 Rich Robertson 1.00 .45
❑ 230 Brooks Robinson 15.00 6.75
❑ 231 Luis Tiant 2.00 .90
❑ 232 Bob Didier 1.00 .45
❑ 233 Lew Krausse 1.00 .45
❑ 234 Tommy Dean 1.00 .45
❑ 235 Mike Epstein 1.00 .45
❑ 236 Bob Veale 1.00 .45
❑ 237 Russ Gibson 1.00 .45
❑ 238 Jose Laboy 1.00 .45
❑ 239 Ken Berry 1.00 .45
❑ 240 Ferguson Jenkins 6.00 2.70
❑ 241 Royals Rookies 1.00 .45
Al Fitzmorris
Scott Northey
❑ 242 Walter Alston MG 4.00 1.80
❑ 243 Joe Sparma 1.00 .45
❑ 244A Checklist 3 6.00 1.20
(Red bat on front)
❑ 244B Checklist 3 6.00 1.20
(Brown bat on front)
❑ 245 Leo Cardenas 1.00 .45
❑ 246 Jim McAndrew 1.00 .45
❑ 247 Lou Klimchock 1.00 .45
❑ 248 Jesus Alou 1.00 .45
❑ 249 Bob Locker 1.00 .45
❑ 250 Willie McCovey UER 10.00 4.50
(1963 San Francisci)
❑ 251 Dick Schofield 1.00 .45
❑ 252 Lowell Palmer 1.00 .45
❑ 253 Ron Woods 1.00 .45
❑ 254 Camilo Pascual 1.00 .45
❑ 255 Jim Spencer 1.00 .45
❑ 256 Vic Davalillo 1.00 .45
❑ 257 Dennis Higgins 1.00 .45
❑ 258 Paul Popovich 1.00 .45
❑ 259 Tommie Reynolds 1.00 .45
❑ 260 Claude Osteen 1.00 .45
❑ 261 Curt Motton 1.00 .45
❑ 262 Padres Rookies 1.00 .45
Jerry Morales
Jim Williams
❑ 263 Duane Josephson 1.00 .45
❑ 264 Rich Hebner 1.00 .45
❑ 265 Randy Hundley 1.00 .45
❑ 266 Wally Bunker 1.00 .45
❑ 267 Twins Rookies 1.00 .45
Herman Hill
Paul Ratliff
❑ 268 Claude Raymond 1.00 .45
❑ 269 Cesar Gutierrez 1.00 .45
❑ 270 Chris Short 1.00 .45
❑ 271 Greg Goossen 1.00 .45
❑ 272 Hector Torres 1.00 .45
❑ 273 Ralph Houk MG 2.00 .90
❑ 274 Gerry Arrigo 1.00 .45
❑ 275 Duke Sims 1.00 .45
❑ 276 Ron Hunt 1.00 .45
❑ 277 Paul Doyle 1.00 .45
❑ 278 Tommie Aaron 1.00 .45
❑ 279 Bill Lee RC 2.00 .90
❑ 280 Donn Clendenon 1.00 .45
❑ 281 Casey Cox 1.00 .45
❑ 282 Steve Huntz 1.00 .45
❑ 283 Angel Bravo 1.00 .45
❑ 284 Jack Baldschun 1.00 .45
❑ 285 Paul Blair 2.00 .90
❑ 286 Dodgers Rookies 6.00 2.70
Jack Jenkins
Bill Buckner RC
❑ 287 Fred Talbot 1.00 .45
❑ 288 Larry Hisle 1.00 .45
❑ 289 Gene Brabender 1.00 .45
❑ 290 Rod Carew 18.00 8.00
❑ 291 Leo Durocher MG 4.00 1.80
❑ 292 Eddie Leon 1.00 .45
❑ 293 Bob Bailey 1.00 .45
❑ 294 Jose Azcue 1.00 .45
❑ 295 Cecil Upshaw 1.00 .45
❑ 296 Woody Woodward 1.00 .45
❑ 297 Curt Blefary 1.00 .45
❑ 298 Ken Henderson 1.00 .45
❑ 299 Buddy Bradford 1.00 .45
❑ 300 Tom Seaver 30.00 13.50
❑ 301 Chico Salmon 1.00 .45
❑ 302 Jeff James 1.00 .45
❑ 303 Brant Alyea 1.00 .45
❑ 304 Bill Russell RC 6.00 2.70
❑ 305 Don Buford WS 4.00 1.80
❑ 306 Donn Clendenon WS 4.00 1.80
❑ 307 Tommie Agee WS 4.00 1.80
❑ 308 J.C. Martin WS 4.00 1.80
❑ 309 Jerry Koosman WS 4.00 1.80
❑ 310 World Series Summary 6.00 2.70
Mets whoop it up
❑ 311 Dick Green 1.00 .45
❑ 312 Mike Torrez 1.00 .45
❑ 313 Mayo Smith MG 1.00 .45
❑ 314 Bill McCool 1.00 .45
❑ 315 Luis Aparicio 6.00 2.70
❑ 316 Skip Guinn 1.00 .45
❑ 317 Red Sox Rookies 1.00 .45
Billy Conigliaro
Luis Alvarado
❑ 318 Willie Smith 1.00 .45
❑ 319 Clay Dalrymple 1.00 .45
❑ 320 Jim Maloney 1.00 .45
❑ 321 Lou Piniella 2.00 .90
❑ 322 Luke Walker 1.00 .45
❑ 323 Wayne Comer 1.00 .45
❑ 324 Tony Taylor 1.00 .45
❑ 325 Dave Boswell 1.00 .45
❑ 326 Bill Voss 1.00 .45
❑ 327 Hal King 1.00 .45
❑ 328 George Brunet 1.00 .45
❑ 329 Chris Cannizzaro 1.00 .45
❑ 330 Lou Brock 10.00 4.50
❑ 331 Chuck Dobson 1.00 .45
❑ 332 Bobby Wine 1.00 .45
❑ 333 Bobby Murcer 2.00 .90
❑ 334 Phil Regan 1.00 .45
❑ 335 Bill Freehan 2.00 .90
❑ 336 Del Unser 1.00 .45
❑ 337 Mike McCormick 1.00 .45
❑ 338 Paul Schaal 1.00 .45
❑ 339 Johnny Edwards 1.00 .45
❑ 340 Tony Conigliaro 4.00 1.80
❑ 341 Bill Sudakis 1.00 .45
❑ 342 Wilbur Wood 2.00 .90
❑ 343A Checklist 4 6.00 1.20
(Red bat on front)
❑ 343B Checklist 4 6.00 1.20
(Brown bat on front)
❑ 344 Marcelino Lopez 1.00 .45
❑ 345 Al Ferrara 1.00 .45
❑ 346 Red Schoendienst MG 2.00 .90
❑ 347 Russ Snyder 1.00 .45
❑ 348 Mets Rookies 2.00 .90
Mike Jorgensen
Jesse Hudson
❑ 349 Steve Hamilton 1.00 .45
❑ 350 Roberto Clemente 60.00 27.00
❑ 351 Tom Murphy 1.00 .45
❑ 352 Bob Barton 1.00 .45
❑ 353 Stan Williams 1.00 .45
❑ 354 Amos Otis 2.00 .90
❑ 355 Doug Rader 1.00 .45
❑ 356 Fred Lasher 1.00 .45
❑ 357 Bob Burda 1.00 .45
❑ 358 Pedro Borbon RC 2.00 .90
❑ 359 Phil Roof 1.00 .45
❑ 360 Curt Flood 2.00 .90
❑ 361 Ray Jarvis 1.00 .45
❑ 362 Joe Hague 1.00 .45
❑ 363 Tom Shopay 1.00 .45
❑ 364 Dan McGinn 1.00 .45
❑ 365 Zoilo Versalles 1.00 .45
❑ 366 Barry Moore 1.00 .45
❑ 367 Mike Lum 1.00 .45
❑ 368 Ed Herrmann 1.00 .45
❑ 369 Alan Foster 1.00 .45
❑ 370 Tommy Harper 2.00 .90
❑ 371 Rod Gaspar 1.00 .45
❑ 372 Dave Giusti 1.50 .70
❑ 373 Roy White 2.00 .90
❑ 374 Tommie Sisk 1.50 .70
❑ 375 Johnny Callison 2.00 .90
❑ 376 Lefty Phillips MG 1.50 .70
❑ 377 Bill Butler 1.00 .45
❑ 378 Jim Davenport 1.50 .70
❑ 379 Tom Tischinski 1.50 .70
❑ 380 Tony Perez 6.00 2.70
❑ 381 Athletics Rookies 1.50 .70
Bobby Brooks
Mike Olivo
❑ 382 Jack DiLauro 1.50 .70
❑ 383 Mickey Stanley 2.00 .90
❑ 384 Gary Neibauer 1.50 .70
❑ 385 George Scott 2.00 .90
❑ 386 Bill Dillman 1.50 .70
❑ 387 Baltimore Orioles 3.00 1.35
Team Card
❑ 388 Byron Browne 1.50 .70
❑ 389 Jim Shellenback 1.50 .70
❑ 390 Willie Davis 2.00 .90
❑ 391 Larry Brown 1.50 .70
❑ 392 Walt Hriniak 2.00 .90
❑ 393 John Gelnar 1.50 .70
❑ 394 Gil Hodges MG 4.00 1.80
❑ 395 Walt Williams 1.50 .70
❑ 396 Steve Blass 2.00 .90
❑ 397 Roger Repoz 1.50 .70
❑ 398 Bill Stoneman 1.50 .70
❑ 399 New York Yankees 3.00 1.35
Team Card
❑ 400 Denny McLain 4.00 1.80
❑ 401 Giants Rookies 1.50 .70
John Harrell
Bernie Williams
❑ 402 Ellie Rodriguez 1.50 .70
❑ 403 Jim Bunning 6.00 2.70
❑ 404 Rich Reese 1.50 .70
❑ 405 Bill Hands 1.50 .70
❑ 406 Mike Andrews 1.50 .70
❑ 407 Bob Watson 2.00 .90
❑ 408 Paul Lindblad 1.50 .70
❑ 409 Bob Tolan 2.00 .90
❑ 410 Boog Powell 4.00 1.80
❑ 411 Los Angeles Dodgers 3.00 1.35
Team Card
❑ 412 Larry Burchart 1.50 .70
❑ 413 Sonny Jackson 1.50 .70
❑ 414 Paul Edmondson 1.50 .70
❑ 415 Julian Javier 2.00 .90
❑ 416 Joe Verbanic 1.50 .70
❑ 417 John Bateman 1.50 .70
❑ 418 John Donaldson 1.50 .70
❑ 419 Ron Taylor 1.50 .70
❑ 420 Ken McMullen 2.00 .90
❑ 421 Pat Dobson 2.00 .90
❑ 422 Royals Team 3.00 1.35
❑ 423 Jerry May 1.50 .70
❑ 424 Mike Kilkenny 1.50 .70
(Inconsistent design
card number in
white circle)
❑ 425 Bobby Bonds 6.00 2.70
❑ 426 Bill Rigney MG 1.50 .70
❑ 427 Fred Norman 1.50 .70
❑ 428 Don Buford 1.50 .70
❑ 429 Cubs Rookies 1.50 .70
Randy Bobb
Jim Cosman
❑ 430 Andy Messersmith 2.00 .90
❑ 431 Ron Swoboda 2.00 .90
❑ 432A Checklist 5 6.00 1.20
(Baseball in
yellow letters)
❑ 432B Checklist 5 6.00 1.20
(Baseball in
white letters)
❑ 433 Ron Bryant 1.50 .70
❑ 434 Felipe Alou 2.00 .90
❑ 435 Nelson Briles 2.00 .90
❑ 436 Philadelphia Phillies 3.00 1.35
Team Card
❑ 437 Danny Cater 1.50 .70

| | No. | Card | | |
|---|---|---|---|---|
| ❑ | 438 | Pat Jarvis | 1.50 | .70 |
| ❑ | 439 | Lee Maye | 1.50 | .70 |
| ❑ | 440 | Bill Mazeroski | 4.00 | 1.80 |
| ❑ | 441 | John O'Donoghue | 1.50 | .70 |
| ❑ | 442 | Gene Mauch MG | 2.00 | .90 |
| ❑ | 443 | Al Jackson | 1.50 | .70 |
| ❑ | 444 | White Sox Rookies | 1.50 | .70 |
| | | Billy Farmer | | |
| | | John Matias | | |
| ❑ | 445 | Vada Pinson | 2.00 | .90 |
| ❑ | 446 | Billy Grabarkewitz | 1.50 | .70 |
| ❑ | 447 | Lee Stange | 1.50 | .70 |
| ❑ | 448 | Houston Astros | 3.00 | 1.35 |
| | | Team Card | | |
| ❑ | 449 | Jim Palmer | 12.00 | 5.50 |
| ❑ | 450 | Willie McCovey AS | 6.00 | 2.70 |
| ❑ | 451 | Boog Powell AS | 4.00 | 1.80 |
| ❑ | 452 | Felix Millan AS | 2.00 | .90 |
| ❑ | 453 | Rod Carew AS | 6.00 | 2.70 |
| ❑ | 454 | Ron Santo AS | 4.00 | 1.80 |
| ❑ | 455 | Brooks Robinson AS | 6.00 | 2.70 |
| ❑ | 456 | Don Kessinger AS | 2.00 | .90 |
| ❑ | 457 | Rico Petrocelli AS | 4.00 | 1.80 |
| ❑ | 458 | Pete Rose AS | 14.00 | 6.25 |
| ❑ | 459 | Reggie Jackson AS | 12.00 | 5.50 |
| ❑ | 460 | Matty Alou AS | 3.00 | 1.35 |
| ❑ | 461 | Carl Yastrzemski AS | 10.00 | 4.50 |
| ❑ | 462 | Hank Aaron AS | 15.00 | 6.75 |
| ❑ | 463 | Frank Robinson AS | 7.00 | 3.10 |
| ❑ | 464 | Johnny Bench AS | 15.00 | 6.75 |
| ❑ | 465 | Bill Freehan AS | 3.00 | 1.35 |
| ❑ | 466 | Juan Marichal AS | 5.00 | 2.20 |
| ❑ | 467 | Denny McLain AS | 3.00 | 1.35 |
| ❑ | 468 | Jerry Koosman AS | 3.00 | 1.35 |
| ❑ | 469 | Sam McDowell AS | 3.00 | 1.35 |
| ❑ | 470 | Willie Stargell | 10.00 | 4.50 |
| ❑ | 471 | Chris Zachary | 2.00 | .90 |
| ❑ | 472 | Braves Team | 3.50 | 1.55 |
| ❑ | 473 | Don Bryant | 2.00 | .90 |
| ❑ | 474 | Dick Kelley | 2.00 | .90 |
| ❑ | 475 | Dick McAuliffe | 3.00 | 1.35 |
| ❑ | 476 | Don Shaw | 2.00 | .90 |
| ❑ | 477 | Orioles Rookies | 2.00 | .90 |
| | | Al Severinsen | | |
| | | Roger Freed | | |
| ❑ | 478 | Bobby Heise | 2.00 | .90 |
| ❑ | 479 | Dick Woodson | 2.00 | .90 |
| ❑ | 480 | Glenn Beckert | 3.00 | 1.35 |
| ❑ | 481 | Jose Tartabull | 3.00 | 1.35 |
| ❑ | 482 | Tom Hilgendorf | 2.00 | .90 |
| ❑ | 483 | Gail Hopkins | 2.00 | .90 |
| ❑ | 484 | Gary Nolan | 3.00 | 1.35 |
| ❑ | 485 | Jay Johnstone | 3.00 | 1.35 |
| ❑ | 486 | Terry Harmon | 2.00 | .90 |
| ❑ | 487 | Cisco Carlos | 2.00 | .90 |
| ❑ | 488 | J.C. Martin | 2.00 | .90 |
| ❑ | 489 | Eddie Kasko MG | 2.00 | .90 |
| ❑ | 490 | Bill Singer | 3.00 | 1.35 |
| ❑ | 491 | Graig Nettles | 5.00 | 2.20 |
| ❑ | 492 | Astros Rookies | 2.00 | .90 |
| | | Keith Lampard | | |
| | | Scipio Spinks | | |
| ❑ | 493 | Lindy McDaniel | 3.00 | 1.35 |
| ❑ | 494 | Larry Stahl | 2.00 | .90 |
| ❑ | 495 | Dave Morehead | 2.00 | .90 |
| ❑ | 496 | Steve Whitaker | 2.00 | .90 |
| ❑ | 497 | Eddie Watt | 2.00 | .90 |
| ❑ | 498 | Al Weis | 2.00 | .90 |
| ❑ | 499 | Skip Lockwood | 3.00 | 1.35 |
| ❑ | 500 | Hank Aaron | 50.00 | 22.00 |
| ❑ | 501 | Chicago White Sox | 3.50 | 1.55 |
| | | Team Card | | |
| ❑ | 502 | Rollie Fingers | 10.00 | 4.50 |
| ❑ | 503 | Dal Maxvill | 2.00 | .90 |
| ❑ | 504 | Don Pavletich | 2.00 | .90 |
| ❑ | 505 | Ken Holtzman | 3.00 | 1.35 |
| ❑ | 506 | Ed Stroud | 2.00 | .90 |
| ❑ | 507 | Pat Corrales | 3.00 | 1.35 |
| ❑ | 508 | Joe Niekro | 3.00 | 1.35 |
| ❑ | 509 | Montreal Expos | 3.50 | 1.55 |
| | | Team Card | | |
| ❑ | 510 | Tony Oliva | 5.00 | 2.20 |
| ❑ | 511 | Joe Hoerner | 2.00 | .90 |
| ❑ | 512 | Billy Harris | 2.00 | .90 |
| ❑ | 513 | Preston Gomez MG | 2.00 | .90 |
| ❑ | 514 | Steve Hovley | 2.00 | .90 |
| ❑ | 515 | Don Wilson | 3.00 | 1.35 |
| ❑ | 516 | Yankees Rookies | 2.00 | .90 |
| | | John Ellis | | |
| | | Jim Lyttle | | |
| ❑ | 517 | Joe Gibbon | 2.00 | .90 |
| ❑ | 518 | Bill Melton | 2.00 | .90 |
| ❑ | 519 | Don McMahon | 2.00 | .90 |
| ❑ | 520 | Willie Horton | 3.00 | 1.35 |
| ❑ | 521 | Cal Koonce | 2.00 | .90 |
| ❑ | 522 | Angels Team | 3.50 | 1.55 |
| ❑ | 523 | Jose Pena | 2.00 | .90 |
| ❑ | 524 | Alvin Dark MG | 3.00 | 1.35 |
| ❑ | 525 | Jerry Adair | 2.00 | .90 |
| ❑ | 526 | Ron Herbel | 2.00 | .90 |
| ❑ | 527 | Don Bosch | 2.00 | .90 |
| ❑ | 528 | Elrod Hendricks | 2.00 | .90 |
| ❑ | 529 | Bob Aspromonte | 2.00 | .90 |
| ❑ | 530 | Bob Gibson | 14.00 | 6.25 |
| ❑ | 531 | Ron Clark | 2.00 | .90 |
| ❑ | 532 | Danny Murtaugh MG | 3.00 | 1.35 |
| ❑ | 533 | Buzz Stephen | 2.00 | .90 |
| ❑ | 534 | Minnesota Twins | 3.50 | 1.55 |
| | | Team Card | | |
| ❑ | 535 | Andy Kosco | 2.00 | .90 |
| ❑ | 536 | Mike Kekich | 2.00 | .90 |
| ❑ | 537 | Joe Morgan | 10.00 | 4.50 |
| ❑ | 538 | Bob Humphreys | 2.00 | .90 |
| ❑ | 539 | Phillies Rookies | 8.00 | 3.60 |
| | | Denny Doyle | | |
| | | Larry Bowa RC | | |
| ❑ | 540 | Gary Peters | 2.00 | .90 |
| ❑ | 541 | Bill Heath | 2.00 | .90 |
| ❑ | 542 | Checklist 6 | 6.00 | 1.20 |
| ❑ | 543 | Clyde Wright | 2.00 | .90 |
| ❑ | 544 | Cincinnati Reds | 3.50 | 1.55 |
| | | Team Card | | |
| ❑ | 545 | Ken Harrelson | 3.00 | 1.35 |
| ❑ | 546 | Ron Reed | 2.00 | .90 |
| ❑ | 547 | Rick Monday | 6.00 | 2.70 |
| ❑ | 548 | Howie Reed | 4.00 | 1.80 |
| ❑ | 549 | St. Louis Cardinals | 6.00 | 2.70 |
| | | Team Card | | |
| ❑ | 550 | Frank Howard | 6.00 | 2.70 |
| ❑ | 551 | Dock Ellis | 6.00 | 2.70 |
| ❑ | 552 | Royals Rookies | 4.00 | 1.80 |
| | | Don O'Riley | | |
| | | Dennis Paepke | | |
| | | Fred Rico | | |
| ❑ | 553 | Jim Lefebvre | 6.00 | 2.70 |
| ❑ | 554 | Tom Timmermann | 4.00 | 1.80 |
| ❑ | 555 | Orlando Cepeda | 8.00 | 3.60 |
| ❑ | 556 | Dave Bristol MG | 6.00 | 2.70 |
| ❑ | 557 | Ed Kranepool | 6.00 | 2.70 |
| ❑ | 558 | Vern Fuller | 4.00 | 1.80 |
| ❑ | 559 | Tommy Davis | 6.00 | 2.70 |
| ❑ | 560 | Gaylord Perry | 12.00 | 5.50 |
| ❑ | 561 | Tom McCraw | 4.00 | 1.80 |
| ❑ | 562 | Ted Abernathy | 4.00 | 1.80 |
| ❑ | 563 | Boston Red Sox | 6.00 | 2.70 |
| | | Team Card | | |
| ❑ | 564 | Johnny Briggs | 4.00 | 1.80 |
| ❑ | 565 | Jim Hunter | 12.00 | 5.50 |
| ❑ | 566 | Gene Alley | 6.00 | 2.70 |
| ❑ | 567 | Bob Oliver | 4.00 | 1.80 |
| ❑ | 568 | Stan Bahnsen | 6.00 | 2.70 |
| ❑ | 569 | Cookie Rojas | 6.00 | 2.70 |
| ❑ | 570 | Jim Fregosi | 6.00 | 2.70 |
| | | White Chevy Pickup in Background | | |
| ❑ | 571 | Jim Brewer | 4.00 | 1.80 |
| ❑ | 572 | Frank Quilici MG | 4.00 | 1.80 |
| ❑ | 573 | Padres Rookies | 4.00 | 1.80 |
| | | Mike Corkins | | |
| | | Rafael Robles | | |
| | | Ron Slocum | | |
| ❑ | 574 | Bobby Bolin | 6.00 | 2.70 |
| ❑ | 575 | Cleon Jones | 6.00 | 2.70 |
| ❑ | 576 | Milt Pappas | 6.00 | 2.70 |
| ❑ | 577 | Bernie Allen | 4.00 | 1.80 |
| ❑ | 578 | Tom Griffin | 4.00 | 1.80 |
| ❑ | 579 | Detroit Tigers | 6.00 | 2.70 |
| | | Team Card | | |
| ❑ | 580 | Pete Rose | 50.00 | 22.00 |
| ❑ | 581 | Tom Satriano | 4.00 | 1.80 |
| ❑ | 582 | Mike Paul | 4.00 | 1.80 |
| ❑ | 583 | Hal Lanier | 4.00 | 1.80 |
| ❑ | 584 | Al Downing | 6.00 | 2.70 |
| ❑ | 585 | Rusty Staub | 8.00 | 3.60 |
| ❑ | 586 | Rickey Clark | 4.00 | 1.80 |
| ❑ | 587 | Jose Arcia | 4.00 | 1.80 |
| ❑ | 588A | Checklist 7 ERR | 8.00 | 1.60 |
| | | (666 Adolfo) | | |
| ❑ | 588B | Checklist 7 COR | 6.00 | 1.20 |
| | | (666 Adolpho) | | |
| ❑ | 589 | Joe Keough | 4.00 | 1.80 |
| ❑ | 590 | Mike Cuellar | 6.00 | 2.70 |
| ❑ | 591 | Mike Ryan UER | 4.00 | 1.80 |
| | | (Pitching Record | | |
| | | header on card back) | | |
| ❑ | 592 | Daryl Patterson | 4.00 | 1.80 |
| ❑ | 593 | Chicago Cubs | 8.00 | 3.60 |
| | | Team Card | | |
| ❑ | 594 | Jake Gibbs | 4.00 | 1.80 |
| ❑ | 595 | Maury Wills | 8.00 | 3.60 |
| ❑ | 596 | Mike Hershberger | 6.00 | 2.70 |
| ❑ | 597 | Sonny Siebert | 4.00 | 1.80 |
| ❑ | 598 | Joe Pepitone | 6.00 | 2.70 |
| ❑ | 599 | Senators Rookies | 4.00 | 1.80 |
| | | Dick Stelmaszek | | |
| | | Gene Martin | | |
| | | Dick Such | | |
| ❑ | 600 | Willie Mays | 70.00 | 32.00 |
| ❑ | 601 | Pete Richert | 4.00 | 1.80 |
| ❑ | 602 | Ted Savage | 4.00 | 1.80 |
| ❑ | 603 | Ray Oyler | 4.00 | 1.80 |
| ❑ | 604 | Clarence Gaston | 6.00 | 2.70 |
| ❑ | 605 | Rick Wise | 6.00 | 2.70 |
| ❑ | 606 | Chico Ruiz | 4.00 | 1.80 |
| ❑ | 607 | Gary Waslewski | 4.00 | 1.80 |
| ❑ | 608 | Pittsburgh Pirates | 6.00 | 2.70 |
| | | Team Card | | |
| ❑ | 609 | Buck Martinez RC | 6.00 | 2.70 |
| | | (Inconsistent design | | |
| | | card number in | | |
| | | white circle) | | |
| ❑ | 610 | Jerry Koosman | 8.00 | 3.60 |
| ❑ | 611 | Norm Cash | 6.00 | 2.70 |
| ❑ | 612 | Jim Hickman | 6.00 | 2.70 |
| ❑ | 613 | Dave Baldwin | 6.00 | 2.70 |
| ❑ | 614 | Mike Shannon | 6.00 | 2.70 |
| ❑ | 615 | Mark Belanger | 6.00 | 2.70 |
| ❑ | 616 | Jim Merritt | 4.00 | 1.80 |
| ❑ | 617 | Jim French | 4.00 | 1.80 |
| ❑ | 618 | Billy Wynne | 4.00 | 1.80 |
| ❑ | 619 | Norm Miller | 4.00 | 1.80 |
| ❑ | 620 | Jim Perry | 6.00 | 2.70 |
| ❑ | 621 | Braves Rookies | 12.00 | 5.50 |
| | | Mike McQueen | | |
| | | Darrell Evans RC | | |
| | | Rick Kester | | |
| ❑ | 622 | Don Sutton | 12.00 | 5.50 |
| ❑ | 623 | Horace Clarke | 6.00 | 2.70 |
| ❑ | 624 | Clyde King MG | 4.00 | 1.80 |
| ❑ | 625 | Dean Chance | 4.00 | 1.80 |
| ❑ | 626 | Dave Ricketts | 4.00 | 1.80 |
| ❑ | 627 | Gary Wagner | 4.00 | 1.80 |
| ❑ | 628 | Wayne Garrett | 4.00 | 1.80 |
| ❑ | 629 | Merv Rettenmund | 4.00 | 1.80 |
| ❑ | 630 | Ernie Banks | 50.00 | 22.00 |
| ❑ | 631 | Oakland Athletics | 6.00 | 2.70 |
| | | Team Card | | |
| ❑ | 632 | Gary Sutherland | 4.00 | 1.80 |
| ❑ | 633 | Roger Nelson | 4.00 | 1.80 |
| ❑ | 634 | Bud Harrelson | 15.00 | 6.75 |
| ❑ | 635 | Bob Allison | 15.00 | 6.75 |
| ❑ | 636 | Jim Stewart | 10.00 | 4.50 |
| ❑ | 637 | Cleveland Indians | 12.00 | 5.50 |
| | | Team Card | | |
| ❑ | 638 | Frank Bertaina | 10.00 | 4.50 |
| ❑ | 639 | Dave Campbell | 10.00 | 4.50 |
| ❑ | 640 | Al Kaline | 50.00 | 22.00 |
| ❑ | 641 | Al McBean | 10.00 | 4.50 |
| ❑ | 642 | Angels Rookies | 10.00 | 4.50 |
| | | Greg Garrett | | |
| | | Gordon Lund | | |
| | | Jarvis Tatum | | |
| ❑ | 643 | Jose Pagan | 10.00 | 4.50 |
| ❑ | 644 | Gerry Nyman | 10.00 | 4.50 |
| ❑ | 645 | Don Money | 15.00 | 6.75 |
| ❑ | 646 | Jim Britton | 10.00 | 4.50 |
| ❑ | 647 | Tom Matchick | 10.00 | 4.50 |
| ❑ | 648 | Larry Haney | 10.00 | 4.50 |
| ❑ | 649 | Jimmie Hall | 10.00 | 4.50 |

❑ 650 Sam McDowell ........ 15.00 6.75
❑ 651 Jim Gosger ........ 10.00 4.50
❑ 652 Rich Rollins ........ 15.00 6.75
❑ 653 Moe Drabowsky ........ 10.00 4.50
❑ 654 NL Rookies ........ 15.00 6.75
Oscar Gamble
Boots Day
Angel Mangual RC ! RC ! RC !
❑ 655 John Roseboro ........ 15.00 6.75
❑ 656 Jim Hardin ........ 10.00 4.50
❑ 657 San Diego Padres ...... 12.00 5.50
Team Card
❑ 658 Ken Tatum ........ 10.00 4.50
❑ 659 Pete Ward ........ 10.00 4.50
❑ 660 Johnny Bench ........ 80.00 36.00
❑ 661 Jerry Robertson ........ 10.00 4.50
❑ 662 Frank Lucchesi MG .... 10.00 4.50
❑ 663 Tito Francona ........ 10.00 4.50
❑ 664 Bob Robertson ........ 10.00 4.50
❑ 665 Jim Lonborg ........ 15.00 6.75
❑ 666 Adolpho Phillips ........ 10.00 4.50
❑ 667 Bob Meyer ........ 15.00 6.75
❑ 668 Bob Tillman ........ 10.00 4.50
❑ 669 White Sox Rookies .... 10.00 4.50
Bart Johnson
Dan Lazar
Mickey Scott
❑ 670 Ron Santo ........ 15.00 6.75
❑ 671 Jim Campanis ........ 10.00 4.50
❑ 672 Leon McFadden ........ 10.00 4.50
❑ 673 Ted Uhlaender ........ 10.00 4.50
❑ 674 Dave Leonhard ........ 10.00 4.50
❑ 675 Jose Cardenal ........ 15.00 6.75
❑ 676 Washington Senators 12.00 5.50
Team Card
❑ 677 Woodie Fryman ........ 10.00 4.50
❑ 678 Dave Duncan ........ 15.00 6.75
❑ 679 Ray Sadecki ........ 10.00 4.50
❑ 680 Rico Petrocelli ........ 15.00 6.75
❑ 681 Bob Garibaldi ........ 10.00 4.50
❑ 682 Dalton Jones ........ 10.00 4.50
❑ 683 Reds Rookies ........ 15.00 6.75
Vern Geishert
Hal McRae
Wayne Simpson
❑ 684 Jack Fisher ........ 10.00 4.50
❑ 685 Tom Haller ........ 10.00 4.50
❑ 686 Jackie Hernandez ...... 10.00 4.50
❑ 687 Bob Priddy ........ 10.00 4.50
❑ 688 Ted Kubiak ........ 15.00 6.75
❑ 689 Frank Tepedino ........ 10.00 4.50
❑ 690 Ron Fairly ........ 15.00 6.75
❑ 691 Joe Grzenda ........ 10.00 4.50
❑ 692 Duffy Dyer ........ 10.00 4.50
❑ 693 Bob Johnson ........ 10.00 4.50
❑ 694 Gary Ross ........ 10.00 4.50
❑ 695 Bobby Knoop ........ 10.00 4.50
❑ 696 San Francisco Giants 12.00 5.50
Team Card
❑ 697 Jim Hannan ........ 10.00 4.50
❑ 698 Tom Tresh ........ 15.00 6.75
❑ 699 Hank Aguirre ........ 10.00 4.50
❑ 700 Frank Robinson ........ 50.00 22.00
❑ 701 Jack Billingham ........ 10.00 4.50
❑ 702 AL Rookies ........ 10.00 4.50
Bob Johnson
Ron Klimkowski
Bill Zepp
❑ 703 Lou Marone ........ 10.00 4.50
❑ 704 Frank Baker ........ 10.00 4.50
❑ 705 Tony Cloninger UER .. 10.00 4.50
(Batter headings
on card back)
❑ 706 John McNamara MG .. 10.00 4.50
❑ 707 Kevin Collins ........ 10.00 4.50
❑ 708 Jose Santiago ........ 10.00 4.50
❑ 709 Mike Fiore ........ 10.00 4.50
❑ 710 Felix Millan ........ 10.00 4.50
❑ 711 Ed Brinkman ........ 10.00 4.50
❑ 712 Nolan Ryan ........ 250.00 110.00
❑ 713 Seattle Pilots ........ 25.00 11.00
Team Card
❑ 714 Al Spangler ........ 10.00 4.50
❑ 715 Mickey Lolich ........ 15.00 6.75
❑ 716 Cardinals Rookies ...... 15.00 6.75
Sal Campisi
Reggie Cleveland
Santiago Guzman
❑ 717 Tom Phoebus ........ 10.00 4.50
❑ 718 Ed Spiezio ........ 10.00 4.50
❑ 719 Jim Roland ........ 10.00 4.50
❑ 720 Rick Reichardt ........ 15.00 5.00

## 1971 Topps

| | NRMT | VG-E |
|---|---|---|
| COMPLETE SET (752) | 2000.00 | 900.00 |
| COMMON CARD (1-393) | 1.50 | .70 |
| COMMON CARD (394-523) | 2.50 | 1.10 |
| COMMON CARD (524-643) | 4.00 | 1.80 |
| COMMON CARD (644-752) | 8.00 | 3.60 |
| COMMON SP (644-752) | 12.00 | 5.50 |
| WRAPPER (10-CENT) | 15.00 | 6.75 |

❑ 1 Baltimore Orioles ........ 15.00 5.00
Team Card
❑ 2 Dock Ellis ........ 1.50 .70
❑ 3 Dick McAuliffe ........ 1.50 .70
❑ 4 Vic Davalillo ........ 1.50 .70
❑ 5 Thurman Munson ........ 18.00 8.00
❑ 6 Ed Spiezio ........ 1.50 .70
❑ 7 Jim Holt ........ 1.50 .70
❑ 8 Mike McQueen ........ 1.50 .70
❑ 9 George Scott ........ 2.00 .90
❑ 10 Claude Osteen ........ 1.50 .70
❑ 11 Elliott Maddox ........ 1.50 .70
❑ 12 Johnny Callison ........ 1.50 .70
❑ 13 White Sox Rookies ........ 1.50 .70
Charlie Brinkman
Dick Moloney
❑ 14 Dave Concepcion RC .. 15.00 6.75
❑ 15 Andy Messersmith ........ 2.00 .90
❑ 16 Ken Singleton RC ........ 4.00 1.80
❑ 17 Billy Sorrell ........ 1.50 .70
❑ 18 Norm Miller ........ 1.50 .70
❑ 19 Skip Pitlock ........ 1.50 .70
❑ 20 Reggie Jackson ........ 30.00 13.50
❑ 21 Dan McGinn ........ 1.50 .70
❑ 22 Phil Roof ........ 1.50 .70
❑ 23 Oscar Gamble ........ 1.50 .70
❑ 24 Rich Hand ........ 1.50 .70
❑ 25 Clarence Gaston ........ 2.00 .90
❑ 26 Bert Blyleven RC ........ 8.00 3.60
❑ 27 Pirates Rookies ........ 1.50 .70
Fred Cambria
Gene Clines
❑ 28 Ron Klimkowski ........ 1.50 .70
❑ 29 Don Buford ........ 1.50 .70
❑ 30 Phil Niekro ........ 6.00 2.70
❑ 31 Eddie Kasko MG ........ 1.50 .70
❑ 32 Jerry DaVanon ........ 1.50 .70
❑ 33 Del Unser ........ 1.50 .70
❑ 34 Sandy Vance ........ 1.50 .70
❑ 35 Lou Piniella ........ 2.00 .90
❑ 36 Dean Chance ........ 1.50 .70
❑ 37 Rich McKinney ........ 1.50 .70
❑ 38 Jim Colborn ........ 1.50 .70
❑ 39 Tiger Rookies ........ 1.50 .70
Lerrin LaGrow
Gene Lamont RC
❑ 40 Lee May ........ 2.00 .90
❑ 41 Rick Austin ........ 1.50 .70
❑ 42 Boots Day ........ 1.50 .70
❑ 43 Steve Kealey ........ 1.50 .70
❑ 44 Johnny Edwards ........ 1.50 .70
❑ 45 Jim Hunter ........ 6.00 2.70
❑ 46 Dave Campbell ........ 1.50 .70
❑ 47 Johnny Jeter ........ 1.50 .70
❑ 48 Dave Baldwin ........ 1.50 .70
❑ 49 Don Money ........ 1.50 .70
❑ 50 Willie McCovey ........ 8.00 3.60
❑ 51 Steve Kline ........ 1.50 .70
❑ 52 Braves Rookies ........ 1.50 .70
Oscar Brown
Earl Williams RC
❑ 53 Paul Blair ........ 2.00 .90
❑ 54 Checklist 1 ........ 11.00 2.20
❑ 55 Steve Carlton ........ 15.00 6.75
❑ 56 Duane Josephson ........ 1.50 .70
❑ 57 Von Joshua ........ 1.50 .70
❑ 58 Bill Lee ........ 2.00 .90
❑ 59 Gene Mauch MG ........ 2.00 .90
❑ 60 Dick Bosman ........ 1.50 .70
❑ 61 AL Batting Leaders ........ 4.00 1.80
Alex Johnson
Carl Yastrzemski
Tony Oliva
❑ 62 NL Batting Leaders ........ 2.00 .90
Rico Carty
Joe Torre
Manny Sanguillen
❑ 63 AL RBI Leaders ........ 4.00 1.80
Frank Howard
Tony Conigliaro
Boog Powell
❑ 64 NL RBI Leaders ........ 6.00 2.70
Johnny Bench
Tony Perez
Billy Williams
❑ 65 AL HR Leaders ........ 4.00 1.80
Frank Howard
Harmon Killebrew
Carl Yastrzemski
❑ 66 NL HR Leaders ........ 6.00 2.70
Johnny Bench
Billy Williams
Tony Perez
❑ 67 AL ERA Leaders ........ 4.00 1.80
Diego Segui
Jim Palmer
Clyde Wright
❑ 68 NL ERA Leaders ........ 4.00 1.80
Tom Seaver
Wayne Simpson
Luke Walker
❑ 69 AL Pitching Leaders ...... 2.00 .90
Mike Cuellar
Dave McNally
Jim Perry
❑ 70 NL Pitching Leaders ...... 6.00 2.70
Bob Gibson
Gaylord Perry
Fergie Jenkins
❑ 71 AL Strikeout Leaders ...... 2.00 .90
Sam McDowell
Mickey Lolich
Bob Johnson
❑ 72 NL Strikeout Leaders .... 6.00 2.70
Tom Seaver
Bob Gibson
Fergie Jenkins
❑ 73 George Brunet ........ 1.50 .70
❑ 74 Twins Rookies ........ 1.50 .70
Pete Hamm
Jim Nettles
❑ 75 Gary Nolan ........ 2.00 .90
❑ 76 Ted Savage ........ 1.50 .70
❑ 77 Mike Compton ........ 1.50 .70
❑ 78 Jim Spencer ........ 1.50 .70
❑ 79 Wade Blasingame ........ 1.50 .70
❑ 80 Bill Melton ........ 1.50 .70
❑ 81 Felix Millan ........ 1.50 .70
❑ 82 Casey Cox ........ 1.50 .70
❑ 83 Met Rookies ........ 1.50 .70
Tim Foli RC
Randy Bobb
❑ 84 Marcel Lachemann RC .. 1.50 .70
❑ 85 Billy Grabarkewitz ........ 1.50 .70
❑ 86 Mike Kilkenny ........ 1.50 .70
❑ 87 Jack Heidemann ........ 1.50 .70

| | | | |
|---|---|---|---|
| ❑ 88 | Hal King | 1.50 | .70 |
| ❑ 89 | Ken Brett | 1.50 | .70 |
| ❑ 90 | Joe Pepitone | 2.00 | .90 |
| ❑ 91 | Bob Lemon MG | 2.00 | .90 |
| ❑ 92 | Fred Wenz | 1.50 | .70 |
| ❑ 93 | Senators Rookies | 1.50 | .70 |
| | Norm McRae | | |
| | Denny Riddleberger | | |
| ❑ 94 | Don Hahn | 1.50 | .70 |
| ❑ 95 | Luis Tiant | 2.00 | .90 |
| ❑ 96 | Joe Hague | 1.50 | .70 |
| ❑ 97 | Floyd Wicker | 1.50 | .70 |
| ❑ 98 | Joe Decker | 1.50 | .70 |
| ❑ 99 | Mark Belanger | 2.00 | .90 |
| ❑ 100 | Pete Rose | 40.00 | 18.00 |
| ❑ 101 | Les Cain | 1.50 | .70 |
| ❑ 102 | Astros Rookies | 2.00 | .90 |
| | Ken Forsch | | |
| | Larry Howard | | |
| ❑ 103 | Rich Severson | 1.50 | .70 |
| ❑ 104 | Dan Frisella | 1.50 | .70 |
| ❑ 105 | Tony Conigliaro | 2.00 | .90 |
| ❑ 106 | Tom Dukes | 1.50 | .70 |
| ❑ 107 | Roy Foster | 1.50 | .70 |
| ❑ 108 | John Cumberland | 1.50 | .70 |
| ❑ 109 | Steve Hovley | 1.50 | .70 |
| ❑ 110 | Bill Mazeroski | 2.00 | .90 |
| ❑ 111 | Yankee Rookies | 1.50 | .70 |
| | Loyd Colson | | |
| | Bobby Mitchell | | |
| ❑ 112 | Manny Mota | 2.00 | .90 |
| ❑ 113 | Jerry Crider | 1.50 | .70 |
| ❑ 114 | Billy Conigliaro | 2.00 | .90 |
| ❑ 115 | Donn Clendenon | 2.00 | .90 |
| ❑ 116 | Ken Sanders | 1.50 | .70 |
| ❑ 117 | Ted Simmons RC | 8.00 | 3.60 |
| ❑ 118 | Cookie Rojas | 2.00 | .90 |
| ❑ 119 | Frank Lucchesi MG | 1.50 | .70 |
| ❑ 120 | Willie Horton | 2.00 | .90 |
| ❑ 121 | Cubs Rookies | 1.50 | .70 |
| | Jim Dunegan | | |
| | Roe Skidmore | | |
| ❑ 122 | Eddie Watt | 1.50 | .70 |
| ❑ 123A | Checklist 2 | 11.00 | 2.20 |
| | (Card number at bottom right) | | |
| ❑ 123B | Checklist 2 | 11.00 | 2.20 |
| | (Card number centered) | | |
| ❑ 124 | Don Gullett RC | 2.00 | .90 |
| ❑ 125 | Ray Fosse | 2.00 | .90 |
| ❑ 126 | Danny Coombs | 1.50 | .70 |
| ❑ 127 | Danny Thompson | 2.00 | .90 |
| ❑ 128 | Frank Johnson | 1.50 | .70 |
| ❑ 129 | Aurelio Monteagudo | 1.50 | .70 |
| ❑ 130 | Denis Menke | 1.50 | .70 |
| ❑ 131 | Curt Blefary | 1.50 | .70 |
| ❑ 132 | Jose Laboy | 1.50 | .70 |
| ❑ 133 | Mickey Lolich | 2.00 | .90 |
| ❑ 134 | Jose Arcia | 1.50 | .70 |
| ❑ 135 | Rick Monday | 2.00 | .90 |
| ❑ 136 | Duffy Dyer | 1.50 | .70 |
| ❑ 137 | Marcelino Lopez | 1.50 | .70 |
| ❑ 138 | Phillies Rookies | 2.00 | .90 |
| | Joe Lis | | |
| | Willie Montanez | | |
| ❑ 139 | Paul Casanova | 1.50 | .70 |
| ❑ 140 | Gaylord Perry | 6.00 | 2.70 |
| ❑ 141 | Frank Quilici | 1.50 | .70 |
| ❑ 142 | Mack Jones | 1.50 | .70 |
| ❑ 143 | Steve Blass | 2.00 | .90 |
| ❑ 144 | Jackie Hernandez | 1.50 | .70 |
| ❑ 145 | Bill Singer | 2.00 | .90 |
| ❑ 146 | Ralph Houk MG | 2.00 | .90 |
| ❑ 147 | Bob Priddy | 1.50 | .70 |
| ❑ 148 | John Mayberry | 2.00 | .90 |
| ❑ 149 | Mike Hershberger | 1.50 | .70 |
| ❑ 150 | Sam McDowell | 2.00 | .90 |
| ❑ 151 | Tommy Davis | 2.00 | .90 |
| ❑ 152 | Angels Rookies | 1.50 | .70 |
| | Lloyd Allen | | |
| | Winston Llenas | | |
| ❑ 153 | Gary Ross | 1.50 | .70 |
| ❑ 154 | Cesar Gutierrez | 1.50 | .70 |
| ❑ 155 | Ken Henderson | 1.50 | .70 |
| ❑ 156 | Bart Johnson | 1.50 | .70 |
| ❑ 157 | Bob Bailey | 1.50 | .70 |
| ❑ 158 | Jerry Reuss | 2.00 | .90 |
| ❑ 159 | Jarvis Tatum | 1.50 | .70 |
| ❑ 160 | Tom Seaver | 25.00 | 11.00 |
| ❑ 161 | Coin Checklist | 11.00 | 2.20 |
| ❑ 162 | Jack Billingham | 1.50 | .70 |
| ❑ 163 | Buck Martinez | 2.00 | .90 |
| ❑ 164 | Reds Rookies | 2.00 | .90 |
| | Frank Duffy | | |
| | Milt Wilcox | | |
| ❑ 165 | Cesar Tovar | 1.50 | .70 |
| ❑ 166 | Joe Hoerner | 1.50 | .70 |
| ❑ 167 | Tom Grieve RC | 2.00 | .90 |
| ❑ 168 | Bruce Dal Canton | 1.50 | .70 |
| ❑ 169 | Ed Herrmann | 1.50 | .70 |
| ❑ 170 | Mike Cuellar | 2.00 | .90 |
| ❑ 171 | Bobby Wine | 1.50 | .70 |
| ❑ 172 | Duke Sims | 1.50 | .70 |
| ❑ 173 | Gil Garrido | 1.50 | .70 |
| ❑ 174 | Dave LaRoche | 1.50 | .70 |
| ❑ 175 | Jim Hickman | 1.50 | .70 |
| ❑ 176 | Red Sox Rookies | 2.00 | .90 |
| | Bob Montgomery RC | | |
| | Doug Griffin | | |
| ❑ 177 | Hal McRae | 2.00 | .90 |
| ❑ 178 | Dave Duncan | 1.50 | .70 |
| ❑ 179 | Mike Corkins | 1.50 | .70 |
| ❑ 180 | Al Kaline UER | 20.00 | 9.00 |
| | (Home instead of Birth) | | |
| ❑ 181 | Hal Lanier | 1.50 | .70 |
| ❑ 182 | Al Downing | 2.00 | .90 |
| ❑ 183 | Gil Hodges MG | 4.00 | 1.80 |
| ❑ 184 | Stan Bahnsen | 1.50 | .70 |
| ❑ 185 | Julian Javier | 2.00 | .90 |
| ❑ 186 | Bob Spence | 1.50 | .70 |
| ❑ 187 | Ted Abernathy | 1.50 | .70 |
| ❑ 188 | Dodgers Rookies | 6.00 | 2.70 |
| | Bob Valentine RC | | |
| | Mike Strahler | | |
| ❑ 189 | George Mitterwald | 1.50 | .70 |
| ❑ 190 | Bob Tolan | 2.00 | .90 |
| ❑ 191 | Mike Andrews | 1.50 | .70 |
| ❑ 192 | Billy Wilson | 1.50 | .70 |
| ❑ 193 | Bob Grich RC | 4.00 | 1.80 |
| ❑ 194 | Mike Lum | 1.50 | .70 |
| ❑ 195 | Boog Powell ALCS | 2.00 | .90 |
| ❑ 196 | Dave McNally ALCS | 2.00 | .90 |
| ❑ 197 | Jim Palmer ALCS | 4.00 | 1.80 |
| ❑ 198 | AL Playoff Summary | 2.00 | .90 |
| | Orioles celebrate | | |
| ❑ 199 | Ty Cline NLCS | 2.00 | .90 |
| ❑ 200 | Bobby Tolan NLCS | 2.00 | .90 |
| ❑ 201 | Ty Cline NLCS | 2.00 | .90 |
| ❑ 202 | NL Playoff Summary | 2.00 | .90 |
| | Reds celebrate | | |
| ❑ 203 | Larry Gura | 2.00 | .90 |
| ❑ 204 | Brewers Rookies | 1.50 | .70 |
| | Bernie Smith | | |
| | George Kopacz | | |
| ❑ 205 | Gerry Moses | 1.50 | .70 |
| ❑ 206 | Checklist 3 | 11.00 | 2.20 |
| ❑ 207 | Alan Foster | 1.50 | .70 |
| ❑ 208 | Billy Martin MG | 4.00 | 1.80 |
| ❑ 209 | Steve Renko | 1.50 | .70 |
| ❑ 210 | Rod Carew | 15.00 | 6.75 |
| ❑ 211 | Phil Hennigan | 1.50 | .70 |
| ❑ 212 | Rich Hebner | 2.00 | .90 |
| ❑ 213 | Frank Baker | 1.50 | .70 |
| ❑ 214 | Al Ferrara | 1.50 | .70 |
| ❑ 215 | Diego Segui | 1.50 | .70 |
| ❑ 216 | Cards Rookies | 1.50 | .70 |
| | Reggie Cleveland | | |
| | Luis Melendez | | |
| ❑ 217 | Ed Stroud | 1.50 | .70 |
| ❑ 218 | Tony Cloninger | 1.50 | .70 |
| ❑ 219 | Elrod Hendricks | 1.50 | .70 |
| ❑ 220 | Ron Santo | 2.00 | .90 |
| ❑ 221 | Dave Morehead | 1.50 | .70 |
| ❑ 222 | Bob Watson | 2.00 | .90 |
| ❑ 223 | Cecil Upshaw | 1.50 | .70 |
| ❑ 224 | Alan Gallagher | 1.50 | .70 |
| ❑ 225 | Gary Peters | 1.50 | .70 |
| ❑ 226 | Bill Russell | 2.00 | .90 |
| ❑ 227 | Floyd Weaver | 1.50 | .70 |
| ❑ 228 | Wayne Garrett | 1.50 | .70 |
| ❑ 229 | Jim Hannan | 1.50 | .70 |
| ❑ 230 | Willie Stargell | 8.00 | 3.60 |
| ❑ 231 | Indians Rookies | 1.50 | .70 |
| | Vince Colbert | | |
| | John Lowenstein RC | | |
| ❑ 232 | John Strohmayer | 1.50 | .70 |
| ❑ 233 | Larry Bowa | 2.00 | .90 |
| ❑ 234 | Jim Lyttle | 1.50 | .70 |
| ❑ 235 | Nate Colbert | 1.50 | .70 |
| ❑ 236 | Bob Humphreys | 1.50 | .70 |
| ❑ 237 | Cesar Cedeno RC | 2.00 | .90 |
| ❑ 238 | Chuck Dobson | 1.50 | .70 |
| ❑ 239 | Red Schoendienst MG | 2.00 | .90 |
| ❑ 240 | Clyde Wright | 1.50 | .70 |
| ❑ 241 | Dave Nelson | 1.50 | .70 |
| ❑ 242 | Jim Ray | 1.50 | .70 |
| ❑ 243 | Carlos May | 2.00 | .90 |
| ❑ 244 | Bob Tillman | 1.50 | .70 |
| ❑ 245 | Jim Kaat | 2.00 | .90 |
| ❑ 246 | Tony Taylor | 2.00 | .90 |
| ❑ 247 | Royals Rookies | 2.00 | .90 |
| | Jerry Cram | | |
| | Paul Splittorff | | |
| ❑ 248 | Hoyt Wilhelm | 4.00 | 1.80 |
| ❑ 249 | Chico Salmon | 1.50 | .70 |
| ❑ 250 | Johnny Bench | 25.00 | 11.00 |
| ❑ 251 | Frank Reberger | 1.50 | .70 |
| ❑ 252 | Eddie Leon | 1.50 | .70 |
| ❑ 253 | Bill Sudakis | 1.50 | .70 |
| ❑ 254 | Cal Koonce | 1.50 | .70 |
| ❑ 255 | Bob Robertson | 2.00 | .90 |
| ❑ 256 | Tony Gonzalez | 1.50 | .70 |
| ❑ 257 | Nelson Briles | 1.50 | .70 |
| ❑ 258 | Dick Green | 1.50 | .70 |
| ❑ 259 | Dave Marshall | 1.50 | .70 |
| ❑ 260 | Tommy Harper | 2.00 | .90 |
| ❑ 261 | Darold Knowles | 1.50 | .70 |
| ❑ 262 | Padres Rookies | 1.50 | .70 |
| | Jim Williams | | |
| | Dave Robinson | | |
| ❑ 263 | John Ellis | 1.50 | .70 |
| ❑ 264 | Joe Morgan | 8.00 | 3.60 |
| ❑ 265 | Jim Northrup | 2.00 | .90 |
| ❑ 266 | Bill Stoneman | 1.50 | .70 |
| ❑ 267 | Rich Morales | 1.50 | .70 |
| ❑ 268 | Philadelphia Phillies | 4.00 | 1.80 |
| | Team Card | | |
| ❑ 269 | Gail Hopkins | 1.50 | .70 |
| ❑ 270 | Rico Carty | 2.00 | .90 |
| ❑ 271 | Bill Zepp | 1.50 | .70 |
| ❑ 272 | Tommy Helms | 2.00 | .90 |
| ❑ 273 | Pete Richert | 1.50 | .70 |
| ❑ 274 | Ron Slocum | 1.50 | .70 |
| ❑ 275 | Vada Pinson | 2.00 | .90 |
| ❑ 276 | Giants Rookies | 8.00 | 3.60 |
| | Mike Davison | | |
| | George Foster RC | | |
| ❑ 277 | Gary Waslewski | 1.50 | .70 |
| ❑ 278 | Jerry Grote | 1.50 | .70 |
| ❑ 279 | Lefty Phillips MG | 1.50 | .70 |
| ❑ 280 | Ferguson Jenkins | 6.00 | 2.70 |
| ❑ 281 | Danny Walton | 1.50 | .70 |
| ❑ 282 | Jose Pagan | 1.50 | .70 |
| ❑ 283 | Dick Such | 1.50 | .70 |
| ❑ 284 | Jim Gosger | 1.50 | .70 |
| ❑ 285 | Sal Bando | 2.00 | .90 |
| ❑ 286 | Jerry McNertney | 1.50 | .70 |
| ❑ 287 | Mike Fiore | 1.50 | .70 |
| ❑ 288 | Joe Moeller | 1.50 | .70 |
| ❑ 289 | Chicago White Sox | 2.00 | .90 |
| | Team Card | | |
| ❑ 290 | Tony Oliva | 2.00 | .90 |
| ❑ 291 | George Culver | 1.50 | .70 |
| ❑ 292 | Jay Johnstone | 2.00 | .90 |
| ❑ 293 | Pat Corrales | 2.00 | .90 |
| ❑ 294 | Steve Dunning | 1.50 | .70 |
| ❑ 295 | Bobby Bonds | 4.00 | 1.80 |
| ❑ 296 | Tom Timmermann | 1.50 | .70 |
| ❑ 297 | Johnny Briggs | 1.50 | .70 |
| ❑ 298 | Jim Nelson | 1.50 | .70 |
| ❑ 299 | Ed Kirkpatrick | 1.50 | .70 |
| ❑ 300 | Brooks Robinson | 20.00 | 9.00 |
| ❑ 301 | Earl Wilson | 1.50 | .70 |
| ❑ 302 | Phil Gagliano | 1.50 | .70 |
| ❑ 303 | Lindy McDaniel | 2.00 | .90 |
| ❑ 304 | Ron Brand | 1.50 | .70 |

❑ 305 Reggie Smith 2.00 .90
❑ 306 Jim Nash 1.50 .70
❑ 307 Don Wert 1.50 .70
❑ 308 St. Louis Cardinals 2.00 .90
Team Card
❑ 309 Dick Ellsworth 1.50 .70
❑ 310 Tommie Agee 2.00 .90
❑ 311 Lee Stange 1.50 .70
❑ 312 Harry Walker MG 1.50 .70
❑ 313 Tom Hall 1.50 .70
❑ 314 Jeff Torborg 2.00 .90
❑ 315 Ron Fairly 2.00 .90
❑ 316 Fred Scherman 1.50 .70
❑ 317 Athletic Rookies 1.50 .70
Jim Driscoll
Angel Mangual
❑ 318 Rudy May 1.50 .70
❑ 319 Ty Cline 1.50 .70
❑ 320 Dave McNally 2.00 .90
❑ 321 Tom Matchick 1.50 .70
❑ 322 Jim Beauchamp 1.50 .70
❑ 323 Billy Champion 1.50 .70
❑ 324 Graig Nettles 2.00 .90
❑ 325 Juan Marichal 6.00 2.70
❑ 326 Richie Scheinblum 1.50 .70
❑ 327 Boog Powell WS 2.00 .90
❑ 328 Don Buford WS 2.00 .90
❑ 329 Frank Robinson WS 4.00 1.80
❑ 330 World Series Game 4 2.00 .90
Reds stay alive
❑ 331 Brooks Robinson WS 6.00 2.70
Commits robbery
❑ 332 World Series Summary 2.00 .90
Orioles celebrate
❑ 333 Clay Kirby 1.50 .70
❑ 334 Roberto Pena 1.50 .70
❑ 335 Jerry Koosman 2.00 .90
❑ 336 Detroit Tigers 2.00 .90
Team Card
❑ 337 Jesus Alou 1.50 .70
❑ 338 Gene Tenace 2.00 .90
❑ 339 Wayne Simpson 1.50 .70
❑ 340 Rico Petrocelli 2.00 .90
❑ 341 Steve Garvey RC ! 30.00 13.50
❑ 342 Frank Tepedino 1.50 .70
❑ 343 Pirates Rookies 1.50 .70
Ed Acosta
Milt May RC
❑ 344 Ellie Rodriguez 1.50 .70
❑ 345 Joel Horlen 1.50 .70
❑ 346 Lum Harris MG 1.50 .70
❑ 347 Ted Uhlaender 1.50 .70
❑ 348 Fred Norman 1.50 .70
❑ 349 Rich Reese 1.50 .70
❑ 350 Billy Williams 6.00 2.70
❑ 351 Jim Shellenback 1.50 .70
❑ 352 Denny Doyle 1.50 .70
❑ 353 Carl Taylor 1.50 .70
❑ 354 Don McMahon 1.50 .70
❑ 355 Bud Harrelson 4.00 1.80
(Nolan Ryan in photo)
❑ 356 Bob Locker 1.50 .70
❑ 357 Cincinnati Reds 2.00 .90
Team Card
❑ 358 Danny Cater 1.50 .70
❑ 359 Ron Reed 1.50 .70
❑ 360 Jim Fregosi 2.00 .90
❑ 361 Don Sutton 6.00 2.70
❑ 362 Orioles Rookies 1.50 .70
Mike Adamson
Roger Freed
❑ 363 Mike Nagy 1.50 .70
❑ 364 Tommy Dean 1.50 .70
❑ 365 Bob Johnson 1.50 .70
❑ 366 Ron Stone 1.50 .70
❑ 367 Dalton Jones 1.50 .70
❑ 368 Bob Veale 2.00 .90
❑ 369 Checklist 4 11.00 2.20
❑ 370 Joe Torre 2.00 .90
❑ 371 Jack Hiatt 1.50 .70
❑ 372 Lew Krausse 1.50 .70
❑ 373 Tom McCraw 1.50 .70
❑ 374 Clete Boyer 2.00 .90
❑ 375 Steve Hargan 1.50 .70
❑ 376 Expos Rookies 1.50 .70
Clyde Mashore
Ernie McAnally
❑ 377 Greg Garrett 1.50 .70
❑ 378 Tito Fuentes 1.50 .70
❑ 379 Wayne Granger 1.50 .70
❑ 380 Ted Williams MG 12.00 5.50
❑ 381 Fred Gladding 1.50 .70
❑ 382 Jake Gibbs 1.50 .70
❑ 383 Rod Gaspar 1.50 .70
❑ 384 Rollie Fingers 6.00 2.70
❑ 385 Maury Wills 2.00 .90
❑ 386 Boston Red Sox 2.00 .90
Team Card
❑ 387 Ron Herbel 1.50 .70
❑ 388 Al Oliver 2.00 .90
❑ 389 Ed Brinkman 1.50 .70
❑ 390 Glenn Beckert 2.00 .90
❑ 391 Twins Rookies 2.00 .90
Steve Brye
Cotton Nash
❑ 392 Grant Jackson 1.50 .70
❑ 393 Merv Rettenmund 2.00 .90
❑ 394 Clay Carroll 2.50 1.10
❑ 395 Roy White 4.00 1.80
❑ 396 Dick Schofield 2.50 1.10
❑ 397 Alvin Dark MG 4.00 1.80
❑ 398 Howie Reed 2.50 1.10
❑ 399 Jim French 2.50 1.10
❑ 400 Hank Aaron 50.00 22.00
❑ 401 Tom Murphy 2.50 1.10
❑ 402 Los Angeles Dodgers 6.00 2.70
Team Card
❑ 403 Joe Coleman 2.50 1.10
❑ 404 Astros Rookies 2.50 1.10
Buddy Harris
Roger Metzger
❑ 405 Leo Cardenas 2.50 1.10
❑ 406 Ray Sadecki 2.50 1.10
❑ 407 Joe Rudi 4.00 1.80
❑ 408 Rafael Robles 2.50 1.10
❑ 409 Don Pavletich 2.50 1.10
❑ 410 Ken Holtzman 4.00 1.80
❑ 411 George Spriggs 2.50 1.10
❑ 412 Jerry Johnson 2.50 1.10
❑ 413 Pat Kelly 2.50 1.10
❑ 414 Woodie Fryman 2.50 1.10
❑ 415 Mike Hegan 2.50 1.10
❑ 416 Gene Alley 2.50 1.10
❑ 417 Dick Hall 2.50 1.10
❑ 418 Adolfo Phillips 2.50 1.10
❑ 419 Ron Hansen 2.50 1.10
❑ 420 Jim Merritt 2.50 1.10
❑ 421 John Stephenson 2.50 1.10
❑ 422 Frank Bertaina 2.50 1.10
❑ 423 Tigers Rookies 2.50 1.10
Dennis Saunders
Tim Marting
❑ 424 Roberto Rodriquez 2.50 1.10
❑ 425 Doug Rader 2.50 1.10
❑ 426 Chris Cannizzaro 2.50 1.10
❑ 427 Bernie Allen 2.50 1.10
❑ 428 Jim McAndrew 2.50 1.10
❑ 429 Chuck Hinton 2.50 1.10
❑ 430 Wes Parker 2.50 1.10
❑ 431 Tom Burgmeier 2.50 1.10
❑ 432 Bob Didier 2.50 1.10
❑ 433 Skip Lockwood 2.50 1.10
❑ 434 Gary Sutherland 2.50 1.10
❑ 435 Jose Cardenal 4.00 1.80
❑ 436 Wilbur Wood 2.50 1.10
❑ 437 Danny Murtaugh MG 4.00 1.80
❑ 438 Mike McCormick 4.00 1.80
❑ 439 Phillies Rookies 6.00 2.70
Greg Luzinski RC
Scott Reid
❑ 440 Bert Campaneris 4.00 1.80
❑ 441 Milt Pappas 4.00 1.80
❑ 442 California Angels 4.00 1.80
Team Card
❑ 443 Rich Robertson 2.50 1.10
❑ 444 Jimmie Price 2.50 1.10
❑ 445 Art Shamsky 2.50 1.10
❑ 446 Bobby Bolin 2.50 1.10
❑ 447 Cesar Geronimo 4.00 1.80
❑ 448 Dave Roberts 2.50 1.10
❑ 449 Brant Alyea 2.50 1.10
❑ 450 Bob Gibson 15.00 6.75
❑ 451 Joe Keough 2.50 1.10
❑ 452 John Boccabella 2.50 1.10
❑ 453 Terry Crowley 2.50 1.10
❑ 454 Mike Paul 2.50 1.10
❑ 455 Don Kessinger 4.00 1.80
❑ 456 Bob Meyer 2.50 1.10
❑ 457 Willie Smith 2.50 1.10
❑ 458 White Sox Rookies 2.50 1.10
Ron Lolich
Dave Lemonds
❑ 459 Jim Lefebvre 2.50 1.10
❑ 460 Fritz Peterson 2.50 1.10
❑ 461 Jim Ray Hart 2.50 1.10
❑ 462 Washington Senators 6.00 2.70
Team Card
❑ 463 Tom Kelley 2.50 1.10
❑ 464 Aurelio Rodriguez 2.50 1.10
❑ 465 Tim McCarver 6.00 2.70
❑ 466 Ken Berry 2.50 1.10
❑ 467 Al Santorini 2.50 1.10
❑ 468 Frank Fernandez 2.50 1.10
❑ 469 Bob Aspromonte 2.50 1.10
❑ 470 Bob Oliver 2.50 1.10
❑ 471 Tom Griffin 2.50 1.10
❑ 472 Ken Rudolph 2.50 1.10
❑ 473 Gary Wagner 2.50 1.10
❑ 474 Jim Fairey 2.50 1.10
❑ 475 Ron Perranoski 2.50 1.10
❑ 476 Dal Maxvill 2.50 1.10
❑ 477 Earl Weaver MG 6.00 2.70
❑ 478 Bernie Carbo 2.50 1.10
❑ 479 Dennis Higgins 2.50 1.10
❑ 480 Manny Sanguillen 4.00 1.80
❑ 481 Daryl Patterson 2.50 1.10
❑ 482 San Diego Padres 6.00 2.70
Team Card
❑ 483 Gene Michael 4.00 1.80
❑ 484 Don Wilson 2.50 1.10
❑ 485 Ken McMullen 2.50 1.10
❑ 486 Steve Huntz 2.50 1.10
❑ 487 Paul Schaal 2.50 1.10
❑ 488 Jerry Stephenson 2.50 1.10
❑ 489 Luis Alvarado 2.50 1.10
❑ 490 Deron Johnson 4.00 1.80
❑ 491 Jim Hardin 2.50 1.10
❑ 492 Ken Boswell 2.50 1.10
❑ 493 Dave May 2.50 1.10
❑ 494 Braves Rookies 4.00 1.80
Ralph Garr
Rick Kester
❑ 495 Felipe Alou 4.00 1.80
❑ 496 Woody Woodward 2.50 1.10
❑ 497 Horacio Pina 2.50 1.10
❑ 498 John Kennedy 2.50 1.10
❑ 499 Checklist 5 11.00 2.20
❑ 500 Jim Perry 4.00 1.80
❑ 501 Andy Etchebarren 2.50 1.10
❑ 502 Chicago Cubs 5.00 2.20
Team Card
❑ 503 Gates Brown 4.00 1.80
❑ 504 Ken Wright 2.50 1.10
❑ 505 Ollie Brown 2.50 1.10
❑ 506 Bobby Knoop 2.50 1.10
❑ 507 George Stone 2.50 1.10
❑ 508 Roger Repoz 2.50 1.10
❑ 509 Jim Grant 2.50 1.10
❑ 510 Ken Harrelson 4.00 1.80
❑ 511 Chris Short 4.00 1.80
(Pete Rose leading off second)
❑ 512 Red Sox Rookies 2.50 1.10
Dick Mills
Mike Garman
❑ 513 Nolan Ryan 150.00 70.00
❑ 514 Ron Woods 2.50 1.10
❑ 515 Carl Morton 2.50 1.10
❑ 516 Ted Kubiak 2.50 1.10
❑ 517 Charlie Fox MG 2.50 1.10
❑ 518 Joe Grzenda 2.50 1.10
❑ 519 Willie Crawford 2.50 1.10
❑ 520 Tommy John 6.00 2.70
❑ 521 Leron Lee 2.50 1.10
❑ 522 Minnesota Twins 6.00 2.70
Team Card
❑ 523 John Odom 2.50 1.10
❑ 524 Mickey Stanley 6.00 2.70
❑ 525 Ernie Banks 50.00 22.00

❑ 526 Ray Jarvis 4.00 1.80
❑ 527 Cleon Jones 6.00 2.70
❑ 528 Wally Bunker 4.00 1.80
❑ 529 NL Rookie Infielders 6.00 2.70
Enzo Hernandez
Bill Buckner
Marty Perez
❑ 530 Carl Yastrzemski 30.00 13.50
❑ 531 Mike Torrez 4.00 1.80
❑ 532 Bill Rigney MG 4.00 1.80
❑ 533 Mike Ryan 4.00 1.80
❑ 534 Luke Walker 4.00 1.80
❑ 535 Curt Flood 6.00 2.70
❑ 536 Claude Raymond 6.00 2.70
❑ 537 Tom Egan 4.00 1.80
❑ 538 Angel Bravo 4.00 1.80
❑ 539 Larry Brown 4.00 1.80
❑ 540 Larry Dierker 6.00 2.70
❑ 541 Bob Burda 4.00 1.80
❑ 542 Bob Miller 4.00 1.80
❑ 543 New York Yankees 10.00 4.50
Team Card
❑ 544 Vida Blue 6.00 2.70
❑ 545 Dick Dietz 4.00 1.80
❑ 546 John Matias 4.00 1.80
❑ 547 Pat Dobson 6.00 2.70
❑ 548 Don Mason 4.00 1.80
❑ 549 Jim Brewer 6.00 2.70
❑ 550 Harmon Killebrew 25.00 11.00
❑ 551 Frank Linzy 4.00 1.80
❑ 552 Buddy Bradford 4.00 1.80
❑ 553 Kevin Collins 4.00 1.80
❑ 554 Lowell Palmer 4.00 1.80
❑ 555 Walt Williams 4.00 1.80
❑ 556 Jim McGlothlin 4.00 1.80
❑ 557 Tom Satriano 4.00 1.80
❑ 558 Hector Torres 4.00 1.80
❑ 559 AL Rookie Pitchers 4.00 1.80
Terry Cox
Bill Gogolewski
Gary Jones
❑ 560 Rusty Staub 6.00 2.70
❑ 561 Syd O'Brien 4.00 1.80
❑ 562 Dave Giusti 4.00 1.80
❑ 563 San Francisco Giants 8.00 3.60
Team Card
❑ 564 Al Fitzmorris 4.00 1.80
❑ 565 Jim Wynn 6.00 2.70
❑ 566 Tim Cullen 4.00 1.80
❑ 567 Walt Alston MG 6.00 2.70
❑ 568 Sal Campisi 4.00 1.80
❑ 569 Ivan Murrell 4.00 1.80
❑ 570 Jim Palmer 30.00 13.50
❑ 571 Ted Sizemore 4.00 1.80
❑ 572 Jerry Kenney 4.00 1.80
❑ 573 Ed Kranepool 6.00 2.70
❑ 574 Jim Bunning 8.00 3.60
❑ 575 Bill Freehan 6.00 2.70
❑ 576 Cubs Rookies 4.00 1.80
Adrian Garrett
Brock Davis
Garry Jestadt
❑ 577 Jim Lonborg 6.00 2.70
❑ 578 Ron Hunt 4.00 1.80
❑ 579 Marty Pattin 4.00 1.80
❑ 580 Tony Perez 20.00 9.00
❑ 581 Roger Nelson 4.00 1.80
❑ 582 Dave Cash 6.00 2.70
❑ 583 Ron Cook 4.00 1.80
❑ 584 Cleveland Indians 8.00 3.60
Team Card
❑ 585 Willie Davis 6.00 2.70
❑ 586 Dick Woodson 4.00 1.80
❑ 587 Sonny Jackson 4.00 1.80
❑ 588 Tom Bradley 4.00 1.80
❑ 589 Bob Barton 4.00 1.80
❑ 590 Alex Johnson 6.00 2.70
❑ 591 Jackie Brown 4.00 1.80
❑ 592 Randy Hundley 6.00 2.70
❑ 593 Jack Aker 4.00 1.80
❑ 594 Cards Rookies 6.00 2.70
Bob Chlupsa
Bob Stinson
Al Hrabosky RC
❑ 595 Dave Johnson 6.00 2.70
❑ 596 Mike Jorgensen 4.00 1.80
❑ 597 Ken Suarez 4.00 1.80
❑ 598 Rick Wise 6.00 2.70
❑ 599 Norm Cash 6.00 2.70
❑ 600 Willie Mays 100.00 45.00
❑ 601 Ken Tatum 4.00 1.80
❑ 602 Marty Martinez 4.00 1.80
❑ 603 Pittsburgh Pirates 8.00 3.60
Team Card
❑ 604 John Gelnar 4.00 1.80
❑ 605 Orlando Cepeda 8.00 3.60
❑ 606 Chuck Taylor 4.00 1.80
❑ 607 Paul Ratliff 4.00 1.80
❑ 608 Mike Wegener 4.00 1.80
❑ 609 Leo Durocher MG 8.00 3.60
❑ 610 Amos Otis 6.00 2.70
❑ 611 Tom Phoebus 4.00 1.80
❑ 612 Indians Rookies 4.00 1.80
Lou Camilli
Ted Ford
Steve Mingori
❑ 613 Pedro Borbon 4.00 1.80
❑ 614 Billy Cowan 4.00 1.80
❑ 615 Mel Stottlemyre 6.00 2.70
❑ 616 Larry Hisle 6.00 2.70
❑ 617 Clay Dalrymple 4.00 1.80
❑ 618 Tug McGraw 6.00 2.70
❑ 619A Checklist 6 ERR 11.00 2.20
(No copyright)
❑ 619B Checklist 6 COR 6.00 1.20
(Copyright on back)
❑ 620 Frank Howard 6.00 2.70
❑ 621 Ron Bryant 4.00 1.80
❑ 622 Joe Lahoud 4.00 1.80
❑ 623 Pat Jarvis 4.00 1.80
❑ 624 Oakland Athletics 8.00 3.60
Team Card
❑ 625 Lou Brock 30.00 13.50
❑ 626 Freddie Patek 6.00 2.70
❑ 627 Steve Hamilton 4.00 1.80
❑ 628 John Bateman 4.00 1.80
❑ 629 John Hiller 6.00 2.70
❑ 630 Roberto Clemente 125.00 55.00
❑ 631 Eddie Fisher 4.00 1.80
❑ 632 Darrel Chaney 4.00 1.80
❑ 633 AL Rookie Outfielders 4.00 1.80
Bobby Brooks
Pete Koegel
Scott Northey
❑ 634 Phil Regan 6.00 2.70
❑ 635 Bobby Murcer 6.00 2.70
❑ 636 Denny Lemaster 4.00 1.80
❑ 637 Dave Bristol MG 4.00 1.80
❑ 638 Stan Williams 4.00 1.80
❑ 639 Tom Haller 4.00 1.80
❑ 640 Frank Robinson 40.00 18.00
❑ 641 New York Mets 15.00 6.75
Team Card
❑ 642 Jim Roland 4.00 1.80
❑ 643 Rick Reichardt 6.00 2.70
❑ 644 Jim Stewart SP 12.00 5.50
❑ 645 Jim Maloney SP 15.00 6.75
❑ 646 Bobby Floyd SP 12.00 5.50
❑ 647 Juan Pizarro 8.00 3.60
❑ 648 Mets Rookies SP 25.00 11.00
Rich Folkers
Ted Martinez
John Matlack RC
❑ 649 Sparky Lyle SP 15.00 6.75
❑ 650 Rich Allen SP 30.00 13.50
❑ 651 Jerry Robertson SP 12.00 5.50
❑ 652 Atlanta Braves 12.00 5.50
Team Card
❑ 653 Russ Snyder SP 12.00 5.50
❑ 654 Don Shaw SP 12.00 5.50
❑ 655 Mike Epstein SP 12.00 5.50
❑ 656 Gerry Nyman SP 12.00 5.50
❑ 657 Jose Azcue 8.00 3.60
❑ 658 Paul Lindblad SP 12.00 5.50
❑ 659 Byron Browne SP 12.00 5.50
❑ 660 Ray Culp 8.00 3.60
❑ 661 Chuck Tanner MG SP 15.00 6.75
❑ 662 Mike Hedlund SP 12.00 5.50
❑ 663 Marv Staehle 8.00 3.60
❑ 664 Rookie Pitchers SP 15.00 6.75
Archie Reynolds
Bob Reynolds
Ken Reynolds
❑ 665 Ron Swoboda SP 15.00 6.75
❑ 666 Gene Brabender SP 12.00 5.50
❑ 667 Pete Ward 8.00 3.60
❑ 668 Gary Neibauer 8.00 3.60
❑ 669 Ike Brown SP 15.00 6.75
❑ 670 Bill Hands 8.00 3.60
❑ 671 Bill Voss SP 12.00 5.50
❑ 672 Ed Crosby SP 12.00 5.50
❑ 673 Gerry Janeski SP 12.00 5.50
❑ 674 Montreal Expos 12.00 5.50
Team Card
❑ 675 Dave Boswell 8.00 3.60
❑ 676 Tommie Reynolds 8.00 3.60
❑ 677 Jack DiLauro SP 12.00 5.50
❑ 678 George Thomas 8.00 3.60
❑ 679 Don O'Riley 8.00 3.60
❑ 680 Don Mincher SP 12.00 5.50
❑ 681 Bill Butler 8.00 3.60
❑ 682 Terry Harmon 8.00 3.60
❑ 683 Bill Burbach SP 12.00 5.50
❑ 684 Curt Motton 8.00 3.60
❑ 685 Moe Drabowsky 8.00 3.60
❑ 686 Chico Ruiz SP 12.00 5.50
❑ 687 Ron Taylor SP 12.00 5.50
❑ 688 Sparky Anderson MG SP 30.00 13.50
❑ 689 Frank Baker 8.00 3.60
❑ 690 Bob Moose 8.00 3.60
❑ 691 Bobby Heise 8.00 3.60
❑ 692 AL Rookie Pitchers SP 12.00 5.50
Hal Haydel
Rogelio Moret
Wayne Twitchell
❑ 693 Jose Pena SP 12.00 5.50
❑ 694 Rick Renick SP 12.00 5.50
❑ 695 Joe Niekro 12.00 5.50
❑ 696 Jerry Morales 8.00 3.60
❑ 697 Rickey Clark SP 12.00 5.50
❑ 698 M. Brewers SP 20.00 9.00
Team Card
❑ 699 Jim Britton 8.00 3.60
❑ 700 Boog Powell SP 25.00 11.00
❑ 701 Bob Garibaldi 8.00 3.60
❑ 702 Milt Ramirez 8.00 3.60
❑ 703 Mike Kekich 8.00 3.60
❑ 704 J.C. Martin SP 12.00 5.50
❑ 705 Dick Selma SP 12.00 5.50
❑ 706 Joe Foy SP 12.00 5.50
❑ 707 Fred Lasher 8.00 3.60
❑ 708 Russ Nagelson SP 12.00 5.50
❑ 709 Rookie Outfielders SP 80.00 36.00
Dusty Baker RC !
Don Baylor
Tom Paciorek
❑ 710 Sonny Siebert 8.00 3.60
❑ 711 Larry Stahl SP 12.00 5.50
❑ 712 Jose Martinez 8.00 3.60
❑ 713 Mike Marshall SP 15.00 6.75
❑ 714 Dick Williams MG SP 15.00 6.75
❑ 715 Horace Clarke SP 15.00 6.75
❑ 716 Dave Leonhard 8.00 3.60
❑ 717 Tommie Aaron SP 12.00 5.50
❑ 718 Billy Wynne 8.00 3.60
❑ 719 Jerry May SP 12.00 5.50
❑ 720 Matty Alou 12.00 5.50
❑ 721 John Morris 8.00 3.60
❑ 722 Houston Astros SP 20.00 9.00
Team Card
❑ 723 Vicente Romo SP 12.00 5.50
❑ 724 Tom Tischinski SP 12.00 5.50
❑ 725 Gary Gentry SP 12.00 5.50
❑ 726 Paul Popovich 8.00 3.60
❑ 727 Ray Lamb SP 12.00 5.50
❑ 728 NL Rookie Outfielders 8.00 3.60
Wayne Redmond
Keith Lampard
Bernie Williams
❑ 729 Dick Billings 8.00 3.60
❑ 730 Jim Rooker 8.00 3.60
❑ 731 Jim Qualls SP 12.00 5.50
❑ 732 Bob Reed 8.00 3.60
❑ 733 Lee Maye SP 12.00 5.50
❑ 734 Rob Gardner SP 12.00 5.50
❑ 735 Mike Shannon SP 15.00 6.75
❑ 736 Mel Queen SP 12.00 5.50
❑ 737 Preston Gomez SP MG 12.00 5.50

❑ 738 Russ Gibson SP ........ 12.00 5.50
❑ 739 Barry Lersch SP ........ 12.00 5.50
❑ 740 Luis Aparicio SP UER 30.00 13.50
(Led AL in steals
from 1965 to 1964;
should be 1956 to 1964)
❑ 741 Skip Guinn.................. 8.00 3.60
❑ 742 Kansas City Royals.... 12.00 5.50
Team Card
❑ 743 John O'Donoghue SP 12.00 5.50
❑ 744 Chuck Manuel SP ...... 12.00 5.50
❑ 745 Sandy Alomar SP ...... 12.00 5.50
❑ 746 Andy Kosco................. 8.00 3.60
❑ 747 NL Rookie Pitchers ...... 8.00 3.60
Al Severinsen
Scipio Spinks
Balor Moore
❑ 748 John Purdin SP .......... 12.00 5.50
❑ 749 Ken Szotkiewicz .......... 8.00 3.60
❑ 750 Denny McLain SP ...... 25.00 11.00
❑ 751 Al Weis SP ............... 15.00 6.75
❑ 752 Dick Drago ............... 12.00 2.90

## 1972 Topps

| | NRMT | VG-E |
|---|---|---|
| COMPLETE SET (787) ...... | 1600.00 | 700.00 |
| COMMON CARD (1-132) .......... | .60 | .25 |
| COMMON CARD (133-263) ...... | 1.00 | .45 |
| COMMON CARD (264-394) ...... | 1.25 | .55 |
| COMMON CARD (395-525) ...... | 1.50 | .70 |
| COMMON CARD (526-656) ...... | 4.00 | 1.80 |
| COMMON CARD (657-787) .... | 12.00 | 5.50 |
| WRAPPER (10-CENT) .......... | 15.00 | 6.75 |

❑ 1 Pittsburgh Pirates ........... 8.00 2.90
Team Card
❑ 2 Ray Culp .......................... .60 .25
❑ 3 Bob Tolan .......................... .60 .25
❑ 4 Checklist 1-132 ................. 6.00 1.20
❑ 5 John Bateman .................. .60 .25
❑ 6 Fred Scherman .................. .60 .25
❑ 7 Enzo Hernandez ................. .60 .25
❑ 8 Ron Swoboda ................. 1.25 .55
❑ 9 Stan Williams .................. .60 .25
❑ 10 Amos Otis ...................... 1.25 .55
❑ 11 Bobby Valentine ............ 1.25 .55
❑ 12 Jose Cardenal ................. .60 .25
❑ 13 Joe Grzenda .................. .60 .25
❑ 14 Phillies Rookies ............... .60 .25
Pete Koegel
Mike Anderson
Wayne Twitchell
❑ 15 Walt Williams.................. .60 .25
❑ 16 Mike Jorgensen................ .60 .25
❑ 17 Dave Duncan .................. .60 .25
❑ 18A Juan Pizarro ................. .60 .25
(Yellow underline
C and S of Cubs)
❑ 18B Juan Pizarro ............... 5.00 2.20
(Green underline
C and S of Cubs)
❑ 19 Billy Cowan ..................... .60 .25
❑ 20 Don Wilson ...................... .60 .25
❑ 21 Atlanta Braves................ 1.50 .70
Team Card
❑ 22 Rob Gardner ..................... .60 .25
❑ 23 Ted Kubiak ....................... .60 .25
❑ 24 Ted Ford .......................... .60 .25
❑ 25 Bill Singer ........................ .60 .25
❑ 26 Andy Etchebarren ............ .60 .25
❑ 27 Bob Johnson ................... .60 .25
❑ 28 Twins Rookies.................. .60 .25
Bob Gebhard
Steve Brye
Hal Haydel
❑ 29A Bill Bonham.................... .60 .25
(Yellow underline
C and S of Cubs)
❑ 29B Bill Bonham................. 5.00 2.20
(Green underline
C and S of Cubs)
❑ 30 Rico Petrocelli ............... 1.25 .55
❑ 31 Cleon Jones ................. 1.25 .55
❑ 32 Cleon Jones IA ................ .60 .25
❑ 33 Billy Martin MG ............. 4.00 1.80
❑ 34 Billy Martin IA .............. 2.50 1.10
❑ 35 Jerry Johnson ................ .60 .25
❑ 36 Jerry Johnson IA............. .60 .25
❑ 37 Carl Yastrzemski .......... 10.00 4.50
❑ 38 Carl Yastrzemski IA........ 6.00 2.70
❑ 39 Bob Barton ..................... .60 .25
❑ 40 Bob Barton IA ................. .60 .25
❑ 41 Tommy Davis ............... 1.25 .55
❑ 42 Tommy Davis IA ............. .60 .25
❑ 43 Rick Wise ..................... 1.25 .55
❑ 44 Rick Wise IA ................... .60 .25
❑ 45A Glenn Beckert............ 1.25 .55
(Yellow underline
C and S of Cubs)
❑ 45B Glenn Beckert............. 5.00 2.20
(Green underline
C and S of Cubs)
❑ 46 Glenn Beckert IA............. .60 .25
❑ 47 John Ellis........................ .60 .25
❑ 48 John Ellis IA ................... .60 .25
❑ 49 Willie Mays ................ 30.00 13.50
❑ 50 Willie Mays IA ............. 14.00 6.25
❑ 51 Harmon Killebrew .......... 7.00 3.10
❑ 52 Harmon Killebrew IA ...... 4.00 1.80
❑ 53 Bud Harrelson .............. 1.25 .55
❑ 54 Bud Harrelson IA............. .60 .25
❑ 55 Clyde Wright ................... .60 .25
❑ 56 Rich Chiles ..................... .60 .25
❑ 57 Bob Oliver ....................... .60 .25
❑ 58 Ernie McAnally ................ .60 .25
❑ 59 Fred Stanley ................... .60 .25
❑ 60 Manny Sanguillen .......... 1.25 .55
❑ 61 Cubs Rookies ............... 1.25 .55
Burt Hooton RC
Gene Hiser
Earl Stephenson
❑ 62 Angel Mangual ................ .60 .25
❑ 63 Duke Sims....................... .60 .25
❑ 64 Pete Broberg.................... .60 .25
❑ 65 Cesar Cedeno .............. 1.25 .55
❑ 66 Ray Corbin ..................... .60 .25
❑ 67 Red Schoendienst MG .. 1.25 .55
❑ 68 Jim York ......................... .60 .25
❑ 69 Roger Freed .................... .60 .25
❑ 70 Mike Cuellar ................. 1.25 .55
❑ 71 California Angels........... 1.50 .70
Team Card
❑ 72 Bruce Kison RC................ .60 .25
❑ 73 Steve Huntz..................... .60 .25
❑ 74 Cecil Upshaw ................... .60 .25
❑ 75 Bert Campaneris ........... 1.25 .55
❑ 76 Don Carrithers.................. .60 .25
❑ 77 Ron Theobald .................. .60 .25
❑ 78 Steve Arlin....................... .60 .25
❑ 79 Red Sox Rookies ........ 50.00 22.00
Mike Garman
Cecil Cooper
Carlton Fisk RC !
❑ 80 Tony Perez .................. 4.00 1.80
❑ 81 Mike Hedlund ................. .60 .25
❑ 82 Ron Woods ..................... .60 .25
❑ 83 Dalton Jones ................... .60 .25
❑ 84 Vince Colbert................... .60 .25
❑ 85 NL Batting Leaders ........ 2.50 1.10
Joe Torre
Ralph Garr
Glenn Beckert
❑ 86 AL Batting Leaders ........ 2.50 1.10
Tony Oliva
Bobby Murcer
Merv Rettenmund
❑ 87 NL RBI Leaders............. 4.00 1.80
Joe Torre
Willie Stargell
Hank Aaron
❑ 88 AL RBI Leaders............. 4.00 1.80
Harmon Killebrew
Frank Robinson
Reggie Smith
❑ 89 NL Home Run Leaders .. 2.50 1.10
Willie Stargell
Hank Aaron
Lee May
❑ 90 AL Home Run Leaders .. 2.50 1.10
Bill Melton
Norm Cash
Reggie Jackson
❑ 91 NL ERA Leaders ........... 2.50 1.10
Tom Seaver
Dave Roberts UER
(Photo actually
Danny Coombs)
Don Wilson
❑ 92 AL ERA Leaders ........... 2.50 1.10
Vida Blue
Wilbur Wood
Jim Palmer
❑ 93 NL Pitching Leaders ...... 4.00 1.80
Fergie Jenkins
Steve Carlton
Al Downing
Tom Seaver
❑ 94 AL Pitching Leaders ...... 2.50 1.10
Mickey Lolich
Vida Blue
Wilbur Wood
❑ 95 NL Strikeout Leaders .... 4.00 1.80
Tom Seaver
Fergie Jenkins
Bill Stoneman
❑ 96 AL Strikeout Leaders...... 2.50 1.10
Mickey Lolich
Vida Blue
Joe Coleman
❑ 97 Tom Kelley ...................... .60 .25
❑ 98 Chuck Tanner MG ......... 1.25 .55
❑ 99 Ross Grimsley.................. .60 .25
❑ 100 Frank Robinson........... 8.00 3.60
❑ 101 Astros Rookies ........... 1.50 .70
Bill Greif
J.R. Richard RC
Ray Busse
❑ 102 Lloyd Allen.................... .60 .25
❑ 103 Checklist 133-263 ........ 6.00 1.20
❑ 104 Toby Harrah RC .......... 1.25 .55
❑ 105 Gary Gentry.................... .60 .25
❑ 106 Milwaukee Brewers...... 1.50 .70
Team Card
❑ 107 Jose Cruz RC ............. 1.25 .55
❑ 108 Gary Waslewski ............ .60 .25
❑ 109 Jerry May ...................... .60 .25
❑ 110 Ron Hunt ....................... .60 .25
❑ 111 Jim Grant....................... .60 .25
❑ 112 Greg Luzinski ............. 1.25 .55
❑ 113 Rogelio Moret ................ .60 .25
❑ 114 Bill Buckner ................ 1.25 .55
❑ 115 Jim Fregosi ................. 1.25 .55
❑ 116 Ed Farmer ...................... .60 .25
❑ 117A Cleo James.................. .60 .25
(Yellow underline
C and S of Cubs)
❑ 117B Cleo James............... 5.00 2.20
(Green underline
C and S of Cubs)
❑ 118 Skip Lockwood .............. .60 .25
❑ 119 Marty Perez................... .60 .25
❑ 120 Bill Freehan................. 1.25 .55
❑ 121 Ed Sprague ................... .60 .25
❑ 122 Larry Biittner ................ .60 .25
❑ 123 Ed Acosta ..................... .60 .25
❑ 124 Yankees Rookies .......... .60 .25
Alan Closter
Rusty Torres
Roger Hambright

❑ 125 Dave Cash 1.25 .55
❑ 126 Bart Johnson .60 .25
❑ 127 Duffy Dyer .60 .25
❑ 128 Eddie Watt .60 .25
❑ 129 Charlie Fox MG .60 .25
❑ 130 Bob Gibson 8.00 3.60
❑ 131 Jim Nettles .60 .25
❑ 132 Joe Morgan 6.00 2.70
❑ 133 Joe Keough 1.00 .45
❑ 134 Carl Morton 1.00 .45
❑ 135 Vada Pinson 2.00 .90
❑ 136 Darrel Chaney 1.00 .45
❑ 137 Dick Williams MG 2.00 .90
❑ 138 Mike Kekich 1.00 .45
❑ 139 Tim McCarver 2.00 .90
❑ 140 Pat Dobson 2.00 .90
❑ 141 Mets Rookies 2.00 .90
Buzz Capra
Lee Stanton
Jon Matlack
❑ 142 Chris Chambliss RC 4.00 1.80
❑ 143 Garry Jestadt 1.00 .45
❑ 144 Marty Pattin 1.00 .45
❑ 145 Don Kessinger 2.00 .90
❑ 146 Steve Kealey 1.00 .45
❑ 147 Dave Kingman RC 6.00 2.70
❑ 148 Dick Billings 1.00 .45
❑ 149 Gary Neibauer 1.00 .45
❑ 150 Norm Cash 2.00 .90
❑ 151 Jim Brewer 1.00 .45
❑ 152 Gene Clines 1.00 .45
❑ 153 Rick Auerbach 1.00 .45
❑ 154 Ted Simmons 4.00 1.80
❑ 155 Larry Dierker 2.00 .90
❑ 156 Minnesota Twins 2.00 .90
Team Card
❑ 157 Don Gullett 1.00 .45
❑ 158 Jerry Kenney 1.00 .45
❑ 159 John Boccabella 1.00 .45
❑ 160 Andy Messersmith 2.00 .90
❑ 161 Brock Davis 1.00 .45
❑ 162 Brewers Rookies UER 2.00 .90
Jerry Bell
Darrell Porter RC
Bob Reynolds
(Porter and Bell photos switched)
❑ 163 Tug McGraw 2.00 .90
❑ 164 Tug McGraw IA 2.00 .90
❑ 165 Chris Speier RC 2.00 .90
❑ 166 Chris Speier IA 2.00 .90
❑ 167 Deron Johnson 1.00 .45
❑ 168 Deron Johnson IA 1.00 .45
❑ 169 Vida Blue 2.00 .90
❑ 170 Vida Blue IA 2.00 .90
❑ 171 Darrell Evans 2.00 .90
❑ 172 Darrell Evans IA 2.00 .90
❑ 173 Clay Kirby 1.00 .45
❑ 174 Clay Kirby IA 1.00 .45
❑ 175 Tom Haller 1.00 .45
❑ 176 Tom Haller IA 1.00 .45
❑ 177 Paul Schaal 1.00 .45
❑ 178 Paul Schaal IA 1.00 .45
❑ 179 Dock Ellis 1.00 .45
❑ 180 Dock Ellis IA 1.00 .45
❑ 181 Ed Kranepool 1.00 .45
❑ 182 Ed Kranepool IA 1.00 .45
❑ 183 Bill Melton 1.00 .45
❑ 184 Bill Melton IA 1.00 .45
❑ 185 Ron Bryant 1.00 .45
❑ 186 Ron Bryant IA 1.00 .45
❑ 187 Gates Brown 1.00 .45
❑ 188 Frank Lucchesi MG 1.00 .45
❑ 189 Gene Tenace 2.00 .90
❑ 190 Dave Giusti 1.00 .45
❑ 191 Jeff Burroughs RC 2.00 .90
❑ 192 Chicago Cubs 2.00 .90
Team Card
❑ 193 Kurt Bevacqua 1.00 .45
❑ 194 Fred Norman 1.00 .45
❑ 195 Orlando Cepeda 6.00 2.70
❑ 196 Mel Queen 1.00 .45
❑ 197 Johnny Briggs 1.00 .45
❑ 198 Dodgers Rookies 4.00 1.80
Charlie Hough RC
Bob O'Brien
Mike Strahler
❑ 199 Mike Fiore 1.00 .45
❑ 200 Lou Brock 7.00 3.10
❑ 201 Phil Roof 1.00 .45
❑ 202 Scipio Spinks 1.00 .45
❑ 203 Ron Blomberg 1.00 .45
❑ 204 Tommy Helms 1.00 .45
❑ 205 Dick Drago 1.00 .45
❑ 206 Dal Maxvill 1.00 .45
❑ 207 Tom Egan 1.00 .45
❑ 208 Milt Pappas 2.00 .90
❑ 209 Joe Rudi 2.00 .90
❑ 210 Denny McLain 2.00 .90
❑ 211 Gary Sutherland 1.00 .45
❑ 212 Grant Jackson 1.00 .45
❑ 213 Angels Rookies 1.00 .45
Billy Parker
Art Kusnyer
Tom Silverio
❑ 214 Mike McQueen 1.00 .45
❑ 215 Alex Johnson 2.00 .90
❑ 216 Joe Niekro 2.00 .90
❑ 217 Roger Metzger 1.00 .45
❑ 218 Eddie Kasko MG 1.00 .45
❑ 219 Rennie Stennett 2.00 .90
❑ 220 Jim Perry 2.00 .90
❑ 221 NL Playoffs 2.00 .90
Bucs champs
❑ 222 Brooks Robinson ALCS 4.00 1.80
❑ 223 Dave McNally WS 2.00 .90
❑ 224 Dave Johnson WS 2.00 .90
Mark Belanger
❑ 225 Manny Sanguillen WS 2.00 .90
❑ 226 Roberto Clemente WS 8.00 3.60
❑ 227 Nellie Briles WS 2.00 .90
❑ 228 Frank Robinson WS 2.00 .90
Manny Sanguillen
❑ 229 Steve Blass WS 2.00 .90
❑ 230 World Series Summary 2.00 .90
(Pirates celebrate)
❑ 231 Casey Cox 1.00 .45
❑ 232 Giants Rookies 1.00 .45
Chris Arnold
Jim Barr
Dave Rader
❑ 233 Jay Johnstone 2.00 .90
❑ 234 Ron Taylor 1.00 .45
❑ 235 Merv Rettenmund 1.00 .45
❑ 236 Jim McGlothlin 1.00 .45
❑ 237 New York Yankees 2.00 .90
Team Card
❑ 238 Leron Lee 1.00 .45
❑ 239 Tom Timmermann 1.00 .45
❑ 240 Rich Allen 2.00 .90
❑ 241 Rollie Fingers 6.00 2.70
❑ 242 Don Mincher 2.00 .90
❑ 243 Frank Linzy 1.00 .45
❑ 244 Steve Braun 1.00 .45
❑ 245 Tommie Agee 2.00 .90
❑ 246 Tom Burgmeier 1.00 .45
❑ 247 Milt May 1.00 .45
❑ 248 Tom Bradley 1.00 .45
❑ 249 Harry Walker MG 1.00 .45
❑ 250 Boog Powell 2.00 .90
❑ 251 Checklist 264-394 6.00 1.20
❑ 252 Ken Reynolds 1.00 .45
❑ 253 Sandy Alomar 2.00 .90
❑ 254 Boots Day 1.00 .45
❑ 255 Jim Lonborg 2.00 .90
❑ 256 George Foster 2.00 .90
❑ 257 Tigers Rookies 1.00 .45
Jim Foor
Tim Hosley
Paul Jata
❑ 258 Randy Hundley 2.00 .90
❑ 259 Sparky Lyle 2.00 .90
❑ 260 Ralph Garr 2.00 .90
❑ 261 Steve Mingori 1.00 .45
❑ 262 San Diego Padres 2.00 .90
Team Card
❑ 263 Felipe Alou 2.00 .90
❑ 264 Tommy John 2.00 .90
❑ 265 Wes Parker 2.00 .90
❑ 266 Bobby Bolin 1.25 .55
❑ 267 Dave Concepcion 4.00 1.80
❑ 268 A's Rookies 1.25 .55
Dwain Anderson
Chris Floethe
❑ 269 Don Hahn 1.25 .55
❑ 270 Jim Palmer 8.00 3.60
❑ 271 Ken Rudolph 1.25 .55
❑ 272 Mickey Rivers RC 2.00 .90
❑ 273 Bobby Floyd 1.25 .55
❑ 274 Al Severinsen 1.25 .55
❑ 275 Cesar Tovar 1.25 .55
❑ 276 Gene Mauch MG 2.00 .90
❑ 277 Elliott Maddox 1.25 .55
❑ 278 Dennis Higgins 1.25 .55
❑ 279 Larry Brown 1.25 .55
❑ 280 Willie McCovey 7.00 3.10
❑ 281 Bill Parsons 1.25 .55
❑ 282 Houston Astros 2.00 .90
Team Card
❑ 283 Darrell Brandon 1.25 .55
❑ 284 Ike Brown 1.25 .55
❑ 285 Gaylord Perry 6.00 2.70
❑ 286 Gene Alley 2.00 .90
❑ 287 Jim Hardin 1.25 .55
❑ 288 Johnny Jeter 1.25 .55
❑ 289 Syd O'Brien 1.25 .55
❑ 290 Sonny Siebert 1.25 .55
❑ 291 Hal McRae 2.00 .90
❑ 292 Hal McRae IA 2.00 .90
❑ 293 Dan Frisella 1.25 .55
❑ 294 Dan Frisella IA 1.25 .55
❑ 295 Dick Dietz 1.25 .55
❑ 296 Dick Dietz IA 1.25 .55
❑ 297 Claude Osteen 2.00 .90
❑ 298 Claude Osteen IA 1.25 .55
❑ 299 Hank Aaron 40.00 18.00
❑ 300 Hank Aaron IA 20.00 9.00
❑ 301 George Mitterwald 1.25 .55
❑ 302 George Mitterwald IA 1.25 .55
❑ 303 Joe Pepitone 2.00 .90
❑ 304 Joe Pepitone IA 1.25 .55
❑ 305 Ken Boswell 1.25 .55
❑ 306 Ken Boswell IA 1.25 .55
❑ 307 Steve Renko 1.25 .55
❑ 308 Steve Renko IA 1.25 .55
❑ 309 Roberto Clemente 60.00 27.00
❑ 310 Roberto Clemente IA 30.00 13.50
❑ 311 Clay Carroll 1.25 .55
❑ 312 Clay Carroll IA 1.25 .55
❑ 313 Luis Aparicio 6.00 2.70
❑ 314 Luis Aparicio IA 2.00 .90
❑ 315 Paul Splittorff 1.25 .55
❑ 316 Cardinals Rookies 2.00 .90
Jim Bibby
Jorge Roque
Santiago Guzman
❑ 317 Rich Hand 1.25 .55
❑ 318 Sonny Jackson 1.25 .55
❑ 319 Aurelio Rodriguez 1.25 .55
❑ 320 Steve Blass 2.00 .90
❑ 321 Joe Lahoud 1.25 .55
❑ 322 Jose Pena 1.25 .55
❑ 323 Earl Weaver MG 4.00 1.80
❑ 324 Mike Ryan 1.25 .55
❑ 325 Mel Stottlemyre 2.00 .90
❑ 326 Pat Kelly 1.25 .55
❑ 327 Steve Stone RC 2.00 .90
❑ 328 Boston Red Sox 2.00 .90
Team Card
❑ 329 Roy Foster 1.25 .55
❑ 330 Jim Hunter 6.00 2.70
❑ 331 Stan Swanson 1.25 .55
❑ 332 Buck Martinez 1.25 .55
❑ 333 Steve Barber 1.25 .55
❑ 334 Rangers Rookies 1.25 .55
Bill Fahey
Jim Mason
Tom Ragland
❑ 335 Bill Hands 1.25 .55
❑ 336 Marty Martinez 1.25 .55
❑ 337 Mike Kilkenny 1.25 .55
❑ 338 Bob Grich 2.00 .90
❑ 339 Ron Cook 1.25 .55
❑ 340 Roy White 2.00 .90
❑ 341 Joe Torre KP 1.25 .55
❑ 342 Wilbur Wood KP 1.25 .55
❑ 343 Willie Stargell KP 2.00 .90
❑ 344 Dave McNally KP 1.25 .55

❑ 345 Rick Wise KP 1.25 .55
❑ 346 Jim Fregosi KP 1.25 .55
❑ 347 Tom Seaver KP 4.00 1.80
❑ 348 Sal Bando KP 1.25 .55
❑ 349 Al Fitzmorris 1.25 .55
❑ 350 Frank Howard 2.00 .90
❑ 351 Braves Rookies 2.00 .90
Tom House
Rick Kester
Jimmy Britton
❑ 352 Dave LaRoche 1.25 .55
❑ 353 Art Shamsky 1.25 .55
❑ 354 Tom Murphy 1.25 .55
❑ 355 Bob Watson 2.00 .90
❑ 356 Gerry Moses 1.25 .55
❑ 357 Woody Fryman 1.25 .55
❑ 358 Sparky Anderson MG 4.00 1.80
❑ 359 Don Pavletich 1.25 .55
❑ 360 Dave Roberts 1.25 .55
❑ 361 Mike Andrews 2.00 .90
❑ 362 New York Mets 2.00 .90
Team Card
❑ 363 Ron Klimkowski 1.25 .55
❑ 364 Johnny Callison 2.00 .90
❑ 365 Dick Bosman 2.00 .90
❑ 366 Jimmy Rosario 1.25 .55
❑ 367 Ron Perranoski 2.00 .90
❑ 368 Danny Thompson 1.25 .55
❑ 369 Jim Lefebvre 2.00 .90
❑ 370 Don Buford 1.25 .55
❑ 371 Denny Lemaster 1.25 .55
❑ 372 Royals Rookies 1.25 .55
Lance Clemons
Monty Montgomery
❑ 373 John Mayberry 2.00 .90
❑ 374 Jack Heidemann 1.25 .55
❑ 375 Reggie Cleveland 1.25 .55
❑ 376 Andy Kosco 1.25 .55
❑ 377 Terry Harmon 1.25 .55
❑ 378 Checklist 395-525 6.00 1.20
❑ 379 Ken Berry 1.25 .55
❑ 380 Earl Williams 1.25 .55
❑ 381 Chicago White Sox 2.00 .90
Team Card
❑ 382 Joe Gibbon 1.25 .55
❑ 383 Brant Alyea 1.25 .55
❑ 384 Dave Campbell 2.00 .90
❑ 385 Mickey Stanley 2.00 .90
❑ 386 Jim Colborn 1.25 .55
❑ 387 Horace Clarke 2.00 .90
❑ 388 Charlie Williams 1.25 .55
❑ 389 Bill Rigney MG 1.25 .55
❑ 390 Willie Davis 2.00 .90
❑ 391 Ken Sanders 1.25 .55
❑ 392 Pirates Rookies 2.00 .90
Fred Cambria
Richie Zisk
❑ 393 Curt Motton 1.25 .55
❑ 394 Ken Forsch 2.00 .90
❑ 395 Matty Alou 2.00 .90
❑ 396 Paul Lindblad 1.50 .70
❑ 397 Philadelphia Phillies 2.00 .90
Team Card
❑ 398 Larry Hisle 2.00 .90
❑ 399 Milt Wilcox 1.50 .70
❑ 400 Tony Oliva 4.00 1.80
❑ 401 Jim Nash 1.50 .70
❑ 402 Bobby Heise 1.50 .70
❑ 403 John Cumberland 1.50 .70
❑ 404 Jeff Torborg 2.00 .90
❑ 405 Ron Fairly 2.00 .90
❑ 406 George Hendrick RC 2.00 .90
❑ 407 Chuck Taylor 1.00 .45
❑ 408 Jim Northrup 2.00 .90
❑ 409 Frank Baker 1.00 .45
❑ 410 Ferguson Jenkins 6.00 2.70
❑ 411 Bob Montgomery 1.00 .45
❑ 412 Dick Kelley 1.00 .45
❑ 413 White Sox Rookies 1.00 .45
Don Eddy
Dave Lemonds
❑ 414 Bob Miller 1.00 .45
❑ 415 Cookie Rojas 2.00 .90
❑ 416 Johnny Edwards 1.00 .45
❑ 417 Tom Hall 1.00 .45
❑ 418 Tom Shopay 1.00 .45
❑ 419 Jim Spencer 1.00 .45
❑ 420 Steve Carlton 18.00 8.00
❑ 421 Ellie Rodriguez 1.00 .45
❑ 422 Ray Lamb 1.00 .45
❑ 423 Oscar Gamble 2.00 .90
❑ 424 Bill Gogolewski 1.00 .45
❑ 425 Ken Singleton 2.00 .90
❑ 426 Ken Singleton IA 1.00 .45
❑ 427 Tito Fuentes 1.00 .45
❑ 428 Tito Fuentes IA 1.00 .45
❑ 429 Bob Robertson 1.00 .45
❑ 430 Bob Robertson IA 1.00 .45
❑ 431 Clarence Gaston 2.00 .90
❑ 432 Clarence Gaston IA 2.00 .90
❑ 433 Johnny Bench 25.00 11.00
❑ 434 Johnny Bench IA 15.00 6.75
❑ 435 Reggie Jackson 30.00 13.50
❑ 436 Reggie Jackson IA 12.00 5.50
❑ 437 Maury Wills 2.00 .90
❑ 438 Maury Wills IA 2.00 .90
❑ 439 Billy Williams 6.00 2.70
❑ 440 Billy Williams IA 4.00 1.80
❑ 441 Thurman Munson 15.00 6.75
❑ 442 Thurman Munson IA 8.00 3.60
❑ 443 Ken Henderson 1.50 .70
❑ 444 Ken Henderson IA 1.50 .70
❑ 445 Tom Seaver 30.00 13.50
❑ 446 Tom Seaver IA 15.00 6.75
❑ 447 Willie Stargell 8.00 3.60
❑ 448 Willie Stargell IA 4.00 1.80
❑ 449 Bob Lemon MG 2.00 .90
❑ 450 Mickey Lolich 2.00 .90
❑ 451 Tony LaRussa 4.00 1.80
❑ 452 Ed Herrmann 1.50 .70
❑ 453 Barry Lersch 1.50 .70
❑ 454 Oakland A's 2.00 .90
Team Card
❑ 455 Tommy Harper 2.00 .90
❑ 456 Mark Belanger 2.00 .90
❑ 457 Padres Rookies 1.50 .70
Darcy Fast
Derrel Thomas
Mike Ivie
❑ 458 Aurelio Monteagudo 1.50 .70
❑ 459 Rick Renick 1.50 .70
❑ 460 Al Downing 1.50 .70
❑ 461 Tim Cullen 1.50 .70
❑ 462 Rickey Clark 1.50 .70
❑ 463 Bernie Carbo 1.50 .70
❑ 464 Jim Roland 1.50 .70
❑ 465 Gil Hodges MG 4.00 1.80
❑ 466 Norm Miller 1.50 .70
❑ 467 Steve Kline 1.50 .70
❑ 468 Richie Scheinblum 1.50 .70
❑ 469 Ron Herbel 1.50 .70
❑ 470 Ray Fosse 1.50 .70
❑ 471 Luke Walker 1.50 .70
❑ 472 Phil Gagliano 1.50 .70
❑ 473 Dan McGinn 1.50 .70
❑ 474 Orioles Rookies 15.00 6.75
Don Baylor
Roric Harrison
Johnny Oates RC
❑ 475 Gary Nolan 2.00 .90
❑ 476 Lee Richard 1.50 .70
❑ 477 Tom Phoebus 1.50 .70
❑ 478 Checklist 526-656 6.00 1.20
❑ 479 Don Shaw 1.50 .70
❑ 480 Lee May 2.00 .90
❑ 481 Billy Conigliaro 2.00 .90
❑ 482 Joe Hoerner 1.50 .70
❑ 483 Ken Suarez 1.50 .70
❑ 484 Lum Harris MG 1.50 .70
❑ 485 Phil Regan 2.00 .90
❑ 486 John Lowenstein 1.50 .70
❑ 487 Detroit Tigers 2.00 .90
Team Card
❑ 488 Mike Nagy 1.50 .70
❑ 489 Expos Rookies 1.50 .70
Terry Humphrey
Keith Lampard
❑ 490 Dave McNally 2.00 .90
❑ 491 Lou Piniella KP 2.00 .90
❑ 492 Mel Stottlemyre KP 2.00 .90
❑ 493 Bob Bailey KP 2.00 .90
❑ 494 Willie Horton KP 2.00 .90
❑ 495 Bill Melton KP 2.00 .90
❑ 496 Bud Harrelson KP 2.00 .90
❑ 497 Jim Perry KP 2.00 .90
❑ 498 Brooks Robinson KP 4.00 1.80
❑ 499 Vicente Romo 1.50 .70
❑ 500 Joe Torre 4.00 1.80
❑ 501 Pete Hamm 1.50 .70
❑ 502 Jackie Hernandez 1.50 .70
❑ 503 Gary Peters 1.50 .70
❑ 504 Ed Spiezio 1.50 .70
❑ 505 Mike Marshall 2.00 .90
❑ 506 Indians Rookies 1.50 .70
Terry Ley
Jim Moyer
Dick Tidrow
❑ 507 Fred Gladding 1.50 .70
❑ 508 Elrod Hendricks 1.50 .70
❑ 509 Don McMahon 1.50 .70
❑ 510 Ted Williams MG 12.00 5.50
❑ 511 Tony Taylor 2.00 .90
❑ 512 Paul Popovich 1.50 .70
❑ 513 Lindy McDaniel 2.00 .90
❑ 514 Ted Sizemore 1.50 .70
❑ 515 Bert Blyleven 4.00 1.80
❑ 516 Oscar Brown 1.00 .45
❑ 517 Ken Brett 1.00 .45
❑ 518 Wayne Garrett 1.00 .45
❑ 519 Ted Abernathy 1.00 .45
❑ 520 Larry Bowa 2.00 .90
❑ 521 Alan Foster 1.00 .45
❑ 522 Los Angeles Dodgers 2.00 .90
Team Card
❑ 523 Chuck Dobson 1.00 .45
❑ 524 Reds Rookies 1.00 .45
Ed Armbrister
Mel Behney
❑ 525 Carlos May 2.00 .90
❑ 526 Bob Bailey 6.00 2.70
❑ 527 Dave Leonhard 4.00 1.80
❑ 528 Ron Stone 4.00 1.80
❑ 529 Dave Nelson 6.00 2.70
❑ 530 Don Sutton 8.00 3.60
❑ 531 Freddie Patek 6.00 2.70
❑ 532 Fred Kendall 4.00 1.80
❑ 533 Ralph Houk MG 6.00 2.70
❑ 534 Jim Hickman 6.00 2.70
❑ 535 Ed Brinkman 4.00 1.80
❑ 536 Doug Rader 6.00 2.70
❑ 537 Bob Locker 4.00 1.80
❑ 538 Charlie Sands 4.00 1.80
❑ 539 Terry Forster RC 6.00 2.70
❑ 540 Felix Millan 4.00 1.80
❑ 541 Roger Repoz 4.00 1.80
❑ 542 Jack Billingham 4.00 1.80
❑ 543 Duane Josephson 4.00 1.80
❑ 544 Ted Martinez 4.00 1.80
❑ 545 Wayne Granger 4.00 1.80
❑ 546 Joe Hague 4.00 1.80
❑ 547 Cleveland Indians 8.00 3.60
Team Card
❑ 548 Frank Reberger 4.00 1.80
❑ 549 Dave May 4.00 1.80
❑ 550 Brooks Robinson 25.00 11.00
❑ 551 Ollie Brown 4.00 1.80
❑ 552 Ollie Brown IA 4.00 1.80
❑ 553 Wilbur Wood 6.00 2.70
❑ 554 Wilbur Wood IA 4.00 1.80
❑ 555 Ron Santo 8.00 3.60
❑ 556 Ron Santo IA 6.00 2.70
❑ 557 John Odom 4.00 1.80
❑ 558 John Odom IA 4.00 1.80
❑ 559 Pete Rose 50.00 22.00
❑ 560 Pete Rose IA 20.00 9.00
❑ 561 Leo Cardenas 4.00 1.80
❑ 562 Leo Cardenas IA 4.00 1.80
❑ 563 Ray Sadecki 4.00 1.80
❑ 564 Ray Sadecki IA 4.00 1.80
❑ 565 Reggie Smith 6.00 2.70
❑ 566 Reggie Smith IA 4.00 1.80
❑ 567 Juan Marichal 12.00 5.50
❑ 568 Juan Marichal IA 6.00 2.70
❑ 569 Ed Kirkpatrick 4.00 1.80
❑ 570 Ed Kirkpatrick IA 4.00 1.80
❑ 571 Nate Colbert 4.00 1.80
❑ 572 Nate Colbert IA 4.00 1.80
❑ 573 Fritz Peterson 4.00 1.80

❑ 574 Fritz Peterson IA 4.00 1.80
❑ 575 Al Oliver 8.00 3.60
❑ 576 Leo Durocher MG 6.00 2.70
❑ 577 Mike Paul 6.00 2.70
❑ 578 Billy Grabarkewitz 4.00 1.80
❑ 579 Doyle Alexander RC 6.00 2.70
❑ 580 Lou Piniella 6.00 2.70
❑ 581 Wade Blasingame 4.00 1.80
❑ 582 Montreal Expos 8.00 3.60
Team Card
❑ 583 Darold Knowles 4.00 1.80
❑ 584 Jerry McNertney 4.00 1.80
❑ 585 George Scott 6.00 2.70
❑ 586 Denis Menke 4.00 1.80
❑ 587 Billy Wilson 4.00 1.80
❑ 588 Jim Holt 4.00 1.80
❑ 589 Hal Lanier 4.00 1.80
❑ 590 Graig Nettles 8.00 3.60
❑ 591 Paul Casanova 4.00 1.80
❑ 592 Lew Krausse 4.00 1.80
❑ 593 Rich Morales 4.00 1.80
❑ 594 Jim Beauchamp 4.00 1.80
❑ 595 Nolan Ryan 150.00 70.00
❑ 596 Manny Mota 6.00 2.70
❑ 597 Jim Magnuson 4.00 1.80
❑ 598 Hal King 6.00 2.70
❑ 599 Billy Champion 4.00 1.80
❑ 600 Al Kaline 25.00 11.00
❑ 601 George Stone 4.00 1.80
❑ 602 Dave Bristol MG 4.00 1.80
❑ 603 Jim Ray 4.00 1.80
❑ 604A Checklist 657-787 12.00 2.40
(Copyright on back bottom right)
❑ 604B Checklist 657-787 12.00 2.40
(Copyright on back bottom left)
❑ 605 Nelson Briles 6.00 2.70
❑ 606 Luis Melendez 4.00 1.80
❑ 607 Frank Duffy 4.00 1.80
❑ 608 Mike Corkins 4.00 1.80
❑ 609 Tom Grieve 6.00 2.70
❑ 610 Bill Stoneman 6.00 2.70
❑ 611 Rich Reese 4.00 1.80
❑ 612 Joe Decker 4.00 1.80
❑ 613 Mike Ferraro 4.00 1.80
❑ 614 Ted Uhlaender 4.00 1.80
❑ 615 Steve Hargan 4.00 1.80
❑ 616 Joe Ferguson RC 6.00 2.70
❑ 617 Kansas City Royals 8.00 3.60
Team Card
❑ 618 Rich Robertson 4.00 1.80
❑ 619 Rich McKinney 4.00 1.80
❑ 620 Phil Niekro 12.00 5.50
❑ 621 Commissioners Award 8.00 3.60
❑ 622 MVP Award 8.00 3.60
❑ 623 Cy Young Award 8.00 3.60
❑ 624 Minor League Player of the Year 8.00 3.60
❑ 625 Rookie of the Year 8.00 3.60
❑ 626 Babe Ruth Award 8.00 3.60
❑ 627 Moe Drabowsky 4.00 1.80
❑ 628 Terry Crowley 4.00 1.80
❑ 629 Paul Doyle 4.00 1.80
❑ 630 Rich Hebner 6.00 2.70
❑ 631 John Strohmayer 4.00 1.80
❑ 632 Mike Hegan 4.00 1.80
❑ 633 Jack Hiatt 4.00 1.80
❑ 634 Dick Woodson 4.00 1.80
❑ 635 Don Money 6.00 2.70
❑ 636 Bill Lee 6.00 2.70
❑ 637 Preston Gomez MG 4.00 1.80
❑ 638 Ken Wright 4.00 1.80
❑ 639 J.C. Martin 4.00 1.80
❑ 640 Joe Coleman 4.00 1.80
❑ 641 Mike Lum 4.00 1.80
❑ 642 Dennis Riddleberger 4.00 1.80
❑ 643 Russ Gibson 4.00 1.80
❑ 644 Bernie Allen 4.00 1.80
❑ 645 Jim Maloney 6.00 2.70
❑ 646 Chico Salmon 4.00 1.80
❑ 647 Bob Moose 4.00 1.80
❑ 648 Jim Lyttle 4.00 1.80
❑ 649 Pete Richert 4.00 1.80
❑ 650 Sal Bando 6.00 2.70
❑ 651 Cincinnati Reds 8.00 3.60
Team Card
❑ 652 Marcelino Lopez 4.00 1.80
❑ 653 Jim Fairey 4.00 1.80
❑ 654 Horacio Pina 6.00 2.70
❑ 655 Jerry Grote 4.00 1.80
❑ 656 Rudy May 4.00 1.80
❑ 657 Bobby Wine 12.00 5.50
❑ 658 Steve Dunning 12.00 5.50
❑ 659 Bob Aspromonte 12.00 5.50
❑ 660 Paul Blair 15.00 6.75
❑ 661 Bill Virdon MG 12.00 5.50
❑ 662 Stan Bahnsen 12.00 5.50
❑ 663 Fran Healy 15.00 6.75
❑ 664 Bobby Knoop 12.00 5.50
❑ 665 Chris Short 12.00 5.50
❑ 666 Hector Torres 12.00 5.50
❑ 667 Ray Newman 12.00 5.50
❑ 668 Texas Rangers 30.00 13.50
Team Card
❑ 669 Willie Crawford 12.00 5.50
❑ 670 Ken Holtzman 15.00 6.75
❑ 671 Donn Clendenon 15.00 6.75
❑ 672 Archie Reynolds 12.00 5.50
❑ 673 Dave Marshall 12.00 5.50
❑ 674 John Kennedy 12.00 5.50
❑ 675 Pat Jarvis 12.00 5.50
❑ 676 Danny Cater 12.00 5.50
❑ 677 Ivan Murrell 12.00 5.50
❑ 678 Steve Luebber 12.00 5.50
❑ 679 Astros Rookies 12.00 5.50
Bob Fenwick
Bob Stinson
❑ 680 Dave Johnson 15.00 6.75
❑ 681 Bobby Pfeil 12.00 5.50
❑ 682 Mike McCormick 15.00 6.75
❑ 683 Steve Hovley 12.00 5.50
❑ 684 Hal Breeden 12.00 5.50
❑ 685 Joel Horlen 12.00 5.50
❑ 686 Steve Garvey 40.00 18.00
❑ 687 Del Unser 12.00 5.50
❑ 688 St. Louis Cardinals 20.00 9.00
Team Card
❑ 689 Eddie Fisher 12.00 5.50
❑ 690 Willie Montanez 15.00 6.75
❑ 691 Curt Blefary 12.00 5.50
❑ 692 Curt Blefary IA 12.00 5.50
❑ 693 Alan Gallagher 12.00 5.50
❑ 694 Alan Gallagher IA 12.00 5.50
❑ 695 Rod Carew 50.00 22.00
❑ 696 Rod Carew IA 30.00 13.50
❑ 697 Jerry Koosman 15.00 6.75
❑ 698 Jerry Koosman IA 15.00 6.75
❑ 699 Bobby Murcer 15.00 6.75
❑ 700 Bobby Murcer IA 15.00 6.75
❑ 701 Jose Pagan 12.00 5.50
❑ 702 Jose Pagan IA 12.00 5.50
❑ 703 Doug Griffin 12.00 5.50
❑ 704 Doug Griffin IA 12.00 5.50
❑ 705 Pat Corrales 15.00 6.75
❑ 706 Pat Corrales IA 12.00 5.50
❑ 707 Tim Foli 12.00 5.50
❑ 708 Tim Foli IA 12.00 5.50
❑ 709 Jim Kaat 15.00 6.75
❑ 710 Jim Kaat IA 15.00 6.75
❑ 711 Bobby Bonds 20.00 9.00
❑ 712 Bobby Bonds IA 15.00 6.75
❑ 713 Gene Michael 20.00 9.00
❑ 714 Gene Michael IA 15.00 6.75
❑ 715 Mike Epstein 12.00 5.50
❑ 716 Jesus Alou 12.00 5.50
❑ 717 Bruce Dal Canton 12.00 5.50
❑ 718 Del Rice MG 12.00 5.50
❑ 719 Cesar Geronimo 12.00 5.50
❑ 720 Sam McDowell 15.00 6.75
❑ 721 Eddie Leon 12.00 5.50
❑ 722 Bill Sudakis 12.00 5.50
❑ 723 Al Santorini 12.00 5.50
❑ 724 AL Rookie Pitchers 12.00 5.50
John Curtis
Rich Hinton
Mickey Scott RC
❑ 725 Dick McAuliffe 15.00 6.75
❑ 726 Dick Selma 12.00 5.50
❑ 727 Jose Laboy 12.00 5.50
❑ 728 Gail Hopkins 12.00 5.50
❑ 729 Bob Veale 15.00 6.75
❑ 730 Rick Monday 15.00 6.75
❑ 731 Baltimore Orioles 20.00 9.00
Team Card
❑ 732 George Culver 12.00 5.50
❑ 733 Jim Ray Hart 15.00 6.75
❑ 734 Bob Burda 12.00 5.50
❑ 735 Diego Segui 12.00 5.50
❑ 736 Bill Russell 15.00 6.75
❑ 737 Len Randle 15.00 6.75
❑ 738 Jim Merritt 12.00 5.50
❑ 739 Don Mason 12.00 5.50
❑ 740 Rico Carty 15.00 6.75
❑ 741 Rookie First Basemen 15.00 6.75
Tom Hutton
John Milner
Rick Miller RC
❑ 742 Jim Rooker 12.00 5.50
❑ 743 Cesar Gutierrez 12.00 5.50
❑ 744 Jim Slaton 12.00 5.50
❑ 745 Julian Javier 15.00 6.75
❑ 746 Lowell Palmer 12.00 5.50
❑ 747 Jim Stewart 12.00 5.50
❑ 748 Phil Hennigan 12.00 5.50
❑ 749 Walter Alston MG 20.00 9.00
❑ 750 Willie Horton 12.00 5.50
❑ 751 Steve Carlton TR 40.00 18.00
❑ 752 Joe Morgan TR 45.00 20.00
❑ 753 Denny McLain TR 20.00 9.00
❑ 754 Frank Robinson TR 45.00 20.00
❑ 755 Jim Fregosi TR 15.00 6.75
❑ 756 Rick Wise TR 15.00 6.75
❑ 757 Jose Cardenal TR 15.00 6.75
❑ 758 Gil Garrido 12.00 5.50
❑ 759 Chris Cannizzaro 12.00 5.50
❑ 760 Bill Mazeroski 20.00 9.00
❑ 761 Rookie Outfielders 25.00 11.00
Ben Oglivie
Ron Cey RC
Bernie Williams
❑ 762 Wayne Simpson 12.00 5.50
❑ 763 Ron Hansen 12.00 5.50
❑ 764 Dusty Baker 20.00 9.00
❑ 765 Ken McMullen 12.00 5.50
❑ 766 Steve Hamilton 12.00 5.50
❑ 767 Tom McCraw 15.00 6.75
❑ 768 Denny Doyle 12.00 5.50
❑ 769 Jack Aker 12.00 5.50
❑ 770 Jim Wynn 15.00 6.75
❑ 771 San Francisco Giants 20.00 9.00
Team Card
❑ 772 Ken Tatum 12.00 5.50
❑ 773 Ron Brand 12.00 5.50
❑ 774 Luis Alvarado 12.00 5.50
❑ 775 Jerry Reuss 15.00 6.75
❑ 776 Bill Voss 12.00 5.50
❑ 777 Hoyt Wilhelm 25.00 11.00
❑ 778 Twins Rookies 20.00 9.00
Vic Albury
Rick Dempsey RC
Jim Strickland
❑ 779 Tony Cloninger 12.00 5.50
❑ 780 Dick Green 12.00 5.50
❑ 781 Jim McAndrew 12.00 5.50
❑ 782 Larry Stahl 12.00 5.50
❑ 783 Les Cain 12.00 5.50
❑ 784 Ken Aspromonte 12.00 5.50
❑ 785 Vic Davalillo 12.00 5.50
❑ 786 Chuck Brinkman 12.00 5.50
❑ 787 Ron Reed 15.00 5.25

## 1973 Topps

| | NRMT | VG-E |
|---|---|---|
| COMPLETE SET (660) | 700.00 | 325.00 |
| COMMON CARD (1-264) | .50 | .23 |
| COMMON CARD (265-396) | .75 | .35 |
| COMMON CARD (397-528) | 1.25 | .55 |
| COMMON CARD (529-660) | 3.50 | 1.55 |
| WRAPPER (10-CENT, BAT) | 15.00 | 6.75 |
| WRAPPER (10-CENT) | 15.00 | 6.75 |

❑ 1 All-Time HR Leaders 40.00 11.50
Babe Ruth 714
Hank Aaron 673
Willie Mays 654
❑ 2 Rich Hebner 1.50 .70

❑ 3 Jim Lonborg .......... 1.50 .70
❑ 4 John Milner .......... .50 .23
❑ 5 Ed Brinkman .......... .50 .23
❑ 6 Mac Scarce .......... .50 .23
❑ 7 Texas Rangers .......... 2.00 .90
Team Card
❑ 8 Tom Hall .......... .50 .23
❑ 9 Johnny Oates .......... .50 .23
❑ 10 Don Sutton .......... 2.50 1.10
❑ 11 Chris Chambliss .......... 1.50 .70
❑ 12A Padres Leaders .......... 3.00 1.35
Don Zimmer MG
Dave Garcia CO
Johnny Podres CO
Bob Skinner CO
Whitey Wietelmann CO
(Podres no right ear)
❑ 12B Padres Leaders .......... .75 .35
(Podres has right ear)
❑ 13 George Hendrick .......... 1.50 .70
❑ 14 Sonny Siebert .......... .50 .23
❑ 15 Ralph Garr .......... 1.50 .70
❑ 16 Steve Braun .......... .50 .23
❑ 17 Fred Gladding .......... .50 .23
❑ 18 Leroy Stanton .......... .50 .23
❑ 19 Tim Foli .......... .50 .23
❑ 20 Stan Bahnsen .......... .50 .23
❑ 21 Randy Hundley .......... 1.50 .70
❑ 22 Ted Abernathy .......... .50 .23
❑ 23 Dave Kingman .......... 1.50 .70
❑ 24 Al Santorini .......... .50 .23
❑ 25 Roy White .......... 1.50 .70
❑ 26 Pittsburgh Pirates .......... 2.00 .90
Team Card
❑ 27 Bill Gogolewski .......... .50 .23
❑ 28 Hal McRae .......... 1.50 .70
❑ 29 Tony Taylor .......... 1.50 .70
❑ 30 Tug McGraw .......... 1.50 .70
❑ 31 Buddy Bell RC .......... 2.50 1.10
❑ 32 Fred Norman .......... .50 .23
❑ 33 Jim Breazeale .......... .50 .23
❑ 34 Pat Dobson .......... .50 .23
❑ 35 Willie Davis .......... 1.50 .70
❑ 36 Steve Barber .......... .50 .23
❑ 37 Bill Robinson .......... 1.50 .70
❑ 38 Mike Epstein .......... .50 .23
❑ 39 Dave Roberts .......... .50 .23
❑ 40 Reggie Smith .......... 1.50 .70
❑ 41 Tom Walker .......... .50 .23
❑ 42 Mike Andrews .......... .50 .23
❑ 43 Randy Moffitt .......... .50 .23
❑ 44 Rick Monday .......... 1.50 .70
❑ 45 Ellie Rodriguez UER .......... .50 .23
(Photo actually
John Felske)
❑ 46 Lindy McDaniel .......... 1.50 .70
❑ 47 Luis Melendez .......... .50 .23
❑ 48 Paul Splittorff .......... .50 .23
❑ 49A Twins Leaders .......... 3.00 1.35
Frank Quilici MG
Vern Morgan CO
Bob Rodgers CO
Ralph Rowe CO
Al Worthington CO
(Solid backgrounds)
❑ 49B Twins Leaders .......... .75 .35
(Natural backgrounds)
❑ 50 Roberto Clemente .......... 60.00 27.00
❑ 51 Chuck Seelbach .......... .50 .23
❑ 52 Denis Menke .......... .50 .23
❑ 53 Steve Dunning .......... .50 .23
❑ 54 Checklist 1-132 .......... 3.00 .60
❑ 55 Jon Matlack .......... 1.50 .70
❑ 56 Merv Rettenmund .......... .50 .23
❑ 57 Derrel Thomas .......... .50 .23
❑ 58 Mike Paul .......... .50 .23
❑ 59 Steve Yeager RC .......... 1.50 .70
❑ 60 Ken Holtzman .......... 1.50 .70
❑ 61 Batting Leaders .......... 2.50 1.10
Billy Williams
Rod Carew
❑ 62 Home Run Leaders .......... 2.50 1.10
Johnny Bench
Dick Allen
❑ 63 RBI Leaders .......... 2.50 1.10
Johnny Bench
Dick Allen
❑ 64 Stolen Base Leaders .......... 1.50 .70
Lou Brock
Bert Campaneris
❑ 65 ERA Leaders .......... 1.50 .70
Steve Carlton
Luis Tiant
❑ 66 Victory Leaders .......... 1.50 .70
Steve Carlton
Gaylord Perry
Wilbur Wood
❑ 67 Strikeout Leaders .......... 30.00 13.50
Steve Carlton
Nolan Ryan
❑ 68 Leading Firemen .......... 1.50 .70
Clay Carroll
Sparky Lyle
❑ 69 Phil Gagliano .......... .50 .23
❑ 70 Milt Pappas .......... 1.50 .70
❑ 71 Johnny Briggs .......... .50 .23
❑ 72 Ron Reed .......... .50 .23
❑ 73 Ed Herrmann .......... .50 .23
❑ 74 Billy Champion .......... .50 .23
❑ 75 Vada Pinson .......... 1.50 .70
❑ 76 Doug Rader .......... .50 .23
❑ 77 Mike Torrez .......... 1.50 .70
❑ 78 Richie Scheinblum .......... .50 .23
❑ 79 Jim Willoughby .......... .50 .23
❑ 80 Tony Oliva UER .......... 1.50 .70
(Minnseota on front)
❑ 81A Cubs Leaders .......... 1.50 .70
Whitey Lockman MG
Hank Aguirre CO
Ernie Banks CO
Larry Jansen CO
Pete Reiser CO
(Solid backgrounds)
❑ 81B Cubs Leaders .......... 1.50 .70
(Natural backgrounds)
❑ 82 Fritz Peterson .......... .50 .23
❑ 83 Leron Lee .......... .50 .23
❑ 84 Rollie Fingers .......... 4.00 1.80
❑ 85 Ted Simmons .......... 1.50 .70
❑ 86 Tom McCraw .......... .50 .23
❑ 87 Ken Boswell .......... .50 .23
❑ 88 Mickey Stanley .......... 1.50 .70
❑ 89 Jack Billingham .......... .50 .23
❑ 90 Brooks Robinson .......... 7.00 3.10
❑ 91 Los Angeles Dodgers .......... 2.00 .90
Team Card
❑ 92 Jerry Bell .......... .50 .23
❑ 93 Jesus Alou .......... .50 .23
❑ 94 Dick Billings .......... .50 .23
❑ 95 Steve Blass .......... 1.50 .70
❑ 96 Doug Griffin .......... .50 .23
❑ 97 Willie Montanez .......... 1.50 .70
❑ 98 Dick Woodson .......... .50 .23
❑ 99 Carl Taylor .......... .50 .23
❑ 100 Hank Aaron .......... 25.00 11.00
❑ 101 Ken Henderson .......... .50 .23
❑ 102 Rudy May .......... .50 .23
❑ 103 Celerino Sanchez .......... .50 .23
❑ 104 Reggie Cleveland .......... .50 .23
❑ 105 Carlos May .......... .50 .23
❑ 106 Terry Humphrey .......... .50 .23
❑ 107 Phil Hennigan .......... .50 .23
❑ 108 Bill Russell .......... 1.50 .70
❑ 109 Doyle Alexander .......... 1.50 .70
❑ 110 Bob Watson .......... 1.50 .70
❑ 111 Dave Nelson .......... .50 .23
❑ 112 Gary Ross .......... .50 .23
❑ 113 Jerry Grote .......... .50 .23
❑ 114 Lynn McGlothen .......... .50 .23
❑ 115 Ron Santo .......... 1.50 .70
❑ 116A Yankees Leaders .......... 3.00 1.35
Ralph Houk MG
Jim Hegan CO
Elston Howard CO
Dick Howser CO
Jim Turner CO
(Solid backgrounds)
❑ 116B Yankees Leaders .......... .75 .35
(Natural backgrounds)
❑ 117 Ramon Hernandez .......... .50 .23
❑ 118 John Mayberry .......... 1.50 .70
❑ 119 Larry Bowa .......... 1.50 .70
❑ 120 Joe Coleman .......... .50 .23
❑ 121 Dave Rader .......... .50 .23
❑ 122 Jim Strickland .......... .50 .23
❑ 123 Sandy Alomar .......... 1.50 .70
❑ 124 Jim Hardin .......... .50 .23
❑ 125 Ron Fairly .......... 1.50 .70
❑ 126 Jim Brewer .......... .50 .23
❑ 127 Milwaukee Brewers .......... 2.00 .90
Team Card
❑ 128 Ted Sizemore .......... .50 .23
❑ 129 Terry Forster .......... 1.50 .70
❑ 130 Pete Rose .......... 20.00 9.00
❑ 131A Red Sox Leaders .......... 3.00 1.35
Eddie Kasko MG
Doug Camilli CO
Don Lenhardt CO
Eddie Popowski CO
(No right ear)
Lee Stange CO
❑ 131B Red Sox Leaders .......... 1.50 .70
(Popowski has right
ear showing)
❑ 132 Matty Alou .......... 1.50 .70
❑ 133 Dave Roberts .......... .50 .23
❑ 134 Milt Wilcox .......... .50 .23
❑ 135 Lee May UER .......... 1.50 .70
(Career average .000)
❑ 136A Orioles Leaders .......... 2.00 .90
Earl Weaver MG
George Bamberger CO
Jim Frey CO
Billy Hunter CO
George Staller CO
(Orange backgrounds)
❑ 136B Orioles Leaders .......... 3.00 1.35
(Dark pale
backgrounds)
❑ 137 Jim Beauchamp .......... .50 .23
❑ 138 Horacio Pina .......... .50 .23
❑ 139 Carmen Fanzone .......... .50 .23
❑ 140 Lou Piniella .......... 1.50 .70
❑ 141 Bruce Kison .......... .50 .23
❑ 142 Thurman Munson .......... 6.00 2.70
❑ 143 John Curtis .......... .50 .23
❑ 144 Marty Perez .......... .50 .23
❑ 145 Bobby Bonds .......... 1.50 .70
❑ 146 Woodie Fryman .......... .50 .23
❑ 147 Mike Anderson .......... .50 .23
❑ 148 Dave Goltz .......... .50 .23
❑ 149 Ron Hunt .......... .50 .23
❑ 150 Wilbur Wood .......... 1.50 .70
❑ 151 Wes Parker .......... 1.50 .70
❑ 152 Dave May .......... .50 .23
❑ 153 Al Hrabosky .......... 1.50 .70
❑ 154 Jeff Torborg .......... 1.50 .70
❑ 155 Sal Bando .......... 1.50 .70
❑ 156 Cesar Geronimo .......... .50 .23
❑ 157 Denny Riddleberger .......... .50 .23
❑ 158 Houston Astros .......... 2.00 .90
Team Card
❑ 159 Clarence Gaston .......... 1.50 .70
❑ 160 Jim Palmer .......... 7.00 3.10
❑ 161 Ted Martinez .......... .50 .23
❑ 162 Pete Broberg .......... .50 .23
❑ 163 Vic Davalillo .......... .50 .23
❑ 164 Monty Montgomery .......... .50 .23
❑ 165 Luis Aparicio .......... 4.00 1.80
❑ 166 Terry Harmon .......... .50 .23

❑ 167 Steve Stone 1.50 .70
❑ 168 Jim Northrup 1.50 .70
❑ 169 Ron Schueler RC .50 .23
❑ 170 Harmon Killebrew 5.00 2.20
❑ 171 Bernie Carbo .50 .23
❑ 172 Steve Kline .50 .23
❑ 173 Hal Breeden .50 .23
❑ 174 Rich Gossage RC 6.00 2.70
❑ 175 Frank Robinson 7.00 3.10
❑ 176 Chuck Taylor .50 .23
❑ 177 Bill Plummer .50 .23
❑ 178 Don Rose .50 .23
❑ 179A A's Leaders 4.00 1.80
Dick Williams MG
Jerry Adair CO
Vern Hoscheit CO
Irv Noren CO
Wes Stock CO
(Hoscheit left ear showing)
❑ 179B A's Leaders 1.50 .70
(Hoscheit left ear not showing)
❑ 180 Ferguson Jenkins 4.00 1.80
❑ 181 Jack Brohamer .50 .23
❑ 182 Mike Caldwell 1.50 .70
❑ 183 Don Buford .50 .23
❑ 184 Jerry Koosman 1.50 .70
❑ 185 Jim Wynn 1.50 .70
❑ 186 Bill Fahey .50 .23
❑ 187 Luke Walker .50 .23
❑ 188 Cookie Rojas 1.50 .70
❑ 189 Greg Luzinski 1.50 .70
❑ 190 Bob Gibson 7.00 3.10
❑ 191 Detroit Tigers 2.50 1.10
Team Card
❑ 192 Pat Jarvis .50 .23
❑ 193 Carlton Fisk 10.00 4.50
❑ 194 Jorge Orta .50 .23
❑ 195 Clay Carroll .50 .23
❑ 196 Ken McMullen .50 .23
❑ 197 Ed Goodson .50 .23
❑ 198 Horace Clarke .50 .23
❑ 199 Bert Blyleven 1.50 .70
❑ 200 Billy Williams 4.00 1.80
❑ 201 George Hendrick ALCS 1.50 .70
❑ 202 George Foster NLCS 1.50 .70
❑ 203 Gene Tenace WS 1.50 .70
❑ 204 World Series Game 2 1.50 .70
A's two straight
❑ 205 Tony Perez WS 2.50 1.10
❑ 206 Gene Tenace WS 1.50 .70
❑ 207 Blue Moon Odom WS 1.50 .70
❑ 208 Johnny Bench WS6 5.00 2.20
❑ 209 Bert Campaneris WS 1.50 .70
❑ 210 World Series Summary .50 .23
World champions:
A's Win
❑ 211 Balor Moore .50 .23
❑ 212 Joe Lahoud .50 .23
❑ 213 Steve Garvey 5.00 2.20
❑ 214 Steve Hamilton .50 .23
❑ 215 Dusty Baker 1.50 .70
❑ 216 Toby Harrah 1.50 .70
❑ 217 Don Wilson .50 .23
❑ 218 Aurelio Rodriguez .50 .23
❑ 219 St. Louis Cardinals 2.50 1.10
Team Card
❑ 220 Nolan Ryan 60.00 27.00
❑ 221 Fred Kendall .50 .23
❑ 222 Rob Gardner .50 .23
❑ 223 Bud Harrelson 1.50 .70
❑ 224 Bill Lee 1.50 .70
❑ 225 Al Oliver 1.50 .70
❑ 226 Ray Fosse .50 .23
❑ 227 Wayne Twitchell .50 .23
❑ 228 Bobby Darwin .50 .23
❑ 229 Roric Harrison .50 .23
❑ 230 Joe Morgan 6.00 2.70
❑ 231 Bill Parsons .50 .23
❑ 232 Ken Singleton 1.50 .70
❑ 233 Ed Kirkpatrick .50 .23
❑ 234 Bill North .50 .23
❑ 235 Jim Hunter 4.00 1.80
❑ 236 Tito Fuentes .50 .23
❑ 237A Braves Leaders 1.50 .70
Eddie Mathews MG
Lew Burdette CO
Jim Busby CO
Roy Hartsfield CO
Ken Silvestri CO
(Burdette right ear showing)
❑ 237B Braves Leaders 3.00 1.35
(Burdette right ear not showing)
❑ 238 Tony Muser .50 .23
❑ 239 Pete Richert .50 .23
❑ 240 Bobby Murcer 1.50 .70
❑ 241 Dwain Anderson .50 .23
❑ 242 George Culver .50 .23
❑ 243 California Angels 2.50 1.10
Team Card
❑ 244 Ed Acosta .50 .23
❑ 245 Carl Yastrzemski 8.00 3.60
❑ 246 Ken Sanders .50 .23
❑ 247 Del Unser .50 .23
❑ 248 Jerry Johnson .50 .23
❑ 249 Larry Biittner .50 .23
❑ 250 Manny Sanguillen 1.50 .70
❑ 251 Roger Nelson .50 .23
❑ 252A Giants Leaders 4.00 1.80
Charlie Fox MG
Joe Amalfitano CO
Andy Gilbert CO
Don McMahon CO
John McNamara CO
(Orange backgrounds)
❑ 252B Giants Leaders 1.50 .70
(Dark pale backgrounds)
❑ 253 Mark Belanger 1.50 .70
❑ 254 Bill Stoneman .50 .23
❑ 255 Reggie Jackson 15.00 6.75
❑ 256 Chris Zachary .50 .23
❑ 257A Mets Leaders 2.50 1.10
Yogi Berra MG
Roy McMillan CO
Joe Pignatano CO
Rube Walker CO
Eddie Yost CO
(Orange backgrounds)
❑ 257B Mets Leaders 5.00 2.20
(Dark pale backgrounds)
❑ 258 Tommy John 1.50 .70
❑ 259 Jim Holt .50 .23
❑ 260 Gary Nolan 1.50 .70
❑ 261 Pat Kelly .50 .23
❑ 262 Jack Aker .50 .23
❑ 263 George Scott 1.50 .70
❑ 264 Checklist 133-264 3.00 .60
❑ 265 Gene Michael 1.50 .70
❑ 266 Mike Lum .50 .23
❑ 267 Lloyd Allen .50 .23
❑ 268 Jerry Morales .50 .23
❑ 269 Tim McCarver 1.50 .70
❑ 270 Luis Tiant 1.50 .70
❑ 271 Tom Hutton .50 .23
❑ 272 Ed Farmer .50 .23
❑ 273 Chris Speier .50 .23
❑ 274 Darold Knowles .50 .23
❑ 275 Tony Perez 4.00 1.80
❑ 276 Joe Lovitto .50 .23
❑ 277 Bob Miller .50 .23
❑ 278 Baltimore Orioles 1.50 .70
Team Card
❑ 279 Mike Strahler .50 .23
❑ 280 Al Kaline 7.00 3.10
❑ 281 Mike Jorgensen .50 .23
❑ 282 Steve Hovley .50 .23
❑ 283 Ray Sadecki .50 .23
❑ 284 Glenn Borgmann .50 .23
❑ 285 Don Kessinger .50 .23
❑ 286 Frank Linzy .50 .23
❑ 287 Eddie Leon .50 .23
❑ 288 Gary Gentry .50 .23
❑ 289 Bob Oliver .50 .23
❑ 290 Cesar Cedeno 1.50 .70
❑ 291 Rogelio Moret .50 .23
❑ 292 Jose Cruz 1.50 .70
❑ 293 Bernie Allen .50 .23
❑ 294 Steve Arlin .50 .23
❑ 295 Bert Campaneris 1.50 .70
❑ 296 Reds Leaders 2.50 1.10
Sparky Anderson MG
Alex Grammas CO
Ted Kluszewski CO
George Scherger CO
Larry Shepard CO
❑ 297 Walt Williams .50 .23
❑ 298 Ron Bryant .50 .23
❑ 299 Ted Ford .50 .23
❑ 300 Steve Carlton 10.00 4.50
❑ 301 Billy Grabarkewitz .50 .23
❑ 302 Terry Crowley .50 .23
❑ 303 Nelson Briles .50 .23
❑ 304 Duke Sims .50 .23
❑ 305 Willie Mays 40.00 18.00
❑ 306 Tom Burgmeier .50 .23
❑ 307 Boots Day .50 .23
❑ 308 Skip Lockwood .50 .23
❑ 309 Paul Popovich .50 .23
❑ 310 Dick Allen 1.50 .70
❑ 311 Joe Decker .50 .23
❑ 312 Oscar Brown .50 .23
❑ 313 Jim Ray .50 .23
❑ 314 Ron Swoboda .50 .23
❑ 315 John Odom .50 .23
❑ 316 San Diego Padres 1.50 .70
Team Card
❑ 317 Danny Cater .50 .23
❑ 318 Jim McGlothlin .50 .23
❑ 319 Jim Spencer .50 .23
❑ 320 Lou Brock 7.00 3.10
❑ 321 Rich Hinton .50 .23
❑ 322 Garry Maddox RC 1.50 .70
❑ 323 Tigers Leaders 1.50 .70
Billy Martin MG
Art Fowler CO
Charlie Silvera CO
Dick Tracewski CO
❑ 324 Al Downing .50 .23
❑ 325 Boog Powell 1.50 .70
❑ 326 Darrell Brandon .50 .23
❑ 327 John Lowenstein .50 .23
❑ 328 Bill Bonham .50 .23
❑ 329 Ed Kranepool .50 .23
❑ 330 Rod Carew 7.00 3.10
❑ 331 Carl Morton .50 .23
❑ 332 John Felske .50 .23
❑ 333 Gene Clines .50 .23
❑ 334 Freddie Patek .50 .23
❑ 335 Bob Tolan .50 .23
❑ 336 Tom Bradley .50 .23
❑ 337 Dave Duncan .50 .23
❑ 338 Checklist 265-396 3.00 .60
❑ 339 Dick Tidrow .50 .23
❑ 340 Nate Colbert .50 .23
❑ 341 Jim Palmer KP 2.50 1.10
❑ 342 Sam McDowell KP .50 .23
❑ 343 Bobby Murcer KP .50 .23
❑ 344 Jim Hunter KP 2.50 1.10
❑ 345 Chris Speier KP .50 .23
❑ 346 Gaylord Perry KP 1.50 .70
❑ 347 Kansas City Royals 1.50 .70
Team Card
❑ 348 Rennie Stennett .50 .23
❑ 349 Dick McAuliffe .50 .23
❑ 350 Tom Seaver 12.00 5.50
❑ 351 Jimmy Stewart .50 .23
❑ 352 Don Stanhouse .50 .23
❑ 353 Steve Brye .50 .23
❑ 354 Billy Parker .50 .23
❑ 355 Mike Marshall 1.50 .70
❑ 356 White Sox Leaders .50 .23
Chuck Tanner MG
Joe Lonnett CO
Jim Mahoney CO
Al Monchak CO
Johnny Sain CO
❑ 357 Ross Grimsley .50 .23
❑ 358 Jim Nettles .50 .23
❑ 359 Cecil Upshaw .50 .23
❑ 360 Joe Rudi UER 1.50 .70
(Photo actually Gene Tenace)
❑ 361 Fran Healy .50 .23

- ❑ 362 Eddie Watt .50 .23
- ❑ 363 Jackie Hernandez .50 .23
- ❑ 364 Rick Wise .50 .23
- ❑ 365 Rico Petrocelli 1.50 .70
- ❑ 366 Brock Davis .50 .23
- ❑ 367 Burt Hooton .50 .23
- ❑ 368 Bill Buckner 1.50 .70
- ❑ 369 Lerrin LaGrow .50 .23
- ❑ 370 Willie Stargell 5.00 2.20
- ❑ 371 Mike Kekich .50 .23
- ❑ 372 Oscar Gamble .50 .23
- ❑ 373 Clyde Wright .50 .23
- ❑ 374 Darrell Evans 1.50 .70
- ❑ 375 Larry Dierker 1.50 .70
- ❑ 376 Frank Duffy .50 .23
- ❑ 377 Expos Leaders .50 .23
  Gene Mauch MG
  Dave Bristol CO
  Larry Doby CO
  Cal McLish CO
  Jerry Zimmerman CO
- ❑ 378 Len Randle .50 .23
- ❑ 379 Cy Acosta .50 .23
- ❑ 380 Johnny Bench 12.00 5.50
- ❑ 381 Vicente Romo .50 .23
- ❑ 382 Mike Hegan .50 .23
- ❑ 383 Diego Segui .50 .23
- ❑ 384 Don Baylor 4.00 1.80
- ❑ 385 Jim Perry 1.50 .70
- ❑ 386 Don Money .50 .23
- ❑ 387 Jim Barr .50 .23
- ❑ 388 Ben Oglivie 1.50 .70
- ❑ 389 New York Mets 4.00 1.80
  Team Card
- ❑ 390 Mickey Lolich 1.50 .70
- ❑ 391 Lee Lacy RC .50 .23
- ❑ 392 Dick Drago .50 .23
- ❑ 393 Jose Cardenal .50 .23
- ❑ 394 Sparky Lyle 1.50 .70
- ❑ 395 Roger Metzger .50 .23
- ❑ 396 Grant Jackson .50 .23
- ❑ 397 Dave Cash 1.25 .55
- ❑ 398 Rich Hand 1.25 .55
- ❑ 399 George Foster 2.00 .90
- ❑ 400 Gaylord Perry 5.00 2.20
- ❑ 401 Clyde Mashore 1.25 .55
- ❑ 402 Jack Hiatt 1.25 .55
- ❑ 403 Sonny Jackson 1.25 .55
- ❑ 404 Chuck Brinkman 1.25 .55
- ❑ 405 Cesar Tovar 1.25 .55
- ❑ 406 Paul Lindblad 1.25 .55
- ❑ 407 Felix Millan 1.25 .55
- ❑ 408 Jim Colborn 1.25 .55
- ❑ 409 Ivan Murrell 1.25 .55
- ❑ 410 Willie McCovey 6.00 2.70
  (Bench behind plate)
- ❑ 411 Ray Corbin 1.25 .55
- ❑ 412 Manny Mota 2.00 .90
- ❑ 413 Tom Timmermann 1.25 .55
- ❑ 414 Ken Rudolph 1.25 .55
- ❑ 415 Marty Pattin 1.25 .55
- ❑ 416 Paul Schaal 1.25 .55
- ❑ 417 Scipio Spinks 1.25 .55
- ❑ 418 Bob Grich 2.00 .90
- ❑ 419 Casey Cox 1.25 .55
- ❑ 420 Tommie Agee 1.25 .55
- ❑ 421A Angels Leaders 1.50 .70
  Bobby Winkles MG
  Tom Morgan CO
  Salty Parker CO
  Jimmie Reese CO
  John Roseboro CO
  (Orange backgrounds)
- ❑ 421B Angels Leaders 1.50 .70
  (Dark pale
  backgrounds)
- ❑ 422 Bob Robertson 1.25 .55
- ❑ 423 Johnny Jeter 1.25 .55
- ❑ 424 Denny Doyle 1.25 .55
- ❑ 425 Alex Johnson 1.25 .55
- ❑ 426 Dave LaRoche 1.25 .55
- ❑ 427 Rick Auerbach 1.25 .55
- ❑ 428 Wayne Simpson 1.25 .55
- ❑ 429 Jim Fairey 1.25 .55
- ❑ 430 Vida Blue 2.00 .90
- ❑ 431 Gerry Moses 1.25 .55
- ❑ 432 Dan Frisella 1.25 .55
- ❑ 433 Willie Horton 2.00 .90
- ❑ 434 San Francisco Giants 3.00 1.35
  Team Card
- ❑ 435 Rico Carty 2.00 .90
- ❑ 436 Jim McAndrew 1.25 .55
- ❑ 437 John Kennedy 1.25 .55
- ❑ 438 Enzo Hernandez 1.25 .55
- ❑ 439 Eddie Fisher 1.25 .55
- ❑ 440 Glenn Beckert 1.25 .55
- ❑ 441 Gail Hopkins 1.25 .55
- ❑ 442 Dick Dietz 1.25 .55
- ❑ 443 Danny Thompson 1.25 .55
- ❑ 444 Ken Brett 1.25 .55
- ❑ 445 Ken Berry 1.25 .55
- ❑ 446 Jerry Reuss 2.00 .90
- ❑ 447 Joe Hague 1.25 .55
- ❑ 448 John Hiller 1.25 .55
- ❑ 449A Indians Leaders 4.00 1.80
  Ken Aspromonte MG
  Rocky Colavito CO
  Joe Lutz CO
  Warren Spahn CO
  (Spahn's right
  ear pointed)
- ❑ 449B Indians Leaders 4.00 1.80
  (Spahn's right
  ear round)
- ❑ 450 Joe Torre 2.00 .90
- ❑ 451 John Vukovich 1.25 .55
- ❑ 452 Paul Casanova 1.25 .55
- ❑ 453 Checklist 397-528 3.00 .60
- ❑ 454 Tom Haller 1.25 .55
- ❑ 455 Bill Melton 1.25 .55
- ❑ 456 Dick Green 1.25 .55
- ❑ 457 John Strohmayer 1.25 .55
- ❑ 458 Jim Mason 1.25 .55
- ❑ 459 Jimmy Howarth 1.25 .55
- ❑ 460 Bill Freehan 2.00 .90
- ❑ 461 Mike Corkins 1.25 .55
- ❑ 462 Ron Blomberg 1.25 .55
- ❑ 463 Ken Tatum 1.25 .55
- ❑ 464 Chicago Cubs 3.00 1.35
  Team Card
- ❑ 465 Dave Giusti 1.25 .55
- ❑ 466 Jose Arcia 1.25 .55
- ❑ 467 Mike Ryan 1.25 .55
- ❑ 468 Tom Griffin 1.25 .55
- ❑ 469 Dan Monzon 1.25 .55
- ❑ 470 Mike Cuellar 2.00 .90
- ❑ 471 Ty Cobb ATL 10.00 4.50
  4191 Hits
- ❑ 472 Lou Gehrig ATL 15.00 6.75
  23 Grand Slams
- ❑ 473 Hank Aaron ATL 10.00 4.50
  6172 Total Bases
- ❑ 474 Babe Ruth ATL 20.00 9.00
  2209 RBI
- ❑ 475 Ty Cobb ATL 8.00 3.60
  .367 Batting Average
- ❑ 476 Walter Johnson ATL 3.00 1.35
  113 Shutouts
- ❑ 477 Cy Young ATL 3.00 1.35
  511 Victories
- ❑ 478 Walter Johnson ATL 3.00 1.35
  3508 Strikeouts
- ❑ 479 Hal Lanier 1.25 .55
- ❑ 480 Juan Marichal 5.00 2.20
- ❑ 481 Chicago White Sox 3.00 1.35
  Team Card
- ❑ 482 Rick Reuschel RC 3.00 1.35
- ❑ 483 Dal Maxvill 1.25 .55
- ❑ 484 Ernie McAnally 1.25 .55
- ❑ 485 Norm Cash 2.00 .90
- ❑ 486A Phillies Leaders 1.50 .70
  Danny Ozark MG
  Carroll Beringer CO
  Billy DeMars CO
  Ray Rippelmeyer CO
  Bobby Wine CO
  (Orange backgrounds)
- ❑ 486B Phillies Leaders 1.50 .70
  (Dark pale
  backgrounds)
- ❑ 487 Bruce Dal Canton 1.25 .55
- ❑ 488 Dave Campbell 2.00 .90
- ❑ 489 Jeff Burroughs 2.00 .90
- ❑ 490 Claude Osteen 1.25 .55
- ❑ 491 Bob Montgomery 1.25 .55
- ❑ 492 Pedro Borbon 1.25 .55
- ❑ 493 Duffy Dyer 1.25 .55
- ❑ 494 Rich Morales 1.25 .55
- ❑ 495 Tommy Helms 1.25 .55
- ❑ 496 Ray Lamb 1.25 .55
- ❑ 497A Cardinals Leaders 2.00 .90
  Red Schoendienst MG
  Vern Benson CO
  George Kissell CO
  Barney Schultz CO
  (Orange backgrounds)
- ❑ 497B Cardinals Leaders 3.00 1.35
  (Dark pale
  backgrounds)
- ❑ 498 Graig Nettles 3.00 1.35
- ❑ 499 Bob Moose 1.25 .55
- ❑ 500 Oakland A's 3.00 1.35
  Team Card
- ❑ 501 Larry Gura 1.25 .55
- ❑ 502 Bobby Valentine 3.00 1.35
- ❑ 503 Phil Niekro 5.00 2.20
- ❑ 504 Earl Williams 1.25 .55
- ❑ 505 Bob Bailey 1.25 .55
- ❑ 506 Bart Johnson 1.25 .55
- ❑ 507 Darrel Chaney 1.25 .55
- ❑ 508 Gates Brown 1.25 .55
- ❑ 509 Jim Nash 1.25 .55
- ❑ 510 Amos Otis 2.00 .90
- ❑ 511 Sam McDowell 2.00 .90
- ❑ 512 Dalton Jones 1.25 .55
- ❑ 513 Dave Marshall 1.25 .55
- ❑ 514 Jerry Kenney 1.25 .55
- ❑ 515 Andy Messersmith 2.00 .90
- ❑ 516 Danny Walton 1.25 .55
- ❑ 517A Pirates Leaders 1.50 .70
  Bill Virdon MG
  Don Leppert CO
  Bill Mazeroski CO
  Dave Ricketts CO
  Mel Wright CO
  (Mazeroski has
  no right ear)
- ❑ 517B Pirates Leaders 1.50 .70
  (Mazeroski has
  right ear)
- ❑ 518 Bob Veale 1.25 .55
- ❑ 519 Johnny Edwards 1.25 .55
- ❑ 520 Mel Stottlemyre 2.00 .90
- ❑ 521 Atlanta Braves 3.00 1.35
  Team Card
- ❑ 522 Leo Cardenas 1.25 .55
- ❑ 523 Wayne Granger 1.25 .55
- ❑ 524 Gene Tenace 2.00 .90
- ❑ 525 Jim Fregosi 2.00 .90
- ❑ 526 Ollie Brown 1.25 .55
- ❑ 527 Dan McGinn 1.25 .55
- ❑ 528 Paul Blair 1.25 .55
- ❑ 529 Milt May 3.50 1.55
- ❑ 530 Jim Kaat 5.00 2.20
- ❑ 531 Ron Woods 3.50 1.55
- ❑ 532 Steve Mingori 3.50 1.55
- ❑ 533 Larry Stahl 3.50 1.55
- ❑ 534 Dave Lemonds 3.50 1.55
- ❑ 535 Johnny Callison 5.00 2.20
- ❑ 536 Philadelphia Phillies 6.00 2.70
  Team Card
- ❑ 537 Bill Slayback 3.50 1.55
- ❑ 538 Jim Ray Hart 5.00 2.20
- ❑ 539 Tom Murphy 3.50 1.55
- ❑ 540 Cleon Jones 5.00 2.20
- ❑ 541 Bob Bolin 3.50 1.55
- ❑ 542 Pat Corrales 5.00 2.20
- ❑ 543 Alan Foster 3.50 1.55
- ❑ 544 Von Joshua 3.50 1.55
- ❑ 545 Orlando Cepeda 8.00 3.60
- ❑ 546 Jim York 3.50 1.55
- ❑ 547 Bobby Heise 3.50 1.55
- ❑ 548 Don Durham 3.50 1.55
- ❑ 549 Rangers Leaders 5.00 2.20
  Whitey Herzog MG
  Chuck Estrada CO
  Chuck Hiller CO
  Jackie Moore CO

❑ 550 Dave Johnson .......... 5.00 2.20
❑ 551 Mike Kilkenny .......... 3.50 1.55
❑ 552 J.C. Martin .......... 3.50 1.55
❑ 553 Mickey Scott .......... 3.50 1.55
❑ 554 Dave Concepcion .......... 5.00 2.20
❑ 555 Bill Hands .......... 3.50 1.55
❑ 556 New York Yankees .......... 8.00 3.60
Team Card
❑ 557 Bernie Williams .......... 3.50 1.55
❑ 558 Jerry May .......... 3.50 1.55
❑ 559 Barry Lersch .......... 3.50 1.55
❑ 560 Frank Howard .......... 5.00 2.20
❑ 561 Jim Geddes .......... 3.50 1.55
❑ 562 Wayne Garrett .......... 3.50 1.55
❑ 563 Larry Haney .......... 3.50 1.55
❑ 564 Mike Thompson .......... 3.50 1.55
❑ 565 Jim Hickman .......... 3.50 1.55
❑ 566 Lew Krausse .......... 3.50 1.55
❑ 567 Bob Fenwick .......... 3.50 1.55
❑ 568 Ray Newman .......... 3.50 1.55
❑ 569 Dodgers Leaders .......... 5.00 2.20
Walt Alston MG
Red Adams CO
Monty Basgall CO
Jim Gilliam CO
Tom Lasorda CO
❑ 570 Bill Singer .......... 5.00 2.20
❑ 571 Rusty Torres .......... 3.50 1.55
❑ 572 Gary Sutherland .......... 3.50 1.55
❑ 573 Fred Beene .......... 3.50 1.55
❑ 574 Bob Didier .......... 3.50 1.55
❑ 575 Dock Ellis .......... 3.50 1.55
❑ 576 Montreal Expos .......... 6.00 2.70
Team Card
❑ 577 Eric Soderholm .......... 3.50 1.55
❑ 578 Ken Wright .......... 3.50 1.55
❑ 579 Tom Grieve .......... 5.00 2.20
❑ 580 Joe Pepitone .......... 5.00 2.20
❑ 581 Steve Kealey .......... 3.50 1.55
❑ 582 Darrell Porter .......... 5.00 2.20
❑ 583 Bill Grief .......... 3.50 1.55
❑ 584 Chris Arnold .......... 3.50 1.55
❑ 585 Joe Niekro .......... 5.00 2.20
❑ 586 Bill Sudakis .......... 3.50 1.55
❑ 587 Rich McKinney .......... 3.50 1.55
❑ 588 Checklist 529-660 .......... 20.00 4.00
❑ 589 Ken Forsch .......... 3.50 1.55
❑ 590 Deron Johnson .......... 5.00 2.20
❑ 591 Mike Hedlund .......... 3.50 1.55
❑ 592 John Boccabella .......... 3.50 1.55
❑ 593 Royals Leaders .......... 3.50 1.55
Jack McKeon MG
Galen Cisco CO
Harry Dunlop CO
Charlie Lau CO
❑ 594 Vic Harris .......... 3.50 1.55
❑ 595 Don Gullett .......... 5.00 2.20
❑ 596 Boston Red Sox .......... 6.00 2.70
Team Card
❑ 597 Mickey Rivers .......... 5.00 2.20
❑ 598 Phil Roof .......... 3.50 1.55
❑ 599 Ed Crosby .......... 3.50 1.55
❑ 600 Dave McNally .......... 5.00 2.20
❑ 601 Rookie Catchers .......... 5.00 2.20
Sergio Robles
George Pena
Rick Stelmaszek
❑ 602 Rookie Pitchers .......... 5.00 2.20
Mel Behney
Ralph Garcia
Doug Rau
❑ 603 Rookie 3rd Basemen .......... 5.00 2.20
Terry Hughes
Bill McNulty
Ken Reitz
❑ 604 Rookie Pitchers .......... 5.00 2.20
Jesse Jefferson
Dennis O'Toole
Bob Strampe
❑ 605 Rookie 1st Basemen .......... 5.00 2.20
Enos Cabell RC
Pat Bourque
Gonzalo Marquez
❑ 606 Rookie Outfielders .......... 5.00 2.20
Gary Matthews RC
Tom Paciorek
Jorge Roque
❑ 607 Rookie Shortstops .......... 5.00 2.20
Pepe Frias
Ray Busse
Mario Guerrero
❑ 608 Rookie Pitchers .......... 5.00 2.20
Steve Busby RC
Dick Colpaert
George Medich
❑ 609 Rookie 2nd Basemen .......... 5.00 2.20
Larvell Blanks
Pedro Garcia
Dave Lopes RC
❑ 610 Rookie Pitchers .......... 5.00 2.20
Jimmy Freeman
Charlie Hough
Hank Webb
❑ 611 Rookie Outfielders .......... 5.00 2.20
Rich Coggins
Jim Wohlford
Richie Zisk
❑ 612 Rookie Pitchers .......... 5.00 2.20
Steve Lawson
Bob Reynolds
Brent Strom
❑ 613 Rookie Catchers .......... 15.00 6.75
Bob Boone RC
Skip Jutze
Mike Ivie
❑ 614 Rookie Outfielders .......... 18.00 8.00
Al Bumbry
Dwight Evans RC
Charlie Spikes
❑ 615 Rookie 3rd Basemen 200.00 90.00
Ron Cey
John Hilton
Mike Schmidt RC !
❑ 616 Rookie Pitchers .......... 5.00 2.20
Norm Angelini
Steve Blateric
Mike Garman
❑ 617 Rich Chiles .......... 3.50 1.55
❑ 618 Andy Etchebarren .......... 3.50 1.55
❑ 619 Billy Wilson .......... 3.50 1.55
❑ 620 Tommy Harper .......... 5.00 2.20
❑ 621 Joe Ferguson .......... 5.00 2.20
❑ 622 Larry Hisle .......... 5.00 2.20
❑ 623 Steve Renko .......... 3.50 1.55
❑ 624 Astros Leaders .......... 5.00 2.20
Leo Durocher MG
Preston Gomez CO
Grady Hatton CO
Hub Kittle CO
Jim Owens CO
❑ 625 Angel Mangual .......... 3.50 1.55
❑ 626 Bob Barton .......... 3.50 1.55
❑ 627 Luis Alvarado .......... 3.50 1.55
❑ 628 Jim Slaton .......... 3.50 1.55
❑ 629 Cleveland Indians .......... 6.00 2.70
Team Card
❑ 630 Denny McLain .......... 8.00 3.60
❑ 631 Tom Matchick .......... 3.50 1.55
❑ 632 Dick Selma .......... 3.50 1.55
❑ 633 Ike Brown .......... 3.50 1.55
❑ 634 Alan Closter .......... 3.50 1.55
❑ 635 Gene Alley .......... 5.00 2.20
❑ 636 Rickey Clark .......... 3.50 1.55
❑ 637 Norm Miller .......... 3.50 1.55
❑ 638 Ken Reynolds .......... 3.50 1.55
❑ 639 Willie Crawford .......... 3.50 1.55
❑ 640 Dick Bosman .......... 3.50 1.55
❑ 641 Cincinnati Reds .......... 6.00 2.70
Team Card
❑ 642 Jose Laboy .......... 3.50 1.55
❑ 643 Al Fitzmorris .......... 3.50 1.55
❑ 644 Jack Heidemann .......... 3.50 1.55
❑ 645 Bob Locker .......... 3.50 1.55
❑ 646 Brewers Leaders .......... 3.50 1.55
Del Crandall MG
Harvey Kuenn CO
Joe Nossek CO
Bob Shaw CO
Jim Walton CO
❑ 647 George Stone .......... 3.50 1.55
❑ 648 Tom Egan .......... 3.50 1.55
❑ 649 Rich Folkers .......... 3.50 1.55
❑ 650 Felipe Alou .......... 5.00 2.20
❑ 651 Don Carrithers .......... 3.50 1.55
❑ 652 Ted Kubiak .......... 3.50 1.55
❑ 653 Joe Hoerner .......... 3.50 1.55
❑ 654 Minnesota Twins .......... 6.00 2.70
Team Card
❑ 655 Clay Kirby .......... 3.50 1.55
❑ 656 John Ellis .......... 3.50 1.55
❑ 657 Bob Johnson .......... 3.50 1.55
❑ 658 Elliott Maddox .......... 3.50 1.55
❑ 659 Jose Pagan .......... 3.50 1.55
❑ 660 Fred Scherman .......... 5.00 1.95

## 1974 Topps

| | NRMT | VG-E |
|---|---|---|
| COMPLETE SET (660) | 400.00 | 180.00 |
| COMP.FACT.SET (660) | 600.00 | 275.00 |
| WRAPPERS (10-CENTS) | 10.00 | 4.50 |

❑ 1 Hank Aaron .......... 40.00 12.00
All-Time Home Run King
(Complete ML record)
❑ 2 Aaron Special 54-57 .......... 6.00 2.70
(Records on back)
❑ 3 Aaron Special 58-61 .......... 6.00 2.70
(Memorable homers)
❑ 4 Aaron Special 62-65 .......... 6.00 2.70
(Life in ML's 1954-63)
❑ 5 Aaron Special 66-69 .......... 6.00 2.70
(Life in ML's 1964-73)
❑ 6 Aaron Special 70-73 .......... 6.00 2.70
(Milestone homers)
❑ 7 Jim Hunter .......... 4.00 1.80
❑ 8 George Theodore .......... .50 .23
❑ 9 Mickey Lolich .......... 1.00 .45
❑ 10 Johnny Bench .......... 15.00 6.75
❑ 11 Jim Bibby .......... .50 .23
❑ 12 Dave May .......... .50 .23
❑ 13 Tom Hilgendorf .......... .50 .23
❑ 14 Paul Popovich .......... .50 .23
❑ 15 Joe Torre .......... 2.00 .90
❑ 16 Baltimore Orioles .......... 1.00 .45
Team Card
❑ 17 Doug Bird .......... .50 .23
❑ 18 Gary Thomasson .......... .50 .23
❑ 19 Gerry Moses .......... .50 .23
❑ 20 Nolan Ryan .......... 40.00 18.00
❑ 21 Bob Gallagher .......... .50 .23
❑ 22 Cy Acosta .......... .50 .23
❑ 23 Craig Robinson .......... .50 .23
❑ 24 John Hiller .......... 1.00 .45
❑ 25 Ken Singleton .......... 1.00 .45
❑ 26 Bill Campbell .......... .50 .23
❑ 27 George Scott .......... 1.00 .45
❑ 28 Manny Sanguillen .......... 1.00 .45
❑ 29 Phil Niekro .......... 3.00 1.35
❑ 30 Bobby Bonds .......... 2.00 .90
❑ 31 Astros Leaders .......... 1.00 .45
Preston Gomez MG
Roger Craig CO
Hub Kittle CO
Grady Hatton CO
Bob Lillis CO
❑ 32A Johnny Grubb SD .......... 1.00 .45
❑ 32B Johnny Grubb WASH .......... 4.00 1.80
❑ 33 Don Newhauser .......... .50 .23
❑ 34 Andy Kosco .......... .50 .23

❑ 35 Gaylord Perry 3.00 1.35
❑ 36 St. Louis Cardinals 1.00 .45
Team Card
❑ 37 Dave Sells .50 .23
❑ 38 Don Kessinger 1.00 .45
❑ 39 Ken Suarez .50 .23
❑ 40 Jim Palmer 6.00 2.70
❑ 41 Bobby Floyd .50 .23
❑ 42 Claude Osteen 1.00 .45
❑ 43 Jim Wynn 1.00 .45
❑ 44 Mel Stottlemyre 1.00 .45
❑ 45 Dave Johnson 1.00 .45
❑ 46 Pat Kelly .50 .23
❑ 47 Dick Ruthven .50 .23
❑ 48 Dick Sharon .50 .23
❑ 49 Steve Renko .50 .23
❑ 50 Rod Carew 8.00 3.60
❑ 51 Bobby Heise .50 .23
❑ 52 Al Oliver .50 .23
❑ 53A Fred Kendall SD 1.00 .45
❑ 53B Fred Kendall WASH 4.00 1.80
❑ 54 Elias Sosa .50 .23
❑ 55 Frank Robinson 6.00 2.70
❑ 56 New York Mets 1.00 .45
Team Card
❑ 57 Darold Knowles .50 .23
❑ 58 Charlie Spikes .50 .23
❑ 59 Ross Grimsley .50 .23
❑ 60 Lou Brock 6.00 2.70
❑ 61 Luis Aparicio 3.00 1.35
❑ 62 Bob Locker .50 .23
❑ 63 Bill Sudakis .50 .23
❑ 64 Doug Rau .50 .23
❑ 65 Amos Otis 1.00 .45
❑ 66 Sparky Lyle 1.00 .45
❑ 67 Tommy Helms .50 .23
❑ 68 Grant Jackson .50 .23
❑ 69 Del Unser .50 .23
❑ 70 Dick Allen 2.00 .90
❑ 71 Dan Frisella .50 .23
❑ 72 Aurelio Rodriguez .50 .23
❑ 73 Mike Marshall 2.00 .90
❑ 74 Minnesota Twins 1.00 .45
Team Card
❑ 75 Jim Colborn .50 .23
❑ 76 Mickey Rivers 1.00 .45
❑ 77A Rich Troedson SD 4.00 1.80
❑ 77B Rich Troedson WASH 1.00 .45
❑ 78 Giants Leaders 1.00 .45
Charlie Fox MG
John McNamara CO
Joe Amalfitano CO
Andy Gilbert CO
Don McMahon CO
❑ 79 Gene Tenace 1.00 .45
❑ 80 Tom Seaver 15.00 6.75
❑ 81 Frank Duffy .50 .23
❑ 82 Dave Giusti .50 .23
❑ 83 Orlando Cepeda 3.00 1.35
❑ 84 Rick Wise .50 .23
❑ 85 Joe Morgan 6.00 2.70
❑ 86 Joe Ferguson 1.00 .45
❑ 87 Fergie Jenkins 3.00 1.35
❑ 88 Freddie Patek 1.00 .45
❑ 89 Jackie Brown .50 .23
❑ 90 Bobby Murcer 1.00 .45
❑ 91 Ken Forsch .50 .23
❑ 92 Paul Blair 1.00 .45
❑ 93 Rod Gilbreath .50 .23
❑ 94 Detroit Tigers 1.00 .45
Team Card
❑ 95 Steve Carlton 8.00 3.60
❑ 96 Jerry Hairston .50 .23
❑ 97 Bob Bailey .50 .23
❑ 98 Bert Blyleven 2.00 .90
❑ 99 Brewers Leaders 1.00 .45
Del Crandall MG
Harvey Kuenn CO
Joe Nossek CO
Jim Walton CO
Al Widmar CO
❑ 100 Willie Stargell 4.00 1.80
❑ 101 Bobby Valentine 1.00 .45
❑ 102A Bill Greif SD 1.00 .45
❑ 102B Bill Greif WASH 4.00 1.80
❑ 103 Sal Bando 1.00 .45
❑ 104 Ron Bryant .50 .23
❑ 105 Carlton Fisk 8.00 3.60
❑ 106 Harry Parker .50 .23
❑ 107 Alex Johnson .50 .23
❑ 108 Al Hrabosky 1.00 .45
❑ 109 Bob Grich 1.00 .45
❑ 110 Billy Williams 3.00 1.35
❑ 111 Clay Carroll .50 .23
❑ 112 Dave Lopes 2.00 .90
❑ 113 Dick Drago .50 .23
❑ 114 Angels Team 1.00 .45
❑ 115 Willie Horton 1.00 .45
❑ 116 Jerry Reuss 1.00 .45
❑ 117 Ron Blomberg .50 .23
❑ 118 Bill Lee 1.00 .45
❑ 119 Phillies Leaders 1.00 .45
Danny Ozark MG
Ray Ripplemeyer CO
Bobby Wine CO
Carroll Beringer CO
Billy DeMars CO
❑ 120 Wilbur Wood .50 .23
❑ 121 Larry Lintz .50 .23
❑ 122 Jim Holt .50 .23
❑ 123 Nelson Briles 1.00 .45
❑ 124 Bobby Coluccio .50 .23
❑ 125A Nate Colbert SD 1.00 .45
❑ 125B Nate Colbert WASH 4.00 1.80
❑ 126 Checklist 1-132 3.00 .60
❑ 127 Tom Paciorek 1.00 .45
❑ 128 John Ellis .50 .23
❑ 129 Chris Speier .50 .23
❑ 130 Reggie Jackson 15.00 6.75
❑ 131 Bob Boone 2.00 .90
❑ 132 Felix Millan .50 .23
❑ 133 David Clyde 1.00 .45
❑ 134 Denis Menke .50 .23
❑ 135 Roy White 1.00 .45
❑ 136 Rick Reuschel 1.00 .45
❑ 137 Al Bumbry 1.00 .45
❑ 138 Eddie Brinkman .50 .23
❑ 139 Aurelio Monteagudo .50 .23
❑ 140 Darrell Evans 2.00 .90
❑ 141 Pat Bourque .50 .23
❑ 142 Pedro Garcia .50 .23
❑ 143 Dick Woodson .50 .23
❑ 144 Dodgers Leaders 2.00 .90
Walter Alston MG
Tom Lasorda CO
Jim Gilliam CO
Red Adams CO
Monty Basgall CO
❑ 145 Dock Ellis .50 .23
❑ 146 Ron Fairly 1.00 .45
❑ 147 Bart Johnson .50 .23
❑ 148A Dave Hilton SD 1.00 .45
❑ 148B Dave Hilton WASH 4.00 1.80
❑ 149 Mac Scarce .50 .23
❑ 150 John Mayberry 1.00 .45
❑ 151 Diego Segui .50 .23
❑ 152 Oscar Gamble 1.00 .45
❑ 153 Jon Matlack 1.00 .45
❑ 154 Houston Astros 1.00 .45
Team Card
❑ 155 Bert Campaneris 1.00 .45
❑ 156 Randy Moffitt .50 .23
❑ 157 Vic Harris .50 .23
❑ 158 Jack Billingham .50 .23
❑ 159 Jim Ray Hart 1.00 .45
❑ 160 Brooks Robinson 6.00 2.70
❑ 161 Ray Burris UER 1.00 .45
(Card number is
printed sideways)
❑ 162 Bill Freehan 1.00 .45
❑ 163 Ken Berry .50 .23
❑ 164 Tom House .50 .23
❑ 165 Willie Davis 1.00 .45
❑ 166 Royals Leaders 1.00 .45
Jack McKeon MG
Charlie Lau CO
Harry Dunlop CO
Galen Cisco CO
❑ 167 Luis Tiant 2.00 .90
❑ 168 Danny Thompson .50 .23
❑ 169 Steve Rogers 2.00 .90
❑ 170 Bill Melton .50 .23
❑ 171 Eduardo Rodriguez .50 .23
❑ 172 Gene Clines .50 .23
❑ 173A Randy Jones SD RC 2.00 .90
❑ 173B Randy Jones WASH 5.00 2.20
❑ 174 Bill Robinson 1.00 .45
❑ 175 Reggie Cleveland .50 .23
❑ 176 John Lowenstein .50 .23
❑ 177 Dave Roberts .50 .23
❑ 178 Garry Maddox 1.00 .45
❑ 179 Mets Leaders 5.00 2.20
Yogi Berra MG
Rube Walker CO
Eddie Yost CO
Roy McMillan CO
Joe Pignatano CO
❑ 180 Ken Holtzman 1.00 .45
❑ 181 Cesar Geronimo .50 .23
❑ 182 Lindy McDaniel 1.00 .45
❑ 183 Johnny Oates 1.00 .45
❑ 184 Texas Rangers 1.00 .45
Team Card
❑ 185 Jose Cardenal .50 .23
❑ 186 Fred Scherman .50 .23
❑ 187 Don Baylor 2.00 .90
❑ 188 Rudy Meoli .50 .23
❑ 189 Jim Brewer .50 .23
❑ 190 Tony Oliva 2.00 .90
❑ 191 Al Fitzmorris .50 .23
❑ 192 Mario Guerrero .50 .23
❑ 193 Tom Walker .50 .23
❑ 194 Darrell Porter 1.00 .45
❑ 195 Carlos May .50 .23
❑ 196 Jim Fregosi 1.00 .45
❑ 197A Vicente Romo SD 1.00 .45
❑ 197B Vicente Romo WASH 4.00 1.80
❑ 198 Dave Cash .50 .23
❑ 199 Mike Kekich .50 .23
❑ 200 Cesar Cedeno 1.00 .45
❑ 201 Batting Leaders 5.00 2.20
Rod Carew
Pete Rose
❑ 202 Home Run Leaders 4.00 1.80
Reggie Jackson
Willie Stargell
❑ 203 RBI Leaders 5.00 2.20
Reggie Jackson
Willie Stargell
❑ 204 Stolen Base Leaders 2.00 .90
Tommy Harper
Lou Brock
❑ 205 Victory Leaders 1.00 .45
Wilbur Wood
Ron Bryant
❑ 206 ERA Leaders 5.00 2.20
Jim Palmer
Tom Seaver
❑ 207 Strikeout Leaders 12.00 5.50
Nolan Ryan
Tom Seaver
❑ 208 Firemen Leaders 1.00 .45
John Hiller
Mike Marshall
❑ 209 Ted Sizemore .50 .23
❑ 210 Bill Singer .50 .23
❑ 211 Chicago Cubs 1.00 .45
Team Card
❑ 212 Rollie Fingers 3.00 1.35
❑ 213 Dave Rader .50 .23
❑ 214 Billy Grabarkewitz .50 .23
❑ 215 Al Kaline UER 8.00 3.60
(No copyright on back)
❑ 216 Ray Sadecki .50 .23
❑ 217 Tim Foli .50 .23
❑ 218 Johnny Briggs .50 .23
❑ 219 Doug Griffin .50 .23
❑ 220 Don Sutton 3.00 1.35
❑ 221 White Sox Leaders 1.00 .45
Chuck Tanner MG
Jim Mahoney CO
Alex Monchak CO
Johnny Sain CO
Joe Lonnett CO
❑ 222 Ramon Hernandez .50 .23
❑ 223 Jeff Burroughs 2.00 .90
❑ 224 Roger Metzger .50 .23
❑ 225 Paul Splittorff .50 .23

| | No. | Card | | |
|---|---|---|---|---|
| ❑ | 226A | San Diego Padres Team Card San Diego Variation | 2.00 | .90 |
| ❑ | 226B | San Diego Padres Team Card Washington Variation | | |
| ❑ | 227 | Mike Lum | .50 | .23 |
| ❑ | 228 | Ted Kubiak | .50 | .23 |
| ❑ | 229 | Fritz Peterson | .50 | .23 |
| ❑ | 230 | Tony Perez | 3.00 | 1.35 |
| ❑ | 231 | Dick Tidrow | .50 | .23 |
| ❑ | 232 | Steve Brye | .50 | .23 |
| ❑ | 233 | Jim Barr | .50 | .23 |
| ❑ | 234 | John Milner | .50 | .23 |
| ❑ | 235 | Dave McNally | 1.00 | .45 |
| ❑ | 236 | Cardinals Leaders<br>Red Schoendienst MG<br>Barney Schultz CO<br>George Kissell CO<br>Johnny Lewis CO<br>Vern Benson CO | 2.00 | .90 |
| ❑ | 237 | Ken Brett | .50 | .23 |
| ❑ | 238 | Fran Healy HOR (Munson sliding in background) | 2.00 | .90 |
| ❑ | 239 | Bill Russell | 1.00 | .45 |
| ❑ | 240 | Joe Coleman | .50 | .23 |
| ❑ | 241A | Glenn Beckert SD | 1.00 | .45 |
| ❑ | 241B | Glenn Beckert WASH | 4.00 | 1.80 |
| ❑ | 242 | Bill Gogolewski | .50 | .23 |
| ❑ | 243 | Bob Oliver | .50 | .23 |
| ❑ | 244 | Carl Morton | .50 | .23 |
| ❑ | 245 | Cleon Jones | .50 | .23 |
| ❑ | 246 | Oakland Athletics Team Card | 2.00 | .90 |
| ❑ | 247 | Rick Miller | .50 | .23 |
| ❑ | 248 | Tom Hall | .50 | .23 |
| ❑ | 249 | George Mitterwald | .50 | .23 |
| ❑ | 250A | Willie McCovey SD | 6.00 | 2.70 |
| ❑ | 250B | Willie McCovey WASH | 30.00 | 13.50 |
| ❑ | 251 | Graig Nettles | 2.00 | .90 |
| ❑ | 252 | Dave Parker RC | 10.00 | 4.50 |
| ❑ | 253 | John Boccabella | .50 | .23 |
| ❑ | 254 | Stan Bahnsen | .50 | .23 |
| ❑ | 255 | Larry Bowa | 1.00 | .45 |
| ❑ | 256 | Tom Griffin | .50 | .23 |
| ❑ | 257 | Buddy Bell | 2.00 | .90 |
| ❑ | 258 | Jerry Morales | .50 | .23 |
| ❑ | 259 | Bob Reynolds | .50 | .23 |
| ❑ | 260 | Ted Simmons | 2.00 | .90 |
| ❑ | 261 | Jerry Bell | .50 | .23 |
| ❑ | 262 | Ed Kirkpatrick | .50 | .23 |
| ❑ | 263 | Checklist 133-264 | 3.00 | .60 |
| ❑ | 264 | Joe Rudi | 1.00 | .45 |
| ❑ | 265 | Tug McGraw | 2.00 | .90 |
| ❑ | 266 | Jim Northrup | 1.00 | .45 |
| ❑ | 267 | Andy Messersmith | 1.00 | .45 |
| ❑ | 268 | Tom Grieve | 1.00 | .45 |
| ❑ | 269 | Bob Johnson | .50 | .23 |
| ❑ | 270 | Ron Santo | 2.00 | .90 |
| ❑ | 271 | Bill Hands | .50 | .23 |
| ❑ | 272 | Paul Casanova | .50 | .23 |
| ❑ | 273 | Checklist 265-396 | 3.00 | .60 |
| ❑ | 274 | Fred Beene | .50 | .23 |
| ❑ | 275 | Ron Hunt | .50 | .23 |
| ❑ | 276 | Angels Leaders<br>Bobby Winkles MG<br>John Roseboro CO<br>Tom Morgan CO<br>Jimmie Reese CO<br>Salty Parker CO | 1.00 | .45 |
| ❑ | 277 | Gary Nolan | 1.00 | .45 |
| ❑ | 278 | Cookie Rojas | 1.00 | .45 |
| ❑ | 279 | Jim Crawford | .50 | .23 |
| ❑ | 280 | Carl Yastrzemski | 10.00 | 4.50 |
| ❑ | 281 | San Francisco Giants Team Card | 1.00 | .45 |
| ❑ | 282 | Doyle Alexander | 1.00 | .45 |
| ❑ | 283 | Mike Schmidt | 30.00 | 13.50 |
| ❑ | 284 | Dave Duncan | 1.00 | .45 |
| ❑ | 285 | Reggie Smith | 1.00 | .45 |
| ❑ | 286 | Tony Muser | .50 | .23 |
| ❑ | 287 | Clay Kirby | .50 | .23 |
| ❑ | 288 | Gorman Thomas RC | 2.00 | .90 |
| ❑ | 289 | Rick Auerbach | .50 | .23 |
| ❑ | 290 | Vida Blue | 1.00 | .45 |
| ❑ | 291 | Don Hahn | .50 | .23 |
| ❑ | 292 | Chuck Seelbach | .50 | .23 |
| ❑ | 293 | Milt May | .50 | .23 |
| ❑ | 294 | Steve Foucault | .50 | .23 |
| ❑ | 295 | Rick Monday | 1.00 | .45 |
| ❑ | 296 | Ray Corbin | .50 | .23 |
| ❑ | 297 | Hal Breeden | .50 | .23 |
| ❑ | 298 | Roric Harrison | .50 | .23 |
| ❑ | 299 | Gene Michael | 1.00 | .45 |
| ❑ | 300 | Pete Rose | 25.00 | 11.00 |
| ❑ | 301 | Bob Montgomery | .50 | .23 |
| ❑ | 302 | Rudy May | .50 | .23 |
| ❑ | 303 | George Hendrick | 1.00 | .45 |
| ❑ | 304 | Don Wilson | .50 | .23 |
| ❑ | 305 | Tito Fuentes | .50 | .23 |
| ❑ | 306 | Orioles Leaders<br>Earl Weaver MG<br>Jim Frey CO<br>George Bamberger CO<br>Billy Hunter CO<br>George Staller CO | 2.00 | .90 |
| ❑ | 307 | Luis Melendez | .50 | .23 |
| ❑ | 308 | Bruce Dal Canton | .50 | .23 |
| ❑ | 309A | Dave Roberts SD | 1.00 | .45 |
| ❑ | 309B | Dave Roberts WASH | | |
| ❑ | 310 | Terry Forster | 1.00 | .45 |
| ❑ | 311 | Jerry Grote | .50 | .23 |
| ❑ | 312 | Deron Johnson | 1.00 | .45 |
| ❑ | 313 | Barry Lersch | .50 | .23 |
| ❑ | 314 | Milwaukee Brewers Team Card | 1.00 | .45 |
| ❑ | 315 | Ron Cey | 2.00 | .90 |
| ❑ | 316 | Jim Perry | 1.00 | .45 |
| ❑ | 317 | Richie Zisk | 1.00 | .45 |
| ❑ | 318 | Jim Merritt | .50 | .23 |
| ❑ | 319 | Randy Hundley | 1.00 | .45 |
| ❑ | 320 | Dusty Baker | 2.00 | .90 |
| ❑ | 321 | Steve Braun | .50 | .23 |
| ❑ | 322 | Ernie McAnally | .50 | .23 |
| ❑ | 323 | Richie Scheinblum | .50 | .23 |
| ❑ | 324 | Steve Kline | .50 | .23 |
| ❑ | 325 | Tommy Harper | 2.00 | .90 |
| ❑ | 326 | Reds Leaders<br>Sparky Anderson MG<br>Larry Shepard CO<br>George Scherger CO<br>Alex Grammas CO<br>Ted Kluszewski CO | 3.00 | 1.35 |
| ❑ | 327 | Tom Timmermann | .50 | .23 |
| ❑ | 328 | Skip Jutze | .50 | .23 |
| ❑ | 329 | Mark Belanger | 1.00 | .45 |
| ❑ | 330 | Juan Marichal | 4.00 | 1.80 |
| ❑ | 331 | All-Star Catchers<br>Carlton Fisk<br>Johnny Bench | 5.00 | 2.20 |
| ❑ | 332 | All-Star 1B<br>Dick Allen<br>Hank Aaron | 8.00 | 3.60 |
| ❑ | 333 | All-Star 2B<br>Rod Carew<br>Joe Morgan | 4.00 | 1.80 |
| ❑ | 334 | All-Star 3B<br>Brooks Robinson<br>Ron Santo | 3.00 | 1.35 |
| ❑ | 335 | All-Star SS<br>Bert Campaneris<br>Chris Speier | 1.00 | .45 |
| ❑ | 336 | All-Star LF<br>Bobby Murcer<br>Pete Rose | 5.00 | 2.20 |
| ❑ | 337 | All-Star CF<br>Amos Otis<br>Cesar Cedeno | 1.00 | .45 |
| ❑ | 338 | All-Star RF<br>Reggie Jackson<br>Billy Williams | 5.00 | 2.20 |
| ❑ | 339 | All-Star Pitchers<br>Jim Hunter<br>Rick Wise | 3.00 | 1.35 |
| ❑ | 340 | Thurman Munson | 6.00 | 2.70 |
| ❑ | 341 | Dan Driessen RC | 1.00 | .45 |
| ❑ | 342 | Jim Lonborg | 1.00 | .45 |
| ❑ | 343 | Royals Team | 1.00 | .45 |
| ❑ | 344 | Mike Caldwell | .50 | .23 |
| ❑ | 345 | Bill North | .50 | .23 |
| ❑ | 346 | Ron Reed | .50 | .23 |
| ❑ | 347 | Sandy Alomar | 1.00 | .45 |
| ❑ | 348 | Pete Richert | .50 | .23 |
| ❑ | 349 | John Vukovich | .50 | .23 |
| ❑ | 350 | Bob Gibson | 6.00 | 2.70 |
| ❑ | 351 | Dwight Evans | 3.00 | 1.35 |
| ❑ | 352 | Bill Stoneman | .50 | .23 |
| ❑ | 353 | Rich Coggins | .50 | .23 |
| ❑ | 354 | Cubs Leaders<br>Whitey Lockman MG<br>J.C. Martin CO<br>Hank Aguirre CO<br>Al Spangler CO<br>Jim Marshall CO | 1.00 | .45 |
| ❑ | 355 | Dave Nelson | .50 | .23 |
| ❑ | 356 | Jerry Koosman | 1.00 | .45 |
| ❑ | 357 | Buddy Bradford | .50 | .23 |
| ❑ | 358 | Dal Maxvill | .50 | .23 |
| ❑ | 359 | Brent Strom | .50 | .23 |
| ❑ | 360 | Greg Luzinski | 2.00 | .90 |
| ❑ | 361 | Don Carrithers | .50 | .23 |
| ❑ | 362 | Hal King | .50 | .23 |
| ❑ | 363 | New York Yankees Team Card | 2.00 | .90 |
| ❑ | 364A | Cito Gaston SD | 2.00 | .90 |
| ❑ | 364B | Cito Gaston WASH | 8.00 | 3.60 |
| ❑ | 365 | Steve Busby | .50 | .23 |
| ❑ | 366 | Larry Hisle | 1.00 | .45 |
| ❑ | 367 | Norm Cash | 2.00 | .90 |
| ❑ | 368 | Manny Mota | 1.00 | .45 |
| ❑ | 369 | Paul Lindblad | .50 | .23 |
| ❑ | 370 | Bob Watson | 1.00 | .45 |
| ❑ | 371 | Jim Slaton | .50 | .23 |
| ❑ | 372 | Ken Reitz | .50 | .23 |
| ❑ | 373 | John Curtis | .50 | .23 |
| ❑ | 374 | Marty Perez | .50 | .23 |
| ❑ | 375 | Earl Williams | .50 | .23 |
| ❑ | 376 | Jorge Orta | .50 | .23 |
| ❑ | 377 | Ron Woods | .50 | .23 |
| ❑ | 378 | Burt Hooton | 1.00 | .45 |
| ❑ | 379 | Rangers Leaders<br>Billy Martin MG<br>Frank Lucchesi CO<br>Art Fowler CO<br>Charlie Silvera CO<br>Jackie Moore CO | 2.00 | .90 |
| ❑ | 380 | Bud Harrelson | 1.00 | .45 |
| ❑ | 381 | Charlie Sands | .50 | .23 |
| ❑ | 382 | Bob Moose | .50 | .23 |
| ❑ | 383 | Philadelphia Phillies Team Card | 1.00 | .45 |
| ❑ | 384 | Chris Chambliss | 1.00 | .45 |
| ❑ | 385 | Don Gullett | 1.00 | .45 |
| ❑ | 386 | Gary Matthews | 2.00 | .90 |
| ❑ | 387A | Rich Morales SD | 1.00 | .45 |
| ❑ | 387B | Rich Morales WASH | | |
| ❑ | 388 | Phil Roof | .50 | .23 |
| ❑ | 389 | Gates Brown | .50 | .23 |
| ❑ | 390 | Lou Piniella | 2.00 | .90 |
| ❑ | 391 | Billy Champion | .50 | .23 |
| ❑ | 392 | Dick Green | .50 | .23 |
| ❑ | 393 | Orlando Pena | .50 | .23 |
| ❑ | 394 | Ken Henderson | .50 | .23 |
| ❑ | 395 | Doug Rader | .50 | .23 |
| ❑ | 396 | Tommy Davis | 1.00 | .45 |
| ❑ | 397 | George Stone | .50 | .23 |
| ❑ | 398 | Duke Sims | .50 | .23 |
| ❑ | 399 | Mike Paul | .50 | .23 |
| ❑ | 400 | Harmon Killebrew | 6.00 | 2.70 |
| ❑ | 401 | Elliott Maddox | .50 | .23 |
| ❑ | 402 | Jim Rooker | .50 | .23 |
| ❑ | 403 | Red Sox Leaders<br>Darrell Johnson MG<br>Eddie Popowski CO<br>Lee Stange CO<br>Don Zimmer CO<br>Don Bryant CO | 1.00 | .45 |
| ❑ | 404 | Jim Howarth | .50 | .23 |
| ❑ | 405 | Ellie Rodriguez | .50 | .23 |
| ❑ | 406 | Steve Arlin | .50 | .23 |
| ❑ | 407 | Jim Wohlford | .50 | .23 |
| ❑ | 408 | Charlie Hough | 1.00 | .45 |
| ❑ | 409 | Ike Brown | .50 | .23 |
| ❑ | 410 | Pedro Borbon | .50 | .23 |
| ❑ | 411 | Frank Baker | .50 | .23 |
| ❑ | 412 | Chuck Taylor | .50 | .23 |
| ❑ | 413 | Don Money | 1.00 | .45 |
| ❑ | 414 | Checklist 397-528 | 3.00 | .60 |
| ❑ | 415 | Gary Gentry | .50 | .23 |

❑ 416 Chicago White Sox ...... 1.00 .45
Team Card
❑ 417 Rich Folkers .................. .50 .23
❑ 418 Walt Williams................. .50 .23
❑ 419 Wayne Twitchell ............ .50 .23
❑ 420 Ray Fosse....................... .50 .23
❑ 421 Dan Fife.......................... .50 .23
❑ 422 Gonzalo Marquez .......... .50 .23
❑ 423 Fred Stanley .................. .50 .23
❑ 424 Jim Beauchamp ............ .50 .23
❑ 425 Pete Broberg.................. .50 .23
❑ 426 Rennie Stennett ............ .50 .23
❑ 427 Bobby Bolin.................... .50 .23
❑ 428 Gary Sutherland ............ .50 .23
❑ 429 Dick Lange .................... .50 .23
❑ 430 Matty Alou .................. 1.00 .45
❑ 431 Gene Garber RC ......... 1.00 .45
❑ 432 Chris Arnold .................. .50 .23
❑ 433 Lerrin LaGrow ................ .50 .23
❑ 434 Ken McMullen ................ .50 .23
❑ 435 Dave Concepcion ........ 2.00 .90
❑ 436 Don Hood ...................... .50 .23
❑ 437 Jim Lyttle ........................ .50 .23
❑ 438 Ed Herrmann.................. .50 .23
❑ 439 Norm Miller .................... .50 .23
❑ 440 Jim Kaat ...................... 2.00 .90
❑ 441 Tom Ragland.................. .50 .23
❑ 442 Alan Foster .................... .50 .23
❑ 443 Tom Hutton .................... .50 .23
❑ 444 Vic Davalillo.................... .50 .23
❑ 445 George Medich .............. .50 .23
❑ 446 Len Randle .................... .50 .23
❑ 447 Twins Leaders............. 1.00 .45
Frank Quilici MG
Ralph Rowe CO
Bob Rodgers CO
Vern Morgan CO
❑ 448 Ron Hodges .................. .50 .23
❑ 449 Tom McCraw.................. .50 .23
❑ 450 Rich Hebner ................ 1.00 .45
❑ 451 Tommy John ................ 2.00 .90
❑ 452 Gene Hiser .................... .50 .23
❑ 453 Balor Moore.................... .50 .23
❑ 454 Kurt Bevacqua................ .50 .23
❑ 455 Tom Bradley .................. .50 .23
❑ 456 Dave Winfield RC ...... 40.00 18.00
❑ 457 Chuck Goggin ................ .50 .23
❑ 458 Jim Ray .......................... .50 .23
❑ 459 Cincinnati Reds............ 2.00 .90
Team Card
❑ 460 Boog Powell ................ 2.00 .90
❑ 461 John Odom .................... .50 .23
❑ 462 Luis Alvarado ................ .50 .23
❑ 463 Pat Dobson .................... .50 .23
❑ 464 Jose Cruz .................... 2.00 .90
❑ 465 Dick Bosman.................. .50 .23
❑ 466 Dick Billings.................... .50 .23
❑ 467 Winston Llenas .............. .50 .23
❑ 468 Pepe Frias...................... .50 .23
❑ 469 Joe Decker .................... .50 .23
❑ 470 Reggie Jackson ALCS 6.00 2.70
❑ 471 Jon Matlack NLCS ...... 1.00 .45
❑ 472 Darold Knowles WS1 .. 1.00 .45
❑ 473 Willie Mays WS ............ 8.00 3.60
❑ 474 Bert Campaneris WS3 1.00 .45
❑ 475 Rusty Staub WS4 ........ 1.00 .45
❑ 476 Cleon Jones WS5 ........ 1.00 .45
❑ 477 Reggie Jackson WS .... 6.00 2.70
❑ 478 Bert Campaneris WS7 1.00 .45
❑ 479 World Series Summary 1.00 .45
A's celebrate; win
2nd consecutive
championship
❑ 480 Willie Crawford .............. .50 .23
❑ 481 Jerry Terrell.................... .50 .23
❑ 482 Bob Didier ...................... .50 .23
❑ 483 Atlanta Braves............ 1.00 .45
Team Card
❑ 484 Carmen Fanzone .......... .50 .23
❑ 485 Felipe Alou .................. 2.00 .90
❑ 486 Steve Stone.................. 1.00 .45
❑ 487 Ted Martinez .................. .50 .23
❑ 488 Andy Etchebarren .......... .50 .23
❑ 489 Pirates Leaders ........... 1.00 .45
Danny Murtaugh MG
Don Osborn CO
Don Leppert CO
Bill Mazeroski CO
Bob Skinner CO
❑ 490 Vada Pinson ................ 2.00 .90
❑ 491 Roger Nelson ................ .50 .23
❑ 492 Mike Rogodzinski .......... .50 .23
❑ 493 Joe Hoerner .................. .50 .23
❑ 494 Ed Goodson .................. .50 .23
❑ 495 Dick McAuliffe ............ 1.00 .45
❑ 496 Tom Murphy.................... .50 .23
❑ 497 Bobby Mitchell................ .50 .23
❑ 498 Pat Corrales .................. .50 .23
❑ 499 Rusty Torres .................. .50 .23
❑ 500 Lee May ...................... 1.00 .45
❑ 501 Eddie Leon .................... .50 .23
❑ 502 Dave LaRoche ................ .50 .23
❑ 503 Eric Soderholm .............. .50 .23
❑ 504 Joe Niekro .................. 1.00 .45
❑ 505 Bill Buckner ................ 1.00 .45
❑ 506 Ed Farmer ...................... .50 .23
❑ 507 Larry Stahl...................... .50 .23
❑ 508 Montreal Expos .......... 1.00 .45
Team Card
❑ 509 Jesse Jefferson .............. .50 .23
❑ 510 Wayne Garrett................ .50 .23
❑ 511 Toby Harrah ................ 1.00 .45
❑ 512 Joe Lahoud .................... .50 .23
❑ 513 Jim Campanis ................ .50 .23
❑ 514 Paul Schaal .................... .50 .23
❑ 515 Willie Montanez.............. .50 .23
❑ 516 Horacio Pina .................. .50 .23
❑ 517 Mike Hegan .................... .50 .23
❑ 518 Derrel Thomas .............. .50 .23
❑ 519 Bill Sharp........................ .50 .23
❑ 520 Tim McCarver .............. 2.00 .90
❑ 521 Indians Leaders........... 1.00 .45
Ken Aspromonte MG
Clay Bryant CO
Tony Pacheco CO
❑ 522 J.R. Richard ................ 2.00 .90
❑ 523 Cecil Cooper ................ 2.00 .90
❑ 524 Bill Plummer .................. .50 .23
❑ 525 Clyde Wright .................. .50 .23
❑ 526 Frank Tepedino.............. .50 .23
❑ 527 Bobby Darwin ................ .50 .23
❑ 528 Bill Bonham.................... .50 .23
❑ 529 Horace Clarke .............. 1.00 .45
❑ 530 Mickey Stanley ............ 1.00 .45
❑ 531 Expos Leaders ............ 1.00 .45
Gene Mauch MG
Dave Bristol CO
Cal McLish CO
Larry Doby CO
Jerry Zimmerman CO
❑ 532 Skip Lockwood .............. .50 .23
❑ 533 Mike Phillips .................. .50 .23
❑ 534 Eddie Watt...................... .50 .23
❑ 535 Bob Tolan ...................... .50 .23
❑ 536 Duffy Dyer ...................... .50 .23
❑ 537 Steve Mingori ................ .50 .23
❑ 538 Cesar Tovar .................. .50 .23
❑ 539 Lloyd Allen...................... .50 .23
❑ 540 Bob Robertson .............. .50 .23
❑ 541 Cleveland Indians ........ 1.00 .45
Team Card
❑ 542 Rich Gossage .............. 2.00 .90
❑ 543 Danny Cater .................. .50 .23
❑ 544 Ron Schueler ................ .50 .23
❑ 545 Billy Conigliaro ............ 1.00 .45
❑ 546 Mike Corkins .................. .50 .23
❑ 547 Glenn Borgmann............ .50 .23
❑ 548 Sonny Siebert ................ .50 .23
❑ 549 Mike Jorgensen.............. .50 .23
❑ 550 Sam McDowell ............ 1.00 .45
❑ 551 Von Joshua .................... .50 .23
❑ 552 Denny Doyle .................. .50 .23
❑ 553 Jim Willoughby .............. .50 .23
❑ 554 Tim Johnson .................. .50 .23
❑ 555 Woodie Fryman.............. .50 .23
❑ 556 Dave Campbell .............. .50 .23
❑ 557 Jim McGlothlin................ .50 .23
❑ 558 Bill Fahey ........................ .50 .23
❑ 559 Darrel Chaney................ .50 .23
❑ 560 Mike Cuellar ................ 1.00 .45
❑ 561 Ed Kranepool .............. 1.00 .45
❑ 562 Jack Aker ...................... .50 .23
❑ 563 Hal McRae .................. 1.00 .45
❑ 564 Mike Ryan ...................... .50 .23
❑ 565 Milt Wilcox...................... .50 .23
❑ 566 Jackie Hernandez .......... .50 .23
❑ 567 Boston Red Sox .......... 1.00 .45
Team Card
❑ 568 Mike Torrez.................. 1.00 .45
❑ 569 Rick Dempsey.............. 1.00 .45
❑ 570 Ralph Garr.................... 1.00 .45
❑ 571 Rich Hand ...................... .50 .23
❑ 572 Enzo Hernandez ............ .50 .23
❑ 573 Mike Adams .................. .50 .23
❑ 574 Bill Parsons.................... .50 .23
❑ 575 Steve Garvey .............. 3.00 1.35
❑ 576 Scipio Spinks.................. .50 .23
❑ 577 Mike Sadek .................... .50 .23
❑ 578 Ralph Houk MG............ 1.00 .45
❑ 579 Cecil Upshaw ................ .50 .23
❑ 580 Jim Spencer .................. .50 .23
❑ 581 Fred Norman .................. .50 .23
❑ 582 Bucky Dent RC ............ 4.00 1.80
❑ 583 Marty Pattin.................... .50 .23
❑ 584 Ken Rudolph .................. .50 .23
❑ 585 Merv Rettenmund .......... .50 .23
❑ 586 Jack Brohamer .............. .50 .23
❑ 587 Larry Christenson .......... .50 .23
❑ 588 Hal Lanier ...................... .50 .23
❑ 589 Boots Day ...................... .50 .23
❑ 590 Roger Moret .................. .50 .23
❑ 591 Sonny Jackson .............. .50 .23
❑ 592 Ed Bane .......................... .50 .23
❑ 593 Steve Yeager .............. 1.00 .45
❑ 594 Leroy Stanton ................ .50 .23
❑ 595 Steve Blass .................... .50 .23
❑ 596 Rookie Pitchers.............. .50 .23
Wayne Garland
Fred Holdsworth
Mark Littell
Dick Pole
❑ 597 Rookie Shortstops........ 1.00 .45
Dave Chalk
John Gamble
Pete MacKanin
Manny Trillo RC
❑ 598 Rookie Outfielders...... 12.00 5.50
Dave Augustine
Ken Griffey RC
Steve Ontiveros
Jim Tyrone
❑ 599A Rookie Pitchers WAS 2.00 .90
Ron Diorio
Dave Freisleben
Frank Riccelli
Greg Shanahan
❑ 599B Rookie Pitchers SD.... 3.00 1.35
(SD in large print)
❑ 599C Rookie Pitchers SD .. 6.00 2.70
(SD in small print)
❑ 600 Rookie Infielders .......... 5.00 2.20
Ron Cash
Jim Cox
Bill Madlock RC
Reggie Sanders
❑ 601 Rookie Outfielders........ 3.00 1.35
Ed Armbrister
Rich Bladt
Brian Downing RC
Bake McBride
❑ 602 Rookie Pitchers............ 1.00 .45
Glen Abbott
Rick Henninger
Craig Swan
Dan Vossler
❑ 603 Rookie Catchers .......... 1.00 .45
Barry Foote
Tom Lundstedt
Charlie Moore RC
Sergio Robles
❑ 604 Rookie Infielders .......... 5.00 2.20
Terry Hughes
John Knox
Andre Thornton
Frank White RC
❑ 605 Rookie Pitchers............ 4.00 1.80
Vic Albury
Ken Frailing

Kevin Kobel
Frank Tanana RC
❑ 606 Rookie Outfielders ........ 1.00 .45
Jim Fuller
Wilbur Howard
Tommy Smith
Otto Velez
❑ 607 Rookie Shortstops ........ 1.00 .45
Leo Foster
Tom Heintzelman
Dave Rosello
Frank Taveras RC
❑ 608A Rookie Pitchers: ERR 2.00 .90
Bob Apodaco (sic)
Dick Baney
John D'Acquisto
Mike Wallace
❑ 608B Rookie Pitchers: COR 1.00 .45
Bob Apodaca
Dick Baney
John D'Acquisto
Mike Wallace
❑ 609 Rico Petrocelli ........ 1.00 .45
❑ 610 Dave Kingman ........ 2.00 .90
❑ 611 Rich Stelmaszek ........ .50 .23
❑ 612 Luke Walker ........ .50 .23
❑ 613 Dan Monzon ........ .50 .23
❑ 614 Adrian Devine ........ .50 .23
❑ 615 Johnny Jeter UER ........ .50 .23
(Misspelled Johnnie
on card back)
❑ 616 Larry Gura ........ .50 .23
❑ 617 Ted Ford ........ .50 .23
❑ 618 Jim Mason ........ .50 .23
❑ 619 Mike Anderson ........ .50 .23
❑ 620 Al Downing ........ .50 .23
❑ 621 Bernie Carbo ........ .50 .23
❑ 622 Phil Gagliano ........ .50 .23
❑ 623 Celerino Sanchez ........ .50 .23
❑ 624 Bob Miller ........ .50 .23
❑ 625 Ollie Brown ........ .50 .23
❑ 626 Pittsburgh Pirates ........ 1.00 .45
Team Card
❑ 627 Carl Taylor ........ .50 .23
❑ 628 Ivan Murrell ........ .50 .23
❑ 629 Rusty Staub ........ 2.00 .90
❑ 630 Tommie Agee ........ 1.00 .45
❑ 631 Steve Barber ........ .50 .23
❑ 632 George Culver ........ .50 .23
❑ 633 Dave Hamilton ........ .50 .23
❑ 634 Braves Leaders ........ 2.00 .90
Eddie Mathews MG
Herm Starrette CO
Connie Ryan CO
Jim Busby CO
Ken Silvestri CO
❑ 635 Johnny Edwards ........ .50 .23
❑ 636 Dave Goltz ........ .50 .23
❑ 637 Checklist 529-660 ........ 3.00 .60
❑ 638 Ken Sanders ........ .50 .23
❑ 639 Joe Lovitto ........ .50 .23
❑ 640 Milt Pappas ........ 1.00 .45
❑ 641 Chuck Brinkman ........ .50 .23
❑ 642 Terry Harmon ........ .50 .23
❑ 643 Dodgers Team ........ 1.00 .45
❑ 644 Wayne Granger ........ .50 .23
❑ 645 Ken Boswell ........ .50 .23
❑ 646 George Foster ........ 2.00 .90
❑ 647 Juan Beniquez ........ .50 .23
❑ 648 Terry Crowley ........ .50 .23
❑ 649 Fernando Gonzalez ........ .50 .23
❑ 650 Mike Epstein ........ .50 .23
❑ 651 Leron Lee ........ .50 .23
❑ 652 Gail Hopkins ........ .50 .23
❑ 653 Bob Stinson ........ .50 .23
❑ 654A Jesus Alou ERR ........ 1.00 .45
(No position)
❑ 654B Jesus Alou COR ........ 4.00 1.80
(Outfield)
❑ 655 Mike Tyson ........ .50 .23
❑ 656 Adrian Garrett ........ .50 .23
❑ 657 Jim Shellenback ........ .50 .23
❑ 658 Lee Lacy ........ .50 .23
❑ 659 Joe Lis ........ .50 .23
❑ 660 Larry Dierker ........ 2.00 .50

## 1974 Topps Traded

NRMT VG-E
COMPLETE SET (44) ........ 20.00 9.00

❑ 23T Craig Robinson ........ .50 .23
❑ 42T Claude Osteen ........ .75 .35
❑ 43T Jim Wynn ........ .75 .35
❑ 51T Bobby Heise ........ .50 .23
❑ 59T Ross Grimsley ........ .50 .23
❑ 62T Bob Locker ........ .50 .23
❑ 63T Bill Sudakis ........ .50 .23
❑ 73T Mike Marshall ........ .75 .35
❑ 123T Nelson Briles ........ .75 .35
❑ 139T Aurelio Monteagudo ........ .50 .23
❑ 151T Diego Segui ........ .50 .23
❑ 165T Willie Davis ........ .75 .35
❑ 175T Reggie Cleveland ........ .50 .23
❑ 182T Lindy McDaniel ........ .75 .35
❑ 186T Fred Scherman ........ .50 .23
❑ 249T George Mitterwald ........ .50 .23
❑ 262T Ed Kirkpatrick ........ .50 .23
❑ 269T Bob Johnson ........ .50 .23
❑ 270T Ron Santo ........ 1.00 .45
❑ 313T Barry Lersch ........ .50 .23
❑ 319T Randy Hundley ........ .75 .35
❑ 330T Juan Marichal ........ 2.00 .90
❑ 348T Pete Richert ........ .50 .23
❑ 373T John Curtis ........ .50 .23
❑ 390T Lou Piniella ........ 1.00 .45
❑ 428T Gary Sutherland ........ .50 .23
❑ 454T Kurt Bevacqua ........ .50 .23
❑ 458T Jim Ray ........ .50 .23
❑ 485T Felipe Alou ........ 1.00 .45
❑ 486T Steve Stone ........ .75 .35
❑ 496T Tom Murphy ........ .50 .23
❑ 516T Horacio Pina ........ .50 .23
❑ 534T Eddie Watt ........ .50 .23
❑ 538T Cesar Tovar ........ .50 .23
❑ 544T Ron Schueler ........ .50 .23
❑ 579T Cecil Upshaw ........ .50 .23
❑ 585T Merv Rettenmund ........ .50 .23
❑ 612T Luke Walker ........ .50 .23
❑ 616T Larry Gura ........ .75 .35
❑ 618T Jim Mason ........ .50 .23
❑ 630T Tommie Agee ........ .75 .35
❑ 648T Terry Crowley ........ .50 .23
❑ 649T Fernando Gonzalez ........ .50 .23
❑ NNO Traded Checklist ........ 1.50 .30

## 1975 Topps

NRMT VG-E
COMPLETE SET (660) ........ 600.00 275.00
WRAPPER (15-CENT) ........

❑ 1 Hank Aaron RB ........ 25.00 8.25
Sets Homer Mark
❑ 2 Lou Brock RB ........ 3.00 1.35
118 Stolen Bases
❑ 3 Bob Gibson RB ........ 3.00 1.35
3000th Strikeout
❑ 4 Al Kaline RB ........ 6.00 2.70
3000 Hit Club
❑ 5 Nolan Ryan RB ........ 20.00 9.00
Fans 300 for
3rd Year in a Row
❑ 6 Mike Marshall HL ........ 1.00 .45
Hurls 106 Games
❑ 7 Steve Busby HL ........ 10.00 4.50
Dick Bosman
Nolan Ryan
❑ 8 Rogelio Moret ........ .50 .23
❑ 9 Frank Tepedino ........ .50 .23
❑ 10 Willie Davis ........ 1.00 .45
❑ 11 Bill Melton ........ .50 .23
❑ 12 David Clyde ........ .50 .23
❑ 13 Gene Locklear RC ........ 1.00 .45
❑ 14 Milt Wilcox ........ .50 .23
❑ 15 Jose Cardenal ........ 1.00 .45
❑ 16 Frank Tanana ........ 2.00 .90
❑ 17 Dave Concepcion ........ 2.00 .90
❑ 18 Tigers: Team/Mgr. ........ 2.00 .40
Ralph Houk
(Checklist back)
❑ 19 Jerry Koosman ........ 1.00 .45
❑ 20 Thurman Munson ........ 6.00 2.70
❑ 21 Rollie Fingers ........ 3.00 1.35
❑ 22 Dave Cash ........ .50 .23
❑ 23 Bill Russell ........ 1.00 .45
❑ 24 Al Fitzmorris ........ .50 .23
❑ 25 Lee May ........ 1.00 .45
❑ 26 Dave McNally ........ 1.00 .45
❑ 27 Ken Reitz ........ .50 .23
❑ 28 Tom Murphy ........ .50 .23
❑ 29 Dave Parker ........ 3.00 1.35
❑ 30 Bert Blyleven ........ 2.00 .90
❑ 31 Dave Rader ........ .50 .23
❑ 32 Reggie Cleveland ........ .50 .23
❑ 33 Dusty Baker ........ 2.00 .90
❑ 34 Steve Renko ........ .50 .23
❑ 35 Ron Santo ........ 1.00 .45
❑ 36 Joe Lovitto ........ .50 .23
❑ 37 Dave Freisleben ........ .50 .23
❑ 38 Buddy Bell ........ 2.00 .90
❑ 39 Andre Thornton ........ 1.00 .45
❑ 40 Bill Singer ........ .50 .23
❑ 41 Cesar Geronimo ........ 1.00 .45
❑ 42 Joe Coleman ........ .50 .23
❑ 43 Cleon Jones ........ 1.00 .45
❑ 44 Pat Dobson ........ .50 .23
❑ 45 Joe Rudi ........ 1.00 .45
❑ 46 Phillies: Team/Mgr. ........ 2.00 .40
Danny Ozark UER
(Checklist back)
(Terry Harmon listed as 339
instead of 399)
❑ 47 Tommy John ........ 2.00 .90
❑ 48 Freddie Patek ........ 1.00 .45
❑ 49 Larry Dierker ........ 1.00 .45
❑ 50 Brooks Robinson ........ 6.00 2.70
❑ 51 Bob Forsch RC ........ 1.00 .45
❑ 52 Darrell Porter ........ 1.00 .45
❑ 53 Dave Giusti ........ .50 .23
❑ 54 Eric Soderholm ........ .50 .23
❑ 55 Bobby Bonds ........ 2.00 .90
❑ 56 Rick Wise ........ 1.00 .45
❑ 57 Dave Johnson ........ 1.00 .45
❑ 58 Chuck Taylor ........ .50 .23
❑ 59 Ken Henderson ........ .50 .23
❑ 60 Fergie Jenkins ........ 3.00 1.35
❑ 61 Dave Winfield ........ 20.00 9.00
❑ 62 Fritz Peterson ........ .50 .23
❑ 63 Steve Swisher ........ .50 .23
❑ 64 Dave Chalk ........ .50 .23
❑ 65 Don Gullett ........ 1.00 .45
❑ 66 Willie Horton ........ 1.00 .45
❑ 67 Tug McGraw ........ 1.00 .45

❑ 68 Ron Blomberg .50 .23
❑ 69 John Odom .50 .23
❑ 70 Mike Schmidt 25.00 11.00
❑ 71 Charlie Hough 1.00 .45
❑ 72 Royals: Team/Mgr. 2.00 .40
Jack McKeon
(Checklist back)
❑ 73 J.R. Richard 1.00 .45
❑ 74 Mark Belanger 1.00 .45
❑ 75 Ted Simmons 2.00 .90
❑ 76 Ed Sprague .50 .23
❑ 77 Richie Zisk 1.00 .45
❑ 78 Ray Corbin .50 .23
❑ 79 Gary Matthews 1.00 .45
❑ 80 Carlton Fisk 6.00 2.70
❑ 81 Ron Reed .50 .23
❑ 82 Pat Kelly .50 .23
❑ 83 Jim Merritt .50 .23
❑ 84 Enzo Hernandez .50 .23
❑ 85 Bill Bonham .50 .23
❑ 86 Joe Lis .50 .23
❑ 87 George Foster 2.00 .90
❑ 88 Tom Egan .50 .23
❑ 89 Jim Ray .50 .23
❑ 90 Rusty Staub 2.00 .90
❑ 91 Dick Green .50 .23
❑ 92 Cecil Upshaw .50 .23
❑ 93 Dave Lopes 2.00 .90
❑ 94 Jim Lonborg 1.00 .45
❑ 95 John Mayberry 1.00 .45
❑ 96 Mike Cosgrove .50 .23
❑ 97 Earl Williams .50 .23
❑ 98 Rich Folkers .50 .23
❑ 99 Mike Hegan .50 .23
❑ 100 Willie Stargell 4.00 1.80
❑ 101 Expos: Team/Mgr. 2.00 .40
Gene Mauch
(Checklist back)
❑ 102 Joe Decker .50 .23
❑ 103 Rick Miller .50 .23
❑ 104 Bill Madlock 2.00 .90
❑ 105 Buzz Capra .50 .23
❑ 106 Mike Hargrove RC 3.00 1.35
❑ 107 Jim Barr .50 .23
❑ 108 Tom Hall .50 .23
❑ 109 George Hendrick 1.00 .45
❑ 110 Wilbur Wood .50 .23
❑ 111 Wayne Garrett .50 .23
❑ 112 Larry Hardy .50 .23
❑ 113 Elliott Maddox .50 .23
❑ 114 Dick Lange .50 .23
❑ 115 Joe Ferguson .50 .23
❑ 116 Lerrin LaGrow .50 .23
❑ 117 Orioles: Team/Mgr. 3.00 .60
Earl Weaver
(Checklist back)
❑ 118 Mike Anderson .50 .23
❑ 119 Tommy Helms .50 .23
❑ 120 Steve Busby UER 1.00 .45
(Photo actually
Fran Healy)
❑ 121 Bill North .50 .23
❑ 122 Al Hrabosky 1.00 .45
❑ 123 Johnny Briggs .50 .23
❑ 124 Jerry Reuss 1.00 .45
❑ 125 Ken Singleton 1.00 .45
❑ 126 Checklist 1-132 3.00 .60
❑ 127 Glenn Borgmann .50 .23
❑ 128 Bill Lee 1.00 .45
❑ 129 Rick Monday 1.00 .45
❑ 130 Phil Niekro 3.00 1.35
❑ 131 Toby Harrah 1.00 .45
❑ 132 Randy Moffitt .50 .23
❑ 133 Dan Driessen 1.00 .45
❑ 134 Ron Hodges .50 .23
❑ 135 Charlie Spikes .50 .23
❑ 136 Jim Mason .50 .23
❑ 137 Terry Forster 1.00 .45
❑ 138 Del Unser .50 .23
❑ 139 Horacio Pina .50 .23
❑ 140 Steve Garvey 3.00 1.35
❑ 141 Mickey Stanley 1.00 .45
❑ 142 Bob Reynolds .50 .23
❑ 143 Cliff Johnson 1.00 .45
❑ 144 Jim Wohlford .50 .23
❑ 145 Ken Holtzman 1.00 .45
❑ 146 Padres: Team/Mgr. 2.00 .40
John McNamara
(Checklist back)
❑ 147 Pedro Garcia .50 .23
❑ 148 Jim Rooker .50 .23
❑ 149 Tim Foli .50 .23
❑ 150 Bob Gibson 6.00 2.70
❑ 151 Steve Brye .50 .23
❑ 152 Mario Guerrero .50 .23
❑ 153 Rick Reuschel 1.00 .45
❑ 154 Mike Lum .50 .23
❑ 155 Jim Bibby .50 .23
❑ 156 Dave Kingman 2.00 .90
❑ 157 Pedro Borbon 1.00 .45
❑ 158 Jerry Grote .50 .23
❑ 159 Steve Arlin .50 .23
❑ 160 Graig Nettles 2.00 .90
❑ 161 Stan Bahnsen .50 .23
❑ 162 Willie Montanez .50 .23
❑ 163 Jim Brewer .50 .23
❑ 164 Mickey Rivers 1.00 .45
❑ 165 Doug Rader 1.00 .45
❑ 166 Woodie Fryman .50 .23
❑ 167 Rich Coggins .50 .23
❑ 168 Bill Greif .50 .23
❑ 169 Cookie Rojas 1.00 .45
❑ 170 Bert Campaneris 1.00 .45
❑ 171 Ed Kirkpatrick .50 .23
❑ 172 Red Sox: Team/Mgr. 3.00 .60
Darrell Johnson
(Checklist back)
❑ 173 Steve Rogers 1.00 .45
❑ 174 Bake McBride 1.00 .45
❑ 175 Don Money 1.00 .45
❑ 176 Burt Hooton 1.00 .45
❑ 177 Vic Correll .50 .23
❑ 178 Cesar Tovar .50 .23
❑ 179 Tom Bradley .50 .23
❑ 180 Joe Morgan 6.00 2.70
❑ 181 Fred Beene .50 .23
❑ 182 Don Hahn .50 .23
❑ 183 Mel Stottlemyre 1.00 .45
❑ 184 Jorge Orta .50 .23
❑ 185 Steve Carlton 8.00 3.60
❑ 186 Willie Crawford .50 .23
❑ 187 Denny Doyle .50 .23
❑ 188 Tom Griffin .50 .23
❑ 189 1951 MVP's 4.00 1.80
Larry (Yogi) Berra
Roy Campanella
(Campy never issued)
❑ 190 1952 MVP's 2.00 .90
Bobby Shantz
Hank Sauer
❑ 191 1953 MVP's 2.00 .90
Al Rosen
Roy Campanella
❑ 192 1954 MVP's 4.00 1.80
Yogi Berra
Willie Mays
❑ 193 1955 MVP's UER 3.00 1.35
Yogi Berra
Roy Campanella
(Campy card never
issued, pictured
with LA cap)
❑ 194 1956 MVP's 15.00 6.75
Mickey Mantle
Don Newcombe
❑ 195 1957 MVP's 20.00 9.00
Mickey Mantle
Hank Aaron
❑ 196 1958 MVP's 2.00 .90
Jackie Jensen
Ernie Banks
❑ 197 1959 MVP's 2.00 .90
Nellie Fox
Ernie Banks
❑ 198 1960 MVP's 2.00 .90
Roger Maris
Dick Groat
❑ 199 1961 MVP's 3.00 1.35
Roger Maris
Frank Robinson
❑ 200 1962 MVP's 15.00 6.75
Mickey Mantle
Maury Wills
(Wills never issued)
❑ 201 1963 MVP's 2.00 .90
Elston Howard
Sandy Koufax
❑ 202 1964 MVP's 2.00 .90
Brooks Robinson
Ken Boyer
❑ 203 1965 MVP's 2.00 .90
Zoilo Versalles
Willie Mays
❑ 204 1966 MVP's 8.00 3.60
Frank Robinson
Bob Clemente
❑ 205 1967 MVP's 2.00 .90
Carl Yastrzemski
Orlando Cepeda
❑ 206 1968 MVP's 2.00 .90
Denny McLain
Bob Gibson
❑ 207 1969 MVP's 2.00 .90
Harmon Killebrew
Willie McCovey
❑ 208 1970 MVP's 2.00 .90
Boog Powell
Johnny Bench
❑ 209 1971 MVP's 2.00 .90
Vida Blue
Joe Torre
❑ 210 1972 MVP's 2.00 .90
Rich Allen
Johnny Bench
❑ 211 1973 MVP's 6.00 2.70
Reggie Jackson
Pete Rose
❑ 212 1974 MVP's 2.00 .90
Jeff Burroughs
Steve Garvey
❑ 213 Oscar Gamble 1.00 .45
❑ 214 Harry Parker .50 .23
❑ 215 Bobby Valentine 1.00 .45
❑ 216 Giants: Team/Mgr. 2.00 .40
Wes Westrum
(Checklist back)
❑ 217 Lou Piniella 2.00 .90
❑ 218 Jerry Johnson .50 .23
❑ 219 Ed Herrmann .50 .23
❑ 220 Don Sutton 3.00 1.35
❑ 221 Aurelio Rodriguez .50 .23
❑ 222 Dan Spillner .50 .23
❑ 223 Robin Yount RC 50.00 22.00
❑ 224 Ramon Hernandez .50 .23
❑ 225 Bob Grich 1.00 .45
❑ 226 Bill Campbell .50 .23
❑ 227 Bob Watson 1.00 .45
❑ 228 George Brett RC 80.00 36.00
❑ 229 Barry Foote .50 .23
❑ 230 Jim Hunter 4.00 1.80
❑ 231 Mike Tyson .50 .23
❑ 232 Diego Segui .50 .23
❑ 233 Billy Grabarkewitz .50 .23
❑ 234 Tom Grieve 1.00 .45
❑ 235 Jack Billingham 1.00 .45
❑ 236 Angels: Team/Mgr. 2.00 .40
Dick Williams
(Checklist back)
❑ 237 Carl Morton .50 .23
❑ 238 Dave Duncan .50 .23
❑ 239 George Stone .50 .23
❑ 240 Garry Maddox 1.00 .45
❑ 241 Dick Tidrow .50 .23
❑ 242 Jay Johnstone 1.00 .45
❑ 243 Jim Kaat 2.00 .90
❑ 244 Bill Buckner 1.00 .45
❑ 245 Mickey Lolich 2.00 .90
❑ 246 Cardinals: Team/Mgr. 2.00 .40
Red Schoendienst
(Checklist back)
❑ 247 Enos Cabell .50 .23
❑ 248 Randy Jones 2.00 .90
❑ 249 Danny Thompson .50 .23
❑ 250 Ken Brett .50 .23
❑ 251 Fran Healy .50 .23
❑ 252 Fred Scherman .50 .23
❑ 253 Jesus Alou .50 .23
❑ 254 Mike Torrez 1.00 .45

- ❑ 255 Dwight Evans 2.00 .90
- ❑ 256 Billy Champion .50 .23
- ❑ 257 Checklist: 133-264 3.00 .60
- ❑ 258 Dave LaRoche .50 .23
- ❑ 259 Len Randle .50 .23
- ❑ 260 Johnny Bench 15.00 6.75
- ❑ 261 Andy Hassler .50 .23
- ❑ 262 Rowland Office .50 .23
- ❑ 263 Jim Perry 1.00 .45
- ❑ 264 John Milner .50 .23
- ❑ 265 Ron Bryant .50 .23
- ❑ 266 Sandy Alomar 1.00 .45
- ❑ 267 Dick Ruthven .50 .23
- ❑ 268 Hal McRae 1.00 .45
- ❑ 269 Doug Rau .50 .23
- ❑ 270 Ron Fairly 1.00 .45
- ❑ 271 Gerry Moses .50 .23
- ❑ 272 Lynn McGlothen .50 .23
- ❑ 273 Steve Braun .50 .23
- ❑ 274 Vicente Romo .50 .23
- ❑ 275 Paul Blair 1.00 .45
- ❑ 276 White Sox Team/Mgr. 2.00 .40
  Chuck Tanner
  (Checklist back)
- ❑ 277 Frank Taveras .50 .23
- ❑ 278 Paul Lindblad .50 .23
- ❑ 279 Milt May .50 .23
- ❑ 280 Carl Yastrzemski 10.00 4.50
- ❑ 281 Jim Slaton .50 .23
- ❑ 282 Jerry Morales .50 .23
- ❑ 283 Steve Foucault .50 .23
- ❑ 284 Ken Griffey 4.00 1.80
- ❑ 285 Ellie Rodriguez .50 .23
- ❑ 286 Mike Jorgensen .50 .23
- ❑ 287 Roric Harrison .50 .23
- ❑ 288 Bruce Ellingsen .50 .23
- ❑ 289 Ken Rudolph .50 .23
- ❑ 290 Jon Matlack .50 .23
- ❑ 291 Bill Sudakis .50 .23
- ❑ 292 Ron Schueler .50 .23
- ❑ 293 Dick Sharon .50 .23
- ❑ 294 Geoff Zahn .50 .23
- ❑ 295 Vada Pinson 2.00 .90
- ❑ 296 Alan Foster .50 .23
- ❑ 297 Craig Kusick .50 .23
- ❑ 298 Johnny Grubb .50 .23
- ❑ 299 Bucky Dent 2.00 .90
- ❑ 300 Reggie Jackson 15.00 6.75
- ❑ 301 Dave Roberts .50 .23
- ❑ 302 Rick Burleson 1.00 .45
- ❑ 303 Grant Jackson .50 .23
- ❑ 304 Pirates: Team/Mgr. 2.00 .40
  Danny Murtaugh
  (Checklist back)
- ❑ 305 Jim Colborn .50 .23
- ❑ 306 Batting Leaders 2.00 .90
  Rod Carew
  Ralph Garr
- ❑ 307 Home Run Leaders 4.00 1.80
  Dick Allen
  Mike Schmidt
- ❑ 308 RBI Leaders 2.00 .90
  Jeff Burroughs
  Johnny Bench
- ❑ 309 Stolen Base Leaders 2.00 .90
  Bill North
  Lou Brock
- ❑ 310 Victory Leaders 2.00 .90
  Jim Hunter
  Fergie Jenkins
  Andy Messersmith
  Phil Niekro
- ❑ 311 ERA Leaders 2.00 .90
  Jim Hunter
  Buzz Capra
- ❑ 312 Strikeout Leaders 12.00 5.50
  Nolan Ryan
  Steve Carlton
- ❑ 313 Firemen Leaders 1.00 .45
  Terry Forster
  Mike Marshall
- ❑ 314 Buck Martinez .50 .23
- ❑ 315 Don Kessinger 1.00 .45
- ❑ 316 Jackie Brown .50 .23
- ❑ 317 Joe Lahoud .50 .23
- ❑ 318 Ernie McAnally .50 .23
- ❑ 319 Johnny Oates 1.00 .45
- ❑ 320 Pete Rose 30.00 13.50
- ❑ 321 Rudy May .50 .23
- ❑ 322 Ed Goodson .50 .23
- ❑ 323 Fred Holdsworth .50 .23
- ❑ 324 Ed Kranepool 1.00 .45
- ❑ 325 Tony Oliva 2.00 .90
- ❑ 326 Wayne Twitchell .50 .23
- ❑ 327 Jerry Hairston .50 .23
- ❑ 328 Sonny Siebert .50 .23
- ❑ 329 Ted Kubiak .50 .23
- ❑ 330 Mike Marshall 1.00 .45
- ❑ 331 Indians: Team/Mgr. 2.00 .40
  Frank Robinson
  (Checklist back)
- ❑ 332 Fred Kendall .50 .23
- ❑ 333 Dick Drago .50 .23
- ❑ 334 Greg Gross .50 .23
- ❑ 335 Jim Palmer 6.00 2.70
- ❑ 336 Rennie Stennett .50 .23
- ❑ 337 Kevin Kobel .50 .23
- ❑ 338 Rich Stelmaszek .50 .23
- ❑ 339 Jim Fregosi 1.00 .45
- ❑ 340 Paul Splittorff .50 .23
- ❑ 341 Hal Breeden .50 .23
- ❑ 342 Leroy Stanton .50 .23
- ❑ 343 Danny Frisella .50 .23
- ❑ 344 Ben Oglivie 1.00 .45
- ❑ 345 Clay Carroll 1.00 .45
- ❑ 346 Bobby Darwin .50 .23
- ❑ 347 Mike Caldwell .50 .23
- ❑ 348 Tony Muser .50 .23
- ❑ 349 Ray Sadecki .50 .23
- ❑ 350 Bobby Murcer 1.00 .45
- ❑ 351 Bob Boone 2.00 .90
- ❑ 352 Darold Knowles .50 .23
- ❑ 353 Luis Melendez .50 .23
- ❑ 354 Dick Bosman .50 .23
- ❑ 355 Chris Cannizzaro .50 .23
- ❑ 356 Rico Petrocelli 1.00 .45
- ❑ 357 Ken Forsch .50 .23
- ❑ 358 Al Bumbry 1.00 .45
- ❑ 359 Paul Popovich .50 .23
- ❑ 360 George Scott 1.00 .45
- ❑ 361 Dodgers: Team/Mgr. 2.00 .40
  Walter Alston
  (Checklist back)
- ❑ 362 Steve Hargan .50 .23
- ❑ 363 Carmen Fanzone .50 .23
- ❑ 364 Doug Bird .50 .23
- ❑ 365 Bob Bailey .50 .23
- ❑ 366 Ken Sanders .50 .23
- ❑ 367 Craig Robinson .50 .23
- ❑ 368 Vic Albury .50 .23
- ❑ 369 Merv Rettenmund .50 .23
- ❑ 370 Tom Seaver 15.00 6.75
- ❑ 371 Gates Brown .50 .23
- ❑ 372 John D'Acquisto .50 .23
- ❑ 373 Bill Sharp .50 .23
- ❑ 374 Eddie Watt .50 .23
- ❑ 375 Roy White 1.00 .45
- ❑ 376 Steve Yeager 1.00 .45
- ❑ 377 Tom Hilgendorf .50 .23
- ❑ 378 Derrel Thomas .50 .23
- ❑ 379 Bernie Carbo .50 .23
- ❑ 380 Sal Bando 1.00 .45
- ❑ 381 John Curtis .50 .23
- ❑ 382 Don Baylor 2.00 .90
- ❑ 383 Jim York .50 .23
- ❑ 384 Brewers: Team/Mgr. 2.00 .40
  Del Crandall
  (Checklist back)
- ❑ 385 Dock Ellis .50 .23
- ❑ 386 Checklist: 265-396 3.00 .60
- ❑ 387 Jim Spencer .50 .23
- ❑ 388 Steve Stone 1.00 .45
- ❑ 389 Tony Solaita .50 .23
- ❑ 390 Ron Cey 2.00 .90
- ❑ 391 Don DeMola .50 .23
- ❑ 392 Bruce Bochte 1.00 .45
- ❑ 393 Gary Gentry .50 .23
- ❑ 394 Larvell Blanks .50 .23
- ❑ 395 Bud Harrelson 1.00 .45
- ❑ 396 Fred Norman 1.00 .45
- ❑ 397 Bill Freehan 1.00 .45
- ❑ 398 Elias Sosa .50 .23
- ❑ 399 Terry Harmon .50 .23
- ❑ 400 Dick Allen 2.00 .90
- ❑ 401 Mike Wallace .50 .23
- ❑ 402 Bob Tolan .50 .23
- ❑ 403 Tom Buskey .50 .23
- ❑ 404 Ted Sizemore .50 .23
- ❑ 405 John Montague .50 .23
- ❑ 406 Bob Gallagher .50 .23
- ❑ 407 Herb Washington RC 2.00 .90
- ❑ 408 Clyde Wright .50 .23
- ❑ 409 Bob Robertson .50 .23
- ❑ 410 Mike Cueller UER 1.00 .45
  (Sic, Cuellar)
- ❑ 411 George Mitterwald .50 .23
- ❑ 412 Bill Hands .50 .23
- ❑ 413 Marty Pattin .50 .23
- ❑ 414 Manny Mota 1.00 .45
- ❑ 415 John Hiller 1.00 .45
- ❑ 416 Larry Lintz .50 .23
- ❑ 417 Skip Lockwood .50 .23
- ❑ 418 Leo Foster .50 .23
- ❑ 419 Dave Goltz .50 .23
- ❑ 420 Larry Bowa 2.00 .90
- ❑ 421 Mets: Team/Mgr. 3.00 .60
  Yogi Berra
  (Checklist back)
- ❑ 422 Brian Downing 1.00 .45
- ❑ 423 Clay Kirby .50 .23
- ❑ 424 John Lowenstein .50 .23
- ❑ 425 Tito Fuentes .50 .23
- ❑ 426 George Medich .50 .23
- ❑ 427 Clarence Gaston 1.00 .45
- ❑ 428 Dave Hamilton .50 .23
- ❑ 429 Jim Dwyer .50 .23
- ❑ 430 Luis Tiant 2.00 .90
- ❑ 431 Rod Gilbreath .50 .23
- ❑ 432 Ken Berry .50 .23
- ❑ 433 Larry Demery .50 .23
- ❑ 434 Bob Locker .50 .23
- ❑ 435 Dave Nelson .50 .23
- ❑ 436 Ken Frailing .50 .23
- ❑ 437 Al Cowens 1.00 .45
- ❑ 438 Don Carrithers .50 .23
- ❑ 439 Ed Brinkman .50 .23
- ❑ 440 Andy Messersmith 1.00 .45
- ❑ 441 Bobby Heise .50 .23
- ❑ 442 Maximino Leon .50 .23
- ❑ 443 Twins: Team/Mgr. 2.00 .40
  Frank Quilici
  (Checklist back)
- ❑ 444 Gene Garber 1.00 .45
- ❑ 445 Felix Millan .50 .23
- ❑ 446 Bart Johnson .50 .23
- ❑ 447 Terry Crowley .50 .23
- ❑ 448 Frank Duffy .50 .23
- ❑ 449 Charlie Williams .50 .23
- ❑ 450 Willie McCovey 6.00 2.70
- ❑ 451 Rick Dempsey 1.00 .45
- ❑ 452 Angel Mangual .50 .23
- ❑ 453 Claude Osteen 1.00 .45
- ❑ 454 Doug Griffin .50 .23
- ❑ 455 Don Wilson .50 .23
- ❑ 456 Bob Coluccio .50 .23
- ❑ 457 Mario Mendoza .50 .23
- ❑ 458 Ross Grimsley .50 .23
- ❑ 459 1974 AL Champs 1.00 .45
  A's over Orioles
  (Second base action
  pictured)
- ❑ 460 Steve Garvey NLCS 2.00 .90
  Frank Taveras
- ❑ 461 Reggie Jackson WS 6.00 2.70
- ❑ 462 World Series Game 2 1.00 .45
  (Dodger dugout)
- ❑ 463 Rollie Fingers WS 2.00 .90
- ❑ 464 World Series Game 4 1.00 .45
  (A's batter)
- ❑ 465 Joe Rudi WS5 1.00 .45
- ❑ 466 World Series Summary 2.00 .90
  A's do it again;
  win third straight
  (A's group picture)
- ❑ 467 Ed Halicki .50 .23
- ❑ 468 Bobby Mitchell .50 .23
- ❑ 469 Tom Dettore .50 .23
- ❑ 470 Jeff Burroughs 1.00 .45

❑ 471 Bob Stinson .50 .23
❑ 472 Bruce Dal Canton .50 .23
❑ 473 Ken McMullen .50 .23
❑ 474 Luke Walker .50 .23
❑ 475 Darrell Evans 1.00 .45
❑ 476 Ed Figueroa .50 .23
❑ 477 Tom Hutton .50 .23
❑ 478 Tom Burgmeier .50 .23
❑ 479 Ken Boswell .50 .23
❑ 480 Carlos May .50 .23
❑ 481 Will McEnaney 1.00 .45
❑ 482 Tom McCraw .50 .23
❑ 483 Steve Ontiveros .50 .23
❑ 484 Glenn Beckert 1.00 .45
❑ 485 Sparky Lyle 1.00 .45
❑ 486 Ray Fosse .50 .23
❑ 487 Astros: Team/Mgr. 2.00 .40
Preston Gomez
(Checklist back)
❑ 488 Bill Travers .50 .23
❑ 489 Cecil Cooper 2.00 .90
❑ 490 Reggie Smith 1.00 .45
❑ 491 Doyle Alexander 1.00 .45
❑ 492 Rich Hebner 1.00 .45
❑ 493 Don Stanhouse .50 .23
❑ 494 Pete LaCock .50 .23
❑ 495 Nelson Briles 1.00 .45
❑ 496 Pepe Frias .50 .23
❑ 497 Jim Nettles .50 .23
❑ 498 Al Downing .50 .23
❑ 499 Marty Perez .50 .23
❑ 500 Nolan Ryan 50.00 22.00
❑ 501 Bill Robinson 1.00 .45
❑ 502 Pat Bourque .50 .23
❑ 503 Fred Stanley .50 .23
❑ 504 Buddy Bradford .50 .23
❑ 505 Chris Speier .50 .23
❑ 506 Leron Lee .50 .23
❑ 507 Tom Carroll .50 .23
❑ 508 Bob Hansen .50 .23
❑ 509 Dave Hilton .50 .23
❑ 510 Vida Blue 1.00 .45
❑ 511 Rangers: Team/Mgr. 2.00 .40
Billy Martin
(Checklist back)
❑ 512 Larry Milbourne .50 .23
❑ 513 Dick Pole .50 .23
❑ 514 Jose Cruz 2.00 .90
❑ 515 Manny Sanguillen 1.00 .45
❑ 516 Don Hood .50 .23
❑ 517 Checklist: 397-528 3.00 .60
❑ 518 Leo Cardenas .50 .23
❑ 519 Jim Todd .50 .23
❑ 520 Amos Otis 1.00 .45
❑ 521 Dennis Blair .50 .23
❑ 522 Gary Sutherland .50 .23
❑ 523 Tom Paciorek 1.00 .45
❑ 524 John Doherty .50 .23
❑ 525 Tom House .50 .23
❑ 526 Larry Hisle 1.00 .45
❑ 527 Mac Scarce .50 .23
❑ 528 Eddie Leon .50 .23
❑ 529 Gary Thomasson .50 .23
❑ 530 Gaylord Perry 3.00 1.35
❑ 531 Reds: Team/Mgr. 5.00 1.00
Sparky Anderson
(Checklist back)
❑ 532 Gorman Thomas 1.00 .45
❑ 533 Rudy Meoli .50 .23
❑ 534 Alex Johnson .50 .23
❑ 535 Gene Tenace 1.00 .45
❑ 536 Bob Moose .50 .23
❑ 537 Tommy Harper 1.00 .45
❑ 538 Duffy Dyer .50 .23
❑ 539 Jesse Jefferson .50 .23
❑ 540 Lou Brock 6.00 2.70
❑ 541 Roger Metzger .50 .23
❑ 542 Pete Broberg .50 .23
❑ 543 Larry Biittner .50 .23
❑ 544 Steve Mingori .50 .23
❑ 545 Billy Williams 3.00 1.35
❑ 546 John Knox .50 .23
❑ 547 Von Joshua .50 .23
❑ 548 Charlie Sands .50 .23
❑ 549 Bill Butler .50 .23
❑ 550 Ralph Garr 1.00 .45
❑ 551 Larry Christenson .50 .23
❑ 552 Jack Brohamer .50 .23
❑ 553 John Boccabella .50 .23
❑ 554 Rich Gossage 2.00 .90
❑ 555 Al Oliver 2.00 .90
❑ 556 Tim Johnson .50 .23
❑ 557 Larry Gura .50 .23
❑ 558 Dave Roberts .50 .23
❑ 559 Bob Montgomery .50 .23
❑ 560 Tony Perez 3.00 1.35
❑ 561 A's: Team/Mgr. 2.00 .40
Alvin Dark
(Checklist back)
❑ 562 Gary Nolan 1.00 .45
❑ 563 Wilbur Howard .50 .23
❑ 564 Tommy Davis 1.00 .45
❑ 565 Joe Torre 2.00 .90
❑ 566 Ray Burris .50 .23
❑ 567 Jim Sundberg RC 2.00 .90
❑ 568 Dale Murray .50 .23
❑ 569 Frank White 1.00 .45
❑ 570 Jim Wynn 1.00 .45
❑ 571 Dave Lemanczyk .50 .23
❑ 572 Roger Nelson .50 .23
❑ 573 Orlando Pena .50 .23
❑ 574 Tony Taylor 1.00 .45
❑ 575 Gene Clines .50 .23
❑ 576 Phil Roof .50 .23
❑ 577 John Morris .50 .23
❑ 578 Dave Tomlin .50 .23
❑ 579 Skip Pitlock .50 .23
❑ 580 Frank Robinson 6.00 2.70
❑ 581 Darrel Chaney .50 .23
❑ 582 Eduardo Rodriguez .50 .23
❑ 583 Andy Etchebarren .50 .23
❑ 584 Mike Garman .50 .23
❑ 585 Chris Chambliss 1.00 .45
❑ 586 Tim McCarver 2.00 .90
❑ 587 Chris Ward .50 .23
❑ 588 Rick Auerbach .50 .23
❑ 589 Braves: Team/Mgr. 2.00 .40
Clyde King
(Checklist back)
❑ 590 Cesar Cedeno 1.00 .45
❑ 591 Glenn Abbott .50 .23
❑ 592 Balor Moore .50 .23
❑ 593 Gene Lamont .50 .23
❑ 594 Jim Fuller .50 .23
❑ 595 Joe Niekro 1.00 .45
❑ 596 Ollie Brown .50 .23
❑ 597 Winston Llenas .50 .23
❑ 598 Bruce Kison .50 .23
❑ 599 Nate Colbert .50 .23
❑ 600 Rod Carew 8.00 3.60
❑ 601 Juan Beniquez .50 .23
❑ 602 John Vukovich .50 .23
❑ 603 Lew Krausse .50 .23
❑ 604 Oscar Zamora .50 .23
❑ 605 John Ellis .50 .23
❑ 606 Bruce Miller .50 .23
❑ 607 Jim Holt .50 .23
❑ 608 Gene Michael 1.00 .45
❑ 609 Elrod Hendricks .50 .23
❑ 610 Ron Hunt .50 .23
❑ 611 Yankees: Team/Mgr. 2.00 .40
Bill Virdon
(Checklist back)
❑ 612 Terry Hughes .50 .23
❑ 613 Bill Parsons .50 .23
❑ 614 Rookie Pitchers 1.00 .45
Jack Kucek
Dyar Miller
Vern Ruhle
Paul Siebert
❑ 615 Rookie Pitchers 2.00 .90
Pat Darcy
Dennis Leonard RC
Tom Underwood
Hank Webb
❑ 616 Rookie Outfielders 10.00 4.50
Dave Augustine
Pepe Mangual
Jim Rice RC
John Scott
❑ 617 Rookie Infielders 2.00 .90
Mike Cubbage
Doug DeCinces RC
Reggie Sanders
Manny Trillo
❑ 618 Rookie Pitchers 1.00 .45
Jamie Easterly
Tom Johnson
Scott McGregor RC
Rick Rhoden
❑ 619 Rookie Outfielders 1.00 .45
Benny Ayala
Nyls Nyman
Tommy Smith
Jerry Turner
❑ 620 Rookie Catcher/OF 20.00 9.00
Gary Carter RC
Marc Hill
Danny Meyer
Leon Roberts
❑ 621 Rookie Pitchers 2.00 .90
John Denny RC
Rawly Eastwick
Jim Kern
Juan Veintidos
❑ 622 Rookie Outfielders 6.00 2.70
Ed Armbrister
Fred Lynn RC
Tom Poquette
Terry Whitfield UER
(Listed as Ney York)
❑ 623 Rookie Infielders 6.00 2.70
Phil Garner
Keith Hernandez RC UER
(Sic, bats right)
Bob Sheldon
Tom Veryzer
❑ 624 Rookie Pitchers 1.00 .45
Doug Konieczny
Gary Lavelle
Jim Otten
Eddie Solomon
❑ 625 Boog Powell 2.00 .90
❑ 626 Larry Haney UER .50 .23
(Photo actually
Dave Duncan)
❑ 627 Tom Walker .50 .23
❑ 628 Ron LeFlore RC 1.00 .45
❑ 629 Joe Hoerner .50 .23
❑ 630 Greg Luzinski 2.00 .90
❑ 631 Lee Lacy .50 .23
❑ 632 Morris Nettles .50 .23
❑ 633 Paul Casanova .50 .23
❑ 634 Cy Acosta .50 .23
❑ 635 Chuck Dobson .50 .23
❑ 636 Charlie Moore .50 .23
❑ 637 Ted Martinez .50 .23
❑ 638 Cubs: Team/Mgr. 2.00 .40
Jim Marshall
(Checklist back)
❑ 639 Steve Kline .50 .23
❑ 640 Harmon Killebrew 6.00 2.70
❑ 641 Jim Northrup .50 .23
❑ 642 Mike Phillips .50 .23
❑ 643 Brent Strom .50 .23
❑ 644 Bill Fahey .50 .23
❑ 645 Danny Cater .50 .23
❑ 646 Checklist: 529-660 3.00 .60
❑ 647 Claudell Washington RC 2.00 .90
❑ 648 Dave Pagan .50 .23
❑ 649 Jack Heidemann .50 .23
❑ 650 Dave May .50 .23
❑ 651 John Morlan .50 .23
❑ 652 Lindy McDaniel 1.00 .45
❑ 653 Lee Richard UER .50 .23
(Listed as Richards
on card front)
❑ 654 Jerry Terrell .50 .23
❑ 655 Rico Carty 1.00 .45
❑ 656 Bill Plummer .50 .23
❑ 657 Bob Oliver .50 .23
❑ 658 Vic Harris .50 .23
❑ 659 Bob Apodaca .50 .23
❑ 660 Hank Aaron 30.00 9.00

## 1976 Topps

| | NRMT | VG-E |
|---|---|---|
| COMPLETE SET (660) | 300.00 | 135.00 |
| COMMON CARD (1-660) | .40 | .18 |

❏ 1 Hank Aaron RB ............. 15.00 4.70
  2262 Career RBIs
❏ 2 Bobby Bonds RB ............. 1.50 .70
  Most leadoff HR's 32;
  plus three seasons
  30 homers/30 steals
❏ 3 Mickey Lolich RB ............. .75 .35
  Most Lefthanded Strikeouts: 2679
❏ 4 Dave Lopes RB ............. .75 .35
  Most Consecutive SB's: 38
❏ 5 Tom Seaver RB ............. 6.00 2.70
  Most Consecutive seasons
  with 200 Strikeouts
❏ 6 Rennie Stennett RB ......... .75 .35
  7 Hits in a 9 inning game
❏ 7 Jim Umbarger ............. .40 .18
❏ 8 Tito Fuentes ............. .40 .18
❏ 9 Paul Lindblad ............. .40 .18
❏ 10 Lou Brock ............. 5.00 2.20
❏ 11 Jim Hughes ............. .40 .18
❏ 12 Richie Zisk ............. .75 .35
❏ 13 John Wockenfuss ............. .40 .18
❏ 14 Gene Garber ............. .75 .35
❏ 15 George Scott ............. .75 .35
❏ 16 Bob Apodaca ............. .40 .18
❏ 17 New York Yankees ....... 1.50 .30
  Team Card;
  Billy Martin MG
  (Checklist back)
❏ 18 Dale Murray ............. .40 .18
❏ 19 George Brett ............. 30.00 13.50
❏ 20 Bob Watson ............. .75 .35
❏ 21 Dave LaRoche ............. .40 .18
❏ 22 Bill Russell ............. .75 .35
❏ 23 Brian Downing ............. .40 .18
❏ 24 Cesar Geronimo ............. .75 .35
❏ 25 Mike Torrez ............. .75 .35
❏ 26 Andre Thornton ............. .75 .35
❏ 27 Ed Figueroa ............. .40 .18
❏ 28 Dusty Baker ............. 1.50 .70
❏ 29 Rick Burleson ............. .75 .35
❏ 30 John Montefusco ............. .75 .35
❏ 31 Len Randle ............. .40 .18
❏ 32 Danny Frisella ............. .40 .18
❏ 33 Bill North ............. .40 .18
❏ 34 Mike Garman ............. .40 .18
❏ 35 Tony Oliva ............. 1.50 .70
❏ 36 Frank Taveras ............. .40 .18
❏ 37 John Hiller ............. .75 .35
❏ 38 Garry Maddox ............. .75 .35
❏ 39 Pete Broberg ............. .40 .18
❏ 40 Dave Kingman ............. 1.50 .70
❏ 41 Tippy Martinez ............. .75 .35
❏ 42 Barry Foote ............. .40 .18
❏ 43 Paul Splittorff ............. .40 .18
❏ 44 Doug Rader ............. .75 .35
❏ 45 Boog Powell ............. 1.50 .70
❏ 46 Los Angeles Dodgers .... 1.50 .30
  Team Card;
  Walter Alston MG
  (Checklist back)
❏ 47 Jesse Jefferson ............. .40 .18
❏ 48 Dave Concepcion .......... 1.50 .70
❏ 49 Dave Duncan ............. .40 .18
❏ 50 Fred Lynn ............. 1.50 .70
❏ 51 Ray Burris ............. .40 .18
❏ 52 Dave Chalk ............. .40 .18
❏ 53 Mike Beard ............. .40 .18
❏ 54 Dave Rader ............. .40 .18
❏ 55 Gaylord Perry ............. 2.50 1.10
❏ 56 Bob Tolan ............. .40 .18
❏ 57 Phil Garner ............. .75 .35
❏ 58 Ron Reed ............. .40 .18
❏ 59 Larry Hisle ............. .75 .35
❏ 60 Jerry Reuss ............. .75 .35
❏ 61 Ron LeFlore ............. .75 .35
❏ 62 Johnny Oates ............. .75 .35
❏ 63 Bobby Darwin ............. .40 .18
❏ 64 Jerry Koosman ............. .75 .35
❏ 65 Chris Chambliss ............. .75 .35
❏ 66 Gus Bell FS ............. .75 .35
  Buddy Bell
❏ 67 Ray Boone FS ............. .75 .35
  Bob Boone
❏ 68 Joe Coleman FS ............. .40 .18
  Joe Coleman Jr.
❏ 69 Jim Hegan FS ............. .40 .18
  Mike Hegan
❏ 70 Roy Smalley FS ............. .75 .35
  Roy Smalley Jr.
❏ 71 Steve Rogers ............. .75 .35
❏ 72 Hal McRae ............. .75 .35
❏ 73 Baltimore Orioles ........... 1.50 .30
  Team Card;
  Earl Weaver MG
  (Checklist back)
❏ 74 Oscar Gamble ............. .75 .35
❏ 75 Larry Dierker ............. .75 .35
❏ 76 Willie Crawford ............. .40 .18
❏ 77 Pedro Borbon ............. .75 .35
❏ 78 Cecil Cooper ............. .75 .35
❏ 79 Jerry Morales ............. .40 .18
❏ 80 Jim Kaat ............. 1.50 .70
❏ 81 Darrell Evans ............. .75 .35
❏ 82 Von Joshua ............. .40 .18
❏ 83 Jim Spencer ............. .40 .18
❏ 84 Brent Strom ............. .40 .18
❏ 85 Mickey Rivers ............. .75 .35
❏ 86 Mike Tyson ............. .40 .18
❏ 87 Tom Burgmeier ............. .40 .18
❏ 88 Duffy Dyer ............. .40 .18
❏ 89 Vern Ruhle ............. .40 .18
❏ 90 Sal Bando ............. .75 .35
❏ 91 Tom Hutton ............. .40 .18
❏ 92 Eduardo Rodriguez ............. .40 .18
❏ 93 Mike Phillips ............. .40 .18
❏ 94 Jim Dwyer ............. .40 .18
❏ 95 Brooks Robinson ............. 5.00 2.20
❏ 96 Doug Bird ............. .40 .18
❏ 97 Wilbur Howard ............. .40 .18
❏ 98 Dennis Eckersley RC ! 30.00 13.50
❏ 99 Lee Lacy ............. .40 .18
❏ 100 Jim Hunter ............. 3.00 1.35
❏ 101 Pete LaCock ............. .40 .18
❏ 102 Jim Willoughby ............. .40 .18
❏ 103 Biff Pocoroba ............. .40 .18
❏ 104 Cincinnati Reds ........... 2.50 .50
  Team Card;
  Sparky Anderson MG
  (Checklist back)
❏ 105 Gary Lavelle ............. .40 .18
❏ 106 Tom Grieve ............. .40 .18
❏ 107 Dave Roberts ............. .40 .18
❏ 108 Don Kirkwood ............. .40 .18
❏ 109 Larry Lintz ............. .40 .18
❏ 110 Carlos May ............. .40 .18
❏ 111 Danny Thompson ............. .40 .18
❏ 112 Kent Tekulve RC ............. 1.50 .70
❏ 113 Gary Sutherland ............. .40 .18
❏ 114 Jay Johnstone ............. .75 .35
❏ 115 Ken Holtzman ............. .75 .35
❏ 116 Charlie Moore ............. .40 .18
❏ 117 Mike Jorgensen ............. .40 .18
❏ 118 Boston Red Sox ............. 1.50 .30
  Team Card;
  Darrell Johnson MG
  (Checklist back)
❏ 119 Checklist 1-132 ............. 1.50 .30
❏ 120 Rusty Staub ............. .75 .35
❏ 121 Tony Solaita ............. .40 .18
❏ 122 Mike Cosgrove ............. .40 .18
❏ 123 Walt Williams ............. .40 .18
❏ 124 Doug Rau ............. .40 .18
❏ 125 Don Baylor ............. 1.50 .70
❏ 126 Tom Dettore ............. .40 .18
❏ 127 Larvell Blanks ............. .40 .18
❏ 128 Ken Griffey Sr. ............. 2.50 1.10
❏ 129 Andy Etchebarren ............. .40 .18
❏ 130 Luis Tiant ............. 1.50 .70
❏ 131 Bill Stein ............. .40 .18
❏ 132 Don Hood ............. .40 .18
❏ 133 Gary Matthews ............. .75 .35
❏ 134 Mike Ivie ............. .40 .18
❏ 135 Bake McBride ............. .75 .35
❏ 136 Dave Goltz ............. .40 .18
❏ 137 Bill Robinson ............. .75 .35
❏ 138 Lerrin LaGrow ............. .40 .18
❏ 139 Gorman Thomas ............. .75 .35
❏ 140 Vida Blue ............. .75 .35
❏ 141 Larry Parrish RC ............. 1.50 .70
❏ 142 Dick Drago ............. .40 .18
❏ 143 Jerry Grote ............. .40 .18
❏ 144 Al Fitzmorris ............. .40 .18
❏ 145 Larry Bowa ............. .75 .35
❏ 146 George Medich ............. .40 .18
❏ 147 Houston Astros ............. 1.50 .30
  Team Card;
  Bill Virdon MG
  (Checklist back)
❏ 148 Stan Thomas ............. .40 .18
❏ 149 Tommy Davis ............. .75 .35
❏ 150 Steve Garvey ............. 2.50 1.10
❏ 151 Bill Bonham ............. .40 .18
❏ 152 Leroy Stanton ............. .40 .18
❏ 153 Buzz Capra ............. .40 .18
❏ 154 Bucky Dent ............. .75 .35
❏ 155 Jack Billingham ............. .75 .35
❏ 156 Rico Carty ............. .75 .35
❏ 157 Mike Caldwell ............. .40 .18
❏ 158 Ken Reitz ............. .40 .18
❏ 159 Jerry Terrell ............. .40 .18
❏ 160 Dave Winfield ............. 10.00 4.50
❏ 161 Bruce Kison ............. .40 .18
❏ 162 Jack Pierce ............. .40 .18
❏ 163 Jim Slaton ............. .40 .18
❏ 164 Pepe Mangual ............. .40 .18
❏ 165 Gene Tenace ............. .75 .35
❏ 166 Skip Lockwood ............. .40 .18
❏ 167 Freddie Patek ............. .75 .35
❏ 168 Tom Hilgendorf ............. .40 .18
❏ 169 Graig Nettles ............. 1.50 .70
❏ 170 Rick Wise ............. .40 .18
❏ 171 Greg Gross ............. .40 .18
❏ 172 Texas Rangers ............. 1.50 .30
  Team Card;
  Frank Lucchesi MG
  (Checklist back)
❏ 173 Steve Swisher ............. .40 .18
❏ 174 Charlie Hough ............. .75 .35
❏ 175 Ken Singleton ............. .75 .35
❏ 176 Dick Lange ............. .40 .18
❏ 177 Marty Perez ............. .40 .18
❏ 178 Tom Buskey ............. .40 .18
❏ 179 George Foster ............. 1.50 .70
❏ 180 Rich Gossage ............. 1.50 .70
❏ 181 Willie Montanez ............. .40 .18
❏ 182 Harry Rasmussen ............. .40 .18
❏ 183 Steve Braun ............. .40 .18
❏ 184 Bill Greif ............. .40 .18
❏ 185 Dave Parker ............. 1.50 .70
❏ 186 Tom Walker ............. .40 .18
❏ 187 Pedro Garcia ............. .40 .18
❏ 188 Fred Scherman ............. .40 .18
❏ 189 Claudell Washington ..... .75 .35
❏ 190 Jon Matlack ............. .40 .18
❏ 191 NL Batting Leaders ............. .75 .35
  Bill Madlock
  Ted Simmons
  Manny Sanguillen
❏ 192 AL Batting Leaders ...... 2.50 1.10
  Rod Carew
  Fred Lynn
  Thurman Munson
❏ 193 NL Home Run Leaders 3.00 1.35

Mike Schmidt
Dave Kingman
Greg Luzinski
❑ 194 AL Home Run Leaders 3.00 1.35
Reggie Jackson
George Scott
John Mayberry
❑ 195 NL RBI Leaders 1.50 .70
Greg Luzinski
Johnny Bench
Tony Perez
❑ 196 AL RBI Leaders .75 .35
George Scott
John Mayberry
Fred Lynn
❑ 197 NL Stolen Base Leaders 1.50 .70
Dave Lopes
Joe Morgan
Lou Brock
❑ 198 AL Stolen Base Leaders .75 .35
Mickey Rivers
Claudell Washington
Amos Otis
❑ 199 NL Victory Leaders 2.50 1.10
Tom Seaver
Randy Jones
Andy Messersmith
❑ 200 AL Victory Leaders 1.50 .70
Jim Hunter
Jim Palmer
Vida Blue
❑ 201 NL ERA Leaders 1.50 .70
Randy Jones
Andy Messersmith
Tom Seaver
❑ 202 AL ERA Leaders 3.00 1.35
Jim Palmer
Jim Hunter
Dennis Eckersley
❑ 203 NL Strikeout Leaders 2.50 1.10
Tom Seaver
John Montefusco
Andy Messersmith
❑ 204 AL Strikeout Leaders .75 .35
Frank Tanana
Bert Blyleven
Gaylord Perry
❑ 205 Leading Firemen .75 .35
Al Hrabosky
Rich Gossage
❑ 206 Manny Trillo .40 .18
❑ 207 Andy Hassler .40 .18
❑ 208 Mike Lum .40 .18
❑ 209 Alan Ashby .75 .35
❑ 210 Lee May .75 .35
❑ 211 Clay Carroll .75 .35
❑ 212 Pat Kelly .40 .18
❑ 213 Dave Heaverlo .40 .18
❑ 214 Eric Soderholm .40 .18
❑ 215 Reggie Smith .75 .35
❑ 216 Montreal Expos 1.50 .30
Team Card;
Karl Kuehl MG
(Checklist back)
❑ 217 Dave Freisleben .40 .18
❑ 218 John Knox .40 .18
❑ 219 Tom Murphy .40 .18
❑ 220 Manny Sanguillen .75 .35
❑ 221 Jim Todd .40 .18
❑ 222 Wayne Garrett .40 .18
❑ 223 Ollie Brown .40 .18
❑ 224 Jim York .40 .18
❑ 225 Roy White .75 .35
❑ 226 Jim Sundberg .75 .35
❑ 227 Oscar Zamora .40 .18
❑ 228 John Hale .40 .18
❑ 229 Jerry Remy .40 .18
❑ 230 Carl Yastrzemski 8.00 3.60
❑ 231 Tom House .40 .18
❑ 232 Frank Duffy .40 .18
❑ 233 Grant Jackson .40 .18
❑ 234 Mike Sadek .40 .18
❑ 235 Bert Blyleven 1.50 .70
❑ 236 Kansas City Royals 1.50 .30
Team Card;
Whitey Herzog MG
(Checklist back)
❑ 237 Dave Hamilton .40 .18
❑ 238 Larry Biittner .40 .18
❑ 239 John Curtis .40 .18
❑ 240 Pete Rose 25.00 11.00
❑ 241 Hector Torres .40 .18
❑ 242 Dan Meyer .40 .18
❑ 243 Jim Rooker .40 .18
❑ 244 Bill Sharp .40 .18
❑ 245 Felix Millan .40 .18
❑ 246 Cesar Tovar .40 .18
❑ 247 Terry Harmon .40 .18
❑ 248 Dick Tidrow .40 .18
❑ 249 Cliff Johnson .75 .35
❑ 250 Fergie Jenkins 2.50 1.10
❑ 251 Rick Monday .75 .35
❑ 252 Tim Nordbrook .40 .18
❑ 253 Bill Buckner .75 .35
❑ 254 Rudy Meoli .40 .18
❑ 255 Fritz Peterson .40 .18
❑ 256 Rowland Office .40 .18
❑ 257 Ross Grimsley .40 .18
❑ 258 Nyls Nyman .40 .18
❑ 259 Darrel Chaney .40 .18
❑ 260 Steve Busby .40 .18
❑ 261 Gary Thomasson .40 .18
❑ 262 Checklist 133-264 1.50 .30
❑ 263 Lyman Bostock RC 1.50 .70
❑ 264 Steve Renko .40 .18
❑ 265 Willie Davis .75 .35
❑ 266 Alan Foster .40 .18
❑ 267 Aurelio Rodriguez .40 .18
❑ 268 Del Unser .40 .18
❑ 269 Rick Austin .40 .18
❑ 270 Willie Stargell 3.00 1.35
❑ 271 Jim Lonborg .75 .35
❑ 272 Rick Dempsey .75 .35
❑ 273 Joe Niekro .75 .35
❑ 274 Tommy Harper .75 .35
❑ 275 Rick Manning .40 .18
❑ 276 Mickey Scott .40 .18
❑ 277 Chicago Cubs 1.50 .30
Team Card;
Jim Marshall MG
(Checklist back)
❑ 278 Bernie Carbo .40 .18
❑ 279 Roy Howell .40 .18
❑ 280 Burt Hooton .75 .35
❑ 281 Dave May .40 .18
❑ 282 Dan Osborn .40 .18
❑ 283 Merv Rettenmund .40 .18
❑ 284 Steve Ontiveros .40 .18
❑ 285 Mike Cuellar .75 .35
❑ 286 Jim Wohlford .40 .18
❑ 287 Pete Mackanin .40 .18
❑ 288 Bill Campbell .40 .18
❑ 289 Enzo Hernandez .40 .18
❑ 290 Ted Simmons .75 .35
❑ 291 Ken Sanders .40 .18
❑ 292 Leon Roberts .40 .18
❑ 293 Bill Castro .40 .18
❑ 294 Ed Kirkpatrick .40 .18
❑ 295 Dave Cash .40 .18
❑ 296 Pat Dobson .40 .18
❑ 297 Roger Metzger .40 .18
❑ 298 Dick Bosman .40 .18
❑ 299 Champ Summers .40 .18
❑ 300 Johnny Bench 12.00 5.50
❑ 301 Jackie Brown .40 .18
❑ 302 Rick Miller .40 .18
❑ 303 Steve Foucault .40 .18
❑ 304 California Angels 1.50 .30
Team Card;
Dick Williams MG
(Checklist back)
❑ 305 Andy Messersmith .75 .35
❑ 306 Rod Gilbreath .40 .18
❑ 307 Al Bumbry .75 .35
❑ 308 Jim Barr .40 .18
❑ 309 Bill Melton .40 .18
❑ 310 Randy Jones .75 .35
❑ 311 Cookie Rojas .75 .35
❑ 312 Don Carrithers .40 .18
❑ 313 Dan Ford .40 .18
❑ 314 Ed Kranepool .40 .18
❑ 315 Al Hrabosky .75 .35
❑ 316 Robin Yount 15.00 6.75
❑ 317 John Candelaria RC 1.50 .70
❑ 318 Bob Boone 1.50 .70
❑ 319 Larry Gura .40 .18
❑ 320 Willie Horton .75 .35
❑ 321 Jose Cruz 1.50 .70
❑ 322 Glenn Abbott .40 .18
❑ 323 Rob Sperring .40 .18
❑ 324 Jim Bibby .40 .18
❑ 325 Tony Perez 2.50 1.10
❑ 326 Dick Pole .40 .18
❑ 327 Dave Moates .40 .18
❑ 328 Carl Morton .40 .18
❑ 329 Joe Ferguson .40 .18
❑ 330 Nolan Ryan 30.00 13.50
❑ 331 San Diego Padres 1.50 .30
Team Card;
John McNamara MG
(Checklist back)
❑ 332 Charlie Williams .40 .18
❑ 333 Bob Coluccio .40 .18
❑ 334 Dennis Leonard .75 .35
❑ 335 Bob Grich .75 .35
❑ 336 Vic Albury .40 .18
❑ 337 Bud Harrelson .75 .35
❑ 338 Bob Bailey .40 .18
❑ 339 John Denny .75 .35
❑ 340 Jim Rice 2.50 1.10
❑ 341 Lou Gehrig ATG 15.00 6.75
❑ 342 Rogers Hornsby ATG 3.00 1.35
❑ 343 Pie Traynor ATG 1.50 .70
❑ 344 Honus Wagner ATG 5.00 2.20
❑ 345 Babe Ruth ATG 20.00 9.00
❑ 346 Ty Cobb ATG 12.00 5.50
❑ 347 Ted Williams ATG 15.00 6.75
❑ 348 Mickey Cochrane ATG 1.50 .70
❑ 349 Walter Johnson ATG 5.00 2.20
❑ 350 Lefty Grove ATG 1.50 .70
❑ 351 Randy Hundley .75 .35
❑ 352 Dave Giusti .40 .18
❑ 353 Sixto Lezcano .75 .35
❑ 354 Ron Blomberg .40 .18
❑ 355 Steve Carlton 6.00 2.70
❑ 356 Ted Martinez .40 .18
❑ 357 Ken Forsch .40 .18
❑ 358 Buddy Bell .75 .35
❑ 359 Rick Reuschel .75 .35
❑ 360 Jeff Burroughs .75 .35
❑ 361 Detroit Tigers 1.50 .30
Team Card;
Ralph Houk MG
(Checklist back)
❑ 362 Will McEnaney .75 .35
❑ 363 Dave Collins RC .75 .35
❑ 364 Elias Sosa .40 .18
❑ 365 Carlton Fisk 5.00 2.20
❑ 366 Bobby Valentine .75 .35
❑ 367 Bruce Miller .40 .18
❑ 368 Wilbur Wood .40 .18
❑ 369 Frank White .75 .35
❑ 370 Ron Cey .75 .35
❑ 371 Elrod Hendricks .40 .18
❑ 372 Rick Baldwin .40 .18
❑ 373 Johnny Briggs .40 .18
❑ 374 Dan Warthen .40 .18
❑ 375 Ron Fairly .75 .35
❑ 376 Rich Hebner .75 .35
❑ 377 Mike Hegan .40 .18
❑ 378 Steve Stone .75 .35
❑ 379 Ken Boswell .40 .18
❑ 380 Bobby Bonds 1.50 .70
❑ 381 Denny Doyle .40 .18
❑ 382 Matt Alexander .40 .18
❑ 383 John Ellis .40 .18
❑ 384 Philadelphia Phillies 1.50 .30
Team Card;
Danny Ozark MG
(Checklist back)
❑ 385 Mickey Lolich .75 .35
❑ 386 Ed Goodson .40 .18
❑ 387 Mike Miley .40 .18
❑ 388 Stan Perzanowski .40 .18
❑ 389 Glenn Adams .40 .18
❑ 390 Don Gullett .75 .35
❑ 391 Jerry Hairston .40 .18
❑ 392 Checklist 265-396 1.50 .30

❑ 393 Paul Mitchell .40 .18
❑ 394 Fran Healy .40 .18
❑ 395 Jim Wynn .75 .35
❑ 396 Bill Lee .40 .18
❑ 397 Tim Foli .40 .18
❑ 398 Dave Tomlin .40 .18
❑ 399 Luis Melendez .40 .18
❑ 400 Rod Carew 6.00 2.70
❑ 401 Ken Brett .40 .18
❑ 402 Don Money .75 .35
❑ 403 Geoff Zahn .40 .18
❑ 404 Enos Cabell .40 .18
❑ 405 Rollie Fingers 2.50 1.10
❑ 406 Ed Herrmann .40 .18
❑ 407 Tom Underwood .40 .18
❑ 408 Charlie Spikes .40 .18
❑ 409 Dave Lemanczyk .40 .18
❑ 410 Ralph Garr .75 .35
❑ 411 Bill Singer .40 .18
❑ 412 Toby Harrah .75 .35
❑ 413 Pete Varney .40 .18
❑ 414 Wayne Garland .40 .18
❑ 415 Vada Pinson 1.50 .70
❑ 416 Tommy John 1.50 .70
❑ 417 Gene Clines .40 .18
❑ 418 Jose Morales RC .40 .18
❑ 419 Reggie Cleveland .40 .18
❑ 420 Joe Morgan 5.00 2.20
❑ 421 Oakland A's 1.50 .30
Team Card;
(No MG on front;
checklist back)
❑ 422 Johnny Grubb .40 .18
❑ 423 Ed Halicki .40 .18
❑ 424 Phil Roof .40 .18
❑ 425 Rennie Stennett .40 .18
❑ 426 Bob Forsch .40 .18
❑ 427 Kurt Bevacqua .40 .18
❑ 428 Jim Crawford .40 .18
❑ 429 Fred Stanley .40 .18
❑ 430 Jose Cardenal .75 .35
❑ 431 Dick Ruthven .40 .18
❑ 432 Tom Veryzer .40 .18
❑ 433 Rick Waits .40 .18
❑ 434 Morris Nettles .40 .18
❑ 435 Phil Niekro 2.50 1.10
❑ 436 Bill Fahey .40 .18
❑ 437 Terry Forster .40 .18
❑ 438 Doug DeCinces .75 .35
❑ 439 Rick Rhoden .75 .35
❑ 440 John Mayberry .75 .35
❑ 441 Gary Carter 4.00 1.80
❑ 442 Hank Webb .40 .18
❑ 443 San Francisco Giants 1.50 .30
Team Card;
(No MG on front;
checklist back)
❑ 444 Gary Nolan .75 .35
❑ 445 Rico Petrocelli .75 .35
❑ 446 Larry Haney .40 .18
❑ 447 Gene Locklear .75 .35
❑ 448 Tom Johnson .40 .18
❑ 449 Bob Robertson .40 .18
❑ 450 Jim Palmer 5.00 2.20
❑ 451 Buddy Bradford .40 .18
❑ 452 Tom Hausman .40 .18
❑ 453 Lou Piniella 1.50 .70
❑ 454 Tom Griffin .40 .18
❑ 455 Dick Allen 1.50 .70
❑ 456 Joe Coleman .40 .18
❑ 457 Ed Crosby .40 .18
❑ 458 Earl Williams .40 .18
❑ 459 Jim Brewer .40 .18
❑ 460 Cesar Cedeno .75 .35
❑ 461 NL and AL Champs .75 .35
Reds sweep Bucs,
Bosox surprise A's
❑ 462 '75 World Series .75 .35
Reds Champs
❑ 463 Steve Hargan .40 .18
❑ 464 Ken Henderson .40 .18
❑ 465 Mike Marshall .75 .35
❑ 466 Bob Stinson .40 .18
❑ 467 Woodie Fryman .40 .18
❑ 468 Jesus Alou .40 .18
❑ 469 Rawly Eastwick .75 .35
❑ 470 Bobby Murcer .75 .35
❑ 471 Jim Burton .40 .18
❑ 472 Bob Davis .40 .18
❑ 473 Paul Blair .75 .35
❑ 474 Ray Corbin .40 .18
❑ 475 Joe Rudi .75 .35
❑ 476 Bob Moose .40 .18
❑ 477 Cleveland Indians 1.50 .30
Team Card;
Frank Robinson MG
(Checklist back)
❑ 478 Lynn McGlothen .40 .18
❑ 479 Bobby Mitchell .40 .18
❑ 480 Mike Schmidt 15.00 6.75
❑ 481 Rudy May .40 .18
❑ 482 Tim Hosley .40 .18
❑ 483 Mickey Stanley .40 .18
❑ 484 Eric Raich .40 .18
❑ 485 Mike Hargrove .75 .35
❑ 486 Bruce Dal Canton .40 .18
❑ 487 Leron Lee .40 .18
❑ 488 Claude Osteen .75 .35
❑ 489 Skip Jutze .40 .18
❑ 490 Frank Tanana .75 .35
❑ 491 Terry Crowley .40 .18
❑ 492 Marty Pattin .40 .18
❑ 493 Derrel Thomas .40 .18
❑ 494 Craig Swan .75 .35
❑ 495 Nate Colbert .40 .18
❑ 496 Juan Beniquez .40 .18
❑ 497 Joe McIntosh .40 .18
❑ 498 Glenn Borgmann .40 .18
❑ 499 Mario Guerrero .40 .18
❑ 500 Reggie Jackson 12.00 5.50
❑ 501 Billy Champion .40 .18
❑ 502 Tim McCarver 1.50 .70
❑ 503 Elliott Maddox .40 .18
❑ 504 Pittsburgh Pirates 1.50 .30
Team Card;
Danny Murtaugh MG
(Checklist back)
❑ 505 Mark Belanger .75 .35
❑ 506 George Mitterwald .40 .18
❑ 507 Ray Bare .40 .18
❑ 508 Duane Kuiper .40 .18
❑ 509 Bill Hands .40 .18
❑ 510 Amos Otis .75 .35
❑ 511 Jamie Easterley .40 .18
❑ 512 Ellie Rodriguez .40 .18
❑ 513 Bart Johnson .40 .18
❑ 514 Dan Driessen .75 .35
❑ 515 Steve Yeager .75 .35
❑ 516 Wayne Granger .40 .18
❑ 517 John Milner .40 .18
❑ 518 Doug Flynn .40 .18
❑ 519 Steve Brye .40 .18
❑ 520 Willie McCovey 5.00 2.20
❑ 521 Jim Colborn .40 .18
❑ 522 Ted Sizemore .40 .18
❑ 523 Bob Montgomery .40 .18
❑ 524 Pete Falcone .40 .18
❑ 525 Billy Williams 2.50 1.10
❑ 526 Checklist 397-528 1.50 .30
❑ 527 Mike Anderson .40 .18
❑ 528 Dock Ellis .40 .18
❑ 529 Deron Johnson .75 .35
❑ 530 Don Sutton 2.50 1.10
❑ 531 New York Mets 1.50 .30
Team Card;
Joe Frazier MG
(Checklist back)
❑ 532 Milt May .40 .18
❑ 533 Lee Richard .40 .18
❑ 534 Stan Bahnsen .40 .18
❑ 535 Dave Nelson .40 .18
❑ 536 Mike Thompson .40 .18
❑ 537 Tony Muser .40 .18
❑ 538 Pat Darcy .40 .18
❑ 539 John Balaz .75 .35
❑ 540 Bill Freehan .75 .35
❑ 541 Steve Mingori .40 .18
❑ 542 Keith Hernandez 1.50 .70
❑ 543 Wayne Twitchell .40 .18
❑ 544 Pepe Frias .40 .18
❑ 545 Sparky Lyle .75 .35
❑ 546 Dave Rosello .40 .18
❑ 547 Roric Harrison .40 .18
❑ 548 Manny Mota .75 .35
❑ 549 Randy Tate .40 .18
❑ 550 Hank Aaron 25.00 11.00
❑ 551 Jerry DaVanon .40 .18
❑ 552 Terry Humphrey .40 .18
❑ 553 Randy Moffitt .40 .18
❑ 554 Ray Fosse .40 .18
❑ 555 Dyar Miller .40 .18
❑ 556 Minnesota Twins 1.50 .30
Team Card;
Gene Mauch MG
(Checklist back)
❑ 557 Dan Spillner .40 .18
❑ 558 Clarence Gaston .75 .35
❑ 559 Clyde Wright .40 .18
❑ 560 Jorge Orta .40 .18
❑ 561 Tom Carroll .40 .18
❑ 562 Adrian Garrett .40 .18
❑ 563 Larry Demery .40 .18
❑ 564 Bubble Gum Champ 1.50 .70
Kurt Bevacqua
❑ 565 Tug McGraw .75 .35
❑ 566 Ken McMullen .40 .18
❑ 567 George Stone .40 .18
❑ 568 Rob Andrews .40 .18
❑ 569 Nelson Briles .75 .35
❑ 570 George Hendrick .75 .35
❑ 571 Don DeMola .40 .18
❑ 572 Rich Coggins .40 .18
❑ 573 Bill Travers .40 .18
❑ 574 Don Kessinger .75 .35
❑ 575 Dwight Evans 1.50 .70
❑ 576 Maximino Leon .40 .18
❑ 577 Marc Hill .40 .18
❑ 578 Ted Kubiak .40 .18
❑ 579 Clay Kirby .40 .18
❑ 580 Bert Campaneris .75 .35
❑ 581 St. Louis Cardinals 1.50 .30
Team Card;
Red Schoendienst MG
(Checklist back)
❑ 582 Mike Kekich .40 .18
❑ 583 Tommy Helms .40 .18
❑ 584 Stan Wall .40 .18
❑ 585 Joe Torre 1.50 .70
❑ 586 Ron Schueler .40 .18
❑ 587 Leo Cardenas .40 .18
❑ 588 Kevin Kobel .40 .18
❑ 589 Rookie Pitchers 1.50 .70
Santo Alcala
Mike Flanagan RC
Joe Pactwa
Pablo Torrealba
❑ 590 Rookie Outfielders .75 .35
Henry Cruz
Chet Lemon RC
Ellis Valentine
Terry Whitfield
❑ 591 Rookie Pitchers .75 .35
Steve Grilli
Craig Mitchell
Jose Sosa
George Throop
❑ 592 Rookie Infielders 6.00 2.70
Willie Randolph RC
Dave McKay
Jerry Royster
Roy Staiger
❑ 593 Rookie Pitchers .75 .35
Larry Anderson
Ken Crosby
Mark Littell
Butch Metzger
❑ 594 Rookie Catchers/OF .75 .35
Andy Merchant
Ed Ott
Royle Stillman
Jerry White
❑ 595 Rookie Pitchers .75 .35
Art DeFillipis
Randy Lerch
Sid Monge
Steve Barr
❑ 596 Rookie Infielders .75 .35
Craig Reynolds

| Card | NRMT | VG-E |
|---|---|---|
| Lamar Johnson | | |
| Johnnie LeMaster | | |
| Jerry Manuel | | |
| ❑ 597 Rookie Pitchers | .75 | .35 |
| Don Aase | | |
| Jack Kucek | | |
| Frank LaCorte | | |
| Mike Pazik | | |
| ❑ 598 Rookie Outfielders | .75 | .35 |
| Hector Cruz | | |
| Jamie Quirk | | |
| Jerry Turner | | |
| Joe Wallis | | |
| ❑ 599 Rookie Pitchers | 6.00 | 2.70 |
| Rob Dressler | | |
| Ron Guidry RC | | |
| Bob McClure | | |
| Pat Zachry | | |
| ❑ 600 Tom Seaver | 12.00 | 5.50 |
| ❑ 601 Ken Rudolph | .40 | .18 |
| ❑ 602 Doug Konieczny | .40 | .18 |
| ❑ 603 Jim Holt | .40 | .18 |
| ❑ 604 Joe Lovitto | .40 | .18 |
| ❑ 605 Al Downing | .40 | .18 |
| ❑ 606 Milwaukee Brewers | 1.50 | .30 |
| Team Card; | | |
| Alex Grammas MG | | |
| (Checklist back) | | |
| ❑ 607 Rich Hinton | .40 | .18 |
| ❑ 608 Vic Correll | .40 | .18 |
| ❑ 609 Fred Norman | .75 | .35 |
| ❑ 610 Greg Luzinski | 1.50 | .70 |
| ❑ 611 Rich Folkers | .40 | .18 |
| ❑ 612 Joe Lahoud | .40 | .18 |
| ❑ 613 Tim Johnson | .40 | .18 |
| ❑ 614 Fernando Arroyo | .40 | .18 |
| ❑ 615 Mike Cubbage | .40 | .18 |
| ❑ 616 Buck Martinez | .40 | .18 |
| ❑ 617 Darold Knowles | .40 | .18 |
| ❑ 618 Jack Brohamer | .40 | .18 |
| ❑ 619 Bill Butler | .40 | .18 |
| ❑ 620 Al Oliver | .75 | .35 |
| ❑ 621 Tom Hall | .40 | .18 |
| ❑ 622 Rick Auerbach | .40 | .18 |
| ❑ 623 Bob Allietta | .40 | .18 |
| ❑ 624 Tony Taylor | .75 | .35 |
| ❑ 625 J.R. Richard | .75 | .35 |
| ❑ 626 Bob Sheldon | .40 | .18 |
| ❑ 627 Bill Plummer | .40 | .18 |
| ❑ 628 John D'Acquisto | .40 | .18 |
| ❑ 629 Sandy Alomar | .75 | .35 |
| ❑ 630 Chris Speier | .40 | .18 |
| ❑ 631 Atlanta Braves | 1.50 | .30 |
| Team Card; | | |
| Dave Bristol MG | | |
| (Checklist back) | | |
| ❑ 632 Rogelio Moret | .40 | .18 |
| ❑ 633 John Stearns RC | .75 | .35 |
| ❑ 634 Larry Christenson | .40 | .18 |
| ❑ 635 Jim Fregosi | .75 | .35 |
| ❑ 636 Joe Decker | .40 | .18 |
| ❑ 637 Bruce Bochte | .40 | .18 |
| ❑ 638 Doyle Alexander | .75 | .35 |
| ❑ 639 Fred Kendall | .40 | .18 |
| ❑ 640 Bill Madlock | 1.50 | .70 |
| ❑ 641 Tom Paciorek | .75 | .35 |
| ❑ 642 Dennis Blair | .40 | .18 |
| ❑ 643 Checklist 529-660 | 1.50 | .30 |
| ❑ 644 Tom Bradley | .40 | .18 |
| ❑ 645 Darrell Porter | .75 | .35 |
| ❑ 646 John Lowenstein | .40 | .18 |
| ❑ 647 Ramon Hernandez | .40 | .18 |
| ❑ 648 Al Cowens | .40 | .18 |
| ❑ 649 Dave Roberts | .40 | .18 |
| ❑ 650 Thurman Munson | 5.00 | 2.20 |
| ❑ 651 John Odom | .40 | .18 |
| ❑ 652 Ed Armbrister | .40 | .18 |
| ❑ 653 Mike Norris | .75 | .35 |
| ❑ 654 Doug Griffin | .40 | .18 |
| ❑ 655 Mike Vail | .40 | .18 |
| ❑ 656 Chicago White Sox | 1.50 | .30 |
| Team Card; | | |
| Chuck Tanner MG | | |
| (Checklist back) | | |
| ❑ 657 Roy Smalley RC | .75 | .35 |
| ❑ 658 Jerry Johnson | .40 | .18 |
| ❑ 659 Ben Oglivie | .75 | .35 |
| ❑ 660 Dave Lopes | 1.50 | .30 |

## 1976 Topps Traded

| | NRMT | VG-E |
|---|---|---|
| COMPLETE SET (44) | 30.00 | 13.50 |
| ❑ 27T Ed Figueroa | .40 | .18 |
| ❑ 28T Dusty Baker | 1.50 | .70 |
| ❑ 44T Doug Rader | .75 | .35 |
| ❑ 58T Ron Reed | .40 | .18 |
| ❑ 74T Oscar Gamble | 1.50 | .70 |
| ❑ 80T Jim Kaat | 1.50 | .70 |
| ❑ 83T Jim Spencer | .40 | .18 |
| ❑ 85T Mickey Rivers | .75 | .35 |
| ❑ 99T Lee Lacy | .40 | .18 |
| ❑ 120T Rusty Staub | .75 | .35 |
| ❑ 127T Larvell Blanks | .40 | .18 |
| ❑ 146T George Medich | .40 | .18 |
| ❑ 158T Ken Reitz | .40 | .18 |
| ❑ 208T Mike Lum | .40 | .18 |
| ❑ 211T Clay Carroll | .40 | .18 |
| ❑ 231T Tom House | .40 | .18 |
| ❑ 250T Fergie Jenkins | 3.00 | 1.35 |
| ❑ 259T Darrel Chaney | .40 | .18 |
| ❑ 292T Leon Roberts | .40 | .18 |
| ❑ 296T Pat Dobson | .40 | .18 |
| ❑ 309T Bill Melton | .40 | .18 |
| ❑ 338T Bob Bailey | .40 | .18 |
| ❑ 380T Bobby Bonds | 1.50 | .70 |
| ❑ 383T John Ellis | .40 | .18 |
| ❑ 385T Mickey Lolich | .75 | .35 |
| ❑ 401T Ken Brett | .40 | .18 |
| ❑ 410T Ralph Garr | .40 | .18 |
| ❑ 411T Bill Singer | .40 | .18 |
| ❑ 428T Jim Crawford | .40 | .18 |
| ❑ 434T Morris Nettles | .40 | .18 |
| ❑ 464T Ken Henderson | .40 | .18 |
| ❑ 497T Joe McIntosh | .40 | .18 |
| ❑ 524T Pete Falcone | .40 | .18 |
| ❑ 527T Mike Anderson | .40 | .18 |
| ❑ 528T Dock Ellis | .40 | .18 |
| ❑ 532T Milt May | .40 | .18 |
| ❑ 554T Ray Fosse | .40 | .18 |
| ❑ 579T Clay Kirby | .40 | .18 |
| ❑ 583T Tommy Helms | .40 | .18 |
| ❑ 592T Willie Randolph | 5.00 | 2.20 |
| ❑ 618T Jack Brohamer | .40 | .18 |
| ❑ 632T Rogelio Moret | .40 | .18 |
| ❑ 649T Dave Roberts | .40 | .18 |
| ❑ NNO Traded Checklist | 2.00 | .40 |

## 1977 Topps

| | NRMT | VG-E |
|---|---|---|
| COMPLETE SET (660) | 250.00 | 110.00 |
| ❑ 1 Batting Leaders | 8.00 | 2.30 |
| George Brett | | |
| Bill Madlock | | |
| ❑ 2 Home Run Leaders | 2.50 | 1.10 |
| Graig Nettles | | |
| Mike Schmidt | | |
| ❑ 3 RBI Leaders | 1.50 | .70 |
| Lee May | | |
| George Foster | | |
| ❑ 4 Stolen Base Leaders | .75 | .35 |

| Card | NRMT | VG-E |
|---|---|---|
| Bill North | | |
| Dave Lopes | | |
| ❑ 5 Victory Leaders | 1.50 | .70 |
| Jim Palmer | | |
| Randy Jones | | |
| ❑ 6 Strikeout Leaders | 15.00 | 6.75 |
| Nolan Ryan | | |
| Tom Seaver | | |
| ❑ 7 ERA Leaders | .75 | .35 |
| Mark Fidrych | | |
| John Denny | | |
| ❑ 8 Firemen Leaders | .75 | .35 |
| Bill Campbell | | |
| Rawly Eastwick | | |
| ❑ 9 Doug Rader | .30 | .14 |
| ❑ 10 Reggie Jackson | 10.00 | 4.50 |
| ❑ 11 Rob Dressler | .30 | .14 |
| ❑ 12 Larry Haney | .30 | .14 |
| ❑ 13 Luis Gomez | .30 | .14 |
| ❑ 14 Tommy Smith | .30 | .14 |
| ❑ 15 Don Gullett | .75 | .35 |
| ❑ 16 Bob Jones | .30 | .14 |
| ❑ 17 Steve Stone | .75 | .35 |
| ❑ 18 Indians Team/Mgr. | 1.50 | .30 |
| Frank Robinson | | |
| (Checklist back) | | |
| ❑ 19 John D'Acquisto | .30 | .14 |
| ❑ 20 Graig Nettles | 1.50 | .70 |
| ❑ 21 Ken Forsch | .30 | .14 |
| ❑ 22 Bill Freehan | .75 | .35 |
| ❑ 23 Dan Driessen | .30 | .14 |
| ❑ 24 Carl Morton | .30 | .14 |
| ❑ 25 Dwight Evans | 1.50 | .70 |
| ❑ 26 Ray Sadecki | .30 | .14 |
| ❑ 27 Bill Buckner | .75 | .35 |
| ❑ 28 Woodie Fryman | .30 | .14 |
| ❑ 29 Bucky Dent | .75 | .35 |
| ❑ 30 Greg Luzinski | 1.50 | .70 |
| ❑ 31 Jim Todd | .30 | .14 |
| ❑ 32 Checklist 1-132 | 1.50 | .30 |
| ❑ 33 Wayne Garland | .30 | .14 |
| ❑ 34 Angels Team/Mgr. | 1.50 | .30 |
| Norm Sherry | | |
| (Checklist back) | | |
| ❑ 35 Rennie Stennett | .30 | .14 |
| ❑ 36 John Ellis | .30 | .14 |
| ❑ 37 Steve Hargan | .30 | .14 |
| ❑ 38 Craig Kusick | .30 | .14 |
| ❑ 39 Tom Griffin | .30 | .14 |
| ❑ 40 Bobby Murcer | .75 | .35 |
| ❑ 41 Jim Kern | .30 | .14 |
| ❑ 42 Jose Cruz | .75 | .35 |
| ❑ 43 Ray Bare | .30 | .14 |
| ❑ 44 Bud Harrelson | .75 | .35 |
| ❑ 45 Rawly Eastwick | .30 | .14 |
| ❑ 46 Buck Martinez | .30 | .14 |
| ❑ 47 Lynn McGlothen | .30 | .14 |
| ❑ 48 Tom Paciorek | .75 | .35 |
| ❑ 49 Grant Jackson | .30 | .14 |
| ❑ 50 Ron Cey | .75 | .35 |
| ❑ 51 Brewers Team/Mgr. | 1.50 | .30 |
| Alex Grammas | | |
| (Checklist back) | | |
| ❑ 52 Ellis Valentine | .30 | .14 |
| ❑ 53 Paul Mitchell | .30 | .14 |
| ❑ 54 Sandy Alomar | .75 | .35 |
| ❑ 55 Jeff Burroughs | .75 | .35 |
| ❑ 56 Rudy May | .30 | .14 |

❑ 57 Marc Hill .30 .14
❑ 58 Chet Lemon .75 .35
❑ 59 Larry Christenson .30 .14
❑ 60 Jim Rice 2.50 1.10
❑ 61 Manny Sanguillen .75 .35
❑ 62 Eric Raich .30 .14
❑ 63 Tito Fuentes .30 .14
❑ 64 Larry Biittner .30 .14
❑ 65 Skip Lockwood .30 .14
❑ 66 Roy Smalley .75 .35
❑ 67 Joaquin Andujar RC .75 .35
❑ 68 Bruce Bochte .30 .14
❑ 69 Jim Crawford .30 .14
❑ 70 Johnny Bench 10.00 4.50
❑ 71 Dock Ellis .30 .14
❑ 72 Mike Anderson .30 .14
❑ 73 Charlie Williams .30 .14
❑ 74 A's Team/Mgr. 1.50 .30
Jack McKeon
(Checklist back)
❑ 75 Dennis Leonard .75 .35
❑ 76 Tim Foli .30 .14
❑ 77 Dyar Miller .30 .14
❑ 78 Bob Davis .30 .14
❑ 79 Don Money .75 .35
❑ 80 Andy Messersmith .75 .35
❑ 81 Juan Beniquez .30 .14
❑ 82 Jim Rooker .30 .14
❑ 83 Kevin Bell .30 .14
❑ 84 Ollie Brown .30 .14
❑ 85 Duane Kuiper .30 .14
❑ 86 Pat Zachry .30 .14
❑ 87 Glenn Borgmann .30 .14
❑ 88 Stan Wall .30 .14
❑ 89 Butch Hobson RC .75 .35
❑ 90 Cesar Cedeno .75 .35
❑ 91 John Verhoeven .30 .14
❑ 92 Dave Rosello .30 .14
❑ 93 Tom Poquette .30 .14
❑ 94 Craig Swan .30 .14
❑ 95 Keith Hernandez .75 .35
❑ 96 Lou Piniella .75 .35
❑ 97 Dave Heaverlo .30 .14
❑ 98 Milt May .30 .14
❑ 99 Tom Hausman .30 .14
❑ 100 Joe Morgan 4.00 1.80
❑ 101 Dick Bosman .30 .14
❑ 102 Jose Morales .30 .14
❑ 103 Mike Bacsik .30 .14
❑ 104 Omar Moreno .75 .35
❑ 105 Steve Yeager .75 .35
❑ 106 Mike Flanagan .75 .35
❑ 107 Bill Melton .30 .14
❑ 108 Alan Foster .30 .14
❑ 109 Jorge Orta .30 .14
❑ 110 Steve Carlton 5.00 2.20
❑ 111 Rico Petrocelli .75 .35
❑ 112 Bill Greif .30 .14
❑ 113 Blue Jays Leaders 1.50 .30
Roy Hartsfield MG
Don Leppert CO
Bob Miller CO
Jackie Moore CO
Harry Warner CO
(Checklist back)
❑ 114 Bruce Dal Canton .30 .14
❑ 115 Rick Manning .30 .14
❑ 116 Joe Niekro .75 .35
❑ 117 Frank White .75 .35
❑ 118 Rick Jones .30 .14
❑ 119 John Stearns .30 .14
❑ 120 Rod Carew 5.00 2.20
❑ 121 Gary Nolan .30 .14
❑ 122 Ben Oglivie .75 .35
❑ 123 Fred Stanley .30 .14
❑ 124 George Mitterwald .30 .14
❑ 125 Bill Travers .30 .14
❑ 126 Rod Gilbreath .30 .14
❑ 127 Ron Fairly .75 .35
❑ 128 Tommy John 1.50 .70
❑ 129 Mike Sadek .30 .14
❑ 130 Al Oliver .75 .35
❑ 131 Orlando Ramirez .30 .14
❑ 132 Chip Lang .30 .14
❑ 133 Ralph Garr .75 .35
❑ 134 Padres Team/Mgr. 1.50 .30
John McNamara
(Checklist back)
❑ 135 Mark Belanger .75 .35
❑ 136 Jerry Mumphrey .75 .35
❑ 137 Jeff Terpko .30 .14
❑ 138 Bob Stinson .30 .14
❑ 139 Fred Norman .30 .14
❑ 140 Mike Schmidt 12.00 5.50
❑ 141 Mark Littell .30 .14
❑ 142 Steve Dillard .30 .14
❑ 143 Ed Herrmann .30 .14
❑ 144 Bruce Sutter RC 3.00 1.35
❑ 145 Tom Veryzer .30 .14
❑ 146 Dusty Baker 1.50 .70
❑ 147 Jackie Brown .30 .14
❑ 148 Fran Healy .30 .14
❑ 149 Mike Cubbage .30 .14
❑ 150 Tom Seaver 10.00 4.50
❑ 151 Johnny LeMaster .30 .14
❑ 152 Gaylord Perry 2.50 1.10
❑ 153 Ron Jackson .30 .14
❑ 154 Dave Giusti .30 .14
❑ 155 Joe Rudi .75 .35
❑ 156 Pete Mackanin .30 .14
❑ 157 Ken Brett .30 .14
❑ 158 Ted Kubiak .30 .14
❑ 159 Bernie Carbo .30 .14
❑ 160 Will McEnaney .30 .14
❑ 161 Garry Templeton RC 1.50 .70
❑ 162 Mike Cuellar .75 .35
❑ 163 Dave Hilton .30 .14
❑ 164 Tug McGraw .75 .35
❑ 165 Jim Wynn .75 .35
❑ 166 Bill Campbell .30 .14
❑ 167 Rich Hebner .75 .35
❑ 168 Charlie Spikes .30 .14
❑ 169 Darold Knowles .30 .14
❑ 170 Thurman Munson 4.00 1.80
❑ 171 Ken Sanders .30 .14
❑ 172 John Milner .30 .14
❑ 173 Chuck Scrivener .30 .14
❑ 174 Nelson Briles .75 .35
❑ 175 Butch Wynegar .75 .35
❑ 176 Bob Robertson .30 .14
❑ 177 Bart Johnson .30 .14
❑ 178 Bombo Rivera .30 .14
❑ 179 Paul Hartzell .30 .14
❑ 180 Dave Lopes .75 .35
❑ 181 Ken McMullen .30 .14
❑ 182 Dan Spillner .30 .14
❑ 183 Cardinals Team/Mgr. 1.50 .30
Vern Rapp
(Checklist back)
❑ 184 Bo McLaughlin .30 .14
❑ 185 Sixto Lezcano .30 .14
❑ 186 Doug Flynn .30 .14
❑ 187 Dick Pole .30 .14
❑ 188 Bob Tolan .30 .14
❑ 189 Rick Dempsey .75 .35
❑ 190 Ray Burris .30 .14
❑ 191 Doug Griffin .30 .14
❑ 192 Clarence Gaston .75 .35
❑ 193 Larry Gura .30 .14
❑ 194 Gary Matthews .75 .35
❑ 195 Ed Figueroa .30 .14
❑ 196 Len Randle .30 .14
❑ 197 Ed Ott .30 .14
❑ 198 Wilbur Wood .30 .14
❑ 199 Pepe Frias .30 .14
❑ 200 Frank Tanana .75 .35
❑ 201 Ed Kranepool .30 .14
❑ 202 Tom Johnson .30 .14
❑ 203 Ed Armbrister .30 .14
❑ 204 Jeff Newman .30 .14
❑ 205 Pete Falcone .30 .14
❑ 206 Boog Powell 1.50 .70
❑ 207 Glenn Abbott .30 .14
❑ 208 Checklist 133-264 1.50 .30
❑ 209 Rob Andrews .30 .14
❑ 210 Fred Lynn .75 .15
❑ 211 Giants Team/Mgr. 1.50 .70
Joe Altobelli
(Checklist back)
❑ 212 Jim Mason .30 .14
❑ 213 Maximino Leon .30 .14
❑ 214 Darrell Porter .75 .35
❑ 215 Butch Metzger .30 .14
❑ 216 Doug DeCinces .75 .35
❑ 217 Tom Underwood .30 .14
❑ 218 John Wathan RC .30 .14
❑ 219 Joe Coleman .30 .14
❑ 220 Chris Chambliss .75 .35
❑ 221 Bob Bailey .30 .14
❑ 222 Francisco Barrios .30 .14
❑ 223 Earl Williams .30 .14
❑ 224 Rusty Torres .30 .14
❑ 225 Bob Apodaca .30 .14
❑ 226 Leroy Stanton .75 .35
❑ 227 Joe Sambito .30 .14
❑ 228 Twins Team/Mgr. 1.50 .30
Gene Mauch
(Checklist back)
❑ 229 Don Kessinger .75 .35
❑ 230 Vida Blue .75 .35
❑ 231 George Brett RB 8.00 3.60
Most consecutive games
3 or more hits
❑ 232 Minnie Minoso RB .75 .35
Oldest to hit safely
❑ 233 Jose Morales RB .30 .14
Most pinch-hits season
❑ 234 Nolan Ryan RB 15.00 6.75
Most seasons, 300 strikeouts
❑ 235 Cecil Cooper .75 .35
❑ 236 Tom Buskey .30 .14
❑ 237 Gene Clines .30 .14
❑ 238 Tippy Martinez .30 .14
❑ 239 Bill Plummer .30 .14
❑ 240 Ron LeFlore .75 .35
❑ 241 Dave Tomlin .30 .14
❑ 242 Ken Henderson .30 .14
❑ 243 Ron Reed .30 .14
❑ 244 John Mayberry .75 .35
(Cartoon mentions
T206 Wagner)
❑ 245 Rick Rhoden .75 .35
❑ 246 Mike Vail .30 .14
❑ 247 Chris Knapp .30 .14
❑ 248 Wilbur Howard .30 .14
❑ 249 Pete Redfern .30 .14
❑ 250 Bill Madlock .75 .35
❑ 251 Tony Muser .30 .14
❑ 252 Dale Murray .30 .14
❑ 253 John Hale .30 .14
❑ 254 Doyle Alexander .30 .14
❑ 255 George Scott .75 .35
❑ 256 Joe Hoerner .30 .14
❑ 257 Mike Miley .30 .14
❑ 258 Luis Tiant .75 .35
❑ 259 Mets Team/Mgr. 1.50 .30
Joe Frazier
(Checklist back)
❑ 260 J.R. Richard .75 .35
❑ 261 Phil Garner .75 .35
❑ 262 Al Cowens .30 .14
❑ 263 Mike Marshall .75 .35
❑ 264 Tom Hutton .30 .14
❑ 265 Mark Fidrych RC 3.00 1.35
❑ 266 Derrel Thomas .30 .14
❑ 267 Ray Fosse .30 .14
❑ 268 Rick Sawyer .30 .14
❑ 269 Joe Lis .30 .14
❑ 270 Dave Parker 1.50 .70
❑ 271 Terry Forster .30 .14
❑ 272 Lee Lacy .30 .14
❑ 273 Eric Soderholm .30 .14
❑ 274 Don Stanhouse .30 .14
❑ 275 Mike Hargrove .75 .35
❑ 276 Chris Chambliss ALCS 1.50 .70
homer decides it
❑ 277 Pete Rose NLCS 5.00 2.20
❑ 278 Danny Frisella .30 .14
❑ 279 Joe Wallis .30 .14
❑ 280 Jim Hunter 2.50 1.10
❑ 281 Roy Staiger .30 .14
❑ 282 Sid Monge .30 .14
❑ 283 Jerry DaVanon .30 .14
❑ 284 Mike Norris .30 .14
❑ 285 Brooks Robinson 4.00 1.80
❑ 286 Johnny Grubb .30 .06
❑ 287 Reds Team/Mgr. 1.50 .70
Sparky Anderson

(Checklist back)
❑ 288 Bob Montgomery .30 .14
❑ 289 Gene Garber .75 .35
❑ 290 Amos Otis .75 .35
❑ 291 Jason Thompson RC .75 .35
❑ 292 Rogelio Moret .30 .14
❑ 293 Jack Brohamer .30 .14
❑ 294 George Medich .30 .14
❑ 295 Gary Carter 2.50 1.10
❑ 296 Don Hood .30 .14
❑ 297 Ken Reitz .30 .14
❑ 298 Charlie Hough .75 .35
❑ 299 Otto Velez .75 .35
❑ 300 Jerry Koosman .75 .35
❑ 301 Toby Harrah .75 .35
❑ 302 Mike Garman .30 .14
❑ 303 Gene Tenace .75 .35
❑ 304 Jim Hughes .30 .14
❑ 305 Mickey Rivers .75 .35
❑ 306 Rick Waits .30 .14
❑ 307 Gary Sutherland .30 .14
❑ 308 Gene Pentz .30 .14
❑ 309 Red Sox Team/Mgr. 1.50 .30
Don Zimmer
(Checklist back)
❑ 310 Larry Bowa .75 .35
❑ 311 Vern Ruhle .30 .14
❑ 312 Rob Belloir .30 .14
❑ 313 Paul Blair .75 .35
❑ 314 Steve Mingori .30 .14
❑ 315 Dave Chalk .30 .14
❑ 316 Steve Rogers .30 .14
❑ 317 Kurt Bevacqua .30 .14
❑ 318 Duffy Dyer .30 .14
❑ 319 Rich Gossage 1.50 .70
❑ 320 Ken Griffey 1.50 .70
❑ 321 Dave Goltz .30 .14
❑ 322 Bill Russell .75 .35
❑ 323 Larry Lintz .30 .14
❑ 324 John Curtis .30 .14
❑ 325 Mike Ivie .30 .14
❑ 326 Jesse Jefferson .30 .14
❑ 327 Astros Team/Mgr. 1.50 .30
Bill Virdon
(Checklist back)
❑ 328 Tommy Boggs .30 .14
❑ 329 Ron Hodges .30 .14
❑ 330 George Hendrick .75 .35
❑ 331 Jim Colborn .30 .14
❑ 332 Elliott Maddox .30 .14
❑ 333 Paul Reuschel .30 .14
❑ 334 Bill Stein .30 .14
❑ 335 Bill Robinson .75 .35
❑ 336 Denny Doyle .30 .14
❑ 337 Ron Schueler .30 .14
❑ 338 Dave Duncan .30 .14
❑ 339 Adrian Devine .30 .14
❑ 340 Hal McRae .75 .35
❑ 341 Joe Kerrigan .30 .14
❑ 342 Jerry Remy .30 .14
❑ 343 Ed Halicki .30 .14
❑ 344 Brian Downing .75 .35
❑ 345 Reggie Smith .75 .35
❑ 346 Bill Singer .30 .14
❑ 347 George Foster 1.50 .70
❑ 348 Brent Strom .30 .14
❑ 349 Jim Holt .30 .14
❑ 350 Larry Dierker .75 .35
❑ 351 Jim Sundberg .75 .35
❑ 352 Mike Phillips .30 .14
❑ 353 Stan Thomas .30 .14
❑ 354 Pirates Team/Mgr. 1.50 .30
Chuck Tanner
(Checklist back)
❑ 355 Lou Brock 4.00 1.80
❑ 356 Checklist 265-396 1.50 .30
❑ 357 Tim McCarver 1.50 .70
❑ 358 Tom House .30 .14
❑ 359 Willie Randolph 1.50 .70
❑ 360 Rick Monday .75 .35
❑ 361 Eduardo Rodriguez .30 .14
❑ 362 Tommy Davis .75 .35
❑ 363 Dave Roberts .30 .14
❑ 364 Vic Correll .30 .14
❑ 365 Mike Torrez .75 .35
❑ 366 Ted Sizemore .30 .14
❑ 367 Dave Hamilton .30 .14
❑ 368 Mike Jorgensen .30 .14
❑ 369 Terry Humphrey .30 .14
❑ 370 John Montefusco .30 .14
❑ 371 Royals Team/Mgr. 1.50 .30
Whitey Herzog
(Checklist back)
❑ 372 Rich Folkers .30 .14
❑ 373 Bert Campaneris .75 .35
❑ 374 Kent Tekulve .75 .35
❑ 375 Larry Hisle .75 .35
❑ 376 Nino Espinosa .30 .14
❑ 377 Dave McKay .30 .14
❑ 378 Jim Umbarger .30 .14
❑ 379 Larry Cox .30 .14
❑ 380 Lee May .75 .35
❑ 381 Bob Forsch .30 .14
❑ 382 Charlie Moore .30 .14
❑ 383 Stan Bahnsen .30 .14
❑ 384 Darrel Chaney .30 .14
❑ 385 Dave LaRoche .30 .14
❑ 386 Manny Mota .75 .35
❑ 387 Yankees Team/Mgr. 2.50 .50
Billy Martin
(Checklist back)
❑ 388 Terry Harmon .30 .14
❑ 389 Ken Kravec .30 .14
❑ 390 Dave Winfield 6.00 2.70
❑ 391 Dan Warthen .30 .14
❑ 392 Phil Roof .30 .14
❑ 393 John Lowenstein .30 .14
❑ 394 Bill Laxton .30 .14
❑ 395 Manny Trillo .30 .14
❑ 396 Tom Murphy .30 .14
❑ 397 Larry Herndon RC .75 .35
❑ 398 Tom Burgmeier .30 .14
❑ 399 Bruce Boisclair .30 .14
❑ 400 Steve Garvey 2.50 1.10
❑ 401 Mickey Scott .30 .14
❑ 402 Tommy Helms .30 .14
❑ 403 Tom Grieve .75 .35
❑ 404 Eric Rasmussen .30 .14
❑ 405 Claudell Washington .75 .35
❑ 406 Tim Johnson .30 .14
❑ 407 Dave Freisleben .30 .14
❑ 408 Cesar Tovar .30 .14
❑ 409 Pete Broberg .30 .14
❑ 410 Willie Montanez .30 .14
❑ 411 Joe Morgan WS 2.50 1.10
Johnny Bench
❑ 412 Johnny Bench WS 2.50 1.10
❑ 413 World Series Summary .75 .35
Cincy wins 2nd
straight series
❑ 414 Tommy Harper .75 .35
❑ 415 Jay Johnstone .75 .35
❑ 416 Chuck Hartenstein .30 .14
❑ 417 Wayne Garrett .30 .14
❑ 418 White Sox Team/Mgr. 1.50 .30
Bob Lemon
(Checklist back)
❑ 419 Steve Swisher .30 .14
❑ 420 Rusty Staub 1.50 .70
❑ 421 Doug Rau .30 .14
❑ 422 Freddie Patek .75 .35
❑ 423 Gary Lavelle .30 .14
❑ 424 Steve Brye .30 .14
❑ 425 Joe Torre 1.50 .70
❑ 426 Dick Drago .30 .14
❑ 427 Dave Rader .30 .14
❑ 428 Rangers Team/Mgr. 1.50 .30
Frank Lucchesi
(Checklist back)
❑ 429 Ken Boswell .30 .14
❑ 430 Fergie Jenkins 2.50 1.10
❑ 431 Dave Collins UER .75 .35
(Photo actually
Bobby Jones)
❑ 432 Buzz Capra .30 .14
❑ 433 Nate Colbert TBC .30 .14
(5 HR, 13 RBI)
❑ 434 Carl Yastrzemski TBC 1.50 .70
'67 Triple Crown
❑ 435 Maury Wills TBC .75 .35
104 steals
❑ 436 Bob Keegan TBC .30 .14
Majors' only no-hitter
❑ 437 Ralph Kiner TBC 1.50 .70
Leads NL in HR's
7th straight year
❑ 438 Marty Perez .30 .14
❑ 439 Gorman Thomas .75 .35
❑ 440 Jon Matlack .30 .14
❑ 441 Larvell Blanks .30 .14
❑ 442 Braves Team/Mgr. 1.50 .30
Dave Bristol
(Checklist back)
❑ 443 Lamar Johnson .30 .14
❑ 444 Wayne Twitchell .30 .14
❑ 445 Ken Singleton .75 .35
❑ 446 Bill Bonham .30 .14
❑ 447 Jerry Turner .30 .14
❑ 448 Ellie Rodriguez .30 .14
❑ 449 Al Fitzmorris .30 .14
❑ 450 Pete Rose 20.00 9.00
❑ 451 Checklist 397-528 1.50 .30
❑ 452 Mike Caldwell .30 .14
❑ 453 Pedro Garcia .30 .14
❑ 454 Andy Etchebarren .30 .14
❑ 455 Rick Wise .30 .14
❑ 456 Leon Roberts .30 .14
❑ 457 Steve Luebber .30 .14
❑ 458 Leo Foster .30 .14
❑ 459 Steve Foucault .30 .14
❑ 460 Willie Stargell 2.50 1.10
❑ 461 Dick Tidrow .30 .14
❑ 462 Don Baylor 1.50 .70
❑ 463 Jamie Quirk .30 .14
❑ 464 Randy Moffitt .30 .14
❑ 465 Rico Carty .75 .35
❑ 466 Fred Holdsworth .30 .14
❑ 467 Phillies Team/Mgr. 1.50 .30
Danny Ozark
(Checklist back)
❑ 468 Ramon Hernandez .30 .14
❑ 469 Pat Kelly .30 .14
❑ 470 Ted Simmons .75 .35
❑ 471 Del Unser .30 .14
❑ 472 Rookie Pitchers .30 .14
Don Aase
Bob McClure
Gil Patterson
Dave Wehrmeister
❑ 473 Rookie Outfielders 20.00 9.00
Andre Dawson RC
Gene Richards
John Scott
Denny Walling
❑ 474 Rookie Shortstops .75 .35
Bob Bailor
Kiko Garcia
Craig Reynolds
Alex Taveras
❑ 475 Rookie Pitchers .75 .35
Chris Batton
Rick Camp
Scott McGregor
Manny Sarmiento
❑ 476 Rookie Catchers 20.00 9.00
Gary Alexander
Rick Cerone
Dale Murphy RC
Kevin Pasley
❑ 477 Rookie Infielders .75 .35
Doug Ault
Rich Dauer
Orlando Gonzalez
Phil Mankowski
❑ 478 Rookie Pitchers .75 .35
Jim Gideon
Leon Hooten
Dave Johnson
Mark Lemongello
❑ 479 Rookie Outfielders .75 .35
Brian Asselstine
Wayne Gross
Sam Mejias
Alvis Woods
❑ 480 Carl Yastrzemski 6.00 2.70
❑ 481 Roger Metzger .30 .14
❑ 482 Tony Solaita .30 .14
❑ 483 Richie Zisk .30 .14

❑ 484 Burt Hooton .75 .35
❑ 485 Roy White .75 .35
❑ 486 Ed Bane .30 .14
❑ 487 Rookie Pitchers .75 .35
Larry Anderson
Ed Glynn
Joe Henderson
Greg Terlecky
❑ 488 Rookie Outfielders 3.00 1.35
Jack Clark RC
Ruppert Jones
Lee Mazzilli
Dan Thomas
❑ 489 Rookie Pitchers .75 .35
Len Barker RC
Randy Lerch
Greg Minton
Mike Overy
❑ 490 Rookie Shortstops .75 .35
Billy Almon
Mickey Klutts
Tommy McMillan
Mark Wagner
❑ 491 Rookie Pitchers 5.00 2.20
Mike Dupree
Dennis Martinez RC
Craig Mitchell
Bob Sykes
❑ 492 Rookie Outfielders .75 .35
Tony Armas
Steve Kemp RC
Carlos Lopez
Gary Woods
❑ 493 Rookie Pitchers .75 .35
Mike Krukow
Jim Otten
Gary Wheelock
Mike Willis
❑ 494 Rookie Infielders 1.50 .70
Juan Bernhardt
Mike Champion
Jim Gantner RC
Bump Wills
❑ 495 Al Hrabosky .30 .14
❑ 496 Gary Thomasson .30 .14
❑ 497 Clay Carroll .30 .14
❑ 498 Sal Bando .75 .35
❑ 499 Pablo Torrealba .30 .14
❑ 500 Dave Kingman 1.50 .70
❑ 501 Jim Bibby .30 .14
❑ 502 Randy Hundley .30 .14
❑ 503 Bill Lee .30 .14
❑ 504 Dodgers Team/Mgr. 1.50 .30
Tom Lasorda
(Checklist back)
❑ 505 Oscar Gamble .75 .35
❑ 506 Steve Grilli .30 .14
❑ 507 Mike Hegan .30 .14
❑ 508 Dave Pagan .30 .14
❑ 509 Cookie Rojas .75 .35
❑ 510 John Candelaria .30 .14
❑ 511 Bill Fahey .30 .14
❑ 512 Jack Billingham .30 .14
❑ 513 Jerry Terrell .30 .14
❑ 514 Cliff Johnson .30 .14
❑ 515 Chris Speier .30 .14
❑ 516 Bake McBride .75 .35
❑ 517 Pete Vuckovich RC .75 .35
❑ 518 Cubs Team/Mgr. 1.50 .30
Herman Franks
(Checklist back)
❑ 519 Don Kirkwood .30 .14
❑ 520 Garry Maddox .30 .14
❑ 521 Bob Grich .75 .35
❑ 522 Enzo Hernandez .30 .14
❑ 523 Rollie Fingers 2.50 1.10
❑ 524 Rowland Office .30 .14
❑ 525 Dennis Eckersley 5.00 2.20
❑ 526 Larry Parrish .75 .35
❑ 527 Dan Meyer .75 .35
❑ 528 Bill Castro .30 .14
❑ 529 Jim Essian .30 .14
❑ 530 Rick Reuschel .75 .35
❑ 531 Lyman Bostock .75 .35
❑ 532 Jim Willoughby .30 .14
❑ 533 Mickey Stanley .30 .14
❑ 534 Paul Splittorff .30 .14
❑ 535 Cesar Geronimo .30 .14
❑ 536 Vic Albury .30 .14
❑ 537 Dave Roberts .30 .14
❑ 538 Frank Taveras .30 .14
❑ 539 Mike Wallace .30 .14
❑ 540 Bob Watson .75 .35
❑ 541 John Denny .75 .35
❑ 542 Frank Duffy .30 .14
❑ 543 Ron Blomberg .30 .14
❑ 544 Gary Ross .30 .14
❑ 545 Bob Boone .75 .35
❑ 546 Orioles Team/Mgr. 1.50 .30
Earl Weaver
(Checklist back)
❑ 547 Willie McCovey 4.00 1.80
❑ 548 Joel Youngblood .30 .14
❑ 549 Jerry Royster .30 .14
❑ 550 Randy Jones .30 .14
❑ 551 Bill North .30 .14
❑ 552 Pepe Mangual .30 .14
❑ 553 Jack Heidemann .30 .14
❑ 554 Bruce Kimm .30 .14
❑ 555 Dan Ford .30 .14
❑ 556 Doug Bird .30 .14
❑ 557 Jerry White .30 .14
❑ 558 Elias Sosa .30 .14
❑ 559 Alan Bannister .30 .14
❑ 560 Dave Concepcion 1.50 .70
❑ 561 Pete LaCock .30 .14
❑ 562 Checklist 529-660 1.50 .30
❑ 563 Bruce Kison .30 .14
❑ 564 Alan Ashby .75 .35
❑ 565 Mickey Lolich .75 .35
❑ 566 Rick Miller .30 .14
❑ 567 Enos Cabell .30 .14
❑ 568 Carlos May .30 .14
❑ 569 Jim Lonborg .75 .35
❑ 570 Bobby Bonds 1.50 .70
❑ 571 Darrell Evans .75 .35
❑ 572 Ross Grimsley .30 .14
❑ 573 Joe Ferguson .30 .14
❑ 574 Aurelio Rodriguez .30 .14
❑ 575 Dick Ruthven .30 .14
❑ 576 Fred Kendall .30 .14
❑ 577 Jerry Augustine .30 .14
❑ 578 Bob Randall .30 .14
❑ 579 Don Carrithers .30 .14
❑ 580 George Brett 15.00 6.75
❑ 581 Pedro Borbon .30 .14
❑ 582 Ed Kirkpatrick .30 .14
❑ 583 Paul Lindblad .30 .14
❑ 584 Ed Goodson .30 .14
❑ 585 Rick Burleson .75 .35
❑ 586 Steve Renko .30 .14
❑ 587 Rick Baldwin .30 .14
❑ 588 Dave Moates .30 .14
❑ 589 Mike Cosgrove .30 .14
❑ 590 Buddy Bell .75 .35
❑ 591 Chris Arnold .30 .14
❑ 592 Dan Briggs .30 .14
❑ 593 Dennis Blair .30 .14
❑ 594 Biff Pocoroba .30 .14
❑ 595 John Hiller .30 .14
❑ 596 Jerry Martin .30 .14
❑ 597 Mariners Leaders 1.50 .30
Darrell Johnson MG
Don Bryant CO
Jim Busby CO
Vada Pinson CO
Wes Stock CO
(Checklist back)
❑ 598 Sparky Lyle .75 .35
❑ 599 Mike Tyson .30 .14
❑ 600 Jim Palmer 4.00 1.80
❑ 601 Mike Lum .30 .14
❑ 602 Andy Hassler .30 .14
❑ 603 Willie Davis .75 .35
❑ 604 Jim Slaton .30 .14
❑ 605 Felix Millan .30 .14
❑ 606 Steve Braun .30 .14
❑ 607 Larry Demery .30 .14
❑ 608 Roy Howell .30 .14
❑ 609 Jim Barr .30 .14
❑ 610 Jose Cardenal .75 .35
❑ 611 Dave Lemanczyk .30 .14
❑ 612 Barry Foote .30 .14
❑ 613 Reggie Cleveland .30 .14
❑ 614 Greg Gross .30 .14
❑ 615 Phil Niekro 2.50 1.10
❑ 616 Tommy Sandt .30 .14
❑ 617 Bobby Darwin .30 .14
❑ 618 Pat Dobson .30 .14
❑ 619 Johnny Oates .75 .35
❑ 620 Don Sutton 2.50 1.10
❑ 621 Tigers Team/Mgr. 1.50 .30
Ralph Houk
(Checklist back)
❑ 622 Jim Wohlford .30 .14
❑ 623 Jack Kucek .30 .14
❑ 624 Hector Cruz .30 .14
❑ 625 Ken Holtzman .75 .35
❑ 626 Al Bumbry .75 .35
❑ 627 Bob Myrick .30 .14
❑ 628 Mario Guerrero .30 .14
❑ 629 Bobby Valentine .30 .14
❑ 630 Bert Blyleven 1.50 .70
❑ 631 George Brett 6.00 2.70
Ken Brett
❑ 632 Bob Forsch .75 .35
Ken Forsch
❑ 633 Lee May .75 .35
Carlos May
❑ 634 Paul Reuschel .75 .35
Rick Reuschel UER
(Photos switched)
❑ 635 Robin Yount 8.00 3.60
❑ 636 Santo Alcala .30 .14
❑ 637 Alex Johnson .30 .14
❑ 638 Jim Kaat 1.50 .70
❑ 639 Jerry Morales .30 .14
❑ 640 Carlton Fisk 4.00 1.80
❑ 641 Dan Larson .30 .14
❑ 642 Willie Crawford .30 .14
❑ 643 Mike Pazik .30 .14
❑ 644 Matt Alexander .30 .14
❑ 645 Jerry Reuss .75 .35
❑ 646 Andres Mora .30 .14
❑ 647 Expos Team/Mgr. 1.50 .30
Dick Williams
(Checklist back)
❑ 648 Jim Spencer .30 .14
❑ 649 Dave Cash .30 .14
❑ 650 Nolan Ryan 30.00 13.50
❑ 651 Von Joshua .30 .14
❑ 652 Tom Walker .30 .14
❑ 653 Diego Segui .75 .35
❑ 654 Ron Pruitt .30 .14
❑ 655 Tony Perez 2.50 1.10
❑ 656 Ron Guidry 1.50 .70
❑ 657 Mick Kelleher .30 .14
❑ 658 Marty Pattin .30 .14
❑ 659 Merv Rettenmund .30 .14
❑ 660 Willie Horton 1.50 .30

# 1978 Topps

| | NRMT | VG-E |
|---|---|---|
| COMPLETE SET (726) | 200.00 | 90.00 |
| COMMON CARD (1-726) | .25 | .11 |
| COMMON CARD DP | .15 | .07 |

❑ 1 Lou Brock RB 3.00 .90
Most lifetime steals

❑ 2 Sparky Lyle RB .60 .25
Most career games pure relief
❑ 3 Willie McCovey RB 2.50 1.10
Most times 2 HR's in inning
❑ 4 Brooks Robinson RB 2.50 1.10
Most consecutive
seasons with one club
❑ 5 Pete Rose RB 8.00 3.60
Most lifetime switch-hitter hits
❑ 6 Nolan Ryan RB 15.00 6.75
Most games 10 or more strikeouts
❑ 7 Reggie Jackson RB 4.00 1.80
Most homers,
one World Series
❑ 8 Mike Sadek .25 .11
❑ 9 Doug DeCinces .60 .25
❑ 10 Phil Niekro 2.50 1.10
❑ 11 Rick Manning .25 .11
❑ 12 Don Aase .25 .11
❑ 13 Art Howe RC .60 .25
❑ 14 Lerrin LaGrow .25 .11
❑ 15 Tony Perez DP 1.25 .55
❑ 16 Roy White .60 .25
❑ 17 Mike Krukow .25 .11
❑ 18 Bob Grich .60 .25
❑ 19 Darrell Porter .60 .25
❑ 20 Pete Rose DP 12.00 5.50
❑ 21 Steve Kemp .25 .11
❑ 22 Charlie Hough .60 .25
❑ 23 Bump Wills .25 .11
❑ 24 Don Money DP .15 .07
❑ 25 Jon Matlack .25 .11
❑ 26 Rich Hebner .60 .25
❑ 27 Geoff Zahn .25 .11
❑ 28 Ed Ott .25 .11
❑ 29 Bob Lacey .25 .11
❑ 30 George Hendrick .60 .25
❑ 31 Glenn Abbott .25 .11
❑ 32 Garry Templeton .60 .25
❑ 33 Dave Lemanczyk .25 .11
❑ 34 Willie McCovey 3.00 1.35
❑ 35 Sparky Lyle .60 .25
❑ 36 Eddie Murray RC ! 80.00 36.00
❑ 37 Rick Waits .25 .11
❑ 38 Willie Montanez .25 .11
❑ 39 Floyd Bannister RC .25 .11
❑ 40 Carl Yastrzemski 5.00 2.20
❑ 41 Burt Hooton .60 .25
❑ 42 Jorge Orta .25 .11
❑ 43 Bill Atkinson .25 .11
❑ 44 Toby Harrah .60 .25
❑ 45 Mark Fidrych 2.50 1.10
❑ 46 Al Cowens .25 .11
❑ 47 Jack Billingham .25 .11
❑ 48 Don Baylor 1.25 .55
❑ 49 Ed Kranepool .60 .25
❑ 50 Rick Reuschel .60 .25
❑ 51 Charlie Moore DP .15 .07
❑ 52 Jim Lonborg .25 .11
❑ 53 Phil Garner DP .25 .11
❑ 54 Tom Johnson .25 .11
❑ 55 Mitchell Page .25 .11
❑ 56 Randy Jones .25 .11
❑ 57 Dan Meyer .25 .11
❑ 58 Bob Forsch .25 .11
❑ 59 Otto Velez .25 .11
❑ 60 Thurman Munson 3.00 1.35
❑ 61 Larvell Blanks .25 .11
❑ 62 Jim Barr .25 .11
❑ 63 Don Zimmer MG .60 .25
❑ 64 Gene Pentz .25 .11
❑ 65 Ken Singleton .60 .25
❑ 66 Chicago White Sox 1.25 .25
Team Card
(Checklist back)
❑ 67 Claudell Washington .60 .25
❑ 68 Steve Foucault DP .15 .07
❑ 69 Mike Vail .25 .11
❑ 70 Rich Gossage 1.25 .55
❑ 71 Terry Humphrey .25 .11
❑ 72 Andre Dawson 5.00 2.20
❑ 73 Andy Hassler .25 .11
❑ 74 Checklist 1-121 1.25 .25
❑ 75 Dick Ruthven .25 .11
❑ 76 Steve Ontiveros .25 .11
❑ 77 Ed Kirkpatrick .25 .11
❑ 78 Pablo Torrealba .25 .11
❑ 79 Darrell Johnson DP MG .15 .07
❑ 80 Ken Griffey Sr. 1.25 .55
❑ 81 Pete Redfern .25 .11
❑ 82 San Francisco Giants 1.25 .25
Team Card
(Checklist back)
❑ 83 Bob Montgomery .25 .11
❑ 84 Kent Tekulve .60 .25
❑ 85 Ron Fairly .60 .25
❑ 86 Dave Tomlin .25 .11
❑ 87 John Lowenstein .25 .11
❑ 88 Mike Phillips .25 .11
❑ 89 Ken Clay .25 .11
❑ 90 Larry Bowa 1.25 .55
❑ 91 Oscar Zamora .25 .11
❑ 92 Adrian Devine .25 .11
❑ 93 Bobby Cox DP .25 .11
❑ 94 Chuck Scrivener .25 .11
❑ 95 Jamie Quirk .25 .11
❑ 96 Baltimore Orioles 1.25 .25
Team Card
(Checklist back)
❑ 97 Stan Bahnsen .25 .11
❑ 98 Jim Essian .60 .25
❑ 99 Willie Hernandez RC 1.25 .55
❑ 100 George Brett 15.00 6.75
❑ 101 Sid Monge .25 .11
❑ 102 Matt Alexander .25 .11
❑ 103 Tom Murphy .25 .11
❑ 104 Lee Lacy .25 .11
❑ 105 Reggie Cleveland .25 .11
❑ 106 Bill Plummer .25 .11
❑ 107 Ed Halicki .25 .11
❑ 108 Von Joshua .25 .11
❑ 109 Joe Torre MG .60 .25
❑ 110 Richie Zisk .25 .11
❑ 111 Mike Tyson .25 .11
❑ 112 Houston Astros 1.25 .25
Team Card
(Checklist back)
❑ 113 Don Carrithers .25 .11
❑ 114 Paul Blair .60 .25
❑ 115 Gary Nolan .25 .11
❑ 116 Tucker Ashford .25 .11
❑ 117 John Montague .25 .11
❑ 118 Terry Harmon .25 .11
❑ 119 Dennis Martinez 2.50 1.10
❑ 120 Gary Carter 2.50 1.10
❑ 121 Alvis Woods .25 .11
❑ 122 Dennis Eckersley 4.00 1.80
❑ 123 Manny Trillo .25 .11
❑ 124 Dave Rozema .25 .11
❑ 125 George Scott .60 .25
❑ 126 Paul Moskau .25 .11
❑ 127 Chet Lemon .60 .25
❑ 128 Bill Russell .60 .25
❑ 129 Jim Colborn .25 .11
❑ 130 Jeff Burroughs .60 .25
❑ 131 Bert Blyleven 1.25 .55
❑ 132 Enos Cabell .25 .11
❑ 133 Jerry Augustine .25 .11
❑ 134 Steve Henderson .25 .11
❑ 135 Ron Guidry DP 1.25 .55
❑ 136 Ted Sizemore .25 .11
❑ 137 Craig Kusick .25 .11
❑ 138 Larry Demery .25 .11
❑ 139 Wayne Gross .25 .11
❑ 140 Rollie Fingers 2.50 1.10
❑ 141 Ruppert Jones .25 .11
❑ 142 John Montefusco .25 .11
❑ 143 Keith Hernandez .60 .25
❑ 144 Jesse Jefferson .25 .11
❑ 145 Rick Monday .60 .25
❑ 146 Doyle Alexander .25 .11
❑ 147 Lee Mazzilli .25 .11
❑ 148 Andre Thornton .60 .25
❑ 149 Dale Murray .25 .11
❑ 150 Bobby Bonds 1.25 .55
❑ 151 Milt Wilcox .25 .11
❑ 152 Ivan DeJesus .25 .11
❑ 153 Steve Stone .60 .25
❑ 154 Cecil Cooper DP .25 .11
❑ 155 Butch Hobson .25 .11
❑ 156 Andy Messersmith .60 .25
❑ 157 Pete LaCock DP .15 .07
❑ 158 Joaquin Andujar .60 .25
❑ 159 Lou Piniella .60 .25
❑ 160 Jim Palmer 3.00 1.35
❑ 161 Bob Boone 1.25 .55
❑ 162 Paul Thormodsgard .25 .11
❑ 163 Bill North .25 .11
❑ 164 Bob Owchinko .25 .11
❑ 165 Rennie Stennett .25 .11
❑ 166 Carlos Lopez .25 .11
❑ 167 Tim Foli .25 .11
❑ 168 Reggie Smith .60 .25
❑ 169 Jerry Johnson .25 .11
❑ 170 Lou Brock 3.00 1.35
❑ 171 Pat Zachry .25 .11
❑ 172 Mike Hargrove .60 .25
❑ 173 Robin Yount UER 6.00 2.70
(Played for Newark
in 1973, not 1971)
❑ 174 Wayne Garland .25 .11
❑ 175 Jerry Morales .25 .11
❑ 176 Milt May .25 .11
❑ 177 Gene Garber DP .25 .11
❑ 178 Dave Chalk .25 .11
❑ 179 Dick Tidrow .25 .11
❑ 180 Dave Concepcion 1.25 .55
❑ 181 Ken Forsch .25 .11
❑ 182 Jim Spencer .25 .11
❑ 183 Doug Bird .25 .11
❑ 184 Checklist 122-242 1.25 .25
❑ 185 Ellis Valentine .25 .11
❑ 186 Bob Stanley DP .25 .11
❑ 187 Jerry Royster DP .15 .07
❑ 188 Al Bumbry .60 .25
❑ 189 Tom Lasorda MG 2.50 1.10
❑ 190 John Candelaria .60 .25
❑ 191 Rodney Scott .25 .11
❑ 192 San Diego Padres 1.25 .25
Team Card
(Checklist back)
❑ 193 Rich Chiles .25 .11
❑ 194 Derrel Thomas .25 .11
❑ 195 Larry Dierker .60 .25
❑ 196 Bob Bailor .25 .11
❑ 197 Nino Espinosa .25 .11
❑ 198 Ron Pruitt .25 .11
❑ 199 Craig Reynolds .25 .11
❑ 200 Reggie Jackson 8.00 3.60
❑ 201 Batting Leaders 1.25 .55
Dave Parker
Rod Carew
❑ 202 Home Run Leaders DP .60 .25
George Foster
Jim Rice
❑ 203 RBI Leaders .60 .25
George Foster
Larry Hisle
❑ 204 Stolen Base Leaders DP .25 .11
Frank Taveras
Freddie Patek
❑ 205 Victory Leaders 2.50 1.10
Steve Carlton
Dave Goltz
Dennis Leonard
Jim Palmer
❑ 206 Strikeout Leaders DP 6.00 2.70
Phil Niekro
Nolan Ryan
❑ 207 ERA Leaders DP .60 .25
John Candelaria
Frank Tanana
❑ 208 Firemen Leaders 1.25 .55
Rollie Fingers
Bill Campbell
❑ 209 Dock Ellis .25 .11
❑ 210 Jose Cardenal .25 .11
❑ 211 Earl Weaver MG DP 1.25 .55
❑ 212 Mike Caldwell .25 .11
❑ 213 Alan Bannister .25 .11
❑ 214 California Angels 1.25 .25
Team Card
(Checklist back)
❑ 215 Darrell Evans .60 .25
❑ 216 Mike Paxton .25 .11
❑ 217 Rod Gilbreath .25 .11
❑ 218 Marty Pattin .25 .11
❑ 219 Mike Cubbage .25 .11

❑ 220 Pedro Borbon .25 .11
❑ 221 Chris Speier .25 .11
❑ 222 Jerry Martin .25 .11
❑ 223 Bruce Kison .25 .11
❑ 224 Jerry Tabb .25 .11
❑ 225 Don Gullett DP .25 .11
❑ 226 Joe Ferguson .25 .11
❑ 227 Al Fitzmorris .25 .11
❑ 228 Manny Mota DP .25 .11
❑ 229 Leo Foster .25 .11
❑ 230 Al Hrabosky .25 .11
❑ 231 Wayne Nordhagen .25 .11
❑ 232 Mickey Stanley .25 .11
❑ 233 Dick Pole .25 .11
❑ 234 Herman Franks MG .25 .11
❑ 235 Tim McCarver .60 .25
❑ 236 Terry Whitfield .25 .11
❑ 237 Rich Dauer .25 .11
❑ 238 Juan Beniquez .25 .11
❑ 239 Dyar Miller .25 .11
❑ 240 Gene Tenace .60 .25
❑ 241 Pete Vuckovich .60 .25
❑ 242 Barry Bonnell DP .15 .07
❑ 243 Bob McClure .25 .11
❑ 244 Montreal Expos .60 .12
Team Card DP
(Checklist back)
❑ 245 Rick Burleson .60 .25
❑ 246 Dan Driessen .25 .11
❑ 247 Larry Christenson .25 .11
❑ 248 Frank White DP .60 .25
❑ 249 Dave Goltz DP .15 .07
❑ 250 Graig Nettles DP .60 .25
❑ 251 Don Kirkwood .25 .11
❑ 252 Steve Swisher DP .15 .07
❑ 253 Jim Kern .25 .11
❑ 254 Dave Collins .60 .25
❑ 255 Jerry Reuss .60 .25
❑ 256 Joe Altobelli MG .25 .11
❑ 257 Hector Cruz .25 .11
❑ 258 John Hiller .25 .11
❑ 259 Los Angeles Dodgers .. 1.25 .25
Team Card
(Checklist back)
❑ 260 Bert Campaneris .60 .25
❑ 261 Tim Hosley .25 .11
❑ 262 Rudy May .25 .11
❑ 263 Danny Walton .25 .11
❑ 264 Jamie Easterly .25 .11
❑ 265 Sal Bando DP .60 .25
❑ 266 Bob Shirley .25 .11
❑ 267 Doug Ault .25 .11
❑ 268 Gil Flores .25 .11
❑ 269 Wayne Twitchell .25 .11
❑ 270 Carlton Fisk 3.00 1.35
❑ 271 Randy Lerch DP .15 .07
❑ 272 Royle Stillman .25 .11
❑ 273 Fred Norman .25 .11
❑ 274 Freddie Patek .60 .25
❑ 275 Dan Ford .25 .11
❑ 276 Bill Bonham DP .15 .07
❑ 277 Bruce Boisclair .25 .11
❑ 278 Enrique Romo .25 .11
❑ 279 Bill Virdon MG .25 .11
❑ 280 Buddy Bell .60 .25
❑ 281 Eric Rasmussen DP .15 .07
❑ 282 New York Yankees 2.50 .50
Team Card
(Checklist back)
❑ 283 Omar Moreno .25 .11
❑ 284 Randy Moffitt .25 .11
❑ 285 Steve Yeager DP .60 .25
❑ 286 Ben Oglivie .60 .25
❑ 287 Kiko Garcia .25 .11
❑ 288 Dave Hamilton .25 .11
❑ 289 Checklist 243-363 1.25 .25
❑ 290 Willie Horton .60 .25
❑ 291 Gary Ross .25 .11
❑ 292 Gene Richards .25 .11
❑ 293 Mike Willis .25 .11
❑ 294 Larry Parrish .60 .25
❑ 295 Bill Lee .25 .11
❑ 296 Biff Pocoroba .25 .11
❑ 297 Warren Brusstar DP .15 .07
❑ 298 Tony Armas .60 .25
❑ 299 Whitey Herzog MG .60 .25
❑ 300 Joe Morgan 3.00 1.35
❑ 301 Buddy Schultz .25 .11
❑ 302 Chicago Cubs 1.25 .25
Team Card
(Checklist back)
❑ 303 Sam Hinds .25 .11
❑ 304 John Milner .25 .11
❑ 305 Rico Carty .60 .25
❑ 306 Joe Niekro .60 .25
❑ 307 Glenn Borgmann .25 .11
❑ 308 Jim Rooker .25 .11
❑ 309 Cliff Johnson .25 .11
❑ 310 Don Sutton 2.50 1.10
❑ 311 Jose Baez DP .15 .07
❑ 312 Greg Minton .25 .11
❑ 313 Andy Etchebarren .25 .11
❑ 314 Paul Lindblad .25 .11
❑ 315 Mark Belanger .60 .25
❑ 316 Henry Cruz DP .15 .07
❑ 317 Dave Johnson .25 .11
❑ 318 Tom Griffin .25 .11
❑ 319 Alan Ashby .25 .11
❑ 320 Fred Lynn .60 .25
❑ 321 Santo Alcala .25 .11
❑ 322 Tom Paciorek .60 .25
❑ 323 Jim Fregosi DP .25 .11
❑ 324 Vern Rapp MG .25 .11
❑ 325 Bruce Sutter 1.25 .55
❑ 326 Mike Lum DP .15 .07
❑ 327 Rick Langford DP .15 .07
❑ 328 Milwaukee Brewers 1.25 .25
Team Card
(Checklist back)
❑ 329 John Verhoeven .25 .11
❑ 330 Bob Watson .60 .25
❑ 331 Mark Littell .25 .11
❑ 332 Duane Kuiper .25 .11
❑ 333 Jim Todd .25 .11
❑ 334 John Stearns .25 .11
❑ 335 Bucky Dent .60 .25
❑ 336 Steve Busby .25 .11
❑ 337 Tom Grieve .60 .25
❑ 338 Dave Heaverlo .25 .11
❑ 339 Mario Guerrero .25 .11
❑ 340 Bake McBride .60 .25
❑ 341 Mike Flanagan .60 .25
❑ 342 Aurelio Rodriguez .25 .11
❑ 343 John Wathan DP .15 .07
❑ 344 Sam Ewing .25 .11
❑ 345 Luis Tiant .60 .25
❑ 346 Larry Biittner .25 .11
❑ 347 Terry Forster .25 .11
❑ 348 Del Unser .25 .11
❑ 349 Rick Camp DP .15 .07
❑ 350 Steve Garvey 2.50 1.10
❑ 351 Jeff Torborg .60 .25
❑ 352 Tony Scott .25 .11
❑ 353 Doug Bair .25 .11
❑ 354 Cesar Geronimo .25 .11
❑ 355 Bill Travers .25 .11
❑ 356 New York Mets 1.25 .25
Team Card
(Checklist back)
❑ 357 Tom Poquette .25 .11
❑ 358 Mark Lemongello .25 .11
❑ 359 Marc Hill .25 .11
❑ 360 Mike Schmidt 10.00 4.50
❑ 361 Chris Knapp .25 .11
❑ 362 Dave May .25 .11
❑ 363 Bob Randall .25 .11
❑ 364 Jerry Turner .25 .11
❑ 365 Ed Figueroa .25 .11
❑ 366 Larry Milbourne DP .15 .07
❑ 367 Rick Dempsey .60 .25
❑ 368 Balor Moore .25 .11
❑ 369 Tim Nordbrook .25 .11
❑ 370 Rusty Staub 1.25 .55
❑ 371 Ray Burris .25 .11
❑ 372 Brian Asselstine .25 .11
❑ 373 Jim Willoughby .25 .11
❑ 374 Jose Morales .25 .11
❑ 375 Tommy John 1.25 .55
❑ 376 Jim Wohlford .25 .11
❑ 377 Manny Sarmiento .25 .11
❑ 378 Bobby Winkles MG .25 .11
❑ 379 Skip Lockwood .25 .11
❑ 380 Ted Simmons .60 .25
❑ 381 Philadelphia Phillies 1.25 .25
Team Card
(Checklist back)
❑ 382 Joe Lahoud .25 .11
❑ 383 Mario Mendoza .25 .11
❑ 384 Jack Clark 1.25 .55
❑ 385 Tito Fuentes .25 .11
❑ 386 Bob Gorinski .25 .11
❑ 387 Ken Holtzman .60 .25
❑ 388 Bill Fahey DP .15 .07
❑ 389 Julio Gonzalez .25 .11
❑ 390 Oscar Gamble .60 .25
❑ 391 Larry Haney .25 .11
❑ 392 Billy Almon .25 .11
❑ 393 Tippy Martinez .60 .25
❑ 394 Roy Howell DP .15 .07
❑ 395 Jim Hughes .25 .11
❑ 396 Bob Stinson DP .15 .07
❑ 397 Greg Gross .25 .11
❑ 398 Don Hood .25 .11
❑ 399 Pete Mackanin .25 .11
❑ 400 Nolan Ryan 30.00 13.50
❑ 401 Sparky Anderson MG .60 .25
❑ 402 Dave Campbell .25 .11
❑ 403 Bud Harrelson .60 .25
❑ 404 Detroit Tigers 1.25 .25
Team Card
(Checklist back)
❑ 405 Rawly Eastwick .25 .11
❑ 406 Mike Jorgensen .25 .11
❑ 407 Odell Jones .25 .11
❑ 408 Joe Zdeb .25 .11
❑ 409 Ron Schueler .25 .11
❑ 410 Bill Madlock .60 .25
❑ 411 AL Champs .60 .25
Willie Randolph
❑ 412 NL Champs .60 .25
Davey Lopes
❑ 413 World Series 4.00 1.80
Reggie Jackson
❑ 414 Darold Knowles DP .15 .07
❑ 415 Ray Fosse .25 .11
❑ 416 Jack Brohamer .25 .11
❑ 417 Mike Garman DP .15 .07
❑ 418 Tony Muser .25 .11
❑ 419 Jerry Garvin .25 .11
❑ 420 Greg Luzinski 1.25 .55
❑ 421 Junior Moore .25 .11
❑ 422 Steve Braun .25 .11
❑ 423 Dave Rosello .25 .11
❑ 424 Boston Red Sox 1.25 .25
Team Card
(Checklist back)
❑ 425 Steve Rogers DP .25 .11
❑ 426 Fred Kendall .25 .11
❑ 427 Mario Soto RC .60 .25
❑ 428 Joel Youngblood .25 .11
❑ 429 Mike Barlow .25 .11
❑ 430 Al Oliver .60 .25
❑ 431 Butch Metzger .25 .11
❑ 432 Terry Bulling .25 .11
❑ 433 Fernando Gonzalez .25 .11
❑ 434 Mike Norris .25 .11
❑ 435 Checklist 364-484 1.25 .25
❑ 436 Vic Harris DP .15 .07
❑ 437 Bo McLaughlin .25 .11
❑ 438 John Ellis .25 .11
❑ 439 Ken Kravec .25 .11
❑ 440 Dave Lopes .60 .25
❑ 441 Larry Gura .25 .11
❑ 442 Elliott Maddox .25 .11
❑ 443 Darrel Chaney .25 .11
❑ 444 Roy Hartsfield MG .25 .11
❑ 445 Mike Ivie .25 .11
❑ 446 Tug McGraw .60 .25
❑ 447 Leroy Stanton .25 .11
❑ 448 Bill Castro .25 .11
❑ 449 Tim Blackwell DP .15 .07
❑ 450 Tom Seaver 8.00 3.60
❑ 451 Minnesota Twins 1.25 .25
Team Card
(Checklist back)
❑ 452 Jerry Mumphrey .25 .11
❑ 453 Doug Flynn .25 .11
❑ 454 Dave LaRoche .25 .11

❑ 455 Bill Robinson .60 .25
❑ 456 Vern Ruhle .25 .11
❑ 457 Bob Bailey .25 .11
❑ 458 Jeff Newman .25 .11
❑ 459 Charlie Spikes .25 .11
❑ 460 Jim Hunter 2.50 1.10
❑ 461 Rob Andrews DP .15 .07
❑ 462 Rogelio Moret .25 .11
❑ 463 Kevin Bell .25 .11
❑ 464 Jerry Grote .25 .11
❑ 465 Hal McRae .60 .25
❑ 466 Dennis Blair .25 .11
❑ 467 Alvin Dark MG .60 .25
❑ 468 Warren Cromartie RC .60 .25
❑ 469 Rick Cerone .60 .25
❑ 470 J.R. Richard .60 .25
❑ 471 Roy Smalley .60 .25
❑ 472 Ron Reed .25 .11
❑ 473 Bill Buckner .60 .25
❑ 474 Jim Slaton .25 .11
❑ 475 Gary Matthews .60 .25
❑ 476 Bill Stein .25 .11
❑ 477 Doug Capilla .25 .11
❑ 478 Jerry Remy .25 .11
❑ 479 St. Louis Cardinals 1.25 .25
Team Card
(Checklist back)
❑ 480 Ron LeFlore .60 .25
❑ 481 Jackson Todd .25 .11
❑ 482 Rick Miller .25 .11
❑ 483 Ken Macha .25 .11
❑ 484 Jim Norris .25 .11
❑ 485 Chris Chambliss .60 .25
❑ 486 John Curtis .25 .11
❑ 487 Jim Tyrone .25 .11
❑ 488 Dan Spillner .25 .11
❑ 489 Rudy Meoli .25 .11
❑ 490 Amos Otis .60 .25
❑ 491 Scott McGregor .60 .25
❑ 492 Jim Sundberg .60 .25
❑ 493 Steve Renko .25 .11
❑ 494 Chuck Tanner MG .60 .25
❑ 495 Dave Cash .25 .11
❑ 496 Jim Clancy DP .15 .07
❑ 497 Glenn Adams .25 .11
❑ 498 Joe Sambito .25 .11
❑ 499 Seattle Mariners 1.25 .25
Team Card
(Checklist back)
❑ 500 George Foster 1.25 .55
❑ 501 Dave Roberts .25 .11
❑ 502 Pat Rockett .25 .11
❑ 503 Ike Hampton .25 .11
❑ 504 Roger Freed .25 .11
❑ 505 Felix Millan .25 .11
❑ 506 Ron Blomberg .25 .11
❑ 507 Willie Crawford .25 .11
❑ 508 Johnny Oates .60 .25
❑ 509 Brent Strom .25 .11
❑ 510 Willie Stargell 2.50 1.10
❑ 511 Frank Duffy .25 .11
❑ 512 Larry Herndon .25 .11
❑ 513 Barry Foote .25 .11
❑ 514 Rob Sperring .25 .11
❑ 515 Tim Corcoran .25 .11
❑ 516 Gary Beare .25 .11
❑ 517 Andres Mora .25 .11
❑ 518 Tommy Boggs DP .15 .07
❑ 519 Brian Downing .60 .25
❑ 520 Larry Hisle .25 .11
❑ 521 Steve Staggs .25 .11
❑ 522 Dick Williams MG .60 .25
❑ 523 Donnie Moore .25 .11
❑ 524 Bernie Carbo .25 .11
❑ 525 Jerry Terrell .25 .11
❑ 526 Cincinnati Reds 1.25 .25
Team Card
(Checklist back)
❑ 527 Vic Correll .25 .11
❑ 528 Rob Picciolo .25 .11
❑ 529 Paul Hartzell .25 .11
❑ 530 Dave Winfield 5.00 2.20
❑ 531 Tom Underwood .25 .11
❑ 532 Skip Jutze .25 .11
❑ 533 Sandy Alomar .60 .25
❑ 534 Wilbur Howard .25 .11
❑ 535 Checklist 485-605 1.25 .25
❑ 536 Roric Harrison .25 .11
❑ 537 Bruce Bochte .25 .11
❑ 538 Johnny LeMaster .25 .11
❑ 539 Vic Davalillo DP .15 .07
❑ 540 Steve Carlton 4.00 1.80
❑ 541 Larry Cox .25 .11
❑ 542 Tim Johnson .25 .11
❑ 543 Larry Harlow DP .15 .07
❑ 544 Len Randle DP .15 .07
❑ 545 Bill Campbell .25 .11
❑ 546 Ted Martinez .25 .11
❑ 547 John Scott .25 .11
❑ 548 Billy Hunter DP MG .15 .07
❑ 549 Joe Kerrigan .25 .11
❑ 550 John Mayberry .60 .25
❑ 551 Atlanta Braves 1.25 .25
Team Card
(Checklist back)
❑ 552 Francisco Barrios .25 .11
❑ 553 Terry Puhl .60 .25
❑ 554 Joe Coleman .25 .11
❑ 555 Butch Wynegar .25 .11
❑ 556 Ed Armbrister .25 .11
❑ 557 Tony Solaita .25 .11
❑ 558 Paul Mitchell .25 .11
❑ 559 Phil Mankowski .25 .11
❑ 560 Dave Parker 1.25 .55
❑ 561 Charlie Williams .25 .11
❑ 562 Glenn Burke .25 .11
❑ 563 Dave Rader .25 .11
❑ 564 Mick Kelleher .25 .11
❑ 565 Jerry Koosman .60 .25
❑ 566 Merv Rettenmund .25 .11
❑ 567 Dick Drago .25 .11
❑ 568 Tom Hutton .25 .11
❑ 569 Lary Sorensen .25 .11
❑ 570 Dave Kingman 1.25 .55
❑ 571 Buck Martinez .25 .11
❑ 572 Rick Wise .25 .11
❑ 573 Luis Gomez .25 .11
❑ 574 Bob Lemon MG 1.25 .55
❑ 575 Pat Dobson .25 .11
❑ 576 Sam Mejias .25 .11
❑ 577 Oakland A's 1.25 .25
Team Card
(Checklist back)
❑ 578 Buzz Capra .25 .11
❑ 579 Rance Mulliniks .25 .11
❑ 580 Rod Carew 4.00 1.80
❑ 581 Lynn McGlothen .25 .11
❑ 582 Fran Healy .25 .11
❑ 583 George Medich .25 .11
❑ 584 John Hale .25 .11
❑ 585 Woodie Fryman DP .15 .07
❑ 586 Ed Goodson .25 .11
❑ 587 John Urrea .25 .11
❑ 588 Jim Mason .25 .11
❑ 589 Bob Knepper .25 .11
❑ 590 Bobby Murcer .60 .25
❑ 591 George Zeber .25 .11
❑ 592 Bob Apodaca .25 .11
❑ 593 Dave Skaggs .25 .11
❑ 594 Dave Freisleben .25 .11
❑ 595 Sixto Lezcano .25 .11
❑ 596 Gary Wheelock .25 .11
❑ 597 Steve Dillard .25 .11
❑ 598 Eddie Solomon .25 .11
❑ 599 Gary Woods .25 .11
❑ 600 Frank Tanana .60 .25
❑ 601 Gene Mauch MG .60 .25
❑ 602 Eric Soderholm .25 .11
❑ 603 Will McEnaney .25 .11
❑ 604 Earl Williams .25 .11
❑ 605 Rick Rhoden .60 .25
❑ 606 Pittsburgh Pirates 1.25 .25
Team Card
(Checklist back)
❑ 607 Fernando Arroyo .25 .11
❑ 608 Johnny Grubb .25 .11
❑ 609 John Denny .25 .11
❑ 610 Garry Maddox .60 .25
❑ 611 Pat Scanlon .25 .11
❑ 612 Ken Henderson .25 .11
❑ 613 Marty Perez .25 .11
❑ 614 Joe Wallis .25 .11
❑ 615 Clay Carroll .25 .11
❑ 616 Pat Kelly .25 .11
❑ 617 Joe Nolan .25 .11
❑ 618 Tommy Helms .25 .11
❑ 619 Thad Bosley DP .15 .07
❑ 620 Willie Randolph 1.25 .55
❑ 621 Craig Swan DP .15 .07
❑ 622 Champ Summers .25 .11
❑ 623 Eduardo Rodriguez .25 .11
❑ 624 Gary Alexander DP .15 .07
❑ 625 Jose Cruz .60 .25
❑ 626 Toronto Blue Jays 1.25 .25
Team Card DP
(Checklist back)
❑ 627 David Johnson .25 .11
❑ 628 Ralph Garr .60 .25
❑ 629 Don Stanhouse .25 .11
❑ 630 Ron Cey 1.25 .55
❑ 631 Danny Ozark MG .25 .11
❑ 632 Rowland Office .25 .11
❑ 633 Tom Veryzer .25 .11
❑ 634 Len Barker .25 .11
❑ 635 Joe Rudi .60 .25
❑ 636 Jim Bibby .25 .11
❑ 637 Duffy Dyer .25 .11
❑ 638 Paul Splittorff .25 .11
❑ 639 Gene Clines .25 .11
❑ 640 Lee May DP .25 .11
❑ 641 Doug Rau .25 .11
❑ 642 Denny Doyle .25 .11
❑ 643 Tom House .25 .11
❑ 644 Jim Dwyer .25 .11
❑ 645 Mike Torrez .60 .25
❑ 646 Rick Auerbach DP .15 .07
❑ 647 Steve Dunning .25 .11
❑ 648 Gary Thomasson .25 .11
❑ 649 Moose Haas .25 .11
❑ 650 Cesar Cedeno .60 .25
❑ 651 Doug Rader .25 .11
❑ 652 Checklist 606-726 1.25 .25
❑ 653 Ron Hodges DP .15 .07
❑ 654 Pepe Frias .25 .11
❑ 655 Lyman Bostock .60 .25
❑ 656 Dave Garcia MG .25 .11
❑ 657 Bombo Rivera .25 .11
❑ 658 Manny Sanguillen .60 .25
❑ 659 Texas Rangers 1.25 .25
Team Card
(Checklist back)
❑ 660 Jason Thompson .60 .25
❑ 661 Grant Jackson .25 .11
❑ 662 Paul Dade .25 .11
❑ 663 Paul Reuschel .25 .11
❑ 664 Fred Stanley .25 .11
❑ 665 Dennis Leonard .60 .25
❑ 666 Billy Smith .25 .11
❑ 667 Jeff Byrd .25 .11
❑ 668 Dusty Baker 1.25 .55
❑ 669 Pete Falcone .25 .11
❑ 670 Jim Rice 1.25 .55
❑ 671 Gary Lavelle .25 .11
❑ 672 Don Kessinger .60 .25
❑ 673 Steve Brye .25 .11
❑ 674 Ray Knight RC 2.50 1.10
❑ 675 Jay Johnstone .60 .25
❑ 676 Bob Myrick .25 .11
❑ 677 Ed Herrmann .25 .11
❑ 678 Tom Burgmeier .25 .11
❑ 679 Wayne Garrett .25 .11
❑ 680 Vida Blue .60 .25
❑ 681 Rob Belloir .25 .11
❑ 682 Ken Brett .25 .11
❑ 683 Mike Champion .25 .11
❑ 684 Ralph Houk MG .60 .25
❑ 685 Frank Taveras .25 .11
❑ 686 Gaylord Perry 2.50 1.10
❑ 687 Julio Cruz .25 .11
❑ 688 George Mitterwald .25 .11
❑ 689 Cleveland Indians 1.25 .25
Team Card
(Checklist back)
❑ 690 Mickey Rivers .60 .25
❑ 691 Ross Grimsley .25 .11
❑ 692 Ken Reitz .25 .11
❑ 693 Lamar Johnson .25 .11
❑ 694 Elias Sosa .25 .11

- ❑ 695 Dwight Evans .......... 1.25 .55
- ❑ 696 Steve Mingori .......... .25 .11
- ❑ 697 Roger Metzger .......... .25 .11
- ❑ 698 Juan Bernhardt .......... .25 .11
- ❑ 699 Jackie Brown .......... .25 .11
- ❑ 700 Johnny Bench .......... 8.00 3.60
- ❑ 701 Rookie Pitchers .......... .60 .25
  Tom Hume
  Larry Landreth
  Steve McCatty
  Bruce Taylor
- ❑ 702 Rookie Catchers .......... .60 .25
  Bill Nahorodny
  Kevin Pasley
  Rick Sweet
  Don Werner
- ❑ 703 Rookie Pitchers DP ...... 5.00 2.20
  Larry Andersen
  Tim Jones
  Mickey Mahler
  Jack Morris RC
- ❑ 704 Rookie 2nd Basemen .. 8.00 3.60
  Garth Iorg
  Dave Oliver
  Sam Perlozzo
  Lou Whitaker RC
- ❑ 705 Rookie Outfielders ........ 1.25 .55
  Dave Bergman
  Miguel Dilone
  Clint Hurdle
  Willie Norwood
- ❑ 706 Rookie 1st Basemen ...... .60 .25
  Wayne Cage
  Ted Cox
  Pat Putnam
  Dave Revering
- ❑ 707 Rookie Shortstops ...... 80.00 36.00
  Mickey Klutts
  Paul Molitor
  Alan Trammell
  U.L. Washington RC ! RC ! RC ! RC !
- ❑ 708 Rookie Catchers .......... 5.00 2.20
  Bo Diaz
  Dale Murphy
  Lance Parrish RC
  Ernie Whitt
- ❑ 709 Rookie Pitchers .......... .60 .25
  Steve Burke
  Matt Keough
  Lance Rautzhan
  Dan Schatzeder
- ❑ 710 Rookie Outfielders ........ 1.25 .55
  Dell Alston
  Rick Bosetti
  Mike Easler
  Keith Smith
- ❑ 711 Rookie Pitchers DP ........ .25 .11
  Cardell Camper
  Dennis Lamp
  Craig Mitchell
  Roy Thomas
- ❑ 712 Bobby Valentine .......... .60 .25
- ❑ 713 Bob Davis .......... .25 .11
- ❑ 714 Mike Anderson .......... .25 .11
- ❑ 715 Jim Kaat .......... 1.25 .55
- ❑ 716 Clarence Gaston .......... .60 .25
- ❑ 717 Nelson Briles .......... .25 .11
- ❑ 718 Ron Jackson .......... .25 .11
- ❑ 719 Randy Elliott .......... .25 .11
- ❑ 720 Fergie Jenkins .......... 2.50 1.10
- ❑ 721 Billy Martin MG .......... 1.25 .55
- ❑ 722 Pete Broberg .......... .25 .11
- ❑ 723 John Wockenfuss .......... .25 .11
- ❑ 724 Kansas City Royals ...... 1.25 .25
  Team Card
  (Checklist back)
- ❑ 725 Kurt Bevacqua .......... .25 .11
- ❑ 726 Wilbur Wood .......... 1.25 .30

## 1979 Topps

| | NRMT | VG-E |
|---|---|---|
| COMPLETE SET (726) | 150.00 | 70.00 |
| COMMON CARD (1-726) | .25 | .11 |
| COMMON CARD DP | .10 | .05 |

- ❑ 1 Batting Leaders .......... 2.50 .50
  Rod Carew
  Dave Parker
- ❑ 2 Home Run Leaders .......... 1.00 .45
  Jim Rice
  George Foster
- ❑ 3 RBI Leaders .......... 1.00 .45
  Jim Rice
  George Foster
- ❑ 4 Stolen Base Leaders .......... .50 .23
  Ron LeFlore
  Omar Moreno
- ❑ 5 Victory Leaders .......... .50 .23
  Ron Guidry
  Gaylord Perry
- ❑ 6 Strikeout Leaders .......... 6.00 2.70
  Nolan Ryan
  J.R. Richard
- ❑ 7 ERA Leaders .......... .50 .23
  Ron Guidry
  Craig Swan
- ❑ 8 Leading Firemen .......... 1.00 .45
  Rich Gossage
  Rollie Fingers
- ❑ 9 Dave Campbell .......... .25 .11
- ❑ 10 Lee May .......... .50 .23
- ❑ 11 Marc Hill .......... .25 .11
- ❑ 12 Dick Drago .......... .25 .11
- ❑ 13 Paul Dade .......... .25 .11
- ❑ 14 Rafael Landestoy .......... .25 .11
- ❑ 15 Ross Grimsley .......... .25 .11
- ❑ 16 Fred Stanley .......... .25 .11
- ❑ 17 Donnie Moore .......... .25 .11
- ❑ 18 Tony Solaita .......... .25 .11
- ❑ 19 Larry Gura DP .......... .10 .05
- ❑ 20 Joe Morgan DP .......... 2.00 .90
- ❑ 21 Kevin Kobel .......... .25 .11
- ❑ 22 Mike Jorgensen .......... .25 .11
- ❑ 23 Terry Forster .......... .25 .11
- ❑ 24 Paul Molitor .......... 15.00 6.75
- ❑ 25 Steve Carlton .......... 3.00 1.35
- ❑ 26 Jamie Quirk .......... .25 .11
- ❑ 27 Dave Goltz .......... .25 .11
- ❑ 28 Steve Brye .......... .25 .11
- ❑ 29 Rick Langford .......... .25 .11
- ❑ 30 Dave Winfield .......... 4.00 1.80
- ❑ 31 Tom House DP .......... .10 .05
- ❑ 32 Jerry Mumphrey .......... .25 .11
- ❑ 33 Dave Rozema .......... .25 .11
- ❑ 34 Rob Andrews .......... .25 .11
- ❑ 35 Ed Figueroa .......... .25 .11
- ❑ 36 Alan Ashby .......... .25 .11
- ❑ 37 Joe Kerrigan DP .......... .10 .05
- ❑ 38 Bernie Carbo .......... .25 .11
- ❑ 39 Dale Murphy .......... 3.00 1.35
- ❑ 40 Dennis Eckersley .......... 2.00 .90
- ❑ 41 Twins Team/Mgr. .......... 1.00 .20
  Gene Mauch
  (Checklist back)
- ❑ 42 Ron Blomberg .......... .25 .11
- ❑ 43 Wayne Twitchell .......... .25 .11
- ❑ 44 Kurt Bevacqua .......... .25 .11
- ❑ 45 Al Hrabosky .......... .25 .11
- ❑ 46 Ron Hodges .......... .25 .11
- ❑ 47 Fred Norman .......... .25 .11
- ❑ 48 Merv Rettenmund .......... .25 .11
- ❑ 49 Vern Ruhle .......... .25 .11
- ❑ 50 Steve Garvey DP .......... 1.00 .45
- ❑ 51 Ray Fosse DP .......... .10 .05
- ❑ 52 Randy Lerch .......... .25 .11
- ❑ 53 Mick Kelleher .......... .25 .11
- ❑ 54 Dell Alston DP .......... .10 .05
- ❑ 55 Willie Stargell .......... 2.00 .90
- ❑ 56 John Hale .......... .25 .11
- ❑ 57 Eric Rasmussen .......... .25 .11
- ❑ 58 Bob Randall DP .......... .10 .05
- ❑ 59 John Denny DP .......... .25 .11
- ❑ 60 Mickey Rivers .......... .50 .23
- ❑ 61 Bo Diaz .......... .25 .11
- ❑ 62 Randy Moffitt .......... .25 .11
- ❑ 63 Jack Brohamer .......... .25 .11
- ❑ 64 Tom Underwood .......... .25 .11
- ❑ 65 Mark Belanger .......... .50 .23
- ❑ 66 Tigers Team/Mgr. .......... 1.00 .20
  Les Moss
  (Checklist back)
- ❑ 67 Jim Mason DP .......... .10 .05
- ❑ 68 Joe Niekro DP .......... .25 .11
- ❑ 69 Elliott Maddox .......... .25 .11
- ❑ 70 John Candelaria .......... .50 .23
- ❑ 71 Brian Downing .......... .50 .23
- ❑ 72 Steve Mingori .......... .25 .11
- ❑ 73 Ken Henderson .......... .25 .11
- ❑ 74 Shane Rawley .......... .25 .11
- ❑ 75 Steve Yeager .......... .50 .23
- ❑ 76 Warren Cromartie .......... .50 .23
- ❑ 77 Dan Briggs DP .......... .10 .05
- ❑ 78 Elias Sosa .......... .25 .11
- ❑ 79 Ted Cox .......... .25 .11
- ❑ 80 Jason Thompson .......... .50 .23
- ❑ 81 Roger Erickson .......... .25 .11
- ❑ 82 Mets Team/Mgr. .......... 1.00 .20
  Joe Torre
  (Checklist back)
- ❑ 83 Fred Kendall .......... .25 .11
- ❑ 84 Greg Minton .......... .25 .11
- ❑ 85 Gary Matthews .......... .50 .23
- ❑ 86 Rodney Scott .......... .25 .11
- ❑ 87 Pete Falcone .......... .25 .11
- ❑ 88 Bob Molinaro .......... .25 .11
- ❑ 89 Dick Tidrow .......... .25 .11
- ❑ 90 Bob Boone .......... 1.00 .45
- ❑ 91 Terry Crowley .......... .25 .11
- ❑ 92 Jim Bibby .......... .25 .11
- ❑ 93 Phil Mankowski .......... .25 .11
- ❑ 94 Len Barker .......... .25 .11
- ❑ 95 Robin Yount .......... 5.00 2.20
- ❑ 96 Indians Team/Mgr. .......... 1.00 .20
  Jeff Torborg
  (Checklist back)
- ❑ 97 Sam Mejias .......... .25 .11
- ❑ 98 Ray Burris .......... .25 .11
- ❑ 99 John Wathan .......... .50 .23
- ❑ 100 Tom Seaver DP .......... 5.00 2.20
- ❑ 101 Roy Howell .......... .25 .11
- ❑ 102 Mike Anderson .......... .25 .11
- ❑ 103 Jim Todd .......... .25 .11
- ❑ 104 Johnny Oates DP .......... .25 .11
- ❑ 105 Rick Camp DP .......... .10 .05
- ❑ 106 Frank Duffy .......... .25 .11
- ❑ 107 Jesus Alou DP .......... .10 .05
- ❑ 108 Eduardo Rodriguez .......... .25 .11
- ❑ 109 Joel Youngblood .......... .25 .11
- ❑ 110 Vida Blue .......... .50 .23
- ❑ 111 Roger Freed .......... .25 .11
- ❑ 112 Phillies Team/Mgr. .......... 1.00 .20
  Danny Ozark
  (Checklist back)
- ❑ 113 Pete Redfern .......... .25 .11
- ❑ 114 Cliff Johnson .......... .25 .11
- ❑ 115 Nolan Ryan .......... 25.00 11.00
- ❑ 116 Ozzie Smith RC ! .......... 80.00 36.00
- ❑ 117 Grant Jackson .......... .25 .11
- ❑ 118 Bud Harrelson .......... .50 .23
- ❑ 119 Don Stanhouse .......... .25 .11
- ❑ 120 Jim Sundberg .......... .50 .23
- ❑ 121 Checklist 1-121 DP .......... .50 .10
- ❑ 122 Mike Paxton .......... .25 .11
- ❑ 123 Lou Whitaker .......... 2.50 1.10
- ❑ 124 Dan Schatzeder .......... .25 .11
- ❑ 125 Rick Burleson .......... .25 .11
- ❑ 126 Doug Bair .......... .25 .11
- ❑ 127 Thad Bosley .......... .25 .11
- ❑ 128 Ted Martinez .......... .25 .11

❑ 129 Marty Pattin DP .10 .05
❑ 130 Bob Watson DP .25 .11
❑ 131 Jim Clancy .25 .11
❑ 132 Rowland Office .25 .11
❑ 133 Bill Castro .25 .11
❑ 134 Alan Bannister .25 .11
❑ 135 Bobby Murcer .50 .23
❑ 136 Jim Kaat .50 .23
❑ 137 Larry Wolfe DP .10 .05
❑ 138 Mark Lee .25 .11
❑ 139 Luis Pujols .25 .11
❑ 140 Don Gullett .50 .23
❑ 141 Tom Paciorek .50 .23
❑ 142 Charlie Williams .25 .11
❑ 143 Tony Scott .25 .11
❑ 144 Sandy Alomar .25 .11
❑ 145 Rick Rhoden .25 .11
❑ 146 Duane Kuiper .25 .11
❑ 147 Dave Hamilton .25 .11
❑ 148 Bruce Boisclair .25 .11
❑ 149 Manny Sarmiento .25 .11
❑ 150 Wayne Cage .25 .11
❑ 151 John Hiller .25 .11
❑ 152 Rick Cerone .25 .11
❑ 153 Dennis Lamp .25 .11
❑ 154 Jim Gantner DP .25 .11
❑ 155 Dwight Evans 1.00 .45
❑ 156 Buddy Solomon .25 .11
❑ 157 U.L. Washington UER .25 .11
(Sic, bats left;
should be right)
❑ 158 Joe Sambito .25 .11
❑ 159 Roy White .50 .23
❑ 160 Mike Flanagan 1.00 .45
❑ 161 Barry Foote .25 .11
❑ 162 Tom Johnson .25 .11
❑ 163 Glenn Burke .25 .11
❑ 164 Mickey Lolich .50 .23
❑ 165 Frank Taveras .25 .11
❑ 166 Leon Roberts .25 .11
❑ 167 Roger Metzger DP .10 .05
❑ 168 Dave Freisleben .25 .11
❑ 169 Bill Nahorodny .25 .11
❑ 170 Don Sutton 2.00 .90
❑ 171 Gene Clines .25 .11
❑ 172 Mike Bruhert .25 .11
❑ 173 John Lowenstein .25 .11
❑ 174 Rick Auerbach .25 .11
❑ 175 George Hendrick 1.00 .45
❑ 176 Aurelio Rodriguez .25 .11
❑ 177 Ron Reed .25 .11
❑ 178 Alvis Woods .25 .11
❑ 179 Jim Beattie DP .25 .11
❑ 180 Larry Hisle .25 .11
❑ 181 Mike Garman .25 .11
❑ 182 Tim Johnson .25 .11
❑ 183 Paul Splittorff .25 .11
❑ 184 Darrel Chaney .25 .11
❑ 185 Mike Torrez .50 .23
❑ 186 Eric Soderholm .25 .11
❑ 187 Mark Lemongello .25 .11
❑ 188 Pat Kelly .25 .11
❑ 189 Eddie Whitson RC .25 .11
❑ 190 Ron Cey .50 .23
❑ 191 Mike Norris .25 .11
❑ 192 Cardinals Team/Mgr. 1.00 .20
Ken Boyer
(Checklist back)
❑ 193 Glenn Adams .25 .11
❑ 194 Randy Jones .25 .11
❑ 195 Bill Madlock .50 .23
❑ 196 Steve Kemp DP .25 .11
❑ 197 Bob Apodaca .25 .11
❑ 198 Johnny Grubb .25 .11
❑ 199 Larry Milbourne .25 .11
❑ 200 Johnny Bench DP 5.00 2.20
❑ 201 RB: Mike Edwards .25 .11
Most unassisted DP's,
second base
❑ 202 RB: Ron Guidry, 1.00 .45
Most strikeouts, left-hander,
nine innings
❑ 203 RB: J.R. Richard .25 .11
Most strikeouts,
season, right-hander
❑ 204 Pete Rose RB 6.00 2.70
Most hits NL season
❑ 205 RB: John Stearns .25 .11
Most SB's by
catcher, season
❑ 206 RB: Sammy Stewart .25 .11
7 straight SO's,
first ML game
❑ 207 Dave Lemanczyk .25 .11
❑ 208 Clarence Gaston .25 .11
❑ 209 Reggie Cleveland .25 .11
❑ 210 Larry Bowa .50 .23
❑ 211 Denny Martinez 2.00 .90
❑ 212 Carney Lansford RC 1.00 .45
❑ 213 Bill Travers .25 .11
❑ 214 Red Sox Team/Mgr. 1.00 .20
Don Zimmer
(Checklist back)
❑ 215 Willie McCovey 2.50 1.10
❑ 216 Wilbur Wood .25 .11
❑ 217 Steve Dillard .25 .11
❑ 218 Dennis Leonard .50 .23
❑ 219 Roy Smalley .50 .23
❑ 220 Cesar Geronimo .25 .11
❑ 221 Jesse Jefferson .25 .11
❑ 222 Bob Beall .25 .11
❑ 223 Kent Tekulve .50 .23
❑ 224 Dave Revering .25 .11
❑ 225 Rich Gossage 1.00 .45
❑ 226 Ron Pruitt .25 .11
❑ 227 Steve Stone .50 .23
❑ 228 Vic Davalillo .25 .11
❑ 229 Doug Flynn .25 .11
❑ 230 Bob Forsch .25 .11
❑ 231 John Wockenfuss .25 .11
❑ 232 Jimmy Sexton .25 .11
❑ 233 Paul Mitchell .25 .11
❑ 234 Toby Harrah .50 .23
❑ 235 Steve Rogers .25 .11
❑ 236 Jim Dwyer .25 .11
❑ 237 Billy Smith .25 .11
❑ 238 Balor Moore .25 .11
❑ 239 Willie Horton .50 .23
❑ 240 Rick Reuschel .50 .23
❑ 241 Checklist 122-242 DP .50 .10
❑ 242 Pablo Torrealba .25 .11
❑ 243 Buck Martinez DP .10 .05
❑ 244 Pirates Team/Mgr. 1.00 .20
Chuck Tanner
(Checklist back)
❑ 245 Jeff Burroughs .50 .23
❑ 246 Darrell Jackson .25 .11
❑ 247 Tucker Ashford DP .10 .05
❑ 248 Pete LaCock .25 .11
❑ 249 Paul Thormodsgard .25 .11
❑ 250 Willie Randolph .50 .23
❑ 251 Jack Morris 2.00 .90
❑ 252 Bob Stinson .25 .11
❑ 253 Rick Wise .25 .11
❑ 254 Luis Gomez .25 .11
❑ 255 Tommy John 1.00 .45
❑ 256 Mike Sadek .25 .11
❑ 257 Adrian Devine .25 .11
❑ 258 Mike Phillips .25 .11
❑ 259 Reds Team/Mgr. 1.00 .20
Sparky Anderson
(Checklist back)
❑ 260 Richie Zisk .25 .11
❑ 261 Mario Guerrero .25 .11
❑ 262 Nelson Briles .25 .11
❑ 263 Oscar Gamble .50 .23
❑ 264 Don Robinson RC .25 .11
❑ 265 Don Money .25 .11
❑ 266 Jim Willoughby .25 .11
❑ 267 Joe Rudi .50 .23
❑ 268 Julio Gonzalez .25 .11
❑ 269 Woodie Fryman .25 .11
❑ 270 Butch Hobson .50 .23
❑ 271 Rawly Eastwick .25 .11
❑ 272 Tim Corcoran .25 .11
❑ 273 Jerry Terrell .25 .11
❑ 274 Willie Norwood .25 .11
❑ 275 Junior Moore .25 .11
❑ 276 Jim Colborn .25 .11
❑ 277 Tom Grieve .50 .23
❑ 278 Andy Messersmith .50 .23
❑ 279 Jerry Grote DP .10 .05
❑ 280 Andre Thornton .50 .23
❑ 281 Vic Correll DP .10 .05
❑ 282 Blue Jays Team/Mgr. .50 .10
Roy Hartsfield
(Checklist back)
❑ 283 Ken Kravec .25 .11
❑ 284 Johnnie LeMaster .25 .11
❑ 285 Bobby Bonds 1.00 .45
❑ 286 Duffy Dyer .25 .11
❑ 287 Andres Mora .25 .11
❑ 288 Milt Wilcox .25 .11
❑ 289 Jose Cruz 1.00 .45
❑ 290 Dave Lopes .50 .23
❑ 291 Tom Griffin .25 .11
❑ 292 Don Reynolds .25 .11
❑ 293 Jerry Garvin .25 .11
❑ 294 Pepe Frias .25 .11
❑ 295 Mitchell Page .25 .11
❑ 296 Preston Hanna .25 .11
❑ 297 Ted Sizemore .25 .11
❑ 298 Rich Gale .25 .11
❑ 299 Steve Ontiveros .25 .11
❑ 300 Rod Carew 3.00 1.35
❑ 301 Tom Hume .25 .11
❑ 302 Braves Team/Mgr. 1.00 .20
Bobby Cox
(Checklist back)
❑ 303 Lary Sorensen DP .10 .05
❑ 304 Steve Swisher .25 .11
❑ 305 Willie Montanez .25 .11
❑ 306 Floyd Bannister .25 .11
❑ 307 Larvell Blanks .25 .11
❑ 308 Bert Blyleven 1.00 .45
❑ 309 Ralph Garr .50 .23
❑ 310 Thurman Munson 2.50 1.10
❑ 311 Gary Lavelle .25 .11
❑ 312 Bob Robertson .25 .11
❑ 313 Dyar Miller .25 .11
❑ 314 Larry Harlow .25 .11
❑ 315 Jon Matlack .25 .11
❑ 316 Milt May .25 .11
❑ 317 Jose Cardenal .50 .23
❑ 318 Bob Welch RC 2.00 .90
❑ 319 Wayne Garrett .25 .11
❑ 320 Carl Yastrzemski 4.00 1.80
❑ 321 Gaylord Perry 2.00 .90
❑ 322 Danny Goodwin .25 .11
❑ 323 Lynn McGlothen .25 .11
❑ 324 Mike Tyson .25 .11
❑ 325 Cecil Cooper .50 .23
❑ 326 Pedro Borbon .25 .11
❑ 327 Art Howe DP .25 .11
❑ 328 Oakland A's Team/Mgr. 1.00 .20
Jack McKeon
(Checklist back)
❑ 329 Joe Coleman .25 .11
❑ 330 George Brett 12.00 5.50
❑ 331 Mickey Mahler .25 .11
❑ 332 Gary Alexander .25 .11
❑ 333 Chet Lemon .50 .23
❑ 334 Craig Swan .25 .11
❑ 335 Chris Chambliss .50 .23
❑ 336 Bobby Thompson .25 .11
❑ 337 John Montague .25 .11
❑ 338 Vic Harris .25 .11
❑ 339 Ron Jackson .25 .11
❑ 340 Jim Palmer 2.50 1.10
❑ 341 Willie Upshaw .50 .23
❑ 342 Dave Roberts .25 .11
❑ 343 Ed Glynn .25 .11
❑ 344 Jerry Royster .25 .11
❑ 345 Tug McGraw .50 .23
❑ 346 Bill Buckner .50 .23
❑ 347 Doug Rau .25 .11
❑ 348 Andre Dawson 3.00 1.35
❑ 349 Jim Wright .25 .11
❑ 350 Garry Templeton .50 .23
❑ 351 Wayne Nordhagen DP .10 .05
❑ 352 Steve Renko .25 .11
❑ 353 Checklist 243-363 1.00 .20
❑ 354 Bill Bonham .25 .11
❑ 355 Lee Mazzilli .25 .11
❑ 356 Giants Team/Mgr. 1.00 .20
Joe Altobelli
(Checklist back)
❑ 357 Jerry Augustine .25 .11

❑ 358 Alan Trammell 3.00 1.35
❑ 359 Dan Spillner DP .10 .05
❑ 360 Amos Otis .50 .23
❑ 361 Tom Dixon .25 .11
❑ 362 Mike Cubbage .25 .11
❑ 363 Craig Skok .25 .11
❑ 364 Gene Richards .25 .11
❑ 365 Sparky Lyle .50 .23
❑ 366 Juan Bernhardt .25 .11
❑ 367 Dave Skaggs .25 .11
❑ 368 Don Aase .25 .11
❑ 369A Bump Wills ERR
(Blue Jays)
❑ 369B Bump Wills COR
(Rangers)
❑ 370 Dave Kingman 1.00 .45
❑ 371 Jeff Holly .25 .11
❑ 372 Lamar Johnson .25 .11
❑ 373 Lance Rautzhan .25 .11
❑ 374 Ed Herrmann .25 .11
❑ 375 Bill Campbell .25 .11
❑ 376 Gorman Thomas .50 .23
❑ 377 Paul Moskau .25 .11
❑ 378 Rob Picciolo DP .10 .05
❑ 379 Dale Murray .25 .11
❑ 380 John Mayberry .50 .23
❑ 381 Astros Team/Mgr. 1.00 .20
Bill Virdon
(Checklist back)
❑ 382 Jerry Martin .25 .11
❑ 383 Phil Garner .50 .23
❑ 384 Tommy Boggs .25 .11
❑ 385 Dan Ford .25 .11
❑ 386 Francisco Barrios .25 .11
❑ 387 Gary Thomasson .25 .11
❑ 388 Jack Billingham .25 .11
❑ 389 Joe Zdeb .25 .11
❑ 390 Rollie Fingers 2.00 .90
❑ 391 Al Oliver .50 .23
❑ 392 Doug Ault .25 .11
❑ 393 Scott McGregor .50 .23
❑ 394 Randy Stein .25 .11
❑ 395 Dave Cash .25 .11
❑ 396 Bill Plummer .25 .11
❑ 397 Sergio Ferrer .25 .11
❑ 398 Ivan DeJesus .25 .11
❑ 399 David Clyde .25 .11
❑ 400 Jim Rice 1.00 .45
❑ 401 Ray Knight .50 .23
❑ 402 Paul Hartzell .25 .11
❑ 403 Tim Foli .25 .11
❑ 404 White Sox Team/Mgr .. 1.00 .20
Don Kessinger
(Checklist back)
❑ 405 Butch Wynegar DP .10 .05
❑ 406 Joe Wallis DP .10 .05
❑ 407 Pete Vuckovich .50 .23
❑ 408 Charlie Moore DP .10 .05
❑ 409 Willie Wilson RC 1.00 .45
❑ 410 Darrell Evans 1.00 .45
❑ 411 George Sisler ATL 2.50 1.10
Ty Cobb
❑ 412 Hack Wilson ATL 2.50 1.10
Hank Aaron
❑ 413 Roger Maris ATL 3.00 1.35
Hank Aaron
❑ 414 Rogers Hornsby ATL 2.50 1.10
Ty Cobb
❑ 415 Lou Brock ATL 1.00 .45
❑ 416 Jack Chesbro ATL .50 .23
Cy Young
❑ 417 Nolan Ryan ATL DP 5.00 2.20
Walter Johnson
❑ 418 Dutch Leonard ATL DP .. .25 .11
Walter Johnson
❑ 419 Dick Ruthven .25 .11
❑ 420 Ken Griffey Sr. .50 .23
❑ 421 Doug DeCinces .50 .23
❑ 422 Ruppert Jones .25 .11
❑ 423 Bob Montgomery .25 .11
❑ 424 Angels Team/Mgr. 1.00 .20
Jim Fregosi
(Checklist back)
❑ 425 Rick Manning .25 .11
❑ 426 Chris Speier .25 .11
❑ 427 Andy Replogle .25 .11
❑ 428 Bobby Valentine .50 .23
❑ 429 John Urrea DP .10 .05
❑ 430 Dave Parker .50 .23
❑ 431 Glenn Borgmann .25 .11
❑ 432 Dave Heaverlo .25 .11
❑ 433 Larry Biittner .25 .11
❑ 434 Ken Clay .25 .11
❑ 435 Gene Tenace .50 .23
❑ 436 Hector Cruz .25 .11
❑ 437 Rick Williams .25 .11
❑ 438 Horace Speed .25 .11
❑ 439 Frank White .50 .23
❑ 440 Rusty Staub 1.00 .45
❑ 441 Lee Lacy .25 .11
❑ 442 Doyle Alexander .25 .11
❑ 443 Bruce Bochte .25 .11
❑ 444 Aurelio Lopez .25 .11
❑ 445 Steve Henderson .25 .11
❑ 446 Jim Lonborg .50 .23
❑ 447 Manny Sanguillen .50 .23
❑ 448 Moose Haas .25 .11
❑ 449 Bombo Rivera .25 .11
❑ 450 Dave Concepcion 1.00 .45
❑ 451 Royals Team/Mgr. 1.00 .20
Whitey Herzog
(Checklist back)
❑ 452 Jerry Morales .25 .11
❑ 453 Chris Knapp .25 .11
❑ 454 Len Randle .25 .11
❑ 455 Bill Lee DP .10 .05
❑ 456 Chuck Baker .25 .11
❑ 457 Bruce Sutter .50 .23
❑ 458 Jim Essian .25 .11
❑ 459 Sid Monge .25 .11
❑ 460 Graig Nettles 1.00 .45
❑ 461 Jim Barr DP .10 .05
❑ 462 Otto Velez .25 .11
❑ 463 Steve Comer .25 .11
❑ 464 Joe Nolan .25 .11
❑ 465 Reggie Smith .50 .23
❑ 466 Mark Littell .25 .11
❑ 467 Don Kessinger DP .25 .11
❑ 468 Stan Bahnsen DP .10 .05
❑ 469 Lance Parrish 1.00 .45
❑ 470 Garry Maddox DP .25 .11
❑ 471 Joaquin Andujar .50 .23
❑ 472 Craig Kusick .25 .11
❑ 473 Dave Roberts .25 .11
❑ 474 Dick Davis .25 .11
❑ 475 Dan Driessen .25 .11
❑ 476 Tom Poquette .25 .11
❑ 477 Bob Grich .50 .23
❑ 478 Juan Beniquez .25 .11
❑ 479 Padres Team/Mgr. 1.00 .20
Roger Craig
(Checklist back)
❑ 480 Fred Lynn .50 .23
❑ 481 Skip Lockwood .25 .11
❑ 482 Craig Reynolds .25 .11
❑ 483 Checklist 364-484 DP .50 .10
❑ 484 Rick Waits .25 .11
❑ 485 Bucky Dent .50 .23
❑ 486 Bob Knepper .25 .11
❑ 487 Miguel Dilone .25 .11
❑ 488 Bob Owchinko .25 .11
❑ 489 Larry Cox UER .25 .11
(Photo actually
Dave Rader)
❑ 490 Al Cowens .25 .11
❑ 491 Tippy Martinez .25 .11
❑ 492 Bob Bailor .25 .11
❑ 493 Larry Christenson .25 .11
❑ 494 Jerry White .25 .11
❑ 495 Tony Perez 2.00 .90
❑ 496 Barry Bonnell DP .10 .05
❑ 497 Glenn Abbott .25 .11
❑ 498 Rich Chiles .25 .11
❑ 499 Rangers Team/Mgr. 1.00 .20
Pat Corrales
(Checklist back)
❑ 500 Ron Guidry .50 .23
❑ 501 Junior Kennedy .25 .11
❑ 502 Steve Braun .25 .11
❑ 503 Terry Humphrey .25 .11
❑ 504 Larry McWilliams .25 .11
❑ 505 Ed Kranepool .25 .11
❑ 506 John D'Acquisto .25 .11
❑ 507 Tony Armas .50 .23
❑ 508 Charlie Hough .50 .23
❑ 509 Mario Mendoza UER .25 .11
(Career BA .278,
should say .204)
❑ 510 Ted Simmons 1.00 .45
❑ 511 Paul Reuschel DP .10 .05
❑ 512 Jack Clark .50 .23
❑ 513 Dave Johnson .50 .23
❑ 514 Mike Proly .25 .11
❑ 515 Enos Cabell .25 .11
❑ 516 Champ Summers DP .10 .05
❑ 517 Al Bumbry .50 .23
❑ 518 Jim Umbarger .25 .11
❑ 519 Ben Oglivie .50 .23
❑ 520 Gary Carter 2.00 .90
❑ 521 Sam Ewing .25 .11
❑ 522 Ken Holtzman .50 .23
❑ 523 John Milner .25 .11
❑ 524 Tom Burgmeier .25 .11
❑ 525 Freddie Patek .25 .11
❑ 526 Dodgers Team/Mgr. 1.00 .20
Tom Lasorda
(Checklist back)
❑ 527 Lerrin LaGrow .25 .11
❑ 528 Wayne Gross DP .10 .05
❑ 529 Brian Asselstine .25 .11
❑ 530 Frank Tanana .50 .23
❑ 531 Fernando Gonzalez .25 .11
❑ 532 Buddy Schultz .25 .11
❑ 533 Leroy Stanton .25 .11
❑ 534 Ken Forsch .25 .11
❑ 535 Ellis Valentine .25 .11
❑ 536 Jerry Reuss .50 .23
❑ 537 Tom Veryzer .25 .11
❑ 538 Mike Ivie DP .10 .05
❑ 539 John Ellis .25 .11
❑ 540 Greg Luzinski .50 .23
❑ 541 Jim Slaton .25 .11
❑ 542 Rick Bosetti .25 .11
❑ 543 Kiko Garcia .25 .11
❑ 544 Fergie Jenkins 2.00 .90
❑ 545 John Stearns .25 .11
❑ 546 Bill Russell .50 .23
❑ 547 Clint Hurdle .25 .11
❑ 548 Enrique Romo .25 .11
❑ 549 Bob Bailey .25 .11
❑ 550 Sal Bando .50 .23
❑ 551 Cubs Team/Mgr. 1.00 .20
Herman Franks
(Checklist back)
❑ 552 Jose Morales .25 .11
❑ 553 Denny Walling .25 .11
❑ 554 Matt Keough .25 .11
❑ 555 Biff Pocoroba .25 .11
❑ 556 Mike Lum .25 .11
❑ 557 Ken Brett .25 .11
❑ 558 Jay Johnstone .50 .23
❑ 559 Greg Pryor .25 .11
❑ 560 John Montefusco .25 .11
❑ 561 Ed Ott .25 .11
❑ 562 Dusty Baker 1.00 .45
❑ 563 Roy Thomas .25 .11
❑ 564 Jerry Turner .25 .11
❑ 565 Rico Carty .50 .23
❑ 566 Nino Espinosa .25 .11
❑ 567 Richie Hebner .50 .23
❑ 568 Carlos Lopez .25 .11
❑ 569 Bob Sykes .25 .11
❑ 570 Cesar Cedeno .50 .23
❑ 571 Darrell Porter .50 .23
❑ 572 Rod Gilbreath .25 .11
❑ 573 Jim Kern .25 .11
❑ 574 Claudell Washington .50 .23
❑ 575 Luis Tiant .50 .23
❑ 576 Mike Parrott .25 .11
❑ 577 Brewers Team/Mgr. 1.00 .20
George Bamberger
(Checklist back)
❑ 578 Pete Broberg .25 .11
❑ 579 Greg Gross .25 .11
❑ 580 Ron Fairly .50 .23
❑ 581 Darold Knowles .25 .11
❑ 582 Paul Blair .50 .23
❑ 583 Julio Cruz .25 .11

❑ 584 Jim Rooker .25 .11
❑ 585 Hal McRae 1.00 .45
❑ 586 Bob Horner RC 1.00 .45
❑ 587 Ken Reitz .25 .11
❑ 588 Tom Murphy .25 .11
❑ 589 Terry Whitfield .25 .11
❑ 590 J.R. Richard .50 .23
❑ 591 Mike Hargrove .50 .23
❑ 592 Mike Krukow .25 .11
❑ 593 Rick Dempsey .50 .23
❑ 594 Bob Shirley .25 .11
❑ 595 Phil Niekro 2.00 .90
❑ 596 Jim Wohlford .25 .11
❑ 597 Bob Stanley .25 .11
❑ 598 Mark Wagner .25 .11
❑ 599 Jim Spencer .25 .11
❑ 600 George Foster .50 .23
❑ 601 Dave LaRoche .25 .11
❑ 602 Checklist 485-605 1.00 .20
❑ 603 Rudy May .25 .11
❑ 604 Jeff Newman .25 .11
❑ 605 Rick Monday DP .25 .11
❑ 606 Expos Team/Mgr. 1.00 .20
Dick Williams
(Checklist back)
❑ 607 Omar Moreno .25 .11
❑ 608 Dave McKay .25 .11
❑ 609 Silvio Martinez .25 .11
❑ 610 Mike Schmidt 8.00 3.60
❑ 611 Jim Norris .25 .11
❑ 612 Rick Honeycutt RC .50 .23
❑ 613 Mike Edwards .25 .11
❑ 614 Willie Hernandez .50 .23
❑ 615 Ken Singleton .50 .23
❑ 616 Billy Almon .25 .11
❑ 617 Terry Puhl .25 .11
❑ 618 Jerry Remy .25 .11
❑ 619 Ken Landreaux .50 .23
❑ 620 Bert Campaneris .50 .23
❑ 621 Pat Zachry .25 .11
❑ 622 Dave Collins .50 .23
❑ 623 Bob McClure .25 .11
❑ 624 Larry Herndon .25 .11
❑ 625 Mark Fidrych 2.00 .90
❑ 626 Yankees Team/Mgr. 1.00 .20
Bob Lemon
(Checklist back)
❑ 627 Gary Serum .25 .11
❑ 628 Del Unser .25 .11
❑ 629 Gene Garber .50 .23
❑ 630 Bake McBride .50 .23
❑ 631 Jorge Orta .25 .11
❑ 632 Don Kirkwood .25 .11
❑ 633 Rob Wilfong DP .10 .05
❑ 634 Paul Lindblad .25 .11
❑ 635 Don Baylor 1.00 .45
❑ 636 Wayne Garland .25 .11
❑ 637 Bill Robinson .50 .23
❑ 638 Al Fitzmorris .25 .11
❑ 639 Manny Trillo .25 .11
❑ 640 Eddie Murray 15.00 6.75
❑ 641 Bobby Castillo .25 .11
❑ 642 Wilbur Howard DP .10 .05
❑ 643 Tom Hausman .25 .11
❑ 644 Manny Mota .50 .23
❑ 645 George Scott DP .25 .11
❑ 646 Rick Sweet .25 .11
❑ 647 Bob Lacey .25 .11
❑ 648 Lou Piniella .50 .23
❑ 649 John Curtis .25 .11
❑ 650 Pete Rose 12.00 5.50
❑ 651 Mike Caldwell .25 .11
❑ 652 Stan Papi .25 .11
❑ 653 Warren Brusstar DP .10 .05
❑ 654 Rick Miller .25 .11
❑ 655 Jerry Koosman .50 .23
❑ 656 Hosken Powell .25 .11
❑ 657 George Medich .25 .11
❑ 658 Taylor Duncan .25 .11
❑ 659 Mariners Team/Mgr. 1.00 .20
Darrell Johnson
(Checklist back)
❑ 660 Ron LeFlore DP .25 .11
❑ 661 Bruce Kison .25 .11
❑ 662 Kevin Bell .25 .11
❑ 663 Mike Vail .25 .11
❑ 664 Doug Bird .25 .11
❑ 665 Lou Brock 2.50 1.10
❑ 666 Rich Dauer .25 .11
❑ 667 Don Hood .25 .11
❑ 668 Bill North .25 .11
❑ 669 Checklist 606-726 1.00 .20
❑ 670 Jim Hunter DP 1.00 .45
❑ 671 Joe Ferguson DP .10 .05
❑ 672 Ed Halicki .25 .11
❑ 673 Tom Hutton .25 .11
❑ 674 Dave Tomlin .25 .11
❑ 675 Tim McCarver 1.00 .45
❑ 676 Johnny Sutton .25 .11
❑ 677 Larry Parrish .50 .23
❑ 678 Geoff Zahn .25 .11
❑ 679 Derrel Thomas .25 .11
❑ 680 Carlton Fisk 2.50 1.10
❑ 681 John Henry Johnson .25 .11
❑ 682 Dave Chalk .25 .11
❑ 683 Dan Meyer DP .10 .05
❑ 684 Jamie Easterly DP .10 .05
❑ 685 Sixto Lezcano .25 .11
❑ 686 Ron Schueler DP .10 .05
❑ 687 Rennie Stennett .25 .11
❑ 688 Mike Willis .25 .11
❑ 689 Orioles Team/Mgr. 1.00 .20
Earl Weaver
(Checklist back)
❑ 690 Buddy Bell DP .25 .11
❑ 691 Dock Ellis DP .10 .05
❑ 692 Mickey Stanley .25 .11
❑ 693 Dave Rader .25 .11
❑ 694 Burt Hooton .50 .23
❑ 695 Keith Hernandez 1.00 .45
❑ 696 Andy Hassler .25 .11
❑ 697 Dave Bergman .25 .11
❑ 698 Bill Stein .25 .11
❑ 699 Hal Dues .25 .11
❑ 700 Reggie Jackson DP 5.00 2.20
❑ 701 Orioles Prospects .50 .23
Mark Corey
John Flinn
Sammy Stewart
❑ 702 Red Sox Prospects .50 .23
Joel Finch
Garry Hancock
Allen Ripley
❑ 703 Angels Prospects .50 .23
Jim Anderson
Dave Frost
Bob Slater
❑ 704 White Sox Prospects .50 .23
Ross Baumgarten
Mike Colbern
Mike Squires
❑ 705 Indians Prospects 1.00 .45
Alfredo Griffin
Tim Norrid
Dave Oliver
❑ 706 Tigers Prospects .50 .23
Dave Stegman
Dave Tobik
Kip Young
❑ 707 Royals Prospects 1.00 .45
Randy Bass
Jim Gaudet
Randy McGilberry
❑ 708 Brewers Prospects 1.00 .45
Kevin Bass
Eddie Romero
Ned Yost
❑ 709 Twins Prospects .50 .23
Sam Perlozzo
Rick Sofield
Kevin Stanfield
❑ 710 Yankees Prospects .50 .23
Brian Doyle
Mike Heath
Dave Rajsich
❑ 711 A's Prospects 1.00 .45
Dwayne Murphy
Bruce Robinson
Alan Wirth
❑ 712 Mariners Prospects .50 .23
Bud Anderson
Greg Biercevicz
Byron McLaughlin
❑ 713 Rangers Prospects 1.00 .45
Danny Darwin
Pat Putnam
Billy Sample
❑ 714 Blue Jays Prospects .50 .23
Victor Cruz
Pat Kelly
Ernie Whitt
❑ 715 Braves Prospects 1.00 .45
Bruce Benedict
Glenn Hubbard
Larry Whisenton
❑ 716 Cubs Prospects .50 .23
Dave Geisel
Karl Pagel
Scot Thompson
❑ 717 Reds Prospects .50 .23
Mike LaCoss
Ron Oester
Harry Spilman
❑ 718 Astros Prospects .50 .23
Bruce Bochy
Mike Fischlin
Don Pisker
❑ 719 Dodgers Prospects 1.00 .45
Pedro Guerrero
Rudy Law
Joe Simpson
❑ 720 Expos Prospects 1.00 .45
Jerry Fry
Jerry Pirtle
Scott Sanderson
❑ 721 Mets Prospects .50 .23
Juan Berenguer
Dwight Bernard
Dan Norman
❑ 722 Phillies Prospects 1.00 .45
Jim Morrison
Lonnie Smith
Jim Wright
❑ 723 Pirates Prospects .50 .23
Dale Berra
Eugenio Cotes
Ben Wiltbank
❑ 724 Cardinals Prospects 1.00 .45
Tom Bruno
George Frazier
Terry Kennedy
❑ 725 Padres Prospects .50 .23
Jim Beswick
Steve Mura
Broderick Perkins
❑ 726 Giants Prospects .50 .10
Greg Johnston
Joe Strain
John Tamargo

## 1980 Topps

| | NRMT | VG-E |
|---|---|---|
| COMPLETE SET (726) | 120.00 | 55.00 |
| COMMON CARD (1-726) | .25 | .11 |
| COMMON CARD DP | .10 | .05 |

❑ 1 Lou Brock HL 2.50 .50
Carl Yastrzemski
Enter 3000 hit circle

❑ 2 Willie McCovey HL .75 .35
512th homer sets new
mark for NL lefties
❑ 3 Manny Mota HL .25 .11
All-time pinch-hits, 145
❑ 4 Pete Rose HL 3.00 1.35
Career Record 10th season
with 200 or more hits
❑ 5 Garry Templeton HL .40 .18
First with 100 hits
from each side of plate
❑ 6 Del Unser HL .40 .18
3 consecutive
pinch homers
❑ 7 Mike Lum .25 .11
❑ 8 Craig Swan .25 .11
❑ 9 Steve Braun .25 .11
❑ 10 Dennis Martinez 1.25 .55
❑ 11 Jimmy Sexton .25 .11
❑ 12 John Curtis DP .10 .05
❑ 13 Ron Pruitt .25 .11
❑ 14 Dave Cash .25 .11
❑ 15 Bill Campbell .25 .11
❑ 16 Jerry Narron .25 .11
❑ 17 Bruce Sutter .75 .35
❑ 18 Ron Jackson .25 .11
❑ 19 Balor Moore .25 .11
❑ 20 Dan Ford .25 .11
❑ 21 Manny Sarmiento .25 .11
❑ 22 Pat Putnam .25 .11
❑ 23 Derrel Thomas .25 .11
❑ 24 Jim Slaton .25 .11
❑ 25 Lee Mazzilli .40 .18
❑ 26 Marty Pattin .25 .11
❑ 27 Del Unser .25 .11
❑ 28 Bruce Kison .25 .11
❑ 29 Mark Wagner .25 .11
❑ 30 Vida Blue .75 .35
❑ 31 Jay Johnstone .40 .18
❑ 32 Julio Cruz DP .10 .05
❑ 33 Tony Scott .25 .11
❑ 34 Jeff Newman DP .10 .05
❑ 35 Luis Tiant .40 .18
❑ 36 Rusty Torres .25 .11
❑ 37 Kiko Garcia .25 .11
❑ 38 Dan Spillner DP .10 .05
❑ 39 Rowland Office .25 .11
❑ 40 Carlton Fisk 1.50 .70
❑ 41 Rangers Team/Mgr. .75 .15
Pat Corrales
(Checklist back)
❑ 42 David Palmer .25 .11
❑ 43 Bombo Rivera .25 .11
❑ 44 Bill Fahey .25 .11
❑ 45 Frank White .75 .35
❑ 46 Rico Carty .40 .18
❑ 47 Bill Bonham DP .10 .05
❑ 48 Rick Miller .25 .11
❑ 49 Mario Guerrero .25 .11
❑ 50 J.R. Richard .40 .18
❑ 51 Joe Ferguson DP .10 .05
❑ 52 Warren Brusstar .25 .11
❑ 53 Ben Oglivie .40 .18
❑ 54 Dennis Lamp .25 .11
❑ 55 Bill Madlock .40 .18
❑ 56 Bobby Valentine .40 .18
❑ 57 Pete Vuckovich .25 .11
❑ 58 Doug Flynn .25 .11
❑ 59 Eddy Putman .25 .11
❑ 60 Bucky Dent .40 .18
❑ 61 Gary Serum .25 .11
❑ 62 Mike Ivie .25 .11
❑ 63 Bob Stanley .25 .11
❑ 64 Joe Nolan .25 .11
❑ 65 Al Bumbry .40 .18
❑ 66 Royals Team/Mgr. .75 .15
Jim Frey
(Checklist back)
❑ 67 Doyle Alexander .25 .11
❑ 68 Larry Harlow .25 .11
❑ 69 Rick Williams .25 .11
❑ 70 Gary Carter 1.25 .55
❑ 71 John Milner DP .10 .05
❑ 72 Fred Howard DP .10 .05
❑ 73 Dave Collins .25 .11
❑ 74 Sid Monge .25 .11
❑ 75 Bill Russell .40 .18
❑ 76 John Stearns .25 .11
❑ 77 Dave Stieb RC 1.25 .55
❑ 78 Ruppert Jones .25 .11
❑ 79 Bob Owchinko .25 .11
❑ 80 Ron LeFlore .40 .18
❑ 81 Ted Sizemore .25 .11
❑ 82 Astros Team/Mgr. .75 .15
Bill Virdon
(Checklist back)
❑ 83 Steve Trout .25 .11
❑ 84 Gary Lavelle .25 .11
❑ 85 Ted Simmons .40 .18
❑ 86 Dave Hamilton .25 .11
❑ 87 Pepe Frias .25 .11
❑ 88 Ken Landreaux .25 .11
❑ 89 Don Hood .25 .11
❑ 90 Manny Trillo .40 .18
❑ 91 Rick Dempsey .40 .18
❑ 92 Rick Rhoden .25 .11
❑ 93 Dave Roberts DP .10 .05
❑ 94 Neil Allen .40 .18
❑ 95 Cecil Cooper .40 .18
❑ 96 A's Team/Mgr. .75 .15
Jim Marshall
(Checklist back)
❑ 97 Bill Lee .40 .18
❑ 98 Jerry Terrell .25 .11
❑ 99 Victor Cruz .25 .11
❑ 100 Johnny Bench 4.00 1.80
❑ 101 Aurelio Lopez .25 .11
❑ 102 Rich Dauer .25 .11
❑ 103 Bill Caudill .25 .11
❑ 104 Manny Mota .40 .18
❑ 105 Frank Tanana .40 .18
❑ 106 Jeff Leonard RC .75 .35
❑ 107 Francisco Barrios .25 .11
❑ 108 Bob Horner .40 .18
❑ 109 Bill Travers .25 .11
❑ 110 Fred Lynn DP .40 .18
❑ 111 Bob Knepper .25 .11
❑ 112 White Sox Team/Mgr. .75 .15
Tony LaRussa
(Checklist back)
❑ 113 Geoff Zahn .25 .11
❑ 114 Juan Beniquez .25 .11
❑ 115 Sparky Lyle .40 .18
❑ 116 Larry Cox .25 .11
❑ 117 Dock Ellis .25 .11
❑ 118 Phil Garner .40 .18
❑ 119 Sammy Stewart .25 .11
❑ 120 Greg Luzinski .40 .18
❑ 121 Checklist 1-121 .75 .15
❑ 122 Dave Rosello DP .10 .05
❑ 123 Lynn Jones .25 .11
❑ 124 Dave Lemanczyk .25 .11
❑ 125 Tony Perez 1.25 .55
❑ 126 Dave Tomlin .25 .11
❑ 127 Gary Thomasson .25 .11
❑ 128 Tom Burgmeier .25 .11
❑ 129 Craig Reynolds .25 .11
❑ 130 Amos Otis .40 .18
❑ 131 Paul Mitchell .25 .11
❑ 132 Biff Pocoroba .25 .11
❑ 133 Jerry Turner .25 .11
❑ 134 Matt Keough .25 .11
❑ 135 Bill Buckner .40 .18
❑ 136 Dick Ruthven .25 .11
❑ 137 John Castino .25 .11
❑ 138 Ross Baumgarten .25 .11
❑ 139 Dane Iorg .25 .11
❑ 140 Rich Gossage .75 .35
❑ 141 Gary Alexander .25 .11
❑ 142 Phil Huffman .25 .11
❑ 143 Bruce Bochte DP .10 .05
❑ 144 Steve Comer .25 .11
❑ 145 Darrell Evans .40 .18
❑ 146 Bob Welch .40 .18
❑ 147 Terry Puhl .25 .11
❑ 148 Manny Sanguillen .40 .18
❑ 149 Tom Hume .25 .11
❑ 150 Jason Thompson .25 .11
❑ 151 Tom Hausman DP .10 .05
❑ 152 John Fulgham .25 .11
❑ 153 Tim Blackwell .25 .11
❑ 154 Lary Sorensen .25 .11
❑ 155 Jerry Remy .25 .11
❑ 156 Tony Brizzolara .25 .11
❑ 157 Willie Wilson DP .40 .18
❑ 158 Rob Picciolo DP .10 .05
❑ 159 Ken Clay .25 .11
❑ 160 Eddie Murray 6.00 2.70
❑ 161 Larry Christenson .25 .11
❑ 162 Bob Randall .25 .11
❑ 163 Steve Swisher .25 .11
❑ 164 Greg Pryor .25 .11
❑ 165 Omar Moreno .25 .11
❑ 166 Glenn Abbott .25 .11
❑ 167 Jack Clark .40 .18
❑ 168 Rick Waits .25 .11
❑ 169 Luis Gomez .25 .11
❑ 170 Burt Hooton .25 .11
❑ 171 Fernando Gonzalez .25 .11
❑ 172 Ron Hodges .25 .11
❑ 173 John Henry Johnson .25 .11
❑ 174 Ray Knight .40 .18
❑ 175 Rick Reuschel .40 .18
❑ 176 Champ Summers .25 .11
❑ 177 Dave Heaverlo .25 .11
❑ 178 Tim McCarver .75 .35
❑ 179 Ron Davis .25 .11
❑ 180 Warren Cromartie .25 .11
❑ 181 Moose Haas .25 .11
❑ 182 Ken Reitz .25 .11
❑ 183 Jim Anderson DP .10 .05
❑ 184 Steve Renko DP .10 .05
❑ 185 Hal McRae .40 .18
❑ 186 Junior Moore .25 .11
❑ 187 Alan Ashby .25 .11
❑ 188 Terry Crowley .25 .11
❑ 189 Kevin Kobel .25 .11
❑ 190 Buddy Bell .40 .18
❑ 191 Ted Martinez .25 .11
❑ 192 Braves Team/Mgr. .75 .15
Bobby Cox
(Checklist back)
❑ 193 Dave Goltz .25 .11
❑ 194 Mike Easler .25 .11
❑ 195 John Montefusco .25 .11
❑ 196 Lance Parrish .40 .18
❑ 197 Byron McLaughlin .25 .11
❑ 198 Dell Alston DP .10 .05
❑ 199 Mike LaCoss .25 .11
❑ 200 Jim Rice .40 .18
❑ 201 Batting Leaders .75 .35
Keith Hernandez
Fred Lynn
❑ 202 Home Run Leaders .75 .35
Dave Kingman
Gorman Thomas
❑ 203 RBI Leaders 1.25 .55
Dave Winfield
Don Baylor
❑ 204 Stolen Base Leaders .40 .18
Omar Moreno
Willie Wilson
❑ 205 Victory Leaders .75 .35
Joe Niekro
Phil Niekro
Mike Flanagan
❑ 206 Strikeout Leaders 5.00 2.20
J.R. Richard
Nolan Ryan
❑ 207 ERA Leaders .75 .35
J.R. Richard
Ron Guidry
❑ 208 Wayne Cage .25 .11
❑ 209 Von Joshua .25 .11
❑ 210 Steve Carlton 2.00 .90
❑ 211 Dave Skaggs DP .10 .05
❑ 212 Dave Roberts .25 .11
❑ 213 Mike Jorgensen DP .10 .05
❑ 214 Angels Team/Mgr. .75 .15
Jim Fregosi
(Checklist back)
❑ 215 Sixto Lezcano .25 .11
❑ 216 Phil Mankowski .25 .11
❑ 217 Ed Halicki .25 .11
❑ 218 Jose Morales .25 .11
❑ 219 Steve Mingori .25 .11
❑ 220 Dave Concepcion .75 .35
❑ 221 Joe Cannon .25 .11

| No. | Player | Nr Mt | Ex-Mt |
|---|---|---|---|
| ❑ 222 | Ron Hassey | .25 | .11 |
| ❑ 223 | Bob Sykes | .25 | .11 |
| ❑ 224 | Willie Montanez | .25 | .11 |
| ❑ 225 | Lou Piniella | .75 | .35 |
| ❑ 226 | Bill Stein | .25 | .11 |
| ❑ 227 | Len Barker | .25 | .11 |
| ❑ 228 | Johnny Oates | .40 | .18 |
| ❑ 229 | Jim Bibby | .25 | .11 |
| ❑ 230 | Dave Winfield | 2.50 | 1.10 |
| ❑ 231 | Steve McCatty | .25 | .11 |
| ❑ 232 | Alan Trammell | 1.25 | .55 |
| ❑ 233 | LaRue Washington | .25 | .11 |
| ❑ 234 | Vern Ruhle | .25 | .11 |
| ❑ 235 | Andre Dawson | 1.50 | .70 |
| ❑ 236 | Marc Hill | .25 | .11 |
| ❑ 237 | Scott McGregor | .25 | .11 |
| ❑ 238 | Rob Wilfong | .25 | .11 |
| ❑ 239 | Don Aase | .25 | .11 |
| ❑ 240 | Dave Kingman | .75 | .35 |
| ❑ 241 | Checklist 122-242 | .75 | .15 |
| ❑ 242 | Lamar Johnson | .25 | .11 |
| ❑ 243 | Jerry Augustine | .25 | .11 |
| ❑ 244 | Cardinals Team/Mgr. Ken Boyer (Checklist back) | .75 | .15 |
| ❑ 245 | Phil Niekro | 1.25 | .55 |
| ❑ 246 | Tim Foli DP | .10 | .05 |
| ❑ 247 | Frank Riccelli | .25 | .11 |
| ❑ 248 | Jamie Quirk | .25 | .11 |
| ❑ 249 | Jim Clancy | .25 | .11 |
| ❑ 250 | Jim Kaat | .75 | .35 |
| ❑ 251 | Kip Young | .25 | .11 |
| ❑ 252 | Ted Cox | .25 | .11 |
| ❑ 253 | John Montague | .25 | .11 |
| ❑ 254 | Paul Dade DP | .10 | .05 |
| ❑ 255 | Dusty Baker DP | .40 | .18 |
| ❑ 256 | Roger Erickson | .25 | .11 |
| ❑ 257 | Larry Herndon | .25 | .11 |
| ❑ 258 | Paul Moskau | .25 | .11 |
| ❑ 259 | Mets Team/Mgr. Joe Torre (Checklist back) | .75 | .15 |
| ❑ 260 | Al Oliver | .75 | .35 |
| ❑ 261 | Dave Chalk | .25 | .11 |
| ❑ 262 | Benny Ayala | .25 | .11 |
| ❑ 263 | Dave LaRoche DP | .10 | .05 |
| ❑ 264 | Bill Robinson | .25 | .11 |
| ❑ 265 | Robin Yount | 3.00 | 1.35 |
| ❑ 266 | Bernie Carbo | .25 | .11 |
| ❑ 267 | Dan Schatzeder | .25 | .11 |
| ❑ 268 | Rafael Landestoy | .25 | .11 |
| ❑ 269 | Dave Tobik | .25 | .11 |
| ❑ 270 | Mike Schmidt DP | 3.00 | 1.35 |
| ❑ 271 | Dick Drago DP | .40 | .18 |
| ❑ 272 | Ralph Garr | .40 | .18 |
| ❑ 273 | Eduardo Rodriguez | .25 | .11 |
| ❑ 274 | Dale Murphy | 1.25 | .55 |
| ❑ 275 | Jerry Koosman | .40 | .18 |
| ❑ 276 | Tom Veryzer | .25 | .11 |
| ❑ 277 | Rick Bosetti | .25 | .11 |
| ❑ 278 | Jim Spencer | .25 | .11 |
| ❑ 279 | Rob Andrews | .25 | .11 |
| ❑ 280 | Gaylord Perry | 1.25 | .55 |
| ❑ 281 | Paul Blair | .40 | .18 |
| ❑ 282 | Mariners Team/Mgr. Darrell Johnson (Checklist back) | .75 | .15 |
| ❑ 283 | John Ellis | .25 | .11 |
| ❑ 284 | Larry Murray DP | .10 | .05 |
| ❑ 285 | Don Baylor | .75 | .35 |
| ❑ 286 | Darold Knowles DP | .10 | .05 |
| ❑ 287 | John Lowenstein | .25 | .11 |
| ❑ 288 | Dave Rozema | .25 | .11 |
| ❑ 289 | Bruce Bochy | .25 | .11 |
| ❑ 290 | Steve Garvey | 1.25 | .55 |
| ❑ 291 | Randy Scarberry | .25 | .11 |
| ❑ 292 | Dale Berra | .25 | .11 |
| ❑ 293 | Elias Sosa | .25 | .11 |
| ❑ 294 | Charlie Spikes | .25 | .11 |
| ❑ 295 | Larry Gura | .25 | .11 |
| ❑ 296 | Dave Rader | .25 | .11 |
| ❑ 297 | Tim Johnson | .25 | .11 |
| ❑ 298 | Ken Holtzman | .40 | .18 |
| ❑ 299 | Steve Henderson | .25 | .11 |
| ❑ 300 | Ron Guidry | .40 | .18 |
| ❑ 301 | Mike Edwards | .25 | .11 |
| ❑ 302 | Dodgers Team/Mgr. Tom Lasorda (Checklist back) | .75 | .15 |
| ❑ 303 | Bill Castro | .25 | .11 |
| ❑ 304 | Butch Wynegar | .25 | .11 |
| ❑ 305 | Randy Jones | .25 | .11 |
| ❑ 306 | Denny Walling | .25 | .11 |
| ❑ 307 | Rick Honeycutt | .25 | .11 |
| ❑ 308 | Mike Hargrove | .40 | .18 |
| ❑ 309 | Larry McWilliams | .25 | .11 |
| ❑ 310 | Dave Parker | .75 | .35 |
| ❑ 311 | Roger Metzger | .25 | .11 |
| ❑ 312 | Mike Barlow | .25 | .11 |
| ❑ 313 | Johnny Grubb | .25 | .11 |
| ❑ 314 | Tim Stoddard | .25 | .11 |
| ❑ 315 | Steve Kemp | .25 | .11 |
| ❑ 316 | Bob Lacey | .25 | .11 |
| ❑ 317 | Mike Anderson DP | .10 | .05 |
| ❑ 318 | Jerry Reuss | .40 | .18 |
| ❑ 319 | Chris Speier | .25 | .11 |
| ❑ 320 | Dennis Eckersley | .75 | .35 |
| ❑ 321 | Keith Hernandez | .40 | .18 |
| ❑ 322 | Claudell Washington | .40 | .18 |
| ❑ 323 | Mick Kelleher | .25 | .11 |
| ❑ 324 | Tom Underwood | .25 | .11 |
| ❑ 325 | Dan Driessen | .25 | .11 |
| ❑ 326 | Bo McLaughlin | .25 | .11 |
| ❑ 327 | Ray Fosse DP | .10 | .05 |
| ❑ 328 | Twins Team/Mgr. Gene Mauch (Checklist back) | .75 | .15 |
| ❑ 329 | Bert Roberge | .25 | .11 |
| ❑ 330 | Al Cowens | .25 | .11 |
| ❑ 331 | Richie Hebner | .40 | .18 |
| ❑ 332 | Enrique Romo | .25 | .11 |
| ❑ 333 | Jim Norris DP | .10 | .05 |
| ❑ 334 | Jim Beattie | .25 | .11 |
| ❑ 335 | Willie McCovey | 1.50 | .70 |
| ❑ 336 | George Medich | .25 | .11 |
| ❑ 337 | Carney Lansford | .40 | .18 |
| ❑ 338 | John Wockenfuss | .25 | .11 |
| ❑ 339 | John D'Acquisto | .25 | .11 |
| ❑ 340 | Ken Singleton | .40 | .18 |
| ❑ 341 | Jim Essian | .25 | .11 |
| ❑ 342 | Odell Jones | .25 | .11 |
| ❑ 343 | Mike Vail | .25 | .11 |
| ❑ 344 | Randy Lerch | .25 | .11 |
| ❑ 345 | Larry Parrish | .40 | .18 |
| ❑ 346 | Buddy Solomon | .25 | .11 |
| ❑ 347 | Harry Chappas | .25 | .11 |
| ❑ 348 | Checklist 243-363 | .75 | .15 |
| ❑ 349 | Jack Brohamer | .25 | .11 |
| ❑ 350 | George Hendrick | .40 | .18 |
| ❑ 351 | Bob Davis | .25 | .11 |
| ❑ 352 | Dan Briggs | .25 | .11 |
| ❑ 353 | Andy Hassler | .25 | .11 |
| ❑ 354 | Rick Auerbach | .25 | .11 |
| ❑ 355 | Gary Matthews | .40 | .18 |
| ❑ 356 | Padres Team/Mgr. Jerry Coleman (Checklist back) | .75 | .15 |
| ❑ 357 | Bob McClure | .25 | .11 |
| ❑ 358 | Lou Whitaker | 1.25 | .55 |
| ❑ 359 | Randy Moffitt | .25 | .11 |
| ❑ 360 | Darrell Porter DP | .25 | .11 |
| ❑ 361 | Wayne Garland | .25 | .11 |
| ❑ 362 | Danny Goodwin | .25 | .11 |
| ❑ 363 | Wayne Gross | .25 | .11 |
| ❑ 364 | Ray Burris | .25 | .11 |
| ❑ 365 | Bobby Murcer | .40 | .18 |
| ❑ 366 | Rob Dressler | .25 | .11 |
| ❑ 367 | Billy Smith | .25 | .11 |
| ❑ 368 | Willie Aikens | .25 | .11 |
| ❑ 369 | Jim Kern | .25 | .11 |
| ❑ 370 | Cesar Cedeno | .40 | .18 |
| ❑ 371 | Jack Morris | .75 | .35 |
| ❑ 372 | Joel Youngblood | .25 | .11 |
| ❑ 373 | Dan Petry RC DP | .25 | .11 |
| ❑ 374 | Jim Gantner | .40 | .18 |
| ❑ 375 | Ross Grimsley | .25 | .11 |
| ❑ 376 | Gary Allenson | .25 | .11 |
| ❑ 377 | Junior Kennedy | .25 | .11 |
| ❑ 378 | Jerry Mumphrey | .25 | .11 |
| ❑ 379 | Kevin Bell | .25 | .11 |
| ❑ 380 | Garry Maddox | .40 | .18 |
| ❑ 381 | Cubs Team/Mgr. Preston Gomez (Checklist back) | .75 | .15 |
| ❑ 382 | Dave Freisleben | .25 | .11 |
| ❑ 383 | Ed Ott | .25 | .11 |
| ❑ 384 | Joey McLaughlin | .25 | .11 |
| ❑ 385 | Enos Cabell | .25 | .11 |
| ❑ 386 | Darrell Jackson | .25 | .11 |
| ❑ 387A | Fred Stanley YL | 2.00 | .90 |
| ❑ 387B | Fred Stanley (Red name on front) | .25 | .11 |
| ❑ 388 | Mike Paxton | .25 | .11 |
| ❑ 389 | Pete LaCock | .25 | .11 |
| ❑ 390 | Fergie Jenkins | 1.25 | .55 |
| ❑ 391 | Tony Armas DP | .25 | .11 |
| ❑ 392 | Milt Wilcox | .25 | .11 |
| ❑ 393 | Ozzie Smith | 12.00 | 5.50 |
| ❑ 394 | Reggie Cleveland | .25 | .11 |
| ❑ 395 | Ellis Valentine | .25 | .11 |
| ❑ 396 | Dan Meyer | .25 | .11 |
| ❑ 397 | Roy Thomas DP | .10 | .05 |
| ❑ 398 | Barry Foote | .25 | .11 |
| ❑ 399 | Mike Proly DP | .10 | .05 |
| ❑ 400 | George Foster | .40 | .18 |
| ❑ 401 | Pete Falcone | .25 | .11 |
| ❑ 402 | Merv Rettenmund | .25 | .11 |
| ❑ 403 | Pete Redfern DP | .10 | .05 |
| ❑ 404 | Orioles Team/Mgr. Earl Weaver (Checklist back) | .75 | .15 |
| ❑ 405 | Dwight Evans | .40 | .18 |
| ❑ 406 | Paul Molitor | 6.00 | 2.70 |
| ❑ 407 | Tony Solaita | .25 | .11 |
| ❑ 408 | Bill North | .25 | .11 |
| ❑ 409 | Paul Splittorff | .25 | .11 |
| ❑ 410 | Bobby Bonds | .75 | .35 |
| ❑ 411 | Frank LaCorte | .25 | .11 |
| ❑ 412 | Thad Bosley | .25 | .11 |
| ❑ 413 | Allen Ripley | .25 | .11 |
| ❑ 414 | George Scott | .40 | .18 |
| ❑ 415 | Bill Atkinson | .25 | .11 |
| ❑ 416 | Tom Brookens | .25 | .11 |
| ❑ 417 | Craig Chamberlain DP | .10 | .05 |
| ❑ 418 | Roger Freed DP | .10 | .05 |
| ❑ 419 | Vic Correll | .25 | .11 |
| ❑ 420 | Butch Hobson | .25 | .11 |
| ❑ 421 | Doug Bird | .25 | .11 |
| ❑ 422 | Larry Milbourne | .25 | .11 |
| ❑ 423 | Dave Frost | .25 | .11 |
| ❑ 424 | Yankees Team/Mgr. Dick Howser (Checklist back) | .75 | .15 |
| ❑ 425 | Mark Belanger | .40 | .18 |
| ❑ 426 | Grant Jackson | .25 | .11 |
| ❑ 427 | Tom Hutton DP | .10 | .05 |
| ❑ 428 | Pat Zachry | .25 | .11 |
| ❑ 429 | Duane Kuiper | .25 | .11 |
| ❑ 430 | Larry Hisle DP | .10 | .05 |
| ❑ 431 | Mike Krukow | .25 | .11 |
| ❑ 432 | Willie Norwood | .25 | .11 |
| ❑ 433 | Rich Gale | .25 | .11 |
| ❑ 434 | Johnnie LeMaster | .25 | .11 |
| ❑ 435 | Don Gullett | .40 | .18 |
| ❑ 436 | Billy Almon | .25 | .11 |
| ❑ 437 | Joe Niekro | .40 | .18 |
| ❑ 438 | Dave Revering | .25 | .11 |
| ❑ 439 | Mike Phillips | .25 | .11 |
| ❑ 440 | Don Sutton | 1.25 | .55 |
| ❑ 441 | Eric Soderholm | .25 | .11 |
| ❑ 442 | Jorge Orta | .25 | .11 |
| ❑ 443 | Mike Parrott | .25 | .11 |
| ❑ 444 | Alvis Woods | .25 | .11 |
| ❑ 445 | Mark Fidrych | 1.25 | .55 |
| ❑ 446 | Duffy Dyer | .25 | .11 |
| ❑ 447 | Nino Espinosa | .25 | .11 |
| ❑ 448 | Jim Wohlford | .25 | .11 |
| ❑ 449 | Doug Bair | .25 | .11 |
| ❑ 450 | George Brett | 8.00 | 3.60 |
| ❑ 451 | Indians Team/Mgr. Dave Garcia (Checklist back) | .40 | .08 |
| ❑ 452 | Steve Dillard | .25 | .11 |
| ❑ 453 | Mike Bacsik | .25 | .11 |
| ❑ 454 | Tom Donohue | .25 | .11 |
| ❑ 455 | Mike Torrez | .25 | .11 |
| ❑ 456 | Frank Taveras | .25 | .11 |
| ❑ 457 | Bert Blyleven | .75 | .35 |

❑ 458 Billy Sample .25 .11
❑ 459 Mickey Lolich DP .25 .11
❑ 460 Willie Randolph .40 .18
❑ 461 Dwayne Murphy .25 .11
❑ 462 Mike Sadek DP .10 .05
❑ 463 Jerry Royster .25 .11
❑ 464 John Denny .25 .11
❑ 465 Rick Monday .25 .11
❑ 466 Mike Squires .25 .11
❑ 467 Jesse Jefferson .25 .11
❑ 468 Aurelio Rodriguez .25 .11
❑ 469 Randy Niemann DP .10 .05
❑ 470 Bob Boone .75 .35
❑ 471 Hosken Powell DP .10 .05
❑ 472 Willie Hernandez .40 .18
❑ 473 Bump Wills .25 .11
❑ 474 Steve Busby .25 .11
❑ 475 Cesar Geronimo .25 .11
❑ 476 Bob Shirley .25 .11
❑ 477 Buck Martinez .25 .11
❑ 478 Gil Flores .25 .11
❑ 479 Expos Team/Mgr. .75 .15
Dick Williams
(Checklist back)
❑ 480 Bob Watson .40 .18
❑ 481 Tom Paciorek .40 .18
❑ 482 Rickey Henderson RC UER 70.00 32.00
(7 steals at Modesto;
should be at Fresno)
❑ 483 Bo Diaz .25 .11
❑ 484 Checklist 364-484 .75 .15
❑ 485 Mickey Rivers .40 .18
❑ 486 Mike Tyson DP .10 .05
❑ 487 Wayne Nordhagen .25 .11
❑ 488 Roy Howell .25 .11
❑ 489 Preston Hanna DP .10 .05
❑ 490 Lee May .40 .18
❑ 491 Steve Mura DP .10 .05
❑ 492 Todd Cruz .25 .11
❑ 493 Jerry Martin .25 .11
❑ 494 Craig Minetto .25 .11
❑ 495 Bake McBride .25 .11
❑ 496 Silvio Martinez .25 .11
❑ 497 Jim Mason .25 .11
❑ 498 Danny Darwin .25 .11
❑ 499 Giants Team/Mgr. .75 .15
Dave Bristol
(Checklist back)
❑ 500 Tom Seaver 4.00 1.80
❑ 501 Rennie Stennett .25 .11
❑ 502 Rich Wortham DP .10 .05
❑ 503 Mike Cubbage .25 .11
❑ 504 Gene Garber .40 .18
❑ 505 Bert Campaneris .40 .18
❑ 506 Tom Buskey .25 .11
❑ 507 Leon Roberts .25 .11
❑ 508 U.L. Washington .25 .11
❑ 509 Ed Glynn .25 .11
❑ 510 Ron Cey .75 .35
❑ 511 Eric Wilkins .25 .11
❑ 512 Jose Cardenal .25 .11
❑ 513 Tom Dixon DP .10 .05
❑ 514 Steve Ontiveros .25 .11
❑ 515 Mike Caldwell UER .25 .11
(1979 loss total reads
96 instead of 69)
❑ 516 Hector Cruz .25 .11
❑ 517 Don Stanhouse .25 .11
❑ 518 Nelson Norman .25 .11
❑ 519 Steve Nicosia .25 .11
❑ 520 Steve Rogers .25 .11
❑ 521 Ken Brett .25 .11
❑ 522 Jim Morrison .25 .11
❑ 523 Ken Henderson .25 .11
❑ 524 Jim Wright DP .10 .05
❑ 525 Clint Hurdle .25 .11
❑ 526 Phillies Team/Mgr. .75 .15
Dallas Green
(Checklist back)
❑ 527 Doug Rau DP .10 .05
❑ 528 Adrian Devine .25 .11
❑ 529 Jim Barr .25 .11
❑ 530 Jim Sundberg DP .25 .11
❑ 531 Eric Rasmussen .25 .11
❑ 532 Willie Horton .40 .18
❑ 533 Checklist 485-605 .75 .15
❑ 534 Andre Thornton .40 .18
❑ 535 Bob Forsch .25 .11
❑ 536 Lee Lacy .25 .11
❑ 537 Alex Trevino .25 .11
❑ 538 Joe Strain .25 .11
❑ 539 Rudy May .25 .11
❑ 540 Pete Rose 8.00 3.60
❑ 541 Miguel Dilone .25 .11
❑ 542 Joe Coleman .25 .11
❑ 543 Pat Kelly .25 .11
❑ 544 Rick Sutcliffe RC .75 .35
❑ 545 Jeff Burroughs .40 .18
❑ 546 Rick Langford .25 .11
❑ 547 John Wathan .25 .11
❑ 548 Dave Rajsich .25 .11
❑ 549 Larry Wolfe .25 .11
❑ 550 Ken Griffey Sr. .75 .35
❑ 551 Pirates Team/Mgr. .75 .15
Chuck Tanner
(Checklist back)
❑ 552 Bill Nahorodny .25 .11
❑ 553 Dick Davis .25 .11
❑ 554 Art Howe .40 .18
❑ 555 Ed Figueroa .25 .11
❑ 556 Joe Rudi .40 .18
❑ 557 Mark Lee .25 .11
❑ 558 Alfredo Griffin .25 .11
❑ 559 Dale Murray .25 .11
❑ 560 Dave Lopes .40 .18
❑ 561 Eddie Whitson .25 .11
❑ 562 Joe Wallis .25 .11
❑ 563 Will McEnaney .25 .11
❑ 564 Rick Manning .25 .11
❑ 565 Dennis Leonard .40 .18
❑ 566 Bud Harrelson .40 .18
❑ 567 Skip Lockwood .25 .11
❑ 568 Gary Roenicke .40 .18
❑ 569 Terry Kennedy .40 .18
❑ 570 Roy Smalley .25 .11
❑ 571 Joe Sambito .25 .11
❑ 572 Jerry Morales DP .10 .05
❑ 573 Kent Tekulve .40 .18
❑ 574 Scot Thompson .25 .11
❑ 575 Ken Kravec .25 .11
❑ 576 Jim Dwyer .25 .11
❑ 577 Blue Jays Team/Mgr. .75 .15
Bobby Mattick
(Checklist back)
❑ 578 Scott Sanderson .40 .18
❑ 579 Charlie Moore .25 .11
❑ 580 Nolan Ryan 20.00 9.00
❑ 581 Bob Bailor .25 .11
❑ 582 Brian Doyle .25 .11
❑ 583 Bob Stinson .25 .11
❑ 584 Kurt Bevacqua .25 .11
❑ 585 Al Hrabosky .25 .11
❑ 586 Mitchell Page .25 .11
❑ 587 Garry Templeton .25 .11
❑ 588 Greg Minton .25 .11
❑ 589 Chet Lemon .40 .18
❑ 590 Jim Palmer 1.50 .70
❑ 591 Rick Cerone .25 .11
❑ 592 Jon Matlack .25 .11
❑ 593 Jesus Alou .25 .11
❑ 594 Dick Tidrow .25 .11
❑ 595 Don Money .25 .11
❑ 596 Rick Matula .25 .11
❑ 597 Tom Poquette .25 .11
❑ 598 Fred Kendall DP .10 .05
❑ 599 Mike Norris .25 .11
❑ 600 Reggie Jackson 4.00 1.80
❑ 601 Buddy Schultz .25 .11
❑ 602 Brian Downing .25 .11
❑ 603 Jack Billingham DP .10 .05
❑ 604 Glenn Adams .25 .11
❑ 605 Terry Forster .25 .11
❑ 606 Reds Team/Mgr. .75 .15
John McNamara
(Checklist back)
❑ 607 Woodie Fryman .25 .11
❑ 608 Alan Bannister .25 .11
❑ 609 Ron Reed .25 .11
❑ 610 Willie Stargell 1.25 .55
❑ 611 Jerry Garvin DP .10 .05
❑ 612 Cliff Johnson .25 .11
❑ 613 Randy Stein .25 .11
❑ 614 John Hiller .25 .11
❑ 615 Doug DeCinces .40 .18
❑ 616 Gene Richards .25 .11
❑ 617 Joaquin Andujar .40 .18
❑ 618 Bob Montgomery DP .40 .18
❑ 619 Sergio Ferrer .25 .11
❑ 620 Richie Zisk .25 .11
❑ 621 Bob Grich .40 .18
❑ 622 Mario Soto .25 .11
❑ 623 Gorman Thomas .40 .18
❑ 624 Lerrin LaGrow .25 .11
❑ 625 Chris Chambliss .40 .18
❑ 626 Tigers Team/Mgr. .75 .15
Sparky Anderson
(Checklist back)
❑ 627 Pedro Borbon .25 .11
❑ 628 Doug Capilla .25 .11
❑ 629 Jim Todd .25 .11
❑ 630 Larry Bowa .40 .18
❑ 631 Mark Littell .25 .11
❑ 632 Barry Bonnell .25 .11
❑ 633 Bob Apodaca .25 .11
❑ 634 Glenn Borgmann DP .10 .05
❑ 635 John Candelaria .40 .18
❑ 636 Toby Harrah .40 .18
❑ 637 Joe Simpson .25 .11
❑ 638 Mark Clear .25 .11
❑ 639 Larry Biittner .25 .11
❑ 640 Mike Flanagan .40 .18
❑ 641 Ed Kranepool .25 .11
❑ 642 Ken Forsch DP .10 .05
❑ 643 John Mayberry .40 .18
❑ 644 Charlie Hough .40 .18
❑ 645 Rick Burleson .25 .11
❑ 646 Checklist 606-726 .75 .15
❑ 647 Milt May .25 .11
❑ 648 Roy White .25 .11
❑ 649 Tom Griffin .25 .11
❑ 650 Joe Morgan 1.50 .70
❑ 651 Rollie Fingers 1.25 .55
❑ 652 Mario Mendoza .25 .11
❑ 653 Stan Bahnsen .25 .11
❑ 654 Bruce Boisclair DP .10 .05
❑ 655 Tug McGraw .40 .18
❑ 656 Larvell Blanks .25 .11
❑ 657 Dave Edwards .25 .11
❑ 658 Chris Knapp .25 .11
❑ 659 Brewers Team/Mgr. .75 .15
George Bamberger
(Checklist back)
❑ 660 Rusty Staub .40 .18
❑ 661 Orioles Rookies .40 .18
Mark Corey
Dave Ford
Wayne Krenchicki
❑ 662 Red Sox Rookies .40 .18
Joel Finch
Mike O'Berry
Chuck Rainey
❑ 663 Angels Rookies .75 .35
Ralph Botting
Bob Clark
Dickie Thon
❑ 664 White Sox Rookies .40 .18
Mike Colbern
Guy Hoffman
Dewey Robinson
❑ 665 Indians Rookies .75 .35
Larry Andersen
Bobby Cuellar
Sandy Wihtol
❑ 666 Tigers Rookies .40 .18
Mike Chris
Al Greene
Bruce Robbins
❑ 667 Royals Rookies .75 .35
Renie Martin
Bill Paschall
Dan Quisenberry
❑ 668 Brewers Rookies .40 .18
Danny Boitano
Willie Mueller
Lenn Sakata
❑ 669 Twins Rookies .40 .18
Dan Graham

Rick Sofield
Gary Ward
❑ 670 Yankees Rookies .......... .40 .18
Bobby Brown
Brad Gulden
Darryl Jones
❑ 671 A's Rookies .................. 1.25 .55
Derek Bryant
Brian Kingman
Mike Morgan
❑ 672 Mariners Rookies .......... .40 .18
Charlie Beamon
Rodney Craig
Rafael Vasquez
❑ 673 Rangers Rookies............ .40 .18
Brian Allard
Jerry Don Gleaton
Greg Mahlberg
❑ 674 Blue Jays Rookies.......... .40 .18
Butch Edge
Pat Kelly
Ted Wilborn
❑ 675 Braves Rookies.............. .40 .18
Bruce Benedict
Larry Bradford
Eddie Miller
❑ 676 Cubs Rookies ................ .40 .18
Dave Geisel
Steve Macko
Karl Pagel
❑ 677 Reds Rookies ................ .40 .18
Art DeFreites
Frank Pastore
Harry Spilman
❑ 678 Astros Rookies .............. .40 .18
Reggie Baldwin
Alan Knicely
Pete Ladd
❑ 679 Dodgers Rookies............ .75 .35
Joe Beckwith
Mickey Hatcher
Dave Patterson
❑ 680 Expos Rookies .............. .75 .35
Tony Bernazard
Randy Miller
John Tamargo
❑ 681 Mets Rookies ................ .40 .18
Dan Norman
Jesse Orosco
Mike Scott
❑ 682 Phillies Rookies.............. .40 .18
Ramon Aviles
Dickie Noles
Kevin Saucier
❑ 683 Pirates Rookies.............. .40 .18
Dorian Boyland
Alberto Lois
Harry Saferight
❑ 684 Cardinals Rookies.......... .75 .35
George Frazier
Tom Herr
Dan O'Brien
❑ 685 Padres Rookies.............. .40 .18
Tim Flannery
Brian Greer
Jim Wilhelm
❑ 686 Giants Rookies .............. .40 .18
Greg Johnston
Dennis Littlejohn
Phil Nastu
❑ 687 Mike Heath DP .............. .10 .05
❑ 688 Steve Stone.................... .40 .18
❑ 689 Red Sox Team/Mgr. ....... .75 .15
Don Zimmer
(Checklist back)
❑ 690 Tommy John .................. .75 .35
❑ 691 Ivan DeJesus ................ .25 .11
❑ 692 Rawly Eastwick DP ........ .10 .05
❑ 693 Craig Kusick .................. .25 .11
❑ 694 Jim Rooker .................... .25 .11
❑ 695 Reggie Smith.................. .40 .18
❑ 696 Julio Gonzalez................ .25 .11
❑ 697 David Clyde.................... .25 .11
❑ 698 Oscar Gamble................ .40 .18
❑ 699 Floyd Bannister.............. .25 .11
❑ 700 Rod Carew DP ............ 1.50 .70
❑ 701 Ken Oberkfell ............... .25 .11
❑ 702 Ed Farmer...................... .25 .11
❑ 703 Otto Velez ..................... .25 .11
❑ 704 Gene Tenace ................ .40 .18
❑ 705 Freddie Patek ............... .25 .11
❑ 706 Tippy Martinez............... .25 .11
❑ 707 Elliott Maddox ............... .25 .11
❑ 708 Bob Tolan ...................... .25 .11
❑ 709 Pat Underwood .............. .25 .11
❑ 710 Graig Nettles.................. .75 .35
❑ 711 Bob Galasso .................. .25 .11
❑ 712 Rodney Scott.................. .25 .11
❑ 713 Terry Whitfield................ .25 .11
❑ 714 Fred Norman .................. .25 .11
❑ 715 Sal Bando ...................... .40 .18
❑ 716 Lynn McGlothen ............. .25 .11
❑ 717 Mickey Klutts DP ........... .10 .05
❑ 718 Greg Gross .................... .25 .11
❑ 719 Don Robinson ................. .40 .18
❑ 720 Carl Yastrzemski DP .... 2.00 .90
❑ 721 Paul Hartzell .................. .25 .11
❑ 722 Jose Cruz ....................... .40 .18
❑ 723 Shane Rawley................. .25 .11
❑ 724 Jerry White .................... .25 .11
❑ 725 Rick Wise ....................... .25 .11
❑ 726 Steve Yeager ................. .75 .15

## 1981 Topps

| | NRMT | VG-E |
|---|---|---|
| COMPLETE SET (726) .......... | 50.00 | 22.00 |
| COMMON CARD (1-726)............ | .15 | .07 |
| COMMON CARD DP .................. | .07 | .03 |

❑ 1 Batting Leaders................. 2.50 1.10
George Brett
Bill Buckner
❑ 2 Home Run Leaders.......... 1.50 .70
Reggie Jackson
Ben Oglivie
Mike Schmidt
❑ 3 RBI Leaders ..................... 1.50 .70
Cecil Cooper
Mike Schmidt
❑ 4 Stolen Base Leaders........ 2.50 1.10
Rickey Henderson
Ron LeFlore
❑ 5 Victory Leaders................. 1.50 .70
Steve Stone
Steve Carlton
❑ 6 Strikeout Leaders ............ 1.50 .70
Len Barker
Steve Carlton
❑ 7 ERA Leaders...................... .75 .35
Rudy May
Don Sutton
❑ 8 Leading Firemen ............... .75 .35
Dan Quisenberry
Rollie Fingers
Tom Hume
❑ 9 Pete LaCock DP ................ .07 .03
❑ 10 Mike Flanagan.................. .40 .18
❑ 11 Jim Wohlford DP .............. .07 .03
❑ 12 Mark Clear......................... .15 .07
❑ 13 Joe Charboneau RC ....... 1.50 .70
❑ 14 John Tudor RC ................ .40 .18
❑ 15 Larry Parrish ..................... .15 .07
❑ 16 Ron Davis .......................... .15 .07
❑ 17 Cliff Johnson ..................... .15 .07
❑ 18 Glenn Adams .................... .15 .07
❑ 19 Jim Clancy......................... .15 .07
❑ 20 Jeff Burroughs.................. .15 .07
❑ 21 Ron Oester ........................ .15 .07
❑ 22 Danny Darwin ................... .15 .07
❑ 23 Alex Trevino ...................... .15 .07
❑ 24 Don Stanhouse ................. .15 .07
❑ 25 Sixto Lezcano ................... .15 .07
❑ 26 U.L. Washington ............... .15 .07
❑ 27 Champ Summers DP ...... .07 .03
❑ 28 Enrique Romo ................... .15 .07
❑ 29 Gene Tenace .................... .40 .18
❑ 30 Jack Clark .......................... .40 .18
❑ 31 Checklist 1-121 DP .......... .15 .07
❑ 32 Ken Oberkfell .................... .15 .07
❑ 33 Rick Honeycutt ................. .15 .07
❑ 34 Aurelio Rodriguez ............ .15 .07
❑ 35 Mitchell Page..................... .15 .07
❑ 36 Ed Farmer.......................... .15 .07
❑ 37 Gary Roenicke .................. .15 .07
❑ 38 Win Remmerswaal ........... .15 .07
❑ 39 Tom Veryzer ...................... .15 .07
❑ 40 Tug McGraw ..................... .40 .18
❑ 41 Ranger Rookies ............... .15 .07
Bob Babcock
John Butcher
Jerry Don Gleaton
❑ 42 Jerry White DP ................. .07 .03
❑ 43 Jose Morales..................... .15 .07
❑ 44 Larry McWilliams.............. .15 .07
❑ 45 Enos Cabell....................... .15 .07
❑ 46 Rick Bosetti ...................... .15 .07
❑ 47 Ken Brett............................ .15 .07
❑ 48 Dave Skaggs..................... .15 .07
❑ 49 Bob Shirley ....................... .15 .07
❑ 50 Dave Lopes....................... .40 .18
❑ 51 Bill Robinson DP .............. .15 .07
❑ 52 Hector Cruz....................... .15 .07
❑ 53 Kevin Saucier .................... .15 .07
❑ 54 Ivan DeJesus .................... .15 .07
❑ 55 Mike Norris ........................ .15 .07
❑ 56 Buck Martinez ................... .15 .07
❑ 57 Dave Roberts .................... .15 .07
❑ 58 Joel Youngblood ............... .15 .07
❑ 59 Dan Petry ........................... .15 .07
❑ 60 Willie Randolph ................ .40 .18
❑ 61 Butch Wynegar ................ .15 .07
❑ 62 Joe Pettini ......................... .15 .07
❑ 63 Steve Renko DP .............. .07 .03
❑ 64 Brian Asselstine ................ .15 .07
❑ 65 Scott McGregor ................ .15 .07
❑ 66 Royals Rookies ................ .15 .07
Manny Castillo
Tim Ireland
Mike Jones
❑ 67 Ken Kravec ........................ .15 .07
❑ 68 Matt Alexander DP ........... .07 .03
❑ 69 Ed Halicki ........................... .15 .07
❑ 70 Al Oliver DP....................... .40 .18
❑ 71 Hal Dues ............................ .15 .07
❑ 72 Barry Evans DP ................ .07 .03
❑ 73 Doug Bair .......................... .15 .07
❑ 74 Mike Hargrove.................. .40 .18
❑ 75 Reggie Smith..................... .40 .18
❑ 76 Mario Mendoza ................. .15 .07
❑ 77 Mike Barlow....................... .15 .07
❑ 78 Steve Dillard ..................... .15 .07
❑ 79 Bruce Robbins................... .15 .07
❑ 80 Rusty Staub....................... .40 .18
❑ 81 Dave Stapleton ................. .15 .07
❑ 82 Astros Rookies DP .......... .15 .07
Danny Heep
Alan Knicely
Bobby Sprowl
❑ 83 Mike Proly ......................... .15 .07
❑ 84 Johnnie LeMaster ............ .15 .07
❑ 85 Mike Caldwell ................... .15 .07
❑ 86 Wayne Gross .................... .15 .07
❑ 87 Rick Camp.......................... .15 .07
❑ 88 Joe Lefebvre ..................... .15 .07
❑ 89 Darrell Jackson ................. .15 .07
❑ 90 Bake McBride ................... .15 .07
❑ 91 Tim Stoddard DP.............. .07 .03
❑ 92 Mike Easler ........................ .15 .07
❑ 93 Ed Glynn DP ..................... .07 .03

❑ 94 Harry Spilman DP .......... .07 .03
❑ 95 Jim Sundberg .......... .40 .18
❑ 96 A's Rookies .......... .15 .07
Dave Beard
Ernie Camacho
Pat Dempsey
❑ 97 Chris Speier .......... .15 .07
❑ 98 Clint Hurdle .......... .15 .07
❑ 99 Eric Wilkins .......... .15 .07
❑ 100 Rod Carew .......... 1.50 .70
❑ 101 Benny Ayala .......... .15 .07
❑ 102 Dave Tobik .......... .15 .07
❑ 103 Jerry Martin .......... .15 .07
❑ 104 Terry Forster .......... .15 .07
❑ 105 Jose Cruz .......... .40 .18
❑ 106 Don Money .......... .15 .07
❑ 107 Rich Wortham .......... .15 .07
❑ 108 Bruce Benedict .......... .15 .07
❑ 109 Mike Scott .......... .40 .18
❑ 110 Carl Yastrzemski .......... 1.50 .70
❑ 111 Greg Minton .......... .15 .07
❑ 112 White Sox Rookies .......... .15 .07
Rusty Kuntz
Fran Mullins
Leo Sutherland
❑ 113 Mike Phillips .......... .15 .07
❑ 114 Tom Underwood .......... .15 .07
❑ 115 Roy Smalley .......... .15 .07
❑ 116 Joe Simpson .......... .15 .07
❑ 117 Pete Falcone .......... .15 .07
❑ 118 Kurt Bevacqua .......... .15 .07
❑ 119 Tippy Martinez .......... .15 .07
❑ 120 Larry Bowa .......... .40 .18
❑ 121 Larry Harlow .......... .15 .07
❑ 122 John Denny .......... .15 .07
❑ 123 Al Cowens .......... .15 .07
❑ 124 Jerry Garvin .......... .15 .07
❑ 125 Andre Dawson .......... .75 .35
❑ 126 Charlie Leibrandt RC .......... .75 .35
❑ 127 Rudy Law .......... .15 .07
❑ 128 Gary Allenson DP .......... .07 .03
❑ 129 Art Howe .......... .40 .18
❑ 130 Larry Gura .......... .15 .07
❑ 131 Keith Moreland .......... .40 .18
❑ 132 Tommy Boggs .......... .15 .07
❑ 133 Jeff Cox .......... .15 .07
❑ 134 Steve Mura .......... .15 .07
❑ 135 Gorman Thomas .......... .40 .18
❑ 136 Doug Capilla .......... .15 .07
❑ 137 Hosken Powell .......... .15 .07
❑ 138 Rich Dotson DP .......... .15 .07
❑ 139 Oscar Gamble .......... .15 .07
❑ 140 Bob Forsch .......... .15 .07
❑ 141 Miguel Dilone .......... .15 .07
❑ 142 Jackson Todd .......... .15 .07
❑ 143 Dan Meyer .......... .15 .07
❑ 144 Allen Ripley .......... .15 .07
❑ 145 Mickey Rivers .......... .40 .18
❑ 146 Bobby Castillo .......... .15 .07
❑ 147 Dale Berra .......... .15 .07
❑ 148 Randy Niemann .......... .15 .07
❑ 149 Joe Nolan .......... .15 .07
❑ 150 Mark Fidrych .......... 1.50 .70
❑ 151 Claudell Washington .......... .15 .07
❑ 152 John Urrea .......... .15 .07
❑ 153 Tom Poquette .......... .15 .07
❑ 154 Rick Langford .......... .15 .07
❑ 155 Chris Chambliss .......... .40 .18
❑ 156 Bob McClure .......... .15 .07
❑ 157 John Wathan .......... .15 .07
❑ 158 Fergie Jenkins .......... 1.50 .70
❑ 159 Brian Doyle .......... .15 .07
❑ 160 Garry Maddox .......... .15 .07
❑ 161 Dan Graham .......... .15 .07
❑ 162 Doug Corbett .......... .15 .07
❑ 163 Bill Almon .......... .15 .07
❑ 164 LaMarr Hoyt RC .......... .40 .18
❑ 165 Tony Scott .......... .15 .07
❑ 166 Floyd Bannister .......... .15 .07
❑ 167 Terry Whitfield .......... .15 .07
❑ 168 Don Robinson DP .......... .07 .03
❑ 169 John Mayberry .......... .15 .07
❑ 170 Ross Grimsley .......... .15 .07
❑ 171 Gene Richards .......... .15 .07
❑ 172 Gary Woods .......... .15 .07
❑ 173 Bump Wills .......... .15 .07
❑ 174 Doug Rau .......... .15 .07
❑ 175 Dave Collins .......... .15 .07
❑ 176 Mike Krukow .......... .15 .07
❑ 177 Rick Peters .......... .15 .07
❑ 178 Jim Essian DP .......... .07 .03
❑ 179 Rudy May .......... .15 .07
❑ 180 Pete Rose .......... 5.00 2.20
❑ 181 Elias Sosa .......... .15 .07
❑ 182 Bob Grich .......... .40 .18
❑ 183 Dick Davis DP .......... .07 .03
❑ 184 Jim Dwyer .......... .15 .07
❑ 185 Dennis Leonard .......... .15 .07
❑ 186 Wayne Nordhagen .......... .15 .07
❑ 187 Mike Parrott .......... .15 .07
❑ 188 Doug DeCinces .......... .40 .18
❑ 189 Craig Swan .......... .15 .07
❑ 190 Cesar Cedeno .......... .40 .18
❑ 191 Rick Sutcliffe .......... .40 .18
❑ 192 Braves Rookies .......... .40 .18
Terry Harper
Ed Miller
Rafael Ramirez
❑ 193 Pete Vuckovich .......... .40 .18
❑ 194 Rod Scurry .......... .15 .07
❑ 195 Rich Murray .......... .15 .07
❑ 196 Duffy Dyer .......... .15 .07
❑ 197 Jim Kern .......... .15 .07
❑ 198 Jerry Dybzinski .......... .15 .07
❑ 199 Chuck Rainey .......... .15 .07
❑ 200 George Foster .......... .40 .18
❑ 201 Johnny Bench RB .......... .75 .35
Most homers catchers
❑ 202 Steve Carlton RB .......... .75 .35
Most strikeouts,
lefthander, lifetime
❑ 203 Bill Gullickson RB .......... .75 .35
Most SO's, game, rookie
❑ 204 Ron LeFlore RB .......... .40 .18
Rodney Scott RB
Most stolen bases
teammates, season
❑ 205 Pete Rose RB .......... 1.50 .70
Most cons. seasons
600 or more at-bats
❑ 206 Mike Schmidt RB .......... .75 .35
Most homers, 3rd baseman, season
❑ 207 Ozzie Smith RB .......... 2.00 .90
Most assists,
season, shortstop
❑ 208 Willie Wilson RB .......... .40 .18
Most AB's season
❑ 209 Dickie Thon DP .......... .40 .18
❑ 210 Jim Palmer .......... 1.50 .70
❑ 211 Derrel Thomas .......... .15 .07
❑ 212 Steve Nicosia .......... .15 .07
❑ 213 Al Holland .......... .15 .07
❑ 214 Angels Rookies .......... .15 .07
Ralph Botting
Jim Dorsey
John Harris
❑ 215 Larry Hisle .......... .15 .07
❑ 216 John Henry Johnson .......... .15 .07
❑ 217 Rich Hebner .......... .15 .07
❑ 218 Paul Splittorff .......... .15 .07
❑ 219 Ken Landreaux .......... .15 .07
❑ 220 Tom Seaver .......... 2.50 1.10
❑ 221 Bob Davis .......... .15 .07
❑ 222 Jorge Orta .......... .15 .07
❑ 223 Roy Lee Jackson .......... .15 .07
❑ 224 Pat Zachry .......... .15 .07
❑ 225 Ruppert Jones .......... .15 .07
❑ 226 Manny Sanguillen DP .......... .07 .03
❑ 227 Fred Martinez .......... .15 .07
❑ 228 Tom Paciorek .......... .40 .18
❑ 229 Rollie Fingers .......... 1.50 .70
❑ 230 George Hendrick .......... .40 .18
❑ 231 Joe Beckwith .......... .15 .07
❑ 232 Mickey Klutts .......... .15 .07
❑ 233 Skip Lockwood .......... .15 .07
❑ 234 Lou Whitaker .......... 1.50 .70
❑ 235 Scott Sanderson .......... .15 .07
❑ 236 Mike Ivie .......... .15 .07
❑ 237 Charlie Moore .......... .15 .07
❑ 238 Willie Hernandez .......... .40 .18
❑ 239 Rick Miller DP .......... .07 .03
❑ 240 Nolan Ryan .......... 8.00 3.60
❑ 241 Checklist 122-242 DP .......... .15 .07
❑ 242 Chet Lemon .......... .15 .07
❑ 243 Sal Butera .......... .15 .07
❑ 244 Cardinals Rookies .......... .15 .07
Tito Landrum
Al Olmsted
Andy Rincon
❑ 245 Ed Figueroa .......... .15 .07
❑ 246 Ed Ott DP .......... .07 .03
❑ 247 Glenn Hubbard DP .......... .07 .03
❑ 248 Joey McLaughlin .......... .15 .07
❑ 249 Larry Cox .......... .15 .07
❑ 250 Ron Guidry .......... .40 .18
❑ 251 Tom Brookens .......... .15 .07
❑ 252 Victor Cruz .......... .15 .07
❑ 253 Dave Bergman .......... .15 .07
❑ 254 Ozzie Smith .......... 5.00 2.20
❑ 255 Mark Littell .......... .15 .07
❑ 256 Bombo Rivera .......... .15 .07
❑ 257 Rennie Stennett .......... .15 .07
❑ 258 Joe Price .......... .15 .07
❑ 259 Mets Rookies .......... 1.50 .70
Juan Berenguer
Hubie Brooks RC
Mookie Wilson
❑ 260 Ron Cey .......... .40 .18
❑ 261 Rickey Henderson .......... 8.00 3.60
❑ 262 Sammy Stewart .......... .15 .07
❑ 263 Brian Downing .......... .40 .18
❑ 264 Jim Norris .......... .15 .07
❑ 265 John Candelaria .......... .40 .18
❑ 266 Tom Herr .......... .40 .18
❑ 267 Stan Bahnsen .......... .15 .07
❑ 268 Jerry Royster .......... .15 .07
❑ 269 Ken Forsch .......... .15 .07
❑ 270 Greg Luzinski .......... .40 .18
❑ 271 Bill Castro .......... .15 .07
❑ 272 Bruce Kimm .......... .15 .07
❑ 273 Stan Papi .......... .15 .07
❑ 274 Craig Chamberlain .......... .15 .07
❑ 275 Dwight Evans .......... .75 .35
❑ 276 Dan Spillner .......... .15 .07
❑ 277 Alfredo Griffin .......... .15 .07
❑ 278 Rick Sofield .......... .15 .07
❑ 279 Bob Knepper .......... .15 .07
❑ 280 Ken Griffey .......... .75 .35
❑ 281 Fred Stanley .......... .15 .07
❑ 282 Mariners Rookies .......... .15 .07
Rick Anderson
Greg Biercevicz
Rodney Craig
❑ 283 Billy Sample .......... .15 .07
❑ 284 Brian Kingman .......... .15 .07
❑ 285 Jerry Turner .......... .15 .07
❑ 286 Dave Frost .......... .15 .07
❑ 287 Lenn Sakata .......... .15 .07
❑ 288 Bob Clark .......... .15 .07
❑ 289 Mickey Hatcher .......... .40 .18
❑ 290 Bob Boone DP .......... .40 .18
❑ 291 Aurelio Lopez .......... .15 .07
❑ 292 Mike Squires .......... .15 .07
❑ 293 Charlie Lea .......... .15 .07
❑ 294 Mike Tyson DP .......... .07 .03
❑ 295 Hal McRae .......... .40 .18
❑ 296 Bill Nahorodny DP .......... .07 .03
❑ 297 Bob Bailor .......... .15 .07
❑ 298 Buddy Solomon .......... .15 .07
❑ 299 Elliott Maddox .......... .15 .07
❑ 300 Paul Molitor .......... 3.00 1.35
❑ 301 Matt Keough .......... .15 .07
❑ 302 Dodgers Rookies .......... 3.00 1.35
Jack Perconte
Mike Scioscia
Fernando Valenzuela RC
❑ 303 Johnny Oates .......... .40 .18
❑ 304 John Castino .......... .15 .07
❑ 305 Ken Clay .......... .15 .07
❑ 306 Juan Beniquez DP .......... .07 .03
❑ 307 Gene Garber .......... .15 .07
❑ 308 Rick Manning .......... .15 .07
❑ 309 Luis Salazar .......... .15 .07
❑ 310 Vida Blue DP .......... .15 .07
❑ 311 Freddie Patek .......... .15 .07
❑ 312 Rick Rhoden .......... .15 .07
❑ 313 Luis Pujols .......... .15 .07
❑ 314 Rich Dauer .......... .15 .07

❑ 315 Kirk Gibson RC 3.00 1.35
❑ 316 Craig Minetto .15 .07
❑ 317 Lonnie Smith .40 .18
❑ 318 Steve Yeager .15 .07
❑ 319 Rowland Office .15 .07
❑ 320 Tom Burgmeier .15 .07
❑ 321 Leon Durham .40 .18
❑ 322 Neil Allen .15 .07
❑ 323 Jim Morrison DP .07 .03
❑ 324 Mike Willis .15 .07
❑ 325 Ray Knight .40 .18
❑ 326 Biff Pocoroba .15 .07
❑ 327 Moose Haas .15 .07
❑ 328 Twins Rookies .15 .07
Dave Engle
Greg Johnston
Gary Ward
❑ 329 Joaquin Andujar .40 .18
❑ 330 Frank White .40 .18
❑ 331 Dennis Lamp .15 .07
❑ 332 Lee Lacy DP .07 .03
❑ 333 Sid Monge .15 .07
❑ 334 Dane Iorg .15 .07
❑ 335 Rick Cerone .15 .07
❑ 336 Eddie Whitson .15 .07
❑ 337 Lynn Jones .15 .07
❑ 338 Checklist 243-363 .75 .35
❑ 339 John Ellis .15 .07
❑ 340 Bruce Kison .15 .07
❑ 341 Dwayne Murphy .15 .07
❑ 342 Eric Rasmussen DP .07 .03
❑ 343 Frank Taveras .15 .07
❑ 344 Byron McLaughlin .15 .07
❑ 345 Warren Cromartie .15 .07
❑ 346 Larry Christenson DP .07 .03
❑ 347 Harold Baines RC 8.00 3.60
❑ 348 Bob Sykes .15 .07
❑ 349 Glenn Hoffman .15 .07
❑ 350 J.R. Richard .40 .18
❑ 351 Otto Velez .15 .07
❑ 352 Dick Tidrow DP .07 .03
❑ 353 Terry Kennedy .15 .07
❑ 354 Mario Soto .15 .07
❑ 355 Bob Horner .40 .18
❑ 356 Padres Rookies .15 .07
George Stablein
Craig Stimac
Tom Tellmann
❑ 357 Jim Slaton .15 .07
❑ 358 Mark Wagner .15 .07
❑ 359 Tom Hausman .15 .07
❑ 360 Willie Wilson .40 .18
❑ 361 Joe Strain .15 .07
❑ 362 Bo Diaz .15 .07
❑ 363 Geoff Zahn .15 .07
❑ 364 Mike Davis .15 .07
❑ 365 Graig Nettles DP .40 .18
❑ 366 Mike Ramsey .15 .07
❑ 367 Dennis Martinez .75 .35
❑ 368 Leon Roberts .15 .07
❑ 369 Frank Tanana .40 .18
❑ 370 Dave Winfield 1.50 .70
❑ 371 Charlie Hough .40 .18
❑ 372 Jay Johnstone .40 .18
❑ 373 Pat Underwood .15 .07
❑ 374 Tommy Hutton .15 .07
❑ 375 Dave Concepcion .40 .18
❑ 376 Ron Reed .15 .07
❑ 377 Jerry Morales .15 .07
❑ 378 Dave Rader .15 .07
❑ 379 Lary Sorensen .15 .07
❑ 380 Willie Stargell 1.50 .70
❑ 381 Cubs Rookies .15 .07
Carlos Lezcano
Steve Macko
Randy Martz
❑ 382 Paul Mirabella .15 .07
❑ 383 Eric Soderholm DP .07 .03
❑ 384 Mike Sadek .15 .07
❑ 385 Joe Sambito .15 .07
❑ 386 Dave Edwards .15 .07
❑ 387 Phil Niekro 1.50 .70
❑ 388 Andre Thornton .40 .18
❑ 389 Marty Pattin .15 .07
❑ 390 Cesar Geronimo .15 .07
❑ 391 Dave Lemanczyk DP .07 .03
❑ 392 Lance Parrish .40 .18
❑ 393 Broderick Perkins .15 .07
❑ 394 Woodie Fryman .15 .07
❑ 395 Scot Thompson .15 .07
❑ 396 Bill Campbell .15 .07
❑ 397 Julio Cruz .15 .07
❑ 398 Ross Baumgarten .15 .07
❑ 399 Orioles Rookies 1.50 .70
Mike Boddicker RC
Mark Corey
Floyd Rayford
❑ 400 Reggie Jackson 2.00 .90
❑ 401 George Brett ALCS 2.00 .90
❑ 402 NL Champs .75 .35
Phillies squeak
past Astros
(Phillies celebrating)
❑ 403 Larry Bowa WS .75 .35
❑ 404 Tug McGraw WS .75 .35
❑ 405 Nino Espinosa .15 .07
❑ 406 Dickie Noles .15 .07
❑ 407 Ernie Whitt .15 .07
❑ 408 Fernando Arroyo .15 .07
❑ 409 Larry Herndon .15 .07
❑ 410 Bert Campaneris .40 .18
❑ 411 Terry Puhl .15 .07
❑ 412 Britt Burns .15 .07
❑ 413 Tony Bernazard .15 .07
❑ 414 John Pacella DP .07 .03
❑ 415 Ben Oglivie .40 .18
❑ 416 Gary Alexander .15 .07
❑ 417 Dan Schatzeder .15 .07
❑ 418 Bobby Brown .15 .07
❑ 419 Tom Hume .15 .07
❑ 420 Keith Hernandez .40 .18
❑ 421 Bob Stanley .15 .07
❑ 422 Dan Ford .15 .07
❑ 423 Shane Rawley .15 .07
❑ 424 Yankees Rookies .15 .07
Tim Lollar
Bruce Robinson
Dennis Werth
❑ 425 Al Bumbry .40 .18
❑ 426 Warren Brusstar .15 .07
❑ 427 John D'Acquisto .15 .07
❑ 428 John Stearns .15 .07
❑ 429 Mick Kelleher .15 .07
❑ 430 Jim Bibby .15 .07
❑ 431 Dave Roberts .15 .07
❑ 432 Len Barker .15 .07
❑ 433 Rance Mulliniks .15 .07
❑ 434 Roger Erickson .15 .07
❑ 435 Jim Spencer .15 .07
❑ 436 Gary Lucas .15 .07
❑ 437 Mike Heath DP .07 .03
❑ 438 John Montefusco .15 .07
❑ 439 Denny Walling .15 .07
❑ 440 Jerry Reuss .40 .18
❑ 441 Ken Reitz .15 .07
❑ 442 Ron Pruitt .15 .07
❑ 443 Jim Beattie DP .07 .03
❑ 444 Garth Iorg .15 .07
❑ 445 Ellis Valentine .15 .07
❑ 446 Checklist 364-484 .75 .35
❑ 447 Junior Kennedy DP .07 .03
❑ 448 Tim Corcoran .15 .07
❑ 449 Paul Mitchell .15 .07
❑ 450 Dave Kingman DP .40 .18
❑ 451 Indians Rookies .15 .07
Chris Bando
Tom Brennan
Sandy Wihtol
❑ 452 Renie Martin .15 .07
❑ 453 Rob Wilfong DP .40 .18
❑ 454 Andy Hassler .15 .07
❑ 455 Rick Burleson .15 .07
❑ 456 Jeff Reardon RC 1.50 .70
❑ 457 Mike Lum .15 .07
❑ 458 Randy Jones .15 .07
❑ 459 Greg Gross .15 .07
❑ 460 Rich Gossage .75 .35
❑ 461 Dave McKay .15 .07
❑ 462 Jack Brohamer .15 .07
❑ 463 Milt May .15 .07
❑ 464 Adrian Devine .15 .07
❑ 465 Bill Russell .40 .18
❑ 466 Bob Molinaro .15 .07
❑ 467 Dave Stieb .40 .18
❑ 468 John Wockenfuss .15 .07
❑ 469 Jeff Leonard .40 .18
❑ 470 Manny Trillo .15 .07
❑ 471 Mike Vail .15 .07
❑ 472 Dyar Miller DP .07 .03
❑ 473 Jose Cardenal .15 .07
❑ 474 Mike LaCoss .15 .07
❑ 475 Buddy Bell .40 .18
❑ 476 Jerry Koosman .40 .18
❑ 477 Luis Gomez .15 .07
❑ 478 Juan Eichelberger .15 .07
❑ 479 Expos Rookies 3.00 1.35
Tim Raines RC
Roberto Ramos
Bobby Pate
❑ 480 Carlton Fisk 1.50 .70
❑ 481 Bob Lacey DP .07 .03
❑ 482 Jim Gantner .40 .18
❑ 483 Mike Griffin .15 .07
❑ 484 Max Venable DP .07 .03
❑ 485 Garry Templeton .15 .07
❑ 486 Marc Hill .15 .07
❑ 487 Dewey Robinson .15 .07
❑ 488 Damaso Garcia .15 .07
❑ 489 John Littlefield .15 .07
(Photo on card believed to
be Mark Riggins)
❑ 490 Eddie Murray 3.00 1.35
❑ 491 Gordy Pladson .15 .07
❑ 492 Barry Foote .15 .07
❑ 493 Dan Quisenberry .40 .18
❑ 494 Bob Walk RC .40 .18
❑ 495 Dusty Baker .75 .35
❑ 496 Paul Dade .15 .07
❑ 497 Fred Norman .15 .07
❑ 498 Pat Putnam .15 .07
❑ 499 Frank Pastore .15 .07
❑ 500 Jim Rice .40 .18
❑ 501 Tim Foli DP .40 .18
❑ 502 Giants Rookies .15 .07
Chris Bourjos
Al Hargesheimer
Mike Rowland
❑ 503 Steve McCatty .15 .07
❑ 504 Dale Murphy 1.50 .70
❑ 505 Jason Thompson .15 .07
❑ 506 Phil Huffman .15 .07
❑ 507 Jamie Quirk .15 .07
❑ 508 Rob Dressler .15 .07
❑ 509 Pete Mackanin .15 .07
❑ 510 Lee Mazzilli .15 .07
❑ 511 Wayne Garland .15 .07
❑ 512 Gary Thomasson .15 .07
❑ 513 Frank LaCorte .15 .07
❑ 514 George Riley .15 .07
❑ 515 Robin Yount 1.50 .70
❑ 516 Doug Bird .15 .07
❑ 517 Richie Zisk .15 .07
❑ 518 Grant Jackson .15 .07
❑ 519 John Tamargo DP .40 .18
❑ 520 Steve Stone .40 .18
❑ 521 Sam Mejias .15 .07
❑ 522 Mike Colbern .15 .07
❑ 523 John Fulgham .15 .07
❑ 524 Willie Aikens .15 .07
❑ 525 Mike Torrez .15 .07
❑ 526 Phillies Rookies .15 .07
Marty Bystrom
Jay Loviglio
Jim Wright
❑ 527 Danny Goodwin .15 .07
❑ 528 Gary Matthews .40 .18
❑ 529 Dave LaRoche .15 .07
❑ 530 Steve Garvey .75 .35
❑ 531 John Curtis .15 .07
❑ 532 Bill Stein .15 .07
❑ 533 Jesus Figueroa .15 .07
❑ 534 Dave Smith RC .40 .18
❑ 535 Omar Moreno .15 .07
❑ 536 Bob Owchinko DP .07 .03
❑ 537 Ron Hodges .15 .07
❑ 538 Tom Griffin .15 .07
❑ 539 Rodney Scott .15 .07
❑ 540 Mike Schmidt DP 2.00 .90

❑ 541 Steve Swisher .15 .07
❑ 542 Larry Bradford DP .07 .03
❑ 543 Terry Crowley .15 .07
❑ 544 Rich Gale .15 .07
❑ 545 Johnny Grubb .15 .07
❑ 546 Paul Moskau .15 .07
❑ 547 Mario Guerrero .15 .07
❑ 548 Dave Goltz .15 .07
❑ 549 Jerry Remy .15 .07
❑ 550 Tommy John .75 .35
❑ 551 Pirates Rookies 1.50 .70
Vance Law
Tony Pena
Pascual Perez RC
❑ 552 Steve Trout .15 .07
❑ 553 Tim Blackwell .15 .07
❑ 554 Bert Blyleven UER .75 .35
(1 is missing from
1980 on card back)
❑ 555 Cecil Cooper .40 .18
❑ 556 Jerry Mumphrey .15 .07
❑ 557 Chris Knapp .15 .07
❑ 558 Barry Bonnell .15 .07
❑ 559 Willie Montanez .15 .07
❑ 560 Joe Morgan 1.50 .70
❑ 561 Dennis Littlejohn .15 .07
❑ 562 Checklist 485-605 .75 .35
❑ 563 Jim Kaat .40 .18
❑ 564 Ron Hassey DP .07 .03
❑ 565 Burt Hooton .15 .07
❑ 566 Del Unser .15 .07
❑ 567 Mark Bomback .15 .07
❑ 568 Dave Revering .15 .07
❑ 569 Al Williams DP .07 .03
❑ 570 Ken Singleton .40 .18
❑ 571 Todd Cruz .15 .07
❑ 572 Jack Morris 1.50 .70
❑ 573 Phil Garner .40 .18
❑ 574 Bill Caudill .15 .07
❑ 575 Tony Perez 1.50 .70
❑ 576 Reggie Cleveland .15 .07
❑ 577 Blue Jays Rookies .15 .07
Luis Leal
Brian Milner
Ken Schrom
❑ 578 Bill Gullickson RC .75 .35
❑ 579 Tim Flannery .15 .07
❑ 580 Don Baylor .75 .35
❑ 581 Roy Howell .15 .07
❑ 582 Gaylord Perry 1.50 .70
❑ 583 Larry Milbourne .15 .07
❑ 584 Randy Lerch .15 .07
❑ 585 Amos Otis .40 .18
❑ 586 Silvio Martinez .15 .07
❑ 587 Jeff Newman .15 .07
❑ 588 Gary Lavelle .15 .07
❑ 589 Lamar Johnson .15 .07
❑ 590 Bruce Sutter .40 .18
❑ 591 John Lowenstein .15 .07
❑ 592 Steve Comer .15 .07
❑ 593 Steve Kemp .15 .07
❑ 594 Preston Hanna DP .07 .03
❑ 595 Butch Hobson .15 .07
❑ 596 Jerry Augustine .15 .07
❑ 597 Rafael Landestoy .15 .07
❑ 598 George Vukovich DP .07 .03
❑ 599 Dennis Kinney .15 .07
❑ 600 Johnny Bench 2.50 1.10
❑ 601 Don Aase .15 .07
❑ 602 Bobby Murcer .40 .18
❑ 603 John Verhoeven .15 .07
❑ 604 Rob Picciolo .15 .07
❑ 605 Don Sutton 1.50 .70
❑ 606 Reds Rookies DP .15 .07
Bruce Berenyi
Geoff Combe
Paul Householder
❑ 607 David Palmer .15 .07
❑ 608 Greg Pryor .15 .07
❑ 609 Lynn McGlothen .15 .07
❑ 610 Darrell Porter .15 .07
❑ 611 Rick Matula DP .07 .03
❑ 612 Duane Kuiper .15 .07
❑ 613 Jim Anderson .15 .07
❑ 614 Dave Rozema .15 .07
❑ 615 Rick Dempsey .40 .18
❑ 616 Rick Wise .15 .07
❑ 617 Craig Reynolds .15 .07
❑ 618 John Milner .15 .07
❑ 619 Steve Henderson .15 .07
❑ 620 Dennis Eckersley 1.50 .70
❑ 621 Tom Donohue .15 .07
❑ 622 Randy Moffitt .15 .07
❑ 623 Sal Bando .40 .18
❑ 624 Bob Welch .40 .18
❑ 625 Bill Buckner .40 .18
❑ 626 Tigers Rookies .15 .07
Dave Steffen
Jerry Ujdur
Roger Weaver
❑ 627 Luis Tiant .40 .18
❑ 628 Vic Correll .15 .07
❑ 629 Tony Armas .40 .18
❑ 630 Steve Carlton 1.50 .70
❑ 631 Ron Jackson .15 .07
❑ 632 Alan Bannister .15 .07
❑ 633 Bill Lee .40 .18
❑ 634 Doug Flynn .15 .07
❑ 635 Bobby Bonds .40 .18
❑ 636 Al Hrabosky .15 .07
❑ 637 Jerry Narron .15 .07
❑ 638 Checklist 606-726 .75 .35
❑ 639 Carney Lansford .40 .18
❑ 640 Dave Parker .40 .18
❑ 641 Mark Belanger .40 .18
❑ 642 Vern Ruhle .15 .07
❑ 643 Lloyd Moseby .40 .18
❑ 644 Ramon Aviles DP .07 .03
❑ 645 Rick Reuschel .40 .18
❑ 646 Marvis Foley .15 .07
❑ 647 Dick Drago .15 .07
❑ 648 Darrell Evans .40 .18
❑ 649 Manny Sarmiento .15 .07
❑ 650 Bucky Dent .40 .18
❑ 651 Pedro Guerrero .75 .35
❑ 652 John Montague .15 .07
❑ 653 Bill Fahey .15 .07
❑ 654 Ray Burris .15 .07
❑ 655 Dan Driessen .15 .07
❑ 656 Jon Matlack .15 .07
❑ 657 Mike Cubbage DP .07 .03
❑ 658 Milt Wilcox .15 .07
❑ 659 Brewers Rookies .15 .07
John Flinn
Ed Romero
Ned Yost
❑ 660 Gary Carter .75 .35
❑ 661 Orioles Team/Mgr. .75 .35
Earl Weaver
❑ 662 Red Sox Team/Mgr. .75 .35
Ralph Houk
❑ 663 Angels Team/Mgr. .75 .35
Jim Fregosi
❑ 664 White Sox Team/Mgr. .75 .35
Tony LaRussa
❑ 665 Indians Team/Mgr. .75 .35
Dave Garcia
❑ 666 Tigers Team/Mgr. .75 .35
Sparky Anderson
❑ 667 Royals Team/Mgr. .75 .35
Jim Frey
❑ 668 Brewers Team/Mgr. .75 .35
Bob Rodgers
❑ 669 Twins Team/Mgr. .75 .35
John Goryl
❑ 670 Yankees Team/Mgr. .75 .35
Gene Michael
❑ 671 A's Team/Mgr. .75 .35
Billy Martin
❑ 672 Mariners Team/Mgr. .75 .35
Maury Wills
❑ 673 Rangers Team/Mgr. .75 .35
Don Zimmer
❑ 674 Blue Jays Team/Mgr. .75 .35
Bobby Mattick
❑ 675 Braves Team/Mgr. .75 .35
Bobby Cox
❑ 676 Cubs Team/Mgr. .75 .35
Joe Amalfitano
❑ 677 Reds Team/Mgr. .75 .35
John McNamara
❑ 678 Astros Team/Mgr. .75 .35
Bill Virdon
❑ 679 Dodgers Team/Mgr. .75 .35
Tom Lasorda
❑ 680 Expos Team/Mgr. .75 .35
Dick Williams
❑ 681 Mets Team/Mgr. .75 .35
Joe Torre
❑ 682 Phillies Team/Mgr. .75 .35
Dallas Green
❑ 683 Pirates Team/Mgr. .75 .35
Chuck Tanner
❑ 684 Cardinals Team/Mgr. .75 .35
Whitey Herzog
❑ 685 Padres Team/Mgr. .75 .35
Frank Howard
❑ 686 Giants Team/Mgr. .75 .35
Dave Bristol
❑ 687 Jeff Jones .15 .07
❑ 688 Kiko Garcia .15 .07
❑ 689 Red Sox Rookies 1.50 .70
Bruce Hurst RC
Keith MacWhorter
Reid Nichols
❑ 690 Bob Watson .40 .18
❑ 691 Dick Ruthven .15 .07
❑ 692 Lenny Randle .15 .07
❑ 693 Steve Howe .40 .18
❑ 694 Bud Harrelson DP .15 .07
❑ 695 Kent Tekulve .40 .18
❑ 696 Alan Ashby .15 .07
❑ 697 Rick Waits .15 .07
❑ 698 Mike Jorgensen .15 .07
❑ 699 Glenn Abbott .15 .07
❑ 700 George Brett 4.00 1.80
❑ 701 Joe Rudi .40 .18
❑ 702 George Medich .15 .07
❑ 703 Alvis Woods .15 .07
❑ 704 Bill Travers DP .07 .03
❑ 705 Ted Simmons .40 .18
❑ 706 Dave Ford .15 .07
❑ 707 Dave Cash .15 .07
❑ 708 Doyle Alexander .15 .07
❑ 709 Alan Trammell DP .75 .35
❑ 710 Ron LeFlore DP .15 .07
❑ 711 Joe Ferguson .15 .07
❑ 712 Bill Bonham .15 .07
❑ 713 Bill North .15 .07
❑ 714 Pete Redfern .15 .07
❑ 715 Bill Madlock .40 .18
❑ 716 Glenn Borgmann .15 .07
❑ 717 Jim Barr DP .07 .03
❑ 718 Larry Biittner .15 .07
❑ 719 Sparky Lyle .40 .18
❑ 720 Fred Lynn .40 .18
❑ 721 Toby Harrah .40 .18
❑ 722 Joe Niekro .40 .18
❑ 723 Bruce Bochte .15 .07
❑ 724 Lou Piniella .40 .18
❑ 725 Steve Rogers .15 .07
❑ 726 Rick Monday .40 .18

## 1981 Topps Traded

| | NRMT | VG-E |
|---|---|---|
| COMP.FACT.SET (132) | 25.00 | 11.00 |
| ❑ 727 Danny Ainge XRC | 5.00 | 2.20 |
| ❑ 728 Doyle Alexander | .25 | .11 |

❑ 729 Gary Alexander .25 .11
❑ 730 Bill Almon .25 .11
❑ 731 Joaquin Andujar 1.00 .45
❑ 732 Bob Bailor .25 .11
❑ 733 Juan Beniquez .25 .11
❑ 734 Dave Bergman .25 .11
❑ 735 Tony Bernazard .25 .11
❑ 736 Larry Biittner .25 .11
❑ 737 Doug Bird .25 .11
❑ 738 Bert Blyleven 1.50 .70
❑ 739 Mark Bomback .25 .11
❑ 740 Bobby Bonds 1.00 .45
❑ 741 Rick Bosetti .25 .11
❑ 742 Hubie Brooks 1.00 .45
❑ 743 Rick Burleson .25 .11
❑ 744 Ray Burris .25 .11
❑ 745 Jeff Burroughs .25 .11
❑ 746 Enos Cabell .25 .11
❑ 747 Ken Clay .25 .11
❑ 748 Mark Clear .25 .11
❑ 749 Larry Cox .25 .11
❑ 750 Hector Cruz .25 .11
❑ 751 Victor Cruz .25 .11
❑ 752 Mike Cubbage .25 .11
❑ 753 Dick Davis .25 .11
❑ 754 Brian Doyle .25 .11
❑ 755 Dick Drago .25 .11
❑ 756 Leon Durham 1.00 .45
❑ 757 Jim Dwyer .25 .11
❑ 758 Dave Edwards UER .25 .11
(No birthdate on card)
❑ 759 Jim Essian .25 .11
❑ 760 Bill Fahey .25 .11
❑ 761 Rollie Fingers 2.50 1.10
❑ 762 Carlton Fisk 5.00 2.20
❑ 763 Barry Foote .25 .11
❑ 764 Ken Forsch .25 .11
❑ 765 Kiko Garcia .25 .11
❑ 766 Cesar Geronimo .25 .11
❑ 767 Gary Gray .25 .11
❑ 768 Mickey Hatcher 1.00 .45
❑ 769 Steve Henderson .25 .11
❑ 770 Marc Hill .25 .11
❑ 771 Butch Hobson .25 .11
❑ 772 Rick Honeycutt .25 .11
❑ 773 Roy Howell .25 .11
❑ 774 Mike Ivie .25 .11
❑ 775 Roy Lee Jackson .25 .11
❑ 776 Cliff Johnson .25 .11
❑ 777 Randy Jones .25 .11
❑ 778 Ruppert Jones .25 .11
❑ 779 Mick Kelleher .25 .11
❑ 780 Terry Kennedy .25 .11
❑ 781 Dave Kingman 1.50 .70
❑ 782 Bob Knepper .25 .11
❑ 783 Ken Kravec .25 .11
❑ 784 Bob Lacey .25 .11
❑ 785 Dennis Lamp .25 .11
❑ 786 Rafael Landestoy .25 .11
❑ 787 Ken Landreaux .25 .11
❑ 788 Carney Lansford 1.00 .45
❑ 789 Dave LaRoche .25 .11
❑ 790 Joe Lefebvre .25 .11
❑ 791 Ron LeFlore 1.00 .45
❑ 792 Randy Lerch .25 .11
❑ 793 Sixto Lezcano .25 .11
❑ 794 John Littlefield .25 .11
❑ 795 Mike Lum .25 .11
❑ 796 Greg Luzinski 1.00 .45
❑ 797 Fred Lynn 1.00 .45
❑ 798 Jerry Martin .25 .11
❑ 799 Buck Martinez .25 .11
❑ 800 Gary Matthews 1.00 .45
❑ 801 Mario Mendoza .25 .11
❑ 802 Larry Milbourne .25 .11
❑ 803 Rick Miller .25 .11
❑ 804 John Montefusco .25 .11
❑ 805 Jerry Morales .25 .11
❑ 806 Jose Morales .25 .11
❑ 807 Joe Morgan 2.50 1.10
❑ 808 Jerry Mumphrey .25 .11
❑ 809 Gene Nelson .25 .11
❑ 810 Ed Ott .25 .11
❑ 811 Bob Owchinko .25 .11
❑ 812 Gaylord Perry 2.50 1.10
❑ 813 Mike Phillips .25 .11
❑ 814 Darrell Porter .25 .11
❑ 815 Mike Proly .25 .11
❑ 816 Tim Raines 5.00 2.20
❑ 817 Lenny Randle .25 .11
❑ 818 Doug Rau .25 .11
❑ 819 Jeff Reardon 2.50 1.10
❑ 820 Ken Reitz .25 .11
❑ 821 Steve Renko .25 .11
❑ 822 Rick Reuschel 1.00 .45
❑ 823 Dave Revering .25 .11
❑ 824 Dave Roberts .25 .11
❑ 825 Leon Roberts .25 .11
❑ 826 Joe Rudi 1.00 .45
❑ 827 Kevin Saucier .25 .11
❑ 828 Tony Scott .25 .11
❑ 829 Bob Shirley .25 .11
❑ 830 Ted Simmons 1.00 .45
❑ 831 Lary Sorensen .25 .11
❑ 832 Jim Spencer .25 .11
❑ 833 Harry Spilman .25 .11
❑ 834 Fred Stanley .25 .11
❑ 835 Rusty Staub 1.00 .45
❑ 836 Bill Stein .25 .11
❑ 837 Joe Strain .25 .11
❑ 838 Bruce Sutter 1.00 .45
❑ 839 Don Sutton 2.50 1.10
❑ 840 Steve Swisher .25 .11
❑ 841 Frank Tanana 1.00 .45
❑ 842 Gene Tenace 1.00 .45
❑ 843 Jason Thompson .25 .11
❑ 844 Dickie Thon 1.00 .45
❑ 845 Bill Travers .25 .11
❑ 846 Tom Underwood .25 .11
❑ 847 John Urrea .25 .11
❑ 848 Mike Vail .25 .11
❑ 849 Ellis Valentine .25 .11
❑ 850 Fernando Valenzuela 5.00 2.20
❑ 851 Pete Vuckovich 1.00 .45
❑ 852 Mark Wagner .25 .11
❑ 853 Bob Walk 1.00 .45
❑ 854 Claudell Washington .25 .11
❑ 855 Dave Winfield 5.00 2.20
❑ 856 Geoff Zahn .25 .11
❑ 857 Richie Zisk .25 .11
❑ 858 Checklist 727-858 .25 .11

## 1982 Topps

| | NRMT | VG-E |
|---|---|---|
| COMPLETE SET (792) | 100.00 | 45.00 |

❑ 1 Steve Carlton HL 1.25 .55
Sets new NL strikeout record
❑ 2 Ron Davis HL .15 .07
Fans 8 straight in relief
❑ 3 Tim Raines HL .60 .25
71 steals as rookie
❑ 4 Pete Rose HL .60 .25
Sets NL hit mark
❑ 5 Nolan Ryan HL 3.00 1.35
Pitches fifth no-hitter
❑ 6 Fernando Valenzuela HL .60 .25
8 shutouts as rookie
❑ 7 Scott Sanderson .15 .07
❑ 8 Rich Dauer .15 .07
❑ 9 Ron Guidry .30 .14
❑ 10 Ron Guidry SA .15 .07
❑ 11 Gary Alexander .15 .07
❑ 12 Moose Haas .15 .07
❑ 13 Lamar Johnson .15 .07
❑ 14 Steve Howe .15 .07
❑ 15 Ellis Valentine .15 .07
❑ 16 Steve Comer .15 .07
❑ 17 Darrell Evans .30 .14
❑ 18 Fernando Arroyo .15 .07
❑ 19 Ernie Whitt .15 .07
❑ 20 Garry Maddox .15 .07
❑ 21 Orioles Rookies 75.00 34.00
Bob Bonner
Cal Ripken
Jeff Schneider RC
❑ 22 Jim Beattie .15 .07
❑ 23 Willie Hernandez .30 .14
❑ 24 Dave Frost .15 .07
❑ 25 Jerry Remy .15 .07
❑ 26 Jorge Orta .15 .07
❑ 27 Tom Herr .30 .14
❑ 28 John Urrea .15 .07
❑ 29 Dwayne Murphy .15 .07
❑ 30 Tom Seaver 2.00 .90
❑ 31 Tom Seaver SA .60 .25
❑ 32 Gene Garber .15 .07
❑ 33 Jerry Morales .15 .07
❑ 34 Joe Sambito .15 .07
❑ 35 Willie Aikens .15 .07
❑ 36 Rangers TL .60 .25
BA: Al Oliver
Pitching: Doc Medich
❑ 37 Dan Graham .15 .07
❑ 38 Charlie Lea .15 .07
❑ 39 Lou Whitaker 1.25 .55
❑ 40 Dave Parker .30 .14
❑ 41 Dave Parker SA .15 .07
❑ 42 Rick Sofield .15 .07
❑ 43 Mike Cubbage .15 .07
❑ 44 Britt Burns .15 .07
❑ 45 Rick Cerone .15 .07
❑ 46 Jerry Augustine .15 .07
❑ 47 Jeff Leonard .15 .07
❑ 48 Bobby Castillo .15 .07
❑ 49 Alvis Woods .15 .07
❑ 50 Buddy Bell .30 .14
❑ 51 Cubs Rookies .60 .25
Jay Howell RC
Carlos Lezcano
Ty Waller
❑ 52 Larry Andersen .15 .07
❑ 53 Greg Gross .15 .07
❑ 54 Ron Hassey .15 .07
❑ 55 Rick Burleson .15 .07
❑ 56 Mark Littell .15 .07
❑ 57 Craig Reynolds .15 .07
❑ 58 John D'Acquisto .15 .07
❑ 59 Rich Gedman .30 .14
❑ 60 Tony Armas .15 .07
❑ 61 Tommy Boggs .15 .07
❑ 62 Mike Tyson .15 .07
❑ 63 Mario Soto .15 .07
❑ 64 Lynn Jones .15 .07
❑ 65 Terry Kennedy .15 .07
❑ 66 Astros TL 2.00 .90
BA: Art Howe
Pitching: Nolan Ryan
❑ 67 Rich Gale .15 .07
❑ 68 Roy Howell .15 .07
❑ 69 Al Williams .15 .07
❑ 70 Tim Raines 1.25 .55
❑ 71 Roy Lee Jackson .15 .07
❑ 72 Rick Auerbach .15 .07
❑ 73 Buddy Solomon .15 .07
❑ 74 Bob Clark .15 .07
❑ 75 Tommy John .60 .25
❑ 76 Greg Pryor .15 .07
❑ 77 Miguel Dilone .15 .07
❑ 78 George Medich .15 .07
❑ 79 Bob Bailor .15 .07
❑ 80 Jim Palmer 1.25 .55
❑ 81 Jim Palmer SA .60 .25
❑ 82 Bob Welch .30 .14
❑ 83 Yankees Rookies .60 .25
Steve Balboni RC
Andy McGaffigan
Andre Robertson
❑ 84 Rennie Stennett .15 .07

❑ 85 Lynn McGlothen .15 .07
❑ 86 Dane Iorg .15 .07
❑ 87 Matt Keough .15 .07
❑ 88 Biff Pocoroba .15 .07
❑ 89 Steve Henderson .15 .07
❑ 90 Nolan Ryan 6.00 2.70
❑ 91 Carney Lansford .30 .14
❑ 92 Brad Havens .15 .07
❑ 93 Larry Hisle .15 .07
❑ 94 Andy Hassler .15 .07
❑ 95 Ozzie Smith 2.50 1.10
❑ 96 Royals TL 1.25 .55
BA: George Brett
Pitching: Larry Gura
❑ 97 Paul Moskau .15 .07
❑ 98 Terry Bulling .15 .07
❑ 99 Barry Bonnell .15 .07
❑ 100 Mike Schmidt 2.50 1.10
❑ 101 Mike Schmidt SA .60 .25
❑ 102 Dan Briggs .15 .07
❑ 103 Bob Lacey .15 .07
❑ 104 Rance Mulliniks .15 .07
❑ 105 Kirk Gibson 1.25 .55
❑ 106 Enrique Romo .15 .07
❑ 107 Wayne Krenchicki .15 .07
❑ 108 Bob Sykes .15 .07
❑ 109 Dave Revering .15 .07
❑ 110 Carlton Fisk 1.25 .55
❑ 111 Carlton Fisk SA .60 .25
❑ 112 Billy Sample .15 .07
❑ 113 Steve McCatty .15 .07
❑ 114 Ken Landreaux .15 .07
❑ 115 Gaylord Perry 1.25 .55
❑ 116 Jim Wohlford .15 .07
❑ 117 Rawly Eastwick .15 .07
❑ 118 Expos Rookies .30 .14
Terry Francona
Brad Mills
Bryn Smith RC
❑ 119 Joe Pittman .15 .07
❑ 120 Gary Lucas .15 .07
❑ 121 Ed Lynch .15 .07
❑ 122 Jamie Easterly UER .15 .07
(Photo actually
Reggie Cleveland)
❑ 123 Danny Goodwin .15 .07
❑ 124 Reid Nichols .15 .07
❑ 125 Danny Ainge 1.50 .70
❑ 126 Braves TL .60 .25
BA: Claudell Washington
Pitching: Rick Mahler
❑ 127 Lonnie Smith .30 .14
❑ 128 Frank Pastore .15 .07
❑ 129 Checklist 1-132 .60 .25
❑ 130 Julio Cruz .15 .07
❑ 131 Stan Bahnsen .15 .07
❑ 132 Lee May .30 .14
❑ 133 Pat Underwood .15 .07
❑ 134 Dan Ford .15 .07
❑ 135 Andy Rincon .15 .07
❑ 136 Lenn Sakata .15 .07
❑ 137 George Cappuzzello .15 .07
❑ 138 Tony Pena .30 .14
❑ 139 Jeff Jones .15 .07
❑ 140 Ron LeFlore .30 .14
❑ 141 Indians Rookies .30 .14
Chris Bando
Tom Brennan
Von Hayes
❑ 142 Dave LaRoche .15 .07
❑ 143 Mookie Wilson .30 .14
❑ 144 Fred Breining .15 .07
❑ 145 Bob Horner .30 .14
❑ 146 Mike Griffin .15 .07
❑ 147 Denny Walling .15 .07
❑ 148 Mickey Klutts .15 .07
❑ 149 Pat Putnam .15 .07
❑ 150 Ted Simmons .30 .14
❑ 151 Dave Edwards .15 .07
❑ 152 Ramon Aviles .15 .07
❑ 153 Roger Erickson .15 .07
❑ 154 Dennis Werth .15 .07
❑ 155 Otto Velez .15 .07
❑ 156 Oakland A's TL .60 .25
BA: Rickey Henderson
Pitching: Steve McCatty
❑ 157 Steve Crawford .15 .07
❑ 158 Brian Downing .15 .07
❑ 159 Larry Biittner .15 .07
❑ 160 Luis Tiant .30 .14
❑ 161 Batting Leaders .30 .14
Bill Madlock
Carney Lansford
❑ 162 Home Run Leaders 1.25 .55
Mike Schmidt
Tony Armas
Dwight Evans
Bobby Grich
Eddie Murray
❑ 163 RBI Leaders 1.25 .55
Mike Schmidt
Eddie Murray
❑ 164 Stolen Base Leaders 1.25 .55
Tim Raines
Rickey Henderson
❑ 165 Victory Leaders .60 .25
Tom Seaver
Denny Martinez
Steve McCatty
Jack Morris
Pete Vuckovich
❑ 166 Strikeout Leaders .30 .14
Fernando Valenzuela
Len Barker
❑ 167 ERA Leaders 2.00 .90
Nolan Ryan
Steve McCatty
❑ 168 Leading Firemen .60 .25
Bruce Sutter
Rollie Fingers
❑ 169 Charlie Leibrandt .15 .07
❑ 170 Jim Bibby .15 .07
❑ 171 Giants Rookies 3.00 1.35
Bob Brenly
Chili Davis RC
Bob Tufts
❑ 172 Bill Gullickson .15 .07
❑ 173 Jamie Quirk .15 .07
❑ 174 Dave Ford .15 .07
❑ 175 Jerry Mumphrey .15 .07
❑ 176 Dewey Robinson .15 .07
❑ 177 John Ellis .15 .07
❑ 178 Dyar Miller .15 .07
❑ 179 Steve Garvey .60 .25
❑ 180 Steve Garvey SA .30 .14
❑ 181 Silvio Martinez .15 .07
❑ 182 Larry Herndon .15 .07
❑ 183 Mike Proly .15 .07
❑ 184 Mick Kelleher .15 .07
❑ 185 Phil Niekro 1.25 .55
❑ 186 Cardinals TL .60 .25
BA: Keith Hernandez
Pitching: Bob Forsch
❑ 187 Jeff Newman .15 .07
❑ 188 Randy Martz .15 .07
❑ 189 Glenn Hoffman .15 .07
❑ 190 J.R. Richard .30 .14
❑ 191 Tim Wallach RC .60 .25
❑ 192 Broderick Perkins .15 .07
❑ 193 Darrell Jackson .15 .07
❑ 194 Mike Vail .15 .07
❑ 195 Paul Molitor 1.50 .70
❑ 196 Willie Upshaw .15 .07
❑ 197 Shane Rawley .15 .07
❑ 198 Chris Speier .15 .07
❑ 199 Don Aase .15 .07
❑ 200 George Brett 2.50 1.10
❑ 201 George Brett SA 1.25 .55
❑ 202 Rick Manning .15 .07
❑ 203 Blue Jays Rookies .60 .25
Jesse Barfield RC
Brian Milner
Boomer Wells
❑ 204 Gary Roenicke .15 .07
❑ 205 Neil Allen .15 .07
❑ 206 Tony Bernazard .15 .07
❑ 207 Rod Scurry .15 .07
❑ 208 Bobby Murcer .30 .14
❑ 209 Gary Lavelle .15 .07
❑ 210 Keith Hernandez .30 .14
❑ 211 Dan Petry .15 .07
❑ 212 Mario Mendoza .15 .07
❑ 213 Dave Stewart RC 1.50 .70
❑ 214 Brian Asselstine .15 .07
❑ 215 Mike Krukow .15 .07
❑ 216 White Sox TL .60 .25
BA: Chet Lemon
Pitching: Dennis Lamp
❑ 217 Bo McLaughlin .15 .07
❑ 218 Dave Roberts .15 .07
❑ 219 John Curtis .15 .07
❑ 220 Manny Trillo .15 .07
❑ 221 Jim Slaton .15 .07
❑ 222 Butch Wynegar .15 .07
❑ 223 Lloyd Moseby .15 .07
❑ 224 Bruce Bochte .15 .07
❑ 225 Mike Torrez .15 .07
❑ 226 Checklist 133-264 .60 .25
❑ 227 Ray Burris .15 .07
❑ 228 Sam Mejias .15 .07
❑ 229 Geoff Zahn .15 .07
❑ 230 Willie Wilson .30 .14
❑ 231 Phillies Rookies .60 .25
Mark Davis RC
Bob Dernier
Ozzie Virgil
❑ 232 Terry Crowley .15 .07
❑ 233 Duane Kuiper .15 .07
❑ 234 Ron Hodges .15 .07
❑ 235 Mike Easler .15 .07
❑ 236 John Martin .15 .07
❑ 237 Rusty Kuntz .15 .07
❑ 238 Kevin Saucier .15 .07
❑ 239 Jon Matlack .15 .07
❑ 240 Bucky Dent .30 .14
❑ 241 Bucky Dent SA .15 .07
❑ 242 Milt May .15 .07
❑ 243 Bob Owchinko .15 .07
❑ 244 Rufino Linares .15 .07
❑ 245 Ken Reitz .15 .07
❑ 246 New York Mets TL .60 .25
BA: Hubie Brooks
Pitching: Mike Scott
❑ 247 Pedro Guerrero .30 .14
❑ 248 Frank LaCorte .15 .07
❑ 249 Tim Flannery .15 .07
❑ 250 Tug McGraw .30 .14
❑ 251 Fred Lynn .30 .14
❑ 252 Fred Lynn SA .15 .07
❑ 253 Chuck Baker .15 .07
❑ 254 Jorge Bell RC 1.25 .55
❑ 255 Tony Perez 1.25 .55
❑ 256 Tony Perez SA .60 .25
❑ 257 Larry Harlow .15 .07
❑ 258 Bo Diaz .15 .07
❑ 259 Rodney Scott .15 .07
❑ 260 Bruce Sutter .30 .14
❑ 261 Tigers Rookies UER .15 .07
Howard Bailey
Marty Castillo
Dave Rucker
(Rucker photo act-
ally Roger Weaver)
❑ 262 Doug Bair .15 .07
❑ 263 Victor Cruz .15 .07
❑ 264 Dan Quisenberry .30 .14
❑ 265 Al Bumbry .15 .07
❑ 266 Rick Leach .15 .07
❑ 267 Kurt Bevacqua .15 .07
❑ 268 Rickey Keeton .15 .07
❑ 269 Jim Essian .15 .07
❑ 270 Rusty Staub .30 .14
❑ 271 Larry Bradford .15 .07
❑ 272 Bump Wills .15 .07
❑ 273 Doug Bird .15 .07
❑ 274 Bob Ojeda RC .60 .25
❑ 275 Bob Watson .30 .14
❑ 276 Angels TL .60 .25
BA: Rod Carew
Pitching: Ken Forsch
❑ 277 Terry Puhl .15 .07
❑ 278 John Littlefield .15 .07
❑ 279 Bill Russell .15 .07
❑ 280 Ben Oglivie .30 .14
❑ 281 John Verhoeven .15 .07
❑ 282 Ken Macha .15 .07
❑ 283 Brian Allard .15 .07
❑ 284 Bobby Grich .30 .14

❑ 285 Sparky Lyle .30 .14
❑ 286 Bill Fahey .15 .07
❑ 287 Alan Bannister .15 .07
❑ 288 Garry Templeton .15 .07
❑ 289 Bob Stanley .15 .07
❑ 290 Ken Singleton .30 .14
❑ 291 Pirates Rookies .30 .14
Vance Law
Bob Long
Johnny Ray
❑ 292 David Palmer .15 .07
❑ 293 Rob Picciolo .15 .07
❑ 294 Mike LaCoss .15 .07
❑ 295 Jason Thompson .15 .07
❑ 296 Bob Walk .15 .07
❑ 297 Clint Hurdle .15 .07
❑ 298 Danny Darwin .15 .07
❑ 299 Steve Trout .15 .07
❑ 300 Reggie Jackson 1.50 .70
❑ 301 Reggie Jackson SA .60 .25
❑ 302 Doug Flynn .15 .07
❑ 303 Bill Caudill .15 .07
❑ 304 Johnnie LeMaster .15 .07
❑ 305 Don Sutton 1.25 .55
❑ 306 Don Sutton SA .60 .25
❑ 307 Randy Bass RC .15 .07
❑ 308 Charlie Moore .15 .07
❑ 309 Pete Redfern .15 .07
❑ 310 Mike Hargrove .30 .14
❑ 311 Dodgers TL .60 .25
BA: Dusty Baker
Pitching: Burt Hooton
❑ 312 Lenny Randle .15 .07
❑ 313 John Harris .15 .07
❑ 314 Buck Martinez .15 .07
❑ 315 Burt Hooton .15 .07
❑ 316 Steve Braun .15 .07
❑ 317 Dick Ruthven .15 .07
❑ 318 Mike Heath .15 .07
❑ 319 Dave Rozema .15 .07
❑ 320 Chris Chambliss .30 .14
❑ 321 Chris Chambliss SA .15 .07
❑ 322 Garry Hancock .15 .07
❑ 323 Bill Lee .30 .14
❑ 324 Steve Dillard .15 .07
❑ 325 Jose Cruz .30 .14
❑ 326 Pete Falcone .15 .07
❑ 327 Joe Nolan .15 .07
❑ 328 Ed Farmer .15 .07
❑ 329 U.L. Washington .15 .07
❑ 330 Rick Wise .15 .07
❑ 331 Benny Ayala .15 .07
❑ 332 Don Robinson .15 .07
❑ 333 Brewers Rookies .15 .07
Frank DiPino
Marshall Edwards
Chuck Porter
❑ 334 Aurelio Rodriguez .15 .07
❑ 335 Jim Sundberg .15 .07
❑ 336 Mariners TL .60 .25
BA: Tom Paciorek
Pitching: Glenn Abbott
❑ 337 Pete Rose AS .60 .25
❑ 338 Dave Lopes AS .15 .07
❑ 339 Mike Schmidt AS .60 .25
❑ 340 Dave Concepcion AS .15 .07
❑ 341 Andre Dawson AS .30 .14
❑ 342A George Foster AS .30 .14
(With autograph)
❑ 342B George Foster AS 1.25 .55
(W/o autograph)
❑ 343 Dave Parker AS .15 .07
❑ 344 Gary Carter AS .30 .14
❑ 345 Fernando Valenzuela AS .60 .25
❑ 346 Tom Seaver AS ERR 1.25 .55
("t ed")
❑ 346B Tom Seaver AS COR 1.25 .55
("tied")
❑ 347 Bruce Sutter AS .15 .07
❑ 348 Derrel Thomas .15 .07
❑ 349 George Frazier .15 .07
❑ 350 Thad Bosley .15 .07
❑ 351 Reds Rookies .15 .07
Scott Brown
Geoff Combe
Paul Householder

❑ 352 Dick Davis .15 .07
❑ 353 Jack O'Connor .15 .07
❑ 354 Roberto Ramos .15 .07
❑ 355 Dwight Evans .60 .25
❑ 356 Denny Lewallyn .15 .07
❑ 357 Butch Hobson .15 .07
❑ 358 Mike Parrott .15 .07
❑ 359 Jim Dwyer .15 .07
❑ 360 Len Barker .15 .07
❑ 361 Rafael Landestoy .15 .07
❑ 362 Jim Wright UER .15 .07
(Wrong Jim Wright
pictured)
❑ 363 Bob Molinaro .15 .07
❑ 364 Doyle Alexander .15 .07
❑ 365 Bill Madlock .30 .14
❑ 366 Padres TL .60 .25
BA: Luis Salazar
Pitching: Juan
Eichelberger
❑ 367 Jim Kaat .30 .14
❑ 368 Alex Trevino .15 .07
❑ 369 Champ Summers .15 .07
❑ 370 Mike Norris .15 .07
❑ 371 Jerry Don Gleaton .15 .07
❑ 372 Luis Gomez .15 .07
❑ 373 Gene Nelson .15 .07
❑ 374 Tim Blackwell .15 .07
❑ 375 Dusty Baker .60 .25
❑ 376 Chris Welsh .15 .07
❑ 377 Kiko Garcia .15 .07
❑ 378 Mike Caldwell .15 .07
❑ 379 Rob Wilfong .15 .07
❑ 380 Dave Stieb .30 .14
❑ 381 Red Sox Rookies .30 .14
Bruce Hurst
Dave Schmidt
Julio Valdez
❑ 382 Joe Simpson .15 .07
❑ 383A Pascual Perez ERR 5.00 2.20
(No position
on front)
❑ 383B Pascual Perez COR .30 .14
❑ 384 Keith Moreland .15 .07
❑ 385 Ken Forsch .15 .07
❑ 386 Jerry White .15 .07
❑ 387 Tom Veryzer .15 .07
❑ 388 Joe Rudi .15 .07
❑ 389 George Vukovich .15 .07
❑ 390 Eddie Murray 1.50 .70
❑ 391 Dave Tobik .15 .07
❑ 392 Rick Bosetti .15 .07
❑ 393 Al Hrabosky .15 .07
❑ 394 Checklist 265-396 .60 .25
❑ 395 Omar Moreno .15 .07
❑ 396 Twins TL .60 .25
BA: John Castino
Fernando Arroyo
❑ 397 Ken Brett .15 .07
❑ 398 Mike Squires .15 .07
❑ 399 Pat Zachry .15 .07
❑ 400 Johnny Bench 2.00 .90
❑ 401 Johnny Bench SA .60 .25
❑ 402 Bill Stein .15 .07
❑ 403 Jim Tracy .15 .07
❑ 404 Dickie Thon .15 .07
❑ 405 Rick Reuschel .30 .14
❑ 406 Al Holland .15 .07
❑ 407 Danny Boone .15 .07
❑ 408 Ed Romero .15 .07
❑ 409 Don Cooper .15 .07
❑ 410 Ron Cey .30 .14
❑ 411 Ron Cey SA .15 .07
❑ 412 Luis Leal .15 .07
❑ 413 Dan Meyer .15 .07
❑ 414 Elias Sosa .15 .07
❑ 415 Don Baylor .60 .25
❑ 416 Marty Bystrom .15 .07
❑ 417 Pat Kelly .15 .07
❑ 418 Rangers Rookies .15 .07
John Butcher
Bobby Johnson
Dave Schmidt
❑ 419 Steve Stone .30 .14
❑ 420 George Hendrick .15 .07
❑ 421 Mark Clear .15 .07

❑ 422 Cliff Johnson .15 .07
❑ 423 Stan Papi .15 .07
❑ 424 Bruce Benedict .15 .07
❑ 425 John Candelaria .15 .07
❑ 426 Orioles TL .60 .25
BA: Eddie Murray
Pitching: Sammy Stewart
❑ 427 Ron Oester .15 .07
❑ 428 LaMarr Hoyt .15 .07
❑ 429 John Wathan .15 .07
❑ 430 Vida Blue .30 .14
❑ 431 Vida Blue SA .15 .07
❑ 432 Mike Scott .30 .14
❑ 433 Alan Ashby .15 .07
❑ 434 Joe Lefebvre .15 .07
❑ 435 Robin Yount 1.25 .55
❑ 436 Joe Strain .15 .07
❑ 437 Juan Berenguer .15 .07
❑ 438 Pete Mackanin .15 .07
❑ 439 Dave Righetti RC 1.25 .55
❑ 440 Jeff Burroughs .15 .07
❑ 441 Astros Rookies .15 .07
Danny Heep
Billy Smith
Bobby Sprowl
❑ 442 Bruce Kison .15 .07
❑ 443 Mark Wagner .15 .07
❑ 444 Terry Forster .15 .07
❑ 445 Larry Parrish .15 .07
❑ 446 Wayne Garland .15 .07
❑ 447 Darrell Porter .30 .14
❑ 448 Darrell Porter SA .15 .07
❑ 449 Luis Aguayo .15 .07
❑ 450 Jack Morris .30 .14
❑ 451 Ed Miller .15 .07
❑ 452 Lee Smith RC 3.00 1.35
❑ 453 Art Howe .30 .14
❑ 454 Rick Langford .15 .07
❑ 455 Tom Burgmeier .15 .07
❑ 456 Chicago Cubs TL .60 .25
BA: Bill Buckner
Pitching: Randy Martz
❑ 457 Tim Stoddard .15 .07
❑ 458 Willie Montanez .15 .07
❑ 459 Bruce Berenyi .15 .07
❑ 460 Jack Clark .30 .14
❑ 461 Rich Dotson .15 .07
❑ 462 Dave Chalk .15 .07
❑ 463 Jim Kern .15 .07
❑ 464 Juan Bonilla .15 .07
❑ 465 Lee Mazzilli .15 .07
❑ 466 Randy Lerch .15 .07
❑ 467 Mickey Hatcher .15 .07
❑ 468 Floyd Bannister .15 .07
❑ 469 Ed Ott .15 .07
❑ 470 John Mayberry .15 .07
❑ 471 Royals Rookies .15 .07
Atlee Hammaker
Mike Jones
Darryl Motley
❑ 472 Oscar Gamble .15 .07
❑ 473 Mike Stanton .15 .07
❑ 474 Ken Oberkfell .15 .07
❑ 475 Alan Trammell .60 .25
❑ 476 Brian Kingman .15 .07
❑ 477 Steve Yeager .15 .07
❑ 478 Ray Searage .15 .07
❑ 479 Rowland Office .15 .07
❑ 480 Steve Carlton 1.25 .55
❑ 481 Steve Carlton SA .60 .25
❑ 482 Glenn Hubbard .15 .07
❑ 483 Gary Woods .15 .07
❑ 484 Ivan DeJesus .15 .07
❑ 485 Kent Tekulve .30 .14
❑ 486 Yankees TL .30 .14
BA: Jerry Mumphrey
Pitching: Tommy John
❑ 487 Bob McClure .15 .07
❑ 488 Ron Jackson .15 .07
❑ 489 Rick Dempsey .30 .14
❑ 490 Dennis Eckersley 1.25 .55
❑ 491 Checklist 397-528 .60 .25
❑ 492 Joe Price .15 .07
❑ 493 Chet Lemon .15 .07
❑ 494 Hubie Brooks .30 .14
❑ 495 Dennis Leonard .15 .07

| No. | Card | | |
|---|---|---|---|
| ❑ 496 | Johnny Grubb | .15 | .07 |
| ❑ 497 | Jim Anderson | .15 | .07 |
| ❑ 498 | Dave Bergman | .15 | .07 |
| ❑ 499 | Paul Mirabella | .15 | .07 |
| ❑ 500 | Rod Carew | 1.25 | .55 |
| ❑ 501 | Rod Carew SA | .60 | .25 |
| ❑ 502 | Braves Rookies | 1.50 | .70 |
| | Steve Bedrosian UER | | |
| | (Photo actually | | |
| | Larry Owen) | | |
| | Brett Butler RC | | |
| | Larry Owen | | |
| ❑ 503 | Julio Gonzalez | .15 | .07 |
| ❑ 504 | Rick Peters | .15 | .07 |
| ❑ 505 | Graig Nettles | .30 | .14 |
| ❑ 506 | Graig Nettles SA | .15 | .07 |
| ❑ 507 | Terry Harper | .15 | .07 |
| ❑ 508 | Jody Davis | .15 | .07 |
| ❑ 509 | Harry Spilman | .15 | .07 |
| ❑ 510 | Fernando Valenzuela | 1.25 | .55 |
| ❑ 511 | Ruppert Jones | .15 | .07 |
| ❑ 512 | Jerry Dybzinski | .15 | .07 |
| ❑ 513 | Rick Rhoden | .15 | .07 |
| ❑ 514 | Joe Ferguson | .15 | .07 |
| ❑ 515 | Larry Bowa | .30 | .14 |
| ❑ 516 | Larry Bowa SA | .15 | .07 |
| ❑ 517 | Mark Brouhard | .15 | .07 |
| ❑ 518 | Garth Iorg | .15 | .07 |
| ❑ 519 | Glenn Adams | .15 | .07 |
| ❑ 520 | Mike Flanagan | .30 | .14 |
| ❑ 521 | Bill Almon | .15 | .07 |
| ❑ 522 | Chuck Rainey | .15 | .07 |
| ❑ 523 | Gary Gray | .15 | .07 |
| ❑ 524 | Tom Hausman | .15 | .07 |
| ❑ 525 | Ray Knight | .30 | .14 |
| ❑ 526 | Expos TL | .60 | .25 |
| | BA: Warren Cromartie | | |
| | Pitching: Bill Gullickson | | |
| ❑ 527 | John Henry Johnson | .15 | .07 |
| ❑ 528 | Matt Alexander | .15 | .07 |
| ❑ 529 | Allen Ripley | .15 | .07 |
| ❑ 530 | Dickie Noles | .15 | .07 |
| ❑ 531 | A's Rookies | .15 | .07 |
| | Rich Bordi | | |
| | Mark Budaska | | |
| | Kelvin Moore | | |
| ❑ 532 | Toby Harrah | .30 | .14 |
| ❑ 533 | Joaquin Andujar | .30 | .14 |
| ❑ 534 | Dave McKay | .15 | .07 |
| ❑ 535 | Lance Parrish | .60 | .25 |
| ❑ 536 | Rafael Ramirez | .15 | .07 |
| ❑ 537 | Doug Capilla | .15 | .07 |
| ❑ 538 | Lou Piniella | .30 | .14 |
| ❑ 539 | Vern Ruhle | .15 | .07 |
| ❑ 540 | Andre Dawson | .60 | .25 |
| ❑ 541 | Barry Evans | .15 | .07 |
| ❑ 542 | Ned Yost | .15 | .07 |
| ❑ 543 | Bill Robinson | .15 | .07 |
| ❑ 544 | Larry Christenson | .15 | .07 |
| ❑ 545 | Reggie Smith | .30 | .14 |
| ❑ 546 | Reggie Smith SA | .15 | .07 |
| ❑ 547 | Rod Carew AS | 1.25 | .55 |
| ❑ 548 | Willie Randolph AS | .30 | .14 |
| ❑ 549 | George Brett AS | 1.25 | .55 |
| ❑ 550 | Bucky Dent AS | .15 | .07 |
| ❑ 551 | Reggie Jackson AS | .60 | .25 |
| ❑ 552 | Ken Singleton AS | .15 | .07 |
| ❑ 553 | Dave Winfield AS | .30 | .14 |
| ❑ 554 | Carlton Fisk AS | .60 | .25 |
| ❑ 555 | Scott McGregor AS | .15 | .07 |
| ❑ 556 | Jack Morris AS | .15 | .07 |
| ❑ 557 | Rich Gossage AS | .30 | .14 |
| ❑ 558 | John Tudor | .15 | .07 |
| ❑ 559 | Indians TL | .30 | .14 |
| | BA: Mike Hargrove | | |
| | Pitching: Bert Blyleven | | |
| ❑ 560 | Doug Corbett | .15 | .07 |
| ❑ 561 | Cardinals Rookies | .15 | .07 |
| | Glenn Brummer | | |
| | Luis DeLeon | | |
| | Gene Roof | | |
| ❑ 562 | Mike O'Berry | .15 | .07 |
| ❑ 563 | Ross Baumgarten | .15 | .07 |
| ❑ 564 | Doug DeCinces | .30 | .14 |
| ❑ 565 | Jackson Todd | .15 | .07 |
| ❑ 566 | Mike Jorgensen | .15 | .07 |
| ❑ 567 | Bob Babcock | .15 | .07 |
| ❑ 568 | Joe Pettini | .15 | .07 |
| ❑ 569 | Willie Randolph | .30 | .14 |
| ❑ 570 | Willie Randolph SA | .30 | .14 |
| ❑ 571 | Glenn Abbott | .15 | .07 |
| ❑ 572 | Juan Beniquez | .15 | .07 |
| ❑ 573 | Rick Waits | .15 | .07 |
| ❑ 574 | Mike Ramsey | .15 | .07 |
| ❑ 575 | Al Cowens | .15 | .07 |
| ❑ 576 | Giants TL | .60 | .25 |
| | BA: Milt May | | |
| | Pitching: Vida Blue | | |
| ❑ 577 | Rick Monday | .15 | .07 |
| ❑ 578 | Shooty Babitt | .15 | .07 |
| ❑ 579 | Rick Mahler | .15 | .07 |
| ❑ 580 | Bobby Bonds | .30 | .14 |
| ❑ 581 | Ron Reed | .15 | .07 |
| ❑ 582 | Luis Pujols | .15 | .07 |
| ❑ 583 | Tippy Martinez | .15 | .07 |
| ❑ 584 | Hosken Powell | .15 | .07 |
| ❑ 585 | Rollie Fingers | 1.25 | .55 |
| ❑ 586 | Rollie Fingers SA | .60 | .25 |
| ❑ 587 | Tim Lollar | .15 | .07 |
| ❑ 588 | Dale Berra | .15 | .07 |
| ❑ 589 | Dave Stapleton | .15 | .07 |
| ❑ 590 | Al Oliver | .30 | .14 |
| ❑ 591 | Al Oliver SA | .15 | .07 |
| ❑ 592 | Craig Swan | .15 | .07 |
| ❑ 593 | Billy Smith | .15 | .07 |
| ❑ 594 | Renie Martin | .15 | .07 |
| ❑ 595 | Dave Collins | .15 | .07 |
| ❑ 596 | Damaso Garcia | .15 | .07 |
| ❑ 597 | Wayne Nordhagen | .15 | .07 |
| ❑ 598 | Bob Galasso | .15 | .07 |
| ❑ 599 | White Sox Rookies | .15 | .07 |
| | Jay Loviglio | | |
| | Reggie Patterson | | |
| | Leo Sutherland | | |
| ❑ 600 | Dave Winfield | 1.25 | .55 |
| ❑ 601 | Sid Monge | .15 | .07 |
| ❑ 602 | Freddie Patek | .15 | .07 |
| ❑ 603 | Rich Hebner | .30 | .14 |
| ❑ 604 | Orlando Sanchez | .15 | .07 |
| ❑ 605 | Steve Rogers | .15 | .07 |
| ❑ 606 | Blue Jays TL | .60 | .25 |
| | BA: John Mayberry | | |
| | Pitching: Dave Stieb | | |
| ❑ 607 | Leon Durham | .15 | .07 |
| ❑ 608 | Jerry Royster | .15 | .07 |
| ❑ 609 | Rick Sutcliffe | .30 | .14 |
| ❑ 610 | Rickey Henderson | 3.00 | 1.35 |
| ❑ 611 | Joe Niekro | .30 | .14 |
| ❑ 612 | Gary Ward | .15 | .07 |
| ❑ 613 | Jim Gantner | .30 | .14 |
| ❑ 614 | Juan Eichelberger | .15 | .07 |
| ❑ 615 | Bob Boone | .30 | .14 |
| ❑ 616 | Bob Boone SA | .15 | .07 |
| ❑ 617 | Scott McGregor | .15 | .07 |
| ❑ 618 | Tim Foli | .15 | .07 |
| ❑ 619 | Bill Campbell | .15 | .07 |
| ❑ 620 | Ken Griffey | .30 | .14 |
| ❑ 621 | Ken Griffey SA | .15 | .07 |
| ❑ 622 | Dennis Lamp | .15 | .07 |
| ❑ 623 | Mets Rookies | .60 | .25 |
| | Ron Gardenhire | | |
| | Terry Leach | | |
| | Tim Leary RC | | |
| ❑ 624 | Fergie Jenkins | 1.25 | .55 |
| ❑ 625 | Hal McRae | .30 | .14 |
| ❑ 626 | Randy Jones | .15 | .07 |
| ❑ 627 | Enos Cabell | .15 | .07 |
| ❑ 628 | Bill Travers | .15 | .07 |
| ❑ 629 | John Wockenfuss | .15 | .07 |
| ❑ 630 | Joe Charboneau | .30 | .14 |
| ❑ 631 | Gene Tenace | .30 | .14 |
| ❑ 632 | Bryan Clark | .15 | .07 |
| ❑ 633 | Mitchell Page | .15 | .07 |
| ❑ 634 | Checklist 529-660 | .60 | .25 |
| ❑ 635 | Ron Davis | .15 | .07 |
| ❑ 636 | Phillies TL | 1.25 | .55 |
| | BA: Pete Rose | | |
| | Pitching: Steve Carlton | | |
| ❑ 637 | Rick Camp | .15 | .07 |
| ❑ 638 | John Milner | .15 | .07 |
| ❑ 639 | Ken Kravec | .15 | .07 |
| ❑ 640 | Cesar Cedeno | .30 | .14 |
| ❑ 641 | Steve Mura | .15 | .07 |
| ❑ 642 | Mike Scioscia | .30 | .14 |
| ❑ 643 | Pete Vuckovich | .15 | .07 |
| ❑ 644 | John Castino | .15 | .07 |
| ❑ 645 | Frank White | .30 | .14 |
| ❑ 646 | Frank White SA | .15 | .07 |
| ❑ 647 | Warren Brusstar | .15 | .07 |
| ❑ 648 | Jose Morales | .15 | .07 |
| ❑ 649 | Ken Clay | .15 | .07 |
| ❑ 650 | Carl Yastrzemski | 1.25 | .55 |
| ❑ 651 | Carl Yastrzemski SA | .60 | .25 |
| ❑ 652 | Steve Nicosia | .15 | .07 |
| ❑ 653 | Angels Rookies | .60 | .25 |
| | Tom Brunansky RC | | |
| | Luis Sanchez | | |
| | Daryl Sconiers | | |
| ❑ 654 | Jim Morrison | .15 | .07 |
| ❑ 655 | Joel Youngblood | .15 | .07 |
| ❑ 656 | Eddie Whitson | .15 | .07 |
| ❑ 657 | Tom Poquette | .15 | .07 |
| ❑ 658 | Tito Landrum | .15 | .07 |
| ❑ 659 | Fred Martinez | .15 | .07 |
| ❑ 660 | Dave Concepcion | .30 | .14 |
| ❑ 661 | Dave Concepcion SA | .15 | .07 |
| ❑ 662 | Luis Salazar | .15 | .07 |
| ❑ 663 | Hector Cruz | .15 | .07 |
| ❑ 664 | Dan Spillner | .15 | .07 |
| ❑ 665 | Jim Clancy | .15 | .07 |
| ❑ 666 | Tigers TL | .60 | .25 |
| | BA: Steve Kemp | | |
| | Pitching: Dan Petry | | |
| ❑ 667 | Jeff Reardon | .60 | .25 |
| ❑ 668 | Dale Murphy | 1.25 | .55 |
| ❑ 669 | Larry Milbourne | .15 | .07 |
| ❑ 670 | Steve Kemp | .15 | .07 |
| ❑ 671 | Mike Davis | .15 | .07 |
| ❑ 672 | Bob Knepper | .15 | .07 |
| ❑ 673 | Keith Drumwright | .15 | .07 |
| ❑ 674 | Dave Goltz | .15 | .07 |
| ❑ 675 | Cecil Cooper | .30 | .14 |
| ❑ 676 | Sal Butera | .15 | .07 |
| ❑ 677 | Alfredo Griffin | .15 | .07 |
| ❑ 678 | Tom Paciorek | .30 | .14 |
| ❑ 679 | Sammy Stewart | .15 | .07 |
| ❑ 680 | Gary Matthews | .30 | .14 |
| ❑ 681 | Dodgers Rookies | 1.25 | .55 |
| | Mike Marshall | | |
| | Ron Roenicke | | |
| | Steve Sax RC | | |
| ❑ 682 | Jesse Jefferson | .15 | .07 |
| ❑ 683 | Phil Garner | .30 | .14 |
| ❑ 684 | Harold Baines | 1.25 | .55 |
| ❑ 685 | Bert Blyleven | .60 | .25 |
| ❑ 686 | Gary Allenson | .15 | .07 |
| ❑ 687 | Greg Minton | .15 | .07 |
| ❑ 688 | Leon Roberts | .15 | .07 |
| ❑ 689 | Lary Sorensen | .15 | .07 |
| ❑ 690 | Dave Kingman | .30 | .14 |
| ❑ 691 | Dan Schatzeder | .15 | .07 |
| ❑ 692 | Wayne Gross | .15 | .07 |
| ❑ 693 | Cesar Geronimo | .15 | .07 |
| ❑ 694 | Dave Wehrmeister | .15 | .07 |
| ❑ 695 | Warren Cromartie | .15 | .07 |
| ❑ 696 | Pirates TL | .60 | .25 |
| | BA: Bill Madlock | | |
| | Pitching: Eddie Solomon | | |
| ❑ 697 | John Montefusco | .15 | .07 |
| ❑ 698 | Tony Scott | .15 | .07 |
| ❑ 699 | Dick Tidrow | .15 | .07 |
| ❑ 700 | George Foster | .30 | .14 |
| ❑ 701 | George Foster SA | .15 | .07 |
| ❑ 702 | Steve Renko | .15 | .07 |
| ❑ 703 | Brewers TL | .60 | .25 |
| | BA: Cecil Cooper | | |
| | Pitching: Pete Vuckovich | | |
| ❑ 704 | Mickey Rivers | .15 | .07 |
| ❑ 705 | Mickey Rivers SA | .15 | .07 |
| ❑ 706 | Barry Foote | .15 | .07 |
| ❑ 707 | Mark Bomback | .15 | .07 |
| ❑ 708 | Gene Richards | .15 | .07 |
| ❑ 709 | Don Money | .15 | .07 |
| ❑ 710 | Jerry Reuss | .30 | .14 |
| ❑ 711 | Mariners Rookies | .60 | .25 |
| | Dave Edler | | |
| | Dave Henderson RC | | |
| | Reggie Walton | | |

❑ 712 Dennis Martinez .60 .25
❑ 713 Del Unser .15 .07
❑ 714 Jerry Koosman .30 .14
❑ 715 Willie Stargell 1.25 .55
❑ 716 Willie Stargell SA .60 .25
❑ 717 Rick Miller .15 .07
❑ 718 Charlie Hough .30 .14
❑ 719 Jerry Narron .15 .07
❑ 720 Greg Luzinski .30 .14
❑ 721 Greg Luzinski SA .15 .07
❑ 722 Jerry Martin .15 .07
❑ 723 Junior Kennedy .15 .07
❑ 724 Dave Rosello .15 .07
❑ 725 Amos Otis .30 .14
❑ 726 Amos Otis SA .15 .07
❑ 727 Sixto Lezcano .15 .07
❑ 728 Aurelio Lopez .15 .07
❑ 729 Jim Spencer .15 .07
❑ 730 Gary Carter .60 .25
❑ 731 Padres Rookies .15 .07
Mike Armstrong
Doug Gwosdz
Fred Kuhaulua
❑ 732 Mike Lum .15 .07
❑ 733 Larry McWilliams .15 .07
❑ 734 Mike Ivie .15 .07
❑ 735 Rudy May .15 .07
❑ 736 Jerry Turner .15 .07
❑ 737 Reggie Cleveland .15 .07
❑ 738 Dave Engle .15 .07
❑ 739 Joey McLaughlin .15 .07
❑ 740 Dave Lopes .30 .14
❑ 741 Dave Lopes SA .15 .07
❑ 742 Dick Drago .15 .07
❑ 743 John Stearns .15 .07
❑ 744 Mike Witt .30 .14
❑ 745 Bake McBride .15 .07
❑ 746 Andre Thornton .15 .07
❑ 747 John Lowenstein .15 .07
❑ 748 Marc Hill .15 .07
❑ 749 Bob Shirley .15 .07
❑ 750 Jim Rice .30 .14
❑ 751 Rick Honeycutt .15 .07
❑ 752 Lee Lacy .15 .07
❑ 753 Tom Brookens .15 .07
❑ 754 Joe Morgan 1.25 .55
❑ 755 Joe Morgan SA .60 .25
❑ 756 Reds TL .60 .25
BA: Ken Griffey
Pitching: Tom Seaver
❑ 757 Tom Underwood .15 .07
❑ 758 Claudell Washington .15 .07
❑ 759 Paul Splittorff .15 .07
❑ 760 Bill Buckner .30 .14
❑ 761 Dave Smith .15 .07
❑ 762 Mike Phillips .15 .07
❑ 763 Tom Hume .15 .07
❑ 764 Steve Swisher .15 .07
❑ 765 Gorman Thomas .30 .14
❑ 766 Twins Rookies 1.50 .70
Lenny Faedo
Kent Hrbek RC
Tim Laudner
❑ 767 Roy Smalley .15 .07
❑ 768 Jerry Garvin .15 .07
❑ 769 Richie Zisk .15 .07
❑ 770 Rich Gossage .60 .25
❑ 771 Rich Gossage SA .30 .14
❑ 772 Bert Campaneris .30 .14
❑ 773 John Denny .15 .07
❑ 774 Jay Johnstone .30 .14
❑ 775 Bob Forsch .15 .07
❑ 776 Mark Belanger .15 .07
❑ 777 Tom Griffin .15 .07
❑ 778 Kevin Hickey .15 .07
❑ 779 Grant Jackson .15 .07
❑ 780 Pete Rose 4.00 1.80
❑ 781 Pete Rose SA 1.25 .55
❑ 782 Frank Taveras .15 .07
❑ 783 Greg Harris RC .15 .07
❑ 784 Milt Wilcox .15 .07
❑ 785 Dan Driessen .15 .07
❑ 786 Red Sox TL .60 .25
BA: Carney Lansford
Pitching: Mike Torrez
❑ 787 Fred Stanley .15 .07
❑ 788 Woodie Fryman .15 .07
❑ 789 Checklist 661-792 .60 .25
❑ 790 Larry Gura .15 .07
❑ 791 Bobby Brown .15 .07
❑ 792 Frank Tanana .30 .14

## 1982 Topps Traded

| | NRMT | VG-E |
|---|---|---|
| COMP.FACT.SET (132) | 300.00 | 135.00 |

❑ 1T Doyle Alexander .50 .23
❑ 2T Jesse Barfield 1.00 .45
❑ 3T Ross Baumgarten .50 .23
❑ 4T Steve Bedrosian 1.00 .45
❑ 5T Mark Belanger 1.00 .45
❑ 6T Kurt Bevacqua .50 .23
❑ 7T Tim Blackwell .50 .23
❑ 8T Vida Blue 1.00 .45
❑ 9T Bob Boone 1.00 .45
❑ 10T Larry Bowa 1.00 .45
❑ 11T Dan Briggs .50 .23
❑ 12T Bobby Brown .50 .23
❑ 13T Tom Brunansky 1.00 .45
❑ 14T Jeff Burroughs .50 .23
❑ 15T Enos Cabell .50 .23
❑ 16T Bill Campbell .50 .23
❑ 17T Bobby Castillo .50 .23
❑ 18T Bill Caudill .50 .23
❑ 19T Cesar Cedeno 1.00 .45
❑ 20T Dave Collins .50 .23
❑ 21T Doug Corbett .50 .23
❑ 22T Al Cowens .50 .23
❑ 23T Chili Davis 8.00 3.60
❑ 24T Dick Davis .50 .23
❑ 25T Ron Davis .50 .23
❑ 26T Doug DeCinces 1.00 .45
❑ 27T Ivan DeJesus .50 .23
❑ 28T Bob Dernier .50 .23
❑ 29T Bo Diaz .50 .23
❑ 30T Roger Erickson .50 .23
❑ 31T Jim Essian .50 .23
❑ 32T Ed Farmer .50 .23
❑ 33T Doug Flynn .50 .23
❑ 34T Tim Foli .50 .23
❑ 35T Dan Ford .50 .23
❑ 36T George Foster 1.00 .45
❑ 37T Dave Frost .50 .23
❑ 38T Rich Gale .50 .23
❑ 39T Ron Gardenhire .50 .23
❑ 40T Ken Griffey 1.00 .45
❑ 41T Greg Harris .50 .23
❑ 42T Von Hayes 1.00 .45
❑ 43T Larry Herndon .50 .23
❑ 44T Kent Hrbek 2.00 .90
❑ 45T Mike Ivie .50 .23
❑ 46T Grant Jackson .50 .23
❑ 47T Reggie Jackson 8.00 3.60
❑ 48T Ron Jackson .50 .23
❑ 49T Fergie Jenkins 4.00 1.80
❑ 50T Lamar Johnson .50 .23
❑ 51T Randy Johnson .50 .23
❑ 52T Jay Johnstone 1.00 .45
❑ 53T Mick Kelleher .50 .23
❑ 54T Steve Kemp .50 .23
❑ 55T Junior Kennedy .50 .23
❑ 56T Jim Kern .50 .23
❑ 57T Ray Knight 1.00 .45
❑ 58T Wayne Krenchicki .50 .23
❑ 59T Mike Krukow .50 .23
❑ 60T Duane Kuiper .50 .23
❑ 61T Mike LaCoss .50 .23
❑ 62T Chet Lemon .50 .23
❑ 63T Sixto Lezcano .50 .23
❑ 64T Dave Lopes 1.00 .45
❑ 65T Jerry Martin .50 .23
❑ 66T Renie Martin .50 .23
❑ 67T John Mayberry .50 .23
❑ 68T Lee Mazzilli .50 .23
❑ 69T Bake McBride .50 .23
❑ 70T Dan Meyer .50 .23
❑ 71T Larry Milbourne .50 .23
❑ 72T Eddie Milner .50 .23
❑ 73T Sid Monge .50 .23
❑ 74T John Montefusco .50 .23
❑ 75T Jose Morales .50 .23
❑ 76T Keith Moreland .50 .23
❑ 77T Jim Morrison .50 .23
❑ 78T Rance Mulliniks .50 .23
❑ 79T Steve Mura .50 .23
❑ 80T Gene Nelson .50 .23
❑ 81T Joe Nolan .50 .23
❑ 82T Dickie Noles .50 .23
❑ 83T Al Oliver 1.00 .45
❑ 84T Jorge Orta .50 .23
❑ 85T Tom Paciorek 1.00 .45
❑ 86T Larry Parrish .50 .23
❑ 87T Jack Perconte .50 .23
❑ 88T Gaylord Perry 4.00 1.80
❑ 89T Rob Picciolo .50 .23
❑ 90T Joe Pittman .50 .23
❑ 91T Hosken Powell .50 .23
❑ 92T Mike Proly .50 .23
❑ 93T Greg Pryor .50 .23
❑ 94T Charlie Puleo .50 .23
❑ 95T Shane Rawley .50 .23
❑ 96T Johnny Ray 1.00 .45
❑ 97T Dave Revering .50 .23
❑ 98T Cal Ripken 200.00 90.00
❑ 99T Allen Ripley .50 .23
❑ 100T Bill Robinson .50 .23
❑ 101T Aurelio Rodriguez .50 .23
❑ 102T Joe Rudi .50 .23
❑ 103T Steve Sax 4.00 1.80
❑ 104T Dan Schatzeder .50 .23
❑ 105T Bob Shirley .50 .23
❑ 106T Eric Show 1.00 .45
❑ 107T Roy Smalley .50 .23
❑ 108T Lonnie Smith 1.00 .45
❑ 109T Ozzie Smith 15.00 6.75
❑ 110T Reggie Smith 1.00 .45
❑ 111T Lary Sorensen .50 .23
❑ 112T Elias Sosa .50 .23
❑ 113T Mike Stanton .50 .23
❑ 114T Steve Stroughter .50 .23
❑ 115T Champ Summers .50 .23
❑ 116T Rick Sutcliffe 1.00 .45
❑ 117T Frank Tanana 1.00 .45
❑ 118T Frank Taveras .50 .23
❑ 119T Garry Templeton .50 .23
❑ 120T Alex Trevino .50 .23
❑ 121T Jerry Turner .50 .23
❑ 122T Ed VandeBerg .50 .23
❑ 123T Tom Veryzer .50 .23
❑ 124T Ron Washington .50 .23
❑ 125T Bob Watson 1.00 .45
❑ 126T Dennis Werth .50 .23
❑ 127T Eddie Whitson .50 .23
❑ 128T Rob Wilfong .50 .23
❑ 129T Bump Wills .50 .23
❑ 130T Gary Woods .50 .23
❑ 131T Butch Wynegar .50 .23
❑ 132T Checklist: 1-132 .50 .23

## 1983 Topps

| | NRMT | VG-E |
|---|---|---|
| COMPLETE SET (792) | 120.00 | 55.00 |

❑ 1 Tony Armas RB .30 .14
❑ 2 Rickey Henderson RB .60 .25
Sets modern SB record
❑ 3 Greg Minton RB .15 .07
269 1/3 homerless

innings streak
❑ 4 Lance Parrish RB .15 .07
❑ 5 Manny Trillo RB .15 .07
479 consecutive
errorless chances,
second baseman
❑ 6 John Wathan RB .15 .07
ML catcher steals, season
❑ 7 Gene Richards .15 .07
❑ 8 Steve Balboni .15 .07
❑ 9 Joey McLaughlin .15 .07
❑ 10 Gorman Thomas .15 .07
❑ 11 Billy Gardner MG .15 .07
❑ 12 Paul Mirabella .15 .07
❑ 13 Larry Herndon .15 .07
❑ 14 Frank LaCorte .15 .07
❑ 15 Ron Cey .30 .14
❑ 16 George Vukovich .15 .07
❑ 17 Kent Tekulve .30 .14
❑ 18 Kent Tekulve SV .15 .07
❑ 19 Oscar Gamble .15 .07
❑ 20 Carlton Fisk 1.25 .55
❑ 21 Baltimore Orioles TL .60 .25
BA: Eddie Murray
ERA: Jim Palmer
❑ 22 Randy Martz .15 .07
❑ 23 Mike Heath .15 .07
❑ 24 Steve Mura .15 .07
❑ 25 Hal McRae .30 .14
❑ 26 Jerry Royster .15 .07
❑ 27 Doug Corbett .15 .07
❑ 28 Bruce Bochte .15 .07
❑ 29 Randy Jones .15 .07
❑ 30 Jim Rice .30 .14
❑ 31 Bill Gullickson .15 .07
❑ 32 Dave Bergman .15 .07
❑ 33 Jack O'Connor .15 .07
❑ 34 Paul Householder .15 .07
❑ 35 Rollie Fingers 1.25 .55
❑ 36 Rollie Fingers SV .60 .25
❑ 37 Darrell Johnson MG .15 .07
❑ 38 Tim Flannery .15 .07
❑ 39 Terry Puhl .15 .07
❑ 40 Fernando Valenzuela .60 .25
❑ 41 Jerry Turner .15 .07
❑ 42 Dale Murray .15 .07
❑ 43 Bob Dernier .15 .07
❑ 44 Don Robinson .15 .07
❑ 45 John Mayberry .15 .07
❑ 46 Richard Dotson .15 .07
❑ 47 Dave McKay .15 .07
❑ 48 Lary Sorensen .15 .07
❑ 49 Willie McGee RC 3.00 1.35
❑ 50 Bob Horner UER .15 .07
('82 RBI total 7)
❑ 51 Chicago Cubs TL .30 .14
BA: Leon Durham
ERA: Fergie Jenkins
❑ 52 Onix Concepcion .15 .07
❑ 53 Mike Witt .15 .07
❑ 54 Jim Maler .15 .07
❑ 55 Mookie Wilson .30 .14
❑ 56 Chuck Rainey .15 .07
❑ 57 Tim Blackwell .15 .07
❑ 58 Al Holland .15 .07
❑ 59 Benny Ayala .15 .07
❑ 60 Johnny Bench 2.00 .90
❑ 61 Johnny Bench SV .60 .25
❑ 62 Bob McClure .15 .07
❑ 63 Rick Monday .15 .07
❑ 64 Bill Stein .15 .07
❑ 65 Jack Morris .30 .14
❑ 66 Bob Lillis MG .15 .07
❑ 67 Sal Butera .15 .07
❑ 68 Eric Show .15 .07
❑ 69 Lee Lacy .15 .07
❑ 70 Steve Carlton 1.25 .55
❑ 71 Steve Carlton SV .60 .25
❑ 72 Tom Paciorek .30 .14
❑ 73 Allen Ripley .15 .07
❑ 74 Julio Gonzalez .15 .07
❑ 75 Amos Otis .30 .14
❑ 76 Rick Mahler .15 .07
❑ 77 Hosken Powell .15 .07
❑ 78 Bill Caudill .15 .07
❑ 79 Mick Kelleher .15 .07
❑ 80 George Foster .30 .14
❑ 81 Yankees TL .30 .14
BA: Jerry Mumphrey
ERA: Dave Righetti
❑ 82 Bruce Hurst .15 .07
❑ 83 Ryne Sandberg RC 20.00 9.00
❑ 84 Milt May .15 .07
❑ 85 Ken Singleton .15 .07
❑ 86 Tom Hume .15 .07
❑ 87 Joe Rudi .15 .07
❑ 88 Jim Gantner .15 .07
❑ 89 Leon Roberts .15 .07
❑ 90 Jerry Reuss .30 .14
❑ 91 Larry Milbourne .15 .07
❑ 92 Mike LaCoss .15 .07
❑ 93 John Castino .15 .07
❑ 94 Dave Edwards .15 .07
❑ 95 Alan Trammell .60 .25
❑ 96 Dick Howser MG .15 .07
❑ 97 Ross Baumgarten .15 .07
❑ 98 Vance Law .15 .07
❑ 99 Dickie Noles .15 .07
❑ 100 Pete Rose 4.00 1.80
❑ 101 Pete Rose SV 1.25 .55
❑ 102 Dave Beard .15 .07
❑ 103 Darrell Porter .15 .07
❑ 104 Bob Walk .15 .07
❑ 105 Don Baylor .60 .25
❑ 106 Gene Nelson .15 .07
❑ 107 Mike Jorgensen .15 .07
❑ 108 Glenn Hoffman .15 .07
❑ 109 Luis Leal .15 .07
❑ 110 Ken Griffey .30 .14
❑ 111 Montreal Expos TL .30 .14
BA: Al Oliver
ERA: Steve Rogers
❑ 112 Bob Shirley .15 .07
❑ 113 Ron Roenicke .15 .07
❑ 114 Jim Slaton .15 .07
❑ 115 Chili Davis 1.25 .55
❑ 116 Dave Schmidt .15 .07
❑ 117 Alan Knicely .15 .07
❑ 118 Chris Welsh .15 .07
❑ 119 Tom Brookens .15 .07
❑ 120 Len Barker .15 .07
❑ 121 Mickey Hatcher .15 .07
❑ 122 Jimmy Smith .15 .07
❑ 123 George Frazier .15 .07
❑ 124 Marc Hill .15 .07
❑ 125 Leon Durham .15 .07
❑ 126 Joe Torre MG .30 .14
❑ 127 Preston Hanna .15 .07
❑ 128 Mike Ramsey .15 .07
❑ 129 Checklist: 1-132 .30 .14
❑ 130 Dave Stieb .30 .14
❑ 131 Ed Ott .15 .07
❑ 132 Todd Cruz .15 .07
❑ 133 Jim Barr .15 .07
❑ 134 Hubie Brooks .30 .14
❑ 135 Dwight Evans .30 .14
❑ 136 Willie Aikens .15 .07
❑ 137 Woodie Fryman .15 .07
❑ 138 Rick Dempsey .30 .14
❑ 139 Bruce Berenyi .15 .07
❑ 140 Willie Randolph .30 .14
❑ 141 Indians TL .30 .14
BA: Toby Harrah
ERA: Rick Sutcliffe
❑ 142 Mike Caldwell .15 .07
❑ 143 Joe Pettini .15 .07
❑ 144 Mark Wagner .15 .07
❑ 145 Don Sutton 1.25 .55
❑ 146 Don Sutton SV .60 .25
❑ 147 Rick Leach .15 .07
❑ 148 Dave Roberts .15 .07
❑ 149 Johnny Ray .15 .07
❑ 150 Bruce Sutter .30 .14
❑ 151 Bruce Sutter SV .15 .07
❑ 152 Jay Johnstone .30 .14
❑ 153 Jerry Koosman .30 .14
❑ 154 Johnnie LeMaster .15 .07
❑ 155 Dan Quisenberry .30 .14
❑ 156 Billy Martin MG .30 .14
❑ 157 Steve Bedrosian .30 .14
❑ 158 Rob Wilfong .15 .07
❑ 159 Mike Stanton .15 .07
❑ 160 Dave Kingman .60 .25
❑ 161 Dave Kingman SV .30 .14
❑ 162 Mark Clear .15 .07
❑ 163 Cal Ripken 12.00 5.50
❑ 164 David Palmer .15 .07
❑ 165 Dan Driessen .15 .07
❑ 166 John Pacella .15 .07
❑ 167 Mark Brouhard .15 .07
❑ 168 Juan Eichelberger .15 .07
❑ 169 Doug Flynn .15 .07
❑ 170 Steve Howe .15 .07
❑ 171 Giants TL .60 .25
BA: Joe Morgan
ERA: Bill Laskey
❑ 172 Vern Ruhle .15 .07
❑ 173 Jim Morrison .15 .07
❑ 174 Jerry Ujdur .15 .07
❑ 175 Bo Diaz .15 .07
❑ 176 Dave Righetti .30 .14
❑ 177 Harold Baines 1.25 .55
❑ 178 Luis Tiant .30 .14
❑ 179 Luis Tiant SV .15 .07
❑ 180 Rickey Henderson 2.00 .90
❑ 181 Terry Felton .15 .07
❑ 182 Mike Fischlin .15 .07
❑ 183 Ed VandeBerg .15 .07
❑ 184 Bob Clark .15 .07
❑ 185 Tim Lollar .15 .07
❑ 186 Whitey Herzog MG .30 .14
❑ 187 Terry Leach .15 .07
❑ 188 Rick Miller .15 .07
❑ 189 Dan Schatzeder .15 .07
❑ 190 Cecil Cooper .30 .14
❑ 191 Joe Price .15 .07
❑ 192 Floyd Rayford .15 .07
❑ 193 Harry Spilman .15 .07
❑ 194 Cesar Geronimo .15 .07
❑ 195 Bob Stoddard .15 .07
❑ 196 Bill Fahey .15 .07
❑ 197 Jim Eisenreich RC 1.25 .55
❑ 198 Kiko Garcia .15 .07
❑ 199 Marty Bystrom .15 .07
❑ 200 Rod Carew 1.25 .55
❑ 201 Rod Carew SV .60 .25
❑ 202 Blue Jays TL .30 .14
BA: Damaso Garcia
ERA: Dave Stieb
❑ 203 Mike Morgan .15 .07
❑ 204 Junior Kennedy .15 .07
❑ 205 Dave Parker .30 .14
❑ 206 Ken Oberkfell .15 .07
❑ 207 Rick Camp .15 .07
❑ 208 Dan Meyer .15 .07
❑ 209 Mike Moore RC .30 .14
❑ 210 Jack Clark .30 .14
❑ 211 John Denny .15 .07
❑ 212 John Stearns .15 .07
❑ 213 Tom Burgmeier .15 .07
❑ 214 Jerry White .15 .07
❑ 215 Mario Soto .15 .07
❑ 216 Tony LaRussa MG .30 .14
❑ 217 Tim Stoddard .15 .07
❑ 218 Roy Howell .15 .07
❑ 219 Mike Armstrong .15 .07
❑ 220 Dusty Baker .30 .14
❑ 221 Joe Niekro .30 .14
❑ 222 Damaso Garcia .15 .07
❑ 223 John Montefusco .15 .07

❑ 224 Mickey Rivers .15 .07
❑ 225 Enos Cabell .15 .07
❑ 226 Enrique Romo .15 .07
❑ 227 Chris Bando .15 .07
❑ 228 Joaquin Andujar .15 .07
❑ 229 Phillies TL .60 .25
BA: Bo Diaz
ERA: Steve Carlton
❑ 230 Fergie Jenkins 1.25 .55
❑ 231 Fergie Jenkins SV .60 .25
❑ 232 Tom Brunansky .30 .14
❑ 233 Wayne Gross .15 .07
❑ 234 Larry Andersen .15 .07
❑ 235 Claudell Washington .15 .07
❑ 236 Steve Renko .15 .07
❑ 237 Dan Norman .15 .07
❑ 238 Bud Black RC .30 .14
❑ 239 Dave Stapleton .15 .07
❑ 240 Rich Gossage .60 .25
❑ 241 Rich Gossage SV .30 .14
❑ 242 Joe Nolan .15 .07
❑ 243 Duane Walker .15 .07
❑ 244 Dwight Bernard .15 .07
❑ 245 Steve Sax .30 .14
❑ 246 George Bamberger MG .15 .07
❑ 247 Dave Smith .15 .07
❑ 248 Bake McBride .15 .07
❑ 249 Checklist: 133-264 .30 .14
❑ 250 Bill Buckner .30 .14
❑ 251 Alan Wiggins .15 .07
❑ 252 Luis Aguayo .15 .07
❑ 253 Larry McWilliams .15 .07
❑ 254 Rick Cerone .15 .07
❑ 255 Gene Garber .15 .07
❑ 256 Gene Garber SV .15 .07
❑ 257 Jesse Barfield .30 .14
❑ 258 Manny Castillo .15 .07
❑ 259 Jeff Jones .15 .07
❑ 260 Steve Kemp .15 .07
❑ 261 Tigers TL .30 .14
BA: Larry Herndon
ERA: Dan Petry
❑ 262 Ron Jackson .15 .07
❑ 263 Renie Martin .15 .07
❑ 264 Jamie Quirk .15 .07
❑ 265 Joel Youngblood .15 .07
❑ 266 Paul Boris .15 .07
❑ 267 Terry Francona .15 .07
❑ 268 Storm Davis RC .15 .07
❑ 269 Ron Oester .15 .07
❑ 270 Dennis Eckersley 1.25 .55
❑ 271 Ed Romero .15 .07
❑ 272 Frank Tanana .30 .14
❑ 273 Mark Belanger .15 .07
❑ 274 Terry Kennedy .15 .07
❑ 275 Ray Knight .30 .14
❑ 276 Gene Mauch MG .15 .07
❑ 277 Rance Mulliniks .15 .07
❑ 278 Kevin Hickey .15 .07
❑ 279 Greg Gross .15 .07
❑ 280 Bert Blyleven .60 .25
❑ 281 Andre Robertson .15 .07
❑ 282 Reggie Smith 1.25 .55
(Ryne Sandberg
ducking back)
❑ 283 Reggie Smith SV .15 .07
❑ 284 Jeff Lahti .15 .07
❑ 285 Lance Parrish .30 .14
❑ 286 Rick Langford .15 .07
❑ 287 Bobby Brown .15 .07
❑ 288 Joe Cowley .15 .07
❑ 289 Jerry Dybzinski .15 .07
❑ 290 Jeff Reardon .30 .14
❑ 291 Pirates TL .30 .14
BA: Bill Madlock
ERA: John Candelaria
❑ 292 Craig Swan .15 .07
❑ 293 Glenn Gulliver .15 .07
❑ 294 Dave Engle .15 .07
❑ 295 Jerry Remy .15 .07
❑ 296 Greg Harris .15 .07
❑ 297 Ned Yost .15 .07
❑ 298 Floyd Chiffer .15 .07
❑ 299 George Wright .15 .07
❑ 300 Mike Schmidt 2.50 1.10
❑ 301 Mike Schmidt SV 1.25 .55

❑ 302 Ernie Whitt .15 .07
❑ 303 Miguel Dilone .15 .07
❑ 304 Dave Rucker .15 .07
❑ 305 Larry Bowa .30 .14
❑ 306 Tom Lasorda MG .60 .25
❑ 307 Lou Piniella .30 .14
❑ 308 Jesus Vega .15 .07
❑ 309 Jeff Leonard .15 .07
❑ 310 Greg Luzinski .30 .14
❑ 311 Glenn Brummer .15 .07
❑ 312 Brian Kingman .15 .07
❑ 313 Gary Gray .15 .07
❑ 314 Ken Dayley .15 .07
❑ 315 Rick Burleson .15 .07
❑ 316 Paul Splittorff .15 .07
❑ 317 Gary Rajsich .15 .07
❑ 318 John Tudor .15 .07
❑ 319 Lenn Sakata .15 .07
❑ 320 Steve Rogers .15 .07
❑ 321 Brewers TL .60 .25
BA: Robin Yount
ERA: Pete Vuckovich
❑ 322 Dave Van Gorder .15 .07
❑ 323 Luis DeLeon .15 .07
❑ 324 Mike Marshall .15 .07
❑ 325 Von Hayes .30 .14
❑ 326 Garth Iorg .15 .07
❑ 327 Bobby Castillo .15 .07
❑ 328 Craig Reynolds .15 .07
❑ 329 Randy Niemann .15 .07
❑ 330 Buddy Bell .30 .14
❑ 331 Mike Krukow .15 .07
❑ 332 Glenn Wilson .30 .14
❑ 333 Dave LaRoche .15 .07
❑ 334 Dave LaRoche SV .15 .07
❑ 335 Steve Henderson .15 .07
❑ 336 Rene Lachemann MG .15 .07
❑ 337 Tito Landrum .15 .07
❑ 338 Bob Owchinko .15 .07
❑ 339 Terry Harper .15 .07
❑ 340 Larry Gura .15 .07
❑ 341 Doug DeCinces .30 .14
❑ 342 Atlee Hammaker .15 .07
❑ 343 Bob Bailor .15 .07
❑ 344 Roger LaFrancois .15 .07
❑ 345 Jim Clancy .15 .07
❑ 346 Joe Pittman .15 .07
❑ 347 Sammy Stewart .15 .07
❑ 348 Alan Bannister .15 .07
❑ 349 Checklist: 265-396 .30 .14
❑ 350 Robin Yount 1.25 .55
❑ 351 Reds TL .30 .14
BA: Cesar Cedeno
ERA: Mario Soto
❑ 352 Mike Scioscia .30 .14
❑ 353 Steve Comer .15 .07
❑ 354 Randy Johnson .15 .07
❑ 355 Jim Bibby .15 .07
❑ 356 Gary Woods .15 .07
❑ 357 Len Matuszek .15 .07
❑ 358 Jerry Garvin .15 .07
❑ 359 Dave Collins .15 .07
❑ 360 Nolan Ryan 6.00 2.70
❑ 361 Nolan Ryan SV 3.00 1.35
❑ 362 Bill Almon .15 .07
❑ 363 John Stuper .15 .07
❑ 364 Brett Butler 1.25 .55
❑ 365 Dave Lopes .30 .14
❑ 366 Dick Williams MG .15 .07
❑ 367 Bud Anderson .15 .07
❑ 368 Richie Zisk .15 .07
❑ 369 Jesse Orosco .15 .07
❑ 370 Gary Carter .60 .25
❑ 371 Mike Richardt .15 .07
❑ 372 Terry Crowley .15 .07
❑ 373 Kevin Saucier .15 .07
❑ 374 Wayne Krenchicki .15 .07
❑ 375 Pete Vuckovich .15 .07
❑ 376 Ken Landreaux .15 .07
❑ 377 Lee May .30 .14
❑ 378 Lee May SV .15 .07
❑ 379 Guy Sularz .15 .07
❑ 380 Ron Davis .15 .07
❑ 381 Red Sox TL .30 .14
BA: Jim Rice
ERA: Bob Stanley

❑ 382 Bob Knepper .15 .07
❑ 383 Ozzie Virgil .15 .07
❑ 384 Dave Dravecky RC 1.25 .55
❑ 385 Mike Easler .15 .07
❑ 386 Rod Carew AS .60 .25
❑ 387 Bob Grich AS .15 .07
❑ 388 George Brett AS 1.25 .55
❑ 389 Robin Yount AS .60 .25
❑ 390 Reggie Jackson AS .60 .25
❑ 391 Rickey Henderson AS .60 .25
❑ 392 Fred Lynn AS .15 .07
❑ 393 Carlton Fisk AS .60 .25
❑ 394 Pete Vuckovich AS .15 .07
❑ 395 Larry Gura AS .15 .07
❑ 396 Dan Quisenberry AS .15 .07
❑ 397 Pete Rose AS .60 .25
❑ 398 Manny Trillo AS .15 .07
❑ 399 Mike Schmidt AS .60 .25
❑ 400 Dave Concepcion AS .15 .07
❑ 401 Dale Murphy AS .60 .25
❑ 402 Andre Dawson AS .30 .14
❑ 403 Tim Raines AS .30 .14
❑ 404 Gary Carter AS .30 .14
❑ 405 Steve Rogers AS .15 .07
❑ 406 Steve Carlton AS .60 .25
❑ 407 Bruce Sutter AS .15 .07
❑ 408 Rudy May .15 .07
❑ 409 Marvis Foley .15 .07
❑ 410 Phil Niekro 1.25 .55
❑ 411 Phil Niekro SV .60 .25
❑ 412 Rangers TL .30 .14
BA: Buddy Bell
ERA: Charlie Hough
❑ 413 Matt Keough .15 .07
❑ 414 Julio Cruz .15 .07
❑ 415 Bob Forsch .15 .07
❑ 416 Joe Ferguson .15 .07
❑ 417 Tom Hausman .15 .07
❑ 418 Greg Pryor .15 .07
❑ 419 Steve Crawford .15 .07
❑ 420 Al Oliver .30 .14
❑ 421 Al Oliver SV .15 .07
❑ 422 George Cappuzzello .15 .07
❑ 423 Tom Lawless .15 .07
❑ 424 Jerry Augustine .15 .07
❑ 425 Pedro Guerrero .30 .14
❑ 426 Earl Weaver MG .60 .25
❑ 427 Roy Lee Jackson .15 .07
❑ 428 Champ Summers .15 .07
❑ 429 Eddie Whitson .15 .07
❑ 430 Kirk Gibson 1.25 .55
❑ 431 Gary Gaetti RC 1.25 .55
❑ 432 Porfirio Altamirano .15 .07
❑ 433 Dale Berra .15 .07
❑ 434 Dennis Lamp .15 .07
❑ 435 Tony Armas .15 .07
❑ 436 Bill Campbell .15 .07
❑ 437 Rick Sweet .15 .07
❑ 438 Dave LaPoint .15 .07
❑ 439 Rafael Ramirez .15 .07
❑ 440 Ron Guidry .30 .14
❑ 441 Astros TL .30 .14
BA: Ray Knight
ERA: Joe Niekro
❑ 442 Brian Downing .15 .07
❑ 443 Don Hood .15 .07
❑ 444 Wally Backman .15 .07
❑ 445 Mike Flanagan .30 .14
❑ 446 Reid Nichols .15 .07
❑ 447 Bryn Smith .15 .07
❑ 448 Darrell Evans .30 .14
❑ 449 Eddie Milner .15 .07
❑ 450 Ted Simmons .30 .14
❑ 451 Ted Simmons SV .15 .07
❑ 452 Lloyd Moseby .15 .07
❑ 453 Lamar Johnson .15 .07
❑ 454 Bob Welch .30 .14
❑ 455 Sixto Lezcano .15 .07
❑ 456 Lee Elia MG .15 .07
❑ 457 Milt Wilcox .15 .07
❑ 458 Ron Washington .15 .07
❑ 459 Ed Farmer .15 .07
❑ 460 Roy Smalley .15 .07
❑ 461 Steve Trout .15 .07
❑ 462 Steve Nicosia .15 .07
❑ 463 Gaylord Perry 1.25 .55

❑ 464 Gaylord Perry SV .60 .25
❑ 465 Lonnie Smith .15 .07
❑ 466 Tom Underwood .15 .07
❑ 467 Rufino Linares .15 .07
❑ 468 Dave Goltz .15 .07
❑ 469 Ron Gardenhire .15 .07
❑ 470 Greg Minton .15 .07
❑ 471 Kansas City Royals TL .30 .14
BA: Willie Wilson
ERA: Vida Blue
❑ 472 Gary Allenson .15 .07
❑ 473 John Lowenstein .15 .07
❑ 474 Ray Burris .15 .07
❑ 475 Cesar Cedeno .30 .14
❑ 476 Rob Picciolo .15 .07
❑ 477 Tom Niedenfuer .15 .07
❑ 478 Phil Garner .30 .14
❑ 479 Charlie Hough .30 .14
❑ 480 Toby Harrah .15 .07
❑ 481 Scot Thompson .15 .07
❑ 482 Tony Gwynn UER 50.00 22.00
(No Topps logo under
card number on back) RC !
❑ 483 Lynn Jones .15 .07
❑ 484 Dick Ruthven .15 .07
❑ 485 Omar Moreno .15 .07
❑ 486 Clyde King MG .15 .07
❑ 487 Jerry Hairston .15 .07
❑ 488 Alfredo Griffin .15 .07
❑ 489 Tom Herr .30 .14
❑ 490 Jim Palmer 1.25 .55
❑ 491 Jim Palmer SV .60 .25
❑ 492 Paul Serna .15 .07
❑ 493 Steve McCatty .15 .07
❑ 494 Bob Brenly .15 .07
❑ 495 Warren Cromartie .15 .07
❑ 496 Tom Veryzer .15 .07
❑ 497 Rick Sutcliffe .30 .14
❑ 498 Wade Boggs RC 25.00 11.00
❑ 499 Jeff Little .15 .07
❑ 500 Reggie Jackson 1.50 .70
❑ 501 Reggie Jackson SV .60 .25
❑ 502 Atlanta Braves TL .30 .14
BA: Dale Murphy
ERA: Phil Niekro
❑ 503 Moose Haas .15 .07
❑ 504 Don Werner .15 .07
❑ 505 Garry Templeton .15 .07
❑ 506 Jim Gott RC .15 .07
❑ 507 Tony Scott .15 .07
❑ 508 Tom Filer .15 .07
❑ 509 Lou Whitaker .60 .25
❑ 510 Tug McGraw .30 .14
❑ 511 Tug McGraw SV .15 .07
❑ 512 Doyle Alexander .15 .07
❑ 513 Fred Stanley .15 .07
❑ 514 Rudy Law .15 .07
❑ 515 Gene Tenace .30 .14
❑ 516 Bill Virdon MG .15 .07
❑ 517 Gary Ward .15 .07
❑ 518 Bill Laskey .15 .07
❑ 519 Terry Bulling .15 .07
❑ 520 Fred Lynn .30 .14
❑ 521 Bruce Benedict .15 .07
❑ 522 Pat Zachry .15 .07
❑ 523 Carney Lansford .30 .14
❑ 524 Tom Brennan .15 .07
❑ 525 Frank White .30 .14
❑ 526 Checklist: 397-528 .30 .14
❑ 527 Larry Biittner .15 .07
❑ 528 Jamie Easterly .15 .07
❑ 529 Tim Laudner .15 .07
❑ 530 Eddie Murray 1.50 .70
❑ 531 Oakland A's TL .60 .25
BA: Rickey Henderson
ERA: Rick Langford
❑ 532 Dave Stewart .30 .14
❑ 533 Luis Salazar .15 .07
❑ 534 John Butcher .15 .07
❑ 535 Manny Trillo .15 .07
❑ 536 John Wockenfuss .15 .07
❑ 537 Rod Scurry .15 .07
❑ 538 Danny Heep .15 .07
❑ 539 Roger Erickson .15 .07
❑ 540 Ozzie Smith 2.00 .90
❑ 541 Britt Burns .15 .07
❑ 542 Jody Davis .15 .07
❑ 543 Alan Fowlkes .15 .07
❑ 544 Larry Whisenton .15 .07
❑ 545 Floyd Bannister .15 .07
❑ 546 Dave Garcia MG .15 .07
❑ 547 Geoff Zahn .15 .07
❑ 548 Brian Giles .15 .07
❑ 549 Charlie Puleo .15 .07
❑ 550 Carl Yastrzemski 1.25 .55
❑ 551 Carl Yastrzemski SV .60 .25
❑ 552 Tim Wallach .30 .14
❑ 553 Dennis Martinez .30 .14
❑ 554 Mike Vail .15 .07
❑ 555 Steve Yeager .15 .07
❑ 556 Willie Upshaw .15 .07
❑ 557 Rick Honeycutt .15 .07
❑ 558 Dickie Thon .15 .07
❑ 559 Pete Redfern .15 .07
❑ 560 Ron LeFlore .15 .07
❑ 561 Cardinals TL .30 .14
BA: Lonnie Smith
ERA: Joaquin Andujar
❑ 562 Dave Rozema .15 .07
❑ 563 Juan Bonilla .15 .07
❑ 564 Sid Monge .15 .07
❑ 565 Bucky Dent .30 .14
❑ 566 Manny Sarmiento .15 .07
❑ 567 Joe Simpson .15 .07
❑ 568 Willie Hernandez .30 .14
❑ 569 Jack Perconte .15 .07
❑ 570 Vida Blue .30 .14
❑ 571 Mickey Klutts .15 .07
❑ 572 Bob Watson .30 .14
❑ 573 Andy Hassler .15 .07
❑ 574 Glenn Adams .15 .07
❑ 575 Neil Allen .15 .07
❑ 576 Frank Robinson MG .60 .25
❑ 577 Luis Aponte .15 .07
❑ 578 David Green .15 .07
❑ 579 Rich Dauer .15 .07
❑ 580 Tom Seaver 2.00 .90
❑ 581 Tom Seaver SV .60 .25
❑ 582 Marshall Edwards .15 .07
❑ 583 Terry Forster .15 .07
❑ 584 Dave Hostetler .15 .07
❑ 585 Jose Cruz .30 .14
❑ 586 Frank Viola RC 1.25 .55
❑ 587 Ivan DeJesus .15 .07
❑ 588 Pat Underwood .15 .07
❑ 589 Alvis Woods .15 .07
❑ 590 Tony Pena .15 .07
❑ 591 White Sox TL .30 .14
BA: Greg Luzinski
ERA: LaMarr Hoyt
❑ 592 Shane Rawley .15 .07
❑ 593 Broderick Perkins .15 .07
❑ 594 Eric Rasmussen .15 .07
❑ 595 Tim Raines 1.25 .55
❑ 596 Randy Johnson .15 .07
❑ 597 Mike Proly .15 .07
❑ 598 Dwayne Murphy .15 .07
❑ 599 Don Aase .15 .07
❑ 600 George Brett 2.50 1.10
❑ 601 Ed Lynch .15 .07
❑ 602 Rich Gedman .15 .07
❑ 603 Joe Morgan 1.25 .55
❑ 604 Joe Morgan SV .60 .25
❑ 605 Gary Roenicke .15 .07
❑ 606 Bobby Cox MG .30 .14
❑ 607 Charlie Leibrandt .15 .07
❑ 608 Don Money .15 .07
❑ 609 Danny Darwin .15 .07
❑ 610 Steve Garvey .60 .25
❑ 611 Bert Roberge .15 .07
❑ 612 Steve Swisher .15 .07
❑ 613 Mike Ivie .15 .07
❑ 614 Ed Glynn .15 .07
❑ 615 Garry Maddox .15 .07
❑ 616 Bill Nahorodny .15 .07
❑ 617 Butch Wynegar .15 .07
❑ 618 LaMarr Hoyt .30 .14
❑ 619 Keith Moreland .15 .07
❑ 620 Mike Norris .15 .07
❑ 621 New York Mets TL .30 .14
BA: Mookie Wilson
ERA: Craig Swan
❑ 622 Dave Edler .15 .07
❑ 623 Luis Sanchez .15 .07
❑ 624 Glenn Hubbard .15 .07
❑ 625 Ken Forsch .15 .07
❑ 626 Jerry Martin .15 .07
❑ 627 Doug Bair .15 .07
❑ 628 Julio Valdez .15 .07
❑ 629 Charlie Lea .15 .07
❑ 630 Paul Molitor 1.50 .70
❑ 631 Tippy Martinez .15 .07
❑ 632 Alex Trevino .15 .07
❑ 633 Vicente Romo .15 .07
❑ 634 Max Venable .15 .07
❑ 635 Graig Nettles .30 .14
❑ 636 Graig Nettles SV .15 .07
❑ 637 Pat Corrales MG .15 .07
❑ 638 Dan Petry .15 .07
❑ 639 Art Howe .30 .14
❑ 640 Andre Thornton .15 .07
❑ 641 Billy Sample .15 .07
❑ 642 Checklist: 529-660 .30 .14
❑ 643 Bump Wills .15 .07
❑ 644 Joe Lefebvre .15 .07
❑ 645 Bill Madlock .30 .14
❑ 646 Jim Essian .15 .07
❑ 647 Bobby Mitchell .15 .07
❑ 648 Jeff Burroughs .15 .07
❑ 649 Tommy Boggs .15 .07
❑ 650 George Hendrick .15 .07
❑ 651 Angels TL .60 .25
BA: Rod Carew
ERA: Mike Witt
❑ 652 Butch Hobson .15 .07
❑ 653 Ellis Valentine .15 .07
❑ 654 Bob Ojeda .15 .07
❑ 655 Al Bumbry .15 .07
❑ 656 Dave Frost .15 .07
❑ 657 Mike Gates .15 .07
❑ 658 Frank Pastore .15 .07
❑ 659 Charlie Moore .15 .07
❑ 660 Mike Hargrove .30 .14
❑ 661 Bill Russell .15 .07
❑ 662 Joe Sambito .15 .07
❑ 663 Tom O'Malley .15 .07
❑ 664 Bob Molinaro .15 .07
❑ 665 Jim Sundberg .30 .14
❑ 666 Sparky Anderson MG .30 .14
❑ 667 Dick Davis .15 .07
❑ 668 Larry Christenson .15 .07
❑ 669 Mike Squires .15 .07
❑ 670 Jerry Mumphrey .15 .07
❑ 671 Lenny Faedo .15 .07
❑ 672 Jim Kaat .30 .14
❑ 673 Jim Kaat SV .15 .07
❑ 674 Kurt Bevacqua .15 .07
❑ 675 Jim Beattie .15 .07
❑ 676 Biff Pocoroba .15 .07
❑ 677 Dave Revering .15 .07
❑ 678 Juan Beniquez .15 .07
❑ 679 Mike Scott .30 .14
❑ 680 Andre Dawson .60 .25
❑ 681 Dodgers Leaders .30 .14
BA: Pedro Guerrero
ERA: Fernando Valenzuela
❑ 682 Bob Stanley .15 .07
❑ 683 Dan Ford .15 .07
❑ 684 Rafael Landestoy .15 .07
❑ 685 Lee Mazzilli .15 .07
❑ 686 Randy Lerch .15 .07
❑ 687 U.L. Washington .15 .07
❑ 688 Jim Wohlford .15 .07
❑ 689 Ron Hassey .15 .07
❑ 690 Kent Hrbek .30 .14
❑ 691 Dave Tobik .15 .07
❑ 692 Denny Walling .15 .07
❑ 693 Sparky Lyle .30 .14
❑ 694 Sparky Lyle SV .15 .07
❑ 695 Ruppert Jones .15 .07
❑ 696 Chuck Tanner MG .15 .07
❑ 697 Barry Foote .15 .07
❑ 698 Tony Bernazard .15 .07
❑ 699 Lee Smith 1.25 .55
❑ 700 Keith Hernandez .30 .14
❑ 701 Batting Leaders .30 .14
AL: Willie Wilson
NL: Al Oliver

❑ 702 Home Run Leaders .60 .25
AL: Reggie Jackson
AL: Gorman Thomas
NL: Dave Kingman
❑ 703 RBI Leaders .30 .14
AL: Hal McRae
NL: Dale Murphy
NL: Al Oliver
❑ 704 SB Leaders 1.25 .55
AL: Rickey Henderson
NL: Tim Raines
❑ 705 Victory Leaders .60 .25
AL: LaMarr Hoyt
NL: Steve Carlton
❑ 706 Strikeout Leaders .60 .25
AL: Floyd Bannister
NL: Steve Carlton
❑ 707 ERA Leaders .30 .14
AL: Rick Sutcliffe
NL: Steve Rogers
❑ 708 Leading Firemen .30 .14
AL: Dan Quisenberry
NL: Bruce Sutter
❑ 709 Jimmy Sexton .15 .07
❑ 710 Willie Wilson .30 .14
❑ 711 Mariners TL .30 .14
BA: Bruce Bochte
ERA: Jim Beattie
❑ 712 Bruce Kison .15 .07
❑ 713 Ron Hodges .15 .07
❑ 714 Wayne Nordhagen .15 .07
❑ 715 Tony Perez 1.25 .55
❑ 716 Tony Perez SV .60 .25
❑ 717 Scott Sanderson .15 .07
❑ 718 Jim Dwyer .15 .07
❑ 719 Rich Gale .15 .07
❑ 720 Dave Concepcion .30 .14
❑ 721 John Martin .15 .07
❑ 722 Jorge Orta .15 .07
❑ 723 Randy Moffitt .15 .07
❑ 724 Johnny Grubb .15 .07
❑ 725 Dan Spillner .15 .07
❑ 726 Harvey Kuenn MG .15 .07
❑ 727 Chet Lemon .15 .07
❑ 728 Ron Reed .15 .07
❑ 729 Jerry Morales .15 .07
❑ 730 Jason Thompson .15 .07
❑ 731 Al Williams .15 .07
❑ 732 Dave Henderson .15 .07
❑ 733 Buck Martinez .15 .07
❑ 734 Steve Braun .15 .07
❑ 735 Tommy John .60 .25
❑ 736 Tommy John SV .30 .14
❑ 737 Mitchell Page .15 .07
❑ 738 Tim Foli .15 .07
❑ 739 Rick Ownbey .15 .07
❑ 740 Rusty Staub .30 .14
❑ 741 Rusty Staub SV .15 .07
❑ 742 Padres TL .30 .14
BA: Terry Kennedy
ERA: Tim Lollar
❑ 743 Mike Torrez .15 .07
❑ 744 Brad Mills .15 .07
❑ 745 Scott McGregor .15 .07
❑ 746 John Wathan .15 .07
❑ 747 Fred Breining .15 .07
❑ 748 Derrel Thomas .15 .07
❑ 749 Jon Matlack .15 .07
❑ 750 Ben Oglivie .15 .07
❑ 751 Brad Havens .15 .07
❑ 752 Luis Pujols .15 .07
❑ 753 Elias Sosa .15 .07
❑ 754 Bill Robinson .15 .07
❑ 755 John Candelaria .15 .07
❑ 756 Russ Nixon MG .15 .07
❑ 757 Rick Manning .15 .07
❑ 758 Aurelio Rodriguez .15 .07
❑ 759 Doug Bird .15 .07
❑ 760 Dale Murphy 1.25 .55
❑ 761 Gary Lucas .15 .07
❑ 762 Cliff Johnson .15 .07
❑ 763 Al Cowens .15 .07
❑ 764 Pete Falcone .15 .07
❑ 765 Bob Boone .30 .14
❑ 766 Barry Bonnell .15 .07
❑ 767 Duane Kuiper .15 .07
❑ 768 Chris Speier .15 .07
❑ 769 Checklist: 661-792 .30 .14
❑ 770 Dave Winfield 1.25 .55
❑ 771 Twins TL .30 .14
BA: Kent Hrbek
ERA: Bobby Castillo
❑ 772 Jim Kern .15 .07
❑ 773 Larry Hisle .15 .07
❑ 774 Alan Ashby .15 .07
❑ 775 Burt Hooton .15 .07
❑ 776 Larry Parrish .15 .07
❑ 777 John Curtis .15 .07
❑ 778 Rich Hebner .30 .14
❑ 779 Rick Waits .15 .07
❑ 780 Gary Matthews .30 .14
❑ 781 Rick Rhoden .15 .07
❑ 782 Bobby Murcer .30 .14
❑ 783 Bobby Murcer SV .15 .07
❑ 784 Jeff Newman .15 .07
❑ 785 Dennis Leonard .15 .07
❑ 786 Ralph Houk MG .15 .07
❑ 787 Dick Tidrow .15 .07
❑ 788 Dane Iorg .15 .07
❑ 789 Bryan Clark .15 .07
❑ 790 Bob Grich .30 .14
❑ 791 Gary Lavelle .15 .07
❑ 792 Chris Chambliss .30 .14
❑ XX Game Insert Card

## 1983 Topps Traded

| | NRMT | VG-E |
|---|---|---|
| COMP.FACT.SET (132) | 25.00 | 11.00 |

❑ 1T Neil Allen .25 .11
❑ 2T Bill Almon .25 .11
❑ 3T Joe Altobelli MG .25 .11
❑ 4T Tony Armas .25 .11
❑ 5T Doug Bair .25 .11
❑ 6T Steve Baker .25 .11
❑ 7T Floyd Bannister .25 .11
❑ 8T Don Baylor 2.00 .90
❑ 9T Tony Bernazard .25 .11
❑ 10T Larry Biittner .25 .11
❑ 11T Dann Bilardello .25 .11
❑ 12T Doug Bird .25 .11
❑ 13T Steve Boros MG .25 .11
❑ 14T Greg Brock .25 .11
❑ 15T Mike C. Brown .25 .11
❑ 16T Tom Burgmeier .25 .11
❑ 17T Randy Bush .25 .11
❑ 18T Bert Campaneris 1.00 .45
❑ 19T Ron Cey 1.00 .45
❑ 20T Chris Codiroli .25 .11
❑ 21T Dave Collins .25 .11
❑ 22T Terry Crowley .25 .11
❑ 23T Julio Cruz .25 .11
❑ 24T Mike Davis .25 .11
❑ 25T Frank DiPino .25 .11
❑ 26T Bill Doran XRC 1.00 .45
❑ 27T Jerry Dybzinski .25 .11
❑ 28T Jamie Easterly .25 .11
❑ 29T Juan Eichelberger .25 .11
❑ 30T Jim Essian .25 .11
❑ 31T Pete Falcone .25 .11
❑ 32T Mike Ferraro MG .25 .11
❑ 33T Terry Forster .25 .11
❑ 34T Julio Franco XRC 4.00 1.80
❑ 35T Rich Gale .25 .11
❑ 36T Kiko Garcia .25 .11
❑ 37T Steve Garvey 2.00 .90
❑ 38T Johnny Grubb .25 .11
❑ 39T Mel Hall XRC* 1.00 .45
❑ 40T Von Hayes 1.00 .45
❑ 41T Danny Heep .25 .11
❑ 42T Steve Henderson .25 .11
❑ 43T Keith Hernandez 2.00 .90
❑ 44T Leo Hernandez .25 .11
❑ 45T Willie Hernandez 1.00 .45
❑ 46T Al Holland .25 .11
❑ 47T Frank Howard MG 1.00 .45
❑ 48T Bobby Johnson .25 .11
❑ 49T Cliff Johnson .25 .11
❑ 50T Odell Jones .25 .11
❑ 51T Mike Jorgensen .25 .11
❑ 52T Bob Kearney .25 .11
❑ 53T Steve Kemp .25 .11
❑ 54T Matt Keough .25 .11
❑ 55T Ron Kittle XRC* 2.00 .90
❑ 56T Mickey Klutts .25 .11
❑ 57T Alan Knicely .25 .11
❑ 58T Mike Krukow .25 .11
❑ 59T Rafael Landestoy .25 .11
❑ 60T Carney Lansford 1.00 .45
❑ 61T Joe Lefebvre .25 .11
❑ 62T Bryan Little .25 .11
❑ 63T Aurelio Lopez .25 .11
❑ 64T Mike Madden .25 .11
❑ 65T Rick Manning .25 .11
❑ 66T Billy Martin MG 1.00 .45
❑ 67T Lee Mazzilli .25 .11
❑ 68T Andy McGaffigan .25 .11
❑ 69T Craig McMurtry .25 .11
❑ 70T John McNamara MG .25 .11
❑ 71T Orlando Mercado .25 .11
❑ 72T Larry Milbourne .25 .11
❑ 73T Randy Moffitt .25 .11
❑ 74T Sid Monge .25 .11
❑ 75T Jose Morales .25 .11
❑ 76T Omar Moreno .25 .11
❑ 77T Joe Morgan 2.00 .90
❑ 78T Mike Morgan .25 .11
❑ 79T Dale Murray .25 .11
❑ 80T Jeff Newman .25 .11
❑ 81T Pete O'Brien XRC 1.00 .45
❑ 82T Jorge Orta .25 .11
❑ 83T Alejandro Pena XRC 1.00 .45
❑ 84T Pascual Perez .25 .11
❑ 85T Tony Perez 2.00 .90
❑ 86T Broderick Perkins .25 .11
❑ 87T Tony Phillips XRC 2.00 .90
❑ 88T Charlie Puleo .25 .11
❑ 89T Pat Putnam .25 .11
❑ 90T Jamie Quirk .25 .11
❑ 91T Doug Rader MG .25 .11
❑ 92T Chuck Rainey .25 .11
❑ 93T Bobby Ramos .25 .11
❑ 94T Gary Redus XRC 1.00 .45
❑ 95T Steve Renko .25 .11
❑ 96T Leon Roberts .25 .11
❑ 97T Aurelio Rodriguez .25 .11
❑ 98T Dick Ruthven .25 .11
❑ 99T Daryl Sconiers .25 .11
❑ 100T Mike Scott 1.00 .45
❑ 101T Tom Seaver 5.00 2.20
❑ 102T John Shelby .25 .11
❑ 103T Bob Shirley .25 .11
❑ 104T Joe Simpson .25 .11
❑ 105T Doug Sisk .25 .11
❑ 106T Mike Smithson .25 .11
❑ 107T Elias Sosa .25 .11
❑ 108T Darryl Strawberry XRC 10.00 4.50
❑ 109T Tom Tellmann .25 .11
❑ 110T Gene Tenace 1.00 .45
❑ 111T Gorman Thomas .25 .11
❑ 112T Dick Tidrow .25 .11
❑ 113T Dave Tobik .25 .11
❑ 114T Wayne Tolleson .25 .11
❑ 115T Mike Torrez .25 .11
❑ 116T Manny Trillo .25 .11
❑ 117T Steve Trout .25 .11
❑ 118T Lee Tunnell .25 .11
❑ 119T Mike Vail .25 .11
❑ 120T Ellis Valentine .25 .11

| | | NRMT | VG-E |
|---|---|---|---|
| ❑ | 121T Tom Veryzer | .25 | .11 |
| ❑ | 122T George Vukovich | .25 | .11 |
| ❑ | 123T Rick Waits | .25 | .11 |
| ❑ | 124T Greg Walker | 1.00 | .45 |
| ❑ | 125T Chris Welsh | .25 | .11 |
| ❑ | 126T Len Whitehouse | .25 | .11 |
| ❑ | 127T Eddie Whitson | .25 | .11 |
| ❑ | 128T Jim Wohlford | .25 | .11 |
| ❑ | 129T Matt Young | .25 | .11 |
| ❑ | 130T Joel Youngblood | .25 | .11 |
| ❑ | 131T Pat Zachry | .25 | .11 |
| ❑ | 132T Checklist 1T-132T | .25 | .11 |

## 1984 Topps

| | | NRMT | VG-E |
|---|---|---|---|
| | COMPLETE SET (792) | 40.00 | 18.00 |
| ❑ | 1 Steve Carlton HL<br>300th win and<br>all-time SO king | .60 | .25 |
| ❑ | 2 Rickey Henderson HL<br>100 stolen bases<br>three times | .40 | .18 |
| ❑ | 3 Dan Quisenberry HL<br>Sets save record | .15 | .07 |
| ❑ | 4 Nolan Ryan HL<br>Steve Carlton<br>Gaylord Perry<br>All surpass Johnson | 1.00 | .45 |
| ❑ | 5 Dave Righetti HL<br>Bob Forsch<br>Mike Warren<br>All pitch no-hitters | .25 | .11 |
| ❑ | 6 Johnny Bench HL<br>Gaylord Perry<br>Carl Yastrzemski<br>Superstars retire | .60 | .25 |
| ❑ | 7 Gary Lucas | .15 | .07 |
| ❑ | 8 Don Mattingly RC | 8.00 | 3.60 |
| ❑ | 9 Jim Gott | .15 | .07 |
| ❑ | 10 Robin Yount | .60 | .25 |
| ❑ | 11 Minnesota Twins TL<br>Kent Hrbek<br>Ken Schrom | .25 | .11 |
| ❑ | 12 Billy Sample | .15 | .07 |
| ❑ | 13 Scott Holman | .15 | .07 |
| ❑ | 14 Tom Brookens | .25 | .11 |
| ❑ | 15 Burt Hooton | .15 | .07 |
| ❑ | 16 Omar Moreno | .15 | .07 |
| ❑ | 17 John Denny | .15 | .07 |
| ❑ | 18 Dale Berra | .15 | .07 |
| ❑ | 19 Ray Fontenot | .15 | .07 |
| ❑ | 20 Greg Luzinski | .25 | .11 |
| ❑ | 21 Joe Altobelli MG | .15 | .07 |
| ❑ | 22 Bryan Clark | .15 | .07 |
| ❑ | 23 Keith Moreland | .15 | .07 |
| ❑ | 24 John Martin | .15 | .07 |
| ❑ | 25 Glenn Hubbard | .15 | .07 |
| ❑ | 26 Bud Black | .15 | .07 |
| ❑ | 27 Daryl Sconiers | .15 | .07 |
| ❑ | 28 Frank Viola | .40 | .18 |
| ❑ | 29 Danny Heep | .15 | .07 |
| ❑ | 30 Wade Boggs | 2.00 | .90 |
| ❑ | 31 Andy McGaffigan | .15 | .07 |
| ❑ | 32 Bobby Ramos | .15 | .07 |
| ❑ | 33 Tom Burgmeier | .15 | .07 |
| ❑ | 34 Eddie Milner | .15 | .07 |
| ❑ | 35 Don Sutton | .60 | .25 |
| ❑ | 36 Denny Walling | .15 | .07 |
| ❑ | 37 Texas Rangers TL<br>Buddy Bell<br>Rick Honeycutt | .25 | .11 |
| ❑ | 38 Luis DeLeon | .15 | .07 |
| ❑ | 39 Garth Iorg | .15 | .07 |
| ❑ | 40 Dusty Baker | .25 | .11 |
| ❑ | 41 Tony Bernazard | .15 | .07 |
| ❑ | 42 Johnny Grubb | .15 | .07 |
| ❑ | 43 Ron Reed | .15 | .07 |
| ❑ | 44 Jim Morrison | .15 | .07 |
| ❑ | 45 Jerry Mumphrey | .15 | .07 |
| ❑ | 46 Ray Smith | .15 | .07 |
| ❑ | 47 Rudy Law | .15 | .07 |
| ❑ | 48 Julio Franco | .40 | .18 |
| ❑ | 49 John Stuper | .15 | .07 |
| ❑ | 50 Chris Chambliss | .25 | .11 |
| ❑ | 51 Jim Frey MG | .15 | .07 |
| ❑ | 52 Paul Splittorff | .15 | .07 |
| ❑ | 53 Juan Beniquez | .15 | .07 |
| ❑ | 54 Jesse Orosco | .15 | .07 |
| ❑ | 55 Dave Concepcion | .25 | .11 |
| ❑ | 56 Gary Allenson | .15 | .07 |
| ❑ | 57 Dan Schatzeder | .15 | .07 |
| ❑ | 58 Max Venable | .15 | .07 |
| ❑ | 59 Sammy Stewart | .15 | .07 |
| ❑ | 60 Paul Molitor UER<br>('83 stats .272, 613,<br>167; should be .270,<br>608, 164) | .60 | .25 |
| ❑ | 61 Chris Codiroli | .15 | .07 |
| ❑ | 62 Dave Hostetler | .15 | .07 |
| ❑ | 63 Ed VandeBerg | .15 | .07 |
| ❑ | 64 Mike Scioscia | .15 | .07 |
| ❑ | 65 Kirk Gibson | .60 | .25 |
| ❑ | 66 Houston Astros TL<br>Jose Cruz<br>Nolan Ryan | 1.00 | .45 |
| ❑ | 67 Gary Ward | .15 | .07 |
| ❑ | 68 Luis Salazar | .15 | .07 |
| ❑ | 69 Rod Scurry | .15 | .07 |
| ❑ | 70 Gary Matthews | .25 | .11 |
| ❑ | 71 Leo Hernandez | .15 | .07 |
| ❑ | 72 Mike Squires | .15 | .07 |
| ❑ | 73 Jody Davis | .15 | .07 |
| ❑ | 74 Jerry Martin | .15 | .07 |
| ❑ | 75 Bob Forsch | .15 | .07 |
| ❑ | 76 Alfredo Griffin | .15 | .07 |
| ❑ | 77 Brett Butler | .40 | .18 |
| ❑ | 78 Mike Torrez | .15 | .07 |
| ❑ | 79 Rob Wilfong | .15 | .07 |
| ❑ | 80 Steve Rogers | .15 | .07 |
| ❑ | 81 Billy Martin MG | .25 | .11 |
| ❑ | 82 Doug Bird | .15 | .07 |
| ❑ | 83 Richie Zisk | .15 | .07 |
| ❑ | 84 Lenny Faedo | .15 | .07 |
| ❑ | 85 Atlee Hammaker | .15 | .07 |
| ❑ | 86 John Shelby | .15 | .07 |
| ❑ | 87 Frank Pastore | .15 | .07 |
| ❑ | 88 Rob Picciolo | .15 | .07 |
| ❑ | 89 Mike Smithson | .15 | .07 |
| ❑ | 90 Pedro Guerrero | .25 | .11 |
| ❑ | 91 Dan Spillner | .15 | .07 |
| ❑ | 92 Lloyd Moseby | .15 | .07 |
| ❑ | 93 Bob Knepper | .15 | .07 |
| ❑ | 94 Mario Ramirez | .15 | .07 |
| ❑ | 95 Aurelio Lopez | .25 | .11 |
| ❑ | 96 Kansas City Royals TL<br>Hal McRae<br>Larry Gura | .25 | .11 |
| ❑ | 97 LaMarr Hoyt | .15 | .07 |
| ❑ | 98 Steve Nicosia | .15 | .07 |
| ❑ | 99 Craig Lefferts RC | .15 | .07 |
| ❑ | 100 Reggie Jackson | .75 | .35 |
| ❑ | 101 Porfirio Altamirano | .15 | .07 |
| ❑ | 102 Ken Oberkfell | .15 | .07 |
| ❑ | 103 Dwayne Murphy | .15 | .07 |
| ❑ | 104 Ken Dayley | .15 | .07 |
| ❑ | 105 Tony Armas | .15 | .07 |
| ❑ | 106 Tim Stoddard | .15 | .07 |
| ❑ | 107 Ned Yost | .15 | .07 |
| ❑ | 108 Randy Moffitt | .15 | .07 |
| ❑ | 109 Brad Wellman | .15 | .07 |
| ❑ | 110 Ron Guidry | .25 | .11 |
| ❑ | 111 Bill Virdon MG | .15 | .07 |
| ❑ | 112 Tom Niedenfuer | .15 | .07 |
| ❑ | 113 Kelly Paris | .15 | .07 |
| ❑ | 114 Checklist 1-132 | .25 | .11 |
| ❑ | 115 Andre Thornton | .15 | .07 |
| ❑ | 116 George Bjorkman | .15 | .07 |
| ❑ | 117 Tom Veryzer | .15 | .07 |
| ❑ | 118 Charlie Hough | .25 | .11 |
| ❑ | 119 John Wockenfuss | .15 | .07 |
| ❑ | 120 Keith Hernandez | .25 | .11 |
| ❑ | 121 Pat Sheridan | .15 | .07 |
| ❑ | 122 Cecilio Guante | .15 | .07 |
| ❑ | 123 Butch Wynegar | .15 | .07 |
| ❑ | 124 Damaso Garcia | .15 | .07 |
| ❑ | 125 Britt Burns | .15 | .07 |
| ❑ | 126 Atlanta Braves TL<br>Dale Murphy<br>Craig McMurtry | .40 | .18 |
| ❑ | 127 Mike Madden | .15 | .07 |
| ❑ | 128 Rick Manning | .15 | .07 |
| ❑ | 129 Bill Laskey | .15 | .07 |
| ❑ | 130 Ozzie Smith | .75 | .35 |
| ❑ | 131 Batting Leaders<br>Bill Madlock<br>Wade Boggs | .75 | .35 |
| ❑ | 132 Home Run Leaders<br>Mike Schmidt<br>Jim Rice | .60 | .25 |
| ❑ | 133 RBI Leaders<br>Dale Murphy<br>Cecil Cooper<br>Jim Rice | .60 | .25 |
| ❑ | 134 Stolen Base Leaders<br>Tim Raines<br>Rickey Henderson | .60 | .25 |
| ❑ | 135 Victory Leaders<br>John Denny<br>LaMarr Hoyt | .60 | .25 |
| ❑ | 136 Strikeout Leaders<br>Steve Carlton<br>Jack Morris | .60 | .25 |
| ❑ | 137 ERA Leaders<br>Atlee Hammaker<br>Rick Honeycutt | .25 | .11 |
| ❑ | 138 Leading Firemen<br>Al Holland<br>Dan Quisenberry | .25 | .11 |
| ❑ | 139 Bert Campaneris | .25 | .11 |
| ❑ | 140 Storm Davis | .15 | .07 |
| ❑ | 141 Pat Corrales MG | .15 | .07 |
| ❑ | 142 Rich Gale | .15 | .07 |
| ❑ | 143 Jose Morales | .15 | .07 |
| ❑ | 144 Brian Harper RC | .25 | .11 |
| ❑ | 145 Gary Lavelle | .15 | .07 |
| ❑ | 146 Ed Romero | .15 | .07 |
| ❑ | 147 Dan Petry | .25 | .11 |
| ❑ | 148 Joe Lefebvre | .15 | .07 |
| ❑ | 149 Jon Matlack | .15 | .07 |
| ❑ | 150 Dale Murphy | .60 | .25 |
| ❑ | 151 Steve Trout | .15 | .07 |
| ❑ | 152 Glenn Brummer | .15 | .07 |
| ❑ | 153 Dick Tidrow | .15 | .07 |
| ❑ | 154 Dave Henderson | .25 | .11 |
| ❑ | 155 Frank White | .25 | .11 |
| ❑ | 156 Oakland A's TL<br>Rickey Henderson<br>Tim Conroy | .60 | .25 |
| ❑ | 157 Gary Gaetti | .40 | .18 |
| ❑ | 158 John Curtis | .15 | .07 |
| ❑ | 159 Darryl Cias | .15 | .07 |
| ❑ | 160 Mario Soto | .15 | .07 |
| ❑ | 161 Junior Ortiz | .15 | .07 |
| ❑ | 162 Bob Ojeda | .15 | .07 |
| ❑ | 163 Lorenzo Gray | .15 | .07 |
| ❑ | 164 Scott Sanderson | .15 | .07 |
| ❑ | 165 Ken Singleton | .15 | .07 |
| ❑ | 166 Jamie Nelson | .15 | .07 |
| ❑ | 167 Marshall Edwards | .15 | .07 |
| ❑ | 168 Juan Bonilla | .15 | .07 |
| ❑ | 169 Larry Parrish | .15 | .07 |
| ❑ | 170 Jerry Reuss | .15 | .07 |
| ❑ | 171 Frank Robinson MG | .40 | .18 |
| ❑ | 172 Frank DiPino | .15 | .07 |
| ❑ | 173 Marvell Wynne | .15 | .07 |
| ❑ | 174 Juan Berenguer | .15 | .07 |
| ❑ | 175 Graig Nettles | .25 | .11 |
| ❑ | 176 Lee Smith | .60 | .25 |

❑ 177 Jerry Hairston .15 .07
❑ 178 Bill Krueger RC .15 .07
❑ 179 Buck Martinez .15 .07
❑ 180 Manny Trillo .15 .07
❑ 181 Roy Thomas .15 .07
❑ 182 Darryl Strawberry RC 1.00 .45
❑ 183 Al Williams .15 .07
❑ 184 Mike O'Berry .15 .07
❑ 185 Sixto Lezcano .15 .07
❑ 186 Cardinal TL .25 .11
Lonnie Smith
John Stuper
❑ 187 Luis Aponte .15 .07
❑ 188 Bryan Little .15 .07
❑ 189 Tim Conroy .15 .07
❑ 190 Ben Oglivie .15 .07
❑ 191 Mike Boddicker .15 .07
❑ 192 Nick Esasky .15 .07
❑ 193 Darrell Brown .15 .07
❑ 194 Domingo Ramos .15 .07
❑ 195 Jack Morris .60 .25
❑ 196 Don Slaught .25 .11
❑ 197 Garry Hancock .15 .07
❑ 198 Bill Doran RC* .25 .11
❑ 199 Willie Hernandez .25 .11
❑ 200 Andre Dawson .40 .18
❑ 201 Bruce Kison .15 .07
❑ 202 Bobby Cox MG .25 .11
❑ 203 Matt Keough .15 .07
❑ 204 Bobby Meacham .15 .07
❑ 205 Greg Minton .15 .07
❑ 206 Andy Van Slyke RC .60 .25
❑ 207 Donnie Moore .15 .07
❑ 208 Jose Oquendo RC .25 .11
❑ 209 Manny Sarmiento .15 .07
❑ 210 Joe Morgan .60 .25
❑ 211 Rick Sweet .15 .07
❑ 212 Broderick Perkins .15 .07
❑ 213 Bruce Hurst .15 .07
❑ 214 Paul Householder .15 .07
❑ 215 Tippy Martinez .15 .07
❑ 216 White Sox TL .60 .25
Carlton Fisk
Richard Dotson
❑ 217 Alan Ashby .15 .07
❑ 218 Rick Waits .15 .07
❑ 219 Joe Simpson .15 .07
❑ 220 Fernando Valenzuela .25 .11
❑ 221 Cliff Johnson .15 .07
❑ 222 Rick Honeycutt .15 .07
❑ 223 Wayne Krenchicki .15 .07
❑ 224 Sid Monge .15 .07
❑ 225 Lee Mazzilli .15 .07
❑ 226 Juan Eichelberger .15 .07
❑ 227 Steve Braun .15 .07
❑ 228 John Rabb .15 .07
❑ 229 Paul Owens MG .15 .07
❑ 230 Rickey Henderson 1.00 .45
❑ 231 Gary Woods .15 .07
❑ 232 Tim Wallach .25 .11
❑ 233 Checklist 133-264 .25 .11
❑ 234 Rafael Ramirez .15 .07
❑ 235 Matt Young .15 .07
❑ 236 Ellis Valentine .15 .07
❑ 237 John Castino .15 .07
❑ 238 Reid Nichols .15 .07
❑ 239 Jay Howell .15 .07
❑ 240 Eddie Murray .60 .25
❑ 241 Bill Almon .15 .07
❑ 242 Alex Trevino .15 .07
❑ 243 Pete Ladd .15 .07
❑ 244 Candy Maldonado .15 .07
❑ 245 Rick Sutcliffe .25 .11
❑ 246 New York Mets TL .60 .25
Mookie Wilson
Tom Seaver
❑ 247 Onix Concepcion .15 .07
❑ 248 Bill Dawley .15 .07
❑ 249 Jay Johnstone .25 .11
❑ 250 Bill Madlock .25 .11
❑ 251 Tony Gwynn 3.00 1.35
❑ 252 Larry Christenson .15 .07
❑ 253 Jim Wohlford .15 .07
❑ 254 Shane Rawley .15 .07
❑ 255 Bruce Benedict .15 .07
❑ 256 Dave Geisel .15 .07
❑ 257 Julio Cruz .15 .07
❑ 258 Luis Sanchez .15 .07
❑ 259 Sparky Anderson MG .40 .18
❑ 260 Scott McGregor .15 .07
❑ 261 Bobby Brown .15 .07
❑ 262 Tom Candiotti RC .60 .25
❑ 263 Jack Fimple .15 .07
❑ 264 Doug Frobel .15 .07
❑ 265 Donnie Hill .15 .07
❑ 266 Steve Lubratich .15 .07
❑ 267 Carmelo Martinez .15 .07
❑ 268 Jack O'Connor .15 .07
❑ 269 Aurelio Rodriguez .15 .07
❑ 270 Jeff Russell RC .25 .11
❑ 271 Moose Haas .15 .07
❑ 272 Rick Dempsey .15 .07
❑ 273 Charlie Puleo .15 .07
❑ 274 Rick Monday .15 .07
❑ 275 Len Matuszek .15 .07
❑ 276 Angels TL .60 .25
Rod Carew
Geoff Zahn
❑ 277 Eddie Whitson .15 .07
❑ 278 Jorge Bell .40 .18
❑ 279 Ivan DeJesus .15 .07
❑ 280 Floyd Bannister .15 .07
❑ 281 Larry Milbourne .15 .07
❑ 282 Jim Barr .15 .07
❑ 283 Larry Biittner .15 .07
❑ 284 Howard Bailey .15 .07
❑ 285 Darrell Porter .15 .07
❑ 286 Lary Sorensen .15 .07
❑ 287 Warren Cromartie .15 .07
❑ 288 Jim Beattie .15 .07
❑ 289 Randy Johnson .15 .07
❑ 290 Dave Dravecky .25 .11
❑ 291 Chuck Tanner MG .15 .07
❑ 292 Tony Scott .15 .07
❑ 293 Ed Lynch .15 .07
❑ 294 U.L. Washington .15 .07
❑ 295 Mike Flanagan .15 .07
❑ 296 Jeff Newman .15 .07
❑ 297 Bruce Berenyi .15 .07
❑ 298 Jim Gantner .15 .07
❑ 299 John Butcher .15 .07
❑ 300 Pete Rose 2.00 .90
❑ 301 Frank LaCorte .15 .07
❑ 302 Barry Bonnell .15 .07
❑ 303 Marty Castillo .15 .07
❑ 304 Warren Brusstar .15 .07
❑ 305 Roy Smalley .15 .07
❑ 306 Dodgers TL .25 .11
Pedro Guerrero
Bob Welch
❑ 307 Bobby Mitchell .15 .07
❑ 308 Ron Hassey .15 .07
❑ 309 Tony Phillips RC .60 .25
❑ 310 Willie McGee .40 .18
❑ 311 Jerry Koosman .25 .11
❑ 312 Jorge Orta .15 .07
❑ 313 Mike Jorgensen .15 .07
❑ 314 Orlando Mercado .15 .07
❑ 315 Bobby Grich .25 .11
❑ 316 Mark Bradley .15 .07
❑ 317 Greg Pryor .15 .07
❑ 318 Bill Gullickson .15 .07
❑ 319 Al Bumbry .15 .07
❑ 320 Bob Stanley .15 .07
❑ 321 Harvey Kuenn MG .25 .11
❑ 322 Ken Schrom .15 .07
❑ 323 Alan Knicely .15 .07
❑ 324 Alejandro Pena RC* .25 .11
❑ 325 Darrell Evans .25 .11
❑ 326 Bob Kearney .15 .07
❑ 327 Ruppert Jones .15 .07
❑ 328 Vern Ruhle .15 .07
❑ 329 Pat Tabler .15 .07
❑ 330 John Candelaria .15 .07
❑ 331 Bucky Dent .25 .11
❑ 332 Kevin Gross RC .15 .07
❑ 333 Larry Herndon .25 .11
❑ 334 Chuck Rainey .15 .07
❑ 335 Don Baylor .40 .18
❑ 336 Seattle Mariners TL .25 .11
Pat Putnam
Matt Young
❑ 337 Kevin Hagen .15 .07
❑ 338 Mike Warren .15 .07
❑ 339 Roy Lee Jackson .15 .07
❑ 340 Hal McRae .25 .11
❑ 341 Dave Tobik .15 .07
❑ 342 Tim Foli .15 .07
❑ 343 Mark Davis .15 .07
❑ 344 Rick Miller .15 .07
❑ 345 Kent Hrbek .25 .11
❑ 346 Kurt Bevacqua .15 .07
❑ 347 Allan Ramirez .15 .07
❑ 348 Toby Harrah .25 .11
❑ 349 Bob L. Gibson .15 .07
❑ 350 George Foster .25 .11
❑ 351 Russ Nixon MG .15 .07
❑ 352 Dave Stewart .25 .11
❑ 353 Jim Anderson .15 .07
❑ 354 Jeff Burroughs .15 .07
❑ 355 Jason Thompson .15 .07
❑ 356 Glenn Abbott .15 .07
❑ 357 Ron Cey .25 .11
❑ 358 Bob Dernier .15 .07
❑ 359 Jim Acker .15 .07
❑ 360 Willie Randolph .25 .11
❑ 361 Dave Smith .15 .07
❑ 362 David Green .15 .07
❑ 363 Tim Laudner .15 .07
❑ 364 Scott Fletcher .15 .07
❑ 365 Steve Bedrosian .15 .07
❑ 366 Padres TL .25 .11
Terry Kennedy
Dave Dravecky
❑ 367 Jamie Easterly .15 .07
❑ 368 Hubie Brooks .15 .07
❑ 369 Steve McCatty .15 .07
❑ 370 Tim Raines .40 .18
❑ 371 Dave Gumpert .15 .07
❑ 372 Gary Roenicke .15 .07
❑ 373 Bill Scherrer .15 .07
❑ 374 Don Money .15 .07
❑ 375 Dennis Leonard .15 .07
❑ 376 Dave Anderson .15 .07
❑ 377 Danny Darwin .15 .07
❑ 378 Bob Brenly .15 .07
❑ 379 Checklist 265-396 .25 .11
❑ 380 Steve Garvey .40 .18
❑ 381 Ralph Houk MG .25 .11
❑ 382 Chris Nyman .15 .07
❑ 383 Terry Puhl .15 .07
❑ 384 Lee Tunnell .15 .07
❑ 385 Tony Perez .60 .25
❑ 386 George Hendrick AS .15 .07
❑ 387 Johnny Ray AS .15 .07
❑ 388 Mike Schmidt AS .40 .18
❑ 389 Ozzie Smith AS .60 .25
❑ 390 Tim Raines AS .25 .11
❑ 391 Dale Murphy AS .40 .18
❑ 392 Andre Dawson AS .25 .11
❑ 393 Gary Carter AS .25 .11
❑ 394 Steve Rogers AS .15 .07
❑ 395 Steve Carlton AS .40 .18
❑ 396 Jesse Orosco AS .15 .07
❑ 397 Eddie Murray AS .40 .18
❑ 398 Lou Whitaker AS .25 .11
❑ 399 George Brett AS .60 .25
❑ 400 Cal Ripken AS 2.00 .90
❑ 401 Jim Rice AS .15 .07
❑ 402 Dave Winfield AS .25 .11
❑ 403 Lloyd Moseby AS .15 .07
❑ 404 Ted Simmons AS .15 .07
❑ 405 LaMarr Hoyt AS .15 .07
❑ 406 Ron Guidry AS .15 .07
❑ 407 Dan Quisenberry AS .15 .07
❑ 408 Lou Piniella .25 .11
❑ 409 Juan Agosto .15 .07
❑ 410 Claudell Washington .15 .07
❑ 411 Houston Jimenez .15 .07
❑ 412 Doug Rader MG .15 .07
❑ 413 Spike Owen RC .25 .11
❑ 414 Mitchell Page .15 .07
❑ 415 Tommy John .40 .18
❑ 416 Dane Iorg .15 .07
❑ 417 Mike Armstrong .15 .07
❑ 418 Ron Hodges .15 .07
❑ 419 John Henry Johnson .15 .07
❑ 420 Cecil Cooper .25 .11

❑ 421 Charlie Lea .15 .07
❑ 422 Jose Cruz .25 .11
❑ 423 Mike Morgan .15 .07
❑ 424 Dann Bilardello .15 .07
❑ 425 Steve Howe .15 .07
❑ 426 Orioles TL 1.50 .70
Cal Ripken
Mike Boddicker
❑ 427 Rick Leach .15 .07
❑ 428 Fred Breining .15 .07
❑ 429 Randy Bush .15 .07
❑ 430 Rusty Staub .25 .11
❑ 431 Chris Bando .15 .07
❑ 432 Charles Hudson .15 .07
❑ 433 Rich Hebner .15 .07
❑ 434 Harold Baines .60 .25
❑ 435 Neil Allen .15 .07
❑ 436 Rick Peters .15 .07
❑ 437 Mike Proly .15 .07
❑ 438 Biff Pocoroba .15 .07
❑ 439 Bob Stoddard .15 .07
❑ 440 Steve Kemp .15 .07
❑ 441 Bob Lillis MG .15 .07
❑ 442 Byron McLaughlin .15 .07
❑ 443 Benny Ayala .15 .07
❑ 444 Steve Renko .15 .07
❑ 445 Jerry Remy .15 .07
❑ 446 Luis Pujols .15 .07
❑ 447 Tom Brunansky .25 .11
❑ 448 Ben Hayes .15 .07
❑ 449 Joe Pettini .15 .07
❑ 450 Gary Carter .40 .18
❑ 451 Bob Jones .15 .07
❑ 452 Chuck Porter .15 .07
❑ 453 Willie Upshaw .15 .07
❑ 454 Joe Beckwith .15 .07
❑ 455 Terry Kennedy .15 .07
❑ 456 Chicago Cubs TL .40 .18
Keith Moreland
Fergie Jenkins
❑ 457 Dave Rozema .15 .07
❑ 458 Kiko Garcia .15 .07
❑ 459 Kevin Hickey .15 .07
❑ 460 Dave Winfield .60 .25
❑ 461 Jim Maler .15 .07
❑ 462 Lee Lacy .15 .07
❑ 463 Dave Engle .15 .07
❑ 464 Jeff A. Jones .15 .07
❑ 465 Mookie Wilson .25 .11
❑ 466 Gene Garber .15 .07
❑ 467 Mike Ramsey .15 .07
❑ 468 Geoff Zahn .15 .07
❑ 469 Tom O'Malley .15 .07
❑ 470 Nolan Ryan 3.00 1.35
❑ 471 Dick Howser MG .15 .07
❑ 472 Mike G. Brown .15 .07
❑ 473 Jim Dwyer .15 .07
❑ 474 Greg Bargar .15 .07
❑ 475 Gary Redus RC* .15 .07
❑ 476 Tom Tellmann .15 .07
❑ 477 Rafael Landestoy .15 .07
❑ 478 Alan Bannister .15 .07
❑ 479 Frank Tanana .25 .11
❑ 480 Ron Kittle .15 .07
❑ 481 Mark Thurmond .15 .07
❑ 482 Enos Cabell .15 .07
❑ 483 Fergie Jenkins .60 .25
❑ 484 Ozzie Virgil .15 .07
❑ 485 Rick Rhoden .15 .07
❑ 486 N.Y. Yankees TL .60 .25
Don Baylor
Ron Guidry
❑ 487 Ricky Adams .15 .07
❑ 488 Jesse Barfield .25 .11
❑ 489 Dave Von Ohlen .15 .07
❑ 490 Cal Ripken 4.00 1.80
❑ 491 Bobby Castillo .15 .07
❑ 492 Tucker Ashford .15 .07
❑ 493 Mike Norris .15 .07
❑ 494 Chili Davis .40 .18
❑ 495 Rollie Fingers .60 .25
❑ 496 Terry Francona .15 .07
❑ 497 Bud Anderson .15 .07
❑ 498 Rich Gedman .15 .07
❑ 499 Mike Witt .15 .07
❑ 500 George Brett 1.25 .55
❑ 501 Steve Henderson .15 .07
❑ 502 Joe Torre MG .25 .11
❑ 503 Elias Sosa .15 .07
❑ 504 Mickey Rivers .15 .07
❑ 505 Pete Vuckovich .15 .07
❑ 506 Ernie Whitt .15 .07
❑ 507 Mike LaCoss .15 .07
❑ 508 Mel Hall .25 .11
❑ 509 Brad Havens .15 .07
❑ 510 Alan Trammell .40 .18
❑ 511 Marty Bystrom .15 .07
❑ 512 Oscar Gamble .15 .07
❑ 513 Dave Beard .15 .07
❑ 514 Floyd Rayford .15 .07
❑ 515 Gorman Thomas .15 .07
❑ 516 Montreal Expos TL .25 .11
Al Oliver
Charlie Lea
❑ 517 John Moses .15 .07
❑ 518 Greg Walker .25 .11
❑ 519 Ron Davis .15 .07
❑ 520 Bob Boone .25 .11
❑ 521 Pete Falcone .15 .07
❑ 522 Dave Bergman .15 .07
❑ 523 Glenn Hoffman .15 .07
❑ 524 Carlos Diaz .15 .07
❑ 525 Willie Wilson .15 .07
❑ 526 Ron Oester .15 .07
❑ 527 Checklist 397-528 .25 .11
❑ 528 Mark Brouhard .15 .07
❑ 529 Keith Atherton .15 .07
❑ 530 Dan Ford .15 .07
❑ 531 Steve Boros MG .15 .07
❑ 532 Eric Show .15 .07
❑ 533 Ken Landreaux .15 .07
❑ 534 Pete O'Brien RC* .25 .11
❑ 535 Bo Diaz .15 .07
❑ 536 Doug Bair .15 .07
❑ 537 Johnny Ray .15 .07
❑ 538 Kevin Bass .15 .07
❑ 539 George Frazier .15 .07
❑ 540 George Hendrick .15 .07
❑ 541 Dennis Lamp .15 .07
❑ 542 Duane Kuiper .15 .07
❑ 543 Craig McMurtry .15 .07
❑ 544 Cesar Geronimo .15 .07
❑ 545 Bill Buckner .25 .11
❑ 546 Indians TL .25 .11
Mike Hargrove
Lary Sorensen
❑ 547 Mike Moore .15 .07
❑ 548 Ron Jackson .15 .07
❑ 549 Walt Terrell .15 .07
❑ 550 Jim Rice .25 .11
❑ 551 Scott Ullger .15 .07
❑ 552 Ray Burris .15 .07
❑ 553 Joe Nolan .15 .07
❑ 554 Ted Power .15 .07
❑ 555 Greg Brock .15 .07
❑ 556 Joey McLaughlin .15 .07
❑ 557 Wayne Tolleson .15 .07
❑ 558 Mike Davis .15 .07
❑ 559 Mike Scott .25 .11
❑ 560 Carlton Fisk .60 .25
❑ 561 Whitey Herzog MG .25 .11
❑ 562 Manny Castillo .15 .07
❑ 563 Glenn Wilson .25 .11
❑ 564 Al Holland .15 .07
❑ 565 Leon Durham .15 .07
❑ 566 Jim Bibby .15 .07
❑ 567 Mike Heath .15 .07
❑ 568 Pete Filson .15 .07
❑ 569 Bake McBride .15 .07
❑ 570 Dan Quisenberry .15 .07
❑ 571 Bruce Bochy .15 .07
❑ 572 Jerry Royster .15 .07
❑ 573 Dave Kingman .40 .18
❑ 574 Brian Downing .15 .07
❑ 575 Jim Clancy .15 .07
❑ 576 Giants TL .25 .11
Jeff Leonard
Atlee Hammaker
❑ 577 Mark Clear .15 .07
❑ 578 Lenn Sakata .15 .07
❑ 579 Bob James .15 .07
❑ 580 Lonnie Smith .15 .07
❑ 581 Jose DeLeon .15 .07
❑ 582 Bob McClure .15 .07
❑ 583 Derrel Thomas .15 .07
❑ 584 Dave Schmidt .15 .07
❑ 585 Dan Driessen .15 .07
❑ 586 Joe Niekro .25 .11
❑ 587 Von Hayes .15 .07
❑ 588 Milt Wilcox .15 .07
❑ 589 Mike Easler .15 .07
❑ 590 Dave Stieb .15 .07
❑ 591 Tony LaRussa MG .25 .11
❑ 592 Andre Robertson .15 .07
❑ 593 Jeff Lahti .15 .07
❑ 594 Gene Richards .15 .07
❑ 595 Jeff Reardon .25 .11
❑ 596 Ryne Sandberg 2.00 .90
❑ 597 Rick Camp .15 .07
❑ 598 Rusty Kuntz .15 .07
❑ 599 Doug Sisk .15 .07
❑ 600 Rod Carew .60 .25
❑ 601 John Tudor .15 .07
❑ 602 John Wathan .15 .07
❑ 603 Renie Martin .15 .07
❑ 604 John Lowenstein .15 .07
❑ 605 Mike Caldwell .15 .07
❑ 606 Blue Jays TL .25 .11
Lloyd Moseby
Dave Stieb
❑ 607 Tom Hume .15 .07
❑ 608 Bobby Johnson .15 .07
❑ 609 Dan Meyer .15 .07
❑ 610 Steve Sax .25 .11
❑ 611 Chet Lemon .15 .07
❑ 612 Harry Spilman .15 .07
❑ 613 Greg Gross .15 .07
❑ 614 Len Barker .15 .07
❑ 615 Garry Templeton .15 .07
❑ 616 Don Robinson .15 .07
❑ 617 Rick Cerone .15 .07
❑ 618 Dickie Noles .15 .07
❑ 619 Jerry Dybzinski .15 .07
❑ 620 Al Oliver .25 .11
❑ 621 Frank Howard MG .25 .11
❑ 622 Al Cowens .15 .07
❑ 623 Ron Washington .15 .07
❑ 624 Terry Harper .15 .07
❑ 625 Larry Gura .15 .07
❑ 626 Bob Clark .15 .07
❑ 627 Dave LaPoint .15 .07
❑ 628 Ed Jurak .15 .07
❑ 629 Rick Langford .15 .07
❑ 630 Ted Simmons .25 .11
❑ 631 Dennis Martinez .25 .11
❑ 632 Tom Foley .15 .07
❑ 633 Mike Krukow .15 .07
❑ 634 Mike Marshall .15 .07
❑ 635 Dave Righetti .25 .11
❑ 636 Pat Putnam .15 .07
❑ 637 Phillies TL .25 .11
Gary Matthews
John Denny
❑ 638 George Vukovich .15 .07
❑ 639 Rick Lysander .15 .07
❑ 640 Lance Parrish .40 .18
❑ 641 Mike Richardt .15 .07
❑ 642 Tom Underwood .15 .07
❑ 643 Mike C. Brown .15 .07
❑ 644 Tim Lollar .15 .07
❑ 645 Tony Pena .15 .07
❑ 646 Checklist 529-660 .25 .11
❑ 647 Ron Roenicke .15 .07
❑ 648 Len Whitehouse .15 .07
❑ 649 Tom Herr .25 .11
❑ 650 Phil Niekro .60 .25
❑ 651 John McNamara MG .15 .07
❑ 652 Rudy May .15 .07
❑ 653 Dave Stapleton .15 .07
❑ 654 Bob Bailor .15 .07
❑ 655 Amos Otis .25 .11
❑ 656 Bryn Smith .15 .07
❑ 657 Thad Bosley .15 .07
❑ 658 Jerry Augustine .15 .07
❑ 659 Duane Walker .15 .07
❑ 660 Ray Knight .25 .11
❑ 661 Steve Yeager .15 .07
❑ 662 Tom Brennan .15 .07

❑ 663 Johnnie LeMaster .......... .15 .07
❑ 664 Dave Stegman .......... .15 .07
❑ 665 Buddy Bell .......... .25 .11
❑ 666 Detroit Tigers TL .......... .60 .25
Lou Whitaker
Jack Morris
❑ 667 Vance Law .......... .15 .07
❑ 668 Larry McWilliams .......... .15 .07
❑ 669 Dave Lopes .......... .25 .11
❑ 670 Rich Gossage .......... .40 .18
❑ 671 Jamie Quirk .......... .15 .07
❑ 672 Ricky Nelson .......... .15 .07
❑ 673 Mike Walters .......... .15 .07
❑ 674 Tim Flannery .......... .15 .07
❑ 675 Pascual Perez .......... .15 .07
❑ 676 Brian Giles .......... .15 .07
❑ 677 Doyle Alexander .......... .15 .07
❑ 678 Chris Speier .......... .15 .07
❑ 679 Art Howe .......... .25 .11
❑ 680 Fred Lynn .......... .25 .11
❑ 681 Tom Lasorda MG .......... .40 .18
❑ 682 Dan Morogiello .......... .15 .07
❑ 683 Marty Barrett .......... .25 .11
❑ 684 Bob Shirley .......... .15 .07
❑ 685 Willie Aikens .......... .15 .07
❑ 686 Joe Price .......... .15 .07
❑ 687 Roy Howell .......... .15 .07
❑ 688 George Wright .......... .15 .07
❑ 689 Mike Fischlin .......... .15 .07
❑ 690 Jack Clark .......... .25 .11
❑ 691 Steve Lake .......... .15 .07
❑ 692 Dickie Thon .......... .15 .07
❑ 693 Alan Wiggins .......... .15 .07
❑ 694 Mike Stanton .......... .15 .07
❑ 695 Lou Whitaker .......... .60 .25
❑ 696 Pirates TL .......... .25 .11
Bill Madlock
Rick Rhoden
❑ 697 Dale Murray .......... .15 .07
❑ 698 Marc Hill .......... .15 .07
❑ 699 Dave Rucker .......... .15 .07
❑ 700 Mike Schmidt .......... 1.25 .55
❑ 701 NL Active Batting .......... .60 .25
Bill Madlock
Pete Rose
Dave Parker
❑ 702 NL Active Hits .......... .60 .25
Pete Rose
Rusty Staub
Tony Perez
❑ 703 NL Active Home Run .......... .60 .25
Mike Schmidt
Tony Perez
Dave Kingman
❑ 704 NL Active RBI .......... .60 .25
Tony Perez
Rusty Staub
Al Oliver
❑ 705 NL Active Steals .......... .60 .25
Joe Morgan
Cesar Cedeno
Larry Bowa
❑ 706 NL Active Victory .......... .60 .25
Steve Carlton
Fergie Jenkins
Tom Seaver
❑ 707 NL Active Strikeout .......... 1.50 .70
Steve Carlton
Nolan Ryan
Tom Seaver
❑ 708 NL Active ERA .......... .60 .25
Tom Seaver
Steve Carlton
Steve Rogers
❑ 709 NL Active Save .......... .25 .11
Bruce Sutter
Tug McGraw
Gene Garber
❑ 710 AL Active Batting .......... .60 .25
Rod Carew
George Brett
Cecil Cooper
❑ 711 AL Active Hits .......... .60 .25
Rod Carew
Bert Campaneris
Reggie Jackson
❑ 712 AL Active Home Run .......... .60 .25
Reggie Jackson
Graig Nettles
Greg Luzinski
❑ 713 AL Active RBI .......... .60 .25
Reggie Jackson
Ted Simmons
Graig Nettles
❑ 714 AL Active Steals .......... .25 .11
Bert Campaneris
Dave Lopes
Omar Moreno
❑ 715 AL Active Victory .......... .60 .25
Jim Palmer
Don Sutton
Tommy John
❑ 716 AL Active Strikeout .......... .60 .25
Don Sutton
Bert Blyleven
Jerry Koosman
❑ 717 AL Active ERA .......... .60 .25
Jim Palmer
Rollie Fingers
Ron Guidry
❑ 718 AL Active Save .......... .60 .25
Rollie Fingers
Rich Gossage
Dan Quisenberry
❑ 719 Andy Hassler .......... .15 .07
❑ 720 Dwight Evans .......... .25 .11
❑ 721 Del Crandall MG .......... .15 .07
❑ 722 Bob Welch .......... .15 .07
❑ 723 Rich Dauer .......... .15 .07
❑ 724 Eric Rasmussen .......... .15 .07
❑ 725 Cesar Cedeno .......... .25 .11
❑ 726 Brewers TL .......... .25 .11
Ted Simmons
Moose Haas
❑ 727 Joel Youngblood .......... .15 .07
❑ 728 Tug McGraw .......... .25 .11
❑ 729 Gene Tenace .......... .25 .11
❑ 730 Bruce Sutter .......... .25 .11
❑ 731 Lynn Jones .......... .15 .07
❑ 732 Terry Crowley .......... .15 .07
❑ 733 Dave Collins .......... .15 .07
❑ 734 Odell Jones .......... .15 .07
❑ 735 Rick Burleson .......... .15 .07
❑ 736 Dick Ruthven .......... .15 .07
❑ 737 Jim Essian .......... .15 .07
❑ 738 Bill Schroeder .......... .15 .07
❑ 739 Bob Watson .......... .25 .11
❑ 740 Tom Seaver .......... 1.00 .45
❑ 741 Wayne Gross .......... .15 .07
❑ 742 Dick Williams MG .......... .25 .11
❑ 743 Don Hood .......... .15 .07
❑ 744 Jamie Allen .......... .15 .07
❑ 745 Dennis Eckersley .......... .60 .25
❑ 746 Mickey Hatcher .......... .15 .07
❑ 747 Pat Zachry .......... .15 .07
❑ 748 Jeff Leonard .......... .15 .07
❑ 749 Doug Flynn .......... .15 .07
❑ 750 Jim Palmer .......... .60 .25
❑ 751 Charlie Moore .......... .15 .07
❑ 752 Phil Garner .......... .25 .11
❑ 753 Doug Gwosdz .......... .15 .07
❑ 754 Kent Tekulve .......... .25 .11
❑ 755 Garry Maddox .......... .15 .07
❑ 756 Reds TL .......... .25 .11
Ron Oester
Mario Soto
❑ 757 Larry Bowa .......... .25 .11
❑ 758 Bill Stein .......... .15 .07
❑ 759 Richard Dotson .......... .15 .07
❑ 760 Bob Horner .......... .15 .07
❑ 761 John Montefusco .......... .15 .07
❑ 762 Rance Mulliniks .......... .15 .07
❑ 763 Craig Swan .......... .15 .07
❑ 764 Mike Hargrove .......... .25 .11
❑ 765 Ken Forsch .......... .15 .07
❑ 766 Mike Vail .......... .15 .07
❑ 767 Carney Lansford .......... .25 .11
❑ 768 Champ Summers .......... .15 .07
❑ 769 Bill Caudill .......... .15 .07
❑ 770 Ken Griffey .......... .25 .11
❑ 771 Billy Gardner MG .......... .15 .07
❑ 772 Jim Slaton .......... .15 .07
❑ 773 Todd Cruz .......... .15 .07
❑ 774 Tom Gorman .......... .15 .07
❑ 775 Dave Parker .......... .25 .11
❑ 776 Craig Reynolds .......... .15 .07
❑ 777 Tom Paciorek .......... .25 .11
❑ 778 Andy Hawkins .......... .15 .07
❑ 779 Jim Sundberg .......... .25 .11
❑ 780 Steve Carlton .......... .60 .25
❑ 781 Checklist 661-792 .......... .25 .11
❑ 782 Steve Balboni .......... .15 .07
❑ 783 Luis Leal .......... .15 .07
❑ 784 Leon Roberts .......... .15 .07
❑ 785 Joaquin Andujar .......... .15 .07
❑ 786 Red Sox TL .......... .60 .25
Wade Boggs
Bob Ojeda
❑ 787 Bill Campbell .......... .15 .07
❑ 788 Milt May .......... .15 .07
❑ 789 Bert Blyleven .......... .25 .11
❑ 790 Doug DeCinces .......... .15 .07
❑ 791 Terry Forster .......... .15 .07
❑ 792 Bill Russell .......... .15 .07

## 1984 Topps Traded

| | NRMT | VG-E |
|---|---|---|
| COMP.FACT.SET (132) | 30.00 | 13.50 |

❑ 1T Willie Aikens .......... .40 .18
❑ 2T Luis Aponte .......... .40 .18
❑ 3T Mike Armstrong .......... .40 .18
❑ 4T Bob Bailor .......... .40 .18
❑ 5T Dusty Baker .......... .60 .25
❑ 6T Steve Balboni .......... .40 .18
❑ 7T Alan Bannister .......... .40 .18
❑ 8T Dave Beard .......... .40 .18
❑ 9T Joe Beckwith .......... .40 .18
❑ 10T Bruce Berenyi .......... .40 .18
❑ 11T Dave Bergman .......... .40 .18
❑ 12T Tony Bernazard .......... .40 .18
❑ 13T Yogi Berra MG .......... 1.50 .70
❑ 14T Barry Bonnell .......... .40 .18
❑ 15T Phil Bradley .......... .60 .25
❑ 16T Fred Breining .......... .40 .18
❑ 17T Bill Buckner .......... .60 .25
❑ 18T Ray Burris .......... .40 .18
❑ 19T John Butcher .......... .40 .18
❑ 20T Brett Butler .......... 1.00 .45
❑ 21T Enos Cabell .......... .40 .18
❑ 22T Bill Campbell .......... .40 .18
❑ 23T Bill Caudill .......... .40 .18
❑ 24T Bob Clark .......... .40 .18
❑ 25T Bryan Clark .......... .40 .18
❑ 26T Jaime Cocanower .......... .40 .18
❑ 27T Ron Darling XRC* .......... 1.00 .45
❑ 28T Alvin Davis XRC .......... .60 .25
❑ 29T Ken Dayley .......... .40 .18
❑ 30T Jeff Dedmon .......... .40 .18
❑ 31T Bob Dernier .......... .40 .18
❑ 32T Carlos Diaz .......... .40 .18
❑ 33T Mike Easler .......... .40 .18
❑ 34T Dennis Eckersley .......... .60 .25
❑ 35T Jim Essian .......... .40 .18
❑ 36T Darrell Evans .......... .60 .25
❑ 37T Mike Fitzgerald .......... .40 .18
❑ 38T Tim Foli .......... .40 .18
❑ 39T George Frazier .......... .40 .18
❑ 40T Rich Gale .......... .40 .18

- ❑ 41T Barbaro Garbey .40 .18
- ❑ 42T Dwight Gooden XRC 5.00 2.20
- ❑ 43T Rich Gossage 1.00 .45
- ❑ 44T Wayne Gross .40 .18
- ❑ 45T Mark Gubicza XRC .60 .25
- ❑ 46T Jackie Gutierrez .40 .18
- ❑ 47T Mel Hall .60 .25
- ❑ 48T Toby Harrah .60 .25
- ❑ 49T Ron Hassey .40 .18
- ❑ 50T Rich Hebner .40 .18
- ❑ 51T Willie Hernandez .60 .25
- ❑ 52T Ricky Horton .40 .18
- ❑ 53T Art Howe .60 .25
- ❑ 54T Dane Iorg .40 .18
- ❑ 55T Brook Jacoby .60 .25
- ❑ 56T Mike Jeffcoat .40 .18
- ❑ 57T Dave Johnson MG .60 .25
- ❑ 58T Lynn Jones .40 .18
- ❑ 59T Ruppert Jones .40 .18
- ❑ 60T Mike Jorgensen .40 .18
- ❑ 61T Bob Kearney .40 .18
- ❑ 62T Jimmy Key XRC 1.00 .45
- ❑ 63T Dave Kingman 1.00 .45
- ❑ 64T Jerry Koosman .60 .25
- ❑ 65T Wayne Krenchicki .40 .18
- ❑ 66T Rusty Kuntz .40 .18
- ❑ 67T Rene Lachemann MG .40 .18
- ❑ 68T Frank LaCorte .40 .18
- ❑ 69T Dennis Lamp .40 .18
- ❑ 70T Mark Langston XRC 1.00 .45
- ❑ 71T Rick Leach .40 .18
- ❑ 72T Craig Lefferts .60 .25
- ❑ 73T Gary Lucas .40 .18
- ❑ 74T Jerry Martin .40 .18
- ❑ 75T Carmelo Martinez .40 .18
- ❑ 76T Mike Mason .40 .18
- ❑ 77T Gary Matthews .60 .25
- ❑ 78T Andy McGaffigan .40 .18
- ❑ 79T Larry Milbourne .40 .18
- ❑ 80T Sid Monge .40 .18
- ❑ 81T Jackie Moore MG .40 .18
- ❑ 82T Joe Morgan 1.50 .70
- ❑ 83T Graig Nettles .60 .25
- ❑ 84T Phil Niekro 1.50 .70
- ❑ 85T Ken Oberkfell .40 .18
- ❑ 86T Mike O'Berry .40 .18
- ❑ 87T Al Oliver .60 .25
- ❑ 88T Jorge Orta .40 .18
- ❑ 89T Amos Otis .60 .25
- ❑ 90T Dave Parker .60 .25
- ❑ 91T Tony Perez 1.50 .70
- ❑ 92T Gerald Perry .60 .25
- ❑ 93T Gary Pettis .40 .18
- ❑ 94T Rob Picciolo .40 .18
- ❑ 95T Vern Rapp MG .40 .18
- ❑ 96T Floyd Rayford .40 .18
- ❑ 97T Randy Ready XRC .60 .25
- ❑ 98T Ron Reed .40 .18
- ❑ 99T Gene Richards .40 .18
- ❑ 100T Jose Rijo XRC 1.50 .70
- ❑ 101T Jeff D. Robinson .40 .18
- ❑ 102T Ron Romanick .40 .18
- ❑ 103T Pete Rose 5.00 2.20
- ❑ 104T Bret Saberhagen XRC 3.00 1.35
- ❑ 105T Juan Samuel XRC* 1.00 .45
- ❑ 106T Scott Sanderson .40 .18
- ❑ 107T Dick Schofield XRC* .60 .25
- ❑ 108T Tom Seaver 2.50 1.10
- ❑ 109T Jim Slaton .40 .18
- ❑ 110T Mike Smithson .40 .18
- ❑ 111T Lary Sorensen .40 .18
- ❑ 112T Tim Stoddard .40 .18
- ❑ 113T Champ Summers .40 .18
- ❑ 114T Jim Sundberg .60 .25
- ❑ 115T Rick Sutcliffe .60 .25
- ❑ 116T Craig Swan .40 .18
- ❑ 117T Tim Teufel XRC* .40 .18
- ❑ 118T Derrel Thomas .40 .18
- ❑ 119T Gorman Thomas .40 .18
- ❑ 120T Alex Trevino .40 .18
- ❑ 121T Manny Trillo .40 .18
- ❑ 122T John Tudor .40 .18
- ❑ 123T Tom Underwood .40 .18
- ❑ 124T Mike Vail .40 .18
- ❑ 125T Tom Waddell .40 .18
- ❑ 126T Gary Ward .40 .18
- ❑ 127T Curtis Wilkerson .40 .18
- ❑ 128T Frank Williams .40 .18
- ❑ 129T Glenn Wilson .40 .18
- ❑ 130T John Wockenfuss .40 .18
- ❑ 131T Ned Yost .40 .18
- ❑ 132T Checklist 1T-132T .40 .18

## 1985 Topps

| | NRMT | VG-E |
|---|---|---|
| COMPLETE SET (792) | 200.00 | 90.00 |
| COMP.FACT.SET (792) | 400.00 | 180.00 |

- ❑ 1 Carlton Fisk RB .25 .11
  Longest game by catcher
- ❑ 2 Steve Garvey RB .25 .11
  Consecutive errorless games, 1B
- ❑ 3 Dwight Gooden RB .60 .25
  Most rookie strikeouts
- ❑ 4 Cliff Johnson RB .15 .07
  Most pinch-hit homers
- ❑ 5 Joe Morgan RB .25 .11
  Most homers 2B, lifetime
- ❑ 6 Pete Rose RB .40 .18
  Most career singles
- ❑ 7 Nolan Ryan RB 1.50 .70
  Most career strikeouts
- ❑ 8 Juan Samuel RB .15 .07
  Most SB's, rookie season
- ❑ 9 Bruce Sutter RB .15 .07
  Most NL season saves
- ❑ 10 Don Sutton RB .25 .11
  Most seasons 100 or more K's
- ❑ 11 Ralph Houk MG .15 .07
- ❑ 12 Dave Lopes .25 .11
  (Now with Cubs on card front)
- ❑ 13 Tim Lollar .15 .07
- ❑ 14 Chris Bando .15 .07
- ❑ 15 Jerry Koosman .25 .11
- ❑ 16 Bobby Meacham .15 .07
- ❑ 17 Mike Scott .15 .07
- ❑ 18 Mickey Hatcher .15 .07
- ❑ 19 George Frazier .15 .07
- ❑ 20 Chet Lemon .15 .07
- ❑ 21 Lee Tunnell .15 .07
- ❑ 22 Duane Kuiper .15 .07
- ❑ 23 Bret Saberhagen RC .50 .23
- ❑ 24 Jesse Barfield .15 .07
- ❑ 25 Steve Bedrosian .15 .07
- ❑ 26 Roy Smalley .15 .07
- ❑ 27 Bruce Berenyi .15 .07
- ❑ 28 Dann Bilardello .15 .07
- ❑ 29 Odell Jones .15 .07
- ❑ 30 Cal Ripken 3.00 1.35
- ❑ 31 Terry Whitfield .15 .07
- ❑ 32 Chuck Porter .15 .07
- ❑ 33 Tito Landrum .15 .07
- ❑ 34 Ed Nunez .15 .07
- ❑ 35 Graig Nettles .25 .11
- ❑ 36 Fred Breining .15 .07
- ❑ 37 Reid Nichols .15 .07
- ❑ 38 Jackie Moore MG .15 .07
- ❑ 39 John Wockenfuss .15 .07
- ❑ 40 Phil Niekro .60 .25
- ❑ 41 Mike Fischlin .15 .07
- ❑ 42 Luis Sanchez .15 .07
- ❑ 43 Andre David .15 .07
- ❑ 44 Dickie Thon .15 .07
- ❑ 45 Greg Minton .15 .07
- ❑ 46 Gary Woods .15 .07
- ❑ 47 Dave Rozema .15 .07
- ❑ 48 Tony Fernandez .25 .11
- ❑ 49 Butch Davis .15 .07
- ❑ 50 John Candelaria .15 .07
- ❑ 51 Bob Watson .25 .11
- ❑ 52 Jerry Dybzinski .15 .07
- ❑ 53 Tom Gorman .15 .07
- ❑ 54 Cesar Cedeno .25 .11
- ❑ 55 Frank Tanana .15 .07
- ❑ 56 Jim Dwyer .15 .07
- ❑ 57 Pat Zachry .15 .07
- ❑ 58 Orlando Mercado .15 .07
- ❑ 59 Rick Waits .15 .07
- ❑ 60 George Hendrick .15 .07
- ❑ 61 Curt Kaufman .15 .07
- ❑ 62 Mike Ramsey .15 .07
- ❑ 63 Steve McCatty .15 .07
- ❑ 64 Mark Bailey .15 .07
- ❑ 65 Bill Buckner .25 .11
- ❑ 66 Dick Williams MG .25 .11
- ❑ 67 Rafael Santana .15 .07
- ❑ 68 Von Hayes .15 .07
- ❑ 69 Jim Winn .15 .07
- ❑ 70 Don Baylor .25 .11
- ❑ 71 Tim Laudner .15 .07
- ❑ 72 Rick Sutcliffe .25 .11
- ❑ 73 Rusty Kuntz .15 .07
- ❑ 74 Mike Krukow .15 .07
- ❑ 75 Willie Upshaw .15 .07
- ❑ 76 Alan Bannister .15 .07
- ❑ 77 Joe Beckwith .15 .07
- ❑ 78 Scott Fletcher .15 .07
- ❑ 79 Rick Mahler .15 .07
- ❑ 80 Keith Hernandez .25 .11
- ❑ 81 Lenn Sakata .15 .07
- ❑ 82 Joe Price .15 .07
- ❑ 83 Charlie Moore .15 .07
- ❑ 84 Spike Owen .15 .07
- ❑ 85 Mike Marshall .15 .07
- ❑ 86 Don Aase .15 .07
- ❑ 87 David Green .15 .07
- ❑ 88 Bryn Smith .15 .07
- ❑ 89 Jackie Gutierrez .15 .07
- ❑ 90 Rich Gossage .25 .11
- ❑ 91 Jeff Burroughs .15 .07
- ❑ 92 Paul Owens MG .15 .07
- ❑ 93 Don Schulze .15 .07
- ❑ 94 Toby Harrah .15 .07
- ❑ 95 Jose Cruz .25 .11
- ❑ 96 Johnny Ray .15 .07
- ❑ 97 Pete Filson .15 .07
- ❑ 98 Steve Lake .15 .07
- ❑ 99 Milt Wilcox .15 .07
- ❑ 100 George Brett 1.25 .55
- ❑ 101 Jim Acker .15 .07
- ❑ 102 Tommy Dunbar .15 .07
- ❑ 103 Randy Lerch .15 .07
- ❑ 104 Mike Fitzgerald .15 .07
- ❑ 105 Ron Kittle .15 .07
- ❑ 106 Pascual Perez .15 .07
- ❑ 107 Tom Foley .15 .07
- ❑ 108 Darnell Coles .15 .07
- ❑ 109 Gary Roenicke .15 .07
- ❑ 110 Alejandro Pena .15 .07
- ❑ 111 Doug DeCinces .15 .07
- ❑ 112 Tom Tellmann .15 .07
- ❑ 113 Tom Herr .15 .07
- ❑ 114 Bob James .15 .07
- ❑ 115 Rickey Henderson .75 .35
- ❑ 116 Dennis Boyd .15 .07
- ❑ 117 Greg Gross .15 .07
- ❑ 118 Eric Show .15 .07
- ❑ 119 Pat Corrales MG .15 .07
- ❑ 120 Steve Kemp .15 .07
- ❑ 121 Checklist: 1-132 .15 .07
- ❑ 122 Tom Brunansky .25 .11
- ❑ 123 Dave Smith .15 .07
- ❑ 124 Rich Hebner .15 .07
- ❑ 125 Kent Tekulve .15 .07
- ❑ 126 Ruppert Jones .15 .07
- ❑ 127 Mark Gubicza RC* .25 .11

❑ 128 Ernie Whitt .15 .07
❑ 129 Gene Garber .15 .07
❑ 130 Al Oliver .25 .11
❑ 131 Buddy Bell FS .25 .11
Gus Bell
❑ 132 Dale Berra FS .25 .11
Yogi Berra
❑ 133 Bob Boone FS .15 .07
Ray Boone
❑ 134 Terry Francona FS .15 .07
Tito Francona
❑ 135 Terry Kennedy FS .15 .07
Bob Kennedy
❑ 136 Jeff Kunkel FS .15 .07
Bill Kunkel
❑ 137 Vance Law FS .25 .11
Vern Law
❑ 138 Dick Schofield FS .15 .07
Dick Schofield
❑ 139 Joel Skinner FS .15 .07
Bob Skinner
❑ 140 Roy Smalley Jr. FS .15 .07
Roy Smalley
❑ 141 Mike Stenhouse FS .15 .07
Dave Stenhouse
❑ 142 Steve Trout FS .15 .07
Dizzy Trout
❑ 143 Ozzie Virgil FS .15 .07
Ossie Virgil
❑ 144 Ron Gardenhire .15 .07
❑ 145 Alvin Davis RC* .25 .11
❑ 146 Gary Redus .15 .07
❑ 147 Bill Swaggerty .15 .07
❑ 148 Steve Yeager .15 .07
❑ 149 Dickie Noles .15 .07
❑ 150 Jim Rice .25 .11
❑ 151 Moose Haas .15 .07
❑ 152 Steve Braun .15 .07
❑ 153 Frank LaCorte .15 .07
❑ 154 Argenis Salazar .15 .07
❑ 155 Yogi Berra MG .40 .18
❑ 156 Craig Reynolds .15 .07
❑ 157 Tug McGraw .25 .11
❑ 158 Pat Tabler .15 .07
❑ 159 Carlos Diaz .15 .07
❑ 160 Lance Parrish .25 .11
❑ 161 Ken Schrom .15 .07
❑ 162 Benny Distefano .15 .07
❑ 163 Dennis Eckersley .60 .25
❑ 164 Jorge Orta .15 .07
❑ 165 Dusty Baker .25 .11
❑ 166 Keith Atherton .15 .07
❑ 167 Rufino Linares .15 .07
❑ 168 Garth Iorg .15 .07
❑ 169 Dan Spillner .15 .07
❑ 170 George Foster .25 .11
❑ 171 Bill Stein .15 .07
❑ 172 Jack Perconte .15 .07
❑ 173 Mike Young .15 .07
❑ 174 Rick Honeycutt .15 .07
❑ 175 Dave Parker .25 .11
❑ 176 Bill Schroeder .15 .07
❑ 177 Dave Von Ohlen .15 .07
❑ 178 Miguel Dilone .15 .07
❑ 179 Tommy John .40 .18
❑ 180 Dave Winfield .60 .25
❑ 181 Roger Clemens RC 20.00 9.00
❑ 182 Tim Flannery .15 .07
❑ 183 Larry McWilliams .15 .07
❑ 184 Carmen Castillo .15 .07
❑ 185 Al Holland .15 .07
❑ 186 Bob Lillis MG .15 .07
❑ 187 Mike Walters .15 .07
❑ 188 Greg Pryor .15 .07
❑ 189 Warren Brusstar .15 .07
❑ 190 Rusty Staub .25 .11
❑ 191 Steve Nicosia .15 .07
❑ 192 Howard Johnson .25 .11
❑ 193 Jimmy Key RC .60 .25
❑ 194 Dave Stegman .15 .07
❑ 195 Glenn Hubbard .15 .07
❑ 196 Pete O'Brien .15 .07
❑ 197 Mike Warren .15 .07
❑ 198 Eddie Milner .15 .07
❑ 199 Dennis Martinez .25 .11
❑ 200 Reggie Jackson .75 .35
❑ 201 Burt Hooton .15 .07
❑ 202 Gorman Thomas .15 .07
❑ 203 Bob McClure .15 .07
❑ 204 Art Howe .15 .07
❑ 205 Steve Rogers .15 .07
❑ 206 Phil Garner .25 .11
❑ 207 Mark Clear .15 .07
❑ 208 Champ Summers .15 .07
❑ 209 Bill Campbell .15 .07
❑ 210 Gary Matthews .15 .07
❑ 211 Clay Christiansen .15 .07
❑ 212 George Vukovich .15 .07
❑ 213 Billy Gardner MG .25 .11
❑ 214 John Tudor .15 .07
❑ 215 Bob Brenly .15 .07
❑ 216 Jerry Don Gleaton .15 .07
❑ 217 Leon Roberts .15 .07
❑ 218 Doyle Alexander .15 .07
❑ 219 Gerald Perry .15 .07
❑ 220 Fred Lynn .25 .11
❑ 221 Ron Reed .15 .07
❑ 222 Hubie Brooks .15 .07
❑ 223 Tom Hume .15 .07
❑ 224 Al Cowens .15 .07
❑ 225 Mike Boddicker .15 .07
❑ 226 Juan Beniquez .15 .07
❑ 227 Danny Darwin .15 .07
❑ 228 Dion James .15 .07
❑ 229 Dave LaPoint .15 .07
❑ 230 Gary Carter .40 .18
❑ 231 Dwayne Murphy .15 .07
❑ 232 Dave Beard .15 .07
❑ 233 Ed Jurak .15 .07
❑ 234 Jerry Narron .15 .07
❑ 235 Garry Maddox .15 .07
❑ 236 Mark Thurmond .15 .07
❑ 237 Julio Franco .40 .18
❑ 238 Jose Rijo RC .40 .18
❑ 239 Tim Teufel .15 .07
❑ 240 Dave Stieb .25 .11
❑ 241 Jim Frey MG .15 .07
❑ 242 Greg Harris .15 .07
❑ 243 Barbaro Garbey .15 .07
❑ 244 Mike Jones .15 .07
❑ 245 Chili Davis .25 .11
❑ 246 Mike Norris .15 .07
❑ 247 Wayne Tolleson .15 .07
❑ 248 Terry Forster .15 .07
❑ 249 Harold Baines .25 .11
❑ 250 Jesse Orosco .15 .07
❑ 251 Brad Gulden .15 .07
❑ 252 Dan Ford .15 .07
❑ 253 Sid Bream RC .25 .11
❑ 254 Pete Vuckovich .15 .07
❑ 255 Lonnie Smith .15 .07
❑ 256 Mike Stanton .15 .07
❑ 257 Bryan Little UER .15 .07
(Name spelled Brian on front)
❑ 258 Mike C. Brown .15 .07
❑ 259 Gary Allenson .15 .07
❑ 260 Dave Righetti .25 .11
❑ 261 Checklist: 133-264 .15 .07
❑ 262 Greg Booker .15 .07
❑ 263 Mel Hall .15 .07
❑ 264 Joe Sambito .15 .07
❑ 265 Juan Samuel .15 .07
❑ 266 Frank Viola .25 .11
❑ 267 Henry Cotto RC .15 .07
❑ 268 Chuck Tanner MG .25 .11
❑ 269 Doug Baker .15 .07
❑ 270 Dan Quisenberry .25 .11
❑ 271 Tim Foli FDP68 .15 .07
❑ 272 Jeff Burroughs FDP69 .15 .07
❑ 273 Bill Almon FDP74 .15 .07
❑ 274 Floyd Bannister FDP76 .15 .07
❑ 275 Harold Baines FDP77 .15 .07
❑ 276 Bob Horner FDP78 .15 .07
❑ 277 Al Chambers FDP79 .15 .07
❑ 278 Darryl Strawberry .25 .11
FDP80
❑ 279 Mike Moore FDP81 .15 .07
❑ 280 Shawon Dunston FDP82 RC .50 .23
❑ 281 Tim Belcher RC FDP83 .60 .25
❑ 282 Shawn Abner FDP84 .15 .07
❑ 283 Fran Mullins .15 .07
❑ 284 Marty Bystrom .15 .07
❑ 285 Dan Driessen .15 .07
❑ 286 Rudy Law .15 .07
❑ 287 Walt Terrell .15 .07
❑ 288 Jeff Kunkel .15 .07
❑ 289 Tom Underwood .15 .07
❑ 290 Cecil Cooper .25 .11
❑ 291 Bob Welch .15 .07
❑ 292 Brad Komminsk .15 .07
❑ 293 Curt Young .15 .07
❑ 294 Tom Nieto .15 .07
❑ 295 Joe Niekro .15 .07
❑ 296 Ricky Nelson .15 .07
❑ 297 Gary Lucas .15 .07
❑ 298 Marty Barrett .15 .07
❑ 299 Andy Hawkins .15 .07
❑ 300 Rod Carew .60 .25
❑ 301 John Montefusco .15 .07
❑ 302 Tim Corcoran .15 .07
❑ 303 Mike Jeffcoat .15 .07
❑ 304 Gary Gaetti .25 .11
❑ 305 Dale Berra .15 .07
❑ 306 Rick Reuschel .15 .07
❑ 307 Sparky Anderson MG .25 .11
❑ 308 John Wathan .15 .07
❑ 309 Mike Witt .15 .07
❑ 310 Manny Trillo .15 .07
❑ 311 Jim Gott .15 .07
❑ 312 Marc Hill .15 .07
❑ 313 Dave Schmidt .15 .07
❑ 314 Ron Oester .15 .07
❑ 315 Doug Sisk .15 .07
❑ 316 John Lowenstein .15 .07
❑ 317 Jack Lazorko .15 .07
❑ 318 Ted Simmons .25 .11
❑ 319 Jeff Jones .15 .07
❑ 320 Dale Murphy .60 .25
❑ 321 Ricky Horton .15 .07
❑ 322 Dave Stapleton .15 .07
❑ 323 Andy McGaffigan .15 .07
❑ 324 Bruce Bochy .15 .07
❑ 325 John Denny .15 .07
❑ 326 Kevin Bass .15 .07
❑ 327 Brook Jacoby .15 .07
❑ 328 Bob Shirley .15 .07
❑ 329 Ron Washington .15 .07
❑ 330 Leon Durham .15 .07
❑ 331 Bill Laskey .15 .07
❑ 332 Brian Harper .15 .07
❑ 333 Willie Hernandez .15 .07
❑ 334 Dick Howser MG .25 .11
❑ 335 Bruce Benedict .15 .07
❑ 336 Rance Mulliniks .15 .07
❑ 337 Billy Sample .15 .07
❑ 338 Britt Burns .15 .07
❑ 339 Danny Heep .15 .07
❑ 340 Robin Yount .60 .25
❑ 341 Floyd Rayford .15 .07
❑ 342 Ted Power .15 .07
❑ 343 Bill Russell .15 .07
❑ 344 Dave Henderson .15 .07
❑ 345 Charlie Lea .15 .07
❑ 346 Terry Pendleton RC .60 .25
❑ 347 Rick Langford .15 .07
❑ 348 Bob Boone .25 .11
❑ 349 Domingo Ramos .15 .07
❑ 350 Wade Boggs 1.00 .45
❑ 351 Juan Agosto .15 .07
❑ 352 Joe Morgan .60 .25
❑ 353 Julio Solano .15 .07
❑ 354 Andre Robertson .15 .07
❑ 355 Bert Blyleven .25 .11
❑ 356 Dave Meier .15 .07
❑ 357 Rich Bordi .15 .07
❑ 358 Tony Pena .15 .07
❑ 359 Pat Sheridan .15 .07
❑ 360 Steve Carlton .60 .25
❑ 361 Alfredo Griffin .15 .07
❑ 362 Craig McMurtry .15 .07
❑ 363 Ron Hodges .15 .07
❑ 364 Richard Dotson .15 .07
❑ 365 Danny Ozark MG .15 .07
❑ 366 Todd Cruz .15 .07
❑ 367 Keefe Cato .15 .07
❑ 368 Dave Bergman .15 .07
❑ 369 R.J. Reynolds .15 .07
❑ 370 Bruce Sutter .25 .11

❑ 371 Mickey Rivers .15 .07
❑ 372 Roy Howell .15 .07
❑ 373 Mike Moore .15 .07
❑ 374 Brian Downing .15 .07
❑ 375 Jeff Reardon .25 .11
❑ 376 Jeff Newman .15 .07
❑ 377 Checklist: 265-396 .15 .07
❑ 378 Alan Wiggins .15 .07
❑ 379 Charles Hudson .15 .07
❑ 380 Ken Griffey .25 .11
❑ 381 Roy Smith .15 .07
❑ 382 Denny Walling .15 .07
❑ 383 Rick Lysander .15 .07
❑ 384 Jody Davis .15 .07
❑ 385 Jose DeLeon .15 .07
❑ 386 Dan Gladden RC .25 .11
❑ 387 Buddy Biancalana .15 .07
❑ 388 Bert Roberge .15 .07
❑ 389 Rod Dedeaux OLY CO .25 .11
❑ 390 Sid Akins OLY .15 .07
❑ 391 Flavio Alfaro OLY .15 .07
❑ 392 Don August OLY .15 .07
❑ 393 Scott Bankhead RC OLY .15 .07
❑ 394 Bob Caffrey OLY .15 .07
❑ 395 Mike Dunne OLY .25 .11
❑ 396 Gary Green OLY .15 .07
❑ 397 John Hoover OLY .15 .07
❑ 398 Shane Mack RC OLY .60 .25
❑ 399 John Marzano OLY .25 .11
❑ 400 Oddibe McDowell RC OLY .25 .11
❑ 401 Mark McGwire OLY RC ! 150.00 70.00
❑ 402 Pat Pacillo OLY .25 .11
❑ 403 Cory Snyder RC OLY .40 .18
❑ 404 Billy Swift OLY RC .40 .18
❑ 405 Tom Veryzer .15 .07
❑ 406 Len Whitehouse .15 .07
❑ 407 Bobby Ramos .15 .07
❑ 408 Sid Monge .15 .07
❑ 409 Brad Wellman .15 .07
❑ 410 Bob Horner .15 .07
❑ 411 Bobby Cox MG .15 .07
❑ 412 Bud Black .15 .07
❑ 413 Vance Law .15 .07
❑ 414 Gary Ward .15 .07
❑ 415 Ron Darling UER .25 .11
(No trivia answer)
❑ 416 Wayne Gross .15 .07
❑ 417 John Franco RC .60 .25
❑ 418 Ken Landreaux .15 .07
❑ 419 Mike Caldwell .15 .07
❑ 420 Andre Dawson
❑ 421 Dave Rucker .15 .07
❑ 422 Carney Lansford .25 .11
❑ 423 Barry Bonnell .15 .07
❑ 424 Al Nipper .15 .07
❑ 425 Mike Hargrove .25 .11
❑ 426 Vern Ruhle .15 .07
❑ 427 Mario Ramirez .15 .07
❑ 428 Larry Andersen .15 .07
❑ 429 Rick Cerone .15 .07
❑ 430 Ron Davis .15 .07
❑ 431 U.L. Washington .15 .07
❑ 432 Thad Bosley .15 .07
❑ 433 Jim Morrison .15 .07
❑ 434 Gene Richards .15 .07
❑ 435 Dan Petry .15 .07
❑ 436 Willie Aikens .15 .07
❑ 437 Al Jones .15 .07
❑ 438 Joe Torre MG .40 .18
❑ 439 Junior Ortiz .15 .07
❑ 440 Fernando Valenzuela .25 .11
❑ 441 Duane Walker .15 .07
❑ 442 Ken Forsch .15 .07
❑ 443 George Wright .15 .07
❑ 444 Tony Phillips .15 .07
❑ 445 Tippy Martinez .15 .07
❑ 446 Jim Sundberg .15 .07
❑ 447 Jeff Lahti .15 .07
❑ 448 Derrel Thomas .15 .07
❑ 449 Phil Bradley .25 .11
❑ 450 Steve Garvey .40 .18
❑ 451 Bruce Hurst .15 .07
❑ 452 John Castino .15 .07
❑ 453 Tom Waddell .15 .07
❑ 454 Glenn Wilson .15 .07
❑ 455 Bob Knepper .15 .07
❑ 456 Tim Foli .15 .07
❑ 457 Cecilio Guante .15 .07
❑ 458 Randy Johnson .15 .07
❑ 459 Charlie Leibrandt .15 .07
❑ 460 Ryne Sandberg 1.25 .55
❑ 461 Marty Castillo .15 .07
❑ 462 Gary Lavelle .15 .07
❑ 463 Dave Collins .15 .07
❑ 464 Mike Mason .15 .07
❑ 465 Bobby Grich .25 .11
❑ 466 Tony LaRussa MG .40 .18
❑ 467 Ed Lynch .15 .07
❑ 468 Wayne Krenchicki .15 .07
❑ 469 Sammy Stewart .15 .07
❑ 470 Steve Sax .15 .07
❑ 471 Pete Ladd .15 .07
❑ 472 Jim Essian .15 .07
❑ 473 Tim Wallach .25 .11
❑ 474 Kurt Kepshire .15 .07
❑ 475 Andre Thornton .15 .07
❑ 476 Jeff Stone .15 .07
❑ 477 Bob Ojeda .15 .07
❑ 478 Kurt Bevacqua .15 .07
❑ 479 Mike Madden .15 .07
❑ 480 Lou Whitaker .40 .18
❑ 481 Dale Murray .15 .07
❑ 482 Harry Spilman .15 .07
❑ 483 Mike Smithson .15 .07
❑ 484 Larry Bowa .25 .11
❑ 485 Matt Young .15 .07
❑ 486 Steve Balboni .15 .07
❑ 487 Frank Williams .15 .07
❑ 488 Joel Skinner .15 .07
❑ 489 Bryan Clark .15 .07
❑ 490 Jason Thompson .15 .07
❑ 491 Rick Camp .15 .07
❑ 492 Dave Johnson MG .25 .11
❑ 493 Orel Hershiser RC .75 .35
❑ 494 Rich Dauer .15 .07
❑ 495 Mario Soto .15 .07
❑ 496 Donnie Scott .15 .07
❑ 497 Gary Pettis UER .15 .07
(Photo actually
Gary's little
brother Lynn)
❑ 498 Ed Romero .15 .07
❑ 499 Danny Cox .15 .07
❑ 500 Mike Schmidt 1.25 .55
❑ 501 Dan Schatzeder .15 .07
❑ 502 Rick Miller .15 .07
❑ 503 Tim Conroy .15 .07
❑ 504 Jerry Willard .15 .07
❑ 505 Jim Beattie .15 .07
❑ 506 Franklin Stubbs .15 .07
❑ 507 Ray Fontenot .15 .07
❑ 508 John Shelby .15 .07
❑ 509 Milt May .15 .07
❑ 510 Kent Hrbek .25 .11
❑ 511 Lee Smith .40 .18
❑ 512 Tom Brookens .15 .07
❑ 513 Lynn Jones .15 .07
❑ 514 Jeff Cornell .15 .07
❑ 515 Dave Concepcion .25 .11
❑ 516 Roy Lee Jackson .15 .07
❑ 517 Jerry Martin .15 .07
❑ 518 Chris Chambliss .25 .11
❑ 519 Doug Rader MG .15 .07
❑ 520 LaMarr Hoyt .15 .07
❑ 521 Rick Dempsey .15 .07
❑ 522 Paul Molitor .60 .25
❑ 523 Candy Maldonado .15 .07
❑ 524 Rob Wilfong .15 .07
❑ 525 Darrell Porter .15 .07
❑ 526 David Palmer .15 .07
❑ 527 Checklist: 397-528 .15 .07
❑ 528 Bill Krueger .15 .07
❑ 529 Rich Gedman .15 .07
❑ 530 Dave Dravecky .25 .11
❑ 531 Joe Lefebvre .15 .07
❑ 532 Frank DiPino .15 .07
❑ 533 Tony Bernazard .15 .07
❑ 534 Brian Dayett .15 .07
❑ 535 Pat Putnam .15 .07
❑ 536 Kirby Puckett RC 8.00 3.60
❑ 537 Don Robinson .15 .07
❑ 538 Keith Moreland .15 .07
❑ 539 Aurelio Lopez .15 .07
❑ 540 Claudell Washington .15 .07
❑ 541 Mark Davis .15 .07
❑ 542 Don Slaught .15 .07
❑ 543 Mike Squires .15 .07
❑ 544 Bruce Kison .15 .07
❑ 545 Lloyd Moseby .15 .07
❑ 546 Brent Gaff .15 .07
❑ 547 Pete Rose MG .40 .18
❑ 548 Larry Parrish .15 .07
❑ 549 Mike Scioscia .15 .07
❑ 550 Scott McGregor .15 .07
❑ 551 Andy Van Slyke .25 .11
❑ 552 Chris Codiroli .15 .07
❑ 553 Bob Clark .15 .07
❑ 554 Doug Flynn .15 .07
❑ 555 Bob Stanley .15 .07
❑ 556 Sixto Lezcano .15 .07
❑ 557 Len Barker .15 .07
❑ 558 Carmelo Martinez .15 .07
❑ 559 Jay Howell .15 .07
❑ 560 Bill Madlock .25 .11
❑ 561 Darryl Motley .15 .07
❑ 562 Houston Jimenez .15 .07
❑ 563 Dick Ruthven .15 .07
❑ 564 Alan Ashby .15 .07
❑ 565 Kirk Gibson .25 .11
❑ 566 Ed VandeBerg .15 .07
❑ 567 Joel Youngblood .15 .07
❑ 568 Cliff Johnson .15 .07
❑ 569 Ken Oberkfell .15 .07
❑ 570 Darryl Strawberry .60 .25
❑ 571 Charlie Hough .25 .11
❑ 572 Tom Paciorek .25 .11
❑ 573 Jay Tibbs .15 .07
❑ 574 Joe Altobelli MG .15 .07
❑ 575 Pedro Guerrero .25 .11
❑ 576 Jaime Cocanower .15 .07
❑ 577 Chris Speier .15 .07
❑ 578 Terry Francona .15 .07
❑ 579 Ron Romanick .15 .07
❑ 580 Dwight Evans .25 .11
❑ 581 Mark Wagner .15 .07
❑ 582 Ken Phelps .15 .07
❑ 583 Bobby Brown .15 .07
❑ 584 Kevin Gross .15 .07
❑ 585 Butch Wynegar .15 .07
❑ 586 Bill Scherrer .15 .07
❑ 587 Doug Frobel .15 .07
❑ 588 Bobby Castillo .15 .07
❑ 589 Bob Dernier .15 .07
❑ 590 Ray Knight .15 .07
❑ 591 Larry Herndon .15 .07
❑ 592 Jeff D. Robinson .15 .07
❑ 593 Rick Leach .15 .07
❑ 594 Curt Wilkerson .15 .07
❑ 595 Larry Gura .15 .07
❑ 596 Jerry Hairston .15 .07
❑ 597 Brad Lesley .15 .07
❑ 598 Jose Oquendo .15 .07
❑ 599 Storm Davis .15 .07
❑ 600 Pete Rose 1.50 .70
❑ 601 Tom Lasorda MG .40 .18
❑ 602 Jeff Dedmon .15 .07
❑ 603 Rick Manning .15 .07
❑ 604 Daryl Sconiers .15 .07
❑ 605 Ozzie Smith .75 .35
❑ 606 Rich Gale .15 .07
❑ 607 Bill Almon .15 .07
❑ 608 Craig Lefferts .15 .07
❑ 609 Broderick Perkins .15 .07
❑ 610 Jack Morris .25 .11
❑ 611 Ozzie Virgil .15 .07
❑ 612 Mike Armstrong .15 .07
❑ 613 Terry Puhl .15 .07
❑ 614 Al Williams .15 .07
❑ 615 Marvell Wynne .15 .07
❑ 616 Scott Sanderson .15 .07
❑ 617 Willie Wilson .15 .07
❑ 618 Pete Falcone .15 .07
❑ 619 Jeff Leonard .15 .07
❑ 620 Dwight Gooden RC .75 .35
❑ 621 Marvis Foley .15 .07
❑ 622 Luis Leal .15 .07
❑ 623 Greg Walker .15 .07
❑ 624 Benny Ayala .15 .07

| No. | Player | NRMT | VG-E |
|---|---|---|---|
| 625 | Mark Langston RC | .40 | .18 |
| 626 | German Rivera | .15 | .07 |
| 627 | Eric Davis RC | 1.00 | .45 |
| 628 | Rene Lachemann MG | .15 | .07 |
| 629 | Dick Schofield | .15 | .07 |
| 630 | Tim Raines | .25 | .11 |
| 631 | Bob Forsch | .15 | .07 |
| 632 | Bruce Bochte | .15 | .07 |
| 633 | Glenn Hoffman | .15 | .07 |
| 634 | Bill Dawley | .15 | .07 |
| 635 | Terry Kennedy | .15 | .07 |
| 636 | Shane Rawley | .15 | .07 |
| 637 | Brett Butler | .25 | .11 |
| 638 | Mike Pagliarulo | .15 | .07 |
| 639 | Ed Hodge | .15 | .07 |
| 640 | Steve Henderson | .15 | .07 |
| 641 | Rod Scurry | .15 | .07 |
| 642 | Dave Owen | .15 | .07 |
| 643 | Johnny Grubb | .15 | .07 |
| 644 | Mark Huismann | .15 | .07 |
| 645 | Damaso Garcia | .15 | .07 |
| 646 | Scot Thompson | .15 | .07 |
| 647 | Rafael Ramirez | .15 | .07 |
| 648 | Bob Jones | .15 | .07 |
| 649 | Sid Fernandez | .25 | .11 |
| 650 | Greg Luzinski | .25 | .11 |
| 651 | Jeff Russell | .15 | .07 |
| 652 | Joe Nolan | .15 | .07 |
| 653 | Mark Brouhard | .15 | .07 |
| 654 | Dave Anderson | .15 | .07 |
| 655 | Joaquin Andujar | .15 | .07 |
| 656 | Chuck Cottier MG | .15 | .07 |
| 657 | Jim Slaton | .15 | .07 |
| 658 | Mike Stenhouse | .15 | .07 |
| 659 | Checklist: 529-660 | .15 | .07 |
| 660 | Tony Gwynn | 2.00 | .90 |
| 661 | Steve Crawford | .15 | .07 |
| 662 | Mike Heath | .15 | .07 |
| 663 | Luis Aguayo | .15 | .07 |
| 664 | Steve Farr RC | .25 | .11 |
| 665 | Don Mattingly | 1.50 | .70 |
| 666 | Mike LaCoss | .15 | .07 |
| 667 | Dave Engle | .15 | .07 |
| 668 | Steve Trout | .15 | .07 |
| 669 | Lee Lacy | .15 | .07 |
| 670 | Tom Seaver | 1.00 | .45 |
| 671 | Dane Iorg | .15 | .07 |
| 672 | Juan Berenguer | .15 | .07 |
| 673 | Buck Martinez | .15 | .07 |
| 674 | Atlee Hammaker | .15 | .07 |
| 675 | Tony Perez | .60 | .25 |
| 676 | Albert Hall | .15 | .07 |
| 677 | Wally Backman | .15 | .07 |
| 678 | Joey McLaughlin | .15 | .07 |
| 679 | Bob Kearney | .15 | .07 |
| 680 | Jerry Reuss | .15 | .07 |
| 681 | Ben Oglivie | .15 | .07 |
| 682 | Doug Corbett | .15 | .07 |
| 683 | Whitey Herzog MG | .25 | .11 |
| 684 | Bill Doran | .15 | .07 |
| 685 | Bill Caudill | .15 | .07 |
| 686 | Mike Easler | .15 | .07 |
| 687 | Bill Gullickson | .15 | .07 |
| 688 | Len Matuszek | .15 | .07 |
| 689 | Luis DeLeon | .15 | .07 |
| 690 | Alan Trammell | .40 | .18 |
| 691 | Dennis Rasmussen | .15 | .07 |
| 692 | Randy Bush | .15 | .07 |
| 693 | Tim Stoddard | .15 | .07 |
| 694 | Joe Carter | .60 | .25 |
| 695 | Rick Rhoden | .15 | .07 |
| 696 | John Rabb | .15 | .07 |
| 697 | Onix Concepcion | .15 | .07 |
| 698 | Jorge Bell | .25 | .11 |
| 699 | Donnie Moore | .15 | .07 |
| 700 | Eddie Murray | .60 | .25 |
| 701 | Eddie Murray AS | .25 | .11 |
| 702 | Damaso Garcia AS | .15 | .07 |
| 703 | George Brett AS | .60 | .25 |
| 704 | Cal Ripken AS | 1.50 | .70 |
| 705 | Dave Winfield AS | .25 | .11 |
| 706 | Rickey Henderson AS | .25 | .11 |
| 707 | Tony Armas AS | .15 | .07 |
| 708 | Lance Parrish AS | .15 | .07 |
| 709 | Mike Boddicker AS | .15 | .07 |
| 710 | Frank Viola AS | .15 | .07 |
| 711 | Dan Quisenberry AS | .15 | .07 |
| 712 | Keith Hernandez AS | .15 | .07 |
| 713 | Ryne Sandberg AS | .60 | .25 |
| 714 | Mike Schmidt AS | .40 | .18 |
| 715 | Ozzie Smith AS | .40 | .18 |
| 716 | Dale Murphy AS | .25 | .11 |
| 717 | Tony Gwynn AS | 1.25 | .55 |
| 718 | Jeff Leonard AS | .15 | .07 |
| 719 | Gary Carter AS | .25 | .11 |
| 720 | Rick Sutcliffe AS | .15 | .07 |
| 721 | Bob Knepper AS | .15 | .07 |
| 722 | Bruce Sutter AS | .15 | .07 |
| 723 | Dave Stewart | .25 | .11 |
| 724 | Oscar Gamble | .15 | .07 |
| 725 | Floyd Bannister | .15 | .07 |
| 726 | Al Bumbry | .15 | .07 |
| 727 | Frank Pastore | .15 | .07 |
| 728 | Bob Bailor | .15 | .07 |
| 729 | Don Sutton | .60 | .25 |
| 730 | Dave Kingman | .25 | .11 |
| 731 | Neil Allen | .15 | .07 |
| 732 | John McNamara MG | .15 | .07 |
| 733 | Tony Scott | .15 | .07 |
| 734 | John Henry Johnson | .15 | .07 |
| 735 | Garry Templeton | .15 | .07 |
| 736 | Jerry Mumphrey | .15 | .07 |
| 737 | Bo Diaz | .15 | .07 |
| 738 | Omar Moreno | .15 | .07 |
| 739 | Ernie Camacho | .15 | .07 |
| 740 | Jack Clark | .25 | .11 |
| 741 | John Butcher | .15 | .07 |
| 742 | Ron Hassey | .15 | .07 |
| 743 | Frank White | .25 | .11 |
| 744 | Doug Bair | .15 | .07 |
| 745 | Buddy Bell | .25 | .11 |
| 746 | Jim Clancy | .15 | .07 |
| 747 | Alex Trevino | .15 | .07 |
| 748 | Lee Mazzilli | .15 | .07 |
| 749 | Julio Cruz | .15 | .07 |
| 750 | Rollie Fingers | .60 | .25 |
| 751 | Kelvin Chapman | .15 | .07 |
| 752 | Bob Owchinko | .15 | .07 |
| 753 | Greg Brock | .15 | .07 |
| 754 | Larry Milbourne | .15 | .07 |
| 755 | Ken Singleton | .15 | .07 |
| 756 | Rob Picciolo | .15 | .07 |
| 757 | Willie McGee | .25 | .11 |
| 758 | Ray Burris | .15 | .07 |
| 759 | Jim Fanning MG | .15 | .07 |
| 760 | Nolan Ryan | 3.00 | 1.35 |
| 761 | Jerry Remy | .15 | .07 |
| 762 | Eddie Whitson | .15 | .07 |
| 763 | Kiko Garcia | .15 | .07 |
| 764 | Jamie Easterly | .15 | .07 |
| 765 | Willie Randolph | .25 | .11 |
| 766 | Paul Mirabella | .15 | .07 |
| 767 | Darrell Brown | .15 | .07 |
| 768 | Ron Cey | .25 | .11 |
| 769 | Joe Cowley | .15 | .07 |
| 770 | Carlton Fisk | .60 | .25 |
| 771 | Geoff Zahn | .15 | .07 |
| 772 | Johnnie LeMaster | .15 | .07 |
| 773 | Hal McRae | .25 | .11 |
| 774 | Dennis Lamp | .15 | .07 |
| 775 | Mookie Wilson | .25 | .11 |
| 776 | Jerry Royster | .15 | .07 |
| 777 | Ned Yost | .15 | .07 |
| 778 | Mike Davis | .15 | .07 |
| 779 | Nick Esasky | .15 | .07 |
| 780 | Mike Flanagan | .15 | .07 |
| 781 | Jim Gantner | .15 | .07 |
| 782 | Tom Niedenfuer | .15 | .07 |
| 783 | Mike Jorgensen | .15 | .07 |
| 784 | Checklist: 661-792 | .15 | .07 |
| 785 | Tony Armas | .15 | .07 |
| 786 | Enos Cabell | .15 | .07 |
| 787 | Jim Wohlford | .15 | .07 |
| 788 | Steve Comer | .15 | .07 |
| 789 | Luis Salazar | .15 | .07 |
| 790 | Ron Guidry | .25 | .11 |
| 791 | Ivan DeJesus | .15 | .07 |
| 792 | Darrell Evans | .25 | .11 |

## 1985 Topps Traded

| | NRMT | VG-E |
|---|---|---|
| COMP.FACT.SET (132) | 6.00 | 2.70 |

| No. | Player | NRMT | VG-E |
|---|---|---|---|
| 1T | Don Aase | .15 | .07 |
| 2T | Bill Almon | .15 | .07 |
| 3T | Benny Ayala | .15 | .07 |
| 4T | Dusty Baker | .40 | .18 |
| 5T | George Bamberger MG | .15 | .07 |
| 6T | Dale Berra | .15 | .07 |
| 7T | Rich Bordi | .15 | .07 |
| 8T | Daryl Boston XRC* | .15 | .07 |
| 9T | Hubie Brooks | .15 | .07 |
| 10T | Chris Brown | .15 | .07 |
| 11T | Tom Browning XRC* | .40 | .18 |
| 12T | Al Bumbry | .15 | .07 |
| 13T | Ray Burris | .15 | .07 |
| 14T | Jeff Burroughs | .15 | .07 |
| 15T | Bill Campbell | .15 | .07 |
| 16T | Don Carman | .15 | .07 |
| 17T | Gary Carter | .75 | .35 |
| 18T | Bobby Castillo | .15 | .07 |
| 19T | Bill Caudill | .15 | .07 |
| 20T | Rick Cerone | .15 | .07 |
| 21T | Bryan Clark | .15 | .07 |
| 22T | Jack Clark | .40 | .18 |
| 23T | Pat Clements | .15 | .07 |
| 24T | Vince Coleman XRC | 1.00 | .45 |
| 25T | Dave Collins | .15 | .07 |
| 26T | Danny Darwin | .15 | .07 |
| 27T | Jim Davenport MG | .15 | .07 |
| 28T | Jerry Davis | .15 | .07 |
| 29T | Brian Dayett | .15 | .07 |
| 30T | Ivan DeJesus | .15 | .07 |
| 31T | Ken Dixon | .15 | .07 |
| 32T | Mariano Duncan XRC | 1.00 | .45 |
| 33T | John Felske MG | .15 | .07 |
| 34T | Mike Fitzgerald | .15 | .07 |
| 35T | Ray Fontenot | .15 | .07 |
| 36T | Greg Gagne XRC* | .40 | .18 |
| 37T | Oscar Gamble | .15 | .07 |
| 38T | Scott Garrelts | .15 | .07 |
| 39T | Bob L. Gibson | .15 | .07 |
| 40T | Jim Gott | .15 | .07 |
| 41T | David Green | .15 | .07 |
| 42T | Alfredo Griffin | .15 | .07 |
| 43T | Ozzie Guillen XRC | 1.00 | .45 |
| 44T | Eddie Haas MG | .15 | .07 |
| 45T | Terry Harper | .15 | .07 |
| 46T | Toby Harrah | .15 | .07 |
| 47T | Greg Harris | .15 | .07 |
| 48T | Ron Hassey | .15 | .07 |
| 49T | Rickey Henderson | 2.00 | .90 |
| 50T | Steve Henderson | .15 | .07 |
| 51T | George Hendrick | .15 | .07 |
| 52T | Joe Hesketh | .15 | .07 |
| 53T | Teddy Higuera XRC | .40 | .18 |
| 54T | Donnie Hill | .15 | .07 |
| 55T | Al Holland | .15 | .07 |
| 56T | Burt Hooton | .15 | .07 |
| 57T | Jay Howell | .15 | .07 |
| 58T | Ken Howell | .15 | .07 |
| 59T | LaMarr Hoyt | .15 | .07 |
| 60T | Tim Hulett XRC* | .15 | .07 |
| 61T | Bob James | .15 | .07 |
| 62T | Steve Jeltz | .15 | .07 |
| 63T | Cliff Johnson | .15 | .07 |

❑ 64T Howard Johnson .40 .18
❑ 65T Ruppert Jones .15 .07
❑ 66T Steve Kemp .15 .07
❑ 67T Bruce Kison .15 .07
❑ 68T Alan Knicely .15 .07
❑ 69T Mike LaCoss .15 .07
❑ 70T Lee Lacy .15 .07
❑ 71T Dave LaPoint .15 .07
❑ 72T Gary Lavelle .15 .07
❑ 73T Vance Law .15 .07
❑ 74T Johnnie LeMaster .15 .07
❑ 75T Sixto Lezcano .15 .07
❑ 76T Tim Lollar .15 .07
❑ 77T Fred Lynn .40 .18
❑ 78T Billy Martin MG .40 .18
❑ 79T Ron Mathis .15 .07
❑ 80T Len Matuszek .15 .07
❑ 81T Gene Mauch MG .40 .18
❑ 82T Oddibe McDowell .40 .18
❑ 83T Roger McDowell XRC .40 .18
❑ 84T John McNamara MG .15 .07
❑ 85T Donnie Moore .15 .07
❑ 86T Gene Nelson .15 .07
❑ 87T Steve Nicosia .15 .07
❑ 88T Al Oliver .40 .18
❑ 89T Joe Orsulak XRC .40 .18
❑ 90T Rob Picciolo .15 .07
❑ 91T Chris Pittaro .15 .07
❑ 92T Jim Presley .40 .18
❑ 93T Rick Reuschel .15 .07
❑ 94T Bert Roberge .15 .07
❑ 95T Bob Rodgers MG .15 .07
❑ 96T Jerry Royster .15 .07
❑ 97T Dave Rozema .15 .07
❑ 98T Dave Rucker .15 .07
❑ 99T Vern Ruhle .15 .07
❑ 100T Paul Runge .15 .07
❑ 101T Mark Salas .15 .07
❑ 102T Luis Salazar .15 .07
❑ 103T Joe Sambito .15 .07
❑ 104T Rick Schu .15 .07
❑ 105T Donnie Scott .15 .07
❑ 106T Larry Sheets .15 .07
❑ 107T Don Slaught .15 .07
❑ 108T Roy Smalley .15 .07
❑ 109T Lonnie Smith .15 .07
❑ 110T Nate Snell UER .15 .07
(Headings on back for a batter)
❑ 111T Chris Speier .15 .07
❑ 112T Mike Stenhouse .15 .07
❑ 113T Tim Stoddard .15 .07
❑ 114T Jim Sundberg .15 .07
❑ 115T Bruce Sutter .40 .18
❑ 116T Don Sutton 1.00 .45
❑ 117T Kent Tekulve .15 .07
❑ 118T Tom Tellmann .15 .07
❑ 119T Walt Terrell .15 .07
❑ 120T Mickey Tettleton XRC 1.00 .45
❑ 121T Derrel Thomas .15 .07
❑ 122T Rich Thompson .15 .07
❑ 123T Alex Trevino .15 .07
❑ 124T John Tudor .15 .07
❑ 125T Jose Uribe .15 .07
❑ 126T Bobby Valentine MG .15 .07
❑ 127T Dave Von Ohlen .15 .07
❑ 128T U.L. Washington .15 .07
❑ 129T Earl Weaver MG .75 .35
❑ 130T Eddie Whitson .15 .07
❑ 131T Herm Winningham .15 .07
❑ 132T Checklist 1-132 .15 .07

## 1986 Topps

| | MINT | NRMT |
|---|---|---|
| COMPLETE SET (792) | 25.00 | 11.00 |
| COMP.FACT.SET (792) | 40.00 | 18.00 |

❑ 1 Pete Rose 1.25 .55
❑ 2 Rose Special: '63-'66 .25 .11
❑ 3 Rose Special: '67-'70 .25 .11
❑ 4 Rose Special: '71-'74 .25 .11
❑ 5 Rose Special: '75-'78 .25 .11
❑ 6 Rose Special: '79-'82 .25 .11
❑ 7 Rose Special: '83-'85 .25 .11
❑ 8 Dwayne Murphy .10 .05
❑ 9 Roy Smith .10 .05
❑ 10 Tony Gwynn .75 .35
❑ 11 Bob Ojeda .10 .05
❑ 12 Jose Uribe .10 .05
❑ 13 Bob Kearney .10 .05
❑ 14 Julio Cruz .10 .05
❑ 15 Eddie Whitson .10 .05
❑ 16 Rick Schu .10 .05
❑ 17 Mike Stenhouse .10 .05
❑ 18 Brent Gaff .10 .05
❑ 19 Rich Hebner .10 .05
❑ 20 Lou Whitaker .15 .07
❑ 21 George Bamberger MG .10 .05
❑ 22 Duane Walker .10 .05
❑ 23 Manny Lee RC* .10 .05
❑ 24 Len Barker .10 .05
❑ 25 Willie Wilson .10 .05
❑ 26 Frank DiPino .10 .05
❑ 27 Ray Knight .15 .07
❑ 28 Eric Davis .25 .11
❑ 29 Tony Phillips .10 .05
❑ 30 Eddie Murray .40 .18
❑ 31 Jamie Easterly .10 .05
❑ 32 Steve Yeager .10 .05
❑ 33 Jeff Lahti .10 .05
❑ 34 Ken Phelps .10 .05
❑ 35 Jeff Reardon .10 .05
❑ 36 Lance Parrish TL .15 .07
❑ 37 Mark Thurmond .10 .05
❑ 38 Glenn Hoffman .10 .05
❑ 39 Dave Rucker .10 .05
❑ 40 Ken Griffey .15 .07
❑ 41 Brad Wellman .10 .05
❑ 42 Geoff Zahn .10 .05
❑ 43 Dave Engle .10 .05
❑ 44 Lance McCullers .10 .05
❑ 45 Damaso Garcia .10 .05
❑ 46 Billy Hatcher .10 .05
❑ 47 Juan Berenguer .10 .05
❑ 48 Bill Almon .10 .05
❑ 49 Rick Manning .10 .05
❑ 50 Dan Quisenberry .10 .05
❑ 51 Bobby Wine MG ERR .10 .05
(Number of card on back is actually 57)
❑ 52 Chris Welsh .10 .05
❑ 53 Len Dykstra RC .75 .35
❑ 54 John Franco .40 .18
❑ 55 Fred Lynn .15 .07
❑ 56 Tom Niedenfuer .10 .05
❑ 57 Bill Doran .10 .05
(See also 51)
❑ 58 Bill Krueger .10 .05
❑ 59 Andre Thornton .10 .05
❑ 60 Dwight Evans .15 .07
❑ 61 Karl Best .10 .05
❑ 62 Bob Boone .15 .07
❑ 63 Ron Roenicke .10 .05
❑ 64 Floyd Bannister .10 .05
❑ 65 Dan Driessen .10 .05
❑ 66 Bob Forsch TL .10 .05
❑ 67 Carmelo Martinez .10 .05
❑ 68 Ed Lynch .10 .05
❑ 69 Luis Aguayo .10 .05
❑ 70 Dave Winfield .40 .18
❑ 71 Ken Schrom .10 .05
❑ 72 Shawon Dunston .15 .07
❑ 73 Randy O'Neal .10 .05
❑ 74 Rance Mulliniks .10 .05
❑ 75 Jose DeLeon .10 .05
❑ 76 Dion James .10 .05
❑ 77 Charlie Leibrandt .10 .05
❑ 78 Bruce Benedict .10 .05
❑ 79 Dave Schmidt .10 .05
❑ 80 Darryl Strawberry .40 .18
❑ 81 Gene Mauch MG .15 .07
❑ 82 Tippy Martinez .10 .05
❑ 83 Phil Garner .15 .07
❑ 84 Curt Young .10 .05
❑ 85 Tony Perez .40 .18
(Eric Davis also shown on card)
❑ 86 Tom Waddell .10 .05
❑ 87 Candy Maldonado .10 .05
❑ 88 Tom Nieto .10 .05
❑ 89 Randy St.Claire .10 .05
❑ 90 Garry Templeton .10 .05
❑ 91 Steve Crawford .10 .05
❑ 92 Al Cowens .10 .05
❑ 93 Scot Thompson .10 .05
❑ 94 Rich Bordi .10 .05
❑ 95 Ozzie Virgil .10 .05
❑ 96 Jim Clancy TL .10 .05
❑ 97 Gary Gaetti .15 .07
❑ 98 Dick Ruthven .10 .05
❑ 99 Buddy Biancalana .10 .05
❑ 100 Nolan Ryan 2.00 .90
❑ 101 Dave Bergman .10 .05
❑ 102 Joe Orsulak RC* .10 .05
❑ 103 Luis Salazar .10 .05
❑ 104 Sid Fernandez .15 .07
❑ 105 Gary Ward .10 .05
❑ 106 Ray Burris .10 .05
❑ 107 Rafael Ramirez .10 .05
❑ 108 Ted Power .10 .05
❑ 109 Len Matuszek .10 .05
❑ 110 Scott McGregor .10 .05
❑ 111 Roger Craig MG .15 .07
❑ 112 Bill Campbell .10 .05
❑ 113 U.L. Washington .10 .05
❑ 114 Mike C. Brown .10 .05
❑ 115 Jay Howell .10 .05
❑ 116 Brook Jacoby .10 .05
❑ 117 Bruce Kison .10 .05
❑ 118 Jerry Royster .10 .05
❑ 119 Barry Bonnell .10 .05
❑ 120 Steve Carlton .40 .18
❑ 121 Nelson Simmons .10 .05
❑ 122 Pete Filson .10 .05
❑ 123 Greg Walker .10 .05
❑ 124 Luis Sanchez .10 .05
❑ 125 Dave Lopes .15 .07
❑ 126 Mookie Wilson TL .10 .05
❑ 127 Jack Howell .10 .05
❑ 128 John Wathan .10 .05
❑ 129 Jeff Dedmon .10 .05
❑ 130 Alan Trammell .25 .11
❑ 131 Checklist: 1-132 .15 .07
❑ 132 Razor Shines .10 .05
❑ 133 Andy McGaffigan .10 .05
❑ 134 Carney Lansford .15 .07
❑ 135 Joe Niekro .10 .05
❑ 136 Mike Hargrove .15 .07
❑ 137 Charlie Moore .10 .05
❑ 138 Mark Davis .10 .05
❑ 139 Daryl Boston .10 .05
❑ 140 John Candelaria .10 .05
❑ 141 Chuck Cottier MG .10 .05
(See also 171)
❑ 142 Bob Jones .10 .05
❑ 143 Dave Van Gorder .10 .05
❑ 144 Doug Sisk .10 .05
❑ 145 Pedro Guerrero .15 .07
❑ 146 Jack Perconte .10 .05
❑ 147 Larry Sheets .10 .05
❑ 148 Mike Heath .10 .05
❑ 149 Brett Butler .15 .07
❑ 150 Joaquin Andujar .10 .05
❑ 151 Dave Stapleton .10 .05
❑ 152 Mike Morgan .10 .05
❑ 153 Ricky Adams .10 .05
❑ 154 Bert Roberge .10 .05
❑ 155 Bobby Grich .15 .07
❑ 156 Richard Dotson TL .10 .05

| ❑ | Card | | |
|---|---|---|---|
| ❑ | 157 Ron Hassey | .10 | .05 |
| ❑ | 158 Derrel Thomas | .10 | .05 |
| ❑ | 159 Orel Hershiser UER | .40 | .18 |
| | (82 Alburquerque) | | |
| ❑ | 160 Chet Lemon | .10 | .05 |
| ❑ | 161 Lee Tunnell | .10 | .05 |
| ❑ | 162 Greg Gagne | .10 | .05 |
| ❑ | 163 Pete Ladd | .10 | .05 |
| ❑ | 164 Steve Balboni | .10 | .05 |
| ❑ | 165 Mike Davis | .10 | .05 |
| ❑ | 166 Dickie Thon | .10 | .05 |
| ❑ | 167 Zane Smith | .10 | .05 |
| ❑ | 168 Jeff Burroughs | .10 | .05 |
| ❑ | 169 George Wright | .10 | .05 |
| ❑ | 170 Gary Carter | .25 | .11 |
| ❑ | 171 Bob Rodgers MG ERR | .10 | .05 |
| | Number of card on back actually 141) | | |
| ❑ | 172 Jerry Reed | .10 | .05 |
| ❑ | 173 Wayne Gross | .10 | .05 |
| ❑ | 174 Brian Snyder | .10 | .05 |
| ❑ | 175 Steve Sax | .10 | .05 |
| ❑ | 176 Jay Tibbs | .10 | .05 |
| ❑ | 177 Joel Youngblood | .10 | .05 |
| ❑ | 178 Ivan DeJesus | .10 | .05 |
| ❑ | 179 Stu Cliburn | .10 | .05 |
| ❑ | 180 Don Mattingly | 1.00 | .45 |
| ❑ | 181 Al Nipper | .10 | .05 |
| ❑ | 182 Bobby Brown | .10 | .05 |
| ❑ | 183 Larry Andersen | .10 | .05 |
| ❑ | 184 Tim Laudner | .10 | .05 |
| ❑ | 185 Rollie Fingers | .40 | .18 |
| ❑ | 186 Jose Cruz TL | .10 | .05 |
| ❑ | 187 Scott Fletcher | .10 | .05 |
| ❑ | 188 Bob Dernier | .10 | .05 |
| ❑ | 189 Mike Mason | .10 | .05 |
| ❑ | 190 George Hendrick | .10 | .05 |
| ❑ | 191 Wally Backman | .10 | .05 |
| ❑ | 192 Milt Wilcox | .10 | .05 |
| ❑ | 193 Daryl Sconiers | .10 | .05 |
| ❑ | 194 Craig McMurtry | .10 | .05 |
| ❑ | 195 Dave Concepcion | .15 | .07 |
| ❑ | 196 Doyle Alexander | .10 | .05 |
| ❑ | 197 Enos Cabell | .10 | .05 |
| ❑ | 198 Ken Dixon | .10 | .05 |
| ❑ | 199 Dick Howser MG | .15 | .07 |
| ❑ | 200 Mike Schmidt | .75 | .35 |
| ❑ | 201 Vince Coleman RB | .15 | .07 |
| | Most SB's rookie season | | |
| ❑ | 202 Dwight Gooden RB | .15 | .07 |
| | Youngest 20 game winner | | |
| ❑ | 203 Keith Hernandez RB | .10 | .05 |
| | Most game-winning RBI's | | |
| ❑ | 204 Phil Niekro RB | .15 | .07 |
| | Oldest shutout pitcher | | |
| ❑ | 205 Tony Perez RB | .15 | .07 |
| | Oldest grand slammer | | |
| ❑ | 206 Pete Rose RB | .40 | .18 |
| | Most lifetime hits | | |
| ❑ | 207 Fernando Valenzuela RB | .15 | .07 |
| | Most cons. innings start of season, no earned runs | | |
| ❑ | 208 Ramon Romero | .10 | .05 |
| ❑ | 209 Randy Ready | .10 | .05 |
| ❑ | 210 Calvin Schiraldi | .10 | .05 |
| ❑ | 211 Ed Wojna | .10 | .05 |
| ❑ | 212 Chris Speier | .10 | .05 |
| ❑ | 213 Bob Shirley | .10 | .05 |
| ❑ | 214 Randy Bush | .10 | .05 |
| ❑ | 215 Frank White | .15 | .07 |
| ❑ | 216 Dwayne Murphy TL | .10 | .05 |
| ❑ | 217 Bill Scherrer | .10 | .05 |
| ❑ | 218 Randy Hunt | .10 | .05 |
| ❑ | 219 Dennis Lamp | .10 | .05 |
| ❑ | 220 Bob Horner | .10 | .05 |
| ❑ | 221 Dave Henderson | .10 | .05 |
| ❑ | 222 Craig Gerber | .10 | .05 |
| ❑ | 223 Atlee Hammaker | .10 | .05 |
| ❑ | 224 Cesar Cedeno | .15 | .07 |
| ❑ | 225 Ron Darling | .10 | .05 |
| ❑ | 226 Lee Lacy | .10 | .05 |
| ❑ | 227 Al Jones | .10 | .05 |
| ❑ | 228 Tom Lawless | .10 | .05 |
| ❑ | 229 Bill Gullickson | .10 | .05 |
| ❑ | 230 Terry Kennedy | .10 | .05 |
| ❑ | 231 Jim Frey MG | .10 | .05 |
| ❑ | 232 Rick Rhoden | .10 | .05 |
| ❑ | 233 Steve Lyons | .10 | .05 |
| ❑ | 234 Doug Corbett | .10 | .05 |
| ❑ | 235 Butch Wynegar | .10 | .05 |
| ❑ | 236 Frank Eufemia | .10 | .05 |
| ❑ | 237 Ted Simmons | .15 | .07 |
| ❑ | 238 Larry Parrish | .10 | .05 |
| ❑ | 239 Joel Skinner | .10 | .05 |
| ❑ | 240 Tommy John | .40 | .18 |
| ❑ | 241 Tony Fernandez | .10 | .05 |
| ❑ | 242 Rich Thompson | .10 | .05 |
| ❑ | 243 Johnny Grubb | .10 | .05 |
| ❑ | 244 Craig Lefferts | .10 | .05 |
| ❑ | 245 Jim Sundberg | .10 | .05 |
| ❑ | 246 Steve Carlton TL | .15 | .07 |
| ❑ | 247 Terry Harper | .10 | .05 |
| ❑ | 248 Spike Owen | .10 | .05 |
| ❑ | 249 Rob Deer | .15 | .07 |
| ❑ | 250 Dwight Gooden | .40 | .18 |
| ❑ | 251 Rich Dauer | .10 | .05 |
| ❑ | 252 Bobby Castillo | .10 | .05 |
| ❑ | 253 Dann Bilardello | .10 | .05 |
| ❑ | 254 Ozzie Guillen RC* | .25 | .11 |
| ❑ | 255 Tony Armas | .10 | .05 |
| ❑ | 256 Kurt Kepshire | .10 | .05 |
| ❑ | 257 Doug DeCinces | .10 | .05 |
| ❑ | 258 Tim Burke | .10 | .05 |
| ❑ | 259 Dan Pasqua | .10 | .05 |
| ❑ | 260 Tony Pena | .10 | .05 |
| ❑ | 261 Bobby Valentine MG | .15 | .07 |
| ❑ | 262 Mario Ramirez | .10 | .05 |
| ❑ | 263 Checklist: 133-264 | .15 | .07 |
| ❑ | 264 Darren Daulton RC | .75 | .35 |
| ❑ | 265 Ron Davis | .10 | .05 |
| ❑ | 266 Keith Moreland | .10 | .05 |
| ❑ | 267 Paul Molitor | .40 | .18 |
| ❑ | 268 Mike Scott | .10 | .05 |
| ❑ | 269 Dane Iorg | .10 | .05 |
| ❑ | 270 Jack Morris | .15 | .07 |
| ❑ | 271 Dave Collins | .10 | .05 |
| ❑ | 272 Tim Tolman | .10 | .05 |
| ❑ | 273 Jerry Willard | .10 | .05 |
| ❑ | 274 Ron Gardenhire | .10 | .05 |
| ❑ | 275 Charlie Hough | .15 | .07 |
| ❑ | 276 Willie Randolph TL | .15 | .07 |
| ❑ | 277 Jaime Cocanower | .10 | .05 |
| ❑ | 278 Sixto Lezcano | .10 | .05 |
| ❑ | 279 Al Pardo | .10 | .05 |
| ❑ | 280 Tim Raines | .15 | .07 |
| ❑ | 281 Steve Mura | .10 | .05 |
| ❑ | 282 Jerry Mumphrey | .10 | .05 |
| ❑ | 283 Mike Fischlin | .10 | .05 |
| ❑ | 284 Brian Dayett | .10 | .05 |
| ❑ | 285 Buddy Bell | .15 | .07 |
| ❑ | 286 Luis DeLeon | .10 | .05 |
| ❑ | 287 John Christensen | .10 | .05 |
| ❑ | 288 Don Aase | .10 | .05 |
| ❑ | 289 Johnnie LeMaster | .10 | .05 |
| ❑ | 290 Carlton Fisk | .40 | .18 |
| ❑ | 291 Tom Lasorda MG | .25 | .11 |
| ❑ | 292 Chuck Porter | .10 | .05 |
| ❑ | 293 Chris Chambliss | .15 | .07 |
| ❑ | 294 Danny Cox | .10 | .05 |
| ❑ | 295 Kirk Gibson | .15 | .07 |
| ❑ | 296 Geno Petralli | .10 | .05 |
| ❑ | 297 Tim Lollar | .10 | .05 |
| ❑ | 298 Craig Reynolds | .10 | .05 |
| ❑ | 299 Bryn Smith | .10 | .05 |
| ❑ | 300 George Brett | .75 | .35 |
| ❑ | 301 Dennis Rasmussen | .10 | .05 |
| ❑ | 302 Greg Gross | .10 | .05 |
| ❑ | 303 Curt Wardle | .10 | .05 |
| ❑ | 304 Mike Gallego RC | .15 | .07 |
| ❑ | 305 Phil Bradley | .10 | .05 |
| ❑ | 306 Terry Kennedy TL | .10 | .05 |
| ❑ | 307 Dave Sax | .10 | .05 |
| ❑ | 308 Ray Fontenot | .10 | .05 |
| ❑ | 309 John Shelby | .10 | .05 |
| ❑ | 310 Greg Minton | .10 | .05 |
| ❑ | 311 Dick Schofield | .10 | .05 |
| ❑ | 312 Tom Filer | .10 | .05 |
| ❑ | 313 Joe DeSa | .10 | .05 |
| ❑ | 314 Frank Pastore | .10 | .05 |
| ❑ | 315 Mookie Wilson | .15 | .07 |
| ❑ | 316 Sammy Khalifa | .10 | .05 |
| ❑ | 317 Ed Romero | .10 | .05 |
| ❑ | 318 Terry Whitfield | .10 | .05 |
| ❑ | 319 Rick Camp | .10 | .05 |
| ❑ | 320 Jim Rice | .15 | .07 |
| ❑ | 321 Earl Weaver MG | .40 | .18 |
| ❑ | 322 Bob Forsch | .10 | .05 |
| ❑ | 323 Jerry Davis | .10 | .05 |
| ❑ | 324 Dan Schatzeder | .10 | .05 |
| ❑ | 325 Juan Beniquez | .10 | .05 |
| ❑ | 326 Kent Tekulve | .10 | .05 |
| ❑ | 327 Mike Pagliarulo | .10 | .05 |
| ❑ | 328 Pete O'Brien | .10 | .05 |
| ❑ | 329 Kirby Puckett | 1.25 | .55 |
| ❑ | 330 Rick Sutcliffe | .15 | .07 |
| ❑ | 331 Alan Ashby | .10 | .05 |
| ❑ | 332 Darryl Motley | .10 | .05 |
| ❑ | 333 Tom Henke | .15 | .07 |
| ❑ | 334 Ken Oberkfell | .10 | .05 |
| ❑ | 335 Don Sutton | .40 | .18 |
| ❑ | 336 Andre Thornton TL | .15 | .07 |
| ❑ | 337 Darnell Coles | .10 | .05 |
| ❑ | 338 Jorge Bell | .15 | .07 |
| ❑ | 339 Bruce Berenyi | .10 | .05 |
| ❑ | 340 Cal Ripken | 1.50 | .70 |
| ❑ | 341 Frank Williams | .10 | .05 |
| ❑ | 342 Gary Redus | .10 | .05 |
| ❑ | 343 Carlos Diaz | .10 | .05 |
| ❑ | 344 Jim Wohlford | .10 | .05 |
| ❑ | 345 Donnie Moore | .10 | .05 |
| ❑ | 346 Bryan Little | .10 | .05 |
| ❑ | 347 Teddy Higuera RC* | .15 | .07 |
| ❑ | 348 Cliff Johnson | .10 | .05 |
| ❑ | 349 Mark Clear | .10 | .05 |
| ❑ | 350 Jack Clark | .15 | .07 |
| ❑ | 351 Chuck Tanner MG | .10 | .05 |
| ❑ | 352 Harry Spilman | .10 | .05 |
| ❑ | 353 Keith Atherton | .10 | .05 |
| ❑ | 354 Tony Bernazard | .10 | .05 |
| ❑ | 355 Lee Smith | .25 | .11 |
| ❑ | 356 Mickey Hatcher | .10 | .05 |
| ❑ | 357 Ed VandeBerg | .10 | .05 |
| ❑ | 358 Rick Dempsey | .10 | .05 |
| ❑ | 359 Mike LaCoss | .10 | .05 |
| ❑ | 360 Lloyd Moseby | .10 | .05 |
| ❑ | 361 Shane Rawley | .10 | .05 |
| ❑ | 362 Tom Paciorek | .15 | .07 |
| ❑ | 363 Terry Forster | .10 | .05 |
| ❑ | 364 Reid Nichols | .10 | .05 |
| ❑ | 365 Mike Flanagan | .10 | .05 |
| ❑ | 366 Dave Concepcion TL | .15 | .07 |
| ❑ | 367 Aurelio Lopez | .10 | .05 |
| ❑ | 368 Greg Brock | .10 | .05 |
| ❑ | 369 Al Holland | .10 | .05 |
| ❑ | 370 Vince Coleman RC* | .40 | .18 |
| ❑ | 371 Bill Stein | .10 | .05 |
| ❑ | 372 Ben Oglivie | .10 | .05 |
| ❑ | 373 Urbano Lugo | .10 | .05 |
| ❑ | 374 Terry Francona | .10 | .05 |
| ❑ | 375 Rich Gedman | .10 | .05 |
| ❑ | 376 Bill Dawley | .10 | .05 |
| ❑ | 377 Joe Carter | .40 | .18 |
| ❑ | 378 Bruce Bochte | .10 | .05 |
| ❑ | 379 Bobby Meacham | .10 | .05 |
| ❑ | 380 LaMarr Hoyt | .10 | .05 |
| ❑ | 381 Ray Miller MG | .10 | .05 |
| ❑ | 382 Ivan Calderon RC* | .15 | .07 |
| ❑ | 383 Chris Brown | .10 | .05 |
| ❑ | 384 Steve Trout | .10 | .05 |
| ❑ | 385 Cecil Cooper | .15 | .07 |
| ❑ | 386 Cecil Fielder RC | .75 | .35 |
| ❑ | 387 Steve Kemp | .10 | .05 |
| ❑ | 388 Dickie Noles | .10 | .05 |
| ❑ | 389 Glenn Davis | .15 | .07 |
| ❑ | 390 Tom Seaver | .60 | .25 |
| ❑ | 391 Julio Franco | .15 | .07 |
| ❑ | 392 John Russell | .10 | .05 |
| ❑ | 393 Chris Pittaro | .10 | .05 |
| ❑ | 394 Checklist: 265-396 | .15 | .07 |
| ❑ | 395 Scott Garrelts | .10 | .05 |
| ❑ | 396 Dwight Evans TL | .15 | .07 |
| ❑ | 397 Steve Buechele RC | .15 | .07 |
| ❑ | 398 Earnie Riles | .10 | .05 |
| ❑ | 399 Bill Swift | .10 | .05 |
| ❑ | 400 Rod Carew | .40 | .18 |
| ❑ | 401 Fernando Valenzuela | .15 | .07 |

TBC '81
❑ 402 Tom Seaver TBC '76 .15 .07
❑ 403 Willie Mays TBC '71 .25 .11
❑ 404 Frank Robinson .15 .07
TBC '66
❑ 405 Roger Maris TBC '61 .15 .07
❑ 406 Scott Sanderson .10 .05
❑ 407 Sal Butera .10 .05
❑ 408 Dave Smith .10 .05
❑ 409 Paul Runge .10 .05
❑ 410 Dave Kingman .15 .07
❑ 411 Sparky Anderson MG .25 .11
❑ 412 Jim Clancy .10 .05
❑ 413 Tim Flannery .10 .05
❑ 414 Tom Gorman .10 .05
❑ 415 Hal McRae .15 .07
❑ 416 Dennis Martinez .15 .07
❑ 417 R.J. Reynolds .10 .05
❑ 418 Alan Knicely .10 .05
❑ 419 Frank Wills .10 .05
❑ 420 Von Hayes .10 .05
❑ 421 David Palmer .10 .05
❑ 422 Mike Jorgensen .10 .05
❑ 423 Dan Spillner .10 .05
❑ 424 Rick Miller .10 .05
❑ 425 Larry McWilliams .10 .05
❑ 426 Charlie Moore TL .10 .05
❑ 427 Joe Cowley .10 .05
❑ 428 Max Venable .10 .05
❑ 429 Greg Booker .10 .05
❑ 430 Kent Hrbek .15 .07
❑ 431 George Frazier .10 .05
❑ 432 Mark Bailey .10 .05
❑ 433 Chris Codiroli .10 .05
❑ 434 Curt Wilkerson .10 .05
❑ 435 Bill Caudill .10 .05
❑ 436 Doug Flynn .10 .05
❑ 437 Rick Mahler .10 .05
❑ 438 Clint Hurdle .10 .05
❑ 439 Rick Honeycutt .10 .05
❑ 440 Alvin Davis .10 .05
❑ 441 Whitey Herzog MG .25 .11
❑ 442 Ron Robinson .10 .05
❑ 443 Bill Buckner .15 .07
❑ 444 Alex Trevino .10 .05
❑ 445 Bert Blyleven .15 .07
❑ 446 Lenn Sakata .10 .05
❑ 447 Jerry Don Gleaton .10 .05
❑ 448 Herm Winningham .10 .05
❑ 449 Rod Scurry .10 .05
❑ 450 Graig Nettles .15 .07
❑ 451 Mark Brown .10 .05
❑ 452 Bob Clark .10 .05
❑ 453 Steve Jeltz .10 .05
❑ 454 Burt Hooton .10 .05
❑ 455 Willie Randolph .15 .07
❑ 456 Dale Murphy TL .15 .07
❑ 457 Mickey Tettleton RC .15 .07
❑ 458 Kevin Bass .10 .05
❑ 459 Luis Leal .10 .05
❑ 460 Leon Durham .10 .05
❑ 461 Walt Terrell .10 .05
❑ 462 Domingo Ramos .10 .05
❑ 463 Jim Gott .10 .05
❑ 464 Ruppert Jones .10 .05
❑ 465 Jesse Orosco .10 .05
❑ 466 Tom Foley .10 .05
❑ 467 Bob James .10 .05
❑ 468 Mike Scioscia .10 .05
❑ 469 Storm Davis .10 .05
❑ 470 Bill Madlock .10 .05
❑ 471 Bobby Cox MG .15 .07
❑ 472 Joe Hesketh .10 .05
❑ 473 Mark Brouhard .10 .05
❑ 474 John Tudor .10 .05
❑ 475 Juan Samuel .10 .05
❑ 476 Ron Mathis .10 .05
❑ 477 Mike Easler .10 .05
❑ 478 Andy Hawkins .10 .05
❑ 479 Bob Melvin .10 .05
❑ 480 Oddibe McDowell .10 .05
❑ 481 Scott Bradley .10 .05
❑ 482 Rick Lysander .10 .05
❑ 483 George Vukovich .10 .05
❑ 484 Donnie Hill .10 .05
❑ 485 Gary Matthews .10 .05
❑ 486 Bobby Grich TL .10 .05
❑ 487 Bret Saberhagen .15 .07
❑ 488 Lou Thornton .10 .05
❑ 489 Jim Winn .10 .05
❑ 490 Jeff Leonard .10 .05
❑ 491 Pascual Perez .10 .05
❑ 492 Kelvin Chapman .10 .05
❑ 493 Gene Nelson .10 .05
❑ 494 Gary Roenicke .10 .05
❑ 495 Mark Langston .10 .05
❑ 496 Jay Johnstone .15 .07
❑ 497 John Stuper .10 .05
❑ 498 Tito Landrum .10 .05
❑ 499 Bob L. Gibson .10 .05
❑ 500 Rickey Henderson .50 .23
❑ 501 Dave Johnson MG .15 .07
❑ 502 Glen Cook .10 .05
❑ 503 Mike Fitzgerald .10 .05
❑ 504 Denny Walling .10 .05
❑ 505 Jerry Koosman .15 .07
❑ 506 Bill Russell .10 .05
❑ 507 Steve Ontiveros RC .15 .07
❑ 508 Alan Wiggins .10 .05
❑ 509 Ernie Camacho .10 .05
❑ 510 Wade Boggs .50 .23
❑ 511 Ed Nunez .10 .05
❑ 512 Thad Bosley .10 .05
❑ 513 Ron Washington .10 .05
❑ 514 Mike Jones .10 .05
❑ 515 Darrell Evans .15 .07
❑ 516 Greg Minton TL .10 .05
❑ 517 Milt Thompson RC .15 .07
❑ 518 Buck Martinez .10 .05
❑ 519 Danny Darwin .10 .05
❑ 520 Keith Hernandez .15 .07
❑ 521 Nate Snell .10 .05
❑ 522 Bob Bailor .10 .05
❑ 523 Joe Price .10 .05
❑ 524 Darrell Miller .10 .05
❑ 525 Marvell Wynne .10 .05
❑ 526 Charlie Lea .10 .05
❑ 527 Checklist: 397-528 .15 .07
❑ 528 Terry Pendleton .15 .07
❑ 529 Marc Sullivan .10 .05
❑ 530 Rich Gossage .15 .07
❑ 531 Tony LaRussa MG .15 .07
❑ 532 Don Carman .10 .05
❑ 533 Billy Sample .10 .05
❑ 534 Jeff Calhoun .10 .05
❑ 535 Toby Harrah .10 .05
❑ 536 Jose Rijo .10 .05
❑ 537 Mark Salas .10 .05
❑ 538 Dennis Eckersley .40 .18
❑ 539 Glenn Hubbard .10 .05
❑ 540 Dan Petry .10 .05
❑ 541 Jorge Orta .10 .05
❑ 542 Don Schulze .10 .05
❑ 543 Jerry Narron .10 .05
❑ 544 Eddie Milner .10 .05
❑ 545 Jimmy Key .40 .18
❑ 546 Dave Henderson TL .10 .05
❑ 547 Roger McDowell RC* .15 .07
❑ 548 Mike Young .10 .05
❑ 549 Bob Welch .10 .05
❑ 550 Tom Herr .10 .05
❑ 551 Dave LaPoint .10 .05
❑ 552 Marc Hill .10 .05
❑ 553 Jim Morrison .10 .05
❑ 554 Paul Householder .10 .05
❑ 555 Hubie Brooks .10 .05
❑ 556 John Denny .10 .05
❑ 557 Gerald Perry .10 .05
❑ 558 Tim Stoddard .10 .05
❑ 559 Tommy Dunbar .10 .05
❑ 560 Dave Righetti .10 .05
❑ 561 Bob Lillis MG .10 .05
❑ 562 Joe Beckwith .10 .05
❑ 563 Alejandro Sanchez .10 .05
❑ 564 Warren Brusstar .10 .05
❑ 565 Tom Brunansky .10 .05
❑ 566 Alfredo Griffin .10 .05
❑ 567 Jeff Barkley .10 .05
❑ 568 Donnie Scott .10 .05
❑ 569 Jim Acker .10 .05
❑ 570 Rusty Staub .15 .07
❑ 571 Mike Jeffcoat .10 .05
❑ 572 Paul Zuvella .10 .05
❑ 573 Tom Hume .10 .05
❑ 574 Ron Kittle .10 .05
❑ 575 Mike Boddicker .10 .05
❑ 576 Andre Dawson TL .15 .07
❑ 577 Jerry Reuss .10 .05
❑ 578 Lee Mazzilli .10 .05
❑ 579 Jim Slaton .10 .05
❑ 580 Willie McGee .15 .07
❑ 581 Bruce Hurst .10 .05
❑ 582 Jim Gantner .10 .05
❑ 583 Al Bumbry .10 .05
❑ 584 Brian Fisher .10 .05
❑ 585 Garry Maddox .10 .05
❑ 586 Greg Harris .10 .05
❑ 587 Rafael Santana .10 .05
❑ 588 Steve Lake .10 .05
❑ 589 Sid Bream .10 .05
❑ 590 Bob Knepper .10 .05
❑ 591 Jackie Moore MG .10 .05
❑ 592 Frank Tanana .10 .05
❑ 593 Jesse Barfield .10 .05
❑ 594 Chris Bando .10 .05
❑ 595 Dave Parker .15 .07
❑ 596 Onix Concepcion .10 .05
❑ 597 Sammy Stewart .10 .05
❑ 598 Jim Presley .10 .05
❑ 599 Rick Aguilera RC .40 .18
❑ 600 Dale Murphy .40 .18
❑ 601 Gary Lucas .10 .05
❑ 602 Mariano Duncan RC* .40 .18
❑ 603 Bill Laskey .10 .05
❑ 604 Gary Pettis .10 .05
❑ 605 Dennis Boyd .10 .05
❑ 606 Hal McRae TL .15 .07
❑ 607 Ken Dayley .10 .05
❑ 608 Bruce Bochy .10 .05
❑ 609 Barbaro Garbey .10 .05
❑ 610 Ron Guidry .15 .07
❑ 611 Gary Woods .10 .05
❑ 612 Richard Dotson .10 .05
❑ 613 Roy Smalley .10 .05
❑ 614 Rick Waits .10 .05
❑ 615 Johnny Ray .10 .05
❑ 616 Glenn Brummer .10 .05
❑ 617 Lonnie Smith .10 .05
❑ 618 Jim Pankovits .10 .05
❑ 619 Danny Heep .10 .05
❑ 620 Bruce Sutter .15 .07
❑ 621 John Felske MG .10 .05
❑ 622 Gary Lavelle .10 .05
❑ 623 Floyd Rayford .10 .05
❑ 624 Steve McCatty .10 .05
❑ 625 Bob Brenly .10 .05
❑ 626 Roy Thomas .10 .05
❑ 627 Ron Oester .10 .05
❑ 628 Kirk McCaskill RC .15 .07
❑ 629 Mitch Webster .10 .05
❑ 630 Fernando Valenzuela .15 .07
❑ 631 Steve Braun .10 .05
❑ 632 Dave Von Ohlen .10 .05
❑ 633 Jackie Gutierrez .10 .05
❑ 634 Roy Lee Jackson .10 .05
❑ 635 Jason Thompson .10 .05
❑ 636 Lee Smith TL .15 .07
❑ 637 Rudy Law .10 .05
❑ 638 John Butcher .10 .05
❑ 639 Bo Diaz .10 .05
❑ 640 Jose Cruz .15 .07
❑ 641 Wayne Tolleson .10 .05
❑ 642 Ray Searage .10 .05
❑ 643 Tom Brookens .10 .05
❑ 644 Mark Gubicza .10 .05
❑ 645 Dusty Baker .15 .07
❑ 646 Mike Moore .10 .05
❑ 647 Mel Hall .10 .05
❑ 648 Steve Bedrosian .10 .05
❑ 649 Ronn Reynolds .10 .05
❑ 650 Dave Stieb .10 .05
❑ 651 Billy Martin MG .15 .07
❑ 652 Tom Browning .10 .05
❑ 653 Jim Dwyer .10 .05
❑ 654 Ken Howell .10 .05
❑ 655 Manny Trillo .10 .05
❑ 656 Brian Harper .10 .05
❑ 657 Juan Agosto .10 .05

| No. | Player | MINT | NRMT |
|---|---|---|---|
| ❑ 658 | Rob Wilfong | .10 | .05 |
| ❑ 659 | Checklist: 529-660 | .15 | .07 |
| ❑ 660 | Steve Garvey | .25 | .11 |
| ❑ 661 | Roger Clemens | 1.50 | .70 |
| ❑ 662 | Bill Schroeder | .10 | .05 |
| ❑ 663 | Neil Allen | .10 | .05 |
| ❑ 664 | Tim Corcoran | .10 | .05 |
| ❑ 665 | Alejandro Pena | .10 | .05 |
| ❑ 666 | Charlie Hough TL | .15 | .07 |
| ❑ 667 | Tim Teufel | .10 | .05 |
| ❑ 668 | Cecilio Guante | .10 | .05 |
| ❑ 669 | Ron Cey | .15 | .07 |
| ❑ 670 | Willie Hernandez | .10 | .05 |
| ❑ 671 | Lynn Jones | .10 | .05 |
| ❑ 672 | Rob Picciolo | .10 | .05 |
| ❑ 673 | Ernie Whitt | .10 | .05 |
| ❑ 674 | Pat Tabler | .10 | .05 |
| ❑ 675 | Claudell Washington | .10 | .05 |
| ❑ 676 | Matt Young | .10 | .05 |
| ❑ 677 | Nick Esasky | .10 | .05 |
| ❑ 678 | Dan Gladden | .10 | .05 |
| ❑ 679 | Britt Burns | .10 | .05 |
| ❑ 680 | George Foster | .15 | .07 |
| ❑ 681 | Dick Williams MG | .15 | .07 |
| ❑ 682 | Junior Ortiz | .10 | .05 |
| ❑ 683 | Andy Van Slyke | .15 | .07 |
| ❑ 684 | Bob McClure | .10 | .05 |
| ❑ 685 | Tim Wallach | .10 | .05 |
| ❑ 686 | Jeff Stone | .10 | .05 |
| ❑ 687 | Mike Trujillo | .10 | .05 |
| ❑ 688 | Larry Herndon | .10 | .05 |
| ❑ 689 | Dave Stewart | .15 | .07 |
| ❑ 690 | Ryne Sandberg UER (No Topps logo on front) | .50 | .23 |
| ❑ 691 | Mike Madden | .10 | .05 |
| ❑ 692 | Dale Berra | .10 | .05 |
| ❑ 693 | Tom Tellmann | .10 | .05 |
| ❑ 694 | Garth Iorg | .10 | .05 |
| ❑ 695 | Mike Smithson | .10 | .05 |
| ❑ 696 | Bill Russell TL | .15 | .07 |
| ❑ 697 | Bud Black | .10 | .05 |
| ❑ 698 | Brad Komminsk | .10 | .05 |
| ❑ 699 | Pat Corrales MG | .10 | .05 |
| ❑ 700 | Reggie Jackson | .50 | .23 |
| ❑ 701 | Keith Hernandez AS | .10 | .05 |
| ❑ 702 | Tom Herr AS | .10 | .05 |
| ❑ 703 | Tim Wallach AS | .10 | .05 |
| ❑ 704 | Ozzie Smith AS | .25 | .11 |
| ❑ 705 | Dale Murphy AS | .15 | .07 |
| ❑ 706 | Pedro Guerrero AS | .10 | .05 |
| ❑ 707 | Willie McGee AS | .10 | .05 |
| ❑ 708 | Gary Carter AS | .15 | .07 |
| ❑ 709 | Dwight Gooden AS | .15 | .07 |
| ❑ 710 | John Tudor AS | .10 | .05 |
| ❑ 711 | Jeff Reardon AS | .10 | .05 |
| ❑ 712 | Don Mattingly AS | .40 | .18 |
| ❑ 713 | Damaso Garcia AS | .10 | .05 |
| ❑ 714 | George Brett AS | .40 | .18 |
| ❑ 715 | Cal Ripken AS | .40 | .18 |
| ❑ 716 | Rickey Henderson AS | .15 | .07 |
| ❑ 717 | Dave Winfield AS | .15 | .07 |
| ❑ 718 | George Bell AS | .10 | .05 |
| ❑ 719 | Carlton Fisk AS | .15 | .07 |
| ❑ 720 | Bret Saberhagen AS | .10 | .05 |
| ❑ 721 | Ron Guidry AS | .15 | .07 |
| ❑ 722 | Dan Quisenberry AS | .10 | .05 |
| ❑ 723 | Marty Bystrom | .10 | .05 |
| ❑ 724 | Tim Hulett | .10 | .05 |
| ❑ 725 | Mario Soto | .10 | .05 |
| ❑ 726 | Rick Dempsey TL | .15 | .07 |
| ❑ 727 | David Green | .10 | .05 |
| ❑ 728 | Mike Marshall | .10 | .05 |
| ❑ 729 | Jim Beattie | .10 | .05 |
| ❑ 730 | Ozzie Smith | .50 | .23 |
| ❑ 731 | Don Robinson | .10 | .05 |
| ❑ 732 | Floyd Youmans | .10 | .05 |
| ❑ 733 | Ron Romanick | .10 | .05 |
| ❑ 734 | Marty Barrett | .10 | .05 |
| ❑ 735 | Dave Dravecky | .15 | .07 |
| ❑ 736 | Glenn Wilson | .10 | .05 |
| ❑ 737 | Pete Vuckovich | .10 | .05 |
| ❑ 738 | Andre Robertson | .10 | .05 |
| ❑ 739 | Dave Rozema | .10 | .05 |
| ❑ 740 | Lance Parrish | .15 | .07 |
| ❑ 741 | Pete Rose MG | .40 | .18 |
| ❑ 742 | Frank Viola | .15 | .07 |
| ❑ 743 | Pat Sheridan | .10 | .05 |
| ❑ 744 | Lary Sorensen | .10 | .05 |
| ❑ 745 | Willie Upshaw | .10 | .05 |
| ❑ 746 | Denny Gonzalez | .10 | .05 |
| ❑ 747 | Rick Cerone | .10 | .05 |
| ❑ 748 | Steve Henderson | .10 | .05 |
| ❑ 749 | Ed Jurak | .10 | .05 |
| ❑ 750 | Gorman Thomas | .10 | .05 |
| ❑ 751 | Howard Johnson | .15 | .07 |
| ❑ 752 | Mike Krukow | .10 | .05 |
| ❑ 753 | Dan Ford | .10 | .05 |
| ❑ 754 | Pat Clements | .10 | .05 |
| ❑ 755 | Harold Baines | .25 | .11 |
| ❑ 756 | Rick Rhoden TL | .10 | .05 |
| ❑ 757 | Darrell Porter | .15 | .07 |
| ❑ 758 | Dave Anderson | .10 | .05 |
| ❑ 759 | Moose Haas | .10 | .05 |
| ❑ 760 | Andre Dawson | .25 | .11 |
| ❑ 761 | Don Slaught | .10 | .05 |
| ❑ 762 | Eric Show | .10 | .05 |
| ❑ 763 | Terry Puhl | .10 | .05 |
| ❑ 764 | Kevin Gross | .10 | .05 |
| ❑ 765 | Don Baylor | .25 | .11 |
| ❑ 766 | Rick Langford | .10 | .05 |
| ❑ 767 | Jody Davis | .10 | .05 |
| ❑ 768 | Vern Ruhle | .10 | .05 |
| ❑ 769 | Harold Reynolds RC | .40 | .18 |
| ❑ 770 | Vida Blue | .15 | .07 |
| ❑ 771 | John McNamara MG | .10 | .05 |
| ❑ 772 | Brian Downing | .10 | .05 |
| ❑ 773 | Greg Pryor | .10 | .05 |
| ❑ 774 | Terry Leach | .10 | .05 |
| ❑ 775 | Al Oliver | .15 | .07 |
| ❑ 776 | Gene Garber | .10 | .05 |
| ❑ 777 | Wayne Krenchicki | .10 | .05 |
| ❑ 778 | Jerry Hairston | .10 | .05 |
| ❑ 779 | Rick Reuschel | .10 | .05 |
| ❑ 780 | Robin Yount | .40 | .18 |
| ❑ 781 | Joe Nolan | .10 | .05 |
| ❑ 782 | Ken Landreaux | .10 | .05 |
| ❑ 783 | Ricky Horton | .10 | .05 |
| ❑ 784 | Alan Bannister | .10 | .05 |
| ❑ 785 | Bob Stanley | .10 | .05 |
| ❑ 786 | Mickey Hatcher TL | .10 | .05 |
| ❑ 787 | Vance Law | .10 | .05 |
| ❑ 788 | Marty Castillo | .10 | .05 |
| ❑ 789 | Kurt Bevacqua | .10 | .05 |
| ❑ 790 | Phil Niekro | .40 | .18 |
| ❑ 791 | Checklist: 661-792 | .15 | .07 |
| ❑ 792 | Charles Hudson | .10 | .05 |

## 1986 Topps Traded

| No. | Player | MINT | NRMT |
|---|---|---|---|
| | COMP.FACT.SET (132) | 20.00 | 9.00 |
| ❑ 1T | Andy Allanson | .10 | .05 |
| ❑ 2T | Neil Allen | .10 | .05 |
| ❑ 3T | Joaquin Andujar | .10 | .05 |
| ❑ 4T | Paul Assenmacher | .10 | .05 |
| ❑ 5T | Scott Bailes | .10 | .05 |
| ❑ 6T | Don Baylor | .25 | .11 |
| ❑ 7T | Steve Bedrosian | .10 | .05 |
| ❑ 8T | Juan Beniquez | .10 | .05 |
| ❑ 9T | Juan Berenguer | .10 | .05 |
| ❑ 10T | Mike Bielecki | .10 | .05 |
| ❑ 11T | Barry Bonds XRC ! | 10.00 | 4.50 |
| ❑ 12T | Bobby Bonilla XRC | .60 | .25 |
| ❑ 13T | Juan Bonilla | .10 | .05 |
| ❑ 14T | Rich Bordi | .10 | .05 |
| ❑ 15T | Steve Boros MG | .10 | .05 |
| ❑ 16T | Rick Burleson | .10 | .05 |
| ❑ 17T | Bill Campbell | .10 | .05 |
| ❑ 18T | Tom Candiotti | .10 | .05 |
| ❑ 19T | John Cangelosi | .10 | .05 |
| ❑ 20T | Jose Canseco XRC | 5.00 | 2.20 |
| ❑ 21T | Carmen Castillo | .10 | .05 |
| ❑ 22T | Rick Cerone | .10 | .05 |
| ❑ 23T | John Cerutti | .10 | .05 |
| ❑ 24T | Will Clark XRC | 1.25 | .55 |
| ❑ 25T | Mark Clear | .10 | .05 |
| ❑ 26T | Darnell Coles | .10 | .05 |
| ❑ 27T | Dave Collins | .10 | .05 |
| ❑ 28T | Tim Conroy | .10 | .05 |
| ❑ 29T | Joe Cowley | .10 | .05 |
| ❑ 30T | Joel Davis | .10 | .05 |
| ❑ 31T | Rob Deer | .10 | .05 |
| ❑ 32T | John Denny | .10 | .05 |
| ❑ 33T | Mike Easler | .10 | .05 |
| ❑ 34T | Mark Eichhorn | .10 | .05 |
| ❑ 35T | Steve Farr | .10 | .05 |
| ❑ 36T | Scott Fletcher | .10 | .05 |
| ❑ 37T | Terry Forster | .10 | .05 |
| ❑ 38T | Terry Francona | .10 | .05 |
| ❑ 39T | Jim Fregosi MG | .10 | .05 |
| ❑ 40T | Andres Galarraga XRC | 1.25 | .55 |
| ❑ 41T | Ken Griffey | .15 | .07 |
| ❑ 42T | Bill Gullickson | .10 | .05 |
| ❑ 43T | Jose Guzman XRC* | .10 | .05 |
| ❑ 44T | Moose Haas | .10 | .05 |
| ❑ 45T | Billy Hatcher | .10 | .05 |
| ❑ 46T | Mike Heath | .10 | .05 |
| ❑ 47T | Tom Hume | .10 | .05 |
| ❑ 48T | Pete Incaviglia XRC | .40 | .18 |
| ❑ 49T | Dane Iorg | .10 | .05 |
| ❑ 50T | Bo Jackson XRC | 1.00 | .45 |
| ❑ 51T | Wally Joyner XRC | .40 | .18 |
| ❑ 52T | Charlie Kerfeld | .10 | .05 |
| ❑ 53T | Eric King | .10 | .05 |
| ❑ 54T | Bob Kipper | .10 | .05 |
| ❑ 55T | Wayne Krenchicki | .10 | .05 |
| ❑ 56T | John Kruk XRC | .40 | .18 |
| ❑ 57T | Mike LaCoss | .10 | .05 |
| ❑ 58T | Pete Ladd | .10 | .05 |
| ❑ 59T | Mike Laga | .10 | .05 |
| ❑ 60T | Hal Lanier MG | .10 | .05 |
| ❑ 61T | Dave LaPoint | .10 | .05 |
| ❑ 62T | Rudy Law | .10 | .05 |
| ❑ 63T | Rick Leach | .10 | .05 |
| ❑ 64T | Tim Leary | .10 | .05 |
| ❑ 65T | Dennis Leonard | .10 | .05 |
| ❑ 66T | Jim Leyland MG XRC | .10 | .05 |
| ❑ 67T | Steve Lyons | .10 | .05 |
| ❑ 68T | Mickey Mahler | .10 | .05 |
| ❑ 69T | Candy Maldonado | .10 | .05 |
| ❑ 70T | Roger Mason XRC* | .10 | .05 |
| ❑ 71T | Bob McClure | .10 | .05 |
| ❑ 72T | Andy McGaffigan | .10 | .05 |
| ❑ 73T | Gene Michael MG | .10 | .05 |
| ❑ 74T | Kevin Mitchell XRC | .40 | .18 |
| ❑ 75T | Omar Moreno | .10 | .05 |
| ❑ 76T | Jerry Mumphrey | .10 | .05 |
| ❑ 77T | Phil Niekro | .40 | .18 |
| ❑ 78T | Randy Niemann | .10 | .05 |
| ❑ 79T | Juan Nieves | .10 | .05 |
| ❑ 80T | Otis Nixon XRC* | .15 | .07 |
| ❑ 81T | Bob Ojeda | .10 | .05 |
| ❑ 82T | Jose Oquendo | .10 | .05 |
| ❑ 83T | Tom Paciorek | .15 | .07 |
| ❑ 84T | David Palmer | .10 | .05 |
| ❑ 85T | Frank Pastore | .10 | .05 |
| ❑ 86T | Lou Piniella MG | .15 | .07 |
| ❑ 87T | Dan Plesac | .10 | .05 |
| ❑ 88T | Darrell Porter | .15 | .07 |
| ❑ 89T | Rey Quinones | .10 | .05 |
| ❑ 90T | Gary Redus | .10 | .05 |
| ❑ 91T | Bip Roberts XRC | .40 | .18 |
| ❑ 92T | Billy Joe Robidoux | .10 | .05 |
| ❑ 93T | Jeff D. Robinson | .10 | .05 |
| ❑ 94T | Gary Roenicke | .10 | .05 |
| ❑ 95T | Ed Romero | .10 | .05 |
| ❑ 96T | Argenis Salazar | .10 | .05 |
| ❑ 97T | Joe Sambito | .10 | .05 |
| ❑ 98T | Billy Sample | .10 | .05 |

❑ 99T Dave Schmidt .10 .05
❑ 100T Ken Schrom .10 .05
❑ 101T Tom Seaver .60 .25
❑ 102T Ted Simmons .15 .07
❑ 103T Sammy Stewart .10 .05
❑ 104T Kurt Stillwell .10 .05
❑ 105T Franklin Stubbs .10 .05
❑ 106T Dale Sveum .10 .05
❑ 107T Chuck Tanner MG .10 .05
❑ 108T Danny Tartabull XRC** .15 .07
❑ 109T Tim Teufel .10 .05
❑ 110T Bob Tewksbury XRC .15 .07
❑ 111T Andres Thomas .10 .05
❑ 112T Milt Thompson .10 .05
❑ 113T Robby Thompson XRC .15 .07
❑ 114T Jay Tibbs .10 .05
❑ 115T Wayne Tolleson .10 .05
❑ 116T Alex Trevino .10 .05
❑ 117T Manny Trillo .10 .05
❑ 118T Ed VandeBerg .10 .05
❑ 119T Ozzie Virgil .10 .05
❑ 120T Bob Walk .10 .05
❑ 121T Gene Walter .10 .05
❑ 122T Claudell Washington .10 .05
❑ 123T Bill Wegman XRC* .10 .05
❑ 124T Dick Williams MG .15 .07
❑ 125T Mitch Williams XRC .15 .07
❑ 126T Bobby Witt XRC .25 .11
❑ 127T Todd Worrell XRC* .40 .18
❑ 128T George Wright .10 .05
❑ 129T Ricky Wright .10 .05
❑ 130T Steve Yeager .10 .05
❑ 131T Paul Zuvella .10 .05
❑ 132T Checklist 1T-132T .10 .05

## 1987 Topps

| | MINT | NRMT |
|---|---|---|
| COMPLETE SET (792) | 20.00 | 9.00 |
| COMP.HOBBY SET (792) | 30.00 | 13.50 |
| COMP.X-MAS.SET (792) | 30.00 | 13.50 |

❑ 1 Roger Clemens RB .25 .11
Most K's 9-inning game
❑ 2 Jim Deshaies RB .05 .02
Most cons. K's, start of game
❑ 3 Dwight Evans RB .10 .05
Earliest home run
❑ 4 Davey Lopes RB .05 .02
Most steals season, 40-year-old
❑ 5 Dave Righetti RB .05 .02
Most saves season
❑ 6 Ruben Sierra RB .05 .02
Youngest player to switch hit HR's, game
❑ 7 Todd Worrell RB .05 .02
Most saves rookie season
❑ 8 Terry Pendleton .10 .05
❑ 9 Jay Tibbs .05 .02
❑ 10 Cecil Cooper .10 .05
❑ 11 Indians Team .05 .02
(Mound conference)
❑ 12 Jeff Sellers .05 .02
❑ 13 Nick Esasky .05 .02
❑ 14 Dave Stewart .10 .05
❑ 15 Claudell Washington .05 .02
❑ 16 Pat Clements .05 .02
❑ 17 Pete O'Brien .05 .02
❑ 18 Dick Howser MG .05 .02
❑ 19 Matt Young .05 .02
❑ 20 Gary Carter .15 .07
❑ 21 Mark Davis .05 .02
❑ 22 Doug DeCinces .05 .02
❑ 23 Lee Smith .15 .07
❑ 24 Tony Walker .05 .02
❑ 25 Bert Blyleven .10 .05
❑ 26 Greg Brock .05 .02
❑ 27 Joe Cowley .05 .02
❑ 28 Rick Dempsey .10 .05
❑ 29 Jimmy Key .10 .05
❑ 30 Tim Raines .10 .05
❑ 31 Braves Team .05 .02
(Glenn Hubbard and Rafael Ramirez)
❑ 32 Tim Leary .05 .02
❑ 33 Andy Van Slyke .10 .05
❑ 34 Jose Rijo .05 .02
❑ 35 Sid Bream .05 .02
❑ 36 Eric King .05 .02
❑ 37 Marvell Wynne .05 .02
❑ 38 Dennis Leonard .05 .02
❑ 39 Marty Barrett .05 .02
❑ 40 Dave Righetti .05 .02
❑ 41 Bo Diaz .05 .02
❑ 42 Gary Redus .05 .02
❑ 43 Gene Michael MG .05 .02
❑ 44 Greg Harris .05 .02
❑ 45 Jim Presley .05 .02
❑ 46 Dan Gladden .05 .02
❑ 47 Dennis Powell .05 .02
❑ 48 Wally Backman .05 .02
❑ 49 Terry Harper .05 .02
❑ 50 Dave Smith .05 .02
❑ 51 Mel Hall .05 .02
❑ 52 Keith Atherton .05 .02
❑ 53 Ruppert Jones .05 .02
❑ 54 Bill Dawley .05 .02
❑ 55 Tim Wallach .05 .02
❑ 56 Brewers Team .05 .02
(Mound conference)
❑ 57 Scott Nielsen .05 .02
❑ 58 Thad Bosley .05 .02
❑ 59 Ken Dayley .05 .02
❑ 60 Tony Pena .05 .02
❑ 61 Bobby Thigpen RC .10 .05
❑ 62 Bobby Meacham .05 .02
❑ 63 Fred Toliver .05 .02
❑ 64 Harry Spilman .05 .02
❑ 65 Tom Browning .05 .02
❑ 66 Marc Sullivan .05 .02
❑ 67 Bill Swift .05 .02
❑ 68 Tony LaRussa MG .10 .05
❑ 69 Lonnie Smith .05 .02
❑ 70 Charlie Hough .10 .05
❑ 71 Mike Aldrete .05 .02
❑ 72 Walt Terrell .05 .02
❑ 73 Dave Anderson .05 .02
❑ 74 Dan Pasqua .05 .02
❑ 75 Ron Darling .05 .02
❑ 76 Rafael Ramirez .05 .02
❑ 77 Bryan Oelkers .05 .02
❑ 78 Tom Foley .05 .02
❑ 79 Juan Nieves .05 .02
❑ 80 Wally Joyner RC .20 .09
❑ 81 Padres Team .05 .02
(Andy Hawkins and Terry Kennedy)
❑ 82 Rob Murphy .05 .02
❑ 83 Mike Davis .05 .02
❑ 84 Steve Lake .05 .02
❑ 85 Kevin Bass .05 .02
❑ 86 Nate Snell .05 .02
❑ 87 Mark Salas .05 .02
❑ 88 Ed Wojna .05 .02
❑ 89 Ozzie Guillen .10 .05
❑ 90 Dave Stieb .05 .02
❑ 91 Harold Reynolds .10 .05
❑ 92A Urbano Lugo .20 .09
ERR (no trademark)
❑ 92B Urbano Lugo COR .05 .02
❑ 93 Jim Leyland MG RC* .10 .05
❑ 94 Calvin Schiraldi .05 .02
❑ 95 Oddibe McDowell .05 .02
❑ 96 Frank Williams .05 .02
❑ 97 Glenn Wilson .05 .02
❑ 98 Bill Scherrer .05 .02
❑ 99 Darryl Motley .05 .02
(Now with Braves on card front)
❑ 100 Steve Garvey .15 .07
❑ 101 Carl Willis RC .05 .02
❑ 102 Paul Zuvella .05 .02
❑ 103 Rick Aguilera .10 .05
❑ 104 Billy Sample .05 .02
❑ 105 Floyd Youmans .05 .02
❑ 106 Blue Jays Team .05 .02
(George Bell and Jesse Barfield)
❑ 107 John Butcher .05 .02
❑ 108 Jim Gantner UER .05 .02
(Brewers logo reversed)
❑ 109 R.J. Reynolds .05 .02
❑ 110 John Tudor .05 .02
❑ 111 Alfredo Griffin .05 .02
❑ 112 Alan Ashby .05 .02
❑ 113 Neil Allen .05 .02
❑ 114 Billy Beane .05 .02
❑ 115 Donnie Moore .05 .02
❑ 116 Bill Russell .05 .02
❑ 117 Jim Beattie .05 .02
❑ 118 Bobby Valentine MG .05 .02
❑ 119 Ron Robinson .05 .02
❑ 120 Eddie Murray .20 .09
❑ 121 Kevin Romine .05 .02
❑ 122 Jim Clancy .05 .02
❑ 123 John Kruk RC* .20 .09
❑ 124 Ray Fontenot .05 .02
❑ 125 Bob Brenly .05 .02
❑ 126 Mike Loynd .05 .02
❑ 127 Vance Law .05 .02
❑ 128 Checklist 1-132 .05 .02
❑ 129 Rick Cerone .05 .02
❑ 130 Dwight Gooden .15 .07
❑ 131 Pirates Team .05 .02
(Sid Bream and Tony Pena)
❑ 132 Paul Assenmacher .15 .07
❑ 133 Jose Oquendo .05 .02
❑ 134 Rich Yett .05 .02
❑ 135 Mike Easler .05 .02
❑ 136 Ron Romanick .05 .02
❑ 137 Jerry Willard .05 .02
❑ 138 Roy Lee Jackson .05 .02
❑ 139 Devon White RC .25 .11
❑ 140 Bret Saberhagen .10 .05
❑ 141 Herm Winningham .05 .02
❑ 142 Rick Sutcliffe .10 .05
❑ 143 Steve Boros MG .05 .02
❑ 144 Mike Scioscia .05 .02
❑ 145 Charlie Kerfeld .05 .02
❑ 146 Tracy Jones .05 .02
❑ 147 Randy Niemann .05 .02
❑ 148 Dave Collins .05 .02
❑ 149 Ray Searage .05 .02
❑ 150 Wade Boggs .25 .11
❑ 151 Mike LaCoss .05 .02
❑ 152 Toby Harrah .05 .02
❑ 153 Duane Ward RC* .10 .05
❑ 154 Tom O'Malley .05 .02
❑ 155 Eddie Whitson .05 .02
❑ 156 Mariners Team .05 .02
(Mound conference)
❑ 157 Danny Darwin .05 .02
❑ 158 Tim Teufel .05 .02
❑ 159 Ed Olwine .05 .02
❑ 160 Julio Franco .10 .05
❑ 161 Steve Ontiveros .05 .02
❑ 162 Mike LaValliere RC* .05 .02
❑ 163 Kevin Gross .05 .02
❑ 164 Sammy Khalifa .05 .02
❑ 165 Jeff Reardon .10 .05
❑ 166 Bob Boone .10 .05
❑ 167 Jim Deshaies RC* .05 .02
❑ 168 Lou Piniella MG .10 .05
❑ 169 Ron Washington .05 .02
❑ 170 Bo Jackson RC .40 .18
❑ 171 Chuck Cary .05 .02

- ❑ 172 Ron Oester .05 .02
- ❑ 173 Alex Trevino .05 .02
- ❑ 174 Henry Cotto .05 .02
- ❑ 175 Bob Stanley .05 .02
- ❑ 176 Steve Buechele .05 .02
- ❑ 177 Keith Moreland .05 .02
- ❑ 178 Cecil Fielder .15 .07
- ❑ 179 Bill Wegman .05 .02
- ❑ 180 Chris Brown .05 .02
- ❑ 181 Cardinals Team .05 .02 (Mound conference)
- ❑ 182 Lee Lacy .05 .02
- ❑ 183 Andy Hawkins .05 .02
- ❑ 184 Bobby Bonilla RC .25 .11
- ❑ 185 Roger McDowell .05 .02
- ❑ 186 Bruce Benedict .05 .02
- ❑ 187 Mark Huismann .05 .02
- ❑ 188 Tony Phillips .05 .02
- ❑ 189 Joe Hesketh .05 .02
- ❑ 190 Jim Sundberg .05 .02
- ❑ 191 Charles Hudson .05 .02
- ❑ 192 Cory Snyder .05 .02
- ❑ 193 Roger Craig MG .05 .02
- ❑ 194 Kirk McCaskill .05 .02
- ❑ 195 Mike Pagliarulo .05 .02
- ❑ 196 Randy O'Neal UER .05 .02 (Wrong ML career W-L totals)
- ❑ 197 Mark Bailey .05 .02
- ❑ 198 Lee Mazzilli .05 .02
- ❑ 199 Mariano Duncan .05 .02
- ❑ 200 Pete Rose .60 .25
- ❑ 201 John Cangelosi .05 .02
- ❑ 202 Ricky Wright .05 .02
- ❑ 203 Mike Kingery RC .05 .02
- ❑ 204 Sammy Stewart .05 .02
- ❑ 205 Graig Nettles .10 .05
- ❑ 206 Twins Team .05 .02 (Frank Viola and Tim Laudner)
- ❑ 207 George Frazier .05 .02
- ❑ 208 John Shelby .05 .02
- ❑ 209 Rick Schu .05 .02
- ❑ 210 Lloyd Moseby .05 .02
- ❑ 211 John Morris .05 .02
- ❑ 212 Mike Fitzgerald .05 .02
- ❑ 213 Randy Myers RC .20 .09
- ❑ 214 Omar Moreno .05 .02
- ❑ 215 Mark Langston .05 .02
- ❑ 216 B.J. Surhoff RC .40 .18
- ❑ 217 Chris Codiroli .05 .02
- ❑ 218 Sparky Anderson MG .10 .05
- ❑ 219 Cecilio Guante .05 .02
- ❑ 220 Joe Carter .20 .09
- ❑ 221 Vern Ruhle .05 .02
- ❑ 222 Denny Walling .05 .02
- ❑ 223 Charlie Leibrandt .05 .02
- ❑ 224 Wayne Tolleson .05 .02
- ❑ 225 Mike Smithson .05 .02
- ❑ 226 Max Venable .05 .02
- ❑ 227 Jamie Moyer RC .15 .07
- ❑ 228 Curt Wilkerson .05 .02
- ❑ 229 Mike Birkbeck .05 .02
- ❑ 230 Don Baylor .10 .05
- ❑ 231 Giants Team .05 .02 (Bob Brenly and Jim Gott)
- ❑ 232 Reggie Williams .05 .02
- ❑ 233 Russ Morman .05 .02
- ❑ 234 Pat Sheridan .05 .02
- ❑ 235 Alvin Davis .05 .02
- ❑ 236 Tommy John .10 .05
- ❑ 237 Jim Morrison .05 .02
- ❑ 238 Bill Krueger .05 .02
- ❑ 239 Juan Espino .05 .02
- ❑ 240 Steve Balboni .05 .02
- ❑ 241 Danny Heep .05 .02
- ❑ 242 Rick Mahler .05 .02
- ❑ 243 Whitey Herzog MG .10 .05
- ❑ 244 Dickie Noles .05 .02
- ❑ 245 Willie Upshaw .05 .02
- ❑ 246 Jim Dwyer .05 .02
- ❑ 247 Jeff Reed .05 .02
- ❑ 248 Gene Walter .05 .02
- ❑ 249 Jim Pankovits .05 .02
- ❑ 250 Teddy Higuera .05 .02
- ❑ 251 Rob Wilfong .05 .02
- ❑ 252 Dennis Martinez .10 .05
- ❑ 253 Eddie Milner .05 .02
- ❑ 254 Bob Tewksbury RC* .10 .05
- ❑ 255 Juan Samuel .05 .02
- ❑ 256 Royals Team .15 .07 (George Brett and Frank White)
- ❑ 257 Bob Forsch .05 .02
- ❑ 258 Steve Yeager .05 .02
- ❑ 259 Mike Greenwell RC .20 .09
- ❑ 260 Vida Blue .10 .05
- ❑ 261 Ruben Sierra RC .20 .09
- ❑ 262 Jim Winn .05 .02
- ❑ 263 Stan Javier .05 .02
- ❑ 264 Checklist 133-264 .05 .02
- ❑ 265 Darrell Evans .10 .05
- ❑ 266 Jeff Hamilton .05 .02
- ❑ 267 Howard Johnson .05 .02
- ❑ 268 Pat Corrales MG .10 .05
- ❑ 269 Cliff Speck .05 .02
- ❑ 270 Jody Davis .05 .02
- ❑ 271 Mike G. Brown .05 .02
- ❑ 272 Andres Galarraga .20 .09
- ❑ 273 Gene Nelson .05 .02
- ❑ 274 Jeff Hearron UER .05 .02 (Duplicate 1986 stat line on back)
- ❑ 275 LaMarr Hoyt .05 .02
- ❑ 276 Jackie Gutierrez .05 .02
- ❑ 277 Juan Agosto .05 .02
- ❑ 278 Gary Pettis .05 .02
- ❑ 279 Dan Plesac .05 .02
- ❑ 280 Jeff Leonard .05 .02
- ❑ 281 Reds Team .20 .09 (Pete Rose, Bo Diaz, and Bill Gullickson)
- ❑ 282 Jeff Calhoun .05 .02
- ❑ 283 Doug Drabek RC* .20 .09
- ❑ 284 John Moses .05 .02
- ❑ 285 Dennis Boyd .05 .02
- ❑ 286 Mike Woodard .05 .02
- ❑ 287 Dave Von Ohlen .05 .02
- ❑ 288 Tito Landrum .05 .02
- ❑ 289 Bob Kipper .05 .02
- ❑ 290 Leon Durham .05 .02
- ❑ 291 Mitch Williams RC* .10 .05
- ❑ 292 Franklin Stubbs .05 .02
- ❑ 293 Bob Rodgers MG .05 .02
- ❑ 294 Steve Jeltz .05 .02
- ❑ 295 Len Dykstra .15 .07
- ❑ 296 Andres Thomas .05 .02
- ❑ 297 Don Schulze .05 .02
- ❑ 298 Larry Herndon .05 .02
- ❑ 299 Joel Davis .05 .02
- ❑ 300 Reggie Jackson .25 .11
- ❑ 301 Luis Aquino UER .05 .02 (No trademark; never corrected)
- ❑ 302 Bill Schroeder .05 .02
- ❑ 303 Juan Berenguer .05 .02
- ❑ 304 Phil Garner .05 .02
- ❑ 305 John Franco .10 .05
- ❑ 306 Red Sox Team .10 .05 (Tom Seaver, John McNamara MG, and Rich Gedman)
- ❑ 307 Lee Guetterman .05 .02
- ❑ 308 Don Slaught .05 .02
- ❑ 309 Mike Young .05 .02
- ❑ 310 Frank Viola .05 .02
- ❑ 311 Rickey Henderson .10 .05 TBC '82
- ❑ 312 Reggie Jackson .20 .09 TBC '77
- ❑ 313 Roberto Clemente .25 .11 TBC '72
- ❑ 314 Carl Yastrzemski UER .20 .09 TBC '67 (Sic, 112 RBI's on back)
- ❑ 315 Maury Wills TBC '62 .10 .05
- ❑ 316 Brian Fisher .05 .02
- ❑ 317 Clint Hurdle .05 .02
- ❑ 318 Jim Fregosi MG .05 .02
- ❑ 319 Greg Swindell RC .20 .09
- ❑ 320 Barry Bonds RC 3.00 1.35
- ❑ 321 Mike Laga .05 .02
- ❑ 322 Chris Bando .05 .02
- ❑ 323 Al Newman .05 .02
- ❑ 324 David Palmer .05 .02
- ❑ 325 Garry Templeton .05 .02
- ❑ 326 Mark Gubicza .05 .02
- ❑ 327 Dale Sveum .05 .02
- ❑ 328 Bob Welch .05 .02
- ❑ 329 Ron Roenicke .05 .02
- ❑ 330 Mike Scott .05 .02
- ❑ 331 Mets Team .10 .05 (Gary Carter and Darryl Strawberry)
- ❑ 332 Joe Price .05 .02
- ❑ 333 Ken Phelps .05 .02
- ❑ 334 Ed Correa .05 .02
- ❑ 335 Candy Maldonado .05 .02
- ❑ 336 Allan Anderson .05 .02
- ❑ 337 Darrell Miller .05 .02
- ❑ 338 Tim Conroy .05 .02
- ❑ 339 Donnie Hill .05 .02
- ❑ 340 Roger Clemens .50 .23
- ❑ 341 Mike C. Brown .05 .02
- ❑ 342 Bob James .05 .02
- ❑ 343 Hal Lanier MG .05 .02
- ❑ 344A Joe Niekro .05 .02 (Copyright inside righthand border)
- ❑ 344B Joe Niekro .05 .02 (Copyright outside righthand border)
- ❑ 345 Andre Dawson .15 .07
- ❑ 346 Shawon Dunston .05 .02
- ❑ 347 Mickey Brantley .05 .02
- ❑ 348 Carmelo Martinez .05 .02
- ❑ 349 Storm Davis .05 .02
- ❑ 350 Keith Hernandez .10 .05
- ❑ 351 Gene Garber .05 .02
- ❑ 352 Mike Felder .05 .02
- ❑ 353 Ernie Camacho .05 .02
- ❑ 354 Jamie Quirk .05 .02
- ❑ 355 Don Carman .05 .02
- ❑ 356 White Sox Team .05 .02 (Mound conference)
- ❑ 357 Steve Fireovid .05 .02
- ❑ 358 Sal Butera .05 .02
- ❑ 359 Doug Corbett .05 .02
- ❑ 360 Pedro Guerrero .05 .02
- ❑ 361 Mark Thurmond .05 .02
- ❑ 362 Luis Quinones .05 .02
- ❑ 363 Jose Guzman .05 .02
- ❑ 364 Randy Bush .05 .02
- ❑ 365 Rick Rhoden .05 .02
- ❑ 366 Mark McGwire 6.00 2.70
- ❑ 367 Jeff Lahti .05 .02
- ❑ 368 John McNamara MG .05 .02
- ❑ 369 Brian Dayett .05 .02
- ❑ 370 Fred Lynn .10 .05
- ❑ 371 Mark Eichhorn .05 .02
- ❑ 372 Jerry Mumphrey .05 .02
- ❑ 373 Jeff Dedmon .05 .02
- ❑ 374 Glenn Hoffman .05 .02
- ❑ 375 Ron Guidry .10 .05
- ❑ 376 Scott Bradley .05 .02
- ❑ 377 John Henry Johnson .05 .02
- ❑ 378 Rafael Santana .05 .02
- ❑ 379 John Russell .05 .02
- ❑ 380 Rich Gossage .10 .05
- ❑ 381 Expos Team .05 .02 (Mound conference)
- ❑ 382 Rudy Law .05 .02
- ❑ 383 Ron Davis .05 .02
- ❑ 384 Johnny Grubb .05 .02
- ❑ 385 Orel Hershiser .10 .05
- ❑ 386 Dickie Thon .05 .02
- ❑ 387 T.R. Bryden .05 .02
- ❑ 388 Geno Petralli .05 .02
- ❑ 389 Jeff D. Robinson .05 .02
- ❑ 390 Gary Matthews .05 .02
- ❑ 391 Jay Howell .05 .02
- ❑ 392 Checklist 265-396 .05 .02
- ❑ 393 Pete Rose MG .15 .07
- ❑ 394 Mike Bielecki .05 .02
- ❑ 395 Damaso Garcia .05 .02
- ❑ 396 Tim Lollar .05 .02
- ❑ 397 Greg Walker .05 .02

❑ 398 Brad Havens .05 .02
❑ 399 Curt Ford .05 .02
❑ 400 George Brett .40 .18
❑ 401 Billy Joe Robidoux .05 .02
❑ 402 Mike Trujillo .05 .02
❑ 403 Jerry Royster .05 .02
❑ 404 Doug Sisk .05 .02
❑ 405 Brook Jacoby .05 .02
❑ 406 Yankees Team .20 .09
(Rickey Henderson and
Don Mattingly)
❑ 407 Jim Acker .05 .02
❑ 408 John Mizerock .05 .02
❑ 409 Milt Thompson .05 .02
❑ 410 Fernando Valenzuela .10 .05
❑ 411 Darnell Coles .05 .02
❑ 412 Eric Davis .15 .07
❑ 413 Moose Haas .05 .02
❑ 414 Joe Orsulak .05 .02
❑ 415 Bobby Witt RC .10 .05
❑ 416 Tom Nieto .05 .02
❑ 417 Pat Perry .05 .02
❑ 418 Dick Williams MG .10 .05
❑ 419 Mark Portugal RC* .10 .05
❑ 420 Will Clark RC .75 .35
❑ 421 Jose DeLeon .05 .02
❑ 422 Jack Howell .05 .02
❑ 423 Jaime Cocanower .05 .02
❑ 424 Chris Speier .05 .02
❑ 425 Tom Seaver UER .20 .09
(Earned runs amount is wrong
for 86 Red Sox and career.
Also the ERA is wrong for 86 and
career)
❑ 426 Floyd Rayford .05 .02
❑ 427 Edwin Nunez .05 .02
❑ 428 Bruce Bochy .05 .02
❑ 429 Tim Pyznarski .05 .02
❑ 430 Mike Schmidt .40 .18
❑ 431 Dodgers Team .05 .02
(Mound conference)
❑ 432 Jim Slaton .05 .02
❑ 433 Ed Hearn .05 .02
❑ 434 Mike Fischlin .05 .02
❑ 435 Bruce Sutter .05 .02
❑ 436 Andy Allanson .05 .02
❑ 437 Ted Power .05 .02
❑ 438 Kelly Downs RC .05 .02
❑ 439 Karl Best .05 .02
❑ 440 Willie McGee .10 .05
❑ 441 Dave Leiper .05 .02
❑ 442 Mitch Webster .05 .02
❑ 443 John Felske MG .05 .02
❑ 444 Jeff Russell .05 .02
❑ 445 Dave Lopes .10 .05
❑ 446 Chuck Finley RC .40 .18
❑ 447 Bill Almon .05 .02
❑ 448 Chris Bosio RC .10 .05
❑ 449 Pat Dodson .05 .02
❑ 450 Kirby Puckett .50 .23
❑ 451 Joe Sambito .05 .02
❑ 452 Dave Henderson .05 .02
❑ 453 Scott Terry .05 .02
❑ 454 Luis Salazar .05 .02
❑ 455 Mike Boddicker .05 .02
❑ 456 A's Team .05 .02
(Mound conference)
❑ 457 Len Matuszek .05 .02
❑ 458 Kelly Gruber .05 .02
❑ 459 Dennis Eckersley .20 .09
❑ 460 Darryl Strawberry .15 .07
❑ 461 Craig McMurtry .05 .02
❑ 462 Scott Fletcher .05 .02
❑ 463 Tom Candiotti .05 .02
❑ 464 Butch Wynegar .05 .02
❑ 465 Todd Worrell .10 .05
❑ 466 Kal Daniels .05 .02
❑ 467 Randy St.Claire .05 .02
❑ 468 George Bamberger MG .05 .02
❑ 469 Mike Diaz .05 .02
❑ 470 Dave Dravecky .10 .05
❑ 471 Ronn Reynolds .05 .02
❑ 472 Bill Doran .05 .02
❑ 473 Steve Farr .05 .02
❑ 474 Jerry Narron .05 .02
❑ 475 Scott Garrelts .05 .02
❑ 476 Danny Tartabull .05 .02
❑ 477 Ken Howell .05 .02
❑ 478 Tim Laudner .05 .02
❑ 479 Bob Sebra .05 .02
❑ 480 Jim Rice .10 .05
❑ 481 Phillies Team .05 .02
(Glenn Wilson
Juan Samuel and
Von Hayes)
❑ 482 Daryl Boston .05 .02
❑ 483 Dwight Lowry .05 .02
❑ 484 Jim Traber .05 .02
❑ 485 Tony Fernandez .05 .02
❑ 486 Otis Nixon .05 .02
❑ 487 Dave Gumpert .05 .02
❑ 488 Ray Knight .05 .02
❑ 489 Bill Gullickson .05 .02
❑ 490 Dale Murphy .20 .09
❑ 491 Ron Karkovice RC .10 .05
❑ 492 Mike Heath .05 .02
❑ 493 Tom Lasorda MG .10 .05
❑ 494 Barry Jones .05 .02
❑ 495 Gorman Thomas .05 .02
❑ 496 Bruce Bochte .05 .02
❑ 497 Dale Mohorcic .05 .02
❑ 498 Bob Kearney .05 .02
❑ 499 Bruce Ruffin .05 .02
❑ 500 Don Mattingly .50 .23
❑ 501 Craig Lefferts .05 .02
❑ 502 Dick Schofield .05 .02
❑ 503 Larry Andersen .05 .02
❑ 504 Mickey Hatcher .05 .02
❑ 505 Bryn Smith .05 .02
❑ 506 Orioles Team .05 .02
(Mound conference)
❑ 507 Dave L. Stapleton .05 .02
❑ 508 Scott Bankhead .05 .02
❑ 509 Enos Cabell .05 .02
❑ 510 Tom Henke .05 .02
❑ 511 Steve Lyons .05 .02
❑ 512 Dave Magadan RC .10 .05
❑ 513 Carmen Castillo .05 .02
❑ 514 Orlando Mercado .05 .02
❑ 515 Willie Hernandez .05 .02
❑ 516 Ted Simmons .10 .05
❑ 517 Mario Soto .05 .02
❑ 518 Gene Mauch MG .10 .05
❑ 519 Curt Young .05 .02
❑ 520 Jack Clark .10 .05
❑ 521 Rick Reuschel .05 .02
❑ 522 Checklist 397-528 .05 .02
❑ 523 Earnie Riles .05 .02
❑ 524 Bob Shirley .05 .02
❑ 525 Phil Bradley .05 .02
❑ 526 Roger Mason .05 .02
❑ 527 Jim Wohlford .05 .02
❑ 528 Ken Dixon .05 .02
❑ 529 Alvaro Espinoza RC .05 .02
❑ 530 Tony Gwynn .40 .18
❑ 531 Astros Team .10 .05
(Yogi Berra conference)
❑ 532 Jeff Stone .05 .02
❑ 533 Argenis Salazar .05 .02
❑ 534 Scott Sanderson .05 .02
❑ 535 Tony Armas .05 .02
❑ 536 Terry Mulholland RC .10 .05
❑ 537 Rance Mulliniks .05 .02
❑ 538 Tom Niedenfuer .05 .02
❑ 539 Reid Nichols .05 .02
❑ 540 Terry Kennedy .05 .02
❑ 541 Rafael Belliard RC .05 .02
❑ 542 Ricky Horton .05 .02
❑ 543 Dave Johnson MG .10 .05
❑ 544 Zane Smith .05 .02
❑ 545 Buddy Bell .10 .05
❑ 546 Mike Morgan .05 .02
❑ 547 Rob Deer .05 .02
❑ 548 Bill Mooneyham .05 .02
❑ 549 Bob Melvin .05 .02
❑ 550 Pete Incaviglia RC* .10 .05
❑ 551 Frank Wills .05 .02
❑ 552 Larry Sheets .05 .02
❑ 553 Mike Maddux .05 .02
❑ 554 Buddy Biancalana .05 .02
❑ 555 Dennis Rasmussen .05 .02
❑ 556 Angels Team .05 .02
(Rene Lachemann CO,
Mike Witt, and
Bob Boone)
❑ 557 John Cerutti .05 .02
❑ 558 Greg Gagne .05 .02
❑ 559 Lance McCullers .05 .02
❑ 560 Glenn Davis .05 .02
❑ 561 Rey Quinones .05 .02
❑ 562 Bryan Clutterbuck .05 .02
❑ 563 John Stefero .05 .02
❑ 564 Larry McWilliams .05 .02
❑ 565 Dusty Baker .10 .05
❑ 566 Tim Hulett .05 .02
❑ 567 Greg Mathews .05 .02
❑ 568 Earl Weaver MG .20 .09
❑ 569 Wade Rowdon .05 .02
❑ 570 Sid Fernandez .05 .02
❑ 571 Ozzie Virgil .05 .02
❑ 572 Pete Ladd .05 .02
❑ 573 Hal McRae .10 .05
❑ 574 Manny Lee .05 .02
❑ 575 Pat Tabler .05 .02
❑ 576 Frank Pastore .05 .02
❑ 577 Dann Bilardello .05 .02
❑ 578 Billy Hatcher .05 .02
❑ 579 Rick Burleson .05 .02
❑ 580 Mike Krukow .05 .02
❑ 581 Cubs Team .05 .02
(Ron Cey and
Steve Trout)
❑ 582 Bruce Berenyi .05 .02
❑ 583 Junior Ortiz .05 .02
❑ 584 Ron Kittle .05 .02
❑ 585 Scott Bailes .05 .02
❑ 586 Ben Oglivie .05 .02
❑ 587 Eric Plunk .05 .02
❑ 588 Wallace Johnson .05 .02
❑ 589 Steve Crawford .05 .02
❑ 590 Vince Coleman .05 .02
❑ 591 Spike Owen .05 .02
❑ 592 Chris Welsh .05 .02
❑ 593 Chuck Tanner MG .05 .02
❑ 594 Rick Anderson .05 .02
❑ 595 Keith Hernandez AS .05 .02
❑ 596 Steve Sax AS .05 .02
❑ 597 Mike Schmidt AS .15 .07
❑ 598 Ozzie Smith AS .15 .07
❑ 599 Tony Gwynn AS .20 .09
❑ 600 Dave Parker AS .05 .02
❑ 601 Darryl Strawberry AS .10 .05
❑ 602 Gary Carter AS .10 .05
❑ 603A Dwight Gooden AS .15 .07
ERR (no trademark)
❑ 603B Dwight Gooden AS COR .15 .07
❑ 604 Fernando Valenzuela AS .10 .05
❑ 605 Todd Worrell AS .10 .05
❑ 606B Don Mattingly AS COR .20 .09
❑ 606A Don Mattingly AS .75 .35
ERR (no trademark)
❑ 607 Tony Bernazard AS .05 .02
❑ 608 Wade Boggs AS .10 .05
❑ 609 Cal Ripken AS .20 .09
❑ 610 Jim Rice AS .05 .02
❑ 611 Kirby Puckett AS .20 .09
❑ 612 George Bell AS .05 .02
❑ 613 Lance Parrish AS UER .10 .05
(Pitcher heading
on back)
❑ 614 Roger Clemens AS .20 .09
❑ 615 Teddy Higuera AS .05 .02
❑ 616 Dave Righetti AS .05 .02
❑ 617 Al Nipper .05 .02
❑ 618 Tom Kelly MG .05 .02
❑ 619 Jerry Reed .05 .02
❑ 620 Jose Canseco .75 .35
❑ 621 Danny Cox .05 .02
❑ 622 Glenn Braggs RC .05 .02
❑ 623 Kurt Stillwell .05 .02
❑ 624 Tim Burke .05 .02
❑ 625 Mookie Wilson .10 .05
❑ 626 Joel Skinner .05 .02
❑ 627 Ken Oberkfell .05 .02
❑ 628 Bob Walk .05 .02
❑ 629 Larry Parrish .05 .02
❑ 630 John Candelaria .05 .02
❑ 631 Tigers Team .05 .02

(Mound conference)
❑ 632 Rob Woodward .05 .02
❑ 633 Jose Uribe .05 .02
❑ 634 Rafael Palmeiro RC 2.00 .90
❑ 635 Ken Schrom .05 .02
❑ 636 Darren Daulton .15 .07
❑ 637 Bip Roberts RC* .20 .09
❑ 638 Rich Bordi .05 .02
❑ 639 Gerald Perry .05 .02
❑ 640 Mark Clear .05 .02
❑ 641 Domingo Ramos .05 .02
❑ 642 Al Pulido .05 .02
❑ 643 Ron Shepherd .05 .02
❑ 644 John Denny .05 .02
❑ 645 Dwight Evans .10 .05
❑ 646 Mike Mason .05 .02
❑ 647 Tom Lawless .05 .02
❑ 648 Barry Larkin RC 1.00 .45
❑ 649 Mickey Tettleton .05 .02
❑ 650 Hubie Brooks .05 .02
❑ 651 Benny Distefano .05 .02
❑ 652 Terry Forster .05 .02
❑ 653 Kevin Mitchell RC* .15 .07
❑ 654 Checklist 529-660 .10 .05
❑ 655 Jesse Barfield .05 .02
❑ 656 Rangers Team .05 .02
(Bobby Valentine MG
and Ricky Wright)
❑ 657 Tom Waddell .05 .02
❑ 658 Robby Thompson RC* .10 .05
❑ 659 Aurelio Lopez .05 .02
❑ 660 Bob Horner .05 .02
❑ 661 Lou Whitaker .10 .05
❑ 662 Frank DiPino .05 .02
❑ 663 Cliff Johnson .05 .02
❑ 664 Mike Marshall .05 .02
❑ 665 Rod Scurry .05 .02
❑ 666 Von Hayes .05 .02
❑ 667 Ron Hassey .05 .02
❑ 668 Juan Bonilla .05 .02
❑ 669 Bud Black .05 .02
❑ 670 Jose Cruz .10 .05
❑ 671A Ray Soff ERR .05 .02
(No D* before
copyright line)
❑ 671B Ray Soff COR .05 .02
(D* before
copyright line)
❑ 672 Chili Davis .15 .07
❑ 673 Don Sutton .20 .09
❑ 674 Bill Campbell .05 .02
❑ 675 Ed Romero .05 .02
❑ 676 Charlie Moore .05 .02
❑ 677 Bob Grich .10 .05
❑ 678 Carney Lansford .10 .05
❑ 679 Kent Hrbek .10 .05
❑ 680 Ryne Sandberg .25 .11
❑ 681 George Bell .05 .02
❑ 682 Jerry Reuss .05 .02
❑ 683 Gary Roenicke .05 .02
❑ 684 Kent Tekulve .05 .02
❑ 685 Jerry Hairston .05 .02
❑ 686 Doyle Alexander .05 .02
❑ 687 Alan Trammell .15 .07
❑ 688 Juan Beniquez .05 .02
❑ 689 Darrell Porter .05 .02
❑ 690 Dane Iorg .05 .02
❑ 691 Dave Parker .10 .05
❑ 692 Frank White .10 .05
❑ 693 Terry Puhl .05 .02
❑ 694 Phil Niekro .20 .09
❑ 695 Chico Walker .05 .02
❑ 696 Gary Lucas .05 .02
❑ 697 Ed Lynch .05 .02
❑ 698 Ernie Whitt .05 .02
❑ 699 Ken Landreaux .05 .02
❑ 700 Dave Bergman .05 .02
❑ 701 Willie Randolph .10 .05
❑ 702 Greg Gross .05 .02
❑ 703 Dave Schmidt .05 .02
❑ 704 Jesse Orosco .05 .02
❑ 705 Bruce Hurst .05 .02
❑ 706 Rick Manning .05 .02
❑ 707 Bob McClure .05 .02
❑ 708 Scott McGregor .05 .02
❑ 709 Dave Kingman .10 .05
❑ 710 Gary Gaetti .10 .05
❑ 711 Ken Griffey .10 .05
❑ 712 Don Robinson .05 .02
❑ 713 Tom Brookens .05 .02
❑ 714 Dan Quisenberry .05 .02
❑ 715 Bob Dernier .05 .02
❑ 716 Rick Leach .05 .02
❑ 717 Ed VandeBerg .05 .02
❑ 718 Steve Carlton .20 .09
❑ 719 Tom Hume .05 .02
❑ 720 Richard Dotson .05 .02
❑ 721 Tom Herr .05 .02
❑ 722 Bob Knepper .05 .02
❑ 723 Brett Butler .10 .05
❑ 724 Greg Minton .05 .02
❑ 725 George Hendrick .05 .02
❑ 726 Frank Tanana .05 .02
❑ 727 Mike Moore .05 .02
❑ 728 Tippy Martinez .05 .02
❑ 729 Tom Paciorek .10 .05
❑ 730 Eric Show .05 .02
❑ 731 Dave Concepcion .10 .05
❑ 732 Manny Trillo .05 .02
❑ 733 Bill Caudill .05 .02
❑ 734 Bill Madlock .10 .05
❑ 735 Rickey Henderson .25 .11
❑ 736 Steve Bedrosian .05 .02
❑ 737 Floyd Bannister .05 .02
❑ 738 Jorge Orta .05 .02
❑ 739 Chet Lemon .05 .02
❑ 740 Rich Gedman .05 .02
❑ 741 Paul Molitor .20 .09
❑ 742 Andy McGaffigan .05 .02
❑ 743 Dwayne Murphy .05 .02
❑ 744 Roy Smalley .05 .02
❑ 745 Glenn Hubbard .05 .02
❑ 746 Bob Ojeda .05 .02
❑ 747 Johnny Ray .05 .02
❑ 748 Mike Flanagan .05 .02
❑ 749 Ozzie Smith .25 .11
❑ 750 Steve Trout .05 .02
❑ 751 Garth Iorg .05 .02
❑ 752 Dan Petry .05 .02
❑ 753 Rick Honeycutt .05 .02
❑ 754 Dave LaPoint .05 .02
❑ 755 Luis Aguayo .05 .02
❑ 756 Carlton Fisk .20 .09
❑ 757 Nolan Ryan 1.00 .45
❑ 758 Tony Bernazard .05 .02
❑ 759 Joel Youngblood .05 .02
❑ 760 Mike Witt .05 .02
❑ 761 Greg Pryor .05 .02
❑ 762 Gary Ward .05 .02
❑ 763 Tim Flannery .05 .02
❑ 764 Bill Buckner .10 .05
❑ 765 Kirk Gibson .10 .05
❑ 766 Don Aase .05 .02
❑ 767 Ron Cey .10 .05
❑ 768 Dennis Lamp .05 .02
❑ 769 Steve Sax .05 .02
❑ 770 Dave Winfield .20 .09
❑ 771 Shane Rawley .05 .02
❑ 772 Harold Baines .10 .05
❑ 773 Robin Yount .20 .09
❑ 774 Wayne Krenchicki .05 .02
❑ 775 Joaquin Andujar .05 .02
❑ 776 Tom Brunansky .05 .02
❑ 777 Chris Chambliss .10 .05
❑ 778 Jack Morris .10 .05
❑ 779 Craig Reynolds .05 .02
❑ 780 Andre Thornton .05 .02
❑ 781 Atlee Hammaker .05 .02
❑ 782 Brian Downing .05 .02
❑ 783 Willie Wilson .10 .05
❑ 784 Cal Ripken .75 .35
❑ 785 Terry Francona .10 .05
❑ 786 Jimy Williams MG .05 .02
❑ 787 Alejandro Pena .05 .02
❑ 788 Tim Stoddard .05 .02
❑ 789 Dan Schatzeder .05 .02
❑ 790 Julio Cruz .05 .02
❑ 791 Lance Parrish UER .10 .05
(No trademark;
never corrected)
❑ 792 Checklist 661-792 .05 .02

# 1987 Topps Traded

| | MINT | NRMT |
|---|---|---|
| COMP.FACT.SET (132) | 8.00 | 3.60 |

❑ 1T Bill Almon .05 .02
❑ 2T Scott Bankhead .05 .02
❑ 3T Eric Bell .05 .02
❑ 4T Juan Beniquez .05 .02
❑ 5T Juan Berenguer .05 .02
❑ 6T Greg Booker .05 .02
❑ 7T Thad Bosley .05 .02
❑ 8T Larry Bowa MG .10 .05
❑ 9T Greg Brock .05 .02
❑ 10T Bob Brower .05 .02
❑ 11T Jerry Browne .05 .02
❑ 12T Ralph Bryant .05 .02
❑ 13T DeWayne Buice .05 .02
❑ 14T Ellis Burks XRC .50 .23
❑ 15T Ivan Calderon .05 .02
❑ 16T Jeff Calhoun .05 .02
❑ 17T Casey Candaele .05 .02
❑ 18T John Cangelosi .05 .02
❑ 19T Steve Carlton .20 .09
❑ 20T Juan Castillo .05 .02
❑ 21T Rick Cerone .05 .02
❑ 22T Ron Cey .10 .05
❑ 23T John Christensen .05 .02
❑ 24T David Cone XRC .75 .35
❑ 25T Chuck Crim .05 .02
❑ 26T Storm Davis .05 .02
❑ 27T Andre Dawson .15 .07
❑ 28T Rick Dempsey .10 .05
❑ 29T Doug Drabek .20 .09
❑ 30T Mike Dunne .05 .02
❑ 31T Dennis Eckersley .20 .09
❑ 32T Lee Elia MG .05 .02
❑ 33T Brian Fisher .05 .02
❑ 34T Terry Francona .10 .05
❑ 35T Willie Fraser .05 .02
❑ 36T Billy Gardner MG .05 .02
❑ 37T Ken Gerhart .05 .02
❑ 38T Dan Gladden .05 .02
❑ 39T Jim Gott .05 .02
❑ 40T Cecilio Guante .05 .02
❑ 41T Albert Hall .05 .02
❑ 42T Terry Harper .05 .02
❑ 43T Mickey Hatcher .05 .02
❑ 44T Brad Havens .05 .02
❑ 45T Neal Heaton .05 .02
❑ 46T Mike Henneman XRC .15 .07
❑ 47T Donnie Hill .05 .02
❑ 48T Guy Hoffman .05 .02
❑ 49T Brian Holton .05 .02
❑ 50T Charles Hudson .05 .02
❑ 51T Danny Jackson .05 .02
❑ 52T Reggie Jackson .25 .11
❑ 53T Chris James XRC* .05 .02
❑ 54T Dion James .05 .02
❑ 55T Stan Jefferson .05 .02
❑ 56T Joe Johnson .05 .02
❑ 57T Terry Kennedy .05 .02
❑ 58T Mike Kingery .05 .02
❑ 59T Ray Knight .05 .02
❑ 60T Gene Larkin XRC .05 .02
❑ 61T Mike LaValliere .05 .02
❑ 62T Jack Lazorko .05 .02
❑ 63T Terry Leach .05 .02

| Card | | MINT | NRMT |
|---|---|---|---|
| ❑ 64T | Tim Leary | .05 | .02 |
| ❑ 65T | Jim Lindeman | .05 | .02 |
| ❑ 66T | Steve Lombardozzi | .05 | .02 |
| ❑ 67T | Bill Long | .05 | .02 |
| ❑ 68T | Barry Lyons | .05 | .02 |
| ❑ 69T | Shane Mack | .10 | .05 |
| ❑ 70T | Greg Maddux XRC | 5.00 | 2.20 |
| ❑ 71T | Bill Madlock | .10 | .05 |
| ❑ 72T | Joe Magrane XRC | .05 | .02 |
| ❑ 73T | Dave Martinez XRC* | .10 | .05 |
| ❑ 74T | Fred McGriff | .40 | .18 |
| ❑ 75T | Mark McLemore XRC* | .10 | .05 |
| ❑ 76T | Kevin McReynolds | .05 | .02 |
| ❑ 77T | Dave Meads | .05 | .02 |
| ❑ 78T | Eddie Milner | .05 | .02 |
| ❑ 79T | Greg Minton | .05 | .02 |
| ❑ 80T | John Mitchell | .05 | .02 |
| ❑ 81T | Kevin Mitchell | .15 | .07 |
| ❑ 82T | Charlie Moore | .05 | .02 |
| ❑ 83T | Jeff Musselman | .05 | .02 |
| ❑ 84T | Gene Nelson | .05 | .02 |
| ❑ 85T | Graig Nettles | .10 | .05 |
| ❑ 86T | Al Newman | .05 | .02 |
| ❑ 87T | Reid Nichols | .05 | .02 |
| ❑ 88T | Tom Niedenfuer | .05 | .02 |
| ❑ 89T | Joe Niekro | .05 | .02 |
| ❑ 90T | Tom Nieto | .05 | .02 |
| ❑ 91T | Matt Nokes XRC | .10 | .05 |
| ❑ 92T | Dickie Noles | .05 | .02 |
| ❑ 93T | Pat Pacillo | .05 | .02 |
| ❑ 94T | Lance Parrish | .10 | .05 |
| ❑ 95T | Tony Pena | .05 | .02 |
| ❑ 96T | Luis Polonia XRC | .10 | .05 |
| ❑ 97T | Randy Ready | .05 | .02 |
| ❑ 98T | Jeff Reardon | .10 | .05 |
| ❑ 99T | Gary Redus | .05 | .02 |
| ❑ 100T | Jeff Reed | .05 | .02 |
| ❑ 101T | Rick Rhoden | .05 | .02 |
| ❑ 102T | Cal Ripken Sr. MG | .05 | .02 |
| ❑ 103T | Wally Ritchie | .05 | .02 |
| ❑ 104T | Jeff M. Robinson | .05 | .02 |
| ❑ 105T | Gary Roenicke | .05 | .02 |
| ❑ 106T | Jerry Royster | .05 | .02 |
| ❑ 107T | Mark Salas | .05 | .02 |
| ❑ 108T | Luis Salazar | .05 | .02 |
| ❑ 109T | Benny Santiago XRC** | .10 | .05 |
| ❑ 110T | Dave Schmidt | .05 | .02 |
| ❑ 111T | Kevin Seitzer XRC* | .20 | .09 |
| ❑ 112T | John Shelby | .05 | .02 |
| ❑ 113T | Steve Shields | .05 | .02 |
| ❑ 114T | John Smiley XRC | .05 | .02 |
| ❑ 115T | Chris Speier | .05 | .02 |
| ❑ 116T | Mike Stanley XRC* | .20 | .09 |
| ❑ 117T | Terry Steinbach XRC | .20 | .09 |
| ❑ 118T | Les Straker | .05 | .02 |
| ❑ 119T | Jim Sundberg | .05 | .02 |
| ❑ 120T | Danny Tartabull | .05 | .02 |
| ❑ 121T | Tom Trebelhorn MG | .05 | .02 |
| ❑ 122T | Dave Valle XRC** | .05 | .02 |
| ❑ 123T | Ed VandeBerg | .05 | .02 |
| ❑ 124T | Andy Van Slyke | .10 | .05 |
| ❑ 125T | Gary Ward | .05 | .02 |
| ❑ 126T | Alan Wiggins | .05 | .02 |
| ❑ 127T | Bill Wilkinson | .05 | .02 |
| ❑ 128T | Frank Williams | .05 | .02 |
| ❑ 129T | Matt Williams XRC | 1.00 | .45 |
| ❑ 130T | Jim Winn | .05 | .02 |
| ❑ 131T | Matt Young | .05 | .02 |
| ❑ 132T | Checklist 1T-132T | .05 | .02 |

## 1988 Topps

| | MINT | NRMT |
|---|---|---|
| COMPLETE SET (792) | 15.00 | 6.75 |
| COMP.FACT.SET (792) | 20.00 | 9.00 |

| Card | | MINT | NRMT |
|---|---|---|---|
| ❑ 1 | Vince Coleman RB<br>100 Steals for<br>Third Cons. Season | .05 | .02 |
| ❑ 2 | Don Mattingly RB<br>Six Grand Slams | .15 | .07 |
| ❑ 3 | Mark McGwire RB<br>Rookie Homer Record<br>(No white spot) | 1.00 | .45 |
| ❑ 3A | Mark McGwire RB<br>Rookie Homer Record<br>(White spot behind<br>left foot) | .25 | .11 |
| ❑ 4 | Eddie Murray RB<br>Switch Home Runs,<br>Two Straight Games<br>(No caption on front) | .10 | .05 |
| ❑ 4A | Eddie Murray RB<br>Switch Home Runs,<br>Two Straight Games<br>(Caption in box<br>on card front) | .40 | .18 |
| ❑ 5 | Phil Niekro<br>Joe Niekro RB<br>Brothers Win Record | .10 | .05 |
| ❑ 6 | Nolan Ryan RB<br>11th 200 K's Season | .20 | .09 |
| ❑ 7 | Benito Santiago RB<br>34-Game Hitting Streak<br>Rookie Record | .05 | .02 |
| ❑ 8 | Kevin Elster | .05 | .02 |
| ❑ 9 | Andy Hawkins | .05 | .02 |
| ❑ 10 | Ryne Sandberg | .25 | .11 |
| ❑ 11 | Mike Young | .05 | .02 |
| ❑ 12 | Bill Schroeder | .05 | .02 |
| ❑ 13 | Andres Thomas | .05 | .02 |
| ❑ 14 | Sparky Anderson MG | .10 | .05 |
| ❑ 15 | Chili Davis | .15 | .07 |
| ❑ 16 | Kirk McCaskill | .05 | .02 |
| ❑ 17 | Ron Oester | .05 | .02 |
| ❑ 18A | Al Leiter RC ERR<br>(Photo actually<br>Steve George,<br>right ear visible) | .20 | .09 |
| ❑ 18B | Al Leiter RC COR<br>(Left ear visible) | .40 | .18 |
| ❑ 19 | Mark Davidson | .05 | .02 |
| ❑ 20 | Kevin Gross | .05 | .02 |
| ❑ 21 | Red Sox TL<br>Wade Boggs and<br>Spike Owen | .10 | .05 |
| ❑ 22 | Greg Swindell | .05 | .02 |
| ❑ 23 | Ken Landreaux | .05 | .02 |
| ❑ 24 | Jim Deshaies | .05 | .02 |
| ❑ 25 | Andres Galarraga | .15 | .07 |
| ❑ 26 | Mitch Williams | .05 | .02 |
| ❑ 27 | R.J. Reynolds | .05 | .02 |
| ❑ 28 | Jose Nunez | .05 | .02 |
| ❑ 29 | Argenis Salazar | .05 | .02 |
| ❑ 30 | Sid Fernandez | .05 | .02 |
| ❑ 31 | Bruce Bochy | .05 | .02 |
| ❑ 32 | Mike Morgan | .05 | .02 |
| ❑ 33 | Rob Deer | .05 | .02 |
| ❑ 34 | Ricky Horton | .05 | .02 |
| ❑ 35 | Harold Baines | .10 | .05 |
| ❑ 36 | Jamie Moyer | .05 | .02 |
| ❑ 37 | Ed Romero | .05 | .02 |
| ❑ 38 | Jeff Calhoun | .05 | .02 |
| ❑ 39 | Gerald Perry | .05 | .02 |
| ❑ 40 | Orel Hershiser | .10 | .05 |
| ❑ 41 | Bob Melvin | .05 | .02 |
| ❑ 42 | Bill Landrum | .05 | .02 |
| ❑ 43 | Dick Schofield | .05 | .02 |
| ❑ 44 | Lou Piniella MG | .10 | .05 |
| ❑ 45 | Kent Hrbek | .10 | .05 |
| ❑ 46 | Darnell Coles | .05 | .02 |
| ❑ 47 | Joaquin Andujar | .05 | .02 |
| ❑ 48 | Alan Ashby | .05 | .02 |
| ❑ 49 | Dave Clark | .05 | .02 |
| ❑ 50 | Hubie Brooks | .05 | .02 |
| ❑ 51 | Orioles TL<br>Eddie Murray and<br>Cal Ripken | .40 | .18 |
| ❑ 52 | Don Robinson | .05 | .02 |
| ❑ 53 | Curt Wilkerson | .05 | .02 |
| ❑ 54 | Jim Clancy | .05 | .02 |
| ❑ 55 | Phil Bradley | .05 | .02 |
| ❑ 56 | Ed Hearn | .05 | .02 |
| ❑ 57 | Tim Crews RC | .05 | .02 |
| ❑ 58 | Dave Magadan | .05 | .02 |
| ❑ 59 | Danny Cox | .05 | .02 |
| ❑ 60 | Rickey Henderson | .25 | .11 |
| ❑ 61 | Mark Knudson | .05 | .02 |
| ❑ 62 | Jeff Hamilton | .05 | .02 |
| ❑ 63 | Jimmy Jones | .05 | .02 |
| ❑ 64 | Ken Caminiti RC | .50 | .23 |
| ❑ 65 | Leon Durham | .05 | .02 |
| ❑ 66 | Shane Rawley | .05 | .02 |
| ❑ 67 | Ken Oberkfell | .05 | .02 |
| ❑ 68 | Dave Dravecky | .10 | .05 |
| ❑ 69 | Mike Hart | .05 | .02 |
| ❑ 70 | Roger Clemens | .40 | .18 |
| ❑ 71 | Gary Pettis | .05 | .02 |
| ❑ 72 | Dennis Eckersley | .10 | .05 |
| ❑ 73 | Randy Bush | .05 | .02 |
| ❑ 74 | Tom Lasorda MG | .20 | .09 |
| ❑ 75 | Joe Carter | .20 | .09 |
| ❑ 76 | Dennis Martinez | .10 | .05 |
| ❑ 77 | Tom O'Malley | .05 | .02 |
| ❑ 78 | Dan Petry | .05 | .02 |
| ❑ 79 | Ernie Whitt | .05 | .02 |
| ❑ 80 | Mark Langston | .05 | .02 |
| ❑ 81 | Reds TL<br>Ron Robinson<br>and John Franco | .05 | .02 |
| ❑ 82 | Darrel Akerfelds | .05 | .02 |
| ❑ 83 | Jose Oquendo | .05 | .02 |
| ❑ 84 | Cecilio Guante | .05 | .02 |
| ❑ 85 | Howard Johnson | .05 | .02 |
| ❑ 86 | Ron Karkovice | .05 | .02 |
| ❑ 87 | Mike Mason | .05 | .02 |
| ❑ 88 | Earnie Riles | .05 | .02 |
| ❑ 89 | Gary Thurman | .05 | .02 |
| ❑ 90 | Dale Murphy | .20 | .09 |
| ❑ 91 | Joey Cora RC | .20 | .09 |
| ❑ 92 | Len Matuszek | .05 | .02 |
| ❑ 93 | Bob Sebra | .05 | .02 |
| ❑ 94 | Chuck Jackson | .05 | .02 |
| ❑ 95 | Lance Parrish | .05 | .02 |
| ❑ 96 | Todd Benzinger RC* | .05 | .02 |
| ❑ 97 | Scott Garrelts | .05 | .02 |
| ❑ 98 | Rene Gonzales RC | .05 | .02 |
| ❑ 99 | Chuck Finley | .15 | .07 |
| ❑ 100 | Jack Clark | .10 | .05 |
| ❑ 101 | Allan Anderson | .05 | .02 |
| ❑ 102 | Barry Larkin | .20 | .09 |
| ❑ 103 | Curt Young | .05 | .02 |
| ❑ 104 | Dick Williams MG | .10 | .05 |
| ❑ 105 | Jesse Orosco | .05 | .02 |
| ❑ 106 | Jim Walewander | .05 | .02 |
| ❑ 107 | Scott Bailes | .05 | .02 |
| ❑ 108 | Steve Lyons | .05 | .02 |
| ❑ 109 | Joel Skinner | .05 | .02 |
| ❑ 110 | Teddy Higuera | .05 | .02 |
| ❑ 111 | Expos TL<br>Hubie Brooks and<br>Vance Law | .05 | .02 |
| ❑ 112 | Les Lancaster | .05 | .02 |
| ❑ 113 | Kelly Gruber | .05 | .02 |
| ❑ 114 | Jeff Russell | .05 | .02 |
| ❑ 115 | Johnny Ray | .05 | .02 |
| ❑ 116 | Jerry Don Gleaton | .05 | .02 |
| ❑ 117 | James Steels | .05 | .02 |
| ❑ 118 | Bob Welch | .05 | .02 |
| ❑ 119 | Robbie Wine | .05 | .02 |
| ❑ 120 | Kirby Puckett | .50 | .23 |
| ❑ 121 | Checklist 1-132 | .05 | .02 |
| ❑ 122 | Tony Bernazard | .05 | .02 |
| ❑ 123 | Tom Candiotti | .05 | .02 |
| ❑ 124 | Ray Knight | .05 | .02 |
| ❑ 125 | Bruce Hurst | .05 | .02 |
| ❑ 126 | Steve Jeltz | .05 | .02 |
| ❑ 127 | Jim Gott | .05 | .02 |
| ❑ 128 | Johnny Grubb | .05 | .02 |
| ❑ 129 | Greg Minton | .05 | .02 |

❑ 130 Buddy Bell .10 .05
❑ 131 Don Schulze .05 .02
❑ 132 Donnie Hill .05 .02
❑ 133 Greg Mathews .05 .02
❑ 134 Chuck Tanner MG .10 .05
❑ 135 Dennis Rasmussen .05 .02
❑ 136 Brian Dayett .05 .02
❑ 137 Chris Bosio .05 .02
❑ 138 Mitch Webster .05 .02
❑ 139 Jerry Browne .05 .02
❑ 140 Jesse Barfield .05 .02
❑ 141 Royals TL .20 .09
George Brett and
Bret Saberhagen
❑ 142 Andy Van Slyke .10 .05
❑ 143 Mickey Tettleton .05 .02
❑ 144 Don Gordon .05 .02
❑ 145 Bill Madlock .10 .05
❑ 146 Donell Nixon .05 .02
❑ 147 Bill Buckner .10 .05
❑ 148 Carmelo Martinez .05 .02
❑ 149 Ken Howell .05 .02
❑ 150 Eric Davis .10 .05
❑ 151 Bob Knepper .05 .02
❑ 152 Jody Reed RC .10 .05
❑ 153 John Habyan .05 .02
❑ 154 Jeff Stone .05 .02
❑ 155 Bruce Sutter .10 .05
❑ 156 Gary Matthews .05 .02
❑ 157 Atlee Hammaker .05 .02
❑ 158 Tim Hulett .05 .02
❑ 159 Brad Arnsberg .05 .02
❑ 160 Willie McGee .10 .05
❑ 161 Bryn Smith .05 .02
❑ 162 Mark McLemore .05 .02
❑ 163 Dale Mohorcic .05 .02
❑ 164 Dave Johnson MG .10 .05
❑ 165 Robin Yount .20 .09
❑ 166 Rick Rodriquez .05 .02
❑ 167 Rance Mulliniks .05 .02
❑ 168 Barry Jones .05 .02
❑ 169 Ross Jones .05 .02
❑ 170 Rich Gossage .10 .05
❑ 171 Cubs TL .05 .02
Shawon Dunston
and Manny Trillo
❑ 172 Lloyd McClendon .05 .02
❑ 173 Eric Plunk .05 .02
❑ 174 Phil Garner .05 .02
❑ 175 Kevin Bass .05 .02
❑ 176 Jeff Reed .05 .02
❑ 177 Frank Tanana .05 .02
❑ 178 Dwayne Henry .05 .02
❑ 179 Charlie Puleo .05 .02
❑ 180 Terry Kennedy .05 .02
❑ 181 David Cone .10 .05
❑ 182 Ken Phelps .05 .02
❑ 183 Tom Lawless .05 .02
❑ 184 Ivan Calderon .05 .02
❑ 185 Rick Rhoden .05 .02
❑ 186 Rafael Palmeiro .40 .18
❑ 187 Steve Kiefer .05 .02
❑ 188 John Russell .05 .02
❑ 189 Wes Gardner .05 .02
❑ 190 Candy Maldonado .05 .02
❑ 191 John Cerutti .05 .02
❑ 192 Devon White .10 .05
❑ 193 Brian Fisher .05 .02
❑ 194 Tom Kelly MG .05 .02
❑ 195 Dan Quisenberry .05 .02
❑ 196 Dave Engle .05 .02
❑ 197 Lance McCullers .05 .02
❑ 198 Franklin Stubbs .05 .02
❑ 199 Dave Meads .05 .02
❑ 200 Wade Boggs .25 .11
❑ 201 Rangers TL .05 .02
Bobby Valentine MG
Pete O'Brien,
Pete Incaviglia and
Steve Buechele
❑ 202 Glenn Hoffman .05 .02
❑ 203 Fred Toliver .05 .02
❑ 204 Paul O'Neill .15 .07
❑ 205 Nelson Liriano .05 .02
❑ 206 Domingo Ramos .05 .02
❑ 207 John Mitchell .05 .02
❑ 208 Steve Lake .05 .02
❑ 209 Richard Dotson .05 .02
❑ 210 Willie Randolph .10 .05
❑ 211 Frank DiPino .05 .02
❑ 212 Greg Brock .05 .02
❑ 213 Albert Hall .05 .02
❑ 214 Dave Schmidt .05 .02
❑ 215 Von Hayes .05 .02
❑ 216 Jerry Reuss .05 .02
❑ 217 Harry Spilman .05 .02
❑ 218 Dan Schatzeder .05 .02
❑ 219 Mike Stanley .10 .05
❑ 220 Tom Henke .05 .02
❑ 221 Rafael Belliard .05 .02
❑ 222 Steve Farr .05 .02
❑ 223 Stan Jefferson .05 .02
❑ 224 Tom Trebelhorn MG .05 .02
❑ 225 Mike Scioscia .05 .02
❑ 226 Dave Lopes .10 .05
❑ 227 Ed Correa .05 .02
❑ 228 Wallace Johnson .05 .02
❑ 229 Jeff Musselman .05 .02
❑ 230 Pat Tabler .05 .02
❑ 231 Pirates TL .10 .05
Barry Bonds and
Bobby Bonilla
❑ 232 Bob James .05 .02
❑ 233 Rafael Santana .05 .02
❑ 234 Ken Dayley .05 .02
❑ 235 Gary Ward .05 .02
❑ 236 Ted Power .05 .02
❑ 237 Mike Heath .05 .02
❑ 238 Luis Polonia RC* .05 .02
❑ 239 Roy Smalley .05 .02
❑ 240 Lee Smith .10 .05
❑ 241 Damaso Garcia .05 .02
❑ 242 Tom Niedenfuer .05 .02
❑ 243 Mark Ryal .05 .02
❑ 244 Jeff D. Robinson .05 .02
❑ 245 Rich Gedman .05 .02
❑ 246 Mike Campbell .05 .02
❑ 247 Thad Bosley .05 .02
❑ 248 Storm Davis .05 .02
❑ 249 Mike Marshall .05 .02
❑ 250 Nolan Ryan 1.00 .45
❑ 251 Tom Foley .05 .02
❑ 252 Bob Brower .05 .02
❑ 253 Checklist 133-264 .05 .02
❑ 254 Lee Elia MG .05 .02
❑ 255 Mookie Wilson .10 .05
❑ 256 Ken Schrom .05 .02
❑ 257 Jerry Royster .05 .02
❑ 258 Ed Nunez .05 .02
❑ 259 Ron Kittle .05 .02
❑ 260 Vince Coleman .05 .02
❑ 261 Giants TL .05 .02
(Five players)
❑ 262 Drew Hall .05 .02
❑ 263 Glenn Braggs .05 .02
❑ 264 Les Straker .05 .02
❑ 265 Bo Diaz .05 .02
❑ 266 Paul Assenmacher .05 .02
❑ 267 Billy Bean .05 .02
❑ 268 Bruce Ruffin .05 .02
❑ 269 Ellis Burks RC .25 .11
❑ 270 Mike Witt .05 .02
❑ 271 Ken Gerhart .05 .02
❑ 272 Steve Ontiveros .05 .02
❑ 273 Garth Iorg .05 .02
❑ 274 Junior Ortiz .05 .02
❑ 275 Kevin Seitzer .10 .05
❑ 276 Luis Salazar .05 .02
❑ 277 Alejandro Pena .05 .02
❑ 278 Jose Cruz .05 .02
❑ 279 Randy St.Claire .05 .02
❑ 280 Pete Incaviglia .05 .02
❑ 281 Jerry Hairston .05 .02
❑ 282 Pat Perry .05 .02
❑ 283 Phil Lombardi .05 .02
❑ 284 Larry Bowa MG .05 .02
❑ 285 Jim Presley .05 .02
❑ 286 Chuck Crim .05 .02
❑ 287 Manny Trillo .05 .02
❑ 288 Pat Pacillo .05 .02
(Chris Sabo in
background of photo)
❑ 289 Dave Bergman .05 .02
❑ 290 Tony Fernandez .05 .02
❑ 291 Astros TL .05 .02
Billy Hatcher
and Kevin Bass
❑ 292 Carney Lansford .10 .05
❑ 293 Doug Jones RC .20 .09
❑ 294 Al Pedrique .05 .02
❑ 295 Bert Blyleven .10 .05
❑ 296 Floyd Rayford .05 .02
❑ 297 Zane Smith .05 .02
❑ 298 Milt Thompson .05 .02
❑ 299 Steve Crawford .05 .02
❑ 300 Don Mattingly .50 .23
❑ 301 Bud Black .05 .02
❑ 302 Jose Uribe .05 .02
❑ 303 Eric Show .05 .02
❑ 304 George Hendrick .05 .02
❑ 305 Steve Sax .05 .02
❑ 306 Billy Hatcher .05 .02
❑ 307 Mike Trujillo .05 .02
❑ 308 Lee Mazzilli .05 .02
❑ 309 Bill Long .05 .02
❑ 310 Tom Herr .05 .02
❑ 311 Scott Sanderson .05 .02
❑ 312 Joey Meyer .05 .02
❑ 313 Bob McClure .05 .02
❑ 314 Jimy Williams MG .05 .02
❑ 315 Dave Parker .10 .05
❑ 316 Jose Rijo .05 .02
❑ 317 Tom Nieto .05 .02
❑ 318 Mel Hall .05 .02
❑ 319 Mike Loynd .05 .02
❑ 320 Alan Trammell .15 .07
❑ 321 White Sox TL .10 .05
Harold Baines and
Carlton Fisk
❑ 322 Vicente Palacios .05 .02
❑ 323 Rick Leach .05 .02
❑ 324 Danny Jackson .05 .02
❑ 325 Glenn Hubbard .05 .02
❑ 326 Al Nipper .05 .02
❑ 327 Larry Sheets .05 .02
❑ 328 Greg Cadaret .05 .02
❑ 329 Chris Speier .05 .02
❑ 330 Eddie Whitson .05 .02
❑ 331 Brian Downing .05 .02
❑ 332 Jerry Reed .05 .02
❑ 333 Wally Backman .05 .02
❑ 334 Dave LaPoint .05 .02
❑ 335 Claudell Washington .05 .02
❑ 336 Ed Lynch .05 .02
❑ 337 Jim Gantner .05 .02
❑ 338 Brian Holton UER .05 .02
(1987 ERA .389;
should be 3.89)
❑ 339 Kurt Stillwell .05 .02
❑ 340 Jack Morris .10 .05
❑ 341 Carmen Castillo .05 .02
❑ 342 Larry Andersen .05 .02
❑ 343 Greg Gagne .05 .02
❑ 344 Tony LaRussa MG .10 .05
❑ 345 Scott Fletcher .05 .02
❑ 346 Vance Law .05 .02
❑ 347 Joe Johnson .05 .02
❑ 348 Jim Eisenreich .20 .09
❑ 349 Bob Walk .05 .02
❑ 350 Will Clark .25 .11
❑ 351 Cardinals TL .10 .05
Red Schoendienst CO
and Tony Pena
❑ 352 Bill Ripken RC* .05 .02
❑ 353 Ed Olwine .05 .02
❑ 354 Marc Sullivan .05 .02
❑ 355 Roger McDowell .05 .02
❑ 356 Luis Aguayo .05 .02
❑ 357 Floyd Bannister .05 .02
❑ 358 Rey Quinones .05 .02
❑ 359 Tim Stoddard .05 .02
❑ 360 Tony Gwynn .40 .18
❑ 361 Greg Maddux 1.00 .45
❑ 362 Juan Castillo .05 .02
❑ 363 Willie Fraser .05 .02
❑ 364 Nick Esasky .05 .02
❑ 365 Floyd Youmans .05 .02
❑ 366 Chet Lemon .05 .02

❑ 367 Tim Leary .05 .02
❑ 368 Gerald Young .05 .02
❑ 369 Greg Harris .05 .02
❑ 370 Jose Canseco .40 .18
❑ 371 Joe Hesketh .05 .02
❑ 372 Matt Williams RC .75 .35
❑ 373 Checklist 265-396 .05 .02
❑ 374 Doc Edwards MG .05 .02
❑ 375 Tom Brunansky .05 .02
❑ 376 Bill Wilkinson .05 .02
❑ 377 Sam Horn RC .05 .02
❑ 378 Todd Frohwirth .05 .02
❑ 379 Rafael Ramirez .05 .02
❑ 380 Joe Magrane RC* .05 .02
❑ 381 Angels TL .10 .05
Wally Joyner and
Jack Howell
❑ 382 Keith A. Miller RC .05 .02
❑ 383 Eric Bell .05 .02
❑ 384 Neil Allen .05 .02
❑ 385 Carlton Fisk .20 .09
❑ 386 Don Mattingly AS .15 .07
❑ 387 Willie Randolph AS .05 .02
❑ 388 Wade Boggs AS .10 .05
❑ 389 Alan Trammell AS .05 .02
❑ 390 George Bell AS .05 .02
❑ 391 Kirby Puckett AS .25 .11
❑ 392 Dave Winfield AS .20 .09
❑ 393 Matt Nokes AS .05 .02
❑ 394 Roger Clemens AS .20 .09
❑ 395 Jimmy Key AS .05 .02
❑ 396 Tom Henke AS .05 .02
❑ 397 Jack Clark AS .10 .05
❑ 398 Juan Samuel AS .05 .02
❑ 399 Tim Wallach AS .05 .02
❑ 400 Ozzie Smith AS .15 .07
❑ 401 Andre Dawson AS .10 .05
❑ 402 Tony Gwynn AS .20 .09
❑ 403 Tim Raines AS .10 .05
❑ 404 Benny Santiago AS .05 .02
❑ 405 Dwight Gooden AS .10 .05
❑ 406 Shane Rawley AS .05 .02
❑ 407 Steve Bedrosian AS .05 .02
❑ 408 Dion James .05 .02
❑ 409 Joel McKeon .05 .02
❑ 410 Tony Pena .05 .02
❑ 411 Wayne Tolleson .05 .02
❑ 412 Randy Myers .15 .07
❑ 413 John Christensen .05 .02
❑ 414 John McNamara MG .05 .02
❑ 415 Don Carman .05 .02
❑ 416 Keith Moreland .05 .02
❑ 417 Mark Ciardi .05 .02
❑ 418 Joel Youngblood .05 .02
❑ 419 Scott McGregor .05 .02
❑ 420 Wally Joyner .15 .07
❑ 421 Ed VandeBerg .05 .02
❑ 422 Dave Concepcion .10 .05
❑ 423 John Smiley RC* .10 .05
❑ 424 Dwayne Murphy .05 .02
❑ 425 Jeff Reardon .10 .05
❑ 426 Randy Ready .05 .02
❑ 427 Paul Kilgus .05 .02
❑ 428 John Shelby .05 .02
❑ 429 Tigers TL .05 .02
Alan Trammell and
Kirk Gibson
❑ 430 Glenn Davis .05 .02
❑ 431 Casey Candaele .05 .02
❑ 432 Mike Moore .05 .02
❑ 433 Bill Pecota RC* .05 .02
❑ 434 Rick Aguilera .10 .05
❑ 435 Mike Pagliarulo .05 .02
❑ 436 Mike Bielecki .05 .02
❑ 437 Fred Manrique .05 .02
❑ 438 Rob Ducey .05 .02
❑ 439 Dave Martinez .05 .02
❑ 440 Steve Bedrosian .05 .02
❑ 441 Rick Manning .05 .02
❑ 442 Tom Bolton .05 .02
❑ 443 Ken Griffey .10 .05
❑ 444 Cal Ripken Sr. MG UER .05 .02
(Two copyrights)
❑ 445 Mike Krukow .05 .02
❑ 446 Doug DeCinces .05 .02
(Now with Cardinals
on card front)
❑ 447 Jeff Montgomery RC .20 .09
❑ 448 Mike Davis .05 .02
❑ 449 Jeff M. Robinson .05 .02
❑ 450 Barry Bonds .60 .25
❑ 451 Keith Atherton .05 .02
❑ 452 Willie Wilson .05 .02
❑ 453 Dennis Powell .05 .02
❑ 454 Marvell Wynne .05 .02
❑ 455 Shawn Hillegas .05 .02
❑ 456 Dave Anderson .05 .02
❑ 457 Terry Leach .05 .02
❑ 458 Ron Hassey .05 .02
❑ 459 Yankees TL .20 .09
Dave Winfield and
Willie Randolph
❑ 460 Ozzie Smith .25 .11
❑ 461 Danny Darwin .05 .02
❑ 462 Don Slaught .05 .02
❑ 463 Fred McGriff .20 .09
❑ 464 Jay Tibbs .05 .02
❑ 465 Paul Molitor .20 .09
❑ 466 Jerry Mumphrey .05 .02
❑ 467 Don Aase .05 .02
❑ 468 Darren Daulton .10 .05
❑ 469 Jeff Dedmon .05 .02
❑ 470 Dwight Evans .10 .05
❑ 471 Donnie Moore .05 .02
❑ 472 Robby Thompson .05 .02
❑ 473 Joe Niekro .05 .02
❑ 474 Tom Brookens .05 .02
❑ 475 Pete Rose MG .50 .23
❑ 476 Dave Stewart .10 .05
❑ 477 Jamie Quirk .05 .02
❑ 478 Sid Bream .05 .02
❑ 479 Brett Butler .10 .05
❑ 480 Dwight Gooden .10 .05
❑ 481 Mariano Duncan .05 .02
❑ 482 Mark Davis .05 .02
❑ 483 Rod Booker .05 .02
❑ 484 Pat Clements .05 .02
❑ 485 Harold Reynolds .10 .05
❑ 486 Pat Keedy .05 .02
❑ 487 Jim Pankovits .05 .02
❑ 488 Andy McGaffigan .05 .02
❑ 489 Dodgers TL .05 .02
Pedro Guerrero and
Fernando Valenzuela
❑ 490 Larry Parrish .05 .02
❑ 491 B.J. Surhoff .10 .05
❑ 492 Doyle Alexander .05 .02
❑ 493 Mike Greenwell .05 .02
❑ 494 Wally Ritchie .05 .02
❑ 495 Eddie Murray .20 .09
❑ 496 Guy Hoffman .05 .02
❑ 497 Kevin Mitchell .10 .05
❑ 498 Bob Boone .10 .05
❑ 499 Eric King .05 .02
❑ 500 Andre Dawson .15 .07
❑ 501 Tim Birtsas .05 .02
❑ 502 Dan Gladden .05 .02
❑ 503 Junior Noboa .05 .02
❑ 504 Bob Rodgers MG .05 .02
❑ 505 Willie Upshaw .05 .02
❑ 506 John Cangelosi .05 .02
❑ 507 Mark Gubicza .05 .02
❑ 508 Tim Teufel .05 .02
❑ 509 Bill Dawley .05 .02
❑ 510 Dave Winfield .20 .09
❑ 511 Joel Davis .05 .02
❑ 512 Alex Trevino .05 .02
❑ 513 Tim Flannery .05 .02
❑ 514 Pat Sheridan .05 .02
❑ 515 Juan Nieves .05 .02
❑ 516 Jim Sundberg .05 .02
❑ 517 Ron Robinson .05 .02
❑ 518 Greg Gross .05 .02
❑ 519 Mariners TL .05 .02
Harold Reynolds and
Phil Bradley
❑ 520 Dave Smith .05 .02
❑ 521 Jim Dwyer .05 .02
❑ 522 Bob Patterson .05 .02
❑ 523 Gary Roenicke .05 .02
❑ 524 Gary Lucas .05 .02
❑ 525 Marty Barrett .05 .02
❑ 526 Juan Berenguer .05 .02
❑ 527 Steve Henderson .05 .02
❑ 528A Checklist 397-528 .20 .09
ERR (455 S. Carlton)
❑ 528B Checklist 397-528 .10 .05
COR (455 S. Hillegas)
❑ 529 Tim Burke .05 .02
❑ 530 Gary Carter .15 .07
❑ 531 Rich Yett .05 .02
❑ 532 Mike Kingery .05 .02
❑ 533 John Farrell .05 .02
❑ 534 John Wathan MG .05 .02
❑ 535 Ron Guidry .05 .02
❑ 536 John Morris .05 .02
❑ 537 Steve Buechele .05 .02
❑ 538 Bill Wegman .05 .02
❑ 539 Mike LaValliere .05 .02
❑ 540 Bret Saberhagen .10 .05
❑ 541 Juan Beniquez .05 .02
❑ 542 Paul Noce .05 .02
❑ 543 Kent Tekulve .05 .02
❑ 544 Jim Traber .05 .02
❑ 545 Don Baylor .10 .05
❑ 546 John Candelaria .05 .02
❑ 547 Felix Fermin .05 .02
❑ 548 Shane Mack .05 .02
❑ 549 Braves TL .05 .02
Albert Hall,
Dale Murphy,
Ken Griffey
and Dion James
❑ 550 Pedro Guerrero .05 .02
❑ 551 Terry Steinbach .10 .05
❑ 552 Mark Thurmond .05 .02
❑ 553 Tracy Jones .05 .02
❑ 554 Mike Smithson .05 .02
❑ 555 Brook Jacoby .05 .02
❑ 556 Stan Clarke .05 .02
❑ 557 Craig Reynolds .05 .02
❑ 558 Bob Ojeda .05 .02
❑ 559 Ken Williams .05 .02
❑ 560 Tim Wallach .05 .02
❑ 561 Rick Cerone .05 .02
❑ 562 Jim Lindeman .05 .02
❑ 563 Jose Guzman .05 .02
❑ 564 Frank Lucchesi MG .05 .02
❑ 565 Lloyd Moseby .05 .02
❑ 566 Charlie O'Brien .05 .02
❑ 567 Mike Diaz .05 .02
❑ 568 Chris Brown .05 .02
❑ 569 Charlie Leibrandt .05 .02
❑ 570 Jeffrey Leonard .05 .02
❑ 571 Mark Williamson .05 .02
❑ 572 Chris James .05 .02
❑ 573 Bob Stanley .05 .02
❑ 574 Graig Nettles .10 .05
❑ 575 Don Sutton .20 .09
❑ 576 Tommy Hinzo .05 .02
❑ 577 Tom Browning .05 .02
❑ 578 Gary Gaetti .10 .05
❑ 579 Mets TL .05 .02
Gary Carter and
Kevin McReynolds
❑ 580 Mark McGwire 2.00 .90
❑ 581 Tito Landrum .05 .02
❑ 582 Mike Henneman RC* .10 .05
❑ 583 Dave Valle .05 .02
❑ 584 Steve Trout .05 .02
❑ 585 Ozzie Guillen .05 .02
❑ 586 Bob Forsch .05 .02
❑ 587 Terry Puhl .05 .02
❑ 588 Jeff Parrett .05 .02
❑ 589 Geno Petralli .05 .02
❑ 590 George Bell .05 .02
❑ 591 Doug Drabek .05 .02
❑ 592 Dale Sveum .05 .02
❑ 593 Bob Tewksbury .05 .02
❑ 594 Bobby Valentine MG .10 .05
❑ 595 Frank White .10 .05
❑ 596 John Kruk .10 .05
❑ 597 Gene Garber .05 .02
❑ 598 Lee Lacy .05 .02
❑ 599 Calvin Schiraldi .05 .02
❑ 600 Mike Schmidt .40 .18
❑ 601 Jack Lazorko .05 .02
❑ 602 Mike Aldrete .05 .02

❑ 603 Rob Murphy .05 .02
❑ 604 Chris Bando .05 .02
❑ 605 Kirk Gibson .10 .05
❑ 606 Moose Haas .05 .02
❑ 607 Mickey Hatcher .05 .02
❑ 608 Charlie Kerfeld .05 .02
❑ 609 Twins TL .10 .05
Gary Gaetti and
Kent Hrbek
❑ 610 Keith Hernandez .10 .05
❑ 611 Tommy John .10 .05
❑ 612 Curt Ford .05 .02
❑ 613 Bobby Thigpen .05 .02
❑ 614 Herm Winningham .05 .02
❑ 615 Jody Davis .05 .02
❑ 616 Jay Aldrich .05 .02
❑ 617 Oddibe McDowell .05 .02
❑ 618 Cecil Fielder .15 .07
❑ 619 Mike Dunne .05 .02
(Inconsistent design,
black name on front)
❑ 620 Cory Snyder .05 .02
❑ 621 Gene Nelson .05 .02
❑ 622 Kal Daniels .05 .02
❑ 623 Mike Flanagan .05 .02
❑ 624 Jim Leyland MG .10 .05
❑ 625 Frank Viola .05 .02
❑ 626 Glenn Wilson .05 .02
❑ 627 Joe Boever .05 .02
❑ 628 Dave Henderson .05 .02
❑ 629 Kelly Downs .05 .02
❑ 630 Darrell Evans .10 .05
❑ 631 Jack Howell .05 .02
❑ 632 Steve Shields .05 .02
❑ 633 Barry Lyons .05 .02
❑ 634 Jose DeLeon .05 .02
❑ 635 Terry Pendleton .10 .05
❑ 636 Charles Hudson .05 .02
❑ 637 Jay Bell RC .50 .23
❑ 638 Steve Balboni .05 .02
❑ 639 Brewers TL .05 .02
Glenn Braggs
and Tony Muser CO
❑ 640 Garry Templeton .05 .02
(Inconsistent design,
green border)
❑ 641 Rick Honeycutt .05 .02
❑ 642 Bob Dernier .05 .02
❑ 643 Rocky Childress .05 .02
❑ 644 Terry McGriff .05 .02
❑ 645 Matt Nokes RC* .05 .02
❑ 646 Checklist 529-660 .05 .02
❑ 647 Pascual Perez .05 .02
❑ 648 Al Newman .05 .02
❑ 649 DeWayne Buice .05 .02
❑ 650 Cal Ripken .75 .35
❑ 651 Mike Jackson RC* .10 .05
❑ 652 Bruce Benedict .05 .02
❑ 653 Jeff Sellers .05 .02
❑ 654 Roger Craig MG .10 .05
❑ 655 Len Dykstra .10 .05
❑ 656 Lee Guetterman .05 .02
❑ 657 Gary Redus .05 .02
❑ 658 Tim Conroy .05 .02
(Inconsistent design,
name in white)
❑ 659 Bobby Meacham .05 .02
❑ 660 Rick Reuschel .05 .02
❑ 661 Nolan Ryan TBC '83 .50 .23
❑ 662 Jim Rice TBC .05 .02
❑ 663 Ron Blomberg TBC .05 .02
❑ 664 Bob Gibson TBC '68 .25 .11
❑ 665 Stan Musial TBC '63 .25 .11
❑ 666 Mario Soto .05 .02
❑ 667 Luis Quinones .05 .02
❑ 668 Walt Terrell .05 .02
❑ 669 Phillies TL .05 .02
Lance Parrish
and Mike Ryan CO
❑ 670 Dan Plesac .05 .02
❑ 671 Tim Laudner .05 .02
❑ 672 John Davis .05 .02
❑ 673 Tony Phillips .05 .02
❑ 674 Mike Fitzgerald .05 .02
❑ 675 Jim Rice .10 .05
❑ 676 Ken Dixon .05 .02
❑ 677 Eddie Milner .05 .02
❑ 678 Jim Acker .05 .02
❑ 679 Darrell Miller .05 .02
❑ 680 Charlie Hough .10 .05
❑ 681 Bobby Bonilla .10 .05
❑ 682 Jimmy Key .10 .05
❑ 683 Julio Franco .05 .02
❑ 684 Hal Lanier MG .05 .02
❑ 685 Ron Darling .05 .02
❑ 686 Terry Francona .05 .02
❑ 687 Mickey Brantley .05 .02
❑ 688 Jim Winn .05 .02
❑ 689 Tom Pagnozzi RC .05 .02
❑ 690 Jay Howell .05 .02
❑ 691 Dan Pasqua .05 .02
❑ 692 Mike Birkbeck .05 .02
❑ 693 Benito Santiago .05 .02
❑ 694 Eric Nolte .05 .02
❑ 695 Shawon Dunston .05 .02
❑ 696 Duane Ward .05 .02
❑ 697 Steve Lombardozzi .05 .02
❑ 698 Brad Havens .05 .02
❑ 699 Padres TL .10 .05
Benito Santiago
and Tony Gwynn
❑ 700 George Brett .40 .18
❑ 701 Sammy Stewart .05 .02
❑ 702 Mike Gallego .05 .02
❑ 703 Bob Brenly .05 .02
❑ 704 Dennis Boyd .05 .02
❑ 705 Juan Samuel .05 .02
❑ 706 Rick Mahler .05 .02
❑ 707 Fred Lynn .05 .02
❑ 708 Gus Polidor .05 .02
❑ 709 George Frazier .05 .02
❑ 710 Darryl Strawberry .10 .05
❑ 711 Bill Gullickson .05 .02
❑ 712 John Moses .05 .02
❑ 713 Willie Hernandez .05 .02
❑ 714 Jim Fregosi MG .05 .02
❑ 715 Todd Worrell .10 .05
❑ 716 Lenn Sakata .05 .02
❑ 717 Jay Baller .05 .02
❑ 718 Mike Felder .05 .02
❑ 719 Denny Walling .05 .02
❑ 720 Tim Raines .10 .05
❑ 721 Pete O'Brien .05 .02
❑ 722 Manny Lee .05 .02
❑ 723 Bob Kipper .05 .02
❑ 724 Danny Tartabull .05 .02
❑ 725 Mike Boddicker .05 .02
❑ 726 Alfredo Griffin .05 .02
❑ 727 Greg Booker .05 .02
❑ 728 Andy Allanson .05 .02
❑ 729 Blue Jays TL .10 .05
George Bell and
Fred McGriff
❑ 730 John Franco .10 .05
❑ 731 Rick Schu .05 .02
❑ 732 David Palmer .05 .02
❑ 733 Spike Owen .05 .02
❑ 734 Craig Lefferts .05 .02
❑ 735 Kevin McReynolds .05 .02
❑ 736 Matt Young .05 .02
❑ 737 Butch Wynegar .05 .02
❑ 738 Scott Bankhead .05 .02
❑ 739 Daryl Boston .05 .02
❑ 740 Rick Sutcliffe .10 .05
❑ 741 Mike Easler .05 .02
❑ 742 Mark Clear .05 .02
❑ 743 Larry Herndon .05 .02
❑ 744 Whitey Herzog MG .10 .05
❑ 745 Bill Doran .05 .02
❑ 746 Gene Larkin RC* .05 .02
❑ 747 Bobby Witt .05 .02
❑ 748 Reid Nichols .05 .02
❑ 749 Mark Eichhorn .05 .02
❑ 750 Bo Jackson .20 .09
❑ 751 Jim Morrison .05 .02
❑ 752 Mark Grant .05 .02
❑ 753 Danny Heep .05 .02
❑ 754 Mike LaCoss .05 .02
❑ 755 Ozzie Virgil .05 .02
❑ 756 Mike Maddux .05 .02
❑ 757 John Marzano .05 .02
❑ 758 Eddie Williams RC .10 .05
❑ 759 A's TL UER 1.00 .45
Mark McGwire
and Jose Canseco
(Two copyrights)
❑ 760 Mike Scott .05 .02
❑ 761 Tony Armas .05 .02
❑ 762 Scott Bradley .05 .02
❑ 763 Doug Sisk .05 .02
❑ 764 Greg Walker .05 .02
❑ 765 Neal Heaton .05 .02
❑ 766 Henry Cotto .05 .02
❑ 767 Jose Lind RC .05 .02
❑ 768 Dickie Noles .05 .02
(Now with Tigers
on card front)
❑ 769 Cecil Cooper .10 .05
❑ 770 Lou Whitaker .10 .05
❑ 771 Ruben Sierra .05 .02
❑ 772 Sal Butera .05 .02
❑ 773 Frank Williams .05 .02
❑ 774 Gene Mauch MG .10 .05
❑ 775 Dave Stieb .05 .02
❑ 776 Checklist 661-792 .05 .02
❑ 777 Lonnie Smith .05 .02
❑ 778A Keith Comstock ERR 2.00 .90
(White "Padres")
❑ 778B Keith Comstock COR .05 .02
(Blue "Padres")
❑ 779 Tom Glavine RC 1.25 .55
❑ 780 Fernando Valenzuela .10 .05
❑ 781 Keith Hughes .05 .02
❑ 782 Jeff Ballard .05 .02
❑ 783 Ron Roenicke .05 .02
❑ 784 Joe Sambito .05 .02
❑ 785 Alvin Davis .05 .02
❑ 786 Joe Price .05 .02
(Inconsistent design,
orange team name)
❑ 787 Bill Almon .05 .02
❑ 788 Ray Searage .05 .02
❑ 789 Indians' TL .10 .05
Joe Carter and
Cory Snyder
❑ 790 Dave Righetti .05 .02
❑ 791 Ted Simmons .10 .05
❑ 792 John Tudor .05 .02

## 1988 Topps Traded

| | MINT | NRMT |
|---|---|---|
| COMP.FACT.SET (132) | 10.00 | 4.50 |
| ❑ 1T Jim Abbott OLY XRC | .50 | .23 |
| ❑ 2T Juan Agosto | .10 | .05 |
| ❑ 3T Luis Alicea XRC | .20 | .09 |
| ❑ 4T Roberto Alomar XRC | 3.00 | 1.35 |
| ❑ 5T Brady Anderson XRC | 1.00 | .45 |
| ❑ 6T Jack Armstrong XRC | .10 | .05 |
| ❑ 7T Don August | .10 | .05 |
| ❑ 8T Floyd Bannister | .10 | .05 |
| ❑ 9T Bret Barberie OLY XRC | .20 | .09 |
| ❑ 10T Jose Bautista | .10 | .05 |
| ❑ 11T Don Baylor | .20 | .09 |
| ❑ 12T Tim Belcher | .20 | .09 |
| ❑ 13T Buddy Bell | .20 | .09 |
| ❑ 14T Andy Benes OLY XRC | .50 | .23 |
| ❑ 15T Damon Berryhill XRC* | .10 | .05 |
| ❑ 16T Bud Black | .10 | .05 |

❑ 17T Pat Borders XRC .20 .09
❑ 18T Phil Bradley .10 .05
❑ 19T Jeff Branson XRC OLY .20 .09
❑ 20T Tom Brunansky .10 .05
❑ 21T Jay Buhner XRC .75 .35
❑ 22T Brett Butler .20 .09
❑ 23T Jim Campanis OLY .10 .05
❑ 24T Sil Campusano .10 .05
❑ 25T John Candelaria .10 .05
❑ 26T Jose Cecena .10 .05
❑ 27T Rick Cerone .10 .05
❑ 28T Jack Clark .20 .09
❑ 29T Kevin Coffman .10 .05
❑ 30T Pat Combs XRC OLY .10 .05
❑ 31T Henry Cotto .10 .05
❑ 32T Chili Davis .30 .14
❑ 33T Mike Davis .10 .05
❑ 34T Jose DeLeon .10 .05
❑ 35T Richard Dotson .10 .05
❑ 36T Cecil Espy .10 .05
❑ 37T Tom Filer .10 .05
❑ 38T Mike Fiore OLY .10 .05
❑ 39T Ron Gant XRC .50 .23
❑ 40T Kirk Gibson .50 .23
❑ 41T Rich Gossage .20 .09
❑ 42T Mark Grace XRC 1.50 .70
❑ 43T Alfredo Griffin .10 .05
❑ 44T Ty Griffin OLY .10 .05
❑ 45T Bryan Harvey XRC .20 .09
❑ 46T Ron Hassey .10 .05
❑ 47T Ray Hayward .10 .05
❑ 48T Dave Henderson .10 .05
❑ 49T Tom Herr .10 .05
❑ 50T Bob Horner .10 .05
❑ 51T Ricky Horton .10 .05
❑ 52T Jay Howell .10 .05
❑ 53T Glenn Hubbard .10 .05
❑ 54T Jeff Innis .10 .05
❑ 55T Danny Jackson .10 .05
❑ 56T Darrin Jackson XRC* .20 .09
❑ 57T Roberto Kelly XRC* .50 .23
❑ 58T Ron Kittle .10 .05
❑ 59T Ray Knight .10 .05
❑ 60T Vance Law .10 .05
❑ 61T Jeffrey Leonard .10 .05
❑ 62T Mike Macfarlane XRC .10 .05
❑ 63T Scotti Madison .10 .05
❑ 64T Kirt Manwaring .10 .05
❑ 65T Mark Marquess OLY CO .10 .05
❑ 66T Tino Martinez OLY XRC 2.50 1.10
❑ 67T Billy Masse OLY XRC .10 .05
❑ 68T Jack McDowell XRC .50 .23
❑ 69T Jack McKeon MG .10 .05
❑ 70T Larry McWilliams .10 .05
❑ 71T Mickey Morandini OLY XRC .50 .23
❑ 72T Keith Moreland .10 .05
❑ 73T Mike Morgan .10 .05
❑ 74T Charles Nagy OLY XRC .50 .23
❑ 75T Al Nipper .10 .05
❑ 76T Russ Nixon MG .10 .05
❑ 77T Jesse Orosco .10 .05
❑ 78T Joe Orsulak .10 .05
❑ 79T Dave Palmer .10 .05
❑ 80T Mark Parent .10 .05
❑ 81T Dave Parker .20 .09
❑ 82T Dan Pasqua .10 .05
❑ 83T Melido Perez XRC* .10 .05
❑ 84T Steve Peters .10 .05
❑ 85T Dan Petry .10 .05
❑ 86T Gary Pettis .10 .05
❑ 87T Jeff Pico .10 .05
❑ 88T Jim Poole XRC OLY .20 .09
❑ 89T Ted Power .10 .05
❑ 90T Rafael Ramirez .10 .05
❑ 91T Dennis Rasmussen .10 .05
❑ 92T Jose Rijo .10 .05
❑ 93T Ernie Riles .10 .05
❑ 94T Luis Rivera .10 .05
❑ 95T Doug Robbins XRC OLY .10 .05
❑ 96T Frank Robinson MG .30 .14
❑ 97T Cookie Rojas MG .10 .05
❑ 98T Chris Sabo XRC .20 .09
❑ 99T Mark Salas .10 .05
❑ 100T Luis Salazar .10 .05
❑ 101T Rafael Santana .10 .05
❑ 102T Nelson Santovenia .10 .05
❑ 103T Mackey Sasser XRC* .10 .05
❑ 104T Calvin Schiraldi .10 .05
❑ 105T Mike Schooler .10 .05
❑ 106T Scott Servais XRC OLY .10 .05
❑ 107T Dave Silvestri XRC OLY .10 .05
❑ 108T Don Slaught .10 .05
❑ 109T Joe Slusarski XRC OLY .10 .05
❑ 110T Lee Smith .20 .09
❑ 111T Pete Smith XRC* .10 .05
❑ 112T Jim Snyder MG .10 .05
❑ 113T Ed Sprague OLY XRC .50 .23
❑ 114T Pete Stanicek .10 .05
❑ 115T Kurt Stillwell .10 .05
❑ 116T Todd Stottlemyre XRC .50 .23
❑ 117T Bill Swift .10 .05
❑ 118T Pat Tabler .10 .05
❑ 119T Scott Terry .10 .05
❑ 120T Mickey Tettleton .10 .05
❑ 121T Dickie Thon .10 .05
❑ 122T Jeff Treadway XRC* .10 .05
❑ 123T Willie Upshaw .10 .05
❑ 124T Robin Ventura OLY XRC 4.00 1.80
❑ 125T Ron Washington .10 .05
❑ 126T Walt Weiss XRC* .50 .23
❑ 127T Bob Welch .10 .05
❑ 128T David Wells XRC 2.00 .90
❑ 129T Glenn Wilson .10 .05
❑ 130T Ted Wood XRC OLY .10 .05
❑ 131T Don Zimmer MG .20 .09
❑ 132T Checklist 1T-132T .10 .05

## 1989 Topps

| | MINT | NRMT |
|---|---|---|
| COMPLETE SET (792) | 15.00 | 6.75 |
| COMP.FACT.SET (792) | 20.00 | 9.00 |

❑ 1 George Bell RB .05 .02
Slams 3 Opening Day HR's
❑ 2 Wade Boggs RB .10 .05
200 Hits 6th Straight Season
❑ 3 Gary Carter RB .10 .05
Career Putouts Record
❑ 4 Andre Dawson RB .10 .05
Logs Double Figures
in HR and SB
❑ 5 Orel Hershiser RB .10 .05
59 Scoreless Innings
❑ 6 Doug Jones RB UER .05 .02
Earns His 15th
Straight Save
(Photo actually
Chris Codiroli)
❑ 7 Kevin McReynolds RB .05 .02
Steals 21 Without
Being Caught
❑ 8 Dave Eiland .05 .02
❑ 9 Tim Teufel .05 .02
❑ 10 Andre Dawson .15 .07
❑ 11 Bruce Sutter .05 .02
❑ 12 Dale Sveum .05 .02
❑ 13 Doug Sisk .05 .02
❑ 14 Tom Kelly MG .05 .02
❑ 15 Robby Thompson .05 .02
❑ 16 Ron Robinson .05 .02
❑ 17 Brian Downing .05 .02
❑ 18 Rick Rhoden .05 .02
❑ 19 Greg Gagne .05 .02
❑ 20 Steve Bedrosian .05 .02
❑ 21 Chicago White Sox TL .05 .02
Greg Walker
❑ 22 Tim Crews .05 .02
❑ 23 Mike Fitzgerald .05 .02
❑ 24 Larry Andersen .05 .02
❑ 25 Frank White .10 .05
❑ 26 Dale Mohorcic .05 .02
❑ 27A Orestes Destrade .05 .02
(F* next to copyright) RC*
❑ 27B Orestes Destrade .05 .02
(E*F* next to
copyright) RC*
❑ 28 Mike Moore .05 .02
❑ 29 Kelly Gruber .05 .02
❑ 30 Dwight Gooden .10 .05
❑ 31 Terry Francona .10 .05
❑ 32 Dennis Rasmussen .05 .02
❑ 33 B.J. Surhoff .10 .05
❑ 34 Ken Williams .05 .02
❑ 35 John Tudor UER .05 .02
(With Red Sox in '84;should
be Pirates)
❑ 36 Mitch Webster .05 .02
❑ 37 Bob Stanley .05 .02
❑ 38 Paul Runge .05 .02
❑ 39 Mike Maddux .05 .02
❑ 40 Steve Sax .05 .02
❑ 41 Terry Mulholland .05 .02
❑ 42 Jim Eppard .05 .02
❑ 43 Guillermo Hernandez .05 .02
❑ 44 Jim Snyder MG .05 .02
❑ 45 Kal Daniels .05 .02
❑ 46 Mark Portugal .05 .02
❑ 47 Carney Lansford .10 .05
❑ 48 Tim Burke .05 .02
❑ 49 Craig Biggio RC .75 .35
❑ 50 George Bell .05 .02
❑ 51 California Angels TL .05 .02
Mark McLemore
❑ 52 Bob Brenly .05 .02
❑ 53 Ruben Sierra .05 .02
❑ 54 Steve Trout .05 .02
❑ 55 Julio Franco .05 .02
❑ 56 Pat Tabler .05 .02
❑ 57 Alejandro Pena .05 .02
❑ 58 Lee Mazzilli .05 .02
❑ 59 Mark Davis .05 .02
❑ 60 Tom Brunansky .05 .02
❑ 61 Neil Allen .05 .02
❑ 62 Alfredo Griffin .05 .02
❑ 63 Mark Clear .05 .02
❑ 64 Alex Trevino .05 .02
❑ 65 Rick Reuschel .05 .02
❑ 66 Manny Trillo .05 .02
❑ 67 Dave Palmer .05 .02
❑ 68 Darrell Miller .05 .02
❑ 69 Jeff Ballard .05 .02
❑ 70 Mark McGwire 1.00 .45
❑ 71 Mike Boddicker .05 .02
❑ 72 John Moses .05 .02
❑ 73 Pascual Perez .05 .02
❑ 74 Nick Leyva MG .05 .02
❑ 75 Tom Henke .05 .02
❑ 76 Terry Blocker .05 .02
❑ 77 Doyle Alexander .05 .02
❑ 78 Jim Sundberg .05 .02
❑ 79 Scott Bankhead .05 .02
❑ 80 Cory Snyder .05 .02
❑ 81 Montreal Expos TL .10 .05
Tim Raines
❑ 82 Dave Leiper .05 .02
❑ 83 Jeff Blauser .10 .05
❑ 84 Bill Bene FDP .05 .02
❑ 85 Kevin McReynolds .05 .02
❑ 86 Al Nipper .05 .02
❑ 87 Larry Owen .05 .02
❑ 88 Darryl Hamilton RC* .05 .02
❑ 89 Dave LaPoint .05 .02
❑ 90 Vince Coleman UER .05 .02
(Wrong birth year)
❑ 91 Floyd Youmans .05 .02
❑ 92 Jeff Kunkel .05 .02
❑ 93 Ken Howell .05 .02
❑ 94 Chris Speier .05 .02
❑ 95 Gerald Young .05 .02

| | | | |
|---|---|---|---|
| ❑ | 96 Rick Cerone | .05 | .02 |
| ❑ | 97 Greg Mathews | .05 | .02 |
| ❑ | 98 Larry Sheets | .05 | .02 |
| ❑ | 99 Sherman Corbett | .05 | .02 |
| ❑ | 100 Mike Schmidt | .40 | .18 |
| ❑ | 101 Les Straker | .05 | .02 |
| ❑ | 102 Mike Gallego | .05 | .02 |
| ❑ | 103 Tim Birtsas | .05 | .02 |
| ❑ | 104 Dallas Green MG | .05 | .02 |
| ❑ | 105 Ron Darling | .05 | .02 |
| ❑ | 106 Willie Upshaw | .05 | .02 |
| ❑ | 107 Jose DeLeon | .05 | .02 |
| ❑ | 108 Fred Manrique | .05 | .02 |
| ❑ | 109 Hipolito Pena | .05 | .02 |
| ❑ | 110 Paul Molitor | .20 | .09 |
| ❑ | 111 Cincinnati Reds TL | .05 | .02 |
| | Eric Davis | | |
| | (Swinging bat) | | |
| ❑ | 112 Jim Presley | .05 | .02 |
| ❑ | 113 Lloyd Moseby | .05 | .02 |
| ❑ | 114 Bob Kipper | .05 | .02 |
| ❑ | 115 Jody Davis | .05 | .02 |
| ❑ | 116 Jeff Montgomery | .10 | .05 |
| ❑ | 117 Dave Anderson | .05 | .02 |
| ❑ | 118 Checklist 1-132 | .05 | .02 |
| ❑ | 119 Terry Puhl | .05 | .02 |
| ❑ | 120 Frank Viola | .05 | .02 |
| ❑ | 121 Garry Templeton | .05 | .02 |
| ❑ | 122 Lance Johnson | .10 | .05 |
| ❑ | 123 Spike Owen | .05 | .02 |
| ❑ | 124 Jim Traber | .05 | .02 |
| ❑ | 125 Mike Krukow | .05 | .02 |
| ❑ | 126 Sid Bream | .05 | .02 |
| ❑ | 127 Walt Terrell | .05 | .02 |
| ❑ | 128 Milt Thompson | .05 | .02 |
| ❑ | 129 Terry Clark | .05 | .02 |
| ❑ | 130 Gerald Perry | .05 | .02 |
| ❑ | 131 Dave Otto | .05 | .02 |
| ❑ | 132 Curt Ford | .05 | .02 |
| ❑ | 133 Bill Long | .05 | .02 |
| ❑ | 134 Don Zimmer MG | .05 | .02 |
| ❑ | 135 Jose Rijo | .05 | .02 |
| ❑ | 136 Joey Meyer | .05 | .02 |
| ❑ | 137 Geno Petralli | .05 | .02 |
| ❑ | 138 Wallace Johnson | .05 | .02 |
| ❑ | 139 Mike Flanagan | .05 | .02 |
| ❑ | 140 Shawon Dunston | .05 | .02 |
| ❑ | 141 Cleveland Indians TL | .05 | .02 |
| | Brook Jacoby | | |
| ❑ | 142 Mike Diaz | .05 | .02 |
| ❑ | 143 Mike Campbell | .05 | .02 |
| ❑ | 144 Jay Bell | .15 | .07 |
| ❑ | 145 Dave Stewart | .10 | .05 |
| ❑ | 146 Gary Pettis | .05 | .02 |
| ❑ | 147 DeWayne Buice | .05 | .02 |
| ❑ | 148 Bill Pecota | .05 | .02 |
| ❑ | 149 Doug Dascenzo | .05 | .02 |
| ❑ | 150 Fernando Valenzuela | .10 | .05 |
| ❑ | 151 Terry McGriff | .05 | .02 |
| ❑ | 152 Mark Thurmond | .05 | .02 |
| ❑ | 153 Jim Pankovits | .05 | .02 |
| ❑ | 154 Don Carman | .05 | .02 |
| ❑ | 155 Marty Barrett | .05 | .02 |
| ❑ | 156 Dave Gallagher | .05 | .02 |
| ❑ | 157 Tom Glavine | .20 | .09 |
| ❑ | 158 Mike Aldrete | .05 | .02 |
| ❑ | 159 Pat Clements | .05 | .02 |
| ❑ | 160 Jeffrey Leonard | .05 | .02 |
| ❑ | 161 Gregg Olson RC FDP UER | .20 | .09 |
| | (Born Scribner, NE, | | |
| | should be Omaha, NE) | | |
| ❑ | 162 John Davis | .05 | .02 |
| ❑ | 163 Bob Forsch | .05 | .02 |
| ❑ | 164 Hal Lanier MG | .05 | .02 |
| ❑ | 165 Mike Dunne | .05 | .02 |
| ❑ | 166 Doug Jennings | .05 | .02 |
| ❑ | 167 Steve Searcy FS | .05 | .02 |
| ❑ | 168 Willie Wilson | .05 | .02 |
| ❑ | 169 Mike Jackson | .05 | .02 |
| ❑ | 170 Tony Fernandez | .05 | .02 |
| ❑ | 171 Atlanta Braves TL | .05 | .02 |
| | Andres Thomas | | |
| ❑ | 172 Frank Williams | .05 | .02 |
| ❑ | 173 Mel Hall | .05 | .02 |
| ❑ | 174 Todd Burns | .05 | .02 |
| ❑ | 175 John Shelby | .05 | .02 |
| ❑ | 176 Jeff Parrett | .05 | .02 |
| ❑ | 177 Monty Fariss FDP | .05 | .02 |
| ❑ | 178 Mark Grant | .05 | .02 |
| ❑ | 179 Ozzie Virgil | .05 | .02 |
| ❑ | 180 Mike Scott | .05 | .02 |
| ❑ | 181 Craig Worthington | .05 | .02 |
| ❑ | 182 Bob McClure | .05 | .02 |
| ❑ | 183 Oddibe McDowell | .05 | .02 |
| ❑ | 184 John Costello | .05 | .02 |
| ❑ | 185 Claudell Washington | .05 | .02 |
| ❑ | 186 Pat Perry | .05 | .02 |
| ❑ | 187 Darren Daulton | .10 | .05 |
| ❑ | 188 Dennis Lamp | .05 | .02 |
| ❑ | 189 Kevin Mitchell | .10 | .05 |
| ❑ | 190 Mike Witt | .05 | .02 |
| ❑ | 191 Sil Campusano | .05 | .02 |
| ❑ | 192 Paul Mirabella | .05 | .02 |
| ❑ | 193 Sparky Anderson MG | .10 | .05 |
| | UER (553 Salazer) | | |
| ❑ | 194 Greg W. Harris RC | .05 | .02 |
| ❑ | 195 Ozzie Guillen | .05 | .02 |
| ❑ | 196 Denny Walling | .05 | .02 |
| ❑ | 197 Neal Heaton | .05 | .02 |
| ❑ | 198 Danny Heep | .05 | .02 |
| ❑ | 199 Mike Schooler RC* | .05 | .02 |
| ❑ | 200 George Brett | .40 | .18 |
| ❑ | 201 Blue Jays TL | .05 | .02 |
| | Kelly Gruber | | |
| ❑ | 202 Brad Moore | .05 | .02 |
| ❑ | 203 Rob Ducey | .05 | .02 |
| ❑ | 204 Brad Havens | .05 | .02 |
| ❑ | 205 Dwight Evans | .10 | .05 |
| ❑ | 206 Roberto Alomar | .30 | .14 |
| ❑ | 207 Terry Leach | .05 | .02 |
| ❑ | 208 Tom Pagnozzi | .05 | .02 |
| ❑ | 209 Jeff Bittiger | .05 | .02 |
| ❑ | 210 Dale Murphy | .20 | .09 |
| ❑ | 211 Mike Pagliarulo | .05 | .02 |
| ❑ | 212 Scott Sanderson | .05 | .02 |
| ❑ | 213 Rene Gonzales | .05 | .02 |
| ❑ | 214 Charlie O'Brien | .05 | .02 |
| ❑ | 215 Kevin Gross | .05 | .02 |
| ❑ | 216 Jack Howell | .05 | .02 |
| ❑ | 217 Joe Price | .05 | .02 |
| ❑ | 218 Mike LaValliere | .05 | .02 |
| ❑ | 219 Jim Clancy | .05 | .02 |
| ❑ | 220 Gary Gaetti | .10 | .05 |
| ❑ | 221 Cecil Espy | .05 | .02 |
| ❑ | 222 Mark Lewis FDP RC | .10 | .05 |
| ❑ | 223 Jay Buhner | .10 | .05 |
| ❑ | 224 Tony LaRussa MG | .10 | .05 |
| ❑ | 225 Ramon Martinez RC | .25 | .11 |
| ❑ | 226 Bill Doran | .05 | .02 |
| ❑ | 227 John Farrell | .05 | .02 |
| ❑ | 228 Nelson Santovenia | .05 | .02 |
| ❑ | 229 Jimmy Key | .10 | .05 |
| ❑ | 230 Ozzie Smith | .25 | .11 |
| ❑ | 231 San Diego Padres TL | .20 | .09 |
| | Roberto Alomar | | |
| | (Gary Carter at plate) | | |
| ❑ | 232 Ricky Horton | .05 | .02 |
| ❑ | 233 Gregg Jefferies FS | .10 | .05 |
| ❑ | 234 Tom Browning | .05 | .02 |
| ❑ | 235 John Kruk | .10 | .05 |
| ❑ | 236 Charles Hudson | .05 | .02 |
| ❑ | 237 Glenn Hubbard | .05 | .02 |
| ❑ | 238 Eric King | .05 | .02 |
| ❑ | 239 Tim Laudner | .05 | .02 |
| ❑ | 240 Greg Maddux | .60 | .25 |
| ❑ | 241 Brett Butler | .10 | .05 |
| ❑ | 242 Ed VandeBerg | .05 | .02 |
| ❑ | 243 Bob Boone | .10 | .05 |
| ❑ | 244 Jim Acker | .05 | .02 |
| ❑ | 245 Jim Rice | .10 | .05 |
| ❑ | 246 Rey Quinones | .05 | .02 |
| ❑ | 247 Shawn Hillegas | .05 | .02 |
| ❑ | 248 Tony Phillips | .05 | .02 |
| ❑ | 249 Tim Leary | .05 | .02 |
| ❑ | 250 Cal Ripken | .75 | .35 |
| ❑ | 251 John Dopson | .05 | .02 |
| ❑ | 252 Billy Hatcher | .05 | .02 |
| ❑ | 253 Jose Alvarez | .05 | .02 |
| ❑ | 254 Tom Lasorda MG | .20 | .09 |
| ❑ | 255 Ron Guidry | .10 | .05 |
| ❑ | 256 Benny Santiago | .05 | .02 |
| ❑ | 257 Rick Aguilera | .10 | .05 |
| ❑ | 258 Checklist 133-264 | .05 | .02 |
| ❑ | 259 Larry McWilliams | .05 | .02 |
| ❑ | 260 Dave Winfield | .20 | .09 |
| ❑ | 261 St.Louis Cardinals TL | .05 | .02 |
| | Tom Brunansky | | |
| | (With Luis Alicea) | | |
| ❑ | 262 Jeff Pico | .05 | .02 |
| ❑ | 263 Mike Felder | .05 | .02 |
| ❑ | 264 Rob Dibble RC* | .10 | .05 |
| ❑ | 265 Kent Hrbek | .10 | .05 |
| ❑ | 266 Luis Aquino | .05 | .02 |
| ❑ | 267 Jeff M. Robinson | .05 | .02 |
| ❑ | 268 N. Keith Miller | .05 | .02 |
| ❑ | 269 Tom Bolton | .05 | .02 |
| ❑ | 270 Wally Joyner | .10 | .05 |
| ❑ | 271 Jay Tibbs | .05 | .02 |
| ❑ | 272 Ron Hassey | .05 | .02 |
| ❑ | 273 Jose Lind | .05 | .02 |
| ❑ | 274 Mark Eichhorn | .05 | .02 |
| ❑ | 275 Danny Tartabull UER | .05 | .02 |
| | (Born San Juan, PR; | | |
| | should be Miami, FL) | | |
| ❑ | 276 Paul Kilgus | .05 | .02 |
| ❑ | 277 Mike Davis | .05 | .02 |
| ❑ | 278 Andy McGaffigan | .05 | .02 |
| ❑ | 279 Scott Bradley | .05 | .02 |
| ❑ | 280 Bob Knepper | .05 | .02 |
| ❑ | 281 Gary Redus | .05 | .02 |
| ❑ | 282 Cris Carpenter RC* | .05 | .02 |
| ❑ | 283 Andy Allanson | .05 | .02 |
| ❑ | 284 Jim Leyland MG | .10 | .05 |
| ❑ | 285 John Candelaria | .05 | .02 |
| ❑ | 286 Darrin Jackson | .05 | .02 |
| ❑ | 287 Juan Nieves | .05 | .02 |
| ❑ | 288 Pat Sheridan | .05 | .02 |
| ❑ | 289 Ernie Whitt | .05 | .02 |
| ❑ | 290 John Franco | .10 | .05 |
| ❑ | 291 New York Mets TL | .10 | .05 |
| | Darryl Strawberry | | |
| | (With Keith Hernandez | | |
| | and Kevin McReynolds) | | |
| ❑ | 292 Jim Corsi | .05 | .02 |
| ❑ | 293 Glenn Wilson | .05 | .02 |
| ❑ | 294 Juan Berenguer | .05 | .02 |
| ❑ | 295 Scott Fletcher | .05 | .02 |
| ❑ | 296 Ron Gant | .10 | .05 |
| ❑ | 297 Oswald Peraza | .05 | .02 |
| ❑ | 298 Chris James | .05 | .02 |
| ❑ | 299 Steve Ellsworth | .05 | .02 |
| ❑ | 300 Darryl Strawberry | .10 | .05 |
| ❑ | 301 Charlie Leibrandt | .05 | .02 |
| ❑ | 302 Gary Ward | .05 | .02 |
| ❑ | 303 Felix Fermin | .05 | .02 |
| ❑ | 304 Joel Youngblood | .05 | .02 |
| ❑ | 305 Dave Smith | .05 | .02 |
| ❑ | 306 Tracy Woodson | .05 | .02 |
| ❑ | 307 Lance McCullers | .05 | .02 |
| ❑ | 308 Ron Karkovice | .05 | .02 |
| ❑ | 309 Mario Diaz | .05 | .02 |
| ❑ | 310 Rafael Palmeiro | .25 | .11 |
| ❑ | 311 Chris Bosio | .05 | .02 |
| ❑ | 312 Tom Lawless | .05 | .02 |
| ❑ | 313 Dennis Martinez | .10 | .05 |
| ❑ | 314 Bobby Valentine MG | .05 | .02 |
| ❑ | 315 Greg Swindell | .05 | .02 |
| ❑ | 316 Walt Weiss | .05 | .02 |
| ❑ | 317 Jack Armstrong RC* | .05 | .02 |
| ❑ | 318 Gene Larkin | .05 | .02 |
| ❑ | 319 Greg Booker | .05 | .02 |
| ❑ | 320 Lou Whitaker | .10 | .05 |
| ❑ | 321 Boston Red Sox TL | .05 | .02 |
| | Jody Reed | | |
| ❑ | 322 John Smiley | .05 | .02 |
| ❑ | 323 Gary Thurman | .05 | .02 |
| ❑ | 324 Bob Milacki | .05 | .02 |
| ❑ | 325 Jesse Barfield | .05 | .02 |
| ❑ | 326 Dennis Boyd | .05 | .02 |
| ❑ | 327 Mark Lemke RC | .15 | .07 |
| ❑ | 328 Rick Honeycutt | .05 | .02 |
| ❑ | 329 Bob Melvin | .05 | .02 |
| ❑ | 330 Eric Davis | .10 | .05 |
| ❑ | 331 Curt Wilkerson | .05 | .02 |
| ❑ | 332 Tony Armas | .05 | .02 |
| ❑ | 333 Bob Ojeda | .05 | .02 |
| ❑ | 334 Steve Lyons | .05 | .02 |
| ❑ | 335 Dave Righetti | .05 | .02 |

❑ 336 Steve Balboni .05 .02
❑ 337 Calvin Schiraldi .05 .02
❑ 338 Jim Adduci .05 .02
❑ 339 Scott Bailes .05 .02
❑ 340 Kirk Gibson .10 .05
❑ 341 Jim Deshaies .05 .02
❑ 342 Tom Brookens .05 .02
❑ 343 Gary Sheffield FS RC .. 1.25 .55
❑ 344 Tom Trebelhorn MG .05 .02
❑ 345 Charlie Hough .10 .05
❑ 346 Rex Hudler .05 .02
❑ 347 John Cerutti .05 .02
❑ 348 Ed Hearn .05 .02
❑ 349 Ron Jones .05 .02
❑ 350 Andy Van Slyke .10 .05
❑ 351 San Fran. Giants TL .05 .02
Bob Melvin
(With Bill Fahey CO)
❑ 352 Rick Schu .05 .02
❑ 353 Marvell Wynne .05 .02
❑ 354 Larry Parrish .05 .02
❑ 355 Mark Langston .05 .02
❑ 356 Kevin Elster .05 .02
❑ 357 Jerry Reuss .05 .02
❑ 358 Ricky Jordan RC* .10 .05
❑ 359 Tommy John .10 .05
❑ 360 Ryne Sandberg .25 .11
❑ 361 Kelly Downs .05 .02
❑ 362 Jack Lazorko .05 .02
❑ 363 Rich Yett .05 .02
❑ 364 Rob Deer .05 .02
❑ 365 Mike Henneman .05 .02
❑ 366 Herm Winningham .05 .02
❑ 367 Johnny Paredes .05 .02
❑ 368 Brian Holton .05 .02
❑ 369 Ken Caminiti .10 .05
❑ 370 Dennis Eckersley .15 .07
❑ 371 Manny Lee .05 .02
❑ 372 Craig Lefferts .05 .02
❑ 373 Tracy Jones .05 .02
❑ 374 John Wathan MG .05 .02
❑ 375 Terry Pendleton .10 .05
❑ 376 Steve Lombardozzi .05 .02
❑ 377 Mike Smithson .05 .02
❑ 378 Checklist 265-396 .05 .02
❑ 379 Tim Flannery .05 .02
❑ 380 Rickey Henderson .25 .11
❑ 381 Baltimore Orioles TL .05 .02
Larry Sheets
❑ 382 John Smoltz RC .40 .18
❑ 383 Howard Johnson .05 .02
❑ 384 Mark Salas .05 .02
❑ 385 Von Hayes .05 .02
❑ 386 Andres Galarraga AS .05 .02
❑ 387 Ryne Sandberg AS .15 .07
❑ 388 Bobby Bonilla AS .10 .05
❑ 389 Ozzie Smith AS .15 .07
❑ 390 Darryl Strawberry AS .05 .02
❑ 391 Andre Dawson AS .10 .05
❑ 392 Andy Van Slyke AS .05 .02
❑ 393 Gary Carter AS .10 .05
❑ 394 Orel Hershiser AS .10 .05
❑ 395 Danny Jackson AS .05 .02
❑ 396 Kirk Gibson AS .10 .05
❑ 397 Don Mattingly AS .15 .07
❑ 398 Julio Franco AS .05 .02
❑ 399 Wade Boggs AS .10 .05
❑ 400 Alan Trammell AS .05 .02
❑ 401 Jose Canseco AS .10 .05
❑ 402 Mike Greenwell AS .05 .02
❑ 403 Kirby Puckett AS .25 .11
❑ 404 Bob Boone AS .05 .02
❑ 405 Roger Clemens AS .20 .09
❑ 406 Frank Viola AS .05 .02
❑ 407 Dave Winfield AS .10 .05
❑ 408 Greg Walker .05 .02
❑ 409 Ken Dayley .05 .02
❑ 410 Jack Clark .05 .02
❑ 411 Mitch Williams .05 .02
❑ 412 Barry Lyons .05 .02
❑ 413 Mike Kingery .05 .02
❑ 414 Jim Fregosi MG .05 .02
❑ 415 Rich Gossage .10 .05
❑ 416 Fred Lynn .05 .02
❑ 417 Mike LaCoss .05 .02
❑ 418 Bob Dernier .05 .02
❑ 419 Tom Filer .05 .02
❑ 420 Joe Carter .15 .07
❑ 421 Kirk McCaskill .05 .02
❑ 422 Bo Diaz .05 .02
❑ 423 Brian Fisher .05 .02
❑ 424 Luis Polonia UER .05 .02
(Wrong birthdate)
❑ 425 Jay Howell .05 .02
❑ 426 Dan Gladden .05 .02
❑ 427 Eric Show .05 .02
❑ 428 Craig Reynolds .05 .02
❑ 429 Minnesota Twins TL .05 .02
Greg Gagne
(Taking throw at 2nd)
❑ 430 Mark Gubicza .05 .02
❑ 431 Luis Rivera .05 .02
❑ 432 Chad Kreuter RC .05 .02
❑ 433 Albert Hall .05 .02
❑ 434 Ken Patterson .05 .02
❑ 435 Len Dykstra .10 .05
❑ 436 Bobby Meacham .05 .02
❑ 437 Andy Benes FDP RC .25 .11
❑ 438 Greg Gross .05 .02
❑ 439 Frank DiPino .05 .02
❑ 440 Bobby Bonilla .10 .05
❑ 441 Jerry Reed .05 .02
❑ 442 Jose Oquendo .05 .02
❑ 443 Rod Nichols .05 .02
❑ 444 Moose Stubing MG .05 .02
❑ 445 Matt Nokes .05 .02
❑ 446 Rob Murphy .05 .02
❑ 447 Donell Nixon .05 .02
❑ 448 Eric Plunk .05 .02
❑ 449 Carmelo Martinez .05 .02
❑ 450 Roger Clemens .40 .18
❑ 451 Mark Davidson .05 .02
❑ 452 Israel Sanchez .05 .02
❑ 453 Tom Prince .05 .02
❑ 454 Paul Assenmacher .05 .02
❑ 455 Johnny Ray .05 .02
❑ 456 Tim Belcher .05 .02
❑ 457 Mackey Sasser .05 .02
❑ 458 Donn Pall .05 .02
❑ 459 Seattle Mariners TL .05 .02
Dave Valle
❑ 460 Dave Stieb .05 .02
❑ 461 Buddy Bell .10 .05
❑ 462 Jose Guzman .05 .02
❑ 463 Steve Lake .05 .02
❑ 464 Bryn Smith .05 .02
❑ 465 Mark Grace .20 .09
❑ 466 Chuck Crim .05 .02
❑ 467 Jim Walewander .05 .02
❑ 468 Henry Cotto .05 .02
❑ 469 Jose Bautista .05 .02
❑ 470 Lance Parrish .05 .02
❑ 471 Steve Curry .05 .02
❑ 472 Brian Harper .05 .02
❑ 473 Don Robinson .05 .02
❑ 474 Bob Rodgers MG .05 .02
❑ 475 Dave Parker .10 .05
❑ 476 Jon Perlman .05 .02
❑ 477 Dick Schofield .05 .02
❑ 478 Doug Drabek .05 .02
❑ 479 Mike Macfarlane RC* .05 .02
❑ 480 Keith Hernandez .10 .05
❑ 481 Chris Brown .05 .02
❑ 482 Steve Peters .05 .02
❑ 483 Mickey Hatcher .05 .02
❑ 484 Steve Shields .05 .02
❑ 485 Hubie Brooks .05 .02
❑ 486 Jack McDowell .10 .05
❑ 487 Scott Lusader .05 .02
❑ 488 Kevin Coffman .05 .02
Now with Cubs
❑ 489 Phila. Phillies TL .10 .05
Mike Schmidt
❑ 490 Chris Sabo RC* .05 .02
❑ 491 Mike Birkbeck .05 .02
❑ 492 Alan Ashby .05 .02
❑ 493 Todd Benzinger .05 .02
❑ 494 Shane Rawley .05 .02
❑ 495 Candy Maldonado .05 .02
❑ 496 Dwayne Henry .05 .02
❑ 497 Pete Stanicek .05 .02
❑ 498 Dave Valle .05 .02
❑ 499 Don Heinkel .05 .02
❑ 500 Jose Canseco .25 .11
❑ 501 Vance Law .05 .02
❑ 502 Duane Ward .05 .02
❑ 503 Al Newman .05 .02
❑ 504 Bob Walk .05 .02
❑ 505 Pete Rose MG .50 .23
❑ 506 Kirt Manwaring .05 .02
❑ 507 Steve Farr .05 .02
❑ 508 Wally Backman .05 .02
❑ 509 Bud Black .05 .02
❑ 510 Bob Horner .05 .02
❑ 511 Richard Dotson .05 .02
❑ 512 Donnie Hill .05 .02
❑ 513 Jesse Orosco .05 .02
❑ 514 Chet Lemon .05 .02
❑ 515 Barry Larkin .20 .09
❑ 516 Eddie Whitson .05 .02
❑ 517 Greg Brock .05 .02
❑ 518 Bruce Ruffin .05 .02
❑ 519 New York Yankees TL .. .05 .02
Willie Randolph
❑ 520 Rick Sutcliffe .10 .05
❑ 521 Mickey Tettleton .05 .02
❑ 522 Randy Kramer .05 .02
❑ 523 Andres Thomas .05 .02
❑ 524 Checklist 397-528 .05 .02
❑ 525 Chili Davis .10 .05
❑ 526 Wes Gardner .05 .02
❑ 527 Dave Henderson .05 .02
❑ 528 Luis Medina .05 .02
(Lower left front
has white triangle)
❑ 529 Tom Foley .05 .02
❑ 530 Nolan Ryan 1.00 .45
❑ 531 Dave Hengel .05 .02
❑ 532 Jerry Browne .05 .02
❑ 533 Andy Hawkins .05 .02
❑ 534 Doc Edwards MG .05 .02
❑ 535 Todd Worrell UER .05 .02
(4 wins in '88,
should be 5)
❑ 536 Joel Skinner .05 .02
❑ 537 Pete Smith .05 .02
❑ 538 Juan Castillo .05 .02
❑ 539 Barry Jones .05 .02
❑ 540 Bo Jackson .15 .07
❑ 541 Cecil Fielder .10 .05
❑ 542 Todd Frohwirth .05 .02
❑ 543 Damon Berryhill .05 .02
❑ 544 Jeff Sellers .05 .02
❑ 545 Mookie Wilson .10 .05
❑ 546 Mark Williamson .05 .02
❑ 547 Mark McLemore .05 .02
❑ 548 Bobby Witt .05 .02
❑ 549 Chicago Cubs TL .05 .02
Jamie Moyer
(Pitching)
❑ 550 Orel Hershiser .10 .05
❑ 551 Randy Ready .05 .02
❑ 552 Greg Cadaret .05 .02
❑ 553 Luis Salazar .05 .02
❑ 554 Nick Esasky .05 .02
❑ 555 Bert Blyleven .10 .05
❑ 556 Bruce Fields .05 .02
❑ 557 Keith A. Miller .05 .02
❑ 558 Dan Pasqua .05 .02
❑ 559 Juan Agosto .05 .02
❑ 560 Tim Raines .10 .05
❑ 561 Luis Aguayo .05 .02
❑ 562 Danny Cox .05 .02
❑ 563 Bill Schroeder .05 .02
❑ 564 Russ Nixon MG .05 .02
❑ 565 Jeff Russell .05 .02
❑ 566 Al Pedrique .05 .02
❑ 567 David Wells UER .10 .05
(Complete Pitching
Recor)
❑ 568 Mickey Brantley .05 .02
❑ 569 German Jimenez .05 .02
❑ 570 Tony Gwynn UER .40 .18
('88 average should
be italicized as
league leader)
❑ 571 Billy Ripken .05 .02
❑ 572 Atlee Hammaker .05 .02

❑ 573 Jim Abbott FDP RC* .20 .09
❑ 574 Dave Clark .05 .02
❑ 575 Juan Samuel .05 .02
❑ 576 Greg Minton .05 .02
❑ 577 Randy Bush .05 .02
❑ 578 John Morris .05 .02
❑ 579 Houston Astros TL .05 .02
Glenn Davis
(Batting stance)
❑ 580 Harold Reynolds .05 .02
❑ 581 Gene Nelson .05 .02
❑ 582 Mike Marshall .05 .02
❑ 583 Paul Gibson .05 .02
❑ 584 Randy Velarde UER .05 .02
(Signed 1935;
should be 1985)
❑ 585 Harold Baines .10 .05
❑ 586 Joe Boever .05 .02
❑ 587 Mike Stanley .05 .02
❑ 588 Luis Alicea RC* .05 .02
❑ 589 Dave Meads .05 .02
❑ 590 Andres Galarraga .15 .07
❑ 591 Jeff Musselman .05 .02
❑ 592 John Cangelosi .05 .02
❑ 593 Drew Hall .05 .02
❑ 594 Jimy Williams MG .05 .02
❑ 595 Teddy Higuera .05 .02
❑ 596 Kurt Stillwell .05 .02
❑ 597 Terry Taylor .05 .02
❑ 598 Ken Gerhart .05 .02
❑ 599 Tom Candiotti .05 .02
❑ 600 Wade Boggs .25 .11
❑ 601 Dave Dravecky .10 .05
❑ 602 Devon White .10 .05
❑ 603 Frank Tanana .05 .02
❑ 604 Paul O'Neill .10 .05
❑ 605A Bob Welch ERR 2.00 .90
(Missing line on back;
Complete M.L. Pitching Record)
❑ 605B Bob Welch COR .05 .02
❑ 606 Rick Dempsey .05 .02
❑ 607 Willie Ansley FDP RC .05 .02
❑ 608 Phil Bradley .05 .02
❑ 609 Detroit Tigers TL .05 .02
Frank Tanana
(With Alan Trammell
and Mike Heath)
❑ 610 Randy Myers .10 .05
❑ 611 Don Slaught .05 .02
❑ 612 Dan Quisenberry .05 .02
❑ 613 Gary Varsho .05 .02
❑ 614 Joe Hesketh .05 .02
❑ 615 Robin Yount .20 .09
❑ 616 Steve Rosenberg .05 .02
❑ 617 Mark Parent .05 .02
❑ 618 Rance Mulliniks .05 .02
❑ 619 Checklist 529-660 .05 .02
❑ 620 Barry Bonds .50 .23
❑ 621 Rick Mahler .05 .02
❑ 622 Stan Javier .05 .02
❑ 623 Fred Toliver .05 .02
❑ 624 Jack McKeon MG .05 .02
❑ 625 Eddie Murray .20 .09
❑ 626 Jeff Reed .05 .02
❑ 627 Greg A. Harris .05 .02
❑ 628 Matt Williams .15 .07
❑ 629 Pete O'Brien .05 .02
❑ 630 Mike Greenwell .05 .02
❑ 631 Dave Bergman .05 .02
❑ 632 Bryan Harvey RC* .05 .02
❑ 633 Daryl Boston .05 .02
❑ 634 Marvin Freeman .05 .02
❑ 635 Willie Randolph .10 .05
❑ 636 Bill Wilkinson .05 .02
❑ 637 Carmen Castillo .05 .02
❑ 638 Floyd Bannister .05 .02
❑ 639 Oakland A's TL .05 .02
Walt Weiss
❑ 640 Willie McGee .10 .05
❑ 641 Curt Young .05 .02
❑ 642 Argenis Salazar .05 .02
❑ 643 Louie Meadows .05 .02
❑ 644 Lloyd McClendon .05 .02
❑ 645 Jack Morris .10 .05
❑ 646 Kevin Bass .05 .02
❑ 647 Randy Johnson RC 2.00 .90
❑ 648 Sandy Alomar FS RC .25 .11
❑ 649 Stewart Cliburn .05 .02
❑ 650 Kirby Puckett .50 .23
❑ 651 Tom Niedenfuer .05 .02
❑ 652 Rich Gedman .05 .02
❑ 653 Tommy Barrett .05 .02
❑ 654 Whitey Herzog MG .05 .02
❑ 655 Dave Magadan .05 .02
❑ 656 Ivan Calderon .05 .02
❑ 657 Joe Magrane .05 .02
❑ 658 R.J. Reynolds .05 .02
❑ 659 Al Leiter .20 .09
❑ 660 Will Clark .20 .09
❑ 661 Dwight Gooden TBC84 .05 .02
❑ 662 Lou Brock TBC79 .20 .09
❑ 663 Hank Aaron TBC74 .20 .09
❑ 664 Gil Hodges TBC69 .15 .07
❑ 665A Tony Oliva TBC64 2.00 .90
ERR (Fabricated card
is enlarged version
of Oliva's 64T card;
Topps copyright
missing)
❑ 665B Tony Oliva TBC64 .10 .05
COR (Fabricated
card)
❑ 666 Randy St.Claire .05 .02
❑ 667 Dwayne Murphy .05 .02
❑ 668 Mike Bielecki .05 .02
❑ 669 L.A. Dodgers TL .10 .05
Orel Hershiser
(Mound conference
with Mike Scioscia)
❑ 670 Kevin Seitzer .05 .02
❑ 671 Jim Gantner .05 .02
❑ 672 Allan Anderson .05 .02
❑ 673 Don Baylor .10 .05
❑ 674 Otis Nixon .05 .02
❑ 675 Bruce Hurst .05 .02
❑ 676 Ernie Riles .05 .02
❑ 677 Dave Schmidt .05 .02
❑ 678 Dion James .05 .02
❑ 679 Willie Fraser .05 .02
❑ 680 Gary Carter .15 .07
❑ 681 Jeff D. Robinson .05 .02
❑ 682 Rick Leach .05 .02
❑ 683 Jose Cecena .05 .02
❑ 684 Dave Johnson MG .05 .02
❑ 685 Jeff Treadway .05 .02
❑ 686 Scott Terry .05 .02
❑ 687 Alvin Davis .05 .02
❑ 688 Zane Smith .05 .02
❑ 689A Stan Jefferson .05 .02
(Pink triangle on
front bottom left)
❑ 689B Stan Jefferson .05 .02
(Violet triangle on
front bottom left)
❑ 690 Doug Jones .05 .02
❑ 691 Roberto Kelly UER .05 .02
(83 Oneonita)
❑ 692 Steve Ontiveros .05 .02
❑ 693 Pat Borders RC* .10 .05
❑ 694 Les Lancaster .05 .02
❑ 695 Carlton Fisk .20 .09
❑ 696 Don August .05 .02
❑ 697A Franklin Stubbs .05 .02
(Team name on front
in white)
❑ 697B Franklin Stubbs .05 .02
(Team name on front
in gray)
❑ 698 Keith Atherton .05 .02
❑ 699 Pittsburgh Pirates TL .05 .02
Al Pedrique
(Tony Gwynn sliding)
❑ 700 Don Mattingly .50 .23
❑ 701 Storm Davis .05 .02
❑ 702 Jamie Quirk .05 .02
❑ 703 Scott Garrelts .05 .02
❑ 704 Carlos Quintana RC .05 .02
❑ 705 Terry Kennedy .05 .02
❑ 706 Pete Incaviglia .05 .02
❑ 707 Steve Jeltz .05 .02
❑ 708 Chuck Finley .10 .05
❑ 709 Tom Herr .05 .02
❑ 710 David Cone .10 .05
❑ 711 Candy Sierra .05 .02
❑ 712 Bill Swift .05 .02
❑ 713 Ty Griffin FDP .05 .02
❑ 714 Joe Morgan MG .05 .02
❑ 715 Tony Pena .05 .02
❑ 716 Wayne Tolleson .05 .02
❑ 717 Jamie Moyer .05 .02
❑ 718 Glenn Braggs .05 .02
❑ 719 Danny Darwin .05 .02
❑ 720 Tim Wallach .05 .02
❑ 721 Ron Tingley .05 .02
❑ 722 Todd Stottlemyre .15 .07
❑ 723 Rafael Belliard .05 .02
❑ 724 Jerry Don Gleaton .05 .02
❑ 725 Terry Steinbach .10 .05
❑ 726 Dickie Thon .05 .02
❑ 727 Joe Orsulak .05 .02
❑ 728 Charlie Puleo .05 .02
❑ 729 Texas Rangers TL .05 .02
Steve Buechele
(Inconsistent design,
team name on front
surrounded by black;
should be white)
❑ 730 Danny Jackson .05 .02
❑ 731 Mike Young .05 .02
❑ 732 Steve Buechele .05 .02
❑ 733 Randy Bockus .05 .02
❑ 734 Jody Reed .05 .02
❑ 735 Roger McDowell .05 .02
❑ 736 Jeff Hamilton .05 .02
❑ 737 Norm Charlton RC .10 .05
❑ 738 Darnell Coles .05 .02
❑ 739 Brook Jacoby .05 .02
❑ 740 Dan Plesac .05 .02
❑ 741 Ken Phelps .05 .02
❑ 742 Mike Harkey FS RC .05 .02
❑ 743 Mike Heath .05 .02
❑ 744 Roger Craig MG .05 .02
❑ 745 Fred McGriff .20 .09
❑ 746 German Gonzalez UER .05 .02
(Wrong birthdate)
❑ 747 Wil Tejada .05 .02
❑ 748 Jimmy Jones .05 .02
❑ 749 Rafael Ramirez .05 .02
❑ 750 Bret Saberhagen .10 .05
❑ 751 Ken Oberkfell .05 .02
❑ 752 Jim Gott .05 .02
❑ 753 Jose Uribe .05 .02
❑ 754 Bob Brower .05 .02
❑ 755 Mike Scioscia .05 .02
❑ 756 Scott Medvin .05 .02
❑ 757 Brady Anderson RC .40 .18
❑ 758 Gene Walter .05 .02
❑ 759 Milwaukee Brewers TL .05 .02
Rob Deer
❑ 760 Lee Smith .10 .05
❑ 761 Dante Bichette RC .40 .18
❑ 762 Bobby Thigpen .05 .02
❑ 763 Dave Martinez .05 .02
❑ 764 Robin Ventura FDP RC .75 .35
❑ 765 Glenn Davis .05 .02
❑ 766 Cecilio Guante .05 .02
❑ 767 Mike Capel .05 .02
❑ 768 Bill Wegman .05 .02
❑ 769 Junior Ortiz .05 .02
❑ 770 Alan Trammell .15 .07
❑ 771 Ron Kittle .05 .02
❑ 772 Ron Oester .05 .02
❑ 773 Keith Moreland .05 .02
❑ 774 Frank Robinson MG .20 .09
❑ 775 Jeff Reardon .10 .05
❑ 776 Nelson Liriano .05 .02
❑ 777 Ted Power .05 .02
❑ 778 Bruce Benedict .05 .02
❑ 779 Craig McMurtry .05 .02
❑ 780 Pedro Guerrero .05 .02
❑ 781 Greg Briley .05 .02
❑ 782 Checklist 661-792 .05 .02
❑ 783 Trevor Wilson RC .05 .02
❑ 784 Steve Avery FDP RC .20 .09
❑ 785 Ellis Burks .15 .07
❑ 786 Melido Perez .05 .02
❑ 787 Dave West RC .05 .02
❑ 788 Mike Morgan .05 .02

| Card | Mint | NrMt |
|---|---|---|
| ❑ 789 Kansas City Royals TL Bo Jackson (Throwing) | .20 | .09 |
| ❑ 790 Sid Fernandez | .05 | .02 |
| ❑ 791 Jim Lindeman | .05 | .02 |
| ❑ 792 Rafael Santana | .05 | .02 |

## 1989 Topps Traded

| | MINT | NRMT |
|---|---|---|
| COMP.FACT.SET (132) | 25.00 | 11.00 |
| ❑ 1T Don Aase | .05 | .02 |
| ❑ 2T Jim Abbott | .20 | .09 |
| ❑ 3T Kent Anderson | .05 | .02 |
| ❑ 4T Keith Atherton | .05 | .02 |
| ❑ 5T Wally Backman | .05 | .02 |
| ❑ 6T Steve Balboni | .05 | .02 |
| ❑ 7T Jesse Barfield | .05 | .02 |
| ❑ 8T Steve Bedrosian | .05 | .02 |
| ❑ 9T Todd Benzinger | .05 | .02 |
| ❑ 10T Geronimo Berroa | .05 | .02 |
| ❑ 11T Bert Blyleven | .10 | .05 |
| ❑ 12T Bob Boone | .10 | .05 |
| ❑ 13T Phil Bradley | .05 | .02 |
| ❑ 14T Jeff Brantley RC | .15 | .07 |
| ❑ 15T Kevin Brown | .40 | .18 |
| ❑ 16T Jerry Browne | .05 | .02 |
| ❑ 17T Chuck Cary | .05 | .02 |
| ❑ 18T Carmen Castillo | .05 | .02 |
| ❑ 19T Jim Clancy | .05 | .02 |
| ❑ 20T Jack Clark | .05 | .02 |
| ❑ 21T Bryan Clutterbuck | .05 | .02 |
| ❑ 22T Jody Davis | .05 | .02 |
| ❑ 23T Mike Devereaux | .05 | .02 |
| ❑ 24T Frank DiPino | .05 | .02 |
| ❑ 25T Benny Distefano | .05 | .02 |
| ❑ 26T John Dopson | .05 | .02 |
| ❑ 27T Len Dykstra | .10 | .05 |
| ❑ 28T Jim Eisenreich | .05 | .02 |
| ❑ 29T Nick Esasky | .05 | .02 |
| ❑ 30T Alvaro Espinoza | .05 | .02 |
| ❑ 31T Darrell Evans UER (Stat headings on back are for a pitcher) | .10 | .05 |
| ❑ 32T Junior Felix RC | .05 | .02 |
| ❑ 33T Felix Fermin | .05 | .02 |
| ❑ 34T Julio Franco | .05 | .02 |
| ❑ 35T Terry Francona | .10 | .05 |
| ❑ 36T Cito Gaston MG | .10 | .05 |
| ❑ 37T Bob Geren UER (Photo actually Mike Fennell) | .05 | .02 |
| ❑ 38T Tom Gordon RC | .20 | .09 |
| ❑ 39T Tommy Gregg | .05 | .02 |
| ❑ 40T Ken Griffey Sr. | .10 | .05 |
| ❑ 41T Ken Griffey Jr. RC ! | 20.00 | 9.00 |
| ❑ 42T Kevin Gross | .05 | .02 |
| ❑ 43T Lee Guetterman | .05 | .02 |
| ❑ 44T Mel Hall | .05 | .02 |
| ❑ 45T Erik Hanson RC | .10 | .05 |
| ❑ 46T Gene Harris RC | .05 | .02 |
| ❑ 47T Andy Hawkins | .05 | .02 |
| ❑ 48T Rickey Henderson | .25 | .11 |
| ❑ 49T Tom Herr | .05 | .02 |
| ❑ 50T Ken Hill RC | .20 | .09 |
| ❑ 51T Brian Holman RC* | .05 | .02 |
| ❑ 52T Brian Holton | .05 | .02 |
| ❑ 53T Art Howe MG | .05 | .02 |
| ❑ 54T Ken Howell | .05 | .02 |
| ❑ 55T Bruce Hurst | .05 | .02 |
| ❑ 56T Chris James | .05 | .02 |
| ❑ 57T Randy Johnson | 1.50 | .70 |
| ❑ 58T Jimmy Jones | .05 | .02 |
| ❑ 59T Terry Kennedy | .05 | .02 |
| ❑ 60T Paul Kilgus | .05 | .02 |
| ❑ 61T Eric King | .05 | .02 |
| ❑ 62T Ron Kittle | .05 | .02 |
| ❑ 63T John Kruk | .10 | .05 |
| ❑ 64T Randy Kutcher | .05 | .02 |
| ❑ 65T Steve Lake | .05 | .02 |
| ❑ 66T Mark Langston | .05 | .02 |
| ❑ 67T Dave LaPoint | .05 | .02 |
| ❑ 68T Rick Leach | .05 | .02 |
| ❑ 69T Terry Leach | .05 | .02 |
| ❑ 70T Jim Lefebvre MG | .05 | .02 |
| ❑ 71T Al Leiter | .20 | .09 |
| ❑ 72T Jeffrey Leonard | .05 | .02 |
| ❑ 73T Derek Lilliquist RC | .05 | .02 |
| ❑ 74T Rick Mahler | .05 | .02 |
| ❑ 75T Tom McCarthy | .05 | .02 |
| ❑ 76T Lloyd McClendon | .05 | .02 |
| ❑ 77T Lance McCullers | .05 | .02 |
| ❑ 78T Oddibe McDowell | .05 | .02 |
| ❑ 79T Roger McDowell | .05 | .02 |
| ❑ 80T Larry McWilliams | .05 | .02 |
| ❑ 81T Randy Milligan | .05 | .02 |
| ❑ 82T Mike Moore | .05 | .02 |
| ❑ 83T Keith Moreland | .05 | .02 |
| ❑ 84T Mike Morgan | .05 | .02 |
| ❑ 85T Jamie Moyer | .05 | .02 |
| ❑ 86T Rob Murphy | .05 | .02 |
| ❑ 87T Eddie Murray | .20 | .09 |
| ❑ 88T Pete O'Brien | .05 | .02 |
| ❑ 89T Gregg Olson | .20 | .09 |
| ❑ 90T Steve Ontiveros | .05 | .02 |
| ❑ 91T Jesse Orosco | .05 | .02 |
| ❑ 92T Spike Owen | .05 | .02 |
| ❑ 93T Rafael Palmeiro | .25 | .11 |
| ❑ 94T Clay Parker | .05 | .02 |
| ❑ 95T Jeff Parrett | .05 | .02 |
| ❑ 96T Lance Parrish | .05 | .02 |
| ❑ 97T Dennis Powell | .05 | .02 |
| ❑ 98T Rey Quinones | .05 | .02 |
| ❑ 99T Doug Rader MG | .05 | .02 |
| ❑ 100T Willie Randolph | .10 | .05 |
| ❑ 101T Shane Rawley | .05 | .02 |
| ❑ 102T Randy Ready | .05 | .02 |
| ❑ 103T Bip Roberts | .10 | .05 |
| ❑ 104T Kenny Rogers RC | .20 | .09 |
| ❑ 105T Ed Romero | .05 | .02 |
| ❑ 106T Nolan Ryan | 2.00 | .90 |
| ❑ 107T Luis Salazar | .05 | .02 |
| ❑ 108T Juan Samuel | .05 | .02 |
| ❑ 109T Alex Sanchez | .05 | .02 |
| ❑ 110T Deion Sanders RC | .50 | .23 |
| ❑ 111T Steve Sax | .05 | .02 |
| ❑ 112T Rick Schu | .05 | .02 |
| ❑ 113T Dwight Smith RC | .10 | .05 |
| ❑ 114T Lonnie Smith | .05 | .02 |
| ❑ 115T Billy Spiers RC | .05 | .02 |
| ❑ 116T Kent Tekulve | .05 | .02 |
| ❑ 117T Walt Terrell | .05 | .02 |
| ❑ 118T Milt Thompson | .05 | .02 |
| ❑ 119T Dickie Thon | .05 | .02 |
| ❑ 120T Jeff Torborg MG | .05 | .02 |
| ❑ 121T Jeff Treadway | .05 | .02 |
| ❑ 122T Omar Vizquel RC | .50 | .23 |
| ❑ 123T Jerome Walton | .20 | .09 |
| ❑ 124T Gary Ward | .05 | .02 |
| ❑ 125T Claudell Washington | .05 | .02 |
| ❑ 126T Curt Wilkerson | .05 | .02 |
| ❑ 127T Eddie Williams | .05 | .02 |
| ❑ 128T Frank Williams | .05 | .02 |
| ❑ 129T Ken Williams | .05 | .02 |
| ❑ 130T Mitch Williams | .05 | .02 |
| ❑ 131T Steve Wilson | .05 | .02 |
| ❑ 132T Checklist 1T-132T | .05 | .02 |

## 1990 Topps

| | MINT | NRMT |
|---|---|---|
| COMPLETE SET (792) | 20.00 | 9.00 |
| COMP.FACT.SET (792) | 25.00 | 11.00 |

| | MINT | NRMT |
|---|---|---|
| COMP.X-MAS.SET (792) | 25.00 | 11.00 |
| ❑ 1 Nolan Ryan | 1.00 | .45 |
| ❑ 2 Nolan Ryan Salute New York Mets | .40 | .18 |
| ❑ 3 Nolan Ryan Salute California Angels | .40 | .18 |
| ❑ 4 Nolan Ryan Salute Houston Astros | .40 | .18 |
| ❑ 5 Nolan Ryan Salute Texas Rangers UER (Says Texas Stadium rather than Arlington Stadium) | .40 | .18 |
| ❑ 6 Vince Coleman RB (50 consecutive SB's) | .05 | .02 |
| ❑ 7 Rickey Henderson RB (40 career leadoff HR's) | .10 | .05 |
| ❑ 8 Cal Ripken RB (20 or more homers for 8 consecutive years, record for shortstops) | .20 | .09 |
| ❑ 9 Eric Plunk | .05 | .02 |
| ❑ 10 Barry Larkin | .20 | .09 |
| ❑ 11 Paul Gibson | .05 | .02 |
| ❑ 12 Joe Girardi | .15 | .07 |
| ❑ 13 Mark Williamson | .05 | .02 |
| ❑ 14 Mike Fetters RC | .05 | .02 |
| ❑ 15 Teddy Higuera | .05 | .02 |
| ❑ 16 Kent Anderson | .05 | .02 |
| ❑ 17 Kelly Downs | .05 | .02 |
| ❑ 18 Carlos Quintana | .05 | .02 |
| ❑ 19 Al Newman | .05 | .02 |
| ❑ 20 Mark Gubicza | .05 | .02 |
| ❑ 21 Jeff Torborg MG | .05 | .02 |
| ❑ 22 Bruce Ruffin | .05 | .02 |
| ❑ 23 Randy Velarde | .05 | .02 |
| ❑ 24 Joe Hesketh | .05 | .02 |
| ❑ 25 Willie Randolph | .10 | .05 |
| ❑ 26 Don Slaught | .05 | .02 |
| ❑ 27 Rick Leach | .05 | .02 |
| ❑ 28 Duane Ward | .05 | .02 |
| ❑ 29 John Cangelosi | .05 | .02 |
| ❑ 30 David Cone | .10 | .05 |
| ❑ 31 Henry Cotto | .05 | .02 |
| ❑ 32 John Farrell | .05 | .02 |
| ❑ 33 Greg Walker | .05 | .02 |
| ❑ 34 Tony Fossas | .05 | .02 |
| ❑ 35 Benito Santiago | .05 | .02 |
| ❑ 36 John Costello | .05 | .02 |
| ❑ 37 Domingo Ramos | .05 | .02 |
| ❑ 38 Wes Gardner | .05 | .02 |
| ❑ 39 Curt Ford | .05 | .02 |
| ❑ 40 Jay Howell | .05 | .02 |
| ❑ 41 Matt Williams | .15 | .07 |
| ❑ 42 Jeff M. Robinson | .05 | .02 |
| ❑ 43 Dante Bichette | .20 | .09 |
| ❑ 44 Roger Salkeld FDP RC | .05 | .02 |
| ❑ 45 Dave Parker UER (Born in Jackson, not Calhoun) | .10 | .05 |
| ❑ 46 Rob Dibble | .05 | .02 |
| ❑ 47 Brian Harper | .05 | .02 |
| ❑ 48 Zane Smith | .05 | .02 |
| ❑ 49 Tom Lawless | .05 | .02 |
| ❑ 50 Glenn Davis | .05 | .02 |
| ❑ 51 Doug Rader MG | .05 | .02 |
| ❑ 52 Jack Daugherty | .05 | .02 |

❑ 53 Mike LaCoss .05 .02
❑ 54 Joel Skinner .05 .02
❑ 55 Darrell Evans UER .10 .05
(HR total should be 414, not 424)
❑ 56 Franklin Stubbs .05 .02
❑ 57 Greg Vaughn .25 .11
❑ 58 Keith Miller .05 .02
❑ 59 Ted Power .05 .02
❑ 60 George Brett .40 .18
❑ 61 Deion Sanders .20 .09
❑ 62 Ramon Martinez .05 .02
❑ 63 Mike Pagliarulo .05 .02
❑ 64 Danny Darwin .05 .02
❑ 65 Devon White .05 .02
❑ 66 Greg Litton .05 .02
❑ 67 Scott Sanderson .05 .02
❑ 68 Dave Henderson .05 .02
❑ 69 Todd Frohwirth .05 .02
❑ 70 Mike Greenwell .05 .02
❑ 71 Allan Anderson .05 .02
❑ 72 Jeff Huson RC .05 .02
❑ 73 Bob Milacki .05 .02
❑ 74 Jeff Jackson FDP RC .05 .02
❑ 75 Doug Jones .05 .02
❑ 76 Dave Valle .05 .02
❑ 77 Dave Bergman .05 .02
❑ 78 Mike Flanagan .05 .02
❑ 79 Ron Kittle .05 .02
❑ 80 Jeff Russell .05 .02
❑ 81 Bob Rodgers MG .05 .02
❑ 82 Scott Terry .05 .02
❑ 83 Hensley Meulens .05 .02
❑ 84 Ray Searage .05 .02
❑ 85 Juan Samuel .05 .02
❑ 86 Paul Kilgus .05 .02
❑ 87 Rick Luecken .05 .02
❑ 88 Glenn Braggs .05 .02
❑ 89 Clint Zavaras .05 .02
❑ 90 Jack Clark .10 .05
❑ 91 Steve Frey .05 .02
❑ 92 Mike Stanley .05 .02
❑ 93 Shawn Hillegas .05 .02
❑ 94 Herm Winningham .05 .02
❑ 95 Todd Worrell .05 .02
❑ 96 Jody Reed .05 .02
❑ 97 Curt Schilling .10 .05
❑ 98 Jose Gonzalez .05 .02
❑ 99 Rich Monteleone .05 .02
❑ 100 Will Clark .20 .09
❑ 101 Shane Rawley .05 .02
❑ 102 Stan Javier .05 .02
❑ 103 Marvin Freeman .05 .02
❑ 104 Bob Knepper .05 .02
❑ 105 Randy Myers .10 .05
❑ 106 Charlie O'Brien .05 .02
❑ 107 Fred Lynn .05 .02
❑ 108 Rod Nichols .05 .02
❑ 109 Roberto Kelly .05 .02
❑ 110 Tommy Helms MG .05 .02
❑ 111 Ed Whited .05 .02
❑ 112 Glenn Wilson .05 .02
❑ 113 Manny Lee .05 .02
❑ 114 Mike Bielecki .05 .02
❑ 115 Tony Pena .05 .02
❑ 116 Floyd Bannister .05 .02
❑ 117 Mike Sharperson .05 .02
❑ 118 Erik Hanson .05 .02
❑ 119 Billy Hatcher .05 .02
❑ 120 John Franco .10 .05
❑ 121 Robin Ventura .20 .09
❑ 122 Shawn Abner .05 .02
❑ 123 Rich Gedman .05 .02
❑ 124 Dave Dravecky .10 .05
❑ 125 Kent Hrbek .10 .05
❑ 126 Randy Kramer .05 .02
❑ 127 Mike Devereaux .05 .02
❑ 128 Checklist 1 .05 .02
❑ 129 Ron Jones .05 .02
❑ 130 Bert Blyleven .10 .05
❑ 131 Matt Nokes .05 .02
❑ 132 Lance Blankenship .05 .02
❑ 133 Ricky Horton .05 .02
❑ 134 Earl Cunningham FDP RC .05 .02
❑ 135 Dave Magadan .05 .02
❑ 136 Kevin Brown .20 .09
❑ 137 Marty Pevey .05 .02
❑ 138 Al Leiter .20 .09
❑ 139 Greg Brock .05 .02
❑ 140 Andre Dawson .15 .07
❑ 141 John Hart MG .05 .02
❑ 142 Jeff Wetherby .05 .02
❑ 143 Rafael Belliard .05 .02
❑ 144 Bud Black .05 .02
❑ 145 Terry Steinbach .05 .02
❑ 146 Rob Richie .05 .02
❑ 147 Chuck Finley .10 .05
❑ 148 Edgar Martinez .15 .07
❑ 149 Steve Farr .05 .02
❑ 150 Kirk Gibson .10 .05
❑ 151 Rick Mahler .05 .02
❑ 152 Lonnie Smith .05 .02
❑ 153 Randy Milligan .05 .02
❑ 154 Mike Maddux .05 .02
❑ 155 Ellis Burks .15 .07
❑ 156 Ken Patterson .05 .02
❑ 157 Craig Biggio .15 .07
❑ 158 Craig Lefferts .05 .02
❑ 159 Mike Felder .05 .02
❑ 160 Dave Righetti .05 .02
❑ 161 Harold Reynolds .05 .02
❑ 162 Todd Zeile .10 .05
❑ 163 Phil Bradley .05 .02
❑ 164 Jeff Juden FDP RC .05 .02
❑ 165 Walt Weiss .05 .02
❑ 166 Bobby Witt .05 .02
❑ 167 Kevin Appier .15 .07
❑ 168 Jose Lind .05 .02
❑ 169 Richard Dotson .05 .02
❑ 170 George Bell .05 .02
❑ 171 Russ Nixon MG .05 .02
❑ 172 Tom Lampkin .05 .02
❑ 173 Tim Belcher .05 .02
❑ 174 Jeff Kunkel .05 .02
❑ 175 Mike Moore .05 .02
❑ 176 Luis Quinones .05 .02
❑ 177 Mike Henneman .05 .02
❑ 178 Chris James .05 .02
❑ 179 Brian Holton .05 .02
❑ 180 Tim Raines .10 .05
❑ 181 Juan Agosto .05 .02
❑ 182 Mookie Wilson .10 .05
❑ 183 Steve Lake .05 .02
❑ 184 Danny Cox .05 .02
❑ 185 Ruben Sierra .05 .02
❑ 186 Dave LaPoint .05 .02
❑ 187 Rick Wrona .05 .02
❑ 188 Mike Smithson .05 .02
❑ 189 Dick Schofield .05 .02
❑ 190 Rick Reuschel .05 .02
❑ 191 Pat Borders .05 .02
❑ 192 Don August .05 .02
❑ 193 Andy Benes .05 .02
❑ 194 Glenallen Hill .05 .02
❑ 195 Tim Burke .05 .02
❑ 196 Gerald Young .05 .02
❑ 197 Doug Drabek .05 .02
❑ 198 Mike Marshall .05 .02
❑ 199 Sergio Valdez .05 .02
❑ 200 Don Mattingly .50 .23
❑ 201 Cito Gaston MG .05 .02
❑ 202 Mike Macfarlane .05 .02
❑ 203 Mike Roesler .05 .02
❑ 204 Bob Dernier .05 .02
❑ 205 Mark Davis .05 .02
❑ 206 Nick Esasky .05 .02
❑ 207 Bob Ojeda .05 .02
❑ 208 Brook Jacoby .05 .02
❑ 209 Greg Mathews .05 .02
❑ 210 Ryne Sandberg .25 .11
❑ 211 John Cerutti .05 .02
❑ 212 Joe Orsulak .05 .02
❑ 213 Scott Bankhead .05 .02
❑ 214 Terry Francona .10 .05
❑ 215 Kirk McCaskill .05 .02
❑ 216 Ricky Jordan .05 .02
❑ 217 Don Robinson .05 .02
❑ 218 Wally Backman .05 .02
❑ 219 Donn Pall .05 .02
❑ 220 Barry Bonds .30 .14
❑ 221 Gary Mielke .05 .02
❑ 222 Kurt Stillwell UER .05 .02
(Graduate misspelled as gradute)
❑ 223 Tommy Gregg .05 .02
❑ 224 Delino DeShields RC .20 .09
❑ 225 Jim Deshaies .05 .02
❑ 226 Mickey Hatcher .05 .02
❑ 227 Kevin Tapani RC .10 .05
❑ 228 Dave Martinez .05 .02
❑ 229 David Wells .10 .05
❑ 230 Keith Hernandez .10 .05
❑ 231 Jack McKeon MG .05 .02
❑ 232 Darnell Coles .05 .02
❑ 233 Ken Hill .10 .05
❑ 234 Mariano Duncan .05 .02
❑ 235 Jeff Reardon .10 .05
❑ 236 Hal Morris .05 .02
❑ 237 Kevin Ritz .05 .02
❑ 238 Felix Jose .05 .02
❑ 239 Eric Show .05 .02
❑ 240 Mark Grace .20 .09
❑ 241 Mike Krukow .05 .02
❑ 242 Fred Manrique .05 .02
❑ 243 Barry Jones .05 .02
❑ 244 Bill Schroeder .05 .02
❑ 245 Roger Clemens .40 .18
❑ 246 Jim Eisenreich .05 .02
❑ 247 Jerry Reed .05 .02
❑ 248 Dave Anderson .05 .02
❑ 249 Mike(Texas) Smith .05 .02
❑ 250 Jose Canseco .25 .11
❑ 251 Jeff Blauser .05 .02
❑ 252 Otis Nixon .05 .02
❑ 253 Mark Portugal .05 .02
❑ 254 Francisco Cabrera .05 .02
❑ 255 Bobby Thigpen .05 .02
❑ 256 Marvell Wynne .05 .02
❑ 257 Jose DeLeon .05 .02
❑ 258 Barry Lyons .05 .02
❑ 259 Lance McCullers .05 .02
❑ 260 Eric Davis .10 .05
❑ 261 Whitey Herzog MG .10 .05
❑ 262 Checklist 2 .05 .02
❑ 263 Mel Stottlemyre Jr. .05 .02
❑ 264 Bryan Clutterbuck .05 .02
❑ 265 Pete O'Brien .05 .02
❑ 266 German Gonzalez .05 .02
❑ 267 Mark Davidson .05 .02
❑ 268 Rob Murphy .05 .02
❑ 269 Dickie Thon .05 .02
❑ 270 Dave Stewart .10 .05
❑ 271 Chet Lemon .05 .02
❑ 272 Bryan Harvey .05 .02
❑ 273 Bobby Bonilla .10 .05
❑ 274 Mauro Gozzo .05 .02
❑ 275 Mickey Tettleton .05 .02
❑ 276 Gary Thurman .05 .02
❑ 277 Lenny Harris .05 .02
❑ 278 Pascual Perez .05 .02
❑ 279 Steve Buechele .05 .02
❑ 280 Lou Whitaker .10 .05
❑ 281 Kevin Bass .05 .02
❑ 282 Derek Lilliquist .05 .02
❑ 283 Joey Belle .75 .35
❑ 284 Mark Gardner RC .05 .02
❑ 285 Willie McGee .10 .05
❑ 286 Lee Guetterman .05 .02
❑ 287 Vance Law .05 .02
❑ 288 Greg Briley .05 .02
❑ 289 Norm Charlton .05 .02
❑ 290 Robin Yount .20 .09
❑ 291 Dave Johnson MG .10 .05
❑ 292 Jim Gott .05 .02
❑ 293 Mike Gallego .05 .02
❑ 294 Craig McMurtry .05 .02
❑ 295 Fred McGriff .20 .09
❑ 296 Jeff Ballard .05 .02
❑ 297 Tommy Herr .05 .02
❑ 298 Dan Gladden .05 .02
❑ 299 Adam Peterson .05 .02
❑ 300 Bo Jackson .10 .05
❑ 301 Don Aase .05 .02
❑ 302 Marcus Lawton .05 .02
❑ 303 Rick Cerone .05 .02
❑ 304 Marty Clary .05 .02
❑ 305 Eddie Murray .20 .09
❑ 306 Tom Niedenfuer .05 .02

❑ 307 Bip Roberts .05 .02
❑ 308 Jose Guzman .05 .02
❑ 309 Eric Yelding .05 .02
❑ 310 Steve Bedrosian .05 .02
❑ 311 Dwight Smith .05 .02
❑ 312 Dan Quisenberry .05 .02
❑ 313 Gus Polidor .05 .02
❑ 314 Donald Harris FDP .05 .02
❑ 315 Bruce Hurst .05 .02
❑ 316 Carney Lansford .10 .05
❑ 317 Mark Guthrie .05 .02
❑ 318 Wallace Johnson .05 .02
❑ 319 Dion James .05 .02
❑ 320 Dave Stieb .10 .05
❑ 321 Joe Morgan MG .05 .02
❑ 322 Junior Ortiz .05 .02
❑ 323 Willie Wilson .05 .02
❑ 324 Pete Harnisch .05 .02
❑ 325 Robby Thompson .05 .02
❑ 326 Tom McCarthy .05 .02
❑ 327 Ken Williams .05 .02
❑ 328 Curt Young .05 .02
❑ 329 Oddibe McDowell .05 .02
❑ 330 Ron Darling .05 .02
❑ 331 Juan Gonzalez RC 1.25 .55
❑ 332 Paul O'Neill .10 .05
❑ 333 Bill Wegman .05 .02
❑ 334 Johnny Ray .05 .02
❑ 335 Andy Hawkins .05 .02
❑ 336 Ken Griffey Jr. 2.00 .90
❑ 337 Lloyd McClendon .05 .02
❑ 338 Dennis Lamp .05 .02
❑ 339 Dave Clark .05 .02
❑ 340 Fernando Valenzuela .10 .05
❑ 341 Tom Foley .05 .02
❑ 342 Alex Trevino .05 .02
❑ 343 Frank Tanana .05 .02
❑ 344 George Canale .05 .02
❑ 345 Harold Baines .10 .05
❑ 346 Jim Presley .05 .02
❑ 347 Junior Felix .05 .02
❑ 348 Gary Wayne .05 .02
❑ 349 Steve Finley .10 .05
❑ 350 Bret Saberhagen .10 .05
❑ 351 Roger Craig MG .05 .02
❑ 352 Bryn Smith .05 .02
❑ 353 Sandy Alomar Jr. .10 .05
(Not listed as Jr. on card front)
❑ 354 Stan Belinda RC .05 .02
❑ 355 Marty Barrett .05 .02
❑ 356 Randy Ready .05 .02
❑ 357 Dave West .05 .02
❑ 358 Andres Thomas .05 .02
❑ 359 Jimmy Jones .05 .02
❑ 360 Paul Molitor .20 .09
❑ 361 Randy McCament .05 .02
❑ 362 Damon Berryhill .05 .02
❑ 363 Dan Petry .05 .02
❑ 364 Rolando Roomes .05 .02
❑ 365 Ozzie Guillen .05 .02
❑ 366 Mike Heath .05 .02
❑ 367 Mike Morgan .05 .02
❑ 368 Bill Doran .05 .02
❑ 369 Todd Burns .05 .02
❑ 370 Tim Wallach .05 .02
❑ 371 Jimmy Key .10 .05
❑ 372 Terry Kennedy .05 .02
❑ 373 Alvin Davis .05 .02
❑ 374 Steve Cummings .05 .02
❑ 375 Dwight Evans .10 .05
❑ 376 Checklist 3 UER .05 .02
(Higuera misalphabet-ized in Brewer list)
❑ 377 Mickey Weston .05 .02
❑ 378 Luis Salazar .05 .02
❑ 379 Steve Rosenberg .05 .02
❑ 380 Dave Winfield .20 .09
❑ 381 Frank Robinson MG .15 .07
❑ 382 Jeff Musselman .05 .02
❑ 383 John Morris .05 .02
❑ 384 Pat Combs .05 .02
❑ 385 Fred McGriff AS .10 .05
❑ 386 Julio Franco AS .05 .02
❑ 387 Wade Boggs AS .10 .05
❑ 388 Cal Ripken AS .40 .18
❑ 389 Robin Yount AS .10 .05
❑ 390 Ruben Sierra AS .05 .02
❑ 391 Kirby Puckett AS .20 .09
❑ 392 Carlton Fisk AS .10 .05
❑ 393 Bret Saberhagen AS .05 .02
❑ 394 Jeff Ballard AS .05 .02
❑ 395 Jeff Russell AS .05 .02
❑ 396 A.Bartlett Giamatti RC .20 .09
COMM MEM
❑ 397 Will Clark AS .10 .05
❑ 398 Ryne Sandberg AS .20 .09
❑ 399 Howard Johnson AS .05 .02
❑ 400 Ozzie Smith AS .20 .09
❑ 401 Kevin Mitchell AS .05 .02
❑ 402 Eric Davis AS .05 .02
❑ 403 Tony Gwynn AS .20 .09
❑ 404 Craig Biggio AS .10 .05
❑ 405 Mike Scott AS .05 .02
❑ 406 Joe Magrane AS .05 .02
❑ 407 Mark Davis AS .05 .02
❑ 408 Trevor Wilson .05 .02
❑ 409 Tom Brunansky .05 .02
❑ 410 Joe Boever .05 .02
❑ 411 Ken Phelps .05 .02
❑ 412 Jamie Moyer .05 .02
❑ 413 Brian DuBois .05 .02
❑ 414A Frank Thomas FDP 800.00 350.00
ERR (Name missing on card front)
❑ 414B F. Thomas FDP COR RC 3.00 1.35
❑ 415 Shawon Dunston .05 .02
❑ 416 Dave Johnson (P) .05 .02
❑ 417 Jim Gantner .05 .02
❑ 418 Tom Browning .05 .02
❑ 419 Beau Allred .05 .02
❑ 420 Carlton Fisk .20 .09
❑ 421 Greg Minton .05 .02
❑ 422 Pat Sheridan .05 .02
❑ 423 Fred Toliver .05 .02
❑ 424 Jerry Reuss .05 .02
❑ 425 Bill Landrum .05 .02
❑ 426 Jeff Hamilton UER .05 .02
(Stats say he fanned 197 times in 1987, but he only had 147 at bats)
❑ 427 Carmen Castillo .05 .02
❑ 428 Steve Davis .05 .02
❑ 429 Tom Kelly MG .05 .02
❑ 430 Pete Incaviglia .05 .02
❑ 431 Randy Johnson .40 .18
❑ 432 Damaso Garcia .05 .02
❑ 433 Steve Olin RC .10 .05
❑ 434 Mark Carreon .05 .02
❑ 435 Kevin Seitzer .05 .02
❑ 436 Mel Hall .05 .02
❑ 437 Les Lancaster .05 .02
❑ 438 Greg Myers .05 .02
❑ 439 Jeff Parrett .05 .02
❑ 440 Alan Trammell .15 .07
❑ 441 Bob Kipper .05 .02
❑ 442 Jerry Browne .05 .02
❑ 443 Cris Carpenter .05 .02
❑ 444 Kyle Abbott FDP .05 .02
❑ 445 Danny Jackson .05 .02
❑ 446 Dan Pasqua .05 .02
❑ 447 Atlee Hammaker .05 .02
❑ 448 Greg Gagne .05 .02
❑ 449 Dennis Rasmussen .05 .02
❑ 450 Rickey Henderson .25 .11
❑ 451 Mark Lemke .05 .02
❑ 452 Luis DeLosSantos .05 .02
❑ 453 Jody Davis .05 .02
❑ 454 Jeff King .05 .02
❑ 455 Jeffrey Leonard .05 .02
❑ 456 Chris Gwynn .05 .02
❑ 457 Gregg Jefferies .10 .05
❑ 458 Bob McClure .05 .02
❑ 459 Jim Lefebvre MG .05 .02
❑ 460 Mike Scott .05 .02
❑ 461 Carlos Martinez .05 .02
❑ 462 Denny Walling .05 .02
❑ 463 Drew Hall .05 .02
❑ 464 Jerome Walton .05 .02
❑ 465 Kevin Gross .05 .02
❑ 466 Rance Mulliniks .05 .02
❑ 467 Juan Nieves .05 .02
❑ 468 Bill Ripken .05 .02
❑ 469 John Kruk .10 .05
❑ 470 Frank Viola .05 .02
❑ 471 Mike Brumley .05 .02
❑ 472 Jose Uribe .05 .02
❑ 473 Joe Price .05 .02
❑ 474 Rich Thompson .05 .02
❑ 475 Bob Welch .05 .02
❑ 476 Brad Komminsk .05 .02
❑ 477 Willie Fraser .05 .02
❑ 478 Mike LaValliere .05 .02
❑ 479 Frank White .10 .05
❑ 480 Sid Fernandez .05 .02
❑ 481 Garry Templeton .05 .02
❑ 482 Steve Carter .05 .02
❑ 483 Alejandro Pena .05 .02
❑ 484 Mike Fitzgerald .05 .02
❑ 485 John Candelaria .05 .02
❑ 486 Jeff Treadway .05 .02
❑ 487 Steve Searcy .05 .02
❑ 488 Ken Oberkfell .05 .02
❑ 489 Nick Leyva MG .05 .02
❑ 490 Dan Plesac .05 .02
❑ 491 Dave Cochrane .05 .02
❑ 492 Ron Oester .05 .02
❑ 493 Jason Grimsley RC .05 .02
❑ 494 Terry Puhl .05 .02
❑ 495 Lee Smith .10 .05
❑ 496 Cecil Espy UER .05 .02
('88 stats have 3 SB's; should be 33)
❑ 497 Dave Schmidt .05 .02
❑ 498 Rick Schu .05 .02
❑ 499 Bill Long .05 .02
❑ 500 Kevin Mitchell .05 .02
❑ 501 Matt Young .05 .02
❑ 502 Mitch Webster .05 .02
❑ 503 Randy St.Claire .05 .02
❑ 504 Tom O'Malley .05 .02
❑ 505 Kelly Gruber .05 .02
❑ 506 Tom Glavine .20 .09
❑ 507 Gary Redus .05 .02
❑ 508 Terry Leach .05 .02
❑ 509 Tom Pagnozzi .05 .02
❑ 510 Dwight Gooden .10 .05
❑ 511 Clay Parker .05 .02
❑ 512 Gary Pettis .05 .02
❑ 513 Mark Eichhorn .05 .02
❑ 514 Andy Allanson .05 .02
❑ 515 Len Dykstra .10 .05
❑ 516 Tim Leary .05 .02
❑ 517 Roberto Alomar .20 .09
❑ 518 Bill Krueger .05 .02
❑ 519 Bucky Dent MG .05 .02
❑ 520 Mitch Williams .05 .02
❑ 521 Craig Worthington .05 .02
❑ 522 Mike Dunne .05 .02
❑ 523 Jay Bell .10 .05
❑ 524 Daryl Boston .05 .02
❑ 525 Wally Joyner .10 .05
❑ 526 Checklist 4 .05 .02
❑ 527 Ron Hassey .05 .02
❑ 528 Kevin Wickander UER .05 .02
(Monthly scoreboard strikeout total was 2.2, that was his innings pitched total)
❑ 529 Greg A. Harris .05 .02
❑ 530 Mark Langston .05 .02
❑ 531 Ken Caminiti .10 .05
❑ 532 Cecilio Guante .05 .02
❑ 533 Tim Jones .05 .02
❑ 534 Louie Meadows .05 .02
❑ 535 John Smoltz .10 .05
❑ 536 Bob Geren .05 .02
❑ 537 Mark Grant .05 .02
❑ 538 Bill Spiers UER .05 .02
(Photo actually George Canale)
❑ 539 Neal Heaton .05 .02
❑ 540 Danny Tartabull .05 .02
❑ 541 Pat Perry .05 .02
❑ 542 Darren Daulton .10 .05
❑ 543 Nelson Liriano .05 .02
❑ 544 Dennis Boyd .05 .02
❑ 545 Kevin McReynolds .05 .02

❑ 546 Kevin Hickey .05 .02
❑ 547 Jack Howell .05 .02
❑ 548 Pat Clements .05 .02
❑ 549 Don Zimmer MG .05 .02
❑ 550 Julio Franco .05 .02
❑ 551 Tim Crews .05 .02
❑ 552 Mike(Miss.) Smith .05 .02
❑ 553 Scott Scudder UER .05 .02
(Cedar Rap1ds)
❑ 554 Jay Buhner .10 .05
❑ 555 Jack Morris .10 .05
❑ 556 Gene Larkin .05 .02
❑ 557 Jeff Innis .05 .02
❑ 558 Rafael Ramirez .05 .02
❑ 559 Andy McGaffigan .05 .02
❑ 560 Steve Sax .05 .02
❑ 561 Ken Dayley .05 .02
❑ 562 Chad Kreuter .05 .02
❑ 563 Alex Sanchez .05 .02
❑ 564 Tyler Houston FDP RC .15 .07
❑ 565 Scott Fletcher .05 .02
❑ 566 Mark Knudson .05 .02
❑ 567 Ron Gant .10 .05
❑ 568 John Smiley .05 .02
❑ 569 Ivan Calderon .05 .02
❑ 570 Cal Ripken .75 .35
❑ 571 Brett Butler .10 .05
❑ 572 Greg W. Harris .05 .02
❑ 573 Danny Heep .05 .02
❑ 574 Bill Swift .05 .02
❑ 575 Lance Parrish .05 .02
❑ 576 Mike Dyer .05 .02
❑ 577 Charlie Hayes .05 .02
❑ 578 Joe Magrane .05 .02
❑ 579 Art Howe MG .05 .02
❑ 580 Joe Carter .10 .05
❑ 581 Ken Griffey Sr. .10 .05
❑ 582 Rick Honeycutt .05 .02
❑ 583 Bruce Benedict .05 .02
❑ 584 Phil Stephenson .05 .02
❑ 585 Kal Daniels .05 .02
❑ 586 Edwin Nunez .05 .02
❑ 587 Lance Johnson .05 .02
❑ 588 Rick Rhoden .05 .02
❑ 589 Mike Aldrete .05 .02
❑ 590 Ozzie Smith .25 .11
❑ 591 Todd Stottlemyre .10 .05
❑ 592 R.J. Reynolds .05 .02
❑ 593 Scott Bradley .05 .02
❑ 594 Luis Sojo .05 .02
❑ 595 Greg Swindell .05 .02
❑ 596 Jose DeJesus .05 .02
❑ 597 Chris Bosio .05 .02
❑ 598 Brady Anderson .20 .09
❑ 599 Frank Williams .05 .02
❑ 600 Darryl Strawberry .10 .05
❑ 601 Luis Rivera .05 .02
❑ 602 Scott Garrelts .05 .02
❑ 603 Tony Armas .05 .02
❑ 604 Ron Robinson .05 .02
❑ 605 Mike Scioscia .05 .02
❑ 606 Storm Davis .05 .02
❑ 607 Steve Jeltz .05 .02
❑ 608 Eric Anthony RC .05 .02
❑ 609 Sparky Anderson MG .10 .05
❑ 610 Pedro Guerrero .05 .02
❑ 611 Walt Terrell .05 .02
❑ 612 Dave Gallagher .05 .02
❑ 613 Jeff Pico .05 .02
❑ 614 Nelson Santovenia .05 .02
❑ 615 Rob Deer .05 .02
❑ 616 Brian Holman .05 .02
❑ 617 Geronimo Berroa .05 .02
❑ 618 Ed Whitson .05 .02
❑ 619 Rob Ducey .05 .02
❑ 620 Tony Castillo .05 .02
❑ 621 Melido Perez .05 .02
❑ 622 Sid Bream .05 .02
❑ 623 Jim Corsi .05 .02
❑ 624 Darrin Jackson .05 .02
❑ 625 Roger McDowell .05 .02
❑ 626 Bob Melvin .05 .02
❑ 627 Jose Rijo .05 .02
❑ 628 Candy Maldonado .05 .02
❑ 629 Eric Hetzel .05 .02
❑ 630 Gary Gaetti .10 .05
❑ 631 John Wetteland .20 .09
❑ 632 Scott Lusader .05 .02
❑ 633 Dennis Cook .05 .02
❑ 634 Luis Polonia .05 .02
❑ 635 Brian Downing .05 .02
❑ 636 Jesse Orosco .05 .02
❑ 637 Craig Reynolds .05 .02
❑ 638 Jeff Montgomery .10 .05
❑ 639 Tony LaRussa MG .10 .05
❑ 640 Rick Sutcliffe .10 .05
❑ 641 Doug Strange .05 .02
❑ 642 Jack Armstrong .05 .02
❑ 643 Alfredo Griffin .05 .02
❑ 644 Paul Assenmacher .05 .02
❑ 645 Jose Oquendo .05 .02
❑ 646 Checklist 5 .05 .02
❑ 647 Rex Hudler .05 .02
❑ 648 Jim Clancy .05 .02
❑ 649 Dan Murphy RC .05 .02
❑ 650 Mike Witt .05 .02
❑ 651 Rafael Santana .05 .02
❑ 652 Mike Boddicker .05 .02
❑ 653 John Moses .05 .02
❑ 654 Paul Coleman FDP RC .05 .02
❑ 655 Gregg Olson .10 .05
❑ 656 Mackey Sasser .05 .02
❑ 657 Terry Mulholland .05 .02
❑ 658 Donell Nixon .05 .02
❑ 659 Greg Cadaret .05 .02
❑ 660 Vince Coleman .05 .02
❑ 661 Dick Howser TBC'85 .05 .02
UER (Seaver's 300th
on 7/11/85; should
be 8/4/85)
❑ 662 Mike Schmidt TBC'80 .20 .09
❑ 663 Fred Lynn TBC'75 .05 .02
❑ 664 Johnny Bench TBC'70 .20 .09
❑ 665 Sandy Koufax TBC'65 .25 .11
❑ 666 Brian Fisher .05 .02
❑ 667 Curt Wilkerson .05 .02
❑ 668 Joe Oliver .05 .02
❑ 669 Tom Lasorda MG .20 .09
❑ 670 Dennis Eckersley .15 .07
❑ 671 Bob Boone .10 .05
❑ 672 Roy Smith .05 .02
❑ 673 Joey Meyer .05 .02
❑ 674 Spike Owen .05 .02
❑ 675 Jim Abbott .15 .07
❑ 676 Randy Kutcher .05 .02
❑ 677 Jay Tibbs .05 .02
❑ 678 Kirt Manwaring UER .05 .02
('88 Phoenix stats
repeated)
❑ 679 Gary Ward .05 .02
❑ 680 Howard Johnson .05 .02
❑ 681 Mike Schooler .05 .02
❑ 682 Dann Bilardello .05 .02
❑ 683 Kenny Rogers .10 .05
❑ 684 Julio Machado .05 .02
❑ 685 Tony Fernandez .05 .02
❑ 686 Carmelo Martinez .05 .02
❑ 687 Tim Birtsas .05 .02
❑ 688 Milt Thompson .05 .02
❑ 689 Rich Yett .05 .02
❑ 690 Mark McGwire .75 .35
❑ 691 Chuck Cary .05 .02
❑ 692 Sammy Sosa RC 5.00 2.20
❑ 693 Calvin Schiraldi .05 .02
❑ 694 Mike Stanton RC .05 .02
❑ 695 Tom Henke .05 .02
❑ 696 B.J. Surhoff .10 .05
❑ 697 Mike Davis .05 .02
❑ 698 Omar Vizquel .20 .09
❑ 699 Jim Leyland MG .05 .02
❑ 700 Kirby Puckett .50 .23
❑ 701 Bernie Williams RC 1.50 .70
❑ 702 Tony Phillips .05 .02
❑ 703 Jeff Brantley .05 .02
❑ 704 Chip Hale .05 .02
❑ 705 Claudell Washington .05 .02
❑ 706 Geno Petralli .05 .02
❑ 707 Luis Aquino .05 .02
❑ 708 Larry Sheets .05 .02
❑ 709 Juan Berenguer .05 .02
❑ 710 Von Hayes .05 .02
❑ 711 Rick Aguilera .10 .05
❑ 712 Todd Benzinger .05 .02
❑ 713 Tim Drummond .05 .02
❑ 714 Marquis Grissom RC .25 .11
❑ 715 Greg Maddux .50 .23
❑ 716 Steve Balboni .05 .02
❑ 717 Ron Karkovice .05 .02
❑ 718 Gary Sheffield .25 .11
❑ 719 Wally Whitehurst .05 .02
❑ 720 Andres Galarraga .15 .07
❑ 721 Lee Mazzilli .05 .02
❑ 722 Felix Fermin .05 .02
❑ 723 Jeff D. Robinson .05 .02
❑ 724 Juan Bell .05 .02
❑ 725 Terry Pendleton .10 .05
❑ 726 Gene Nelson .05 .02
❑ 727 Pat Tabler .05 .02
❑ 728 Jim Acker .05 .02
❑ 729 Bobby Valentine MG .05 .02
❑ 730 Tony Gwynn .40 .18
❑ 731 Don Carman .05 .02
❑ 732 Ernest Riles .05 .02
❑ 733 John Dopson .05 .02
❑ 734 Kevin Elster .05 .02
❑ 735 Charlie Hough .10 .05
❑ 736 Rick Dempsey .05 .02
❑ 737 Chris Sabo .05 .02
❑ 738 Gene Harris .05 .02
❑ 739 Dale Sveum .05 .02
❑ 740 Jesse Barfield .05 .02
❑ 741 Steve Wilson .05 .02
❑ 742 Ernie Whitt .05 .02
❑ 743 Tom Candiotti .05 .02
❑ 744 Kelly Mann .05 .02
❑ 745 Hubie Brooks .05 .02
❑ 746 Dave Smith .05 .02
❑ 747 Randy Bush .05 .02
❑ 748 Doyle Alexander .05 .02
❑ 749 Mark Parent UER .05 .02
('87 BA .80;
should be .080)
❑ 750 Dale Murphy .20 .09
❑ 751 Steve Lyons .05 .02
❑ 752 Tom Gordon .10 .05
❑ 753 Chris Speier .05 .02
❑ 754 Bob Walk .05 .02
❑ 755 Rafael Palmeiro .20 .09
❑ 756 Ken Howell .05 .02
❑ 757 Larry Walker RC .75 .35
❑ 758 Mark Thurmond .05 .02
❑ 759 Tom Trebelhorn MG .05 .02
❑ 760 Wade Boggs .25 .11
❑ 761 Mike Jackson .05 .02
❑ 762 Doug Dascenzo .05 .02
❑ 763 Dennis Martinez .10 .05
❑ 764 Tim Teufel .05 .02
❑ 765 Chili Davis .10 .05
❑ 766 Brian Meyer .05 .02
❑ 767 Tracy Jones .05 .02
❑ 768 Chuck Crim .05 .02
❑ 769 Greg Hibbard RC .05 .02
❑ 770 Cory Snyder .05 .02
❑ 771 Pete Smith .05 .02
❑ 772 Jeff Reed .05 .02
❑ 773 Dave Leiper .05 .02
❑ 774 Ben McDonald RC .10 .05
❑ 775 Andy Van Slyke .10 .05
❑ 776 Charlie Leibrandt .05 .02
❑ 777 Tim Laudner .05 .02
❑ 778 Mike Jeffcoat .05 .02
❑ 779 Lloyd Moseby .05 .02
❑ 780 Orel Hershiser .10 .05
❑ 781 Mario Diaz .05 .02
❑ 782 Jose Alvarez .05 .02
❑ 783 Checklist 6 .05 .02
❑ 784 Scott Bailes .05 .02
❑ 785 Jim Rice .10 .05
❑ 786 Eric King .05 .02
❑ 787 Rene Gonzales .05 .02
❑ 788 Frank DiPino .05 .02
❑ 789 John Wathan MG .05 .02
❑ 790 Gary Carter .15 .07
❑ 791 Alvaro Espinoza .05 .02
❑ 792 Gerald Perry .05 .02
❑ XX George Bush PRES

## 1990 Topps Traded

| | MINT | NRMT |
|---|---|---|
| COMPLETE SET (132) | 2.50 | 1.10 |
| COMP.FACT.SET (132) | 3.00 | 1.35 |
| ❑ 1T Darrel Akerfelds | .05 | .02 |
| ❑ 2T Sandy Alomar Jr. | .10 | .05 |
| ❑ 3T Brad Arnsberg | .05 | .02 |
| ❑ 4T Steve Avery | .05 | .02 |
| ❑ 5T Wally Backman | .05 | .02 |
| ❑ 6T Carlos Baerga RC | .10 | .05 |
| ❑ 7T Kevin Bass | .05 | .02 |
| ❑ 8T Willie Blair RC | .05 | .02 |
| ❑ 9T Mike Blowers RC | .10 | .05 |
| ❑ 10T Shawn Boskie RC | .05 | .02 |
| ❑ 11T Daryl Boston | .05 | .02 |
| ❑ 12T Dennis Boyd | .05 | .02 |
| ❑ 13T Glenn Braggs | .05 | .02 |
| ❑ 14T Hubie Brooks | .05 | .02 |
| ❑ 15T Tom Brunansky | .05 | .02 |
| ❑ 16T John Burkett | .05 | .02 |
| ❑ 17T Casey Candaele | .05 | .02 |
| ❑ 18T John Candelaria | .05 | .02 |
| ❑ 19T Gary Carter | .15 | .07 |
| ❑ 20T Joe Carter | .10 | .05 |
| ❑ 21T Rick Cerone | .05 | .02 |
| ❑ 22T Scott Coolbaugh | .05 | .02 |
| ❑ 23T Bobby Cox MG | .10 | .05 |
| ❑ 24T Mark Davis | .05 | .02 |
| ❑ 25T Storm Davis | .05 | .02 |
| ❑ 26T Edgar Diaz | .05 | .02 |
| ❑ 27T Wayne Edwards | .05 | .02 |
| ❑ 28T Mark Eichhorn | .05 | .02 |
| ❑ 29T Scott Erickson RC | .25 | .11 |
| ❑ 30T Nick Esasky | .05 | .02 |
| ❑ 31T Cecil Fielder | .10 | .05 |
| ❑ 32T John Franco | .10 | .05 |
| ❑ 33T Travis Fryman RC | .25 | .11 |
| ❑ 34T Bill Gullickson | .05 | .02 |
| ❑ 35T Darryl Hamilton | .05 | .02 |
| ❑ 36T Mike Harkey | .05 | .02 |
| ❑ 37T Bud Harrelson MG | .05 | .02 |
| ❑ 38T Billy Hatcher | .05 | .02 |
| ❑ 39T Keith Hernandez | .10 | .05 |
| ❑ 40T Joe Hesketh | .05 | .02 |
| ❑ 41T Dave Hollins RC | .20 | .09 |
| ❑ 42T Sam Horn | .05 | .02 |
| ❑ 43T Steve Howard | .05 | .02 |
| ❑ 44T Todd Hundley RC | .40 | .18 |
| ❑ 45T Jeff Huson | .05 | .02 |
| ❑ 46T Chris James | .05 | .02 |
| ❑ 47T Stan Javier | .05 | .02 |
| ❑ 48T Dave Justice RC | 1.00 | .45 |
| ❑ 49T Jeff Kaiser | .05 | .02 |
| ❑ 50T Dana Kiecker | .05 | .02 |
| ❑ 51T Joe Klink | .05 | .02 |
| ❑ 52T Brent Knackert RC | .05 | .02 |
| ❑ 53T Brad Komminsk | .05 | .02 |
| ❑ 54T Mark Langston | .05 | .02 |
| ❑ 55T Tim Layana | .05 | .02 |
| ❑ 56T Rick Leach | .05 | .02 |
| ❑ 57T Terry Leach | .05 | .02 |
| ❑ 58T Tim Leary | .05 | .02 |
| ❑ 59T Craig Lefferts | .05 | .02 |
| ❑ 60T Charlie Leibrandt | .05 | .02 |
| ❑ 61T Jim Leyritz RC | .25 | .11 |
| ❑ 62T Fred Lynn | .05 | .02 |
| ❑ 63T Kevin Maas RC | .10 | .05 |
| ❑ 64T Shane Mack | .05 | .02 |
| ❑ 65T Candy Maldonado | .05 | .02 |
| ❑ 66T Fred Manrique | .05 | .02 |
| ❑ 67T Mike Marshall | .05 | .02 |
| ❑ 68T Carmelo Martinez | .05 | .02 |
| ❑ 69T John Marzano | .05 | .02 |
| ❑ 70T Ben McDonald | .05 | .02 |
| ❑ 71T Jack McDowell | .05 | .02 |
| ❑ 72T John McNamara MG | .05 | .02 |
| ❑ 73T Orlando Mercado | .05 | .02 |
| ❑ 74T Stump Merrill MG | .05 | .02 |
| ❑ 75T Alan Mills RC | .05 | .02 |
| ❑ 76T Hal Morris | .05 | .02 |
| ❑ 77T Lloyd Moseby | .05 | .02 |
| ❑ 78T Randy Myers | .10 | .05 |
| ❑ 79T Tim Naehring RC | .10 | .05 |
| ❑ 80T Junior Noboa | .05 | .02 |
| ❑ 81T Matt Nokes | .05 | .02 |
| ❑ 82T Pete O'Brien | .05 | .02 |
| ❑ 83T John Olerud RC | .60 | .25 |
| ❑ 84T Greg Olson RC | .05 | .02 |
| ❑ 85T Junior Ortiz | .05 | .02 |
| ❑ 86T Dave Parker | .10 | .05 |
| ❑ 87T Rick Parker | .05 | .02 |
| ❑ 88T Bob Patterson | .05 | .02 |
| ❑ 89T Alejandro Pena | .05 | .02 |
| ❑ 90T Tony Pena | .05 | .02 |
| ❑ 91T Pascual Perez | .05 | .02 |
| ❑ 92T Gerald Perry | .05 | .02 |
| ❑ 93T Dan Petry | .05 | .02 |
| ❑ 94T Gary Pettis | .05 | .02 |
| ❑ 95T Tony Phillips | .05 | .02 |
| ❑ 96T Lou Piniella MG | .10 | .05 |
| ❑ 97T Luis Polonia | .05 | .02 |
| ❑ 98T Jim Presley | .05 | .02 |
| ❑ 99T Scott Radinsky RC | .05 | .02 |
| ❑ 100T Willie Randolph | .10 | .05 |
| ❑ 101T Jeff Reardon | .10 | .05 |
| ❑ 102T Greg Riddoch MG | .05 | .02 |
| ❑ 103T Jeff Robinson | .05 | .02 |
| ❑ 104T Ron Robinson | .05 | .02 |
| ❑ 105T Kevin Romine | .05 | .02 |
| ❑ 106T Scott Ruskin | .05 | .02 |
| ❑ 107T John Russell | .05 | .02 |
| ❑ 108T Bill Sampen | .05 | .02 |
| ❑ 109T Juan Samuel | .05 | .02 |
| ❑ 110T Scott Sanderson | .05 | .02 |
| ❑ 111T Jack Savage | .05 | .02 |
| ❑ 112T Dave Schmidt | .05 | .02 |
| ❑ 113T Red Schoendienst MG | .20 | .09 |
| ❑ 114T Terry Shumpert | .05 | .02 |
| ❑ 115T Matt Sinatro | .05 | .02 |
| ❑ 116T Don Slaught | .05 | .02 |
| ❑ 117T Bryn Smith | .05 | .02 |
| ❑ 118T Lee Smith | .10 | .05 |
| ❑ 119T Paul Sorrento RC | .15 | .07 |
| ❑ 120T Franklin Stubbs UER | .05 | .02 |
| ('84 says '99 and has the same stats as '89; '83 stats are missing) | | |
| ❑ 121T Russ Swan RC | .05 | .02 |
| ❑ 122T Bob Tewksbury | .05 | .02 |
| ❑ 123T Wayne Tolleson | .05 | .02 |
| ❑ 124T John Tudor | .05 | .02 |
| ❑ 125T Randy Veres | .05 | .02 |
| ❑ 126T Hector Villanueva RC | .05 | .02 |
| ❑ 127T Mitch Webster | .05 | .02 |
| ❑ 128T Ernie Whitt | .05 | .02 |
| ❑ 129T Frank Wills | .05 | .02 |
| ❑ 130T Dave Winfield | .20 | .09 |
| ❑ 131T Matt Young | .05 | .02 |
| ❑ 132T Checklist 1T-132T | .05 | .02 |

## 1991 Topps

| | MINT | NRMT |
|---|---|---|
| COMPLETE SET (792) | 20.00 | 9.00 |
| COMP.FACT.SET (792) | 30.00 | 13.50 |
| ❑ 1 Nolan Ryan | 1.00 | .45 |
| ❑ 2 George Brett RB | .20 | .09 |
| Batting Title, 3 decades | | |
| ❑ 3 Carlton Fisk RB | .10 | .05 |
| Catcher HR Record | | |
| ❑ 4 Kevin Maas RB | .05 | .02 |
| Quickest to 10 HR's | | |
| ❑ 5 Cal Ripken RB | .40 | .09 |
| Most cons. errorless games | | |
| ❑ 6 Nolan Ryan RB | .50 | .18 |
| Oldest pitcher, no-hitter | | |
| ❑ 7 Ryne Sandberg RB | .20 | .09 |
| Most cons. errorless games | | |
| ❑ 8 Bobby Thigpen RB | .05 | .02 |
| Most saves, season | | |
| ❑ 9 Darrin Fletcher | .05 | .02 |
| ❑ 10 Gregg Olson | .05 | .02 |
| ❑ 11 Roberto Kelly | .05 | .02 |
| ❑ 12 Paul Assenmacher | .05 | .02 |
| ❑ 13 Mariano Duncan | .05 | .02 |
| ❑ 14 Dennis Lamp | .05 | .02 |
| ❑ 15 Von Hayes | .05 | .02 |
| ❑ 16 Mike Heath | .05 | .02 |
| ❑ 17 Jeff Brantley | .05 | .02 |
| ❑ 18 Nelson Liriano | .05 | .02 |
| ❑ 19 Jeff D. Robinson | .05 | .02 |
| ❑ 20 Pedro Guerrero | .05 | .02 |
| ❑ 21 Joe Morgan MG | .05 | .02 |
| ❑ 22 Storm Davis | .05 | .02 |
| ❑ 23 Jim Gantner | .05 | .02 |
| ❑ 24 Dave Martinez | .05 | .02 |
| ❑ 25 Tim Belcher | .05 | .02 |
| ❑ 26 Luis Sojo UER | .05 | .02 |
| (Born in Barquisimento, not Carquis) | | |
| ❑ 27 Bobby Witt | .05 | .02 |
| ❑ 28 Alvaro Espinoza | .05 | .02 |
| ❑ 29 Bob Walk | .05 | .02 |
| ❑ 30 Gregg Jefferies | .05 | .02 |
| ❑ 31 Colby Ward | .05 | .02 |
| ❑ 32 Mike Simms | .05 | .02 |
| ❑ 33 Barry Jones | .05 | .02 |
| ❑ 34 Atlee Hammaker | .05 | .02 |
| ❑ 35 Greg Maddux | .50 | .23 |
| ❑ 36 Donnie Hill | .05 | .02 |
| ❑ 37 Tom Bolton | .05 | .02 |
| ❑ 38 Scott Bradley | .05 | .02 |
| ❑ 39 Jim Neidlinger | .05 | .02 |
| ❑ 40 Kevin Mitchell | .05 | .02 |
| ❑ 41 Ken Dayley | .05 | .02 |
| ❑ 42 Chris Hoiles | .05 | .02 |
| ❑ 43 Roger McDowell | .05 | .02 |
| ❑ 44 Mike Felder | .05 | .02 |
| ❑ 45 Chris Sabo | .05 | .02 |
| ❑ 46 Tim Drummond | .05 | .02 |
| ❑ 47 Brook Jacoby | .05 | .02 |
| ❑ 48 Dennis Boyd | .05 | .02 |
| ❑ 49A Pat Borders ERR | .20 | .09 |
| (40 steals at Kinston in '86) | | |
| ❑ 49B Pat Borders COR | .05 | .02 |
| (0 steals at Kinston in '86) | | |
| ❑ 50 Bob Welch | .05 | .02 |
| ❑ 51 Art Howe MG | .05 | .02 |
| ❑ 52 Francisco Oliveras | .05 | .02 |
| ❑ 53 Mike Sharperson UER | .05 | .02 |
| (Born in 1961, not 1960) | | |
| ❑ 54 Gary Mielke | .05 | .02 |
| ❑ 55 Jeffrey Leonard | .05 | .02 |
| ❑ 56 Jeff Parrett | .05 | .02 |
| ❑ 57 Jack Howell | .05 | .02 |
| ❑ 58 Mel Stottlemyre Jr. | .05 | .02 |
| ❑ 59 Eric Yelding | .05 | .02 |

| No. | Player | | |
|---|---|---|---|
| 60 | Frank Viola | .05 | .02 |
| 61 | Stan Javier | .05 | .02 |
| 62 | Lee Guetterman | .05 | .02 |
| 63 | Milt Thompson | .05 | .02 |
| 64 | Tom Herr | .05 | .02 |
| 65 | Bruce Hurst | .05 | .02 |
| 66 | Terry Kennedy | .05 | .02 |
| 67 | Rick Honeycutt | .05 | .02 |
| 68 | Gary Sheffield | .20 | .09 |
| 69 | Steve Wilson | .05 | .02 |
| 70 | Ellis Burks | .10 | .05 |
| 71 | Jim Acker | .05 | .02 |
| 72 | Junior Ortiz | .05 | .02 |
| 73 | Craig Worthington | .05 | .02 |
| 74 | Shane Andrews RC | .25 | .11 |
| 75 | Jack Morris | .10 | .05 |
| 76 | Jerry Browne | .05 | .02 |
| 77 | Drew Hall | .05 | .02 |
| 78 | Geno Petralli | .05 | .02 |
| 79 | Frank Thomas | .50 | .23 |
| 80A | Fernando Valenzuela ERR (104 earned runs in '90 tied for league lead) | .10 | .05 |
| 80B | Fernando Valenzuela COR (104 earned runs in '90 led league; 20 CG's in 1986 now italicized) | .10 | .05 |
| 81 | Cito Gaston MG | .05 | .02 |
| 82 | Tom Glavine | .20 | .09 |
| 83 | Daryl Boston | .05 | .02 |
| 84 | Bob McClure | .05 | .02 |
| 85 | Jesse Barfield | .05 | .02 |
| 86 | Les Lancaster | .05 | .02 |
| 87 | Tracy Jones | .05 | .02 |
| 88 | Bob Tewksbury | .05 | .02 |
| 89 | Darren Daulton | .10 | .05 |
| 90 | Danny Tartabull | .05 | .02 |
| 91 | Greg Colbrunn RC | .05 | .02 |
| 92 | Danny Jackson | .05 | .02 |
| 93 | Ivan Calderon | .05 | .02 |
| 94 | John Dopson | .05 | .02 |
| 95 | Paul Molitor | .20 | .09 |
| 96 | Trevor Wilson | .05 | .02 |
| 97A | Brady Anderson ERR (September, 2 RBI and 3 hits, should be 3 RBI and 14 hits | .20 | .09 |
| 97B | Brady Anderson COR | .20 | .09 |
| 98 | Sergio Valdez | .05 | .02 |
| 99 | Chris Gwynn | .05 | .02 |
| 100 | Don Mattingly COR (101 hits in 1990) | .50 | .23 |
| 100A | Don Mattingly ERR (10 hits in 1990) | 1.00 | .35 |
| 101 | Rob Ducey | .05 | .02 |
| 102 | Gene Larkin | .05 | .02 |
| 103 | Tim Costo RC | .05 | .02 |
| 104 | Don Robinson | .05 | .02 |
| 105 | Kevin McReynolds | .05 | .02 |
| 106 | Ed Nunez | .05 | .02 |
| 107 | Luis Polonia | .05 | .02 |
| 108 | Matt Young | .05 | .02 |
| 109 | Greg Riddoch MG | .05 | .02 |
| 110 | Tom Henke | .05 | .02 |
| 111 | Andres Thomas | .05 | .02 |
| 112 | Frank DiPino | .05 | .02 |
| 113 | Carl Everett RC | 1.00 | .45 |
| 114 | Lance Dickson RC | .05 | .02 |
| 115 | Hubie Brooks | .05 | .02 |
| 116 | Mark Davis | .05 | .02 |
| 117 | Dion James | .05 | .02 |
| 118 | Tom Edens | .05 | .02 |
| 119 | Carl Nichols | .05 | .02 |
| 120 | Joe Carter | .10 | .05 |
| 121 | Eric King | .05 | .02 |
| 122 | Paul O'Neill | .10 | .05 |
| 123 | Greg A. Harris | .05 | .02 |
| 124 | Randy Bush | .05 | .02 |
| 125 | Steve Bedrosian | .05 | .02 |
| 126 | Bernard Gilkey | .10 | .05 |
| 127 | Joe Price | .05 | .02 |
| 128 | Travis Fryman (Front has SS; back has SS-3B) | .20 | .09 |
| 129 | Mark Eichhorn | .05 | .02 |
| 130 | Ozzie Smith | .25 | .11 |
| 131A | Checklist 1 ERR 727 Phil Bradley | .20 | .09 |
| 131B | Checklist 1 COR 717 Phil Bradley | .05 | .02 |
| 132 | Jamie Quirk | .05 | .02 |
| 133 | Greg Briley | .05 | .02 |
| 134 | Kevin Elster | .05 | .02 |
| 135 | Jerome Walton | .05 | .02 |
| 136 | Dave Schmidt | .05 | .02 |
| 137 | Randy Ready | .05 | .02 |
| 138 | Jamie Moyer | .05 | .02 |
| 139 | Jeff Treadway | .05 | .02 |
| 140 | Fred McGriff | .20 | .09 |
| 141 | Nick Leyva MG | .05 | .02 |
| 142 | Curt Wilkerson | .05 | .02 |
| 143 | John Smiley | .05 | .02 |
| 144 | Dave Henderson | .05 | .02 |
| 145 | Lou Whitaker | .10 | .05 |
| 146 | Dan Plesac | .05 | .02 |
| 147 | Carlos Baerga | .05 | .02 |
| 148 | Rey Palacios | .05 | .02 |
| 149 | Al Osuna UER (Shown throwing right, but bio says lefty) | .05 | .02 |
| 150 | Cal Ripken | .75 | .35 |
| 151 | Tom Browning | .05 | .02 |
| 152 | Mickey Hatcher | .05 | .02 |
| 153 | Bryan Harvey | .05 | .02 |
| 154 | Jay Buhner | .10 | .05 |
| 155A | Dwight Evans ERR (Led league with 162 games in '82) | .20 | .09 |
| 155B | Dwight Evans COR (Tied for lead with 162 games in '82) | .10 | .05 |
| 156 | Carlos Martinez | .05 | .02 |
| 157 | John Smoltz | .10 | .05 |
| 158 | Jose Uribe | .05 | .02 |
| 159 | Joe Boever | .05 | .02 |
| 160 | Vince Coleman UER (Wrong birth year; born 9/22/60) | .05 | .02 |
| 161 | Tim Leary | .05 | .02 |
| 162 | Ozzie Canseco | .05 | .02 |
| 163 | Dave Johnson | .05 | .02 |
| 164 | Edgar Diaz | .05 | .02 |
| 165 | Sandy Alomar Jr. | .10 | .05 |
| 166 | Harold Baines | .10 | .05 |
| 167A | Randy Tomlin RC ERR (Harriburg) | .20 | .09 |
| 167B | Randy Tomlin RC COR (Harrisburg) | .05 | .02 |
| 168 | John Olerud | .15 | .07 |
| 169 | Luis Aquino | .05 | .02 |
| 170 | Carlton Fisk | .20 | .09 |
| 171 | Tony LaRussa MG | .10 | .05 |
| 172 | Pete Incaviglia | .05 | .02 |
| 173 | Jason Grimsley | .05 | .02 |
| 174 | Ken Caminiti | .10 | .05 |
| 175 | Jack Armstrong | .05 | .02 |
| 176 | John Orton | .05 | .02 |
| 177 | Reggie Harris | .05 | .02 |
| 178 | Dave Valle | .05 | .02 |
| 179 | Pete Harnisch | .05 | .02 |
| 180 | Tony Gwynn | .40 | .18 |
| 181 | Duane Ward | .05 | .02 |
| 182 | Junior Noboa | .05 | .02 |
| 183 | Clay Parker | .05 | .02 |
| 184 | Gary Green | .05 | .02 |
| 185 | Joe Magrane | .05 | .02 |
| 186 | Rod Booker | .05 | .02 |
| 187 | Greg Cadaret | .05 | .02 |
| 188 | Damon Berryhill | .05 | .02 |
| 189 | Daryl Irvine | .05 | .02 |
| 190 | Matt Williams | .15 | .07 |
| 191 | Willie Blair | .05 | .02 |
| 192 | Rob Deer | .05 | .02 |
| 193 | Felix Fermin | .05 | .02 |
| 194 | Xavier Hernandez | .05 | .02 |
| 195 | Wally Joyner | .10 | .05 |
| 196 | Jim Vatcher | .05 | .02 |
| 197 | Chris Nabholz | .05 | .02 |
| 198 | R.J. Reynolds | .05 | .02 |
| 199 | Mike Hartley | .05 | .02 |
| 200 | Darryl Strawberry | .10 | .05 |
| 201 | Tom Kelly MG | .05 | .02 |
| 202 | Jim Leyritz | .05 | .02 |
| 203 | Gene Harris | .05 | .02 |
| 204 | Herm Winningham | .05 | .02 |
| 205 | Mike Perez RC | .05 | .02 |
| 206 | Carlos Quintana | .05 | .02 |
| 207 | Gary Wayne | .05 | .02 |
| 208 | Willie Wilson | .05 | .02 |
| 209 | Ken Howell | .05 | .02 |
| 210 | Lance Parrish | .05 | .02 |
| 211 | Brian Barnes | .05 | .02 |
| 212 | Steve Finley | .10 | .05 |
| 213 | Frank Wills | .05 | .02 |
| 214 | Joe Girardi | .10 | .05 |
| 215 | Dave Smith | .05 | .02 |
| 216 | Greg Gagne | .05 | .02 |
| 217 | Chris Bosio | .05 | .02 |
| 218 | Rick Parker | .05 | .02 |
| 219 | Jack McDowell | .05 | .02 |
| 220 | Tim Wallach | .05 | .02 |
| 221 | Don Slaught | .05 | .02 |
| 222 | Brian McRae RC | .10 | .05 |
| 223 | Allan Anderson | .05 | .02 |
| 224 | Juan Gonzalez | .25 | .11 |
| 225 | Randy Johnson | .30 | .14 |
| 226 | Alfredo Griffin | .05 | .02 |
| 227 | Steve Avery UER (Pitched 13 games for Durham in 1989, not 2) | .05 | .02 |
| 228 | Rex Hudler | .05 | .02 |
| 229 | Rance Mulliniks | .05 | .02 |
| 230 | Sid Fernandez | .05 | .02 |
| 231 | Doug Rader MG | .05 | .02 |
| 232 | Jose DeJesus | .05 | .02 |
| 233 | Al Leiter | .10 | .05 |
| 234 | Scott Erickson | .05 | .02 |
| 235 | Dave Parker | .10 | .05 |
| 236A | Frank Tanana ERR (Tied for lead with 269 K's in '75) | .10 | .05 |
| 236B | Frank Tanana COR (Led league with 269 K's in '75) | .05 | .02 |
| 237 | Rick Cerone | .05 | .02 |
| 238 | Mike Dunne | .05 | .02 |
| 239 | Darren Lewis | .10 | .05 |
| 240 | Mike Scott | .05 | .02 |
| 241 | Dave Clark UER (Career totals 19 HR and 5 3B; should be 22 and 3) | .05 | .02 |
| 242 | Mike LaCoss | .05 | .02 |
| 243 | Lance Johnson | .05 | .02 |
| 244 | Mike Jeffcoat | .05 | .02 |
| 245 | Kal Daniels | .05 | .02 |
| 246 | Kevin Wickander | .05 | .02 |
| 247 | Jody Reed | .05 | .02 |
| 248 | Tom Gordon | .05 | .02 |
| 249 | Bob Melvin | .05 | .02 |
| 250 | Dennis Eckersley | .10 | .05 |
| 251 | Mark Lemke | .05 | .02 |
| 252 | Mel Rojas | .10 | .05 |
| 253 | Garry Templeton | .05 | .02 |
| 254 | Shawn Boskie | .05 | .02 |
| 255 | Brian Downing | .05 | .02 |
| 256 | Greg Hibbard | .05 | .02 |
| 257 | Tom O'Malley | .05 | .02 |
| 258 | Chris Hammond | .05 | .02 |
| 259 | Hensley Meulens | .05 | .02 |
| 260 | Harold Reynolds | .05 | .02 |
| 261 | Bud Harrelson MG | .05 | .02 |
| 262 | Tim Jones | .05 | .02 |
| 263 | Checklist 2 | .05 | .02 |
| 264 | Dave Hollins | .05 | .02 |
| 265 | Mark Gubicza | .05 | .02 |
| 266 | Carmelo Castillo | .05 | .02 |
| 267 | Mark Knudson | .05 | .02 |
| 268 | Tom Brookens | .05 | .02 |
| 269 | Joe Hesketh | .05 | .02 |
| 270 | Mark McGwire COR (1987 Slugging Pctg. listed as .618) | .75 | .35 |
| 270A | Mark McGwire ERR (1987 Slugging Pctg. listed as 618) | 1.50 | |

❑ 271 Omar Olivares RC .05 .02
❑ 272 Jeff King .05 .02
❑ 273 Johnny Ray .05 .02
❑ 274 Ken Williams .05 .02
❑ 275 Alan Trammell .15 .07
❑ 276 Bill Swift .05 .02
❑ 277 Scott Coolbaugh .05 .02
❑ 278 Alex Fernandez UER .10 .05
(No '90 White Sox stats)
❑ 279A Jose Gonzalez ERR .05 .02
(Photo actually
Billy Bean)
❑ 279B Jose Gonzalez COR .05 .02
❑ 280 Bret Saberhagen .10 .05
❑ 281 Larry Sheets .05 .02
❑ 282 Don Carman .05 .02
❑ 283 Marquis Grissom .05 .02
❑ 284 Billy Spiers .05 .02
❑ 285 Jim Abbott .10 .05
❑ 286 Ken Oberkfell .05 .02
❑ 287 Mark Grant .05 .02
❑ 288 Derrick May .05 .02
❑ 289 Tim Birtsas .05 .02
❑ 290 Steve Sax .05 .02
❑ 291 John Wathan MG .05 .02
❑ 292 Bud Black .05 .02
❑ 293 Jay Bell .10 .05
❑ 294 Mike Moore .05 .02
❑ 295 Rafael Palmeiro .20 .09
❑ 296 Mark Williamson .05 .02
❑ 297 Manny Lee .05 .02
❑ 298 Omar Vizquel .20 .09
❑ 299 Scott Radinsky .05 .02
❑ 300 Kirby Puckett .50 .23
❑ 301 Steve Farr .05 .02
❑ 302 Tim Teufel .05 .02
❑ 303 Mike Boddicker .05 .02
❑ 304 Kevin Reimer .05 .02
❑ 305 Mike Scioscia .05 .02
❑ 306A Lonnie Smith ERR .20 .09
(136 games in '90)
❑ 306B Lonnie Smith COR .05 .02
(135 games in '90)
❑ 307 Andy Benes .05 .02
❑ 308 Tom Pagnozzi .05 .02
❑ 309 Norm Charlton .05 .02
❑ 310 Gary Carter .15 .07
❑ 311 Jeff Pico .05 .02
❑ 312 Charlie Hayes .05 .02
❑ 313 Ron Robinson .05 .02
❑ 314 Gary Pettis .05 .02
❑ 315 Roberto Alomar .20 .09
❑ 316 Gene Nelson .05 .02
❑ 317 Mike Fitzgerald .05 .02
❑ 318 Rick Aguilera .10 .05
❑ 319 Jeff McKnight .05 .02
❑ 320 Tony Fernandez .05 .02
❑ 321 Bob Rodgers MG .05 .02
❑ 322 Terry Shumpert .05 .02
❑ 323 Cory Snyder .05 .02
❑ 324A Ron Kittle ERR .20 .09
(Set another
standard ...)
❑ 324B Ron Kittle COR .05 .02
(Tied another
standard ...)
❑ 325 Brett Butler .10 .05
❑ 326 Ken Patterson .05 .02
❑ 327 Ron Hassey .05 .02
❑ 328 Walt Terrell .05 .02
❑ 329 Dave Justice UER .20 .09
(Drafted third round
on card, should say
fourth pick)
❑ 330 Dwight Gooden .10 .05
❑ 331 Eric Anthony .05 .02
❑ 332 Kenny Rogers .05 .02
❑ 333 Chipper Jones FDP RC 4.00 1.80
❑ 334 Todd Benzinger .05 .02
❑ 335 Mitch Williams .05 .02
❑ 336 Matt Nokes .05 .02
❑ 337A Keith Comstock ERR .20 .09
(Cubs logo on front)
❑ 337B Keith Comstock COR .05 .02
(Mariners logo on front)
❑ 338 Luis Rivera .05 .02

❑ 339 Larry Walker .20 .09
❑ 340 Ramon Martinez .05 .02
❑ 341 John Moses .05 .02
❑ 342 Mickey Morandini .05 .02
❑ 343 Jose Oquendo .05 .02
❑ 344 Jeff Russell .05 .02
❑ 345 Len Dykstra .10 .05
❑ 346 Jesse Orosco .05 .02
❑ 347 Greg Vaughn .20 .09
❑ 348 Todd Stottlemyre .10 .05
❑ 349 Dave Gallagher .05 .02
❑ 350 Glenn Davis .05 .02
❑ 351 Joe Torre MG .10 .05
❑ 352 Frank White .10 .05
❑ 353 Tony Castillo .05 .02
❑ 354 Sid Bream .05 .02
❑ 355 Chili Davis .10 .05
❑ 356 Mike Marshall .05 .02
❑ 357 Jack Savage .05 .02
❑ 358 Mark Parent .05 .02
❑ 359 Chuck Cary .05 .02
❑ 360 Tim Raines .10 .05
❑ 361 Scott Garrelts .05 .02
❑ 362 Hector Villenueva .05 .02
❑ 363 Rick Mahler .05 .02
❑ 364 Dan Pasqua .05 .02
❑ 365 Mike Schooler .05 .02
❑ 366A Checklist 3 ERR .20 .09
19 Carl Nichols
❑ 366B Checklist 3 COR .05 .02
119 Carl Nichols
❑ 367 Dave Walsh .05 .02
❑ 368 Felix Jose .05 .02
❑ 369 Steve Searcy .05 .02
❑ 370 Kelly Gruber .05 .02
❑ 371 Jeff Montgomery .10 .05
❑ 372 Spike Owen .05 .02
❑ 373 Darrin Jackson .05 .02
❑ 374 Larry Casian .05 .02
❑ 375 Tony Pena .05 .02
❑ 376 Mike Harkey .05 .02
❑ 377 Rene Gonzales .05 .02
❑ 378A Wilson Alvarez ERR .75 .35
('89 Port Charlotte
and '90 Birmingham
stat lines omitted)
❑ 378B Wilson Alvarez COR .05 .02
(Text still says 143
K's in 1988, whereas
stats say 134)
❑ 379 Randy Velarde .05 .02
❑ 380 Willie McGee .10 .05
❑ 381 Jim Leyland MG .05 .02
❑ 382 Mackey Sasser .05 .02
❑ 383 Pete Smith .05 .02
❑ 384 Gerald Perry .05 .02
❑ 385 Mickey Tettleton .05 .02
❑ 386 Cecil Fielder AS .05 .02
❑ 387 Julio Franco AS .05 .02
❑ 388 Kelly Gruber AS .05 .02
❑ 389 Alan Trammell AS .05 .02
❑ 390 Jose Canseco AS .10 .05
❑ 391 Rickey Henderson AS .10 .05
❑ 392 Ken Griffey Jr. AS .50 .35
❑ 393 Carlton Fisk AS .10 .05
❑ 394 Bob Welch AS .05 .02
❑ 395 Chuck Finley AS .05 .02
❑ 396 Bobby Thigpen AS .05 .02
❑ 397 Eddie Murray AS .10 .05
❑ 398 Ryne Sandberg AS .20 .09
❑ 399 Matt Williams AS .10 .05
❑ 400 Barry Larkin AS .10 .05
❑ 401 Barry Bonds AS .20 .09
❑ 402 Darryl Strawberry AS .05 .02
❑ 403 Bobby Bonilla AS .05 .02
❑ 404 Mike Scioscia AS .05 .02
❑ 405 Doug Drabek AS .05 .02
❑ 406 Frank Viola AS .05 .02
❑ 407 John Franco AS .05 .02
❑ 408 Earnest Riles .05 .02
❑ 409 Mike Stanley .05 .02
❑ 410 Dave Righetti .05 .02
❑ 411 Lance Blankenship .05 .02
❑ 412 Dave Bergman .05 .02
❑ 413 Terry Mulholland .05 .02
❑ 414 Sammy Sosa .50 .23

❑ 415 Rick Sutcliffe .10 .05
❑ 416 Randy Milligan .05 .02
❑ 417 Bill Krueger .05 .02
❑ 418 Nick Esasky .05 .02
❑ 419 Jeff Reed .05 .02
❑ 420 Bobby Thigpen .05 .02
❑ 421 Alex Cole .05 .02
❑ 422 Rick Reuschel .05 .02
❑ 423 Rafael Ramirez UER .05 .02
(Born 1959, not 1958)
❑ 424 Calvin Schiraldi .05 .02
❑ 425 Andy Van Slyke .10 .05
❑ 426 Joe Grahe RC .05 .02
❑ 427 Rick Dempsey .05 .02
❑ 428 John Barfield .05 .02
❑ 429 Stump Merrill MG .05 .02
❑ 430 Gary Gaetti .10 .05
❑ 431 Paul Gibson .05 .02
❑ 432 Delino DeShields .10 .05
❑ 433 Pat Tabler .05 .02
❑ 434 Julio Machado .05 .02
❑ 435 Kevin Maas .05 .02
❑ 436 Scott Bankhead .05 .02
❑ 437 Doug Dascenzo .05 .02
❑ 438 Vicente Palacios .05 .02
❑ 439 Dickie Thon .05 .02
❑ 440 George Bell .05 .02
❑ 441 Zane Smith .05 .02
❑ 442 Charlie O'Brien .05 .02
❑ 443 Jeff Innis .05 .02
❑ 444 Glenn Braggs .05 .02
❑ 445 Greg Swindell .05 .02
❑ 446 Craig Grebeck .05 .02
❑ 447 John Burkett .05 .02
❑ 448 Craig Lefferts .05 .02
❑ 449 Juan Berenguer .05 .02
❑ 450 Wade Boggs .25 .11
❑ 451 Neal Heaton .05 .02
❑ 452 Bill Schroeder .05 .02
❑ 453 Lenny Harris .05 .02
❑ 454A Kevin Appier ERR .10 .05
('90 Omaha stat
line omitted)
❑ 454B Kevin Appier COR .10 .05
❑ 455 Walt Weiss .05 .02
❑ 456 Charlie Leibrandt .05 .02
❑ 457 Todd Hundley .05 .02
❑ 458 Brian Holman .05 .02
❑ 459 Tom Trebelhorn MG UER .05 .02
(Pitching and batting
columns switched)
❑ 460 Dave Stieb .05 .02
❑ 461 Robin Ventura .20 .09
❑ 462 Steve Frey .05 .02
❑ 463 Dwight Smith .05 .02
❑ 464 Steve Buechele .05 .02
❑ 465 Ken Griffey Sr. .10 .05
❑ 466 Charles Nagy .05 .02
❑ 467 Dennis Cook .05 .02
❑ 468 Tim Hulett .05 .02
❑ 469 Chet Lemon .05 .02
❑ 470 Howard Johnson .05 .02
❑ 471 Mike Lieberthal RC .50 .23
❑ 472 Kirt Manwaring .05 .02
❑ 473 Curt Young .05 .02
❑ 474 Phil Plantier RC .05 .02
❑ 475 Ted Higuera .05 .02
❑ 476 Glenn Wilson .05 .02
❑ 477 Mike Fetters .05 .02
❑ 478 Kurt Stillwell .05 .02
❑ 479 Bob Patterson UER .05 .02
(Has a decimal point
between 7 and 9)
❑ 480 Dave Magadan .05 .02
❑ 481 Eddie Whitson .05 .02
❑ 482 Tino Martinez .10 .05
❑ 483 Mike Aldrete .05 .02
❑ 484 Dave LaPoint .05 .02
❑ 485 Terry Pendleton .10 .05
❑ 486 Tommy Greene .05 .02
❑ 487 Rafael Belliard .05 .02
❑ 488 Jeff Manto .05 .02
❑ 489 Bobby Valentine MG .05 .02
❑ 490 Kirk Gibson .10 .05
❑ 491 Kurt Miller RC .05 .02
❑ 492 Ernie Whitt .05 .02

❑ 493 Jose Rijo .05 .02
❑ 494 Chris James .05 .02
❑ 495 Charlie Hough .10 .05
❑ 496 Marty Barrett .05 .02
❑ 497 Ben McDonald .05 .02
❑ 498 Mark Salas .05 .02
❑ 499 Melido Perez .05 .02
❑ 500 Will Clark .20 .09
❑ 501 Mike Bielecki .05 .02
❑ 502 Carney Lansford .10 .05
❑ 503 Roy Smith .05 .02
❑ 504 Julio Valera .05 .02
❑ 505 Chuck Finley .10 .05
❑ 506 Darnell Coles .05 .02
❑ 507 Steve Jeltz .05 .02
❑ 508 Mike York .05 .02
❑ 509 Glenallen Hill .05 .02
❑ 510 John Franco .10 .05
❑ 511 Steve Balboni .05 .02
❑ 512 Jose Mesa .05 .02
❑ 513 Jerald Clark .05 .02
❑ 514 Mike Stanton .05 .02
❑ 515 Alvin Davis .05 .02
❑ 516 Karl Rhodes .05 .02
❑ 517 Joe Oliver .05 .02
❑ 518 Cris Carpenter .05 .02
❑ 519 Sparky Anderson MG .10 .05
❑ 520 Mark Grace .20 .09
❑ 521 Joe Orsulak .05 .02
❑ 522 Stan Belinda .05 .02
❑ 523 Rodney McCray .05 .02
❑ 524 Darrel Akerfelds .05 .02
❑ 525 Willie Randolph .10 .05
❑ 526A Moises Alou ERR .50 .23
(37 runs in 2 games
for '90 Pirates)
❑ 526B Moises Alou COR .20 .09
(0 runs in 2 games
for '90 Pirates)
❑ 527A Checklist 4 ERR .20 .09
105 Keith Miller
719 Kevin McReynolds
❑ 527B Checklist 4 COR .05 .02
105 Kevin McReynolds
719 Keith Miller
❑ 528 Dennis Martinez .10 .05
❑ 529 Marc Newfield RC .05 .02
❑ 530 Roger Clemens .40 .18
❑ 531 Dave Rohde .05 .02
❑ 532 Kirk McCaskill .05 .02
❑ 533 Oddibe McDowell .05 .02
❑ 534 Mike Jackson .05 .02
❑ 535 Ruben Sierra UER .05 .02
(Back reads 100 Runs
amd 100 RBI's)
❑ 536 Mike Witt .05 .02
❑ 537 Jose Lind .05 .02
❑ 538 Bip Roberts .05 .02
❑ 539 Scott Terry .05 .02
❑ 540 George Brett .40 .18
❑ 541 Domingo Ramos .05 .02
❑ 542 Rob Murphy .05 .02
❑ 543 Junior Felix .05 .02
❑ 544 Alejandro Pena .05 .02
❑ 545 Dale Murphy .20 .09
❑ 546 Jeff Ballard .05 .02
❑ 547 Mike Pagliarulo .05 .02
❑ 548 Jaime Navarro .05 .02
❑ 549 John McNamara MG .05 .02
❑ 550 Eric Davis .10 .05
❑ 551 Bob Kipper .05 .02
❑ 552 Jeff Hamilton .05 .02
❑ 553 Joe Klink .05 .02
❑ 554 Brian Harper .05 .02
❑ 555 Turner Ward RC .05 .02
❑ 556 Gary Ward .05 .02
❑ 557 Wally Whitehurst .05 .02
❑ 558 Otis Nixon .05 .02
❑ 559 Adam Peterson .05 .02
❑ 560 Greg Smith .05 .02
❑ 561 Tim McIntosh .05 .02
❑ 562 Jeff Kunkel .05 .02
❑ 563 Brent Knackert .05 .02
❑ 564 Dante Bichette .20 .09
❑ 565 Craig Biggio .15 .07
❑ 566 Craig Wilson .05 .02
❑ 567 Dwayne Henry .05 .02
❑ 568 Ron Karkovice .05 .02
❑ 569 Curt Schilling .10 .05
❑ 570 Barry Bonds .30 .14
❑ 571 Pat Combs .05 .02
❑ 572 Dave Anderson .05 .02
❑ 573 Rich Rodriguez UER .05 .02
(Stats say drafted 4th,
but bio says 9th round)
❑ 574 John Marzano .05 .02
❑ 575 Robin Yount .20 .09
❑ 576 Jeff Kaiser .05 .02
❑ 577 Bill Doran .05 .02
❑ 578 Dave West .05 .02
❑ 579 Roger Craig MG .05 .02
❑ 580 Dave Stewart .10 .05
❑ 581 Luis Quinones .05 .02
❑ 582 Marty Clary .05 .02
❑ 583 Tony Phillips .05 .02
❑ 584 Kevin Brown .15 .07
❑ 585 Pete O'Brien .05 .02
❑ 586 Fred Lynn .05 .02
❑ 587 Jose Offerman UER .05 .02
(Text says he signed
7/24/86, but bio
says 1988)
❑ 588 Mark Whiten .05 .02
❑ 589 Scott Ruskin .05 .02
❑ 590 Eddie Murray .20 .09
❑ 591 Ken Hill .05 .02
❑ 592 B.J. Surhoff .10 .05
❑ 593A Mike Walker ERR .20 .09
('90 Canton-Akron
stat line omitted)
❑ 593B Mike Walker COR .05 .02
❑ 594 Rich Garces RC .05 .02
❑ 595 Bill Landrum .05 .02
❑ 596 Ronnie Walden RC .05 .02
❑ 597 Jerry Don Gleaton .05 .02
❑ 598 Sam Horn .05 .02
❑ 599A Greg Myers ERR .20 .09
('90 Syracuse
stat line omitted)
❑ 599B Greg Myers COR .05 .02
❑ 600 Bo Jackson .10 .05
❑ 601 Bob Ojeda .05 .02
❑ 602 Casey Candaele .05 .02
❑ 603A Wes Chamberlain RC ERR .20 .09
(Photo actually
Louie Meadows)
❑ 603B Wes Chamberlain RC COR .05 .02
❑ 604 Billy Hatcher .05 .02
❑ 605 Jeff Reardon .10 .05
❑ 606 Jim Gott .05 .02
❑ 607 Edgar Martinez .15 .07
❑ 608 Todd Burns .05 .02
❑ 609 Jeff Torborg MG .05 .02
❑ 610 Andres Galarraga .15 .07
❑ 611 Dave Eiland .05 .02
❑ 612 Steve Lyons .05 .02
❑ 613 Eric Show .05 .02
❑ 614 Luis Salazar .05 .02
❑ 615 Bert Blyleven .10 .05
❑ 616 Todd Zeile .10 .05
❑ 617 Bill Wegman .05 .02
❑ 618 Sil Campusano .05 .02
❑ 619 David Wells .10 .05
❑ 620 Ozzie Guillen .05 .02
❑ 621 Ted Power .05 .02
❑ 622 Jack Daugherty .05 .02
❑ 623 Jeff Blauser .05 .02
❑ 624 Tom Candiotti .05 .02
❑ 625 Terry Steinbach .10 .05
❑ 626 Gerald Young .05 .02
❑ 627 Tim Layana .05 .02
❑ 628 Greg Litton .05 .02
❑ 629 Wes Gardner .05 .02
❑ 630 Dave Winfield .20 .09
❑ 631 Mike Morgan .05 .02
❑ 632 Lloyd Moseby .05 .02
❑ 633 Kevin Tapani .05 .02
❑ 634 Henry Cotto .05 .02
❑ 635 Andy Hawkins .05 .02
❑ 636 Geronimo Pena .05 .02
❑ 637 Bruce Ruffin .05 .02
❑ 638 Mike Macfarlane .05 .02
❑ 639 Frank Robinson MG .15 .07
❑ 640 Andre Dawson .15 .07
❑ 641 Mike Henneman .05 .02
❑ 642 Hal Morris .05 .02
❑ 643 Jim Presley .05 .02
❑ 644 Chuck Crim .05 .02
❑ 645 Juan Samuel .05 .02
❑ 646 Andujar Cedeno .05 .02
❑ 647 Mark Portugal .05 .02
❑ 648 Lee Stevens .10 .05
❑ 649 Bill Sampen .05 .02
❑ 650 Jack Clark .10 .05
❑ 651 Alan Mills .05 .02
❑ 652 Kevin Romine .05 .02
❑ 653 Anthony Telford .05 .02
❑ 654 Paul Sorrento .10 .05
❑ 655 Erik Hanson .05 .02
❑ 656A Checklist 5 ERR .20 .09
348 Vicente Palacios
381 Jose Lind
537 Mike LaValliere
665 Jim Leyland
❑ 656B Checklist 5 ERR .20 .09
433 Vicente Palacios
(Palacios should be 438)
537 Jose Lind
665 Mike LaValliere
381 Jim Leyland
❑ 656C Checklist 5 COR .20 .09
438 Vicente Palacios
537 Jose Lind
665 Mike LaValliere
381 Jim Leyland
❑ 657 Mike Kingery .05 .02
❑ 658 Scott Aldred .05 .02
❑ 659 Oscar Azocar .05 .02
❑ 660 Lee Smith .10 .05
❑ 661 Steve Lake .05 .02
❑ 662 Ron Dibble .05 .02
❑ 663 Greg Brock .05 .02
❑ 664 John Farrell .05 .02
❑ 665 Mike LaValliere .05 .02
❑ 666 Danny Darwin .05 .02
❑ 667 Kent Anderson .05 .02
❑ 668 Bill Long .05 .02
❑ 669 Lou Piniella MG .10 .05
❑ 670 Rickey Henderson .25 .11
❑ 671 Andy McGaffigan .05 .02
❑ 672 Shane Mack .05 .02
❑ 673 Greg Olson UER .05 .02
(6 RBI in '88 at Tidewater
and 2 RBI in '87;
should be 48 and 15)
❑ 674A Kevin Gross ERR .20 .09
(89 BB with Phillies
in '88 tied for
league lead)
❑ 674B Kevin Gross COR .05 .02
(89 BB with Phillies
in '88 led league)
❑ 675 Tom Brunansky .05 .02
❑ 676 Scott Chiamparino .05 .02
❑ 677 Billy Ripken .05 .02
❑ 678 Mark Davidson .05 .02
❑ 679 Bill Bathe .05 .02
❑ 680 David Cone .10 .05
❑ 681 Jeff Schaefer .05 .02
❑ 682 Ray Lankford .20 .09
❑ 683 Derek Lilliquist .05 .02
❑ 684 Milt Cuyler .05 .02
❑ 685 Doug Drabek .05 .02
❑ 686 Mike Gallego .05 .02
❑ 687A John Cerutti ERR .20 .09
(4.46 ERA in '90)
❑ 687B John Cerutti COR .05 .02
(4.76 ERA in '90)
❑ 688 Rosario Rodriguez .05 .02
❑ 689 John Kruk .10 .05
❑ 690 Orel Hershiser .10 .05
❑ 691 Mike Blowers .05 .02
❑ 692A Efrain Valdez ERR .20 .09
(Born 6/11/66)
❑ 692B Efrain Valdez COR .05 .02
(Born 7/11/66 and two
lines of text added)
❑ 693 Francisco Cabrera .05 .02

❑ 694 Randy Veres .05 .02
❑ 695 Kevin Seitzer .05 .02
❑ 696 Steve Olin .05 .02
❑ 697 Shawn Abner .05 .02
❑ 698 Mark Guthrie .05 .02
❑ 699 Jim Lefebvre MG .05 .02
❑ 700 Jose Canseco .25 .11
❑ 701 Pascual Perez .05 .02
❑ 702 Tim Naehring .05 .02
❑ 703 Juan Agosto .05 .02
❑ 704 Devon White .05 .02
❑ 705 Robby Thompson .05 .02
❑ 706A Brad Arnsberg ERR .20 .09
(68.2 IP in '90)
❑ 706B Brad Arnsberg COR .05 .02
(62.2 IP in '90)
❑ 707 Jim Eisenreich .05 .02
❑ 708 John Mitchell .05 .02
❑ 709 Matt Sinatro .05 .02
❑ 710 Kent Hrbek .10 .05
❑ 711 Jose DeLeon .05 .02
❑ 712 Ricky Jordan .05 .02
❑ 713 Scott Scudder .05 .02
❑ 714 Marvell Wynne .05 .02
❑ 715 Tim Burke .05 .02
❑ 716 Bob Geren .05 .02
❑ 717 Phil Bradley .05 .02
❑ 718 Steve Crawford .05 .02
❑ 719 Keith Miller .05 .02
❑ 720 Cecil Fielder .10 .05
❑ 721 Mark Lee .05 .02
❑ 722 Wally Backman .05 .02
❑ 723 Candy Maldonado .05 .02
❑ 724 David Segui .05 .02
❑ 725 Ron Gant .10 .05
❑ 726 Phil Stephenson .05 .02
❑ 727 Mookie Wilson .10 .05
❑ 728 Scott Sanderson .05 .02
❑ 729 Don Zimmer MG .05 .02
❑ 730 Barry Larkin .20 .09
❑ 731 Jeff Gray .05 .02
❑ 732 Franklin Stubbs .05 .02
❑ 733 Kelly Downs .05 .02
❑ 734 John Russell .05 .02
❑ 735 Ron Darling .05 .02
❑ 736 Dick Schofield .05 .02
❑ 737 Tim Crews .05 .02
❑ 738 Mel Hall .05 .02
❑ 739 Russ Swan .05 .02
❑ 740 Ryne Sandberg .25 .11
❑ 741 Jimmy Key .10 .05
❑ 742 Tommy Gregg .05 .02
❑ 743 Bryn Smith .05 .02
❑ 744 Nelson Santovenia .05 .02
❑ 745 Doug Jones .05 .02
❑ 746 John Shelby .05 .02
❑ 747 Tony Fossas .05 .02
❑ 748 Al Newman .05 .02
❑ 749 Greg W. Harris .05 .02
❑ 750 Bobby Bonilla .10 .05
❑ 751 Wayne Edwards .05 .02
❑ 752 Kevin Bass .05 .02
❑ 753 Paul Marak UER .05 .02
(Stats say drafted in Jan. but bio says May)
❑ 754 Bill Pecota .05 .02
❑ 755 Mark Langston .05 .02
❑ 756 Jeff Huson .05 .02
❑ 757 Mark Gardner .05 .02
❑ 758 Mike Devereaux .05 .02
❑ 759 Bobby Cox MG .05 .02
❑ 760 Benny Santiago .05 .02
❑ 761 Larry Andersen .05 .02
❑ 762 Mitch Webster .05 .02
❑ 763 Dana Kiecker .05 .02
❑ 764 Mark Carreon .05 .02
❑ 765 Shawon Dunston .05 .02
❑ 766 Jeff Robinson .05 .02
❑ 767 Dan Wilson RC .20 .09
❑ 768 Don Pall .05 .02
❑ 769 Tim Sherrill .05 .02
❑ 770 Jay Howell .05 .02
❑ 771 Gary Redus UER .05 .02
(Born in Tanner, should say Athens)
❑ 772 Kent Mercker UER .05 .02
(Born in Indianapolis, should say Dublin, Ohio)
❑ 773 Tom Foley .05 .02
❑ 774 Dennis Rasmussen .05 .02
❑ 775 Julio Franco .05 .02
❑ 776 Brent Mayne .05 .02
❑ 777 John Candelaria .05 .02
❑ 778 Dan Gladden .05 .02
❑ 779 Carmelo Martinez .05 .02
❑ 780A Randy Myers ERR .05 .02
(15 career losses)
❑ 780B Randy Myers COR .05 .02
(19 career losses)
❑ 781 Darryl Hamilton .05 .02
❑ 782 Jim Deshaies .05 .02
❑ 783 Joel Skinner .05 .02
❑ 784 Willie Fraser .05 .02
❑ 785 Scott Fletcher .05 .02
❑ 786 Eric Plunk .05 .02
❑ 787 Checklist 6 .05 .02
❑ 788 Bob Milacki .05 .02
❑ 789 Tom Lasorda MG .20 .09
❑ 790 Ken Griffey Jr. 1.00 .45
❑ 791 Mike Benjamin .05 .02
❑ 792 Mike Greenwell .05 .02

## 1991 Topps Traded

| | MINT | NRMT |
|---|---|---|
| COMPLETE SET (132) | 15.00 | 6.75 |
| COMP.FACT.SET (132) | 15.00 | 6.75 |

❑ 1T Juan Agosto .05 .02
❑ 2T Roberto Alomar .20 .09
❑ 3T Wally Backman .05 .02
❑ 4T Jeff Bagwell RC 3.00 1.35
❑ 5T Skeeter Barnes .05 .02
❑ 6T Steve Bedrosian .05 .02
❑ 7T Derek Bell .10 .05
❑ 8T George Bell .05 .02
❑ 9T Rafael Belliard .05 .02
❑ 10T Dante Bichette .20 .09
❑ 11T Bud Black .05 .02
❑ 12T Mike Boddicker .05 .02
❑ 13T Sid Bream .05 .02
❑ 14T Hubie Brooks .05 .02
❑ 15T Brett Butler .10 .05
❑ 16T Ivan Calderon .05 .02
❑ 17T John Candelaria .05 .02
❑ 18T Tom Candiotti .05 .02
❑ 19T Gary Carter .15 .07
❑ 20T Joe Carter .10 .05
❑ 21T Rick Cerone .05 .02
❑ 22T Jack Clark .10 .05
❑ 23T Vince Coleman .05 .02
❑ 24T Scott Coolbaugh .05 .02
❑ 25T Danny Cox .05 .02
❑ 26T Danny Darwin .05 .02
❑ 27T Chili Davis .10 .05
❑ 28T Glenn Davis .05 .02
❑ 29T Steve Decker .05 .02
❑ 30T Rob Deer .05 .02
❑ 31T Rich DeLucia .05 .02
❑ 32T John Dettmer USA RC .05 .02
❑ 33T Brian Downing .05 .02
❑ 34T Darren Dreifort USA RC .50 .23
❑ 35T Kirk Dressendorfer RC .05 .02
❑ 36T Jim Essian MG .05 .02
❑ 37T Dwight Evans .10 .05
❑ 38T Steve Farr .05 .02
❑ 39T Jeff Fassero RC .10 .05
❑ 40T Junior Felix .05 .02
❑ 41T Tony Fernandez .05 .02
❑ 42T Steve Finley .10 .05
❑ 43T Jim Fregosi MG .05 .02
❑ 44T Gary Gaetti .10 .05
❑ 45T Jason Giambi USA RC 8.00 3.60
❑ 46T Kirk Gibson .10 .05
❑ 47T Leo Gomez .05 .02
❑ 48T Luis Gonzalez RC .75 .35
❑ 49T Jeff Granger USA RC .10 .05
❑ 50T Todd Greene USA RC .10 .05
❑ 51T Jeffrey Hammonds USA RC 1.00 .45
❑ 52T Mike Hargrove MG .05 .02
❑ 53T Pete Harnisch .05 .02
❑ 54T Rick Helling RC USA UER .50 .23
(Misspelled Hellings on card back)
❑ 55T Glenallen Hill .05 .02
❑ 56T Charlie Hough .10 .05
❑ 57T Pete Incaviglia .05 .02
❑ 58T Bo Jackson .10 .05
❑ 59T Danny Jackson .05 .02
❑ 60T Reggie Jefferson .15 .07
❑ 61T Charles Johnson USA RC .50 .23
❑ 62T Jeff Johnson .05 .02
❑ 63T Todd Johnson USA RC .05 .02
❑ 64T Barry Jones .05 .02
❑ 65T Chris Jones RC .05 .02
❑ 66T Scott Kamieniecki RC .05 .02
❑ 67T Pat Kelly RC .05 .02
❑ 68T Darryl Kile .10 .05
❑ 69T Chuck Knoblauch .10 .05
❑ 70T Bill Krueger .05 .02
❑ 71T Scott Leius .05 .02
❑ 72T Donnie Leshnock USA RC .05 .02
❑ 73T Mark Lewis .05 .02
❑ 74T Candy Maldonado .05 .02
❑ 75T Jason McDonald USA RC .05 .02
❑ 76T Willie McGee .10 .05
❑ 77T Fred McGriff .20 .09
❑ 78T Billy McMillon USA RC .05 .02
❑ 79T Hal McRae MG .05 .02
❑ 80T Dan Melendez USA RC .05 .02
❑ 81T Orlando Merced RC .05 .02
❑ 82T Jack Morris .10 .05
❑ 83T Phil Nevin USA RC 1.00 .45
❑ 84T Otis Nixon .05 .02
❑ 85T Johnny Oates MG .05 .02
❑ 86T Bob Ojeda .05 .02
❑ 87T Mike Pagliarulo .05 .02
❑ 88T Dean Palmer .10 .05
❑ 89T Dave Parker .10 .05
❑ 90T Terry Pendleton .10 .05
❑ 91T Tony Phillips (P) USA RC .05 .02
❑ 92T Doug Piatt .05 .02
❑ 93T Ron Polk USA CO .05 .02
❑ 94T Tim Raines .10 .05
❑ 95T Willie Randolph .10 .05
❑ 96T Dave Righetti .05 .02
❑ 97T Ernie Riles .05 .02
❑ 98T Chris Roberts USA RC .20 .09
❑ 99T Jeff D. Robinson .05 .02
❑ 100T Jeff M. Robinson .05 .02
❑ 101T Ivan Rodriguez RC 3.00 1.35
❑ 102T Steve Rodriguez USA RC .05 .02
❑ 103T Tom Runnells MG .05 .02
❑ 104T Scott Sanderson .05 .02
❑ 105T Bob Scanlan .05 .02
❑ 106T Pete Schourek RC .10 .05
❑ 107T Gary Scott .05 .02
❑ 108T Paul Shuey USA RC .10 .05
❑ 109T Doug Simons .05 .02
❑ 110T Dave Smith .05 .02
❑ 111T Cory Snyder .05 .02
❑ 112T Luis Sojo .05 .02
❑ 113T Kennie Steenstra USA RC .05 .02
❑ 114T Darryl Strawberry .10 .05
❑ 115T Franklin Stubbs .05 .02
❑ 116T Todd Taylor USA RC .05 .02
❑ 117T Wade Taylor .05 .02
❑ 118T Garry Templeton .05 .02
❑ 119T Mickey Tettleton .05 .02
❑ 120T Tim Teufel .05 .02

❑ 121T Mike Timlin RC .05 .02
❑ 122T David Tuttle USA RC .05 .02
❑ 123T Mo Vaughn .10 .05
❑ 124T Jeff Ware USA RC .05 .02
❑ 125T Devon White .05 .02
❑ 126T Mark Whiten .05 .02
❑ 127T Mitch Williams .05 .02
❑ 128T Craig Wilson USA RC .05 .02
❑ 129T Willie Wilson .05 .02
❑ 130T Chris Wimmer USA RC .05 .02
❑ 131T Ivan Zweig USA RC .05 .02
❑ 132T Checklist 1T-132T .05 .02

## 1992 Topps

| | MINT | NRMT |
|---|---|---|
| COMPLETE SET (792) | 30.00 | 13.50 |
| COMP.FACT.SET (802) | 35.00 | 16.00 |
| COMP.HOLIDAY SET (811) | 40.00 | 18.00 |

❑ 1 Nolan Ryan 1.00 .45
❑ 2 Ricky Henderson RB .10 .05
Most career SB's
(Some cards have print marks that show 1.991 on the front)
❑ 3 Jeff Reardon RB .05 .02
10 seasons, 20 or more saves
❑ 4 Nolan Ryan RB .50 .09
22 cons. 100 K seasons
❑ 5 Dave Winfield RB .10 .05
Oldest player, cycle
❑ 6 Brien Taylor RC .05 .02
❑ 7 Jim Olander .05 .02
❑ 8 Bryan Hickerson RC .05 .02
❑ 9 Jon Farrell RC .05 .02
❑ 10 Wade Boggs .25 .11
❑ 11 Jack McDowell .05 .02
❑ 12 Luis Gonzalez .15 .07
❑ 13 Mike Scioscia .05 .02
❑ 14 Wes Chamberlain .05 .02
❑ 15 Dannis Martinez .10 .05
❑ 16 Jeff Montgomery .10 .05
❑ 17 Randy Milligan .05 .02
❑ 18 Greg Cadaret .05 .02
❑ 19 Jamie Quirk .05 .02
❑ 20 Bip Roberts .05 .02
❑ 21 Buck Rodgers MG .05 .02
❑ 22 Bill Wegman .05 .02
❑ 23 Chuck Knoblauch .10 .05
❑ 24 Randy Myers .10 .05
❑ 25 Ron Gant .10 .05
❑ 26 Mike Bielecki .05 .02
❑ 27 Juan Gonzalez .20 .09
❑ 28 Mike Schooler .05 .02
❑ 29 Mickey Tettleton .05 .02
❑ 30 John Kruk .10 .05
❑ 31 Bryn Smith .05 .02
❑ 32 Chris Nabholz .05 .02
❑ 33 Carlos Baerga .05 .02
❑ 34 Jeff Juden .05 .02
❑ 35 Dave Righetti .05 .02
❑ 36 Scott Ruffcorn RC .05 .02
❑ 37 Luis Polonia .05 .02
❑ 38 Tom Candiotti .05 .02
❑ 39 Greg Olson .05 .02
❑ 40 Cal Ripken 2.00 .90
❑ 41 Craig Lefferts .05 .02
❑ 42 Mike Macfarlane .05 .02
❑ 43 Jose Lind .05 .02
❑ 44 Rick Aguilera .10 .05
❑ 45 Gary Carter .15 .07
❑ 46 Steve Farr .05 .02
❑ 47 Rex Hudler .05 .02
❑ 48 Scott Scudder .05 .02
❑ 49 Damon Berryhill .05 .02
❑ 50 Ken Griffey Jr. .75 .35
❑ 51 Tom Runnells MG .05 .02
❑ 52 Juan Bell .05 .02
❑ 53 Tommy Gregg .05 .02
❑ 54 David Wells .10 .05
❑ 55 Rafael Palmeiro .20 .09
❑ 56 Charlie O'Brien .05 .02
❑ 57 Donn Pall .05 .02
❑ 58 1992 Prospects C .25 .11
Brad Ausmus RC
Jim Campanis Jr.
Dave Nilsson
Doug Robbins
❑ 59 Mo Vaughn .10 .05
❑ 60 Tony Fernandez .05 .02
❑ 61 Paul O'Neill .10 .05
❑ 62 Gene Nelson .05 .02
❑ 63 Randy Ready .05 .02
❑ 64 Bob Kipper .05 .02
❑ 65 Willie McGee .10 .05
❑ 66 Scott Stahoviak RC .05 .02
❑ 67 Luis Salazar .05 .02
❑ 68 Marvin Freeman .05 .02
❑ 69 Kenny Lofton .25 .11
❑ 70 Gary Gaetti .10 .05
❑ 71 Erik Hanson .05 .02
❑ 72 Eddie Zosky .05 .02
❑ 73 Brian Barnes .05 .02
❑ 74 Scott Leius .05 .02
❑ 75 Bret Saberhagen .10 .05
❑ 76 Mike Gallego .05 .02
❑ 77 Jack Armstrong .05 .02
❑ 78 Ivan Rodriguez .40 .18
❑ 79 Jesse Orosco .05 .02
❑ 80 David Justice .15 .07
❑ 81 Ced Landrum .05 .02
❑ 82 Doug Simons .05 .02
❑ 83 Tommy Greene .05 .02
❑ 84 Leo Gomez .05 .02
❑ 85 Jose DeLeon .05 .02
❑ 86 Steve Finley .10 .05
❑ 87 Bob MacDonald .05 .02
❑ 88 Darrin Jackson .05 .02
❑ 89 Neal Heaton .05 .02
❑ 90 Robin Yount .20 .09
❑ 91 Jeff Reed .05 .02
❑ 92 Lenny Harris .05 .02
❑ 93 Reggie Jefferson .10 .05
❑ 94 Sammy Sosa .40 .18
❑ 95 Scott Bailes .05 .02
❑ 96 Tom McKinnon RC .05 .02
❑ 97 Luis Rivera .05 .02
❑ 98 Mike Harkey .05 .02
❑ 99 Jeff Treadway .05 .02
❑ 100 Jose Canseco .25 .11
❑ 101 Omar Vizquel .10 .05
❑ 102 Scott Kamieniecki .05 .02
❑ 103 Ricky Jordan .05 .02
❑ 104 Jeff Ballard .05 .02
❑ 105 Felix Jose .05 .02
❑ 106 Mike Boddicker .05 .02
❑ 107 Dan Pasqua .05 .02
❑ 108 Mike Timlin .05 .02
❑ 109 Roger Craig MG .05 .02
❑ 110 Ryne Sandberg .25 .11
❑ 111 Mark Carreon .05 .02
❑ 112 Oscar Azocar .05 .02
❑ 113 Mike Greenwell .05 .02
❑ 114 Mark Portugal .05 .02
❑ 115 Terry Pendleton .10 .05
❑ 116 Willie Randolph .10 .05
❑ 117 Scott Terry .05 .02
❑ 118 Chili Davis .10 .05
❑ 119 Mark Gardner .05 .02
❑ 120 Alan Trammell .15 .07
❑ 121 Derek Bell .10 .05
❑ 122 Gary Varsho .05 .02
❑ 123 Bob Ojeda .05 .02
❑ 124 Shawn Livsey RC .05 .02
❑ 125 Chris Hoiles .05 .02
❑ 126 1992 Prospects 1B .25 .11
Ryan Klesko
John Jaha RC
Rico Brogna
Dave Staton
❑ 127 Carlos Quintana .05 .02
❑ 128 Kurt Stillwell .05 .02
❑ 129 Melido Perez .05 .02
❑ 130 Alvin Davis .05 .02
❑ 131 Checklist 1-132 .05 .02
❑ 132 Eric Show .05 .02
❑ 133 Rance Mulliniks .05 .02
❑ 134 Darryl Kile .10 .05
❑ 135 Von Hayes .05 .02
❑ 136 Bill Doran .05 .02
❑ 137 Jeff D. Robinson .05 .02
❑ 138 Monty Fariss .05 .02
❑ 139 Jeff Innis .05 .02
❑ 140 Mark Grace UER .20 .09
(Home Calie.; should be Calif.)
❑ 141 Jim Leyland MG UER .10 .05
(No closed parenthesis after East in 1991)
❑ 142 Todd Van Poppel .05 .02
❑ 143 Paul Gibson .05 .02
❑ 144 Bill Swift .05 .02
❑ 145 Danny Tartabull .05 .02
❑ 146 Al Newman .05 .02
❑ 147 Cris Carpenter .05 .02
❑ 148 Anthony Young .05 .02
❑ 149 Brian Bohanon .05 .02
❑ 150 Roger Clemens UER .40 .18
(League leading ERA in 1990 not italicized)
❑ 151 Jeff Hamilton .05 .02
❑ 152 Charlie Leibrandt .05 .02
❑ 153 Ron Karkovice .05 .02
❑ 154 Hensley Meulens .05 .02
❑ 155 Scott Bankhead .05 .02
❑ 156 Manny Ramirez RC 1.50 .70
❑ 157 Keith Miller .05 .02
❑ 158 Todd Frohwirth .05 .02
❑ 159 Darrin Fletcher .05 .02
❑ 160 Bobby Bonilla .10 .05
❑ 161 Casey Candaele .05 .02
❑ 162 Paul Faries .05 .02
❑ 163 Dana Kiecker .05 .02
❑ 164 Shane Mack .05 .02
❑ 165 Mark Langston .05 .02
❑ 166 Geronimo Pena .05 .02
❑ 167 Andy Allanson .05 .02
❑ 168 Dwight Smith .05 .02
❑ 169 Chuck Crim .05 .02
❑ 170 Alex Cole .05 .02
❑ 171 Bill Plummer MG .05 .02
❑ 172 Juan Berenguer .05 .02
❑ 173 Brian Downing .05 .02
❑ 174 Steve Frey .05 .02
❑ 175 Orel Hershiser .10 .05
❑ 176 Ramon Garcia .05 .02
❑ 177 Dan Gladden .05 .02
❑ 178 Jim Acker .05 .02
❑ 179 1992 Prospects 2B .05 .02
Bobby DeJardin
Cesar Bernhardt
Armando Moreno
Andy Stankiewicz
❑ 180 Kevin Mitchell .10 .05
❑ 181 Hector Villanueva .05 .02
❑ 182 Jeff Reardon .10 .05
❑ 183 Brent Mayne .05 .02
❑ 184 Jimmy Jones .05 .02
❑ 185 Benito Santiago .05 .02
❑ 186 Cliff Floyd RC .50 .23
❑ 187 Ernie Riles .05 .02
❑ 188 Jose Guzman .05 .02
❑ 189 Junior Felix .05 .02
❑ 190 Glenn Davis .05 .02
❑ 191 Charlie Hough .10 .05
❑ 192 Dave Fleming .05 .02
❑ 193 Omar Olivares .05 .02
❑ 194 Eric Karros .20 .09
❑ 195 David Cone .10 .05

❑ 196 Frank Castillo .05 .02
❑ 197 Glenn Braggs .05 .02
❑ 198 Scott Aldred .05 .02
❑ 199 Jeff Blauser .05 .02
❑ 200 Len Dykstra .10 .05
❑ 201 Buck Showalter RC MG .20 .09
❑ 202 Rick Honeycutt .05 .02
❑ 203 Greg Myers .05 .02
❑ 204 Trevor Wilson .05 .02
❑ 205 Jay Howell .05 .02
❑ 206 Luis Sojo .05 .02
❑ 207 Jack Clark .10 .05
❑ 208 Julio Machado .05 .02
❑ 209 Lloyd McClendon .05 .02
❑ 210 Ozzie Guillen .05 .02
❑ 211 Jeremy Hernandez RC .05 .02
❑ 212 Randy Velarde .05 .02
❑ 213 Les Lancaster .05 .02
❑ 214 Andy Mota .05 .02
❑ 215 Rich Gossage .10 .05
❑ 216 Brent Gates RC .05 .02
❑ 217 Brian Harper .05 .02
❑ 218 Mike Flanagan .05 .02
❑ 219 Jerry Browne .05 .02
❑ 220 Jose Rijo .05 .02
❑ 221 Skeeter Barnes .05 .02
❑ 222 Jaime Navarro .05 .02
❑ 223 Mel Hall .05 .02
❑ 224 Bret Barberie .05 .02
❑ 225 Roberto Alomar .20 .09
❑ 226 Pete Smith .05 .02
❑ 227 Daryl Boston .05 .02
❑ 228 Eddie Whitson .05 .02
❑ 229 Shawn Boskie .05 .02
❑ 230 Dick Schofield .05 .02
❑ 231 Brian Drahman .05 .02
❑ 232 John Smiley .05 .02
❑ 233 Mitch Webster .05 .02
❑ 234 Terry Steinbach .05 .02
❑ 235 Jack Morris .10 .05
❑ 236 Bill Pecota .05 .02
❑ 237 Jose Hernandez RC .05 .02
❑ 238 Greg Litton .05 .02
❑ 239 Brian Holman .05 .02
❑ 240 Andres Galarraga .15 .07
❑ 241 Gerald Young .05 .02
❑ 242 Mike Mussina .30 .14
❑ 243 Alvaro Espinoza .05 .02
❑ 244 Darren Daulton .10 .05
❑ 245 John Smoltz .10 .05
❑ 246 Jason Pruitt RC .05 .02
❑ 247 Chuck Finley .10 .05
❑ 248 Jim Gantner .05 .02
❑ 249 Tony Fossas .05 .02
❑ 250 Ken Griffey Sr. .10 .05
❑ 251 Kevin Elster .05 .02
❑ 252 Dennis Rasmussen .05 .02
❑ 253 Terry Kennedy .05 .02
❑ 254 Ryan Bowen .05 .02
❑ 255 Robin Ventura .10 .05
❑ 256 Mike Aldrete .05 .02
❑ 257 Jeff Russell .05 .02
❑ 258 Jim Lindeman .05 .02
❑ 259 Ron Darling .05 .02
❑ 260 Devon White .05 .02
❑ 261 Tom Lasorda MG .10 .05
❑ 262 Terry Lee .05 .02
❑ 263 Bob Patterson .05 .02
❑ 264 Checklist 133-264 .05 .02
❑ 265 Teddy Higuera .05 .02
❑ 266 Roberto Kelly .05 .02
❑ 267 Steve Bedrosian .05 .02
❑ 268 Brady Anderson .15 .07
❑ 269 Ruben Amaro .05 .02
❑ 270 Tony Gwynn .40 .18
❑ 271 Tracy Jones .05 .02
❑ 272 Jerry Don Gleaton .05 .02
❑ 273 Craig Grebeck .05 .02
❑ 274 Bob Scanlan .05 .02
❑ 275 Todd Zeile .05 .02
❑ 276 Shawn Green RC 1.50 .70
❑ 277 Scott Chiamparino .05 .02
❑ 278 Darryl Hamilton .05 .02
❑ 279 Jim Clancy .05 .02
❑ 280 Carlos Martinez .05 .02
❑ 281 Kevin Appier .10 .05
❑ 282 John Wehner .05 .02
❑ 283 Reggie Sanders .05 .02
❑ 284 Gene Larkin .05 .02
❑ 285 Bob Welch .05 .02
❑ 286 Gilberto Reyes .05 .02
❑ 287 Pete Schourek .05 .02
❑ 288 Andujar Cedeno .05 .02
❑ 289 Mike Morgan .05 .02
❑ 290 Bo Jackson .10 .05
❑ 291 Phil Garner MG .05 .02
❑ 292 Ray Lankford .20 .09
❑ 293 Mike Henneman .05 .02
❑ 294 Dave Valle .05 .02
❑ 295 Alonzo Powell .05 .02
❑ 296 Tom Brunansky .05 .02
❑ 297 Kevin Brown .15 .07
❑ 298 Kelly Gruber .05 .02
❑ 299 Charles Nagy .05 .02
❑ 300 Don Mattingly .50 .23
❑ 301 Kirk McCaskill .05 .02
❑ 302 Joey Cora .05 .02
❑ 303 Dan Plesac .05 .02
❑ 304 Joe Oliver .05 .02
❑ 305 Tom Glavine .15 .07
❑ 306 Al Shirley RC .05 .02
❑ 307 Bruce Ruffin .05 .02
❑ 308 Craig Shipley .05 .02
❑ 309 Dave Martinez .05 .02
❑ 310 Jose Mesa .05 .02
❑ 311 Henry Cotto .05 .02
❑ 312 Mike LaValliere .05 .02
❑ 313 Kevin Tapani .05 .02
❑ 314 Jeff Huson .05 .02
(Shows Jose Canseco sliding into second)
❑ 315 Juan Samuel .05 .02
❑ 316 Curt Schilling .10 .05
❑ 317 Mike Bordick .05 .02
❑ 318 Steve Howe .05 .02
❑ 319 Tony Phillips .05 .02
❑ 320 George Bell .05 .02
❑ 321 Lou Piniella MG .10 .05
❑ 322 Tim Burke .05 .02
❑ 323 Milt Thompson .05 .02
❑ 324 Danny Darwin .05 .02
❑ 325 Joe Orsulak .05 .02
❑ 326 Eric King .05 .02
❑ 327 Jay Buhner .10 .05
❑ 328 Joel Johnston .05 .02
❑ 329 Franklin Stubbs .05 .02
❑ 330 Will Clark .20 .09
❑ 331 Steve Lake .05 .02
❑ 332 Chris Jones .05 .02
❑ 333 Pat Tabler .05 .02
❑ 334 Kevin Gross .05 .02
❑ 335 Dave Henderson .05 .02
❑ 336 Greg Anthony RC .05 .02
❑ 337 Alejandro Pena .05 .02
❑ 338 Shawn Abner .05 .02
❑ 339 Tom Browning .05 .02
❑ 340 Otis Nixon .05 .02
❑ 341 Bob Geren .05 .02
❑ 342 Tim Spehr .05 .02
❑ 343 John Vander Wal .05 .02
❑ 344 Jack Daugherty .05 .02
❑ 345 Zane Smith .05 .02
❑ 346 Rheal Cormier .05 .02
❑ 347 Kent Hrbek .10 .05
❑ 348 Rick Wilkins .05 .02
❑ 349 Steve Lyons .05 .02
❑ 350 Gregg Olson .05 .02
❑ 351 Greg Riddoch MG .05 .02
❑ 352 Ed Nunez .05 .02
❑ 353 Braulio Castillo .05 .02
❑ 354 Dave Bergman .05 .02
❑ 355 Warren Newson .05 .02
❑ 356 Luis Quinones .05 .02
❑ 357 Mike Witt .05 .02
❑ 358 Ted Wood .05 .02
❑ 359 Mike Moore .05 .02
❑ 360 Lance Parrish .05 .02
❑ 361 Barry Jones .05 .02
❑ 362 Javier Ortiz .05 .02
❑ 363 John Candelaria .05 .02
❑ 364 Glenallen Hill .05 .02
❑ 365 Duane Ward .05 .02
❑ 366 Checklist 265-396 .05 .02
❑ 367 Rafael Belliard .05 .02
❑ 368 Bill Krueger .05 .02
❑ 369 Steve Whitaker RC .05 .02
❑ 370 Shawon Dunston .05 .02
❑ 371 Dante Bichette .15 .07
❑ 372 Kip Gross .05 .02
❑ 373 Don Robinson .05 .02
❑ 374 Bernie Williams .20 .09
❑ 375 Bert Blyleven .10 .05
❑ 376 Chris Donnels .05 .02
❑ 377 Bob Zupcic RC .05 .02
❑ 378 Joel Skinner .05 .02
❑ 379 Steve Chitren .05 .02
❑ 380 Barry Bonds .30 .14
❑ 381 Sparky Anderson MG .10 .05
❑ 382 Sid Fernandez .05 .02
❑ 383 Dave Hollins .05 .02
❑ 384 Mark Lee .05 .02
❑ 385 Tim Wallach .05 .02
❑ 386 Will Clark AS .10 .05
❑ 387 Ryne Sandberg AS .20 .09
❑ 388 Howard Johnson AS .05 .02
❑ 389 Barry Larkin AS .15 .07
❑ 390 Barry Bonds AS .20 .09
❑ 391 Ron Gant AS .05 .02
❑ 392 Bobby Bonilla AS .05 .02
❑ 393 Craig Biggio AS .15 .07
❑ 394 Dennis Martinez AS .05 .02
❑ 395 Tom Glavine AS .10 .05
❑ 396 Lee Smith AS .05 .02
❑ 397 Cecil Fielder AS .05 .02
❑ 398 Julio Franco AS .05 .02
❑ 399 Wade Boggs AS .10 .05
❑ 400 Cal Ripken AS .40 .09
❑ 401 Jose Canseco AS .10 .05
❑ 402 Joe Carter AS .05 .02
❑ 403 Ruben Sierra AS .05 .02
❑ 404 Matt Nokes AS .05 .02
❑ 405 Roger Clemens AS .20 .09
❑ 406 Jim Abbott AS .05 .02
❑ 407 Bryan Harvey AS .05 .02
❑ 408 Bob Milacki .05 .02
❑ 409 Gene Petralli .05 .02
❑ 410 Dave Stewart .10 .05
❑ 411 Mike Jackson .05 .02
❑ 412 Luis Aquino .05 .02
❑ 413 Tim Teufel .05 .02
❑ 414 Jeff Ware .05 .02
❑ 415 Jim Deshaies .05 .02
❑ 416 Ellis Burks .10 .05
❑ 417 Allan Anderson .05 .02
❑ 418 Alfredo Griffin .05 .02
❑ 419 Wally Whitehurst .05 .02
❑ 420 Sandy Alomar Jr. .10 .05
❑ 421 Juan Agosto .05 .02
❑ 422 Sam Horn .05 .02
❑ 423 Jeff Fassero .05 .02
❑ 424 Paul McClellan .05 .02
❑ 425 Cecil Fielder .10 .05
❑ 426 Tim Raines .10 .05
❑ 427 Eddie Taubensee RC .10 .05
❑ 428 Dennis Boyd .05 .02
❑ 429 Tony LaRussa MG .10 .05
❑ 430 Steve Sax .05 .02
❑ 431 Tom Gordon .05 .02
❑ 432 Billy Hatcher .05 .02
❑ 433 Cal Eldred .05 .02
❑ 434 Wally Backman .05 .02
❑ 435 Mark Eichhorn .05 .02
❑ 436 Mookie Wilson .10 .05
❑ 437 Scott Servais .05 .02
❑ 438 Mike Maddux .05 .02
❑ 439 Chico Walker .05 .02
❑ 440 Doug Drabek .05 .02
❑ 441 Rob Deer .05 .02
❑ 442 Dave West .05 .02
❑ 443 Spike Owen .05 .02
❑ 444 Tyrone Hill RC .05 .02
❑ 445 Matt Williams .15 .07
❑ 446 Mark Lewis .05 .02
❑ 447 David Segui .05 .02
❑ 448 Tom Pagnozzi .05 .02
❑ 449 Jeff Johnson .05 .02
❑ 450 Mark McGwire .75 .35
❑ 451 Tom Henke .05 .02

| No. | Player | Price | Price |
|---|---|---|---|
| ❑ 452 | Wilson Alvarez | .05 | .02 |
| ❑ 453 | Gary Redus | .05 | .02 |
| ❑ 454 | Darren Holmes | .05 | .02 |
| ❑ 455 | Pete O'Brien | .05 | .02 |
| ❑ 456 | Pat Combs | .05 | .02 |
| ❑ 457 | Hubie Brooks | .05 | .02 |
| ❑ 458 | Frank Tanana | .05 | .02 |
| ❑ 459 | Tom Kelly MG | .05 | .02 |
| ❑ 460 | Andre Dawson | .15 | .07 |
| ❑ 461 | Doug Jones | .05 | .02 |
| ❑ 462 | Rich Rodriguez | .05 | .02 |
| ❑ 463 | Mike Simms | .05 | .02 |
| ❑ 464 | Mike Jeffcoat | .05 | .02 |
| ❑ 465 | Barry Larkin | .15 | .07 |
| ❑ 466 | Stan Belinda | .05 | .02 |
| ❑ 467 | Lonnie Smith | .05 | .02 |
| ❑ 468 | Greg Harris | .05 | .02 |
| ❑ 469 | Jim Eisenreich | .05 | .02 |
| ❑ 470 | Pedro Guerrero | .05 | .02 |
| ❑ 471 | Jose DeJesus | .05 | .02 |
| ❑ 472 | Rich Rowland RC | .05 | .02 |
| ❑ 473 | 1992 Prospects 3B UER | .20 | .09 |
| | Frank Bolick | | |
| | Craig Paquette | | |
| | Tom Redington | | |
| | Paul Russo | | |
| | (Line around top border) | | |
| ❑ 474 | Mike Rossiter RC | .05 | .02 |
| ❑ 475 | Robby Thompson | .05 | .02 |
| ❑ 476 | Randy Bush | .05 | .02 |
| ❑ 477 | Greg Hibbard | .05 | .02 |
| ❑ 478 | Dale Sveum | .05 | .02 |
| ❑ 479 | Chito Martinez | .05 | .02 |
| ❑ 480 | Scott Sanderson | .05 | .02 |
| ❑ 481 | Tino Martinez | .10 | .05 |
| ❑ 482 | Jimmy Key | .10 | .05 |
| ❑ 483 | Terry Shumpert | .05 | .02 |
| ❑ 484 | Mike Hartley | .05 | .02 |
| ❑ 485 | Chris Sabo | .05 | .02 |
| ❑ 486 | Bob Walk | .05 | .02 |
| ❑ 487 | John Cerutti | .05 | .02 |
| ❑ 488 | Scott Cooper | .05 | .02 |
| ❑ 489 | Bobby Cox MG | .10 | .05 |
| ❑ 490 | Julio Franco | .05 | .02 |
| ❑ 491 | Jeff Brantley | .05 | .02 |
| ❑ 492 | Mike Devereaux | .05 | .02 |
| ❑ 493 | Jose Offerman | .05 | .02 |
| ❑ 494 | Gary Thurman | .05 | .02 |
| ❑ 495 | Carney Lansford | .10 | .05 |
| ❑ 496 | Joe Grahe | .05 | .02 |
| ❑ 497 | Andy Ashby | .10 | .05 |
| ❑ 498 | Gerald Perry | .05 | .02 |
| ❑ 499 | Dave Otto | .05 | .02 |
| ❑ 500 | Vince Coleman | .05 | .02 |
| ❑ 501 | Rob Mallicoat | .05 | .02 |
| ❑ 502 | Greg Briley | .05 | .02 |
| ❑ 503 | Pascual Perez | .05 | .02 |
| ❑ 504 | Aaron Sele RC | .50 | .23 |
| ❑ 505 | Bobby Thigpen | .05 | .02 |
| ❑ 506 | Todd Benzinger | .05 | .02 |
| ❑ 507 | Candy Maldonado | .05 | .02 |
| ❑ 508 | Bill Gullickson | .05 | .02 |
| ❑ 509 | Doug Dascenzo | .05 | .02 |
| ❑ 510 | Frank Viola | .05 | .02 |
| ❑ 511 | Kenny Rogers | .05 | .02 |
| ❑ 512 | Mike Heath | .05 | .02 |
| ❑ 513 | Kevin Bass | .05 | .02 |
| ❑ 514 | Kim Batiste | .05 | .02 |
| ❑ 515 | Delino DeShields | .10 | .05 |
| ❑ 516 | Ed Sprague | .05 | .02 |
| ❑ 517 | Jim Gott | .05 | .02 |
| ❑ 518 | Jose Melendez | .05 | .02 |
| ❑ 519 | Hal McRae MG | .05 | .02 |
| ❑ 520 | Jeff Bagwell | .40 | .18 |
| ❑ 521 | Joe Hesketh | .05 | .02 |
| ❑ 522 | Milt Cuyler | .05 | .02 |
| ❑ 523 | Shawn Hillegas | .05 | .02 |
| ❑ 524 | Don Slaught | .05 | .02 |
| ❑ 525 | Randy Johnson | .25 | .11 |
| ❑ 526 | Doug Piatt | .05 | .02 |
| ❑ 527 | Checklist 397-528 | .05 | .02 |
| ❑ 528 | Steve Foster | .05 | .02 |
| ❑ 529 | Joe Girardi | .10 | .05 |
| ❑ 530 | Jim Abbott | .10 | .05 |
| ❑ 531 | Larry Walker | .15 | .07 |
| ❑ 532 | Mike Huff | .05 | .02 |
| ❑ 533 | Mackey Sasser | .05 | .02 |
| ❑ 534 | Benji Gil RC | .05 | .02 |
| ❑ 535 | Dave Stieb | .05 | .02 |
| ❑ 536 | Willie Wilson | .05 | .02 |
| ❑ 537 | Mark Leiter | .05 | .02 |
| ❑ 538 | Jose Uribe | .05 | .02 |
| ❑ 539 | Thomas Howard | .05 | .02 |
| ❑ 540 | Ben McDonald | .05 | .02 |
| ❑ 541 | Jose Tolentino | .05 | .02 |
| ❑ 542 | Keith Mitchell | .05 | .02 |
| ❑ 543 | Jerome Walton | .05 | .02 |
| ❑ 544 | Cliff Brantley | .05 | .02 |
| ❑ 545 | Andy Van Slyke | .10 | .05 |
| ❑ 546 | Paul Sorrento | .05 | .02 |
| ❑ 547 | Herm Winningham | .05 | .02 |
| ❑ 548 | Mark Guthrie | .05 | .02 |
| ❑ 549 | Joe Torre MG | .10 | .05 |
| ❑ 550 | Darryl Strawberry | .10 | .05 |
| ❑ 551 | 1992 Prospects SS UER | 1.25 | .55 |
| | Wilfredo Cordero | | |
| | Chipper Jones | | |
| | Manny Alexander | | |
| | Alex Arias | | |
| | (No line around top border) | | |
| ❑ 552 | Dave Gallagher | .05 | .02 |
| ❑ 553 | Edgar Martinez | .15 | .07 |
| ❑ 554 | Donald Harris | .05 | .02 |
| ❑ 555 | Frank Thomas | .40 | .18 |
| ❑ 556 | Storm Davis | .05 | .02 |
| ❑ 557 | Dickie Thon | .05 | .02 |
| ❑ 558 | Scott Garrelts | .05 | .02 |
| ❑ 559 | Steve Olin | .05 | .02 |
| ❑ 560 | Rickey Henderson | .25 | .11 |
| ❑ 561 | Jose Vizcaino | .05 | .02 |
| ❑ 562 | Wade Taylor | .05 | .02 |
| ❑ 563 | Pat Borders | .05 | .02 |
| ❑ 564 | Jimmy Gonzalez RC | .05 | .02 |
| ❑ 565 | Lee Smith | .10 | .05 |
| ❑ 566 | Bill Sampen | .05 | .02 |
| ❑ 567 | Dean Palmer | .10 | .05 |
| ❑ 568 | Bryan Harvey | .05 | .02 |
| ❑ 569 | Tony Pena | .05 | .02 |
| ❑ 570 | Lou Whitaker | .10 | .05 |
| ❑ 571 | Randy Tomlin | .05 | .02 |
| ❑ 572 | Greg Vaughn | .15 | .07 |
| ❑ 573 | Kelly Downs | .05 | .02 |
| ❑ 574 | Steve Avery UER | .05 | .02 |
| | (Should be 13 games for Durham in 1989) | | |
| ❑ 575 | Kirby Puckett | .50 | .23 |
| ❑ 576 | Heathcliff Slocumb | .05 | .02 |
| ❑ 577 | Kevin Seitzer | .05 | .02 |
| ❑ 578 | Lee Guetterman | .05 | .02 |
| ❑ 579 | Johnny Oates MG | .05 | .02 |
| ❑ 580 | Greg Maddux | .50 | .23 |
| ❑ 581 | Stan Javier | .05 | .02 |
| ❑ 582 | Vicente Palacios | .05 | .02 |
| ❑ 583 | Mel Rojas | .05 | .02 |
| ❑ 584 | Wayne Rosenthal RC | .05 | .02 |
| ❑ 585 | Lenny Webster | .05 | .02 |
| ❑ 586 | Rod Nichols | .05 | .02 |
| ❑ 587 | Mickey Morandini | .05 | .02 |
| ❑ 588 | Russ Swan | .05 | .02 |
| ❑ 589 | Mariano Duncan | .05 | .02 |
| ❑ 590 | Howard Johnson | .05 | .02 |
| ❑ 591 | 1992 Prospects OF | .20 | .09 |
| | Jeromy Burnitz | | |
| | Jacob Brumfield | | |
| | Alan Cockrell | | |
| | D.J. Dozier | | |
| ❑ 592 | Denny Neagle | .15 | .07 |
| ❑ 593 | Steve Decker | .05 | .02 |
| ❑ 594 | Brian Barber RC | .05 | .02 |
| ❑ 595 | Bruce Hurst | .05 | .02 |
| ❑ 596 | Kent Mercker | .05 | .02 |
| ❑ 597 | Mike Magnante RC | .05 | .02 |
| ❑ 598 | Jody Reed | .05 | .02 |
| ❑ 599 | Steve Searcy | .05 | .02 |
| ❑ 600 | Paul Molitor | .20 | .09 |
| ❑ 601 | Dave Smith | .05 | .02 |
| ❑ 602 | Mike Fetters | .05 | .02 |
| ❑ 603 | Luis Mercedes | .05 | .02 |
| ❑ 604 | Chris Gwynn | .05 | .02 |
| ❑ 605 | Scott Erickson | .05 | .02 |
| ❑ 606 | Brook Jacoby | .05 | .02 |
| ❑ 607 | Todd Stottlemyre | .10 | .05 |
| ❑ 608 | Scott Bradley | .05 | .02 |
| ❑ 609 | Mike Hargrove MG | .10 | .05 |
| ❑ 610 | Eric Davis | .10 | .05 |
| ❑ 611 | Brian Hunter | .05 | .02 |
| ❑ 612 | Pat Kelly | .05 | .02 |
| ❑ 613 | Pedro Munoz | .05 | .02 |
| ❑ 614 | Al Osuna | .05 | .02 |
| ❑ 615 | Matt Merullo | .05 | .02 |
| ❑ 616 | Larry Andersen | .05 | .02 |
| ❑ 617 | Junior Ortiz | .05 | .02 |
| ❑ 618 | 1992 Prospects OF | .05 | .02 |
| | Cesar Hernandez | | |
| | Steve Hosey | | |
| | Jeff McNeely | | |
| | Dan Peltier | | |
| ❑ 619 | Danny Jackson | .05 | .02 |
| ❑ 620 | George Brett | .40 | .18 |
| ❑ 621 | Dan Gakeler | .05 | .02 |
| ❑ 622 | Steve Buechele | .05 | .02 |
| ❑ 623 | Bob Tewksbury | .05 | .02 |
| ❑ 624 | Shawn Estes RC | .40 | .18 |
| ❑ 625 | Kevin McReynolds | .05 | .02 |
| ❑ 626 | Chris Haney | .05 | .02 |
| ❑ 627 | Mike Sharperson | .05 | .02 |
| ❑ 628 | Mark Williamson | .05 | .02 |
| ❑ 629 | Wally Joyner | .10 | .05 |
| ❑ 630 | Carlton Fisk | .20 | .09 |
| ❑ 631 | Armando Reynoso RC | .05 | .02 |
| ❑ 632 | Felix Fermin | .05 | .02 |
| ❑ 633 | Mitch Williams | .05 | .02 |
| ❑ 634 | Manuel Lee | .05 | .02 |
| ❑ 635 | Harold Baines | .10 | .05 |
| ❑ 636 | Greg Harris | .05 | .02 |
| ❑ 637 | Orlando Merced | .05 | .02 |
| ❑ 638 | Chris Bosio | .05 | .02 |
| ❑ 639 | Wayne Housie | .05 | .02 |
| ❑ 640 | Xavier Hernandez | .05 | .02 |
| ❑ 641 | David Howard | .05 | .02 |
| ❑ 642 | Tim Crews | .05 | .02 |
| ❑ 643 | Rick Cerone | .05 | .02 |
| ❑ 644 | Terry Leach | .05 | .02 |
| ❑ 645 | Deion Sanders | .20 | .09 |
| ❑ 646 | Craig Wilson | .05 | .02 |
| ❑ 647 | Marquis Grissom | .05 | .02 |
| ❑ 648 | Scott Fletcher | .05 | .02 |
| ❑ 649 | Norm Charlton | .05 | .02 |
| ❑ 650 | Jesse Barfield | .05 | .02 |
| ❑ 651 | Joe Slusarski | .05 | .02 |
| ❑ 652 | Bobby Rose | .05 | .02 |
| ❑ 653 | Dennis Lamp | .05 | .02 |
| ❑ 654 | Allen Watson RC | .05 | .02 |
| ❑ 655 | Brett Butler | .10 | .05 |
| ❑ 656 | 1992 Prospects OF | .05 | .02 |
| | Rudy Pemberton | | |
| | Henry Rodriguez | | |
| | Lee Tinsley RC | | |
| | Gerald Williams | | |
| ❑ 657 | Dave Johnson | .05 | .02 |
| ❑ 658 | Checklist 529-660 | .05 | .02 |
| ❑ 659 | Brian McRae | .05 | .02 |
| ❑ 660 | Fred McGriff | .15 | .07 |
| ❑ 661 | Bill Landrum | .05 | .02 |
| ❑ 662 | Juan Guzman | .05 | .02 |
| ❑ 663 | Greg Gagne | .05 | .02 |
| ❑ 664 | Ken Hill | .05 | .02 |
| ❑ 665 | Dave Haas | .05 | .02 |
| ❑ 666 | Tom Foley | .05 | .02 |
| ❑ 667 | Roberto Hernandez | .05 | .02 |
| ❑ 668 | Dwayne Henry | .05 | .02 |
| ❑ 669 | Jim Fregosi MG | .05 | .02 |
| ❑ 670 | Harold Reynolds | .05 | .02 |
| ❑ 671 | Mark Whiten | .05 | .02 |
| ❑ 672 | Eric Plunk | .05 | .02 |
| ❑ 673 | Todd Hundley | .05 | .02 |
| ❑ 674 | Mo Sanford | .05 | .02 |
| ❑ 675 | Bobby Witt | .05 | .02 |
| ❑ 676 | 1992 Prospects P | .05 | .02 |
| | Sam Militello | | |
| | Pat Mahomes RC | | |
| | Turk Wendell | | |
| | Roger Salkeld | | |
| ❑ 677 | John Marzano | .05 | .02 |
| ❑ 678 | Joe Klink | .05 | .02 |
| ❑ 679 | Pete Incaviglia | .05 | .02 |
| ❑ 680 | Dale Murphy | .20 | .09 |

❑ 681 Rene Gonzales .05 .02
❑ 682 Andy Benes .05 .02
❑ 683 Jim Poole .05 .02
❑ 684 Trever Miller RC .05 .02
❑ 685 Scott Livingstone .05 .02
❑ 686 Rich DeLucia .05 .02
❑ 687 Harvey Pulliam .05 .02
❑ 688 Tim Belcher .05 .02
❑ 689 Mark Lemke .05 .02
❑ 690 John Franco .10 .05
❑ 691 Walt Weiss .05 .02
❑ 692 Scott Ruskin .05 .02
❑ 693 Jeff King .05 .02
❑ 694 Mike Gardiner .05 .02
❑ 695 Gary Sheffield .20 .09
❑ 696 Joe Boever .05 .02
❑ 697 Mike Felder .05 .02
❑ 698 John Habyan .05 .02
❑ 699 Cito Gaston MG .05 .02
❑ 700 Ruben Sierra .05 .02
❑ 701 Scott Radinsky .05 .02
❑ 702 Lee Stevens .10 .05
❑ 703 Mark Wohlers .05 .02
❑ 704 Curt Young .05 .02
❑ 705 Dwight Evans .10 .05
❑ 706 Rob Murphy .05 .02
❑ 707 Gregg Jefferies .05 .02
❑ 708 Tom Bolton .05 .02
❑ 709 Chris James .05 .02
❑ 710 Kevin Maas .05 .02
❑ 711 Ricky Bones .05 .02
❑ 712 Curt Wilkerson .05 .02
❑ 713 Roger McDowell .05 .02
❑ 714 Pokey Reese RC .50 .23
❑ 715 Craig Biggio .15 .07
❑ 716 Kirk Dressendorfer .05 .02
❑ 717 Ken Dayley .05 .02
❑ 718 B.J. Surhoff .10 .05
❑ 719 Terry Mulholland .05 .02
❑ 720 Kirk Gibson .10 .05
❑ 721 Mike Pagliarulo .05 .02
❑ 722 Walt Terrell .05 .02
❑ 723 Jose Oquendo .05 .02
❑ 724 Kevin Morton .05 .02
❑ 725 Dwight Gooden .10 .05
❑ 726 Kirt Manwaring .05 .02
❑ 727 Chuck McElroy .05 .02
❑ 728 Dave Burba .05 .02
❑ 729 Art Howe MG .05 .02
❑ 730 Ramon Martinez .05 .02
❑ 731 Donnie Hill .05 .02
❑ 732 Nelson Santovenia .05 .02
❑ 733 Bob Melvin .05 .02
❑ 734 Scott Hatteberg RC .05 .02
❑ 735 Greg Swindell .05 .02
❑ 736 Lance Johnson .05 .02
❑ 737 Kevin Reimer .05 .02
❑ 738 Dennis Eckersley .10 .05
❑ 739 Rob Ducey .05 .02
❑ 740 Ken Caminiti .10 .05
❑ 741 Mark Gubicza .05 .02
❑ 742 Bill Spiers .05 .02
❑ 743 Darren Lewis .05 .02
❑ 744 Chris Hammond .05 .02
❑ 745 Dave Magadan .05 .02
❑ 746 Bernard Gilkey .10 .05
❑ 747 Willie Banks .05 .02
❑ 748 Matt Nokes .05 .02
❑ 749 Jerald Clark .05 .02
❑ 750 Travis Fryman .10 .05
❑ 751 Steve Wilson .05 .02
❑ 752 Billy Ripken .05 .02
❑ 753 Paul Assenmacher .05 .02
❑ 754 Charlie Hayes .05 .02
❑ 755 Alex Fernandez .10 .05
❑ 756 Gary Pettis .05 .02
❑ 757 Rob Dibble .05 .02
❑ 758 Tim Naehring .05 .02
❑ 759 Jeff Torborg MG .05 .02
❑ 760 Ozzie Smith .25 .11
❑ 761 Mike Fitzgerald .05 .02
❑ 762 John Burkett .05 .02
❑ 763 Kyle Abbott .05 .02
❑ 764 Tyler Green RC .05 .02
❑ 765 Pete Harnisch .05 .02
❑ 766 Mark Davis .05 .02
❑ 767 Kal Daniels .05 .02
❑ 768 Jim Thome .40 .18
❑ 769 Jack Howell .05 .02
❑ 770 Sid Bream .05 .02
❑ 771 Arthur Rhodes .05 .02
❑ 772 Garry Templeton UER .05 .02
(Stat heading in for pitchers)
❑ 773 Hal Morris .05 .02
❑ 774 Bud Black .05 .02
❑ 775 Ivan Calderon .05 .02
❑ 776 Doug Henry RC .05 .02
❑ 777 John Olerud .10 .05
❑ 778 Tim Leary .05 .02
❑ 779 Jay Bell .10 .05
❑ 780 Eddie Murray .20 .09
❑ 781 Paul Abbott .05 .02
❑ 782 Phil Plantier .05 .02
❑ 783 Joe Magrane .05 .02
❑ 784 Ken Patterson .05 .02
❑ 785 Albert Belle .15 .07
❑ 786 Royce Clayton .05 .02
❑ 787 Checklist 661-792 .05 .02
❑ 788 Mike Stanton .05 .02
❑ 789 Bobby Valentine MG .05 .02
❑ 790 Joe Carter .10 .05
❑ 791 Danny Cox .05 .02
❑ 792 Dave Winfield .20 .09

## 1992 Topps Traded

| | MINT | NRMT |
|---|---|---|
| COMP.FACT.SET (132) | 120.00 | 55.00 |

❑ 1T Willie Adams USA RC .10 .05
❑ 2T Jeff Alkire USA RC .10 .05
❑ 3T Felipe Alou MG .10 .05
❑ 4T Moises Alou .75 .35
❑ 5T Ruben Amaro .10 .05
❑ 6T Jack Armstrong .10 .05
❑ 7T Scott Bankhead .10 .05
❑ 8T Tim Belcher .10 .05
❑ 9T George Bell .10 .05
❑ 10T Freddie Benavides .10 .05
❑ 11T Todd Benzinger .10 .05
❑ 12T Joe Boever .10 .05
❑ 13T Ricky Bones .10 .05
❑ 14T Bobby Bonilla .20 .09
❑ 15T Hubie Brooks .10 .05
❑ 16T Jerry Browne .10 .05
❑ 17T Jim Bullinger .10 .05
❑ 18T Dave Burba .10 .05
❑ 19T Kevin Campbell .10 .05
❑ 20T Tom Candiotti .10 .05
❑ 21T Mark Carreon .10 .05
❑ 22T Gary Carter .25 .11
❑ 23T Archi Cianfrocco RC .10 .05
❑ 24T Phil Clark .10 .05
❑ 25T Chad Curtis RC .40 .18
❑ 26T Eric Davis .20 .09
❑ 27T Tim Davis USA RC .10 .05
❑ 28T Gary DiSarcina .10 .05
❑ 29T Darren Dreifort USA .20 .09
❑ 30T Mariano Duncan .10 .05
❑ 31T Mike Fitzgerald .10 .05
❑ 32T John Flaherty .10 .05
❑ 33T Darrin Fletcher .10 .05
❑ 34T Scott Fletcher .10 .05
❑ 35T Ron Fraser CO USA RC .10 .05
❑ 36T Andres Galarraga .25 .11
❑ 37T Dave Gallagher .10 .05
❑ 38T Mike Gallego .10 .05
❑ 39T Nomar Garciaparra USA RC ! 100.00 45.00
❑ 40T Jason Giambi USA 1.50 .70
❑ 41T Danny Gladden .10 .05
❑ 42T Rene Gonzales .10 .05
❑ 43T Jeff Granger USA .10 .05
❑ 44T Rick Greene USA RC .10 .05
❑ 45T Jeffrey Hammonds USA .50 .23
❑ 46T Charlie Hayes .10 .05
❑ 47T Von Hayes .10 .05
❑ 48T Rick Helling USA .20 .09
❑ 49T Butch Henry RC .10 .05
❑ 50T Carlos Hernandez .10 .05
❑ 51T Ken Hill .10 .05
❑ 52T Butch Hobson .10 .05
❑ 53T Vince Horsman .10 .05
❑ 54T Pete Incaviglia .10 .05
❑ 55T Gregg Jefferies .10 .05
❑ 56T Charles Johnson USA .50 .23
❑ 57T Doug Jones .10 .05
❑ 58T Brian Jordan RC 4.00 1.80
❑ 59T Wally Joyner .20 .09
❑ 60T Daron Kirkreit USA RC .10 .05
❑ 61T Bill Krueger .10 .05
❑ 62T Gene Lamont MG .10 .05
❑ 63T Jim Lefebvre MG .10 .05
❑ 64T Danny Leon .10 .05
❑ 65T Pat Listach RC .10 .05
❑ 66T Kenny Lofton .75 .35
❑ 67T Dave Martinez .10 .05
❑ 68T Derrick May .10 .05
❑ 69T Kirk McCaskill .10 .05
❑ 70T Chad McConnell USA RC .20 .09
❑ 71T Kevin McReynolds .10 .05
❑ 72T Rusty Meacham .10 .05
❑ 73T Keith Miller .10 .05
❑ 74T Kevin Mitchell .20 .09
❑ 75T Jason Moler USA RC .10 .05
❑ 76T Mike Morgan .10 .05
❑ 77T Jack Morris .20 .09
❑ 78T Calvin Murray USA RC .10 .05
❑ 79T Eddie Murray .40 .18
❑ 80T Randy Myers .20 .09
❑ 81T Denny Neagle .25 .11
❑ 82T Phil Nevin USA .50 .23
❑ 83T Dave Nilsson .20 .09
❑ 84T Junior Ortiz .10 .05
❑ 85T Donovan Osborne .10 .05
❑ 86T Bill Pecota .10 .05
❑ 87T Melido Perez .10 .05
❑ 88T Mike Perez .10 .05
❑ 89T Hipolito Pichardo RC .10 .05
❑ 90T Willie Randolph .20 .09
❑ 91T Darren Reed .10 .05
❑ 92T Bip Roberts .10 .05
❑ 93T Chris Roberts USA .10 .05
❑ 94T Steve Rodriguez USA .10 .05
❑ 95T Bruce Ruffin .10 .05
❑ 96T Scott Ruskin .10 .05
❑ 97T Bret Saberhagen .20 .09
❑ 98T Rey Sanchez RC .10 .05
❑ 99T Steve Sax .10 .05
❑ 100T Curt Schilling .20 .09
❑ 101T Dick Schofield .10 .05
❑ 102T Gary Scott .10 .05
❑ 103T Kevin Seitzer .10 .05
❑ 104T Frank Seminara RC .10 .05
❑ 105T Gary Sheffield .40 .18
❑ 106T John Smiley .10 .05
❑ 107T Cory Snyder .10 .05
❑ 108T Paul Sorrento .10 .05
❑ 109T Sammy Sosa 1.25 .55
❑ 110T Matt Stairs RC 1.00 .45
❑ 111T Andy Stankiewicz .10 .05
❑ 112T Kurt Stillwell .10 .05
❑ 113T Rick Sutcliffe .20 .09
❑ 114T Bill Swift .10 .05
❑ 115T Jeff Tackett .10 .05
❑ 116T Danny Tartabull .10 .05
❑ 117T Eddie Taubensee .20 .09
❑ 118T Dickie Thon .10 .05
❑ 119T Michael Tucker USA RC .75 .35
❑ 120T Scooter Tucker .10 .05
❑ 121T Marc Valdes USA RC .10 .05

❑ 122T Julio Valera .10 .05
❑ 123T Jason Varitek USA RC 4.00 1.80
❑ 124T Ron Villone USA RC .10 .05
❑ 125T Frank Viola .10 .05
❑ 126T B.J. Wallace USA RC .20 .09
❑ 127T Dan Walters .10 .05
❑ 128T Craig Wilson USA .10 .05
❑ 129T Chris Wimmer USA .10 .05
❑ 130T Dave Winfield .40 .18
❑ 131T Herm Winningham .10 .05
❑ 132T Checklist 1T-132T .10 .05

## 1993 Topps

| | MINT | NRMT |
|---|---|---|
| COMPLETE SET (825) | 35.00 | 16.00 |
| COMP.HOBBY.SET (847) | 60.00 | 27.00 |
| COMP.RETAIL.SET (838) | 40.00 | 18.00 |
| COMPLETE SERIES 1 (396) | 20.00 | 9.00 |
| COMPLETE SERIES 2 (429) | 15.00 | 6.75 |

❑ 1 Robin Yount .25 .11
❑ 2 Barry Bonds .60 .25
❑ 3 Ryne Sandberg .50 .23
❑ 4 Roger Clemens .75 .35
❑ 5 Tony Gwynn .75 .35
❑ 6 Jeff Tackett .10 .05
❑ 7 Pete Incaviglia .10 .05
❑ 8 Mark Wohlers .10 .05
❑ 9 Kent Hrbek .20 .09
❑ 10 Will Clark .40 .18
❑ 11 Eric Karros .25 .11
❑ 12 Lee Smith .20 .09
❑ 13 Esteban Beltre .10 .05
❑ 14 Greg Briley .10 .05
❑ 15 Marquis Grissom .10 .05
❑ 16 Dan Plesac .10 .05
❑ 17 Dave Hollins .10 .05
❑ 18 Terry Steinbach .10 .05
❑ 19 Ed Nunez .10 .05
❑ 20 Tim Salmon .20 .09
❑ 21 Luis Salazar .10 .05
❑ 22 Jim Eisenreich .10 .05
❑ 23 Todd Stottlemyre .10 .05
❑ 24 Tim Naehring .10 .05
❑ 25 John Franco .20 .09
❑ 26 Skeeter Barnes .10 .05
❑ 27 Carlos Garcia .10 .05
❑ 28 Joe Orsulak .10 .05
❑ 29 Dwayne Henry .10 .05
❑ 30 Fred McGriff .25 .11
❑ 31 Derek Lilliquist .10 .05
❑ 32 Don Mattingly 1.00 .45
❑ 33 B.J. Wallace .10 .05
❑ 34 Juan Gonzalez .40 .18
❑ 35 John Smoltz .20 .09
❑ 36 Scott Servais .10 .05
❑ 37 Lenny Webster .10 .05
❑ 38 Chris James .10 .05
❑ 39 Roger McDowell .10 .05
❑ 40 Ozzie Smith .50 .23
❑ 41 Alex Fernandez .20 .09
❑ 42 Spike Owen .10 .05
❑ 43 Ruben Amaro .10 .05
❑ 44 Kevin Seitzer .10 .05
❑ 45 Dave Fleming .10 .05
❑ 46 Eric Fox .10 .05
❑ 47 Bob Scanlan .10 .05
❑ 48 Bert Blyleven .20 .09
❑ 49 Brian McRae .10 .05
❑ 50 Roberto Alomar .40 .18
❑ 51 Mo Vaughn .20 .09
❑ 52 Bobby Bonilla .20 .09
❑ 53 Frank Tanana .10 .05
❑ 54 Mike LaValliere .10 .05
❑ 55 Mark McLemore .10 .05
❑ 56 Chad Mottola RC .10 .05
❑ 57 Norm Charlton .10 .05
❑ 58 Jose Melendez .10 .05
❑ 59 Carlos Martinez .10 .05
❑ 60 Roberto Kelly .10 .05
❑ 61 Gene Larkin .10 .05
❑ 62 Rafael Belliard .10 .05
❑ 63 Al Osuna .10 .05
❑ 64 Scott Chiamparino .10 .05
❑ 65 Brett Butler .20 .09
❑ 66 John Burkett .10 .05
❑ 67 Felix Jose .10 .05
❑ 68 Omar Vizquel .20 .09
❑ 69 John Vander Wal .10 .05
❑ 70 Roberto Hernandez .10 .05
❑ 71 Ricky Bones .10 .05
❑ 72 Jeff Grotewold .10 .05
❑ 73 Mike Moore .10 .05
❑ 74 Steve Buechele .10 .05
❑ 75 Juan Guzman .10 .05
❑ 76 Kevin Appier .20 .09
❑ 77 Junior Felix .10 .05
❑ 78 Greg W. Harris .10 .05
❑ 79 Dick Schofield .10 .05
❑ 80 Cecil Fielder .20 .09
❑ 81 Lloyd McClendon .10 .05
❑ 82 David Segui .10 .05
❑ 83 Reggie Sanders .10 .05
❑ 84 Kurt Stillwell .10 .05
❑ 85 Sandy Alomar Jr. .20 .09
❑ 86 John Habyan .10 .05
❑ 87 Kevin Reimer .10 .05
❑ 88 Mike Stanton .10 .05
❑ 89 Eric Anthony .10 .05
❑ 90 Scott Erickson .10 .05
❑ 91 Craig Colbert .10 .05
❑ 92 Tom Pagnozzi .10 .05
❑ 93 Pedro Astacio .20 .09
❑ 94 Lance Johnson .10 .05
❑ 95 Larry Walker .20 .09
❑ 96 Russ Swan .10 .05
❑ 97 Scott Fletcher .10 .05
❑ 98 Derek Jeter RC 10.00 4.50
❑ 99 Mike Williams .10 .05
❑ 100 Mark McGwire 1.50 .70
❑ 101 Jim Bullinger .10 .05
❑ 102 Brian Hunter .10 .05
❑ 103 Jody Reed .10 .05
❑ 104 Mike Butcher .10 .05
❑ 105 Gregg Jefferies .10 .05
❑ 106 Howard Johnson .10 .05
❑ 107 John Kiely .10 .05
❑ 108 Jose Lind .10 .05
❑ 109 Sam Horn .10 .05
❑ 110 Barry Larkin .40 .18
❑ 111 Bruce Hurst .10 .05
❑ 112 Brian Barnes .10 .05
❑ 113 Thomas Howard .10 .05
❑ 114 Mel Hall .10 .05
❑ 115 Robby Thompson .10 .05
❑ 116 Mark Lemke .10 .05
❑ 117 Eddie Taubensee .10 .05
❑ 118 David Hulse RC .10 .05
❑ 119 Pedro Munoz .10 .05
❑ 120 Ramon Martinez .10 .05
❑ 121 Todd Worrell .10 .05
❑ 122 Joey Cora .10 .05
❑ 123 Moises Alou .20 .09
❑ 124 Franklin Stubbs .10 .05
❑ 125 Pete O'Brien .10 .05
❑ 126 Bob Ayrault .10 .05
❑ 127 Carney Lansford .20 .09
❑ 128 Kal Daniels .10 .05
❑ 129 Joe Grahe .10 .05
❑ 130 Jeff Montgomery .20 .09
❑ 131 Dave Winfield .40 .18
❑ 132 Preston Wilson RC .75 .35
❑ 133 Steve Wilson .10 .05
❑ 134 Lee Guetterman .10 .05
❑ 135 Mickey Tettleton .10 .05
❑ 136 Jeff King .10 .05
❑ 137 Alan Mills .10 .05
❑ 138 Joe Oliver .10 .05
❑ 139 Gary Gaetti .20 .09
❑ 140 Gary Sheffield .40 .18
❑ 141 Dennis Cook .10 .05
❑ 142 Charlie Hayes .10 .05
❑ 143 Jeff Huson .10 .05
❑ 144 Kent Mercker .10 .05
❑ 145 Eric Young .10 .05
❑ 146 Scott Leius .10 .05
❑ 147 Bryan Hickerson .10 .05
❑ 148 Steve Finley .20 .09
❑ 149 Rheal Cormier .10 .05
❑ 150 Frank Thomas UER .75 .35
(Categories leading league are italicized but not printed in red)
❑ 151 Archi Cianfrocco .10 .05
❑ 152 Rich DeLucia .10 .05
❑ 153 Greg Vaughn .20 .09
❑ 154 Wes Chamberlain .10 .05
❑ 155 Dennis Eckersley .20 .09
❑ 156 Sammy Sosa .75 .35
❑ 157 Gary DiSarcina .10 .05
❑ 158 Kevin Koslofski .10 .05
❑ 159 Doug Linton .10 .05
❑ 160 Lou Whitaker .20 .09
❑ 161 Chad McConnell .10 .05
❑ 162 Joe Hesketh .10 .05
❑ 163 Tim Wakefield .10 .05
❑ 164 Leo Gomez .10 .05
❑ 165 Jose Rijo .10 .05
❑ 166 Tim Scott .10 .05
❑ 167 Steve Olin UER .10 .05
(Born 10/4/65; should say 10/10/65)
❑ 168 Kevin Maas .10 .05
❑ 169 Kenny Rogers .10 .05
❑ 170 David Justice .25 .11
❑ 171 Doug Jones .10 .05
❑ 172 Jeff Reboulet .10 .05
❑ 173 Andres Galarraga .25 .11
❑ 174 Randy Velarde .10 .05
❑ 175 Kirk McCaskill .10 .05
❑ 176 Darren Lewis .10 .05
❑ 177 Lenny Harris .10 .05
❑ 178 Jeff Fassero .10 .05
❑ 179 Ken Griffey Jr. 1.50 .70
❑ 180 Darren Daulton .20 .09
❑ 181 John Jaha .10 .05
❑ 182 Ron Darling .10 .05
❑ 183 Greg Maddux 1.00 .45
❑ 184 Damion Easley .10 .05
❑ 185 Jack Morris .20 .09
❑ 186 Mike Magnante .10 .05
❑ 187 John Dopson .10 .05
❑ 188 Sid Fernandez .10 .05
❑ 189 Tony Phillips .10 .05
❑ 190 Doug Drabek .10 .05
❑ 191 Sean Lowe RC .10 .05
❑ 192 Bob Milacki .10 .05
❑ 193 Steve Foster .10 .05
❑ 194 Jerald Clark .10 .05
❑ 195 Pete Harnisch .10 .05
❑ 196 Pat Kelly .10 .05
❑ 197 Jeff Frye .10 .05
❑ 198 Alejandro Pena .10 .05
❑ 199 Junior Ortiz .10 .05
❑ 200 Kirby Puckett 1.00 .45
❑ 201 Jose Uribe .10 .05
❑ 202 Mike Scioscia .10 .05
❑ 203 Bernard Gilkey .10 .05
❑ 204 Dan Pasqua .10 .05
❑ 205 Gary Carter .25 .11
❑ 206 Henry Cotto .10 .05
❑ 207 Paul Molitor .40 .18
❑ 208 Mike Hartley .10 .05
❑ 209 Jeff Parrett .10 .05
❑ 210 Mark Langston .10 .05
❑ 211 Doug Dascenzo .10 .05
❑ 212 Rick Reed .10 .05
❑ 213 Candy Maldonado .10 .05
❑ 214 Danny Darwin .10 .05

- ❑ 215 Pat Howell .10 .05
- ❑ 216 Mark Leiter .10 .05
- ❑ 217 Kevin Mitchell .20 .09
- ❑ 218 Ben McDonald .10 .05
- ❑ 219 Bip Roberts .10 .05
- ❑ 220 Benny Santiago .10 .05
- ❑ 221 Carlos Baerga .10 .05
- ❑ 222 Bernie Williams .40 .18
- ❑ 223 Roger Pavlik .10 .05
- ❑ 224 Sid Bream .10 .05
- ❑ 225 Matt Williams .25 .11
- ❑ 226 Willie Banks .10 .05
- ❑ 227 Jeff Bagwell .50 .23
- ❑ 228 Tom Goodwin .10 .05
- ❑ 229 Mike Perez .10 .05
- ❑ 230 Carlton Fisk .40 .18
- ❑ 231 John Wetteland .20 .09
- ❑ 232 Tino Martinez .20 .09
- ❑ 233 Rick Greene .10 .05
- ❑ 234 Tim McIntosh .10 .05
- ❑ 235 Mitch Williams .10 .05
- ❑ 236 Kevin Campbell .10 .05
- ❑ 237 Jose Vizcaino .10 .05
- ❑ 238 Chris Donnels .10 .05
- ❑ 239 Mike Boddicker .10 .05
- ❑ 240 John Olerud .25 .11
- ❑ 241 Mike Gardiner .10 .05
- ❑ 242 Charlie O'Brien .10 .05
- ❑ 243 Rob Deer .10 .05
- ❑ 244 Denny Neagle .20 .09
- ❑ 245 Chris Sabo .10 .05
- ❑ 246 Gregg Olson .10 .05
- ❑ 247 Frank Seminara UER .10 .05
  (Acquired 12/3/98)
- ❑ 248 Scott Scudder .10 .05
- ❑ 249 Tim Burke .10 .05
- ❑ 250 Chuck Knoblauch .20 .09
- ❑ 251 Mike Bielecki .10 .05
- ❑ 252 Xavier Hernandez .10 .05
- ❑ 253 Jose Guzman .10 .05
- ❑ 254 Cory Snyder .10 .05
- ❑ 255 Orel Hershiser .20 .09
- ❑ 256 Wil Cordero .10 .05
- ❑ 257 Luis Alicea .10 .05
- ❑ 258 Mike Schooler .10 .05
- ❑ 259 Craig Grebeck .10 .05
- ❑ 260 Duane Ward .10 .05
- ❑ 261 Bill Wegman .10 .05
- ❑ 262 Mickey Morandini .10 .05
- ❑ 263 Vince Horsman .10 .05
- ❑ 264 Paul Sorrento .10 .05
- ❑ 265 Andre Dawson .25 .11
- ❑ 266 Rene Gonzales .10 .05
- ❑ 267 Keith Miller .10 .05
- ❑ 268 Derek Bell .10 .05
- ❑ 269 Todd Steverson RC .10 .05
- ❑ 270 Frank Viola .10 .05
- ❑ 271 Wally Whitehurst .10 .05
- ❑ 272 Kurt Knudsen .10 .05
- ❑ 273 Dan Walters .10 .05
- ❑ 274 Rick Sutcliffe .20 .09
- ❑ 275 Andy Van Slyke .20 .09
- ❑ 276 Paul O'Neill .20 .09
- ❑ 277 Mark Whiten .10 .05
- ❑ 278 Chris Nabholz .10 .05
- ❑ 279 Todd Burns .10 .05
- ❑ 280 Tom Glavine .25 .11
- ❑ 281 Butch Henry .10 .05
- ❑ 282 Shane Mack .10 .05
- ❑ 283 Mike Jackson .10 .05
- ❑ 284 Henry Rodriguez .10 .05
- ❑ 285 Bob Tewksbury .10 .05
- ❑ 286 Ron Karkovice .10 .05
- ❑ 287 Mike Gallego .10 .05
- ❑ 288 Dave Cochrane .10 .05
- ❑ 289 Jesse Orosco .10 .05
- ❑ 290 Dave Stewart .20 .09
- ❑ 291 Tommy Greene .10 .05
- ❑ 292 Rey Sanchez .10 .05
- ❑ 293 Rob Ducey .10 .05
- ❑ 294 Brent Mayne .10 .05
- ❑ 295 Dave Stieb .10 .05
- ❑ 296 Luis Rivera .10 .05
- ❑ 297 Jeff Innis .10 .05
- ❑ 298 Scott Livingstone .10 .05
- ❑ 299 Bob Patterson .10 .05
- ❑ 300 Cal Ripken 1.50 .70
- ❑ 301 Cesar Hernandez .10 .05
- ❑ 302 Randy Myers .20 .09
- ❑ 303 Brook Jacoby .10 .05
- ❑ 304 Melido Perez .10 .05
- ❑ 305 Rafael Palmeiro .40 .18
- ❑ 306 Damon Berryhill .10 .05
- ❑ 307 Dan Serafini RC .10 .05
- ❑ 308 Darryl Kile .20 .09
- ❑ 309 J.T. Bruett .10 .05
- ❑ 310 Dave Righetti .10 .05
- ❑ 311 Jay Howell .10 .05
- ❑ 312 Geronimo Pena .10 .05
- ❑ 313 Greg Hibbard .10 .05
- ❑ 314 Mark Gardner .10 .05
- ❑ 315 Edgar Martinez .25 .11
- ❑ 316 Dave Nilsson .20 .09
- ❑ 317 Kyle Abbott .10 .05
- ❑ 318 Willie Wilson .10 .05
- ❑ 319 Paul Assenmacher .10 .05
- ❑ 320 Tim Fortugno .10 .05
- ❑ 321 Rusty Meacham .10 .05
- ❑ 322 Pat Borders .10 .05
- ❑ 323 Mike Greenwell .10 .05
- ❑ 324 Willie Randolph .20 .09
- ❑ 325 Bill Gullickson .10 .05
- ❑ 326 Gary Varsho .10 .05
- ❑ 327 Tim Hulett .10 .05
- ❑ 328 Scott Ruskin .10 .05
- ❑ 329 Mike Maddux .10 .05
- ❑ 330 Danny Tartabull .10 .05
- ❑ 331 Kenny Lofton .20 .09
- ❑ 332 Geno Petralli .10 .05
- ❑ 333 Otis Nixon .10 .05
- ❑ 334 Jason Kendall RC 1.50 .70
- ❑ 335 Mark Portugal .10 .05
- ❑ 336 Mike Pagliarulo .10 .05
- ❑ 337 Kirt Manwaring .10 .05
- ❑ 338 Bob Ojeda .10 .05
- ❑ 339 Mark Clark .10 .05
- ❑ 340 John Kruk .20 .09
- ❑ 341 Mel Rojas .10 .05
- ❑ 342 Erik Hanson .10 .05
- ❑ 343 Doug Henry .10 .05
- ❑ 344 Jack McDowell .10 .05
- ❑ 345 Harold Baines .20 .09
- ❑ 346 Chuck McElroy .10 .05
- ❑ 347 Luis Sojo .10 .05
- ❑ 348 Andy Stankiewicz .10 .05
- ❑ 349 Hipolito Pichardo .10 .05
- ❑ 350 Joe Carter .20 .09
- ❑ 351 Ellis Burks .20 .09
- ❑ 352 Pete Schourek .10 .05
- ❑ 353 Bubby Groom .10 .05
- ❑ 354 Jay Bell .20 .09
- ❑ 355 Brady Anderson .20 .09
- ❑ 356 Freddie Benavides .10 .05
- ❑ 357 Phil Stephenson .10 .05
- ❑ 358 Kevin Wickander .10 .05
- ❑ 359 Mike Stanley .10 .05
- ❑ 360 Ivan Rodriguez .50 .23
- ❑ 361 Scott Bankhead .10 .05
- ❑ 362 Luis Gonzalez .20 .09
- ❑ 363 John Smiley .10 .05
- ❑ 364 Trevor Wilson .10 .05
- ❑ 365 Tom Candiotti .10 .05
- ❑ 366 Craig Wilson .10 .05
- ❑ 367 Steve Sax .10 .05
- ❑ 368 Delino DeShields .20 .09
- ❑ 369 Jaime Navarro .10 .05
- ❑ 370 Dave Valle .10 .05
- ❑ 371 Mariano Duncan .10 .05
- ❑ 372 Rod Nichols .10 .05
- ❑ 373 Mike Morgan .10 .05
- ❑ 374 Julio Valera .10 .05
- ❑ 375 Wally Joyner .20 .09
- ❑ 376 Tom Henke .10 .05
- ❑ 377 Herm Winningham .10 .05
- ❑ 378 Orlando Merced .10 .05
- ❑ 379 Mike Munoz .10 .05
- ❑ 380 Todd Hundley .10 .05
- ❑ 381 Mike Flanagan .10 .05
- ❑ 382 Tim Belcher .10 .05
- ❑ 383 Jerry Browne .10 .05
- ❑ 384 Mike Benjamin .10 .05
- ❑ 385 Jim Leyritz .10 .05
- ❑ 386 Ray Lankford .25 .11
- ❑ 387 Devon White .10 .05
- ❑ 388 Jeremy Hernandez .10 .05
- ❑ 389 Brian Harper .10 .05
- ❑ 390 Wade Boggs .50 .23
- ❑ 391 Derrick May .10 .05
- ❑ 392 Travis Fryman .20 .09
- ❑ 393 Ron Gant .20 .09
- ❑ 394 Checklist 1-132 .10 .05
- ❑ 395 Checklist 133-264 UER .10 .05
  (Eckerlsey)
- ❑ 396 Checklist 265-396 .10 .05
- ❑ 397 George Brett .75 .35
- ❑ 398 Bobby Witt .10 .05
- ❑ 399 Daryl Boston .10 .05
- ❑ 400 Bo Jackson .20 .09
- ❑ 401 Fred McGriff .40 .18
  Frank Thomas
- ❑ 402 Ryne Sandberg .10 .05
  Carlos Baerga
- ❑ 403 Gary Sheffield .20 .09
  Edgar Martinez
- ❑ 404 Barry Larkin .20 .09
  Travis Fryman
- ❑ 405 Andy Van Slyke .50 .23
  Ken Griffey Jr.
- ❑ 406 Larry Walker .40 .18
  Kirby Puckett
- ❑ 407 Barry Bonds .20 .09
  Joe Carter
- ❑ 408 Darren Daulton .20 .09
  Brian Harper
- ❑ 409 Greg Maddux .50 .23
  Roger Clemens
- ❑ 410 Tom Glavine .20 .09
  Dave Fleming
- ❑ 411 Lee Smith .20 .09
  Dennis Eckersley
- ❑ 412 Jamie McAndrew .10 .05
- ❑ 413 Pete Smith .10 .05
- ❑ 414 Juan Guerrero .10 .05
- ❑ 415 Todd Frohwirth .10 .05
- ❑ 416 Randy Tomlin .10 .05
- ❑ 417 B.J. Surhoff .20 .09
- ❑ 418 Jim Gott .10 .05
- ❑ 419 Mark Thompson RC .10 .05
- ❑ 420 Kevin Tapani .10 .05
- ❑ 421 Curt Schilling .20 .09
- ❑ 422 J.T. Snow RC .50 .23
- ❑ 423 1993 Prospects .40 .18
  Ryan Klesko
  Ivan Cruz
  Bubba Smith
  Larry Sutton
- ❑ 424 John Valentin .10 .05
- ❑ 425 Joe Girardi .20 .09
- ❑ 426 Nigel Wilson .10 .05
- ❑ 427 Bob MacDonald .10 .05
- ❑ 428 Todd Zeile .10 .05
- ❑ 429 Milt Cuyler .10 .05
- ❑ 430 Eddie Murray .40 .18
- ❑ 431 Rich Amaral .10 .05
- ❑ 432 Pete Young .10 .05
- ❑ 433 Roger Bailey RC and .10 .05
  Tom Schmidt
- ❑ 434 Jack Armstrong .10 .05
- ❑ 435 Willie McGee .20 .09
- ❑ 436 Greg W. Harris .10 .05
- ❑ 437 Chris Hammond .10 .05
- ❑ 438 Ritchie Moody RC .10 .05
- ❑ 439 Bryan Harvey .10 .05
- ❑ 440 Ruben Sierra .10 .05
- ❑ 441 Don Lemon and .10 .05
  Todd Pridy RC
- ❑ 442 Kevin McReynolds .10 .05
- ❑ 443 Terry Leach .10 .05
- ❑ 444 David Nied .10 .05
- ❑ 445 Dale Murphy .25 .11
- ❑ 446 Luis Mercedes .10 .05
- ❑ 447 Keith Shepherd RC .10 .05
- ❑ 448 Ken Caminiti .20 .09
- ❑ 449 James Austin .10 .05
- ❑ 450 Darryl Strawberry .20 .09
- ❑ 451 1993 Prospects .20 .09
  Ramon Caraballo
  Jon Shave RC

Brent Gates
Quinton McCracken
❑ 452 Bob Wickman .10 .05
❑ 453 Victor Cole .10 .05
❑ 454 John Johnstone RC .10 .05
❑ 455 Chili Davis .20 .09
❑ 456 Scott Taylor .10 .05
❑ 457 Tracy Woodson .10 .05
❑ 458 David Wells .20 .09
❑ 459 Derek Wallace RC .10 .05
❑ 460 Randy Johnson .50 .23
❑ 461 Steve Reed RC .10 .05
❑ 462 Felix Fermin .10 .05
❑ 463 Scott Aldred .10 .05
❑ 464 Greg Colbrunn .10 .05
❑ 465 Tony Fernandez .10 .05
❑ 466 Mike Felder .10 .05
❑ 467 Lee Stevens .20 .09
❑ 468 Matt Whiteside RC .10 .05
❑ 469 Dave Hansen .10 .05
❑ 470 Rob Dibble .10 .05
❑ 471 Dave Gallagher .10 .05
❑ 472 Chris Gwynn .10 .05
❑ 473 Dave Henderson .10 .05
❑ 474 Ozzie Guillen .10 .05
❑ 475 Jeff Reardon .20 .09
❑ 476 Mark Voisard and .10 .05
Will Scalzitti RC
❑ 477 Jimmy Jones .10 .05
❑ 478 Greg Cadaret .10 .05
❑ 479 Todd Pratt RC .25 .11
❑ 480 Pat Listach .10 .05
❑ 481 Ryan Luzinski RC .10 .05
❑ 482 Darren Reed .10 .05
❑ 483 Brian Griffiths RC .10 .05
❑ 484 John Wehner .10 .05
❑ 485 Glenn Davis .10 .05
❑ 486 Eric Wedge RC .10 .05
❑ 487 Jesse Hollins .10 .05
❑ 488 Manuel Lee .10 .05
❑ 489 Scott Fredrickson RC .10 .05
❑ 490 Omar Olivares .10 .05
❑ 491 Shawn Hare .10 .05
❑ 492 Tom Lampkin .10 .05
❑ 493 Jeff Nelson .10 .05
❑ 494 1993 Prospects .20 .09
Kevin Young
Adell Davenport
Eduardo Perez
Lou Lucca RC
❑ 495 Ken Hill .10 .05
❑ 496 Reggie Jefferson .20 .09
❑ 497 Matt Petersen and .10 .05
Willie Brown RC
❑ 498 Bud Black .10 .05
❑ 499 Chuck Crim .10 .05
❑ 500 Jose Canseco .50 .23
❑ 501 Johnny Oates MG .20 .09
Bobby Cox MG
❑ 502 Butch Hobson MG .10 .05
Jim Lefebvre MG
❑ 503 Buck Rodgers MG .20 .09
Tony Perez MG
❑ 504 Gene Lamont MG .20 .09
Don Baylor MG
❑ 505 Mike Hargrove MG .20 .09
Rene Lachemann MG
❑ 506 Sparky Anderson MG .20 .09
Art Howe MG
❑ 507 Hal McRae MG .20 .09
Tom Lasorda MG
❑ 508 Phil Garner MG .20 .09
Felipe Alou MG
❑ 509 Tom Kelly MG .10 .05
Jeff Torborg MG
❑ 510 Buck Showalter MG .20 .09
Jim Fregosi MG
❑ 511 Tony LaRussa MG .20 .09
Jim Leyland MG
❑ 512 Lou Piniella MG .20 .09
Joe Torre MG
❑ 513 Kevin Kennedy MG .10 .05
Jim Riggleman MG
❑ 514 Cito Gaston MG .10 .05
Dusty Baker MG
❑ 515 Greg Swindell .10 .05
❑ 516 Alex Arias .10 .05
❑ 517 Bill Pecota .10 .05
❑ 518 Benji Grigsby RC UER .10 .05
(Misspelled Bengi
on card front)
❑ 519 David Howard .10 .05
❑ 520 Charlie Hough .20 .09
❑ 521 Kevin Flora .10 .05
❑ 522 Shane Reynolds .10 .05
❑ 523 Doug Bochtler RC .10 .05
❑ 524 Chris Hoiles .10 .05
❑ 525 Scott Sanderson .10 .05
❑ 526 Mike Sharperson .10 .05
❑ 527 Mike Fetters .10 .05
❑ 528 Paul Quantrill .10 .05
❑ 529 1993 Prospects 1.25 .55
Dave Silvestri
Chipper Jones
Benji Gil
Jeff Patzke
❑ 530 Sterling Hitchcock RC .20 .09
❑ 531 Joe Millette .10 .05
❑ 532 Tom Brunansky .10 .05
❑ 533 Frank Castillo .10 .05
❑ 534 Randy Knorr .10 .05
❑ 535 Jose Oquendo .10 .05
❑ 536 Dave Haas .10 .05
❑ 537 Jason Hutchins RC and .10 .05
Ryan Turner
❑ 538 Jimmy Baron RC .10 .05
❑ 539 Kerry Woodson .10 .05
❑ 540 Ivan Calderon .10 .05
❑ 541 Denis Boucher .10 .05
❑ 542 Royce Clayton .10 .05
❑ 543 Reggie Williams .10 .05
❑ 544 Steve Decker .10 .05
❑ 545 Dean Palmer .20 .09
❑ 546 Hal Morris .10 .05
❑ 547 Ryan Thompson .10 .05
❑ 548 Lance Blankenship .10 .05
❑ 549 Hensley Meulens .10 .05
❑ 550 Scott Radinsky .10 .05
❑ 551 Eric Young .10 .05
❑ 552 Jeff Blauser .10 .05
❑ 553 Andujar Cedeno .10 .05
❑ 554 Arthur Rhodes .10 .05
❑ 555 Terry Mulholland .10 .05
❑ 556 Darryl Hamilton .10 .05
❑ 557 Pedro Martinez 1.00 .45
❑ 558 Ryan Whitman RC and .10 .05
Mark Skeels
❑ 559 Jamie Arnold RC .10 .05
❑ 560 Zane Smith .10 .05
❑ 561 Matt Nokes .10 .05
❑ 562 Bob Zupcic .10 .05
❑ 563 Shawn Boskie .10 .05
❑ 564 Mike Timlin .10 .05
❑ 565 Jerald Clark .10 .05
❑ 566 Rod Brewer .10 .05
❑ 567 Mark Carreon .10 .05
❑ 568 Andy Benes .10 .05
❑ 569 Shawn Barton RC .10 .05
❑ 570 Tim Wallach .10 .05
❑ 571 Dave Mlicki .10 .05
❑ 572 Trevor Hoffman .40 .18
❑ 573 John Patterson .10 .05
❑ 574 De Shawn Warren RC .10 .05
❑ 575 Monty Fariss .10 .05
❑ 576 1993 Prospects .20 .09
Darrell Sherman
Damon Buford
Cliff Floyd
Michael Moore
❑ 577 Tim Costo .10 .05
❑ 578 Dave Magadan .10 .05
❑ 579 Neil Garret and .10 .05
Jason Bates RC
❑ 580 Walt Weiss .10 .05
❑ 581 Chris Haney .10 .05
❑ 582 Shawn Abner .10 .05
❑ 583 Marvin Freeman .10 .05
❑ 584 Casey Candaele .10 .05
❑ 585 Ricky Jordan .10 .05
❑ 586 Jeff Tabaka RC .10 .05
❑ 587 Manny Alexander .10 .05
❑ 588 Mike Trombley .10 .05
❑ 589 Carlos Hernandez .10 .05
❑ 590 Cal Eldred .10 .05
❑ 591 Alex Cole .10 .05
❑ 592 Phil Plantier .10 .05
❑ 593 Brett Merriman RC .10 .05
❑ 594 Jerry Nielsen .10 .05
❑ 595 Shawon Dunston .10 .05
❑ 596 Jimmy Key .20 .09
❑ 597 Gerald Perry .10 .05
❑ 598 Rico Brogna .20 .09
❑ 599 Clemente Nunez and .10 .05
Daniel Robinson
❑ 600 Bret Saberhagen .20 .09
❑ 601 Craig Shipley .10 .05
❑ 602 Henry Mercedes .10 .05
❑ 603 Jim Thome .25 .11
❑ 604 Rod Beck .10 .05
❑ 605 Chuck Finley .20 .09
❑ 606 J. Owens RC .10 .05
❑ 607 Dan Smith .10 .05
❑ 608 Bill Doran .10 .05
❑ 609 Lance Parrish .10 .05
❑ 610 Dennis Martinez .20 .09
❑ 611 Tom Gordon .10 .05
❑ 612 Byron Mathews RC .10 .05
❑ 613 Joel Adamson RC .10 .05
❑ 614 Brian Williams .10 .05
❑ 615 Steve Avery .10 .05
❑ 616 1993 Prospects .10 .05
Matt Mieske
Tracy Sanders
Midre Cummings RC
Ryan Freeburg
❑ 617 Craig Lefferts .10 .05
❑ 618 Tony Pena .10 .05
❑ 619 Billy Spiers .10 .05
❑ 620 Todd Benzinger .10 .05
❑ 621 Mike Kotarski and .10 .05
Greg Boyd RC
❑ 622 Ben Rivera .10 .05
❑ 623 Al Martin .10 .05
❑ 624 Sam Militello UER .10 .05
(Profile says drafted
in 1988; bio says
drafted in 1990)
❑ 625 Rick Aguilera .10 .05
❑ 626 Dan Gladden .10 .05
❑ 627 Andres Berumen RC .10 .05
❑ 628 Kelly Gruber .10 .05
❑ 629 Cris Carpenter .10 .05
❑ 630 Mark Grace .40 .18
❑ 631 Jeff Brantley .10 .05
❑ 632 Chris Widger RC .25 .11
❑ 633 Three Russians UER .10 .05
Rudolf Razjigaev
Eugneyi Puchkov
Ilya Bogatyrev
(Bogatyrev is a shortstop,
card has pitching header)
❑ 634 Mo Sanford .10 .05
❑ 635 Albert Belle .25 .11
❑ 636 Tim Teufel .10 .05
❑ 637 Greg Myers .10 .05
❑ 638 Brian Bohanon .10 .05
❑ 639 Mike Bordick .10 .05
❑ 640 Dwight Gooden .20 .09
❑ 641 Pat Leahy and .10 .05
Gavin Baugh RC
❑ 642 Milt Hill .10 .05
❑ 643 Luis Aquino .10 .05
❑ 644 Dante Bichette .20 .09
❑ 645 Bobby Thigpen .10 .05
❑ 646 Rich Scheid RC .10 .05
❑ 647 Brian Sackinsky RC .10 .05
❑ 648 Ryan Hawblitzel .10 .05
❑ 649 Tom Marsh .10 .05
❑ 650 Terry Pendleton .20 .09
❑ 651 Rafael Bournigal .10 .05
❑ 652 Dave West .10 .05
❑ 653 Steve Hosey .10 .05
❑ 654 Gerald Williams .10 .05
❑ 655 Scott Cooper .10 .05
❑ 656 Gary Scott .10 .05
❑ 657 Mike Harkey .10 .05
❑ 658 1993 Prospects .10 .05
Jeromy Burnitz

Melvin Nieves
Rich Becker
Shon Walker RC
❑ 659 Ed Sprague .10 .05
❑ 660 Alan Trammell .25 .11
❑ 661 Garvin Alston RCand .10 .05
Michael Case
❑ 662 Donovan Osborne .10 .05
❑ 663 Jeff Gardner .10 .05
❑ 664 Calvin Jones .10 .05
❑ 665 Darrin Fletcher .10 .05
❑ 666 Glenallen Hill .10 .05
❑ 667 Jim Rosenbohm RC .10 .05
❑ 668 Scott Lewis .10 .05
❑ 669 Kip Yaughn RC .10 .05
❑ 670 Julio Franco .10 .05
❑ 671 Dave Martinez .10 .05
❑ 672 Kevin Bass .10 .05
❑ 673 Todd Van Poppel .10 .05
❑ 674 Mark Gubicza .10 .05
❑ 675 Tim Raines .20 .09
❑ 676 Rudy Seanez .10 .05
❑ 677 Charlie Leibrandt .10 .05
❑ 678 Randy Milligan .10 .05
❑ 679 Kim Batiste .10 .05
❑ 680 Craig Biggio .25 .11
❑ 681 Darren Holmes .10 .05
❑ 682 John Candelaria .10 .05
❑ 683 Jerry Stafford and .20 .09
Eddie Christian RC
❑ 684 Pat Mahomes .10 .05
❑ 685 Bob Walk .10 .05
❑ 686 Russ Springer .10 .05
❑ 687 Tony Sheffield RC .10 .05
❑ 688 Dwight Smith .10 .05
❑ 689 Eddie Zosky .10 .05
❑ 690 Bien Figueroa .10 .05
❑ 691 Jim Tatum RC .10 .05
❑ 692 Chad Kreuter .10 .05
❑ 693 Rich Rodriguez .10 .05
❑ 694 Shane Turner .10 .05
❑ 695 Kent Bottenfield .10 .05
❑ 696 Jose Mesa .10 .05
❑ 697 Darrell Whitmore RC .10 .05
❑ 698 Ted Wood .10 .05
❑ 699 Chad Curtis .10 .05
❑ 700 Nolan Ryan 2.00 .90
❑ 701 1993 Prospects 2.00 .90
Mike Piazza
Brook Fordyce
Carlos Delgado
Donnie Leshnock
❑ 702 Tim Pugh RC .10 .05
❑ 703 Jeff Kent .40 .18
❑ 704 Jon Goodrich and .20 .09
Danny Figueroa RC
❑ 705 Bob Welch .10 .05
❑ 706 Sherard Clinkscales RC .10 .05
❑ 707 Donn Pall .10 .05
❑ 708 Greg Olson .10 .05
❑ 709 Jeff Juden .10 .05
❑ 710 Mike Mussina .40 .18
❑ 711 Scott Chiamparino .10 .05
❑ 712 Stan Javier .10 .05
❑ 713 John Doherty .10 .05
❑ 714 Kevin Gross .10 .05
❑ 715 Greg Gagne .10 .05
❑ 716 Steve Cooke .10 .05
❑ 717 Steve Farr .10 .05
❑ 718 Jay Buhner .20 .09
❑ 719 Butch Henry .10 .05
❑ 720 David Cone .20 .09
❑ 721 Rick Wilkins .10 .05
❑ 722 Chuck Carr .10 .05
❑ 723 Kenny Felder RC .10 .05
❑ 724 Guillermo Velasquez .10 .05
❑ 725 Billy Hatcher .10 .05
❑ 726 Mike Veneziale RC and .20 .09
Ken Kendrena
❑ 727 Jonathan Hurst .10 .05
❑ 728 Steve Frey .10 .05
❑ 729 Mark Leonard .10 .05
❑ 730 Charles Nagy .10 .05
❑ 731 Donald Harris .10 .05
❑ 732 Travis Buckley RC .10 .05
❑ 733 Tom Browning .10 .05
❑ 734 Anthony Young .10 .05
❑ 735 Steve Shifflett .10 .05
❑ 736 Jeff Russell .10 .05
❑ 737 Wilson Alvarez .10 .05
❑ 738 Lance Painter RC .10 .05
❑ 739 Dave Weathers .10 .05
❑ 740 Len Dykstra .20 .09
❑ 741 Mike Devereaux .10 .05
❑ 742 1993 Prospects .10 .05
Rene Arocha
Alan Embree
Brien Taylor
Tim Crabtree
❑ 743 Dave Landaker RC .10 .05
❑ 744 Chris George .10 .05
❑ 745 Eric Davis .20 .09
❑ 746 Mark Strittmatter and .20 .09
Lamarr Rogers RC
❑ 747 Carl Willis .10 .05
❑ 748 Stan Belinda .10 .05
❑ 749 Scott Kamieniecki .10 .05
❑ 750 Rickey Henderson .50 .23
❑ 751 Eric Hillman .10 .05
❑ 752 Pat Hentgen .10 .05
❑ 753 Jim Corsi .10 .05
❑ 754 Brian Jordan .20 .09
❑ 755 Bill Swift .10 .05
❑ 756 Mike Henneman .10 .05
❑ 757 Harold Reynolds .10 .05
❑ 758 Sean Berry .10 .05
❑ 759 Charlie Hayes .10 .05
❑ 760 Luis Polonia .10 .05
❑ 761 Darrin Jackson .10 .05
❑ 762 Mark Lewis .10 .05
❑ 763 Rob Maurer .10 .05
❑ 764 Willie Greene .10 .05
❑ 765 Vince Coleman .10 .05
❑ 766 Todd Revenig .10 .05
❑ 767 Rich Ireland RC .10 .05
❑ 768 Mike Macfarlane .10 .05
❑ 769 Francisco Cabrera .10 .05
❑ 770 Robin Ventura .20 .09
❑ 771 Kevin Ritz .10 .05
❑ 772 Chito Martinez .10 .05
❑ 773 Cliff Brantley .10 .05
❑ 774 Curt Leskanic RC .10 .05
❑ 775 Chris Bosio .10 .05
❑ 776 Jose Offerman .10 .05
❑ 777 Mark Guthrie .10 .05
❑ 778 Don Slaught .10 .05
❑ 779 Rich Monteleone .10 .05
❑ 780 Jim Abbott .20 .09
❑ 781 Jack Clark .10 .05
❑ 782 Reynol Mendoza and .20 .09
Dan Homan RC
❑ 783 Heathcliff Slocumb .10 .05
❑ 784 Jeff Branson .10 .05
❑ 785 Kevin Brown .25 .11
❑ 786 1993 Prospects .20 .09
Mike Christopher
Ken Ryan
Aaron Taylor
Gus Gandarillas RC
❑ 787 Mike Matthews RC .10 .05
❑ 788 Mackey Sasser .10 .05
❑ 789 Jeff Conine UER .10 .05
(No inclusion of 1990
stats in career total)
❑ 790 George Bell .10 .05
❑ 791 Pat Rapp .10 .05
❑ 792 Joe Boever .10 .05
❑ 793 Jim Poole .10 .05
❑ 794 Andy Ashby .20 .09
❑ 795 Deion Sanders .25 .11
❑ 796 Scott Brosius .20 .09
❑ 797 Brad Pennington .10 .05
❑ 798 Greg Blosser .10 .05
❑ 799 Jim Edmonds RC 3.00 1.35
❑ 800 Shawn Jeter .10 .05
❑ 801 Jesse Levis .10 .05
❑ 802 Phil Clark UER .10 .05
(Word "a" is missing in
sentence beginning
with "In 1992 ...")
❑ 803 Ed Pierce RC .10 .05
❑ 804 Jose Valentin RC .40 .18
❑ 805 Terry Jorgensen .10 .05
❑ 806 Mark Hutton .10 .05
❑ 807 Troy Neel .10 .05
❑ 808 Bret Boone .20 .09
❑ 809 Cris Colon .10 .05
❑ 810 Domingo Martinez RC .10 .05
❑ 811 Javier Lopez .20 .09
❑ 812 Matt Walbeck RC .10 .05
❑ 813 Dan Wilson .20 .09
❑ 814 Scooter Tucker .10 .05
❑ 815 Billy Ashley .10 .05
❑ 816 Tim Laker RC .10 .05
❑ 817 Bobby Jones .20 .09
❑ 818 Brad Brink .10 .05
❑ 819 William Pennyfeather .10 .05
❑ 820 Stan Royer .10 .05
❑ 821 Doug Brocail .10 .05
❑ 822 Kevin Rogers .10 .05
❑ 823 Checklist 397-540 .10 .05
❑ 824 Checklist 541-691 .10 .05
❑ 825 Checklist 692-825 .10 .05

## 1993 Topps Traded

| | MINT | NRMT |
|---|---|---|
| COMP.FACT.SET (132) | 50.00 | 22.00 |

❑ 1T Barry Bonds .80 .35
❑ 2T Rich Renteria .15 .07
❑ 3T Aaron Sele .50 .23
❑ 4T Carlton Loewer USA RC 1.00 .45
❑ 5T Erik Pappas .15 .07
❑ 6T Greg McMichael RC .15 .07
❑ 7T Freddie Benavides .15 .07
❑ 8T Kirk Gibson .25 .11
❑ 9T Tony Fernandez .15 .07
❑ 10T Jay Gainer RC .15 .07
❑ 11T Orestes Destrade .15 .07
❑ 12T A.J. Hinch USA RC 1.00 .45
❑ 13T Bobby Munoz .15 .07
❑ 14T Tom Henke .15 .07
❑ 15T Rob Butler .15 .07
❑ 16T Gary Wayne .15 .07
❑ 17T David McCarty .15 .07
❑ 18T Walt Weiss .15 .07
❑ 19T Todd Helton USA RC 30.00 13.50
❑ 20T Mark Whiten .15 .07
❑ 21T Ricky Gutierrez .15 .07
❑ 22T Dustin Hermanson USA RC 1.50 .70
❑ 23T Sherman Obando RC .15 .07
❑ 24T Mike Piazza 2.50 1.10
❑ 25T Jeff Russell .15 .07
❑ 26T Jason Bere .15 .07
❑ 27T Jack Voigt RC .15 .07
❑ 28T Chris Bosio .15 .07
❑ 29T Phil Hiatt .15 .07
❑ 30T Matt Beaumont USA RC .15 .07
❑ 31T Andres Galarraga .20 .09
❑ 32T Greg Swindell .15 .07
❑ 33T Vinny Castilla 2.00 .90
❑ 34T Pat Clougherty RC USA .15 .07
❑ 35T Greg Briley .15 .07
❑ 36T Dallas Green MG .15 .07
Davey Johnson MG
❑ 37T Tyler Green .15 .07
❑ 38T Craig Paquette .15 .07
❑ 39T Danny Sheaffer RC .15 .07
❑ 40T Jim Converse RC .15 .07

| Card | MINT | NRMT |
|---|---|---|
| ❑ 41T Terry Harvey RC USA | .15 | .07 |
| ❑ 42T Phil Plantier | .15 | .07 |
| ❑ 43T Doug Saunders RC | .15 | .07 |
| ❑ 44T Benny Santiago | .15 | .07 |
| ❑ 45T Dante Powell USA RC | 1.00 | .45 |
| ❑ 46T Jeff Parrett | .15 | .07 |
| ❑ 47T Wade Boggs | .50 | .25 |
| ❑ 48T Paul Molitor | .50 | .23 |
| ❑ 49T Turk Wendell | .15 | .07 |
| ❑ 50T David Wells | .25 | .11 |
| ❑ 51T Gary Sheffield | .50 | .23 |
| ❑ 52T Kevin Young | .25 | .11 |
| ❑ 53T Nelson Liriano | .15 | .07 |
| ❑ 54T Greg Maddux | 1.00 | .55 |
| ❑ 55T Derek Bell | .15 | .07 |
| ❑ 56T Matt Turner RC | .15 | .07 |
| ❑ 57T Charlie Nelson RC USA | .15 | .07 |
| ❑ 58T Mike Hampton | .50 | .23 |
| ❑ 59T Troy O'Leary RC | 1.00 | .45 |
| ❑ 60T Benji Gil | .15 | .07 |
| ❑ 61T Mitch Lyden RC | .15 | .07 |
| ❑ 62T J.T. Snow | .50 | .23 |
| ❑ 63T Damon Buford | .15 | .07 |
| ❑ 64T Gene Harris | .15 | .07 |
| ❑ 65T Randy Myers | .25 | .11 |
| ❑ 66T Felix Jose | .15 | .07 |
| ❑ 67T Todd Dunn USA RC | .15 | .07 |
| ❑ 68T Jimmy Key | .25 | .11 |
| ❑ 69T Pedro Castellano | .15 | .07 |
| ❑ 70T Mark Merila USA RC | .15 | .07 |
| ❑ 71T Rich Rodriguez | .15 | .07 |
| ❑ 72T Matt Mieske | .15 | .07 |
| ❑ 73T Pete Incaviglia | .15 | .07 |
| ❑ 74T Carl Everett | .25 | .11 |
| ❑ 75T Jim Abbott | .25 | .11 |
| ❑ 76T Luis Aquino | .15 | .07 |
| ❑ 77T Rene Arocha | .15 | .07 |
| ❑ 78T Jon Shave | .15 | .07 |
| ❑ 79T Todd Walker USA RC | 1.50 | .70 |
| ❑ 80T Jack Armstrong | .15 | .07 |
| ❑ 81T Jeff Richardson | .15 | .07 |
| ❑ 82T Blas Minor | .15 | .07 |
| ❑ 83T Dave Winfield | .50 | .23 |
| ❑ 84T Paul O'Neill | .25 | .11 |
| ❑ 85T Steve Reich RC USA | .15 | .07 |
| ❑ 86T Chris Hammond | .15 | .07 |
| ❑ 87T Hilly Hathaway RC | .15 | .07 |
| ❑ 88T Fred McGriff | .20 | .09 |
| ❑ 89T Dave Telgheder RC | .15 | .07 |
| ❑ 90T Richie Lewis RC | .15 | .07 |
| ❑ 91T Brent Gates | .15 | .07 |
| ❑ 92T Andre Dawson | .20 | .09 |
| ❑ 93T Andy Barkett RC USA | .15 | .07 |
| ❑ 94T Doug Drabek | .15 | .07 |
| ❑ 95T Joe Klink | .15 | .07 |
| ❑ 96T Willie Blair | .15 | .07 |
| ❑ 97T Danny Graves USA RC | 2.00 | .90 |
| ❑ 98T Pat Meares RC | .15 | .07 |
| ❑ 99T Mike Lansing RC | .25 | .11 |
| ❑ 100T Marcos Armas RC | .15 | .07 |
| ❑ 101T Darren Grass RC USA | .15 | .07 |
| ❑ 102T Chris Jones | .15 | .07 |
| ❑ 103T Ken Ryan RC | .15 | .07 |
| ❑ 104T Ellis Burks | .25 | .11 |
| ❑ 105T Roberto Kelly | .15 | .07 |
| ❑ 106T Dave Magadan | .15 | .07 |
| ❑ 107T Paul Wilson USA RC | .20 | .09 |
| ❑ 108T Rob Natal | .15 | .07 |
| ❑ 109T Paul Wagner | .15 | .07 |
| ❑ 110T Jeromy Burnitz | .25 | .11 |
| ❑ 111T Monty Fariss | .15 | .07 |
| ❑ 112T Kevin Mitchell | .25 | .11 |
| ❑ 113T Scott Pose RC | .15 | .07 |
| ❑ 114T Dave Stewart | .25 | .11 |
| ❑ 115T Russ Johnson USA RC | .50 | .23 |
| ❑ 116T Armando Reynoso | .15 | .07 |
| ❑ 117T Geronimo Berroa | .15 | .07 |
| ❑ 118T Woody Williams RC | .20 | .09 |
| ❑ 119T Tim Bogar RC | .15 | .07 |
| ❑ 120T Bob Scafa RC USA | .15 | .07 |
| ❑ 121T Henry Cotto | .15 | .07 |
| ❑ 122T Gregg Jefferies | .15 | .07 |
| ❑ 123T Norm Charlton | .15 | .07 |
| ❑ 124T Bret Wagner USA RC | .50 | .23 |
| ❑ 125T David Cone | .25 | .11 |
| ❑ 126T Daryl Boston | .15 | .07 |
| ❑ 127T Tim Wallach | .15 | .07 |
| ❑ 128T Mike Martin USA RC | .15 | .07 |
| ❑ 129T John Cummings RC | .15 | .07 |
| ❑ 130T Ryan Bowen | .15 | .07 |
| ❑ 131T John Powell RC USA | .15 | .07 |
| ❑ 132T Checklist 1-132 | .15 | .07 |

## 1994 Topps

| | MINT | NRMT |
|---|---|---|
| COMPLETE SET (792) | 40.00 | 18.00 |
| COMP.FACT.SET (808) | 60.00 | 27.00 |
| COMP.BAKER SET (818) | 60.00 | 27.00 |
| COMPLETE SERIES 1 (396) | 20.00 | 9.00 |
| COMPLETE SERIES 2 (396) | 20.00 | 9.00 |
| COMMON CARD (1-792) | .10 | .05 |

| Card | MINT | NRMT |
|---|---|---|
| ❑ 1 Mike Piazza | 1.25 | .55 |
| ❑ 2 Bernie Williams | .40 | .18 |
| ❑ 3 Kevin Rogers | .10 | .05 |
| ❑ 4 Paul Carey | .10 | .05 |
| ❑ 5 Ozzie Guillen | .10 | .05 |
| ❑ 6 Derrick May | .10 | .05 |
| ❑ 7 Jose Mesa | .10 | .05 |
| ❑ 8 Todd Hundley | .10 | .05 |
| ❑ 9 Chris Haney | .10 | .05 |
| ❑ 10 John Olerud | .20 | .09 |
| ❑ 11 Andujar Cedeno | .10 | .05 |
| ❑ 12 John Smiley | .10 | .05 |
| ❑ 13 Phil Plantier | .10 | .05 |
| ❑ 14 Willie Banks | .10 | .05 |
| ❑ 15 Jay Bell | .20 | .09 |
| ❑ 16 Doug Henry | .10 | .05 |
| ❑ 17 Lance Blankenship | .10 | .05 |
| ❑ 18 Greg W. Harris | .10 | .05 |
| ❑ 19 Scott Livingstone | .10 | .05 |
| ❑ 20 Bryan Harvey | .10 | .05 |
| ❑ 21 Wil Cordero | .10 | .05 |
| ❑ 22 Roger Pavlik | .10 | .05 |
| ❑ 23 Mark Lemke | .10 | .05 |
| ❑ 24 Jeff Nelson | .10 | .05 |
| ❑ 25 Todd Zeile | .10 | .05 |
| ❑ 26 Billy Hatcher | .10 | .05 |
| ❑ 27 Joe Magrane | .10 | .05 |
| ❑ 28 Tony Longmire | .10 | .05 |
| ❑ 29 Omar Daal | .10 | .05 |
| ❑ 30 Kirt Manwaring | .10 | .05 |
| ❑ 31 Melido Perez | .10 | .05 |
| ❑ 32 Tim Hulett | .10 | .05 |
| ❑ 33 Jeff Schwartz | .10 | .05 |
| ❑ 34 Nolan Ryan | 2.00 | .90 |
| ❑ 35 Jose Guzman | .10 | .05 |
| ❑ 36 Felix Fermin | .10 | .05 |
| ❑ 37 Jeff Innis | .10 | .05 |
| ❑ 38 Brett Mayne | .10 | .05 |
| ❑ 39 Huck Flener RC | .10 | .05 |
| ❑ 40 Jeff Bagwell | .50 | .23 |
| ❑ 41 Kevin Wickander | .10 | .05 |
| ❑ 42 Ricky Gutierrez | .10 | .05 |
| ❑ 43 Pat Mahomes | .10 | .05 |
| ❑ 44 Jeff King | .10 | .05 |
| ❑ 45 Cal Eldred | .10 | .05 |
| ❑ 46 Craig Paquette | .10 | .05 |
| ❑ 47 Richie Lewis | .10 | .05 |
| ❑ 48 Tony Phillips | .10 | .05 |
| ❑ 49 Armando Reynoso | .10 | .05 |
| ❑ 50 Moises Alou | .20 | .09 |
| ❑ 51 Manuel Lee | .10 | .05 |
| ❑ 52 Otis Nixon | .10 | .05 |
| ❑ 53 Billy Ashley | .10 | .05 |
| ❑ 54 Mark Whiten | .10 | .05 |
| ❑ 55 Jeff Russell | .10 | .05 |
| ❑ 56 Chad Curtis | .10 | .05 |
| ❑ 57 Kevin Stocker | .10 | .05 |
| ❑ 58 Mike Jackson | .10 | .05 |
| ❑ 59 Matt Nokes | .10 | .05 |
| ❑ 60 Chris Bosio | .10 | .05 |
| ❑ 61 Damon Buford | .10 | .05 |
| ❑ 62 Tim Belcher | .10 | .05 |
| ❑ 63 Glenallen Hill | .10 | .05 |
| ❑ 64 Bill Wertz | .10 | .05 |
| ❑ 65 Eddie Murray | .40 | .18 |
| ❑ 66 Tom Gordon | .10 | .05 |
| ❑ 67 Alex Gonzalez | .10 | .05 |
| ❑ 68 Eddie Taubensee | .10 | .05 |
| ❑ 69 Jacob Brumfield | .10 | .05 |
| ❑ 70 Andy Benes | .10 | .05 |
| ❑ 71 Rich Becker | .10 | .05 |
| ❑ 72 Steve Cooke | .10 | .05 |
| ❑ 73 Billy Spiers | .10 | .05 |
| ❑ 74 Scott Brosius | .20 | .09 |
| ❑ 75 Alan Trammell | .20 | .09 |
| ❑ 76 Luis Aquino | .10 | .05 |
| ❑ 77 Jerald Clark | .10 | .05 |
| ❑ 78 Mel Rojas | .10 | .05 |
| ❑ 79 Outfield Prospects<br>Billy Masse<br>Stanton Cameron<br>Tim Clark<br>Craig McClure RC | .10 | .05 |
| ❑ 80 Jose Canseco | .50 | .23 |
| ❑ 81 Greg McMichael | .10 | .05 |
| ❑ 82 Brian Turang RC | .10 | .05 |
| ❑ 83 Tom Urbani | .10 | .05 |
| ❑ 84 Garret Anderson | .40 | .18 |
| ❑ 85 Tony Pena | .10 | .05 |
| ❑ 86 Ricky Jordan | .10 | .05 |
| ❑ 87 Jim Gott | .10 | .05 |
| ❑ 88 Pat Kelly | .10 | .05 |
| ❑ 89 Bud Black | .10 | .05 |
| ❑ 90 Robin Ventura | .20 | .09 |
| ❑ 91 Rick Sutcliffe | .20 | .09 |
| ❑ 92 Jose Bautista | .10 | .05 |
| ❑ 93 Bob Ojeda | .10 | .05 |
| ❑ 94 Phil Hiatt | .10 | .05 |
| ❑ 95 Tim Pugh | .10 | .05 |
| ❑ 96 Randy Knorr | .10 | .05 |
| ❑ 97 Todd Jones | .10 | .05 |
| ❑ 98 Ryan Thompson | .10 | .05 |
| ❑ 99 Tim Mauser | .10 | .05 |
| ❑ 100 Kirby Puckett | 1.00 | .45 |
| ❑ 101 Mark Dewey | .10 | .05 |
| ❑ 102 B.J. Surhoff | .20 | .09 |
| ❑ 103 Sterling Hitchcock | .10 | .05 |
| ❑ 104 Alex Arias | .10 | .05 |
| ❑ 105 David Wells | .20 | .09 |
| ❑ 106 Daryl Boston | .10 | .05 |
| ❑ 107 Mike Stanton | .10 | .05 |
| ❑ 108 Gary Redus | .10 | .05 |
| ❑ 109 Delino DeShields | .10 | .05 |
| ❑ 110 Lee Smith | .20 | .09 |
| ❑ 111 Greg Litton | .10 | .05 |
| ❑ 112 Frankie Rodriguez | .10 | .05 |
| ❑ 113 Russ Springer | .10 | .05 |
| ❑ 114 Mitch Williams | .10 | .05 |
| ❑ 115 Eric Karros | .20 | .09 |
| ❑ 116 Jeff Brantley | .10 | .05 |
| ❑ 117 Jack Voigt | .10 | .05 |
| ❑ 118 Jason Bere | .10 | .05 |
| ❑ 119 Kevin Roberson | .10 | .05 |
| ❑ 120 Jimmy Key | .20 | .09 |
| ❑ 121 Reggie Jefferson | .10 | .05 |
| ❑ 122 Jeromy Burnitz | .20 | .09 |
| ❑ 123 Billy Brewer | .10 | .05 |
| ❑ 124 Willie Canate | .10 | .05 |
| ❑ 125 Greg Swindell | .10 | .05 |
| ❑ 126 Hal Morris | .10 | .05 |
| ❑ 127 Brad Ausmus | .10 | .05 |
| ❑ 128 George Tsamis | .10 | .05 |
| ❑ 129 Denny Neagle | .10 | .05 |
| ❑ 130 Pat Listach | .10 | .05 |
| ❑ 131 Steve Karsay | .10 | .05 |
| ❑ 132 Bret Barberie | .10 | .05 |
| ❑ 133 Mark Leiter | .10 | .05 |

❑ 134 Greg Colbrunn .10 .05
❑ 135 David Nied .10 .05
❑ 136 Dean Palmer .20 .09
❑ 137 Steve Avery .10 .05
❑ 138 Bill Haselman .10 .05
❑ 139 Tripp Cromer .10 .05
❑ 140 Frank Viola .10 .05
❑ 141 Rene Gonzales .10 .05
❑ 142 Curt Schilling .20 .09
❑ 143 Tim Wallach .10 .05
❑ 144 Bobby Munoz .10 .05
❑ 145 Brady Anderson .20 .09
❑ 146 Rod Beck .10 .05
❑ 147 Mike LaValliere .10 .05
❑ 148 Greg Hibbard .10 .05
❑ 149 Kenny Lofton .20 .09
❑ 150 Dwight Gooden .20 .09
❑ 151 Greg Gagne .10 .05
❑ 152 Ray McDavid .10 .05
❑ 153 Chris Donnels .10 .05
❑ 154 Dan Wilson .10 .05
❑ 155 Todd Stottlemyre .10 .05
❑ 156 David McCarty .10 .05
❑ 157 Paul Wagner .10 .05
❑ 158 Shortstop Prospects 2.00 .90
Orlando Miller
Brandon Wilson
Derek Jeter
Mike Neal
❑ 159 Mike Fetters .10 .05
❑ 160 Scott Lydy .10 .05
❑ 161 Darrell Whitmore .10 .05
❑ 162 Bob MacDonald .10 .05
❑ 163 Vinny Castilla .20 .09
❑ 164 Denis Boucher .10 .05
❑ 165 Ivan Rodriguez .50 .23
❑ 166 Ron Gant .20 .09
❑ 167 Tim Davis .10 .05
❑ 168 Steve Dixon .10 .05
❑ 160 Scott Fletcher .10 .05
❑ 170 Terry Mulholland .10 .05
❑ 171 Greg Myers .10 .05
❑ 172 Brett Butler .20 .09
❑ 173 Rob Wickman .10 .05
❑ 174 Dave Martinez .10 .05
❑ 175 Fernando Valenzuela .20 .09
❑ 176 Craig Grebeck .10 .05
❑ 177 Shawn Boskie .10 .05
❑ 178 Albie Lopez .10 .05
❑ 179 Dutch Huskey .10 .05
❑ 180 George Brett .75 .35
❑ 181 Juan Guzman .10 .05
❑ 182 Eric Anthony .10 .05
❑ 183 Rob Dibble .10 .05
❑ 184 Craig Shipley .10 .05
❑ 185 Kevin Tapani .10 .05
❑ 186 Marcus Moore .10 .05
❑ 187 Graeme Lloyd .10 .05
❑ 188 Mike Bordick .10 .05
❑ 189 Chris Hammond .10 .05
❑ 190 Cecil Fielder .20 .09
❑ 191 Curt Leskanic .10 .05
❑ 192 Lou Frazier .10 .05
❑ 193 Steve Dreyer RC .10 .05
❑ 194 Javier Lopez .20 .09
❑ 195 Edgar Martinez .20 .09
❑ 196 Allen Watson .10 .05
❑ 197 John Flaherty .10 .05
❑ 198 Kurt Stillwell .10 .05
❑ 199 Danny Jackson .10 .05
❑ 200 Cal Ripken 1.50 .70
❑ 201 Mike Bell FDP RC .10 .05
❑ 202 Alan Benes FDP RC .20 .09
❑ 203 Matt Farner FDP RC .10 .05
❑ 204 Jeff Granger .10 .05
❑ 205 Brooks Kieschnick FDP RC .10 .05
❑ 206 Jeremy Lee FDP RC .20 .09
❑ 207 Charles Peterson FDP RC .20 .09
❑ 208 Alan Rice FDP RC .10 .05
❑ 209 Billy Wagner FDP RC .40 .18
❑ 210 Kelly Wunsch FDP RC .20 .09
❑ 211 Tom Candiotti .10 .05
❑ 212 Domingo Jean .10 .05
❑ 213 John Burkett .10 .05
❑ 214 George Bell .10 .05
❑ 215 Dan Plesac .10 .05
❑ 216 Manny Ramirez .60 .25
❑ 217 Mike Maddux .10 .05
❑ 218 Kevin McReynolds .10 .05
❑ 219 Pat Borders .10 .05
❑ 220 Doug Drabek .10 .05
❑ 221 Larry Luebbers RC .10 .05
❑ 222 Trevor Hoffman .20 .09
❑ 223 Pat Meares .10 .05
❑ 224 Danny Miceli .10 .05
❑ 225 Greg Vaughn .20 .09
❑ 226 Scott Hemond .10 .05
❑ 227 Pat Rapp .10 .05
❑ 228 Kirk Gibson .20 .09
❑ 229 Lance Painter .10 .05
❑ 230 Larry Walker .20 .09
❑ 231 Benji Gil .10 .05
❑ 232 Mark Wohlers .10 .05
❑ 233 Rich Amaral .10 .05
❑ 234 Eric Pappas .10 .05
❑ 235 Scott Cooper .10 .05
❑ 236 Mike Butcher .10 .05
❑ 237 Outfield Prospects .50 .23
Curtis Pride
Shawn Green
Mark Sweeney
Eddie Davis
❑ 238 Kim Batiste .10 .05
❑ 239 Paul Assenmacher .10 .05
❑ 240 Will Clark .40 .18
❑ 241 Jose Offerman .10 .05
❑ 242 Todd Frohwirth .10 .05
❑ 243 Tim Raines .20 .09
❑ 244 Rick Wilkins .10 .05
❑ 245 Bret Saberhagen .20 .09
❑ 246 Thomas Howard .10 .05
❑ 247 Stan Belinda .10 .05
❑ 248 Rickey Henderson .50 .23
❑ 249 Brian Williams .10 .05
❑ 250 Barry Larkin .40 .18
❑ 251 Jose Valentin .10 .05
❑ 252 Lenny Webster .10 .05
❑ 253 Blas Minor .10 .05
❑ 254 Tim Teufel .10 .05
❑ 255 Bobby Witt .10 .05
❑ 256 Walt Weiss .10 .05
❑ 257 Chad Kreuter .10 .05
❑ 258 Roberto Mejia .10 .05
❑ 259 Cliff Floyd .20 .09
❑ 260 Julio Franco .10 .05
❑ 261 Rafael Belliard .10 .05
❑ 262 Marc Newfield .10 .05
❑ 263 Gerald Perry .10 .05
❑ 264 Ken Ryan .10 .05
❑ 265 Chili Davis .20 .09
❑ 266 Dave West .10 .05
❑ 267 Royce Clayton .10 .05
❑ 268 Pedro Martinez .60 .25
❑ 269 Mark Hutton .10 .05
❑ 270 Frank Thomas .75 .35
❑ 271 Brad Pennington .10 .05
❑ 272 Mike Harkey .10 .05
❑ 273 Sandy Alomar Jr. .20 .09
❑ 274 Dave Gallagher .10 .05
❑ 275 Wally Joyner .20 .09
❑ 276 Ricky Trlicek .10 .05
❑ 277 Al Osuna .10 .05
❑ 278 Pokey Reese .20 .09
❑ 279 Kevin Higgins .10 .05
❑ 280 Rick Aguilera .10 .05
❑ 281 Orlando Merced .10 .05
❑ 282 Mike Mohler .10 .05
❑ 283 John Jaha .10 .05
❑ 284 Robb Nen .10 .05
❑ 285 Travis Fryman .20 .09
❑ 286 Mark Thompson .10 .05
❑ 287 Mike Lansing .10 .05
❑ 288 Craig Lefferts .10 .05
❑ 289 Damon Berryhill .10 .05
❑ 290 Randy Johnson .50 .23
❑ 291 Jeff Reed .10 .05
❑ 292 Danny Darwin .10 .05
❑ 293 J.T. Snow .20 .09
❑ 294 Tyler Green .10 .05
❑ 295 Chris Hoiles .10 .05
❑ 296 Roger McDowell .10 .05
❑ 297 Spike Owen .10 .05
❑ 298 Salomon Torres .10 .05
❑ 299 Wilson Alvarez .10 .05
❑ 300 Ryne Sandberg .50 .23
❑ 301 Derek Lilliquist .10 .05
❑ 302 Howard Johnson .10 .05
❑ 303 Greg Cadaret .10 .05
❑ 304 Pat Hentgen .10 .05
❑ 305 Craig Biggio .20 .09
❑ 306 Scott Service .10 .05
❑ 307 Melvin Nieves .10 .05
❑ 308 Mike Trombley .10 .05
❑ 309 Carlos Garcia .10 .05
❑ 310 Robin Yount UER .40 .18
(Listed with 111 triples in 1988; should be 11)
❑ 311 Marcos Armas .10 .05
❑ 312 Rich Rodriguez .10 .05
❑ 313 Justin Thompson .10 .05
❑ 314 Danny Sheaffer .10 .05
❑ 315 Ken Hill .10 .05
❑ 316 Pitching Prospects .20 .09
Chad Ogea
Duff Brumley
Terrell Wade RC
Chris Michalak
❑ 317 Cris Carpenter .10 .05
❑ 318 Jeff Blauser .10 .05
❑ 319 Ted Power .10 .05
❑ 320 Ozzie Smith .50 .23
❑ 321 John Dopson .10 .05
❑ 322 Chris Turner .10 .05
❑ 323 Pete Incaviglia .10 .05
❑ 324 Alan Mills .10 .05
❑ 325 Jody Reed .10 .05
❑ 326 Rich Monteleone .10 .05
❑ 327 Mark Carreon .10 .05
❑ 328 Donn Pall .10 .05
❑ 329 Matt Walbeck .10 .05
❑ 330 Charles Nagy .10 .05
❑ 331 Jeff McKnight .10 .05
❑ 332 Jose Lind .10 .05
❑ 333 Mike Timlin .10 .05
❑ 334 Doug Jones .10 .05
❑ 335 Kevin Mitchell .10 .05
❑ 000 Luis Lopez .10 .05
❑ 337 Shane Mack .10 .05
❑ 338 Randy Tomlin .10 .05
❑ 339 Matt Mieske .10 .05
❑ 340 Mark McGwire 1.50 .70
❑ 341 Nigel Wilson .10 .05
❑ 342 Danny Gladden .10 .05
❑ 343 Mo Sanford .10 .05
❑ 344 Sean Berry .10 .05
❑ 345 Kevin Brown .20 .09
❑ 346 Greg Olson .10 .05
❑ 347 Dave Magadan .10 .05
❑ 348 Rene Arocha .10 .05
❑ 349 Carlos Quintana .10 .05
❑ 350 Jim Abbott .20 .09
❑ 351 Gary DiSarcina .10 .05
❑ 352 Ben Rivera .10 .05
❑ 353 Carlos Hernandez .10 .05
❑ 354 Darren Lewis .10 .05
❑ 355 Harold Reynolds .10 .05
❑ 356 Scott Ruffcorn .10 .05
❑ 357 Mark Gubicza .10 .05
❑ 358 Paul Sorrento .10 .05
❑ 359 Anthony Young .10 .05
❑ 360 Mark Grace .40 .18
❑ 361 Rob Butler .10 .05
❑ 362 Kevin Bass .10 .05
❑ 363 Eric Helfand .10 .05
❑ 364 Derek Bell .10 .05
❑ 365 Scott Erickson .10 .05
❑ 366 Al Martin .10 .05
❑ 367 Ricky Bones .10 .05
❑ 368 Jeff Branson .10 .05
❑ 369 Third Base Prospects .50 .23
Luis Ortiz
David Bell RC
Jason Giambi
George Arias
❑ 370 Benito Santiago .10 .05
(See also 379)
❑ 371 John Doherty .10 .05
❑ 372 Joe Girardi .10 .05

| No. | Player | | |
|---|---|---|---|
| ❑ 373 | Tim Scott | .10 | .05 |
| ❑ 374 | Marvin Freeman | .10 | .05 |
| ❑ 375 | Deion Sanders | .20 | .09 |
| ❑ 376 | Roger Salkeld | .10 | .05 |
| ❑ 377 | Bernard Gilkey | .10 | .05 |
| ❑ 378 | Tony Fossas | .10 | .05 |
| ❑ 379 | Mark McLemore UER | .10 | .05 |
| | (Card number is 370) | | |
| ❑ 380 | Darren Daulton | .20 | .09 |
| ❑ 381 | Chuck Finley | .20 | .09 |
| ❑ 382 | Mitch Webster | .10 | .05 |
| ❑ 383 | Gerald Williams | .10 | .05 |
| ❑ 384 | Frank Thomas AS | .40 | .18 |
| | Fred McGriff AS | | |
| ❑ 385 | Roberto Alomar AS | .20 | .09 |
| | Robby Thompson AS | | |
| ❑ 386 | Wade Boggs AS | .20 | .09 |
| | Matt Williams AS | | |
| ❑ 387 | Cal Ripken AS | .40 | .18 |
| | Jeff Blauser AS | | |
| ❑ 388 | Ken Griffey Jr. AS | .40 | .18 |
| | Len Dykstra AS | | |
| ❑ 389 | Juan Gonzalez AS | .20 | .09 |
| | David Justice AS | | |
| ❑ 390 | George Belle AS | .20 | .09 |
| | Bobby Bonds AS | | |
| ❑ 391 | Mike Stanley AS | .40 | .18 |
| | Mike Piazza AS | | |
| ❑ 392 | Jack McDowell AS | .20 | .09 |
| | Greg Maddux AS | | |
| ❑ 393 | Jimmy Key AS | .20 | .09 |
| | Tom Glavine AS | | |
| ❑ 394 | Jeff Montgomery AS | .10 | .05 |
| | Randy Myers AS | | |
| ❑ 395 | Checklist 1-198 | .10 | .05 |
| ❑ 396 | Checklist 199-396 | .10 | .05 |
| ❑ 397 | Tim Salmon | .20 | .09 |
| ❑ 398 | Todd Benzinger | .10 | .05 |
| ❑ 399 | Frank Castillo | .10 | .05 |
| ❑ 400 | Ken Griffey Jr. | 1.50 | .70 |
| ❑ 401 | John Kruk | .20 | .09 |
| ❑ 402 | Dave Telgheder | .10 | .05 |
| ❑ 403 | Gary Gaetti | .20 | .09 |
| ❑ 404 | Jim Edmonds | .50 | .23 |
| ❑ 405 | Don Slaught | .10 | .05 |
| ❑ 406 | Jose Oquendo | .10 | .05 |
| ❑ 407 | Bruce Ruffin | .10 | .05 |
| ❑ 408 | Phil Clark | .10 | .05 |
| ❑ 409 | Joe Klink | .10 | .05 |
| ❑ 410 | Lou Whitaker | .20 | .09 |
| ❑ 411 | Kevin Seitzer | .10 | .05 |
| ❑ 412 | Darrin Fletcher | .10 | .05 |
| ❑ 413 | Kenny Rogers | .10 | .05 |
| ❑ 414 | Bill Pecota | .10 | .05 |
| ❑ 415 | Dave Fleming | .10 | .05 |
| ❑ 416 | Luis Alicea | .10 | .05 |
| ❑ 417 | Paul Quantrill | .10 | .05 |
| ❑ 418 | Damion Easley | .10 | .05 |
| ❑ 419 | Wes Chamberlain | .10 | .05 |
| ❑ 420 | Harold Baines | .20 | .09 |
| ❑ 421 | Scott Radinsky | .10 | .05 |
| ❑ 422 | Rey Sanchez | .10 | .05 |
| ❑ 423 | Junior Ortiz | .10 | .05 |
| ❑ 424 | Jeff Kent | .20 | .09 |
| ❑ 425 | Brian McRae | .10 | .05 |
| ❑ 426 | Ed Sprague | .10 | .05 |
| ❑ 427 | Tom Edens | .10 | .05 |
| ❑ 428 | Willie Greene | .10 | .05 |
| ❑ 429 | Bryan Hickerson | .10 | .05 |
| ❑ 430 | Dave Winfield | .40 | .18 |
| ❑ 431 | Pedro Astacio | .10 | .05 |
| ❑ 432 | Mike Gallego | .10 | .05 |
| ❑ 433 | Dave Burba | .10 | .05 |
| ❑ 434 | Bob Walk | .10 | .05 |
| ❑ 435 | Darryl Hamilton | .10 | .05 |
| ❑ 436 | Vince Horsman | .10 | .05 |
| ❑ 437 | Bob Natal | .10 | .05 |
| ❑ 438 | Mike Henneman | .10 | .05 |
| ❑ 439 | Willie Blair | .10 | .05 |
| ❑ 440 | Dennis Martinez | .20 | .09 |
| ❑ 441 | Dan Peltier | .10 | .05 |
| ❑ 442 | Tony Tarasco | .10 | .05 |
| ❑ 443 | John Cummings | .10 | .05 |
| ❑ 444 | Geronimo Pena | .10 | .05 |
| ❑ 445 | Aaron Sele | .20 | .09 |
| ❑ 446 | Stan Javier | .10 | .05 |
| ❑ 447 | Mike Williams | .10 | .05 |
| ❑ 448 | First Base Prospects | .20 | .09 |
| | Greg Pirkl | | |
| | Roberto Petagine | | |
| | D.J.Boston | | |
| | Shawn Wooten RC | | |
| ❑ 449 | Jim Poole | .10 | .05 |
| ❑ 450 | Carlos Baerga | .10 | .05 |
| ❑ 451 | Bob Scanlan | .10 | .05 |
| ❑ 452 | Lance Johnson | .10 | .05 |
| ❑ 453 | Eric Hillman | .10 | .05 |
| ❑ 454 | Keith Miller | .10 | .05 |
| ❑ 455 | Dave Stewart | .20 | .09 |
| ❑ 456 | Pete Harnisch | .10 | .05 |
| ❑ 457 | Roberto Kelly | .10 | .05 |
| ❑ 458 | Tim Worrell | .10 | .05 |
| ❑ 459 | Pedro Munoz | .10 | .05 |
| ❑ 460 | Orel Hershiser | .20 | .09 |
| ❑ 461 | Randy Velarde | .10 | .05 |
| ❑ 462 | Trevor Wilson | .10 | .05 |
| ❑ 463 | Jerry Goff | .10 | .05 |
| ❑ 464 | Bill Wegman | .10 | .05 |
| ❑ 465 | Dennis Eckersley | .20 | .09 |
| ❑ 466 | Jeff Conine | .10 | .05 |
| ❑ 467 | Joe Boever | .10 | .05 |
| ❑ 468 | Dante Bichette | .20 | .09 |
| ❑ 469 | Jeff Shaw | .10 | .05 |
| ❑ 470 | Rafael Palmeiro | .40 | .18 |
| ❑ 471 | Phil Leftwich RC | .10 | .05 |
| ❑ 472 | Jay Buhner | .20 | .09 |
| ❑ 473 | Bob Tewksbury | .10 | .05 |
| ❑ 474 | Tim Naehring | .10 | .05 |
| ❑ 475 | Tom Glavine | .40 | .18 |
| ❑ 476 | Dave Hollins | .10 | .05 |
| ❑ 477 | Arthur Rhodes | .10 | .05 |
| ❑ 478 | Joey Cora | .10 | .05 |
| ❑ 479 | Mike Morgan | .10 | .05 |
| ❑ 480 | Albert Belle | .20 | .09 |
| ❑ 481 | John Franco | .20 | .09 |
| ❑ 482 | Hipolito Pichardo | .10 | .05 |
| ❑ 483 | Duane Ward | .10 | .05 |
| ❑ 484 | Luis Gonzalez | .20 | .09 |
| ❑ 485 | Joe Oliver | .10 | .05 |
| ❑ 486 | Wally Whitehurst | .10 | .05 |
| ❑ 487 | Mike Benjamin | .10 | .05 |
| ❑ 488 | Eric Davis | .20 | .09 |
| ❑ 489 | Scott Kamieniecki | .10 | .05 |
| ❑ 490 | Kent Hrbek | .20 | .09 |
| ❑ 491 | John Hope RC | .10 | .05 |
| ❑ 492 | Jesse Orosco | .10 | .05 |
| ❑ 493 | Troy Neel | .10 | .05 |
| ❑ 494 | Ryan Bowen | .10 | .05 |
| ❑ 495 | Mickey Tettleton | .10 | .05 |
| ❑ 496 | Chris Jones | .10 | .05 |
| ❑ 497 | John Wetteland | .20 | .09 |
| ❑ 498 | David Hulse | .10 | .05 |
| ❑ 499 | Greg Maddux | 1.00 | .45 |
| ❑ 500 | Bo Jackson | .20 | .09 |
| ❑ 501 | Donovan Osborne | .10 | .05 |
| ❑ 502 | Mike Greenwell | .10 | .05 |
| ❑ 503 | Steve Frey | .10 | .05 |
| ❑ 504 | Jim Eisenreich | .10 | .05 |
| ❑ 505 | Robby Thompson | .10 | .05 |
| ❑ 506 | Leo Gomez | .10 | .05 |
| ❑ 507 | Dave Staton | .10 | .05 |
| ❑ 508 | Wayne Kirby | .10 | .05 |
| ❑ 509 | Tim Bogar | .10 | .05 |
| ❑ 510 | David Cone | .20 | .09 |
| ❑ 511 | Devon White | .10 | .05 |
| ❑ 512 | Xavier Hernandez | .10 | .05 |
| ❑ 513 | Tim Costo | .10 | .05 |
| ❑ 514 | Gene Harris | .10 | .05 |
| ❑ 515 | Jack McDowell | .10 | .05 |
| ❑ 516 | Kevin Gross | .10 | .05 |
| ❑ 517 | Scott Leius | .10 | .05 |
| ❑ 518 | Lloyd McClendon | .10 | .05 |
| ❑ 519 | Alex Diaz RC | .10 | .05 |
| ❑ 520 | Wade Boggs | .50 | .23 |
| ❑ 521 | Bob Welch | .10 | .05 |
| ❑ 522 | Henry Cotto | .10 | .05 |
| ❑ 523 | Mike Moore | .10 | .05 |
| ❑ 524 | Tim Laker | .10 | .05 |
| ❑ 525 | Andres Galarraga | .20 | .09 |
| ❑ 526 | Jamie Moyer | .10 | .05 |
| ❑ 527 | Second Base Prospects | .20 | .09 |
| | Norberto Martin | | |
| | Ruben Santana | | |
| | Jason Hardtke | | |
| | Chris Sexton RC | | |
| ❑ 528 | Sid Bream | .10 | .05 |
| ❑ 529 | Erik Hanson | .10 | .05 |
| ❑ 530 | Ray Lankford | .20 | .09 |
| ❑ 531 | Rob Deer | .10 | .05 |
| ❑ 532 | Rod Correia | .10 | .05 |
| ❑ 533 | Roger Mason | .10 | .05 |
| ❑ 534 | Mike Devereaux | .10 | .05 |
| ❑ 535 | Jeff Montgomery | .10 | .05 |
| ❑ 536 | Dwight Smith | .10 | .05 |
| ❑ 537 | Jeremy Hernandez | .10 | .05 |
| ❑ 538 | Ellis Burks | .20 | .09 |
| ❑ 539 | Bobby Jones | .10 | .05 |
| ❑ 540 | Paul Molitor | .40 | .18 |
| ❑ 541 | Jeff Juden | .10 | .05 |
| ❑ 542 | Chris Sabo | .10 | .05 |
| ❑ 543 | Larry Casian | .10 | .05 |
| ❑ 544 | Jeff Gardner | .10 | .05 |
| ❑ 545 | Ramon Martinez | .10 | .05 |
| ❑ 546 | Paul O'Neill | .20 | .09 |
| ❑ 547 | Steve Hosey | .10 | .05 |
| ❑ 548 | Dave Nilsson | .10 | .05 |
| ❑ 549 | Ron Darling | .10 | .05 |
| ❑ 550 | Matt Williams | .20 | .09 |
| ❑ 551 | Jack Armstrong | .10 | .05 |
| ❑ 552 | Bill Krueger | .10 | .05 |
| ❑ 553 | Freddie Benavides | .10 | .05 |
| ❑ 554 | Jeff Fassero | .10 | .05 |
| ❑ 555 | Chuck Knoblauch | .20 | .09 |
| ❑ 556 | Guillermo Velasquez | .10 | .05 |
| ❑ 557 | Joel Johnston | .10 | .05 |
| ❑ 558 | Tom Lampkin | .10 | .05 |
| ❑ 559 | Todd Van Poppel | .10 | .05 |
| ❑ 560 | Gary Sheffield | .40 | .18 |
| ❑ 561 | Skeeter Barnes | .10 | .05 |
| ❑ 562 | Darren Holmes | .10 | .05 |
| ❑ 563 | John Vander Wal | .10 | .05 |
| ❑ 564 | Mike Ignasiak | .10 | .05 |
| ❑ 565 | Fred McGriff | .20 | .09 |
| ❑ 566 | Luis Polonia | .10 | .05 |
| ❑ 567 | Mike Perez | .10 | .05 |
| ❑ 568 | John Valentin | .10 | .05 |
| ❑ 569 | Mike Felder | .10 | .05 |
| ❑ 570 | Tommy Greene | .10 | .05 |
| ❑ 571 | David Segui | .10 | .05 |
| ❑ 572 | Roberto Hernandez | .10 | .05 |
| ❑ 573 | Steve Wilson | .10 | .05 |
| ❑ 574 | Willie McGee | .20 | .09 |
| ❑ 575 | Randy Myers | .10 | .05 |
| ❑ 576 | Darrin Jackson | .10 | .05 |
| ❑ 577 | Eric Plunk | .10 | .05 |
| ❑ 578 | Mike Macfarlane | .10 | .05 |
| ❑ 579 | Doug Brocail | .10 | .05 |
| ❑ 580 | Steve Finley | .20 | .09 |
| ❑ 581 | John Roper | .10 | .05 |
| ❑ 582 | Danny Cox | .10 | .05 |
| ❑ 583 | Chip Hale | .10 | .05 |
| ❑ 584 | Scott Bullett | .10 | .05 |
| ❑ 585 | Kevin Reimer | .10 | .05 |
| ❑ 586 | Brent Gates | .10 | .05 |
| ❑ 587 | Matt Turner | .10 | .05 |
| ❑ 588 | Rich Rowland | .10 | .05 |
| ❑ 589 | Kent Bottenfield | .10 | .05 |
| ❑ 590 | Marquis Grissom | .10 | .05 |
| ❑ 591 | Doug Strange | .10 | .05 |
| ❑ 592 | Jay Howell | .10 | .05 |
| ❑ 593 | Omar Vizquel | .20 | .09 |
| ❑ 594 | Rheal Cormier | .10 | .05 |
| ❑ 595 | Andre Dawson | .20 | .09 |
| ❑ 596 | Hilly Hathaway | .10 | .05 |
| ❑ 597 | Todd Pratt | .10 | .05 |
| ❑ 598 | Mike Mussina | .40 | .18 |
| ❑ 599 | Alex Fernandez | .10 | .05 |
| ❑ 600 | Don Mattingly | 1.00 | .45 |
| ❑ 601 | Frank Thomas ST | .40 | .18 |
| ❑ 602 | Ryne Sandberg ST | .20 | .09 |
| ❑ 603 | Wade Boggs ST | .40 | .18 |
| ❑ 604 | Cal Ripken ST | .75 | .35 |
| ❑ 605 | Barry Bonds ST | .40 | .18 |
| ❑ 606 | Ken Griffey Jr. ST | .75 | .35 |
| ❑ 607 | Kirby Puckett ST | .50 | .23 |
| ❑ 608 | Darren Daulton ST | .10 | .05 |
| ❑ 609 | Paul Molitor ST | .20 | .09 |
| ❑ 610 | Terry Steinbach | .10 | .05 |

❑ 611 Todd Worrell .10 .05
❑ 612 Jim Thome .20 .09
❑ 613 Chuck McElroy .10 .05
❑ 614 John Habyan .10 .05
❑ 615 Sid Fernandez .10 .05
❑ 616 Outfield Prospects .20 .09
Eddie Zambrano
Glenn Murray
Chad Mottola
Jermaine Allensworth RC
❑ 617 Steve Bedrosian .10 .05
❑ 618 Rob Ducey .10 .05
❑ 619 Tom Browning .10 .05
❑ 620 Tony Gwynn .75 .35
❑ 621 Carl Willis .10 .05
❑ 622 Kevin Young .10 .05
❑ 623 Rafael Novoa .10 .05
❑ 624 Jerry Browne .10 .05
❑ 625 Charlie Hough .20 .09
❑ 626 Chris Gomez .10 .05
❑ 627 Steve Reed .10 .05
❑ 628 Kirk Rueter .10 .05
❑ 629 Matt Whiteside .10 .05
❑ 630 David Justice .20 .09
❑ 631 Brad Holman .10 .05
❑ 632 Brian Jordan .20 .09
❑ 633 Scott Bankhead .10 .05
❑ 634 Torey Lovullo .10 .05
❑ 635 Len Dykstra .20 .09
❑ 636 Ben McDonald .10 .05
❑ 637 Steve Howe .10 .05
❑ 638 Jose Vizcaino .10 .05
❑ 639 Bill Swift .10 .05
❑ 640 Darryl Strawberry .20 .09
❑ 641 Steve Farr .10 .05
❑ 642 Tom Kramer .10 .05
❑ 643 Joe Orsulak .10 .05
❑ 644 Tom Henke .10 .05
❑ 645 Joe Carter .20 .09
❑ 646 Ken Caminiti .20 .09
❑ 647 Reggie Sanders .10 .05
❑ 648 Andy Ashby .10 .05
❑ 649 Derek Parks .10 .05
❑ 650 Andy Van Slyke .20 .09
❑ 651 Juan Bell .10 .05
❑ 652 Roger Smithberg .10 .05
❑ 653 Chuck Carr .10 .05
❑ 654 Bill Gullickson .10 .05
❑ 655 Charlie Hayes .10 .05
❑ 656 Chris Nabholz .10 .05
❑ 657 Karl Rhodes .10 .05
❑ 658 Pete Smith .10 .05
❑ 659 Bret Boone .20 .09
❑ 660 Gregg Jefferies .10 .05
❑ 661 Bob Zupcic .10 .05
❑ 662 Steve Sax .10 .05
❑ 663 Mariano Duncan .10 .05
❑ 664 Jeff Tackett .10 .05
❑ 665 Mark Langston .10 .05
❑ 666 Steve Buechele .10 .05
❑ 667 Candy Maldonado .10 .05
❑ 668 Woody Williams .10 .05
❑ 669 Tim Wakefield .10 .05
❑ 670 Danny Tartabull .10 .05
❑ 671 Charlie O'Brien .10 .05
❑ 672 Felix Jose .10 .05
❑ 673 Bobby Ayala .10 .05
❑ 674 Scott Servais .10 .05
❑ 675 Roberto Alomar .40 .18
❑ 676 Pedro A.Martinez RC .10 .05
❑ 677 Eddie Guardado .10 .05
❑ 678 Mark Lewis .10 .05
❑ 679 Jaime Navarro .10 .05
❑ 680 Ruben Sierrra .10 .05
❑ 681 Rick Renteria .10 .05
❑ 682 Storm Davis .10 .05
❑ 683 Cory Snyder .10 .05
❑ 684 Ron Karkovice .10 .05
❑ 685 Juan Gonzalez .40 .18
❑ 686 Catchers Prospects 1.00 .45
Chris Howard
Carlos Delgado
Jason Kendall
Paul Bako
❑ 687 John Smoltz .20 .09
❑ 688 Brian Dorsett .10 .05
❑ 689 Omar Olivares .10 .05
❑ 690 Mo Vaughn .20 .09
❑ 691 Joe Grahe .10 .05
❑ 692 Mickey Morandini .10 .05
❑ 693 Tino Martinez .20 .09
❑ 694 Brian Barnes .10 .05
❑ 695 Mike Stanley .10 .05
❑ 696 Mark Clark .10 .05
❑ 697 Dave Hansen .10 .05
❑ 698 Willie Wilson .10 .05
❑ 699 Pete Schourek .10 .05
❑ 700 Barry Bonds .60 .25
❑ 701 Kevin Appier .20 .09
❑ 702 Tony Fernandez .10 .05
❑ 703 Darryl Kile .20 .09
❑ 704 Archi Cianfrocco .10 .05
❑ 705 Jose Rijo .10 .05
❑ 706 Brian Harper .10 .05
❑ 707 Zane Smith .10 .05
❑ 708 Dave Henderson .10 .05
❑ 709 Angel Miranda UER .10 .05
(No Topps logo on back)
❑ 710 Orestes Destrade .10 .05
❑ 711 Greg Gohr .10 .05
❑ 712 Eric Young .10 .05
❑ 713 Relief Pitchers .10 .05
Prospects
Todd Williams
Ron Watson
Kirk Bullinger
Mike Welch
❑ 714 Tim Spehr .10 .05
❑ 715 Hank Aaron 715 HR .50 .23
❑ 716 Nate Minchey .10 .05
❑ 717 Mike Blowers .10 .05
❑ 718 Kent Mercker .10 .05
❑ 719 Tom Pagnozzi .10 .05
❑ 720 Roger Clemens .75 .35
❑ 721 Eduardo Perez .10 .05
❑ 722 Milt Thompson .10 .05
❑ 723 Gregg Olson .10 .05
❑ 724 Kirk McCaskill .10 .05
❑ 725 Sammy Sosa .75 .35
❑ 726 Alvaro Espinoza .10 .05
❑ 727 Henry Rodriguez .10 .05
❑ 728 Jim Leyritz .10 .05
❑ 729 Steve Scarsone .10 .05
❑ 730 Bobby Bonilla .20 .09
❑ 731 Chris Gwynn .10 .05
❑ 732 Al Leiter .20 .09
❑ 733 Bip Roberts .10 .05
❑ 734 Mark Portugal .10 .05
❑ 735 Terry Pendleton .20 .09
❑ 736 Dave Valle .10 .05
❑ 737 Paul Kilgus .10 .05
❑ 738 Greg A. Harris .10 .05
❑ 739 Jon Ratliff DP RC .10 .05
❑ 740 Kirk Presley DP RC .10 .05
❑ 741 Josue Estrada DP RC .20 .09
❑ 742 Wayne Gomes DP RC .10 .05
❑ 743 Pat Watkins DP RC .20 .09
❑ 744 Jamey Wright DP RC .20 .09
❑ 745 Jay Powell DP RC .20 .09
❑ 746 Ryan McGuire DP RC .20 .09
❑ 747 Marc Barcelo DP RC .20 .09
❑ 748 Sloan Smith DP RC .10 .05
❑ 749 John Wasdin DP RC .20 .09
❑ 750 Marc Vlades .10 .05
❑ 751 Dan Ehler DP RC .10 .05
❑ 752 Andre King DP RC .10 .05
❑ 753 Greg Keagle DP RC .10 .05
❑ 754 Jason Myers DP RC .10 .05
❑ 755 Dax Winslett DP RC .10 .05
❑ 756 Casey Whitten DP RC .20 .09
❑ 757 Tony Fuduric DP RC .10 .05
❑ 758 Greg Norton DP RC .20 .09
❑ 759 Jeff D'Amico DP RC .50 .23
❑ 760 Ryan Hancock DP RC .10 .05
❑ 761 David Cooper DP RC .10 .05
❑ 762 Kevin Orie DP RC .20 .09
❑ 763 John O'Donoghue .10 .05
Mike Oquist
❑ 764 Cory Bailey RC .10 .05
Scott Hatteberg
❑ 765 Mark Holzemer .10 .05
Paul Swingle
❑ 766 James Baldwin .20 .09
Rod Bolton
❑ 767 Jerry Di Poto .10 .05
Julian Tavarez RC
❑ 768 Danny Bautista .10 .05
Sean Bergman
❑ 769 Bob Hamelin .10 .05
Joe Vitiello
❑ 770 Mark Kiefer .10 .05
Troy O'Leary
❑ 771 Denny Hocking .20 .09
Oscar Munoz RC
❑ 772 Russ Davis .10 .05
Brien Taylor
❑ 773 Kyle Abbott RC .10 .05
Miguel Jimenez
❑ 774 Kevin King .10 .05
Eric Plantenberg RC
❑ 775 Jon Shave .10 .05
Desi Wilson
❑ 776 Domingo Cedeno .10 .05
Paul Spoljaric
❑ 777 Chipper Jones 1.00 .45
Ryan Klesko
❑ 778 Steve Trachsel .10 .05
Turk Wendell
❑ 779 Johnny Ruffin .10 .05
Jerry Spradlin RC
❑ 780 Jason Bates .10 .05
John Burke
❑ 781 Carl Everett .20 .09
Dave Weathers
❑ 782 Gary Mota .20 .09
James Mouton
❑ 783 Raul Mondesi .20 .09
Ben Van Ryn
❑ 784 Gabe White .20 .09
Rondell White
❑ 785 Brook Fordyce .20 .09
Bill Pulsipher
❑ 786 Kevin Foste RCr .10 .05
Gene Schall
❑ 787 Rich Aude RC .10 .05
Midre Cummings
❑ 788 Brian Barber .20 .09
Rich Batchelor
❑ 789 Brian Johnson RC .10 .05
Scott Sanders
❑ 790 Ricky Faneyte .10 .05
J.R. Phillips
❑ 791 Checklist 3 .10 .05
❑ 792 Checklist 4 .10 .05

## 1994 Topps Traded

| | MINT | NRMT |
|---|---|---|
| COMP.FACT.SET (140) | 50.00 | 22.00 |

❑ 1T Paul Wilson .25 .11
❑ 2T Bill Taylor RC .15 .07
❑ 3T Dan Wilson .15 .07
❑ 4T Mark Smith .15 .07
❑ 5T Toby Borland RC .15 .07
❑ 6T Dave Clark .15 .07
❑ 7T Dennis Martinez .25 .11
❑ 8T Dave Gallagher .15 .07
❑ 9T Josias Manzanillo .15 .07
❑ 10T Brian Anderson RC 1.00 .45

❑ 11T Damon Berryhill .15 .07
❑ 12T Alex Cole .15 .07
❑ 13T Jacob Shumate RC .25 .11
❑ 14T Oddibe McDowell .15 .07
❑ 15T Willie Banks .15 .07
❑ 16T Jerry Browne .15 .07
❑ 17T Donnie Elliott .15 .07
❑ 18T Ellis Burks .25 .11
❑ 19T Chuck McElroy .15 .07
❑ 20T Luis Polonia .15 .07
❑ 21T Brian Harper .15 .07
❑ 22T Mark Portugal .15 .07
❑ 23T Dave Henderson .15 .07
❑ 24T Mark Acre RC .15 .07
❑ 25T Julio Franco .15 .07
❑ 26T Darren Hall RC .15 .07
❑ 27T Eric Anthony .15 .07
❑ 28T Sid Fernandez .15 .07
❑ 29T Rusty Greer RC 3.00 1.35
❑ 30T Riccardo Ingram RC .15 .07
❑ 31T Gabe White .15 .07
❑ 32T Tim Belcher .15 .07
❑ 33T Terrence Long RC 8.00 3.60
❑ 34T Mark Dalesandro RC .15 .07
❑ 35T Mike Kelly .15 .07
❑ 36T Jack Morris .25 .11
❑ 37T Jeff Brantley .15 .07
❑ 38T Larry Barnes RC .25 .11
❑ 39T Brian R. Hunter .15 .07
❑ 40T Otis Nixon .15 .07
❑ 41T Bret Wagner .15 .07
❑ 42T Pedro Martinez TR 1.00 .45
Delino Deshields
❑ 43T Heathcliff Slocumb .15 .07
❑ 44T Ben Grieve RC 20.00 9.00
❑ 45T John Hudek RC .15 .07
❑ 46T Shawon Dunston .15 .07
❑ 47T Greg Colbrunn .15 .07
❑ 48T Joey Hamilton .15 .07
❑ 49T Marvin Freeman .15 .07
❑ 50T Terry Mulholland .15 .07
❑ 51T Keith Mitchell .15 .07
❑ 52T Dwight Smith .15 .07
❑ 53T Shawn Boskie .15 .07
❑ 54T Kevin Witt RC 1.00 .45
❑ 55T Ron Gant .25 .11
❑ 56T 1994 Prospects 1.00 .45
Trenidad Hubbard
Jason Schmidt RC
Larry Sutton
Stephen Larkin
❑ 57T Jody Reed .15 .07
❑ 58T Rick Helling .25 .11
❑ 59T John Powell .25 .11
❑ 60T Eddie Murray .50 .23
❑ 61T Joe Hall RC .15 .07
❑ 62T Jorge Fabregas .15 .07
❑ 63T Mike Mordecai RC .15 .07
❑ 64T Ed Vosberg .15 .07
❑ 65T Rickey Henderson .60 .25
❑ 66T Tim Grieve RC .15 .07
❑ 67T Jon Lieber .15 .07
❑ 68T Chris Howard .15 .07
❑ 69T Matt Walbeck .15 .07
❑ 70T Chan Ho Park RC 4.00 1.80
❑ 71T Bryan Eversgerd RC .15 .07
❑ 72T John Dettmer .15 .07
❑ 73T Erik Hanson .15 .07
❑ 74T Mike Thurman RC .15 .07
❑ 75T Bobby Ayala .15 .07
❑ 76T Rafael Palmeiro .50 .23
❑ 77T Bret Boone .25 .11
❑ 78T Paul Shuey .15 .07
❑ 79T Kevin Foster RC .15 .07
❑ 80T Dave Magadan .15 .07
❑ 81T Bip Roberts .15 .07
❑ 82T Howard Johnson .15 .07
❑ 83T Xavier Hernandez .15 .07
❑ 84T Ross Powell RC .15 .07
❑ 85T Doug Million RC .15 .07
❑ 86T Geronimo Berroa .15 .07
❑ 87T Mark Farris RC .25 .11
❑ 88T Butch Henry .15 .07
❑ 89T Junior Felix .15 .07
❑ 90T Bo Jackson .25 .11
❑ 91T Hector Carrasco .15 .07
❑ 92T Charlie O'Brien .15 .07
❑ 93T Omar Vizquel .25 .11
❑ 94T David Segui .15 .07
❑ 95T Dustin Hermanson .25 .11
❑ 96T Gar Finnvold RC .15 .07
❑ 97T Dave Stevens .15 .07
❑ 98T Corey Pointer RC .15 .07
❑ 99T Felix Fermin .15 .07
❑ 100T Lee Smith .25 .11
❑ 101T Reid Ryan RC .25 .11
❑ 102T Bobby Munoz .15 .07
❑ 103T Deion Sanders TR .25 .11
Roberto Kelly
❑ 104T Turner Ward .15 .07
❑ 105T W.VanLandingham RC .15 .07
❑ 106T Vince Coleman .15 .07
❑ 107T Stan Javier .15 .07
❑ 108T Darrin Jackson .15 .07
❑ 109T C.J. Nitkowski RC .15 .07
❑ 110T Anthony Young .15 .07
❑ 111T Kurt Miller .15 .07
❑ 112T Paul Konerko RC 8.00 3.60
❑ 113T Walt Weiss .15 .07
❑ 114T Daryl Boston .15 .07
❑ 115T Will Clark .50 .23
❑ 116T Matt Smith RC .25 .11
❑ 117T Mark Leiter .15 .07
❑ 118T Gregg Olson .15 .07
❑ 119T Tony Pena .15 .07
❑ 120T Jose Vizcaino .15 .07
❑ 121T Rick White RC .15 .07
❑ 122T Rich Rowland .15 .07
❑ 123T Jeff Reboulet .15 .07
❑ 124T Greg Hibbard .15 .07
❑ 125T Chris Sabo .15 .07
❑ 126T Doug Jones .15 .07
❑ 127T Tony Fernandez .15 .07
❑ 128T Carlos Reyes RC .15 .07
❑ 129T Kevin L.Brown RC .50 .23
❑ 130T Ryne Sandberg 1.00 .45
Farewell
❑ 131T Ryne Sandberg 1.00 .45
Farewell
❑ 132T Checklist 1-132 .15 .07

## 1995 Topps

| | MINT | NRMT |
|---|---|---|
| COMPLETE SET (660) | 60.00 | 27.00 |
| COMP.HOBBY SET (677) | 100.00 | 45.00 |
| COMP.RETAIL SET (677) | 80.00 | 36.00 |
| COMPLETE SERIES 1 (396) | 30.00 | 13.50 |
| COMPLETE SERIES 2 (264) | 30.00 | 13.50 |
| COMMON CARD (1-660) | .15 | .07 |

❑ 1 Frank Thomas 1.25 .55
❑ 2 Mickey Morandini .15 .07
❑ 3 Babe Ruth 100th B-Day 2.00 .90
❑ 4 Scott Cooper .15 .07
❑ 5 David Cone .25 .11
❑ 6 Jacob Shumate .15 .07
❑ 7 Trevor Hoffman .25 .11
❑ 8 Shane Mack .15 .07
❑ 9 Delino DeShields .15 .07
❑ 10 Matt Williams .40 .18
❑ 11 Sammy Sosa 1.25 .55
❑ 12 Gary DiSarcina .15 .07
❑ 13 Kenny Rogers .15 .07
❑ 14 Jose Vizcaino .15 .07
❑ 15 Lou Whitaker .25 .11
❑ 16 Ron Darling .15 .07
❑ 17 Dave Nilsson .15 .07
❑ 18 Chris Hammond .15 .07
❑ 19 Sid Bream .15 .07
❑ 20 Denny Martinez .25 .11
❑ 21 Orlando Merced .15 .07
❑ 22 John Wetteland .25 .11
❑ 23 Mike Devereaux .15 .07
❑ 24 Rene Arocha .15 .07
❑ 25 Jay Buhner .25 .11
❑ 26 Darren Holmes .15 .07
❑ 27 Hal Morris .15 .07
❑ 28 Brian Buchanan RC .15 .07
❑ 29 Keith Miller .15 .07
❑ 30 Paul Molitor .60 .25
❑ 31 Dave West .15 .07
❑ 32 Tony Tarasco .15 .07
❑ 33 Scott Sanders .15 .07
❑ 34 Eddie Zambrano .15 .07
❑ 35 Ricky Bones .15 .07
❑ 36 John Valentin .15 .07
❑ 37 Kevin Tapani .15 .07
❑ 38 Tim Wallach .15 .07
❑ 39 Darren Lewis .15 .07
❑ 40 Travis Fryman .25 .11
❑ 41 Mark Leiter .15 .07
❑ 42 Jose Bautista .15 .07
❑ 43 Pete Smith .15 .07
❑ 44 Bret Barberie .15 .07
❑ 45 Dennis Eckersley .25 .11
❑ 46 Ken Hill .15 .07
❑ 47 Chad Ogea .15 .07
❑ 48 Pete Harnisch .15 .07
❑ 49 James Baldwin .25 .11
❑ 50 Mike Mussina .60 .25
❑ 51 Al Martin .15 .07
❑ 52 Mark Thompson .15 .07
❑ 53 Matt Smith .15 .07
❑ 54 Joey Hamilton .15 .07
❑ 55 Edgar Martinez .40 .18
❑ 56 John Smiley .15 .07
❑ 57 Rey Sanchez .15 .07
❑ 58 Mike Timlin .15 .07
❑ 59 Ricky Bottalico .15 .07
❑ 60 Jim Abbott .25 .11
❑ 61 Mike Kelly .15 .07
❑ 62 Brian Jordan .25 .11
❑ 63 Ken Ryan .15 .07
❑ 64 Matt Mieske .15 .07
❑ 65 Rick Aguilera .15 .07
❑ 66 Ismael Valdes .15 .07
❑ 67 Royce Clayton .15 .07
❑ 68 Junior Felix .15 .07
❑ 69 Harold Reynolds .15 .07
❑ 70 Juan Gonzalez .60 .25
❑ 71 Kelly Stinnett .15 .07
❑ 72 Carlos Reyes .15 .07
❑ 73 Dave Weathers .15 .07
❑ 74 Mel Rojas .15 .07
❑ 75 Doug Drabek .15 .07
❑ 76 Charles Nagy .15 .07
❑ 77 Tim Raines .25 .11
❑ 78 Midre Cummings .15 .07
❑ 79 First Base Prospects .15 .07
Gene Schall
Scott Talanoa
Harold Williams
Ray Brown RC
❑ 80 Rafael Palmeiro .60 .25
❑ 81 Charlie Hayes .15 .07
❑ 82 Ray Lankford .25 .11
❑ 83 Tim Davis .15 .07
❑ 84 C.J. Nitkowski .15 .07
❑ 85 Andy Ashby .15 .07
❑ 86 Gerald Williams .15 .07
❑ 87 Terry Shumpert .15 .07
❑ 88 Heathcliff Slocumb .15 .07
❑ 89 Domingo Cedeno .15 .07
❑ 90 Mark Grace .60 .25
❑ 91 Brad Woodall RC .15 .07
❑ 92 Gar Finnvold .15 .07
❑ 93 Jaime Navarro .15 .07
❑ 94 Carlos Hernandez .15 .07
❑ 95 Mark Langston .15 .07

❑ 96 Chuck Carr .15 .07
❑ 97 Mike Gardiner .15 .07
❑ 98 Dave McCarty .15 .07
❑ 99 Cris Carpenter .15 .07
❑ 100 Barry Bonds 1.00 .45
❑ 101 David Segui .15 .07
❑ 102 Scott Brosius .25 .11
❑ 103 Mariano Duncan .15 .07
❑ 104 Kenny Lofton .25 .11
❑ 105 Ken Caminiti .25 .11
❑ 106 Darrin Jackson .15 .07
❑ 107 Jim Poole .15 .07
❑ 108 Wil Cordero .15 .07
❑ 109 Danny Miceli .15 .07
❑ 110 Walt Weiss .15 .07
❑ 111 Tom Pagnozzi .15 .07
❑ 112 Terrence Long .60 .25
❑ 113 Bret Boone .25 .11
❑ 114 Daryl Boston .15 .07
❑ 115 Wally Joyner .25 .11
❑ 116 Rob Butler .15 .07
❑ 117 Rafael Belliard .15 .07
❑ 118 Luis Lopez .15 .07
❑ 119 Tony Fossas .15 .07
❑ 120 Len Dykstra .25 .11
❑ 121 Mike Morgan .15 .07
❑ 122 Denny Hocking .15 .07
❑ 123 Kevin Gross .15 .07
❑ 124 Todd Benzinger .15 .07
❑ 125 John Doherty .15 .07
❑ 126 Eduardo Perez .15 .07
❑ 127 Dan Smith .15 .07
❑ 128 Joe Orsulak .15 .07
❑ 129 Brent Gates .15 .07
❑ 130 Jeff Conine .15 .07
❑ 131 Doug Henry .15 .07
❑ 132 Paul Sorrento .15 .07
❑ 133 Mike Hampton .25 .11
❑ 134 Tim Spehr .15 .07
❑ 135 Julio Franco .25 .11
❑ 136 Mike Dyer .15 .07
❑ 137 Chris Sabo .15 .07
❑ 138 Rheal Cormier .15 .07
❑ 139 Paul Konerko .60 .25
❑ 140 Dante Bichette .25 .11
❑ 141 Chuck McElroy .15 .07
❑ 142 Mike Stanley .15 .07
❑ 143 Bob Hamelin .15 .07
❑ 144 Tommy Greene .15 .07
❑ 145 John Smoltz .25 .11
❑ 146 Ed Sprague .15 .07
❑ 147 Ray McDavid .15 .07
❑ 148 Otis Nixon .15 .07
❑ 149 Turk Wendell .15 .07
❑ 150 Chris James .15 .07
❑ 151 Derek Parks .15 .07
❑ 152 Jose Offerman .15 .07
❑ 153 Tony Clark .25 .11
❑ 154 Chad Curtis .15 .07
❑ 155 Mark Portugal .15 .07
❑ 156 Bill Pulsipher .15 .07
❑ 157 Troy Neel .15 .07
❑ 158 Dave Winfield .60 .25
❑ 159 Bill Wegman .15 .07
❑ 160 Benito Santiago .15 .07
❑ 161 Jose Mesa .15 .07
❑ 162 Luis Gonzalez .25 .11
❑ 163 Alex Fernandez .15 .07
❑ 164 Freddie Benavides .15 .07
❑ 165 Ben McDonald .15 .07
❑ 166 Blas Minor .15 .07
❑ 167 Bret Wagner .15 .07
❑ 168 Mac Suzuki .15 .07
❑ 169 Roberto Mejia .15 .07
❑ 170 Wade Boggs .75 .35
❑ 171 Pokey Reese .25 .11
❑ 172 Hipolito Pichardo .15 .07
❑ 173 Kim Batiste .15 .07
❑ 174 Darren Hall .15 .07
❑ 175 Tom Glavine .60 .25
❑ 176 Phil Plantier .15 .07
❑ 177 Chris Howard .15 .07
❑ 178 Karl Rhodes .15 .07
❑ 179 LaTroy Hawkins .15 .07
❑ 180 Raul Mondesi .25 .11
❑ 181 Jeff Reed .15 .07
❑ 182 Milt Cuyler .15 .07
❑ 183 Jim Edmonds .60 .25
❑ 184 Hector Fajardo .15 .07
❑ 185 Jeff Kent .40 .18
❑ 186 Wilson Alvarez .15 .07
❑ 187 Geronimo Berroa .15 .07
❑ 188 Billy Spiers .15 .07
❑ 189 Derek Lilliquist .15 .07
❑ 190 Craig Biggio .40 .18
❑ 191 Roberto Hernandez .15 .07
❑ 192 Bob Natal .15 .07
❑ 193 Bobby Ayala .15 .07
❑ 194 Travis Miller RC .15 .07
❑ 195 Bob Tewksbury .15 .07
❑ 196 Rondell White .25 .11
❑ 197 Steve Cooke .15 .07
❑ 198 Jeff Branson .15 .07
❑ 199 Derek Jeter 2.50 1.10
❑ 200 Tim Salmon .25 .11
❑ 201 Steve Frey .15 .07
❑ 202 Kent Mercker .15 .07
❑ 203 Randy Johnson .75 .35
❑ 204 Todd Worrell .15 .07
❑ 205 Mo Vaughn .25 .11
❑ 206 Howard Johnson .15 .07
❑ 207 John Wasdin .15 .07
❑ 208 Eddie Williams .15 .07
❑ 209 Tim Belcher .15 .07
❑ 210 Jeff Montgomery .15 .07
❑ 211 Kirt Manwaring .15 .07
❑ 212 Ben Grieve 1.00 .45
❑ 213 Pat Hentgen .15 .07
❑ 214 Shawon Dunston .15 .07
❑ 215 Mike Greenwell .15 .07
❑ 216 Alex Diaz .15 .07
❑ 217 Pat Mahomes .15 .07
❑ 218 Dave Hansen .15 .07
❑ 219 Kevin Rogers .15 .07
❑ 220 Cecil Fielder .25 .11
❑ 221 Andrew Lorraine .15 .07
❑ 222 Jack Armstrong .15 .07
❑ 223 Todd Hundley .15 .07
❑ 224 Mark Acre .15 .07
❑ 225 Darrell Whitmore .15 .07
❑ 226 Randy Milligan .15 .07
❑ 227 Wayne Kirby .15 .07
❑ 228 Darryl Kile .25 .11
❑ 229 Bob Zupcic .15 .07
❑ 230 Jay Bell .25 .11
❑ 231 Dustin Hermanson .15 .07
❑ 232 Harold Baines .25 .11
❑ 233 Alan Benes .15 .07
❑ 234 Felix Fermin .15 .07
❑ 235 Ellis Burks .25 .11
❑ 236 Jeff Brantley .15 .07
❑ 237 Outfield Prospects .25 .11
Brian Hunter
Jose Malave
Karim Garcia RC
Shane Pullen
❑ 238 Matt Nokes .15 .07
❑ 239 Ben Rivera .15 .07
❑ 240 Joe Carter .25 .11
❑ 241 Jeff Granger .15 .07
❑ 242 Terry Pendleton .25 .11
❑ 243 Melvin Nieves .15 .07
❑ 244 Frankie Rodriguez .15 .07
❑ 245 Darryl Hamilton .15 .07
❑ 246 Brooks Kieschnick .15 .07
❑ 247 Todd Hollandsworth .15 .07
❑ 248 Joe Rosselli .15 .07
❑ 249 Bill Gullickson .15 .07
❑ 250 Chuck Knoblauch .25 .11
❑ 251 Kurt Miller .15 .07
❑ 252 Bobby Jones .15 .07
❑ 253 Lance Blankenship .15 .07
❑ 254 Matt Whiteside .15 .07
❑ 255 Darrin Fletcher .15 .07
❑ 256 Eric Plunk .15 .07
❑ 257 Shane Reynolds .15 .07
❑ 258 Norberto Martin .15 .07
❑ 259 Mike Thurman .15 .07
❑ 260 Andy Van Slyke .25 .11
❑ 261 Dwight Smith .15 .07
❑ 262 Allen Watson .15 .07
❑ 263 Dan Wilson .15 .07
❑ 264 Brent Mayne .15 .07
❑ 265 Bip Roberts .15 .07
❑ 266 Sterling Hitchcock .15 .07
❑ 267 Alex Gonzalez .15 .07
❑ 268 Greg Harris .15 .07
❑ 269 Ricky Jordan .15 .07
❑ 270 Johnny Ruffin .15 .07
❑ 271 Mike Stanton .15 .07
❑ 272 Rich Rowland .15 .07
❑ 273 Steve Trachsel .15 .07
❑ 274 Pedro Munoz .15 .07
❑ 275 Ramon Martinez .15 .07
❑ 276 Dave Henderson .15 .07
❑ 277 Chris Gomez .15 .07
❑ 278 Joe Grahe .15 .07
❑ 279 Rusty Greer .25 .11
❑ 280 John Franco .25 .11
❑ 281 Mike Bordick .15 .07
❑ 282 Jeff D'Amico .25 .11
❑ 283 Dave Magadan .15 .07
❑ 284 Tony Pena .15 .07
❑ 285 Greg Swindell .15 .07
❑ 286 Doug Million .15 .07
❑ 287 Gabe White .15 .07
❑ 288 Trey Beamon .15 .07
❑ 289 Arthur Rhodes .15 .07
❑ 290 Juan Guzman .15 .07
❑ 291 Jose Oquendo .15 .07
❑ 292 Willie Blair .15 .07
❑ 293 Eddie Taubensee .15 .07
❑ 294 Steve Howe .15 .07
❑ 295 Greg Maddux 1.50 .70
❑ 296 Mike Macfarlane .15 .07
❑ 297 Curt Schilling .25 .11
❑ 298 Phil Clark .15 .07
❑ 299 Woody Williams .15 .07
❑ 300 Jose Canseco .75 .35
❑ 301 Aaron Sele .25 .11
❑ 302 Carl Willis .15 .07
❑ 303 Steve Buechele .15 .07
❑ 304 Dave Burba .15 .07
❑ 305 Orel Hershiser .25 .11
❑ 306 Damion Easley .15 .07
❑ 307 Mike Henneman .15 .07
❑ 308 Josias Manzanillo .15 .07
❑ 309 Kevin Seitzer .15 .07
❑ 310 Ruben Sierra .15 .07
❑ 311 Bryan Harvey .15 .07
❑ 312 Jim Thome .40 .18
❑ 313 Ramon Castro RC .25 .11
❑ 314 Lance Johnson .15 .07
❑ 315 Marquis Grissom .15 .07
❑ 316 Starting Pitcher .15 .07
Prospects
Terrell Wade
Juan Acevedo
Matt Arrandale
Eddie Priest RC
❑ 317 Paul Wagner .15 .07
❑ 318 Jamie Moyer .15 .07
❑ 319 Todd Zeile .15 .07
❑ 320 Chris Bosio .15 .07
❑ 321 Steve Reed .15 .07
❑ 322 Erik Hanson .15 .07
❑ 323 Luis Polonia .15 .07
❑ 324 Ryan Klesko .25 .11
❑ 325 Kevin Appier .25 .11
❑ 326 Jim Eisenreich .15 .07
❑ 327 Randy Knorr .15 .07
❑ 328 Craig Shipley .15 .07
❑ 329 Tim Naehring .15 .07
❑ 330 Randy Myers .15 .07
❑ 331 Alex Cole .15 .07
❑ 332 Jim Gott .15 .07
❑ 333 Mike Jackson .15 .07
❑ 334 John Flaherty .15 .07
❑ 335 Chili Davis .25 .11
❑ 336 Benji Gil .15 .07
❑ 337 Jason Jacome .15 .07
❑ 338 Stan Javier .15 .07
❑ 339 Mike Fetters .15 .07
❑ 340 Rich Renteria .15 .07
❑ 341 Kevin Witt .25 .11
❑ 342 Scott Servais .15 .07
❑ 343 Craig Grebeck .15 .07
❑ 344 Kirk Rueter .15 .07

| No. | Card | | |
|---|---|---|---|
| ❑ 345 | Don Slaught | .15 | .07 |
| ❑ 346 | Armando Benitez | .25 | .11 |
| ❑ 347 | Ozzie Smith | .75 | .35 |
| ❑ 348 | Mike Blowers | .15 | .07 |
| ❑ 349 | Armando Reynoso | .15 | .07 |
| ❑ 350 | Barry Larkin | .60 | .25 |
| ❑ 351 | Mike Williams | .15 | .07 |
| ❑ 352 | Scott Kamieniecki | .15 | .07 |
| ❑ 353 | Gary Gaetti | .25 | .11 |
| ❑ 354 | Todd Stottlemyre | .15 | .07 |
| ❑ 355 | Fred McGriff | .40 | .18 |
| ❑ 356 | Tim Mauser | .15 | .07 |
| ❑ 357 | Chris Gwynn | .15 | .07 |
| ❑ 358 | Frank Castillo | .15 | .07 |
| ❑ 359 | Jeff Reboulet | .15 | .07 |
| ❑ 360 | Roger Clemens | 1.25 | .55 |
| ❑ 361 | Mark Carreon | .15 | .07 |
| ❑ 362 | Chad Kreuter | .15 | .07 |
| ❑ 363 | Mark Farris | .15 | .07 |
| ❑ 364 | Bob Welch | .15 | .07 |
| ❑ 365 | Dean Palmer | .25 | .11 |
| ❑ 366 | Jeromy Burnitz | .25 | .11 |
| ❑ 367 | B.J. Surhoff | .25 | .11 |
| ❑ 368 | Mike Butcher | .15 | .07 |
| ❑ 369 | Relief Pitcher | .25 | .11 |
| | Prospects | | |
| | Brad Clontz | | |
| | Steve Phoenix | | |
| | Scott Gentile | | |
| | Bucky Buckles RC | | |
| ❑ 370 | Eddie Murray | .60 | .25 |
| ❑ 371 | Orlando Miller | .15 | .07 |
| ❑ 372 | Ron Karkovice | .15 | .07 |
| ❑ 373 | Richie Lewis | .15 | .07 |
| ❑ 374 | Lenny Webster | .15 | .07 |
| ❑ 375 | Jeff Tackett | .15 | .07 |
| ❑ 376 | Tom Urbani | .15 | .07 |
| ❑ 377 | Tino Martinez | .25 | .11 |
| ❑ 378 | Mark Dewey | .15 | .07 |
| ❑ 379 | Charles O'Brien | .15 | .07 |
| ❑ 380 | Terry Mulholland | .15 | .07 |
| ❑ 381 | Thomas Howard | .15 | .07 |
| ❑ 382 | Chris Haney | .15 | .07 |
| ❑ 383 | Billy Hatcher | .15 | .07 |
| ❑ 384 | Jeff Bagwell AS | .60 | .25 |
| | Frank Thomas AS | | |
| ❑ 385 | Bret Boone AS | .15 | .07 |
| | Carlos Baerga AS | | |
| ❑ 386 | Matt Williams AS | .40 | .18 |
| | Wade Boggs AS | | |
| ❑ 387 | Wil Cordero AS | .60 | .25 |
| | Cal Ripken AS | | |
| ❑ 388 | Barry Bonds AS | .60 | .25 |
| | Ken Griffey AS | | |
| ❑ 389 | Tony Gwynn AS | .25 | .11 |
| | Albert Belle AS | | |
| ❑ 390 | Dante Bichette AS | .60 | .25 |
| | Kirby Puckett AS | | |
| ❑ 391 | Mike Piazza AS | .60 | .25 |
| | Mike Stanley AS | | |
| ❑ 392 | Greg Maddux AS | .25 | .11 |
| | David Cone AS | | |
| ❑ 393 | Danny Jackson AS | .15 | .07 |
| | Jimmy Key AS | | |
| ❑ 394 | John Franco AS | .15 | .07 |
| | Lee Smith AS | | |
| ❑ 395 | Checklist 1-198 | .15 | .07 |
| ❑ 396 | Checklist 199-396 | .15 | .07 |
| ❑ 397 | Ken Griffey Jr. | 2.50 | 1.10 |
| ❑ 398 | Rick Heiserman RC | .15 | .07 |
| ❑ 399 | Don Mattingly | 1.50 | .70 |
| ❑ 400 | Henry Rodriguez | .15 | .07 |
| ❑ 401 | Lenny Harris | .15 | .07 |
| ❑ 402 | Ryan Thompson | .15 | .07 |
| ❑ 403 | Darren Oliver | .15 | .07 |
| ❑ 404 | Omar Vizquel | .25 | .11 |
| ❑ 405 | Jeff Bagwell | .75 | .35 |
| ❑ 406 | Doug Webb RC | .15 | .07 |
| ❑ 407 | Todd Van Poppel | .15 | .07 |
| ❑ 408 | Leo Gomez | .15 | .07 |
| ❑ 409 | Mark Whiten | .15 | .07 |
| ❑ 410 | Pedro A.Martinez | .15 | .07 |
| ❑ 411 | Reggie Sanders | .15 | .07 |
| ❑ 412 | Kevin Foster | .15 | .07 |
| ❑ 413 | Danny Tartabull | .15 | .07 |
| ❑ 414 | Jeff Blauser | .15 | .07 |
| ❑ 415 | Mike Magnante | .15 | .07 |
| ❑ 416 | Tom Candiotti | .15 | .07 |
| ❑ 417 | Rod Beck | .15 | .07 |
| ❑ 418 | Jody Reed | .15 | .07 |
| ❑ 419 | Vince Coleman | .15 | .07 |
| ❑ 420 | Danny Jackson | .15 | .07 |
| ❑ 421 | Ryan Nye RC | .15 | .07 |
| ❑ 422 | Larry Walker | .25 | .11 |
| ❑ 423 | Russ Johnson DP | .15 | .07 |
| ❑ 424 | Pat Borders | .15 | .07 |
| ❑ 425 | Lee Smith | .25 | .11 |
| ❑ 426 | Paul O'Neill | .25 | .11 |
| ❑ 427 | Devon White | .25 | .11 |
| ❑ 428 | Jim Bullinger | .15 | .07 |
| ❑ 429 | Starting Pitchers | .15 | .07 |
| | Prospects | | |
| | Greg Hansell | | |
| | Brian Sackinsky | | |
| | Carey Paige | | |
| | Rob Welch RC | | |
| ❑ 430 | Steve Avery | .15 | .07 |
| ❑ 431 | Tony Gwynn | 1.25 | .55 |
| ❑ 432 | Pat Meares | .15 | .07 |
| ❑ 433 | Bill Swift | .15 | .07 |
| ❑ 434 | David Wells | .25 | .11 |
| ❑ 435 | John Briscoe | .15 | .07 |
| ❑ 436 | Roger Pavlik | .15 | .07 |
| ❑ 437 | Jayson Peterson RC | .15 | .07 |
| ❑ 438 | Roberto Alomar | .60 | .25 |
| ❑ 439 | Billy Brewer | .15 | .07 |
| ❑ 440 | Gary Sheffield | .60 | .25 |
| ❑ 441 | Lou Frazier | .15 | .07 |
| ❑ 442 | Terry Steinbach | .15 | .07 |
| ❑ 443 | Jay Payton RC | 1.50 | .70 |
| ❑ 444 | Jason Bere | .15 | .07 |
| ❑ 445 | Denny Neagle | .25 | .11 |
| ❑ 446 | Andres Galarraga | .40 | .18 |
| ❑ 447 | Hector Carrasco | .15 | .07 |
| ❑ 448 | Bill Risley | .15 | .07 |
| ❑ 449 | Andy Benes | .15 | .07 |
| ❑ 450 | Jim Leyritz | .15 | .07 |
| ❑ 451 | Jose Oliva | .15 | .07 |
| ❑ 452 | Greg Vaughn | .25 | .11 |
| ❑ 453 | Rich Monteleone | .15 | .07 |
| ❑ 454 | Tony Eusebio | .15 | .07 |
| ❑ 455 | Chuck Finley | .25 | .11 |
| ❑ 456 | Kevin Brown | .25 | .11 |
| ❑ 457 | Joe Boever | .15 | .07 |
| ❑ 458 | Bobby Munoz | .15 | .07 |
| ❑ 459 | Bret Saberhagen | .25 | .11 |
| ❑ 460 | Kurt Abbott | .15 | .07 |
| ❑ 461 | Bobby Witt | .15 | .07 |
| ❑ 462 | Cliff Floyd | .25 | .11 |
| ❑ 463 | Mark Clark | .15 | .07 |
| ❑ 464 | Andujar Cedeno | .15 | .07 |
| ❑ 465 | Marvin Freeman | .15 | .07 |
| ❑ 466 | Mike Piazza | 2.00 | .90 |
| ❑ 467 | Willie Greene | .15 | .07 |
| ❑ 468 | Pat Kelly | .15 | .07 |
| ❑ 469 | Carlos Delgado | .60 | .25 |
| ❑ 470 | Willie Banks | .15 | .07 |
| ❑ 471 | Matt Walbeck | .15 | .07 |
| ❑ 472 | Mark McGwire | 2.50 | 1.10 |
| ❑ 473 | McKay Christensen RC | .15 | .07 |
| ❑ 474 | Alan Trammell | .40 | .18 |
| ❑ 475 | Tom Gordon | .15 | .07 |
| ❑ 476 | Greg Colbrunn | .15 | .07 |
| ❑ 477 | Darren Daulton | .25 | .11 |
| ❑ 478 | Albie Lopez | .15 | .07 |
| ❑ 479 | Robin Ventura | .25 | .11 |
| ❑ 480 | Catcher Prospects | .50 | .23 |
| | Eddie Perez RC | | |
| | Jason Kendall | | |
| | Einar Diaz | | |
| | Bret Hemphill | | |
| ❑ 481 | Bryan Eversgerd | .15 | .07 |
| ❑ 482 | Dave Fleming | .15 | .07 |
| ❑ 483 | Scott Livingstone | .15 | .07 |
| ❑ 484 | Pete Schourek | .15 | .07 |
| ❑ 485 | Bernie Williams | .60 | .25 |
| ❑ 486 | Mark Lemke | .15 | .07 |
| ❑ 487 | Eric Karros | .25 | .11 |
| ❑ 488 | Scott Ruffcorn | .15 | .07 |
| ❑ 489 | Billy Ashley | .15 | .07 |
| ❑ 490 | Rico Brogna | .15 | .07 |
| ❑ 491 | John Burkett | .15 | .07 |
| ❑ 492 | Cade Gaspar RC | .15 | .07 |
| ❑ 493 | Jorge Fabregas | .15 | .07 |
| ❑ 494 | Greg Gagne | .15 | .07 |
| ❑ 495 | Doug Jones | .15 | .07 |
| ❑ 496 | Troy O'Leary | .15 | .07 |
| ❑ 497 | Pat Rapp | .15 | .07 |
| ❑ 498 | Butch Henry | .15 | .07 |
| ❑ 499 | John Olerud | .25 | .11 |
| ❑ 500 | John Hudek | .15 | .07 |
| ❑ 501 | Jeff King | .15 | .07 |
| ❑ 502 | Bobby Bonilla | .25 | .11 |
| ❑ 503 | Albert Belle | .40 | .18 |
| ❑ 504 | Rick Wilkins | .15 | .07 |
| ❑ 505 | John Jaha | .15 | .07 |
| ❑ 506 | Nigel Wilson | .15 | .07 |
| ❑ 507 | Sid Fernandez | .15 | .07 |
| ❑ 508 | Deion Sanders | .25 | .11 |
| ❑ 509 | Gil Heredia | .15 | .07 |
| ❑ 510 | Scott Elarton RC | 1.50 | .70 |
| ❑ 511 | Melido Perez | .15 | .07 |
| ❑ 512 | Greg McMichael | .15 | .07 |
| ❑ 513 | Rusty Meacham | .15 | .07 |
| ❑ 514 | Shawn Green | .60 | .25 |
| ❑ 515 | Carlos Garcia | .15 | .07 |
| ❑ 516 | Dave Stevens | .15 | .07 |
| ❑ 517 | Eric Young | .15 | .07 |
| ❑ 518 | Omar Daal | .15 | .07 |
| ❑ 519 | Kirk Gibson | .25 | .11 |
| ❑ 520 | Spike Owen | .15 | .07 |
| ❑ 521 | Jacob Cruz RC | .25 | .11 |
| ❑ 522 | Sandy Alomar Jr. | .25 | .11 |
| ❑ 523 | Steve Bedrosian | .15 | .07 |
| ❑ 524 | Ricky Gutierrez | .15 | .07 |
| ❑ 525 | Dave Veres | .15 | .07 |
| ❑ 526 | Gregg Jefferies | .15 | .07 |
| ❑ 527 | Jose Valentin | .15 | .07 |
| ❑ 528 | Robb Nen | .15 | .07 |
| ❑ 529 | Jose Rijo | .15 | .07 |
| ❑ 530 | Sean Berry | .15 | .07 |
| ❑ 531 | Mike Gallego | .15 | .07 |
| ❑ 532 | Roberto Kelly | .15 | .07 |
| ❑ 533 | Kevin Stocker | .15 | .07 |
| ❑ 534 | Kirby Puckett | 1.50 | .70 |
| ❑ 535 | Chipper Jones | 1.50 | .70 |
| ❑ 536 | Russ Davis | .15 | .07 |
| ❑ 537 | Jon Lieber | .15 | .07 |
| ❑ 538 | Trey Moore RC | .15 | .07 |
| ❑ 539 | Joe Girardi | .15 | .07 |
| ❑ 540 | Second Base Prospects | .50 | .23 |
| | Quilvio Veras | | |
| | Arquimedez Pozo | | |
| | Miguel Cairo RC | | |
| | Jason Camilli | | |
| ❑ 541 | Tony Phillips | .15 | .07 |
| ❑ 542 | Brian Anderson | .15 | .07 |
| ❑ 543 | Ivan Rodriguez | .75 | .35 |
| ❑ 544 | Jeff Cirillo | .25 | .11 |
| ❑ 545 | Joey Cora | .15 | .07 |
| ❑ 546 | Chris Hoiles | .15 | .07 |
| ❑ 547 | Bernard Gilkey | .15 | .07 |
| ❑ 548 | Mike Lansing | .15 | .07 |
| ❑ 549 | Jimmy Key | .25 | .11 |
| ❑ 550 | Mark Wohlers | .15 | .07 |
| ❑ 551 | Chris Clemons RC | .15 | .07 |
| ❑ 552 | Vinny Castilla | .25 | .11 |
| ❑ 553 | Mark Guthrie | .15 | .07 |
| ❑ 554 | Mike Lieberthal | .25 | .11 |
| ❑ 555 | Tommy Davis RC | .15 | .07 |
| ❑ 556 | Robby Thompson | .15 | .07 |
| ❑ 557 | Danny Bautista | .15 | .07 |
| ❑ 558 | Will Clark | .60 | .25 |
| ❑ 559 | Rickey Henderson | .75 | .35 |
| ❑ 560 | Todd Jones | .15 | .07 |
| ❑ 561 | Jack McDowell | .15 | .07 |
| ❑ 562 | Carlos Rodriguez | .15 | .07 |
| ❑ 563 | Mark Eichhorn | .15 | .07 |
| ❑ 564 | Jeff Nelson | .15 | .07 |
| ❑ 565 | Eric Anthony | .15 | .07 |
| ❑ 566 | Randy Velarde | .15 | .07 |
| ❑ 567 | Javier Lopez | .25 | .11 |
| ❑ 568 | Kevin Mitchell | .15 | .07 |
| ❑ 569 | Steve Karsay | .15 | .07 |
| ❑ 570 | Brian Meadows RC | .25 | .11 |
| ❑ 571 | Rey Ordonez RC | .75 | .35 |
| | Mike Metcalfe | | |
| | Kevin Orie | | |

Ray Holbert
❑ 572 John Kruk .25 .11
❑ 573 Scott Leius .15 .07
❑ 574 John Patterson .15 .07
❑ 575 Kevin Brown .25 .11
❑ 576 Mike Moore .15 .07
❑ 577 Manny Ramirez .75 .35
❑ 578 Jose Lind .15 .07
❑ 579 Derrick May .15 .07
❑ 580 Cal Eldred .15 .07
❑ 581 Third Base Prospects .25 .11
David Bell
Joel Chelmis
Lino Diaz
Aaron Boone RC
❑ 582 J.T. Snow .25 .11
❑ 583 Luis Sojo .15 .07
❑ 584 Moises Alou .25 .11
❑ 585 Dave Clark .15 .07
❑ 586 Dave Hollins .15 .07
❑ 587 Nomar Garciaparra 4.00 1.80
❑ 588 Cal Ripken 2.50 1.10
❑ 589 Pedro Astacio .15 .07
❑ 590 J.R. Phillips .15 .07
❑ 591 Jeff Frye .15 .07
❑ 592 Bo Jackson .25 .11
❑ 593 Steve Ontiveros .15 .07
❑ 594 David Nied .15 .07
❑ 595 Brad Ausmus .15 .07
❑ 596 Carlos Baerga .15 .07
❑ 597 James Mouton .15 .07
❑ 598 Ozzie Guillen .15 .07
❑ 599 Outfield Prospects .15 .07
Ozzie Timmons
Curtis Goodwin
Johnny Damon
Jeff Abbott RC
❑ 600 Yorkis Perez .15 .07
❑ 601 Rich Rodriguez .15 .07
❑ 602 Mark McLemore .15 .07
❑ 603 Jeff Fassero .15 .07
❑ 604 John Hoper .15 .07
❑ 605 Mark Johnson RC .25 .11
❑ 606 Wes Chamberlain .15 .07
❑ 607 Felix Jose .15 .07
❑ 608 Tony Longmire .15 .07
❑ 609 Duane Ward .15 .07
❑ 610 Brett Butler .25 .11
❑ 611 William VanLandingham .15 .07
❑ 612 Mickey Tettleton .15 .07
❑ 613 Brady Anderson .25 .11
❑ 614 Reggie Jefferson .15 .07
❑ 615 Mike Kingery .15 .07
❑ 616 Derek Bell .15 .07
❑ 617 Scott Erickson .15 .07
❑ 618 Bob Wickman .15 .07
❑ 619 Phil Leftwich .15 .07
❑ 620 David Justice .40 .18
❑ 621 Paul Wilson .15 .07
❑ 622 Pedro Martinez .75 .35
❑ 623 Terry Mathews .15 .07
❑ 624 Brian McRae .15 .07
❑ 625 Bruce Ruffin .15 .07
❑ 626 Steve Finley .25 .11
❑ 627 Ron Gant .15 .07
❑ 628 Rafael Bournigal .15 .07
❑ 629 Darryl Strawberry .25 .11
❑ 630 Luis Alicea .15 .07
❑ 631 Orioles Prospects .15 .07
Mark Smith
Scott Klingenbeck
❑ 632 Red Sox Prospects .15 .07
Cory Bailey
Scott Hatteberg
❑ 633 Angels Prospects .15 .07
Todd Greene
Troy Percival
❑ 634 White Sox Prospects .15 .07
Rod Bolton
Olmedo Saenz
❑ 635 Indians Prospects .15 .07
Steve Kline
Herb Perry
❑ 636 Tigers Prospects .15 .07
Sean Bergman
Shannon Penn
❑ 637 Royals Prospects .15 .07
Joe Randa
Joe Vitiello
❑ 638 Brewers Prospects .15 .07
Jose Mercedes
Duane Singleton
❑ 639 Twins Prospects .15 .07
Marc Barcelo
Marty Cordova
❑ 640 Yankees Prospects .15 .07
Andy Pettitte
Ruben Rivera
❑ 641 Athletics Prospects .15 .07
Willie Adams
Scott Spiezio
❑ 642 Mariners Prospects .15 .07
Eddy Diaz RC
Desi Relaford
❑ 643 Rangers Prospects .15 .07
Terrell Lowery
Jon Shave
❑ 644 Blue Jays Prospects .15 .07
Angel Martinez
Paul Spoljaric
❑ 645 Braves Prospects .15 .07
Tony Graffanino
Damon Hollins
❑ 646 Cubs Prospects .15 .07
Darron Cox
Doug Glanville
❑ 647 Reds Prospects .15 .07
Tim Belk
Pat Watkins
❑ 648 Rockies Propsects .15 .07
Rod Pedraza
Phil Schneider
❑ 649 Marlins Prospects .15 .07
Vic Darensbourg
Marc Valdes
❑ 650 Astros Prospects .15 .07
Rick Huisman
Roberto Petagine
❑ 651 Dodgers Prospects .50 .23
Roger Cedeno
Ron Coomer RC
❑ 652 Expos Prospects .25 .11
Shane Andrews
Carlos Perez RC
❑ 653 Mets Prospects .25 .11
Jason Isringhausen
Chris Roberts
❑ 654 Phillies Prospects .15 .07
Wayne Gomes
Kevin Jordan
❑ 655 Pirates Prospects .15 .07
Esteban Loiaza
Steve Pegues
❑ 656 Cardinals Prospects .15 .07
Terry Bradshaw
John Frascatore
❑ 657 Padres Prospects .15 .07
Andres Berumen
Bryce Florie
❑ 658 Giants Prospects .15 .07
Dan Carlson
Keith Williams
❑ 659 Checklist .15 .07
❑ 660 Checklist .15 .07

## 1995 Topps Traded

| | MINT | NRMT |
|---|---|---|
| COMPLETE SET (165) | 40.00 | 18.00 |

❑ 1T Frank Thomas ATB .60 .25
❑ 2T Ken Griffey Jr. ATB 1.25 .55
❑ 3T Barry Bonds ATB .30 .14
❑ 4T Albert Belle ATB .30 .14
❑ 5T Cal Ripken ATB 1.25 .55
❑ 6T Mike Piazza ATB 1.00 .45
❑ 7T Tony Gwynn ATB .60 .25
❑ 8T Jeff Bagwell ATB .60 .25
❑ 9T Mo Vaughn ATB .30 .14
❑ 10T Matt Williams ATB .30 .14
❑ 11T Ray Durham .30 .14
❑ 12T Juan LeBron 2.00 .90
(Card pictures Carlos Beltran instead of Juan LeBron) RC
❑ 13T Shawn Green .60 .25
❑ 14T Kevin Gross .15 .07
❑ 15T Jon Nunnally .15 .07
❑ 16T Brian Maxcy RC .15 .07
❑ 17T Mark Kiefer .15 .07
❑ 18T Carlos Beltran UER 8.00 3.60
(Card pictures Juan LeBron instead of Carlos Beltran) RC.
❑ 19T Mike Mimbs RC .15 .07
❑ 20T Larry Walker .30 .14
❑ 21T Chad Curtis .15 .07
❑ 22T Jeff Barry .15 .07
❑ 23T Joe Oliver .15 .07
❑ 24T Tomas Perez RC .15 .07
❑ 25T Michael Barrett RC 2.00 .90
❑ 26T Brian McRae .15 .07
❑ 27T Derek Bell .15 .07
❑ 28T Ray Durham .30 .14
❑ 29T Todd Williams .15 .07
❑ 30T Ryan Jaroncyk RC .15 .07
❑ 31T Todd Steverson .15 .07
❑ 32T Mike Devereaux .15 .07
❑ 33T Rheal Cormier .15 .07
❑ 34T Benny Santiago .15 .07
❑ 35T Bobby Higginson RC 1.50 .70
❑ 36T Jack McDowell .15 .07
❑ 37T Mike Macfarlane .15 .07
❑ 38T Tony McKnight RC .15 .07
❑ 39T Brian Hunter .15 .07
❑ 40T Hideo Nomo RC 2.50 1.10
❑ 41T Brett Butler .30 .14
❑ 42T Donovan Osborne .15 .07
❑ 43T Scott Karl .15 .07
❑ 44T Tony Phillips .15 .07
❑ 45T Marty Cordova .15 .07
❑ 46T Dave Mlicki .15 .07
❑ 47T Bronson Arroyo RC 1.00 .45
❑ 48T John Burkett .15 .07
❑ 49T J.D. Smart RC .15 .07
❑ 50T Mickey Tettleton .15 .07
❑ 51T Todd Stottlemyre .15 .07
❑ 52T Mike Perez .15 .07
❑ 53T Terry Mulholland .15 .07
❑ 54T Edgardo Alfonzo .60 .25
❑ 55T Zane Smith .15 .07
❑ 56T Jacob Brumfield .15 .07
❑ 57T Andujar Cedeno .15 .07
❑ 58T Jose Parra .15 .07
❑ 59T Manny Alexander .15 .07
❑ 60T Tony Tarasco .15 .07
❑ 61T Orel Hershiser .30 .14
❑ 62T Tim Scott .15 .07
❑ 63T Felix Rodriguez RC .15 .07
❑ 64T Ken Hill .15 .07
❑ 65T Marquis Grissom .15 .07
❑ 66T Lee Smith .30 .14
❑ 67T Jason Bates .15 .07
❑ 68T Felipe Lira .15 .07
❑ 69T Alex Hernandez RC 1.00 .45
❑ 70T Tony Fernandez .15 .07
❑ 71T Scott Radinsky .15 .07
❑ 72T Jose Canseco .75 .35
❑ 73T Mark Grudzielanek RC .30 .14
❑ 74T Ben Davis RC 2.00 .90
❑ 75T Jim Abbott .30 .14
❑ 76T Roger Bailey .15 .07

❑ 77T Gregg Jefferies .15 .07
❑ 78T Erik Hanson .15 .07
❑ 79T Brad Radke RC 1.50 .70
❑ 80T Jaime Navarro .15 .07
❑ 81T John Wetteland .30 .14
❑ 82T Chad Fonville RC .15 .07
❑ 83T John Mabry .15 .07
❑ 84T Glenallen Hill .15 .07
❑ 85T Ken Caminiti .30 .14
❑ 86T Tom Goodwin .15 .07
❑ 87T Darren Bragg .15 .07
❑ 88T Pitching Prospects 3.00 1.35
Pat Ahearne
Gary Rath
Larry Wimberly
Robbie Bell RC
❑ 89T Jeff Russell .15 .07
❑ 90T Dave Gallagher .15 .07
❑ 91T Steve Finley .30 .14
❑ 92T Vaughn Eshelman .15 .07
❑ 93T Kevin Jarvis .15 .07
❑ 94T Mark Gubicza .15 .07
❑ 95T Tim Wakefield .15 .07
❑ 96T Bob Tewksbury .15 .07
❑ 97T Sid Roberson RC .15 .07
❑ 98T Tom Henke .15 .07
❑ 99T Michael Tucker .15 .07
❑ 100T Jason Bates .15 .07
❑ 101T Otis Nixon .15 .07
❑ 102T Mark Whiten .15 .07
❑ 103T Dilson Torres RC .15 .07
❑ 104T Melvin Bunch RC .15 .07
❑ 105T Terry Pendleton .30 .14
❑ 106T Corey Jenkins RC .60 .25
❑ 107T Glenn Dishman RC .15 .07
Rob Grable
❑ 108T Reggie Taylor RC 1.00 .45
❑ 109T Curtis Goodwin .15 .07
❑ 110T David Cone .30 .14
❑ 111T Antonio Osuna .15 .07
❑ 112T Paul Shuey .15 .07
❑ 113T Doug Jones .15 .07
❑ 114T Mark McLemore .15 .07
❑ 115T Kevin Ritz .15 .07
❑ 116T John Kruk .30 .14
❑ 117T Trevor Wilson .15 .07
❑ 118T Jerald Clark .15 .07
❑ 119T Julian Tavarez .15 .07
❑ 120T Tim Pugh .15 .07
❑ 121T Todd Zeile .15 .07
❑ 122T Prospects 5.00 2.20
Mark Sweeney UER
George Arias
Richie Sexson RC
Brian Schneider
❑ 123T Bobby Witt .15 .07
❑ 124T Hideo Nomo 1.00 .45
❑ 125T Joey Cora .15 .07
❑ 126T Jim Scharrer RC .15 .07
❑ 127T Paul Quantrill .15 .07
❑ 128T Chipper Jones ROY 1.25 .55
❑ 129T Kenny James RC .15 .07
❑ 130T Lyle Mouton .30 .14
Mariano Rivera
❑ 131T Tyler Green .15 .07
❑ 132T Brad Clontz .15 .07
❑ 133T Jon Nunnally .15 .07
❑ 134T Dave Magadan .15 .07
❑ 135T Al Leiter .30 .14
❑ 136T Bret Barberie .15 .07
❑ 137T Bill Swift .15 .07
❑ 138T Scott Cooper .15 .07
❑ 139T Roberto Kelly .15 .07
❑ 140T Charlie Hayes .15 .07
❑ 141T Pete Harnisch .15 .07
❑ 142T Rich Amaral .15 .07
❑ 143T Rudy Seanez .15 .07
❑ 144T Pat Listach .15 .07
❑ 145T Quilvio Veras .15 .07
❑ 146T Jose Olmeda RC .15 .07
❑ 147T Roberto Petagine .15 .07
❑ 148T Kevin Brown .30 .14
❑ 149T Phil Plantier .15 .07
❑ 150T Carlos Perez .30 .14
❑ 151T Pat Borders .15 .07
❑ 152T Tyler Green .15 .07
❑ 153T Stan Belinda .15 .07
❑ 154T Dave Stewart .30 .14
❑ 155T Andre Dawson .30 .14
❑ 156T Frank Thomas AS .60 .25
Fred McGriff UER
(McGriff's team shown as Blue Jays)
❑ 157T Carlos Baerga AS .30 .14
Craig Biggio
❑ 158T Wade Boggs AS .30 .14
Matt Williams
❑ 159T Cal Ripken AS .60 .25
Ozzie Smith
❑ 160T Ken Griffey Jr. AS .60 .25
Tony Gwynn
❑ 161T Albert Belle AS .30 .14
Barry Bonds
❑ 162T Kirby Puckett .60 .25
Len Dykstra
❑ 163T Ivan Rodriguez AS .60 .25
Mike Piazza
❑ 164T Randy Johnson AS 1.00 .45
Hideo Nomo
❑ 165T Checklist .15 .07

## 1996 Topps

| | MINT | NRMT |
|---|---|---|
| COMPLETE SET (440) | 50.00 | 22.00 |
| COMP.HOBBY SET (449) | 60.00 | 27.00 |
| COMP.CEREAL SET (444) | 50.00 | 22.00 |
| COMPLETE SERIES 1 (220) | 30.00 | 13.50 |
| COMPLETE SERIES 2 (220) | 20.00 | 9.00 |

❑ 1 Tony Gwynn STP .40 .18
❑ 2 Mike Piazza STP .60 .25
❑ 3 Greg Maddux STP .60 .25
❑ 4 Jeff Bagwell STP .25 .11
❑ 5 Larry Walker STP .10 .05
❑ 6 Barry Larkin STP .15 .07
❑ 7 Mickey Mantle 4.00 1.80
❑ 8 Tom Glavine STP UER .15 .07
(Won 21 games in June 95)
❑ 9 Craig Biggio STP .15 .07
❑ 10 Barry Bonds STP .40 .18
❑ 11 Heathcliff Slocumb STP .10 .05
❑ 12 Matt Williams STP .15 .07
❑ 13 Todd Helton 2.00 .90
❑ 14 Mark Redman .15 .07
❑ 15 Michael Barrett .15 .07
❑ 16 Ben Davis .15 .07
❑ 17 Juan LeBron .10 .05
❑ 18 Tony McKnight .10 .05
❑ 19 Ryan Jaroncyk .10 .05
❑ 20 Corey Jenkins .10 .05
❑ 21 Jim Scharrer .10 .05
❑ 22 Mark Bellhorn RC .25 .11
❑ 23 Jarrod Washburn RC .25 .11
❑ 24 Geoff Jenkins RC 2.00 .90
❑ 25 Sean Casey RC 8.00 3.60
❑ 26 Brett Tomko RC .25 .11
❑ 27 Tony Fernandez .10 .05
❑ 28 Rich Becker .10 .05
❑ 29 Andujar Cedeno .10 .05
❑ 30 Paul Molitor .40 .18
❑ 31 Brent Gates .10 .05
❑ 32 Glenallen Hill .10 .05
❑ 33 Mike Macfarlane .10 .05
❑ 34 Manny Alexander .10 .05
❑ 35 Todd Zeile .10 .05
❑ 36 Joe Girardi .10 .05
❑ 37 Tony Tarasco .10 .05
❑ 38 Tim Belcher .10 .05
❑ 39 Tom Goodwin .10 .05
❑ 40 Orel Hershiser .15 .07
❑ 41 Tripp Cromer .10 .05
❑ 42 Sean Bergman .10 .05
❑ 43 Troy Percival .10 .05
❑ 44 Kevin Stocker .10 .05
❑ 45 Albert Belle .25 .11
❑ 46 Tony Eusebio .10 .05
❑ 47 Sid Roberson .10 .05
❑ 48 Todd Hollandsworth .10 .05
❑ 49 Mark Wohlers .10 .05
❑ 50 Kirby Puckett 1.00 .45
❑ 51 Darren Holmes .10 .05
❑ 52 Ron Karkovice .10 .05
❑ 53 Al Martin .10 .05
❑ 54 Pat Rapp .10 .05
❑ 55 Mark Grace .40 .18
❑ 56 Greg Gagne .10 .05
❑ 57 Stan Javier .10 .05
❑ 58 Scott Sanders .10 .05
❑ 59 J.T. Snow .15 .07
❑ 60 David Justice .25 .11
❑ 61 Royce Clayton .10 .05
❑ 62 Kevin Foster .10 .05
❑ 63 Tim Naehring .10 .05
❑ 64 Orlando Miller .10 .05
❑ 65 Mike Mussina .40 .18
❑ 66 Jim Eisenreich .10 .05
❑ 67 Felix Fermin .10 .05
❑ 68 Bernie Williams .40 .18
❑ 69 Robb Nen .10 .05
❑ 70 Ron Gant .10 .05
❑ 71 Felipe Lira .10 .05
❑ 72 Jacob Brumfield .10 .05
❑ 73 John Mabry .10 .05
❑ 74 Mark Carreon .10 .05
❑ 75 Carlos Baerga .10 .05
❑ 76 Jim Dougherty .10 .05
❑ 77 Ryan Thompson .10 .05
❑ 78 Scott Leius .10 .05
❑ 79 Roger Pavlik .10 .05
❑ 80 Gary Sheffield .40 .18
❑ 81 Julian Tavarez .10 .05
❑ 82 Andy Ashby .10 .05
❑ 83 Mark Lemke .10 .05
❑ 84 Omar Vizquel .15 .07
❑ 85 Darren Daulton .15 .07
❑ 86 Mike Lansing .10 .05
❑ 87 Rusty Greer .15 .07
❑ 88 Dave Stevens .10 .05
❑ 89 Jose Offerman .10 .05
❑ 90 Tom Henke .10 .05
❑ 91 Troy O'Leary .10 .05
❑ 92 Michael Tucker .10 .05
❑ 93 Marvin Freeman .10 .05
❑ 94 Alex Diaz .10 .05
❑ 95 John Wetteland .15 .07
❑ 96 Cal Ripken 2131 2.00 .90
❑ 97 Mike Mimbs .10 .05
❑ 98 Bobby Higginson .15 .07
❑ 99 Edgardo Alfonzo .15 .07
❑ 100 Frank Thomas .75 .35
❑ 101 Steve Gibralter .50 .23
Bob Abreu
❑ 102 Brian Givens .10 .05
T.J. Mathews
❑ 103 Chris Pritchett .10 .05
Trenidad Hubbard
❑ 104 Eric Owens .10 .05
Butch Huskey
❑ 105 Doug Drabek .10 .05
❑ 106 Tomas Perez .10 .05
❑ 107 Mark Leiter .10 .05
❑ 108 Joe Oliver .10 .05
❑ 109 Tony Castillo .10 .05
❑ 110 Checklist (1-110) .10 .05
❑ 111 Kevin Seitzer .10 .05
❑ 112 Pete Schourek .10 .05
❑ 113 Sean Berry .10 .05
❑ 114 Todd Stottlemyre .10 .05
❑ 115 Joe Carter .15 .07
❑ 116 Jeff King .10 .05

- ❑ 117 Dan Wilson .10 .05
- ❑ 118 Kurt Abbott .10 .05
- ❑ 119 Lyle Mouton .10 .05
- ❑ 120 Jose Rijo .10 .05
- ❑ 121 Curtis Goodwin .10 .05
- ❑ 122 Jose Valentin .10 .05
- ❑ 123 Ellis Burks .15 .07
- ❑ 124 David Cone .15 .07
- ❑ 125 Eddie Murray .40 .18
- ❑ 126 Brian Jordan .15 .07
- ❑ 127 Darrin Fletcher .10 .05
- ❑ 128 Curt Schilling .15 .07
- ❑ 129 Ozzie Guillen .10 .05
- ❑ 130 Kenny Rogers .10 .05
- ❑ 131 Tom Pagnozzi .10 .05
- ❑ 132 Garret Anderson .15 .07
- ❑ 133 Bobby Jones .10 .05
- ❑ 134 Chris Gomez .10 .05
- ❑ 135 Mike Stanley .10 .05
- ❑ 136 Hideo Nomo .40 .18
- ❑ 137 Jon Nunnally .10 .05
- ❑ 138 Tim Wakefield .10 .05
- ❑ 139 Steve Finley .15 .07
- ❑ 140 Ivan Rodriguez .50 .23
- ❑ 141 Quilvio Veras .10 .05
- ❑ 142 Mike Fetters .10 .05
- ❑ 143 Mike Greenwell .10 .05
- ❑ 144 Bill Pulsipher .10 .05
- ❑ 145 Mark McGwire 1.50 .70
- ❑ 146 Frank Castillo .10 .05
- ❑ 147 Greg Vaughn .15 .07
- ❑ 148 Pat Hentgen .10 .05
- ❑ 149 Walt Weiss .10 .05
- ❑ 150 Randy Johnson .50 .23
- ❑ 151 David Segui .10 .05
- ❑ 152 Benji Gil .10 .05
- ❑ 153 Tom Candiotti .10 .05
- ❑ 154 Geronimo Berroa .10 .05
- ❑ 155 John Franco .15 .07
- ❑ 156 Jay Bell .15 .07
- ❑ 157 Mark Gubicza .10 .05
- ❑ 158 Hal Morris .10 .05
- ❑ 159 Wilson Alvarez .10 .05
- ❑ 160 Derek Bell .10 .05
- ❑ 161 Ricky Bottalico .10 .05
- ❑ 162 Bret Boone .15 .07
- ❑ 163 Brad Radke .15 .07
- ❑ 164 John Valentin .10 .05
- ❑ 165 Steve Avery .10 .05
- ❑ 166 Mark McLemore .10 .05
- ❑ 167 Danny Jackson .10 .05
- ❑ 168 Tino Martinez .15 .07
- ❑ 169 Shane Reynolds .10 .05
- ❑ 170 Terry Pendleton .15 .07
- ❑ 171 Jim Edmonds .40 .18
- ❑ 172 Esteban Loaiza .10 .05
- ❑ 173 Ray Durham .15 .07
- ❑ 174 Carlos Perez .10 .05
- ❑ 175 Raul Mondesi .15 .07
- ❑ 176 Steve Ontiveros .10 .05
- ❑ 177 Chipper Jones 1.00 .45
- ❑ 178 Otis Nixon .10 .05
- ❑ 179 John Burkett .10 .05
- ❑ 180 Gregg Jefferies .10 .05
- ❑ 181 Denny Martinez .15 .07
- ❑ 182 Ken Caminiti .15 .07
- ❑ 183 Doug Jones .10 .05
- ❑ 184 Brian McRae .10 .05
- ❑ 185 Don Mattingly 1.00 .45
- ❑ 186 Mel Rojas .10 .05
- ❑ 187 Marty Cordova .10 .05
- ❑ 188 Vinny Castilla .15 .07
- ❑ 189 John Smoltz .15 .07
- ❑ 190 Travis Fryman .15 .07
- ❑ 191 Chris Hoiles .10 .05
- ❑ 192 Chuck Finley .15 .07
- ❑ 193 Ryan Klesko .15 .07
- ❑ 194 Alex Fernandez .10 .05
- ❑ 195 Dante Bichette .15 .07
- ❑ 196 Eric Karros .15 .07
- ❑ 197 Roger Clemens .75 .35
- ❑ 198 Randy Myers .10 .05
- ❑ 199 Tony Phillips .10 .05
- ❑ 200 Cal Ripken 1.50 .70
- ❑ 201 Rod Beck .10 .05
- ❑ 202 Chad Curtis .10 .05
- ❑ 203 Jack McDowell .10 .05
- ❑ 204 Gary Gaetti .15 .07
- ❑ 205 Ken Griffey Jr. 1.50 .70
- ❑ 206 Ramon Martinez .10 .05
- ❑ 207 Jeff Kent .25 .11
- ❑ 208 Brad Ausmus .10 .05
- ❑ 209 Devon White .15 .07
- ❑ 210 Jason Giambi .40 .18
- ❑ 211 Nomar Garciaparra 1.25 .55
- ❑ 212 Billy Wagner .10 .05
- ❑ 213 Todd Greene .10 .05
- ❑ 214 Paul Wilson .10 .05
- ❑ 215 Johnny Damon .15 .07
- ❑ 216 Alan Benes .10 .05
- ❑ 217 Karim Garcia .10 .05
- ❑ 218 Dustin Hermanson .10 .05
- ❑ 219 Derek Jeter 1.50 .70
- ❑ 220 Checklist (111-220) .10 .05
- ❑ 221 Kirby Puckett STP .50 .23
- ❑ 222 Cal Ripken STP .75 .35
- ❑ 223 Albert Belle STP .15 .07
- ❑ 224 Randy Johnson STP .25 .11
- ❑ 225 Wade Boggs STP .25 .11
- ❑ 226 Carlos Baerga STP .10 .05
- ❑ 227 Ivan Rodriguez STP .25 .11
- ❑ 228 Mike Mussina STP .15 .07
- ❑ 229 Frank Thomas STP .40 .18
- ❑ 230 Ken Griffey Jr. STP 1.00 .45
- ❑ 231 Jose Mesa STP .10 .05
- ❑ 232 Matt Morris RC .25 .11
- ❑ 233 Craig Wilson RC .10 .05
- ❑ 234 Alvie Shepherd .10 .05
- ❑ 235 Randy Winn RC .25 .11
- ❑ 236 David Yocum RC .10 .05
- ❑ 237 Jason Brester RC .25 .11
- ❑ 238 Shane Monahan RC .10 .05
- ❑ 239 Brian McNichol RC .25 .11
- ❑ 240 Reggie Taylor .10 .05
- ❑ 241 Garrett Long .10 .05
- ❑ 242 Jonathan Johnson .10 .05
- ❑ 243 Jeff Liefer RC .25 .11
- ❑ 244 Brian Powell .10 .05
- ❑ 245 Brian Buchanan .10 .05
- ❑ 246 Mike Piazza 1.25 .55
- ❑ 247 Edgar Martinez .25 .11
- ❑ 248 Chuck Knoblauch .15 .07
- ❑ 249 Andres Galarraga .25 .11
- ❑ 250 Tony Gwynn .75 .35
- ❑ 251 Lee Smith .15 .07
- ❑ 252 Sammy Sosa .75 .35
- ❑ 253 Jim Thome .25 .11
- ❑ 254 Frank Rodriguez .10 .05
- ❑ 255 Charlie Hayes .10 .05
- ❑ 256 Bernard Gilkey .10 .05
- ❑ 257 John Smiley .10 .05
- ❑ 258 Brady Anderson .15 .07
- ❑ 259 Rico Brogna .10 .05
- ❑ 260 Kirt Manwaring .10 .05
- ❑ 261 Len Dykstra .15 .07
- ❑ 262 Tom Glavine .40 .18
- ❑ 263 Vince Coleman .10 .05
- ❑ 264 John Olerud .15 .07
- ❑ 265 Orlando Merced .10 .05
- ❑ 266 Kent Mercker .10 .05
- ❑ 267 Terry Steinbach .10 .05
- ❑ 268 Brian L. Hunter .10 .05
- ❑ 269 Jeff Fassero .10 .05
- ❑ 270 Jay Buhner .15 .07
- ❑ 271 Jeff Brantley .10 .05
- ❑ 272 Tim Raines .15 .07
- ❑ 273 Jimmy Key .15 .07
- ❑ 274 Mo Vaughn .15 .07
- ❑ 275 Andre Dawson .25 .11
- ❑ 276 Jose Mesa .10 .05
- ❑ 277 Brett Butler .15 .07
- ❑ 278 Luis Gonzalez .15 .07
- ❑ 279 Steve Sparks .10 .05
- ❑ 280 Chili Davis .15 .07
- ❑ 281 Carl Everett .15 .07
- ❑ 282 Jeff Cirillo .15 .07
- ❑ 283 Thomas Howard .10 .05
- ❑ 284 Paul O'Neill .15 .07
- ❑ 285 Pat Meares .10 .05
- ❑ 286 Mickey Tettleton .10 .05
- ❑ 287 Rey Sanchez .10 .05
- ❑ 288 Bip Roberts .10 .05
- ❑ 289 Roberto Alomar .40 .18
- ❑ 290 Ruben Sierra .10 .05
- ❑ 291 John Flaherty .10 .05
- ❑ 292 Bret Saberhagen .15 .07
- ❑ 293 Barry Larkin .40 .18
- ❑ 294 Sandy Alomar Jr. .15 .07
- ❑ 295 Ed Sprague .10 .05
- ❑ 296 Gary DiSarcina .10 .05
- ❑ 297 Marquis Grissom .10 .05
- ❑ 298 John Frascatore .10 .05
- ❑ 299 Will Clark .40 .18
- ❑ 300 Barry Bonds .60 .25
- ❑ 301 Ozzie Smith UER .50 .23 (Padres is listed as Padre)
- ❑ 302 Dave Nilsson .10 .05
- ❑ 303 Pedro Martinez .50 .23
- ❑ 304 Joey Cora .10 .05
- ❑ 305 Rick Aguilera .10 .05
- ❑ 306 Craig Biggio .25 .11
- ❑ 307 Jose Vizcaino .10 .05
- ❑ 308 Jeff Montgomery .10 .05
- ❑ 309 Moises Alou .15 .07
- ❑ 310 Robin Ventura .15 .07
- ❑ 311 David Wells .15 .07
- ❑ 312 Delino DeShields .10 .05
- ❑ 313 Trevor Hoffman .15 .07
- ❑ 314 Andy Benes .10 .05
- ❑ 315 Deion Sanders .15 .07
- ❑ 316 Jim Bullinger .10 .05
- ❑ 317 John Jaha .10 .05
- ❑ 318 Greg Maddux 1.00 .45
- ❑ 319 Tim Salmon .15 .07
- ❑ 320 Ben McDonald .10 .05
- ❑ 321 Sandy Martinez .10 .05
- ❑ 322 Dan Miceli .10 .05
- ❑ 323 Wade Boggs .50 .23
- ❑ 324 Ismael Valdes .10 .05
- ❑ 325 Juan Gonzalez .40 .18
- ❑ 326 Charles Nagy .10 .05
- ❑ 327 Ray Lankford .15 .07
- ❑ 328 Mark Portugal .10 .05
- ❑ 329 Bobby Bonilla .15 .07
- ❑ 330 Reggie Sanders .10 .05
- ❑ 331 Jamie Brewington RC .10 .05
- ❑ 332 Aaron Sele .15 .07
- ❑ 333 Pete Harnisch .10 .05
- ❑ 334 Cliff Floyd .15 .07
- ❑ 335 Cal Eldred .10 .05
- ❑ 336 Jason Bates .10 .05
- ❑ 337 Tony Clark .10 .05
- ❑ 338 Jose Herrera .10 .05
- ❑ 339 Alex Ochoa .10 .05
- ❑ 340 Mark Loretta .10 .05
- ❑ 341 Donne Wall .10 .05
- ❑ 342 Jason Kendall .15 .07
- ❑ 343 Shannon Stewart .15 .07
- ❑ 344 Brooks Kieschnick .10 .05
- ❑ 345 Chris Snopek .10 .05
- ❑ 346 Ruben Rivera .10 .05
- ❑ 347 Jeff Suppan .10 .05
- ❑ 348 Phil Nevin .15 .07
- ❑ 349 John Wasdin .10 .05
- ❑ 350 Jay Payton .15 .07
- ❑ 351 Tim Crabtree .10 .05
- ❑ 352 Rick Krivda .10 .05
- ❑ 353 Bob Wolcott .10 .05
- ❑ 354 Jimmy Haynes .10 .05
- ❑ 355 Herb Perry .10 .05
- ❑ 356 Ryne Sandberg .50 .23
- ❑ 357 Harold Baines .15 .07
- ❑ 358 Chad Ogea .10 .05
- ❑ 359 Lee Tinsley .10 .05
- ❑ 360 Matt Williams .25 .11
- ❑ 361 Randy Velarde .10 .05
- ❑ 362 Jose Canseco .50 .23
- ❑ 363 Larry Walker .15 .07
- ❑ 364 Kevin Appier .15 .07
- ❑ 365 Darryl Hamilton .10 .05
- ❑ 366 Jose Lima .10 .05
- ❑ 367 Javy Lopez .15 .07
- ❑ 368 Dennis Eckersley .15 .07
- ❑ 369 Jason Isringhausen .15 .07
- ❑ 370 Mickey Morandini .10 .05
- ❑ 371 Scott Cooper .10 .05
- ❑ 372 Jim Abbott .15 .07
- ❑ 373 Paul Sorrento .10 .05

| Card | Player | Mint | NRMT |
|---|---|---|---|
| ❑ 374 | Chris Hammond | .10 | .05 |
| ❑ 375 | Lance Johnson | .10 | .05 |
| ❑ 376 | Kevin Brown | .15 | .07 |
| ❑ 377 | Luis Alicea | .10 | .05 |
| ❑ 378 | Andy Pettitte | .15 | .07 |
| ❑ 379 | Dean Palmer | .15 | .07 |
| ❑ 380 | Jeff Bagwell | .50 | .23 |
| ❑ 381 | Jaime Navarro | .10 | .05 |
| ❑ 382 | Rondell White | .15 | .07 |
| ❑ 383 | Erik Hanson | .10 | .05 |
| ❑ 384 | Pedro Munoz | .10 | .05 |
| ❑ 385 | Heathcliff Slocumb | .10 | .05 |
| ❑ 386 | Wally Joyner | .15 | .07 |
| ❑ 387 | Bob Tewksbury | .10 | .05 |
| ❑ 388 | David Bell | .10 | .05 |
| ❑ 389 | Fred McGriff | .25 | .11 |
| ❑ 390 | Mike Henneman | .10 | .05 |
| ❑ 391 | Robby Thompson | .10 | .05 |
| ❑ 392 | Norm Charlton | .10 | .05 |
| ❑ 393 | Cecil Fielder | .15 | .07 |
| ❑ 394 | Benito Santiago | .10 | .05 |
| ❑ 395 | Rafael Palmeiro | .40 | .18 |
| ❑ 396 | Ricky Bones | .10 | .05 |
| ❑ 397 | Rickey Henderson | .50 | .23 |
| ❑ 398 | C.J. Nitkowski | .10 | .05 |
| ❑ 399 | Shawon Dunston | .10 | .05 |
| ❑ 400 | Manny Ramirez | .50 | .23 |
| ❑ 401 | Bill Swift | .10 | .05 |
| ❑ 402 | Chad Fonville | .10 | .05 |
| ❑ 403 | Joey Hamilton | .10 | .05 |
| ❑ 404 | Alex Gonzalez | .10 | .05 |
| ❑ 405 | Roberto Hernandez | .10 | .05 |
| ❑ 406 | Jeff Blauser | .10 | .05 |
| ❑ 407 | LaTroy Hawkins | .10 | .05 |
| ❑ 408 | Greg Colbrunn | .10 | .05 |
| ❑ 409 | Todd Hundley | .10 | .05 |
| ❑ 410 | Glenn Dishman | .10 | .05 |
| ❑ 411 | Joe Vitiello | .10 | .05 |
| ❑ 412 | Todd Worrell | .10 | .05 |
| ❑ 413 | Wil Cordero | .10 | .05 |
| ❑ 414 | Ken Hill | .10 | .05 |
| ❑ 415 | Carlos Garcia | .10 | .05 |
| ❑ 416 | Bryan Rekar | .10 | .05 |
| ❑ 417 | Shawn Green | .40 | .18 |
| ❑ 418 | Tyler Green | .10 | .05 |
| ❑ 419 | Mike Blowers | .10 | .05 |
| ❑ 420 | Kenny Lofton | .15 | .07 |
| ❑ 421 | Denny Neagle | .15 | .07 |
| ❑ 422 | Jeff Conine | .10 | .05 |
| ❑ 423 | Mark Langston | .10 | .05 |
| ❑ 424 | Steve Cox | .15 | .07 |
| | Jesse Ibarra | | |
| | Derrek Lee | | |
| | Ron Wright RC | | |
| ❑ 425 | Jim Bonnici | 3.00 | 1.35 |
| | Billy Owens | | |
| | Richie Sexson | | |
| | Daryle Ward RC | | |
| ❑ 426 | Kevin Jordan | .10 | .05 |
| | Bobby Morris | | |
| | Desi Relaford | | |
| | Adam Riggs RC | | |
| ❑ 427 | Tim Harkrider | .10 | .05 |
| | Rey Ordonez | | |
| | Neifi Perez | | |
| | Enrique Wilson | | |
| ❑ 428 | Bartolo Colon | .15 | .07 |
| | Doug Million | | |
| | Rafael Orellano | | |
| | Ray Ricken | | |
| ❑ 429 | Jeff D'Amico | .10 | .05 |
| | Marty Janzen RC | | |
| | Gary Rath | | |
| | Clint Sodowsky | | |
| ❑ 430 | Matt Drews | .10 | .05 |
| | Rich Hunter RC | | |
| | Matt Ruebel | | |
| | Bret Wagner | | |
| ❑ 431 | Jaime Bluma | .10 | .05 |
| | David Coggin | | |
| | Steve Montgomery | | |
| | Brandon Reed RC | | |
| ❑ 432 | Mike Figga | .15 | .07 |
| | Raul Ibanez | | |
| | Paul Konerko | | |
| | Julio Mosquera | | |
| ❑ 433 | Brian Barber | .10 | .05 |
| | Marc Kroon | | |
| | Marc Valdes | | |
| | Don Wengert | | |
| ❑ 434 | George Arias | .75 | .35 |
| | Chris Haas RC | | |
| | Scott Rolen | | |
| | Scott Spiezio | | |
| ❑ 435 | Brian Banks | 3.00 | 1.35 |
| | Vladimir Guerrero | | |
| | Andruw Jones | | |
| | Billy McMillon | | |
| ❑ 436 | Roger Cedeno | .75 | .35 |
| | Derrick Gibson | | |
| | Ben Grieve | | |
| | Shane Spencer RC | | |
| ❑ 437 | Anton French | .10 | .05 |
| | Demond Smith | | |
| | DaRond Stovall RC | | |
| | Keith Williams | | |
| ❑ 438 | Michael Coleman RC | .15 | .07 |
| | Jacob Cruz | | |
| | Richard Hidalgo | | |
| | Charles Peterson | | |
| ❑ 439 | Trey Beamon | .15 | .07 |
| | Yamil Benitez | | |
| | Jermaine Dye | | |
| | Angel Echevarria | | |
| ❑ 440 | Checklist | .10 | .05 |
| ❑ F7 | Mickey Mantle Last Day | 15.00 | 6.75 |

## 1997 Topps

| | MINT | NRMT |
|---|---|---|
| COMPLETE SET (495) | 60.00 | 27.00 |
| COMPLETE SERIES 1 (276) | 30.00 | 13.50 |
| COMPLETE SERIES 2 (220) | 30.00 | 13.50 |

| Card | Player | Mint | NRMT |
|---|---|---|---|
| ❑ 1 | Barry Bonds | .60 | .25 |
| ❑ 2 | Tom Pagnozzi | .10 | .05 |
| ❑ 3 | Terrell Wade | .10 | .05 |
| ❑ 4 | Jose Valentin | .10 | .05 |
| ❑ 5 | Mark Clark | .10 | .05 |
| ❑ 6 | Brady Anderson | .15 | .07 |
| ❑ 8 | Wade Boggs | .50 | .23 |
| ❑ 9 | Scott Stahoviak | .10 | .05 |
| ❑ 10 | Andres Galarraga | .25 | .11 |
| ❑ 11 | Steve Avery | .10 | .05 |
| ❑ 12 | Rusty Greer | .15 | .07 |
| ❑ 13 | Derek Jeter | 1.50 | .70 |
| ❑ 14 | Ricky Bottalico | .10 | .05 |
| ❑ 15 | Andy Ashby | .10 | .05 |
| ❑ 16 | Paul Shuey | .10 | .05 |
| ❑ 17 | F.P. Santangelo | .10 | .05 |
| ❑ 18 | Royce Clayton | .10 | .05 |
| ❑ 19 | Mike Mohler | .10 | .05 |
| ❑ 20 | Mike Piazza | 1.25 | .55 |
| ❑ 21 | Jaime Navarro | .10 | .05 |
| ❑ 22 | Billy Wagner | .10 | .05 |
| ❑ 23 | Mike Timlin | .10 | .05 |
| ❑ 24 | Garret Anderson | .15 | .07 |
| ❑ 25 | Ben McDonald | .10 | .05 |
| ❑ 26 | Mel Rojas | .10 | .05 |
| ❑ 27 | John Burkett | .10 | .05 |
| ❑ 28 | Jeff King | .10 | .05 |
| ❑ 29 | Reggie Jefferson | .10 | .05 |
| ❑ 30 | Kevin Appier | .15 | .07 |
| ❑ 31 | Felipe Lira | .10 | .05 |
| ❑ 32 | Kevin Tapani | .10 | .05 |
| ❑ 33 | Mark Portugal | .10 | .05 |
| ❑ 34 | Carlos Garcia | .10 | .05 |
| ❑ 35 | Joey Cora | .10 | .05 |
| ❑ 36 | David Segui | .10 | .05 |
| ❑ 37 | Mark Grace | .40 | .18 |
| ❑ 38 | Erik Hanson | .10 | .05 |
| ❑ 39 | Jeff D'Amico | .10 | .05 |
| ❑ 40 | Jay Buhner | .15 | .07 |
| ❑ 41 | B.J. Surhoff | .15 | .07 |
| ❑ 42 | Jackie Robinson TRIB | 2.00 | .90 |
| ❑ 43 | Roger Pavlik | .10 | .05 |
| ❑ 44 | Hal Morris | .10 | .05 |
| ❑ 45 | Mariano Duncan | .10 | .05 |
| ❑ 46 | Harold Baines | .15 | .07 |
| ❑ 47 | Jorge Fabregas | .10 | .05 |
| ❑ 48 | Jose Herrera | .10 | .05 |
| ❑ 49 | Jeff Cirillo | .15 | .07 |
| ❑ 50 | Tom Glavine | .40 | .18 |
| ❑ 51 | Pedro Astacio | .10 | .05 |
| ❑ 52 | Mark Gardner | .10 | .05 |
| ❑ 53 | Arthur Rhodes | .10 | .05 |
| ❑ 54 | Troy O'Leary | .10 | .05 |
| ❑ 55 | Bip Roberts | .10 | .05 |
| ❑ 56 | Mike Lieberthal | .15 | .07 |
| ❑ 57 | Shane Andrews | .10 | .05 |
| ❑ 58 | Scott Karl | .10 | .05 |
| ❑ 59 | Gary DiSarcina | .10 | .05 |
| ❑ 60 | Andy Pettitte | .15 | .07 |
| ❑ 61 | Kevin Elster | .10 | .05 |
| ❑ 62 | Mark McGwire | 1.50 | .70 |
| ❑ 63 | Dan Wilson | .10 | .05 |
| ❑ 64 | Mickey Morandini | .10 | .05 |
| ❑ 65 | Chuck Knoblauch | .15 | .07 |
| ❑ 66 | Tim Wakefield | .10 | .05 |
| ❑ 67 | Raul Mondesi | .15 | .07 |
| ❑ 68 | Todd Jones | .10 | .05 |
| ❑ 69 | Albert Belle | .25 | .11 |
| ❑ 70 | Trevor Hoffman | .15 | .07 |
| ❑ 71 | Eric Young | .10 | .05 |
| ❑ 72 | Robert Perez | .10 | .05 |
| ❑ 73 | Butch Huskey | .10 | .05 |
| ❑ 74 | Brian McRae | .10 | .05 |
| ❑ 75 | Jim Edmonds | .40 | .18 |
| ❑ 76 | Mike Henneman | .10 | .05 |
| ❑ 77 | Frank Rodriguez | .10 | .05 |
| ❑ 78 | Danny Tartabull | .10 | .05 |
| ❑ 79 | Robb Nen | .10 | .05 |
| ❑ 80 | Reggie Sanders | .10 | .05 |
| ❑ 81 | Ron Karkovice | .10 | .05 |
| ❑ 82 | Benito Santiago | .10 | .05 |
| ❑ 83 | Mike Lansing | .10 | .05 |
| ❑ 84 | Mike Fetters UER | .10 | .05 |
| | (Card numbered 61) | | |
| ❑ 85 | Craig Biggio | .25 | .11 |
| ❑ 86 | Mike Bordick | .10 | .05 |
| ❑ 87 | Ray Lankford | .15 | .07 |
| ❑ 88 | Charles Nagy | .10 | .05 |
| ❑ 89 | Paul Wilson | .10 | .05 |
| ❑ 90 | John Wetteland | .15 | .07 |
| ❑ 91 | Tom Candiotti | .10 | .05 |
| ❑ 92 | Carlos Delgado | .40 | .18 |
| ❑ 93 | Derek Bell | .10 | .05 |
| ❑ 94 | Mark Lemke | .10 | .05 |
| ❑ 95 | Edgar Martinez | .25 | .11 |
| ❑ 96 | Rickey Henderson | .50 | .23 |
| ❑ 97 | Greg Myers | .10 | .05 |
| ❑ 98 | Jim Leyritz | .10 | .05 |
| ❑ 99 | Mark Johnson | .10 | .05 |
| ❑ 100 | Dwight Gooden HL | .10 | .05 |
| ❑ 101 | Al Leiter HL | .10 | .05 |
| ❑ 102 | John Mabry HL | .10 | .05 |
| ❑ 103 | Alex Ochoa HL | .10 | .05 |
| ❑ 104 | Mike Piazza HL | .60 | .25 |
| ❑ 105 | Jim Thome | .25 | .11 |
| ❑ 106 | Ricky Otero | .10 | .05 |
| ❑ 107 | Jamey Wright | .10 | .05 |
| ❑ 108 | Frank Thomas | .75 | .35 |
| ❑ 109 | Jody Reed | .10 | .05 |
| ❑ 110 | Orel Hershiser | .15 | .07 |
| ❑ 111 | Terry Steinbach | .10 | .05 |
| ❑ 112 | Mark Loretta | .10 | .05 |
| ❑ 113 | Turk Wendell | .10 | .05 |
| ❑ 114 | Marvin Benard | .10 | .05 |
| ❑ 115 | Kevin Brown | .15 | .07 |
| ❑ 116 | Robert Person | .10 | .05 |

❑ 117 Joey Hamilton .10 .05
❑ 118 Francisco Cordova .10 .05
❑ 119 John Smiley .10 .05
❑ 120 Travis Fryman .15 .07
❑ 121 Jimmy Key .15 .07
❑ 122 Tom Goodwin .10 .05
❑ 123 Mike Greenwell .10 .05
❑ 124 Juan Gonzalez .40 .18
❑ 125 Pete Harnisch .10 .05
❑ 126 Roger Cedeno .10 .05
❑ 127 Ron Gant .10 .05
❑ 128 Mark Langston .10 .05
❑ 129 Tim Crabtree .10 .05
❑ 130 Greg Maddux 1.00 .45
❑ 131 William VanLandingham .10 .05
❑ 132 Wally Joyner .15 .07
❑ 133 Randy Myers .10 .05
❑ 134 John Valentin .10 .05
❑ 135 Bret Boone .15 .07
❑ 136 Bruce Ruffin .10 .05
❑ 137 Chris Snopek .10 .05
❑ 138 Paul Molitor .40 .18
❑ 139 Mark McLemore .10 .05
❑ 140 Rafael Palmeiro .40 .18
❑ 141 Herb Perry .10 .05
❑ 142 Luis Gonzalez .15 .07
❑ 143 Doug Drabek .10 .05
❑ 144 Ken Ryan .10 .05
❑ 145 Todd Hundley .10 .05
❑ 146 Ellis Burks .15 .07
❑ 147 Ozzie Guillen .10 .05
❑ 148 Rich Becker .10 .05
❑ 149 Sterling Hitchcock .10 .05
❑ 150 Bernie Williams .40 .18
❑ 151 Mike Stanley .10 .05
❑ 152 Roberto Alomar .40 .18
❑ 153 Jose Mesa .10 .05
❑ 154 Steve Trachsel .10 .05
❑ 155 Alex Gonzalez .10 .05
❑ 156 Troy Percival .10 .05
❑ 157 John Smoltz .15 .07
❑ 158 Pedro Martinez .50 .23
❑ 159 Jeff Conine .10 .05
❑ 160 Bernard Gilkey .10 .05
❑ 161 Jim Eisenreich .10 .05
❑ 162 Mickey Tettleton .10 .05
❑ 163 Justin Thompson .10 .05
❑ 164 Jose Offerman .10 .05
❑ 165 Tony Phillips .10 .05
❑ 166 Ismael Valdes .10 .05
❑ 167 Ryne Sandberg .50 .23
❑ 168 Matt Mieske .10 .05
❑ 169 Geronimo Berroa .10 .05
❑ 170 Otis Nixon .10 .05
❑ 171 John Mabry .10 .05
❑ 172 Shawon Dunston .10 .05
❑ 173 Omar Vizquel .15 .07
❑ 174 Chris Hoiles .10 .05
❑ 175 Dwight Gooden .15 .07
❑ 176 Wilson Alvarez .10 .05
❑ 177 Todd Hollandsworth .10 .05
❑ 178 Roger Salkeld .10 .05
❑ 179 Rey Sanchez .10 .05
❑ 180 Rey Ordonez .10 .05
❑ 181 Denny Martinez .15 .07
❑ 182 Ramon Martinez .10 .05
❑ 183 Dave Nilsson .10 .05
❑ 184 Marquis Grissom .10 .05
❑ 185 Randy Velarde .10 .05
❑ 186 Ron Coomer .10 .05
❑ 187 Tino Martinez .15 .07
❑ 188 Jeff Brantley .10 .05
❑ 189 Steve Finley .15 .07
❑ 190 Andy Benes .10 .05
❑ 191 Terry Adams .10 .05
❑ 192 Mike Blowers .10 .05
❑ 193 Russ Davis .10 .05
❑ 194 Darryl Hamilton .10 .05
❑ 195 Jason Kendall .15 .07
❑ 196 Johnny Damon .15 .07
❑ 197 Dave Martinez .10 .05
❑ 198 Mike Macfarlane .10 .05
❑ 199 Norm Charlton .10 .05
❑ 200 Doug Million RC .10 .05
Damian Moss
Bobby Rodgers
❑ 201 Geoff Jenkins .15 .07
Raul Ibanez
Mike Cameron
❑ 202 Sean Casey .50 .23
Jim Bonnici
Dmitri Young
❑ 203 Jed Hansen .10 .05
Homer Bush
Felipe Crespo
❑ 204 Kevin Orie .10 .05
Gabe Alvarez
Aaron Boone
❑ 205 Ben Davis .10 .05
Kevin Brown
Bobby Estalella
❑ 206 Billy McMillon RC .15 .07
Bubba Trammell
Dante Powell
❑ 207 Jarrod Washburn .10 .05
Marc Wilkins RC
Glendon Rusch
❑ 208 Brian Hunter .10 .05
❑ 209 Jason Giambi .40 .18
❑ 210 Henry Rodriguez .10 .05
❑ 211 Edgar Renteria .15 .07
❑ 212 Edgardo Alfonzo .15 .07
❑ 213 Fernando Vina .10 .05
❑ 214 Shawn Green .40 .18
❑ 215 Ray Durham .15 .07
❑ 216 Joe Randa .10 .05
❑ 217 Armando Reynoso .10 .05
❑ 218 Eric Davis .15 .07
❑ 219 Bob Tewksbury .10 .05
❑ 220 Jacob Cruz .10 .05
❑ 221 Glenallen Hill .10 .05
❑ 222 Gary Gaetti .15 .07
❑ 223 Donne Wall .10 .05
❑ 224 Brad Clontz .10 .05
❑ 225 Marty Janzen .10 .05
❑ 226 Todd Worrell .10 .05
❑ 227 John Franco .15 .07
❑ 228 David Wells .15 .07
❑ 229 Gregg Jefferies .10 .05
❑ 230 Tim Naehring .10 .05
❑ 231 Thomas Howard .10 .05
❑ 232 Roberto Hernandez .10 .05
❑ 233 Kevin Ritz .10 .05
❑ 234 Julian Tavarez .10 .05
❑ 235 Ken Hill .10 .05
❑ 236 Greg Gagne .10 .05
❑ 237 Bobby Chouinard .10 .05
❑ 238 Joe Carter .15 .07
❑ 239 Jermaine Dye .15 .07
❑ 240 Antonio Osuna .10 .05
❑ 241 Julio Franco .15 .07
❑ 242 Mike Grace .10 .05
❑ 243 Aaron Sele .15 .07
❑ 244 David Justice .25 .11
❑ 245 Sandy Alomar Jr. .15 .07
❑ 246 Jose Canseco .50 .23
❑ 247 Paul O'Neill .15 .07
❑ 248 Sean Berry .10 .05
❑ 249 Nick Bierbrodt .40 .18
Kevin Sweeney RC
❑ 250 Larry Rodriguez RC .25 .11
Vladimir Nunez RC
❑ 251 Ron Hartman .15 .07
David Hayman RC
❑ 252 Alex Sanchez .25 .11
Matthew Quatraro RC
❑ 253 Ronni Seberino RC .25 .11
Pablo Ortego RC
❑ 254 Rex Hudler .10 .05
❑ 255 Orlando Miller .10 .05
❑ 256 Mariano Rivera .15 .07
❑ 257 Brad Radke .15 .07
❑ 258 Bobby Higginson .15 .07
❑ 259 Jay Bell .15 .07
❑ 260 Mark Grudzielanek .10 .05
❑ 261 Lance Johnson .10 .05
❑ 262 Ken Caminiti .15 .07
❑ 263 J.T. Snow .15 .07
❑ 264 Gary Sheffield .40 .18
❑ 265 Darrin Fletcher .10 .05
❑ 266 Eric Owens .10 .05
❑ 267 Luis Castillo .15 .07
❑ 268 Scott Rolen .40 .18
❑ 269 Todd Noel .25 .11
John Oliver RC
❑ 270 Robert Stratton RC .50 .23
Corey Lee RC
❑ 271 Gil Meche 1.00 .45
Matt Halloran RC
❑ 272 Eric Milton RC 1.00 .45
Dermal Brown
❑ 273 Josh Garrett .25 .11
Chris Reitsma RC
❑ 274 A.J.Zapp RC .40 .18
Jason Marquis
❑ 275 Checklist .10 .05
❑ 276 Checklist .10 .05
❑ 277 Chipper Jones UER 1.00 .45
(Incorrectly numbered 276)
❑ 278 Orlando Merced .10 .05
❑ 279 Ariel Prieto .10 .05
❑ 280 Al Leiter .15 .07
❑ 281 Pat Meares .10 .05
❑ 282 Darryl Strawberry .15 .07
❑ 283 Jamie Moyer .10 .05
❑ 284 Scott Servais .10 .05
❑ 285 Delino DeShields .10 .05
❑ 286 Danny Graves .10 .05
❑ 287 Gerald Williams .10 .05
❑ 288 Todd Greene .10 .05
❑ 289 Rico Brogna .10 .05
❑ 290 Derrick Gibson .10 .05
❑ 291 Joe Girardi .10 .05
❑ 292 Darren Lewis .10 .05
❑ 293 Nomar Garciaparra 1.25 .55
❑ 294 Greg Colbrunn .10 .05
❑ 295 Jeff Bagwell .50 .23
❑ 296 Brent Gates .10 .05
❑ 297 Jose Vizcaino .10 .05
❑ 298 Alex Ochoa .10 .05
❑ 299 Sid Fernandez .10 .05
❑ 300 Ken Griffey Jr. 1.50 .70
❑ 301 Chris Gomez .10 .05
❑ 302 Wendell Magee .10 .05
❑ 303 Darren Oliver .10 .05
❑ 304 Mel Nieves .10 .05
❑ 305 Sammy Sosa .75 .35
❑ 306 George Arias .10 .05
❑ 307 Jack McDowell .10 .05
❑ 308 Stan Javier .10 .05
❑ 309 Kimera Bartee .10 .05
❑ 310 James Baldwin .15 .07
❑ 311 Rocky Coppinger .10 .05
❑ 312 Keith Lockhart .10 .05
❑ 313 C.J. Nitkowski .10 .05
❑ 314 Allen Watson .10 .05
❑ 315 Darryl Kile .15 .07
❑ 316 Amaury Telemaco .10 .05
❑ 317 Jason Isringhausen .10 .05
❑ 318 Manny Ramirez .50 .23
❑ 319 Terry Pendleton .15 .07
❑ 320 Tim Salmon .15 .07
❑ 321 Eric Karros .15 .07
❑ 322 Mark Whiten .10 .05
❑ 323 Rick Krivda .10 .05
❑ 324 Brett Butler .15 .07
❑ 325 Randy Johnson .50 .23
❑ 326 Eddie Taubensee .10 .05
❑ 327 Mark Leiter .10 .05
❑ 328 Kevin Gross .10 .05
❑ 329 Ernie Young .10 .05
❑ 330 Pat Hentgen .10 .05
❑ 331 Rondell White .15 .07
❑ 332 Bobby Witt .10 .05
❑ 333 Eddie Murray .40 .18
❑ 334 Tim Raines .15 .07
❑ 335 Jeff Fassero .10 .05
❑ 336 Chuck Finley .15 .07
❑ 337 Willie Adams .10 .05
❑ 338 Chan Ho Park .15 .07
❑ 339 Jay Powell .10 .05
❑ 340 Ivan Rodriguez .50 .23
❑ 341 Jermaine Allensworth .10 .05
❑ 342 Jay Payton .15 .07
❑ 343 T.J. Mathews .10 .05
❑ 344 Tony Batista .40 .18
❑ 345 Ed Sprague .10 .05
❑ 346 Jeff Kent .25 .11

| | | | |
|---|---|---|---|
| ❑ 347 | Scott Erickson | .10 | .05 |
| ❑ 348 | Jeff Suppan | .10 | .05 |
| ❑ 349 | Pete Schourek | .10 | .05 |
| ❑ 350 | Kenny Lofton | .15 | .07 |
| ❑ 351 | Alan Benes | .10 | .05 |
| ❑ 352 | Fred McGriff | .25 | .11 |
| ❑ 353 | Charlie O'Brien | .10 | .05 |
| ❑ 354 | Darren Bragg | .10 | .05 |
| ❑ 355 | Alex Fernandez | .10 | .05 |
| ❑ 356 | Al Martin | .10 | .05 |
| ❑ 357 | Bob Wells | .10 | .05 |
| ❑ 358 | Chad Mottola | .10 | .05 |
| ❑ 359 | Devon White | .15 | .07 |
| ❑ 360 | David Cone | .15 | .07 |
| ❑ 361 | Bobby Jones | .10 | .05 |
| ❑ 362 | Scott Sanders | .10 | .05 |
| ❑ 363 | Karim Garcia | .10 | .05 |
| ❑ 364 | Kirt Manwaring | .10 | .05 |
| ❑ 365 | Chili Davis | .15 | .07 |
| ❑ 366 | Mike Hampton | .15 | .07 |
| ❑ 367 | Chad Ogea | .10 | .05 |
| ❑ 368 | Curt Schilling | .15 | .07 |
| ❑ 369 | Phil Nevin | .15 | .07 |
| ❑ 370 | Roger Clemens | .75 | .35 |
| ❑ 371 | Willie Greene | .10 | .05 |
| ❑ 372 | Kenny Rogers | .10 | .05 |
| ❑ 373 | Jose Rijo | .10 | .05 |
| ❑ 374 | Bobby Bonilla | .15 | .07 |
| ❑ 375 | Mike Mussina | .40 | .18 |
| ❑ 376 | Curtis Pride | .10 | .05 |
| ❑ 377 | Todd Walker | .10 | .05 |
| ❑ 378 | Jason Bere | .10 | .05 |
| ❑ 379 | Heathcliff Slocumb | .10 | .05 |
| ❑ 380 | Dante Bichette | .15 | .07 |
| ❑ 381 | Carlos Baerga | .10 | .05 |
| ❑ 382 | Livan Hernandez | .15 | .07 |
| ❑ 383 | Jason Schmidt | .10 | .05 |
| ❑ 384 | Kevin Stocker | .10 | .05 |
| ❑ 385 | Matt Williams | .25 | .11 |
| ❑ 386 | Bartolo Colon | .15 | .07 |
| ❑ 387 | Will Clark | .40 | .18 |
| ❑ 388 | Dennis Eckersley | .15 | .07 |
| ❑ 389 | Brooks Kieschnick | .10 | .05 |
| ❑ 390 | Ryan Klesko | .15 | .07 |
| ❑ 391 | Mark Carreon | .10 | .05 |
| ❑ 392 | Tim Worrell | .10 | .05 |
| ❑ 393 | Dean Palmer | .15 | .07 |
| ❑ 394 | Wil Cordero | .10 | .05 |
| ❑ 395 | Javy Lopez | .15 | .07 |
| ❑ 396 | Rich Aurilia | .15 | .07 |
| ❑ 397 | Greg Vaughn | .15 | .07 |
| ❑ 398 | Vinny Castilla | .15 | .07 |
| ❑ 399 | Jeff Montgomery | .10 | .05 |
| ❑ 400 | Cal Ripken | 1.50 | .70 |
| ❑ 401 | Walt Weiss | .10 | .05 |
| ❑ 402 | Brad Ausmus | .10 | .05 |
| ❑ 403 | Ruben Rivera | .10 | .05 |
| ❑ 404 | Mark Wohlers | .10 | .05 |
| ❑ 405 | Rick Aguilera | .10 | .05 |
| ❑ 406 | Tony Clark | .10 | .05 |
| ❑ 407 | Lyle Mouton | .10 | .05 |
| ❑ 408 | Bill Pulsipher | .10 | .05 |
| ❑ 409 | Jose Rosado | .10 | .05 |
| ❑ 410 | Tony Gwynn | .75 | .35 |
| ❑ 411 | Cecil Fielder | .15 | .07 |
| ❑ 412 | John Flaherty | .10 | .05 |
| ❑ 413 | Lenny Dykstra | .15 | .07 |
| ❑ 414 | Ugueth Urbina | .10 | .05 |
| ❑ 415 | Brian Jordan | .15 | .07 |
| ❑ 416 | Bob Abreu | .15 | .07 |
| ❑ 417 | Craig Paquette | .10 | .05 |
| ❑ 418 | Sandy Martinez | .10 | .05 |
| ❑ 419 | Jeff Blauser | .10 | .05 |
| ❑ 420 | Barry Larkin | .40 | .18 |
| ❑ 421 | Kevin Seitzer | .10 | .05 |
| ❑ 422 | Tim Belcher | .10 | .05 |
| ❑ 423 | Paul Sorrento | .10 | .05 |
| ❑ 424 | Cal Eldred | .10 | .05 |
| ❑ 425 | Robin Ventura | .15 | .07 |
| ❑ 426 | John Olerud | .15 | .07 |
| ❑ 427 | Bob Wolcott | .10 | .05 |
| ❑ 428 | Matt Lawton | .15 | .07 |
| ❑ 429 | Rod Beck | .10 | .05 |
| ❑ 430 | Shane Reynolds | .10 | .05 |
| ❑ 431 | Mike James | .10 | .05 |
| ❑ 432 | Steve Wojciechowski | .10 | .05 |
| ❑ 433 | Vladimir Guerrero | .75 | .35 |
| ❑ 434 | Dustin Hermanson | .10 | .05 |
| ❑ 435 | Marty Cordova | .10 | .05 |
| ❑ 436 | Marc Newfield | .10 | .05 |
| ❑ 437 | Todd Stottlemyre | .10 | .05 |
| ❑ 438 | Jeffrey Hammonds | .15 | .07 |
| ❑ 439 | Dave Stevens | .10 | .05 |
| ❑ 440 | Hideo Nomo | .40 | .18 |
| ❑ 441 | Mark Thompson | .10 | .05 |
| ❑ 442 | Mark Lewis | .10 | .05 |
| ❑ 443 | Quinton McCracken | .10 | .05 |
| ❑ 444 | Cliff Floyd | .15 | .07 |
| ❑ 445 | Denny Neagle | .15 | .07 |
| ❑ 446 | John Jaha | .10 | .05 |
| ❑ 447 | Mike Sweeney | .15 | .07 |
| ❑ 448 | John Wasdin | .10 | .05 |
| ❑ 449 | Chad Curtis | .10 | .05 |
| ❑ 450 | Mo Vaughn | .15 | .07 |
| ❑ 451 | Donovan Osborne | .10 | .05 |
| ❑ 452 | Ruben Sierra | .10 | .05 |
| ❑ 453 | Michael Tucker | .10 | .05 |
| ❑ 454 | Kurt Abbott | .10 | .05 |
| ❑ 455 | Andruw Jones UER | .50 | .23 |
| | (Birthdate is incorrectly listed as 1-22-67; should be 1-22-77) | | |
| ❑ 456 | Shannon Stewart | .15 | .07 |
| ❑ 457 | Scott Brosius | .15 | .07 |
| ❑ 458 | Juan Guzman | .10 | .05 |
| ❑ 459 | Ron Villone | .10 | .05 |
| ❑ 460 | Moises Alou | .15 | .07 |
| ❑ 461 | Larry Walker | .15 | .07 |
| ❑ 462 | Eddie Murray SH | .15 | .07 |
| ❑ 463 | Paul Molitor SH | .15 | .07 |
| ❑ 464 | Hideo Nomo SH | .15 | .07 |
| ❑ 465 | Barry Bonds SH | .40 | .18 |
| ❑ 466 | Todd Hundley SH | .10 | .05 |
| ❑ 467 | Rheal Cormier | .10 | .05 |
| ❑ 468 | Jason Conti RC | .25 | .11 |
| | Jhensy Sandoval | | |
| ❑ 469 | Rod Barajas | .25 | .11 |
| | Jackie Rexrode RC | | |
| ❑ 470 | Cedric Bowers RC | .25 | .11 |
| | Jared Sandberg | | |
| ❑ 471 | Chei Gunner RC | .10 | .05 |
| | Paul Wilder | | |
| ❑ 472 | Mike Decelle | .10 | .05 |
| | Marcus McCain RC | | |
| ❑ 473 | Todd Zeile | .10 | .05 |
| ❑ 474 | Neifi Perez | .10 | .05 |
| ❑ 475 | Jeromy Burnitz | .15 | .07 |
| ❑ 476 | Trey Beamon | .10 | .05 |
| ❑ 477 | Braden Looper RC | .40 | .18 |
| | John Patterson | | |
| ❑ 478 | Danny Peoples | .25 | .11 |
| | Jake Westbrook RC | | |
| ❑ 479 | Eric Chavez | 1.50 | .70 |
| | Adam Eaton RC | | |
| ❑ 480 | Joe Lawrence RC | .40 | .18 |
| | Pete Tucci | | |
| ❑ 481 | Kris Benson | 1.25 | .55 |
| | Billy Koch RC | | |
| ❑ 482 | John Nicholson | .25 | .11 |
| | Andy Prater RC | | |
| ❑ 483 | Mark Johnson RC | .40 | .18 |
| | Mark Kotsay | | |
| ❑ 484 | Armando Benitez | .10 | .05 |
| ❑ 485 | Mike Matheny | .10 | .05 |
| ❑ 486 | Jeff Reed | .10 | .05 |
| ❑ 487 | Mark Bellhorn | .10 | .05 |
| | Russ Johnson | | |
| | Enrique Wilson | | |
| ❑ 488 | Ben Grieve | .10 | .05 |
| | Richard Hidalgo | | |
| | Scott Morgan RC | | |
| ❑ 489 | Paul Konerko | .15 | .07 |
| | Derrek Lee UER spelled Derek on back | | |
| | Ron Wright | | |
| ❑ 490 | Wes Helms RC | .25 | .11 |
| | Bill Mueller | | |
| | Brad Seitzer | | |
| ❑ 491 | Jeff Abbott | .10 | .05 |
| | Shane Monahan | | |
| | Edgard Velazquez | | |
| ❑ 492 | Jimmy Anderson RC | .25 | .11 |
| | Ron Blazier | | |
| | Gerald Witasick | | |
| ❑ 493 | Darin Blood | .25 | .11 |
| | Heath Murray | | |
| | Carl Pavano | | |
| ❑ 494 | Nelson Figueroa RC | .25 | .11 |
| | Mark Redman | | |
| | Mike Villano | | |
| ❑ 495 | Checklist | .10 | .05 |
| ❑ 496 | Checklist | .10 | .05 |
| ❑ NNO | Derek Jeter AU | 150.00 | 70.00 |

## 1998 Topps

| | MINT | NRMT |
|---|---|---|
| COMPLETE SET (503) | 50.00 | 22.00 |
| COMP.HOBBY SET (511) | 100.00 | 45.00 |
| COMP.RETAIL SET (511) | 80.00 | 36.00 |
| COMPLETE SERIES 1 (282) | 25.00 | 11.00 |
| COMPLETE SERIES 2 (221) | 25.00 | 11.00 |
| COMMON CARD (1-504) | .10 | .05 |

| | | | |
|---|---|---|---|
| ❑ 1 | Tony Gwynn | .75 | .35 |
| ❑ 2 | Larry Walker | .15 | .07 |
| ❑ 3 | Billy Wagner | .10 | .05 |
| ❑ 4 | Denny Neagle | .10 | .05 |
| ❑ 5 | Vladimir Guerrero | .60 | .25 |
| ❑ 6 | Kevin Brown | .25 | .11 |
| ❑ 8 | Mariano Rivera | .15 | .07 |
| ❑ 9 | Tony Clark | .10 | .05 |
| ❑ 10 | Deion Sanders | .15 | .07 |
| ❑ 11 | Francisco Cordova | .10 | .05 |
| ❑ 12 | Matt Williams | .25 | .11 |
| ❑ 13 | Carlos Baerga | .10 | .05 |
| ❑ 14 | Mo Vaughn | .15 | .07 |
| ❑ 15 | Bobby Witt | .10 | .05 |
| ❑ 16 | Matt Stairs | .10 | .05 |
| ❑ 17 | Chan Ho Park | .15 | .07 |
| ❑ 18 | Mike Bordick | .10 | .05 |
| ❑ 19 | Michael Tucker | .10 | .05 |
| ❑ 20 | Frank Thomas | .75 | .35 |
| ❑ 21 | Roberto Clemente | 1.00 | .45 |
| ❑ 22 | Dmitri Young | .15 | .07 |
| ❑ 23 | Steve Trachsel | .10 | .05 |
| ❑ 24 | Jeff Kent | .25 | .11 |
| ❑ 25 | Scott Rolen | .40 | .18 |
| ❑ 26 | John Thomson | .10 | .05 |
| ❑ 27 | Joe Vitiello | .10 | .05 |
| ❑ 28 | Eddie Guardado | .10 | .05 |
| ❑ 29 | Charlie Hayes | .10 | .05 |
| ❑ 30 | Juan Gonzalez | .40 | .18 |
| ❑ 31 | Garret Anderson | .15 | .07 |
| ❑ 32 | John Jaha | .15 | .07 |
| ❑ 33 | Omar Vizquel | .15 | .07 |
| ❑ 34 | Brian Hunter | .10 | .05 |
| ❑ 35 | Jeff Bagwell | .50 | .23 |
| ❑ 36 | Mark Lemke | .10 | .05 |
| ❑ 37 | Doug Glanville | .10 | .05 |
| ❑ 38 | Dan Wilson | .10 | .05 |
| ❑ 39 | Steve Cooke | .10 | .05 |
| ❑ 40 | Chili Davis | .15 | .07 |
| ❑ 41 | Mike Cameron | .15 | .07 |
| ❑ 42 | F.P. Santangelo | .10 | .05 |
| ❑ 43 | Brad Ausmus | .10 | .05 |
| ❑ 44 | Gary DiSarcina | .10 | .05 |
| ❑ 45 | Pat Hentgen | .10 | .05 |
| ❑ 46 | Wilton Guerrero | .10 | .05 |
| ❑ 47 | Devon White | .10 | .05 |
| ❑ 48 | Danny Patterson | .10 | .05 |

❑ 49 Pat Meares .10 .05
❑ 50 Rafael Palmeiro .40 .18
❑ 51 Mark Gardner .10 .05
❑ 52 Jeff Blauser .10 .05
❑ 53 Dave Hollins .10 .05
❑ 54 Carlos Garcia .10 .05
❑ 55 Ben McDonald .10 .05
❑ 56 John Mabry .10 .05
❑ 57 Trevor Hoffman .15 .07
❑ 58 Tony Fernandez .10 .05
❑ 59 Rich Loiselle .15 .07
❑ 60 Mark Leiter .10 .05
❑ 61 Pat Kelly .10 .05
❑ 62 John Flaherty .10 .05
❑ 63 Roger Bailey .10 .05
❑ 64 Tom Gordon .15 .07
❑ 65 Ryan Klesko .15 .07
❑ 66 Darryl Hamilton .10 .05
❑ 67 Jim Eisenreich .10 .05
❑ 68 Butch Huskey .10 .05
❑ 69 Mark Grudzielanek .10 .05
❑ 70 Marquis Grissom .10 .05
❑ 71 Mark McLemore .10 .05
❑ 72 Gary Gaetti .15 .07
❑ 73 Greg Gagne .10 .05
❑ 74 Lyle Mouton .10 .05
❑ 75 Jim Edmonds .40 .18
❑ 76 Shawn Green .40 .18
❑ 77 Greg Vaughn .15 .07
❑ 78 Terry Adams .10 .05
❑ 79 Kevin Polcovich .10 .05
❑ 80 Troy O'Leary .10 .05
❑ 81 Jeff Shaw .10 .05
❑ 82 Rich Becker .10 .05
❑ 83 David Wells .15 .07
❑ 84 Steve Karsay .10 .05
❑ 85 Charles Nagy .10 .05
❑ 86 B.J. Surhoff .15 .07
❑ 87 Jamey Wright .10 .05
❑ 88 James Baldwin .10 .05
❑ 89 Edgardo Alfonzo .15 .07
❑ 90 Jay Buhner .15 .07
❑ 91 Brady Anderson .15 .07
❑ 92 Scott Servais .10 .05
❑ 93 Edgar Renteria .10 .05
❑ 94 Mike Lieberthal .15 .07
❑ 95 Rick Aguilera .10 .05
❑ 96 Walt Weiss .15 .07
❑ 97 Deivi Cruz .10 .05
❑ 98 Kurt Abbott .10 .05
❑ 99 Henry Rodriguez .10 .05
❑ 100 Mike Piazza 1.25 .55
❑ 101 Bill Taylor .10 .05
❑ 102 Todd Zeile .15 .07
❑ 103 Rey Ordonez .10 .05
❑ 104 Willie Greene .10 .05
❑ 105 Tony Womack .10 .05
❑ 106 Mike Sweeney .15 .07
❑ 107 Jeffrey Hammonds .15 .07
❑ 108 Kevin Orie .10 .05
❑ 109 Alex Gonzalez .10 .05
❑ 110 Jose Canseco .50 .23
❑ 111 Paul Sorrento .10 .05
❑ 112 Joey Hamilton .10 .05
❑ 113 Brad Radke .15 .07
❑ 114 Steve Avery .10 .05
❑ 115 Esteban Loaiza .10 .05
❑ 116 Stan Javier .10 .05
❑ 117 Chris Gomez .10 .05
❑ 118 Royce Clayton .10 .05
❑ 119 Orlando Merced .10 .05
❑ 120 Kevin Appier .15 .07
❑ 121 Mel Nieves .10 .05
❑ 122 Joe Girardi .10 .05
❑ 123 Rico Brogna .10 .05
❑ 124 Kent Mercker .10 .05
❑ 125 Manny Ramirez .50 .23
❑ 126 Jeromy Burnitz .15 .07
❑ 127 Kevin Foster .10 .05
❑ 128 Matt Morris .10 .05
❑ 129 Jason Dickson .10 .05
❑ 130 Tom Glavine .40 .18
❑ 131 Wally Joyner .15 .07
❑ 132 Rick Reed .10 .05
❑ 133 Todd Jones .10 .05
❑ 134 Dave Martinez .10 .05
❑ 135 Sandy Alomar Jr. .15 .07
❑ 136 Mike Lansing .10 .05
❑ 137 Sean Berry .10 .05
❑ 138 Doug Jones .10 .05
❑ 139 Todd Stottlemyre .10 .05
❑ 140 Jay Bell .15 .07
❑ 141 Jaime Navarro .10 .05
❑ 142 Chris Hoiles .10 .05
❑ 143 Joey Cora .10 .05
❑ 144 Scott Spiezio .10 .05
❑ 145 Joe Carter .15 .07
❑ 146 Jose Guillen .10 .05
❑ 147 Damion Easley .10 .05
❑ 148 Lee Stevens .10 .05
❑ 149 Alex Fernandez .10 .05
❑ 150 Randy Johnson .50 .23
❑ 151 J.T. Snow .15 .07
❑ 152 Chuck Finley .15 .07
❑ 153 Bernard Gilkey .10 .05
❑ 154 David Segui .10 .05
❑ 155 Dante Bichette .15 .07
❑ 156 Kevin Stocker .10 .05
❑ 157 Carl Everett .15 .07
❑ 158 Jose Valentin .10 .05
❑ 159 Pokey Reese .15 .07
❑ 160 Derek Jeter 1.50 .70
❑ 161 Roger Pavlik .10 .05
❑ 162 Mark Wohlers .10 .05
❑ 163 Ricky Bottalico .10 .05
❑ 164 Ozzie Guillen .10 .05
❑ 165 Mike Mussina .40 .18
❑ 166 Gary Sheffield .40 .18
❑ 167 Hideo Nomo .40 .18
❑ 168 Mark Grace .40 .18
❑ 169 Aaron Sele .15 .07
❑ 170 Darryl Kile .15 .07
❑ 171 Shawn Estes .10 .05
❑ 172 Vinny Castilla .15 .07
❑ 173 Ron Coomer .10 .05
❑ 174 Jose Rosado .10 .05
❑ 175 Kenny Lofton .15 .07
❑ 176 Jason Giambi .40 .18
❑ 177 Hal Morris .10 .05
❑ 178 Darren Bragg .10 .05
❑ 179 Orel Hershiser .15 .07
❑ 180 Ray Lankford .15 .07
❑ 181 Hideki Irabu .10 .05
❑ 182 Kevin Young .15 .07
❑ 183 Javy Lopez .15 .07
❑ 184 Jeff Montgomery .10 .05
❑ 185 Mike Holtz .10 .05
❑ 186 George Williams .10 .05
❑ 187 Cal Eldred .10 .05
❑ 188 Tom Candiotti .10 .05
❑ 189 Glenallen Hill .10 .05
❑ 190 Brian Giles .15 .07
❑ 191 Dave Mlicki .10 .05
❑ 192 Garrett Stephenson .10 .05
❑ 193 Jeff Frye .10 .05
❑ 194 Joe Oliver .10 .05
❑ 195 Bob Hamelin .10 .05
❑ 196 Luis Sojo .10 .05
❑ 197 LaTroy Hawkins .10 .05
❑ 198 Kevin Elster .10 .05
❑ 199 Jeff Reed .10 .05
❑ 200 Dennis Eckersley .15 .07
❑ 201 Bill Mueller .10 .05
❑ 202 Russ Davis .10 .05
❑ 203 Armando Benitez .10 .05
❑ 204 Quilvio Veras .10 .05
❑ 205 Tim Naehring .10 .05
❑ 206 Quinton McCracken .10 .05
❑ 207 Raul Casanova .10 .05
❑ 208 Matt Lawton .10 .05
❑ 209 Luis Alicea .10 .05
❑ 210 Luis Gonzalez .15 .07
❑ 211 Allen Watson .10 .05
❑ 212 Gerald Williams .10 .05
❑ 213 David Bell .10 .05
❑ 214 Todd Hollandsworth .10 .05
❑ 215 Wade Boggs .50 .23
❑ 216 Jose Mesa .10 .05
❑ 217 Jamie Moyer .10 .05
❑ 218 Darren Daulton .15 .07
❑ 219 Mickey Morandini .10 .05
❑ 220 Rusty Greer .15 .07
❑ 221 Jim Bullinger .10 .05
❑ 222 Jose Offerman .10 .05
❑ 223 Matt Karchner .10 .05
❑ 224 Woody Williams .10 .05
❑ 225 Mark Loretta .10 .05
❑ 226 Mike Hampton .15 .07
❑ 227 Willie Adams .10 .05
❑ 228 Scott Hatteberg .10 .05
❑ 229 Rich Amaral .10 .05
❑ 230 Terry Steinbach .10 .05
❑ 231 Glendon Rusch .10 .05
❑ 232 Bret Boone .15 .07
❑ 233 Robert Person .10 .05
❑ 234 Jose Hernandez .10 .05
❑ 235 Doug Drabek .10 .05
❑ 236 Jason McDonald .10 .05
❑ 237 Chris Widger .10 .05
❑ 238 Tom Martin .10 .05
❑ 239 Dave Burba .10 .05
❑ 240 Pete Rose Jr. .15 .07
❑ 241 Bobby Ayala .10 .05
❑ 242 Tim Wakefield .10 .05
❑ 243 Dennis Springer .10 .05
❑ 244 Tim Belcher .10 .05
❑ 245 Jon Garland .10 .05
Geoff Goetz
❑ 246 Glenn Davis .25 .11
Lance Berkman
❑ 247 Vernon Wells .25 .11
Aaron Akin
❑ 248 Adam Kennedy .15 .07
Jason Romano
❑ 249 Jason Dellaero .10 .05
Troy Cameron
❑ 250 Alex Sanchez .10 .05
Jared Sandberg
❑ 251 Pablo Ortega .10 .05
James Manias
❑ 252 Jason Conti RC .10 .05
Mike Stoner
❑ 253 John Patterson .10 .05
Larry Rodriguez
❑ 254 Adrian Beltre .25 .11
Ryan Minor RC
Aaron Boone
❑ 255 Ben Grieve .15 .07
Brian Buchanan
Dermal Brown
❑ 256 Kerry Wood .40 .18
Carl Pavano
Gil Meche
❑ 257 David Ortiz .15 .07
Daryle Ward
Richie Sexson
❑ 258 Randy Winn .15 .07
Juan Encarnacion
Andrew Vessel
❑ 259 Kris Benson RC .10 .05
Travis Smith
Courtney Duncan
❑ 260 Chad Hermansen RC .40 .18
Brent Butler
Warren Morris
❑ 261 Ben Davis .10 .05
Eli Marrero
Ramon Hernandez
❑ 262 Eric Chavez .15 .07
Russell Branyan
Russ Johnson
❑ 263 Todd Dunwoody RC .15 .07
John Barnes
Ryan Jackson
❑ 264 Matt Clement RC .25 .11
Roy Halladay
Brian Fuentes
❑ 265 Randy Johnson SH .15 .07
❑ 266 Kevin Brown SH .15 .07
❑ 267 Ricardo Rincon SH .10 .05
Francisco Cordova
❑ 268 Nomar Garciaparra SH .40 .18
❑ 269 Tino Martinez SH .10 .05
❑ 270 Chuck Knoblauch IL .10 .05
❑ 271 Pedro Martinez IL .25 .11
❑ 272 Denny Neagle IL .10 .05
❑ 273 Juan Gonzalez IL .15 .07
❑ 274 Andres Galarraga IL .10 .05

| No. | Player | | |
|---|---|---|---|
| ❑ 275 | Checklist | .10 | .05 |
| ❑ 276 | Checklist | .10 | .05 |
| ❑ 277 | Moises Alou WS | .10 | .05 |
| ❑ 278 | Sandy Alomar Jr. WS | .10 | .05 |
| ❑ 279 | Gary Sheffield WS | .15 | .07 |
| ❑ 280 | Matt Williams WS | .15 | .07 |
| ❑ 281 | Livan Hernandez WS | .10 | .05 |
| ❑ 282 | Chad Ogea WS | .10 | .05 |
| ❑ 283 | Marlins Champs | .10 | .05 |
| ❑ 284 | Tino Martinez | .15 | .07 |
| ❑ 285 | Roberto Alomar | .40 | .18 |
| ❑ 286 | Jeff King | .10 | .05 |
| ❑ 287 | Brian Jordan | .15 | .07 |
| ❑ 288 | Darin Erstad | .40 | .18 |
| ❑ 289 | Ken Caminiti | .15 | .07 |
| ❑ 290 | Jim Thome | .25 | .11 |
| ❑ 291 | Paul Molitor | .40 | .18 |
| ❑ 292 | Ivan Rodriguez | .50 | .23 |
| ❑ 293 | Bernie Williams | .40 | .18 |
| ❑ 294 | Todd Hundley | .10 | .05 |
| ❑ 295 | Andres Galarraga | .25 | .11 |
| ❑ 296 | Greg Maddux | 1.00 | .45 |
| ❑ 297 | Edgar Martinez | .25 | .11 |
| ❑ 298 | Ron Gant | .15 | .07 |
| ❑ 299 | Derek Bell | .10 | .05 |
| ❑ 300 | Roger Clemens | .75 | .35 |
| ❑ 301 | Rondell White | .15 | .07 |
| ❑ 302 | Barry Larkin | .40 | .18 |
| ❑ 303 | Robin Ventura | .15 | .07 |
| ❑ 304 | Jason Kendall | .15 | .07 |
| ❑ 305 | Chipper Jones | 1.00 | .45 |
| ❑ 306 | John Franco | .15 | .07 |
| ❑ 307 | Sammy Sosa | .75 | .35 |
| ❑ 308 | Troy Percival | .10 | .05 |
| ❑ 309 | Chuck Knoblauch | .15 | .07 |
| ❑ 310 | Ellis Burks | .15 | .07 |
| ❑ 311 | Al Martin | .10 | .05 |
| ❑ 312 | Tim Salmon | .15 | .07 |
| ❑ 313 | Moises Alou | .15 | .07 |
| ❑ 314 | Lance Johnson | .10 | .05 |
| ❑ 315 | Justin Thompson | .10 | .05 |
| ❑ 316 | Will Clark | .40 | .18 |
| ❑ 317 | Barry Bonds | .60 | .25 |
| ❑ 318 | Craig Biggio | .25 | .11 |
| ❑ 319 | John Smoltz | .15 | .07 |
| ❑ 320 | Cal Ripken | 1.50 | .70 |
| ❑ 321 | Ken Griffey Jr. | 1.50 | .70 |
| ❑ 322 | Paul O'Neill | .15 | .07 |
| ❑ 323 | Todd Helton | .50 | .23 |
| ❑ 324 | John Olerud | .15 | .07 |
| ❑ 325 | Mark McGwire | 1.50 | .70 |
| ❑ 326 | Jose Cruz Jr. | .15 | .07 |
| ❑ 327 | Jeff Cirillo | .15 | .07 |
| ❑ 328 | Dean Palmer | .15 | .07 |
| ❑ 329 | John Wetteland | .15 | .07 |
| ❑ 330 | Steve Finley | .15 | .07 |
| ❑ 331 | Albert Belle | .25 | .11 |
| ❑ 332 | Curt Schilling | .15 | .07 |
| ❑ 333 | Raul Mondesi | .15 | .07 |
| ❑ 334 | Andruw Jones | .40 | .18 |
| ❑ 335 | Nomar Garciaparra | 1.25 | .55 |
| ❑ 336 | David Justice | .25 | .11 |
| ❑ 337 | Andy Pettitte | .15 | .07 |
| ❑ 338 | Pedro Martinez | .50 | .23 |
| ❑ 339 | Travis Miller | .10 | .05 |
| ❑ 340 | Chris Stynes | .10 | .05 |
| ❑ 341 | Gregg Jefferies | .10 | .05 |
| ❑ 342 | Jeff Fassero | .10 | .05 |
| ❑ 343 | Craig Counsell | .10 | .05 |
| ❑ 344 | Wilson Alvarez | .10 | .05 |
| ❑ 345 | Bip Roberts | .10 | .05 |
| ❑ 346 | Kelvim Escobar | .10 | .05 |
| ❑ 347 | Mark Bellhorn | .10 | .05 |
| ❑ 348 | Cory Lidle | .10 | .05 |
| ❑ 349 | Fred McGriff | .25 | .11 |
| ❑ 350 | Chuck Carr | .10 | .05 |
| ❑ 351 | Bob Abreu | .15 | .07 |
| ❑ 352 | Juan Guzman | .10 | .05 |
| ❑ 353 | Fernando Vina | .10 | .05 |
| ❑ 354 | Andy Benes | .10 | .05 |
| ❑ 355 | Dave Nilsson | .10 | .05 |
| ❑ 356 | Bobby Bonilla | .15 | .07 |
| ❑ 357 | Ismael Valdes | .10 | .05 |
| ❑ 358 | Carlos Perez | .10 | .05 |
| ❑ 359 | Kirk Rueter | .10 | .05 |
| ❑ 360 | Bartolo Colon | .15 | .07 |
| ❑ 361 | Mel Rojas | .10 | .05 |
| ❑ 362 | Johnny Damon | .15 | .07 |
| ❑ 363 | Geronimo Berroa | .10 | .05 |
| ❑ 364 | Reggie Sanders | .10 | .05 |
| ❑ 365 | Jermaine Allensworth | .10 | .05 |
| ❑ 366 | Orlando Cabrera | .10 | .05 |
| ❑ 367 | Jorge Fabregas | .10 | .05 |
| ❑ 368 | Scott Stahoviak | .10 | .05 |
| ❑ 369 | Ken Cloude | .10 | .05 |
| ❑ 370 | Donovan Osborne | .10 | .05 |
| ❑ 371 | Roger Cedeno | .10 | .05 |
| ❑ 372 | Neifi Perez | .10 | .05 |
| ❑ 373 | Chris Holt | .10 | .05 |
| ❑ 374 | Cecil Fielder | .15 | .07 |
| ❑ 375 | Marty Cordova | .10 | .05 |
| ❑ 376 | Tom Goodwin | .10 | .05 |
| ❑ 377 | Jeff Suppan | .10 | .05 |
| ❑ 378 | Jeff Brantley | .10 | .05 |
| ❑ 379 | Mark Langston | .10 | .05 |
| ❑ 380 | Shane Reynolds | .10 | .05 |
| ❑ 381 | Mike Fetters | .10 | .05 |
| ❑ 382 | Todd Greene | .10 | .05 |
| ❑ 383 | Ray Durham | .15 | .07 |
| ❑ 384 | Carlos Delgado | .40 | .18 |
| ❑ 385 | Jeff D'Amico | .10 | .05 |
| ❑ 386 | Brian McRae | .10 | .05 |
| ❑ 387 | Alan Benes | .10 | .05 |
| ❑ 388 | Heathcliff Slocumb | .10 | .05 |
| ❑ 389 | Eric Young | .10 | .05 |
| ❑ 390 | Travis Fryman | .15 | .07 |
| ❑ 391 | David Cone | .15 | .07 |
| ❑ 392 | Otis Nixon | .10 | .05 |
| ❑ 393 | Jeremi Gonzalez | .10 | .05 |
| ❑ 394 | Jeff Juden | .10 | .05 |
| ❑ 395 | Jose Vizcaino | .10 | .05 |
| ❑ 396 | Ugueth Urbina | .10 | .05 |
| ❑ 397 | Ramon Martinez | .10 | .05 |
| ❑ 398 | Robb Nen | .10 | .05 |
| ❑ 399 | Harold Baines | .15 | .07 |
| ❑ 400 | Delino DeShields | .10 | .05 |
| ❑ 401 | John Burkett | .10 | .05 |
| ❑ 402 | Sterling Hitchcock | .10 | .05 |
| ❑ 403 | Mark Clark | .10 | .05 |
| ❑ 404 | Terrell Wade | .10 | .05 |
| ❑ 405 | Scott Brosius | .15 | .07 |
| ❑ 406 | Chad Curtis | .10 | .05 |
| ❑ 407 | Brian Johnson | .10 | .05 |
| ❑ 408 | Roberto Kelly | .10 | .05 |
| ❑ 409 | Dave Dellucci RC | .10 | .05 |
| ❑ 410 | Michael Tucker | .10 | .05 |
| ❑ 411 | Mark Kotsay | .15 | .07 |
| ❑ 412 | Mark Lewis | .10 | .05 |
| ❑ 413 | Ryan McGuire | .10 | .05 |
| ❑ 414 | Shawon Dunston | .10 | .05 |
| ❑ 415 | Brad Rigby | .10 | .05 |
| ❑ 416 | Scott Erickson | .10 | .05 |
| ❑ 417 | Bobby Jones | .10 | .05 |
| ❑ 418 | Darren Oliver | .10 | .05 |
| ❑ 419 | John Smiley | .10 | .05 |
| ❑ 420 | T.J. Mathews | .10 | .05 |
| ❑ 421 | Dustin Hermanson | .10 | .05 |
| ❑ 422 | Mike Timlin | .10 | .05 |
| ❑ 423 | Willie Blair | .10 | .05 |
| ❑ 424 | Manny Alexander | .10 | .05 |
| ❑ 425 | Bob Tewksbury | .10 | .05 |
| ❑ 426 | Pete Schourek | .10 | .05 |
| ❑ 427 | Reggie Jefferson | .10 | .05 |
| ❑ 428 | Ed Sprague | .10 | .05 |
| ❑ 429 | Jeff Conine | .10 | .05 |
| ❑ 430 | Roberto Hernandez | .10 | .05 |
| ❑ 431 | Tom Pagnozzi | .10 | .05 |
| ❑ 432 | Jaret Wright | .10 | .05 |
| ❑ 433 | Livan Hernandez | .10 | .05 |
| ❑ 434 | Andy Ashby | .10 | .05 |
| ❑ 435 | Todd Dunn | .10 | .05 |
| ❑ 436 | Bobby Higginson | .15 | .07 |
| ❑ 437 | Rod Beck | .10 | .05 |
| ❑ 438 | Jim Leyritz | .10 | .05 |
| ❑ 439 | Matt Williams | .25 | .11 |
| ❑ 440 | Brett Tomko | .10 | .05 |
| ❑ 441 | Joe Randa | .10 | .05 |
| ❑ 442 | Chris Carpenter | .15 | .07 |
| ❑ 443 | Dennis Reyes | .10 | .05 |
| ❑ 444 | Al Leiter | .15 | .07 |
| ❑ 445 | Jason Schmidt | .10 | .05 |
| ❑ 446 | Ken Hill | .10 | .05 |
| ❑ 447 | Shannon Stewart | .15 | .07 |
| ❑ 448 | Enrique Wilson | .10 | .05 |
| ❑ 449 | Fernando Tatis | .15 | .07 |
| ❑ 450 | Jimmy Key | .15 | .07 |
| ❑ 451 | Darrin Fletcher | .10 | .05 |
| ❑ 452 | John Valentin | .10 | .05 |
| ❑ 453 | Kevin Tapani | .10 | .05 |
| ❑ 454 | Eric Karros | .15 | .07 |
| ❑ 455 | Jay Bell | .15 | .07 |
| ❑ 456 | Walt Weiss | .15 | .07 |
| ❑ 457 | Devon White | .10 | .05 |
| ❑ 458 | Carl Pavano | .10 | .05 |
| ❑ 459 | Mike Lansing | .10 | .05 |
| ❑ 460 | John Flaherty | .10 | .05 |
| ❑ 461 | Richard Hidalgo | .15 | .07 |
| ❑ 462 | Quinton McCracken | .10 | .05 |
| ❑ 463 | Karim Garcia | .10 | .05 |
| ❑ 464 | Miguel Cairo | .10 | .05 |
| ❑ 465 | Edwin Diaz | .10 | .05 |
| ❑ 466 | Bobby Smith | .10 | .05 |
| ❑ 467 | Yamil Benitez | .10 | .05 |
| ❑ 468 | Rich Butler | .10 | .05 |
| ❑ 469 | Ben Ford RC | .15 | .07 |
| ❑ 470 | Bubba Trammell | .10 | .05 |
| ❑ 471 | Brent Brede | .10 | .05 |
| ❑ 472 | Brooks Kieschnick | .10 | .05 |
| ❑ 473 | Carlos Castillo | .10 | .05 |
| ❑ 474 | Brad Radke SH | .10 | .05 |
| ❑ 475 | Roger Clemens SH | .40 | .18 |
| ❑ 476 | Curt Schilling SH | .15 | .07 |
| ❑ 477 | John Olerud SH | .10 | .05 |
| ❑ 478 | Mark McGwire SH | .75 | .35 |
| ❑ 479 | Mike Piazza<br>Ken Griffey Jr. IL | .75 | .35 |
| ❑ 480 | Jeff Bagwell<br>Frank Thomas IL | .25 | .11 |
| ❑ 481 | Chipper Jones<br>Nomar Garciaparra IL | .60 | .25 |
| ❑ 482 | Larry Walker<br>Juan Gonzalez IL | .15 | .07 |
| ❑ 483 | Gary Sheffield<br>Tino Martinez IL | .15 | .07 |
| ❑ 484 | Derrick Gibson<br>Michael Coleman<br>Norm Hutchins | .10 | .05 |
| ❑ 485 | Braden Looper<br>Cliff Politte<br>Brian Rose | .10 | .05 |
| ❑ 486 | Eric Milton<br>Jason Marquis<br>Corey Lee | .15 | .07 |
| ❑ 487 | A.J.Hinch<br>Mark Osborne RC<br>Robert Fick | .40 | .18 |
| ❑ 488 | Aramis Ramirez<br>Alex Gonzalez<br>Sean Casey | .10 | .05 |
| ❑ 489 | Donnie Bridges<br>Tim Drew RC | .30 | .14 |
| ❑ 490 | Ntema Ndungidi RC<br>Darnell McDonald | .40 | .18 |
| ❑ 491 | Ryan Anderson RC<br>Mark Mangum | 1.50 | .70 |
| ❑ 492 | J.J.Davis<br>Troy Glaus RC | 2.50 | 1.10 |
| ❑ 493 | Jayson Werth RC<br>Dan Reichert | .40 | .18 |
| ❑ 494 | John Curtice RC<br>Michael Cuddyer | .50 | .23 |
| ❑ 495 | Jack Cust RC<br>Jason Standridge | .75 | .35 |
| ❑ 496 | Brian Anderson | .10 | .05 |
| ❑ 497 | Tony Saunders | .10 | .05 |
| ❑ 498 | Vladimir Nunez<br>Jhensy Sandoval | .10 | .05 |
| ❑ 499 | Brad Penny<br>Nick Bierbrodt | .15 | .07 |
| ❑ 500 | Dustin Carr<br>Luis Cruz RC | .25 | .11 |
| ❑ 501 | Cedric Bowers<br>Marcus McCain | .15 | .07 |
| ❑ 502 | Checklist | .10 | .05 |
| ❑ 503 | Checklist | .10 | .05 |
| ❑ 504 | Alex Rodriguez | 2.50 | 1.10 |

## 1999 Topps

| | MINT | NRMT |
|---|---|---|
| COMPLETE SET (462) | 55.00 | 25.00 |
| COMP.HOBBY SET (462) | 60.00 | 27.00 |
| COMP.X-MAS SET (463) | 60.00 | 27.00 |
| COMPLETE SERIES 1 (241) | 30.00 | 13.50 |
| COMPLETE SERIES 2 (221) | 25.00 | 11.00 |
| COMP.MCGWIRE HR SET (70) | 1000.00 | 450.00 |
| COMP.SOSA HR SET (66) | 400.00 | 180.00 |

❑ 1 Roger Clemens .75 .35
❑ 2 Andres Galarraga .25 .11
❑ 3 Scott Brosius .15 .07
❑ 4 John Flaherty .10 .05
❑ 5 Jim Leyritz .10 .05
❑ 6 Ray Durham .15 .07
❑ 8 Jose Vizcaino .10 .05
❑ 9 Will Clark .40 .18
❑ 10 David Wells .15 .07
❑ 11 Jose Guillen .10 .05
❑ 12 Scott Hatteberg .10 .05
❑ 13 Edgardo Alfonzo .15 .07
❑ 14 Mike Bordick .10 .05
❑ 15 Manny Ramirez .50 .23
❑ 16 Greg Maddux 1.00 .45
❑ 17 David Segui .10 .05
❑ 18 Darryl Strawberry .15 .07
❑ 19 Brad Radke .15 .07
❑ 20 Kerry Wood .15 .07
❑ 21 Matt Anderson .10 .05
❑ 22 Derrek Lee .10 .05
❑ 23 Mickey Morandini .10 .05
❑ 24 Paul Konerko .15 .07
❑ 25 Travis Lee .10 .05
❑ 26 Ken Hill .10 .05
❑ 27 Kenny Rogers .10 .05
❑ 28 Paul Sorrento .10 .05
❑ 29 Quilvio Veras .10 .05
❑ 30 Todd Walker .10 .05
❑ 31 Ryan Jackson .10 .05
❑ 32 John Olerud .15 .07
❑ 33 Doug Glanville .10 .05
❑ 34 Nolan Ryan 2.50 1.10
❑ 35 Ray Lankford .15 .07
❑ 36 Mark Loretta .10 .05
❑ 37 Jason Dickson .10 .05
❑ 38 Sean Bergman .10 .05
❑ 39 Quinton McCracken .10 .05
❑ 40 Bartolo Colon .15 .07
❑ 41 Brady Anderson .15 .07
❑ 42 Chris Stynes .10 .05
❑ 43 Jorge Posada .15 .07
❑ 44 Justin Thompson .10 .05
❑ 45 Johnny Damon .15 .07
❑ 46 Armando Benitez .10 .05
❑ 47 Brant Brown .10 .05
❑ 48 Charlie Hayes .10 .05
❑ 49 Darren Dreifort .10 .05
❑ 50 Juan Gonzalez .40 .18
❑ 51 Chuck Knoblauch .15 .07
❑ 52 Todd Helton .50 .23
❑ 53 Rick Reed .10 .05
❑ 54 Chris Gomez .10 .05
❑ 55 Gary Sheffield .40 .18
❑ 56 Rod Beck .10 .05
❑ 57 Rey Sanchez .10 .05
❑ 58 Garret Anderson .15 .07
❑ 59 Jimmy Haynes .10 .05
❑ 60 Steve Woodard .10 .05
❑ 61 Rondell White .15 .07
❑ 62 Vladimir Guerrero .60 .25
❑ 63 Eric Karros .15 .07
❑ 64 Russ Davis .10 .05
❑ 65 Mo Vaughn .15 .07
❑ 66 Sammy Sosa .75 .35
❑ 67 Troy Percival .10 .05
❑ 68 Kenny Lofton .15 .07
❑ 69 Bill Taylor .10 .05
❑ 70 Mark McGwire 1.50 .70
❑ 71 Roger Cedeno .10 .05
❑ 72 Javy Lopez .15 .07
❑ 73 Damion Easley .10 .05
❑ 74 Andy Pettitte .15 .07
❑ 75 Tony Gwynn .75 .35
❑ 76 Ricardo Rincon .10 .05
❑ 77 F.P. Santangelo .10 .05
❑ 78 Jay Bell .15 .07
❑ 79 Scott Servais .10 .05
❑ 80 Jose Canseco .50 .23
❑ 81 Roberto Hernandez .10 .05
❑ 82 Todd Dunwoody .10 .05
❑ 83 John Wetteland .15 .07
❑ 84 Mike Caruso .10 .05
❑ 85 Derek Jeter 1.50 .70
❑ 86 Aaron Sele .15 .07
❑ 87 Jose Lima .10 .05
❑ 88 Ryan Christenson .10 .05
❑ 89 Jeff Cirillo .15 .07
❑ 90 Jose Hernandez .10 .05
❑ 91 Mark Kotsay .10 .05
❑ 92 Darren Bragg .10 .05
❑ 93 Albert Belle .25 .11
❑ 94 Matt Lawton .15 .07
❑ 95 Pedro Martinez .50 .23
❑ 96 Greg Vaughn .15 .07
❑ 97 Neifi Perez .10 .05
❑ 98 Gerald Williams .10 .05
❑ 99 Derek Bell .10 .05
❑ 100 Ken Griffey Jr. 1.50 .70
❑ 101 David Cone .15 .07
❑ 102 Brian Johnson .10 .05
❑ 103 Dean Palmer .15 .07
❑ 104 Javier Valentin .10 .05
❑ 105 Trevor Hoffman .15 .07
❑ 106 Butch Huskey .10 .05
❑ 107 Dave Martinez .10 .05
❑ 108 Billy Wagner .10 .05
❑ 109 Shawn Green .40 .18
❑ 110 Ben Grieve .15 .07
❑ 111 Tom Goodwin .10 .05
❑ 112 Jaret Wright .10 .05
❑ 113 Aramis Ramirez .10 .05
❑ 114 Dmitri Young .15 .07
❑ 115 Hideki Irabu .10 .05
❑ 116 Roberto Kelly .10 .05
❑ 117 Jeff Fassero .10 .05
❑ 118 Mark Clark UER .10 .05
(1997 and Career Victory totals are wrong)
❑ 119 Jason McDonald .10 .05
❑ 120 Matt Williams .25 .11
❑ 121 Dave Burba .10 .05
❑ 122 Bret Saberhagen .15 .07
❑ 123 Deivi Cruz .10 .05
❑ 124 Chad Curtis .10 .05
❑ 125 Scott Rolen .40 .18
❑ 126 Lee Stevens .10 .05
❑ 127 J.T. Snow .15 .07
❑ 128 Rusty Greer .15 .07
❑ 129 Brian Meadows .10 .05
❑ 130 Jim Edmonds .40 .18
❑ 131 Ron Gant .15 .07
❑ 132 A.J. Hinch .10 .05
❑ 133 Shannon Stewart .15 .07
❑ 134 Brad Fullmer .15 .07
❑ 135 Cal Eldred .10 .05
❑ 136 Matt Walbeck .10 .05
❑ 137 Carl Everett .15 .07
❑ 138 Walt Weiss .10 .05
❑ 139 Fred McGriff .25 .11
❑ 140 Darin Erstad .40 .18
❑ 141 Dave Nilsson .10 .05
❑ 142 Eric Young .10 .05
❑ 143 Dan Wilson .10 .05
❑ 144 Jeff Reed .10 .05
❑ 145 Brett Tomko .10 .05
❑ 146 Terry Steinbach .10 .05
❑ 147 Seth Greisinger .10 .05
❑ 148 Pat Meares .10 .05
❑ 149 Livan Hernandez .10 .05
❑ 150 Jeff Bagwell .50 .23
❑ 151 Bob Wickman .10 .05
❑ 152 Omar Vizquel .15 .07
❑ 153 Eric Davis .15 .07
❑ 154 Larry Sutton .10 .05
❑ 155 Magglio Ordonez .25 .11
❑ 156 Eric Milton .10 .05
❑ 157 Darren Lewis .10 .05
❑ 158 Rick Aguilera .10 .05
❑ 159 Mike Lieberthal .15 .07
❑ 160 Robb Nen .10 .05
❑ 161 Brian Giles .15 .07
❑ 162 Jeff Brantley .10 .05
❑ 163 Gary DiSarcina .10 .05
❑ 164 John Valentin .10 .05
❑ 165 David Dellucci .10 .05
❑ 166 Chan Ho Park .15 .07
❑ 167 Masato Yoshii .15 .07
❑ 168 Jason Schmidt .10 .05
❑ 169 LaTroy Hawkins .10 .05
❑ 170 Bret Boone .15 .07
❑ 171 Jerry DiPoto .10 .05
❑ 172 Mariano Rivera .15 .07
❑ 173 Mike Cameron .10 .05
❑ 174 Scott Erickson .10 .05
❑ 175 Charles Johnson .15 .07
❑ 176 Bobby Jones .10 .05
❑ 177 Francisco Cordova .10 .05
❑ 178 Todd Jones .10 .05
❑ 179 Jeff Montgomery .10 .05
❑ 180 Mike Mussina .40 .18
❑ 181 Bob Abreu .15 .07
❑ 182 Ismael Valdes .10 .05
❑ 183 Andy Fox .10 .05
❑ 184 Woody Williams .10 .05
❑ 185 Denny Neagle .10 .05
❑ 186 Jose Valentin .10 .05
❑ 187 Darrin Fletcher .10 .05
❑ 188 Gabe Alvarez .10 .05
❑ 189 Eddie Taubensee .10 .05
❑ 190 Edgar Martinez .25 .11
❑ 191 Jason Kendall .15 .07
❑ 192 Darryl Kile .15 .07
❑ 193 Jeff King .10 .05
❑ 194 Rey Ordonez .10 .05
❑ 195 Andruw Jones .40 .18
❑ 196 Tony Fernandez .10 .05
❑ 197 Jamey Wright .10 .05
❑ 198 B.J. Surhoff .15 .07
❑ 199 Vinny Castilla .15 .07
❑ 200 David Wells HL .10 .05
❑ 201 Mark McGwire HL .75 .35
❑ 202 Sammy Sosa HL .40 .18
❑ 203 Roger Clemens HL .40 .18
❑ 204 Kerry Wood HL .15 .07
❑ 205 Lance Berkman .15 .07
Mike Frank
Gabe Kapler
❑ 206 Alex Escobar RC .75 .35
Ricky Ledee
Mike Stoner
❑ 207 Peter Bergeron RC .40 .18
Jeremy Giambi
George Lombard
❑ 208 Michael Barrett .10 .05
Ben Davis
Robert Fick
❑ 209 Pat Cline .10 .05
Ramon Hernandez
Jayson Werth
❑ 210 Bruce Chen .15 .07
Chris Enochs
Ryan Anderson
❑ 211 Mike Lincoln .10 .05
Octavio Dotel
Brad Penny
❑ 212 Chuck Abbott RC .10 .05
Brent Butler
Danny Klassen

❑ 213 Chris C.Jones .25 .11
Jeff Urban RC
❑ 214 Arturo McDowell RC .40 .18
Tony Torcato
❑ 215 Josh McKinley RC .40 .18
Jason Tyner
❑ 216 Matt Burch .25 .11
Seth Etheron RC
UER back Etherton
❑ 217 Mamon Tucker RC .25 .11
Rick Elder
❑ 218 J.M.Gold .25 .11
Ryan Mills RC
❑ 219 Adam Brown .40 .18
Choo Freeman RC
❑ 220A Mark McGwire HR 1 40.00 18.00
❑ 220B Mark McGwire HR 2 20.00 9.00
❑ 220C Mark McGwire HR 3 20.00 9.00
❑ 220D Mark McGwire HR 4 20.00 9.00
❑ 220E Mark McGwire HR 5 20.00 9.00
❑ 220F Mark McGwire HR 6 20.00 9.00
❑ 220G Mark McGwire HR 7 20.00 9.00
❑ 220H Mark McGwire HR 8 20.00 9.00
❑ 220I Mark McGwire HR 9 20.00 9.00
❑ 220J Mark McGwire HR 10 20.00 9.00
❑ 220K Mark McGwire HR 11 20.00 9.00
❑ 220L Mark McGwire HR 12 20.00 9.00
❑ 220M Mark McGwire HR 13 20.00 9.00
❑ 220N Mark McGwire HR 14 20.00 9.00
❑ 220O Mark McGwire HR 15 20.00 9.00
❑ 220P Mark McGwire HR 16 20.00 9.00
❑ 220Q Mark McGwire HR 17 20.00 9.00
❑ 220R Mark McGwire HR 18 20.00 9.00
❑ 220S Mark McGwire HR 19 20.00 9.00
❑ 220T Mark McGwire HR 20 20.00 9.00
❑ 220U Mark McGwire HR 21 20.00 9.00
❑ 220V Mark McGwire HR 22 20.00 9.00
❑ 220W Mark McGwire HR 23 20.00 9.00
❑ 220X Mark McGwire HR 24 20.00 9.00
❑ 220Y Mark McGwire HR 25 20.00 9.00
❑ 220Z Mark McGwire HR 26 20.00 9.00
❑ 220AA Mark McGwire HR 27 20.00 9.00
❑ 220AB Mark McGwire HR 28 20.00 9.00
❑ 220AC Mark McGwire HR 29 20.00 9.00
❑ 220AD Mark McGwire HR 30 20.00 9.00
❑ 220AE Mark McGwire HR 31 20.00 9.00
❑ 220AF Mark McGwire HR 32 20.00 9.00
❑ 220AG Mark McGwire HR 33 20.00 9.00
❑ 220AH Mark McGwire HR 34 20.00 9.00
❑ 220AI Mark McGwire HR 35 20.00 9.00
❑ 220AJ Mark McGwire HR 36 20.00 9.00
❑ 220AK Mark McGwire HR 37 20.00 9.00
❑ 220AL Mark McGwire HR 38 20.00 9.00
❑ 220AM Mark McGwire HR 39 20.00 9.00
❑ 220AN Mark McGwire HR 40 20.00 9.00
❑ 220AO Mark McGwire HR 41 20.00 9.00
❑ 220AP Mark McGwire HR 42 20.00 9.00
❑ 220AQ Mark McGwire HR 43 20.00 9.00
❑ 220AR Mark McGwire HR 44 20.00 9.00
❑ 220AS Mark McGwire HR 45 20.00 9.00
❑ 220AT Mark McGwire HR 46 20.00 9.00
❑ 220AU Mark McGwire HR 47 20.00 9.00
❑ 220AV Mark McGwire HR 48 20.00 9.00
❑ 220AW Mark McGwire HR 49 20.00 9.00
❑ 220AX Mark McGwire HR 50 20.00 9.00
❑ 220AY Mark McGwire HR 51 20.00 9.00
❑ 220AZ Mark McGwire HR 52 20.00 9.00
❑ 220BB Mark McGwire HR 53 20.00 9.00
❑ 220CC Mark McGwire HR 54 20.00 9.00
❑ 220DD Mark McGwire HR 55 20.00 9.00
❑ 220EE Mark McGwire HR 56 20.00 9.00
❑ 220FF Mark McGwire HR 57 20.00 9.00
❑ 220GG Mark McGwire HR 58 20.00 9.00
❑ 220HH Mark McGwire HR 59 20.00 9.00
❑ 220II Mark McGwire HR 60 20.00 9.00
❑ 220JJ Mark McGwire HR 61 40.00 18.00
❑ 220KK Mark McGwire HR 62 60.00 27.00
❑ 220LL Mark McGwire HR 63 20.00 9.00
❑ 220MM Mark McGwire HR 64 20.00 9.00
❑ 220NN Mark McGwire HR 65 20.00 9.00
❑ 220OO Mark McGwire HR 66 20.00 9.00
❑ 220PP Mark McGwire HR 67 20.00 9.00
❑ 220QQ Mark McGwire HR 68 20.00 9.00
❑ 220RR Mark McGwire HR 69 20.00 9.00
❑ 220SS Mark McGwire HR 70 125.00 55.00
❑ 221 Larry Walker LL .15 .07
❑ 222 Bernie Williams LL .15 .07
❑ 223 Mark McGwire LL .75 .35
❑ 224 Ken Griffey Jr. LL .75 .35
❑ 225 Sammy Sosa LL .40 .18
❑ 226 Juan Gonzalez LL .15 .07
❑ 227 Dante Bichette LL .10 .05
❑ 228 Alex Rodriguez LL .60 .25
❑ 229 Sammy Sosa LL .40 .18
❑ 230 Derek Jeter LL .75 .35
❑ 231 Greg Maddux LL .50 .23
❑ 232 Roger Clemens LL .40 .18
❑ 233 Ricky Ledee WS .10 .05
❑ 234 Chuck Knoblauch WS .15 .07
❑ 235 Bernie Williams WS .15 .07
❑ 236 Tino Martinez WS .10 .05
❑ 237 Orlando Hernandez WS .15 .07
❑ 238 Scott Brosius WS .10 .05
❑ 239 Andy Pettitte WS .10 .05
❑ 240 Mariano Rivera WS .15 .07
❑ 241 Checklist 1 .10 .05
❑ 242 Checklist 2 .10 .05
❑ 243 Tom Glavine .40 .18
❑ 244 Andy Benes .10 .05
❑ 245 Sandy Alomar Jr. .15 .07
❑ 246 Wilton Guerrero .10 .05
❑ 247 Alex Gonzalez .10 .05
❑ 248 Roberto Alomar .40 .18
❑ 249 Ruben Rivera .10 .05
❑ 250 Eric Chavez .15 .07
❑ 251 Ellis Burks .15 .07
❑ 252 Richie Sexson .15 .07
❑ 253 Steve Finley .15 .07
❑ 254 Dwight Gooden .15 .07
❑ 255 Dustin Hermanson .10 .05
❑ 256 Kirk Rueter .10 .05
❑ 257 Steve Trachsel .10 .05
❑ 258 Gregg Jefferies .10 .05
❑ 259 Matt Stairs .10 .05
❑ 260 Shane Reynolds .10 .05
❑ 261 Gregg Olson .10 .05
❑ 262 Kevin Tapani .10 .05
❑ 263 Matt Morris .10 .05
❑ 264 Carl Pavano .10 .05
❑ 265 Nomar Garciaparra 1.25 .55
❑ 266 Kevin Young .15 .07
❑ 267 Rick Helling .15 .07
❑ 268 Matt Franco .10 .05
❑ 269 Brian McRae .10 .05
❑ 270 Cal Ripken 1.50 .70
❑ 271 Jeff Abbott .10 .05
❑ 272 Tony Batista .15 .07
❑ 273 Bill Simas .10 .05
❑ 274 Brian Hunter .10 .05
❑ 275 John Franco .15 .07
❑ 276 Devon White .10 .05
❑ 277 Rickey Henderson .50 .23
❑ 278 Chuck Finley .15 .07
❑ 279 Mike Blowers .10 .05
❑ 280 Mark Grace .40 .18
❑ 281 Randy Winn .10 .05
❑ 282 Bobby Bonilla .15 .07
❑ 283 David Justice .25 .11
❑ 284 Shane Monahan .10 .05
❑ 285 Kevin Brown .25 .11
❑ 286 Todd Zeile .15 .07
❑ 287 Al Martin .10 .05
❑ 288 Troy O'Leary .10 .05
❑ 289 Darryl Hamilton .10 .05
❑ 290 Tino Martinez .15 .07
❑ 291 David Ortiz .10 .05
❑ 292 Tony Clark .10 .05
❑ 293 Ryan Minor .10 .05
❑ 294 Mark Leiter .10 .05
❑ 295 Wally Joyner .15 .07
❑ 296 Cliff Floyd .15 .07
❑ 297 Shawn Estes .10 .05
❑ 298 Pat Hentgen .10 .05
❑ 299 Scott Elarton .15 .07
❑ 300 Alex Rodriguez 1.25 .55
❑ 301 Ozzie Guillen .10 .05
❑ 302 Hideo Nomo .40 .18
❑ 303 Ryan McGuire .10 .05
❑ 304 Brad Ausmus .10 .05
❑ 305 Alex Gonzalez .10 .05
❑ 306 Brian Jordan .15 .07
❑ 307 John Jaha .10 .05
❑ 308 Mark Grudzielanek .10 .05
❑ 309 Juan Guzman .10 .05
❑ 310 Tony Womack .10 .05
❑ 311 Dennis Reyes .10 .05
❑ 312 Marty Cordova .10 .05
❑ 313 Ramiro Mendoza .10 .05
❑ 314 Robin Ventura .15 .07
❑ 315 Rafael Palmeiro .40 .18
❑ 316 Ramon Martinez .10 .05
❑ 317 Pedro Astacio .10 .05
❑ 318 Dave Hollins .10 .05
❑ 319 Tom Candiotti .10 .05
❑ 320 Al Leiter .15 .07
❑ 321 Rico Brogna .10 .05
❑ 322 Reggie Jefferson .10 .05
❑ 323 Bernard Gilkey .10 .05
❑ 324 Jason Giambi .40 .18
❑ 325 Craig Biggio .25 .11
❑ 326 Troy Glaus .60 .25
❑ 327 Delino DeShields .10 .05
❑ 328 Fernando Vina .10 .05
❑ 329 John Smoltz .15 .07
❑ 330 Jeff Kent .25 .11
❑ 331 Roy Halladay .10 .05
❑ 332 Andy Ashby .10 .05
❑ 333 Tim Wakefield .10 .05
❑ 334 Roger Clemens .75 .35
❑ 335 Bernie Williams .40 .18
❑ 336 Desi Relaford .10 .05
❑ 337 John Burkett .10 .05
❑ 338 Mike Hampton .15 .07
❑ 339 Royce Clayton .10 .05
❑ 340 Mike Piazza 1.25 .55
❑ 341 Jeremi Gonzalez .10 .05
❑ 342 Mike Lansing .10 .05
❑ 343 Jamie Moyer .10 .05
❑ 344 Ron Coomer .10 .05
❑ 345 Barry Larkin .40 .18
❑ 346 Fernando Tatis .15 .07
❑ 347 Chili Davis .15 .07
❑ 348 Bobby Higginson .15 .07
❑ 349 Hal Morris .10 .05
❑ 350 Larry Walker .15 .07
❑ 351 Carlos Guillen .10 .05
❑ 352 Miguel Tejada .15 .07
❑ 353 Travis Fryman .15 .07
❑ 354 Jarrod Washburn .10 .05
❑ 355 Chipper Jones 1.00 .45
❑ 356 Todd Stottlemyre .10 .05
❑ 357 Henry Rodriguez .10 .05
❑ 358 Eli Marrero .10 .05
❑ 359 Alan Benes .10 .05
❑ 360 Tim Salmon .15 .07
❑ 361 Luis Gonzalez .15 .07
❑ 362 Scott Spiezio .10 .05
❑ 363 Chris Carpenter .10 .05
❑ 364 Bobby Howry .10 .05
❑ 365 Raul Mondesi .15 .07
❑ 366 Ugueth Urbina .10 .05
❑ 367 Tom Evans .10 .05
❑ 368 Kerry Ligtenberg RC .25 .11
❑ 369 Adrian Beltre .15 .07
❑ 370 Ryan Klesko .15 .07
❑ 371 Wilson Alvarez .10 .05
❑ 372 John Thomson .10 .05
❑ 373 Tony Saunders .10 .05
❑ 374 Dave Mlicki .10 .05
❑ 375 Ken Caminiti .15 .07
❑ 376 Jay Buhner .15 .07
❑ 377 Bill Mueller .10 .05
❑ 378 Jeff Blauser .10 .05
❑ 379 Edgar Renteria .10 .05
❑ 380 Jim Thome .25 .11
❑ 381 Joey Hamilton .10 .05
❑ 382 Calvin Pickering .10 .05
❑ 383 Marquis Grissom .10 .05
❑ 384 Omar Daal .10 .05
❑ 385 Curt Schilling .15 .07
❑ 386 Jose Cruz Jr. .15 .07
❑ 387 Chris Widger .10 .05
❑ 388 Pete Harnisch .10 .05
❑ 389 Charles Nagy .10 .05
❑ 390 Tom Gordon .10 .05
❑ 391 Bobby Smith .10 .05
❑ 392 Derrick Gibson .10 .05
❑ 393 Jeff Conine .10 .05

❑ 394 Carlos Perez .10 .05
❑ 395 Barry Bonds .60 .25
❑ 396 Mark McLemore .10 .05
❑ 397 Juan Encarnacion .15 .07
❑ 398 Wade Boggs .50 .23
❑ 399 Ivan Rodriguez .50 .23
❑ 400 Moises Alou .15 .07
❑ 401 Jeromy Burnitz .15 .07
❑ 402 Sean Casey .15 .07
❑ 403 Jose Offerman .10 .05
❑ 404 Joe Fontenot .10 .05
❑ 405 Kevin Millwood .15 .07
❑ 406 Lance Johnson .10 .05
❑ 407 Richard Hidalgo .15 .07
❑ 408 Mike Jackson .10 .05
❑ 409 Brian Anderson .10 .05
❑ 410 Jeff Shaw .10 .05
❑ 411 Preston Wilson .15 .07
❑ 412 Todd Hundley .10 .05
❑ 413 Jim Parque .10 .05
❑ 414 Justin Baughman .10 .05
❑ 415 Dante Bichette .15 .07
❑ 416 Paul O'Neill .15 .07
❑ 417 Miguel Cairo .10 .05
❑ 418 Randy Johnson .50 .23
❑ 419 Jesus Sanchez .10 .05
❑ 420 Carlos Delgado .40 .18
❑ 421 Ricky Ledee .10 .05
❑ 422 Orlando Hernandez .15 .07
❑ 423 Frank Thomas .75 .35
❑ 424 Pokey Reese .15 .07
❑ 425 Carlos Lee .25 .11
Mike Lowell
Kit Pellow RC
❑ 426 Michael Cuddyer .10 .05
Mark DeRosa
Jerry Hairston Jr.
❑ 427 Marlon Anderson .10 .05
Ron Belliard
Orlando Cabrera
❑ 428 Micah Bowie .10 .05
Phil Norton RC
Randy Wolf
❑ 429 Jack Cressend RC .25 .11
Jason Rakers
John Rocker
❑ 430 Ruben Mateo .10 .05
Scott Morgan
Mike Zywica RC
❑ 431 Jason LaRue .10 .05
Matt LeCroy
Mitch Meluskey
❑ 432 Gabe Kapler .10 .05
Armando Rios
Fernando Seguignol
❑ 433 Adam Kennedy .10 .05
Mickey Lopez RC
Jackie Rexrode
❑ 434 Jose Fernandez RC .10 .05
Jeff Liefer
Chris Truby
❑ 435 Corey Koskie .25 .11
Doug Mientkiewicz RC
Damon Minor
❑ 436 Roosevelt Brown RC .25 .11
Dernell Stenson
Vernon Wells
❑ 437 A.J. Burnett RC .40 .18
Billy Koch
John Nicholson
❑ 438 Matt Belisle .40 .18
Matt Roney RC
❑ 439 Austin Kearns .75 .35
Chris George RC
❑ 440 Nate Bump RC .25 .11
Nate Cornejo
❑ 441 Brad Lidge .25 .11
Mike Nannini RC
❑ 442 Matt Holliday .40 .18
Jeff Winchester RC
❑ 443 Adam Everett .40 .18
Chip Ambres RC
❑ 444 Pat Burrell 2.00 .90
Eric Valent RC
❑ 445 Roger Clemens SK .40 .18
❑ 446 Kerry Wood SK .15 .07
❑ 447 Curt Schilling SK .10 .05
❑ 448 Randy Johnson SK .15 .07
❑ 449 Pedro Martinez SK .25 .11
❑ 450 Jeff Bagwell AT .75 .35
Andres Galarraga
Mark McGwire
❑ 451 John Olerud AT .15 .07
Jim Thome
Tino Martinez
❑ 452 Alex Rodriguez AT .75 .35
Nomar Garciaparra
Derek Jeter
❑ 453 Vinny Castilla AT .40 .18
Chipper Jones
Scott Rolen
❑ 454 Sammy Sosa AT .75 .35
Ken Griffey Jr.
Juan Gonzalez
❑ 455 Barry Bonds AT .15 .07
Manny Ramirez
Larry Walker
❑ 456 Frank Thomas AT .40 .18
Tim Salmon
David Justice
❑ 457 Travis Lee AT .40 .18
Todd Helton
Ben Grieve
❑ 458 Vladimir Guerrero AT .40 .18
Greg Vaughn
Bernie Williams
❑ 459 Mike Piazza AT .40 .18
Ivan Rodriguez
Jason Kendall
❑ 460 Roger Clemens AT .40 .18
Kerry Wood
Greg Maddux
❑ 461A Sammy Sosa HR 1 20.00 9.00
❑ 461B Sammy Sosa HR 2 8.00 3.60
❑ 461C Sammy Sosa HR 3 8.00 3.60
❑ 461D Sammy Sosa HR 4 8.00 3.60
❑ 461E Sammy Sosa HR 5 8.00 3.60
❑ 461F Sammy Sosa HR 6 8.00 3.60
❑ 461G Sammy Sosa HR 7 8.00 3.60
❑ 461H Sammy Sosa HR 8 8.00 3.60
❑ 461I Sammy Sosa HR 9 8.00 3.60
❑ 461J Sammy Sosa HR 10 8.00 3.60
❑ 461K Sammy Sosa HR 11 8.00 3.60
❑ 461L Sammy Sosa HR 12 8.00 3.60
❑ 461M Sammy Sosa HR 13 8.00 3.60
❑ 461N Sammy Sosa HR 14 8.00 3.60
❑ 461O Sammy Sosa HR 15 8.00 3.60
❑ 461P Sammy Sosa HR 16 8.00 3.60
❑ 461Q Sammy Sosa HR 17 8.00 3.60
❑ 461R Sammy Sosa HR 18 8.00 3.60
❑ 461S Sammy Sosa HR 19 8.00 3.60
❑ 461T Sammy Sosa HR 20 8.00 3.60
❑ 461U Sammy Sosa HR 21 8.00 3.60
❑ 461V Sammy Sosa HR 22 8.00 3.60
❑ 461W Sammy Sosa HR 23 8.00 3.60
❑ 461X Sammy Sosa HR 24 8.00 3.60
❑ 461Y Sammy Sosa HR 25 8.00 3.60
❑ 461Z Sammy Sosa HR 26 8.00 3.60
❑ 461AA Sammy Sosa HR 27 8.00 3.60
❑ 461AB Sammy Sosa HR 28 8.00 3.60
❑ 461AC Sammy Sosa HR 29 8.00 3.60
❑ 461AD Sammy Sosa HR 30 8.00 3.60
❑ 461AE Sammy Sosa HR 31 8.00 3.60
❑ 461AF Sammy Sosa HR 32 8.00 3.60
❑ 461AG Sammy Sosa HR 33 8.00 3.60
❑ 461AH Sammy Sosa HR 34 8.00 3.60
❑ 461AI Sammy Sosa HR 35 8.00 3.60
❑ 461AJ Sammy Sosa HR 36 8.00 3.60
❑ 461AK Sammy Sosa HR 37 8.00 3.60
❑ 461AL Sammy Sosa HR 38 8.00 3.60
❑ 461AM Sammy Sosa HR 39 8.00 3.60
❑ 461AN Sammy Sosa HR 40 8.00 3.60
❑ 461AO Sammy Sosa HR 41 8.00 3.60
❑ 461AP Sammy Sosa HR 42 8.00 3.60
❑ 461AQ Sammy Sosa HR 43 8.00 3.60
❑ 461AS Sammy Sosa HR 44 8.00 3.60
❑ 461AT Sammy Sosa HR 45 8.00 3.60
❑ 461AU Sammy Sosa HR 46 8.00 3.60
❑ 461AV Sammy Sosa HR 47 8.00 3.60
❑ 461AW Sammy Sosa HR 48 8.00 3.60
❑ 461AX Sammy Sosa HR 49 8.00 3.60
❑ 461AY Sammy Sosa HR 50 8.00 3.60
❑ 461AZ Sammy Sosa HR 51 8.00 3.60
❑ 461BB Sammy Sosa HR 52 8.00 3.60
❑ 461CC Sammy Sosa HR 53 8.00 3.60
❑ 461DD Sammy Sosa HR 54 8.00 3.60
❑ 461EE Sammy Sosa HR 55 8.00 3.60
❑ 461FF Sammy Sosa HR 56 8.00 3.60
❑ 461GG Sammy Sosa HR 57 8.00 3.60
❑ 461HH Sammy Sosa HR 58 8.00 3.60
❑ 461II Sammy Sosa HR 59 8.00 3.60
❑ 461JJ Sammy Sosa HR 60 8.00 3.60
❑ 461KK Sammy Sosa HR 61 20.00 9.00
❑ 461LL Sammy Sosa HR 62 25.00 11.00
❑ 461MM Sammy Sosa HR 63 10.00 4.50
❑ 461NN Sammy Sosa HR 64 10.00 4.50
❑ 461OO Sammy Sosa HR 65 10.00 4.50
❑ 461PP Sammy Sosa HR 66 30.00 13.50
❑ 462 Checklist .10 .05
❑ 463 Checklist .10 .05

## 1999 Topps Traded

| | MINT | NRMT |
|---|---|---|
| COMP.FACT.SET (122) | 30.00 | 13.50 |
| COMPLETE SET (121) | 20.00 | 9.00 |

❑ T1 Seth Etherton .15 .07
❑ T2 Mark Harriger RC .25 .11
❑ T3 Matt Wise RC .25 .11
❑ T4 Carlos Hernandez RC .25 .11
❑ T5 Julio Lugo RC .40 .18
❑ T6 Mike Nannini .15 .07
❑ T7 Justin Bowles RC .10 .05
❑ T8 Mark Mulder RC .60 .25
❑ T9 Roberto Vaz RC .25 .11
❑ T10 Felipe Lopez RC .60 .25
❑ T11 Matt Belisle .50 .23
❑ T12 Micah Bowie .10 .05
❑ T13 Ruben Quevedo RC .40 .18
❑ T14 Jose Garcia RC .25 .11
❑ T15 David Kelton RC .60 .25
❑ T16 Phil Norton .15 .07
❑ T17 Corey Patterson RC 3.00 1.35
❑ T18 Ron Walker RC .25 .11
❑ T19 Paul Hoover RC .25 .11
❑ T20 Ryan Rupe RC .40 .18
❑ T21 J.D. Closser RC .40 .18
❑ T22 Rob Ryan RC .10 .05
❑ T23 Steve Colyer RC .25 .11
❑ T24 Bubba Crosby RC .25 .11
❑ T25 Luke Prokopec RC .50 .23
❑ T26 Matt Blank RC .25 .11
❑ T27 Josh McKinley .15 .07
❑ T28 Nate Bump .15 .07
❑ T29 Giuseppe Chiaramonte RC .40 .18
❑ T30 Arturo McDowell .40 .18
❑ T31 Tony Torcato .60 .25
❑ T32 Dave Roberts RC .10 .05
❑ T33 C.C. Sabathia RC 1.25 .55
❑ T34 Sean Spencer RC .25 .11
❑ T35 Chip Ambres .40 .18
❑ T36 A.J. Burnett .50 .23
❑ T37 Mo Bruce RC .25 .11
❑ T38 Jason Tyner .50 .23
❑ T39 Mamon Tucker .40 .18
❑ T40 Sean Burroughs RC 2.00 .90
❑ T41 Kevin Eberwein RC .40 .18
❑ T42 Junior Herndon RC .25 .11
❑ T43 Bryan Wolff RC .10 .05

| | | | |
|---|---|---|---|
| ❑ | T44 Pat Burrell | 3.00 | 1.35 |
| ❑ | T45 Eric Valent | .60 | .25 |
| ❑ | T46 Carlos Pena RC | 1.25 | .55 |
| ❑ | T47 Mike Zywica | .15 | .07 |
| ❑ | T48 Adam Everett | .40 | .18 |
| ❑ | T49 Juan Pena RC | .25 | .11 |
| ❑ | T50 Adam Dunn RC | 1.25 | .55 |
| ❑ | T51 Austin Kearns | 1.25 | .55 |
| ❑ | T52 Jacobo Sequea RC | .25 | .11 |
| ❑ | T53 Choo Freeman | .40 | .18 |
| ❑ | T54 Jeff Winchester | .15 | .07 |
| ❑ | T55 Matt Burch | .15 | .07 |
| ❑ | T56 Chris George | .50 | .23 |
| ❑ | T57 Scott Mullen RC | .10 | .05 |
| ❑ | T58 Kit Pellow | .25 | .11 |
| ❑ | T59 Mark Quinn RC | 1.00 | .45 |
| ❑ | T60 Nate Cornejo | .40 | .18 |
| ❑ | T61 Ryan Mills | .15 | .07 |
| ❑ | T62 Kevin Beirne RC | .10 | .05 |
| ❑ | T63 Kip Wells RC | .50 | .23 |
| ❑ | T64 Juan Rivera RC | .60 | .25 |
| ❑ | T65 Alfonso Soriano RC | 1.25 | .55 |
| ❑ | T66 Josh Hamilton RC | 3.00 | 1.35 |
| ❑ | T67 Josh Girdley RC | .50 | .23 |
| ❑ | T68 Kyle Snyder RC | .25 | .11 |
| ❑ | T69 Mike Paradis RC | .25 | .11 |
| ❑ | T70 Jason Jennings RC | .40 | .18 |
| ❑ | T71 David Walling RC | .40 | .18 |
| ❑ | T72 Omar Ortiz RC | .25 | .11 |
| ❑ | T73 Jay Gehrke RC | .25 | .11 |
| ❑ | T74 Casey Burns RC | .25 | .11 |
| ❑ | T75 Carl Crawford RC | .75 | .35 |
| ❑ | T76 Reggie Sanders | .10 | .05 |
| ❑ | T77 Will Clark | .40 | .18 |
| ❑ | T78 David Wells | .15 | .07 |
| ❑ | T79 Paul Konerko | .15 | .07 |
| ❑ | T80 Armando Benitez | .10 | .05 |
| ❑ | T81 Brant Brown | .10 | .05 |
| ❑ | T82 Mo Vaughn | .15 | .07 |
| ❑ | T83 Jose Canseco | .50 | .23 |
| ❑ | T84 Albert Belle | .25 | .11 |
| ❑ | T85 Dean Palmer | .15 | .07 |
| ❑ | T86 Greg Vaughn | .15 | .07 |
| ❑ | T87 Mark Clark | .10 | .05 |
| ❑ | T88 Pat Meares | .10 | .05 |
| ❑ | T89 Eric Davis | .15 | .07 |
| ❑ | T90 Brian Giles | .15 | .07 |
| ❑ | T91 Jeff Brantley | .10 | .05 |
| ❑ | T92 Bret Boone | .15 | .07 |
| ❑ | T93 Ron Gant | .15 | .07 |
| ❑ | T94 Mike Cameron | .10 | .05 |
| ❑ | T95 Charles Johnson | .15 | .07 |
| ❑ | T96 Denny Neagle | .10 | .05 |
| ❑ | T97 Brian Hunter | .10 | .05 |
| ❑ | T98 Jose Hernandez | .10 | .05 |
| ❑ | T99 Rick Aguilera | .10 | .05 |
| ❑ | T100 Tony Batista | .15 | .07 |
| ❑ | T101 Roger Cedeno | .10 | .05 |
| ❑ | T102 Creighton Gubanich RC | .10 | .05 |
| ❑ | T103 Tim Belcher | .10 | .05 |
| ❑ | T104 Bruce Aven | .10 | .05 |
| ❑ | T105 Brian Daubach RC | .50 | .23 |
| ❑ | T106 Ed Sprague | .10 | .05 |
| ❑ | T107 Michael Tucker | .10 | .05 |
| ❑ | T108 Homer Bush | .10 | .05 |
| ❑ | T109 Armando Reynoso | .10 | .05 |
| ❑ | T110 Brook Fordyce | .10 | .05 |
| ❑ | T111 Matt Mantei | .10 | .05 |
| ❑ | T112 Dave Mlicki | .10 | .05 |
| ❑ | T113 Kenny Rogers | .10 | .05 |
| ❑ | T114 Livan Hernandez | .10 | .05 |
| ❑ | T115 Butch Huskey | .10 | .05 |
| ❑ | T116 David Segui | .10 | .05 |
| ❑ | T117 Darryl Hamilton | .10 | .05 |
| ❑ | T118 Terry Mulholland | .10 | .05 |
| ❑ | T119 Randy Velarde | .10 | .05 |
| ❑ | T120 Bill Taylor | .10 | .05 |
| ❑ | T121 Kevin Appier | .15 | .07 |

## 2000 Topps

| | MINT | NRMT |
|---|---|---|
| COMPLETE SET (478) | 60.00 | 27.00 |
| COMP.HOBBY SET (478) | 65.00 | 29.00 |
| COMPLETE SERIES 1 (239) | 30.00 | 13.50 |
| COMPLETE SERIES 2 (240) | 30.00 | 13.50 |

| | | |
|---|---|---|
| MCGWIRE MM SET (5) | 20.00 | 9.00 |
| AARON MM SET (5) | 10.00 | 4.50 |
| RIPKEN MM SET (5) | 15.00 | 6.75 |
| BOGGS MM SET (5) | 5.00 | 2.20 |
| GWYNN MM SET (5) | 8.00 | 3.60 |
| GRIFFEY MM SET (5) | 15.00 | 6.75 |
| BONDS MM SET (5) | 6.00 | 2.70 |
| SOSA MM SET (5) | 10.00 | 4.50 |
| JETER MM SET (5) | 15.00 | 6.75 |
| A.ROD MM SET (5) | 12.00 | 5.50 |

| | | | |
|---|---|---|---|
| ❑ | 1 Mark McGwire | 1.50 | .70 |
| ❑ | 2 Tony Gwynn | .75 | .35 |
| ❑ | 3 Wade Boggs | .50 | .23 |
| ❑ | 4 Cal Ripken | 1.50 | .70 |
| ❑ | 5 Matt Williams | .25 | .11 |
| ❑ | 6 Jay Buhner | .15 | .07 |
| ❑ | 7 Does Not Exist | .10 | .05 |
| ❑ | 8 Jeff Conine | .10 | .05 |
| ❑ | 9 Todd Greene | .10 | .05 |
| ❑ | 10 Mike Lieberthal | .15 | .07 |
| ❑ | 11 Steve Avery | .10 | .05 |
| ❑ | 12 Bret Saberhagen | .15 | .07 |
| ❑ | 13 Magglio Ordonez | .15 | .07 |
| ❑ | 14 Brad Radke | .15 | .07 |
| ❑ | 15 Derek Jeter | 1.50 | .70 |
| ❑ | 16 Javy Lopez | .15 | .07 |
| ❑ | 17 Russ Davis | .10 | .05 |
| ❑ | 18 Armando Benitez | .15 | .07 |
| ❑ | 19 B.J. Surhoff | .15 | .07 |
| ❑ | 20 Darryl Kile | .15 | .07 |
| ❑ | 21 Mark Lewis | .10 | .05 |
| ❑ | 22 Mike Williams | .10 | .05 |
| ❑ | 23 Mark McLemore | .10 | .05 |
| ❑ | 24 Sterling Hitchcock | .10 | .05 |
| ❑ | 25 Darin Erstad | .40 | .18 |
| ❑ | 26 Ricky Gutierrez | .10 | .05 |
| ❑ | 27 John Jaha | .10 | .05 |
| ❑ | 28 Homer Bush | .10 | .05 |
| ❑ | 29 Darrin Fletcher | .10 | .05 |
| ❑ | 30 Mark Grace | .40 | .18 |
| ❑ | 31 Fred McGriff | .25 | .11 |
| ❑ | 32 Omar Daal | .10 | .05 |
| ❑ | 33 Eric Karros | .15 | .07 |
| ❑ | 34 Orlando Cabrera | .10 | .05 |
| ❑ | 35 J.T. Snow | .15 | .07 |
| ❑ | 36 Luis Castillo | .15 | .07 |
| ❑ | 37 Rey Ordonez | .10 | .05 |
| ❑ | 38 Bob Abreu | .15 | .07 |
| ❑ | 39 Warren Morris | .10 | .05 |
| ❑ | 40 Juan Gonzalez | .40 | .18 |
| ❑ | 41 Mike Lansing | .10 | .05 |
| ❑ | 42 Chili Davis | .15 | .07 |
| ❑ | 43 Dean Palmer | .15 | .07 |
| ❑ | 44 Hank Aaron | .75 | .35 |
| ❑ | 45 Jeff Bagwell | .50 | .23 |
| ❑ | 46 Jose Valentin | .10 | .05 |
| ❑ | 47 Shannon Stewart | .15 | .07 |
| ❑ | 48 Kent Bottenfield | .10 | .05 |
| ❑ | 49 Jeff Shaw | .10 | .05 |
| ❑ | 50 Sammy Sosa | .75 | .35 |
| ❑ | 51 Randy Johnson | .50 | .23 |
| ❑ | 52 Benny Agbayani | .10 | .05 |
| ❑ | 53 Dante Bichette | .15 | .07 |
| ❑ | 54 Pete Harnisch | .10 | .05 |
| ❑ | 55 Frank Thomas | .75 | .35 |
| ❑ | 56 Jorge Posada | .15 | .07 |
| ❑ | 57 Todd Walker | .10 | .05 |
| ❑ | 58 Juan Encarnacion | .15 | .07 |
| ❑ | 59 Mike Sweeney | .15 | .07 |
| ❑ | 60 Pedro Martinez | .50 | .23 |
| ❑ | 61 Lee Stevens | .10 | .05 |
| ❑ | 62 Brian Giles | .15 | .07 |
| ❑ | 63 Chad Ogea | .10 | .05 |
| ❑ | 64 Ivan Rodriguez | .50 | .23 |
| ❑ | 65 Roger Cedeno | .10 | .05 |
| ❑ | 66 David Justice | .25 | .11 |
| ❑ | 67 Steve Trachsel | .10 | .05 |
| ❑ | 68 Eli Marrero | .10 | .05 |
| ❑ | 69 Dave Nilsson | .10 | .05 |
| ❑ | 70 Ken Caminiti | .15 | .07 |
| ❑ | 71 Tim Raines | .15 | .07 |
| ❑ | 72 Brian Jordan | .15 | .07 |
| ❑ | 73 Jeff Blauser | .10 | .05 |
| ❑ | 74 Bernard Gilkey | .10 | .05 |
| ❑ | 75 John Flaherty | .10 | .05 |
| ❑ | 76 Brent Mayne | .10 | .05 |
| ❑ | 77 Jose Vidro | .10 | .05 |
| ❑ | 78 David Bell | .10 | .05 |
| ❑ | 79 Bruce Aven | .10 | .05 |
| ❑ | 80 John Olerud | .15 | .07 |
| ❑ | 81 Pokey Reese | .15 | .07 |
| ❑ | 82 Woody Williams | .10 | .05 |
| ❑ | 83 Ed Sprague | .10 | .05 |
| ❑ | 84 Joe Girardi | .10 | .05 |
| ❑ | 85 Barry Larkin | .40 | .18 |
| ❑ | 86 Mike Caruso | .10 | .05 |
| ❑ | 87 Bobby Higginson | .10 | .05 |
| ❑ | 88 Roberto Kelly | .10 | .05 |
| ❑ | 89 Edgar Martinez | .25 | .11 |
| ❑ | 90 Mark Kotsay | .10 | .05 |
| ❑ | 91 Paul Sorrento | .10 | .05 |
| ❑ | 92 Eric Young | .10 | .05 |
| ❑ | 93 Carlos Delgado | .40 | .18 |
| ❑ | 94 Troy Glaus | .50 | .23 |
| ❑ | 95 Ben Grieve | .15 | .07 |
| ❑ | 96 Jose Lima | .10 | .05 |
| ❑ | 97 Garret Anderson | .15 | .07 |
| ❑ | 98 Luis Gonzalez | .15 | .07 |
| ❑ | 99 Carl Pavano | .10 | .05 |
| ❑ | 100 Alex Rodriguez | 1.25 | .55 |
| ❑ | 101 Preston Wilson | .15 | .07 |
| ❑ | 102 Ron Gant | .15 | .07 |
| ❑ | 103 Brady Anderson | .15 | .07 |
| ❑ | 104 Rickey Henderson | .50 | .23 |
| ❑ | 105 Gary Sheffield | .40 | .18 |
| ❑ | 106 Mickey Morandini | .10 | .05 |
| ❑ | 107 Jim Edmonds | .40 | .18 |
| ❑ | 108 Kris Benson | .15 | .07 |
| ❑ | 109 Adrian Beltre | .15 | .07 |
| ❑ | 110 Alex Fernandez | .10 | .05 |
| ❑ | 111 Dan Wilson | .10 | .05 |
| ❑ | 112 Mark Clark | .10 | .05 |
| ❑ | 113 Greg Vaughn | .15 | .07 |
| ❑ | 114 Neifi Perez | .10 | .05 |
| ❑ | 115 Paul O'Neill | .15 | .07 |
| ❑ | 116 Jermaine Dye | .15 | .07 |
| ❑ | 117 Todd Jones | .10 | .05 |
| ❑ | 118 Terry Steinbach | .10 | .05 |
| ❑ | 119 Greg Norton | .10 | .05 |
| ❑ | 120 Curt Schilling | .15 | .07 |
| ❑ | 121 Todd Zeile | .15 | .07 |
| ❑ | 122 Edgardo Alfonzo | .15 | .07 |
| ❑ | 123 Ryan McGuire | .10 | .05 |
| ❑ | 124 Rich Aurilia | .10 | .05 |
| ❑ | 125 John Smoltz | .15 | .07 |
| ❑ | 126 Bob Wickman | .10 | .05 |
| ❑ | 127 Richard Hidalgo | .15 | .07 |
| ❑ | 128 Chuck Finley | .15 | .07 |
| ❑ | 129 Billy Wagner | .10 | .05 |
| ❑ | 130 Todd Hundley | .10 | .05 |
| ❑ | 131 Dwight Gooden | .15 | .07 |
| ❑ | 132 Russ Ortiz | .15 | .07 |
| ❑ | 133 Mike Lowell | .10 | .05 |
| ❑ | 134 Reggie Sanders | .10 | .05 |
| ❑ | 135 John Valentin | .10 | .05 |
| ❑ | 136 Brad Ausmus | .10 | .05 |
| ❑ | 137 Chad Kreuter | .10 | .05 |
| ❑ | 138 David Cone | .15 | .07 |
| ❑ | 139 Brook Fordyce | .10 | .05 |
| ❑ | 140 Roberto Alomar | .40 | .18 |
| ❑ | 141 Charles Nagy | .10 | .05 |
| ❑ | 142 Brian Hunter | .10 | .05 |
| ❑ | 143 Mike Mussina | .40 | .18 |

| | | | |
|---|---|---|---|
| ❑ 144 | Robin Ventura | .25 | .11 |
| ❑ 145 | Kevin Brown | .25 | .11 |
| ❑ 146 | Pat Hentgen | .10 | .05 |
| ❑ 147 | Ryan Klesko | .15 | .07 |
| ❑ 148 | Derek Bell | .10 | .05 |
| ❑ 149 | Andy Sheets | .10 | .05 |
| ❑ 150 | Larry Walker | .15 | .07 |
| ❑ 151 | Scott Williamson | .10 | .05 |
| ❑ 152 | Jose Offerman | .10 | .05 |
| ❑ 153 | Doug Mientkiewicz | .10 | .05 |
| ❑ 154 | John Snyder RC | .25 | .11 |
| ❑ 155 | Sandy Alomar Jr. | .10 | .05 |
| ❑ 156 | Joe Nathan | .10 | .05 |
| ❑ 157 | Lance Johnson | .10 | .05 |
| ❑ 158 | Odalis Perez | .10 | .05 |
| ❑ 159 | Hideo Nomo | .40 | .18 |
| ❑ 160 | Steve Finley | .15 | .07 |
| ❑ 161 | Dave Martinez | .10 | .05 |
| ❑ 162 | Matt Walbeck | .10 | .05 |
| ❑ 163 | Bill Spiers | .10 | .05 |
| ❑ 164 | Fernando Tatis | .15 | .07 |
| ❑ 165 | Kenny Lofton | .15 | .07 |
| ❑ 166 | Paul Byrd | .10 | .05 |
| ❑ 167 | Aaron Sele | .10 | .05 |
| ❑ 168 | Eddie Taubensee | .10 | .05 |
| ❑ 169 | Reggie Jefferson | .10 | .05 |
| ❑ 170 | Roger Clemens | .75 | .35 |
| ❑ 171 | Francisco Cordova | .10 | .05 |
| ❑ 172 | Mike Bordick | .10 | .05 |
| ❑ 173 | Wally Joyner | .15 | .07 |
| ❑ 174 | Marvin Benard | .10 | .05 |
| ❑ 175 | Jason Kendall | .15 | .07 |
| ❑ 176 | Mike Stanley | .10 | .05 |
| ❑ 177 | Chad Allen | .10 | .05 |
| ❑ 178 | Carlos Beltran | .15 | .07 |
| ❑ 179 | Deivi Cruz | .10 | .05 |
| ❑ 180 | Chipper Jones | 1.00 | .45 |
| ❑ 181 | Vladimir Guerrero | .60 | .25 |
| ❑ 182 | Dave Burba | .10 | .05 |
| ❑ 183 | Tom Goodwin | .10 | .05 |
| ❑ 184 | Brian Daubach | .10 | .05 |
| ❑ 185 | Jay Bell | .15 | .07 |
| ❑ 186 | Roy Halladay | .10 | .05 |
| ❑ 187 | Miguel Tejada | .15 | .07 |
| ❑ 188 | Armando Rios | .10 | .05 |
| ❑ 189 | Fernando Vina | .10 | .05 |
| ❑ 190 | Eric Davis | .15 | .07 |
| ❑ 191 | Henry Rodriguez | .10 | .05 |
| ❑ 192 | Joe McEwing | .10 | .05 |
| ❑ 193 | Jeff Kent | .25 | .11 |
| ❑ 194 | Mike Jackson | .10 | .05 |
| ❑ 195 | Mike Morgan | .10 | .05 |
| ❑ 196 | Jeff Montgomery | .10 | .05 |
| ❑ 197 | Jeff Zimmerman | .10 | .05 |
| ❑ 198 | Tony Fernandez | .10 | .05 |
| ❑ 199 | Jason Giambi | .40 | .18 |
| ❑ 200 | Jose Canseco | .50 | .23 |
| ❑ 201 | Alex Gonzalez | .10 | .05 |
| ❑ 202 | Jack Cust | .15 | .07 |
| | Mike Colangelo | | |
| | Dee Brown | | |
| ❑ 203 | Felipe Lopez | .15 | .07 |
| | Alfonso Soriano | | |
| | Pablo Ozuna | | |
| ❑ 204 | Erubiel Durazo | .60 | .25 |
| | Pat Burrell | | |
| | Nick Johnson | | |
| ❑ 205 | John Sneed RC | .25 | .11 |
| | Kip Wells | | |
| | Matt Blank | | |
| ❑ 206 | Josh Kalinowski | .25 | .11 |
| | Michael Tejera | | |
| | Chris Mears RC | | |
| ❑ 207 | Roosevelt Brown | .60 | .25 |
| | Corey Patterson | | |
| | Lance Berkman | | |
| ❑ 208 | Kit Pellow | .10 | .05 |
| | Kevin Barker | | |
| | Russ Branyan | | |
| ❑ 209 | B.J. Garbe | .75 | .35 |
| | Larry Bigbie RC | | |
| ❑ 210 | Eric Munson | 1.25 | .55 |
| | Bobby Bradley RC | | |
| ❑ 211 | Josh Girdley | .15 | .07 |
| | Kyle Snyder | | |
| ❑ 212 | Chance Caple RC | .40 | .18 |
| | Jason Jennings | | |
| ❑ 213 | Ryan Christianson | .60 | .25 |
| | Brett Myers RC | | |
| ❑ 214 | Jason Stumm | .50 | .23 |
| | Rob Purvis RC | | |
| ❑ 215 | David Walling | .10 | .05 |
| | Mike Paradis | | |
| ❑ 216 | Omar Ortiz | .10 | .05 |
| | Jay Gehrke | | |
| ❑ 217 | David Cone HL | .15 | .07 |
| ❑ 218 | Jose Jimenez HL | .10 | .05 |
| ❑ 219 | Chris Singleton HL | .10 | .05 |
| ❑ 220 | Fernando Tatis HL | .10 | .05 |
| ❑ 221 | Todd Helton HL | .40 | .18 |
| ❑ 222 | Kevin Millwood DIV | .10 | .05 |
| ❑ 223 | Todd Pratt DIV | .10 | .05 |
| ❑ 224 | Orlando Hernandez DIV | .10 | .05 |
| ❑ 225 | Pedro Martinez DIV | .50 | .23 |
| ❑ 226 | Tom Glavine LCS | .15 | .07 |
| ❑ 227 | Bernie Williams LCS | .15 | .07 |
| ❑ 228 | Mariano Rivera WS | .10 | .05 |
| ❑ 229 | Tony Gwynn 20CB | .75 | .35 |
| ❑ 230 | Wade Boggs 20CB | .50 | .23 |
| ❑ 231 | Lance Johnson CB | .10 | .05 |
| ❑ 232 | Mark McGwire 20CB | 1.50 | .70 |
| ❑ 233 | Rickey Henderson 20CB | .50 | .23 |
| ❑ 234 | Rickey Henderson 20CB | .50 | .23 |
| ❑ 235 | Roger Clemens 20CB | .75 | .35 |
| ❑ 236A | M.McGwire MM 1st HR | 5.00 | 2.20 |
| ❑ 236B | M.McGwire MM 1987 ROY | 5.00 | 2.20 |
| ❑ 236C | M.McGwire MM 62nd HR | 5.00 | 2.20 |
| ❑ 236D | M.McGwire MM 70th HR | 5.00 | 2.20 |
| ❑ 236E | M.McGwire MM 500th HR | 5.00 | 2.20 |
| ❑ 237A | H.Aaron MM 1st Career HR | 2.00 | .90 |
| ❑ 237B | H.Aaron MM 1957 MVP | 2.00 | .90 |
| ❑ 237C | H.Aaron MM 3000th Hit | 2.00 | .90 |
| ❑ 237D | H.Aaron MM 715th HR | 2.00 | .90 |
| ❑ 237E | H.Aaron MM 755th HR | 2.00 | .90 |
| ❑ 238A | C.Ripken MM 1982 ROY | 4.00 | 1.80 |
| ❑ 238B | C.Ripken MM 1991 MVP | 4.00 | 1.80 |
| ❑ 238C | C.Ripken MM 2131 Game | 4.00 | 1.80 |
| ❑ 238D | C.Ripken MM Streak Ends | 4.00 | 1.80 |
| ❑ 238E | C.Ripken MM 400th HR | 4.00 | 1.80 |
| ❑ 239A | W.Boggs MM 1983 Batting | 1.25 | .55 |
| ❑ 239B | W.Boggs MM 1988 Batting | 1.25 | .55 |
| ❑ 239C | W.Boggs MM 2000th Hit | 1.25 | .55 |
| ❑ 239D | W.Boggs MM 1996 Champs | 1.25 | .55 |
| ❑ 239E | W.Boggs MM 3000th Hit | 1.25 | .55 |
| ❑ 240A | T.Gwynn MM 1984 Batting | 2.00 | .90 |
| ❑ 240B | T.Gwynn MM 1984 NLCS | 2.00 | .90 |
| ❑ 240C | T.Gwynn MM 1995 Batting | 2.00 | .90 |
| ❑ 240D | T.Gwynn MM 1998 NLCS | 2.00 | .90 |
| ❑ 240E | T.Gwynn MM 3000th Hit | 2.00 | .90 |
| ❑ 241 | Tom Glavine | .40 | .18 |
| ❑ 242 | David Wells | .15 | .07 |
| ❑ 243 | Kevin Appier | .10 | .05 |
| ❑ 244 | Troy Percival | .10 | .05 |
| ❑ 245 | Ray Lankford | .15 | .07 |
| ❑ 246 | Marquis Grissom | .10 | .05 |
| ❑ 247 | Randy Winn | .10 | .05 |
| ❑ 248 | Miguel Batista | .10 | .05 |
| ❑ 249 | Darren Dreifort | .10 | .05 |
| ❑ 250 | Barry Bonds | .60 | .25 |
| ❑ 251 | Harold Baines | .15 | .07 |
| ❑ 252 | Cliff Floyd | .15 | .07 |
| ❑ 253 | Freddy Garcia | .15 | .07 |
| ❑ 254 | Kenny Rogers | .10 | .05 |
| ❑ 255 | Ben Davis | .10 | .05 |
| ❑ 256 | Charles Johnson | .15 | .07 |
| ❑ 257 | Bubba Trammell | .10 | .05 |
| ❑ 258 | Desi Relaford | .10 | .05 |
| ❑ 259 | Al Martin | .10 | .05 |
| ❑ 260 | Andy Pettitte | .15 | .07 |
| ❑ 261 | Carlos Lee | .15 | .07 |
| ❑ 262 | Matt Lawton | .10 | .05 |
| ❑ 263 | Andy Fox | .10 | .05 |
| ❑ 264 | Chan Ho Park | .15 | .07 |
| ❑ 265 | Billy Koch | .15 | .07 |
| ❑ 266 | Dave Roberts | .10 | .05 |
| ❑ 267 | Carl Everett | .15 | .07 |
| ❑ 268 | Orel Hershiser | .15 | .07 |
| ❑ 269 | Trot Nixon | .15 | .07 |
| ❑ 270 | Rusty Greer | .15 | .07 |
| ❑ 271 | Will Clark | .40 | .18 |
| ❑ 272 | Quilvio Veras | .10 | .05 |
| ❑ 273 | Rico Brogna | .10 | .05 |
| ❑ 274 | Devon White | .10 | .05 |
| ❑ 275 | Tim Hudson | .40 | .18 |
| ❑ 276 | Mike Hampton | .15 | .07 |
| ❑ 277 | Miguel Cairo | .10 | .05 |
| ❑ 278 | Darren Oliver | .10 | .05 |
| ❑ 279 | Jeff Cirillo | .15 | .07 |
| ❑ 280 | Al Leiter | .10 | .05 |
| ❑ 281 | Shane Andrews | .10 | .05 |
| ❑ 282 | Carlos Febles | .10 | .05 |
| ❑ 283 | Pedro Astacio | .10 | .05 |
| ❑ 284 | Juan Guzman | .10 | .05 |
| ❑ 285 | Orlando Hernandez | .15 | .07 |
| ❑ 286 | Paul Konerko | .15 | .07 |
| ❑ 287 | Tony Clark | .10 | .05 |
| ❑ 288 | Aaron Boone | .10 | .05 |
| ❑ 289 | Ismael Valdes | .10 | .05 |
| ❑ 290 | Moises Alou | .15 | .07 |
| ❑ 291 | Kevin Tapani | .10 | .05 |
| ❑ 292 | John Franco | .15 | .07 |
| ❑ 293 | Todd Zeile | .15 | .07 |
| ❑ 294 | Jason Schmidt | .10 | .05 |
| ❑ 295 | Johnny Damon | .15 | .07 |
| ❑ 296 | Scott Brosius | .15 | .07 |
| ❑ 297 | Travis Fryman | .15 | .07 |
| ❑ 298 | Jose Vizcaino | .10 | .05 |
| ❑ 299 | Eric Chavez | .15 | .07 |
| ❑ 300 | Mike Piazza | 1.25 | .55 |
| ❑ 301 | Matt Clement | .10 | .05 |
| ❑ 302 | Cristian Guzman | .10 | .05 |
| ❑ 303 | C.J. Nitkowski | .10 | .05 |
| ❑ 304 | Michael Tucker | .10 | .05 |
| ❑ 305 | Brett Tomko | .10 | .05 |
| ❑ 306 | Mike Lansing | .10 | .05 |
| ❑ 307 | Eric Owens | .10 | .05 |
| ❑ 308 | Livan Hernandez | .10 | .05 |
| ❑ 309 | Rondell White | .15 | .07 |
| ❑ 310 | Todd Stottlemyre | .10 | .05 |
| ❑ 311 | Chris Carpenter | .10 | .05 |
| ❑ 312 | Ken Hill | .10 | .05 |
| ❑ 313 | Mark Loretta | .10 | .05 |
| ❑ 314 | John Rocker | .15 | .07 |
| ❑ 315 | Richie Sexson | .15 | .07 |
| ❑ 316 | Ruben Mateo | .15 | .07 |
| ❑ 317 | Joe Randa | .10 | .05 |
| ❑ 318 | Mike Sirotka | .10 | .05 |
| ❑ 319 | Jose Rosado | .10 | .05 |
| ❑ 320 | Matt Mantei | .10 | .05 |
| ❑ 321 | Kevin Millwood | .15 | .07 |
| ❑ 322 | Gary DiSarcina | .10 | .05 |
| ❑ 323 | Dustin Hermanson | .10 | .05 |
| ❑ 324 | Mike Stanton | .10 | .05 |
| ❑ 325 | Kirk Rueter | .10 | .05 |
| ❑ 326 | Damian Miller | .10 | .05 |
| ❑ 327 | Doug Glanville | .10 | .05 |
| ❑ 328 | Scott Rolen | .40 | .18 |
| ❑ 329 | Ray Durham | .15 | .07 |
| ❑ 330 | Butch Huskey | .10 | .05 |
| ❑ 331 | Mariano Rivera | .15 | .07 |
| ❑ 332 | Darren Lewis | .10 | .05 |
| ❑ 333 | Mike Timlin | .10 | .05 |
| ❑ 334 | Mark Grudzielanek | .10 | .05 |
| ❑ 335 | Mike Cameron | .10 | .05 |
| ❑ 336 | Kelvim Escobar | .10 | .05 |
| ❑ 337 | Bret Boone | .10 | .05 |
| ❑ 338 | Mo Vaughn | .15 | .07 |
| ❑ 339 | Craig Biggio | .25 | .11 |
| ❑ 340 | Michael Barrett | .10 | .05 |
| ❑ 341 | Marlon Anderson | .10 | .05 |
| ❑ 342 | Bobby Jones | .10 | .05 |
| ❑ 343 | John Halama | .10 | .05 |
| ❑ 344 | Todd Ritchie | .10 | .05 |
| ❑ 345 | Chuck Knoblauch | .15 | .07 |
| ❑ 346 | Rick Reed | .10 | .05 |
| ❑ 347 | Kelly Stinnett | .10 | .05 |
| ❑ 348 | Tim Salmon | .15 | .07 |
| ❑ 349 | A.J. Hinch | .10 | .05 |
| ❑ 350 | Jose Cruz Jr. | .15 | .07 |
| ❑ 351 | Roberto Hernandez | .10 | .05 |
| ❑ 352 | Edgar Renteria | .10 | .05 |
| ❑ 353 | Jose Hernandez | .10 | .05 |
| ❑ 354 | Brad Fullmer | .15 | .07 |
| ❑ 355 | Trevor Hoffman | .15 | .07 |
| ❑ 356 | Troy O'Leary | .10 | .05 |
| ❑ 357 | Justin Thompson | .10 | .05 |
| ❑ 358 | Kevin Young | .10 | .05 |
| ❑ 359 | Hideki Irabu | .10 | .05 |

❑ 360 Jim Thome .25 .11
❑ 361 Steve Karsay .10 .05
❑ 362 Octavio Dotel .10 .05
❑ 363 Omar Vizquel .15 .07
❑ 364 Raul Mondesi .15 .07
❑ 365 Shane Reynolds .10 .05
❑ 366 Bartolo Colon .15 .07
❑ 367 Chris Widger .10 .05
❑ 368 Gabe Kapler .15 .07
❑ 369 Bill Simas .10 .05
❑ 370 Tino Martinez .15 .07
❑ 371 John Thomson .10 .05
❑ 372 Delino DeShields .10 .05
❑ 373 Carlos Perez .10 .05
❑ 374 Eddie Perez .10 .05
❑ 375 Jeromy Burnitz .15 .07
❑ 376 Jimmy Haynes .10 .05
❑ 377 Travis Lee .10 .05
❑ 378 Darryl Hamilton .10 .05
❑ 379 Jamie Moyer .10 .05
❑ 380 Alex Gonzalez .10 .05
❑ 381 John Wetteland .15 .07
❑ 382 Vinny Castilla .15 .07
❑ 383 Jeff Suppan .10 .05
❑ 384 Jim Leyritz .10 .05
❑ 385 Robb Nen .10 .05
❑ 386 Wilson Alvarez .10 .05
❑ 007 Andreo Galarroga .25 .11
❑ 388 Mike Remlinger .10 .05
❑ 389 Geoff Jenkins .15 .07
❑ 390 Matt Stairs .10 .05
❑ 391 Bill Mueller .10 .05
❑ 392 Mike Lowell .10 .05
❑ 393 Andy Ashby .10 .05
❑ 394 Ruben Rivera .10 .05
❑ 395 Todd Helton .50 .23
❑ 396 Bernie Williams .40 .18
❑ 397 Royce Clayton .10 .05
❑ 398 Manny Ramirez .50 .23
❑ 399 Kerry Wood .15 .07
❑ 400 Ken Griffey Jr. 1.50 .70
❑ 401 Enrique Wilson .10 .05
❑ 402 Joey Hamilton .10 .05
❑ 403 Shawn Estes .10 .05
❑ 404 Ugueth Urbina .10 .05
❑ 405 Albert Belle .25 .11
❑ 406 Rick Helling .15 .07
❑ 407 Steve Parris .10 .05
❑ 408 Eric Milton .10 .05
❑ 409 Dave Mlicki .10 .05
❑ 410 Shawn Green .40 .18
❑ 411 Jaret Wright .10 .05
❑ 412 Tony Womack .10 .05
❑ 413 Vernon Wells .15 .07
❑ 414 Ron Belliard .10 .05
❑ 415 Ellis Burks .15 .07
❑ 416 Scott Erickson .10 .05
❑ 417 Rafael Palmeiro .40 .18
❑ 418 Damion Easley .10 .05
❑ 419 Jamey Wright .10 .05
❑ 420 Corey Koskie .10 .05
❑ 421 Bobby Howry .10 .05
❑ 422 Ricky Ledee .10 .05
❑ 423 Dmitri Young .15 .07
❑ 424 Sidney Ponson .10 .05
❑ 425 Greg Maddux 1.00 .45
❑ 426 Jose Guillen .10 .05
❑ 427 Jon Lieber .10 .05
❑ 428 Andy Benes .10 .05
❑ 429 Randy Velarde .10 .05
❑ 430 Sean Casey .15 .07
❑ 431 Torii Hunter .10 .05
❑ 432 Ryan Rupe .10 .05
❑ 433 David Segui .10 .05
❑ 434 Todd Pratt .10 .05
❑ 435 Nomar Garciaparra 1.25 .55
❑ 436 Denny Neagle .10 .05
❑ 437 Ron Coomer .10 .05
❑ 438 Chris Singleton .15 .07
❑ 439 Tony Batista .15 .07
❑ 440 Andruw Jones .40 .18
❑ 441 Aubrey Huff .40 .18
Sean Burroughs
Adam Piatt
❑ 442 Rafael Furcal 1.00 .45
Travis Dawkins
Jason Dellaero
❑ 443 Mike Lamb RC .50 .23
Joe Crede
Wilton Veras
❑ 444 Julio Zuleta RC .25 .11
Jorge Toca
Dernell Stenson
❑ 445 Garry Maddox Jr. RC .25 .11
Gary Matthews Jr.
Tim Raines Jr.
❑ 446 Mark Mulder .15 .07
C.C. Sabathia
Matt Riley
❑ 447 Scott Downs RC .25 .11
Chris George
Matt Belisle
❑ 448 Doug Mirabelli .10 .05
Ben Petrick
Jayson Werth
❑ 449 Josh Hamilton .60 .25
Corey Myers RC
❑ 450 Ben Christensen RC .60 .25
Richard Stahl RC
❑ 451 Ben Sheets RC 2.50 1.10
Barry Zito
❑ 452 Kurt Ainsworth .60 .25
Ty Howington RC
❑ 453 Vince Faison RC 2.00 .90
Rick Asadoorian
❑ 454 Keith Reed RC .50 .23
Jeff Heaverlo
❑ 455 Mike MacDougal .60 .25
Brad Baker RC
❑ 456 Mark McGwire SH .75 .35
❑ 457 Cal Ripken SH .75 .35
❑ 458 Wade Boggs SH .25 .11
❑ 459 Tony Gwynn SH .40 .18
❑ 460 Jesse Orosco SH .10 .05
❑ 461 Larry Walker .40 .18
Nomar Garciaparra LL
❑ 462 Ken Griffey Jr. .75 .35
Mark McGwire LL
❑ 463 Manny Ramirez .50 .23
Mark McGwire LL
❑ 464 Pedro Martinez .25 .11
Randy Johnson LL
❑ 465 Pedro Martinez .25 .11
Randy Johnson LL
❑ 466 Derek Jeter .50 .23
Luis Gonzalez LL
❑ 467 Larry Walker .15 .07
Manny Ramirez LL
❑ 468 Tony Gwynn 20CB .75 .35
❑ 469 Mark McGwire 20CB 1.50 .70
❑ 470 Frank Thomas 20CB .75 .35
❑ 471 Harold Baines 20CB .15 .07
❑ 472 Roger Clemens 20CB .75 .35
❑ 473 John Franco 20CB .15 .07
❑ 474 John Franco 20CB .15 .07
❑ 475A K.Griffey Jr. MM 350th HR 4.00 1.80
❑ 475B K.Griffey Jr. MM 1997 MVP 4.00 1.80
❑ 475C K.Griffey Jr. MM HR Dad 4.00 1.80
❑ 475D K.Griffey Jr. MM 1992 AS MVP 4.00 1.80
❑ 475E K.Griffey Jr. MM 50 HR 1997 4.00 1.80
❑ 476A B.Bonds MM 400HR/400SB 1.50 .70
❑ 476B B.Bonds MM 40HR/40SB 1.50 .70
❑ 476C B.Bonds MM 1993 MVP 1.50 .70
❑ 476D B.Bonds MM 1990 MVP 1.50 .70
❑ 476E B.Bonds MM 1992 MVP 1.50 .70
❑ 477A S.Sosa MM 20 HR June 2.50 1.10
❑ 477B S.Sosa MM 66 HR 1998 2.50 1.10
❑ 477C S.Sosa MM 60 HR 1999 2.50 1.10
❑ 477D S.Sosa MM 1998 MVP 2.50 1.10
❑ 477E S.Sosa MM HR's 61/62 2.50 1.10
❑ 478A D.Jeter MM 1996 ROY 4.00 1.80
❑ 478B D.Jeter MM Wins 1999 WS 4.00 1.80
❑ 478C D.Jeter MM Wins 1998 WS 4.00 1.80
❑ 478D D.Jeter MM Wins 1996 WS 4.00 1.80
❑ 478E D.Jeter MM 17 GM Hit Streak 4.001.80
❑ 479A A.Rodriguez MM 40HR/40SB 3.00 1.35
❑ 479B A.Rodriguez MM 100th HR 3.00 1.35
❑ 479C A.Rodriguez MM 1996 POY 3.00 1.35
❑ 479D A.Rodriguez MM Wins 1 Million 3.00 1.35
❑ 479E A.Rodriguez MM 3.00 1.35
1996 Batting Leader
❑ NNO Mark McGwire 85 Reprint 6.00 2.70

## 2000 Topps Limited

| | MINT | NRMT |
|---|---|---|
| COMP.FACT.SET (619) | 275.00 | 125.00 |
| COMPLETE SET (478) | 150.00 | 70.00 |

*STARS: 2.5X TO 6X BASIC CARDS
*YNG.STARS: 2.5X TO 6X BASIC CARDS
*ROOKIES: 4X TO 10X BASIC CARDS
*MAGIC MOMENTS: 1.25X TO 3X BASIC MM

## 2000 Topps Traded

| | MINT | NRMT |
|---|---|---|
| COMP.FACT.SET (136) | 30.00 | 13.50 |
| COMPLETE SET (135) | 20.00 | 9.00 |

❑ T1 Mike MacDougal .25 .11
❑ T2 Andy Tracy RC .25 .11
❑ T3 Brandon Phillips RC .40 .18
❑ T4 Brandon Inge RC .60 .25
❑ T5 Robbie Morrison RC .25 .11
❑ T6 Josh Pressley RC .40 .18
❑ T7 Todd Moser RC .25 .11
❑ T8 Rob Purvis .25 .11
❑ T9 Chance Caple .25 .11
❑ T10 Ben Sheets 2.00 .90
❑ T11 Russ Jacobson RC .40 .18
❑ T12 Brian Cole RC .75 .35
❑ T13 Brad Baker .60 .25
❑ T14 Alex Cintron RC .50 .23
❑ T15 Lyle Overbay RC .75 .35
❑ T16 Mike Edwards RC .25 .11
❑ T17 Sean McGowan RC .50 .23
❑ T18 Jose Molina .15 .07
❑ T19 Marcos Castillo RC .25 .11
❑ T20 Josue Espada RC .25 .11
❑ T21 Alex Gordon RC .50 .23
❑ T22 Rob Pugmire RC .25 .11
❑ T23 Jason Stumm .40 .18
❑ T24 Ty Howington .40 .18
❑ T25 Brett Myers .40 .18
❑ T26 Maicer Izturis RC .25 .11
❑ T27 John McDonald .15 .07
❑ T28 Wilfredo Rodriguez RC .50 .23
❑ T29 Carlos Zambrano RC .60 .25
❑ T30 Alejandro Diaz RC .40 .18
❑ T31 Geraldo Guzman RC .25 .11
❑ T32 J.R. House RC 2.00 .90
❑ T33 Elvin Nina RC .25 .11
❑ T34 Juan Pierre RC .50 .23
❑ T35 Ben Johnson RC .75 .35

| Card | Mint | NrMt |
|---|---|---|
| ❑ T36 Jeff Bailey RC | .25 | .11 |
| ❑ T37 Miguel Olivo RC | .40 | .18 |
| ❑ T38 Francisco Rodriguez RC | .40 | .18 |
| ❑ T39 Tony Pena Jr. RC | .50 | .23 |
| ❑ T40 Miguel Cabrera RC | .40 | .18 |
| ❑ T41 Asdrubal Oropeza RC | .40 | .18 |
| ❑ T42 Junior Zamora RC | .25 | .11 |
| ❑ T43 Jovanny Cedeno RC | .50 | .23 |
| ❑ T44 John Sneed | .25 | .11 |
| ❑ T45 Josh Kalinowski | .25 | .11 |
| ❑ T46 Mike Young RC | .40 | .18 |
| ❑ T47 Rico Washington RC | .40 | .18 |
| ❑ T48 Chad Durbin RC | .25 | .11 |
| ❑ T49 Junior Brignac RC | .40 | .18 |
| ❑ T50 Carlos Hernandez RC | .40 | .18 |
| ❑ T51 Cesar Izturis RC | .40 | .18 |
| ❑ T52 Oscar Salazar RC | .40 | .18 |
| ❑ T53 Pat Strange RC | .75 | .35 |
| ❑ T54 Rick Asadoorian | 1.25 | .55 |
| ❑ T55 Keith Reed | .40 | .18 |
| ❑ T56 Leo Estrella RC | .25 | .11 |
| ❑ T57 Wascar Serrano RC | .40 | .18 |
| ❑ T58 Richard Gomez RC | .50 | .23 |
| ❑ T59 Ramon Santiago RC | .50 | .23 |
| ❑ T60 Jovanny Sosa RC | .50 | .23 |
| ❑ T61 Aaron Rowand RC | .60 | .25 |
| ❑ T62 Junior Guerrero RC | .25 | .11 |
| ❑ T63 Luis Terrero RC | .40 | .18 |
| ❑ T64 Brian Sanches RC | .25 | .11 |
| ❑ T65 Scott Sobkowiak RC | .40 | .18 |
| ❑ T66 Gary Majewski RC | .40 | .18 |
| ❑ T67 Barry Zito | 2.00 | .90 |
| ❑ T68 Ryan Christianson | .60 | .25 |
| ❑ T69 Cristian Guerrero RC | 2.00 | .90 |
| ❑ T70 Tomas De La Rosa RC | .25 | .11 |
| ❑ T71 Andrew Beinbrink RC | .25 | .11 |
| ❑ T72 Ryan Knox RC | .40 | .18 |
| ❑ T73 Alex Graman RC | .60 | .25 |
| ❑ T74 Juan Guzman RC | .25 | .11 |
| ❑ T75 Ruben Salazar RC | .60 | .25 |
| ❑ T76 Luis Matos RC | .60 | .25 |
| ❑ T77 Tony Mota RC | .25 | .11 |
| ❑ T78 Doug Davis | .15 | .07 |
| ❑ T79 Ben Christensen | .60 | .25 |
| ❑ T80 Mike Lamb | .40 | .18 |
| ❑ T81 Adrian Gonzalez RC | 1.50 | .70 |
| ❑ T82 Mike Stodolka RC | .50 | .23 |
| ❑ T83 Adam Johnson RC | .60 | .25 |
| ❑ T84 Matt Wheatland RC | .75 | .35 |
| ❑ T85 Corey Smith RC | .60 | .25 |
| ❑ T86 Rocco Baldelli RC | 1.00 | .45 |
| ❑ T87 Keith Bucktrot RC | .40 | .18 |
| ❑ T88 Adam Wainwright RC | .75 | .35 |
| ❑ T89 Scott Thorman RC | .40 | .18 |
| ❑ T90 Tripper Johnson RC | .50 | .23 |
| ❑ T91 Jim Edmonds | .60 | .25 |
| ❑ T92 Masato Yoshii | .15 | .07 |
| ❑ T93 Adam Kennedy | .25 | .11 |
| ❑ T94 Darryl Kile | .25 | .11 |
| ❑ T95 Mark McLemore | .15 | .07 |
| ❑ T96 Ricky Gutierrez | .15 | .07 |
| ❑ T97 Juan Gonzalez | .60 | .25 |
| ❑ T98 Melvin Mora | .15 | .07 |
| ❑ T99 Dante Bichette | .25 | .11 |
| ❑ T100 Lee Stevens | .15 | .07 |
| ❑ T101 Roger Cedeno | .15 | .07 |
| ❑ T102 John Olerud | .25 | .11 |
| ❑ T103 Eric Young | .15 | .07 |
| ❑ T104 Mickey Morandini | .15 | .07 |
| ❑ T105 Travis Lee | .15 | .07 |
| ❑ T106 Greg Vaughn | .25 | .11 |
| ❑ T107 Todd Zeile | .25 | .11 |
| ❑ T108 Chuck Finley | .25 | .11 |
| ❑ T109 Ismael Valdes | .15 | .07 |
| ❑ T110 Reggie Sanders | .15 | .07 |
| ❑ T111 Pat Hentgen | .15 | .07 |
| ❑ T112 Ryan Klesko | .25 | .11 |
| ❑ T113 Derek Bell | .15 | .07 |
| ❑ T114 Hideo Nomo | .60 | .25 |
| ❑ T115 Aaron Sele | .25 | .11 |
| ❑ T116 Fernando Vina | .15 | .07 |
| ❑ T117 Wally Joyner | .25 | .11 |
| ❑ T118 Brian Hunter | .15 | .07 |
| ❑ T119 Joe Girardi | .15 | .07 |
| ❑ T120 Omar Daal | .15 | .07 |
| ❑ T121 Brook Fordyce | .15 | .07 |
| ❑ T122 Jose Valentin | .15 | .07 |
| ❑ T123 Curt Schilling | .25 | .11 |
| ❑ T124 B.J. Surhoff | .25 | .11 |
| ❑ T125 Henry Rodriguez | .15 | .07 |
| ❑ T126 Mike Bordick | .15 | .07 |
| ❑ T127 David Justice | .40 | .18 |
| ❑ T128 Charles Johnson | .25 | .11 |
| ❑ T129 Will Clark | .60 | .25 |
| ❑ T130 Dwight Gooden | .25 | .11 |
| ❑ T131 David Segui | .15 | .07 |
| ❑ T132 Denny Neagle | .25 | .11 |
| ❑ T133 Jose Canseco | .75 | .35 |
| ❑ T134 Bruce Chen | .25 | .11 |
| ❑ T135 Jason Bere | .15 | .07 |

## 2001 Topps

| | MINT | NRMT |
|---|---|---|
| COMPLETE SERIES 1 (405) | 50.00 | 22.00 |
| COMMON CARD (1-6/8-406) | .10 | .05 |
| COMMON PROSPECT (352-376) | .25 | .11 |

| Card | Mint | NrMt |
|---|---|---|
| ❑ 1 Cal Ripken | 1.50 | .70 |
| ❑ 2 Chipper Jones | 1.00 | .45 |
| ❑ 3 Roger Cedeno | .10 | .05 |
| ❑ 4 Garret Anderson | .15 | .07 |
| ❑ 5 Robin Ventura | .15 | .07 |
| ❑ 6 Daryle Ward | .10 | .05 |
| ❑ 7 Does Not Exist | | |
| ❑ 8 Craig Paquette | .10 | .05 |
| ❑ 9 Phil Nevin | .15 | .07 |
| ❑ 10 Jermaine Dye | .15 | .07 |
| ❑ 11 Chris Singleton | .15 | .07 |
| ❑ 12 Mike Stanton | .10 | .05 |
| ❑ 13 Brian Hunter | .10 | .05 |
| ❑ 14 Mike Redmond | .10 | .05 |
| ❑ 15 Jim Thome | .25 | .11 |
| ❑ 16 Brian Jordan | .15 | .07 |
| ❑ 17 Joe Girardi | .10 | .05 |
| ❑ 18 Steve Woodard | .10 | .05 |
| ❑ 19 Dustin Hermanson | .10 | .05 |
| ❑ 20 Shawn Green | .40 | .18 |
| ❑ 21 Todd Stottlemyre | .10 | .05 |
| ❑ 22 Dan Wilson | .10 | .05 |
| ❑ 23 Todd Pratt | .10 | .05 |
| ❑ 24 Derek Lowe | .10 | .05 |
| ❑ 25 Juan Gonzalez | .40 | .18 |
| ❑ 26 Clay Bellinger | .10 | .05 |
| ❑ 27 Jeff Fassero | .10 | .05 |
| ❑ 28 Pat Meares | .10 | .05 |
| ❑ 29 Eddie Taubensee | .10 | .05 |
| ❑ 30 Paul O'Neill | .15 | .07 |
| ❑ 31 Jeffrey Hammonds | .15 | .07 |
| ❑ 32 Pokey Reese | .15 | .07 |
| ❑ 33 Mike Mussina | .40 | .18 |
| ❑ 34 Rico Brogna | .10 | .05 |
| ❑ 35 Jay Buhner | .15 | .07 |
| ❑ 36 Steve Cox | .10 | .05 |
| ❑ 37 Quilvio Veras | .10 | .05 |
| ❑ 38 Marquis Grissom | .10 | .05 |
| ❑ 39 Shigetoshi Hasegawa | .15 | .07 |
| ❑ 40 Shane Reynolds | .10 | .05 |
| ❑ 41 Adam Piatt | .15 | .07 |
| ❑ 42 Luis Polonia | .10 | .05 |
| ❑ 43 Brook Fordyce | .10 | .05 |
| ❑ 44 Preston Wilson | .15 | .07 |
| ❑ 45 Ellis Burks | .15 | .07 |
| ❑ 46 Armando Rios | .10 | .05 |
| ❑ 47 Chuck Finley | .15 | .07 |
| ❑ 48 Dan Plesac | .10 | .05 |
| ❑ 49 Shannon Stewart | .15 | .07 |
| ❑ 50 Mark McGwire | 1.50 | .70 |
| ❑ 51 Mark Loretta | .10 | .05 |
| ❑ 52 Gerald Williams | .10 | .05 |
| ❑ 53 Eric Young | .10 | .05 |
| ❑ 54 Peter Bergeron | .10 | .05 |
| ❑ 55 Dave Hansen | .10 | .05 |
| ❑ 56 Arthur Rhodes | .10 | .05 |
| ❑ 57 Bobby Jones | .10 | .05 |
| ❑ 58 Matt Clement | .10 | .05 |
| ❑ 59 Mike Benjamin | .10 | .05 |
| ❑ 60 Pedro Martinez | .50 | .23 |
| ❑ 61 Jose Canseco | .50 | .23 |
| ❑ 62 Matt Anderson | .10 | .05 |
| ❑ 63 Torii Hunter | .10 | .05 |
| ❑ 64 Carlos Lee | .15 | .07 |
| ❑ 65 David Cone | .15 | .07 |
| ❑ 66 Rey Sanchez | .10 | .05 |
| ❑ 67 Eric Chavez | .15 | .07 |
| ❑ 68 Rick Helling | .15 | .07 |
| ❑ 69 Manny Alexander | .10 | .05 |
| ❑ 70 John Franco | .15 | .07 |
| ❑ 71 Mike Bordick | .10 | .05 |
| ❑ 72 Andres Galarraga | .25 | .11 |
| ❑ 73 Jose Cruz Jr. | .15 | .07 |
| ❑ 74 Mike Matheny | .10 | .05 |
| ❑ 75 Randy Johnson | .50 | .23 |
| ❑ 76 Richie Sexson | .15 | .07 |
| ❑ 77 Vladimir Nunez | .10 | .05 |
| ❑ 78 Harold Baines | .15 | .07 |
| ❑ 79 Aaron Boone | .10 | .05 |
| ❑ 80 Darin Erstad | .40 | .18 |
| ❑ 81 Alex Gonzalez | .10 | .05 |
| ❑ 82 Gil Heredia | .10 | .05 |
| ❑ 83 Shane Andrews | .10 | .05 |
| ❑ 84 Todd Hundley | .10 | .05 |
| ❑ 85 Bill Mueller | .10 | .05 |
| ❑ 86 Mark McLemore | .10 | .05 |
| ❑ 87 Scott Spiezio | .10 | .05 |
| ❑ 88 Kevin McGlinchy | .10 | .05 |
| ❑ 89 Bubba Trammell | .10 | .05 |
| ❑ 90 Manny Ramirez | .50 | .23 |
| ❑ 91 Mike Lamb | .10 | .05 |
| ❑ 92 Scott Karl | .10 | .05 |
| ❑ 93 Brian Buchanan | .10 | .05 |
| ❑ 94 Chris Turner | .10 | .05 |
| ❑ 95 Mike Sweeney | .15 | .07 |
| ❑ 96 John Wetteland | .15 | .07 |
| ❑ 97 Rob Bell | .10 | .05 |
| ❑ 98 Pat Rapp | .10 | .05 |
| ❑ 99 John Burkett | .10 | .05 |
| ❑ 100 Derek Jeter | 1.50 | .70 |
| ❑ 101 J.D. Drew | .40 | .18 |
| ❑ 102 Jose Offerman | .10 | .05 |
| ❑ 103 Rick Reed | .10 | .05 |
| ❑ 104 Will Clark | .40 | .18 |
| ❑ 105 Rickey Henderson | .50 | .23 |
| ❑ 106 Dave Berg | .10 | .05 |
| ❑ 107 Kirk Rueter | .10 | .05 |
| ❑ 108 Lee Stevens | .10 | .05 |
| ❑ 109 Jay Bell | .15 | .07 |
| ❑ 110 Fred McGriff | .25 | .11 |
| ❑ 111 Julio Zuleta | .10 | .05 |
| ❑ 112 Brian Anderson | .10 | .05 |
| ❑ 113 Orlando Cabrera | .10 | .05 |
| ❑ 114 Alex Fernandez | .10 | .05 |
| ❑ 115 Derek Bell | .10 | .05 |
| ❑ 116 Eric Owens | .10 | .05 |
| ❑ 117 Brian Bohanon | .10 | .05 |
| ❑ 118 Dennys Reyes | .10 | .05 |
| ❑ 119 Mike Stanley | .10 | .05 |
| ❑ 120 Jorge Posada | .15 | .07 |
| ❑ 121 Rich Becker | .10 | .05 |
| ❑ 122 Paul Konerko | .15 | .07 |
| ❑ 123 Mike Remlinger | .10 | .05 |
| ❑ 124 Travis Lee | .10 | .05 |
| ❑ 125 Ken Caminiti | .15 | .07 |
| ❑ 126 Kevin Barker | .10 | .05 |
| ❑ 127 Paul Quantrill | .10 | .05 |
| ❑ 128 Ozzie Guillen | .10 | .05 |
| ❑ 129 Kevin Tapani | .10 | .05 |
| ❑ 130 Mark Johnson | .10 | .05 |
| ❑ 131 Randy Wolf | .10 | .05 |
| ❑ 132 Michael Tucker | .10 | .05 |
| ❑ 133 Darren Lewis | .10 | .05 |
| ❑ 134 Joe Randa | .10 | .05 |

❑ 135 Jeff Cirillo .15 .07
❑ 136 David Ortiz .10 .05
❑ 137 Herb Perry .10 .05
❑ 138 Jeff Nelson .10 .05
❑ 139 Chris Stynes .10 .05
❑ 140 Johnny Damon .15 .07
❑ 141 Jeff Reboulet .10 .05
❑ 142 Jason Schmidt .10 .05
❑ 143 Charles Johnson .10 .05
❑ 144 Pat Burrell .40 .18
❑ 145 Gary Sheffield .40 .18
❑ 146 Tom Glavine .40 .18
❑ 147 Jason Isringhausen .10 .05
❑ 148 Chris Carpenter .10 .05
❑ 149 Jeff Suppan .10 .05
❑ 150 Ivan Rodriguez .50 .23
❑ 151 Luis Sojo .10 .05
❑ 152 Ron Villone .10 .05
❑ 153 Mike Sirotka .10 .05
❑ 154 Chuck Knoblauch .15 .07
❑ 155 Jason Kendall .15 .07
❑ 156 Dennis Cook .10 .05
❑ 157 Bobby Estalella .10 .05
❑ 158 Jose Guillen .10 .05
❑ 159 Thomas Howard .10 .05
❑ 160 Carlos Delgado .40 .18
❑ 161 Benji Gil .10 .05
❑ 162 Tim Bogar .10 .05
❑ 163 Kevin Elster .10 .05
❑ 164 Einar Diaz .10 .05
❑ 165 Andy Benes .10 .05
❑ 166 Adrian Beltre .15 .07
❑ 167 David Bell .10 .05
❑ 168 Turk Wendell .10 .05
❑ 169 Pete Harnisch .10 .05
❑ 170 Roger Clemens .75 .35
❑ 171 Scott Williamson .10 .05
❑ 172 Kevin Jordan .10 .05
❑ 173 Brad Penny .15 .07
❑ 174 John Flaherty .10 .05
❑ 175 Troy Glaus .50 .23
❑ 176 Kevin Appier .15 .07
❑ 177 Walt Weiss .10 .05
❑ 178 Tyler Houston .10 .05
❑ 179 Michael Barrett .10 .05
❑ 180 Mike Hampton .15 .07
❑ 181 Francisco Cordova .10 .05
❑ 182 Mike Jackson .10 .05
❑ 183 David Segui .10 .05
❑ 184 Carlos Febles .10 .05
❑ 185 Roy Halladay .10 .05
❑ 186 Seth Etherton .10 .05
❑ 187 Charlie Hayes .10 .05
❑ 188 Fernando Tatis .15 .07
❑ 189 Steve Trachsel .10 .05
❑ 190 Livan Hernandez .10 .05
❑ 191 Joe Oliver .10 .05
❑ 192 Stan Javier .10 .05
❑ 193 B.J. Surhoff .15 .07
❑ 194 Rob Ducey .10 .05
❑ 195 Barry Larkin .40 .18
❑ 196 Danny Patterson .10 .05
❑ 197 Bobby Howry .10 .05
❑ 198 Dmitri Young .15 .07
❑ 199 Brian Hunter .10 .05
❑ 200 Alex Rodriguez 1.25 .55
❑ 201 Hideo Nomo .40 .18
❑ 202 Luis Alicea .10 .05
❑ 203 Warren Morris .10 .05
❑ 204 Antonio Alfonseca .10 .05
❑ 205 Edgardo Alfonzo .15 .07
❑ 206 Mark Grudzielanek .10 .05
❑ 207 Fernando Vina .10 .05
❑ 208 Willie Greene .10 .05
❑ 209 Homer Bush .10 .05
❑ 210 Jason Giambi .40 .18
❑ 211 Mike Morgan .10 .05
❑ 212 Steve Karsay .10 .05
❑ 213 Matt Lawton .15 .07
❑ 214 Wendell Magee Jr. .10 .05
❑ 215 Rusty Greer .15 .07
❑ 216 Keith Lockhart .10 .05
❑ 217 Billy Koch .15 .07
❑ 218 Todd Hollandsworth .10 .05
❑ 219 Raul Ibanez .10 .05
❑ 220 Tony Gwynn .75 .35
❑ 221 Carl Everett .15 .07
❑ 222 Hector Carrasco .10 .05
❑ 223 Jose Valentin .10 .05
❑ 224 Deivi Cruz .10 .05
❑ 225 Bret Boone .10 .05
❑ 226 Kurt Abbott .10 .05
❑ 227 Melvin Mora .10 .05
❑ 228 Danny Graves .10 .05
❑ 229 Jose Jimenez .10 .05
❑ 230 James Baldwin .15 .07
❑ 231 C.J. Nitkowski .10 .05
❑ 232 Jeff Zimmerman .10 .05
❑ 233 Mike Lowell .10 .05
❑ 234 Hideki Irabu .10 .05
❑ 235 Greg Vaughn .15 .07
❑ 236 Omar Daal .10 .05
❑ 237 Darren Dreifort .10 .05
❑ 238 Gil Meche .10 .05
❑ 239 Damian Jackson .10 .05
❑ 240 Frank Thomas .75 .35
❑ 241 Travis Miller .10 .05
❑ 242 Jeff Frye .10 .05
❑ 243 Dave Magadan .10 .05
❑ 244 Luis Castillo .15 .07
❑ 245 Bartolo Colon .15 .07
❑ 246 Steve Kline .10 .05
❑ 247 Shawon Dunston .10 .05
❑ 248 Rick Aguilera .10 .05
❑ 249 Omar Olivares .10 .05
❑ 250 Craig Biggio .25 .11
❑ 251 Scott Schoeneweis .10 .05
❑ 252 Dave Veres .10 .05
❑ 253 Ramon Martinez .10 .05
❑ 254 Jose Vidro .15 .07
❑ 255 Todd Helton .50 .23
❑ 256 Greg Norton .10 .05
❑ 257 Jacque Jones .15 .07
❑ 258 Jason Grimsley .10 .05
❑ 259 Dan Reichert .10 .05
❑ 260 Robb Nen .10 .05
❑ 261 Mark Clark .10 .05
❑ 262 Scott Hatteberg .10 .05
❑ 263 Doug Brocail .10 .05
❑ 264 Mark Johnson .10 .05
❑ 265 Eric Davis .15 .07
❑ 266 Terry Shumpert .10 .05
❑ 267 Kevin Millar .10 .05
❑ 268 Ismael Valdes .10 .05
❑ 269 Richard Hidalgo .15 .07
❑ 270 Randy Velarde .10 .05
❑ 271 Bengie Molina .15 .07
❑ 272 Tony Womack .10 .05
❑ 273 Enrique Wilson .10 .05
❑ 274 Jeff Brantley .10 .05
❑ 275 Rick Ankiel .50 .23
❑ 276 Terry Mulholland .10 .05
❑ 277 Ron Belliard .10 .05
❑ 278 Terrence Long .15 .07
❑ 279 Alberto Castillo .10 .05
❑ 280 Royce Clayton .10 .05
❑ 281 Joe McEwing .10 .05
❑ 282 Jason McDonald .10 .05
❑ 283 Ricky Bottalico .10 .05
❑ 284 Keith Foulke .10 .05
❑ 285 Brad Radke .15 .07
❑ 286 Gabe Kapler .15 .07
❑ 287 Pedro Astacio .10 .05
❑ 288 Armando Reynoso .10 .05
❑ 289 Darryl Kile .15 .07
❑ 290 Reggie Sanders .10 .05
❑ 291 Esteban Yan .10 .05
❑ 292 Joe Nathan .10 .05
❑ 293 Jay Payton .15 .07
❑ 294 Francisco Cordero .10 .05
❑ 295 Gregg Jefferies .10 .05
❑ 296 LaTroy Hawkins .10 .05
❑ 297 Jeff Tam RC .25 .11
❑ 298 Jacob Cruz .10 .05
❑ 299 Chris Holt .10 .05
❑ 300 Vladimir Guerrero .60 .25
❑ 301 Marvin Benard .10 .05
❑ 302 Alex Ramirez .10 .05
❑ 303 Mike Williams .10 .05
❑ 304 Sean Bergman .10 .05
❑ 305 Juan Encarnacion .15 .07
❑ 306 Russ Davis .10 .05
❑ 307 Hanley Frias .10 .05
❑ 308 Ramon Hernandez .10 .05
❑ 309 Matt Walbeck .10 .05
❑ 310 Bill Spiers .10 .05
❑ 311 Bob Wickman .10 .05
❑ 312 Sandy Alomar Jr. .15 .07
❑ 313 Eddie Guardado .10 .05
❑ 314 Shane Halter .10 .05
❑ 315 Geoff Jenkins .15 .07
❑ 316 Brian Meadows .10 .05
❑ 317 Damian Miller .10 .05
❑ 318 Darrin Fletcher .10 .05
❑ 319 Rafael Furcal .60 .25
❑ 320 Mark Grace .40 .18
❑ 321 Mark Mulder .15 .07
❑ 322 Joe Torre MG .15 .07
❑ 323 Bobby Cox MG .10 .05
❑ 324 Mike Scioscia MG .10 .05
❑ 325 Mike Hargrove MG .10 .05
❑ 326 Jimy Williams MG .10 .05
❑ 327 Jerry Manuel MG .10 .05
❑ 328 Buck Showalter MG .10 .05
❑ 329 Charlie Manuel MG .10 .05
❑ 330 Don Baylor MG .15 .07
❑ 331 Phil Garner MG .10 .05
❑ 332 Jack McKeon MG .10 .05
❑ 333 Tony Muser MG .10 .05
❑ 334 Buddy Bell MG .15 .07
❑ 335 Tom Kelly MG .10 .05
❑ 336 John Boles MG .10 .05
❑ 337 Art Howe MG .10 .05
❑ 338 Larry Dierker MG .10 .05
❑ 339 Lou Piniella MG .15 .07
❑ 340 Davey Johnson MG .10 .05
❑ 341 Larry Rothschild MG .10 .05
❑ 342 Davey Lopes MG .15 .07
❑ 343 Johnny Oates MG .10 .05
❑ 344 Felipe Alou MG .10 .05
❑ 345 Jim Fregosi MG .10 .05
❑ 346 Bobby Valentine MG .10 .05
❑ 347 Terry Francona MG .10 .05
❑ 348 Gene Lamont MG .10 .05
❑ 349 Tony LaRussa MG .10 .05
❑ 350 Bruce Bochy MG .10 .05
❑ 351 Dusty Baker MG .15 .07
❑ 352 Adrian Gonzalez .75 .35
Adam Johnson
❑ 353 Matt Wheatland .50 .23
Bryan Digby
❑ 354 Tripper Johnson .50 .23
Scott Thorman
❑ 355 Phil Dumatrait .50 .23
Adam Wainwright
❑ 356 Scott Heard 1.00 .45
David Parrish RC
❑ 357 Rocco Baldelli .75 .35
Mark Folsom RC
❑ 358 Dominic Rich RC .50 .23
Aaron Herr
❑ 359 Mike Stodolka .50 .23
Sean Burnett
❑ 360 Derek Thompson .50 .23
Corey Smith
❑ 361 Danny Borrell RC .50 .23
Jason Bourgeois RC
❑ 362 Chin-Feng Chen 1.00 .45
Corey Patterson
Josh Hamilton
❑ 363 Ryan Anderson 1.00 .45
Barry Zito
C.C. Sabathia
❑ 364 Scott Sobkowiak .75 .35
David Walling
Ben Sheets
❑ 365 Ty Howington .25 .11
Josh Kalinowski
Josh Girdley
❑ 366 Hee Seop Choi RC 1.00 .45
Aaron McNeal
Jason Hart
❑ 367 Bobby Bradley 1.00 .45
Kurt Ainsworth
Chin-Hui Tsao
❑ 368 Mike Glendenning .50 .23
Kenny Kelly
Juan Silvestri

| No. | Player | | |
|---|---|---|---|
| ❑ 369 | J.R. House<br>Ramon Castro<br>Ben Davis | 1.00 | .45 |
| ❑ 370 | Chance Caple<br>Rafael Soriano RC<br>Pascual Coco | .50 | .23 |
| ❑ 371 | Travis Hafner<br>Eric Munson<br>Bucky Jacobsen | .50 | .23 |
| ❑ 372 | Jason Conti<br>Chris Wakeland<br>Brian Cole | .50 | .23 |
| ❑ 373 | Scott Seabol<br>Aubrey Huff<br>Joe Crede | .50 | .23 |
| ❑ 374 | Adam Everett<br>Jose Ortiz<br>Keith Ginter | .50 | .23 |
| ❑ 375 | Carlos Hernandez<br>Geraldo Guzman<br>Adam Eaton | .50 | .23 |
| ❑ 376 | Bobby Kielty<br>Milton Bradley<br>Juan Rivera | .50 | .23 |
| ❑ 377 | Mark McGwire GM | .75 | .35 |
| ❑ 378 | Don Larsen GM | .15 | .07 |
| ❑ 379 | Bobby Thomson GM | .15 | .07 |
| ❑ 380 | Bill Mazeroski GM | .15 | .07 |
| ❑ 381 | Reggie Jackson GM | .40 | .18 |
| ❑ 382 | Kirk Gibson GM | .15 | .07 |
| ❑ 383 | Roger Maris GM | .40 | .18 |
| ❑ 384 | Cal Ripken GM | .75 | .35 |
| ❑ 385 | Hank Aaron GM | .50 | .23 |
| ❑ 386 | Joe Carter GM | .15 | .07 |
| ❑ 387 | Cal Ripken SH | 1.50 | .70 |
| ❑ 388 | Randy Johnson SH | .50 | .23 |
| ❑ 389 | Ken Griffey Jr. SH | 1.50 | .70 |
| ❑ 390 | Troy Glaus SH | .50 | .23 |
| ❑ 391 | Kazuhiro Sasaki SH | 1.00 | .45 |
| ❑ 392 | Sammy Sosa<br>Troy Glaus | .40 | .18 |
| ❑ 393 | Todd Helton<br>Edgar Martinez | .25 | .11 |
| ❑ 394 | Todd Helton<br>Nomar Garicaparra | .75 | .35 |
| ❑ 395 | Barry Bonds<br>Jason Giambi | .25 | .11 |
| ❑ 396 | Todd Helton<br>Manny Ramirez | .25 | .11 |
| ❑ 397 | Todd Helton<br>Darin Erstad | .25 | .11 |
| ❑ 398 | Kevin Brown<br>Pedro Martinez | .25 | .11 |
| ❑ 399 | Randy Johnson<br>Pedro Martinez | .25 | .11 |
| ❑ 400 | Will Clark HL | .50 | .23 |
| ❑ 401 | New York Mets HL | .50 | .23 |
| ❑ 402 | New York Yankees HL | .75 | .35 |
| ❑ 403 | Seattle Mariners HL | .50 | .23 |
| ❑ 404 | Mike Hampton HL | .50 | .23 |
| ❑ 405 | New York Yankees HL | 1.00 | .45 |
| ❑ 406 | New York Yankees Champs | 2.00 | .90 |
| ❑ NNO | Bobby Thomson<br>Ralph Branca<br>1991 Bowman Autograph | 150.00 | 70.00 |

## 1996 Topps Chrome

| | | MINT | NRMT |
|---|---|---|---|
| | COMPLETE SET (165) | 80.00 | 36.00 |
| ❑ 1 | Tony Gwynn STP | 1.50 | .70 |
| ❑ 2 | Mike Piazza STP | 2.50 | 1.10 |
| ❑ 3 | Greg Maddux STP | 2.00 | .90 |
| ❑ 4 | Jeff Bagwell STP | 1.50 | .70 |
| ❑ 5 | Larry Walker STP | .60 | .25 |
| ❑ 6 | Barry Larkin STP | .40 | .18 |
| ❑ 7 | Mickey Mantle COMM | 10.00 | 4.50 |
| ❑ 8 | Tom Glavine STP | .60 | .25 |
| ❑ 9 | Craig Biggio STP | .60 | .25 |
| ❑ 10 | Barry Bonds STP | 1.00 | .45 |
| ❑ 11 | Heathcliff Slocumb STP | .40 | .18 |
| ❑ 12 | Matt Williams STP | 1.00 | .45 |
| ❑ 13 | Todd Helton | 6.00 | 2.70 |
| ❑ 14 | Paul Molitor | 1.50 | .70 |
| ❑ 15 | Glenallen Hill | .40 | .18 |
| ❑ 16 | Troy Percival | .40 | .18 |
| ❑ 17 | Albert Belle | 1.00 | .45 |
| ❑ 18 | Mark Wohlers | .40 | .18 |
| ❑ 19 | Kirby Puckett | 4.00 | 1.80 |
| ❑ 20 | Mark Grace | 1.50 | .70 |
| ❑ 21 | J.T. Snow | .60 | .25 |
| ❑ 22 | David Justice | 1.00 | .45 |
| ❑ 23 | Mike Mussina | 1.50 | .70 |
| ❑ 24 | Bernie Williams | 1.50 | .70 |
| ❑ 25 | Ron Gant | .40 | .18 |
| ❑ 26 | Carlos Baerga | .40 | .18 |
| ❑ 27 | Gary Sheffield | 1.50 | .70 |
| ❑ 28 | Cal Ripken 2131 | 6.00 | 2.70 |
| ❑ 29 | Frank Thomas | 3.00 | 1.35 |
| ❑ 30 | Kevin Seitzer | .40 | .18 |
| ❑ 31 | Joe Carter | .60 | .25 |
| ❑ 32 | Jeff King | .40 | .18 |
| ❑ 33 | David Cone | .60 | .25 |
| ❑ 34 | Eddie Murray | 1.50 | .70 |
| ❑ 35 | Brian Jordan | .60 | .25 |
| ❑ 36 | Garret Anderson | .60 | .25 |
| ❑ 37 | Hideo Nomo | 1.50 | .70 |
| ❑ 38 | Steve Finley | .60 | .25 |
| ❑ 39 | Ivan Rodriguez | 2.00 | .90 |
| ❑ 40 | Quilvio Veras | .40 | .18 |
| ❑ 41 | Mark McGwire | 6.00 | 2.70 |
| ❑ 42 | Greg Vaughn | .60 | .25 |
| ❑ 43 | Randy Johnson | 2.00 | .90 |
| ❑ 44 | David Segui | .40 | .18 |
| ❑ 45 | Derek Bell | .40 | .18 |
| ❑ 46 | John Valentin | .40 | .18 |
| ❑ 47 | Steve Avery | .40 | .18 |
| ❑ 48 | Tino Martinez | .60 | .25 |
| ❑ 49 | Shane Reynolds | .40 | .18 |
| ❑ 50 | Jim Edmonds | 1.50 | .70 |
| ❑ 51 | Raul Mondesi | .60 | .25 |
| ❑ 52 | Chipper Jones | 4.00 | 1.80 |
| ❑ 53 | Gregg Jefferies | .40 | .18 |
| ❑ 54 | Ken Caminiti | .60 | .25 |
| ❑ 55 | Brian McRae | .40 | .18 |
| ❑ 56 | Don Mattingly | 4.00 | 1.80 |
| ❑ 57 | Marty Cordova | .40 | .18 |
| ❑ 58 | Vinny Castilla | .60 | .25 |
| ❑ 59 | John Smoltz | .60 | .25 |
| ❑ 60 | Travis Fryman | .60 | .25 |
| ❑ 61 | Ryan Klesko | .60 | .25 |
| ❑ 62 | Alex Fernandez | .40 | .18 |
| ❑ 63 | Dante Bichette | .60 | .25 |
| ❑ 64 | Eric Karros | .60 | .25 |
| ❑ 65 | Roger Clemens | 3.00 | 1.35 |
| ❑ 66 | Randy Myers | .40 | .18 |
| ❑ 67 | Cal Ripken | 6.00 | 2.70 |
| ❑ 68 | Rod Beck | .40 | .18 |
| ❑ 69 | Jack McDowell | .40 | .18 |
| ❑ 70 | Ken Griffey Jr. | 6.00 | 2.70 |
| ❑ 71 | Ramon Martinez | .40 | .18 |
| ❑ 72 | Jason Giambi | 1.50 | .70 |
| ❑ 73 | Nomar Garciaparra FS | 5.00 | 2.20 |
| ❑ 74 | Billy Wagner | .40 | .18 |
| ❑ 75 | Todd Greene | .40 | .18 |
| ❑ 76 | Paul Wilson | .40 | .18 |
| ❑ 77 | Johnny Damon | 1.00 | .45 |
| ❑ 78 | Alan Benes | .40 | .18 |
| ❑ 79 | Karim Garcia FS | .40 | .18 |
| ❑ 80 | Derek Jeter FS | 6.00 | 2.70 |
| ❑ 81 | Kirby Puckett STP | 2.00 | .90 |
| ❑ 82 | Cal Ripken STP | 3.00 | 1.35 |
| ❑ 83 | Albert Belle STP | .40 | .18 |

| | | | |
|---|---|---|---|
| ❑ 84 | Randy Johnson STP | .60 | .25 |
| ❑ 85 | Wade Boggs STP | .60 | .25 |
| ❑ 86 | Carlos Baerga STP | .40 | .18 |
| ❑ 87 | Ivan Rodriguez STP | 1.00 | .45 |
| ❑ 88 | Mike Mussina STP | .60 | .25 |
| ❑ 89 | Frank Thomas STP | 1.50 | .70 |
| ❑ 90 | Ken Griffey Jr. STP | 3.00 | 1.35 |
| ❑ 91 | Jose Mesa STP | .40 | .18 |
| ❑ 92 | Matt Morris RC | 1.00 | .45 |
| ❑ 93 | Mike Piazza | 5.00 | 2.20 |
| ❑ 94 | Edgar Martinez | 1.00 | .45 |
| ❑ 95 | Chuck Knoblauch | .60 | .25 |
| ❑ 96 | Andres Galarraga | 1.00 | .45 |
| ❑ 97 | Tony Gwynn | 3.00 | 1.35 |
| ❑ 98 | Lee Smith | .60 | .25 |
| ❑ 99 | Sammy Sosa | 3.00 | 1.35 |
| ❑ 100 | Jim Thome | 1.00 | .45 |
| ❑ 101 | Bernard Gilkey | .40 | .18 |
| ❑ 102 | Brady Anderson | .60 | .25 |
| ❑ 103 | Rico Brogna | .40 | .18 |
| ❑ 104 | Len Dykstra | .60 | .25 |
| ❑ 105 | Tom Glavine | 1.50 | .70 |
| ❑ 106 | John Olerud | .60 | .25 |
| ❑ 107 | Terry Steinbach | .40 | .18 |
| ❑ 108 | Brian Hunter | .40 | .18 |
| ❑ 109 | Jay Buhner | .60 | .25 |
| ❑ 110 | Mo Vaughn | .60 | .25 |
| ❑ 111 | Jose Mesa | .40 | .18 |
| ❑ 112 | Brett Butler | .60 | .25 |
| ❑ 113 | Chili Davis | .60 | .25 |
| ❑ 114 | Paul O'Neill | .60 | .25 |
| ❑ 115 | Roberto Alomar | 1.50 | .70 |
| ❑ 116 | Barry Larkin | 1.50 | .70 |
| ❑ 117 | Marquis Grissom | .40 | .18 |
| ❑ 118 | Will Clark | 1.50 | .70 |
| ❑ 119 | Barry Bonds | 2.50 | 1.10 |
| ❑ 120 | Ozzie Smith | 2.00 | .90 |
| ❑ 121 | Pedro Martinez | 2.00 | .90 |
| ❑ 122 | Craig Biggio | 1.00 | .45 |
| ❑ 123 | Moises Alou | .60 | .25 |
| ❑ 124 | Robin Ventura | .60 | .25 |
| ❑ 125 | Greg Maddux | 4.00 | 1.80 |
| ❑ 126 | Tim Salmon | .60 | .25 |
| ❑ 127 | Wade Boggs | 2.00 | .90 |
| ❑ 128 | Ismael Valdes | .40 | .18 |
| ❑ 129 | Juan Gonzalez | 1.50 | .70 |
| ❑ 130 | Ray Lankford | .60 | .25 |
| ❑ 131 | Bobby Bonilla | .60 | .25 |
| ❑ 132 | Reggie Sanders | .40 | .18 |
| ❑ 133 | Alex Ochoa | .40 | .18 |
| ❑ 134 | Mark Loretta | .40 | .18 |
| ❑ 135 | Jason Kendall | .60 | .25 |
| ❑ 136 | Brooks Kieschnick | .40 | .18 |
| ❑ 137 | Chris Snopek | .40 | .18 |
| ❑ 138 | Ruben Rivera NOW | .40 | .18 |
| ❑ 139 | Jeff Suppan | .40 | .18 |
| ❑ 140 | John Wasdin | .40 | .18 |
| ❑ 141 | Jay Payton | .60 | .25 |
| ❑ 142 | Rick Krivda | .40 | .18 |
| ❑ 143 | Jimmy Haynes | .40 | .18 |
| ❑ 144 | Ryne Sandberg | 2.00 | .90 |
| ❑ 145 | Matt Williams | 1.00 | .45 |
| ❑ 146 | Jose Canseco | 2.00 | .90 |
| ❑ 147 | Larry Walker | .60 | .25 |
| ❑ 148 | Kevin Appier | .60 | .25 |
| ❑ 149 | Javy Lopez | .60 | .25 |
| ❑ 150 | Dennis Eckersley | .60 | .25 |
| ❑ 151 | Jason Isringhausen | .60 | .25 |
| ❑ 152 | Dean Palmer | .60 | .25 |
| ❑ 153 | Jeff Bagwell | 2.00 | .90 |
| ❑ 154 | Rondell White | .60 | .25 |
| ❑ 155 | Wally Joyner | .60 | .25 |
| ❑ 156 | Fred McGriff | 1.00 | .45 |
| ❑ 157 | Cecil Fielder | .60 | .25 |
| ❑ 158 | Rafael Palmeiro | 1.50 | .70 |
| ❑ 159 | Rickey Henderson | 2.00 | .90 |
| ❑ 160 | Shawon Dunston | .40 | .18 |
| ❑ 161 | Manny Ramirez | 2.00 | .90 |
| ❑ 162 | Alex Gonzalez | .40 | .18 |
| ❑ 163 | Shawn Green | 1.50 | .70 |
| ❑ 164 | Kenny Lofton | .60 | .25 |
| ❑ 165 | Jeff Conine | .40 | .18 |

## 1997 Topps Chrome

| | MINT | NRMT |
|---|---|---|
| COMPLETE SET (165) | 70.00 | 32.00 |

| Card | MINT | NRMT |
|---|---|---|
| ❑ 1 Barry Bonds | 2.50 | 1.10 |
| ❑ 2 Jose Valentin | .40 | .18 |
| ❑ 3 Brady Anderson | .60 | .25 |
| ❑ 4 Wade Boggs | 2.00 | .90 |
| ❑ 5 Andres Galarraga | 1.00 | .45 |
| ❑ 5 Rusty Greer | .60 | .25 |
| ❑ 7 Derek Jeter | 6.00 | 2.70 |
| ❑ 8 Ricky Bottalico | .40 | .18 |
| ❑ 9 Mike Piazza | 5.00 | 2.20 |
| ❑ 10 Garret Anderson | .60 | .25 |
| ❑ 11 Jeff King | .40 | .18 |
| ❑ 12 Kevin Appier | .60 | .25 |
| ❑ 13 Mark Grace | 1.50 | .70 |
| ❑ 14 Jeff D'Amico | .40 | .18 |
| ❑ 15 Jay Buhner | .60 | .25 |
| ❑ 16 Hal Morris | .40 | .18 |
| ❑ 17 Harold Baines | .60 | .25 |
| ❑ 18 Jeff Cirillo | .60 | .25 |
| ❑ 19 Tom Glavine | 1.50 | .70 |
| ❑ 20 Andy Pettitte | .60 | .25 |
| ❑ 21 Mark McGwire | 6.00 | 2.70 |
| ❑ 22 Chuck Knoblauch | .60 | .25 |
| ❑ 23 Raul Mondesi | .60 | .25 |
| ❑ 24 Albert Belle | 1.00 | .45 |
| ❑ 25 Trevor Hoffman | .60 | .25 |
| ❑ 26 Eric Young | .40 | .18 |
| ❑ 27 Brian McRae | .40 | .18 |
| ❑ 28 Jim Edmonds | 1.50 | .70 |
| ❑ 29 Robb Nen | .40 | .18 |
| ❑ 30 Reggie Sanders | .40 | .18 |
| ❑ 31 Mike Lansing | .40 | .18 |
| ❑ 32 Craig Biggio | 1.00 | .45 |
| ❑ 33 Ray Lankford | .60 | .25 |
| ❑ 34 Charles Nagy | .40 | .18 |
| ❑ 35 Paul Wilson | .40 | .18 |
| ❑ 36 John Wetteland | .60 | .25 |
| ❑ 37 Derek Bell | .40 | .18 |
| ❑ 38 Edgar Martinez | 1.00 | .45 |
| ❑ 39 Rickey Henderson | 2.00 | .90 |
| ❑ 40 Jim Thome | 1.00 | .45 |
| ❑ 41 Frank Thomas | 3.00 | 1.35 |
| ❑ 42 Jackie Robinson | 5.00 | 2.20 |
| ❑ 43 Terry Steinbach | .40 | .18 |
| ❑ 44 Kevin Brown | 1.00 | .45 |
| ❑ 45 Joey Hamilton | .40 | .18 |
| ❑ 46 Travis Fryman | .60 | .25 |
| ❑ 47 Juan Gonzalez | 1.50 | .70 |
| ❑ 48 Ron Gant | .40 | .18 |
| ❑ 49 Greg Maddux | 4.00 | 1.80 |
| ❑ 50 Wally Joyner | .60 | .25 |
| ❑ 51 John Valentin | .40 | .18 |
| ❑ 52 Bret Boone | .60 | .25 |
| ❑ 53 Paul Molitor | 1.50 | .70 |
| ❑ 54 Rafael Palmeiro | 1.50 | .70 |
| ❑ 55 Todd Hundley | .40 | .18 |
| ❑ 56 Ellis Burks | .60 | .25 |
| ❑ 57 Bernie Williams | 1.50 | .70 |
| ❑ 58 Roberto Alomar | 1.50 | .70 |
| ❑ 59 Jose Mesa | .40 | .18 |
| ❑ 60 Troy Percival | .40 | .18 |
| ❑ 61 John Smoltz | .60 | .25 |
| ❑ 62 Jeff Conine | .40 | .18 |
| ❑ 63 Bernard Gilkey | .40 | .18 |
| ❑ 64 Mickey Tettleton | .40 | .18 |
| ❑ 65 Justin Thompson | .40 | .18 |
| ❑ 66 Tony Phillips | .40 | .18 |
| ❑ 67 Ryne Sandberg | 2.00 | .90 |
| ❑ 68 Geronimo Berroa | .40 | .18 |
| ❑ 69 Todd Hollandsworth | .40 | .18 |
| ❑ 70 Rey Ordonez | .40 | .18 |
| ❑ 71 Marquis Grissom | .40 | .18 |
| ❑ 72 Tino Martinez | .60 | .25 |
| ❑ 73 Steve Finley | .60 | .25 |
| ❑ 74 Andy Benes | .40 | .18 |
| ❑ 75 Jason Kendall | .60 | .25 |
| ❑ 76 Johnny Damon | .60 | .25 |
| ❑ 77 Jason Giambi | 1.50 | .70 |
| ❑ 78 Henry Rodriguez | .40 | .18 |
| ❑ 79 Edgar Renteria | .40 | .18 |
| ❑ 80 Ray Durham | .60 | .25 |
| ❑ 81 Gregg Jefferies | .40 | .18 |
| ❑ 82 Roberto Hernandez | .40 | .18 |
| ❑ 83 Joe Carter | .60 | .25 |
| ❑ 84 Jermaine Dye | .60 | .25 |
| ❑ 85 Julio Franco | .60 | .25 |
| ❑ 86 David Justice | 1.00 | .45 |
| ❑ 87 Jose Canseco | 2.00 | .90 |
| ❑ 88 Paul O'Neill | .60 | .25 |
| ❑ 89 Mariano Rivera | .60 | .25 |
| ❑ 90 Bobby Higginson | .60 | .25 |
| ❑ 91 Mark Grudzielanek | .40 | .18 |
| ❑ 92 Lance Johnson | .40 | .18 |
| ❑ 93 Ken Caminiti | .60 | .25 |
| ❑ 94 Gary Sheffield | 1.50 | .70 |
| ❑ 95 Luis Castillo | .60 | .25 |
| ❑ 96 Scott Rolen | 1.50 | .70 |
| ❑ 97 Chipper Jones | 4.00 | 1.80 |
| ❑ 98 Darryl Strawberry | .60 | .25 |
| ❑ 99 Nomar Garciaparra | 5.00 | 2.20 |
| ❑ 100 Jeff Bagwell | 2.00 | .90 |
| ❑ 101 Ken Griffey Jr. | 6.00 | 2.70 |
| ❑ 102 Sammy Sosa | 3.00 | 1.35 |
| ❑ 103 Jack McDowell | .40 | .18 |
| ❑ 104 James Baldwin | .60 | .25 |
| ❑ 105 Rocky Coppinger | .40 | .18 |
| ❑ 106 Manny Ramirez | 2.00 | .90 |
| ❑ 107 Tim Salmon | .60 | .25 |
| ❑ 108 Eric Karros | .60 | .25 |
| ❑ 109 Brett Butler | .60 | .25 |
| ❑ 110 Randy Johnson | 2.00 | .90 |
| ❑ 111 Pat Hentgen | .40 | .18 |
| ❑ 112 Rondell White | .60 | .25 |
| ❑ 113 Eddie Murray | 1.50 | .70 |
| ❑ 114 Ivan Rodriguez | 2.00 | .90 |
| ❑ 115 Jermaine Allensworth | .40 | .18 |
| ❑ 116 Ed Sprague | .40 | .18 |
| ❑ 117 Kenny Lofton | .60 | .25 |
| ❑ 118 Alan Benes | .40 | .18 |
| ❑ 119 Fred McGriff | 1.00 | .45 |
| ❑ 120 Alex Fernandez | .40 | .18 |
| ❑ 121 Al Martin | .40 | .18 |
| ❑ 122 Devon White | .60 | .25 |
| ❑ 123 David Cone | .60 | .25 |
| ❑ 124 Karim Garcia | .40 | .18 |
| ❑ 125 Chili Davis | .60 | .25 |
| ❑ 126 Roger Clemens | 3.00 | 1.35 |
| ❑ 127 Bobby Bonilla | .60 | .25 |
| ❑ 128 Mike Mussina | 1.50 | .70 |
| ❑ 129 Todd Walker | .40 | .18 |
| ❑ 130 Dante Bichette | .60 | .25 |
| ❑ 131 Carlos Baerga | .40 | .18 |
| ❑ 132 Matt Williams | 1.00 | .45 |
| ❑ 133 Will Clark | 1.50 | .70 |
| ❑ 134 Dennis Eckersley | .60 | .25 |
| ❑ 135 Ryan Klesko | .60 | .25 |
| ❑ 136 Dean Palmer | .60 | .25 |
| ❑ 137 Javy Lopez | .60 | .25 |
| ❑ 138 Greg Vaughn | .60 | .25 |
| ❑ 139 Vinny Castilla | .60 | .25 |
| ❑ 140 Cal Ripken | 6.00 | 2.70 |
| ❑ 141 Ruben Rivera | .40 | .18 |
| ❑ 142 Mark Wohlers | .40 | .18 |
| ❑ 143 Tony Clark | .40 | .18 |
| ❑ 144 Jose Rosado | .40 | .18 |
| ❑ 145 Tony Gwynn | 3.00 | 1.35 |
| ❑ 146 Cecil Fielder | .60 | .25 |
| ❑ 147 Brian Jordan | .60 | .25 |
| ❑ 148 Bob Abreu | .60 | .25 |
| ❑ 149 Barry Larkin | 1.50 | .70 |
| ❑ 150 Robin Ventura | .60 | .25 |
| ❑ 151 John Olerud | .60 | .25 |
| ❑ 152 Rod Beck | .40 | .18 |
| ❑ 153 Vladimir Guerrero | 3.00 | 1.35 |
| ❑ 154 Marty Cordova | .40 | .18 |
| ❑ 155 Todd Stottlemyre | .40 | .18 |
| ❑ 156 Hideo Nomo | 1.50 | .70 |
| ❑ 157 Denny Neagle | .60 | .25 |
| ❑ 158 John Jaha | .40 | .18 |
| ❑ 159 Mo Vaughn | .60 | .25 |
| ❑ 160 Andruw Jones | 2.00 | .90 |
| ❑ 161 Moises Alou | .60 | .25 |
| ❑ 162 Larry Walker | .60 | .25 |
| ❑ 163 Eddie Murray SH | .60 | .25 |
| ❑ 164 Paul Molitor SH | .60 | .25 |
| ❑ 165 Checklist | .40 | .18 |

## 1998 Topps Chrome

| | MINT | NRMT |
|---|---|---|
| COMPLETE SET (503) | 350.00 | 160.00 |
| COMPLETE SERIES 1 (282) | 200.00 | 90.00 |
| COMPLETE SERIES 2 (221) | 150.00 | 70.00 |
| COMMON CARD (1-504) | .40 | .18 |

| Card | MINT | NRMT |
|---|---|---|
| ❑ 1 Tony Gwynn | 3.00 | 1.35 |
| ❑ 2 Larry Walker | .60 | .25 |
| ❑ 3 Billy Wagner | .40 | .18 |
| ❑ 4 Denny Neagle | .40 | .18 |
| ❑ 5 Vladimir Guerrero | 2.50 | 1.10 |
| ❑ 6 Kevin Brown | 1.00 | .45 |
| ❑ 8 Mariano Rivera | .60 | .25 |
| ❑ 9 Tony Clark | .40 | .18 |
| ❑ 10 Deion Sanders | .60 | .25 |
| ❑ 11 Francisco Cordova | .40 | .18 |
| ❑ 12 Matt Williams | 1.00 | .45 |
| ❑ 13 Carlos Baerga | .40 | .18 |
| ❑ 14 Mo Vaughn | .60 | .25 |
| ❑ 15 Bobby Witt | .40 | .18 |
| ❑ 16 Matt Stairs | .40 | .18 |
| ❑ 17 Chan Ho Park | .60 | .25 |
| ❑ 18 Mike Bordick | .40 | .18 |
| ❑ 19 Michael Tucker | .40 | .18 |
| ❑ 20 Frank Thomas | 3.00 | 1.35 |
| ❑ 21 Roberto Clemente | 5.00 | 2.20 |
| ❑ 22 Dmitri Young | .60 | .25 |
| ❑ 23 Steve Trachsel | .40 | .18 |
| ❑ 24 Jeff Kent | 1.00 | .45 |
| ❑ 25 Scott Rolen | 1.50 | .70 |
| ❑ 26 John Thomson | .40 | .18 |
| ❑ 27 Joe Vitiello | .40 | .18 |
| ❑ 28 Eddie Guardado | .40 | .18 |
| ❑ 29 Charlie Hayes | .40 | .18 |
| ❑ 30 Juan Gonzalez | 1.50 | .70 |
| ❑ 31 Garret Anderson | .60 | .25 |
| ❑ 32 John Jaha | .60 | .25 |
| ❑ 33 Omar Vizquel | .60 | .25 |
| ❑ 34 Brian Hunter | .40 | .18 |
| ❑ 35 Jeff Bagwell | 2.00 | .90 |
| ❑ 36 Mark Lemke | .40 | .18 |
| ❑ 37 Doug Glanville | .40 | .18 |
| ❑ 38 Dan Wilson | .40 | .18 |
| ❑ 39 Steve Cooke | .40 | .18 |
| ❑ 40 Chili Davis | .60 | .25 |
| ❑ 41 Mike Cameron | .60 | .25 |
| ❑ 42 F.P. Santangelo | .40 | .18 |
| ❑ 43 Brad Ausmus | .40 | .18 |
| ❑ 44 Gary DiSarcina | .40 | .18 |
| ❑ 45 Pat Hentgen | .40 | .18 |

| | No. | Player | | |
|---|---|---|---|---|
| ❑ | 46 | Wilton Guerrero | .40 | .18 |
| ❑ | 47 | Devon White | .40 | .18 |
| ❑ | 48 | Danny Patterson | .40 | .18 |
| ❑ | 49 | Pat Meares | .40 | .18 |
| ❑ | 50 | Rafael Palmeiro | 1.50 | .70 |
| ❑ | 51 | Mark Gardner | .40 | .18 |
| ❑ | 52 | Jeff Blauser | .40 | .18 |
| ❑ | 53 | Dave Hollins | .40 | .18 |
| ❑ | 54 | Carlos Garcia | .40 | .18 |
| ❑ | 55 | Ben McDonald | .40 | .18 |
| ❑ | 56 | John Mabry | .40 | .18 |
| ❑ | 57 | Trevor Hoffman | .60 | .25 |
| ❑ | 58 | Tony Fernandez | .40 | .18 |
| ❑ | 59 | Rich Loiselle RC | .60 | .25 |
| ❑ | 60 | Mark Leiter | .40 | .18 |
| ❑ | 61 | Pat Kelly | .40 | .18 |
| ❑ | 62 | John Flaherty | .40 | .18 |
| ❑ | 63 | Roger Bailey | .40 | .18 |
| ❑ | 64 | Tom Gordon | .60 | .25 |
| ❑ | 65 | Ryan Klesko | .60 | .25 |
| ❑ | 66 | Darryl Hamilton | .40 | .18 |
| ❑ | 67 | Jim Eisenreich | .40 | .18 |
| ❑ | 68 | Butch Huskey | .40 | .18 |
| ❑ | 69 | Mark Grudzielanek | .40 | .18 |
| ❑ | 70 | Marquis Grissom | .40 | .18 |
| ❑ | 71 | Mark McLemore | .40 | .18 |
| ❑ | 72 | Gary Gaetti | .60 | .25 |
| ❑ | 73 | Greg Gagne | .40 | .18 |
| ❑ | 74 | Lyle Mouton | .40 | .18 |
| ❑ | 75 | Jim Edmonds | 1.50 | .70 |
| ❑ | 76 | Shawn Green | 1.50 | .70 |
| ❑ | 77 | Greg Vaughn | .60 | .25 |
| ❑ | 78 | Terry Adams | .40 | .18 |
| ❑ | 79 | Kevin Polcovich | .40 | .18 |
| ❑ | 80 | Troy O'Leary | .40 | .18 |
| ❑ | 81 | Jeff Shaw | .40 | .18 |
| ❑ | 82 | Rich Becker | .40 | .18 |
| ❑ | 83 | David Wells | .60 | .25 |
| ❑ | 84 | Steve Karsay | .40 | .18 |
| ❑ | 85 | Charles Nagy | .40 | .18 |
| ❑ | 86 | B.J. Surhoff | .60 | .25 |
| ❑ | 87 | Jamey Wright | .40 | .18 |
| ❑ | 88 | James Baldwin | .40 | .18 |
| ❑ | 89 | Edgardo Alfonzo | .60 | .25 |
| ❑ | 90 | Jay Buhner | .60 | .25 |
| ❑ | 91 | Brady Anderson | .60 | .25 |
| ❑ | 92 | Scott Servais | .40 | .18 |
| ❑ | 93 | Edgar Renteria | .40 | .18 |
| ❑ | 94 | Mike Lieberthal | .60 | .25 |
| ❑ | 95 | Rick Aguilera | .40 | .18 |
| ❑ | 96 | Walt Weiss | .60 | .25 |
| ❑ | 97 | Deivi Cruz | .40 | .18 |
| ❑ | 98 | Kurt Abbott | .40 | .18 |
| ❑ | 99 | Henry Rodriguez | .40 | .18 |
| ❑ | 100 | Mike Piazza | 5.00 | 2.20 |
| ❑ | 101 | Billy Taylor | .40 | .18 |
| ❑ | 102 | Todd Zeile | .60 | .25 |
| ❑ | 103 | Rey Ordonez | .40 | .18 |
| ❑ | 104 | Willie Greene | .40 | .18 |
| ❑ | 105 | Tony Womack | .40 | .18 |
| ❑ | 106 | Mike Sweeney | .60 | .25 |
| ❑ | 107 | Jeffrey Hammonds | .60 | .25 |
| ❑ | 108 | Kevin Orie | .40 | .18 |
| ❑ | 109 | Alex Gonzalez | .40 | .18 |
| ❑ | 110 | Jose Canseco | 2.00 | .90 |
| ❑ | 111 | Paul Sorrento | .40 | .18 |
| ❑ | 112 | Joey Hamilton | .40 | .18 |
| ❑ | 113 | Brad Radke | .60 | .25 |
| ❑ | 114 | Steve Avery | .40 | .18 |
| ❑ | 115 | Esteban Loaiza | .40 | .18 |
| ❑ | 116 | Stan Javier | .40 | .18 |
| ❑ | 117 | Chris Gomez | .40 | .18 |
| ❑ | 118 | Royce Clayton | .40 | .18 |
| ❑ | 119 | Orlando Merced | .40 | .18 |
| ❑ | 120 | Kevin Appier | .60 | .25 |
| ❑ | 121 | Mel Nieves | .40 | .18 |
| ❑ | 122 | Joe Girardi | .40 | .18 |
| ❑ | 123 | Rico Brogna | .40 | .18 |
| ❑ | 124 | Kent Mercker | .40 | .18 |
| ❑ | 125 | Manny Ramirez | 2.00 | .90 |
| ❑ | 126 | Jeromy Burnitz | .60 | .25 |
| ❑ | 127 | Kevin Foster | .40 | .18 |
| ❑ | 128 | Matt Morris | .40 | .18 |
| ❑ | 129 | Jason Dickson | .40 | .18 |
| ❑ | 130 | Tom Glavine | 1.50 | .70 |
| ❑ | 131 | Wally Joyner | .60 | .25 |
| ❑ | 132 | Rick Reed | .40 | .18 |
| ❑ | 133 | Todd Jones | .40 | .18 |
| ❑ | 134 | Dave Martinez | .40 | .18 |
| ❑ | 135 | Sandy Alomar Jr. | .60 | .25 |
| ❑ | 136 | Mike Lansing | .40 | .18 |
| ❑ | 137 | Sean Berry | .40 | .18 |
| ❑ | 138 | Doug Jones | .40 | .18 |
| ❑ | 139 | Todd Stottlemyre | .40 | .18 |
| ❑ | 140 | Jay Bell | .60 | .25 |
| ❑ | 141 | Jaime Navarro | .40 | .18 |
| ❑ | 142 | Chris Hoiles | .40 | .18 |
| ❑ | 143 | Joey Cora | .40 | .18 |
| ❑ | 144 | Scott Spiezio | .40 | .18 |
| ❑ | 145 | Joe Carter | .60 | .25 |
| ❑ | 146 | Jose Guillen | .40 | .18 |
| ❑ | 147 | Damion Easley | .40 | .18 |
| ❑ | 148 | Lee Stevens | .40 | .18 |
| ❑ | 149 | Alex Fernandez | .40 | .18 |
| ❑ | 150 | Randy Johnson | 2.00 | .90 |
| ❑ | 151 | J.T. Snow | .60 | .25 |
| ❑ | 152 | Chuck Finley | .60 | .25 |
| ❑ | 153 | Bernard Gilkey | .40 | .18 |
| ❑ | 154 | David Segui | .40 | .18 |
| ❑ | 155 | Dante Bichette | .60 | .25 |
| ❑ | 156 | Kevin Stocker | .40 | .18 |
| ❑ | 157 | Carl Everett | .60 | .25 |
| ❑ | 158 | Jose Valentin | .40 | .18 |
| ❑ | 159 | Pokey Reese | .60 | .25 |
| ❑ | 160 | Derek Jeter | 6.00 | 2.70 |
| ❑ | 161 | Roger Pavlik | .40 | .18 |
| ❑ | 162 | Mark Wohlers | .40 | .18 |
| ❑ | 163 | Ricky Bottalico | .40 | .18 |
| ❑ | 164 | Ozzie Guillen | .40 | .18 |
| ❑ | 165 | Mike Mussina | 1.50 | .70 |
| ❑ | 166 | Gary Sheffield | 1.50 | .70 |
| ❑ | 167 | Hideo Nomo | 1.50 | .70 |
| ❑ | 168 | Mark Grace | 1.50 | .70 |
| ❑ | 169 | Aaron Sele | .60 | .25 |
| ❑ | 170 | Darryl Kile | .60 | .25 |
| ❑ | 171 | Shawn Estes | .40 | .18 |
| ❑ | 172 | Vinny Castilla | .60 | .25 |
| ❑ | 173 | Ron Coomer | .40 | .18 |
| ❑ | 174 | Jose Rosado | .40 | .18 |
| ❑ | 175 | Kenny Lofton | .60 | .25 |
| ❑ | 176 | Jason Giambi | 1.50 | .70 |
| ❑ | 177 | Hal Morris | .40 | .18 |
| ❑ | 178 | Darren Bragg | .40 | .18 |
| ❑ | 179 | Orel Hershiser | .60 | .25 |
| ❑ | 180 | Ray Lankford | .60 | .25 |
| ❑ | 181 | Hideki Irabu | .40 | .18 |
| ❑ | 182 | Kevin Young | .60 | .25 |
| ❑ | 183 | Javy Lopez | .60 | .25 |
| ❑ | 184 | Jeff Montgomery | .40 | .18 |
| ❑ | 185 | Mike Holtz | .40 | .18 |
| ❑ | 186 | George Williams | .40 | .18 |
| ❑ | 187 | Cal Eldred | .40 | .18 |
| ❑ | 188 | Tom Candiotti | .40 | .18 |
| ❑ | 189 | Glenallen Hill | .40 | .18 |
| ❑ | 190 | Brian Giles | .60 | .25 |
| ❑ | 191 | Dave Mlicki | .40 | .18 |
| ❑ | 192 | Garrett Stephenson | .40 | .18 |
| ❑ | 193 | Jeff Frye | .40 | .18 |
| ❑ | 194 | Joe Oliver | .40 | .18 |
| ❑ | 195 | Bob Hamelin | .40 | .18 |
| ❑ | 196 | Luis Sojo | .40 | .18 |
| ❑ | 197 | LaTroy Hawkins | .40 | .18 |
| ❑ | 198 | Kevin Elster | .40 | .18 |
| ❑ | 199 | Jeff Reed | .40 | .18 |
| ❑ | 200 | Dennis Eckersley | .60 | .25 |
| ❑ | 201 | Bill Mueller | .40 | .18 |
| ❑ | 202 | Russ Davis | .40 | .18 |
| ❑ | 203 | Armando Benitez | .40 | .18 |
| ❑ | 204 | Quilvio Veras | .40 | .18 |
| ❑ | 205 | Tim Naehring | .40 | .18 |
| ❑ | 206 | Quinton McCracken | .40 | .18 |
| ❑ | 207 | Raul Casanova | .40 | .18 |
| ❑ | 208 | Matt Lawton | .40 | .18 |
| ❑ | 209 | Luis Alicea | .40 | .18 |
| ❑ | 210 | Luis Gonzalez | .60 | .25 |
| ❑ | 211 | Allen Watson | .40 | .18 |
| ❑ | 212 | Gerald Williams | .40 | .18 |
| ❑ | 213 | David Bell | .40 | .18 |
| ❑ | 214 | Todd Hollandsworth | .40 | .18 |
| ❑ | 215 | Wade Boggs | 2.00 | .90 |
| ❑ | 216 | Jose Mesa | .40 | .18 |
| ❑ | 217 | Jamie Moyer | .40 | .18 |
| ❑ | 218 | Darren Daulton | .60 | .25 |
| ❑ | 219 | Mickey Morandini | .40 | .18 |
| ❑ | 220 | Rusty Greer | .60 | .25 |
| ❑ | 221 | Jim Bullinger | .40 | .18 |
| ❑ | 222 | Jose Offerman | .40 | .18 |
| ❑ | 223 | Matt Karchner | .40 | .18 |
| ❑ | 224 | Woody Williams | .40 | .18 |
| ❑ | 225 | Mark Loretta | .40 | .18 |
| ❑ | 226 | Mike Hampton | .60 | .25 |
| ❑ | 227 | Willie Adams | .40 | .18 |
| ❑ | 228 | Scott Hatteberg | .40 | .18 |
| ❑ | 229 | Rich Amaral | .40 | .18 |
| ❑ | 230 | Terry Steinbach | .40 | .18 |
| ❑ | 231 | Glendon Rusch | .40 | .18 |
| ❑ | 232 | Bret Boone | .60 | .25 |
| ❑ | 233 | Robert Person | .40 | .18 |
| ❑ | 234 | Jose Hernandez | .40 | .18 |
| ❑ | 235 | Doug Drabek | .40 | .18 |
| ❑ | 236 | Jason McDonald | .40 | .18 |
| ❑ | 237 | Chris Widger | .40 | .18 |
| ❑ | 238 | Tom Martin | .40 | .18 |
| ❑ | 239 | Dave Burba | .40 | .18 |
| ❑ | 240 | Pete Rose Jr. RC | .60 | .25 |
| ❑ | 241 | Bobby Ayala | .40 | .18 |
| ❑ | 242 | Tim Wakefield | .40 | .18 |
| ❑ | 243 | Dennis Springer | .40 | .18 |
| ❑ | 244 | Tim Belcher | .40 | .18 |
| ❑ | 245 | Jon Garland | 1.00 | .45 |
| | | Geoff Goetz | | |
| ❑ | 246 | Glenn Davis | 1.50 | .70 |
| | | Lance Berkman | | |
| ❑ | 247 | Vernon Wells | 1.50 | .70 |
| | | Aaron Akin | | |
| ❑ | 248 | Adam Kennedy | 1.50 | .70 |
| | | Jason Romano | | |
| ❑ | 249 | Jason Dellaero | 1.00 | .45 |
| | | Troy Cameron | | |
| ❑ | 250 | Alex Sanchez | 1.00 | .45 |
| | | Jared Sandberg | | |
| ❑ | 251 | Pablo Ortega | 1.00 | .45 |
| | | James Manias | | |
| ❑ | 252 | Jason Conti RC | 1.00 | .45 |
| | | Mike Stoner | | |
| ❑ | 253 | John Patterson | 1.00 | .45 |
| | | Larry Rodriguez | | |
| ❑ | 254 | Adrian Beltre | 1.50 | .70 |
| | | Ryan Minor RC | | |
| | | Aaron Boone | | |
| ❑ | 255 | Ben Grieve | 1.50 | .70 |
| | | Brian Buchanan | | |
| | | Dermal Brown | | |
| ❑ | 256 | Kerry Wood | | |
| | | Carl Pavano | | |
| | | Gil Meche | | |
| ❑ | 257 | David Ortiz | 1.50 | .70 |
| | | Daryle Ward | | |
| | | Richie Sexson | | |
| ❑ | 258 | Randy Winn | 1.50 | .70 |
| | | Juan Encarnacion | | |
| | | Andrew Vessel | | |
| ❑ | 259 | Kris Benson RC | 1.00 | .45 |
| | | Travis Smith | | |
| | | Courtney Duncan | | |
| ❑ | 260 | Chad Hermansen RC | 2.00 | .90 |
| | | Brent Butler | | |
| | | Warren Morris | | |
| ❑ | 261 | Ben Davis | 1.00 | .45 |
| | | Eli Marrero | | |
| | | Ramon Hernandez | | |
| ❑ | 262 | Eric Chavez | 1.50 | .70 |
| | | Russell Branyan | | |
| | | Russ Johnson | | |
| ❑ | 263 | Todd Dunwoody RC | 1.50 | .70 |
| | | John Barnes | | |
| | | Ryan Jackson | | |
| ❑ | 264 | Matt Clement RC | 1.00 | .45 |
| | | Roy Halladay | | |
| | | Brian Fuentes | | |
| ❑ | 265 | Randy Johnson SH | .60 | .25 |
| ❑ | 266 | Kevin Brown SH | .60 | .25 |
| ❑ | 267 | Ricardo Rincon SH | .40 | .18 |
| ❑ | 268 | Nomar Garciaparra SH | 2.50 | 1.10 |
| ❑ | 269 | Tino Martinez SH | .40 | .18 |
| ❑ | 270 | Chuck Knoblauch IL | .40 | .18 |
| ❑ | 271 | Pedro Martinez IL | 1.00 | .45 |
| ❑ | 272 | Denny Neagle IL | .40 | .18 |

| | | | |
|---|---|---|---|
| ❑ 273 | Juan Gonzalez IL | .60 | .25 |
| ❑ 274 | Andres Galarraga IL | .40 | .18 |
| ❑ 275 | Checklist | .40 | .18 |
| ❑ 276 | Checklist | .40 | .18 |
| ❑ 277 | Moises Alou WS | .40 | .18 |
| ❑ 278 | Sandy Alomar Jr. WS | .60 | .25 |
| ❑ 279 | Gary Sheffield WS | .60 | .25 |
| ❑ 280 | Matt Williams WS | 1.00 | .45 |
| ❑ 281 | Livan Hernandez WS | .40 | .18 |
| ❑ 282 | Chad Ogea WS | .40 | .18 |
| ❑ 283 | Marlins Champs | .60 | .25 |
| ❑ 284 | Tino Martinez | .60 | .25 |
| ❑ 285 | Roberto Alomar | 1.50 | .70 |
| ❑ 286 | Jeff King | .40 | .18 |
| ❑ 287 | Brian Jordan | .60 | .25 |
| ❑ 288 | Darin Erstad | 1.50 | .70 |
| ❑ 289 | Ken Caminiti | .60 | .25 |
| ❑ 290 | Jim Thome | 1.00 | .45 |
| ❑ 291 | Paul Molitor | 1.50 | .70 |
| ❑ 292 | Ivan Rodriguez | 2.00 | .90 |
| ❑ 293 | Bernie Williams | 1.50 | .70 |
| ❑ 294 | Todd Hundley | .40 | .18 |
| ❑ 295 | Andres Galarraga | 1.00 | .45 |
| ❑ 296 | Greg Maddux | 4.00 | 1.80 |
| ❑ 297 | Edgar Martinez | 1.00 | .45 |
| ❑ 298 | Ron Gant | .60 | .25 |
| ❑ 299 | Derek Bell | .40 | .18 |
| ❑ 300 | Roger Clemens | 3.00 | 1.35 |
| ❑ 301 | Rondell White | .60 | .25 |
| ❑ 302 | Barry Larkin | 1.50 | .70 |
| ❑ 303 | Robin Ventura | .60 | .25 |
| ❑ 304 | Jason Kendall | .60 | .25 |
| ❑ 305 | Chipper Jones | 4.00 | 1.80 |
| ❑ 306 | John Franco | .60 | .25 |
| ❑ 307 | Sammy Sosa | 3.00 | 1.35 |
| ❑ 308 | Troy Percival | .40 | .18 |
| ❑ 309 | Chuck Knoblauch | .60 | .25 |
| ❑ 310 | Ellis Burks | .60 | .25 |
| ❑ 311 | Al Martin | .40 | .18 |
| ❑ 312 | Tim Salmon | .60 | .25 |
| ❑ 313 | Moises Alou | .60 | .25 |
| ❑ 314 | Lance Johnson | .40 | .18 |
| ❑ 315 | Justin Thompson | .40 | .18 |
| ❑ 316 | Will Clark | 1.50 | .70 |
| ❑ 317 | Barry Bonds | 2.50 | 1.10 |
| ❑ 318 | Craig Biggio | 1.00 | .45 |
| ❑ 319 | John Smoltz | .60 | .25 |
| ❑ 320 | Cal Ripken | 6.00 | 2.70 |
| ❑ 321 | Ken Griffey Jr. | 6.00 | 2.70 |
| ❑ 322 | Paul O'Neill | .60 | .25 |
| ❑ 323 | Todd Helton | 2.00 | .90 |
| ❑ 324 | John Olerud | .60 | .25 |
| ❑ 325 | Mark McGwire | 6.00 | 2.70 |
| ❑ 326 | Jose Cruz Jr. | .60 | .25 |
| ❑ 327 | Jeff Cirillo | .60 | .25 |
| ❑ 328 | Dean Palmer | .60 | .25 |
| ❑ 329 | John Wetteland | .60 | .25 |
| ❑ 330 | Steve Finley | .60 | .25 |
| ❑ 331 | Albert Belle | 1.00 | .45 |
| ❑ 332 | Curt Schilling | .60 | .25 |
| ❑ 333 | Raul Mondesi | .60 | .25 |
| ❑ 334 | Andruw Jones | 1.50 | .70 |
| ❑ 335 | Nomar Garciaparra | 5.00 | 2.20 |
| ❑ 336 | David Justice | 1.00 | .45 |
| ❑ 337 | Andy Pettitte | .60 | .25 |
| ❑ 338 | Pedro Martinez | 2.00 | .90 |
| ❑ 339 | Travis Miller | .40 | .18 |
| ❑ 340 | Chris Stynes | .40 | .18 |
| ❑ 341 | Gregg Jefferies | .40 | .18 |
| ❑ 342 | Jeff Fassero | .40 | .18 |
| ❑ 343 | Craig Counsell | .40 | .18 |
| ❑ 344 | Wilson Alvarez | .40 | .18 |
| ❑ 345 | Bip Roberts | .40 | .18 |
| ❑ 346 | Kelvim Escobar | .40 | .18 |
| ❑ 347 | Mark Bellhorn | .40 | .18 |
| ❑ 348 | Cory Lidle | .40 | .18 |
| ❑ 349 | Fred McGriff | 1.00 | .45 |
| ❑ 350 | Chuck Carr | .40 | .18 |
| ❑ 351 | Bob Abreu | .60 | .25 |
| ❑ 352 | Juan Guzman | .40 | .18 |
| ❑ 353 | Fernando Vina | .40 | .18 |
| ❑ 354 | Andy Benes | .40 | .18 |
| ❑ 355 | Dave Nilsson | .40 | .18 |
| ❑ 356 | Bobby Bonilla | .60 | .25 |
| ❑ 357 | Ismael Valdes | .40 | .18 |
| ❑ 358 | Carlos Perez | .40 | .18 |
| ❑ 359 | Kirk Rueter | .40 | .18 |
| ❑ 360 | Bartolo Colon | .60 | .25 |
| ❑ 361 | Mel Rojas | .40 | .18 |
| ❑ 362 | Johnny Damon | .60 | .25 |
| ❑ 363 | Geronimo Berroa | .40 | .18 |
| ❑ 364 | Reggie Sanders | .40 | .18 |
| ❑ 365 | Jermaine Allensworth | .40 | .18 |
| ❑ 366 | Orlando Cabrera | .40 | .18 |
| ❑ 367 | Jorge Fabregas | .40 | .18 |
| ❑ 368 | Scott Stahoviak | .40 | .18 |
| ❑ 369 | Ken Cloude | .40 | .18 |
| ❑ 370 | Donovan Osborne | .40 | .18 |
| ❑ 371 | Roger Cedeno | .40 | .18 |
| ❑ 372 | Neifi Perez | .40 | .18 |
| ❑ 373 | Chris Holt | .40 | .18 |
| ❑ 374 | Cecil Fielder | .60 | .25 |
| ❑ 375 | Marty Cordova | .40 | .18 |
| ❑ 376 | Tom Goodwin | .40 | .18 |
| ❑ 377 | Jeff Suppan | .40 | .18 |
| ❑ 378 | Jeff Brantley | .40 | .18 |
| ❑ 379 | Mark Langston | .40 | .18 |
| ❑ 380 | Shane Reynolds | .40 | .18 |
| ❑ 381 | Mike Fetters | .40 | .18 |
| ❑ 382 | Todd Greene | .40 | .18 |
| ❑ 383 | Ray Durham | .60 | .25 |
| ❑ 384 | Carlos Delgado | 1.50 | .70 |
| ❑ 385 | Jeff D'Amico | .40 | .18 |
| ❑ 386 | Brian McRae | .40 | .18 |
| ❑ 387 | Alan Benes | .40 | .18 |
| ❑ 388 | Heathcliff Slocumb | .40 | .18 |
| ❑ 389 | Eric Young | .40 | .18 |
| ❑ 390 | Travis Fryman | .60 | .25 |
| ❑ 391 | David Cone | .60 | .25 |
| ❑ 392 | Otis Nixon | .40 | .18 |
| ❑ 393 | Jeremi Gonzalez | .40 | .18 |
| ❑ 394 | Jeff Juden | .40 | .18 |
| ❑ 395 | Jose Vizcaino | .40 | .18 |
| ❑ 396 | Ugueth Urbina | .40 | .18 |
| ❑ 397 | Ramon Martinez | .40 | .18 |
| ❑ 398 | Robb Nen | .40 | .18 |
| ❑ 399 | Harold Baines | .60 | .25 |
| ❑ 400 | Delino DeShields | .40 | .18 |
| ❑ 401 | John Burkett | .40 | .18 |
| ❑ 402 | Sterling Hitchcock | .40 | .18 |
| ❑ 403 | Mark Clark | .40 | .18 |
| ❑ 404 | Terrell Wade | .40 | .18 |
| ❑ 405 | Scott Brosius | .60 | .25 |
| ❑ 406 | Chad Curtis | .40 | .18 |
| ❑ 407 | Brian Johnson | .40 | .18 |
| ❑ 408 | Roberto Kelly | .40 | .18 |
| ❑ 409 | Dave Dellucci RC | .40 | .18 |
| ❑ 410 | Michael Tucker | .40 | .18 |
| ❑ 411 | Mark Kotsay | .60 | .25 |
| ❑ 412 | Mark Lewis | .40 | .18 |
| ❑ 413 | Ryan McGuire | .40 | .18 |
| ❑ 414 | Shawon Dunston | .40 | .18 |
| ❑ 415 | Brad Rigby | .40 | .18 |
| ❑ 416 | Scott Erickson | .40 | .18 |
| ❑ 417 | Bobby Jones | .40 | .18 |
| ❑ 418 | Darren Oliver | .40 | .18 |
| ❑ 419 | John Smiley | .40 | .18 |
| ❑ 420 | T.J. Mathews | .40 | .18 |
| ❑ 421 | Dustin Hermanson | .40 | .18 |
| ❑ 422 | Mike Timlin | .40 | .18 |
| ❑ 423 | Willie Blair | .40 | .18 |
| ❑ 424 | Manny Alexander | .40 | .18 |
| ❑ 425 | Bob Tewksbury | .40 | .18 |
| ❑ 426 | Pete Schourek | .40 | .18 |
| ❑ 427 | Reggie Jefferson | .40 | .18 |
| ❑ 428 | Ed Sprague | .40 | .18 |
| ❑ 429 | Jeff Conine | .40 | .18 |
| ❑ 430 | Roberto Hernandez | .40 | .18 |
| ❑ 431 | Tom Pagnozzi | .40 | .18 |
| ❑ 432 | Jaret Wright | .40 | .18 |
| ❑ 433 | Livan Hernandez | .40 | .18 |
| ❑ 434 | Andy Ashby | .40 | .18 |
| ❑ 435 | Todd Dunn | .40 | .18 |
| ❑ 436 | Bobby Higginson | .60 | .25 |
| ❑ 437 | Rod Beck | .40 | .18 |
| ❑ 438 | Jim Leyritz | .40 | .18 |
| ❑ 439 | Matt Williams | 1.00 | .45 |
| ❑ 440 | Brett Tomko | .40 | .18 |
| ❑ 441 | Joe Randa | .40 | .18 |
| ❑ 442 | Chris Carpenter | .60 | .25 |
| ❑ 443 | Dennis Reyes | .40 | .18 |
| ❑ 444 | Al Leiter | .60 | .25 |
| ❑ 445 | Jason Schmidt | .40 | .18 |
| ❑ 446 | Ken Hill | .40 | .18 |
| ❑ 447 | Shannon Stewart | .60 | .25 |
| ❑ 448 | Enrique Wilson | .40 | .18 |
| ❑ 449 | Fernando Tatis | .60 | .25 |
| ❑ 450 | Jimmy Key | .60 | .25 |
| ❑ 451 | Darrin Fletcher | .40 | .18 |
| ❑ 452 | John Valentin | .40 | .18 |
| ❑ 453 | Kevin Tapani | .40 | .18 |
| ❑ 454 | Eric Karros | .60 | .25 |
| ❑ 455 | Jay Bell | .60 | .25 |
| ❑ 456 | Walt Weiss | .60 | .25 |
| ❑ 457 | Devon White | .40 | .18 |
| ❑ 458 | Carl Pavano | .40 | .18 |
| ❑ 459 | Mike Lansing | .40 | .18 |
| ❑ 460 | John Flaherty | .40 | .18 |
| ❑ 461 | Richard Hidalgo | .60 | .25 |
| ❑ 462 | Quinton McCracken | .40 | .18 |
| ❑ 463 | Karim Garcia | .40 | .18 |
| ❑ 464 | Miguel Cairo | .40 | .18 |
| ❑ 465 | Edwin Diaz | .40 | .18 |
| ❑ 466 | Bobby Smith | .40 | .18 |
| ❑ 467 | Yamil Benitez | .40 | .18 |
| ❑ 468 | Rich Butler RC | .40 | .18 |
| ❑ 469 | Ben Ford RC | .60 | .25 |
| ❑ 470 | Bubba Trammell | .40 | .18 |
| ❑ 471 | Brent Brede | .40 | .18 |
| ❑ 472 | Brooks Kieschnick | .40 | .18 |
| ❑ 473 | Carlos Castillo | .40 | .18 |
| ❑ 474 | Brad Radke SH | .40 | .18 |
| ❑ 475 | Roger Clemens SH | 1.50 | .70 |
| ❑ 476 | Curt Schilling SH | .60 | .25 |
| ❑ 477 | John Olerud SH | .40 | .18 |
| ❑ 478 | Mark McGwire SH | 3.00 | 1.35 |
| ❑ 479 | Mike Piazza IL<br>Ken Griffey Jr. | 3.00 | 1.35 |
| ❑ 480 | Jeff Bagwell<br>Frank Thomas | 1.50 | .70 |
| ❑ 481 | Chipper Jones<br>Nomar Garciaparra IL | 2.50 | 1.10 |
| ❑ 482 | Larry Walker IL<br>Juan Gonzalez IL | .60 | .25 |
| ❑ 483 | Gary Sheffield IL<br>Tino Martinez IL | .60 | .25 |
| ❑ 484 | Derrick Gibson<br>Michael Coleman<br>Norm Hutchins | 1.00 | .45 |
| ❑ 485 | Braden Looper<br>Cliff Politte<br>Brian Rose | 1.00 | .45 |
| ❑ 486 | Eric Milton<br>Jason Marquis<br>Corey Lee | 1.50 | .70 |
| ❑ 487 | A.J.Hinch<br>Mark Osborne RC<br>Robert Fick | 2.00 | .90 |
| ❑ 488 | Aramis Ramirez<br>Alex Gonzalez<br>Sean Casey | 1.00 | .45 |
| ❑ 489 | Donnie Bridges<br>Tim Drew RC | 2.00 | .90 |
| ❑ 490 | Ntema Ndungidi RC<br>Darnell McDonald | 2.50 | 1.10 |
| ❑ 491 | Ryan Anderson RC<br>Mark Mangum | 10.00 | 4.50 |
| ❑ 492 | J.J.Davis<br>Troy Glaus RC | 15.00 | 6.75 |
| ❑ 493 | Jayson Werth RC<br>Dan Reichert | 2.00 | .90 |
| ❑ 494 | John Curtice RC<br>Michael Cuddyer | 3.00 | 1.35 |
| ❑ 495 | Jack Cust RC<br>Jason Standridge | 5.00 | 2.20 |
| ❑ 496 | Brian Anderson | 1.00 | .45 |
| ❑ 497 | Tony Saunders | 1.00 | .45 |
| ❑ 498 | Vladimir Nunez<br>Jhensy Sandoval | 1.00 | .45 |
| ❑ 499 | Brad Penny<br>Nick Bierbrodt | 1.50 | .70 |
| ❑ 500 | Dustin Carr<br>Luis Cruz RC | 1.00 | .45 |
| ❑ 501 | Cedric Bowers<br>Marcus McCain | 1.50 | .70 |
| ❑ 502 | Checklist | .40 | .18 |
| ❑ 503 | Checklist | .40 | .18 |
| ❑ 504 | Alex Rodriguez | 5.00 | 2.20 |

## 1999 Topps Chrome

| | MINT | NRMT |
|---|---|---|
| COMPLETE SET (462) | 300.00 | 135.00 |
| COMPLETE SERIES 1 (241) | 150.00 | 70.00 |
| COMPLETE SERIES 2 (221) | 150.00 | 70.00 |
| COMMON CARD (1-6/8-463) | .40 | .18 |
| COMMON PROS. (205-212/425-437) | 1.00 | .45 |
| COMP.MCGWIRE HR SET (70) | 3000.00 | 1350.00 |
| COMP.SOSA HR SET (66) | 1100.00 | 500.00 |

| | Card | MINT | NRMT |
|---|---|---|---|
| ❑ | 1 Roger Clemens | 3.00 | 1.35 |
| ❑ | 2 Andres Galarraga | 1.00 | .45 |
| ❑ | 3 Scott Brosius | .60 | .25 |
| ❑ | 4 John Flaherty | .40 | .18 |
| ❑ | 5 Jim Leyritz | .40 | .18 |
| ❑ | 6 Ray Durham | .60 | .25 |
| ❑ | 8 Jose Vizcaino | .40 | .18 |
| ❑ | 9 Will Clark | 1.50 | .70 |
| ❑ | 10 David Wells | .60 | .25 |
| ❑ | 11 Jose Guillen | .40 | .18 |
| ❑ | 12 Scott Hatteberg | .40 | .18 |
| ❑ | 13 Edgardo Alfonzo | .60 | .25 |
| ❑ | 14 Mike Bordick | .40 | .18 |
| ❑ | 15 Manny Ramirez | 2.00 | .90 |
| ❑ | 16 Greg Maddux | 4.00 | 1.80 |
| ❑ | 17 David Segui | .40 | .18 |
| ❑ | 18 Darryl Strawberry | .60 | .25 |
| ❑ | 19 Brad Radke | .60 | .25 |
| ❑ | 20 Kerry Wood | .60 | .25 |
| ❑ | 21 Matt Anderson | .40 | .18 |
| ❑ | 22 Derrek Lee | .40 | .18 |
| ❑ | 23 Mickey Morandini | .40 | .18 |
| ❑ | 24 Paul Konerko | .60 | .25 |
| ❑ | 25 Travis Lee | .40 | .18 |
| ❑ | 26 Ken Hill | .40 | .18 |
| ❑ | 27 Kenny Rogers | .40 | .18 |
| ❑ | 28 Paul Sorrento | .40 | .18 |
| ❑ | 29 Quilvio Veras | .40 | .18 |
| ❑ | 30 Todd Walker | .40 | .18 |
| ❑ | 31 Ryan Jackson | .40 | .18 |
| ❑ | 32 John Olerud | .60 | .25 |
| ❑ | 33 Doug Glanville | .40 | .18 |
| ❑ | 34 Nolan Ryan | 8.00 | 3.60 |
| ❑ | 35 Ray Lankford | .60 | .25 |
| ❑ | 36 Mark Loretta | .40 | .18 |
| ❑ | 37 Jason Dickson | .40 | .18 |
| ❑ | 38 Sean Bergman | .40 | .18 |
| ❑ | 39 Quinton McCracken | .40 | .18 |
| ❑ | 40 Bartolo Colon | .60 | .25 |
| ❑ | 41 Brady Anderson | .60 | .25 |
| ❑ | 42 Chris Stynes | .40 | .18 |
| ❑ | 43 Jorge Posada | .60 | .25 |
| ❑ | 44 Justin Thompson | .40 | .18 |
| ❑ | 45 Johnny Damon | .60 | .25 |
| ❑ | 46 Armando Benitez | .40 | .18 |
| ❑ | 47 Brant Brown | .40 | .18 |
| ❑ | 48 Charlie Hayes | .40 | .18 |
| ❑ | 49 Darren Dreifort | .40 | .18 |
| ❑ | 50 Juan Gonzalez | 1.50 | .70 |
| ❑ | 51 Chuck Knoblauch | .60 | .25 |
| ❑ | 52 Todd Helton | 2.00 | .90 |
| ❑ | 53 Rick Reed | .40 | .18 |
| ❑ | 54 Chris Gomez | .40 | .18 |
| ❑ | 55 Gary Sheffield | 1.50 | .70 |
| ❑ | 56 Rod Beck | .40 | .18 |
| ❑ | 57 Rey Sanchez | .40 | .18 |
| ❑ | 58 Garret Anderson | .60 | .25 |
| ❑ | 59 Jimmy Haynes | .40 | .18 |
| ❑ | 60 Steve Woodard | .40 | .18 |
| ❑ | 61 Rondell White | .60 | .25 |
| ❑ | 62 Vladimir Guerrero | 2.50 | 1.10 |
| ❑ | 63 Eric Karros | .60 | .25 |
| ❑ | 64 Russ Davis | .40 | .18 |
| ❑ | 65 Mo Vaughn | .60 | .25 |
| ❑ | 66 Sammy Sosa | 3.00 | 1.35 |
| ❑ | 67 Troy Percival | .40 | .18 |
| ❑ | 68 Kenny Lofton | .60 | .25 |
| ❑ | 69 Bill Taylor | .40 | .18 |
| ❑ | 70 Mark McGwire | 6.00 | 2.70 |
| ❑ | 71 Roger Cedeno | .40 | .18 |
| ❑ | 72 Javy Lopez | .60 | .25 |
| ❑ | 73 Damion Easley | .40 | .18 |
| ❑ | 74 Andy Pettitte | .60 | .25 |
| ❑ | 75 Tony Gwynn | 3.00 | 1.35 |
| ❑ | 76 Ricardo Rincon | .40 | .18 |
| ❑ | 77 F.P. Santangelo | .40 | .18 |
| ❑ | 78 Jay Bell | .60 | .25 |
| ❑ | 79 Scott Servais | .40 | .18 |
| ❑ | 80 Jose Canseco | 2.00 | .90 |
| ❑ | 81 Roberto Hernandez | .40 | .18 |
| ❑ | 82 Todd Dunwoody | .40 | .18 |
| ❑ | 83 John Wetteland | .60 | .25 |
| ❑ | 84 Mike Caruso | .40 | .18 |
| ❑ | 85 Derek Jeter | 6.00 | 2.70 |
| ❑ | 86 Aaron Sele | .60 | .25 |
| ❑ | 87 Jose Lima | .40 | .18 |
| ❑ | 88 Ryan Christenson | .40 | .18 |
| ❑ | 89 Jeff Cirillo | .60 | .25 |
| ❑ | 90 Jose Hernandez | .40 | .18 |
| ❑ | 91 Mark Kotsay | .40 | .18 |
| ❑ | 92 Darren Bragg | .40 | .18 |
| ❑ | 93 Albert Belle | 1.00 | .45 |
| ❑ | 94 Matt Lawton | .60 | .25 |
| ❑ | 95 Pedro Martinez | 2.00 | .90 |
| ❑ | 96 Greg Vaughn | .60 | .25 |
| ❑ | 97 Neifi Perez | .40 | .18 |
| ❑ | 98 Gerald Williams | .40 | .18 |
| ❑ | 99 Derek Bell | .40 | .18 |
| ❑ | 100 Ken Griffey Jr. | 6.00 | 2.70 |
| ❑ | 101 David Cone | .60 | .25 |
| ❑ | 102 Brian Johnson | .40 | .18 |
| ❑ | 103 Dean Palmer | .60 | .25 |
| ❑ | 104 Javier Valentin | .40 | .18 |
| ❑ | 105 Trevor Hoffman | .60 | .25 |
| ❑ | 106 Butch Huskey | .40 | .18 |
| ❑ | 107 Dave Martinez | .40 | .18 |
| ❑ | 108 Billy Wagner | .40 | .18 |
| ❑ | 109 Shawn Green | 1.50 | .70 |
| ❑ | 110 Ben Grieve | .60 | .25 |
| ❑ | 111 Tom Goodwin | .40 | .18 |
| ❑ | 112 Jaret Wright | .40 | .18 |
| ❑ | 113 Aramis Ramirez | .40 | .18 |
| ❑ | 114 Dmitri Young | .60 | .25 |
| ❑ | 115 Hideki Irabu | .40 | .18 |
| ❑ | 116 Roberto Kelly | .40 | .18 |
| ❑ | 117 Jeff Fassero | .40 | .18 |
| ❑ | 118 Mark Clark | .40 | .18 |
| ❑ | 119 Jason McDonald | .40 | .18 |
| ❑ | 120 Matt Williams | 1.00 | .45 |
| ❑ | 121 Dave Burba | .40 | .18 |
| ❑ | 122 Bret Saberhagen | .60 | .25 |
| ❑ | 123 Deivi Cruz | .40 | .18 |
| ❑ | 124 Chad Curtis | .40 | .18 |
| ❑ | 125 Scott Rolen | 1.50 | .70 |
| ❑ | 126 Lee Stevens | .40 | .18 |
| ❑ | 127 J.T. Snow | .60 | .25 |
| ❑ | 128 Rusty Greer | .60 | .25 |
| ❑ | 129 Brian Meadows | .40 | .18 |
| ❑ | 130 Jim Edmonds | 1.50 | .70 |
| ❑ | 131 Ron Gant | .60 | .25 |
| ❑ | 132 A.J. Hinch | .40 | .18 |
| ❑ | 133 Shannon Stewart | .60 | .25 |
| ❑ | 134 Brad Fullmer | .60 | .25 |
| ❑ | 135 Cal Eldred | .40 | .18 |
| ❑ | 136 Matt Walbeck | .40 | .18 |
| ❑ | 137 Carl Everett | .60 | .25 |
| ❑ | 138 Walt Weiss | .40 | .18 |
| ❑ | 139 Fred McGriff | 1.00 | .45 |
| ❑ | 140 Darin Erstad | 1.50 | .70 |
| ❑ | 141 Dave Nilsson | .40 | .18 |
| ❑ | 142 Eric Young | .40 | .18 |
| ❑ | 143 Dan Wilson | .40 | .18 |
| ❑ | 144 Jeff Reed | .40 | .18 |
| ❑ | 145 Brett Tomko | .40 | .18 |
| ❑ | 146 Terry Steinbach | .40 | .18 |
| ❑ | 147 Seth Greisinger | .40 | .18 |
| ❑ | 148 Pat Meares | .40 | .18 |
| ❑ | 149 Livan Hernandez | .40 | .18 |
| ❑ | 150 Jeff Bagwell | 2.00 | .90 |
| ❑ | 151 Bob Wickman | .40 | .18 |
| ❑ | 152 Omar Vizquel | .60 | .25 |
| ❑ | 153 Eric Davis | .60 | .25 |
| ❑ | 154 Larry Sutton | .40 | .18 |
| ❑ | 155 Magglio Ordonez | 1.00 | .45 |
| ❑ | 156 Eric Milton | .40 | .18 |
| ❑ | 157 Darren Lewis | .40 | .18 |
| ❑ | 158 Rick Aguilera | .40 | .18 |
| ❑ | 159 Mike Lieberthal | .60 | .25 |
| ❑ | 160 Robb Nen | .40 | .18 |
| ❑ | 161 Brian Giles | .60 | .25 |
| ❑ | 162 Jeff Brantley | .40 | .18 |
| ❑ | 163 Gary DiSarcina | .40 | .18 |
| ❑ | 164 John Valentin | .40 | .18 |
| ❑ | 165 Dave Dellucci | .40 | .18 |
| ❑ | 166 Chan Ho Park | .60 | .25 |
| ❑ | 167 Masato Yoshii | .60 | .25 |
| ❑ | 168 Jason Schmidt | .40 | .18 |
| ❑ | 169 LaTroy Hawkins | .40 | .18 |
| ❑ | 170 Bret Boone | .60 | .25 |
| ❑ | 171 Jerry DiPoto | .40 | .18 |
| ❑ | 172 Mariano Rivera | .60 | .25 |
| ❑ | 173 Mike Cameron | .40 | .18 |
| ❑ | 174 Scott Erickson | .40 | .18 |
| ❑ | 175 Charles Johnson | .60 | .25 |
| ❑ | 176 Bobby Jones | .40 | .18 |
| ❑ | 177 Francisco Cordova | .40 | .18 |
| ❑ | 178 Todd Jones | .40 | .18 |
| ❑ | 179 Jeff Montgomery | .40 | .18 |
| ❑ | 180 Mike Mussina | 1.50 | .70 |
| ❑ | 181 Bob Abreu | .60 | .25 |
| ❑ | 182 Ismael Valdes | .40 | .18 |
| ❑ | 183 Andy Fox | .40 | .18 |
| ❑ | 184 Woody Williams | .40 | .18 |
| ❑ | 185 Denny Neagle | .40 | .18 |
| ❑ | 186 Jose Valentin | .40 | .18 |
| ❑ | 187 Darrin Fletcher | .40 | .18 |
| ❑ | 188 Gabe Alvarez | .40 | .18 |
| ❑ | 189 Eddie Taubensee | .40 | .18 |
| ❑ | 190 Edgar Martinez | 1.00 | .45 |
| ❑ | 191 Jason Kendall | .60 | .25 |
| ❑ | 192 Darryl Kile | .60 | .25 |
| ❑ | 193 Jeff King | .40 | .18 |
| ❑ | 194 Rey Ordonez | .40 | .18 |
| ❑ | 195 Andruw Jones | 1.50 | .70 |
| ❑ | 196 Tony Fernandez | .40 | .18 |
| ❑ | 197 Jamey Wright | .40 | .18 |
| ❑ | 198 B.J. Surhoff | .60 | .25 |
| ❑ | 199 Vinny Castilla | .60 | .25 |
| ❑ | 200 David Wells HL | .40 | .18 |
| ❑ | 201 Mark McGwire HL | 3.00 | 1.35 |
| ❑ | 202 Sammy Sosa HL | 1.50 | .70 |
| ❑ | 203 Roger Clemens HL | 1.50 | .70 |
| ❑ | 204 Kerry Wood HL | .60 | .25 |
| ❑ | 205 Gabe Kapler<br>Lance Berkman<br>Mike Frank | .60 | .25 |
| ❑ | 206 Alex Escobar RC<br>Ricky Ledee<br>Mike Stoner | 5.00 | 2.20 |
| ❑ | 207 Peter Bergeron RC<br>Jeremy Giambi<br>George Lombard | 2.00 | .90 |
| ❑ | 208 Michael Barrett<br>Ben Davis<br>Robert Fick | 1.00 | .45 |
| ❑ | 209 Jayson Werth<br>Ramon Hernandez<br>Pat Cline | 1.00 | .45 |
| ❑ | 210 Ryan Anderson<br>Bruce Chen<br>Chris Enochs | 1.25 | .55 |
| ❑ | 211 Brad Penny<br>Octavio Dotel<br>Mike Lincoln | 1.00 | .45 |
| ❑ | 212 Chuck Abbott RC<br>Brent Butler<br>Danny Klassen | 1.00 | .45 |
| ❑ | 213 Chris C.Jones<br>Jeff Urban RC | 1.25 | .55 |

❑ 214 Arturo McDowell RC 2.50 1.10
Tony Torcato
❑ 215 Josh McKinley RC 2.00 .90
Jason Tyner
❑ 216 Matt Burch 1.25 .55
Seth Etheron RC
❑ 217 Mamon Tucker RC 1.25 .55
Rick Elder
❑ 218 J.M.Gold 1.25 .55
Ryan Mills RC
❑ 219 Andy Brown 2.00 .90
Choo Freeman RC
❑ 220A Mark McGwire HR 1 80.00 36.00
❑ 220B Mark McGwire HR 2 50.00 22.00
❑ 220C Mark McGwire HR 3 50.00 22.00
❑ 220D Mark McGwire HR 4 50.00 22.00
❑ 220E Mark McGwire HR 5 50.00 22.00
❑ 220F Mark McGwire HR 6 50.00 22.00
❑ 220G Mark McGwire HR 7 50.00 22.00
❑ 220H Mark McGwire HR 8 50.00 22.00
❑ 220I Mark McGwire HR 9 50.00 22.00
❑ 220J Mark McGwire HR 10 50.00 22.00
❑ 220K Mark McGwire HR 11 50.00 22.00
❑ 220L Mark McGwire HR 12 50.00 22.00
❑ 220M Mark McGwire HR 13 50.00 22.00
❑ 220N Mark McGwire HR 14 50.00 22.00
❑ 220O Mark McGwire HR 15 50.00 22.00
❑ 220P Mark McGwire HR 16 50.00 22.00
❑ 220Q Mark McGwire HR 17 50.00 22.00
❑ 220R Mark McGwire HR 18 50.00 22.00
❑ 220S Mark McGwire HR 19 50.00 22.00
❑ 220T Mark McGwire HR 20 50.00 22.00
❑ 220U Mark McGwire HR 21 50.00 22.00
❑ 220V Mark McGwire HR 22 50.00 22.00
❑ 220W Mark McGwire HR 23 50.00 22.00
❑ 220X Mark McGwire HR 24 50.00 22.00
❑ 220Y Mark McGwire HR 25 50.00 22.00
❑ 220Z Mark McGwire HR 26 50.00 22.00
❑ 220AA Mark McGwire HR 27 50.00 22.00
❑ 220AB Mark McGwire HR 28 50.00 22.00
❑ 220AC Mark McGwire HR 29 50.00 22.00
❑ 220AD Mark McGwire HR 30 50.00 22.00
❑ 220AE Mark McGwire HR 31 50.00 22.00
❑ 220AF Mark McGwire HR 32 50.00 22.00
❑ 220AG Mark McGwire HR 33 50.00 22.00
❑ 220AH Mark McGwire HR 34 50.00 22.00
❑ 220AI Mark McGwire HR 35 50.00 22.00
❑ 220AJ Mark McGwire HR 36 50.00 22.00
❑ 220AK Mark McGwire HR 37 50.00 22.00
❑ 220AL Mark McGwire HR 38 50.00 22.00
❑ 220AM Mark McGwire HR 39 50.00 22.00
❑ 220AN Mark McGwire HR 40 50.00 22.00
❑ 220AO Mark McGwire HR 41 50.00 22.00
❑ 220AP Mark McGwire HR 42 50.00 22.00
❑ 220AQ Mark McGwire HR 43 50.00 22.00
❑ 220AR Mark McGwire HR 44 50.00 22.00
❑ 220AS Mark McGwire HR 45 50.00 22.00
❑ 220AT Mark McGwire HR 46 50.00 22.00
❑ 220AU Mark McGwire HR 47 50.00 22.00
❑ 220AV Mark McGwire HR 48 50.00 22.00
❑ 220AW Mark McGwire HR 49 50.00 22.00
❑ 220AX Mark McGwire HR 50 50.00 22.00
❑ 220AY Mark McGwire HR 51 50.00 22.00
❑ 220AZ Mark McGwire HR 52 50.00 22.00
❑ 220BB Mark McGwire HR 53 50.00 22.00
❑ 220CC Mark McGwire HR 54 50.00 22.00
❑ 220DD Mark McGwire HR 55 50.00 22.00
❑ 220EE Mark McGwire HR 56 50.00 22.00
❑ 220FF Mark McGwire HR 57 50.00 22.00
❑ 220GG Mark McGwire HR 58 50.00 22.00
❑ 220HH Mark McGwire HR 59 50.00 22.00
❑ 220II Mark McGwire HR 60 50.00 22.00
❑ 220JJ Mark McGwire HR 61 80.00 36.00
❑ 220KK Mark McGwire HR 62 120.00 55.00
❑ 220LL Mark McGwire HR 63 60.00 27.00
❑ 220MM Mark McGwire HR 64 60.00 27.00
❑ 220NN Mark McGwire HR 65 60.00 27.00
❑ 220OO Mark McGwire HR 66 60.00 27.00
❑ 220PP Mark McGwire HR 67 60.00 27.00
❑ 220QQ Mark McGwire HR 68 60.00 27.00
❑ 220RR Mark McGwire HR 69 60.00 27.00
❑ 220SS Mark McGwire HR 70 300.00 135.00
❑ 221 Larry Walker LL .60 .25
❑ 222 Bernie Williams LL .60 .25
❑ 223 Mark McGwire LL 3.00 1.35
❑ 224 Ken Griffey Jr. LL 3.00 1.35
❑ 225 Sammy Sosa LL 1.50 .70
❑ 226 Juan Gonzalez LL 1.00 .45
❑ 227 Dante Bichette LL .40 .18
❑ 228 Alex Rodriguez LL 2.50 1.10
❑ 229 Sammy Sosa LL 1.50 .70
❑ 230 Derek Jeter LL 3.00 1.35
❑ 231 Greg Maddux LL 2.00 .90
❑ 232 Roger Clemens LL 1.50 .70
❑ 233 Ricky Ledee WS .40 .18
❑ 234 Chuck Knoblauch WS .60 .25
❑ 235 Bernie Williams WS .60 .25
❑ 236 Tino Martinez WS .40 .18
❑ 237 Orlando Hernandez WS .60 .25
❑ 238 Scott Brosius WS .40 .18
❑ 239 Andy Pettitte WS .40 .18
❑ 240 Mariano Rivera WS .60 .25
❑ 241 Checklist .40 .18
❑ 242 Checklist .40 .18
❑ 243 Tom Glavine 1.50 .70
❑ 244 Andy Benes .40 .18
❑ 245 Sandy Alomar Jr. .60 .25
❑ 246 Wilton Guerrero .40 .18
❑ 247 Alex Gonzalez .40 .18
❑ 248 Roberto Alomar 1.50 .70
❑ 249 Ruben Rivera .40 .18
❑ 250 Eric Chavez .60 .25
❑ 251 Ellis Burks .60 .25
❑ 252 Richie Sexson .60 .25
❑ 253 Steve Finley .60 .25
❑ 254 Dwight Gooden .60 .25
❑ 255 Dustin Hermanson .40 .18
❑ 256 Kirk Rueter .40 .18
❑ 257 Steve Trachsel .40 .18
❑ 258 Gregg Jefferies .40 .18
❑ 259 Matt Stairs .40 .18
❑ 260 Shane Reynolds .40 .18
❑ 261 Gregg Olson .40 .18
❑ 262 Kevin Tapani .40 .18
❑ 263 Matt Morris .40 .18
❑ 264 Carl Pavano .40 .18
❑ 265 Nomar Garciaparra 5.00 2.20
❑ 266 Kevin Young .60 .25
❑ 267 Rick Helling .60 .25
❑ 268 Matt Franco .40 .18
❑ 269 Brian McRae .40 .18
❑ 270 Cal Ripken 6.00 2.70
❑ 271 Jeff Abbott .40 .18
❑ 272 Tony Batista .60 .25
❑ 273 Bill Simas .40 .18
❑ 274 Brian Hunter .40 .18
❑ 275 John Franco .60 .25
❑ 276 Devon White .40 .18
❑ 277 Rickey Henderson 2.00 .90
❑ 278 Chuck Finley .60 .25
❑ 279 Mike Blowers .40 .18
❑ 280 Mark Grace 1.50 .70
❑ 281 Randy Winn .40 .18
❑ 282 Bobby Bonilla .60 .25
❑ 283 David Justice 1.00 .45
❑ 284 Shane Monahan .40 .18
❑ 285 Kevin Brown 1.00 .45
❑ 286 Todd Zeile .60 .25
❑ 287 Al Martin .40 .18
❑ 288 Troy O'Leary .40 .18
❑ 289 Darryl Hamilton .40 .18
❑ 290 Tino Martinez .60 .25
❑ 291 David Ortiz .40 .18
❑ 292 Tony Clark .40 .18
❑ 293 Ryan Minor .40 .18
❑ 294 Mark Leiter .40 .18
❑ 295 Wally Joyner .60 .25
❑ 296 Cliff Floyd .60 .25
❑ 297 Shawn Estes .40 .18
❑ 298 Pat Hentgen .40 .18
❑ 299 Scott Elarton .60 .25
❑ 300 Alex Rodriguez 5.00 2.20
❑ 301 Ozzie Guillen .40 .18
❑ 302 Hideo Nomo 1.50 .70
❑ 303 Ryan McGuire .40 .18
❑ 304 Brad Ausmus .40 .18
❑ 305 Alex Gonzalez .40 .18
❑ 306 Brian Jordan .60 .25
❑ 307 John Jaha .40 .18
❑ 308 Mark Grudzielanek .40 .18
❑ 309 Juan Guzman .40 .18
❑ 310 Tony Womack .40 .18
❑ 311 Dennis Reyes .40 .18
❑ 312 Marty Cordova .40 .18
❑ 313 Ramiro Mendoza .40 .18
❑ 314 Robin Ventura .60 .25
❑ 315 Rafael Palmeiro 1.50 .70
❑ 316 Ramon Martinez .40 .18
❑ 317 Pedro Astacio .40 .18
❑ 318 Dave Hollins .40 .18
❑ 319 Tom Candiotti .40 .18
❑ 320 Al Leiter .60 .25
❑ 321 Rico Brogna .40 .18
❑ 322 Reggie Jefferson .40 .18
❑ 323 Bernard Gilkey .40 .18
❑ 324 Jason Giambi 1.50 .70
❑ 325 Craig Biggio 1.00 .45
❑ 326 Troy Glaus 2.50 1.10
❑ 327 Delino DeShields .40 .18
❑ 328 Fernando Vina .40 .18
❑ 329 John Smoltz .60 .25
❑ 330 Jeff Kent 1.00 .45
❑ 331 Roy Halladay .40 .18
❑ 332 Andy Ashby .40 .18
❑ 333 Tim Wakefield .40 .18
❑ 334 Roger Clemens 3.00 1.35
❑ 335 Bernie Williams 1.50 .70
❑ 336 Desi Relaford .40 .18
❑ 337 John Burkett .40 .18
❑ 338 Mike Hampton .60 .25
❑ 339 Royce Clayton .40 .18
❑ 340 Mike Piazza 5.00 2.20
❑ 341 Jeremi Gonzalez .40 .18
❑ 342 Mike Lansing .40 .18
❑ 343 Jamie Moyer .40 .18
❑ 344 Ron Coomer .40 .18
❑ 345 Barry Larkin 1.50 .70
❑ 346 Fernando Tatis .60 .25
❑ 347 Chili Davis .60 .25
❑ 348 Bobby Higginson .60 .25
❑ 349 Hal Morris .40 .18
❑ 350 Larry Walker .60 .25
❑ 351 Carlos Guillen .40 .18
❑ 352 Miguel Tejada .60 .25
❑ 353 Travis Fryman .60 .25
❑ 354 Jarrod Washburn .40 .18
❑ 355 Chipper Jones 4.00 1.80
❑ 356 Todd Stottlemyre .40 .18
❑ 357 Henry Rodriguez .40 .18
❑ 358 Eli Marrero .40 .18
❑ 359 Alan Benes .40 .18
❑ 360 Tim Salmon .60 .25
❑ 361 Luis Gonzalez .60 .25
❑ 362 Scott Spiezio .40 .18
❑ 363 Chris Carpenter .40 .18
❑ 364 Bobby Howry .40 .18
❑ 365 Raul Mondesi .60 .25
❑ 366 Ugueth Urbina .40 .18
❑ 367 Tom Evans .40 .18
❑ 368 Kerry Ligtenberg RC 1.00 .45
❑ 369 Adrian Beltre .60 .25
❑ 370 Ryan Klesko .60 .25
❑ 371 Wilson Alvarez .40 .18
❑ 372 John Thomson .40 .18
❑ 373 Tony Saunders .40 .18
❑ 374 Dave Mlicki .40 .18
❑ 375 Ken Caminiti .60 .25
❑ 376 Jay Buhner .60 .25
❑ 377 Bill Mueller .40 .18
❑ 378 Jeff Blauser .40 .18
❑ 379 Edgar Renteria .40 .18
❑ 380 Jim Thome 1.00 .45
❑ 381 Joey Hamilton .40 .18
❑ 382 Calvin Pickering .40 .18
❑ 383 Marquis Grissom .40 .18
❑ 384 Omar Daal .40 .18
❑ 385 Curt Schilling .60 .25
❑ 386 Jose Cruz Jr. .60 .25
❑ 387 Chris Widger .40 .18
❑ 388 Pete Harnisch .40 .18
❑ 389 Charles Nagy .40 .18
❑ 390 Tom Gordon .40 .18
❑ 391 Bobby Smith .40 .18
❑ 392 Derrick Gibson .40 .18
❑ 393 Jeff Conine .40 .18
❑ 394 Carlos Perez .40 .18
❑ 395 Barry Bonds 2.50 1.10
❑ 396 Mark McLemore .40 .18

| | Card | | |
|---|---|---|---|
| ❑ 397 | Juan Encarnacion | .60 | .25 |
| ❑ 398 | Wade Boggs | 2.00 | .90 |
| ❑ 399 | Ivan Rodriguez | 2.00 | .90 |
| ❑ 400 | Moises Alou | .60 | .25 |
| ❑ 401 | Jeromy Burnitz | .60 | .25 |
| ❑ 402 | Sean Casey | .60 | .25 |
| ❑ 403 | Jose Offerman | .40 | .18 |
| ❑ 404 | Joe Fontenot | .40 | .18 |
| ❑ 405 | Kevin Millwood | .60 | .25 |
| ❑ 406 | Lance Johnson | .40 | .18 |
| ❑ 407 | Richard Hidalgo | .60 | .25 |
| ❑ 408 | Mike Jackson | .40 | .18 |
| ❑ 409 | Brian Anderson | .40 | .18 |
| ❑ 410 | Jeff Shaw | .40 | .18 |
| ❑ 411 | Preston Wilson | .60 | .25 |
| ❑ 412 | Todd Hundley | .40 | .18 |
| ❑ 413 | Jim Parque | .40 | .18 |
| ❑ 414 | Justin Baughman | .40 | .18 |
| ❑ 415 | Dante Bichette | .60 | .25 |
| ❑ 416 | Paul O'Neill | .60 | .25 |
| ❑ 417 | Miguel Cairo | .40 | .18 |
| ❑ 418 | Randy Johnson | 2.00 | .90 |
| ❑ 419 | Jesus Sanchez | .40 | .18 |
| ❑ 420 | Carlos Delgado | 1.50 | .70 |
| ❑ 421 | Ricky Ledee | .40 | .18 |
| ❑ 422 | Orlando Hernandez | .60 | .25 |
| ❑ 423 | Frank Thomas | 3.00 | 1.35 |
| ❑ 424 | Pokey Reese | .60 | .25 |
| ❑ 425 | Carlos Lee | 1.00 | .45 |
| | Mike Lowell | | |
| | Kit Pellow RC | | |
| ❑ 426 | Michael Cuddyer | 1.00 | .45 |
| | Mark DeRosa | | |
| | Jerry Hairston Jr. | | |
| ❑ 427 | Marlon Anderson | 1.00 | .45 |
| | Ron Belliard | | |
| | Orlando Cabrera | | |
| ❑ 428 | Micah Bowie | 1.00 | .45 |
| | Phil Norton RC | | |
| | Randy Wolf | | |
| ❑ 429 | Jack Cressend RC | 1.00 | .45 |
| | Jason Rakers | | |
| | John Rocker | | |
| ❑ 430 | Ruben Mateo | 1.00 | .45 |
| | Scott Morgan | | |
| | Mike Zywica RC | | |
| ❑ 431 | Jason LaRue | 1.00 | .45 |
| | Matt LeCroy | | |
| | Mitch Meluskey | | |
| ❑ 432 | Gabe Kapler | 1.00 | .45 |
| | Armando Rios | | |
| | Fernando Seguignol | | |
| ❑ 433 | Adam Kennedy | 1.00 | .45 |
| | Mickey Lopez RC | | |
| | Jackie Rexrode | | |
| ❑ 434 | Jose Fernandez RC | 1.00 | .45 |
| | Jeff Liefer | | |
| | Chris Truby | | |
| ❑ 435 | Corey Koskie | 1.00 | .45 |
| | Doug Mientkiewicz RC | | |
| | Damon Minor | | |
| ❑ 436 | Roosevelt Brown RC | 1.25 | .55 |
| | Dernell Stenson | | |
| | Vernon Wells | | |
| ❑ 437 | A.J. Burnett RC | 2.00 | .90 |
| | Billy Koch | | |
| | John Nicholson | | |
| ❑ 438 | Matt Belisle | 2.00 | .90 |
| | Matt Roney RC | | |
| ❑ 439 | Austin Kearns | 5.00 | 2.20 |
| | Chris George RC | | |
| ❑ 440 | Nate Bump RC | 1.25 | .55 |
| | Nate Cornejo | | |
| ❑ 441 | Brad Lidge | 1.25 | .55 |
| | Mike Nannini RC | | |
| ❑ 442 | Matt Holliday | 2.00 | .90 |
| | Jeff Winchester RC | | |
| ❑ 443 | Adam Everett | 1.50 | .70 |
| | Chip Ambres RC | | |
| ❑ 444 | Pat Burrell | 12.00 | 5.50 |
| | Eric Valent RC | | |
| ❑ 445 | Roger Clemens SK | 1.50 | .70 |
| ❑ 446 | Kerry Wood SK | .60 | .25 |
| ❑ 447 | Curt Schilling SK | .40 | .18 |
| ❑ 448 | Randy Johnson SK | .60 | .25 |
| ❑ 449 | Pedro Martinez SK | 1.00 | .45 |

| | Card | | |
|---|---|---|---|
| ❑ 450 | Jeff Bagwell AT | 3.00 | 1.35 |
| | Andres Galarraga | | |
| | Mark McGwire | | |
| ❑ 451 | John Olerud AT | .60 | .25 |
| | Jim Thome | | |
| | Tino Martinez | | |
| ❑ 452 | Alex Rodriguez AT | 3.00 | 1.35 |
| | Nomar Garciaparra | | |
| | Derek Jeter | | |
| ❑ 453 | Vinny Castilla AT | 1.50 | .70 |
| | Chipper Jones | | |
| | Scott Rolen | | |
| ❑ 454 | Sammy Sosa AT | 3.00 | 1.35 |
| | Ken Griffey Jr. | | |
| | Juan Gonzalez | | |
| ❑ 455 | Barry Bonds AT | 1.00 | .45 |
| | Manny Ramirez | | |
| | Larry Walker | | |
| ❑ 456 | Frank Thomas AT | 1.50 | .70 |
| | Tim Salmon | | |
| | David Justice | | |
| ❑ 457 | Travis Lee AT | 1.50 | .70 |
| | Todd Helton | | |
| | Ben Grieve | | |
| ❑ 458 | Vladimir Guerrero AT | 1.50 | .70 |
| | Greg Vaughn | | |
| | Bernie Williams | | |
| ❑ 459 | Mike Piazza AT | 1.50 | .70 |
| | Ivan Rodriguez | | |
| | Jason Kendall | | |
| ❑ 460 | Roger Clemens AT | 1.50 | .70 |
| | Kerry Wood | | |
| | Greg Maddux | | |
| ❑ 461A | Sammy Sosa HR 1 | 30.00 | 13.50 |
| ❑ 461B | Sammy Sosa HR 2 | 15.00 | 6.75 |
| ❑ 461C | Sammy Sosa HR 3 | 15.00 | 6.75 |
| ❑ 461D | Sammy Sosa HR 4 | 15.00 | 6.75 |
| ❑ 461E | Sammy Sosa HR 5 | 15.00 | 6.75 |
| ❑ 461F | Sammy Sosa HR 6 | 15.00 | 6.75 |
| ❑ 461G | Sammy Sosa HR 7 | 15.00 | 6.75 |
| ❑ 461H | Sammy Sosa HR 8 | 15.00 | 6.75 |
| ❑ 461I | Sammy Sosa HR 9 | 15.00 | 6.75 |
| ❑ 461J | Sammy Sosa HR 10 | 15.00 | 6.75 |
| ❑ 461K | Sammy Sosa HR 11 | 15.00 | 6.75 |
| ❑ 461L | Sammy Sosa HR 12 | 15.00 | 6.75 |
| ❑ 461M | Sammy Sosa HR 13 | 15.00 | 6.75 |
| ❑ 461N | Sammy Sosa HR 14 | 15.00 | 6.75 |
| ❑ 461O | Sammy Sosa HR 15 | 15.00 | 6.75 |
| ❑ 461P | Sammy Sosa HR 16 | 15.00 | 6.75 |
| ❑ 461Q | Sammy Sosa HR 17 | 15.00 | 6.75 |
| ❑ 461R | Sammy Sosa HR 18 | 15.00 | 6.75 |
| ❑ 461S | Sammy Sosa HR 19 | 15.00 | 6.75 |
| ❑ 461T | Sammy Sosa HR 20 | 15.00 | 6.75 |
| ❑ 461U | Sammy Sosa HR 21 | 15.00 | 6.75 |
| ❑ 461V | Sammy Sosa HR 22 | 15.00 | 6.75 |
| ❑ 461W | Sammy Sosa HR 23 | 15.00 | 6.75 |
| ❑ 461X | Sammy Sosa HR 24 | 15.00 | 6.75 |
| ❑ 461Y | Sammy Sosa HR 25 | 15.00 | 6.75 |
| ❑ 461Z | Sammy Sosa HR 26 | 15.00 | 6.75 |
| ❑ 461AA | Sammy Sosa HR 27 | 15.00 | 6.75 |
| ❑ 461AB | Sammy Sosa HR 28 | 15.00 | 6.75 |
| ❑ 461AC | Sammy Sosa HR 29 | 15.00 | 6.75 |
| ❑ 461AD | Sammy Sosa HR 30 | 15.00 | 6.75 |
| ❑ 461AE | Sammy Sosa HR 31 | 15.00 | 6.75 |
| ❑ 461AF | Sammy Sosa HR 32 | 15.00 | 6.75 |
| ❑ 461AG | Sammy Sosa HR 33 | 15.00 | 6.75 |
| ❑ 461AH | Sammy Sosa HR 34 | 15.00 | 6.75 |
| ❑ 461AI | Sammy Sosa HR 35 | 15.00 | 6.75 |
| ❑ 461AJ | Sammy Sosa HR 36 | 15.00 | 6.75 |
| ❑ 461AK | Sammy Sosa HR 37 | 15.00 | 6.75 |
| ❑ 461AL | Sammy Sosa HR 38 | 15.00 | 6.75 |
| ❑ 461AM | Sammy Sosa HR 39 | 15.00 | 6.75 |
| ❑ 461AN | Sammy Sosa HR 40 | 15.00 | 6.75 |
| ❑ 461AO | Sammy Sosa HR 41 | 15.00 | 6.75 |
| ❑ 461AP | Sammy Sosa HR 42 | 15.00 | 6.75 |
| ❑ 461AR | Sammy Sosa HR 43 | 15.00 | 6.75 |
| ❑ 461AS | Sammy Sosa HR 44 | 15.00 | 6.75 |
| ❑ 461AT | Sammy Sosa HR 45 | 15.00 | 6.75 |
| ❑ 461AU | Sammy Sosa HR 46 | 15.00 | 6.75 |
| ❑ 461AV | Sammy Sosa HR 47 | 15.00 | 6.75 |
| ❑ 461AW | Sammy Sosa HR 48 | 15.00 | 6.75 |
| ❑ 461AX | Sammy Sosa HR 49 | 15.00 | 6.75 |
| ❑ 461AY | Sammy Sosa HR 50 | 15.00 | 6.75 |
| ❑ 461AZ | Sammy Sosa HR 51 | 15.00 | 6.75 |
| ❑ 461BB | Sammy Sosa HR 52 | 15.00 | 6.75 |
| ❑ 461CC | Sammy Sosa HR 53 | 15.00 | 6.75 |
| ❑ 461DD | Sammy Sosa HR 54 | 15.00 | 6.75 |
| ❑ 461EE | Sammy Sosa HR 55 | 15.00 | 6.75 |
| ❑ 461FF | Sammy Sosa HR 56 | 15.00 | 6.75 |
| ❑ 461GG | Sammy Sosa HR 57 | 15.00 | 6.75 |
| ❑ 461HH | Sammy Sosa HR 58 | 15.00 | 6.75 |
| ❑ 461II | Sammy Sosa HR 59 | 15.00 | 6.75 |
| ❑ 461JJ | Sammy Sosa HR 60 | 15.00 | 6.75 |
| ❑ 461KK | Sammy Sosa HR 61 | 30.00 | 13.50 |
| ❑ 461LL | Sammy Sosa HR 62 | 50.00 | 22.00 |
| ❑ 461MM | Sammy Sosa HR 63 | 20.00 | 9.00 |
| ❑ 461NN | Sammy Sosa HR 64 | 20.00 | 9.00 |
| ❑ 461OO | Sammy Sosa HR 65 | 20.00 | 9.00 |
| ❑ 461PP | Sammy Sosa HR 66 | 80.00 | 36.00 |
| ❑ 462 | Checklist | .40 | .18 |
| ❑ 463 | Checklist | .40 | .18 |

## 1999 Topps Chrome Traded

| | | MINT | NRMT |
|---|---|---|---|
| COMP.FACT SET (121) | | 120.00 | 55.00 |
| ❑ T1 | Seth Etherton | 2.00 | .90 |
| ❑ T2 | Mark Harriger RC | 1.50 | .70 |
| ❑ T3 | Matt Wise RC | 1.50 | .70 |
| ❑ T4 | Carlos Hernandez RC | 1.50 | .70 |
| ❑ T5 | Julio Lugo RC | 2.00 | .90 |
| ❑ T6 | Mike Nannini | 2.50 | 1.10 |
| ❑ T7 | Justin Bowles RC | .40 | .18 |
| ❑ T8 | Mark Mulder RC | 4.00 | 1.80 |
| ❑ T9 | Roberto Vaz RC | 1.50 | .70 |
| ❑ T10 | Felipe Lopez RC | 4.00 | 1.80 |
| ❑ T11 | Matt Belisle | 3.00 | 1.35 |
| ❑ T12 | Micah Bowie | .40 | .18 |
| ❑ T13 | Ruben Quevedo RC | 2.00 | .90 |
| ❑ T14 | Jose Garcia RC | 1.50 | .70 |
| ❑ T15 | David Kelton RC | 4.00 | 1.80 |
| ❑ T16 | Phil Norton | 1.50 | .70 |
| ❑ T17 | Corey Patterson RC | [illegible] | [illegible] |
| ❑ T18 | Ron Walker RC | 1.50 | .70 |
| ❑ T19 | Paul Hoover RC | 1.50 | .70 |
| ❑ T20 | Ryan Rupe RC | 2.00 | .90 |
| ❑ T21 | J.D. Closser RC | 2.00 | .90 |
| ❑ T22 | Rob Ryan RC | .40 | .18 |
| ❑ T23 | Steve Colyer RC | 1.50 | .70 |
| ❑ T24 | Bubba Crosby RC | 1.50 | .70 |
| ❑ T25 | Luke Prokopec RC | 3.00 | 1.35 |
| ❑ T26 | Matt Blank RC | 1.50 | .70 |
| ❑ T27 | Josh McKinley | 2.00 | .90 |
| ❑ T28 | Nate Bump | 1.50 | .70 |
| ❑ T29 | Giuseppe Chiaramonte RC | 2.50 | 1.10 |
| ❑ T30 | Arturo McDowell | 2.00 | .90 |
| ❑ T31 | Tony Torcato | 4.00 | 1.80 |
| ❑ T32 | Dave Roberts RC | .40 | .18 |
| ❑ T33 | C.C. Sabathia RC | 8.00 | 3.60 |
| ❑ T34 | Sean Spencer RC | 1.50 | .70 |
| ❑ T35 | Chip Ambres | 2.50 | 1.10 |
| ❑ T36 | A.J. Burnett | 3.00 | 1.35 |
| ❑ T37 | Mo Bruce RC | 1.50 | .70 |
| ❑ T38 | Jason Tyner | 3.00 | 1.35 |
| ❑ T39 | Mamon Tucker | 2.00 | .90 |
| ❑ T40 | Sean Burroughs RC | 12.00 | 5.50 |
| ❑ T41 | Kevin Eberwein RC | 2.00 | .90 |
| ❑ T42 | Junior Herndon RC | 1.50 | .70 |
| ❑ T43 | Bryan Wolff RC | .40 | .18 |
| ❑ T44 | Pat Burrell | 15.00 | 6.75 |
| ❑ T45 | Eric Valent | 4.00 | 1.80 |
| ❑ T46 | Carlos Pena RC | 8.00 | 3.60 |

| | Card | Player | Mint | Nrmt |
|---|---|---|---|---|
| ❑ | T47 | Mike Zywica | .40 | .18 |
| ❑ | T48 | Adam Everett | 2.50 | 1.10 |
| ❑ | T49 | Juan Pena RC | 1.50 | .70 |
| ❑ | T50 | Adam Dunn RC | 6.00 | 2.70 |
| ❑ | T51 | Austin Kearns | 8.00 | 3.60 |
| ❑ | T52 | Jacobo Sequea RC | 1.50 | .70 |
| ❑ | T53 | Choo Freeman | 2.50 | 1.10 |
| ❑ | T54 | Jeff Winchester | 3.00 | 1.35 |
| ❑ | T55 | Matt Burch | 1.50 | .70 |
| ❑ | T56 | Chris George | 3.00 | 1.35 |
| ❑ | T57 | Scott Mullen RC | .40 | .18 |
| ❑ | T58 | Kit Pellow | 1.50 | .70 |
| ❑ | T59 | Mark Quinn RC | 5.00 | 2.20 |
| ❑ | T60 | Nate Cornejo | 2.00 | .90 |
| ❑ | T61 | Ryan Mills | 1.50 | .70 |
| ❑ | T62 | Kevin Beirne RC | .40 | .18 |
| ❑ | T63 | Kip Wells RC | 3.00 | 1.35 |
| ❑ | T64 | Juan Rivera RC | 4.00 | 1.80 |
| ❑ | T65 | Alfonso Soriano RC | 6.00 | 2.70 |
| ❑ | T66 | Josh Hamilton RC | 20.00 | 9.00 |
| ❑ | T67 | Josh Girdley RC | 3.00 | 1.35 |
| ❑ | T68 | Kyle Snyder RC | 1.50 | .70 |
| ❑ | T69 | Mike Paradis RC | 1.50 | .70 |
| ❑ | T70 | Jason Jennings RC | 2.50 | 1.10 |
| ❑ | T71 | David Walling RC | 2.00 | .90 |
| ❑ | T72 | Omar Ortiz RC | 1.50 | .70 |
| ❑ | T73 | Jay Gehrke RC | 1.50 | .70 |
| ❑ | T74 | Casey Burns RC | 1.50 | .70 |
| ❑ | T75 | Carl Crawford RC | 5.00 | 2.20 |
| ❑ | T76 | Reggie Sanders | .40 | .18 |
| ❑ | T77 | Will Clark | 1.50 | .70 |
| ❑ | T78 | David Wells | .60 | .25 |
| ❑ | T79 | Paul Konerko | .60 | .25 |
| ❑ | T80 | Armando Benitez | .40 | .18 |
| ❑ | T81 | Brant Brown | .40 | .18 |
| ❑ | T82 | Mo Vaughn | .60 | .25 |
| ❑ | T83 | Jose Canseco | 2.00 | .90 |
| ❑ | T84 | Albert Belle | 1.00 | .45 |
| ❑ | T85 | Dean Palmer | .60 | .25 |
| ❑ | T86 | Greg Vaughn | .60 | .25 |
| ❑ | T87 | Mark Clark | .40 | .18 |
| ❑ | T88 | Pat Meares | .40 | .18 |
| ❑ | T89 | Eric Davis | .60 | .25 |
| ❑ | T90 | Brian Giles | .60 | .25 |
| ❑ | T91 | Jeff Brantley | .40 | .18 |
| ❑ | T92 | Bret Boone | .60 | .25 |
| ❑ | T93 | Ron Gant | .60 | .25 |
| ❑ | T94 | Mike Cameron | .40 | .18 |
| ❑ | T95 | Charles Johnson | .60 | .25 |
| ❑ | T96 | Denny Neagle | .40 | .18 |
| ❑ | T97 | Brian Hunter | .40 | .18 |
| ❑ | T98 | Jose Hernandez | .40 | .18 |
| ❑ | T99 | Rick Aguilera | .40 | .18 |
| ❑ | T100 | Tony Batista | .60 | .25 |
| ❑ | T101 | Roger Cedeno | .40 | .18 |
| ❑ | T102 | Creighton Gubanich RC | .40 | .18 |
| ❑ | T103 | Tim Belcher | .40 | .18 |
| ❑ | T104 | Bruce Aven | .40 | .18 |
| ❑ | T105 | Brian Daubach RC | 3.00 | 1.35 |
| ❑ | T106 | Ed Sprague | .40 | .18 |
| ❑ | T107 | Michael Tucker | .40 | .18 |
| ❑ | T108 | Homer Bush | .40 | .18 |
| ❑ | T109 | Armando Reynoso | .40 | .18 |
| ❑ | T110 | Brook Fordyce | .40 | .18 |
| ❑ | T111 | Matt Mantei | .40 | .18 |
| ❑ | T112 | Dave Mlicki | .40 | .18 |
| ❑ | T113 | Kenny Rogers | .40 | .18 |
| ❑ | T114 | Livan Hernandez | .40 | .18 |
| ❑ | T115 | Butch Huskey | .40 | .18 |
| ❑ | T116 | David Segui | .40 | .18 |
| ❑ | T117 | Darryl Hamilton | .40 | .18 |
| ❑ | T118 | Terry Mulholland | .40 | .18 |
| ❑ | T119 | Randy Velarde | .40 | .18 |
| ❑ | T120 | Bill Taylor | .40 | .18 |
| ❑ | T121 | Kevin Appier | .60 | .25 |

## 2000 Topps Chrome

| | MINT | NRMT |
|---|---|---|
| COMPLETE SET (478) | 400.00 | 180.00 |
| COMPLETE SERIES 1 (239) | 200.00 | 90.00 |
| COMPLETE SERIES 2 (240) | 200.00 | 90.00 |
| MCGWIRE MM SET (5) | 80.00 | 36.00 |
| AARON MM SET (5) | 40.00 | 18.00 |
| RIPKEN MM SET (5) | 60.00 | 27.00 |
| BOGGS MM SET (5) | 20.00 | 9.00 |

| | MINT | NRMT |
|---|---|---|
| GWYNN MM SET (5) | 30.00 | 13.50 |
| GRIFFEY MM SET (5) | 60.00 | 27.00 |
| BONDS MM SET (5) | 25.00 | 11.00 |
| SOSA MM SET (5) | 40.00 | 18.00 |
| JETER MM SET (5) | 60.00 | 27.00 |
| A.ROD MM SET (5) | 50.00 | 22.00 |

| | Card | Player | Mint | Nrmt |
|---|---|---|---|---|
| ❑ | 1 | Mark McGwire | 6.00 | 2.70 |
| ❑ | 2 | Tony Gwynn | 3.00 | 1.35 |
| ❑ | 3 | Wade Boggs | 2.00 | .90 |
| ❑ | 4 | Cal Ripken | 6.00 | 2.70 |
| ❑ | 5 | Matt Williams | 1.00 | .45 |
| ❑ | 6 | Jay Buhner | .60 | .25 |
| ❑ | 7 | Does Not Exist | | .18 |
| ❑ | 8 | Jeff Conine | .40 | .18 |
| ❑ | 9 | Todd Greene | .40 | .18 |
| ❑ | 10 | Mike Lieberthal | .60 | .25 |
| ❑ | 11 | Steve Avery | .40 | .18 |
| ❑ | 12 | Bret Saberhagen | .60 | .25 |
| ❑ | 13 | Magglio Ordonez | .60 | .25 |
| ❑ | 14 | Brad Radke | .60 | .25 |
| ❑ | 15 | Derek Jeter | 6.00 | 2.70 |
| ❑ | 16 | Javy Lopez | .60 | .25 |
| ❑ | 17 | Russ Davis | .40 | .18 |
| ❑ | 18 | Armando Benitez | .60 | .25 |
| ❑ | 19 | B.J. Surhoff | .60 | .25 |
| ❑ | 20 | Darryl Kile | .60 | .25 |
| ❑ | 21 | Mark Lewis | .40 | .18 |
| ❑ | 22 | Mike Williams | .40 | .18 |
| ❑ | 23 | Mark McLemore | .40 | .18 |
| ❑ | 24 | Sterling Hitchcock | .40 | .18 |
| ❑ | 25 | Darin Erstad | 1.50 | .70 |
| ❑ | 26 | Ricky Gutierrez | .40 | .18 |
| ❑ | 27 | John Jaha | .40 | .18 |
| ❑ | 28 | Homer Bush | .40 | .18 |
| ❑ | 29 | Darrin Fletcher | .40 | .18 |
| ❑ | 30 | Mark Grace | 1.50 | .70 |
| ❑ | 31 | Fred McGriff | 1.00 | .45 |
| ❑ | 32 | Omar Daal | .40 | .18 |
| ❑ | 33 | Eric Karros | .60 | .25 |
| ❑ | 34 | Orlando Cabrera | .40 | .18 |
| ❑ | 35 | J.T. Snow | .60 | .25 |
| ❑ | 36 | Luis Castillo | .60 | .25 |
| ❑ | 37 | Rey Ordonez | .40 | .18 |
| ❑ | 38 | Bob Abreu | .60 | .25 |
| ❑ | 39 | Warren Morris | .40 | .18 |
| ❑ | 40 | Juan Gonzalez | 1.50 | .70 |
| ❑ | 41 | Mike Lansing | .40 | .18 |
| ❑ | 42 | Chili Davis | .60 | .25 |
| ❑ | 43 | Dean Palmer | .60 | .25 |
| ❑ | 44 | Hank Aaron | 4.00 | 1.80 |
| ❑ | 45 | Jeff Bagwell | 2.00 | .90 |
| ❑ | 46 | Jose Valentin | .40 | .18 |
| ❑ | 47 | Shannon Stewart | .60 | .25 |
| ❑ | 48 | Kent Bottenfield | .40 | .18 |
| ❑ | 49 | Jeff Shaw | .40 | .18 |
| ❑ | 50 | Sammy Sosa | 3.00 | 1.35 |
| ❑ | 51 | Randy Johnson | 2.00 | .90 |
| ❑ | 52 | Benny Agbayani | .40 | .18 |
| ❑ | 53 | Dante Bichette | .60 | .25 |
| ❑ | 54 | Pete Harnisch | .40 | .18 |
| ❑ | 55 | Frank Thomas | 3.00 | 1.35 |
| ❑ | 56 | Jorge Posada | .60 | .25 |
| ❑ | 57 | Todd Walker | .40 | .18 |
| ❑ | 58 | Juan Encarnacion | .60 | .25 |
| ❑ | 59 | Mike Sweeney | .60 | .25 |
| ❑ | 60 | Pedro Martinez | 2.00 | .90 |
| ❑ | 61 | Lee Stevens | .40 | .18 |
| ❑ | 62 | Brian Giles | .60 | .25 |
| ❑ | 63 | Chad Ogea | .40 | .18 |
| ❑ | 64 | Ivan Rodriguez | 2.00 | .90 |
| ❑ | 65 | Roger Cedeno | .40 | .18 |
| ❑ | 66 | David Justice | 1.00 | .45 |
| ❑ | 67 | Steve Trachsel | .40 | .18 |
| ❑ | 68 | Eli Marrero | .40 | .18 |
| ❑ | 69 | Dave Nilsson | .40 | .18 |
| ❑ | 70 | Ken Caminiti | .60 | .25 |
| ❑ | 71 | Tim Raines | .60 | .25 |
| ❑ | 72 | Brian Jordan | .60 | .25 |
| ❑ | 73 | Jeff Blauser | .40 | .18 |
| ❑ | 74 | Bernard Gilkey | .40 | .18 |
| ❑ | 75 | John Flaherty | .40 | .18 |
| ❑ | 76 | Brent Mayne | .40 | .18 |
| ❑ | 77 | Jose Vidro | .40 | .18 |
| ❑ | 78 | David Bell | .40 | .18 |
| ❑ | 79 | Bruce Aven | .40 | .18 |
| ❑ | 80 | John Olerud | .60 | .25 |
| ❑ | 81 | Pokey Reese | .60 | .25 |
| ❑ | 82 | Woody Williams | .40 | .18 |
| ❑ | 83 | Ed Sprague | .40 | .18 |
| ❑ | 84 | Joe Girardi | .40 | .18 |
| ❑ | 85 | Barry Larkin | 1.50 | .70 |
| ❑ | 86 | Mike Caruso | .40 | .18 |
| ❑ | 87 | Bobby Higginson | .40 | .18 |
| ❑ | 88 | Roberto Kelly | .40 | .18 |
| ❑ | 89 | Edgar Martinez | 1.00 | .45 |
| ❑ | 90 | Mark Kotsay | .40 | .18 |
| ❑ | 91 | Paul Sorrento | .40 | .18 |
| ❑ | 92 | Eric Young | .40 | .18 |
| ❑ | 93 | Carlos Delgado | 1.50 | .70 |
| ❑ | 94 | Troy Glaus | 2.00 | .90 |
| ❑ | 95 | Ben Grieve | .60 | .25 |
| ❑ | 96 | Jose Lima | .40 | .18 |
| ❑ | 97 | Garret Anderson | .60 | .25 |
| ❑ | 98 | Luis Gonzalez | .60 | .25 |
| ❑ | 99 | Carl Pavano | .40 | .18 |
| ❑ | 100 | Alex Rodriguez | 5.00 | 2.20 |
| ❑ | 101 | Preston Wilson | .60 | .25 |
| ❑ | 102 | Ron Gant | .60 | .25 |
| ❑ | 103 | Brady Anderson | .60 | .25 |
| ❑ | 104 | Rickey Henderson | 2.00 | .90 |
| ❑ | 105 | Gary Sheffield | 1.50 | .70 |
| ❑ | 106 | Mickey Morandini | .40 | .18 |
| ❑ | 107 | Jim Edmonds | 1.50 | .70 |
| ❑ | 108 | Kris Benson | .60 | .25 |
| ❑ | 109 | Adrian Beltre | .60 | .25 |
| ❑ | 110 | Alex Fernandez | .40 | .18 |
| ❑ | 111 | Dan Wilson | .40 | .18 |
| ❑ | 112 | Mark Clark | .40 | .18 |
| ❑ | 113 | Greg Vaughn | .60 | .25 |
| ❑ | 114 | Neifi Perez | .40 | .18 |
| ❑ | 115 | Paul O'Neill | .60 | .25 |
| ❑ | 116 | Jermaine Dye | .60 | .25 |
| ❑ | 117 | Todd Jones | .40 | .18 |
| ❑ | 118 | Terry Steinbach | .40 | .18 |
| ❑ | 119 | Greg Norton | .40 | .18 |
| ❑ | 120 | Curt Schilling | .60 | .25 |
| ❑ | 121 | Todd Zeile | .60 | .25 |
| ❑ | 122 | Edgardo Alfonzo | .60 | .25 |
| ❑ | 123 | Ryan McGuire | .40 | .18 |
| ❑ | 124 | Rich Aurilia | .40 | .18 |
| ❑ | 125 | John Smoltz | .60 | .25 |
| ❑ | 126 | Bob Wickman | .40 | .18 |
| ❑ | 127 | Richard Hidalgo | .60 | .25 |
| ❑ | 128 | Chuck Finley | .60 | .25 |
| ❑ | 129 | Billy Wagner | .40 | .18 |
| ❑ | 130 | Todd Hundley | .40 | .18 |
| ❑ | 131 | Dwight Gooden | .60 | .25 |
| ❑ | 132 | Russ Ortiz | .60 | .25 |
| ❑ | 133 | Mike Lowell | .40 | .18 |
| ❑ | 134 | Reggie Sanders | .40 | .18 |
| ❑ | 135 | John Valentin | .40 | .18 |
| ❑ | 136 | Brad Ausmus | .40 | .18 |
| ❑ | 137 | Chad Kreuter | .40 | .18 |
| ❑ | 138 | David Cone | .60 | .25 |
| ❑ | 139 | Brook Fordyce | .40 | .18 |
| ❑ | 140 | Roberto Alomar | 1.50 | .70 |
| ❑ | 141 | Charles Nagy | .40 | .18 |
| ❑ | 142 | Brian Hunter | .40 | .18 |
| ❑ | 143 | Mike Mussina | 1.50 | .70 |
| ❑ | 144 | Robin Ventura | 1.00 | .45 |
| ❑ | 145 | Kevin Brown | 1.00 | .45 |
| ❑ | 146 | Pat Hentgen | .40 | .18 |
| ❑ | 147 | Ryan Klesko | .60 | .25 |

| | | | |
|---|---|---|---|
| ❑ 148 | Derek Bell | .40 | .18 |
| ❑ 149 | Andy Sheets | .40 | .18 |
| ❑ 150 | Larry Walker | .60 | .25 |
| ❑ 151 | Scott Williamson | .40 | .18 |
| ❑ 152 | Jose Offerman | .40 | .18 |
| ❑ 153 | Doug Mientkiewicz | .40 | .18 |
| ❑ 154 | John Snyder RC | 1.25 | .55 |
| ❑ 155 | Sandy Alomar Jr. | .40 | .18 |
| ❑ 156 | Joe Nathan | .40 | .18 |
| ❑ 157 | Lance Johnson | .40 | .18 |
| ❑ 158 | Odalis Perez | .40 | .18 |
| ❑ 159 | Hideo Nomo | 1.50 | .70 |
| ❑ 160 | Steve Finley | .60 | .25 |
| ❑ 161 | Dave Martinez | .40 | .18 |
| ❑ 162 | Matt Walbeck | .40 | .18 |
| ❑ 163 | Bill Spiers | .40 | .18 |
| ❑ 164 | Fernando Tatis | .60 | .25 |
| ❑ 165 | Kenny Lofton | .60 | .25 |
| ❑ 166 | Paul Byrd | .40 | .18 |
| ❑ 167 | Aaron Sele | .40 | .18 |
| ❑ 168 | Eddie Taubensee | .40 | .18 |
| ❑ 169 | Reggie Jefferson | .40 | .18 |
| ❑ 170 | Roger Clemens | 3.00 | 1.35 |
| ❑ 171 | Francisco Cordova | .40 | .18 |
| ❑ 172 | Mike Bordick | .40 | .18 |
| ❑ 173 | Wally Joyner | .60 | .25 |
| ❑ 174 | Marvin Benard | .40 | .18 |
| ❑ 175 | Jason Kendall | .60 | .25 |
| ❑ 176 | Mike Stanley | .40 | .18 |
| ❑ 177 | Chad Allen | .40 | .18 |
| ❑ 178 | Carlos Beltran | .60 | .25 |
| ❑ 179 | Deivi Cruz | .40 | .18 |
| ❑ 180 | Chipper Jones | 4.00 | 1.80 |
| ❑ 181 | Vladimir Guerrero | 2.50 | 1.10 |
| ❑ 182 | Dave Burba | .40 | .18 |
| ❑ 183 | Tom Goodwin | .40 | .18 |
| ❑ 184 | Brian Daubach | .40 | .18 |
| ❑ 185 | Jay Bell | .60 | .25 |
| ❑ 186 | Roy Halladay | .40 | .18 |
| ❑ 187 | Miguel Tejada | .60 | .25 |
| ❑ 188 | Armando Rios | .40 | .18 |
| ❑ 189 | Fernando Vina | .40 | .18 |
| ❑ 190 | Eric Davis | .00 | .25 |
| ❑ 191 | Henry Rodriguez | .40 | .18 |
| ❑ 192 | Joe McEwing | .40 | .18 |
| ❑ 193 | Jeff Kent | 1.00 | .45 |
| ❑ 194 | Mike Jackson | .40 | .18 |
| ❑ 195 | Mike Morgan | .40 | .18 |
| ❑ 196 | Jeff Montgomery | .40 | .18 |
| ❑ 197 | Jeff Zimmerman | .40 | .18 |
| ❑ 198 | Tony Fernandez | .40 | .18 |
| ❑ 199 | Jason Giambi | 1.50 | .70 |
| ❑ 200 | Jose Canseco | 2.00 | .90 |
| ❑ 201 | Alex Gonzalez | .40 | .18 |
| ❑ 202 | Jack Cust | .60 | .25 |
| | Mike Colangelo | | |
| | Dee Brown | | |
| ❑ 203 | Felipe Lopez | .60 | .25 |
| | Alfonso Soriano | | |
| | Pablo Ozuna | | |
| ❑ 204 | Erubiel Durazo | 2.50 | 1.10 |
| | Pat Burrell | | |
| | Nick Johnson | | |
| ❑ 205 | John Sneed RC | 1.00 | .45 |
| | Kip Wells | | |
| | Matt Blank | | |
| ❑ 206 | Josh Kalinowski | 1.00 | .45 |
| | Michael Tejera | | |
| | Chris Mears RC | | |
| ❑ 207 | Roosevelt Brown | 2.50 | 1.10 |
| | Corey Patterson | | |
| | Lance Berkman | | |
| ❑ 208 | Kit Pellow | .40 | .18 |
| | Kevin Barker | | |
| | Russ Branyan | | |
| ❑ 209 | B.J. Garbe | 2.50 | 1.10 |
| | Larry Bigbie RC | | |
| ❑ 210 | Eric Munson | 4.00 | 1.80 |
| | Bobby Bradley RC | | |
| ❑ 211 | Josh Girdley | .60 | .25 |
| | Kyle Snyder | | |
| ❑ 212 | Chance Caple RC | 1.50 | .70 |
| | Jason Jennings | | |
| ❑ 213 | Ryan Christianson | 2.00 | .90 |
| | Brett Myers RC | | |
| ❑ 214 | Jason Stumm | 1.50 | .70 |
| | Rob Purvis RC | | |
| ❑ 215 | David Walling | .60 | .25 |
| | Mike Paradis | | |
| ❑ 216 | Omar Ortiz | .60 | .25 |
| | Jay Gehrke | | |
| ❑ 217 | David Cone HL | .60 | .25 |
| ❑ 218 | Jose Jimenez HL | .40 | .18 |
| ❑ 219 | Chris Singleton HL | .40 | .18 |
| ❑ 220 | Fernando Tatis HL | .40 | .18 |
| ❑ 221 | Todd Helton HL | 1.50 | .70 |
| ❑ 222 | Kevin Millwood DIV | .40 | .18 |
| ❑ 223 | Todd Pratt DIV | .40 | .18 |
| ❑ 224 | Orlando Hernandez DIV | .40 | .18 |
| ❑ 225 | Pedro Martinez DIV | 1.00 | .45 |
| ❑ 226 | Tom Glavine LCS | .60 | .25 |
| ❑ 227 | Bernie Williams LCS | .60 | .25 |
| ❑ 228 | Mariano Rivera WS | .40 | .18 |
| ❑ 229 | Tony Gwynn 20CB | 3.00 | 1.35 |
| ❑ 230 | Wade Boggs 20CB | 2.00 | .90 |
| ❑ 231 | Lance Johnson CB | .40 | .18 |
| ❑ 232 | Mark McGwire 20CB | 6.00 | 2.70 |
| ❑ 233 | Rickey Henderson 20CB | 2.00 | .90 |
| ❑ 234 | Rickey Henderson 20CB | 2.00 | .90 |
| ❑ 235 | Roger Clemens 20CB | 3.00 | 1.35 |
| ❑ 236A | M.McGwire MM 1st HR | 20.00 | 9.00 |
| ❑ 236B | M.McGwire MM 1987 ROY | 20.00 | 9.00 |
| ❑ 236C | M.McGwire MM 62nd HR | 20.00 | 9.00 |
| ❑ 236D | M.McGwire MM 70th HR | 20.00 | 9.00 |
| ❑ 236E | M.McGwire MM 500th HR | 20.00 | 9.00 |
| ❑ 237A | H.Aaron MM 1st Career HR | 10.00 | 4.50 |
| ❑ 237B | H.Aaron MM 1957 MVP | 10.00 | 4.50 |
| ❑ 237C | H.Aaron MM 3000th Hit | 10.00 | 4.50 |
| ❑ 237D | H.Aaron MM 715th HR | 10.00 | 4.50 |
| ❑ 237E | H.Aaron MM 755th HR | 10.00 | 4.50 |
| ❑ 238A | C.Ripken MM 1982 ROY | 15.00 | 6.75 |
| ❑ 238B | C.Ripken MM 1991 MVP | 15.00 | 6.75 |
| ❑ 238C | C.Ripken MM 2131 Game | 15.00 | 6.75 |
| ❑ 238D | C.Ripken MM Streak Ends | 15.00 | 6.75 |
| ❑ 238E | C.Ripken MM 400th HR | 15.00 | 6.75 |
| ❑ 239A | W.Boggs MM 1983 Batting | 5.00 | 2.20 |
| ❑ 239B | W.Boggs MM 1988 Batting | 5.00 | 2.20 |
| ❑ 239C | W.Boggs MM 2000th Hit | 5.00 | 2.20 |
| ❑ 239D | W.Boggs MM 1996 Champs | 5.00 | 2.20 |
| ❑ 239E | W.Boggs MM 3000th Hit | 5.00 | 2.20 |
| ❑ 240A | T.Gwynn MM 1984 Batting | 8.00 | 3.60 |
| ❑ 240B | T.Gwynn MM 1984 NLCS | 8.00 | 3.60 |
| ❑ 240C | T.Gwynn MM 1995 Batting | 8.00 | 3.60 |
| ❑ 240D | T.Gwynn MM 1998 NLCS | 8.00 | 3.60 |
| ❑ 240E | T.Gwynn MM 3000th Hit | 8.00 | 3.60 |
| ❑ 241 | Tom Glavine | 1.50 | .70 |
| ❑ 242 | David Wells | .60 | .25 |
| ❑ 243 | Kevin Appier | .40 | .18 |
| ❑ 244 | Troy Percival | .40 | .18 |
| ❑ 245 | Ray Lankford | .60 | .25 |
| ❑ 246 | Marquis Grissom | .40 | .18 |
| ❑ 247 | Randy Winn | .40 | .18 |
| ❑ 248 | Miguel Batista | .40 | .18 |
| ❑ 249 | Darren Dreifort | .40 | .18 |
| ❑ 250 | Barry Bonds | 2.00 | .90 |
| ❑ 251 | Harold Baines | .60 | .25 |
| ❑ 252 | Cliff Floyd | .60 | .25 |
| ❑ 253 | Freddy Garcia | .60 | .25 |
| ❑ 254 | Kenny Rogers | .40 | .18 |
| ❑ 255 | Ben Davis | .40 | .18 |
| ❑ 256 | Charles Johnson | .60 | .25 |
| ❑ 257 | Bubba Trammell | .40 | .18 |
| ❑ 258 | Desi Relaford | .40 | .18 |
| ❑ 259 | Al Martin | .40 | .18 |
| ❑ 260 | Andy Pettitte | .60 | .25 |
| ❑ 261 | Carlos Lee | .60 | .25 |
| ❑ 262 | Matt Lawton | .40 | .18 |
| ❑ 263 | Andy Fox | .40 | .18 |
| ❑ 264 | Chan Ho Park | .60 | .25 |
| ❑ 265 | Billy Koch | .60 | .25 |
| ❑ 266 | Dave Roberts | .40 | .18 |
| ❑ 267 | Carl Everett | .60 | .25 |
| ❑ 268 | Orel Hershiser | .60 | .25 |
| ❑ 269 | Trot Nixon | .60 | .25 |
| ❑ 270 | Rusty Greer | .60 | .25 |
| ❑ 271 | Will Clark | 1.50 | .70 |
| ❑ 272 | Quilvio Veras | .40 | .18 |
| ❑ 273 | Rico Brogna | .40 | .18 |
| ❑ 274 | Devon White | .40 | .18 |
| ❑ 275 | Tim Hudson | 1.50 | .70 |
| ❑ 276 | Mike Hampton | .60 | .25 |
| ❑ 277 | Miguel Cairo | .40 | .18 |
| ❑ 278 | Darren Oliver | .40 | .18 |
| ❑ 279 | Jeff Cirillo | .60 | .25 |
| ❑ 280 | Al Leiter | .40 | .18 |
| ❑ 281 | Shane Andrews | .40 | .18 |
| ❑ 282 | Carlos Febles | .40 | .18 |
| ❑ 283 | Pedro Astacio | .40 | .18 |
| ❑ 284 | Juan Guzman | .40 | .18 |
| ❑ 285 | Orlando Hernandez | .60 | .25 |
| ❑ 286 | Paul Konerko | .60 | .25 |
| ❑ 287 | Tony Clark | .40 | .18 |
| ❑ 288 | Aaron Boone | .40 | .18 |
| ❑ 289 | Ismael Valdes | .40 | .18 |
| ❑ 290 | Moises Alou | .60 | .25 |
| ❑ 291 | Kevin Tapani | .40 | .18 |
| ❑ 292 | John Franco | .60 | .25 |
| ❑ 293 | Todd Zeile | .60 | .25 |
| ❑ 294 | Jason Schmidt | .40 | .18 |
| ❑ 295 | Johnny Damon | .60 | .25 |
| ❑ 296 | Scott Brosius | .60 | .25 |
| ❑ 297 | Travis Fryman | .60 | .25 |
| ❑ 298 | Jose Vizcaino | .40 | .18 |
| ❑ 299 | Eric Chavez | .60 | .25 |
| ❑ 300 | Mike Piazza | 5.00 | 2.20 |
| ❑ 301 | Matt Clement | .40 | .18 |
| ❑ 302 | Cristian Guzman | .40 | .18 |
| ❑ 303 | C.J. Nitkowski | .40 | .18 |
| ❑ 304 | Michael Tucker | .40 | .18 |
| ❑ 305 | Brett Tomko | .40 | .18 |
| ❑ 306 | Mike Lansing | .40 | .18 |
| ❑ 307 | Eric Owens | .40 | .18 |
| ❑ 308 | Livan Hernandez | .40 | .18 |
| ❑ 309 | Rondell White | .60 | .25 |
| ❑ 310 | Todd Stottlemyre | .40 | .18 |
| ❑ 311 | Chris Carpenter | .40 | .18 |
| ❑ 312 | Ken Hill | .40 | .18 |
| ❑ 313 | Mark Loretta | .40 | .18 |
| ❑ 314 | John Rocker | .60 | .25 |
| ❑ 315 | Richie Sexson | .60 | .25 |
| ❑ 316 | Ruben Mateo | .60 | .25 |
| ❑ 317 | Joe Randa | .40 | .18 |
| ❑ 318 | Mike Sirotka | .40 | .18 |
| ❑ 319 | Jose Rosado | .40 | .18 |
| ❑ 320 | Matt Mantei | .40 | .18 |
| ❑ 321 | Kevin Millwood | .60 | .25 |
| ❑ 322 | Gary DiSarcina | .40 | .18 |
| ❑ 323 | Dustin Hermanson | .40 | .18 |
| ❑ 324 | Mike Stanton | .40 | .18 |
| ❑ 325 | Kirk Rueter | .40 | .18 |
| ❑ 326 | Damian Miller | .40 | .18 |
| ❑ 327 | Doug Glanville | .40 | .18 |
| ❑ 328 | Scott Rolen | 1.50 | .70 |
| ❑ 329 | Ray Durham | .60 | .25 |
| ❑ 330 | Butch Huskey | .40 | .18 |
| ❑ 331 | Mariano Rivera | .60 | .25 |
| ❑ 332 | Darren Lewis | .40 | .18 |
| ❑ 333 | Mike Timlin | .40 | .18 |
| ❑ 334 | Mark Grudzielanek | .40 | .18 |
| ❑ 335 | Mike Cameron | .40 | .18 |
| ❑ 336 | Kelvim Escobar | .40 | .18 |
| ❑ 337 | Bret Boone | .40 | .18 |
| ❑ 338 | Mo Vaughn | .60 | .25 |
| ❑ 339 | Craig Biggio | 1.00 | .45 |
| ❑ 340 | Michael Barrett | .40 | .18 |
| ❑ 341 | Marlon Anderson | .40 | .18 |
| ❑ 342 | Bobby Jones | .40 | .18 |
| ❑ 343 | John Halama | .40 | .18 |
| ❑ 344 | Todd Ritchie | .40 | .18 |
| ❑ 345 | Chuck Knoblauch | .60 | .25 |
| ❑ 346 | Rick Reed | .40 | .18 |
| ❑ 347 | Kelly Stinnett | .40 | .18 |
| ❑ 348 | Tim Salmon | .60 | .25 |
| ❑ 349 | A.J. Hinch | .40 | .18 |
| ❑ 350 | Jose Cruz Jr. | .60 | .25 |
| ❑ 351 | Roberto Hernandez | .40 | .18 |
| ❑ 352 | Edgar Renteria | .40 | .18 |
| ❑ 353 | Jose Hernandez | .40 | .18 |
| ❑ 354 | Brad Fullmer | .60 | .25 |
| ❑ 355 | Trevor Hoffman | .60 | .25 |
| ❑ 356 | Troy O'Leary | .40 | .18 |
| ❑ 357 | Justin Thompson | .40 | .18 |
| ❑ 358 | Kevin Young | .40 | .18 |
| ❑ 359 | Hideki Irabu | .40 | .18 |
| ❑ 360 | Jim Thome | 1.00 | .45 |
| ❑ 361 | Steve Karsay | .40 | .18 |
| ❑ 362 | Octavio Dotel | .40 | .18 |
| ❑ 363 | Omar Vizquel | .60 | .25 |

❑ 364 Raul Mondesi .60 .25
❑ 365 Shane Reynolds .40 .18
❑ 366 Bartolo Colon .60 .25
❑ 367 Chris Widger .40 .18
❑ 368 Gabe Kapler .60 .25
❑ 369 Bill Simas .40 .18
❑ 370 Tino Martinez .60 .25
❑ 371 John Thomson .40 .18
❑ 372 Delino DeShields .40 .18
❑ 373 Carlos Perez .40 .18
❑ 374 Eddie Perez .40 .18
❑ 375 Jeromy Burnitz .60 .25
❑ 376 Jimmy Haynes .40 .18
❑ 377 Travis Lee .40 .18
❑ 378 Darryl Hamilton .40 .18
❑ 379 Jamie Moyer .40 .18
❑ 380 Alex Gonzalez .40 .18
❑ 381 John Wetteland .60 .25
❑ 382 Vinny Castilla .60 .25
❑ 383 Jeff Suppan .40 .18
❑ 384 Jim Leyritz .40 .18
❑ 385 Robb Nen .40 .18
❑ 386 Wilson Alvarez .40 .18
❑ 387 Andres Galarraga 1.00 .45
❑ 388 Mike Remlinger .40 .18
❑ 389 Geoff Jenkins .60 .25
❑ 390 Matt Stairs .40 .18
❑ 391 Bill Mueller .40 .18
❑ 392 Mike Lowell .40 .18
❑ 393 Andy Ashby .40 .18
❑ 394 Ruben Rivera .40 .18
❑ 395 Todd Helton 2.00 .90
❑ 396 Bernie Williams 1.50 .70
❑ 397 Royce Clayton .40 .18
❑ 398 Manny Ramirez 2.00 .90
❑ 399 Kerry Wood .60 .25
❑ 400 Ken Griffey Jr. 6.00 2.70
❑ 401 Enrique Wilson .40 .18
❑ 402 Joey Hamilton .40 .18
❑ 403 Shawn Estes .40 .18
❑ 404 Ugueth Urbina .40 .18
❑ 405 Albert Belle 1.00 .45
❑ 406 Rick Helling .60 .25
❑ 407 Steve Parris .40 .18
❑ 408 Eric Milton .40 .18
❑ 409 Dave Mlicki .40 .18
❑ 410 Shawn Green 1.50 .70
❑ 411 Jaret Wright .40 .18
❑ 412 Tony Womack .40 .18
❑ 413 Vernon Wells .60 .25
❑ 414 Ron Belliard .40 .18
❑ 415 Ellis Burks .60 .25
❑ 416 Scott Erickson .40 .18
❑ 417 Rafael Palmeiro 1.50 .70
❑ 418 Damion Easley .40 .18
❑ 419 Jamey Wright .40 .18
❑ 420 Corey Koskie .40 .18
❑ 421 Bobby Howry .40 .18
❑ 422 Ricky Ledee .40 .18
❑ 423 Dmitri Young .60 .25
❑ 424 Sidney Ponson .40 .18
❑ 425 Greg Maddux 4.00 1.80
❑ 426 Jose Guillen .40 .18
❑ 427 Jon Lieber .40 .18
❑ 428 Andy Benes .40 .18
❑ 429 Randy Velarde .40 .18
❑ 430 Sean Casey .60 .25
❑ 431 Torii Hunter .40 .18
❑ 432 Ryan Rupe .40 .18
❑ 433 David Segui .40 .18
❑ 434 Todd Pratt .40 .18
❑ 435 Nomar Garciaparra 5.00 2.20
❑ 436 Denny Neagle .40 .18
❑ 437 Ron Coomer .40 .18
❑ 438 Chris Singleton .60 .25
❑ 439 Tony Batista .60 .25
❑ 440 Andruw Jones 1.50 .70
❑ 441 Aubrey Huff 1.50 .70
Sean Burroughs
Adam Piatt
❑ 442 Rafael Furcal 4.00 1.80
Travis Dawkins
Jason Dellaero
❑ 443 Mike Lamb RC 1.50 .70
Joe Crede
Wilton Veras
❑ 444 Julio Zuleta RC 1.00 .45
Jorge Toca
Dernell Stenson
❑ 445 Garry Maddox Jr. RC 1.00 .45
Gary Matthews Jr.
Tim Raines Jr.
❑ 446 Mark Mulder .60 .25
C.C. Sabathia
Matt Riley
❑ 447 Scott Downs RC 1.00 .45
Chris George
Matt Belisle
❑ 448 Doug Mirabelli .40 .18
Ben Petrick
Jayson Werth
❑ 449 Josh Hamilton 2.50 1.10
Corey Myers RC
❑ 450 Ben Christensen RC 2.00 .90
Richard Stahl
❑ 451 Ben Sheets RC 15.00 6.75
Barry Zito
❑ 452 Kurt Ainsworth 2.00 .90
Ty Howington RC
❑ 453 Vince Faison RC 6.00 2.70
Rick Asadoorian
❑ 454 Keith Reed RC 1.50 .70
Jeff Heaverlo
❑ 455 Mike MacDougal 2.00 .90
Brad Baker RC
❑ 456 Mark McGwire SH 3.00 1.35
❑ 457 Cal Ripken SH 3.00 1.35
❑ 458 Wade Boggs SH 1.00 .45
❑ 459 Tony Gwynn SH 1.50 .70
❑ 460 Jesse Orosco SH .40 .18
❑ 461 Larry Walker 1.50 .70
Nomar Garciaparra LL
❑ 462 Ken Griffey Jr. 2.50 1.10
Mark McGwire LL
❑ 463 Manny Ramirez 1.50 .70
Mark McGwire LL
❑ 464 Pedro Martinez 1.00 .45
Randy Johnson LL
❑ 465 Pedro Martinez 1.00 .45
Randy Johnson LL
❑ 466 Derek Jeter 2.00 .90
Luis Gonzalez LL
❑ 467 Larry Walker .60 .25
Manny Ramirez LL
❑ 468 Tony Gwynn 20CB 3.00 1.35
❑ 469 Mark McGwire 20CB 6.00 2.70
❑ 470 Frank Thomas 20CB 3.00 1.35
❑ 471 Harold Baines 20CB .60 .25
❑ 472 Roger Clemens 20CB 3.00 1.35
❑ 473 John Franco 20CB .60 .25
❑ 474 John Franco 20CB .60 .25
❑ 475A K.Griffey Jr. MM 350th HR 15.00 6.75
❑ 475B K.Griffey Jr. MM 1997 MVP 15.00 6.75
❑ 475C K.Griffey Jr. MM HR Dad 15.00 6.75
❑ 475D K.Griffey Jr. MM 1992 AS MVP 15.00 6.75
❑ 475E K.Griffey Jr. MM 50 HR 1997 15.00 6.75
❑ 476A B.Bonds MM 400HR/400SB 6.00 2.70
❑ 476B B.Bonds MM 40HR/40SB 6.00 2.70
❑ 476C B.Bonds MM 1993 MVP 6.00 2.70
❑ 476D B.Bonds MM 1990 MVP 6.00 2.70
❑ 476E B.Bonds MM 1992 MVP 6.00 2.70
❑ 477A S.Sosa MM 20 HR June 10.00 4.50
❑ 477B S.Sosa MM 66 HR 1998 10.00 4.50
❑ 477C S.Sosa MM 60 HR 1999 10.00 4.50
❑ 477D S.Sosa MM 1998 MVP 10.00 4.50
❑ 477E S.Sosa MM HR's 61/62 10.00 4.50
❑ 478A D.Jeter MM 1996 ROY 15.00 6.75
❑ 478B D.Jeter MM Wins 1999 WS 15.00 6.75
❑ 478C D.Jeter MM Wins 1998 WS 15.00 6.75
❑ 478D D.Jeter MM Wins 1996 WS 15.00 6.75
❑ 478E D.Jeter MM 17 GM Hit Streak 15.00 6.75
❑ 479A A.Rodriguez MM 40HR/40SB 12.00 5.50
❑ 479B A.Rodriguez MM 100th HR 12.00 5.50
❑ 479C A.Rodriguez MM 1996 POY 12.00 5.50
❑ 479D A.Rodriguez MM Wins 1 Million 12.00 5.50
❑ 479E A.Rodriguez MM 1996 Batting Leader 12.00 5.50
❑ NNO Mark McGwire 85 Reprint 8.00 3.60

## 2000 Topps Chrome Traded

| | MINT | NRMT |
|---|---|---|
| COMP.FACT.SET (135) | 100.00 | 45.00 |
| MINOR STARS | .60 | .25 |
| SEMISTARS | 1.00 | .45 |
| UNLISTED STARS | 1.50 | .70 |

❑ T1 Mike MacDougal .60 .25
❑ T2 Andy Tracy RC 1.00 .45
❑ T3 Brandon Phillips RC 2.00 .90
❑ T4 Brandon Inge RC 3.00 1.35
❑ T5 Robbie Morrison RC 1.00 .45
❑ T6 Josh Pressley RC 2.00 .90
❑ T7 Todd Moser RC 1.00 .45
❑ T8 Rob Purvis .60 .25
❑ T9 Chance Caple .60 .25
❑ T10 Ben Sheets 5.00 2.20
❑ T11 Russ Jacobson RC 2.00 .90
❑ T12 Brian Cole RC 4.00 1.80
❑ T13 Brad Baker 3.00 1.35
❑ T14 Alex Cintron RC 2.50 1.10
❑ T15 Lyle Overbay RC 4.00 1.80
❑ T16 Mike Edwards RC 1.00 .45
❑ T17 Sean McGowan RC 2.50 1.10
❑ T18 Jose Molina .40 .18
❑ T19 Marcos Castillo RC 1.00 .45
❑ T20 Josue Espada RC 1.00 .45
❑ T21 Alex Gordon RC 2.50 1.10
❑ T22 Rob Pugmire RC 1.00 .45
❑ T23 Jason Stumm 2.00 .90
❑ T24 Ty Howington 2.00 .90
❑ T25 Brett Myers 2.00 .90
❑ T26 Maicer Izturis RC 1.00 .45
❑ T27 John McDonald .40 .18
❑ T28 Wilfredo Rodriguez RC 2.50 1.10
❑ T29 Carlos Zambrano RC 3.00 1.35
❑ T30 Alejandro Diaz RC 2.00 .90
❑ T31 Geraldo Guzman RC 1.00 .45
❑ T32 J.R. House RC 10.00 4.50
❑ T33 Elvin Nina RC 1.00 .45
❑ T34 Juan Pierre RC 2.50 1.10
❑ T35 Ben Johnson RC 4.00 1.80
❑ T36 Jeff Bailey RC 1.00 .45
❑ T37 Miguel Olivo RC 2.00 .90
❑ T38 Francisco Rodriguez RC 2.00 .90
❑ T39 Tony Pena Jr. RC 2.50 1.10
❑ T40 Miguel Cabrera RC 2.00 .90
❑ T41 Asdrubal Oropeza RC 2.00 .90
❑ T42 Junior Zamora RC 1.00 .45
❑ T43 Jovanny Cedeno RC 2.50 1.10
❑ T44 John Sneed .60 .25
❑ T45 Josh Kalinowski .60 .25
❑ T46 Mike Young RC 2.00 .90
❑ T47 Rico Washington RC 1.50 .70
❑ T48 Chad Durbin RC 1.00 .45
❑ T49 Junior Brignac RC 2.00 .90
❑ T50 Carlos Hernandez RC 2.00 .90
❑ T51 Cesar Izturis RC 2.00 .90
❑ T52 Oscar Salazar RC 2.00 .90
❑ T53 Pat Strange RC 4.00 1.80
❑ T54 Rick Asadoorian 6.00 2.70
❑ T55 Keith Reed 2.00 .90
❑ T56 Leo Estrella RC 1.00 .45
❑ T57 Wascar Serrano RC 2.00 .90
❑ T58 Richard Gomez RC 2.50 1.10
❑ T59 Ramon Santiago RC 2.50 1.10

| Card | Player | Mint | NrMt |
|---|---|---|---|
| T60 | Jovanny Sosa RC | 2.50 | 1.10 |
| T61 | Aaron Rowand RC | 3.00 | 1.35 |
| T62 | Junior Guerrero RC | 1.00 | .45 |
| T63 | Luis Terrero RC | 2.00 | .90 |
| T64 | Brian Sanches RC | 1.00 | .45 |
| T65 | Scott Sobkowiak RC | 2.00 | .90 |
| T66 | Gary Majewski RC | 2.00 | .90 |
| T67 | Barry Zito | 5.00 | 2.20 |
| T68 | Ryan Christianson | 3.00 | 1.35 |
| T69 | Cristian Guerrero RC | 10.00 | 4.50 |
| T70 | Tomas De La Rosa RC | 1.00 | .45 |
| T71 | Andrew Beinbrink RC | 1.00 | .45 |
| T72 | Ryan Knox RC | 2.00 | .90 |
| T73 | Alex Graman RC | 3.00 | 1.35 |
| T74 | Juan Guzman RC | 1.00 | .45 |
| T75 | Ruben Salazar RC | 3.00 | 1.35 |
| T76 | Luis Matos RC | 3.00 | 1.35 |
| T77 | Tony Mota RC | 1.00 | .45 |
| T78 | Doug Davis | .40 | .18 |
| T79 | Ben Christensen | 3.00 | 1.35 |
| T80 | Mike Lamb | 2.50 | 1.10 |
| T81 | Adrian Gonzalez RC | 8.00 | 3.60 |
| T82 | Mike Stodolka RC | 2.50 | 1.10 |
| T83 | Adam Johnson RC | 3.00 | 1.35 |
| T84 | Matt Wheatland RC | 4.00 | 1.80 |
| T85 | Corey Smith RC | 3.00 | 1.35 |
| T86 | Rocco Baldelli RC | 5.00 | 2.20 |
| T87 | Keith Bucktrot RC | 2.00 | .90 |
| T88 | Adam Wainwright RC | 4.00 | 1.80 |
| T89 | Scott Thorman RC | 2.00 | .90 |
| T90 | Tripper Johnson RC | 2.50 | 1.10 |
| T91 | Jim Edmonds | 1.50 | .70 |
| T92 | Masato Yoshii | .40 | .18 |
| T93 | Adam Kennedy | .60 | .25 |
| T94 | Darryl Kile | .60 | .25 |
| T95 | Mark McLemore | .40 | .18 |
| T96 | Ricky Gutierrez | .40 | .18 |
| T97 | Juan Gonzalez | 1.50 | .70 |
| T98 | Melvin Mora | .40 | .18 |
| T99 | Dante Bichette | .60 | .25 |
| T100 | Lee Stevens | .40 | .18 |
| T101 | Roger Cedeno | .40 | .18 |
| T102 | John Olerud | .60 | .25 |
| T103 | Eric Young | .40 | .18 |
| T104 | Mickey Morandini | .40 | .18 |
| T105 | Travis Lee | .40 | .18 |
| T106 | Greg Vaughn | .60 | .25 |
| T107 | Todd Zeile | .60 | .25 |
| T108 | Chuck Finley | .60 | .25 |
| T109 | Ismael Valdes | .40 | .18 |
| T110 | Reggie Sanders | .40 | .18 |
| T111 | Pat Hentgen | .40 | .18 |
| T112 | Ryan Klesko | .60 | .25 |
| T113 | Derek Bell | .40 | .18 |
| T114 | Hideo Nomo | 1.50 | .70 |
| T115 | Aaron Sele | .60 | .25 |
| T116 | Fernando Vina | .40 | .18 |
| T117 | Wally Joyner | .60 | .25 |
| T118 | Brian Hunter | .40 | .18 |
| T119 | Joe Girardi | .40 | .18 |
| T120 | Omar Daal | .40 | .18 |
| T121 | Brook Fordyce | .40 | .18 |
| T122 | Jose Valentin | .40 | .18 |
| T123 | Curt Schilling | .60 | .25 |
| T124 | B.J. Surhoff | .60 | .25 |
| T125 | Henry Rodriguez | .40 | .18 |
| T126 | Mike Bordick | .40 | .18 |
| T127 | David Justice | 1.00 | .45 |
| T128 | Charles Johnson | .60 | .25 |
| T129 | Will Clark | 1.50 | .70 |
| T130 | Dwight Gooden | .60 | .25 |
| T131 | David Segui | .40 | .18 |
| T132 | Denny Neagle | .60 | .25 |
| T133 | Jose Canseco | 2.00 | .90 |
| T134 | Bruce Chen | .60 | .25 |
| T135 | Jason Bere | .40 | .18 |

## 1996 Topps Gallery

| | MINT | NRMT |
|---|---|---|
| COMPLETE SET (180) | 40.00 | 18.00 |
| COMMON CARD (1-180) | .25 | .11 |

| Card | Player | Mint | NrMt |
|---|---|---|---|
| 1 | Tom Glavine | 1.00 | .45 |
| 2 | Carlos Baerga | .25 | .11 |
| 3 | Dante Bichette | .50 | .23 |
| 4 | Mark Langston | .25 | .11 |
| 5 | Ray Lankford | .50 | .23 |
| 6 | Moises Alou | .50 | .23 |
| 7 | Marquis Grissom | .25 | .11 |
| 8 | Ramon Martinez | .25 | .11 |
| 9 | Steve Finley | .50 | .23 |
| 10 | Todd Hundley | .25 | .11 |
| 11 | Brady Anderson | .50 | .23 |
| 12 | John Valentin | .25 | .11 |
| 13 | Heathcliff Slocumb | .25 | .11 |
| 14 | Ruben Sierra | .25 | .11 |
| 15 | Jeff Conine | .25 | .11 |
| 16 | Jay Buhner | .50 | .23 |
| 17 | Sammy Sosa | 2.00 | .90 |
| 18 | Doug Drabek | .25 | .11 |
| 19 | Jose Mesa | .25 | .11 |
| 20 | Jeff King | .25 | .11 |
| 21 | Mickey Tettleton | .25 | .11 |
| 22 | Jeff Montgomery | .25 | .11 |
| 23 | Alex Fernandez | .25 | .11 |
| 24 | Greg Vaughn | .50 | .23 |
| 25 | Chuck Finley | .50 | .23 |
| 26 | Terry Steinbach | .25 | .11 |
| 27 | Rod Beck | .25 | .11 |
| 28 | Jack McDowell | .25 | .11 |
| 29 | Mark Wohlers | .25 | .11 |
| 30 | Len Dykstra | .50 | .23 |
| 31 | Bernie Williams | 1.00 | .45 |
| 32 | Travis Fryman | .50 | .23 |
| 33 | Jose Canseco | 1.25 | .55 |
| 34 | Ken Caminiti | .50 | .23 |
| 35 | Devon White | .50 | .23 |
| 36 | Bobby Bonilla | .50 | .23 |
| 37 | Paul Sorrento | .25 | .11 |
| 38 | Ryne Sandberg | 1.25 | .55 |
| 39 | Derek Bell | .25 | .11 |
| 40 | Bobby Jones | .25 | .11 |
| 41 | J.T. Snow | .50 | .23 |
| 42 | Denny Neagle | .50 | .23 |
| 43 | Tim Wakefield | .25 | .11 |
| 44 | Andres Galarraga | .50 | .23 |
| 45 | David Segui | .25 | .11 |
| 46 | Lee Smith | .50 | .23 |
| 47 | Mel Rojas | .25 | .11 |
| 48 | John Franco | .50 | .23 |
| 49 | Pete Schourek | .25 | .11 |
| 50 | John Wetteland | .50 | .23 |
| 51 | Paul Molitor | 1.00 | .45 |
| 52 | Ivan Rodriguez | 1.25 | .55 |
| 53 | Chris Hoiles | .25 | .11 |
| 54 | Mike Greenwell | .25 | .11 |
| 55 | Orel Hershiser | .50 | .23 |
| 56 | Brian McRae | .25 | .11 |
| 57 | Geronimo Berroa | .25 | .11 |
| 58 | Craig Biggio | .50 | .23 |
| 59 | David Justice | .50 | .23 |
| 60 | Lance Johnson | .25 | .11 |
| 61 | Andy Ashby | .25 | .11 |
| 62 | Randy Myers | .25 | .11 |
| 63 | Gregg Jefferies | .25 | .11 |
| 64 | Kevin Appier | .50 | .23 |
| 65 | Rick Aguilera | .25 | .11 |
| 66 | Shane Reynolds | .25 | .11 |
| 67 | John Smoltz | .50 | .23 |
| 68 | Ron Gant | .25 | .11 |
| 69 | Eric Karros | .50 | .23 |
| 70 | Jim Thome | .50 | .23 |
| 71 | Terry Pendleton | .50 | .23 |
| 72 | Kenny Rogers | .25 | .11 |
| 73 | Robin Ventura | .50 | .23 |
| 74 | Dave Nilsson | .25 | .11 |
| 75 | Brian Jordan | .50 | .23 |
| 76 | Glenallen Hill | .25 | .11 |
| 77 | Greg Colbrunn | .25 | .11 |
| 78 | Roberto Alomar | 1.00 | .45 |
| 79 | Rickey Henderson | 1.25 | .55 |
| 80 | Carlos Garcia | .25 | .11 |
| 81 | Dean Palmer | .50 | .23 |
| 82 | Mike Stanley | .25 | .11 |
| 83 | Hal Morris | .25 | .11 |
| 84 | Wade Boggs | 1.25 | .55 |
| 85 | Chad Curtis | .25 | .11 |
| 86 | Roberto Hernandez | .25 | .11 |
| 87 | John Olerud | .50 | .23 |
| 88 | Frank Castillo | .25 | .11 |
| 89 | Rafael Palmeiro | 1.00 | .45 |
| 90 | Trevor Hoffman | .50 | .23 |
| 91 | Marty Cordova | .25 | .11 |
| 92 | Hideo Nomo | 1.00 | .45 |
| 93 | Johnny Damon | .50 | .23 |
| 94 | Bill Pulsipher | .25 | .11 |
| 95 | Garret Anderson | .50 | .23 |
| 96 | Ray Durham | .50 | .23 |
| 97 | Ricky Bottalico | .25 | .11 |
| 98 | Carlos Perez | .25 | .11 |
| 99 | Troy Percival | .25 | .11 |
| 100 | Chipper Jones | 2.50 | 1.10 |
| 101 | Esteban Loaiza | .25 | .11 |
| 102 | John Mabry | .25 | .11 |
| 103 | Jon Nunnally | .25 | .11 |
| 104 | Andy Pettitte | .50 | .23 |
| 105 | Lyle Mouton | .25 | .11 |
| 106 | Jason Isringhausen | .50 | .23 |
| 107 | Brian L.Hunter | .25 | .11 |
| 108 | Quilvio Veras | .25 | .11 |
| 109 | Jim Edmonds | 1.00 | .45 |
| 110 | Ryan Klesko | .50 | .23 |
| 111 | Pedro Martinez | 1.25 | .55 |
| 112 | Joey Hamilton | .25 | .11 |
| 113 | Vinny Castilla | .50 | .23 |
| 114 | Alex Gonzalez | .25 | .11 |
| 115 | Raul Mondesi | .50 | .23 |
| 116 | Rondell White | .50 | .23 |
| 117 | Dan Miceli | .25 | .11 |
| 118 | Tom Goodwin | .25 | .11 |
| 119 | Bret Boone | .50 | .23 |
| 120 | Shawn Green | 1.00 | .45 |
| 121 | Jeff Cirillo | .50 | .23 |
| 122 | Rico Brogna | .25 | .11 |
| 123 | Chris Gomez | .25 | .11 |
| 124 | Ismael Valdes | .25 | .11 |
| 125 | Javy Lopez | .50 | .23 |
| 126 | Manny Ramirez | 1.25 | .55 |
| 127 | Paul Wilson | .25 | .11 |
| 128 | Billy Wagner | .25 | .11 |
| 129 | Eric Owens | .25 | .11 |
| 130 | Todd Greene | .25 | .11 |
| 131 | Karim Garcia | .25 | .11 |
| 132 | Jimmy Haynes | .25 | .11 |
| 133 | Michael Tucker | .25 | .11 |
| 134 | John Wasdin | .25 | .11 |
| 135 | Brooks Kieschnick | .25 | .11 |
| 136 | Alex Ochoa | .25 | .11 |
| 137 | Ariel Prieto | .25 | .11 |
| 138 | Tony Clark | .25 | .11 |
| 139 | Mark Loretta | .25 | .11 |
| 140 | Rey Ordonez | .50 | .23 |
| 141 | Chris Snopek | .25 | .11 |
| 142 | Roger Cedeno | .25 | .11 |
| 143 | Derek Jeter | 4.00 | 1.80 |
| 144 | Jeff Suppan | .25 | .11 |
| 145 | Greg Maddux | 2.50 | 1.10 |
| 146 | Ken Griffey Jr. | 4.00 | 1.80 |
| 147 | Tony Gwynn | 2.00 | .90 |
| 148 | Darren Daulton | .50 | .23 |
| 149 | Will Clark | 1.00 | .45 |
| 150 | Mo Vaughn | .50 | .23 |
| 151 | Reggie Sanders | .25 | .11 |
| 152 | Kirby Puckett | 2.50 | 1.10 |
| 153 | Paul O'Neill | .50 | .23 |
| 154 | Tim Salmon | .50 | .23 |
| 155 | Mark McGwire | 4.00 | 1.80 |
| 156 | Barry Bonds | 1.50 | .70 |
| 157 | Albert Belle | .50 | .23 |

| Card | Mint | NrMt |
|---|---|---|
| ❑ 158 Edgar Martinez | .50 | .23 |
| ❑ 159 Mike Mussina | 1.00 | .45 |
| ❑ 160 Cecil Fielder | .50 | .23 |
| ❑ 161 Kenny Lofton | .50 | .23 |
| ❑ 162 Randy Johnson | 1.25 | .55 |
| ❑ 163 Juan Gonzalez | 1.00 | .45 |
| ❑ 164 Jeff Bagwell | 1.25 | .55 |
| ❑ 165 Joe Carter | .50 | .23 |
| ❑ 166 Mike Piazza | 3.00 | 1.35 |
| ❑ 167 Eddie Murray | 1.00 | .45 |
| ❑ 168 Cal Ripken | 4.00 | 1.80 |
| ❑ 169 Barry Larkin | 1.00 | .45 |
| ❑ 170 Chuck Knoblauch | .50 | .23 |
| ❑ 171 Chili Davis | .50 | .23 |
| ❑ 172 Fred McGriff | .50 | .23 |
| ❑ 173 Matt Williams | .50 | .23 |
| ❑ 174 Roger Clemens | 2.00 | .90 |
| ❑ 175 Frank Thomas | 2.00 | .90 |
| ❑ 176 Dennis Eckersley | .50 | .23 |
| ❑ 177 Gary Sheffield | 1.00 | .45 |
| ❑ 178 David Cone | .50 | .23 |
| ❑ 179 Larry Walker | .50 | .23 |
| ❑ 180 Mark Grace | 1.00 | .45 |
| ❑ NNO M. Mantle Masterpiece | 20.00 | 9.00 |

## 1997 Topps Gallery

| | MINT | NRMT |
|---|---|---|
| COMPLETE SET (180) | 50.00 | 22.00 |
| ❑ 1 Paul Molitor | 1.00 | .45 |
| ❑ 2 Devon White | .40 | .18 |
| ❑ 3 Andres Galarraga | .60 | .25 |
| ❑ 4 Cal Ripken | 4.00 | 1.80 |
| ❑ 5 Tony Gwynn | 2.00 | .90 |
| ❑ 6 Mike Stanley | .25 | .11 |
| ❑ 7 Orel Hershiser | .40 | .18 |
| ❑ 8 Jose Canseco | 1.25 | .55 |
| ❑ 9 Chili Davis | .40 | .18 |
| ❑ 10 Harold Baines | .40 | .18 |
| ❑ 11 Rickey Henderson | 1.25 | .55 |
| ❑ 12 Darryl Strawberry | .40 | .18 |
| ❑ 13 Todd Worrell | .25 | .11 |
| ❑ 14 Cecil Fielder | .40 | .18 |
| ❑ 15 Gary Gaetti | .40 | .18 |
| ❑ 16 Bobby Bonilla | .40 | .18 |
| ❑ 17 Will Clark | 1.00 | .45 |
| ❑ 18 Kevin Brown | .40 | .18 |
| ❑ 19 Tom Glavine | 1.00 | .45 |
| ❑ 20 Wade Boggs | 1.25 | .55 |
| ❑ 21 Edgar Martinez | .60 | .25 |
| ❑ 22 Lance Johnson | .25 | .11 |
| ❑ 23 Gregg Jefferies | .25 | .11 |
| ❑ 24 Bip Roberts | .25 | .11 |
| ❑ 25 Tony Phillips | .25 | .11 |
| ❑ 26 Greg Maddux | 2.50 | 1.10 |
| ❑ 27 Mickey Tettleton | .25 | .11 |
| ❑ 28 Terry Steinbach | .25 | .11 |
| ❑ 29 Ryne Sandberg | 1.25 | .55 |
| ❑ 30 Wally Joyner | .40 | .18 |
| ❑ 31 Joe Carter | .40 | .18 |
| ❑ 32 Ellis Burks | .40 | .18 |
| ❑ 33 Fred McGriff | .60 | .25 |
| ❑ 34 Barry Larkin | 1.00 | .45 |
| ❑ 35 John Franco | .40 | .18 |
| ❑ 36 Rafael Palmeiro | 1.00 | .45 |
| ❑ 37 Mark McGwire | 4.00 | 1.80 |
| ❑ 38 Ken Caminiti | .40 | .18 |
| ❑ 39 David Cone | .40 | .18 |
| ❑ 40 Julio Franco | .40 | .18 |
| ❑ 41 Roger Clemens | 2.00 | .90 |
| ❑ 42 Barry Bonds | 1.50 | .70 |
| ❑ 43 Dennis Eckersley | .40 | .18 |
| ❑ 44 Eddie Murray | 1.00 | .45 |
| ❑ 45 Paul O'Neill | .40 | .18 |
| ❑ 46 Craig Biggio | .60 | .25 |
| ❑ 47 Roberto Alomar | 1.00 | .45 |
| ❑ 48 Mark Grace | 1.00 | .45 |
| ❑ 49 Matt Williams | .60 | .25 |
| ❑ 50 Jay Buhner | .40 | .18 |
| ❑ 51 John Smoltz | .40 | .18 |
| ❑ 52 Randy Johnson | 1.25 | .55 |
| ❑ 53 Ramon Martinez | .25 | .11 |
| ❑ 54 Curt Schilling | .40 | .18 |
| ❑ 55 Gary Sheffield | 1.00 | .45 |
| ❑ 56 Jack McDowell | .25 | .11 |
| ❑ 57 Brady Anderson | .40 | .18 |
| ❑ 58 Dante Bichette | .40 | .18 |
| ❑ 59 Ron Gant | .25 | .11 |
| ❑ 60 Alex Fernandez | .25 | .11 |
| ❑ 61 Moises Alou | .40 | .18 |
| ❑ 62 Travis Fryman | .40 | .18 |
| ❑ 63 Dean Palmer | .40 | .18 |
| ❑ 64 Todd Hundley | .25 | .11 |
| ❑ 65 Jeff Brantley | .25 | .11 |
| ❑ 66 Bernard Gilkey | .25 | .11 |
| ❑ 67 Geronimo Berroa | .25 | .11 |
| ❑ 68 John Wetteland | .40 | .18 |
| ❑ 69 Robin Ventura | .40 | .18 |
| ❑ 70 Ray Lankford | .40 | .18 |
| ❑ 71 Kevin Appier | .40 | .18 |
| ❑ 72 Larry Walker | .40 | .18 |
| ❑ 73 Juan Gonzalez | 1.00 | .45 |
| ❑ 74 Jeff King | .25 | .11 |
| ❑ 75 Greg Vaughn | .40 | .18 |
| ❑ 76 Steve Finley | .40 | .18 |
| ❑ 77 Brian McRae | .25 | .11 |
| ❑ 78 Paul Sorrento | .25 | .11 |
| ❑ 79 Ken Griffey Jr. | 4.00 | 1.80 |
| ❑ 80 Omar Vizquel | .40 | .18 |
| ❑ 81 Jose Mesa | .25 | .11 |
| ❑ 82 Albert Belle | .60 | .25 |
| ❑ 83 Glenallen Hill | .25 | .11 |
| ❑ 84 Sammy Sosa | 2.00 | .90 |
| ❑ 85 Andy Benes | .25 | .11 |
| ❑ 86 David Justice | .60 | .25 |
| ❑ 87 Marquis Grissom | .25 | .11 |
| ❑ 88 John Olerud | .40 | .18 |
| ❑ 89 Tino Martinez | .40 | .18 |
| ❑ 90 Frank Thomas | 2.00 | .90 |
| ❑ 91 Raul Mondesi | .40 | .18 |
| ❑ 92 Steve Trachsel | .25 | .11 |
| ❑ 93 Jim Edmonds | 1.00 | .45 |
| ❑ 94 Rusty Greer | .40 | .18 |
| ❑ 95 Joey Hamilton | .25 | .11 |
| ❑ 96 Ismael Valdes | .25 | .11 |
| ❑ 97 Dave Nilsson | .25 | .11 |
| ❑ 98 John Jaha | .25 | .11 |
| ❑ 99 Alex Gonzalez | .25 | .11 |
| ❑ 100 Javy Lopez | .40 | .18 |
| ❑ 101 Ryan Klesko | .40 | .18 |
| ❑ 102 Tim Salmon | .40 | .18 |
| ❑ 103 Bernie Williams | 1.00 | .45 |
| ❑ 104 Roberto Hernandez | .25 | .11 |
| ❑ 105 Chuck Knoblauch | .40 | .18 |
| ❑ 106 Mike Lansing | .25 | .11 |
| ❑ 107 Vinny Castilla | .40 | .18 |
| ❑ 108 Reggie Sanders | .25 | .11 |
| ❑ 109 Mo Vaughn | .40 | .18 |
| ❑ 110 Rondell White | .40 | .18 |
| ❑ 111 Ivan Rodriguez | 1.25 | .55 |
| ❑ 112 Mike Mussina | 1.00 | .45 |
| ❑ 113 Carlos Baerga | .25 | .11 |
| ❑ 114 Jeff Conine | .25 | .11 |
| ❑ 115 Jim Thome | .60 | .25 |
| ❑ 116 Manny Ramirez | 1.25 | .55 |
| ❑ 117 Kenny Lofton | .40 | .18 |
| ❑ 118 Wilson Alvarez | .25 | .11 |
| ❑ 119 Eric Karros | .40 | .18 |
| ❑ 120 Robb Nen | .25 | .11 |
| ❑ 121 Mark Wohlers | .25 | .11 |
| ❑ 122 Ed Sprague | .25 | .11 |
| ❑ 123 Pat Hentgen | .25 | .11 |
| ❑ 124 Juan Guzman | .25 | .11 |
| ❑ 125 Derek Bell | .25 | .11 |
| ❑ 126 Jeff Bagwell | 1.25 | .55 |
| ❑ 127 Eric Young | .25 | .11 |
| ❑ 128 John Valentin | .25 | .11 |
| ❑ 129 Al Martin UER<br>Picture of Javy Lopez | .25 | .11 |
| ❑ 130 Trevor Hoffman | .40 | .18 |
| ❑ 131 Henry Rodriguez | .25 | .11 |
| ❑ 132 Pedro Martinez | 1.25 | .55 |
| ❑ 133 Mike Piazza | 3.00 | 1.35 |
| ❑ 134 Brian Jordan | .40 | .18 |
| ❑ 135 Jose Valentin | .25 | .11 |
| ❑ 136 Jeff Cirillo | .40 | .18 |
| ❑ 137 Chipper Jones | 2.50 | 1.10 |
| ❑ 138 Ricky Bottalico | .25 | .11 |
| ❑ 139 Hideo Nomo | 1.00 | .45 |
| ❑ 140 Troy Percival | .25 | .11 |
| ❑ 141 Rey Ordonez | .25 | .11 |
| ❑ 142 Edgar Renteria | .40 | .18 |
| ❑ 143 Luis Castillo | .40 | .18 |
| ❑ 144 Vladimir Guerrero | 2.00 | .90 |
| ❑ 145 Jeff D'Amico | .25 | .11 |
| ❑ 146 Andruw Jones | 1.25 | .55 |
| ❑ 147 Darin Erstad | 1.25 | .55 |
| ❑ 148 Bob Abreu | .40 | .18 |
| ❑ 149 Carlos Delgado | 1.00 | .45 |
| ❑ 150 Jamey Wright | .25 | .11 |
| ❑ 151 Nomar Garciaparra | 3.00 | 1.35 |
| ❑ 152 Jason Kendall | .40 | .18 |
| ❑ 153 Jermaine Allensworth | .25 | .11 |
| ❑ 154 Scott Rolen | 1.00 | .45 |
| ❑ 155 Rocky Coppinger | .25 | .11 |
| ❑ 156 Paul Wilson | .25 | .11 |
| ❑ 157 Garret Anderson | .40 | .18 |
| ❑ 158 Mariano Rivera | .40 | .18 |
| ❑ 159 Ruben Rivera | .25 | .11 |
| ❑ 160 Andy Pettitte | .40 | .18 |
| ❑ 161 Derek Jeter | 4.00 | 1.80 |
| ❑ 162 Neifi Perez | .25 | .11 |
| ❑ 163 Ray Durham | .40 | .18 |
| ❑ 164 James Baldwin | .40 | .18 |
| ❑ 165 Marty Cordova | .25 | .11 |
| ❑ 166 Tony Clark | .25 | .11 |
| ❑ 167 Michael Tucker | .25 | .11 |
| ❑ 168 Mike Sweeney | .40 | .18 |
| ❑ 169 Johnny Damon | .40 | .18 |
| ❑ 170 Jermaine Dye | .40 | .18 |
| ❑ 171 Alex Ochoa | .25 | .11 |
| ❑ 172 Jason Isringhausen | .25 | .11 |
| ❑ 173 Mark Grudzielanek | .25 | .11 |
| ❑ 174 Jose Rosado | .25 | .11 |
| ❑ 175 Todd Hollandsworth | .25 | .11 |
| ❑ 176 Alan Benes | .25 | .11 |
| ❑ 177 Jason Giambi | 1.00 | .45 |
| ❑ 178 Billy Wagner | .25 | .11 |
| ❑ 179 Justin Thompson | .25 | .11 |
| ❑ 180 Todd Walker | .25 | .11 |

## 1998 Topps Gallery

| | MINT | NRMT |
|---|---|---|
| COMPLETE SET (150) | 55.00 | 25.00 |
| ❑ 1 Andruw Jones | 1.00 | .45 |
| ❑ 2 Fred McGriff | .60 | .25 |
| ❑ 3 Wade Boggs | 1.25 | .55 |
| ❑ 4 Pedro Martinez | 1.25 | .55 |
| ❑ 5 Matt Williams | .60 | .25 |

- ❑ 6 Wilson Alvarez .25 .11
- ❑ 7 Henry Rodriguez .25 .11
- ❑ 8 Jay Bell .40 .18
- ❑ 9 Marquis Grissom .25 .11
- ❑ 10 Darryl Kile .40 .18
- ❑ 11 Chuck Knoblauch .40 .18
- ❑ 12 Kenny Lofton .40 .18
- ❑ 13 Quinton McCracken .25 .11
- ❑ 14 Andres Galarraga .60 .25
- ❑ 15 Brian Jordan .40 .18
- ❑ 16 Mike Lansing .25 .11
- ❑ 17 Travis Fryman .40 .18
- ❑ 18 Tony Saunders .25 .11
- ❑ 19 Moises Alou .40 .18
- ❑ 20 Travis Lee .40 .18
- ❑ 21 Garret Anderson .40 .18
- ❑ 22 Ken Caminiti .40 .18
- ❑ 23 Pedro Astacio .25 .11
- ❑ 24 Ellis Burks .40 .18
- ❑ 25 Albert Belle .60 .25
- ❑ 26 Alan Benes .25 .11
- ❑ 27 Jay Buhner .40 .18
- ❑ 28 Derek Bell .25 .11
- ❑ 29 Jeromy Burnitz .40 .18
- ❑ 30 Kevin Appier .40 .18
- ❑ 31 Jeff Cirillo .40 .18
- ❑ 32 Bernard Gilkey .25 .11
- ❑ 33 David Cone .40 .18
- ❑ 34 Jason Dickson .25 .11
- ❑ 35 Jose Cruz Jr. .40 .18
- ❑ 36 Marty Cordova .25 .11
- ❑ 37 Ray Durham .40 .18
- ❑ 38 Jaret Wright .25 .11
- ❑ 39 Billy Wagner .25 .11
- ❑ 40 Roger Clemens 2.00 .90
- ❑ 41 Juan Gonzalez 1.00 .45
- ❑ 42 Jeremi Gonzalez .25 .11
- ❑ 43 Mark Grudzielanek .25 .11
- ❑ 44 Tom Glavine 1.00 .45
- ❑ 45 Barry Larkin 1.00 .45
- ❑ 46 Lance Johnson .25 .11
- ❑ 47 Bobby Higginson .40 .18
- ❑ 48 Mike Mussina 1.00 .45
- ❑ 49 Al Martin .25 .11
- ❑ 50 Mark McGwire 4.00 1.80
- ❑ 51 Todd Hundley .25 .11
- ❑ 52 Ray Lankford .40 .18
- ❑ 53 Jason Kendall .40 .18
- ❑ 54 Javy Lopez .40 .18
- ❑ 55 Ben Grieve .40 .18
- ❑ 56 Randy Johnson 1.25 .55
- ❑ 57 Jeff King .25 .11
- ❑ 58 Mark Grace 1.00 .45
- ❑ 59 Rusty Greer .40 .18
- ❑ 60 Greg Maddux 2.50 1.10
- ❑ 61 Jeff Kent .60 .25
- ❑ 62 Rey Ordonez .25 .11
- ❑ 63 Hideo Nomo 1.00 .45
- ❑ 64 Charles Nagy .25 .11
- ❑ 65 Rondell White .40 .18
- ❑ 66 Todd Helton 1.25 .55
- ❑ 67 Jim Thome .60 .25
- ❑ 68 Denny Neagle .25 .11
- ❑ 69 Ivan Rodriguez 1.25 .55
- ❑ 70 Vladimir Guerrero 1.50 .70
- ❑ 71 Jorge Posada .25 .11
- ❑ 72 J.T. Snow .40 .18
- ❑ 73 Reggie Sanders .25 .11
- ❑ 74 Scott Rolen 1.00 .45
- ❑ 75 Robin Ventura .40 .18
- ❑ 76 Mariano Rivera .40 .18
- ❑ 77 Cal Ripken 4.00 1.80
- ❑ 78 Justin Thompson .25 .11
- ❑ 79 Mike Piazza 3.00 1.35
- ❑ 80 Kevin Brown .60 .25
- ❑ 81 Sandy Alomar Jr. .40 .18
- ❑ 82 Craig Biggio .60 .25
- ❑ 83 Vinny Castilla .40 .18
- ❑ 84 Eric Young .25 .11
- ❑ 85 Bernie Williams 1.00 .45
- ❑ 86 Brady Anderson .40 .18
- ❑ 87 Bobby Bonilla .40 .18
- ❑ 88 Tony Clark .25 .11
- ❑ 89 Dan Wilson .25 .11
- ❑ 90 John Wetteland .40 .18
- ❑ 91 Barry Bonds 1.50 .70
- ❑ 92 Chan Ho Park .40 .18
- ❑ 93 Carlos Delgado 1.00 .45
- ❑ 94 David Justice .60 .25
- ❑ 95 Chipper Jones 2.50 1.10
- ❑ 96 Shawn Estes .25 .11
- ❑ 97 Jason Giambi 1.00 .45
- ❑ 98 Ron Gant .40 .18
- ❑ 99 John Olerud .40 .18
- ❑ 100 Frank Thomas 2.00 .90
- ❑ 101 Jose Guillen .25 .11
- ❑ 102 Brad Radke .40 .18
- ❑ 103 Troy Percival .25 .11
- ❑ 104 John Smoltz .40 .18
- ❑ 105 Edgardo Alfonzo .40 .18
- ❑ 106 Dante Bichette .40 .18
- ❑ 107 Larry Walker .40 .18
- ❑ 108 John Valentin .25 .11
- ❑ 109 Roberto Alomar 1.00 .45
- ❑ 110 Mike Cameron .40 .18
- ❑ 111 Eric Davis .40 .18
- ❑ 112 Johnny Damon .40 .18
- ❑ 113 Darin Erstad 1.00 .45
- ❑ 114 Omar Vizquel .40 .18
- ❑ 115 Derek Jeter 4.00 1.80
- ❑ 116 Tony Womack .25 .11
- ❑ 117 Edgar Renteria .25 .11
- ❑ 118 Raul Mondesi .40 .18
- ❑ 119 Tony Gwynn 2.00 .90
- ❑ 120 Ken Griffey Jr. 4.00 1.80
- ❑ 121 Jim Edmonds 1.00 .45
- ❑ 122 Brian Hunter .25 .11
- ❑ 123 Neifi Perez .25 .11
- ❑ 124 Dean Palmer .40 .18
- ❑ 125 Alex Rodriguez 3.00 1.35
- ❑ 126 Tim Salmon .40 .18
- ❑ 127 Curt Schilling .40 .18
- ❑ 128 Kevin Orie .25 .11
- ❑ 129 Andy Pettitte .40 .18
- ❑ 130 Gary Sheffield 1.00 .45
- ❑ 131 Jose Rosado .25 .11
- ❑ 132 Manny Ramirez 1.25 .55
- ❑ 133 Rafael Palmeiro 1.00 .45
- ❑ 134 Sammy Sosa 2.00 .90
- ❑ 135 Jeff Bagwell 1.25 .55
- ❑ 136 Delino DeShields .25 .11
- ❑ 137 Ryan Klesko .40 .18
- ❑ 138 Mo Vaughn .40 .18
- ❑ 139 Steve Finley .40 .18
- ❑ 140 Nomar Garciaparra 3.00 1.35
- ❑ 141 Paul Molitor 1.00 .45
- ❑ 142 Pat Hentgen .25 .11
- ❑ 143 Eric Karros .40 .18
- ❑ 144 Bobby Jones .25 .11
- ❑ 145 Tino Martinez .40 .18
- ❑ 146 Matt Morris .25 .11
- ❑ 147 Livan Hernandez .25 .11
- ❑ 148 Edgar Martinez .60 .25
- ❑ 149 Paul O'Neill .40 .18
- ❑ 150 Checklist .25 .11

## 1999 Topps Gallery

| | MINT | NRMT |
|---|---|---|
| COMPLETE SET (150) | 100.00 | 45.00 |
| COMP.SET w/o SP's (100) | 25.00 | 11.00 |
| COMMON CARD (1-100) | .15 | .07 |
| COMMON CARD (101-150) | .50 | .23 |

- ❑ 1 Mark McGwire 2.50 1.10
- ❑ 2 Jim Thome .40 .18
- ❑ 3 Bernie Williams .60 .25
- ❑ 4 Larry Walker .25 .11
- ❑ 5 Juan Gonzalez .60 .25
- ❑ 6 Ken Griffey Jr. 2.50 1.10
- ❑ 7 Raul Mondesi .25 .11
- ❑ 8 Sammy Sosa 1.25 .55
- ❑ 9 Greg Maddux 1.50 .70
- ❑ 10 Jeff Bagwell .75 .35
- ❑ 11 Vladimir Guerrero 1.00 .45
- ❑ 12 Scott Rolen .60 .25
- ❑ 13 Nomar Garciaparra 2.00 .90
- ❑ 14 Mike Piazza 2.00 .90
- ❑ 15 Travis Lee .15 .07
- ❑ 16 Carlos Delgado .60 .25
- ❑ 17 Darin Erstad .60 .25
- ❑ 18 David Justice .40 .18
- ❑ 19 Cal Ripken 2.50 1.10
- ❑ 20 Derek Jeter 2.50 1.10
- ❑ 21 Tony Clark .15 .07
- ❑ 22 Barry Larkin .60 .25
- ❑ 23 Greg Vaughn .25 .11
- ❑ 24 Jeff Kent .40 .18
- ❑ 25 Wade Boggs .75 .35
- ❑ 26 Andres Galarraga .40 .18
- ❑ 27 Ken Caminiti .25 .11
- ❑ 28 Jason Kendall .25 .11
- ❑ 29 Todd Helton .75 .35
- ❑ 30 Chuck Knoblauch .25 .11
- ❑ 31 Roger Clemens 1.25 .55
- ❑ 32 Jeromy Burnitz .25 .11
- ❑ 33 Javy Lopez .25 .11
- ❑ 34 Roberto Alomar .60 .25
- ❑ 35 Eric Karros .25 .11
- ❑ 36 Ben Grieve .25 .11
- ❑ 37 Eric Davis .25 .11
- ❑ 38 Rondell White .25 .11
- ❑ 39 Dmitri Young .25 .11
- ❑ 40 Ivan Rodriguez .75 .35
- ❑ 41 Paul O'Neill .25 .11
- ❑ 42 Jeff Cirillo .25 .11
- ❑ 43 Kerry Wood .25 .11
- ❑ 44 Albert Belle .40 .10
- ❑ 45 Frank Thomas 1.25 .55
- ❑ 46 Manny Ramirez .75 .35
- ❑ 47 Tom Glavine .60 .25
- ❑ 48 Mo Vaughn .25 .11
- ❑ 49 Jose Cruz Jr. .25 .11
- ❑ 50 Sandy Alomar Jr. .25 .11
- ❑ 51 Edgar Martinez .40 .18
- ❑ 52 John Olerud .25 .11
- ❑ 53 Todd Walker .15 .07
- ❑ 54 Tim Salmon .25 .11
- ❑ 55 Derek Bell .15 .07
- ❑ 56 Matt Williams .40 .18
- ❑ 57 Alex Rodriguez 2.00 .90
- ❑ 58 Rusty Greer .25 .11
- ❑ 59 Vinny Castilla .25 .11
- ❑ 60 Jason Giambi .60 .25
- ❑ 61 Mark Grace .60 .25
- ❑ 62 Jose Canseco .75 .35
- ❑ 63 Gary Sheffield .60 .25
- ❑ 64 Brad Fullmer .25 .11
- ❑ 65 Trevor Hoffman .25 .11
- ❑ 66 Mark Kotsay .15 .07
- ❑ 67 Mike Mussina .60 .25
- ❑ 68 Johnny Damon .25 .11
- ❑ 69 Tino Martinez .25 .11
- ❑ 70 Curt Schilling .25 .11
- ❑ 71 Jay Buhner .25 .11
- ❑ 72 Kenny Lofton .25 .11
- ❑ 73 Randy Johnson .75 .35
- ❑ 74 Kevin Brown .40 .18
- ❑ 75 Brian Jordan .25 .11
- ❑ 76 Craig Biggio .40 .18
- ❑ 77 Barry Bonds 1.00 .45
- ❑ 78 Tony Gwynn 1.25 .55
- ❑ 79 Jim Edmonds .60 .25
- ❑ 80 Shawn Green .60 .25
- ❑ 81 Todd Hundley .15 .07
- ❑ 82 Cliff Floyd .25 .11
- ❑ 83 Jose Guillen .15 .07
- ❑ 84 Dante Bichette .25 .11
- ❑ 85 Moises Alou .25 .11
- ❑ 86 Chipper Jones 1.50 .70

| Card | MINT | NRMT |
|---|---|---|
| ❑ 87 Ray Lankford | .25 | .11 |
| ❑ 88 Fred McGriff | .40 | .18 |
| ❑ 89 Rod Beck | .15 | .07 |
| ❑ 90 Dean Palmer | .25 | .11 |
| ❑ 91 Pedro Martinez | .75 | .35 |
| ❑ 92 Andruw Jones | .60 | .25 |
| ❑ 93 Robin Ventura | .25 | .11 |
| ❑ 94 Ugueth Urbina | .15 | .07 |
| ❑ 95 Orlando Hernandez | .25 | .11 |
| ❑ 96 Sean Casey | .25 | .11 |
| ❑ 97 Denny Neagle | .15 | .07 |
| ❑ 98 Troy Glaus | 1.00 | .45 |
| ❑ 99 John Smoltz | .25 | .11 |
| ❑ 100 Al Leiter | .25 | .11 |
| ❑ 101 Ken Griffey Jr. MAS | 5.00 | 2.20 |
| ❑ 102 Frank Thomas MAS | 2.50 | 1.10 |
| ❑ 103 Mark McGwire MAS | 5.00 | 2.20 |
| ❑ 104 Sammy Sosa MAS | 2.50 | 1.10 |
| ❑ 105 Chipper Jones MAS | 3.00 | 1.35 |
| ❑ 106 Alex Rodriguez MAS | 4.00 | 1.80 |
| ❑ 107 Nomar Garciaparra MAS | 4.00 | 1.80 |
| ❑ 108 Juan Gonzalez MAS | 1.25 | .55 |
| ❑ 109 Derek Jeter MAS | 5.00 | 2.20 |
| ❑ 110 Mike Piazza MAS | 4.00 | 1.80 |
| ❑ 111 Barry Bonds MAS | 2.00 | .90 |
| ❑ 112 Tony Gwynn MAS | 2.50 | 1.10 |
| ❑ 113 Cal Ripken MAS | 5.00 | 2.20 |
| ❑ 114 Greg Maddux MAS | 3.00 | 1.35 |
| ❑ 115 Roger Clemens MAS | 2.50 | 1.10 |
| ❑ 116 Brad Fullmer ART | .60 | .25 |
| ❑ 117 Kerry Wood ART | .60 | .25 |
| ❑ 118 Ben Grieve ART | .60 | .25 |
| ❑ 119 Todd Helton ART | 1.50 | .70 |
| ❑ 120 Kevin Millwood ART | .60 | .25 |
| ❑ 121 Sean Casey ART | .60 | .25 |
| ❑ 122 Vladimir Guerrero ART | 2.00 | .90 |
| ❑ 123 Travis Lee ART | .50 | .23 |
| ❑ 124 Troy Glaus ART | 2.00 | .90 |
| ❑ 125 Bartolo Colon ART | .60 | .25 |
| ❑ 126 Andruw Jones ART | 1.25 | .55 |
| ❑ 127 Scott Rolen ART | 1.25 | .55 |
| ❑ 128 Alfonso Soriano APP RC | 4.00 | 1.80 |
| ❑ 129 Nick Johnson APP RC | 4.00 | 1.80 |
| ❑ 130 Matt Belisle APP RC | 1.50 | .70 |
| ❑ 131 Jorge Toca APP RC | 1.00 | .45 |
| ❑ 132 Masao Kida APP RC | .60 | .25 |
| ❑ 133 Carlos Pena APP RC | 4.00 | 1.80 |
| ❑ 134 Adrian Beltre APP | .60 | .25 |
| ❑ 135 Eric Chavez APP | .60 | .25 |
| ❑ 136 Carlos Beltran APP | .60 | .25 |
| ❑ 137 Alex Gonzalez APP | .50 | .23 |
| ❑ 138 Ryan Anderson APP | .60 | .25 |
| ❑ 139 Ruben Mateo APP | .60 | .25 |
| ❑ 140 Bruce Chen APP | .50 | .23 |
| ❑ 141 Pat Burrell APP RC | 10.00 | 4.50 |
| ❑ 142 Michael Barrett APP | .50 | .23 |
| ❑ 143 Carlos Lee APP | .60 | .25 |
| ❑ 144 Mark Mulder APP RC | 2.00 | .90 |
| ❑ 145 Choo Freeman APP RC | 1.25 | .55 |
| ❑ 146 Gabe Kapler APP | .60 | .25 |
| ❑ 147 Juan Encarnacion APP | .60 | .25 |
| ❑ 148 Jeremy Giambi APP | .50 | .23 |
| ❑ 149 Jason Tyner APP RC | 1.50 | .70 |
| ❑ 150 George Lombard APP | .50 | .23 |

## 2000 Topps Gallery

| | MINT | NRMT |
|---|---|---|
| COMPLETE SET (150) | 100.00 | 45.00 |
| COMP.SET w/o SP's (100) | 25.00 | 11.00 |
| COMMON CARD (1-100) | .15 | .07 |
| COMMON CARD (101-150) | 1.00 | .45 |

| Card | MINT | NRMT |
|---|---|---|
| ❑ 1 Nomar Garciaparra | 2.00 | .90 |
| ❑ 2 Kevin Millwood | .25 | .11 |
| ❑ 3 Jay Bell | .25 | .11 |
| ❑ 4 Rusty Greer | .25 | .11 |
| ❑ 5 Bernie Williams | .60 | .25 |
| ❑ 6 Barry Larkin | .60 | .25 |
| ❑ 7 Carlos Beltran | .25 | .11 |
| ❑ 8 Damion Easley | .15 | .07 |
| ❑ 9 Magglio Ordonez | .25 | .11 |
| ❑ 10 Matt Williams | .40 | .18 |
| ❑ 11 Shannon Stewart | .25 | .11 |
| ❑ 12 Ray Lankford | .25 | .11 |
| ❑ 13 Vinny Castilla | .25 | .11 |
| ❑ 14 Miguel Tejada | .25 | .11 |
| ❑ 15 Craig Biggio | .40 | .18 |
| ❑ 16 Chipper Jones | 1.50 | .70 |
| ❑ 17 Albert Belle | .40 | .18 |
| ❑ 18 Doug Glanville | .15 | .07 |
| ❑ 19 Brian Giles | .25 | .11 |
| ❑ 20 Shawn Green | .60 | .25 |
| ❑ 21 Bret Boone | .15 | .07 |
| ❑ 22 Luis Gonzalez | .25 | .11 |
| ❑ 23 Carlos Delgado | .60 | .25 |
| ❑ 24 J.D. Drew | .60 | .25 |
| ❑ 25 Ivan Rodriguez | .75 | .35 |
| ❑ 26 Tino Martinez | .25 | .11 |
| ❑ 27 Erubiel Durazo | .25 | .11 |
| ❑ 28 Scott Rolen | .60 | .25 |
| ❑ 29 Gary Sheffield | .60 | .25 |
| ❑ 30 Manny Ramirez | .75 | .35 |
| ❑ 31 Luis Castillo | .25 | .11 |
| ❑ 32 Fernando Tatis | .25 | .11 |
| ❑ 33 Darin Erstad | .60 | .25 |
| ❑ 34 Tim Hudson | .60 | .25 |
| ❑ 35 Sammy Sosa | 1.25 | .55 |
| ❑ 36 Jason Kendall | .25 | .11 |
| ❑ 37 Todd Walker | .15 | .07 |
| ❑ 38 Orlando Hernandez | .25 | .11 |
| ❑ 39 Pokey Reese | .25 | .11 |
| ❑ 40 Mike Piazza | 2.00 | .90 |
| ❑ 41 B.J. Surhoff | .25 | .11 |
| ❑ 42 Tony Gwynn | 1.25 | .55 |
| ❑ 43 Kevin Brown | .25 | .11 |
| ❑ 44 Preston Wilson | .25 | .11 |
| ❑ 45 Kenny Lofton | .25 | .11 |
| ❑ 46 Rondell White | .25 | .11 |
| ❑ 47 Frank Thomas | 1.25 | .55 |
| ❑ 48 Neifi Perez | .15 | .07 |
| ❑ 49 Edgardo Alfonzo | .15 | .07 |
| ❑ 50 Ken Griffey Jr. | 2.50 | 1.10 |
| ❑ 51 Barry Bonds | 1.00 | .45 |
| ❑ 52 Brian Jordan | .25 | .11 |
| ❑ 53 Raul Mondesi | .25 | .11 |
| ❑ 54 Troy Glaus | .75 | .35 |
| ❑ 55 Curt Schilling | .25 | .11 |
| ❑ 56 Mike Mussina | .60 | .25 |
| ❑ 57 Brian Daubach | .15 | .07 |
| ❑ 58 Roger Clemens | 1.25 | .55 |
| ❑ 59 Carlos Febles | .15 | .07 |
| ❑ 60 Todd Helton | .75 | .35 |
| ❑ 61 Mark Grace | .60 | .25 |
| ❑ 62 Randy Johnson | .75 | .35 |
| ❑ 63 Jeff Bagwell | .75 | .35 |
| ❑ 64 Tom Glavine | .60 | .25 |
| ❑ 65 Adrian Beltre | .25 | .11 |
| ❑ 66 Rafael Palmeiro | .60 | .25 |
| ❑ 67 Paul O'Neill | .25 | .11 |
| ❑ 68 Robin Ventura | .25 | .11 |
| ❑ 69 Ray Durham | .25 | .11 |
| ❑ 70 Mark McGwire | 2.50 | 1.10 |
| ❑ 71 Greg Vaughn | .25 | .11 |
| ❑ 72 Javy Lopez | .25 | .11 |
| ❑ 73 Ryan Klesko | .25 | .11 |
| ❑ 74 Mike Lieberthal | .25 | .11 |
| ❑ 75 Cal Ripken | 2.50 | 1.10 |
| ❑ 76 Juan Gonzalez | .60 | .25 |
| ❑ 77 Sean Casey | .25 | .11 |
| ❑ 78 Jermaine Dye | .25 | .11 |
| ❑ 79 John Olerud | .25 | .11 |
| ❑ 80 Jose Canseco | .75 | .35 |
| ❑ 81 Eric Karros | .25 | .11 |
| ❑ 82 Roberto Alomar | .60 | .25 |
| ❑ 83 Ben Grieve | .25 | .11 |
| ❑ 84 Greg Maddux | 1.50 | .70 |
| ❑ 85 Pedro Martinez | .75 | .35 |
| ❑ 86 Tony Clark | .15 | .07 |
| ❑ 87 Richie Sexson | .25 | .11 |
| ❑ 88 Cliff Floyd | .25 | .11 |
| ❑ 89 Eric Chavez | .25 | .11 |
| ❑ 90 Andruw Jones | .60 | .25 |
| ❑ 91 Vladimir Guerrero | 1.00 | .45 |
| ❑ 92 Alex Gonzalez | .15 | .07 |
| ❑ 93 Jim Thome | .40 | .18 |
| ❑ 94 Bob Abreu | .25 | .11 |
| ❑ 95 Derek Jeter | 2.50 | 1.10 |
| ❑ 96 Larry Walker | .25 | .11 |
| ❑ 97 Mike Hampton | .25 | .11 |
| ❑ 98 Mo Vaughn | .25 | .11 |
| ❑ 99 Jason Giambi | .60 | .25 |
| ❑ 100 Alex Rodriguez | 2.00 | .90 |
| ❑ 101 Mark McGwire MAS | 5.00 | 2.20 |
| ❑ 102 Sammy Sosa MAS | 2.50 | 1.10 |
| ❑ 103 Alex Rodriguez MAS | 4.00 | 1.80 |
| ❑ 104 Derek Jeter MAS | 5.00 | 2.20 |
| ❑ 105 Greg Maddux MAS | 3.00 | 1.35 |
| ❑ 106 Jeff Bagwell MAS | 1.50 | .70 |
| ❑ 107 Nomar Garciaparra MAS | 4.00 | 1.80 |
| ❑ 108 Mike Piazza MAS | 4.00 | 1.80 |
| ❑ 109 Pedro Martinez MAS | 1.50 | .70 |
| ❑ 110 Chipper Jones MAS | 3.00 | 1.35 |
| ❑ 111 Randy Johnson MAS | 1.50 | .70 |
| ❑ 112 Barry Bonds MAS | 2.00 | .90 |
| ❑ 113 Ken Griffey Jr. MAS | 5.00 | 2.20 |
| ❑ 114 Manny Ramirez MAS | 1.50 | .70 |
| ❑ 115 Ivan Rodriguez MAS | 1.50 | .70 |
| ❑ 116 Juan Gonzalez MAS | 2.00 | .90 |
| ❑ 117 Vladimir Guerrero MAS | 2.00 | .90 |
| ❑ 118 Tony Gwynn MAS | 2.50 | 1.10 |
| ❑ 119 Larry Walker MAS | 1.00 | .45 |
| ❑ 120 Cal Ripken MAS | 5.00 | 2.20 |
| ❑ 121 Josh Hamilton SG | 3.00 | 1.35 |
| ❑ 122 Corey Patterson SG | 3.00 | 1.35 |
| ❑ 123 Pat Burrell SG | 3.00 | 1.35 |
| ❑ 124 Nick Johnson SG | 1.00 | .45 |
| ❑ 125 Adam Piatt SG | 2.00 | .90 |
| ❑ 126 Rick Ankiel SG | 4.00 | 1.80 |
| ❑ 127 A.J. Burnett SG | 1.00 | .45 |
| ❑ 128 Ben Petrick SG | 1.00 | .45 |
| ❑ 129 Rafael Furcal SG | 5.00 | 2.20 |
| ❑ 130 Alfonso Soriano SG | 1.00 | .45 |
| ❑ 131 Dee Brown SG | 1.00 | .45 |
| ❑ 132 Ruben Mateo SG | 1.00 | .45 |
| ❑ 133 Pablo Ozuna SG | 1.00 | .45 |
| ❑ 134 Sean Burroughs SG UER<br>Eric Munson's bio on back | 2.00 | .90 |
| ❑ 135 Mark Mulder SG | 1.00 | .45 |
| ❑ 136 Jason Jennings SG | 1.00 | .45 |
| ❑ 137 Eric Munson SG | 2.00 | .90 |
| ❑ 138 Vernon Wells SG | 1.00 | .45 |
| ❑ 139 Brett Myers SG RC | 1.50 | .70 |
| ❑ 140 Ben Christensen SG RC | 2.00 | .90 |
| ❑ 141 Bobby Bradley SG RC | 4.00 | 1.80 |
| ❑ 142 Ruben Salazar SG RC | 2.00 | .90 |
| ❑ 143 Ryan Christianson SG RC | 2.00 | .90 |
| ❑ 144 Corey Myers SG RC | 1.25 | .55 |
| ❑ 145 Aaron Rowand SG RC | 2.00 | .90 |
| ❑ 146 Julio Zuleta SG RC | 1.00 | .45 |
| ❑ 147 Kurt Ainsworth SG RC | 2.50 | 1.10 |
| ❑ 148 Scott Downs SG RC | 1.00 | .45 |
| ❑ 149 Larry Bigbie SG RC | 1.50 | .70 |
| ❑ 150 Chance Caple SG RC | 1.25 | .55 |

## 1998 Topps Gold Label Class 1

| | MINT | NRMT |
|---|---|---|
| COMP.GOLD SET (100) | 60.00 | 27.00 |

*CLASS 1 RED RC's: 8X TO 20X HI

| Card | MINT | NRMT |
|---|---|---|
| ❑ 1 Kevin Brown | .60 | .25 |
| ❑ 2 Greg Maddux | 2.50 | 1.10 |
| ❑ 3 Albert Belle | .60 | .25 |
| ❑ 4 Andres Galarraga | .60 | .25 |
| ❑ 5 Craig Biggio | .60 | .25 |
| ❑ 6 Matt Williams | .60 | .25 |

❑ 7 Derek Jeter ...... 4.00 1.80
❑ 8 Randy Johnson ...... 1.25 .55
❑ 9 Jay Bell ...... .40 .18
❑ 10 Jim Thome ...... .60 .25
❑ 11 Roberto Alomar ...... 1.00 .45
❑ 12 Tom Glavine ...... 1.00 .45
❑ 13 Reggie Sanders ...... .25 .11
❑ 14 Tony Gwynn ...... 2.00 .90
❑ 15 Mark McGwire ...... 4.00 1.80
❑ 16 Jeromy Burnitz ...... .40 .18
❑ 17 Andruw Jones ...... 1.00 .45
❑ 18 Jay Buhner ...... .40 .18
❑ 19 Robin Ventura ...... .40 .18
❑ 20 Jeff Bagwell ...... 1.25 .55
❑ 21 Roger Clemens ...... 2.00 .90
❑ 22 Masato Yoshii RC ...... 1.00 .45
❑ 23 Travis Fryman ...... .40 .18
❑ 24 Rafael Palmeiro ...... 1.00 .45
❑ 25 Alex Rodriguez ...... 3.00 1.35
❑ 26 Sandy Alomar Jr. ...... .40 .18
❑ 27 Chipper Jones ...... 2.50 1.10
❑ 28 Rusty Greer ...... .40 .18
❑ 29 Cal Ripken ...... 4.00 1.80
❑ 30 Tony Clark ...... .25 .11
❑ 31 Derek Bell ...... .25 .11
❑ 32 Fred McGriff ...... .60 .25
❑ 33 Paul O'Neill ...... .40 .18
❑ 34 Moises Alou ...... .40 .18
❑ 35 Henry Rodriguez ...... .25 .11
❑ 36 Steve Finley ...... .40 .18
❑ 37 Marquis Grissom ...... .25 .11
❑ 38 Jason Giambi ...... 1.00 .45
❑ 39 Javy Lopez ...... .40 .18
❑ 40 Damion Easley ...... .25 .11
❑ 41 Mariano Rivera ...... .40 .18
❑ 42 Mo Vaughn ...... .40 .18
❑ 43 Mike Mussina ...... 1.00 .45
❑ 44 Jason Kendall ...... .40 .18
❑ 45 Pedro Martinez ...... 1.25 .55
❑ 46 Frank Thomas ...... 2.00 .90
❑ 47 Jim Edmonds ...... 1.00 .45
❑ 48 Hideki Irabu ...... .25 .11
❑ 49 Eric Karros ...... .40 .18
❑ 50 Juan Gonzalez ...... 1.00 .45
❑ 51 Ellis Burks ...... .40 .18
❑ 52 Dean Palmer ...... .40 .18
❑ 53 Scott Rolen ...... 1.00 .45
❑ 54 Raul Mondesi ...... .40 .18
❑ 55 Quinton McCracken ...... .25 .11
❑ 56 John Olerud ...... .40 .18
❑ 57 Ken Caminiti ...... .40 .18
❑ 58 Brian Jordan ...... .40 .18
❑ 59 Wade Boggs ...... 1.25 .55
❑ 60 Mike Piazza ...... 3.00 1.35
❑ 61 Darin Erstad ...... 1.00 .45
❑ 62 Curt Schilling ...... .40 .18
❑ 63 David Justice ...... .60 .25
❑ 64 Kenny Lofton ...... .40 .18
❑ 65 Barry Bonds ...... 1.50 .70
❑ 66 Ray Lankford ...... .40 .18
❑ 67 Brian Hunter ...... .25 .11
❑ 68 Chuck Knoblauch ...... .40 .18
❑ 69 Vinny Castilla ...... .40 .18
❑ 70 Vladimir Guerrero ...... 1.50 .70
❑ 71 Tim Salmon ...... .40 .18
❑ 72 Larry Walker ...... .40 .18
❑ 73 Paul Molitor ...... 1.00 .45
❑ 74 Barry Larkin ...... 1.00 .45
❑ 75 Edgar Martinez ...... .60 .25
❑ 76 Bernie Williams ...... 1.00 .45
❑ 77 Dante Bichette ...... .40 .18
❑ 78 Nomar Garciaparra ...... 3.00 1.35
❑ 79 Ben Grieve ...... .40 .18
❑ 80 Ivan Rodriguez ...... 1.25 .55
❑ 81 Todd Helton ...... 1.25 .55
❑ 82 Ryan Klesko ...... .40 .18
❑ 83 Sammy Sosa ...... 2.00 .90
❑ 84 Travis Lee ...... .40 .18
❑ 85 Jose Cruz Jr. ...... .40 .18
❑ 86 Mark Kotsay ...... .40 .18
❑ 87 Richard Hidalgo ...... .40 .18
❑ 88 Rondell White ...... .40 .18
❑ 89 Greg Vaughn ...... .40 .18
❑ 90 Gary Sheffield ...... 1.00 .45
❑ 91 Paul Konerko ...... .40 .18
❑ 92 Mark Grace ...... 1.00 .45
❑ 93 Kevin Millwood RC ...... 2.00 .90
❑ 94 Manny Ramirez ...... 1.25 .55
❑ 95 Tino Martinez ...... .40 .18
❑ 96 Brad Fullmer ...... .40 .18
❑ 97 Todd Walker ...... .25 .11
❑ 98 Carlos Delgado ...... 1.00 .45
❑ 99 Kerry Wood ...... 1.00 .45
❑ 100 Ken Griffey Jr. ...... 4.00 1.80

## 1999 Topps Gold Label Class 1

| | MINT | NRMT |
|---|---|---|
| COMP.GOLD SET (100) | 60.00 | 27.00 |
| COMMON BLACK (1-100) | 1.00 | .45 |

*CLASS 1 BLACK STARS: 1.5X TO 4X HI
*CLASS 1 BLACK RC'S: 1.25X TO 3X HI
CLASS 1 BLACK ODDS 1:12 RETAIL, 1:8 HTA

| | | |
|---|---|---|
| COMMON RED (1-100) | 8.00 | 3.60 |

*CLASS 1 RED STARS: 12.5X TO 30X HI
*CLASS 1 RED RC'S: 8X TO 20X HI
CLASS 1 RED ODDS 1:148 RETAIL, 1:118 HTA
CLASS 1 RED PRINT RUN 100 SERIAL #'d SETS
NINE DIFF.ONE TO ONE PARALLELS EXIST
ONE TO ONE ODDS 1:1587 RETAIL, 1:1271 HTA

❑ 1 Mike Piazza ...... 3.00 1.35
❑ 2 Andres Galarraga ...... .60 .25
❑ 3 Mark Grace ...... 1.00 .45
❑ 4 Tony Clark ...... .25 .11
❑ 5 Jim Thome ...... .60 .25
❑ 6 Tony Gwynn ...... 2.00 .90
❑ 7 Kelly Dransfeldt RC ...... .50 .23
❑ 8 Eric Chavez ...... .40 .18
❑ 9 Brian Jordan ...... .40 .18
❑ 10 Todd Hundley ...... .25 .11
❑ 11 Rondell White ...... .40 .18
❑ 12 Dmitri Young ...... .40 .18
❑ 13 Jeff Kent ...... .60 .25
❑ 14 Derek Bell ...... .25 .11
❑ 15 Todd Helton ...... 1.25 .55
❑ 16 Chipper Jones ...... 2.50 1.10
❑ 17 Albert Belle ...... .60 .25
❑ 18 Barry Larkin ...... 1.00 .45
❑ 19 Dante Bichette ...... .40 .18
❑ 20 Gary Sheffield ...... 1.00 .45
❑ 21 Cliff Floyd ...... .40 .18
❑ 22 Derek Jeter ...... 4.00 1.80
❑ 23 Jason Giambi ...... 1.00 .45
❑ 24 Ray Lankford ...... .40 .18
❑ 25 Alex Rodriguez ...... 3.00 1.35
❑ 26 Ruben Mateo ...... .40 .18
❑ 27 Wade Boggs ...... 1.25 .55
❑ 28 Carlos Delgado ...... 1.00 .45
❑ 29 Tim Salmon ...... .40 .18
❑ 30 Alfonso Soriano RC ...... 2.00 .90
❑ 31 Javy Lopez ...... .40 .18
❑ 32 Jason Kendall ...... .40 .18
❑ 33 Nick Johnson RC ...... 2.00 .90
❑ 34 A.J. Burnett RC ...... .75 .35
❑ 35 Troy Glaus ...... 1.50 .70
❑ 36 Pat Burrell RC ...... 5.00 2.20
❑ 37 Jeff Cirillo ...... .40 .18
❑ 38 David Justice ...... .60 .25
❑ 39 Ivan Rodriguez ...... 1.25 .55
❑ 40 Bernie Williams ...... 1.00 .45
❑ 41 Jay Buhner ...... .40 .18
❑ 42 Mo Vaughn ...... .40 .18
❑ 43 Randy Johnson ...... 1.25 .55
❑ 44 Pedro Martinez ...... 1.25 .55
❑ 45 Larry Walker ...... .40 .18
❑ 46 Todd Walker ...... .25 .11
❑ 47 Roberto Alomar ...... 1.00 .45
❑ 48 Kevin Brown ...... .60 .25
❑ 49 Mike Mussina ...... 1.00 .45
❑ 50 Tom Glavine ...... 1.00 .45
❑ 51 Curt Schilling ...... .40 .18
❑ 52 Ken Caminiti ...... .40 .18
❑ 53 Brad Fullmer ...... .40 .18
❑ 54 Bobby Seay RC ...... .60 .25
❑ 55 Orlando Hernandez ...... .40 .18
❑ 56 Sean Casey ...... .40 .18
❑ 57 Al Leiter ...... .40 .18
❑ 58 Sandy Alomar Jr. ...... .40 .18
❑ 59 Mark Kotsay ...... .25 .11
❑ 60 Matt Williams ...... .60 .25
❑ 61 Raul Mondesi ...... .40 .18
❑ 62 Joe Crede RC ...... 15.00 6.75
❑ 63 Jim Edmonds ...... 1.00 .45
❑ 64 Jose Cruz Jr. ...... .40 .18
❑ 65 Juan Gonzalez ...... 1.00 .45
❑ 66 Sammy Sosa ...... 2.00 .90
❑ 67 Cal Ripken ...... 4.00 1.80
❑ 68 Vinny Castilla ...... .40 .18
❑ 69 Craig Biggio ...... .60 .25
❑ 70 Mark McGwire ...... 4.00 1.80
❑ 71 Greg Vaughn ...... .40 .18
❑ 72 Greg Maddux ...... 2.50 1.10
❑ 73 Paul O'Neill ...... .40 .18
❑ 74 Scott Rolen ...... 1.00 .45
❑ 75 Ben Grieve ...... .40 .18
❑ 76 Vladimir Guerrero ...... 1.50 .70
❑ 77 John Olerud ...... .40 .18
❑ 78 Eric Karros ...... .40 .18
❑ 79 Jeromy Burnitz ...... .40 .18
❑ 80 Jeff Bagwell ...... 1.25 .55
❑ 81 Kenny Lofton ...... .40 .18
❑ 82 Manny Ramirez ...... 1.25 .55
❑ 83 Andruw Jones ...... 1.00 .45
❑ 84 Travis Lee ...... .25 .11
❑ 85 Darin Erstad ...... 1.00 .45
❑ 86 Nomar Garciaparra ...... 3.00 1.35
❑ 87 Frank Thomas ...... 2.00 .90
❑ 88 Moises Alou ...... .40 .18
❑ 89 Tino Martinez ...... .40 .18
❑ 90 Carlos Pena RC ...... 2.00 .90
❑ 91 Shawn Green ...... 1.00 .45
❑ 92 Rusty Greer ...... .40 .18
❑ 93 Matt Belisle RC ...... .75 .35
❑ 94 Adrian Beltre ...... .40 .18
❑ 95 Roger Clemens ...... 2.00 .90
❑ 96 John Smoltz ...... .40 .18
❑ 97 Mark Mulder RC ...... 1.00 .45
❑ 98 Kerry Wood ...... .40 .18
❑ 99 Barry Bonds ...... 1.50 .70
❑ 100 Ken Griffey Jr. ...... 4.00 1.80

## 2000 Topps Gold Label Class 1

| | MINT | NRMT |
|---|---|---|
| COMPLETE SET (100) | 100.00 | 45.00 |

❑ 1 Sammy Sosa ...... 2.00 .90
❑ 2 Greg Maddux ...... 2.50 1.10

| | | MINT | NRMT |
|---|---|---|---|
| ❑ 3 | Mark Quinn | .40 | .18 |
| ❑ 4 | Rondell White | .40 | .18 |
| ❑ 5 | Fernando Tatis | .40 | .18 |
| ❑ 6 | Troy Glaus | 1.25 | .55 |
| ❑ 7 | Nick Johnson | .40 | .18 |
| ❑ 8 | Albert Belle | .60 | .25 |
| ❑ 9 | Scott Rolen | 1.00 | .45 |
| ❑ 10 | Rafael Palmeiro | 1.00 | .45 |
| ❑ 11 | Tony Gwynn | 2.00 | .90 |
| ❑ 12 | Kevin Brown | .40 | .18 |
| ❑ 13 | Roberto Alomar | 1.00 | .45 |
| ❑ 14 | John Olerud | .40 | .18 |
| ❑ 15 | Rick Ankiel | 2.00 | .90 |
| ❑ 16 | Chipper Jones | 2.50 | 1.10 |
| ❑ 17 | Craig Biggio | .60 | .25 |
| ❑ 18 | Mark Mulder | .40 | .18 |
| ❑ 19 | Carlos Delgado | 1.00 | .45 |
| ❑ 20 | Alex Gonzalez | .25 | .11 |
| ❑ 21 | Gabe Kapler | .40 | .18 |
| ❑ 22 | Derek Jeter | 4.00 | 1.80 |
| ❑ 23 | Carlos Beltran | .40 | .18 |
| ❑ 24 | Todd Helton | 1.25 | .55 |
| ❑ 25 | Mark McGwire | 4.00 | 1.80 |
| ❑ 26 | Ben Grieve | .40 | .18 |
| ❑ 27 | Rafael Furcal | 2.50 | 1.10 |
| ❑ 28 | Vernon Wells | .40 | .18 |
| ❑ 29 | Greg Vaughn | .40 | .18 |
| ❑ 30 | Vladimir Guerrero | 1.50 | .70 |
| ❑ 31 | Mike Piazza | 3.00 | 1.35 |
| ❑ 32 | Roger Clemens | 2.00 | .90 |
| ❑ 33 | Barry Larkin | 1.00 | .45 |
| ❑ 34 | Pedro Martinez | 1.25 | .55 |
| ❑ 35 | Matt Williams | .60 | .25 |
| ❑ 36 | Mo Vaughn | .40 | .18 |
| ❑ 37 | Tim Hudson | .25 | .11 |
| ❑ 38 | Andruw Jones | 1.00 | .45 |
| ❑ 39 | Vinny Castilla | .40 | .18 |
| ❑ 40 | Frank Thomas | 2.00 | .90 |
| ❑ 41 | Pokey Reese | .40 | .18 |
| ❑ 42 | Corey Patterson | 1.50 | .70 |
| ❑ 43 | Jeromy Burnitz | .40 | .18 |
| ❑ 44 | Preston Wilson | .40 | .18 |
| ❑ 45 | Juan Gonzalez | 1.00 | .45 |
| ❑ 46 | Brian Giles | .40 | .18 |
| ❑ 47 | Todd Walker | .25 | .11 |
| ❑ 48 | Magglio Ordonez | .40 | .18 |
| ❑ 49 | Alfonso Soriano | .40 | .18 |
| ❑ 50 | Ken Griffey Jr. | 4.00 | 1.80 |
| ❑ 51 | Michael Barrett | .25 | .11 |
| ❑ 52 | Shawn Green | 1.00 | .45 |
| ❑ 53 | Erubiel Durazo | .40 | .18 |
| ❑ 54 | Adam Piatt | 1.00 | .45 |
| ❑ 55 | Pat Burrell | 1.50 | .70 |
| ❑ 56 | Mike Mussina | 1.00 | .45 |
| ❑ 57 | Bernie Williams | 1.00 | .45 |
| ❑ 58 | Sean Casey | .40 | .18 |
| ❑ 59 | Randy Johnson | 1.25 | .55 |
| ❑ 60 | Jeff Bagwell | 1.25 | .55 |
| ❑ 61 | Eric Chavez | .40 | .18 |
| ❑ 62 | Josh Hamilton | 1.50 | .70 |
| ❑ 63 | A.J. Burnett | .40 | .18 |
| ❑ 64 | Jim Thome | .60 | .25 |
| ❑ 65 | Raul Mondesi | .40 | .18 |
| ❑ 66 | Jason Kendall | .40 | .18 |
| ❑ 67 | Mike Lieberthal | .40 | .18 |
| ❑ 68 | Robin Ventura | .40 | .18 |
| ❑ 69 | Ivan Rodriguez | 1.25 | .55 |
| ❑ 70 | Larry Walker | .40 | .18 |
| ❑ 71 | Eric Munson | 1.00 | .45 |
| ❑ 72 | Brian Jordan | .40 | .18 |
| ❑ 73 | Edgardo Alfonzo | .40 | .18 |
| ❑ 74 | Curt Schilling | .40 | .18 |
| ❑ 75 | Nomar Garciaparra | 3.00 | 1.35 |
| ❑ 76 | Mark Grace | 1.00 | .45 |
| ❑ 77 | Shannon Stewart | .40 | .18 |
| ❑ 78 | J.D. Drew | 1.00 | .45 |
| ❑ 79 | Jack Cust | .40 | .18 |
| ❑ 80 | Cal Ripken | 4.00 | 1.80 |
| ❑ 81 | Bob Abreu | .40 | .18 |
| ❑ 82 | Ruben Mateo | .40 | .18 |
| ❑ 83 | Orlando Hernandez | .40 | .18 |
| ❑ 84 | Kris Benson | .40 | .18 |
| ❑ 85 | Barry Bonds | 1.50 | .70 |
| ❑ 86 | Manny Ramirez | 1.25 | .55 |
| ❑ 87 | Jose Canseco | 1.25 | .55 |
| ❑ 88 | Sean Burroughs | 1.00 | .45 |
| ❑ 89 | Kevin Millwood | .40 | .18 |
| ❑ 90 | Alex Rodriguez | 3.00 | 1.35 |
| ❑ 91 | Brett Myers RC | 1.00 | .45 |
| ❑ 92 | Rick Asadoorian RC | 3.00 | 1.35 |
| ❑ 93 | Ben Christensen RC | 1.25 | .55 |
| ❑ 94 | Bobby Bradley RC | 2.50 | 1.10 |
| ❑ 95 | Chris Wakeland RC | .75 | .35 |
| ❑ 96 | Brad Baisley RC | .75 | .35 |
| ❑ 97 | Aaron McNeal RC | 1.25 | .55 |
| ❑ 98 | Aaron Rowand RC | 1.25 | .55 |
| ❑ 99 | Scott Downs RC | .60 | .25 |
| ❑ 100 | Michael Tejera RC | .75 | .35 |
| ❑ NNO | D.Jeter AU Sheet/40 EXCH | | |

## 2000 Topps HD

| | | MINT | NRMT |
|---|---|---|---|
| COMPLETE SET (100) | | 100.00 | 45.00 |
| ❑ 1 | Derek Jeter | 5.00 | 2.20 |
| ❑ 2 | Andruw Jones | 1.25 | .55 |
| ❑ 3 | Ben Grieve | .50 | .23 |
| ❑ 4 | Carlos Beltran | .50 | .23 |
| ❑ 5 | Randy Johnson | 1.50 | .70 |
| ❑ 6 | Javy Lopez | .50 | .23 |
| ❑ 7 | Gary Sheffield | 1.25 | .55 |
| ❑ 8 | John Olerud | .50 | .23 |
| ❑ 9 | Vinny Castilla | .50 | .23 |
| ❑ 10 | Barry Larkin | 1.25 | .55 |
| ❑ 11 | Tony Clark | .30 | .14 |
| ❑ 12 | Roberto Alomar | 1.25 | .55 |
| ❑ 13 | Brian Jordan | .50 | .23 |
| ❑ 14 | Wade Boggs | 1.50 | .70 |
| ❑ 15 | Carlos Febles | .30 | .14 |
| ❑ 16 | Alfonso Soriano | .50 | .23 |
| ❑ 17 | A.J. Burnett | .50 | .23 |
| ❑ 18 | Matt Williams | .75 | .35 |
| ❑ 19 | Alex Gonzalez | .30 | .14 |
| ❑ 20 | Larry Walker | .50 | .23 |
| ❑ 21 | Jeff Bagwell | 1.50 | .70 |
| ❑ 22 | Al Leiter | .30 | .14 |
| ❑ 23 | Ken Griffey Jr. | 5.00 | 2.20 |
| ❑ 24 | Ruben Mateo | .50 | .23 |
| ❑ 25 | Mark Grace | 1.25 | .55 |
| ❑ 26 | Carlos Delgado | 1.25 | .55 |
| ❑ 27 | Vladimir Guerrero | 2.00 | .90 |
| ❑ 28 | Kenny Lofton | .50 | .23 |
| ❑ 29 | Rusty Greer | .50 | .23 |
| ❑ 30 | Pedro Martinez | 1.50 | .70 |
| ❑ 31 | Todd Helton | 1.00 | .45 |
| ❑ 32 | Ray Lankford | .50 | .23 |
| ❑ 33 | Jose Canseco | 1.50 | .70 |
| ❑ 34 | Raul Mondesi | .50 | .23 |
| ❑ 35 | Mo Vaughn | .50 | .23 |
| ❑ 36 | Eric Chavez | .50 | .23 |
| ❑ 37 | Manny Ramirez | 1.50 | .70 |
| ❑ 38 | Jason Kendall | .50 | .23 |
| ❑ 39 | Mike Mussina | 1.25 | .55 |
| ❑ 40 | Dante Bichette | .50 | .23 |
| ❑ 41 | Troy Glaus | 1.50 | .70 |
| ❑ 42 | Rickey Henderson | 1.50 | .70 |
| ❑ 43 | Pablo Ozuna | .30 | .14 |
| ❑ 44 | Michael Barrett | .30 | .14 |
| ❑ 45 | Tony Gwynn | 2.50 | 1.10 |
| ❑ 46 | John Smoltz | .50 | .23 |
| ❑ 47 | Rafael Palmeiro | 1.25 | .55 |
| ❑ 48 | Curt Schilling | .50 | .23 |
| ❑ 49 | Todd Walker | .30 | .14 |
| ❑ 50 | Greg Vaughn | .50 | .23 |
| ❑ 51 | Orlando Hernandez | .50 | .23 |
| ❑ 52 | Jim Thome | .75 | .35 |
| ❑ 53 | Pat Burrell | 2.00 | .90 |
| ❑ 54 | Tim Salmon | .50 | .23 |
| ❑ 55 | Tom Glavine | 1.25 | .55 |
| ❑ 56 | Travis Lee | .30 | .14 |
| ❑ 57 | Gabe Kapler | .50 | .23 |
| ❑ 58 | Greg Maddux | 3.00 | 1.35 |
| ❑ 59 | Scott Rolen | 1.25 | .55 |
| ❑ 60 | Cal Ripken | 5.00 | 2.20 |
| ❑ 61 | Preston Wilson | .50 | .23 |
| ❑ 62 | Ivan Rodriguez | 1.50 | .70 |
| ❑ 63 | Johnny Damon | .50 | .23 |
| ❑ 64 | Bernie Williams | 1.25 | .55 |
| ❑ 65 | Barry Bonds | 2.00 | .90 |
| ❑ 66 | Sammy Sosa | 2.50 | 1.10 |
| ❑ 67 | Robin Ventura | .75 | .35 |
| ❑ 68 | Tony Fernandez | .30 | .14 |
| ❑ 69 | Jay Bell | .50 | .23 |
| ❑ 70 | Mark McGwire | 5.00 | 2.20 |
| ❑ 71 | Jeromy Burnitz | .50 | .23 |
| ❑ 72 | Chipper Jones | 3.00 | 1.35 |
| ❑ 73 | Josh Hamilton | 2.00 | .90 |
| ❑ 74 | Darin Erstad | 1.25 | .55 |
| ❑ 75 | Alex Rodriguez | 4.00 | 1.80 |
| ❑ 76 | Sean Casey | .50 | .23 |
| ❑ 77 | Tino Martinez | .50 | .23 |
| ❑ 78 | Juan Gonzalez | 1.25 | .55 |
| ❑ 79 | Cliff Floyd | .50 | .23 |
| ❑ 80 | Craig Biggio | .75 | .35 |
| ❑ 81 | Shawn Green | 1.25 | .55 |
| ❑ 82 | Adrian Beltre | .50 | .23 |
| ❑ 83 | Mike Piazza | 4.00 | 1.80 |
| ❑ 84 | Nomar Garciaparra | 4.00 | 1.80 |
| ❑ 85 | Kevin Brown | .75 | .35 |
| ❑ 86 | Roger Clemens | 2.50 | 1.10 |
| ❑ 87 | Frank Thomas | 2.50 | 1.10 |
| ❑ 88 | Albert Belle | .75 | .35 |
| ❑ 89 | Erubiel Durazo | .50 | .23 |
| ❑ 90 | David Walling | .50 | .23 |
| ❑ 91 | John Sneed RC | .75 | .35 |
| ❑ 92 | Larry Bigbie RC | 2.00 | .90 |
| ❑ 93 | B.J. Garbe RC | 3.00 | 1.35 |
| ❑ 94 | Bobby Bradley RC | 5.00 | 2.20 |
| ❑ 95 | Ryan Christianson RC | 2.50 | 1.10 |
| ❑ 96 | Jay Gehrke | .30 | .14 |
| ❑ 97 | Jason Stumm RC | 2.00 | .90 |
| ❑ 98 | Brett Myers RC | 2.00 | .90 |
| ❑ 99 | Chance Caple RC | 1.50 | .70 |
| ❑ 100 | Corey Myers RC | 1.50 | .70 |

## 1998 Topps Opening Day

| | | MINT | NRMT |
|---|---|---|---|
| COMPLETE SET (165) | | 50.00 | 22.00 |
| ❑ 1 | Tony Gwynn | 1.50 | .70 |
| ❑ 2 | Larry Walker | .30 | .14 |
| ❑ 3 | Billy Wagner | .20 | .09 |
| ❑ 4 | Denny Neagle | .20 | .09 |
| ❑ 5 | Vladimir Guerrero | 1.25 | .55 |
| ❑ 6 | Kevin Brown | .50 | .23 |
| ❑ 7 | Mariano Rivera | .30 | .14 |
| ❑ 8 | Tony Clark | .20 | .09 |
| ❑ 9 | Deion Sanders | .30 | .14 |
| ❑ 10 | Matt Williams | .50 | .23 |
| ❑ 11 | Carlos Baerga | .20 | .09 |
| ❑ 12 | Mo Vaughn | .30 | .14 |

| | | MINT | NRMT |
|---|---|---|---|
| ❑ 13 | Chan Ho Park | .30 | .14 |
| ❑ 14 | Frank Thomas | 1.50 | .70 |
| ❑ 15 | John Jaha | .30 | .14 |
| ❑ 16 | Steve Trachsel | .20 | .09 |
| ❑ 17 | Jeff Kent | .50 | .23 |
| ❑ 18 | Scott Rolen | .75 | .35 |
| ❑ 19 | Juan Gonzalez | .75 | .35 |
| ❑ 20 | Garret Anderson | .30 | .14 |
| ❑ 21 | Roberto Clemente | 2.00 | .90 |
| ❑ 22 | Omar Vizquel | .30 | .14 |
| ❑ 23 | Brian Hunter | .20 | .09 |
| ❑ 24 | Jeff Bagwell | 1.00 | .45 |
| ❑ 25 | Chili Davis | .30 | .14 |
| ❑ 26 | Mike Cameron | .30 | .14 |
| ❑ 27 | Pat Hentgen | .20 | .09 |
| ❑ 28 | Wilton Guerrero | .20 | .09 |
| ❑ 29 | Devon White | .20 | .09 |
| ❑ 30 | Rafael Palmeiro | .75 | .35 |
| ❑ 31 | Jeff Blauser | .20 | .09 |
| ❑ 32 | Dave Hollins | .20 | .09 |
| ❑ 33 | Trevor Hoffman | .30 | .14 |
| ❑ 34 | Ryan Klesko | .30 | .14 |
| ❑ 35 | Butch Huskey | .20 | .09 |
| ❑ 36 | Mark Grudzielanek | .20 | .09 |
| ❑ 37 | Marquis Grissom | .20 | .09 |
| ❑ 38 | Jim Edmonds | .75 | .35 |
| ❑ 39 | Greg Vaughn | .30 | .14 |
| ❑ 40 | David Wells | .30 | .14 |
| ❑ 41 | Charles Nagy | .20 | .09 |
| ❑ 42 | B.J. Surhoff | .30 | .14 |
| ❑ 43 | Edgardo Alfonzo | .30 | .14 |
| ❑ 44 | Jay Buhner | .30 | .14 |
| ❑ 45 | Brady Anderson | .30 | .14 |
| ❑ 46 | Edgar Renteria | .20 | .09 |
| ❑ 47 | Rick Aguilera | .20 | .09 |
| ❑ 48 | Henry Rodriguez | .20 | .09 |
| ❑ 49 | Mike Piazza | 2.50 | 1.10 |
| ❑ 50 | Todd Zeile | .30 | .14 |
| ❑ 51 | Rey Ordonez | .20 | .09 |
| ❑ 52 | Tony Womack | .20 | .09 |
| ❑ 53 | Mike Sweeney | .30 | .14 |
| ❑ 54 | Jeffrey Hammonds | .30 | .14 |
| ❑ 55 | Kevin Orie | .20 | .09 |
| ❑ 56 | Alex Gonzalez | .20 | .09 |
| ❑ 57 | Jose Canseco | 1.00 | .45 |
| ❑ 58 | Joey Hamilton | .20 | .09 |
| ❑ 59 | Brad Radke | .30 | .14 |
| ❑ 60 | Kevin Appier | .30 | .14 |
| ❑ 61 | Manny Ramirez | 1.00 | .45 |
| ❑ 62 | Jeromy Burnitz | .30 | .14 |
| ❑ 63 | Matt Morris | .20 | .09 |
| ❑ 64 | Jason Dickson | .20 | .09 |
| ❑ 65 | Tom Glavine | .75 | .35 |
| ❑ 66 | Wally Joyner | .30 | .14 |
| ❑ 67 | Todd Jones | .20 | .09 |
| ❑ 68 | Sandy Alomar Jr. | .30 | .14 |
| ❑ 69 | Mike Lansing | .20 | .09 |
| ❑ 70 | Todd Stottlemyre | .20 | .09 |
| ❑ 71 | Jay Bell | .30 | .14 |
| ❑ 72 | Joey Cora | .20 | .09 |
| ❑ 73 | Scott Spiezio | .20 | .09 |
| ❑ 74 | Joe Carter | .30 | .14 |
| ❑ 75 | Jose Guillen | .20 | .09 |
| ❑ 76 | Damion Easley | .20 | .09 |
| ❑ 77 | Alex Fernandez | .20 | .09 |
| ❑ 78 | Randy Johnson | 1.00 | .45 |
| ❑ 79 | J.T. Snow | .30 | .14 |
| ❑ 80 | Bernard Gilkey | .20 | .09 |
| ❑ 81 | David Segui | .20 | .09 |
| ❑ 82 | Dante Bichette | .30 | .14 |
| ❑ 83 | Derek Jeter | 3.00 | 1.35 |
| ❑ 84 | Mark Wohlers | .20 | .09 |
| ❑ 85 | Ricky Bottalico | .20 | .09 |
| ❑ 86 | Mike Mussina | .75 | .35 |
| ❑ 87 | Gary Sheffield | .75 | .35 |
| ❑ 88 | Hideo Nomo | .75 | .35 |
| ❑ 89 | Mark Grace | .75 | .35 |
| ❑ 90 | Darryl Kile | .30 | .14 |
| ❑ 91 | Shawn Estes | .20 | .09 |
| ❑ 92 | Vinny Castilla | .30 | .14 |
| ❑ 93 | Jose Rosado | .20 | .09 |
| ❑ 94 | Kenny Lofton | .30 | .14 |
| ❑ 95 | Jason Giambi | .75 | .35 |
| ❑ 96 | Ray Lankford | .30 | .14 |
| ❑ 97 | Hideki Irabu | .20 | .09 |
| ❑ 98 | Javy Lopez | .30 | .14 |
| ❑ 99 | Jeff Montgomery | .20 | .09 |
| ❑ 100 | Dennis Eckersley | .30 | .14 |
| ❑ 101 | Armando Benitez | .20 | .09 |
| ❑ 102 | Tim Naehring | .20 | .09 |
| ❑ 103 | Luis Gonzalez | .30 | .14 |
| ❑ 104 | Todd Hollandsworth | .20 | .09 |
| ❑ 105 | Wade Boggs | 1.00 | .45 |
| ❑ 106 | Mickey Morandini | .20 | .09 |
| ❑ 107 | Rusty Greer | .30 | .14 |
| ❑ 108 | Terry Steinbach | .20 | .09 |
| ❑ 109 | Pete Rose Jr. | .30 | .14 |
| ❑ 110 | Checklist | .20 | .09 |
| ❑ 111 | Tino Martinez | .30 | .14 |
| ❑ 112 | Roberto Alomar | .75 | .35 |
| ❑ 113 | Jeff King | .20 | .09 |
| ❑ 114 | Brian Jordan | .30 | .14 |
| ❑ 115 | Darin Erstad | .75 | .35 |
| ❑ 116 | Ken Caminiti | .30 | .14 |
| ❑ 117 | Jim Thome | .50 | .23 |
| ❑ 118 | Paul Molitor | .75 | .35 |
| ❑ 119 | Ivan Rodriguez | 1.00 | .45 |
| ❑ 120 | Bernie Williams | .75 | .35 |
| ❑ 121 | Todd Hundley | .20 | .09 |
| ❑ 122 | Andres Galarraga | .50 | .23 |
| ❑ 123 | Greg Maddux | 2.00 | .90 |
| ❑ 124 | Edgar Martinez | .50 | .23 |
| ❑ 125 | Ron Gant | .30 | .14 |
| ❑ 126 | Derek Bell | .20 | .09 |
| ❑ 127 | Roger Clemens | 1.50 | .70 |
| ❑ 128 | Rondell White | .30 | .14 |
| ❑ 129 | Barry Larkin | .75 | .35 |
| ❑ 130 | Robin Ventura | .30 | .14 |
| ❑ 131 | Jason Kendall | .30 | .14 |
| ❑ 132 | Chipper Jones | 2.00 | .90 |
| ❑ 133 | John Franco | .30 | .14 |
| ❑ 134 | Sammy Sosa | 1.25 | .55 |
| ❑ 135 | Chuck Knoblauch | .30 | .14 |
| ❑ 136 | Ellis Burks | .30 | .14 |
| ❑ 137 | Al Martin | .20 | .09 |
| ❑ 138 | Tim Salmon | .30 | .14 |
| ❑ 139 | Moises Alou | .30 | .14 |
| ❑ 140 | Lance Johnson | .20 | .09 |
| ❑ 141 | Justin Thompson | .20 | .09 |
| ❑ 142 | Will Clark | .75 | .35 |
| ❑ 143 | Barry Bonds | 1.25 | .55 |
| ❑ 144 | Craig Biggio | .50 | .23 |
| ❑ 145 | John Smoltz | .30 | .14 |
| ❑ 146 | Cal Ripken | 3.00 | 1.35 |
| ❑ 147 | Ken Griffey Jr. | 3.00 | 1.35 |
| ❑ 148 | Paul O'Neill | .30 | .14 |
| ❑ 149 | Todd Helton | 1.00 | .45 |
| ❑ 150 | John Olerud | .30 | .14 |
| ❑ 151 | Mark McGwire | 3.00 | 1.35 |
| ❑ 152 | Jose Cruz Jr. | .30 | .14 |
| ❑ 153 | Jeff Cirillo | .30 | .14 |
| ❑ 154 | Dean Palmer | .30 | .14 |
| ❑ 155 | John Wetteland | .30 | .14 |
| ❑ 156 | Eric Karros | .30 | .14 |
| ❑ 157 | Steve Finley | .30 | .14 |
| ❑ 158 | Albert Belle | .50 | .23 |
| ❑ 159 | Curt Schilling | .30 | .14 |
| ❑ 160 | Raul Mondesi | .30 | .14 |
| ❑ 161 | Andruw Jones | .75 | .35 |
| ❑ 162 | Nomar Garciaparra | 2.50 | 1.10 |
| ❑ 163 | David Justice | .50 | .23 |
| ❑ 164 | Andy Pettitte | .30 | .14 |
| ❑ 165 | Pedro Martinez | 1.00 | .45 |

## 1999 Topps Opening Day

| | | MINT | NRMT |
|---|---|---|---|
| COMPLETE SET (165) | | 45.00 | 20.00 |
| ❑ 1 | Hank Aaron | 2.50 | 1.10 |
| ❑ 2 | Roger Clemens | 1.50 | .70 |
| ❑ 3 | Andres Galarraga UER | .50 | .23 |
| | Card erroneously numbered 2 | | |
| ❑ 4 | Scott Brosius | .30 | .14 |
| ❑ 5 | Ray Durham | .30 | .14 |
| ❑ 6 | Will Clark | .75 | .35 |
| ❑ 7 | David Wells | .30 | .14 |
| ❑ 8 | Jose Guillen | .20 | .09 |
| ❑ 9 | Edgardo Alfonzo | .30 | .14 |
| ❑ 10 | Manny Ramirez | 1.00 | .45 |
| ❑ 11 | Greg Maddux | 2.00 | .90 |
| ❑ 12 | David Segui | .20 | .09 |
| ❑ 13 | Darryl Strawberry | .30 | .14 |
| ❑ 14 | Brad Radke | .30 | .14 |
| ❑ 15 | Kerry Wood | .30 | .14 |
| ❑ 16 | Paul Konerko | .30 | .14 |
| ❑ 17 | Travis Lee | .20 | .09 |
| ❑ 18 | Kenny Rogers | .20 | .09 |
| ❑ 19 | Todd Walker | .20 | .09 |
| ❑ 20 | John Olerud | .30 | .14 |
| ❑ 21 | Nolan Ryan | 5.00 | 2.20 |
| ❑ 22 | Ray Lankford | .30 | .14 |
| ❑ 23 | Bartolo Colon | .30 | .14 |
| ❑ 24 | Brady Anderson | .30 | .14 |
| ❑ 25 | Jorge Posada | .30 | .14 |
| ❑ 26 | Justin Thompson | .20 | .09 |
| ❑ 27 | Juan Gonzalez | .75 | .35 |
| ❑ 28 | Chuck Knoblauch | .30 | .14 |
| ❑ 29 | Todd Helton | 1.00 | .45 |
| ❑ 30 | Gary Sheffield | .75 | .35 |
| ❑ 31 | Rod Beck | .20 | .09 |
| ❑ 32 | Garret Anderson | .30 | .14 |
| ❑ 33 | Rondell White | .30 | .14 |
| ❑ 34 | Vladimir Guerrero | 1.25 | .55 |
| ❑ 35 | Eric Karros | .30 | .14 |
| ❑ 36 | Mo Vaughn | .30 | .14 |
| ❑ 37 | Sammy Sosa | 1.50 | .70 |
| ❑ 38 | Kenny Lofton | .30 | .14 |
| ❑ 39 | Mark McGwire | 3.00 | 1.35 |
| ❑ 40 | Javy Lopez | .30 | .14 |
| ❑ 41 | Damion Easley | .20 | .09 |
| ❑ 42 | Andy Pettitte | .30 | .14 |
| ❑ 43 | Tony Gwynn | 1.50 | .70 |
| ❑ 44 | Jay Bell | .30 | .14 |
| ❑ 45 | Jose Canseco | 1.00 | .45 |
| ❑ 46 | John Wetteland | .30 | .14 |
| ❑ 47 | Mike Caruso | .20 | .09 |
| ❑ 48 | Derek Jeter | 3.00 | 1.35 |
| ❑ 49 | Aaron Sele | .30 | .14 |
| ❑ 50 | Jeff Cirillo | .30 | .14 |
| ❑ 51 | Mark Kotsay | .20 | .09 |
| ❑ 52 | Albert Belle | .50 | .23 |
| ❑ 53 | Matt Lawton | .30 | .14 |
| ❑ 54 | Pedro Martinez | 1.00 | .45 |
| ❑ 55 | Greg Vaughn | .30 | .14 |
| ❑ 56 | Neifi Perez | .20 | .09 |
| ❑ 57 | Derek Bell | .20 | .09 |
| ❑ 58 | Ken Griffey Jr. | 3.00 | 1.35 |
| ❑ 59 | David Cone | .30 | .14 |
| ❑ 60 | Dean Palmer | .30 | .14 |
| ❑ 61 | Trevor Hoffman | .30 | .14 |

| | | |
|---|---|---|
| ❑ 62 Billy Wagner | .20 | .09 |
| ❑ 63 Shawn Green | .75 | .35 |
| ❑ 64 Ben Grieve | .30 | .14 |
| ❑ 65 Tom Goodwin | .20 | .09 |
| ❑ 66 Jaret Wright | .20 | .09 |
| ❑ 67 Dmitri Young | .30 | .14 |
| ❑ 68 Hideki Irabu | .20 | .09 |
| ❑ 69 Jeff Fassero | .20 | .09 |
| ❑ 70 Matt Williams | .50 | .23 |
| ❑ 71 Bret Saberhagen | .30 | .14 |
| ❑ 72 Chad Curtis | .20 | .09 |
| ❑ 73 Scott Rolen | .75 | .35 |
| ❑ 74 J.T. Snow | .30 | .14 |
| ❑ 75 Rusty Greer | .30 | .14 |
| ❑ 76 Jim Edmonds | .75 | .35 |
| ❑ 77 Ron Gant | .30 | .14 |
| ❑ 78 A.J. Hinch | .20 | .09 |
| ❑ 79 Shannon Stewart | .30 | .14 |
| ❑ 80 Brad Fullmer | .30 | .14 |
| ❑ 81 Walt Weiss | .20 | .09 |
| ❑ 82 Fred McGriff | .50 | .23 |
| ❑ 83 Darin Erstad | .75 | .35 |
| ❑ 84 Eric Young | .20 | .09 |
| ❑ 85 Livan Hernandez | .20 | .09 |
| ❑ 86 Jeff Bagwell | 1.00 | .45 |
| ❑ 87 Omar Vizquel | .30 | .14 |
| ❑ 88 Eric Davis | .30 | .14 |
| ❑ 89 Magglio Ordonez | .50 | .23 |
| ❑ 90 John Valentin | .20 | .09 |
| ❑ 91 Dave Dellucci | .20 | .09 |
| ❑ 92 Chan Ho Park | .30 | .14 |
| ❑ 93 Masato Yoshii | .30 | .14 |
| ❑ 94 Bret Boone | .30 | .14 |
| ❑ 95 Mariano Rivera | .30 | .14 |
| ❑ 96 Bobby Jones | .20 | .09 |
| ❑ 97 Francisco Cordova | .20 | .09 |
| ❑ 98 Mike Mussina | .75 | .35 |
| ❑ 99 Denny Neagle | .20 | .09 |
| ❑ 100 Edgar Martinez | .50 | .23 |
| ❑ 101 Jason Kendall | .30 | .14 |
| ❑ 102 Jeff King | .20 | .09 |
| ❑ 103 Rey Ordonez | .20 | .09 |
| ❑ 104 Andruw Jones | .75 | .35 |
| ❑ 105 Vinny Castilla | .30 | .14 |
| ❑ 106 Troy Glaus | 1.25 | .55 |
| ❑ 107 Tom Glavine | .75 | .35 |
| ❑ 108 Moises Alou | .30 | .14 |
| ❑ 109 Carlos Delgado | .75 | .35 |
| ❑ 110 Raul Mondesi | .30 | .14 |
| ❑ 111 Shane Reynolds | .20 | .09 |
| ❑ 112 Jason Giambi | .75 | .35 |
| ❑ 113 Jose Cruz Jr. | .30 | .14 |
| ❑ 114 Craig Biggio | .50 | .23 |
| ❑ 115 Tim Salmon | .30 | .14 |
| ❑ 116 Chipper Jones | 2.00 | .90 |
| ❑ 117 Andy Benes | .20 | .09 |
| ❑ 118 John Smoltz | .30 | .14 |
| ❑ 119 Jeromy Burnitz | .30 | .14 |
| ❑ 120 Randy Johnson | 1.00 | .45 |
| ❑ 121 Mark Grace | .75 | .35 |
| ❑ 122 Henry Rodriguez | .20 | .09 |
| ❑ 123 Ryan Klesko | .30 | .14 |
| ❑ 124 Kevin Milwood | .30 | .14 |
| ❑ 125 Sean Casey | .30 | .14 |
| ❑ 126 Brian Jordan | .30 | .14 |
| ❑ 127 Kevin Brown | .50 | .23 |
| ❑ 128 Orlando Hernandez | .30 | .14 |
| ❑ 129 Barry Bonds | 1.25 | .55 |
| ❑ 130 David Justice | .50 | .23 |
| ❑ 131 Carlos Perez | .20 | .09 |
| ❑ 132 Andy Ashby | .20 | .09 |
| ❑ 133 Paul O'Neill | .30 | .14 |
| ❑ 134 Curt Schilling | .30 | .14 |
| ❑ 135 Alex Rodriguez | 2.50 | 1.10 |
| ❑ 136 Cliff Floyd | .30 | .14 |
| ❑ 137 Rafael Palmeiro | .75 | .35 |
| ❑ 138 Nomar Garciaparra | 2.50 | 1.10 |
| ❑ 139 Mike Piazza | 2.50 | 1.10 |
| ❑ 140 Roberto Alomar | .75 | .35 |
| ❑ 141 Todd Hundley | .20 | .09 |
| ❑ 142 Jeff Kent | .50 | .23 |
| ❑ 143 Barry Larkin | .75 | .35 |
| ❑ 144 Cal Ripken | 3.00 | 1.35 |
| ❑ 145 Jay Buhner | .30 | .14 |
| ❑ 146 Kevin Young | .30 | .14 |
| ❑ 147 Ivan Rodriguez | 1.00 | .45 |
| ❑ 148 Al Leiter | .30 | .14 |
| ❑ 149 Sandy Alomar Jr. | .30 | .14 |
| ❑ 150 Bernie Williams | .75 | .35 |
| ❑ 151 Ellis Burks | .30 | .14 |
| ❑ 152 Wally Joyner | .30 | .14 |
| ❑ 153 Bobby Higginson | .30 | .14 |
| ❑ 154 Tony Clark | .20 | .09 |
| ❑ 155 Larry Walker | .30 | .14 |
| ❑ 156 Frank Thomas | 1.50 | .70 |
| ❑ 157 Tino Martinez | .30 | .14 |
| ❑ 158 Jim Thome | .50 | .23 |
| ❑ 159 Dante Bichette | .30 | .14 |
| ❑ 160 David Wells HL | .20 | .09 |
| ❑ 161 Roger Clemens HL | .75 | .35 |
| ❑ 162 Kerry Wood HL | .30 | .14 |
| ❑ 163 Mark McGwire HR 70 | 8.00 | 3.60 |
| ❑ 164 Sammy Sosa HR 66 | 4.00 | 1.80 |
| ❑ 165 Checklist | .20 | .09 |
| ❑ NNO Hank Aaron AU | 300.00 | 135.00 |

## 2000 Topps Opening Day

| | MINT | NRMT |
|---|---|---|
| COMPLETE SET (165) | 50.00 | 22.00 |
| ❑ 1 Mark McGwire | 3.00 | 1.35 |
| ❑ 2 Tony Gwynn | 1.50 | .70 |
| ❑ 3 Wade Boggs | 1.00 | .45 |
| ❑ 4 Cal Ripken | 3.00 | 1.35 |
| ❑ 5 Matt Williams | .50 | .23 |
| ❑ 6 Jay Buhner | .30 | .14 |
| ❑ 7 Mike Lieberthal | .30 | .14 |
| ❑ 8 Magglio Ordonez | .30 | .14 |
| ❑ 9 Derek Jeter | 3.00 | 1.35 |
| ❑ 10 Javy Lopez | .30 | .14 |
| ❑ 11 Armando Benitez | .30 | .14 |
| ❑ 12 Darin Erstad | .75 | .35 |
| ❑ 13 Mark Grace | .75 | .35 |
| ❑ 14 Eric Karros | .30 | .14 |
| ❑ 15 J.T. Snow | .30 | .14 |
| ❑ 16 Luis Castillo | .30 | .14 |
| ❑ 17 Rey Ordonez | .20 | .09 |
| ❑ 18 Bob Abreu | .30 | .14 |
| ❑ 19 Warren Morris | .20 | .09 |
| ❑ 20 Juan Gonzalez | .75 | .35 |
| ❑ 21 Dean Palmer | .30 | .14 |
| ❑ 22 Hank Aaron | 2.00 | .90 |
| ❑ 23 Jeff Bagwell | 1.00 | .45 |
| ❑ 24 Sammy Sosa | 1.50 | .70 |
| ❑ 25 Randy Johnson | 1.00 | .45 |
| ❑ 26 Dante Bichette | .30 | .14 |
| ❑ 27 Frank Thomas | 1.50 | .70 |
| ❑ 28 Pedro Martinez | 1.00 | .45 |
| ❑ 29 Brain Giles | .30 | .14 |
| ❑ 30 Ivan Rodriguez | 1.00 | .45 |
| ❑ 31 Roger Cedeno | .20 | .09 |
| ❑ 32 David Justice | .50 | .23 |
| ❑ 33 Ken Caminiti | .30 | .14 |
| ❑ 34 Brian Jordan | .30 | .14 |
| ❑ 35 John Olerud | .30 | .14 |
| ❑ 36 Pokey Reese | .30 | .14 |
| ❑ 37 Barry Larkin | .75 | .35 |
| ❑ 38 Edgar Martinez | .50 | .23 |
| ❑ 39 Carlos Delgado | .75 | .35 |
| ❑ 40 Troy Glaus | 1.00 | .45 |
| ❑ 41 Ben Grieve | .30 | .14 |
| ❑ 42 Jose Lima | .20 | .09 |
| ❑ 43 Luis Gonzalez | .30 | .14 |
| ❑ 44 Alex Rodriguez | 2.50 | 1.10 |
| ❑ 45 Preston Wilson | .30 | .14 |
| ❑ 46 Rickey Henderson | 1.00 | .45 |
| ❑ 47 Gary Sheffield | .75 | .35 |
| ❑ 48 Jim Edmonds | .75 | .35 |
| ❑ 49 Greg Vaughn | .30 | .14 |
| ❑ 50 Neifi Perez | .20 | .09 |
| ❑ 51 Paul O'Neill | .30 | .14 |
| ❑ 52 Jermaine Dye | .30 | .14 |
| ❑ 53 Curt Schilling | .30 | .14 |
| ❑ 54 Edgardo Alfonzo | .30 | .14 |
| ❑ 55 John Smoltz | .30 | .14 |
| ❑ 56 Chuck Finley | .30 | .14 |
| ❑ 57 Billy Wagner | .20 | .09 |
| ❑ 58 David Cone | .30 | .14 |
| ❑ 59 Roberto Alomar | .75 | .35 |
| ❑ 60 Charles Nagy | .20 | .09 |
| ❑ 61 Mike Mussina | .75 | .35 |
| ❑ 62 Robin Ventura | .50 | .23 |
| ❑ 63 Kevin Brown | .50 | .23 |
| ❑ 64 Pat Hentgen | .20 | .09 |
| ❑ 65 Ryan Klesko | .30 | .14 |
| ❑ 66 Derek Bell | .20 | .09 |
| ❑ 67 Larry Walker | .30 | .14 |
| ❑ 68 Scott Williamson | .20 | .09 |
| ❑ 69 Jose Offerman | .20 | .09 |
| ❑ 70 Doug Mientkiewicz | .20 | .09 |
| ❑ 71 John Snyder RC | .50 | .23 |
| ❑ 72 Sandy Alomar Jr. | .20 | .09 |
| ❑ 73 Joe Nathan | .20 | .09 |
| ❑ 74 Steve Finley | .30 | .14 |
| ❑ 75 Dave Martinez | .20 | .09 |
| ❑ 76 Fernando Tatis | .30 | .14 |
| ❑ 77 Kenny Lofton | .30 | .14 |
| ❑ 78 Paul Byrd | .20 | .09 |
| ❑ 79 Aaron Sele | .20 | .09 |
| ❑ 80 Roger Clemens | 1.50 | .70 |
| ❑ 81 Francisco Cordova | .20 | .09 |
| ❑ 82 Wally Joyner | .30 | .14 |
| ❑ 83 Jason Kendall | .30 | .14 |
| ❑ 84 Carlos Beltran | .30 | .14 |
| ❑ 85 Chipper Jones | 2.00 | .90 |
| ❑ 86 Vladimir Guerrero | 1.25 | .55 |
| ❑ 87 Tom Goodwin | .20 | .09 |
| ❑ 88 Brian Daubach | .20 | .09 |
| ❑ 89 Jay Bell | .30 | .14 |
| ❑ 90 Roy Halladay | .20 | .09 |
| ❑ 91 Miguel Tejada | .30 | .14 |
| ❑ 92 Eric Davis | .30 | .14 |
| ❑ 93 Henry Rodriguez | .20 | .09 |
| ❑ 94 Joe McEwing | .20 | .09 |
| ❑ 95 Jeff Kent | .50 | .23 |
| ❑ 96 Jeff Zimmerman | .20 | .09 |
| ❑ 97 Tony Fernandez | .20 | .09 |
| ❑ 98 Jason Giambi | .75 | .35 |
| ❑ 99 Jose Canseco | 1.00 | .45 |
| ❑ 100 Alex Gonzalez | .20 | .09 |
| ❑ 101 Erubiel Durazo<br>Pat Burrell<br>Nick Johnson | 1.25 | .55 |
| ❑ 102 Lance Berkman<br>Corey Patterson<br>Roosevelt Brown | 1.25 | .55 |
| ❑ 103 Bobby Bradley RC<br>Eric Munson | 2.00 | .90 |
| ❑ 104 Josh Hamilton<br>Corey Myers RC | 1.25 | .55 |
| ❑ 105 M.McGwire MM 70th HR | 3.00 | 1.35 |
| ❑ 106 H.Aaron MM 715th HR | 2.00 | .90 |
| ❑ 107 C.Ripken MM 2131st Game | 3.00 | 1.35 |
| ❑ 108 W.Boggs MM 3000th Hit | 1.00 | .45 |
| ❑ 109 T.Gwynn MM 3000th Hit | 1.50 | .70 |
| ❑ 110 Hank Aaron 1954 UER128 | 4.00 | 1.80 |
| ❑ 111 Tom Glavine | .75 | .35 |
| ❑ 112 Mo Vaughn | .30 | .14 |
| ❑ 113 Tino Martinez | .30 | .14 |
| ❑ 114 Craig Biggio | .50 | .23 |
| ❑ 115 Tim Hudson | .75 | .35 |
| ❑ 116 John Wetteland | .30 | .14 |
| ❑ 117 Ellis Burks | .30 | .14 |
| ❑ 118 David Wells | .30 | .14 |
| ❑ 119 Rico Brogna | .20 | .09 |
| ❑ 120 Greg Maddux | 2.00 | .90 |
| ❑ 121 Jeromy Burnitz | .30 | .14 |
| ❑ 122 Raul Mondesi | .30 | .14 |

| | | MINT | NRMT |
|---|---|---|---|
| ❑ | 123 Rondell White | .30 | .14 |
| ❑ | 124 Barry Bonds | 1.25 | .55 |
| ❑ | 125 Orlando Hernandez | .30 | .14 |
| ❑ | 126 Bartolo Colon | .30 | .14 |
| ❑ | 127 Tim Salmon | .30 | .14 |
| ❑ | 128 Kevin Young | .20 | .09 |
| ❑ | 129 Troy O'Leary | .20 | .09 |
| ❑ | 130 Jim Thome | .50 | .23 |
| ❑ | 131 Ray Durham | .30 | .14 |
| ❑ | 132 Tony Clark | .20 | .09 |
| ❑ | 133 Mariano Rivera | .30 | .14 |
| ❑ | 134 Omar Vizquel | .30 | .14 |
| ❑ | 135 Ken Griffey Jr. | 3.00 | 1.35 |
| ❑ | 136 Shawn Green | .75 | .35 |
| ❑ | 137 Cliff Floyd | .30 | .14 |
| ❑ | 138 Al Leiter | .20 | .09 |
| ❑ | 139 Mike Hampton | .30 | .14 |
| ❑ | 140 Mike Piazza | 2.50 | 1.10 |
| ❑ | 141 Andy Pettitte | .30 | .14 |
| ❑ | 142 Albert Belle | .50 | .23 |
| ❑ | 143 Scott Rolen | .75 | .35 |
| ❑ | 144 Rusty Greer | .30 | .14 |
| ❑ | 145 Kevin Millwood | .30 | .14 |
| ❑ | 146 Sean Casey | .30 | .14 |
| ❑ | 147 Nomar Garciaparra | 2.50 | 1.10 |
| ❑ | 148 Denny Neagle | .20 | .09 |
| ❑ | 149 Manny Ramirez | 1.00 | .45 |
| ❑ | 150 Vinny Castilla | .30 | .14 |
| ❑ | 151 Andruw Jones | .75 | .35 |
| ❑ | 152 Johnny Damon | .30 | .14 |
| ❑ | 153 Eric Milton | .20 | .09 |
| ❑ | 154 Todd Helton | 1.00 | .45 |
| ❑ | 155 Rafael Palmeiro | .75 | .35 |
| ❑ | 156 Damion Easley | .20 | .09 |
| ❑ | 157 Carlos Febles | .20 | .09 |
| ❑ | 158 Paul Konerko | .30 | .14 |
| ❑ | 159 Bernie Williams | .75 | .35 |
| ❑ | 160 K.Griffey Jr. MM HR Dad | 3.00 | 1.35 |
| ❑ | 161 B.Bonds MM 400/400 | 1.25 | .55 |
| ❑ | 162 S.Sosa MM 20 HR June | 1.50 | .70 |
| ❑ | 163 D.Jeter MM 96 AL ROY | 3.00 | 1.35 |
| ❑ | 164 A.Rodriguez MM 40/40 | 2.50 | 1.10 |
| ❑ | 165 Checklist | .20 | .09 |

## 1997 Topps Stars

| | | MINT | NRMT |
|---|---|---|---|
| | COMPLETE SET (125) | 60.00 | 27.00 |
| ❑ | 1 Larry Walker | .25 | .11 |
| ❑ | 2 Tino Martinez | .25 | .11 |
| ❑ | 3 Cal Ripken | 2.50 | 1.10 |
| ❑ | 4 Ken Griffey Jr. | 2.50 | 1.10 |
| ❑ | 5 Chipper Jones | 1.50 | .70 |
| ❑ | 6 David Justice | .40 | .18 |
| ❑ | 7 Mike Piazza | 2.00 | .90 |
| ❑ | 8 Jeff Bagwell | .75 | .35 |
| ❑ | 9 Ron Gant | .15 | .07 |
| ❑ | 10 Sammy Sosa | 1.25 | .55 |
| ❑ | 11 Tony Gwynn | 1.25 | .55 |
| ❑ | 12 Carlos Baerga | .15 | .07 |
| ❑ | 13 Frank Thomas | 1.25 | .55 |
| ❑ | 14 Moises Alou | .25 | .11 |
| ❑ | 15 Barry Larkin | .60 | .25 |
| ❑ | 16 Ivan Rodriguez | .75 | .35 |
| ❑ | 17 Greg Maddux | 1.50 | .70 |
| ❑ | 18 Jim Edmonds | .60 | .25 |
| ❑ | 19 Jose Canseco | .75 | .35 |
| ❑ | 20 Rafael Palmeiro | .60 | .25 |
| ❑ | 21 Paul Molitor | .60 | .25 |
| ❑ | 22 Kevin Appier | .25 | .11 |
| ❑ | 23 Raul Mondesi | .25 | .11 |
| ❑ | 24 Lance Johnson | .15 | .07 |
| ❑ | 25 Edgar Martinez | .40 | .18 |
| ❑ | 26 Andres Galarraga | .40 | .18 |
| ❑ | 27 Mo Vaughn | .25 | .11 |
| ❑ | 28 Ken Caminiti | .25 | .11 |
| ❑ | 29 Cecil Fielder | .25 | .11 |
| ❑ | 30 Harold Baines | .25 | .11 |
| ❑ | 31 Roberto Alomar | .60 | .25 |
| ❑ | 32 Shawn Estes | .25 | .11 |
| ❑ | 33 Tom Glavine | .60 | .25 |
| ❑ | 34 Dennis Eckersley | .25 | .11 |
| ❑ | 35 Manny Ramirez | .75 | .35 |
| ❑ | 36 John Olerud | .25 | .11 |
| ❑ | 37 Juan Gonzalez | .60 | .25 |
| ❑ | 38 Chuck Knoblauch | .25 | .11 |
| ❑ | 39 Albert Belle | .40 | .18 |
| ❑ | 40 Vinny Castilla | .25 | .11 |
| ❑ | 41 John Smoltz | .25 | .11 |
| ❑ | 42 Barry Bonds | 1.00 | .45 |
| ❑ | 43 Randy Johnson | .75 | .35 |
| ❑ | 44 Brady Anderson | .25 | .11 |
| ❑ | 45 Jeff Blauser | .15 | .07 |
| ❑ | 46 Craig Biggio | .40 | .18 |
| ❑ | 47 Jeff Conine | .15 | .07 |
| ❑ | 48 Marquis Grissom | .15 | .07 |
| ❑ | 49 Mark Grace | .60 | .25 |
| ❑ | 50 Roger Clemens | 1.25 | .55 |
| ❑ | 51 Mark McGwire | 2.50 | 1.10 |
| ❑ | 52 Fred McGriff | .40 | .18 |
| ❑ | 53 Gary Sheffield | .60 | .25 |
| ❑ | 54 Bobby Jones | .15 | .07 |
| ❑ | 55 Eric Young | .15 | .07 |
| ❑ | 56 Robin Ventura | .25 | .11 |
| ❑ | 57 Wade Boggs | .75 | .35 |
| ❑ | 58 Joe Carter | .25 | .11 |
| ❑ | 59 Ryne Sandberg | .75 | .35 |
| ❑ | 60 Matt Williams | .40 | .18 |
| ❑ | 61 Todd Hundley | .15 | .07 |
| ❑ | 62 Dante Bichette | .25 | .11 |
| ❑ | 63 Chili Davis | .25 | .11 |
| ❑ | 64 Kenny Lofton | .25 | .11 |
| ❑ | 65 Jay Buhner | .25 | .11 |
| ❑ | 66 Will Clark | .60 | .25 |
| ❑ | 67 Travis Fryman | .25 | .11 |
| ❑ | 68 Pat Hentgen | .15 | .07 |
| ❑ | 69 Ellis Burks | .25 | .11 |
| ❑ | 70 Mike Mussina | .60 | .25 |
| ❑ | 71 Hideo Nomo | .60 | .25 |
| ❑ | 72 Sandy Alomar Jr. | .25 | .11 |
| ❑ | 73 Bobby Bonilla | .25 | .11 |
| ❑ | 74 Rickey Henderson | .75 | .35 |
| ❑ | 75 David Cone | .25 | .11 |
| ❑ | 76 Terry Steinbach | .15 | .07 |
| ❑ | 77 Pedro Martinez | .75 | .35 |
| ❑ | 78 Jim Thome | .40 | .18 |
| ❑ | 79 Rod Beck | .15 | .07 |
| ❑ | 80 Randy Myers | .15 | .07 |
| ❑ | 81 Charles Nagy | .15 | .07 |
| ❑ | 82 Mark Wohlers | .15 | .07 |
| ❑ | 83 Paul O'Neill | .25 | .11 |
| ❑ | 84 Curt Schilling | .25 | .11 |
| ❑ | 85 Joey Cora | .15 | .07 |
| ❑ | 86 John Franco | .25 | .11 |
| ❑ | 87 Kevin Brown | .25 | .11 |
| ❑ | 88 Benito Santiago | .15 | .07 |
| ❑ | 89 Ray Lankford | .25 | .11 |
| ❑ | 90 Bernie Williams | .60 | .25 |
| ❑ | 91 Jason Dickson | .15 | .07 |
| ❑ | 92 Jeff Cirillo | .25 | .11 |
| ❑ | 93 Nomar Garciaparra | 2.00 | .90 |
| ❑ | 94 Mariano Rivera | .25 | .11 |
| ❑ | 95 Javy Lopez | .25 | .11 |
| ❑ | 96 Tony Womack RC | 2.00 | .90 |
| ❑ | 97 Jose Rosado | .15 | .07 |
| ❑ | 98 Denny Neagle | .25 | .11 |
| ❑ | 99 Darryl Kile | .25 | .11 |
| ❑ | 100 Justin Thompson | .15 | .07 |
| ❑ | 101 Juan Encarnacion | .25 | .11 |
| ❑ | 102 Brad Fullmer | .25 | .11 |
| ❑ | 103 Kris Benson RC | 5.00 | 2.20 |
| ❑ | 104 Todd Helton | 1.00 | .45 |
| ❑ | 105 Paul Konerko | .25 | .11 |
| ❑ | 106 Travis Lee RC | 2.00 | .90 |
| ❑ | 107 Todd Greene | .15 | .07 |
| ❑ | 108 Mark Kotsay RC | 1.50 | .70 |
| ❑ | 109 Carl Pavano | .25 | .11 |
| ❑ | 110 Kerry Wood RC | 8.00 | 3.60 |
| ❑ | 111 Jason Romano RC | 3.00 | 1.35 |
| ❑ | 112 Geoff Goetz RC | .60 | .25 |
| ❑ | 113 Scott Hodges RC | 1.25 | .55 |
| ❑ | 114 Aaron Akin RC | .60 | .25 |
| ❑ | 115 Vernon Wells RC | 4.00 | 1.80 |
| ❑ | 116 Chris Stowe RC | .15 | .07 |
| ❑ | 117 Brett Caradonna RC | .60 | .25 |
| ❑ | 118 Adam Kennedy RC | 2.50 | 1.10 |
| ❑ | 119 Jayson Werth RC | 1.25 | .55 |
| ❑ | 120 Glenn Davis RC | .60 | .25 |
| ❑ | 121 Troy Cameron RC | .75 | .35 |
| ❑ | 122 J.J. Davis RC | 2.00 | .90 |
| ❑ | 123 Jason Dellaero RC | .60 | .25 |
| ❑ | 124 Jason Standridge RC | 1.00 | .45 |
| ❑ | 125 Lance Berkman RC | 5.00 | 2.20 |
| ❑ | NNO Checklist | .15 | .07 |

## 1998 Topps Stars

| | | MINT | NRMT |
|---|---|---|---|
| | COMP.RED SET (150) | 80.00 | 36.00 |
| ❑ | 1 Greg Maddux | 4.00 | 1.80 |
| ❑ | 2 Darryl Kile | .60 | .25 |
| ❑ | 3 Rod Beck | .40 | .18 |
| ❑ | 4 Ellis Burks | .60 | .25 |
| ❑ | 5 Gary Sheffield | 1.50 | .70 |
| ❑ | 6 David Ortiz | .40 | .18 |
| ❑ | 7 Marquis Grissom | .40 | .18 |
| ❑ | 8 Tony Womack | .40 | .18 |
| ❑ | 9 Mike Mussina | 1.50 | .70 |
| ❑ | 10 Bernie Williams | 1.50 | .70 |
| ❑ | 11 Andy Benes | .40 | .18 |
| ❑ | 12 Rusty Greer | .60 | .25 |
| ❑ | 13 Carlos Delgado | 1.50 | .70 |
| ❑ | 14 Jim Edmonds | 1.50 | .70 |
| ❑ | 15 Raul Mondesi | .60 | .25 |
| ❑ | 16 Andres Galarraga | 1.00 | .45 |
| ❑ | 17 Wade Boggs | 2.00 | .90 |
| ❑ | 18 Paul O'Neill | .60 | .25 |
| ❑ | 19 Edgar Renteria | .40 | .18 |
| ❑ | 20 Tony Clark | .40 | .18 |
| ❑ | 21 Vladimir Guerrero | 2.50 | 1.10 |
| ❑ | 22 Moises Alou | .60 | .25 |
| ❑ | 23 Bernard Gilkey | .40 | .18 |
| ❑ | 24 Lance Johnson | .40 | .18 |
| ❑ | 25 Ben Grieve | .60 | .25 |
| ❑ | 26 Sandy Alomar Jr. | .60 | .25 |
| ❑ | 27 Ray Durham | .60 | .25 |
| ❑ | 28 Shawn Estes | .40 | .18 |
| ❑ | 29 David Segui | .40 | .18 |
| ❑ | 30 Javy Lopez | .60 | .25 |
| ❑ | 31 Steve Finley | .60 | .25 |
| ❑ | 32 Rey Ordonez | .40 | .18 |
| ❑ | 33 Derek Jeter | 6.00 | 2.70 |
| ❑ | 34 Henry Rodriguez | .40 | .18 |
| ❑ | 35 Mo Vaughn | .60 | .25 |
| ❑ | 36 Richard Hidalgo | .60 | .25 |
| ❑ | 37 Omar Vizquel | .60 | .25 |
| ❑ | 38 Johnny Damon | .60 | .25 |
| ❑ | 39 Brian Hunter | .40 | .18 |
| ❑ | 40 Matt Williams | 1.00 | .45 |
| ❑ | 41 Chuck Finley | .60 | .25 |

| | | |
|---|---|---|
| ❑ 42 Jeromy Burnitz | .60 | .25 |
| ❑ 43 Livan Hernandez | .40 | .18 |
| ❑ 44 Delino DeShields | .40 | .18 |
| ❑ 45 Charles Nagy | .40 | .18 |
| ❑ 46 Scott Rolen | 1.50 | .70 |
| ❑ 47 Neifi Perez | .40 | .18 |
| ❑ 48 John Wetteland | .60 | .25 |
| ❑ 49 Eric Milton | .40 | .18 |
| ❑ 50 Mike Piazza | 5.00 | 2.20 |
| ❑ 51 Cal Ripken | 6.00 | 2.70 |
| ❑ 52 Mariano Rivera | .60 | .25 |
| ❑ 53 Butch Huskey | .40 | .18 |
| ❑ 54 Quinton McCracken | .40 | .18 |
| ❑ 55 Jose Cruz Jr. | .60 | .25 |
| ❑ 56 Brian Jordan | .60 | .25 |
| ❑ 57 Hideo Nomo | 1.50 | .70 |
| ❑ 58 Masato Yoshii RC | 1.25 | .55 |
| ❑ 59 Cliff Floyd | .60 | .25 |
| ❑ 60 Jose Guillen | .40 | .18 |
| ❑ 61 Jeff Shaw | .40 | .18 |
| ❑ 62 Edgar Martinez | 1.00 | .45 |
| ❑ 63 Rondell White | .60 | .25 |
| ❑ 64 Hal Morris | .40 | .18 |
| ❑ 65 Barry Larkin | 1.50 | .70 |
| ❑ 66 Eric Young | .40 | .18 |
| ❑ 67 Ray Lankford | .60 | .25 |
| ❑ 68 Derek Bell | .40 | .18 |
| ❑ 69 Charles Johnson | .60 | .25 |
| ❑ 70 Robin Ventura | .60 | .25 |
| ❑ 71 Chuck Knoblauch | .60 | .25 |
| ❑ 72 Kevin Brown | 1.00 | .45 |
| ❑ 73 Jose Valentin | .40 | .18 |
| ❑ 74 Jay Buhner | .60 | .25 |
| ❑ 75 Tony Gwynn | 3.00 | 1.35 |
| ❑ 76 Andy Pettitte | .60 | .25 |
| ❑ 77 Edgardo Alfonzo | .60 | .25 |
| ❑ 78 Kerry Wood | 1.50 | .70 |
| ❑ 79 Darin Erstad | 1.50 | .70 |
| ❑ 80 Paul Konerko | .60 | .25 |
| ❑ 81 Jason Kendall | .60 | .25 |
| ❑ 82 Tino Martinez | .60 | .25 |
| ❑ 83 Brad Radke | .60 | .25 |
| ❑ 84 Jeff King | .40 | .18 |
| ❑ 85 Travis Lee | .60 | .25 |
| ❑ 86 Jeff Kent | 1.00 | .45 |
| ❑ 87 Trevor Hoffman | .60 | .25 |
| ❑ 88 David Cone | .60 | .25 |
| ❑ 89 Jose Canseco | 2.00 | .90 |
| ❑ 90 Juan Gonzalez | 1.50 | .70 |
| ❑ 91 Todd Hundley | .40 | .18 |
| ❑ 92 John Valentin | .40 | .18 |
| ❑ 93 Sammy Sosa | 3.00 | 1.35 |
| ❑ 94 Jason Giambi | 1.50 | .70 |
| ❑ 95 Chipper Jones | 4.00 | 1.80 |
| ❑ 96 Jeff Blauser | .40 | .18 |
| ❑ 97 Brad Fullmer | .60 | .25 |
| ❑ 98 Derrek Lee | .40 | .18 |
| ❑ 99 Denny Neagle | .40 | .18 |
| ❑ 100 Ken Griffey Jr. | 6.00 | 2.70 |
| ❑ 101 David Justice | 1.00 | .45 |
| ❑ 102 Tim Salmon | .60 | .25 |
| ❑ 103 J.T. Snow | .60 | .25 |
| ❑ 104 Fred McGriff | 1.00 | .45 |
| ❑ 105 Brady Anderson | .60 | .25 |
| ❑ 106 Larry Walker | .60 | .25 |
| ❑ 107 Jeff Cirillo | .60 | .25 |
| ❑ 108 Andruw Jones | 1.50 | .70 |
| ❑ 109 Manny Ramirez | 2.00 | .90 |
| ❑ 110 Justin Thompson | .40 | .18 |
| ❑ 111 Vinny Castilla | .60 | .25 |
| ❑ 112 Chan Ho Park | .60 | .25 |
| ❑ 113 Mark Grudzielanek | .40 | .18 |
| ❑ 114 Mark Grace | 1.50 | .70 |
| ❑ 115 Ken Caminiti | .60 | .25 |
| ❑ 116 Ryan Klesko | .60 | .25 |
| ❑ 117 Rafael Palmeiro | 1.50 | .70 |
| ❑ 118 Pat Hentgen | .40 | .18 |
| ❑ 119 Eric Karros | .60 | .25 |
| ❑ 120 Randy Johnson | 2.00 | .90 |
| ❑ 121 Roberto Alomar | 1.50 | .70 |
| ❑ 122 John Olerud | .60 | .25 |
| ❑ 123 Paul Molitor | 1.50 | .70 |
| ❑ 124 Dean Palmer | .60 | .25 |
| ❑ 125 Nomar Garciaparra | 5.00 | 2.20 |
| ❑ 126 Curt Schilling | .60 | .25 |
| ❑ 127 Jay Bell | .60 | .25 |
| ❑ 128 Craig Biggio | 1.00 | .45 |
| ❑ 129 Marty Cordova | .40 | .18 |
| ❑ 130 Ivan Rodriguez | 2.00 | .90 |
| ❑ 131 Todd Helton | 2.00 | .90 |
| ❑ 132 Jim Thome | 1.00 | .45 |
| ❑ 133 Albert Belle | 1.00 | .45 |
| ❑ 134 Mike Lansing | .40 | .18 |
| ❑ 135 Mark McGwire | 6.00 | 2.70 |
| ❑ 136 Roger Clemens | 3.00 | 1.35 |
| ❑ 137 Tom Glavine | 1.50 | .70 |
| ❑ 138 Ron Gant | .60 | .25 |
| ❑ 139 Alex Rodriguez | 5.00 | 2.20 |
| ❑ 140 Jeff Bagwell | 2.00 | .90 |
| ❑ 141 John Smoltz | .60 | .25 |
| ❑ 142 Kenny Lofton | .60 | .25 |
| ❑ 143 Dante Bichette | .60 | .25 |
| ❑ 144 Pedro Martinez | 2.00 | .90 |
| ❑ 145 Barry Bonds | 2.50 | 1.10 |
| ❑ 146 Travis Fryman | .60 | .25 |
| ❑ 147 Bobby Jones | .40 | .18 |
| ❑ 148 Bobby Higginson | .60 | .25 |
| ❑ 149 Reggie Sanders | .40 | .18 |
| ❑ 150 Frank Thomas | 3.00 | 1.35 |

## 1999 Topps Stars

| | MINT | NRMT |
|---|---|---|
| COMPLETE SET (180) | 120.00 | 55.00 |
| ❑ 1 Ken Griffey Jr. | 5.00 | 2.20 |
| ❑ 2 Chipper Jones | 3.00 | 1.35 |
| ❑ 3 Mike Piazza | 4.00 | 1.80 |
| ❑ 4 Nomar Garciaparra | 4.00 | 1.80 |
| ❑ 5 Derek Jeter | 5.00 | 2.20 |
| ❑ 6 Frank Thomas | 2.50 | 1.10 |
| ❑ 7 Ben Grieve | .50 | .23 |
| ❑ 8 Mark McGwire | 5.00 | 2.20 |
| ❑ 9 Sammy Sosa | 2.50 | 1.10 |
| ❑ 10 Alex Rodriguez | 4.00 | 1.80 |
| ❑ 11 Troy Glaus | 2.00 | .90 |
| ❑ 12 Eric Chavez | .50 | .23 |
| ❑ 13 Kerry Wood | .50 | .23 |
| ❑ 14 Barry Bonds | 2.00 | .90 |
| ❑ 15 Vladimir Guerrero | 2.00 | .90 |
| ❑ 16 Albert Belle | .75 | .35 |
| ❑ 17 Juan Gonzalez | 1.25 | .55 |
| ❑ 18 Roger Clemens | 2.50 | 1.10 |
| ❑ 19 Ruben Mateo | .50 | .23 |
| ❑ 20 Cal Ripken | 5.00 | 2.20 |
| ❑ 21 Darin Erstad | 1.25 | .55 |
| ❑ 22 Jeff Bagwell | 1.50 | .70 |
| ❑ 23 Roy Halladay | .30 | .14 |
| ❑ 24 Todd Helton | 1.50 | .70 |
| ❑ 25 Michael Barrett | .30 | .14 |
| ❑ 26 Manny Ramirez | 1.50 | .70 |
| ❑ 27 Fernando Seguignol | .30 | .14 |
| ❑ 28 Pat Burrell RC | 5.00 | 2.20 |
| ❑ 29 Andruw Jones | 1.25 | .55 |
| ❑ 30 Randy Johnson | 1.50 | .70 |
| ❑ 31 Jose Canseco | 1.50 | .70 |
| ❑ 32 Brad Fullmer | .50 | .23 |
| ❑ 33 Alex Escobar RC | 2.00 | .90 |
| ❑ 34 Alfonso Soriano RC | 2.00 | .90 |
| ❑ 35 Larry Walker | .50 | .23 |
| ❑ 36 Matt Clement | .30 | .14 |
| ❑ 37 Mo Vaughn | .50 | .23 |
| ❑ 38 Bruce Chen | .30 | .14 |
| ❑ 39 Travis Lee | .30 | .14 |
| ❑ 40 Adrian Beltre | .50 | .23 |
| ❑ 41 Alex Gonzalez | .30 | .14 |
| ❑ 42 Jason Tyner RC | .75 | .35 |
| ❑ 43 George Lombard | .30 | .14 |
| ❑ 44 Scott Rolen | 1.25 | .55 |
| ❑ 45 Mark Mulder RC | 1.00 | .45 |
| ❑ 46 Gabe Kapler | .50 | .23 |
| ❑ 47 Choo Freeman RC | .60 | .25 |
| ❑ 48 Tony Gwynn | 2.50 | 1.10 |
| ❑ 49 A.J. Burnett RC | .75 | .35 |
| ❑ 50 Matt Belisle RC | .75 | .35 |
| ❑ 51 Greg Maddux | 3.00 | 1.35 |
| ❑ 52 John Smoltz | .50 | .23 |
| ❑ 53 Mark Grace | 1.25 | .55 |
| ❑ 54 Wade Boggs | 1.50 | .70 |
| ❑ 55 Bernie Williams | 1.25 | .55 |
| ❑ 56 Pedro Martinez | 1.50 | .70 |
| ❑ 57 Barry Larkin | 1.25 | .55 |
| ❑ 58 Orlando Hernandez | .50 | .23 |
| ❑ 59 Jason Kendall | .50 | .23 |
| ❑ 60 Mark Kotsay | .30 | .14 |
| ❑ 61 Jim Thome | .75 | .35 |
| ❑ 62 Gary Sheffield | 1.25 | .55 |
| ❑ 63 Preston Wilson | .50 | .23 |
| ❑ 64 Rafael Palmeiro | 1.25 | .55 |
| ❑ 65 David Wells | .50 | .23 |
| ❑ 66 Shawn Green | 1.25 | .55 |
| ❑ 67 Tom Glavine | 1.25 | .55 |
| ❑ 68 Jeromy Burnitz | .50 | .23 |
| ❑ 69 Kevin Brown | .75 | .35 |
| ❑ 70 Rondell White | .50 | .23 |
| ❑ 71 Roberto Alomar | 1.25 | .55 |
| ❑ 72 Cliff Floyd | .50 | .23 |
| ❑ 73 Craig Biggio | .75 | .35 |
| ❑ 74 Greg Vaughn | .50 | .23 |
| ❑ 75 Ivan Rodriguez | 1.50 | .70 |
| ❑ 76 Vinny Castilla | .50 | .23 |
| ❑ 77 Todd Walker | .30 | .14 |
| ❑ 78 Paul Konerko | .50 | .23 |
| ❑ 79 Andy Brown RC | .75 | .35 |
| ❑ 80 Todd Hundley | .30 | .14 |
| ❑ 81 Dmitri Young | .50 | .23 |
| ❑ 82 Tony Clark | .30 | .14 |
| ❑ 83 Nick Johnson RC | 2.00 | .90 |
| ❑ 84 Mike Caruso | .30 | .14 |
| ❑ 85 David Ortiz | .30 | .14 |
| ❑ 86 Matt Williams | .75 | .35 |
| ❑ 87 Raul Mondesi | .50 | .23 |
| ❑ 88 Kenny Lofton | .50 | .23 |
| ❑ 89 Miguel Tejada | .50 | .23 |
| ❑ 90 Dante Bichette | .50 | .23 |
| ❑ 91 Jorge Posada | .50 | .23 |
| ❑ 92 Carlos Beltran | .50 | .23 |
| ❑ 93 Carlos Delgado | 1.25 | .55 |
| ❑ 94 Javy Lopez | .50 | .23 |
| ❑ 95 Aramis Ramirez | .30 | .14 |
| ❑ 96 Neifi Perez | .30 | .14 |
| ❑ 97 Marlon Anderson | .30 | .14 |
| ❑ 98 David Cone | .50 | .23 |
| ❑ 99 Moises Alou | .50 | .23 |
| ❑ 100 John Olerud | .50 | .23 |
| ❑ 101 Tim Salmon | .50 | .23 |
| ❑ 102 Jason Giambi | 1.25 | .55 |
| ❑ 103 Sandy Alomar Jr. | .50 | .23 |
| ❑ 104 Curt Schilling | .50 | .23 |
| ❑ 105 Andres Galarraga | .75 | .35 |
| ❑ 106 Rusty Greer | .50 | .23 |
| ❑ 107 Bobby Seay RC | .60 | .25 |
| ❑ 108 Eric Young | .30 | .14 |
| ❑ 109 Brian Jordan | .50 | .23 |
| ❑ 110 Eric Davis | .50 | .23 |
| ❑ 111 Will Clark | 1.25 | .55 |
| ❑ 112 Andy Ashby | .30 | .14 |
| ❑ 113 Edgardo Alfonzo | .50 | .23 |
| ❑ 114 Paul O'Neill | .50 | .23 |
| ❑ 115 Denny Neagle | .30 | .14 |
| ❑ 116 Eric Karros | .50 | .23 |
| ❑ 117 Ken Caminiti | .50 | .23 |
| ❑ 118 Garret Anderson | .50 | .23 |
| ❑ 119 Todd Stottlemyre | .30 | .14 |
| ❑ 120 David Justice | .75 | .35 |
| ❑ 121 Francisco Cordova | .30 | .14 |
| ❑ 122 Robin Ventura | .50 | .23 |
| ❑ 123 Mike Mussina | 1.25 | .55 |
| ❑ 124 Hideki Irabu | .30 | .14 |
| ❑ 125 Justin Thompson | .30 | .14 |

- ❑ 126 Mariano Rivera .50 .23
- ❑ 127 Delino DeShields .30 .14
- ❑ 128 Steve Finley .50 .23
- ❑ 129 Jose Cruz Jr. .50 .23
- ❑ 130 Ray Lankford .50 .23
- ❑ 131 Jim Edmonds 1.25 .55
- ❑ 132 Charles Johnson .50 .23
- ❑ 133 Al Leiter .50 .23
- ❑ 134 Jose Offerman .30 .14
- ❑ 135 Eric Milton .30 .14
- ❑ 136 Dean Palmer .50 .23
- ❑ 137 Johnny Damon .50 .23
- ❑ 138 Andy Pettitte .50 .23
- ❑ 139 Ray Durham .50 .23
- ❑ 140 Ugueth Urbina .30 .14
- ❑ 141 Marquis Grissom .30 .14
- ❑ 142 Ryan Klesko .50 .23
- ❑ 143 Brady Anderson .50 .23
- ❑ 144 Bobby Higginson .50 .23
- ❑ 145 Chuck Knoblauch .50 .23
- ❑ 146 Rickey Henderson 1.50 .70
- ❑ 147 Kevin Millwood .50 .23
- ❑ 148 Fred McGriff .75 .35
- ❑ 149 Damion Easley .30 .14
- ❑ 150 Tino Martinez .50 .23
- ❑ 151 Greg Maddux LUM 1.50 .70
- ❑ 152 Scott Rolen LUM 1.25 .55
- ❑ 153 Pat Burrell LUM 1.50 .70
- ❑ 154 Roger Clemens LUM 1.25 .55
- ❑ 155 Albert Belle LUM .30 .14
- ❑ 156 Troy Glaus LUM 1.25 .55
- ❑ 157 Cal Ripken LUM 2.50 1.10
- ❑ 158 Alfonso Soriano LUM .60 .25
- ❑ 159 Manny Ramirez LUM .75 .35
- ❑ 160 Eric Chavez LUM .50 .23
- ❑ 161 Kerry Wood LUM .50 .23
- ❑ 162 Tony Gwynn LUM 1.25 .55
- ❑ 163 Barry Bonds LUM .75 .35
- ❑ 164 Ruben Mateo LUM .50 .23
- ❑ 165 Todd Helton LUM 1.25 .55
- ❑ 166 Darin Erstad LUM 1.25 .55
- ❑ 167 Jeff Bagwell LUM .75 .35
- ❑ 168 Juan Gonzalez LUM .50 .23
- ❑ 169 Mo Vaughn LUM .50 .23
- ❑ 170 Vladimir Guerrero LUM .75 .35
- ❑ 171 Nomar Garciaparra SUP [illegible] [illegible]
- ❑ 172 Derek Jeter SUP 2.50 1.10
- ❑ 173 Alex Rodriguez SUP 2.00 .90
- ❑ 174 Ben Grieve SUP .50 .23
- ❑ 175 Mike Piazza SUP 2.00 .90
- ❑ 176 Chipper Jones SUP 1.50 .70
- ❑ 177 Frank Thomas SUP 1.25 .55
- ❑ 178 Ken Griffey Jr. SUP 2.50 1.10
- ❑ 179 Sammy Sosa SUP 1.25 .55
- ❑ 180 Mark McGwire SUP 2.50 1.10

## 2000 Topps Stars

| | MINT | NRMT |
|---|---|---|
| COMPLETE SET (200) | 80.00 | 36.00 |
| MINOR STARS | .40 | .18 |

- ❑ 1 Vladimir Guerrero 1.50 .70
- ❑ 2 Eric Karros .40 .18
- ❑ 3 Omar Vizquel .40 .18
- ❑ 4 Ken Griffey Jr. 4.00 1.80
- ❑ 5 Preston Wilson .40 .18
- ❑ 6 Albert Belle .60 .25
- ❑ 7 Ryan Klesko .40 .18
- ❑ 8 Bob Abreu .40 .18
- ❑ 9 Warren Morris .25 .11
- ❑ 10 Rafael Palmeiro 1.00 .45
- ❑ 11 Nomar Garciaparra 3.00 1.35
- ❑ 12 Dante Bichette .40 .18
- ❑ 13 Jeff Cirillo .40 .18
- ❑ 14 Carlos Beltran .40 .18
- ❑ 15 Tony Clark .25 .11
- ❑ 16 Ray Durham .40 .18
- ❑ 17 Mark McGwire 4.00 1.80
- ❑ 18 Jim Thome .60 .25
- ❑ 19 Todd Walker .25 .11
- ❑ 20 Richie Sexson .40 .18
- ❑ 21 Adrian Beltre .40 .18
- ❑ 22 Jay Bell .40 .18
- ❑ 23 Craig Biggio .60 .25
- ❑ 24 Ben Grieve .40 .18
- ❑ 25 Greg Maddux 2.50 1.10
- ❑ 26 Fernando Tatis .40 .18
- ❑ 27 Jeromy Burnitz .40 .18
- ❑ 28 Vinny Castilla .40 .18
- ❑ 29 Mark Grace 1.00 .45
- ❑ 30 Derek Jeter 4.00 1.80
- ❑ 31 Larry Walker .40 .18
- ❑ 32 Ivan Rodriguez 1.25 .55
- ❑ 33 Curt Schilling .40 .18
- ❑ 34 Mike Lamb RC .75 .35
- ❑ 35 Kevin Brown .40 .18
- ❑ 36 Andruw Jones 1.00 .45
- ❑ 37 Chris Mears RC .50 .23
- ❑ 38 Bartolo Colon .40 .18
- ❑ 39 Edgardo Alfonzo .40 .18
- ❑ 40 Brady Anderson .40 .18
- ❑ 41 Andres Galarraga .60 .25
- ❑ 42 Scott Rolen 1.00 .45
- ❑ 43 Manny Ramirez 1.25 .55
- ❑ 44 Carlos Delgado 1.00 .45
- ❑ 45 David Cone .40 .18
- ❑ 46 Carl Everett .40 .18
- ❑ 47 Chipper Jones 2.50 1.10
- ❑ 48 Barry Bonds 1.50 .70
- ❑ 49 Dean Palmer .40 .18
- ❑ 50 Frank Thomas 2.00 .90
- ❑ 51 Paul O'Neill .40 .18
- ❑ 52 Mo Vaughn .40 .18
- ❑ 53 Todd Helton 1.25 .55
- ❑ 54 Jason Giambi 1.00 .45
- ❑ 55 Brian Jordan .40 .18
- ❑ 56 Luis Gonzalez .40 .18
- ❑ 57 Alex Rodriguez 3.00 1.35
- ❑ 58 J.D. Drew 1.00 .45
- ❑ 59 Javy Lopez .40 .18
- ❑ 60 Tony Gwynn 2.00 .90
- ❑ 61 Jason Kendall .40 .18
- ❑ 62 Pedro Martinez 1.25 .55
- ❑ 63 Matt Williams .60 .25
- ❑ 64 Gary Sheffield 1.00 .45
- ❑ 65 Roberto Alomar 1.00 .45
- ❑ 66 Lyle Overbay RC 1.25 .55
- ❑ 67 Jeff Bagwell 1.25 .55
- ❑ 68 Tim Hudson 1.00 .45
- ❑ 69 Sammy Sosa 2.00 .90
- ❑ 70 Keith Reed RC .75 .35
- ❑ 71 Robin Ventura .40 .18
- ❑ 72 Cal Ripken 4.00 1.80
- ❑ 73 Alex Gonzalez .25 .11
- ❑ 74 Aaron McNeal RC 1.00 .45
- ❑ 75 Mike Lieberthal .40 .18
- ❑ 76 Brian Giles .40 .18
- ❑ 77 Kevin Millwood .40 .18
- ❑ 78 Troy O'Leary .25 .11
- ❑ 79 Raul Mondesi .40 .18
- ❑ 80 John Olerud .40 .18
- ❑ 81 David Justice .60 .25
- ❑ 82 Erubiel Durazo .40 .18
- ❑ 83 Shawn Green 1.00 .45
- ❑ 84 Tino Martinez .40 .18
- ❑ 85 Greg Vaughn .40 .18
- ❑ 86 Tom Glavine 1.00 .45
- ❑ 87 Jose Canseco 1.25 .55
- ❑ 88 Kenny Lofton .40 .18
- ❑ 89 Brian Daubach .25 .11
- ❑ 90 Mike Piazza 3.00 1.35
- ❑ 91 Randy Johnson 1.25 .55
- ❑ 92 Pokey Reese .40 .18
- ❑ 93 Troy Glaus 1.25 .55
- ❑ 94 Kerry Wood .40 .18
- ❑ 95 Sean Casey .40 .18
- ❑ 96 Magglio Ordonez .40 .18
- ❑ 97 Bernie Williams 1.00 .45
- ❑ 98 Juan Gonzalez 1.00 .45
- ❑ 99 Barry Larkin 1.00 .45
- ❑ 100 Orlando Hernandez .40 .18
- ❑ 101 Roger Clemens 2.00 .90
- ❑ 102 Bob Gibson 1.00 .45
- ❑ 103 Gary Carter .60 .25
- ❑ 104 Willie Stargell .60 .25
- ❑ 105 Joe Morgan 1.00 .45
- ❑ 106 Brooks Robinson 1.00 .45
- ❑ 107 Ozzie Smith 1.25 .55
- ❑ 108 Carl Yastrzemski 1.50 .70
- ❑ 109 Al Kaline 1.25 .55
- ❑ 110 Frank Robinson 1.00 .45
- ❑ 111 Lance Berkman .40 .18
- ❑ 112 Adam Piatt 1.00 .45
- ❑ 113 Vernon Wells .40 .18
- ❑ 114 Rafael Furcal 2.50 1.10
- ❑ 115 Rick Ankiel 2.00 .90
- ❑ 116 Corey Patterson 1.50 .70
- ❑ 117 Josh Hamilton 1.50 .70
- ❑ 118 Jack Cust .40 .18
- ❑ 119 Josh Girdley .25 .11
- ❑ 120 Pablo Ozuna .25 .11
- ❑ 121 Sean Burroughs 1.00 .45
- ❑ 122 Pat Burrell 1.50 .70
- ❑ 123 Chad Hermansen .25 .11
- ❑ 124 Ruben Mateo .40 .18
- ❑ 125 Ben Petrick .25 .11
- ❑ 126 Dee Brown .40 .18
- ❑ 127 Eric Munson 1.00 .45
- ❑ 128 Ruben Salazar RC 1.00 .45
- ❑ 129 Kip Wells .40 .18
- ❑ 130 Alfonso Soriano .40 .18
- ❑ 131 Mark Mulder .40 .18
- ❑ 132 Roosevelt Brown .25 .11
- ❑ 133 Nick Johnson .40 .18
- ❑ 134 Kyle Snyder .25 .11
- ❑ 135 David Walling .25 .11
- ❑ 136 Geraldo Guzman RC .40 .18
- ❑ 137 John Sneed RC .40 .18
- ❑ 138 Ben Christensen RC 1.00 .45
- ❑ 139 Corey Myers RC .60 .25
- ❑ 140 Jose Ortiz RC 10.00 4.50
- ❑ 141 Ryan Christianson RC 1.00 .45
- ❑ 142 Brett Myers RC .75 .35
- ❑ 143 Bobby Bradley RC 2.00 .90
- ❑ 144 Rick Asadoorian RC 2.50 1.10
- ❑ 145 Julio Zuleta RC .50 .23
- ❑ 146 Ty Howington RC .75 .35
- ❑ 147 Josh Kalinowski RC .50 .23
- ❑ 148 B.J. Garbe RC 1.25 .55
- ❑ 149 Scott Downs RC .50 .23
- ❑ 150 Dan Wright RC [illegible] [illegible]
- ❑ 151 Jeff Bagwell SPOT .60 .25
- ❑ 152 Vladimir Guerrero SPOT 1.00 .45
- ❑ 153 Mike Piazza SPOT 2.00 .90
- ❑ 154 Juan Gonzalez SPOT .40 .18
- ❑ 155 Ivan Rodriguez SPOT .60 .25
- ❑ 156 Manny Ramirez SPOT .60 .25
- ❑ 157 Sammy Sosa SPOT 1.25 .55
- ❑ 158 Chipper Jones SPOT 1.50 .70
- ❑ 159 Shawn Green SPOT .40 .18
- ❑ 160 Ken Griffey Jr. SPOT 2.50 1.10
- ❑ 161 Cal Ripken SPOT 2.50 1.10
- ❑ 162 Nomar Garciaparra SPOT 2.00 .90
- ❑ 163 Derek Jeter SPOT 2.50 1.10
- ❑ 164 Barry Bonds SPOT 1.00 .45
- ❑ 165 Greg Maddux SPOT 1.50 .70
- ❑ 166 Mark McGwire SPOT 2.50 1.10
- ❑ 167 Roberto Alomar SPOT .40 .18
- ❑ 168 Alex Rodriguez SPOT 2.00 .90
- ❑ 169 Randy Johnson SPOT .60 .25
- ❑ 170 Tony Gwynn SPOT 1.25 .55
- ❑ 171 Pedro Martinez SPOT .60 .25
- ❑ 172 Bob Gibson SPOT .60 .25
- ❑ 173 Gary Carter SPOT .40 .18
- ❑ 174 Willie Stargell SPOT .40 .18
- ❑ 175 Joe Morgan SPOT .60 .25
- ❑ 176 Brooks Robinson SPOT .60 .25
- ❑ 177 Ozzie Smith SPOT .60 .25
- ❑ 178 Carl Yastrzemski SPOT .60 .25

| Card | MINT | NRMT |
|---|---|---|
| 179 Al Kaline SPOT | .60 | .25 |
| 180 Frank Robinson SPOT | .60 | .25 |
| 181 Adam Piatt SPOT | .40 | .18 |
| 182 Alfonso Soriano SPOT | .40 | .18 |
| 183 Corey Patterson SPOT | 1.00 | .45 |
| 184 Vernon Wells SPOT | .40 | .18 |
| 185 Pat Burrell SPOT | 1.00 | .45 |
| 186 Mark Mulder SPOT | .40 | .18 |
| 187 Eric Munson SPOT | .40 | .18 |
| 188 Rafael Furcal SPOT | 1.50 | .70 |
| 189 Rick Ankiel SPOT | 1.25 | .55 |
| 190 Ruben Mateo SPOT | .40 | .18 |
| 191 Sean Burroughs SPOT | .40 | .18 |
| 192 Josh Hamilton SPOT | 1.00 | .45 |
| 193 Brett Myers SPOT | .50 | .23 |
| 194 Ben Christensen SPOT | .60 | .25 |
| 195 Ty Howington SPOT | .50 | .23 |
| 196 Rick Asadoorian SPOT | 1.50 | .70 |
| 197 Josh Kalinowski SPOT | .40 | .18 |
| 198 Corey Myers SPOT | .40 | .18 |
| 199 Ryan Christianson SPOT | .60 | .25 |
| 200 John Sneed SPOT | .25 | .11 |

## 1998 Topps Tek

| | MINT | NRMT |
|---|---|---|
| COMPLETE SET (90) | 150.00 | 70.00 |
| 1 Ben Grieve | .75 | .35 |
| 2 Kerry Wood | 2.00 | .90 |
| 3 Barry Bonds | 3.00 | 1.35 |
| 4 John Olerud | .75 | .35 |
| 5 Ivan Rodriguez | 2.50 | 1.10 |
| 6 Frank Thomas | 4.00 | 1.80 |
| 7 Bernie Williams | 2.00 | .90 |
| 8 Dante Bichette | .75 | .35 |
| 9 Alex Rodriguez | 6.00 | 2.70 |
| 10 Tom Glavine | 2.00 | .90 |
| 11 Eric Karros | .75 | .35 |
| 12 Craig Biggio | 1.25 | .55 |
| 13 Mark McGwire | 8.00 | 3.60 |
| 14 Derek Jeter | 8.00 | 3.60 |
| 15 Nomar Garciaparra | 6.00 | 2.70 |
| 16 Brady Anderson | .75 | .35 |
| 17 Vladimir Guerrero | 3.00 | 1.35 |
| 18 David Justice | 1.25 | .55 |
| 19 Chipper Jones | 5.00 | 2.20 |
| 20 Jim Edmonds | 2.00 | .90 |
| 21 Roger Clemens | 4.00 | 1.80 |
| 22 Mark Kotsay | .75 | .35 |
| 23 Tony Gwynn | 4.00 | 1.80 |
| 24 Todd Walker | .50 | .23 |
| 25 Tino Martinez | .75 | .35 |
| 26 Andruw Jones | 2.00 | .90 |
| 27 Sandy Alomar Jr. | .75 | .35 |
| 28 Sammy Sosa | 4.00 | 1.80 |
| 29 Gary Sheffield | 2.00 | .90 |
| 30 Ken Griffey Jr. | 8.00 | 3.60 |
| 31 Aramis Ramirez | .75 | .35 |
| 32 Curt Schilling | .75 | .35 |
| 33 Robin Ventura | .75 | .35 |
| 34 Larry Walker | .75 | .35 |
| 35 Darin Erstad | 2.00 | .90 |
| 36 Todd Dunwoody | .50 | .23 |
| 37 Paul O'Neill | .75 | .35 |
| 38 Vinny Castilla | .75 | .35 |
| 39 Randy Johnson | 2.50 | 1.10 |
| 40 Rafael Palmeiro | 2.00 | .90 |
| 41 Pedro Martinez | 2.50 | 1.10 |
| 42 Derek Bell | .50 | .23 |
| 43 Carlos Delgado | 2.00 | .90 |
| 44 Matt Williams | 1.25 | .55 |
| 45 Kenny Lofton | .75 | .35 |
| 46 Edgar Renteria | .50 | .23 |
| 47 Albert Belle | 1.25 | .55 |
| 48 Jeromy Burnitz | .75 | .35 |
| 49 Adrian Beltre | .75 | .35 |
| 50 Greg Maddux | 5.00 | 2.20 |
| 51 Cal Ripken | 8.00 | 3.60 |
| 52 Jason Kendall | .75 | .35 |
| 53 Ellis Burks | .75 | .35 |
| 54 Paul Molitor | 2.00 | .90 |
| 55 Moises Alou | .75 | .35 |
| 56 Raul Mondesi | .75 | .35 |
| 57 Barry Larkin | 2.00 | .90 |
| 58 Tony Clark | .50 | .23 |
| 59 Travis Lee | .75 | .35 |
| 60 Juan Gonzalez | 2.00 | .90 |
| 61 Troy Glaus RC | 5.00 | 2.20 |
| 62 Jose Cruz Jr. | .75 | .35 |
| 63 Paul Konerko | .75 | .35 |
| 64 Edgar Martinez | 1.25 | .55 |
| 65 Javy Lopez | .75 | .35 |
| 66 Manny Ramirez | 2.50 | 1.10 |
| 67 Roberto Alomar | 2.00 | .90 |
| 68 Ken Caminiti | .75 | .35 |
| 69 Todd Helton | 2.50 | 1.10 |
| 70 Chuck Knoblauch | .75 | .35 |
| 71 Kevin Brown | 1.25 | .55 |
| 72 Tim Salmon | .75 | .35 |
| 73 Orlando Hernandez RC | 1.50 | .70 |
| 74 Jeff Bagwell | 2.50 | 1.10 |
| 75 Brian Jordan | .75 | .35 |
| 76 Derrek Lee | .50 | .23 |
| 77 Brad Fullmer | .75 | .35 |
| 78 Mark Grace | 2.00 | .90 |
| 79 Jeff King | .50 | .23 |
| 80 Mike Mussina | 2.00 | .90 |
| 81 Jay Buhner | .75 | .35 |
| 82 Quinton McCracken | .50 | .23 |
| 83 A.J. Hinch | .50 | .23 |
| 84 Richard Hidalgo | .75 | .35 |
| 85 Andres Galarraga | 1.25 | .55 |
| 86 Mike Piazza | 6.00 | 2.70 |
| 87 Mo Vaughn | .75 | .35 |
| 88 Scott Rolen | 2.00 | .90 |
| 89 Jim Thome | 1.25 | .55 |
| 90 Ray Lankford | .75 | .35 |

## 1999 Topps Tek

| | MINT | NRMT |
|---|---|---|
| COMPLETE SET (90) | 100.00 | 45.00 |
| 1A Ben Grieve | .75 | .35 |
| 1B Ben Grieve Away | .75 | .35 |
| 2A Andres Galarraga | 1.00 | .45 |
| 2B Andres Galarraga Away | 1.00 | .45 |
| 3A Travis Lee | .75 | .35 |
| 3B Travis Lee Away | .75 | .35 |
| 4A Larry Walker | .75 | .35 |
| 4B Larry Walker Away | .75 | .35 |
| 5A Ken Griffey Jr. | 6.00 | 2.70 |
| 5B Ken Griffey Jr. Away | 6.00 | 2.70 |
| 6A Sammy Sosa | 3.00 | 1.35 |
| 6B Sammy Sosa Away | 3.00 | 1.35 |
| 7A Mark McGwire | 6.00 | 2.70 |
| 7B Mark McGwire Away | 6.00 | 2.70 |
| 8A Roberto Alomar | 1.50 | .70 |
| 8B Roberto Alomar Away | 1.50 | .70 |
| 9A Wade Boggs | 2.00 | .90 |
| 9B Wade Boggs Away | 2.00 | .90 |
| 10A Troy Glaus | 2.50 | 1.10 |
| 10B Troy Glaus Away | 2.50 | 1.10 |
| 11A Craig Biggio | 1.00 | .45 |
| 11B Craig Biggio Away | 1.00 | .45 |
| 12A Kerry Wood | .75 | .35 |
| 12B Kerry Wood Away | .75 | .35 |
| 13A Vladimir Guerrero | 2.50 | 1.10 |
| 13B Vladimir Guerrero Away | 2.50 | 1.10 |
| 14A Albert Belle | 1.00 | .45 |
| 14B Albert Belle Away | 1.00 | .45 |
| 15A Mike Piazza | 5.00 | 2.20 |
| 15B Mike Piazza Away | 5.00 | 2.20 |
| 16A Chipper Jones | 4.00 | 1.80 |
| 16B Chipper Jones Away | 4.00 | 1.80 |
| 17A Randy Johnson | 2.00 | .90 |
| 17B Randy Johnson Away | 2.00 | .90 |
| 18A Adrian Beltre | .75 | .35 |
| 18B Adrian Beltre Away | .75 | .35 |
| 19A Barry Bonds | 2.50 | 1.10 |
| 19B Barry Bonds Away | 2.50 | 1.10 |
| 20A Jim Thome | 1.00 | .45 |
| 20B Jim Thome Away | 1.00 | .45 |
| 21A Greg Vaughn | .75 | .35 |
| 21B Greg Vaughn Away | .75 | .35 |
| 22A Scott Rolen | 1.50 | .70 |
| 22B Scott Rolen Away | 1.50 | .70 |
| 23A Ivan Rodriguez | 2.00 | .90 |
| 23B Ivan Rodriguez Away | 2.00 | .90 |
| 24A Derek Jeter | 6.00 | 2.70 |
| 24B Derek Jeter Away | 6.00 | 2.70 |
| 25A Cal Ripken | 6.00 | 2.70 |
| 25B Cal Ripken Away | 6.00 | 2.70 |
| 26A Mark Grace | 1.50 | .70 |
| 26B Mark Grace Away | 1.50 | .70 |
| 27A Bernie Williams | 1.50 | .70 |
| 27B Bernie Williams Away | 1.50 | .70 |
| 28A Darin Erstad | 1.50 | .70 |
| 28B Darin Erstad Away | 1.50 | .70 |
| 29A Eric Chavez | .75 | .35 |
| 29B Eric Chavez Away | .75 | .35 |
| 30A Tom Glavine | 1.50 | .70 |
| 30B Tom Glavine Away | 1.50 | .70 |
| 31A Jeff Bagwell | 2.00 | .90 |
| 31B Jeff Bagwell Away | 2.00 | .90 |
| 32A Manny Ramirez | 2.00 | .90 |
| 32B Manny Ramirez Away | 2.00 | .90 |
| 33A Tino Martinez | .75 | .35 |
| 33B Tino Martinez Away | .75 | .35 |
| 34A Todd Helton | 2.00 | .90 |
| 34B Todd Helton Away | 2.00 | .90 |
| 35A Jason Kendall | .75 | .35 |
| 35B Jason Kendall Away | .75 | .35 |
| 36A Pat Burrell RC | 5.00 | 2.20 |
| 36B Pat Burrell Away RC | 5.00 | 2.20 |
| 37A Tony Gwynn | 3.00 | 1.35 |
| 37B Tony Gwynn Away | 3.00 | 1.35 |
| 38A Nomar Garciaparra | 5.00 | 2.20 |
| 38B Nomar Garciaparra Away | 5.00 | 2.20 |
| 39A Frank Thomas | 3.00 | 1.35 |
| 39B Frank Thomas Away | 3.00 | 1.35 |
| 40A Orlando Hernandez | .75 | .35 |
| 40B Orlando Hernandez Away | .75 | .35 |
| 41A Juan Gonzalez | 1.50 | .70 |
| 41B Juan Gonzalez Away | 1.50 | .70 |
| 42A Alex Rodriguez | 5.00 | 2.20 |
| 42B Alex Rodriguez Away | 5.00 | 2.20 |
| 43A Greg Maddux | 4.00 | 1.80 |
| 43B Greg Maddux Away | 4.00 | 1.80 |
| 44A Mo Vaughn | .75 | .35 |
| 44B Mo Vaughn Away | .75 | .35 |
| 45A Roger Clemens | 3.00 | 1.35 |
| 45B Roger Clemens Away | 3.00 | 1.35 |

## 2000 Topps Tek

| | MINT | NRMT |
|---|---|---|
| COMPLETE SET (45) | 50.00 | 22.00 |
| COMMON CARD (1-40) | .40 | .18 |
| COMMON ROOKIE (41-45) | 1.00 | .45 |

| Card | MINT | NRMT |
|---|---|---|
| ❑ 1 Mike Piazza | 3.00 | 1.35 |
| ❑ 2 Chipper Jones | 2.50 | 1.10 |
| ❑ 3 Juan Gonzalez | 1.00 | .45 |
| ❑ 4 Ivan Rodriguez | 1.25 | .55 |
| ❑ 5 Cal Ripken | 4.00 | 1.80 |
| ❑ 6 A.J. Burnett | .40 | .18 |
| ❑ 7 Jim Thome | .60 | .25 |
| ❑ 8 Mo Vaughn | .40 | .18 |
| ❑ 9 Andruw Jones | 1.00 | .45 |
| ❑ 10 Mark McGwire | 4.00 | 1.80 |
| ❑ 11 Jose Canseco | 1.25 | .55 |
| ❑ 12 Shawn Green | 1.00 | .45 |
| ❑ 13 Barry Bonds | 1.50 | .70 |
| ❑ 14 Bernie Williams | 1.00 | .45 |
| ❑ 15 Manny Ramirez | 1.25 | .55 |
| ❑ 16 Greg Maddux | 2.50 | 1.10 |
| ❑ 17 Carlos Beltran | .40 | .18 |
| ❑ 18 Pedro Martinez | 1.25 | .55 |
| ❑ 19 Jeff Bagwell | 1.25 | .55 |
| ❑ 20 Sammy Sosa | 2.00 | .90 |
| ❑ 21 J.D. Drew | 1.00 | .45 |
| ❑ 22 Randy Johnson | 1.25 | .55 |
| ❑ 23 Larry Walker | .40 | .18 |
| ❑ 24 Frank Thomas | 2.00 | .90 |
| ❑ 25 Orlando Hernandez | .40 | .18 |
| ❑ 26 Scott Rolen | .75 | .35 |
| ❑ 27 Tony Gwynn | 2.00 | .90 |
| ❑ 28 Rick Ankiel | 2.00 | .90 |
| ❑ 29 Roberto Alomar | 1.00 | .45 |
| ❑ 30 Ken Griffey Jr. | 4.00 | 1.80 |
| ❑ 31 Vladimir Guerrero | 1.50 | .70 |
| ❑ 32 Derek Jeter | 4.00 | 1.80 |
| ❑ 33 Nomar Garciaparra | 3.00 | 1.35 |
| ❑ 34 Alex Rodriguez | 3.00 | 1.35 |
| ❑ 35 Sean Casey | .40 | .18 |
| ❑ 36 Adam Piatt | 1.00 | .45 |
| ❑ 37 Corey Patterson | 1.50 | .70 |
| ❑ 38 Josh Hamilton | 1.50 | .70 |
| ❑ 39 Pat Burrell | 1.50 | .70 |
| ❑ 40 Eric Munson | 1.00 | .45 |
| ❑ 41 Ruben Salazar 1-5 RC | 2.00 | .90 |
| ❑ 41 Ruben Salazar 6-10 RC | 2.00 | .90 |
| ❑ 41 Ruben Salazar 11-15 RC | 2.00 | .90 |
| ❑ 42 John Sneed 1-5 RC | 1.00 | .45 |
| ❑ 42 John Sneed 6-10 RC | 1.00 | .45 |
| ❑ 42 John Sneed 11-15 RC | 1.00 | .45 |
| ❑ 43 Josh Girdley 1-5 | 1.00 | .45 |
| ❑ 43 Josh Girdley 6-10 | 1.00 | .45 |
| ❑ 43 Josh Girdley 11-15 | 1.00 | .45 |
| ❑ 44 Brett Myers 1-5 RC | 1.50 | .70 |
| ❑ 44 Brett Myers 6-10 RC | 1.50 | .70 |
| ❑ 44 Brett Myers 11-15 RC | 1.50 | .70 |
| ❑ 45 Rick Asadoorian 1-5 RC | 5.00 | 2.20 |
| ❑ 45 Rick Asadoorian 6-10 RC | 5.00 | 2.20 |
| ❑ 45 Rick Asadoorian 11-15 RC | 5.00 | 2.20 |

## 1997 UD3

| | MINT | NRMT |
|---|---|---|
| COMPLETE SET (60) | 50.00 | 22.00 |
| ❑ 1 Mark McGwire | 5.00 | 2.20 |
| ❑ 2 Brady Anderson | .60 | .25 |
| ❑ 3 Ken Griffey Jr. | 5.00 | 2.20 |
| ❑ 4 Albert Belle | .75 | .35 |
| ❑ 5 Andres Galarraga | .75 | .35 |
| ❑ 6 Juan Gonzalez | 1.25 | .55 |
| ❑ 7 Jay Buhner | .60 | .25 |
| ❑ 8 Mo Vaughn | .60 | .25 |
| ❑ 9 Barry Bonds | 2.00 | .90 |
| ❑ 10 Gary Sheffield | 1.25 | .55 |
| ❑ 11 Todd Hundley | .50 | .23 |
| ❑ 12 Ellis Burks | .60 | .25 |
| ❑ 13 Ken Caminiti | .60 | .25 |
| ❑ 14 Vinny Castilla | .60 | .25 |
| ❑ 15 Sammy Sosa | 2.50 | 1.10 |
| ❑ 16 Frank Thomas | 2.50 | 1.10 |
| ❑ 17 Rafael Palmeiro | 1.25 | .55 |
| ❑ 18 Mike Piazza | 4.00 | 1.80 |
| ❑ 19 Matt Williams | .75 | .35 |
| ❑ 20 Eddie Murray | 1.25 | .55 |
| ❑ 21 Roger Clemens | 2.50 | 1.10 |
| ❑ 22 Tim Salmon | .60 | .25 |
| ❑ 23 Robin Ventura | .60 | .25 |
| ❑ 24 Ron Gant | .50 | .23 |
| ❑ 25 Cal Ripken | 5.00 | 2.20 |
| ❑ 26 Bernie Williams | 1.25 | .55 |
| ❑ 27 Hideo Nomo | 1.25 | .55 |
| ❑ 28 Ivan Rodriguez | 1.50 | .70 |
| ❑ 29 John Smoltz | .60 | .25 |
| ❑ 30 Paul Molitor | 1.25 | .55 |
| ❑ 31 Greg Maddux | 3.00 | 1.35 |
| ❑ 32 Raul Mondesi | .60 | .25 |
| ❑ 33 Roberto Alomar | 1.25 | .55 |
| ❑ 34 Barry Larkin | 1.25 | .55 |
| ❑ 35 Tony Gwynn | 2.50 | 1.10 |
| ❑ 36 Jim Thome | .75 | .35 |
| ❑ 37 Kenny Lofton | .60 | .25 |
| ❑ 38 Jeff Bagwell | 1.50 | .70 |
| ❑ 39 Ozzie Smith | 1.50 | .70 |
| ❑ 40 Kirby Puckett | 3.00 | 1.35 |
| ❑ 41 Andruw Jones | 1.50 | .70 |
| ❑ 42 Vladimir Guerrero | 2.50 | 1.10 |
| ❑ 43 Edgar Renteria | .60 | .25 |
| ❑ 44 Luis Castillo | .60 | .25 |
| ❑ 45 Darin Erstad | 1.50 | .70 |
| ❑ 46 Nomar Garciaparra | 4.00 | 1.80 |
| ❑ 47 Todd Greene | .50 | .23 |
| ❑ 48 Jason Kendall | .60 | .25 |
| ❑ 49 Rey Ordonez | .50 | .23 |
| ❑ 50 Alex Rodriguez | 4.00 | 1.80 |
| ❑ 51 Manny Ramirez | 1.50 | .70 |
| ❑ 52 Todd Walker | .50 | .23 |
| ❑ 53 Ruben Rivera | .50 | .23 |
| ❑ 54 Andy Pettitte | .60 | .25 |
| ❑ 55 Derek Jeter | 5.00 | 2.20 |
| ❑ 56 Todd Hollandsworth | .50 | .23 |
| ❑ 57 Rocky Coppinger | .50 | .23 |
| ❑ 58 Scott Rolen | 1.25 | .55 |
| ❑ 59 Jermaine Dye | .60 | .25 |
| ❑ 60 Chipper Jones | 3.00 | 1.35 |

## 1998 UD3

| | MINT | NRMT |
|---|---|---|
| COMP.FUTURE FX SET (30) | 80.00 | 36.00 |
| COMMON FUTURE FX (1-30) | .75 | .35 |
| COMP.POWER FX SET (30) | 40.00 | 18.00 |
| COMMON POWER FX (31-60) | .25 | .11 |
| COMP.EST.FX SET (30) | 60.00 | 27.00 |
| COMMON EST.FX (61-90) | .60 | .25 |
| COMP.FUTURE EMB.SET (30) | 50.00 | 22.00 |
| COM.FUTURE EMB. (91-120) | .50 | .23 |
| COMP.POWER EMB.SET (30) | 60.00 | 27.00 |
| COM.POWER EMB. (121-150) | .40 | .18 |
| COMP.EST.EMB.SET (30) | 20.00 | 9.00 |
| COMMON EST.EMB. (151-180) | .20 | .09 |
| COMP.FUTURE RBW.SET (30) | 25.00 | 11.00 |
| COM.FUTURE RBW (181-210) | .25 | .11 |
| COMP.POWER RBW.SET (30) | 200.00 | 90.00 |
| COM.POWER RBW (211-240) | 1.25 | .55 |
| COMP.EST.RBW.SET (30) | 200.00 | 90.00 |
| COMMON EST.RBW (241-270) | 2.00 | .90 |
| ❑ 1 Travis Lee FF | 1.25 | .55 |
| ❑ 2 A.J. Hinch FF | .75 | .35 |
| ❑ 3 Mike Caruso FF | .75 | .35 |
| ❑ 4 Miguel Tejada FF | 3.00 | 1.35 |
| ❑ 5 Brad Fullmer FF | 1.25 | .55 |
| ❑ 6 Eric Milton FF | .75 | .35 |
| ❑ 7 Mark Kotsay FF | 1.25 | .55 |
| ❑ 8 Darin Erstad FF | 3.00 | 1.35 |
| ❑ 9 Magglio Ordonez FF | 10.00 | 4.50 |
| ❑ 10 Ben Grieve FF | 1.25 | .55 |
| ❑ 11 Brett Tomko FF | .75 | .35 |
| ❑ 12 Mike Kinkade FF | 3.00 | 1.35 |
| ❑ 13 Rolando Arrojo FF | 3.00 | 1.35 |
| ❑ 14 Todd Helton FF | 4.00 | 1.80 |
| ❑ 15 Scott Rolen FF | 3.00 | 1.35 |
| ❑ 16 Bruce Chen FF | .75 | .35 |
| ❑ 17 Daryle Ward FF | 1.25 | .55 |
| ❑ 18 Jaret Wright FF | .75 | .35 |
| ❑ 19 Sean Casey FF | 1.25 | .55 |
| ❑ 20 Paul Konerko FF | 1.25 | .55 |
| ❑ 21 Kerry Wood FF | 3.00 | 1.35 |
| ❑ 22 Russell Branyan FF | 1.25 | .55 |
| ❑ 23 Gabe Alvarez FF | .75 | .35 |
| ❑ 24 Juan Encarnacion FF | 1.25 | .55 |
| ❑ 25 Andruw Jones FF | 3.00 | 1.35 |
| ❑ 26 Vladimir Guerrero FF | 5.00 | 2.20 |
| ❑ 27 Eli Marrero FF | .75 | .35 |
| ❑ 28 Matt Clement FF | 1.25 | .55 |
| ❑ 29 Gary Matthews Jr. FF | 3.00 | 1.35 |
| ❑ 30 Derrek Lee FF | .75 | .35 |
| ❑ 31 Ken Caminiti PF | .40 | .18 |
| ❑ 32 Gary Sheffield PF | 1.00 | .45 |
| ❑ 33 Jay Buhner PF | .40 | .18 |
| ❑ 34 Ryan Klesko PF | .40 | .18 |
| ❑ 35 Nomar Garciaparra PF | 3.00 | 1.35 |
| ❑ 36 Vinny Castilla PF | .40 | .18 |
| ❑ 37 Tony Clark PF | .25 | .11 |
| ❑ 38 Sammy Sosa PF | 2.00 | .90 |
| ❑ 39 Tino Martinez PF | .40 | .18 |
| ❑ 40 Mike Piazza PF | 3.00 | 1.35 |
| ❑ 41 Manny Ramirez PF | 1.25 | .55 |
| ❑ 42 Larry Walker PF | .40 | .18 |
| ❑ 43 Jose Cruz Jr. PF | .40 | .18 |
| ❑ 44 Matt Williams PF | .60 | .25 |
| ❑ 45 Frank Thomas PF | 2.00 | .90 |
| ❑ 46 Jim Edmonds PF | 1.00 | .45 |
| ❑ 47 Raul Mondesi PF | .40 | .18 |
| ❑ 48 Alex Rodriguez PF | 3.00 | 1.35 |
| ❑ 49 Albert Belle PF | .60 | .25 |
| ❑ 50 Mark McGwire PF | 4.00 | 1.80 |
| ❑ 51 Tim Salmon PF | .40 | .18 |
| ❑ 52 Andres Galarraga PF | .60 | .25 |
| ❑ 53 Jeff Bagwell PF | 1.25 | .55 |
| ❑ 54 Jim Thome PF | .60 | .25 |
| ❑ 55 Barry Bonds PF | 1.50 | .70 |
| ❑ 56 Carlos Delgado PF | 1.00 | .45 |
| ❑ 57 Mo Vaughn PF | .40 | .18 |
| ❑ 58 Chipper Jones PF | 2.50 | 1.10 |
| ❑ 59 Juan Gonzalez PF | .40 | .18 |
| ❑ 60 Ken Griffey Jr. PF | 4.00 | 1.80 |
| ❑ 61 David Cone EF | 1.00 | .45 |
| ❑ 62 Hideo Nomo EF | 2.50 | 1.10 |
| ❑ 63 Edgar Martinez EF | 1.50 | .70 |
| ❑ 64 Fred McGriff EF | 1.50 | .70 |
| ❑ 65 Cal Ripken EF | 10.00 | 4.50 |
| ❑ 66 Todd Hundley EF | .60 | .25 |
| ❑ 67 Barry Larkin EF | 2.50 | 1.10 |
| ❑ 68 Dennis Eckersley EF | 1.00 | .45 |
| ❑ 69 Randy Johnson EF | 3.00 | 1.35 |
| ❑ 70 Paul Molitor EF | 2.50 | 1.10 |
| ❑ 71 Eric Karros EF | 1.00 | .45 |
| ❑ 72 Rafael Palmeiro EF | 2.50 | 1.10 |
| ❑ 73 Chuck Knoblauch EF | 1.00 | .45 |
| ❑ 74 Ivan Rodriguez EF | 3.00 | 1.35 |
| ❑ 75 Greg Maddux EF | 6.00 | 2.70 |
| ❑ 76 Dante Bichette EF | 1.00 | .45 |
| ❑ 77 Brady Anderson EF | 1.00 | .45 |
| ❑ 78 Craig Biggio EF | 1.50 | .70 |

| Card | Mint | Nrmt |
|---|---|---|
| ❑ 79 Derek Jeter EF | 10.00 | 4.50 |
| ❑ 80 Roger Clemens EF | 5.00 | 2.20 |
| ❑ 81 Roberto Alomar EF | 2.50 | 1.10 |
| ❑ 82 Wade Boggs EF | 3.00 | 1.35 |
| ❑ 83 Charles Johnson EF | 1.00 | .45 |
| ❑ 84 Mark Grace EF | 2.50 | 1.10 |
| ❑ 85 Kenny Lofton EF | 1.00 | .45 |
| ❑ 86 Mike Mussina EF | 2.50 | 1.10 |
| ❑ 87 Pedro Martinez EF | 3.00 | 1.35 |
| ❑ 88 Curt Schilling EF | 1.00 | .45 |
| ❑ 89 Bernie Williams EF | 2.50 | 1.10 |
| ❑ 90 Tony Gwynn EF | 5.00 | 2.20 |
| ❑ 91 Travis Lee FE | .75 | .35 |
| ❑ 92 A.J. Hinch FE | .50 | .23 |
| ❑ 93 Mike Caruso FE | .50 | .23 |
| ❑ 94 Miguel Tejada FE | 2.00 | .90 |
| ❑ 95 Brad Fullmer FE | .75 | .35 |
| ❑ 96 Eric Milton FE | .50 | .23 |
| ❑ 97 Mark Kotsay FE | .75 | .35 |
| ❑ 98 Darin Erstad FE | 2.00 | .90 |
| ❑ 99 Magglio Ordonez FE | 6.00 | 2.70 |
| ❑ 100 Ben Grieve FE | .75 | .35 |
| ❑ 101 Brett Tomko FE | .50 | .23 |
| ❑ 102 Mike Kinkade FE | 2.00 | .90 |
| ❑ 103 Rolando Arrojo FE | 2.00 | .90 |
| ❑ 104 Todd Helton FE | 2.50 | 1.10 |
| ❑ 105 Scott Rolen FE | 2.00 | .90 |
| ❑ 106 Bruce Chen FE | .50 | .23 |
| ❑ 107 Daryle Ward FE | .75 | .35 |
| ❑ 108 Jaret Wright FE | .50 | .23 |
| ❑ 109 Sean Casey FE | .75 | .35 |
| ❑ 110 Paul Konerko FE | .75 | .35 |
| ❑ 111 Kerry Wood FE | 2.00 | .90 |
| ❑ 112 Russell Branyan FE | .75 | .35 |
| ❑ 113 Gabe Alvarez FE | .50 | .23 |
| ❑ 114 Juan Encarnacion FE | .75 | .35 |
| ❑ 115 Andruw Jones FE | 2.00 | .90 |
| ❑ 116 Vladimir Guerrero FE | 3.00 | 1.35 |
| ❑ 117 Eli Marrero FE | .50 | .23 |
| ❑ 118 Matt Clement FE | .75 | .35 |
| ❑ 119 Gary Matthews Jr. FE | 2.00 | .90 |
| ❑ 120 Derrek Lee FE | .50 | .23 |
| ❑ 121 Ken Caminiti PE | .60 | .25 |
| ❑ 122 Gary Sheffield PE | 1.50 | .70 |
| ❑ 123 Jay Buhner PE | .60 | .25 |
| ❑ 124 Ryan Klesko PE | .60 | .25 |
| ❑ 125 Nomar Garciaparra PE | 5.00 | 2.20 |
| ❑ 126 Vinny Castilla PE | .60 | .25 |
| ❑ 127 Tony Clark PE | .40 | .18 |
| ❑ 128 Sammy Sosa PE | 3.00 | 1.35 |
| ❑ 129 Tino Martinez PE | .60 | .25 |
| ❑ 130 Mike Piazza PE | 5.00 | 2.20 |
| ❑ 131 Manny Ramirez PE | 2.00 | .90 |
| ❑ 132 Larry Walker PE | .60 | .25 |
| ❑ 133 Jose Cruz Jr. PE | .60 | .25 |
| ❑ 134 Matt Williams PE | 1.00 | .45 |
| ❑ 135 Frank Thomas PE | 3.00 | 1.35 |
| ❑ 136 Jim Edmonds PE | 1.50 | .70 |
| ❑ 137 Raul Mondesi PE | .60 | .25 |
| ❑ 138 Alex Rodriguez PE | 5.00 | 2.20 |
| ❑ 139 Albert Belle PE | 1.00 | .45 |
| ❑ 140 Mark McGwire PE | 6.00 | 2.70 |
| ❑ 141 Tim Salmon PE | .60 | .25 |
| ❑ 142 Andres Galarraga PE | 1.00 | .45 |
| ❑ 143 Jeff Bagwell PE | 2.00 | .90 |
| ❑ 144 Jim Thome PE | 1.00 | .45 |
| ❑ 145 Barry Bonds PE | 2.50 | 1.10 |
| ❑ 146 Carlos Delgado PE | 1.50 | .70 |
| ❑ 147 Mo Vaughn PE | .60 | .25 |
| ❑ 148 Chipper Jones PE | 4.00 | 1.80 |
| ❑ 149 Juan Gonzalez PE | 1.50 | .70 |
| ❑ 150 Ken Griffey Jr. PE | 6.00 | 2.70 |
| ❑ 151 David Cone EE | .30 | .14 |
| ❑ 152 Hideo Nomo EE | .75 | .35 |
| ❑ 153 Edgar Martinez EE | .50 | .23 |
| ❑ 154 Fred McGriff EE | .50 | .23 |
| ❑ 155 Cal Ripken EE | 3.00 | 1.35 |
| ❑ 156 Todd Hundley EE | .20 | .09 |
| ❑ 157 Barry Larkin EE | .75 | .35 |
| ❑ 158 Dennis Eckersley EE | .30 | .14 |
| ❑ 159 Randy Johnson EE | 1.00 | .45 |
| ❑ 160 Paul Molitor EE | .75 | .35 |
| ❑ 161 Eric Karros EE | .30 | .14 |
| ❑ 162 Rafael Palmeiro EE | .75 | .35 |
| ❑ 163 Chuck Knoblauch EE | .30 | .14 |
| ❑ 164 Ivan Rodriguez EE | 1.00 | .45 |
| ❑ 165 Greg Maddux EE | 2.00 | .90 |
| ❑ 166 Dante Bichette EE | .30 | .14 |
| ❑ 167 Brady Anderson EE | .30 | .14 |
| ❑ 168 Craig Biggio EE | .50 | .23 |
| ❑ 169 Derek Jeter EE | 3.00 | 1.35 |
| ❑ 170 Roger Clemens EE | 1.50 | .70 |
| ❑ 171 Roberto Alomar EE | .75 | .35 |
| ❑ 172 Wade Boggs EE | 1.00 | .45 |
| ❑ 173 Charles Johnson EE | .30 | .14 |
| ❑ 174 Mark Grace EE | .75 | .35 |
| ❑ 175 Kenny Lofton EE | .30 | .14 |
| ❑ 176 Mike Mussina EE | .75 | .35 |
| ❑ 177 Pedro Martinez EE | 1.00 | .45 |
| ❑ 178 Curt Schilling EE | .30 | .14 |
| ❑ 179 Bernie Williams EE | .75 | .35 |
| ❑ 180 Tony Gwynn EE | 1.50 | .70 |
| ❑ 181 Travis Lee FR | .40 | .18 |
| ❑ 182 A.J. Hinch FR | .25 | .11 |
| ❑ 183 Mike Caruso FR | .25 | .11 |
| ❑ 184 Miguel Tejada FR | 1.00 | .45 |
| ❑ 185 Brad Fullmer FR | .40 | .18 |
| ❑ 186 Eric Milton FR | .25 | .11 |
| ❑ 187 Mark Kotsay FR | .40 | .18 |
| ❑ 188 Darin Erstad FR | 1.00 | .45 |
| ❑ 189 Magglio Ordonez FR RC | 3.00 | 1.35 |
| ❑ 190 Ben Grieve FR | .40 | .18 |
| ❑ 191 Brett Tomko FR | .25 | .11 |
| ❑ 192 Mike Kinkade FR RC | .60 | .25 |
| ❑ 193 Rolando Arrojo FR RC | .75 | .35 |
| ❑ 194 Todd Helton FR | 1.25 | .55 |
| ❑ 195 Scott Rolen FR | 1.00 | .45 |
| ❑ 196 Bruce Chen FR | .25 | .11 |
| ❑ 197 Daryle Ward FR | .40 | .18 |
| ❑ 198 Jaret Wright FR | .25 | .11 |
| ❑ 199 Sean Casey FR | .40 | .18 |
| ❑ 200 Paul Konerko FR | .40 | .18 |
| ❑ 201 Kerry Wood FR | 1.00 | .45 |
| ❑ 202 Russell Branyan FR | .40 | .18 |
| ❑ 203 Gabe Alvarez FR | .25 | .11 |
| ❑ 204 Juan Encarnacion FR | .40 | .18 |
| ❑ 205 Andruw Jones FR | 1.00 | .45 |
| ❑ 206 Vladimir Guerrero FR | 1.50 | .70 |
| ❑ 207 Eli Marrero FR | .25 | .11 |
| ❑ 208 Matt Clement FR | .40 | .18 |
| ❑ 209 Gary Matthews Jr. FR RC | .40 | .18 |
| ❑ 210 Derrek Lee FR | .25 | .11 |
| ❑ 211 Ken Caminiti PR | 2.00 | .90 |
| ❑ 212 Gary Sheffield PR | 5.00 | 2.20 |
| ❑ 213 Jay Buhner PR | 2.00 | .90 |
| ❑ 214 Ryan Klesko PR | 2.00 | .90 |
| ❑ 215 Nomar Garciaparra PR | 15.00 | 6.75 |
| ❑ 216 Vinny Castilla PR | 2.00 | .90 |
| ❑ 217 Tony Clark PR | 1.25 | .55 |
| ❑ 218 Sammy Sosa PR | 10.00 | 4.50 |
| ❑ 219 Tino Martinez PR | 2.00 | .90 |
| ❑ 220 Mike Piazza PR | 15.00 | 6.75 |
| ❑ 221 Manny Ramirez PR | 6.00 | 2.70 |
| ❑ 222 Larry Walker PR | 2.00 | .90 |
| ❑ 223 Jose Cruz Jr. PR | 2.00 | .90 |
| ❑ 224 Matt Williams PR | 3.00 | 1.35 |
| ❑ 225 Frank Thomas PR | 10.00 | 4.50 |
| ❑ 226 Jim Edmonds PR | 5.00 | 2.20 |
| ❑ 227 Raul Mondesi PR | 2.00 | .90 |
| ❑ 228 Alex Rodriguez PR | 15.00 | 6.75 |
| ❑ 229 Albert Belle PR | 3.00 | 1.35 |
| ❑ 230 Mark McGwire PR | 20.00 | 9.00 |
| ❑ 231 Tim Salmon PR | 2.00 | .90 |
| ❑ 232 Andres Galarraga PR | 3.00 | 1.35 |
| ❑ 233 Jeff Bagwell PR | 6.00 | 2.70 |
| ❑ 234 Jim Thome PR | 3.00 | 1.35 |
| ❑ 235 Barry Bonds PR | 8.00 | 3.60 |
| ❑ 236 Carlos Delgado PR | 5.00 | 2.20 |
| ❑ 237 Mo Vaughn PR | 2.00 | .90 |
| ❑ 238 Chipper Jones PR | 12.00 | 5.50 |
| ❑ 239 Juan Gonzalez PR | 5.00 | 2.20 |
| ❑ 240 Ken Griffey Jr. PR | 20.00 | 9.00 |
| ❑ 241 David Cone ER | 3.00 | 1.35 |
| ❑ 242 Hideo Nomo ER | 8.00 | 3.60 |
| ❑ 243 Edgar Martinez ER | 5.00 | 2.20 |
| ❑ 244 Fred McGriff ER | 5.00 | 2.20 |
| ❑ 245 Cal Ripken ER | 30.00 | 13.50 |
| ❑ 246 Todd Hundley ER | 2.00 | .90 |
| ❑ 247 Barry Larkin ER | 8.00 | 3.60 |
| ❑ 248 Dennis Eckersley ER | 3.00 | 1.35 |
| ❑ 249 Randy Johnson ER | 10.00 | 4.50 |
| ❑ 250 Paul Molitor ER | 8.00 | 3.60 |
| ❑ 251 Eric Karros ER | 3.00 | 1.35 |
| ❑ 252 Rafael Palmeiro ER | 8.00 | 3.60 |
| ❑ 253 Chuck Knoblauch ER | 3.00 | 1.35 |
| ❑ 254 Ivan Rodriguez ER | 10.00 | 4.50 |
| ❑ 255 Greg Maddux ER | 20.00 | 9.00 |
| ❑ 256 Dante Bichette ER | 3.00 | 1.35 |
| ❑ 257 Brady Anderson ER | 3.00 | 1.35 |
| ❑ 258 Craig Biggio ER | 5.00 | 2.20 |
| ❑ 259 Derek Jeter ER | 30.00 | 13.50 |
| ❑ 260 Roger Clemens ER | 15.00 | 6.75 |
| ❑ 261 Roberto Alomar ER | 8.00 | 3.60 |
| ❑ 262 Wade Boggs ER | 10.00 | 4.50 |
| ❑ 263 Charles Johnson ER | 3.00 | 1.35 |
| ❑ 264 Mark Grace ER | 8.00 | 3.60 |
| ❑ 265 Kenny Lofton ER | 3.00 | 1.35 |
| ❑ 266 Mike Mussina ER | 8.00 | 3.60 |
| ❑ 267 Pedro Martinez ER | 10.00 | 4.50 |
| ❑ 268 Curt Schilling ER | 3.00 | 1.35 |
| ❑ 269 Bernie Williams ER | 8.00 | 3.60 |
| ❑ 270 Tony Gwynn ER | 15.00 | 6.75 |
| ❑ S1 Ken Griffey Jr. PE Sample | 3.00 | 1.35 |

## 1999 UD Ionix

| | MINT | NRMT |
|---|---|---|
| COMPLETE SET (90) | 150.00 | 70.00 |
| COMP.SET w/o SP's (60) | 30.00 | 13.50 |
| COMMON CARD (1-60) | .20 | .09 |
| COMMON TECH (61-90) | 2.00 | .90 |
| ❑ 1 Troy Glaus | 1.25 | .55 |
| ❑ 2 Darin Erstad | .75 | .35 |
| ❑ 3 Travis Lee | .20 | .09 |
| ❑ 4 Matt Williams | .50 | .23 |
| ❑ 5 Chipper Jones | 2.00 | .90 |
| ❑ 6 Greg Maddux | 2.00 | .90 |
| ❑ 7 Andruw Jones | .75 | .35 |
| ❑ 8 Andres Galarraga | .50 | .23 |
| ❑ 9 Tom Glavine | .75 | .35 |
| ❑ 10 Cal Ripken | 3.00 | 1.35 |
| ❑ 11 Ryan Minor | .20 | .09 |
| ❑ 12 Nomar Garciaparra | 2.50 | 1.10 |
| ❑ 13 Mo Vaughn | .30 | .14 |
| ❑ 14 Pedro Martinez | 1.00 | .45 |
| ❑ 15 Sammy Sosa | 1.50 | .70 |
| ❑ 16 Kerry Wood | .30 | .14 |
| ❑ 17 Albert Belle | .50 | .23 |
| ❑ 18 Frank Thomas | 1.50 | .70 |
| ❑ 19 Sean Casey | .30 | .14 |
| ❑ 20 Kenny Lofton | .30 | .14 |
| ❑ 21 Manny Ramirez | 1.00 | .45 |
| ❑ 22 Jim Thome | .50 | .23 |
| ❑ 23 Bartolo Colon | .30 | .14 |
| ❑ 24 Jaret Wright | .20 | .09 |
| ❑ 25 Larry Walker | .30 | .14 |
| ❑ 26 Tony Clark | .20 | .09 |
| ❑ 27 Gabe Kapler | .30 | .14 |
| ❑ 28 Edgar Renteria | .20 | .09 |
| ❑ 29 Randy Johnson | 1.00 | .45 |
| ❑ 30 Craig Biggio | .50 | .23 |
| ❑ 31 Jeff Bagwell | 1.00 | .45 |
| ❑ 32 Moises Alou | .30 | .14 |
| ❑ 33 Johnny Damon | .30 | .14 |
| ❑ 34 Adrian Beltre | .30 | .14 |
| ❑ 35 Jeromy Burnitz | .30 | .14 |
| ❑ 36 Todd Walker | .20 | .09 |
| ❑ 37 Corey Koskie | .20 | .09 |
| ❑ 38 Vladimir Guerrero | 1.25 | .55 |

| | | |
|---|---|---|
| ❑ 39 Mike Piazza | 2.50 | 1.10 |
| ❑ 40 Hideo Nomo | .75 | .35 |
| ❑ 41 Derek Jeter | 3.00 | 1.35 |
| ❑ 42 Tino Martinez | .30 | .14 |
| ❑ 43 Orlando Hernandez | .30 | .14 |
| ❑ 44 Ben Grieve | .30 | .14 |
| ❑ 45 Rickey Henderson | 1.00 | .45 |
| ❑ 46 Scott Rolen | .75 | .35 |
| ❑ 47 Curt Schilling | .30 | .14 |
| ❑ 48 Aramis Ramirez | .20 | .09 |
| ❑ 49 Tony Gwynn | 1.50 | .70 |
| ❑ 50 Kevin Brown | .30 | .14 |
| ❑ 51 Barry Bonds | 1.25 | .55 |
| ❑ 52 Ken Griffey Jr. | 3.00 | 1.35 |
| ❑ 53 Alex Rodriguez | 2.50 | 1.10 |
| ❑ 54 Mark McGwire | 3.00 | 1.35 |
| ❑ 55 J.D. Drew | .75 | .35 |
| ❑ 56 Rolando Arrojo | .20 | .09 |
| ❑ 57 Ivan Rodriguez | 1.00 | .45 |
| ❑ 58 Juan Gonzalez | .75 | .35 |
| ❑ 59 Roger Clemens | 1.50 | .70 |
| ❑ 60 Jose Cruz Jr. | .30 | .14 |
| ❑ 61 Travis Lee TECH | 2.00 | .90 |
| ❑ 62 Andres Galarraga TECH | 2.00 | .90 |
| ❑ 63 Andruw Jones TECH | 3.00 | 1.35 |
| ❑ 64 Chipper Jones TECH | 8.00 | 3.60 |
| ❑ 65 Greg Maddux TECH | 8.00 | 3.60 |
| ❑ 66 Cal Ripken TECH | 12.00 | 5.50 |
| ❑ 67 Nomar Garciaparra TECH | 10.00 | 4.50 |
| ❑ 68 Mo Vaughn TECH | 2.00 | .90 |
| ❑ 69 Sammy Sosa TECH | 6.00 | 2.70 |
| ❑ 70 Frank Thomas TECH | 6.00 | 2.70 |
| ❑ 71 Kerry Wood TECH | 2.00 | .90 |
| ❑ 72 Kenny Lofton TECH | 2.00 | .90 |
| ❑ 73 Manny Ramirez TECH | 4.00 | 1.80 |
| ❑ 74 Larry Walker TECH | 2.00 | .90 |
| ❑ 75 Jeff Bagwell TECH | 4.00 | 1.80 |
| ❑ 76 Randy Johnson TECH | 4.00 | 1.80 |
| ❑ 77 Paul Molitor TECH | 3.00 | 1.35 |
| ❑ 78 Derek Jeter TECH | 12.00 | 5.50 |
| ❑ 79 Tino Martinez TECH | 2.00 | .90 |
| ❑ 80 Mike Piazza TECH | 10.00 | 4.50 |
| ❑ 81 Ben Grieve TECH | 2.00 | .90 |
| ❑ 82 Scott Rolen TECH | 3.00 | 1.35 |
| ❑ 83 Mark McGwire TECH | 12.00 | 5.50 |
| ❑ 84 Tony Gwynn TECH | 6.00 | 2.70 |
| ❑ 85 Barry Bonds TECH | 5.00 | 2.20 |
| ❑ 86 Ken Griffey Jr. TECH | 12.00 | 5.50 |
| ❑ 87 Alex Rodriguez TECH | 10.00 | 4.50 |
| ❑ 88 Juan Gonzalez TECH | 3.00 | 1.35 |
| ❑ 89 Roger Clemens TECH | 6.00 | 2.70 |
| ❑ 90 J.D. Drew TECH | 3.00 | 1.35 |
| ❑ S100 Ken Griffey Jr. Sample | 3.00 | 1.35 |

## 2000 UD Ionix

| | MINT | NRMT |
|---|---|---|
| COMPLETE SET (90) | 120.00 | 55.00 |
| COMP.SET w/o SP's (60) | 30.00 | 13.50 |
| COMMON CARD (1-60) | .20 | .09 |
| COMMON FUTURE (61-90) | 2.00 | .90 |

| | | |
|---|---|---|
| ❑ 1 Mo Vaughn | .30 | .14 |
| ❑ 2 Troy Glaus | 1.00 | .45 |
| ❑ 3 Jeff Bagwell | 1.00 | .45 |
| ❑ 4 Craig Biggio | .50 | .23 |
| ❑ 5 Jose Lima | .20 | .09 |
| ❑ 6 Jason Giambi | .75 | .35 |
| ❑ 7 Tim Hudson | .75 | .35 |
| ❑ 8 Shawn Green | .75 | .35 |
| ❑ 9 Carlos Delgado | .75 | .35 |
| ❑ 10 Chipper Jones | 2.00 | .90 |
| ❑ 11 Andruw Jones | .75 | .35 |
| ❑ 12 Greg Maddux | 2.00 | .90 |
| ❑ 13 Jeromy Burnitz | .30 | .14 |
| ❑ 14 Mark McGwire | 3.00 | 1.35 |
| ❑ 15 J.D. Drew | .75 | .35 |
| ❑ 16 Sammy Sosa | 1.50 | .70 |
| ❑ 17 Jose Canseco | 1.00 | .45 |
| ❑ 18 Fred McGriff | .50 | .23 |
| ❑ 19 Randy Johnson | 1.00 | .45 |
| ❑ 20 Matt Williams | .50 | .23 |
| ❑ 21 Kevin Brown | .50 | .23 |
| ❑ 22 Gary Sheffield | .75 | .35 |
| ❑ 23 Vladimir Guerrero | 1.25 | .55 |
| ❑ 24 Barry Bonds | 1.25 | .55 |
| ❑ 25 Jim Thome | .50 | .23 |
| ❑ 26 Manny Ramirez | 1.00 | .45 |
| ❑ 27 Roberto Alomar | .75 | .35 |
| ❑ 28 Kenny Lofton | .30 | .14 |
| ❑ 29 Ken Griffey Jr. | 3.00 | 1.35 |
| ❑ 30 Alex Rodriguez | 2.50 | 1.10 |
| ❑ 31 Alex Gonzalez | .20 | .09 |
| ❑ 32 Preston Wilson | .30 | .14 |
| ❑ 33 Mike Piazza | 2.50 | 1.10 |
| ❑ 34 Robin Ventura | .50 | .23 |
| ❑ 35 Cal Ripken | 3.00 | 1.35 |
| ❑ 36 Albert Belle | .50 | .23 |
| ❑ 37 Tony Gwynn | 1.50 | .70 |
| ❑ 38 Scott Rolen | .75 | .35 |
| ❑ 39 Curt Schilling | .30 | .14 |
| ❑ 40 Brian Giles | .30 | .14 |
| ❑ 41 Juan Gonzalez | .75 | .35 |
| ❑ 42 Ivan Rodriguez | 1.00 | .45 |
| ❑ 43 Rafael Palmeiro | .75 | .35 |
| ❑ 44 Pedro Martinez | 1.00 | .45 |
| ❑ 45 Nomar Garciaparra | 2.50 | 1.10 |
| ❑ 46 Sean Casey | .30 | .14 |
| ❑ 47 Aaron Boone | .20 | .09 |
| ❑ 48 Barry Larkin | .75 | .35 |
| ❑ 49 Larry Walker | .30 | .14 |
| ❑ 50 Vinny Castilla | .30 | .14 |
| ❑ 51 Carlos Beltran | .30 | .14 |
| ❑ 52 Gabe Kapler | .30 | .14 |
| ❑ 53 Dean Palmer | .30 | .14 |
| ❑ 54 Eric Milton | .20 | .09 |
| ❑ 55 Corey Koskie | .20 | .09 |
| ❑ 56 Frank Thomas | 1.50 | .70 |
| ❑ 57 Magglio Ordonez | .30 | .14 |
| ❑ 58 Roger Clemens | 1.50 | .70 |
| ❑ 59 Bernie Williams | .75 | .35 |
| ❑ 60 Derek Jeter | 3.00 | 1.35 |
| ❑ 61 Josh Beckett FUT | .75 | .35 |
| ❑ 62 Eric Munson FUT | .75 | .35 |
| ❑ 63 Rick Ankiel FUT | 8.00 | 3.60 |
| ❑ 64 Matt Riley FUT | 2.00 | .90 |
| ❑ 65 Rob Ramsay FUT | 2.00 | .90 |
| ❑ 66 Vernon Wells FUT | 2.00 | .90 |
| ❑ 67 Eric Gagne FUT | 2.00 | .90 |
| ❑ 68 Robert Fick FUT | 2.00 | .90 |
| ❑ 69 Mark Quinn FUT | 2.00 | .90 |
| ❑ 70 Kip Wells FUT | 2.00 | .90 |
| ❑ 71 Peter Bergeron FUT | 2.00 | .90 |
| ❑ 72 Ed Yarnall FUT | 2.00 | .90 |
| ❑ 73 Jorge Toca FUT | 2.00 | .90 |
| ❑ 74 Alfonso Soriano FUT | 2.00 | .90 |
| ❑ 75 Calvin Murray FUT | 2.00 | .90 |
| ❑ 76 Ramon Ortiz FUT | 2.00 | .90 |
| ❑ 77 Chad Meyers FUT | 2.00 | .90 |
| ❑ 78 Jason LaRue FUT | 2.00 | .90 |
| ❑ 79 Pat Burrell FUT | 6.00 | 2.70 |
| ❑ 80 Chad Hermansen FUT | 2.00 | .90 |
| ❑ 81 Lance Berkman FUT | 2.00 | .90 |
| ❑ 82 Erubiel Durazo FUT | 2.00 | .90 |
| ❑ 83 Juan Pena FUT | 2.00 | .90 |
| ❑ 84 Adam Kennedy FUT | 2.00 | .90 |
| ❑ 85 Ben Petrick FUT | 2.00 | .90 |
| ❑ 86 Kevin Barker FUT | 2.00 | .90 |
| ❑ 87 Bruce Chen FUT | 2.00 | .90 |
| ❑ 88 Jerry Hairston Jr. FUT | 2.00 | .90 |
| ❑ 89 A.J. Burnett FUT | 2.00 | .90 |
| ❑ 90 Gary Matthews Jr. FUT | 2.00 | .90 |

## 1991 Ultra

| | MINT | NRMT |
|---|---|---|
| COMPLETE SET (400) | 20.00 | 9.00 |

| | | |
|---|---|---|
| ❑ 1 Steve Avery | .10 | .05 |
| ❑ 2 Jeff Blauser | .10 | .05 |
| ❑ 3 Francisco Cabrera | .10 | .05 |
| ❑ 4 Ron Gant | .20 | .09 |
| ❑ 5 Tom Glavine | .40 | .18 |
| ❑ 6 Tommy Gregg | .10 | .05 |
| ❑ 7 Dave Justice | .40 | .18 |
| ❑ 8 Oddibe McDowell | .10 | .05 |
| ❑ 9 Greg Olson | .10 | .05 |
| ❑ 10 Terry Pendleton | .20 | .09 |
| ❑ 11 Lonnie Smith | .10 | .05 |
| ❑ 12 John Smoltz | .20 | .09 |
| ❑ 13 Jeff Treadway | .10 | .05 |
| ❑ 14 Glenn Davis | .10 | .05 |
| ❑ 15 Mike Devereaux | .10 | .05 |
| ❑ 16 Leo Gomez | .10 | .05 |
| ❑ 17 Chris Hoiles | .10 | .05 |
| ❑ 18 Dave Johnson | .10 | .05 |
| ❑ 19 Ben McDonald | .10 | .05 |
| ❑ 20 Randy Milligan | .10 | .05 |
| ❑ 21 Gregg Olson | .10 | .05 |
| ❑ 22 Joe Orsulak | .10 | .05 |
| ❑ 23 Bill Ripken | .10 | .05 |
| ❑ 24 Cal Ripken | 1.50 | .70 |
| ❑ 25 David Segui | .10 | .05 |
| ❑ 26 Craig Worthington | .10 | .05 |
| ❑ 27 Wade Boggs | .50 | .23 |
| ❑ 28 Tom Bolton | .10 | .05 |
| ❑ 29 Tom Brunansky | .10 | .05 |
| ❑ 30 Ellis Burks | .20 | .09 |
| ❑ 31 Roger Clemens | .75 | .35 |
| ❑ 32 Mike Greenwell | .10 | .05 |
| ❑ 33 Greg A. Harris | .10 | .05 |
| ❑ 34 Daryl Irvine | .10 | .05 |
| ❑ 35 Mike Marshall UER (1990 in stats is shown as 990) | .10 | .05 |
| ❑ 36 Tim Naehring | .10 | .05 |
| ❑ 37 Tony Pena | .10 | .05 |
| ❑ 38 Phil Plantier RC | .10 | .05 |
| ❑ 39 Carlos Quintana | .10 | .05 |
| ❑ 40 Jeff Reardon | .20 | .09 |
| ❑ 41 Jody Reed | .10 | .05 |
| ❑ 42 Luis Rivera | .10 | .05 |
| ❑ 43 Jim Abbott | .20 | .09 |
| ❑ 44 Chuck Finley | .20 | .09 |
| ❑ 45 Bryan Harvey | .10 | .05 |
| ❑ 46 Donnie Hill | .10 | .05 |
| ❑ 47 Jack Howell | .10 | .05 |
| ❑ 48 Wally Joyner | .20 | .09 |
| ❑ 49 Mark Langston | .10 | .05 |
| ❑ 50 Kirk McCaskill | .10 | .05 |
| ❑ 51 Lance Parrish | .10 | .05 |
| ❑ 52 Dick Schofield | .10 | .05 |
| ❑ 53 Lee Stevens | .20 | .09 |
| ❑ 54 Dave Winfield | .40 | .18 |
| ❑ 55 George Bell | .10 | .05 |
| ❑ 56 Damon Berryhill | .10 | .05 |
| ❑ 57 Mike Bielecki | .10 | .05 |
| ❑ 58 Andre Dawson | .20 | .09 |
| ❑ 59 Shawon Dunston | .10 | .05 |
| ❑ 60 Joe Girardi UER (Bats right, LH hitter) | .20 | .09 |

shown is Doug Dascenzo)
❑ 61 Mark Grace .40 .18
❑ 62 Mike Harkey .10 .05
❑ 63 Les Lancaster .10 .05
❑ 64 Greg Maddux 1.00 .45
❑ 65 Derrick May .10 .05
❑ 66 Ryne Sandberg .50 .23
❑ 67 Luis Salazar .10 .05
❑ 68 Dwight Smith .10 .05
❑ 69 Hector Villanueva .10 .05
❑ 70 Jerome Walton .10 .05
❑ 71 Mitch Williams .10 .05
❑ 72 Carlton Fisk .40 .18
❑ 73 Scott Fletcher .10 .05
❑ 74 Ozzie Guillen .10 .05
❑ 75 Greg Hibbard .10 .05
❑ 76 Lance Johnson .10 .05
❑ 77 Steve Lyons .10 .05
❑ 78 Jack McDowell .10 .05
❑ 79 Dan Pasqua .10 .05
❑ 80 Melido Perez .10 .05
❑ 81 Tim Raines .20 .09
❑ 82 Sammy Sosa 1.00 .45
❑ 83 Cory Snyder .10 .05
❑ 84 Bobby Thigpen .10 .05
❑ 85 Frank Thomas 1.00 .45
(Card says he is
an outfielder)
❑ 86 Robin Ventura .40 .18
❑ 87 Todd Benzinger .10 .05
❑ 88 Glenn Braggs .10 .05
❑ 89 Tom Browning UER .10 .05
(Front photo actually
Norm Charlton)
❑ 90 Norm Charlton .10 .05
❑ 91 Eric Davis .20 .09
❑ 92 Rob Dibble .10 .05
❑ 93 Bill Doran .10 .05
❑ 94 Mariano Duncan UER .10 .05
(Right back photo
is Billy Hatcher)
❑ 95 Billy Hatcher .10 .05
❑ 96 Barry Larkin .40 .18
❑ 97 Randy Myers .20 .09
❑ 98 Hal Morris .10 .05
❑ 99 Joe Oliver .10 .05
❑ 100 Paul O'Neill .20 .09
❑ 101 Jeff Reed .10 .05
(See also 104)
❑ 102 Jose Rijo .10 .05
❑ 103 Chris Sabo .10 .05
(See also 106)
❑ 104 Beau Allred UER .10 .05
(Card number is 101)
❑ 105 Sandy Alomar Jr. .20 .09
❑ 106 Carlos Baerga UER .10 .05
(Card number is 103)
❑ 107 Albert Belle .20 .09
❑ 108 Jerry Browne .10 .05
❑ 109 Tom Candiotti .10 .05
❑ 110 Alex Cole .10 .05
❑ 111 John Farrell .10 .05
(See also 114)
❑ 112 Felix Fermin .10 .05
❑ 113 Brook Jacoby .10 .05
❑ 114 Chris James UER .10 .05
(Card number is 111)
❑ 115 Doug Jones .10 .05
❑ 116 Steve Olin .10 .05
(See also 119)
❑ 117 Greg Swindell .10 .05
❑ 118 Turner Ward RC .10 .05
❑ 119 Mitch Webster UER .10 .05
(Card number is 116)
❑ 120 Dave Bergman .10 .05
❑ 121 Cecil Fielder .20 .09
❑ 122 Travis Fryman .40 .18
❑ 123 Mike Henneman .10 .05
❑ 124 Lloyd Moseby .10 .05
❑ 125 Dan Petry .10 .05
❑ 126 Tony Phillips .10 .05
❑ 127 Mark Salas .10 .05
❑ 128 Frank Tanana .10 .05
❑ 129 Alan Trammell .20 .09
❑ 130 Lou Whitaker .20 .09
❑ 131 Eric Anthony .10 .05
❑ 132 Craig Biggio .20 .09
❑ 133 Ken Caminiti .20 .09
❑ 134 Casey Candaele .10 .05
❑ 135 Andujar Cedeno .10 .05
❑ 136 Mark Davidson .10 .05
❑ 137 Jim Deshaies .10 .05
❑ 138 Mark Portugal .10 .05
❑ 139 Rafael Ramirez .10 .05
❑ 140 Mike Scott .10 .05
❑ 141 Eric Yelding .10 .05
❑ 142 Gerald Young .10 .05
❑ 143 Kevin Appier .20 .09
❑ 144 George Brett .75 .35
❑ 145 Jeff Conine RC .40 .18
❑ 146 Jim Eisenreich .10 .05
❑ 147 Tom Gordon .10 .05
❑ 148 Mark Gubicza .10 .05
❑ 149 Bo Jackson .20 .09
❑ 150 Brent Mayne .10 .05
❑ 151 Mike Macfarlane .10 .05
❑ 152 Brian McRae RC .20 .09
❑ 153 Jeff Montgomery .20 .09
❑ 154 Bret Saberhagen .20 .09
❑ 155 Kevin Seitzer .10 .05
❑ 156 Terry Shumpert .10 .05
❑ 157 Kurt Stillwell .10 .05
❑ 158 Danny Tartabull .10 .05
❑ 159 Tim Belcher .10 .05
❑ 160 Kal Daniels .10 .05
❑ 161 Alfredo Griffin .10 .05
❑ 162 Lenny Harris .10 .05
❑ 163 Jay Howell .10 .05
❑ 164 Ramon Martinez .10 .05
❑ 165 Mike Morgan .10 .05
❑ 166 Eddie Murray .40 .18
❑ 167 Jose Offerman .10 .05
❑ 168 Juan Samuel .10 .05
❑ 169 Mike Scioscia .10 .05
❑ 170 Mike Sharperson .10 .05
❑ 171 Darryl Strawberry .20 .09
❑ 172 Greg Brock .10 .05
❑ 173 Chuck Crim .10 .05
❑ 174 Jim Gantner .10 .05
❑ 175 Ted Higuera .10 .05
❑ 176 Mark Knudson .10 .05
❑ 177 Tim McIntosh .10 .05
❑ 178 Paul Molitor .40 .18
❑ 179 Dan Plesac .10 .05
❑ 180 Gary Sheffield .40 .18
❑ 181 Bill Spiers .10 .05
❑ 182 B.J. Surhoff .20 .09
❑ 183 Greg Vaughn .40 .18
❑ 184 Robin Yount .40 .18
❑ 185 Rick Aguilera .20 .09
❑ 186 Greg Gagne .10 .05
❑ 187 Dan Gladden .10 .05
❑ 188 Brian Harper .10 .05
❑ 189 Kent Hrbek .20 .09
❑ 190 Gene Larkin .10 .05
❑ 191 Shane Mack .10 .05
❑ 192 Pedro Munoz RC .10 .05
❑ 193 Al Newman .10 .05
❑ 194 Junior Ortiz .10 .05
❑ 195 Kirby Puckett 1.00 .45
❑ 196 Kevin Tapani .10 .05
❑ 197 Dennis Boyd .10 .05
❑ 198 Tim Burke .10 .05
❑ 199 Ivan Calderon .10 .05
❑ 200 Delino DeShields .20 .09
❑ 201 Mike Fitzgerald .10 .05
❑ 202 Steve Frey .10 .05
❑ 203 Andres Galarraga .20 .09
❑ 204 Marquis Grissom .10 .05
❑ 205 Dave Martinez .10 .05
❑ 206 Dennis Martinez .20 .09
❑ 207 Junior Noboa .10 .05
❑ 208 Spike Owen .10 .05
❑ 209 Scott Ruskin .10 .05
❑ 210 Tim Wallach .10 .05
❑ 211 Daryl Boston .10 .05
❑ 212 Vince Coleman .10 .05
❑ 213 David Cone .20 .09
❑ 214 Ron Darling .10 .05
❑ 215 Kevin Elster .10 .05
❑ 216 Sid Fernandez .10 .05
❑ 217 John Franco .20 .09
❑ 218 Dwight Gooden .20 .09
❑ 219 Tom Herr .10 .05
❑ 220 Todd Hundley .10 .05
❑ 221 Gregg Jefferies .10 .05
❑ 222 Howard Johnson .10 .05
❑ 223 Dave Magadan .10 .05
❑ 224 Kevin McReynolds .10 .05
❑ 225 Keith Miller .10 .05
❑ 226 Mackey Sasser .10 .05
❑ 227 Frank Viola .10 .05
❑ 228 Jesse Barfield .10 .05
❑ 229 Greg Cadaret .10 .05
❑ 230 Alvaro Espinoza .10 .05
❑ 231 Bob Geren .10 .05
❑ 232 Lee Guetterman .10 .05
❑ 233 Mel Hall .10 .05
❑ 234 Andy Hawkins UER .10 .05
(Back center photo
is not him)
❑ 235 Roberto Kelly .10 .05
❑ 236 Tim Leary .10 .05
❑ 237 Jim Leyritz .10 .05
❑ 238 Kevin Maas .10 .05
❑ 239 Don Mattingly 1.00 .45
❑ 240 Hensley Meulens .10 .05
❑ 241 Eric Plunk .10 .05
❑ 242 Steve Sax .10 .05
❑ 243 Todd Burns .10 .05
❑ 244 Jose Canseco .50 .23
❑ 245 Dennis Eckersley .20 .09
❑ 246 Mike Gallego .10 .05
❑ 247 Dave Henderson .10 .05
❑ 248 Rickey Henderson .50 .23
❑ 249 Rick Honeycutt .10 .05
❑ 250 Carney Lansford .20 .09
❑ 251 Mark McGwire 1.50 .70
❑ 252 Mike Moore .10 .05
❑ 253 Terry Steinbach .20 .09
❑ 254 Dave Stewart .20 .09
❑ 255 Walt Weiss .10 .05
❑ 256 Bob Welch .10 .05
❑ 257 Curt Young .10 .05
❑ 258 Wes Chamberlain RC .10 .05
❑ 259 Pat Combs .10 .05
❑ 260 Darren Daulton .20 .09
❑ 261 Jose DeJesus .10 .05
❑ 262 Len Dykstra .20 .09
❑ 263 Charlie Hayes .10 .05
❑ 264 Von Hayes .10 .05
❑ 265 Ken Howell .10 .05
❑ 266 John Kruk .20 .09
❑ 267 Roger McDowell .10 .05
❑ 268 Mickey Morandini .10 .05
❑ 269 Terry Mulholland .10 .05
❑ 270 Dale Murphy .40 .18
❑ 271 Randy Ready .10 .05
❑ 272 Dickie Thon .10 .05
❑ 273 Stan Belinda .10 .05
❑ 274 Jay Bell .20 .09
❑ 275 Barry Bonds .60 .25
❑ 276 Bobby Bonilla .20 .09
❑ 277 Doug Drabek .10 .05
❑ 278 Carlos Garcia RC .10 .05
❑ 279 Neal Heaton .10 .05
❑ 280 Jeff King .10 .05
❑ 281 Bill Landrum .10 .05
❑ 282 Mike LaValliere .10 .05
❑ 283 Jose Lind .10 .05
❑ 284 Orlando Merced RC .10 .05
❑ 285 Gary Redus .10 .05
❑ 286 Don Slaught .10 .05
❑ 287 Andy Van Slyke .20 .09
❑ 288 Jose DeLeon .10 .05
❑ 289 Pedro Guerrero .10 .05
❑ 290 Ray Lankford .40 .18
❑ 291 Joe Magrane .10 .05
❑ 292 Jose Oquendo .10 .05
❑ 293 Tom Pagnozzi .10 .05
❑ 294 Bryn Smith .10 .05
❑ 295 Lee Smith .20 .09
❑ 296 Ozzie Smith UER .50 .23
(Born 12-26, 54,
should have hyphen)
❑ 297 Milt Thompson .10 .05
❑ 298 Craig Wilson .10 .05
❑ 299 Todd Zeile .20 .09

| | | MINT | NRMT |
|---|---|---|---|
| ❑ 300 | Shawn Abner | .10 | .05 |
| ❑ 301 | Andy Benes | .10 | .05 |
| ❑ 302 | Paul Faries | .10 | .05 |
| ❑ 303 | Tony Gwynn | .75 | .35 |
| ❑ 304 | Greg W. Harris | .10 | .05 |
| ❑ 305 | Thomas Howard | .10 | .05 |
| ❑ 306 | Bruce Hurst | .10 | .05 |
| ❑ 307 | Craig Lefferts | .10 | .05 |
| ❑ 308 | Fred McGriff | .40 | .18 |
| ❑ 309 | Dennis Rasmussen | .10 | .05 |
| ❑ 310 | Bip Roberts | .10 | .05 |
| ❑ 311 | Benito Santiago | .10 | .05 |
| ❑ 312 | Garry Templeton | .10 | .05 |
| ❑ 313 | Ed Whitson | .10 | .05 |
| ❑ 314 | Dave Anderson | .10 | .05 |
| ❑ 315 | Kevin Bass | .10 | .05 |
| ❑ 316 | Jeff Brantley | .10 | .05 |
| ❑ 317 | John Burkett | .10 | .05 |
| ❑ 318 | Will Clark | .40 | .18 |
| ❑ 319 | Steve Decker | .10 | .05 |
| ❑ 320 | Scott Garrelts | .10 | .05 |
| ❑ 321 | Terry Kennedy | .10 | .05 |
| ❑ 322 | Mark Leonard | .10 | .05 |
| ❑ 323 | Darren Lewis | .20 | .09 |
| ❑ 324 | Greg Litton | .10 | .05 |
| ❑ 325 | Willie McGee | .20 | .09 |
| ❑ 326 | Kevin Mitchell | .10 | .05 |
| ❑ 327 | Don Robinson | .10 | .05 |
| ❑ 328 | Andres Santana | .10 | .05 |
| ❑ 329 | Robby Thompson | .10 | .05 |
| ❑ 330 | Jose Uribe | .10 | .05 |
| ❑ 331 | Matt Williams | .20 | .09 |
| ❑ 332 | Scott Bradley | .10 | .05 |
| ❑ 333 | Henry Cotto | .10 | .05 |
| ❑ 334 | Alvin Davis | .10 | .05 |
| ❑ 335 | Ken Griffey Sr. | .20 | .09 |
| ❑ 336 | Ken Griffey Jr. | 2.00 | .90 |
| ❑ 337 | Erik Hanson | .10 | .05 |
| ❑ 338 | Brian Holman | .10 | .05 |
| ❑ 339 | Randy Johnson | .60 | .25 |
| ❑ 340 | Edgar Martinez UER (Listed as playing SS) | .20 | .09 |
| ❑ 341 | Tino Martinez | .20 | .09 |
| ❑ 342 | Pete O'Brien | .10 | .05 |
| ❑ 343 | Harold Reynolds | .10 | .05 |
| ❑ 344 | Dave Valle | .10 | .05 |
| ❑ 345 | Omar Vizquel | .40 | .18 |
| ❑ 346 | Brad Arnsberg | .10 | .05 |
| ❑ 347 | Kevin Brown | .20 | .09 |
| ❑ 348 | Julio Franco | .10 | .05 |
| ❑ 349 | Jeff Huson | .10 | .05 |
| ❑ 350 | Rafael Palmeiro | .40 | .18 |
| ❑ 351 | Geno Petralli | .10 | .05 |
| ❑ 352 | Gary Pettis | .10 | .05 |
| ❑ 353 | Kenny Rogers | .10 | .05 |
| ❑ 354 | Jeff Russell | .10 | .05 |
| ❑ 355 | Nolan Ryan | 2.00 | .90 |
| ❑ 356 | Ruben Sierra | .10 | .05 |
| ❑ 357 | Bobby Witt | .10 | .05 |
| ❑ 358 | Roberto Alomar | .40 | .18 |
| ❑ 359 | Pat Borders | .10 | .05 |
| ❑ 360 | Joe Carter UER (Reverse negative on back photo) | .20 | .09 |
| ❑ 361 | Kelly Gruber | .10 | .05 |
| ❑ 362 | Tom Henke | .10 | .05 |
| ❑ 363 | Glenallen Hill | .10 | .05 |
| ❑ 364 | Jimmy Key | .20 | .09 |
| ❑ 365 | Manny Lee | .10 | .05 |
| ❑ 366 | Rance Mulliniks | .10 | .05 |
| ❑ 367 | John Olerud UER (Throwing left on card; back has throws right; he does throw lefty) | .20 | .09 |
| ❑ 368 | Dave Stieb | .10 | .05 |
| ❑ 369 | Duane Ward | .10 | .05 |
| ❑ 370 | David Wells | .20 | .09 |
| ❑ 371 | Mark Whiten | .10 | .05 |
| ❑ 372 | Mookie Wilson | .20 | .09 |
| ❑ 373 | Willie Banks MLP | .10 | .05 |
| ❑ 374 | Steve Carter MLP | .10 | .05 |
| ❑ 375 | Scott Chiamparino MLP | .10 | .05 |
| ❑ 376 | Steve Chitren MLP | .10 | .05 |
| ❑ 377 | Darrin Fletcher MLP | .10 | .05 |
| ❑ 378 | Rich Garces MLP RC | .10 | .05 |
| ❑ 379 | Reggie Jefferson MLP | .20 | .09 |
| ❑ 380 | Eric Karros MLP RC | .75 | .35 |
| ❑ 381 | Pat Kelly MLP RC | .10 | .05 |
| ❑ 382 | Chuck Knoblauch MLP | .20 | .09 |
| ❑ 383 | Denny Neagle MLP RC | .50 | .23 |
| ❑ 384 | Dan Opperman MLP | .10 | .05 |
| ❑ 385 | John Ramos MLP | .10 | .05 |
| ❑ 386 | Henry Rodriguez MLP RC | .40 | .18 |
| ❑ 387 | Mo Vaughn MLP | .50 | .23 |
| ❑ 388 | Gerald Williams MLP RC | .40 | .18 |
| ❑ 389 | Mike York MLP | .10 | .05 |
| ❑ 390 | Eddie Zosky MLP | .10 | .05 |
| ❑ 391 | Barry Bonds EP | .40 | .18 |
| ❑ 392 | Cecil Fielder EP | .10 | .05 |
| ❑ 393 | Rickey Henderson EP | .20 | .09 |
| ❑ 394 | Dave Justice EP | .20 | .09 |
| ❑ 395 | Nolan Ryan EP | 1.00 | .45 |
| ❑ 396 | Bobby Thigpen EP | .10 | .05 |
| ❑ 397 | Gregg Jefferies CL | .10 | .05 |
| ❑ 398 | Von Hayes CL | .10 | .05 |
| ❑ 399 | Terry Kennedy CL | .10 | .05 |
| ❑ 400 | Nolan Ryan CL | .40 | .18 |

## 1991 Ultra Update

| | | MINT | NRMT |
|---|---|---|---|
| COMP.FACT.SET (120) | | 50.00 | 22.00 |
| ❑ 1 | Dwight Evans | .50 | .23 |
| ❑ 2 | Chito Martinez | .25 | .11 |
| ❑ 3 | Bob Melvin | .25 | .11 |
| ❑ 4 | Mike Mussina RC | 6.00 | 2.70 |
| ❑ 5 | Jack Clark | .50 | .23 |
| ❑ 6 | Dana Kiecker | .25 | .11 |
| ❑ 7 | Steve Lyons | .25 | .11 |
| ❑ 8 | Gary Gaetti | .50 | .23 |
| ❑ 9 | Dave Gallagher | .25 | .11 |
| ❑ 10 | Dave Parker | .50 | .23 |
| ❑ 11 | Luis Polonia | .25 | .11 |
| ❑ 12 | Luis Sojo | .25 | .11 |
| ❑ 13 | Wilson Alvarez | .25 | .11 |
| ❑ 14 | Alex Fernandez | .50 | .23 |
| ❑ 15 | Craig Grebeck | .25 | .11 |
| ❑ 16 | Ron Karkovice | .25 | .11 |
| ❑ 17 | Warren Newson | .25 | .11 |
| ❑ 18 | Scott Radinsky | .25 | .11 |
| ❑ 19 | Glenallen Hill | .25 | .11 |
| ❑ 20 | Charles Nagy | .25 | .11 |
| ❑ 21 | Mark Whiten | .25 | .11 |
| ❑ 22 | Milt Cuyler | .25 | .11 |
| ❑ 23 | Paul Gibson | .25 | .11 |
| ❑ 24 | Mickey Tettleton | .25 | .11 |
| ❑ 25 | Todd Benzinger | .25 | .11 |
| ❑ 26 | Storm Davis | .25 | .11 |
| ❑ 27 | Kirk Gibson | .50 | .23 |
| ❑ 28 | Bill Pecota | .25 | .11 |
| ❑ 29 | Gary Thurman | .25 | .11 |
| ❑ 30 | Darryl Hamilton | .25 | .11 |
| ❑ 31 | Jaime Navarro | .25 | .11 |
| ❑ 32 | Willie Randolph | .50 | .23 |
| ❑ 33 | Bill Wegman | .25 | .11 |
| ❑ 34 | Randy Bush | .25 | .11 |
| ❑ 35 | Chili Davis | .50 | .23 |
| ❑ 36 | Scott Erickson | .25 | .11 |
| ❑ 37 | Chuck Knoblauch | .50 | .23 |
| ❑ 38 | Scott Leius | .25 | .11 |
| ❑ 39 | Jack Morris | .50 | .23 |
| ❑ 40 | John Habyan | .25 | .11 |
| ❑ 41 | Pat Kelly | .25 | .11 |
| ❑ 42 | Matt Nokes | .25 | .11 |
| ❑ 43 | Scott Sanderson | .25 | .11 |
| ❑ 44 | Bernie Williams | 5.00 | 2.20 |
| ❑ 45 | Harold Baines | .50 | .23 |
| ❑ 46 | Brook Jacoby | .25 | .11 |
| ❑ 47 | Earnest Riles | .25 | .11 |
| ❑ 48 | Willie Wilson | .25 | .11 |
| ❑ 49 | Jay Buhner | .50 | .23 |
| ❑ 50 | Rich DeLucia | .25 | .11 |
| ❑ 51 | Mike Jackson | .25 | .11 |
| ❑ 52 | Bill Krueger | .25 | .11 |
| ❑ 53 | Bill Swift | .25 | .11 |
| ❑ 54 | Brian Downing | .25 | .11 |
| ❑ 55 | Juan Gonzalez | 8.00 | 3.60 |
| ❑ 56 | Dean Palmer | 1.50 | .70 |
| ❑ 57 | Kevin Reimer | .25 | .11 |
| ❑ 58 | Ivan Rodriguez RC | 15.00 | 6.75 |
| ❑ 59 | Tom Candiotti | .25 | .11 |
| ❑ 60 | Juan Guzman RC | .50 | .23 |
| ❑ 61 | Bob MacDonald | .25 | .11 |
| ❑ 62 | Greg Myers | .25 | .11 |
| ❑ 63 | Ed Sprague | .25 | .11 |
| ❑ 64 | Devon White | .25 | .11 |
| ❑ 65 | Rafael Belliard | .25 | .11 |
| ❑ 66 | Juan Berenguer | .25 | .11 |
| ❑ 67 | Brian R. Hunter RC | .50 | .23 |
| ❑ 68 | Kent Mercker | .25 | .11 |
| ❑ 69 | Otis Nixon | .25 | .11 |
| ❑ 70 | Danny Jackson | .25 | .11 |
| ❑ 71 | Chuck McElroy | .25 | .11 |
| ❑ 72 | Gary Scott | .25 | .11 |
| ❑ 73 | Heathcliff Slocumb RC | .25 | .11 |
| ❑ 74 | Chico Walker | .25 | .11 |
| ❑ 75 | Rick Wilkins RC | .25 | .11 |
| ❑ 76 | Chris Hammond | .25 | .11 |
| ❑ 77 | Luis Quinones | .25 | .11 |
| ❑ 78 | Herm Winningham | .25 | .11 |
| ❑ 79 | Jeff Bagwell RC | 15.00 | 6.75 |
| ❑ 80 | Jim Corsi | .25 | .11 |
| ❑ 81 | Steve Finley | .50 | .23 |
| ❑ 82 | Luis Gonzalez RC | 2.00 | .90 |
| ❑ 83 | Pete Harnisch | .25 | .11 |
| ❑ 84 | Darryl Kile | .50 | .23 |
| ❑ 85 | Brett Butler | .50 | .23 |
| ❑ 86 | Gary Carter | .75 | .35 |
| ❑ 87 | Tim Crews | .25 | .11 |
| ❑ 88 | Orel Hershiser | .50 | .23 |
| ❑ 89 | Bob Ojeda | .25 | .11 |
| ❑ 90 | Bret Barberie RC** | .25 | .11 |
| ❑ 91 | Barry Jones | .25 | .11 |
| ❑ 92 | Gilberto Reyes | .25 | .11 |
| ❑ 93 | Larry Walker | 1.00 | .45 |
| ❑ 94 | Hubie Brooks | .25 | .11 |
| ❑ 95 | Tim Burke | .25 | .11 |
| ❑ 96 | Rick Cerone | .25 | .11 |
| ❑ 97 | Jeff Innis | .25 | .11 |
| ❑ 98 | Wally Backman | .25 | .11 |
| ❑ 99 | Tommy Greene | .25 | .11 |
| ❑ 100 | Ricky Jordan | .25 | .11 |
| ❑ 101 | Mitch Williams | .25 | .11 |
| ❑ 102 | John Smiley | .25 | .11 |
| ❑ 103 | Randy Tomlin RC | .25 | .11 |
| ❑ 104 | Gary Varsho | .25 | .11 |
| ❑ 105 | Cris Carpenter | .25 | .11 |
| ❑ 106 | Ken Hill | .25 | .11 |
| ❑ 107 | Felix Jose | .25 | .11 |
| ❑ 108 | Omar Olivares RC | .25 | .11 |
| ❑ 109 | Gerald Perry | .25 | .11 |
| ❑ 110 | Jerald Clark | .25 | .11 |
| ❑ 111 | Tony Fernandez | .25 | .11 |
| ❑ 112 | Darrin Jackson | .25 | .11 |
| ❑ 113 | Mike Maddux | .25 | .11 |
| ❑ 114 | Tim Teufel | .25 | .11 |
| ❑ 115 | Bud Black | .25 | .11 |
| ❑ 116 | Kelly Downs | .25 | .11 |
| ❑ 117 | Mike Felder | .25 | .11 |
| ❑ 118 | Willie McGee | .50 | .23 |
| ❑ 119 | Trevor Wilson | .25 | .11 |
| ❑ 120 | Checklist 1-120 | .25 | .11 |

## 1992 Ultra

| | MINT | NRMT |
|---|---|---|
| COMPLETE SET (600) | 30.00 | 13.50 |
| COMPLETE SERIES 1 (300) | 20.00 | 9.00 |
| COMPLETE SERIES 2 (300) | 10.00 | 4.50 |

❑ 1 Glenn Davis .10 .05
❑ 2 Mike Devereaux .10 .05
❑ 3 Dwight Evans .20 .09
❑ 4 Leo Gomez .10 .05
❑ 5 Chris Hoiles .10 .05
❑ 6 Sam Horn .10 .05
❑ 7 Chito Martinez .10 .05
❑ 8 Randy Milligan .10 .05
❑ 9 Mike Mussina .60 .25
❑ 10 Billy Ripken .10 .05
❑ 11 Cal Ripken 1.50 .70
❑ 12 Tom Brunansky .10 .05
❑ 13 Ellis Burks .20 .09
❑ 14 Jack Clark .20 .09
❑ 15 Roger Clemens .75 .35
❑ 16 Mike Greenwell .10 .05
❑ 17 Joe Hesketh .10 .05
❑ 18 Tony Pena .10 .05
❑ 19 Carlos Quintana .10 .05
❑ 20 Jeff Reardon .20 .09
❑ 21 Jody Reed .10 .05
❑ 22 Luis Rivera .10 .05
❑ 23 Mo Vaughn .20 .09
❑ 24 Gary DiSarcina .10 .05
❑ 25 Chuck Finley .20 .09
❑ 26 Gary Gaetti .20 .09
❑ 27 Bryan Harvey .10 .05
❑ 28 Lance Parrish .10 .05
❑ 29 Luis Polonia .10 .05
❑ 30 Dick Schofield .10 .05
❑ 31 Luis Sojo .10 .05
❑ 32 Wilson Alvarez .10 .05
❑ 33 Carlton Fisk .40 .18
❑ 34 Craig Grebeck .10 .05
❑ 35 Ozzie Guillen .10 .05
❑ 36 Greg Hibbard .10 .05
❑ 37 Charlie Hough .20 .09
❑ 38 Lance Johnson .10 .05
❑ 39 Ron Karkovice .10 .05
❑ 40 Jack McDowell .10 .05
❑ 41 Donn Pall .10 .05
❑ 42 Melido Perez .10 .05
❑ 43 Tim Raines .20 .09
❑ 44 Frank Thomas .75 .35
❑ 45 Sandy Alomar Jr. .20 .09
❑ 46 Carlos Baerga .10 .05
❑ 47 Albert Belle .20 .09
❑ 48 Jerry Browne UER .10 .05
(Reversed negative on card back)
❑ 49 Felix Fermin .10 .05
❑ 50 Reggie Jefferson UER .20 .09
(Born 1968; not 1966)
❑ 51 Mark Lewis .10 .05
❑ 52 Carlos Martinez .10 .05
❑ 53 Steve Olin .10 .05
❑ 54 Jim Thome .75 .35
❑ 55 Mark Whiten .10 .05
❑ 56 Dave Bergman .10 .05
❑ 57 Milt Cuyler .10 .05
❑ 58 Rob Deer .10 .05
❑ 59 Cecil Fielder .20 .09
❑ 60 Travis Fryman .20 .09
❑ 61 Scott Livingstone .10 .05
❑ 62 Tony Phillips .10 .05
❑ 63 Mickey Tettleton .10 .05
❑ 64 Alan Trammell .20 .09
❑ 65 Lou Whitaker .20 .09
❑ 66 Kevin Appier .20 .09
❑ 67 Mike Boddicker .10 .05
❑ 68 George Brett .75 .35
❑ 69 Jim Eisenreich .10 .05
❑ 70 Mark Gubicza .10 .05
❑ 71 David Howard .10 .05
❑ 72 Joel Johnson .10 .05
❑ 73 Mike Macfarlane .10 .05
❑ 74 Brent Mayne .10 .05
❑ 75 Brian McRae .10 .05
❑ 76 Jeff Montgomery .20 .09
❑ 77 Danny Tartabull .10 .05
❑ 78 Don August .10 .05
❑ 79 Dante Bichette .20 .09
❑ 80 Ted Higuera .10 .05
❑ 81 Paul Molitor .40 .18
❑ 82 Jaime Navarro .10 .05
❑ 83 Gary Sheffield .40 .18
❑ 84 Bill Spiers .10 .05
❑ 85 B.J. Surhoff .20 .09
❑ 86 Greg Vaughn .20 .09
❑ 87 Robin Yount .40 .18
❑ 88 Rick Aguilera .20 .09
❑ 89 Chili Davis .20 .09
❑ 90 Scott Erickson .10 .05
❑ 91 Brian Harper .10 .05
❑ 92 Kent Hrbek .20 .09
❑ 93 Chuck Knoblauch .20 .09
❑ 94 Scott Leius .10 .05
❑ 95 Shane Mack .10 .05
❑ 96 Mike Pagliarulo .10 .05
❑ 97 Kirby Puckett 1.00 .45
❑ 98 Kevin Tapani .10 .05
❑ 99 Jesse Barfield .10 .05
❑ 100 Alvaro Espinoza .10 .05
❑ 101 Mel Hall .10 .05
❑ 102 Pat Kelly .10 .05
❑ 103 Roberto Kelly .10 .05
❑ 104 Kevin Maas .10 .05
❑ 105 Don Mattingly 1.00 .45
❑ 106 Hensley Meulens .10 .05
❑ 107 Matt Nokes .10 .05
❑ 108 Steve Sax .10 .05
❑ 109 Harold Baines .20 .09
❑ 110 Jose Canseco .50 .23
❑ 111 Ron Darling .10 .05
❑ 112 Mike Gallego .10 .05
❑ 113 Dave Henderson .10 .05
❑ 114 Rickey Henderson .50 .23
❑ 115 Mark McGwire 1.50 .70
❑ 116 Terry Steinbach .10 .05
❑ 117 Dave Stewart .20 .09
❑ 118 Todd Van Poppel .10 .05
❑ 119 Bob Welch .10 .05
❑ 120 Greg Briley .10 .05
❑ 121 Jay Buhner .20 .09
❑ 122 Rick DeLucia .10 .05
❑ 123 Ken Griffey Jr. 1.50 .70
❑ 124 Erik Hanson .10 .05
❑ 125 Randy Johnson .50 .23
❑ 126 Edgar Martinez .20 .09
❑ 127 Tino Martinez .20 .09
❑ 128 Pete O'Brien .10 .05
❑ 129 Harold Reynolds .10 .05
❑ 130 Dave Valle .10 .05
❑ 131 Julio Franco .10 .05
❑ 132 Juan Gonzalez .40 .18
❑ 133 Jeff Huson .20 .09
(Shows Jose Canseco sliding into second)
❑ 134 Mike Jeffcoat .10 .05
❑ 135 Terry Mathews .10 .05
❑ 136 Rafael Palmeiro .40 .18
❑ 137 Dean Palmer .20 .09
❑ 138 Geno Petralli .10 .05
❑ 139 Ivan Rodriguez .75 .35
❑ 140 Jeff Russell .10 .05
❑ 141 Nolan Ryan 2.00 .90
❑ 142 Ruben Sierra .10 .05
❑ 143 Roberto Alomar .40 .18
❑ 144 Pat Borders .10 .05
❑ 145 Joe Carter .20 .09
❑ 146 Kelly Gruber .10 .05
❑ 147 Jimmy Key .20 .09
❑ 148 Manny Lee .10 .05
❑ 149 Rance Mulliniks .10 .05
❑ 150 Greg Myers .10 .05
❑ 151 John Olerud .20 .09
❑ 152 Dave Stieb .10 .05
❑ 153 Todd Stottlemyre .20 .09
❑ 154 Duane Ward .10 .05
❑ 155 Devon White .10 .05
❑ 156 Eddie Zosky .10 .05
❑ 157 Steve Avery .10 .05
❑ 158 Rafael Belliard .10 .05
❑ 159 Jeff Blauser .10 .05
❑ 160 Sid Bream .10 .05
❑ 161 Ron Gant .20 .09
❑ 162 Tom Glavine .20 .09
❑ 163 Brian Hunter .10 .05
❑ 164 Dave Justice .20 .09
❑ 165 Mark Lemke .10 .05
❑ 166 Greg Olson .10 .05
❑ 167 Terry Pendleton .20 .09
❑ 168 Lonnie Smith .10 .05
❑ 169 John Smoltz .20 .09
❑ 170 Mike Stanton .10 .05
❑ 171 Jeff Treadway .10 .05
❑ 172 Paul Assenmacher .10 .05
❑ 173 George Bell .10 .05
❑ 174 Shawon Dunston .10 .05
❑ 175 Mark Grace .40 .18
❑ 176 Danny Jackson .10 .05
❑ 177 Les Lancaster .10 .05
❑ 178 Greg Maddux 1.00 .45
❑ 179 Luis Salazar .10 .05
❑ 180 Rey Sanchez RC .10 .05
❑ 181 Ryne Sandberg .50 .23
❑ 182 Jose Vizcaino .10 .05
❑ 183 Chico Walker .10 .05
❑ 184 Jerome Walton .10 .05
❑ 185 Glenn Braggs .10 .05
❑ 186 Tom Browning .10 .05
❑ 187 Rob Dibble .10 .05
❑ 188 Bill Doran .10 .05
❑ 189 Chris Hammond .10 .05
❑ 190 Billy Hatcher .10 .05
❑ 191 Barry Larkin .20 .09
❑ 192 Hal Morris .10 .05
❑ 193 Joe Oliver .10 .05
❑ 194 Paul O'Neill .20 .09
❑ 195 Jeff Reed .10 .05
❑ 196 Jose Rijo .10 .05
❑ 197 Chris Sabo .10 .05
❑ 198 Jeff Bagwell .75 .35
❑ 199 Craig Biggio .20 .09
❑ 200 Ken Caminiti .20 .09
❑ 201 Andujar Cedeno .10 .05
❑ 202 Steve Finley .20 .09
❑ 203 Luis Gonzalez .20 .09
❑ 204 Pete Harnisch .10 .05
❑ 205 Xavier Hernandez .10 .05
❑ 206 Darryl Kile .20 .09
❑ 207 Al Osuna .10 .05
❑ 208 Curt Schilling .20 .09
❑ 209 Brett Butler .20 .09
❑ 210 Kal Daniels .10 .05
❑ 211 Lenny Harris .10 .05
❑ 212 Stan Javier .10 .05
❑ 213 Ramon Martinez .10 .05
❑ 214 Roger McDowell .10 .05
❑ 215 Jose Offerman .10 .05
❑ 216 Juan Samuel .10 .05
❑ 217 Mike Scioscia .10 .05
❑ 218 Mike Sharperson .10 .05
❑ 219 Darryl Strawberry .20 .09
❑ 220 Delino DeShields .20 .09
❑ 221 Tom Foley .10 .05
❑ 222 Steve Frey .10 .05
❑ 223 Dennis Martinez .20 .09
❑ 224 Spike Owen .10 .05
❑ 225 Gilberto Reyes .10 .05
❑ 226 Tim Wallach .10 .05
❑ 227 Daryl Boston .10 .05
❑ 228 Tim Burke .10 .05
❑ 229 Vince Coleman .10 .05
❑ 230 David Cone .20 .09
❑ 231 Kevin Elster .10 .05
❑ 232 Dwight Gooden .20 .09
❑ 233 Todd Hundley .10 .05
❑ 234 Jeff Innis .10 .05
❑ 235 Howard Johnson .10 .05

- ❑ 236 Dave Magadan .10 .05
- ❑ 237 Mackey Sasser .10 .05
- ❑ 238 Anthony Young .10 .05
- ❑ 239 Wes Chamberlain .10 .05
- ❑ 240 Darren Daulton .20 .09
- ❑ 241 Len Dykstra .20 .09
- ❑ 242 Tommy Greene .10 .05
- ❑ 243 Charlie Hayes .10 .05
- ❑ 244 Dave Hollins .10 .05
- ❑ 245 Ricky Jordan .10 .05
- ❑ 246 John Kruk .20 .09
- ❑ 247 Mickey Morandini .10 .05
- ❑ 248 Terry Mulholland .10 .05
- ❑ 249 Dale Murphy .40 .18
- ❑ 250 Jay Bell .20 .09
- ❑ 251 Barry Bonds .60 .25
- ❑ 252 Steve Buechele .10 .05
- ❑ 253 Doug Drabek .10 .05
- ❑ 254 Mike LaValliere .10 .05
- ❑ 255 Jose Lind .10 .05
- ❑ 256 Lloyd McClendon .10 .05
- ❑ 257 Orlando Merced .10 .05
- ❑ 258 Don Slaught .10 .05
- ❑ 259 John Smiley .10 .05
- ❑ 260 Zane Smith .10 .05
- ❑ 261 Randy Tomlin .10 .05
- ❑ 262 Andy Van Slyke .20 .09
- ❑ 263 Pedro Guerrero .10 .05
- ❑ 264 Felix Jose .10 .05
- ❑ 265 Ray Lankford .40 .18
- ❑ 266 Omar Olivares .10 .05
- ❑ 267 Jose Oquendo .10 .05
- ❑ 268 Tom Pagnozzi .10 .05
- ❑ 269 Bryn Smith .10 .05
- ❑ 270 Lee Smith UER .20 .09
  (1991 record listed as 61-61)
- ❑ 271 Ozzie Smith UER .50 .23
  (Comma before year of birth on card back)
- ❑ 272 Milt Thompson .10 .05
- ❑ 273 Todd Zeile .10 .05
- ❑ 274 Andy Benes .10 .05
- ❑ 275 Jerald Clark .10 .05
- ❑ 276 Tony Fernandez .10 .05
- ❑ 277 Tony Gwynn .75 .35
- ❑ 278 Greg W. Harris .10 .05
- ❑ 279 Thomas Howard .10 .05
- ❑ 280 Bruce Hurst .10 .05
- ❑ 281 Mike Maddux .10 .05
- ❑ 282 Fred McGriff .20 .09
- ❑ 283 Benito Santiago .10 .05
- ❑ 284 Kevin Bass .10 .05
- ❑ 285 Jeff Brantley .10 .05
- ❑ 286 John Burkett .10 .05
- ❑ 287 Will Clark .40 .18
- ❑ 288 Royce Clayton .10 .05
- ❑ 289 Steve Decker .10 .05
- ❑ 290 Kelly Downs .10 .05
- ❑ 291 Mike Felder .10 .05
- ❑ 292 Darren Lewis .10 .05
- ❑ 293 Kirt Manwaring .10 .05
- ❑ 294 Willie McGee .20 .09
- ❑ 295 Robby Thompson .10 .05
- ❑ 296 Matt Williams .20 .09
- ❑ 297 Trevor Wilson .10 .05
- ❑ 298 Checklist 1-100 .10 .05
- ❑ 299 Checklist 101-200 .10 .05
- ❑ 300 Checklist 201-300 .10 .05
- ❑ 301 Brady Anderson .20 .09
- ❑ 302 Todd Frohwirth .10 .05
- ❑ 303 Ben McDonald .10 .05
- ❑ 304 Mark McLemore .10 .05
- ❑ 305 Jose Mesa .10 .05
- ❑ 306 Bob Milacki .10 .05
- ❑ 307 Gregg Olson .10 .05
- ❑ 308 David Segui .10 .05
- ❑ 309 Rick Sutcliffe .20 .09
- ❑ 310 Jeff Tackett .10 .05
- ❑ 311 Wade Boggs .50 .23
- ❑ 312 Scott Cooper .10 .05
- ❑ 313 John Flaherty .10 .05
- ❑ 314 Wayne Housie .10 .05
- ❑ 315 Peter Hoy .10 .05
- ❑ 316 John Marzano .10 .05
- ❑ 317 Tim Naehring .10 .05
- ❑ 318 Phil Plantier .10 .05
- ❑ 319 Frank Viola .10 .05
- ❑ 320 Matt Young .10 .05
- ❑ 321 Jim Abbott .20 .09
- ❑ 322 Hubie Brooks .10 .05
- ❑ 323 Chad Curtis RC .40 .18
- ❑ 324 Alvin Davis .10 .05
- ❑ 325 Junior Felix .10 .05
- ❑ 326 Von Hayes .10 .05
- ❑ 327 Mark Langston .10 .05
- ❑ 328 Scott Lewis .10 .05
- ❑ 329 Don Robinson .10 .05
- ❑ 330 Bobby Rose .10 .05
- ❑ 331 Lee Stevens .20 .09
- ❑ 332 George Bell .10 .05
- ❑ 333 Esteban Beltre .10 .05
- ❑ 334 Joey Cora .10 .05
- ❑ 335 Alex Fernandez .20 .09
- ❑ 336 Roberto Hernandez .10 .05
- ❑ 337 Mike Huff .10 .05
- ❑ 338 Kirk McCaskill .10 .05
- ❑ 339 Dan Pasqua .10 .05
- ❑ 340 Scott Radinsky .10 .05
- ❑ 341 Steve Sax .10 .05
- ❑ 342 Bobby Thigpen .10 .05
- ❑ 343 Robin Ventura .20 .09
- ❑ 344 Jack Armstrong .10 .05
- ❑ 345 Alex Cole .10 .05
- ❑ 346 Dennis Cook .10 .05
- ❑ 347 Glenallen Hill .10 .05
- ❑ 348 Thomas Howard .10 .05
- ❑ 349 Brook Jacoby .10 .05
- ❑ 350 Kenny Lofton .50 .23
- ❑ 351 Charles Nagy .10 .05
- ❑ 352 Rod Nichols .10 .05
- ❑ 353 Junior Ortiz .10 .05
- ❑ 354 Dave Otto .10 .05
- ❑ 355 Tony Perezchica .10 .05
- ❑ 356 Scott Scudder .10 .05
- ❑ 357 Paul Sorrento .10 .05
- ❑ 358 Skeeter Barnes .10 .05
- ❑ 359 Mark Carreon .10 .05
- ❑ 360 John Doherty RC .10 .05
- ❑ 361 Dan Gladden .10 .05
- ❑ 362 Bill Gullickson .10 .05
- ❑ 363 Shawn Hare RC .10 .05
- ❑ 364 Mike Henneman .10 .05
- ❑ 365 Chad Kreuter .10 .05
- ❑ 366 Mark Leiter .10 .05
- ❑ 367 Mike Munoz .10 .05
- ❑ 368 Kevin Ritz .10 .05
- ❑ 369 Mark Davis .10 .05
- ❑ 370 Tom Gordon .10 .05
- ❑ 371 Chris Gwynn .10 .05
- ❑ 372 Gregg Jefferies .10 .05
- ❑ 373 Wally Joyner .20 .09
- ❑ 374 Kevin McReynolds .10 .05
- ❑ 375 Keith Miller .10 .05
- ❑ 376 Rico Rossy .10 .05
- ❑ 377 Curtis Wilkerson .10 .05
- ❑ 378 Ricky Bones .10 .05
- ❑ 379 Chris Bosio .10 .05
- ❑ 380 Cal Eldred .10 .05
- ❑ 381 Scott Fletcher .10 .05
- ❑ 382 Jim Gantner .10 .05
- ❑ 383 Darryl Hamilton .10 .05
- ❑ 384 Doug Henry RC .10 .05
- ❑ 385 Pat Listach RC .10 .05
- ❑ 386 Tim McIntosh .10 .05
- ❑ 387 Edwin Nunez .10 .05
- ❑ 388 Dan Plesac .10 .05
- ❑ 389 Kevin Seitzer .10 .05
- ❑ 390 Franklin Stubbs .10 .05
- ❑ 391 William Suero .10 .05
- ❑ 392 Bill Wegman .10 .05
- ❑ 393 Willie Banks .10 .05
- ❑ 394 Jarvis Brown .10 .05
- ❑ 395 Greg Gagne .10 .05
- ❑ 396 Mark Guthrie .10 .05
- ❑ 397 Bill Krueger .10 .05
- ❑ 398 Pat Mahomes RC .10 .05
- ❑ 399 Pedro Munoz .10 .05
- ❑ 400 John Smiley .10 .05
- ❑ 401 Gary Wayne .10 .05
- ❑ 402 Lenny Webster .10 .05
- ❑ 403 Carl Willis .10 .05
- ❑ 404 Greg Cadaret .10 .05
- ❑ 405 Steve Farr .10 .05
- ❑ 406 Mike Gallego .10 .05
- ❑ 407 Charlie Hayes .10 .05
- ❑ 408 Steve Howe .10 .05
- ❑ 409 Dion James .10 .05
- ❑ 410 Jeff Johnson .10 .05
- ❑ 411 Tim Leary .10 .05
- ❑ 412 Jim Leyritz .10 .05
- ❑ 413 Melido Perez .10 .05
- ❑ 414 Scott Sanderson .10 .05
- ❑ 415 Andy Stankiewicz .10 .05
- ❑ 416 Mike Stanley .10 .05
- ❑ 417 Danny Tartabull .10 .05
- ❑ 418 Lance Blankenship .10 .05
- ❑ 419 Mike Bordick .10 .05
- ❑ 420 Scott Brosius RC .50 .23
- ❑ 421 Dennis Eckersley .20 .09
- ❑ 422 Scott Hemond .10 .05
- ❑ 423 Carney Lansford .20 .09
- ❑ 424 Henry Mercedes .10 .05
- ❑ 425 Mike Moore .10 .05
- ❑ 426 Gene Nelson .10 .05
- ❑ 427 Randy Ready .10 .05
- ❑ 428 Bruce Walton .10 .05
- ❑ 429 Willie Wilson .10 .05
- ❑ 430 Rich Amaral .10 .05
- ❑ 431 Dave Cochrane .10 .05
- ❑ 432 Henry Cotto .10 .05
- ❑ 433 Calvin Jones .10 .05
- ❑ 434 Kevin Mitchell .20 .09
- ❑ 435 Clay Parker .10 .05
- ❑ 436 Omar Vizquel .20 .09
- ❑ 437 Floyd Bannister .10 .05
- ❑ 438 Kevin Brown .20 .09
- ❑ 439 John Cangelosi .10 .05
- ❑ 440 Brian Downing .10 .05
- ❑ 441 Monty Fariss .10 .05
- ❑ 442 Jose Guzman .10 .05
- ❑ 443 Donald Harris .10 .05
- ❑ 444 Kevin Reimer .10 .05
- ❑ 445 Kenny Rogers .10 .05
- ❑ 446 Wayne Rosenthal .10 .05
- ❑ 447 Dickie Thon .10 .05
- ❑ 448 Derek Bell .20 .09
- ❑ 449 Juan Guzman .10 .05
- ❑ 450 Tom Henke .10 .05
- ❑ 451 Candy Maldonado .10 .05
- ❑ 452 Jack Morris .20 .00
- ❑ 453 David Wells .20 .09
- ❑ 454 Dave Winfield .40 .18
- ❑ 455 Juan Berenguer .10 .05
- ❑ 456 Damon Berryhill .10 .05
- ❑ 457 Mike Bielecki .10 .05
- ❑ 458 Marvin Freeman .10 .05
- ❑ 459 Charlie Leibrandt .10 .05
- ❑ 460 Kent Mercker .10 .05
- ❑ 461 Otis Nixon .10 .05
- ❑ 462 Alejandro Pena .10 .05
- ❑ 463 Ben Rivera .10 .05
- ❑ 464 Deion Sanders .40 .18
- ❑ 465 Mark Wohlers .10 .05
- ❑ 466 Shawn Boskie .10 .05
- ❑ 467 Frank Castillo .10 .05
- ❑ 468 Andre Dawson .20 .09
- ❑ 469 Joe Girardi .20 .09
- ❑ 470 Chuck McElroy .10 .05
- ❑ 471 Mike Morgan .10 .05
- ❑ 472 Ken Patterson .10 .05
- ❑ 473 Bob Scanlan .10 .05
- ❑ 474 Gary Scott .10 .05
- ❑ 475 Dave Smith .10 .05
- ❑ 476 Sammy Sosa .75 .35
- ❑ 477 Hector Villanueva .10 .05
- ❑ 478 Scott Bankhead .10 .05
- ❑ 479 Tim Belcher .10 .05
- ❑ 480 Freddie Benavides .10 .05
- ❑ 481 Jacob Brumfield .10 .05
- ❑ 482 Norm Charlton .10 .05
- ❑ 483 Dwayne Henry .10 .05
- ❑ 484 Dave Martinez .10 .05
- ❑ 485 Bip Roberts .10 .05
- ❑ 486 Reggie Sanders .10 .05
- ❑ 487 Greg Swindell .10 .05
- ❑ 488 Ryan Bowen .10 .05
- ❑ 489 Casey Candaele .10 .05

❑ 490 Juan Guerrero UER .10 .05
(Photo on front is Andujar Cedeno)
❑ 491 Pete Incaviglia .10 .05
❑ 492 Jeff Juden .10 .05
❑ 493 Rob Murphy .10 .05
❑ 494 Mark Portugal .10 .05
❑ 495 Rafael Ramirez .10 .05
❑ 496 Scott Servais .10 .05
❑ 497 Ed Taubensee RC .20 .09
❑ 498 Brian Williams RC .10 .05
❑ 499 Todd Benzinger .10 .05
❑ 500 John Candelaria .10 .05
❑ 501 Tom Candiotti .10 .05
❑ 502 Tim Crews .10 .05
❑ 503 Eric Davis .20 .09
❑ 504 Jim Gott .10 .05
❑ 505 Dave Hansen .10 .05
❑ 506 Carlos Hernandez .10 .05
❑ 507 Orel Hershiser .20 .09
❑ 508 Eric Karros .40 .18
❑ 509 Bob Ojeda .10 .05
❑ 510 Steve Wilson .10 .05
❑ 511 Moises Alou .40 .18
❑ 512 Bret Barberie .10 .05
❑ 513 Ivan Calderon .10 .05
❑ 514 Gary Carter .20 .09
❑ 515 Archi Cianfrocco RC .10 .05
❑ 516 Jeff Fassero .10 .05
❑ 517 Darrin Fletcher .10 .05
❑ 518 Marquis Grissom .10 .05
❑ 519 Chris Haney .10 .05
❑ 520 Ken Hill .10 .05
❑ 521 Chris Nabholz .10 .05
❑ 522 Bill Sampen .10 .05
❑ 523 John Vander Wal .10 .05
❑ 524 Dave Wainhouse .10 .05
❑ 525 Larry Walker .20 .09
❑ 526 John Wetteland .20 .09
❑ 527 Bobby Bonilla .20 .09
❑ 528 Sid Fernandez .10 .05
❑ 529 John Franco .20 .09
❑ 530 Dave Gallagher .10 .05
❑ 531 Paul Gibson .10 .05
❑ 532 Eddie Murray .40 .18
❑ 533 Junior Noboa .10 .05
❑ 534 Charlie O'Brien .10 .05
❑ 535 Bill Pecota .10 .05
❑ 536 Willie Randolph .20 .09
❑ 537 Bret Saberhagen .20 .09
❑ 538 Dick Schofield .10 .05
❑ 539 Pete Schourek .10 .05
❑ 540 Ruben Amaro .10 .05
❑ 541 Andy Ashby .20 .09
❑ 542 Kim Batiste .10 .05
❑ 543 Cliff Brantley .10 .05
❑ 544 Mariano Duncan .10 .05
❑ 545 Jeff Grotewold .10 .05
❑ 546 Barry Jones .10 .05
❑ 547 Julio Peguero .10 .05
❑ 548 Curt Schilling .20 .09
❑ 549 Mitch Williams .10 .05
❑ 550 Stan Belinda .10 .05
❑ 551 Scott Bullett RC .10 .05
❑ 552 Cecil Espy .10 .05
❑ 553 Jeff King .10 .05
❑ 554 Roger Mason .10 .05
❑ 555 Paul Miller .10 .05
❑ 556 Denny Neagle .20 .09
❑ 557 Vicente Palacios .10 .05
❑ 558 Bob Patterson .10 .05
❑ 559 Tom Prince .10 .05
❑ 560 Gary Redus .10 .05
❑ 561 Gary Varsho .10 .05
❑ 562 Juan Agosto .10 .05
❑ 563 Cris Carpenter .10 .05
❑ 564 Mark Clark RC .10 .05
❑ 565 Jose DeLeon .10 .05
❑ 566 Rich Gedman .10 .05
❑ 567 Bernard Gilkey .20 .09
❑ 568 Rex Hudler .10 .05
❑ 569 Tim Jones .10 .05
❑ 570 Donovan Osborne .10 .05
❑ 571 Mike Perez .10 .05
❑ 572 Gerald Perry .10 .05
❑ 573 Bob Tewksbury .10 .05
❑ 574 Todd Worrell .10 .05
❑ 575 Dave Eiland .10 .05
❑ 576 Jeremy Hernandez RC .10 .05
❑ 577 Craig Lefferts .10 .05
❑ 578 Jose Melendez .10 .05
❑ 579 Randy Myers .20 .09
❑ 580 Gary Pettis .10 .05
❑ 581 Rich Rodriguez .10 .05
❑ 582 Gary Sheffield .40 .18
❑ 583 Craig Shipley .10 .05
❑ 584 Kurt Stillwell .10 .05
❑ 585 Tim Teufel .10 .05
❑ 586 Rod Beck RC .40 .18
❑ 587 Dave Burba .10 .05
❑ 588 Craig Colbert .10 .05
❑ 589 Bryan Hickerson RC .10 .05
❑ 590 Mike Jackson .10 .05
❑ 591 Mark Leonard .10 .05
❑ 592 Jim McNamara .10 .05
❑ 593 John Patterson .10 .05
❑ 594 Dave Righetti .10 .05
❑ 595 Cory Snyder .10 .05
❑ 596 Bill Swift .10 .05
❑ 597 Ted Wood .10 .05
❑ 598 Checklist 301-400 .10 .05
❑ 599 Checklist 401-500 .10 .05
❑ 600 Checklist 501-600 .10 .05

## 1993 Ultra

| | MINT | NRMT |
|---|---|---|
| COMPLETE SET (650) | 30.00 | 13.50 |
| COMPLETE SERIES 1 (300) | 15.00 | 6.75 |
| COMPLETE SERIES 2 (350) | 15.00 | 6.75 |

❑ 1 Steve Avery .15 .07
❑ 2 Rafael Belliard .15 .07
❑ 3 Damon Berryhill .15 .07
❑ 4 Sid Bream .15 .07
❑ 5 Ron Gant .30 .14
❑ 6 Tom Glavine .30 .14
❑ 7 Ryan Klesko .60 .25
❑ 8 Mark Lemke .15 .07
❑ 9 Javier Lopez .30 .14
❑ 10 Greg Olson .15 .07
❑ 11 Terry Pendleton .30 .14
❑ 12 Deion Sanders .30 .14
❑ 13 Mike Stanton .15 .07
❑ 14 Paul Assenmacher .15 .07
❑ 15 Steve Buechele .15 .07
❑ 16 Frank Castillo .15 .07
❑ 17 Shawon Dunston .15 .07
❑ 18 Mark Grace .60 .25
❑ 19 Derrick May .15 .07
❑ 20 Chuck McElroy .15 .07
❑ 21 Mike Morgan .15 .07
❑ 22 Bob Scanlan .15 .07
❑ 23 Dwight Smith .15 .07
❑ 24 Sammy Sosa 1.25 .55
❑ 25 Rick Wilkins .15 .07
❑ 26 Tim Belcher .15 .07
❑ 27 Jeff Branson .15 .07
❑ 28 Bill Doran .15 .07
❑ 29 Chris Hammond .15 .07
❑ 30 Barry Larkin .60 .25
❑ 31 Hal Morris .15 .07
❑ 32 Joe Oliver .15 .07
❑ 33 Jose Rijo .15 .07
❑ 34 Bip Roberts .15 .07
❑ 35 Chris Sabo .15 .07
❑ 36 Reggie Sanders .15 .07
❑ 37 Craig Biggio .30 .14
❑ 38 Ken Caminiti .30 .14
❑ 39 Steve Finley .30 .14
❑ 40 Luis Gonzalez .30 .14
❑ 41 Juan Guerrero .15 .07
❑ 42 Pete Harnisch .15 .07
❑ 43 Xavier Hernandez .15 .07
❑ 44 Doug Jones .15 .07
❑ 45 Al Osuna .15 .07
❑ 46 Eddie Taubensee .15 .07
❑ 47 Scooter Tucker .15 .07
❑ 48 Brian Williams .15 .07
❑ 49 Pedro Astacio .30 .14
❑ 50 Rafael Bournigal .15 .07
❑ 51 Brett Butler .30 .14
❑ 52 Tom Candiotti .15 .07
❑ 53 Eric Davis .30 .14
❑ 54 Lenny Harris .15 .07
❑ 55 Orel Hershiser .30 .14
❑ 56 Eric Karros .30 .14
❑ 57 Pedro Martinez 1.50 .70
❑ 58 Roger McDowell .15 .07
❑ 59 Jose Offerman .15 .07
❑ 60 Mike Piazza 3.00 1.35
❑ 61 Moises Alou .30 .14
❑ 62 Kent Bottenfield .15 .07
❑ 63 Archi Cianfrocco .15 .07
❑ 64 Greg Colbrunn .15 .07
❑ 65 Wil Cordero .15 .07
❑ 66 Delino DeShields .30 .14
❑ 67 Darrin Fletcher .15 .07
❑ 68 Ken Hill .15 .07
❑ 69 Chris Nabholz .15 .07
❑ 70 Mel Rojas .15 .07
❑ 71 Larry Walker .30 .14
❑ 72 Sid Fernandez .15 .07
❑ 73 John Franco .30 .14
❑ 74 Dave Gallagher .15 .07
❑ 75 Todd Hundley .15 .07
❑ 76 Howard Johnson .15 .07
❑ 77 Jeff Kent .60 .25
❑ 78 Eddie Murray .60 .25
❑ 79 Bret Saberhagen .30 .14
❑ 80 Chico Walker .15 .07
❑ 81 Anthony Young .15 .07
❑ 82 Kyle Abbott .15 .07
❑ 83 Ruben Amaro .15 .07
❑ 84 Juan Bell .15 .07
❑ 85 Wes Chamberlain .15 .07
❑ 86 Darren Daulton .30 .14
❑ 87 Mariano Duncan .15 .07
❑ 88 Dave Hollins .15 .07
❑ 89 Ricky Jordan .15 .07
❑ 90 John Kruk .30 .14
❑ 91 Mickey Morandini .15 .07
❑ 92 Terry Mulholland .15 .07
❑ 93 Ben Rivera .15 .07
❑ 94 Mike Williams .15 .07
❑ 95 Stan Belinda .15 .07
❑ 96 Jay Bell .30 .14
❑ 97 Jeff King .15 .07
❑ 98 Mike LaValliere .15 .07
❑ 99 Lloyd McClendon .15 .07
❑ 100 Orlando Merced .15 .07
❑ 101 Zane Smith .15 .07
❑ 102 Randy Tomlin .15 .07
❑ 103 Andy Van Slyke .30 .14
❑ 104 Tim Wakefield .15 .07
❑ 105 John Wehner .15 .07
❑ 106 Bernard Gilkey .15 .07
❑ 107 Brian Jordan .30 .14
❑ 108 Ray Lankford .30 .14
❑ 109 Donovan Osborne .15 .07
❑ 110 Tom Pagnozzi .15 .07
❑ 111 Mike Perez .15 .07
❑ 112 Lee Smith .30 .14
❑ 113 Ozzie Smith .75 .35
❑ 114 Bob Tewksbury .15 .07
❑ 115 Todd Zeile .15 .07
❑ 116 Andy Benes .15 .07
❑ 117 Greg W. Harris .15 .07
❑ 118 Darrin Jackson .15 .07
❑ 119 Fred McGriff .30 .14
❑ 120 Rich Rodriguez .15 .07

❑ 121 Frank Seminara .15 .07
❑ 122 Gary Sheffield .60 .25
❑ 123 Craig Shipley .15 .07
❑ 124 Kurt Stillwell .15 .07
❑ 125 Dan Walters .15 .07
❑ 126 Rod Beck .15 .07
❑ 127 Mike Benjamin .15 .07
❑ 128 Jeff Brantley .15 .07
❑ 129 John Burkett .15 .07
❑ 130 Will Clark .60 .25
❑ 131 Royce Clayton .15 .07
❑ 132 Steve Hosey .15 .07
❑ 133 Mike Jackson .15 .07
❑ 134 Darren Lewis .15 .07
❑ 135 Kirt Manwaring .15 .07
❑ 136 Bill Swift .15 .07
❑ 137 Robby Thompson .15 .07
❑ 138 Brady Anderson .30 .14
❑ 139 Glenn Davis .15 .07
❑ 140 Leo Gomez .15 .07
❑ 141 Chito Martinez .15 .07
❑ 142 Ben McDonald .15 .07
❑ 143 Alan Mills .15 .07
❑ 144 Mike Mussina .60 .25
❑ 145 Gregg Olson .15 .07
❑ 146 David Segui .15 .07
❑ 147 Jeff Tackett .15 .07
❑ 148 Jack Clark .15 .07
❑ 149 Scott Cooper .15 .07
❑ 150 Danny Darwin .15 .07
❑ 151 John Dopson .15 .07
❑ 152 Mike Greenwell .15 .07
❑ 153 Tim Naehring .15 .07
❑ 154 Tony Pena .15 .07
❑ 155 Paul Quantrill .15 .07
❑ 156 Mo Vaughn .30 .14
❑ 157 Frank Viola .15 .07
❑ 158 Bob Zupcic .15 .07
❑ 159 Chad Curtis .15 .07
❑ 160 Gary DiSarcina .15 .07
❑ 161 Damion Easley .15 .07
❑ 162 Chuck Finley .30 .14
❑ 163 Tim Fortugno .15 .07
❑ 164 Rene Gonzales .15 .07
❑ 165 Joe Grahe .15 .07
❑ 166 Mark Langston .15 .07
❑ 167 John Orton .15 .07
❑ 168 Luis Polonia .15 .07
❑ 169 Julio Valera .15 .07
❑ 170 Wilson Alvarez .15 .07
❑ 171 George Bell .15 .07
❑ 172 Joey Cora .15 .07
❑ 173 Alex Fernandez .30 .14
❑ 174 Lance Johnson .15 .07
❑ 175 Ron Karkovice .15 .07
❑ 176 Jack McDowell .15 .07
❑ 177 Scott Radinsky .15 .07
❑ 178 Tim Raines .30 .14
❑ 179 Steve Sax .15 .07
❑ 180 Bobby Thigpen .15 .07
❑ 181 Frank Thomas 1.25 .55
❑ 182 Sandy Alomar Jr. .30 .14
❑ 183 Carlos Baerga .15 .07
❑ 184 Felix Fermin .15 .07
❑ 185 Thomas Howard .15 .07
❑ 186 Mark Lewis .15 .07
❑ 187 Derek Lilliquist .15 .07
❑ 188 Carlos Martinez .15 .07
❑ 189 Charles Nagy .15 .07
❑ 190 Scott Scudder .15 .07
❑ 191 Paul Sorrento .15 .07
❑ 192 Jim Thome .30 .14
❑ 193 Mark Whiten .15 .07
❑ 194 Milt Cuyler UER .15 .07
(Reversed negative on card front)
❑ 195 Rob Deer .15 .07
❑ 196 John Doherty .15 .07
❑ 197 Travis Fryman .30 .14
❑ 198 Dan Gladden .15 .07
❑ 199 Mike Henneman .15 .07
❑ 200 John Kiely .15 .07
❑ 201 Chad Kreuter .15 .07
❑ 202 Scott Livingstone .15 .07
❑ 203 Tony Phillips .15 .07
❑ 204 Alan Trammell .30 .14
❑ 205 Mike Boddicker .15 .07
❑ 206 George Brett 1.25 .55
❑ 207 Tom Gordon .15 .07
❑ 208 Mark Gubicza .15 .07
❑ 209 Gregg Jefferies .15 .07
❑ 210 Wally Joyner .30 .14
❑ 211 Kevin Koslofski .15 .07
❑ 212 Brent Mayne .15 .07
❑ 213 Brian McRae .15 .07
❑ 214 Kevin McReynolds .15 .07
❑ 215 Rusty Meacham .15 .07
❑ 216 Steve Shifflett .15 .07
❑ 217 James Austin .15 .07
❑ 218 Cal Eldred .15 .07
❑ 219 Darryl Hamilton .15 .07
❑ 220 Doug Henry .15 .07
❑ 221 John Jaha .15 .07
❑ 222 Dave Nilsson .30 .14
❑ 223 Jesse Orosco .15 .07
❑ 224 B.J. Surhoff .30 .14
❑ 225 Greg Vaughn .30 .14
❑ 226 Bill Wegman .15 .07
❑ 227 Robin Yount UER .30 .14
(Born in Illinois, not in Virginia)
❑ 228 Rick Aguilera .15 .07
❑ 229 J.T. Bruett .15 .07
❑ 230 Scott Erickson .15 .07
❑ 231 Kent Hrbek .30 .14
❑ 232 Terry Jorgensen .15 .07
❑ 233 Scott Leius .15 .07
❑ 234 Pat Mahomes .15 .07
❑ 235 Pedro Munoz .15 .07
❑ 236 Kirby Puckett 1.50 .70
❑ 237 Kevin Tapani .15 .07
❑ 238 Lenny Webster .15 .07
❑ 239 Carl Willis .15 .07
❑ 240 Mike Gallego .15 .07
❑ 241 John Habyan .15 .07
❑ 242 Pat Kelly .15 .07
❑ 243 Kevin Maas .15 .07
❑ 244 Don Mattingly 1.50 .70
❑ 245 Hensley Meulens .15 .07
❑ 246 Sam Militello .15 .07
❑ 247 Matt Nokes .15 .07
❑ 248 Melido Perez .15 .07
❑ 249 Andy Stankiewicz .15 .07
❑ 250 Randy Velarde .15 .07
❑ 251 Bob Wickman .15 .07
❑ 252 Bernie Williams .60 .25
❑ 253 Lance Blankenship .15 .07
❑ 254 Mike Bordick .15 .07
❑ 255 Jerry Browne .15 .07
❑ 256 Ron Darling .15 .07
❑ 257 Dennis Eckersley .30 .14
❑ 258 Rickey Henderson .75 .35
❑ 259 Vince Horsman .15 .07
❑ 260 Troy Neel .15 .07
❑ 261 Jeff Parrett .15 .07
❑ 262 Terry Steinbach .15 .07
❑ 263 Bob Welch .15 .07
❑ 264 Bobby Witt .15 .07
❑ 265 Rich Amaral .15 .07
❑ 266 Bret Boone .30 .14
❑ 267 Jay Buhner .30 .14
❑ 268 Dave Fleming .15 .07
❑ 269 Randy Johnson .75 .35
❑ 270 Edgar Martinez .30 .14
❑ 271 Mike Schooler .15 .07
❑ 272 Russ Swan .15 .07
❑ 273 Dave Valle .15 .07
❑ 274 Omar Vizquel .30 .14
❑ 275 Kerry Woodson .15 .07
❑ 276 Kevin Brown .30 .14
❑ 277 Julio Franco .15 .07
❑ 278 Jeff Frye .15 .07
❑ 279 Juan Gonzalez .60 .25
❑ 280 Jeff Huson .15 .07
❑ 281 Rafael Palmeiro .60 .25
❑ 282 Dean Palmer .30 .14
❑ 283 Roger Pavlik .15 .07
❑ 284 Ivan Rodriguez .75 .35
❑ 285 Kenny Rogers .15 .07
❑ 286 Derek Bell .15 .07
❑ 287 Pat Borders .15 .07
❑ 288 Joe Carter .30 .14
❑ 289 Bob MacDonald .15 .07
❑ 290 Jack Morris .30 .14
❑ 291 John Olerud .30 .14
❑ 292 Ed Sprague .15 .07
❑ 293 Todd Stottlemyre .15 .07
❑ 294 Mike Timlin .15 .07
❑ 295 Duane Ward .15 .07
❑ 296 David Wells .30 .14
❑ 297 Devon White .15 .07
❑ 298 Ray Lankford CL .30 .14
❑ 299 Bobby Witt CL .15 .07
❑ 300 Mike Piazza CL .60 .25
❑ 301 Steve Bedrosian .15 .07
❑ 302 Jeff Blauser .15 .07
❑ 303 Francisco Cabrera .15 .07
❑ 304 Marvin Freeman .15 .07
❑ 305 Brian Hunter .15 .07
❑ 306 David Justice .30 .14
❑ 307 Greg Maddux 1.50 .70
❑ 308 Greg McMichael RC .15 .07
❑ 309 Kent Mercker .15 .07
❑ 310 Otis Nixon .15 .07
❑ 311 Pete Smith .15 .07
❑ 312 John Smoltz .30 .14
❑ 313 Jose Guzman .15 .07
❑ 314 Mike Harkey .15 .07
❑ 315 Greg Hibbard .15 .07
❑ 316 Candy Maldonado .15 .07
❑ 317 Randy Myers .30 .14
❑ 318 Dan Plesac .15 .07
❑ 319 Rey Sanchez .15 .07
❑ 320 Ryne Sandberg .75 .35
❑ 321 Tommy Shields .15 .07
❑ 322 Jose Vizcaino .15 .07
❑ 323 Matt Walbeck RC .15 .07
❑ 324 Willie Wilson .15 .07
❑ 325 Tom Browning .15 .07
❑ 326 Tim Costo .15 .07
❑ 327 Rob Dibble .15 .07
❑ 328 Steve Foster .15 .07
❑ 329 Roberto Kelly .15 .07
❑ 330 Randy Milligan .15 .07
❑ 331 Kevin Mitchell .30 .14
❑ 332 Tim Pugh RC .15 .07
❑ 333 Jeff Reardon .30 .14
❑ 334 John Roper .15 .07
❑ 335 Juan Samuel .15 .07
❑ 336 John Smiley .15 .07
❑ 337 Dan Wilson .30 .14
❑ 338 Scott Aldred .15 .07
❑ 339 Andy Ashby .30 .14
❑ 340 Freddie Benavides .15 .07
❑ 341 Dante Bichette .30 .14
❑ 342 Willie Blair .15 .07
❑ 343 Daryl Boston .15 .07
❑ 344 Vinny Castilla .75 .35
❑ 345 Jerald Clark .15 .07
❑ 346 Alex Cole .15 .07
❑ 347 Andres Galarraga .30 .14
❑ 348 Joe Girardi .30 .14
❑ 349 Ryan Hawblitzel .15 .07
❑ 350 Charlie Hayes .15 .07
❑ 351 Butch Henry .15 .07
❑ 352 Darren Holmes .15 .07
❑ 353 Dale Murphy .30 .14
❑ 354 David Nied .15 .07
❑ 355 Jeff Parrett .15 .07
❑ 356 Steve Reed RC .15 .07
❑ 357 Bruce Ruffin .15 .07
❑ 358 Danny Sheaffer RC .15 .07
❑ 359 Bryn Smith .15 .07
❑ 360 Jim Tatum RC .15 .07
❑ 361 Eric Young .15 .07
❑ 362 Gerald Young .15 .07
❑ 363 Luis Aquino .15 .07
❑ 364 Alex Arias .15 .07
❑ 365 Jack Armstrong .15 .07
❑ 366 Bret Barberie .15 .07
❑ 367 Ryan Bowen .15 .07
❑ 368 Greg Briley .15 .07
❑ 369 Cris Carpenter .15 .07
❑ 370 Chuck Carr .15 .07
❑ 371 Jeff Conine .15 .07
❑ 372 Steve Decker .15 .07
❑ 373 Orestes Destrade .15 .07
❑ 374 Monty Fariss .15 .07

❑ 375 Junior Felix .15 .07
❑ 376 Chris Hammond .15 .07
❑ 377 Bryan Harvey .15 .07
❑ 378 Trevor Hoffman .60 .25
❑ 379 Charlie Hough .30 .14
❑ 380 Joe Klink .15 .07
❑ 381 Richie Lewis RC .15 .07
❑ 382 Dave Magadan .15 .07
❑ 383 Bob McClure .15 .07
❑ 384 Scott Pose RC .15 .07
❑ 385 Rich Renteria .15 .07
❑ 386 Benito Santiago .15 .07
❑ 387 Walt Weiss .15 .07
❑ 388 Nigel Wilson .15 .07
❑ 389 Eric Anthony .15 .07
❑ 390 Jeff Bagwell .75 .35
❑ 391 Andujar Cedeno .15 .07
❑ 392 Doug Drabek .15 .07
❑ 393 Darryl Kile .30 .14
❑ 394 Mark Portugal .15 .07
❑ 395 Karl Rhodes .15 .07
❑ 396 Scott Servais .15 .07
❑ 397 Greg Swindell .15 .07
❑ 398 Tom Goodwin .15 .07
❑ 399 Kevin Gross .15 .07
❑ 400 Carlos Hernandez .15 .07
❑ 401 Ramon Martinez .15 .07
❑ 402 Raul Mondesi .30 .14
❑ 403 Jody Reed .15 .07
❑ 404 Mike Sharperson .15 .07
❑ 405 Cory Snyder .15 .07
❑ 406 Darryl Strawberry .30 .14
❑ 407 Rick Trlicek .15 .07
❑ 408 Tim Wallach .15 .07
❑ 409 Todd Worrell .15 .07
❑ 410 Tavo Alvarez .15 .07
❑ 411 Sean Berry .15 .07
❑ 412 Frank Bolick .15 .07
❑ 413 Cliff Floyd .30 .14
❑ 414 Mike Gardiner .15 .07
❑ 415 Marquis Grissom .15 .07
❑ 416 Tim Laker RC .15 .07
❑ 417 Mike Lansing RC .30 .14
❑ 418 Dennis Martinez .30 .14
❑ 419 John Vander Wal .15 .07
❑ 420 John Wetteland .30 .14
❑ 421 Rondell White .30 .14
❑ 422 Bobby Bonilla .30 .14
❑ 423 Jeromy Burnitz .30 .14
❑ 424 Vince Coleman .15 .07
❑ 425 Mike Draper .15 .07
❑ 426 Tony Fernandez .15 .07
❑ 427 Dwight Gooden .30 .14
❑ 428 Jeff Innis .15 .07
❑ 429 Bobby Jones .30 .14
❑ 430 Mike Maddux .15 .07
❑ 431 Charlie O'Brien .15 .07
❑ 432 Joe Orsulak .15 .07
❑ 433 Pete Schourek .15 .07
❑ 434 Frank Tanana .15 .07
❑ 435 Ryan Thompson .15 .07
❑ 436 Kim Batiste .15 .07
❑ 437 Mark Davis .15 .07
❑ 438 Jose DeLeon .15 .07
❑ 439 Len Dykstra .30 .14
❑ 440 Jim Eisenreich .15 .07
❑ 441 Tommy Greene .15 .07
❑ 442 Pete Incaviglia .15 .07
❑ 443 Danny Jackson .15 .07
❑ 444 Todd Pratt RC .40 .18
❑ 445 Curt Schilling .30 .14
❑ 446 Milt Thompson .15 .07
❑ 447 David West .15 .07
❑ 448 Mitch Williams .15 .07
❑ 449 Steve Cooke .15 .07
❑ 450 Carlos Garcia .15 .07
❑ 451 Al Martin .15 .07
❑ 452 Blas Minor .15 .07
❑ 453 Dennis Moeller .15 .07
❑ 454 Denny Neagle .30 .14
❑ 455 Don Slaught .15 .07
❑ 456 Lonnie Smith .15 .07
❑ 457 Paul Wagner .15 .07
❑ 458 Bob Walk .15 .07
❑ 459 Kevin Young .30 .14
❑ 460 Rene Arocha RC .15 .07
❑ 461 Brian Barber .15 .07
❑ 462 Rheal Cormier .15 .07
❑ 463 Gregg Jefferies .15 .07
❑ 464 Joe Magrane .15 .07
❑ 465 Omar Olivares .15 .07
❑ 466 Geronimo Pena .15 .07
❑ 467 Allen Watson .15 .07
❑ 468 Mark Whiten .15 .07
❑ 469 Derek Bell .15 .07
❑ 470 Phil Clark .15 .07
❑ 471 Pat Gomez RC .15 .07
❑ 472 Tony Gwynn 1.25 .55
❑ 473 Jeremy Hernandez .15 .07
❑ 474 Bruce Hurst .15 .07
❑ 475 Phil Plantier .15 .07
❑ 476 Scott Sanders RC .15 .07
❑ 477 Tim Scott .15 .07
❑ 478 Darrell Sherman RC .15 .07
❑ 479 Guillermo Velasquez .15 .07
❑ 480 Tim Worrell RC .15 .07
❑ 481 Todd Benzinger .15 .07
❑ 482 Bud Black .15 .07
❑ 483 Barry Bonds 1.00 .45
❑ 484 Dave Burba .15 .07
❑ 485 Bryan Hickerson .15 .07
❑ 486 Dave Martinez .15 .07
❑ 487 Willie McGee .30 .14
❑ 488 Jeff Reed .15 .07
❑ 489 Kevin Rogers .15 .07
❑ 490 Matt Williams .30 .14
❑ 491 Trevor Wilson .15 .07
❑ 492 Harold Baines .30 .14
❑ 493 Mike Devereaux .15 .07
❑ 494 Todd Frohwirth .15 .07
❑ 495 Chris Hoiles .15 .07
❑ 496 Luis Mercedes .15 .07
❑ 497 Sherman Obando RC .15 .07
❑ 498 Brad Pennington .15 .07
❑ 499 Harold Reynolds .15 .07
❑ 500 Arthur Rhodes .15 .07
❑ 501 Cal Ripken 2.50 1.10
❑ 502 Rick Sutcliffe .30 .14
❑ 503 Fernando Valenzuela .30 .14
❑ 504 Mark Williamson .15 .07
❑ 505 Scott Bankhead .15 .07
❑ 506 Greg Blosser .15 .07
❑ 507 Ivan Calderon .15 .07
❑ 508 Roger Clemens 1.25 .55
❑ 509 Andre Dawson .30 .14
❑ 510 Scott Fletcher .15 .07
❑ 511 Greg A. Harris .15 .07
❑ 512 Billy Hatcher .15 .07
❑ 513 Bob Melvin .15 .07
❑ 514 Carlos Quintana .15 .07
❑ 515 Luis Rivera .15 .07
❑ 516 Jeff Russell .15 .07
❑ 517 Ken Ryan RC .15 .07
❑ 518 Chili Davis .30 .14
❑ 519 Jim Edmonds RC 5.00 2.20
❑ 520 Gary Gaetti .30 .14
❑ 521 Torey Lovullo .15 .07
❑ 522 Troy Percival .15 .07
❑ 523 Tim Salmon .30 .14
❑ 524 Scott Sanderson .15 .07
❑ 525 J.T. Snow RC .75 .35
❑ 526 Jerome Walton .15 .07
❑ 527 Jason Bere .15 .07
❑ 528 Rod Bolton .15 .07
❑ 529 Ellis Burks .30 .14
❑ 530 Carlton Fisk .60 .25
❑ 531 Craig Grebeck .15 .07
❑ 532 Ozzie Guillen .15 .07
❑ 533 Roberto Hernandez .15 .07
❑ 534 Bo Jackson .30 .14
❑ 535 Kirk McCaskill .15 .07
❑ 536 Dave Stieb .15 .07
❑ 537 Robin Ventura .30 .14
❑ 538 Albert Belle .30 .14
❑ 539 Mike Bielecki .15 .07
❑ 540 Glenallen Hill .15 .07
❑ 541 Reggie Jefferson .30 .14
❑ 542 Kenny Lofton .30 .14
❑ 543 Jeff Mutis .15 .07
❑ 544 Junior Ortiz .15 .07
❑ 545 Manny Ramirez 1.50 .70
❑ 546 Jeff Treadway .15 .07
❑ 547 Kevin Wickander .15 .07
❑ 548 Cecil Fielder .30 .14
❑ 549 Kirk Gibson .30 .14
❑ 550 Greg Gohr .15 .07
❑ 551 David Haas .15 .07
❑ 552 Bill Krueger .15 .07
❑ 553 Mike Moore .15 .07
❑ 554 Mickey Tettleton .15 .07
❑ 555 Lou Whitaker .30 .14
❑ 556 Kevin Appier .30 .14
❑ 557 Billy Brewer .15 .07
❑ 558 David Cone .30 .14
❑ 559 Greg Gagne .15 .07
❑ 560 Mark Gardner .15 .07
❑ 561 Phil Hiatt .15 .07
❑ 562 Felix Jose .15 .07
❑ 563 Jose Lind .15 .07
❑ 564 Mike Macfarlane .15 .07
❑ 565 Keith Miller .15 .07
❑ 566 Jeff Montgomery .30 .14
❑ 567 Hipolito Pichardo .15 .07
❑ 568 Ricky Bones .15 .07
❑ 569 Tom Brunansky .15 .07
❑ 570 Joe Kmak .15 .07
❑ 571 Pat Listach .15 .07
❑ 572 Graeme Lloyd RC .15 .07
❑ 573 Carlos Maldonado .15 .07
❑ 574 Josias Manzanillo .15 .07
❑ 575 Matt Mieske .15 .07
❑ 576 Kevin Reimer .15 .07
❑ 577 Bill Spiers .15 .07
❑ 578 Dickie Thon .15 .07
❑ 579 Willie Banks .15 .07
❑ 580 Jim Deshaies .15 .07
❑ 581 Mark Guthrie .15 .07
❑ 582 Brian Harper .15 .07
❑ 583 Chuck Knoblauch .30 .14
❑ 584 Gene Larkin .15 .07
❑ 585 Shane Mack .15 .07
❑ 586 David McCarty .15 .07
❑ 587 Mike Pagliarulo .15 .07
❑ 588 Mike Trombley .15 .07
❑ 589 Dave Winfield .60 .25
❑ 590 Jim Abbott .30 .14
❑ 591 Wade Boggs .75 .35
❑ 592 Russ Davis RC .30 .14
❑ 593 Steve Farr .15 .07
❑ 594 Steve Howe .15 .07
❑ 595 Mike Humphreys .15 .07
❑ 596 Jimmy Key .30 .14
❑ 597 Jim Leyritz .15 .07
❑ 598 Bobby Munoz .15 .07
❑ 599 Paul O'Neill .30 .14
❑ 600 Spike Owen .15 .07
❑ 601 Mike Stanley .15 .07
❑ 602 Danny Tartabull .15 .07
❑ 603 Scott Brosius .30 .14
❑ 604 Storm Davis .15 .07
❑ 605 Eric Fox .15 .07
❑ 606 Rich Gossage .30 .14
❑ 607 Scott Hemond .15 .07
❑ 608 Dave Henderson .15 .07
❑ 609 Mark McGwire 2.50 1.10
❑ 610 Mike Mohler RC .15 .07
❑ 611 Edwin Nunez .15 .07
❑ 612 Kevin Seitzer .15 .07
❑ 613 Ruben Sierra .15 .07
❑ 614 Chris Bosio .15 .07
❑ 615 Norm Charlton .15 .07
❑ 616 Jim Converse RC .15 .07
❑ 617 John Cummings RC .15 .07
❑ 618 Mike Felder .15 .07
❑ 619 Ken Griffey Jr. 2.50 1.10
❑ 620 Mike Hampton .60 .25
❑ 621 Erik Hanson .15 .07
❑ 622 Bill Haselman .15 .07
❑ 623 Tino Martinez .30 .14
❑ 624 Lee Tinsley .15 .07
❑ 625 Fernando Vina RC .50 .23
❑ 626 David Wainhouse .15 .07
❑ 627 Jose Canseco .75 .35
❑ 628 Benji Gil .15 .07
❑ 629 Tom Henke .15 .07
❑ 630 David Hulse RC .15 .07
❑ 631 Manuel Lee .15 .07
❑ 632 Craig Lefferts .15 .07

| | Card | MINT | NRMT |
|---|---|---|---|
| ❑ | 633 Robb Nen | .30 | .14 |
| ❑ | 634 Gary Redus | .15 | .07 |
| ❑ | 635 Bill Ripken | .15 | .07 |
| ❑ | 636 Nolan Ryan | 3.00 | 1.35 |
| ❑ | 637 Dan Smith | .15 | .07 |
| ❑ | 638 Matt Whiteside RC | .15 | .07 |
| ❑ | 639 Roberto Alomar | .60 | .25 |
| ❑ | 640 Juan Guzman | .15 | .07 |
| ❑ | 641 Pat Hentgen | .15 | .07 |
| ❑ | 642 Darrin Jackson | .15 | .07 |
| ❑ | 643 Randy Knorr | .15 | .07 |
| ❑ | 644 Domingo Martinez RC | .15 | .07 |
| ❑ | 645 Paul Molitor | .60 | .25 |
| ❑ | 646 Dick Schofield | .15 | .07 |
| ❑ | 647 Dave Stewart | .30 | .14 |
| ❑ | 648 Rey Sanchez CL | .15 | .07 |
| ❑ | 649 Jeremy Hernandez CL | .15 | .07 |
| ❑ | 650 Junior Ortiz CL | .15 | .07 |

## 1994 Ultra

| | | MINT | NRMT |
|---|---|---|---|
| | COMPLETE SET (600) | 30.00 | 13.50 |
| | COMPLETE SERIES 1 (300) | 15.00 | 6.75 |
| | COMPLETE SERIES 2 (300) | 15.00 | 6.75 |
| ❑ | 1 Jeffrey Hammonds | .25 | .11 |
| ❑ | 2 Chris Hoiles | .15 | .07 |
| ❑ | 3 Ben McDonald | .15 | .07 |
| ❑ | 4 Mark McLemore | .15 | .07 |
| ❑ | 5 Alan Mills | .15 | .07 |
| ❑ | 6 Jamie Moyer | .15 | .07 |
| ❑ | 7 Brad Pennington | .15 | .07 |
| ❑ | 8 Jim Poole | .15 | .07 |
| ❑ | 9 Cal Ripken Jr. | 2.50 | 1.10 |
| ❑ | 10 Jack Voigt | .15 | .07 |
| ❑ | 11 Roger Clemens | 1.25 | .55 |
| ❑ | 12 Danny Darwin | .15 | .07 |
| ❑ | 13 Andre Dawson | .40 | .18 |
| ❑ | 14 Scott Fletcher | .15 | .07 |
| ❑ | 15 Greg A. Harris | .15 | .07 |
| ❑ | 16 Billy Hatcher | .15 | .07 |
| ❑ | 17 Jeff Russell | .15 | .07 |
| ❑ | 18 Aaron Sele | .25 | .11 |
| ❑ | 19 Mo Vaughn | .25 | .11 |
| ❑ | 20 Mike Butcher | .15 | .07 |
| ❑ | 21 Rod Correia | .15 | .07 |
| ❑ | 22 Steve Frey | .15 | .07 |
| ❑ | 23 Phil Leftwich RC | .15 | .07 |
| ❑ | 24 Torey Lovullo | .15 | .07 |
| ❑ | 25 Ken Patterson | .15 | .07 |
| ❑ | 26 Eduardo Perez UER (Listed as Twin instead of Angel) | .15 | .07 |
| ❑ | 27 Tim Salmon | .25 | .11 |
| ❑ | 28 J.T. Snow | .25 | .11 |
| ❑ | 29 Chris Turner | .15 | .07 |
| ❑ | 30 Wilson Alvarez | .15 | .07 |
| ❑ | 31 Jason Bere | .15 | .07 |
| ❑ | 32 Joey Cora | .15 | .07 |
| ❑ | 33 Alex Fernandez | .15 | .07 |
| ❑ | 34 Roberto Hernandez | .15 | .07 |
| ❑ | 35 Lance Johnson | .15 | .07 |
| ❑ | 36 Ron Karkovice | .15 | .07 |
| ❑ | 37 Kirk McCaskill | .15 | .07 |
| ❑ | 38 Jeff Schwarz | .15 | .07 |
| ❑ | 39 Frank Thomas | 1.25 | .55 |
| ❑ | 40 Sandy Alomar Jr. | .25 | .11 |
| ❑ | 41 Albert Belle | .40 | .18 |
| ❑ | 42 Felix Fermin | .15 | .07 |
| ❑ | 43 Wayne Kirby | .15 | .07 |
| ❑ | 44 Tom Kramer | .15 | .07 |
| ❑ | 45 Kenny Lofton | .25 | .11 |
| ❑ | 46 Jose Mesa | .15 | .07 |
| ❑ | 47 Eric Plunk | .15 | .07 |
| ❑ | 48 Paul Sorrento | .15 | .07 |
| ❑ | 49 Jim Thome | .40 | .18 |
| ❑ | 50 Bill Wertz | .15 | .07 |
| ❑ | 51 John Doherty | .15 | .07 |
| ❑ | 52 Cecil Fielder | .25 | .11 |
| ❑ | 53 Travis Fryman | .25 | .11 |
| ❑ | 54 Chris Gomez | .15 | .07 |
| ❑ | 55 Mike Henneman | .15 | .07 |
| ❑ | 56 Chad Kreuter | .15 | .07 |
| ❑ | 57 Bob MacDonald | .15 | .07 |
| ❑ | 58 Mike Moore | .15 | .07 |
| ❑ | 59 Tony Phillips | .15 | .07 |
| ❑ | 60 Lou Whitaker | .25 | .11 |
| ❑ | 61 Kevin Appier | .25 | .11 |
| ❑ | 62 Greg Gagne | .15 | .07 |
| ❑ | 63 Chris Gwynn | .15 | .07 |
| ❑ | 64 Bob Hamelin | .15 | .07 |
| ❑ | 65 Chris Haney | .15 | .07 |
| ❑ | 66 Phil Hiatt | .15 | .07 |
| ❑ | 67 Felix Jose | .15 | .07 |
| ❑ | 68 Jose Lind | .15 | .07 |
| ❑ | 69 Mike Macfarlane | .15 | .07 |
| ❑ | 70 Jeff Montgomery | .15 | .07 |
| ❑ | 71 Hipolito Pichardo | .15 | .07 |
| ❑ | 72 Juan Bell | .15 | .07 |
| ❑ | 73 Cal Eldred | .15 | .07 |
| ❑ | 74 Darryl Hamilton | .15 | .07 |
| ❑ | 75 Doug Henry | .15 | .07 |
| ❑ | 76 Mike Ignasiak | .15 | .07 |
| ❑ | 77 John Jaha | .15 | .07 |
| ❑ | 78 Graeme Lloyd | .15 | .07 |
| ❑ | 79 Angel Miranda | .15 | .07 |
| ❑ | 80 Dave Nilsson | .15 | .07 |
| ❑ | 81 Troy O'Leary | .15 | .07 |
| ❑ | 82 Kevin Reimer | .15 | .07 |
| ❑ | 83 Willie Banks | .15 | .07 |
| ❑ | 84 Larry Casian | .15 | .07 |
| ❑ | 85 Scott Erickson | .15 | .07 |
| ❑ | 86 Eddie Guardado | .15 | .07 |
| ❑ | 87 Kent Hrbek | .25 | .11 |
| ❑ | 88 Terry Jorgensen | .15 | .07 |
| ❑ | 89 Chuck Knoblauch | .25 | .11 |
| ❑ | 90 Pat Meares | .15 | .07 |
| ❑ | 91 Mike Trombley | .15 | .07 |
| ❑ | 92 Dave Winfield | .60 | .25 |
| ❑ | 93 Wade Boggs | .75 | .35 |
| ❑ | 94 Scott Kamieniecki | .15 | .07 |
| ❑ | 95 Pat Kelly | .15 | .07 |
| ❑ | 96 Jimmy Key | .25 | .11 |
| ❑ | 97 Jim Leyritz | .15 | .07 |
| ❑ | 98 Bobby Munoz | .15 | .07 |
| ❑ | 99 Paul O'Neill | .25 | .11 |
| ❑ | 100 Melido Perez | .15 | .07 |
| ❑ | 101 Mike Stanley | .15 | .07 |
| ❑ | 102 Danny Tartabull | .15 | .07 |
| ❑ | 103 Bernie Williams | .60 | .25 |
| ❑ | 104 Kurt Abbott RC | .25 | .11 |
| ❑ | 105 Mike Bordick | .15 | .07 |
| ❑ | 106 Ron Darling | .15 | .07 |
| ❑ | 107 Brent Gates | .15 | .07 |
| ❑ | 108 Miguel Jimenez | .15 | .07 |
| ❑ | 109 Steve Karsay | .15 | .07 |
| ❑ | 110 Scott Lydy | .15 | .07 |
| ❑ | 111 Mark McGwire | 2.50 | 1.10 |
| ❑ | 112 Troy Neel | .15 | .07 |
| ❑ | 113 Craig Paquette | .15 | .07 |
| ❑ | 114 Bob Welch | .15 | .07 |
| ❑ | 115 Bobby Witt | .15 | .07 |
| ❑ | 116 Rich Amaral | .15 | .07 |
| ❑ | 117 Mike Blowers | .15 | .07 |
| ❑ | 118 Jay Buhner | .25 | .11 |
| ❑ | 119 Dave Fleming | .15 | .07 |
| ❑ | 120 Ken Griffey Jr. | 2.50 | 1.10 |
| ❑ | 121 Tino Martinez | .25 | .11 |
| ❑ | 122 Marc Newfield | .15 | .07 |
| ❑ | 123 Ted Power | .15 | .07 |
| ❑ | 124 Mackey Sasser | .15 | .07 |
| ❑ | 125 Omar Vizquel | .25 | .11 |
| ❑ | 126 Kevin Brown | .25 | .11 |
| ❑ | 127 Juan Gonzalez | .60 | .25 |
| ❑ | 128 Tom Henke | .15 | .07 |
| ❑ | 129 David Hulse | .15 | .07 |
| ❑ | 130 Dean Palmer | .25 | .11 |
| ❑ | 131 Roger Pavlik | .15 | .07 |
| ❑ | 132 Ivan Rodriguez | .75 | .35 |
| ❑ | 133 Kenny Rogers | .15 | .07 |
| ❑ | 134 Doug Strange | .15 | .07 |
| ❑ | 135 Pat Borders | .15 | .07 |
| ❑ | 136 Joe Carter | .25 | .11 |
| ❑ | 137 Darnell Coles | .15 | .07 |
| ❑ | 138 Pat Hentgen | .15 | .07 |
| ❑ | 139 Al Leiter | .25 | .11 |
| ❑ | 140 Paul Molitor | .60 | .25 |
| ❑ | 141 John Olerud | .25 | .11 |
| ❑ | 142 Ed Sprague | .15 | .07 |
| ❑ | 143 Dave Stewart | .25 | .11 |
| ❑ | 144 Mike Timlin | .15 | .07 |
| ❑ | 145 Duane Ward | .15 | .07 |
| ❑ | 146 Devon White | .15 | .07 |
| ❑ | 147 Steve Avery | .15 | .07 |
| ❑ | 148 Steve Bedrosian | .15 | .07 |
| ❑ | 149 Damon Berryhill | .15 | .07 |
| ❑ | 150 Jeff Blauser | .15 | .07 |
| ❑ | 151 Tom Glavine | .60 | .25 |
| ❑ | 152 Chipper Jones | 1.50 | .70 |
| ❑ | 153 Mark Lemke | .15 | .07 |
| ❑ | 154 Fred McGriff | .40 | .18 |
| ❑ | 155 Greg McMichael | .15 | .07 |
| ❑ | 156 Deion Sanders | .25 | .11 |
| ❑ | 157 John Smoltz | .25 | .11 |
| ❑ | 158 Mark Wohlers | .15 | .07 |
| ❑ | 159 Jose Bautista | .15 | .07 |
| ❑ | 160 Steve Buechele | .15 | .07 |
| ❑ | 161 Mike Harkey | .15 | .07 |
| ❑ | 162 Greg Hibbard | .15 | .07 |
| ❑ | 163 Chuck McElroy | .15 | .07 |
| ❑ | 164 Mike Morgan | .15 | .07 |
| ❑ | 165 Kevin Roberson | .15 | .07 |
| ❑ | 166 Ryne Sandberg | .75 | .35 |
| ❑ | 167 Jose Vizcaino | .15 | .07 |
| ❑ | 168 Rick Wilkins | .15 | .07 |
| ❑ | 169 Willie Wilson | .15 | .07 |
| ❑ | 170 Willie Greene | .15 | .07 |
| ❑ | 171 Roberto Kelly | .15 | .07 |
| ❑ | 172 Larry Luebbers RC | .15 | .07 |
| ❑ | 173 Kevin Mitchell | .15 | .07 |
| ❑ | 174 Joe Oliver | .15 | .07 |
| ❑ | 175 John Roper | .15 | .07 |
| ❑ | 176 Johnny Ruffin | .15 | .07 |
| ❑ | 177 Reggie Sanders | .15 | .07 |
| ❑ | 178 John Smiley | .15 | .07 |
| ❑ | 179 Jerry Spradlin RC | .15 | .07 |
| ❑ | 180 Freddie Benavides | .15 | .07 |
| ❑ | 181 Dante Bichette | .25 | .11 |
| ❑ | 182 Willie Blair | .15 | .07 |
| ❑ | 183 Kent Bottenfield | .15 | .07 |
| ❑ | 184 Jerald Clark | .15 | .07 |
| ❑ | 185 Joe Girardi | .15 | .07 |
| ❑ | 186 Roberto Mejia | .15 | .07 |
| ❑ | 187 Steve Reed | .15 | .07 |
| ❑ | 188 Armando Reynoso | .15 | .07 |
| ❑ | 189 Bruce Ruffin | .15 | .07 |
| ❑ | 190 Eric Young | .15 | .07 |
| ❑ | 191 Luis Aquino | .15 | .07 |
| ❑ | 192 Bret Barberie | .15 | .07 |
| ❑ | 193 Ryan Bowen | .15 | .07 |
| ❑ | 194 Chuck Carr | .15 | .07 |
| ❑ | 195 Orestes Destrade | .15 | .07 |
| ❑ | 196 Richie Lewis | .15 | .07 |
| ❑ | 197 Dave Magadan | .15 | .07 |
| ❑ | 198 Bob Natal | .15 | .07 |
| ❑ | 199 Gary Sheffield | .60 | .25 |
| ❑ | 200 Matt Turner | .15 | .07 |
| ❑ | 201 Darrell Whitmore | .15 | .07 |
| ❑ | 202 Eric Anthony | .15 | .07 |
| ❑ | 203 Jeff Bagwell | .75 | .35 |
| ❑ | 204 Andujar Cedeno | .15 | .07 |
| ❑ | 205 Luis Gonzalez | .25 | .11 |
| ❑ | 206 Xavier Hernandez | .15 | .07 |
| ❑ | 207 Doug Jones | .15 | .07 |
| ❑ | 208 Darryl Kile | .25 | .11 |
| ❑ | 209 Scott Servais | .15 | .07 |
| ❑ | 210 Greg Swindell | .15 | .07 |
| ❑ | 211 Brian Williams | .15 | .07 |
| ❑ | 212 Pedro Astacio | .15 | .07 |

❑ 213 Brett Butler .25 .11
❑ 214 Omar Daal .15 .07
❑ 215 Jim Gott .15 .07
❑ 216 Raul Mondesi .25 .11
❑ 217 Jose Offerman .15 .07
❑ 218 Mike Piazza 2.00 .90
❑ 219 Cory Snyder .15 .07
❑ 220 Tim Wallach .15 .07
❑ 221 Todd Worrell .15 .07
❑ 222 Moises Alou .25 .11
❑ 223 Sean Berry .15 .07
❑ 224 Wil Cordero .15 .07
❑ 225 Jeff Fassero .15 .07
❑ 226 Darrin Fletcher .15 .07
❑ 227 Cliff Floyd .25 .11
❑ 228 Marquis Grissom .15 .07
❑ 229 Ken Hill .15 .07
❑ 230 Mike Lansing .15 .07
❑ 231 Kirk Rueter .15 .07
❑ 232 John Wetteland .25 .11
❑ 233 Rondell White .25 .11
❑ 234 Tim Bogar .15 .07
❑ 235 Jeromy Burnitz .25 .11
❑ 236 Dwight Gooden .25 .11
❑ 237 Todd Hundley .15 .07
❑ 238 Jeff Kent .40 .18
❑ 239 Josias Manzanillo .15 .07
❑ 240 Joe Orsulak .15 .07
❑ 241 Ryan Thompson .15 .07
❑ 242 Kim Batiste .15 .07
❑ 243 Darren Daulton .25 .11
❑ 244 Tommy Greene .15 .07
❑ 245 Dave Hollins .15 .07
❑ 246 Pete Incaviglia .15 .07
❑ 247 Danny Jackson .15 .07
❑ 248 Ricky Jordan .15 .07
❑ 249 John Kruk .25 .11
❑ 250 Mickey Morandini .15 .07
❑ 251 Terry Mulholland .15 .07
❑ 252 Ben Rivera .15 .07
❑ 253 Kevin Stocker .15 .07
❑ 254 Jay Bell .25 .11
❑ 255 Steve Cooke .15 .07
❑ 256 Jeff King .15 .07
❑ 257 Al Martin .15 .07
❑ 258 Danny Miceli .15 .07
❑ 259 Blas Minor .15 .07
❑ 260 Don Slaught .15 .07
❑ 261 Paul Wagner .15 .07
❑ 262 Tim Wakefield .15 .07
❑ 263 Kevin Young .15 .07
❑ 264 Rene Arocha .15 .07
❑ 265 Richard Batchelor RC .15 .07
❑ 266 Gregg Jefferies .15 .07
❑ 267 Brian Jordan .25 .11
❑ 268 Jose Oquendo .15 .07
❑ 269 Donovan Osborne .15 .07
❑ 270 Erik Pappas .15 .07
❑ 271 Mike Perez .15 .07
❑ 272 Bob Tewksbury .15 .07
❑ 273 Mark Whiten .15 .07
❑ 274 Todd Zeile .15 .07
❑ 275 Andy Ashby .15 .07
❑ 276 Brad Ausmus .15 .07
❑ 277 Phil Clark .15 .07
❑ 278 Jeff Gardner .15 .07
❑ 279 Ricky Gutierrez .15 .07
❑ 280 Tony Gwynn 1.25 .55
❑ 281 Tim Mauser .15 .07
❑ 282 Scott Sanders .15 .07
❑ 283 Frank Seminara .15 .07
❑ 284 Wally Whitehurst .15 .07
❑ 285 Rod Beck .15 .07
❑ 286 Barry Bonds 1.00 .45
❑ 287 Dave Burba .15 .07
❑ 288 Mark Carreon .15 .07
❑ 289 Royce Clayton .15 .07
❑ 290 Mike Jackson .15 .07
❑ 291 Darren Lewis .15 .07
❑ 292 Kirt Manwaring .15 .07
❑ 293 Dave Martinez .15 .07
❑ 294 Billy Swift .15 .07
❑ 295 Salomon Torres .15 .07
❑ 296 Matt Williams .40 .18
❑ 297 Checklist 1-75 .15 .07
❑ 298 Checklist 76-150 .15 .07
❑ 299 Checklist 151-225 .15 .07
❑ 300 Checklist 226-300 .15 .07
❑ 301 Brady Anderson .25 .11
❑ 302 Harold Baines .25 .11
❑ 303 Damon Buford .15 .07
❑ 304 Mike Devereaux .15 .07
❑ 305 Sid Fernandez .15 .07
❑ 306 Rick Krivda RC .15 .07
❑ 307 Mike Mussina .60 .25
❑ 308 Rafael Palmeiro .60 .25
❑ 309 Arthur Rhodes .15 .07
❑ 310 Chris Sabo .15 .07
❑ 311 Lee Smith .25 .11
❑ 312 Gregg Zaun RC .15 .07
❑ 313 Scott Cooper .15 .07
❑ 314 Mike Greenwell .15 .07
❑ 315 Tim Naehring .15 .07
❑ 316 Otis Nixon .15 .07
❑ 317 Paul Quantrill .15 .07
❑ 318 John Valentin .15 .07
❑ 319 Dave Valle .15 .07
❑ 320 Frank Viola .25 .11
❑ 321 Brian Anderson RC .25 .11
❑ 322 Garret Anderson .25 .11
❑ 323 Chad Curtis .15 .07
❑ 324 Chili Davis .25 .11
❑ 325 Gary DiSarcina .15 .07
❑ 326 Damion Easley .15 .07
❑ 327 Jim Edmonds .75 .35
❑ 328 Chuck Finley .25 .11
❑ 329 Joe Grahe .15 .07
❑ 330 Bo Jackson .25 .11
❑ 331 Mark Langston .15 .07
❑ 332 Harold Reynolds .15 .07
❑ 333 James Baldwin .25 .11
❑ 334 Ray Durham RC 1.50 .70
❑ 335 Julio Franco .25 .11
❑ 336 Craig Grebeck .15 .07
❑ 337 Ozzie Guillen .15 .07
❑ 338 Joe Hall RC .15 .07
❑ 339 Darrin Jackson .15 .07
❑ 340 Jack McDowell .15 .07
❑ 341 Tim Raines .25 .11
❑ 342 Robin Ventura .25 .11
❑ 343 Carlos Baerga .15 .07
❑ 344 Derek Lilliquist .15 .07
❑ 345 Dennis Martinez .25 .11
❑ 346 Jack Morris .25 .11
❑ 347 Eddie Murray .60 .25
❑ 348 Chris Nabholz .15 .07
❑ 349 Charles Nagy .15 .07
❑ 350 Chad Ogea .15 .07
❑ 351 Manny Ramirez 1.00 .45
❑ 352 Omar Vizquel .25 .11
❑ 353 Tim Belcher .15 .07
❑ 354 Eric Davis .25 .11
❑ 355 Kirk Gibson .25 .11
❑ 356 Rick Greene .15 .07
❑ 357 Mickey Tettleton .15 .07
❑ 358 Alan Trammell .40 .18
❑ 359 David Wells .25 .11
❑ 360 Stan Belinda .15 .07
❑ 361 Vince Coleman .15 .07
❑ 362 David Cone .25 .11
❑ 363 Gary Gaetti .25 .11
❑ 364 Tom Gordon .15 .07
❑ 365 Dave Henderson .15 .07
❑ 366 Wally Joyner .25 .11
❑ 367 Brent Mayne .15 .07
❑ 368 Brian McRae .15 .07
❑ 369 Michael Tucker .15 .07
❑ 370 Ricky Bones .15 .07
❑ 371 Brian Harper .15 .07
❑ 372 Tyrone Hill .15 .07
❑ 373 Mark Kiefer .15 .07
❑ 374 Pat Listach .15 .07
❑ 375 Mike Matheny RC .15 .07
❑ 376 Jose Mercedes RC .15 .07
❑ 377 Jody Reed .15 .07
❑ 378 Kevin Seitzer .15 .07
❑ 379 B.J. Surhoff .25 .11
❑ 380 Greg Vaughn .25 .11
❑ 381 Turner Ward .15 .07
❑ 382 Wes Weger RC .15 .07
❑ 383 Bill Wegman .15 .07
❑ 384 Rick Aguilera .15 .07
❑ 385 Rich Becker .15 .07
❑ 386 Alex Cole .15 .07
❑ 387 Steve Dunn .15 .07
❑ 388 Keith Garagozzo RC .15 .07
❑ 389 LaTroy Hawkins RC .25 .11
❑ 390 Shane Mack .15 .07
❑ 391 David McCarty .15 .07
❑ 392 Pedro Munoz .15 .07
❑ 393 Derek Parks .15 .07
❑ 394 Kirby Puckett 1.50 .70
❑ 395 Kevin Tapani .15 .07
❑ 396 Matt Walbeck .15 .07
❑ 397 Jim Abbott .25 .11
❑ 398 Mike Gallego .15 .07
❑ 399 Xavier Hernandez .15 .07
❑ 400 Don Mattingly 1.50 .70
❑ 401 Terry Mulholland .15 .07
❑ 402 Matt Nokes .15 .07
❑ 403 Luis Polonia .15 .07
❑ 404 Bob Wickman .15 .07
❑ 405 Mark Acre RC .15 .07
❑ 406 Fausto Cruz RC .15 .07
❑ 407 Dennis Eckersley .25 .11
❑ 408 Rickey Henderson .75 .35
❑ 409 Stan Javier .15 .07
❑ 410 Carlos Reyes RC .15 .07
❑ 411 Ruben Sierra .15 .07
❑ 412 Terry Steinbach .15 .07
❑ 413 Bill Taylor RC .25 .11
❑ 414 Todd Van Poppel .15 .07
❑ 415 Eric Anthony .15 .07
❑ 416 Bobby Ayala .15 .07
❑ 417 Chris Bosio .15 .07
❑ 418 Tim Davis .15 .07
❑ 419 Randy Johnson .75 .35
❑ 420 Kevin King RC .15 .07
❑ 421 Anthony Manahan RC .15 .07
❑ 422 Edgar Martinez .40 .18
❑ 423 Keith Mitchell .15 .07
❑ 424 Roger Salkeld .15 .07
❑ 425 Mac Suzuki RC .25 .11
❑ 426 Dan Wilson .15 .07
❑ 427 Duff Brumley RC .15 .07
❑ 428 Jose Canseco .75 .35
❑ 429 Will Clark .60 .25
❑ 430 Steve Dreyer RC .15 .07
❑ 431 Rick Helling .25 .11
❑ 432 Chris James .15 .07
❑ 433 Matt Whiteside .15 .07
❑ 434 Roberto Alomar .60 .25
❑ 435 Scott Brow .15 .07
❑ 436 Domingo Cedeno .15 .07
❑ 437 Carlos Delgado 1.00 .45
❑ 438 Juan Guzman .15 .07
❑ 439 Paul Spoljaric .15 .07
❑ 440 Todd Stottlemyre .15 .07
❑ 441 Woody Williams .15 .07
❑ 442 David Justice .40 .18
❑ 443 Mike Kelly .15 .07
❑ 444 Ryan Klesko .25 .11
❑ 445 Javier Lopez .25 .11
❑ 446 Greg Maddux 1.50 .70
❑ 447 Kent Mercker .15 .07
❑ 448 Charlie O'Brien .15 .07
❑ 449 Terry Pendleton .25 .11
❑ 450 Mike Stanton .15 .07
❑ 451 Tony Tarasco .15 .07
❑ 452 Terrell Wade RC .15 .07
❑ 453 Willie Banks .15 .07
❑ 454 Shawon Dunston .15 .07
❑ 455 Mark Grace .60 .25
❑ 456 Jose Guzman .15 .07
❑ 457 Jose Hernandez .15 .07
❑ 458 Glenallen Hill .15 .07
❑ 459 Blaise Ilsley RC .15 .07
❑ 460 Brooks Kieschnick RC .15 .07
❑ 461 Derrick May .15 .07
❑ 462 Randy Myers .15 .07
❑ 463 Karl Rhodes .15 .07
❑ 464 Sammy Sosa 1.25 .55
❑ 465 Steve Trachsel .15 .07
❑ 466 Anthony Young .15 .07
❑ 467 Eddie Zambrano RC .15 .07
❑ 468 Bret Boone .25 .11
❑ 469 Tom Browning .15 .07
❑ 470 Hector Carrasco .15 .07

❑ 471 Rob Dibble .15 .07
❑ 472 Erik Hanson .15 .07
❑ 473 Thomas Howard .15 .07
❑ 474 Barry Larkin .60 .25
❑ 475 Hal Morris .15 .07
❑ 476 Jose Rijo .15 .07
❑ 477 John Burke .15 .07
❑ 478 Ellis Burks .25 .11
❑ 479 Marvin Freeman .15 .07
❑ 480 Andres Galarraga .40 .18
❑ 481 Greg W. Harris .15 .07
❑ 482 Charlie Hayes .15 .07
❑ 483 Darren Holmes .15 .07
❑ 484 Howard Johnson .15 .07
❑ 485 Marcus Moore .15 .07
❑ 486 David Nied .15 .07
❑ 487 Mark Thompson .15 .07
❑ 488 Walt Weiss .15 .07
❑ 489 Kurt Abbott .25 .11
❑ 490 Matias Carrillo RC .15 .07
❑ 491 Jeff Conine .15 .07
❑ 492 Chris Hammond .15 .07
❑ 493 Bryan Harvey .15 .07
❑ 494 Charlie Hough .25 .11
❑ 495 Yorkis Perez .15 .07
❑ 496 Pat Rapp .15 .07
❑ 497 Benito Santiago .15 .07
❑ 498 David Weathers .15 .07
❑ 499 Craig Biggio .40 .18
❑ 500 Ken Caminiti .25 .11
❑ 501 Doug Drabek .15 .07
❑ 502 Tony Eusebio .15 .07
❑ 503 Steve Finley .25 .11
❑ 504 Pete Harnisch .15 .07
❑ 505 Brian L. Hunter .15 .07
❑ 506 Domingo Jean .15 .07
❑ 507 Todd Jones .15 .07
❑ 508 Orlando Miller .15 .07
❑ 509 James Mouton .15 .07
❑ 510 Roberto Petagine .15 .07
❑ 511 Shane Reynolds .15 .07
❑ 512 Mitch Williams .15 .07
❑ 513 Billy Ashley .15 .07
❑ 514 Tom Candiotti .15 .07
❑ 515 Delino DeShields .15 .07
❑ 516 Kevin Gross .15 .07
❑ 517 Orel Hershiser .25 .11
❑ 518 Eric Karros .25 .11
❑ 519 Ramon Martinez .15 .07
❑ 520 Chan Ho Park RC .75 .35
❑ 521 Henry Rodriguez .15 .07
❑ 522 Joey Eischen .15 .07
❑ 523 Rod Henderson .15 .07
❑ 524 Pedro Martinez 1.00 .45
❑ 525 Mel Rojas .15 .07
❑ 526 Larry Walker .25 .11
❑ 527 Gabe White .15 .07
❑ 528 Bobby Bonilla .25 .11
❑ 529 Jonathan Hurst .15 .07
❑ 530 Bobby Jones .15 .07
❑ 531 Kevin McReynolds .15 .07
❑ 532 Bill Pulsipher .25 .11
❑ 533 Bret Saberhagen .25 .11
❑ 534 David Segui .15 .07
❑ 535 Pete Smith .15 .07
❑ 536 Kelly Stinnett RC .25 .11
❑ 537 Dave Telgheder .15 .07
❑ 538 Quilvio Veras .15 .07
❑ 539 Jose Vizcaino .15 .07
❑ 540 Pete Walker RC .15 .07
❑ 541 Ricky Bottalico RC .25 .11
❑ 542 Wes Chamberlain .15 .07
❑ 543 Mariano Duncan .15 .07
❑ 544 Lenny Dykstra .25 .11
❑ 545 Jim Eisenreich .15 .07
❑ 546 Phil Geisler RC .15 .07
❑ 547 Wayne Gomes RC .15 .07
❑ 548 Doug Jones .15 .07
❑ 549 Jeff Juden .15 .07
❑ 550 Mike Lieberthal .25 .11
❑ 551 Tony Longmire .15 .07
❑ 552 Tom Marsh .15 .07
❑ 553 Bobby Munoz .15 .07
❑ 554 Curt Schilling .25 .11
❑ 555 Carlos Garcia .15 .07
❑ 556 Ravelo Manzanillo RC .15 .07
❑ 557 Orlando Merced .15 .07
❑ 558 Will Pennyfeather .15 .07
❑ 559 Zane Smith .15 .07
❑ 560 Andy Van Slyke .25 .11
❑ 561 Rick White .15 .07
❑ 562 Luis Alicea .15 .07
❑ 563 Brian Barber .15 .07
❑ 564 Clint Davis RC .15 .07
❑ 565 Bernard Gilkey .15 .07
❑ 566 Ray Lankford .25 .11
❑ 567 Tom Pagnozzi .15 .07
❑ 568 Ozzie Smith .75 .35
❑ 569 Rick Sutcliffe .25 .11
❑ 570 Allen Watson .15 .07
❑ 571 Dmitri Young .25 .11
❑ 572 Derek Bell .15 .07
❑ 573 Andy Benes .15 .07
❑ 574 Archi Cianfrocco .15 .07
❑ 575 Joey Hamilton .15 .07
❑ 576 Gene Harris .15 .07
❑ 577 Trevor Hoffman .25 .11
❑ 578 Tim Hyers RC .15 .07
❑ 579 Brian Johnson RC .15 .07
❑ 580 Keith Lockhart RC .25 .11
❑ 581 Pedro A. Martinez RC .15 .07
❑ 582 Ray McDavid .15 .07
❑ 583 Phil Plantier .15 .07
❑ 584 Bip Roberts .15 .07
❑ 585 Dave Staton .15 .07
❑ 586 Todd Benzinger .15 .07
❑ 587 John Burkett .15 .07
❑ 588 Bryan Hickerson .15 .07
❑ 589 Willie McGee .25 .11
❑ 590 John Patterson .15 .07
❑ 591 Mark Portugal .15 .07
❑ 592 Kevin Rogers .15 .07
❑ 593 Joe Rosselli .15 .07
❑ 594 Steve Soderstrom RC .15 .07
❑ 595 Robby Thompson .15 .07
❑ 596 125th Anniversary Card .15 .07
❑ 597 Checklist .15 .07
❑ 598 Checklist .15 .07
❑ 599 Checklist .15 .07
❑ 600 Checklist .15 .07
❑ P243 Darren Daulton Promo 2.00 .90
❑ P249 John Kruk Promo 2.00 .90

## 1995 Ultra

| | MINT | NRMT |
|---|---|---|
| COMPLETE SET (450) | 30.00 | 13.50 |
| COMPLETE SERIES 1 (250) | 18.00 | 8.00 |
| COMPLETE SERIES 2 (200) | 12.00 | 5.50 |

❑ 1 Brady Anderson .30 .14
❑ 2 Sid Fernandez .15 .07
❑ 3 Jeffrey Hammonds .30 .14
❑ 4 Chris Hoiles .15 .07
❑ 5 Ben McDonald .15 .07
❑ 6 Mike Mussina .60 .25
❑ 7 Rafael Palmeiro .60 .25
❑ 8 Jack Voigt .15 .07
❑ 9 Wes Chamberlain .15 .07
❑ 10 Roger Clemens 1.25 .55
❑ 11 Chris Howard .15 .07
❑ 12 Tim Naehring .15 .07
❑ 13 Otis Nixon .15 .07
❑ 14 Rich Rowland .15 .07
❑ 15 Ken Ryan .15 .07
❑ 16 John Valentin .15 .07
❑ 17 Mo Vaughn .30 .14
❑ 18 Brian Anderson .15 .07
❑ 19 Chili Davis .30 .14
❑ 20 Damion Easley .15 .07
❑ 21 Jim Edmonds .60 .25
❑ 22 Mark Langston .15 .07
❑ 23 Tim Salmon .30 .14
❑ 24 J.T. Snow .30 .14
❑ 25 Chris Turner .15 .07
❑ 26 Wilson Alvarez .15 .07
❑ 27 Joey Cora .15 .07
❑ 28 Alex Fernandez .15 .07
❑ 29 Roberto Hernandez .15 .07
❑ 30 Lance Johnson .15 .07
❑ 31 Ron Karkovice .15 .07
❑ 32 Kirk McCaskill .15 .07
❑ 33 Tim Raines .30 .14
❑ 34 Frank Thomas 1.25 .55
❑ 35 Sandy Alomar Jr. .30 .14
❑ 36 Albert Belle .30 .14
❑ 37 Mark Clark .15 .07
❑ 38 Kenny Lofton .30 .14
❑ 39 Eddie Murray .60 .25
❑ 40 Eric Plunk .15 .07
❑ 41 Manny Ramirez .75 .35
❑ 42 Jim Thome .30 .14
❑ 43 Omar Vizquel .30 .14
❑ 44 Danny Bautista .15 .07
❑ 45 Junior Felix .15 .07
❑ 46 Cecil Fielder .30 .14
❑ 47 Chris Gomez .15 .07
❑ 48 Chad Kreuter .15 .07
❑ 49 Mike Moore .15 .07
❑ 50 Tony Phillips .15 .07
❑ 51 Alan Trammell .30 .14
❑ 52 David Wells .30 .14
❑ 53 Kevin Appier .30 .14
❑ 54 Billy Brewer .15 .07
❑ 55 David Cone .30 .14
❑ 56 Greg Gagne .15 .07
❑ 57 Bob Hamelin .15 .07
❑ 58 Jose Lind .15 .07
❑ 59 Brent Mayne .15 .07
❑ 60 Brian McRae .15 .07
❑ 61 Terry Shumpert .15 .07
❑ 62 Ricky Bones .15 .07
❑ 63 Mike Fetters .15 .07
❑ 64 Darryl Hamilton .15 .07
❑ 65 John Jaha .15 .07
❑ 66 Graeme Lloyd .15 .07
❑ 67 Matt Mieske .15 .07
❑ 68 Kevin Seitzer .15 .07
❑ 69 Jose Valentin .15 .07
❑ 70 Turner Ward .15 .07
❑ 71 Rick Aguilera .15 .07
❑ 72 Rich Becker .15 .07
❑ 73 Alex Cole .15 .07
❑ 74 Scott Leius .15 .07
❑ 75 Pat Meares .15 .07
❑ 76 Kirby Puckett 1.50 .70
❑ 77 Dave Stevens .15 .07
❑ 78 Kevin Tapani .15 .07
❑ 79 Matt Walbeck .15 .07
❑ 80 Wade Boggs .75 .35
❑ 81 Scott Kamieniecki .15 .07
❑ 82 Pat Kelly .15 .07
❑ 83 Jimmy Key .30 .14
❑ 84 Paul O'Neill .30 .14
❑ 85 Luis Polonia .15 .07
❑ 86 Mike Stanley .15 .07
❑ 87 Danny Tartabull .15 .07
❑ 88 Bob Wickman .15 .07
❑ 89 Mark Acre .15 .07
❑ 90 Geronimo Berroa .15 .07
❑ 91 Mike Bordick .15 .07
❑ 92 Ron Darling .15 .07
❑ 93 Stan Javier .15 .07
❑ 94 Mark McGwire 2.50 1.10
❑ 95 Troy Neel .15 .07
❑ 96 Ruben Sierra .15 .07
❑ 97 Terry Steinbach .15 .07
❑ 98 Eric Anthony .15 .07
❑ 99 Chris Bosio .15 .07

| No. | Player | | |
|---|---|---|---|
| ❑ 100 | Dave Fleming | .15 | .07 |
| ❑ 101 | Ken Griffey Jr. | 2.50 | 1.10 |
| ❑ 102 | Reggie Jefferson | .15 | .07 |
| ❑ 103 | Randy Johnson | .75 | .35 |
| ❑ 104 | Edgar Martinez | .30 | .14 |
| ❑ 105 | Bill Risley | .15 | .07 |
| ❑ 106 | Dan Wilson | .15 | .07 |
| ❑ 107 | Cris Carpenter | .15 | .07 |
| ❑ 108 | Will Clark | .60 | .25 |
| ❑ 109 | Juan Gonzalez | .60 | .25 |
| ❑ 110 | Rusty Greer | .30 | .14 |
| ❑ 111 | David Hulse | .15 | .07 |
| ❑ 112 | Roger Pavlik | .15 | .07 |
| ❑ 113 | Ivan Rodriguez | .75 | .35 |
| ❑ 114 | Doug Strange | .15 | .07 |
| ❑ 115 | Matt Whiteside | .15 | .07 |
| ❑ 116 | Roberto Alomar | .60 | .25 |
| ❑ 117 | Brad Cornett | .15 | .07 |
| ❑ 118 | Carlos Delgado | .60 | .25 |
| ❑ 119 | Alex Gonzalez | .15 | .07 |
| ❑ 120 | Darren Hall | .15 | .07 |
| ❑ 121 | Pat Hentgen | .15 | .07 |
| ❑ 122 | Paul Molitor | .60 | .25 |
| ❑ 123 | Ed Sprague | .15 | .07 |
| ❑ 124 | Devon White | .30 | .14 |
| ❑ 125 | Tom Glavine | .60 | .25 |
| ❑ 126 | David Justice | .30 | .14 |
| ❑ 127 | Roberto Kelly | .15 | .07 |
| ❑ 128 | Mark Lemke | .15 | .07 |
| ❑ 129 | Greg Maddux | 1.50 | .70 |
| ❑ 130 | Greg McMichael | .15 | .07 |
| ❑ 131 | Kent Mercker | .15 | .07 |
| ❑ 132 | Charlie O'Brien | .15 | .07 |
| ❑ 133 | John Smoltz | .30 | .14 |
| ❑ 134 | Willie Banks | .15 | .07 |
| ❑ 135 | Steve Buechele | .15 | .07 |
| ❑ 136 | Kevin Foster | .15 | .07 |
| ❑ 137 | Glenallen Hill | .15 | .07 |
| ❑ 138 | Rey Sanchez | .15 | .07 |
| ❑ 139 | Sammy Sosa | 1.25 | .55 |
| ❑ 140 | Steve Trachsel | .15 | .07 |
| ❑ 141 | Rick Wilkins | .15 | .07 |
| ❑ 142 | Jeff Brantley | .15 | .07 |
| ❑ 143 | Hector Carrasco | .15 | .07 |
| ❑ 144 | Kevin Jarvis | .15 | .07 |
| ❑ 145 | Barry Larkin | .60 | .25 |
| ❑ 146 | Chuck McElroy | .15 | .07 |
| ❑ 147 | Jose Rijo | .15 | .07 |
| ❑ 148 | Johnny Ruffin | .15 | .07 |
| ❑ 149 | Deion Sanders | .30 | .14 |
| ❑ 150 | Eddie Taubensee | .15 | .07 |
| ❑ 151 | Dante Bichette | .30 | .14 |
| ❑ 152 | Ellis Burks | .30 | .14 |
| ❑ 153 | Joe Girardi | .15 | .07 |
| ❑ 154 | Charlie Hayes | .15 | .07 |
| ❑ 155 | Mike Kingery | .15 | .07 |
| ❑ 156 | Steve Reed | .15 | .07 |
| ❑ 157 | Kevin Ritz | .15 | .07 |
| ❑ 158 | Bruce Ruffin | .15 | .07 |
| ❑ 159 | Eric Young | .15 | .07 |
| ❑ 160 | Kurt Abbott | .15 | .07 |
| ❑ 161 | Chuck Carr | .15 | .07 |
| ❑ 162 | Chris Hammond | .15 | .07 |
| ❑ 163 | Bryan Harvey | .15 | .07 |
| ❑ 164 | Terry Mathews | .15 | .07 |
| ❑ 165 | Yorkis Perez | .15 | .07 |
| ❑ 166 | Pat Rapp | .15 | .07 |
| ❑ 167 | Gary Sheffield | .60 | .25 |
| ❑ 168 | Dave Weathers | .15 | .07 |
| ❑ 169 | Jeff Bagwell | .75 | .35 |
| ❑ 170 | Ken Caminiti | .30 | .14 |
| ❑ 171 | Doug Drabek | .15 | .07 |
| ❑ 172 | Steve Finley | .30 | .14 |
| ❑ 173 | John Hudek | .15 | .07 |
| ❑ 174 | Todd Jones | .15 | .07 |
| ❑ 175 | James Mouton | .15 | .07 |
| ❑ 176 | Shane Reynolds | .15 | .07 |
| ❑ 177 | Scott Servais | .15 | .07 |
| ❑ 178 | Tom Candiotti | .15 | .07 |
| ❑ 179 | Omar Daal | .15 | .07 |
| ❑ 180 | Darren Dreifort | .30 | .14 |
| ❑ 181 | Eric Karros | .30 | .14 |
| ❑ 182 | Ramon J.Martinez | .15 | .07 |
| ❑ 183 | Raul Mondesi | .30 | .14 |
| ❑ 184 | Henry Rodriguez | .15 | .07 |
| ❑ 185 | Todd Worrell | .15 | .07 |
| ❑ 186 | Moises Alou | .30 | .14 |
| ❑ 187 | Sean Berry | .15 | .07 |
| ❑ 188 | Wil Cordero | .15 | .07 |
| ❑ 189 | Jeff Fassero | .15 | .07 |
| ❑ 190 | Darrin Fletcher | .15 | .07 |
| ❑ 191 | Butch Henry | .15 | .07 |
| ❑ 192 | Ken Hill | .15 | .07 |
| ❑ 193 | Mel Rojas | .15 | .07 |
| ❑ 194 | John Wetteland | .30 | .14 |
| ❑ 195 | Bobby Bonilla | .30 | .14 |
| ❑ 196 | Rico Brogna | .15 | .07 |
| ❑ 197 | Bobby Jones | .15 | .07 |
| ❑ 198 | Jeff Kent | .30 | .14 |
| ❑ 199 | Josias Manzanillo | .15 | .07 |
| ❑ 200 | Kelly Stinnett | .15 | .07 |
| ❑ 201 | Ryan Thompson | .15 | .07 |
| ❑ 202 | Jose Vizcaino | .15 | .07 |
| ❑ 203 | Lenny Dykstra | .30 | .14 |
| ❑ 204 | Jim Eisenreich | .15 | .07 |
| ❑ 205 | Dave Hollins | .15 | .07 |
| ❑ 206 | Mike Lieberthal | .30 | .14 |
| ❑ 207 | Mickey Morandini | .15 | .07 |
| ❑ 208 | Bobby Munoz | .15 | .07 |
| ❑ 209 | Curt Schilling | .30 | .14 |
| ❑ 210 | Heathcliff Slocumb | .15 | .07 |
| ❑ 211 | David West | .30 | .14 |
| ❑ 212 | Dave Clark | .15 | .07 |
| ❑ 213 | Steve Cooke | .15 | .07 |
| ❑ 214 | Midre Cummings | .15 | .07 |
| ❑ 215 | Carlos Garcia | .15 | .07 |
| ❑ 216 | Jeff King | .15 | .07 |
| ❑ 217 | Jon Lieber | .15 | .07 |
| ❑ 218 | Orlando Merced | .15 | .07 |
| ❑ 219 | Don Slaught | .15 | .07 |
| ❑ 220 | Rick White | .15 | .07 |
| ❑ 221 | Rene Arocha | .15 | .07 |
| ❑ 222 | Bernard Gilkey | .15 | .07 |
| ❑ 223 | Brian Jordan | .30 | .14 |
| ❑ 224 | Tom Pagnozzi | .15 | .07 |
| ❑ 225 | Vicente Palacios | .15 | .07 |
| ❑ 226 | Geronimo Pena | .15 | .07 |
| ❑ 227 | Ozzie Smith | .75 | .35 |
| ❑ 228 | Allen Watson | .15 | .07 |
| ❑ 229 | Mark Whiten | .15 | .07 |
| ❑ 230 | Brad Ausmus | .15 | .07 |
| ❑ 231 | Derek Bell | .15 | .07 |
| ❑ 232 | Andy Benes | .15 | .07 |
| ❑ 233 | Tony Gwynn | 1.25 | .55 |
| ❑ 234 | Joey Hamilton | .15 | .07 |
| ❑ 235 | Luis Lopez | .15 | .07 |
| ❑ 236 | Pedro A.Martinez | .15 | .07 |
| ❑ 237 | Scott Sanders | .15 | .07 |
| ❑ 238 | Eddie Williams | .15 | .07 |
| ❑ 239 | Rod Beck | .15 | .07 |
| ❑ 240 | Dave Burba | .15 | .07 |
| ❑ 241 | Darren Lewis | .15 | .07 |
| ❑ 242 | Kirt Manwaring | .15 | .07 |
| ❑ 243 | Mark Portugal | .15 | .07 |
| ❑ 244 | Darryl Strawberry | .30 | .14 |
| ❑ 245 | Robby Thompson | .15 | .07 |
| ❑ 246 | Wm.VanLandingham | .15 | .07 |
| ❑ 247 | Matt Williams | .30 | .14 |
| ❑ 248 | Checklist | .15 | .07 |
| ❑ 249 | Checklist | .15 | .07 |
| ❑ 250 | Checklist | .15 | .07 |
| ❑ 251 | Harold Baines | .30 | .14 |
| ❑ 252 | Bret Barberie | .15 | .07 |
| ❑ 253 | Armando Benitez | .30 | .14 |
| ❑ 254 | Mike Devereaux | .15 | .07 |
| ❑ 255 | Leo Gomez | .15 | .07 |
| ❑ 256 | Jamie Moyer | .15 | .07 |
| ❑ 257 | Arthur Rhodes | .15 | .07 |
| ❑ 258 | Cal Ripken | 2.50 | 1.10 |
| ❑ 259 | Luis Alicea | .15 | .07 |
| ❑ 260 | Jose Canseco | .75 | .35 |
| ❑ 261 | Scott Cooper | .15 | .07 |
| ❑ 262 | Andre Dawson | .30 | .14 |
| ❑ 263 | Mike Greenwell | .15 | .07 |
| ❑ 264 | Aaron Sele | .30 | .14 |
| ❑ 265 | Garret Anderson | .30 | .14 |
| ❑ 266 | Chad Curtis | .15 | .07 |
| ❑ 267 | Gary DiSarcina | .15 | .07 |
| ❑ 268 | Chuck Finley | .30 | .14 |
| ❑ 269 | Rex Hudler | .15 | .07 |
| ❑ 270 | Andrew Lorraine | .15 | .07 |
| ❑ 271 | Spike Owen | .15 | .07 |
| ❑ 272 | Lee Smith | .30 | .14 |
| ❑ 273 | Jason Bere | .15 | .07 |
| ❑ 274 | Ozzie Guillen | .15 | .07 |
| ❑ 275 | Norberto Martin | .15 | .07 |
| ❑ 276 | Scott Ruffcorn | .15 | .07 |
| ❑ 277 | Robin Ventura | .30 | .14 |
| ❑ 278 | Carlos Baerga | .15 | .07 |
| ❑ 279 | Jason Grimsley | .15 | .07 |
| ❑ 280 | Dennis Martinez | .30 | .14 |
| ❑ 281 | Charles Nagy | .15 | .07 |
| ❑ 282 | Paul Sorrento | .15 | .07 |
| ❑ 283 | Dave Winfield | .60 | .25 |
| ❑ 284 | John Doherty | .15 | .07 |
| ❑ 285 | Travis Fryman | .30 | .14 |
| ❑ 286 | Kirk Gibson | .30 | .14 |
| ❑ 287 | Lou Whitaker | .30 | .14 |
| ❑ 288 | Gary Gaetti | .30 | .14 |
| ❑ 289 | Tom Gordon | .15 | .07 |
| ❑ 290 | Mark Gubicza | .15 | .07 |
| ❑ 291 | Wally Joyner | .30 | .14 |
| ❑ 292 | Mike Macfarlane | .15 | .07 |
| ❑ 293 | Jeff Montgomery | .15 | .07 |
| ❑ 294 | Jeff Cirillo | .30 | .14 |
| ❑ 295 | Cal Eldred | .15 | .07 |
| ❑ 296 | Pat Listach | .15 | .07 |
| ❑ 297 | Jose Mercedes | .15 | .07 |
| ❑ 298 | Dave Nilsson | .15 | .07 |
| ❑ 299 | Duane Singleton | .15 | .07 |
| ❑ 300 | Greg Vaughn | .30 | .14 |
| ❑ 301 | Scott Erickson | .15 | .07 |
| ❑ 302 | Denny Hocking | .15 | .07 |
| ❑ 303 | Chuck Knoblauch | .30 | .14 |
| ❑ 304 | Pat Mahomes | .15 | .07 |
| ❑ 305 | Pedro Munoz | .15 | .07 |
| ❑ 306 | Erik Schullstrom | .15 | .07 |
| ❑ 307 | Jim Abbott | .30 | .14 |
| ❑ 308 | Tony Fernandez | .15 | .07 |
| ❑ 309 | Sterling Hitchcock | .15 | .07 |
| ❑ 310 | Jim Leyritz | .15 | .07 |
| ❑ 311 | Don Mattingly | 1.50 | .70 |
| ❑ 312 | Jack McDowell | .15 | .07 |
| ❑ 313 | Melido Perez | .15 | .07 |
| ❑ 314 | Bernie Williams | .60 | .25 |
| ❑ 315 | Scott Brosius | .30 | .14 |
| ❑ 316 | Dennis Eckersley | .30 | .14 |
| ❑ 317 | Brent Gates | .15 | .07 |
| ❑ 318 | Rickey Henderson | .75 | .35 |
| ❑ 319 | Steve Karsay | .15 | .07 |
| ❑ 320 | Steve Ontiveros | .15 | .07 |
| ❑ 321 | Bill Taylor | .15 | .07 |
| ❑ 322 | Todd Van Poppel | .15 | .07 |
| ❑ 323 | Bob Welch | .15 | .07 |
| ❑ 324 | Bobby Ayala | .15 | .07 |
| ❑ 325 | Mike Blowers | .15 | .07 |
| ❑ 326 | Jay Buhner | .30 | .14 |
| ❑ 327 | Felix Fermin | .15 | .07 |
| ❑ 328 | Tino Martinez | .30 | .14 |
| ❑ 329 | Marc Newfield | .15 | .07 |
| ❑ 330 | Greg Pirkl | .15 | .07 |
| ❑ 331 | Alex Rodriguez | 2.50 | 1.10 |
| ❑ 332 | Kevin Brown | .30 | .14 |
| ❑ 333 | John Burkett | .15 | .07 |
| ❑ 334 | Jeff Frye | .15 | .07 |
| ❑ 335 | Kevin Gross | .15 | .07 |
| ❑ 336 | Dean Palmer | .30 | .14 |
| ❑ 337 | Joe Carter | .30 | .14 |
| ❑ 338 | Shawn Green | .60 | .25 |
| ❑ 339 | Juan Guzman | .15 | .07 |
| ❑ 340 | Mike Huff | .15 | .07 |
| ❑ 341 | Al Leiter | .30 | .14 |
| ❑ 342 | John Olerud | .30 | .14 |
| ❑ 343 | Dave Stewart | .30 | .14 |
| ❑ 344 | Todd Stottlemyre | .15 | .07 |
| ❑ 345 | Steve Avery | .15 | .07 |
| ❑ 346 | Jeff Blauser | .15 | .07 |
| ❑ 347 | Chipper Jones | 1.50 | .70 |
| ❑ 348 | Mike Kelly | .15 | .07 |
| ❑ 349 | Ryan Klesko | .30 | .14 |
| ❑ 350 | Javier Lopez | .30 | .14 |
| ❑ 351 | Fred McGriff | .30 | .14 |
| ❑ 352 | Jose Oliva | .15 | .07 |
| ❑ 353 | Terry Pendleton | .30 | .14 |
| ❑ 354 | Mike Stanton | .15 | .07 |
| ❑ 355 | Tony Tarasco | .15 | .07 |
| ❑ 356 | Mark Wohlers | .15 | .07 |
| ❑ 357 | Jim Bullinger | .15 | .07 |

| | No. | Player | Mint | NRMT |
|---|---|---|---|---|
| ❑ | 358 | Shawon Dunston | .15 | .07 |
| ❑ | 359 | Mark Grace | .60 | .25 |
| ❑ | 360 | Derrick May | .15 | .07 |
| ❑ | 361 | Randy Myers | .15 | .07 |
| ❑ | 362 | Karl Rhodes | .15 | .07 |
| ❑ | 363 | Bret Boone | .30 | .14 |
| ❑ | 364 | Brian Dorsett | .15 | .07 |
| ❑ | 365 | Ron Gant | .15 | .07 |
| ❑ | 366 | Brian R.Hunter | .15 | .07 |
| ❑ | 367 | Hal Morris | .15 | .07 |
| ❑ | 368 | Jack Morris | .30 | .14 |
| ❑ | 369 | John Roper | .15 | .07 |
| ❑ | 370 | Reggie Sanders | .15 | .07 |
| ❑ | 371 | Pete Schourek | .15 | .07 |
| ❑ | 372 | John Smiley | .15 | .07 |
| ❑ | 373 | Marvin Freeman | .15 | .07 |
| ❑ | 374 | Andres Galarraga | .30 | .14 |
| ❑ | 375 | Mike Munoz | .15 | .07 |
| ❑ | 376 | David Nied | .15 | .07 |
| ❑ | 377 | Walt Weiss | .15 | .07 |
| ❑ | 378 | Greg Colbrunn | .15 | .07 |
| ❑ | 379 | Jeff Conine | .15 | .07 |
| ❑ | 380 | Charles Johnson | .30 | .14 |
| ❑ | 381 | Kurt Miller | .15 | .07 |
| ❑ | 382 | Robb Nen | .15 | .07 |
| ❑ | 383 | Benito Santiago | .15 | .07 |
| ❑ | 384 | Craig Biggio | .30 | .14 |
| ❑ | 385 | Tony Eusebio | .15 | .07 |
| ❑ | 386 | Luis Gonzalez | .15 | .07 |
| ❑ | 387 | Brian L.Hunter | .15 | .07 |
| ❑ | 388 | Darryl Kile | .30 | .14 |
| ❑ | 389 | Orlando Miller | .15 | .07 |
| ❑ | 390 | Phil Plantier | .15 | .07 |
| ❑ | 391 | Greg Swindell | .15 | .07 |
| ❑ | 392 | Billy Ashley | .15 | .07 |
| ❑ | 393 | Pedro Astacio | .15 | .07 |
| ❑ | 394 | Brett Butler | .30 | .14 |
| ❑ | 395 | Delino DeShields | .15 | .07 |
| ❑ | 396 | Orel Hershiser | .30 | .14 |
| ❑ | 397 | Garey Ingram | .15 | .07 |
| ❑ | 398 | Chan Ho Park | .30 | .14 |
| ❑ | 399 | Mike Piazza | 2.00 | .90 |
| ❑ | 400 | Ismael Valdes | .15 | .07 |
| ❑ | 401 | Tim Wallach | .15 | .07 |
| ❑ | 402 | Cliff Floyd | .30 | .14 |
| ❑ | 403 | Marquis Grissom | .15 | .07 |
| ❑ | 404 | Mike Lansing | .15 | .07 |
| ❑ | 405 | Pedro Martinez | .75 | .35 |
| ❑ | 406 | Kirk Rueter | .15 | .07 |
| ❑ | 407 | Tim Scott | .15 | .07 |
| ❑ | 408 | Jeff Shaw | .15 | .07 |
| ❑ | 409 | Larry Walker | .30 | .14 |
| ❑ | 410 | Rondell White | .30 | .14 |
| ❑ | 411 | John Franco | .30 | .14 |
| ❑ | 412 | Todd Hundley | .15 | .07 |
| ❑ | 413 | Jason Jacome | .15 | .07 |
| ❑ | 414 | Joe Orsulak | .15 | .07 |
| ❑ | 415 | Bret Saberhagen | .30 | .14 |
| ❑ | 416 | David Segui | .15 | .07 |
| ❑ | 417 | Darren Daulton | .30 | .14 |
| ❑ | 418 | Mariano Duncan | .15 | .07 |
| ❑ | 419 | Tommy Greene | .15 | .07 |
| ❑ | 420 | Gregg Jefferies | .15 | .07 |
| ❑ | 421 | John Kruk | .30 | .14 |
| ❑ | 422 | Kevin Stocker | .15 | .07 |
| ❑ | 423 | Jay Bell | .30 | .14 |
| ❑ | 424 | Al Martin | .15 | .07 |
| ❑ | 425 | Denny Neagle | .30 | .14 |
| ❑ | 426 | Zane Smith | .15 | .07 |
| ❑ | 427 | Andy Van Slyke | .30 | .14 |
| ❑ | 428 | Paul Wagner | .15 | .07 |
| ❑ | 429 | Tom Henke | .15 | .07 |
| ❑ | 430 | Danny Jackson | .15 | .07 |
| ❑ | 431 | Ray Lankford | .30 | .14 |
| ❑ | 432 | John Mabry | .15 | .07 |
| ❑ | 433 | Bob Tewksbury | .15 | .07 |
| ❑ | 434 | Todd Zeile | .15 | .07 |
| ❑ | 435 | Andy Ashby | .15 | .07 |
| ❑ | 436 | Andujar Cedeno | .15 | .07 |
| ❑ | 437 | Donnie Elliott | .15 | .07 |
| ❑ | 438 | Bryce Florie | .15 | .07 |
| ❑ | 439 | Trevor Hoffman | .30 | .14 |
| ❑ | 440 | Melvin Nieves | .15 | .07 |
| ❑ | 441 | Bip Roberts | .15 | .07 |
| ❑ | 442 | Barry Bonds | 1.00 | .45 |
| ❑ | 443 | Royce Clayton | .15 | .07 |
| ❑ | 444 | Mike Jackson | .15 | .07 |
| ❑ | 445 | John Patterson | .15 | .07 |
| ❑ | 446 | J.R. Phillips | .15 | .07 |
| ❑ | 447 | Bill Swift | .15 | .07 |
| ❑ | 448 | Checklist | .15 | .07 |
| ❑ | 449 | Checklist | .15 | .07 |
| ❑ | 450 | Checklist | .15 | .07 |

## 1996 Ultra

| | MINT | NRMT |
|---|---|---|
| COMPLETE SET (600) | 60.00 | 27.00 |
| COMPLETE SERIES 1 (300) | 30.00 | 13.50 |
| COMPLETE SERIES 2 (300) | 30.00 | 13.50 |

| | No. | Player | Mint | NRMT |
|---|---|---|---|---|
| ❑ | 1 | Manny Alexander | .15 | .07 |
| ❑ | 2 | Brady Anderson | .25 | .11 |
| ❑ | 3 | Bobby Bonilla | .25 | .11 |
| ❑ | 4 | Scott Erickson | .15 | .07 |
| ❑ | 5 | Curtis Goodwin | .15 | .07 |
| ❑ | 6 | Chris Hoiles | .15 | .07 |
| ❑ | 7 | Doug Jones | .15 | .07 |
| ❑ | 8 | Jeff Manto | .15 | .07 |
| ❑ | 9 | Mike Mussina | .60 | .25 |
| ❑ | 10 | Rafael Palmeiro | .60 | .25 |
| ❑ | 11 | Cal Ripken | 2.50 | 1.10 |
| ❑ | 12 | Rick Aguilera | .15 | .07 |
| ❑ | 13 | Luis Alicea | .15 | .07 |
| ❑ | 14 | Stan Belinda | .15 | .07 |
| ❑ | 15 | Jose Canseco | .75 | .35 |
| ❑ | 16 | Roger Clemens | 1.25 | .55 |
| ❑ | 17 | Mike Greenwell | .15 | .07 |
| ❑ | 18 | Mike Macfarlane | .15 | .07 |
| ❑ | 19 | Tim Naehring | .15 | .07 |
| ❑ | 20 | Troy O'Leary | .15 | .07 |
| ❑ | 21 | John Valentin | .15 | .07 |
| ❑ | 22 | Mo Vaughn | .25 | .11 |
| ❑ | 23 | Tim Wakefield | .15 | .07 |
| ❑ | 24 | Brian Anderson | .15 | .07 |
| ❑ | 25 | Garret Anderson | .25 | .11 |
| ❑ | 26 | Chili Davis | .25 | .11 |
| ❑ | 27 | Gary DiSarcina | .15 | .07 |
| ❑ | 28 | Jim Edmonds | .60 | .25 |
| ❑ | 29 | Jorge Fabregas | .15 | .07 |
| ❑ | 30 | Chuck Finley | .25 | .11 |
| ❑ | 31 | Mark Langston | .15 | .07 |
| ❑ | 32 | Troy Percival | .15 | .07 |
| ❑ | 33 | Tim Salmon | .25 | .11 |
| ❑ | 34 | Lee Smith | .25 | .11 |
| ❑ | 35 | Wilson Alvarez | .15 | .07 |
| ❑ | 36 | Ray Durham | .25 | .11 |
| ❑ | 37 | Alex Fernandez | .15 | .07 |
| ❑ | 38 | Ozzie Guillen | .15 | .07 |
| ❑ | 39 | Roberto Hernandez | .15 | .07 |
| ❑ | 40 | Lance Johnson | .15 | .07 |
| ❑ | 41 | Ron Karkovice | .15 | .07 |
| ❑ | 42 | Lyle Mouton | .15 | .07 |
| ❑ | 43 | Tim Raines | .25 | .11 |
| ❑ | 44 | Frank Thomas | 1.25 | .55 |
| ❑ | 45 | Carlos Baerga | .15 | .07 |
| ❑ | 46 | Albert Belle | .40 | .18 |
| ❑ | 47 | Orel Hershiser | .25 | .11 |
| ❑ | 48 | Kenny Lofton | .25 | .11 |
| ❑ | 49 | Dennis Martinez | .25 | .11 |
| ❑ | 50 | Jose Mesa | .15 | .07 |
| ❑ | 51 | Eddie Murray | .60 | .25 |
| ❑ | 52 | Chad Ogea | .15 | .07 |
| ❑ | 53 | Manny Ramirez | .75 | .35 |
| ❑ | 54 | Jim Thome | .40 | .18 |
| ❑ | 55 | Omar Vizquel | .25 | .11 |
| ❑ | 56 | Dave Winfield | .60 | .25 |
| ❑ | 57 | Chad Curtis | .15 | .07 |
| ❑ | 58 | Cecil Fielder | .25 | .11 |
| ❑ | 59 | John Flaherty | .15 | .07 |
| ❑ | 60 | Travis Fryman | .25 | .11 |
| ❑ | 61 | Chris Gomez | .15 | .07 |
| ❑ | 62 | Bob Higginson | .25 | .11 |
| ❑ | 63 | Felipe Lira | .15 | .07 |
| ❑ | 64 | Brian Maxcy | .15 | .07 |
| ❑ | 65 | Alan Trammell | .40 | .18 |
| ❑ | 66 | Lou Whitaker | .25 | .11 |
| ❑ | 67 | Kevin Appier | .25 | .11 |
| ❑ | 68 | Gary Gaetti | .25 | .11 |
| ❑ | 69 | Tom Goodwin | .15 | .07 |
| ❑ | 70 | Tom Gordon | .15 | .07 |
| ❑ | 71 | Jason Jacome | .15 | .07 |
| ❑ | 72 | Wally Joyner | .25 | .11 |
| ❑ | 73 | Brent Mayne | .15 | .07 |
| ❑ | 74 | Jeff Montgomery | .15 | .07 |
| ❑ | 75 | Jon Nunnally | .15 | .07 |
| ❑ | 76 | Joe Vitiello | .15 | .07 |
| ❑ | 77 | Ricky Bones | .15 | .07 |
| ❑ | 78 | Jeff Cirillo | .25 | .11 |
| ❑ | 79 | Mike Fetters | .15 | .07 |
| ❑ | 80 | Darryl Hamilton | .15 | .07 |
| ❑ | 81 | David Hulse | .15 | .07 |
| ❑ | 82 | Dave Nilsson | .15 | .07 |
| ❑ | 83 | Kevin Seitzer | .15 | .07 |
| ❑ | 84 | Steve Sparks | .15 | .07 |
| ❑ | 85 | B.J. Surhoff | .25 | .11 |
| ❑ | 86 | Jose Valentin | .15 | .07 |
| ❑ | 87 | Greg Vaughn | .25 | .11 |
| ❑ | 88 | Marty Cordova | .15 | .07 |
| ❑ | 89 | Chuck Knoblauch | .25 | .11 |
| ❑ | 90 | Pat Meares | .15 | .07 |
| ❑ | 91 | Pedro Munoz | .15 | .07 |
| ❑ | 92 | Kirby Puckett | 1.50 | .70 |
| ❑ | 93 | Brad Radke | .25 | .11 |
| ❑ | 94 | Scott Stahoviak | .15 | .07 |
| ❑ | 95 | Dave Stevens | .15 | .07 |
| ❑ | 96 | Mike Trombley | .15 | .07 |
| ❑ | 97 | Matt Walbeck | .15 | .07 |
| ❑ | 98 | Wade Boggs | .75 | .35 |
| ❑ | 99 | Russ Davis | .15 | .07 |
| ❑ | 100 | Jim Leyritz | .15 | .07 |
| ❑ | 101 | Don Mattingly | 1.50 | .70 |
| ❑ | 102 | Jack McDowell | .15 | .07 |
| ❑ | 103 | Paul O'Neill | .25 | .11 |
| ❑ | 104 | Andy Pettitte | .25 | .11 |
| ❑ | 105 | Mariano Rivera | .25 | .11 |
| ❑ | 106 | Ruben Sierra | .15 | .07 |
| ❑ | 107 | Darryl Strawberry | .25 | .11 |
| ❑ | 108 | John Wetteland | .25 | .11 |
| ❑ | 109 | Bernie Williams | .60 | .25 |
| ❑ | 110 | Geronimo Berroa | .15 | .07 |
| ❑ | 111 | Scott Brosius | .25 | .11 |
| ❑ | 112 | Dennis Eckersley | .25 | .11 |
| ❑ | 113 | Brent Gates | .15 | .07 |
| ❑ | 114 | Rickey Henderson | .75 | .35 |
| ❑ | 115 | Mark McGwire | 2.50 | 1.10 |
| ❑ | 116 | Ariel Prieto | .15 | .07 |
| ❑ | 117 | Terry Steinbach | .15 | .07 |
| ❑ | 118 | Todd Stottlemyre | .15 | .07 |
| ❑ | 119 | Todd Van Poppel | .15 | .07 |
| ❑ | 120 | Steve Wojciechowski | .15 | .07 |
| ❑ | 121 | Rich Amaral | .15 | .07 |
| ❑ | 122 | Bobby Ayala | .15 | .07 |
| ❑ | 123 | Mike Blowers | .15 | .07 |
| ❑ | 124 | Chris Bosio | .15 | .07 |
| ❑ | 125 | Joey Cora | .15 | .07 |
| ❑ | 126 | Ken Griffey Jr. | 2.50 | 1.10 |
| ❑ | 127 | Randy Johnson | .75 | .35 |
| ❑ | 128 | Edgar Martinez | .40 | .18 |
| ❑ | 129 | Tino Martinez | .25 | .11 |
| ❑ | 130 | Alex Rodriguez | 2.00 | .90 |
| ❑ | 131 | Dan Wilson | .15 | .07 |
| ❑ | 132 | Will Clark | .60 | .25 |
| ❑ | 133 | Jeff Frye | .15 | .07 |
| ❑ | 134 | Benji Gil | .15 | .07 |
| ❑ | 135 | Juan Gonzalez | .60 | .25 |
| ❑ | 136 | Rusty Greer | .25 | .11 |
| ❑ | 137 | Mark McLemore | .15 | .07 |
| ❑ | 138 | Roger Pavlik | .15 | .07 |
| ❑ | 139 | Ivan Rodriguez | .75 | .35 |

❑ 140 Kenny Rogers .15 .07
❑ 141 Mickey Tettleton .15 .07
❑ 142 Roberto Alomar .60 .25
❑ 143 Joe Carter .25 .11
❑ 144 Tony Castillo .15 .07
❑ 145 Alex Gonzalez .15 .07
❑ 146 Shawn Green .60 .25
❑ 147 Pat Hentgen .15 .07
❑ 148 Sandy Martinez .15 .07
❑ 149 Paul Molitor .60 .25
❑ 150 John Olerud .25 .11
❑ 151 Ed Sprague .15 .07
❑ 152 Jeff Blauser .15 .07
❑ 153 Brad Clontz .15 .07
❑ 154 Tom Glavine .60 .25
❑ 155 Marquis Grissom .15 .07
❑ 156 Chipper Jones 1.50 .70
❑ 157 David Justice .40 .18
❑ 158 Ryan Klesko .25 .11
❑ 159 Javier Lopez .25 .11
❑ 160 Greg Maddux 1.50 .70
❑ 161 John Smoltz .25 .11
❑ 162 Mark Wohlers .15 .07
❑ 163 Jim Bullinger .15 .07
❑ 164 Frank Castillo .15 .07
❑ 165 Shawon Dunston .15 .07
❑ 166 Kevin Foster .15 .07
❑ 167 Luis Gonzalez .25 .11
❑ 168 Mark Grace .60 .25
❑ 169 Rey Sanchez .15 .07
❑ 170 Scott Servais .15 .07
❑ 171 Sammy Sosa 1.25 .55
❑ 172 Ozzie Timmons .15 .07
❑ 173 Steve Trachsel .15 .07
❑ 174 Bret Boone .25 .11
❑ 175 Jeff Branson .15 .07
❑ 176 Jeff Brantley .15 .07
❑ 177 Dave Burba .15 .07
❑ 178 Ron Gant .15 .07
❑ 179 Barry Larkin .60 .25
❑ 180 Darren Lewis .15 .07
❑ 181 Mark Portugal .15 .07
❑ 182 Reggie Sanders .15 .07
❑ 183 Pete Schourek .15 .07
❑ 184 John Smiley .15 .07
❑ 185 Jason Bates .15 .07
❑ 186 Dante Bichette .25 .11
❑ 187 Ellis Burks .25 .11
❑ 188 Vinny Castilla .25 .11
❑ 189 Andres Galarraga .40 .18
❑ 190 Darren Holmes .15 .07
❑ 191 Armando Reynoso .15 .07
❑ 192 Kevin Ritz .15 .07
❑ 193 Bill Swift .15 .07
❑ 194 Larry Walker .25 .11
❑ 195 Kurt Abbott .15 .07
❑ 196 John Burkett .15 .07
❑ 197 Greg Colbrunn .15 .07
❑ 198 Jeff Conine .15 .07
❑ 199 Andre Dawson .40 .18
❑ 200 Chris Hammond .15 .07
❑ 201 Charles Johnson .25 .11
❑ 202 Robb Nen .15 .07
❑ 203 Terry Pendleton .25 .11
❑ 204 Quilvio Veras .15 .07
❑ 205 Jeff Bagwell .75 .35
❑ 206 Derek Bell .15 .07
❑ 207 Doug Drabek .15 .07
❑ 208 Tony Eusebio .15 .07
❑ 209 Mike Hampton .25 .11
❑ 210 Brian L. Hunter .15 .07
❑ 211 Todd Jones .15 .07
❑ 212 Orlando Miller .15 .07
❑ 213 James Mouton .15 .07
❑ 214 Shane Reynolds .15 .07
❑ 215 Dave Veres .15 .07
❑ 216 Billy Ashley .15 .07
❑ 217 Brett Butler .25 .11
❑ 218 Chad Fonville .15 .07
❑ 219 Todd Hollandsworth .15 .07
❑ 220 Eric Karros .25 .11
❑ 221 Ramon Martinez .15 .07
❑ 222 Raul Mondesi .25 .11
❑ 223 Hideo Nomo .60 .25
❑ 224 Mike Piazza 2.00 .90
❑ 225 Kevin Tapani .15 .07
❑ 226 Ismael Valdes .15 .07
❑ 227 Todd Worrell .15 .07
❑ 228 Moises Alou .25 .11
❑ 229 Wil Cordero .15 .07
❑ 230 Jeff Fassero .15 .07
❑ 231 Darrin Fletcher .15 .07
❑ 232 Mike Lansing .15 .07
❑ 233 Pedro Martinez .75 .35
❑ 234 Carlos Perez .15 .07
❑ 235 Mel Rojas .15 .07
❑ 236 David Segui .15 .07
❑ 237 Tony Tarasco .15 .07
❑ 238 Rondell White .25 .11
❑ 239 Edgardo Alfonzo .25 .11
❑ 240 Rico Brogna .15 .07
❑ 241 Carl Everett .25 .11
❑ 242 Todd Hundley .15 .07
❑ 243 Butch Huskey .15 .07
❑ 244 Jason Isringhausen .25 .11
❑ 245 Bobby Jones .15 .07
❑ 246 Jeff Kent .40 .18
❑ 247 Bill Pulsipher .15 .07
❑ 248 Jose Vizcaino .15 .07
❑ 249 Ricky Bottalico .15 .07
❑ 250 Darren Daulton .25 .11
❑ 251 Jim Eisenreich .15 .07
❑ 252 Tyler Green .15 .07
❑ 253 Charlie Hayes .15 .07
❑ 254 Gregg Jefferies .15 .07
❑ 255 Tony Longmire .15 .07
❑ 256 Michael Mimbs .15 .07
❑ 257 Mickey Morandini .15 .07
❑ 258 Paul Quantrill .15 .07
❑ 259 Heathcliff Slocumb .15 .07
❑ 260 Jay Bell .25 .11
❑ 261 Jacob Brumfield .15 .07
❑ 262 Angelo Encarnacion RC .15 .07
❑ 263 John Ericks .15 .07
❑ 264 Mark Johnson .15 .07
❑ 265 Esteban Loaiza .15 .07
❑ 266 Al Martin .15 .07
❑ 267 Orlando Merced .15 .07
❑ 268 Dan Miceli .15 .07
❑ 269 Denny Neagle .25 .11
❑ 270 Brian Barber .15 .07
❑ 271 Scott Cooper .15 .07
❑ 272 Tripp Cromer .15 .07
❑ 273 Bernard Gilkey .15 .07
❑ 274 Tom Henke .15 .07
❑ 275 Brian Jordan .25 .11
❑ 276 John Mabry .15 .07
❑ 277 Tom Pagnozzi .15 .07
❑ 278 Mark Petkovsek .15 .07
❑ 279 Ozzie Smith .75 .35
❑ 280 Andy Ashby .15 .07
❑ 281 Brad Ausmus .15 .07
❑ 282 Ken Caminiti .25 .11
❑ 283 Glenn Dishman .15 .07
❑ 284 Tony Gwynn 1.25 .55
❑ 285 Joey Hamilton .15 .07
❑ 286 Trevor Hoffman .25 .11
❑ 287 Phil Plantier .15 .07
❑ 288 Jody Reed .15 .07
❑ 289 Eddie Williams .15 .07
❑ 290 Barry Bonds 1.00 .45
❑ 291 Jamie Brewington RC .15 .07
❑ 292 Mark Carreon .15 .07
❑ 293 Royce Clayton .15 .07
❑ 294 Glenallen Hill .15 .07
❑ 295 Mark Leiter .15 .07
❑ 296 Kirt Manwaring .15 .07
❑ 297 J.R. Phillips .15 .07
❑ 298 Deion Sanders .25 .11
❑ 299 Wm. VanLandingham .15 .07
❑ 300 Matt Williams .40 .18
❑ 301 Roberto Alomar .60 .25
❑ 302 Armando Benitez .15 .07
❑ 303 Mike Devereaux .15 .07
❑ 304 Jeffrey Hammonds .25 .11
❑ 305 Jimmy Haynes .15 .07
❑ 306 Scott McClain .15 .07
❑ 307 Kent Mercker .15 .07
❑ 308 Randy Myers .15 .07
❑ 309 B.J. Surhoff .25 .11
❑ 310 Tony Tarasco .15 .07
❑ 311 David Wells .25 .11
❑ 312 Wil Cordero .15 .07
❑ 313 Alex Delgado .15 .07
❑ 314 Tom Gordon .15 .07
❑ 315 Dwayne Hosey .15 .07
❑ 316 Jose Malave .15 .07
❑ 317 Kevin Mitchell .15 .07
❑ 318 Jamie Moyer .15 .07
❑ 319 Aaron Sele .25 .11
❑ 320 Heathcliff Slocumb .15 .07
❑ 321 Mike Stanley .15 .07
❑ 322 Jeff Suppan .15 .07
❑ 323 Jim Abbott .25 .11
❑ 324 George Arias .15 .07
❑ 325 Todd Greene .15 .07
❑ 326 Bryan Harvey .15 .07
❑ 327 J.T. Snow .25 .11
❑ 328 Randy Velarde .15 .07
❑ 329 Tim Wallach .15 .07
❑ 330 Harold Baines .25 .11
❑ 331 Jason Bere .15 .07
❑ 332 Darren Lewis .15 .07
❑ 333 Norberto Martin .15 .07
❑ 334 Tony Phillips .15 .07
❑ 335 Bill Simas .15 .07
❑ 336 Chris Snopek .15 .07
❑ 337 Kevin Tapani .15 .07
❑ 338 Danny Tartabull .15 .07
❑ 339 Robin Ventura .25 .11
❑ 340 Sandy Alomar Jr. .25 .11
❑ 341 Julio Franco .25 .11
❑ 342 Jack McDowell .15 .07
❑ 343 Charles Nagy .15 .07
❑ 344 Julian Tavarez .15 .07
❑ 345 Kimera Bartee .15 .07
❑ 346 Greg Keagle .15 .07
❑ 347 Mark Lewis .15 .07
❑ 348 Jose Lima .15 .07
❑ 349 Melvin Nieves .15 .07
❑ 350 Mark Parent .15 .07
❑ 351 Eddie Williams .15 .07
❑ 352 Johnny Damon .25 .11
❑ 353 Sal Fasano .15 .07
❑ 354 Mark Gubicza .15 .07
❑ 355 Bob Hamelin .15 .07
❑ 356 Chris Haney .15 .07
❑ 357 Keith Lockhart .15 .07
❑ 358 Mike Macfarlane .15 .07
❑ 359 Jose Offerman .15 .07
❑ 360 Bip Roberts .15 .07
❑ 361 Michael Tucker .15 .07
❑ 362 Chuck Carr .15 .07
❑ 363 Bobby Hughes .15 .07
❑ 364 John Jaha .15 .07
❑ 365 Mark Loretta .15 .07
❑ 366 Mike Matheny .15 .07
❑ 367 Ben McDonald .15 .07
❑ 368 Matt Mieske .15 .07
❑ 369 Angel Miranda .15 .07
❑ 370 Fernando Vina .15 .07
❑ 371 Rick Aguilera .15 .07
❑ 372 Rich Becker .15 .07
❑ 373 LaTroy Hawkins .15 .07
❑ 374 Dave Hollins .15 .07
❑ 375 Roberto Kelly .15 .07
❑ 376 Matt Lawton RC .75 .35
❑ 377 Paul Molitor .60 .25
❑ 378 Dan Naulty .15 .07
❑ 379 Rich Robertson .15 .07
❑ 380 Frank Rodriguez .15 .07
❑ 381 David Cone .25 .11
❑ 382 Mariano Duncan .15 .07
❑ 383 Andy Fox .15 .07
❑ 384 Joe Girardi .15 .07
❑ 385 Dwight Gooden .25 .11
❑ 386 Derek Jeter 2.50 1.10
❑ 387 Pat Kelly .15 .07
❑ 388 Jimmy Key .25 .11
❑ 389 Matt Luke .15 .07
❑ 390 Tino Martinez .25 .11
❑ 391 Jeff Nelson .15 .07
❑ 392 Melido Perez .15 .07
❑ 393 Tim Raines .25 .11
❑ 394 Ruben Rivera .15 .07
❑ 395 Kenny Rogers .15 .07
❑ 396 Tony Batista RC 5.00 2.20
❑ 397 Allen Battle .15 .07

❑ 398 Mike Bordick .15 .07
❑ 399 Steve Cox .15 .07
❑ 400 Jason Giambi .60 .25
❑ 401 Doug Johns .15 .07
❑ 402 Pedro Munoz .15 .07
❑ 403 Phil Plantier .15 .07
❑ 404 Scott Spiezio .15 .07
❑ 405 George Williams .15 .07
❑ 406 Ernie Young .15 .07
❑ 407 Darren Bragg .15 .07
❑ 408 Jay Buhner .25 .11
❑ 409 Norm Charlton .15 .07
❑ 410 Russ Davis .15 .07
❑ 411 Sterling Hitchcock .15 .07
❑ 412 Edwin Hurtado .15 .07
❑ 413 Raul Ibanez RC .15 .07
❑ 414 Mike Jackson .15 .07
❑ 415 Luis Sojo .15 .07
❑ 416 Paul Sorrento .15 .07
❑ 417 Bob Wolcott .15 .07
❑ 418 Damon Buford .15 .07
❑ 419 Kevin Gross .15 .07
❑ 420 Darryl Hamilton UER .15 .07
❑ 421 Mike Henneman .15 .07
❑ 422 Ken Hill .15 .07
❑ 423 Dean Palmer .25 .11
❑ 424 Bobby Witt .15 .07
❑ 425 Tilson Brito RC .15 .07
❑ 426 Giovanni Carrara RC .15 .07
❑ 427 Domingo Cedeno .15 .07
❑ 428 Felipe Crespo .15 .07
❑ 429 Carlos Delgado .60 .25
❑ 430 Juan Guzman .15 .07
❑ 431 Erik Hanson .15 .07
❑ 432 Marty Janzen .15 .07
❑ 433 Otis Nixon .15 .07
❑ 434 Robert Perez .15 .07
❑ 435 Paul Quantrill .15 .07
❑ 436 Bill Risley .15 .07
❑ 437 Steve Avery .15 .07
❑ 438 Jermaine Dye .25 .11
❑ 439 Mark Lemke .15 .07
❑ 440 Marty Malloy RC .15 .07
❑ 441 Fred McGriff .40 .18
❑ 442 Greg McMichael .15 .07
❑ 443 Wonderful Monds RC .15 .07
❑ 444 Eddie Perez .15 .07
❑ 445 Jason Schmidt .15 .07
❑ 446 Terrell Wade .15 .07
❑ 447 Terry Adams .15 .07
❑ 448 Scott Bullett .15 .07
❑ 449 Robin Jennings .15 .07
❑ 450 Doug Jones .15 .07
❑ 451 Brooks Kieschnick .15 .07
❑ 452 Dave Magadan .15 .07
❑ 453 Jason Maxwell RC .15 .07
❑ 454 Brian McRae .15 .07
❑ 455 Rodney Myers RC .15 .07
❑ 456 Jaime Navarro .15 .07
❑ 457 Ryne Sandberg .75 .35
❑ 458 Vince Coleman .15 .07
❑ 459 Eric Davis .25 .11
❑ 460 Steve Gibralter .15 .07
❑ 461 Thomas Howard .15 .07
❑ 462 Mike Kelly .15 .07
❑ 463 Hal Morris .15 .07
❑ 464 Eric Owens .15 .07
❑ 465 Jose Rijo .15 .07
❑ 466 Chris Sabo .15 .07
❑ 467 Eddie Taubensee .15 .07
❑ 468 Trenidad Hubbard .15 .07
❑ 469 Curt Leskanic .15 .07
❑ 470 Quinton McCracken .15 .07
❑ 471 Jayhawk Owens .15 .07
❑ 472 Steve Reed .15 .07
❑ 473 Bryan Rekar .15 .07
❑ 474 Bruce Ruffin .15 .07
❑ 475 Bret Saberhagen .25 .11
❑ 476 Walt Weiss .15 .07
❑ 477 Eric Young .15 .07
❑ 478 Kevin Brown .25 .11
❑ 479 Al Leiter .25 .11
❑ 480 Pat Rapp .15 .07
❑ 481 Gary Sheffield .60 .25
❑ 482 Devon White .25 .11
❑ 483 Bob Abreu .75 .35
❑ 484 Sean Berry .15 .07
❑ 485 Craig Biggio .40 .18
❑ 486 Jim Dougherty .15 .07
❑ 487 Richard Hidalgo .25 .11
❑ 488 Darryl Kile .25 .11
❑ 489 Derrick May .15 .07
❑ 490 Greg Swindell .15 .07
❑ 491 Rick Wilkins .15 .07
❑ 492 Mike Blowers .15 .07
❑ 493 Tom Candiotti .15 .07
❑ 494 Roger Cedeno .15 .07
❑ 495 Delino DeShields .15 .07
❑ 496 Greg Gagne .15 .07
❑ 497 Karim Garcia .15 .07
❑ 498 Wilton Guerrero RC .40 .18
❑ 499 Chan Ho Park .25 .11
❑ 500 Israel Alcantara .15 .07
❑ 501 Shane Andrews .15 .07
❑ 502 Yamil Benitez .15 .07
❑ 503 Cliff Floyd .25 .11
❑ 504 Mark Grudzielanek .15 .07
❑ 505 Ryan McGuire .15 .07
❑ 506 Sherman Obando .15 .07
❑ 507 Jose Paniagua .15 .07
❑ 508 Henry Rodriguez .15 .07
❑ 509 Kirk Rueter .15 .07
❑ 510 Juan Acevedo .15 .07
❑ 511 John Franco .25 .11
❑ 512 Bernard Gilkey .15 .07
❑ 513 Lance Johnson .15 .07
❑ 514 Rey Ordonez .15 .07
❑ 515 Robert Person .15 .07
❑ 516 Paul Wilson .15 .07
❑ 517 Toby Borland .15 .07
❑ 518 David Doster RC .15 .07
❑ 519 Lenny Dykstra .25 .11
❑ 520 Sid Fernandez .15 .07
❑ 521 Mike Grace RC .15 .07
❑ 522 Rich Hunter .15 .07
❑ 523 Benito Santiago .15 .07
❑ 524 Gene Schall .15 .07
❑ 525 Curt Schilling .25 .11
❑ 526 Kevin Sefcik RC .15 .07
❑ 527 Lee Tinsley .15 .07
❑ 528 David West .15 .07
❑ 529 Mark Whiten .15 .07
❑ 530 Todd Zeile .15 .07
❑ 531 Carlos Garcia .15 .07
❑ 532 Charlie Hayes .15 .07
❑ 533 Jason Kendall .25 .11
❑ 534 Jeff King .15 .07
❑ 535 Mike Kingery .15 .07
❑ 536 Nelson Liriano .15 .07
❑ 537 Dan Plesac .15 .07
❑ 538 Paul Wagner .15 .07
❑ 539 Luis Alicea .15 .07
❑ 540 David Bell .15 .07
❑ 541 Alan Benes .15 .07
❑ 542 Andy Benes .15 .07
❑ 543 Mike Busby RC .15 .07
❑ 544 Royce Clayton .15 .07
❑ 545 Dennis Eckersley .25 .11
❑ 546 Gary Gaetti .25 .11
❑ 547 Ron Gant .15 .07
❑ 548 Aaron Holbert .15 .07
❑ 549 Ray Lankford .25 .11
❑ 550 T.J. Mathews .15 .07
❑ 551 Willie McGee .25 .11
❑ 552 Miguel Mejia .15 .07
❑ 553 Todd Stottlemyre .15 .07
❑ 554 Sean Bergman .15 .07
❑ 555 Willie Blair .15 .07
❑ 556 Andujar Cedeno .15 .07
❑ 557 Steve Finley .25 .11
❑ 558 Rickey Henderson .75 .35
❑ 559 Wally Joyner .25 .11
❑ 560 Scott Livingstone .15 .07
❑ 561 Marc Newfield .15 .07
❑ 562 Bob Tewksbury .15 .07
❑ 563 Fernando Valenzuela .25 .11
❑ 564 Rod Beck .15 .07
❑ 565 Doug Creek .15 .07
❑ 566 Shawon Dunston .15 .07
❑ 567 Osvaldo Fernandez RC .15 .07
❑ 568 Stan Javier .15 .07
❑ 569 Marcus Jensen .15 .07
❑ 570 Steve Scarsone .15 .07
❑ 571 Robby Thompson .15 .07
❑ 572 Allen Watson .15 .07
❑ 573 Roberto Alomar STA .25 .11
❑ 574 Jeff Bagwell STA .40 .18
❑ 575 Albert Belle STA .25 .11
❑ 576 Wade Boggs STA .40 .18
❑ 577 Barry Bonds STA .60 .25
❑ 578 Juan Gonzalez STA .25 .11
❑ 579 Ken Griffey Jr. STA 1.25 .55
❑ 580 Tony Gwynn STA .60 .25
❑ 581 Randy Johnson STA .40 .18
❑ 582 Chipper Jones STA .75 .35
❑ 583 Barry Larkin STA .25 .11
❑ 584 Kenny Lofton STA .15 .07
❑ 585 Greg Maddux STA .75 .35
❑ 586 Raul Mondesi STA .15 .07
❑ 587 Mike Piazza STA 1.00 .45
❑ 588 Cal Ripken STA 1.25 .55
❑ 589 Tim Salmon STA .15 .07
❑ 590 Frank Thomas STA .60 .25
❑ 591 Mo Vaughn STA .15 .07
❑ 592 Matt Williams STA .25 .11
❑ 593 Marty Cordova RAW .15 .07
❑ 594 Jim Edmonds RAW .25 .11
❑ 595 Cliff Floyd RAW .15 .07
❑ 596 Chipper Jones RAW .75 .35
❑ 597 Ryan Klesko RAW .15 .07
❑ 598 Raul Mondesi RAW .15 .07
❑ 599 Manny Ramirez RAW .40 .18
❑ 600 Ruben Rivera RAW .15 .07
❑ DD1 C. Ripken Diamond Dust 25.00 11.00
Issued through dealers
Serial numbered to 2131
❑ DD2 Cal Ripken Diamond Dust 15.00 6.75
Issued through a wrapper redemption

## 1997 Ultra

| | MINT | NRMT |
|---|---|---|
| COMPLETE SET (553) | 60.00 | 27.00 |
| COMPLETE SERIES 1 (300) | 30.00 | 13.50 |
| COMPLETE SERIES 2 (253) | 30.00 | 13.50 |
| COMMON CARD (1-450) | .15 | .07 |
| COMMON CARD (451-553) | .20 | .09 |

❑ 1 Roberto Alomar .60 .25
❑ 2 Brady Anderson .25 .11
❑ 3 Rocky Coppinger .15 .07
❑ 4 Jeffrey Hammonds .25 .11
❑ 5 Chris Hoiles .15 .07
❑ 6 Eddie Murray .60 .25
❑ 7 Mike Mussina .60 .25
❑ 8 Jimmy Myers .15 .07
❑ 9 Randy Myers .15 .07
❑ 10 Arthur Rhodes .15 .07
❑ 11 Cal Ripken 2.50 1.10
❑ 12 Jose Canseco .75 .35
❑ 13 Roger Clemens 1.25 .55
❑ 14 Tom Gordon .15 .07
❑ 15 Jose Malave .15 .07
❑ 16 Tim Naehring .15 .07
❑ 17 Troy O'Leary .15 .07
❑ 18 Bill Selby .15 .07
❑ 19 Heathcliff Slocumb .15 .07
❑ 20 Mike Stanley .15 .07
❑ 21 Mo Vaughn .25 .11
❑ 22 Garret Anderson .25 .11

❑ 23 George Arias .15 .07
❑ 24 Chili Davis .25 .11
❑ 25 Jim Edmonds .60 .25
❑ 26 Darin Erstad .75 .35
❑ 27 Chuck Finley .25 .11
❑ 28 Todd Greene .15 .07
❑ 29 Troy Percival .15 .07
❑ 30 Tim Salmon .25 .11
❑ 31 Jeff Schmidt .15 .07
❑ 32 Randy Velarde .15 .07
❑ 33 Shad Williams .15 .07
❑ 34 Wilson Alvarez .15 .07
❑ 35 Harold Baines .25 .11
❑ 36 James Baldwin .25 .11
❑ 37 Mike Cameron .25 .11
❑ 38 Ray Durham .25 .11
❑ 39 Ozzie Guillen .15 .07
❑ 40 Roberto Hernandez .15 .07
❑ 41 Darren Lewis .15 .07
❑ 42 Jose Munoz .15 .07
❑ 43 Tony Phillips .15 .07
❑ 44 Frank Thomas 1.25 .55
❑ 45 Sandy Alomar Jr. .25 .11
❑ 46 Albert Belle .40 .18
❑ 47 Mark Carreon .15 .07
❑ 48 Julio Franco .25 .11
❑ 49 Orel Hershiser .25 .11
❑ 50 Kenny Lofton .25 .11
❑ 51 Jack McDowell .15 .07
❑ 52 Jose Mesa .15 .07
❑ 53 Charles Nagy .15 .07
❑ 54 Manny Ramirez .75 .35
❑ 55 Julian Tavarez .15 .07
❑ 56 Omar Vizquel .25 .11
❑ 57 Raul Casanova .15 .07
❑ 58 Tony Clark .15 .07
❑ 59 Travis Fryman .25 .11
❑ 60 Bob Higginson .25 .11
❑ 61 Melvin Nieves .15 .07
❑ 62 Curtis Pride .15 .07
❑ 63 Justin Thompson .15 .07
❑ 64 Alan Trammell .40 .18
❑ 65 Kevin Appier .25 .11
❑ 66 Johnny Damon .25 .11
❑ 67 Keith Lockhart .15 .07
❑ 68 Jeff Montgomery .15 .07
❑ 69 Jose Offerman .15 .07
❑ 70 Bip Roberts .15 .07
❑ 71 Jose Rosado .15 .07
❑ 72 Chris Stynes .15 .07
❑ 73 Mike Sweeney .25 .11
❑ 74 Jeff Cirillo .25 .11
❑ 75 Jeff D'Amico .15 .07
❑ 76 John Jaha .15 .07
❑ 77 Scott Karl .15 .07
❑ 78 Mike Matheny .15 .07
❑ 79 Ben McDonald .15 .07
❑ 80 Matt Mieske .15 .07
❑ 81 Marc Newfield .15 .07
❑ 82 Dave Nilsson .15 .07
❑ 83 Jose Valentin .15 .07
❑ 84 Fernando Vina .15 .07
❑ 85 Rick Aguilera .15 .07
❑ 86 Marty Cordova .15 .07
❑ 87 Chuck Knoblauch .25 .11
❑ 88 Matt Lawton .25 .11
❑ 89 Pat Meares .15 .07
❑ 90 Paul Molitor .60 .25
❑ 91 Greg Myers .15 .07
❑ 92 Dan Naulty .15 .07
❑ 93 Kirby Puckett 1.50 .70
❑ 94 Frank Rodriguez .15 .07
❑ 95 Wade Boggs .75 .35
❑ 96 Cecil Fielder .25 .11
❑ 97 Joe Girardi .15 .07
❑ 98 Dwight Gooden .25 .11
❑ 99 Derek Jeter 2.50 1.10
❑ 100 Tino Martinez .25 .11
❑ 101 Ramiro Mendoza RC .50 .23
❑ 102 Andy Pettitte .25 .11
❑ 103 Mariano Rivera .25 .11
❑ 104 Ruben Rivera .15 .07
❑ 105 Kenny Rogers .15 .07
❑ 106 Darryl Strawberry .25 .11
❑ 107 Bernie Williams .60 .25
❑ 108 Tony Batista .60 .25
❑ 109 Geronimo Berroa .15 .07
❑ 110 Bobby Chouinard .15 .07
❑ 111 Brent Gates .15 .07
❑ 112 Jason Giambi .60 .25
❑ 113 Damon Mashore .15 .07
❑ 114 Mark McGwire 2.50 1.10
❑ 115 Scott Spiezio .15 .07
❑ 116 John Wasdin .15 .07
❑ 117 Steve Wojciechowski .15 .07
❑ 118 Ernie Young .15 .07
❑ 119 Norm Charlton .15 .07
❑ 120 Joey Cora .15 .07
❑ 121 Ken Griffey Jr. 2.50 1.10
❑ 122 Sterling Hitchcock .15 .07
❑ 123 Raul Ibanez .15 .07
❑ 124 Randy Johnson .75 .35
❑ 125 Edgar Martinez .40 .18
❑ 126 Alex Rodriguez 2.00 .90
❑ 127 Matt Wagner .15 .07
❑ 128 Bob Wells .15 .07
❑ 129 Dan Wilson .15 .07
❑ 130 Will Clark .60 .25
❑ 131 Kevin Elster .15 .07
❑ 132 Juan Gonzalez .60 .25
❑ 133 Rusty Greer .25 .11
❑ 134 Darryl Hamilton .15 .07
❑ 135 Mike Henneman .15 .07
❑ 136 Ken Hill .15 .07
❑ 137 Mark McLemore .15 .07
❑ 138 Dean Palmer .25 .11
❑ 139 Roger Pavlik .15 .07
❑ 140 Ivan Rodriguez .75 .35
❑ 141 Joe Carter .25 .11
❑ 142 Carlos Delgado .60 .25
❑ 143 Alex Gonzalez .15 .07
❑ 144 Juan Guzman .15 .07
❑ 145 Pat Hentgen .15 .07
❑ 146 Marty Janzen .15 .07
❑ 147 Otis Nixon .15 .07
❑ 148 Charlie O'Brien .15 .07
❑ 149 John Olerud .25 .11
❑ 150 Robert Perez .15 .07
❑ 151 Jermaine Dye .25 .11
❑ 152 Tom Glavine .60 .25
❑ 153 Andruw Jones .75 .35
❑ 154 Chipper Jones 1.50 .70
❑ 155 Ryan Klesko .25 .11
❑ 156 Javier Lopez .25 .11
❑ 157 Greg Maddux 1.50 .70
❑ 158 Fred McGriff .40 .18
❑ 159 Wonderful Monds .15 .07
❑ 160 John Smoltz .25 .11
❑ 161 Terrell Wade .15 .07
❑ 162 Mark Wohlers .15 .07
❑ 163 Brant Brown .15 .07
❑ 164 Mark Grace .60 .25
❑ 165 Tyler Houston .15 .07
❑ 166 Robin Jennings .15 .07
❑ 167 Jason Maxwell .15 .07
❑ 168 Ryne Sandberg .75 .35
❑ 169 Sammy Sosa 1.25 .55
❑ 170 Amaury Telemaco .15 .07
❑ 171 Steve Trachsel .15 .07
❑ 172 Pedro Valdes RC .15 .07
❑ 173 Tim Belk .15 .07
❑ 174 Bret Boone .25 .11
❑ 175 Jeff Brantley .15 .07
❑ 176 Eric Davis .25 .11
❑ 177 Barry Larkin .60 .25
❑ 178 Chad Mottola .15 .07
❑ 179 Mark Portugal .15 .07
❑ 180 Reggie Sanders .15 .07
❑ 181 John Smiley .15 .07
❑ 182 Eddie Taubensee .15 .07
❑ 183 Dante Bichette .25 .11
❑ 184 Ellis Burks .25 .11
❑ 185 Andres Galarraga .40 .18
❑ 186 Curt Leskanic .15 .07
❑ 187 Quinton McCracken .15 .07
❑ 188 Jeff Reed .15 .07
❑ 189 Kevin Ritz .15 .07
❑ 190 Walt Weiss .15 .07
❑ 191 Jamey Wright .15 .07
❑ 192 Eric Young .15 .07
❑ 193 Kevin Brown .25 .11
❑ 194 Luis Castillo .25 .11
❑ 195 Jeff Conine .15 .07
❑ 196 Andre Dawson .40 .18
❑ 197 Charles Johnson .25 .11
❑ 198 Al Leiter .25 .11
❑ 199 Ralph Milliard .15 .07
❑ 200 Robb Nen .15 .07
❑ 201 Edgar Renteria .25 .11
❑ 202 Gary Sheffield .60 .25
❑ 203 Bob Abreu .25 .11
❑ 204 Jeff Bagwell .75 .35
❑ 205 Derek Bell .15 .07
❑ 206 Sean Berry .15 .07
❑ 207 Richard Hidalgo .25 .11
❑ 208 Todd Jones .15 .07
❑ 209 Darryl Kile .25 .11
❑ 210 Orlando Miller .15 .07
❑ 211 Shane Reynolds .15 .07
❑ 212 Billy Wagner .15 .07
❑ 213 Donne Wall .15 .07
❑ 214 Roger Cedeno .15 .07
❑ 215 Greg Gagne .15 .07
❑ 216 Karim Garcia .15 .07
❑ 217 Wilton Guerrero .15 .07
❑ 218 Todd Hollandsworth .15 .07
❑ 219 Ramon Martinez .15 .07
❑ 220 Raul Mondesi .25 .11
❑ 221 Hideo Nomo .60 .25
❑ 222 Chan Ho Park .25 .11
❑ 223 Mike Piazza 2.00 .90
❑ 224 Ismael Valdes .15 .07
❑ 225 Moises Alou .25 .11
❑ 226 Derek Aucoin .15 .07
❑ 227 Yamil Benitez .15 .07
❑ 228 Jeff Fassero .15 .07
❑ 229 Darrin Fletcher .15 .07
❑ 230 Mark Grudzielanek .15 .07
❑ 231 Barry Manuel .15 .07
❑ 232 Pedro Martinez .75 .35
❑ 233 Henry Rodriguez .15 .07
❑ 234 Ugueth Urbina .15 .07
❑ 235 Rondell White .25 .11
❑ 236 Carlos Baerga .15 .07
❑ 237 John Franco .25 .11
❑ 238 Bernard Gilkey .15 .07
❑ 239 Todd Hundley .15 .07
❑ 240 Butch Huskey .15 .07
❑ 241 Jason Isringhausen .15 .07
❑ 242 Lance Johnson .15 .07
❑ 243 Bobby Jones .15 .07
❑ 244 Alex Ochoa .15 .07
❑ 245 Rey Ordonez .15 .07
❑ 246 Paul Wilson .15 .07
❑ 247 Ron Blazier .15 .07
❑ 248 David Doster .15 .07
❑ 249 Jim Eisenreich .15 .07
❑ 250 Mike Grace .15 .07
❑ 251 Mike Lieberthal .25 .11
❑ 252 Wendell Magee .15 .07
❑ 253 Mickey Morandini .15 .07
❑ 254 Ricky Otero .15 .07
❑ 255 Scott Rolen .60 .25
❑ 256 Curt Schilling .25 .11
❑ 257 Todd Zeile .15 .07
❑ 258 Jermaine Allensworth .15 .07
❑ 259 Trey Beamon .15 .07
❑ 260 Carlos Garcia .15 .07
❑ 261 Mark Johnson .15 .07
❑ 262 Jason Kendall .25 .11
❑ 263 Jeff King .15 .07
❑ 264 Al Martin .15 .07
❑ 265 Denny Neagle .25 .11
❑ 266 Matt Ruebel .15 .07
❑ 267 Marc Wilkins .15 .07
❑ 268 Alan Benes .15 .07
❑ 269 Dennis Eckersley .25 .11
❑ 270 Ron Gant .15 .07
❑ 271 Aaron Holbert .15 .07
❑ 272 Brian Jordan .25 .11
❑ 273 Ray Lankford .25 .11
❑ 274 John Mabry .15 .07
❑ 275 T.J. Mathews .15 .07
❑ 276 Ozzie Smith .75 .35
❑ 277 Todd Stottlemyre .15 .07
❑ 278 Mark Sweeney .15 .07
❑ 279 Andy Ashby .15 .07
❑ 280 Steve Finley .25 .11

❑ 281 John Flaherty .15 .07
❑ 282 Chris Gomez .15 .07
❑ 283 Tony Gwynn 1.25 .55
❑ 284 Joey Hamilton .15 .07
❑ 285 Rickey Henderson .75 .35
❑ 286 Trevor Hoffman .25 .11
❑ 287 Jason Thompson .15 .07
❑ 288 Fernando Valenzuela .25 .11
❑ 289 Greg Vaughn .25 .11
❑ 290 Barry Bonds 1.00 .45
❑ 291 Jay Canizaro .15 .07
❑ 292 Jacob Cruz .15 .07
❑ 293 Shawon Dunston .15 .07
❑ 294 Shawn Estes .25 .11
❑ 295 Mark Gardner .15 .07
❑ 296 Marcus Jensen .15 .07
❑ 297 Bill Mueller RC .40 .18
❑ 298 Chris Singleton .25 .11
❑ 299 Allen Watson .15 .07
❑ 300 Matt Williams .40 .18
❑ 301 Rod Beck .15 .07
❑ 302 Jay Bell .25 .11
❑ 303 Shawon Dunston .15 .07
❑ 304 Reggie Jefferson .15 .07
❑ 305 Darren Oliver .15 .07
❑ 306 Benito Santiago .15 .07
❑ 307 Gerald Williams .15 .07
❑ 308 Damon Buford .15 .07
❑ 309 Jeromy Burnitz .25 .11
❑ 310 Sterling Hitchcock .15 .07
❑ 311 Dave Hollins .15 .07
❑ 312 Mel Rojas .15 .07
❑ 313 Robin Ventura .25 .11
❑ 314 David Wells .25 .11
❑ 315 Cal Eldred .15 .07
❑ 316 Gary Gaetti .25 .11
❑ 317 John Hudek .15 .07
❑ 318 Brian Johnson .15 .07
❑ 319 Denny Neagle .25 .11
❑ 320 Larry Walker .25 .11
❑ 321 Russ Davis .15 .07
❑ 322 Delino DeShields .15 .07
❑ 323 Charlie Hayes .15 .07
❑ 324 Jermaine Dye .25 .11
❑ 325 John Ericks .15 .07
❑ 326 Jeff Fassero .15 .07
❑ 327 Nomar Garciaparra 2.00 .90
❑ 328 Willie Greene .15 .07
❑ 329 Greg McMichael .15 .07
❑ 330 Damion Easley .15 .07
❑ 331 Ricky Bones .15 .07
❑ 332 John Burkett .15 .07
❑ 333 Royce Clayton .15 .07
❑ 334 Greg Colbrunn .15 .07
❑ 335 Tony Eusebio .15 .07
❑ 336 Gregg Jefferies .15 .07
❑ 337 Wally Joyner .25 .11
❑ 338 Jim Leyritz .15 .07
❑ 339 Paul O'Neill .25 .11
❑ 340 Bruce Ruffin .15 .07
❑ 341 Michael Tucker .15 .07
❑ 342 Andy Benes .15 .07
❑ 343 Craig Biggio .40 .18
❑ 344 Rex Hudler .15 .07
❑ 345 Brad Radke .25 .11
❑ 346 Deion Sanders .25 .11
❑ 347 Moises Alou .25 .11
❑ 348 Brad Ausmus .15 .07
❑ 349 Armando Benitez .15 .07
❑ 350 Mark Gubicza .15 .07
❑ 351 Terry Steinbach .15 .07
❑ 352 Mark Whiten .15 .07
❑ 353 Ricky Bottalico .15 .07
❑ 354 Brian Giles RC 2.50 1.10
❑ 355 Eric Karros .25 .11
❑ 356 Jimmy Key .25 .11
❑ 357 Carlos Perez .15 .07
❑ 358 Alex Fernandez .15 .07
❑ 359 J.T. Snow .25 .11
❑ 360 Bobby Bonilla .25 .11
❑ 361 Scott Brosius .25 .11
❑ 362 Greg Swindell .15 .07
❑ 363 Jose Vizcaino .15 .07
❑ 364 Matt Williams .40 .18
❑ 365 Darren Daulton .25 .11
❑ 366 Shane Andrews .15 .07
❑ 367 Jim Eisenreich .15 .07
❑ 368 Ariel Prieto .15 .07
❑ 369 Bob Tewksbury .15 .07
❑ 370 Mike Bordick .15 .07
❑ 371 Rheal Cormier .15 .07
❑ 372 Cliff Floyd .25 .11
❑ 373 David Justice .40 .18
❑ 374 John Wetteland .25 .11
❑ 375 Mike Blowers .15 .07
❑ 376 Jose Canseco .75 .35
❑ 377 Roger Clemens 1.25 .55
❑ 378 Kevin Mitchell .15 .07
❑ 379 Todd Zeile .15 .07
❑ 380 Jim Thome .40 .18
❑ 381 Turk Wendell .15 .07
❑ 382 Rico Brogna .15 .07
❑ 383 Eric Davis .25 .11
❑ 384 Mike Lansing .15 .07
❑ 385 Devon White .25 .11
❑ 386 Marquis Grissom .15 .07
❑ 387 Todd Worrell .15 .07
❑ 388 Jeff Kent .40 .18
❑ 389 Mickey Tettleton .15 .07
❑ 390 Steve Avery .15 .07
❑ 391 David Cone .25 .11
❑ 392 Scott Cooper .15 .07
❑ 393 Lee Stevens .15 .07
❑ 394 Kevin Elster .15 .07
❑ 395 Tom Goodwin .15 .07
❑ 396 Shawn Green .60 .25
❑ 397 Pete Harnisch .15 .07
❑ 398 Eddie Murray .60 .25
❑ 399 Joe Randa .15 .07
❑ 400 Scott Sanders .15 .07
❑ 401 John Valentin .15 .07
❑ 402 Todd Jones .15 .07
❑ 403 Terry Adams .15 .07
❑ 404 Brian Hunter .15 .07
❑ 405 Pat Listach .15 .07
❑ 406 Kenny Lofton .25 .11
❑ 407 Hal Morris .15 .07
❑ 408 Ed Sprague .15 .07
❑ 409 Rich Becker .15 .07
❑ 410 Edgardo Alfonzo .25 .11
❑ 411 Albert Belle .50 .23
❑ 412 Jeff King .15 .07
❑ 413 Kirt Manwaring .15 .07
❑ 414 Jason Schmidt .15 .07
❑ 415 Allen Watson .15 .07
❑ 416 Lee Tinsley .15 .07
❑ 417 Brett Butler .25 .11
❑ 418 Carlos Garcia .15 .07
❑ 419 Mark Lemke .15 .07
❑ 420 Jaime Navarro .15 .07
❑ 421 David Segui .15 .07
❑ 422 Ruben Sierra .15 .07
❑ 423 B.J. Surhoff .25 .11
❑ 424 Julian Tavarez .15 .07
❑ 425 Billy Taylor .15 .07
❑ 426 Ken Caminiti .25 .11
❑ 427 Chuck Carr .15 .07
❑ 428 Benji Gil .15 .07
❑ 429 Terry Mulholland .15 .07
❑ 430 Mike Stanton .15 .07
❑ 431 Wil Cordero .15 .07
❑ 432 Chili Davis .25 .11
❑ 433 Mariano Duncan .15 .07
❑ 434 Orlando Merced .15 .07
❑ 435 Kent Mercker .15 .07
❑ 436 John Olerud .25 .11
❑ 437 Quilvio Veras .15 .07
❑ 438 Mike Fetters .15 .07
❑ 439 Glenallen Hill .15 .07
❑ 440 Bill Swift .15 .07
❑ 441 Tim Wakefield .15 .07
❑ 442 Pedro Astacio .15 .07
❑ 443 Vinny Castilla .25 .11
❑ 444 Doug Drabek .15 .07
❑ 445 Alan Embree .15 .07
❑ 446 Lee Smith .25 .11
❑ 447 Darryl Hamilton .15 .07
❑ 448 Brian McRae .15 .07
❑ 449 Mike Timlin .15 .07
❑ 450 Bob Wickman .15 .07
❑ 451 Jason Dickson .20 .09
❑ 452 Chad Curtis .20 .09
❑ 453 Mark Leiter .20 .09
❑ 454 Damon Berryhill .20 .09
❑ 455 Kevin Orie .20 .09
❑ 456 Dave Burba .20 .09
❑ 457 Chris Holt .20 .09
❑ 458 Ricky Ledee RC .75 .35
❑ 459 Mike Devereaux .20 .09
❑ 460 Pokey Reese .30 .14
❑ 461 Tim Raines .30 .14
❑ 462 Ryan Jones .20 .09
❑ 463 Shane Mack .20 .09
❑ 464 Darren Dreifort .30 .14
❑ 465 Mark Parent .20 .09
❑ 466 Mark Portugal .20 .09
❑ 467 Dante Powell .20 .09
❑ 468 Craig Grebeck .20 .09
❑ 469 Ron Villone .20 .09
❑ 470 Dmitri Young .30 .14
❑ 471 Shannon Stewart .30 .14
❑ 472 Rick Helling .30 .14
❑ 473 Bill Haselman .20 .09
❑ 474 Albie Lopez .20 .09
❑ 475 Glendon Rusch .20 .09
❑ 476 Derrick May .20 .09
❑ 477 Chad Ogea .20 .09
❑ 478 Kirk Rueter .20 .09
❑ 479 Chris Hammond .20 .09
❑ 480 Russ Johnson .20 .09
❑ 481 James Mouton .20 .09
❑ 482 Mike Macfarlane .20 .09
❑ 483 Scott Ruffcorn .20 .09
❑ 484 Jeff Frye .20 .09
❑ 485 Richie Sexson .30 .14
❑ 486 Emil Brown RC .20 .09
❑ 487 Desi Wilson .20 .09
❑ 488 Brent Gates .20 .09
❑ 489 Tony Graffanino .20 .09
❑ 490 Dan Miceli .20 .09
❑ 491 Orlando Cabrera RC .50 .23
❑ 492 Tony Womack RC 1.00 .45
❑ 493 Jerome Walton .20 .09
❑ 494 Mark Thompson .20 .09
❑ 495 Jose Guillen .20 .09
❑ 496 Willie Blair .20 .09
❑ 497 T.J. Staton RC .20 .09
❑ 498 Scott Kamieniecki .20 .09
❑ 499 Vince Coleman .20 .09
❑ 500 Jeff Abbott .20 .09
❑ 501 Chris Widger .20 .09
❑ 502 Kevin Tapani .20 .09
❑ 503 Carlos Castillo RC .20 .09
❑ 504 Luis Gonzalez .30 .14
❑ 505 Tim Belcher .20 .09
❑ 506 Armando Reynoso .20 .09
❑ 507 Jamie Moyer .20 .09
❑ 508 Randall Simon RC .50 .23
❑ 509 Vladimir Guerrero 1.50 .70
❑ 510 Wady Almonte RC .20 .09
❑ 511 Dustin Hermanson .20 .09
❑ 512 Deivi Cruz RC 1.00 .45
❑ 513 Luis Alicea .20 .09
❑ 514 Felix Heredia RC .20 .09
❑ 515 Don Slaught .20 .09
❑ 516 Shigetoshi Hasegawa RC .50 .23
❑ 517 Matt Walbeck .20 .09
❑ 518 David Arias-Ortiz RC 1.00 .45
❑ 519 Brady Raggio RC .20 .09
❑ 520 Rudy Pemberton .20 .09
❑ 521 Wayne Kirby .20 .09
❑ 522 Calvin Maduro .20 .09
❑ 523 Mark Lewis .20 .09
❑ 524 Mike Jackson .20 .09
❑ 525 Sid Fernandez .20 .09
❑ 526 Mike Bielecki .20 .09
❑ 527 Bubba Trammell RC .30 .14
❑ 528 Brent Brede RC .20 .09
❑ 529 Matt Morris .20 .09
❑ 530 Joe Borowski RC .20 .09
❑ 531 Orlando Miller .20 .09
❑ 532 Jim Bullinger .20 .09
❑ 533 Robert Person .20 .09
❑ 534 Doug Glanville .20 .09
❑ 535 Terry Pendleton .30 .14
❑ 536 Jorge Posada .30 .14
❑ 537 Marc Sagmoen RC .20 .09
❑ 538 Fernando Tatis RC 2.00 .90

| Card | MINT | NRMT |
|---|---|---|
| ❑ 539 Aaron Sele | .30 | .14 |
| ❑ 540 Brian Banks | .20 | .09 |
| ❑ 541 Derrek Lee | .20 | .09 |
| ❑ 542 John Wasdin | .20 | .09 |
| ❑ 543 Justin Towle RC | .20 | .09 |
| ❑ 544 Pat Cline | .20 | .09 |
| ❑ 545 Dave Magadan | .20 | .09 |
| ❑ 546 Jeff Blauser | .20 | .09 |
| ❑ 547 Phil Nevin | .30 | .14 |
| ❑ 548 Todd Walker | .20 | .09 |
| ❑ 549 Eli Marrero | .20 | .09 |
| ❑ 550 Bartolo Colon | .30 | .14 |
| ❑ 551 Jose Cruz Jr. RC | 2.00 | .90 |
| ❑ 552 Todd Dunwoody | .20 | .09 |
| ❑ 553 Hideki Irabu RC | .60 | .25 |
| ❑ P11 Cal Ripken Promo Three Card Strip | 2.00 | .90 |

## 1998 Ultra

| | MINT | NRMT |
|---|---|---|
| COMPLETE SET (501) | 250.00 | 110.00 |
| COMPLETE SERIES 1 (250) | 150.00 | 70.00 |
| COMPLETE SERIES 2 (251) | 100.00 | 45.00 |
| COMP.SER.1 w/o SP's (210) | 15.00 | 6.75 |
| COMP.SER.2 w/o SP's (226) | 15.00 | 6.75 |
| COMMON 1 (1-220/246-250) | .15 | .07 |
| COMMON 2 (251-475/501) | .15 | .07 |
| COMMON SC (211-220) | 2.50 | 1.10 |
| COMMON PROS (221-245) | 3.00 | 1.35 |
| COMMON PZ (476-500) | .75 | .35 |

| Card | MINT | NRMT |
|---|---|---|
| ❑ 1 Ken Griffey Jr. | 2.50 | 1.10 |
| ❑ 2 Matt Morris | .15 | .07 |
| ❑ 3 Roger Clemens | 1.25 | .55 |
| ❑ 4 Matt Williams | .40 | .18 |
| ❑ 5 Roberto Hernandez | .15 | .07 |
| ❑ 6 Rondell White | .25 | .11 |
| ❑ 7 Tim Salmon | .25 | .11 |
| ❑ 8 Brad Radke | .25 | .11 |
| ❑ 9 Brett Butler | .25 | .11 |
| ❑ 10 Carl Everett | .25 | .11 |
| ❑ 11 Chili Davis | .25 | .11 |
| ❑ 12 Chuck Finley | .25 | .11 |
| ❑ 13 Darryl Kile | .25 | .11 |
| ❑ 14 Deivi Cruz | .15 | .07 |
| ❑ 15 Gary Gaetti | .25 | .11 |
| ❑ 16 Matt Stairs | .15 | .07 |
| ❑ 17 Pat Meares | .15 | .07 |
| ❑ 18 Will Cunnane | .15 | .07 |
| ❑ 19 Steve Woodard | .15 | .07 |
| ❑ 20 Andy Ashby | .15 | .07 |
| ❑ 21 Bobby Higginson | .25 | .11 |
| ❑ 22 Brian Jordan | .25 | .11 |
| ❑ 23 Craig Biggio | .40 | .18 |
| ❑ 24 Jim Edmonds | .60 | .25 |
| ❑ 25 Ryan McGuire | .15 | .07 |
| ❑ 26 Scott Hatteberg | .15 | .07 |
| ❑ 27 Willie Greene | .15 | .07 |
| ❑ 28 Albert Belle | .40 | .18 |
| ❑ 29 Ellis Burks | .25 | .11 |
| ❑ 30 Hideo Nomo | .60 | .25 |
| ❑ 31 Jeff Bagwell | .75 | .35 |
| ❑ 32 Kevin Brown | .40 | .18 |
| ❑ 33 Nomar Garciaparra | 2.00 | .90 |
| ❑ 34 Pedro Martinez | .75 | .35 |
| ❑ 35 Raul Mondesi | .25 | .11 |
| ❑ 36 Ricky Bottalico | .15 | .07 |
| ❑ 37 Shawn Estes | .15 | .07 |
| ❑ 38 Otis Nixon | .15 | .07 |
| ❑ 39 Terry Steinbach | .15 | .07 |
| ❑ 40 Tom Glavine | .60 | .25 |
| ❑ 41 Todd Dunwoody | .15 | .07 |
| ❑ 42 Deion Sanders | .25 | .11 |
| ❑ 43 Gary Sheffield | .60 | .25 |
| ❑ 44 Mike Lansing | .15 | .07 |
| ❑ 45 Mike Lieberthal | .25 | .11 |
| ❑ 46 Paul Sorrento | .15 | .07 |
| ❑ 47 Paul O'Neill | .25 | .11 |
| ❑ 48 Tom Goodwin | .15 | .07 |
| ❑ 49 Andruw Jones | .60 | .25 |
| ❑ 50 Barry Bonds | 1.00 | .45 |
| ❑ 51 Bernie Williams | .60 | .25 |
| ❑ 52 Jeremi Gonzalez | .15 | .07 |
| ❑ 53 Mike Piazza | 2.00 | .90 |
| ❑ 54 Russ Davis | .15 | .07 |
| ❑ 55 Vinny Castilla | .25 | .11 |
| ❑ 56 Rod Beck | .15 | .07 |
| ❑ 57 Andres Galarraga | .40 | .18 |
| ❑ 58 Ben McDonald | .15 | .07 |
| ❑ 59 Billy Wagner | .15 | .07 |
| ❑ 60 Charles Johnson | .25 | .11 |
| ❑ 61 Fred McGriff | .40 | .18 |
| ❑ 62 Dean Palmer | .25 | .11 |
| ❑ 63 Frank Thomas | 1.25 | .55 |
| ❑ 64 Ismael Valdes | .15 | .07 |
| ❑ 65 Mark Bellhorn | .15 | .07 |
| ❑ 66 Jeff King | .15 | .07 |
| ❑ 67 John Wetteland | .25 | .11 |
| ❑ 68 Mark Grace | .60 | .25 |
| ❑ 69 Mark Kotsay | .25 | .11 |
| ❑ 70 Scott Rolen | .60 | .25 |
| ❑ 71 Todd Hundley | .15 | .07 |
| ❑ 72 Todd Worrell | .15 | .07 |
| ❑ 73 Wilson Alvarez | .15 | .07 |
| ❑ 74 Bobby Jones | .15 | .07 |
| ❑ 75 Jose Canseco | .75 | .35 |
| ❑ 76 Kevin Appier | .25 | .11 |
| ❑ 77 Neifi Perez | .15 | .07 |
| ❑ 78 Paul Molitor | .60 | .25 |
| ❑ 79 Quilvio Veras | .15 | .07 |
| ❑ 80 Randy Johnson | .75 | .35 |
| ❑ 81 Glendon Rusch | .15 | .07 |
| ❑ 82 Curt Schilling | .25 | .11 |
| ❑ 83 Alex Rodriguez | 2.00 | .90 |
| ❑ 84 Rey Ordonez | .15 | .07 |
| ❑ 85 Jeff Juden | .15 | .07 |
| ❑ 86 Mike Cameron | .25 | .11 |
| ❑ 87 Ryan Klesko | .25 | .11 |
| ❑ 88 Trevor Hoffman | .25 | .11 |
| ❑ 89 Chuck Knoblauch | .25 | .11 |
| ❑ 90 Larry Walker | .25 | .11 |
| ❑ 91 Mark McLemore | .15 | .07 |
| ❑ 92 B.J. Surhoff | .25 | .11 |
| ❑ 93 Darren Daulton | .25 | .11 |
| ❑ 94 Ray Durham | .25 | .11 |
| ❑ 95 Sammy Sosa | 1.25 | .55 |
| ❑ 96 Eric Young | .15 | .07 |
| ❑ 97 Gerald Williams | .15 | .07 |
| ❑ 98 Javy Lopez | .25 | .11 |
| ❑ 99 John Smiley | .15 | .07 |
| ❑ 100 Juan Gonzalez | .60 | .25 |
| ❑ 101 Shawn Green | .60 | .25 |
| ❑ 102 Charles Nagy | .15 | .07 |
| ❑ 103 David Justice | .40 | .18 |
| ❑ 104 Joey Hamilton | .15 | .07 |
| ❑ 105 Pat Hentgen | .15 | .07 |
| ❑ 106 Raul Casanova | .15 | .07 |
| ❑ 107 Tony Phillips | .15 | .07 |
| ❑ 108 Tony Gwynn | 1.25 | .55 |
| ❑ 109 Will Clark | .60 | .25 |
| ❑ 110 Jason Giambi | .60 | .25 |
| ❑ 111 Jay Bell | .25 | .11 |
| ❑ 112 Johnny Damon | .25 | .11 |
| ❑ 113 Alan Benes | .15 | .07 |
| ❑ 114 Jeff Suppan | .15 | .07 |
| ❑ 115 Kevin Polcovich | .15 | .07 |
| ❑ 116 Shigetoshi Hasegawa | .25 | .11 |
| ❑ 117 Steve Finley | .25 | .11 |
| ❑ 118 Tony Clark | .15 | .07 |
| ❑ 119 David Cone | .25 | .11 |
| ❑ 120 Jose Guillen | .15 | .07 |
| ❑ 121 Kevin Millwood RC | 1.00 | .45 |
| ❑ 122 Greg Maddux | 1.50 | .70 |
| ❑ 123 Dave Nilsson | .15 | .07 |
| ❑ 124 Hideki Irabu | .15 | .07 |
| ❑ 125 Jason Kendall | .25 | .11 |
| ❑ 126 Jim Thome | .40 | .18 |
| ❑ 127 Delino DeShields | .15 | .07 |
| ❑ 128 Edgar Renteria | .15 | .07 |
| ❑ 129 Edgardo Alfonzo | .25 | .11 |
| ❑ 130 J.T. Snow | .25 | .11 |
| ❑ 131 Jeff Abbott | .15 | .07 |
| ❑ 132 Jeffrey Hammonds | .25 | .11 |
| ❑ 133 Todd Greene | .15 | .07 |
| ❑ 134 Vladimir Guerrero | 1.00 | .45 |
| ❑ 135 Jay Buhner | .25 | .11 |
| ❑ 136 Jeff Cirillo | .25 | .11 |
| ❑ 137 Jeromy Burnitz | .25 | .11 |
| ❑ 138 Mickey Morandini | .15 | .07 |
| ❑ 139 Tino Martinez | .25 | .11 |
| ❑ 140 Jeff Shaw | .15 | .07 |
| ❑ 141 Rafael Palmeiro | .60 | .25 |
| ❑ 142 Bobby Bonilla | .25 | .11 |
| ❑ 143 Cal Ripken | 2.50 | 1.10 |
| ❑ 144 Chad Fox RC | .15 | .07 |
| ❑ 145 Dante Bichette | .25 | .11 |
| ❑ 146 Dennis Eckersley | .25 | .11 |
| ❑ 147 Mariano Rivera | .25 | .11 |
| ❑ 148 Mo Vaughn | .25 | .11 |
| ❑ 149 Reggie Sanders | .15 | .07 |
| ❑ 150 Derek Jeter | 2.50 | 1.10 |
| ❑ 151 Rusty Greer | .25 | .11 |
| ❑ 152 Brady Anderson | .25 | .11 |
| ❑ 153 Brett Tomko | .15 | .07 |
| ❑ 154 Jaime Navarro | .15 | .07 |
| ❑ 155 Kevin Orie | .15 | .07 |
| ❑ 156 Roberto Alomar | .60 | .25 |
| ❑ 157 Edgar Martinez | .40 | .18 |
| ❑ 158 John Olerud | .25 | .11 |
| ❑ 159 John Smoltz | .25 | .11 |
| ❑ 160 Ryne Sandberg | .75 | .35 |
| ❑ 161 Billy Taylor | .15 | .07 |
| ❑ 162 Chris Holt | .15 | .07 |
| ❑ 163 Damion Easley | .15 | .07 |
| ❑ 164 Darin Erstad | .60 | .25 |
| ❑ 165 Joe Carter | .25 | .11 |
| ❑ 166 Kelvim Escobar | .15 | .07 |
| ❑ 167 Ken Caminiti | .25 | .11 |
| ❑ 168 Pokey Reese | .25 | .11 |
| ❑ 169 Ray Lankford | .25 | .11 |
| ❑ 170 Livan Hernandez | .15 | .07 |
| ❑ 171 Steve Kline | .15 | .07 |
| ❑ 172 Tom Gordon | .25 | .11 |
| ❑ 173 Travis Fryman | .25 | .11 |
| ❑ 174 Al Martin | .15 | .07 |
| ❑ 175 Andy Pettitte | .25 | .11 |
| ❑ 176 Jeff Kent | .40 | .18 |
| ❑ 177 Jimmy Key | .25 | .11 |
| ❑ 178 Mark Grudzielanek | .15 | .07 |
| ❑ 179 Tony Saunders | .15 | .07 |
| ❑ 180 Barry Larkin | .60 | .25 |
| ❑ 181 Bubba Trammell | .15 | .07 |
| ❑ 182 Carlos Delgado | .60 | .25 |
| ❑ 183 Carlos Baerga | .15 | .07 |
| ❑ 184 Derek Bell | .15 | .07 |
| ❑ 185 Henry Rodriguez | .15 | .07 |
| ❑ 186 Jason Dickson | .15 | .07 |
| ❑ 187 Ron Gant | .25 | .11 |
| ❑ 188 Tony Womack | .15 | .07 |
| ❑ 189 Justin Thompson | .15 | .07 |
| ❑ 190 Fernando Tatis | .25 | .11 |
| ❑ 191 Mark Wohlers | .15 | .07 |
| ❑ 192 Takashi Kashiwada | .25 | .11 |
| ❑ 193 Garret Anderson | .25 | .11 |
| ❑ 194 Jose Cruz Jr. | .25 | .11 |
| ❑ 195 Ricardo Rincon | .15 | .07 |
| ❑ 196 Tim Naehring | .15 | .07 |
| ❑ 197 Moises Alou | .25 | .11 |
| ❑ 198 Eric Karros | .25 | .11 |
| ❑ 199 John Jaha | .25 | .11 |
| ❑ 200 Marty Cordova | .15 | .07 |
| ❑ 201 Ken Hill | .15 | .07 |
| ❑ 202 Chipper Jones | 1.50 | .70 |
| ❑ 203 Kenny Lofton | .25 | .11 |
| ❑ 204 Mike Mussina | .60 | .25 |
| ❑ 205 Manny Ramirez | .75 | .35 |
| ❑ 206 Todd Hollandsworth | .15 | .07 |
| ❑ 207 Cecil Fielder | .25 | .11 |
| ❑ 208 Mark McGwire | 2.50 | 1.10 |

❑ 209 Jim Leyritz .15 .07
❑ 210 Ivan Rodriguez .75 .35
❑ 211 Jeff Bagwell SC 3.00 1.35
❑ 212 Barry Bonds SC 4.00 1.80
❑ 213 Roger Clemens SC 5.00 2.20
❑ 214 Nomar Garciaparra SC 8.00 3.60
❑ 215 Ken Griffey Jr. SC 10.00 4.50
❑ 216 Tony Gwynn SC 6.00 2.70
❑ 217 Randy Johnson SC 3.00 1.35
❑ 218 Mark McGwire SC 10.00 4.50
❑ 219 Scott Rolen SC 2.50 1.10
❑ 220 Frank Thomas SC 5.00 2.20
❑ 221 Matt Perisho PROS 3.00 1.35
❑ 222 Wes Helms PROS 3.00 1.35
❑ 223 Dave Dellucci PROS RC 3.00 1.35
❑ 224 Todd Helton PROS 6.00 2.70
❑ 225 Brian Rose PROS 3.00 1.35
❑ 226 Aaron Boone PROS 3.00 1.35
❑ 227 Keith Foulke PROS 3.00 1.35
❑ 228 Homer Bush PROS 3.00 1.35
❑ 229 Shannon Stewart PROS 3.00 1.35
❑ 230 Richard Hidalgo PROS 3.00 1.35
❑ 231 Russ Johnson PROS 3.00 1.35
❑ 232 Henry Blanco PROS RC 3.00 1.35
❑ 233 Paul Konerko PROS 3.00 1.35
❑ 234 Antone Williamson PROS 3.00 1.35
❑ 235 Shane Bowers PROS RC 3.00 1.35
❑ 236 Jose Vidro PROS 3.00 1.35
❑ 237 Derek Wallace PROS 3.00 1.35
❑ 238 Ricky Ledee PROS SP 4.00 1.80
❑ 239 Ben Grieve PROS 3.00 1.35
❑ 240 Lou Collier PROS 3.00 1.35
❑ 241 Derrek Lee PROS 3.00 1.35
❑ 242 Ruben Rivera PROS 3.00 1.35
❑ 243 Jorge Velandia PROS SP 4.00 1.80
❑ 244 Andrew Vessel PROS 3.00 1.35
❑ 245 Chris Carpenter PROS 3.00 1.35
❑ 246 Ken Griffey Jr. CL 1.25 .55
❑ 247 Alex Rodriguez CL 1.00 .45
❑ 248 Diamond Ink CL .15 .07
❑ 249 Frank Thomas CL .60 .25
❑ 250 Cal Ripken CL 1.25 .55
❑ 251 Carlos Perez .15 .07
❑ 252 Larry Sutton .15 .07
❑ 253 Gary Sheffield .60 .25
❑ 254 Wally Joyner .25 .11
❑ 255 Todd Stottlemyre .15 .07
❑ 256 Nerio Rodriguez .15 .07
❑ 257 Charles Johnson .25 .11
❑ 258 Pedro Astacio .15 .07
❑ 259 Cal Eldred .15 .07
❑ 260 Chili Davis .25 .11
❑ 261 Freddy Garcia .15 .07
❑ 262 Bobby Witt .15 .07
❑ 263 Michael Coleman .15 .07
❑ 264 Mike Caruso .15 .07
❑ 265 Mike Lansing .15 .07
❑ 266 Dennis Reyes .15 .07
❑ 267 F.P. Santangelo .15 .07
❑ 268 Darryl Hamilton .15 .07
❑ 269 Mike Fetters .15 .07
❑ 270 Charlie Hayes .15 .07
❑ 271 Royce Clayton .15 .07
❑ 272 Doug Drabek .15 .07
❑ 273 James Baldwin .15 .07
❑ 274 Brian Hunter .15 .07
❑ 275 Chan Ho Park .25 .11
❑ 276 John Franco .25 .11
❑ 277 David Wells .25 .11
❑ 278 Eli Marrero .15 .07
❑ 279 Kerry Wood .60 .25
❑ 280 Donnie Sadler .15 .07
❑ 281 Scott Winchester RC .15 .07
❑ 282 Hal Morris .15 .07
❑ 283 Brad Fullmer .25 .11
❑ 284 Bernard Gilkey .15 .07
❑ 285 Ramiro Mendoza .15 .07
❑ 286 Kevin Brown .40 .18
❑ 287 David Segui .15 .07
❑ 288 Willie McGee .25 .11
❑ 289 Darren Oliver .15 .07
❑ 290 Antonio Alfonseca .15 .07
❑ 291 Eric Davis .25 .11
❑ 292 Mickey Morandini .15 .07
❑ 293 Frank Catalanotto RC .40 .18
❑ 294 Derrek Lee .15 .07
❑ 295 Todd Zeile .25 .11
❑ 296 Chuck Knoblauch .25 .11
❑ 297 Wilson Delgado .15 .07
❑ 298 Bobby Bonilla .25 .11
❑ 299 Orel Hershiser .25 .11
❑ 300 Ozzie Guillen .15 .07
❑ 301 Aaron Sele .25 .11
❑ 302 Joe Carter .25 .11
❑ 303 Darryl Kile .25 .11
❑ 304 Shane Reynolds .15 .07
❑ 305 Todd Dunn .15 .07
❑ 306 Bob Abreu .25 .11
❑ 307 Doug Strange .15 .07
❑ 308 Jose Canseco .75 .35
❑ 309 Lance Johnson .15 .07
❑ 310 Harold Baines .25 .11
❑ 311 Todd Pratt .15 .07
❑ 312 Greg Colbrunn .15 .07
❑ 313 Masato Yoshii RC .50 .23
❑ 314 Felix Heredia .15 .07
❑ 315 Dennis Martinez .25 .11
❑ 316 Geronimo Berroa .15 .07
❑ 317 Darren Lewis .15 .07
❑ 318 Bill Ripken .15 .07
❑ 319 Enrique Wilson .15 .07
❑ 320 Alex Ochoa .15 .07
❑ 321 Doug Glanville .15 .07
❑ 322 Mike Stanley .15 .07
❑ 323 Gerald Williams .15 .07
❑ 324 Pedro Martinez .75 .35
❑ 325 Jaret Wright .15 .07
❑ 326 Terry Pendleton .25 .11
❑ 327 LaTroy Hawkins .15 .07
❑ 328 Emil Brown .15 .07
❑ 329 Walt Weiss .25 .11
❑ 330 Omar Vizquel .25 .11
❑ 331 Carl Everett .25 .11
❑ 332 Fernando Vina .15 .07
❑ 333 Mike Blowers .15 .07
❑ 334 Dwight Gooden .15 .07
❑ 335 Mark Lewis .15 .07
❑ 336 Jim Leyritz .15 .07
❑ 337 Kenny Lofton .25 .11
❑ 338 John Halama RC .50 .23
❑ 339 Jose Valentin .15 .07
❑ 340 Desi Relaford .15 .07
❑ 341 Dante Powell .15 .07
❑ 342 Ed Sprague .15 .07
❑ 343 Reggie Jefferson .15 .07
❑ 344 Mike Hampton .25 .11
❑ 345 Marquis Grissom .15 .07
❑ 346 Heathcliff Slocumb .15 .07
❑ 347 Francisco Cordova .15 .07
❑ 348 Ken Cloude .15 .07
❑ 349 Benito Santiago .15 .07
❑ 350 Denny Neagle .15 .07
❑ 351 Sean Casey .25 .11
❑ 352 Robb Nen .15 .07
❑ 353 Orlando Merced .15 .07
❑ 354 Adrian Brown .15 .07
❑ 355 Gregg Jefferies .15 .07
❑ 356 Otis Nixon .15 .07
❑ 357 Michael Tucker .15 .07
❑ 358 Eric Milton .15 .07
❑ 359 Travis Fryman .25 .11
❑ 360 Gary DiSarcina .15 .07
❑ 361 Mario Valdez .15 .07
❑ 362 Craig Counsell .15 .07
❑ 363 Jose Offerman .15 .07
❑ 364 Tony Fernandez .15 .07
❑ 365 Jason McDonald .15 .07
❑ 366 Sterling Hitchcock .15 .07
❑ 367 Donovan Osborne .15 .07
❑ 368 Troy Percival .15 .07
❑ 369 Henry Rodriguez .15 .07
❑ 370 Dmitri Young .25 .11
❑ 371 Jay Powell .15 .07
❑ 372 Jeff Conine .15 .07
❑ 373 Orlando Cabrera .15 .07
❑ 374 Butch Huskey .15 .07
❑ 375 Mike Lowell RC .75 .35
❑ 376 Kevin Young .25 .11
❑ 377 Jamie Moyer .15 .07
❑ 378 Jeff D'Amico .15 .07
❑ 379 Scott Erickson .15 .07
❑ 380 Magglio Ordonez RC 2.50 1.10
❑ 381 Melvin Nieves .15 .07
❑ 382 Ramon Martinez .15 .07
❑ 383 A.J. Hinch .15 .07
❑ 384 Jeff Brantley .15 .07
❑ 385 Kevin Elster .15 .07
❑ 386 Allen Watson .15 .07
❑ 387 Moises Alou .25 .11
❑ 388 Jeff Blauser .15 .07
❑ 389 Pete Harnisch .15 .07
❑ 390 Shane Andrews .15 .07
❑ 391 Rico Brogna .15 .07
❑ 392 Stan Javier .15 .07
❑ 393 David Howard .15 .07
❑ 394 Darryl Strawberry .25 .11
❑ 395 Kent Mercker .15 .07
❑ 396 Juan Encarnacion .25 .11
❑ 397 Sandy Alomar Jr. .25 .11
❑ 398 Al Leiter .25 .11
❑ 399 Tony Graffanino .15 .07
❑ 400 Terry Adams .15 .07
❑ 401 Bruce Aven .15 .07
❑ 402 Derrick Gibson .15 .07
❑ 403 Jose Cabrera RC .15 .07
❑ 404 Rich Becker .15 .07
❑ 405 David Ortiz .15 .07
❑ 406 Brian McRae .15 .07
❑ 407 Bobby Estalella .15 .07
❑ 408 Bill Mueller .15 .07
❑ 409 Dennis Eckersley .25 .11
❑ 410 Sandy Martinez .15 .07
❑ 411 Jose Vizcaino .15 .07
❑ 412 Jermaine Allensworth .15 .07
❑ 413 Miguel Tejada .60 .25
❑ 414 Turner Ward .15 .07
❑ 415 Glenallen Hill .15 .07
❑ 416 Lee Stevens .15 .07
❑ 417 Cecil Fielder .25 .11
❑ 418 Ruben Sierra .15 .07
❑ 419 Jon Nunnally .15 .07
❑ 420 Rod Myers .15 .07
❑ 421 Dustin Hermanson .15 .07
❑ 422 James Mouton .15 .07
❑ 423 Dan Wilson .15 .07
❑ 424 Roberto Kelly .15 .07
❑ 425 Antonio Osuna .15 .07
❑ 426 Jacob Cruz .15 .07
❑ 427 Brent Mayne .15 .07
❑ 428 Matt Karchner .15 .07
❑ 429 Damian Jackson .15 .07
❑ 430 Roger Cedeno .15 .07
❑ 431 Rickey Henderson .75 .35
❑ 432 Joe Randa .15 .07
❑ 433 Greg Vaughn .25 .11
❑ 434 Andres Galarraga .40 .18
❑ 435 Rod Beck .15 .07
❑ 436 Curtis Goodwin .15 .07
❑ 437 Brad Ausmus .15 .07
❑ 438 Bob Hamelin .15 .07
❑ 439 Todd Walker .15 .07
❑ 440 Scott Brosius .25 .11
❑ 441 Len Dykstra .25 .11
❑ 442 Abraham Nunez .15 .07
❑ 443 Brian Johnson .15 .07
❑ 444 Randy Myers .25 .11
❑ 445 Bret Boone .25 .11
❑ 446 Oscar Henriquez .15 .07
❑ 447 Mike Sweeney .25 .11
❑ 448 Kenny Rogers .15 .07
❑ 449 Mark Langston .15 .07
❑ 450 Luis Gonzalez .25 .11
❑ 451 John Burkett .15 .07
❑ 452 Bip Roberts .15 .07
❑ 453 Travis Lee .25 .11
❑ 454 Felix Rodriguez .15 .07
❑ 455 Andy Benes .15 .07
❑ 456 Willie Blair .15 .07
❑ 457 Brian Anderson .15 .07
❑ 458 Jay Bell .25 .11
❑ 459 Matt Williams .40 .18
❑ 460 Devon White .15 .07
❑ 461 Karim Garcia .15 .07
❑ 462 Jorge Fabregas .15 .07
❑ 463 Wilson Alvarez .15 .07
❑ 464 Roberto Hernandez .15 .07
❑ 465 Tony Saunders .15 .07
❑ 466 Rolando Arrojo RC .50 .23

| | Player | MINT | NRMT |
|---|---|---|---|
| ❑ 467 | Wade Boggs | .75 | .35 |
| ❑ 468 | Fred McGriff | .40 | .18 |
| ❑ 469 | Paul Sorrento | .15 | .07 |
| ❑ 470 | Kevin Stocker | .15 | .07 |
| ❑ 471 | Bubba Trammell | .15 | .07 |
| ❑ 472 | Quinton McCracken | .15 | .07 |
| ❑ 473 | Ken Griffey Jr. CL | 1.25 | .55 |
| ❑ 474 | Cal Ripken CL | 1.25 | .55 |
| ❑ 475 | Frank Thomas CL | .60 | .25 |
| ❑ 476 | Ken Griffey Jr. PZ | 8.00 | 3.60 |
| ❑ 477 | Cal Ripken PZ | 8.00 | 3.60 |
| ❑ 478 | Frank Thomas PZ | 4.00 | 1.80 |
| ❑ 479 | Alex Rodriguez PZ | 6.00 | 2.70 |
| ❑ 480 | Nomar Garciaparra PZ | 6.00 | 2.70 |
| ❑ 481 | Derek Jeter PZ | 8.00 | 3.60 |
| ❑ 482 | Andruw Jones PZ | 2.00 | .90 |
| ❑ 483 | Chipper Jones PZ | 5.00 | 2.20 |
| ❑ 484 | Greg Maddux PZ | 5.00 | 2.20 |
| ❑ 485 | Mike Piazza PZ | 6.00 | 2.70 |
| ❑ 486 | Juan Gonzalez PZ | .60 | .25 |
| ❑ 487 | Jose Cruz Jr. PZ | 1.00 | .45 |
| ❑ 488 | Jaret Wright PZ | .75 | .35 |
| ❑ 489 | Hideo Nomo PZ | 2.00 | .90 |
| ❑ 490 | Scott Rolen PZ | 2.00 | .90 |
| ❑ 491 | Tony Gwynn PZ | 4.00 | 1.80 |
| ❑ 492 | Roger Clemens PZ | 4.00 | 1.80 |
| ❑ 493 | Darin Erstad PZ | 2.00 | .90 |
| ❑ 494 | Mark McGwire PZ | 8.00 | 3.60 |
| ❑ 495 | Jeff Bagwell PZ | 2.50 | 1.10 |
| ❑ 496 | Mo Vaughn PZ | 1.00 | .45 |
| ❑ 497 | Albert Belle PZ | 1.25 | .55 |
| ❑ 498 | Kenny Lofton PZ | 1.00 | .45 |
| ❑ 499 | Ben Grieve PZ | 1.00 | .45 |
| ❑ 500 | Barry Bonds PZ | 3.00 | 1.35 |
| ❑ 501 | Mike Piazza | 2.00 | .90 |
| ❑ S100 | Alex Rodriguez AU/750 | 120.00 | 55.00 |

## 1999 Ultra

| | MINT | NRMT |
|---|---|---|
| COMPLETE SET (250) | 80.00 | 36.00 |
| COMP.SET w/o SP's (215) | 20.00 | 9.00 |
| COMMON CARD (1-215) | .15 | .07 |
| COMMON SC (216-225) | 1.00 | .45 |
| COMMON PROSPECT (226-250) | 2.00 | .90 |

| | Player | MINT | NRMT |
|---|---|---|---|
| ❑ 1 | Greg Maddux | 1.50 | .70 |
| ❑ 2 | Greg Vaughn | .25 | .11 |
| ❑ 3 | John Wetteland | .25 | .11 |
| ❑ 4 | Tino Martinez | .25 | .11 |
| ❑ 5 | Todd Walker | .15 | .07 |
| ❑ 6 | Troy O'Leary | .15 | .07 |
| ❑ 7 | Barry Larkin | .60 | .25 |
| ❑ 8 | Mike Lansing | .15 | .07 |
| ❑ 9 | Delino DeShields | .15 | .07 |
| ❑ 10 | Brett Tomko | .15 | .07 |
| ❑ 11 | Carlos Perez | .15 | .07 |
| ❑ 12 | Mark Langston | .15 | .07 |
| ❑ 13 | Jamie Moyer | .15 | .07 |
| ❑ 14 | Jose Guillen | .15 | .07 |
| ❑ 15 | Bartolo Colon | .25 | .11 |
| ❑ 16 | Brady Anderson | .25 | .11 |
| ❑ 17 | Walt Weiss | .15 | .07 |
| ❑ 18 | Shane Reynolds | .15 | .07 |
| ❑ 19 | David Segui | .15 | .07 |
| ❑ 20 | Vladimir Guerrero | 1.00 | .45 |
| ❑ 21 | Freddy Garcia | .15 | .07 |
| ❑ 22 | Carl Everett | .25 | .11 |
| ❑ 23 | Jose Cruz Jr. | .25 | .11 |
| ❑ 24 | David Ortiz | .15 | .07 |
| ❑ 25 | Andruw Jones | .60 | .25 |
| ❑ 26 | Darren Lewis | .15 | .07 |
| ❑ 27 | Ray Lankford | .25 | .11 |
| ❑ 28 | Wally Joyner | .25 | .11 |
| ❑ 29 | Charles Johnson | .25 | .11 |
| ❑ 30 | Derek Jeter | 2.50 | 1.10 |
| ❑ 31 | Sean Casey | .25 | .11 |
| ❑ 32 | Bobby Bonilla | .25 | .11 |
| ❑ 33 | Todd Zeile | .25 | .11 |
| ❑ 34 | Todd Helton | .75 | .35 |
| ❑ 35 | David Wells | .25 | .11 |
| ❑ 36 | Darin Erstad | .60 | .25 |
| ❑ 37 | Ivan Rodriguez | .75 | .35 |
| ❑ 38 | Antonio Osuna | .15 | .07 |
| ❑ 39 | Mickey Morandini | .15 | .07 |
| ❑ 40 | Rusty Greer | .25 | .11 |
| ❑ 41 | Rod Beck | .15 | .07 |
| ❑ 42 | Larry Sutton | .15 | .07 |
| ❑ 43 | Edgar Renteria | .15 | .07 |
| ❑ 44 | Otis Nixon | .15 | .07 |
| ❑ 45 | Eli Marrero | .15 | .07 |
| ❑ 46 | Reggie Jefferson | .15 | .07 |
| ❑ 47 | Trevor Hoffman | .25 | .11 |
| ❑ 48 | Andres Galarraga | .40 | .18 |
| ❑ 49 | Scott Brosius | .25 | .11 |
| ❑ 50 | Vinny Castilla | .25 | .11 |
| ❑ 51 | Bret Boone | .25 | .11 |
| ❑ 52 | Masato Yoshii | .15 | .07 |
| ❑ 53 | Matt Williams | .40 | .18 |
| ❑ 54 | Robin Ventura | .25 | .11 |
| ❑ 55 | Jay Powell | .15 | .07 |
| ❑ 56 | Dean Palmer | .25 | .11 |
| ❑ 57 | Eric Milton | .15 | .07 |
| ❑ 58 | Willie McGee | .25 | .11 |
| ❑ 59 | Tony Gwynn | 1.25 | .55 |
| ❑ 60 | Tom Gordon | .15 | .07 |
| ❑ 61 | Dante Bichette | .25 | .11 |
| ❑ 62 | Jaret Wright | .15 | .07 |
| ❑ 63 | Devon White | .15 | .07 |
| ❑ 64 | Frank Thomas | 1.25 | .55 |
| ❑ 65 | Mike Piazza | 2.00 | .90 |
| ❑ 66 | Jose Offerman | .15 | .07 |
| ❑ 67 | Pat Meares | .15 | .07 |
| ❑ 68 | Brian Meadows | .15 | .07 |
| ❑ 69 | Nomar Garciaparra | 2.00 | .90 |
| ❑ 70 | Mark McGwire | 2.50 | 1.10 |
| ❑ 71 | Tony Graffanino | .15 | .07 |
| ❑ 72 | Ken Griffey Jr. | 2.50 | 1.10 |
| ❑ 73 | Ken Caminiti | .25 | .11 |
| ❑ 74 | Todd Jones | .15 | .07 |
| ❑ 75 | A.J. Hinch | .15 | .07 |
| ❑ 76 | Marquis Grissom | .15 | .07 |
| ❑ 77 | Jay Buhner | .25 | .11 |
| ❑ 78 | Albert Belle | .40 | .18 |
| ❑ 79 | Brian Anderson | .15 | .07 |
| ❑ 80 | Quinton McCracken | .15 | .07 |
| ❑ 81 | Omar Vizquel | .25 | .11 |
| ❑ 82 | Todd Stottlemyre | .15 | .07 |
| ❑ 83 | Cal Ripken | 2.50 | 1.10 |
| ❑ 84 | Magglio Ordonez | .40 | .18 |
| ❑ 85 | John Olerud | .25 | .11 |
| ❑ 86 | Hal Morris | .15 | .07 |
| ❑ 87 | Derrek Lee | .15 | .07 |
| ❑ 88 | Doug Glanville | .15 | .07 |
| ❑ 89 | Marty Cordova | .15 | .07 |
| ❑ 90 | Kevin Brown | .25 | .11 |
| ❑ 91 | Kevin Young | .25 | .11 |
| ❑ 92 | Rico Brogna | .15 | .07 |
| ❑ 93 | Wilson Alvarez | .15 | .07 |
| ❑ 94 | Bob Wickman | .15 | .07 |
| ❑ 95 | Jim Thome | .40 | .18 |
| ❑ 96 | Mike Mussina | .60 | .25 |
| ❑ 97 | Al Leiter | .25 | .11 |
| ❑ 98 | Travis Lee | .15 | .07 |
| ❑ 99 | Jeff King | .15 | .07 |
| ❑ 100 | Kerry Wood | .25 | .11 |
| ❑ 101 | Cliff Floyd | .25 | .11 |
| ❑ 102 | Jose Valentin | .15 | .07 |
| ❑ 103 | Manny Ramirez | .75 | .35 |
| ❑ 104 | Butch Huskey | .15 | .07 |
| ❑ 105 | Scott Erickson | .15 | .07 |
| ❑ 106 | Ray Durham | .25 | .11 |
| ❑ 107 | Johnny Damon | .25 | .11 |
| ❑ 108 | Craig Counsell | .15 | .07 |
| ❑ 109 | Rolando Arrojo | .15 | .07 |
| ❑ 110 | Bob Abreu | .25 | .11 |
| ❑ 111 | Tony Womack | .15 | .07 |
| ❑ 112 | Mike Stanley | .15 | .07 |
| ❑ 113 | Kenny Lofton | .25 | .11 |
| ❑ 114 | Eric Davis | .25 | .11 |
| ❑ 115 | Jeff Conine | .15 | .07 |
| ❑ 116 | Carlos Baerga | .15 | .07 |
| ❑ 117 | Rondell White | .25 | .11 |
| ❑ 118 | Billy Wagner | .15 | .07 |
| ❑ 119 | Ed Sprague | .15 | .07 |
| ❑ 120 | Jason Schmidt | .15 | .07 |
| ❑ 121 | Edgar Martinez | .40 | .18 |
| ❑ 122 | Travis Fryman | .25 | .11 |
| ❑ 123 | Armando Benitez | .15 | .07 |
| ❑ 124 | Matt Stairs | .15 | .07 |
| ❑ 125 | Roberto Hernandez | .15 | .07 |
| ❑ 126 | Jay Bell | .25 | .11 |
| ❑ 127 | Justin Thompson | .15 | .07 |
| ❑ 128 | John Jaha | .15 | .07 |
| ❑ 129 | Mike Caruso | .15 | .07 |
| ❑ 130 | Miguel Tejada | .25 | .11 |
| ❑ 131 | Geoff Jenkins | .25 | .11 |
| ❑ 132 | Wade Boggs | .75 | .35 |
| ❑ 133 | Andy Benes | .15 | .07 |
| ❑ 134 | Aaron Sele | .25 | .11 |
| ❑ 135 | Bret Saberhagen | .25 | .11 |
| ❑ 136 | Mariano Rivera | .25 | .11 |
| ❑ 137 | Neifi Perez | .15 | .07 |
| ❑ 138 | Paul Konerko | .25 | .11 |
| ❑ 139 | Barry Bonds | 1.00 | .45 |
| ❑ 140 | Garret Anderson | .25 | .11 |
| ❑ 141 | Bernie Williams | .60 | .25 |
| ❑ 142 | Gary Sheffield | .60 | .25 |
| ❑ 143 | Rafael Palmeiro | .60 | .25 |
| ❑ 144 | Orel Hershiser | .25 | .11 |
| ❑ 145 | Craig Biggio | .40 | .18 |
| ❑ 146 | Dmitri Young | .25 | .11 |
| ❑ 147 | Damion Easley | .15 | .07 |
| ❑ 148 | Henry Rodriguez | .15 | .07 |
| ❑ 149 | Brad Radke | .25 | .11 |
| ❑ 150 | Pedro Martinez | .75 | .35 |
| ❑ 151 | Mike Lieberthal | .25 | .11 |
| ❑ 152 | Jim Leyritz | .15 | .07 |
| ❑ 153 | Chuck Knoblauch | .25 | .11 |
| ❑ 154 | Darryl Kile | .25 | .11 |
| ❑ 155 | Brian Jordan | .25 | .11 |
| ❑ 156 | Chipper Jones | 1.50 | .70 |
| ❑ 157 | Pete Harnisch | .15 | .07 |
| ❑ 158 | Moises Alou | .25 | .11 |
| ❑ 159 | Ismael Valdes | .15 | .07 |
| ❑ 160 | Stan Javier | .15 | .07 |
| ❑ 161 | Mark Grace | .60 | .25 |
| ❑ 162 | Jason Giambi | .60 | .25 |
| ❑ 163 | Chuck Finley | .25 | .11 |
| ❑ 164 | Juan Encarnacion | .25 | .11 |
| ❑ 165 | Chan Ho Park | .25 | .11 |
| ❑ 166 | Randy Johnson | .75 | .35 |
| ❑ 167 | J.T. Snow | .25 | .11 |
| ❑ 168 | Tim Salmon | .25 | .11 |
| ❑ 169 | Brian L.Hunter | .15 | .07 |
| ❑ 170 | Rickey Henderson | .75 | .35 |
| ❑ 171 | Cal Eldred | .15 | .07 |
| ❑ 172 | Curt Schilling | .25 | .11 |
| ❑ 173 | Alex Rodriguez | 2.00 | .90 |
| ❑ 174 | Dustin Hermanson | .15 | .07 |
| ❑ 175 | Mike Hampton | .25 | .11 |
| ❑ 176 | Shawn Green | .60 | .25 |
| ❑ 177 | Roberto Alomar | .60 | .25 |
| ❑ 178 | Sandy Alomar Jr. | .25 | .11 |
| ❑ 179 | Larry Walker | .25 | .11 |
| ❑ 180 | Mo Vaughn | .25 | .11 |
| ❑ 181 | Raul Mondesi | .25 | .11 |
| ❑ 182 | Hideki Irabu | .15 | .07 |
| ❑ 183 | Jim Edmonds | .60 | .25 |
| ❑ 184 | Shawn Estes | .15 | .07 |
| ❑ 185 | Tony Clark | .15 | .07 |
| ❑ 186 | Dan Wilson | .15 | .07 |
| ❑ 187 | Michael Tucker | .15 | .07 |
| ❑ 188 | Jeff Shaw | .15 | .07 |
| ❑ 189 | Mark Grudzielanek | .15 | .07 |
| ❑ 190 | Roger Clemens | 1.25 | .55 |
| ❑ 191 | Juan Gonzalez | .60 | .25 |
| ❑ 192 | Sammy Sosa | 1.25 | .55 |
| ❑ 193 | Troy Percival | .15 | .07 |
| ❑ 194 | Robb Nen | .15 | .07 |

| | No. | Player | MINT | NRMT |
|---|---|---|---|---|
| ❑ | 195 | Bill Mueller | .15 | .07 |
| ❑ | 196 | Ben Grieve | .25 | .11 |
| ❑ | 197 | Luis Gonzalez | .25 | .11 |
| ❑ | 198 | Will Clark | .60 | .25 |
| ❑ | 199 | Jeff Cirillo | .25 | .11 |
| ❑ | 200 | Scott Rolen | .60 | .25 |
| ❑ | 201 | Reggie Sanders | .15 | .07 |
| ❑ | 202 | Fred McGriff | .40 | .18 |
| ❑ | 203 | Denny Neagle | .15 | .07 |
| ❑ | 204 | Brad Fullmer | .25 | .11 |
| ❑ | 205 | Royce Clayton | .15 | .07 |
| ❑ | 206 | Jose Canseco | .75 | .35 |
| ❑ | 207 | Jeff Bagwell | .75 | .35 |
| ❑ | 208 | Hideo Nomo | .60 | .25 |
| ❑ | 209 | Karim Garcia | .15 | .07 |
| ❑ | 210 | Kenny Rogers | .15 | .07 |
| ❑ | 211 | Kerry Wood CL | .25 | .11 |
| ❑ | 212 | Alex Rodriguez CL | 1.00 | .45 |
| ❑ | 213 | Cal Ripken CL | 1.25 | .55 |
| ❑ | 214 | Frank Thomas CL | .60 | .25 |
| ❑ | 215 | Ken Griffey Jr. CL | 1.25 | .55 |
| ❑ | 216 | Alex Rodriguez SC | 5.00 | 2.20 |
| ❑ | 217 | Greg Maddux SC | 4.00 | 1.80 |
| ❑ | 218 | Juan Gonzalez SC | 1.50 | .70 |
| ❑ | 219 | Ken Griffey Jr. SC | 6.00 | 2.70 |
| ❑ | 220 | Kerry Wood SC | 1.00 | .45 |
| ❑ | 221 | Mark McGwire SC | 6.00 | 2.70 |
| ❑ | 222 | Mike Piazza SC | 5.00 | 2.20 |
| ❑ | 223 | Rickey Henderson SC | 2.00 | .90 |
| ❑ | 224 | Sammy Sosa SC | 3.00 | 1.35 |
| ❑ | 225 | Travis Lee SC | 1.00 | .45 |
| ❑ | 226 | Gabe Alvarez PROS | 2.00 | .90 |
| ❑ | 227 | Matt Anderson PROS | 2.00 | .90 |
| ❑ | 228 | Adrian Beltre PROS | 2.00 | .90 |
| ❑ | 229 | Orlando Cabrera PROS | 2.00 | .90 |
| ❑ | 230 | Orl. Hernandez PROS | 2.00 | .90 |
| ❑ | 231 | Aramis Ramirez PROS | 2.00 | .90 |
| ❑ | 232 | Troy Glaus PROS | 8.00 | 3.60 |
| ❑ | 233 | Gabe Kapler PROS | 2.00 | .90 |
| ❑ | 234 | Jeremy Giambi PROS | 2.00 | .90 |
| ❑ | 235 | Derrick Gibson PROS | 2.00 | .90 |
| ❑ | 236 | Carlton Loewer PROS | 2.00 | .90 |
| ❑ | 237 | Mike Frank PROS | 2.00 | .90 |
| ❑ | 238 | Carlos Guillen PROS | 2.00 | .90 |
| ❑ | 239 | Alex Gonzalez PROS | 2.00 | .90 |
| ❑ | 240 | Enrique Wilson PROS | 2.00 | .90 |
| ❑ | 241 | J.D. Drew PROS | 5.00 | 2.20 |
| ❑ | 242 | Bruce Chen PROS | 2.00 | .90 |
| ❑ | 243 | Ryan Minor PROS | 2.00 | .90 |
| ❑ | 244 | Preston Wilson PROS | 2.00 | .90 |
| ❑ | 245 | Josh Booty PROS | 2.00 | .90 |
| ❑ | 246 | Luis Ordaz PROS | 2.00 | .90 |
| ❑ | 247 | George Lombard PROS | 2.00 | .90 |
| ❑ | 248 | Matt Clement PROS | 2.00 | .90 |
| ❑ | 249 | Eric Chavez PROS | 2.00 | .90 |
| ❑ | 250 | Corey Koskie PROS | 2.00 | .90 |

## 2000 Ultra

| | MINT | NRMT |
|---|---|---|
| COMPLETE SET (300) | 250.00 | 110.00 |
| COMP.SET w/o SP's (250) | 25.00 | 11.00 |
| COMMON CARD (1-250) | .15 | .07 |
| COMMON PROSPECT (251-300) | 4.00 | 1.80 |

| | No. | Player | MINT | NRMT |
|---|---|---|---|---|
| ❑ | 1 | Alex Rodriguez | 2.00 | .90 |
| ❑ | 2 | Shawn Green | .60 | .25 |
| ❑ | 3 | Magglio Ordonez | .25 | .11 |
| ❑ | 4 | Tony Gwynn | 1.25 | .55 |
| ❑ | 5 | Joe McEwing | .15 | .07 |
| ❑ | 6 | Jose Rosado | .15 | .07 |
| ❑ | 7 | Sammy Sosa | 1.25 | .55 |
| ❑ | 8 | Gary Sheffield | .60 | .25 |
| ❑ | 9 | Mickey Morandini | .15 | .07 |
| ❑ | 10 | Mo Vaughn | .25 | .11 |
| ❑ | 11 | Todd Hollandsworth | .15 | .07 |
| ❑ | 12 | Tom Gordon | .15 | .07 |
| ❑ | 13 | Charles Johnson | .25 | .11 |
| ❑ | 14 | Derek Bell | .15 | .07 |
| ❑ | 15 | Kevin Young | .15 | .07 |
| ❑ | 16 | Jay Buhner | .25 | .11 |
| ❑ | 17 | J.T. Snow | .25 | .11 |
| ❑ | 18 | Jay Bell | .25 | .11 |
| ❑ | 19 | John Rocker | .25 | .11 |
| ❑ | 20 | Ivan Rodriguez | .75 | .35 |
| ❑ | 21 | Pokey Reese | .25 | .11 |
| ❑ | 22 | Paul O'Neill | .25 | .11 |
| ❑ | 23 | Ronnie Belliard | .15 | .07 |
| ❑ | 24 | Ryan Rupe | .15 | .07 |
| ❑ | 25 | Travis Fryman | .25 | .11 |
| ❑ | 26 | Trot Nixon | .25 | .11 |
| ❑ | 27 | Wally Joyner | .25 | .11 |
| ❑ | 28 | Andy Pettitte | .25 | .11 |
| ❑ | 29 | Dan Wilson | .15 | .07 |
| ❑ | 30 | Orlando Hernandez | .25 | .11 |
| ❑ | 31 | Dmitri Young | .25 | .11 |
| ❑ | 32 | Edgar Renteria | .15 | .07 |
| ❑ | 33 | Eric Karros | .25 | .11 |
| ❑ | 34 | Fernando Seguignol | .15 | .07 |
| ❑ | 35 | Jason Kendall | .25 | .11 |
| ❑ | 36 | Jeff Shaw | .15 | .07 |
| ❑ | 37 | Matt Lawton | .15 | .07 |
| ❑ | 38 | Robin Ventura | .40 | .18 |
| ❑ | 39 | Scott Williamson | .15 | .07 |
| ❑ | 40 | Ben Grieve | .25 | .11 |
| ❑ | 41 | Billy Wagner | .15 | .07 |
| ❑ | 42 | Javy Lopez | .25 | .11 |
| ❑ | 43 | Joe Randa | .15 | .07 |
| ❑ | 44 | Neifi Perez | .15 | .07 |
| ❑ | 45 | David Justice | .40 | .18 |
| ❑ | 46 | Ray Durham | .25 | .11 |
| ❑ | 47 | Dustin Hermanson | .15 | .07 |
| ❑ | 48 | Andres Galarraga | .40 | .18 |
| ❑ | 49 | Brad Fullmer | .25 | .11 |
| ❑ | 50 | Nomar Garciaparra | 2.00 | .90 |
| ❑ | 51 | David Cone | .25 | .11 |
| ❑ | 52 | David Nilsson | .15 | .07 |
| ❑ | 53 | David Wells | .25 | .11 |
| ❑ | 54 | Miguel Tejada | .25 | .11 |
| ❑ | 55 | Ismael Valdes | .15 | .07 |
| ❑ | 56 | Jose Lima | .15 | .07 |
| ❑ | 57 | Juan Encarnacion | .25 | .11 |
| ❑ | 58 | Fred McGriff | .40 | .18 |
| ❑ | 59 | Kenny Rogers | .15 | .07 |
| ❑ | 60 | Vladimir Guerrero | 1.00 | .45 |
| ❑ | 61 | Benito Santiago | .15 | .07 |
| ❑ | 62 | Chris Singleton | .25 | .11 |
| ❑ | 63 | Carlos Lee | .25 | .11 |
| ❑ | 64 | Sean Casey | .25 | .11 |
| ❑ | 65 | Tom Goodwin | .15 | .07 |
| ❑ | 66 | Todd Hundley | .15 | .07 |
| ❑ | 67 | Ellis Burks | .25 | .11 |
| ❑ | 68 | Tim Hudson | .60 | .25 |
| ❑ | 69 | Matt Stairs | .15 | .07 |
| ❑ | 70 | Chipper Jones UER (Dodgers logo on the back) | 1.50 | .70 |
| ❑ | 71 | Craig Biggio | .40 | .18 |
| ❑ | 72 | Brian Rose | .15 | .07 |
| ❑ | 73 | Carlos Delgado | .60 | .25 |
| ❑ | 74 | Eddie Taubensee | .15 | .07 |
| ❑ | 75 | John Smoltz | .25 | .11 |
| ❑ | 76 | Ken Caminiti | .25 | .11 |
| ❑ | 77 | Rafael Palmeiro | .60 | .25 |
| ❑ | 78 | Sidney Ponson | .15 | .07 |
| ❑ | 79 | Todd Helton | .75 | .35 |
| ❑ | 80 | Juan Gonzalez | .60 | .25 |
| ❑ | 81 | Bruce Aven | .15 | .07 |
| ❑ | 82 | Desi Relaford | .15 | .07 |
| ❑ | 83 | Johnny Damon | .25 | .11 |
| ❑ | 84 | Albert Belle | .40 | .18 |
| ❑ | 85 | Mark McGwire | 2.50 | 1.10 |
| ❑ | 86 | Rico Brogna | .15 | .07 |
| ❑ | 87 | Tom Glavine | .60 | .25 |
| ❑ | 88 | Harold Baines | .25 | .11 |
| ❑ | 89 | Chad Allen | .15 | .07 |
| ❑ | 90 | Barry Bonds | 1.00 | .45 |
| ❑ | 91 | Mark Grace | .60 | .25 |
| ❑ | 92 | Paul Byrd | .15 | .07 |
| ❑ | 93 | Roberto Alomar | .60 | .25 |
| ❑ | 94 | Roberto Hernandez | .15 | .07 |
| ❑ | 95 | Steve Finley | .25 | .11 |
| ❑ | 96 | Bret Boone | .15 | .07 |
| ❑ | 97 | Charles Nagy | .15 | .07 |
| ❑ | 98 | Eric Chavez | .25 | .11 |
| ❑ | 99 | Jamie Moyer | .15 | .07 |
| ❑ | 100 | Ken Griffey Jr. | 2.50 | 1.10 |
| ❑ | 101 | J.D. Drew | .60 | .25 |
| ❑ | 102 | Todd Stottlemyre | .15 | .07 |
| ❑ | 103 | Tony Fernandez | .15 | .07 |
| ❑ | 104 | Jeromy Burnitz | .25 | .11 |
| ❑ | 105 | Jeremy Giambi | .15 | .07 |
| ❑ | 106 | Livan Hernandez | .15 | .07 |
| ❑ | 107 | Marlon Anderson | .15 | .07 |
| ❑ | 108 | Troy Glaus | .75 | .35 |
| ❑ | 109 | Troy O'Leary | .15 | .07 |
| ❑ | 110 | Scott Rolen | .60 | .25 |
| ❑ | 111 | Bernard Gilkey | .15 | .07 |
| ❑ | 112 | Brady Anderson | .25 | .11 |
| ❑ | 113 | Chuck Knoblauch | .25 | .11 |
| ❑ | 114 | Jeff Weaver | .15 | .07 |
| ❑ | 115 | B.J. Surhoff | .25 | .11 |
| ❑ | 116 | Alex Gonzalez | .15 | .07 |
| ❑ | 117 | Vinny Castilla | .25 | .11 |
| ❑ | 118 | Tim Salmon | .25 | .11 |
| ❑ | 119 | Brian Jordan | .25 | .11 |
| ❑ | 120 | Corey Koskie | .15 | .07 |
| ❑ | 121 | Dean Palmer | .25 | .11 |
| ❑ | 122 | Gabe Kapler | .25 | .11 |
| ❑ | 123 | Jim Edmonds | .60 | .25 |
| ❑ | 124 | John Jaha | .15 | .07 |
| ❑ | 125 | Mark Grudzielanek | .15 | .07 |
| ❑ | 126 | Mike Bordick | .15 | .07 |
| ❑ | 127 | Mike Lieberthal | .25 | .11 |
| ❑ | 128 | Pete Harnisch | .15 | .07 |
| ❑ | 129 | Russ Ortiz | .25 | .11 |
| ❑ | 130 | Kevin Brown | .40 | .18 |
| ❑ | 131 | Troy Percival | .15 | .07 |
| ❑ | 132 | Alex Gonzalez | .15 | .07 |
| ❑ | 133 | Bartolo Colon | .25 | .11 |
| ❑ | 134 | John Valentin | .15 | .07 |
| ❑ | 135 | Jose Hernandez | .15 | .07 |
| ❑ | 136 | Marquis Grissom | .15 | .07 |
| ❑ | 137 | Wade Boggs | .75 | .35 |
| ❑ | 138 | Dante Bichette | .25 | .11 |
| ❑ | 139 | Bobby Higginson | .15 | .07 |
| ❑ | 140 | Frank Thomas | 1.25 | .55 |
| ❑ | 141 | Geoff Jenkins | .25 | .11 |
| ❑ | 142 | Jason Giambi | .60 | .25 |
| ❑ | 143 | Jeff Cirillo | .25 | .11 |
| ❑ | 144 | Sandy Alomar Jr. | .15 | .07 |
| ❑ | 145 | Luis Gonzalez | .25 | .11 |
| ❑ | 146 | Preston Wilson | .25 | .11 |
| ❑ | 147 | Carlos Beltran | .25 | .11 |
| ❑ | 148 | Greg Vaughn | .25 | .11 |
| ❑ | 149 | Carlos Febles | .15 | .07 |
| ❑ | 150 | Jose Canseco | .75 | .35 |
| ❑ | 151 | Kris Benson | .25 | .11 |
| ❑ | 152 | Chuck Finley | .25 | .11 |
| ❑ | 153 | Michael Barrett | .15 | .07 |
| ❑ | 154 | Rey Ordonez | .15 | .07 |
| ❑ | 155 | Adrian Beltre | .25 | .11 |
| ❑ | 156 | Andruw Jones | .60 | .25 |
| ❑ | 157 | Barry Larkin | .60 | .25 |
| ❑ | 158 | Brian Giles | .25 | .11 |
| ❑ | 159 | Carl Everett | .25 | .11 |
| ❑ | 160 | Manny Ramirez | .75 | .35 |
| ❑ | 161 | Darryl Kile | .25 | .11 |
| ❑ | 162 | Edgar Martinez | .40 | .18 |
| ❑ | 163 | Jeff Kent | .40 | .18 |
| ❑ | 164 | Matt Williams | .40 | .18 |
| ❑ | 165 | Mike Piazza | 2.00 | .90 |
| ❑ | 166 | Pedro Martinez | .75 | .35 |
| ❑ | 167 | Ray Lankford | .25 | .11 |
| ❑ | 168 | Roger Cedeno | .15 | .07 |
| ❑ | 169 | Ron Coomer | .15 | .07 |
| ❑ | 170 | Cal Ripken | 2.50 | 1.10 |
| ❑ | 171 | Jose Offerman | .15 | .07 |
| ❑ | 172 | Kenny Lofton | .25 | .11 |
| ❑ | 173 | Kent Bottenfield | .15 | .07 |
| ❑ | 174 | Kevin Millwood | .25 | .11 |

| Card | Mint | NrMt |
|---|---|---|
| ❑ 175 Omar Daal | .15 | .07 |
| ❑ 176 Orlando Cabrera | .15 | .07 |
| ❑ 177 Pat Hentgen | .15 | .07 |
| ❑ 178 Tino Martinez | .25 | .11 |
| ❑ 179 Tony Clark | .15 | .07 |
| ❑ 180 Roger Clemens | 1.25 | .55 |
| ❑ 181 Brad Radke | .25 | .11 |
| ❑ 182 Darin Erstad | .60 | .25 |
| ❑ 183 Jose Jimenez | .15 | .07 |
| ❑ 184 Jim Thome | .40 | .18 |
| ❑ 185 John Wetteland | .25 | .11 |
| ❑ 186 Justin Thompson | .15 | .07 |
| ❑ 187 John Halama | .15 | .07 |
| ❑ 188 Lee Stevens | .15 | .07 |
| ❑ 189 Miguel Cairo | .15 | .07 |
| ❑ 190 Mike Mussina | .60 | .25 |
| ❑ 191 Raul Mondesi | .25 | .11 |
| ❑ 192 Armando Rios | .15 | .07 |
| ❑ 193 Trevor Hoffman | .25 | .11 |
| ❑ 194 Tony Batista | .25 | .11 |
| ❑ 195 Will Clark | .60 | .25 |
| ❑ 196 Brad Ausmus | .15 | .07 |
| ❑ 197 Chili Davis | .25 | .11 |
| ❑ 198 Cliff Floyd | .25 | .11 |
| ❑ 199 Curt Schilling | .25 | .11 |
| ❑ 200 Derek Jeter | 2.50 | 1.10 |
| ❑ 201 Henry Rodriguez | .15 | .07 |
| ❑ 202 Jose Cruz Jr. | .25 | .11 |
| ❑ 203 Omar Vizquel | .25 | .11 |
| ❑ 204 Randy Johnson | .75 | .35 |
| ❑ 205 Reggie Sanders | .15 | .07 |
| ❑ 206 Al Leiter | .15 | .07 |
| ❑ 207 Damion Easley | .15 | .07 |
| ❑ 208 David Bell | .15 | .07 |
| ❑ 209 Fernando Tatis | .25 | .11 |
| ❑ 210 Kerry Wood | .25 | .11 |
| ❑ 211 Kevin Appier | .15 | .07 |
| ❑ 212 Mariano Rivera | .25 | .11 |
| ❑ 213 Mike Caruso | .15 | .07 |
| ❑ 214 Moises Alou | .25 | .11 |
| ❑ 215 Randy Winn | .15 | .07 |
| ❑ 216 Roy Halladay | .15 | .07 |
| ❑ 217 Shannon Stewart | .25 | .11 |
| ❑ 218 Todd Walker | .15 | .07 |
| ❑ 219 Jim Parque | .15 | .07 |
| ❑ 220 Travis Lee | .15 | .07 |
| ❑ 221 Andy Ashby | .15 | .07 |
| ❑ 222 Ed Sprague | .15 | .07 |
| ❑ 223 Larry Walker | .25 | .11 |
| ❑ 224 Rick Helling | .25 | .11 |
| ❑ 225 Rusty Greer | .25 | .11 |
| ❑ 226 Todd Zeile | .25 | .11 |
| ❑ 227 Freddy Garcia | .25 | .11 |
| ❑ 228 Hideo Nomo | .60 | .25 |
| ❑ 229 Marty Cordova | .15 | .07 |
| ❑ 230 Greg Maddux | 1.50 | .70 |
| ❑ 231 Rondell White | .25 | .11 |
| ❑ 232 Paul Konerko | .25 | .11 |
| ❑ 233 Warren Morris | .15 | .07 |
| ❑ 234 Bernie Williams | .60 | .25 |
| ❑ 235 Bob Abreu | .25 | .11 |
| ❑ 236 John Olerud | .25 | .11 |
| ❑ 237 Doug Glanville | .15 | .07 |
| ❑ 238 Eric Young | .15 | .07 |
| ❑ 239 Robb Nen | .15 | .07 |
| ❑ 240 Jeff Bagwell | .75 | .35 |
| ❑ 241 Sterling Hitchcock | .15 | .07 |
| ❑ 242 Todd Greene | .15 | .07 |
| ❑ 243 Bill Mueller | .15 | .07 |
| ❑ 244 Rickey Henderson | .75 | .35 |
| ❑ 245 Chan Ho Park | .25 | .11 |
| ❑ 246 Jason Schmidt | .15 | .07 |
| ❑ 247 Jeff Zimmerman | .15 | .07 |
| ❑ 248 Jermaine Dye | .25 | .11 |
| ❑ 249 Randall Simon | .15 | .07 |
| ❑ 250 Richie Sexson | .25 | .11 |
| ❑ 251 Micah Bowie PROS | 4.00 | 1.80 |
| ❑ 252 Joe Nathan PROS | 4.00 | 1.80 |
| ❑ 253 Chris Woodward PROS | 4.00 | 1.80 |
| ❑ 254 Lance Berkman PROS | 6.00 | 2.70 |
| ❑ 255 Ruben Mateo PROS | 4.00 | 1.80 |
| ❑ 256 Russell Branyan PROS | 4.00 | 1.80 |
| ❑ 257 Randy Wolf PROS | 4.00 | 1.80 |
| ❑ 258 A.J. Burnett PROS | 4.00 | 1.80 |
| ❑ 259 Mark Quinn PROS | 4.00 | 1.80 |
| ❑ 260 Buddy Carlyle PROS | 4.00 | 1.80 |
| ❑ 261 Ben Davis PROS | 4.00 | 1.80 |
| ❑ 262 Yamid Haad PROS | 4.00 | 1.80 |
| ❑ 263 Mike Colangelo PROS | 4.00 | 1.80 |
| ❑ 264 Rick Ankiel PROS | 12.00 | 5.50 |
| ❑ 265 Jacque Jones PROS | 4.00 | 1.80 |
| ❑ 266 Kelly Dransfeldt PROS | 4.00 | 1.80 |
| ❑ 267 Matt Riley PROS | 4.00 | 1.80 |
| ❑ 268 Adam Kennedy PROS | 4.00 | 1.80 |
| ❑ 269 Octavio Dotel PROS | 4.00 | 1.80 |
| ❑ 270 Francisco Cordero PROS | 4.00 | 1.80 |
| ❑ 271 Wilton Veras PROS | 4.00 | 1.80 |
| ❑ 272 Calvin Pickering PROS | 4.00 | 1.80 |
| ❑ 273 Alex Sanchez PROS | 4.00 | 1.80 |
| ❑ 274 Tony Armas Jr. PROS | 4.00 | 1.80 |
| ❑ 275 Pat Burrell PROS | 10.00 | 4.50 |
| ❑ 276 Chad Meyers PROS | 4.00 | 1.80 |
| ❑ 277 Ben Petrick PROS | 4.00 | 1.80 |
| ❑ 278 Ramon Hernandez PROS | 4.00 | 1.80 |
| ❑ 279 Ed Yarnall PROS | 4.00 | 1.80 |
| ❑ 280 Erubiel Durazo PROS | 4.00 | 1.80 |
| ❑ 281 Vernon Wells PROS | 4.00 | 1.80 |
| ❑ 282 Gary Matthews Jr. PROS | 4.00 | 1.80 |
| ❑ 283 Kip Wells PROS | 4.00 | 1.80 |
| ❑ 284 Peter Bergeron PROS | 4.00 | 1.80 |
| ❑ 285 Travis Dawkins PROS | 4.00 | 1.80 |
| ❑ 286 Jorge Toca PROS | 4.00 | 1.80 |
| ❑ 287 Cole Liniak PROS | 4.00 | 1.80 |
| ❑ 288 Chad Hermansen PROS | 4.00 | 1.80 |
| ❑ 289 Eric Gagne PROS | 4.00 | 1.80 |
| ❑ 290 Chad Hutchinson PROS | 4.00 | 1.80 |
| ❑ 291 Eric Munson PROS | 6.00 | 2.70 |
| ❑ 292 Wiki Gonzalez PROS | 4.00 | 1.80 |
| ❑ 293 Alfonso Soriano PROS | 4.00 | 1.80 |
| ❑ 294 Trent Durrington PROS | 4.00 | 1.80 |
| ❑ 295 Ben Molina PROS | 4.00 | 1.80 |
| ❑ 296 Aaron Myette PROS | 4.00 | 1.80 |
| ❑ 297 Wily Pena PROS | 4.00 | 1.80 |
| ❑ 298 Kevin Barker PROS | 4.00 | 1.80 |
| ❑ 299 Geoff Blum PROS | 4.00 | 1.80 |
| ❑ 300 Josh Beckett PROS | 6.00 | 2.70 |
| ❑ P1 Alex Rodriguez Promo | 2.00 | .90 |
| ❑ P2 Alex Rodriguez Promo 3-D | 5.00 | 2.20 |

## 2001 Ultra

| | MINT | NRMT |
|---|---|---|
| COMPLETE SET (275) | 120.00 | 55.00 |
| COMP.SET w/o SP's (250) | 25.00 | 11.00 |
| COMMON CARD (1-250) | .15 | .07 |
| COMMON PROSPECT (251-275) | 3.00 | 1.35 |

| Card | Mint | NrMt |
|---|---|---|
| ❑ 1 Pedro Martinez | .75 | .35 |
| ❑ 2 Derek Jeter | 2.50 | 1.10 |
| ❑ 3 Cal Ripken | 2.50 | 1.10 |
| ❑ 4 Alex Rodriguez | 2.00 | .90 |
| ❑ 5 Vladimir Guerrero | 1.00 | .45 |
| ❑ 6 Troy Glaus | .75 | .35 |
| ❑ 7 Sammy Sosa | 1.25 | .55 |
| ❑ 8 Mike Piazza | 2.00 | .90 |
| ❑ 9 Tony Gwynn | 1.25 | .55 |
| ❑ 10 Tim Hudson | .50 | .23 |
| ❑ 11 John Flaherty | .15 | .07 |
| ❑ 12 Jeff Cirillo | .25 | .11 |
| ❑ 13 Ellis Burks | .25 | .11 |
| ❑ 14 Carlos Lee | .25 | .11 |
| ❑ 15 Carlos Beltran | .25 | .11 |
| ❑ 16 Ruben Rivera | .15 | .07 |
| ❑ 17 Richard Hidalgo | .25 | .11 |
| ❑ 18 Omar Vizquel | .25 | .11 |
| ❑ 19 Michael Barrett | .15 | .07 |
| ❑ 20 Jose Canseco | .75 | .35 |
| ❑ 21 Jason Giambi | .60 | .25 |
| ❑ 22 Greg Maddux | 1.50 | .70 |
| ❑ 23 Charles Johnson | .25 | .11 |
| ❑ 24 Sandy Alomar Jr. | .25 | .11 |
| ❑ 25 Rick Ankiel | .75 | .35 |
| ❑ 26 Richie Sexson | .25 | .11 |
| ❑ 27 Matt Williams | .40 | .18 |
| ❑ 28 Joe Girardi | .15 | .07 |
| ❑ 29 Jason Kendall | .25 | .11 |
| ❑ 30 Brad Fullmer | .25 | .11 |
| ❑ 31 Alex Gonzalez | .15 | .07 |
| ❑ 32 Rick Helling | .25 | .11 |
| ❑ 33 Mike Mussina | .60 | .25 |
| ❑ 34 Joe Randa | .15 | .07 |
| ❑ 35 J.T. Snow | .25 | .11 |
| ❑ 36 Edgardo Alfonzo | .25 | .11 |
| ❑ 37 Dante Bichette | .25 | .11 |
| ❑ 38 Brad Ausmus | .15 | .07 |
| ❑ 39 Bobby Abreu | .25 | .11 |
| ❑ 40 Warren Morris | .15 | .07 |
| ❑ 41 Tony Womack | .15 | .07 |
| ❑ 42 Russell Branyan | .25 | .11 |
| ❑ 43 Mike Lowell | .25 | .11 |
| ❑ 44 Mark Grace | .60 | .25 |
| ❑ 45 Jeromy Burnitz | .25 | .11 |
| ❑ 46 J.D. Drew | | |
| ❑ 47 David Justice | .40 | .18 |
| ❑ 48 Alex Gonzalez | .15 | .07 |
| ❑ 49 Tino Martinez | .25 | .11 |
| ❑ 50 Raul Mondesi | .25 | .11 |
| ❑ 51 Rafael Furcal | 1.00 | .45 |
| ❑ 52 Marquis Grissom | .15 | .07 |
| ❑ 53 Kevin Young | .15 | .07 |
| ❑ 54 Jon Lieber | .15 | .07 |
| ❑ 55 Henry Rodriguez | .15 | .07 |
| ❑ 56 Dave Burba | .15 | .07 |
| ❑ 57 Shannon Stewart | .25 | .11 |
| ❑ 58 Preston Wilson | .25 | .11 |
| ❑ 59 Paul O'Neill | .25 | .11 |
| ❑ 60 Jimmy Haynes | .15 | .07 |
| ❑ 61 Darryl Kile | .25 | .11 |
| ❑ 62 Bret Boone | .25 | .11 |
| ❑ 63 Bartolo Colon | .25 | .11 |
| ❑ 64 Andres Galarraga | .40 | .18 |
| ❑ 65 Trot Nixon | .25 | .11 |
| ❑ 66 Steve Finley | .25 | .11 |
| ❑ 67 Shawn Green | .50 | .23 |
| ❑ 68 Robert Person | .15 | .07 |
| ❑ 69 Kenny Rogers | .15 | .07 |
| ❑ 70 Bobby Higginson | .25 | .11 |
| ❑ 71 Barry Larkin | .50 | .23 |
| ❑ 72 Al Martin | .15 | .07 |
| ❑ 73 Tom Glavine | .50 | .23 |
| ❑ 74 Rondell White | .25 | .11 |
| ❑ 75 Ray Lankford | .25 | .11 |
| ❑ 76 Moises Alou | .25 | .11 |
| ❑ 77 Matt Clement | .15 | .07 |
| ❑ 78 Geoff Jenkins | .25 | .11 |
| ❑ 79 David Wells | .25 | .11 |
| ❑ 80 Chuck Finley | .25 | .11 |
| ❑ 81 Andy Pettitte | .25 | .11 |
| ❑ 82 Travis Fryman | .25 | .11 |
| ❑ 83 Ron Coomer | .15 | .07 |
| ❑ 84 Mark McGwire | 2.50 | 1.10 |
| ❑ 85 Kerry Wood | .25 | .11 |
| ❑ 86 Jorge Posada | .25 | .11 |
| ❑ 87 Jeff Bagwell | .75 | .35 |
| ❑ 88 Andruw Jones | .60 | .25 |
| ❑ 89 Ryan Klesko | .25 | .11 |
| ❑ 90 Mariano Rivera | .25 | .11 |
| ❑ 91 Lance Berkman | .25 | .11 |
| ❑ 92 Kenny Lofton | .25 | .11 |
| ❑ 93 Jacque Jones | .25 | .11 |
| ❑ 94 Eric Young | .15 | .07 |
| ❑ 95 Edgar Renteria | .15 | .07 |
| ❑ 96 Chipper Jones | 1.50 | .70 |
| ❑ 97 Todd Helton | .75 | .35 |
| ❑ 98 Shawn Estes | .15 | .07 |
| ❑ 99 Mark Mulder | .25 | .11 |
| ❑ 100 Lee Stevens | .15 | .07 |
| ❑ 101 Jermaine Dye | .25 | .11 |
| ❑ 102 Greg Vaughn | .25 | .11 |
| ❑ 103 Chris Singleton | .25 | .11 |

❑ 104 Brady Anderson .25 .11
❑ 105 Terrence Long .25 .11
❑ 106 Quilvio Veras .15 .07
❑ 107 Magglio Ordonez .25 .11
❑ 108 Johnny Damon .25 .11
❑ 109 Jeffrey Hammonds .25 .11
❑ 110 Fred McGriff .40 .18
❑ 111 Carl Pavano .15 .07
❑ 112 Bobby Estalella .15 .07
❑ 113 Todd Hundley .15 .07
❑ 114 Scott Rolen .50 .23
❑ 115 Robin Ventura .25 .11
❑ 116 Pokey Reese .25 .11
❑ 117 Luis Gonzalez .25 .11
❑ 118 Jose Offerman .15 .07
❑ 119 Edgar Martinez .40 .18
❑ 120 Dean Palmer .25 .11
❑ 121 David Segui .15 .07
❑ 122 Troy O'Leary .15 .07
❑ 123 Tony Batista .25 .11
❑ 124 Todd Zeile .25 .11
❑ 125 Randy Johnson .75 .35
❑ 126 Luis Castillo .25 .11
❑ 127 Kris Benson .25 .11
❑ 128 John Olerud .25 .11
❑ 129 Eric Karros .25 .11
❑ 130 Eddie Taubensee .15 .07
❑ 131 Neifi Perez .15 .07
❑ 132 Matt Stairs .15 .07
❑ 133 Luis Alicea .15 .07
❑ 134 Jeff Kent .40 .18
❑ 135 Javier Vazquez .15 .07
❑ 136 Garret Anderson .25 .11
❑ 137 Frank Thomas 1.25 .55
❑ 138 Carlos Febles .15 .07
❑ 139 Albert Belle .40 .18
❑ 140 Tony Clark .15 .07
❑ 141 Pat Burrell .60 .25
❑ 142 Mike Sweeney .25 .11
❑ 143 Jay Buhner .25 .11
❑ 144 Gabe Kapler .25 .11
❑ 145 Derek Bell .15 .07
❑ 146 B.J. Surhoff .25 .11
❑ 147 Adam Kennedy .25 .11
❑ 148 Aaron Boone .15 .07
❑ 149 Todd Stottlemyre .15 .07
❑ 150 Roberto Alomar .60 .25
❑ 151 Orlando Hernandez .25 .11
❑ 152 Jason Varitek .25 .11
❑ 153 Gary Sheffield .50 .23
❑ 154 Cliff Floyd .25 .11
❑ 155 Chad Hermansen .15 .07
❑ 156 Carlos Delgado .60 .25
❑ 157 Aaron Sele .25 .11
❑ 158 Sean Casey .25 .11
❑ 159 Ruben Mateo .25 .11
❑ 160 Mike Bordick .15 .07
❑ 161 Mike Cameron .25 .11
❑ 162 Doug Glanville .15 .07
❑ 163 Damion Easley .15 .07
❑ 164 Carl Everett .25 .11
❑ 165 Bengie Molina .25 .11
❑ 166 Adrian Beltre .25 .11
❑ 167 Tom Goodwin .15 .07
❑ 168 Rickey Henderson .75 .35
❑ 169 Mo Vaughn .25 .11
❑ 170 Mike Lieberthal .25 .11
❑ 171 Ken Griffey Jr. 2.50 1.10
❑ 172 Juan Gonzalez .50 .23
❑ 173 Ivan Rodriguez .75 .35
❑ 174 Al Leiter .25 .11
❑ 175 Vinny Castilla .25 .11
❑ 176 Peter Bergeron .15 .07
❑ 177 Pedro Astacio .15 .07
❑ 178 Paul Konerko .25 .11
❑ 179 Mitch Meluskey .15 .07
❑ 180 Kevin Millwood .25 .11
❑ 181 Ben Grieve .25 .11
❑ 182 Barry Bonds 1.00 .45
❑ 183 Rusty Greer .25 .11
❑ 184 Miguel Tejada .25 .11
❑ 185 Mark Quinn .25 .11
❑ 186 Larry Walker .25 .11
❑ 187 Jose Valentin .15 .07
❑ 188 Jose Vidro .25 .11
❑ 189 Delino DeShields .15 .07
❑ 190 Darin Erstad .60 .25
❑ 191 Bill Mueller .15 .07
❑ 192 Ray Durham .25 .11
❑ 193 Ken Caminiti .25 .11
❑ 194 Jim Thome .40 .18
❑ 195 Javy Lopez .25 .11
❑ 196 Fernando Vina .15 .07
❑ 197 Eric Chavez .25 .11
❑ 198 Eric Owens .15 .07
❑ 199 Brad Radke .25 .11
❑ 200 Travis Lee .15 .07
❑ 201 Tim Salmon .25 .11
❑ 202 Rafael Palmeiro .50 .23
❑ 203 Nomar Garciaparra 2.00 .90
❑ 204 Mike Hampton .25 .11
❑ 205 Keith Brown .25 .11
❑ 206 Juan Encarnacion .25 .11
❑ 207 Danny Graves .15 .07
❑ 208 Carlos Guillen .15 .07
❑ 209 Phil Nevin .25 .11
❑ 210 Matt Lawton .25 .11
❑ 211 Manny Ramirez .75 .35
❑ 212 James Baldwin .25 .11
❑ 213 Fernando Tatis .25 .11
❑ 214 Craig Biggio .40 .18
❑ 215 Brian Jordan .25 .11
❑ 216 Bernie Williams .50 .23
❑ 217 Ryan Dempster .25 .11
❑ 218 Roger Clemens 1.25 .55
❑ 219 Jose Cruz Jr. .25 .11
❑ 220 John Valentin .15 .07
❑ 221 Dmitri Young .25 .11
❑ 222 Curt Schilling .25 .11
❑ 223 Jim Edmonds .50 .23
❑ 224 Chan Ho Park .25 .11
❑ 225 Brian Giles .25 .11
❑ 226 Jimmy Anderson .15 .07
Tike Redman
❑ 227 Adam Piatt .75 .35
Jose Ortiz
❑ 228 Kenny Kelly .25 .11
Aubrey Huff
❑ 229 Randy Choate .15 .07
Craig Dingman
❑ 230 Eric Cammack .15 .07
Grant Roberts
❑ 231 Yovanny Lara .15 .07
Andy Tracy
❑ 232 Wayne Franklin .15 .07
Scott Linebrink
❑ 233 Cameron Cairncross .15 .07
Chan Perry
❑ 234 J.C. Romero .15 .07
Matt LeCroy
❑ 235 Geraldo Guzman .15 .07
Jason Conti
❑ 236 Morgan Burkhart .15 .07
Paxton Crawford
❑ 237 Pasqual Coco .15 .07
Leo Estrella
❑ 238 John Parrish .15 .07
Fernando Lunar
❑ 239 Keith McDonald .15 .07
Justin Brunette
❑ 240 Carlos Casimiro .15 .07
Ivanon Coffie
❑ 241 Daniel Garibay .15 .07
Ruben Quevedo
❑ 242 Sang-Hoon Lee .25 .11
Tomo Ohka
❑ 243 Hector Ortiz .15 .07
Jeff D'Amico
❑ 244 Jeff Sparks .15 .07
Travis Harper
❑ 245 Jason Boyd .15 .07
David Coggin
❑ 246 Mark Buehrle .15 .07
Lorenzo Barcelo
❑ 247 Adam Melhuse .15 .07
Ben Petrick
❑ 248 Kane Davis .15 .07
Paul Rigdon
❑ 249 Mike Darr .15 .07
Kory DeHaan
❑ 250 Vicente Padilla .15 .07
Mark Brownson
❑ 251 Barry Zito PROS 8.00 3.60
❑ 252 Tim Drew PROS 3.00 1.35
❑ 253 Luis Matos PROS 4.00 1.80
❑ 254 Alex Cabrera PROS 4.00 1.80
❑ 255 Jon Garland PROS 4.00 1.80
❑ 256 Milton Bradley PROS 4.00 1.80
❑ 257 Juan Pierre PROS 4.00 1.80
❑ 258 Ismael Villegas PROS 3.00 1.35
❑ 259 Eric Munson PROS 4.00 1.80
❑ 260 Tomas De la Rosa PROS 3.00 1.35
❑ 261 Chris Richard PROS 4.00 1.80
❑ 262 Jason Tyner PROS 3.00 1.35
❑ 263 B.J. Waszgis PROS 3.00 1.35
❑ 264 Jason Marquis PROS 3.00 1.35
❑ 265 Dusty Allen PROS 3.00 1.35
❑ 266 Corey Patterson PROS 5.00 2.20
❑ 267 Eric Byrnes PROS 4.00 1.80
❑ 268 Xavier Nady PROS 10.00 4.50
❑ 269 George Lombard PROS 3.00 1.35
❑ 270 Timo Perez PROS 5.00 2.20
❑ 271 Gary Matthews Jr. PROS 3.00 1.35
❑ 272 Chad Durbin PROS 3.00 1.35
❑ 273 Tony Armas Jr. PROS 4.00 1.80
❑ 274 Francisco Cordero PROS 3.00 1.35
❑ 275 Alfonso Soriano PROS 4.00 1.80

## 1989 Upper Deck

| | MINT | NRMT |
|---|---|---|
| COMPLETE SET (800) | 200.00 | 90.00 |
| COMP.FACT.SET (800) | 250.00 | 110.00 |
| COMPLETE LO SET (700) | 140.00 | 65.00 |
| COMPLETE HI SET (100) | 10.00 | 4.50 |
| COMP.HI FACT.SET (100) | 8.00 | 3.60 |

❑ 1 Ken Griffey Jr. RC ! 150.00 70.00
❑ 2 Luis Medina .20 .09
❑ 3 Tony Chance .20 .09
❑ 4 Dave Otto .20 .09
❑ 5 Sandy Alomar Jr. RC UER 1.00 .45
(Born 6/16/66;
should be 6/18/66)
❑ 6 Rolando Roomes .20 .09
❑ 7 Dave West RC .20 .09
❑ 8 Cris Carpenter RC* .20 .09
❑ 9 Gregg Jefferies .30 .14
❑ 10 Doug Dascenzo .20 .09
❑ 11 Ron Jones .20 .09
❑ 12 Luis DeLosSantos .20 .09
❑ 13 Gary Sheffield COR RC 6.00 2.70
❑ 13A Gary Sheffield RC ERR .75 .35
(SS upside down
on card front)
❑ 14 Mike Harkey RC .20 .09
❑ 15 Lance Blankenship RC .20 .09
❑ 16 William Brennan .20 .09
❑ 17 John Smoltz RC 2.00 .90
❑ 18 Ramon Martinez RC 1.00 .45
❑ 19 Mark Lemke RC .50 .23
❑ 20 Juan Bell RC .20 .09
❑ 21 Rey Palacios .20 .09
❑ 22 Felix Jose RC .20 .09
❑ 23 Van Snider .20 .09
❑ 24 Dante Bichette RC 2.00 .90
❑ 25 Randy Johnson RC 12.00 5.50
❑ 26 Carlos Quintana RC .20 .09
❑ 27 Star Rookie CL .20 .09
❑ 28 Mike Schooler .20 .09

❑ 29 Randy St.Claire .20 .09
❑ 30 Jerald Clark RC .20 .09
❑ 31 Kevin Gross .20 .09
❑ 32 Dan Firova .20 .09
❑ 33 Jeff Calhoun .20 .09
❑ 34 Tommy Hinzo .20 .09
❑ 35 Ricky Jordan RC* .30 .14
❑ 36 Larry Parrish .20 .09
❑ 37 Bret Saberhagen UER .30 .14
(Hit total 931;
should be 1031)
❑ 38 Mike Smithson .20 .09
❑ 39 Dave Dravecky .30 .14
❑ 40 Ed Romero .20 .09
❑ 41 Jeff Musselman .20 .09
❑ 42 Ed Hearn .20 .09
❑ 43 Rance Mulliniks .20 .09
❑ 44 Jim Eisenreich .20 .09
❑ 45 Sil Campusano .20 .09
❑ 46 Mike Krukow .20 .09
❑ 47 Paul Gibson .20 .09
❑ 48 Mike LaCoss .20 .09
❑ 49 Larry Herndon .20 .09
❑ 50 Scott Garrelts .20 .09
❑ 51 Dwayne Henry .20 .09
❑ 52 Jim Acker .20 .09
❑ 53 Steve Sax .20 .09
❑ 54 Pete O'Brien .20 .09
❑ 55 Paul Runge .20 .09
❑ 56 Rick Rhoden .20 .09
❑ 57 John Dopson .20 .09
❑ 58 Casey Candaele UER .20 .09
(No stats for Astros
for '88 season)
❑ 59 Dave Righetti .20 .09
❑ 60 Joe Hesketh .20 .09
❑ 61 Frank DiPino .20 .09
❑ 62 Tim Laudner .20 .09
❑ 63 Jamie Moyer .20 .09
❑ 64 Fred Toliver .20 .09
❑ 65 Mitch Webster .20 .09
❑ 66 John Tudor .20 .09
❑ 67 John Cangelosi .20 .09
❑ 68 Mike Devereaux .20 .09
❑ 69 Brian Fisher .20 .09
❑ 70 Mike Marshall .20 .09
❑ 71 Zane Smith .20 .09
❑ 72A Brian Holton ERR .75 .35
(Photo actually
Shawn Hillegas)
❑ 72B Brian Holton COR .30 .14
❑ 73 Jose Guzman .20 .09
❑ 74 Rick Mahler .20 .09
❑ 75 John Shelby .20 .09
❑ 76 Jim Deshaies .20 .09
❑ 77 Bobby Meacham .20 .09
❑ 78 Bryn Smith .20 .09
❑ 79 Joaquin Andujar .20 .09
❑ 80 Richard Dotson .20 .09
❑ 81 Charlie Lea .20 .09
❑ 82 Calvin Schiraldi .20 .09
❑ 83 Les Straker .20 .09
❑ 84 Les Lancaster .20 .09
❑ 85 Allan Anderson .20 .09
❑ 86 Junior Ortiz .20 .09
❑ 87 Jesse Orosco .20 .09
❑ 88 Felix Fermin .20 .09
❑ 89 Dave Anderson .20 .09
❑ 90 Rafael Belliard UER .20 .09
(Born '61, not '51)
❑ 91 Franklin Stubbs .20 .09
❑ 92 Cecil Espy .20 .09
❑ 93 Albert Hall .20 .09
❑ 94 Tim Leary .20 .09
❑ 95 Mitch Williams .20 .09
❑ 96 Tracy Jones .20 .09
❑ 97 Danny Darwin .20 .09
❑ 98 Gary Ward .20 .09
❑ 99 Neal Heaton .20 .09
❑ 100 Jim Pankovits .20 .09
❑ 101 Bill Doran .20 .09
❑ 102 Tim Wallach .20 .09
❑ 103 Joe Magrane .20 .09
❑ 104 Ozzie Virgil .20 .09
❑ 105 Alvin Davis .20 .09
❑ 106 Tom Brookens .20 .09
❑ 107 Shawon Dunston .20 .09
❑ 108 Tracy Woodson .20 .09
❑ 109 Nelson Liriano .20 .09
❑ 110 Devon White UER .30 .14
(Doubles total 46,
should be 56)
❑ 111 Steve Balboni .20 .09
❑ 112 Buddy Bell .30 .14
❑ 113 German Jimenez .20 .09
❑ 114 Ken Dayley .20 .09
❑ 115 Andres Galarraga .50 .23
❑ 116 Mike Scioscia .20 .09
❑ 117 Gary Pettis .20 .09
❑ 118 Ernie Whitt .20 .09
❑ 119 Bob Boone .30 .14
❑ 120 Ryne Sandberg 1.00 .45
❑ 121 Bruce Benedict .20 .09
❑ 122 Hubie Brooks .20 .09
❑ 123 Mike Moore .20 .09
❑ 124 Wallace Johnson .20 .09
❑ 125 Bob Horner .20 .09
❑ 126 Chili Davis .30 .14
❑ 127 Manny Trillo .20 .09
❑ 128 Chet Lemon .20 .09
❑ 129 John Cerutti .20 .09
❑ 130 Orel Hershiser .30 .14
❑ 131 Terry Pendleton .20 .09
❑ 132 Jeff Blauser .30 .14
❑ 133 Mike Fitzgerald .20 .09
❑ 134 Henry Cotto .20 .09
❑ 135 Gerald Young .20 .09
❑ 136 Luis Salazar .20 .09
❑ 137 Alejandro Pena .20 .09
❑ 138 Jack Howell .20 .09
❑ 139 Tony Fernandez .20 .09
❑ 140 Mark Grace .75 .35
❑ 141 Ken Caminiti 1.00 .45
❑ 142 Mike Jackson .20 .09
❑ 143 Larry McWilliams .20 .09
❑ 144 Andres Thomas .20 .09
❑ 145 Nolan Ryan 3X 4.00 1.80
❑ 146 Mike Davis .20 .09
❑ 147 DeWayne Buice .20 .09
❑ 148 Jody Davis .20 .09
❑ 149 Jesse Barfield .20 .09
❑ 150 Matt Nokes .20 .09
❑ 151 Jerry Reuss .20 .09
❑ 152 Rick Cerone .20 .09
❑ 153 Storm Davis .20 .09
❑ 154 Marvell Wynne .20 .09
❑ 155 Will Clark .75 .35
❑ 156 Luis Aguayo .20 .09
❑ 157 Willie Upshaw .20 .09
❑ 158 Randy Bush .20 .09
❑ 159 Ron Darling .20 .09
❑ 160 Kal Daniels .20 .09
❑ 161 Spike Owen .20 .09
❑ 162 Luis Polonia .20 .09
❑ 163 Kevin Mitchell UER .30 .14
('88/total HR's 18/52;
should be 19/53)
❑ 164 Dave Gallagher .20 .09
❑ 165 Benito Santiago .20 .09
❑ 166 Greg Gagne .20 .09
❑ 167 Ken Phelps .20 .09
❑ 168 Sid Fernandez .20 .09
❑ 169 Bo Diaz .20 .09
❑ 170 Cory Snyder .20 .09
❑ 171 Eric Show .20 .09
❑ 172 Robby Thompson .20 .09
❑ 173 Marty Barrett .20 .09
❑ 174 Dave Henderson .20 .09
❑ 175 Ozzie Guillen .20 .09
❑ 176 Barry Lyons .20 .09
❑ 177 Kelvin Torve .20 .09
❑ 178 Don Slaught .20 .09
❑ 179 Steve Lombardozzi .20 .09
❑ 180 Chris Sabo RC* .20 .09
❑ 181 Jose Uribe .20 .09
❑ 182 Shane Mack .20 .09
❑ 183 Ron Karkovice .20 .09
❑ 184 Todd Benzinger .20 .09
❑ 185 Dave Stewart .30 .14
❑ 186 Julio Franco .20 .09
❑ 187 Ron Robinson .20 .09
❑ 188 Wally Backman .20 .09
❑ 189 Randy Velarde .20 .09
❑ 190 Joe Carter .50 .23
❑ 191 Bob Welch .20 .09
❑ 192 Kelly Paris .20 .09
❑ 193 Chris Brown .20 .09
❑ 194 Rick Reuschel .20 .09
❑ 195 Roger Clemens 1.50 .70
❑ 196 Dave Concepcion .30 .14
❑ 197 Al Newman .20 .09
❑ 198 Brook Jacoby .20 .09
❑ 199 Mookie Wilson .30 .14
❑ 200 Don Mattingly 2.00 .90
❑ 201 Dick Schofield .20 .09
❑ 202 Mark Gubicza .20 .09
❑ 203 Gary Gaetti .30 .14
❑ 204 Dan Pasqua .20 .09
❑ 205 Andre Dawson .50 .23
❑ 206 Chris Speier .20 .09
❑ 207 Kent Tekulve .20 .09
❑ 208 Rod Scurry .20 .09
❑ 209 Scott Bailes .20 .09
❑ 210 Rickey Henderson UER 1.00 .45
(Throws Right)
❑ 211 Harold Baines .30 .14
❑ 212 Tony Armas .20 .09
❑ 213 Kent Hrbek .30 .14
❑ 214 Darrin Jackson .20 .09
❑ 215 George Brett 1.50 .70
❑ 216 Rafael Santana .20 .09
❑ 217 Andy Allanson .20 .09
❑ 218 Brett Butler .30 .14
❑ 219 Steve Jeltz .20 .09
❑ 220 Jay Buhner .30 .14
❑ 221 Bo Jackson .50 .23
❑ 222 Angel Salazar .20 .09
❑ 223 Kirk McCaskill .20 .09
❑ 224 Steve Lyons .20 .09
❑ 225 Bert Blyleven .30 .14
❑ 226 Scott Bradley .20 .09
❑ 227 Bob Melvin .20 .09
❑ 228 Ron Kittle .20 .09
❑ 229 Phil Bradley .20 .09
❑ 230 Tommy John .30 .14
❑ 231 Greg Walker .20 .09
❑ 232 Juan Berenguer .20 .09
❑ 233 Pat Tabler .20 .09
❑ 234 Terry Clark .20 .09
❑ 235 Rafael Palmeiro 1.00 .45
❑ 236 Paul Zuvella .20 .09
❑ 237 Willie Randolph .30 .14
❑ 238 Bruce Fields .20 .09
❑ 239 Mike Aldrete .20 .09
❑ 240 Lance Parrish .20 .09
❑ 241 Greg Maddux 3.00 1.35
❑ 242 John Moses .20 .09
❑ 243 Melido Perez .20 .09
❑ 244 Willie Wilson .20 .09
❑ 245 Mark McLemore .20 .09
❑ 246 Von Hayes .20 .09
❑ 247 Matt Williams .50 .23
❑ 248 John Candelaria UER .20 .09
(Listed as Yankee for
part of '87;
should be Mets)
❑ 249 Harold Reynolds .20 .09
❑ 250 Greg Swindell .20 .09
❑ 251 Juan Agosto .20 .09
❑ 252 Mike Felder .20 .09
❑ 253 Vince Coleman .20 .09
❑ 254 Larry Sheets .20 .09
❑ 255 George Bell .20 .09
❑ 256 Terry Steinbach .30 .14
❑ 257 Jack Armstrong RC* .20 .09
❑ 258 Dickie Thon .20 .09
❑ 259 Ray Knight .20 .09
❑ 260 Darryl Strawberry .30 .14
❑ 261 Doug Sisk .20 .09
❑ 262 Alex Trevino .20 .09
❑ 263 Jeffrey Leonard .20 .09
❑ 264 Tom Henke .20 .09
❑ 265 Ozzie Smith 1.00 .45
❑ 266 Dave Bergman .20 .09
❑ 267 Tony Phillips .20 .09
❑ 268 Mark Davis .20 .09
❑ 269 Kevin Elster .20 .09
❑ 270 Barry Larkin .75 .35

❑ 271 Manny Lee .20 .09
❑ 272 Tom Brunansky .20 .09
❑ 273 Craig Biggio RC 4.00 1.80
❑ 274 Jim Gantner .20 .09
❑ 275 Eddie Murray .75 .35
❑ 276 Jeff Reed .20 .09
❑ 277 Tim Teufel .20 .09
❑ 278 Rick Honeycutt .20 .09
❑ 279 Guillermo Hernandez .20 .09
❑ 280 John Kruk .30 .14
❑ 281 Luis Alicea RC* .20 .09
❑ 282 Jim Clancy .20 .09
❑ 283 Billy Ripken .20 .09
❑ 284 Craig Reynolds .20 .09
❑ 285 Robin Yount .75 .35
❑ 286 Jimmy Jones .20 .09
❑ 287 Ron Oester .20 .09
❑ 288 Terry Leach .20 .09
❑ 289 Dennis Eckersley .50 .23
❑ 290 Alan Trammell .50 .23
❑ 291 Jimmy Key .30 .14
❑ 292 Chris Bosio .20 .09
❑ 293 Jose DeLeon .20 .09
❑ 294 Jim Traber .20 .09
❑ 295 Mike Scott .20 .09
❑ 296 Roger McDowell .20 .09
❑ 297 Garry Templeton .20 .09
❑ 298 Doyle Alexander .20 .09
❑ 299 Nick Esasky .20 .09
❑ 300 Mark McGwire UER 5.00 2.20
(Doubles total 52;
should be 51)
❑ 301 Darryl Hamilton RC* .20 .09
❑ 302 Dave Smith .20 .09
❑ 303 Rick Sutcliffe .30 .14
❑ 304 Dave Stapleton .20 .09
❑ 305 Alan Ashby .20 .09
❑ 306 Pedro Guerrero .20 .09
❑ 307 Ron Guidry .30 .14
❑ 308 Steve Farr .20 .09
❑ 309 Curt Ford .20 .09
❑ 310 Claudell Washington .20 .09
❑ 311 Tom Prince .20 .09
❑ 312 Chad Kreuter RC .20 .09
❑ 313 Ken Oberkfell .20 .09
❑ 314 Jerry Browne .20 .09
❑ 315 R.J. Reynolds .20 .09
❑ 316 Scott Bankhead .20 .09
❑ 317 Milt Thompson .20 .09
❑ 318 Mario Diaz .20 .09
❑ 319 Bruce Ruffin .20 .09
❑ 320 Dave Valle .20 .09
❑ 321A Gary Varsho ERR 2.00 .90
(Back photo actually
Mike Bielecki bunting)
❑ 321B Gary Varsho COR .20 .09
(In road uniform)
❑ 322 Paul Mirabella .20 .09
❑ 323 Chuck Jackson .20 .09
❑ 324 Drew Hall .20 .09
❑ 325 Don August .20 .09
❑ 326 Israel Sanchez .20 .09
❑ 327 Denny Walling .20 .09
❑ 328 Joel Skinner .20 .09
❑ 329 Danny Tartabull .20 .09
❑ 330 Tony Pena .20 .09
❑ 331 Jim Sundberg .20 .09
❑ 332 Jeff D. Robinson .20 .09
❑ 333 Oddibe McDowell .20 .09
❑ 334 Jose Lind .20 .09
❑ 335 Paul Kilgus .20 .09
❑ 336 Juan Samuel .20 .09
❑ 337 Mike Campbell .20 .09
❑ 338 Mike Maddux .20 .09
❑ 339 Darnell Coles .20 .09
❑ 340 Bob Dernier .20 .09
❑ 341 Rafael Ramirez .20 .09
❑ 342 Scott Sanderson .20 .09
❑ 343 B.J. Surhoff .30 .14
❑ 344 Billy Hatcher .20 .09
❑ 345 Pat Perry .20 .09
❑ 346 Jack Clark .20 .09
❑ 347 Gary Thurman .20 .09
❑ 348 Tim Jones .20 .09
❑ 349 Dave Winfield .75 .35
❑ 350 Frank White .30 .14
❑ 351 Dave Collins .20 .09
❑ 352 Jack Morris .30 .14
❑ 353 Eric Plunk .20 .09
❑ 354 Leon Durham .20 .09
❑ 355 Ivan DeJesus .20 .09
❑ 356 Brian Holman RC* .20 .09
❑ 357A Dale Murphy ERR 35.00 16.00
(Front has
reverse negative)
❑ 357B Dale Murphy COR .30 .14
❑ 358 Mark Portugal .20 .09
❑ 359 Andy McGaffigan .20 .09
❑ 360 Tom Glavine .75 .35
❑ 361 Keith Moreland .20 .09
❑ 362 Todd Stottlemyre .50 .23
❑ 363 Dave Leiper .20 .09
❑ 364 Cecil Fielder .30 .14
❑ 365 Carmelo Martinez .20 .09
❑ 366 Dwight Evans .30 .14
❑ 367 Kevin McReynolds .20 .09
❑ 368 Rich Gedman .20 .09
❑ 369 Len Dykstra .30 .14
❑ 370 Jody Reed .20 .09
❑ 371 Jose Canseco UER 1.00 .45
(Strikeout total 391;
should be 491)
❑ 372 Rob Murphy .20 .09
❑ 373 Mike Henneman .20 .09
❑ 374 Walt Weiss .20 .09
❑ 375 Rob Dibble RC* .30 .14
❑ 376 Kirby Puckett 2.00 .90
(Mark McGwire
in background)
❑ 377 Dennis Martinez .30 .14
❑ 378 Ron Gant .30 .14
❑ 379 Brian Harper .20 .09
❑ 380 Nelson Santovenia .20 .09
❑ 381 Lloyd Moseby .20 .09
❑ 382 Lance McCullers .20 .09
❑ 383 Dave Stieb .20 .09
❑ 384 Tony Gwynn 1.50 .70
❑ 385 Mike Flanagan .20 .09
❑ 386 Bob Ojeda .20 .09
❑ 387 Bruce Hurst .20 .09
❑ 388 Dave Magadan .20 .09
❑ 389 Wade Boggs 1.00 .45
❑ 390 Gary Carter .50 .23
❑ 391 Frank Tanana .20 .09
❑ 392 Curt Young .20 .09
❑ 393 Jeff Treadway .20 .09
❑ 394 Darrell Evans .30 .14
❑ 395 Glenn Hubbard .20 .09
❑ 396 Chuck Cary .20 .09
❑ 397 Frank Viola .20 .09
❑ 398 Jeff Parrett .20 .09
❑ 399 Terry Blocker .20 .09
❑ 400 Dan Gladden .20 .09
❑ 401 Louie Meadows .20 .09
❑ 402 Tim Raines .30 .14
❑ 403 Joey Meyer .20 .09
❑ 404 Larry Andersen .20 .09
❑ 405 Rex Hudler .20 .09
❑ 406 Mike Schmidt 1.50 .70
❑ 407 John Franco .30 .14
❑ 408 Brady Anderson RC 2.00 .90
❑ 409 Don Carman .20 .09
❑ 410 Eric Davis .30 .14
❑ 411 Bob Stanley .20 .09
❑ 412 Pete Smith .20 .09
❑ 413 Jim Rice .30 .14
❑ 414 Bruce Sutter .20 .09
❑ 415 Oil Can Boyd .20 .09
❑ 416 Ruben Sierra .20 .09
❑ 417 Mike LaValliere .20 .09
❑ 418 Steve Buechele .20 .09
❑ 419 Gary Redus .20 .09
❑ 420 Scott Fletcher .20 .09
❑ 421 Dale Sveum .20 .09
❑ 422 Bob Knepper .20 .09
❑ 423 Luis Rivera .20 .09
❑ 424 Ted Higuera .20 .09
❑ 425 Kevin Bass .20 .09
❑ 426 Ken Gerhart .20 .09
❑ 427 Shane Rawley .20 .09
❑ 428 Paul O'Neill .30 .14
❑ 429 Joe Orsulak .20 .09
❑ 430 Jackie Gutierrez .20 .09
❑ 431 Gerald Perry .20 .09
❑ 432 Mike Greenwell .20 .09
❑ 433 Jerry Royster .20 .09
❑ 434 Ellis Burks .50 .23
❑ 435 Ed Olwine .20 .09
❑ 436 Dave Rucker .20 .09
❑ 437 Charlie Hough .30 .14
❑ 438 Bob Walk .20 .09
❑ 439 Bob Brower .20 .09
❑ 440 Barry Bonds 2.00 .90
❑ 441 Tom Foley .20 .09
❑ 442 Rob Deer .20 .09
❑ 443 Glenn Davis .20 .09
❑ 444 Dave Martinez .20 .09
❑ 445 Bill Wegman .20 .09
❑ 446 Lloyd McClendon .20 .09
❑ 447 Dave Schmidt .20 .09
❑ 448 Darren Daulton .30 .14
❑ 449 Frank Williams .20 .09
❑ 450 Don Aase .20 .09
❑ 451 Lou Whitaker .30 .14
❑ 452 Rich Gossage .30 .14
❑ 453 Ed Whitson .20 .09
❑ 454 Jim Walewander .20 .09
❑ 455 Damon Berryhill .20 .09
❑ 456 Tim Burke .20 .09
❑ 457 Barry Jones .20 .09
❑ 458 Joel Youngblood .20 .09
❑ 459 Floyd Youmans .20 .09
❑ 460 Mark Salas .20 .09
❑ 461 Jeff Russell .20 .09
❑ 462 Darrell Miller .20 .09
❑ 463 Jeff Kunkel .20 .09
❑ 464 Sherman Corbett .20 .09
❑ 465 Curtis Wilkerson .20 .09
❑ 466 Bud Black .20 .09
❑ 467 Cal Ripken 3.00 1.35
❑ 468 John Farrell .20 .09
❑ 469 Terry Kennedy .20 .09
❑ 470 Tom Candiotti .20 .09
❑ 471 Roberto Alomar 1.25 .55
❑ 472 Jeff M. Robinson .20 .09
❑ 473 Vance Law .20 .09
❑ 474 Randy Ready UER .20 .09
(Strikeout total 136;
should be 115)
❑ 475 Walt Terrell .20 .09
❑ 476 Kelly Downs .20 .09
❑ 477 Johnny Paredes .20 .09
❑ 478 Shawn Hillegas .20 .09
❑ 479 Bob Brenly .20 .09
❑ 480 Otis Nixon .20 .09
❑ 481 Johnny Ray .20 .09
❑ 482 Geno Petralli .20 .09
❑ 483 Stu Cliburn .20 .09
❑ 484 Pete Incaviglia .20 .09
❑ 485 Brian Downing .20 .09
❑ 486 Jeff Stone .20 .09
❑ 487 Carmen Castillo .20 .09
❑ 488 Tom Niedenfuer .20 .09
❑ 489 Jay Bell .50 .23
❑ 490 Rick Schu .20 .09
❑ 491 Jeff Pico .20 .09
❑ 492 Mark Parent .20 .09
❑ 493 Eric King .20 .09
❑ 494 Al Nipper .20 .09
❑ 495 Andy Hawkins .20 .09
❑ 496 Daryl Boston .20 .09
❑ 497 Ernie Riles .20 .09
❑ 498 Pascual Perez .20 .09
❑ 499 Bill Long UER .20 .09
(Games started total
70; should be 44)
❑ 500 Kirt Manwaring .20 .09
❑ 501 Chuck Crim .20 .09
❑ 502 Candy Maldonado .20 .09
❑ 503 Dennis Lamp .20 .09
❑ 504 Glenn Braggs .20 .09
❑ 505 Joe Price .20 .09
❑ 506 Ken Williams .20 .09
❑ 507 Bill Pecota .20 .09
❑ 508 Rey Quinones .20 .09
❑ 509 Jeff Bittiger .20 .09
❑ 510 Kevin Seitzer .20 .09
❑ 511 Steve Bedrosian .20 .09

❑ 512 Todd Worrell .30 .14
❑ 513 Chris James .20 .09
❑ 514 Jose Oquendo .20 .09
❑ 515 David Palmer .20 .09
❑ 516 John Smiley .20 .09
❑ 517 Dave Clark .20 .09
❑ 518 Mike Dunne .20 .09
❑ 519 Ron Washington .20 .09
❑ 520 Bob Kipper .20 .09
❑ 521 Lee Smith .30 .14
❑ 522 Juan Castillo .20 .09
❑ 523 Don Robinson .20 .09
❑ 524 Kevin Romine .20 .09
❑ 525 Paul Molitor .75 .35
❑ 526 Mark Langston .20 .09
❑ 527 Donnie Hill .20 .09
❑ 528 Larry Owen .20 .09
❑ 529 Jerry Reed .20 .09
❑ 530 Jack McDowell .30 .14
❑ 531 Greg Mathews .20 .09
❑ 532 John Russell .20 .09
❑ 533 Dan Quisenberry .20 .09
❑ 534 Greg Gross .20 .09
❑ 535 Danny Cox .20 .09
❑ 536 Terry Francona .30 .14
❑ 537 Andy Van Slyke .30 .14
❑ 538 Mel Hall .20 .09
❑ 539 Jim Gott .20 .09
❑ 540 Doug Jones .20 .09
❑ 541 Craig Lefferts .20 .09
❑ 542 Mike Boddicker .20 .09
❑ 543 Greg Brock .20 .09
❑ 544 Atlee Hammaker .20 .09
❑ 545 Tom Bolton .20 .09
❑ 546 Mike Macfarlane RC* .20 .09
❑ 547 Rich Renteria .20 .09
❑ 548 John Davis .20 .09
❑ 549 Floyd Bannister .20 .09
❑ 550 Mickey Brantley .20 .09
❑ 551 Duane Ward .20 .09
❑ 552 Dan Petry .20 .09
❑ 553 Mickey Tettleton UER .20 .09
(Walks total 175;
should be 136)
❑ 554 Rick Leach .20 .09
❑ 555 Mike Witt .20 .09
❑ 556 Sid Bream .20 .09
❑ 557 Bobby Witt .20 .09
❑ 558 Tommy Herr .20 .09
❑ 559 Randy Milligan .20 .09
❑ 560 Jose Cecena .20 .09
❑ 561 Mackey Sasser .20 .09
❑ 562 Carney Lansford .30 .14
❑ 563 Rick Aguilera .30 .14
❑ 564 Ron Hassey .20 .09
❑ 565 Dwight Gooden .30 .14
❑ 566 Paul Assenmacher .20 .09
❑ 567 Neil Allen .20 .09
❑ 568 Jim Morrison .20 .09
❑ 569 Mike Pagliarulo .20 .09
❑ 570 Ted Simmons .30 .14
❑ 571 Mark Thurmond .20 .09
❑ 572 Fred McGriff .75 .35
❑ 573 Wally Joyner .30 .14
❑ 574 Jose Bautista .20 .09
❑ 575 Kelly Gruber .20 .09
❑ 576 Cecilio Guante .20 .09
❑ 577 Mark Davidson .20 .09
❑ 578 Bobby Bonilla UER .30 .14
(Total steals 2 in '87;
should be 3)
❑ 579 Mike Stanley .20 .09
❑ 580 Gene Larkin .20 .09
❑ 581 Stan Javier .20 .09
❑ 582 Howard Johnson .20 .09
❑ 583A Mike Gallego ERR .75 .35
(Front reversed
negative)
❑ 583B Mike Gallego COR .75 .35
❑ 584 David Cone .30 .14
❑ 585 Doug Jennings .20 .09
❑ 586 Charles Hudson .20 .09
❑ 587 Dion James .20 .09
❑ 588 Al Leiter .75 .35
❑ 589 Charlie Puleo .20 .09
❑ 590 Roberto Kelly .30 .14
❑ 591 Thad Bosley .20 .09
❑ 592 Pete Stanicek .20 .09
❑ 593 Pat Borders RC* .30 .14
❑ 594 Bryan Harvey RC* .20 .09
❑ 595 Jeff Ballard .20 .09
❑ 596 Jeff Reardon .30 .14
❑ 597 Doug Drabek .20 .09
❑ 598 Edwin Correa .20 .09
❑ 599 Keith Atherton .20 .09
❑ 600 Dave LaPoint .20 .09
❑ 601 Don Baylor .30 .14
❑ 602 Tom Pagnozzi .20 .09
❑ 603 Tim Flannery .20 .09
❑ 604 Gene Walter .20 .09
❑ 605 Dave Parker .30 .14
❑ 606 Mike Diaz .20 .09
❑ 607 Chris Gwynn .20 .09
❑ 608 Odell Jones .20 .09
❑ 609 Carlton Fisk .75 .35
❑ 610 Jay Howell .20 .09
❑ 611 Tim Crews .20 .09
❑ 612 Keith Hernandez .30 .14
❑ 613 Willie Fraser .20 .09
❑ 614 Jim Eppard .20 .09
❑ 615 Jeff Hamilton .20 .09
❑ 616 Kurt Stillwell .20 .09
❑ 617 Tom Browning .20 .09
❑ 618 Jeff Montgomery .30 .14
❑ 619 Jose Rijo .20 .09
❑ 620 Jamie Quirk .20 .09
❑ 621 Willie McGee .30 .14
❑ 622 Mark Grant UER .20 .09
(Glove on wrong hand)
❑ 623 Bill Swift .20 .09
❑ 624 Orlando Mercado .20 .09
❑ 625 John Costello .20 .09
❑ 626 Jose Gonzalez .20 .09
❑ 627A Bill Schroeder ERR .75 .35
(Back photo actually
Ronn Reynolds buckling
shin guards)
❑ 627B Bill Schroeder COR .75 .35
❑ 628A Fred Manrique ERR .75 .35
(Back photo actually
Ozzie Guillen throwing)
❑ 628B Fred Manrique COR .20 .09
(Swinging bat on back)
❑ 629 Ricky Horton .20 .09
❑ 630 Dan Plesac .20 .09
❑ 631 Alfredo Griffin .20 .09
❑ 632 Chuck Finley .30 .14
❑ 633 Kirk Gibson .30 .14
❑ 634 Randy Myers .30 .14
❑ 635 Greg Minton .20 .09
❑ 636A Herm Winningham .75 .35
ERR (W1nningham
on back)
❑ 636B Herm Winningham COR .20 .09
❑ 637 Charlie Leibrandt .20 .09
❑ 638 Tim Birtsas .20 .09
❑ 639 Bill Buckner .30 .14
❑ 640 Danny Jackson .20 .09
❑ 641 Greg Booker .20 .09
❑ 642 Jim Presley .20 .09
❑ 643 Gene Nelson .20 .09
❑ 644 Rod Booker .20 .09
❑ 645 Dennis Rasmussen .20 .09
❑ 646 Juan Nieves .20 .09
❑ 647 Bobby Thigpen .20 .09
❑ 648 Tim Belcher .20 .09
❑ 649 Mike Young .20 .09
❑ 650 Ivan Calderon .20 .09
❑ 651 Oswaldo Peraza .20 .09
❑ 652A Pat Sheridan ERR 2.00 .90
(No position on front)
❑ 652B Pat Sheridan COR .20 .09
❑ 653 Mike Morgan .20 .09
❑ 654 Mike Heath .20 .09
❑ 655 Jay Tibbs .20 .09
❑ 656 Fernando Valenzuela .30 .14
❑ 657 Lee Mazzilli .20 .09
❑ 658 Frank Viola AL CY .20 .09
❑ 659A Jose Canseco AL MVP .30 .14
(Eagle logo in black)
❑ 659B Jose Canseco AL MVP .30 .14
(Eagle logo in blue)
❑ 660 Walt Weiss AL ROY .20 .09
❑ 661 Orel Hershiser NL CY .30 .14
❑ 662 Kirk Gibson NL MVP .20 .09
❑ 663 Chris Sabo NL ROY .20 .09
❑ 664 Dennis Eckersley .20 .09
ALCS MVP
❑ 665 Orel Hershiser .30 .14
NLCS MVP
❑ 666 Kirk Gibson WS .75 .35
❑ 667 Orel Hershiser WS MVP .30 .14
❑ 668 Wally Joyner TC .20 .09
❑ 669 Nolan Ryan TC 1.25 .55
❑ 670 Jose Canseco TC .30 .14
❑ 671 Fred McGriff TC .30 .14
❑ 672 Dale Murphy TC .30 .14
❑ 673 Paul Molitor TC .30 .14
❑ 674 Ozzie Smith TC .50 .23
❑ 675 Ryne Sandberg TC .50 .23
❑ 676 Kirk Gibson TC .20 .09
❑ 677 Andres Galarraga TC .20 .09
❑ 678 Will Clark TC .30 .14
❑ 679 Cory Snyder TC .20 .09
❑ 680 Alvin Davis TC .20 .09
❑ 681 Darryl Strawberry TC .20 .09
❑ 682 Cal Ripken TC 1.00 .45
❑ 683 Tony Gwynn TC .75 .35
❑ 684 Mike Schmidt TC .30 .14
❑ 685 Andy Van Slyke TC UER .20 .09
(96 Junior Ortiz)
❑ 686 Ruben Sierra TC .20 .09
❑ 687 Wade Boggs TC .30 .14
❑ 688 Eric Davis TC .20 .09
❑ 689 George Brett TC .75 .35
❑ 690 Alan Trammell TC .20 .09
❑ 691 Frank Viola TC .20 .09
❑ 692 Harold Baines TC .20 .09
❑ 693 Don Mattingly TC .50 .23
❑ 694 Checklist 1-100 .20 .09
❑ 695 Checklist 101-200 .20 .09
❑ 696 Checklist 201-300 .20 .09
❑ 697 Checklist 301-400 .20 .09
❑ 698 Checklist 401-500 UER .20 .09
(467 Cal Ripkin Jr.)
❑ 699 Checklist 501-600 UER .20 .09
(543 Greg Booker)
❑ 700 Checklist 601-700 .20 .09
❑ 701 Checklist 701-800 .20 .09
❑ 702 Jesse Barfield .20 .09
❑ 703 Walt Terrell .20 .09
❑ 704 Dickie Thon .20 .09
❑ 705 Al Leiter .75 .35
❑ 706 Dave LaPoint .20 .09
❑ 707 Charlie Hayes RC .75 .35
❑ 708 Andy Hawkins .20 .09
❑ 709 Mickey Hatcher .20 .09
❑ 710 Lance McCullers .20 .09
❑ 711 Ron Kittle .20 .09
❑ 712 Bert Blyleven .30 .14
❑ 713 Rick Dempsey .20 .09
❑ 714 Ken Williams .20 .09
❑ 715 Steve Rosenberg .20 .09
❑ 716 Joe Skalski .20 .09
❑ 717 Spike Owen .20 .09
❑ 718 Todd Burns .20 .09
❑ 719 Kevin Gross .20 .09
❑ 720 Tommy Herr .20 .09
❑ 721 Rob Ducey .20 .09
❑ 722 Gary Green .20 .09
❑ 723 Gregg Olson RC .75 .35
❑ 724 Greg W. Harris RC .20 .09
❑ 725 Craig Worthington .20 .09
❑ 726 Tom Howard RC .20 .09
❑ 727 Dale Mohorcic .20 .09
❑ 728 Rich Yett .20 .09
❑ 729 Mel Hall .20 .09
❑ 730 Floyd Youmans .20 .09
❑ 731 Lonnie Smith .20 .09
❑ 732 Wally Backman .20 .09
❑ 733 Trevor Wilson RC .20 .09
❑ 734 Jose Alvarez .20 .09
❑ 735 Bob Milacki .20 .09
❑ 736 Tom Gordon RC .75 .35
❑ 737 Wally Whitehurst RC .20 .09
❑ 738 Mike Aldrete .20 .09
❑ 739 Keith Miller .20 .09
❑ 740 Randy Milligan .20 .09

❑ 741 Jeff Parrett .20 .09
❑ 742 Steve Finley RC 2.50 1.10
❑ 743 Junior Felix RC .20 .09
❑ 744 Pete Harnisch RC 1.00 .45
❑ 745 Bill Spiers RC .20 .09
❑ 746 Hensley Meulens RC .20 .09
❑ 747 Juan Bell .20 .09
❑ 748 Steve Sax .20 .09
❑ 749 Phil Bradley .20 .09
❑ 750 Rey Quinones .20 .09
❑ 751 Tommy Gregg .20 .09
❑ 752 Kevin Brown 1.50 .70
❑ 753 Derek Lilliquist RC .20 .09
❑ 754 Todd Zeile RC 1.00 .45
❑ 755 Jim Abbott RC* .75 .35
(Triple exposure)
❑ 756 Ozzie Canseco .20 .09
❑ 757 Nick Esasky .20 .09
❑ 758 Mike Moore .20 .09
❑ 759 Rob Murphy .20 .09
❑ 760 Rick Mahler .20 .09
❑ 761 Fred Lynn .20 .09
❑ 762 Kevin Blankenship .20 .09
❑ 763 Eddie Murray .75 .35
❑ 764 Steve Searcy .20 .09
❑ 765 Jerome Walton RC .75 .35
❑ 766 Erik Hanson RC .30 .14
❑ 767 Bob Boone .30 .14
❑ 768 Edgar Martinez .50 .23
❑ 769 Jose DeJesus .20 .09
❑ 770 Greg Briley .20 .09
❑ 771 Steve Peters .20 .09
❑ 772 Rafael Palmeiro 1.00 .45
❑ 773 Jack Clark .20 .09
❑ 774 Nolan Ryan 4.00 1.80
(Throwing football)
❑ 775 Lance Parrish .20 .09
❑ 776 Joe Girardi RC .75 .35
❑ 777 Willie Randolph .30 .14
❑ 778 Mitch Williams .20 .09
❑ 779 Dennis Cook RC .20 .09
❑ 780 Dwight Smith RC .30 .14
❑ 781 Lenny Harris RC .30 .14
❑ 782 Torey Lovullo RC .20 .09
❑ 783 Norm Charlton RC .30 .14
❑ 784 Chris Brown .20 .09
❑ 785 Todd Benzinger .20 .09
❑ 786 Shane Rawley .20 .09
❑ 787 Omar Vizquel RC 2.50 1.10
❑ 788 LaVel Freeman .20 .09
❑ 789 Jeffrey Leonard .20 .09
❑ 790 Eddie Williams .20 .09
❑ 791 Jamie Moyer .20 .09
❑ 792 Bruce Hurst UER .20 .09
(Workd Series)
❑ 793 Julio Franco .20 .09
❑ 794 Claudell Washington .20 .09
❑ 795 Jody Davis .20 .09
❑ 796 Oddibe McDowell .20 .09
❑ 797 Paul Kilgus .20 .09
❑ 798 Tracy Jones .20 .09
❑ 799 Steve Wilson .20 .09
❑ 800 Pete O'Brien .20 .09

## 1990 Upper Deck

| | MINT | NRMT |
|---|---|---|
| COMPLETE SET (800) | 30.00 | 13.50 |
| COMP.FACT.SET (800) | 30.00 | 13.50 |
| COMPLETE LO SET (700) | 25.00 | 11.00 |
| COMPLETE HI SET (100) | 5.00 | 2.20 |
| COMP.HI FACT.SET (100) | 4.00 | 1.80 |

❑ 1 Star Rookie Checklist .10 .05
❑ 2 Randy Nosek .10 .05
❑ 3 Tom Drees UER .10 .05
(11th line, hulred;
should be hurled)
❑ 4 Curt Young .10 .05
❑ 5 Devon White TC .10 .05
❑ 6 Luis Salazar .10 .05
❑ 7 Von Hayes TC .10 .05
❑ 8 Jose Bautista .10 .05
❑ 9 Marquis Grissom RC .50 .23
❑ 10 Orel Hershiser TC .10 .05
❑ 11 Rick Aguilera .20 .09
❑ 12 Benito Santiago TC .10 .05
❑ 13 Deion Sanders .40 .18
❑ 14 Marvell Wynne .10 .05
❑ 15 Dave West .10 .05
❑ 16 Bobby Bonilla TC .10 .05
❑ 17 Sammy Sosa RC 8.00 3.60
❑ 18 Steve Sax TC .10 .05
❑ 19 Jack Howell .10 .05
❑ 20 Mike Schmidt Special .75 .35
UER (Suprising;
should be surprising)
❑ 21 Robin Ventura UER .40 .18
(Samta Maria)
❑ 22 Brian Meyer .10 .05
❑ 23 Blaine Beatty .10 .05
❑ 24 Ken Griffey Jr. TC 1.00 .45
❑ 25 Greg Vaughn UER .50 .23
(Association misspelled
as assiocation)
❑ 26 Xavier Hernandez RC .10 .05
❑ 27 Jason Grimsley RC .10 .05
❑ 28 Eric Anthony RC UER .10 .05
(Ashville; should
be Asheville)
❑ 29 Tim Raines TC UER .10 .05
(Wallach listed before Walker)
❑ 30 David Wells .20 .09
❑ 31 Hal Morris .10 .05
❑ 32 Bo Jackson TC .20 .09
❑ 33 Kelly Mann .10 .05
❑ 34 Nolan Ryan Special 1.00 .45
❑ 35 Scott Service UER .10 .05
(Born Cincinatti on
7/27/67; should be
Cincinnati 2/27)
❑ 36 Mark McGwire TC
❑ 37 Tino Martinez .50 .23
❑ 38 Chili Davis .20 .09
❑ 39 Scott Sanderson .10 .05
❑ 40 Kevin Mitchell TC .10 .05
❑ 41 Lou Whitaker TC .10 .05
❑ 42 Scott Coolbaugh UER .10 .05
(Definately)
❑ 43 Jose Cano UER .10 .05
(Born 9/7/62; should
be 3/7/62)
❑ 44 Jose Vizcaino RC .25 .11
❑ 45 Bob Hamelin RC .40 .18
❑ 46 Jose Offerman RC UER .50 .23
(Posesses)
❑ 47 Kevin Blankenship .10 .05
❑ 48 Kirby Puckett TC .50 .23
❑ 49 Tommy Greene RC UER .10 .05
(Livest, should be
liveliest)
❑ 50 Will Clark Special .20 .09
UER (Perenial, should
be perennial)
❑ 51 Rob Nelson .10 .05
❑ 52 Chris Hammond RC UER .10 .05
(Chatanooga)
❑ 53 Joe Carter TC .10 .05
❑ 54A Ben McDonald RC ERR 2.00 .90
(No Rookie designation
on card front)
❑ 54B Ben McDonald COR RC .25 .11
❑ 55 Andy Benes UER .10 .05
(Whichita)
❑ 56 John Olerud RC 1.00 .45
❑ 57 Roger Clemens TC .40 .18
❑ 58 Tony Armas .10 .05
❑ 59 George Canale .10 .05
❑ 60A Mickey Tettleton TC 2.00 .90
ERR (683 Jamie Weston)
❑ 60B Mickey Tettleton TC .10 .05
COR (683 Mickey Weston)
❑ 61 Mike Stanton RC .10 .05
❑ 62 Dwight Gooden TC .10 .05
❑ 63 Kent Mercker RC UER .10 .05
(Albuguerque)
❑ 64 Francisco Cabrera .10 .05
❑ 65 Steve Avery UER .10 .05
(Born NJ; should be MI;
Merker should be Mercker)
❑ 66 Jose Canseco .50 .23
❑ 67 Matt Merullo .10 .05
❑ 68 Vince Coleman TC UER .10 .05
(Guererro)
❑ 69 Ron Karkovice .10 .05
❑ 70 Kevin Maas RC .20 .09
❑ 71 Dennis Cook UER .10 .05
(Shown with righty
glove on card back)
❑ 72 Juan Gonzalez RC UER 2.00 .90
(135 games for Tulsa
in '89; should be 133)
❑ 73 Andre Dawson TC .20 .09
❑ 74 Dean Palmer RC UER .75 .35
(Permanent misspelled
as perminant)
❑ 75 Bo Jackson Special .20 .09
UER (Monsterous,
should be monstrous)
❑ 76 Rob Richie .10 .05
❑ 77 Bobby Rose UER .10 .05
(Pickin, should
be pick in)
❑ 78 Brian DuBois UER .10 .05
(Commiting)
❑ 79 Ozzie Guillen TC .10 .05
❑ 80 Gene Nelson .10 .05
❑ 81 Bob McClure .10 .05
❑ 82 Julio Franco TC .10 .05
❑ 83 Greg Minton .10 .05
❑ 84 John Smoltz TC UER .10 .05
(Oddibe not Odibbe)
❑ 85 Willie Fraser .10 .05
❑ 86 Neal Heaton .10 .05
❑ 87 Kevin Tapani RC UER .20 .09
(24th line has excpet;
should be except)
❑ 88 Mike Scott TC .10 .05
❑ 89A Jim Gott ERR 2.00 .90
(Photo actually
Rick Reed)
❑ 89B Jim Gott COR .10 .05
❑ 90 Lance Johnson .10 .05
❑ 91 Robin Yount TC UER .20 .09
(Checklist on back has
178 Rob Deer and
176 Mike Felder)
❑ 92 Jeff Parrett .10 .05
❑ 93 Julio Machado UER .10 .05
(Valenzuelan, should
be Venezuelan)
❑ 94 Ron Jones .10 .05
❑ 95 George Bell TC .10 .05
❑ 96 Jerry Reuss .10 .05
❑ 97 Brian Fisher .10 .05
❑ 98 Kevin Ritz UER .10 .05
(Amercian)
❑ 99 Barry Larkin TC .20 .09
❑ 100 Checklist 1-100 .10 .05
❑ 101 Gerald Perry .10 .05
❑ 102 Kevin Appier .25 .11
❑ 103 Julio Franco .10 .05
❑ 104 Craig Biggio .25 .11
❑ 105 Bo Jackson UER .20 .09
('89 BA wrong,
should be .256)
❑ 106 Junior Felix .10 .05
❑ 107 Mike Harkey .10 .05
❑ 108 Fred McGriff .40 .18
❑ 109 Rick Sutcliffe .20 .09

| No. | Card | | |
|---|---|---|---|
| ❑ 110 | Pete O'Brien | .10 | .05 |
| ❑ 111 | Kelly Gruber | .10 | .05 |
| ❑ 112 | Dwight Evans | .20 | .09 |
| ❑ 113 | Pat Borders | .10 | .05 |
| ❑ 114 | Dwight Gooden | .20 | .09 |
| ❑ 115 | Kevin Batiste | .10 | .05 |
| ❑ 116 | Eric Davis | .20 | .09 |
| ❑ 117 | Kevin Mitchell UER (Career HR total 99; should be 100) | .10 | .05 |
| ❑ 118 | Ron Oester | .10 | .05 |
| ❑ 119 | Brett Butler | .20 | .09 |
| ❑ 120 | Danny Jackson | .10 | .05 |
| ❑ 121 | Tommy Gregg | .10 | .05 |
| ❑ 122 | Ken Caminiti | .20 | .09 |
| ❑ 123 | Kevin Brown | .40 | .18 |
| ❑ 124 | George Brett UER (133 runs; should be 1300) | .75 | .35 |
| ❑ 125 | Mike Scott | .10 | .05 |
| ❑ 126 | Cory Snyder | .10 | .05 |
| ❑ 127 | George Bell | .10 | .05 |
| ❑ 128 | Mark Grace | .40 | .18 |
| ❑ 129 | Devon White | .10 | .05 |
| ❑ 130 | Tony Fernandez | .10 | .05 |
| ❑ 131 | Don Aase | .10 | .05 |
| ❑ 132 | Rance Mulliniks | .10 | .05 |
| ❑ 133 | Marty Barrett | .10 | .05 |
| ❑ 134 | Nelson Liriano | .10 | .05 |
| ❑ 135 | Mark Carreon | .10 | .05 |
| ❑ 136 | Candy Maldonado | .10 | .05 |
| ❑ 137 | Tim Birtsas | .10 | .05 |
| ❑ 138 | Tom Brookens | .10 | .05 |
| ❑ 139 | John Franco | .20 | .09 |
| ❑ 140 | Mike LaCoss | .10 | .05 |
| ❑ 141 | Jeff Treadway | .10 | .05 |
| ❑ 142 | Pat Tabler | .10 | .05 |
| ❑ 143 | Darrell Evans | .20 | .09 |
| ❑ 144 | Rafael Ramirez | .10 | .05 |
| ❑ 145 | Oddibe McDowell UER (Misspelled Odibbe) | .10 | .05 |
| ❑ 146 | Brian Downing | .10 | .05 |
| ❑ 147 | Curt Wilkerson | .10 | .05 |
| ❑ 148 | Ernie Whitt | .10 | .05 |
| ❑ 149 | Bill Schroeder | .10 | .05 |
| ❑ 150 | Domingo Ramos UER (Says throws right, but shows him throwing lefty) | .10 | .05 |
| ❑ 151 | Rick Honeycutt | .10 | .05 |
| ❑ 152 | Don Slaught | .10 | .05 |
| ❑ 153 | Mitch Webster | .10 | .05 |
| ❑ 154 | Tony Phillips | .10 | .05 |
| ❑ 155 | Paul Kilgus | .10 | .05 |
| ❑ 156 | Ken Griffey Jr. UER (Simultaniously) | 3.00 | 1.35 |
| ❑ 157 | Gary Sheffield | .50 | .23 |
| ❑ 158 | Wally Backman | .10 | .05 |
| ❑ 159 | B.J. Surhoff | .20 | .09 |
| ❑ 160 | Louie Meadows | .10 | .05 |
| ❑ 161 | Paul O'Neill | .20 | .09 |
| ❑ 162 | Jeff McKnight | .10 | .05 |
| ❑ 163 | Alvaro Espinoza | .10 | .05 |
| ❑ 164 | Scott Scudder | .10 | .05 |
| ❑ 165 | Jeff Reed | .10 | .05 |
| ❑ 166 | Gregg Jefferies | .20 | .09 |
| ❑ 167 | Barry Larkin | .40 | .18 |
| ❑ 168 | Gary Carter | .25 | .11 |
| ❑ 169 | Robby Thompson | .10 | .05 |
| ❑ 170 | Rolando Roomes | .10 | .05 |
| ❑ 171 | Mark McGwire UER (Total games 427 and hits 479; should be 467 and 427) | 1.50 | .70 |
| ❑ 172 | Steve Sax | .10 | .05 |
| ❑ 173 | Mark Williamson | .10 | .05 |
| ❑ 174 | Mitch Williams | .10 | .05 |
| ❑ 175 | Brian Holton | .10 | .05 |
| ❑ 176 | Rob Deer | .10 | .05 |
| ❑ 177 | Tim Raines | .20 | .09 |
| ❑ 178 | Mike Felder | .10 | .05 |
| ❑ 179 | Harold Reynolds | .10 | .05 |
| ❑ 180 | Terry Francona | .20 | .09 |
| ❑ 181 | Chris Sabo | .10 | .05 |
| ❑ 182 | Darryl Strawberry | .20 | .09 |
| ❑ 183 | Willie Randolph | .20 | .09 |
| ❑ 184 | Bill Ripken | .10 | .05 |
| ❑ 185 | Mackey Sasser | .10 | .05 |
| ❑ 186 | Todd Benzinger | .10 | .05 |
| ❑ 187 | Kevin Elster UER (16 homers in 1989; should be 10) | .10 | .05 |
| ❑ 188 | Jose Uribe | .10 | .05 |
| ❑ 189 | Tom Browning | .10 | .05 |
| ❑ 190 | Keith Miller | .10 | .05 |
| ❑ 191 | Don Mattingly | 1.00 | .45 |
| ❑ 192 | Dave Parker | .20 | .09 |
| ❑ 193 | Roberto Kelly UER (96 RBI; should be 62) | .10 | .05 |
| ❑ 194 | Phil Bradley | .10 | .05 |
| ❑ 195 | Ron Hassey | .10 | .05 |
| ❑ 196 | Gerald Young | .10 | .05 |
| ❑ 197 | Hubie Brooks | .10 | .05 |
| ❑ 198 | Bill Doran | .10 | .05 |
| ❑ 199 | Al Newman | .10 | .05 |
| ❑ 200 | Checklist 101-200 | .10 | .05 |
| ❑ 201 | Terry Puhl | .10 | .05 |
| ❑ 202 | Frank DiPino | .10 | .05 |
| ❑ 203 | Jim Clancy | .10 | .05 |
| ❑ 204 | Bob Ojeda | .10 | .05 |
| ❑ 205 | Alex Trevino | .10 | .05 |
| ❑ 206 | Dave Henderson | .10 | .05 |
| ❑ 207 | Henry Cotto | .10 | .05 |
| ❑ 208 | Rafael Belliard UER (Born 1961, not 1951) | .10 | .05 |
| ❑ 209 | Stan Javier | .10 | .05 |
| ❑ 210 | Jerry Reed | .10 | .05 |
| ❑ 211 | Doug Dascenzo | .10 | .05 |
| ❑ 212 | Andres Thomas | .10 | .05 |
| ❑ 213 | Greg Maddux | 1.00 | .45 |
| ❑ 214 | Mike Schooler | .10 | .05 |
| ❑ 215 | Lonnie Smith | .10 | .05 |
| ❑ 216 | Jose Rijo | .10 | .05 |
| ❑ 217 | Greg Gagne | .10 | .05 |
| ❑ 218 | Jim Gantner | .10 | .05 |
| ❑ 219 | Allan Anderson | .10 | .05 |
| ❑ 220 | Rick Mahler | .10 | .05 |
| ❑ 221 | Jim Deshaies | .10 | .05 |
| ❑ 222 | Keith Hernandez | .20 | .09 |
| ❑ 223 | Vince Coleman | .10 | .05 |
| ❑ 224 | David Cone | .20 | .09 |
| ❑ 225 | Ozzie Smith | .50 | .23 |
| ❑ 226 | Matt Nokes | .10 | .05 |
| ❑ 227 | Barry Bonds | .60 | .25 |
| ❑ 228 | Felix Jose | .10 | .05 |
| ❑ 229 | Dennis Powell | .10 | .05 |
| ❑ 230 | Mike Gallego | .10 | .05 |
| ❑ 231 | Shawon Dunston UER ('89 stats are Andre Dawson's) | .10 | .05 |
| ❑ 232 | Ron Gant | .20 | .09 |
| ❑ 233 | Omar Vizquel | .40 | .18 |
| ❑ 234 | Derek Lilliquist | .10 | .05 |
| ❑ 235 | Erik Hanson | .10 | .05 |
| ❑ 236 | Kirby Puckett UER (824 games; should be 924) | 1.00 | .45 |
| ❑ 237 | Bill Spiers | .10 | .05 |
| ❑ 238 | Dan Gladden | .10 | .05 |
| ❑ 239 | Bryan Clutterbuck | .10 | .05 |
| ❑ 240 | John Moses | .10 | .05 |
| ❑ 241 | Ron Darling | .10 | .05 |
| ❑ 242 | Joe Magrane | .10 | .05 |
| ❑ 243 | Dave Magadan | .10 | .05 |
| ❑ 244 | Pedro Guerrero UER (Misspelled Guererro) | .10 | .05 |
| ❑ 245 | Glenn Davis | .10 | .05 |
| ❑ 246 | Terry Steinbach | .10 | .05 |
| ❑ 247 | Fred Lynn | .10 | .05 |
| ❑ 248 | Gary Redus | .10 | .05 |
| ❑ 249 | Ken Williams | .10 | .05 |
| ❑ 250 | Sid Bream | .10 | .05 |
| ❑ 251 | Bob Welch UER (2587 career strike-outs; should be 1587) | .10 | .05 |
| ❑ 252 | Bill Buckner | .10 | .05 |
| ❑ 253 | Carney Lansford | .20 | .09 |
| ❑ 254 | Paul Molitor | .40 | .18 |
| ❑ 255 | Jose DeJesus | .10 | .05 |
| ❑ 256 | Orel Hershiser | .20 | .09 |
| ❑ 257 | Tom Brunansky | .10 | .05 |
| ❑ 258 | Mike Davis | .10 | .05 |
| ❑ 259 | Jeff Ballard | .10 | .05 |
| ❑ 260 | Scott Terry | .10 | .05 |
| ❑ 261 | Sid Fernandez | .10 | .05 |
| ❑ 262 | Mike Marshall | .10 | .05 |
| ❑ 263 | Howard Johnson UER (192 SO; should be 592) | .10 | .05 |
| ❑ 264 | Kirk Gibson UER (659 runs; should be 669) | .20 | .09 |
| ❑ 265 | Kevin McReynolds | .10 | .05 |
| ❑ 266 | Cal Ripken | 1.50 | .70 |
| ❑ 267 | Ozzie Guillen UER (Career triples 27; should be 29) | .10 | .05 |
| ❑ 268 | Jim Traber | .10 | .05 |
| ❑ 269 | Bobby Thigpen UER (31 saves in 1989; should be 34) | .10 | .05 |
| ❑ 270 | Joe Orsulak | .10 | .05 |
| ❑ 271 | Bob Boone | .20 | .09 |
| ❑ 272 | Dave Stewart UER (Totals wrong due to omission of '86 stats) | .20 | .09 |
| ❑ 273 | Tim Wallach | .10 | .05 |
| ❑ 274 | Luis Aquino UER (Says throws lefty, but shows him throwing righty) | .10 | .05 |
| ❑ 275 | Mike Moore | .10 | .05 |
| ❑ 276 | Tony Pena | .10 | .05 |
| ❑ 277 | Eddie Murray UER (Several typos in career total stats) | .40 | .18 |
| ❑ 278 | Milt Thompson | .10 | .05 |
| ❑ 279 | Alejandro Pena | .10 | .05 |
| ❑ 280 | Ken Dayley | .10 | .05 |
| ❑ 281 | Carmen Castillo | .10 | .05 |
| ❑ 282 | Tom Henke | .10 | .05 |
| ❑ 283 | Mickey Hatcher | .10 | .05 |
| ❑ 284 | Roy Smith | .10 | .05 |
| ❑ 285 | Manny Lee | .10 | .05 |
| ❑ 286 | Dan Pasqua | .10 | .05 |
| ❑ 287 | Larry Sheets | .10 | .05 |
| ❑ 288 | Garry Templeton | .10 | .05 |
| ❑ 289 | Eddie Williams | .10 | .05 |
| ❑ 290 | Brady Anderson UER (Home: Silver Springs, not Siver Springs) | .40 | .18 |
| ❑ 291 | Spike Owen | .10 | .05 |
| ❑ 292 | Storm Davis | .10 | .05 |
| ❑ 293 | Chris Bosio | .10 | .05 |
| ❑ 294 | Jim Eisenreich | .10 | .05 |
| ❑ 295 | Don August | .10 | .05 |
| ❑ 296 | Jeff Hamilton | .10 | .05 |
| ❑ 297 | Mickey Tettleton | .10 | .05 |
| ❑ 298 | Mike Scioscia | .10 | .05 |
| ❑ 299 | Kevin Hickey | .10 | .05 |
| ❑ 300 | Checklist 201-300 | .10 | .05 |
| ❑ 301 | Shawn Abner | .10 | .05 |
| ❑ 302 | Kevin Bass | .10 | .05 |
| ❑ 303 | Bip Roberts | .10 | .05 |
| ❑ 304 | Joe Girardi | .25 | .11 |
| ❑ 305 | Danny Darwin | .10 | .05 |
| ❑ 306 | Mike Heath | .10 | .05 |
| ❑ 307 | Mike Macfarlane | .10 | .05 |
| ❑ 308 | Ed Whitson | .10 | .05 |
| ❑ 309 | Tracy Jones | .10 | .05 |
| ❑ 310 | Scott Fletcher | .10 | .05 |
| ❑ 311 | Darnell Coles | .10 | .05 |
| ❑ 312 | Mike Brumley | .10 | .05 |
| ❑ 313 | Bill Swift | .10 | .05 |
| ❑ 314 | Charlie Hough | .20 | .09 |
| ❑ 315 | Jim Presley | .10 | .05 |
| ❑ 316 | Luis Polonia | .10 | .05 |
| ❑ 317 | Mike Morgan | .10 | .05 |
| ❑ 318 | Lee Guetterman | .10 | .05 |
| ❑ 319 | Jose Oquendo | .10 | .05 |
| ❑ 320 | Wayne Tolleson | .10 | .05 |
| ❑ 321 | Jody Reed | .10 | .05 |
| ❑ 322 | Damon Berryhill | .10 | .05 |
| ❑ 323 | Roger Clemens | .75 | .35 |
| ❑ 324 | Ryne Sandberg | .50 | .23 |
| ❑ 325 | Benito Santiago UER (Misspelled Santago on card back) | .10 | .05 |
| ❑ 326 | Bret Saberhagen UER | .20 | .09 |

(1140 hits; should be 1240; 56 CG, should be 52)
❑ 327 Lou Whitaker .20 .09
❑ 328 Dave Gallagher .10 .05
❑ 329 Mike Pagliarulo .10 .05
❑ 330 Doyle Alexander .10 .05
❑ 331 Jeffrey Leonard .10 .05
❑ 332 Torey Lovullo .10 .05
❑ 333 Pete Incaviglia .10 .05
❑ 334 Rickey Henderson .50 .23
❑ 335 Rafael Palmeiro .40 .18
❑ 336 Ken Hill .20 .09
❑ 337 Dave Winfield UER .40 .18
(1418 RBI's; should be 1438)
❑ 338 Alfredo Griffin .10 .05
❑ 339 Andy Hawkins .10 .05
❑ 340 Ted Power .10 .05
❑ 341 Steve Wilson .10 .05
❑ 342 Jack Clark UER .20 .09
(916 BB; should be 1006; 1142 SO, should be 1130)
❑ 343 Ellis Burks .25 .11
❑ 344 Tony Gwynn UER .75 .35
(Doubles stats on card back are wrong)
❑ 345 Jerome Walton UER .10 .05
(Total At Bats 476; should be 475)
❑ 346 Roberto Alomar UER .40 .18
(61 doubles; should be 51)
❑ 347 Carlos Martinez UER .10 .05
(Born 8/11/64; should be 8/11/65)
❑ 348 Chet Lemon .10 .05
❑ 349 Willie Wilson .10 .05
❑ 350 Greg Walker .10 .05
❑ 351 Tom Bolton .10 .05
❑ 352 German Gonzalez .10 .05
❑ 353 Harold Baines .20 .09
❑ 354 Mike Greenwell .10 .05
❑ 355 Ruben Sierra .10 .05
❑ 356 Andres Galarraga .25 .11
❑ 357 Andre Dawson .25 .11
❑ 358 Jeff Brantley .10 .05
❑ 359 Mike Bielecki .10 .05
❑ 360 Ken Oberkfell .10 .05
❑ 361 Kurt Stillwell .10 .05
❑ 362 Brian Holman .10 .05
❑ 363 Kevin Seitzer UER .10 .05
(Career triples total does not add up)
❑ 364 Alvin Davis .10 .05
❑ 365 Tom Gordon .20 .09
❑ 366 Bobby Bonilla UER .20 .09
(Two steals in 1987; should be 3)
❑ 367 Carlton Fisk .40 .18
❑ 368 Steve Carter UER .10 .05
(Charlotesville)
❑ 369 Joel Skinner .10 .05
❑ 370 John Cangelosi .10 .05
❑ 371 Cecil Espy .10 .05
❑ 372 Gary Wayne .10 .05
❑ 373 Jim Rice .20 .09
❑ 374 Mike Dyer .10 .05
❑ 375 Joe Carter .20 .09
❑ 376 Dwight Smith .10 .05
❑ 377 John Wetteland .40 .18
❑ 378 Earnie Riles .10 .05
❑ 379 Otis Nixon .10 .05
❑ 380 Vance Law .10 .05
❑ 381 Dave Bergman .10 .05
❑ 382 Frank White .20 .09
❑ 383 Scott Bradley .10 .05
❑ 384 Israel Sanchez UER .10 .05
(Totals don't include '89 stats)
❑ 385 Gary Pettis .10 .05
❑ 386 Donn Pall .10 .05
❑ 387 John Smiley .10 .05
❑ 388 Tom Candiotti .10 .05
❑ 389 Junior Ortiz .10 .05
❑ 390 Steve Lyons .10 .05
❑ 391 Brian Harper .10 .05
❑ 392 Fred Manrique .10 .05
❑ 393 Lee Smith .20 .09
❑ 394 Jeff Kunkel .10 .05
❑ 395 Claudell Washington .10 .05
❑ 396 John Tudor .10 .05
❑ 397 Terry Kennedy UER .10 .05
(Career totals all wrong)
❑ 398 Lloyd McClendon .10 .05
❑ 399 Craig Lefferts .10 .05
❑ 400 Checklist 301-400 .10 .05
❑ 401 Keith Moreland .10 .05
❑ 402 Rich Gedman .10 .05
❑ 403 Jeff D. Robinson .10 .05
❑ 404 Randy Ready .10 .05
❑ 405 Rick Cerone .10 .05
❑ 406 Jeff Blauser .10 .05
❑ 407 Larry Andersen .10 .05
❑ 408 Joe Boever .10 .05
❑ 409 Felix Fermin .10 .05
❑ 410 Glenn Wilson .10 .05
❑ 411 Rex Hudler .10 .05
❑ 412 Mark Grant .10 .05
❑ 413 Dennis Martinez .20 .09
❑ 414 Darrin Jackson .10 .05
❑ 415 Mike Aldrete .10 .05
❑ 416 Roger McDowell .10 .05
❑ 417 Jeff Reardon .20 .09
❑ 418 Darren Daulton .20 .09
❑ 419 Tim Laudner .10 .05
❑ 420 Don Carman .10 .05
❑ 421 Lloyd Moseby .10 .05
❑ 422 Doug Drabek .10 .05
❑ 423 Lenny Harris UER .10 .05
(Walks 2 in '80; should be 20)
❑ 424 Jose Lind .10 .05
❑ 425 Dave Johnson (P) .10 .05
❑ 426 Jerry Browne .10 .05
❑ 427 Eric Yelding .10 .05
❑ 428 Brad Komminsk .10 .05
❑ 429 Jody Davis .10 .05
❑ 430 Mariano Duncan .10 .05
❑ 431 Mark Davis .10 .05
❑ 432 Nelson Santovenia .10 .05
❑ 433 Bruce Hurst .10 .05
❑ 434 Jeff Huson RC .10 .05
❑ 435 Chris James .10 .05
❑ 436 Mark Guthrie .10 .05
❑ 437 Charlie Hayes .10 .05
❑ 438 Shane Rawley .10 .05
❑ 439 Dickie Thon .10 .05
❑ 440 Juan Berenguer .10 .05
❑ 441 Kevin Romine .10 .05
❑ 442 Bill Landrum .10 .05
❑ 443 Todd Frohwirth .10 .05
❑ 444 Craig Worthington .10 .05
❑ 445 Fernando Valenzuela .20 .09
❑ 446 Joey Belle 1.00 .45
❑ 447 Ed Whited UER .10 .05
(Ashville, should be Asheville)
❑ 448 Dave Smith .10 .05
❑ 449 Dave Clark .10 .05
❑ 450 Juan Agosto .10 .05
❑ 451 Dave Valle .10 .05
❑ 452 Kent Hrbek .20 .09
❑ 453 Von Hayes .10 .05
❑ 454 Gary Gaetti .20 .09
❑ 455 Greg Briley .10 .05
❑ 456 Glenn Braggs .10 .05
❑ 457 Kirt Manwaring .10 .05
❑ 458 Mel Hall .10 .05
❑ 459 Brook Jacoby .10 .05
❑ 460 Pat Sheridan .10 .05
❑ 461 Rob Murphy .10 .05
❑ 462 Jimmy Key .20 .09
❑ 463 Nick Esasky .10 .05
❑ 464 Rob Ducey .10 .05
❑ 465 Carlos Quintana UER .10 .05
(Internatinoal)
❑ 466 Larry Walker RC 1.25 .55
❑ 467 Todd Worrell .10 .05
❑ 468 Kevin Gross .10 .05
❑ 469 Terry Pendleton .20 .09
❑ 470 Dave Martinez .10 .05
❑ 471 Gene Larkin .10 .05
❑ 472 Len Dykstra UER .20 .09
('89 and total runs understated by 10)
❑ 473 Barry Lyons .10 .05
❑ 474 Terry Mulholland .10 .05
❑ 475 Chip Hale .10 .05
❑ 476 Jesse Barfield .10 .05
❑ 477 Dan Plesac .10 .05
❑ 478A Scott Garrelts ERR 2.00 .90
(Photo actually Bill Bathe)
❑ 478B Scott Garrelts COR .10 .05
❑ 479 Dave Righetti .10 .05
❑ 480 Gus Polidor UER .10 .05
(Wearing 14 on front, but 10 on back)
❑ 481 Mookie Wilson .20 .09
❑ 482 Luis Rivera .10 .05
❑ 483 Mike Flanagan .10 .05
❑ 484 Dennis Boyd .10 .05
❑ 485 John Cerutti .10 .05
❑ 486 John Costello .10 .05
❑ 487 Pascual Perez .10 .05
❑ 488 Tommy Herr .10 .05
❑ 489 Tom Foley .10 .05
❑ 490 Curt Ford .10 .05
❑ 491 Steve Lake .10 .05
❑ 492 Tim Teufel .10 .05
❑ 493 Randy Bush .10 .05
❑ 494 Mike Jackson .10 .05
❑ 495 Steve Jeltz .10 .05
❑ 496 Paul Gibson .10 .05
❑ 497 Steve Balboni .10 .05
❑ 498 Bud Black .10 .05
❑ 499 Dale Sveum .10 .05
❑ 500 Checklist 401-500 .10 .05
❑ 501 Tim Jones .10 .05
❑ 502 Mark Portugal .10 .05
❑ 503 Ivan Calderon .10 .05
❑ 504 Rick Rhoden .10 .05
❑ 505 Willie McGee .20 .09
❑ 506 Kirk McCaskill .10 .05
❑ 507 Dave LaPoint .10 .05
❑ 508 Jay Howell .10 .05
❑ 509 Johnny Ray .10 .05
❑ 510 Dave Anderson .10 .05
❑ 511 Chuck Crim .10 .05
❑ 512 Joe Hesketh .10 .05
❑ 513 Dennis Eckersley .25 .11
❑ 514 Greg Brock .10 .05
❑ 515 Tim Burke .10 .05
❑ 516 Frank Tanana .10 .05
❑ 517 Jay Bell .20 .09
❑ 518 Guillermo Hernandez .10 .05
❑ 519 Randy Kramer UER .10 .05
(Codiroli misspelled as Codoroli)
❑ 520 Charles Hudson .10 .05
❑ 521 Jim Corsi .10 .05
(Word originally is misspelled on back)
❑ 522 Steve Rosenberg .10 .05
❑ 523 Cris Carpenter .10 .05
❑ 524 Matt Winters .10 .05
❑ 525 Melido Perez .10 .05
❑ 526 Chris Gwynn UER .10 .05
(Albeguergue)
❑ 527 Bert Blyleven UER .20 .09
(Games career total is wrong; should be 644)
❑ 528 Chuck Cary .10 .05
❑ 529 Daryl Boston .10 .05
❑ 530 Dale Mohorcic .10 .05
❑ 531 Geronimo Berroa .10 .05
❑ 532 Edgar Martinez .25 .11
❑ 533 Dale Murphy .40 .18
❑ 534 Jay Buhner .20 .09
❑ 535 John Smoltz UER .20 .09
(HEA Stadium)
❑ 536 Andy Van Slyke .20 .09
❑ 537 Mike Henneman .10 .05
❑ 538 Miguel Garcia .10 .05
❑ 539 Frank Williams .10 .05

❑ 540 R.J. Reynolds ................ .10 .05
❑ 541 Shawn Hillegas ............. .10 .05
❑ 542 Walt Weiss .................... .10 .05
❑ 543 Greg Hibbard RC .......... .10 .05
❑ 544 Nolan Ryan .................. 2.00 .90
❑ 545 Todd Zeile ...................... .20 .09
❑ 546 Hensley Meulens............ .10 .05
❑ 547 Tim Belcher .................... .10 .05
❑ 548 Mike Witt ........................ .10 .05
❑ 549 Greg Cadaret UER ........ .10 .05
(Aquiring, should
be Acquiring)
❑ 550 Franklin Stubbs ............. .10 .05
❑ 551 Tony Castillo .................. .10 .05
❑ 552 Jeff M. Robinson ............ .10 .05
❑ 553 Steve Olin RC ................ .20 .09
❑ 554 Alan Trammell ................ .25 .11
❑ 555 Wade Boggs 4X ............ .50 .23
(Bo Jackson
in background)
❑ 556 Will Clark ........................ .40 .18
❑ 557 Jeff King ........................ .10 .05
❑ 558 Mike Fitzgerald .............. .10 .05
❑ 559 Ken Howell ..................... .10 .05
❑ 560 Bob Kipper ..................... .10 .05
❑ 561 Scott Bankhead .............. .10 .05
❑ 562A Jeff Innis ERR............ 2.00 .90
(Photo actually
David West)
❑ 562B Jeff Innis COR ............ .10 .05
❑ 563 Randy Johnson .............. .75 .35
❑ 564 Wally Whitehurst ............ .10 .05
❑ 565 Gene Harris..................... .10 .05
❑ 566 Norm Charlton ................ .10 .05
❑ 567 Robin Yount UER .......... .20 .09
(7602 career hits,
should be 2606)
❑ 568 Joe Oliver UER .............. .10 .05
(Fl.orida)
❑ 569 Mark Parent.................... .10 .05
❑ 570 John Farrell UER............ .10 .05
(Loss total added wrong)
❑ 571 Tom Glavine ................... .40 .18
❑ 572 Rod Nichols..................... .10 .05
❑ 573 Jack Morris ..................... .20 .09
❑ 574 Greg Swindell ................ .10 .05
❑ 575 Steve Searcy.................. .10 .05
❑ 576 Ricky Jordan .................. .10 .05
❑ 577 Matt Williams.................. .25 .11
❑ 578 Mike LaValliere .............. .10 .05
❑ 579 Bryn Smith...................... .10 .05
❑ 580 Bruce Ruffin ................... .10 .05
❑ 581 Randy Myers.................. .20 .09
❑ 582 Rick Wrona ..................... .10 .05
❑ 583 Juan Samuel .................. .10 .05
❑ 584 Les Lancaster ................ .10 .05
❑ 585 Jeff Musselman .............. .10 .05
❑ 586 Rob Dibble ..................... .10 .05
❑ 587 Eric Show ....................... .10 .05
❑ 588 Jesse Orosco ................ .10 .05
❑ 589 Herm Winningham ........ .10 .05
❑ 590 Andy Allanson ................ .10 .05
❑ 591 Dion James .................... .10 .05
❑ 592 Carmelo Martinez .......... .10 .05
❑ 593 Luis Quinones ................ .10 .05
❑ 594 Dennis Rasmussen........ .10 .05
❑ 595 Rich Yett ........................ .10 .05
❑ 596 Bob Walk......................... .10 .05
❑ 597A Andy McGaffigan ERR .20 .09
(Photo actually
Rich Thompson)
❑ 597B Andy McGaffigan COR .10 .05
❑ 598 Billy Hatcher .................. .10 .05
❑ 599 Bob Knepper .................. .10 .05
❑ 600 Checklist 501-600 UER.. .10 .05
(599 Bob Kneppers)
❑ 601 Joey Cora ...................... .20 .09
❑ 602 Steve Finley ................... .20 .09
❑ 603 Kal Daniels UER ............ .10 .05
(12 hits in '87, should
be 123; 335 runs,
should be 235)
❑ 604 Gregg Olson .................. .20 .09
❑ 605 Dave Stieb...................... .20 .09
❑ 606 Kenny Rogers ................ .20 .09
(Shown catching
football)
❑ 607 Zane Smith ..................... .10 .05
❑ 608 Bob Geren UER ............ .10 .05
(Origionally)
❑ 609 Chad Kreuter.................. .10 .05
❑ 610 Mike Smithson................ .10 .05
❑ 611 Jeff Wetherby ................ .10 .05
❑ 612 Gary Mielke.................... .10 .05
❑ 613 Pete Smith....................... .10 .05
❑ 614 Jack Daugherty UER...... .10 .05
(Born 7/30/60; should
be 7/3/60)
❑ 615 Lance McCullers ............ .10 .05
❑ 616 Don Robinson ................ .10 .05
❑ 617 Jose Guzman ................ .10 .05
❑ 618 Steve Bedrosian ............ .10 .05
❑ 619 Jamie Moyer .................. .10 .05
❑ 620 Atlee Hammaker ............ .10 .05
❑ 621 Rick Luecken UER ........ .10 .05
(Innings pitched wrong)
❑ 622 Greg W. Harris .............. .10 .05
❑ 623 Pete Harnisch ................ .10 .05
❑ 624 Jerald Clark.................... .10 .05
❑ 625 Jack McDowell UER ...... .10 .05
(Career totals for Games
and GS don't include
1987 season)
❑ 626 Frank Viola .................... .10 .05
❑ 627 Teddy Higuera................ .10 .05
❑ 628 Marty Pevey .................. .10 .05
❑ 629 Bill Wegman .................. .10 .05
❑ 630 Eric Plunk ...................... .10 .05
❑ 631 Drew Hall........................ .10 .05
❑ 632 Doug Jones .................... .10 .05
❑ 633 Geno Petralli UER.......... .10 .05
(Sacremento)
❑ 634 Jose Alvarez .................. .10 .05
❑ 635 Bob Milacki .................... .10 .05
❑ 636 Bobby Witt...................... .10 .05
❑ 637 Trevor Wilson ................ .10 .05
❑ 638 Jeff Russell UER ........... .10 .05
(Shutout stats wrong)
❑ 639 Mike Krukow .................. .10 .05
❑ 640 Rick Leach ..................... .10 .05
❑ 641 Dave Schmidt ................ .10 .05
❑ 642 Terry Leach .................... .10 .05
❑ 643 Calvin Schiraldi ............. .10 .05
❑ 644 Bob Melvin ..................... .10 .05
❑ 645 Jim Abbott....................... .25 .11
❑ 646 Jaime Navarro................. .10 .05
❑ 647 Mark Langston UER ...... .10 .05
(Several errors in
stats totals)
❑ 648 Juan Nieves ................... .10 .05
❑ 649 Damaso Garcia .............. .10 .05
❑ 650 Charlie O'Brien .............. .10 .05
❑ 651 Eric King ........................ .10 .05
❑ 652 Mike Boddicker .............. .10 .05
❑ 653 Duane Ward ................... .10 .05
❑ 654 Bob Stanley.................... .10 .05
❑ 655 Sandy Alomar Jr............. .20 .09
❑ 656 Danny Tartabull UER .... .10 .05
(395 BB; should be 295)
❑ 657 Randy McCament .......... .10 .05
❑ 658 Charlie Leibrandt............ .10 .05
❑ 659 Dan Quisenberry ............ .10 .05
❑ 660 Paul Assenmacher ........ .10 .05
❑ 661 Walt Terrell ..................... .10 .05
❑ 662 Tim Leary ....................... .10 .05
❑ 663 Randy Milligan................ .10 .05
❑ 664 Bo Diaz ........................... .10 .05
❑ 665 Mark Lemke UER .......... .10 .05
(Richmond misspelled
as Richomond)
❑ 666 Jose Gonzalez ................ .10 .05
❑ 667 Chuck Finley UER.......... .20 .09
(Born 11/16/62; should
be 11/26/62)
❑ 668 John Kruk ....................... .20 .09
❑ 669 Dick Schofield ................ .10 .05
❑ 670 Tim Crews....................... .10 .05
❑ 671 John Dopson .................. .10 .05
❑ 672 John Orton RC ............... .10 .05
❑ 673 Eric Hetzel...................... .10 .05
❑ 674 Lance Parrish ................. .10 .05
❑ 675 Ramon Martinez ............ .10 .05
❑ 676 Mark Gubicza ................ .10 .05
❑ 677 Greg Litton ..................... .10 .05
❑ 678 Greg Mathews................ .10 .05
❑ 679 Dave Dravecky .............. .20 .09
❑ 680 Steve Farr ....................... .10 .05
❑ 681 Mike Devereaux ............ .10 .05
❑ 682 Ken Griffey Sr.................. .20 .09
❑ 683A Mickey Weston ERR.. 2.00 .90
(Listed as Jamie
on card)
❑ 683B Mickey Weston COR .. .10 .05
(Technically still an
error as birthdate is
listed as 3/26/81)
❑ 684 Jack Armstrong .............. .10 .05
❑ 685 Steve Buechele.............. .10 .05
❑ 686 Bryan Harvey ................ .10 .05
❑ 687 Lance Blankenship ........ .10 .05
❑ 688 Dante Bichette................ .40 .18
❑ 689 Todd Burns .................... .10 .05
❑ 690 Dan Petry ....................... .10 .05
❑ 691 Kent Anderson .............. .10 .05
❑ 692 Todd Stottlemyre............ .20 .09
❑ 693 Wally Joyner UER.......... .20 .09
(Several stats errors)
❑ 694 Mike Rochford ................ .10 .05
❑ 695 Floyd Bannister .............. .10 .05
❑ 696 Rick Reuschel ................ .10 .05
❑ 697 Jose DeLeon .................. .10 .05
❑ 698 Jeff Montgomery ........... .20 .09
❑ 699 Kelly Downs ................... .10 .05
❑ 700A Checklist 601-700 ...... 2.00 .90
(683 Jamie Weston)
❑ 700B Checklist 601-700 ........ .10 .05
(683 Mickey Weston)
❑ 701 Jim Gott........................... .10 .05
❑ 702 Rookie Threats .............. .50 .23
Delino DeShields
Marquis Grissom
Larry Walker
❑ 703 Alejandro Pena .............. .10 .05
❑ 704 Willie Randolph ............. .20 .09
❑ 705 Tim Leary ....................... .10 .05
❑ 706 Chuck McElroy RC ........ .10 .05
❑ 707 Gerald Perry ................... .10 .05
❑ 708 Tom Brunansky .............. .10 .05
❑ 709 John Franco ................... .20 .09
❑ 710 Mark Davis ..................... .10 .05
❑ 711 David Justice RC......... 1.50 .70
❑ 712 Storm Davis.................... .10 .05
❑ 713 Scott Ruskin ................... .10 .05
❑ 714 Glenn Braggs ................ .10 .05
❑ 715 Kevin Bearse.................. .10 .05
❑ 716 Jose Nunez .................... .10 .05
❑ 717 Tim Layana .................... .10 .05
❑ 718 Greg Myers .................... .10 .05
❑ 719 Pete O'Brien .................. .10 .05
❑ 720 John Candelaria ............ .10 .05
❑ 721 Craig Grebeck RC.......... .10 .05
❑ 722 Shawn Boskie RC ......... .10 .05
❑ 723 Jim Leyritz RC................ .50 .23
❑ 724 Bill Sampen.................... .10 .05
❑ 725 Scott Radinsky RC ....... .10 .05
❑ 726 Todd Hundley RC .......... .50 .23
❑ 727 Scott Hemond RC.......... .10 .05
❑ 728 Lenny Webster RC ........ .10 .05
❑ 729 Jeff Reardon .................. .20 .09
❑ 730 Mitch Webster ................ .10 .05
❑ 731 Brian Bohanon RC ........ .10 .05
❑ 732 Rick Parker ..................... .10 .05
❑ 733 Terry Shumpert .............. .10 .05
❑ 734A Ryan's 6th No-Hitter .. 3.00 1.35
(No stripe on front)
❑ 734B Ryan's 6th No-Hitter .. 1.00 .45
(Stripe added on card
front for 300th win)
❑ 735 John Burkett ................... .10 .05
❑ 736 Derrick May RC.............. .20 .09
❑ 737 Carlos Baerga RC.......... .20 .09
❑ 738 Greg Smith ..................... .10 .05
❑ 739 Scott Sanderson ............ .10 .05
❑ 740 Joe Kraemer .................. .10 .05
❑ 741 Hector Villanueva RC .... .10 .05
❑ 742 Mike Fetters RC ............ .10 .05
❑ 743 Mark Gardner RC .......... .10 .05
❑ 744 Matt Nokes ..................... .10 .05

❑ 745 Dave Winfield .40 .18
❑ 746 Delino DeShields RC .40 .18
❑ 747 Dann Howitt .10 .05
❑ 748 Tony Pena .10 .05
❑ 749 Oil Can Boyd .10 .05
❑ 750 Mike Benjamin .10 .05
❑ 751 Alex Cole RC .10 .05
❑ 752 Eric Gunderson .10 .05
❑ 753 Howard Farmer .10 .05
❑ 754 Joe Carter .20 .09
❑ 755 Ray Lankford RC .75 .35
❑ 756 Sandy Alomar Jr. .20 .09
❑ 757 Alex Sanchez .10 .05
❑ 758 Nick Esasky .10 .05
❑ 759 Stan Belinda RC .10 .05
❑ 760 Jim Presley .10 .05
❑ 761 Gary DiSarcina RC .25 .11
❑ 762 Wayne Edwards .10 .05
❑ 763 Pat Combs .10 .05
❑ 764 Mickey Pina .10 .05
❑ 765 Wilson Alvarez RC .20 .09
❑ 766 Dave Parker .20 .09
❑ 767 Mike Blowers RC .20 .09
❑ 768 Tony Phillips .10 .05
❑ 769 Pascual Perez .10 .05
❑ 770 Gary Pettis .10 .05
❑ 771 Fred Lynn .10 .05
❑ 772 Mel Rojas RC .20 .09
❑ 773 David Segui RC .75 .35
❑ 774 Gary Carter .25 .11
❑ 775 Rafael Valdez .10 .05
❑ 776 Glenallen Hill .10 .05
❑ 777 Keith Hernandez .20 .09
❑ 778 Billy Hatcher .10 .05
❑ 779 Marty Clary .10 .05
❑ 780 Candy Maldonado .10 .05
❑ 781 Mike Marshall .10 .05
❑ 782 Billy Joe Robidoux .10 .05
❑ 783 Mark Langston .10 .05
❑ 784 Paul Sorrento RC .25 .11
❑ 785 Dave Hollins RC .40 .18
❑ 786 Cecil Fielder .20 .09
❑ 787 Matt Young .10 .05
❑ 788 Jeff Huson .10 .05
❑ 789 Lloyd Moseby .10 .05
❑ 790 Ron Kittle .10 .05
❑ 791 Hubie Brooks .10 .05
❑ 792 Craig Lefferts .10 .05
❑ 793 Kevin Bass .10 .05
❑ 794 Bryn Smith .10 .05
❑ 795 Juan Samuel .10 .05
❑ 796 Sam Horn .10 .05
❑ 797 Randy Myers .20 .09
❑ 798 Chris James .10 .05
❑ 799 Bill Gullickson .10 .05
❑ 800 Checklist 701-800 .10 .05

## 1991 Upper Deck

| | MINT | NRMT |
|---|---|---|
| COMPLETE SET (800) | 20.00 | 9.00 |
| COMP.FACT.SET (800) | 25.00 | 11.00 |
| COMPLETE LO SET (700) | 16.00 | 7.25 |
| COMPLETE HI SET (100) | 4.00 | 1.80 |

❑ 1 Star Rookie Checklist .05 .02
❑ 2 Phil Plantier RC .05 .02
❑ 3 D.J. Dozier .05 .02
❑ 4 Dave Hansen .05 .02
❑ 5 Maurice Vaughn .10 .05
❑ 6 Leo Gomez .05 .02
❑ 7 Scott Aldred .05 .02
❑ 8 Scott Chiamparino .05 .02
❑ 9 Lance Dickson RC .05 .02
❑ 10 Sean Berry RC .10 .05
❑ 11 Bernie Williams .25 .11
❑ 12 Brian Barnes UER .05 .02
(Photo either not him
or in wrong jersey)
❑ 13 Narciso Elvira .05 .02
❑ 14 Mike Gardiner .05 .02
❑ 15 Greg Colbrunn RC .05 .02
❑ 16 Bernard Gilkey .10 .05
❑ 17 Mark Lewis .05 .02
❑ 18 Mickey Morandini .05 .02
❑ 19 Charles Nagy .05 .02
❑ 20 Geronimo Pena .05 .02
❑ 21 Henry Rodriguez RC .25 .11
❑ 22 Scott Cooper .05 .02
❑ 23 Andujar Cedeno UER .05 .02
(Shown batting left,
back says right)
❑ 24 Eric Karros RC .50 .23
❑ 25 Steve Decker UER .05 .02
(Lewis-Clark State
College, not Lewis
and Clark)
❑ 26 Kevin Belcher .05 .02
❑ 27 Jeff Conino RC .20 .09
❑ 28 Dave Stewart TC .05 .02
❑ 29 Carlton Fisk TC .10 .05
❑ 30 Rafael Palmeiro TC .10 .05
❑ 31 Chuck Finley TC .05 .02
❑ 32 Harold Reynolds TC .05 .02
❑ 33 Bret Saberhagen TC .05 .02
❑ 34 Gary Gaetti TC .05 .02
❑ 35 Scott Leius .05 .02
❑ 36 Neal Heaton .05 .02
❑ 37 Terry Lee .05 .02
❑ 38 Gary Redus .05 .02
❑ 39 Barry Jones .05 .02
❑ 40 Chuck Knoblauch .10 .05
❑ 41 Larry Andersen .05 .02
❑ 42 Darryl Hamilton .05 .02
❑ 43 Mike Greenwell TC .05 .02
❑ 44 Kelly Gruber TC .05 .02
❑ 45 Jack Morris TC .05 .02
❑ 46 Sandy Alomar Jr. TC .05 .02
❑ 47 Gregg Olson TC .05 .02
❑ 48 Dave Parker TC .05 .02
❑ 49 Roberto Kelly TC .05 .02
❑ 50 Top Prospect Checklist .05 .02
❑ 51 Kyle Abbott .05 .02
❑ 52 Jeff Juden .05 .02
❑ 53 Todd Van Poppel UER RC .05 .02
(Born Arlington and
attended John Martin HS;
should say Hinsdale and
James Martin HS)
❑ 54 Steve Karsay RC .25 .11
❑ 55 Chipper Jones RC 4.00 1.80
❑ 56 Chris Johnson RC UER .05 .02
(Called Tim on back)
❑ 57 John Ericks .05 .02
❑ 58 Gary Scott .05 .02
❑ 59 Kiki Jones .05 .02
❑ 60 Wil Cordero RC .05 .02
❑ 61 Royce Clayton .10 .05
❑ 62 Tim Costo RC .05 .02
❑ 63 Roger Salkeld .05 .02
❑ 64 Brook Fordyce RC .05 .02
❑ 65 Mike Mussina RC 1.25 .55
❑ 66 Dave Staton RC .05 .02
❑ 67 Mike Lieberthal RC .50 .23
❑ 68 Kurt Miller RC .05 .02
❑ 69 Dan Peltier RC .05 .02
❑ 70 Greg Blosser .05 .02
❑ 71 Reggie Sanders RC .25 .11
❑ 72 Brent Mayne .05 .02
❑ 73 Rico Brogna .10 .05
❑ 74 Willie Banks .05 .02
❑ 75 Len Brutcher .05 .02
❑ 76 Pat Kelly RC .05 .02
❑ 77 Chris Sabo TC .05 .02
❑ 78 Ramon Martinez TC .05 .02
❑ 79 Matt Williams TC .10 .05
❑ 80 Roberto Alomar TC .10 .05
❑ 81 Glenn Davis TC .05 .02
❑ 82 Ron Gant TC .05 .02
❑ 83 Cecil Fielder FEAT .05 .02
❑ 84 Orlando Merced RC .05 .02
❑ 85 Domingo Ramos .05 .02
❑ 86 Tom Bolton .05 .02
❑ 87 Andres Santana .05 .02
❑ 88 John Dopson .05 .02
❑ 89 Kenny Williams .05 .02
❑ 90 Marty Barrett .05 .02
❑ 91 Tom Pagnozzi .05 .02
❑ 92 Carmelo Martinez .05 .02
❑ 93 Bobby Thigpen SAVE .05 .02
❑ 94 Barry Bonds TC .20 .09
❑ 95 Gregg Jefferies TC .05 .02
❑ 96 Tim Wallach TC .05 .02
❑ 97 Len Dykstra TC .05 .02
❑ 98 Pedro Guerrero TC .05 .02
❑ 99 Mark Grace TC .10 .05
❑ 100 Checklist 1-100 .05 .02
❑ 101 Kevin Elster .05 .02
❑ 102 Tom Brookens .05 .02
❑ 103 Mackey Sasser .05 .02
❑ 104 Felix Fermin .05 .02
❑ 105 Kevin McReynolds .05 .02
❑ 106 Dave Stieb .05 .02
❑ 107 Jeffrey Leonard .05 .02
❑ 108 Dave Henderson .05 .02
❑ 109 Sid Bream .05 .02
❑ 110 Henry Cotto .05 .02
❑ 111 Shawon Dunston .05 .02
❑ 112 Mariano Duncan .05 .02
❑ 113 Joe Girardi .10 .05
❑ 114 Billy Hatcher .05 .02
❑ 115 Greg Maddux .50 .23
❑ 116 Jerry Browne .05 .02
❑ 117 Juan Samuel .05 .02
❑ 118 Steve Olin .05 .02
❑ 119 Alfredo Griffin .05 .02
❑ 120 Mitch Webster .05 .02
❑ 121 Joel Skinner .05 .02
❑ 122 Frank Viola .05 .02
❑ 123 Cory Snyder .05 .02
❑ 124 Howard Johnson .05 .02
❑ 125 Carlos Baerga .05 .02
❑ 126 Tony Fernandez .05 .02
❑ 127 Dave Stewart .10 .05
❑ 128 Jay Buhner .10 .05
❑ 129 Mike LaValliere .05 .02
❑ 130 Scott Bradley .05 .02
❑ 131 Tony Phillips .05 .02
❑ 132 Ryne Sandberg .25 .11
❑ 133 Paul O'Neill .10 .05
❑ 134 Mark Grace .20 .09
❑ 135 Chris Sabo .05 .02
❑ 136 Ramon Martinez .05 .02
❑ 137 Brook Jacoby .05 .02
❑ 138 Candy Maldonado .05 .02
❑ 139 Mike Scioscia .05 .02
❑ 140 Chris James .05 .02
❑ 141 Craig Worthington .05 .02
❑ 142 Manny Lee .05 .02
❑ 143 Tim Raines .10 .05
❑ 144 Sandy Alomar Jr. .10 .05
❑ 145 John Olerud .10 .05
❑ 146 Ozzie Canseco .10 .05
(With Jose)
❑ 147 Pat Borders .05 .02
❑ 148 Harold Reynolds .05 .02
❑ 149 Tom Henke .05 .02
❑ 150 R.J. Reynolds .05 .02
❑ 151 Mike Gallego .05 .02
❑ 152 Bobby Bonilla .10 .05
❑ 153 Terry Steinbach .10 .05
❑ 154 Barry Bonds .30 .14
❑ 155 Jose Canseco .25 .11
❑ 156 Gregg Jefferies .05 .02
❑ 157 Matt Williams .10 .05
❑ 158 Craig Biggio .10 .05
❑ 159 Daryl Boston .05 .02
❑ 160 Ricky Jordan .05 .02
❑ 161 Stan Belinda .05 .02
❑ 162 Ozzie Smith .25 .11

❑ 163 Tom Brunansky .05 .02
❑ 164 Todd Zeile .10 .05
❑ 165 Mike Greenwell .05 .02
❑ 166 Kal Daniels .05 .02
❑ 167 Kent Hrbek .10 .05
❑ 168 Franklin Stubbs .05 .02
❑ 169 Dick Schofield .05 .02
❑ 170 Junior Ortiz .05 .02
❑ 171 Hector Villanueva .05 .02
❑ 172 Dennis Eckersley .10 .05
❑ 173 Mitch Williams .05 .02
❑ 174 Mark McGwire .75 .35
❑ 175 Fernando Valenzuela 3X .10 .05
❑ 176 Gary Carter .10 .05
❑ 177 Dave Magadan .05 .02
❑ 178 Robby Thompson .05 .02
❑ 179 Bob Ojeda .05 .02
❑ 180 Ken Caminiti .10 .05
❑ 181 Don Slaught .05 .02
❑ 182 Luis Rivera .05 .02
❑ 183 Jay Bell .10 .05
❑ 184 Jody Reed .05 .02
❑ 185 Wally Backman .05 .02
❑ 186 Dave Martinez .05 .02
❑ 187 Luis Polonia .05 .02
❑ 188 Shane Mack .05 .02
❑ 189 Spike Owen .05 .02
❑ 190 Scott Bailes .05 .02
❑ 191 John Russell .05 .02
❑ 192 Walt Weiss .05 .02
❑ 193 Jose Oquendo .05 .02
❑ 194 Carney Lansford .10 .05
❑ 195 Jeff Huson .05 .02
❑ 196 Keith Miller .05 .02
❑ 197 Eric Yelding .05 .02
❑ 198 Ron Darling .05 .02
❑ 199 John Kruk .10 .05
❑ 200 Checklist 101-200 .05 .02
❑ 201 John Shelby .05 .02
❑ 202 Bob Geren .05 .02
❑ 203 Lance McCullers .05 .02
❑ 204 Alvaro Espinoza .05 .02
❑ 205 Mark Salas .05 .02
❑ 206 Mike Pagliarulo .05 .02
❑ 207 Jose Uribe .05 .02
❑ 208 Jim Deshaies .05 .02
❑ 209 Ron Karkovice .05 .02
❑ 210 Rafael Ramirez .05 .02
❑ 211 Donnie Hill .05 .02
❑ 212 Brian Harper .05 .02
❑ 213 Jack Howell .05 .02
❑ 214 Wes Gardner .05 .02
❑ 215 Tim Burke .05 .02
❑ 216 Doug Jones .05 .02
❑ 217 Hubie Brooks .05 .02
❑ 218 Tom Candiotti .05 .02
❑ 219 Gerald Perry .05 .02
❑ 220 Jose DeLeon .05 .02
❑ 221 Wally Whitehurst .05 .02
❑ 222 Alan Mills .05 .02
❑ 223 Alan Trammell .10 .05
❑ 224 Dwight Gooden .10 .05
❑ 225 Travis Fryman .20 .09
❑ 226 Joe Carter .10 .05
❑ 227 Julio Franco .05 .02
❑ 228 Craig Lefferts .05 .02
❑ 229 Gary Pettis .05 .02
❑ 230 Dennis Rasmussen .05 .02
❑ 231A Brian Downing ERR .05 .02
(No position on front)
❑ 231B Brian Downing COR .10 .05
(DH on front)
❑ 232 Carlos Quintana .05 .02
❑ 233 Gary Gaetti .10 .05
❑ 234 Mark Langston .05 .02
❑ 235 Tim Wallach .05 .02
❑ 236 Greg Swindell .05 .02
❑ 237 Eddie Murray .20 .09
❑ 238 Jeff Manto .05 .02
❑ 239 Lenny Harris .05 .02
❑ 240 Jesse Orosco .05 .02
❑ 241 Scott Lusader .05 .02
❑ 242 Sid Fernandez .05 .02
❑ 243 Jim Leyritz .05 .02
❑ 244 Cecil Fielder .10 .05
❑ 245 Darryl Strawberry .10 .05
❑ 246 Frank Thomas UER .50 .23
(Comiskey Park
misspelled Comisky)
❑ 247 Kevin Mitchell .05 .02
❑ 248 Lance Johnson .05 .02
❑ 249 Rick Reuschel .05 .02
❑ 250 Mark Portugal .05 .02
❑ 251 Derek Lilliquist .05 .02
❑ 252 Brian Holman .05 .02
❑ 253 Rafael Valdez UER .05 .02
(Born 4/17/68;
should be 12/17/67)
❑ 254 B.J. Surhoff .10 .05
❑ 255 Tony Gwynn .40 .18
❑ 256 Andy Van Slyke .10 .05
❑ 257 Todd Stottlemyre .10 .05
❑ 258 Jose Lind .05 .02
❑ 259 Greg Myers .05 .02
❑ 260 Jeff Ballard .05 .02
❑ 261 Bobby Thigpen .05 .02
❑ 262 Jimmy Kremers .05 .02
❑ 263 Robin Ventura .20 .09
❑ 264 John Smoltz .10 .05
❑ 265 Sammy Sosa .50 .23
❑ 266 Gary Sheffield .20 .09
❑ 267 Len Dykstra .10 .05
❑ 268 Bill Spiers .05 .02
❑ 269 Charlie Hayes .05 .02
❑ 270 Brett Butler .10 .05
❑ 271 Bip Roberts .05 .02
❑ 272 Rob Deer .05 .02
❑ 273 Fred Lynn .05 .02
❑ 274 Dave Parker .10 .05
❑ 275 Andy Benes .05 .02
❑ 276 Glenallen Hill .05 .02
❑ 277 Steve Howard .05 .02
❑ 278 Doug Drabek .05 .02
❑ 279 Joe Oliver .05 .02
❑ 280 Todd Benzinger .05 .02
❑ 281 Eric King .05 .02
❑ 282 Jim Presley .05 .02
❑ 283 Ken Patterson .05 .02
❑ 284 Jack Daugherty .05 .02
❑ 285 Ivan Calderon .05 .02
❑ 286 Edgar Diaz .05 .02
❑ 287 Kevin Bass .05 .02
❑ 288 Don Carman .05 .02
❑ 289 Greg Brock .05 .02
❑ 290 John Franco .10 .05
❑ 291 Joey Cora .05 .02
❑ 292 Bill Wegman .05 .02
❑ 293 Eric Show .05 .02
❑ 294 Scott Bankhead .05 .02
❑ 295 Garry Templeton .05 .02
❑ 296 Mickey Tettleton .10 .05
❑ 297 Luis Sojo .05 .02
❑ 298 Jose Rijo .05 .02
❑ 299 Dave Johnson .05 .02
❑ 300 Checklist 201-300 .05 .02
❑ 301 Mark Grant .05 .02
❑ 302 Pete Harnisch .05 .02
❑ 303 Greg Olson .05 .02
❑ 304 Anthony Telford .05 .02
❑ 305 Lonnie Smith .05 .02
❑ 306 Chris Hoiles .05 .02
❑ 307 Bryn Smith .05 .02
❑ 308 Mike Devereaux .05 .02
❑ 309A Milt Thompson ERR .20 .09
(Under yr information
has print dot)
❑ 309B Milt Thompson COR .05 .02
(Under yr information
says 86)
❑ 310 Bob Melvin .05 .02
❑ 311 Luis Salazar .05 .02
❑ 312 Ed Whitson .05 .02
❑ 313 Charlie Hough .10 .05
❑ 314 Dave Clark .05 .02
❑ 315 Eric Gunderson .05 .02
❑ 316 Dan Petry .05 .02
❑ 317 Dante Bichette UER .20 .09
(Assists misspelled
as assissts)
❑ 318 Mike Heath .05 .02
❑ 319 Damon Berryhill .05 .02
❑ 320 Walt Terrell .05 .02
❑ 321 Scott Fletcher .05 .02
❑ 322 Dan Plesac .05 .02
❑ 323 Jack McDowell .05 .02
❑ 324 Paul Molitor .20 .09
❑ 325 Ozzie Guillen .05 .02
❑ 326 Gregg Olson .05 .02
❑ 327 Pedro Guerrero .05 .02
❑ 328 Bob Milacki .05 .02
❑ 329 John Tudor UER .05 .02
('90 Cardinals;
should be '90 Dodgers)
❑ 330 Steve Finley UER .20 .09
(Born 3/12/65;
should be 5/12)
❑ 331 Jack Clark .10 .05
❑ 332 Jerome Walton .05 .02
❑ 333 Andy Hawkins .05 .02
❑ 334 Derrick May .05 .02
❑ 335 Roberto Alomar .20 .09
❑ 336 Jack Morris .10 .05
❑ 337 Dave Winfield .20 .09
❑ 338 Steve Searcy .05 .02
❑ 339 Chili Davis .10 .05
❑ 340 Larry Sheets .05 .02
❑ 341 Ted Higuera .05 .02
❑ 342 David Segui .05 .02
❑ 343 Greg Cadaret .05 .02
❑ 344 Robin Yount .20 .09
❑ 345 Nolan Ryan 1.00 .45
❑ 346 Ray Lankford .20 .09
❑ 347 Cal Ripken .75 .35
❑ 348 Lee Smith .10 .05
❑ 349 Brady Anderson .20 .09
❑ 350 Frank DiPino .05 .02
❑ 351 Hal Morris .05 .02
❑ 352 Deion Sanders .10 .05
❑ 353 Barry Larkin .20 .09
❑ 354 Don Mattingly .50 .23
❑ 355 Eric Davis .10 .05
❑ 356 Jose Offerman .05 .02
❑ 357 Mel Rojas .10 .05
❑ 358 Rudy Seanez .05 .02
❑ 359 Oil Can Boyd .05 .02
❑ 360 Nelson Liriano .05 .02
❑ 361 Ron Gant .10 .05
❑ 362 Howard Farmer .05 .02
❑ 363 David Justice .20 .09
❑ 364 Delino DeShields .10 .05
❑ 365 Steve Avery .05 .02
❑ 366 David Cone .10 .05
❑ 367 Lou Whitaker .10 .05
❑ 368 Von Hayes .05 .02
❑ 369 Frank Tanana .05 .02
❑ 370 Tim Teufel .05 .02
❑ 371 Randy Myers .10 .05
❑ 372 Roberto Kelly .05 .02
❑ 373 Jack Armstrong .05 .02
❑ 374 Kelly Gruber .05 .02
❑ 375 Kevin Maas .05 .02
❑ 376 Randy Johnson .30 .14
❑ 377 David West .05 .02
❑ 378 Brent Knackert .05 .02
❑ 379 Rick Honeycutt .05 .02
❑ 380 Kevin Gross .05 .02
❑ 381 Tom Foley .05 .02
❑ 382 Jeff Blauser .05 .02
❑ 383 Scott Ruskin .05 .02
❑ 384 Andres Thomas .05 .02
❑ 385 Dennis Martinez .10 .05
❑ 386 Mike Henneman .05 .02
❑ 387 Felix Jose .05 .02
❑ 388 Alejandro Pena .05 .02
❑ 389 Chet Lemon .05 .02
❑ 390 Craig Wilson .05 .02
❑ 391 Chuck Crim .05 .02
❑ 392 Mel Hall .05 .02
❑ 393 Mark Knudson .05 .02
❑ 394 Norm Charlton .05 .02
❑ 395 Mike Felder .05 .02
❑ 396 Tim Layana .05 .02
❑ 397 Steve Frey .05 .02
❑ 398 Bill Doran .05 .02
❑ 399 Dion James .05 .02
❑ 400 Checklist 301-400 .05 .02
❑ 401 Ron Hassey .05 .02
❑ 402 Don Robinson .05 .02

| No. | Player | | |
|---|---|---|---|
| 403 | Gene Nelson | .05 | .02 |
| 404 | Terry Kennedy | .05 | .02 |
| 405 | Todd Burns | .05 | .02 |
| 406 | Roger McDowell | .05 | .02 |
| 407 | Bob Kipper | .05 | .02 |
| 408 | Darren Daulton | .10 | .05 |
| 409 | Chuck Cary | .05 | .02 |
| 410 | Bruce Ruffin | .05 | .02 |
| 411 | Juan Berenguer | .05 | .02 |
| 412 | Gary Ward | .05 | .02 |
| 413 | Al Newman | .05 | .02 |
| 414 | Danny Jackson | .05 | .02 |
| 415 | Greg Gagne | .05 | .02 |
| 416 | Tom Herr | .05 | .02 |
| 417 | Jeff Parrett | .05 | .02 |
| 418 | Jeff Reardon | .10 | .05 |
| 419 | Mark Lemke | .05 | .02 |
| 420 | Charlie O'Brien | .05 | .02 |
| 421 | Willie Randolph | .10 | .05 |
| 422 | Steve Bedrosian | .05 | .02 |
| 423 | Mike Moore | .05 | .02 |
| 424 | Jeff Brantley | .05 | .02 |
| 425 | Bob Welch | .05 | .02 |
| 426 | Terry Mulholland | .05 | .02 |
| 427 | Willie Blair | .05 | .02 |
| 428 | Darrin Fletcher | .05 | .02 |
| 429 | Mike Witt | .05 | .02 |
| 430 | Joe Boever | .05 | .02 |
| 431 | Tom Gordon | .05 | .02 |
| 432 | Pedro Munoz RC | .05 | .02 |
| 433 | Kevin Seitzer | .05 | .02 |
| 434 | Kevin Tapani | .05 | .02 |
| 435 | Bret Saberhagen | .10 | .05 |
| 436 | Ellis Burks | .10 | .05 |
| 437 | Chuck Finley | .10 | .05 |
| 438 | Mike Boddicker | .05 | .02 |
| 439 | Francisco Cabrera | .05 | .02 |
| 440 | Todd Hundley | .05 | .02 |
| 441 | Kelly Downs | .05 | .02 |
| 442 | Dann Howitt | .05 | .02 |
| 443 | Scott Garrelts | .05 | .02 |
| 444 | Rickey Henderson 3X | .25 | .11 |
| 445 | Will Clark | .20 | .09 |
| 446 | Ben McDonald | .05 | .02 |
| 447 | Dale Murphy | .20 | .09 |
| 448 | Dave Righetti | .05 | .02 |
| 449 | Dickie Thon | .05 | .02 |
| 450 | Ted Power | .05 | .02 |
| 451 | Scott Coolbaugh | .05 | .02 |
| 452 | Dwight Smith | .05 | .02 |
| 453 | Pete Incaviglia | .05 | .02 |
| 454 | Andre Dawson | .10 | .05 |
| 455 | Ruben Sierra | .05 | .02 |
| 456 | Andres Galarraga | .10 | .05 |
| 457 | Alvin Davis | .05 | .02 |
| 458 | Tony Castillo | .05 | .02 |
| 459 | Pete O'Brien | .05 | .02 |
| 460 | Charlie Leibrandt | .05 | .02 |
| 461 | Vince Coleman | .05 | .02 |
| 462 | Steve Sax | .05 | .02 |
| 463 | Omar Olivares RC | .05 | .02 |
| 464 | Oscar Azocar | .05 | .02 |
| 465 | Joe Magrane | .05 | .02 |
| 466 | Karl Rhodes | .05 | .02 |
| 467 | Benito Santiago | .05 | .02 |
| 468 | Joe Klink | .05 | .02 |
| 469 | Sil Campusano | .05 | .02 |
| 470 | Mark Parent | .05 | .02 |
| 471 | Shawn Boskie UER (Depleted misspelled as depleated) | .05 | .02 |
| 472 | Kevin Brown | .10 | .05 |
| 473 | Rick Sutcliffe | .10 | .05 |
| 474 | Rafael Palmeiro | .20 | .09 |
| 475 | Mike Harkey | .05 | .02 |
| 476 | Jaime Navarro | .05 | .02 |
| 477 | Marquis Grissom UER (DeShields misspelled as DeSheilds) | .05 | .02 |
| 478 | Marty Clary | .05 | .02 |
| 479 | Greg Briley | .05 | .02 |
| 480 | Tom Glavine | .20 | .09 |
| 481 | Lee Guetterman | .05 | .02 |
| 482 | Rex Hudler | .05 | .02 |
| 483 | Dave LaPoint | .05 | .02 |
| 484 | Terry Pendleton | .10 | .05 |
| 485 | Jesse Barfield | .05 | .02 |
| 486 | Jose DeJesus | .05 | .02 |
| 487 | Paul Abbott | .05 | .02 |
| 488 | Ken Howell | .05 | .02 |
| 489 | Greg W. Harris | .05 | .02 |
| 490 | Roy Smith | .05 | .02 |
| 491 | Paul Assenmacher | .05 | .02 |
| 492 | Geno Petralli | .05 | .02 |
| 493 | Steve Wilson | .05 | .02 |
| 494 | Kevin Reimer | .05 | .02 |
| 495 | Bill Long | .05 | .02 |
| 496 | Mike Jackson | .05 | .02 |
| 497 | Oddibe McDowell | .05 | .02 |
| 498 | Bill Swift | .05 | .02 |
| 499 | Jeff Treadway | .05 | .02 |
| 500 | Checklist 401-500 | .05 | .02 |
| 501 | Gene Larkin | .05 | .02 |
| 502 | Bob Boone | .10 | .05 |
| 503 | Allan Anderson | .05 | .02 |
| 504 | Luis Aquino | .05 | .02 |
| 505 | Mark Guthrie | .05 | .02 |
| 506 | Joe Orsulak | .05 | .02 |
| 507 | Dana Kiecker | .05 | .02 |
| 508 | Dave Gallagher | .05 | .02 |
| 509 | Greg A. Harris | .05 | .02 |
| 510 | Mark Williamson | .05 | .02 |
| 511 | Casey Candaele | .05 | .02 |
| 512 | Mookie Wilson | .10 | .05 |
| 513 | Dave Smith | .05 | .02 |
| 514 | Chuck Carr | .05 | .02 |
| 515 | Glenn Wilson | .05 | .02 |
| 516 | Mike Fitzgerald | .05 | .02 |
| 517 | Devon White | .05 | .02 |
| 518 | Dave Hollins | .05 | .02 |
| 519 | Mark Eichhorn | .05 | .02 |
| 520 | Otis Nixon | .05 | .02 |
| 521 | Terry Shumpert | .05 | .02 |
| 522 | Scott Erickson | .05 | .02 |
| 523 | Danny Tartabull | .05 | .02 |
| 524 | Orel Hershiser | .10 | .05 |
| 525 | George Brett | .40 | .18 |
| 526 | Greg Vaughn | .20 | .09 |
| 527 | Tim Naehring | .05 | .02 |
| 528 | Curt Schilling | .10 | .05 |
| 529 | Chris Bosio | .05 | .02 |
| 530 | Sam Horn | .05 | .02 |
| 531 | Mike Scott | .05 | .02 |
| 532 | George Bell | .05 | .02 |
| 533 | Eric Anthony | .05 | .02 |
| 534 | Julio Valera | .05 | .02 |
| 535 | Glenn Davis | .05 | .02 |
| 536 | Larry Walker UER (Should have comma after Expos in text) | .20 | .09 |
| 537 | Pat Combs | .05 | .02 |
| 538 | Chris Nabholz | .05 | .02 |
| 539 | Kirk McCaskill | .05 | .02 |
| 540 | Randy Ready | .05 | .02 |
| 541 | Mark Gubicza | .05 | .02 |
| 542 | Rick Aguilera | .10 | .05 |
| 543 | Brian McRae RC | .10 | .05 |
| 544 | Kirby Puckett | .50 | .23 |
| 545 | Bo Jackson | .10 | .05 |
| 546 | Wade Boggs | .25 | .11 |
| 547 | Tim McIntosh | .05 | .02 |
| 548 | Randy Milligan | .05 | .02 |
| 549 | Dwight Evans | .10 | .05 |
| 550 | Billy Ripken | .05 | .02 |
| 551 | Erik Hanson | .05 | .02 |
| 552 | Lance Parrish | .05 | .02 |
| 553 | Tino Martinez | .10 | .05 |
| 554 | Jim Abbott | .10 | .05 |
| 555 | Ken Griffey Jr. UER (Second most votes for 1991 All-Star Game) | 1.00 | .45 |
| 556 | Milt Cuyler | .05 | .02 |
| 557 | Mark Leonard | .05 | .02 |
| 558 | Jay Howell | .05 | .02 |
| 559 | Lloyd Moseby | .05 | .02 |
| 560 | Chris Gwynn | .05 | .02 |
| 561 | Mark Whiten | .05 | .02 |
| 562 | Harold Baines | .10 | .05 |
| 563 | Junior Felix | .05 | .02 |
| 564 | Darren Lewis | .10 | .05 |
| 565 | Fred McGriff | .20 | .09 |
| 566 | Kevin Appier | .10 | .05 |
| 567 | Luis Gonzalez RC | .50 | .23 |
| 568 | Frank White | .10 | .05 |
| 569 | Juan Agosto | .05 | .02 |
| 570 | Mike Macfarlane | .05 | .02 |
| 571 | Bert Blyleven | .10 | .05 |
| 572 | Ken Griffey Sr. Ken Griffey Jr. | .50 | .18 |
| 573 | Lee Stevens | .10 | .05 |
| 574 | Edgar Martinez | .10 | .05 |
| 575 | Wally Joyner | .10 | .05 |
| 576 | Tim Belcher | .05 | .02 |
| 577 | John Burkett | .05 | .02 |
| 578 | Mike Morgan | .05 | .02 |
| 579 | Paul Gibson | .05 | .02 |
| 580 | Jose Vizcaino | .05 | .02 |
| 581 | Duane Ward | .05 | .02 |
| 582 | Scott Sanderson | .05 | .02 |
| 583 | David Wells | .10 | .05 |
| 584 | Willie McGee | .10 | .05 |
| 585 | John Cerutti | .05 | .02 |
| 586 | Danny Darwin | .05 | .02 |
| 587 | Kurt Stillwell | .05 | .02 |
| 588 | Rich Gedman | .05 | .02 |
| 589 | Mark Davis | .05 | .02 |
| 590 | Bill Gullickson | .05 | .02 |
| 591 | Matt Young | .05 | .02 |
| 592 | Bryan Harvey | .05 | .02 |
| 593 | Omar Vizquel | .20 | .09 |
| 594 | Scott Lewis RC | .05 | .02 |
| 595 | Dave Valle | .05 | .02 |
| 596 | Tim Crews | .05 | .02 |
| 597 | Mike Bielecki | .05 | .02 |
| 598 | Mike Sharperson | .05 | .02 |
| 599 | Dave Bergman | .05 | .02 |
| 600 | Checklist 501-600 | .05 | .02 |
| 601 | Steve Lyons | .05 | .02 |
| 602 | Bruce Hurst | .05 | .02 |
| 603 | Donn Pall | .05 | .02 |
| 604 | Jim Vatcher | .05 | .02 |
| 605 | Dan Pasqua | .05 | .02 |
| 606 | Kenny Rogers | .05 | .02 |
| 607 | Jeff Schulz | .05 | .02 |
| 608 | Brad Arnsberg | .05 | .02 |
| 609 | Willie Wilson | .05 | .02 |
| 610 | Jamie Moyer | .05 | .02 |
| 611 | Ron Oester | .05 | .02 |
| 612 | Dennis Cook | .05 | .02 |
| 613 | Rick Mahler | .05 | .02 |
| 614 | Bill Landrum | .05 | .02 |
| 615 | Scott Scudder | .05 | .02 |
| 616 | Tom Edens | .05 | .02 |
| 617 | 1917 Revisited (White Sox vintage uniforms) | .10 | .05 |
| 618 | Jim Gantner | .05 | .02 |
| 619 | Darrel Akerfelds | .05 | .02 |
| 620 | Ron Robinson | .05 | .02 |
| 621 | Scott Radinsky | .05 | .02 |
| 622 | Pete Smith | .05 | .02 |
| 623 | Melido Perez | .05 | .02 |
| 624 | Jerald Clark | .05 | .02 |
| 625 | Carlos Martinez | .05 | .02 |
| 626 | Wes Chamberlain RC | .05 | .02 |
| 627 | Bobby Witt | .05 | .02 |
| 628 | Ken Dayley | .05 | .02 |
| 629 | John Barfield | .05 | .02 |
| 630 | Bob Tewksbury | .05 | .02 |
| 631 | Glenn Braggs | .05 | .02 |
| 632 | Jim Neidlinger | .05 | .02 |
| 633 | Tom Browning | .05 | .02 |
| 634 | Kirk Gibson | .10 | .05 |
| 635 | Rob Dibble | .05 | .02 |
| 636 | Rickey Henderson SB Lou Brock (May 1, 1991 on front) | .20 | .09 |
| 636A | Rickey Henderson SB Lou Brock (No date on card) | .25 | .11 |
| 637 | Jeff Montgomery | .10 | .05 |
| 638 | Mike Schooler | .05 | .02 |
| 639 | Storm Davis | .05 | .02 |
| 640 | Rich Rodriguez | .05 | .02 |
| 641 | Phil Bradley | .05 | .02 |
| 642 | Kent Mercker | .05 | .02 |
| 643 | Carlton Fisk | .20 | .09 |
| 644 | Mike Bell | .05 | .02 |
| 645 | Alex Fernandez | .10 | .05 |

❑ 646 Juan Gonzalez .25 .11
❑ 647 Ken Hill .05 .02
❑ 648 Jeff Russell .05 .02
❑ 649 Chuck Malone .05 .02
❑ 650 Steve Buechele .05 .02
❑ 651 Mike Benjamin .05 .02
❑ 652 Tony Pena .05 .02
❑ 653 Trevor Wilson .05 .02
❑ 654 Alex Cole .05 .02
❑ 655 Roger Clemens .40 .18
❑ 656 Mark McGwire BASH .40 .18
❑ 657 Joe Grahe RC .05 .02
❑ 658 Jim Eisenreich .05 .02
❑ 659 Dan Gladden .05 .02
❑ 660 Steve Farr .05 .02
❑ 661 Bill Sampen .05 .02
❑ 662 Dave Rohde .05 .02
❑ 663 Mark Gardner .05 .02
❑ 664 Mike Simms .05 .02
❑ 665 Moises Alou .20 .09
❑ 666 Mickey Hatcher .05 .02
❑ 667 Jimmy Key .10 .05
❑ 668 John Wetteland .20 .09
❑ 669 John Smiley .05 .02
❑ 670 Jim Acker .05 .02
❑ 671 Pascual Perez .05 .02
❑ 672 Reggie Harris UER .05 .02
(Opportunity misspelled
as oppurtinty)
❑ 673 Matt Nokes .05 .02
❑ 674 Rafael Novoa .05 .02
❑ 675 Hensley Meulens .05 .02
❑ 676 Jeff M. Robinson .05 .02
❑ 677 Ground Breaking .10 .05
(New Comiskey Park;
Carlton Fisk and
Robin Ventura)
❑ 678 Johnny Ray .05 .02
❑ 679 Greg Hibbard .05 .02
❑ 680 Paul Sorrento .10 .05
❑ 681 Mike Marshall .05 .02
❑ 682 Jim Clancy .05 .02
❑ 683 Rob Murphy .05 .02
❑ 684 Dave Schmidt .05 .02
❑ 685 Jeff Gray .05 .02
❑ 686 Mike Hartley .05 .02
❑ 687 Jeff King .05 .02
❑ 688 Stan Javier .05 .02
❑ 689 Bob Walk .05 .02
❑ 690 Jim Gott .05 .02
❑ 691 Mike LaCoss .05 .02
❑ 692 John Farrell .05 .02
❑ 693 Tim Leary .05 .02
❑ 694 Mike Walker .05 .02
❑ 695 Eric Plunk .05 .02
❑ 696 Mike Fetters .05 .02
❑ 697 Wayne Edwards .05 .02
❑ 698 Tim Drummond .05 .02
❑ 699 Willie Fraser .05 .02
❑ 700 Checklist 601-700 .05 .02
❑ 701 Mike Heath .05 .02
❑ 702 Rookie Threats .50 .23
Luis Gonzalez
Karl Rhodes
Jeff Bagwell
❑ 703 Jose Mesa .05 .02
❑ 704 Dave Smith .05 .02
❑ 705 Danny Darwin .05 .02
❑ 706 Rafael Belliard .05 .02
❑ 707 Rob Murphy .05 .02
❑ 708 Terry Pendleton .10 .05
❑ 709 Mike Pagliarulo .05 .02
❑ 710 Sid Bream .05 .02
❑ 711 Junior Felix .05 .02
❑ 712 Dante Bichette .20 .09
❑ 713 Kevin Gross .05 .02
❑ 714 Luis Sojo .05 .02
❑ 715 Bob Ojeda .05 .02
❑ 716 Julio Machado .05 .02
❑ 717 Steve Farr .05 .02
❑ 718 Franklin Stubbs .05 .02
❑ 719 Mike Boddicker .05 .02
❑ 720 Willie Randolph .10 .05
❑ 721 Willie McGee .10 .05
❑ 722 Chili Davis .10 .05
❑ 723 Danny Jackson .05 .02
❑ 724 Cory Snyder .05 .02
❑ 725 MVP Lineup .10 .05
Andre Dawson
George Bell
Ryne Sandberg
❑ 726 Rob Deer .05 .02
❑ 727 Rich DeLucia .05 .02
❑ 728 Mike Perez RC .05 .02
❑ 729 Mickey Tettleton .05 .02
❑ 730 Mike Blowers .05 .02
❑ 731 Gary Gaetti .10 .05
❑ 732 Brett Butler .10 .05
❑ 733 Dave Parker .10 .05
❑ 734 Eddie Zosky .05 .02
❑ 735 Jack Clark .10 .05
❑ 736 Jack Morris .10 .05
❑ 737 Kirk Gibson .10 .05
❑ 738 Steve Bedrosian .05 .02
❑ 739 Candy Maldonado .05 .02
❑ 740 Matt Young .05 .02
❑ 741 Rich Garces RC .05 .02
❑ 742 George Bell .05 .02
❑ 743 Deion Sanders .10 .05
❑ 744 Bo Jackson .10 .05
❑ 745 Luis Mercedes RC .05 .02
❑ 746 Reggie Jefferson UER .10 .05
(Throwing left on card;
back has throws right)
❑ 747 Pete Incaviglia .05 .02
❑ 748 Chris Hammond .05 .02
❑ 749 Mike Stanton .05 .02
❑ 750 Scott Sanderson .05 .02
❑ 751 Paul Faries .05 .02
❑ 752 Al Osuna RC .05 .02
❑ 753 Steve Chitren .05 .02
❑ 754 Tony Fernandez .05 .02
❑ 755 Jeff Bagwell RC UER 2.50 1.10
(Strikeout and walk
totals reversed)
❑ 756 Kirk Dressendorfer RC .05 .02
❑ 757 Glenn Davis .05 .02
❑ 758 Gary Carter .10 .05
❑ 759 Zane Smith .05 .02
❑ 760 Vance Law .05 .02
❑ 761 Denis Boucher RC .05 .02
❑ 762 Turner Ward RC .05 .02
❑ 763 Roberto Alomar .20 .09
❑ 764 Albert Belle .10 .05
❑ 765 Joe Carter .10 .05
❑ 766 Pete Schourek RC .10 .05
❑ 767 Heathcliff Slocumb RC .05 .02
❑ 768 Vince Coleman .05 .02
❑ 769 Mitch Williams .05 .02
❑ 770 Brian Downing .05 .02
❑ 771 Dana Allison .05 .02
❑ 772 Pete Harnisch .05 .02
❑ 773 Tim Raines .10 .05
❑ 774 Darryl Kile .10 .05
❑ 775 Fred McGriff .20 .09
❑ 776 Dwight Evans .10 .05
❑ 777 Joe Slusarski .05 .02
❑ 778 Dave Righetti .05 .02
❑ 779 Jeff Hamilton .05 .02
❑ 780 Ernest Riles .05 .02
❑ 781 Ken Dayley .05 .02
❑ 782 Eric King .05 .02
❑ 783 Devon White .05 .02
❑ 784 Beau Allred .05 .02
❑ 785 Mike Timlin RC .05 .02
❑ 786 Ivan Calderon .05 .02
❑ 787 Hubie Brooks .05 .02
❑ 788 Juan Agosto .05 .02
❑ 789 Barry Jones .05 .02
❑ 790 Wally Backman .05 .02
❑ 791 Jim Presley .05 .02
❑ 792 Charlie Hough .10 .05
❑ 793 Larry Andersen .05 .02
❑ 794 Steve Finley .20 .09
❑ 795 Shawn Abner .05 .02
❑ 796 Jeff M. Robinson .05 .02
❑ 797 Joe Bitker .05 .02
❑ 798 Eric Show .05 .02
❑ 799 Bud Black .05 .02
❑ 800 Checklist 701-800 .05 .02
❑ HH1 Hank Aaron Hologram 1.50 .70
❑ SP1 Michael Jordan SP 10.00 4.50
(Shown batting in
White Sox uniform)
❑ SP2 Rickey Henderson 2.00 .90
Nolan Ryan
May 1, 1991 Records

## 1991 Upper Deck Final Edition

| | MINT | NRMT |
|---|---|---|
| COMP.FACT.SET (100) | 20.00 | 9.00 |

❑ 1F Ryan Klesko CL .10 .05
Reggie Sanders
❑ 2F Pedro Martinez RC 12.00 5.50
❑ 3F Lance Dickson .05 .02
❑ 4F Royce Clayton .10 .05
❑ 5F Scott Bryant .05 .02
❑ 6F Dan Wilson RC .20 .09
❑ 7F Dmitri Young RC .40 .18
❑ 8F Ryan Klesko RC .40 .18
❑ 9F Tom Goodwin .10 .05
❑ 10F Rondell White RC .40 .18
❑ 11F Reggie Sanders .10 .05
❑ 12F Todd Van Poppel .05 .02
❑ 13F Arthur Rhodes RC .10 .05
❑ 14F Eddie Zosky .05 .02
❑ 15F Gerald Williams RC .25 .11
❑ 16F Robert Eenhoorn RC .05 .02
❑ 17F Jim Thome RC .75 .35
❑ 18F Marc Newfield RC .05 .02
❑ 19F Kerwin Moore RC .05 .02
❑ 20F Jeff McNeely RC .05 .02
❑ 21F Frankie Rodriguez RC .10 .05
❑ 22F Andy Mota .05 .02
❑ 23F Chris Haney RC .05 .02
❑ 24F Kenny Lofton RC .50 .23
❑ 25F Dave Nilsson RC .25 .11
❑ 26F Derek Bell .10 .05
❑ 27F Frank Castillo RC .25 .11
❑ 28F Candy Maldonado .05 .02
❑ 29F Chuck McElroy .05 .02
❑ 30F Chito Martinez .05 .02
❑ 31F Steve Howe .05 .02
❑ 32F Freddie Benavides .05 .02
❑ 33F Scott Kamieniecki RC .05 .02
❑ 34F Denny Neagle RC .25 .11
❑ 35F Mike Humphreys RC .05 .02
❑ 36F Mike Remlinger .05 .02
❑ 37F Scott Coolbaugh .05 .02
❑ 38F Darren Lewis .10 .05
❑ 39F Thomas Howard .05 .02
❑ 40F John Candelaria .05 .02
❑ 41F Todd Benzinger .05 .02
❑ 42F Wilson Alvarez .05 .02
❑ 43F Patrick Lennon RC .05 .02
❑ 44F Rusty Meacham RC .05 .02
❑ 45F Ryan Bowen RC .05 .02
❑ 46F Rick Wilkins RC .05 .02
❑ 47F Ed Sprague .05 .02
❑ 48F Bob Scanlan .05 .02
❑ 49F Tom Candiotti .05 .02
❑ 50F Dennis Martinez .05 .02
(Perfecto)
❑ 51F Oil Can Boyd .05 .02
❑ 52F Glenallen Hill .05 .02
❑ 53F Scott Livingstone RC .05 .02
❑ 54F Brian R. Hunter RC .10 .05

| | | | |
|---|---|---|---|
| ❑ 55F | Ivan Rodriguez RC | 2.00 | .90 |
| ❑ 56F | Keith Mitchell RC | .05 | .02 |
| ❑ 57F | Roger McDowell | .05 | .02 |
| ❑ 58F | Otis Nixon | .05 | .02 |
| ❑ 59F | Juan Bell | .05 | .02 |
| ❑ 60F | Bill Krueger | .05 | .02 |
| ❑ 61F | Chris Donnels | .05 | .02 |
| ❑ 62F | Tommy Greene | .05 | .02 |
| ❑ 63F | Doug Simons | .05 | .02 |
| ❑ 64F | Andy Ashby RC | .25 | .09 |
| ❑ 65F | Anthony Young RC | .05 | .02 |
| ❑ 66F | Kevin Morton | .05 | .02 |
| ❑ 67F | Bret Barberie RC** | .05 | .02 |
| ❑ 68F | Scott Servais RC | .05 | .02 |
| ❑ 69F | Ron Darling | .05 | .02 |
| ❑ 70F | Tim Burke | .05 | .02 |
| ❑ 71F | Vicente Palacios | .05 | .02 |
| ❑ 72F | Gerald Alexander | .05 | .02 |
| ❑ 73F | Reggie Jefferson | .10 | .05 |
| ❑ 74F | Dean Palmer | .10 | .05 |
| ❑ 75F | Mark Whiten | .05 | .02 |
| ❑ 76F | Randy Tomlin RC | .05 | .02 |
| ❑ 77F | Mark Wohlers RC | .10 | .05 |
| ❑ 78F | Brook Jacoby | .05 | .02 |
| ❑ 79F | Ken Griffey Jr. CL | .40 | .18 |
| | Ryne Sandberg | | |
| ❑ 80F | Jack Morris AS | .05 | .02 |
| ❑ 81F | Sandy Alomar Jr. AS | .05 | .02 |
| ❑ 82F | Cecil Fielder AS | .05 | .02 |
| ❑ 83F | Roberto Alomar AS | .10 | .05 |
| ❑ 84F | Wade Boggs AS | .10 | .05 |
| ❑ 85F | Cal Ripken AS | .40 | .18 |
| ❑ 86F | Rickey Henderson AS | .10 | .05 |
| ❑ 87F | Ken Griffey Jr. AS | .50 | .35 |
| ❑ 88F | Dave Henderson AS | .05 | .02 |
| ❑ 89F | Danny Tartabull AS | .05 | .02 |
| ❑ 90F | Tom Glavine AS | .10 | .05 |
| ❑ 91F | Benito Santiago AS | .05 | .02 |
| ❑ 92F | Will Clark AS | .10 | .05 |
| ❑ 93F | Ryne Sandberg AS | .20 | .09 |
| ❑ 94F | Chris Sabo AS | .05 | .02 |
| ❑ 95F | Ozzie Smith AS | .20 | .09 |
| ❑ 96F | Ivan Calderon AS | .05 | .02 |
| ❑ 97F | Tony Gwynn AS | .20 | .09 |
| ❑ 98F | Andre Dawson AS | .10 | .05 |
| ❑ 99F | Bobby Bonilla AS | .10 | .05 |
| ❑ 100F | Checklist 1-100 | .05 | .02 |

## 1992 Upper Deck

| | MINT | NRMT |
|---|---|---|
| COMPLETE SET (800) | 15.00 | 6.75 |
| COMP.FACT.SET (800) | 20.00 | 9.00 |
| COMPLETE LO SET (700) | 12.00 | 5.50 |
| COMPLETE HI SET (100) | 3.00 | 1.35 |

| | | | |
|---|---|---|---|
| ❑ 1 | Ryan Klesko CL | .25 | .11 |
| | Jim Thome | | |
| ❑ 2 | Royce Clayton SR | .05 | .02 |
| ❑ 3 | Brian Jordan SR RC | .50 | .23 |
| ❑ 4 | Dave Fleming SR | .05 | .02 |
| ❑ 5 | Jim Thome SR | .40 | .18 |
| ❑ 6 | Jeff Juden SR | .05 | .02 |
| ❑ 7 | Roberto Hernandez SR | .05 | .02 |
| ❑ 8 | Kyle Abbott SR | .05 | .02 |
| ❑ 9 | Chris George SR | .05 | .02 |
| ❑ 10 | Rob Maurer SR | .05 | .02 |
| ❑ 11 | Donald Harris SR | .05 | .02 |
| ❑ 12 | Ted Wood SR | .05 | .02 |
| ❑ 13 | Patrick Lennon SR | .05 | .02 |
| ❑ 14 | Willie Banks SR | .05 | .02 |
| ❑ 15 | Roger Salkeld SR UER | .05 | .02 |
| | (Bill was his grand-father, not his father) | | |
| ❑ 16 | Wil Cordero SR | .05 | .02 |
| ❑ 17 | Arthur Rhodes SR | .05 | .02 |
| ❑ 18 | Pedro Martinez SR | 2.00 | .90 |
| ❑ 19 | Andy Ashby SR | .10 | .05 |
| ❑ 20 | Tom Goodwin SR | .05 | .02 |
| ❑ 21 | Braulio Castillo SR | .05 | .02 |
| ❑ 22 | Todd Van Poppel SR | .05 | .02 |
| ❑ 23 | Brian Williams SR RC | .05 | .02 |
| ❑ 24 | Ryan Klesko SR | .20 | .09 |
| ❑ 25 | Kenny Lofton SR | .25 | .11 |
| ❑ 26 | Derek Bell SR | .10 | .05 |
| ❑ 27 | Reggie Sanders SR | .05 | .02 |
| ❑ 28 | Dave Winfield's 400th | .10 | .05 |
| ❑ 29 | David Justice TC | .10 | .05 |
| ❑ 30 | Rob Dibble TC | .05 | .02 |
| ❑ 31 | Craig Biggio TC | .10 | .05 |
| ❑ 32 | Eddie Murray TC | .10 | .05 |
| ❑ 33 | Fred McGriff TC | .10 | .05 |
| ❑ 34 | Willie McGee TC | .05 | .02 |
| ❑ 35 | Shawon Dunston TC | .05 | .02 |
| ❑ 36 | Delino DeShields TC | .05 | .02 |
| ❑ 37 | Howard Johnson TC | .05 | .02 |
| ❑ 38 | John Kruk TC | .05 | .02 |
| ❑ 39 | Doug Drabek TC | .05 | .02 |
| ❑ 40 | Todd Zeile TC | .05 | .02 |
| ❑ 41 | Steve Avery | .05 | .02 |
| | Playoff Perfection | | |
| ❑ 42 | Jeremy Hernandez RC | .05 | .02 |
| ❑ 43 | Doug Henry RC | .05 | .02 |
| ❑ 44 | Chris Donnels | .05 | .02 |
| ❑ 45 | Mo Sanford | .05 | .02 |
| ❑ 46 | Scott Kamieniecki | .05 | .02 |
| ❑ 47 | Mark Lemke | .05 | .02 |
| ❑ 48 | Steve Farr | .05 | .02 |
| ❑ 49 | Francisco Oliveras | .05 | .02 |
| ❑ 50 | Ced Landrum | .05 | .02 |
| ❑ 51 | Rondell White CL | .20 | .09 |
| | Mark Newfield | | |
| ❑ 52 | Eduardo Perez TP RC | .05 | .02 |
| ❑ 53 | Tom Nevers TP | .05 | .02 |
| ❑ 54 | David Zancanaro TP | .05 | .02 |
| ❑ 55 | Shawn Green TP RC | 1.50 | .70 |
| ❑ 56 | Mark Wohlers TP | .05 | .02 |
| ❑ 57 | Dave Nilsson TP | .10 | .05 |
| ❑ 58 | Dmitri Young TP | .10 | .05 |
| ❑ 59 | Ryan Hawblitzel TP RC | .05 | .02 |
| ❑ 60 | Raul Mondesi TP | .40 | .18 |
| ❑ 61 | Rondell White TP | .20 | .09 |
| ❑ 62 | Steve Hosey TP | .05 | .02 |
| ❑ 63 | Manny Ramirez TP RC | 1.50 | .70 |
| ❑ 64 | Marc Newfield TP | .05 | .02 |
| ❑ 65 | Jeromy Burnitz TP | .20 | .09 |
| ❑ 66 | Mark Smith TP RC | .05 | .02 |
| ❑ 67 | Joey Hamilton TP RC | .25 | .11 |
| ❑ 68 | Tyler Green TP RC | .05 | .02 |
| ❑ 69 | Jon Farrell TP RC | .05 | .02 |
| ❑ 70 | Kurt Miller TP | .05 | .02 |
| ❑ 71 | Jeff Plympton TP | .05 | .02 |
| ❑ 72 | Dan Wilson TP | .10 | .05 |
| ❑ 73 | Joe Vitiello TP RC | .05 | .02 |
| ❑ 74 | Rico Brogna TP | .10 | .05 |
| ❑ 75 | David McCarty TP RC | .05 | .02 |
| ❑ 76 | Bob Wickman TP | .05 | .02 |
| ❑ 77 | Carlos Rodriguez TP | .05 | .02 |
| ❑ 78 | Jim Abbott | .05 | .02 |
| | Stay In School | | |
| ❑ 79 | Ramon Martinez | .20 | .09 |
| | Pedro Martinez | | |
| ❑ 80 | Kevin Mitchell | .05 | .02 |
| | Keith Mitchell | | |
| ❑ 81 | Sandy Alomar Jr. | .20 | .09 |
| | Roberto Alomar | | |
| ❑ 82 | Cal Ripken | .50 | .23 |
| | Billy Ripken | | |
| ❑ 83 | Tony Gwynn | .20 | .09 |
| | Chris Gwynn | | |
| ❑ 84 | Dwight Gooden | .20 | .09 |
| | Gary Sheffield | | |
| ❑ 85 | Ken Griffey Sr. | .50 | .23 |
| | Ken Griffey Jr. | | |
| | Craig Griffey | | |
| ❑ 86 | Jim Abbott TC | .05 | .02 |
| ❑ 87 | Frank Thomas TC | .20 | .09 |
| ❑ 88 | Danny Tartabull TC | .05 | .02 |
| ❑ 89 | Scott Erickson TC | .05 | .02 |
| ❑ 90 | Rickey Henderson TC | .10 | .05 |
| ❑ 91 | Edgar Martinez TC | .10 | .05 |
| ❑ 92 | Nolan Ryan TC | .50 | .09 |
| ❑ 93 | Ben McDonald TC | .05 | .02 |
| ❑ 94 | Ellis Burks TC | .05 | .02 |
| ❑ 95 | Greg Swindell TC | .05 | .02 |
| ❑ 96 | Cecil Fielder TC | .05 | .02 |
| ❑ 97 | Greg Vaughn TC | .05 | .02 |
| ❑ 98 | Kevin Maas TC | .05 | .02 |
| ❑ 99 | Dave Stieb TC | .05 | .02 |
| ❑ 100 | Checklist 1-100 | .05 | .02 |
| ❑ 101 | Joe Oliver | .05 | .02 |
| ❑ 102 | Hector Villanueva | .05 | .02 |
| ❑ 103 | Ed Whitson | .05 | .02 |
| ❑ 104 | Danny Jackson | .05 | .02 |
| ❑ 105 | Chris Hammond | .05 | .02 |
| ❑ 106 | Ricky Jordan | .05 | .02 |
| ❑ 107 | Kevin Bass | .05 | .02 |
| ❑ 108 | Darrin Fletcher | .05 | .02 |
| ❑ 109 | Junior Ortiz | .05 | .02 |
| ❑ 110 | Tom Bolton | .05 | .02 |
| ❑ 111 | Jeff King | .05 | .02 |
| ❑ 112 | Dave Magadan | .05 | .02 |
| ❑ 113 | Mike LaValliere | .05 | .02 |
| ❑ 114 | Hubie Brooks | .05 | .02 |
| ❑ 115 | Jay Bell | .10 | .05 |
| ❑ 116 | David Wells | .10 | .05 |
| ❑ 117 | Jim Leyritz | .05 | .02 |
| ❑ 118 | Manuel Lee | .05 | .02 |
| ❑ 119 | Alvaro Espinoza | .05 | .02 |
| ❑ 120 | B.J. Surhoff | .10 | .05 |
| ❑ 121 | Hal Morris | .05 | .02 |
| ❑ 122 | Shawon Dawson | .05 | .02 |
| ❑ 123 | Chris Sabo | .05 | .02 |
| ❑ 124 | Andre Dawson | .10 | .05 |
| ❑ 125 | Eric Davis | .10 | .05 |
| ❑ 126 | Chili Davis | .10 | .05 |
| ❑ 127 | Dale Murphy | .20 | .09 |
| ❑ 128 | Kirk McCaskill | .05 | .02 |
| ❑ 129 | Terry Mulholland | .05 | .02 |
| ❑ 130 | Rick Aguilera | .10 | .05 |
| ❑ 131 | Vince Coleman | .05 | .02 |
| ❑ 132 | Andy Van Slyke | .10 | .05 |
| ❑ 133 | Gregg Jefferies | .05 | .02 |
| ❑ 134 | Barry Bonds | .30 | .14 |
| ❑ 135 | Dwight Gooden | .10 | .05 |
| ❑ 136 | Dave Stieb | .05 | .02 |
| ❑ 137 | Albert Belle | .10 | .05 |
| ❑ 138 | Teddy Higuera | .05 | .02 |
| ❑ 139 | Jesse Barfield | .05 | .02 |
| ❑ 140 | Pat Borders | .05 | .02 |
| ❑ 141 | Bip Roberts | .05 | .02 |
| ❑ 142 | Rob Dibble | .05 | .02 |
| ❑ 143 | Mark Grace | .20 | .09 |
| ❑ 144 | Barry Larkin | .10 | .05 |
| ❑ 145 | Ryne Sandberg | .25 | .11 |
| ❑ 146 | Scott Erickson | .05 | .02 |
| ❑ 147 | Luis Polonia | .05 | .02 |
| ❑ 148 | John Burkett | .05 | .02 |
| ❑ 149 | Luis Sojo | .05 | .02 |
| ❑ 150 | Dickie Thon | .05 | .02 |
| ❑ 151 | Walt Weiss | .05 | .02 |
| ❑ 152 | Mike Scioscia | .05 | .02 |
| ❑ 153 | Mark McGwire | .75 | .35 |
| ❑ 154 | Matt Williams | .10 | .05 |
| ❑ 155 | Rickey Henderson | .25 | .11 |
| ❑ 156 | Sandy Alomar Jr. | .10 | .05 |
| ❑ 157 | Brian McRae | .05 | .02 |
| ❑ 158 | Harold Baines | .10 | .05 |
| ❑ 159 | Kevin Appier | .10 | .05 |
| ❑ 160 | Felix Fermin | .05 | .02 |
| ❑ 161 | Leo Gomez | .05 | .02 |
| ❑ 162 | Craig Biggio | .10 | .05 |
| ❑ 163 | Ben McDonald | .05 | .02 |
| ❑ 164 | Randy Johnson | .25 | .11 |
| ❑ 165 | Cal Ripken | .75 | .35 |
| ❑ 166 | Frank Thomas | .40 | .18 |
| ❑ 167 | Delino DeShields | .10 | .05 |
| ❑ 168 | Greg Gagne | .05 | .02 |
| ❑ 169 | Ron Karkovice | .05 | .02 |
| ❑ 170 | Charlie Leibrandt | .05 | .02 |

❑ 171 Dave Righetti .05 .02
❑ 172 Dave Henderson .05 .02
❑ 173 Steve Decker .05 .02
❑ 174 Darryl Strawberry .10 .05
❑ 175 Will Clark .20 .09
❑ 176 Ruben Sierra .05 .02
❑ 177 Ozzie Smith .25 .11
❑ 178 Charles Nagy .05 .02
❑ 179 Gary Pettis .05 .02
❑ 180 Kirk Gibson .10 .05
❑ 181 Randy Milligan .05 .02
❑ 182 Dave Valle .05 .02
❑ 183 Chris Hoiles .05 .02
❑ 184 Tony Phillips .05 .02
❑ 185 Brady Anderson .10 .05
❑ 186 Scott Fletcher .05 .02
❑ 187 Gene Larkin .05 .02
❑ 188 Lance Johnson .05 .02
❑ 189 Greg Olson .05 .02
❑ 190 Melido Perez .05 .02
❑ 191 Lenny Harris .05 .02
❑ 192 Terry Kennedy .05 .02
❑ 193 Mike Gallego .05 .02
❑ 194 Willie McGee .10 .05
❑ 195 Juan Samuel .05 .02
❑ 196 Jeff Huson .10 .05
(Shows Jose Canseco sliding into second)
❑ 197 Alex Cole .05 .02
❑ 198 Ron Robinson .05 .02
❑ 199 Joel Skinner .05 .02
❑ 200 Checklist 101-200 .05 .02
❑ 201 Kevin Reimer .05 .02
❑ 202 Stan Belinda .05 .02
❑ 203 Pat Tabler .05 .02
❑ 204 Jose Guzman .05 .02
❑ 205 Jose Lind .05 .02
❑ 206 Spike Owen .05 .02
❑ 207 Joe Orsulak .05 .02
❑ 208 Charlie Hayes .05 .02
❑ 209 Mike Devereaux .05 .02
❑ 210 Mike Fitzgerald .05 .02
❑ 211 Willie Randolph .10 .05
❑ 212 Rod Nichols .05 .02
❑ 213 Mike Boddicker .05 .02
❑ 214 Bill Spiers .05 .02
❑ 215 Steve Olin .05 .02
❑ 216 David Howard .05 .02
❑ 217 Gary Varsho .05 .02
❑ 218 Mike Harkey .05 .02
❑ 219 Luis Aquino .05 .02
❑ 220 Chuck McElroy .05 .02
❑ 221 Doug Drabek .05 .02
❑ 222 Dave Winfield .20 .09
❑ 223 Rafael Palmeiro .20 .09
❑ 224 Joe Carter .10 .05
❑ 225 Bobby Bonilla .10 .05
❑ 226 Ivan Calderon .05 .02
❑ 227 Gregg Olson .05 .02
❑ 228 Tim Wallach .05 .02
❑ 229 Terry Pendleton .10 .05
❑ 230 Gilberto Reyes .05 .02
❑ 231 Carlos Baerga .05 .02
❑ 232 Greg Vaughn .10 .05
❑ 233 Bret Saberhagen .10 .05
❑ 234 Gary Sheffield .20 .09
❑ 235 Mark Lewis .05 .02
❑ 236 George Bell .05 .02
❑ 237 Danny Tartabull .05 .02
❑ 238 Willie Wilson .05 .02
❑ 239 Doug Dascenzo .05 .02
❑ 240 Bill Pecota .05 .02
❑ 241 Julio Franco .05 .02
❑ 242 Ed Sprague .05 .02
❑ 243 Juan Gonzalez .20 .09
❑ 244 Chuck Finley .10 .05
❑ 245 Ivan Rodriguez .40 .18
❑ 246 Len Dykstra .10 .05
❑ 247 Deion Sanders .20 .09
❑ 248 Dwight Evans .10 .05
❑ 249 Larry Walker .10 .05
❑ 250 Billy Ripken .05 .02
❑ 251 Mickey Tettleton .05 .02
❑ 252 Tony Pena .05 .02
❑ 253 Benito Santiago .05 .02
❑ 254 Kirby Puckett .50 .23
❑ 255 Cecil Fielder .10 .05
❑ 256 Howard Johnson .05 .02
❑ 257 Andujar Cedeno .05 .02
❑ 258 Jose Rijo .05 .02
❑ 259 Al Osuna .05 .02
❑ 260 Todd Hundley .05 .02
❑ 261 Orel Hershiser .10 .05
❑ 262 Ray Lankford .20 .09
❑ 263 Robin Ventura .10 .05
❑ 264 Felix Jose .05 .02
❑ 265 Eddie Murray .20 .09
❑ 266 Kevin Mitchell .10 .05
❑ 267 Gary Carter .10 .05
❑ 268 Mike Benjamin .05 .02
❑ 269 Dick Schofield .05 .02
❑ 270 Jose Uribe .05 .02
❑ 271 Pete Incaviglia .05 .02
❑ 272 Tony Fernandez .05 .02
❑ 273 Alan Trammell .10 .05
❑ 274 Tony Gwynn .40 .18
❑ 275 Mike Greenwell .05 .02
❑ 276 Jeff Bagwell .40 .18
❑ 277 Frank Viola .05 .02
❑ 278 Randy Myers .10 .05
❑ 279 Ken Caminiti .10 .05
❑ 280 Bill Doran .05 .02
❑ 281 Dan Pasqua .05 .02
❑ 282 Alfredo Griffin .05 .02
❑ 283 Jose Oquendo .05 .02
❑ 284 Kal Daniels .05 .02
❑ 285 Bobby Thigpen .05 .02
❑ 286 Robby Thompson .05 .02
❑ 287 Mark Eichhorn .05 .02
❑ 288 Mike Felder .05 .02
❑ 289 Dave Gallagher .05 .02
❑ 290 Dave Anderson .05 .02
❑ 291 Mel Hall .05 .02
❑ 292 Jerald Clark .05 .02
❑ 293 Al Newman .05 .02
❑ 294 Rob Deer .05 .02
❑ 295 Matt Nokes .05 .02
❑ 296 Jack Armstrong .05 .02
❑ 297 Jim Deshaies .05 .02
❑ 298 Jeff Innis .05 .02
❑ 299 Jeff Reed .05 .02
❑ 300 Checklist 201-300 .05 .02
❑ 301 Lonnie Smith .05 .02
❑ 302 Jimmy Key .10 .05
❑ 303 Junior Felix .05 .02
❑ 304 Mike Heath .05 .02
❑ 305 Mark Langston .05 .02
❑ 306 Greg W. Harris .05 .02
❑ 307 Brett Butler .10 .05
❑ 308 Luis Rivera .05 .02
❑ 309 Bruce Ruffin .05 .02
❑ 310 Paul Faries .05 .02
❑ 311 Terry Leach .05 .02
❑ 312 Scott Brosius RC .25 .11
❑ 313 Scott Leius .05 .02
❑ 314 Harold Reynolds .05 .02
❑ 315 Jack Morris .10 .05
❑ 316 David Segui .05 .02
❑ 317 Bill Gullickson .05 .02
❑ 318 Todd Frohwirth .05 .02
❑ 319 Mark Leiter .05 .02
❑ 320 Jeff M. Robinson .05 .02
❑ 321 Gary Gaetti .10 .05
❑ 322 John Smoltz .10 .05
❑ 323 Andy Benes .05 .02
❑ 324 Kelly Gruber .05 .02
❑ 325 Jim Abbott .10 .05
❑ 326 John Kruk .10 .05
❑ 327 Kevin Seitzer .05 .02
❑ 328 Darrin Jackson .05 .02
❑ 329 Kurt Stillwell .05 .02
❑ 330 Mike Maddux .05 .02
❑ 331 Dennis Eckersley .10 .05
❑ 332 Dan Gladden .05 .02
❑ 333 Jose Canseco .25 .11
❑ 334 Kent Hrbek .10 .05
❑ 335 Ken Griffey Sr. .10 .05
❑ 336 Greg Swindell .05 .02
❑ 337 Trevor Wilson .05 .02
❑ 338 Sam Horn .05 .02
❑ 339 Mike Henneman .05 .02
❑ 340 Jerry Browne .05 .02
❑ 341 Glenn Braggs .05 .02
❑ 342 Tom Glavine .10 .05
❑ 343 Wally Joyner .10 .05
❑ 344 Fred McGriff .10 .05
❑ 345 Ron Gant .10 .05
❑ 346 Ramon Martinez .05 .02
❑ 347 Wes Chamberlain .05 .02
❑ 348 Terry Shumpert .05 .02
❑ 349 Tim Teufel .05 .02
❑ 350 Wally Backman .05 .02
❑ 351 Joe Girardi .10 .05
❑ 352 Devon White .05 .02
❑ 353 Greg Maddux .50 .23
❑ 354 Ryan Bowen .05 .02
❑ 355 Roberto Alomar .20 .09
❑ 356 Don Mattingly .50 .23
❑ 357 Pedro Guerrero .05 .02
❑ 358 Steve Sax .05 .02
❑ 359 Joey Cora .05 .02
❑ 360 Jim Gantner .05 .02
❑ 361 Brian Barnes .05 .02
❑ 362 Kevin McReynolds .05 .02
❑ 363 Bret Barberie .05 .02
❑ 364 David Cone .10 .05
❑ 365 Dennis Martinez .10 .05
❑ 366 Brian Hunter .05 .02
❑ 367 Edgar Martinez .10 .05
❑ 368 Steve Finley .10 .05
❑ 369 Greg Briley .05 .02
❑ 370 Jeff Blauser .05 .02
❑ 371 Todd Stottlemyre .10 .05
❑ 372 Luis Gonzalez .10 .05
❑ 373 Rick Wilkins .05 .02
❑ 374 Darryl Kile .10 .05
❑ 375 John Olerud .10 .05
❑ 376 Lee Smith .10 .05
❑ 377 Kevin Maas .05 .02
❑ 378 Dante Bichette .10 .05
❑ 379 Tom Pagnozzi .05 .02
❑ 380 Mike Flanagan .05 .02
❑ 381 Charlie O'Brien .05 .02
❑ 382 Dave Martinez .05 .02
❑ 383 Keith Miller .05 .02
❑ 384 Scott Ruskin .05 .02
❑ 385 Kevin Elster .05 .02
❑ 386 Alvin Davis .05 .02
❑ 387 Casey Candaele .05 .02
❑ 388 Pete O'Brien .05 .02
❑ 389 Jeff Treadway .05 .02
❑ 390 Scott Bradley .05 .02
❑ 391 Mookie Wilson .10 .05
❑ 392 Jimmy Jones .05 .02
❑ 393 Candy Maldonado .05 .02
❑ 394 Eric Yelding .05 .02
❑ 395 Tom Henke .05 .02
❑ 396 Franklin Stubbs .05 .02
❑ 397 Milt Thompson .05 .02
❑ 398 Mark Carreon .05 .02
❑ 399 Randy Velarde .05 .02
❑ 400 Checklist 301-400 .05 .02
❑ 401 Omar Vizquel .10 .05
❑ 402 Joe Boever .05 .02
❑ 403 Bill Krueger .05 .02
❑ 404 Jody Reed .05 .02
❑ 405 Mike Schooler .05 .02
❑ 406 Jason Grimsley .05 .02
❑ 407 Greg Myers .05 .02
❑ 408 Randy Ready .05 .02
❑ 409 Mike Timlin .05 .02
❑ 410 Mitch Williams .05 .02
❑ 411 Garry Templeton .05 .02
❑ 412 Greg Cadaret .05 .02
❑ 413 Donnie Hill .05 .02
❑ 414 Wally Whitehurst .05 .02
❑ 415 Scott Sanderson .05 .02
❑ 416 Thomas Howard .05 .02
❑ 417 Neal Heaton .05 .02
❑ 418 Charlie Hough .10 .05
❑ 419 Jack Howell .05 .02
❑ 420 Greg Hibbard .05 .02
❑ 421 Carlos Quintana .05 .02
❑ 422 Kim Batiste .05 .02
❑ 423 Paul Molitor .20 .09
❑ 424 Ken Griffey Jr. .75 .35
❑ 425 Phil Plantier .05 .02
❑ 426 Denny Neagle .10 .05

❑ 427 Von Hayes .05 .02
❑ 428 Shane Mack .05 .02
❑ 429 Darren Daulton .10 .05
❑ 430 Dwayne Henry .05 .02
❑ 431 Lance Parrish .05 .02
❑ 432 Mike Humphreys .05 .02
❑ 433 Tim Burke .05 .02
❑ 434 Bryan Harvey .05 .02
❑ 435 Pat Kelly .05 .02
❑ 436 Ozzie Guillen .05 .02
❑ 437 Bruce Hurst .05 .02
❑ 438 Sammy Sosa .40 .18
❑ 439 Dennis Rasmussen .05 .02
❑ 440 Ken Patterson .05 .02
❑ 441 Jay Buhner .10 .05
❑ 442 Pat Combs .05 .02
❑ 443 Wade Boggs .25 .11
❑ 444 George Brett .40 .18
❑ 445 Mo Vaughn .10 .05
❑ 446 Chuck Knoblauch .10 .05
❑ 447 Tom Candiotti .05 .02
❑ 448 Mark Portugal .05 .02
❑ 449 Mickey Morandini .05 .02
❑ 450 Duane Ward .05 .02
❑ 451 Otis Nixon .05 .02
❑ 452 Bob Welch .05 .02
❑ 453 Rusty Meacham .05 .02
❑ 454 Keith Mitchell .05 .02
❑ 455 Marquis Grissom .05 .02
❑ 456 Robin Yount .20 .09
❑ 457 Harvey Pulliam .05 .02
❑ 458 Jose DeLeon .05 .02
❑ 459 Mark Gubicza .05 .02
❑ 460 Darryl Hamilton .05 .02
❑ 461 Tom Browning .05 .02
❑ 462 Monty Fariss .05 .02
❑ 463 Jerome Walton .05 .02
❑ 464 Paul O'Neill .10 .05
❑ 465 Dean Palmer .10 .05
❑ 466 Travis Fryman .10 .05
❑ 467 John Smiley .05 .02
❑ 468 Lloyd Moseby .05 .02
❑ 469 John Wehner .05 .02
❑ 470 Skeeter Barnes .05 .02
❑ 471 Steve Chitren .05 .02
❑ 472 Kent Mercker .05 .02
❑ 473 Terry Steinbach .05 .02
❑ 474 Andres Galarraga .10 .05
❑ 475 Steve Avery .05 .02
❑ 476 Tom Gordon .05 .02
❑ 477 Cal Eldred .05 .02
❑ 478 Omar Olivares .05 .02
❑ 479 Julio Machado .05 .02
❑ 480 Bob Milacki .05 .02
❑ 481 Les Lancaster .05 .02
❑ 482 John Candelaria .05 .02
❑ 483 Brian Downing .05 .02
❑ 484 Roger McDowell .05 .02
❑ 485 Scott Scudder .05 .02
❑ 486 Zane Smith .05 .02
❑ 487 John Cerutti .05 .02
❑ 488 Steve Buechele .05 .02
❑ 489 Paul Gibson .05 .02
❑ 490 Curtis Wilkerson .05 .02
❑ 491 Marvin Freeman .05 .02
❑ 492 Tom Foley .05 .02
❑ 493 Juan Berenguer .05 .02
❑ 494 Ernest Riles .05 .02
❑ 495 Sid Bream .05 .02
❑ 496 Chuck Crim .05 .02
❑ 497 Mike Macfarlane .05 .02
❑ 498 Dale Sveum .05 .02
❑ 499 Storm Davis .05 .02
❑ 500 Checklist 401-500 .05 .02
❑ 501 Jeff Reardon .10 .05
❑ 502 Shawn Abner .05 .02
❑ 503 Tony Fossas .05 .02
❑ 504 Cory Snyder .05 .02
❑ 505 Matt Young .05 .02
❑ 506 Allan Anderson .05 .02
❑ 507 Mark Lee .05 .02
❑ 508 Gene Nelson .05 .02
❑ 509 Mike Pagliarulo .05 .02
❑ 510 Rafael Belliard .05 .02
❑ 511 Jay Howell .05 .02
❑ 512 Bob Tewksbury .05 .02
❑ 513 Mike Morgan .05 .02
❑ 514 John Franco .10 .05
❑ 515 Kevin Gross .05 .02
❑ 516 Lou Whitaker .10 .05
❑ 517 Orlando Merced .05 .02
❑ 518 Todd Benzinger .05 .02
❑ 519 Gary Redus .05 .02
❑ 520 Walt Terrell .05 .02
❑ 521 Jack Clark .10 .05
❑ 522 Dave Parker .10 .05
❑ 523 Tim Naehring .05 .02
❑ 524 Mark Whiten .05 .02
❑ 525 Ellis Burks .10 .05
❑ 526 Frank Castillo .05 .02
❑ 527 Brian Harper .05 .02
❑ 528 Brook Jacoby .05 .02
❑ 529 Rick Sutcliffe .10 .05
❑ 530 Joe Klink .05 .02
❑ 531 Terry Bross .05 .02
❑ 532 Jose Offerman .05 .02
❑ 533 Todd Zeile .05 .02
❑ 534 Eric Karros .20 .09
❑ 535 Anthony Young .05 .02
❑ 536 Milt Cuyler .05 .02
❑ 537 Randy Tomlin .05 .02
❑ 538 Scott Livingstone .05 .02
❑ 539 Jim Eisenreich .05 .02
❑ 540 Don Slaught .05 .02
❑ 541 Scott Cooper .05 .02
❑ 542 Joe Grahe .05 .02
❑ 543 Tom Brunansky .05 .02
❑ 544 Eddie Zosky .05 .02
❑ 545 Roger Clemens .40 .18
❑ 546 David Justice .05 .02
❑ 547 Dave Stewart .10 .05
❑ 548 David West .05 .02
❑ 549 Dave Smith .05 .02
❑ 550 Dan Plesac .05 .02
❑ 551 Alex Fernandez .10 .05
❑ 552 Bernard Gilkey .10 .05
❑ 553 Jack McDowell .05 .02
❑ 554 Tino Martinez .10 .05
❑ 555 Bo Jackson .10 .05
❑ 556 Bernie Williams .20 .09
❑ 557 Mark Gardner .05 .02
❑ 558 Glenallen Hill .05 .02
❑ 559 Oil Can Boyd .05 .02
❑ 560 Chris James .05 .02
❑ 561 Scott Servais .05 .02
❑ 562 Rey Sanchez RC .05 .02
❑ 563 Paul McClellan .05 .02
❑ 564 Andy Mota .05 .02
❑ 565 Darren Lewis .05 .02
❑ 566 Jose Melendez .05 .02
❑ 567 Tommy Greene .05 .02
❑ 568 Rich Rodriguez .05 .02
❑ 569 Heathcliff Slocumb .05 .02
❑ 570 Joe Hesketh .05 .02
❑ 571 Carlton Fisk .20 .09
❑ 572 Erik Hanson .05 .02
❑ 573 Wilson Alvarez .05 .02
❑ 574 Rheal Cormier .05 .02
❑ 575 Tim Raines .10 .05
❑ 576 Bobby Witt .05 .02
❑ 577 Roberto Kelly .05 .02
❑ 578 Kevin Brown .10 .05
❑ 579 Chris Nabholz .05 .02
❑ 580 Jesse Orosco .05 .02
❑ 581 Jeff Brantley .05 .02
❑ 582 Rafael Ramirez .05 .02
❑ 583 Kelly Downs .05 .02
❑ 584 Mike Simms .05 .02
❑ 585 Mike Remlinger .05 .02
❑ 586 Dave Hollins .05 .02
❑ 587 Larry Andersen .05 .02
❑ 588 Mike Gardiner .05 .02
❑ 589 Craig Lefferts .05 .02
❑ 590 Paul Assenmacher .05 .02
❑ 591 Bryn Smith .05 .02
❑ 592 Donn Pall .05 .02
❑ 593 Mike Jackson .05 .02
❑ 594 Scott Radinsky .05 .02
❑ 595 Brian Holman .05 .02
❑ 596 Geronimo Pena .05 .02
❑ 597 Mike Jeffcoat .05 .02
❑ 598 Carlos Martinez .05 .02
❑ 599 Geno Petralli .05 .02
❑ 600 Checklist 501-600 .05 .02
❑ 601 Jerry Don Gleaton .05 .02
❑ 602 Adam Peterson .05 .02
❑ 603 Craig Grebeck .05 .02
❑ 604 Mark Guthrie .05 .02
❑ 605 Frank Tanana .05 .02
❑ 606 Hensley Meulens .05 .02
❑ 607 Mark Davis .05 .02
❑ 608 Eric Plunk .05 .02
❑ 609 Mark Williamson .05 .02
❑ 610 Lee Guetterman .05 .02
❑ 611 Bobby Rose .05 .02
❑ 612 Bill Wegman .05 .02
❑ 613 Mike Hartley .05 .02
❑ 614 Chris Beasley .05 .02
❑ 615 Chris Bosio .05 .02
❑ 616 Henry Cotto .05 .02
❑ 617 Chico Walker .05 .02
❑ 618 Russ Swan .05 .02
❑ 619 Bob Walk .05 .02
❑ 620 Bill Swift .05 .02
❑ 621 Warren Newson .05 .02
❑ 622 Steve Bedrosian .05 .02
❑ 623 Ricky Bones .05 .02
❑ 624 Kevin Tapani .05 .02
❑ 625 Juan Guzman .05 .02
❑ 626 Jeff Johnson .05 .02
❑ 627 Jeff Montgomery .10 .05
❑ 628 Ken Hill .05 .02
❑ 629 Gary Thurman .05 .02
❑ 630 Steve Howe .05 .02
❑ 631 Jose DeJesus .05 .02
❑ 632 Kirk Dressendorfer .05 .02
❑ 633 Jaime Navarro .05 .02
❑ 634 Lee Stevens .10 .05
❑ 635 Pete Harnisch .05 .02
❑ 636 Bill Landrum .05 .02
❑ 637 Rich DeLucia .05 .02
❑ 638 Luis Salazar .05 .02
❑ 639 Rob Murphy .05 .02
❑ 640 Jose Canseco CL .20 .09
Rickey Henderson
❑ 641 Roger Clemens DS .20 .09
❑ 642 Jim Abbott DS .05 .02
❑ 643 Travis Fryman DS .05 .02
❑ 644 Jesse Barfield DS .05 .02
❑ 645 Cal Ripken DS .40 .18
❑ 646 Wade Boggs DS .10 .05
❑ 647 Cecil Fielder DS .05 .02
❑ 648 Rickey Henderson DS .10 .05
❑ 649 Jose Canseco DS .10 .05
❑ 650 Ken Griffey Jr. DS .60 .25
❑ 651 Kenny Rogers .05 .02
❑ 652 Luis Mercedes .05 .02
❑ 653 Mike Stanton .05 .02
❑ 654 Glenn Davis .05 .02
❑ 655 Nolan Ryan 1.00 .45
❑ 656 Reggie Jefferson .10 .05
❑ 657 Javier Ortiz .05 .02
❑ 658 Greg A. Harris .05 .02
❑ 659 Mariano Duncan .05 .02
❑ 660 Jeff Shaw .05 .02
❑ 661 Mike Moore .05 .02
❑ 662 Chris Haney .05 .02
❑ 663 Joe Slusarski .05 .02
❑ 664 Wayne Housie .05 .02
❑ 665 Carlos Garcia .05 .02
❑ 666 Bob Ojeda .05 .02
❑ 667 Bryan Hickerson RC .05 .02
❑ 668 Tim Belcher .05 .02
❑ 669 Ron Darling .05 .02
❑ 670 Rex Hudler .05 .02
❑ 671 Sid Fernandez .05 .02
❑ 672 Chito Martinez .05 .02
❑ 673 Pete Schourek .05 .02
❑ 674 Armando Reynoso RC .05 .02
❑ 675 Mike Mussina .30 .14
❑ 676 Kevin Morton .05 .02
❑ 677 Norm Charlton .05 .02
❑ 678 Danny Darwin .05 .02
❑ 679 Eric King .05 .02
❑ 680 Ted Power .05 .02
❑ 681 Barry Jones .05 .02
❑ 682 Carney Lansford .10 .05
❑ 683 Mel Rojas .05 .02

| | Card | | |
|---|---|---|---|
| ❑ 684 | Rick Honeycutt | .05 | .02 |
| ❑ 685 | Jeff Fassero | .05 | .02 |
| ❑ 686 | Cris Carpenter | .05 | .02 |
| ❑ 687 | Tim Crews | .05 | .02 |
| ❑ 688 | Scott Terry | .05 | .02 |
| ❑ 689 | Chris Gwynn | .05 | .02 |
| ❑ 690 | Gerald Perry | .05 | .02 |
| ❑ 691 | John Barfield | .05 | .02 |
| ❑ 692 | Bob Melvin | .05 | .02 |
| ❑ 693 | Juan Agosto | .05 | .02 |
| ❑ 694 | Alejandro Pena | .05 | .02 |
| ❑ 695 | Jeff Russell | .05 | .02 |
| ❑ 696 | Carmelo Martinez | .05 | .02 |
| ❑ 697 | Bud Black | .05 | .02 |
| ❑ 698 | Dave Otto | .05 | .02 |
| ❑ 699 | Billy Hatcher | .05 | .02 |
| ❑ 700 | Checklist 601-700 | .05 | .02 |
| ❑ 701 | Clemente Nunez RC | .10 | .05 |
| ❑ 702 | Rookie Threats | .05 | .02 |
| | Mark Clark | | |
| | Donovan Osborne | | |
| | Brian Jordan | | |
| ❑ 703 | Mike Morgan | .05 | .02 |
| ❑ 704 | Keith Miller | .05 | .02 |
| ❑ 705 | Kurt Stillwell | .05 | .02 |
| ❑ 706 | Damon Berryhill | .05 | .02 |
| ❑ 707 | Von Hayes | .05 | .02 |
| ❑ 708 | Rick Sutcliffe | .10 | .05 |
| ❑ 709 | Hubie Brooks | .05 | .02 |
| ❑ 710 | Ryan Turner RC | .05 | .02 |
| ❑ 711 | Barry Bonds CL | .10 | .05 |
| | Andy Van Slyke | | |
| ❑ 712 | Jose Rijo DS | .05 | .02 |
| ❑ 713 | Tom Glavine DS | .10 | .05 |
| ❑ 714 | Shawon Dunston DS | .05 | .02 |
| ❑ 715 | Andy Van Slyke DS | .05 | .02 |
| ❑ 716 | Ozzie Smith DS | .20 | .09 |
| ❑ 717 | Tony Gwynn DS | .20 | .09 |
| ❑ 718 | Will Clark DS | .10 | .05 |
| ❑ 719 | Marquis Grissom DS | .05 | .02 |
| ❑ 720 | Howard Johnson DS | .05 | .02 |
| ❑ 721 | Barry Bonds DS | .20 | .09 |
| ❑ 722 | Kirk McCaskill | .05 | .02 |
| ❑ 723 | Sammy Sosa | .75 | .35 |
| ❑ 724 | George Bell | .05 | .02 |
| ❑ 725 | Gregg Jefferies | .05 | .02 |
| ❑ 726 | Gary DiSarcina | .05 | .02 |
| ❑ 727 | Mike Bordick | .05 | .02 |
| ❑ 728 | Eddie Murray | .10 | .05 |
| | 400 Home Run Club | | |
| ❑ 729 | Rene Gonzales | .05 | .02 |
| ❑ 730 | Mike Bielecki | .05 | .02 |
| ❑ 731 | Calvin Jones | .05 | .02 |
| ❑ 732 | Jack Morris | .10 | .05 |
| ❑ 733 | Frank Viola | .05 | .02 |
| ❑ 734 | Dave Winfield | .20 | .09 |
| ❑ 735 | Kevin Mitchell | .10 | .05 |
| ❑ 736 | Bill Swift | .05 | .02 |
| ❑ 737 | Dan Gladden | .05 | .02 |
| ❑ 738 | Mike Jackson | .05 | .02 |
| ❑ 739 | Mark Carreon | .05 | .02 |
| ❑ 740 | Kirt Manwaring | .05 | .02 |
| ❑ 741 | Randy Myers | .10 | .05 |
| ❑ 742 | Kevin McReynolds | .05 | .02 |
| ❑ 743 | Steve Sax | .05 | .02 |
| ❑ 744 | Wally Joyner | .10 | .05 |
| ❑ 745 | Gary Sheffield | .20 | .09 |
| ❑ 746 | Danny Tartabull | .05 | .02 |
| ❑ 747 | Julio Valera | .05 | .02 |
| ❑ 748 | Denny Neagle | .10 | .05 |
| ❑ 749 | Lance Blankenship | .05 | .02 |
| ❑ 750 | Mike Gallego | .05 | .02 |
| ❑ 751 | Bret Saberhagen | .10 | .05 |
| ❑ 752 | Ruben Amaro | .05 | .02 |
| ❑ 753 | Eddie Murray | .20 | .09 |
| ❑ 754 | Kyle Abbott | .05 | .02 |
| ❑ 755 | Bobby Bonilla | .10 | .05 |
| ❑ 756 | Eric Davis | .10 | .05 |
| ❑ 757 | Eddie Taubensee RC | .10 | .05 |
| ❑ 758 | Andres Galarraga | .10 | .05 |
| ❑ 759 | Pete Incaviglia | .05 | .02 |
| ❑ 760 | Tom Candiotti | .05 | .02 |
| ❑ 761 | Tim Belcher | .05 | .02 |
| ❑ 762 | Ricky Bones | .05 | .02 |
| ❑ 763 | Bip Roberts | .05 | .02 |
| ❑ 764 | Pedro Munoz | .05 | .02 |
| ❑ 765 | Greg Swindell | .05 | .02 |
| ❑ 766 | Kenny Lofton | .25 | .11 |
| ❑ 767 | Gary Carter | .10 | .05 |
| ❑ 768 | Charlie Hayes | .05 | .02 |
| ❑ 769 | Dickie Thon | .05 | .02 |
| ❑ 770 | Donovan Osborne DD CL | .05 | .02 |
| ❑ 771 | Bret Boone DD | .20 | .09 |
| ❑ 772 | Archi Cianfrocco DD RC | .05 | .02 |
| ❑ 773 | Mark Clark DD RC | .05 | .02 |
| ❑ 774 | Chad Curtis DD RC | .25 | .11 |
| ❑ 775 | Pat Listach DD RC | .05 | .02 |
| ❑ 776 | Pat Mahomes DD RC | .05 | .02 |
| ❑ 777 | Donovan Osborne DD | .05 | .02 |
| ❑ 778 | John Patterson DD | .05 | .02 |
| ❑ 779 | Andy Stankiewicz DD | .05 | .02 |
| ❑ 780 | Turk Wendell DD RC | .10 | .05 |
| ❑ 781 | Bill Krueger | .05 | .02 |
| ❑ 782 | Rickey Henderson | .10 | .05 |
| | Grand Theft | | |
| ❑ 783 | Kevin Seitzer | .05 | .02 |
| ❑ 784 | Dave Martinez | .05 | .02 |
| ❑ 785 | John Smiley | .05 | .02 |
| ❑ 786 | Matt Stairs RC | .25 | .11 |
| ❑ 787 | Scott Scudder | .05 | .02 |
| ❑ 788 | John Wetteland | .10 | .05 |
| ❑ 789 | Jack Armstrong | .05 | .02 |
| ❑ 790 | Ken Hill | .05 | .02 |
| ❑ 791 | Dick Schofield | .05 | .02 |
| ❑ 792 | Mariano Duncan | .05 | .02 |
| ❑ 793 | Bill Pecota | .05 | .02 |
| ❑ 794 | Mike Kelly RC | .05 | .02 |
| ❑ 795 | Willie Randolph | .10 | .05 |
| ❑ 796 | Butch Henry | .05 | .02 |
| ❑ 797 | Carlos Hernandez | .05 | .02 |
| ❑ 798 | Doug Jones | .05 | .02 |
| ❑ 799 | Melido Perez | .05 | .02 |
| ❑ 800 | Checklist 701-800 | .05 | .02 |
| ❑ HH2 | Ted Williams Hologram | 2.00 | .90 |
| | (Top left corner says | | |
| | 91 Upper Deck 92) | | |
| ❑ SP3 | Deion Sanders FB/BB | .50 | .23 |
| ❑ SP4 | Tom Selleck | 1.00 | .45 |
| | Frank Thomas SP | | |
| | (Mr. Baseball) | | |

## 1993 Upper Deck

| | MINT | NRMT |
|---|---|---|
| COMPLETE SET (840) | 50.00 | 22.00 |
| COMP.FACT.SET (840) | 40.00 | 18.00 |
| COMPLETE SERIES 1 (420) | 15.00 | 6.75 |
| COMPLETE SERIES 2 (420) | 20.00 | 9.00 |

| | Card | | |
|---|---|---|---|
| ❑ 1 | Tim Salmon CL | .10 | .05 |
| ❑ 2 | Mike Piazza SR | 2.00 | .90 |
| ❑ 3 | Rene Arocha SR RC | .10 | .05 |
| ❑ 4 | Willie Greene SR | .10 | .05 |
| ❑ 5 | Manny Alexander | .10 | .05 |
| ❑ 6 | Dan Wilson | .20 | .09 |
| ❑ 7 | Dan Smith | .10 | .05 |
| ❑ 8 | Kevin Rogers | .10 | .05 |
| ❑ 9 | Kurt Miller SR | .10 | .05 |
| ❑ 10 | Joe Vitko | .10 | .05 |
| ❑ 11 | Tim Costo | .10 | .05 |
| ❑ 12 | Alan Embree SR | .10 | .05 |
| ❑ 13 | Jim Tatum SR RC | .10 | .05 |
| ❑ 14 | Cris Colon | .10 | .05 |
| ❑ 15 | Steve Hosey | .10 | .05 |
| ❑ 16 | Sterling Hitchcock SR RC | .20 | .09 |
| ❑ 17 | Dave Mlicki | .10 | .05 |
| ❑ 18 | Jessie Hollins | .10 | .05 |
| ❑ 19 | Bobby Jones SR | .20 | .09 |
| ❑ 20 | Kurt Miller | .10 | .05 |
| ❑ 21 | Melvin Nieves SR | .10 | .05 |
| ❑ 22 | Billy Ashley SR | .10 | .05 |
| ❑ 23 | J.T. Snow SR RC | .50 | .23 |
| ❑ 24 | Chipper Jones SR | 1.25 | .55 |
| ❑ 25 | Tim Salmon SR | .20 | .09 |
| ❑ 26 | Tim Pugh SR RC | .10 | .05 |
| ❑ 27 | David Nied SR | .10 | .05 |
| ❑ 28 | Mike Trombley | .10 | .05 |
| ❑ 29 | Javier Lopez SR | .20 | .09 |
| ❑ 30 | Jim Abbott CH CL | .10 | .05 |
| ❑ 31 | Jim Abbott CH | .10 | .05 |
| ❑ 32 | Dale Murphy CH | .20 | .09 |
| ❑ 33 | Tony Pena CH | .10 | .05 |
| ❑ 34 | Kirby Puckett CH | .50 | .23 |
| ❑ 35 | Harold Reynolds CH | .10 | .05 |
| ❑ 36 | Cal Ripken CH | .75 | .35 |
| ❑ 37 | Nolan Ryan CH | 1.00 | .45 |
| ❑ 38 | Ryne Sandberg CH | .20 | .09 |
| ❑ 39 | Dave Stewart CH | .10 | .05 |
| ❑ 40 | Dave Winfield CH | .20 | .09 |
| ❑ 41 | Joe Carter CL | .40 | .18 |
| | Mark McGwire | | |
| ❑ 42 | Blockbuster Trade | .40 | .18 |
| | Joe Carter | | |
| | Roberto Alomar | | |
| ❑ 43 | Brew Crew | .40 | .18 |
| | Paul Molitor | | |
| | Pat Listach | | |
| | Robin Yount | | |
| ❑ 44 | Iron and Steel | .40 | .18 |
| | Cal Ripken | | |
| | Brady Anderson | | |
| ❑ 45 | Youthful Tribe | .10 | .05 |
| | Albert Belle | | |
| | Sandy Alomar Jr. | | |
| | Jim Thome | | |
| | Carlos Baerga | | |
| | Kenny Lofton | | |
| ❑ 46 | Motown Mashers | .10 | .05 |
| | Cecil Fielder | | |
| | Mickey Tettleton | | |
| ❑ 47 | Yankee Pride | .20 | .09 |
| | Roberto Kelly | | |
| | Don Mattingly | | |
| ❑ 48 | Boston Cy Sox | .20 | .09 |
| | Frank Viola | | |
| | Roger Clemens | | |
| ❑ 49 | Bash Brothers | .20 | .09 |
| | Ruben Sierra | | |
| | Mark McGwire | | |
| ❑ 50 | Twin Titles | .20 | .09 |
| | Kent Hrbek | | |
| | Kirby Puckett | | |
| ❑ 51 | Southside Sluggers | .40 | .18 |
| | Robin Ventura | | |
| | Frank Thomas | | |
| ❑ 52 | Latin Stars | .20 | .09 |
| | Juan Gonzalez | | |
| | Jose Canseco | | |
| | Ivan Rodriguez | | |
| | Rafael Palmeiro | | |
| ❑ 53 | Lethal Lefties | .10 | .05 |
| | Mark Langston | | |
| | Jim Abbott | | |
| | Chuck Finley | | |
| ❑ 54 | Royal Family | .10 | .05 |
| | Wally Joyner | | |
| | Gregg Jefferies | | |
| | George Brett | | |
| ❑ 55 | Pacific Sock Exchange | .40 | .18 |
| | Kevin Mitchell | | |
| | Ken Griffey Jr. | | |
| | Jay Buhner | | |
| ❑ 56 | George Brett | .75 | .35 |
| ❑ 57 | Scott Cooper | .10 | .05 |
| ❑ 58 | Mike Maddux | .10 | .05 |
| ❑ 59 | Rusty Meacham | .10 | .05 |
| ❑ 60 | Wil Cordero | .10 | .05 |
| ❑ 61 | Tim Teufel | .10 | .05 |
| ❑ 62 | Jeff Montgomery | .20 | .09 |
| ❑ 63 | Scott Livingstone | .10 | .05 |

❑ 64 Doug Dascenzo .10 .05
❑ 65 Bret Boone .20 .09
❑ 66 Tim Wakefield .10 .05
❑ 67 Curt Schilling .20 .09
❑ 68 Frank Tanana .10 .05
❑ 69 Len Dykstra .20 .09
❑ 70 Derek Lilliquist .10 .05
❑ 71 Anthony Young .10 .05
❑ 72 Hipolito Pichardo .10 .05
❑ 73 Rod Beck .10 .05
❑ 74 Kent Hrbek .20 .09
❑ 75 Tom Glavine .20 .09
❑ 76 Kevin Brown .20 .09
❑ 77 Chuck Finley .20 .09
❑ 78 Bob Walk .10 .05
❑ 79 Rheal Cormier UER .10 .05
(Born in New Brunswick, not British Columbia)
❑ 80 Rick Sutcliffe .20 .09
❑ 81 Harold Baines .20 .09
❑ 82 Lee Smith .20 .09
❑ 83 Geno Petralli .10 .05
❑ 84 Jose Oquendo .10 .05
❑ 85 Mark Gubicza .10 .05
❑ 86 Mickey Tettleton .10 .05
❑ 87 Bobby Witt .10 .05
❑ 88 Mark Lewis .10 .05
❑ 89 Kevin Appier .20 .09
❑ 90 Mike Stanton .10 .05
❑ 91 Rafael Belliard .10 .05
❑ 92 Kenny Rogers .10 .05
❑ 93 Randy Velarde .10 .05
❑ 94 Luis Sojo .10 .05
❑ 95 Mark Leiter .10 .05
❑ 96 Jody Reed .10 .05
❑ 97 Pete Harnisch .10 .05
❑ 98 Tom Candiotti .10 .05
❑ 99 Mark Portugal .10 .05
❑ 100 Dave Valle .10 .05
❑ 101 Shawon Dunston .10 .05
❑ 102 B.J. Surhoff .20 .09
❑ 103 Jay Bell .20 .09
❑ 104 Sid Bream .10 .05
❑ 105 Frank Thomas CL .40 .18
❑ 106 Mike Morgan .10 .05
❑ 107 Bill Doran .10 .05
❑ 108 Lance Blankenship .10 .05
❑ 109 Mark Lemke .10 .05
❑ 110 Brian Harper .10 .05
❑ 111 Brady Anderson .20 .09
❑ 112 Bip Roberts .10 .05
❑ 113 Mitch Williams .10 .05
❑ 114 Craig Biggio .20 .09
❑ 115 Eddie Murray .40 .18
❑ 116 Matt Nokes .10 .05
❑ 117 Lance Parrish .10 .05
❑ 118 Bill Swift .10 .05
❑ 119 Jeff Innis .10 .05
❑ 120 Mike LaValliere .10 .05
❑ 121 Hal Morris .10 .05
❑ 122 Walt Weiss .10 .05
❑ 123 Ivan Rodriguez .50 .23
❑ 124 Andy Van Slyke .20 .09
❑ 125 Roberto Alomar .40 .18
❑ 126 Robby Thompson .10 .05
❑ 127 Sammy Sosa .75 .35
❑ 128 Mark Langston .10 .05
❑ 129 Jerry Browne .10 .05
❑ 130 Chuck McElroy .10 .05
❑ 131 Frank Viola .10 .05
❑ 132 Leo Gomez .10 .05
❑ 133 Ramon Martinez .10 .05
❑ 134 Don Mattingly 1.00 .45
❑ 135 Roger Clemens .75 .35
❑ 136 Rickey Henderson .50 .23
❑ 137 Darren Daulton .20 .09
❑ 138 Ken Hill .10 .05
❑ 139 Ozzie Guillen .10 .05
❑ 140 Jerald Clark .10 .05
❑ 141 Dave Fleming .10 .05
❑ 142 Delino DeShields .20 .09
❑ 143 Matt Williams .20 .09
❑ 144 Larry Walker .20 .09
❑ 145 Ruben Sierra .10 .05
❑ 146 Ozzie Smith .50 .23
❑ 147 Chris Sabo .10 .05
❑ 148 Carlos Hernandez .10 .05
❑ 149 Pat Borders .10 .05
❑ 150 Orlando Merced .10 .05
❑ 151 Royce Clayton .10 .05
❑ 152 Kurt Stillwell .10 .05
❑ 153 Dave Hollins .10 .05
❑ 154 Mike Greenwell .10 .05
❑ 155 Nolan Ryan 2.00 .90
❑ 156 Felix Jose .10 .05
❑ 157 Junior Felix .10 .05
❑ 158 Derek Bell .10 .05
❑ 159 Steve Buechele .10 .05
❑ 160 John Burkett .10 .05
❑ 161 Pat Howell .10 .05
❑ 162 Milt Cuyler .10 .05
❑ 163 Terry Pendleton .20 .09
❑ 164 Jack Morris .20 .09
❑ 165 Tony Gwynn .75 .35
❑ 166 Deion Sanders .20 .09
❑ 167 Mike Devereaux .10 .05
❑ 168 Ron Darling .10 .05
❑ 169 Orel Hershiser .20 .09
❑ 170 Mike Jackson .10 .05
❑ 171 Doug Jones .10 .05
❑ 172 Dan Walters .10 .05
❑ 173 Darren Lewis .10 .05
❑ 174 Carlos Baerga .10 .05
❑ 175 Ryne Sandberg .50 .23
❑ 176 Gregg Jefferies .10 .05
❑ 177 John Jaha .10 .05
❑ 178 Luis Polonia .10 .05
❑ 179 Kirt Manwaring .10 .05
❑ 180 Mike Magnante .10 .05
❑ 181 Billy Ripken .10 .05
❑ 182 Mike Moore .10 .05
❑ 183 Eric Anthony .10 .05
❑ 184 Lenny Harris .10 .05
❑ 185 Tony Pena .10 .05
❑ 186 Mike Felder .10 .05
❑ 187 Greg Olson .10 .05
❑ 188 Rene Gonzales .10 .05
❑ 189 Mike Bordick .10 .05
❑ 190 Mel Rojas .10 .05
❑ 191 Todd Frohwirth .10 .05
❑ 192 Darryl Hamilton .10 .05
❑ 193 Mike Fetters .10 .05
❑ 194 Omar Olivares .10 .05
❑ 195 Tony Phillips .10 .05
❑ 196 Paul Sorrento .10 .05
❑ 197 Trevor Wilson .10 .05
❑ 198 Kevin Gross .10 .05
❑ 199 Ron Karkovice .10 .05
❑ 200 Brook Jacoby .10 .05
❑ 201 Mariano Duncan .10 .05
❑ 202 Dennis Cook .10 .05
❑ 203 Daryl Boston .10 .05
❑ 204 Mike Perez .10 .05
❑ 205 Manuel Lee .10 .05
❑ 206 Steve Olin .10 .05
❑ 207 Charlie Hough .20 .09
❑ 208 Scott Scudder .10 .05
❑ 209 Charlie O'Brien .10 .05
❑ 210 Barry Bonds CL .40 .18
❑ 211 Jose Vizcaino .10 .05
❑ 212 Scott Leius .10 .05
❑ 213 Kevin Mitchell .20 .09
❑ 214 Brian Barnes .10 .05
❑ 215 Pat Kelly .10 .05
❑ 216 Chris Hammond .10 .05
❑ 217 Rob Deer .10 .05
❑ 218 Cory Snyder .10 .05
❑ 219 Gary Carter .20 .09
❑ 220 Danny Darwin .10 .05
❑ 221 Tom Gordon .10 .05
❑ 222 Gary Sheffield .20 .09
❑ 223 Joe Carter .20 .09
❑ 224 Jay Buhner .20 .09
❑ 225 Jose Offerman .10 .05
❑ 226 Jose Rijo .10 .05
❑ 227 Mark Whiten .10 .05
❑ 228 Randy Milligan .10 .05
❑ 229 Bud Black .10 .05
❑ 230 Gary DiSarcina .10 .05
❑ 231 Steve Finley .20 .09
❑ 232 Dennis Martinez .20 .09
❑ 233 Mike Mussina .40 .18
❑ 234 Joe Oliver .10 .05
❑ 235 Chad Curtis .10 .05
❑ 236 Shane Mack .10 .05
❑ 237 Jaime Navarro .10 .05
❑ 238 Brian McRae .10 .05
❑ 239 Chili Davis .20 .09
❑ 240 Jeff King .10 .05
❑ 241 Dean Palmer .20 .09
❑ 242 Danny Tartabull .10 .05
❑ 243 Charles Nagy .10 .05
❑ 244 Ray Lankford .20 .09
❑ 245 Barry Larkin .40 .18
❑ 246 Steve Avery .10 .05
❑ 247 John Kruk .20 .09
❑ 248 Derrick May .10 .05
❑ 249 Stan Javier .10 .05
❑ 250 Roger McDowell .10 .05
❑ 251 Dan Gladden .10 .05
❑ 252 Wally Joyner .20 .09
❑ 253 Pat Listach .10 .05
❑ 254 Chuck Knoblauch .20 .09
❑ 255 Sandy Alomar Jr. .20 .09
❑ 256 Jeff Bagwell .50 .23
❑ 257 Andy Stankiewicz .10 .05
❑ 258 Darrin Jackson .10 .05
❑ 259 Brett Butler .20 .09
❑ 260 Joe Orsulak .10 .05
❑ 261 Andy Benes .10 .05
❑ 262 Kenny Lofton .20 .09
❑ 263 Robin Ventura .20 .09
❑ 264 Ron Gant .20 .09
❑ 265 Ellis Burks .20 .09
❑ 266 Juan Guzman .10 .05
❑ 267 Wes Chamberlain .10 .05
❑ 268 John Smiley .10 .05
❑ 269 Franklin Stubbs .10 .05
❑ 270 Tom Browning .10 .05
❑ 271 Dennis Eckersley .20 .09
❑ 272 Carlton Fisk .40 .18
❑ 273 Lou Whitaker .20 .09
❑ 274 Phil Plantier .10 .05
❑ 275 Bobby Bonilla .20 .09
❑ 276 Ben McDonald .10 .05
❑ 277 Bob Zupcic .10 .05
❑ 278 Terry Steinbach .10 .05
❑ 279 Terry Mulholland .10 .05
❑ 280 Lance Johnson .10 .05
❑ 281 Willie McGee .20 .09
❑ 282 Bret Saberhagen .20 .09
❑ 283 Randy Myers .20 .09
❑ 284 Randy Tomlin .10 .05
❑ 285 Mickey Morandini .10 .05
❑ 286 Brian Williams .10 .05
❑ 287 Tino Martinez .20 .09
❑ 288 Jose Melendez .10 .05
❑ 289 Jeff Huson .10 .05
❑ 290 Joe Grahe .10 .05
❑ 291 Mel Hall .10 .05
❑ 292 Otis Nixon .10 .05
❑ 293 Todd Hundley .10 .05
❑ 294 Casey Candaele .10 .05
❑ 295 Kevin Seitzer .10 .05
❑ 296 Eddie Taubensee .10 .05
❑ 297 Moises Alou .20 .09
❑ 298 Scott Radinsky .10 .05
❑ 299 Thomas Howard .10 .05
❑ 300 Kyle Abbott .10 .05
❑ 301 Omar Vizquel .20 .09
❑ 302 Keith Miller .10 .05
❑ 303 Rick Aguilera .10 .05
❑ 304 Bruce Hurst .10 .05
❑ 305 Ken Caminiti .20 .09
❑ 306 Mike Pagliarulo .10 .05
❑ 307 Frank Seminara .10 .05
❑ 308 Andre Dawson .20 .09
❑ 309 Jose Lind .10 .05
❑ 310 Joe Boever .10 .05
❑ 311 Jeff Parrett .10 .05
❑ 312 Alan Mills .10 .05
❑ 313 Kevin Tapani .10 .05
❑ 314 Darryl Kile .20 .09
❑ 315 Will Clark CL .20 .09
❑ 316 Mike Sharperson .10 .05
❑ 317 John Orton .10 .05
❑ 318 Bob Tewksbury .10 .05
❑ 319 Xavier Hernandez .10 .05

| No. | Card | Price | Price |
|---|---|---|---|
| ❑ 320 | Paul Assenmacher | .10 | .05 |
| ❑ 321 | John Franco | .20 | .09 |
| ❑ 322 | Mike Timlin | .10 | .05 |
| ❑ 323 | Jose Guzman | .10 | .05 |
| ❑ 324 | Pedro Martinez | 1.00 | .45 |
| ❑ 325 | Bill Spiers | .10 | .05 |
| ❑ 326 | Melido Perez | .10 | .05 |
| ❑ 327 | Mike Macfarlane | .10 | .05 |
| ❑ 328 | Ricky Bones | .10 | .05 |
| ❑ 329 | Scott Bankhead | .10 | .05 |
| ❑ 330 | Rich Rodriguez | .10 | .05 |
| ❑ 331 | Geronimo Pena | .10 | .05 |
| ❑ 332 | Bernie Williams | .40 | .18 |
| ❑ 333 | Paul Molitor | .40 | .18 |
| ❑ 334 | Carlos Garcia | .10 | .05 |
| ❑ 335 | David Cone | .20 | .09 |
| ❑ 336 | Randy Johnson | .50 | .23 |
| ❑ 337 | Pat Mahomes | .10 | .05 |
| ❑ 338 | Erik Hanson | .10 | .05 |
| ❑ 339 | Duane Ward | .10 | .05 |
| ❑ 340 | Al Martin | .10 | .05 |
| ❑ 341 | Pedro Munoz | .10 | .05 |
| ❑ 342 | Greg Colbrunn | .10 | .05 |
| ❑ 343 | Julio Valera | .10 | .05 |
| ❑ 344 | John Olerud | .20 | .09 |
| ❑ 345 | George Bell | .10 | .05 |
| ❑ 346 | Devon White | .10 | .05 |
| ❑ 347 | Donovan Osborne | .10 | .05 |
| ❑ 348 | Mark Gardner | .10 | .05 |
| ❑ 349 | Zane Smith | .10 | .05 |
| ❑ 350 | Wilson Alvarez | .10 | .05 |
| ❑ 351 | Kevin Koslofski | .10 | .05 |
| ❑ 352 | Roberto Hernandez | .10 | .05 |
| ❑ 353 | Glenn Davis | .10 | .05 |
| ❑ 354 | Reggie Sanders | .10 | .05 |
| ❑ 355 | Ken Griffey Jr. | 1.50 | .70 |
| ❑ 356 | Marquis Grissom | .10 | .05 |
| ❑ 357 | Jack McDowell | .10 | .05 |
| ❑ 358 | Jimmy Key | .20 | .09 |
| ❑ 359 | Stan Belinda | .10 | .05 |
| ❑ 360 | Gerald Williams | .10 | .05 |
| ❑ 361 | Sid Fernandez | .10 | .05 |
| ❑ 362 | Alex Fernandez | .20 | .09 |
| ❑ 363 | John Smoltz | .20 | .09 |
| ❑ 364 | Travis Fryman | .20 | .09 |
| ❑ 365 | Jose Canseco | .50 | .23 |
| ❑ 366 | David Justice | .20 | .09 |
| ❑ 367 | Pedro Astacio | .20 | .09 |
| ❑ 368 | Tim Belcher | .10 | .05 |
| ❑ 369 | Steve Sax | .10 | .05 |
| ❑ 370 | Gary Gaetti | .20 | .09 |
| ❑ 371 | Jeff Frye | .10 | .05 |
| ❑ 372 | Bob Wickman | .10 | .05 |
| ❑ 373 | Ryan Thompson | .10 | .05 |
| ❑ 374 | David Hulse RC | .10 | .05 |
| ❑ 375 | Cal Eldred | .10 | .05 |
| ❑ 376 | Ryan Klesko | .40 | .18 |
| ❑ 377 | Damion Easley | .10 | .05 |
| ❑ 378 | John Kiely | .10 | .05 |
| ❑ 379 | Jim Bullinger | .10 | .05 |
| ❑ 380 | Brian Bohanon | .10 | .05 |
| ❑ 381 | Rod Brewer | .10 | .05 |
| ❑ 382 | Fernando Ramsey RC | .10 | .05 |
| ❑ 383 | Sam Militello | .10 | .05 |
| ❑ 384 | Arthur Rhodes | .10 | .05 |
| ❑ 385 | Eric Karros | .20 | .09 |
| ❑ 386 | Rico Brogna | .20 | .09 |
| ❑ 387 | John Valentin | .10 | .05 |
| ❑ 388 | Kerry Woodson | .10 | .05 |
| ❑ 389 | Ben Rivera | .10 | .05 |
| ❑ 390 | Matt Whiteside RC | .10 | .05 |
| ❑ 391 | Henry Rodriguez | .10 | .05 |
| ❑ 392 | John Wetteland | .20 | .09 |
| ❑ 393 | Kent Mercker | .10 | .05 |
| ❑ 394 | Bernard Gilkey | .10 | .05 |
| ❑ 395 | Doug Henry | .10 | .05 |
| ❑ 396 | Mo Vaughn | .20 | .09 |
| ❑ 397 | Scott Erickson | .10 | .05 |
| ❑ 398 | Bill Gullickson | .10 | .05 |
| ❑ 399 | Mark Guthrie | .10 | .05 |
| ❑ 400 | Dave Martinez | .10 | .05 |
| ❑ 401 | Jeff Kent | .40 | .18 |
| ❑ 402 | Chris Hoiles | .10 | .05 |
| ❑ 403 | Mike Henneman | .10 | .05 |
| ❑ 404 | Chris Nabholz | .10 | .05 |
| ❑ 405 | Tom Pagnozzi | .10 | .05 |
| ❑ 406 | Kelly Gruber | .10 | .05 |
| ❑ 407 | Bob Welch | .10 | .05 |
| ❑ 408 | Frank Castillo | .10 | .05 |
| ❑ 409 | John Dopson | .10 | .05 |
| ❑ 410 | Steve Farr | .10 | .05 |
| ❑ 411 | Henry Cotto | .10 | .05 |
| ❑ 412 | Bob Patterson | .10 | .05 |
| ❑ 413 | Todd Stottlemyre | .10 | .05 |
| ❑ 414 | Greg A. Harris | .10 | .05 |
| ❑ 415 | Denny Neagle | .20 | .09 |
| ❑ 416 | Bill Wegman | .10 | .05 |
| ❑ 417 | Willie Wilson | .10 | .05 |
| ❑ 418 | Terry Leach | .10 | .05 |
| ❑ 419 | Willie Randolph | .20 | .09 |
| ❑ 420 | Mark McGwire CL | .40 | .18 |
| ❑ 421 | Calvin Murray CL | .10 | .05 |
| ❑ 422 | Pete Janicki TP RC | .10 | .05 |
| ❑ 423 | Todd Jones TP | .20 | .09 |
| ❑ 424 | Mike Neill TP | .10 | .05 |
| ❑ 425 | Carlos Delgado TP | .75 | .35 |
| ❑ 426 | Jose Oliva TP | .10 | .05 |
| ❑ 427 | Tyrone Hill TP | .10 | .05 |
| ❑ 428 | Dmitri Young TP | .20 | .09 |
| ❑ 429 | Derek Wallace TP RC | .10 | .05 |
| ❑ 430 | Michael Moore TP RC | .10 | .05 |
| ❑ 431 | Cliff Floyd TP | .20 | .09 |
| ❑ 432 | Calvin Murray TP | .10 | .05 |
| ❑ 433 | Manny Ramirez TP | 1.00 | .45 |
| ❑ 434 | Marc Newfield TP | .10 | .05 |
| ❑ 435 | Charles Johnson TP | .40 | .18 |
| ❑ 436 | Butch Huskey TP | .10 | .05 |
| ❑ 437 | Brad Pennington TP | .10 | .05 |
| ❑ 438 | Ray McDavid TP RC | .10 | .05 |
| ❑ 439 | Chad McConnell TP | .10 | .05 |
| ❑ 440 | Midre Cummings TP RC | .10 | .05 |
| ❑ 441 | Benji Gil TP | .10 | .05 |
| ❑ 442 | Frankie Rodriguez TP | .10 | .05 |
| ❑ 443 | Chad Mottola TP RC | .10 | .05 |
| ❑ 444 | John Burke TP RC | .10 | .05 |
| ❑ 445 | Michael Tucker TP | .40 | .18 |
| ❑ 446 | Rick Greene TP | .10 | .05 |
| ❑ 447 | Rich Becker TP | .10 | .05 |
| ❑ 448 | Mike Robertson TP | .10 | .05 |
| ❑ 449 | Derek Jeter TP RC ! | 10.00 | 4.50 |
| ❑ 450 | Ivan Rodriguez CL | .20 | .09 |
| | David McCarty | | |
| ❑ 451 | Jim Abbott IN | .10 | .05 |
| ❑ 452 | Jeff Bagwell IN | .20 | .09 |
| ❑ 453 | Jason Bere IN | .10 | .05 |
| ❑ 454 | Delino DeShields IN | .10 | .05 |
| ❑ 455 | Travis Fryman IN | .10 | .05 |
| ❑ 456 | Alex Gonzalez IN | .20 | .09 |
| ❑ 457 | Phil Hiatt IN | .10 | .05 |
| ❑ 458 | Dave Hollins IN | .10 | .05 |
| ❑ 459 | Chipper Jones IN | .60 | .25 |
| ❑ 460 | David Justice IN | .10 | .05 |
| ❑ 461 | Ray Lankford IN | .20 | .09 |
| ❑ 462 | David McCarty IN | .10 | .05 |
| ❑ 463 | Mike Mussina IN | .20 | .09 |
| ❑ 464 | Jose Offerman IN | .10 | .05 |
| ❑ 465 | Dean Palmer IN | .10 | .05 |
| ❑ 466 | Geronimo Pena IN | .10 | .05 |
| ❑ 467 | Eduardo Perez IN | .10 | .05 |
| ❑ 468 | Ivan Rodriguez IN | .20 | .09 |
| ❑ 469 | Reggie Sanders IN | .10 | .05 |
| ❑ 470 | Bernie Williams IN | .40 | .18 |
| ❑ 471 | Barry Bonds CL | .20 | .09 |
| | Matt Williams | | |
| | Will Clark | | |
| ❑ 472 | Strike Force | .40 | .18 |
| | Greg Maddux | | |
| | Steve Avery | | |
| | John Smoltz | | |
| | Tom Glavine | | |
| ❑ 473 | Red October | .10 | .05 |
| | Jose Rijo | | |
| | Rob Dibble | | |
| | Roberto Kelly | | |
| | Reggie Sanders | | |
| | Barry Larkin | | |
| ❑ 474 | Four Corners | .40 | .18 |
| | Gary Sheffield | | |
| | Phil Plantier | | |
| | Tony Gwynn | | |
| | Fred McGriff | | |
| ❑ 475 | Shooting Stars | .10 | .05 |
| | Doug Drabek | | |
| | Craig Biggio | | |
| | Jeff Bagwell | | |
| ❑ 476 | Giant Sticks | .20 | .09 |
| | Will Clark | | |
| | Barry Bonds | | |
| | Matt Williams | | |
| ❑ 477 | Boyhood Friends | .20 | .09 |
| | Eric Davis | | |
| | Darryl Strawberry | | |
| ❑ 478 | Rock Solid Foundation | .20 | .09 |
| | Dante Bichette | | |
| | David Nied | | |
| | Andres Galarraga | | |
| ❑ 479 | Inaugural Catch | .10 | .05 |
| | Dave Magadan | | |
| | Orestes Destrade | | |
| | Bret Barberie | | |
| | Jeff Conine | | |
| ❑ 480 | Steel City Champions | .10 | .05 |
| | Tim Wakefield | | |
| | Andy Van Slyke | | |
| | Jay Bell | | |
| ❑ 481 | Les Grandes Etoiles | .10 | .05 |
| | Marquis Grissom | | |
| | Delino DeShields | | |
| | Dennis Martinez | | |
| | Larry Walker | | |
| ❑ 482 | Runnin' Redbirds | .20 | .09 |
| | Geronimo Pena | | |
| | Ray Lankford | | |
| | Ozzie Smith | | |
| | Bernard Gilkey | | |
| ❑ 483 | Ivy Leaguers | .20 | .09 |
| | Randy Myers | | |
| | Ryne Sandberg | | |
| | Mark Grace | | |
| ❑ 484 | Big Apple Power Switch | .10 | .05 |
| | Eddie Murray | | |
| | Howard Johnson | | |
| | Bobby Bonilla | | |
| ❑ 485 | Hammers and Nails | .10 | .05 |
| | John Kruk | | |
| | Dave Hollins | | |
| | Darren Daulton | | |
| | Len Dykstra | | |
| ❑ 486 | Barry Bonds AW | .40 | .18 |
| ❑ 487 | Dennis Eckersley AW | .10 | .05 |
| ❑ 488 | Greg Maddux AW | .50 | .23 |
| ❑ 489 | Dennis Eckersley AW | .10 | .05 |
| ❑ 490 | Eric Karros AW | .10 | .05 |
| ❑ 491 | Pat Listach AW | .10 | .05 |
| ❑ 492 | Gary Sheffield AW | .20 | .09 |
| ❑ 493 | Mark McGwire AW | .75 | .35 |
| ❑ 494 | Gary Sheffield AW | .20 | .09 |
| ❑ 495 | Edgar Martinez AW | .20 | .09 |
| ❑ 496 | Fred McGriff AW | .20 | .09 |
| ❑ 497 | Juan Gonzalez AW | .20 | .09 |
| ❑ 498 | Darren Daulton AW | .10 | .05 |
| ❑ 499 | Cecil Fielder AW | .10 | .05 |
| ❑ 500 | Brent Gates CL | .10 | .05 |
| ❑ 501 | Tavo Alvarez DD | .10 | .05 |
| ❑ 502 | Rod Bolton | .10 | .05 |
| ❑ 503 | John Cummings DD RC | .10 | .05 |
| ❑ 504 | Brent Gates DD | .10 | .05 |
| ❑ 505 | Tyler Green | .10 | .05 |
| ❑ 506 | Jose Martinez DD RC | .10 | .05 |
| ❑ 507 | Troy Percival | .10 | .05 |
| ❑ 508 | Kevin Stocker DD | .10 | .05 |
| ❑ 509 | Matt Walbeck DD RC | .10 | .05 |
| ❑ 510 | Rondell White DD | .20 | .09 |
| ❑ 511 | Billy Ripken | .10 | .05 |
| ❑ 512 | Mike Moore | .10 | .05 |
| ❑ 513 | Jose Lind | .10 | .05 |
| ❑ 514 | Chito Martinez | .10 | .05 |
| ❑ 515 | Jose Guzman | .10 | .05 |
| ❑ 516 | Kim Batiste | .10 | .05 |
| ❑ 517 | Jeff Tackett | .10 | .05 |
| ❑ 518 | Charlie Hough | .20 | .09 |
| ❑ 519 | Marvin Freeman | .10 | .05 |
| ❑ 520 | Carlos Martinez | .10 | .05 |
| ❑ 521 | Eric Young | .10 | .05 |
| ❑ 522 | Pete Incaviglia | .10 | .05 |
| ❑ 523 | Scott Fletcher | .10 | .05 |
| ❑ 524 | Orestes Destrade | .10 | .05 |
| ❑ 525 | Ken Griffey Jr. CL | .40 | .18 |

- ❑ 526 Ellis Burks .20 .09
- ❑ 527 Juan Samuel .10 .05
- ❑ 528 Dave Magadan .10 .05
- ❑ 529 Jeff Parrett .10 .05
- ❑ 530 Bill Krueger .10 .05
- ❑ 531 Frank Bolick .10 .05
- ❑ 532 Alan Trammell .20 .09
- ❑ 533 Walt Weiss .10 .05
- ❑ 534 David Cone .20 .09
- ❑ 535 Greg Maddux 1.00 .45
- ❑ 536 Kevin Young .20 .09
- ❑ 537 Dave Hansen .10 .05
- ❑ 538 Alex Cole .10 .05
- ❑ 539 Greg Hibbard .10 .05
- ❑ 540 Gene Larkin .10 .05
- ❑ 541 Jeff Reardon .20 .09
- ❑ 542 Felix Jose .10 .05
- ❑ 543 Jimmy Key .20 .09
- ❑ 544 Reggie Jefferson .20 .09
- ❑ 545 Gregg Jefferies .10 .05
- ❑ 546 Dave Stewart .20 .09
- ❑ 547 Tim Wallach .10 .05
- ❑ 548 Spike Owen .10 .05
- ❑ 549 Tommy Greene .10 .05
- ❑ 550 Fernando Valenzuela .20 .09
- ❑ 551 Rich Amaral .10 .05
- ❑ 552 Bret Barberie .10 .05
- ❑ 553 Edgar Martinez .20 .09
- ❑ 554 Jim Abbott .20 .09
- ❑ 555 Frank Thomas .75 .35
- ❑ 556 Wade Boggs .50 .23
- ❑ 557 Tom Henke .10 .05
- ❑ 558 Milt Thompson .10 .05
- ❑ 559 Lloyd McClendon .10 .05
- ❑ 560 Vinny Castilla .50 .23
- ❑ 561 Ricky Jordan .10 .05
- ❑ 562 Andujar Cedeno .10 .05
- ❑ 563 Greg Vaughn .20 .09
- ❑ 564 Cecil Fielder .20 .09
- ❑ 565 Kirby Puckett 1.00 .45
- ❑ 566 Mark McGwire 1.50 .70
- ❑ 567 Barry Bonds .60 .25
- ❑ 568 Jody Reed .10 .05
- ❑ 569 Todd Zeile .10 .05
- ❑ 570 Mark Carreon .10 .05
- ❑ 571 Joe Girardi .20 .09
- ❑ 572 Luis Gonzalez .20 .09
- ❑ 573 Mark Grace .40 .18
- ❑ 574 Rafael Palmeiro .40 .18
- ❑ 575 Darryl Strawberry .20 .09
- ❑ 576 Will Clark .40 .18
- ❑ 577 Fred McGriff .20 .09
- ❑ 578 Kevin Reimer .10 .05
- ❑ 579 Dave Righetti .10 .05
- ❑ 580 Juan Bell .10 .05
- ❑ 581 Jeff Brantley .10 .05
- ❑ 582 Brian Hunter .10 .05
- ❑ 583 Tim Naehring .10 .05
- ❑ 584 Glenallen Hill .10 .05
- ❑ 585 Cal Ripken 1.50 .70
- ❑ 586 Albert Belle .20 .09
- ❑ 587 Robin Yount .20 .09
- ❑ 588 Chris Bosio .10 .05
- ❑ 589 Pete Smith .10 .05
- ❑ 590 Chuck Carr .10 .05
- ❑ 591 Jeff Blauser .10 .05
- ❑ 592 Kevin McReynolds .10 .05
- ❑ 593 Andres Galarraga .20 .09
- ❑ 594 Kevin Maas .10 .05
- ❑ 595 Eric Davis .20 .09
- ❑ 596 Brian Jordan .20 .09
- ❑ 597 Tim Raines .20 .09
- ❑ 598 Rick Wilkins .10 .05
- ❑ 599 Steve Cooke .10 .05
- ❑ 600 Mike Gallego .10 .05
- ❑ 601 Mike Munoz .10 .05
- ❑ 602 Luis Rivera .10 .05
- ❑ 603 Junior Ortiz .10 .05
- ❑ 604 Brent Mayne .10 .05
- ❑ 605 Luis Alicea .10 .05
- ❑ 606 Damon Berryhill .10 .05
- ❑ 607 Dave Henderson .10 .05
- ❑ 608 Kirk McCaskill .10 .05
- ❑ 609 Jeff Fassero .10 .05
- ❑ 610 Mike Harkey .10 .05
- ❑ 611 Francisco Cabrera .10 .05
- ❑ 612 Rey Sanchez .10 .05
- ❑ 613 Scott Servais .10 .05
- ❑ 614 Darrin Fletcher .10 .05
- ❑ 615 Felix Fermin .10 .05
- ❑ 616 Kevin Seitzer .10 .05
- ❑ 617 Bob Scanlan .10 .05
- ❑ 618 Billy Hatcher .10 .05
- ❑ 619 John Vander Wal .10 .05
- ❑ 620 Joe Hesketh .10 .05
- ❑ 621 Hector Villanueva .10 .05
- ❑ 622 Randy Milligan .10 .05
- ❑ 623 Tony Tarasco RC .10 .05
- ❑ 624 Russ Swan .10 .05
- ❑ 625 Willie Wilson .10 .05
- ❑ 626 Frank Tanana .10 .05
- ❑ 627 Pete O'Brien .10 .05
- ❑ 628 Lenny Webster .10 .05
- ❑ 629 Mark Clark .10 .05
- ❑ 630 Roger Clemens CL .40 .18
- ❑ 631 Alex Arias .10 .05
- ❑ 632 Chris Gwynn .10 .05
- ❑ 633 Tom Bolton .10 .05
- ❑ 634 Greg Briley .10 .05
- ❑ 635 Kent Bottenfield .10 .05
- ❑ 636 Kelly Downs .10 .05
- ❑ 637 Manuel Lee .10 .05
- ❑ 638 Al Leiter .20 .09
- ❑ 639 Jeff Gardner .10 .05
- ❑ 640 Mike Gardiner .10 .05
- ❑ 641 Mark Gardner .10 .05
- ❑ 642 Jeff Branson .10 .05
- ❑ 643 Paul Wagner .10 .05
- ❑ 644 Sean Berry .10 .05
- ❑ 645 Phil Hiatt .10 .05
- ❑ 646 Kevin Mitchell .20 .09
- ❑ 647 Charlie Hayes .10 .05
- ❑ 648 Jim Deshaies .10 .05
- ❑ 649 Dan Pasqua .10 .05
- ❑ 650 Mike Maddux .10 .05
- ❑ 651 Domingo Martinez RC .10 .05
- ❑ 652 Greg McMichael RC .10 .05
- ❑ 653 Eric Wedge RC .10 .05
- ❑ 654 Mark Whiten .10 .05
- ❑ 655 Roberto Kelly .10 .05
- ❑ 656 Julio Franco .10 .05
- ❑ 657 Gene Harris .10 .05
- ❑ 658 Pete Schourek .10 .05
- ❑ 659 Mike Bielecki .10 .05
- ❑ 660 Ricky Gutierrez .10 .05
- ❑ 661 Chris Hammond .10 .05
- ❑ 662 Tim Scott .10 .05
- ❑ 663 Norm Charlton .10 .05
- ❑ 664 Doug Drabek .10 .05
- ❑ 665 Dwight Gooden .20 .09
- ❑ 666 Jim Gott .10 .05
- ❑ 667 Randy Myers .20 .09
- ❑ 668 Darren Holmes .10 .05
- ❑ 669 Tim Spehr .10 .05
- ❑ 670 Bruce Ruffin .10 .05
- ❑ 671 Bobby Thigpen .10 .05
- ❑ 672 Tony Fernandez .10 .05
- ❑ 673 Darrin Jackson .10 .05
- ❑ 674 Gregg Olson .10 .05
- ❑ 675 Rob Dibble .10 .05
- ❑ 676 Howard Johnson .10 .05
- ❑ 677 Mike Lansing RC .20 .09
- ❑ 678 Charlie Leibrandt .10 .05
- ❑ 679 Kevin Bass .10 .05
- ❑ 680 Hubie Brooks .10 .05
- ❑ 681 Scott Brosius .20 .09
- ❑ 682 Randy Knorr .10 .05
- ❑ 683 Dante Bichette .20 .09
- ❑ 684 Bryan Harvey .10 .05
- ❑ 685 Greg Gohr .10 .05
- ❑ 686 Willie Banks .10 .05
- ❑ 687 Robb Nen .20 .09
- ❑ 688 Mike Scioscia .10 .05
- ❑ 689 John Farrell .10 .05
- ❑ 690 John Candelaria .10 .05
- ❑ 691 Damon Buford .10 .05
- ❑ 692 Todd Worrell .10 .05
- ❑ 693 Pat Hentgen .10 .05
- ❑ 694 John Smiley .10 .05
- ❑ 695 Greg Swindell .10 .05
- ❑ 696 Derek Bell .10 .05
- ❑ 697 Terry Jorgensen .10 .05
- ❑ 698 Jimmy Jones .10 .05
- ❑ 699 David Wells .20 .09
- ❑ 700 Dave Martinez .10 .05
- ❑ 701 Steve Bedrosian .10 .05
- ❑ 702 Jeff Russell .10 .05
- ❑ 703 Joe Magrane .10 .05
- ❑ 704 Matt Mieske .10 .05
- ❑ 705 Paul Molitor .40 .18
- ❑ 706 Dale Murphy .20 .09
- ❑ 707 Steve Howe .10 .05
- ❑ 708 Greg Gagne .10 .05
- ❑ 709 Dave Eiland .10 .05
- ❑ 710 David West .10 .05
- ❑ 711 Luis Aquino .10 .05
- ❑ 712 Joe Orsulak .10 .05
- ❑ 713 Eric Plunk .10 .05
- ❑ 714 Mike Felder .10 .05
- ❑ 715 Joe Klink .10 .05
- ❑ 716 Lonnie Smith .10 .05
- ❑ 717 Monty Fariss .10 .05
- ❑ 718 Craig Lefferts .10 .05
- ❑ 719 John Habyan .10 .05
- ❑ 720 Willie Blair .10 .05
- ❑ 721 Darnell Coles .10 .05
- ❑ 722 Mark Williamson .10 .05
- ❑ 723 Bryn Smith .10 .05
- ❑ 724 Greg W. Harris .10 .05
- ❑ 725 Graeme Lloyd RC .10 .05
- ❑ 726 Cris Carpenter .10 .05
- ❑ 727 Chico Walker .10 .05
- ❑ 728 Tracy Woodson .10 .05
- ❑ 729 Jose Uribe .10 .05
- ❑ 730 Stan Javier .10 .05
- ❑ 731 Jay Howell .10 .05
- ❑ 732 Freddie Benavides .10 .05
- ❑ 733 Jeff Reboulet .10 .05
- ❑ 734 Scott Sanderson .10 .05
- ❑ 735 Ryne Sandberg CL .20 .09
- ❑ 736 Archi Cianfrocco .10 .05
- ❑ 737 Daryl Boston .10 .05
- ❑ 738 Craig Grebeck .10 .05
- ❑ 739 Doug Dascenzo .10 .05
- ❑ 740 Gerald Young .10 .05
- ❑ 741 Candy Maldonado .10 .05
- ❑ 742 Joey Cora .10 .05
- ❑ 743 Don Slaught .10 .05
- ❑ 744 Steve Decker .10 .05
- ❑ 745 Blas Minor .10 .05
- ❑ 746 Storm Davis .10 .05
- ❑ 747 Carlos Quintana .10 .05
- ❑ 748 Vince Coleman .10 .05
- ❑ 749 Todd Burns .10 .05
- ❑ 750 Steve Frey .10 .05
- ❑ 751 Ivan Calderon .10 .05
- ❑ 752 Steve Reed RC .10 .05
- ❑ 753 Danny Jackson .10 .05
- ❑ 754 Jeff Conine .10 .05
- ❑ 755 Juan Gonzalez .40 .18
- ❑ 756 Mike Kelly .10 .05
- ❑ 757 John Doherty .10 .05
- ❑ 758 Jack Armstrong .10 .05
- ❑ 759 John Wehner .10 .05
- ❑ 760 Scott Bankhead .10 .05
- ❑ 761 Jim Tatum .10 .05
- ❑ 762 Scott Pose RC .10 .05
- ❑ 763 Andy Ashby .20 .09
- ❑ 764 Ed Sprague .10 .05
- ❑ 765 Harold Baines .20 .09
- ❑ 766 Kirk Gibson .20 .09
- ❑ 767 Troy Neel .10 .05
- ❑ 768 Dick Schofield .10 .05
- ❑ 769 Dickie Thon .10 .05
- ❑ 770 Butch Henry .10 .05
- ❑ 771 Junior Felix .10 .05
- ❑ 772 Ken Ryan RC .10 .05
- ❑ 773 Trevor Hoffman .40 .18
- ❑ 774 Phil Plantier .10 .05
- ❑ 775 Bo Jackson .20 .09
- ❑ 776 Benito Santiago .10 .05
- ❑ 777 Andre Dawson .20 .09
- ❑ 778 Bryan Hickerson .10 .05
- ❑ 779 Dennis Moeller .10 .05
- ❑ 780 Ryan Bowen .10 .05
- ❑ 781 Eric Fox .10 .05
- ❑ 782 Joe Kmak .10 .05
- ❑ 783 Mike Hampton .40 .18

| | | | |
|---|---|---|---|
| ❑ 784 | Darrell Sherman RC | .10 | .05 |
| ❑ 785 | J.T. Snow | .40 | .18 |
| ❑ 786 | Dave Winfield | .40 | .18 |
| ❑ 787 | Jim Austin | .10 | .05 |
| ❑ 788 | Craig Shipley | .10 | .05 |
| ❑ 789 | Greg Myers | .10 | .05 |
| ❑ 790 | Todd Benzinger | .10 | .05 |
| ❑ 791 | Cory Snyder | .10 | .05 |
| ❑ 792 | David Segui | .10 | .05 |
| ❑ 793 | Armando Reynoso | .10 | .05 |
| ❑ 794 | Chili Davis | .20 | .09 |
| ❑ 795 | Dave Nilsson | .20 | .09 |
| ❑ 796 | Paul O'Neill | .20 | .09 |
| ❑ 797 | Jerald Clark | .10 | .05 |
| ❑ 798 | Jose Mesa | .10 | .05 |
| ❑ 799 | Brain Holman | .10 | .05 |
| ❑ 800 | Jim Eisenreich | .10 | .05 |
| ❑ 801 | Mark McLemore | .10 | .05 |
| ❑ 802 | Luis Sojo | .10 | .05 |
| ❑ 803 | Harold Reynolds | .10 | .05 |
| ❑ 804 | Dan Plesac | .10 | .05 |
| ❑ 805 | Dave Stieb | .10 | .05 |
| ❑ 806 | Tom Brunansky | .10 | .05 |
| ❑ 807 | Kelly Gruber | .10 | .05 |
| ❑ 808 | Bob Ojeda | .10 | .05 |
| ❑ 809 | Dave Burba | .10 | .05 |
| ❑ 810 | Joe Boever | .10 | .05 |
| ❑ 811 | Jeremy Hernandez | .10 | .05 |
| ❑ 812 | Tim Salmon TC | .20 | .09 |
| ❑ 813 | Jeff Bagwell TC | .20 | .09 |
| ❑ 814 | Dennis Eckersley TC | .10 | .05 |
| ❑ 815 | Roberto Alomar TC | .20 | .09 |
| ❑ 816 | Steve Avery TC | .10 | .05 |
| ❑ 817 | Pat Listach TC | .10 | .05 |
| ❑ 818 | Gregg Jefferies TC | .10 | .05 |
| ❑ 819 | Sammy Sosa TC | .40 | .18 |
| ❑ 820 | Darryl Strawberry TC | .10 | .05 |
| ❑ 821 | Dennis Martinez TC | .10 | .05 |
| ❑ 822 | Robby Thompson TC | .10 | .05 |
| ❑ 823 | Albert Belle TC | .10 | .05 |
| ❑ 824 | Randy Johnson TC | .20 | .09 |
| ❑ 825 | Nigel Wilson TC | .10 | .05 |
| ❑ 826 | Bobby Bonilla TC | .10 | .05 |
| ❑ 827 | Glenn Davis TC | .10 | .05 |
| ❑ 828 | Gary Sheffield TC | .20 | .09 |
| ❑ 829 | Darren Daulton TC | .10 | .05 |
| ❑ 830 | Jay Bell TC | .10 | .05 |
| ❑ 831 | Juan Gonzalez TC | .20 | .09 |
| ❑ 832 | Andre Dawson TC | .20 | .09 |
| ❑ 833 | Hal Morris TC | .10 | .05 |
| ❑ 834 | David Nied TC | .10 | .05 |
| ❑ 835 | Felix Jose TC | .10 | .05 |
| ❑ 836 | Travis Fryman TC | .10 | .05 |
| ❑ 837 | Shane Mack TC | .10 | .05 |
| ❑ 838 | Robin Ventura TC | .20 | .09 |
| ❑ 839 | Danny Tartabull TC | .10 | .05 |
| ❑ 840 | Roberto Alomar CL | .20 | .09 |
| ❑ SP5 | George Brett<br>Robin Yount<br>3,000th Hit | 1.00 | .45 |
| ❑ SP6 | Nolan Ryan | 2.50 | 1.10 |

## 1994 Upper Deck

| | MINT | NRMT |
|---|---|---|
| COMPLETE SET (550) | 50.00 | 22.00 |
| COMPLETE SERIES 1 (280) | 30.00 | 13.50 |
| COMPLETE SERIES 2 (270) | 20.00 | 9.00 |

| | | | |
|---|---|---|---|
| ❑ 1 | Brian Anderson RC | .30 | .14 |
| ❑ 2 | Shane Andrews | .15 | .07 |
| ❑ 3 | James Baldwin | .30 | .14 |
| ❑ 4 | Rich Becker | .15 | .07 |
| ❑ 5 | Greg Blosser | .15 | .07 |
| ❑ 6 | Ricky Bottalico RC | .15 | .07 |
| ❑ 7 | Midre Cummings | .15 | .07 |
| ❑ 8 | Carlos Delgado | .75 | .35 |
| ❑ 9 | Steve Dreyer RC | .15 | .07 |
| ❑ 10 | Joey Eischen | .15 | .07 |
| ❑ 11 | Carl Everett | .30 | .14 |
| ❑ 12 | Cliff Floyd UER<br>(Text indicates he throws left; should be right) | .30 | .14 |
| ❑ 13 | Alex Gonzalez | .15 | .07 |
| ❑ 14 | Jeff Granger | .15 | .07 |
| ❑ 15 | Shawn Green | .75 | .35 |
| ❑ 16 | Brian L. Hunter | .15 | .07 |
| ❑ 17 | Butch Huskey | .15 | .07 |
| ❑ 18 | Mark Hutton | .15 | .07 |
| ❑ 19 | Michael Jordan RC | 10.00 | 4.50 |
| ❑ 20 | Steve Karsay | .15 | .07 |
| ❑ 21 | Jeff McNeely | .15 | .07 |
| ❑ 22 | Marc Newfield | .15 | .07 |
| ❑ 23 | Manny Ramirez | 1.00 | .45 |
| ❑ 24 | Alex Rodriguez RC | 15.00 | 6.75 |
| ❑ 25 | Scott Ruffcorn UER<br>(Photo on back is Robert Ellis) | .15 | .07 |
| ❑ 26 | Paul Spoljaric UER<br>(Expos logo on back) | .15 | .07 |
| ❑ 27 | Salomon Torres | .15 | .07 |
| ❑ 28 | Steve Trachsel | .15 | .07 |
| ❑ 29 | Chris Turner | .15 | .07 |
| ❑ 30 | Gabe White | .15 | .07 |
| ❑ 31 | Randy Johnson FT | .30 | .14 |
| ❑ 32 | John Wetteland FT | .15 | .07 |
| ❑ 33 | Mike Piazza FT | 1.00 | .45 |
| ❑ 34 | Rafael Palmeiro FT | .30 | .14 |
| ❑ 35 | Roberto Alomar FT | .30 | .14 |
| ❑ 36 | Matt Williams FT | .15 | .07 |
| ❑ 37 | Travis Fryman FT | .15 | .07 |
| ❑ 38 | Barry Bonds FT | .60 | .25 |
| ❑ 39 | Marquis Grissom FT | .15 | .07 |
| ❑ 40 | Albert Belle FT | .15 | .07 |
| ❑ 41 | Steve Avery FUT | .15 | .07 |
| ❑ 42 | Jason Bere FUT | .15 | .07 |
| ❑ 43 | Alex Fernandez FUT | .15 | .07 |
| ❑ 44 | Mike Mussina FUT | .30 | .14 |
| ❑ 45 | Aaron Sele FUT | .15 | .07 |
| ❑ 46 | Rod Beck FUT | .15 | .07 |
| ❑ 47 | Mike Piazza FUT | 1.00 | .45 |
| ❑ 48 | John Olerud FUT | .15 | .07 |
| ❑ 49 | Carlos Baerga FUT | .15 | .07 |
| ❑ 50 | Gary Sheffield FUT | .30 | .14 |
| ❑ 51 | Travis Fryman FUT | .15 | .07 |
| ❑ 52 | Juan Gonzalez FUT | .30 | .14 |
| ❑ 53 | Ken Griffey Jr. FUT | 1.25 | .55 |
| ❑ 54 | Tim Salmon FUT | .15 | .07 |
| ❑ 55 | Frank Thomas FUT | .60 | .25 |
| ❑ 56 | Tony Phillips | .15 | .07 |
| ❑ 57 | Julio Franco | .15 | .07 |
| ❑ 58 | Kevin Mitchell | .15 | .07 |
| ❑ 59 | Raul Mondesi | .30 | .14 |
| ❑ 60 | Rickey Henderson | .75 | .35 |
| ❑ 61 | Jay Buhner | .30 | .14 |
| ❑ 62 | Bill Swift | .15 | .07 |
| ❑ 63 | Brady Anderson | .30 | .14 |
| ❑ 64 | Ryan Klesko | .30 | .14 |
| ❑ 65 | Darren Daulton | .30 | .14 |
| ❑ 66 | Damion Easley | .15 | .07 |
| ❑ 67 | Mark McGwire | 2.50 | 1.10 |
| ❑ 68 | John Roper | .15 | .07 |
| ❑ 69 | Dave Telgheder | .15 | .07 |
| ❑ 70 | David Nied | .15 | .07 |
| ❑ 71 | Mo Vaughn | .30 | .14 |
| ❑ 72 | Tyler Green | .15 | .07 |
| ❑ 73 | Dave Magadan | .15 | .07 |
| ❑ 74 | Chili Davis | .30 | .14 |
| ❑ 75 | Archi Cianfrocco | .15 | .07 |
| ❑ 76 | Joe Girardi | .15 | .07 |
| ❑ 77 | Chris Hoiles | .15 | .07 |
| ❑ 78 | Ryan Bowen | .15 | .07 |
| ❑ 79 | Greg Gagne | .15 | .07 |
| ❑ 80 | Aaron Sele | .30 | .14 |
| ❑ 81 | Dave Winfield | .60 | .25 |
| ❑ 82 | Chad Curtis | .15 | .07 |
| ❑ 83 | Andy Van Slyke | .30 | .14 |
| ❑ 84 | Kevin Stocker | .15 | .07 |
| ❑ 85 | Deion Sanders | .30 | .14 |
| ❑ 86 | Bernie Williams | .60 | .25 |
| ❑ 87 | John Smoltz | .30 | .14 |
| ❑ 88 | Ruben Santana | .15 | .07 |
| ❑ 89 | Dave Stewart | .30 | .14 |
| ❑ 90 | Don Mattingly | 1.50 | .70 |
| ❑ 91 | Joe Carter | .30 | .14 |
| ❑ 92 | Ryne Sandberg | .75 | .35 |
| ❑ 93 | Chris Gomez | .15 | .07 |
| ❑ 94 | Tino Martinez | .30 | .14 |
| ❑ 95 | Terry Pendleton | .30 | .14 |
| ❑ 96 | Andre Dawson | .30 | .14 |
| ❑ 97 | Wil Cordero | .15 | .07 |
| ❑ 98 | Kent Hrbek | .30 | .14 |
| ❑ 99 | John Olerud | .30 | .14 |
| ❑ 100 | Kirt Manwaring | .15 | .07 |
| ❑ 101 | Tim Bogar | .15 | .07 |
| ❑ 102 | Mike Mussina | .60 | .25 |
| ❑ 103 | Nigel Wilson | .15 | .07 |
| ❑ 104 | Ricky Gutierrez | .15 | .07 |
| ❑ 105 | Roberto Mejia | .15 | .07 |
| ❑ 106 | Tom Pagnozzi | .15 | .07 |
| ❑ 107 | Mike Macfarlane | .15 | .07 |
| ❑ 108 | Jose Bautista | .15 | .07 |
| ❑ 109 | Luis Ortiz | .15 | .07 |
| ❑ 110 | Brent Gates | .15 | .07 |
| ❑ 111 | Tim Salmon | .30 | .14 |
| ❑ 112 | Wade Boggs | .75 | .35 |
| ❑ 113 | Tripp Cromer | .15 | .07 |
| ❑ 114 | Denny Hocking | .15 | .07 |
| ❑ 115 | Carlos Baerga | .15 | .07 |
| ❑ 116 | J.R. Phillips | .15 | .07 |
| ❑ 117 | Bo Jackson | .30 | .14 |
| ❑ 118 | Lance Johnson | .15 | .07 |
| ❑ 119 | Bobby Jones | .15 | .07 |
| ❑ 120 | Bobby Witt | .15 | .07 |
| ❑ 121 | Ron Karkovice | .15 | .07 |
| ❑ 122 | Jose Vizcaino | .15 | .07 |
| ❑ 123 | Danny Darwin | .15 | .07 |
| ❑ 124 | Eduardo Perez | .15 | .07 |
| ❑ 125 | Brian Looney RC | .15 | .07 |
| ❑ 126 | Pat Hentgen | .15 | .07 |
| ❑ 127 | Frank Viola | .15 | .07 |
| ❑ 128 | Darren Holmes | .15 | .07 |
| ❑ 129 | Wally Whitehurst | .15 | .07 |
| ❑ 130 | Matt Walbeck | .15 | .07 |
| ❑ 131 | Albert Belle | .30 | .14 |
| ❑ 132 | Steve Cooke | .15 | .07 |
| ❑ 133 | Kevin Appier | .30 | .14 |
| ❑ 134 | Joe Oliver | .15 | .07 |
| ❑ 135 | Benji Gil | .15 | .07 |
| ❑ 136 | Steve Buechele | .15 | .07 |
| ❑ 137 | Devon White | .15 | .07 |
| ❑ 138 | Sterling Hitchcock UER<br>(Two losses for career; should be four) | .15 | .07 |
| ❑ 139 | Phil Leftwich RC | .15 | .07 |
| ❑ 140 | Jose Canseco | .75 | .35 |
| ❑ 141 | Rick Aguilera | .15 | .07 |
| ❑ 142 | Rod Beck | .15 | .07 |
| ❑ 143 | Jose Rijo | .15 | .07 |
| ❑ 144 | Tom Glavine | .60 | .25 |
| ❑ 145 | Phil Plantier | .15 | .07 |
| ❑ 146 | Jason Bere | .15 | .07 |
| ❑ 147 | Jamie Moyer | .15 | .07 |
| ❑ 148 | Wes Chamberlain | .15 | .07 |
| ❑ 149 | Glenallen Hill | .15 | .07 |
| ❑ 150 | Mark Whiten | .15 | .07 |
| ❑ 151 | Bret Barberie | .15 | .07 |
| ❑ 152 | Chuck Knoblauch | .30 | .14 |
| ❑ 153 | Trevor Hoffman | .30 | .14 |
| ❑ 154 | Rick Wilkins | .15 | .07 |
| ❑ 155 | Juan Gonzalez | .60 | .25 |
| ❑ 156 | Ozzie Guillen | .15 | .07 |
| ❑ 157 | Jim Eisenreich | .15 | .07 |
| ❑ 158 | Pedro Astacio | .15 | .07 |
| ❑ 159 | Joe Magrane | .15 | .07 |
| ❑ 160 | Ryan Thompson | .15 | .07 |
| ❑ 161 | Jose Lind | .15 | .07 |
| ❑ 162 | Jeff Conine | .15 | .07 |
| ❑ 163 | Todd Benzinger | .15 | .07 |
| ❑ 164 | Roger Salkeld | .15 | .07 |
| ❑ 165 | Gary DiSarcina | .15 | .07 |
| ❑ 166 | Kevin Gross | .15 | .07 |
| ❑ 167 | Charlie Hayes | .15 | .07 |
| ❑ 168 | Tim Costo | .15 | .07 |
| ❑ 169 | Wally Joyner | .30 | .14 |
| ❑ 170 | Johnny Ruffin | .15 | .07 |
| ❑ 171 | Kirk Rueter | .15 | .07 |
| ❑ 172 | Lenny Dykstra | .30 | .14 |
| ❑ 173 | Ken Hill | .15 | .07 |
| ❑ 174 | Mike Bordick | .15 | .07 |
| ❑ 175 | Billy Hall | .15 | .07 |
| ❑ 176 | Rob Butler | .15 | .07 |
| ❑ 177 | Jay Bell | .30 | .14 |
| ❑ 178 | Jeff Kent | .30 | .14 |
| ❑ 179 | David Wells | .30 | .14 |
| ❑ 180 | Dean Palmer | .30 | .14 |
| ❑ 181 | Mariano Duncan | .15 | .07 |
| ❑ 182 | Orlando Merced | .15 | .07 |
| ❑ 183 | Brett Butler | .30 | .14 |

❑ 184 Milt Thompson .15 .07
❑ 185 Chipper Jones 1.50 .70
❑ 186 Paul O'Neill .30 .14
❑ 187 Mike Greenwell .15 .07
❑ 188 Harold Baines .30 .14
❑ 189 Todd Stottlemyre .15 .07
❑ 190 Jeromy Burnitz .30 .14
❑ 191 Rene Arocha .15 .07
❑ 192 Jeff Fassero .15 .07
❑ 193 Robby Thompson .15 .07
❑ 194 Greg W. Harris .15 .07
❑ 195 Todd Van Poppel .15 .07
❑ 196 Jose Guzman .15 .07
❑ 197 Shane Mack .15 .07
❑ 198 Carlos Garcia .15 .07
❑ 199 Kevin Roberson .15 .07
❑ 200 David McCarty .15 .07
❑ 201 Alan Trammell .30 .14
❑ 202 Chuck Carr .15 .07
❑ 203 Tommy Greene .15 .07
❑ 204 Wilson Alvarez .15 .07
❑ 205 Dwight Gooden .30 .14
❑ 206 Tony Tarasco .15 .07
❑ 207 Darren Lewis .15 .07
❑ 208 Eric Karros .30 .14
❑ 209 Chris Hammond .15 .07
❑ 210 Jeffrey Hammonds .30 .14
❑ 211 Rich Amaral .15 .07
❑ 212 Danny Tartabull .15 .07
❑ 213 Jeff Russell .15 .07
❑ 214 Dave Staton .15 .07
❑ 215 Kenny Lofton .30 .14
❑ 216 Manuel Lee .15 .07
❑ 217 Brian Koelling .15 .07
❑ 218 Scott Lydy .15 .07
❑ 219 Tony Gwynn 1.25 .55
❑ 220 Cecil Fielder .30 .14
❑ 221 Royce Clayton .15 .07
❑ 222 Reggie Sanders .15 .07
❑ 223 Brian Jordan .30 .14
❑ 224 Ken Griffey Jr. 2.50 1.10
❑ 225 Fred McGriff .30 .14
❑ 226 Felix Jose .15 .07
❑ 227 Brad Pennington .15 .07
❑ 228 Chris Bosio .15 .07
❑ 229 Mike Stanley .15 .07
❑ 230 Willie Greene .15 .07
❑ 231 Alex Fernandez .15 .07
❑ 232 Brad Ausmus .15 .07
❑ 233 Darrell Whitmore .15 .07
❑ 234 Marcus Moore .15 .07
❑ 235 Allen Watson .15 .07
❑ 236 Jose Offerman .15 .07
❑ 237 Rondell White .30 .14
❑ 238 Jeff King .15 .07
❑ 239 Luis Alicea .15 .07
❑ 240 Dan Wilson .15 .07
❑ 241 Ed Sprague .15 .07
❑ 242 Todd Hundley .15 .07
❑ 243 Al Martin .15 .07
❑ 244 Mike Lansing .15 .07
❑ 245 Ivan Rodriguez .75 .35
❑ 246 Dave Fleming .15 .07
❑ 247 John Doherty .15 .07
❑ 248 Mark McLemore .15 .07
❑ 249 Bob Hamelin .15 .07
❑ 250 Curtis Pride RC .15 .07
❑ 251 Zane Smith .15 .07
❑ 252 Eric Young .15 .07
❑ 253 Brian McRae .15 .07
❑ 254 Tim Raines .30 .14
❑ 255 Javier Lopez .30 .14
❑ 256 Melvin Nieves .15 .07
❑ 257 Randy Myers .15 .07
❑ 258 Willie McGee .30 .14
❑ 259 Jimmy Key UER .30 .14
(Birthdate missing on back)
❑ 260 Tom Candiotti .15 .07
❑ 261 Eric Davis .30 .14
❑ 262 Craig Paquette .15 .07
❑ 263 Robin Ventura .30 .14
❑ 264 Pat Kelly .15 .07
❑ 265 Gregg Jefferies .15 .07
❑ 266 Cory Snyder .15 .07
❑ 267 David Justice HFA .15 .07
❑ 268 Sammy Sosa HFA .60 .25
❑ 269 Barry Larkin HFA .30 .14
❑ 270 Andres Galarraga HFA .15 .07
❑ 271 Gary Sheffield HFA .30 .14
❑ 272 Jeff Bagwell HFA .30 .14
❑ 273 Mike Piazza HFA 1.00 .45
❑ 274 Larry Walker HFA .30 .14
❑ 275 Bobby Bonilla HFA .15 .07
❑ 276 John Kruk HFA .15 .07
❑ 277 Jay Bell HFA .15 .07
❑ 278 Ozzie Smith HFA .60 .25
❑ 279 Tony Gwynn HFA .60 .25
❑ 280 Barry Bonds HFA .60 .25
❑ 281 Cal Ripken Jr. HFA 1.25 .55
❑ 282 Mo Vaughn HFA .30 .14
❑ 283 Tim Salmon HFA .15 .07
❑ 284 Frank Thomas HFA .60 .25
❑ 285 Albert Belle HFA .15 .07
❑ 286 Cecil Fielder HFA .15 .07
❑ 287 Wally Joyner HFA .15 .07
❑ 288 Greg Vaughn HFA .15 .07
❑ 289 Kirby Puckett HFA .75 .35
❑ 290 Don Mattingly HFA .75 .14
❑ 291 Terry Steinbach HFA .15 .07
❑ 292 Ken Griffey Jr. HFA 1.25 .55
❑ 293 Juan Gonzalez HFA .30 .14
❑ 294 Paul Molitor HFA .30 .14
❑ 295 Tavo Alvarez UDCA .15 .07
❑ 296 Matt Brunson UDC .15 .07
❑ 297 Shawn Green UDC .30 .14
❑ 298 Alex Rodriguez UDC 2.50 1.10
❑ 299 Shannon Stewart UDCA .60 .25
❑ 300 Frank Thomas 1.25 .55
❑ 301 Mickey Tettleton .15 .07
❑ 302 Pedro Munoz .15 .07
❑ 303 Jose Valentin .15 .07
❑ 304 Orestes Destrade .15 .07
❑ 305 Pat Listach .15 .07
❑ 306 Scott Brosius .30 .14
❑ 307 Kurt Miller .15 .07
❑ 308 Rob Dibble .15 .07
❑ 309 Mike Blowers .15 .07
❑ 310 Jim Abbott .30 .14
❑ 311 Mike Jackson .15 .07
❑ 312 Craig Biggio .30 .14
❑ 313 Kurt Abbott RC .15 .07
❑ 314 Chuck Finley .30 .14
❑ 315 Andres Galarraga .30 .14
❑ 316 Mike Moore .15 .07
❑ 317 Doug Strange .15 .07
❑ 318 Pedro Martinez 1.00 .45
❑ 319 Kevin McReynolds .15 .07
❑ 320 Greg Maddux 1.50 .70
❑ 321 Mike Henneman .15 .07
❑ 322 Scott Leius .15 .07
❑ 323 John Franco .30 .14
❑ 324 Jeff Blauser .15 .07
❑ 325 Kirby Puckett 1.50 .70
❑ 326 Darryl Hamilton .15 .07
❑ 327 John Smiley .15 .07
❑ 328 Derrick May .15 .07
❑ 329 Jose Vizcaino .15 .07
❑ 330 Randy Johnson .75 .35
❑ 331 Jack Morris .30 .14
❑ 332 Graeme Lloyd .15 .07
❑ 333 Dave Valle .15 .07
❑ 334 Greg Myers .15 .07
❑ 335 John Wetteland .30 .14
❑ 336 Jim Gott .15 .07
❑ 337 Tim Naehring .15 .07
❑ 338 Mike Kelly .15 .07
❑ 339 Jeff Montgomery .15 .07
❑ 340 Rafael Palmeiro .60 .25
❑ 341 Eddie Murray .60 .25
❑ 342 Xavier Hernandez .15 .07
❑ 343 Bobby Munoz .15 .07
❑ 344 Bobby Bonilla .30 .14
❑ 345 Travis Fryman .30 .14
❑ 346 Steve Finley .30 .14
❑ 347 Chris Sabo .15 .07
❑ 348 Armando Reynoso .15 .07
❑ 349 Ramon Martinez .15 .07
❑ 350 Will Clark .60 .25
❑ 351 Moises Alou .30 .14
❑ 352 Jim Thome .30 .14
❑ 353 Bob Tewksbury .15 .07
❑ 354 Andujar Cedeno .15 .07
❑ 355 Orel Hershiser .30 .14
❑ 356 Mike Devereaux .15 .07
❑ 357 Mike Perez .15 .07
❑ 358 Dennis Martinez .30 .14
❑ 359 Dave Nilsson .15 .07
❑ 360 Ozzie Smith .75 .35
❑ 361 Eric Anthony .15 .07
❑ 362 Scott Sanders .15 .07
❑ 363 Paul Sorrento .15 .07
❑ 364 Tim Belcher .15 .07
❑ 365 Dennis Eckersley .30 .14
❑ 366 Mel Rojas .15 .07
❑ 367 Tom Henke .15 .07
❑ 368 Randy Tomlin .15 .07
❑ 369 B.J. Surhoff .30 .14
❑ 370 Larry Walker .30 .14
❑ 371 Joey Cora .15 .07
❑ 372 Mike Harkey .15 .07
❑ 373 John Valentin .15 .07
❑ 374 Doug Jones .15 .07
❑ 375 David Justice .30 .14
❑ 376 Vince Coleman .15 .07
❑ 377 David Hulse .15 .07
❑ 378 Kevin Seitzer .15 .07
❑ 379 Pete Harnisch .15 .07
❑ 380 Ruben Sierra .15 .07
❑ 381 Mark Lewis .15 .07
❑ 382 Bip Roberts .15 .07
❑ 383 Paul Wagner .15 .07
❑ 384 Stan Javier .15 .07
❑ 385 Barry Larkin .60 .25
❑ 386 Mark Portugal .15 .07
❑ 387 Roberto Kelly .15 .07
❑ 388 Andy Benes .15 .07
❑ 389 Felix Fermin .15 .07
❑ 390 Marquis Grissom .15 .07
❑ 391 Troy Neel .15 .07
❑ 392 Chad Kreuter .15 .07
❑ 393 Gregg Olson .15 .07
❑ 394 Charles Nagy .15 .07
❑ 395 Jack McDowell .15 .07
❑ 396 Luis Gonzalez .30 .14
❑ 397 Benito Santiago .15 .07
❑ 398 Chris James .15 .07
❑ 399 Terry Mulholland .15 .07
❑ 400 Barry Bonds 1.00 .45
❑ 401 Joe Grahe .15 .07
❑ 402 Duane Ward .15 .07
❑ 403 John Burkett .15 .07
❑ 404 Scott Servais .15 .07
❑ 405 Bryan Harvey .15 .07
❑ 406 Bernard Gilkey .15 .07
❑ 407 Greg McMichael .15 .07
❑ 408 Tim Wallach .15 .07
❑ 409 Ken Caminiti .30 .14
❑ 410 John Kruk .30 .14
❑ 411 Darrin Jackson .15 .07
❑ 412 Mike Gallego .15 .07
❑ 413 David Cone .30 .14
❑ 414 Lou Whitaker .30 .14
❑ 415 Sandy Alomar Jr. .30 .14
❑ 416 Bill Wegman .15 .07
❑ 417 Pat Borders .15 .07
❑ 418 Roger Pavlik .15 .07
❑ 419 Pete Smith .15 .07
❑ 420 Steve Avery .15 .07
❑ 421 David Segui .15 .07
❑ 422 Rheal Cormier .15 .07
❑ 423 Harold Reynolds .15 .07
❑ 424 Edgar Martinez .30 .14
❑ 425 Cal Ripken Jr. 2.50 1.10
❑ 426 Jaime Navarro .15 .07
❑ 427 Sean Berry .15 .07
❑ 428 Bret Saberhagen .30 .14
❑ 429 Bob Welch .15 .07
❑ 430 Juan Guzman .15 .07
❑ 431 Cal Eldred .15 .07
❑ 432 Dave Hollins .15 .07
❑ 433 Sid Fernandez .15 .07
❑ 434 Willie Banks .15 .07
❑ 435 Darryl Kile .30 .14
❑ 436 Henry Rodriguez .15 .07
❑ 437 Tony Fernandez .15 .07
❑ 438 Walt Weiss .15 .07
❑ 439 Kevin Tapani .15 .07
❑ 440 Mark Grace .60 .25

| Card | Player | Mint | NrMt |
|---|---|---|---|
| ❑ 441 | Brian Harper | .15 | .07 |
| ❑ 442 | Kent Mercker | .15 | .07 |
| ❑ 443 | Anthony Young | .15 | .07 |
| ❑ 444 | Todd Zeile | .15 | .07 |
| ❑ 445 | Greg Vaughn | .30 | .14 |
| ❑ 446 | Ray Lankford | .30 | .14 |
| ❑ 447 | Dave Weathers | .15 | .07 |
| ❑ 448 | Bret Boone | .30 | .14 |
| ❑ 449 | Charlie Hough | .30 | .14 |
| ❑ 450 | Roger Clemens | 1.25 | .55 |
| ❑ 451 | Mike Morgan | .15 | .07 |
| ❑ 452 | Doug Drabek | .15 | .07 |
| ❑ 453 | Danny Jackson | .15 | .07 |
| ❑ 454 | Dante Bichette | .30 | .14 |
| ❑ 455 | Roberto Alomar | .60 | .25 |
| ❑ 456 | Ben McDonald | .15 | .07 |
| ❑ 457 | Kenny Rogers | .15 | .07 |
| ❑ 458 | Bill Gullickson | .15 | .07 |
| ❑ 459 | Darrin Fletcher | .15 | .07 |
| ❑ 460 | Curt Schilling | .30 | .14 |
| ❑ 461 | Billy Hatcher | .15 | .07 |
| ❑ 462 | Howard Johnson | .15 | .07 |
| ❑ 463 | Mickey Morandini | .15 | .07 |
| ❑ 464 | Frank Castillo | .15 | .07 |
| ❑ 465 | Delino DeShields | .15 | .07 |
| ❑ 466 | Gary Gaetti | .30 | .14 |
| ❑ 467 | Steve Farr | .15 | .07 |
| ❑ 468 | Roberto Hernandez | .15 | .07 |
| ❑ 469 | Jack Armstrong | .15 | .07 |
| ❑ 470 | Paul Molitor | .60 | .25 |
| ❑ 471 | Melido Perez | .15 | .07 |
| ❑ 472 | Greg Hibbard | .15 | .07 |
| ❑ 473 | Jody Reed | .15 | .07 |
| ❑ 474 | Tom Gordon | .15 | .07 |
| ❑ 475 | Gary Sheffield | .60 | .25 |
| ❑ 476 | John Jaha | .15 | .07 |
| ❑ 477 | Shawon Dunston | .15 | .07 |
| ❑ 478 | Reggie Jefferson | .15 | .07 |
| ❑ 479 | Don Slaught | .15 | .07 |
| ❑ 480 | Jeff Bagwell | .75 | .35 |
| ❑ 481 | Tim Pugh | .15 | .07 |
| ❑ 482 | Kevin Young | .15 | .07 |
| ❑ 483 | Ellis Burks | .30 | .14 |
| ❑ 484 | Greg Swindell | .15 | .07 |
| ❑ 485 | Mark Langston | .15 | .07 |
| ❑ 486 | Omar Vizquel | .30 | .14 |
| ❑ 487 | Kevin Brown | .30 | .14 |
| ❑ 488 | Terry Steinbach | .15 | .07 |
| ❑ 489 | Mark Lemke | .15 | .07 |
| ❑ 490 | Matt Williams | .30 | .14 |
| ❑ 491 | Pete Incaviglia | .15 | .07 |
| ❑ 492 | Karl Rhodes | .15 | .07 |
| ❑ 493 | Shawn Green | .75 | .35 |
| ❑ 494 | Hal Morris | .15 | .07 |
| ❑ 495 | Derek Bell | .15 | .07 |
| ❑ 496 | Luis Polonia | .15 | .07 |
| ❑ 497 | Otis Nixon | .15 | .07 |
| ❑ 498 | Ron Darling | .15 | .07 |
| ❑ 499 | Mitch Williams | .15 | .07 |
| ❑ 500 | Mike Piazza | 2.00 | .90 |
| ❑ 501 | Pat Meares | .15 | .07 |
| ❑ 502 | Scott Cooper | .15 | .07 |
| ❑ 503 | Scott Erickson | .15 | .07 |
| ❑ 504 | Jeff Juden | .15 | .07 |
| ❑ 505 | Lee Smith | .30 | .14 |
| ❑ 506 | Bobby Ayala | .15 | .07 |
| ❑ 507 | Dave Henderson | .15 | .07 |
| ❑ 508 | Erik Hanson | .15 | .07 |
| ❑ 509 | Bob Wickman | .15 | .07 |
| ❑ 510 | Sammy Sosa | 1.25 | .55 |
| ❑ 511 | Hector Carrasco | .15 | .07 |
| ❑ 512 | Tim Davis | .15 | .07 |
| ❑ 513 | Joey Hamilton DD | .15 | .07 |
| ❑ 514 | Robert Eenhoorn | .15 | .07 |
| ❑ 515 | Jorge Fabregas | .15 | .07 |
| ❑ 516 | Tim Hyers RC | .15 | .07 |
| ❑ 517 | John Hudek DD RC | .15 | .07 |
| ❑ 518 | James Mouton DD | .15 | .07 |
| ❑ 519 | Herbert Perry DD RC | .15 | .07 |
| ❑ 520 | Chan Ho Park DD RC | .75 | .35 |
| ❑ 521 | W.Van Landingham DD RC | .15 | .07 |
| ❑ 522 | Paul Shuey DD | .15 | .07 |
| ❑ 523 | Ryan Hancock TP RC | .15 | .07 |
| ❑ 524 | Billy Wagner TP RC | .50 | .23 |
| ❑ 525 | Jason Giambi | .75 | .35 |
| ❑ 526 | Jose Silva TP RC | .15 | .07 |
| ❑ 527 | Terrell Wade TP RC | .15 | .07 |
| ❑ 528 | Todd Dunn TP | .15 | .07 |
| ❑ 529 | Alan Benes TP RC | .30 | .14 |
| ❑ 530 | Brooks Kieschnick TP RC | .15 | .07 |
| ❑ 531 | Todd Hollandsworth TP | .15 | .07 |
| ❑ 532 | Brad Fullmer TP RC | 1.25 | .55 |
| ❑ 533 | Steve Soderstrom TP RC | .15 | .07 |
| ❑ 534 | Daron Kirkreit | .15 | .07 |
| ❑ 535 | Arquimedez Pozo TP RC | .30 | .14 |
| ❑ 536 | Charles Johnson TP | .30 | .14 |
| ❑ 537 | Preston Wilson | .60 | .25 |
| ❑ 538 | Alex Ochoa | .15 | .07 |
| ❑ 539 | Derrek Lee TP RC | .50 | .23 |
| ❑ 540 | Wayne Gomes TP RC | .15 | .07 |
| ❑ 541 | Jermaine Allensworth TP RC | .30 | .14 |
| ❑ 542 | Mike Bell TP RC | .15 | .07 |
| ❑ 543 | Trot Nixon TP RC | 1.25 | .55 |
| ❑ 544 | Pokey Reese | .30 | .14 |
| ❑ 545 | Neifi Perez TP RC | .60 | .25 |
| ❑ 546 | Johnny Damon TP | .60 | .25 |
| ❑ 547 | Matt Brunson TP RC | .15 | .07 |
| ❑ 548 | LaTroy Hawkins TP RC | .30 | .14 |
| ❑ 549 | Eddie Pearson TP RC | .30 | .14 |
| ❑ 550 | Derek Jeter TP | 3.00 | 1.35 |
| ❑ A298 | Alex Rodriguez AU | 300.00 | 135.00 |
| ❑ P224 | Ken Griffey Jr. Promo | 3.00 | |
| ❑ GM1 | Ken Griffey Jr. AU<br>Mickey Mantle AU/1000 | 1800.00 | 800.00 |
| ❑ KG1 | Ken Griffey Jr. AU1000 | 250.00 | 110.00 |
| ❑ MM1 | Mickey Mantle AU1000 | 600.00 | 275.00 |

## 1995 Upper Deck

| | MINT | NRMT |
|---|---|---|
| COMPLETE SET (450) | 80.00 | 36.00 |
| COMPLETE SERIES 1 (225) | 40.00 | 18.00 |
| COMPLETE SERIES 2 (225) | 40.00 | 18.00 |
| COMMON CARD (1-450) | .15 | .07 |
| COMP.TRADE SET (45) | 20.00 | 9.00 |
| COMMON TRADE (451T-495T) | .50 | .23 |

| Card | Player | Mint | NrMt |
|---|---|---|---|
| ❑ 1 | Ruben Rivera | .15 | .07 |
| ❑ 2 | Bill Pulsipher | .15 | .07 |
| ❑ 3 | Ben Grieve | 1.00 | .45 |
| ❑ 4 | Curtis Goodwin | .15 | .07 |
| ❑ 5 | Damon Hollins | .15 | .07 |
| ❑ 6 | Todd Greene | .15 | .07 |
| ❑ 7 | Glenn Williams | .15 | .07 |
| ❑ 8 | Bret Wagner | .15 | .07 |
| ❑ 9 | Karim Garcia RC | .50 | .23 |
| ❑ 10 | Nomar Garciaparra | 4.00 | 1.80 |
| ❑ 11 | Raul Casanova RC | .15 | .07 |
| ❑ 12 | Matt Smith | .15 | .07 |
| ❑ 13 | Paul Wilson | .15 | .07 |
| ❑ 14 | Jason Isringhausen | .30 | .14 |
| ❑ 15 | Reid Ryan | .30 | .14 |
| ❑ 16 | Lee Smith | .30 | .14 |
| ❑ 17 | Chili Davis | .30 | .14 |
| ❑ 18 | Brian Anderson | .15 | .07 |
| ❑ 19 | Gary DiSarcina | .15 | .07 |
| ❑ 20 | Bo Jackson | .30 | .14 |
| ❑ 21 | Chuck Finley | .30 | .14 |
| ❑ 22 | Darryl Kile | .30 | .14 |
| ❑ 23 | Shane Reynolds | .15 | .07 |
| ❑ 24 | Tony Eusebio | .15 | .07 |
| ❑ 25 | Craig Biggio | .30 | .14 |
| ❑ 26 | Doug Drabek | .15 | .07 |
| ❑ 27 | Brian L. Hunter | .15 | .07 |
| ❑ 28 | James Mouton | .15 | .07 |
| ❑ 29 | Geronimo Berroa | .15 | .07 |
| ❑ 30 | Rickey Henderson | .75 | .35 |
| ❑ 31 | Steve Karsay | .15 | .07 |
| ❑ 32 | Steve Ontiveros | .15 | .07 |
| ❑ 33 | Ernie Young | .15 | .07 |
| ❑ 34 | Dennis Eckersley | .30 | .14 |
| ❑ 35 | Mark McGwire | 2.50 | 1.10 |
| ❑ 36 | Dave Stewart | .30 | .14 |
| ❑ 37 | Pat Hentgen | .15 | .07 |
| ❑ 38 | Carlos Delgado | .60 | .25 |
| ❑ 39 | Joe Carter | .30 | .14 |
| ❑ 40 | Roberto Alomar | .60 | .25 |
| ❑ 41 | John Olerud | .30 | .14 |
| ❑ 42 | Devon White | .30 | .14 |
| ❑ 43 | Roberto Kelly | .15 | .07 |
| ❑ 44 | Jeff Blauser | .15 | .07 |
| ❑ 45 | Fred McGriff | .30 | .14 |
| ❑ 46 | Tom Glavine | .60 | .25 |
| ❑ 47 | Mike Kelly | .15 | .07 |
| ❑ 48 | Javier Lopez | .30 | .14 |
| ❑ 49 | Greg Maddux | 1.50 | .70 |
| ❑ 50 | Matt Mieske | .15 | .07 |
| ❑ 51 | Troy O'Leary | .15 | .07 |
| ❑ 52 | Jeff Cirillo | .30 | .14 |
| ❑ 53 | Cal Eldred | .15 | .07 |
| ❑ 54 | Pat Listach | .15 | .07 |
| ❑ 55 | Jose Valentin | .15 | .07 |
| ❑ 56 | John Mabry | .15 | .07 |
| ❑ 57 | Bob Tewksbury | .15 | .07 |
| ❑ 58 | Brian Jordan | .30 | .14 |
| ❑ 59 | Gregg Jefferies | .15 | .07 |
| ❑ 60 | Ozzie Smith | .75 | .35 |
| ❑ 61 | Geronimo Pena | .15 | .07 |
| ❑ 62 | Mark Whiten | .15 | .07 |
| ❑ 63 | Rey Sanchez | .15 | .07 |
| ❑ 64 | Willie Banks | .15 | .07 |
| ❑ 65 | Mark Grace | .60 | .25 |
| ❑ 66 | Randy Myers | .15 | .07 |
| ❑ 67 | Steve Trachsel | .15 | .07 |
| ❑ 68 | Derrick May | .15 | .07 |
| ❑ 69 | Brett Butler | .30 | .14 |
| ❑ 70 | Eric Karros | .30 | .14 |
| ❑ 71 | Tim Wallach | .15 | .07 |
| ❑ 72 | Delino DeShields | .15 | .07 |
| ❑ 73 | Darren Dreifort | .30 | .14 |
| ❑ 74 | Orel Hershiser | .30 | .14 |
| ❑ 75 | Billy Ashley | .15 | .07 |
| ❑ 76 | Sean Berry | .15 | .07 |
| ❑ 77 | Ken Hill | .15 | .07 |
| ❑ 78 | John Wetteland | .30 | .14 |
| ❑ 79 | Moises Alou | .30 | .14 |
| ❑ 80 | Cliff Floyd | .30 | .14 |
| ❑ 81 | Marquis Grissom | .15 | .07 |
| ❑ 82 | Larry Walker | .30 | .14 |
| ❑ 83 | Rondell White | .30 | .14 |
| ❑ 84 | William VanLandingham | .15 | .07 |
| ❑ 85 | Matt Williams | .30 | .14 |
| ❑ 86 | Rod Beck | .15 | .07 |
| ❑ 87 | Darren Lewis | .15 | .07 |
| ❑ 88 | Robby Thompson | .15 | .07 |
| ❑ 89 | Darryl Strawberry | .30 | .14 |
| ❑ 90 | Kenny Lofton | .30 | .14 |
| ❑ 91 | Charles Nagy | .15 | .07 |
| ❑ 92 | Sandy Alomar Jr. | .30 | .14 |
| ❑ 93 | Mark Clark | .15 | .07 |
| ❑ 94 | Dennis Martinez | .30 | .14 |
| ❑ 95 | Dave Winfield | .60 | .25 |
| ❑ 96 | Jim Thome | .30 | .14 |
| ❑ 97 | Manny Ramirez | .75 | .35 |
| ❑ 98 | Goose Gossage | .30 | .14 |
| ❑ 99 | Tino Martinez | .30 | .14 |
| ❑ 100 | Ken Griffey Jr. | 2.50 | 1.10 |
| ❑ 101 | Greg Maddux ANA | .75 | .35 |
| ❑ 102 | Randy Johnson ANA | .30 | .14 |
| ❑ 103 | Barry Bonds ANA | .30 | .14 |
| ❑ 104 | Juan Gonzalez ANA | .30 | .14 |
| ❑ 105 | Frank Thomas ANA | .60 | .25 |
| ❑ 106 | Matt Williams ANA | .30 | .14 |
| ❑ 107 | Paul Molitor ANA | .30 | .14 |
| ❑ 108 | Fred McGriff ANA | .15 | .07 |
| ❑ 109 | Carlos Baerga ANA | .15 | .07 |
| ❑ 110 | Ken Griffey Jr. ANA | 1.25 | .55 |
| ❑ 111 | Reggie Jefferson | .15 | .07 |

| No. | Player | | |
|---|---|---|---|
| 112 | Randy Johnson | .75 | .35 |
| 113 | Marc Newfield | .15 | .07 |
| 114 | Robb Nen | .15 | .07 |
| 115 | Jeff Conine | .15 | .07 |
| 116 | Kurt Abbott | .15 | .07 |
| 117 | Charlie Hough | .30 | .14 |
| 118 | Dave Weathers | .15 | .07 |
| 119 | Juan Castillo | .15 | .07 |
| 120 | Bret Saberhagen | .30 | .14 |
| 121 | Rico Brogna | .15 | .07 |
| 122 | John Franco | .30 | .14 |
| 123 | Todd Hundley | .15 | .07 |
| 124 | Jason Jacome | .15 | .07 |
| 125 | Bobby Jones | .15 | .07 |
| 126 | Bret Barberie | .15 | .07 |
| 127 | Ben McDonald | .15 | .07 |
| 128 | Harold Baines | .30 | .14 |
| 129 | Jeffrey Hammonds | .30 | .14 |
| 130 | Mike Mussina | .60 | .25 |
| 131 | Chris Hoiles | .15 | .07 |
| 132 | Brady Anderson | .30 | .14 |
| 133 | Eddie Williams | .15 | .07 |
| 134 | Andy Benes | .15 | .07 |
| 135 | Tony Gwynn | 1.25 | .55 |
| 136 | Bip Roberts | .15 | .07 |
| 137 | Joey Hamilton | .15 | .07 |
| 138 | Luis Lopez | .15 | .07 |
| 139 | Ray McDavid | .15 | .07 |
| 140 | Lenny Dykstra | .30 | .14 |
| 141 | Mariano Duncan | .15 | .07 |
| 142 | Fernando Valenzuela | .30 | .14 |
| 143 | Bobby Munoz | .15 | .07 |
| 144 | Kevin Stocker | .15 | .07 |
| 145 | John Kruk | .30 | .14 |
| 146 | Jon Lieber | .15 | .07 |
| 147 | Zane Smith | .15 | .07 |
| 148 | Steve Cooke | .15 | .07 |
| 149 | Andy Van Slyke | .30 | .14 |
| 150 | Jay Bell | .30 | .14 |
| 151 | Carlos Garcia | .15 | .07 |
| 152 | John Dettmer | .15 | .07 |
| 153 | Darren Oliver | .15 | .07 |
| 154 | Dean Palmer | .30 | .14 |
| 155 | Otis Nixon | .15 | .07 |
| 156 | Rusty Greer | .30 | .14 |
| 157 | Rick Helling | .30 | .14 |
| 158 | Jose Canseco | .75 | .35 |
| 159 | Roger Clemens | 1.25 | .55 |
| 160 | Andre Dawson | .30 | .14 |
| 161 | Mo Vaughn | .30 | .14 |
| 162 | Aaron Sele | .30 | .14 |
| 163 | John Valentin | .15 | .07 |
| 164 | Brian R. Hunter | .15 | .07 |
| 165 | Bret Boone | .30 | .14 |
| 166 | Hector Carrasco | .15 | .07 |
| 167 | Pete Schourek | .15 | .07 |
| 168 | Willie Greene | .15 | .07 |
| 169 | Kevin Mitchell | .15 | .07 |
| 170 | Deion Sanders | .30 | .14 |
| 171 | John Roper | .15 | .07 |
| 172 | Charlie Hayes | .15 | .07 |
| 173 | David Nied | .15 | .07 |
| 174 | Ellis Burks | .30 | .14 |
| 175 | Dante Bichette | .30 | .14 |
| 176 | Marvin Freeman | .15 | .07 |
| 177 | Eric Young | .15 | .07 |
| 178 | David Cone | .30 | .14 |
| 179 | Greg Gagne | .15 | .07 |
| 180 | Bob Hamelin | .15 | .07 |
| 181 | Wally Joyner | .30 | .14 |
| 182 | Jeff Montgomery | .15 | .07 |
| 183 | Jose Lind | .15 | .07 |
| 184 | Chris Gomez | .15 | .07 |
| 185 | Travis Fryman | .30 | .14 |
| 186 | Kirk Gibson | .30 | .14 |
| 187 | Mike Moore | .15 | .07 |
| 188 | Lou Whitaker | .30 | .14 |
| 189 | Sean Bergman | .15 | .07 |
| 190 | Shane Mack | .15 | .07 |
| 191 | Rick Aguilera | .15 | .07 |
| 192 | Denny Hocking | .15 | .07 |
| 193 | Chuck Knoblauch | .30 | .14 |
| 194 | Kevin Tapani | .15 | .07 |
| 195 | Kent Hrbek | .15 | .07 |
| 196 | Ozzie Guillen | .15 | .07 |
| 197 | Wilson Alvarez | .15 | .07 |
| 198 | Tim Raines | .30 | .14 |
| 199 | Scott Ruffcorn | .15 | .07 |
| 200 | Michael Jordan | 2.50 | 1.10 |
| 201 | Robin Ventura | .30 | .14 |
| 202 | Jason Bere | .15 | .07 |
| 203 | Darrin Jackson | .15 | .07 |
| 204 | Russ Davis | .15 | .07 |
| 205 | Jimmy Key | .30 | .14 |
| 206 | Jack McDowell | .15 | .07 |
| 207 | Jim Abbott | .30 | .14 |
| 208 | Paul O'Neill | .30 | .14 |
| 209 | Bernie Williams | .60 | .25 |
| 210 | Don Mattingly | 1.50 | .70 |
| 211 | Orlando Miller | .15 | .07 |
| 212 | Alex Gonzalez | .15 | .07 |
| 213 | Terrell Wade | .15 | .07 |
| 214 | Jose Oliva | .15 | .07 |
| 215 | Alex Rodriguez | 2.50 | 1.10 |
| 216 | Garret Anderson | .30 | .14 |
| 217 | Alan Benes | .15 | .07 |
| 218 | Armando Benitez | .30 | .14 |
| 219 | Dustin Hermanson | .15 | .07 |
| 220 | Charles Johnson | .30 | .14 |
| 221 | Julian Tavarez | .15 | .07 |
| 222 | Jason Giambi | .60 | .25 |
| 223 | LaTroy Hawkins | .15 | .07 |
| 224 | Todd Hollandsworth | .15 | .07 |
| 225 | Derek Jeter | 2.50 | 1.10 |
| 226 | Hideo Nomo RC | 1.50 | .70 |
| 227 | Tony Clark | .30 | .14 |
| 228 | Roger Cedeno | .15 | .07 |
| 229 | Scott Stahoviak | .15 | .07 |
| 230 | Michael Tucker | .15 | .07 |
| 231 | Joe Rosselli | .15 | .07 |
| 232 | Antonio Osuna | .15 | .07 |
| 233 | Bobby Higginson RC | 1.00 | .45 |
| 234 | Mark Grudzielanek RC | .30 | .14 |
| 235 | Ray Durham | .30 | .14 |
| 236 | Frank Rodriguez | .15 | .07 |
| 237 | Quilvio Veras | .15 | .07 |
| 238 | Darren Bragg | .15 | .07 |
| 239 | Ugueth Urbina | .15 | .07 |
| 240 | Jason Bates | .15 | .07 |
| 241 | David Bell | .15 | .07 |
| 242 | Ron Villone | .15 | .07 |
| 243 | Joe Randa | .15 | .07 |
| 244 | Carlos Perez RC | .30 | .14 |
| 245 | Brad Clontz | .15 | .07 |
| 246 | Steve Rodriguez | .15 | .07 |
| 247 | Joe Vitiello | .15 | .07 |
| 248 | Ozzie Timmons | .15 | .07 |
| 249 | Rudy Pemberton | .15 | .07 |
| 250 | Marty Cordova | .15 | .07 |
| 251 | Tony Graffanino | .15 | .07 |
| 252 | Mark Johnson RC | .15 | .07 |
| 253 | Tomas Perez RC | .15 | .07 |
| 254 | Jimmy Hurst | .15 | .07 |
| 255 | Edgardo Alfonzo | .60 | .25 |
| 256 | Jose Malave | .15 | .07 |
| 257 | Brad Radke RC | 1.00 | .45 |
| 258 | Jon Nunnally | .15 | .07 |
| 259 | Dilson Torres RC | .15 | .07 |
| 260 | Esteban Loaiza | .15 | .07 |
| 261 | Freddy Garcia RC | .15 | .07 |
| 262 | Don Wengert | .15 | .07 |
| 263 | Robert Person RC | .50 | .23 |
| 264 | Tim Unroe RC | .15 | .07 |
| 265 | Juan Acevedo RC | .15 | .07 |
| 266 | Eduardo Perez | .15 | .07 |
| 267 | Tony Phillips | .15 | .07 |
| 268 | Jim Edmonds | .60 | .25 |
| 269 | Jorge Fabregas | .15 | .07 |
| 270 | Tim Salmon | .30 | .14 |
| 271 | Mark Langston | .15 | .07 |
| 272 | J.T. Snow | .30 | .14 |
| 273 | Phil Plantier | .15 | .07 |
| 274 | Derek Bell | .15 | .07 |
| 275 | Jeff Bagwell | .75 | .35 |
| 276 | Luis Gonzalez | .15 | .07 |
| 277 | John Hudek | .15 | .07 |
| 278 | Todd Stottlemyre | .15 | .07 |
| 279 | Mark Acre | .15 | .07 |
| 280 | Ruben Sierra | .15 | .07 |
| 281 | Mike Bordick | .15 | .07 |
| 282 | Ron Darling | .15 | .07 |
| 283 | Brent Gates | .15 | .07 |
| 284 | Todd Van Poppel | .15 | .07 |
| 285 | Paul Molitor | .60 | .25 |
| 286 | Ed Sprague | .15 | .07 |
| 287 | Juan Guzman | .15 | .07 |
| 288 | David Cone | .30 | .14 |
| 289 | Shawn Green | .60 | .25 |
| 290 | Marquis Grissom | .15 | .07 |
| 291 | Kent Mercker | .15 | .07 |
| 292 | Steve Avery | .15 | .07 |
| 293 | Chipper Jones | 1.50 | .70 |
| 294 | John Smoltz | .30 | .14 |
| 295 | David Justice | .30 | .14 |
| 296 | Ryan Klesko | .30 | .14 |
| 297 | Joe Oliver | .15 | .07 |
| 298 | Ricky Bones | .15 | .07 |
| 299 | John Jaha | .15 | .07 |
| 300 | Greg Vaughn | .30 | .14 |
| 301 | Dave Nilsson | .15 | .07 |
| 302 | Kevin Seitzer | .15 | .07 |
| 303 | Bernard Gilkey | .15 | .07 |
| 304 | Allen Battle | .15 | .07 |
| 305 | Ray Lankford | .30 | .14 |
| 306 | Tom Pagnozzi | .15 | .07 |
| 307 | Allen Watson | .15 | .07 |
| 308 | Danny Jackson | .15 | .07 |
| 309 | Ken Hill | .15 | .07 |
| 310 | Todd Zeile | .15 | .07 |
| 311 | Kevin Roberson | .15 | .07 |
| 312 | Steve Buechele | .15 | .07 |
| 313 | Rick Wilkins | .15 | .07 |
| 314 | Kevin Foster | .15 | .07 |
| 315 | Sammy Sosa | 1.25 | .55 |
| 316 | Howard Johnson | .15 | .07 |
| 317 | Greg Hansell | .15 | .07 |
| 318 | Pedro Astacio | .15 | .07 |
| 319 | Rafael Bournigal | .15 | .07 |
| 320 | Mike Piazza | 2.00 | .90 |
| 321 | Ramon Martinez | .15 | .07 |
| 322 | Raul Mondesi | .30 | .14 |
| 323 | Ismael Valdes | .15 | .07 |
| 324 | Wil Cordero | .15 | .07 |
| 325 | Tony Tarasco | .15 | .07 |
| 326 | Roberto Kelly | .15 | .07 |
| 327 | Jeff Fassero | .15 | .07 |
| 328 | Mike Lansing | .15 | .07 |
| 329 | Pedro Martinez | .75 | .35 |
| 330 | Kirk Rueter | .15 | .07 |
| 331 | Glenallen Hill | .15 | .07 |
| 332 | Kirt Manwaring | .15 | .07 |
| 333 | Royce Clayton | .15 | .07 |
| 334 | J.R. Phillips | .15 | .07 |
| 335 | Barry Bonds | 1.00 | .45 |
| 336 | Mark Portugal | .15 | .07 |
| 337 | Terry Mulholland | .15 | .07 |
| 338 | Omar Vizquel | .30 | .14 |
| 339 | Carlos Baerga | .15 | .07 |
| 340 | Albert Belle | .30 | .14 |
| 341 | Eddie Murray | .60 | .25 |
| 342 | Wayne Kirby | .15 | .07 |
| 343 | Chad Ogea | .15 | .07 |
| 344 | Tim Davis | .15 | .07 |
| 345 | Jay Buhner | .30 | .14 |
| 346 | Bobby Ayala | .15 | .07 |
| 347 | Mike Blowers | .15 | .07 |
| 348 | Dave Fleming | .15 | .07 |
| 349 | Edgar Martinez | .30 | .14 |
| 350 | Andre Dawson | .30 | .14 |
| 351 | Darrell Whitmore | .15 | .07 |
| 352 | Chuck Carr | .15 | .07 |
| 353 | John Burkett | .15 | .07 |
| 354 | Chris Hammond | .15 | .07 |
| 355 | Gary Sheffield | .60 | .25 |
| 356 | Pat Rapp | .15 | .07 |
| 357 | Greg Colbrunn | .15 | .07 |
| 358 | David Segui | .15 | .07 |
| 359 | Jeff Kent | .30 | .14 |
| 360 | Bobby Bonilla | .30 | .14 |
| 361 | Pete Harnisch | .15 | .07 |
| 362 | Ryan Thompson | .15 | .07 |
| 363 | Jose Vizcaino | .15 | .07 |
| 364 | Brett Butler | .30 | .14 |
| 365 | Cal Ripken Jr. | 2.50 | 1.10 |
| 366 | Rafael Palmeiro | .60 | .25 |
| 367 | Leo Gomez | .15 | .07 |
| 368 | Andy Van Slyke | .30 | .14 |
| 369 | Arthur Rhodes | .15 | .07 |

❑ 370 Ken Caminiti .30 .14
❑ 371 Steve Finley .30 .14
❑ 372 Melvin Nieves .15 .07
❑ 373 Andujar Cedeno .15 .07
❑ 374 Trevor Hoffman .30 .14
❑ 375 Fernando Valenzuela .30 .14
❑ 376 Ricky Bottalico .15 .07
❑ 377 Dave Hollins .15 .07
❑ 378 Charlie Hayes .15 .07
❑ 379 Tommy Greene .15 .07
❑ 380 Darren Daulton .30 .14
❑ 381 Curt Schilling .30 .14
❑ 382 Midre Cummings .15 .07
❑ 383 Al Martin .15 .07
❑ 384 Jeff King .15 .07
❑ 385 Orlando Merced .15 .07
❑ 386 Denny Neagle .30 .14
❑ 387 Don Slaught .15 .07
❑ 388 Dave Clark .15 .07
❑ 389 Kevin Gross .15 .07
❑ 390 Will Clark .60 .25
❑ 391 Ivan Rodriguez .75 .35
❑ 392 Benji Gil .15 .07
❑ 393 Jeff Frye .15 .07
❑ 394 Kenny Rogers .15 .07
❑ 395 Juan Gonzalez .60 .25
❑ 396 Mike Macfarlane .15 .07
❑ 397 Lee Tinsley .15 .07
❑ 398 Tim Naehring .15 .07
❑ 399 Tim Vanegmond .15 .07
❑ 400 Mike Greenwell .15 .07
❑ 401 Ken Ryan .15 .07
❑ 402 John Smiley .15 .07
❑ 403 Tim Pugh .15 .07
❑ 404 Reggie Sanders .15 .07
❑ 405 Barry Larkin .60 .25
❑ 406 Hal Morris .15 .07
❑ 407 Jose Rijo .15 .07
❑ 408 Lance Painter .15 .07
❑ 409 Joe Girardi .15 .07
❑ 410 Andres Galarraga .30 .14
❑ 411 Mike Kingery .15 .07
❑ 412 Roberto Mejia .15 .07
❑ 413 Walt Weiss .15 .07
❑ 414 Bill Swift .15 .07
❑ 415 Larry Walker .30 .14
❑ 416 Billy Brewer .15 .07
❑ 417 Pat Borders .15 .07
❑ 418 Tom Gordon .15 .07
❑ 419 Kevin Appier .30 .14
❑ 420 Gary Gaetti .30 .14
❑ 421 Greg Gohr .15 .07
❑ 422 Felipe Lira .15 .07
❑ 423 John Doherty .15 .07
❑ 424 Chad Curtis .15 .07
❑ 425 Cecil Fielder .30 .14
❑ 426 Alan Trammell .30 .14
❑ 427 David McCarty .15 .07
❑ 428 Scott Erickson .15 .07
❑ 429 Pat Mahomes .15 .07
❑ 430 Kirby Puckett 1.50 .70
❑ 431 Dave Stevens .15 .07
❑ 432 Pedro Munoz .15 .07
❑ 433 Chris Sabo .15 .07
❑ 434 Alex Fernandez .15 .07
❑ 435 Frank Thomas 1.25 .55
❑ 436 Roberto Hernandez .15 .07
❑ 437 Lance Johnson .15 .07
❑ 438 Jim Abbott .30 .14
❑ 439 John Wetteland .30 .14
❑ 440 Melido Perez .15 .07
❑ 441 Tony Fernandez .15 .07
❑ 442 Pat Kelly .15 .07
❑ 443 Mike Stanley .15 .07
❑ 444 Danny Tartabull .15 .07
❑ 445 Wade Boggs .75 .35
❑ 446 Robin Yount .60 .25
❑ 447 Ryne Sandberg .75 .35
❑ 448 Nolan Ryan 3.00 1.35
❑ 449 George Brett 1.25 .55
❑ 450 Mike Schmidt 1.00 .45
❑ 451 Jim Abbott TRADE 1.00 .45
❑ 452 Danny Tartabull TRADE .50 .23
❑ 453 Ariel Prieto TRADE .50 .23
❑ 454 Scott Cooper TRADE .50 .23
❑ 455 Tom Henke TRADE .50 .23
❑ 456 Todd Zeile TRADE .50 .23
❑ 457 Brian McRae TRADE .50 .23
❑ 458 Luis Gonzalez TRADE 1.00 .45
❑ 459 Jaime Navarro TRADE .50 .23
❑ 460 Todd Worrell TRADE .50 .23
❑ 461 Roberto Kelly TRADE .50 .23
❑ 462 Chad Fonville TRADE .50 .23
❑ 463 Shane Andrews TRADE .50 .23
❑ 464 David Segui TRADE .15 .07
❑ 465 Deion Sanders TRADE 1.00 .45
❑ 466 Orel Hershiser TRADE 1.00 .45
❑ 467 Ken Hill TRADE .50 .23
❑ 468 Andy Benes TRADE .50 .23
❑ 469 Terry Pendleton TRADE .50 .23
❑ 470 Bobby Bonilla TRADE 1.00 .45
❑ 471 Scott Erickson TRADE .50 .23
❑ 472 Kevin Brown TRADE 1.50 .70
❑ 473 Glenn Dishman TRADE .50 .23
❑ 474 Phil Plantier TRADE .50 .23
❑ 475 Gregg Jefferies TRADE .50 .23
❑ 476 Tyler Green TRADE .50 .23
❑ 477 H. Slocumb TRADE .50 .23
❑ 478 Mark Whiten TRADE .50 .23
❑ 479 Mickey Tettleton TRADE .50 .23
❑ 480 Tim Wakefield TRADE .50 .23
❑ 481 V. Eshelman TRADE .50 .23
❑ 482 Rick Aguilera TRADE .50 .23
❑ 483 Erik Hanson TRADE .50 .23
❑ 484 Willie McGee TRADE 1.00 .45
❑ 485 Troy O'Leary TRADE .50 .23
❑ 486 Benito Santiago TRADE .50 .23
❑ 487 Darren Lewis TRADE .50 .23
❑ 488 Dave Burba TRADE .50 .23
❑ 489 Ron Gant TRADE .50 .23
❑ 490 Bret Saberhagen TRADE 1.00 .45
❑ 491 Vinny Castilla TRADE 1.00 .45
❑ 492 Frank Rodriguez TRADE .50 .23
❑ 493 Andy Pettitte TRADE 1.50 .70
❑ 494 Ruben Sierra TRADE .50 .23
❑ 495 David Cone TRADE 1.00 .45
❑ J159 R. Clemens Jumbo AU 40.00 18.00
❑ J215 A. Rodriguez Jumbo AU 80.00 36.00
❑ P100 Ken Griffey Jr. Promo 30.00 1.35

## 1996 Upper Deck

| | MINT | NRMT |
|---|---|---|
| COMPLETE SET (480) | 60.00 | 27.00 |
| COMP.FACT.SET (510) | 80.00 | 36.00 |
| COMPLETE SERIES 1 (240) | 30.00 | 13.50 |
| COMPLETE SERIES 2 (240) | 30.00 | 13.50 |
| COMMON CARD (1-480) | .15 | .07 |
| COMP.UPDATE SET (30) | 20.00 | 9.00 |
| COMMON UPDATE (481U-510U) | .50 | .23 |

❑ 1 Cal Ripken 2131 4.00 1.80
❑ 2 Eddie Murray 3000 Hits .60 .25
❑ 3 Mark Wohlers .15 .07
❑ 4 David Justice .40 .18
❑ 5 Chipper Jones 1.50 .70
❑ 6 Javier Lopez .25 .11
❑ 7 Mark Lemke .15 .07
❑ 8 Marquis Grissom .15 .07
❑ 9 Tom Glavine .60 .25
❑ 10 Greg Maddux 1.50 .70
❑ 11 Manny Alexander .15 .07
❑ 12 Curtis Goodwin .15 .07
❑ 13 Scott Erickson .15 .07
❑ 14 Chris Hoiles .15 .07
❑ 15 Rafael Palmeiro .60 .25
❑ 16 Rick Krivda .15 .07
❑ 17 Jeff Manto .15 .07
❑ 18 Mo Vaughn .25 .11
❑ 19 Tim Wakefield .15 .07
❑ 20 Roger Clemens 1.25 .55
❑ 21 Tim Naehring .15 .07
❑ 22 Troy O'Leary .15 .07
❑ 23 Mike Greenwell .15 .07
❑ 24 Stan Belinda .15 .07
❑ 25 John Valentin .15 .07
❑ 26 J.T. Snow .25 .11
❑ 27 Gary DiSarcina .15 .07
❑ 28 Mark Langston .15 .07
❑ 29 Brian Anderson .15 .07
❑ 30 Jim Edmonds .60 .25
❑ 31 Garret Anderson .25 .11
❑ 32 Orlando Palmeiro .15 .07
❑ 33 Brian McRae .15 .07
❑ 34 Kevin Foster .15 .07
❑ 35 Sammy Sosa 1.25 .55
❑ 36 Todd Zeile .15 .07
❑ 37 Jim Bullinger .15 .07
❑ 38 Luis Gonzalez .25 .11
❑ 39 Lyle Mouton .15 .07
❑ 40 Ray Durham .25 .11
❑ 41 Ozzie Guillen .15 .07
❑ 42 Alex Fernandez .15 .07
❑ 43 Brian Keyser .15 .07
❑ 44 Robin Ventura .25 .11
❑ 45 Reggie Sanders .15 .07
❑ 46 Pete Schourek .15 .07
❑ 47 John Smiley .15 .07
❑ 48 Jeff Brantley .15 .07
❑ 49 Thomas Howard .15 .07
❑ 50 Bret Boone .25 .11
❑ 51 Kevin Jarvis .15 .07
❑ 52 Jeff Branson .15 .07
❑ 53 Carlos Baerga .15 .07
❑ 54 Jim Thome .40 .18
❑ 55 Manny Ramirez .75 .35
❑ 56 Omar Vizquel .25 .11
❑ 57 Jose Mesa .15 .07
❑ 58 Julian Tavarez UER .15 .07
❑ 59 Orel Hershiser .25 .11
❑ 60 Larry Walker .25 .11
❑ 61 Bret Saberhagen .25 .11
❑ 62 Vinny Castilla .25 .11
❑ 63 Eric Young .15 .07
❑ 64 Bryan Rekar .15 .07
❑ 65 Andres Galarraga .40 .18
❑ 66 Steve Reed .15 .07
❑ 67 Chad Curtis .15 .07
❑ 68 Bobby Higginson .25 .11
❑ 69 Phil Nevin .25 .11
❑ 70 Cecil Fielder .25 .11
❑ 71 Felipe Lira .15 .07
❑ 72 Chris Gomez .15 .07
❑ 73 Charles Johnson .25 .11
❑ 74 Quilvio Veras .15 .07
❑ 75 Jeff Conine .15 .07
❑ 76 John Burkett .15 .07
❑ 77 Greg Colbrunn .15 .07
❑ 78 Terry Pendleton .25 .11
❑ 79 Shane Reynolds .15 .07
❑ 80 Jeff Bagwell .75 .35
❑ 81 Orlando Miller .15 .07
❑ 82 Mike Hampton .25 .11
❑ 83 James Mouton .15 .07
❑ 84 Brian L. Hunter .15 .07
❑ 85 Derek Bell .15 .07
❑ 86 Kevin Appier .25 .11
❑ 87 Joe Vitiello .15 .07
❑ 88 Wally Joyner .25 .11
❑ 89 Michael Tucker .15 .07
❑ 90 Johnny Damon .25 .11
❑ 91 Jon Nunnally .15 .07
❑ 92 Jason Jacome .15 .07
❑ 93 Chad Fonville .15 .07
❑ 94 Chan Ho Park .25 .11
❑ 95 Hideo Nomo .60 .25
❑ 96 Ismael Valdes .15 .07
❑ 97 Greg Gagne .15 .07
❑ 98 Diamondbacks-Devil Rays .60 .25
❑ 99 Raul Mondesi .25 .11

❑ 100 Dave Winfield YH .25 .11
❑ 101 Dennis Eckersley YH .15 .07
❑ 102 Andre Dawson YH .25 .11
❑ 103 Dennis Martinez YH .15 .07
❑ 104 Lance Parrish YH .15 .07
❑ 105 Eddie Murray YH .25 .11
❑ 106 Alan Trammell YH .25 .11
❑ 107 Lou Whitaker YH .15 .07
❑ 108 Ozzie Smith YH .40 .18
❑ 109 Paul Molitor YH .25 .11
❑ 110 Rickey Henderson YH .40 .18
❑ 111 Tim Raines YH .15 .07
❑ 112 Harold Baines YH .15 .07
❑ 113 Lee Smith YH .15 .07
❑ 114 Fernando Valenzuela YH .15 .07
❑ 115 Cal Ripken YH 1.25 .55
❑ 116 Tony Gwynn YH .60 .25
❑ 117 Wade Boggs .75 .35
❑ 118 Todd Hollandsworth .15 .07
❑ 119 Dave Nilsson .15 .07
❑ 120 Jose Valentin .15 .07
❑ 121 Steve Sparks .15 .07
❑ 122 Chuck Carr .15 .07
❑ 123 John Jaha .15 .07
❑ 124 Scott Karl .15 .07
❑ 125 Chuck Knoblauch .25 .11
❑ 126 Brad Radke .25 .11
❑ 127 Pat Meares .15 .07
❑ 128 Ron Coomer .15 .07
❑ 129 Pedro Munoz .15 .07
❑ 130 Kirby Puckett 1.50 .70
❑ 131 David Segui .15 .07
❑ 132 Mark Grudzielanek .15 .07
❑ 133 Mike Lansing .15 .07
❑ 134 Sean Berry .15 .07
❑ 135 Rondell White .25 .11
❑ 136 Pedro Martinez .75 .35
❑ 137 Carl Everett .25 .11
❑ 138 Dave Mlicki .15 .07
❑ 139 Bill Pulsipher .15 .07
❑ 140 Jason Isringhausen .25 .11
❑ 141 Rico Brogna .15 .07
❑ 142 Edgardo Alfonzo .25 .11
❑ 143 Jeff Kent .40 .18
❑ 144 Andy Pettitte .25 .11
❑ 145 Mike Piazza BO 1.00 .45
❑ 146 Cliff Floyd BO .15 .07
❑ 147 Jason Isringhausen BO .15 .07
❑ 148 Tim Wakefield BO .15 .07
❑ 149 Chipper Jones BO .75 .35
❑ 150 Hideo Nomo BO .25 .11
❑ 151 Mark McGwire BO 1.25 .55
❑ 152 Ron Gant BO .15 .07
❑ 153 Gary Gaetti BO .15 .07
❑ 154 Don Mattingly 1.50 .70
❑ 155 Paul O'Neill .25 .11
❑ 156 Derek Jeter 2.50 1.10
❑ 157 Joe Girardi .15 .07
❑ 158 Ruben Sierra .15 .07
❑ 159 Jorge Posada .25 .11
❑ 160 Geronimo Berroa .15 .07
❑ 161 Steve Ontiveros .15 .07
❑ 162 George Williams .15 .07
❑ 163 Doug Johns .15 .07
❑ 164 Ariel Prieto .15 .07
❑ 165 Scott Brosius .25 .11
❑ 166 Mike Bordick .15 .07
❑ 167 Tyler Green .15 .07
❑ 168 Mickey Morandini .15 .07
❑ 169 Darren Daulton .25 .11
❑ 170 Gregg Jefferies .15 .07
❑ 171 Jim Eisenreich .15 .07
❑ 172 Heathcliff Slocumb .15 .07
❑ 173 Kevin Stocker .15 .07
❑ 174 Esteban Loaiza .15 .07
❑ 175 Jeff King .15 .07
❑ 176 Mark Johnson .15 .07
❑ 177 Denny Neagle .25 .11
❑ 178 Orlando Merced .15 .07
❑ 179 Carlos Garcia .15 .07
❑ 180 Brian Jordan .25 .11
❑ 181 Mike Morgan .15 .07
❑ 182 Mark Petkovsek .15 .07
❑ 183 Bernard Gilkey .15 .07
❑ 184 John Mabry .15 .07
❑ 185 Tom Henke .15 .07

❑ 186 Glenn Dishman .15 .07
❑ 187 Andy Ashby .15 .07
❑ 188 Bip Roberts .15 .07
❑ 189 Melvin Nieves .15 .07
❑ 190 Ken Caminiti .25 .11
❑ 191 Brad Ausmus .15 .07
❑ 192 Deion Sanders .25 .11
❑ 193 Jamie Brewington RC .15 .07
❑ 194 Glenallen Hill .15 .07
❑ 195 Barry Bonds 1.00 .45
❑ 196 Wm. Van Landingham .15 .07
❑ 197 Mark Carreon .15 .07
❑ 198 Royce Clayton .15 .07
❑ 199 Joey Cora .15 .07
❑ 200 Ken Griffey Jr. 2.50 1.10
❑ 201 Jay Buhner .25 .11
❑ 202 Alex Rodriguez 2.00 .90
❑ 203 Norm Charlton .15 .07
❑ 204 Andy Benes .15 .07
❑ 205 Edgar Martinez .40 .18
❑ 206 Juan Gonzalez .60 .25
❑ 207 Will Clark .60 .25
❑ 208 Kevin Gross .15 .07
❑ 209 Roger Pavlik .15 .07
❑ 210 Ivan Rodriguez .75 .35
❑ 211 Rusty Greer .25 .11
❑ 212 Angel Martinez .15 .07
❑ 213 Tomas Perez .15 .07
❑ 214 Alex Gonzalez .15 .07
❑ 215 Joe Carter .25 .11
❑ 216 Shawn Green .60 .25
❑ 217 Edwin Hurtado .15 .07
❑ 218 Edgar Martinez .15 .07
Tony Pena CL
❑ 219 Chipper Jones .60 .25
Barry Larkin CL
❑ 220 Orel Hershiser CL .15 .07
❑ 221 Mike Devereaux CL .15 .07
❑ 222 Tom Glavine CL .25 .11
❑ 223 Karim Garcia .15 .07
❑ 224 Arquimedez Pozo .15 .07
❑ 225 Billy Wagner .15 .07
❑ 226 John Wasdin .15 .07
❑ 227 Jeff Suppan .15 .07
❑ 228 Steve Gibralter .15 .07
❑ 229 Jimmy Haynes .15 .07
❑ 230 Ruben Rivera .15 .07
❑ 231 Chris Snopek .15 .07
❑ 232 Alex Ochoa .15 .07
❑ 233 Shannon Stewart .25 .11
❑ 234 Quinton McCracken .15 .07
❑ 235 Trey Beamon .15 .07
❑ 236 Billy McMillon .15 .07
❑ 237 Steve Cox .15 .07
❑ 238 George Arias .15 .07
❑ 239 Yamil Benitez .15 .07
❑ 240 Todd Greene .15 .07
❑ 241 Jason Kendall .25 .11
❑ 242 Brooks Kieschnick .15 .07
❑ 243 Osvaldo Fernandez RC .15 .07
❑ 244 Livan Hernandez RC .75 .35
❑ 245 Rey Ordonez .15 .07
❑ 246 Mike Grace RC .15 .07
❑ 247 Jay Canizaro .15 .07
❑ 248 Bob Wolcott .15 .07
❑ 249 Jermaine Dye .25 .11
❑ 250 Jason Schmidt .15 .07
❑ 251 Mike Sweeney RC 2.50 1.10
❑ 252 Marcus Jensen .15 .07
❑ 253 Mendy Lopez .15 .07
❑ 254 Wilton Guerrero RC .40 .18
❑ 255 Paul Wilson .15 .07
❑ 256 Edgar Renteria .25 .11
❑ 257 Richard Hidalgo .25 .11
❑ 258 Bob Abreu .75 .35
❑ 259 Robert Smith RC .40 .18
❑ 260 Sal Fasano .15 .07
❑ 261 Enrique Wilson .15 .07
❑ 262 Rich Hunter RC .15 .07
❑ 263 Sergio Nunez .15 .07
❑ 264 Dan Serafini .15 .07
❑ 265 David Doster .15 .07
❑ 266 Ryan McGuire .15 .07
❑ 267 Scott Spiezio .15 .07
❑ 268 Rafael Orellano .15 .07
❑ 269 Steve Avery .15 .07

❑ 270 Fred McGriff .40 .18
❑ 271 John Smoltz .25 .11
❑ 272 Ryan Klesko .25 .11
❑ 273 Jeff Blauser .15 .07
❑ 274 Brad Clontz .15 .07
❑ 275 Roberto Alomar .60 .25
❑ 276 B.J. Surhoff .25 .11
❑ 277 Jeffrey Hammonds .25 .11
❑ 278 Brady Anderson .25 .11
❑ 279 Bobby Bonilla .25 .11
❑ 280 Cal Ripken 2.50 1.10
❑ 281 Mike Mussina .60 .25
❑ 282 Wil Cordero .15 .07
❑ 283 Mike Stanley .15 .07
❑ 284 Aaron Sele .25 .11
❑ 285 Jose Canseco .75 .35
❑ 286 Tom Gordon .15 .07
❑ 287 Heathcliff Slocumb .15 .07
❑ 288 Lee Smith .25 .11
❑ 289 Troy Percival .15 .07
❑ 290 Tim Salmon .25 .11
❑ 291 Chuck Finley .25 .11
❑ 292 Jim Abbott .25 .11
❑ 293 Chili Davis .25 .11
❑ 294 Steve Trachsel .15 .07
❑ 295 Mark Grace .60 .25
❑ 296 Rey Sanchez .15 .07
❑ 297 Scott Servais .15 .07
❑ 298 Jaime Navarro .15 .07
❑ 299 Frank Castillo .15 .07
❑ 300 Frank Thomas 1.25 .55
❑ 301 Jason Bere .15 .07
❑ 302 Danny Tartabull .15 .07
❑ 303 Darren Lewis .15 .07
❑ 304 Roberto Hernandez .15 .07
❑ 305 Tony Phillips .15 .07
❑ 306 Wilson Alvarez .15 .07
❑ 307 Jose Rijo .15 .07
❑ 308 Hal Morris .15 .07
❑ 309 Mark Portugal .15 .07
❑ 310 Barry Larkin .60 .25
❑ 311 Dave Burba .15 .07
❑ 312 Ed Taubensee .15 .07
❑ 313 Sandy Alomar Jr. .25 .11
❑ 314 Dennis Martinez .25 .11
❑ 315 Albert Belle .40 .18
❑ 316 Eddie Murray .60 .25
❑ 317 Charles Nagy .15 .07
❑ 318 Chad Ogea .15 .07
❑ 319 Kenny Lofton .25 .11
❑ 320 Dante Bichette .25 .11
❑ 321 Armando Reynoso .15 .07
❑ 322 Walt Weiss .15 .07
❑ 323 Ellis Burks .25 .11
❑ 324 Kevin Ritz .15 .07
❑ 325 Bill Swift .15 .07
❑ 326 Jason Bates .15 .07
❑ 327 Tony Clark .15 .07
❑ 328 Travis Fryman .25 .11
❑ 329 Mark Parent .15 .07
❑ 330 Alan Trammell .40 .18
❑ 331 C.J. Nitkowski .15 .07
❑ 332 Jose Lima .15 .07
❑ 333 Phil Plantier .15 .07
❑ 334 Kurt Abbott .15 .07
❑ 335 Andre Dawson .40 .18
❑ 336 Chris Hammond .15 .07
❑ 337 Robb Nen .15 .07
❑ 338 Pat Rapp .15 .07
❑ 339 Al Leiter .25 .11
❑ 340 Gary Sheffield UER .60 .25
(HR total says 17
❑ 341 Todd Jones .15 .07
❑ 342 Doug Drabek .15 .07
❑ 343 Greg Swindell .15 .07
❑ 344 Tony Eusebio .15 .07
❑ 345 Craig Biggio .40 .18
❑ 346 Darryl Kile .25 .11
❑ 347 Mike Macfarlane .15 .07
❑ 348 Jeff Montgomery .15 .07
❑ 349 Chris Haney .15 .07
❑ 350 Bip Roberts .15 .07
❑ 351 Tom Goodwin .15 .07
❑ 352 Mark Gubicza .15 .07
❑ 353 Joe Randa .15 .07
❑ 354 Ramon Martinez .15 .07

❑ 355 Eric Karros .25 .11
❑ 356 Delino DeShields .15 .07
❑ 357 Brett Butler .25 .11
❑ 358 Todd Worrell .15 .07
❑ 359 Mike Blowers .15 .07
❑ 360 Mike Piazza 2.00 .90
❑ 361 Ben McDonald .15 .07
❑ 362 Ricky Bones .15 .07
❑ 363 Greg Vaughn .25 .11
❑ 364 Matt Mieske .15 .07
❑ 365 Kevin Seitzer .15 .07
❑ 366 Jeff Cirillo .25 .11
❑ 367 LaTroy Hawkins .15 .07
❑ 368 Frank Rodriguez .15 .07
❑ 369 Rick Aguilera .15 .07
❑ 370 Roberto Alomar BG .25 .11
❑ 371 Albert Belle BG .25 .11
❑ 372 Wade Boggs BG .40 .18
❑ 373 Barry Bonds BG .60 .25
❑ 374 Roger Clemens BG .60 .25
❑ 375 Dennis Eckersley BG .15 .07
❑ 376 Ken Griffey Jr. BG 1.25 .55
❑ 377 Tony Gwynn BG .60 .25
❑ 378 Rickey Henderson BG .40 .18
❑ 379 Greg Maddux BG .75 .35
❑ 380 Fred McGriff BG .25 .11
❑ 381 Paul Molitor BG .25 .11
❑ 382 Eddie Murray BG .25 .11
❑ 383 Mike Piazza BG 1.00 .45
❑ 384 Kirby Puckett BG .75 .35
❑ 385 Cal Ripken BG 1.25 .55
❑ 386 Ozzie Smith BG .40 .18
❑ 387 Frank Thomas BG .60 .25
❑ 388 Matt Walbeck .15 .07
❑ 389 Dave Stevens .15 .07
❑ 390 Marty Cordova .15 .07
❑ 391 Darrin Fletcher .15 .07
❑ 392 Cliff Floyd .25 .11
❑ 393 Mel Rojas .15 .07
❑ 394 Shane Andrews .15 .07
❑ 395 Moises Alou .25 .11
❑ 396 Carlos Perez .15 .07
❑ 397 Jeff Fassero .15 .07
❑ 398 Bobby Jones .15 .07
❑ 399 Todd Hundley .15 .07
❑ 400 John Franco .25 .11
❑ 401 Jose Vizcaino .15 .07
❑ 402 Bernard Gilkey .15 .07
❑ 403 Pete Harnisch .15 .07
❑ 404 Pat Kelly .15 .07
❑ 405 David Cone .25 .11
❑ 406 Bernie Williams .60 .25
❑ 407 John Wetteland .25 .11
❑ 408 Scott Kamieniecki .15 .07
❑ 409 Tim Raines .25 .11
❑ 410 Wade Boggs .75 .35
❑ 411 Terry Steinbach .15 .07
❑ 412 Jason Giambi .60 .25
❑ 413 Todd Van Poppel .15 .07
❑ 414 Pedro Munoz .15 .07
❑ 415 Eddie Murray SBT .25 .11
❑ 416 Dennis Eckersley SBT .15 .07
❑ 417 Bip Roberts SBT .15 .07
❑ 418 Glenallen Hill SBT .15 .07
❑ 419 John Hudek SBT .15 .07
❑ 420 Derek Bell SBT .15 .07
❑ 421 Larry Walker SBT .15 .07
❑ 422 Greg Maddux SBT .75 .35
❑ 423 Ken Caminiti SBT .15 .07
❑ 424 Brent Gates .15 .07
❑ 425 Mark McGwire 2.50 1.10
❑ 426 Mark Whiten .15 .07
❑ 427 Sid Fernandez .15 .07
❑ 428 Ricky Bottalico .15 .07
❑ 429 Mike Mimbs .15 .07
❑ 430 Lenny Dykstra .25 .11
❑ 431 Todd Zeile .15 .07
❑ 432 Benito Santiago .15 .07
❑ 433 Danny Miceli .15 .07
❑ 434 Al Martin .15 .07
❑ 435 Jay Bell .25 .11
❑ 436 Charlie Hayes .15 .07
❑ 437 Mike Kingery .15 .07
❑ 438 Paul Wagner .15 .07
❑ 439 Tom Pagnozzi .15 .07
❑ 440 Ozzie Smith .75 .35
❑ 441 Ray Lankford .25 .11
❑ 442 Dennis Eckersley .25 .11
❑ 443 Ron Gant .15 .07
❑ 444 Alan Benes .15 .07
❑ 445 Rickey Henderson .75 .35
❑ 446 Jody Reed .15 .07
❑ 447 Trevor Hoffman .25 .11
❑ 448 Andujar Cedeno .15 .07
❑ 449 Steve Finley .25 .11
❑ 450 Tony Gwynn 1.25 .55
❑ 451 Joey Hamilton .15 .07
❑ 452 Mark Leiter .15 .07
❑ 453 Rod Beck .15 .07
❑ 454 Kirt Manwaring .15 .07
❑ 455 Matt Williams .40 .18
❑ 456 Robby Thompson .15 .07
❑ 457 Shawon Dunston .15 .07
❑ 458 Russ Davis .15 .07
❑ 459 Paul Sorrento .15 .07
❑ 460 Randy Johnson .75 .35
❑ 461 Chris Bosio .15 .07
❑ 462 Luis Sojo .15 .07
❑ 463 Sterling Hitchcock .15 .07
❑ 464 Benji Gil .15 .07
❑ 465 Mickey Tettleton .15 .07
❑ 466 Mark McLemore .15 .07
❑ 467 Darryl Hamilton .15 .07
❑ 468 Ken Hill .15 .07
❑ 469 Dean Palmer .25 .11
❑ 470 Carlos Delgado .60 .25
❑ 471 Ed Sprague .15 .07
❑ 472 Otis Nixon .15 .07
❑ 473 Pat Hentgen .15 .07
❑ 474 Juan Guzman .15 .07
❑ 475 John Olerud .25 .11
❑ 476 Buck Showalter CL .15 .07
❑ 477 Bobby Cox CL .15 .07
❑ 478 Tommy Lasorda CL .25 .11
❑ 479 Buck Showalter CL .15 .07
❑ 480 Sparky Anderson CL .25 .11
❑ 481U Randy Myers .50 .23
❑ 482U Kent Mercker .50 .23
❑ 483U David Wells .75 .35
❑ 484U Kevin Mitchell .50 .23
❑ 485U Randy Velarde .50 .23
❑ 486U Ryne Sandberg 2.50 1.10
❑ 487U Doug Jones .50 .23
❑ 488U Terry Adams .50 .23
❑ 489U Kevin Tapani .50 .23
❑ 490U Harold Baines .75 .35
❑ 491U Eric Davis .75 .35
❑ 492U Julio Franco .75 .35
❑ 493U Jack McDowell .50 .23
❑ 494U Devon White .75 .35
❑ 495U Kevin Brown .75 .35
❑ 496U Rick Wilkins .50 .23
❑ 497U Sean Berry .50 .23
❑ 498U Keith Lockhart .50 .23
❑ 499U Mark Loretta .50 .23
❑ 500U Paul Molitor 2.00 .90
❑ 501U Roberto Kelly .50 .23
❑ 502U Lance Johnson .50 .23
❑ 503U Tino Martinez .75 .35
❑ 504U Kenny Rogers .50 .23
❑ 505U Todd Stottlemyre .50 .23
❑ 506U Gary Gaetti .75 .35
❑ 507U Royce Clayton .50 .23
❑ 508U Andy Benes .50 .23
❑ 509U Wally Joyner .75 .35
❑ 510U Erik Hanson .50 .23

## 1997 Upper Deck

| | MINT | NRMT |
|---|---|---|
| COMP.MASTER SET (550) | 230.00 | 105.00 |
| COMPLETE SET (490) | 120.00 | 55.00 |
| COMPLETE SERIES 1 (240) | 40.00 | 18.00 |
| COMPLETE SERIES 2 (250) | 80.00 | 36.00 |
| COMP.SER.2 w/o GHL (240) | 20.00 | 9.00 |
| COMMON (1-240/271-520) | .15 | .07 |
| COMP.UPDATE SET (30) | 80.00 | 36.00 |
| COMMON UPDATE (241-270) | 1.00 | .45 |
| COMMON GHL (415-424) | 1.50 | .70 |
| COMP.TRADE SET (30) | 20.00 | 9.00 |
| COMMON TRADE (521-550) | .50 | .23 |

❑ 1 Jackie Robinson .50 .23
The Beginnings
❑ 2 Jackie Robinson .50 .23
Breaking the Barrier
❑ 3 Jackie Robinson .50 .23
The MVP Season, 1949
❑ 4 Jackie Robinson .50 .23
1951 season
❑ 5 Jackie Robinson .50 .23
1952 and 1953 seasons
❑ 6 Jackie Robinson .50 .23
1954 season
❑ 7 Jackie Robinson .50 .23
1955 season
❑ 8 Jackie Robinson .50 .23
1956 season
❑ 9 Jackie Robinson .50 .23
Hall of Fame
❑ 10 Chipper Jones 1.50 .70
❑ 11 Marquis Grissom .15 .07
❑ 12 Jermaine Dye .25 .11
❑ 13 Mark Lemke .15 .07
❑ 14 Terrell Wade .15 .07
❑ 15 Fred McGriff .40 .18
❑ 16 Tom Glavine .60 .25
❑ 17 Mark Wohlers .15 .07
❑ 18 Randy Myers .15 .07
❑ 19 Roberto Alomar .60 .25
❑ 20 Cal Ripken 2.50 1.10
❑ 21 Rafael Palmeiro .60 .25
❑ 22 Mike Mussina .60 .25
❑ 23 Brady Anderson .25 .11
❑ 24 Jose Canseco .75 .35
❑ 25 Mo Vaughn .25 .11
❑ 26 Roger Clemens 1.25 .55
❑ 27 Tim Naehring .15 .07
❑ 28 Jeff Suppan .15 .07
❑ 29 Troy Percival .15 .07
❑ 30 Sammy Sosa 1.25 .55
❑ 31 Amaury Telemaco .15 .07
❑ 32 Rey Sanchez .15 .07
❑ 33 Scott Servais .15 .07
❑ 34 Steve Trachsel .15 .07
❑ 35 Mark Grace .60 .25
❑ 36 Wilson Alvarez .15 .07
❑ 37 Harold Baines .25 .11
❑ 38 Tony Phillips .15 .07
❑ 39 James Baldwin .25 .11
❑ 40 Frank Thomas UER 1.25 .55
(Bio information is Ken Griffey Jr.'s)
❑ 41 Lyle Mouton .15 .07
❑ 42 Chris Snopek .15 .07
❑ 43 Hal Morris .15 .07
❑ 44 Eric Davis .25 .11
❑ 45 Barry Larkin .60 .25
❑ 46 Reggie Sanders .15 .07
❑ 47 Pete Schourek .15 .07
❑ 48 Lee Smith .25 .11
❑ 49 Charles Nagy .15 .07
❑ 50 Albert Belle .40 .18
❑ 51 Julio Franco .25 .11
❑ 52 Kenny Lofton .25 .11
❑ 53 Orel Hershiser .25 .11
❑ 54 Omar Vizquel .25 .11
❑ 55 Eric Young .15 .07
❑ 56 Curtis Leskanic .15 .07
❑ 57 Quinton McCracken .15 .07
❑ 58 Kevin Ritz .15 .07

❑ 59 Walt Weiss .15 .07
❑ 60 Dante Bichette .25 .11
❑ 61 Mark Lewis .15 .07
❑ 62 Tony Clark .15 .07
❑ 63 Travis Fryman .25 .11
❑ 64 John Smoltz SF .15 .07
❑ 65 Greg Maddux SF .75 .35
❑ 66 Tom Glavine SF .25 .11
❑ 67 Mike Mussina SF .25 .11
❑ 68 Andy Pettitte SF .15 .07
❑ 69 Mariano Rivera SF .15 .07
❑ 70 Hideo Nomo SF .25 .11
❑ 71 Kevin Brown SF .15 .07
❑ 72 Randy Johnson SF .40 .18
❑ 73 Felipe Lira .15 .07
❑ 74 Kimera Bartee .15 .07
❑ 75 Alan Trammell .40 .18
❑ 76 Kevin Brown .25 .11
❑ 77 Edgar Renteria .25 .11
❑ 78 Al Leiter .25 .11
❑ 79 Charles Johnson .25 .11
❑ 80 Andre Dawson .40 .18
❑ 81 Billy Wagner .15 .07
❑ 82 Donne Wall .15 .07
❑ 83 Jeff Bagwell .75 .35
❑ 84 Keith Lockhart .15 .07
❑ 85 Jeff Montgomery .15 .07
❑ 86 Tom Goodwin .15 .07
❑ 87 Tim Belcher .15 .07
❑ 88 Mike Macfarlane .15 .07
❑ 89 Joe Randa .15 .07
❑ 90 Brett Butler .25 .11
❑ 91 Todd Worrell .15 .07
❑ 92 Todd Hollandsworth .15 .07
❑ 93 Ismael Valdes .15 .07
❑ 94 Hideo Nomo .60 .25
❑ 95 Mike Piazza 2.00 .90
❑ 96 Jeff Cirillo .25 .11
❑ 97 Ricky Bones .15 .07
❑ 98 Fernando Vina .15 .07
❑ 99 Ben McDonald .15 .07
❑ 100 John Jaha .15 .07
❑ 101 Mark Loretta .15 .07
❑ 102 Paul Molitor .60 .25
❑ 103 Rick Aguilera .15 .07
❑ 104 Marty Cordova .15 .07
❑ 105 Kirby Puckett 1.50 .70
❑ 106 Dan Naulty .15 .07
❑ 107 Frank Rodriguez .15 .07
❑ 108 Shane Andrews .15 .07
❑ 109 Henry Rodriguez .15 .07
❑ 110 Mark Grudzielanek .15 .07
❑ 111 Pedro Martinez .75 .35
❑ 112 Ugueth Urbina .15 .07
❑ 113 David Segui .15 .07
❑ 114 Rey Ordonez .15 .07
❑ 115 Bernard Gilkey .15 .07
❑ 116 Butch Huskey .15 .07
❑ 117 Paul Wilson .15 .07
❑ 118 Alex Ochoa .15 .07
❑ 119 John Franco .25 .11
❑ 120 Dwight Gooden .25 .11
❑ 121 Ruben Rivera .15 .07
❑ 122 Andy Pettitte .25 .11
❑ 123 Tino Martinez .25 .11
❑ 124 Bernie Williams .60 .25
❑ 125 Wade Boggs .75 .35
❑ 126 Paul O'Neill .25 .11
❑ 127 Scott Brosius .25 .11
❑ 128 Ernie Young .15 .07
❑ 129 Doug Johns .15 .07
❑ 130 Geronimo Berroa .15 .07
❑ 131 Jason Giambi .60 .25
❑ 132 John Wasdin .15 .07
❑ 133 Jim Eisenreich .15 .07
❑ 134 Ricky Otero .15 .07
❑ 135 Ricky Bottalico .15 .07
❑ 136 Mark Langston DG .15 .07
❑ 137 Greg Maddux DG .75 .35
❑ 138 Ivan Rodriguez DG .40 .18
❑ 139 Charles Johnson DG .15 .07
❑ 140 J.T. Snow DG .15 .07
❑ 141 Mark Grace DG .25 .11
❑ 142 Roberto Alomar DG .25 .11
❑ 143 Craig Biggio DG .25 .11
❑ 144 Ken Caminiti DG .15 .07
❑ 145 Matt Williams DG .25 .11
❑ 146 Omar Vizquel DG .15 .07
❑ 147 Cal Ripken DG 1.25 .55
❑ 148 Ozzie Smith DG .40 .18
❑ 149 Rey Ordonez DG .15 .07
❑ 150 Ken Griffey Jr. DG 1.25 .55
❑ 151 Devon White DG .15 .07
❑ 152 Barry Bonds DG .60 .25
❑ 153 Kenny Lofton DG .15 .07
❑ 154 Mickey Morandini .15 .07
❑ 155 Gregg Jefferies .15 .07
❑ 156 Curt Schilling .25 .11
❑ 157 Jason Kendall .25 .11
❑ 158 Francisco Cordova .15 .07
❑ 159 Dennis Eckersley .25 .11
❑ 160 Ron Gant .15 .07
❑ 161 Ozzie Smith .75 .35
❑ 162 Brian Jordan .25 .11
❑ 163 John Mabry .15 .07
❑ 164 Andy Ashby .15 .07
❑ 165 Steve Finley .25 .11
❑ 166 Fernando Valenzuela .25 .11
❑ 167 Archi Cianfrocco .15 .07
❑ 168 Wally Joyner .25 .11
❑ 169 Greg Vaughn .25 .11
❑ 170 Barry Bonds 1.00 .45
❑ 171 William VanLandingham .15 .07
❑ 172 Marvin Benard .15 .07
❑ 173 Rich Aurilia .25 .11
❑ 174 Jay Canizaro .15 .07
❑ 175 Ken Griffey Jr. 2.50 1.10
❑ 176 Bob Wells .15 .07
❑ 177 Jay Buhner .25 .11
❑ 178 Sterling Hitchcock .15 .07
❑ 179 Edgar Martinez .40 .18
❑ 180 Rusty Greer .25 .11
❑ 181 Dave Nilsson GI .15 .07
❑ 182 Larry Walker GI .15 .07
❑ 183 Edgar Renteria GI .15 .07
❑ 184 Rey Ordonez GI .15 .07
❑ 185 Rafael Palmeiro GI .25 .11
❑ 186 Osvaldo Fernandez GI .15 .07
❑ 187 Raul Mondesi GI .15 .07
❑ 188 Manny Ramirez GI .40 .18
❑ 189 Sammy Sosa GI .60 .25
❑ 190 Robert Eenhoorn GI .15 .07
❑ 191 Devon White GI .15 .07
❑ 192 Hideo Nomo GI .25 .11
❑ 193 Mac Suzuki GI .15 .07
❑ 194 Chan Ho Park GI .15 .07
❑ 195 Fernando Valenzuela GI .15 .07
❑ 196 Andruw Jones GI .40 .18
❑ 197 Vinny Castilla GI .15 .07
❑ 198 Dennis Martinez GI .15 .07
❑ 199 Ruben Rivera GI .15 .07
❑ 200 Juan Gonzalez GI .25 .11
❑ 201 Roberto Alomar GI .25 .11
❑ 202 Edgar Martinez GI .25 .11
❑ 203 Ivan Rodriguez GI .40 .18
❑ 204 Carlos Delgado GI .25 .11
❑ 205 Andres Galarraga GI .25 .11
❑ 206 Ozzie Guillen GI .15 .07
❑ 207 Midre Cummings GI .15 .07
❑ 208 Roger Pavlik .15 .07
❑ 209 Darren Oliver .15 .07
❑ 210 Dean Palmer .25 .11
❑ 211 Ivan Rodriguez .75 .35
❑ 212 Otis Nixon .15 .07
❑ 213 Pat Hentgen .15 .07
❑ 214 Ozzie Smith .25 .11
Andre Dawson
Kirby Puckett
HL/CL (1-27)
❑ 215 Barry Bonds .25 .11
Gary Sheffield
Brady Anderson
HL/CL (28-54)
❑ 216 Ken Caminiti SH CL .15 .07
❑ 217 John Smoltz SH CL .15 .07
❑ 218 Eric Young SH CL .15 .07
❑ 219 Juan Gonzalez SH CL .25 .11
❑ 220 Eddie Murray SH CL .25 .11
❑ 221 Tommy Lasorda SH CL .15 .07
❑ 222 Paul Molitor SH CL .25 .11
❑ 223 Luis Castillo .25 .11
❑ 224 Justin Thompson .15 .07
❑ 225 Rocky Coppinger .15 .07
❑ 226 Jermaine Allensworth .15 .07
❑ 227 Jeff D'Amico .15 .07
❑ 228 Jamey Wright .15 .07
❑ 229 Scott Rolen .60 .25
❑ 230 Darin Erstad .75 .35
❑ 231 Marty Janzen .15 .07
❑ 232 Jacob Cruz .15 .07
❑ 233 Raul Ibanez .15 .07
❑ 234 Nomar Garciaparra 2.00 .90
❑ 235 Todd Walker .15 .07
❑ 236 Brian Giles RC 2.00 .90
❑ 237 Matt Beech .15 .07
❑ 238 Mike Cameron .25 .11
❑ 239 Jose Paniagua .15 .07
❑ 240 Andruw Jones .75 .35
❑ 241 Brant Brown UPD 1.00 .45
❑ 242 Robin Jennings UPD 1.00 .45
❑ 243 Willie Adams UPD 1.00 .45
❑ 244 Ken Caminiti UPD 1.50 .70
❑ 245 Brian Jordan UPD 1.50 .70
❑ 246 Chipper Jones UPD 10.00 4.50
❑ 247 Juan Gonzalez UPD 4.00 1.80
❑ 248 Bernie Williams UPD 4.00 1.80
❑ 249 Roberto Alomar UPD 4.00 1.80
❑ 250 Bernie Williams UPD 4.00 1.80
❑ 251 David Wells UPD 1.50 .70
❑ 252 Cecil Fielder UPD 1.50 .70
❑ 253 Darryl Strawberry UPD 1.50 .70
❑ 254 Andy Pettitte UPD 1.50 .70
❑ 255 Javier Lopez UPD 1.50 .70
❑ 256 Gary Gaetti UPD 1.50 .70
❑ 257 Ron Gant UPD 1.00 .45
❑ 258 Brian Jordan UPD 1.50 .70
❑ 259 John Smoltz UPD 1.50 .70
❑ 260 Greg Maddux UPD 10.00 4.50
❑ 261 Tom Glavine UPD 4.00 1.80
❑ 262 Andruw Jones UPD 5.00 2.20
❑ 263 Greg Maddux UPD 10.00 4.50
❑ 264 David Cone UPD 1.50 .70
❑ 265 Jim Leyritz UPD 1.00 .45
❑ 266 Andy Pettitte UPD 1.50 .70
❑ 267 John Wetteland UPD 1.50 .70
❑ 268 Dario Veras UPD 1.00 .45
❑ 269 Neifi Perez UPD 1.00 .45
❑ 270 Bill Mueller UPD 2.50 1.10
❑ 271 Vladimir Guerrero 1.25 .55
❑ 272 Dmitri Young .25 .11
❑ 273 Nerio Rodriguez RC .15 .07
❑ 274 Kevin Orie .15 .07
❑ 275 Felipe Crespo .15 .07
❑ 276 Danny Graves .15 .07
❑ 277 Rod Myers .15 .07
❑ 278 Felix Heredia RC .15 .07
❑ 279 Ralph Milliard .15 .07
❑ 280 Greg Norton .15 .07
❑ 281 Derek Wallace .15 .07
❑ 282 Trot Nixon .25 .11
❑ 283 Bobby Chouinard .15 .07
❑ 284 Jay Witasick .15 .07
❑ 285 Travis Miller .15 .07
❑ 286 Brian Bevil RC .15 .07
❑ 287 Bobby Estalella .15 .07
❑ 288 Steve Soderstrom .15 .07
❑ 289 Mark Langston .15 .07
❑ 290 Tim Salmon .25 .11
❑ 291 Jim Edmonds .60 .25
❑ 292 Garret Anderson .25 .11
❑ 293 George Arias .15 .07
❑ 294 Gary DiSarcina .15 .07
❑ 295 Chuck Finley .25 .11
❑ 296 Todd Greene .15 .07
❑ 297 Randy Velarde .15 .07
❑ 298 David Justice .40 .18
❑ 299 Ryan Klesko .25 .11
❑ 300 John Smoltz .25 .11
❑ 301 Javier Lopez .25 .11
❑ 302 Greg Maddux 1.50 .70
❑ 303 Denny Neagle .25 .11
❑ 304 B.J. Surhoff .25 .11
❑ 305 Chris Hoiles .15 .07
❑ 306 Eric Davis .25 .11
❑ 307 Scott Erickson .15 .07
❑ 308 Mike Bordick .15 .07
❑ 309 John Valentin .15 .07
❑ 310 Heathcliff Slocumb .15 .07

❑ 311 Tom Gordon .15 .07
❑ 312 Mike Stanley .15 .07
❑ 313 Reggie Jefferson .15 .07
❑ 314 Darren Bragg .15 .07
❑ 315 Troy O'Leary .15 .07
❑ 316 John Mabry SH CL .15 .07
❑ 317 Mark Whiten SH CL .15 .07
❑ 318 Edgar Martinez SH CL .25 .11
❑ 319 Alex Rodriguez SH CL 1.00 .45
❑ 320 Mark McGwire SH CL 1.25 .55
❑ 321 Hideo Nomo SH CL .25 .11
❑ 322 Todd Hundley SH CL .15 .07
❑ 323 Barry Bonds SH CL .60 .25
❑ 324 Andruw Jones SH CL .40 .18
❑ 325 Ryne Sandberg .75 .35
❑ 326 Brian McRae .15 .07
❑ 327 Frank Castillo .15 .07
❑ 328 Shawon Dunston .15 .07
❑ 329 Ray Durham .25 .11
❑ 330 Robin Ventura .25 .11
❑ 331 Ozzie Guillen .15 .07
❑ 332 Roberto Hernandez .15 .07
❑ 333 Albert Belle .40 .18
❑ 334 Dave Martinez .15 .07
❑ 335 Willie Greene .15 .07
❑ 336 Jeff Brantley .15 .07
❑ 337 Kevin Jarvis .15 .07
❑ 338 John Smiley .15 .07
❑ 339 Eddie Taubensee .15 .07
❑ 340 Bret Boone .25 .11
❑ 341 Kevin Seitzer .15 .07
❑ 342 Jack McDowell .15 .07
❑ 343 Sandy Alomar Jr. .25 .11
❑ 344 Chad Curtis .15 .07
❑ 345 Manny Ramirez .75 .35
❑ 346 Chad Ogea .15 .07
❑ 347 Jim Thome .40 .18
❑ 348 Mark Thompson .15 .07
❑ 349 Ellis Burks .25 .11
❑ 350 Andres Galarraga .40 .18
❑ 351 Vinny Castilla .25 .11
❑ 352 Kirt Manwaring .15 .07
❑ 353 Larry Walker .25 .11
❑ 354 Omar Olivares .15 .07
❑ 355 Bobby Higginson .25 .11
❑ 356 Melvin Nieves .15 .07
❑ 357 Brian Johnson .15 .07
❑ 358 Devon White .25 .11
❑ 359 Jeff Conine .15 .07
❑ 360 Gary Sheffield .60 .25
❑ 361 Robb Nen .15 .07
❑ 362 Mike Hampton .25 .11
❑ 363 Bob Abreu .25 .11
❑ 364 Luis Gonzalez .25 .11
❑ 365 Derek Bell .15 .07
❑ 366 Sean Berry .15 .07
❑ 367 Craig Biggio .40 .18
❑ 368 Darryl Kile .25 .11
❑ 369 Shane Reynolds .15 .07
❑ 370 Jeff Bagwell CF .40 .18
❑ 371 Ron Gant CF .15 .07
❑ 372 Andy Benes CF .15 .07
❑ 373 Gary Gaetti CF .15 .07
❑ 374 Ramon Martinez CF .15 .07
❑ 375 Raul Mondesi CF .15 .07
❑ 376 Steve Finley CF .15 .07
❑ 377 Ken Caminiti CF .15 .07
❑ 378 Tony Gwynn CF .60 .25
❑ 379 Dario Veras RC .15 .07
❑ 380 Andy Pettitte CF .15 .07
❑ 381 Ruben Rivera CF .15 .07
❑ 382 David Cone CF .15 .07
❑ 383 Roberto Alomar CF .25 .11
❑ 384 Edgar Martinez CF .25 .11
❑ 385 Ken Griffey Jr. CF 1.25 .55
❑ 386 Mark McGwire CF 1.25 .55
❑ 387 Rusty Greer CF .15 .07
❑ 388 Jose Rosado .15 .07
❑ 389 Kevin Appier .25 .11
❑ 390 Johnny Damon .25 .11
❑ 391 Jose Offerman .15 .07
❑ 392 Michael Tucker .15 .07
❑ 393 Craig Paquette .15 .07
❑ 394 Bip Roberts .15 .07
❑ 395 Ramon Martinez .15 .07
❑ 396 Greg Gagne .15 .07
❑ 397 Chan Ho Park .25 .11
❑ 398 Karim Garcia .15 .07
❑ 399 Wilton Guerrero .15 .07
❑ 400 Eric Karros .25 .11
❑ 401 Raul Mondesi .25 .11
❑ 402 Matt Mieske .15 .07
❑ 403 Mike Fetters .15 .07
❑ 404 Dave Nilsson .15 .07
❑ 405 Jose Valentin .15 .07
❑ 406 Scott Karl .15 .07
❑ 407 Marc Newfield .15 .07
❑ 408 Cal Eldred .15 .07
❑ 409 Rich Becker .15 .07
❑ 410 Terry Steinbach .15 .07
❑ 411 Chuck Knoblauch .25 .11
❑ 412 Pat Meares .15 .07
❑ 413 Brad Radke .25 .11
❑ 414 Kirby Puckett UER 1.50 .70
(Card numbered 415)
❑ 415 Andruw Jones GHL SP 3.00 1.35
❑ 416 Chipper Jones GHL SP 6.00 2.70
❑ 417 Mo Vaughn GHL SP 1.50 .70
❑ 418 Frank Thomas GHL SP 5.00 2.20
❑ 419 Albert Belle GHL SP 1.50 .70
❑ 420 Mark McGwire GHL SP 10.00 4.50
❑ 421 Derek Jeter GHL SP 10.00 4.50
❑ 422 Alex Rodriguez GHL SP 8.00 3.60
❑ 423 Juan Gonzalez GHL SP 2.50 1.10
❑ 424 Ken Griffey Jr. GHL SP 10.00 4.50
❑ 425 Rondell White .25 .11
❑ 426 Darrin Fletcher .15 .07
❑ 427 Cliff Floyd .25 .11
❑ 428 Mike Lansing .15 .07
❑ 429 F.P. Santangelo .15 .07
❑ 430 Todd Hundley .15 .07
❑ 431 Mark Clark .15 .07
❑ 432 Pete Harnisch .15 .07
❑ 433 Jason Isringhausen .15 .07
❑ 434 Bobby Jones .15 .07
❑ 435 Lance Johnson .15 .07
❑ 436 Carlos Baerga .15 .07
❑ 437 Mariano Duncan .15 .07
❑ 438 David Cone .25 .11
❑ 439 Mariano Rivera .25 .11
❑ 440 Derek Jeter 2.50 1.10
❑ 441 Joe Girardi .15 .07
❑ 442 Charlie Hayes .15 .07
❑ 443 Tim Raines .25 .11
❑ 444 Darryl Strawberry .25 .11
❑ 445 Cecil Fielder .25 .11
❑ 446 Ariel Prieto .15 .07
❑ 447 Tony Batista .60 .25
❑ 448 Brent Gates .15 .07
❑ 449 Scott Spiezio .15 .07
❑ 450 Mark McGwire 2.50 1.10
❑ 451 Don Wengert .15 .07
❑ 452 Mike Lieberthal .25 .11
❑ 453 Lenny Dykstra .25 .11
❑ 454 Rex Hudler .15 .07
❑ 455 Darren Daulton .25 .11
❑ 456 Kevin Stocker .15 .07
❑ 457 Trey Beamon .15 .07
❑ 458 Midre Cummings .15 .07
❑ 459 Mark Johnson .15 .07
❑ 460 Al Martin .15 .07
❑ 461 Kevin Elster .15 .07
❑ 462 Jon Lieber .15 .07
❑ 463 Jason Schmidt .15 .07
❑ 464 Paul Wagner .15 .07
❑ 465 Andy Benes .15 .07
❑ 466 Alan Benes .15 .07
❑ 467 Royce Clayton .15 .07
❑ 468 Gary Gaetti .25 .11
❑ 469 Curt Lyons RC .15 .07
❑ 470 Eugene Kingsale DD .15 .07
❑ 471 Damian Jackson DD .15 .07
❑ 472 Wendell Magee DD .15 .07
❑ 473 Kevin L. Brown DD .15 .07
❑ 474 Raul Casanova DD .15 .07
❑ 475 Ramiro Mendoza DD RC .50 .23
❑ 476 Todd Dunn DD .15 .07
❑ 477 Chad Mottola DD .15 .07
❑ 478 Andy Larkin DD .15 .07
❑ 479 Jaime Bluma DD .15 .07
❑ 480 Mac Suzuki DD .15 .07
❑ 481 Brian Banks DD .15 .07
❑ 482 Desi Wilson DD .15 .07
❑ 483 Einar Diaz DD .15 .07
❑ 484 Tom Pagnozzi .15 .07
❑ 485 Ray Lankford .25 .11
❑ 486 Todd Stottlemyre .15 .07
❑ 487 Donovan Osborne .15 .07
❑ 488 Trevor Hoffman .25 .11
❑ 489 Chris Gomez .15 .07
❑ 490 Ken Caminiti .25 .11
❑ 491 John Flaherty .15 .07
❑ 492 Tony Gwynn 1.25 .55
❑ 493 Joey Hamilton .15 .07
❑ 494 Rickey Henderson .75 .35
❑ 495 Glenallen Hill .15 .07
❑ 496 Rod Beck .15 .07
❑ 497 Osvaldo Fernandez .15 .07
❑ 498 Rick Wilkins .15 .07
❑ 499 Joey Cora .15 .07
❑ 500 Alex Rodriguez 2.00 .90
❑ 501 Randy Johnson .75 .35
❑ 502 Paul Sorrento .15 .07
❑ 503 Dan Wilson .15 .07
❑ 504 Jamie Moyer .15 .07
❑ 505 Will Clark .60 .25
❑ 506 Mickey Tettleton .15 .07
❑ 507 John Burkett .15 .07
❑ 508 Ken Hill .15 .07
❑ 509 Mark McLemore .15 .07
❑ 510 Juan Gonzalez .60 .25
❑ 511 Bobby Witt .15 .07
❑ 512 Carlos Delgado .60 .25
❑ 513 Alex Gonzalez .15 .07
❑ 514 Shawn Green .60 .25
❑ 515 Joe Carter .25 .11
❑ 516 Juan Guzman .15 .07
❑ 517 Charlie O'Brien .15 .07
❑ 518 Ed Sprague .15 .07
❑ 519 Mike Timlin .15 .07
❑ 520 Roger Clemens 1.25 .55
❑ 521 Eddie Murray TRADE 2.00 .90
❑ 522 Jason Dickson TRADE .50 .23
❑ 523 Jim Leyritz TRADE .50 .23
❑ 524 Michael Tucker TRADE .50 .23
❑ 525 Kenny Lofton TRADE .75 .35
❑ 526 Jimmy Key TRADE .75 .35
❑ 527 Mel Rojas TRADE .50 .23
❑ 528 Deion Sanders TRADE .75 .35
❑ 529 Bartolo Colon TRADE .75 .35
❑ 530 Matt Williams TRADE 1.25 .55
❑ 531 Marquis Grissom TRADE .50 .23
❑ 532 David Justice TRADE .50 .23
❑ 533 Bubba Trammell TRADE .75 .35
❑ 534 Moises Alou TRADE .75 .35
❑ 535 Bobby Bonilla TRADE .75 .35
❑ 536 Alex Fernandez TRADE .50 .23
❑ 537 Jay Bell TRADE .75 .35
❑ 538 Chili Davis TRADE .75 .35
❑ 539 Jeff King TRADE .50 .23
❑ 540 Todd Zeile TRADE .50 .23
❑ 541 John Olerud TRADE .50 .23
❑ 542 Jose Guillen TRADE .50 .23
❑ 543 Derrek Lee TRADE .50 .23
❑ 544 Dante Powell TRADE .50 .23
❑ 545 J.T. Snow TRADE .75 .35
❑ 546 Jeff Kent TRADE 1.25 .55
❑ 547 Jose Cruz Jr. TRADE 5.00 2.20
❑ 548 John Wetteland TRADE .75 .35
❑ 549 Orlando Merced TRADE .50 .23
❑ 550 Hideki Irabu TRADE 1.50 .70

## 1998 Upper Deck

| | MINT | NRMT |
|---|---|---|
| COMPLETE SET (751) | 225.00 | 100.00 |
| COMPLETE SERIES 1 (270) | 50.00 | 22.00 |
| COMPLETE SERIES 2 (270) | 50.00 | 22.00 |
| COMPLETE SERIES 3 (211) | 125.00 | 55.00 |
| COMMON (1-600/631-750) | .15 | .07 |
| COMMON EP (601-630) | 1.50 | .70 |

❑ 1 Tino Martinez HIST .15 .07
❑ 2 Jimmy Key HIST .15 .07
❑ 3 Jay Buhner HIST .15 .07
❑ 4 Mark Gardner HIST .15 .07
❑ 5 Greg Maddux HIST .75 .35
❑ 6 Pedro Martinez HIST .40 .18

| | | | |
|---|---|---|---|
| ❑ 7 | Hideo Nomo HIST | .25 | .11 |
| ❑ 8 | Sammy Sosa HIST | .60 | .25 |
| ❑ 9 | Mark McGwire GHL | 1.25 | .55 |
| ❑ 10 | Ken Griffey Jr. GHL | 1.25 | .55 |
| ❑ 11 | Larry Walker GHL | .25 | .11 |
| ❑ 12 | Tino Martinez GHL | .25 | .11 |
| ❑ 13 | Mike Piazza GHL | 1.00 | .45 |
| ❑ 14 | Jose Cruz Jr. GHL | .25 | .11 |
| ❑ 15 | Tony Gwynn GHL | .60 | .25 |
| ❑ 16 | Greg Maddux GHL | .75 | .35 |
| ❑ 17 | Roger Clemens GHL | .00 | .25 |
| ❑ 18 | Alex Rodriguez GHL | 1.00 | .45 |
| ❑ 19 | Shigetoshi Hasegawa | .25 | .11 |
| ❑ 20 | Eddie Murray | .60 | .25 |
| ❑ 21 | Jason Dickson | .15 | .07 |
| ❑ 22 | Darin Erstad | .60 | .25 |
| ❑ 23 | Chuck Finley | .25 | .11 |
| ❑ 24 | Dave Hollins | .15 | .07 |
| ❑ 25 | Garret Anderson | .25 | .11 |
| ❑ 26 | Michael Tucker | .15 | .07 |
| ❑ 27 | Kenny Lofton | .25 | .11 |
| ❑ 28 | Javier Lopez | .25 | .11 |
| ❑ 29 | Fred McGriff | .40 | .18 |
| ❑ 30 | Greg Maddux | 1.50 | .70 |
| ❑ 31 | Jeff Blauser | .15 | .07 |
| ❑ 32 | John Smoltz | .25 | .11 |
| ❑ 33 | Mark Wohlers | .15 | .07 |
| ❑ 34 | Scott Erickson | .15 | .07 |
| ❑ 35 | Jimmy Key | .25 | .11 |
| ❑ 36 | Harold Baines | .25 | .11 |
| ❑ 37 | Randy Myers | .25 | .11 |
| ❑ 38 | B.J. Surhoff | .25 | .11 |
| ❑ 39 | Eric Davis | .25 | .11 |
| ❑ 40 | Rafael Palmeiro | .60 | .25 |
| ❑ 41 | Jeffrey Hammonds | .25 | .11 |
| ❑ 42 | Mo Vaughn | .25 | .11 |
| ❑ 43 | Tom Gordon | .25 | .11 |
| ❑ 44 | Tim Naehring | .15 | .07 |
| ❑ 45 | Darren Bragg | .15 | .07 |
| ❑ 46 | Aaron Sele | .25 | .11 |
| ❑ 47 | Troy O'Leary | .15 | .07 |
| ❑ 48 | John Valentin | .15 | .07 |
| ❑ 49 | Doug Glanville | .15 | .07 |
| ❑ 50 | Ryne Sandberg | .75 | .35 |
| ❑ 51 | Steve Trachsel | .15 | .07 |
| ❑ 52 | Mark Grace | .60 | .25 |
| ❑ 53 | Kevin Foster | .15 | .07 |
| ❑ 54 | Kevin Tapani | .15 | .07 |
| ❑ 55 | Kevin Orie | .15 | .07 |
| ❑ 56 | Lyle Mouton | .15 | .07 |
| ❑ 57 | Ray Durham | .25 | .11 |
| ❑ 58 | Jaime Navarro | .15 | .07 |
| ❑ 59 | Mike Cameron | .25 | .11 |
| ❑ 60 | Albert Belle | .40 | .18 |
| ❑ 61 | Doug Drabek | .15 | .07 |
| ❑ 62 | Chris Snopek | .15 | .07 |
| ❑ 63 | Ed Taubensee | .15 | .07 |
| ❑ 64 | Terry Pendleton | .25 | .11 |
| ❑ 65 | Barry Larkin | .60 | .25 |
| ❑ 66 | Willie Greene | .15 | .07 |
| ❑ 67 | Deion Sanders | .25 | .11 |
| ❑ 68 | Pokey Reese | .25 | .11 |
| ❑ 69 | Jeff Shaw | .15 | .07 |
| ❑ 70 | Jim Thome | .40 | .18 |
| ❑ 71 | Orel Hershiser | .25 | .11 |
| ❑ 72 | Omar Vizquel | .25 | .11 |
| ❑ 73 | Brian Giles | .25 | .11 |
| ❑ 74 | David Justice | .40 | .18 |
| ❑ 75 | Bartolo Colon | .25 | .11 |
| ❑ 76 | Sandy Alomar Jr. | .25 | .11 |
| ❑ 77 | Neifi Perez | .15 | .07 |
| ❑ 78 | Dante Bichette | .25 | .11 |
| ❑ 79 | Vinny Castilla | .25 | .11 |
| ❑ 80 | Eric Young | .15 | .07 |
| ❑ 81 | Quinton McCracken | .15 | .07 |
| ❑ 82 | Jamey Wright | .15 | .07 |
| ❑ 83 | John Thomson | .15 | .07 |
| ❑ 84 | Damion Easley | .15 | .07 |
| ❑ 85 | Justin Thompson | .15 | .07 |
| ❑ 86 | Willie Blair | .15 | .07 |
| ❑ 87 | Raul Casanova | .15 | .07 |
| ❑ 88 | Bobby Higginson | .25 | .11 |
| ❑ 89 | Bubba Trammell | .15 | .07 |
| ❑ 90 | Tony Clark | .15 | .07 |
| ❑ 91 | Livan Hernandez | .15 | .07 |
| ❑ 92 | Charles Johnson | .25 | .11 |
| ❑ 93 | Edgar Renteria | .15 | .07 |
| ❑ 94 | Alex Fernandez | .15 | .07 |
| ❑ 95 | Gary Sheffield | .60 | .25 |
| ❑ 96 | Moises Alou | .25 | .11 |
| ❑ 97 | Tony Saunders | .15 | .07 |
| ❑ 98 | Robb Nen | .15 | .07 |
| ❑ 99 | Darryl Kile | .25 | .11 |
| ❑ 100 | Craig Biggio | .40 | .18 |
| ❑ 101 | Chris Holt | .15 | .07 |
| ❑ 102 | Bob Abreu | .25 | .11 |
| ❑ 103 | Luis Gonzalez | .25 | .11 |
| ❑ 104 | Billy Wagner | .15 | .07 |
| ❑ 105 | Brad Ausmus | .15 | .07 |
| ❑ 106 | Chili Davis | .25 | .11 |
| ❑ 107 | Tim Belcher | .15 | .07 |
| ❑ 108 | Dean Palmer | .25 | .11 |
| ❑ 109 | Jeff King | .15 | .07 |
| ❑ 110 | Jose Rosado | .15 | .07 |
| ❑ 111 | Mike Macfarlane | .15 | .07 |
| ❑ 112 | Jay Bell | .25 | .11 |
| ❑ 113 | Todd Worrell | .15 | .07 |
| ❑ 114 | Chan Ho Park | .25 | .11 |
| ❑ 115 | Raul Mondesi | .25 | .11 |
| ❑ 116 | Brett Butler | .25 | .11 |
| ❑ 117 | Greg Gagne | .15 | .07 |
| ❑ 118 | Hideo Nomo | .60 | .25 |
| ❑ 119 | Todd Zeile | .25 | .11 |
| ❑ 120 | Eric Karros | .25 | .11 |
| ❑ 121 | Cal Eldred | .15 | .07 |
| ❑ 122 | Jeff D'Amico | .15 | .07 |
| ❑ 123 | Antone Williamson | .15 | .07 |
| ❑ 124 | Doug Jones | .15 | .07 |
| ❑ 125 | Dave Nilsson | .15 | .07 |
| ❑ 126 | Gerald Williams | .15 | .07 |
| ❑ 127 | Fernando Vina | .15 | .07 |
| ❑ 128 | Ron Coomer | .15 | .07 |
| ❑ 129 | Matt Lawton | .15 | .07 |
| ❑ 130 | Paul Molitor | .60 | .25 |
| ❑ 131 | Todd Walker | .15 | .07 |
| ❑ 132 | Rick Aguilera | .15 | .07 |
| ❑ 133 | Brad Radke | .25 | .11 |
| ❑ 134 | Bob Tewksbury | .15 | .07 |
| ❑ 135 | Vladimir Guerrero | 1.00 | .45 |
| ❑ 136 | Tony Gwynn DG | .60 | .25 |
| ❑ 137 | Roger Clemens DG | .60 | .25 |
| ❑ 138 | Dennis Eckersley DG | .15 | .07 |
| ❑ 139 | Brady Anderson DG | .15 | .07 |
| ❑ 140 | Ken Griffey Jr. DG | 1.25 | .55 |
| ❑ 141 | Derek Jeter DG | 1.25 | .55 |
| ❑ 142 | Ken Caminiti DG | .15 | .07 |
| ❑ 143 | Frank Thomas DG | .60 | .25 |
| ❑ 144 | Barry Bonds DG | .40 | .18 |
| ❑ 145 | Cal Ripken DG | 1.25 | .55 |
| ❑ 146 | Alex Rodriguez DG | 1.00 | .45 |
| ❑ 147 | Greg Maddux DG | .75 | .35 |
| ❑ 148 | Kenny Lofton DG | .15 | .07 |
| ❑ 149 | Mike Piazza DG | 1.00 | .45 |
| ❑ 150 | Mark McGwire DG | 1.25 | .55 |
| ❑ 151 | Andruw Jones DG | .25 | .11 |
| ❑ 152 | Rusty Greer DG | .15 | .07 |
| ❑ 153 | F.P. Santangelo DG | .15 | .07 |
| ❑ 154 | Mike Lansing | .15 | .07 |
| ❑ 155 | Lee Smith | .25 | .11 |
| ❑ 156 | Carlos Perez | .15 | .07 |
| ❑ 157 | Pedro Martinez | .75 | .35 |
| ❑ 158 | Ryan McGuire | .15 | .07 |
| ❑ 159 | F.P. Santangelo | .15 | .07 |
| ❑ 160 | Rondell White | .25 | .11 |
| ❑ 161 | Takashi Kashiwada RC | .15 | .07 |
| ❑ 162 | Butch Huskey | .15 | .07 |
| ❑ 163 | Edgardo Alfonzo | .25 | .11 |
| ❑ 164 | John Franco | .25 | .11 |
| ❑ 165 | Todd Hundley | .15 | .07 |
| ❑ 166 | Rey Ordonez | .15 | .07 |
| ❑ 167 | Armando Reynoso | .15 | .07 |
| ❑ 168 | John Olerud | .25 | .11 |
| ❑ 169 | Bernie Williams | .60 | .25 |
| ❑ 170 | Andy Pettitte | .25 | .11 |
| ❑ 171 | Wade Boggs | .75 | .35 |
| ❑ 172 | Paul O'Neill | .25 | .11 |
| ❑ 173 | Cecil Fielder | .25 | .11 |
| ❑ 174 | Charlie Hayes | .15 | .07 |
| ❑ 175 | David Cone | .25 | .11 |
| ❑ 176 | Hideki Irabu | .15 | .07 |
| ❑ 177 | Mark Bellhorn | .15 | .07 |
| ❑ 178 | Steve Karsay | .15 | .07 |
| ❑ 179 | Damon Mashore | .15 | .07 |
| ❑ 180 | Jason McDonald | .15 | .07 |
| ❑ 181 | Scott Spiezio | .15 | .07 |
| ❑ 182 | Ariel Prieto | .15 | .07 |
| ❑ 183 | Jason Giambi | .60 | .25 |
| ❑ 184 | Wendell Magee | .15 | .07 |
| ❑ 185 | Rico Brogna | .15 | .07 |
| ❑ 186 | Garrett Stephenson | .15 | .07 |
| ❑ 187 | Wayne Gomes | .15 | .07 |
| ❑ 188 | Ricky Bottalico | .15 | .07 |
| ❑ 189 | Mickey Morandini | .15 | .07 |
| ❑ 190 | Mike Lieberthal | .25 | .11 |
| ❑ 191 | Kevin Polcovich | .15 | .07 |
| ❑ 192 | Francisco Cordova | .15 | .07 |
| ❑ 193 | Kevin Young | .25 | .11 |
| ❑ 194 | Jon Lieber | .15 | .07 |
| ❑ 195 | Kevin Elster | .15 | .07 |
| ❑ 196 | Tony Womack | .15 | .07 |
| ❑ 197 | Lou Collier | .15 | .07 |
| ❑ 198 | Mike Difelice RC | .15 | .07 |
| ❑ 199 | Gary Gaetti | .25 | .11 |
| ❑ 200 | Dennis Eckersley | .25 | .11 |
| ❑ 201 | Alan Benes | .15 | .07 |
| ❑ 202 | Willie McGee | .25 | .11 |
| ❑ 203 | Ron Gant | .25 | .11 |
| ❑ 204 | Fernando Valenzuela | .25 | .11 |
| ❑ 205 | Mark McGwire | 2.50 | 1.10 |
| ❑ 206 | Archi Cianfrocco | .15 | .07 |
| ❑ 207 | Andy Ashby | .15 | .07 |
| ❑ 208 | Steve Finley | .25 | .11 |
| ❑ 209 | Quilvio Veras | .15 | .07 |
| ❑ 210 | Ken Caminiti | .25 | .11 |
| ❑ 211 | Rickey Henderson | .75 | .35 |
| ❑ 212 | Joey Hamilton | .15 | .07 |
| ❑ 213 | Derrek Lee | .15 | .07 |
| ❑ 214 | Bill Mueller | .15 | .07 |
| ❑ 215 | Shawn Estes | .15 | .07 |
| ❑ 216 | J.T. Snow | .25 | .11 |
| ❑ 217 | Mark Gardner | .15 | .07 |
| ❑ 218 | Terry Mulholland | .15 | .07 |
| ❑ 219 | Dante Powell | .15 | .07 |
| ❑ 220 | Jeff Kent | .40 | .18 |
| ❑ 221 | Jamie Moyer | .15 | .07 |
| ❑ 222 | Joey Cora | .15 | .07 |
| ❑ 223 | Jeff Fassero | .15 | .07 |
| ❑ 224 | Dennis Martinez | .25 | .11 |
| ❑ 225 | Ken Griffey Jr. | 2.50 | 1.10 |
| ❑ 226 | Edgar Martinez | .40 | .18 |
| ❑ 227 | Russ Davis | .15 | .07 |
| ❑ 228 | Dan Wilson | .15 | .07 |
| ❑ 229 | Will Clark | .60 | .25 |
| ❑ 230 | Ivan Rodriguez | .75 | .35 |
| ❑ 231 | Benji Gil | .15 | .07 |
| ❑ 232 | Lee Stevens | .15 | .07 |
| ❑ 233 | Mickey Tettleton | .15 | .07 |
| ❑ 234 | Julio Santana | .15 | .07 |
| ❑ 235 | Rusty Greer | .25 | .11 |
| ❑ 236 | Bobby Witt | .15 | .07 |
| ❑ 237 | Ed Sprague | .15 | .07 |
| ❑ 238 | Pat Hentgen | .15 | .07 |
| ❑ 239 | Kelvim Escobar | .15 | .07 |
| ❑ 240 | Joe Carter | .25 | .11 |
| ❑ 241 | Carlos Delgado | .60 | .25 |
| ❑ 242 | Shannon Stewart | .25 | .11 |
| ❑ 243 | Benito Santiago | .15 | .07 |
| ❑ 244 | Tino Martinez SH | .15 | .07 |
| ❑ 245 | Ken Griffey Jr. SH | 1.25 | .55 |
| ❑ 246 | Kevin Brown SH | .25 | .11 |

| |  |  | | |
|---|---|---|---|---|
| ❑ | 247 | Ryne Sandberg SH | .40 | .18 |
| ❑ | 248 | Mo Vaughn SH | .25 | .11 |
| ❑ | 249 | Darryl Hamilton SH | .15 | .07 |
| ❑ | 250 | Randy Johnson SH | .25 | .11 |
| ❑ | 251 | Steve Finley SH | .15 | .07 |
| ❑ | 252 | Bobby Higginson SH | .15 | .07 |
| ❑ | 253 | Brett Tomko | .15 | .07 |
| ❑ | 254 | Mark Kotsay | .25 | .11 |
| ❑ | 255 | Jose Guillen | .15 | .07 |
| ❑ | 256 | Eli Marrero | .15 | .07 |
| ❑ | 257 | Dennis Reyes | .15 | .07 |
| ❑ | 258 | Richie Sexson | .40 | .18 |
| ❑ | 259 | Pat Cline | .15 | .07 |
| ❑ | 260 | Todd Helton | .75 | .35 |
| ❑ | 261 | Juan Melo | .15 | .07 |
| ❑ | 262 | Matt Morris | .15 | .07 |
| ❑ | 263 | Jeremi Gonzalez | .15 | .07 |
| ❑ | 264 | Jeff Abbott | .15 | .07 |
| ❑ | 265 | Aaron Boone | .15 | .07 |
| ❑ | 266 | Todd Dunwoody | .15 | .07 |
| ❑ | 267 | Jaret Wright | .15 | .07 |
| ❑ | 268 | Derrick Gibson | .15 | .07 |
| ❑ | 269 | Mario Valdez | .15 | .07 |
| ❑ | 270 | Fernando Tatis | .25 | .11 |
| ❑ | 271 | Craig Counsell | .15 | .07 |
| ❑ | 272 | Brad Rigby | .15 | .07 |
| ❑ | 273 | Danny Clyburn | .15 | .07 |
| ❑ | 274 | Brian Rose | .15 | .07 |
| ❑ | 275 | Miguel Tejada | .60 | .25 |
| ❑ | 276 | Jason Varitek | .25 | .11 |
| ❑ | 277 | Dave Dellucci RC | .15 | .07 |
| ❑ | 278 | Michael Coleman | .15 | .07 |
| ❑ | 279 | Adam Riggs | .15 | .07 |
| ❑ | 280 | Ben Grieve | .25 | .11 |
| ❑ | 281 | Brad Fullmer | .25 | .11 |
| ❑ | 282 | Ken Cloude | .15 | .07 |
| ❑ | 283 | Tom Evans | .15 | .07 |
| ❑ | 284 | Kevin Millwood RC | 1.00 | .45 |
| ❑ | 285 | Paul Konerko | .25 | .11 |
| ❑ | 286 | Juan Encarnacion | .25 | .11 |
| ❑ | 287 | Chris Carpenter | .25 | .11 |
| ❑ | 288 | Tom Fordham | .15 | .07 |
| ❑ | 289 | Gary DiSarcina | .15 | .07 |
| ❑ | 290 | Tim Salmon | .25 | .11 |
| ❑ | 291 | Troy Percival | .15 | .07 |
| ❑ | 292 | Todd Greene | .15 | .07 |
| ❑ | 293 | Ken Hill | .15 | .07 |
| ❑ | 294 | Dennis Springer | .15 | .07 |
| ❑ | 295 | Jim Edmonds | .60 | .25 |
| ❑ | 296 | Allen Watson | .15 | .07 |
| ❑ | 297 | Brian Anderson | .15 | .07 |
| ❑ | 298 | Keith Lockhart | .15 | .07 |
| ❑ | 299 | Tom Glavine | .60 | .25 |
| ❑ | 300 | Chipper Jones | 1.50 | .70 |
| ❑ | 301 | Randall Simon | .15 | .07 |
| ❑ | 302 | Mark Lemke | .15 | .07 |
| ❑ | 303 | Ryan Klesko | .25 | .11 |
| ❑ | 304 | Denny Neagle | .15 | .07 |
| ❑ | 305 | Andruw Jones | .60 | .25 |
| ❑ | 306 | Mike Mussina | .60 | .25 |
| ❑ | 307 | Brady Anderson | .25 | .11 |
| ❑ | 308 | Chris Hoiles | .15 | .07 |
| ❑ | 309 | Mike Bordick | .15 | .07 |
| ❑ | 310 | Cal Ripken | 2.50 | 1.10 |
| ❑ | 311 | Geronimo Berroa | .15 | .07 |
| ❑ | 312 | Armando Benitez | .15 | .07 |
| ❑ | 313 | Roberto Alomar | .60 | .25 |
| ❑ | 314 | Tim Wakefield | .15 | .07 |
| ❑ | 315 | Reggie Jefferson | .15 | .07 |
| ❑ | 316 | Jeff Frye | .15 | .07 |
| ❑ | 317 | Scott Hatteberg | .15 | .07 |
| ❑ | 318 | Steve Avery | .15 | .07 |
| ❑ | 319 | Robinson Checo | .15 | .07 |
| ❑ | 320 | Nomar Garciaparra | 2.00 | .90 |
| ❑ | 321 | Lance Johnson | .15 | .07 |
| ❑ | 322 | Tyler Houston | .15 | .07 |
| ❑ | 323 | Mark Clark | .15 | .07 |
| ❑ | 324 | Terry Adams | .15 | .07 |
| ❑ | 325 | Sammy Sosa | 1.25 | .55 |
| ❑ | 326 | Scott Servais | .15 | .07 |
| ❑ | 327 | Manny Alexander | .15 | .07 |
| ❑ | 328 | Norberto Martin | .15 | .07 |
| ❑ | 329 | Scott Eyre | .15 | .07 |
| ❑ | 330 | Frank Thomas | 1.25 | .55 |
| ❑ | 331 | Robin Ventura | .25 | .11 |
| ❑ | 332 | Matt Karchner | .15 | .07 |
| ❑ | 333 | Keith Foulke | .15 | .07 |
| ❑ | 334 | James Baldwin | .15 | .07 |
| ❑ | 335 | Chris Stynes | .15 | .07 |
| ❑ | 336 | Bret Boone | .25 | .11 |
| ❑ | 337 | Jon Nunnally | .15 | .07 |
| ❑ | 338 | Dave Burba | .15 | .07 |
| ❑ | 339 | Eduardo Perez | .15 | .07 |
| ❑ | 340 | Reggie Sanders | .15 | .07 |
| ❑ | 341 | Mike Remlinger | .15 | .07 |
| ❑ | 342 | Pat Watkins | .15 | .07 |
| ❑ | 343 | Chad Ogea | .15 | .07 |
| ❑ | 344 | John Smiley | .15 | .07 |
| ❑ | 345 | Kenny Lofton | .25 | .11 |
| ❑ | 346 | Jose Mesa | .15 | .07 |
| ❑ | 347 | Charles Nagy | .15 | .07 |
| ❑ | 348 | Enrique Wilson | .15 | .07 |
| ❑ | 349 | Bruce Aven | .15 | .07 |
| ❑ | 350 | Manny Ramirez | .75 | .35 |
| ❑ | 351 | Jerry DiPoto | .15 | .07 |
| ❑ | 352 | Ellis Burks | .25 | .11 |
| ❑ | 353 | Kirt Manwaring | .15 | .07 |
| ❑ | 354 | Vinny Castilla | .25 | .11 |
| ❑ | 355 | Larry Walker | .25 | .11 |
| ❑ | 356 | Kevin Ritz | .15 | .07 |
| ❑ | 357 | Pedro Astacio | .15 | .07 |
| ❑ | 358 | Scott Sanders | .15 | .07 |
| ❑ | 359 | Deivi Cruz | .15 | .07 |
| ❑ | 360 | Brian L. Hunter | .15 | .07 |
| ❑ | 361 | Pedro Martinez HM | .40 | .18 |
| ❑ | 362 | Tom Glavine HM | .25 | .11 |
| ❑ | 363 | Willie McGee HM | .15 | .07 |
| ❑ | 364 | J.T. Snow HM | .15 | .07 |
| ❑ | 365 | Rusty Greer HM | .15 | .07 |
| ❑ | 366 | Mike Grace HM | .15 | .07 |
| ❑ | 367 | Tony Clark HM | .15 | .07 |
| ❑ | 368 | Ben Grieve HM | .25 | .11 |
| ❑ | 369 | Gary Sheffield HM | .25 | .11 |
| ❑ | 370 | Joe Oliver | .15 | .07 |
| ❑ | 371 | Todd Jones | .15 | .07 |
| ❑ | 372 | Frank Catalanotto RC | .40 | .18 |
| ❑ | 373 | Brian Moehler | .15 | .07 |
| ❑ | 374 | Cliff Floyd | .25 | .11 |
| ❑ | 375 | Bobby Bonilla | .25 | .11 |
| ❑ | 376 | Al Leiter | .25 | .11 |
| ❑ | 377 | Josh Booty | .15 | .07 |
| ❑ | 378 | Darren Daulton | .25 | .11 |
| ❑ | 379 | Jay Powell | .15 | .07 |
| ❑ | 380 | Felix Heredia | .15 | .07 |
| ❑ | 381 | Jim Eisenreich | .15 | .07 |
| ❑ | 382 | Richard Hidalgo | .25 | .11 |
| ❑ | 383 | Mike Hampton | .25 | .11 |
| ❑ | 384 | Shane Reynolds | .15 | .07 |
| ❑ | 385 | Jeff Bagwell | .75 | .35 |
| ❑ | 386 | Derek Bell | .15 | .07 |
| ❑ | 387 | Ricky Gutierrez | .15 | .07 |
| ❑ | 388 | Bill Spiers | .15 | .07 |
| ❑ | 389 | Jose Offerman | .15 | .07 |
| ❑ | 390 | Johnny Damon | .25 | .11 |
| ❑ | 391 | Jermaine Dye | .25 | .11 |
| ❑ | 392 | Jeff Montgomery | .15 | .07 |
| ❑ | 393 | Glendon Rusch | .15 | .07 |
| ❑ | 394 | Mike Sweeney | .25 | .11 |
| ❑ | 395 | Kevin Appier | .25 | .11 |
| ❑ | 396 | Joe Vitiello | .15 | .07 |
| ❑ | 397 | Ramon Martinez | .15 | .07 |
| ❑ | 398 | Darren Dreifort | .15 | .07 |
| ❑ | 399 | Wilton Guerrero | .15 | .07 |
| ❑ | 400 | Mike Piazza | 2.00 | .90 |
| ❑ | 401 | Eddie Murray | .60 | .25 |
| ❑ | 402 | Ismael Valdes | .15 | .07 |
| ❑ | 403 | Todd Hollandsworth | .15 | .07 |
| ❑ | 404 | Mark Loretta | .15 | .07 |
| ❑ | 405 | Jeromy Burnitz | .25 | .11 |
| ❑ | 406 | Jeff Cirillo | .25 | .11 |
| ❑ | 407 | Scott Karl | .15 | .07 |
| ❑ | 408 | Mike Matheny | .15 | .07 |
| ❑ | 409 | Jose Valentin | .15 | .07 |
| ❑ | 410 | John Jaha | .25 | .11 |
| ❑ | 411 | Terry Steinbach | .15 | .07 |
| ❑ | 412 | Torii Hunter | .15 | .07 |
| ❑ | 413 | Pat Meares | .15 | .07 |
| ❑ | 414 | Marty Cordova | .15 | .07 |
| ❑ | 415 | Jaret Wright PH | .15 | .07 |
| ❑ | 416 | Mike Mussina PH | .25 | .11 |
| ❑ | 417 | John Smoltz PH | .15 | .07 |
| ❑ | 418 | Devon White PH | .15 | .07 |
| ❑ | 419 | Denny Neagle PH | .15 | .07 |
| ❑ | 420 | Livan Hernandez PH | .15 | .07 |
| ❑ | 421 | Kevin Brown PH | .25 | .11 |
| ❑ | 422 | Marquis Grissom PH | .15 | .07 |
| ❑ | 423 | Mike Mussina PH | .25 | .11 |
| ❑ | 424 | Eric Davis PH | .15 | .07 |
| ❑ | 425 | Tony Fernandez PH | .15 | .07 |
| ❑ | 426 | Moises Alou PH | .15 | .07 |
| ❑ | 427 | Sandy Alomar Jr. PH | .15 | .07 |
| ❑ | 428 | Gary Sheffield PH | .25 | .11 |
| ❑ | 429 | Jaret Wright PH | .15 | .07 |
| ❑ | 430 | Livan Hernandez PH | .15 | .07 |
| ❑ | 431 | Chad Ogea PH | .15 | .07 |
| ❑ | 432 | Edgar Renteria PH | .15 | .07 |
| ❑ | 433 | LaTroy Hawkins | .15 | .07 |
| ❑ | 434 | Rich Robertson | .15 | .07 |
| ❑ | 435 | Chuck Knoblauch | .25 | .11 |
| ❑ | 436 | Jose Vidro | .15 | .07 |
| ❑ | 437 | Dustin Hermanson | .15 | .07 |
| ❑ | 438 | Jim Bullinger | .15 | .07 |
| ❑ | 439 | Orlando Cabrera | .15 | .07 |
| ❑ | 440 | Vladimir Guerrero | 1.00 | .45 |
| ❑ | 441 | Ugueth Urbina | .15 | .07 |
| ❑ | 442 | Brian McRae | .15 | .07 |
| ❑ | 443 | Matt Franco | .15 | .07 |
| ❑ | 444 | Bobby Jones | .15 | .07 |
| ❑ | 445 | Bernard Gilkey | .15 | .07 |
| ❑ | 446 | Dave Mlicki | .15 | .07 |
| ❑ | 447 | Brian Bohanon | .15 | .07 |
| ❑ | 448 | Mel Rojas | .15 | .07 |
| ❑ | 449 | Tim Raines | .25 | .11 |
| ❑ | 450 | Derek Jeter | 2.50 | 1.10 |
| ❑ | 451 | Roger Clemens UE | .60 | .25 |
| ❑ | 452 | Nomar Garciaparra UE | 1.00 | .45 |
| ❑ | 453 | Mike Piazza UE | 1.00 | .45 |
| ❑ | 454 | Mark McGwire UE | 1.25 | .55 |
| ❑ | 455 | Ken Griffey Jr. UE | 1.25 | .55 |
| ❑ | 456 | Larry Walker UE | .25 | .11 |
| ❑ | 457 | Alex Rodriguez UE | 1.00 | .45 |
| ❑ | 458 | Tony Gwynn UE | .60 | .25 |
| ❑ | 459 | Frank Thomas UE | .60 | .25 |
| ❑ | 460 | Tino Martinez | .25 | .11 |
| ❑ | 461 | Chad Curtis | .15 | .07 |
| ❑ | 462 | Ramiro Mendoza | .15 | .07 |
| ❑ | 463 | Joe Girardi | .15 | .07 |
| ❑ | 464 | David Wells | .25 | .11 |
| ❑ | 465 | Mariano Rivera | .25 | .11 |
| ❑ | 466 | Willie Adams | .15 | .07 |
| ❑ | 467 | George Williams | .15 | .07 |
| ❑ | 468 | Dave Telgheder | .15 | .07 |
| ❑ | 469 | Dave Magadan | .15 | .07 |
| ❑ | 470 | Matt Stairs | .15 | .07 |
| ❑ | 471 | Bill Taylor | .15 | .07 |
| ❑ | 472 | Jimmy Haynes | .15 | .07 |
| ❑ | 473 | Gregg Jefferies | .15 | .07 |
| ❑ | 474 | Midre Cummings | .15 | .07 |
| ❑ | 475 | Curt Schilling | .25 | .11 |
| ❑ | 476 | Mike Grace | .15 | .07 |
| ❑ | 477 | Mark Leiter | .15 | .07 |
| ❑ | 478 | Matt Beech | .15 | .07 |
| ❑ | 479 | Scott Rolen | .60 | .25 |
| ❑ | 480 | Jason Kendall | .25 | .11 |
| ❑ | 481 | Esteban Loaiza | .15 | .07 |
| ❑ | 482 | Jermaine Allensworth | .15 | .07 |
| ❑ | 483 | Mark Smith | .15 | .07 |
| ❑ | 484 | Jason Schmidt | .15 | .07 |
| ❑ | 485 | Jose Guillen | .15 | .07 |
| ❑ | 486 | Al Martin | .15 | .07 |
| ❑ | 487 | Delino DeShields | .15 | .07 |
| ❑ | 488 | Todd Stottlemyre | .15 | .07 |
| ❑ | 489 | Brian Jordan | .25 | .11 |
| ❑ | 490 | Ray Lankford | .25 | .11 |
| ❑ | 491 | Matt Morris | .15 | .07 |
| ❑ | 492 | Royce Clayton | .15 | .07 |
| ❑ | 493 | John Mabry | .15 | .07 |
| ❑ | 494 | Wally Joyner | .25 | .11 |
| ❑ | 495 | Trevor Hoffman | .25 | .11 |
| ❑ | 496 | Chris Gomez | .15 | .07 |
| ❑ | 497 | Sterling Hitchcock | .15 | .07 |
| ❑ | 498 | Pete Smith | .15 | .07 |
| ❑ | 499 | Greg Vaughn | .25 | .11 |
| ❑ | 500 | Tony Gwynn | 1.25 | .55 |
| ❑ | 501 | Will Cunnane | .15 | .07 |
| ❑ | 502 | Darryl Hamilton | .15 | .07 |
| ❑ | 503 | Brian Johnson | .15 | .07 |
| ❑ | 504 | Kirk Rueter | .15 | .07 |

| No. | Player | Mint | NrMt |
|---|---|---|---|
| ❑ 505 | Barry Bonds | 1.00 | .45 |
| ❑ 506 | Osvaldo Fernandez | .15 | .07 |
| ❑ 507 | Stan Javier | .15 | .07 |
| ❑ 508 | Julian Tavarez | .15 | .07 |
| ❑ 509 | Rich Aurilia | .15 | .07 |
| ❑ 510 | Alex Rodriguez | 2.00 | .90 |
| ❑ 511 | David Segui | .15 | .07 |
| ❑ 512 | Rich Amaral | .15 | .07 |
| ❑ 513 | Raul Ibanez | .15 | .07 |
| ❑ 514 | Jay Buhner | .25 | .11 |
| ❑ 515 | Randy Johnson | .75 | .35 |
| ❑ 516 | Heathcliff Slocumb | .15 | .07 |
| ❑ 517 | Tony Saunders | .15 | .07 |
| ❑ 518 | Kevin Elster | .15 | .07 |
| ❑ 519 | John Burkett | .15 | .07 |
| ❑ 520 | Juan Gonzalez | .60 | .25 |
| ❑ 521 | John Wetteland | .25 | .11 |
| ❑ 522 | Domingo Cedeno | .15 | .07 |
| ❑ 523 | Darren Oliver | .15 | .07 |
| ❑ 524 | Roger Pavlik | .15 | .07 |
| ❑ 525 | Jose Cruz Jr. | .25 | .11 |
| ❑ 526 | Woody Williams | .15 | .07 |
| ❑ 527 | Alex Gonzalez | .15 | .07 |
| ❑ 528 | Robert Person | .15 | .07 |
| ❑ 529 | Juan Guzman | .15 | .07 |
| ❑ 530 | Roger Clemens | 1.25 | .55 |
| ❑ 531 | Shawn Green | .60 | .25 |
| ❑ 532 | Francisco Cordova SH<br>Ricardo Rincon<br>Mark Smith | .15 | .07 |
| ❑ 533 | Nomar Garciaparra SH | 1.00 | .45 |
| ❑ 534 | Roger Clemens SH | .60 | .25 |
| ❑ 535 | Mark McGwire SH | 1.25 | .55 |
| ❑ 536 | Larry Walker SH | .25 | .11 |
| ❑ 537 | Mike Piazza SH | 1.00 | .45 |
| ❑ 538 | Curt Schilling SH | .25 | .11 |
| ❑ 539 | Tony Gwynn SH | .60 | .25 |
| ❑ 540 | Ken Griffey Jr. SH | 1.25 | .55 |
| ❑ 541 | Carl Pavano | .15 | .07 |
| ❑ 542 | Shane Monahan | .15 | .07 |
| ❑ 543 | Gabe Kapler RC | 2.00 | .90 |
| ❑ 544 | Eric Milton | .15 | .07 |
| ❑ 545 | Gary Matthews Jr. RC | .25 | .11 |
| ❑ 546 | Mike Kinkade RC | .40 | .18 |
| ❑ 547 | Ryan Christenson RC | .25 | .11 |
| ❑ 548 | Corey Koskie RC | .60 | .25 |
| ❑ 549 | Norm Hutchins | .15 | .07 |
| ❑ 550 | Russell Branyan | .25 | .11 |
| ❑ 551 | Masato Yoshii RC | .50 | .23 |
| ❑ 552 | Jesus Sanchez RC | .40 | .18 |
| ❑ 553 | Anthony Sanders | .15 | .07 |
| ❑ 554 | Edwin Diaz | .15 | .07 |
| ❑ 555 | Gabe Alvarez | .15 | .07 |
| ❑ 556 | Carlos Lee RC | 1.50 | .70 |
| ❑ 557 | Mike Darr | .25 | .11 |
| ❑ 558 | Kerry Wood | .60 | .25 |
| ❑ 559 | Carlos Guillen | .15 | .07 |
| ❑ 560 | Sean Casey | .25 | .11 |
| ❑ 561 | Manny Aybar RC | .25 | .11 |
| ❑ 562 | Octavio Dotel | .15 | .07 |
| ❑ 563 | Jarrod Washburn | .15 | .07 |
| ❑ 564 | Mark L. Johnson | .15 | .07 |
| ❑ 565 | Ramon Hernandez | .15 | .07 |
| ❑ 566 | Rich Butler RC | .15 | .07 |
| ❑ 567 | Mike Caruso | .15 | .07 |
| ❑ 568 | Cliff Politte | .15 | .07 |
| ❑ 569 | Scott Elarton | .25 | .11 |
| ❑ 570 | Magglio Ordonez RC | 2.50 | 1.10 |
| ❑ 571 | Adam Butler RC | .25 | .11 |
| ❑ 572 | Marlon Anderson | .15 | .07 |
| ❑ 573 | Julio Ramirez RC | .50 | .23 |
| ❑ 574 | Darron Ingram RC | .40 | .18 |
| ❑ 575 | Bruce Chen | .15 | .07 |
| ❑ 576 | Steve Woodard | .15 | .07 |
| ❑ 577 | Hiram Bocachica | .15 | .07 |
| ❑ 578 | Kevin Witt | .15 | .07 |
| ❑ 579 | Javier Vazquez | .15 | .07 |
| ❑ 580 | Alex Gonzalez | .15 | .07 |
| ❑ 581 | Brian Powell | .15 | .07 |
| ❑ 582 | Wes Helms | .15 | .07 |
| ❑ 583 | Ron Wright | .15 | .07 |
| ❑ 584 | Rafael Medina | .15 | .07 |
| ❑ 585 | Daryle Ward | .25 | .11 |
| ❑ 586 | Geoff Jenkins | .25 | .11 |
| ❑ 587 | Preston Wilson | .25 | .11 |
| ❑ 588 | Jim Chamblee RC | .15 | .07 |
| ❑ 589 | Mike Lowell RC | .75 | .35 |
| ❑ 590 | A.J. Hinch | .15 | .07 |
| ❑ 591 | Francisco Cordero RC | .40 | .18 |
| ❑ 592 | Rolando Arrojo RC | .50 | .23 |
| ❑ 593 | Braden Looper | .15 | .07 |
| ❑ 594 | Sidney Ponson | .15 | .07 |
| ❑ 595 | Matt Clement | .25 | .11 |
| ❑ 596 | Carlton Loewer | .15 | .07 |
| ❑ 597 | Brian Meadows | .15 | .07 |
| ❑ 598 | Danny Klassen | .15 | .07 |
| ❑ 599 | Larry Sutton | .15 | .07 |
| ❑ 600 | Travis Lee | .25 | .11 |
| ❑ 601 | Randy Johnson EP | 2.50 | 1.10 |
| ❑ 602 | Greg Maddux EP | 5.00 | 2.20 |
| ❑ 603 | Roger Clemens EP | 4.00 | 1.80 |
| ❑ 604 | Jaret Wright EP | 1.50 | .70 |
| ❑ 605 | Mike Piazza EP | 6.00 | 2.70 |
| ❑ 606 | Tino Martinez EP | 1.50 | .70 |
| ❑ 607 | Frank Thomas EP | 4.00 | 1.80 |
| ❑ 608 | Mo Vaughn EP | 1.50 | .70 |
| ❑ 609 | Todd Helton EP | 2.50 | 1.10 |
| ❑ 610 | Mark McGwire EP | 8.00 | 3.60 |
| ❑ 611 | Jeff Bagwell EP | 2.50 | 1.10 |
| ❑ 612 | Travis Lee EP | 1.50 | .70 |
| ❑ 613 | Scott Rolen EP | 2.00 | .90 |
| ❑ 614 | Cal Ripken EP | 8.00 | 3.60 |
| ❑ 615 | Chipper Jones EP | 5.00 | 2.20 |
| ❑ 616 | Nomar Garciaparra EP | 6.00 | 2.70 |
| ❑ 617 | Alex Rodriguez EP | 6.00 | 2.70 |
| ❑ 618 | Derek Jeter EP | 8.00 | 3.60 |
| ❑ 619 | Tony Gwynn EP | 4.00 | 1.80 |
| ❑ 620 | Ken Griffey Jr. EP | 8.00 | 3.60 |
| ❑ 621 | Kenny Lofton EP | 1.50 | .70 |
| ❑ 622 | Juan Gonzalez EP | 2.00 | .90 |
| ❑ 623 | Jose Cruz Jr. EP | 1.50 | .70 |
| ❑ 624 | Larry Walker EP | 1.50 | .70 |
| ❑ 625 | Barry Bonds EP | 3.00 | 1.35 |
| ❑ 626 | Ben Grieve EP | 1.50 | .70 |
| ❑ 627 | Andruw Jones EP | 2.00 | .90 |
| ❑ 628 | Vladimir Guerrero EP | 3.00 | 1.35 |
| ❑ 629 | Paul Konerko EP | 1.50 | .70 |
| ❑ 630 | Paul Molitor EP | 2.00 | .90 |
| ❑ 631 | Cecil Fielder | .25 | .11 |
| ❑ 632 | Jack McDowell | .15 | .07 |
| ❑ 633 | Mike James | .15 | .07 |
| ❑ 634 | Brian Anderson | .15 | .07 |
| ❑ 635 | Jay Bell | .25 | .11 |
| ❑ 636 | Devon White | .15 | .07 |
| ❑ 637 | Andy Stankiewicz | .15 | .07 |
| ❑ 638 | Tony Batista | .25 | .11 |
| ❑ 639 | Omar Daal | .15 | .07 |
| ❑ 640 | Matt Williams | .40 | .18 |
| ❑ 641 | Brent Brede | .15 | .07 |
| ❑ 642 | Jorge Fabregas | .15 | .07 |
| ❑ 643 | Karim Garcia | .15 | .07 |
| ❑ 644 | Felix Rodriguez | .15 | .07 |
| ❑ 645 | Andy Benes | .15 | .07 |
| ❑ 646 | Willie Blair | .15 | .07 |
| ❑ 647 | Jeff Suppan | .15 | .07 |
| ❑ 648 | Yamil Benitez | .15 | .07 |
| ❑ 649 | Walt Weiss | .25 | .11 |
| ❑ 650 | Andres Galarraga | .40 | .18 |
| ❑ 651 | Doug Drabek | .15 | .07 |
| ❑ 652 | Ozzie Guillen | .15 | .07 |
| ❑ 653 | Joe Carter | .25 | .11 |
| ❑ 654 | Dennis Eckersley | .25 | .11 |
| ❑ 655 | Pedro Martinez | .75 | .35 |
| ❑ 656 | Jim Leyritz | .15 | .07 |
| ❑ 657 | Henry Rodriguez | .15 | .07 |
| ❑ 658 | Rod Beck | .15 | .07 |
| ❑ 659 | Mickey Morandini | .15 | .07 |
| ❑ 660 | Jeff Blauser | .15 | .07 |
| ❑ 661 | Ruben Sierra | .15 | .07 |
| ❑ 662 | Mike Sirotka | .15 | .07 |
| ❑ 663 | Pete Harnisch | .15 | .07 |
| ❑ 664 | Damian Jackson | .15 | .07 |
| ❑ 665 | Dmitri Young | .25 | .11 |
| ❑ 666 | Steve Cooke | .15 | .07 |
| ❑ 667 | Geronimo Berroa | .15 | .07 |
| ❑ 668 | Shawon Dunston | .15 | .07 |
| ❑ 669 | Mike Jackson | .15 | .07 |
| ❑ 670 | Travis Fryman | .25 | .11 |
| ❑ 671 | Dwight Gooden | .15 | .07 |
| ❑ 672 | Paul Assenmacher | .15 | .07 |
| ❑ 673 | Eric Plunk | .15 | .07 |
| ❑ 674 | Mike Lansing | .15 | .07 |
| ❑ 675 | Darryl Kile | .25 | .11 |
| ❑ 676 | Luis Gonzalez | .25 | .11 |
| ❑ 677 | Frank Castillo | .15 | .07 |
| ❑ 678 | Joe Randa | .15 | .07 |
| ❑ 679 | Bip Roberts | .15 | .07 |
| ❑ 680 | Derrek Lee | .15 | .07 |
| ❑ 681 | Mike Piazza SP<br>New York Mets | 5.00 | 2.20 |
| ❑ 681A | Mike Piazza SP<br>Florida Marlins | 5.00 | 2.20 |
| ❑ 682 | Sean Berry | .15 | .07 |
| ❑ 683 | Ramon Garcia | .15 | .07 |
| ❑ 684 | Carl Everett | .25 | .11 |
| ❑ 685 | Moises Alou | .25 | .11 |
| ❑ 686 | Hal Morris | .15 | .07 |
| ❑ 687 | Jeff Conine | .15 | .07 |
| ❑ 688 | Gary Sheffield | .60 | .25 |
| ❑ 689 | Jose Vizcaino | .15 | .07 |
| ❑ 690 | Charles Johnson | .25 | .11 |
| ❑ 691 | Bobby Bonilla | .25 | .11 |
| ❑ 692 | Marquis Grissom | .15 | .07 |
| ❑ 693 | Alex Ochoa | .15 | .07 |
| ❑ 694 | Mike Morgan | .15 | .07 |
| ❑ 695 | Orlando Merced | .15 | .07 |
| ❑ 696 | David Ortiz | .15 | .07 |
| ❑ 697 | Brent Gates | .15 | .07 |
| ❑ 698 | Otis Nixon | .15 | .07 |
| ❑ 699 | Trey Moore | .15 | .07 |
| ❑ 700 | Derrick May | .15 | .07 |
| ❑ 701 | Rich Becker | .15 | .07 |
| ❑ 702 | Al Leiter | .25 | .11 |
| ❑ 703 | Chili Davis | .25 | .11 |
| ❑ 704 | Scott Brosius | .25 | .11 |
| ❑ 705 | Chuck Knoblauch | .25 | .11 |
| ❑ 706 | Kenny Rogers | .15 | .07 |
| ❑ 707 | Mike Blowers | .15 | .07 |
| ❑ 708 | Mike Fetters | .15 | .07 |
| ❑ 709 | Tom Candiotti | .15 | .07 |
| ❑ 710 | Rickey Henderson | .75 | .35 |
| ❑ 711 | Bob Abreu | .25 | .11 |
| ❑ 712 | Mark Lewis | .15 | .07 |
| ❑ 713 | Doug Glanville | .15 | .07 |
| ❑ 714 | Desi Relaford | .15 | .07 |
| ❑ 715 | Kent Mercker | .15 | .07 |
| ❑ 716 | Kevin Brown | .40 | .18 |
| ❑ 717 | James Mouton | .15 | .07 |
| ❑ 718 | Mark Langston | .15 | .07 |
| ❑ 719 | Greg Myers | .15 | .07 |
| ❑ 720 | Orel Hershiser | .25 | .11 |
| ❑ 721 | Charlie Hayes | .15 | .07 |
| ❑ 722 | Robb Nen | .15 | .07 |
| ❑ 723 | Glenallen Hill | .15 | .07 |
| ❑ 724 | Tony Saunders | .15 | .07 |
| ❑ 725 | Wade Boggs | .75 | .35 |
| ❑ 726 | Kevin Stocker | .15 | .07 |
| ❑ 727 | Wilson Alvarez | .15 | .07 |
| ❑ 728 | Albie Lopez | .15 | .07 |
| ❑ 729 | Dave Martinez | .15 | .07 |
| ❑ 730 | Fred McGriff | .40 | .18 |
| ❑ 731 | Quinton McCracken | .15 | .07 |
| ❑ 732 | Bryan Rekar | .15 | .07 |
| ❑ 733 | Paul Sorrento | .15 | .07 |
| ❑ 734 | Roberto Hernandez | .15 | .07 |
| ❑ 735 | Bubba Trammell | .15 | .07 |
| ❑ 736 | Miguel Cairo | .15 | .07 |
| ❑ 737 | John Flaherty | .15 | .07 |
| ❑ 738 | Terrell Wade | .15 | .07 |
| ❑ 739 | Roberto Kelly | .15 | .07 |
| ❑ 740 | Mark McLemore | .15 | .07 |
| ❑ 741 | Danny Patterson | .15 | .07 |
| ❑ 742 | Aaron Sele | .25 | .11 |
| ❑ 743 | Tony Fernandez | .15 | .07 |
| ❑ 744 | Randy Myers | .25 | .11 |
| ❑ 745 | Jose Canseco | .75 | .35 |
| ❑ 746 | Darrin Fletcher | .15 | .07 |
| ❑ 747 | Mike Stanley | .15 | .07 |
| ❑ 748 | Marquis Grissom SH CL | .15 | .07 |
| ❑ 749 | Fred McGriff SH CL | .25 | .11 |
| ❑ 750 | Travis Lee SH CL | .25 | .11 |

## 1999 Upper Deck

| | MINT | NRMT |
|---|---|---|
| COMPLETE SET (525) | 100.00 | 45.00 |
| COMPLETE SERIES 1 (255) | 60.00 | 27.00 |
| COMPLETE SERIES 2 (270) | 40.00 | 18.00 |

| | | |
|---|---|---|
| COMMON (19-255/293-535) | .15 | .07 |
| COMMON SER.2 SR (266-292) | .30 | .14 |
| ❑ 1 Troy Glaus SR | 3.00 | 1.35 |
| ❑ 2 Adrian Beltre SR | .60 | .25 |
| ❑ 3 Matt Anderson SR | .40 | .18 |
| ❑ 4 Eric Chavez SR | .60 | .25 |
| ❑ 5 Jin Ho Cho SR | .40 | .18 |
| ❑ 6 Robert Smith SR | .40 | .18 |
| ❑ 7 George Lombard SR | .40 | .18 |
| ❑ 8 Mike Kinkade SR | .40 | .18 |
| ❑ 9 Seth Greisinger SR | .40 | .18 |
| ❑ 10 J.D. Drew SR | 2.00 | .90 |
| ❑ 11 Aramis Ramirez SR | .40 | .18 |
| ❑ 12 Carlos Guillen SR | .40 | .18 |
| ❑ 13 Justin Baughman SR | .40 | .18 |
| ❑ 14 Jim Parque SR | .40 | .18 |
| ❑ 15 Ryan Jackson SR | .40 | .18 |
| ❑ 16 Ramon E.Martinez SR RC | .40 | .18 |
| ❑ 17 Orlando Hernandez SR | .60 | .25 |
| ❑ 18 Jeremy Giambi SR | .40 | .18 |
| ❑ 19 Gary DiSarcina | .15 | .07 |
| ❑ 20 Darin Erstad | .60 | .25 |
| ❑ 21 Troy Glaus | 1.00 | .45 |
| ❑ 22 Chuck Finley | .25 | .11 |
| ❑ 23 Dave Hollins | .15 | .07 |
| ❑ 24 Troy Percival | .15 | .07 |
| ❑ 25 Tim Salmon | .25 | .11 |
| ❑ 26 Brian Anderson | .15 | .07 |
| ❑ 27 Jay Bell | .25 | .11 |
| ❑ 28 Andy Benes | .15 | .07 |
| ❑ 29 Brent Brede | .15 | .07 |
| ❑ 30 David Dellucci | .15 | .07 |
| ❑ 31 Karim Garcia | .15 | .07 |
| ❑ 32 Travis Lee | .15 | .07 |
| ❑ 33 Andres Galarraga | .40 | .18 |
| ❑ 34 Ryan Klesko | .25 | .11 |
| ❑ 35 Keith Lockhart | .15 | .07 |
| ❑ 36 Kevin Millwood | .25 | .11 |
| ❑ 37 Denny Neagle | .15 | .07 |
| ❑ 38 John Smoltz | .25 | .11 |
| ❑ 39 Michael Tucker | .15 | .07 |
| ❑ 40 Walt Weiss | .15 | .07 |
| ❑ 41 Dennis Martinez | .25 | .11 |
| ❑ 42 Javy Lopez | .25 | .11 |
| ❑ 43 Brady Anderson | .25 | .11 |
| ❑ 44 Harold Baines | .25 | .11 |
| ❑ 45 Mike Bordick | .15 | .07 |
| ❑ 46 Roberto Alomar | .60 | .25 |
| ❑ 47 Scott Erickson | .15 | .07 |
| ❑ 48 Mike Mussina | .60 | .25 |
| ❑ 49 Cal Ripken | 2.50 | 1.10 |
| ❑ 50 Darren Bragg | .15 | .07 |
| ❑ 51 Dennis Eckersley | .25 | .11 |
| ❑ 52 Nomar Garciaparra | 2.00 | .90 |
| ❑ 53 Scott Hatteberg | .15 | .07 |
| ❑ 54 Troy O'Leary | .15 | .07 |
| ❑ 55 Bret Saberhagen | .25 | .11 |
| ❑ 56 John Valentin | .15 | .07 |
| ❑ 57 Rod Beck | .15 | .07 |
| ❑ 58 Jeff Blauser | .15 | .07 |
| ❑ 59 Brant Brown | .15 | .07 |
| ❑ 60 Mark Clark | .15 | .07 |
| ❑ 61 Mark Grace | .60 | .25 |
| ❑ 62 Kevin Tapani | .15 | .07 |
| ❑ 63 Henry Rodriguez | .15 | .07 |
| ❑ 64 Mike Cameron | .15 | .07 |
| ❑ 65 Mike Caruso | .15 | .07 |
| ❑ 66 Ray Durham | .25 | .11 |
| ❑ 67 Jaime Navarro | .15 | .07 |
| ❑ 68 Magglio Ordonez | .40 | .18 |
| ❑ 69 Mike Sirotka | .15 | .07 |
| ❑ 70 Sean Casey | .25 | .11 |
| ❑ 71 Barry Larkin | .60 | .25 |
| ❑ 72 Jon Nunnally | .15 | .07 |
| ❑ 73 Paul Konerko | .25 | .11 |
| ❑ 74 Chris Stynes | .15 | .07 |
| ❑ 75 Brett Tomko | .15 | .07 |
| ❑ 76 Dmitri Young | .25 | .11 |
| ❑ 77 Sandy Alomar Jr. | .25 | .11 |
| ❑ 78 Bartolo Colon | .25 | .11 |
| ❑ 79 Travis Fryman | .25 | .11 |
| ❑ 80 Brian Giles | .25 | .11 |
| ❑ 81 David Justice | .40 | .18 |
| ❑ 82 Omar Vizquel | .25 | .11 |
| ❑ 83 Jaret Wright | .15 | .07 |
| ❑ 84 Jim Thome | .40 | .18 |
| ❑ 85 Charles Nagy | .15 | .07 |
| ❑ 86 Pedro Astacio | .15 | .07 |
| ❑ 87 Todd Helton | .75 | .35 |
| ❑ 88 Darryl Kile | .25 | .11 |
| ❑ 89 Mike Lansing | .15 | .07 |
| ❑ 90 Neifi Perez | .15 | .07 |
| ❑ 91 John Thomson | .15 | .07 |
| ❑ 92 Larry Walker | .25 | .11 |
| ❑ 93 Tony Clark | .15 | .07 |
| ❑ 94 Deivi Cruz | .15 | .07 |
| ❑ 95 Damion Easley | .15 | .07 |
| ❑ 96 Brian L.Hunter | .15 | .07 |
| ❑ 97 Todd Jones | .15 | .07 |
| ❑ 98 Brian Moehler | .15 | .07 |
| ❑ 99 Gabe Alvarez | .15 | .07 |
| ❑ 100 Craig Counsell | .15 | .07 |
| ❑ 101 Cliff Floyd | .25 | .11 |
| ❑ 102 Livan Hernandez | .15 | .07 |
| ❑ 103 Andy Larkin | .15 | .07 |
| ❑ 104 Derrek Lee | .15 | .07 |
| ❑ 105 Brian Meadows | .15 | .07 |
| ❑ 106 Moises Alou | .25 | .11 |
| ❑ 107 Sean Berry | .15 | .07 |
| ❑ 108 Craig Biggio | .40 | .18 |
| ❑ 109 Ricky Gutierrez | .15 | .07 |
| ❑ 110 Mike Hampton | .25 | .11 |
| ❑ 111 Jose Lima | .15 | .07 |
| ❑ 112 Billy Wagner | .15 | .07 |
| ❑ 113 Hal Morris | .15 | .07 |
| ❑ 114 Johnny Damon | .25 | .11 |
| ❑ 115 Jeff King | .15 | .07 |
| ❑ 116 Jeff Montgomery | .15 | .07 |
| ❑ 117 Glendon Rusch | .15 | .07 |
| ❑ 118 Larry Sutton | .15 | .07 |
| ❑ 119 Bobby Bonilla | .25 | .11 |
| ❑ 120 Jim Eisenreich | .15 | .07 |
| ❑ 121 Eric Karros | .25 | .11 |
| ❑ 122 Matt Luke | .15 | .07 |
| ❑ 123 Ramon Martinez | .15 | .07 |
| ❑ 124 Gary Sheffield | .60 | .25 |
| ❑ 125 Eric Young | .15 | .07 |
| ❑ 126 Charles Johnson | .25 | .11 |
| ❑ 127 Jeff Cirillo | .25 | .11 |
| ❑ 128 Marquis Grissom | .15 | .07 |
| ❑ 129 Jeromy Burnitz | .25 | .11 |
| ❑ 130 Bob Wickman | .15 | .07 |
| ❑ 131 Scott Karl | .15 | .07 |
| ❑ 132 Mark Loretta | .15 | .07 |
| ❑ 133 Fernando Vina | .15 | .07 |
| ❑ 134 Matt Lawton | .25 | .11 |
| ❑ 135 Pat Meares | .15 | .07 |
| ❑ 136 Eric Milton | .15 | .07 |
| ❑ 137 Paul Molitor | .60 | .25 |
| ❑ 138 David Ortiz | .15 | .07 |
| ❑ 139 Todd Walker | .15 | .07 |
| ❑ 140 Shane Andrews | .15 | .07 |
| ❑ 141 Brad Fullmer | .25 | .11 |
| ❑ 142 Vladimir Guerrero | 1.00 | .45 |
| ❑ 143 Dustin Hermanson | .15 | .07 |
| ❑ 144 Ryan McGuire | .15 | .07 |
| ❑ 145 Ugueth Urbina | .15 | .07 |
| ❑ 146 John Franco | .25 | .11 |
| ❑ 147 Butch Huskey | .15 | .07 |
| ❑ 148 Bobby Jones | .15 | .07 |
| ❑ 149 John Olerud | .25 | .11 |
| ❑ 150 Rey Ordonez | .15 | .07 |
| ❑ 151 Mike Piazza | 2.00 | .90 |
| ❑ 152 Hideo Nomo | .60 | .25 |
| ❑ 153 Masato Yoshii | .25 | .11 |
| ❑ 154 Derek Jeter | 2.50 | 1.10 |
| ❑ 155 Chuck Knoblauch | .25 | .11 |
| ❑ 156 Paul O'Neill | .25 | .11 |
| ❑ 157 Andy Pettitte | .25 | .11 |
| ❑ 158 Mariano Rivera | .25 | .11 |
| ❑ 159 Darryl Strawberry | .25 | .11 |
| ❑ 160 David Wells | .25 | .11 |
| ❑ 161 Jorge Posada | .25 | .11 |
| ❑ 162 Ramiro Mendoza | .15 | .07 |
| ❑ 163 Miguel Tejada | .25 | .11 |
| ❑ 164 Ryan Christenson | .15 | .07 |
| ❑ 165 Rickey Henderson | .75 | .35 |
| ❑ 166 A.J. Hinch | .15 | .07 |
| ❑ 167 Ben Grieve | .25 | .11 |
| ❑ 168 Kenny Rogers | .15 | .07 |
| ❑ 169 Matt Stairs | .15 | .07 |
| ❑ 170 Bob Abreu | .25 | .11 |
| ❑ 171 Rico Brogna | .15 | .07 |
| ❑ 172 Doug Glanville | .15 | .07 |
| ❑ 173 Mike Grace | .15 | .07 |
| ❑ 174 Desi Relaford | .15 | .07 |
| ❑ 175 Scott Rolen | .60 | .25 |
| ❑ 176 Jose Guillen | .15 | .07 |
| ❑ 177 Francisco Cordova | .15 | .07 |
| ❑ 178 Al Martin | .15 | .07 |
| ❑ 179 Jason Schmidt | .15 | .07 |
| ❑ 180 Turner Ward | .15 | .07 |
| ❑ 181 Kevin Young | .25 | .11 |
| ❑ 182 Mark McGwire | 2.50 | 1.10 |
| ❑ 183 Delino DeShields | .15 | .07 |
| ❑ 184 Eli Marrero | .15 | .07 |
| ❑ 185 Tom Lampkin | .15 | .07 |
| ❑ 186 Ray Lankford | .25 | .11 |
| ❑ 187 Willie McGee | .25 | .11 |
| ❑ 188 Matt Morris | .15 | .07 |
| ❑ 189 Andy Ashby | .15 | .07 |
| ❑ 190 Kevin Brown | .40 | .18 |
| ❑ 191 Ken Caminiti | .25 | .11 |
| ❑ 192 Trevor Hoffman | .25 | .11 |
| ❑ 193 Wally Joyner | .25 | .11 |
| ❑ 194 Greg Vaughn | .25 | .11 |
| ❑ 195 Danny Darwin | .15 | .07 |
| ❑ 196 Shawn Estes | .15 | .07 |
| ❑ 197 Orel Hershiser | .25 | .11 |
| ❑ 198 Jeff Kent | .40 | .18 |
| ❑ 199 Bill Mueller | .15 | .07 |
| ❑ 200 Robb Nen | .15 | .07 |
| ❑ 201 J.T. Snow | .25 | .11 |
| ❑ 202 Ken Cloude | .15 | .07 |
| ❑ 203 Russ Davis | .15 | .07 |
| ❑ 204 Jeff Fassero | .15 | .07 |
| ❑ 205 Ken Griffey Jr. | 2.50 | 1.10 |
| ❑ 206 Shane Monahan | .15 | .07 |
| ❑ 207 David Segui | .15 | .07 |
| ❑ 208 Dan Wilson | .15 | .07 |
| ❑ 209 Wilson Alvarez | .15 | .07 |
| ❑ 210 Wade Boggs | .75 | .35 |
| ❑ 211 Miguel Cairo | .15 | .07 |
| ❑ 212 Bubba Trammell | .15 | .07 |
| ❑ 213 Quinton McCracken | .15 | .07 |
| ❑ 214 Paul Sorrento | .15 | .07 |
| ❑ 215 Kevin Stocker | .15 | .07 |
| ❑ 216 Will Clark | .60 | .25 |
| ❑ 217 Rusty Greer | .25 | .11 |
| ❑ 218 Rick Helling | .25 | .11 |
| ❑ 219 Mark McLemore | .15 | .07 |
| ❑ 220 Ivan Rodriguez | .75 | .35 |
| ❑ 221 John Wetteland | .25 | .11 |
| ❑ 222 Jose Canseco | .75 | .35 |
| ❑ 223 Roger Clemens | 1.25 | .55 |
| ❑ 224 Carlos Delgado | .60 | .25 |
| ❑ 225 Darrin Fletcher | .15 | .07 |
| ❑ 226 Alex Gonzalez | .15 | .07 |
| ❑ 227 Jose Cruz Jr. | .25 | .11 |
| ❑ 228 Shannon Stewart | .25 | .11 |
| ❑ 229 Rolando Arrojo FF | .15 | .07 |
| ❑ 230 Livan Hernandez FF | .15 | .07 |
| ❑ 231 Orlando Hernandez FF | .25 | .11 |
| ❑ 232 Raul Mondesi FF | .25 | .11 |
| ❑ 233 Moises Alou FF | .25 | .11 |
| ❑ 234 Pedro Martinez FF | .75 | .35 |
| ❑ 235 Sammy Sosa FF | 1.25 | .55 |
| ❑ 236 Vladimir Guerrero FF | 1.00 | .45 |
| ❑ 237 Bartolo Colon FF | .25 | .11 |

| | | |
|---|---|---|
| ☐ 238 Miguel Tejada FF | .25 | .11 |
| ☐ 239 Ismael Valdes FF | .15 | .07 |
| ☐ 240 Mariano Rivera FF | .25 | .11 |
| ☐ 241 Jose Cruz Jr. FF | .25 | .11 |
| ☐ 242 Juan Gonzalez FF | .60 | .25 |
| ☐ 243 Ivan Rodriguez FF | .75 | .35 |
| ☐ 244 Sandy Alomar Jr. FF | .25 | .11 |
| ☐ 245 Roberto Alomar FF | .60 | .25 |
| ☐ 246 Magglio Ordonez FF | .40 | .18 |
| ☐ 247 Kerry Wood SH CL | .25 | .11 |
| ☐ 248 Mark McGwire SH CL | 2.50 | 1.10 |
| ☐ 249 David Wells SH CL | .25 | .11 |
| ☐ 250 Rolando Arrojo SH CL | .15 | .07 |
| ☐ 251 Ken Griffey Jr. SH CL | 2.50 | 1.10 |
| ☐ 252 Trevor Hoffman SH CL | .25 | .11 |
| ☐ 253 Travis Lee SH CL | .15 | .07 |
| ☐ 254 Roberto Alomar SH CL | .60 | .25 |
| ☐ 255 Sammy Sosa SH CL | 1.25 | .55 |
| ☐ 266 Pat Burrell SR RC | 4.00 | 1.80 |
| ☐ 267 Shea Hillenbrand SR RC | .50 | .23 |
| ☐ 268 Robert Fick SR | .30 | .14 |
| ☐ 269 Roy Halladay SR | .30 | .14 |
| ☐ 270 Ruben Mateo SR | .50 | .23 |
| ☐ 271 Bruce Chen SR | .30 | .14 |
| ☐ 272 Angel Pena SR | .30 | .14 |
| ☐ 273 Michael Barrett SR | .30 | .14 |
| ☐ 274 Kevin Witt SR | .30 | .14 |
| ☐ 275 Damon Minor SR | .30 | .14 |
| ☐ 276 Ryan Minor SR | .30 | .14 |
| ☐ 277 A.J. Pierzynski SR | .30 | .14 |
| ☐ 278 A.J. Burnett SR RC | .75 | .35 |
| ☐ 279 Dermal Brown SR | .50 | .23 |
| ☐ 280 Joe Lawrence SR | .50 | .23 |
| ☐ 281 Derrick Gibson SR | .30 | .14 |
| ☐ 282 Carlos Febles SR | .30 | .14 |
| ☐ 283 Chris Haas SR | .30 | .14 |
| ☐ 284 Cesar King SR | .30 | .14 |
| ☐ 285 Calvin Pickering SR | .30 | .14 |
| ☐ 286 Mitch Meluskey SR | .30 | .14 |
| ☐ 287 Carlos Beltran SR | .50 | .23 |
| ☐ 288 Ron Belliard SR | .30 | .14 |
| ☐ 289 Jerry Hairston Jr. SR | .50 | .23 |
| ☐ 290 Fernando Seguignol SR | .30 | .14 |
| ☐ 291 Kris Benson SR | .50 | .23 |
| ☐ 292 Chad Hutchinson SR RC | .60 | .25 |
| ☐ 293 Jarrod Washburn | .15 | .07 |
| ☐ 294 Jason Dickson | .15 | .07 |
| ☐ 295 Mo Vaughn | .25 | .11 |
| ☐ 296 Garret Anderson | .25 | .11 |
| ☐ 297 Jim Edmonds | .60 | .25 |
| ☐ 298 Ken Hill | .15 | .07 |
| ☐ 299 Shigetoshi Hasegawa | .15 | .07 |
| ☐ 300 Todd Stottlemyre | .15 | .07 |
| ☐ 301 Randy Johnson | .75 | .35 |
| ☐ 302 Omar Daal | .15 | .07 |
| ☐ 303 Steve Finley | .25 | .11 |
| ☐ 304 Matt Williams | .40 | .18 |
| ☐ 305 Danny Klassen | .15 | .07 |
| ☐ 306 Tony Batista | .25 | .11 |
| ☐ 307 Brian Jordan | .25 | .11 |
| ☐ 308 Greg Maddux | 1.50 | .70 |
| ☐ 309 Chipper Jones | 1.50 | .70 |
| ☐ 310 Bret Boone | .25 | .11 |
| ☐ 311 Ozzie Guillen | .15 | .07 |
| ☐ 312 John Rocker | .25 | .11 |
| ☐ 313 Tom Glavine | .60 | .25 |
| ☐ 314 Andruw Jones | .60 | .25 |
| ☐ 315 Albert Belle | .40 | .18 |
| ☐ 316 Charles Johnson | .25 | .11 |
| ☐ 317 Will Clark | .60 | .25 |
| ☐ 318 B.J. Surhoff | .25 | .11 |
| ☐ 319 Delino DeShields | .15 | .07 |
| ☐ 320 Heathcliff Slocumb | .15 | .07 |
| ☐ 321 Sidney Ponson | .15 | .07 |
| ☐ 322 Juan Guzman | .15 | .07 |
| ☐ 323 Reggie Jefferson | .15 | .07 |
| ☐ 324 Mark Portugal | .15 | .07 |
| ☐ 325 Tim Wakefield | .15 | .07 |
| ☐ 326 Jason Varitek | .25 | .11 |
| ☐ 327 Jose Offerman | .15 | .07 |
| ☐ 328 Pedro Martinez | .75 | .35 |
| ☐ 329 Trot Nixon | .25 | .11 |
| ☐ 330 Kerry Wood | .25 | .11 |
| ☐ 331 Sammy Sosa | 1.25 | .55 |
| ☐ 332 Glenallen Hill | .15 | .07 |
| ☐ 333 Gary Gaetti | .15 | .07 |
| ☐ 334 Mickey Morandini | .15 | .07 |
| ☐ 335 Benito Santiago | .15 | .07 |
| ☐ 336 Jeff Blauser | .15 | .07 |
| ☐ 337 Frank Thomas | 1.25 | .55 |
| ☐ 338 Paul Konerko | .25 | .11 |
| ☐ 339 Jaime Navarro | .15 | .07 |
| ☐ 340 Carlos Lee | .25 | .11 |
| ☐ 341 Brian Simmons | .15 | .07 |
| ☐ 342 Mark Johnson | .15 | .07 |
| ☐ 343 Jeff Abbott | .15 | .07 |
| ☐ 344 Steve Avery | .15 | .07 |
| ☐ 345 Mike Cameron | .15 | .07 |
| ☐ 346 Michael Tucker | .15 | .07 |
| ☐ 347 Greg Vaughn | .25 | .11 |
| ☐ 348 Hal Morris | .15 | .07 |
| ☐ 349 Pete Harnisch | .15 | .07 |
| ☐ 350 Denny Neagle | .15 | .07 |
| ☐ 351 Manny Ramirez | .75 | .35 |
| ☐ 352 Roberto Alomar | .60 | .25 |
| ☐ 353 Dwight Gooden | .25 | .11 |
| ☐ 354 Kenny Lofton | .25 | .11 |
| ☐ 355 Mike Jackson | .15 | .07 |
| ☐ 356 Charles Nagy | .15 | .07 |
| ☐ 357 Enrique Wilson | .15 | .07 |
| ☐ 358 Russ Branyan | .25 | .11 |
| ☐ 359 Richie Sexson | .25 | .11 |
| ☐ 360 Vinny Castilla | .25 | .11 |
| ☐ 361 Dante Bichette | .25 | .11 |
| ☐ 362 Kirt Manwaring | .15 | .07 |
| ☐ 363 Darryl Hamilton | .15 | .07 |
| ☐ 364 Jamey Wright | .15 | .07 |
| ☐ 365 Curtis Leskanic | .15 | .07 |
| ☐ 366 Jeff Reed | .15 | .07 |
| ☐ 367 Bobby Higginson | .25 | .11 |
| ☐ 368 Justin Thompson | .15 | .07 |
| ☐ 369 Brad Ausmus | .15 | .07 |
| ☐ 370 Dean Palmer | .25 | .11 |
| ☐ 371 Gabe Kapler | .25 | .11 |
| ☐ 372 Juan Encarnacion | .25 | .11 |
| ☐ 373 Karim Garcia | .15 | .07 |
| ☐ 374 Alex Gonzalez | .15 | .07 |
| ☐ 375 Braden Looper | .15 | .07 |
| ☐ 376 Preston Wilson | .25 | .11 |
| ☐ 377 Todd Dunwoody | .15 | .07 |
| ☐ 378 Alex Fernandez | .15 | .07 |
| ☐ 379 Mark Kotsay | .15 | .07 |
| ☐ 380 Matt Mantei | .15 | .07 |
| ☐ 381 Ken Caminiti | .25 | .11 |
| ☐ 382 Scott Elarton | .25 | .11 |
| ☐ 383 Jeff Bagwell | .75 | .35 |
| ☐ 384 Derek Bell | .15 | .07 |
| ☐ 385 Ricky Gutierrez | .15 | .07 |
| ☐ 386 Richard Hidalgo | .25 | .11 |
| ☐ 387 Shane Reynolds | .15 | .07 |
| ☐ 388 Carl Everett | .25 | .11 |
| ☐ 389 Scott Service | .15 | .07 |
| ☐ 390 Jeff Suppan | .15 | .07 |
| ☐ 391 Joe Randa | .15 | .07 |
| ☐ 392 Kevin Appier | .25 | .11 |
| ☐ 393 Shane Halter | .15 | .07 |
| ☐ 394 Chad Kreuter | .15 | .07 |
| ☐ 395 Mike Sweeney | .25 | .11 |
| ☐ 396 Kevin Brown | .40 | .18 |
| ☐ 397 Devon White | .15 | .07 |
| ☐ 398 Todd Hollandsworth | .15 | .07 |
| ☐ 399 Todd Hundley | .15 | .07 |
| ☐ 400 Chan Ho Park | .25 | .11 |
| ☐ 401 Mark Grudzielanek | .15 | .07 |
| ☐ 402 Raul Mondesi | .25 | .11 |
| ☐ 403 Ismael Valdes | .15 | .07 |
| ☐ 404 Rafael Roque RC | .25 | .11 |
| ☐ 405 Sean Berry | .15 | .07 |
| ☐ 406 Kevin Barker | .15 | .07 |
| ☐ 407 Dave Nilsson | .15 | .07 |
| ☐ 408 Geoff Jenkins | .25 | .11 |
| ☐ 409 Jim Abbott | .25 | .11 |
| ☐ 410 Bobby Hughes | .15 | .07 |
| ☐ 411 Corey Koskie | .15 | .07 |
| ☐ 412 Rick Aguilera | .15 | .07 |
| ☐ 413 LaTroy Hawkins | .15 | .07 |
| ☐ 414 Ron Coomer | .15 | .07 |
| ☐ 415 Denny Hocking | .15 | .07 |
| ☐ 416 Marty Cordova | .15 | .07 |
| ☐ 417 Terry Steinbach | .15 | .07 |
| ☐ 418 Rondell White | .25 | .11 |
| ☐ 419 Wilton Guerrero | .15 | .07 |
| ☐ 420 Shane Andrews | .15 | .07 |
| ☐ 421 Orlando Cabrera | .15 | .07 |
| ☐ 422 Carl Pavano | .15 | .07 |
| ☐ 423 Javier Vazquez | .15 | .07 |
| ☐ 424 Chris Widger | .15 | .07 |
| ☐ 425 Robin Ventura | .25 | .11 |
| ☐ 426 Rickey Henderson | .75 | .35 |
| ☐ 427 Al Leiter | .25 | .11 |
| ☐ 428 Bobby Jones | .15 | .07 |
| ☐ 429 Brian McRae | .15 | .07 |
| ☐ 430 Roger Cedeno | .15 | .07 |
| ☐ 431 Bobby Bonilla | .25 | .11 |
| ☐ 432 Edgardo Alfonzo | .25 | .11 |
| ☐ 433 Bernie Williams | .60 | .25 |
| ☐ 434 Ricky Ledee | .15 | .07 |
| ☐ 435 Chili Davis | .25 | .11 |
| ☐ 436 Tino Martinez | .25 | .11 |
| ☐ 437 Scott Brosius | .25 | .11 |
| ☐ 438 David Cone | .25 | .11 |
| ☐ 439 Joe Girardi | .15 | .07 |
| ☐ 440 Roger Clemens | 1.25 | .55 |
| ☐ 441 Chad Curtis | .15 | .07 |
| ☐ 442 Hideki Irabu | .15 | .07 |
| ☐ 443 Jason Giambi | .60 | .25 |
| ☐ 444 Scott Spiezio | .15 | .07 |
| ☐ 445 Tony Phillips | .15 | .07 |
| ☐ 446 Ramon Hernandez | .15 | .07 |
| ☐ 447 Mike Macfarlane | .15 | .07 |
| ☐ 448 Tom Candiotti | .15 | .07 |
| ☐ 449 Billy Taylor | .15 | .07 |
| ☐ 450 Bobby Estalella | .15 | .07 |
| ☐ 451 Curt Schilling | .25 | .11 |
| ☐ 452 Carlton Loewer | .15 | .07 |
| ☐ 453 Marlon Anderson | .15 | .07 |
| ☐ 454 Kevin Jordan | .15 | .07 |
| ☐ 455 Ron Gant | .25 | .11 |
| ☐ 456 Chad Ogea | .15 | .07 |
| ☐ 457 Abraham Nunez | .15 | .07 |
| ☐ 458 Jason Kendall | .25 | .11 |
| ☐ 459 Pat Meares | .15 | .07 |
| ☐ 460 Brant Brown | .15 | .07 |
| ☐ 461 Brian Giles | .25 | .11 |
| ☐ 462 Chad Hermansen | .15 | .07 |
| ☐ 463 Freddy Garcia | .15 | .07 |
| ☐ 464 Edgar Renteria | .15 | .07 |
| ☐ 465 Fernando Tatis | .25 | .11 |
| ☐ 466 Eric Davis | .25 | .11 |
| ☐ 467 Darren Bragg | .15 | .07 |
| ☐ 468 Donovan Osborne | .15 | .07 |
| ☐ 469 Manny Aybar | .15 | .07 |
| ☐ 470 Jose Jimenez | .15 | .07 |
| ☐ 471 Kent Mercker | .15 | .07 |
| ☐ 472 Reggie Sanders | .15 | .07 |
| ☐ 473 Ruben Rivera | .15 | .07 |
| ☐ 474 Tony Gwynn | 1.25 | .55 |
| ☐ 475 Jim Leyritz | .15 | .07 |
| ☐ 476 Chris Gomez | .15 | .07 |
| ☐ 477 Matt Clement | .15 | .07 |
| ☐ 478 Carlos Hernandez | .15 | .07 |
| ☐ 479 Sterling Hitchcock | .15 | .07 |
| ☐ 480 Ellis Burks | .25 | .11 |
| ☐ 481 Barry Bonds | 1.00 | .45 |
| ☐ 482 Marvin Benard | .15 | .07 |
| ☐ 483 Kirk Rueter | .15 | .07 |
| ☐ 484 F.P. Santangelo | .15 | .07 |
| ☐ 485 Stan Javier | .15 | .07 |
| ☐ 486 Jeff Kent | .40 | .18 |
| ☐ 487 Alex Rodriguez | 2.00 | .90 |
| ☐ 488 Tom Lampkin | .15 | .07 |
| ☐ 489 Jose Mesa | .15 | .07 |
| ☐ 490 Jay Buhner | .25 | .11 |
| ☐ 491 Edgar Martinez | .40 | .18 |
| ☐ 492 Butch Huskey | .15 | .07 |
| ☐ 493 John Mabry | .15 | .07 |
| ☐ 494 Jamie Moyer | .15 | .07 |
| ☐ 495 Roberto Hernandez | .15 | .07 |
| ☐ 496 Tony Saunders | .15 | .07 |
| ☐ 497 Fred McGriff | .40 | .18 |
| ☐ 498 Dave Martinez | .15 | .07 |
| ☐ 499 Jose Canseco | .75 | .35 |
| ☐ 500 Rolando Arrojo | .15 | .07 |
| ☐ 501 Esteban Yan | .15 | .07 |
| ☐ 502 Juan Gonzalez | .60 | .25 |
| ☐ 503 Rafael Palmeiro | .60 | .25 |
| ☐ 504 Aaron Sele | .25 | .11 |
| ☐ 505 Royce Clayton | .15 | .07 |

| | Card | | |
|---|---|---|---|
| ❑ | 506 Todd Zeile | .25 | .11 |
| ❑ | 507 Tom Goodwin | .15 | .07 |
| ❑ | 508 Lee Stevens | .15 | .07 |
| ❑ | 509 Esteban Loaiza | .15 | .07 |
| ❑ | 510 Joey Hamilton | .15 | .07 |
| ❑ | 511 Homer Bush | .15 | .07 |
| ❑ | 512 Willie Greene | .15 | .07 |
| ❑ | 513 Shawn Green | .60 | .25 |
| ❑ | 514 David Wells | .25 | .11 |
| ❑ | 515 Kelvim Escobar | .15 | .07 |
| ❑ | 516 Tony Fernandez | .15 | .07 |
| ❑ | 517 Pat Hentgen | .15 | .07 |
| ❑ | 518 Mark McGwire AR | 1.25 | .55 |
| ❑ | 519 Ken Griffey Jr. AR | 1.25 | .55 |
| ❑ | 520 Sammy Sosa AR | .60 | .25 |
| ❑ | 521 Juan Gonzalez AR | .25 | .11 |
| ❑ | 522 J.D. Drew AR | .60 | .25 |
| ❑ | 523 Chipper Jones AR | .75 | .35 |
| ❑ | 524 Alex Rodriguez AR | 1.00 | .45 |
| ❑ | 525 Mike Piazza AR | 1.00 | .45 |
| ❑ | 526 Nomar Garciaparra AR | 1.00 | .45 |
| ❑ | 527 Mark McGwire SH CL | 1.25 | .55 |
| ❑ | 528 Sammy Sosa SH CL | .60 | .25 |
| ❑ | 529 Scott Brosius SH CL | .15 | .07 |
| ❑ | 530 Cal Ripken SH CL | 1.25 | .55 |
| ❑ | 531 Barry Bonds SH CL | .40 | .18 |
| ❑ | 532 Roger Clemens SH CL | .60 | .25 |
| ❑ | 533 Ken Griffey Jr. SH CL | 1.25 | .55 |
| ❑ | 534 Alex Rodriguez SH CL | 1.00 | .45 |
| ❑ | 535 Curt Schilling SH CL | .15 | .07 |
| ❑ | NNO K.Griffey Jr. '89 AU/100 | 1500.00 | 700.00 |

## 2000 Upper Deck

| | MINT | NRMT |
|---|---|---|
| COMPLETE SET (540) | 100.00 | 45.00 |
| COMPLETE SERIES 1 (270) | 50.00 | 22.00 |
| COMPLETE SERIES 2 (270) | 50.00 | 22.00 |
| COMMON CARD (1-540) | .15 | .07 |
| COMMON SR (1-28/271-297) | .25 | .11 |

| | Card | | |
|---|---|---|---|
| ❑ | 1 Rick Ankiel SR | 2.00 | .90 |
| ❑ | 2 Vernon Wells SR | .40 | .18 |
| ❑ | 3 Ryan Anderson SR | .40 | .18 |
| ❑ | 4 Ed Yarnall SR | .25 | .11 |
| ❑ | 5 Brian McNichol SR | .25 | .11 |
| ❑ | 6 Ben Petrick SR | .25 | .11 |
| ❑ | 7 Kip Wells SR | .40 | .18 |
| ❑ | 8 Eric Munson SR | 1.00 | .45 |
| ❑ | 9 Matt Riley SR | .40 | .18 |
| ❑ | 10 Peter Bergeron SR | .25 | .11 |
| ❑ | 11 Eric Gagne SR | .25 | .11 |
| ❑ | 12 Ramon Ortiz SR | .40 | .18 |
| ❑ | 13 Josh Beckett SR | 1.00 | .45 |
| ❑ | 14 Alfonso Soriano SR | .40 | .18 |
| ❑ | 15 Jorge Toca SR | .25 | .11 |
| ❑ | 16 Buddy Carlyle SR | .25 | .11 |
| ❑ | 17 Chad Hermansen SR | .25 | .11 |
| ❑ | 18 Matt Perisho SR | .25 | .11 |
| ❑ | 19 Tomokazu Ohka SR RC | 1.00 | .45 |
| ❑ | 20 Jacque Jones SR | .40 | .18 |
| ❑ | 21 Josh Paul SR | .25 | .11 |
| ❑ | 22 Dermal Brown SR | .40 | .18 |
| ❑ | 23 Adam Kennedy SR | .40 | .18 |
| ❑ | 24 Chad Harville SR | .25 | .11 |
| ❑ | 25 Calvin Murray SR | .25 | .11 |
| ❑ | 26 Chad Meyers SR | .25 | .11 |
| ❑ | 27 Brian Cooper SR | .25 | .11 |
| ❑ | 28 Troy Glaus | .75 | .35 |
| ❑ | 29 Ben Molina | .25 | .11 |
| ❑ | 30 Troy Percival | .15 | .07 |
| ❑ | 31 Ken Hill | .15 | .07 |
| ❑ | 32 Chuck Finley | .25 | .11 |
| ❑ | 33 Todd Greene | .15 | .07 |
| ❑ | 34 Tim Salmon | .25 | .11 |
| ❑ | 35 Gary DiSarcina | .15 | .07 |
| ❑ | 36 Luis Gonzalez | .25 | .11 |
| ❑ | 37 Tony Womack | .15 | .07 |
| ❑ | 38 Omar Daal | .15 | .07 |
| ❑ | 39 Randy Johnson | .75 | .35 |
| ❑ | 40 Erubiel Durazo | .25 | .11 |
| ❑ | 41 Jay Bell | .25 | .11 |
| ❑ | 42 Steve Finley | .25 | .11 |
| ❑ | 43 Travis Lee | .15 | .07 |
| ❑ | 44 Greg Maddux | 2.00 | .90 |
| ❑ | 45 Bret Boone | .15 | .07 |
| ❑ | 46 Brian Jordan | .25 | .11 |
| ❑ | 47 Kevin Millwood | .25 | .11 |
| ❑ | 48 Odalis Perez | .15 | .07 |
| ❑ | 49 Javy Lopez | .25 | .11 |
| ❑ | 50 John Smoltz | .25 | .11 |
| ❑ | 51 Bruce Chen | .15 | .07 |
| ❑ | 52 Albert Belle | .40 | .18 |
| ❑ | 53 Jerry Hairston Jr. | .15 | .07 |
| ❑ | 54 Will Clark | .60 | .25 |
| ❑ | 55 Sidney Ponson | .15 | .07 |
| ❑ | 56 Charles Johnson | .25 | .11 |
| ❑ | 57 Cal Ripken | 2.50 | 1.10 |
| ❑ | 58 Ryan Minor | .15 | .07 |
| ❑ | 59 Mike Mussina | .60 | .25 |
| ❑ | 60 Tom Gordon | .15 | .07 |
| ❑ | 61 Jose Offerman | .15 | .07 |
| ❑ | 62 Trot Nixon | .25 | .11 |
| ❑ | 63 Pedro Martinez | .75 | .35 |
| ❑ | 64 John Valentin | .15 | .07 |
| ❑ | 65 Jason Varitek | .25 | .11 |
| ❑ | 66 Juan Pena | .15 | .07 |
| ❑ | 67 Troy O'Leary | .15 | .07 |
| ❑ | 68 Sammy Sosa | 1.25 | .55 |
| ❑ | 69 Henry Rodriguez | .15 | .07 |
| ❑ | 70 Kyle Farnsworth | .15 | .07 |
| ❑ | 71 Glenallen Hill | .15 | .07 |
| ❑ | 72 Lance Johnson | .15 | .07 |
| ❑ | 73 Mickey Morandini | .15 | .07 |
| ❑ | 74 Jon Lieber | .15 | .07 |
| ❑ | 75 Kevin Tapani | .15 | .07 |
| ❑ | 76 Carlos Lee | .25 | .11 |
| ❑ | 77 Ray Durham | .25 | .11 |
| ❑ | 78 Jim Parque | .15 | .07 |
| ❑ | 79 Bob Howry | .15 | .07 |
| ❑ | 80 Magglio Ordonez | .25 | .11 |
| ❑ | 81 Paul Konerko | .25 | .11 |
| ❑ | 82 Mike Caruso | .15 | .07 |
| ❑ | 83 Chris Singleton | .25 | .11 |
| ❑ | 84 Sean Casey | .25 | .11 |
| ❑ | 85 Barry Larkin | .60 | .25 |
| ❑ | 86 Pokey Reese | .25 | .11 |
| ❑ | 87 Eddie Taubensee | .15 | .07 |
| ❑ | 88 Scott Williamson | .15 | .07 |
| ❑ | 89 Jason LaRue | .15 | .07 |
| ❑ | 90 Aaron Boone | .15 | .07 |
| ❑ | 91 Jeffrey Hammonds | .25 | .11 |
| ❑ | 92 Omar Vizquel | .25 | .11 |
| ❑ | 93 Manny Ramirez | .75 | .35 |
| ❑ | 94 Kenny Lofton | .25 | .11 |
| ❑ | 95 Jaret Wright | .15 | .07 |
| ❑ | 96 Einar Diaz | .15 | .07 |
| ❑ | 97 Charles Nagy | .15 | .07 |
| ❑ | 98 David Justice | .40 | .18 |
| ❑ | 99 Richie Sexson | .25 | .11 |
| ❑ | 100 Steve Karsay | .15 | .07 |
| ❑ | 101 Todd Helton | .75 | .35 |
| ❑ | 102 Dante Bichette | .25 | .11 |
| ❑ | 103 Larry Walker | .25 | .11 |
| ❑ | 104 Pedro Astacio | .15 | .07 |
| ❑ | 105 Neifi Perez | .15 | .07 |
| ❑ | 106 Brian Bohanon | .15 | .07 |
| ❑ | 107 Edgard Clemente | .15 | .07 |
| ❑ | 108 Dave Veres | .15 | .07 |
| ❑ | 109 Gabe Kapler | .25 | .11 |
| ❑ | 110 Juan Encarnacion | .25 | .11 |
| ❑ | 111 Jeff Weaver | .15 | .07 |
| ❑ | 112 Damion Easley | .15 | .07 |
| ❑ | 113 Justin Thompson | .15 | .07 |
| ❑ | 114 Brad Ausmus | .15 | .07 |
| ❑ | 115 Frank Catalanotto | .15 | .07 |
| ❑ | 116 Todd Jones | .15 | .07 |
| ❑ | 117 Preston Wilson | .25 | .11 |
| ❑ | 118 Cliff Floyd | .25 | .11 |
| ❑ | 119 Mike Lowell | .15 | .07 |
| ❑ | 120 Antonio Alfonseca | .15 | .07 |
| ❑ | 121 Alex Gonzalez | .15 | .07 |
| ❑ | 122 Braden Looper | .15 | .07 |
| ❑ | 123 Bruce Aven | .15 | .07 |
| ❑ | 124 Richard Hidalgo | .25 | .11 |
| ❑ | 125 Mitch Meluskey | .15 | .07 |
| ❑ | 126 Jeff Bagwell | .75 | .35 |
| ❑ | 127 Jose Lima | .15 | .07 |
| ❑ | 128 Derek Bell | .15 | .07 |
| ❑ | 129 Billy Wagner | .15 | .07 |
| ❑ | 130 Shane Reynolds | .15 | .07 |
| ❑ | 131 Moises Alou | .25 | .11 |
| ❑ | 132 Carlos Beltran | .25 | .11 |
| ❑ | 133 Carlos Febles | .15 | .07 |
| ❑ | 134 Jermaine Dye | .25 | .11 |
| ❑ | 135 Jeremy Giambi | .15 | .07 |
| ❑ | 136 Joe Randa | .15 | .07 |
| ❑ | 137 Jose Rosado | .15 | .07 |
| ❑ | 138 Chad Kreuter | .15 | .07 |
| ❑ | 139 Jose Vizcaino | .15 | .07 |
| ❑ | 140 Adrian Beltre | .25 | .11 |
| ❑ | 141 Kevin Brown | .40 | .18 |
| ❑ | 142 Ismael Valdes | .15 | .07 |
| ❑ | 143 Angel Pena | .15 | .07 |
| ❑ | 144 Chan Ho Park | .25 | .11 |
| ❑ | 145 Mark Grudzielanek | .15 | .07 |
| ❑ | 146 Jeff Shaw | .15 | .07 |
| ❑ | 147 Geoff Jenkins | .25 | .11 |
| ❑ | 148 Jeromy Burnitz | .25 | .11 |
| ❑ | 149 Hideo Nomo | .60 | .25 |
| ❑ | 150 Ron Belliard | .15 | .07 |
| ❑ | 151 Sean Berry | .15 | .07 |
| ❑ | 152 Mark Loretta | .15 | .07 |
| ❑ | 153 Steve Woodard | .15 | .07 |
| ❑ | 154 Joe Mays | .15 | .07 |
| ❑ | 155 Eric Milton | .25 | .11 |
| ❑ | 156 Corey Koskie | .15 | .07 |
| ❑ | 157 Ron Coomer | .15 | .07 |
| ❑ | 158 Brad Radke | .25 | .11 |
| ❑ | 159 Terry Steinbach | .15 | .07 |
| ❑ | 160 Cristian Guzman | .15 | .07 |
| ❑ | 161 Vladimir Guerrero | 1.00 | .45 |
| ❑ | 162 Wilton Guerrero | .15 | .07 |
| ❑ | 163 Michael Barrett | .15 | .07 |
| ❑ | 164 Chris Widger | .15 | .07 |
| ❑ | 165 Fernando Seguignol | .15 | .07 |
| ❑ | 166 Ugueth Urbina | .15 | .07 |
| ❑ | 167 Dustin Hermanson | .15 | .07 |
| ❑ | 168 Kenny Rogers | .15 | .07 |
| ❑ | 169 Edgardo Alfonzo | .25 | .11 |
| ❑ | 170 Orel Hershiser | .25 | .11 |
| ❑ | 171 Robin Ventura | .25 | .11 |
| ❑ | 172 Octavio Dotel | .15 | .07 |
| ❑ | 173 Rickey Henderson | .75 | .35 |
| ❑ | 174 Roger Cedeno | .15 | .07 |
| ❑ | 175 John Olerud | .25 | .11 |
| ❑ | 176 Derek Jeter | 2.50 | 1.10 |
| ❑ | 177 Tino Martinez | .25 | .11 |
| ❑ | 178 Orlando Hernandez | .25 | .11 |
| ❑ | 179 Chuck Knoblauch | .25 | .11 |
| ❑ | 180 Bernie Williams | .60 | .25 |
| ❑ | 181 Chili Davis | .25 | .11 |
| ❑ | 182 David Cone | .25 | .11 |
| ❑ | 183 Ricky Ledee | .15 | .07 |
| ❑ | 184 Paul O'Neill | .25 | .11 |
| ❑ | 185 Jason Giambi | .60 | .25 |
| ❑ | 186 Eric Chavez | .25 | .11 |
| ❑ | 187 Matt Stairs | .15 | .07 |
| ❑ | 188 Miguel Tejada | .25 | .11 |
| ❑ | 189 Olmedo Saenz | .15 | .07 |
| ❑ | 190 Tim Hudson | .60 | .25 |
| ❑ | 191 John Jaha | .15 | .07 |
| ❑ | 192 Randy Velarde | .15 | .07 |
| ❑ | 193 Rico Brogna | .15 | .07 |
| ❑ | 194 Mike Lieberthal | .25 | .11 |
| ❑ | 195 Marlon Anderson | .15 | .07 |
| ❑ | 196 Bob Abreu | .25 | .11 |
| ❑ | 197 Ron Gant | .25 | .11 |
| ❑ | 198 Randy Wolf | .15 | .07 |
| ❑ | 199 Desi Relaford | .15 | .07 |

| No. | Player | | |
|---|---|---|---|
| 200 | Doug Glanville | .15 | .07 |
| 201 | Warren Morris | .15 | .07 |
| 202 | Kris Benson | .25 | .11 |
| 203 | Kevin Young | .15 | .07 |
| 204 | Brian Giles | .25 | .11 |
| 205 | Jason Schmidt | .15 | .07 |
| 206 | Ed Sprague | .15 | .07 |
| 207 | Francisco Cordova | .15 | .07 |
| 208 | Mark McGwire | 3.00 | 1.35 |
| 209 | Jose Jimenez | .15 | .07 |
| 210 | Fernando Tatis | .25 | .11 |
| 211 | Kent Bottenfield | .15 | .07 |
| 212 | Eli Marrero | .15 | .07 |
| 213 | Edgar Renteria | .15 | .07 |
| 214 | Joe McEwing | .15 | .07 |
| 215 | J.D. Drew | .60 | .25 |
| 216 | Tony Gwynn | 1.25 | .55 |
| 217 | Gary Matthews Jr. | .15 | .07 |
| 218 | Eric Owens | .15 | .07 |
| 219 | Damian Jackson | .15 | .07 |
| 220 | Reggie Sanders | .15 | .07 |
| 221 | Trevor Hoffman | .25 | .11 |
| 222 | Ben Davis | .15 | .07 |
| 223 | Shawn Estes | .15 | .07 |
| 224 | F.P. Santangelo | .15 | .07 |
| 225 | Livan Hernandez | .15 | .07 |
| 226 | Ellis Burks | .25 | .11 |
| 227 | J.T. Snow | .25 | .11 |
| 228 | Jeff Kent | .40 | .18 |
| 229 | Robb Nen | .15 | .07 |
| 230 | Marvin Benard | .15 | .07 |
| 231 | Ken Griffey Jr. | 2.50 | 1.10 |
| 232 | John Halama | .15 | .07 |
| 233 | Gil Meche | .25 | .11 |
| 234 | David Bell | .15 | .07 |
| 235 | Brian Hunter | .15 | .07 |
| 236 | Jay Buhner | .25 | .11 |
| 237 | Edgar Martinez | .40 | .18 |
| 238 | Jose Mesa | .15 | .07 |
| 239 | Wilson Alvarez | .15 | .07 |
| 240 | Wade Boggs | .75 | .35 |
| 241 | Fred McGriff | .40 | .18 |
| 242 | Jose Canseco | .75 | .35 |
| 243 | Kevin Stocker | .15 | .07 |
| 244 | Roberto Hernandez | .15 | .07 |
| 245 | Bubba Trammell | .15 | .07 |
| 246 | John Flaherty | .15 | .07 |
| 247 | Ivan Rodriguez | .75 | .35 |
| 248 | Rusty Greer | .25 | .11 |
| 249 | Rafael Palmeiro | .60 | .25 |
| 250 | Jeff Zimmerman | .15 | .07 |
| 251 | Royce Clayton | .15 | .07 |
| 252 | Todd Zeile | .25 | .11 |
| 253 | John Wetteland | .25 | .11 |
| 254 | Ruben Mateo | .25 | .11 |
| 255 | Kelvim Escobar | .15 | .07 |
| 256 | David Wells | .25 | .11 |
| 257 | Shawn Green | .60 | .25 |
| 258 | Homer Bush | .15 | .07 |
| 259 | Shannon Stewart | .25 | .11 |
| 260 | Carlos Delgado | .60 | .25 |
| 261 | Roy Halladay | .15 | .07 |
| 262 | Fernando Tatis SH CL | .15 | .07 |
| 263 | Jose Jimenez SH CL | .15 | .07 |
| 264 | Tony Gwynn SH CL | .60 | .25 |
| 265 | Wade Boggs SH CL | .40 | .18 |
| 266 | Cal Ripken SH CL | 1.25 | .55 |
| 267 | David Cone SH CL | .25 | .11 |
| 268 | Mark McGwire SH CL | 1.50 | .70 |
| 269 | Pedro Martinez SH CL | .40 | .18 |
| 270 | N. Garciaparra SH CL | 1.00 | .45 |
| 271 | Nick Johnson SR | .40 | .18 |
| 272 | Mark Quinn SR | .40 | .18 |
| 273 | Roosevelt Brown SR | .25 | .11 |
| 274 | Terrence Long SR | .40 | .18 |
| 275 | Jason Marquis SR | .40 | .18 |
| 276 | Kazuhiro Sasaki SR RC | 3.00 | 1.35 |
| 277 | Aaron Myette SR | .40 | .18 |
| 278 | Danys Baez SR RC | 1.00 | .45 |
| 279 | Travis Dawkins SR | .40 | .18 |
| 280 | Mark Mulder SR | .40 | .18 |
| 281 | Chris Haas SR | .25 | .11 |
| 282 | Milton Bradley SR | .40 | .18 |
| 283 | Brad Penny SR | .40 | .18 |
| 284 | Rafael Furcal SR | 2.50 | 1.10 |
| 285 | Luis Matos SR RC | 1.00 | .45 |
| 286 | Victor Santos SR RC | .40 | .18 |
| 287 | Rico Washington SR RC | .50 | .23 |
| 288 | Rob Bell SR | .25 | .11 |
| 289 | Joe Crede SR | 1.00 | .45 |
| 290 | Pablo Ozuna SR | .25 | .11 |
| 291 | Wascar Serrano SR RC | .60 | .25 |
| 292 | Sang-Hoon Lee SR RC | .40 | .18 |
| 293 | Chris Wakeland SR RC | .40 | .18 |
| 294 | Luis Rivera SR | .25 | .11 |
| 295 | Mike Lamb SR RC | .75 | .35 |
| 296 | Wily Mo Pena SR | .40 | .18 |
| 297 | Mike Meyers SR RC | .50 | .23 |
| 298 | Mo Vaughn | .25 | .11 |
| 299 | Darin Erstad | .60 | .25 |
| 300 | Garret Anderson | .25 | .11 |
| 301 | Tim Belcher | .15 | .07 |
| 302 | Scott Spiezio | .15 | .07 |
| 303 | Kent Bottenfield | .15 | .07 |
| 304 | Orlando Palmeiro | .15 | .07 |
| 305 | Jason Dickson | .15 | .07 |
| 306 | Matt Williams | .40 | .18 |
| 307 | Brian Anderson | .15 | .07 |
| 308 | Hanley Frias | .15 | .07 |
| 309 | Todd Stottlemyre | .15 | .07 |
| 310 | Matt Mantei | .15 | .07 |
| 311 | David Dellucci | .15 | .07 |
| 312 | Armando Reynoso | .15 | .07 |
| 313 | Bernard Gilkey | .15 | .07 |
| 314 | Chipper Jones | 1.50 | .70 |
| 315 | Tom Glavine | .60 | .25 |
| 316 | Quilvio Veras | .15 | .07 |
| 317 | Andruw Jones | .60 | .25 |
| 318 | Bobby Bonilla | .25 | .11 |
| 319 | Reggie Sanders | .15 | .07 |
| 320 | Andres Galarraga | .40 | .18 |
| 321 | George Lombard | .15 | .07 |
| 322 | John Rocker | .25 | .11 |
| 323 | Wally Joyner | .25 | .11 |
| 324 | B.J. Surhoff | .25 | .11 |
| 325 | Scott Erickson | .15 | .07 |
| 326 | Delino DeShields | .15 | .07 |
| 327 | Jeff Conine | .15 | .07 |
| 328 | Mike Timlin | .15 | .07 |
| 329 | Brady Anderson | .25 | .11 |
| 330 | Mike Bordick | .15 | .07 |
| 331 | Harold Baines | .25 | .11 |
| 332 | Nomar Garciaparra | 2.00 | .90 |
| 333 | Bret Saberhagen | .25 | .11 |
| 334 | Ramon Martinez | .15 | .07 |
| 335 | Donnie Sadler | .15 | .07 |
| 336 | Wilton Veras | .25 | .11 |
| 337 | Mike Stanley | .15 | .07 |
| 338 | Brian Rose | .15 | .07 |
| 339 | Carl Everett | .25 | .11 |
| 340 | Tim Wakefield | .15 | .07 |
| 341 | Mark Grace | .60 | .25 |
| 342 | Kerry Wood | .25 | .11 |
| 343 | Eric Young | .15 | .07 |
| 344 | Jose Nieves | .15 | .07 |
| 345 | Ismael Valdes | .15 | .07 |
| 346 | Joe Girardi | .15 | .07 |
| 347 | Damon Buford | .15 | .07 |
| 348 | Ricky Gutierrez | .15 | .07 |
| 349 | Frank Thomas | 1.25 | .55 |
| 350 | Brian Simmons | .15 | .07 |
| 351 | James Baldwin | .25 | .11 |
| 352 | Brook Fordyce | .15 | .07 |
| 353 | Jose Valentin | .15 | .07 |
| 354 | Mike Sirotka | .15 | .07 |
| 355 | Greg Norton | .15 | .07 |
| 356 | Dante Bichette | .25 | .11 |
| 357 | Deion Sanders | .25 | .11 |
| 358 | Ken Griffey Jr. | 2.50 | 1.10 |
| 359 | Denny Neagle | .25 | .11 |
| 360 | Dmitri Young | .25 | .11 |
| 361 | Pete Harnisch | .15 | .07 |
| 362 | Michael Tucker | .15 | .07 |
| 363 | Roberto Alomar | .60 | .25 |
| 364 | Dave Roberts | .15 | .07 |
| 365 | Jim Thome | .40 | .18 |
| 366 | Bartolo Colon | .25 | .11 |
| 367 | Travis Fryman | .25 | .11 |
| 368 | Chuck Finley | .25 | .11 |
| 369 | Russell Branyan | .25 | .11 |
| 370 | Alex Ramirez | .15 | .07 |
| 371 | Jeff Cirillo | .25 | .11 |
| 372 | Jeffrey Hammonds | .25 | .11 |
| 373 | Scott Karl | .15 | .07 |
| 374 | Brent Mayne | .15 | .07 |
| 375 | Tom Goodwin | .15 | .07 |
| 376 | Jose Jimenez | .15 | .07 |
| 377 | Rolando Arrojo | .15 | .07 |
| 378 | Terry Shumpert | .15 | .07 |
| 379 | Juan Gonzalez | .60 | .25 |
| 380 | Bobby Higginson | .25 | .11 |
| 381 | Tony Clark | .15 | .07 |
| 382 | Dave Mlicki | .15 | .07 |
| 383 | Deivi Cruz | .15 | .07 |
| 384 | Brian Moehler | .15 | .07 |
| 385 | Dean Palmer | .25 | .11 |
| 386 | Luis Castillo | .25 | .11 |
| 387 | Mike Redmond | .15 | .07 |
| 388 | Alex Fernandez | .15 | .07 |
| 389 | Brant Brown | .15 | .07 |
| 390 | Dave Berg | .15 | .07 |
| 391 | A.J. Burnett | .25 | .11 |
| 392 | Mark Kotsay | .15 | .07 |
| 393 | Craig Biggio | .40 | .18 |
| 394 | Daryle Ward | .25 | .11 |
| 395 | Lance Berkman | .25 | .11 |
| 396 | Roger Cedeno | .15 | .07 |
| 397 | Scott Elarton | .25 | .11 |
| 398 | Octavio Dotel | .15 | .07 |
| 399 | Ken Caminiti | .25 | .11 |
| 400 | Johnny Damon | .25 | .11 |
| 401 | Mike Sweeney | .25 | .11 |
| 402 | Jeff Suppan | .15 | .07 |
| 403 | Rey Sanchez | .15 | .07 |
| 404 | Blake Stein | .15 | .07 |
| 405 | Ricky Bottalico | .15 | .07 |
| 406 | Jay Witasick | .15 | .07 |
| 407 | Shawn Green | .60 | .25 |
| 408 | Orel Hershiser | .25 | .11 |
| 409 | Gary Sheffield | .60 | .25 |
| 410 | Todd Hollandsworth | .15 | .07 |
| 411 | Terry Adams | .15 | .07 |
| 412 | Todd Hundley | .15 | .07 |
| 413 | Eric Karros | .25 | .11 |
| 414 | F.P. Santangelo | .15 | .07 |
| 415 | Alex Cora | .15 | .07 |
| 416 | Marquis Grissom | .15 | .07 |
| 417 | Henry Blanco | .15 | .07 |
| 418 | Jose Hernandez | .15 | .07 |
| 419 | Kyle Peterson | .15 | .07 |
| 420 | John Snyder RC | .40 | .18 |
| 421 | Bob Wickman | .15 | .07 |
| 422 | Jamey Wright | .15 | .07 |
| 423 | Chad Allen | .15 | .07 |
| 424 | Todd Walker | .15 | .07 |
| 425 | J.C. Romero RC | .40 | .18 |
| 426 | Butch Huskey | .15 | .07 |
| 427 | Jacque Jones | .25 | .11 |
| 428 | Matt Lawton | .25 | .11 |
| 429 | Rondell White | .25 | .11 |
| 430 | Jose Vidro | .25 | .11 |
| 431 | Hideki Irabu | .15 | .07 |
| 432 | Javier Vazquez | .15 | .07 |
| 433 | Lee Stevens | .15 | .07 |
| 434 | Mike Thurman | .15 | .07 |
| 435 | Geoff Blum | .15 | .07 |
| 436 | Mike Hampton | .25 | .11 |
| 437 | Mike Piazza | 2.00 | .90 |
| 438 | Al Leiter | .25 | .11 |
| 439 | Derek Bell | .15 | .07 |
| 440 | Armando Benitez | .25 | .11 |
| 441 | Rey Ordonez | .15 | .07 |
| 442 | Todd Zeile | .25 | .11 |
| 443 | Roger Clemens | 1.25 | .55 |
| 444 | Ramiro Mendoza | .15 | .07 |
| 445 | Andy Pettitte | .25 | .11 |
| 446 | Scott Brosius | .25 | .11 |
| 447 | Mariano Rivera | .25 | .11 |
| 448 | Jim Leyritz | .15 | .07 |
| 449 | Jorge Posada | .25 | .11 |
| 450 | Omar Olivares | .15 | .07 |
| 451 | Ben Grieve | .25 | .11 |
| 452 | A.J. Hinch | .15 | .07 |
| 453 | Gil Heredia | .15 | .07 |
| 454 | Kevin Appier | .25 | .11 |
| 455 | Ryan Christenson | .15 | .07 |
| 456 | Ramon Hernandez | .15 | .07 |
| 457 | Scott Rolen | .60 | .25 |

| | | |
|---|---|---|
| ❑ 458 Alex Arias | .15 | .07 |
| ❑ 459 Andy Ashby | .15 | .07 |
| ❑ 460 Kevin Jordan UER 474 | .15 | .07 |
| ❑ 461 Robert Person | .15 | .07 |
| ❑ 462 Paul Byrd | .15 | .07 |
| ❑ 463 Curt Schilling | .25 | .11 |
| ❑ 464 Mike Jackson | .15 | .07 |
| ❑ 465 Jason Kendall | .25 | .11 |
| ❑ 466 Pat Meares | .15 | .07 |
| ❑ 467 Bruce Aven | .15 | .07 |
| ❑ 468 Todd Ritchie | .15 | .07 |
| ❑ 469 Wil Cordero | .15 | .07 |
| ❑ 470 Aramis Ramirez | .15 | .07 |
| ❑ 471 Andy Benes | .15 | .07 |
| ❑ 472 Ray Lankford | .25 | .11 |
| ❑ 473 Fernando Vina | .15 | .07 |
| ❑ 474 Jim Edmonds | .60 | .25 |
| ❑ 475 Craig Paquette | .15 | .07 |
| ❑ 476 Pat Hentgen | .15 | .07 |
| ❑ 477 Darryl Kile | .25 | .11 |
| ❑ 478 Sterling Hitchcock | .15 | .07 |
| ❑ 479 Ruben Rivera | .15 | .07 |
| ❑ 480 Ryan Klesko | .25 | .11 |
| ❑ 481 Phil Nevin | .25 | .11 |
| ❑ 482 Woody Williams | .15 | .07 |
| ❑ 483 Carlos Hernandez | .15 | .07 |
| ❑ 484 Brian Meadows | .15 | .07 |
| ❑ 485 Bret Boone | .25 | .11 |
| ❑ 486 Barry Bonds | 1.00 | .45 |
| ❑ 487 Russ Ortiz | .15 | .07 |
| ❑ 488 Bobby Estalella | .15 | .07 |
| ❑ 489 Rich Aurilia | .15 | .07 |
| ❑ 490 Bill Mueller | .15 | .07 |
| ❑ 491 Joe Nathan | .15 | .07 |
| ❑ 492 Russ Davis | .15 | .07 |
| ❑ 493 John Olerud | .25 | .11 |
| ❑ 494 Alex Rodriguez | 2.00 | .90 |
| ❑ 495 Freddy Garcia | .25 | .11 |
| ❑ 496 Carlos Guillen | .15 | .07 |
| ❑ 497 Aaron Sele | .25 | .11 |
| ❑ 498 Brett Tomko | .15 | .07 |
| ❑ 499 Jamie Moyer | .15 | .07 |
| ❑ 500 Mike Cameron | .15 | .07 |
| ❑ 501 Vinny Castilla | .25 | .11 |
| ❑ 502 Gerald Williams | .15 | .07 |
| ❑ 503 Mike DiFelice | .15 | .07 |
| ❑ 504 Ryan Rupe | .15 | .07 |
| ❑ 505 Greg Vaughn | .25 | .11 |
| ❑ 506 Miguel Cairo | .15 | .07 |
| ❑ 507 Juan Guzman | .15 | .07 |
| ❑ 508 Jose Guillen | .15 | .07 |
| ❑ 509 Gabe Kapler | .25 | .11 |
| ❑ 510 Rick Helling | .25 | .11 |
| ❑ 511 David Segui | .15 | .07 |
| ❑ 512 Doug Davis | .15 | .07 |
| ❑ 513 Justin Thompson | .15 | .07 |
| ❑ 514 Chad Curtis | .15 | .07 |
| ❑ 515 Tony Batista | .25 | .11 |
| ❑ 516 Billy Koch | .25 | .11 |
| ❑ 517 Raul Mondesi | .25 | .11 |
| ❑ 518 Joey Hamilton | .15 | .07 |
| ❑ 519 Darrin Fletcher | .15 | .07 |
| ❑ 520 Brad Fullmer | .25 | .11 |
| ❑ 521 Jose Cruz Jr. | .25 | .11 |
| ❑ 522 Kevin Witt | .15 | .07 |
| ❑ 523 Mark McGwire AUT | 1.25 | .55 |
| ❑ 524 Roberto Alomar AUT | .25 | .11 |
| ❑ 525 Chipper Jones AUT | .75 | .35 |
| ❑ 526 Derek Jeter AUT | 1.25 | .55 |
| ❑ 527 Ken Griffey Jr. AUT | 1.25 | .55 |
| ❑ 528 Sammy Sosa AUT | .60 | .25 |
| ❑ 529 Manny Ramirez AUT | .40 | .18 |
| ❑ 530 Ivan Rodriguez AUT | .40 | .18 |
| ❑ 531 Pedro Martinez AUT | .40 | .18 |
| ❑ 532 Mariano Rivera CL | .25 | .11 |
| ❑ 533 Sammy Sosa CL | .60 | .25 |
| ❑ 534 Cal Ripken CL | 1.25 | .55 |
| ❑ 535 Vladimir Guerrero CL | .60 | .25 |
| ❑ 536 Tony Gwynn CL | .60 | .25 |
| ❑ 537 Mark McGwire CL | 1.25 | .55 |
| ❑ 538 Bernie Williams CL | .25 | .11 |
| ❑ 539 Pedro Martinez CL | .40 | .18 |
| ❑ 540 Ken Griffey Jr. CL | 1.25 | .55 |

## 2001 Upper Deck

| | MINT | NRMT |
|---|---|---|
| COMPLETE SERIES 1 (270) | 50.00 | 22.00 |
| COMMON CARD | .15 | .07 |
| COMMON SR (1-50) | .25 | .11 |
| ❑ 1 Jeff DaVanon SR | .25 | .11 |
| ❑ 2 Aubrey Huff SR | .40 | .18 |
| ❑ 3 Pasqual Coco SR | .25 | .11 |
| ❑ 4 Barry Zito SR | 2.00 | .90 |
| ❑ 5 Augie Ojeda SR | .25 | .11 |
| ❑ 6 Chris Richard SR | .25 | .11 |
| ❑ 7 Josh Phelps SR | .25 | .11 |
| ❑ 8 Kevin Nicholson SR | .25 | .11 |
| ❑ 9 Juan Guzman SR | .25 | .11 |
| ❑ 10 Brandon Kolb SR | .25 | .11 |
| ❑ 11 Johan Santana SR | .40 | .18 |
| ❑ 12 Josh Kalinowski SR | .25 | .11 |
| ❑ 13 Tike Redman SR | .25 | .11 |
| ❑ 14 Ivanon Coffie SR | .25 | .11 |
| ❑ 15 Chad Durbin SR | .25 | .11 |
| ❑ 16 Derrick Turnbow SR | .25 | .11 |
| ❑ 17 Scott Downs SR | .25 | .11 |
| ❑ 18 Jason Grilli SR | .25 | .11 |
| ❑ 19 Mark Buehrle SR | .25 | .11 |
| ❑ 20 Paxton Crawford SR | .25 | .11 |
| ❑ 21 Bronson Arroyo SR | .25 | .11 |
| ❑ 22 Tomas De la Rosa SR | .25 | .11 |
| ❑ 23 Paul Rigdon SR | .25 | .11 |
| ❑ 24 Rob Ramsay SR | .25 | .11 |
| ❑ 25 Damian Rolls SR | .25 | .11 |
| ❑ 26 Jason Conti SR | .25 | .11 |
| ❑ 27 John Parrish SR | .25 | .11 |
| ❑ 28 Geraldo Guzman SR | .25 | .11 |
| ❑ 29 Tony Mota SR | .25 | .11 |
| ❑ 30 Luis Rivas SR | .25 | .11 |
| ❑ 31 Brian Tollberg SR | .25 | .11 |
| ❑ 32 Adam Bernero SR | .25 | .11 |
| ❑ 33 Michael Cuddyer SR | .40 | .18 |
| ❑ 34 Josue Espada SR | .25 | .11 |
| ❑ 35 Joe Lawrence SR | .25 | .11 |
| ❑ 36 Chad Moeller SR | .25 | .11 |
| ❑ 37 Nick Bierbrodt SR | .25 | .11 |
| ❑ 38 DeWayne Wise SR | .25 | .11 |
| ❑ 39 Javier Cardona SR | .25 | .11 |
| ❑ 40 Hiram Bocachica SR | .25 | .11 |
| ❑ 41 Giuseppe Chiaramonte SR | .25 | .11 |
| ❑ 42 Alex Cabrera SR | .40 | .18 |
| ❑ 43 Jimmy Rollins SR | .25 | .11 |
| ❑ 44 Pat Flury SR RC | .40 | .18 |
| ❑ 45 Leo Estrella SR | .25 | .11 |
| ❑ 46 Darin Erstad | .60 | .25 |
| ❑ 47 Seth Etherton | .15 | .07 |
| ❑ 48 Troy Glaus | .75 | .35 |
| ❑ 49 Brian Cooper | .15 | .07 |
| ❑ 50 Tim Salmon | .25 | .11 |
| ❑ 51 Adam Kennedy | .25 | .11 |
| ❑ 52 Bengie Molina | .25 | .11 |
| ❑ 53 Jason Giambi | .60 | .25 |
| ❑ 54 Miguel Tejada | .25 | .11 |
| ❑ 55 Tim Hudson | .60 | .25 |
| ❑ 56 Eric Chavez | .25 | .11 |
| ❑ 57 Terrence Long | .25 | .11 |
| ❑ 58 Jason Isringhausen | .15 | .07 |
| ❑ 59 Ramon Hernandez | .15 | .07 |
| ❑ 60 Raul Mondesi | .25 | .11 |
| ❑ 61 David Wells | .25 | .11 |
| ❑ 62 Shannon Stewart | .25 | .11 |
| ❑ 63 Tony Batista | .25 | .11 |
| ❑ 64 Brad Fullmer | .25 | .11 |
| ❑ 65 Chris Carpenter | .15 | .07 |
| ❑ 66 Homer Bush | .15 | .07 |
| ❑ 67 Gerald Williams | .15 | .07 |
| ❑ 68 Miguel Cairo | .15 | .07 |
| ❑ 69 Ryan Rupe | .15 | .07 |
| ❑ 70 Greg Vaughn | .25 | .11 |
| ❑ 71 John Flaherty | .15 | .07 |
| ❑ 72 Dan Wheeler | .15 | .07 |
| ❑ 73 Fred McGriff | .40 | .18 |
| ❑ 74 Roberto Alomar | .60 | .25 |
| ❑ 75 Bartolo Colon | .25 | .11 |
| ❑ 76 Kenny Lofton | .25 | .11 |
| ❑ 77 David Segui | .15 | .07 |
| ❑ 78 Omar Vizquel | .25 | .11 |
| ❑ 79 Russ Branyan | .25 | .11 |
| ❑ 80 Chuck Finley | .25 | .11 |
| ❑ 81 Manny Ramirez UER (Back photo is of David Segui) | .75 | .35 |
| ❑ 82 Alex Rodriguez | 2.00 | .90 |
| ❑ 83 John Halama | .15 | .07 |
| ❑ 84 Mike Cameron | .15 | .07 |
| ❑ 85 David Bell | .15 | .07 |
| ❑ 86 Jay Buhner | .25 | .11 |
| ❑ 87 Aaron Sele | .25 | .11 |
| ❑ 88 Rickey Henderson | .75 | .35 |
| ❑ 89 Brook Fordyce | .15 | .07 |
| ❑ 90 Cal Ripken | 2.50 | 1.10 |
| ❑ 91 Mike Mussina | .60 | .25 |
| ❑ 92 Delino DeShields | .15 | .07 |
| ❑ 93 Melvin Mora | .15 | .07 |
| ❑ 94 Sidney Ponson | .15 | .07 |
| ❑ 95 Brady Anderson | .25 | .11 |
| ❑ 96 Ivan Rodriguez | .75 | .35 |
| ❑ 97 Ricky Ledee | .15 | .07 |
| ❑ 98 Rick Helling | .25 | .11 |
| ❑ 99 Ruben Mateo | .25 | .11 |
| ❑ 100 Luis Alicea | .15 | .07 |
| ❑ 101 John Wetteland | .25 | .11 |
| ❑ 102 Mike Lamb | .15 | .07 |
| ❑ 103 Carl Everett | .25 | .11 |
| ❑ 104 Troy O'Leary | .15 | .07 |
| ❑ 105 Wilton Veras | .15 | .07 |
| ❑ 106 Pedro Martinez | .75 | .35 |
| ❑ 107 Rolando Arrojo | .15 | .07 |
| ❑ 108 Scott Hatteberg | .15 | .07 |
| ❑ 109 Jason Varitek | .25 | .11 |
| ❑ 110 Jose Offerman | .15 | .07 |
| ❑ 111 Carlos Beltran | .25 | .11 |
| ❑ 112 Johnny Damon | .25 | .11 |
| ❑ 113 Mark Quinn | .25 | .11 |
| ❑ 114 Rey Sanchez | .15 | .07 |
| ❑ 115 Mac Suzuki | .15 | .07 |
| ❑ 116 Jermaine Dye | .25 | .11 |
| ❑ 117 Chris Fussell | .15 | .07 |
| ❑ 118 Jeff Weaver | .15 | .07 |
| ❑ 119 Dean Palmer | .25 | .11 |
| ❑ 120 Robert Fick | .15 | .07 |
| ❑ 121 Brian Moehler | .15 | .07 |
| ❑ 122 Damion Easley | .15 | .07 |
| ❑ 123 Juan Encarnacion | .25 | .11 |
| ❑ 124 Tony Clark | .15 | .07 |
| ❑ 125 Cristian Guzman | .15 | .07 |
| ❑ 126 Matt LeCroy | .15 | .07 |
| ❑ 127 Eric Milton | .25 | .11 |
| ❑ 128 Jay Canizaro | .15 | .07 |
| ❑ 129 David Ortiz | .15 | .07 |
| ❑ 130 Brad Radke | .25 | .11 |
| ❑ 131 Jacque Jones | .25 | .11 |
| ❑ 132 Maggio Ordonez | .25 | .11 |
| ❑ 133 Carlos Lee | .25 | .11 |
| ❑ 134 Mike Sirotka | .15 | .07 |
| ❑ 135 Ray Durham | .25 | .11 |
| ❑ 136 Paul Konerko | .25 | .11 |
| ❑ 137 Charles Johnson | .25 | .11 |
| ❑ 138 James Baldwin | .25 | .11 |
| ❑ 139 Jeff Abbott | .15 | .07 |
| ❑ 140 Roger Clemens | 1.25 | .55 |
| ❑ 141 Derek Jeter | 2.50 | 1.10 |
| ❑ 142 David Justice | .40 | .18 |
| ❑ 143 Ramiro Mendoza | .15 | .07 |
| ❑ 144 Chuck Knoblauch | .25 | .11 |
| ❑ 145 Orlando Hernandez | .25 | .11 |
| ❑ 146 Alfonso Soriano | .25 | .11 |

❑ 147 Jeff Bagwell .75 .35
❑ 148 Julio Lugo .15 .07
❑ 149 Mitch Meluskey .15 .07
❑ 150 Jose Lima .15 .07
❑ 151 Richard Hidalgo .25 .11
❑ 152 Moises Alou .25 .11
❑ 153 Scott Elarton .25 .11
❑ 154 Andruw Jones .60 .25
❑ 155 Quilvio Veras .15 .07
❑ 156 Greg Maddux 1.50 .70
❑ 157 Brian Jordan .25 .11
❑ 158 Andres Galarraga .40 .18
❑ 159 Kevin Millwood .25 .11
❑ 160 Rafael Furcal 1.00 .45
❑ 161 Jeromy Burnitz .25 .11
❑ 162 Jimmy Haynes .15 .07
❑ 163 Mark Loretta .15 .07
❑ 164 Ron Belliard .15 .07
❑ 165 Richie Sexson .25 .11
❑ 166 Kevin Barker .15 .07
❑ 167 Jeff D'Amico .15 .07
❑ 168 Rick Ankiel .75 .35
❑ 169 Mark McGwire 2.50 1.10
❑ 170 J.D. Drew .60 .25
❑ 171 Eli Marrero .15 .07
❑ 172 Darryl Kile .25 .11
❑ 173 Edgar Renteria .15 .07
❑ 174 Will Clark .60 .25
❑ 175 Eric Young .15 .07
❑ 176 Mark Grace .60 .25
❑ 177 Jon Lieber .15 .07
❑ 178 Damon Buford .15 .07
❑ 179 Kerry Wood .25 .11
❑ 180 Rondell White .25 .11
❑ 181 Joe Girardi .15 .07
❑ 182 Curt Schilling .25 .11
❑ 183 Randy Johnson .75 .35
❑ 184 Steve Finley .25 .11
❑ 185 Kelly Stinnett .15 .07
❑ 186 Jay Bell .25 .11
❑ 187 Matt Mantei .15 .07
❑ 188 Luis Gonzalez .25 .11
❑ 189 Shawn Green .60 .25
❑ 190 Todd Hundley .15 .07
❑ 191 Chan Ho Park .25 .11
❑ 192 Adrian Beltre .25 .11
❑ 193 Mark Grudzielanek .15 .07
❑ 194 Gary Sheffield .60 .25
❑ 195 Tom Goodwin .15 .07
❑ 196 Lee Stevens .15 .07
❑ 197 Javier Vazquez .15 .07
❑ 198 Milton Bradley .25 .11
❑ 199 Vladimir Guerrero 1.00 .45
❑ 200 Carl Pavano .15 .07
❑ 201 Orlando Cabrera .15 .07
❑ 202 Tony Armas Jr. .25 .11
❑ 203 Jeff Kent .40 .18
❑ 204 Calvin Murray .15 .07
❑ 205 Ellis Burks .25 .11
❑ 206 Barry Bonds 1.00 .45
❑ 207 Russ Ortiz .25 .11
❑ 208 Marvin Benard .15 .07
❑ 209 Joe Nathan .15 .07
❑ 210 Preston Wilson .25 .11
❑ 211 Cliff Floyd .25 .11
❑ 212 Mike Lowell .25 .11
❑ 213 Ryan Dempster .25 .11
❑ 214 Brad Penny .25 .11
❑ 215 Mike Redmond .15 .07
❑ 216 Luis Castillo .25 .11
❑ 217 Derek Bell .15 .07
❑ 218 Mike Hampton .25 .11
❑ 219 Todd Zeile .25 .11
❑ 220 Robin Ventura .25 .11
❑ 221 Mike Piazza 2.00 .90
❑ 222 Al Leiter .25 .11
❑ 223 Edgardo Alfonzo .25 .11
❑ 224 Mike Bordick .15 .07
❑ 225 Phil Nevin .25 .11
❑ 226 Ryan Klesko .25 .11
❑ 227 Adam Eaton .25 .11
❑ 228 Eric Owens .15 .07
❑ 229 Tony Gwynn 1.25 .55
❑ 230 Matt Clement .15 .07
❑ 231 Wiki Gonzalez .15 .07
❑ 232 Robert Person .15 .07
❑ 233 Doug Glanville .15 .07
❑ 234 Scott Rolen .60 .25
❑ 235 Mike Lieberthal .25 .11
❑ 236 Randy Wolf .15 .07
❑ 237 Bob Abreu .25 .11
❑ 238 Pat Burrell .60 .25
❑ 239 Bruce Chen .15 .07
❑ 240 Kevin Young .15 .07
❑ 241 Todd Ritchie .15 .07
❑ 242 Adrian Brown .15 .07
❑ 243 Chad Hermansen .15 .07
❑ 244 Warren Morris .15 .07
❑ 245 Kris Benson .25 .11
❑ 246 Jason Kendall .25 .11
❑ 247 Pokey Reese .25 .11
❑ 248 Rob Bell .15 .07
❑ 249 Ken Griffey Jr. 2.50 1.10
❑ 250 Sean Casey .25 .11
❑ 251 Aaron Boone .15 .07
❑ 252 Pete Harnisch .15 .07
❑ 253 Barry Larkin .60 .25
❑ 254 Dmitri Young .25 .11
❑ 255 Todd Hollandsworth .15 .07
❑ 256 Pedro Astacio .15 .07
❑ 257 Todd Helton .75 .35
❑ 258 Terry Shumpert .15 .07
❑ 259 Neifi Perez .15 .07
❑ 260 Jeffrey Hammonds .25 .11
❑ 261 Ben Petrick .15 .07
❑ 262 Mark McGwire SH 1.25 .55
❑ 263 Derek Jeter SH 1.25 .55
❑ 264 Sammy Sosa SH .60 .25
❑ 265 Cal Ripken SH 1.25 .55
❑ 266 Pedro Martinez SH .40 .18
❑ 267 Barry Bonds SH .60 .25
❑ 268 Fred McGriff SH .25 .11
❑ 269 Randy Johnson SH .40 .18
❑ 270 Darin Erstad SH .25 .11

## 2000 Upper Deck Gold Reserve

| | MINT | NRMT |
|---|---|---|
| COMPLETE SET (300) | 350.00 | 160.00 |
| COMP.SET w/o SP's (270) | 50.00 | 22.00 |
| COMMON (1-267/298-300) | .15 | .07 |
| COMMON CARD (268-297) | 8.00 | 3.60 |

❑ 1 Mo Vaughn .25 .11
❑ 2 Darin Erstad .60 .25
❑ 3 Garret Anderson .25 .11
❑ 4 Troy Glaus .75 .35
❑ 5 Troy Percival .15 .07
❑ 6 Kent Bottenfield .15 .07
❑ 7 Orlando Palmeiro .15 .07
❑ 8 Tim Salmon .25 .11
❑ 9 Jason Giambi .60 .25
❑ 10 Eric Chavez .25 .11
❑ 11 Matt Stairs .15 .07
❑ 12 Miguel Tejada .25 .11
❑ 13 Tim Hudson .60 .25
❑ 14 John Jaha .15 .07
❑ 15 Ben Grieve .25 .11
❑ 16 Kevin Appier .25 .11
❑ 17 David Wells .25 .11
❑ 18 Jose Cruz Jr. .25 .11
❑ 19 Homer Bush .15 .07
❑ 20 Shannon Stewart .25 .11
❑ 21 Carlos Delgado .60 .25
❑ 22 Roy Halladay .15 .07
❑ 23 Tony Batista .25 .11
❑ 24 Raul Mondesi .25 .11
❑ 25 Fred McGriff .40 .18
❑ 26 Jose Canseco .75 .35
❑ 27 Roberto Hernandez UER 73 .15 .07
❑ 28 Vinny Castilla .25 .11
❑ 29 Gerald Williams .15 .07
❑ 30 Ryan Rupe .15 .07
❑ 31 Greg Vaughn .25 .11
❑ 32 Miguel Cairo .15 .07
❑ 33 Roberto Alomar .60 .25
❑ 34 Jim Thome .40 .18
❑ 35 Bartolo Colon .25 .11
❑ 36 Omar Vizquel .25 .11
❑ 37 Manny Ramirez .75 .35
❑ 38 Chuck Finley .25 .11
❑ 39 Travis Fryman .25 .11
❑ 40 Kenny Lofton .25 .11
❑ 41 Richie Sexson .25 .11
❑ 42 Charles Nagy .15 .07
❑ 43 John Halama .15 .07
❑ 44 David Bell .15 .07
❑ 45 Jay Buhner .25 .11
❑ 46 Edgar Martinez .40 .18
❑ 47 Alex Rodriguez 2.00 .90
❑ 48 Freddy Garcia .25 .11
❑ 49 Aaron Sele .25 .11
❑ 50 Jamie Moyer .15 .07
❑ 51 Mike Cameron .15 .07
❑ 52 Albert Belle .40 .18
❑ 53 Jerry Hairston Jr. .15 .07
❑ 54 Sidney Ponson .15 .07
❑ 55 Cal Ripken 2.50 1.10
❑ 56 Mike Mussina .60 .25
❑ 57 B.J. Surhoff .25 .11
❑ 58 Brady Anderson .25 .11
❑ 59 Mike Bordick .15 .07
❑ 60 Ivan Rodriguez .75 .35
❑ 61 Rusty Greer .25 .11
❑ 62 Rafael Palmeiro .60 .25
❑ 63 John Wetteland .25 .11
❑ 64 Ruben Mateo .25 .11
❑ 65 Gabe Kapler .25 .11
❑ 66 David Segui .15 .07
❑ 67 Justin Thompson .15 .07
❑ 68 Rick Helling .25 .11
❑ 69 Jose Offerman .15 .07
❑ 70 Trot Nixon .25 .11
❑ 71 Pedro Martinez .75 .35
❑ 72 Jason Varitek .25 .11
❑ 73 Troy O'Leary .15 .07
❑ 74 Nomar Garciaparra 2.00 .90
❑ 75 Carl Everett .25 .11
❑ 76 Wilton Veras .25 .11
❑ 77 Tim Wakefield .15 .07
❑ 78 Ramon Martinez .15 .07
❑ 79 Johnny Damon .25 .11
❑ 80 Mike Sweeney .25 .11
❑ 81 Rey Sanchez .15 .07
❑ 82 Carlos Beltran .25 .11
❑ 83 Carlos Febles .15 .07
❑ 84 Jermaine Dye .25 .11
❑ 85 Joe Randa .15 .07
❑ 86 Jose Rosado .15 .07
❑ 87 Jeff Suppan .15 .07
❑ 88 Juan Encarnacion .25 .11
❑ 89 Damion Easley .15 .07
❑ 90 Brad Ausmus .15 .07
❑ 91 Todd Jones .15 .07
❑ 92 Juan Gonzalez .60 .25
❑ 93 Bobby Higginson .25 .11
❑ 94 Tony Clark .15 .07
❑ 95 Brian Moehler .15 .07
❑ 96 Dean Palmer .25 .11
❑ 97 Joe Mays .15 .07
❑ 98 Eric Milton .25 .11
❑ 99 Corey Koskie .15 .07
❑ 100 Ron Coomer .15 .07
❑ 101 Brad Radke .15 .07
❑ 102 Todd Walker .15 .07
❑ 103 Butch Huskey .15 .07
❑ 104 Jacque Jones .25 .11
❑ 105 Frank Thomas 1.25 .55

❑ 106 Mike Sirotka .15 .07
❑ 107 Carlos Lee .25 .11
❑ 108 Ray Durham .25 .11
❑ 109 Bob Howry .15 .07
❑ 110 Magglio Ordonez .25 .11
❑ 111 Paul Konerko .25 .11
❑ 112 Chris Singleton .25 .11
❑ 113 James Baldwin .25 .11
❑ 114 Derek Jeter 2.50 1.10
❑ 115 Tino Martinez .25 .11
❑ 116 Orlando Hernandez .25 .11
❑ 117 Chuck Knoblauch .25 .11
❑ 118 Bernie Williams .60 .25
❑ 119 David Cone .25 .11
❑ 120 Paul O'Neill .25 .11
❑ 121 Roger Clemens 1.25 .55
❑ 122 Mariano Rivera .25 .11
❑ 123 Ricky Ledee .15 .07
❑ 124 Richard Hidalgo .25 .11
❑ 125 Jeff Bagwell .75 .35
❑ 126 Jose Lima .15 .07
❑ 127 Billy Wagner .15 .07
❑ 128 Shane Reynolds .15 .07
❑ 129 Moises Alou .25 .11
❑ 130 Craig Biggio .40 .18
❑ 131 Roger Cedeno .15 .07
❑ 132 Octavio Dotel .15 .07
❑ 133 Greg Maddux 1.50 .70
❑ 134 Brian Jordan .25 .11
❑ 135 Kevin Millwood .25 .11
❑ 136 Javy Lopez .25 .11
❑ 137 Bruce Chen .15 .07
❑ 138 Chipper Jones 1.50 .70
❑ 139 Tom Glavine .60 .25
❑ 140 Andruw Jones .60 .25
❑ 141 Andres Galarraga .40 .18
❑ 142 Reggie Sanders .15 .07
❑ 143 Geoff Jenkins .25 .11
❑ 144 Jeromy Burnitz .25 .11
❑ 145 Ron Belliard .15 .07
❑ 146 Mark Loretta .15 .07
❑ 147 Steve Woodard .15 .07
❑ 148 Marquis Grissom .15 .07
❑ 149 Bob Wickman .15 .07
❑ 150 Mark McGwire 2.50 1.10
❑ 151 Fernando Tatis .25 .11
❑ 152 Edgar Renteria .15 .07
❑ 153 J.D. Drew .60 .25
❑ 154 Ray Lankford .25 .11
❑ 155 Fernando Vina .15 .07
❑ 156 Pat Hentgen .15 .07
❑ 157 Jim Edmonds .60 .25
❑ 158 Mark Grace .60 .25
❑ 159 Kerry Wood .25 .11
❑ 160 Eric Young .15 .07
❑ 161 Ismael Valdes .15 .07
❑ 162 Sammy Sosa 1.25 .55
❑ 163 Henry Rodriguez .15 .07
❑ 164 Kyle Farnsworth .15 .07
❑ 165 Glenallen Hill .15 .07
❑ 166 Jon Lieber .15 .07
❑ 167 Luis Gonzalez .25 .11
❑ 168 Tony Womack .15 .07
❑ 169 Omar Daal .15 .07
❑ 170 Randy Johnson .75 .35
❑ 171 Erubiel Durazo .25 .11
❑ 172 Jay Bell .25 .11
❑ 173 Steve Finley .25 .11
❑ 174 Travis Lee .15 .07
❑ 175 Matt Williams .40 .18
❑ 176 Matt Mantei .15 .07
❑ 177 Adrian Beltre .25 .11
❑ 178 Kevin Brown .40 .18
❑ 179 Chan Ho Park .25 .11
❑ 180 Mark Grudzielanek .15 .07
❑ 181 Jeff Shaw .15 .07
❑ 182 Shawn Green .60 .25
❑ 183 Gary Sheffield .60 .25
❑ 184 Todd Hundley .15 .07
❑ 185 Eric Karros .25 .11
❑ 186 Kevin Elster .15 .07
❑ 187 Vladimir Guerrero 1.00 .45
❑ 188 Michael Barrett .15 .07
❑ 189 Chris Widger .15 .07
❑ 190 Ugueth Urbina .15 .07
❑ 191 Dustin Hermanson .15 .07
❑ 192 Rondell White .25 .11
❑ 193 Jose Vidro .25 .11
❑ 194 Hideki Irabu .15 .07
❑ 195 Lee Stevens .15 .07
❑ 196 Livan Hernandez .15 .07
❑ 197 Ellis Burks .15 .07
❑ 198 J.T. Snow .25 .11
❑ 199 Jeff Kent .40 .18
❑ 200 Robb Nen .15 .07
❑ 201 Marvin Benard .15 .07
❑ 202 Barry Bonds 1.00 .45
❑ 203 Russ Ortiz .15 .07
❑ 204 Rich Aurilia .15 .07
❑ 205 Joe Nathan .15 .07
❑ 206 Preston Wilson .25 .11
❑ 207 Cliff Floyd .25 .11
❑ 208 Mike Lowell .25 .11
❑ 209 Ryan Dempster .25 .11
❑ 210 Luis Castillo .25 .11
❑ 211 Alex Fernandez .15 .07
❑ 212 Mark Kotsay .15 .07
❑ 213 Brant Brown .15 .07
❑ 214 Edgardo Alfonzo .25 .11
❑ 215 Robin Ventura .25 .11
❑ 216 Rickey Henderson .75 .35
❑ 217 Mike Hampton .25 .11
❑ 218 Mike Piazza 2.00 .90
❑ 219 Al Leiter .25 .11
❑ 220 Derek Bell .15 .07
❑ 221 Armando Benitez .15 .07
❑ 222 Rey Ordonez .15 .07
❑ 223 Todd Zeile .25 .11
❑ 224 Tony Gwynn 1.25 .55
❑ 225 Eric Owens .15 .07
❑ 226 Damian Jackson .15 .07
❑ 227 Trevor Hoffman .25 .11
❑ 228 Ben Davis .15 .07
❑ 229 Sterling Hitchcock .15 .07
❑ 230 Ruben Rivera .15 .07
❑ 231 Ryan Klesko .25 .11
❑ 232 Phil Nevin .25 .11
❑ 233 Mike Lieberthal .25 .11
❑ 234 Bob Abreu .25 .11
❑ 235 Doug Glanville .15 .07
❑ 236 Rico Brogna .15 .07
❑ 237 Scott Rolen .60 .25
❑ 238 Andy Ashby .15 .07
❑ 239 Robert Person .15 .07
❑ 240 Curt Schilling .25 .11
❑ 241 Mike Jackson .15 .07
❑ 242 Warren Morris .15 .07
❑ 243 Kris Benson .25 .11
❑ 244 Kevin Young .15 .07
❑ 245 Brian Giles .25 .11
❑ 246 Jason Schmidt .15 .07
❑ 247 Jason Kendall .25 .11
❑ 248 Todd Ritchie .15 .07
❑ 249 Wil Cordero .15 .07
❑ 250 Aramis Ramirez .15 .07
❑ 251 Sean Casey .25 .11
❑ 252 Barry Larkin .60 .25
❑ 253 Pokey Reese .25 .11
❑ 254 Scott Williamson .15 .07
❑ 255 Aaron Boone .15 .07
❑ 256 Dante Bichette .25 .11
❑ 257 Ken Griffey Jr. 2.50 1.10
❑ 258 Denny Neagle .15 .07
❑ 259 Dmitri Young .25 .11
❑ 260 Todd Helton .75 .35
❑ 261 Larry Walker .25 .11
❑ 262 Pedro Astacio .15 .07
❑ 263 Neifi Perez .15 .07
❑ 264 Jeff Cirillo .25 .11
❑ 265 Jeffrey Hammonds .25 .11
❑ 266 Tom Goodwin .15 .07
❑ 267 Rolando Arrojo .15 .07
❑ 268 Rick Ankiel FF 20.00 9.00
❑ 269 Pat Burrell FF 15.00 6.75
❑ 270 Eric Munson FF 10.00 4.50
❑ 271 Rafael Furcal FF 25.00 11.00
❑ 272 Brad Penny FF 8.00 3.60
❑ 273 Adam Kennedy FF 8.00 3.60
❑ 274 Mike Lamb FF RC 8.00 3.60
❑ 275 Matt Riley FF 8.00 3.60
❑ 276 Eric Gagne FF 8.00 3.60
❑ 277 Kazuhiro Sasaki FF RC 30.00 13.50
❑ 278 Julio Lugo FF 8.00 3.60
❑ 279 Kip Wells FF 8.00 3.60
❑ 280 Danys Baez FF RC 10.00 4.50
❑ 281 Josh Beckett FF 10.00 4.50
❑ 282 Alfonso Soriano FF 8.00 3.60
❑ 283 Vernon Wells FF 8.00 3.60
❑ 284 Nick Johnson FF 8.00 3.60
❑ 285 Ramon Ortiz FF 8.00 3.60
❑ 286 Peter Bergeron FF 8.00 3.60
❑ 287 Wascar Serrano FF RC 8.00 3.60
❑ 288 Josh Paul FF 8.00 3.60
❑ 289 Mark Quinn FF 8.00 3.60
❑ 290 Jason Marquis FF 8.00 3.60
❑ 291 Rob Bell FF 8.00 3.60
❑ 292 Pablo Ozuna FF 8.00 3.60
❑ 293 Milton Bradley FF 8.00 3.60
❑ 294 Roosevelt Brown FF 8.00 3.60
❑ 295 Terrence Long FF 8.00 3.60
❑ 296 Chad Durbin FF RC 8.00 3.60
❑ 297 Matt LeCroy FF 8.00 3.60
❑ 298 Ken Griffey Jr. CL 1.25 .55
❑ 299 Mark McGwire CL 1.25 .55
❑ 300 Derek Jeter CL 1.25 .55

## 2000 Upper Deck Hitter's Club

| | MINT | NRMT |
|---|---|---|
| COMPLETE SET (90) | 40.00 | 18.00 |

❑ 1 Mo Vaughn .25 .11
❑ 2 Troy Glaus .75 .35
❑ 3 Jeff Bagwell .75 .35
❑ 4 Craig Biggio .40 .18
❑ 5 Jason Giambi .60 .25
❑ 6 Eric Chavez .25 .11
❑ 7 Carlos Delgado .60 .25
❑ 8 Chipper Jones 1.50 .70
❑ 9 Andruw Jones .60 .25
❑ 10 Andres Galarraga .40 .18
❑ 11 Jeromy Burnitz .25 .11
❑ 12 Mark McGwire 2.50 1.10
❑ 13 Mark Grace .60 .25
❑ 14 Sammy Sosa 1.25 .55
❑ 15 Jose Canseco .75 .35
❑ 16 Vinny Castilla .25 .11
❑ 17 Matt Williams .40 .18
❑ 18 Gary Sheffield .60 .25
❑ 19 Shawn Green .60 .25
❑ 20 Vladimir Guerrero 1.00 .45
❑ 21 Barry Bonds 1.00 .45
❑ 22 Manny Ramirez .75 .35
❑ 23 Roberto Alomar .60 .25
❑ 24 Jim Thome .40 .18
❑ 25 Ken Griffey Jr. 2.50 1.10
❑ 26 Alex Rodriguez 2.00 .90
❑ 27 Edgar Martinez .40 .18
❑ 28 Preston Wilson .25 .11
❑ 29 Mike Piazza 2.00 .90
❑ 30 Robin Ventura .40 .18
❑ 31 Albert Belle .40 .18
❑ 32 Cal Ripken 2.50 1.10
❑ 33 Tony Gwynn 1.25 .55
❑ 34 Scott Rolen .60 .25
❑ 35 Bob Abreu .25 .11
❑ 36 Brian Giles .25 .11
❑ 37 Ivan Rodriguez .75 .35
❑ 38 Rafael Palmeiro .60 .25

| Card | MINT | NRMT |
|---|---|---|
| ❑ 39 Nomar Garciaparra | 2.00 | .90 |
| ❑ 40 Sean Casey | .25 | .11 |
| ❑ 41 Larry Walker | .25 | .11 |
| ❑ 42 Todd Helton | .50 | .23 |
| ❑ 43 Carlos Beltran | .25 | .11 |
| ❑ 44 Dean Palmer | .25 | .11 |
| ❑ 45 Juan Gonzalez | .60 | .25 |
| ❑ 46 Corey Koskie | .15 | .07 |
| ❑ 47 Frank Thomas | 1.25 | .55 |
| ❑ 48 Magglio Ordonez | .25 | .11 |
| ❑ 49 Derek Jeter | 2.50 | 1.10 |
| ❑ 50 Bernie Williams | .60 | .25 |
| ❑ 51 Paul Waner W3K | .60 | .25 |
| ❑ 52 Honus Wagner W3K | .75 | .35 |
| ❑ 53 Tris Speaker W3K | .60 | .25 |
| ❑ 54 Nap Lajoie W3K | .75 | .35 |
| ❑ 55 Eddie Collins W3K | .60 | .25 |
| ❑ 56 Roberto Clemente W3K | 1.50 | .70 |
| ❑ 57 Ty Cobb W3K | 1.50 | .70 |
| ❑ 58 Cap Anson W3K | .60 | .25 |
| ❑ 59 Robin Yount W3K | .75 | .35 |
| ❑ 60 Carl Yastrzemski W3K | .75 | .35 |
| ❑ 61 Dave Winfield W3K | .60 | .25 |
| ❑ 62 Stan Musial W3K | 1.00 | .45 |
| ❑ 63 Eddie Murray W3K | .60 | .25 |
| ❑ 64 Paul Molitor W3K | .60 | .25 |
| ❑ 65 Wille Mays W3K | 1.50 | .70 |
| ❑ 66 Al Kaline W3K | .75 | .35 |
| ❑ 67 Tony Gwynn W3K | 1.25 | .55 |
| ❑ 68 Rod Carew W3K | .75 | .35 |
| ❑ 69 Lou Brock W3K | .60 | .25 |
| ❑ 70 George Brett W3K | 1.25 | .55 |
| ❑ 71 Wade Boggs W3K | .75 | .35 |
| ❑ 72 Hank Aaron W3K | 1.50 | .70 |
| ❑ 73 Jorge Toca HS | .25 | .11 |
| ❑ 74 J.D. Drew HS | .60 | .25 |
| ❑ 75 Pat Burrell HS | 1.00 | .45 |
| ❑ 76 Vernon Wells HS | .25 | .11 |
| ❑ 77 Julio Ramirez HS | .15 | .07 |
| ❑ 78 Gabe Kapler HS | .25 | .11 |
| ❑ 79 Erubiel Durazo HS | .25 | .11 |
| ❑ 80 Lance Berkman HS | .25 | .11 |
| ❑ 81 Peter Bergeron HS | .15 | .07 |
| ❑ 82 Alfonso Soriano HS | .25 | .11 |
| ❑ 83 Jacque Jones HS | .25 | .11 |
| ❑ 84 Ben Petrick HS | .15 | .07 |
| ❑ 85 Jerry Hairston Jr. HS | .15 | .07 |
| ❑ 86 Kevin Witt HS | .15 | .07 |
| ❑ 87 Dermal Brown HS | .25 | .11 |
| ❑ 88 Chad Hermansen HS | .15 | .07 |
| ❑ 89 Ruben Mateo HS | .25 | .11 |
| ❑ 90 Ken Griffey Jr. CL | 1.25 | .55 |

## 1999 Upper Deck HoloGrFX

| | MINT | NRMT |
|---|---|---|
| COMPLETE SET (60) | 25.00 | 11.00 |
| ❑ 1 Mo Vaughn | .40 | .18 |
| ❑ 2 Troy Glaus | 1.25 | .55 |
| ❑ 3 Tim Salmon | .40 | .18 |
| ❑ 4 Randy Johnson | 1.00 | .45 |
| ❑ 5 Travis Lee | .30 | .14 |
| ❑ 6 Chipper Jones | 2.00 | .90 |
| ❑ 7 Greg Maddux | 2.00 | .90 |
| ❑ 8 Andruw Jones | .75 | .35 |
| ❑ 9 Tom Glavine | .75 | .35 |
| ❑ 10 Cal Ripken | 3.00 | 1.35 |
| ❑ 11 Albert Belle | .50 | .23 |
| ❑ 12 Nomar Garciaparra | 2.50 | 1.10 |
| ❑ 13 Pedro Martinez | 1.00 | .45 |
| ❑ 14 Sammy Sosa | 1.50 | .70 |
| ❑ 15 Frank Thomas | 1.50 | .70 |
| ❑ 16 Greg Vaughn | .40 | .18 |
| ❑ 17 Kenny Lofton | .40 | .18 |
| ❑ 18 Jim Thome | .50 | .23 |
| ❑ 19 Manny Ramirez | 1.00 | .45 |
| ❑ 20 Todd Helton | 1.00 | .45 |
| ❑ 21 Larry Walker | .40 | .18 |
| ❑ 22 Tony Clark | .30 | .14 |
| ❑ 23 Juan Encarnacion | .40 | .18 |
| ❑ 24 Mark Kotsay | .30 | .14 |
| ❑ 25 Jeff Bagwell | 1.00 | .45 |
| ❑ 26 Craig Biggio | .50 | .23 |
| ❑ 27 Ken Caminiti | .40 | .18 |
| ❑ 28 Carlos Beltran | .40 | .18 |
| ❑ 29 Jeremy Giambi | .30 | .14 |
| ❑ 30 Raul Mondesi | .40 | .18 |
| ❑ 31 Kevin Brown | .50 | .23 |
| ❑ 32 Jeromy Burnitz | .40 | .18 |
| ❑ 33 Corey Koskie | .30 | .14 |
| ❑ 34 Todd Walker | .30 | .14 |
| ❑ 35 Vladimir Guerrero | 1.25 | .55 |
| ❑ 36 Mike Piazza | 2.50 | 1.10 |
| ❑ 37 Robin Ventura | .40 | .18 |
| ❑ 38 Derek Jeter | 3.00 | 1.35 |
| ❑ 39 Roger Clemens | 1.50 | .70 |
| ❑ 40 Bernie Williams | .75 | .35 |
| ❑ 41 Orlando Hernandez | .40 | .18 |
| ❑ 42 Ben Grieve | .40 | .18 |
| ❑ 43 Eric Chavez | .40 | .18 |
| ❑ 44 Scott Rolen | .75 | .35 |
| ❑ 45 Pat Burrell RC | 5.00 | 2.20 |
| ❑ 46 Warren Morris | .30 | .14 |
| ❑ 47 Jason Kendall | .40 | .18 |
| ❑ 48 Mark McGwire | 3.00 | 1.35 |
| ❑ 49 J.D. Drew | .75 | .35 |
| ❑ 50 Tony Gwynn | 1.50 | .70 |
| ❑ 51 Trevor Hoffman | .40 | .18 |
| ❑ 52 Barry Bonds | 1.25 | .55 |
| ❑ 53 Ken Griffey Jr. | 3.00 | 1.35 |
| ❑ 54 Alex Rodriguez | 2.50 | 1.10 |
| ❑ 55 Jose Canseco | 1.00 | .45 |
| ❑ 56 Juan Gonzalez | .75 | .35 |
| ❑ 57 Ivan Rodriguez | 1.00 | .45 |
| ❑ 58 Rafael Palmeiro | .75 | .35 |
| ❑ 59 David Wells | .40 | .18 |
| ❑ 60 Carlos Delgado | .75 | .35 |
| ❑ S60 Ken Griffey Jr. Sample | 3.00 | 1.35 |

## 2000 Upper Deck HoloGrFX

| | MINT | NRMT |
|---|---|---|
| COMPLETE SET (90) | 30.00 | 13.50 |
| ❑ 1 Mo Vaughn | .30 | .14 |
| ❑ 2 Troy Glaus | 1.00 | .45 |
| ❑ 3 Daryle Ward | .30 | .14 |
| ❑ 4 Jeff Bagwell | 1.00 | .45 |
| ❑ 5 Craig Biggio | .50 | .23 |
| ❑ 6 Jose Lima | .20 | .09 |
| ❑ 7 Jason Giambi | .75 | .35 |
| ❑ 8 Eric Chavez | .30 | .14 |
| ❑ 9 Tim Hudson | .75 | .35 |
| ❑ 10 Raul Mondesi | .30 | .14 |
| ❑ 11 Carlos Delgado | .75 | .35 |
| ❑ 12 David Wells | .30 | .14 |
| ❑ 13 Chipper Jones | 2.00 | .90 |
| ❑ 14 Greg Maddux | 2.00 | .90 |
| ❑ 15 Andruw Jones | .75 | .35 |
| ❑ 16 Brian Jordan | .30 | .14 |
| ❑ 17 Jeromy Burnitz | .30 | .14 |
| ❑ 18 Ron Belliard | .20 | .09 |
| ❑ 19 Mark McGwire | 3.00 | 1.35 |
| ❑ 20 Fernando Tatis | .30 | .14 |
| ❑ 21 J.D. Drew | .75 | .35 |
| ❑ 22 Sammy Sosa | 1.50 | .70 |
| ❑ 23 Mark Grace | .75 | .35 |
| ❑ 24 Greg Vaughn | .30 | .14 |
| ❑ 25 Jose Canseco | 1.00 | .45 |
| ❑ 26 Vinny Castilla | .30 | .14 |
| ❑ 27 Fred McGriff | .50 | .23 |
| ❑ 28 Matt Williams | .50 | .23 |
| ❑ 29 Randy Johnson | 1.00 | .45 |
| ❑ 30 Erubiel Durazo | .30 | .14 |
| ❑ 31 Shawn Green | .75 | .35 |
| ❑ 32 Gary Sheffield | .75 | .35 |
| ❑ 33 Kevin Brown | .50 | .23 |
| ❑ 34 Vladimir Guerrero | 1.25 | .55 |
| ❑ 35 Michael Barrett | .20 | .09 |
| ❑ 36 Russ Ortiz | .30 | .14 |
| ❑ 37 Barry Bonds | 1.25 | .55 |
| ❑ 38 Jeff Kent | .50 | .23 |
| ❑ 39 Kenny Lofton | .30 | .14 |
| ❑ 40 Manny Ramirez | 1.00 | .45 |
| ❑ 41 Roberto Alomar | .75 | .35 |
| ❑ 42 Richie Sexson | .30 | .14 |
| ❑ 43 Edgar Martinez | .50 | .23 |
| ❑ 44 Alex Rodriguez | 2.50 | 1.10 |
| ❑ 45 Freddy Garcia | .30 | .14 |
| ❑ 46 Preston Wilson | .30 | .14 |
| ❑ 47 Alex Gonzalez | .20 | .09 |
| ❑ 48 Mike Hampton | .30 | .14 |
| ❑ 49 Mike Piazza | 2.50 | 1.10 |
| ❑ 50 Robin Ventura | .50 | .23 |
| ❑ 51 Edgardo Alfonzo | .30 | .14 |
| ❑ 52 Albert Belle | .50 | .23 |
| ❑ 53 Cal Ripken | 3.00 | 1.35 |
| ❑ 54 B.J. Surhoff | .30 | .14 |
| ❑ 55 Tony Gwynn | 1.50 | .70 |
| ❑ 56 Trevor Hoffman | .30 | .14 |
| ❑ 57 Mike Lieberthal | .30 | .14 |
| ❑ 58 Scott Rolen | .75 | .35 |
| ❑ 59 Bob Abreu | .30 | .14 |
| ❑ 60 Curt Schilling | .30 | .14 |
| ❑ 61 Jason Kendall | .30 | .14 |
| ❑ 62 Brian Giles | .30 | .14 |
| ❑ 63 Kris Benson | .30 | .14 |
| ❑ 64 Rafael Palmeiro | .75 | .35 |
| ❑ 65 Ivan Rodriguez | 1.00 | .45 |
| ❑ 66 Gabe Kapler | .30 | .14 |
| ❑ 67 Nomar Garciaparra | 2.50 | 1.10 |
| ❑ 68 Pedro Martinez | 1.00 | .45 |
| ❑ 69 Troy O'Leary | .20 | .09 |
| ❑ 70 Barry Larkin | .75 | .35 |
| ❑ 71 Dante Bichette | .30 | .14 |
| ❑ 72 Sean Casey | .30 | .14 |
| ❑ 73 Ken Griffey Jr. | 3.00 | 1.35 |
| ❑ 74 Jeff Cirillo | .30 | .14 |
| ❑ 75 Todd Helton | 1.00 | .45 |
| ❑ 76 Larry Walker | .30 | .14 |
| ❑ 77 Carlos Beltran | .30 | .14 |
| ❑ 78 Jermaine Dye | .30 | .14 |
| ❑ 79 Juan Gonzalez | .75 | .35 |
| ❑ 80 Juan Encarnacion | .30 | .14 |
| ❑ 81 Dean Palmer | .30 | .14 |
| ❑ 82 Corey Koskie | .20 | .09 |
| ❑ 83 Eric Milton | .20 | .09 |
| ❑ 84 Frank Thomas | 1.50 | .70 |
| ❑ 85 Magglio Ordonez | .30 | .14 |
| ❑ 86 Carlos Lee | .30 | .14 |
| ❑ 87 Derek Jeter | 3.00 | 1.35 |
| ❑ 88 Tino Martinez | .30 | .14 |
| ❑ 89 Bernie Williams | .75 | .35 |
| ❑ 90 Roger Clemens | 1.50 | .70 |

## 2000 Upper Deck Legends

| | MINT | NRMT |
|---|---|---|
| COMPLETE SET (135) | 150.00 | 70.00 |
| COMP.SET w/o SP'S (90) | 20.00 | 9.00 |
| COMMON CARD (1-90) | .25 | .11 |
| COMMON CARD (91-105) | 2.00 | .90 |
| COMMON CARD (106-135) | 2.00 | .90 |

| | | MINT | NRMT |
|---|---|---|---|
| ❑ 1 | Darin Erstad | .60 | .25 |
| ❑ 2 | Troy Glaus | .75 | .35 |
| ❑ 3 | Mo Vaughn | .30 | .14 |
| ❑ 4 | Craig Biggio | .60 | .25 |
| ❑ 5 | Jeff Bagwell | .75 | .35 |
| ❑ 6 | Reggie Jackson | .75 | .35 |
| ❑ 7 | Tim Hudson | .60 | .25 |
| ❑ 8 | Jason Giambi | .60 | .25 |
| ❑ 9 | Hank Aaron | 1.50 | .70 |
| ❑ 10 | Greg Maddux | 1.50 | .70 |
| ❑ 11 | Chipper Jones | 1.50 | .70 |
| ❑ 12 | Andres Galarraga | .40 | .18 |
| ❑ 13 | Robin Yount | .60 | .25 |
| ❑ 14 | Jeromy Burnitz | .30 | .14 |
| ❑ 15 | Paul Molitor | .60 | .25 |
| ❑ 16 | David Wells | .30 | .14 |
| ❑ 17 | Carlos Delgado | .60 | .25 |
| ❑ 18 | Ernie Banks | .75 | .35 |
| ❑ 19 | Sammy Sosa | 1.25 | .55 |
| ❑ 20 | Kerry Wood | .30 | .14 |
| ❑ 21 | Stan Musial | 1.00 | .45 |
| ❑ 22 | Bob Gibson | .60 | .25 |
| ❑ 23 | Mark McGwire | 2.50 | 1.10 |
| ❑ 24 | Fernando Tatis | .30 | .14 |
| ❑ 25 | Randy Johnson | .75 | .35 |
| ❑ 26 | Matt Williams | .40 | .18 |
| ❑ 27 | Jackie Robinson | 1.25 | .55 |
| ❑ 28 | Sandy Koufax | 2.00 | .90 |
| ❑ 29 | Shawn Green | .60 | .25 |
| ❑ 30 | Kevin Brown | .40 | .18 |
| ❑ 31 | Gary Sheffield | .60 | .25 |
| ❑ 32 | Greg Vaughn | .30 | .14 |
| ❑ 33 | Jose Canseco | .75 | .35 |
| ❑ 34 | Gary Carter | .40 | .18 |
| ❑ 35 | Vladimir Guerrero | 1.00 | .45 |
| ❑ 36 | Willie Mays | 1.50 | .70 |
| ❑ 37 | Barry Bonds | 1.00 | .45 |
| ❑ 38 | Jeff Kent | .40 | .18 |
| ❑ 39 | Bob Feller | .60 | .25 |
| ❑ 40 | Roberto Alomar | .60 | .25 |
| ❑ 41 | Jim Thome | .40 | .18 |
| ❑ 42 | Manny Ramirez | .75 | .35 |
| ❑ 43 | Alex Rodriguez | 2.00 | .90 |
| ❑ 44 | Preston Wilson | .30 | .14 |
| ❑ 45 | Tom Seaver | 1.00 | .45 |
| ❑ 46 | Robin Ventura | .30 | .14 |
| ❑ 47 | Mike Piazza | 2.00 | .90 |
| ❑ 48 | Mike Hampton | .30 | .14 |
| ❑ 49 | Brooks Robinson | .60 | .25 |
| ❑ 50 | Frank Robinson | .60 | .25 |
| ❑ 51 | Cal Ripken | 2.50 | 1.10 |
| ❑ 52 | Albert Belle | .40 | .18 |
| ❑ 53 | Eddie Murray | .60 | .25 |
| ❑ 54 | Tony Gwynn | 1.25 | .55 |
| ❑ 55 | Roberto Clemente | 1.50 | .70 |
| ❑ 56 | Willie Stargell | .40 | .18 |
| ❑ 57 | Brian Giles | .30 | .14 |
| ❑ 58 | Jason Kendall | .30 | .14 |
| ❑ 59 | Mike Schmidt | 1.25 | .55 |
| ❑ 60 | Bob Abreu | .30 | .14 |
| ❑ 61 | Scott Rolen | .60 | .25 |
| ❑ 62 | Curt Schilling | .30 | .14 |
| ❑ 63 | Johnny Bench | 1.00 | .45 |
| ❑ 64 | Sean Casey | .30 | .14 |
| ❑ 65 | Barry Larkin | .60 | .25 |
| ❑ 66 | Ken Griffey Jr. | 2.50 | 1.10 |
| ❑ 67 | George Brett | 1.25 | .55 |
| ❑ 68 | Carlos Beltran | .30 | .14 |
| ❑ 69 | Nolan Ryan | 3.00 | 1.35 |
| ❑ 70 | Ivan Rodriguez | .75 | .35 |
| ❑ 71 | Rafael Palmeiro | .60 | .25 |
| ❑ 72 | Larry Walker | .30 | .14 |
| ❑ 73 | Todd Helton | .75 | .35 |
| ❑ 74 | Jeff Cirillo | .30 | .14 |
| ❑ 75 | Carl Everett | .30 | .14 |
| ❑ 76 | Nomar Garciaparra | 2.00 | .90 |
| ❑ 77 | Pedro Martinez | .75 | .35 |
| ❑ 78 | Harmon Killebrew | .60 | .25 |
| ❑ 79 | Corey Koskie | .25 | .11 |
| ❑ 80 | Ty Cobb | 1.25 | .55 |
| ❑ 81 | Dean Palmer | .30 | .14 |
| ❑ 82 | Juan Gonzalez | .60 | .25 |
| ❑ 83 | Carlton Fisk | .60 | .25 |
| ❑ 84 | Frank Thomas | 1.25 | .55 |
| ❑ 85 | Magglio Ordonez | .30 | .14 |
| ❑ 86 | Lou Gehrig | 2.00 | .90 |
| ❑ 87 | Babe Ruth | 3.00 | 1.35 |
| ❑ 88 | Derek Jeter | 2.50 | 1.10 |
| ❑ 89 | Roger Clemens | 1.25 | .55 |
| ❑ 90 | Bernie Williams | .60 | .25 |
| ❑ 91 | Rick Ankiel Y2K | 5.00 | 2.20 |
| ❑ 92 | Kip Wells Y2K | 2.00 | .90 |
| ❑ 93 | Pat Burrell Y2K | 4.00 | 1.80 |
| ❑ 94 | Mark Quinn Y2K | 2.00 | .90 |
| ❑ 95 | Ruben Mateo Y2K | 2.00 | .90 |
| ❑ 96 | Adam Kennedy Y2K | 2.00 | .90 |
| ❑ 97 | Brad Penny Y2K | 2.00 | .90 |
| ❑ 98 | Kazuhiro Sasaki Y2K RC | 4.00 | 1.80 |
| ❑ 99 | Peter Bergeron Y2K | 2.00 | .90 |
| ❑ 100 | Rafael Furcal Y2K | 6.00 | 2.70 |
| ❑ 101 | Eric Munson Y2K | 2.50 | 1.10 |
| ❑ 102 | Nick Johnson Y2K | 2.00 | .90 |
| ❑ 103 | Rob Bell Y2K | 2.00 | .90 |
| ❑ 104 | Vernon Wells Y2K | 2.00 | .90 |
| ❑ 105 | Ben Petrick Y2K | 2.00 | .90 |
| ❑ 106 | Babe Ruth 20C | 8.00 | 3.60 |
| ❑ 107 | Mark McGwire 20C | 6.00 | 2.70 |
| ❑ 108 | Nolan Ryan 20C | 8.00 | 3.60 |
| ❑ 109 | Hank Aaron 20C | 4.00 | 1.80 |
| ❑ 110 | Barry Bonds 20C | 2.00 | .90 |
| ❑ 111 | Nomar Garciaparra 20C | 5.00 | 2.20 |
| ❑ 112 | Roger Clemens 20C | 3.00 | 1.35 |
| ❑ 113 | Johnny Bench 20C | 2.50 | 1.10 |
| ❑ 114 | Alex Rodriguez 20C | 5.00 | 2.20 |
| ❑ 115 | Cal Ripken 20C | 6.00 | 2.70 |
| ❑ 116 | Willie Mays 20C | 4.00 | 1.80 |
| ❑ 117 | Mike Piazza 20C | 5.00 | 2.20 |
| ❑ 118 | Reggie Jackson 20C | 2.00 | .90 |
| ❑ 119 | Tony Gwynn 20C | 3.00 | 1.35 |
| ❑ 120 | Cy Young 20C | 2.00 | .90 |
| ❑ 121 | George Brett 20C | 3.00 | 1.35 |
| ❑ 122 | Greg Maddux 20C | 4.00 | 1.80 |
| ❑ 123 | Yogi Berra 20C | 2.00 | .90 |
| ❑ 124 | Sammy Sosa 20C | 3.00 | 1.35 |
| ❑ 125 | Randy Johnson 20C | 2.00 | .90 |
| ❑ 126 | Bob Gibson 20C | 2.00 | .90 |
| ❑ 127 | Lou Gehrig 20C | 5.00 | 2.20 |
| ❑ 128 | Ken Griffey Jr. 20C | 6.00 | 2.70 |
| ❑ 129 | Derek Jeter 20C | 6.00 | 2.70 |
| ❑ 130 | Mike Schmidt 20C | 3.00 | 1.35 |
| ❑ 131 | Pedro Martinez 20C | 2.00 | .90 |
| ❑ 132 | Jackie Robinson 20C | 3.00 | 1.35 |
| ❑ 133 | Jose Canseco 20C | 2.00 | .90 |
| ❑ 134 | Ty Cobb 20C | 3.00 | 1.35 |
| ❑ 135 | Stan Musial 20C | 2.50 | 1.10 |

## 1999 Upper Deck MVP

| | MINT | NRMT |
|---|---|---|
| COMPLETE SET (220) | 25.00 | 11.00 |

| | | MINT | NRMT |
|---|---|---|---|
| ❑ 1 | Mo Vaughn | .15 | .07 |
| ❑ 2 | Tim Belcher | .10 | .05 |
| ❑ 3 | Jack McDowell | .10 | .05 |
| ❑ 4 | Troy Glaus | .60 | .25 |
| ❑ 5 | Darin Erstad | .40 | .18 |
| ❑ 6 | Tim Salmon | .15 | .07 |
| ❑ 7 | Jim Edmonds | .40 | .18 |
| ❑ 8 | Randy Johnson | .50 | .23 |
| ❑ 9 | Steve Finley | .15 | .07 |
| ❑ 10 | Travis Lee | .10 | .05 |
| ❑ 11 | Matt Williams | .25 | .11 |
| ❑ 12 | Todd Stottlemyre | .10 | .05 |
| ❑ 13 | Jay Bell | .15 | .07 |
| ❑ 14 | David Dellucci | .10 | .05 |
| ❑ 15 | Chipper Jones | 1.00 | .45 |
| ❑ 16 | Andruw Jones | .40 | .18 |
| ❑ 17 | Greg Maddux | 1.00 | .45 |
| ❑ 18 | Tom Glavine | .40 | .18 |
| ❑ 19 | Javy Lopez | .15 | .07 |
| ❑ 20 | Brian Jordan | .15 | .07 |
| ❑ 21 | George Lombard | .10 | .05 |
| ❑ 22 | John Smoltz | .15 | .07 |
| ❑ 23 | Cal Ripken | 1.50 | .70 |
| ❑ 24 | Charles Johnson | .15 | .07 |
| ❑ 25 | Albert Belle | .25 | .11 |
| ❑ 26 | Brady Anderson | .15 | .07 |
| ❑ 27 | Mike Mussina | .40 | .18 |
| ❑ 28 | Calvin Pickering | .10 | .05 |
| ❑ 29 | Ryan Minor | .10 | .05 |
| ❑ 30 | Jerry Hairston Jr. | .15 | .07 |
| ❑ 31 | Nomar Garciaparra | 1.25 | .55 |
| ❑ 32 | Pedro Martinez | .50 | .23 |
| ❑ 33 | Jason Varitek | .15 | .07 |
| ❑ 34 | Troy O'Leary | .10 | .05 |
| ❑ 35 | Donnie Sadler | .10 | .05 |
| ❑ 36 | Mark Portugal | .10 | .05 |
| ❑ 37 | John Valentin | .10 | .05 |
| ❑ 38 | Kerry Wood | .15 | .07 |
| ❑ 39 | Sammy Sosa | .75 | .35 |
| ❑ 40 | Mark Grace | .40 | .18 |
| ❑ 41 | Henry Rodriguez | .10 | .05 |
| ❑ 42 | Rod Beck | .10 | .05 |
| ❑ 43 | Benito Santiago | .10 | .05 |
| ❑ 44 | Kevin Tapani | .10 | .05 |
| ❑ 45 | Frank Thomas | .75 | .35 |
| ❑ 46 | Mike Caruso | .10 | .05 |
| ❑ 47 | Magglio Ordonez | .25 | .11 |
| ❑ 48 | Paul Konerko | .15 | .07 |
| ❑ 49 | Ray Durham | .15 | .07 |
| ❑ 50 | Jim Parque | .10 | .05 |
| ❑ 51 | Carlos Lee | .15 | .07 |
| ❑ 52 | Denny Neagle | .10 | .05 |
| ❑ 53 | Pete Harnisch | .10 | .05 |
| ❑ 54 | Michael Tucker | .10 | .05 |
| ❑ 55 | Sean Casey | .15 | .07 |
| ❑ 56 | Eddie Taubensee | .10 | .05 |
| ❑ 57 | Barry Larkin | .40 | .18 |
| ❑ 58 | Pokey Reese | .15 | .07 |
| ❑ 59 | Sandy Alomar Jr. | .15 | .07 |
| ❑ 60 | Roberto Alomar | .40 | .18 |
| ❑ 61 | Bartolo Colon | .15 | .07 |
| ❑ 62 | Kenny Lofton | .15 | .07 |
| ❑ 63 | Omar Vizquel | .15 | .07 |
| ❑ 64 | Travis Fryman | .15 | .07 |
| ❑ 65 | Jim Thome | .25 | .11 |
| ❑ 66 | Manny Ramirez | .50 | .23 |
| ❑ 67 | Jaret Wright | .10 | .05 |
| ❑ 68 | Darryl Kile | .15 | .07 |
| ❑ 69 | Kirt Manwaring | .10 | .05 |
| ❑ 70 | Vinny Castilla | .15 | .07 |
| ❑ 71 | Todd Helton | .50 | .23 |

| No. | Player | MINT | NRMT |
|---|---|---|---|
| 72 | Dante Bichette | .15 | .07 |
| 73 | Larry Walker | .15 | .07 |
| 74 | Derrick Gibson | .10 | .05 |
| 75 | Gabe Kapler | .15 | .07 |
| 76 | Dean Palmer | .15 | .07 |
| 77 | Matt Anderson | .10 | .05 |
| 78 | Bobby Higginson | .15 | .07 |
| 79 | Damion Easley | .10 | .05 |
| 80 | Tony Clark | .10 | .05 |
| 81 | Juan Encarnacion | .15 | .07 |
| 82 | Livan Hernandez | .10 | .05 |
| 83 | Alex Gonzalez | .10 | .05 |
| 84 | Preston Wilson | .15 | .07 |
| 85 | Derrek Lee | .10 | .05 |
| 86 | Mark Kotsay | .10 | .05 |
| 87 | Todd Dunwoody | .10 | .05 |
| 88 | Cliff Floyd | .15 | .07 |
| 89 | Ken Caminiti | .15 | .07 |
| 90 | Jeff Bagwell | .50 | .23 |
| 91 | Moises Alou | .15 | .07 |
| 92 | Craig Biggio | .25 | .11 |
| 93 | Billy Wagner | .10 | .05 |
| 94 | Richard Hidalgo | .15 | .07 |
| 95 | Derek Bell | .10 | .05 |
| 96 | Hipolito Pichardo | .10 | .05 |
| 97 | Jeff King | .10 | .05 |
| 98 | Carlos Beltran | .15 | .07 |
| 99 | Jeremy Giambi | .10 | .05 |
| 100 | Larry Sutton | .10 | .05 |
| 101 | Johnny Damon | .15 | .07 |
| 102 | Dee Brown | .15 | .07 |
| 103 | Kevin Brown | .25 | .11 |
| 104 | Chan Ho Park | .15 | .07 |
| 105 | Raul Mondesi | .15 | .07 |
| 106 | Eric Karros | .15 | .07 |
| 107 | Adrian Beltre | .15 | .07 |
| 108 | Devon White | .10 | .05 |
| 109 | Gary Sheffield | .40 | .18 |
| 110 | Sean Berry | .10 | .05 |
| 111 | Alex Ochoa | .10 | .05 |
| 112 | Marquis Grissom | .10 | .05 |
| 113 | Fernando Vina | .10 | .05 |
| 114 | Jeff Cirillo | .15 | .07 |
| 115 | Geoff Jenkins | .15 | .07 |
| 116 | Jeromy Burnitz | .15 | .07 |
| 117 | Brad Radke | .15 | .07 |
| 118 | Eric Milton | .10 | .05 |
| 119 | A.J. Pierzynski | .10 | .05 |
| 120 | Todd Walker | .10 | .05 |
| 121 | David Ortiz | .10 | .05 |
| 122 | Corey Koskie | .10 | .05 |
| 123 | Vladimir Guerrero | .60 | .25 |
| 124 | Rondell White | .15 | .07 |
| 125 | Brad Fullmer | .15 | .07 |
| 126 | Ugueth Urbina | .10 | .05 |
| 127 | Dustin Hermanson | .10 | .05 |
| 128 | Michael Barrett | .10 | .05 |
| 129 | Fernando Seguignol | .10 | .05 |
| 130 | Mike Piazza | 1.25 | .55 |
| 131 | Rickey Henderson | .50 | .23 |
| 132 | Rey Ordonez | .10 | .05 |
| 133 | John Olerud | .15 | .07 |
| 134 | Robin Ventura | .15 | .07 |
| 135 | Hideo Nomo | .40 | .18 |
| 136 | Mike Kinkade | .10 | .05 |
| 137 | Al Leiter | .15 | .07 |
| 138 | Brian McRae | .10 | .05 |
| 139 | Derek Jeter | 1.50 | .70 |
| 140 | Bernie Williams | .40 | .18 |
| 141 | Paul O'Neill | .15 | .07 |
| 142 | Scott Brosius | .15 | .07 |
| 143 | Tino Martinez | .15 | .07 |
| 144 | Roger Clemens | .75 | .35 |
| 145 | Orlando Hernandez | .15 | .07 |
| 146 | Mariano Rivera | .15 | .07 |
| 147 | Ricky Ledee | .10 | .05 |
| 148 | A.J. Hinch | .10 | .05 |
| 149 | Ben Grieve | .15 | .07 |
| 150 | Eric Chavez | .15 | .07 |
| 151 | Miguel Tejada | .15 | .07 |
| 152 | Matt Stairs | .10 | .05 |
| 153 | Ryan Christenson | .10 | .05 |
| 154 | Jason Giambi | .40 | .18 |
| 155 | Curt Schilling | .15 | .07 |
| 156 | Scott Rolen | .40 | .18 |
| 157 | Pat Burrell RC | 2.00 | .90 |
| 158 | Doug Glanville | .10 | .05 |
| 159 | Bobby Abreu | .15 | .07 |
| 160 | Rico Brogna | .10 | .05 |
| 161 | Ron Gant | .15 | .07 |
| 162 | Jason Kendall | .15 | .07 |
| 163 | Aramis Ramirez | .10 | .05 |
| 164 | Jose Guillen | .10 | .05 |
| 165 | Emil Brown | .10 | .05 |
| 166 | Pat Meares | .10 | .05 |
| 167 | Kevin Young | .15 | .07 |
| 168 | Brian Giles | .15 | .07 |
| 169 | Mark McGwire | 1.50 | .70 |
| 170 | J.D. Drew | .40 | .18 |
| 171 | Edgar Renteria | .10 | .05 |
| 172 | Fernando Tatis | .15 | .07 |
| 173 | Matt Morris | .10 | .05 |
| 174 | Eli Marrero | .10 | .05 |
| 175 | Ray Lankford | .15 | .07 |
| 176 | Tony Gwynn | .75 | .35 |
| 177 | Sterling Hitchcock | .10 | .05 |
| 178 | Ruben Rivera | .10 | .05 |
| 179 | Wally Joyner | .15 | .07 |
| 180 | Trevor Hoffman | .15 | .07 |
| 181 | Jim Leyritz | .10 | .05 |
| 182 | Carlos Hernandez | .10 | .05 |
| 183 | Barry Bonds | .60 | .25 |
| 184 | Ellis Burks | .15 | .07 |
| 185 | F.P. Santangelo | .10 | .05 |
| 186 | J.T. Snow | .15 | .07 |
| 187 | Ramon E.Martinez RC | .10 | .05 |
| 188 | Jeff Kent | .25 | .11 |
| 189 | Robb Nen | .10 | .05 |
| 190 | Ken Griffey Jr. | 1.50 | .70 |
| 191 | Alex Rodriguez | 1.25 | .55 |
| 192 | Shane Monahan | .10 | .05 |
| 193 | Carlos Guillen | .10 | .05 |
| 194 | Edgar Martinez | .25 | .11 |
| 195 | David Segui | .10 | .05 |
| 196 | Jose Mesa | .10 | .05 |
| 197 | Jose Canseco | .50 | .23 |
| 198 | Rolando Arrojo | .10 | .05 |
| 199 | Wade Boggs | .50 | .23 |
| 200 | Fred McGriff | .25 | .11 |
| 201 | Quinton McCracken | .10 | .05 |
| 202 | Bobby Smith | .10 | .05 |
| 203 | Bubba Trammell | .10 | .05 |
| 204 | Juan Gonzalez | .40 | .18 |
| 205 | Ivan Rodriguez | .50 | .23 |
| 206 | Rafael Palmeiro | .40 | .18 |
| 207 | Royce Clayton | .10 | .05 |
| 208 | Rick Helling | .15 | .07 |
| 209 | Todd Zeile | .15 | .07 |
| 210 | Rusty Greer | .15 | .07 |
| 211 | David Wells | .15 | .07 |
| 212 | Roy Halladay | .10 | .05 |
| 213 | Carlos Delgado | .40 | .18 |
| 214 | Darrin Fletcher | .10 | .05 |
| 215 | Shawn Green | .40 | .18 |
| 216 | Kevin Witt | .10 | .05 |
| 217 | Jose Cruz Jr. | .15 | .07 |
| 218 | Ken Griffey Jr. CL | .75 | .35 |
| 219 | Sammy Sosa CL | .40 | .18 |
| 220 | Mark McGwire CL | .75 | .35 |
| S3 | Ken Griffey Jr. Sample | 1.00 | .45 |

## 2000 Upper Deck MVP

| | | MINT | NRMT |
|---|---|---|---|
| | COMPLETE SET (220) | 25.00 | 11.00 |
| 1 | Garret Anderson | .15 | .07 |
| 2 | Mo Vaughn | .15 | .07 |
| 3 | Tim Salmon | .15 | .07 |
| 4 | Ramon Ortiz | .15 | .07 |
| 5 | Darin Erstad | .40 | .18 |
| 6 | Troy Glaus | .50 | .23 |
| 7 | Troy Percival | .10 | .05 |
| 8 | Jeff Bagwell | .50 | .23 |
| 9 | Ken Caminiti | .15 | .07 |
| 10 | Daryle Ward | .15 | .07 |
| 11 | Craig Biggio | .25 | .11 |
| 12 | Jose Lima | .10 | .05 |
| 13 | Moises Alou | .15 | .07 |
| 14 | Octavio Dotel | .10 | .05 |
| 15 | Ben Grieve | .15 | .07 |
| 16 | Jason Giambi | .40 | .18 |
| 17 | Tim Hudson | .40 | .18 |
| 18 | Eric Chavez | .15 | .07 |
| 19 | Matt Stairs | .10 | .05 |
| 20 | Miguel Tejada | .15 | .07 |
| 21 | John Jaha | .10 | .05 |
| 22 | Chipper Jones | 1.00 | .45 |
| 23 | Kevin Millwood | .15 | .07 |
| 24 | Brian Jordan | .15 | .07 |
| 25 | Andruw Jones | .40 | .18 |
| 26 | Andres Galarraga | .25 | .11 |
| 27 | Greg Maddux | 1.00 | .45 |
| 28 | Reggie Sanders | .10 | .05 |
| 29 | Javy Lopez | .15 | .07 |
| 30 | Jeromy Burnitz | .15 | .07 |
| 31 | Kevin Barker | .10 | .05 |
| 32 | Jose Hernandez | .10 | .05 |
| 33 | Ron Belliard | .10 | .05 |
| 34 | Henry Blanco | .10 | .05 |
| 35 | Marquis Grissom | .10 | .05 |
| 36 | Geoff Jenkins | .15 | .07 |
| 37 | Carlos Delgado | .40 | .18 |
| 38 | Raul Mondesi | .15 | .07 |
| 39 | Roy Halladay | .10 | .05 |
| 40 | Tony Batista | .15 | .07 |
| 41 | David Wells | .15 | .07 |
| 42 | Shannon Stewart | .15 | .07 |
| 43 | Vernon Wells | .15 | .07 |
| 44 | Sammy Sosa | .75 | .35 |
| 45 | Ismael Valdes | .10 | .05 |
| 46 | Joe Girardi | .10 | .05 |
| 47 | Mark Grace | .40 | .18 |
| 48 | Henry Rodriguez | .10 | .05 |
| 49 | Kerry Wood | .15 | .07 |
| 50 | Eric Young | .10 | .05 |
| 51 | Mark McGwire | 1.50 | .70 |
| 52 | Darryl Kile | .15 | .07 |
| 53 | Fernando Vina | .10 | .05 |
| 54 | Ray Lankford | .15 | .07 |
| 55 | J.D. Drew | .40 | .18 |
| 56 | Fernando Tatis | .15 | .07 |
| 57 | Rick Ankiel | .75 | .35 |
| 58 | Matt Williams | .25 | .11 |
| 59 | Erubiel Durazo | .15 | .07 |
| 60 | Tony Womack | .10 | .05 |
| 61 | Jay Bell | .15 | .07 |
| 62 | Randy Johnson | .50 | .23 |
| 63 | Steve Finley | .15 | .07 |
| 64 | Matt Mantei | .10 | .05 |
| 65 | Luis Gonzalez | .15 | .07 |
| 66 | Gary Sheffield | .40 | .18 |
| 67 | Eric Gagne | .10 | .05 |
| 68 | Adrian Beltre | .15 | .07 |
| 69 | Mark Grudzielanek | .10 | .05 |
| 70 | Kevin Brown | .15 | .07 |
| 71 | Chan Ho Park | .15 | .07 |
| 72 | Shawn Green | .40 | .18 |
| 73 | Vinny Castilla | .15 | .07 |
| 74 | Fred McGriff | .25 | .11 |
| 75 | Wilson Alvarez | .10 | .05 |
| 76 | Greg Vaughn | .15 | .07 |
| 77 | Gerald Williams | .10 | .05 |
| 78 | Ryan Rupe | .10 | .05 |
| 79 | Jose Canseco | .50 | .23 |
| 80 | Vladimir Guerrero | .60 | .25 |
| 81 | Dustin Hermanson | .10 | .05 |
| 82 | Michael Barrett | .10 | .05 |
| 83 | Rondell White | .15 | .07 |

| | | | |
|---|---|---|---|
| ❑ 84 | Tony Armas Jr. | .15 | .07 |
| ❑ 85 | Wilton Guerrero | .10 | .05 |
| ❑ 86 | Jose Vidro | .15 | .07 |
| ❑ 87 | Barry Bonds | .60 | .25 |
| ❑ 88 | Russ Ortiz | .10 | .05 |
| ❑ 89 | Ellis Burks | .15 | .07 |
| ❑ 90 | Jeff Kent | .25 | .11 |
| ❑ 91 | Russ Davis | .10 | .05 |
| ❑ 92 | J.T. Snow | .15 | .07 |
| ❑ 93 | Roberto Alomar | .40 | .18 |
| ❑ 94 | Manny Ramirez | .50 | .23 |
| ❑ 95 | Chuck Finley | .15 | .07 |
| ❑ 96 | Kenny Lofton | .15 | .07 |
| ❑ 97 | Jim Thome | .25 | .11 |
| ❑ 98 | Bartolo Colon | .15 | .07 |
| ❑ 99 | Omar Vizquel | .15 | .07 |
| ❑ 100 | Richie Sexson | .15 | .07 |
| ❑ 101 | Mike Cameron | .10 | .05 |
| ❑ 102 | Brett Tomko | .10 | .05 |
| ❑ 103 | Edgar Martinez | .25 | .11 |
| ❑ 104 | Alex Rodriguez | 1.25 | .55 |
| ❑ 105 | John Olerud | .15 | .07 |
| ❑ 106 | Freddy Garcia | .15 | .07 |
| ❑ 107 | Kazuhiro Sasaki RC | 2.00 | .90 |
| ❑ 108 | Preston Wilson | .15 | .07 |
| ❑ 109 | Luis Castillo | .15 | .07 |
| ❑ 110 | A.J. Burnett | .15 | .07 |
| ❑ 111 | Mike Lowell | .10 | .05 |
| ❑ 112 | Cliff Floyd | .15 | .07 |
| ❑ 113 | Brad Penny | .15 | .07 |
| ❑ 114 | Alex Gonzalez | .10 | .05 |
| ❑ 115 | Mike Piazza | 1.25 | .55 |
| ❑ 116 | Derek Bell | .10 | .05 |
| ❑ 117 | Edgardo Alfonzo | .15 | .07 |
| ❑ 118 | Rickey Henderson | .50 | .23 |
| ❑ 119 | Todd Zeile | .15 | .07 |
| ❑ 120 | Mike Hampton | .15 | .07 |
| ❑ 121 | Al Leiter | .15 | .07 |
| ❑ 122 | Robin Ventura | .15 | .07 |
| ❑ 123 | Cal Ripken | 1.50 | .70 |
| ❑ 124 | Mike Mussina | .40 | .18 |
| ❑ 125 | B.J. Surhoff | .15 | .07 |
| ❑ 126 | Jerry Hairston Jr. | .10 | .05 |
| ❑ 127 | Brady Anderson | .15 | .07 |
| ❑ 128 | Albert Belle | .25 | .11 |
| ❑ 129 | Sidney Ponson | .10 | .05 |
| ❑ 130 | Tony Gwynn | .75 | .35 |
| ❑ 131 | Ryan Klesko | .15 | .07 |
| ❑ 132 | Sterling Hitchcock | .10 | .05 |
| ❑ 133 | Eric Owens | .10 | .05 |
| ❑ 134 | Trevor Hoffman | .15 | .07 |
| ❑ 135 | Al Martin | .10 | .05 |
| ❑ 136 | Bret Boone | .10 | .05 |
| ❑ 137 | Brian Giles | .15 | .07 |
| ❑ 138 | Chad Hermansen | .10 | .05 |
| ❑ 139 | Kevin Young | .10 | .05 |
| ❑ 140 | Kris Benson | .15 | .07 |
| ❑ 141 | Warren Morris | .10 | .05 |
| ❑ 142 | Jason Kendall | .15 | .07 |
| ❑ 143 | Wil Cordero | .10 | .05 |
| ❑ 144 | Scott Rolen | .40 | .18 |
| ❑ 145 | Curt Schilling | .15 | .07 |
| ❑ 146 | Doug Glanville | .10 | .05 |
| ❑ 147 | Mike Lieberthal | .15 | .07 |
| ❑ 148 | Mike Jackson | .10 | .05 |
| ❑ 149 | Rico Brogna | .10 | .05 |
| ❑ 150 | Andy Ashby | .10 | .05 |
| ❑ 151 | Bob Abreu | .15 | .07 |
| ❑ 152 | Sean Casey | .15 | .07 |
| ❑ 153 | Pete Harnisch | .10 | .05 |
| ❑ 154 | Dante Bichette | .15 | .07 |
| ❑ 155 | Pokey Reese | .15 | .07 |
| ❑ 156 | Aaron Boone | .10 | .05 |
| ❑ 157 | Ken Griffey Jr. | 1.50 | .70 |
| ❑ 158 | Barry Larkin | .40 | .18 |
| ❑ 159 | Scott Williamson | .10 | .05 |
| ❑ 160 | Carlos Beltran | .15 | .07 |
| ❑ 161 | Jermaine Dye | .15 | .07 |
| ❑ 162 | Jose Rosado | .10 | .05 |
| ❑ 163 | Joe Randa | .10 | .05 |
| ❑ 164 | Johnny Damon | .15 | .07 |
| ❑ 165 | Mike Sweeney | .15 | .07 |
| ❑ 166 | Mark Quinn | .15 | .07 |
| ❑ 167 | Ivan Rodriguez | .50 | .23 |
| ❑ 168 | Rusty Greer | .15 | .07 |
| ❑ 169 | Ruben Mateo | .15 | .07 |
| ❑ 170 | Doug Davis | .10 | .05 |
| ❑ 171 | Gabe Kapler | .15 | .07 |
| ❑ 172 | Justin Thompson | .10 | .05 |
| ❑ 173 | Rafael Palmeiro | .40 | .18 |
| ❑ 174 | Larry Walker | .15 | .07 |
| ❑ 175 | Neifi Perez | .10 | .05 |
| ❑ 176 | Rolando Arrojo | .10 | .05 |
| ❑ 177 | Jeffrey Hammonds | .15 | .07 |
| ❑ 178 | Todd Helton | .50 | .23 |
| ❑ 179 | Pedro Astacio | .10 | .05 |
| ❑ 180 | Jeff Cirillo | .15 | .07 |
| ❑ 181 | Pedro Martinez | .50 | .23 |
| ❑ 182 | Carl Everett | .15 | .07 |
| ❑ 183 | Troy O'Leary | .10 | .05 |
| ❑ 184 | Nomar Garciaparra | 1.25 | .55 |
| ❑ 185 | Jose Offerman | .10 | .05 |
| ❑ 186 | Bret Saberhagen | .15 | .07 |
| ❑ 187 | Trot Nixon | .15 | .07 |
| ❑ 188 | Jason Varitek | .15 | .07 |
| ❑ 189 | Todd Walker | .10 | .05 |
| ❑ 190 | Eric Milton | .10 | .05 |
| ❑ 191 | Chad Allen | .10 | .05 |
| ❑ 192 | Jacque Jones | .15 | .07 |
| ❑ 193 | Brad Radke | .15 | .07 |
| ❑ 194 | Corey Koskie | .10 | .05 |
| ❑ 195 | Joe Mays | .10 | .05 |
| ❑ 196 | Juan Gonzalez | .40 | .18 |
| ❑ 197 | Jeff Weaver | .10 | .05 |
| ❑ 198 | Juan Encarnacion | .15 | .07 |
| ❑ 199 | Deivi Cruz | .10 | .05 |
| ❑ 200 | Damion Easley | .10 | .05 |
| ❑ 201 | Tony Clark | .10 | .05 |
| ❑ 202 | Dean Palmer | .15 | .07 |
| ❑ 203 | Frank Thomas | .75 | .35 |
| ❑ 204 | Carlos Lee | .15 | .07 |
| ❑ 205 | Mike Sirotka | .10 | .05 |
| ❑ 206 | Kip Wells | .15 | .07 |
| ❑ 207 | Maggio Ordonez | .15 | .07 |
| ❑ 208 | Paul Konerko | .15 | .07 |
| ❑ 209 | Chris Singleton | .15 | .07 |
| ❑ 210 | Derek Jeter | 1.50 | .70 |
| ❑ 211 | Tino Martinez | .15 | .07 |
| ❑ 212 | Mariano Rivera | .15 | .07 |
| ❑ 213 | Roger Clemens | .75 | .35 |
| ❑ 214 | Nick Johnson | .15 | .07 |
| ❑ 215 | Paul O'Neill | .15 | .07 |
| ❑ 216 | Bernie Williams | .40 | .18 |
| ❑ 217 | David Cone | .15 | .07 |
| ❑ 218 | Ken Griffey Jr. CL | .75 | .35 |
| ❑ 219 | Sammy Sosa CL | .40 | .18 |
| ❑ 220 | Mark McGwire CL | .75 | .35 |

## 1999 Upper Deck Ovation

| | MINT | NRMT |
|---|---|---|
| COMPLETE SET (90) | 100.00 | 45.00 |
| COMP.SET w/o SP's (60) | 30.00 | 13.50 |
| COMMON CARD (1-60) | .20 | .09 |
| COMMON WP (61-80) | 1.50 | .70 |
| COMMON SS (81-90) | 2.00 | .90 |

| | | | |
|---|---|---|---|
| ❑ 1 | Ken Griffey Jr. | 3.00 | 1.35 |
| ❑ 2 | Rondell White | .30 | .14 |
| ❑ 3 | Tony Clark | .20 | .09 |
| ❑ 4 | Barry Bonds | 1.25 | .55 |
| ❑ 5 | Larry Walker | .30 | .14 |
| ❑ 6 | Greg Vaughn | .30 | .14 |
| ❑ 7 | Mark Grace | .75 | .35 |
| ❑ 8 | John Olerud | .30 | .14 |
| ❑ 9 | Matt Williams | .50 | .23 |
| ❑ 10 | Craig Biggio | .50 | .23 |
| ❑ 11 | Quinton McCracken | .20 | .09 |
| ❑ 12 | Kerry Wood | .30 | .14 |
| ❑ 13 | Derek Jeter | 3.00 | 1.35 |
| ❑ 14 | Frank Thomas | 1.50 | .70 |
| ❑ 15 | Tino Martinez | .30 | .14 |
| ❑ 16 | Albert Belle | .50 | .23 |
| ❑ 17 | Ben Grieve | .30 | .14 |
| ❑ 18 | Cal Ripken | 3.00 | 1.35 |
| ❑ 19 | Johnny Damon | .30 | .14 |
| ❑ 20 | Jose Cruz Jr. | .30 | .14 |
| ❑ 21 | Barry Larkin | .75 | .35 |
| ❑ 22 | Jason Giambi | .75 | .35 |
| ❑ 23 | Sean Casey | .30 | .14 |
| ❑ 24 | Scott Rolen | .75 | .35 |
| ❑ 25 | Jim Thome | .50 | .23 |
| ❑ 26 | Curt Schilling | .30 | .14 |
| ❑ 27 | Moises Alou | .30 | .14 |
| ❑ 28 | Alex Rodriguez | 2.50 | 1.10 |
| ❑ 29 | Mark Kotsay | .20 | .09 |
| ❑ 30 | Darin Erstad | .75 | .35 |
| ❑ 31 | Mike Mussina | .75 | .35 |
| ❑ 32 | Todd Walker | .20 | .09 |
| ❑ 33 | Nomar Garciaparra | 2.50 | 1.10 |
| ❑ 34 | Vladimir Guerrero | 1.25 | .55 |
| ❑ 35 | Jeff Bagwell | 1.00 | .45 |
| ❑ 36 | Mark McGwire | 3.00 | 1.35 |
| ❑ 37 | Travis Lee | .20 | .09 |
| ❑ 38 | Dean Palmer | .30 | .14 |
| ❑ 39 | Fred McGriff | .50 | .23 |
| ❑ 40 | Sammy Sosa | 1.50 | .70 |
| ❑ 41 | Mike Piazza | 2.50 | 1.10 |
| ❑ 42 | Andres Galarraga | .50 | .23 |
| ❑ 43 | Pedro Martinez | 1.00 | .45 |
| ❑ 44 | Juan Gonzalez | .75 | .35 |
| ❑ 45 | Greg Maddux | 2.00 | .90 |
| ❑ 46 | Jeromy Burnitz | .30 | .14 |
| ❑ 47 | Roger Clemens | 1.50 | .70 |
| ❑ 48 | Vinny Castilla | .30 | .14 |
| ❑ 49 | Kevin Brown | .50 | .23 |
| ❑ 50 | Mo Vaughn | .30 | .14 |
| ❑ 51 | Raul Mondesi | .30 | .14 |
| ❑ 52 | Randy Johnson | 1.00 | .45 |
| ❑ 53 | Ray Lankford | .30 | .14 |
| ❑ 54 | Jaret Wright | .20 | .09 |
| ❑ 55 | Tony Gwynn | 1.50 | .70 |
| ❑ 56 | Chipper Jones | 2.00 | .90 |
| ❑ 57 | Gary Sheffield | .75 | .35 |
| ❑ 58 | Ivan Rodriguez | 1.00 | .45 |
| ❑ 59 | Kenny Lofton | .30 | .14 |
| ❑ 60 | Jason Kendall | .30 | .14 |
| ❑ 61 | J.D. Drew WP | 4.00 | 1.80 |
| ❑ 62 | Gabe Kapler WP | 1.50 | .70 |
| ❑ 63 | Adrian Beltre WP | 1.50 | .70 |
| ❑ 64 | Carlos Beltran WP | 1.50 | .70 |
| ❑ 65 | Eric Chavez WP | 1.50 | .70 |
| ❑ 66 | Mike Lowell WP | 1.50 | .70 |
| ❑ 67 | Troy Glaus WP | 6.00 | 2.70 |
| ❑ 68 | George Lombard WP | 1.50 | .70 |
| ❑ 69 | Alex Gonzalez WP | 1.50 | .70 |
| ❑ 70 | Mike Kinkade WP | 1.50 | .70 |
| ❑ 71 | Jeremy Giambi WP | 1.50 | .70 |
| ❑ 72 | Bruce Chen WP | 1.50 | .70 |
| ❑ 73 | Preston Wilson WP | 1.50 | .70 |
| ❑ 74 | Kevin Witt WP | 1.50 | .70 |
| ❑ 75 | Carlos Guillen WP | 1.50 | .70 |
| ❑ 76 | Ryan Minor WP | 1.50 | .70 |
| ❑ 77 | Corey Koskie WP | 1.50 | .70 |
| ❑ 78 | Robert Fick WP | 1.50 | .70 |
| ❑ 79 | Michael Barrett WP | 1.50 | .70 |
| ❑ 80 | Calvin Pickering WP | 1.50 | .70 |
| ❑ 81 | Ken Griffey Jr. SS | 8.00 | 3.60 |
| ❑ 82 | Mark McGwire SS | 8.00 | 3.60 |
| ❑ 83 | Cal Ripken SS | 8.00 | 3.60 |
| ❑ 84 | Derek Jeter SS | 8.00 | 3.60 |
| ❑ 85 | Chipper Jones SS | 5.00 | 2.20 |
| ❑ 86 | Nomar Garciaparra SS | 6.00 | 2.70 |
| ❑ 87 | Sammy Sosa SS | 4.00 | 1.80 |
| ❑ 88 | Juan Gonzalez SS | 2.00 | .90 |
| ❑ 89 | Mike Piazza SS | 6.00 | 2.70 |
| ❑ 90 | Alex Rodriguez SS | 6.00 | 2.70 |
| ❑ MICL | M.Mantle Legendary Cut/1 | | |

## 2000 Upper Deck Ovation

| | MINT | NRMT |
|---|---|---|
| COMPLETE SET (89) | 120.00 | 55.00 |
| COMP.SET w/o SP's (60) | 25.00 | 11.00 |
| COMMON CARD (1-60) | .20 | .09 |
| COMMON WP (61-80) | 2.00 | .90 |
| COMMON SS (81-90) | 3.00 | 1.35 |
| ❑ 1 Mo Vaughn | .30 | .14 |
| ❑ 2 Troy Glaus | 1.00 | .45 |
| ❑ 3 Jeff Bagwell | 1.00 | .45 |
| ❑ 4 Craig Biggio | .50 | .23 |
| ❑ 5 Mike Hampton | .30 | .14 |
| ❑ 6 Jason Giambi | .75 | .35 |
| ❑ 7 Tim Hudson | .75 | .35 |
| ❑ 8 Chipper Jones | 2.00 | .90 |
| ❑ 9 Greg Maddux | 2.00 | .90 |
| ❑ 10 Kevin Millwood | .30 | .14 |
| ❑ 11 Brian Jordan | .30 | .14 |
| ❑ 12 Jeromy Burnitz | .30 | .14 |
| ❑ 13 David Wells | .30 | .14 |
| ❑ 14 Carlos Delgado | .75 | .35 |
| ❑ 15 Sammy Sosa | 1.50 | .70 |
| ❑ 16 Mark McGwire | 3.00 | 1.35 |
| ❑ 17 Matt Williams | .50 | .23 |
| ❑ 18 Randy Johnson | 1.00 | .45 |
| ❑ 19 Erubiel Durazo | .30 | .14 |
| ❑ 20 Kevin Brown | .50 | .23 |
| ❑ 21 Shawn Green | .75 | .35 |
| ❑ 22 Gary Sheffield | .75 | .35 |
| ❑ 23 Jose Canseco | 1.00 | .45 |
| ❑ 24 Vladimir Guerrero | 1.25 | .55 |
| ❑ 25 Barry Bonds | 1.25 | .55 |
| ❑ 26 Manny Ramirez | 1.00 | .45 |
| ❑ 27 Roberto Alomar | .75 | .35 |
| ❑ 28 Richie Sexson | .30 | .14 |
| ❑ 29 Jim Thome | .50 | .23 |
| ❑ 30 Alex Rodriguez | 2.50 | 1.10 |
| ❑ 31 Ken Griffey Jr. | 3.00 | 1.35 |
| ❑ 32 Preston Wilson | .30 | .14 |
| ❑ 33 Mike Piazza | 2.50 | 1.10 |
| ❑ 34 Al Leiter | .20 | .09 |
| ❑ 35 Robin Ventura | .50 | .23 |
| ❑ 36 Cal Ripken | 3.00 | 1.35 |
| ❑ 37 Albert Belle | .50 | .23 |
| ❑ 38 Tony Gwynn | 1.50 | .70 |
| ❑ 39 Brian Giles | .30 | .14 |
| ❑ 40 Jason Kendall | .30 | .14 |
| ❑ 41 Scott Rolen | .75 | .35 |
| ❑ 42 Bob Abreu | .30 | .14 |
| ❑ 43 Ken Griffey Jr. Reds | 3.00 | 1.35 |
| ❑ 44 Sean Casey | .30 | .14 |
| ❑ 45 Carlos Beltran | .30 | .14 |
| ❑ 46 Gabe Kapler | .30 | .14 |
| ❑ 47 Ivan Rodriguez | 1.00 | .45 |
| ❑ 48 Rafael Palmeiro | .75 | .35 |
| ❑ 49 Larry Walker | .30 | .14 |
| ❑ 50 Nomar Garciaparra | 2.50 | 1.10 |
| ❑ 51 Pedro Martinez | 1.00 | .45 |
| ❑ 52 Eric Milton | .20 | .09 |
| ❑ 53 Juan Gonzalez | .75 | .35 |
| ❑ 54 Tony Clark | .20 | .09 |
| ❑ 55 Frank Thomas | 1.50 | .70 |
| ❑ 56 Magglio Ordonez | .30 | .14 |
| ❑ 57 Roger Clemens | 1.50 | .70 |
| ❑ 58 Derek Jeter | 3.00 | 1.35 |
| ❑ 59 Bernie Williams | .75 | .35 |
| ❑ 60 Orlando Hernandez | .30 | .14 |
| ❑ 61 Rick Ankiel WP | 10.00 | 4.50 |
| ❑ 62 Josh Beckett WP | 5.00 | 2.20 |
| ❑ 63 Vernon Wells WP | 2.50 | 1.10 |
| ❑ 64 Alfonso Soriano WP | 2.50 | 1.10 |
| ❑ 65 Pat Burrell WP | 8.00 | 3.60 |
| ❑ 66 Eric Munson WP | 5.00 | 2.20 |
| ❑ 67 Chad Hutchinson WP | 2.00 | .90 |
| ❑ 68 Eric Gagne WP | 2.00 | .90 |
| ❑ 69 Peter Bergeron WP | 2.00 | .90 |
| ❑ 70 Ryan Anderson WP SP | 250.00 | 110.00 |
| ❑ 71 A.J. Burnett WP | 2.50 | 1.10 |
| ❑ 72 Jorge Toca WP | 2.00 | .90 |
| ❑ 73 Matt Riley WP | 2.50 | 1.10 |
| ❑ 74 Chad Hermansen WP | 2.00 | .90 |
| ❑ 75 Doug Davis WP | 2.00 | .90 |
| ❑ 76 Jim Morris WP | 2.00 | .90 |
| ❑ 77 Ben Petrick WP | 2.00 | .90 |
| ❑ 78 Mark Quinn WP | 2.50 | 1.10 |
| ❑ 79 Ed Yarnall WP | 2.00 | .90 |
| ❑ 80 Ramon Ortiz WP | 2.50 | 1.10 |
| ❑ 81 Ken Griffey Jr. SS | 10.00 | 4.50 |
| ❑ 82 Mark McGwire SS | 10.00 | 4.50 |
| ❑ 83 Derek Jeter SS | 10.00 | 4.50 |
| ❑ 84 Jeff Bagwell SS | 3.00 | 1.35 |
| ❑ 85 Nomar Garciaparra SS | 8.00 | 3.60 |
| ❑ 86 Sammy Sosa SS | 5.00 | 2.20 |
| ❑ 87 Mike Piazza SS | 8.00 | 3.60 |
| ❑ 88 Alex Rodriguez SS | 8.00 | 3.60 |
| ❑ 89 Cal Ripken SS | 10.00 | 4.50 |
| ❑ 90 Pedro Martinez SS | 3.00 | 1.35 |

## 1999 Upper Deck PowerDeck

| | MINT | NRMT |
|---|---|---|
| COMPLETE SET (25) | 125.00 | 55.00 |
| COMMON CD (1-25) | 2.00 | .90 |
| ❑ 1 Ken Griffey Jr. | 12.00 | 5.50 |
| ❑ 2 Mark McGwire | 12.00 | 5.50 |
| ❑ 3 Cal Ripken | 12.00 | 5.50 |
| ❑ 4 Sammy Sosa | 6.00 | 2.70 |
| ❑ 5 Derek Jeter | 12.00 | 5.50 |
| ❑ 6 Mike Piazza | 10.00 | 4.50 |
| ❑ 7 Nomar Garciaparra | 10.00 | 4.50 |
| ❑ 8 Greg Maddux | 8.00 | 3.60 |
| ❑ 9 Tony Gwynn | 6.00 | 2.70 |
| ❑ 10 Roger Clemens | 6.00 | 2.70 |
| ❑ 11 Scott Rolen | 3.00 | 1.35 |
| ❑ 12 Alex Rodriguez | 10.00 | 4.50 |
| ❑ 13 Manny Ramirez | 4.00 | 1.80 |
| ❑ 14 Chipper Jones | 8.00 | 3.60 |
| ❑ 15 Juan Gonzalez | 3.00 | 1.35 |
| ❑ 16 Ivan Rodriguez | 4.00 | 1.80 |
| ❑ 17 Frank Thomas | 6.00 | 2.70 |
| ❑ 18 Mo Vaughn | 2.00 | .90 |
| ❑ 19 Barry Bonds | 5.00 | 2.20 |
| ❑ 20 Vladimir Guerrero | 5.00 | 2.20 |
| ❑ 21 Jose Canseco | 4.00 | 1.80 |
| ❑ 22 Jeff Bagwell | 4.00 | 1.80 |
| ❑ 23 Pedro Martinez | 4.00 | 1.80 |
| ❑ 24 Gabe Kapler | 2.00 | .90 |
| ❑ 25 J.D. Drew | 3.00 | 1.35 |

## 2000 Upper Deck PowerDeck

| | MINT | NRMT |
|---|---|---|
| COMPLETE SET (12) | 60.00 | 27.00 |
| ❑ 1 Sammy Sosa | 4.00 | 1.80 |
| ❑ 2 Ken Griffey Jr | 8.00 | 3.60 |
| ❑ 3 Mark McGwire | 8.00 | 3.60 |
| ❑ 4 Derek Jeter | 8.00 | 3.60 |
| ❑ 5 Alex Rodriguez | 6.00 | 2.70 |
| ❑ 6 Nomar Garciaparra | 6.00 | 2.70 |
| ❑ 7 Mike Piazza | 6.00 | 2.70 |
| ❑ 8 Cal Ripken | 8.00 | 3.60 |
| ❑ 9 Ivan Rodriguez | 4.00 | 1.80 |
| ❑ 10 Chipper Jones | 5.00 | 2.20 |
| ❑ 11 Pedro Martinez | 4.00 | 1.80 |
| ❑ 12 Manny Ramirez | 4.00 | 1.80 |

## 2000 Upper Deck Pros and Prospects

| | MINT | NRMT |
|---|---|---|
| COMPLETE SET (192) | | |
| COMPLETE BASIC SET (132) | 1000.00 | 450.00 |
| COMPLETE UPDATE SET (60) | | |
| COMP.SET w/o SP's (90) | 25.00 | 11.00 |
| COMMON CARD (1-90) | .20 | .09 |
| COMMON PS (91-120) | 15.00 | 6.75 |
| COMMON PF (121-132) | 15.00 | 6.75 |
| COMMON PS (133-162) | | |
| COMMON CARD (163-192) | | |
| ❑ 1 Darin Erstad | .75 | .35 |
| ❑ 2 Troy Glaus | 1.00 | .45 |
| ❑ 3 Mo Vaughn | .30 | .14 |
| ❑ 4 Jason Giambi | .75 | .35 |
| ❑ 5 Tim Hudson | .75 | .35 |
| ❑ 6 Ben Grieve | .30 | .14 |
| ❑ 7 Eric Chavez | .30 | .14 |
| ❑ 8 Shannon Stewart | .30 | .14 |
| ❑ 9 Raul Mondesi | .30 | .14 |
| ❑ 10 Carlos Delgado | .75 | .35 |
| ❑ 11 Jose Canseco | 1.00 | .45 |
| ❑ 12 Fred McGriff | .50 | .23 |
| ❑ 13 Greg Vaughn | .30 | .14 |
| ❑ 14 Manny Ramirez | 1.00 | .45 |
| ❑ 15 Roberto Alomar | .75 | .35 |
| ❑ 16 Jim Thome | .50 | .23 |
| ❑ 17 Alex Rodriguez | 2.50 | 1.10 |

| | Card | | |
|---|---|---|---|
| ❑ | 18 Freddy Garcia | .30 | .14 |
| ❑ | 19 John Olerud | .30 | .14 |
| ❑ | 20 Cal Ripken | 3.00 | 1.35 |
| ❑ | 21 Albert Belle | .50 | .23 |
| ❑ | 22 Mike Mussina | .75 | .35 |
| ❑ | 23 Ivan Rodriguez | 1.00 | .45 |
| ❑ | 24 Rafael Palmeiro | .75 | .35 |
| ❑ | 25 Ruben Mateo | .30 | .14 |
| ❑ | 26 Gabe Kapler | .30 | .14 |
| ❑ | 27 Pedro Martinez | 1.00 | .45 |
| ❑ | 28 Nomar Garciaparra | 2.50 | 1.10 |
| ❑ | 29 Carl Everett | .30 | .14 |
| ❑ | 30 Carlos Beltran | .30 | .14 |
| ❑ | 31 Jermaine Dye | .30 | .14 |
| ❑ | 32 Johnny Damon UER (Picture on front is Joe Randa) | .30 | .14 |
| ❑ | 33 Juan Gonzalez | .75 | .35 |
| ❑ | 34 Juan Encarnacion | .30 | .14 |
| ❑ | 35 Dean Palmer | .30 | .14 |
| ❑ | 36 Jacque Jones | .30 | .14 |
| ❑ | 37 Matt Lawton | .20 | .09 |
| ❑ | 38 Frank Thomas | 1.50 | .70 |
| ❑ | 39 Paul Konerko | .30 | .14 |
| ❑ | 40 Magglio Ordonez | .30 | .14 |
| ❑ | 41 Derek Jeter | 3.00 | 1.35 |
| ❑ | 42 Bernie Williams | .75 | .35 |
| ❑ | 43 Mariano Rivera | .30 | .14 |
| ❑ | 44 Roger Clemens | 1.50 | .70 |
| ❑ | 45 Jeff Bagwell | 1.00 | .45 |
| ❑ | 46 Craig Biggio | .50 | .23 |
| ❑ | 47 Richard Hidalgo | .30 | .14 |
| ❑ | 48 Chipper Jones | 2.00 | .90 |
| ❑ | 49 Andres Galarraga | .50 | .23 |
| ❑ | 50 Andruw Jones | .75 | .35 |
| ❑ | 51 Greg Maddux | 2.00 | .90 |
| ❑ | 52 Jeromy Burnitz | .30 | .14 |
| ❑ | 53 Geoff Jenkins | .30 | .14 |
| ❑ | 54 Mark McGwire | 3.00 | 1.35 |
| ❑ | 55 Jim Edmonds | .75 | .35 |
| ❑ | 56 Fernando Tatis | .30 | .14 |
| ❑ | 57 J.D. Drew | .75 | .35 |
| ❑ | 58 Sammy Sosa | 1.50 | .70 |
| ❑ | 59 Kerry Wood | .30 | .14 |
| ❑ | 60 Randy Johnson | 1.00 | .45 |
| ❑ | 61 Matt Williams | .30 | .14 |
| ❑ | 62 Erubiel Durazo | .30 | .14 |
| ❑ | 63 Shawn Green | .75 | .35 |
| ❑ | 64 Kevin Brown | .30 | .14 |
| ❑ | 65 Gary Sheffield | .75 | .35 |
| ❑ | 66 Adrian Beltre | .30 | .14 |
| ❑ | 67 Vladimir Guerrero | 1.25 | .55 |
| ❑ | 68 Jose Vidro | .30 | .14 |
| ❑ | 69 Barry Bonds | 1.25 | .55 |
| ❑ | 70 Jeff Kent | .50 | .23 |
| ❑ | 71 Preston Wilson | .30 | .14 |
| ❑ | 72 Ryan Dempster | .30 | .14 |
| ❑ | 73 Mike Lowell | .30 | .14 |
| ❑ | 74 Mike Piazza | 2.50 | 1.10 |
| ❑ | 75 Robin Ventura | .30 | .14 |
| ❑ | 76 Edgardo Alfonzo | .30 | .14 |
| ❑ | 77 Derek Bell | .20 | .09 |
| ❑ | 78 Tony Gwynn | 1.50 | .70 |
| ❑ | 79 Matt Clement | .20 | .09 |
| ❑ | 80 Scott Rolen | .50 | .23 |
| ❑ | 81 Bobby Abreu | .30 | .14 |
| ❑ | 82 Curt Schilling | .30 | .14 |
| ❑ | 83 Brian Giles | .30 | .14 |
| ❑ | 84 Jason Kendall | .30 | .14 |
| ❑ | 85 Kris Benson | .30 | .14 |
| ❑ | 86 Ken Griffey Jr. | 3.00 | 1.35 |
| ❑ | 87 Sean Casey | .30 | .14 |
| ❑ | 88 Pokey Reese | .30 | .14 |
| ❑ | 89 Larry Walker | .30 | .14 |
| ❑ | 90 Todd Helton | 1.00 | .45 |
| ❑ | 91 Rick Ankiel PS | 30.00 | 13.50 |
| ❑ | 92 Milton Bradley PS | 15.00 | 6.75 |
| ❑ | 93 Vernon Wells PS | 15.00 | 6.75 |
| ❑ | 94 Rafael Furcal PS | 40.00 | 18.00 |
| ❑ | 95 Kazuhiro Sasaki PS RC | 50.00 | 22.00 |
| ❑ | 96 Joe Torres PS RC | 25.00 | 11.00 |
| ❑ | 97 Adam Kennedy PS | 15.00 | 6.75 |
| ❑ | 98 Adam Piatt PS | 20.00 | 9.00 |
| ❑ | 99 Matt Wheatland PS RC | 30.00 | 13.50 |
| ❑ | 100 Alex Cabrera PS RC | 20.00 | 9.00 |
| ❑ | 101 Barry Zito PS RC | 150.00 | 70.00 |
| ❑ | 102 Mike Lamb PS RC | 15.00 | 6.75 |
| ❑ | 103 Scott Heard PS RC | 25.00 | 11.00 |
| ❑ | 104 Danys Baez PS RC | 20.00 | 9.00 |
| ❑ | 105 Matt Riley PS | 15.00 | 6.75 |
| ❑ | 106 Mark Mulder PS | 15.00 | 6.75 |
| ❑ | 107 Wilfredo Rodriguez PS RC | 15.00 | 6.75 |
| ❑ | 108 Luis Matos PS RC | 25.00 | 11.00 |
| ❑ | 109 Alfonso Soriano PS | 15.00 | 6.75 |
| ❑ | 110 Pat Burrell PS | 25.00 | 11.00 |
| ❑ | 111 Mike Tonis PS RC | 40.00 | 18.00 |
| ❑ | 112 Aaron McNeal PS RC | 20.00 | 9.00 |
| ❑ | 113 Dave Krynzel PS RC | 30.00 | 13.50 |
| ❑ | 114 Josh Beckett PS | 20.00 | 9.00 |
| ❑ | 115 Sean Burnett PS RC | 25.00 | 11.00 |
| ❑ | 116 Eric Munson PS | 20.00 | 9.00 |
| ❑ | 117 Scott Downs PS RC | 15.00 | 6.75 |
| ❑ | 118 Brian Tollberg PS RC | 15.00 | 6.75 |
| ❑ | 119 Nick Johnson PS | 15.00 | 6.75 |
| ❑ | 120 Leo Estrella PS RC | 15.00 | 6.75 |
| ❑ | 121 Ken Griffey Jr. PF | 40.00 | 18.00 |
| ❑ | 122 Frank Thomas PF | 20.00 | 9.00 |
| ❑ | 123 Cal Ripken PF | 40.00 | 18.00 |
| ❑ | 124 Ivan Rodriguez PF | 15.00 | 6.75 |
| ❑ | 125 Derek Jeter PF | 40.00 | 18.00 |
| ❑ | 126 Mark McGwire PF | 40.00 | 18.00 |
| ❑ | 127 Pedro Martinez PF | 15.00 | 6.75 |
| ❑ | 128 Chipper Jones PF | 25.00 | 11.00 |
| ❑ | 129 Sammy Sosa PF | 20.00 | 9.00 |
| ❑ | 130 Alex Rodriguez PF | 30.00 | 13.50 |
| ❑ | 131 Vladimir Guerrero PF | 15.00 | 6.75 |
| ❑ | 132 Jeff Bagwell PF | 15.00 | 6.75 |

## 1999 Upper Deck Ultimate Victory

| | MINT | NRMT |
|---|---|---|
| COMPLETE SET (180) | 300.00 | 135.00 |
| COMP.SET w/o SP's (120) | 40.00 | 18.00 |
| COMMON CARD (1-120) | .20 | .09 |
| COMMON SP (121-150) | 1.50 | .70 |
| COMMON MCGWIRE (151-180) | 3.00 | 1.35 |

| | Card | | |
|---|---|---|---|
| ❑ | 1 Troy Glaus | 1.25 | .55 |
| ❑ | 2 Tim Salmon | .30 | .14 |
| ❑ | 3 Mo Vaughn | .30 | .14 |
| ❑ | 4 Garret Anderson | .30 | .14 |
| ❑ | 5 Darin Erstad | .75 | .35 |
| ❑ | 6 Randy Johnson | 1.00 | .45 |
| ❑ | 7 Matt Williams | .50 | .23 |
| ❑ | 8 Travis Lee | .20 | .09 |
| ❑ | 9 Jay Bell | .30 | .14 |
| ❑ | 10 Steve Finley | .30 | .14 |
| ❑ | 11 Luis Gonzalez | .30 | .14 |
| ❑ | 12 Greg Maddux | 2.00 | .90 |
| ❑ | 13 Chipper Jones | 2.00 | .90 |
| ❑ | 14 Javy Lopez | .30 | .14 |
| ❑ | 15 Tom Glavine | .75 | .35 |
| ❑ | 16 John Smoltz | .30 | .14 |
| ❑ | 17 Cal Ripken | 3.00 | 1.35 |
| ❑ | 18 Charles Johnson | .30 | .14 |
| ❑ | 19 Albert Belle | .50 | .23 |
| ❑ | 20 Mike Mussina | .75 | .35 |
| ❑ | 21 Pedro Martinez | 1.00 | .45 |
| ❑ | 22 Nomar Garciaparra | 2.50 | 1.10 |
| ❑ | 23 Jose Offerman | .20 | .09 |
| ❑ | 24 Sammy Sosa | 1.50 | .70 |
| ❑ | 25 Mark Grace | .75 | .35 |
| ❑ | 26 Kerry Wood | .30 | .14 |
| ❑ | 27 Frank Thomas | 1.50 | .70 |
| ❑ | 28 Ray Durham | .30 | .14 |
| ❑ | 29 Paul Konerko | .30 | .14 |
| ❑ | 30 Pete Harnisch | .20 | .09 |
| ❑ | 31 Greg Vaughn | .30 | .14 |
| ❑ | 32 Sean Casey | .30 | .14 |
| ❑ | 33 Manny Ramirez | 1.00 | .45 |
| ❑ | 34 Jim Thome | .50 | .23 |
| ❑ | 35 Sandy Alomar Jr. | .30 | .14 |
| ❑ | 36 Roberto Alomar | .75 | .35 |
| ❑ | 37 Travis Fryman | .30 | .14 |
| ❑ | 38 Kenny Lofton | .30 | .14 |
| ❑ | 39 Omar Vizquel | .30 | .14 |
| ❑ | 40 Larry Walker | .30 | .14 |
| ❑ | 41 Todd Helton | 1.00 | .45 |
| ❑ | 42 Vinny Castilla | .30 | .14 |
| ❑ | 43 Tony Clark | .20 | .09 |
| ❑ | 44 Juan Encarnacion | .30 | .14 |
| ❑ | 45 Dean Palmer | .30 | .14 |
| ❑ | 46 Damion Easley | .20 | .09 |
| ❑ | 47 Mark Kotsay | .20 | .09 |
| ❑ | 48 Cliff Floyd | .30 | .14 |
| ❑ | 49 Jeff Bagwell | 1.00 | .45 |
| ❑ | 50 Ken Caminiti | .30 | .14 |
| ❑ | 51 Craig Biggio | .50 | .23 |
| ❑ | 52 Moises Alou | .30 | .14 |
| ❑ | 53 Johnny Damon | .30 | .14 |
| ❑ | 54 Larry Sutton | .20 | .09 |
| ❑ | 55 Kevin Brown | .50 | .23 |
| ❑ | 56 Adrian Beltre | .30 | .14 |
| ❑ | 57 Raul Mondesi | .30 | .14 |
| ❑ | 58 Gary Sheffield | .75 | .35 |
| ❑ | 59 Jeromy Burnitz | .30 | .14 |
| ❑ | 60 Sean Berry | .20 | .09 |
| ❑ | 61 Jeff Cirillo | .30 | .14 |
| ❑ | 62 Brad Radke | .30 | .14 |
| ❑ | 63 Todd Walker | .20 | .09 |
| ❑ | 64 Matt Lawton | .30 | .14 |
| ❑ | 65 Vladimir Guerrero | 1.25 | .55 |
| ❑ | 66 Rondell White | .30 | .14 |
| ❑ | 67 Dustin Hermanson | .20 | .09 |
| ❑ | 68 Mike Piazza | 2.50 | 1.10 |
| ❑ | 69 Rickey Henderson | 1.00 | .45 |
| ❑ | 70 Robin Ventura | .30 | .14 |
| ❑ | 71 John Olerud | .30 | .14 |
| ❑ | 72 Derek Jeter | 3.00 | 1.35 |
| ❑ | 73 Roger Clemens | 1.50 | .70 |
| ❑ | 74 Orlando Hernandez | .30 | .14 |
| ❑ | 75 Paul O'Neill | .30 | .14 |
| ❑ | 76 Bernie Williams | .75 | .35 |
| ❑ | 77 Chuck Knoblauch | .30 | .14 |
| ❑ | 78 Tino Martinez | .30 | .14 |
| ❑ | 79 Jason Giambi | .75 | .35 |
| ❑ | 80 Ben Grieve | .30 | .14 |
| ❑ | 81 Matt Stairs | .20 | .09 |
| ❑ | 82 Scott Rolen | .75 | .35 |
| ❑ | 83 Ron Gant | .30 | .14 |
| ❑ | 84 Bobby Abreu | .30 | .14 |
| ❑ | 85 Curt Schilling | .30 | .14 |
| ❑ | 86 Brian Giles | .30 | .14 |
| ❑ | 87 Jason Kendall | .30 | .14 |
| ❑ | 88 Kevin Young | .30 | .14 |
| ❑ | 89 Mark McGwire | 3.00 | 1.35 |
| ❑ | 90 Fernando Tatis | .30 | .14 |
| ❑ | 91 Ray Lankford | .30 | .14 |
| ❑ | 92 Eric Davis | .30 | .14 |
| ❑ | 93 Tony Gwynn | 1.50 | .70 |
| ❑ | 94 Reggie Sanders | .20 | .09 |
| ❑ | 95 Wally Joyner | .30 | .14 |
| ❑ | 96 Trevor Hoffman | .30 | .14 |
| ❑ | 97 Robb Nen | .20 | .09 |
| ❑ | 98 Barry Bonds | 1.25 | .55 |
| ❑ | 99 Jeff Kent | .50 | .23 |
| ❑ | 100 J.T. Snow | .30 | .14 |
| ❑ | 101 Ellis Burks | .30 | .14 |
| ❑ | 102 Ken Griffey Jr. | 3.00 | 1.35 |
| ❑ | 103 Alex Rodriguez | 2.50 | 1.10 |
| ❑ | 104 Jay Buhner | .30 | .14 |
| ❑ | 105 Edgar Martinez | .50 | .23 |
| ❑ | 106 David Bell | .20 | .09 |
| ❑ | 107 Bobby Smith | .20 | .09 |
| ❑ | 108 Wade Boggs | 1.00 | .45 |
| ❑ | 109 Fred McGriff | .50 | .23 |
| ❑ | 110 Rolando Arrojo | .20 | .09 |
| ❑ | 111 Jose Canseco | 1.00 | .45 |
| ❑ | 112 Ivan Rodriguez | 1.00 | .45 |
| ❑ | 113 Juan Gonzalez | .75 | .35 |

| | | MINT | NRMT |
|---|---|---|---|
| ❑ 114 | Rafael Palmeiro | .75 | .35 |
| ❑ 115 | Rusty Greer | .30 | .14 |
| ❑ 116 | Todd Zeile | .30 | .14 |
| ❑ 117 | Jose Cruz Jr. | .30 | .14 |
| ❑ 118 | Carlos Delgado | .75 | .35 |
| ❑ 119 | Shawn Green | .75 | .35 |
| ❑ 120 | David Wells | .30 | .14 |
| ❑ 121 | Eric Munson SP RC ! | 15.00 | 6.75 |
| ❑ 122 | Lance Berkman SP | 2.00 | .90 |
| ❑ 123 | Ed Yarnall SP | 1.50 | .70 |
| ❑ 124 | Jacque Jones SP | 2.00 | .90 |
| ❑ 125 | Kyle Farnsworth SP RC | 2.50 | 1.10 |
| ❑ 126 | Ryan Rupe SP RC | 3.00 | 1.35 |
| ❑ 127 | Jeff Weaver SP RC | 5.00 | 2.20 |
| ❑ 128 | Gabe Kapler SP | 2.00 | .90 |
| ❑ 129 | Alex Gonzalez SP | 1.50 | .70 |
| ❑ 130 | Randy Wolf SP | 1.50 | .70 |
| ❑ 131 | Ben Davis SP | 1.50 | .70 |
| ❑ 132 | Carlos Beltran SP | 2.00 | .90 |
| ❑ 133 | Jim Morris SP RC | 1.50 | .70 |
| ❑ 134 | Jeff Zimmerman SP RC | 2.50 | 1.10 |
| ❑ 135 | Bruce Aven SP | 1.50 | .70 |
| ❑ 136 | Alfonso Soriano SP RC ! | 12.00 | 5.50 |
| ❑ 137 | Tim Hudson SP RC | 50.00 | 22.00 |
| ❑ 138 | Josh Beckett SP RC ! | 25.00 | 11.00 |
| ❑ 139 | Michael Barrett SP | 1.50 | .70 |
| ❑ 140 | Eric Chavez SP | 2.00 | .90 |
| ❑ 141 | Pat Burrell SP RC ! | 30.00 | 13.50 |
| ❑ 142 | Kris Benson SP | 2.00 | .90 |
| ❑ 143 | J.D. Drew SP | 5.00 | 2.20 |
| ❑ 144 | Matt Clement SP | 1.50 | .70 |
| ❑ 145 | Rick Ankiel SP RC ! | 70.00 | 32.00 |
| ❑ 146 | Vernon Wells SP | 2.00 | .90 |
| ❑ 147 | Ruben Mateo SP UER<br>Card is misnumbered | 2.00 | .90 |
| ❑ 148 | Roy Halladay SP | 1.50 | .70 |
| ❑ 149 | Joe McEwing SP RC | 2.50 | 1.10 |
| ❑ 150 | Freddy Garcia SP RC | 10.00 | 4.50 |
| ❑ 151 | Mark McGwire MM | 3.00 | 1.35 |
| ❑ 152 | Mark McGwire MM | 3.00 | 1.35 |
| ❑ 153 | Mark McGwire MM | 3.00 | 1.35 |
| ❑ 154 | Mark McGwire MM | 3.00 | 1.35 |
| ❑ 155 | Mark McGwire MM | 3.00 | 1.35 |
| ❑ 156 | Mark McGwire MM | 3.00 | 1.35 |
| ❑ 157 | Mark McGwire MM | 3.00 | 1.35 |
| ❑ 158 | Mark McGwire MM | 3.00 | 1.35 |
| ❑ 159 | Mark McGwire MM | 3.00 | 1.35 |
| ❑ 160 | Mark McGwire MM | 3.00 | 1.35 |
| ❑ 161 | Mark McGwire MM | 3.00 | 1.35 |
| ❑ 162 | Mark McGwire MM | 3.00 | 1.35 |
| ❑ 163 | Mark McGwire MM | 3.00 | 1.35 |
| ❑ 164 | Mark McGwire MM | 3.00 | 1.35 |
| ❑ 165 | Mark McGwire MM | 3.00 | 1.35 |
| ❑ 166 | Mark McGwire MM | 3.00 | 1.35 |
| ❑ 167 | Mark McGwire MM | 3.00 | 1.35 |
| ❑ 168 | Mark McGwire MM | 3.00 | 1.35 |
| ❑ 169 | Mark McGwire MM | 3.00 | 1.35 |
| ❑ 170 | Mark McGwire MM | 3.00 | 1.35 |
| ❑ 171 | Mark McGwire MM | 3.00 | 1.35 |
| ❑ 172 | Mark McGwire MM | 3.00 | 1.35 |
| ❑ 173 | Mark McGwire MM | 3.00 | 1.35 |
| ❑ 174 | Mark McGwire MM | 3.00 | 1.35 |
| ❑ 175 | Mark McGwire MM | 3.00 | 1.35 |
| ❑ 176 | Mark McGwire MM | 3.00 | 1.35 |
| ❑ 177 | Mark McGwire MM | 3.00 | 1.35 |
| ❑ 178 | Mark McGwire MM | 3.00 | 1.35 |
| ❑ 179 | Mark McGwire MM | 3.00 | 1.35 |
| ❑ 180 | Mark McGwire MM | 3.00 | 1.35 |

## 2000 Upper Deck Ultimate Victory

| | MINT | NRMT |
|---|---|---|
| COMPLETE SET (120) | 850.00 | 375.00 |
| COMP.SET w/o SP's (90) | 25.00 | 11.00 |
| COMMON CARD (1-90) | .15 | .07 |

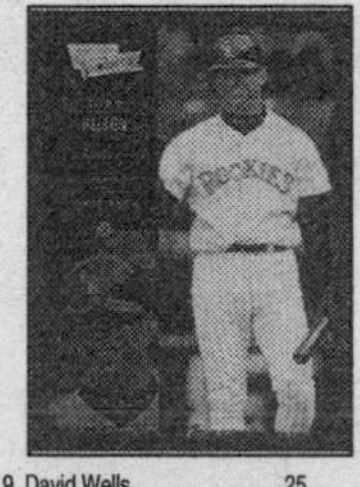

| | | MINT | NRMT |
|---|---|---|---|
| ❑ 1 | Mo Vaughn | .25 | .11 |
| ❑ 2 | Darin Erstad | .60 | .25 |
| ❑ 3 | Troy Glaus | .75 | .35 |
| ❑ 4 | Adam Kennedy | .25 | .11 |
| ❑ 5 | Jason Giambi | .60 | .25 |
| ❑ 6 | Ben Grieve | .25 | .11 |
| ❑ 7 | Terrence Long | .25 | .11 |
| ❑ 8 | Tim Hudson | .60 | .25 |
| ❑ 9 | David Wells | .25 | .11 |
| ❑ 10 | Carlos Delgado | .60 | .25 |
| ❑ 11 | Shannon Stewart | .25 | .11 |
| ❑ 12 | Greg Vaughn | .25 | .11 |
| ❑ 13 | Gerald Williams | .15 | .07 |
| ❑ 14 | Manny Ramirez | .75 | .35 |
| ❑ 15 | Roberto Alomar | .60 | .25 |
| ❑ 16 | Jim Thome | .40 | .18 |
| ❑ 17 | Edgar Martinez | .40 | .18 |
| ❑ 18 | Alex Rodriguez | 2.00 | .90 |
| ❑ 19 | Matt Riley | .25 | .11 |
| ❑ 20 | Cal Ripken | 2.50 | 1.10 |
| ❑ 21 | Mike Mussina | .60 | .25 |
| ❑ 22 | Albert Belle | .40 | .18 |
| ❑ 23 | Ivan Rodriguez | .75 | .35 |
| ❑ 24 | Rafael Palmeiro | .60 | .25 |
| ❑ 25 | Nomar Garciaparra | 2.00 | .90 |
| ❑ 26 | Pedro Martinez | .75 | .35 |
| ❑ 27 | Carl Everett | .25 | .11 |
| ❑ 28 | Tomokazu Ohka RC | 1.00 | .45 |
| ❑ 29 | Jermaine Dye | .25 | .11 |
| ❑ 30 | Johnny Damon | .25 | .11 |
| ❑ 31 | Dean Palmer | .25 | .11 |
| ❑ 32 | Juan Gonzalez | .60 | .25 |
| ❑ 33 | Eric Milton | .15 | .07 |
| ❑ 34 | Matt Lawton | .25 | .11 |
| ❑ 35 | Frank Thomas | 1.25 | .55 |
| ❑ 36 | Paul Konerko | .25 | .11 |
| ❑ 37 | Magglio Ordonez | .25 | .11 |
| ❑ 38 | Jon Garland | .25 | .11 |
| ❑ 39 | Derek Jeter | 2.50 | 1.10 |
| ❑ 40 | Roger Clemens | 1.25 | .55 |
| ❑ 41 | Bernie Williams | .60 | .25 |
| ❑ 42 | Nick Johnson | .25 | .11 |
| ❑ 43 | Julio Lugo | .15 | .07 |
| ❑ 44 | Jeff Bagwell | .75 | .35 |
| ❑ 45 | Richard Hidalgo | .25 | .11 |
| ❑ 46 | Chipper Jones | 1.50 | .70 |
| ❑ 47 | Greg Maddux | 1.50 | .70 |
| ❑ 48 | Andruw Jones | .60 | .25 |
| ❑ 49 | Andres Galarraga | .40 | .18 |
| ❑ 50 | Rafael Furcal | 1.50 | .70 |
| ❑ 51 | Jeromy Burnitz | .25 | .11 |
| ❑ 52 | Geoff Jenkins | .25 | .11 |
| ❑ 53 | Mark McGwire | 2.50 | 1.10 |
| ❑ 54 | Jim Edmonds | .60 | .25 |
| ❑ 55 | Rick Ankiel | 1.25 | .55 |
| ❑ 56 | Sammy Sosa | 1.25 | .55 |
| ❑ 57 | Julio Zuleta RC | .50 | .23 |
| ❑ 58 | Kerry Wood | .25 | .11 |
| ❑ 59 | Randy Johnson | .75 | .35 |
| ❑ 60 | Matt Williams | .40 | .18 |
| ❑ 61 | Steve Finley | .25 | .11 |
| ❑ 62 | Gary Sheffield | .60 | .25 |
| ❑ 63 | Kevin Brown | .25 | .11 |
| ❑ 64 | Shawn Green | .60 | .25 |
| ❑ 65 | Milton Bradley | .25 | .11 |
| ❑ 66 | Vladimir Guerrero | 1.00 | .45 |
| ❑ 67 | Jose Vidro | .25 | .11 |
| ❑ 68 | Barry Bonds | 1.00 | .45 |
| ❑ 69 | Jeff Kent | .40 | .18 |
| ❑ 70 | Preston Wilson | .25 | .11 |
| ❑ 71 | Mike Lowell | .25 | .11 |
| ❑ 72 | Mike Piazza | 2.00 | .90 |
| ❑ 73 | Robin Ventura | .25 | .11 |
| ❑ 74 | Edgardo Alfonzo | .25 | .11 |
| ❑ 75 | Jay Payton | .25 | .11 |
| ❑ 76 | Tony Gwynn | 1.25 | .55 |
| ❑ 77 | Adam Eaton | .25 | .11 |
| ❑ 78 | Phil Nevin | .25 | .11 |
| ❑ 79 | Scott Rolen | .60 | .25 |
| ❑ 80 | Bob Abreu | .25 | .11 |
| ❑ 81 | Pat Burrell | 1.00 | .45 |
| ❑ 82 | Brian Giles | .25 | .11 |
| ❑ 83 | Jason Kendall | .25 | .11 |
| ❑ 84 | Kris Benson | .25 | .11 |
| ❑ 85 | Gookie Dawkins | .25 | .11 |
| ❑ 86 | Ken Griffey Jr. | 2.50 | 1.10 |
| ❑ 87 | Barry Larkin | .60 | .25 |
| ❑ 88 | Larry Walker | .25 | .11 |
| ❑ 89 | Todd Helton | .75 | .35 |
| ❑ 90 | Ben Petrick | .15 | .07 |
| ❑ 91 | Alex Cabrera/3500 RC | 8.00 | 3.60 |
| ❑ 92 | Matt Wheatland/1000 RC | 40.00 | 18.00 |
| ❑ 93 | Joe Torres/1000 RC | 30.00 | 13.50 |
| ❑ 94 | Xavier Nady/1000 RC | 100.00 | 45.00 |
| ❑ 95 | Kenny Kelly/3500 RC | 8.00 | 3.60 |
| ❑ 96 | Matt Ginter/3500 RC | 6.00 | 2.70 |
| ❑ 97 | Ben Diggins/1000 RC | 40.00 | 18.00 |
| ❑ 98 | Danys Baez/3500 RC | 10.00 | 4.50 |
| ❑ 99 | Daylan Holt/2500 RC | 15.00 | 6.75 |
| ❑ 100 | Kazuhiro Sasaki/3500 RC | 25.00 | 11.00 |
| ❑ 101 | Dane Artman/2500 RC | 10.00 | 4.50 |
| ❑ 102 | Mike Tonis/1000 RC | 50.00 | 22.00 |
| ❑ 103 | Timo Perez/2500 RC | 20.00 | 9.00 |
| ❑ 104 | Barry Zito/2500 RC | 60.00 | 27.00 |
| ❑ 105 | Koyie Hill/2500 RC | 10.00 | 4.50 |
| ❑ 106 | Brad Wilkerson/2500 RC | 20.00 | 9.00 |
| ❑ 107 | Juan Pierre/3500 RC | 8.00 | 3.60 |
| ❑ 108 | Aaron McNeal/3500 RC | 10.00 | 4.50 |
| ❑ 109 | Jay Spurgeon/3500 RC | 10.00 | 4.50 |
| ❑ 110 | Sean Burnett/1000 RC | 30.00 | 13.50 |
| ❑ 111 | Luis Matos/3500 RC | 10.00 | 4.50 |
| ❑ 112 | Dave Krynzel/1000 RC | 40.00 | 18.00 |
| ❑ 113 | Scott Heard/1000 RC | 30.00 | 13.50 |
| ❑ 114 | Ben Sheets/2500 RC | 60.00 | 27.00 |
| ❑ 115 | Dane Sardinha/1000 RC | 30.00 | 13.50 |
| ❑ 116 | David Espinosa/1000 RC | 40.00 | 18.00 |
| ❑ 117 | Leo Estrella/3500 RC | 6.00 | 2.70 |
| ❑ 118 | Kurt Ainsworth/2500 RC | 20.00 | 9.00 |
| ❑ 119 | Jon Rauch/2500 RC | 40.00 | 18.00 |
| ❑ 120 | Ryan Franklin/2500 RC | 10.00 | 4.50 |

## 1999 Upper Deck Victory

| | MINT | NRMT |
|---|---|---|
| COMPLETE SET (470) | 75.00 | 34.00 |
| COMMON CARD (1-470) | .10 | .05 |
| COMMON MCGWIRE (421-450) | 1.00 | .45 |

| | | MINT | NRMT |
|---|---|---|---|
| ❑ 1 | Anaheim Angels TC | .10 | .05 |
| ❑ 2 | Mark Harriger RC | .25 | .11 |
| ❑ 3 | Mo Vaughn PT | .15 | .07 |
| ❑ 4 | Darin Erstad BP | .15 | .07 |
| ❑ 5 | Troy Glaus | .50 | .23 |
| ❑ 6 | Tim Salmon | .15 | .07 |
| ❑ 7 | Mo Vaughn | .15 | .07 |
| ❑ 8 | Darin Erstad | .40 | .18 |
| ❑ 9 | Garret Anderson | .15 | .07 |
| ❑ 10 | Todd Greene | .10 | .05 |
| ❑ 11 | Troy Percival | .10 | .05 |
| ❑ 12 | Chuck Finley | .15 | .07 |
| ❑ 13 | Jason Dickson | .10 | .05 |
| ❑ 14 | Jim Edmonds | .40 | .18 |
| ❑ 15 | Arizona Diamondbacks TC | .10 | .05 |

| | No. | Player | Price 1 | Price 2 |
|---|---|---|---|---|
| ❑ | 16 | Randy Johnson | .50 | .23 |
| ❑ | 17 | Matt Williams | .25 | .11 |
| ❑ | 18 | Travis Lee | .10 | .05 |
| ❑ | 19 | Jay Bell | .15 | .07 |
| ❑ | 20 | Tony Womack | .10 | .05 |
| ❑ | 21 | Steve Finley | .15 | .07 |
| ❑ | 22 | Bernard Gilkey | .10 | .05 |
| ❑ | 23 | Tony Batista | .15 | .07 |
| ❑ | 24 | Todd Stottlemyre | .10 | .05 |
| ❑ | 25 | Omar Daal | .10 | .05 |
| ❑ | 26 | Atlanta Braves TC | .10 | .05 |
| ❑ | 27 | Bruce Chen | .10 | .05 |
| ❑ | 28 | George Lombard | .10 | .05 |
| ❑ | 29 | Chipper Jones PT | .50 | .23 |
| ❑ | 30 | Chipper Jones BP | .50 | .23 |
| ❑ | 31 | Greg Maddux | 1.00 | .45 |
| ❑ | 32 | Chipper Jones | 1.00 | .45 |
| ❑ | 33 | Javy Lopez | .15 | .07 |
| ❑ | 34 | Tom Glavine | .40 | .18 |
| ❑ | 35 | John Smoltz | .15 | .07 |
| ❑ | 36 | Andruw Jones | .40 | .18 |
| ❑ | 37 | Brian Jordan | .15 | .07 |
| ❑ | 38 | Walt Weiss | .10 | .05 |
| ❑ | 39 | Bret Boone | .15 | .07 |
| ❑ | 40 | Andres Galarraga | .25 | .11 |
| ❑ | 41 | Baltimore Orioles TC | .10 | .05 |
| ❑ | 42 | Ryan Minor | .10 | .05 |
| ❑ | 43 | Jerry Hairston Jr. | .15 | .07 |
| ❑ | 44 | Calvin Pickering | .10 | .05 |
| ❑ | 45 | Cal Ripken HM | .75 | .35 |
| ❑ | 46 | Cal Ripken | 1.50 | .70 |
| ❑ | 47 | Charles Johnson | .15 | .07 |
| ❑ | 48 | Albert Belle | .25 | .11 |
| ❑ | 49 | Delino DeShields | .10 | .05 |
| ❑ | 50 | Mike Mussina | .40 | .18 |
| ❑ | 51 | Scott Erickson | .10 | .05 |
| ❑ | 52 | Brady Anderson | .15 | .07 |
| ❑ | 53 | B.J. Surhoff | .15 | .07 |
| ❑ | 54 | Harold Baines | .15 | .07 |
| ❑ | 55 | Will Clark | .40 | .18 |
| ❑ | 56 | Boston Red Sox TC | .10 | .05 |
| ❑ | 57 | Shea Hillenbrand RC | .25 | .11 |
| ❑ | 58 | Trot Nixon | .15 | .07 |
| ❑ | 59 | Jin Ho Cho | .10 | .05 |
| ❑ | 60 | Nomar Garciaparra PT | .60 | .25 |
| ❑ | 61 | Nomar Garciaparra BP | .60 | .25 |
| ❑ | 62 | Pedro Martinez | .50 | .23 |
| ❑ | 63 | Nomar Garciaparra | 1.25 | .55 |
| ❑ | 64 | Jose Offerman | .10 | .05 |
| ❑ | 65 | Jason Varitek | .15 | .07 |
| ❑ | 66 | Darren Lewis | .10 | .05 |
| ❑ | 67 | Troy O'Leary | .10 | .05 |
| ❑ | 68 | Donnie Sadler | .10 | .05 |
| ❑ | 69 | John Valentin | .10 | .05 |
| ❑ | 70 | Tim Wakefield | .10 | .05 |
| ❑ | 71 | Bret Saberhagen | .15 | .07 |
| ❑ | 72 | Chicago Cubs TC | .10 | .05 |
| ❑ | 73 | Kyle Farnsworth RC | .25 | .11 |
| ❑ | 74 | Sammy Sosa PT | .40 | .18 |
| ❑ | 75 | Sammy Sosa BP | .40 | .18 |
| ❑ | 76 | Sammy Sosa HM | .40 | .18 |
| ❑ | 77 | Kerry Wood HM | .15 | .07 |
| ❑ | 78 | Sammy Sosa | .75 | .35 |
| ❑ | 79 | Mark Grace | .40 | .18 |
| ❑ | 80 | Kerry Wood | .15 | .07 |
| ❑ | 81 | Kevin Tapani | .10 | .05 |
| ❑ | 82 | Benito Santiago | .10 | .05 |
| ❑ | 83 | Gary Gaetti | .10 | .05 |
| ❑ | 84 | Mickey Morandini | .10 | .05 |
| ❑ | 85 | Glenallen Hill | .10 | .05 |
| ❑ | 86 | Henry Rodriguez | .10 | .05 |
| ❑ | 87 | Rod Beck | .10 | .05 |
| ❑ | 88 | Chicago White Sox TC | .10 | .05 |
| ❑ | 89 | Carlos Lee | .15 | .07 |
| ❑ | 90 | Mark Johnson | .10 | .05 |
| ❑ | 91 | Frank Thomas PT | .40 | .18 |
| ❑ | 92 | Frank Thomas | .75 | .35 |
| ❑ | 93 | Jim Parque | .10 | .05 |
| ❑ | 94 | Mike Sirotka | .10 | .05 |
| ❑ | 95 | Mike Caruso | .10 | .05 |
| ❑ | 96 | Ray Durham | .15 | .07 |
| ❑ | 97 | Magglio Ordonez | .25 | .11 |
| ❑ | 98 | Paul Konerko | .15 | .07 |
| ❑ | 99 | Bob Howry | .10 | .05 |
| ❑ | 100 | Brian Simmons | .10 | .05 |
| ❑ | 101 | Jaime Navarro | .10 | .05 |
| ❑ | 102 | Cincinnati Reds TC | .10 | .05 |
| ❑ | 103 | Denny Neagle | .10 | .05 |
| ❑ | 104 | Pete Harnisch | .10 | .05 |
| ❑ | 105 | Greg Vaughn | .15 | .07 |
| ❑ | 106 | Brett Tomko | .10 | .05 |
| ❑ | 107 | Mike Cameron | .10 | .05 |
| ❑ | 108 | Sean Casey | .15 | .07 |
| ❑ | 109 | Aaron Boone | .10 | .05 |
| ❑ | 110 | Michael Tucker | .10 | .05 |
| ❑ | 111 | Dmitri Young | .15 | .07 |
| ❑ | 112 | Barry Larkin | .40 | .18 |
| ❑ | 113 | Cleveland Indians TC | .10 | .05 |
| ❑ | 114 | Russ Branyan | .15 | .07 |
| ❑ | 115 | Jim Thome PT | .15 | .07 |
| ❑ | 116 | Manny Ramirez PT | .25 | .11 |
| ❑ | 117 | Manny Ramirez | .50 | .23 |
| ❑ | 118 | Jim Thome | .25 | .11 |
| ❑ | 119 | David Justice | .25 | .11 |
| ❑ | 120 | Sandy Alomar Jr. | .15 | .07 |
| ❑ | 121 | Roberto Alomar | .40 | .18 |
| ❑ | 122 | Jaret Wright | .10 | .05 |
| ❑ | 123 | Bartolo Colon | .15 | .07 |
| ❑ | 124 | Travis Fryman | .15 | .07 |
| ❑ | 125 | Kenny Lofton | .15 | .07 |
| ❑ | 126 | Omar Vizquel | .15 | .07 |
| ❑ | 127 | Colorado Rockies TC | .10 | .05 |
| ❑ | 128 | Derrick Gibson | .10 | .05 |
| ❑ | 129 | Larry Walker BP | .15 | .07 |
| ❑ | 130 | Larry Walker | .15 | .07 |
| ❑ | 131 | Dante Bichette | .15 | .07 |
| ❑ | 132 | Todd Helton | .50 | .23 |
| ❑ | 133 | Neifi Perez | .10 | .05 |
| ❑ | 134 | Vinny Castilla | .15 | .07 |
| ❑ | 135 | Darryl Kile | .15 | .07 |
| ❑ | 136 | Pedro Astacio | .10 | .05 |
| ❑ | 137 | Darryl Hamilton | .10 | .05 |
| ❑ | 138 | Mike Lansing | .10 | .05 |
| ❑ | 139 | Kirt Manwaring | .10 | .05 |
| ❑ | 140 | Detroit Tigers TC | .10 | .05 |
| ❑ | 141 | Jeff Weaver RC | .25 | .11 |
| ❑ | 142 | Gabe Kapler | .15 | .07 |
| ❑ | 143 | Tony Clark PT | .10 | .05 |
| ❑ | 144 | Tony Clark | .10 | .05 |
| ❑ | 145 | Juan Encarnacion | .15 | .07 |
| ❑ | 146 | Dean Palmer | .15 | .07 |
| ❑ | 147 | Damion Easley | .10 | .05 |
| ❑ | 148 | Bobby Higginson | .15 | .07 |
| ❑ | 149 | Karim Garcia | .10 | .05 |
| ❑ | 150 | Justin Thompson | .10 | .05 |
| ❑ | 151 | Matt Anderson | .10 | .05 |
| ❑ | 152 | Willie Blair | .10 | .05 |
| ❑ | 153 | Brian Hunter | .10 | .05 |
| ❑ | 154 | Florida Marlins TC | .10 | .05 |
| ❑ | 155 | Alex Gonzalez | .10 | .05 |
| ❑ | 156 | Mark Kotsay | .10 | .05 |
| ❑ | 157 | Livan Hernandez | .10 | .05 |
| ❑ | 158 | Cliff Floyd | .15 | .07 |
| ❑ | 159 | Todd Dunwoody | .10 | .05 |
| ❑ | 160 | Alex Fernandez | .10 | .05 |
| ❑ | 161 | Matt Mantei | .10 | .05 |
| ❑ | 162 | Derrek Lee | .10 | .05 |
| ❑ | 163 | Kevin Orie | .10 | .05 |
| ❑ | 164 | Craig Counsell | .10 | .05 |
| ❑ | 165 | Rafael Medina | .10 | .05 |
| ❑ | 166 | Houston Astros TC | .10 | .05 |
| ❑ | 167 | Daryle Ward | .15 | .07 |
| ❑ | 168 | Mitch Meluskey | .10 | .05 |
| ❑ | 169 | Jeff Bagwell PT | .25 | .11 |
| ❑ | 170 | Jeff Bagwell | .50 | .23 |
| ❑ | 171 | Ken Caminiti | .15 | .07 |
| ❑ | 172 | Craig Biggio | .25 | .11 |
| ❑ | 173 | Derek Bell | .10 | .05 |
| ❑ | 174 | Moises Alou | .15 | .07 |
| ❑ | 175 | Billy Wagner | .10 | .05 |
| ❑ | 176 | Shane Reynolds | .10 | .05 |
| ❑ | 177 | Carl Everett | .15 | .07 |
| ❑ | 178 | Scott Elarton | .15 | .07 |
| ❑ | 179 | Richard Hidalgo | .15 | .07 |
| ❑ | 180 | Kansas City Royals TC | .10 | .05 |
| ❑ | 181 | Carlos Beltran | .15 | .07 |
| ❑ | 182 | Carlos Febles | .10 | .05 |
| ❑ | 183 | Jeremy Giambi | .10 | .05 |
| ❑ | 184 | Johnny Damon | .15 | .07 |
| ❑ | 185 | Joe Randa | .10 | .05 |
| ❑ | 186 | Jeff King | .10 | .05 |
| ❑ | 187 | Hipolito Pichardo | .10 | .05 |
| ❑ | 188 | Kevin Appier | .15 | .07 |
| ❑ | 189 | Chad Kreuter | .10 | .05 |
| ❑ | 190 | Rey Sanchez | .10 | .05 |
| ❑ | 191 | Larry Sutton | .10 | .05 |
| ❑ | 192 | Jeff Montgomery | .10 | .05 |
| ❑ | 193 | Jermaine Dye | .15 | .07 |
| ❑ | 194 | Los Angeles Dodgers TC | .10 | .05 |
| ❑ | 195 | Adam Riggs | .10 | .05 |
| ❑ | 196 | Angel Pena | .10 | .05 |
| ❑ | 197 | Todd Hundley | .10 | .05 |
| ❑ | 198 | Kevin Brown | .25 | .11 |
| ❑ | 199 | Ismael Valdes | .10 | .05 |
| ❑ | 200 | Chan Ho Park | .15 | .07 |
| ❑ | 201 | Adrian Beltre | .15 | .07 |
| ❑ | 202 | Mark Grudzielanek | .10 | .05 |
| ❑ | 203 | Raul Mondesi | .15 | .07 |
| ❑ | 204 | Gary Sheffield | .40 | .18 |
| ❑ | 205 | Eric Karros | .15 | .07 |
| ❑ | 206 | Devon White | .10 | .05 |
| ❑ | 207 | Milwaukee Brewers TC | .10 | .05 |
| ❑ | 208 | Ron Belliard | .10 | .05 |
| ❑ | 209 | Rafael Roque RC | .15 | .07 |
| ❑ | 210 | Jeromy Burnitz | .15 | .07 |
| ❑ | 211 | Fernando Vina | .10 | .05 |
| ❑ | 212 | Scott Karl | .10 | .05 |
| ❑ | 213 | Jim Abbott | .15 | .07 |
| ❑ | 214 | Sean Berry | .10 | .05 |
| ❑ | 215 | Marquis Grissom | .10 | .05 |
| ❑ | 216 | Geoff Jenkins | .15 | .07 |
| ❑ | 217 | Jeff Cirillo | .15 | .07 |
| ❑ | 218 | Dave Nilsson | .10 | .05 |
| ❑ | 219 | Jose Valentin | .10 | .05 |
| ❑ | 220 | Minnesota Twins TC | .10 | .05 |
| ❑ | 221 | Corey Koskie | .10 | .05 |
| ❑ | 222 | Cristian Guzman | .10 | .05 |
| ❑ | 223 | A.J. Pierzynski | .10 | .05 |
| ❑ | 224 | David Ortiz | .10 | .05 |
| ❑ | 225 | Brad Radke | .15 | .07 |
| ❑ | 226 | Todd Walker | .10 | .05 |
| ❑ | 227 | Matt Lawton | .15 | .07 |
| ❑ | 228 | Rick Aguilera | .10 | .05 |
| ❑ | 229 | Eric Milton | .10 | .05 |
| ❑ | 230 | Marty Cordova | .10 | .05 |
| ❑ | 231 | Torii Hunter | .10 | .05 |
| ❑ | 232 | Ron Coomer | .10 | .05 |
| ❑ | 233 | LaTroy Hawkins | .10 | .05 |
| ❑ | 234 | Montreal Expos TC | .10 | .05 |
| ❑ | 235 | Fernando Seguignol | .10 | .05 |
| ❑ | 236 | Michael Barrett | .10 | .05 |
| ❑ | 237 | Vladimir Guerrero BP | .25 | .11 |
| ❑ | 238 | Vladimir Guerrero | .60 | .25 |
| ❑ | 239 | Brad Fullmer | .15 | .07 |
| ❑ | 240 | Rondell White | .15 | .07 |
| ❑ | 241 | Ugueth Urbina | .10 | .05 |
| ❑ | 242 | Dustin Hermanson | .10 | .05 |
| ❑ | 243 | Orlando Cabrera | .10 | .05 |
| ❑ | 244 | Wilton Guerrero | .10 | .05 |
| ❑ | 245 | Carl Pavano | .10 | .05 |
| ❑ | 246 | Javier Vazquez | .10 | .05 |
| ❑ | 247 | Chris Widger | .10 | .05 |
| ❑ | 248 | New York Mets TC | .10 | .05 |
| ❑ | 249 | Mike Kinkade | .10 | .05 |
| ❑ | 250 | Octavio Dotel | .10 | .05 |
| ❑ | 251 | Mike Piazza PT | .60 | .25 |
| ❑ | 252 | Mike Piazza | 1.25 | .55 |
| ❑ | 253 | Rickey Henderson | .50 | .23 |
| ❑ | 254 | Edgardo Alfonzo | .15 | .07 |
| ❑ | 255 | Robin Ventura | .15 | .07 |
| ❑ | 256 | Al Leiter | .15 | .07 |
| ❑ | 257 | Brian McRae | .10 | .05 |
| ❑ | 258 | Rey Ordonez | .10 | .05 |
| ❑ | 259 | Bobby Bonilla | .15 | .07 |
| ❑ | 260 | Orel Hershiser | .15 | .07 |
| ❑ | 261 | John Olerud | .15 | .07 |
| ❑ | 262 | New York Yankees TC | .10 | .05 |
| ❑ | 263 | Ricky Ledee | .10 | .05 |
| ❑ | 264 | Bernie Williams BP | .15 | .07 |
| ❑ | 265 | Derek Jeter BP | .75 | .35 |
| ❑ | 266 | Scott Brosius HM | .10 | .05 |
| ❑ | 267 | Derek Jeter | 1.50 | .70 |
| ❑ | 268 | Roger Clemens | .75 | .35 |
| ❑ | 269 | Orlando Hernandez | .15 | .07 |
| ❑ | 270 | Scott Brosius | .15 | .07 |
| ❑ | 271 | Paul O'Neill | .15 | .07 |
| ❑ | 272 | Bernie Williams | .40 | .18 |
| ❑ | 273 | Chuck Knoblauch | .15 | .07 |

| No. | Card | MINT | NRMT |
|---|---|---|---|
| ❑ 274 | Tino Martinez | .15 | .07 |
| ❑ 275 | Mariano Rivera | .15 | .07 |
| ❑ 276 | Jorge Posada | .15 | .07 |
| ❑ 277 | Oakland Athletics TC | .10 | .05 |
| ❑ 278 | Eric Chavez | .15 | .07 |
| ❑ 279 | Ben Grieve HM | .15 | .07 |
| ❑ 280 | Jason Giambi | .40 | .18 |
| ❑ 281 | John Jaha | .10 | .05 |
| ❑ 282 | Miguel Tejada | .15 | .07 |
| ❑ 283 | Ben Grieve | .15 | .07 |
| ❑ 284 | Matt Stairs | .10 | .05 |
| ❑ 285 | Ryan Christenson | .10 | .05 |
| ❑ 286 | A.J. Hinch | .10 | .05 |
| ❑ 287 | Kenny Rogers | .10 | .05 |
| ❑ 288 | Tom Candiotti | .10 | .05 |
| ❑ 289 | Scott Spiezio | .10 | .05 |
| ❑ 290 | Philadelphia Phillies TC | .10 | .05 |
| ❑ 291 | Pat Burrell RC | 1.50 | .70 |
| ❑ 292 | Marlon Anderson | .10 | .05 |
| ❑ 293 | Scott Rolen BP | .40 | .18 |
| ❑ 294 | Scott Rolen | .40 | .18 |
| ❑ 295 | Doug Glanville | .10 | .05 |
| ❑ 296 | Rico Brogna | .10 | .05 |
| ❑ 297 | Ron Gant | .15 | .07 |
| ❑ 298 | Bobby Abreu | .15 | .07 |
| ❑ 299 | Desi Relaford | .10 | .05 |
| ❑ 300 | Curt Schilling | .15 | .07 |
| ❑ 301 | Chad Ogea | .10 | .05 |
| ❑ 302 | Kevin Jordan | .10 | .05 |
| ❑ 303 | Carlton Loewer | .10 | .05 |
| ❑ 304 | Pittsburgh Pirates TC | .10 | .05 |
| ❑ 305 | Kris Benson | .15 | .07 |
| ❑ 306 | Brian Giles | .15 | .07 |
| ❑ 307 | Jason Kendall | .15 | .07 |
| ❑ 308 | Jose Guillen | .10 | .05 |
| ❑ 309 | Pat Meares | .10 | .05 |
| ❑ 310 | Brant Brown | .10 | .05 |
| ❑ 311 | Kevin Young | .15 | .07 |
| ❑ 312 | Ed Sprague | .10 | .05 |
| ❑ 313 | Francisco Cordova | .10 | .05 |
| ❑ 314 | Aramis Ramirez | .10 | .05 |
| ❑ 315 | Freddy Garcia | .10 | .05 |
| ❑ 316 | St. Louis Cardinals TC | .10 | .05 |
| ❑ 317 | J.D. Drew | .40 | .18 |
| ❑ 318 | Chad Hutchinson RC | .25 | .11 |
| ❑ 319 | Mark McGwire PT | .75 | .35 |
| ❑ 320 | J.D. Drew PT | .40 | .18 |
| ❑ 321 | Mark McGwire BP | .75 | .05 |
| ❑ 322 | Mark McGwire HM | .75 | .35 |
| ❑ 323 | Mark McGwire | 1.50 | .70 |
| ❑ 324 | Fernando Tatis | .15 | .07 |
| ❑ 325 | Edgar Renteria | .10 | .05 |
| ❑ 326 | Ray Lankford | .15 | .07 |
| ❑ 327 | Willie McGee | .15 | .07 |
| ❑ 328 | Ricky Bottalico | .10 | .05 |
| ❑ 329 | Eli Marrero | .10 | .05 |
| ❑ 330 | Matt Morris | .10 | .05 |
| ❑ 331 | Eric Davis | .15 | .07 |
| ❑ 332 | Darren Bragg | .10 | .05 |
| ❑ 333 | San Diego Padres TC | .10 | .05 |
| ❑ 334 | Matt Clement | .10 | .05 |
| ❑ 335 | Ben Davis | .10 | .05 |
| ❑ 336 | Gary Matthews Jr. | .10 | .05 |
| ❑ 337 | Tony Gwynn BP | .40 | .18 |
| ❑ 338 | Tony Gwynn HM | .40 | .18 |
| ❑ 339 | Tony Gwynn | .75 | .35 |
| ❑ 340 | Reggie Sanders | .10 | .05 |
| ❑ 341 | Ruben Rivera | .10 | .05 |
| ❑ 342 | Wally Joyner | .15 | .07 |
| ❑ 343 | Sterling Hitchcock | .10 | .05 |
| ❑ 344 | Carlos Hernandez | .10 | .05 |
| ❑ 345 | Andy Ashby | .10 | .05 |
| ❑ 346 | Trevor Hoffman | .15 | .07 |
| ❑ 347 | Chris Gomez | .10 | .05 |
| ❑ 348 | Jim Leyritz | .10 | .05 |
| ❑ 349 | San Francisco Giants TC | .10 | .05 |
| ❑ 350 | Armando Rios | .10 | .05 |
| ❑ 351 | Barry Bonds PT | .25 | .11 |
| ❑ 352 | Barry Bonds BP | .25 | .11 |
| ❑ 353 | Barry Bonds HM | .25 | .11 |
| ❑ 354 | Robb Nen | .10 | .05 |
| ❑ 355 | Bill Mueller | .10 | .05 |
| ❑ 356 | Barry Bonds | .60 | .25 |
| ❑ 357 | Jeff Kent | .25 | .11 |
| ❑ 358 | J.T. Snow | .15 | .07 |
| ❑ 359 | Ellis Burks | .15 | .07 |
| ❑ 360 | F.P. Santangelo | .10 | .05 |
| ❑ 361 | Marvin Benard | .10 | .05 |
| ❑ 362 | Stan Javier | .10 | .05 |
| ❑ 363 | Shawn Estes | .10 | .05 |
| ❑ 364 | Seattle Mariners TC | .10 | .05 |
| ❑ 365 | Carlos Guillen | .10 | .05 |
| ❑ 366 | Ken Griffey Jr. PT | .75 | .35 |
| ❑ 367 | Alex Rodriguez PT | .60 | .25 |
| ❑ 368 | Ken Griffey Jr. BP | .75 | .35 |
| ❑ 369 | Alex Rodriguez BP | .60 | .25 |
| ❑ 370 | Ken Griffey Jr. HM | .75 | .35 |
| ❑ 371 | Alex Rodriguez HM | .60 | .25 |
| ❑ 372 | Ken Griffey Jr. | 1.50 | .70 |
| ❑ 373 | Alex Rodriguez | 1.25 | .55 |
| ❑ 374 | Jay Buhner | .15 | .07 |
| ❑ 375 | Edgar Martinez | .25 | .11 |
| ❑ 376 | Jeff Fassero | .10 | .05 |
| ❑ 377 | David Bell | .10 | .05 |
| ❑ 378 | David Segui | .10 | .05 |
| ❑ 379 | Russ Davis | .10 | .05 |
| ❑ 380 | Dan Wilson | .10 | .05 |
| ❑ 381 | Jamie Moyer | .10 | .05 |
| ❑ 382 | Tampa Bay Devil Rays TC | .10 | .05 |
| ❑ 383 | Roberto Hernandez | .10 | .05 |
| ❑ 384 | Bobby Smith | .10 | .05 |
| ❑ 385 | Wade Boggs | .50 | .23 |
| ❑ 386 | Fred McGriff | .25 | .11 |
| ❑ 387 | Rolando Arrojo | .10 | .05 |
| ❑ 388 | Jose Canseco | .50 | .23 |
| ❑ 389 | Wilson Alvarez | .10 | .05 |
| ❑ 390 | Kevin Stocker | .10 | .05 |
| ❑ 391 | Miguel Cairo | .10 | .05 |
| ❑ 392 | Quinton McCracken | .10 | .05 |
| ❑ 393 | Texas Rangers TC | .10 | .05 |
| ❑ 394 | Ruben Mateo | .15 | .07 |
| ❑ 395 | Cesar King | .10 | .05 |
| ❑ 396 | Juan Gonzalez PT | .15 | .07 |
| ❑ 397 | Juan Gonzalez BP | .15 | .07 |
| ❑ 398 | Ivan Rodriguez | .50 | .23 |
| ❑ 399 | Juan Gonzalez | .40 | .18 |
| ❑ 400 | Rafael Palmeiro | .40 | .18 |
| ❑ 401 | Rick Helling | .15 | .07 |
| ❑ 402 | Aaron Sele | .15 | .07 |
| ❑ 403 | John Wetteland | .15 | .07 |
| ❑ 404 | Rusty Greer | .15 | .07 |
| ❑ 405 | Todd Zeile | .15 | .07 |
| ❑ 406 | Royce Clayton | .10 | .05 |
| ❑ 407 | Tom Goodwin | .10 | .05 |
| ❑ 408 | Toronto Blue Jays TC | .10 | .05 |
| ❑ 409 | Kevin Witt | .10 | .05 |
| ❑ 410 | Roy Halladay | .10 | .05 |
| ❑ 411 | Jose Cruz Jr. | .15 | .07 |
| ❑ 412 | Carlos Delgado | .40 | .18 |
| ❑ 413 | Willie Greene | .10 | .05 |
| ❑ 414 | Shawn Green | .40 | .18 |
| ❑ 415 | Homer Bush | .10 | .05 |
| ❑ 416 | Shannon Stewart | .15 | .07 |
| ❑ 417 | David Wells | .15 | .07 |
| ❑ 418 | Kelvim Escobar | .10 | .05 |
| ❑ 419 | Joey Hamilton | .10 | .05 |
| ❑ 420 | Alex Gonzalez | .10 | .05 |
| ❑ 421 | Mark McGwire MM | 1.00 | .45 |
| ❑ 422 | Mark McGwire MM | 1.00 | .45 |
| ❑ 423 | Mark McGwire MM | 1.00 | .45 |
| ❑ 424 | Mark McGwire MM | 1.00 | .45 |
| ❑ 425 | Mark McGwire MM | 1.00 | .45 |
| ❑ 426 | Mark McGwire MM | 1.00 | .45 |
| ❑ 427 | Mark McGwire MM | 1.00 | .45 |
| ❑ 428 | Mark McGwire MM | 1.00 | .45 |
| ❑ 429 | Mark McGwire MM | 1.00 | .45 |
| ❑ 430 | Mark McGwire MM | 1.00 | .45 |
| ❑ 431 | Mark McGwire MM | 1.00 | .45 |
| ❑ 432 | Mark McGwire MM | 1.00 | .45 |
| ❑ 433 | Mark McGwire MM | 1.00 | .45 |
| ❑ 434 | Mark McGwire MM | 1.00 | .45 |
| ❑ 435 | Mark McGwire MM | 1.00 | .45 |
| ❑ 436 | Mark McGwire MM | 1.00 | .45 |
| ❑ 437 | Mark McGwire MM | 1.00 | .45 |
| ❑ 438 | Mark McGwire MM | 1.00 | .45 |
| ❑ 439 | Mark McGwire MM | 1.00 | .45 |
| ❑ 440 | Mark McGwire MM | 1.00 | .45 |
| ❑ 441 | Mark McGwire MM | 1.00 | .45 |
| ❑ 442 | Mark McGwire MM | 1.00 | .45 |
| ❑ 443 | Mark McGwire MM | 1.00 | .45 |
| ❑ 444 | Mark McGwire MM | 1.00 | .45 |
| ❑ 445 | Mark McGwire MM | 1.00 | .45 |
| ❑ 446 | Mark McGwire MM | 1.00 | .45 |
| ❑ 447 | Mark McGwire MM | 1.00 | .45 |
| ❑ 448 | Mark McGwire MM | 1.00 | .45 |
| ❑ 449 | Mark McGwire MM | 1.00 | .45 |
| ❑ 450 | Mark McGwire MM | 1.00 | .45 |
| ❑ 451 | Chipper Jones RF | .50 | .23 |
| ❑ 452 | Cal Ripken RF | .75 | .35 |
| ❑ 453 | Roger Clemens RF | .40 | .18 |
| ❑ 454 | Wade Boggs RF | .15 | .07 |
| ❑ 455 | Greg Maddux RF | .50 | .23 |
| ❑ 456 | Frank Thomas RF | .40 | .18 |
| ❑ 457 | Jeff Bagwell RF | .25 | .11 |
| ❑ 458 | Mike Piazza RF | .60 | .25 |
| ❑ 459 | Randy Johnson RF | .15 | .07 |
| ❑ 460 | Mo Vaughn RF | .15 | .07 |
| ❑ 461 | Mark McGwire RF | .75 | .35 |
| ❑ 462 | Rickey Henderson RF | .25 | .11 |
| ❑ 463 | Barry Bonds RF | .25 | .11 |
| ❑ 464 | Tony Gwynn RF | .40 | .18 |
| ❑ 465 | Ken Griffey Jr. RF | .75 | .35 |
| ❑ 466 | Alex Rodriguez RF | .60 | .25 |
| ❑ 467 | Sammy Sosa RF | .40 | .18 |
| ❑ 468 | Juan Gonzalez RF | .15 | .07 |
| ❑ 469 | Kevin Brown RF | .15 | .07 |
| ❑ 470 | Fred McGriff RF | .15 | .07 |

## 2000 Upper Deck Victory

| | MINT | NRMT |
|---|---|---|
| COMPLETE SET (440) | 25.00 | 11.00 |
| COMP.FACT.SET (466) | 35.00 | 16.00 |
| COMMON CARD (1-390) | .10 | .05 |
| COMMON GRIFFEY (391-440) | .50 | .23 |
| COMMON USA (441-466) | .50 | .23 |

| No. | Card | MINT | NRMT |
|---|---|---|---|
| ❑ 1 | Mo Vaughn | .15 | .07 |
| ❑ 2 | Garret Anderson | .15 | .07 |
| ❑ 3 | Tim Salmon | .15 | .07 |
| ❑ 4 | Troy Percival | .10 | .05 |
| ❑ 5 | Orlando Palmeiro | .10 | .05 |
| ❑ 6 | Darin Erstad | .40 | .18 |
| ❑ 7 | Ramon Ortiz | .15 | .07 |
| ❑ 8 | Ben Molina | .15 | .07 |
| ❑ 9 | Troy Glaus | .50 | .23 |
| ❑ 10 | Jim Edmonds | .40 | .18 |
| ❑ 11 | Mo Vaughn<br>Troy Percival CL | .15 | .07 |
| ❑ 12 | Craig Biggio | .25 | .11 |
| ❑ 13 | Roger Cedeno | .10 | .05 |
| ❑ 14 | Shane Reynolds | .10 | .05 |
| ❑ 15 | Jeff Bagwell | .50 | .23 |
| ❑ 16 | Octavio Dotel | .10 | .05 |
| ❑ 17 | Moises Alou | .15 | .07 |
| ❑ 18 | Jose Lima | .10 | .05 |
| ❑ 19 | Ken Caminiti | .15 | .07 |
| ❑ 20 | Richard Hidalgo | .15 | .07 |
| ❑ 21 | Billy Wagner | .10 | .05 |
| ❑ 22 | Lance Berkman | .15 | .07 |
| ❑ 23 | Jeff Bagwell<br>Jose Lima CL | .10 | .05 |
| ❑ 24 | Jason Giambi | .40 | .18 |
| ❑ 25 | Randy Velarde | .10 | .05 |
| ❑ 26 | Miguel Tejada | .15 | .07 |
| ❑ 27 | Matt Stairs | .10 | .05 |
| ❑ 28 | A.J. Hinch | .10 | .05 |
| ❑ 29 | Olmedo Saenz | .10 | .05 |
| ❑ 30 | Ben Grieve | .15 | .07 |

❑ 31 Ryan Christenson .10 .05
❑ 32 Eric Chavez .15 .07
❑ 33 Tim Hudson .40 .18
❑ 34 John Jaha .10 .05
❑ 35 Jason Giambi .40 .18
Matt Stairs CL
❑ 36 Raul Mondesi .15 .07
❑ 37 Tony Batista .15 .07
❑ 38 David Wells .15 .07
❑ 39 Homer Bush .10 .05
❑ 40 Carlos Delgado .40 .18
❑ 41 Billy Koch .15 .07
❑ 42 Darrin Fletcher .10 .05
❑ 43 Tony Fernandez .10 .05
❑ 44 Shannon Stewart .15 .07
❑ 45 Roy Halladay .10 .05
❑ 46 Chris Carpenter .10 .05
❑ 47 Carlos Delgado .15 .07
David Wells CL
❑ 48 Chipper Jones 1.00 .45
❑ 49 Greg Maddux 1.00 .45
❑ 50 Andruw Jones .40 .18
❑ 51 Andres Galarraga .25 .11
❑ 52 Tom Glavine .40 .18
❑ 53 Brian Jordan .15 .07
❑ 54 John Smoltz .15 .07
❑ 55 John Rocker .15 .07
❑ 56 Javy Lopez .15 .07
❑ 57 Eddie Perez .10 .05
❑ 58 Kevin Millwood .15 .07
❑ 59 Chipper Jones .50 .23
Greg Maddux CL
❑ 60 Jeromy Burnitz .15 .07
❑ 61 Steve Woodard .10 .05
❑ 62 Ron Belliard .10 .05
❑ 63 Geoff Jenkins .15 .07
❑ 64 Bob Wickman .10 .05
❑ 65 Marquis Grissom .10 .05
❑ 66 Henry Blanco .10 .05
❑ 67 Mark Loretta .10 .05
❑ 68 Alex Ochoa .10 .05
❑ 69 Marquis Grissom .15 .07
Jeromy Burnitz CL
❑ 70 Mark McGwire 1.50 .70
❑ 71 Edgar Renteria .10 .05
❑ 72 Dave Veres .10 .05
❑ 73 Eli Marrero .10 .05
❑ 74 Fernando Tatis .15 .07
❑ 75 J.D. Drew .40 .18
❑ 76 Ray Lankford .15 .07
❑ 77 Darryl Kile .15 .07
❑ 78 Kent Bottenfield .10 .05
❑ 79 Joe McEwing .10 .05
❑ 80 Mark McGwire .75 .35
Ray Lankford CL
❑ 81 Sammy Sosa .75 .35
❑ 82 Jose Nieves .10 .05
❑ 83 Jon Lieber .10 .05
❑ 84 Henry Rodriguez .10 .05
❑ 85 Mark Grace .40 .18
❑ 86 Eric Young .10 .05
❑ 87 Kerry Wood .15 .07
❑ 88 Ismael Valdes .10 .05
❑ 89 Glenallen Hill .10 .05
❑ 90 Sammy Sosa .40 .18
Mark Grace CL
❑ 91 Greg Vaughn .15 .07
❑ 92 Fred McGriff .25 .11
❑ 93 Ryan Rupe .10 .05
❑ 94 Bubba Trammell .10 .05
❑ 95 Miguel Cairo .10 .05
❑ 96 Roberto Hernandez .10 .05
❑ 97 Jose Canseco .50 .23
❑ 98 Wilson Alvarez .10 .05
❑ 99 John Flaherty .10 .05
❑ 100 Vinny Castilla .15 .07
❑ 101 Jose Canseco .25 .11
Ramon Hernandez CL
❑ 102 Randy Johnson .50 .23
❑ 103 Matt Williams .25 .11
❑ 104 Matt Mantei .10 .05
❑ 105 Steve Finley .15 .07
❑ 106 Luis Gonzalez .15 .07
❑ 107 Travis Lee .10 .05
❑ 108 Omar Daal .10 .05
❑ 109 Jay Bell .15 .07
❑ 110 Erubiel Durazo .15 .07
❑ 111 Tony Womack .10 .05
❑ 112 Todd Stottlemyre .10 .05
❑ 113 Randy Johnson .15 .07
Matt Williams CL
❑ 114 Gary Sheffield .40 .18
❑ 115 Adrian Beltre .15 .07
❑ 116 Kevin Brown .25 .11
❑ 117 Todd Hundley .10 .05
❑ 118 Eric Karros .15 .07
❑ 119 Shawn Green .40 .18
❑ 120 Chan Ho Park .15 .07
❑ 121 Mark Grudzielanek .10 .05
❑ 122 Todd Hollandsworth .10 .05
❑ 123 Jeff Shaw .10 .05
❑ 124 Darren Dreifort .10 .05
❑ 125 Gary Sheffield .40 .18
Kevin Brown CL
❑ 126 Vladimir Guerrero .60 .25
❑ 127 Michael Barrett .10 .05
❑ 128 Dustin Hermanson .10 .05
❑ 129 Jose Vidro .10 .05
❑ 130 Chris Widger .10 .05
❑ 131 Mike Thurman .10 .05
❑ 132 Wilton Guerrero .10 .05
❑ 133 Brad Fullmer .15 .07
❑ 134 Rondell White .15 .07
❑ 135 Ugueth Urbina .10 .05
❑ 136 Vladimir Guerrero .15 .07
Rondell White CL
❑ 137 Barry Bonds .60 .25
❑ 138 Russ Ortiz .15 .07
❑ 139 J.T. Snow .15 .07
❑ 140 Joe Nathan .10 .05
❑ 141 Rich Aurilia .10 .05
❑ 142 Jeff Kent .25 .11
❑ 143 Armando Rios .10 .05
❑ 144 Ellis Burks .15 .07
❑ 145 Robb Nen .10 .05
❑ 146 Marvin Benard .10 .05
❑ 147 Barry Bonds .15 .07
Russ Ortiz CL
❑ 148 Manny Ramirez .50 .23
❑ 149 Bartolo Colon .15 .07
❑ 150 Kenny Lofton .15 .07
❑ 151 Sandy Alomar Jr. .10 .05
❑ 152 Travis Fryman .15 .07
❑ 153 Omar Vizquel .15 .07
❑ 154 Roberto Alomar .40 .18
❑ 155 Richie Sexson .15 .07
❑ 156 David Justice .25 .11
❑ 157 Jim Thome .25 .11
❑ 158 Manny Ramirez .15 .07
Roberto Alomar CL
❑ 159 Ken Griffey Jr. 1.50 .70
❑ 160 Edgar Martinez .25 .11
❑ 161 Freddy Garcia .15 .07
❑ 162 Alex Rodriguez 1.25 .55
❑ 163 John Halama .10 .05
❑ 164 Russ Davis .10 .05
❑ 165 David Bell .10 .05
❑ 166 Gil Meche .15 .07
❑ 167 Jamie Moyer .10 .05
❑ 168 John Olerud .15 .07
❑ 169 Ken Griffey Jr. .75 .35
Freddy Garcia CL
❑ 170 Preston Wilson .15 .07
❑ 171 Antonio Alfonseca .10 .05
❑ 172 A.J. Burnett .15 .07
❑ 173 Luis Castillo .15 .07
❑ 174 Mike Lowell .10 .05
❑ 175 Alex Fernandez .10 .05
❑ 176 Mike Redmond .10 .05
❑ 177 Alex Gonzalez .10 .05
❑ 178 Vladimir Nunez .10 .05
❑ 179 Mark Kotsay .10 .05
❑ 180 Preston Wilson .15 .07
Luis Castillo CL
❑ 181 Mike Piazza 1.25 .55
❑ 182 Darryl Hamilton .10 .05
❑ 183 Al Leiter .10 .05
❑ 184 Robin Ventura .25 .11
❑ 185 Rickey Henderson .50 .23
❑ 186 Rey Ordonez .10 .05
❑ 187 Edgardo Alfonzo .15 .07
❑ 188 Derek Bell .10 .05
❑ 189 Mike Hampton .15 .07
❑ 190 Armando Benitez .15 .07
❑ 191 Mike Piazza .60 .25
Rickey Henderson CL
❑ 192 Cal Ripken 1.50 .70
❑ 193 B.J. Surhoff .15 .07
❑ 194 Mike Mussina .40 .18
❑ 195 Albert Belle .25 .11
❑ 196 Jerry Hairston Jr. .10 .05
❑ 197 Will Clark .40 .18
❑ 198 Sidney Ponson .10 .05
❑ 199 Brady Anderson .15 .07
❑ 200 Scott Erickson .10 .05
❑ 201 Ryan Minor .10 .05
❑ 202 Cal Ripken .75 .35
Albert Belle CL
❑ 203 Tony Gwynn .75 .35
❑ 204 Bret Boone .10 .05
❑ 205 Ryan Klesko .15 .07
❑ 206 Ben Davis .10 .05
❑ 207 Matt Clement .10 .05
❑ 208 Eric Owens .10 .05
❑ 209 Trevor Hoffman .15 .07
❑ 210 Sterling Hitchcock .10 .05
❑ 211 Phil Nevin .15 .07
❑ 212 Tony Gwynn .40 .18
Trevor Hoffman CL
❑ 213 Scott Rolen .40 .18
❑ 214 Bob Abreu .15 .07
❑ 215 Curt Schilling .15 .07
❑ 216 Rico Brogna .10 .05
❑ 217 Robert Person .10 .05
❑ 218 Doug Glanville .10 .05
❑ 219 Mike Lieberthal .15 .07
❑ 220 Andy Ashby .10 .05
❑ 221 Randy Wolf .10 .05
❑ 222 Bob Abreu .15 .07
Curt Schilling CL
❑ 223 Brian Giles .15 .07
❑ 224 Jason Kendall .15 .07
❑ 225 Kris Benson .15 .07
❑ 226 Warren Morris .10 .05
❑ 227 Kevin Young .10 .05
❑ 228 Al Martin .10 .05
❑ 229 Wil Cordero .10 .05
❑ 230 Bruce Aven .10 .05
❑ 231 Todd Ritchie .10 .05
❑ 232 Jason Kendall .10 .05
Brian Giles CL
❑ 233 Ivan Rodriguez .50 .23
❑ 234 Rusty Greer .15 .07
❑ 235 Ruben Mateo .15 .07
❑ 236 Justin Thompson .10 .05
❑ 237 Rafael Palmeiro .40 .18
❑ 238 Chad Curtis .10 .05
❑ 239 Royce Clayton UER .10 .05
(Mark McLemore pictured on back)
❑ 240 Gabe Kapler .15 .07
❑ 241 Jeff Zimmerman .10 .05
❑ 242 John Wetteland .15 .07
❑ 243 Ivan Rodriguez .25 .11
Rafael Palmeiro CL
❑ 244 Nomar Garciaparra 1.25 .55
❑ 245 Pedro Martinez .50 .23
❑ 246 Jose Offerman .10 .05
❑ 247 Jason Varitek .15 .07
❑ 248 Troy O'Leary .10 .05
❑ 249 John Valentin .10 .05
❑ 250 Trot Nixon .15 .07
❑ 251 Carl Everett .15 .07
❑ 252 Wilton Veras .15 .07
❑ 253 Bret Saberhagen .15 .07
❑ 254 Nomar Garciaparra .60 .25
Pedro Martinez CL
❑ 255 Sean Casey .15 .07
❑ 256 Barry Larkin .40 .18
❑ 257 Pokey Reese .15 .07
❑ 258 Pete Harnisch .10 .05
❑ 259 Aaron Boone .10 .05
❑ 260 Dante Bichette .15 .07
❑ 261 Scott Williamson .10 .05
❑ 262 Steve Parris .10 .05
❑ 263 Dmitri Young .15 .07
❑ 264 Mike Cameron .10 .05
❑ 265 Sean Casey .10 .05
Scott Williamson CL

- ❑ 266 Larry Walker .15 .07
- ❑ 267 Rolando Arrojo .10 .05
- ❑ 268 Pedro Astacio .10 .05
- ❑ 269 Todd Helton .50 .23
- ❑ 270 Jeff Cirillo .15 .07
- ❑ 271 Neifi Perez .10 .05
- ❑ 272 Brian Bohanon .10 .05
- ❑ 273 Jeffrey Hammonds .15 .07
- ❑ 274 Tom Goodwin .10 .05
- ❑ 275 Larry Walker .40 .18
  Todd Helton CL
- ❑ 276 Carlos Beltran .15 .07
- ❑ 277 Jermaine Dye .15 .07
- ❑ 278 Mike Sweeney .15 .07
- ❑ 279 Joe Randa .10 .05
- ❑ 280 Jose Rosado .10 .05
- ❑ 281 Carlos Febles .10 .05
- ❑ 282 Jeff Suppan .10 .05
- ❑ 283 Johnny Damon .15 .07
- ❑ 284 Jeremy Giambi .10 .05
- ❑ 285 Mike Sweeney .15 .07
  Carlos Beltran CL
- ❑ 286 Tony Clark .10 .05
- ❑ 287 Damion Easley .10 .05
- ❑ 288 Jeff Weaver .10 .05
- ❑ 289 Dean Palmer .15 .07
- ❑ 290 Juan Gonzalez .40 .18
- ❑ 291 Juan Encarnacion .15 .07
- ❑ 292 Todd Jones .10 .05
- ❑ 293 Karim Garcia .10 .05
- ❑ 294 Deivi Cruz .10 .05
- ❑ 295 Dean Palmer .10 .05
  Juan Encarnacion CL
- ❑ 296 Corey Koskie .10 .05
- ❑ 297 Brad Radke .15 .07
- ❑ 298 Doug Mientkiewicz .10 .05
- ❑ 299 Ron Coomer .10 .05
- ❑ 300 Joe Mays .10 .05
- ❑ 301 Eric Milton .10 .05
- ❑ 302 Jacque Jones .15 .07
- ❑ 303 Chad Allen .10 .05
- ❑ 304 Cristian Guzman .10 .05
- ❑ 305 Jason Ryan .10 .05
- ❑ 306 Todd Walker .10 .05
- ❑ 307 Corey Koskie .10 .05
  Eric Milton CL
- ❑ 308 Frank Thomas .75 [illegible]
- ❑ 309 Paul Konerko .15 .07
- ❑ 310 Mike Sirotka .10 .05
- ❑ 311 Jim Parque .10 .05
- ❑ 312 Magglio Ordonez .15 .07
- ❑ 313 Bob Howry .10 .05
- ❑ 314 Carlos Lee .15 .07
- ❑ 315 Ray Durham .15 .07
- ❑ 316 Chris Singleton .15 .07
- ❑ 317 Brook Fordyce .10 .05
- ❑ 318 Frank Thomas .40 .18
  Magglio Ordonez CL
- ❑ 319 Derek Jeter 1.50 .70
- ❑ 320 Roger Clemens .75 .35
- ❑ 321 Paul O'Neill .15 .07
- ❑ 322 Bernie Williams .40 .18
- ❑ 323 Mariano Rivera .15 .07
- ❑ 324 Tino Martinez .15 .07
- ❑ 325 David Cone .15 .07
- ❑ 326 Chuck Knoblauch .15 .07
- ❑ 327 Darryl Strawberry .15 .07
- ❑ 328 Orlando Hernandez .15 .07
- ❑ 329 Ricky Ledee .10 .05
- ❑ 330 Derek Jeter .75 .35
  Bernie Williams CL
- ❑ 331 Pat Burrell .60 .25
- ❑ 332 Alfonso Soriano .15 .07
- ❑ 333 Josh Beckett .40 .18
- ❑ 334 Matt Riley .15 .07
- ❑ 335 Brian Cooper .10 .05
- ❑ 336 Eric Munson .40 .18
- ❑ 337 Vernon Wells .15 .07
- ❑ 338 Juan Pena .10 .05
- ❑ 339 Mark DeRosa .10 .05
- ❑ 340 Kip Wells .15 .07
- ❑ 341 Roosevelt Brown .10 .05
- ❑ 342 Jason LaRue .10 .05
- ❑ 343 Ben Petrick .10 .05
- ❑ 344 Mark Quinn .15 .07
- ❑ 345 Julio Ramirez .10 .05
- ❑ 346 Rod Barajas .10 .05
- ❑ 347 Robert Fick .10 .05
- ❑ 348 David Newhan .10 .05
- ❑ 349 Eric Gagne .10 .05
- ❑ 350 Jorge Toca .10 .05
- ❑ 351 Mitch Meluskey .10 .05
- ❑ 352 Ed Yarnall .10 .05
- ❑ 353 Chad Hermansen .10 .05
- ❑ 354 Peter Bergeron .10 .05
- ❑ 355 Dermal Brown .15 .07
- ❑ 356 Adam Kennedy .15 .07
- ❑ 357 Kevin Barker .10 .05
- ❑ 358 Francisco Cordero .10 .05
- ❑ 359 Travis Dawkins .15 .07
- ❑ 360 Jeff Williams RC .25 .11
- ❑ 361 Chad Hutchinson .10 .05
- ❑ 362 D'Angelo Jimenez .15 .07
- ❑ 363 Derrick Gibson .10 .05
- ❑ 364 Calvin Murray .10 .05
- ❑ 365 Doug Davis .10 .05
- ❑ 366 Rob Ramsay .10 .05
- ❑ 367 Mark Redman .10 .05
- ❑ 368 Rick Ankiel .75 .35
- ❑ 369 Domingo Guzman RC .25 .11
- ❑ 370 Eugene Kingsale .10 .05
- ❑ 371 Nomar Garciaparra BPM .60 .25
- ❑ 372 Ken Griffey Jr. BPM .75 .35
- ❑ 373 Randy Johnson BPM .25 .11
- ❑ 374 Jeff Bagwell BPM .25 .11
- ❑ 375 Ivan Rodriguez BPM .25 .11
- ❑ 376 Derek Jeter BPM .75 .35
- ❑ 377 Carlos Beltran BPM .15 .07
- ❑ 378 Vladimir Guerrero BPM .25 .11
- ❑ 379 Sammy Sosa BPM .40 .18
- ❑ 380 Barry Bonds BPM .25 .11
- ❑ 381 Pedro Martinez BPM .25 .11
- ❑ 382 Chipper Jones BPM .50 .23
- ❑ 383 Mo Vaughn BPM .15 .07
- ❑ 384 Mike Piazza BPM .60 .25
- ❑ 385 Alex Rodriguez BPM .60 .25
- ❑ 386 Manny Ramirez BPM .25 .11
- ❑ 387 Mark McGwire BPM .75 .35
- ❑ 388 Tony Gwynn BPM .40 .18
- ❑ 389 Sean Casey BPM .15 .07
- ❑ 390 Cal Ripken BPM .75 .35
- ❑ 391 Ken Griffey Jr. JC .50 .23
- ❑ 392 Ken Griffey Jr. JC .50 .23
- ❑ 393 Ken Griffey Jr. JC .50 .23
- ❑ 394 Ken Griffey Jr. JC .50 .23
- ❑ 395 Ken Griffey Jr. JC .50 .23
- ❑ 396 Ken Griffey Jr. JC .50 .23
- ❑ 397 Ken Griffey Jr. JC .50 .23
- ❑ 398 Ken Griffey Jr. JC .50 .23
- ❑ 399 Ken Griffey Jr. JC .50 .23
- ❑ 400 Ken Griffey Jr. JC .50 .23
- ❑ 401 Ken Griffey Jr. JC .50 .23
- ❑ 402 Ken Griffey Jr. JC .50 .23
- ❑ 403 Ken Griffey Jr. JC .50 .23
- ❑ 404 Ken Griffey Jr. JC .50 .23
- ❑ 405 Ken Griffey Jr. JC .50 .23
- ❑ 406 Ken Griffey Jr. JC .50 .23
- ❑ 407 Ken Griffey Jr. JC .50 .23
- ❑ 408 Ken Griffey Jr. JC .50 .23
- ❑ 409 Ken Griffey Jr. JC .50 .23
- ❑ 410 Ken Griffey Jr. JC .50 .23
- ❑ 411 Ken Griffey Jr. JC .50 .23
- ❑ 412 Ken Griffey Jr. JC .50 .23
- ❑ 413 Ken Griffey Jr. JC .50 .23
- ❑ 414 Ken Griffey Jr. JC .50 .23
- ❑ 415 Ken Griffey Jr. JC .50 .23
- ❑ 416 Ken Griffey Jr. JC .50 .23
- ❑ 417 Ken Griffey Jr. JC .50 .23
- ❑ 418 Ken Griffey Jr. JC .50 .23
- ❑ 419 Ken Griffey Jr. JC .50 .23
- ❑ 420 Ken Griffey Jr. JC .50 .23
- ❑ 421 Ken Griffey Jr. JC .50 .23
- ❑ 422 Ken Griffey Jr. JC .50 .23
- ❑ 423 Ken Griffey Jr. JC .50 .23
- ❑ 424 Ken Griffey Jr. JC .50 .23
- ❑ 425 Ken Griffey Jr. JC .50 .23
- ❑ 426 Ken Griffey Jr. JC .50 .23
- ❑ 427 Ken Griffey Jr. JC .50 .23
- ❑ 428 Ken Griffey Jr. JC .50 .23
- ❑ 429 Ken Griffey Jr. JC .50 .23
- ❑ 430 Ken Griffey Jr. JC .50 .23
- ❑ 431 Ken Griffey Jr. JC .50 .23
- ❑ 432 Ken Griffey Jr. JC .50 .23
- ❑ 433 Ken Griffey Jr. JC .50 .23
- ❑ 434 Ken Griffey Jr. JC .50 .23
- ❑ 435 Ken Griffey Jr. JC .50 .23
- ❑ 436 Ken Griffey Jr. JC .50 .23
- ❑ 437 Ken Griffey Jr. JC .50 .23
- ❑ 438 Ken Griffey Jr. JC .50 .23
- ❑ 439 Ken Griffey Jr. JC .50 .23
- ❑ 440 Ken Griffey Jr. JC .50 .23
- ❑ 441 Tommy Lasorda USA MG 1.00 .45
- ❑ 442 Sean Burroughs USA 1.50 .70
- ❑ 443 Rick Krivda USA .50 .23
- ❑ 444 Ben Sheets USA RC 8.00 3.60
- ❑ 445 Pat Borders USA .50 .23
- ❑ 446 Brent Abernathy USA RC 1.50 .70
- ❑ 447 Tim Young USA .50 .23
- ❑ 448 Adam Everett USA 1.00 .45
- ❑ 449 Anthony Sanders USA .50 .23
- ❑ 450 Ernie Young USA .50 .23
- ❑ 451 Brad Wilkerson USA RC 3.00 1.35
- ❑ 452 Kurt Ainsworth USA RC 3.00 1.35
- ❑ 453 Ryan Franklin USA RC 1.00 .45
- ❑ 454 Todd Williams USA .50 .23
- ❑ 455 Jon Rauch USA RC 5.00 2.20
- ❑ 456 Roy Oswalt USA RC 2.00 .90
- ❑ 457 Shane Heams USA RC 1.00 .45
- ❑ 458 Chris George USA 1.00 .45
- ❑ 459 Bobby Seay USA .50 .23
- ❑ 460 Mike Kinkade USA .50 .23
- ❑ 461 Marcus Jensen USA .50 .23
- ❑ 462 Travis Dawkins USA 1.00 .45
- ❑ 463 Doug Mientkiewicz USA .50 .23
- ❑ 464 John Cotton USA RC 1.00 .45
- ❑ 465 Mike Neill USA .50 .23
- ❑ 466 Team Photo USA 3.00 1.35
- ❑ NNO Japanese Product Information .10 .05
- ❑ NNO Japanese Checklist .10 .05

HOCB01

BECKETT GRADING SERVICES

**$4 OFF** *one card grading*

Cut out coupon and attach to BGS submission form. No photocopies or other reproductions accepted. Offer is good at any BGS service level. To receive discount on multiple submissions, one coupon must accompany each card submitted. Offer expires March 15, 2002. Cannot be combined with any other promotional offer. For a submission form, complete submission instructions or more information about Beckett Grading Services, visit our web site at www.beckett.com.

# Notes

# Notes

# Notes